NOTRE DAME, INDIANA

THE EUROPA WORLD YEAR BOOK 2006

THE EUROPA WORLD YEAR BOOK 2006

VOLUME II

KAZAKHSTAN–ZIMBABWE

LONDON AND NEW YORK

First published 1926

© **Routledge 2006**
Haines House, 21 John Street, London, WC1N 2BP, United Kingdom
(Routledge is an imprint of the Taylor & Francis Group, an Informa business)

All rights reserved. No part of this
publication may be photocopied, recorded,
or otherwise reproduced, stored in a retrieval
system or transmitted in any form or by any
electronic or mechanical means without the
prior permission of the copyright owner.

ISBN-10 1-85743-362-9 (The Set)
1-85743-364-5 (Vol. II)
ISBN-13 978-1-85743-362-3 (The Set)
978-1-85743-364-7 (Vol. II)
ISSN 0071-2302
Library of Congress Catalog Card Number 59-2942

Senior Editor: Joanne Maher

Statistics Editor: Philip McIntyre

Regional Editors: Lynn Daniel, Lucy Dean, Iain Frame,
Imogen Gladman, Juliet Love, Jillian O'Brien, Jacqueline West

International Organizations Editors: Catriona Appeatu Holman, Helen Canton

Associate Regional Editor: Elizabeth Kerr

Contributing Regional Editor: Katharine Murison

Assistant Editors: Eleanor Baynes, Camilla Chew, Katie Dawson,
Anthony Gladman, Nicola Gollan, Michael Grayer, Dominic Heaney, Kirstie Macdonald,
Catriona Marcham, Christopher Matthews, James Middleton, Frances Musselwhite, Patrick Raleigh,
Anna Thomas, Christopher Tooke, Edward Tyerman, Daniel Ward

Editorial Clerical Assistant: Charley McCartney

Editorial Director: Paul Kelly

Typeset in New Century Schoolbook

Typeset by Data Standards Limited, Frome, Somerset

Printed and bound in Great Britain by William Clowes Limited, Beccles, Suffolk

FOREWORD

THE EUROPA WORLD YEAR BOOK was first published in 1926. Since 1960 it has appeared in annual two-volume editions, and has become established as an authoritative reference work, providing a wealth of detailed information on the political, economic and commercial institutions of the world.

Volume I contains a comprehensive listing of some 1,900 international organizations and the first part of the alphabetical survey of countries of the world, from Afghanistan to Jordan. Volume II contains countries from Kazakhstan to Zimbabwe. An Index of Territories covered in both volumes is to be be found at the end of Volume II.

Each country is covered by an individual chapter, containing: an introductory survey including recent history, economic affairs, government, defence, education, and public holidays; an economic and demographic survey using the latest available statistics on area and population, health and welfare, agriculture, forestry, fishing, industry, finance, trade, transport, tourism, the media, and education; and a directory section listing names, addresses and other useful facts about organizations in the fields of government, election commissions, political parties, diplomatic representation, judiciary, religions, the media, telecommunications, banking, insurance, trade and industry, development organizations, chambers of commerce, industrial and trade associations, utilities, trade unions, transport, and tourism.

The entire content of the print edition of THE EUROPA WORLD YEAR BOOK is available online at www.europaworld.com. This prestigious resource incorporates sophisticated search and browse functions as well as specially commissioned visual and statistical content. An ongoing programme of updates of key areas of information ensures currency of content, and enhances the richness of the coverage for which THE EUROPA WORLD YEAR BOOK is renowned.

Readers are referred to the nine titles in the Europa Regional Surveys of the World series: AFRICA SOUTH OF THE SAHARA, CENTRAL AND SOUTH-EASTERN EUROPE, EASTERN EUROPE, RUSSIA AND CENTRAL ASIA, THE FAR EAST AND AUSTRALASIA, THE MIDDLE EAST AND NORTH AFRICA, SOUTH AMERICA, CENTRAL AMERICA AND THE CARIBBEAN, SOUTH ASIA, THE USA AND CANADA, and WESTERN EUROPE, available both in print and online, offer comprehensive analysis at regional, sub-regional and country level. More detailed coverage of international organizations is to be found in THE EUROPA DIRECTORY OF INTERNATIONAL ORGANIZATIONS.

The content of THE EUROPA WORLD YEAR BOOK is extensively revised and updated by a variety of methods, including direct mailing to all the institutions listed. Many other sources are used, such as national statistical offices, government departments and diplomatic missions. The editors thank the innumerable individuals and organizations world-wide whose generous co-operation in providing current information for this edition is invaluable in presenting the most accurate and up-to-date material available.

May 2006

ACKNOWLEDGEMENTS

The editors gratefully acknowledge particular indebtedness for permission to reproduce material from the following publications: the United Nations' *Demographic Yearbook*, *Statistical Yearbook*, *Monthly Bulletin of Statistics*, *Industrial Commodity Statistics Yearbook* and *International Trade Statistics Yearbook*; the United Nations Educational, Scientific and Cultural Organization's *Statistical Yearbook*; the Food and Agriculture Organization of the United Nations' statistical database; the International Labour Office's statistical database and *Yearbook of Labour Statistics*; the World Bank's *World Bank Atlas*, *Global Development Finance*, *World Development Report* and *World Development Indicators*; the International Monetary Fund's statistical database, *International Financial Statistics* and *Government Finance Statistics Yearbook*; the World Tourism Organization's *Yearbook of Tourism Statistics*; and *The Military Balance 2005–2006*, a publication of the International Institute for Strategic Studies, Arundel House, 13–15 Arundel Street, London WC2R 3DX.

HEALTH AND WELFARE STATISTICS: SOURCES AND DEFINITIONS

Total fertility rate Source: WHO, *The World Health Report* (2005). The number of children that would be born per woman, assuming no female mortality at child-bearing ages and the age-specific fertility rates of a specified country and reference period.

Under-5 mortality rate Source: UNICEF, *The State of the World's Children* (2005). The ratio of registered deaths of children under 5 years to the total number of registered live births over the same period.

HIV/AIDS Source: UNAIDS. Estimated percentage of adults aged 15 to 49 years living with HIV/AIDS. < indicates 'fewer than'.

Health expenditure Source: WHO, *The World Health Report* (2005).
US $ per head (PPP)
International dollar estimates, derived by dividing local currency units by an estimate of their purchasing-power parity (PPP) compared with the US dollar. PPPs are the rates of currency conversion that equalize the purchasing power of different currencies by eliminating the differences in price levels between countries.
% of GDP
GDP levels for OECD countries follow the most recent UN System of National Accounts. For non-OECD countries a value was estimated by utilizing existing UN, IMF and World Bank data.
Public expenditure
Government health-related outlays plus expenditure by social schemes compulsorily affiliated with a sizeable share of the population, and extrabudgetary funds allocated to health services. Figures include grants or loans provided by international agencies, other national authorities, and sometimes commercial banks.

Access to water and sanitation Source: WHO/UNICEF Joint Monitoring Programme on Water Supply and Sanitation (JMP) (Mid-Term Assessment, 2004). Defined in terms of the percentage of the population using improved facilities in terms of the type of technology and levels of service afforded. For water, this includes house connections, public standpipes, boreholes with hand-pumps, protected dug wells, protected spring and rainwater collection; allowance is also made for other locally defined technologies. Sanitation is defined to include connection to a sewer or septic tank system, pour-flush latrine, simple pit or ventilated improved pit latrine, again with allowance for acceptable local technologies. Access to water and sanitation does not imply that the level of service or quality of water is 'adequate' or 'safe'.

Human Development Index (HDI) Source: UNDP, *Human Development Report* (2005). A summary of human development measured by three basic dimensions: prospects for a long and healthy life, measured by life expectancy at birth; knowledge, measured by adult literacy rate (two-thirds' weight) and the combined gross enrolment ratio in primary, secondary and tertiary education (one-third weight); and standard of living, measured by GDP per head (PPP US $). The index value obtained lies between zero and one. A value above 0.8 indicates high human development, between 0.5 and 0.8 medium human development, and below 0.5 low human development. A centralized data source for all three dimensions was not available for all countries. In some such cases other data sources were used to calculate a substitute value; however, this was excluded from the ranking. Other countries, including non-UNDP members, were excluded from the HDI altogether. In total, 177 countries were ranked for 2003.

CONTENTS

Abbreviations	Page ix	Nicaragua	Page 3256
International Telephone Codes	xiii	Niger	3275
		Nigeria	3294
Kazakhstan	2493	Norway	3321
Kenya	2515	Norwegian External Territories:	
Kiribati	2537	Svalbard	3345
The Democratic People's Republic of Korea (North Korea)	2545	Jan Mayen	3347
The Republic of Korea (South Korea)	2574	Norwegian Dependencies	3347
Kuwait	2611	Oman	3348
Kyrgyzstan	2630	Pakistan	3362
Laos	2648	Palau	3410
Latvia	2664	Palestinian Autonomous Areas	3417
Lebanon	2683	Panama	3440
Lesotho	2711	Papua New Guinea	3458
Liberia	2724	Paraguay	3480
Libya	2741	Peru	3498
Liechtenstein	2759	The Philippines	3522
Lithuania	2767	Poland	3560
Luxembourg	2787	Portugal	3586
The former Yugoslav republic of Macedonia	2799	Qatar	3613
Madagascar	2818	Romania	3624
Malawi	2836	The Russian Federation	3651
Malaysia	2852	Rwanda	3696
The Maldives	2890	Saint Christopher and Nevis	3713
Mali	2901	Saint Lucia	3722
Malta	2918	Saint Vincent and the Grenadines	3733
The Marshall Islands	2929	Samoa	3742
Mauritania	2937	San Marino	3751
Mauritius	2952	São Tomé and Príncipe	3757
Mexico	2967	Saudi Arabia	3767
The Federated States of Micronesia	2998	Senegal	3788
Moldova	3005	Serbia and Montenegro	3813
Monaco	3024	Seychelles	3844
Mongolia	3030	Sierra Leone	3853
Montenegro (see Serbia and Montenegro)		Singapore	3870
Morocco	3053	Slovakia	3896
Mozambique	3077	Slovenia	3915
Myanmar	3096	Solomon Islands	3933
Namibia	3122	Somalia	3946
Nauru	3140	South Africa	3964
Nepal	3148	Spain	3998
The Netherlands	3172	Spanish External Territories:	
Netherlands Dependencies:		Ceuta	4047
Aruba	3198	Melilla	4051
The Netherlands Antilles	3204	Sri Lanka	4056
New Zealand	3216	Sudan	4084
New Zealand's Dependent Territories:		Suriname	4109
Ross Dependency	3239	Swaziland	4121
Tokelau	3239	Sweden	4135
New Zealand's Associated States:		Switzerland	4160
Cook Islands	3243	Syria	4186
Niue	3250	Taiwan (see China, Vol. I)	

vii

CONTENTS

Tajikistan	Page 4209
Tanzania	4228
Thailand	4248
Timor-Leste	4279
Togo	4295
Tonga	4313
Trinidad and Tobago	4323
Tunisia	4341
Turkey	4360
Turkmenistan	4396
Tuvalu	4413
Uganda	4420
Ukraine	4439
The United Arab Emirates	4469
The United Kingdom	4486
United Kingdom Crown Dependencies:	
The Channel Islands	4561
The Isle of Man	4567
United Kingdom Overseas Territories:	
Anguilla	4572
Bermuda	4578
The British Antarctic Territory	4585
The British Indian Ocean Territory	4586
The British Virgin Islands	4587
The Cayman Islands	4593
The Falkland Islands	4600

Gibraltar	Page 4605
Montserrat	4612
Pitcairn Islands	4619
Saint Helena and Dependencies	4621
South Georgia and the South Sandwich Islands	4625
The Turks and Caicos Islands	4626
The United States of America	4632
United States Commonwealth Territories:	
The Northern Mariana Islands	4703
Puerto Rico	4709
United States External Territories:	
American Samoa	4721
Guam	4726
The United States Virgin Islands	4733
Other Territories	4737
Uruguay	4739
Uzbekistan	4757
Vanuatu	4776
The Vatican City	4788
Venezuela	4797
Viet Nam	4823
Yemen	4851
Zambia	4870
Zimbabwe	4888
Index of Territories	4912

ABBREVIATIONS

AB	Aktiebolag (Joint-Stock Company); Alberta
Abog.	Abogado (Lawyer)
Acad.	Academician; Academy
ACP	African, Caribbean and Pacific (countries)
ACT	Australian Capital Territory
AD	anno Domini
ADB	African Development Bank; Asian Development Bank
ADC	aide-de-camp
Adm.	Admiral
admin.	administration
AfDB	African Development Bank
AG	Aktiengesellschaft (Joint-Stock Company)
AH	anno Hegirae
a.i.	ad interim
AID	(US) Agency for International Development
AIDS	acquired immunodeficiency syndrome
AK	Alaska
Al.	Aleja (Alley, Avenue)
AL	Alabama
ALADI	Asociación Latinoamericana de Integración
Alt.	Alternate
AM	Amplitude Modulation
a.m.	ante meridiem (before noon)
amalg.	amalgamated
Apdo	Apartado (Post Box)
APEC	Asia-Pacific Economic Co-operation
approx.	approximately
Apt	Apartment
AR	Arkansas
ARV	advanced retroviral
AŞ	Anonim Şirketi (Joint-Stock Company)
A/S	Aktieselskab (Joint-Stock Company)
ASEAN	Association of South East Asian Nations
asscn	association
assoc.	associate
ASSR	Autonomous Soviet Socialist Republic
asst	assistant
AU	African Union
Aug.	August
auth.	authorized
av., Ave	Avenija, Avenue
Av., Avda	Avenida (Avenue)
Avv.	Avvocato (Lawyer)
AZ	Arizona
b.b.	bez broja (without number)
BC	British Columbia
BC	before Christ
Bd	Board
Bd, Bld, Blv., Blvd	Boulevard
b/d	barrels per day
BFPO	British Forces' Post Office
Bhd	Berhad (Public Limited Company)
Bldg	Building
blk	block
Blvr	Bulevar
BP	Boîte postale (Post Box)
br.(s)	branch(es)
Brig.	Brigadier
BSE	bovine spongiform encephalopathy
BSEC	(Organization of the) Black Sea Economic Co-operation
bte	boîte (box)
BTN	Brussels Tariff Nomenclature
Bul.	Bulvar (boulevard)
bulv.	bulvarīs (boulevard)
C	Centigrade
c.	circa; cuadra(s) (block(s))
CA	California
CACM	Central American Common Market
Cad.	Caddesi (Street)
CAP	Common Agricultural Policy
cap.	capital
Capt.	Captain
CAR	Central African Republic
CARICOM	Caribbean Community and Common Market
CBSS	Council of Baltic Sea States
CCL	Caribbean Congress of Labour
Cdre	Commodore
CEMAC	Communauté économique et monétaire de l'Afrique centrale
Cen.	Central
CEO	Chief Executive Officer
CFA	Communauté Financière Africaine; Coopération Financière en Afrique centrale
CFP	Common Fisheries Policy; Communauté française du Pacifique; Comptoirs français du Pacifique
Chair.	Chairman/person/woman
Chih.	Chihuahua
CI	Channel Islands
Cia	Companhia
Cía	Compañía
Cie	Compagnie
c.i.f.	cost, insurance and freight
C-in-C	Commander-in-Chief
circ.	circulation
CIS	Commonwealth of Independent States
CJD	Creutzfeldt-Jakob disease
cm	centimetre(s)
cnr	corner
CO	Colorado
Co	Company; County
c/o	care of
Coah.	Coahuila
Col	Colonel
Col.	Colima; Colonia
COMESA	Common Market for Eastern and Southern Africa
Comm.	Commission; Commendatore
Commdr	Commander
Commdt	Commandant
Commr	Commissioner
Cond.	Condiminio
Confed.	Confederation
Cont.	Contador (Accountant)
COO	Chief Operating Officer
Corp.	Corporate
Corpn	Corporation
CP	Case Postale, Caixa Postal, Casella Postale (Post Box); Communist Party
CPSU	Communist Party of the Soviet Union
Cres.	Crescent
CSCE	Conference on Security and Cooperation in Europe
CSTAL	Confederación Sindical de los Trabajadores de América Latina
CT	Connecticut
CTCA	Confederación de Trabajadores Centro-americanos
Cttee	Committee
cu	cubic
cwt	hundredweight
DC	District of Columbia; Distrito Capital; Distrito Central
d.d.	delniška družba, dioničko društvo (joint stock company)
DE	Departamento Estatal; Delaware
Dec.	December
Del.	Delegación
Dem.	Democratic; Democrat
Dep.	Deputy
dep.	deposits
Dept	Department
devt	development
DF	Distrito Federal
Dgo	Durango
Diag.	Diagonal
Dir	Director
Div.	Division(al)
DM	Deutsche Mark
DMZ	demilitarized zone
DNA	deoxyribonucleic acid
DN	Distrito Nacional
Doc.	Docent
Dott.	Dottore/essa
DPRK	Democratic People's Republic of Korea
Dr	Doctor
Dr.	Drive
Dra	Doctora
Dr Hab.	Doktor Habilitowany (Assistant Professor)
dr.(e)	drachma(e)
Drs	Doctorandus
DU	depleted uranium
dwt	dead weight tons
E	East; Eastern
EBRD	European Bank for Reconstruction and Development
EC	European Community
ECA	(United Nations) Economic Commission for Africa
ECE	(United Nations) Economic Commission for Europe
ECLAC	(United Nations) Economic Commission for Latin America and the Caribbean
ECO	Economic Co-operation Organization
Econ.	Economist; Economics
ECOSOC	(United Nations) Economic and Social Council
ECOWAS	Economic Community of West African States
ECU	European Currency Unit
Edif.	Edificio (Building)
edn	edition
EEA	European Economic Area
EFTA	European Free Trade Association
e.g.	exempli gratia (for example)
EIB	European Investment Bank
eKv	electron kilovolt
EMS	European Monetary System
EMU	Economic and Monetary Union
eMv	electron megavolt
Eng.	Engineer; Engineering
EP	Empresa Pública
ERM	Exchange Rate Mechanism
ESACA	Emisora de Capital Abierto Sociedad Anónima

ABBREVIATIONS

Esc.	Escuela; Escudos; Escritorio	ICC	International Chamber of Commerce; International Criminal Court	LPG	liquefied petroleum gas
ESCAP	(United Nations) Economic and Social Commission for Asia and the Pacific			Lt, Lieut	Lieutenant
		ICFTU	International Confederation of Free Trade Unions	Ltd	Limited
ESCWA	(United Nations) Economic and Social Commission for Western Asia	ICRC	International Committee of the Red Cross		
				m	metre(s)
esq.	esquina (corner)	ICTR	International Criminal Tribunal for Rwanda	m.	million
est.	established; estimate; estimated			MA	Massachusetts
etc.	et cetera	ICTY	International Criminal Tribunal for the former Yugoslavia	Maj.	Major
EU	European Union			Man.	Manager; managing
eV	eingetragener Verein	ID	Idaho	MB	Manitoba
excl.	excluding	IDA	International Development Association	mbH	mit beschränkter Haftung (with limited liability)
exec.	executive				
Ext.	Extension	IDB	Inter-American Development Bank	MD	Maryland
				MDG	Millennium Development Goal
		IDPs	internally displaced persons	MDRI	multilateral debt relief initiative
F	Fahrenheit	i.e.	id est (that is to say)	ME	Maine
f.	founded	IFC	International Finance Corporation	Me	Maître
FAO	Food and Agriculture Organization			mem.(s)	member(s)
		IGAD	Intergovernmental Authority on Development	MEP	Member of the European Parliament
f.a.s.	free alongside ship				
Feb.	February	IHL	International Humanitarian Law	Mercosul	Mercado Comum do Sul (Southern Common Market)
Fed.	Federation; Federal	IL	Illinois		
FL	Florida	ILO	International Labour Organization/Office	Mercosur	Mercado Común del Sur (Southern Common Market)
FM	frequency modulation				
fmr(ly)	former(ly)	IMF	International Monetary Fund	Méx.	México
f.o.b.	free on board	IML	International Migration Law	MFN	most favoured nation
Fr	Father	in (ins)	inch (inches)	mfrs	manufacturers
Fr.	Franc	IN	Indiana	Mgr	Monseigneur; Monsignor
Fri.	Friday	Inc, Incorp.		MHz	megahertz
FRY	Federal Republic of Yugoslavia	Incd	Incorporated	MI	Michigan
ft	foot (feet)	incl.	including	MIA	missing in action
FYRM	former Yugoslav republic of Macedonia	Ind.	Independent	Mich.	Michoacán
		INF	Intermediate-Range Nuclear Forces	MIGA	Multilateral Investment Guarantee Agency
g	gram(s)	Ing.	Engineer	Mil.	Military
g.	gatve (street)	Insp.	Inspector	Mlle	Mademoiselle
GA	Georgia	Int.	International	mm	millimetre(s)
GATT	General Agreement on Tariffs and Trade	Inzå.	Engineer	Mme	Madame
		IPU	Inter-Parliamentary Union	MN	Minnesota
GCC	Gulf Co-operation Council	Ir	Engineer	mnt.	mante (road)
Gdns	Gardens	IRF	International Road Federation	MO	Missouri
GDP	gross domestic product	irreg.	irregular	Mon.	Monday
Gen.	General	Is	Islands	Mor.	Morelos
GeV	giga electron volts	ISIC	International Standard Industrial Classification	MOU	memorandum of understanding
GM	genetically modified			MP	Member of Parliament
GmbH	Gesellschaft mit beschränkter Haftung (Limited Liability Company)	IT	information technology	MS	Mississippi
		ITU	International Telecommunication Union	MSS	Manuscripts
				MT	Montana
GMO(s)	genetically modified organism(s)	Iur.	Lawyer	MW	megawatt(s); medium wave
GMT	Greenwich Mean Time			MWh	megawatt hour(s)
GNI	gross national income				
GNP	gross national product	Jal.	Jalisco		
Gov.	Governor	Jan.	January		
Govt	Government	Jnr	Junior	N	North; Northern
Gro	Guerrero	Jr	Jonkheer (Esquire); Junior	n.a.	not available
grt	gross registered tons	Jt	Joint	nab.	naberezhnaya (embankment, quai)
GSM	Global System for Mobile Communications				
				NAFTA	North American Free Trade Agreement
Gto	Guanajuato	kg	kilogram(s)		
GWh	gigawatt hours	KG	Kommandit Gesellschaft (Limited Partnership)	nám.	náměstí (square)
				Nat.	National
		kHz	kilohertz	NATO	North Atlantic Treaty Organization
ha	hectares	KK	Kaien Kaisha (Limited Company)		
HE	His/Her Eminence; His/Her Excellency	km	kilometre(s)	Nay.	Nayarit
		kom.	komnata (room)	NB	New Brunswick
hf	hlutafelag (Limited Company)	kor.	korpus (block)	NC	North Carolina
HI	Hawaii	k'och.	k'ochasi (street)	NCD	National Capital District
HIPC	heavily indebted poor country	KS	Kansas	NCO	non-commissioned officer
HIV	human immunodeficiency virus	küç	küçasi (street)	ND	North Dakota
hl	hectolitre(s)	kv.	kvartal (apartment block); kvartira (apartment)	NE	Nebraska; North-East
HM	His/Her Majesty			NEPAD	New Partnership for Africa's Development
Hon.	Honorary, Honourable	kW	kilowatt(s)		
hp	horsepower	kWh	kilowatt hours	NGO	non-governmental organization
HQ	Headquarters	KY	Kentucky	NH	New Hampshire
HRH	His/Her Royal Highness			NJ	New Jersey
HSH	His/Her Serene Highness			NL	Newfoundland and Labrador, Nuevo León
Hwy	Highway	LA	Louisiana		
		lauk	laukums (square)		
		lb	pound(s)	NM	New Mexico
IA	Iowa	LDCs	Least Developed Countries	NMP	net material product
IBRD	International Bank for Reconstruction and Development	Lic.	Licenciado	no	numéro, número (number)
		Licda	Licenciada	no.	number
				Nov.	November
		LNG	liquefied natural gas	nr	near

x

ABBREVIATIONS

nrt	net registered tons	QC	Québec	Sra	Señora
NS	Nova Scotia	QIP	Quick Impact Project	Srl	Società a Responsabilità Limitata (Limited Company)
NSW	New South Wales	Qld	Queensland		
NT	Northwest Territories	Qro	Querétaro	SSR	Soviet Socialist Republic
NU	Nunavut Territory	Q. Roo	Quintana Roo	St	Saint, Sint; Street
NV	Naamloze Vennootschap (Limited Company); Nevada	q.v.	quod vide (to which refer)	Sta	Santa
				Ste	Sainte
NW	North-West			STI(s)	sexually transmitted infection(s)
NY	New York	Rag.	Ragioniere (Accountant)	str.	strada, stradă (street)
NZ	New Zealand	Rd	Road	str-la	stradelă (street)
		R(s)	rand; rupee(s)	subs.	subscriptions; subscribed
		reg., regd	register; registered	Sun.	Sunday
		reorg.	reorganized	Supt	Superintendent
OAPEC	Organization of Arab Petroleum Exporting Countries	Rep.	Republic; Republican; Representative	SUV	sports utility vehicle
				sv.	Saint
OAS	Organization of American States	Repub.	Republic	SW	South-West
OAU	Organization of African Unity	res	reserve(s)		
Oax.	Oaxaca	retd	retired		
Oct.	October	Rev.	Reverend	Tab.	Tabasco
OECD	Organisation for Economic Cooperation and Development	RI	Rhode Island	Tamps	Tamaulipas
		RJ	Rio de Janeiro	TAŞ	Turkiye Anonim Şirketi (Turkish Joint-Stock Company)
OECS	Organisation of Eastern Caribbean States	Rm	Room		
		RN	Royal Navy	Tas	Tasmania
Of.	Oficina (Office)	ro-ro	roll-on roll-off	TD	Teachta Dàla (Member of Parliament)
OH	Ohio	RP	Recette principale		
OIC	Organization of the Islamic Conference	Rp.(s)	rupiah(s)	tech., techn.	technical
		Rpto	Reparto (Estate)	tel.	telephone
OK	Oklahoma	RSFSR	Russian Soviet Federative Socialist Republic	TEU	20-ft equivalent unit
ON	Ontario			Thur.	Thursday
OPEC	Organization of the Petroleum Exporting Countries	Rt	Right	TN	Tennessee
				tř	třída (avenue)
opp.	opposite			Treas.	Treasurer
OR	Oregon	S	South; Southern; San	Tue.	Tuesday
Org.	Organization	SA	Société Anonyme, Sociedad Anónima (Limited Company); South Australia	TV	television
ORIT	Organización Regional Interamericana de Trabajadores			TX	Texas
		SAARC	South Asian Association for Regional Co-operation		
OSCE	Organization for Security and Cooperation in Europe	SACN	South American Community of Nations	u.	utca (street)
				u/a	unit of account
		SAECA	Sociedad Anónima Emisora de Capital Abierto	UAE	United Arab Emirates
				UEE	Unidade Económica Estatal
p.	page	SADC	Southern African Development Community	UEMOA	Union économique et monetaire ouest-africaine
p.a.	per annum				
PA	Palestinian Authority; Pennsylvania	SAR	Special Administrative Region	UK	United Kingdom
		SARL	Sociedade Anônima de Responsabilidade Limitada (Joint-Stock Company of Limited Liability)	ul.	ulica, ulitsa (street)
Parl.	Parliament(ary)			UM	ouguiya
per.	pereulok (lane, alley)			UN	United Nations
PE	Prince Edward Island			UNAIDS	United Nations Joint Programme on HIV/AIDS
Perm.	Rep. Permanent Representative	SARS	Severe Acute Respiratory Syndrome		
PF	Postfach (Post Box)			UNCTAD	United Nations Conference on Trade and Development
PK	Post Box (Turkish)	Sat.	Saturday		
Pl.	Plac, Plads (square)	SC	South Carolina	UNDP	United Nations Development Programme
pl.	platz; place; ploshchad (square)	SD	South Dakota		
PLC	Public Limited Company	Sdn Bhd	Sendirian Berhad (Private Limited Company)	UNEP	United Nations Environment Programme
PLO	Palestine Liberation Organization				
		SDR(s)	Special Drawing Right(s)	UNESCO	United Nations Educational, Scientific and Cultural Organization
p.m.	post meridiem (after noon)	SE	South-East		
PMB	Private Mail Bag	Sec.	Secretary		
PNA	Palestinian National Authority	Secr.	Secretariat	UNHCHR	UN High Commissioner for Human Rights
POB	Post Office Box	Sen.	Senior; Senator		
pp.	pages	Sept.	September	UNHCR	United Nations High Commissioner for Refugees
PPP	purchasing-power parity	SER	Sua Eccellenza Reverendissima (His Eminence)		
PQ	Québec			UNICEF	United Nations Children's Fund
PR	Puerto Rico	SFRY	Socialist Federal Republic of Yugoslavia	Univ.	University
pr.	prospekt, prospekti (avenue)			UNODC	United Nations Office on Drugs and Crime
Pres.	President	Sin.	Sinaloa		
PRGF	Poverty Reduction and Growth Facility	SITC	Standard International Trade Classification	UNRWA	United Nations Relief and Works Agency for Palestine Refugees in the Near East
Prin.	Principal	SJ	Society of Jesus		
Prof.	Professor	SK	Saskatchewan	UNWTO	World Tourism Organization
Propr	Proprietor	SLP	San Luis Potosí	Urb.	Urbanización (District)
Prov.	Province; Provincial; Provinciale (Dutch)	SMEs	small and medium-sized enterprises	USA	United States of America
				USAID	United States Agency for International Development
prov.	provulok (lane)	s/n	sin número (without number)		
pst.	puistotie (avenue)	Soc.	Society	USSR	Union of Soviet Socialist Republics
PT	Perseroan Terbatas (Limited Company)	Sok.	Sokak (Street)		
		Son.	Sonora	UT	Utah
Pte	Private; Puente (Bridge)	Şos.	Şosea (Road)		
Pty	Proprietary	SP	São Paulo		
p.u.	paid up	SpA	Società per Azioni (Joint-Stock Company)	VA	Virginia
publ.	publication; published			VAT	value-added tax
Publr	Publisher	Sq.	Square	VEB	Volkseigener Betrieb (Public Company)
Pue.	Puebla	sq	square (in measurements)		
Pvt.	Private	Sr	Senior; Señor		

xi

ABBREVIATIONS

v-CJD	new variant Creutzfeldt-Jakob disease	W	West; Western	WSSD	World Summit on Sustainable Development
Ven.	Venerable	WA	Western Australia; Washington (State)	WTO	World Trade Organization
Ver.	Veracruz	WCL	World Confederation of Labour	WV	West Virginia
VHF	Very High Frequency	Wed.	Wednesday	WY	Wyoming
VI	(US) Virgin Islands	WEU	Western European Union		
Vic	Victoria	WFP	World Food Programme		
Vn	Veien (Street)	WFTU	World Federation of Trade Unions	yr	year
vol.(s)	volume(s)				
VT	Vermont	WHO	World Health Organization	YT	Yukon Territory
vul.	vulitsa, vulytsa (street)	WI	Wisconsin	Yuc.	Yucatán

INTERNATIONAL TELEPHONE CODES

To make international calls to telephone and fax numbers listed in *The Europa World Year Book*, dial the international code of the country from which you are calling, followed by the appropriate country code for the organization you wish to call (listed below), followed by the area code (if applicable) and telephone or fax number listed in the entry.

	Country code	+ or − GMT*
Afghanistan	93	+4½
Albania	355	+1
Algeria	213	+1
Andorra	376	+1
Angola	244	+1
Antigua and Barbuda	1 268	−4
Argentina	54	−3
Armenia	374	+4
Australia	61	+8 to +10
Australian External Territories:		
Australian Antarctic Territory	672	+3 to +10
Christmas Island	61	+7
Cocos (Keeling) Islands	61	+6½
Norfolk Island	672	+11½
Austria	43	+1
Azerbaijan	994	+5
The Bahamas	1 242	−5
Bahrain	973	+3
Bangladesh	880	+6
Barbados	1 246	−4
Belarus	375	+2
Belgium	32	+1
Belize	501	−6
Benin	229	+1
Bhutan	975	+6
Bolivia	591	−4
Bosnia and Herzegovina	387	+1
Botswana	267	+2
Brazil	55	−3 to −4
Brunei	673	+8
Bulgaria	359	+2
Burkina Faso	226	0
Burundi	257	+2
Cambodia	855	+7
Cameroon	237	+1
Canada	1	−3 to −8
Cape Verde	238	−1
The Central African Republic	236	+1
Chad	235	+1
Chile	56	−4
China, People's Republic	86	+8
Special Administrative Regions:		
Hong Kong	852	+8
Macao	853	+8
China (Taiwan)	886	+8
Colombia	57	−5
The Comoros	269	+3
Congo, Democratic Republic	243	+1
Congo, Republic	242	+1
Costa Rica	506	−6
Côte d'Ivoire	225	0
Croatia	385	+1
Cuba	53	−5
Cyprus	357	+2
'Turkish Republic of Northern Cyprus'	90 392	+2
Czech Republic	420	+1
Denmark	45	+1
Danish External Territories:		
Faroe Islands	298	0
Greenland	299	−1 to −4
Djibouti	253	+3

	Country code	+ or − GMT*
Dominica	1 767	−4
Dominican Republic	1 809	−4
Ecuador	593	−5
Egypt	20	+2
El Salvador	503	−6
Equatorial Guinea	240	+1
Eritrea	291	+3
Estonia	372	+2
Ethiopia	251	+3
Fiji	679	+12
Finland	358	+2
Finnish External Territory:		
Åland Islands	358	+2
France	33	+1
French Overseas Regions and Departments:		
French Guiana	594	−3
Guadeloupe	590	−4
Martinique	596	−4
Réunion	262	+4
French Overseas Collectivities:		
French Polynesia	689	−9 to −10
Mayotte	269	+3
Saint Pierre and Miquelon	508	−3
Wallis and Futuna Islands	681	+12
Other French Overseas Territory:		
New Caledonia	687	+11
Gabon	241	+1
Gambia	220	0
Georgia	995	+4
Germany	49	+1
Ghana	233	0
Greece	30	+2
Grenada	1 473	−4
Guatemala	502	−6
Guinea	224	0
Guinea-Bissau	245	0
Guyana	592	−4
Haiti	509	−5
Honduras	504	−6
Hungary	36	+1
Iceland	354	0
India	91	+5½
Indonesia	62	+7 to +9
Iran	98	+3½
Iraq	964	+3
Ireland	353	0
Israel	972	+2
Italy	39	+1
Jamaica	1 876	−5
Japan	81	+9
Jordan	962	+2
Kazakhstan	7	+6
Kenya	254	+3
Kiribati	686	+12 to +13
Korea, Democratic People's Republic (North Korea)	850	+9
Korea, Republic (South Korea)	82	+9
Kuwait	965	+3
Kyrgyzstan	996	+5
Laos	856	+7

INTERNATIONAL TELEPHONE CODES

	Country code	+ or − GMT*
Latvia	371	+2
Lebanon	961	+2
Lesotho	266	+2
Liberia	231	0
Libya	218	+1
Liechtenstein	423	+1
Lithuania	370	+2
Luxembourg	352	+1
Macedonia, former Yugoslav republic	389	+1
Madagascar	261	+3
Malawi	265	+2
Malaysia	60	+8
Maldives	960	+5
Mali	223	0
Malta	356	+1
Marshall Islands	692	+12
Mauritania	222	0
Mauritius	230	+4
Mexico	52	−6 to −7
Micronesia, Federated States	691	+10 to +11
Moldova	373	+2
Monaco	377	+1
Mongolia	976	+7 to +9
Morocco	212	0
Mozambique	258	+2
Myanmar	95	+6½
Namibia	264	+2
Nauru	674	+12
Nepal	977	+5¾
Netherlands	31	+1
Netherlands Dependencies:		
Aruba	297	−4
Netherlands Antilles	599	−4
New Zealand	64	+12
New Zealand's Dependent and Associated Territories:		
Tokelau	690	−10
Cook Islands	682	−10
Niue	683	−11
Nicaragua	505	−6
Niger	227	+1
Nigeria	234	+1
Norway	47	+1
Norwegian External Territory:		
Svalbard	47	+1
Oman	968	+4
Pakistan	92	+5
Palau	680	+9
Palestinian Autonomous Areas	970 or 972	+2
Panama	507	−5
Papua New Guinea	675	+10
Paraguay	595	−4
Peru	51	−5
The Philippines	63	+8
Poland	48	+1
Portugal	351	0
Qatar	974	+3
Romania	40	+2
Russian Federation	7	+2 to +12
Rwanda	250	+2
Saint Christopher and Nevis	1 869	−4
Saint Lucia	1 758	−4
Saint Vincent and the Grenadines	1 784	−4
Samoa	685	−11
San Marino	378	+1
São Tomé and Príncipe	239	0
Saudi Arabia	966	+3
Senegal	221	0
Serbia and Montenegro	381	+1
Seychelles	248	+4

	Country code	+ or − GMT*
Sierra Leone	232	0
Singapore	65	+8
Slovakia	421	+1
Slovenia	386	+1
Solomon Islands	677	+11
Somalia	252	+3
South Africa	27	+2
Spain	34	+1
Sri Lanka	94	+5½
Sudan	249	+2
Suriname	597	−3
Swaziland	268	+2
Sweden	46	+1
Switzerland	41	+1
Syria	963	+2
Tajikistan	992	+5
Tanzania	255	+3
Thailand	66	+7
Timor-Leste	670	+9
Togo	228	0
Tonga	676	+13
Trinidad and Tobago	1 868	−4
Tunisia	216	+1
Turkey	90	+2
Turkmenistan	993	+5
Tuvalu	688	+12
Uganda	256	+3
Ukraine	380	+2
United Arab Emirates	971	+4
United Kingdom	44	0
United Kingdom Crown Dependencies	44	0
United Kingdom Overseas Territories:		
Anguilla	1 264	−4
Ascension Island	247	0
Bermuda	1 441	−4
British Virgin Islands	1 284	−4
Cayman Islands	1 345	−5
Diego Garcia (British Indian Ocean Territory)	246	+5
Falkland Islands	500	−4
Gibraltar	350	+1
Montserrat	1 664	−4
Pitcairn Islands	872	−8
Saint Helena	290	0
Tristan da Cunha	2 897	0
Turks and Caicos Islands	1 649	−5
United States of America	1	−5 to −10
United States Commonwealth Territories:		
Northern Mariana Islands	1 670	+10
Puerto Rico	1 787	−4
United States External Territories:		
American Samoa	1 684	−11
Guam	1 671	+10
United States Virgin Islands	1 340	−4
Uruguay	598	−3
Uzbekistan	998	+5
Vanuatu	678	+11
Vatican City	39	+1
Venezuela	58	−4
Viet Nam	84	+7
Yemen	967	+3
Zambia	260	+2
Zimbabwe	263	+2

* The times listed compare the standard (winter) times in the various countries. Some countries adopt Summer (Daylight Saving) Time—i.e. +1 hour—for part of the year.

Europa World *Plus*

Free trial available!

Europa World and the Europa Regional Surveys of the World online

www.europaworld.com

Europa World *Plus* enables you to subscribe to Europa World together with as many of the nine Regional Surveys of the World online as you choose, in one simple annual subscription.

The Europa Regional Surveys of the World complement and expand upon the information in Europa World with in-depth, expert analysis at regional, sub-regional and country level.

Providing:
* An interactive online library for all the countries and territories of each of the world regions
* Impartial coverage of issues of regional importance from acknowledged experts
* A vast range of up-to-date economic, political and statistical data
* Book and periodical bibliographies - direct you to further research

* Extensive directory of research institutes specializing in the region
* Ability to search by content type across regions
* Thousands of click-through web links to external sites

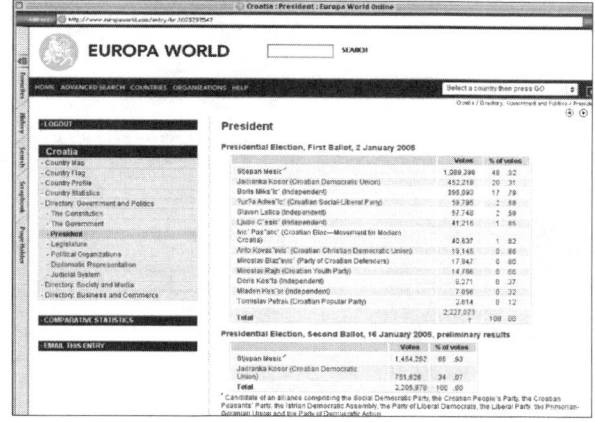

The nine titles that make up the series are as follows: *Africa South of the Sahara*; *Central and South-Eastern Europe*; *Eastern Europe, Russia and Central Asia*; *The Far East and Australasia*; *The Middle East and North Africa*; *South America, Central America and the Caribbean*; *South Asia*; *The USA and Canada*; *Western Europe*.

For further information and to register for a free trial please contact us at:
Tel: + 44 (0) 20 7017 6608/6131
Fax: + 44 (0) 20 7017 6720
E-mail: reference.online@tandf.co.uk

KAZAKHSTAN

Introductory Survey

Location, Climate, Language, Religion, Flag, Capital

The Republic of Kazakhstan (formerly the Kazakh Soviet Socialist Republic) is the second largest of the former Soviet republics, extending some 1,900 km (1,200 miles) from the Volga river in the west to the Altai mountains in the east, and about 1,300 km from the Siberian plain in the north to the Central Asian deserts in the south. To the south it borders Turkmenistan, Uzbekistan and Kyrgyzstan. To the east the border is with the People's Republic of China. There is a long border in the north with Russia and a coastline of 2,320 km on the Caspian Sea in the south-west. The climate is of a strongly continental type, but there are wide variations throughout the territory. Average temperatures in January range from −18°C (0°F) in the north to −3°C (27°F) in the south. In July average temperatures are 19°C (66°F) in the north and 28°C–30°C (82°F–86°F) in the south. Similarly, average annual rainfall in mountainous regions reaches 1,600 mm (63 ins), whereas in the central desert areas it is less than 100 mm (4 ins). The state language is Kazakh; however, Russian is employed officially in state and local government bodies. The predominant religion is Islam, most ethnic Kazakhs being Sunni Muslims of the Hanafi school. Other ethnic groups have their own religious communities, notably the (Christian) Eastern Orthodox Church, which is attended mainly by Slavs. The national flag (proportions 1 by 2) consists of a light blue field, at the centre of which is a yellow sun disc surrounded by 32 rays), framed by the wings of a flying eagle, also in yellow, with a vertical stripe of national ornamentation in yellow near the hoist. In November 1997 the capital is moved from Almaty to Akmola (formerly Tselinograd), now known as Astana.

Recent History

After the February Revolution and the Bolshevik *coup d'état* in Russia in 1917, there was civil war throughout Kazakhstan, which had come under Russian control the first half of the 18th century. Bolshevik forces finally overcame those of the White Army, foreign interventionists and local nationalists. In 1920 the Kyrgyz Autonomous Soviet Socialist Republic (ASSR) was created within the Russian Soviet Federative Socialist Republic (the Russian Federation): the Kazakhs were known to the Russians as Kyrgyz, to distinguish them from unrelated Cossacks. In 1925 the Kyrgyz ASSR was renamed the Kazakh ASSR; the Karakalpak region (now in Uzbekistan, as Qoraqalpog'iston) was detached in 1930, and became an autonomous republic within the Uzbek Soviet Socialist Republic (SSR) in 1936. In December 1936 the Kazakh ASSR became a full Union Republic of the USSR, the Kazakh SSR.

Under Soviet rule parts of Kazakhstan were heavily industrialized. However, more than 1m. people were estimated to have died as a result of the starvation that accompanied the campaign in the early 1930s to collectivize agriculture and settle nomadic peoples. There was severe repression from the 1930s, and Russian immigration greatly increased. Many of those deported from parts of the USSR during the Second World War (including Germans, Crimean Tatars, Baltic and Ukrainian peoples) were sent to Kazakhstan. During Nikita Khrushchev's period in office as Soviet leader (1953–64) large areas of previously uncultivated land in Kazakhstan were transformed into arable land under the 'Virgin Lands' programme. This and other schemes, including nuclear-testing sites in eastern Kazakhstan, the Baikonur space centre and the huge industrial complexes in the north and east, brought large numbers of ethnic Russians to Kazakhstan; the proportion of Russians increased from 1% of the population in 1926 to 42.7% in 1959.

In December 1986 some 3,000 people took part in protests in the capital, Almaty (Alma-Ata), after Gennadii Kolbin, an ethnic Russian, was appointed First Secretary of the Communist Party of Kazakhstan (CPK), in place of the popular but corrupt Dinmukhamed Kunayev, an ethnic Kazakh. In June 1989 Nursultan Nazarbayev, a prominent ethnic Kazakh, who had been Chairman of the republic's Council of Ministers since March 1984, was appointed First Secretary of the CPK. Nazarbayev advocated economic reform, while emphasizing the need for political stability. Political and administrative changes were instituted in September 1989: a permanent Supreme Soviet (Supreme Kenges—Supreme Council—legislature) was to be established, and elections were to be conducted on a multi-candidate basis. In addition, the state duties that had hitherto been the responsibility of the First Secretary of the CPK were transferred to the office of the Chairman of the Kazakhstani Supreme Soviet, to which post Nazarbayev was elected in February 1990. Many candidates stood unopposed at elections to the Supreme Soviet in March, and the system of reserved seats for CPK-affiliated organizations was retained, resulting in a substantial communist majority. In April the new body elected Nazarbayev to the newly established post of President of Kazakhstan.

On 25 October 1990 the Kazakhstani Supreme Soviet declared its sovereignty, asserting republican control over natural resources and the economy. Although the declaration emphasized ethnic equality, there were protests in the predominantly Slav-populated city of Ust-Kamenogorsk; Kazakh nationalist groups, meanwhile, judged the declaration too weak. Nazarbayev strongly supported a redefinition of the respective all-Union and republican powers, and the Kazakhstani Government participated in discussions on the new Union Treaty in early 1991. However, Nazarbayev also sought economic sovereignty for Kazakhstan, where some 90% of enterprises were under all-Union control.

In the referendum on the future of the USSR conducted in nine Soviet republics in March 1991, almost 90% of the electorate voted in Kazakhstan, of whom 94% endorsed the proposal to preserve the USSR as a 'union of sovereign states with equal rights'. In June the Kazakhstani Supreme Soviet voted, in principle, to adopt a draft union treaty. Kazakhstan was to sign the treaty in August, but the event was forestalled by the attempted *coup d'état*, led by conservative communists, in Moscow, the Soviet and Russian capital. As the coup attempt collapsed, Nazarbayev resigned from the Politburo and Central Committee of the Communist Party of the Soviet Union (CPSU), in protest at the open support granted to the putschists by the CPSU leadership. The CPK was ordered to cease activities in state and government organs, and in September the party withdrew from the CPSU; it was re-formed as the independent Socialist Party of Kazakhstan (SPK).

On 1 December 1991 Nazarbayev was elected President of Kazakhstan in direct popular elections, as the sole candidate. On 8 December the leaders of Russia, Ukraine and Belarus signed an agreement establishing the Commonwealth of Independent States (CIS, see p. 201). On 16 December Kazakhstan became the last of the republics to declare independence from the USSR, and was redesignated the Republic of Kazakhstan. The country was formally recognized as a co-founder of the CIS on 21 December, when the leaders of 11 former Soviet countries met in Almaty.

Kazakhstan did not experience the inter-ethnic violence that affected several former Soviet republics, but some unrest was reported during 1992, particularly among Kazakhstan's ethnic Russian community (which at that time constituted an estimated 38% of the total population, while ethnic Kazakhs comprised 40%). The Constitution, adopted in January 1993, invoked legislation adopted in September 1989, denoting Kazakh as the state language, and Russian as a language of inter-ethnic communication. The document also required that the President be fluent in Kazakh. Meanwhile, increased emigration, particularly by ethnic Germans (more than 300,000 of whom left Kazakhstan in the early 1990s) and Russians, was accompanied, albeit on a much smaller scale, by the return of ethnic Kazakhs from, most notably, Kyrgyzstan, Mongolia, Tajikistan and Turkmenistan.

In June 1991 some 5,000 people demonstrated in Almaty against continued communist predominance in the Government and Supreme Council (as the legislature was now styled), demanding the formation of a new, coalition administration. In October the three most prominent nationalist opposition parties (the Azat movement, the Republican Party and the Jeltoqsan National Democratic Party) united to form the Republican Party—Azat (RP—A). The Union of National Unity of Kazakhstan was established in February 1993, with the declared aim of promoting social harmony and countering radical nationalism. Nazarbayev (who had held no party affiliation since August 1991) became Chairman of the Union, which was reorganized as a political party, the People's Unity Party (PUP), later in 1993.

In December 1993 the Supreme Kenges voted to dissolve itself and to grant Nazarbayev the power to rule by decree pending elections to a new standing legislature, which was to be reduced in size from 360 to 177 seats. Kazakhstan's first multi-party elections were duly held on 7 March 1994, with the participation of 74% of the electorate; a number of irregularities were reported by international observers. The final composition of the new legislature was reported to be 59% Kazakh and 28% Russian. The PUP obtained 33 seats, which, when combined with the 42 seats won by candidates from the so-called 'President's List' (candidates nominated by Nazarbayev) and those of pro-Nazarbayev independents, ensured that Nazarbayev's supporters emerged as the strongest force in the assembly. The Confederation of Kazakhstani Trade Unions (CKTU) won 11 seats, the People's Congress Party of Kazakhstan (PCPK) nine and the SPK eight. After several unsuccessful attempts at re-establishment, the CPK was granted legal status in March. In May the CPK (claiming a membership of some 50,000) and other opposition parties, including the SPK, the PCPK and the RP—A, together with the CKTU, formed an opposition bloc in the Supreme Kenges, with the stated aim of acting as a guarantor against 'dictatorship by executive bodies'.

In May 1994 96 members of the Supreme Kenges endorsed a motion expressing 'no confidence' in the Government's economic, social and legal policies, and in June Nazarbayev announced a major government reorganization, in an attempt to stimulate economic reform. The Government of Sergei Tereshchenko (the Prime Minister since 1991) resigned in October 1994, admitting its failure to reform the economy. Akezhan Kazhegeldin, an economist and First Deputy Prime Minister in the outgoing Council of Ministers, was appointed premier.

In February 1995 the Constitutional Court declared the results of the 1994 general election to be null and void, owing to procedural irregularities. Following an unsuccessful attempt by the Supreme Kenges to amend the Constitution in order to overrule the Court's decision, in March 1995 the Government was forced to tender its resignation, on the grounds that it had been approved by an unconstitutional parliament (although it was subsequently reinstated virtually unchanged). Nazarbayev was thus effectively empowered to rule by decree pending further legislative elections. At a national referendum on 29 April more than 95% of voters endorsed the extension of Nazarbayev's five-year mandate until 1 December 2000; the President had asserted that the measure was necessary to ensure political stability.

In May 1995 Nazarbayev ordered the establishment of a special council to prepare (under his guidance) a new constitution. Opposition activists denounced provisions whereby, they considered, the President would be guaranteed 'unchecked rule'. The final draft, which was approved by 89.1% of the electorate in a referendum on 30 August, preserved the President's extensive executive powers. The Supreme Kenges was replaced by a bicameral Parliament, comprising a 47-member Senate (the upper chamber—with 40 members elected by Kazakhstan's regional administrative bodies and seven appointed by the President) and a directly elected, 67-member Majlis (Assembly). The Constitutional Court was replaced by a Constitutional Council, the rulings of which were to be subject to a presidential right of veto.

At elections to the Senate held on 5 December 1995, 38 of the 40 regionally elected seats were filled; Nazarbayev duly appointed seven senators. Direct elections were held to the Majlis on 9 December, with the participation of 80.7% of the electorate; further rounds of voting took place later in the month and in February 1996, in those constituencies where no candidate had obtained the requisite 50% of the votes. Foreign observers reported procedural violations.

Popular dissatisfaction with the Government's economic and social policies became more pronounced in 1996. In April a new opposition movement, Citizen (Azamat), was established. Prolonged delays in payments of wages, owing to the insolvency of numerous state-owned enterprises, were a principal cause of strikes and unauthorized demonstrations throughout 1997 and early 1998. The ongoing reform of pensions legislation also provoked protests. Legislation regulating the pensions system was approved by the Majlis in May 1997 and by Nazarbayev in June. Opponents of the new legislation (effective from January 1998) claimed that it would lead to the curtailment of many social guarantees. Meanwhile, demonstrations were held, in protest at the non-payment of pensions (arrears amounted to some US $500m. in May 1997). Payment of pensions arrears commenced in August, and by February 1998 it was announced that all such arrears had been cleared.

Meanwhile, in late 1996 the relocation of civil servants from Almaty to the northern city of Akmola (formerly Tselinograd) marked the beginning of the transfer of the capital city (in July 1994 the Supreme Kenges had approved a proposal by Nazarbayev to transfer the capital to Akmola by 2000). In November 1997 the new capital was officially inaugurated by Nazarbayev, and a joint session of both chambers of Parliament was held for the first time in Akmola in the following month. However, the costly transfer attracted widespread criticism, and it was reported that the initial stages had been poorly managed. None the less, a ceremony was held in early June 1998 to mark the official opening of the capital under the new name of Astana ('Capital City'—a presidential decree changing the name of the capital had been issued in May).

In March 1997 Nazarbayev reduced the number of ministries and other government agencies from 48 to 25 as part of a major reorganization of the state apparatus. The Ministry of Petroleum and Natural Gas was abolished and replaced by a new state company, KazakhOil. Seven government institutions, including the Ministries of Defence and of Internal Affairs, became directly subordinate to the President, and the structure of regional government was reorganized. The fact that these changes had been made while Kazhegeldin was out of the country led to speculation that the President's confidence in the Prime Minister had begun to decline. In September a Russian newspaper published an admission by Kazhegeldin of his involvement, in the late 1980s, with the former Soviet state security service (KGB). It was announced in October that Kazhegeldin had resigned, ostensibly for health reasons. Nazarbayev appointed Nurlan Balgymbayev, hitherto head of KazakhOil and the former Minister of Petroleum and Natural Gas, as his replacement.

In January 1998, in an apparent attempt to counter increasing opposition to Nazarbayev, 17 political parties and movements signed a 'memorandum mutual understanding and co-operation', pledging their support for the President's policies and reforms. However, political tensions were revived in April, when an opposition leader was sentenced to one year's imprisonment, having been convicted of insulting the President during an unauthorized rally in November 1997.

In September 1998 Nazarbayev outlined proposals for political reforms, including amendments to electoral procedures and enhanced legislative powers. In October, however, a joint session of Parliament rejected Nazarbayev's proposed constitutional reforms, amid apparent concern that the President was attempting to mitigate his penal responsibility in the event of a future economic or political crisis. The session subsequently voted in favour of a parliamentary amendment whereby a presidential election would take place before the expiry of Nazarbayev's extended mandate in 2000. Other amendments included a decrease in the percentage of votes required by parties in order to secure representation in the legislature, from 10% to 7%.

During November 1998 several opposition figures were deemed ineligible to contest the presidency by the Central Electoral Commission accordance with a presidential decree, enacted in May which prevented those convicted of an administrative offence in the 12 months prior to an election from registering as a candidate. The most prominent disqualification was that of Kazhegeldin, who had been widely regarded as Nazarbayev's principal rival: his offence was to have attended a meeting of an unauthorized political organization, the Movement for Honest Elections. Kazhegeldin subsequently established a new political party, the Republican People's Party of Kazakhstan (RPPK) which was inaugurated in December. A number of other opposition parties were formed in late 1998 and early 1999, although many were prevented from registering. Among those to be awarded official status was the pro-presidential Fatherland Republican Political Party (Fatherland—Otan).

The Organization for Security and Co-operation in Europe (OSCE, see p. 27) was among international bodies to express serious concern at conduct of the presidential election, held on 10 January 1999 despite appeals for a postponement. The election, contested four candidates, resulted in victory for the incumbent, with 8% of the votes cast by 88.3% of the registered electorate. Nazarbayev was sworn in on 20 January, and a new Government, headed by Balgymbayev, was appointed two days later.

In August 1999 the President of KazakhOil, Nurlan Kaparov, was dismissed, accused by Nazarbayev of having exceeded his powers. Earlier that month both the Minister of Defence, Gen. Mukhtar Altynbayev, and the Chairman of the National Security Committee (KNB), Nurtai Abykayev, had been dismissed, after admitting responsibility for the attempted illegal sale of military aircraft to the Democratic People's Republic of Korea.

In early September 1999 Kazhegeldin, who had been charged with tax evasion in April, was arrested at Moscow airport, but released following criticism of his detention by the OSCE. Owing to the outstanding charges against him, Kazhegeldin, together with two other leading members of the RPPK, was barred from registering as a candidate for the parliamentary elections in October. (Further charges were brought against him in late February 2000.)

In late September 1999 the RPPK announced that it would boycott the forthcoming elections to the Majlis, in protest at the severe restrictions imposed on opposition parties by the President, although some of the party's members were to stand as independents. In early October Balgymbayev resigned the premiership and resumed his former position as President of KazakhOil. He was replaced as Prime Minister by Kasymzhomart Tokayev, a former Minister of Foreign Affairs. A government reorganization followed. Elections to the Majlis (as well as to municipal and local councils) were held on 10 October. According to official reports, 65 candidates from nine political parties contested 10 seats allocated, for the first time, according to a party-list system, and almost 500 candidates competed for the remaining 67 seats in single-mandate constituencies. Although all of the 10 party-list seats were filled at the first round (with Fatherland winning four seats and the CPK, the Agrarian Party of Kazakhstan and the Civic Party of Kazakhstan—founded in the previous year—each taking two), only 20 of the 67 directly elected seats were filled, and a second round of voting was held on 24 October. Final results indicated that Fatherland was to be the largest political grouping in the new Majlis, with 23 seats; the Civic Party held 13. Three other parties achieved representation, and 34 seats were taken by independent candidates. The rate of participation by voters was reported to be 62.6%. Observers from the OSCE cited numerous breaches of electoral law.

In June 2000 a law was passed awarding President Nazarbayev certain lifetime guarantees and rights, as the first President of Kazakhstan. Despite opposition protests, the Constitutional Court upheld the legislation in the following month.

In June 2001 a month-long amnesty was declared, to allow the return of capital that had been transferred abroad in violation of financial legislation; the Chairman of the National Bank of Kazakhstan (NBK) subsequently announced that US $480m. had been returned to domestic banks. However, the amnesty attracted criticism from Kazhegeldin, who claimed that the sale of petroleum had accounted for some $2,000m. in illegal transfers to Caribbean banks in 2000. In September 2001 Kazhegeldin, who had been tried *in absentia* on charges of abuse of power, tax evasion and the illegal possession of weapons, was sentenced to 10 years' imprisonment; there were allegations that his trial had been politically motivated.

In November 2001 Nazarbayev approved the resignation of Rakhat Aliyev as Deputy Chairman of the KNB, amid accusations of abuse of power. Persistent reports that Aliyev, the husband of Nazarbayev's daughter, Darigha Nazarbayeva, controlled the majority of Kazakhstan's media outlets, and influenced their output, prompted the Akim (governor) of Pavlodar Oblast, Galymzhan Zhakiyanov, and a number of other prominent political and business figures, including the Deputy Prime Minister, Uraz Jandosov, to form a new political movement, the Democratic Choice of Kazakhstan (DCK), in late November. The DCK, which aimed to revive democratic reform, decentralize political power and ensure the freedom of the mass media, criticized the concentration of power among members of Nazarbayev's family and a small group of leading entrepreneurs. Prime Minister Tokayev subsequently announced that two attempts to assassinate the President had been averted, and threatened to tender his resignation unless the President dismissed ministers whom he denounced as disloyal, owing to their involvement in the formation of the DCK. Jandosov, Alikhan Baymenov (the Minister of Labour and Social Security) and two deputy ministers resigned shortly afterwards, announcing that they were unable to work with the Prime Minister; Nazarbayev dismissed Zhakiyanov on the same day. In December the Azamat Democratic Party, the PCPK and the RPPK announced their intention to merge to form the United Democratic Party (UDP). The UDP, which was established in early 2002, declared its main aim to be the creation of a parliamentary republic, with a unicameral legislature and a new constitution, to be adopted by means of a referendum.

Meanwhile, in December 2001 Gen. Mukhtar Altynbayev was reappointed Minister of Defence. In January 2002 amendments to media legislation came into effect, which required 50% of all radio and television programmes to be broadcast in Kazakh, restricted the rebroadcast of foreign (mainly Russian) television programmes, and subjected internet sites to the same controls as print media. In mid-January a further assassination attempt against the President was reported to have been thwarted by the security services. In late January Tokayev announced his resignation. Some observers believed Tokayev's resignation to have been prompted by divisions within the political élite, and others agreed that the high-profile ministerial resignations of November 2001 had discredited the Prime Minister. On 31 January 2002 a new Government was sworn in, led by a former Deputy Prime Minister, Imangali Tasmagambetov; Tokayev was appointed State Secretary and Minister of Foreign Affairs. Meanwhile, divisions emerged within the DCK as a number of its founding members, including Jandosov and Zhakiyanov, formed a new party, Light Road (Ak Zhol), which held its founding congress in March.

Also in March 2002 a warrant was issued for the arrest of Zhakiyanov, on charges of abuse of power during his tenure as Akim of Pavlodar Oblast. He subsequently sought refuge in the French embassy until early April, when agreement was reached between the Government and the ambassadors of France, Germany, the United Kingdom and the USA that Zhakiyanov would be permitted to go free until an investigation into the allegations had been carried out. However, less than one week later he was arrested and flown to Pavlodar, in contravention of the agreement, to assist the police there with their enquiries. In mid-May it was reported that Zhakiyanov had been admitted to hospital following interrogation by security officials. Zhakiyanov's trial commenced in July, and he was sentenced to a seven-year term in early August.

Meanwhile, in early April 2002 Prime Minister Tasmagambetov confirmed allegations that a clandestine state foreign-bank account, funded by the sale of a 20% stake in the large Tengiz oil field, had been established in 1996, reportedly in an attempt to prevent unexpected increases in consumer-price inflation. The Prime Minister stated that the account's foundation had been authorized by Kazhegeldin, and that money from the account had been used to settle pensions arrears in 1997–98. The remaining funds had subsequently been transferred to the National Fund, which was officially established in 2001.

At the end of April 2002 a new National Council was established by presidential decree, to function as an advisory and consultative body. In mid-July Nazarbayev signed into law controversial new legislation on political parties, which required a party to demonstrate that it had at least 50,000 members (rather than the previous 3,000), representing every administrative region of the country, in order to qualify for registration. In the same month a former Minister of Energy, Industry and Trade and founding member of the DCK, Mukhtar Ablyazov, was sentenced to six years' imprisonment, having been found guilty of abuse of office. In late August Nazarbayev carried out a reorganization of the Government. On 8 October partial elections to fill 16 seats in the Senate took place; Fatherland remained the largest grouping in the chamber, accounting for 18 of the 47 senators.

In early January 2003 it was reported that Jandosov had been appointed as an aide to President Nazarbayev, suggesting to many observers that Light Road was in fact supportive of the incumbent leadership. In the same month the DCK's party registration was annulled by the Ministry of Justice, and in mid-January the establishment of a new opposition bloc, Democracy-Elections-Kazakhstan, was announced, with the aim of uniting those parties prevented from re-registering by the new legislation on political parties. By the end of the re-registration period in April, only seven parties had satisfied the criteria for registration.

In late January 2003 Sergei Duvanov, an independent journalist, was convicted of rape and sentenced to more than three years' imprisonment. He had been arrested in October 2002, shortly before he was due to travel to the USA to speak about press freedoms and human rights issues. Duvanov's conviction prompted the US embassy to express concern about judicial procedure during his trial, and in mid-February 2003 the European Parliament adopted a resolution condemning the sentences awarded to Duvanov and the opposition politicians Ablyazov and Zhakiyanov, and demanding that an independent investigation into their trials be carried out. Ablyazov was pardoned in May, and subsequently announced his withdrawal from politics. (Duvanov was released in August 2004, and Zhakiyanov was released on parole in January 2006.) Meanwhile, in March 2003 Nazarbayev's links with US petroleum companies came under scrutiny, when a US businessman was indicted in the USA for allegedly offering financial incentives to Kazakhstani officials, in an attempt to influence the award of important contracts (see below).

In mid-May 2003 the Government defeated a parliamentary vote of 'no confidence', prompted by opposition to government plans to introduce legislation on land reform, which would permit the private ownership of land. However, on 9 June Tasmagambetov tendered his resignation, after it emerged that the results of the 'no confidence' vote had been falsified by supporters of the Government (although it was reported that Tasmagambetov was not implicated in the fraud). A new Government, led by Daniyal Akhmetov, a former Akim of Pavlodar Oblast, was appointed in June, which included more than two-thirds of the ministers of the outgoing administration. The controversial land-reform bill was approved by Parliament on 20 June.

In mid-September 2003 Zautbek Turisbekov was appointed as Minister of Internal Affairs, replacing Col-Gen. Kairbek Suleimonov, after Nazarbayev reportedly decreed that the heads of the law-enforcement and security bodies should be civilian appointments. Elections to local councils took place on 20 September, with further rounds of voting in October–November. The OSCE was again critical of the conduct of the electoral process.

In late October 2003 a new party, Mutual Help (Asar), led by Darigha Nazarbayeva, was officially registered. Some observers speculated that the establishment of the party by Nazarbayev's daughter was part of a long-term strategy to prepare for the succession. However, at the end of January 2004 it was reported that Nazarbayev had stated his intention to stand for re-election. In March Nurtai Abykayev was appointed as Chairman of the Senate. In early May four political parties that had not been granted official registration were declared invalid by a court ruling: Kazakh Ely, the Republican People's Party of Kazakhstan, the Azamat Party and the People's Congress of Kazakhstan. However, in mid-June the Ministry of Justice officially registered the People's Communist Party of Kazakhstan and the Democratic Party of Kazakhstan (DPK).

On 19 September 2004 elections took place to the Majlis, with 'run-off' elections held on 3 October in 22 constituencies where no candidate had received an overall majority of the votes cast. Fatherland emerged as the largest grouping, with 42 seats, giving it an absolute majority in the chamber. The next largest group of deputies was formed by an electoral coalition of the Agrarian Party of Kazakhstan and the Civic Party of Kazakhstan (known as Aist), with 11 seats, while Mutual Help obtained four seats. Light Road and the Democratic Party of Kazakhstan each obtained one seat, and 18 non-partisan candidates were elected. The rate of participation by the electorate was 56.7% in the first round of voting and 45.2% in the second round. Monitors from the OSCE criticized the conduct of the polls, in particular maintaining that media coverage had been biased towards pro-Government parties. Alikhan Baymenov of Light Road, who was effectively the only opposition representative elected to the new legislature, subsequently announced that he would not take up his seat in the Majlis, alleging that the results of the elections had been falsified. The Chairman of the outgoing legislature, Zharmakhan Tuyakbai, resigned from Fatherland in mid-October in order to protest against the conduct of the elections. At the inaugural session of the new Majlis, held on 3 November, Ural Mukhamejanov was elected Chairman.

In early December 2004, apparently in response to mass protests in Ukraine against the alleged falsification of presidential election results in that country (see the chapter on Ukraine), the DCK declared that it regarded the Kazakhstani Government to be illegitimate and urged non-violent civil disobedience. In early January 2005 a court ordered that the DCK be dismantled, alleging that a recent statement by the party had breached national security laws. Later in the month at least 1,000 people took part in an unsanctioned rally organized by Light Road, the DCK and the Communist Party of Kazakhstan (CPK) to protest against the closure of the party; in October 2004 the three parties had established a Co-ordinating Council of Opposition Democratic Forces of Kazakhstan, which aimed to draft a new constitution and create a more influential democratic movement in the country. Seven members of the DCK were fined and sentenced to gaol terms of between two and seven days. In early February 2005 the Co-ordinating Council of Opposition Democratic Forces of Kazakhstan announced that it was establishing a working group to formulate the principles of a new national movement, to be known as For a Just Kazakhstan. In late March former members of the DCK announced the establishment of a new grouping, Forward (Alga), led by Asylbek Kozhakhmetov. (However, in February 2006 the party was refused registration.) In late April 2005 another new party, True Light Road (Naghyz Ak Zhol), held its founding congress, following divisions within Light Road.

In late April 2005 a law was introduced prohibiting demonstrations both during and after elections, and in late June the Majlis approved legislation, which required, *inter alia*, all religious organizations and communities to register with the state authorities. Concern was expressed at an announcement in early July that the security agencies were preparing to use force against any popular unrest that might arise around the time of the forthcoming presidential election: the Minister of Internal Affairs, Zauytbek Turisbekov, asserted that the country would not allow a repetition of the events that had taken place in 2003–05 in Georgia, Ukraine and Kyrgyzstan (where popular revolts, resulting from disputed elections, had led to the collapse of the incumbent regimes). In early August 2005 the For a Just Kazakhstan movement, led by former parliamentary Chairman Zharmakhan Tuyakbai, and comprising the Communist Party of Kazakhstan, Forward, the Generation Pensioners' Movement and True Light Road, was officially registered with the Ministry of Justice.

Meanwhile, in early December 2004 President Nazarbayev had issued a decree allowing village akims to be elected, and providing for 'experimental' elections of akims (who had hitherto been appointed) in several oblasts. Elections were duly held in four oblasts in mid-August 2005. (Elections of village akims had been conducted earlier in the year.) Opposition representatives criticized the small number of administrative units covered. The fact that all of the candidates (who had been proposed by the local authorities) were already akims of various oblasts and, moreover, that the incumbent candidates were all re-elected also attracted criticism.

On 19 August 2005 partial elections to the Senate, originally scheduled to be held in December, took place. Fatherland secured 10 of the 16 seats contested; three seats were won by other pro-Nazarbayev parties and three by independents. In early September the Majlis confirmed that a presidential election would be held on 4 December (rather than in December 2006, as anticipated). Later in September the For a Just Kazakhstan movement elected Tuyakbai to stand as its single opposition candidate in the election. In mid-November 2005 a former Akim of Almaty City and of Almaty Oblast, Zamanbek Nurkadilov, died as a result of gunshot wounds. (In early June Nurkadilov, a supporter of For a Just Kazakhstan, had been found guilty of defamation of the President, and ordered to pay damages.) In late December an official investigation concluded that Nurkadilov had committed suicide.

In the presidential ballot, conducted on 4 December 2005, Nazarbayev was re-elected as President, with 91.2% of the votes cast, according to official preliminary results; his candidacy was supported by an electoral bloc, the Popular Coalition, which included Fatherland, Mutual Help, the DPK, the Agrarian Party of Kazakhstan and the Civic Party of Kazakhstan. Of the four other candidates, Nazarbayev's closest rival was Tuyakbai, who received some 6.6% of the votes. The rate of participation by the electorate was about 76.8%. Monitors from the OSCE declared that the conduct of the election had not satisfied international standards of democracy, but CIS observers announced that the election had been free and fair. Nazarbayev was inaugurated on 11 January 2006, and the Government duly resigned, in accordance with the Constitution. On 18 January the bicameral Parliament unanimously approved Nazarbayev's nomination of Daniyal Akhmetov as Prime Minister. Following Akhmetov's re-appointment, on 19 March Nazarbayev approved his new Government, the composition of which was largely unchanged from the previous administration. New appointments included that of Natalya Korzhova as Minister of Finance.

In mid-February 2006 three men, including Altynbek Sarsenbayev, one of the leaders of True Light Road and a prominent supporter of Tuyakbai's presidential campaign, were shot and killed in Almaty. A special commission was established to investigate Sarsenbayev's murder, which opposition representatives claimed had been politically motivated. Those detained on suspicion of involvement in the case included five KNB officials and the head of the administration of the Senate, Erzhan Utembayev. In late February the head of the KNB, Nartai Dutbayev, tendered his resignation as a result of the investigation (he was replaced by Amangeldy Shabdarbayev in early March). An unsanctioned protest rally was held in Almaty in late February, at which demonstrators urged the authorities to end the persecution of opposition representatives and to bring the murderers to trial; a number of organizers of the demonstration were later imprisoned. In early March it was reported that Utembayev had confessed to organizing the murder, although opposition representatives asserted that the true perpetrators were much more senior officials. Later in March True Light Road was granted official registration.

Relations between Kazakhstan and Russia have periodically been strained by the issue of Kazakhstan's large Russian minority (comprising some 27.2% of the total population in 2004). In early 1997 draft legislation to enhance the status of the Kazakh language attracted criticism from ethnic Russians resident in Kazakhstan. In July Parliament confirmed Kazakh as the state language, although Russian was to retain its parity with Kazakh in state organizations and as a language of inter-ethnic communication. According to official statistics, in 1997 72.4% of emigrants from Kazakhstan departed for Russia. Some 60,000 ethnic Russians were reported to have migrated to Kazakhstan from other CIS states, notably Uzbekistan, in 2003–04.

The issue of the legal status of the Caspian Sea—and the division of the substantial mineral resources believed to be located in the seabed—was a further source of tension between Kazakhstan and Russia, as well as the other littoral states (Azerbaijan, Turkmenistan and Iran). Nevertheless, in July 1998 Nazarbayev and the Russian President, Boris Yeltsin, signed a bilateral agreement on the delineation of their respective boundaries of the Caspian seabed, by which Russia for the first time formally recognized Kazakhstan's claim to, and right to exploit, its offshore petroleum resources, prompting particular criticism from Iran, which continued to assert that partitioning of the seabed required the consensus of all five littoral states. In October 2000 the Presidents of Kazakhstan and Russia signed an additional agreement, on the definition of the legal status of the Caspian Sea, and the 1998 agreement was further augmented in May 2002, when an accord was signed on the equal division of three oilfields in the northern Caspian, prompting condemnation by Iran. Russia and Kazakhstan have also signed a Treaty of Eternal Friendship and Co-operation, which provides for mutual military assistance in the event of aggression by a third party. In November 2001 Kazakhstan concluded a bilateral agreement with Azerbaijan on the two countries' respective mineral rights in the Caspian Sea, which also prompted protests from Iran. In May 2003 Azerbaijan, Kazakhstan and Russia signed a further, trilateral agreement. In November representatives of Azerbaijan, Iran, Kazakhstan, Russia and Turkmenistan, meeting in Tehran, Iran, signed a UN-sponsored framework Convention for the Protection of the Marine Environment of the Caspian Sea, which sought to alleviate environmental damage in the Caspian Sea region. In mid-January 2005 President Nazarbayev and the Russian President, Vladimir Putin, signed a treaty in Moscow defining their 7,500-km land border with Russia.

In the early 1990s the issue of the formerly Soviet, subsequently Russian-controlled, nuclear warheads deployed in Kazakhstan (effectively making the country the fourth largest nuclear power in the world) was the focus of international concern. In September 1992 the Kazakh legislature ratified the first Strategic Arms Reduction Treaty, signed by the USA and the USSR in July 1991, the provisions of which affected Kazakhstan as a (nuclear) successor state to the USSR. In December 1993 the Kazakh legislature ratified the Treaty on the Non-Proliferation of Nuclear Weapons. By April 1995 all nuclear warheads had been transferred to Russia, and in September 1996 Russia and Kazakhstan signed a final protocol governing the withdrawal of military units linked to the Russian nuclear weapons facilities in Kazakhstan. In November 2001 the Kazakh legislature ratified the Comprehensive Nuclear Test Ban Treaty.

In May 2001 the signatories of the CIS Collective Security Treaty (Armenia, Belarus, Kazakhstan, Kyrgyzstan, Russia and Tajikistan) agreed to form a Collective Rapid Reaction Force in Bishkek, Kyrgyzstan, to combat Islamist militancy in Central Asia; in January 2002 it was announced that the force was ready to undertake combat missions. An anti-terrorism centre became operational in Bishkek in August 2001. In late April 2003 a successor organization to the Collective Security Treaty was formed, when Armenia, Belarus, Kazakhstan, Kyrgyzstan, Russia and Tajikistan inaugurated the Collective Security Treaty Organization (CSTO).

In 1992 Kazakhstan joined the Economic Co-operation Organization (ECO, see p. 223), founded originally by Iran, Pakistan and Turkey. In 1994 Kazakhstan, Kyrgyzstan and Uzbekistan formed a trilateral economic area, and in February 1995 an Interstate Council was established to supervise its implementation. Several agreements to expand economic co-operation were signed by the three countries in 1996, and in December 1997 the Council met in Akmola (now Astana) to discuss the possibility of full economic integration. In March 1998 Tajikistan joined the alliance, which was renamed the Central Asian Co-operation Organization in March 2002. Meanwhile, in January 1995 Kazakhstan established a customs union with Russia and Belarus, and in March 1996 the three members of the customs union were joined by Kyrgyzstan; Tajikistan joined the union in April 1998. In October 2000 a new economic body, the Eurasian Economic Community (EurAsEc), was established to supersede the customs union. (In October 2005 EurAsEC announced that it was to merge with the Central Asian Co-operation Organization.) In September 2002 President Nazarbayev and the President of Uzbekistan, Islam Karimov, signed a bilateral agreement on the delimitation of remaining sectors of their common border (another border agreement had been signed in the previous year). A border agreement with Turkmenistan, which had been signed in July 2001, was ratified by the Kazakhstani Senate in June 2003, and in July Nazarbayev signed a number of laws confirming the delimitation of Kazakhstan's borders with Kyrgyzstan, Turkmenistan and Uzbekistan.

However, relations between Kazakhstan and Uzbekistan remained tense. In December 2004 the office of the Prosecutor-General of Uzbekistan announced that three suicide bombers who had launched an attack on the Uzbekistani capital, Tashkent, in July had been Kazakhstani citizens. In January 2005 representatives from the Uzbekistani Ministry of Defence were reported to have described Kazakhstan as a probable military adversary and a base for possible acts of terrorism against Uzbekistan. None the less, in March Presidents Nazarbayev and Karimov agreed to establish a working group to plan and oversee the creation of a free-trade zone, apparently signalling improved relations between the two countries. Nazarbayev described the suppression by government troops of a demonstration in Uzbekistan in mid-May, as a result of which at least 187 people were killed (see the chapter on Uzbekistan), as an appropriate reaction to the unrest. (The Uzbekistani Government's response to the situation had prompted international condemnation.)

In 1995 Nazarbayev made an official visit to the People's Republic of China, where an agreement was signed to improve long-term stability between the two countries, following concerns at Chinese underground nuclear tests near the border with eastern Kazakhstan. Bilateral relations were further strengthened by two accords concluded in 1997, whereby China was granted permission to exploit two of the largest oilfields in Kazakhstan. The agreements, worth an estimated US $9,500m., provided, *inter alia*, for the construction of a petroleum pipeline connecting the two countries, on which work commenced in September 2004. Construction, at an estimated cost of $700m., was completed in November 2005; exports of around 192,000 barrels of petroleum per day were expected to commence in mid-2006. China and Kazakhstan further developed their economic relationship in November 2005, when Kazakhstan agreed to export electricity worth some $10,000m. to China over a period of four to five years. Meanwhile, in late November 1998 Nazarbayev made a state visit to China, which resulted in the signature of a communiqué on the full settlement of outstanding border issues, and of an agreement outlining future bilateral relations. In July 2005 Nazarbayev and Chinese President Hu Jintao signed an agreement on the establishment of a strategic partnership between the two countries. China and Kazakhstan have attended annual summit meetings of the heads of state of the so-called Shanghai Five (also comprising

Kyrgyzstan, Russia and Tajikistan), which aimed to promote economic co-operation and regional co-ordination on border and security issues. Members of the alliance, later known as the Shanghai Forum, and renamed the Shanghai Co-operation Organization (SCO, see p. 398) upon the accession of Uzbekistan in mid-2001, signed the Shanghai Convention on Combating Terrorism, Separatism and Extremism in June 2001. In August 2003 Kazakhstan and China jointly hosted military manoeuvres involving the member states of the SCO. In July 2005, at a summit meeting in Astana, members of the SCO approved anti-terrorist measures, and signed a declaration advocating non-interference in the affairs of sovereign states.

Following the suicide attacks on the USA on 11 September 2001, President Nazarbayev expressed his support for US-led military action against the al-Qa'ida (Base) organization of the Saudi-born militant Islamist, Osama bin Laden, and the regime of its hosts, the Taliban, in Afghanistan (see the chapters on Afghanistan and the USA). The USA acknowledged Kazakhstan's strategic importance, and Kazakhstan offered the USA the use of airports, airspace and military bases. In February 2006 it was announced that US forces were to participate in Kazakhstani-British military exercises in Kazakhstan in September, and were to engage in the command component of the exercises for the first time. Meanwhile, Nazarbayev's links with US petroleum companies were subject to legal scrutiny from late March 2003, when James H. Giffen, a US businessman and former adviser to Nazarbayev, was indicted in the USA under the 1977 Foreign Corrupt Practices Act (which prohibits US companies or individuals from offering financial inducements to foreign officials in order to secure an agreement). He was accused of offering bribes to prominent Kazakhstani politicians, including Nazarbayev and former Prime Minister Nurlan Balgymbayev, in return for securing valuable contracts for US petroleum companies. In April 2004 a US federal court indicted Giffen and a Mobil executive on charges of corrupt business practices. However, in October 2005 a judge allowed Giffen to use classified information in his defence as evidence that the US Government had endorsed his actions: since the information allegedly threatened the security interests of the USA, it was considered possible that the charges against him could be withdrawn.

Government

Under the terms of the 1995 Constitution (to which a number of amendments were made in October 1998), the President of the Republic is Head of State and commander-in-chief of the armed forces, and holds broad executive powers. The President is directly elected by universal adult suffrage for a seven-year term (and may serve a maximum of two consecutive terms). The Government, headed by the Prime Minister, is responsible to the President. The supreme legislative organ is the bicameral Parliament, comprising the 39-member Senate (upper chamber) and the 77-member Majlis (Assembly, lower chamber). Seven Senators are appointed by the President of the Republic, and the remaining 32 are elected for six years by regional assemblies. The deputies of the Majlis are directly elected every six years. One-half of the elected deputies in the Senate are subject to election every three years. The seven-member Constitutional Council is empowered to ensure the correct implementation of the Constitution; its rulings are subject to a presidential right of veto.

For administrative purposes, Kazakhstan is divided into 16 local governments (14 regions and the cities of Almaty and Astana). (The city of Leninsk—now Turatam—serving the Baikonur space centre, and formerly one of Kazakhstan's administrative units, was transferred to Russian jurisdiction in August 1995. In January 2004 President Nazarbayev and the Russian President, Vladimir Putin, signed an agreement permitting Russia's continued use of the Baikonur space centre until 2050.)

Defence

In May 1992 President Nursultan Nazarbayev issued a decree on the establishment of Kazakhstan's armed forces (until independence, Kazakhstan had no armed forces separate from those of the USSR). By August 2005 the estimated strength of the national armed forces was 65,800 (army 46,800 and air force 19,000). In addition, there were 34,500 paramilitary troops (including an estimated 20,000 troops attached to the Ministry of Internal Affairs, and an estimated 12,000 border guards). Kazakhstan participates, with Russia, Azerbaijan and Turkmenistan, in the operation of the Caspian Sea Flotilla, a former Soviet force based, under Russian command, at Astrakhan (Russia). In mid-1992 Kazakhstan signed a Collective Security Treaty with five other members of the Commonwealth of Independent States (CIS, see p. 201); in May 2001 it was announced that the signatory countries were to form a Collective Rapid Reaction Force to combat Islamist militancy in Central Asia. In April 2003 the Collective Security Treaty Organization (CSTO) was inaugurated as the successor to the CIS collective security system, with the participation of Armenia, Belarus, Kazakhstan, Kyrgyzstan, Russia and Tajikistan. A nuclear successor state to the USSR, Kazakhstan undertook to dismantle its nuclear capabilities, ratifying the first Strategic Arms Reduction Treaty in 1992 and the Treaty on the Non-Proliferation of Nuclear Weapons in 1993. All nuclear warheads had been transferred to Russia by mid-1995, and a final protocol for the withdrawal of the Russian strategic-missile troops was signed in September 1996. In July 2000 the Semipalatinsk nuclear facility, once the world's largest nuclear-testing ground, was finally closed. In late 2001 Kazakhstan ratified the Comprehensive Nuclear Test Ban Treaty. In May 1994 Kazakhstan joined the North Atlantic Treaty Organization's (NATO) 'Partnership for Peace' (see p. 316) programme of military co-operation. Kazakhstan became a full member of the UN Conference on Disarmament in August 1999. The defence budget for 2005 was an estimated 54,900m. tenge.

Economic Affairs

In 2004, according to estimates by the World Bank, Kazakhstan's gross national income (GNI), measured at average 2002–04 prices, was US $33,780m., equivalent to $2,260 per head (or $6,980 per head on an international purchasing-power parity basis). During 1995–2004, it was estimated, the population decreased at an average annual rate of 0.8%, while gross domestic product (GDP) per head increased, in real terms, by an average of 6.8% per year. Overall GDP increased, in real terms, at an average annual rate of 6.0% in 1995–2004. Real GDP increased by by 9.4% in both 2004 and 2005.

Agriculture (including forestry and fishing) contributed 7.9% of GDP in 2004, according to provisional figures. The sector provided 35.8% of total employment in 2003. There are large areas of land suitable for agriculture, and Kazakhstan is a major producer and exporter of agricultural products. The principal crops include fruit, sugar beet, vegetables, potatoes, cotton and, most importantly, cereals. Livestock-breeding is also important, and Kazakhstan is a significant producer of karakul and astrakhan wools. The GDP of the agricultural sector increased, in real terms, by an average of 1.2% per year in 1995–2004. According to the Asian Development Bank (ADB, see p. 169), agricultural GDP increased by 0.1% in 2004 and by 6.7% in 2005.

Industry (including mining, manufacturing, construction, and power) contributed 37.1% of GDP in 2004, according to provisional figures. The sector provided 17.2% of total employment in 2003. Measured by the gross value of output, the principal branches of industry in 1997 were the fuel industry (accounting for 27.7% of the total), metal-processing (23.9%), food-processing (15.4%) and electrical power generation (14.1%). Industrial GDP increased, in real terms, at an average annual rate of 7.2% in 1995–2004. According to ADB figures, the GDP of the sector increased by 10.1% in 2004 and by 4.6% in 2005.

Mining and quarrying provided 2.0% of employment in 1998. Kazakhstan possesses immense mineral wealth, and large-scale mining and processing industries have been developed. There are major coalfields (in the Karaganda, Turgai, Ekibastuz and Maikuben basins), as well as substantial deposits of iron ore, lead, zinc ore, titanium, magnesium, chromium, tungsten, molybdenum, gold, silver, copper and manganese. Petroleum is extracted, and Kazakhstan possesses what are believed to be among the world's largest unexploited oilfields (in the Caspian depression) and substantial reserves of natural gas. The discovery of major petroleum reserves at the offshore Kashagan oilfield was announced in mid-2000 (see below). In January 2004 the state-owned hydrocarbons company KazMunaiGaz awarded the Russian energy company LUKoil a 50% stake in a 40-year production-sharing contract for the development of the Tyub-Karagan field in the Caspian Sea, which has petroleum reserves of an estimated 100m. metric tons. In January 2005 the Kazakhstani and Russian Presidents signed an agreement confirming the equal rights of both countries to the Imashevskoye natural gas field, the second largest natural gas field in Kazakhstan, which was to be developed jointly by KazMunaiGaz and the Russian energy company GazProm. Also in 2005 a subsidiary of KazMunaiGaz signed a production-sharing agreement with the Russian state-owned petroleum companies Zarubezneft and

Rosneft to develop the offshore Kurmanagazy oilfield, estimated to contain recoverable reserves of petroleum of between 900m. and 1,000m. metric tons. At the end of 2004 Kazakhstan's proven total reserves (onshore and offshore) of petroleum and natural gas were estimated at 5,400m. metric tons and 3,000,000m. cu m, respectively.

Manufacturing provided 10.2% of employment in 1998, and an estimated 15.6% of GDP in 2004. The GDP of the manufacturing sector increased at an average annual rate of 6.4% in 1995–2004.

In 2002 coal-fired thermal power stations provided about 69.9% of annual domestic electricity production, while hydro-electric power stations accounted for 15.2% of production and natural gas for 10.6%. In 2004 mineral fuels accounted for 14.7% of total imports.

In 2004 the services sector contributed some 55.0% of GDP, according to provisional figures. The sector provided 47.0% of employment in 2003. During 1995–2004 the GDP of the services sector increased, in real terms, at an average annual rate of 5.3%. Services GDP increased by 10.8% in 2004 and by 10.5% in 2005, according to the ADB.

In 2004 Kazakhstan recorded a visible trade surplus of US $6,785.6m., and there was a surplus of $529.6m. on the current account of the balance of payments. In that year the principal source of imports was Russia (accounting for 33.9% of total imports). Other major suppliers were the People's Republic of China (13.6%), Germany (9.7%) and France (6.8%). The principal market for exports in that year was Russia (accounting for 13.5% of total exports). Other important purchasers of exports were Bermuda (13.4%), China (10.4%), Germany (9.2%), Switzerland (9.1%) and France (6.7%). The main exports were mineral products and base metals. The principal imports in that year were machinery and electrical equipment, mineral products, transportation equipment, base metals and chemical products.

In 2004 Kazakhstan recorded a preliminary budgetary deficit of some 44,800m. tenge (equivalent to approximately 0.8% of GDP). At the end of 2003 Kazakhstan's external debt amounted to US $22,835m. of which $3,546m. was long-term public debt. In 2003 the cost of debt-servicing was equivalent to 34.5% of the value of exports of goods and services. The annual rate of inflation averaged 12.1% during 1995–2004. Consumer prices increased by 6.8% in 2004 and by 7.6% in 2005. In 2005, according to the ADB, 7.8% of the labour force were unemployed.

In addition to its membership of the economic bodies of the Commonwealth of Independent States (CIS, see p. 201), Kazakhstan has joined the ADB, is a 'Country of Operations' of the European Bank for Reconstruction and Development (EBRD, see p. 224) and is a member of the Economic Co-operation Organization (ECO, see p. 223).

After independence in 1991, contraction was recorded annually until 1995, when signs of an economic recovery emerged. In 1996 a large-scale privatization programme was extended to include the hydrocarbons and metallurgical sectors. In 1998 the economy was severely affected by the economic crises in Russia and Asia, and the subsequent decline in prices for Kazakhstan's principal exports. However, by mid-2000 Kazakhstan had repaid all debts owed to the IMF, seven years ahead of schedule. A National Oil Fund was created in 2001, to manage the country's wealth and guard against sudden declines in petroleum prices. By June 2005 the Fund's assets amounted to some US $5,200m. Meanwhile, the discovery, announced in July 2000, of substantial petroleum deposits at the offshore Kashagan oilfield (thought to be the world's second largest) was expected to be enormously beneficial to the economy, although in February 2004 it was agreed that commercial petroleum extraction was unlikely to commence before 2008. Nevertheless, petroleum exports had increased significantly following the official opening, in November 2001, of a new, 1,500-km petroleum pipeline, connecting the onshore Tengiz field in western Kazakhstan with Novorossiisk, on the Russian Black Sea coast. In addition, a trilateral agreement, signed with Azerbaijan and Russia in May 2003, on the division of mineral resources in the Caspian seabed, was expected to stimulate petroleum and natural gas extraction. In May 2005 a pipeline constructed to transport petroleum from Baku, Azerbaijan, via Tbilisi, Georgia, to Ceyhan, Turkey, and onto Western markets (known as the BTC pipeline) was officially inaugurated. Kazakhstan expressed an interest in participating in the project, by constructing an undersea pipeline from Aktau to Baku; by early 2006, however, no final agreement had been reached. In October 2005 the Canadian-listed energy company PetroKazakhstan was acquired by an affiliate of the China National Petroleum Company (CNPC), reportedly at a cost of $4,180m.; the Kazakhstani Government reportedly hoped to acquire a 33% stake in PetroKazakhstan in 2006. An IMF report published in January 2006 concluded that, although the non-petroleum-sector had expanded by an average of 8% per year since 1998, further liberalization, accelerated structural reforms and measures to increase regional trade were required to ensure the further diversification of the economy. Overall, however, the country's immense hydrocarbons and other mineral resources meant that Kazakhstan's long-term economic prospects remained highly favourable. Strong economic growth, of 9.4%, was maintained in 2005, owing to increased global prices for commodities, domestic demand and significant foreign investment. An average rate of growth of some 8.5% was anticipated in 2006–08.

Education

General education (primary and secondary) is compulsory, and is fully funded by the state. Primary education begins at seven years of age and lasts for four years. Secondary education, beginning at 11 years of age, lasts for a further seven years, comprising a first cycle of five years and a second of two years. In 2002/03 total enrolment at primary schools was equivalent to 91% of the relevant age-group (males 92%; females 91%), and the comparable ratio for secondary enrolment was 87% (males 87%; females 87%). After completing general education, pupils may continue their studies at specialized secondary schools. In 2004/05 there was a total of 181 higher schools (including universities), with a total enrolment of 747,100 students. Ethnic Kazakhs form a greater proportion (64% in 1995/96) of students in higher education than in general education, since many ethnic Russians choose to study at universities outside Kazakhstan. None the less, the majority of higher-education students (approximately 75% in 1997) are instructed in Russian. The number of private general schools in Kazakhstan increased from 18 in 1994/95 to 199 in 1999, as part of a government programme to encourage the private provision of education, although this figure had declined to 155 by 2003/04. In that year there were 179 private secondary vocational schools and 134 private higher schools (including universities). Government expenditure on education in 2001 was 105,024m. tenge (14.7% of total spending).

Public Holidays

2006: 2–3 January (for New Year), 8 March (International Women's Day), 22 March (Nauryz Meyramy, Spring Holiday), 1 May (Day of Unity of the Peoples of Kazakhstan), 9 May (Victory Day, Day of Remembrance), 30 August (Constitution Day), 25 October (Republic Day), 18–19 December (for Independence Day).

2007: 1–2 January (New Year), 8 March (International Women's Day), 22 March (Nauryz Meyramy, Spring Holiday), 1 May (Day of Unity of the Peoples of Kazakhstan), 9 May (Victory Day, Day of Remembrance), 30 August (Constitution Day), 25 October (Republic Day), 17–18 December (for Independence Day).

Weights and Measures

The metric system is in force.

KAZAKHSTAN

Statistical Survey

Source (unless otherwise stated): Statistical Agency of the Republic of Kazakhstan, 480008 Almaty, pr. Abaya 125; tel. (3272) 61-13-23; fax (3272) 42-08-24; e-mail stat@mail.online.kz; internet www.stat.kz.

Area and Population

AREA, POPULATION AND DENSITY

Area (sq km)	2,724,900*
Population (census results)	
12 January 1989†	16,464,464
25 February–4 March 1999	
Males	7,201,785
Females	7,751,341
Total	14,953,126
Population (official estimates at 1 January)	
2003	14,866,900
2004	14,951,200
2005	15,074,200
Density (per sq km) at 1 January 2005	5.5

* 1,049,150 sq miles.
† Figure refers to the *de jure* population. The *de facto* total was 16,536,511.

PRINCIPAL ETHNIC GROUPS
(official estimates, 1 January 2004)

	Number	%
Kazakh	8,550,986	57.19
Russian	4,072,337	27.24
Ukrainian	469,397	3.14
Uzbek	409,770	2.74
German	237,643	1.59
Tatar	232,735	1.56
Uigur	223,039	1.49
Korean	100,235	0.67
Belarusian	96,221	0.64
Azeri	84,436	0.56
Turkish	82,977	0.55
Total (incl. others)	14,951,200	100.00

ADMINISTRATIVE DIVISIONS
(official estimates, 1 January 2004)

	Area (sq km)	Population	Density (per sq km)	Capital city
Oblasts				
Akmola	146,200	748,900	5.12	Kokshetau
Aktobe	300,600	671,800	2.23	Aktobe
Almaty	224,000	1,571,200	7.01	Taldykorgan
Atyrau	118,600	457,200	3.85	Atyrau
Eastern Kazakhstan	283,200	1,455,400	5.14	Ust-Kamenogorsk
Jambul	144,300	985,600	6.83	Taraz
Karaganda	428,000	1,330,900	3.11	Karaganda
Kostanai	196,000	913,400	4.66	Kostanai
Kzyl-Orda	226,000	607,500	2.69	Kzyl-Orda
Mangystau	165,600	349,700	2.11	Aktau
Northern Kazakhstan	98,000	674,500	6.88	Petropavlovsk
Pavlodar	124,800	745,300	5.97	Pavlodar
Southern Kazakhstan	117,300	2,150,300	18.33	Chimkent
Western Kazakhstan	151,300	603,800	3.99	Oral
Cities				
Almaty	700	1,175,200	1,678.86	—
Astana (capital)	300	510,500	1,701.67	—
Total	2,724,900	14,951,200	5.49	—

PRINCIPAL TOWNS
(population at 1999 census)

Almaty (Alma-Ata)	1,129,400	Petropavlovsk	203,500
Karaganda	436,900	Oral	195,500
Chimkent	360,100	Temirtau	170,500
Taraz*	330,100	Kzyl-Orda	157,400
Astana† (capital)	313,000	Aktau‡	143,400
Ust-Kamenogorsk	311,000	Atyrau§	142,500
Pavlodar	300,500	Ekibastuz	127,200
Semipalatinsk	269,600	Kokchetau	123,400
Aktobe	253,100	Rudniy	109,500
Kustanai	221,400		

* Formerly Jambul.
† Formerly Akmola, and prior to that, Tselinograd.
‡ Formerly Shevchenko.
§ Formerly Guriyev.

Mid-2003 (UN estimate, incl. suburbs): Almaty (Alma-Ata) 1,114,941 (Source: UN, *World Urbanization Prospects: The 2003 Revision*).

BIRTHS, MARRIAGES AND DEATHS

	Registered live births		Registered marriages		Registered deaths	
	Number	Rate (per 1,000)	Number	Rate (per 1,000)	Number	Rate (per 1,000)
1996	253,175	16.3	102,558	6.6	166,028	10.7
1997	232,356	15.2	101,874	6.6	160,138	10.4
1998	222,380	14.8	96,048	6.4	154,314	10.2
1999	271,578	14.5	85,872	5.8	147,416	9.8
2000	222,054	14.9	90,873	6.1	149,778	10.0
2001	221,487	14.9	92,852	6.3	147,876	10.0
2002	227,171	15.3	98,986	6.7	149,381	10.1
2003	247,946	16.6	110,414	7.4	155,277	10.4

Expectation of life (years at birth): 61 (males 56; females 67) in 2003 (Source: WHO, *World Health Report*).

ECONOMICALLY ACTIVE POPULATION
(annual averages, '000 persons)

	2001	2002	2003
Agriculture, forestry and fishing	2,379.4	2,380.2	2,462.6
Industry*	830.4	824.0	855.2
Construction	264.0	268.4	329.5
Trade, restaurants and hotels	1,006.4	1,007.2	1,015.1
Transport, storage and communications	506.3	503.7	503.9
Financing and insurance	45.9	50.1	53.5
Community, social and personal services	1,666.4	1,675.7	1,665.4
Total employed	6,698.8	6,708.9	6,885.2
Unemployed	780.3	690.7	672.1
Total labour force	7,479.1	7,399.6	7,557.3

* Including mining and quarrying, manufacturing, and electricity, gas and water.

KAZAKHSTAN

Health and Welfare

KEY INDICATORS

Total fertility rate (children per woman, 2003)	1.9
Under-5 mortality rate (per 1,000 live births, 2004)	73
HIV/AIDS (% of persons aged 15–49, 2003)	0.2
Physicians (per 1,000 head, 2002)	3.61
Hospital beds (per 1,000 head, 2002)	7.02
Health expenditure (2002): US $ per head (PPP)	261
Health expenditure (2002): % of GDP	3.5
Health expenditure (2002): public (% of total)	53.2
Access to water (% of persons, 2002)	86
Access to sanitation (% of persons, 2002)	72
Human Development Index (2003): ranking	80
Human Development Index (2003): value	0.761

For sources and definitions, see explanatory note on p. vi.

Agriculture

PRINCIPAL CROPS
('000 metric tons)

	2002	2003	2004
Wheat	12,700.0	11,537.4	9,936.9
Rice (paddy)	199.1	273.3	275.8
Barley	2,208.9	2,154.0	1,387.9
Maize	435.2	437.5	457.8
Rye	106.5	42.4	20.3
Oats	183.2	170.9	130.3
Millet	39.2	48.8	50.7
Buckwheat	29.6	48.4	52.4
Other cereals	27.3	25.2*	20.6*
Potatoes	2,268.8	2,308.3	2,260.6
Sugar beet	372.2	423.6	397.9
Dry beans*	3.1	5.0	3.0
Dry peas	26.6	29.3	31.6
Soybeans	25.1	37.9	46.7
Sunflower seed	189.8	292.6	265.5
Safflower seed	37.9	94.8	76.1
Cottonseed*	220.0	240.0	257.0
Cabbages	321.8	328.0	321.5
Tomatoes	448.9	447.9	490.9
Cucumbers and gherkins	246.0*	226.6	260.0
Aubergines (Eggplants)	28.0*	43.7	48.3
Chillies and green peppers	51.7	58.4	73.5
Dry onions	309.9	320.0	327.3
Leeks and other alliaceous vegetables*	15.0	15.5	17.0
Green broad beans*	11.0	11.5	12.0
Carrots	214.5	223.9	236.4
Other vegetables*	212.1	264.5	272.7
Watermelons*	628.8	603.8	666.9
Apples	110.5	93.1	148.9
Pears	9.6	9.3	16.8
Cherries	14.0	11.0	14.6
Plums	6.4	5.0	7.8
Grapes	26.3	28.0	53.2
Other fruits*	64.2	56.1	72.3
Tobacco (leaves)	15.8	15.9	14.3
Cotton (lint)	90.4	132.6	140.1

* Unofficial figure(s).
Source: FAO.

LIVESTOCK
('000 head, year ending September)

	2002	2003	2004
Horses	989.5	1,019.3	1,064.3
Asses*	30.0	30.0	30.0
Cattle	4,293.5	4,559.5	4,871.0
Buffaloes*	9.0	9.0	9.0
Camels	103.8	107.5	114.9
Pigs	1,123.8	1,229.8	1,368.8
Sheep	9,207.5	9,787.5	10,420.1
Goats	1,271.1	1,485.5	1,827.0
Chickens†	20,961	23,600	24,700
Turkeys†	169	191	50
Rabbits*	48,000	50,000	60,000

* FAO estimates.
† Unofficial figures.
Source: FAO.

LIVESTOCK PRODUCTS
('000 metric tons)

	2002	2003	2004
Beef and veal	296.0	311.9	329.7
Mutton and lamb	93.9	96.0	101.6
Goat meat	7.2	7.3*	7.0*
Horse meat*	51.6	53.0	53.0
Pig meat	186.9	184.9*	198.6
Poultry meat	36.1	38.4	41.3
Cows' milk*	4,061.0	4,265.4	4,460.2
Sheeps' milk*	36.6	38.5	40.0
Goats' milk*	12.2	12.8	15.0
Cheese	11.8	14.3	15.8
Butter	9.0	10.6	13.0
Hen eggs*	116.7	126.0	127.0
Wool: greasy	24.8	26.8	28.5
Wool: scoured	14.9	16.1	17.1
Cattle hides (fresh)†	36.1	39.9	41.8
Sheepskins (fresh)†	10.4	10.4	10.9

* Unofficial figure(s).
† FAO estimates.
Source: FAO.

Forestry

ROUNDWOOD REMOVALS
(unofficial figures, cubic metres, excl. bark)

	2001	2002	2003
Sawlogs, veneer logs and logs for sleepers	124,100	116,640	103,920
Pulpwood	15,500	14,580	12,990
Other industrial roundwood	15,500	14,580	12,990
Fuel wood	590,800	347,400	170,900
Total	745,900	493,200	300,800

2004: Figures assumed to be unchanged from 2003 (FAO estimates).
Source: FAO.

SAWNWOOD PRODUCTION
(cubic metres, incl. railway sleepers)

	2002	2003*	2004†
Coniferous (softwood)	215,300	265,084	245,791
Broadleaved (hardwood)	16,900	19,293	19,293
Total	232,200	284,377	265,084

* Unofficial figures.
† FAO estimates.
Source: FAO.

KAZAKHSTAN

Fishing

('000 metric tons, live weight)

	2001	2002	2003
Capture	21.7	24.3	23.1
Freshwater bream	12.6	14.1	16.0
Common carp	0.7	1.4	1.5
Crucian carp	1.7	1.6	—
Roaches	0.6	1.7	1.2
Asp	0.5	0.7	1.0
Northern pike	0.8	0.9	0.6
Wels (Som) catfish	0.8	0.6	1.1
Pike-perch	1.6	1.7	1.4
Aquaculture	0.4	0.8	0.8*
Total catch	22.1	25.0	23.9*

* FAO estimate.
Source: FAO.

Mining

('000 metric tons, unless otherwise indicated)

	2001	2002	2003
Hard coal }	79,315	73,731	84,906
Brown coal (incl. lignite)			
Crude petroleum*	36,060	42,067	45,376
Natural gas (million cu m)	11,610	14,109	16,597
Iron ore (gross weight)	15,886	17,675	19,281
Copper ore (metal content)	470	474	485
Bauxite	3,685	4,377	4,737
Lead ore (metal content)	38	46	38
Zinc ore (metal content)	345	392	394
Manganese ore	1,387	1,835	2,369
Chromite	2,046	2,370	2,928
Silver ore (metal content, metric tons)	981,918	892,614	827,377
Gold (metal content, kg)	25,010	22,402	19,266
Asbestos	271	291	355

* Including gas condensate.

Crude petroleum (incl. gas concentrate, '000 metric tons): 50,582 in 2004 (Source: Asian Development Bank, *Key Indicators of Developing Asian and Pacific Countries*).

Natural gas (million cu m): 21,856 in 2004 (Source: Asian Development Bank, *Key Indicators of Developing Asian and Pacific Countries*).

Coal ('000 metric tons): 86,822 in 2004 (Source: Asian Development Bank, *Key Indicators of Developing Asian and Pacific Countries*).

Iron ore (gross weight) ('000 metric tons): 20,000 in 2004; 19,000 in 2005 (estimate) (Source: US Geological Survey).

Copper ('000 metric tons): 461 in 2004; 400 in 2005 (estimate) (Source: US Geological Survey).

Lead ore (metal content) ('000 metric tons): 40 in 2004; 40 in 2005 (estimate) (Source: US Geological Survey).

Zinc ore (metal content) ('000 metric tons): 360 in 2004; 370 in 2005 (estimate) (Source: US Geological Survey).

Asbestos ('000 metric tons): 347 in 2004; 350 in 2005 (estimate) (Source: US Geological Survey).

Industry

SELECTED PRODUCTS
('000 metric tons, unless otherwise indicated)

	2001	2002	2003
Wheat flour	1,776.1	2,107.1	2,122.7
Raw sugar	346.5	390.5	480.3
Wine ('000 hectolitres)	115	218	200
Beer ('000 hectolitres)	1,732	2,020	2,348
Mineral water ('000 hectolitres)	1,615	2,230	2,615
Cigarettes (million)	21,395.3	23,453.0	25,715.0
Cotton yarn (metric tons)	1,466	2,452	3,759
Woven cotton fabrics (metric tons)	7,615.8	14,204.0	19,979.0
Sulphuric acid (metric tons)	694,652	710,301	743,211
Motor spirit (petrol)	1,582.3	1,692.8	1,841.4
Kerosene	109.3	245.3	309.2
Gas-diesel (distillate fuel) oils	2,244.7	2,304.0	2,754.0
Residual fuel oils	2,736.7	2,796.5	3,069.3
Cement	2,029.2	2,128.5	2,581.1
Pig-iron	3,906.5	4,008.9	4,138.1
Crude steel	4,691	4,866	5,069
Copper (unrefined, metric tons)	433,561	446,198	431,940
Electric energy (million kWh)	55,384.0	58,330.6	63,866.4

Finance

CURRENCY AND EXCHANGE RATES

Monetary Units
100 tein = 1 tenge.

Sterling, Dollar and Euro Equivalents (30 December 2005)
£1 sterling = 230.70 tenge;
US $1 = 133.98 tenge;
€1 = 158.06 tenge;
1,000 tenge = £4.33 = $7.46 = €6.33.

Average Exchange Rate (tenge per US $)
2003 149.58
2004 136.04
2005 132.88

Note: The tenge was introduced on 15 November 1993, replacing the old Russian (formerly Soviet) rouble at an exchange rate of 1 tenge = 500 roubles. On 18 November the rate was adjusted to 250 roubles per tenge. In April 1999 the tenge was allowed to 'float' on foreign exchange markets.

STATE BUDGET
(million tenge)

Revenue	2001	2002	2003
Tax revenue	635,792	752,785	947,251
Other current revenue	70,505	45,573	44,813
Capital revenue	25,363	9,494	12,502
Official transfers	233	—	—
Repayment of debt principal	12,719	13,308	17,690
Total	746,612	821,160	1,022,256

KAZAKHSTAN

Statistical Survey

Expenditure	1999	2000	2001
General public services	28,856	35,114	47,771
Defence	17,198	20,379	32,347
Public order and security	32,507	47,738	63,681
Education	78,491	84,668	105,024
Health care	44,825	54,323	62,238
Social security and social assistance	159,064	171,065	186,641
Recreation and cultural activities	12,237	17,487	18,076
Housing and communal services	6,012	22,106	30,396
Economic affairs and services	48,794	87,761	132,188
Agriculture, forestry, water management, fishing and environmental protection	6,944	11,441	23,113
Mining and minerals (excl. fuel), manufacturing and construction	2,867	7,191	4,558
Transport and communications	12,865	37,804	41,651
Other purposes	19,442	35,541	37,764
Debt interest	19,442	35,541	37,764
Total	447,426	576,182	716,126

Revised expenditure totals (million tenge, rounded figures): Total expenditure (excluding lending minus repayments) 468,400 in 1999; 602,000 in 2000; 759,600 in 2001.

Expenditure in 2002 (million tenge, rounded figures): Total expenditure (excluding lending minus repayments) 834,200 (Defence 37,700; Social and cultural 416,500; Economic 123,800; Public administration 45,600).

Expenditure in 2003 (million tenge, rounded figures): Total expenditure (excluding lending minus repayments) 1,062,600 (Defence 47,500; Social and cultural 511,700; Economic 173,100; Public administration 63,900).

2004 (million tenge, rounded figures, preliminary): Total revenue 1,282,800; Total expenditure (excluding lending minus repayments) 1,327,600 (Source: Asian Development Bank, *Key Indicators of Developing Asian and Pacific Countries*).

INTERNATIONAL RESERVES
(US $ million at 31 December)

	2002	2003	2004
Gold	585.6	725.9	803.6
IMF special drawing rights	1.0	1.2	1.2
Reserve position in IMF	0.0	0.0	0.0
Foreign exchange	2,554.2	4,235.0	8,471.9
Total	3,140.8	4,962.1	9,276.7

Source: IMF, *International Financial Statistics*.

MONEY SUPPLY
(million tenge at 31 December)

	2002	2003	2004
Currency outside banks	161,701	238,545	379,273
Demand deposits at commercial banks	219,423	238,890	373,288
Total money (incl. others)	381,975	479,023	755,296

Source: IMF, *International Financial Statistics*.

COST OF LIVING
(Consumer Price Index; base: 1995 = 100)

	2002	2003	2004
All items	213.8	229.7	245.4

Source: Asian Development Bank, *Key Indicators of Developing Asian and Pacific Countries*.

NATIONAL ACCOUNTS
('000 million tenge at current prices)

Expenditure on the Gross Domestic Product

	2002	2003	2004*
Government final consumption expenditure	435.0	519.2	682.1
Private final consumption expenditure	2,205.9	2,667.3	3,159.0
Increase in stocks	123.3	122.8	74.6
Gross fixed capital formation	907.1	1,072.7	1,256.8
Total domestic expenditure	3,671.4	4,382.0	5,172.5
Exports of goods and services / *Less* Imports of goods and services	33.7	282.3	509.5
Sub-total	3,705.1	4,664.3	5,682.0
Statistical discrepancy†	71.2	−52.3	−139.5
GDP in purchasers' values	3,776.3	4,612.0	5,542.5
GDP at constant 1994 prices	548.4	599.2	655.5

* Provisional figures.
† Referring to the difference between the sum of the expenditure components and official estimates of GDP, compiled from the production approach.

Gross Domestic Product by Economic Activity

	2002	2003	2004*
Agriculture, forestry and fishing	301.9	362.6	439.0
Industry†	1,112.9	1,341.5	1,726.3
Construction	239.4	276.2	328.3
Trade, restaurants and hotels	459.5	536.9	629.3
Transport, storage and communications	437.8	570.8	677.0
Other services / Import duties / *Less* Imputed bank service charges	1,224.7	1,524.0	1,743.1
GDP in purchasers' values	3,776.3	4,612.0	5,542.5

* Provisional figures.
† Including mining and quarrying, manufacturing, and electricity, gas and water.

Source: Asian Development Bank, *Key Indicators of Developing Asian and Pacific Countries*.

BALANCE OF PAYMENTS
(US $ million)

	2002	2003	2004
Exports of goods f.o.b.	10,026.9	13,232.6	20,603.1
Imports of goods f.o.b.	−8,039.8	−9,553.6	−13,817.6
Trade balance	1,987.1	3,679.0	6,785.6
Exports of services	1,540.4	1,712.3	1,999.2
Imports of services	−3,538.3	−3,752.7	−4,982.9
Balance on goods and services	−10.7	1,638.6	3,801.9
Other income received	233.8	255.3	422.5
Other income paid	−1,361.1	−2,001.9	−3,206.6
Balance on goods, services and income	−1,138.1	−108.0	1,017.8
Current transfers received	425.9	278.6	352.9
Current transfers paid	−312.1	−443.3	−841.1
Current balance	−1,024.3	−272.6	529.6
Capital account (net)	−119.8	−27.8	−20.3
Direct investment abroad	−426.4	121.3	1,279.3
Direct investment from abroad	2,590.2	2,092.0	4,104.2
Portfolio investment assets	−1,063.9	−2,073.1	−1,092.1
Portfolio investment liabilities	−182.9	182.1	670.9
Financial derivatives assets	—	—	−44.6
Financial derivatives liabilities	—	15.9	−1.8
Other investment assets	−1,116.8	−977.5	−4,454.6
Other investment liabilities	1,558.8	3,405.0	4,144.4
Net errors and omissions	320.2	−931.9	−1,116.0
Overall balance	535.1	1,533.5	3,999.0

Source: IMF, *International Financial Statistics*.

KAZAKHSTAN

External Trade

PRINCIPAL COMMODITIES
(US $ million)

Imports c.i.f.	2002	2003	2004
Prepared foodstuffs	333.0	426.0	611.1
Mineral products	822.9	1,007.2	1,873.5
Chemical products	715.7	909.6	1,128.3
Plastics and rubber	267.9	362.8	504.2
Base metals and articles thereof	737.9	993.2	1,666.1
Machinery, mechanical appliances and electrical equipment	1,881.7	2,152.5	3,421.9
Transportation equipment	803.2	1,222.8	1,777.2
Total (incl. others)	6,584.0	8,408.7	12,781.2

Exports f.o.b.	2002	2003	2004
Vegetable products	408.2	659.5	640.7
Mineral products	5,917.5	8,316.3	13,727.1
Chemical products	418.6	440.0	634.1
Pearls, precious and semi-precious stones, and metals	269.5	249.9	345.6
Base metals and articles thereof	2,234.1	2,635.1	3,897.2
Total (incl. others)	9,670.3	12,926.7	20,096.2

Source: Asian Development Bank, *Key Indicators of Developing Asian and Pacific Countries*.

PRINCIPAL TRADING PARTNERS
(US $ million)

Imports c.i.f.	2001	2002	2003
Belarus	46.3	54.8	94.9
China, People's Republic	172.0	313.0	523.7
Finland	71.4	73.4	97.2
France	141.6	110.2	196.9
Germany	490.2	586.2	734.2
Italy	268.9	219.1	250.2
Japan	142.0	164.6	212.0
Korea, Republic	110.6	110.2	114.6
Netherlands	85.4	87.5	127.6
Poland	61.3	74.7	117.2
Russia	2,891.9	2,548.8	3,282.1
Switzerland	67.6	60.2	61.7
Turkey	137.0	173.7	209.0
Ukraine	155.0	217.1	324.0
United Kingdom	249.4	259.7	248.6
USA	349.1	461.4	470.4
Uzbekistan	81.1	86.5	89.7
Total (incl. others)	6,446.0	6,584.0	8,408.7

Exports f.o.b.	2001	2002	2003
Bermuda	1,221.2	2,011.3	2,192.6
China, People's Republic	659.6	1,023.0	1,653.1
Finland	56.1	48.8	108.9
Germany	501.8	220.3	146.4
Italy	956.3	904.2	1,013.1
Korea, Republic	43.4	48.9	55.5
Kyrgyzstan	87.0	108.6	156.4
Netherlands	144.2	123.6	186.1
Poland	164.2	320.5	201.0
Russia	1,759.5	1,497.8	1,967.9
Switzerland	408.7	792.4	1,679.9
Tajikistan	61.2	45.7	75.7
Turkey	74.2	97.4	99.2
Ukraine	490.2	291.5	426.2
United Kingdom	294.3	131.8	143.2
USA	159.0	116.9	99.1
Uzbekistan	150.2	101.0	137.9
Total (incl. others)	8,639.1	9,670.3	12,926.7

2004 (US $ million, 2004): *Imports c.i.f.*: China, People's Republic 1,678.2; France 846.9; Germany 1,194.8; Italy 420.4; Japan 204.4; Russia 4,198.0; Turkey 391.1; Ukraine 344.4; United Kingdom 273.0; USA 307.2; Total (incl. others) 12,381.3. *Exports f.o.b.*: Bermuda 2,746.0; China, People's Republic 2,126.0; France 1,364.6; Germany 1,879.1; Iran 472.3; Italy 803.8; Russia 2,777.6; Switzerland 1,865.7; Ukraine 533.8; United Arab Emirates 247.1; Total (incl. others) 20,500.4 (Source: Asian Development Bank, *Key Indicators of Developing Asian and Pacific Countries*).

Transport

RAILWAYS
(estimated traffic)

	2001	2002	2003
Passenger-km (million)	10,384	10,449	10,686
Freight net ton-km (million)	135,653	133,088	147,672

ROAD TRAFFIC
(motor vehicles in use at 31 December)

	2001	2002	2003
Passenger cars	1,057,801	1,062,554	1,148,754
Buses and coaches	50,162	51,367	61,391
Lorries and vans	241,528	251,129	261,327
Motorcycles and mopeds	97,909	80,953	74,756

SHIPPING
Merchant Fleet
(registered at 31 December)

	2002	2003	2004
Number of vessels	20	22	36
Total displacement (grt)	11,845	15,300	25,950

Source: Lloyd's Register-Fairplay, *World Fleet Statistics*.

CIVIL AVIATION
(traffic on scheduled services)

	2001	2002	2003
Passengers carried ('000)	884	1,036	1,275
Passenger-km (million)	1,901	2,179	2,654
Total ton-km (million)	44	53	94

Kilometres flown (million): 20 in 1996; 20 in 1997; 35 in 1998 (Source: UN, *Statistical Yearbook*).

KAZAKHSTAN

Tourism

FOREIGN TOURIST ARRIVALS

Country of residence	2001	2002	2003
Armenia	702	896	9,730
Australia	6,050	1,346	1,465
Austria	1,096	1,223	1,477
Azerbaijan	18,165	19,958	24,690
Belarus	9,067	2,283	6,983
Canada	2,822	3,641	3,646
China, People's Republic	41,116	48,306	57,035
France	2,459	3,249	3,966
Georgia	1,522	1,669	2,656
Germany	44,020	47,994	56,384
Hungary	2,724	1,897	1,494
India	3,633	4,217	4,810
Iran	4,479	6,245	10,347
Israel	2,413	2,493	3,122
Italy	4,653	5,492	6,614
Japan	2,882	2,550	3,071
Korea, Republic	5,396	5,999	6,871
Kyrgyzstan	1,367,370	1,962,465	1,383,314
Lithuania	440	595	1,264
Mongolia	10,228	3,142	3,049
Netherlands	3,427	4,760	5,277
Pakistan	1,145	1,245	1,749
Poland	1,306	1,861	2,525
Romania	444	909	1,050
Russia	145,673	163,784	605,909
Switzerland	1,129	1,058	1,088
Tajikistan	49,719	95,051	202,744
Turkey	15,640	24,671	31,331
United Kingdom	13,772	20,367	16,956
USA	14,131	20,199	18,850
Uzbekistan	877,657	1,181,108	696,327
Total (incl. others)	2,692,590	3,677,921	3,249,344

Tourism receipts (US $ million, incl. passenger transport): 761 in 2001; 864 in 2002; 783 in 2003.

Source: World Tourism Organization.

Communications Media

	1999	2000	2001
Television receivers ('000 in use)	3,900	4,670	5,440
Telephones ('000 main lines in use)	1,759.8	1,834.2	1,939.6
Facsimile machines (number in use)	2,045	n.a.	n.a.
Mobile cellular telephones ('000 subscribers)	49.5	197.3	582.0
Internet users ('000)	70.0	100.0	150.0

Book production (titles, incl. pamphlets): 1,223 in 1999.

Book production (copies, 1996): 21,014,000.

Daily newspapers (1996): Titles 3; Average circulation 500,000.

Radio receivers ('000 in use, 1997): 6,470.

2002: Telephones ('000 main lines in use) 2,081.9; Mobile cellular telephones ('000 subscribers) 1,027.0; Internet users ('000) 250.0.

2003 ('000 main lines in use): Telephones 2,228.4.

Sources: UNESCO, *Statistical Yearbook*; UN, *Statistical Yearbook*; International Telecommunication Union.

Education

(state educational institutions, 2005/06, unless otherwise indicated)

	Institutions	Teachers	Students ('000)
Pre-primary	1,095*	15,412†	147.5*
Primary	8,157	60,509*	2,824.6
Secondary: general		170,190*	
Secondary: vocational	415	27,000	397.6
Professional-technical schools	307	5,900	104.2
Higher‡	181	42,300	747.1

* 2002/03.
† 2001/02.
‡ 2004/05.

Note: In 2003/04 there were, additionally: 155 private primary and secondary-general schools, with 20,000 students; 179 private secondary-vocational schools, with 88,700 students; and 134 non-governmental higher education institutes, with 297,900 students.

Adult literacy rate (UNESCO estimates): 99.4% (males 99.7%; females 99.2%) in 1995–99 (Source: UN Development Programme, *Human Development Report*).

Directory

The Constitution

The Constitution of the Republic of Kazakhstan was endorsed by 89% of the electorate voting in a national referendum on 30 August 1995, and was officially adopted on 6 September, replacing the Constitution of January 1993. A number of constitutional amendments were adopted on 8 October 1998. The following is a summary of the Constitution's main provisions:

GENERAL PROVISIONS

The Republic of Kazakhstan is a democratic, secular, law-based, unitary state with a presidential system of rule. The state ensures the integrity, inviolability and inalienability of its territory. State power belongs to the people, who exercise it directly through referendums and free elections, and also delegate the exercise of their power to state bodies. State power is separated into legislative, executive and judicial branches; these interact, with a system of checks and balances being applied.

Ideological and political diversity are recognized. State and private property are recognized and afforded equal protection. The state language is Kazakh. Russian is employed officially in state bodies and local government bodies on a par with Kazakh. The state creates the conditions necessary for the study and development of the languages of the peoples of Kazakhstan.

HUMAN AND CIVIL RIGHTS AND LIBERTIES

Citizenship of the Republic of Kazakhstan is acquired and terminated in accordance with the law. Citizenship of another state is not recognized for any citizen of Kazakhstan. The rights and liberties of the individual are recognized and guaranteed. No one may be subjected to discrimination on grounds of origin, sex, race, language, religious or other beliefs, or place of residence. No one may be subjected to torture, violence or other treatment or punishment that is cruel or degrading. All are entitled to use their native language and culture. Freedom of speech and creativity are guaranteed. Censorship is prohibited. Citizens are entitled to assemble and to hold meetings, rallies, demonstrations, marches and picket-lines peacefully and without weapons. Defence of the republic is the sacred duty and obligation of every citizen. Human and civil rights and liberties may be restricted only by law and only to the extent that is necessary to defend the constitutional system and to safeguard public order, and human rights and liberties. Any action capable of disrupting inter-ethnic accord is deemed unconstitutional. Restriction of civil rights and liberties on political grounds is not permitted in any form.

THE PRESIDENT OF THE REPUBLIC

The President of the Republic is the Head of State and highest official of Kazakhstan, who determines the main directions of the state's domestic and foreign policy and represents Kazakhstan within the country and in international relations. The President is symbol and guarantor of the unity of people and state power, the permanency of the Constitution and of human and civil rights and liberties. The President is elected for a seven-year term by secret ballot on the basis of general, equal and direct suffrage. No person may be elected to the office for more than two consecutive terms. A citizen of the republic by birth, who is at least 40 years of age, has a fluent command of the state language, and has lived in Kazakhstan for no less than 15 years, may be elected President.

The President addresses an annual message to the people; schedules regular and extraordinary elections to Parliament; signs and promulgates laws submitted by the Senate, or returns draft legislation for further discussion; with the consent of Parliament, appoints the Prime Minister and relieves him of office; on the recommendation of the Prime Minister, determines the structure of the Government, appoints its members to office and relieves them of office; presides at sessions of the Government on matters of particular importance; may cancel or suspend acts of the Government and of the akims (heads of regional administrative bodies); with the consent of Parliament, appoints to and relieves of office the Chairman of the National Bank; with the consent of the Senate, appoints to and relieves of office the Prosecutor-General and the Chairman of the National Security Committee; appoints and recalls the heads of diplomatic missions of the republic; decides on the holding of referendums; negotiates and signs international treaties; is supreme Commander-in-Chief of the armed forces; bestows state awards and confers honours; resolves matters of citizenship and of granting political asylum; in the event of aggression against the republic, imposes martial law or announces a partial or general mobilization; forms the Security Council, the Supreme Judicial Council and other consultative and advisory bodies.

The President may be relieved of office only in the event of his having committed an act of treason or if he exhibits a consistent incapacity to carry out his duties owing to illness. A decision on the President's early dismissal is adopted at a joint sitting of the chambers of Parliament by a majority of no less than three-quarters of the total number of deputies of each chamber. Dismissal of a treason indictment against the President at any stage shall result in the early termination of the powers of the Majlis members who initiated the consideration of the matter. The question of dismissal of the President may not be raised at the same time as he is considering early termination of the authority of Parliament.

PARLIAMENT

Parliament is the supreme representative body of the republic, exercising legislative functions. It consists of two chambers, the Senat (Senate—upper chamber) and the Majlis (Assembly—lower chamber). The Senate comprises 39 members, of whom 32 are elected at joint sittings of the deputies of all representative bodies of the regions and the capital, while the remaining seven deputies are appointed by the President. The Majlis consists of 67 deputies elected from single-mandate constituencies by secret ballot on the basis of general, equal and direct suffrage and 10 elected by party lists. The Senate's term is six years, and that of the Majlis is five years. One-half of the elected deputies in the Senate are subject to election every three years.

THE GOVERNMENT

The Government exercises the executive power of the republic and is responsible to the President. The Government drafts the main areas of the state's socio-economic policy, defence capability, security and public order, and orders their implementation; presents to Parliament the republican budget and the report of its implementation, and ensures that the budget is implemented; submits draft legislation to the Majlis and provides for the implementation of laws; organizes the management of state property; formulates measures for the pursuit of Kazakhstan's foreign policy; directs the activity of Ministries, State Committees and other central and local executive bodies. The Prime Minister organizes and directs the activity of the Government and is personally responsible for its work.

THE CONSTITUTIONAL COUNCIL

The Constitutional Council consists of seven members whose term of office is six years. Former Presidents of the Republic are by right life members of the Constitutional Council. The Chairman and two members of the Council are appointed by the President of the Republic, two members are appointed by the Chairman of the Senate and two by the Chairman of the Majlis. One-half of the members of the Council are replaced every three years. The Council decides whether to hold a presidential or parliamentary election, or a republican referendum; prior to signature by the President, examines laws passed by Parliament for compliance with the Constitution; prior to ratification, examines international treaties.

LOCAL STATE ADMINISTRATION GOVERNMENT

Local state administration is exercised by local representative and executive bodies, which are responsible for the state of affairs on their own territory. The local representative bodies—the councils (maslikhat)—express the will of the population of the corresponding administrative-territorial units and, bearing in mind the overall state interest, define the measures necessary to realize this will and monitor the ways in which these are implemented. Councils are elected for a four-year term by a secret ballot of the public on the basis of general, equal and direct suffrage. The local executive bodies are part of the unified system of executive bodies of Kazakhstan, and ensure that the general state policy of the executive authority is implemented in co-ordination with the interests and development needs of the corresponding territory. Each local executive body is headed by the akim of the corresponding administrative-territorial unit, who is the representative of the President and the Government of the Republic.

The Government

HEAD OF STATE

President: NURSULTAN A. NAZARBAYEV (elected indirectly 24 April 1990; elected unopposed 1 December 1991; re-elected 10 January 1999; re-elected 4 December 2005; inaugurated 11 January 2006).

GOVERNMENT
(April 2006)

Prime Minister: DANIYAL K. AKHMETOV.
Deputy Prime Minister: SAUAT M. MYNBAYEV.
Deputy Prime Minister and Minister of Economy and Budget Planning: KARIM K. MASIMOV.
Head of the Office of the Prime Minister: ALTAI A. TLEUBERDIN.
Minister of Foreign Affairs: KASYMZHOMART K. TOKAYEV.
Minister of Defence: Gen. MUKHTAR K. ALTYNBAYEV.
Minister of Internal Affairs: BAURZHAN A. MUKHAMEJANOV.
Minister of Health: YERBOLAT A. DOSAYEV.
Minister of Industry and Trade: VLADIMIR S. SHKOLNIK.
Minister of Culture and Information: YERMUKHAMET K. YERTYSBAYEV.
Minister of Tourism and Sport: TEMIRKHAN DOSMUKHANBETOV.
Minister of Education and Science: BYRGANYM S. AITIMOVA.
Minister of Environmental Protection: NURLAN A. ISKAKOV.
Minister of Agriculture: AKHMETZHAN S. YESIMOV.
Minister of Transport and Communications: ASKAR U. MAMIN.
Minister of Labour and Social Security: GULZHANA J. KARAGUSOVA.
Minister of Finance: NATALYA A. KORZHOVA.
Minister of Emergency Situations: SHALBAI KULMAKHANOV.
Minister of Energy and Mineral Resources: BAKTYKOZHA S. IZMUKHAMBETOV.
Minister of Justice: ZAGIPA YA. BALIYEVA.

MINISTRIES

Office of the President: 010000 Astana, Beibitshilik 11; tel. (3172) 32-13-99; fax (3172) 32-61-72; internet www.akorda.kz.
Office of the Prime Minister: 010000 Astana, Beibitshilik 11; tel. (3172) 32-31-04; fax (3172) 32-40-89; internet www.government.kz.
Ministry of Agriculture: 010000 Astana, pr. Abaya 49; tel. (3172) 32-37-63; fax (3172) 32-62-99; e-mail mailbox@minagri.kz; internet www.minagri.kz.
Ministry of Culture and Information: 010000 Astana, Transport Tower, 26th Floor; tel. (3172) 24-19-07; fax (3172) 24-17-14.
Ministry of Defence: 010000 Astana, Beibitshilik 51A; tel. and fax (3172) 33-78-89.
Ministry of Economy and Budget Planning: 010000 Astana, Popeda 33; tel. (3172) 71-77-70; fax (3172) 71-77-12; e-mail mineconom@nursat.kz; internet www.minplan.kz.
Ministry of Education and Science: 010000 Astana, Kenesary 83; tel. (3172) 32-25-40; fax (3172) 32-64-82.
Ministry of Emergency Situations: 010000 Astana, Beibitshilik 22; e-mail chs@emer.kz; internet www.ns.emer.kz.

Ministry of Energy and Mineral Resources: 010000 Astana, Beibitshilik 37; tel. (3172) 31-71-33; fax (3172) 31-71-64; e-mail ministr@minenergo.kegoc.kz; internet www.minenergo.kz.

Ministry of Environmental Protection: 010000 Astana, Pobeda 31; tel. (3172) 59-19-44; fax (3172) 59-19-73; internet www.nature.kz.

Ministry of Finance: 010000 Astana, pl. Respubliki 60; tel. (3172) 28-00-65; fax (3172) 32-40-89; internet www.minfin.kz.

Ministry of Foreign Affairs: 010000 Astana, Beibitshilik 11; tel. (3172) 32-76-69; fax (3172) 32-76-67; internet www.mfa.kz.

Ministry of Health: 010000 Astana.

Ministry of Industry and Trade: 010000 Astana.

Ministry of Internal Affairs: 010000 Astana, Manasa 4; tel. (3172) 34-36-01; fax (3172) 34-17-38; internet www.mvd.kz.

Ministry of Justice: 010000 Astana, Pobeda 45; tel. (3172) 39-12-13; fax (3172) 32-15-54; internet www.minjust.kz.

Ministry of Labour and Social Security: 010000 Astana, Manasa 2; tel. (3172) 15-36-02; fax (3172) 15-36-54; e-mail inter@enbek.kz; internet www.enbek.kz.

Ministry of Tourism and Sport: 010000 Astana.

Ministry of Transport and Communications: 010000 Astana, pr. Abaya 49; tel. (3172) 32-62-77; fax (3172) 32-16-96.

President and Legislature

PRESIDENT

Presidential Election, 4 December 2005*

Candidates	Votes	%
Nursultan A. Nazarbayev	6,147,517	91.15
Zharmakhan A. Tuyakbai	445,934	6.61
Alikhan M. Baymenov	108,730	1.61
Yerasyl Abylkasymov	23,252	0.34
Mels Kh. Yeleusizov	18,834	0.28
Total	6,744,267	100.00

* Preliminary official results.

PARLIAMENT

Parliament is a bicameral legislative body, comprising the Senate and the Majlis (Assembly).

Senate

010000 Astana, pr. Abaya 33, Parliament House; tel. (3172) 15-33-76; fax (3172) 33-31-18; e-mail www@parlam.kz; internet www.parlam.kz.

Chairman: NURTAI ABYKAYEV.

The Senate is the upper chamber of Parliament. It comprises 39 members: 32 elected by special electoral colleges (comprising members of local councils) in Kazakhstan's 14 regions and two cities (the country's third city, Baikonur, was transferred to Russian jurisdiction in August 1995, for a period of 20 years), and seven appointed by the President of the Republic. Elections are held every three years for one-half of the elected seats; the term of office for members of the Senate is six years. Partial elections to the Senate were held on 8 October 2002 and 19 August 2005.

Majlis

010000 Astana, Parliament House; tel. (3172) 15-30-19; fax (3172) 33-30-99; e-mail www@parlam.kz; internet www.parlam.kz.

Chairman: URAL MUKHAMEJANOV.

General Election, 19 September and 3 October 2004

Parties and blocs	Party lists % of votes	Seats	Single-member constituency seats	Total seats
Fatherland Republican Political Party (Otan)	60.61	7	35	42
Agrarian Party of Kazakhstan-Civic Party of Kazakhstan bloc (Aist)	7.07	1	10	11
Mutual Help Republican Political Party (Asar)	11.38	1	3	4
Light Road—Democratic Party of Kazakhstan (Ak Zhol)	12.04	1	—	1
Democratic Party of Kazakhstan	0.76	—	1	1
People's Opposition Union of Communists and DVK bloc*	3.44	—	—	—
Communist People's Party of Kazakhstan	1.98	—	—	—
Village Peasants' Social-Democratic Party (Aul)	1.73	—	—	—
Independents	—	—	18	18
Total (incl. others)	100.00	10	67	77

* An electoral alliance comprising the Communist Party of Kazakhstan and Democratic Choice of Kazakhstan.

Election Commission

Ortalyk Sailau Komissiyasy (Central Election Commission): 473000 Astana, Beibitshilik 4; tel. (3172) 152210; fax (3172) 333388; e-mail info@election.kz; internet www.election.kz; Chair. ONALSYN I. ZHUMABEKOV.

Political Organizations

A new law was introduced in July 2002, which required all parties to have a minimum of 50,000 members from among all the country's regions in order to qualify for official registration. At August 2004 12 parties were registered with the Ministry of Justice.

Agrarian Party of Kazakhstan (Kazakstan Agrarlyk partiyasy/Agrarnaya partiya Kazakhstana): 050000 Astana, Zhengis dangghyly 104; tel. and fax (3172) 31-82-21; e-mail agro@agrocenter.kz; f. and registered 1999; re-registered 2002; favours private land ownership, particularly in the agricultural sector; seeks to protect the rights and interests of agricultural workers; centrist; supportive of Pres. Nazarbayev; contested 2004 legislative elections in alliance with the Civic Party of Kazakhstan, as the Aist bloc; Chair. ROMIN R. MADINOV; 52,700 mems (2005).

Civic Party of Kazakhstan (Kazakstan Azamattyk partiyasy/Grazhdanskaya partiya Kazakhstana): 050000 Almaty, Zverev k-si 6A; tel. and fax (3272) 91-34-73; e-mail civicparty@mail.kz; f. 1998; registered 1999 and re-registered 2003; seeks strengthening of state system and improvements in the provision of social welfare; supportive of Pres. Nazarbayev; contested 2004 legislative elections in alliance with the Agrarian Party of Kazakhstan, as the Aist bloc; Chair. AZAT PERUASHEV; 63,500 mems (2005).

Communist Party of Kazakhstan (CPK) (Kazakstan Kommunistik partiyasi/Kommunisticheskaya partiya Kazakhstana): Astana, Beibitshilik 27/49; tel. and fax (3272) 21-32-97; e-mail pravdakz@list.ru; internet www.comparty.kz; f. 1937; suspended Aug. 1991, re-registered Aug. 1998 and March 2003; contested 2004 legislative elections in alliance with Democratic Choice of Kazakhstan, as the People's Opposition Union of Communists and DVK bloc; part of the For a Just Kazakhstan opposition bloc; Chair. SERIKBOLSYN A. ABDILDIN; 54,200 mems (2005).

Communist People's Party of Kazakhstan (KNPK): 010000 Astana; f. 2004; splinter group of the CPK; Leader VLADISLAV KOSAREV; 70,000 mems (2004).

Democratic Party of Kazakhstan (DPK): 050000 Almaty; f. 2004; advocates strong state institutions, rule of law and enhancing the legislative process; Chair. MAKSUT S. NARIKBAYEV; 60,108 mems.

Fatherland Republican Political Party ('Otan' Respublikalyk Sayasi Partiyasy—Otan): 010000 Astana, ul. Kenesary 25; tel. (3172)

23-95-96; fax (3172) 23-60-01; e-mail otan@party.kz; internet www.party.kz; f. 1999; supports regime of President Nazarbayev; merger with People's Co-operative Party of Kazakhstan and the Republican Labour Party reported in 2002; Chair. BAKYTZHAN T. ZHUMAGULOV (acting); 111,100 mems (2005).

For a Just Kazakhstan: f. 2005 as opposition bloc comprising the Communist Party of Kazakhstan, Forward, the Pokoleniye (Generation) Pensioners' Movement and True Light Road; Leader ZHARMAKHAN TUYAKBAI.

Forward (Alga): f. March 2005, on the basis of the Democratic Choice of Kazakhstan, which had been dissolved by court order in Jan. 2005; advocates democratic reform and socially responsible governance; aims to fight corruption and injustices, and uphold citizens' rights; supports a sovereign and independent Kazakhstan; part of the For a Just Kazakhstan Opposition Bloc; denied registration in early 2006; Leader ASYLBEK KOZHAKHMETOV.

Light Road—Democratic Party of Kazakhstan (Ak Zhol): 050004 Almaty, Gogol 111A; tel. (3272) 50-46-25; fax (3272) 50-46-27; e-mail ca@dpkazhol.kz; internet www.dpkakzhol.kz; f. 2002 by former members of the Democratic Choice of Kazakhstan; faction True Light Road separated from main party in 2004; Chair. ALIKHAN M. BAYMENOV.

Mutual Help Republican Political Party ('Asar' Respublikalyk Sayasi Partiyasy—Asar): 050010 Almaty, Kazybek bi 41A; tel. (3272) 78-38-91; e-mail asar@asar.kz; internet www.asar.kz; f. 2003; centrist; Chair. DARIGHA NAZARBAYEVA; 177,000 mems (2004).

Party of Patriots of Kazakhstan (PPK): 050000 Almaty; f. 2000; merged with the Union of Officers in 2004; Chair. GANI YE. KASYMOV; 132,000 mems (2004).

Spirituality Republican Party (Rukhaniyat): 050000 Almaty, Kurmangazy 61; f. 1995 as Renaissance Party of Kazakhstan; re-registered under new name 2003; supports Govt of President Nazarbayev; Chair. ALTYNSHASH K. JAGANOVA; 75,000 mems (2004).

True Light Road—Democratic Party of Kazakhstan (Naghyz Ak Zhol): 050010 Almaty, pr. Dostyk 123/7; tel. (3272) 64-19-99; fax 60-73-34; e-mail info@akzhol-party.kz; internet www.akzhol-party.kz; f. 2004, following split from Light Road; registered in 2006; part of the For a Just Kazakhstan opposition bloc; Leaders BULAT ABILOV, URAZ DZHANDOSOV, TULEGEN T. JUKEYEV.

Village Peasants' Social-Democratic Party (Aul): 050000 Almaty; f. 2000; seeks to strengthen government support for the agricultural sector; Chair. GANI A. KALIYEV; 125,000 mems (2004).

Diplomatic Representation

EMBASSIES IN KAZAKHSTAN

Afghanistan: 050000 Almaty, Mira 12; tel. and fax (3272) 55-27-92; Ambassador SAYD ZAHER SHAH AKHBARI.

Armenia: 480075 Almaty, Seifullina 579; tel. (3272) 69-29-32; fax (3272) 69-29-08; e-mail akod100@hotmail.com; Ambassador GARIK ISRAELIN.

Azerbaijan: 010000 Astana; Ambassador LYATIF QANDILOV.

Belarus: 010000 Astana, pr. Respubliki 17; tel. (3172) 32-18-70; fax (3172) 32-06-65; e-mail kazakhstan@belembassy.org; Ambassador LARISA V. PAKUSH.

Bulgaria: 480002 Almaty, Makatayeva 13A; tel. (3272) 30-27-54; fax (3272) 30-27-55; e-mail dekov@itte.kz; Chargé d'affaires a.i. IVAN PAROV.

Canada: 050010 Almaty, Karasai Batyr 34; tel. (3272) 50-11-51; fax (3272) 58-24-93; e-mail almat@international.gc.ca; internet www.dfait-maeci.gc.ca/canadaeuropa/kazakhstan; Ambassador ANNA BIOLIK.

China, People's Republic: 010000 Astana, Diplomaticheskii gorodok, kottedzh 2; tel. (3172) 24-13-80; fax (3172) 24-13-81; e-mail chinaemb_kz@mfa.gov.cn; internet kz.chineseembassy.org; Ambassador ZHANG XIYUN.

Cuba: 010000 Astana, pr. Kabanbai Batyra 27/2; tel. and fax and fax (3172) 22-14-19; e-mail embacuba@cubakaz.com; internet www.cubakaz.com; Ambassador TERESITA CAPOTE CAMACHO.

Czech Republic: 050051 Almaty, Dostyk 212, POB 26; tel. (3272) 64-16-06; fax (3272) 64-49-97; e-mail almaata@embassy.mzv.cz; internet www.mzv.cz/almaty; Ambassador Dr MILAN SEDLÁČEK.

Egypt: 050010 Almaty, Zenkova 59; tel. (3272) 91-63-58; fax (3272) 91-10-22; e-mail sphinx_emb@nursat.kz; Ambassador ABDEL MAWJOOD AL-HABASHI.

France: 050004 Almaty, Furmanova 173; tel. (3272) 58-25-04; fax (3272) 58-25-09; e-mail ambafrance@mail.kz; Ambassador GÉRARD PERROLET.

Georgia: 050000 Almaty, Bayan Aul Dacha 7; tel. (3272) 56-87-61; Ambassador ZURAB SHURGAYA.

Germany: 050000 Almaty, Vila C-12, Furmanova 173; tel. (3272) 24-15-63; fax (3272) 24-18-30; e-mail zreg@alma.auswaertiges-amt.de; internet www.almaty.diplo.de; Ambassador GERHARDT WEISS.

Greece: 050051 Almaty, pr. Dostyk 216/1; tel. (3272) 50-39-61; fax (3272) 50-39-38; e-mail gr_embassy@kaznet.kz; Ambassador CHRISTOS KONTOVOUNISIOS.

Holy See: 010000 Astana, Zelyonaya Alleya 20; tel. (3172) 24-16-03; fax (3172) 24-16-04; Apostolic Nuncio JÓZEF WESOŁOWSKI (Titular Bishop of Siebte).

Hungary: 050000 Almaty, ul. Musabayeva 4, POB 166; tel. (3272) 55-12-06; fax (3272) 58-18-37; e-mail titkarsagala@mail.online.kz; Ambassador JÁNOS NÉMET.

India: 050000 Almaty, Maulenova 71; tel. (3272) 92-14-11; fax (3272) 92-67-67; e-mail hoc@indembassy.kz; internet www.indembassy.kz; Ambassador Sri ASOKE KUMAR MUKERJI.

Iran: 050000 Almaty, ul. Luganskogo 31–33; tel. (3272) 54-19-74; fax (3272) 54-27-54; e-mail iranembassy@itte.kz; Ambassador RAMIN MEHMAN PARAST.

Israel: 050000 Almaty, ul. Zheltoksan 87, Kaybek bi; tel. (3272) 50-62-84; fax (3272) 50-62-83; e-mail info@almaty.mfa.gov.il; Ambassador YEHUDA YAAKOV.

Italy: 473000 Astana, ul. Kosmonavtov 62; tel. (3272) 91-03-07; fax (3272) 91-03-12; e-mail ambasta@ducatmail.kz; internet sedi.esteri.it/almaty; Ambassador DIEGO LORENZO LONGO.

Japan: 050010 Almaty, Kazybek bi 41; tel. (3272) 98-06-00; fax (3272) 60-86-01; e-mail taishikz@nursat.kz; internet www.kz.emb-japan.go.jp; Ambassador TOSHIO TSUNOZAKI.

Korea, Republic: 050000 Almaty, Jarkentskaya 2/77; tel. (3272) 53-26-60; fax (3272) 50-70-59; e-mail swtae76@mofat.go.kr; Ambassador TAE SUK-WON.

Kyrgyzstan: Astana, 'Karaotkel' A2/1; tel. (3172) 24-20-24; fax (3172) 24-24-12; e-mail kz@mail.online.kz; Ambassador ZHUMAGUL S. SAADANBEKOV.

Libya: 050000 Almaty, ul. Melichnaya 10; tel. (3272) 91-93-31; fax (3272) 98-05-36; e-mail libya@nursat.kz; Chargé d'affaires a.i. RAMADAN BZAMA.

Lithuania: 050059 Almaty, Iskanderova 15; tel. (3272) 93-46-06; fax (3272) 93-51-53; e-mail amb.kz@urm.lt; Ambassador ROMUALDAS VISOKAVIČIUS.

Malaysia: Almaty, Al-Farabi pr. 36/2; tel. (3272) 93-96-41; fax (3272) 93-96-45; e-mail mwalmaty@nursat.kz; Ambassador THAN TAI HING.

Mongolia: Almaty, ul. Al-Farabi, Aubakirova 1; tel. (3272) 20-08-65; fax (3272) 60-17-23; e-mail monkazel@kazmail.asdc.kz; Ambassador RAVDANGIIN KHATANBAATAR.

Netherlands: 480072 Almaty, Nauryzbai Batyr 103; tel. (3272) 50-37-73; fax (3272) 50-37-72; e-mail alm@minbuza.nl; internet www.nlembassy-almaty.org; Ambassador PETER VAN LEEUWEN.

Pakistan: 050004 Almaty, Tulebayeva 25; tel. (3272) 73-15-02; fax (3272) 73-13-00; e-mail parepalmaty@hotmail.com; Ambassador IRFAN-UR-REHMAN RAJA.

Poland: 050059 Almaty, Jarkentskaya 9, c/o Iskanderov 1 1/13; tel. (3272) 58-16-17; fax (3272) 58-15-50; e-mail ambpol@asdc.kz; Ambassador WŁADYSŁAW SOKOŁOWSKI.

Romania: 050010 Almaty, Pushkina 97; tel. (3272) 61-57-72; fax (3272) 58-83-17; e-mail amb@rom.ricc.kz; Ambassador VASILE SOARE.

Russia: Almaty, ul. Jandosov 4; tel. (3272) 74-71-05; fax (3172) 74-71-68; e-mail rfe@nursat.kz; Ambassador VLADIMIR S. BABICHEV.

Saudi Arabia: 050000 Almaty, Gornaya 137; tel. (3272) 50-28-71; fax (3272) 50-28-11; e-mail emb_kz@hotmail.com; Ambassador ALI AL-HAMDAN.

Slovakia: 010000 Astana, Karaotkel 5; tel. (3172) 24-11-91; fax (3172) 24-20-48; Ambassador DUŠAN PODHORSKÝ.

Spain: 050000 Almaty, Baitursinova 102; tel. (3272) 50-09-06; fax (3272) 50-35-30; e-mail embespkz@mail.mae.es; Ambassador SANTIAGO CHAMORRO Y GONZÁLEZ-TABLAS.

Tajikistan: 050000 Almaty, Al Farabi 96; tel. (3272) 93-51-65; fax (3272) 93-51-80; e-mail tajemb-kaz@vitelco.kz; Ambassador IKBARSHO ISHKANDEROV.

Turkey: 050010 Almaty, Tole bi 29; tel. (3272) 91-39-32; fax (3272) 50-62-08; e-mail almatyturk@kaznet.kz; Ambassador TANER SEBEN.

Turkmenistan: 010000 Astana, Otyrar 64; tel. and fax (3172) 28-08-82; e-mail tm_emb@at.kz; Ambassador MUHAMMAD ABALAKOV.

Ukraine: 010000 Astana, Auezova 57; tel. (3172) 32-60-42; fax (3172) 32-68-11; e-mail embassy_ua@kepter.kz; internet ukrembassy.kepter.kz; Ambassador VASYL H. TSYBENKO.

United Kingdom: 050000 Almaty, Furmanova 173; tel. (3272) 50-61-91; fax (3272) 50-62-60; e-mail british-embassy@nursat.kz; internet www.britishembassy.gov.uk/kazakhstan; Ambassador PAUL BRUMMELL.

KAZAKHSTAN

USA: 050000 Almaty, ul. Furmanov 99/97A; tel. (3272) 50-48-02; fax (3272) 50-25-06; e-mail usembassy@freenet.kz; internet www.usembassy-kazakhstan.freenet.kz; Ambassador JOHN M. ORDWAY.

Uzbekistan: 050010 Almaty, Baribayeva 36; tel. (3272) 91-83-16; fax (3272) 91-10-55; Ambassador TURDIKUL BUTAYAROV.

Judicial System

Supreme Court of the Republic of Kazakhstan (Kazakhstan Respublikasynyn Zhogargy Soty): 010000 Astana; tel. (3172) 74-75-00; fax (3172) 74-78-13; internet www.supcourt.kz.
Chairman: KAYRAT A. MAMI.

Constitutional Council of the Republic of Kazakhstan (Kazakstan Respublikasy Konstitutsiyalyk Keneci): 010000 Astana, Levoberezhiye, Verkhovnyi sud, Blok A, dom A; tel. (3172) 74-76-15; fax (3172) 77-76-51; internet www.constcouncil.kz; f. 1995; seven mems; Chair. IGOR I. ROGOV.

Prosecutor-General: RASHID T. TUSUPBEKOV, 010000 Astana, ul. Seifullina 73; e-mail procuror@nursat.kz; internet www.procuror.kz.

Religion

The major religion of the Kazakhs is Islam. They are almost exclusively Sunni Muslims of the Hanafi school. The Russian Orthodox Church is the dominant Christian denomination; it is attended mainly by Slavs. There are also Protestant Churches (mainly Baptists), as well as a Roman Catholic (Latin Rite) presence and a Jewish community. In mid-2005 legislation was introduced, which required all religious organizations and communities to register with the state authorities before engaging in any religious activity.

ISLAM

The Kazakhs were converted to Islam only in the early 19th century, and for many years elements of animist practices remained. Over the period 1985–90 the number of mosques in Kazakhstan increased from 25 to 60, 12 of which were newly built. By 1991 there were an estimated 230 Muslim religious communities functioning in Kazakhstan and an Islamic institute had been opened in Almaty. The Islamic revival intensified following Kazakhstan's independence from the USSR, and during 1991–94 some 4,000 mosques were reported to have been opened.

Mufti of Kazakhstan: ABSATTAR B. haji DERBISALI, Almaty.

CHRISTIANITY

The Roman Catholic Church

In May 2003 the hierarchy of the Roman Catholic Church in Kazakhstan was restructured. The former apostolic administration of Astana was elevated to the status of archdiocese, as the Archdiocese of the Most Holy Virgin Mary at Astana, with authority over the dioceses of the Most Holy Trinity at Almaty (formerly an apostolic administration) and Karaganda, and the apostolic administration of Atyrau. Adherents to the Roman Catholic Church totalled an estimated 182,600 at 31 December 2003.

Archbishop of the Archdiocese of the Most Holy Virgin Mary at Astana: Rt Rev. TOMASZ PETA, 473033 Astana, Tashenova 3, POB 622; tel. (3172) 34-29-35; fax (3172) 34-29-27; e-mail catholic_astana@mail.ru.

The Russian Orthodox Church (Moscow Patriarchate)

Metropolitanate of Astana and Almaty: 050014 Almaty, mikroraion Dorozhnik 29; tel. (3272) 98-94-15; e-mail office@orthodox.kz; internet www.orthodox.kz; f. 2003; three dioceses; Metropolitan MEFODII (NEMTSOV).

JUDAISM

Rabbi of Almaty: Rabbi MENACHEM GERSHOVICH.
Rabbi of Karaganda: Rabbi MEIR SHAINER.

The Press

At July 2001 an estimated 950 newspaper and 342 periodical titles were published in Kazakhstan. In addition, 15 news agencies were operating in the country.

PRINCIPAL DAILY NEWSPAPERS

Almaty Asia Times: 050000 Almaty, Jandosova 60/412; tel. (3272) 44-74-54; fax (3272) 44-78-40.

Almaty Herald: 480009 Almaty, ul. Rozybakiyeva 37; tel. (3272) 41-45-69; fax (3272) 41-40-78; e-mail herald@nursat.kz; Editor-in-Chief OLESSYA IVANOVA.

Ekspress–K: 050044 Almaty, Abdullinykh 6; tel. (3272) 59-60-00; fax (3272) 59-60-39; e-mail daily@express-k.kz; internet www.express-k.kz; f. 1920; 5 a week; in Russian; Editor-in-Chief ADILKHAN NUSUPOV; circ. 19,500.

Kazakhstanskaya Pravda (Kazakhstani Truth): 050044 Almaty, Gogolya 39; tel. (3272) 63-65-65; fax (3272) 50-18-73; tel. (3172) 32-19-44; e-mail kpam@kaznet.kz; internet www.kazpravda.kz; f. 1920; 5 a week; publ. by the Govt; in Russian; Editor-in-Chief V. MIKHAILOV; circ. 34,115.

Khalyk Kenesi (Councils of the People): 010000 Astana; tel. (3272) 33-10-85; f. 1990; 5 a week; publ. by Parliament; in Kazakh; Editor-in-Chief ZH. KENZHALIN.

Navigator: internet www.navi.kz; f. 2000; online only; in Russian.

Vechernii Almaty (Evening Almaty): 050016 Almaty, pr. Abylai khana 2; tel. and fax (3272) 79-28-90; e-mail vecherni_almaty@mail.ru; internet www.vechorka.kz; f. 1968; in Russian; Editor-in-Chief ELMIRA R. PASHINA.

Yegemen Kazakhstan (Sovereign Kazakhstan): 050044 Almaty, Gogolya 39; Astana; tel. and fax (3272) 63-25-46; tel. (3172) 34-16-41; e-mail astegemen@nursat.kz; f. 1919; 6 a week; organ of the Govt; in Kazakh; Editor-in-Chief M. SERKHANOV; circ. 31,840.

OTHER PUBLICATIONS

Akikat (Justice): 050044 Almaty, Gogolya 39; tel. (3272) 63-94-33; fax (3272) 63-94-19; f. 1921; monthly; social and political; circ. 1,484.

Aktsionery (Shareholders): 050044 Almaty, Chaikovskogo 11; tel. (3272) 32-96-09; fax (3272) 39-98-95; f. 1990; in Russian; twice a week; business, investment; Editor-in-Chief VIKTOR SHATSKY.

Ana Tili (Native Language): 050044 Almaty, pr. Dostyk 7; tel. (3272) 33-22-21; fax (3272) 33-34-73; f. 1990; weekly; publ. by the Kazakh Tili society; in Kazakh; Editor-in-Chief ZH. BEISENBAY-ULY; circ. 11,073.

Ara-Shmel (Bumble-bee): 050044 Almaty, Gogolya 39; tel. (3272) 63-59-46; f. 1956; monthly; satirical; in Kazakh and Russian; Editor-in-Chief S. ZHUMABEKOV; circ. 53,799.

Arai (Dawn): 050000 Almaty, Furmanova 53; tel. (3272) 32-29-45; f. 1987; every two months; socio-political; Editor-in-Chief S. KUTTYKADAMOV; circ. 7,500.

Atameken (Fatherland): 050010 Almaty, pr. Dostyk 85; tel. (3272) 63-58-43; f. 1991; ecological; publ. by Ministry of Environmental Protection; circ. 25,063.

Aziya Kino (Asian Cinema): 050000 Almaty; tel. (3272) 61-86-55; f. 1994; monthly; in Russian and Kazakh; Editor-in-Chief G. ABIKEYEVA.

Baldyrgan (Sprout): 050044 Almaty, pr. Zhibek zholy 50; tel. (3272) 33-16-73; f. 1958; monthly; illustrated; for pre-school and first grades of school; in Kazakh; Editor-in-Chief T. MOLDAGALIYEV; circ. 150,000.

Business World: 010000 Astana, Pushkina 166; tel. and fax (3172) 75-19-34; e-mail areket-kz@hotmail.com; f. 1999; weekly; circ. 10,000.

Continent: 050000 Almaty, POB 271; tel. (3272) 50-10-39; fax (3272) 50-10-41; e-mail bzchyt@kaznet.kz; f. 1999; policy and society journal; Editor-in-Chief ANDREI KUKUSHKIN; circ. 10,000.

Delovaya Nedelya (Business Week): 480200 Almaty, pr. Zhibek zholy 64; tel. (3272) 50-62-72; fax (3272) 73-91-48; e-mail rikki@kazmail.asdc.kz; internet www.dn.kz; f. 1992; weekly; in Russian; Editor-in-Chief S.A. KORZHUMBAYEV; circ. 10,600.

Deutsche Allgemeine Zeitung: 050044 Almaty, pr. Zhibek zholy 50/418; tel. (3272) 73-42-69; fax (3272) 73-92-91; e-mail daz@ok.kz; f. 1966; weekly; political, economic, cultural, social; in German; Editor-in-Chief IRINA ZIRENTSCHIKOWA; circ. 1,700.

Ekonomika i Zhizn (Economics and Life): 050000 Almaty; tel. (3272) 63-96-86; f. 1926; monthly; publ. by the Govt; in Russian; Editor-in-Chief MURAT T. SARSENOV; circ. 4,800.

Globe: 050009 Almaty, pr. Abaya 155/13–14; tel. (3272) 50-76-39; fax (3272) 50-63-62; e-mail ipa@mailonline.kz; f. 1995; two a week; in English and Russian; Editor-in-Chief NURLAN ABLYAZOV; circ. 5,550.

Golos Kazakha/Kazakh Uni (Voice of a Kazakh): 050000 Almaty, Zenkov 75; tel. (3272) 61-79-09; fax (3272) 61-94-47; f. 1989; weekly; organ of the Federation of Trade Unions of Kazakhstan; in Russian and Kazakh.

Kakadu (Cockatoo): 050004 Almaty, Chaikovskogo 11; tel. (3272) 39-97-04; f. 1995; monthly; in Russian; Editor-in-Chief L. GERTZY.

KAZAKHSTAN

Karavan (Caravan): Almaty, pl. Respubliki 13; tel. (3272) 32-08-39; fax (3272) 32-97-57; e-mail kaztag@caravan.kz; internet www.caravan.kz; f. 1991; weekly; in Russian; Editor-in-Chief ANDREI SHUKHOV; circ. 250,000.

Kazakh Adebiety (Kazakh Literature): 050000 Almaty, pr. Ablaikhana 105; tel. and fax (3272) 69-54-62; f. 1934; weekly; organ of the Union of Writers of Kazakhstan; in Kazakh; Editor-in-Chief A. ZHAKSYBAYEV; circ. 7,874.

Kazakhstan: 050044 Almaty, pr. Zhibek zholy 50; tel. (3272) 33-13-56; f. 1992; weekly; economic reform; in English; Editor-in-Chief N. ORAZBEKOV.

Kazakhstan Aielderi (Women of Kazakhstan): 050044 Almaty, pr. Zhibek zholy 50; tel. (3272) 33-06-23; fax (3272) 46-15-53; f. 1925; monthly; literary, artistic, social and political; in Kazakh; Editor-in-Chief ALTYNSHASH K. JAGANOVA; circ. 15,200.

Kazakhstan Business: 050044 Almaty, pr. Zhibek zholy 50; tel. (3272) 33-42-56; f. 1991; weekly; in Russian; Editor-in-Chief B. SUKHARBEKOV.

Kazakstan Mektebi (Kazakh School): 0580004 Almaty, pr. Ablaikhana 34; tel. (3272) 39-76-65; f. 1925; monthly; in Kazakh; Editor-in-Chief S. ABISHEVA; circ. 10,000.

Kazakstan Mugalimi (Kazakh Teacher): 050010 Almaty, Jambula 25; tel. (3272) 61-60-58; f. 1935; weekly; in Kazakh; Editor-in-Chief ZH. TEMIRBEKOV; circ. 6,673.

Kazakstan Zaman (Kazakh Time): 050002 Almaty, pr. Dostyk 106G; tel. (3272) 65-07-39; e-mail kazakstanzaman@mail.ru; f. 1992; in Kazakh and Turkish; weekly; publ. by the al-Farabi Foundation; circ. 15,000; Gen. Dir ERSIN DEMIRCI.

Korye Ilbo (Korean News): 050046 Almaty, pr. Zhibek zholy 50; tel. (3272) 33-90-10; fax (3272) 63-25-46; f. 1923; weekly; in Korean and Russian; Editor-in-Chief YAN WON SIK.

Medicina (Medicine): 050000 Almaty, pr. Ablaikhana 63; tel. (3272) 73-48-01; fax (3272) 73-16-90; e-mail zdrav_kz@nursat.kz; f. 2000; monthly; in Kazakh; Editor-in-Chief A. SH. SEYSENBAYEV; circ. 5,000.

Novoye Pokoleniye (New Generation): 050091 Almaty, ul. Bogenbai batyra 139/1–2; tel. (3272) 61-31-06; fax (3272) 50-95-46; e-mail np@host.kz; internet www.np.kz; f. 1998; weekly; in Russian; Editor-in-Chief SERGEI APARIN; circ. 95,000.

Oasis: 484039 Jambul obl., ul. Lenina 31–34; tel. and fax (3262) 23-27-93; e-mail alex@zagribelny.jambyl.kz; organ of the Green Movement Socio-Ecological Centre; environmental matters; Editor-in-Chief ALEKSANDR ZAGRIBELNYI.

Panorama: 050013 Almaty, pl. Respubliki 15/647; tel. (3272) 63-28-34; fax (3272) 63-66-16; e-mail panorama@kazmail.asdc.kz; internet www.panorama.kz; f. 1992; weekly; in Russian; Editor-in-Chief LERA TSOY; circ. 18,500.

Parasat: 180100 Almaty, Aiteke bi 28; tel. (3272) 93-94-71; fax (3272) 93-94-74; f. 1958; monthly; socio-political, literary, illustrated; in Kazakh; Editor-in-Chief BAKKOZHA S. MUKAY; circ. 20,000.

Petroleum of Kazakhstan: 050091 Almaty, Nauryzbai Batyr 58; tel. (3272) 58-28-33; fax (3272) 50-50-82; e-mail office@petroleumjournal.kz; internet www.petroleumjournal.kz; every two months; in Russian and English; Editor-in-Chief OLEG C. CHERVINSKY; circ. 2,000.

Prostor (Expanse): 050091 Almaty, pr. Ablylai khana 105; tel. (3272) 72-61-87; e-mail info@prstr.samal.kz; internet prostor.samal.kz; f. 1933; monthly; literary and artistic; in Russian; Editor-in-Chief VALERII F. MIKHAILOV; circ. 1,800.

Respublika—Delovoye obozreniye (Republic—Business Review): 480100 Almaty, ul. Satpayeva 2/17; tel. and fax (3272) 53-46-71; e-mail assandy@fromru.com; internet www.respublika.kz; weekly; in Russian; Editor-in-Chief IRINA PETRUSHOVA.

Russkii Yazyk i Literatura (Russian Language and Literature): 050091 Almaty, Ablylai khana 34; tel. (3272) 39-76-68; f. 1962; monthly; in Russian; Editor-in-Chief B. S. MUKANOV; circ. 17,465.

Shalkar: 050044 Almaty, pr. Zhibek zholy 50; tel. (3272) 33-86-85; f. 1976; twice a month; in Kazakh (in the Arabic script); Editor-in-Chief A. KAIYRBEKOV; circ. 2,500.

Sovety Kazakhstana (Councils of Kazakhstan): 050002 Almaty, pr. Zhibek zholy 15; tel. (3272) 34-92-19; f. 1990; weekly; publ. by Parliament; in Russian; Editor-in-Chief YU. GURSKII; circ. 30,000.

Turkistan: 050012 Almaty, Bogenbai Batyr 150; tel. (3272) 69-61-54; fax (3272) 62-08-98; f. 1994; weekly; political; in Kazakh; circ. 5,000.

Uigur Avazi (Uigur Voice): 050044 Almaty, pr. Zhibek zholy 50; tel. (3272) 33-84-59; f. 1957; 2 a week; publ. by the Govt; socio-political; in Uigur; Editor-in-Chief I. AZAMATOV; circ. 9,000.

Ukrainskiy Novyny (Ukrainian News): 010000 Astana, pr. Respubliki 17; tel. (3172) 21-74-62; e-mail un_astana@mail.kz; f. 1994; weekly; in Ukrainian; Editor-in-Chief TARAS CHERNEHA; circ. 1,200.

Ulan: 050044 Almaty, pr. Zhibek zholy 50; tel. (3272) 33-80-03; f. 1930; weekly; in Kazakh; Editor-in-Chief S. KALIYEV; circ. 183,014.

Vremya (Time): 050000 Almaty, pr. Raiymbeka 115; tel. and fax (3272) 58-10-06; e-mail isemenko@time.kz; internet www.time.kz; f. 1999; weekly; in Russian; Editor-in-Chief IGOR MELTSER; circ. 250,000 (2004).

Zerde (Intellect): 050044 Almaty, pr. Zhibek zholy 50; tel. (3272) 33-83-81; f. 1960; monthly; popular, scientific, technical; in Kazakh; Editor-in-Chief E. RAUSHAN-ULY; circ. 68,600.

Zhalyn (Flame): 050002 Almaty, pr. Dostyk 7; tel. (3272) 33-22-21; f. 1969; monthly; literary, artistic, social and political; in Kazakh; Editor-in-Chief M. KULKENOV; circ. 2,196.

Zhas Alash (Young Generation): 050044 Almaty, Makatayeva 22; tel. (3272) 30-60-90; fax (3272) 30-24-69; internet www.zhasalash.kz; f. 1921; publ. by the Kazakhstan Youth Union; in Kazakh; Editor-in-Chief ZHUSIPBEK KORGASBEK; circ. 133,000.

Zhuldyz (Star): 050091 Almaty, pr. Ablai-Khan 105; tel. (3272) 62-51-37; f. 1922; monthly; journal of the Union of Writers of Kazakhstan; literary, artistic, socio-political; in Kazakh; Editor-in-Chief MUKHTAR MAGAUIN; circ. 1,539.

NEWS AGENCIES

Khabar News Agency: see Broadcasting and Communications.

National Information Agency (Kazinform): 010000 Astana, Jambul 32A; tel. (3172) 23-83-58; fax (3172) 23-02-83; e-mail info@inform.kz; internet www.kazinform.com; f. 1997; 100% state-owned open jt-stock co; provides information on govt activities in Kazakhstan and abroad; Pres. GADILBEK M. SHALAKHMETOV.

Foreign Bureaux

Agence France-Presse (AFP): 050010 Almaty, Dostyk 29/31; tel. (3272) 91-06-58; fax (3272) 91-06-58.

Anadolu Ajansı (Turkey): 050000 Almaty, Panfilova 83/55; tel. (3272) 33-15-64; fax (3272) 50-79-49; e-mail almati@anadoluajansi.com.tr.

Internews Network Agency (USA): 050091 Almaty, Nauryzbai Batyr 58; tel. (3272) 50-89-50; fax (3272) 50-89-59; e-mail oleg@internews.kz; internet www.internews.kz.

Islamic Republic News Agency (IRNA) (Iran): Almaty; tel. (3272) 68-10-05; e-mail irna@irna.com; internet www.irna.com; Correspondent BAHARVAND ALI RAHMAD.

ITAR—TASS (Information Telegraph Agency of Russia-Telegraphic Agency of the Sovereign Countries) (Russia): Almaty; Astana; tel. (3272) 33-96-81; tel. (3172) 32-42-02.

Reuters (United Kingdom): Astana; tel. (3172) 50-94-10.

RIA—Novosti (Russian Information Agency—News) (Russia): Almaty; tel. (3272) 33-99-50; Correspondent REVMIRA VOSHENKO.

Xinhua (New China) News Agency (People's Republic of China): Almaty; tel. (3272) 24-68-68.

Publishers

Gylym (Science): 050010 Almaty, Pushkina 111–113; tel. (3272) 91-18-77; fax (3272) 61-88-45; f. 1946; books on natural sciences, humanities and scientific research journals; Dir S. G. BAIMENOV.

Kainar (Spring): 050009 Almaty, pr. Abaya 143; tel. (3272) 42-27-96; f. 1962; agriculture, history, culture, religion; Dir ORAZBEK S. SARSENBAYEV.

Kazakhskaya Entsiklopediya (Kazakh Encyclopedia): Almaty; tel. (3272) 62-55-66; f. 1968; Editor-in-Chief R. N. NURGALIYEV.

Kazakhstan Publishing House: 050000 Almaty, pr. Abaya 143; tel. and fax (3272) 42-29-29; f. 1920; political science, economics, medicine, general and social sciences; Dir E. KH. SYZDYKOV; Editors-in-Chief M. D. SITKO, M. A. RASHEV.

Mektep: 050009 Almaty, pr. Abaya 143; tel. (3272) 42-26-24; fax (3272) 77-85-44; e-mail mektep@mail.ru; internet www.mektep.kz; f. 1947; mainly literature for educational institutions; dictionaries, phrase books, children's textbooks, teaching materials, reference books; publishes books in Kazakh, Russian, Uigur and Uzbek; Gen. Dir E. SATYBALDIYEV; Editor-in-Chief SH. GUSAKOVA.

Oner (Art): 050000 Almaty, pr. Abaya 143; tel. (3272) 42-08-88; f. 1980; Dir S. S. ORAZALINOV; Editor-in-Chief A. A. ASKAROV.

Zhazushy (Writer): 050000 Almaty, pr. Abaya 143; tel. (3272) 42-28-49; f. 1934; literature, literary criticism, essays and poetry; Dir D. I. ISABEKOV; Editor-in-Chief A. T. SARAYEV.

KAZAKHSTAN

Broadcasting and Communications

TELECOMMUNICATIONS

Altel: 480002 Almaty, ul. Zhurgeneva 9; tel. (3272) 30-16-30; fax (3272) 30-01-43; e-mail info@altel.kz; internet www.altel.kz; f. 1994; provides mobile cellular communications in Kazakhstan (as Dalacom and PAThWORD).

GSM Kazakhstan: 480099 Almaty, Samal 2/100; tel. (3272) 58-11-48; fax (3272) 58-89-11; e-mail webmaster@kcell.kz; internet www.kcell.kz; f. 1998; 51% owned by Fintur Holdings (Finland/Turkey), 49% by Kazakhtelecom; provides mobile cellular telecommunications services (as K-Cell and Activ) in 180 settlements and along principal roads across Kazakhstan; 2m. subscribers (April 2005).

KaR-tel (K-Mobile): 050000 Almaty, ul. Tole bi 55; tel. (3272) 50-60-60; fax (3272) 95-23-97; e-mail csales@kartel.kz; internet www.k-mobile.kz; f. 1999; 100% subsidiary of VympelKom-Bilain (Russia); provides mobile cellular telecommunications services (as K-Mobile, Excess and Beeline) in more than 100 settlements and along principal roads across Kazakhstan; Gen. Dir DMITRII KROMSKII; 1.6m. subscribers (mid-2005).

Kazakhtelekom: 050000 Almaty, pr. Abylai Khan 86; tel. (3272) 62-05-41; fax (3272) 63-93-95; internet www.itte.kz; f. 1994; national telecommunications corpn; 60% state-owned, 40% owned by Daewoo Corpn (Republic of Korea); Pres. SERIK BURKITBAYEV.

KazTransCom Joint-Stock Co.: 50012 Almaty, ul. Baitursynov 46A; tel. (3272) 70-13-10; fax (3272) 70-13-18; e-mail ktc@kaztranscom.kz; provides telecommunications services to the petroleum and natural gas sectors; won licence in 2004 to provide long-distance and international telephone calls country-wide, thus becoming Kazakhstan's second long-distance provider; 7 brs (2003).

BROADCASTING

Private radio and television stations began operating in Kazakhstan in the 1990s. In mid-2001 there were an estimated 124 radio and television stations.

Kazakh State Television and Radio Broadcasting Corpn: 050013 Almaty, Zheltoksan 175A; tel. (3272) 63-37-16; f. 1920; Pres. YERMEK TURSUNOV.

Radio

Kazakh Radio: 050013 Almaty, Zheltoksan 175 A; tel. (3272) 63-19-68; fax (3272) 65-03-87; e-mail kazradio@astel.kz; internet www.radio.kz; f. 1921; broadcasts in Kazakh, Russian, Uigur, German and other minority languages; Gen. Dir TOREKHAN DANIYAR.

Television

Khabar News Agency: 050013 Almaty, pl. Respubliki 13; tel. (3272) 63-83-69; fax (3272) 50-63-45; e-mail naz@khabar.almaty.kz; internet www.khabar.kz; f. 1959; international broadcasts in Kazakh, Uigur, Russian and German; two television channels; Chair. of the Bd of Dirs MAULEN ASHIMBAYEV; Dir GULNAR IKSANOVA.

KTK (Kazakh Commercial Television): 050013 Almaty, pl. Respubliki 13; tel. (3272) 63-44-28; fax (3272) 50-66-25; e-mail ktkao@kzaira.com; f. 1990; independent; 20% of shares were reported to have been sold to a US investment co in 2001; Gen. Dir ANDREI SHUKHOV; Pres. SHOKAN LAUULIN.

NTK (Association of TV and Radio Broadcasters of Kazakhstan): 050013 Almaty, pl. Respubliki 13, 6th Floor; tel. (3272) 70-01-83; fax (3272) 70-01-85; e-mail kaztvradio@nursat.kz; f. 2000; privately owned; Pres. AIDAR ZHUMABAYEV.

Finance

(cap. = capital; res = reserves; dep. = deposits; m. = million; brs = branches; amounts in tenge, unless otherwise indicated)

BANKING

From 1994 the National Bank of Kazakhstan (NBK) effected a series of measures aimed at rationalizing the banking sector, in order to ensure a sound financial infrastructure. Numerous banks had their licences revoked: between 1995 and 1998 the number of commercial banks declined by almost one-half, and it continued to decline thereafter. By July 2003 the banking system comprised 35 banks, including two state banks and 16 with foreign participation. At 1 July 2003 commercial banks in Kazakhstan had aggregate equity of 183,900m. tenge, and aggregate assets of 1,378,600m. tenge.

Central Bank

National Bank of Kazakhstan (NBK): 050000 Almaty, Koktem-3 21; tel. (3272) 50-46-25; fax (3272) 50-60-90; e-mail hq@nationalbank.kz; internet www.nationalbank.kz; f. 1990; cap. 20,000.0m., res 148,003.8m., dep. 332,144.9m. (Dec. 2003); Chair. ANVAR G. SAIDENOV; 19 brs.

Major Commercial Banks

Abidbank: 050010 Almaty, pr. Dostyka 85 A; tel. and fax (3272) 41-60-67; e-mail herald@mailbox.kz; f. 1993; Chair. ANATOLII P. NEDELIN.

ABN AMRO Bank Kazakhstan: 050000 Almaty, Khadji Mukana 45; tel. (3272) 50-73-00; fax (3272) 50-72-98; e-mail aabk@kz.abnamro.com; internet www.abnamro.kz; f. 1994; 51% owned by ABN AMRO Bank NV (Netherlands); cap. 1,800.0m., res 121m., dep. 26,963m. (Oct. 2001); Chair. DOUGLAS KENNEDY; 3 brs.

Alashbank: 050012 Almaty, Sharipova 84; tel. (3272) 92-60-08; fax (3272) 67-01-44; e-mail alashbnk@online.ru; f. 1992; Pres. MADZHED M. K. ALBSURIY; 1 br.

Alfa Bank Kazakhstan: 050012 Almaty, ul. Masanchi 57A/202; tel. (3272) 92-00-12; fax (3272) 92-00-21; e-mail infokz@alfabank.ru; f. 1994; Chair. A. I. ARTYSHKO; 3 brs.

Almaty Commercial Bank: 050002 Almaty, Nauryzbay Batyr 19; tel. (3272) 58-82-26; fax (3272) 58-82-24; e-mail acb1@kaznet.kz; f. 1993; Chair. YERLAN U. BAYMURATOV.

Astana Bank: 160010 Southern Kazakhstan obl., Turkestan, Aiteke bi 31; tel. (3252) 57-24-39; e-mail astanabnk@shym.kz.

ATF Bank: 050000 Almaty, ul. Furmanova 100; tel. (3272) 58-81-11; fax (3272) 50-19-95; e-mail info@atfbank.kz; internet www.atfbank.kz; f. 1995; present name adopted 2002; cap. 6,239.50m., res 667.2m., dep. 81,908.7m. (Dec. 2003); Chair. TIMUR ISSATAYEV; 10 brs.

Bank Centercredit: 050072 Almaty, Shevchenko 100; tel. (3272) 59-85-46; fax (3272) 50-78-13; e-mail info@centercredit.kz; internet www.centercredit.kz; f. 1988; present name adopted 1996; cap. 5,167.0m., res 2,273.6m., dep. 69,704.5m. (Dec. 2003); Chair. of Council BAKHYTBEK R. BAYSEITOV; Chair. of Bd VLADISLAV S. LI; 19 brs.

Bank TuranAlem: 050000 Almaty, Samal 2, Zholdasbekov 97; tel. (3272) 50-40-70; fax (3272) 50-02-24; e-mail post@bta.kz; internet bta.kz; f. 1997 by merger of Turanbank and Alembank; privatized in 1998; cap. 16,091.0m., res 687.0m., dep. 195,696.0m. (Dec. 2002); Chair. SADUAKAS MAMESHTEGI; 23 brs.

Caspian Bank (Bank Kaspiiskii): 050012 Almaty, Adi Sharipova 90; tel. (3272) 50-85-92; fax (3272) 50-95-96; e-mail office@bankcaspian.kz; internet www.bankcaspian.kz; cap. 3,700.5m., res 521.0m., dep. 48,295.4m. (Dec. 2003); Chair. IGOR KIM; 17 brs.

Central Asian Bank of Co-operation and Development: 050008 Almaty, pr. Abaya 115A; tel. (3272) 33-01-12; fax (3272) 50-62-38; e-mail cab@asdc.kz; f. 1994; Chair. GAMAL K. SOODANBEKOV; 1 br.

Citibank Kazakhstan: 050010 Almaty, Kazybek bi 41 A; tel. (3272) 98-04-00; fax (3272) 98-03-99; e-mail citibank.kazakhstan@citigroup.com; internet www.citibank.kz; f. 1995; cap. US $25m. (1998); Chair. DANIEL J. CONNELLY.

DanaBank: 140000 Pavlodar, Lenina 119; tel. (3182) 32-38-41; fax (3182) 32-04-88; e-mail danabank@db.kz; f. 1992; cap. 1,000m., res 12m., dep. 481m.; Chair. ZHANAR M. ADBYKARIMOVA; 4 brs.

Demır Kazakhstan Bank (de): 050000 Almaty, Kurmangazy 61A; tel. (3272) 50-85-50; fax (3272) 50-85-25; e-mail demirbank@demirbank.kz; internet www.demirbank.kz; f. 1997; cap. 1,000.0m., res 81.3m., dep. 2,801.2m. (Dec. 2003); Chair. IHSAN UGUR.

Development Bank of Kazakhstan: 473000 Astana, pr. Republic 66/1; tel. (3172) 58-08-44; fax (3172) 58-02-69; e-mail info@kdb.kz; internet www.kdb.kz.

Eurasian Bank: 050002 Almaty, Kunayeva 56; tel. (3272) 50-86-07; fax (3272) 50-86-50; e-mail info@eurasian-bank.kz; internet www.eurasian-bank.kz; f. 1994; cap. US $107.5m., res $11.0m., total assets $656.0m. (July 2005); Chair. ALEKSANDR KONOPASSEVICH; 9 brs.

Eximbank Kazakhstan (Export-Import Bank of Kazakhstan): 480100 Almaty, Pushkina 118; tel. (3272) 63-43-00; fax (3272) 50-75-49; e-mail post_mail@eximbank.kz; f. 1994; state-owned; cap. 6,091m. (March 2000); Chair. BEISENBAY IZTELEUOV.

Industrial Bank of Kazakhstan: 050020 Almaty, Amangeldy 70; tel. (3272) 93-59-91; fax (3272) 53-38-43; e-mail info@ibk.kz; f. 1993; cap. 1,000m.; Chair. of Bd NURLAN T. SHAUKEROV; 1 br.

OJSC Kazakhstan International Bank: 480072 Almaty, Seifullina 597; tel. (3272) 92-99-62; fax (3272) 92-90-74; e-mail kib@kib.almaty.kz; f. 1993; cap. 887.8m., res 8.2m.; Chair. ASKAR B. NASENOV.

Kazakstan Halyk Bank/Narodnyi Bank Kazakhstana (People's Bank of Kazakhstan): 050046 Almaty, Rozybakiyeva 97; tel. (3272) 59-00-00; fax (3272) 59-02-71; e-mail halykbank@halykbank.kz; internet www.halykbank.kz; f. 1936 as br. of Savings Bank of USSR; fully privatized in Nov. 2001; cap. 9,896.8m., res 2,544.1m., dep. 217,250.8m. (Dec. 2003); Chair. ASSIYA SYRGABEKOVA; Man. Dir KAIRAT RAKHMANOV; 611 brs.

KAZAKHSTAN

Kazkommertsbank: 050060 Almaty, Zh. Gagarina 135; tel. (3272) 58-52-42; fax (3272) 58-52-81; e-mail mailbox@kkb.kz; internet www.kazkommertsbank.com; f. 1990; total assets US $5,416m., cap. $440.8m., dep. $1,521.7m. (Dec. 2004); Chair. NURZHAN S. SUBKHANBERDIN; Man. Dir ANDREI I. TIMCHENKO; 23 brs.

KZI Bank—Kazakhstan-Ziraat International Bank: 050057 Almaty, Klochkova 132, POB 34; tel. (3272) 50-60-80; fax (3272) 50-60-82; e-mail kzibank@kzibank.com; internet www.kzibank.com; f. 1993; owned by Türkiye Cumhuriyeti Ziraat Bankası (Agricultural Bank of the Turkish Republic); cap. 2,066.3m., res 114.2m., dep. 881.8m. (Dec. 2003); Chair. ZEKI SAYIN; Gen. Man. BEKIR SONMEZ.

Lariba-Bank: 050060 Almaty, Rozibakiyeva 181A; tel. (3272) 49-14-32; fax (3272) 49-64-21; e-mail lariba@kazmail.asdc.kz; f. 1992; Chair. ALEKSANDR G. BOYCHENKO; 1 br.

Neftebank: 090200 Western Kazakhstan obl., Aktau, Microraion 9/23A; tel. (3292) 43-61-61; fax (3292) 43-61-45; e-mail nb@neftebank.kz; cap. 835.8m.; Chair. of Bd G. S. MUSINA; 5 brs.

Nurbank: 050013 Almaty, Zheltoksan 168B; tel. (3272) 50-67-80; fax (3272) 50-16-09; e-mail bank@nurbank.kz; internet www.nurbank.kz; f. 1992; cap. 3,465.0m., dep. 38,494.3m. (June 2004); Chair. ABILMAZHEN KNK. GILIMOV; 11 brs.

Temirbank: 050008 Almaty, pr. Abaya 68/74; tel. (3272) 58-78-88; fax (3272) 50-62-41; e-mail board@temirbank.kz; internet www.temirbank.kz; f. 1992; cap. 6,584.0m., res 555.0m., dep. 29,248.6m. (June 2005); Chair. MURAT YULDASHEV; 15 brs.

Tsesnabank: 010000 Astana, Zhengis dangghyly 29; tel. (3172) 17-02-01; fax (3172) 17-01-95; e-mail tsb@tsb.kz; internet www.tsb.kz; f. 1992; cap. 993.9m., res 150.0m., dep. 18,885.8m. (July 2005); Chair. KUAT KOZHAHMETOV; 9 brs.

Bankers' Organization

Bank Association of Kazakhstan: 010000 Almaty, Panfilova 98; tel. (3272) 73-16-89; fax (3272) 73-90-85; Pres. BAKHYTBEK BAISEITOV.

STOCK AND COMMODITY EXCHANGES

Kazakhstan Stock Exchange (KASE): 050000 Almaty, Aiteke bi 67; tel. (3272) 72-98-98; fax (3272) 72-09-25; e-mail info@kase.kz; internet www.kase.kz; f. 1993; Pres. and Chief Exec. AZAMAT M. DZHOLDASBEKOV.

Ken Dala Central Kazakhstan Commodity Exchange: 100074 Karaganda, pr. Stroitelei 28; tel. (3212) 74-27-80; fax (3212) 74-43-35; f. 1991; auth. cap. 6m.; Pres. MADEGDA PAK.

Kazakhstan also has a Metal Exchange (f. 1992).

INSURANCE

At August 2000 there were 41 licensed insurance companies in Kazakhstan.

Almaty International Insurance Group: 050000 Almaty, ul. Kabanbay Batyr 112; tel. and fax (3272) 50-12-31; e-mail aiig@world2.almaty.kz; internet www.aiig.escort.kz; f. 1994; Chair. SUREN AMBARTSUMIAN.

Dynasty Life Insurance Co: 050000 Almaty, Seifullina 410; tel. (3272) 50-73-95; e-mail dynasty@bta.nursat.kz; Chair. SERIK TEMIRGALEYEV.

Industrial Insurance Group (IIG): 050046 Almaty, Nauryzbai Batyr 65–69; tel. (3272) 50-96-95; fax (3272) 50-96-98; e-mail iig@kaznet.kz; f. 1998; Pres. IVAN MIKHAILOV.

KazAgroPolits Insurance Co: 050000 Almaty, Nauryzbai Batyr 49–61; tel. (3272) 32-13-24; fax (3272) 32-13-26; e-mail kazagropolise@mail.banknet.kz; Chair. YERMEK USPANOV.

Kazakhinstrakh (Kazakh International Insurance Co): 010004 Almaty, Zhibek Zholy 69; tel. (3272) 33-73-49; fax (3272) 50-74-37; e-mail kiscentr@nursat.kz; Chair. NURLAN MOLDAKHMETOV.

Kazkommerts-Polits Insurance Co: 050013 Almaty, Satpayeva 24; tel. (3272) 58-48-08; fax (3272) 92-73-97; e-mail info@kkp.kz; internet www.kkp.kz; f. 1996; non-life; Chair. MEIRAM B. SERGAZIN; Dir TALGAT K. USSENOV.

MSCA (Medical Systems of Central Asia) Interteach: 480091 Almaty, Kabanbai Batyr 122A; tel. and fax (3272) 58-23-32; e-mail interteach@kaznet.kaz; f. 1989; medical and travel insurance, health care, accident and employee liability insurance; 290 employees; 48 brs; Gen. Dir ERNST M. KURLEUTOV.

Western Kazakhstan Insurance Co: 090000 Western Kazakhstan obl., Oral, pr. Lenina 203; tel. (31122) 50-62-94; Chair. BOLAT DJUMAGALIYEV.

Trade and Industry

GOVERNMENT AGENCY

State Committee for Investment: 010000 Astana, Transport Tower; tel. (3172) 24-21-24; fax (3172) 24-21-68; internet www.mit.kz; f. 1997; Chair. ERLAN A. ARINOV.

CHAMBERS OF COMMERCE

Union of Chambers of Commerce and Industry of Kazakhstan: 050000 Almaty, Masanchi 26; tel. (3272) 92-00-52; fax (3272) 50-70-29; e-mail tpprkaz@online.ru; internet www.ccikaz.kz; f. 1959; Chair. ABLAI MYRZAKHMETOV.

Akmola Oblast Chamber of Commerce and Industry: 020000 Kokshatau, Marks 107; tel. (3162) 25-76-68; e-mail tpp@kokc.kz; Chair. TURSUNHAN T. KALIASKAROVA.

Aktobe Oblast Chamber of Commerce and Industry: 030000 Aktobe, Zhubanova 289/1; tel. (3132) 51-02-20; e-mail akbtpp@nursat.kz; Chair. ELENA A. RUDENKO.

Almaty City Chamber of Commerce and Industry: 050000 Almaty, Tole bi 45; tel. (3272) 62-03-01; e-mail alcci@nursat.kz; internet www.atpp.marketcenter.ru; Chair. ZULFIYA K. AKHMETZHANOVA.

Almaty Oblast Chamber of Commerce: 0408000 Taldykorgan, Taulsizdik 101/37; tel. (3282) 7-20-40; Chair. EMMA V. KIM.

Astana City Chamber of Commerce and Industry: 010000 Astana, Auezov 66, POB 1966; tel. (3172) 32-38-33; e-mail akmcci@dan.kz; internet www.chamber.kz; Chair. TATYANA I. KONONOVA.

Jambul Oblast Chamber of Commerce and Industry: 080012 Jambul obl., Taraz, Karakhana 2; tel. (3262) 43-05-98; Chair. ADILKHAN ZHAPARBEKOV.

Karaganda Oblast Chamber of Commerce and Industry: 100000 Karaganda, bulv. Mira 31; tel. (3212) 56-32-32; e-mail ccikr@mail.kz; f. 1994; Chair. NESIP SEITOVA.

Kostanai Oblast Chamber of Commerce and Industry: 110003 Kostanai, Taran 165; tel. (3142) 54-66-72; fax (3142) 54-44-03; e-mail ko_tpp@mail.kz; f. 1973; Chair. VALENTINA N. TRIBUSHNAYA.

Kyzyl-Orda Oblast Chamber of Commerce and Industry: 120014 Kyzyl-Orda, Aiteke bi 24; tel. (3242) 26-24-36; Chair. TAMARA V. HRAMTSOVA.

Pavlodar Oblast Chamber of Commerce and Industry: 140002 Pavlodar, Toraigyrova 95/1; tel. (3182) 75-79-69; e-mail pav-cci@kaznet.kz; Chair. RAJHANGUL SATABAYEVA.

Southern Kazakhstan Oblast Chamber of Commerce and Industry: 160000 Chimkent, Tauke Khan 31; tel. (3252) 21-14-05; Chair. SYRLYBAJ ORDABEKOV.

Western Kazakhstan Oblast Chamber of Commerce and Industry: 090000 Oral, Kuibyshev 67; tel. (3112) 50-44-40; e-mail zktpp@kaznet.kz; Chair. KAIR A. SYUNTIYEV.

EMPLOYERS' ORGANIZATIONS

Confederation of Employers of the Republic of Kazakhstan (KRRK): 050022 Almaty, Abai 42/44; tel. (3272) 93-07-42; fax (3272) 92-27-68; e-mail krrk@krrk.kz; internet www.krrk.kz; Pres. KADYR BAYIKENOV.

Kazakhstan Petroleum Association: 050010 Almaty, pr. Dostyk 43/517; tel. (3272) 50-18-16; fax (3272) 50-18-17; e-mail kpa@arna.kz; internet www.kpa.kz; f. 1998; Chair. Dr SAGINDYK K. NURALIYEV; 49 mem. cos.

UTILITIES

Electricity

Privatization of the electric power sector was undertaken from 1996. Many power stations were withdrawn from the national electricity company and transformed into independent joint-stock companies; several power-supply network companies were established in the region. The state had completed the privatization of virtually all electricity producers and local distribution companies by the end of 2001.

State Committee for Energy Supervision: Chair. MURAT RAMAZANOV.

Kazakhstan Electric Grid Operational Co (KEGOC): 050000 Almaty, ul. Kozybayeva 23; tel. (3272) 71-93-59; internet www.kegoc.kz; f. 1997; technical electricity network operator; Vice-Pres. ESBERGEN ABITAYEV (Operations), ALMASADAM SATKALIYEV (Finance).

Water

Almaty Vodocanal: 050057 Almaty, Jarokova 196; tel. (3272) 44-00-17; fax (3272) 44-84-02; f. 1937; state-owned; responsible for water supply and sewerage in Almaty and surrounding villages; Gen. Dir SHARIPBEK SHARDARBEKOV.

STATE HYDROCARBONS COMPANIES

Aktobemunaigaz: 030000 Aktobe; 25.1% state-owned; 60.3% owned by China National Petroleum Co (CNPC).

KazMunaiGaz National Joint-Stock Co: 473000 Astana, ul. Kabanbai batyra 22; tel. (3172) 97-60-00; fax (3172) 97-60-01; e-mail info@kmg.kz; internet www.kmg.kz; f. 2002 by merger of KazakhOil and Transneftegas; Pres. UZAKBAI S. KARABALIN; First Vice-Pres. TIMUR A. KULIBAYEV.

KazMunaiTeniz Offshore Oil Co: Astana, ul. Kosmonavtov 62; tel. (3172) 97-96-01; fax (3172) 97-96-62; f. 2003; petroleum and natural gas projects in the Kazakhstani sector of the Caspian and Aral Seas, incl. devt of fields, transportation and sale; Dir-Gen. BAKHYTZHAN K. KHASANOV.

KazTransOil: 010000 Astana, pr. Kabanbay Batyr 20B; tel. (3172) 55-56-53; fax (3172) 55-56-52; internet www.kaztransoil.kz; transportation of petroleum; Dir-Gen. ASKAR SMANKULOV.

KazTransGas: e-mail info@intergas.kz; internet www.kaztransgas.kz; transportation of natural gas; Dir-Gen. ABAY SADYKOV.

MunaiTas North-West Pipeline Co: Almaty, ul. Satpayeva 29; fax (3272) 58-84-42; e-mail munaitas@munaitas.kz; internet www.munaitas.com; f. 2001; engineering, financing, construction and operation of Kenkiyak–Atyrau petroleum pipeline, which links oilfields in western Kazakhstan with the Atyrau–Samara export pipeline to the north; jt venture between China National Petroleum Co Int. Kazakhstan (People's Republic of China—49%) and KazMunaiGaz (51%); Gen. Dir ZHANG CHENG WU; First Deputy Gen. Dir KHASSEN SOLTANBAYEV.

Munaigaz: 050000 Almaty; tel. (3272) 69-58-00; fax (3272) 69-52-72; f. 1991; petroleum and gas prospecting and producing; Pres. T. A. KHAZANOV.

Aktyubinskneft: 030000 Aktobe, Atynsarin 8; tel. (3132) 22-47-82; fax (3132) 22-93-21; f. 1993; produces petroleum and natural gas; Pres. S. P. ZIMIN; 10,500 employees.

Mangistaumunaigaz: 130000 Mangistau obl., Aktau, Mikrorayon 1; tel. (3292) 51-45-57; fax (3292) 43-39-19; 60% owned by Central Asian Petroleum (Indonesia), 10% owned by employees; production and transportation of petroleum and natural gas; Gen. Dir V. MIROSHNIKOV.

Pavlodar Petrochemical Joint Stock Co: 140000 Pavlodar, Khimkombinatovskaya 1; tel. (3182) 39-65-20; fax (3182) 39-60-98; e-mail fvg@pnhz.kz; f. 1978; 51% owned by JSC Mangistaumunaigaz; processes petroleum from western Siberia (Russia); produces unleaded petroleum, diesel fuel, petroleum chemical gases, bitumen and petroleum coke; Gen. Dir YURII GINATULIN; Exec. Dir VALERIY FOMIN.

Tengizchevroil (TCO): 060011 Atyrau, Satpayeva 3; tel. (312) 22-71-212; fax (312) 30-26-752; e-mail tiny@tengizchevroil.com; f. 1993; jt venture between ChevronTexaco (USA—50%), ExxonMobil (USA—25%), KazMunaiGaz (20%) and LUKArco (a jt venture between LUKoil of Russia and Atlantic Richfield of the USA—5%); Gen. Dir ALEXANDER CORNELIUS.

TRADE UNIONS

Confederation of Free Trade Unions: f. 1991; fmrly Independent Trade Union Centre of Kazakhstan; 9 regional brs with 2,200 mems; Chair. SERGEI BELKIN.

Confederation of Free Trade Unions of Coal and Mining Industries: 050000 Almaty; Chair. V. GAIPOV.

Federation of Trade Unions of Kazakhstan: 010000 Astana, pr. Abaya 94; tel. (3172) 216-68-14; fax (3172) 21-68-35; e-mail fprkastana@nursat.kz; internet www.fprk.kz; 30 affiliated unions with 2,300,000 mems (2001); Chair. SIYAZBEK MUKASHEV.

Transport

RAILWAYS

In 2003 the total length of rail track in use was 13,601 km (3,661 km of which were electrified). The rail network is most concentrated in the north of the country, where it joins the rail lines of Russia. From the former capital, Almaty, lines run north-east, to join the Trans-Siberian Railway, and west, to Chimkent, and then north-west along the Syr-Dar'ya river, to Orenburg in European Russia. In mid-2003 Kazakhstan and Kyrgyzstan announced that a 100-km railway link was to be built between Almaty and lake Issyk-Kul in Kyrgyzstan. Construction work was expected to be completed by 2008. From Chu lines run to central and northern regions of Kazakhstan, while a main line runs from Chimkent south to Uzbekistan. There is an international line between Druzhba, on the eastern border of Kazakhstan, and Alataw Shankou, in the People's Republic of China.

In the early 2000s construction was under way of the first line of a new underground railway (metro) in Almaty. It was envisaged that the metro system, when completed, would comprise three lines (35.4 km in length). In 2004 it was announced that a major monorail system was being planned for Almaty, to comprise approximately 40 km of track and 44 stations.

In December 2004 a new rail line was opened, linking Altynsarino in the Kostanai oblast and Khromtau in west Kazakhstan, greatly reducing travel time between northern and central parts of the country and its petroleum-producing regions in the west, and eliminating the need for passengers to cross Russia twice in order to travel between central Kazakhstan and western regions of the country. Proposals for a railway line linking the rail system of the People's Republic of China with Europe, via Kazakhstan and other countries in the region, were still in the early stages of discussion in early 2006.

Department of Railways (Ministry of Transport and Communications): 480091 Almaty, Vinogradova 56; tel. (3272) 60-49-06; fax (3272) 39-52-55; Dir-Gen. BAURZHAN BAYMUKHANOV.

Kazakhstan Temir Zholy (Kazakhstan Railways): 473011 Astana, Zhengis dangghyly 98; tel. (3172) 93-44-00; fax (3172) 32-82-30; e-mail temirzhol@railways.kz; internet www.railways.kz; f. 1991; Pres. YERLAN D. ATAMKULOV.

ROADS

In 2002 Kazakhstan's total road network was 82,980 km, including 22,781 km of main roads and 60,199 km of secondary roads. Some 93.9% of the network was hard-surfaced. Kazakhstan is linked by road with Russia (46 border crossings), Kyrgyzstan (seven), Uzbekistan (seven) and, via Uzbekistan and Turkmenistan, with Iran. There are six road connections with the People's Republic of China (including two international crossings, at Korgas and Bakhty). In 2000 the Islamic Development Bank agreed to donate $200m. towards the rehabilitation of the Karaganda–Astana road.

Department of Roads (Ministry of Transport and Communications): 473000 Astana, pr. Abaya 49; tel. (3172) 32-02-08; fax (3172) 32-16-96; Dir S. LARICHEV.

INLAND WATERWAYS

Kazakhstan has an inland waterway network extending over some 4,000 km. The main navigable river is the Irtysh, accounting for approximately 80% of cargo transported by river. The Kazakhstan River Fleet Industrial Association (Kazrechmorflot), comprising 11 water companies, administers river traffic.

Department of Water Transport (Ministry of Transport and Communications): 473000 Astana, pr. Abaya 49; tel. (3172) 32-03-58; fax (3172) 32-10-58; Dir JENYS M. KASYMBEK.

SHIPPING

Kazakhstan's ports of Atyrau and Aktau are situated on the eastern shores of the Caspian Sea. A ferry port was inaugurated at Aktau in September 2001 as part of the Transport Corridor Europa—Caucasus—Asia (TRACECA) programme, with lines to Azerbaijan, Iran and Russia; the port was capable of processing some 10m. tons of petroleum and up to 30m. tons of dry goods per year. At 31 December 2004 Kazakhstan's merchant fleet comprised 36 vessels, with a combined total displacement of 25,950 grt.

Aktau International Commercial Sea Port: 466200 Aktau, Umirzak; tel. (3292) 51-45-49; fax (3292) 44-51-01; e-mail aktauport@aktauport.kz; internet www.portaktau.kz; f. 1963; Dir ZHENIS M. KASSYMBEK; 429 employees.

Atyrauozenporty (Atyrau Port): tel. (3122) 25-45-63; fax (3122) 25-45-16; e-mail atr_info@asdc.kz.

CIVIL AVIATION

There are 18 domestic airports and three airports with international services (at Almaty, Aktau and Atyrau). In 2002 plans were announced for the reconstruction of Atyrau airport, with the help of financial assistance from the European Bank for Reconstruction and Development. In that year 19 of the country's 56 air companies had their activities suspended and their licences revoked, in the interests of safety. Almaty airport has scheduled links with cities in Russia and other former Soviet republics, as well as with destinations in Europe, other parts of Asia and the Middle East.

Department of Aviation (Ministry of Transport and Communications): 010000 Astana, pr. Abaya 49; tel. (3172) 32-63-16; fax (3172) 32-16-96; Dir S. BURANBAYEV.

Aeroservice Kazakhstan Aviakompaniya: 050028 Almaty, Alga basskaya 2A; tel. (3272) 36-69-26; fax (3272) 52-93-45; f. 1991; provides charter services to Europe, the Middle East, Pakistan and the Republic of Korea.

Air Astana: 010000 Astana, Samal Microraion 12, Astana Towers Business Centre, POB 1416; tel. (3172) 58-09-50; fax (3172) 58-09-80; e-mail astana@air-astana.kz; internet www.air-astana.kz; f. 2001 jointly by the Government and BAE Systems (United Kingdom); domestic and international flights; Pres. LLOYD PAXTON.

Asiya Servis Aue Zholy (Asia Service Airlines): 050000 Almaty, Zheltoksan 59; tel. (3272) 33-63-49; operates services between Almaty, Atyrau and Aktau.

Jana-Arka Air: 050012 Almaty, Ninogradova 85; tel. (3272) 63-28-74; fax (3272) 63-19-09; privately owned; domestic and regional flights; Pres. YALKEN VALIN.

Sayakhat Air Co: 050000 Almaty, Bogenbai Batyr 124; tel. (3272) 79-07-63; fax (3272) 79-03-27; e-mail sayakhat@inbox.ru; f. 1989; privately owned; commenced operations in 1991; passenger and cargo services to Asia, the Middle East and Europe; Pres. and Operations and Finance Dir VLADIMIR KOROPATENKO.

Tourism

Tourism is not widely developed in Kazakhstan, owing to its Soviet legacy and infrastructural limitations. However, the country possesses mountain ranges, lakes and a number of historical sites. Chimbulak, above Almaty, is a popular local skiing resort. The Government declared tourism a priority sector in 2001, and launched the Tourism Development Plan 2003–05.

Ministry of Culture and Information: see The Government—Ministries).

Kazakhstan Tourist Association (KTA): 480091 Almaty, ul.Zheltoksan 98; tel. (3272) 73-07-04; fax (3272)73-00-52; e-mail kta@mail.kz; f. 1999; asscn incorporates the Kazakhstan Association of Hotels and Restaurants; more than 70 members.

KENYA

Introductory Survey

Location, Climate, Language, Religion, Flag, Capital

The Republic of Kenya lies astride the equator on the east coast of Africa, with Somalia to the north-east, Ethiopia and Sudan to the north, Uganda to the west and Tanzania to the south. The climate varies with altitude: the coastal region is hot and humid, with temperatures averaging between 20°C and 32°C (69°F–90°F), while inland, at more than 1,500 m (5,000 ft) above sea-level, temperatures average 7°C–27°C (45°F–80°F). The highlands and western areas receive ample rainfall (an annual average of 1,000 mm–1,250 mm) but most of northern Kenya is very dry (about 250 mm). Kiswahili is the official language, while English is widely spoken and 22% and 13% of the population, respectively, speak Kikuyu and Luo as their mother tongue. Most of the country's inhabitants follow traditional beliefs. There is a sizeable Christian community, while Muslims form a smaller proportion of the population. The national flag (proportions 2 by 3) has three broad horizontal stripes, of black, red and green, separated by two narrow white stripes. Superimposed in the centre is a red shield, with black and white markings, upon crossed white spears. The capital is Nairobi.

Recent History

Kenya was formerly a British colony (inland) and protectorate (along the coast). The first significant African nationalist organization was the Kenya African Union (KAU), founded in 1944, which was supported mainly by the Kikuyu, the largest ethnic group in Kenya. In 1947 Jomo Kenyatta, a Kikuyu, became President of the KAU. During 1952 a campaign of terrorism was launched by Mau Mau, a predominantly Kikuyu secret society that aimed to expel European (mainly British) settlers from Kenya. The British authorities declared a state of emergency in October 1952 and banned the KAU in 1953, when Kenyatta was imprisoned for alleged involvement with Mau Mau activities. The terrorist campaign ceased in 1956, and the state of emergency was revoked in January 1960.

Kenyatta was released from prison in 1961 and elected to the Legislative Council in 1962. Following general elections in May 1963, Kenya was granted internal self-government in June. The country became independent, within the Commonwealth, on 12 December 1963, and a republic exactly one year later. Kenyatta, then leader of the Kenya African National Union (KANU), was appointed Prime Minister in June 1963 and became the country's first President in December 1964. (He was subsequently re-elected to the presidency, unopposed, in 1969 and 1974.)

Kenyatta died in August 1978; the Vice-President, Daniel arap Moi, was proclaimed President in October, and was the sole candidate at a presidential election held (concurrently with a KANU-only general election) in November 1979. In June 1982 the National Assembly officially declared Kenya a one-party state. A series of political detentions and increasing press censorship were followed by an attempted coup in August, in which several hundred people were killed. Several cabinet ministers lost their seats at legislative elections in September 1983. Nevertheless, at a simultaneous presidential election Moi was returned unopposed. In August 1986 KANU approved an open 'queue-voting' system to replace the secret ballot in the preliminary stage of a general election. In June 1987 it was announced that only members of the ruling party were to be entitled to vote during the preliminary stages of a general election.

In February 1988 Moi was nominated unopposed to serve a third term as President. In the same month preliminary elections under the 'queue-voting' system produced a KANU-approved list to contest 123 of the 188 elective seats in the National Assembly at a general election held in March (54 candidates received more than 70% of votes cast at the preliminary stage, and were thus deemed to have been elected, while 11 were elected unopposed). In an extensive cabinet reshuffle following the election, the Vice-President, Mwai Kibaki, was replaced by Josephat Karanja. In July the National Assembly adopted constitutional amendments allowing the President to dismiss senior judges at will, and increasing from 24 hours to 14 days the legally permissible period of detention without trial for people suspected of capital offences. In December Kenneth Matiba, the Minister of Transport and Communications, resigned and was expelled from KANU, after criticizing the conduct of the party elections.

In April 1989 the National Assembly unanimously approved a motion of 'no confidence' in Karanja, following allegations that he had abused his position as Vice-President to further his own personal and tribal interests. Karanja, while denying the charges against him, resigned shortly afterwards, and was replaced by the Minister of Finance, Prof. George Saitoti.

In February 1990 the Minister of Foreign Affairs and International Co-operation, Dr Robert Ouko, died in suspicious circumstances. Allegations that the Moi administration was implicated in his death led to anti-Government riots. In response, Moi banned all demonstrations and requested an investigation by British police into Ouko's death; the results of this were presented to the Kenyan authorities in September, and in October Moi ordered a judicial inquiry into the affair. In May a broad alliance of intellectuals, lawyers and clergy, under the leadership of Matiba, began to exert pressure on the Government to legalize political opposition to KANU.

In December 1990 KANU abolished the system of 'queue-voting' and resolved to cease expelling party members, readmitting 31 expelled members in the following month. In August six opposition leaders, including Oginga Odinga (Kenya's Vice-President in 1964–66), formed a new political movement, the Forum for the Restoration of Democracy (FORD); the Government outlawed the grouping, but it continued to operate.

In September 1991 the judicial inquiry into the death of Ouko was presented with evidence that he had been murdered; in November Moi dismissed the Minister of Industry, Nicholas Biwott, in response to widespread suspicion that the latter was implicated in the alleged assassination. Shortly afterwards Moi ordered the dissolution of the judicial inquiry. A suspect was eventually charged with the murder, but was acquitted in July 1994. (Biwott was reappointed to the Cabinet in 1997. In December 2000 Biwott won a libel case against the British authors of a book that implicated him in the murder of Ouko.)

In November 1991 several members of FORD were arrested prior to a planned pro-democracy rally in Nairobi; protesters at the rally (which had been banned by the Government) were dispersed by the security forces. The Kenyan authorities were condemned internationally for suppressing the demonstration, and most of the opposition activists who had been detained were subsequently released. Bilateral and multilateral creditors suspended aid to Kenya indefinitely, pending the acceleration of both economic and political reforms. In December a special conference of KANU delegates acceded to the pressure for reform, resolving to introduce a multi-party political system. The National Assembly subsequently endorsed appropriate amendments to the Constitution. Former Vice-President Kibaki resigned as Minister of Health later in the month, in protest against alleged electoral malpractice by KANU and against the unsatisfactory outcome of the judicial inquiry into the death of Ouko, and founded the Democratic Party (DP).

During the first half of 1992 some 2,000 people were reportedly killed in tribal clashes in western Kenya. In March the Government banned all political rallies, and restrictions were placed on the activities of the press. Following a two-day general strike in April, organized by FORD, the Government ended the ban on political rallies. In August FORD split into two opposing factions, which were registered in October as separate political parties, FORD—Asili and FORD—Kenya, respectively led by Matiba and Odinga.

At multi-party presidential and legislative elections held in December 1992 Moi was elected for a fourth term of office as President, winning 36.3% of the votes cast, ahead of Matiba (26.0%), Kibaki (19.5%) and Odinga (17.5%). Of the 188 elective seats in the National Assembly, KANU won 100 (including 16 uncontested); FORD—Asili and FORD—Kenya secured 31 seats each, and the DP took 23. Votes were cast predominantly in accordance with ethnic affiliations, with the two largest tribes, the Kikuyu and Luo, overwhelmingly rejecting KANU. An extensive reshuffle of cabinet posts was subsequently effected.

Tribal clashes in western regions continued during 1993, escalating significantly in October. In November the human rights organization Africa Watch reiterated persistent accusations by the opposition that the Government was covertly inciting ethnic violence in order to discredit political pluralism in Kenya. During that month several people were arrested and charged with co-ordinating the unrest. Meanwhile, the international donor community agreed to resume the provision of aid to Kenya, in response to what it recognized as the Government's progress in implementing political and economic reforms.

In January 1994 Odinga died; he was succeeded as the Chairman of FORD—Kenya by Michael Wamalwa Kijana, hitherto the party's Vice-President. In June main opposition groups, excluding FORD—Asili, formed a loose coalition, the United National Democratic Alliance, which was, however, subsequently divided by disagreements. Disunity was also becoming apparent within individual opposition parties, with vying factions evident within both FORD—Kenya and FORD—Asili.

In May 1995 leading opposition activists formed a new political organization, Safina. Dr Richard Leakey, a prominent white Kenyan and former Director of the Kenya Wildlife Service (KWS), was appointed as Safina's Secretary-General. The party (which was refused registration) aimed to combat corruption and human rights abuses by the Kenyan authorities and to campaign for the introduction of an electoral system of proportional representation.

During the mid-1990s Kenya's human rights record came under intense domestic and international scrutiny. In April 1995 the country's Roman Catholic bishops accused the Government of eroding judicial independence and of condoning police brutality and endemic corruption. In December the human rights organization Amnesty International alleged that the security forces were systematically torturing criminal suspects and opposition activists. In response to its critics, the Moi administration provisionally withdrew controversial draft legislation in January 1996 that would have severely restricted the freedom of the press and, in July, inaugurated a human rights committee to investigate alleged humanitarian abuses.

Divisions within opposition parties continued to undermine efforts to present a cohesive challenge to Moi and KANU prior to the 1997 elections. A renewed attempt to establish a coalition of opposition organizations, initiated in November 1995, was short-lived. Meanwhile, following an unsuccessful attempt to oust Wamalwa as Chairman of FORD—Kenya, Raila Odinga (the son of Oginga Odinga and a prominent opposition activist) left that party and subsequently became leader of the National Development Party (NDP). In October 1997 Matiba's faction of FORD—Asili registered as an independent party, the Forum for the Restoration of Democracy for the People (FORD—People). During the mid-1990s several opposition deputies, disaffected by these internal rivalries, defected to KANU. Within KANU itself rivalries also began to emerge, not least because the Constitution permitted Moi to stand for only one further term as President.

During the first half of 1997 Moi repeatedly refused to accede to opposition demands for a review of the Constitution prior to the forthcoming elections. Opposition organizations protested that constitutional reforms and a reorganization of the supervisory Electoral Commission were essential in order to eliminate an in-built electoral advantage for the Moi administration. In April the National Convention Executive Council (NCEC) was established as a forum embracing representatives of non-governmental organizations, religious groups and opposition parties (excluding, however, supporters of Matiba and Odinga). In June opposition parliamentarians disrupted the budget speech, in protest at the Moi administration's perceived intransigence, and anti-Government activists demonstrated in Nairobi. Illegal protest rallies in early July were brutally suppressed by the security forces, resulting in several fatalities and provoking strong condemnation from abroad. Eventually, in mid-July, Moi agreed to meet with opposition and religious leaders to discuss constitutional reform. It was subsequently announced that the opposition would henceforth be permitted to organize registered public meetings, and that a constitutional review commission would be established.

At the beginning of August 1997 the IMF suspended assistance to Kenya, pending the implementation of decisive action to eliminate official corruption and to improve the system of revenue collection; the Government consequently announced the inauguration of an anti-corruption body. The NCEC organized a one-day general strike in early August, in support of its demands for constitutional reform. In late August serious unrest erupted in and around Mombasa. While the Government blamed the NCEC for orchestrating the attacks, the NCEC alleged that the Government was inciting inter-ethnic conflict with the aim of depriving opposition supporters from the predominantly Luo region of the opportunity to vote in the forthcoming elections by forcing them to flee their homes. In the following month the National Assembly approved legislation that amended the Constitution with the stated aim of ensuring free and fair democratic elections. All political parties were granted equal access to the media, and detention without trial was prohibited. In addition, the new legislation enabled the opposition to participate in selecting the 12 nominated members of the National Assembly and 10 of the 12 members of the supervisory Electoral Commission.

The presidential and legislative elections, which took place concurrently on 29 December 1997, were undermined by allegations of widespread fraud, as well as by logistical difficulties. Moi was re-elected President, winning 40.6% of the valid votes cast. Mwai Kibaki, the leader of the DP and former Vice-President, came second, with 31.5% of the votes cast. KANU secured 107 of the 210 elected seats in the enlarged National Assembly, while the remainder were divided between nine opposition parties, with the DP taking 39 seats, the NDP 21, FORD—Kenya 17 and the Social Democratic Party 15. Safina (which had finally been registered in November) won five seats. Moi was inaugurated for a fifth (and final) term as President in January 1998. Shortly afterwards Moi appointed a new Cabinet. However, he postponed the designation of a new Vice-President, evidently in order not to give an indication of his preferred successor to the presidency. Following the elections, Kibaki petitioned the High Court to declare Moi's re-election invalid. A group of independent Kenyan observers had, none the less, pronounced the electoral process 'satisfactory'.

In early 1998 inter-ethnic violence erupted once again in the volatile Rift Valley. The Moi administration blamed the conflict on bitterness in the Kikuyu and Luo communities at the outcome of the elections, while the latter alleged persecution both by the security forces and by smaller tribal groups that had voted predominantly for Moi and KANU. In July the authorities organized a judicial inquiry into the causes of the ethnic disturbances of both 1992 and 1998. Tension between the Kikuyu and Kalenjin communities in the Rift valley remained, however, especially over disputed land vacated by the Kikuyu during the clashes.

In early August 1998 a car-bomb exploded at the US embassy in central Nairobi, concurrently with a similar attack on the US mission in Dar es Salaam, Tanzania. Some 254 people were killed in Nairobi, and more than 5,000 suffered injuries. The attacks were believed to have been co-ordinated by international Islamist terrorists, and, in mid-August, the USA retaliated by launching air strikes against targets in Afghanistan and Sudan. In the aftermath of the bomb attacks, evidence emerged that young Kenyan Muslims had been systematically recruited for military training by international Islamist guerrilla groups. Four men were convicted of involvement in the bombings by a court in New York, USA, in May 2001 and were later sentenced to life imprisonment. Other suspects, including Osama bin Laden, the fugitive Saudi-born Islamist activist whom the US authorities held ultimately responsible for the bombings, were still at large.

During early 1998 an apparent *rapprochement* between Odinga and Moi caused considerable disquiet in both the NDP and KANU. A consultative forum on the constitutional review process was inaugurated in April, with the aim of organizing the long-anticipated constitutional review commission. In February 1999 the Cabinet was reorganized. Most significantly the Minister of Finance, Simeon Nyachae, exchanged portfolios with the Minister of Industrial Development, Yekokanda Francis Masakhalia; this effectively represented a demotion for Nyachae, who had played a leading role in ongoing attempts to eliminate corruption and financial mismanagement from the public sector. Nyachae, claiming to have been victimized by senior government figures allegedly involved in corrupt activities, immediately resigned from his new post. In April Saitoti was reappointed to the position of Vice-President (vacant since January 1998). In July Moi appointed Dr Leakey as head of the civil service and Secretary to the Cabinet, with responsibility for combating corruption in the public services. In September Moi effected a major reorganization of the Cabinet, merging several ministries and reducing the number of government ministers from 27 to 15.

In December 1999 the KANU-NDP majority in the National Assembly voted in favour of appointing a parliamentary select committee on constitutional review. However, a rival commission was established by an alliance of opposition and religious groups, known as Ufungamano, which intended to propose its own recommendations for constitutional change. Moi opposed the Ufungamano commission, although many Kenyans appeared to support it. In April 2000 the parliamentary committee, headed by Raila Odinga of the NDP, completed its review, proposing the establishment of a constitutional review commission, comprising 15 members, to be nominated by the National Assembly prior to their appointment by Moi. However, in November, following months of recriminations between the two rival commissions, Prof. Yash Pal Ghai, appointed by Moi to head the parliamentary commission, refused to be sworn into office. Ghai declared that he first wanted to negotiate with Ufungamano in an attempt to unite the two groups. The merger went ahead in May 2001; the new commission comprised 27 members, 12 of whom were drawn from Ufungamano.

In July 2000 the civil service commenced the reduction of its work-force as part of a programme of reforms to be effected over three years. Meanwhile, a parliamentary anti-graft committee sought the adoption by the National Assembly of a report in which the alleged perpetrators of corruption were named. (The Government later deleted the addendum containing the list of names, causing widespread outrage.) The committee also proposed legislation on economic crimes that would allow the anti-corruption authority (which had been established in 1997 at the insistence of the IMF) to prosecute alleged perpetrators of corruption without seeking permission from the Attorney-General. As a result of these measures, the IMF announced that it was to resume lending to Kenya. The Government agreed to a number of conditions, including the introduction of a law binding public officials to declare their wealth and liabilities and the enactment of the legislation on economic crimes. However, less than one month after the resumption of aid the High Court temporarily halted the retrenchment of civil servants, pending the final determination of a lawsuit on the issue, and ruled that all civil servants who had already been retrenched should be reinstated. In January 2001 the IMF and the World Bank expressed concern over the set-backs in the reforms, particularly the failure to approve legislation on public-service ethics and economic crimes, and suspended aid to Kenya until the situation could be resolved. In August Kenyan deputies again refused to approve anti-corruption legislation, and the IMF suspended aid to Kenya indefinitely. Moi subsequently created a new police body to combat corruption. Meanwhile, in March Leakey resigned as head of the civil service and Secretary to the Cabinet (two months before the expiry of his contract) and was replaced by Dr Sally Kosgei, an ally of Moi. Leakey's departure, along with the dismissal of most of his colleagues, prompted a major reshuffle within the senior civil service. Many observers believed that Moi was now intent on gathering loyal followers around him in preparation for the 2002 elections.

In January 2001 Raila Odinga of the Luo-dominated NDP signed a memorandum of understanding with KANU, which allowed Moi to appoint ministers from the NDP. In June 2001 Moi reshuffled the Cabinet and appointed Odinga as Minister of Energy, thereby creating the first coalition Government in Kenya's history. Moi reshuffled the Cabinet again in November, introducing younger KANU ministers in an apparent attempt to provide suitable candidates for his succession; most notably Uhuru Kenyatta (son of the late President Jomo Kenyatta) and Cyrus Jirongo were appointed as Minister for Local Government and Minister for Rural Development, respectively.

The NDP was dissolved and absorbed into KANU in mid-March 2002, despite opposition from elements within both parties; Moi was elected as party Chairman, while Odinga was elected as Secretary-General, when the incumbent, Kamotho, withdrew from the contest. In July some 12 opposition parties, including the DP, FORD—Kenya and the National Party of Kenya, formed an electoral alliance, the National Alliance Party of Kenya (NAK).

In August 2002 Moi publicly announced that he favoured Uhuru Kenyatta as KANU's presidential candidate. However, several senior KANU members, including Vice-President Saitoti and Odinga, subsequently announced their intention to seek the party's presidential nomination and formed the Rainbow Alliance to campaign within KANU for a democratic vote to select its candidate. Moi responded by dismissing the Vice-President. In mid-October, in protest at Moi's attempts to impose his preferred successor, members of the Rainbow Alliance resigned from their posts in the Government and from KANU, together with some 30 KANU deputies. The Rainbow Alliance subsequently boycotted the KANU conference, at which Kenyatta's presidential candidacy was endorsed. It was widely believed that Moi was hoping to extend his rule through Kenyatta, a close family friend of Moi, who was likely to protect Moi's wealth and shield him from prosecution. Later in October the Rainbow Alliance established a new party, the Liberal Democratic Party (LDP), and joined with the NAK to form the National Rainbow Coalition (NARC), with Mwai Kibaki as its presidential candidate. The NARC proposed a vote of no confidence in Moi's Government, stating that the Government was illegally attempting to block the introduction of a new constitution. However, Moi forestalled the tabling of the motion by dissolving the National Assembly on 25 October, thereby ensuring that the elections would be held under the current Constitution.

At the presidential and legislative elections, held concurrently on 27 December 2002, the opposition secured an emphatic victory, with Kibaki winning 62.3% of the votes cast in the presidential election, and the NARC securing 125 of the 210 elected seats in the National Assembly, while Kenyatta received 31.2% of the votes cast for the presidency, and KANU won 64 seats in the legislature. The NARC were allocated a further seven appointed seats, increasing their representation to 132, and KANU a further four seats, bringing their total to 68. The electoral turn-out was 56.1%. Moi stepped down, as promised; he resigned as Chairman of KANU in September 2003.

Following his inauguration as President on 30 December 2002, Kibaki promised reforms, including the adoption of a new constitution, under which certain powers would be transferred from the President to the legislature and the full independence of the judiciary guaranteed, the adoption of anti-corruption legislation, the privatization of state-owned companies and the dismissal of corrupt civil servants. In January 2003 Kibaki appointed a new Cabinet, which included Michael Kijana Wamalwa as Vice-President, Odinga as Minister of Roads, Public Works and Housing, and Saitoti as Minister of Education. However, divisions within the ruling coalition soon became apparent, as a group of 25 LDP deputies accused Kibaki of breaching a power-sharing agreement signed by the constituent parties of the NARC prior to the elections. In May the Anti-Corruption and Economic Crimes Act, which provided for the establishment of the Kenya Anti-Corruption Commission (KACC), and the Public Service (Code of Conduct and Ethics) Act, which required elected officials and senior civil servants to declare their wealth, came into effect.

In February 2003 Kibaki appointed a commission of inquiry into the Goldenberg financial scandal, in which public funds had been paid to the company Goldenberg International in 1990–93 as subsidies for non-existent exports of gold and diamonds. Evidence presented at the inquiry indicated that Goldenberg had initially received some Ks. 13,500m. (around US $180m.) under the Government's export compensation scheme. After thousands of transfers, including dubious foreign-exchange transactions, made with the alleged complicity of officials at the central bank, the payments to Goldenberg increased to Ks. 25,000m. ($600m.), equivalent to more than 10% of Kenya's annual GDP, although it was estimated that the total amount misappropriated could reach $4,000m. The scandal had also contributed to an IMF decision to suspend the disbursement to Kenya of loans worth some $500m. in 1997. The inquiry was halted temporarily in October 2003, when its Vice-Chairman was one of 23 appeals court and high court judges suspended, in response to the publication of a report into corruption in the judiciary; tribunals were established to examine the allegations against the judges, and some 82 magistrates were also placed under investigation. Former President Moi was questioned in connection with the scandal in June 2003; he denied any involvement, but promised to co-operate fully with the inquiry. Public hearings ended in November 2004, and the commission's findings were reported to Kibaki in February 2005. It had initially been expected that prosecutions would follow from the report, however, the Minister of Justice and Constitutional Affairs, Martha Karua, stated that further investigations were necessary before any charges could be brought.

In March 2003 a parliamentary select committee was established to reinvestigate the murder of Robert Ouko in 1990 (see above). Moi and Biwott, who both denied any involvement in the murder, were both summoned to give evidence, as was Ouko's brother, Eston Barrack Mbajah. In his evidence, Mbajah claimed that Moi had attempted to bribe him to make a public statement calling for the initial investigation into Ouko's death to be halted, and that after he had refused the offer, he had been detained by the police and tortured. A British detective who had participated in an earlier inquiry into the case stated that Ouko was probably killed because he was about to expose corruption by ministers, and named one of Ouko's fellow ministers and a senior civil servant, both close allies of Moi, as key suspects. A witness, who claimed to have had intimate relations with Moi, testified in February 2005 that the previous inquiry into Ouko's death had been halted after it had emerged that she was to be called as a witness, as the Government at the time feared her evidence would reveal politically sensitive information. She also alleged that Ouko was preparing to reveal details of corrupt dealings by members of Moi's Cabinet who had sought unduly to benefit from the revival of a molasses plant in Kisumu. Furthermore, she claimed that Biwott had convinced Moi of Ouko's responsibility for providing her with allegations of corruption involving Moi, and that Moi had subsequently ordered her deportation from Kenya. Both Moi and Biwott refused to be questioned by the committee. Moi was instead represented by a lawyer, while Biwott insisted on presenting a written statement; the committee, however, did not accept the evidence thus presented and the inquiry came to an end in March 2005 amid some confusion. The committee presented its findings to the National Assembly later that month. It did not name those responsible for Ouko's death, but recommended that the bodies of several key witnesses, some of whom had died in suspicious circumstances, be exhumed in order to determine the causes of their deaths. The committee also recommended that the roles of Moi and Biwott in the matter be examined further.

Meanwhile, the constitutional review conference opened in April 2003, but divisions over the proposed post of Prime Minister led to an impasse. The LDP advocated an executive Prime Minister with powers to appoint the Cabinet, while Kibaki and his supporters sought to maintain a strong presidency. The ensuing tensions between the NAK and LDP factions of the NARC threatened to split the ruling coalition. In August the death of Vice-President Wamalwa, who had been regarded as a moderating influence within the Government, led to an intensification of the power struggle. President Kibaki faced demands for a successor both from Wamalwa's Luhya ethnic group and from the Luo, who proposed the appointment of Odinga to the vice-presidency. In late September Kibaki named the Minister of Home Affairs, Arthur Moody Awori (a Luhya), as Vice-President and effected a minor government reshuffle. In March 2004 the constitutional review conference voted to reduce the powers vested in the presidency and to create the new post of executive Prime Minister following the next elections, which were scheduled to be held in 2007. Under the recommendations adopted by the conference, greater power was to be accorded to the National Assembly. The Government withdrew from the conference in protest, and a powerful Kikuyu cabal within the Cabinet attempted to block the process; however, the draft constitution was successfully presented to the Attorney-General, after which it was to be considered by the National Assembly. The High Court subsequently ruled that before the document could enter into force it required approval at a referendum. In July 2004 President Kibaki reshuffled the Cabinet; his political rivals and those who had indicated their support for constitutional reform were moved to more junior positions. In December the National Assembly approved the Constitution of Kenya Review (Amendment) Act 2004. The Act allowed the legislature to amend the draft constitution with the approval of a simple majority, rather than the two-thirds majority previously required. KANU and the LDP protested vehemently, as they believed that the President could use the legislation to reduce the proposed power of the Prime Minister.

The amended draft constitution, which was approved by the National Assembly in July 2005, confirmed the opposition's fears and provided for the retention of the executive functions of the President, who would have the power to appoint and dismiss a non-executive Prime Minister. Devolution was to be on two levels (national and provincial), rather than the four levels originally envisaged, while the National Assembly was to remain unicameral.

There followed several months of campaigning punctuated by often violent demonstrations. Support for the draft constitution was largely split along tribal affiliations, while the Cabinet was also divided. Seven ministers announced their opposition to the proposed new constitution, including, most notably, Raila Odinga, whose LDP split from the NARC coalition and joined with KANU to form the Orange Democratic Movement (ODM). At the referendum, held on 21 November 2005, the draft constitution was rejected by 58.12% of voters. Some 53% of the electorate participated in the poll. Kibaki conceded defeat but ignored demands from Odinga and the ODM to hold legislative elections. Instead Kibaki moved swiftly to dismiss the entire Cabinet and in early December he unveiled a new administration, from which those ministers who had opposed the draft constitution were removed.

Security in Kenya was a major concern in 2002–03. In November 2002 two simultaneous terrorist attacks were carried out in Mombasa. Two surface-to-air missiles narrowly missed an Israeli charter aircraft as it took off from Mombasa airport, while in a nearby tourist resort suicide bombers attacked an Israeli-owned hotel, killing 18 people and injuring many more. The militant Islamist al-Qa'ida (Base) organization later claimed responsibility for the attacks. Agents from the US and Israeli intelligence services arrived in Kenya soon afterwards to assist the authorities with their investigations, and by the end of the month 12 people had been arrested. Four Kenyan men were charged with murder in connection with the attacks in June 2003, and their trial began in Nairobi in February 2004. A further three Kenyans were being tried separately, on charges of conspiracy, for their alleged involvement in the Mombasa attacks, the 1998 bombing of the US embassy and an alleged plot to target the new US embassy between November 2002 and June 2003. All seven were acquitted in June 2005 owing to insufficient evidence.

In 2004 it became increasingly apparent that corruption remained endemic in Kenya, despite the NARC Government's pledge to take measures to combat it. Four senior civil servants were suspended in May following their involvement in awarding contracts to supply passport printing equipment to a fictitious British company, Anglo Leasing Ltd. In July the British High Commissioner, Sir Edward Clay, claimed that corruption had cost Kenya some Ks. 15,000m. since Kibaki took office and warned that it could lead to a reduction in donor assistance—indeed, later that month the European Union (see p. 228) withheld substantial aid. Clay subsequently produced a dossier of some 20 allegedly dubious contracts involving corruption in four ministries, and in February 2005 reiterated his criticisms, urging Kibaki to remove corrupt ministers in order that investigations could proceed unhindered. In October 2004 a UN report named Kenya as the most corrupt country in Africa, and in January 2005 a joint survey by the World Bank and the Kenya Institute for Public Policy Research revealed that corruption remained the largest obstacle to conducting business in Kenya.

With public resentment increasing, the issue of corruption became the subject of further attention in February 2005 when the Permanent Secretary for Governance and Ethics in the Office of the President, John Githongo, resigned citing his inability to continue working for the Government. As he reported directly to the President, Githongo's resignation raised questions about Kibaki's own commitment to the fight against corruption. (Moreover, Kibaki did not appoint a replacement for Githongo, and in November 2005 disbanded the Office of Governance and Ethics.) Following Githongo's resignation, the USA and Germany announced that they would withhold anti-corruption aid, and the United Kingdom imposed travel restrictions on government ministers and others implicated in corruption. Awori admitted that there was massive corruption at senior levels, and there were demands from within the Government for the resignations of corrupt ministers. Kibaki subsequently reshuffled the Cabinet, dismissing several high-ranking civil servants and effectively demoting a key presidential aide, the Minister of State for Provincial Administration and National Security in the Office of the President, Christopher Murungaru, to the Ministry of Transport. Kibaki also ordered the KACC to investigate procurement procedures in the National Security department.

Later in February 2005 the Kenya Law Society announced that it was to prosecute senior figures on corruption charges, including Awori, the Attorney-General, Amos Wako, and the Minister of Finance, David Mwiraria. It was also revealed that the four senior civil servants suspended in May 2004 had agreed to act as prosecution witnesses and to testify that they had received instructions from government ministers to pursue the transactions for which they were being prosecuted. However, Wako invoked a provision in the Constitution granting him the power to take over private prosecutions initiated by individuals or institutions and entered a *nolle prosequi* to terminate the case.

In November 2005 Githongo presented Kibaki a dossier detailing his investigations into corruption in Kenya and death threats made against him, as well as accounts of his meetings with allegedly corrupt senior officials. Awori, Mwiraria, Murungaru and Kiraitu Murungi (the Minister of Energy) were implicated by Githongo in the Anglo Leasing scandal. His statement showed that a 'commitment fee' of Ks. 90m. was paid to the fictitious company for work that was never carried out, and that following his investigation much of the money had since been repaid (the Government refused to reveal by whom). Githongo claimed that, in total, the four intended to defraud the exchequer of US $700m. through false military and security contracts. He further alleged that two ministers had admitted that the money was to be used for party political campaigning. Awori, Mwiraria, Murungaru and Murungi were subsequently summoned to appear before the KACC; they all denied the allegations.

In January 2006 Githongo, who considered that Kibaki had failed to act upon the information supplied, released a copy of his dossier to the British media. (Githongo remained in exile in the United Kingdom.) He also released a tape recording of a meeting with Murungi in which the latter allegedly attempted to impede Githongo's investigation. Following Githongo's disclosure, a delegation of deputies representing the parliamentary Public Accounts Committee (PAC) travelled to the United Kingdom and interviewed Githongo at the Kenyan High Commission in London. In early February Mwiraria resigned from the Cabinet. Pressure increased on the Government and later that month Kibaki announced the resignations of Murungi and Saitoti, the Minister of Education. (Saitoti had also been implicated in the Goldenberg scandal—see above.) All three denied any wrongdoing. Kibaki reshuffled the Cabinet following the resignations, with Amos Kimunya assuming the finance portfolio, although Awori retained his position as Vice-President despite growing demands for his resignation. The PAC began questioning Awori, Mwiraria, Murungi and Saitoti in late February. In March Saitoti was also questioned by the police about his role in the Goldenberg affair.

Also in March 2006 police arrested three journalists from *The East African Standard* responsible for a story which alleged that Kibaki had attended a secret meeting with a former cabinet minister, Stephen Kalonzo Musyoka. The three were held for 72 hours before they were charged with 'publishing an alarming report' and released on bail. On the night following their arrest, heavily armed police officers raided the newspaper's offices and printing plant, where they disabled printing presses and destroyed most of the day's newspapers. The security forces also raided the offices of the Kenya Television Network from where they removed computers and transmission equipment, leaving the station unable to broadcast for several hours. The Government initially denied any knowledge of the raids, but subsequently confirmed that they were carried out by police 'to safeguard state security'.

Kenya's relations with Tanzania were strained during the late 1970s. However, the Kenya–Tanzania border, which had been closed prior to the dissolution of the East African Community (EAC) in 1977, was reopened in November 1983, following an agreement on the distribution of EAC assets and liabilities between the three former members (Kenya, Tanzania and Uganda), and in December Kenya and Tanzania agreed to establish full diplomatic relations. Following the seizure of power by the National Resistance Army in Uganda in January 1986, Moi offered full co-operation to the new Ugandan President, Yoweri Museveni. After visits to Kenya by Museveni and President Ali Hassan Mwinyi of Tanzania in June, it was announced that joint commissions were to be formed to enhance co-operation between the three countries. In September, however, Ugandan authorities claimed that Kenya was harbouring anti-Museveni rebels, and stationed troops at the two countries' common border. These claims were denied, and in December, when Ugandan troops allegedly entered Kenya in pursuit of rebels, Ugandan and Kenyan armed forces exchanged fire across the border for several days; at least 15 people were reported to have been killed. Later in December Moi and Museveni agreed to withdraw troops from either side of the border. In July 1988 the Ugandan Government accused Kenya of complicity in smuggling weapons to rebels in Uganda. During 1988–89 the Kenyan authorities repeatedly accused the Ugandan armed forces of making incursions into Kenya. Moi visited Museveni in August 1990, indicating a renewed *détente* between Kenya and Uganda. In November 1994 Moi, Museveni and Mwinyi met in Arusha, Tanzania, and established a commission for co-operation; in March 1996 the Secretariat of the Permanent Tripartite Commission for East African Co-operation was formally inaugurated, with a view to reviving the EAC. A treaty for the re-establishment of the EAC, providing for the promotion of free trade between the member states, the development of the region's infrastructure and economy and the creation of a regional legislative assembly and court, was ratified by the Kenyan, Tanzanian and Ugandan Heads of State in November 1999. The new EAC (see p. 385) was officially inaugurated in Arusha in January 2001. Talks on integrating the economies of the three EAC members followed, and in March 2004 Kibaki, Museveni and President Benjamin Mkapa of Tanzania signed a protocol on the creation of a customs union, eliminating most duties on goods traded within the EAC, which took effect from January 2005.

Relations between Kenya and Sudan deteriorated in mid-1988, as the two countries made mutual accusations of aiding rebel factions. In early 1989 Sudan renewed a long-standing dispute with Kenya over the sovereignty of territory on the Kenyan side of the two countries' common border, known as the 'Elemi triangle'. During the late 1990s Kenya hosted a series of peace talks between the Sudanese Government and opposition leaders, under the auspices of the Intergovernmental Authority on Development (see p. 286), in an attempt to resolve the conflict in southern Sudan. Further negotiations were held in Nairobi in September 2000 and June 2001, and in July 2002 the Sudanese Government and the opposition Sudan People's Liberation Army (SPLA) signed an accord in Machakos, Kenya, which provided for the holding of a referendum on self-determination for southern Sudan after a transitional period of six years. In September 2003 Kenya and Sudan agreed to form a joint border committee. Talks aimed at achieving a final peace settlement between the Sudanese Government and the SPLA continued in Kenya throughout 2003 and early 2004 (see the chapter on Sudan).

Somalia has traditionally laid claim to part of north-eastern Kenya. During 1989 tension developed between the Kenyan authorities and ethnic Somalis from both sides of the Kenya–Somalia border, when Somalis were alleged to be largely responsible for wildlife-poaching and banditry in north-eastern Kenya. In September Moi protested strongly to the Somali Government, following an incursion into Kenya by Somali troops (reportedly pursuing Somali rebels), which resulted in the deaths of four Kenyans. The Kenyan Government closed the two countries' common border in mid-1999, in response to rising insecurity in the area. The border was reopened in April 2000. In September the Kenyan Minister of Foreign Affairs and International Co-operation, Dr Bonaya Godana, stated that, while the Government supported the peace process in Somalia, it had not, as had been reported, officially declared recognition of the interim Somali President, Abdulkasim Hasan, or his Government. Moi later agreed to mediate between the interim Government and opposing rebel factions in Somalia. In July 2001 Kenya again closed the border after numerous clashes were reported on the Somali side, which threatened to spill over into Kenya. However, Moi agreed to reopen the border in November. An IGAD-sponsored Somali reconciliation conference opened in the Kenyan town of Eldoret in October 2002 and was moved to Nairobi in February 2003; the talks continued throughout 2003 and early 2004, despite various disruptions, and in January 2004 representatives from more than 20 factions in attendance reached agreement on the establishment of a new Somali parliament (see the chapter on Somalia).

Relations between the Kenyan and Ethiopian Governments became strained in 1997, owing to an increased incidence of cross-border cattle-rustling, including an attack in March during which 16 members of the Kenyan security forces were killed. A number of communiqués were subsequently signed by representatives of the two countries, agreeing to reinforce border security, to take measures to prevent the smuggling of arms and drugs, and to enhance trade. In November 1998 some 189 people (mainly Somalis) were found to have been massacred in north-eastern Kenya; Ethiopian guerrillas were widely believed to be responsible. In January 1999 the Kenyan Government protested to the Ethiopian authorities, following an incursion into Kenya by Ethiopian security forces, who were alleged to be in pursuit of Ethiopian rebels. Kenya deployed additional troops at the two countries' common frontier in May, following a series of landmine explosions in the region, which had resulted in several fatalities. Ethiopian troops allegedly made a further infiltration into Kenyan territory in July. Bilateral relations deteriorated further during late 2000 after it was reported that some 50 Kenyans had been killed, allegedly by Ethiopian militia forces, in cross-border clashes. In January 2001 representatives from both countries met in Nairobi and agreed to initiate measures aimed at ending border disputes.

In October 1995, despite strong condemnation from foreign Governments, the Kenyan authorities refused to permit the international tribunal that was investigating war crimes committed in Rwanda during 1994 access to alleged Rwandan perpetrators of genocide who had fled to Kenya. In June 1996 the Moi Government closed the Rwandan embassy in Nairobi in protest at the Rwandan Government's refusal to waive diplomatic immunity for an embassy official who was suspected of plotting a murder in Kenya; the diplomat was deported. In September, however, the first arrest in Kenya was made of a Rwandan Hutu suspected of involvement in genocide. Kenya strongly denied accusations, in November, of supplying arms to Rwandan Hutu rebels operating from within Zaire (now the Democratic Republic of the Congo). Following the *coup d'état* in Burundi in July 1996, Kenya, along with other countries of the region, imposed full economic sanctions on the administration of Maj. Pierre Buyoya; these sanctions were subsequently relaxed, and eventually withdrawn in January 1999. In November and December 1996 regional summit meetings were held in Nairobi to discuss the crisis in the Great Lakes region. Relations between the Kenyan and Rwandan Governments improved during 1997, when further Rwandan Hutus were arrested by the Kenyan security forces to stand trial on charges of genocide at the UN tribunal in Arusha, Tanzania. During a visit by Moi to Rwanda in May 2000 the two countries agreed to reopen the Kenyan embassy in Kigali and to establish a joint commission for bilateral relations.

In 1995 Kenya was reportedly sheltering about 200,000 refugees from the conflict in Somalia. The Moi Government, which claimed that the refugees placed an intolerable burden on the country's resources, repeatedly requested the UN to repatriate the total refugee population. By mid-1998 an estimated 155,000 Somalis had been repatriated from Kenya, with assistance from the office of the UN High Commissioner for Refugees. However, continuing instability in Somalia resulted in further influxes of refugees to Kenya. Kenya's total refugee population stood at 239,835 at the end of 2004, including 153,627 from Somalia and 67,556 from Sudan.

Government

Legislative power is vested in the unicameral National Assembly, with 224 members (210 elected by universal adult suffrage, the Attorney-General, the Speaker and 12 nominated members), who serve a term of five years, subject to dissolution. Executive power is held by the President, also directly elected for five years, who is assisted by an appointed Vice-President and Cabinet.

Defence

In August 2005 Kenya's active armed forces numbered 24,120, comprising an army of 20,000, an air force of 2,500 and a navy of 1,620; the paramilitary Police General Service Unit had a membership of 5,000. Military service is voluntary. Defence was allocated an estimated Ks. 22,000m. in the budget for 2005. Military assistance is received from the United Kingdom and from the USA, whose Rapid Deployment Force uses port and onshore facilities in Kenya.

Economic Affairs

In 2004, according to estimates by the World Bank, Kenya's gross national income (GNI), measured at average 2002–04 prices, was US $14,987m., equivalent to $460 per head (or $1,050 per head on an international purchasing-power parity basis). During 1995–2004, it was estimated, the population increased at an average annual rate of 2.2%, while gross domestic product (GDP) per head declined, in real terms, by an average of 0.5% per year. Overall GDP increased, in real terms, at an average annual rate of 1.7% in 1995–2004. Real GDP increased by 2.1% in 2004.

Agriculture (including forestry and fishing) contributed an estimated 16.4% of GDP in 2004 and, according the to FAO, employed 74.1% of the labour force in 2003. The principal cash crops are tea (which contributed 29.3% of total export earnings in 2000) and coffee (accounting for 9.8% of export earnings in 2000). Horticultural produce (Kenya is the world's fourth largest exporter of cut flowers), pyrethrum, sisal, sugar cane and cotton are also important. Maize is the principal subsistence crop. There is a significant dairy industry for domestic consumption and export. During 1995–2004, according to the World Bank, agricultural GDP increased at an average annual rate of 1.4%. Agricultural GDP increased by 2.4% in 2004.

Industry (including mining, manufacturing, construction and power) contributed an estimated 19.0% of GDP in 2004, and, according to the IMF, employed an estimated 19.2% of the total labour force in 2001. During 1995–2004, according to the World Bank, industrial GDP increased at an average annual rate of 1.5%. Industrial GDP increased by 3.3% in 2004.

Mining contributed an estimated 0.2% of GDP in 2003. According to IMF estimates, the sector employed 0.3% of the total labour force in 2001. Soda ash is the principal mineral export. Fluorspar, iron ore, salt, limestone, gold, gemstones (including rubies and sapphires), vermiculite and lead are also mined. Kenya has substantial reserves of titanium.

Manufacturing contributed an estimated 13.0% of GDP in 2004. According to IMF estimates, the sector employed 13.0% of the total labour force in 2001. During 1995–2004, according to the World Bank, manufacturing GDP increased at an average annual rate of 1.5%. Manufacturing GDP increased by 3.5% in 2004.

Hydroelectric power accounted for 68.9% of total electricity generated in 2002. It had accounted for an average of 81.9% during 1990–1998, whereafter recurrent droughts began to affect hydroelectric production. This shortfall was taken up by petroleum, which accounted for 22.6% in 2002 (as opposed to an average of 9.2% during 1990–1998). Kenya does not produce electricity from coal, natural gas or nuclear power. Energy for domestic use is derived principally from fuel wood and charcoal. The prolonged drought led to severe power shortages in 2000 and threatened to affect hydroelectric production in 2005–06. In February 2004 it was announced that the Kenyan and Tanzanian national grids were to be connected to that of Zambia under a cross-border energy project; the first phase of the project, which was to cost some US $300m., was to be commissioned in 2007, followed by a second phase in 2012. In 2003 imports of mineral fuels and lubricants (including crude petroleum intended for refining) comprised 23.1% of the value of total imports.

The services sector contributed an estimated 64.6% of GDP in 2004; according to IMF estimates, it employed 62.0% of the total labour force in 2001. Tourism makes an important contribution to Kenya's economy, and has been the country's principal source of foreign exchange since 1987. In 1998, however, a decline of 10.6% in tourist arrivals, to 894,300, was attributed partly to the effects of civil unrest in coastal areas during 1997. In 1999–2000 there was some recovery in tourism, with arrivals increasing to 1,036,628 in 2000. Following terrorist attacks in 2001, however, and subsequent warnings against travel to Kenya by the United Kingdom and the USA, the tourism industry again experienced difficulties. In 2003 tourist arrivals totalled 1,146,099, while receipts from tourism amounted to US $631m. The GDP of the services sector increased at an average annual rate of 2.2% in 1995–2004, according to the World Bank. Services GDP increased by 2.4% in 2004.

In 2004 Kenya recorded a visible trade deficit of US $1,597.5m., and there was a deficit of $378.5m. on the current account of the balance of payments. In 2004 the principal source of imports was the United Arab Emirates (which supplied 12.4% of total imports in that year); other major suppliers were South Africa, Saudi Arabia, the United Kingdom, Japan and India. Uganda was the principal market for Kenya's exports (purchasing 17.3%) in that year; other important purchasers were the United Kingdom, Tanzania, the Netherlands and Pakistan. The principal exports in 2000 were tea, vegetables and fruit, coffee and refined petroleum products. The principal imports in that year were petroleum and petroleum products, aircraft and parts, cereals and cereal preparations, and road vehicles and parts.

In the financial year ending 30 June 2003 there was a budgetary deficit of Ks. 32,814m., equivalent to 3.2% of GDP. The country's external debt was US $6,766m. at the end of 2003, of which $5,704m. was long-term public debt. In that year the cost of debt-servicing was equivalent to 15.8% of the value of exports of goods and services. The annual rate of inflation averaged 6.3% in 1995–2004; consumer prices increased by an average of 16.8% in 2004. Some 23% of the labour force were estimated to be unemployed in late 2000, and the rate of unemployment was reported to be approaching 30% by October 2001.

Kenya is a member of the Common Market for Eastern and Southern Africa (see p. 191) and, with Tanzania and Uganda, of the East African Community (see p. 385). The International Tea Promotion Association (see p. 383) is based in Kenya.

KENYA

Kenya's economy is reasonably diversified, although most employment is dependent on agriculture. Agricultural development has been intermittently hindered by adverse weather conditions (generally low rainfall, although severe flooding occurred in 1997–98), resulting in sporadic food shortages, and also by rural ethnic unrest. Moreover, the country is highly vulnerable to fluctuations in international prices for its cash crops, most notably tea and coffee. Poverty is widespread, with population growth considerably higher than growth in GNI per head. Hopes that the change in government in December 2002 would lead to a rapid economic recovery were disappointed to a large extent, and performance remained weak in 2003, as the expected resumption of IMF lending, which had been suspended in 2001, was delayed. The Government's failure to fulfil its election promises, and the revelation that large scale corruption remained endemic in Kenya, adversely affected business confidence and investment and led international donors to withhold aid. The tourism sector recovered in 2004 and increased investment in infrastructure, particularly roads and telecommunications, allied with a growth in intermediate imports in the second half of 2004, supported further economic expansion in 2005. During the first five months of 2005 the key sectors of agriculture, tourism and manufacturing all experienced significant growth. However, in late 2005 growth was restricted by food shortages and violent competition for water and pasture in northern Kenya, precipitated by a prolonged drought. In October 2005 reforms were enacted in order to stimulate foreign investment; the minimum investment sum was reduced from US $500,000 to $100,000, and several administrative hinderances were eliminated. In the following month a South African-led consortium won the right to operate the Kenya–Uganda 'Lunatic Express' (a 2,350-km railway linking Mombasa to Kampala) for 25 years. The state-owned line had suffered from poor management—freight levels had halved since 1983 while considerable debts accumulated. However, the privatization stalled in February 2006 when the consortium collapsed. It was estimated in March that some 3.5m. Kenyans urgently required food aid and the Kenyan Government appealed to the international donor community for assistance. Despite these difficulties, GDP was expected to increase by some 5% in 2005/06.

Education

The Government provides, or assists in the provision of, schools. In 2002/03 enrolment at pre-primary level was 33% (32% of boys; 33% of girls). Primary education, which is compulsory, is provided free of charge. The education system involves eight years of primary education (beginning at six years of age), four years at secondary school and four years of university education. Primary enrolment in 2002/03 was 66% (66% of both boys and girls). In the same year, however, secondary enrolment was only 25% (25% of boys; 24% of girls), according to UNESCO estimates. Tertiary enrolment in 2001/02 included just 3% of those in the relevant age group (4% males; 2% females), according to UNESCO estimates. There are five state universities and five chartered private universities. The education sector was allocated Ks. 54,653m. in the budget for 2001/02 (equivalent to 25.6% of total budgetary expenditure by the central Government).

Public Holidays

2006: 1 January (New Year's Day), 10 January*† (Id al Adha, Feast of the Sacrifice), 14–17 April (Easter), 1 May (Labour Day, anniversary of self-government), 1 June (Madaraka Day, anniversary of self-government), 10 October (Moi Day), 20 October (Kenyatta Day), 24 October* (Id al Fitr, end of Ramadan), 12 December (Independence Day), 25–26 December (Christmas), 31 December*† (Id al Adha, Feast of the Sacrifice).

2007: 1 January (New Year's Day), 6–9 April (Easter), 1 May (Labour Day, anniversary of self-government), 1 June (Madaraka Day, anniversary of self-government), 10 October (Moi Day), 20 October (Kenyatta Day), 13 October* (Id al Fitr, end of Ramadan), 12 December (Independence Day), 20 December* (Id al Adha, Feast of the Sacrifice), 25–26 December (Christmas).

* These holidays are determined by the Islamic lunar calendar and may vary by one or two days from the dates given.

† This festival occurs twice (in the Islamic years AH 1426 and 1427) within the same Gregorian year.

Weights and Measures

The metric system is in use.

Statistical Survey

Source (unless otherwise stated): Central Bureau of Statistics, Ministry of Finance and Planning, POB 30266, Nairobi; tel. (20) 333971; fax (20) 333030; internet www.cbs.go.ke.

Area and Population

AREA, POPULATION AND DENSITY

Area (sq km)	580,367*
Population (census results)†	
24 August 1989	21,443,636
24 August 1999	
Males	14,205,589
Females	14,481,018
Total	28,686,607
Population (official estimates at mid-year)	
2002	31,800,000
2003	32,700,000
2004	33,600,000
Density (per sq km) at mid-2004	57.9

* 224,081 sq miles. Total includes 11,230 sq km (4,336 sq miles) of inland water.
† Excluding adjustment for underenumeration.

PRINCIPAL ETHNIC GROUPS
(census of August 1989)

African	21,163,076		European	34,560
Arab	41,595		Other*	115,220
Asian	89,185		**Total**	21,443,636

* Includes persons who did not state 'tribe' or 'race'.

POPULATION BY PROVINCE
(census of August 1999)

Nairobi	2,143,254		Nyanza	4,392,196
Central	3,724,159		Rift Valley	6,987,036
Coast	2,487,264		Western	3,358,776
Eastern	4,631,779		**Total**	28,686,607
North-Eastern	962,143			

PRINCIPAL TOWNS
(estimated population at census of August 1999)

Nairobi (capital)	2,143,020		Meru	78,100
Mombasa	660,800		Kitale	63,245
Nakuru	219,366		Malindi*	53,805
Kisumu*	194,390		Nyeri*	46,969
Eldoret*	167,016		Kericho	30,023
Thika	82,665		Kisii	29,634

* Boundaries extended between 1979 and 1989.

Mid-2003 (UN estimate, incl. suburbs): Nairobi 2,574,847 (Source: UN, *World Urbanization Prospects: The 2003 Revision*).

KENYA

BIRTHS AND DEATHS
(UN estimates, annual averages)

	1990–95	1995–2000	2000–05
Birth rate (per 1,000)	38.5	37.5	38.8
Death rate (per 1,000)	10.3	13.4	15.5

Source: UN, *World Population Prospects: The 2004 Revision*.

Expectation of life (WHO estimates, years at birth): 50 (males 50; females 49) in 2003 (Source: WHO, *World Health Report*).

ECONOMICALLY ACTIVE POPULATION

	1999	2000	2001*
Agriculture and forestry	311,257	312,200	312,500
Mining and quarrying	5,162	5,300	5,200
Manufacturing	219,604	218,700	216,600
Electricity and water	22,713	22,700	21,400
Construction	78,647	78,600	76,800
Wholesale and retail trade	153,629	155,500	156,900
Transport and communications	83,805	84,200	84,300
Finance, insurance, real estate and business services	84,528	85,000	70,300
Community, social and personal services	714,205	733,100	719,600
Total	**1,673,550**	**1,695,300**	**1,663,600**

* Provisional figures.

Source: IMF, *Kenya: Statistical Appendix* (July 2003).

Health and Welfare

KEY INDICATORS

Total fertility rate (children per woman, 2003)	3.9
Under-5 mortality rate (per 1,000 live births, 2004)	120
HIV/AIDS (% of persons aged 15–49, 2003)	6.7
Physicians (per 1,000 head, 1995)	0.13
Hospital beds (per 1,000 head, 1990)	1.65
Health expenditure (2002): US $ per head (PPP)	70
Health expenditure (2002): % of GDP	4.9
Health expenditure (2002): public (% of total)	44.0
Access to water (% of persons, 2002)	62
Access to sanitation (% of persons, 2002)	48
Human Development Index (2003): ranking	154
Human Development Index (2003): value	0.474

For sources and definitions, see explanatory note on p. vi.

Agriculture

PRINCIPAL CROPS
('000 metric tons)

	2002	2003	2004
Wheat	307.2	378.7	379.4
Rice (paddy)	45.0	40.5	49.3
Barley	92.9	26.6	39.2
Maize	2,408.6	2,710.8	2,138.4
Millet	72.2	63.6	50.5
Sorghum	115.6	127.2	69.5
Potatoes	861.6	1,223.5	1,000.0*
Sweet potatoes	434.8	615.5	571.3
Cassava (Manioc)	602.0	423.8	642.9
Sugar cane	4,501.4	4,204.1	4,661.0†
Dry beans	480.8	428.8	277.5
Dry cow peas	59.4	47.0	29.3
Pigeon peas	93.2	98.3	105.6
Cashew nuts	10.0	10.0*	10.0*
Coconuts	60.1	60.0*	60.0*
Seed cotton	20.0	20.0*	20.0*
Cottonseed*	13.0	13.0	13.0
Cabbages	578.1	709.0	550.0*
Tomatoes	284.9	318.6	260.0*
Dry onions	60.5	65.8	58.0*
Carrots	53.8	44.3	40.0*
Other vegetables*	647.2	670.1	668.3

	2002	2003	2004
Bananas	536.5	509.7	510.0*
Plantains	536.5	509.7	510.0*
Citrus fruit*	155.7	168.9	169.4
Mangoes	176.5	129.5	118.0
Avocados	52.4	70.9	70.0*
Pineapples	619.9	399.1	600.0
Papayas	81.8	86.5	86.0*
Other fruits (excl. melons)*	130.0	138.6	143.2
Coffee (green)	51.9	51.9	50.8†
Tea (made)	287.0	293.7	295.0*
Tobacco (leaves)	20.0	20.0*	20.0*
Pyrethrum*	8.0	8.0	8.0
Sisal	23.4	24.4	25.0*

* FAO estimate(s).
† Unofficial figure.

Source: FAO.

LIVESTOCK
('000 head, year ending September)

	2002	2003	2004*
Cattle	11,500.0*	12,531.3	12,000.0
Sheep	8,208.1	9,938.8	10,000.0
Goats	10,959.7	11,945.5	12,000.0
Pigs	335.9	415.2	415.0
Camels*	830.0	830.0	830.0
Chickens	27,902	29,901	26,000

* FAO estimate(s).

Source: FAO.

LIVESTOCK PRODUCTS
('000 metric tons)

	2002	2003	2004
Beef and veal	295.0	305.0*	318.7
Mutton and lamb*	27.6	33.6	34.2
Goats' meat*	34.1	36.3	36.3
Pig meat	11.4	18.5*	18.5*
Poultry meat	54.0	54.0*	54.0*
Game meat*	14.0	14.0	14.0
Camel meat*	19.8	19.8	19.8
Cows' milk	2,812.0	2,819.5	2,812.0
Sheeps' milk*	30.8	31.0	31.0
Goats' milk*	96.0	97.5	97.5
Camels' milk*	25.2	25.2	25.2
Hen eggs*	60.7	60.7	60.7
Honey	22.0	22.0*	21.5
Wool			
Greasy	2.1	2.1*	1.5
Scoured*	1.0	1.0	1.0
Cattle hides*	38.9	41.0	41.0
Goatskins*	10.9	11.6	11.6
Sheepskins*	5.5	6.7	6.8

* FAO estimate(s).

Source: FAO.

Forestry

ROUNDWOOD REMOVALS
('000 cubic metres, excluding bark)

	2002	2003	2004
Sawlogs, veneer logs and logs for sleepers	241.0	251.0	241.0
Pulpwood	441.0	349.0	391.0
Other industrial wood*	1,160.0	1,160.0	1,160.0
Fuel wood*	20,001.5	20,182.4	20,369.6
Total	**21,843.5**	**21,942.4**	**22,161.6**

* FAO estimates.

Source: FAO.

KENYA

SAWNWOOD PRODUCTION
('000 cubic metres, including railway sleepers)

	2000*	2001	2002
Coniferous (softwood)	184	74	70
Broadleaved (hardwood)	1	10	8
Total	185	84	78

* FAO estimates.

2003–04: Production as in 2002.

Source: FAO.

Fishing

('000 metric tons, live weight)

	2001	2002	2003
Capture	164.2	144.5	119.5
Silver cyprinid	41.4	35.5	31.7
Nile tilapia	7.3	16.3	16.0
Other tilapias	19.1	17.4	4.5
Nile perch	78.5	58.4	54.7
Other freshwater fishes	5.2	5.0	1.8
Aquaculture	1.0	0.8	1.0
Total catch	165.2	145.3	120.5

Note: Figures exclude crocodiles, recorded by number rather than by weight. The number of Nile crocodiles caught was: 4,250 in 2001; 3,967 in 2002; 3,811 in 2003.

Source: FAO.

Mining

('000 metric tons)

	2001	2002*	2003*
Soda ash	297.8	304.1	352.6
Fluorspar	118.9	85.0	95.3
Salt	5.7	18.8	19.0
Limestone flux	32	32	32

* Estimates.

Industry

SELECTED PRODUCTS
('000 metric tons, unless otherwise indicated)

	2000	2001	2002
Wheat flour	189	181	188
Raw sugar	402	377	494
Beer ('000 hectolitres)	2,029	1,843	1,919
Cigarettes (million)	6,009	5,850	5,950
Cement	1,366	1,319	1,495
Kerosene and jet fuels	400	320	273
Motor spirit (petrol)	335	273	253
Gas-diesel (distillate fuel) oils	511	436	405
Residual fuel oil	616	535	533
Electric energy (million kWh)	3,958	4,338	4,447

Finance

CURRENCY AND EXCHANGE RATES

Monetary Units
100 cents = 1 Kenya shilling (Ks.).
Ks. 20 = 1 Kenya pound (K£).

Sterling, Dollar and Euro Equivalents (30 December 2005)
£1 sterling = Ks. 124.61;
US $1 = Ks. 72.37;
€1 = Ks. 85.37;
Ks. 1,000 = £8.03 sterling = $13.82 = €11.71.

Average Exchange Rate (Ks. per US $)
2003   75.936
2004   79.174
2005   75.554

Note: The foregoing information refers to the Central Bank's mid-point exchange rate. However, with the introduction of a foreign exchange bearer certificate (FEBC) scheme in October 1991, a dual exchange rate system is in effect. In May 1994 foreign exchange transactions were liberalized and the Kenya shilling became fully convertible against other currencies.

BUDGET
(Ks. million, year ending 30 June)

Revenue	1999/2000	2000/01	2001/02*
Tax revenue	151,359.5	160,771.6	160,394.2
Taxes on income and profits	53,317.0	53,428.9	55,861.9
Taxes on goods and services	69,437.3	78,538.9	82,948.6
Value-added tax	40,944.2	50,220.9	50,871.7
Excise duties	28,493.1	28,317.9	32,076.9
Taxes on international trade	28,605.2	28,803.7	21,583.7
Import duties	28,605.2	28,803.7	21,583.7
Non-tax revenue	27,585.1	26,306.1	25,399.4
Property income	6,482.4	4,786.1	4,105.5
Administrative fees and charges	21,538.1	21,538.1	21,293.9
Total (incl. others)	184,550.9	192,221.0	187,863.8

Expenditure	1999/2000	2000/01	2001/02*
General administration	44,080.7	62,943.3	57,584.5
Defence	10,427.2	14,202.8	16,268.2
Social services	59,670.4	67,611.1	71,953.1
Education	47,726.8	49,611.3	54,653.0
Health	9,188.6	15,629.3	14,336.5
Economic services	28,481.1	39,362.3	38,069.4
General administration	5,101.3	14,085.6	12,696.2
Agriculture, forestry and fishing	8,115.4	8,269.6	7,850.1
Roads	8,848.5	9,458.4	8,856.7
Interest on public debt	28,917.8	24,425.5	29,850.9
Total	171,577.2	208,545.7	213,726.2

* Forecasts.

INTERNATIONAL RESERVES
(US $ million at 31 December)

	2002	2003	2004
IMF special drawing rights	0.8	2.0	0.6
Reserve position in IMF	17.1	18.8	19.7
Foreign exchange	1,050.0	1,461.0	1,499.0
Total	1,067.9	1,481.8	1,519.3

Source: IMF, *International Financial Statistics*.

MONEY SUPPLY
(Ks. million at 31 December)

	2002	2003	2004
Currency outside banks	53,895	55,550	62,728
Demand deposits at commercial banks	86,070	128,297	136,729
Total money (incl. others)	139,965	183,847	199,457

Source: IMF, *International Financial Statistics*.

KENYA

COST OF LIVING
(Consumer Price Index at December; base: October 1997 = 100)

	2000	2001	2002
Food and non-alcoholic beverages	136.3	134.8	142.5
Alcohol and tobacco	120.8	136.3	137.1
Clothing and footwear	109.9	109.8	110.7
Housing	121.6	129.3	133.9
Fuel and power	143.1	154.1	165.8
Household goods and services	117.6	119.0	120.8
Medical goods and services	134.1	152.6	158.8
Transport and communnications	128.4	127.7	130.8
Recreation and education	120.2	129.6	132.8
Personal goods and services	118.2	120.5	122.8
All items (incl. others)	129.0	131.1	136.7

Source: IMF, *Kenya: Statistical Appendix* (July 2003).

NATIONAL ACCOUNTS
(Ks. million at current prices)

Expenditure on the Gross Domestic Product

	2001	2002	2003
Government final consumption expenditure	168,731	184,337	195,467
Private final consumption expenditure	665,208	701,822	805,163
Increase in stocks	5,282	4,542	4,588
Gross fixed capital formation	123,079	124,313	136,567
Total domestic expenditure	962,300	1,015,014	1,141,785
Exports of goods and services	234,176	250,429	271,785
Less Imports of goods and services	317,745	302,758	321,929
GDP in purchasers' values	878,731	962,686	1,091,640

Source: IMF, *International Financial Statistics*.

Gross Domestic Product by Economic Activity

	2001	2002	2003*
Agriculture, forestry and fishing	143,533.7	143,601.3	152,545.5
Mining and quarrying	1,260.2	1,441.7	1,618.6
Manufacturing	96,968.5	110,853.3	131,614.4
Electricity, gas and water	8,892.6	11,227.6	12,590.8
Construction	33,160.8	37,993.1	43,870.4
Trade, restaurants and hotels	193,782.6	224,276.0	250,333.4
Transport, storage and communication	57,972.0	72,550.0	84,665.8
Finance, insurance, real estate and business services	74,174.0	70,099.0	89,041.0
Ownership and dwelling	39,315.3	46,432.0	46,864.4
Government services	101,048.0	111,093.7	129,262.8
Private households	8,932.4	9,222.8	9,926.9
Other services	36,773.9	37,973.3	50,584.7
Sub-total	795,814.0	876,763.3	1,002,918.7
Less Imputed bank service charge	28,433.0	26,776.0	34,495.0
Indirect taxes	111,549.8	112,898.2	123,416.5
Less Subsidies	200.0	200.0	200.0
GDP in market prices	878,730.8	962,686.0	1,091,640.3

* Provisional.
Source: Central Bank of Kenya.

BALANCE OF PAYMENTS
(US $ million)

	2002	2003	2004
Exports of goods f.o.b.	2,162.5	2,412.2	2,722.7
Imports of goods f.o.b.	−3,159.0	−3,554.8	−4,320.2
Trade balance	−996.5	−1,142.6	−1,597.5
Exports of services	1,018.1	1,153.2	1,479.1
Imports of services	−645.9	−670.9	−794.4
Balance on goods and services	−624.2	−660.4	−912.8
Other income received	35.4	59.6	45.0
Other income paid	−178.2	−147.8	−159.4
Balance on goods, services and income	−767.1	−748.5	−1,027.2
Current transfers received	632.1	818.6	649.7
Current transfers paid	−1.9	−2.3	−0.9

—*continued*	2002	2003	2004
Current balance	−136.9	67.7	−378.5
Capital account	81.2	163.0	145.2
Direct investment abroad	−7.4	−2.1	−4.4
Direct investment from abroad	27.6	81.7	46.1
Portfolio investment assets	−10.0	−38.6	−71.7
Portfolio investment liabilities	5.3	0.9	5.4
Other investment assets	−132.6	−67.4	−308.4
Other investment liabilities	−56.7	431.7	372.6
Net errors and omissions	213.2	−211.9	202.7
Overall balance	−16.4	425.2	9.0

Source: IMF, *International Financial Statistics*.

External Trade

PRINCIPAL COMMODITIES
(distribution by SITC, Ks. million)

Imports c.i.f.	1998	1999	2000
Food and live animals	18,905.4	13,132.9	21,332.6
Cereals and cereal preparations	11,071.7	85,114.0	14,353.3
Crude materials (inedible) except fuels	6,299.3	5,791.0	6,364.0
Mineral fuels, lubricants, etc.	32,189.1	30,745.6	64,855.9
Petroleum, petroleum products, etc.	31,828.5	30,224.1	64,358.0
Crude petroleum oils	15,036.6	11,087.0	41,907.2
Refined petroleum products	16,317.9	18,593.0	21,882.6
Animal and vegetable oils, fats and waxes	8,750.1	9,087.8	8,015.8
Chemicals and related products	30,018.1	31,918.4	32,796.7
Medicinal and pharmaceutical products	6,559.4	6,378.6	5,975.8
Artificial resins, plastic materials, etc.	6,108.2	6,006.5	7,134.8
Basic manufactures	25,307.2	28,169.1	27,562.4
Iron and steel	7,899.7	9,136.9	8,603.8
Machinery and transport equipment	63,341.0	59,519.1	72,131.3
Power-generating machinery and equipment	5,160.0	6,011.9	12,142.8
Machinery specialized for particular industries	7,564.8	5,914.4	4,817.6
General industrial machinery, equipment and parts	8,735.8	8,530.4	8,831.9
Electrical machinery, apparatus, etc.	6,310.7	6,390.4	6,685.3
Road vehicles and parts*	17,737.0	14,992.4	12,546.1
Passenger motor cars (excl. buses)	6,458.8	5,290.3	4,763.2
Motor vehicles for goods transport and special purposes	6,062.5	4,805.1	2,798.1
Aircraft, associated equipment and parts*	8,545.7	8,838.5	14,972.7
Miscellaneous manufactured articles	12,002.4	15,193.0	13,353.8
Total (incl. others)	197,788.7	195,003.7	247,803.9

* Data on parts exclude tyres, engines and electrical parts.

KENYA

Statistical Survey

Exports f.o.b.*	1998	1999	2000
Food and live animals	62,850.0	63,471.2	66,953.7
Vegetables and fruit	9,384.0	11,147.8	13,420.8
Fresh or simply preserved vegetables	3,714.6	4,327.0	7,812.7
Coffee, tea, cocoa and spices	46,393.9	45,749.1	47,519.5
Coffee (green and roasted)	12,875.0	12,104.9	11,759.2
Tea	32,970.7	33,065.1	35,149.9
Crude materials (inedible) except fuels	10,196.7	11,578.9	13,575.9
Cut flowers and foliage	5,155.4	5,965.5	6,896.7
Mineral fuels, lubricants, etc.	9,915.1	9,603.1	9,705.4
Petroleum, petroleum products, etc.	9,865.4	9,555.1	9,641.9
Refined petroleum products	9,671.5	9,392.4	9,441.3
Chemicals and related products	7,336.5	7,406.2	6,712.8
Basic manufactures	13,269.4	12,113.7	12,357.3
Iron and steel	3,823.7	2,757.5	2,605.1
Miscellaneous manufactured articles	4,868.4	5,637.6	5,736.1
Total (incl. others)	114,445.3	115,405.5	119,763.7

* Excluding re-exports.

PRINCIPAL TRADING PARTNERS
(Ks. million)

Imports c.i.f.	2002	2003	2004*
Belgium	6,944	6,757	9,686
China, People's Repub.	6,052	8,023	12,785
France	9,712	8,957	12,193
Germany	12,942	10,962	13,127
India	13,810	14,811	22,630
Indonesia	13,080	12,497	7,691
Italy	4,146	5,840	7,145
Japan	17,242	18,611	24,138
Korea, Repub.	2,755	2,966	3,286
Netherlands	5,409	6,256	7,309
Pakistan	4,020	4,456	3,247
Saudi Arabia	13,446	24,305	31,529
Singapore	4,188	2,352	4,452
South Africa	6,863	23,309	34,627
Spain	2,959	2,154	1,989
Sweden	12,259	1,615	2,007
United Arab Emirates	29,060	31,918	45,012
United Kingdom	21,138	19,621	27,124
USA	14,648	14,388	14,400
Total (incl. others)	257,710	281,844	364,205

Exports f.o.b.	2002	2003	2004*
Belgium	2,292	2,332	2,474
Egypt	6,752	5,453	6,918
France	2,374	3,100	3,592
Germany	4,377	5,330	4,574
India	2,543	2,498	4,147
Italy	1,759	1,671	1,766
Japan	1,753	1,215	1,593
Netherlands	11,012	14,139	17,094
Pakistan	8,341	9,153	11,359
Rwanda	4,313	6,012	6,190
Tanzania	14,181	14,588	17,921
Uganda	31,280	30,668	37,060
United Arab Emirates	2,468	2,108	2,396
United Kingdom	19,607	21,525	22,413
USA	3,377	2,796	4,495
Total (incl. others)	169,241	183,154	214,402

* Provisional.

Transport

RAILWAYS
(traffic)

	2000	2001	2002*
Passenger-km (million)	302	216	288
Freight ton-km (million)	1,557	1,603	1,538

* Provisional figures.

ROAD TRAFFIC
(estimates, motor vehicles in use)

	2000	2001	2002*
Motor cars	244,836	255,379	269,925
Light vans	159,450	162,603	166,811
Lorries, trucks and heavy vans	57,796	58,501	59,835
Buses and mini-buses	38,930	42,629	46,606
Motorcycles and autocycles	44,894	46,004	47,451
Other motor vehicles	31,820	32,255	32,724

* Provisional figures.

SHIPPING

Merchant Fleet
(registered at 31 December)

	2002	2003	2004
Number of vessels	36	38	41
Total displacement ('000 grt)	19.1	17.8	18.7

Source: Lloyd's Register-Fairplay, *World Fleet Statistics*.

International Sea-borne Freight Traffic
(estimates, '000 metric tons)

	1999	2000	2001*
Goods loaded	1,845	1,722	1,998
Goods unloaded	6,200	7,209	8,299

* Provisional figures.

CIVIL AVIATION
(traffic on scheduled services)

	1999	2000	2001
Kilometres flown (million)	19	27	27
Passengers carried ('000)	808	973	990
Passenger-km (million)	2,286	3,040	3,522
Total ton-km (million)	271	355	410

Source: UN, *Statistical Yearbook*.

Tourism

FOREIGN TOURIST ARRIVALS
(number of visitors by country of origin)

	2001	2002	2003
Austria	19,929	20,054	22,954
France	47,802	48,101	55,057
Germany	156,414	157,394	180,156
India	23,858	24,007	27,479
Italy	53,328	53,662	61,428
Sweden	34,376	34,591	39,593
Switzerland	39,081	39,326	45,013
Tanzania	111,735	112,435	128,695
Uganda	69,781	70,218	80,373
United Kingdom	153,968	154,933	177,339
USA	65,191	65,599	75,086
Total (incl. others)	993,600	1,001,297	1,146,099

Source: World Tourism Organization, *Yearbook of Tourism Statistics*.

Tourism receipts (US $ million, incl. passenger transport): 536 in 2001; 513 in 2002; 631 in 2003.

Source: World Tourism Organization.

Communications Media

	2002	2003	2004
Telephones ('000 main lines in use)	322	328	299
Mobile cellular telephones ('000 subscribers)	1,187	1,591	2,546
Personal computers ('000 in use)	204	n.a.	441
Internet users ('000)	400	n.a.	1,500

Source: International Telecommunication Union.

Television receivers ('000 in use, 2000): 768.
Radio receivers ('000 in use, 1999): 6,383.
Facsimile machines (number in use, year ending 30 June 1995): 3,800.
Daily newspapers (2000): 4 titles (average circulation 310,000 copies).
Book production (titles, 1994): 300 first editions (excl. pamphlets).
Sources: UNESCO, *Statistical Yearbook*; UN, *Statistical Yearbook*.

Education

(1998/99, unless otherwise indicated)

	Institutions	Teachers	Pupils
Pre-primary	23,977	37,752	1,016,606
Primary	17,611	192,306	5,480,689
Secondary:			
general secondary	3,057	43,694	1,139,569
technical*	36	1,147	11,700
teacher training	26†	808‡	18,992§
Higher	n.a.‖	n.a.‖	61,526

* 1988 figures.
† 1995 figure.
‡ 1985 figure.
§ 1992 figure.
‖ In 1990 there were four universities, with 4,392 teachers.

Sources: Ministry of Education, Nairobi; UNESCO Institute for Statistics.

Adult literacy rate (UNESCO estimates): 73.6% (males 77.7%; females 70.2%) in 2003 (Source: UN Development Programme, *Human Development Report*).

Directory

The Constitution

The Constitution was introduced at independence on 12 December 1963. Subsequent amendments, including the adoption of republican status on 12 December 1964, were consolidated in 1969. A further amendment in December 1991 permitted the establishment of a multi-party system. In September 1997 the National Assembly approved legislation which amended the Constitution with a view to ensuring free and fair democratic elections. All political parties were granted equal access to the media, and detention without trial was prohibited. In addition, the opposition was to participate in selecting the 12 nominated members of the National Assembly and 10 of the 12 members of the supervisory Electoral Commission. An amendment to the Constitution, approved by the National Assembly in November 1999, reduced the level of presidential control over the legislative process. The Constitution can be amended by the affirmative vote on Second and Third Reading of 65% of the membership of the National Assembly (excluding the Speaker and Attorney-General).

The central legislative authority is the unicameral National Assembly, in which there are 210 directly elected Representatives, 12 nominated members and two *ex-officio* members, the Attorney-General and the Speaker. The maximum term of the National Assembly is five years from its first meeting (except in wartime). It can be dissolved by the President at any time, and the National Assembly may force its own dissolution by a vote of 'no confidence', whereupon presidential and Assembly elections have to be held within 90 days.

Executive power is vested in the President, Vice-President and Cabinet. Both the Vice-President and the Cabinet are appointed by the President, who must be a member of the Assembly and at least 35 years of age. Election of the President, for a five-year term, is by direct popular vote; the winning candidate at a presidential election must receive no less than 25% of the votes in at least five of Kenya's eight provinces. If a President dies, or a vacancy otherwise occurs during a President's period of office, the Vice-President becomes interim President for up to 90 days while a successor is elected.

The Government

HEAD OF STATE

President: MWAI KIBAKI (took office 30 December 2002).

CABINET
(March 2006)

Vice-President and Minister of Home Affairs: ARTHUR MOODY AWORI.
Minister of Finance: AMOS KIMUNYA.
Minister of Planning and National Development and Acting Minister of Energy: HENRY ONYANCHA OBWOCHA.
Minister of Foreign Affairs: RAPHAEL TUJU.
Minister of East African and Regional Co-operation: JOHN KOECH.
Minister of Roads and Public Works: SIMEON NYACHAE.
Minister of Science and Technology and Acting Minister of Education: Dr NOAH WEKESA.
Minister of Agriculture: KIPRUTO RONO ARAP KIRWA.
Minister of Livestock and Fisheries Development: JOSEPH KONZOLO MUNYAO.
Minister of Health: CHARITY KALUKI NGILU.
Minister of Tourism and Wildlife: MORRIS DZORO.
Minister of Information and Communications: MUTAHI KAGWE.
Minister of Transport: CHIRAU ALI MAKWERE.
Minister of Local Government: MUSIKARI N. KOMBO.
Minister of Gender, Sports, Culture and Social Services: MAINA KAMANDA.
Minister of Water and Irrigation: J. K. KATUKU.
Minister of Regional Development Authorities: ABDI M. MOHAMED.
Minister of the Environment and Natural Resources and Acting Minister of Lands: Prof. KIVUTHA KIBWANA.
Minister of Labour and Human Resource Development: Dr NEWTON W. KULUNDU.
Minister of Co-operative Development and Marketing: PETER N. NDWIGA.
Minister of Justice and Constitutional Affairs: MARTHA KARUA.
Minister of Housing: SOITA SHITANDA.
Minister of Trade and Industry: Dr MUKHISA KITUYI.
Ministers of State in the Office of the President: JOHN NJOROGE MICHUKI (Provincial Administration and National Security), NJENGA KRUME (Defence), MOSES AKARANGA (Public Service), JOHN MUNYES (Special Programmes), GIDEON KONCHELAH (Immigration and Registration of Persons).
Ministers of State in the Office of the Vice-President: SULEIMAN SHAKOMBO (National Heritage), MOHAMMED ABDI KUTI (Youth Affairs).

The Attorney-General and the Solicitor-General are also members of the Cabinet.

MINISTRIES

Office of the President: Harambee House, Harambee Ave, POB 30510, Nairobi; tel. (20) 227411; internet www.officeofthepresident.go.ke.
Office of the Vice-President and Ministry of Home Affairs: Jogoo House 'A', Taifa Rd, POB 30520, Nairobi; tel. (20) 228411; internet www.vice-president.go.ke.
Ministry of Agriculture: Kilimo House, Cathedral Rd, POB 30028, Nairobi; tel. (20) 718870; fax (20) 720586; internet www.agriculture.go.ke.

KENYA

Ministry of Co-operative Development and Marketing: Reinsurance Plaza, Taifa Rd, POB 30547, 00100 Nairobi; tel. (20) 339650; internet www.co-operative.go.ke.

Ministry of East African and Regional Co-operation: Old Treasury Bldg, 1st Floor, Harambee Ave, POB 30551, Nairobi; tel. (20) 310310; fax (20) 310365.

Ministry of Education, Science and Technology: Jogoo House 'B', Harambee Ave, POB 30040, Nairobi; tel. (20) 334411; e-mail info@education.go.ke; internet www.education.go.ke.

Ministry of Energy: Nyayo House, Kenyatta Ave, POB 30582, Nairobi; tel. (20) 333551; internet www.energy.go.ke.

Ministry of the Environment and Natural Resources: Maji House, Ngong Rd, POB 30521, Nairobi; tel. (20) 2716103; e-mail mec@nbnet.co.ke; internet www.environment.go.ke.

Ministry of Finance: Treasury Bldg, Harambee Ave, POB 30007, Nairobi; tel. (20) 338111; fax (20) 330426; e-mail info@treasury.go.ke; internet www.treasury.go.ke.

Ministry of Foreign Affairs: Old Treasury Bldg, Harambee Ave, POB 30551, Nairobi; tel. (20) 334433; e-mail mfapress@nbnet.co.ke; internet www.mfa.go.ke.

Ministry of Gender, Sports, Culture and Social Services: Jogoo House 'A', Taifa Rd, POB 30520, Nairobi; tel. (20) 228411; internet www.kenya.go.ke/gender.

Ministry of Health: Medical HQ, Afya House, Cathedral Rd, POB 30016, Nairobi; tel. (20) 2717077; fax (20) 2725902; internet www.health.go.ke.

Ministry of Information and Communications: Utalii House, off Uhuru Highway, POB 30027, Nairobi; tel. (20) 333555; fax (20) 318045.

Ministry of Justice and Constitutional Affairs: State Law Office, Harambee Ave, POB 40112, Nairobi; tel. (20) 227461; internet www.kenya.go.ke/justice.

Ministry of Labour and Human Resource Development: Social Security House, Block 'C', Bishop Rd, POB 40326, Nairobi; tel. (20) 2729800; fax (20) 2726497; internet www.labour.go.ke.

Ministry of Lands and Housing: Ardhi House, Ngong Rd, POB 30450, Nairobi; tel. (20) 2718050; internet www.ardhi.go.ke.

Ministry of Livestock and Fisheries Development: Kilimo House, Cathedral Rd, POB 30028, Nairobi; tel. (20) 7118870; fax (20) 2711149; internet www.livestock.go.ke.

Ministry of Local Government: Jogoo House 'A', Taifa Rd, POB 30004, Nairobi; tel. (20) 217475; e-mail mlog@form-net.com; internet www.localgovernment.go.ke.

Ministry of Planning and National Development: Treasury Bldg, Harambee Ave, POB 30007, Nairobi; tel. (20) 338111; internet www.planning.go.ke.

Ministry of Regional Development Authorities: Harambee Ave, POB 62345, Nairobi; tel. (20) 227411; internet www.regional-dev.go.ke.

Ministry of Roads and Public Works: Ministry of Works Bldg, Ngong Rd, POB 30260, Nairobi; tel. (20) 723101; fax (20) 720044; e-mail ps@roadsnet.go.ke; internet www.publicworks.go.ke.

Ministry of Tourism and Wildlife: Utalii House, 5th Floor, off Uhuru Highway, POB 30027, Nairobi; tel. (20) 333555; fax (20) 318045; internet www.tourism.go.ke.

Ministry of Trade and Industry: Teleposta Towers, Kenyatta Ave, POB 30430, Nairobi; tel. (20) 331030; internet www.tradeandindustry.go.ke.

Ministry of Transport: Transcom House, Ngong Rd, POB 52692, Nairobi; tel. (20) 729200; fax (20) 726362; internet www.transport.go.ke.

Ministry of Water: Maji House, Ngong Rd, POB 49720, Nairobi; tel. (20) 2716103; internet www.kenya.go.ke/water.

President and Legislature

PRESIDENT

Election, 27 December 2002

Candidates	Votes	%
Mwai Kibaki (NARC)	3,646,409	62.3
Uhuru Kenyatta (KANU)	1,828,914	31.2
Simeon Nyachae (Ford—People)	345,378	5.9
James Orengo (SDP)	24,537	0.4
David Ng'ethe (CCU)	10,038	0.2
Total	**5,855,276**	**100.0**

NATIONAL ASSEMBLY

Speaker: FRANCIS XAVIER OLE KAPARO.

General Election, 27 December 2002

Party	Seats
NARC	125
KANU	64
FORD—People	14
FORD—Asili	2
Safina	2
SKS	2
SPK	1
Total	**210***

* In addition to the 210 directly elected seats, 12 are held by nominees (NARC 7; KANU 4; FORD—People 1). The Attorney-General and the Speaker are, *ex officio*, members of the National Assembly.

Election Commission

Electoral Commission of Kenya: Anniversary Towers, University Way, POB 45371, Nairobi; tel. (20) 222072; internet www.eck.ke; independent; Chair. SAMUEL KIVUITU.

Political Organizations

Chama Cha Uma (CCU): Nairobi; DAVID NG'ETHE.

Democratic Party of Kenya (DP): Continental House, POB 56396, Nairobi; tel. (20) 340044; f. 1991; Chair. MWAI KIBAKI; Sec. JOSEPH MUNYAO; rival faction led by NGENGI MUIGAI.

Forum for the Restoration of Democracy—Asili (FORD—Asili): Anyany Estate, POB 72595, Nairobi; f. 1992; Chair. GEORGE NTHENGE; Sec. MARTIN J. SHIKUKU.

Forum for the Restoration of Democracy—Kenya (FORD—Kenya): Odinga House, POB 57449, Nairobi; tel. (20) 570361; f. 1992; predominantly Luo support; Chair. MUSKARI KOMBO; Sec. GITOBU IMANYARA.

Forum for the Restoration of Democracy for the People (FORD—People): Nairobi; f. 1997 by fmr mems of FORD—Asili; Chair. KIPKALIA KONES.

Kenya African National Union (KANU): KICC POB 72394, Nairobi; tel. (20) 332383; f. 1960; sole legal party 1982–91; absorbed the National Development Party (f. 1994) in 2002; Pres. UHURU KENYATTA; Sec.-Gen. JULIUS SUNKULI.

Kenya National Congress (KNC): POB 9474, Nairobi; f. 1992; Chair. Prof. KATANA MKANGI; Sec.-Gen. ONESMUS MUSYOKA MBALI.

Kenya National Democratic Alliance (KENDA): Wetithe House, Nkrumah St, POB 1851, Thika; tel. (151) 562304; f. 1991; Chair. JORAM GAINYE KARIUKI; Sec. PATRICK OUMA KANG'ETHE.

Kenya Social Congress (KSC): POB 55318, Nairobi; f. 1992; Chair. GEORGE MOSETI ANYONA; Sec.-Gen. KASHINI MALOBA FAFNA.

Liberal Democratic Party (LDP): Nairobi; f. 2002 by fmr mems of KANU; Leader RAILA ODINGA.

Labour Party Democracy: POB 7905, Nairobi; Chair. GEOFFREY MBURU; Sec. DAVID MBURI NGACHURA.

Liberal Party: Chair. WANGARI MAATHAI.

National Alliance Party of Kenya (NAPK): Nairobi; f. 2002; alliance of some 12 parties, including the DP, FORD—Kenya and the NPK.

National Party of Kenya (NPK): f. 2001; Chair. CHARITY KALUKI NGILU; Sec.-Gen. FIDELIS MWEKE.

New Kanu Alliance: Sec. IMANYARA MUGAMBI.

Party of Independent Candidates of Kenya (PICK): Plot No 299/096 Kenyatta Ave, POB 21821, Nairobi; Chair. G. N. MUSYIMI; Sec. F. NGUGI.

Patriotic Pastoralist Alliance of Kenya: f. 1997; represents the interests of northern Kenyan pastoralist communities; Leaders KHALIF ABDULLAHI, IBRAHIM WOCHE, JACKSON LAISAGOR.

People's Alliance for Change in Kenya (PACK): Nairobi; f. 1999; aims to unite diverse ethnic groups; Sec.-Gen. OLANG SANA.

Safina ('Noah's Ark'): POB 135, Nairobi; f. 1995; aims to combat corruption and human rights abuses and to introduce proportional representation; Chair. CLEMENT MUTURI KIGANO; Sec.-Gen. MWANDAWIRO MGHANGA.

Shirikisho Party of Kenya (SPK): POB 70421, Nairobi; Chair. HAMISI SAIDI JEFFAH; Sec. OMARA ABAE KALASINGHA.

KENYA

Sisi Kwa Sisi (SKS): Nairobi; f. 2001; Leader John Rukenya Kabugua.

Social Democratic Party of Kenya (SDP): POB 55845, Nairobi; tel. (20) 260309; f. 1992; Chair. Justus Nyagaya; Sec.-Gen. Dr Apollo Lugano Njonjo.

United Agri Party of Kenya: f. 2001; Chair. George Kinyua; Sec.-Gen. Simon Mitobio.

United Democratic Movement: Nairobi; Chair. Kipruto Rono arap Kirwa; Sec.-Gen. Stephen Tarus.

United Patriotic Party of Kenya: POB 115, Athi River; Chair. Josephat Gathua Gathiga; Sec. Michael Njuguna Kiganya.

The following organizations are banned:

February Eighteen Resistance Army: believed to operate from Uganda; Leader Brig. John Odongo (also known as Stephen Amoke).

Islamic Party of Kenya (IPK): Mombasa; f. 1992; Islamic fundamentalist; Chair. Sheikh Khalifa Muhammad (acting); Sec.-Gen. Abdulrahman Wandati.

Diplomatic Representation

EMBASSIES AND HIGH COMMISSIONS IN KENYA

Algeria: 37 Muthaiga Rd, POB 53902, Nairobi; tel. (20) 310440; fax (20) 310450; e-mail algerianembassy@mitsuminett.com; Ambassador Muhammad-Hacene Echarif.

Argentina: Posta Sacco, 6th Floor, University Way, POB 30283-00100, Nairobi; tel. (20) 339949; fax (20) 217693; e-mail argentina@form-net.com; Ambassador José Luis Casal.

Australia: ICIPE House, River Side Drive, off Chiromo Rd, POB 39341, Nairobi; tel. (20) 445034; fax (20) 444718; High Commissioner George Atkin.

Austria: City House, 2nd Floor, Wabera St, POB 30560, 00100 Nairobi; tel. and fax (20) 319076; fax (20) 342290; e-mail nairobi-ob@bmaa.gv.at; Ambassador Franz Hörlberger.

Bangladesh: Lenana Rd, POB 41645, Nairobi; tel. (20) 562816; fax (20) 562817; High Commissioner Subir K. Bhattacharyya.

Belgium: Muthaiga, Limuru Rd, POB 30461, Nairobi; tel. (20) 741564; fax (20) 442701; e-mail belgianembke@form-net.com; Ambassador Leo Willems.

Brazil: Jeevan Bharati Bldg, 4th Floor, Harambee Ave, POB 30754-00100, Nairobi; tel. (20) 3753223; fax (20) 3766442; Ambassador Joaquim Augusto Whitaker Salles.

Burundi: Development House, 14th Floor, Moi Ave, POB 44439, Nairobi; tel. (20) 575113; fax (20) 219005; Ambassador Germain Nkeshimana.

Canada: Comcraft House, 6th Floor, Haile Selassie Ave, POB 30481, Nairobi; tel. (20) 214804; fax (20) 226987; High Commissioner Gerry Campbell.

Chile: International House, 5th Floor, Mama Ngina St, POB 45554, Nairobi; tel. (20) 331320; fax (20) 215648; e-mail echileke@form-net.com; Ambassador Dr Vicente Sánchez.

China, People's Republic: POB 30508, Nairobi; tel. (20) 722559; fax (20) 746402; Ambassador Du Qiwen.

Colombia: International House, 8th Floor, POB 48494, Nairobi; tel. (20) 246770; fax (20) 246771; e-mail embcol@form-net.com; Ambassador Dr Germán García-Durán.

Congo, Democratic Republic: Electricity House, Harambee Ave, POB 48106, Nairobi; tel. (20) 229771; fax (20) 334539; Ambassador (vacant).

Cuba: International House, Mama Ngina St, 13th Floor, POB 41931, Nairobi; tel. (20) 241003; fax (20) 241023; e-mail embacuba@swiftkenya.com; Ambassador Pedro Luis Pedroso Cuesta.

Cyprus: Eagle House, 5th Floor, Kimathi St, POB 30739, 00100 Nairobi; tel. (20) 220881; fax (20) 312202; e-mail cyphc@nbnet.co.ke; High Commissioner Constantinos Eliades.

Czech Republic: Jumia Pl., Lenana Rd, POB 48785, 00100 Nairobi; tel. (20) 2731010; fax (20) 2731013; e-mail nairobi@embassy.mzv.cz; internet www.mzv.cz/nairobi; Ambassador Peter Kopøiva.

Denmark: HFCK Bldg, 11th Floor, Kenyatta Ave, POB 40412-00100, Nairobi; tel. (20) 331088; fax (20) 331492; e-mail nboamb@um.dk; Ambassador Finn Thilsted.

Djibouti: Comcraft House, 2nd Floor, Haile Selassie Ave, POB 59528, Nairobi; tel. (20) 339640; Ambassador Saleh Haji Farah.

Egypt: Harambee Plaza, 7th Floor, Haile Selassie Ave, POB 30285, Nairobi; tel. (20) 570360; fax (20) 570383; Ambassador Mohammed Asim Ibrahim.

Eritrea: New Rehema House, 2nd Floor, Westlands, POB 38651, Nairobi; tel. (20) 443164; fax (20) 443165; e-mail eriembk@africaonline.co.ke; Ambassador Mohamed Ali Omaro.

Ethiopia: State House Ave, POB 45198, Nairobi; tel. (20) 723027; fax (20) 723401; e-mail ethembnb@africaonline.co.ke; Ambassador Toshome Toga.

Finland: International House, 2nd Floor, Mama Ngina St, POB 30379-00100, Nairobi; tel. (20) 334777; fax (20) 335986; e-mail finland@form-net.com; Ambassador Lauri Kangas.

France: Barclays Plaza, 9th Floor, Loita St, POB 41784, Nairobi; tel. (20) 339783; fax (20) 339421; e-mail ienkenya@form-net.com; Ambassador Pierre Jacquemot.

Germany: Williamson House, 8th Floor, 4th Ngong Ave, POB 30180, Nairobi; tel. (20) 712527; fax (20) 714886; e-mail ger-emb@form-net.com; Ambassador Jürgen Weerth.

Greece: Nation Centre, 13th Floor, Kimathi St, POB 30543, Nairobi; tel. (20) 340722; fax (20) 216044; Ambassador Ioannis Korinthios.

Holy See: Apostolic Nunciature, Manyani Rd West, Waiyaki Way, POB 14326, 00800 Nairobi; tel. (20) 4442975; fax (20) 4446789; e-mail nunciokenya@kenyaweb.com; Apostolic Nuncio Most Rev. Alain Paul Charles Lebeaupin (Titular Archbishop of Vico Equense).

Hungary: Ole Odume Rd, POB 61146, Nairobi; tel. (20) 560060; fax (20) 560114; e-mail huembnai@africaonline.co.ke; Ambassador András Tóth.

India: Jeevan Bharati Bldg, 2nd Floor, Harambee Ave, POB 30074, Nairobi; tel. (20) 225104; fax (20) 334167; e-mail hcindia@form-net.com; High Commissioner T. P. Sreenivasan.

Indonesia: Menengai House, Upper Hill, POB 48868, Nairobi; tel. (20) 714196; fax (20) 713475; e-mail indonbi@arcc.or.ke; Ambassador Tupuck Sutrisno.

Iran: Dennis Pritt Rd, POB 49170, Nairobi; tel. (20) 711257; fax (20) 339936; Ambassador Sayed Ahmad Sebajzadeh.

Israel: Bishop's Rd, POB 30354, Nairobi; tel. (20) 722182; fax (20) 715966; Ambassador Yaacov Amitai.

Italy: International House, 9th Floor, Mama Ngina St, POB 30107, Nairobi; tel. (20) 337356; fax (20) 337056; e-mail afra@form-net.com; Ambassador Dr Alberto Balboni.

Japan: ICEA Bldg, 15th Floor, Kenyatta Ave, POB 60202, Nairobi; tel. and fax (20) 332955; Ambassador Morihisa Aoki.

Korea, Republic: Anniversary Towers, 15th Floor, University Way, POB 30455, Nairobi; tel. (20) 333581; fax (20) 217772; e-mail emb-ke@mofat.go.kr; Ambassador Kwon Jong Rak.

Kuwait: Muthaiga Rd, POB 42353, Nairobi; tel. (20) 761614; fax (20) 762837; e-mail kuwaitembassy@form-net.com; Chargé d'affaires a.i. Jaber Salem Hussain Ebraheem.

Lesotho: Nairobi; tel. (20) 224876; fax (20) 337493; High Commissioner (vacant).

Mexico: Kibagare Way, off Loresho Ridge, POB 14145, Nairobi; tel. (20) 582850; fax (20) 581500; e-mail mexico@embamexken.co.ke; Ambassador Leandro Arellano.

Morocco: Diamond Trust House, 3rd Floor, Moi Ave, POB 61098, Nairobi; tel. (20) 710647; fax (20) 222364; e-mail embassymorocco@form-net.com; Ambassador Mohamed Chraibi.

Mozambique: Bruce House, 3rd Floor, Standard St, POB 66923, Nairobi; tel. (20) 221979; fax (20) 222446; High Commissioner Paulo Elias Cigarro.

Netherlands: Uchumi House, 6th Floor, Nkrumah Ave, POB 41537, Nairobi; tel. (20) 227111; fax (20) 339155; e-mail holland@form-net.com; Ambassador Ruud J. Treffers.

Nigeria: Lenana Rd, Hurlingham, POB 30516, Nairobi; tel. (20) 564116; fax (20) 564117; High Commissioner N. Tapgun.

Norway: Lion Pl. 1st Floor, Wayiaki Way, POB 46363, 00100 Nairobi; tel. (20) 4451510; fax (20) 4451517; e-mail emb.nairobi@mfa.no; internet www.norway.or.ke; Ambassador Kjell Harald Dalen.

Pakistan: St Michel Rd, Westlands Ave, POB 30045-00100, Nairobi; tel. (20) 443911; fax (20) 446507; High Commissioner H. A. Kidwai.

Poland: Kabarnet Rd, off Ngong Rd, Woodley, POB 30086, 00100 Nairobi; tel. (20) 566288; fax (20) 727701; e-mail polambnairobi@form-net.com; Ambassador Wojciech Jasinski.

Portugal: Reinsurance Plaza, 10th Floor, Aga Khan Walk, POB 34020, Nairobi; tel. (20) 338990; fax (20) 214711; Ambassador José Lameiras.

Romania: POB 63240, Nairobi; tel. (20) 743209; fax (20) 741696; e-mail roembken@wananchi.com; Chargé d'affaires a.i. Paul Finantu.

Russia: Lenana Rd, POB 30049, Nairobi; tel. (20) 728700; fax (20) 721888; e-mail russemb@swiftkenya.com; Ambassador Alexander A. Ignatiev.

Rwanda: International House, 12th Floor, Mama Ngina St, POB 48579, Nairobi; tel. (20) 560178; fax (20) 561932.

Saudi Arabia: Muthaiga Rd, POB 58297, Nairobi; tel. (20) 762781; fax (20) 760939; Ambassador Nbeel Khalaf A. Ashour.

Serbia and Montenegro: State House Ave, Nairobi; tel. (20) 720670.
Slovakia: Milimani Rd, POB 30204, Nairobi; tel. (20) 721896; fax (20) 721898; Ambassador STEFAN MORAVEK.
Somalia: POB 30769, Nairobi; tel. (20) 580165; fax (20) 581683.
South Africa: Lonhro House, 14th Floor, Standard St, POB 42441, Nairobi; tel. (20) 32063100; fax (20) 32063236; e-mail sahc@africaonline.co.ke; High Commissioner L. M. MAKHUBELA.
Spain: Bruce House, 5th Floor, Standard St, POB 45503, Nairobi; tel. (20) 226568; fax (20) 332858; Ambassador L. GARCIA CEREZO.
Sri Lanka: Lenana Rd, POB 48145 GPO, Nairobi; tel. (20) 572627; fax (20) 572141; e-mail slhckeny@africaonline.co.ke; internet www.lk/dipmissionf.html; High Commissioner HABEEB MOHAMMED FAROOK.
Sudan: Minet-ICDC Bldg, 7th Floor, Mamlaka Rd, POB 48784, Nairobi; tel. (20) 720853; fax (20) 721015; Ambassador OMER EL-SHEIKH.
Swaziland: Transnational Plaza, 3rd Floor, Mama Ngina St, POB 41887, Nairobi; tel. (20) 339231; fax (20) 330540; High Commissioner Prince SOLOMON MBILINI N. DLAMINI.
Sweden: Lion Place, 3rd Floor, Waiyaki Way, Westlands, POB 30600, 00100 Nairobi; tel. (20) 4234000; fax (20) 4452008; e-mail ambassaden.nairobi@sida.se; Ambassador BO GÖRANSSON.
Switzerland: International House, 7th Floor, Mama Ngina St, POB 30752, Nairobi; tel. (20) 228735; fax (20) 217388; e-mail vertretung@nai.rep.admin.ch; Ambassador PIERRE COMBERNOUS.
Tanzania: Continental House, Uhuru Highway, POB 47790, Nairobi; tel. (20) 331056; fax (20) 218269; High Commissioner Maj.-Gen. MIRISHO SAM HAGGAI SARAKIKYA.
Thailand: Ambassador House, Rose Ave, POB 58349, Nairobi; tel. (20) 715800; fax (20) 715801; e-mail thainbi@form-net.com; Ambassador PONGSAK DISYATAT.
Turkey: Gigiri Rd, off Limuru Rd, POB 64748, 00620 Nairobi; tel. (20) 522562; fax (20) 522562; e-mail tcbenair@wananchi.com; Ambassador OSMAN M. BUYUKDAVRAS.
Uganda: Uganda House, 5th Floor, Kenyatta Ave, POB 60853, Nairobi; tel. (20) 449096; fax (20) 330970; High Commissioner FRANCIS BUTAGIRA.
United Kingdom: Upper Hill Rd, POB 30465, 00100 Nairobi; tel. (20) 2844000; fax (20) 2844033; e-mail nairobi-chancery@fco.gov.uk; internet www.britishhighcommission.gov.uk/kenya; High Commissioner ADAM WOOD.
USA: United Nations Ave, POB 606, Village Market, 00621 Nairobi; tel. (20) 3636000; fax (20) 537810; e-mail ircnairobi@state.gov; internet usembassy.state.gov/nairobi; Ambassador WILLIAM M. BELLAMY.
Venezuela: Ngong/Kabarnet Rd, POB 34477, Nairobi; tel. (20) 574646; fax (20) 337487; e-mail embavene@africaonline.co.ke; Chargé d'affaires a.i. NOEL D. QUINTERO.
Yemen: cnr Ngong and Kabarnet Rds, POB 44642, Nairobi; tel. (20) 564379; fax (20) 564394; Ambassador AHMAD MAYSARI.
Zambia: Nyerere Rd, POB 48741, Nairobi; tel. (20) 724850; fax (20) 718494; High Commissioner ENESS CHISHALA CHIYENGE.
Zimbabwe: Minet-ICDC Bldg, 6th Floor, Mamlaka Rd, POB 30806, Nairobi; tel. (20) 721071; fax (20) 726503; Ambassador Gen. (retd) ELISHA MUZONZINI.

Judicial System

The Kenya Court of Appeal

POB 30187, Nairobi; The final court of appeal for Kenya in civil and criminal process; sits at Nairobi, Mombasa, Kisumu, Nakuru and Nyeri.
Chief Justice: JOHNSON EVANS GICHERU.
Justices of Appeal: MATHEW MULI, J. M. GACHUHI, J. R. O. MASIME, SAMUEL BOSIRE, R. O. KWACH, EFFIE OWUOR.
The High Court of Kenya: Between Taifa Rd and City Hall Way, POB 30041, Nairobi; tel. (20) 221221; e-mail hck-lib@nbnet.co.ke; has unlimited criminal and civil jurisdiction at first instance, and sits as a court of appeal from subordinate courts in both criminal and civil cases. The High Court is also a court of admiralty. There are three resident puisne judges at Mombasa and at Nakuru, two resident puisne judge at Eldoret, Kisumu and Meru and one resident puisne judge at Bungoma, Embu, Kakamega, Kissi, Kitale, Machakos, Malindi and Nyeri.
Resident Magistrates' Courts: have country-wide jurisdiction, with powers of punishment by imprisonment up to five years or by fine up to K£500. If presided over by a chief magistrate or senior resident magistrate the court is empowered to pass any sentence authorized by law. For certain offences, a resident magistrate may pass minimum sentences authorized by law.
District Magistrates' Courts: of first, second and third class; have jurisdiction within districts and powers of punishment by imprisonment for up to five years, or by fines of up to K£500.
Kadhi's Courts: have jurisdiction within districts, to determine questions of Islamic law.

Religion

According to official government figures, Protestants, the largest religious group, represent approximately 38% of the population. Approximately 25% of the population is Roman Catholic, 7% of the population practices Islam, 1% practices Hinduism and the remainder follows various traditional indigenous religions or offshoots of Christian religions. There are very few atheists. Muslim groups dispute government estimates; most often they claim to represent 15% to 20% of the population, sometimes higher. Members of most religious groups are active throughout the country, although certain religions dominate particular regions. Muslims dominate North-Eastern Province, where the population is chiefly Somali. Muslims also dominate Coast Province, except for the western areas of the province, which predominantly are Christian. Eastern Province is approximately 50% Muslim (mostly in the north) and 50% Christian (mostly in the south). The rest of the country largely is Christian, with some persons following traditional indigenous religions. Many foreign missionary groups operate in the country, the largest of which are the African Inland Mission (Evangelical Protestant), the Southern Baptist Church, the Pentecostal Assembly of Kenya, and the Church Missionary Society of Britain (Anglican). The Government generally has permitted these missionary groups to assist the poor and to operate schools and hospitals. The missionaries openly promote their religious beliefs and have encountered little resistance.

CHRISTIANITY

National Council of Churches of Kenya: Church House, Moi Ave, POB 45009, Nairobi; tel. (20) 242278; fax (20) 224463; f. 1943 as Christian Council of Kenya; 35 full mems and eight assoc. mems; Chair. Rev. JOSEPH WAITHONGA; Sec.-Gen. Rev. MUTAVA MUSYIMI.

The Anglican Communion

Anglicans are adherents of the Church of the Province of Kenya, which was established in 1970. It comprises 28 dioceses, and has about 2.5m. members.
Archbishop of Kenya and Bishop of Nairobi: Most Rev. Dr DAVID M. GITARI, POB 40502, Nairobi; tel. (20) 2714755; fax (20) 2718442; e-mail davidgitari@insightkenya.com.

Greek Orthodox Church

Archbishop of East Africa: NICADEMUS OF IRINOUPOULIS, Nairobi; jurisdiction covers Kenya, Tanzania and Uganda.

The Roman Catholic Church

Kenya comprises four archdioceses, 20 dioceses and one Apostolic Vicariate. At 31 December 2003 an estimated 24.9% of the total population were adherents of the Roman Catholic Church.

Kenya Episcopal Conference

Kenya Catholic Secretariat, POB 13475, Nairobi; tel. (20) 443133; fax (20) 442910; e-mail secgeneral@catholicchurch.or.ke; internet www.catholicchurch.or.ke; f. 1976; Pres. Rt Rev. CORNELIUS K. ARAP KORIR (Bishop of Eldoret).
Archbishop of Kisumu: Most Rev. ZACCHAEUS OKOTH, POB 1728, Kisumu; tel. (57) 43950; fax (57) 42415; e-mail archdiocese-ksm@net2000ke.com.
Archbishop of Mombasa: Most Rev. JOHN NJENGA, Catholic Secretariat, Nyerere Ave, POB 83131, Mombasa; tel. (43) 311526; fax (43) 228217; e-mail devmsa@africaonline.co.ke.
Archbishop of Nairobi: Most Rev. RAPHAEL NDINGI MWANA'A NZEKI, Archbishop's House, POB 14231, 00800 Nairobi; tel. (20) 241391; fax (20) 223799; e-mail arch-nbo@wananchi.com.
Archbishop of Nyeri: Most Rev. NICODEMUS KIRIMA, POB 288, 10100 Nyeri; tel. (61) 2030446; fax (61) 2030435; e-mail adn@wananchi.com.

Other Christian Churches

Africa Inland Church in Kenya: Bishop Rev. Dr TITUS M. KIVUNZI.
African Christian Church and Schools: POB 1365, Thika; tel. (15) 47; f. 1948; Moderator Rt Rev. JOHN NJUNGUNA; Gen. Sec. Rev. SAMUEL MWANGI; 50,000 mems.

KENYA

African Church of the Holy Spirit: POB 183, Kakamega; f. 1927; 20,000 mems.

African Israel Nineveh Church: Nineveh HQ, POB 701, Kisumu; f. 1942; High Priest Rt Rev. JOHN KIVULI, II; Gen. Sec. Rev. JOHN ARAP TONUI; 350,000 mems.

Baptist Convention of Kenya: POB 14907, Nairobi; Pres. Rev. ELIUD MUNGAI.

Church of God in East Africa: Pres. Rev. Dr BYRUM MAKOKHA.

Evangelical Fellowship of Kenya: Co-ordinator Rt Rev. ARTHUR GITONGA; Sec.-Gen. Dr WASHINGTON NG'ENG'I.

Evangelical Lutheran Church in Kenya: POB 874, Kisii; tel. (40) 31231; fax (40) 30475; e-mail elok@africaonline.co.ke; Bishop Rev. FRANCIS NYAMWARO ONDERI; 65,000 mems.

Methodist Church in Kenya: POB 47633, Nairobi; tel. (20) 724841; f. 1862; autonomous since 1967; Presiding Bishop Rev. Dr ZABLON NTHAMBURI; 854,000 mems (2000).

Presbyterian Church of East Africa: POB 48268, Nairobi; tel. (20) 504417; fax (20) 504442; e-mail pcea@africaonline.co.ke; Moderator Rt Rev. Dr JESSE KAMAU; Sec.-Gen. Rev. Dr PATRICK RUKENYA.

Other denominations active in Kenya include the Africa Gospel Church, the African Brotherhood Church, the African Independent Pentecostal Church, the African Interior Church, the Episcopal Church of Kenya, the Free Pentecostal Fellowship of Kenya, the Full Gospel Churches of Kenya, the Lutheran Church in Kenya, the National Independent Church of Africa, the Pentecostal Assemblies of God, the Pentecostal Evangelistic Fellowship of God and the Reformed Church of East Africa.

BAHÁ'Í FAITH

National Spiritual Assembly: POB 47562, Nairobi; tel. (20) 725447; mems resident in 9,654 localities.

ISLAM

Supreme Council of Kenyan Muslims (SUPKEM)
POB 45163, Nairobi; tel. and fax (20) 243109; Nat. Chair. Prof. ABD AL-GHAFUR AL-BUSAIDY; Sec.-Gen. MOHAMMED KHALIF.

Chief Kadhi: NASSOR NAHDI.

The Press

PRINCIPAL DAILIES

Daily Nation: POB 49010, Nairobi; tel. (20) 2221222; fax (20) 2337710; e-mail nation@africaonline.co.ke; internet www.nationaudio.com; f. 1960; English; owned by Nation Media Group; Editor-in-Chief WANGETHI MWANGI; Man. Editor JOSEPH ODINDO; circ. 195,000.

East African Standard: POB 30080, Nairobi; tel. (20) 2540280; fax (20) 2553939; e-mail online@eastandard.net; internet www.eastandard.net; f. 1902; Editor MUTUMA MATHIY; circ. 59,000.

Kenya Leo: POB 30958, Nairobi; tel. (20) 332390; f. 1983; Kiswahili; KANU party newspaper; Group Editor-in-Chief AMBOKA ANDERE; circ. 6,000.

Kenya Times: POB 30958, Nairobi; tel. (20) 2336611; fax (20) 2927348; internet www.timesnews.co.uk; f. 1983; evening; English; KANU party newspaper; Group Editor-in-Chief AMBOKA ANDERE; circ. 10,000.

The People: POB 10296, 00100 Nairobi; tel. (20) 249686; fax (20) 253344; e-mail info@people.co.ke; internet www.people.co.ke; f. 1993; Man. Editor MUGO THEURI; circ. 40,000.

Taifa Leo: POB 49010, Nairobi; tel. (20) 337691; Kiswahili; f. 1960; daily and weekly edns; owned by Nation Media Group; Editor ROBERT MWANGI; circ. 57,000.

Kenya has a thriving vernacular press, but titles are often short-lived. Newspapers in African languages include:

Kihooto (The Truth): Kikuyu; satirical.

Mwaria Ma (Honest Speaker): Nyeri; f. 1997; Publr Canon JAMLICK M. MIANO.

Mwihoko (Hope): POB 734, Muranga; f. 1997; Roman Catholic.

Nam Dar: Luo.

Otit Mach (Firefly): Luo.

SELECTED PERIODICALS
Weeklies and Fortnightlies

The Business Chronicle: POB 53328, Nairobi; tel. (20) 544283; fax (20) 532736; f. 1994; weekly; Man. Editor MUSYOKA KYENDO.

Coastweek: Oriental Bldg, 2nd Floor, Nkrumah Rd, POB 87270, Mombasa; tel. (11) 230125; fax (11) 225003; e-mail coastwk@africaonline.co.ke; internet www.coastweek.com; f. 1978; English; weekly; Editor ADRIAN GRIMWOOD; Man. Dir SHIRAZ D. ALIBHAI; circ. 40,000.

The East African: POB 49010 Nairobi; tel. (20) 221222; fax (20) 2213946; e-mail nation@africaonline.co.ke; internet www.nationaudio.com/news/eastafrican/current; f. 1994; weekly; English; owned by Nation Media Group; Editor-in-Chief JOE ODINDO; Man. Editor MBATAU WA NGAI.

The Herald: POB 30958, Nairobi; tel. (20) 332390; English; sponsored by KANU; Editor JOB MUTUNGI; circ. 8,000.

Kenrail: POB 30121, Nairobi; tel. (20) 2221211; fax (20) 2340049; quarterly; English and Kiswahili; publ. by Kenya Railways Corpn; Editor J. N. LUSENO; circ. 20,000.

Kenya Gazette: POB 30746, Nairobi; tel. (20) 334075; f. 1898; official notices; weekly; circ. 8,000.

Post on Sunday: Nairobi; weekly; independent; Editor-in-Chief TONY GACHOKA.

Sunday Nation: POB 49010, Nairobi; f. 1960; English; owned by Nation Media Group; Man. Editor BERNARD NDERITU; circ. 170,000.

Sunday Standard: POB 30080, Nairobi; tel. (20) 552510; fax (20) 553939; English; Man. Editor DAVID MAKALI; circ. 90,000.

Sunday Times: POB 30958, Nairobi; tel. (20) 337798; Group Editor AMBOKA ANDERE.

Taifa Jumapili: POB 49010, Nairobi; f. 1987; Kiswahili; owned by Nation Media Group; Editor ROBERT K. MWANGI; circ. 56,000.

Taifa Weekly: POB 49010, Nairobi; tel. (20) 337691; f. 1960; Kiswahili; Editor ROBERT K. MWANGI; circ. 68,000.

Trans Nzoia Post: POB 34, Kitale; weekly.

The Weekly Review: Stellacom House, POB 42271, Nairobi; tel. (20) 2251473; fax (20) 2222555; f. 1975; English; Man. Dir JAINDI KISERO; circ. 16,000.

What's On: Rehema House, Nairobi; tel. (20) 27651; Editor NANCY KAIRO; circ. 10,000.

Monthlies

Africa Law Review: Tumaini House, 4th Floor, Nkrumah Ave, POB 53234, Nairobi; tel. (20) 330480; fax (20) 230173; e-mail alr@africalaw.org; f. 1987; English; Editor-in-Chief GITOBU IMANYARA.

East African Medical Journal: POB 41632, 00100 Nairobi; tel. (20) 2712010; fax (20) 2724617; e-mail eamj@ken.healthnet.org; English; f. 1923; Editor-in-Chief Prof. WILLIAM LORE; circ. 4,500.

East African Report on Trade and Industry: POB 30339, Nairobi; journal of Kenya Asscn of Mfrs; Editor GORDON BOY; circ. 3,000.

Executive: POB 47186, Nairobi; tel. (20) 530598; fax (20) 557815; e-mail spacesellers@wananchi.com; f. 1980; business; Publr SYLVIA KING; circ. 25,000.

Kenya Farmer (Journal of the Agricultural Society of Kenya): c/o English Press, POB 30127, Nairobi; tel. (20) 20377; f. 1954; English and Kiswahili; Editor ROBERT IRUNGU; circ. 20,000.

Kenya Yetu: POB 8053, Nairobi; tel. (20) 250083; fax (20) 340659; f. 1965; Kiswahili; publ. by Ministry of Information and Communications; Editor M. NDAVI; circ. 10,000.

Nairobi Handbook: POB 30127, Accra Rd, Nairobi; Editor R. OUMA; circ. 20,000.

News from Kenya: POB 8053, Nairobi; tel. (20) 253083; fax (20) 340659; publ. by Ministry of Information and Communications.

PC World (East Africa): Gilgil House, Monrovia St, Nairobi; tel. (20) 246808; fax (20) 215643; f. 1996; Editor ANDREW KARANJA.

Presence: POB 10988, 00400 Nairobi; tel. (20) 577708; fax (20) 4948840; f. 1984; economics, law, women's issues, fiction.

Sparkle: POB 47186, Nairobi; tel. (20) 530598; fax (20) 557815; e-mail spacesellers@wananchi.com; f. 1990; children's; Editor ANNA NDILA NDUTO.

Today in Africa: POB 60, Kijabe; tel. (25) 64210; English; Man. Editor MWAURA NJOROGE; circ. 13,000.

Other Periodicals

African Ecclesiastical Review: POB 4002, Eldoret; tel. (32) 61218; fax (32) 62570; e-mail gabapubs@net2000ke.com; f. 1969; scripture, religion and development; 6 a year; Editor AGATHA RADOLI; circ. 2,500.

Afya: POB 30125, Nairobi; tel. (20) 501301; fax (20) 506112; e-mail amrefkco@africaonline.co.ke; journal for medical and health workers; quarterly.

Azania: POB 30710, Nairobi; tel. (20) 243721; fax (20) 243365; f. 1966; annual (April); English and French; history, archaeology, ethnography and linguistics of East African region; circ. 750.

Busara: Nairobi; literary; 2 a year; Editor KIMANI GECAU; circ. 3,000.

Defender: AMREF, POB 30125, Nairobi; tel. (20) 201301; f. 1968; quarterly; English; health and fitness; Editor WILLIAM OKEDI; circ. 100,000.

East African Agricultural and Forestry Journal: POB 30148, Nairobi; f. 1935; English; quarterly; Editor J. O. MUGAH; circ. 1,000.

Eastern African Economic Review: POB 30022, Nairobi; f. 1954; 2 a year; Editor J. K. MAITHA.

Economic Review of Agriculture: POB 30028, Nairobi; tel. (20) 728370; f. 1968; publ. by Ministry of Agriculture; quarterly; last issue 1999; Editor OKIYA OKOITI.

Education in Eastern Africa: Nairobi; f. 1970; 2 a year; Editor JOHN C. B. BIGALA; circ. 2,000.

Finance: Nairobi; monthly; Editor-in-Chief NJEHU GATABAKI.

Inside Kenya Today: POB 8053, Nairobi; tel. (20) 340010; fax (20) 340659; English; publ. by Ministry of Tourism; quarterly; Editor M. NDAVI; circ. 10,000.

Kenya Education Journal: Nairobi; f. 1958; English; 3 a year; Editor W. G. BOWMAN; circ. 5,500.

Kenya Statistical Digest: POB 30007, Nairobi; tel. (20) 338111; fax (20) 330426; publ. by Ministry of Finance; quarterly.

Safari: Norwich Bldg, 4th Floor, Mama Ngina St, POB 30339, Nairobi; tel. (20) 2246612; fax (20) 2215127; 6 a year; English.

Target: POB 72839, Nairobi; f. 1964; English; 6 a year; religious; Editor FRANCIS MWANIKI; circ. 17,000.

NEWS AGENCIES

Kenya News Agency (KNA): Information House, POB 8053, Nairobi; tel. (20) 223201; f. 1963; Dir S. MUSANDU.

Foreign Bureaux

Agence France-Presse (AFP): International Life House, Mama Ngina St, POB 30671, 00100 Nairobi; tel. (20) 230613; fax (20) 230649; e-mail afpnai@swiftkenya.com; Bureau Chief GERARD VANDENBERGHE.

Agenzia Nazionale Stampa Associata (ANSA) (Italy): 12 Kyuna Rd, Spring Valley, Morningside, POB 20444, 00220 Nairobi; tel. (20) 583565; fax (20) 229383; e-mail ansake@africaonline.co.ke; Rep. Dr LUCIANO CAUSA.

Associated Press (AP) (USA): Chester House, Koinange St, POB 47590, Nairobi; tel. (20) 250168; fax (20) 221449; e-mail naiburo@ap.org; Bureau Chief SUSAN LINNÉE.

Deutsche Presse-Agentur (dpa) (Germany): Chester House, 1st Floor, Koinange St, POB 48546, 00100 Nairobi; tel. (02) 733633379; e-mail dpa@swiftkenya.com; Bureau Chief Dr ULRIKE KOLTERMANN.

Informatsionnoye Telegrafnoye Agentstvo Rossii—Telegrafnoye Agentstvo Suverennykh Stran (ITAR—TASS) (Russia): Likoni Lane, POB 49602, Nairobi; tel. and fax (20) 721978; e-mail itartass@swiftkenya.com; Correspondent ANDREI K. POLYAKOV.

Inter Press Service (IPS) (Italy): Chester House, 1st Floor, Room 3, Koinange St, POB 42005; tel. (20) 240951; e-mail ipsnrb@iconnect.co.ke; Correspondent JOYCE MULAMA.

Kyodo Tsushin (Japan): Koinange St, POB 58281, Nairobi; tel. (20) 243250; fax (20) 230448; e-mail kyodonew@africaonline.co.ke; Bureau Chief OHNO KEIICHIRO.

Newslink Africa (United Kingdom): POB 3325, Nairobi; tel. (20) 241339; Correspondent PAMPHIL KWEYUH.

Reuters (United Kingdom): Finance House, 12th Floor, Loita St, POB 34043, Nairobi; tel. (20) 330261; fax (20) 338860; e-mail nairobi.newsroom@reuters.com; Bureau Chief DAVID FOX.

United Press International (UPI) (USA): POB 76282, Nairobi; tel. (20) 337349; fax (20) 213625; Correspondent JOE KHAMISI.

Xinhua (New China) News Agency (People's Republic of China): Ngong Rd at Rose Ave, POB 30728, Nairobi; tel. and fax (20) 711685; Pres. and Editor-in-Chief Prof. FLAMINGO Q. M. CHEN.

Publishers

Academy Science Publishers: POB 24916, Nairobi; tel. (20) 884401; fax (20) 884406; e-mail asp@africaonline.co.ke; f. 1989; part of the African Academy of Sciences; Editor-in-Chief Prof. KETO E. MSHIGENI.

Amecea Gaba Publications: Amecea Pastoral Institute, POB 4002, Eldoret; tel. (32) 61218; fax (32) 62570; e-mail gabapubs@net2000ke.com; f. 1989; anthropology, religious; Dir Sister AGATHA RADOLI.

Camerapix Publishers International: POB 45048, Nairobi; tel. (20) 4448923; fax (20) 4448926; e-mail info@camerapix.com; internet www.camerapix.com; f. 1960; travel, topography, natural history; Man. Dir RUKHSANA HAQ.

East African Educational Publishers: cnr Mpaka Rd and Woodvale Grove, Westlands, POB 45314, Nairobi; tel. (20) 222057; fax (20) 448753; e-mail eaep@africaonline.co.ke; internet www.eastafricanpublishers.com; f. 1965 as Heinemann Kenya Ltd; present name adopted 1992; academic, educational, creative writing; some books in Kenyan languages; Man. Dir and Chief Exec. HENRY CHAKAVA.

Evangel Publishing House: Lumumba Drive, off Kamiti Rd, Thika Rd, Private Bag 28963, 00200 Nairobi; tel. (20) 860839; fax (20) 862050; e-mail info@evangelpublishing.org; internet www.evangelpublishing.org; f. 1952; religious; Gen. Man. BARINE A. KIRIMI.

Foundation Books: Nairobi; tel. (20) 765485; f. 1974; biography, poetry; Man. Dir F. O. OKWANYA.

Kenway Publications Ltd: POB 45314, Nairobi; tel. (20) 444700; fax (20) 448753; e-mail eaep@africaonline.co.ke; f. 1981; general, regional interests; Chair. HENRY CHAKAVA.

Kenya Literature Bureau: Bellevue Area, off Mombasa Rd, POB 30022, 00100 Nairobi; tel. (20) 600839; fax (20) 601474; e-mail customer@kenyaliteraturebureau.com; f. 1947; educational and general books; CEO M. A. KARAURI.

Jomo Kenyatta Foundation: Industrial Area, Enterprise Rd, POB 30533, Nairobi; tel. (20) 557222; fax (20) 531966; e-mail publish@jomokenyattaf.com; f. 1966; primary, secondary, university textbooks; Man. Dir F. Z. K. MENJO.

Longman Kenya Ltd: Banda School, Magadi Rd, POB 24722, Nairobi; tel. (20) 891458; fax (20) 891307; f. 1966; textbooks and educational materials; Gen. Man. JANET NJOROGE.

Macmillan Kenya Publishers Ltd: Kijabe St, POB 30797, Nairobi; tel. (20) 220012; fax (20) 212179; e-mail dmuita@macken.co.ke; f. 1970; atlases, children's educational, guide books, literature; Man. Dir DAVID MUITA.

Newspread International: POB 46854, Nairobi; tel. (20) 331402; fax (20) 607252; f. 1971; reference, economic development; Exec. Editor KUL BHUSHAN.

Oxford University Press (Eastern Africa): Waiyaki Way, ABC Place, POB 72532, Nairobi; tel. (20) 440555; fax (20) 443972; f. 1954; children's, educational and general; Regional Man. ABDULLAH ISMAILY.

Paulines Publications-Africa: POB 49026, 00100 Nairobi; tel. (20) 447202; fax (20) 442097; e-mail publications@paulinesafrica.org; internet www.paulinesafrica.org; f. 1985; children's, educational; religious; Pres. Sister MARIA PEZZINI; Dir Sister MARIA ROSA.

Transafrica Press: Kenwood House, Kimathi St, POB 48239, Nairobi; tel. (20) 331762; f. 1976; general, educational and children's; Man. Dir JOHN NOTTINGHAM.

GOVERNMENT PUBLISHING HOUSE

Government Printing Press: POB 30128, Nairobi; tel. (20) 334075.

PUBLISHERS' ORGANIZATION

Kenya Publishers' Association: POB 42767, 00100 Nairobi; tel. (20) 3752344; fax (20) 3754076; e-mail kenyapublishers@wananchi.com; internet www.kenyabooks.org; f. 1971; organizes Nairobi International Book Fair each September; Chair. DAVID MUITA.

Broadcasting and Communications

TELECOMMUNICATIONS

KenCell Communications Ltd: Parkside Towers, City Sq., Mombasa Rd, POB 73146, 00200 Nairobi; e-mail info@kencell.co.ke; internet www.kencell.co.ke; f. 2000; operates a national mobile cellular telephone network; Man. Dir and CEO PHILLIPE VANDEBROUCK.

Telkom Kenya Ltd: Telposta Towers, Kenyatta Ave, POB 30301, Nairobi; tel. (20) 227401; fax (20) 251071; e-mail mdtelkom@kenyaeafix.net; f. 1999; operates a national fixed telephone network; privatization pending; Man. Dir AUGUSTINE CHESEREM.

Safaricom Ltd: Safaricom House, Waiyaki Way, Westlands, POB 46350, Nairobi; e-mail info@safaricom.co.ke; internet www.safaricom.co.ke; f. 1999; owned by Telkom Kenya Ltd and Vodafone Airtouch (UK); operates a national mobile telephone network; Gen. Man. and CEO MICHAEL JOSEPH.

KENYA

Directory

Regulatory Authority

Communications Commission of Kenya (CCK): Kijabe St, Longonot Place, POB 14448, Nairobi; tel. (20) 240165; fax (20) 252547; e-mail info@cck.go.ke; internet www.cck.go.ke; f. 1999; Dir-Gen. and Chief Exec. SAMUEL K. CHEPKONG'A.

BROADCASTING

Radio

Kenya Broadcasting Corpn (KBC): Broadcasting House, Harry Thuku Rd, POB 30456, Nairobi; tel. (20) 334567; fax (20) 220675; e-mail kbc@swiftkenya.com; internet www.kbc.co.ke; f. 1989; state corpn responsible for radio and television services; Chair. Dr JULIUS KIANO; Man. Dir JOE M. KHAMISI.

Radio: National service (Kiswahili); General service (English); Vernacular services (Borana, Burji, Hindustani, Kalenjin, Kikamba, Kikuyu, Kimasai, Kimeru, Kisii, Kuria, Luo, Luhya, Rendile, Somali, Suba, Teso and Turkana).

Capital FM: Lonrho House, Standard St, POB 74933, Nairobi; tel. (20) 210020; fax (20) 332349; e-mail info@capitalfm.co.ke; internet www.capitalfm.co.ke; f. 1999; commercial station broadcasting to Nairobi and environs; Man. Dir LYNDA HOLT.

Citizen Radio: Ambank House, University Way, POB 45897, Nairobi; tel. (20) 249122; fax (20) 249126; commercial radio station broadcasting in Nairobi and its environs; Man. Dir S. K. MACHARIA.

IQRA Broadcasting Network: Bandari Plaza, 7th Floor, Woodvale Grove, Westlands, POB 45163 GPO, Nairobi; tel. (20) 4447624; fax (20) 4443978; e-mail iqrafm@swiftkenya.com; Islamic radio station broadcasting religious programmes in Nairobi; Man. Dir SHARIF HUSSEIN OMAR.

Kameme FM: Longonot Pl., Kijabe St, POB 49640, 00100, Nairobi; tel. (20) 217963; fax (20) 338129; e-mail rroach@kenyaweb.com; commercial radio station broadcasting in Kikuyu in Nairobi and its environs; Man. Dir ROSE KIMOTHO.

Kitambo Communications Ltd: NSSF Bldg, POB 56155, Nairobi; tel. (20) 331770; fax (20) 212847; commercial radio and television station broadcasting Christian programmes in Mombasa and Nairobi; Man. Dir Dr R. AYAH.

Nation FM: Nation Centre, Kimathi St, POB 49010, Nairobi; tel. (20) 32088801; fax (20) 241892; e-mail philmatthews@nation.co.ke; internet www.nationmedia.com; f. 1999; commercial radio station broadcasting in English and Swahili; owned by Nation Media Group; Man. Dir IAN FERNANDES.

Radio Africa Ltd (KISS FM): Safina Towers, 16th Floor, University of Nairobi, POB 45897, Nairobi; tel. (20) 245368; fax (20) 245565; Man. Dir KIPRONO KITTONY.

Sauti ya Raheme RTV Network: POB 4139, Eldoret; Christian, broadcasts in Eldoret and its environs; Man. Dir Rev. ELI ROP.

Television

Kenya Broadcasting Corpn (KBC): see Radio

Television: KBC–TV, financed by licence fees and commercial advertisements; services in Kiswahili and English; operates on five channels for *c*. 50 hours per week. KBC–II: private subscription service.

Citizen TV: POB 45897, Nairobi; tel. (20) 249122; fax (20) 249126; commercial station broadcasting in Nairobi and its environs.

Family TV: NSSF Bldg, POB 56155, Nairobi; tel. (20) 331770; fax (20) 212847.

Kenya Television Network (KTN–TV): Nyayo House, 22nd Floor, POB 56985, Nairobi; tel. (20) 227122; fax (20) 214467; e-mail ktn@form-net.com; f. 1990; commercial station operating in Nairobi and Mombasa; Man. Dir D. J. DAVIES.

Nation TV: POB 49010, Nairobi; e-mail nation@users.co.ke; f. 1999; commercial station; owned by Nation Media Group; Man. Dir CYRILLE NABUTOLA.

Stellagraphics TV (STV): NSSF Bldg, 22nd Floor, POB 42271, Nairobi; tel. (20) 218043; fax (20) 222555; f. 1998; commercial station broadcasting in Nairobi; Man. Dir HILLARY NGWENO.

Finance

(cap. = capital; res = reserves; dep. = deposits; m. = million; brs = branches; amounts in Kenya shillings)

BANKING

Central Bank

Central Bank of Kenya (Banki Kuu Ya Kenya): Haile Selassie Ave, POB 60000, 00200 Nairobi; tel. (20) 226431; fax (20) 217940; e-mail info@centralbank.go.ke; internet www.centralbank.go.ke; f. 1966; bank of issue; cap. 1,500m., res 12,399m., dep. 82,545m. (June 2003); Gov. Dr ANDREW KAVULYA MULLEI.

Commercial Banks

African Banking Corpn Ltd: ABC-Bank House, Mezzanine Floor, Koinange St, POB 46452, Nairobi; tel. (20) 223922; fax (20) 222437; e-mail ho@abcthebank.co.ke; internet www.abcthebank.com; f. 1984 as Consolidated Finance Co; converted to commercial bank and adopted present name 1995; cap. 350m., dep. 2,869m. (Dec. 2002); Exec. Chair. ASHRAF SAVANI; Gen. Man. GHULAM HUSSAIN SHEIKH; 7 brs.

Akiba Bank Ltd: Fedha Towers, 5th Floor, Muindi Mbingu St, POB 49584, 00100 Nairobi; tel. (20) 2883000; fax (20) 2883815; e-mail akiba.ho@akibabank.com; internet www.akibabank.com; cap. 500m., res 75m., dep. 1,800m. (Dec. 2000); Exec. Chair. L. J. PANDIT; Exec. Dir D. L. PANDIT; 3 brs.

Barclays Bank of Kenya Ltd: Barclays Plaza, Loita St, POB 30120, 00100 Nairobi; tel. (20) 332230; fax (20) 213915; e-mail barclays.kenya@barclays.com; f. 1978; cap. 2,037m., res 1,630m., dep. 77,417m. (Dec. 2003); Chair. SAMUEL O. J. AMBUNDO; Man. Dir ADAN MOHAMMED; 87 brs.

CFC Bank Ltd: CFC Centre, Chiromo Rd, POB 72833, 00200 Nairobi; tel. (20) 3752900; fax (20) 3752905; e-mail cfcbank@cfcgroup.co.ke; internet www.cfcbank.co.ke; f. 1955 as Credit Finance Corporation Ltd; became commercial bank and adopted present name 1995; cap. 600m., res 1,616m., dep. 11,090m. (Dec. 2003); Chair. P. K. JANI; Man. Dir R. J. BARRY.

Chase Bank (Kenya) Ltd: Prudential Assurance Bldg, Wabera St, POB 28987, Nairobi; tel. (20) 244035; fax (20) 246334; e-mail info@chasebank.co.ke; cap. 520m. (Dec. 2004); Chair. OSMAN MURGIAN; Man. Dir ZAFRULLAH KHAN.

Commercial Bank of Africa Ltd: Commercial Bank Bldg, cnr Wabera and Standard Sts, POB 30437, Nairobi; tel. (20) 228881; fax (20) 335827; e-mail cba@cba.co.ke; internet www.cba.co.ke; f. 1962; owned by Kenyan shareholders; cap. 1,000m., res 780m., dep. 16,070m. (Dec. 2003); Chair. M. H. DA GAMA-ROSE; Pres. and Man. Dir ISAAC O. AWUONDO; 9 brs.

Consolidated Bank of Kenya Ltd: Consolidated Bank House, Koinange St, POB 51133, Nairobi; tel. (20) 340551; fax (20) 340213; e-mail headoffice@consolidated-bank.com; internet www.consolidated-bank.com; f. 1989; state-owned; cap. 1,120m., res –496m., dep. 1,794m. (Dec. 2002); Chair. PHILIP J. NJUKI; Man. Dir DAVID K. WACHIRA.

Dubai Bank Kenya Ltd: ICEA Bldg, Kenyatta Ave, POB 11129, Nairobi; tel. (20) 330562; fax (20) 245242; e-mail info@dubaibank.co.ke; internet www.dubaibank.co.ke; 25% owned by World of Marble and Granite, Dubai (United Arab Emirates), 25% owned by Abdul Hassan Ahmed, 16% owned by Hassan Bin Hassan Trading Co LLC, Dubai (United Arab Emirates), 15% owned by Ahmed Mohamed Zubeidi; cap. 323m., res 32m., dep. 403m. (Dec. 2003); Chair. ABDULLAH S. DAHIR; Man. Dir AHMED HASSAN ZUBEIDI.

Equatorial Commercial Bank Ltd: Sasini House, Loita St, POB 52467, Nairobi; tel. (20) 331122; fax (20) 331606; e-mail ecb@saamnet.com; internet www.sameer-group.com; cap. 306m. (Dec. 2001); Chair. EDGAR I. MANASSEH; Man. Dir TAHIR N. KHWAJA.

Fidelity Commercial Bank Ltd: IPS Bldg, 7th Floor, Kimathi St, POB 34886, Nairobi; tel. (20) 242348; fax (20) 243389; e-mail customerservice@fidelitybankkenya.com; f. 1993 as Fidelity Finance; present name adopted 1996; CEO SULTAN KHIMJI.

Kenya Commercial Bank Ltd: Kencom House, Moi Ave, POB 48400, Nairobi; tel. (20) 223846; fax (20) 215565; e-mail kcbhq@kcb.co.ke; internet www.kcb.co.ke; f. 1970; 26.2% state-owned; cap. 1,496m., res 535m., dep. 51,635m. (Dec. 2003); CEO and Man. Dir TERRY DAVIDSON; 105 brs and sub-brs.

Middle East Bank Kenya Ltd: Mebank Tower, Milimani Rd, POB 47387, Nairobi; tel. (20) 723120; fax (20) 335168; e-mail info@mebkenya.com; internet www.mebkenya.com; f. 1981; 25% owned by Banque Belgolaise SA (Belgium), 75% owned by Kenyan shareholders; cap. 507m., res 31m., dep. 2,556m. (Dec. 2003); Chair. A. A. K. ESMAIL; Man. Dir DEB GHOSH; 3 brs.

National Bank of Kenya Ltd (Banki ya Taifa La Kenya): National Bank Bldg, Harambee Ave, POB 72866, Nairobi; tel. (20) 339690; fax (20) 330784; e-mail nbkops@nbnet.co.ke; internet www.nationalbank.co.ke; f. 1968; 64.5% state-owned; cap. 6,175m., res –4,021m., dep. 21,621m. (Dec. 2003); Exec. Chair. JOHN P. N. SIMBA; Gen. Man. A. H. AHMED; 25 brs.

Stanbic Bank Kenya Ltd: Stanbic Bank Bldg, Kenyatta Ave, POB 30550, Nairobi; tel. (20) 335888; fax (20) 330227; e-mail stanbickenya@stanbic.com; internet www.stanbic.co.ke; f. 1992; 89.5% owned by Stanbic Africa Holdings Ltd (London), 10.5% state-owned; cap. 1,260m., res 128m., dep. 5,526m. (Dec. 2001); Chair. J. B. WANJUI; Man. Dir P. R. SOUTHEY; 3 brs.

KENYA

Standard Chartered Bank Kenya Ltd: Stanbank House, Moi Ave, POB 30003, Nairobi; tel. (20) 330200; fax (20) 214086; e-mail mds.office@ke.standardchartered.com; internet www.standardchartered.com/ke; f. 1987; 74.5% owned by Standard Chartered Holdings (Africa) BV (Netherlands); cap. 824m., res 3,698m., dep. 34,939m. (Dec. 1999); Chair. HARRINGTON AWORI; CEO LES GIBSON; 43 brs.

Trans-National Bank Ltd: Transnational Plaza, 2nd Floor, Mama Ngina St, POB 34352, 00100 Nairobi; tel. (20) 224234; fax (20) 339227; e-mail tnbl@form-net.com; f. 1985; cap. 558m., res 309m., dep. 523m. (Dec. 2003); Chair. MWAKAI SIO; CEO DHIRENDRA RANA; 5 brs.

Merchant Banks

Diamond Trust Bank of Kenya Ltd: Nation Centre, 8th Floor, Kimathi St, POB 61711-00200, Nairobi; tel. (20) 210988; fax (20) 336836; e-mail user@dtbkenya.co.ke; f. 1945; cap. 398m., res 197m., dep. 6,862m. (Dec. 2003); Chair. ROBERT A. BIRD; Man. Dir NASIM DEVJI.

Kenya Commercial Finance Co Ltd: Kenyan House, 6th Floor, Moi Ave, POB 21984, Nairobi; tel. (20) 339074; fax (20) 215881; e-mail kcfc@kcb.co.ke; internet www.kcb.co.ke; f. 1971; cap. 300m. (Dec. 1999), dep. 4,042m. (1998); Chair. PETER C. J. O. NYAKIAMO; Man. Dir JAMES G. CHEGE.

National Industrial Credit Bank Ltd (NIC): NIC House, Masaba Rd, POB 44599, Nairobi; tel. (20) 718200; fax (20) 718232; e-mail nic@iconnect.co.ke; cap. 412m. (Dec. 2001); Chair. N. MURIUKI MUGWANDIA; Man. Dir M. N. DAVIDSON.

Standard Chartered Financial Services Ltd: International House, 1st Floor, Mama Ngina St, POB 40310, Nairobi; tel. (20) 336333; fax (20) 334934; owned by Standard Chartered Bank Kenya; cap. and res 161.7m., dep. 1,700m. (Dec. 1992); Chair. A. CLEARY; Man. Dir W. VON ISENBURG.

Foreign Banks

Bank of Baroda (Kenya) Ltd (India): Bank of Baroda Bldg, cnr Mandlane St and Tom Mboya St, POB 30033, Nairobi; tel. (20) 2337611; fax (20) 2333089; e-mail md.kenya@bankofbaroda.com; Exec. Chair. C. K. DAIYA; Man. Dir T. K. KRISHMAN; 6 brs.

Bank of India: Kenyatta Ave, POB 30246, 00100 Nairobi; tel. (20) 221414; fax (20) 229462; e-mail boi@calva.com; internet www.bankofindiake.com; CEO G. L. N. SASTRY.

Citibank NA (USA): Citibank House, Upperhill Rd, POB 30711, 00100 Nairobi; tel. (20) 2711221; fax (20) 2711481; internet www.citibank.co.ke; f. 1974; Gen. Man. SRIDHAR SRINIVASAN.

First American Bank of Kenya Ltd (USA): First American Bank Centre, Nyerere Rd, POB 30691, 00100 Nairobi; tel. (20) 2710455; fax (20) 2714511; e-mail fabk@fabk.com; internet www.fabk.com; f. 1987; 20.5% owned by Sameer Investments Ltd; cap. 1,300m., res 25m., dep. 7,515m. (Dec. 2004); Chair. D. G. M. HUTCHINSON; Man. Dir MANLIO BLASETTI; 3 brs.

Habib Bank AG Zurich (Switzerland): Nagina House, Koinange St, POB 30584, 00100 Nairobi; tel. (20) 334984; fax (20) 218699; e-mail habibbank@form-net.com; Country Man. IQBAL A. ALLAWALA.

Co-operative Bank

Co-operative Bank of Kenya Ltd: Co-operative Bank House, POB 48231, Nairobi; tel. (20) 32076000; fax (20) 249474; e-mail md@co-opbank.co.ke; internet www.co-opbank.co.ke; f. 1968; cap. 1,211m., res 589m., dep. 25,084m. (Dec. 2002); Chair. STANLEY C. MUCHIRI; Man. Dir GIDEON MURIUKI; 30 brs.

Development Banks

Development Bank of Kenya Ltd: Finance House, Loita St, POB 30483–00100, Nairobi; tel. (20) 340401; fax (20) 338426; e-mail dbk@africaonline.co.ke; f. 1963 as Development Finance Co of Kenya; current name adopted 1996; owned by Industrial and Commercial Devt Corpn (30.5%), govt agencies of Germany and the Netherlands (28.8% and 22.8% respectively), the Commonwealth Development Corpn (10.7%) and the International Finance Corpn (7.2%); cap. 348m., res 558m., dep. 1,028m. (Dec. 2003); Chair. Prof. HAROUN NGENY KIPKEMBOI MENGECH; Man. Dir SAJAL RAKHIT.

East African Development Bank: Lonrho House, 12th Floor, Standard St, Nairobi; tel. (20) 340656; fax (20) 216651; Dirs J. M. MAGARI, J. B. WANJUI.

Industrial Development Bank Ltd (IDB): National Bank Bldg, 18th Floor, Harambee Ave, POB 44036, Nairobi; tel. (20) 337079; fax (20) 334594; e-mail bizcare@idbkenya.com; f. 1973; 49% state-owned; cap. 272m., res 83m., dep. 190m. (Dec. 2002); Chair. DAVID LANGAT; Man. Dir L. A. MASAVIRU.

STOCK EXCHANGE

Nairobi Stock Exchange (NSE): Nation Centre, 1st Floor, Kimathi St, POB 43633, 00100 Nairobi; tel. (20) 230692; fax (20) 224200; e-mail info@nse.co.ke; internet www.nse.co.ke; f. 1954; Chair. MIRABEAU DA GAMA ROSE; CEO CHRIS MWEBESA.

INSURANCE

American Life Insurance Co (Kenya) Ltd: POB 30364, 00100 Nairobi; tel. (20) 2711242; fax (20) 2711378; e-mail alicolife@alico-kenya.com; internet www.alico-kenya.com; f. 1964; life and general; Man. Dir ERWIN BREWSTER.

Apollo Insurance Co Ltd: POB 30389, Nairobi; tel. (20) 223562; fax (20) 339260; e-mail insurance@apollo.co.ke; f. 1977; life and general; Chief Exec. ASHOK K. M. SHAH.

Blue Shield Insurance Co Ltd: POB 49610, Nairobi; tel. (20) 219592; fax (20) 337808; f. 1983; life and general.

Cannon Assurance (Kenya) Ltd: Haile Selassie Ave, POB 30216, Nairobi; tel. (20) 335478; fax (20) 331235; e-mail info@cannon.co.ke; internet www.cannon.co.ke; f. 1964; life and general; Man. Dir I. J. TALWAR.

Fidelity Shield Insurance Ltd: POB 47435, Nairobi; tel. (20) 430635; fax (20) 445699.

Heritage AII Insurance Co Ltd: CFC Centre, Chiromo Rd, POB 30390, Nairobi; tel. (20) 3749118; fax (20) 3752621; e-mail info@heriaii.com; f. 1976; general; Man. Dir J. H. D. MILNE.

Insurance Co of East Africa Ltd (ICEA): ICEA Bldg, Kenyatta Ave, POB 46143, Nairobi; tel. (20) 221652; fax (20) 338089; e-mail hof@icea.co.ke; internet www.icea.co.ke; life and general; Man. Dir J. K. NDUNGU.

Jubilee Insurance Co Ltd: POB 30376, Nairobi; tel. (20) 340343; fax (20) 216882; f. 1937; life and general; Chair. ABDUL JAFFER.

Kenindia Assurance Co Ltd: Kenindia House, Loita St, POB 44372, Nairobi; tel. (20) 333100; fax (20) 218380; e-mail kenindia@users.africaonline.co.ke; f. 1978; life and general; Exec. Dir R. S. BEDI.

Kenya Reinsurance Corpn Ltd (KenyaRe): Reinsurance Plaza, Taifa Rd, POB 30271, Nairobi; tel. (20) 240188; fax (20) 339161; e-mail kenyare@kenyare.co.ke; internet www.kenyare.co.ke; f. 1970; Man. Dir JOHNSON GITHAKA.

Lion of Kenya Insurance Co Ltd: POB 30190, Nairobi; tel. (20) 710400; fax (20) 711177; e-mail insurance@lionofkenya.com; f. 1978; general; CEO J. P. M. NDEGWA.

Mercantile Life and General Assurance Co Ltd: Nairobi; tel. (20) 218244; fax (20) 215528; e-mail mercantile@form-net.com; Gen. Man. SUPRIYO SEN.

Monarch Insurance Co Ltd: Chester House, 2nd Floor, Koinange St, POB 44003, Nairobi; tel. (20) 330042; fax (20) 340691; e-mail monarch@form-net.com; f. 1975; general; Exec. Dir R. A. VADGAMA.

Pan Africa Insurance Co Ltd: POB 30065, Nairobi; tel. (20) 252168; fax (20) 217675; e-mail insure@pan-africa.com; f. 1946; life and general; Man. Dir WILLIAM OLOTCH.

Phoenix of East Africa Assurance Co Ltd: Ambank House, University Way, POB 30129, Nairobi; tel. (20) 338784; fax (20) 211848; general; Man. Dir D. K. SHARMA.

Prudential Assurance Co of Kenya Ltd: Yaya Centre, Argwings Kodhek Rd, POB 76190, Nairobi; tel. (20) 567374; fax (20) 567433; f. 1979; general; Man. Dir JOSEPH MURAGE.

PTA Reinsurance Co (ZEP-RE): Anniversary Towers, 13th Floor, University Way, POB 42769, Nairobi; tel. (20) 212792; fax (20) 224102; e-mail mail@zep-re.com; internet www.zep-re.com; f. 1992; Man. Dir S. M. LUBASI.

Royal Insurance Co of East Africa Ltd: Mama Ngina St, POB 40001, Nairobi; tel. (20) 717888; fax (20) 712620; f. 1979; general; CEO S. K. KAMAU.

Standard Assurance (Kenya) Ltd: POB 42996, Nairobi; tel. (20) 224721; fax (20) 224862; Man. Dir WILSON K. KAPKOTI.

UAP Provincial Insurance Co of East Africa Ltd: Old Mutual Bldg, Kimathi St, POB 43013, Nairobi; tel. (20) 330173; fax (20) 340483; f. 1980; general; CEO E. C. BATES.

United Insurance Co Ltd: POB 30961, Nairobi; tel. (20) 227345; fax (20) 215609; Man. Dir G. KARRUIKI.

Trade and Industry

GOVERNMENT AGENCIES

Export Processing Zones Authority: POB 50563, Nairobi; tel. (20) 712800; fax (20) 713704; e-mail epzahq@africaonline.co.ke; established by the Govt to promote investment in Export Processing Zones; CEO SILAS ITA.

KENYA

Export Promotion Council: Anniversary Towers, 1st and 16th Floors, University Way, POB 40247, Nairobi; tel. (20) 228534; fax (20) 218013; e-mail chiefexe@epc.or.ke; internet www.cbik.or.ke; f. 1992; promotes exports; CEO MATANDA WABUYELE.

Investment Promotion Centre: National Bank Bldg, 8th Floor, Harambee Ave, POB 55704, 00200 Nairobi; tel. (20) 221401; fax (20) 336663; e-mail info@investmentkenya.com; internet www.investmentkenya.com; f. 1986; promotes and facilitates local and foreign investment; CEO LUKA E. OBBANDA.

Kenya National Trading Corpn Ltd: Yarrow Rd, off Nanyuki Rd, POB 30587, Nairobi; tel. (20) 543121; fax (20) 532800; f. 1965; promotes national control of trade in both locally produced and imported items; exports coffee and sugar; CEO S. W. O. OGESSA.

Settlement Fund Trustees: POB 30449, Nairobi; administers a land purchase programme involving over 1.2m. ha for resettlement of African farmers.

DEVELOPMENT ORGANIZATIONS

Agricultural Development Corpn: POB 47101, Nairobi; tel. (20) 338530; fax (20) 336524; f. 1965 to promote agricultural development and reconstruction; CEO Dr WALTER KILELE.

Agricultural Finance Corpn: POB 30367, Nairobi; tel. (20) 317199; fax (20) 219390; e-mail afc@wananchi.com; a statutory organization providing agricultural loans; Man. Dir OMUREMBE IYADI.

Horticultural Crops Development Authority: POB 42601, Nairobi; tel. (20) 8272601; fax (20) 827264; e-mail hcdamd@wananchi.com; internet www.hcda.or.ke; f. 1968; invests in production, dehydration, processing and freezing of fruit and vegetables; exports of fresh fruit and vegetables; Chair. Prof. ROSALIND W. MUTUA; Man. Dir S. P. GACHANJA.

Housing Finance Co of Kenya Ltd: Rehani House, cnr Kenyatta Ave and Koinange St, POB 30088, 00100 Nairobi; tel. (20) 333910; fax (20) 334670; e-mail hfck@hfck.co.ke; internet www.hfck.co.ke; f. 1965; Chair. RICHARD KEMOLI; Man. Dir PETER LEWIS-JONES.

Industrial and Commercial Development Corpn: Uchumi House, Aga Khan Walk, POB 45519, Nairobi; tel. (20) 229213; fax (20) 333880; e-mail icdcexe@africaonline.co.ke; f. 1954; govt-financed; assists industrial and commercial development; Chair. JOHN NGUTHU MUTIO; Exec. Dir K. ETICH ARAP BETT.

Kenya Fishing Industries Ltd: Nairobi; Man. Dir ABDALLA MBWANA.

Kenya Industrial Estates Ltd: Nairobi Industrial Estate, Likoni Rd, POB 78029, Nairobi; tel. (20) 530551; fax (20) 534625; f. 1967 to finance and develop small-scale industries.

Kenya Industrial Research and Development Institute: POB 30650, Nairobi; tel. (20) 557762; f. 1942; reorg. 1979; restructured 1995; research and development in industrial and allied technologies including engineering, commodity technologies, mining and power resources; Dir Dr H. L. KAANE.

Kenya Tea Development Agency: POB 30213, Nairobi; tel. (20) 221541; fax (20) 211240; e-mail info@ktdateas.com; internet www.ktdateas.com; f. 1964 as Kenya Tea Development Authority; to develop tea growing, manufacturing and marketing among African smallholders; operates 51 factories; privatized in 2000; Chair. STEPHEN M. IMANYARA; Man. Dir ERIC KIMANI.

CHAMBER OF COMMERCE

Kenya National Chamber of Commerce and Industry: Ufanisi House, Haile Selassie Ave, POB 47024, Nairobi; tel. (20) 220867; fax (20) 334293; f. 1965; 69 brs; Nat. Chair. DAVID M. GITHERE; Chief Exec. TITUS G. RUHIU.

INDUSTRIAL AND TRADE ASSOCIATIONS

Central Province Marketing Board: POB 189, Nyeri.

Coffee Board of Kenya: POB 30566, Nairobi; tel. (20) 332896; fax (20) 330546; f. 1947; Chair. JOHN NGARI ZACHARIAH; Gen. Man. AGGREY MURUNGA.

East African Tea Trade Association: Tea Trade Centre, Nyerere Ave, POB 85174–80100, Mombasa; tel. (41) 315687; fax (41) 225823; e-mail info@eatta.co.ke; internet www.eatta.com; f. 1957; organizes Mombasa weekly tea auctions; Exec. Sec. LUCY MICHENI; 264 mems.

Fresh Produce Exporters' Association of Kenya: Nairobi; Chair. JAMES MATHENGE.

Kenya Association of Manufacturers: POB 30225, Nairobi; tel. (20) 746005; fax (20) 746028; e-mail kam@users.africaonline.co.ke; Chair. MANU CHANDARIA; Exec. Sec. LUCY MICHENI; 200 mems.

Kenya Dairy Board: POB 30406, Nairobi.

Kenya Flower Council: POB 24856, Nairobi; tel. and fax (20) 883041; e-mail kfc@africaonline.co.ke; internet www.kenyaflowers.co.ke; regulates production of cut flowers; Exec. Dir MICHAEL MORLAND.

Kenya Meat Corpn: POB 30414, Nairobi; tel. (20) 340750; f. 1953; purchasing, processing and marketing of beef livestock; Chair. H. P. BARCLAY.

Kenya Planters' Co-operative Union Ltd: Nairobi; e-mail gm@kpcu.co.ke; coffee processing and marketing; Chair. J. M. MACHARIA; Gen. Man. RUTH MWANIKI.

Kenya Sisal Board: Mutual Bldg, Kimathi St, POB 41179, Nairobi; tel. (20) 223457; f. 1946; CEO J. H. WAIRAGU; Man. Dir KENNETH MUKUMA.

Kenya Sugar Authority: NSSF Complex, 9th Floor, Bishops Rd, POB 51500, Nairobi; tel. (20) 710600; fax (20) 723903; e-mail ksa@users.africaonline.co.ke; Chair. LUKE R. OBOK; CEO F. M. CHAHONYO.

Mild Coffee Trade Association of Eastern Africa (MCTA): Nairobi; F. J. MWANGI.

National Cereals and Produce Board: POB 30586, Nairobi; tel. (20) 536028; fax (20) 542024; e-mail cereals@africaonline.co.ke; f. 1995; grain marketing and handling, provides drying, weighing, storage and fumigation services to farmers and traders, stores and manages strategic national food reserves, distributes famine relief; Chair. JAMES MUTUA; Man. Dir Maj. W. K. KOITABA.

Pyrethrum Board of Kenya: POB 420, Nakuru; tel. (37) 211567; fax (37) 45274; e-mail pbk@pyrethrum.co.ke; internet www.kenya-pyrethrum.com; f. 1935; 14 mems; Chair. J. O. MARIARIA; CEO J. C. KIPTOON.

Tea Board of Kenya: POB 20064, 00200 Nairobi; tel. (20) 572421; fax (20) 562120; e-mail teaboardk@kenyaweb.com; internet www.teaboard.or.ke; f. 1950; regulates tea industry on all matters of policy, licenses tea processing, carries out research on tea through **Tea Research Foundation of Kenya**, monitors tea planting and trade through registration, promotes Kenyan tea internationally; 16 mems; Chair. NICHOLAS NGANGA; CEO STEPHEN K. NKANATA.

EMPLOYERS' ORGANIZATIONS

Federation of Kenya Employers: Waajiri House, Argwings Kodhek Rd, POB 48311, Nairobi; tel. (20) 721929; fax (20) 721990; Chair. J. P. N. SIMBA; Exec. Dir TOM DIJU OWUOR.

Association of Local Government Employers: POB 52, Muranga; Chair. S. K. ITONGU.

Distributive and Allied Industries Employers' Association: POB 30587, Nairobi; Chair. P. J. MWAURA.

Engineering and Allied Industries Employers' Association: POB 48311, Nairobi; tel. (20) 721929; Chair. D. M. NJOROGE.

Kenya Association of Building and Civil Engineering Contractors: Nairobi; Chair. G. S. HIRANI.

Kenya Association of Hotelkeepers and Caterers: Heidelberg House, Mombasa Rd, POB 9977, 00100 Nairobi; tel. (20) 604419; fax (20) 602539; e-mail info@kahc.co.ke; internet www.kahc.co.ke; f. 1944; CEO KABANDO WA KABANDO.

Kenya Bankers' Association: POB 73100, Nairobi; tel. (20) 221792; e-mail kba@kenyaweb.com; Chair. TERRY DAVIDSON.

Kenya Sugar Employers' Union: Kisumu; Chair. L. OKECH.

Kenya Tea Growers' Association: POB 320, Kericho; tel. (20) 21010; fax (20) 32172; Chair. M. K. A. SANG.

Kenya Vehicle Manufacturers' Association: POB 1436, Thika; Chair. C. PETERSON.

Motor Trade and Allied Industries Employers' Association: POB 48311, Nairobi; tel. (20) 721929; fax (20) 721990; Exec. Sec. G. N. KONDITI.

Sisal Growers' and Employers' Association: POB 47523, Nairobi; tel. (20) 720170; fax (20) 721990; Chair. A. G. COMBOS.

Timber Industries Employers' Association: POB 18070, Nairobi; Chair. H. S. BAMBRAH.

UTILITIES

Electricity

Kenya Electricity Generating Co Ltd (KenGen): Stima Plaza, Phase 3, Kolobot Rd, Parklands, POB 47936, Nairobi; tel. (20) 3666000; fax (20) 248848; e-mail comms@kengen.co.ke; internet www.kengen.co.ke; f. 1997 as Kenya Power Co; present name adopted 1998; generates 82% of Kenya's electricity requirements; Man. Dir EDWARD NJOROGE.

Kenya Power and Lighting Co (KPLC): Stima Plaza, Kolobot Rd, POB 30099, Nairobi; tel. (20) 243366; fax (20) 337351; e-mail isd@form-net.com; state-owned; co-ordinates electricity transmission and distribution; Man. Dir SAMUEL GICHURU.

KENYA
Directory

TRADE UNIONS

Central Organization of Trade Unions (Kenya) (COTU): Solidarity Bldg, Digo St, POB 13000, Nairobi; tel. (20) 761375; fax (20) 762695; f. 1965 as the sole trade union fed.; Chair. PETER G. MUTHEE; Sec.-Gen. JOSEPH J. MUGALLA.

Amalgamated Union of Kenya Metalworkers: POB 73651, Nairobi; tel. (20) 211060; Gen. Sec. F. E. OMIDO.

Bakers', Confectionary Manufacturing and Allied Workers' Union (Kenya): POB 57751, 00200 Nairobi; Lengo House, 3rd Floor, Room 20, Tom Mboya St, opposite Gill House, Nairobi; tel. (20) 330275; fax (20) 222735; e-mail bakers@form-net.com.

Communication Workers' Union of Kenya: POB 48155, Nairobi; tel. (20) 219345; e-mail cowuk@clubinternet.com.

Dockworkers' Union: POB 98207, Mombasa; tel. (11) 491427; f. 1954; Gen. Sec. J. KHAMIS.

Kenya Airline Pilots' Association: POB 57505, Nairobi; tel. (20) 716986.

Kenya Building, Construction, Timber, Furniture and Allied Industries Employees' Union: POB 49628, Nairobi; tel. (20) 336414; Gen. Sec. FRANCIS KARIMI MURAGE.

Kenya Chemical and Allied Workers' Union: POB 73820, Nairobi; tel. (20) 338815; Gen. Sec. WERE DIBI OGUTO.

Kenya Electrical Trades Allied Workers' Union: POB 47060, Nairobi; tel. (20) 334655.

Kenya Engineering Workers' Union: POB 73987, Nairobi; tel. (20) 333745; Gen. Sec. JUSTUS MULEI.

Kenya Game Hunting and Safari Workers' Union: Nairobi; tel. (20) 25049; Gen. Sec. J. M. NDOLO.

Kenya Jockey and Betting Workers' Union: POB 55094, Nairobi; tel. (20) 332120.

Kenya Local Government Workers' Union: POB 55827, Nairobi; tel. (20) 217213; Gen. Sec. WASIKE NDOMBI.

Kenya National Union of Fishermen: POB 83322, Nairobi; tel. (20) 227899.

Kenya Petroleum Oil Workers' Union: POB 48125, Nairobi; tel. (20) 338756; Gen. Sec. JACOB OCHINO.

Kenya Plantation and Agricultural Workers' Union: POB 1161, 20100 Nakuru; tel. and fax (51) 2212310; e-mail kpawu@africaonline.co.ke; Gen. Sec. FRANCIS ATWOLI.

Kenya Quarry and Mine Workers' Union: POB 332120, Nairobi; f. 1961; Gen. Sec. WAFULA WA MUSAMIA.

Kenya Railway Workers' Union: RAHU House, Mfangano St, POB 72029, Nairobi; tel. (20) 340302; f. 1952; Nat. Chair. FRANCIS O'LORE; Sec.-Gen. RICHARD A. KANANI.

Kenya Scientific Research, International Technical and Allied Institutions Workers' Union: Ngumba House, Tom Mboya St, POB 55094, Nairobi; tel. (20) 215713; Sec.-Gen. FRANCIS D. KIRUBI.

Kenya Shipping, Clearing and Warehouse Workers' Union: POB 84067, Mombasa; tel. (11) 312000.

Kenya Shoe and Leather Workers' Union: POB 49629, Nairobi; tel. (20) 533827; Gen. Sec. JAMES AWICH.

Kenya Union of Commercial, Food and Allied Workers: POB 46818, Nairobi; tel. (20) 212545.

Kenya Union of Domestic, Hotel, Educational Institutions, Hospitals and Allied Workers: POB 41763, 00100 Nairobi; tel. (20) 211840.

Kenyan Union of Entertainment and Music Industry Employees: Nairobi; tel. (20) 333745.

Kenya Union of Journalists: POB 47035, 00100 Nairobi; tel. (20) 250888; fax (20) 250880; e-mail info@kujkenya.org; f. 1962; Gen. Sec. and CEO EZEKIEL MUTUA; Chair. TERVIL OKOKO.

Kenya Union of Printing, Publishing, Paper Manufacturers and Allied Workers: POB 72358, Nairobi; tel. (20) 331387; Gen. Sec. JOHN BOSCO.

Kenya Union of Sugar Plantation Workers: POB 36, Kisumu; tel. (35) 22221; Gen. Sec. ONYANGO MIDIKA.

National Seamen's Union of Kenya: Mombasa; tel. (11) 312106; Gen. Sec. I. S. ABDALLAH MWARUA.

Tailors' and Textile Workers' Union: POB 72076, Nairobi; tel. (20) 338836.

Transport and Allied Workers' Union: POB 45171, Nairobi; tel. (20) 545317; Gen. Sec. JULIAS MALII.

Independent Unions

Academic Staff Association: Nairobi; e-mail dorata@uonbi.ac.ke; Interim Chair. Dr KORWA ADAR.

Kenya Medical Practitioners' and Dentists' Union: not officially registered; Nat. Chair. GIBBON ATEKA.

Kenya National Union of Teachers: POB 30407, Nairobi; f. 1957; Sec.-Gen. AMBROSE ADEYA ADONGO.

Transport

RAILWAYS

In 1999 there were some 2,700 km of track open for traffic.

Kenya Railways Corpn: POB 30121, Nairobi; tel. (20) 221211; fax (20) 224156; f. 1977; privatization pending; Man. Dir A. HARIZ.

ROADS

At the end of 2000 there were an estimated 63,942 km of classified roads, of which 6,251 km were main roads and 11,339 km were secondary roads. Only an estimated 12.1% of road surfaces were paved. An all-weather road links Nairobi to Addis Ababa, in Ethiopia, and there is a 590-km road link between Kitale (Kenya) and Juba (Sudan). The rehabilitation of the important internal road link between Nairobi and Mombasa (funded by a US $165m. loan from the World Bank) was undertaken during the late 1990s.

Abamba Public Road Services: POB 40322, Nairobi; tel. (20) 556062; fax (20) 559884; operates bus services from Nairobi to all major towns in Kenya and to Kampala in Uganda.

East African Road Services Ltd: Nairobi; tel. (20) 764622; f. 1947; operates bus services from Nairobi to all major towns in Kenya; Chair. S. H. NATHOO.

Kenya Roads Board: Nairobi; tel. (20) 722865; f. 2000 to coordinate maintenance, rehabilitation and development of the road network; Chair. SHEM ODUOR NOAH.

Nyayo Bus Service Corpn: Nairobi; tel. (20) 803588; f. 1986; operates bus services within and between major towns in Kenya.

Speedways Trans-Africa Freighters: POB 75755, Nairobi; tel. (20) 544267; private road haulier; CEO HASSAN KANYARE.

SHIPPING

The major international seaport of Mombasa has 16 deep-water berths, with a total length of 3,044 m, and facilities for the off-loading of bulk carriers, tankers and container vessels. Mombasa port handled more than 8.5m. metric tons of cargo in 1998. An inland container depot with a potential full capacity of 120,000 20-ft (6-m) equivalent units was opened in Nairobi in 1984.

Kenya Ports Authority: POB 95009, Mombasa; tel. (41) 312211; fax (41) 311867; e-mail md@kpa.co.ke; internet www.kenya.ports.com; f. 1978; sole operator of coastal port facilities, and operates two inland container depots at Nairobi and Kisimu; Chair. Gen. (Retd) JOSEPH KIBWANA; Man. Dir BROWN M. M. ONDEGO.

Inchcape Shipping Services Kenya Ltd: POB 90194, Mombasa; tel. (11) 314245; fax (11) 314224; Man. Dir DAVID MACKAY.

Mackenzie Maritime Ltd: Maritime Centre, Archbishop Makarios Close, POB 90120, Mombasa; tel. (11) 221273; fax (11) 316260; e-mail mml@africaonline.co.ke; shipping agents; Man. Dir M. M. BROWN.

Marship Ltd: Mombasa; tel. (11) 314705; fax (11) 316654; f. 1986; shipbrokers, ship management and chartering agents; Man. Dir MICHELE ESPOSITO.

Mitchell Cotts Kenya Ltd: Cotts House, Wabera St, POB 30182, Nairobi; tel. (20) 221273; fax (20) 214228.

Motaku Shipping Agencies Ltd: Motaku House, Tangana Rd, POB 80419, 80100 Mombasa; tel. (11) 312562; fax (11) 220777; e-mail motaku@motakushipping.com; f. 1977; ship managers and shipping agents; Man. Dir KARIM KUDRATI.

PIL (Kenya) Ltd: POB 43050, Mombasa; tel. (11) 225361; fax (11) 312296.

Shipmarc Ltd: POB 99553, Mombasa; tel. (11) 229241; fax (11) 315673; e-mail shipmarc@form-net.com.

Southern Line Ltd: POB 90102, Mombasa 80107; tel. (11) 229241; fax (11) 221390; e-mail shipmarc@africaonline.co.ke; operating dry cargo and tanker vessels between East African ports, Red Sea ports, the Persian (Arabian) Gulf and Indian Ocean islands.

Spanfreight Shipping Ltd: Cannon Towers, Moi Ave, POB 99760, Mombasa; tel. (11) 315623; fax (11) 312092; e-mail a23ke464@gncomtext.com; Exec. Dir DILIPKUMAR AMRITLAL SHAH.

Star East Africa Co: POB 86725, Mombasa; tel. (11) 314060; fax (11) 312818; shipping agents and brokers; Man. Dir YEUDA FISHER.

CIVIL AVIATION

Jomo Kenyatta International Airport (JKIA), in south-eastern Nairobi, Moi International Airport, at Mombasa, and Eldoret International Airport (which opened in 1997) all service international flights.

KENYA

Wilson Airport, in south-western Nairobi, and airports at Malindi and Kisumu handle internal flights. Kenya has about 150 smaller airfields. The rehabilitation and expansion of JKIA and Moi International Airport was undertaken during the late 1990s. A new cargo handling facility, The Nairobi Cargo Centre, opened at JKIA in June 1999, increasing the airport's capacity for storing horticultural exports.

Kenya Airports Authority: Jomo Kenyatta International Airport, POB 19001, Nairobi; tel. (20) 825400; fax (20) 822078; e-mail info@kenyaairports.co.ke; f. 1991; state-owned; responsible for the provision, management and operation of all airports and private airstrips; Man. Dir GEORGE MUHOHO.

African Airlines International: POB 74772, Nairobi; tel. (20) 824333; fax (20) 823999; placed under receivership mid-1999; CEO Capt. MUSA BULHAN.

Airkenya Aviation: Wilson Airport, POB 30357, Nairobi; tel. (20) 605730; fax (20) 500845; e-mail info@airkenya.com; internet www.airkenya.com; f. 1985; operates internal scheduled and charter passenger services; Man. Dir JOHN BUCKLEY.

Blue Bird Aviation Ltd: Wilson Airport, Langata Rd, POB 52382, Nairobi; tel. (20) 506004; fax (20) 602337; e-mail bbal@form-net.com.

Eagle Aviation (African Eagle): POB 93926, Mombasa; tel. (11) 434502; fax (11) 434249; e-mail eaglemsa@africaonline.co.ke; f. 1986; scheduled regional and domestic passenger and cargo services; Chair. RAJA TANUJ; CEO Capt. KIRAN PATEL.

East African Safari Air: Mombasa; operates charter service.

Kenya Airways Ltd: Jomo Kenyatta International Airport, POB 19002, Nairobi; tel. (20) 823000; fax (20) 823757; e-mail gmurira@kenya-airways.com; internet www.kenya-airways.com; f. 1977; in private-sector ownership since 1996; passenger services to Africa, Asia, Europe and Middle East; freight services to Europe; internal services from Nairobi to Kisumu, Mombasa and Malindi; also operates a freight subsidiary; Chair. EVANSON MWANIKI; Man. Dir and CEO TITUS NAIKUNI.

CIVIL AVIATION AUTHORITY

Kenya Directorate of Civil Aviation: Jomo Kenyatta International Airport, POB 30163, Nairobi; tel. (20) 822950; f. 1948; under Kenya govt control since 1977; responsible for the conduct of civil aviation; advises the Govt on civil aviation policy; Dir J. P. AYUGA.

Kenya Civil Aviation Authority: POB 30163, 00100 Nairobi; tel. (20) 824557; fax (20) 824716; e-mail cav@insightkenya.com; f. 2002; regulatory and advisory services for air navigation; Dir Gen. C. A. KUTO.

Tourism

Kenya's main attractions for visitors are its wildlife, with 25 National Parks and 23 game reserves, the Indian Ocean coast and an equable year-round climate. A decline in the number of visitors in 1996–98 was attributed both to competition from other countries of the region, and to perceptions of high rates of crime and shortcomings in security within Kenya. There was a modest recovery in 1999–2000, with an estimated 1,036,628 foreign tourist arrivals recorded in 2000. In 2003 there were 1,146,099 foreign visitors. Earnings from the sector totalled US $631m. in that year.

Kenya Tourism Board: Nairobi; internet www.kenyatourism.com; f. 1996; promotes Kenya as a tourist destination, monitors the standard of tourist facilities; Chair. UHURU KENYATTA.

Kenya Tourist Development Corpn: Utalii House, 11th Floor, Uhuru Highway, POB 42013, Nairobi; tel. (20) 330820; fax (20) 227815; e-mail info@ktdc.co.ke; internet www.ktdc.co.ke; f. 1965; Chair. PAUL KITOLOLO; Man. Dir JOHN A. M. MALITI.

KIRIBATI

Introductory Survey

Location, Climate, Language, Religion, Flag, Capital

The Republic of Kiribati (pronounced 'Kir-a-bas') comprises 33 atolls, in three principal groups, scattered within an area of about 5m. sq km (2m. sq miles) in the mid-Pacific Ocean. The country extends about 3,870 km (2,400 miles) from east to west and about 2,050 km (1,275 miles) from north to south. Its nearest neighbours are Nauru, to the west, and Tuvalu and Tokelau, to the south. The climate varies between maritime equatorial in the central islands and tropical in the north and south, with daytime temperatures varying between 26°C (79°F) and 32°C (90°F). There is a season of north-westerly trade winds from March to October and a season of rains and gales from October to March. Average annual rainfall, however, varies greatly, from 3,000 mm (118 ins) in the northern islands to 1,500 mm (59 ins) in Tarawa and 700 mm (28 ins) in the Line Islands. Droughts often occur in the central and southern islands. The principal languages are I-Kiribati (Gilbertese) and English, and the islands' inhabitants are mostly Christians. The national flag (proportions 1 by 2) depicts a golden frigate bird in flight, on a red background, above a rising sun and six alternating wavy horizontal lines of blue and white, representing the sea. The capital is the island of Bairiki, in Tarawa Atoll.

Recent History

In 1892 the United Kingdom established a protectorate over the 16 atolls of the Gilbert Islands and the nine Ellice Islands (now Tuvalu). The two groups were administered together by the Western Pacific High Commission (WPHC), which was based in Fiji until its removal to the British Solomon Islands (now Solomon Islands) in 1953. The phosphate-rich Ocean Island (now Banaba), west of the Gilberts, was annexed by the United Kingdom in 1900. The Gilbert and Ellice Islands were annexed in 1915, effective from January 1916, when the protectorate became a colony. The local representative of the WPHC was the Resident Commissioner, based on Tarawa Atoll in the Gilbert group. Later in 1916 the new Gilbert and Ellice Islands Colony (GEIC) was extended to include Ocean Island and two of the Line Islands, far to the east. Christmas Island (now Kiritimati), another of the Line Islands, was added in 1919, and the eight Phoenix Islands (then uninhabited) in 1937. The Line and Phoenix Islands, south of Hawaii, were also claimed by the USA. A joint British-US administration for two of the Phoenix group, Canton (now Kanton) and Enderbury, was agreed in April 1939. During the Second World War the GEIC was invaded by Japanese forces, who occupied the Gilbert Islands in 1942–43. Tarawa Atoll was the scene of some of the fiercest fighting in the Pacific between Japan and the USA.

As part of the British Government's programme to develop its own nuclear weapons, the first test of a British hydrogen bomb was conducted near Christmas Island in May 1957. Two further tests in the same vicinity followed later that year.

In 1963, to prepare the GEIC for self-government, the first of a series of legislative and executive bodies were established. In 1972 a Governor of the GEIC was appointed to assume almost all the functions previously exercised in the colony by the High Commissioner. The five uninhabited Central and Southern Line Islands, previously administered directly by the High Commissioner, became part of the GEIC at this time. In 1974 the Legislative Council was replaced by a House of Assembly, with 28 elected members and three official members. The House elected Naboua Ratieta as Chief Minister.

In October 1975 the Ellice Islands were allowed to secede from the GEIC to form a separate territory, Tuvalu (q.v.). The remainder of the GEIC was renamed the Gilbert Islands, and the House of Assembly's membership was reduced.

In 1975 the British Government refused to recognize as legitimate a demand for independence by the people of Ocean Island (Banaba), who had been in litigation with the British Government since 1971 over revenues derived from exports of phosphate. Open-cast mining had so adversely affected the island's environment that most Banabans had been resettled on Rabi Island, 2,600 km (1,600 miles) away in the Fiji group. The Banabans rejected the British Government's argument that phosphate revenues should be distributed over the whole territory of the Gilbert Islands. In 1976 the British High Court dismissed the Banabans' claim for unpaid royalties but upheld that for damages. An offer made by the British Government in 1977 of an *ex gratia* payment of $A10m., without admission of liability and on condition that no further judicial appeal would be made, was rejected.

The Gilbert Islands obtained internal self-government on 1 January 1977. Later in that year the number of elected members in the House of Assembly was increased to 36, and provision was subsequently made for a member appointed by the Rabi Council of Leaders. Following a general election in 1978, Ieremia Tabai, Leader of the Opposition in the previous House, was elected Chief Minister. On 12 July 1979 the Gilbert Islands became an independent republic within the Commonwealth, under the name of Kiribati. The House of Assembly was renamed the Maneaba ni Maungatabu, and Ieremia Tabai became the country's first President (Beretitenti). In September Kiribati signed a treaty of friendship with the USA, which relinquished its claim to the Line and Phoenix Islands, including Kanton and Enderbury. Kiribati did not become a member of the UN until September 1999, although it had previously joined some of the organization's agencies.

In 1981 the Banaban community on Rabi accepted the British Government's earlier *ex gratia* offer of compensation, but they continued to seek self-government. The 1979 Constitution provided for the establishment of an independent commission of inquiry to review the political status of the Banabans three years after Kiribati had achieved independence, but the inquiry was not commissioned until 1985.

The first general election since independence took place in March–April 1982. The members of the new Maneaba all sat as independents. In accordance with the 1979 Constitution, the legislature nominated from among its members candidates for the country's first presidential election, to be held on the basis of direct popular vote. President Tabai was confirmed in office at the election in May. The Government resigned in December, after the Maneaba had twice rejected proposals to increase salaries for civil servants. The legislature was dissolved, and a general election took place in January 1983. The formation of the new Maneaba necessitated a further presidential election in February, at which Tabai was re-elected for a third term of office. He was returned to office in May 1987 (following a general election in March). The May 1991 legislative election was followed by a presidential election in July, at which the former Vice-President, Teatao Teannaki, narrowly defeated Roniti Teiwaki to replace Tabai, who had served the maximum number of presidential terms permitted by the Constitution.

In 1992 the Maneaba approved an opposition motion urging the Government to seek compensation from Japan for damage caused during the Second World War. The intention to seek compensation was reiterated by President Teburoro Tito (see below) in late 1994.

In May 1994 the Government was defeated on a motion of confidence, following opposition allegations that government ministers had misused travel allowances. The Maneaba was dissolved, and at legislative elections in July five cabinet ministers lost their seats. Of the newly elected members, 13 were supporters of the Maneaban Te Mauri, while only eight were known to support the previously dominant National Progressive Party grouping. At the presidential election in September Teburoro Tito, of the Maneaban Te Mauri, was elected, receiving 51.1% of the total votes. The new President declared that reducing Kiribati's dependence on foreign aid would be a major objective for his Government. He also announced his intention to pursue civil and criminal action against members of the previous administration for alleged misuse of public funds while in office.

In 1995 a committee was created with the aim of assessing public opinion regarding possible amendments to the Constitution. In March 1998 more than 200 delegates attended a Constitutional Review Convention in Bairiki to consider the recommendations of a report presented to the Government in 1996, which included equalizing the status of men and women regarding the citizenship rights of foreigners marrying I-Kiribati and changes to the structure of the Council of State. Leaders of the Banaban community in Rabi, Fiji, were also consulted during 1998 as part of the review process.

A general election, held in September 1998 and contested by a record 191 candidates, failed to produce a conclusive result, necessitating a second round of voting one week later, at which the Government and opposition each lost seven seats. The new Maneaba convened in October, when it selected three presidential candidates. At a presidential election in November Tito was re-elected with 52.3% of total votes cast, defeating Dr Harry Tong, who obtained 45.8% of votes, and Ambreroti Nikora, with 1.8%.

In mid-1999 John Kum Kee, a member of the Maneaba, was sentenced to four years' imprisonment, having been convicted of bribing a customs official and evasion of customs duty. Controversy continued in 1999 regarding the renamed Millennium Island (previously Caroline Island). The island had been renamed in 1997 in an attempt to promote it as a tourist destination for the year 2000. In 1994 Kiribati had moved the international date-line to incorporate the Line and Phoenix Islands groups (including Millennium Island) in the same time zone as the Gilbert group, thus creating a large eastward anomaly in the date-line. Millennium Island's position as the first place to celebrate the New Year, however, was subsequently confirmed. In early 2000, however, opposition politicians severely criticized the Government for failing to attract the predicted numbers of tourists to the islands' millennium celebrations, despite expenditure of more than $A1m. Meanwhile, in April 1999 the Kiribati Government reiterated its desire to acquire Baker, Howland and Jarvis Islands (see US External Territories) from the USA, citing the potential economic value of their fishing resources.

In late 1999 concerns were expressed by a Pacific media organization after a New Zealand journalist working for Agence France-Presse was banned from entering Kiribati. The Kiribati Government claimed that a series of articles by the correspondent, unfavourable to Kiribati, which had been published in a regional magazine, were biased and sensationalist. In December former President Ieremia Tabai and a former member of the Maneaba, Atiera Tetoa, were fined, having been convicted of importing telecommunications equipment without a permit. They had launched Newair FM, an independent commercial radio station, 12 months previously; it had been immediately suspended and a criminal investigation was instigated by the police. Tabai subsequently established Kiribati's first private newspaper, the *Kiribati Newstar*, in an attempt to reduce the Government's control over the media in the islands. Its first published edition coincided with Media Freedom Week in May 2000.

In November 2000 the Vice-President and Minister for Home Affairs and Rural Development, Tewarika Tentoa, collapsed while addressing the Maneaba and died. The post of Vice-President was subsequently combined with the cabinet portfolio of finance and economic planning.

Campaigning for the general election during November 2002 was characterized by numerous allegations of improper conduct. Observers noted that officials from the Chinese embassy in Tarawa, accompanied by government candidates, had been donating gifts to the local community in the weeks preceding the election. (The Government had recently amended the Elections Act to allow gifts to be distributed to the public by candidates during their electoral campaigns, a practice that had been banned hitherto.) The opposition, which had stated its intention to close the Chinese satellite-tracking station (based on South Tarawa—see below) if elected, claimed that this action constituted a clear attempt to influence voters. Moreover, under a newly amended Newspaper Registration Act, Tito ordered police to seize opposition election pamphlets in November. Further allegations that the Government was attempting to stifle freedom of expression were made by former President Iremia Tabai, whoses private radio station was finally granted a licence to broadcast in December, following delays totalling almost four years in issuing the permit.

A total of 176 candidates contested the general election on 29 November 2002. The Government suffered significant losses with 14 of its members (including seven ministers) failing to retain their seats. The presidential election was postponed from its original date and finally took place on 25 February 2003. At the poll Tito received 14,160 votes, while the opposition candidate Taberannang Timeon secured 13,613. Tito was sworn in for his third term as President on 28 February and many of his former opponents in the legislature were expected to cross the floor to support him. However, in late March Tito was narrowly defeated on a motion of 'no confidence' and his Government was replaced by an interim administration, the Council of State (comprising the Speaker, the Chief Justice and the Public Service Commissioner). In accordance with the Constitution, another general election took place on 9 and 14 May, at which supporters of Tito secured a majority of seats. A presidential election took place in early July at which the opposition candidate, Anote Tong, narrowly defeated his brother, Harry Tong. Anote Tong's electoral campaign, which had focused on his pledge to review the lease of the Chinese satellite-tracking station on South Tarawa, had been characterized by a series of personal attacks on his brother.

In early November 2003 President Anote Tong announced the establishment of diplomatic relations with Taiwan. The Government's decision to switch its allegiance from the People's Republic of China to Taiwan caused considerable controversy within Kiribati and the region. Several hundred people staged a protest in Tarawa against the Government's decision, claiming that it had been made in return for Taiwanese funding of Anote Tong's electoral campaign. The President strongly refuted this allegation, but did, however, state that Taiwan had offered extensive development funds to Kiribati for adopting its position. By late November it was reported that Chinese technicians were dismantling the satellite-tracking station, which had played an important role in China's recent first manned space flight. The Chinese embassy, however, remained open while China requested that Kiribati reconsider its decision. Despite its efforts, which, according to many commentators, were motivated largely by the islands' strategic importance to China, in late November that country suspended diplomatic relations with Kiribati. In the same week the police in Kiribati announced the launch of an investigation into the death threats received by President Tong, believed to be from a Chinese source. A Taiwanese embassy was opened in Tarawa in January 2004. The continued presence of Chinese officials in Kiribati (three diplomats remained as caretakers of the Chinese embassy building in Tarawa in mid-2004) caused the authorities some concern. In May 2005, as part of a diplomatic tour of Pacific nations, President Chen Shui-bian of Taiwan reportedly became the first foreign head of state to visit Kiribati in an official capacity.

In November 2004 a 20-strong police riot squad travelled to the island of Butaritari, where a village dispute had led to violent clashes in which one man was killed and six houses burned. Police arrested at least seven people in connection with the riot.

As a result of discussions held at the Pacific Islands Forum summit meeting in Kiribati in October 2000, Japan announced that it was willing to negotiate compensation claims with the islanders for damage caused during the Second World War. Furthermore, a six-day visit by President Tito to Japan in February 2001 resulted in a number of informal agreements aimed at enhancing relations between the two countries. These included a decision to try to resolve a dispute over tuna fishing, caused by Japan's refusal to sign a convention aimed at protecting tuna stocks in the central and western Pacific Ocean and agreements to address their differences over whaling and nuclear-fuel shipments. Tito also appeared to modify his position on nuclear energy following the visit to Japan, stating that emissions of harmful 'greenhouse gases' could be reduced by replacing fossil with nuclear fuel.

In September 1995 Kiribati severed relations with France, in protest at the French Government's decision to renew nuclear-weapons testing at Mururoa Atoll in French Polynesia.

Reports that Palmyra Atoll (a privately owned uninhabited US territory some 200 km north of Kiribati's northern Line Islands) was to be sold and used by a US company for the storage of nuclear waste prompted a unanimous resolution of the Maneaba, in May 1996, urging the Government to convey to the US Government the islanders' concerns over the proposals. The islanders' anxieties centred largely on Palmyra's proximity to Kiribati, coupled with the belief that the atoll's fragility and porous structure made it an unstable environment for the storage of highly toxic materials. In November 2000, however, Palmyra was purchased by The Nature Conservancy, a conservation group that planned to preserve the natural state of the atoll.

Owing to the high rate of population growth within the territory (about 2% per year) and, in particular, the situation of over-population on South Tarawa and its associated social and economic problems, it was announced in 1988 that nearly 5,000 inhabitants were to be resettled on outlying atolls, mainly in the Line Islands. In November 2004 the Government announced a major new initiative, supported by the UN Development Programme and the Asian Development Bank, to establish up to four new urban areas in the outer islands as part of ongoing efforts to ease the overcrowding of South Tarawa.

A Chinese satellite-tracking station was opened on South Tarawa in late 1997 but was dismantled in late 2003 following the suspension of diplomatic relations between the two countries (see above). Sea Launch, an international consortium led by the US Boeing Commercial Space Company, also announced plans to undertake a rocket-launching project from a converted oil-rig near the islands. A prototype satellite was launched in March 1999, and commercial operations began in late 1999. Kiribati, which, together with the South Pacific Regional Environment Programme (SPREP, see p. 394), had expressed concerns regarding the potential negative environmental impact of the site, was not expected to benefit financially from the project, as the consortium had sought to carry out its activities in international waters near the outer limits of the islands' exclusive economic zone. The US authorities dismissed environmental concerns about the negative impact of the site (particularly the dumping of large quantities of waste fuel in the islands' waters), which were expressed by both the Government of Kiribati and SPREP in 1998. These fears were compounded in March 2000 after a rocket launched from the site crashed, and, furthermore, Sea Launch refused to disclose where it had landed. In November 1999 it was announced that the Government of Kiribati and the National Space Development Agency of Japan had reached agreement on the proposed establishment of a space-vehicle launching and landing facility on Kiritimati. In the following year the Japanese organization, which was subsequently renamed the Japan Aerospace Exploration Agency, was also given permission by the Kiribati Government to use land and runway facilities on the island, free of charge, until 2020 and to construct a 100–150-room hotel.

In 1989 a UN report on the 'greenhouse effect' (the heating of the earth's atmosphere, and a resultant rise in sea-level as a consequence of pollution) listed Kiribati as one of the countries that would completely disappear beneath the sea in the 21st century, unless drastic action were taken. None of the land on the islands is more than two metres above sea-level, making the country extremely vulnerable to the effects of climate change. It was feared that a rise in sea-level would not only cause flooding, but would also upset the balance between sea and fresh water (below the coral sands), rendering water supplies undrinkable. In late 1997 President Tito strongly criticized the Australian Government's refusal, at the Conference of the Parties to the Framework Convention on Climate Change (under the auspices of the UN Environment Programme, see p. 58) in Kyoto, Japan, to reduce its emission of gases known to contribute to the 'greenhouse effect'. In April 2001 the USA's decision to reject the Kyoto Protocol to the UN's Framework Convention on Climate Change was widely criticized. In March 2002 Kiribati, Tuvalu and the Maldives announced their decision to take legal action against the USA for its refusal to sign the Kyoto Protocol. In January 2006 the Australian Government reiterated its position, declaring that it believed there to be no evidence to suggest that the populations of the Pacific islands were in any imminent danger of being displaced by rising sea-levels.

A report released by the World Bank in 2000 listed the flooding and loss of low-lying areas, more intense cyclones and droughts, the failure of subsistence crops and coastal fisheries, the death of coral reefs and the spread of mosquito-borne diseases such as malaria and dengue fever as consequences of the 'greenhouse effect' on Pacific island nations. Meanwhile, a state of emergency was declared in Kiribati in early 1999, owing to one of the worst droughts ever recorded in the islands. In mid-1999 it was announced that two of the country's uninhabited coral reefs had been submerged as a result of the 'greenhouse effect'. Concern among the islanders intensified in early 2001 when many of the causeways linking villages on Tarawa atoll were flooded by high tides, and by the mid-2000s increasingly high 'king tides' were reported to be causing regular flooding on the islands.

In March 2006 President Anote Tong announced that one of the world's largest marine reserves was to be established in Kiribati. Commercial fishing was to be banned in the Phoenix Islands Protected Area, which encompassed an area of 184,700 sq km and would afford protection to more than 120 species of coral and to 520 species of fish. A leading US aquarium and an international conservation group were to assist in the creation of the reserve.

Government

Legislative power is vested in the unicameral Maneaba ni Maungatabu. It has 39 members elected by universal adult suffrage for four years (subject to dissolution), one nominated representative of the Banaban community and, if he is not an elected member, the Attorney-General as an *ex-officio* member. The Head of State is the Beretitenti (President), who is also Head of Government. The President is elected by direct popular vote. The President governs with the assistance of the Vice-President and Cabinet, whom he appoints from among members of the Maneaba. Executive authority is vested in the Cabinet, which is responsible to the Maneaba.

Defence

Kiribati has no defence forces: defence assistance is provided by Australia and New Zealand.

Economic Affairs

In 2004, according to estimates by the World Bank, Kiribati's gross national income (GNI), measured at average 2002–04 prices, was US $95.0m., equivalent to US $970 per head. During 1995–2004, it was estimated, the population increased by an average of 2.3% per year, while gross domestic product (GDP) per head increased, in real terms, by an estimated average of 2.0% per year. Overall GDP increased, in real terms, at an average annual rate of 4.3% in 1995–2004. According to estimates by the Asian Development Bank (ADB), GDP contracted by 4.0% in 2003 but expanded by 3.3% in 2004 and by 0.3% in 2005.

According to figures from the ADB, agriculture (including fishing), contributed an estimated 10.3% of monetary GDP in 2004. In 2003, according to FAO, agriculture engaged 26% of the economically active population. The principal cash crop is coconut, yielding copra. Export revenue from copra continued to decline in the early 2000s, decreasing from $A2.5m. in 2000 to less than $A2.0m. in 2001 and to $A0.7m. in 2002. In March 2002, however, construction of a new copra mill, near Betio port, began. Bananas, screw-pine (*Pandanus*), breadfruit and papaya are cultivated as food crops. The cultivation of seaweed began on Tabuaeran in the mid-1980s. In 2002, however, seaweed provided only 2.2% of total export earnings. Pigs and chickens are kept. Fish provided only 1.8% of export earnings in 2000 (compared with 46.2% in 1990). Revenue from fish exports decreased from $A353,000 in 2001 to just $A16,000 in 2002. Pet fish have been a significant export commodity, contributing 13.6% of export earnings in 1999 (although this figure declined to 1.9% in 2000 and to less than 0.3% in 2002). The sale of fishing licences to foreign fleets (notably from South Korea, Japan, the People's Republic of China, Taiwan and the USA) has provided an important source of income: revenue from the sale of fishing licences reached a record $A52m. in 2001 but had declined to $A24.5m. by 2004. The GDP of the agricultural sector increased at an average annual rate of 9.2% in 1995–2004. According to figures from the ADB, agricultural GDP increased by 33.4% in 2003 and by 11.9% in 2004.

Industry (including manufacturing, construction and power) contributed an estimated 13.2% of monetary GDP in 2004. Industrial GDP increased by an average of 12.0% per year in 1995–2004. Compared with the previous year, industrial GDP was estimated by the ADB to have contracted by 1.1% in 2003, before expanding by 1.8% in 2004.

Mining of phosphate rock on the island of Banaba, which ceased in 1979, formerly provided some 80% of export earnings. Interest from a phosphate reserve fund (the Revenue Equalization Reserve Fund—RERF), established in 1956, continues to be an important source of income (see below). The production of solar-evaporated salt for export to other islands of the Pacific (for use on fishing vessels with brine refrigeration systems) began on Kiritimati in 1985.

Manufacturing, which contributed an estimated 0.9% of monetary GDP in 2004, is confined to the small-scale production of coconut-based products, soap, foods, handicrafts, furniture, leather goods and garments. Manufacturing GDP increased by an annual average of 1.9% in 1995–2004. In 2003, compared with the previous year, the GDP of the manufacturing sector increased by an 10.5%, and by 11.5% in 2004.

Production of electrical energy increased from 14.0m. kWh in 2002 to 17.8m. kWh in 2003. Mineral fuels accounted for an estimated 14.0% of total import costs in 2001. In August 2001 the European Union (EU) announced that it planned to fund the introduction of 1,500 new solar energy systems, valued at more than $A6m., to Kiribati. Moreover, in May 2003 the Government announced the completion of a Japanese-funded programme to construct a new power station, to install two new generating units and to upgrade 16 km of power lines. The project, which cost a total of US $11m. to implement, was expected to ensure a power supply sufficient to meet Kiribati's increasing demand.

Services provided 76.5% of monetary GDP in 2004. Tourism makes a significant contribution to the economy: the trade, hotels and bars sector provided an estimated 11.9% of GDP in 2004. Tourist arrivals at Tarawa and Kiritimati declined from 4,842 in 2001, in which year receipts from tourism reached $A3.0m., to 4,288 in 2002 and to 3,676 in 2003. An estimated 2,882 visitors arrived in Kiribati in 2004. The GDP of the services sector increased at an annual average rate of 2.5% in 1995–2004. According to the ADB, the services sector's GDP decreased by 5.7% in 2003 but increased by 3.7% in 2004.

In 2004, according to the ADB, Kiribati recorded a trade deficit of an estimated US $80.5m., and a deficit of $12.8m. on the current account of the balance of payments. In that year Kiribati's trade deficit reached the equivalent of 89.3% of GDP. According to the ADB, the trade deficit increased from US $38m. in 2003 to $42m. in 2004, reaching $43m. in 2005. In 2004 the ADB estimated that the deficit on the current account was equivalent to 3.3%% of GDP, compared with 0.9% in 2003. In 2004 the principal sources of imports were Australia (36.0%) and Fiji (24.7%). The principal recipients of exports in that year were France (45.3%) and Japan (29.1%). The major imports in 2004 were food and live animals (25.1%), machinery and transport equipment (25.3%), manufactures (16.3%), mineral fuels (14.0%), beverages and tobacco (6.0%), and chemicals (3.9%). The major domestic exports were copra, seaweed and shark fins.

Budgetary expenditure for 2002, announced in December 2001, was projected at $A77.9m., 15% less than the revised estimates for 2001, and required a drawdown of $A16.7m. from the RERF. In 2003, according to the ADB, the government deficit increased sharply to reach the equivalent of 28.2% of GDP. In April 2003 the interim administration enacted a budget providing for expenditure of $A32m. over the next five months. The country is reliant on foreign assistance for its development budget. Official development assistance increased from a total of US $12.4m. in 2001 to US $20.9m. in 2002. Australia is a major provider of development assistance, with emphasis on the management of human resources, governance, health, education and improved customs procedures, within the framework of a new co-operation strategy. In 2005/06 aid from Australia was projected at $A12.5m. and aid from New Zealand was expected to total $NZ3.14m. Kiribati's total external debt was estimated by the ADB to have risen from US $21m. in 2004 to $24m. in 2005. In 2004 the cost of debt-servicing was equivalent to 4.1% of revenue from exports of goods and services. The annual rate of inflation averaged 2.2% in 1996–2004. Consumer prices increased by an annual average of 2.6% in 2003 and of 2.5% in 2004. About 1.6% of the labour force were unemployed in 2000. Only around 8,600 people, equivalent to less than 20% of the working-age population, were formally employed in 2001.

Kiribati is a member of the Pacific Community (see p. 350), the Pacific Islands Forum (see p. 352) and the Asian Development Bank (ADB, see p. 169); it is an associate member of the UN Economic and Social Commission for Asia and the Pacific (ESCAP, see p. 33), and is a signatory to the South Pacific Regional Trade and Economic Co-operation Agreement (SPARTECA, see p. 354) and to the Lomé Conventions and successor Cotonou Agreement (see p. 277) with the EU. The Council of Micronesian Government Executives, of which Kiribati was a founder member in 1996, aims to facilitate discussion of economic developments in the region and to examine possibilities for reducing the considerable cost of shipping essential goods between the islands.

According to UN criteria, Kiribati is one of the world's least developed nations. The Government's policy of subsidizing copra producers, following a sharp fall in world prices of the commodity, had a negative impact on the economy; in 2001 these subsidies totalled $A2m. Kiribati remains vulnerable to fluctuations in international copra prices. In the longer term, furthermore, the country is highly vulnerable to rising sea-levels (see Recent History). Kiribati's extremely limited export base and dependence on imports of almost all essential commodities result in a permanent trade deficit, which in most years has been only partially offset by revenue from fishing licence fees, interest earned on the RERF and remittances from I-Kiribati working overseas. The majority of the latter group is comprised of seamen working on foreign ships, particularly Japanese fishing boats and cruise liners. In 2000 there were some 2,000 of these overseas workers. Total remittances from overseas workers were estimated to have reached almost US $6.3m. in 2003. The RERF usually provides the Government with investment income equivalent to around 33% of GDP per year. At the end of 2003 the value of the fund was put at US $513.3m. The Government also holds substantial offshore assets through the Kiribati Provident Fund. In the first quarter of 2005 it was estimated that the country's total official reserves were sufficient to cover the cost of more than four years of imports. In early 2003 Kiribati established a non-government body to secure US $840,000 in EU funding under the Cotonou Agreement, which would be spent on projects over the next five years. In addition to the regular allocations provided by Australia and New Zealand (see above), substantial development finance was expected to be received from Taiwan following the establishment of diplomatic relations in late 2003. By 2005, through the ADB, Taiwan was assisting with various infrastructural projects (as was Japan) and with agricultural training programmes. Attempts to encourage greater investment in the country's private sector, which would allow the creation of jobs and the broadening of the islands' narrow base of exports, continued. The Government's National Development Strategy for 2004–07, released in November 2003, stressed the importance of economic growth, fair distribution, the performance of the public sector, the management of change, the conservation of physical assets and the sustainable use of financial reserves. In its Country Strategy and Program Update on Kiribati (2006–2007), released in January 2006, the ADB reiterated its support for the National Development Strategy. Since 2000 the ADB has increased efforts to assist Kiribati in the development of the outer islands. Initiatives included the establishment of a trust fund and the development of an investment project covering several different sectors in an attempt to promote growth and investment opportunities. The ADB also proposed to offer a loan of US $10m. to assist in the establishment of the Kiritimati Island Growth Center in 2007. Following the creation of the Phoenix Islands Protected Area in 2006 (see Recent History), the sale of fewer fishing licences was expected to lead to a decline in the country's revenue, but it was hoped that this would be offset by payments from an endowment fund established for the purposes of financing the cost of the marine reserve's management. In 2007, furthermore, the Government hoped to expand its sources of revenue through the introduction of a broad-based tax on sales in both the wholesale and retail sectors. The ADB forecast an increase in real GDP of 0.8% in 2006 and of 0.7% in 2007.

Education

Education is compulsory for nine years between the ages of six and 15 years, comprising six years of primary school and three years of junior secondary school, an initiative introduced in 1998. Students may then continue at secondary school for a further three years. Every atoll is provided with at least one primary and junior secondary school. An estimated 92% of children aged six to 12 receive primary education. In 2001 there were 88 primary schools and 14 secondary schools. In 2002/03 there were 14,823 pupils enrolled in primary school and 10,334 students enrolled in secondary school. The Government administers a technical college and training colleges for teachers, nurses and seamen (the last, the Marine Training Centre, trains about 200 seamen each year for employment by overseas shipping companies). An extra-mural centre of the University of the South Pacific (based in Fiji) is located on South Tarawa. In 2001 the Government allocated $A16.1m. (equivalent to 17.5% of total budgetary expenditure) to education.

Public Holidays

2006: 1 January (New Year), 14–17 April (Easter), 18 May (National Health Day), 11 July (National Church Day), 12–16 July (National Day Celebrations), 7 August (Youth Day), 11 December (Human Rights and Peace Day), 25–26 December (Christmas).

2007: 1 January (New Year), 6–9 April (Easter), 18 May (National Health Day), 11 July (National Church Day), 12–16 July (National Day Celebrations), 7 August (Youth Day), 11 December (Human Rights and Peace Day), 25–26 December (Christmas).

Statistical Survey

Source (unless otherwise stated): Statistics Office, Ministry of Finance and Economic Planning, POB 67, Bairiki, Tarawa; tel. 21082; fax 21307.

AREA AND POPULATION

Area: 810.5 sq km (312.9 sq miles). *Principal Atolls* (sq km): Banaba (island) 6.29 Tarawa 31.02 (North 15.26, South 15.76); Abemama 27.37; Tabiteuea 37.63 (North 25.78, South 11.85); Total Gilbert group (incl. others) 285.52; Kanton (Phoenix Is) 9.15; Teraina (Fanning) 33.73; Kiritimati (Christmas—Line Is) 388.39.

Population: 77,658 at census of 7 November 1995; 84,494 (males 41,646, females 42,848) at census of 7 November 2000; 89,700 (estimate) at mid-2004. *Principal Atolls* (2000): Banaba (island) 276; Abaiang 5,794; Tarawa 41,194 (North 4,477, South—including Bairiki, the capital—36,717); Tabiteuea 4,582 (North 3,365, South 1,217); Total Gilbert group (incl. others) 78,158; Kanton (Phoenix Is) 61; Kiritimati 3,431; Total Line and Phoenix Is (incl. others) 6,336. *Mid-2003* (UN estimate, incl. suburbs) South Tarawa (including Bairiki, the capital) 41,530 (Source: UN, *World Urbanization Prospects: The 2003 Revision*).

Density (mid-2004): 110.7 per sq km.

Ethnic Groups (census of 2000): Micronesians 83,452; Polynesians 641; Europeans 154; Others 247; Total 84,494.

Principal Towns: (population in '000, 1990): Bairiki (capital) 18.1; Bikenibeu 5.1; Taburao 3.5; Butaritari 3.2. Source: Stefan Helders, *World Gazetteer* (internet www.world-gazetteer.com). *Mid-2003* (UN estimate, incl. suburbs) South Tarawa (including Bairiki, the capital) 41,530 (Source: UN, *World Urbanization Prospects: The 2003 Revision*).

Births, Marriages and Deaths: Registered live births (1996) 2,299 (birth rate 29.5 per 1,000); Marriages (registrations, 1988) 352 (marriage rate 5.2 per 1,000); Death rate (estimate, 1995) 7 per 1,000.

Expectation of Life (WHO estimates, years at birth): 65 (males 62; females 67) in 2003. Source: WHO, *World Health Report*.

Employment (paid employees, 1995, provisional): Agriculture, hunting, forestry and fishing 487; Manufacturing 104; Electricity, gas and water 182; Construction 215; Trade, restaurants and hotels 1,026; Transport, storage and communications 710; Financing, insurance, real estate and business services 349; Community, social and personal services 4,778; *Total employed* 7,848. Source: UN, *Statistical Yearbook for Asia and the Pacific*. *Mid-2003* (estimates, '000 persons employed): Agriculture, etc. 10; Total 38 (Source: FAO).

HEALTH AND WELFARE
Key Indicators

Total Fertility Rate (children per woman, 2003): 4.0.

Under-5 Mortality Rate (per 1,000 live births, 2004): 65.

Physicians (per 1,000 head, 1998): 0.30.

Hospital Beds (per 1,000 head, 1990): 4.27.

Health Expenditure (2002): US $ per head (PPP): 141.

Health Expenditure (2002): % of GDP: 8.0.

Health Expenditure (2002): public (% of total): 98.8.

Access to Water (% of persons, 2002): 64.

Access to Sanitation (% of persons, 2002): 39.

For sources and definitions, see explanatory note on p. vi.

AGRICULTURE, ETC.

Principal Crops (FAO estimates, '000 metric tons, 2004): Taro (Coco yam) 2.0; Other roots and tubers 7.8; Coconuts 103; Copra 8.5; Vegetables 5.9; Bananas 5.0; Other fruits 1.3.

Livestock (FAO estimates, '000 head, year ending September 2004): Pigs 12.2; Chickens 460.

Livestock Products (FAO estimates, metric tons, 2004): Pig meat 860; Poultry meat 459; Hen eggs 240.

Fishing ('000 metric tons, live weight, 2003): Capture 32.0 (Snappers 3.7; Flyingfishes 0.5; Jacks and crevalles 2.7; Skipjack tuna 3.9; Emperors 2.9; Clupeoids 0.4; Marine molluscs 5.4); Aquaculture 0.0; Total catch 32.0. Figures exclude aquatic plants ('000 metric tons): 3.9 (all aquaculture).

Source: FAO.

INDUSTRY

Copra Production (metric tons): 6,101 in 2002; 10,501 in 2003; 12,334 in 2004.

Electric Energy (million kWh): 15.13 in 2001; 13.98 in 2002; 17.76 in 2003.

Source: Asian Development Bank, *Key Indicators of Developing Asian and Pacific Countries*.

FINANCE

Currency and Exchange Rates: Australian currency: 100 cents = 1 Australian dollar ($A). *Sterling, US Dollar and Euro Equivalents* (30 December 2005): £1 sterling = $A2.3469; US $1 = $A1.3630; €1 = $A1.6079; $A100 = £42.61 = US $73.37 = €62.19. *Average Exchange Rate* (US $ per Australian dollar): 1.5419 in 2003; 1.3598 in 2004; 1.3095 in 2005..

Budget ($A million, 2001): *Revenue*: Tax revenue 25.8; Other current revenue 1.5; Capital revenue 0.0; Total 27.3. *Expenditure*: General public services 8.7; Public order and safety 5.8; Education 16.1; Health 10.4; Welfare and environment 1.4; Community amenities 1.9; Agriculture and fishing 2.5; Construction 2.3; Communication 2.1; Commerce and labour affairs 2.8; Others 37.9; Total 91.8.

Cost of Living (Consumer Price Index for urban areas of Tarawa; base: 1996 = 100): 117.9 in 2002; 121.0 in 2003; 118.7 in 2004.

Expenditure on the Gross Domestic Product ($A million at current prices, 2002): Government final consumption expenditure 21; Private final consumption expenditure 42; Gross fixed capital formation 8; *Total domestic expenditure* 71; Exports of goods and services 56; *Less* Imports of goods and services 31; Statistical discrepancy 2; *GDP in purchasers' values* 98. Source: UN, *Statistical Yearbook for Asia and the Pacific*.

Gross Domestic Product by Economic Activity ($A '000 at current factor cost, 2004): Agriculture (incl. fishing) 7,435; Manufacturing 665; Electricity, gas and water 2,277; Construction 6,600; Trade, hotels and bars 8,608; Transport and communications 3,455; Finance (incl. imputed bank charges) 715; Public administration 37,836; Others (incl. owner-occupied dwelling) 4,795; *Sub-total* 72,386; Indirect taxes, *less* subsidies 17,700; *GDP in market prices* 90,086. Source: Asian Development Bank, *Key Indicators of Developing Asian and Pacific Countries*.

Balance of Payments (US $ '000, 2004, estimates): Exports of goods 8,855; Imports of goods –89,316; *Trade balance* –80,461; Exports of services and income 91,588; Imports of services and income –45,080; *Balance on goods, services and income* –33,953; Current transfers received 23,736; Current transfers paid –2,540; *Current balance* –12,757; Capital account (net) 17,042; Portfolio investment (net) 18,200; Other investments 4,000; Net errors and omissions –42,085; *Overall balance* –15,600. Source: Asian Development Bank, *Key Indicators of Developing Asian and Pacific Countries*.

EXTERNAL TRADE

Principal Commodities (estimates, $A '000): *Imports f.o.b.* (2001): Food and live animals 18,855; Beverages and tobacco 4,504; Mineral fuels, lubricants, etc. 10,515; Chemicals 2,954; Basic manufactures 12,220; Machinery and transport equipment 18,953; Miscellaneous manufactured articles 5,022; Total (incl. others) 75,008. *Exports f.o.b.* (2002): Copra 746; Seaweed 140; Pet fish 16; Shark fins 328; Total (incl. others) 6,322. *2002:* Total imports 91,585. *2003:* Total imports 80,000 (estimate).

Principal Trading Partners (US $ million, 2004): *Imports*: Australia 20.7; Fiji 14.2; Japan 6.3; New Zealand 5.0; Total (incl. others) 57.5. *Exports* (incl. re-exports): France 7.8; Japan 5.0; USA 1.6; Total (incl. others) 17.2.

Source: Asian Development Bank, *Key Indicators of Developing Asian and Pacific Countries*.

TRANSPORT

Road Traffic (motor vehicles registered on South Tarawa, 2000): Motor cycles 702; Passenger cars 477; Buses 10; Trucks 267; Minibuses 392; Others 13; Total 1,861.

Shipping: *Merchant Fleet* (registered, at 31 December 2004): 8 vessels; total displacement 4,198 grt. (Source: Lloyd's Register-Fairplay, *World Fleet Statistics*. *International Sea-borne Freight Traffic* ('000 metric tons, 1990): Goods loaded 15; Goods unloaded 26 (Source: UN, *Monthly Bulletin of Statistics*).

Civil Aviation (traffic on scheduled services, 1998): Passengers carried 28,000; Passenger-km 11 million; Total ton-km 2 million. Source: UN, *Statistical Yearbook*.

KIRIBATI

TOURISM

Foreign Tourist Arrivals (at Tarawa and Kiritimati): 4,288 in 2002; 3,676 in 2003; 2,882 in 2004 (provisional).

Tourism Receipts ($A million): 2.1 in 1999; 2.2 in 2000; 3.0 in 2001.

COMMUNICATIONS MEDIA

Radio Receivers (1997): 17,000 in use.
Television Receivers (1997): 1,000 in use.
Telephones (main lines in use, 2002): 4,000.
Facsimile Machines (1996): 200 in use.
Mobile Cellular Telephones (subscribers, 2002): 545.
Personal Computers ('000 in use, 2001): 2.
Internet Users ('000, 2002): 2.
Non-daily Newspapers (2002): 2; estimated combined circulation 3,600.

Sources: UNESCO, *Statistical Yearbook*; UN, *Statistical Yearbook*; International Telecommunication Union; Australian Press Council.

EDUCATION

Primary (2002 unless otherwise indicated): 88 schools (2001); 14,823 students; 660 teachers.

Secondary (2002 unless otherwise indicated): 14 schools (2001); 10,334 students; 561 teachers.

Teacher-training (2001): 198 students; 22 teachers.

Vocational (2001): 1,303 students; 17 teachers.

Adult Literacy Rate (UNESCO estimates): 92.5% (males 93%; females 92%) in 2001. Source: UNESCO, *Assessment of Resources, Best Practices and Gaps in Gender, Science and Technology in Kiribati*.

Directory

The Constitution

A new Constitution was promulgated at independence on 12 July 1979. The main provisions are as follows:

The Constitution states that Kiribati is a sovereign democratic Republic and that the Constitution is the supreme law. It guarantees protection of all fundamental rights and freedoms of the individual and provides for the determination of citizenship.

The President, known as the Beretitenti, is Head of State and Head of the Government and presides over the Cabinet which consists of the Beretitenti, the Kauoman-ni-Beretitenti (Vice-President), the Attorney-General and not more than eight other ministers appointed by the Beretitenti from an elected parliament known as the Maneaba ni Maungatabu. The Constitution provided that the pre-independence Chief Minister became the first Beretitenti, but that in future the Beretitenti would be elected. After each general election for the Maneaba, the chamber nominates, from among its members, three or four candidates from whom the Beretitenti is elected by universal adult suffrage. Executive authority is vested in the Cabinet, which is directly responsible to the Maneaba ni Maungatabu. The Constitution also provides for a Council of State consisting of the Chairman of the Public Services Commission, the Chief Justice and the Speaker of the Maneaba.

Legislative power resides with the single-chamber Maneaba ni Maungatabu, composed of 40 members elected by universal adult suffrage for four years (subject to dissolution), one nominated member (see below) and the Attorney-General as an *ex-officio* member if he is not elected. The Maneaba is presided over by the Speaker, who is elected by the Maneaba from among persons who are not members of the Maneaba.

One chapter makes special provision for Banaba and the Banabans, stating that one seat in the Maneaba is reserved for a nominated member of the Banaban community. The Banabans' inalienable right to enter and reside in Banaba is guaranteed and, where any right over or interest in land there has been acquired by the Republic of Kiribati or by the Crown before independence, the Republic is required to hand back the land on completion of phosphate extraction. A Banaba Island Council is provided for, as is an independent commission of inquiry to review the provisions relating to Banaba.

The Constitution also makes provision for finance, for a Public Service and for an independent judiciary (see Judicial System).

The Government

HEAD OF STATE

President (Beretitenti): ANOTE TONG (elected 4 July 2003).
Vice-President (Kauoman-ni-Beretitenti): TEIMA ONORIO.

THE CABINET
(April 2006)

President and Minister for Foreign Affairs: ANOTE TONG.
Vice-President and Minister for Education, Youth and Sport Development: TEIMA ONORIO.

Minister for Commerce, Industry and Co-operatives: IOTEBA REDFERN.

Minister for Communications, Transport and Tourism Development: NAATAN TEEWE.

Minister for Environment, Lands and Agricultural Development: MARTIN TOFINGA.

Minister for Finance and Economic Development: NABUTI MWEMWENIKARAWA.

Minister for Health and Medical Services: NATANERA KIRATA.

Minister for Human Resources Development: BAURO TONGAAI.

Minister for Internal Affairs and Social Development: AMBEROTI NIKORA.

Minister for the Line and Phoenix Islands: TAWITA TEMOKU.

Minister for Natural Resources Development: TETABO NAKARA.

Minister for Public Works and Utilities: JAMES TAOM.

MINISTRIES

Office of the President (Beretitenti): POB 68, Bairiki, Tarawa; tel. 21183; fax 21145.

Ministry of Commerce, Industry and Co-operatives: POB 510, Betio, Tarawa; tel. 26158/26157; fax 26233; e-mail commerce@tskl.net.ki.

Ministry of Communications, Transport and Tourism Development: POB 487, Betio, Tarawa; tel. 26003/26435; fax 26193.

Ministry of Education, Youth and Sport Development: POB 263, Bikenibeu, Tarawa; tel. 28091/28033; fax 28222.

Ministry of the Environment, Lands and Agricultural Development: POB 234, Bikenibeu, Tarawa; tel. 28211/28071; fax 28334; e-mail ps@melad.gov.ki.

Ministry of Finance and Economic Development: POB 67, Bairiki, Tarawa; tel. 21802/21805; fax 21307.

Ministry of Foreign Affairs and Immigration: POB 68, Bairiki, Tarawa; tel. 21342; fax 21466; e-mail mfa@tskl.net.ki.

Ministry of Health and Medical Services: POB 268, Bikenibeu, Tarawa; tel. 28100; fax 28152.

Ministry of Human Resources and Development: POB 69, Bairiki, Tarawa; tel. 21068/21071; fax 21452.

Ministry of Internal Affairs and Social Development: POB 75, Bairiki, Tarawa; tel. 21092; fax 21133; e-mail homeaffairs@tskl.net.ki.

Ministry of Line and Phoenix Islands: Kiritimati Island; tel. 21449/81213; fax 81278.

Ministry of Natural Resources Development: POB 64, Bairiki, Tarawa; tel. 21099; fax 21120.

Ministry of Public Works and Utilities: POB 498, Betio, Tarawa; tel. 26192; fax 26172.

KIRIBATI

President and Legislature

PRESIDENT
Election, 4 July 2003

Candidate	Votes
Anote Tong	13,556
Harry Tong	12,457

A third candidate, Banuera Berina, won a small number of votes in the election

MANEABA NI MAUNGATABU
(House of Assembly)

This is a unicameral body comprising 40 elected members (most of whom formally present themselves for election as independent candidates), and one nominated representative of the Banaban community. A general election was held on 29 November 2002. However, in late March 2003, following its defeat on a motion of 'no confidence', the Government was replaced by an interim authority. A further general election was held on 9 and 14 May 2003, at which supporters of former President Teburoro Tito secured a majority of seats.

Speaker: TAOMATI IUTA.

Political Organizations

There are no organized political parties in Kiribati. However, loose groupings of individuals supporting similar policies do exist, the most prominent being the Maneaban Te Mauri (Protect the Maneaba), led by Teburoro Tito, the National Progressive Party, led by Teatao Teannaki, the Liberal Party, led by Tewareka Tentoa, and the Boutokan Te Koaua (Pillars of Truth), led by Dr Harry Tong.

Diplomatic Representation

EMBASSY AND HIGH COMMISSIONS IN KIRIBATI

Australia: POB 77, Bairiki, Tarawa; tel. 21184; fax 21904; e-mail AHC_Tarawa@dfat.gov.au; High Commissioner ANNE QUINANE.

China (Taiwan): Bairiki, Tarawa; tel. 22557; fax 22535; e-mail Kir@mofa.gov.tw; Ambassador SHIH-LIANG (SAMUEL) CHEN.

New Zealand: POB 53, Bairiki, Tarawa; tel. 21400; fax 21402; e-mail nzhc@tskl.net.ki; High Commissioner JOHN GOODMAN.

Judicial System

There are 24 Magistrates' Courts (each consisting of one presiding magistrate and up to eight other magistrates) hearing civil, criminal and land cases. When hearing civil or criminal cases, the presiding magistrate sits with two other magistrates, and when hearing land cases with four other magistrates. A single magistrate has national jurisdiction in civil and criminal matters. Appeal from the Magistrates' Courts lies, in civil and criminal matters, to a single judge of the High Court, and, in matters concerning land, divorce and inheritance, to the High Court's Land Division, which consists of a judge and two Land Appeal Magistrates.

The High Court of Kiribati is a superior court of record and has unlimited jurisdiction. It consists of the Chief Justice and a Puisne Judge. Appeal from a single judge of the High Court, both as a Court of the First Instance and in its appellate capacity, lies to the Kiribati Court of Appeal, which is also a court of record and consists of a panel of three judges.

All judicial appointments are made by the Beretitenti (President).

High Court
POB 501, Betio, Tarawa; tel. 26007; fax 26149; e-mail highcourt@tskl.net.ki.

Chief Justice: ROBIN MILLHOUSE.

Judges of the Kiribati Court of Appeal: ROBIN MILLHOUSE (President), Sir MAURICE CASEY, Sir MICHAEL HARDIE-BOYS, Sir DAVID TOMPKINS, PETER PENLINGTON.

Religion

CHRISTIANITY

Most of the population are Christians: 53.4% Roman Catholic and 39.2% members of the Kiribati Protestant Church, according to the 1990 census.

The Roman Catholic Church

Kiribati forms part of the diocese of Tarawa and Nauru, suffragan to the archdiocese of Suva (Fiji). At 31 December 2003 the diocese contained an estimated 48,908 adherents. The Bishop participates in the Catholic Bishops' Conference of the Pacific, based in Suva (Fiji).

Bishop of Tarawa and Nauru: Most Rev. PAUL EUSEBIUS MEA KAIUEA, Bishop's House, POB 79, Bairiki, Tarawa; fax 21401; e-mail cathchurch@tskl.net.ki.

The Anglican Communion

Kiribati is within the diocese of Polynesia, part of the Anglican Church in Aotearoa, New Zealand and Polynesia. The Bishop in Polynesia is resident in Fiji.

Protestant Church

Kiribati Protestant Church: POB 80, Bairiki, Tarawa; tel. 21195; fax 21453; f. 1988; Moderator Rev. BAITEKE NABETARI; Gen. Sec. Rev. TIAONTIN ARUE; 29,432 mems in 1998.

Other Churches

Seventh-day Adventist, Church of God and Assembly of God communities are also represented, as is the Church of Jesus Christ of Latter-day Saints (Mormon).

BAHÁ'Í FAITH

National Spiritual Assembly: POB 269, Bikenibeu, Tarawa; tel. and fax 28074; e-mail emi@tskl.net.ki; 2,400 mems resident in 100 localities in 1995.

The Press

Butim'aea Manin te Euangkerio: POB 80, Bairiki, Tarawa; tel. 21195; e-mail kpc@tskl.net.ki; f. 1913; Protestant Church newspaper; weekly; a monthly publication Te Kaotan te Ota is also produced; Editor Rev. TOOM TOAKAI.

Kiribati Business Link: Bairiki, Tarawa; English.

Kiribati Newstar: POB 10, Bairiki, Tarawa; tel. 21652; fax 21671; e-mail newstar@tskl.net.ki; internet www.users.bigpond.com/kiribati_newstar; f. 2000; independent; weekly; English and I-Kiribati; Editor-in-Chief NGAUEA UATIOA.

Te Itoi ni Kiribati: POB 231, Bikenibeu, Tarawa; tel. 28138; fax 21341; f. 1914; Roman Catholic Church newsletter; monthly; circ. 2,300.

Te Uekera: Broadcasting and Publications Authority, POB 78, Bairiki, Tarawa; tel. 21162; fax 21096; f. 1945; weekly; English and I-Kiribati; Editor TIBWERE BOBO; circ. 5,000.

Broadcasting and Communications

TELECOMMUNICATIONS

Telecom Kiribati Ltd: Bairiki, Tarawa; Gen. Man. ENOTA INGINTAU.

Telecom Services Kiribati Ltd: POB 72, Bairiki, Tarawa; tel. 21446; fax 21424; e-mail ceo@tskl.net.ki; internet www.tski.net.ki; owned by Govt of Kiribati; Gen. Man. STUART EASTWARD; CEO CLIFF MACALPINE.

BROADCASTING

Regulatory Authority

Broadcasting and Publications Authority: POB 78, Bairiki, Tarawa; tel. 21187; fax 21096.

Radio

Radio Kiribati: Broadcasting and Publications Authority, POB 78, Bairiki, Tarawa; tel. 21187; fax 21096; f. 1954; statutory body; station Radio Kiribati broadcasting on SW and MW transmitters; programmes in I-Kiribati (90%) and English (10%); some advertising; Gen. Man. TANIERI TEIBUAKO.

Television

Television Kiribati: Broadcasting and Publications Authority, POB 78, Bairiki, Tarawa; tel. 21187; fax 21096; in process of establishing services.

Finance

(cap. = capital; dep. = deposits; res = reserves)

BANKING

The Bank of Kiribati Ltd: POB 66, Bairiki, Tarawa; tel. 21095; fax 21200; e-mail bankofkiribati@tskl.net.ki; f. 1984; 75% owned by ANZ Bank, 25% by Govt of Kiribati; dep. $A42.8m., res $A1.3m., total assets $A46.3m. (Sept. 1999); Chair. R. GOUDSWAARD; Pres. and Man. Dir N. OLDHAM; 3 brs.

Development Bank of Kiribati: POB 33, Bairiki, Tarawa; tel. 21345; fax 21297; e-mail dbk@tskl.net.ki; f. 1986; took over the assets of the National Loans Board; identifies, promotes and finances small-scale projects; auth. cap. $A2m.; Gen. Man. KIETAU TABWEBWEITI; 5 brs.

A network of lending entities known as 'village banks' operates throughout the islands, as do a number of credit unions under the management of the Credit Union League. In August 1995 there were 26 credit unions operating in Tarawa and seven in the outer islands with a total membership of 1,808 people.

INSURANCE

Kiribati Insurance Corpn: POB 38, Bairiki, Tarawa; tel. 21260; fax 21426; e-mail kirins@tskl.net.ki; f. 1981; govt-owned; only insurance co; reinsures overseas; Gen. Man. TEAIRO TOOMA.

Trade and Industry

GOVERNMENT AGENCIES

Kiribati Housing Corporation: Bairiki, Tarawa; tel. 21092; operates the Housing Loan and Advice Centre; Chair. TOKOREAUA KAIRORO.

Kiribati Provident Fund: POB 76, Bairiki, Tarawa; tel. 21300; fax 21186; f. 1977; total equity $A56.8m. (Dec. 1998); Gen. Man. TOKAATA NIATA.

CHAMBER OF COMMERCE

Kiribati Chamber of Commerce: POB 550, Betio, Tarawa; tel. 26351; fax 26351; Pres. WAYSANG KUM KEE; Sec.-Gen. TIARITE KWONG.

UTILITIES

Public Utilities Board: POB 443, Betio, Tarawa; tel. 26292; fax 26106; e-mail pub@tskl.net.ki; f. 1977; govt-owned; provides electricity, water and sewerage services in Tarawa; CEO TOKIA GREIG.

Solar Energy Company: Tarawa; e-mail sec@tskl.net.ki; a co-operative administering and implementing solar-generated electricity projects in North Tarawa and the outer islands.

CO-OPERATIVE SOCIETIES

Co-operative societies dominate trading in Tarawa and enjoy a virtual monopoly outside the capital, except for Banaba and Kiritimati.

The Kiribati Copra Co-operative Society Ltd: POB 489, Betio, Tarawa; tel. 26534; fax 26391; f. 1976; the sole exporter of copra; seven cttee mems; 29 mem. socs; Chair. RAIMON TAAKE; CEO RUTIANO BENETITO.

Bobotin Kiribati Ltd: POB 485, Betio, Tarawa; tel. 26092; fax 26224; replaced Kiribati Co-operative Wholesale Society; govt-owned; Gen. Man. AKAU TIARE.

TRADE UNIONS

Kiribati Trades Union Congress (KTUC): POB 502, Betio, Tarawa; tel. 26277; fax 26257; f. 1982; unions and asscns affiliated to the KTUC include the Fishermen's Union, the Co-operative Workers' Union, the Seamen's Union, the Teachers' Union, the Nurses' Assn, the Public Employees' Asscn, the Bankers' Union, Butaritari Rural Workers' Union, Christmas Island Union of Federated Workers, the Pre-School Teachers' Asscn, Makim Island Rural Workers' Org., Nanolelei Retailers' Union, the Plantation Workers' Union of Fanning Island and the Overseas Fishermen's Union (formed in 1998); 2,500 mems; Pres. TATOA KAITEIE; Gen. Sec. TAMARETI TAAU.

Transport

ROADS

Wherever practicable, roads are built on all atolls, and connecting causeways between islets are also being built as funds and labour permit. A programme to construct causeways between North and South Tarawa was completed in the mid-1990s. Kiribati has about 670 km of roads that are suitable for motor vehicles; all-weather roads exist in Tarawa and Kiritimati. In 2000 there were about 1,468 motor vehicles registered in the islands, of which some 48% were motorcycles.

SHIPPING

A major project to rehabilitate the port terminal and facilities at Betio, with finance totalling some US $22m. from Japan, was completed in May 2000. There are other port facilities at Banaba, Kanton and English Harbour.

Kiribati Shipping Services Ltd: POB 495, Betio, Tarawa; tel. 26195; fax 26204; e-mail kssl@tskl.net.ki; operates three passenger/freight vessels on inter-island services and one landing craft; govt-owned; Gen. Man. Capt. ITIBWINNANG AIAIMOA.

MATS Shipping and Transport: POB 413, Betio, Tarawa; tel. 26355; operates a fortnightly passenger and cargo service to the outer islands and occasional longer journeys.

CIVIL AVIATION

There are five international airports (Bonriki on South Tarawa, Cassidy on Kiritimati, Antekana on Butaritari, as well as others on Kanton and Tabuaeran) and several other airfields in Kiribati. The airport at Bonriki was enlarged in the early 1990s, using a loan from the Bank of China. Air Nauru and Air Marshall Islands also operate international services to Tarawa, and Aloha Airlines operates a charter flight service between Kiritimati Island and Honolulu, Hawaii. In December 2001 the Government announced its decision to lease a prop-jet, which it intended to operate from Tarawa to the Marshall Islands, Tuvalu and Fiji.

Air Kiribati Ltd: POB 274, Bonriki, Tarawa; tel. 28088; fax 28216; e-mail airkiribati.admin@tsklnet.ki; f. 1977; fmrly Air Tungaru; national airline; operates scheduled services to 15 outer islands; Chair. TAKEI TAOABA; CEO TANIERA TEIBUAKO.

Tourism

Attempts to establish tourism as a major source of revenue have been impeded by the remoteness of the islands. There were 14,211 visitor arrivals in 1998 (of whom fewer than 40% were tourists). Of total tourist arrivals in 1998, some 58.3% came from Asia and Oceania, and 26.9% came from the Americas. The number of tourist arrivals at Tarawa and Kiritimati airports rose from 3,112 in 1999 to 4,831 in 2001. This figure declined in subsequent years, however, and totalled some 2,882 in 2004. In 2001 the industry earned some $A3.0m. In 1996 there were 201 hotel rooms in the islands. In 1989 the Government adopted a plan to develop hotels in the Line Islands and to exploit sites of Second World War battles. A further Tourism Development Action Plan was introduced in 1997. Game-fishing and 'eco-tourism', particularly bird-watching, were promoted in the late 1990s in an attempt to increase tourist arrivals to Kiritimati. Kiribati also exploited the location of some of its islands in the Line and Phoenix group by marketing the area as a destination for tourists wishing to celebrate the year 2000. In 1997 Caroline Island, situated close to the recently realigned international date-line, was renamed Millennium Island in an attempt to maximize its potential for attracting visitors. In late 2000 an agreement was signed with the Norwegian Shipping Line company allowing large cruise ships to make weekly calls to the Line Islands from the end of 2001.

Kiribati National Tourism Office: Ministry of Communications Transport and Tourism Development, POB 487, Betio, Tarawa; tel. 26003; fax 26193; e-mail sto@mict.gov.ki; internet www.spto.com; Sec. TEBWE IETAAKE; Senior Tourist Officer TARATAAKE TEANNAKI.

THE DEMOCRATIC PEOPLE'S REPUBLIC OF KOREA

Introductory Survey

Location, Climate, Language, Religion, Flag, Capital

The Democratic People's Republic of Korea (North Korea) occupies the northern part of the Korean peninsula, bordered to the north by the People's Republic of China and, for a very short section to the north-east, by the Russian Federation, and to the south by the Republic of Korea. The climate is continental, with cold, dry winters and hot, humid summers; temperatures range from −6°C to 25°C (21°F to 77°F). The language is Korean. Buddhism, Christianity and Chundo Kyo are officially cited as the principal religions. The national flag (proportions 33 by 65) is red, with blue stripes on the upper and lower edges, each separated from the red by a narrow white stripe. Left of centre is a white disc containing a five-pointed red star. The capital is Pyongyang.

Recent History

Korea was formerly an independent monarchy. It was occupied by Japanese forces in 1905 and annexed by Japan in 1910, when the Emperor was deposed. Following Japan's surrender in August 1945, ending the Second World War, Korea was divided at latitude 38°N into military occupation zones, with Soviet forces in the North and US forces in the South. A Provisional People's Committee, led by Kim Il Sung of the Korean Communist Party (KCP), was established in the North in February 1946 and accorded government status by the Soviet occupation forces. In July the KCP merged with another group to form the North Korean Workers' Party. In 1947 a legislative body, the Choe Ko In Min Hoe Ui (Supreme People's Assembly—SPA), was established, and Kim Il Sung became Premier. A new Assembly was elected in August 1948, and the Democratic People's Republic of Korea (DPRK) was proclaimed on 9 September. In the same year the Republic of Korea (q.v.) was proclaimed in the South. Initially, the DPRK was recognized only by the USSR and other communist countries. Soviet forces withdrew from North Korea in December 1948. In the following year, as a result of a merger between communists in the North and South, the Korean Workers' Party (KWP) was formed, under the leadership of Kim Il Sung; it has held power in North Korea ever since.

The two republics each claimed to have legitimate jurisdiction over the whole Korean peninsula. North Korean forces crossed the 38th parallel in June 1950, precipitating a three-year war between North and South. The UN mounted a collective defence action in support of South Korea, and the invasion was repelled. North Korean forces were supported by the People's Republic of China from October 1950. Peace talks began in July 1951 and an armistice agreement was concluded in July 1953. The cease-fire line, which approximately follows the 38th parallel, remains the frontier between North and South Korea. A demilitarized zone (DMZ), supervised by UN forces, separates the two countries.

Through the 'personality cult' of Kim Il Sung (the 'Great Leader') and of his son Kim Jong Il (the 'Dear Leader'), and a policy of strict surveillance of the entire population, overt opposition to the KWP was effectively eliminated. The only organized opposition to the regime (albeit in exile) appeared to be the Salvation Front for the Democratic Unification of Chosun, established by former military and other officials of the DPRK in the early 1990s, with branches in Russia, Japan and the People's Republic of China. International human rights organizations indicated that they believed there to be a number of concentration camps in North Korea, in which as many as 200,000 political prisoners were being held.

A new Constitution, adopted in December 1972, created the office of President, and Kim Il Sung was duly elected to the post. Kim Jong Il was appointed to several key positions within the KWP in 1980. In July 1984 Radio Pyongyang referred to Kim Jong Il, for the first time, as the 'sole successor' to his father, but there were reports of opposition to the President's heir, particularly among older members of the KWP.

Following elections to the eighth SPA, in November 1986 (when the 655 members were returned unopposed), Kim Il Sung was re-elected President, and a new Administration Council (cabinet) was formed. In March 1990 Kim Il Sung was returned to the post of President, and Kim Jong Il was appointed to his first state (as distinct from party) post, as First Vice-Chairman of the National Defence Commission. In February 1991 it was rumoured that there had been an unsuccessful military coup against Kim Jong Il. In December he was appointed Supreme Commander of the Korean People's Army (KPA), in place of his father, and in January 1992 he was reported to have been given control of foreign policy. In April Kim Jong Il was appointed to the rank of Marshal, while his father assumed the title of Grand Marshal.

In what was interpreted as a partial attempt to adapt to the change in international conditions following the collapse of communist regimes world-wide, the SPA (according to South Korean reports) made several amendments to the DPRK's Constitution in April 1992. Principal among these were the deletion of all references to Marxism-Leninism, and the promotion of 'economic openness' to allow limited foreign investment in the DPRK (although the KWP's guiding principle of *juche*, or self-reliance, was strongly emphasized). In September measures to address the deteriorating economic situation included a drastic devaluation of the national currency. The extent of the DPRK's economic difficulties was indicated by the budget proposals for 1993, which envisaged substantial reductions in expenditure, and by persistent reports of food riots. At the fifth session of the ninth SPA in April 1993 Kim Jong Il was elected Chairman of the National Defence Commission. In July Kim Il Sung's younger brother, Kim Yong Ju, unexpectedly returned to political life after a 17-year absence, and was subsequently elevated to the position of Vice-President and to membership of the Central Committee of the KWP's Politburo.

Kim Il Sung died of heart failure on 8 July 1994. One hundred days of national mourning were observed, but, contrary to expectations, Kim Jong Il was not appointed to the leading post of President of the DPRK. Although the official media now referred to Kim Jong Il as the 'Great Leader', he did not appear in public during this period, reviving earlier speculation that he was either in poor health or that a struggle for power was taking place. It was thought that Kim Il Sung's widow, Kim Song Ae, who was the stepmother of Kim Jong Il, favoured her eldest son Kim Pyong Il for the presidency. In February 1995 the Minister of the People's Armed Forces, Marshal O Jin U, died; O had been a significant supporter within the military of Kim Jong Il's succession. Scheduled elections to the SPA did not take place in April 1995, and no session of the Assembly was convened in 1996. Meanwhile, from the mid-1990s, the influence of the KPA expanded significantly, as Kim Jong Il increasingly relied upon the military to maintain his power, and the policy of *Songun* ('military first') was emphasized as the regime's central doctrine. The 50th anniversary of the establishment of the KWP in October 1995 was dominated by the military rather than the party, and several generals were promoted. Kim Jong Il, however, failed to assume any new posts. In February 1996 Sung Hye Rim, a former consort of Kim Jong Il and mother of his eldest son, defected to a western European country. In February 1997 Premier Kang Song San, who had made no public appearance since early 1996, was dismissed, and replaced on an acting basis by Hong Song Nam. Deepening social unrest was indicated by an increase in the rate of defections. In February Hwang Jang Yop, a close adviser to Kim Jong Il, sought political asylum in the South Korean embassy in the People's Republic of China while returning from an official visit to Japan, and warned that the DPRK was preparing to launch a military assault on South Korea. Hwang's defection appeared to precipitate significant changes in the KWP and military high command, as did the deaths of the Minister of the People's Armed Forces, Marshal Choe Kwang, and also of his deputy, Kim Kwang Jin. Many senior figures in the formal hierarchy were replaced, and some 123 generals, including many allies of Kim Jong Il, were promoted in rank in

April. In August two senior North Korean diplomats, including the ambassador to Egypt, defected to the USA. There were also rumours of unrest and coup attempts, and several senior figures disappeared from public view without explanation. The official mourning period for Kim Il Sung was formally declared to be at an end in July 1997, on the third anniversary of his death. It was announced that, henceforth, the country was to use the *Juche* calendar, with 1912, the year of Kim Il Sung's birth, designated the first year of the new calendar. On 8 October 1997, in accordance with the recommendations of recent municipal and provincial conferences of the KWP (including KPA delegates) Kim Jong Il was elected General Secretary of the KWP.

Elections to the SPA finally took place in July 1998, at which the single list of candidates received 100% of the votes cast. Some two-thirds of the 687 deputies were newcomers to the Assembly, while the military reportedly doubled its representation. The first session of the 10th SPA was convened in September, shortly before the 50th anniversary of the establishment of North Korea. However, the anticipated appointment of Kim Jong Il as President of the DPRK did not occur, as the post was effectively abolished under major amendments to the Constitution that extensively revised the structure of government. The deceased Kim Il Sung was designated 'Eternal President', thus remaining *de jure* Head of State, while Kim Jong Il, who had been re-elected to the Chairmanship of the National Defence Commission (now apparently the highest office in the state hierarchy), assumed the role of *de facto* Head of State. Vice-Marshal Jo Myong Rok, the Director of the General Political Bureau of the KPA, was appointed First Vice-Chairman of the Commission, becoming the *de facto* second-ranking official in the DPRK. The Cabinet, as the Administration Council was redesignated, assumed many of the functions of the Central People's Committee, which was abolished. A new Presidium of the SPA was established, the President of which was to represent the State in diplomatic affairs; Kim Yong Nam, hitherto Minister of Foreign Affairs, was appointed to this position. Hong Song Nam was formally appointed Premier of the new Cabinet. Two technocrats, Jo Chang Dok and Kwak Pom Gi, were appointed Vice-Premiers.

Elections to the Local People's Assemblies were held in March 1999; it was reported that all candidates were fully endorsed. In October 2000 the Minister of Finance, Rim Kyong Suk, and the President of the central bank, Jong Song Taek, were dismissed. They were replaced, respectively, by Mun Il Bong and Kim Wan Su. No reasons were given for their dismissal. The replacement of the Minister of Foreign Trade, Kang Chong Mo, in December, by Ri Kwang Gun, was also unexplained. The Minister of Agriculture was replaced in March 2001. Meanwhile, in October 2000 the 55th anniversary of the founding of the KWP was marked by a military parade, attended, *inter alia*, by an invited delegation from South Korea.

In January 2001 the Government urged a 'new way of thinking' to solve the country's economic and domestic problems and to complement the *Kangsong Taeguk* ('prosperous and powerful nation') philosophy adopted in the late 1990s. Meanwhile, the number of people defecting from the North to the South continued to increase, with nearly 650 such persons having settled in the latter since 1996. Several senior officials died or were replaced during 2001, including Ri Song Bok, the Secretary-General of the Party Central Committee and a senior aide to Kim Jong Il, who died in May. In August Vice-Marshal Jo Myong Rok returned to Pyongyang after a kidney transplant operation in Beijing. He subsequently received medical treatment in France in late September.

In February 2002 Kim Jong Il celebrated his 60th birthday, but the commemoration was less grandiose than expected, possibly so as not to overshadow the 90th anniversary of the birth of Kim Il Sung in mid-April. In late March the fifth session of the 10th SPA was held. In addition to announcing a new budget, the SPA also adopted a new land planning law, aimed at improving and intensifying land work. Prime Minister Hong Song Nam also urged improved trade and economic co-operation, including joint ventures with other countries and international organizations. In mid-April Kim Jong Il promoted some 55 military leaders, including Jang Song U, the elder brother of Kim's brother-in-law, Jang Song Taek.

The question of the succession of the next generation leadership became increasingly important during 2002–03, following Kim Jong Il's 60th birthday. Kim was initially believed to have been preparing his eldest son, Kim Jong Nam, to succeed him. Kim Jong Nam had served in the Ministry of Public Security and as head of the country's information technology (IT) industry since the late 1990s; however, in May 2001 he was detained in Tokyo, Japan, on charges of entering the country with a false passport, and subsequently deported to China. The incident discredited Kim Jong Nam, and thenceforth it was reported that Kim Jong Il was preparing Kim Jong Chol, the elder son of Ko Yong Hui, described as Kim Jong Il's unofficial wife. Kim Jong Nam spent much of 2002 in Russia, where his mother, Sung Hye Rim, died in July.

In late September 2002 the Government designated the city of Sinuiju a 'Special Administrative Region' designed to attract foreign investment, and appointed Yang Bin, a Chinese-born Dutch citizen, as its first governor. However, within days of his appointment, Yang was arrested by the Chinese authorities on corruption charges, and he was unable to assume his post. None the less, the creation of the region was a significant development in the country's efforts to open up the economy. Under the 'Basic Law' establishing the region, Sinuiju would have its own government and legal system for a 50-year period, without interference from Pyongyang. (In late 2004, however, there were reports that the Sinuiju project had been abandoned.) In late 2002 the Government also established a special industrial zone in Kaesong, and a special tourist zone in the region of Mount Kumgang, although these did not have the same special status as Sinuiju. Despite these developments, a meeting of senior law enforcement officials was held in Pyongyang in early December during which Premier Hong urged the elimination of 'non-socialist elements'. In early 2003 it was reported that travel restrictions within the country had been reintroduced, in order to improve security.

The sixth session of the 10th SPA was held in late March 2003. Unlike previous sessions, Kim Jong Il did not attend the meeting, and South Korean observers noted that Kim had disappeared from public view for 50 days between February and early April. Furthermore, Vice-Marshal Jo Myong Rok received treatment for kidney disease in Beijing—although his visit was believed to be linked to discussions with China over the situation on the Korean Peninsula (see below). Kim reappeared in early April to make an inspection of a military medical university, and later in that month celebrations took place in Pyongyang to mark the 10th anniversary of Kim's election as Chairman of the National Defence Commission. Further celebrations took place in July to mark the 50th anniversary of the Korean War truce (celebrated as a triumph for the DPRK by the country's media), as well as in September on the occasion of the 55th anniversary of the establishment of the DPRK. In August 2003 elections were held to form the 11th SPA. Voter turn-out was reported to be have been 99.9%, and all 687 candidates were elected unopposed. At the first session of the 11th SPA in September, Kim Jong Il was re-elected as Chairman of the National Defence Commission. In October Kim Yong Sun, a member of the KWP Secretariat and Chairman of the Korea Asia-Pacific Peace Committee, died, reportedly as a result of a traffic accident. Kim Yong Sun had been an important figure in inter-Korean relations (see below). Also in October, it was reported that Kim's consort, Ko Yong Hui, was critically ill. Vice-Marshal Jo Myong Rok was hospitalized in China again in December 2003.

In early 2004 reports from defectors, as well as some documentary evidence, indicated that mistreatment of political prisoners in the DPRK had included human experimentation for the purposes of chemical weapons development. On the occasion of Kim's 62nd birthday in February 2004, there was renewed speculation on the question of his successor. It was rumoured that Kim Jong Un, younger son of Ko Yong Hui, might have emerged as the most likely candidate, having been referred to by some sources as the 'Morning Star King'.

In April 2004 more than 150 people were killed and 1,300 injured by a massive explosion on a railway line at Ryongchon, a town near the border with China. Many children were among the victims of the accident, apparently caused when electric cables ignited chemical and other materials being transported by rail, only hours after a train carrying Kim Jong Il had travelled through the area. The North Korean authorities withheld information on the accident for two days, but subsequently accepted international humanitarian aid, including a donation (made through the Red Cross) from the USA. The railway accident drew attention to the shortcomings of the DPRK's health care system. It was reported that most hospitals lacked basic supplies such as running water and analgesics. Kim Jong Il's reaction to the accident was not reported; he did not appear in public until May.

In July 2004 Ju Sang Song was appointed as Minister of People's Security, replacing Choe Ryong Su. Choe had been removed from his post only one year after being appointed, and the reason for his removal remained unclear. Also in July the 10th anniversary of the death of Kim Il Sung was commemorated. In August Ko Yong Hui, the mother of two of Kim Jong Il's sons (see above), was reported to have died. In November there was speculation that Kim's hold on power might be weakening, following reports that portraits of him had been removed from public locations. It was also noted that official news reports no longer referred to Kim by the honorific title of 'Dear Leader'. Some sources claimed that Kim himself was attempting to diminish the personality cult surrounding him. However, there were tentative suggestions throughout 2004 that a power struggle was taking place in Pyongyang. It was believed that in April Kim had removed his brother-in-law, Jang Song Taek, from his position as vice-director of the KWP Central Committee and placed him under house arrest. Later in the year Jang's wife, Kim Jong Il's sister Kim Kyong Hui, was injured in a traffic accident, which was believed to have been a deliberate attack. The couple were described as the most powerful people in the DPRK after Kim Jong Il. Meanwhile, in April Kim's eldest son Kim Jong Nam (see above) reportedly survived an assassination attempt in Austria, amid suggestions that the attempt on his life had been connected to the issue of leadership succession.

In early 2005 a video smuggled out of the DPRK apparently contained footage of a poster of Kim Jong Il defaced with slogans opposing his dictatorship. However, rumours of challenges to Kim's rule remained unconfirmed. In May South Korean media reported that the North Korean Minister of Post and Telecommunications, Ri Kum Bom, had been dismissed, apparently as a result of his failure to control the revelation of information earlier in the year disclosing that the DPRK was in the process of combating outbreaks of avian influenza ('bird flu'). In July it was announced that his replacement was Ryu Yong Sop. In August an unspecified number of prisoners were granted amnesty to mark the 60th anniversary of the liberation of the Korean peninsula from Japanese rule. In October 2005 the 60th anniversary of the KWP was celebrated. North Korean citizens were reportedly granted four public holidays in honour of the event. On 9 October, the day before the anniversary, the KWP held a national meeting in Pyongyang, at which the primacy of the *Songun* or 'military first' policy was reaffirmed, as was the need for economic development in order to achieve the objective of *Kangsong Taeguk* ('prosperous and powerful nation'). The anniversary itself was commemorated with a large military parade in Pyongyang. Despite speculation, however, Kim Jong Il declined to take advantage of the occasion to announce his successor. In late October it was reported that Yon Hyong Muk, a Vice-Chairman of the National Defence Commission, who was regarded as a close adviser to Kim Jong Il, had died. North Korean media reports in November indicated that Ri Kwang Nam had been replaced as Minister of Extractive Industries by Kang Min Chol, while a report in December implied that Kim Jin Song had become Minister of Culture, replacing Choe Ik Kyu. In January 2006 Jang Song Taek made his first public appearance since 2003, prompting speculation that he had been rehabilitated following his apparent removal from favour in 2004 (see above).

Meanwhile, the DPRK's economic difficulties and widespread food shortages were exacerbated by unusually serious flooding in 1995 and 1996, forcing the country to appeal to the UN and other international organizations for emergency food aid and flood relief. Assistance was provided by the USA, the Republic of Korea and Japan in 1995, but in early 1996 further shipments of cereals were halted, pending a positive response by North Korea to US proposals for peace negotiations (see below). Renewed appeals for emergency aid were issued by the UN in mid-1996, to which the USA, South Korea and Japan responded on humanitarian grounds. In January 1997 it was reported that the People's Republic of China had agreed to provide 500,000 metric tons of rice annually for five years. This was followed, in February, by an unprecedented admission from the DPRK that the country was experiencing 'temporary food problems' and that it had only one-half of the cereals necessary to feed its people.

In April and July 1997 the UN World Food Programme (WFP) issued two further appeals for food and medical supplies. UN representatives sent to the DPRK to assess the extent of the crisis confirmed that chronic malnutrition was widespread, particularly among infants, and that the medical system was no longer able to provide even basic health care. The situation deteriorated in mid-1997, when severe drought devastated most of North Korea's maize crop; further damage was caused by a tidal wave on the western coast, which left many people homeless. In January 1998 WFP issued the largest appeal in the organization's history, requesting emergency aid valued at some US $380m. Agreement was reached with the DPRK whereby additional UN staff were to be permitted to enter the country in order to monitor the distribution of aid, following allegations that supplies had been diverted to the army. Despite the provision of aid, severe food shortages persisted during 1998 and malnutrition was widespread among children. In December the UN issued an appeal for humanitarian aid. In January 1999 WFP announced that substantial food aid would be required for the DPRK in that year. By mid-1999 WFP announced that increased aid had prevented starvation in the country for the time being, although poor infrastructure continued to hamper food distribution, and entry to 49 of the country's 211 counties was still forbidden. In August serious flooding destroyed large areas of farm land and caused severe damage to the communications network.

Severe weather conditions during 2000 exacerbated food shortages in North Korea, leaving it in increased need of international aid. In November 2000 the UN estimated North Korea's food shortage for 2001 at some 1.2m. metric tons. In December 2000 the organization appealed to the international community for aid worth some US $390m., including 810,000 tons of food. The total international assistance received by the DPRK in 2000 was US $220.4m., of which the Republic of Korea provided 52%, including 500,000 tons of rice and corn, and 300,000 tons of fertilizer.

In February 2001 WFP agreed to provide 810,000 tons of food and US $93m. in aid. The UN subsequently urged members to provide $383m. in humanitarian aid in 2002. In April 2001 the head of WFP in the country stated that the most recent winter had been especially severe and could thus result in food shortages comparable to those of 1996–97. In May the South began deliveries of 200,000 tons of agricultural fertilizer, and in June WFP stated that the North had received 389,775 tons of food aid between January and May, but would require an additional 250,000 tons to prevent starvation later in the year. The official state media announced in June, meanwhile, that the country had experienced 100 days of continuous drought since March; WFP subsequently estimated that the 2001 grain harvest would fall to 2.57m. tons as a result, far less than the 4.8m. tons needed overall. The worst-affected drought areas were South Hwanghae, Kangwon, and South Pyongan Provinces. In October WFP delivered emergency food supplies to flood-stricken Kangwon Province, and the Government began land rezoning programmes aimed at modernizing agricultural production in South Hwanghae Province. In November the head of the World Health Organization (WHO), Gro Harlem Brundtland, visited the DPRK and opened a permanent WHO office in Pyongyang. In December 2001 the Government launched an intensive campaign for potato and double-crop growing, in order to ease the famine.

In September–October 2002 representatives of FAO and WFP visited the DPRK and released a special report on the food situation. According to this report, in 2002 the harvest was believed to have improved somewhat, with cereal production 4.9% higher than in the previous year. Overall food production was 49% higher than in 2001, but 6% below the levels of 1995/96. Total cereal production, including potato equivalents, for 2002/03 was expected to reach 3.8m. tons, whereas food requirements were forecast at 4.9m. tons, thus leaving a deficit of 1.1m. tons. Urban residents remained more vulnerable to food shortages than rural residents, and food consumption per caput per day was projected at 270g of cereal in cities, compared with 600g in rural areas. Thus, urban residents were forced to spend 75%–85% of income on food purchases. The introduction in July 2002 of a quasi-market pricing system caused a significant inflation of food prices, despite the concurrent increase in salaries. The FAO-WFP mission therefore recommended concentrating resources on assisting urban areas and vulnerable groups, such as children and pregnant women.

In November 2003 the UN made a new appeal for humanitarian assistance to North Korea, stating that aid of more than US $200m. would be required in order to resolve the 'chronic emergency' in the DPRK. By February 2004 the aid crisis had deepened, with WFP stating that in early 2004 it would be able to give food rations to only 100,000 people, leaving the remainder of the 6.5m. people hitherto supported by WFP vulnerable to food shortages. A survey conducted by WFP in 2004 concluded that 37% of North Korean children aged six years and under were chronically malnourished. In November 2004 the UN stated that, despite relatively good harvests in 2004, 6.4m. people would remain in need of food aid in 2005, owing in part to a dramatic increase in food prices as a consequence of price reforms in 2002 (see above, and Economic Affairs). In January 2005 it was reported that government food rations, upon which approximately two thirds of the population were believed to depend, were to be reduced from 300g of grains per day to 250g. The WFP subsequently appealed for additional funds for food assistance to North Korea, projecting an increase in the number of people who would become dependent on overseas aid. In May the head of the WFP's mission in the DPRK warned that without increased contributions a number of people in the country could face 'famine-like conditions'. In June the USA pledged to supply 50,000 metric tons of food aid, its third successive annual donation, while simultaneously denying that this act was linked to the stalled negotiations on the DPRK's military nuclear programme (see below). In September, however, the North Korean Government announced that it had asked humanitarian aid agencies operating in the DPRK to terminate food aid programmes and withdraw the majority of their foreign staff by the end of the year. The Government asserted that, following a harvest that year reported to be the best in a decade, it was able to feed its people without assistance, and expressed a desire to progress from humanitarian to developmental aid. (Analysts speculated that the Government of the DPRK preferred to rely on food aid from China and the Republic of Korea, as the distribution of aid from these countries was monitored less closely and the political implications of allowing Westerners access to the country were thereby avoided.) Subsequently, WFP terminated its operations in North Korea in January 2006.

In 1971, meanwhile, talks took place for the first time between the Red Cross Societies of North and South Korea. Negotiations were, however, suspended in 1973, and hopes for better relations were undermined by a series of clashes between North and South Korean vessels in disputed waters during 1974. Propaganda campaigns, suspended by agreement in 1972, were resumed by both sides, and minor border incidents continued. In October 1978 the UN Command (UNC—under which troops were stationed in South Korea) accused North Korea of threatening the 1953 truce, after the discovery of an underground tunnel (the third since 1974) beneath the DMZ. During the 1980s the increasing prominence of Kim Jong Il, who advocated an uncompromising policy towards the South, appeared to aggravate the situation. In 1983 some 17 South Koreans, including four government ministers, were killed in a bomb explosion in Burma (now Myanmar), in what appeared to be an assassination attempt on the South Korean President, Chun Doo-Hwan. The DPRK was held responsible for the attack, and Burma severed relations with Pyongyang. In January 1984, none the less, the DPRK suggested tripartite talks on reunification, involving North and South Korea and the USA; however the proposal was rejected by South Korea, which favoured bilateral talks. During 1984 the DPRK's propaganda campaign was moderated, and in September North Korea provided emergency relief to flood-stricken areas of the South. In November the first talks, on possible economic co-operation, were held, and negotiations continued in 1985. However, in February 1986, during the annual South Korean-US 'Team Spirit' military manoeuvres, North Korea suspended all negotiations with the South. The DPRK denied accusations by the South of North Korean involvement in the explosion of a South Korean airliner over Burma in November 1987, despite the subsequent confession of an alleged North Korean agent. In his 1988 New Year message, none the less, Kim Il Sung reiterated proposals for the convening of a joint conference. In August three sessions of talks were held at the 'peace village' of Panmunjom (in the DMZ) between delegates of the legislatures of North and South Korea, although the discussions (the first formal contact between the two countries since 1986) produced no conclusive results. Further negotiations in 1989 were suspended by the DPRK.

Inter-Korean talks resumed in mid-1990, and in September the DPRK Premier visited the South Korean capital, Seoul, for discussions with his counterpart, the highest-level bilateral contact since the end of the Korean War. Subsequent discussions culminated in the signing of an 'Agreement on Reconciliation, Non-aggression and Exchanges and Co-operation between the South and the North', in Seoul in December 1991. Both states pledged, *inter alia*, to desist from mutual slander, vilification and sabotage, to promote economic and other co-operation and the reunion of families separated by the war, and to work towards a full peace treaty to replace the 1953 armistice agreement. In November 1992, however, the DPRK threatened a complete suspension of contacts with the South, in protest at the latter's decision to resume the 'Team Spirit' military exercises in March 1993. (The 1992 exercises had been cancelled, owing to the improvement in relations between the two states.) Relations had also been seriously impaired by the South's announcement, in October 1992, that an extensive North Korean espionage network had been discovered in South Korea, and by the North's repeated refusals to agree to simultaneous nuclear inspections in both countries (see below).

The controversy surrounding the DPRK's suspected nuclear programme prevented any improvement in inter-Korean relations during 1993 and the first half of 1994, and contacts were also strained by the DPRK's withdrawal, in May 1994, of its mission to the Military Armistice Commission (the Panmunjom-based body overseeing the maintenance of the 1953 truce). Following talks between Kim Il Sung and former US President Jimmy Carter, who visited the DPRK (on a private initiative) in June 1994, it was announced that the first summit meeting at presidential level between the two Korean states would be held in Pyongyang in July. However, the death of Kim Il Sung led to the indefinite postponement of the summit meeting. The DPRK was, furthermore, angered by the Republic of Korea's failure to express official condolences at Kim's demise. The signature of the US-DPRK nuclear accord in October (see below) caused South Korea to make renewed efforts to resume the inter-Korean negotiations, and in February 1995 the South announced the cancellation of the annual 'Team Spirit' manoeuvres (for the second consecutive year), as a gesture of goodwill.

Tension increased markedly in April 1996, when the DPRK announced its decision to abandon the 1953 armistice. North Korean troops subsequently made a number of incursions into the DMZ, thereby violating the provisions of the agreement. Later in the month, in an attempt to revitalize the peace process and replace the armistice agreement with a formal peace treaty, President Bill Clinton of the USA and President Kim Young-Sam of the Republic of Korea proposed four-way talks, involving the two Koreas, the USA and the People's Republic of China. China responded positively, but the DPRK declared its willingness to hold discussions only with the USA. Following severe flooding in the DPRK in mid-1996, the USA, the Republic of Korea and Japan agreed to provide additional food aid to North Korea as an inducement to participate in the proposed quadripartite talks. North Korea, however, imposed conditions for its participation. Relations between the two Koreas deteriorated considerably in September, when a submarine from North Korea was discovered abandoned in South Korean waters. One of the two surviving crew members claimed that this was the fourth such mission undertaken by armed North Koreans. South Korea suspended all contact with the DPRK, including the provision of food aid, and the UN Security Council subsequently expressed 'serious concern' at the incident. Following protracted mediation by the USA, an unprecedented apology was broadcast in South Korea by the (North) Korean Central News Agency.

In March 1997 explanatory talks between delegates from the DPRK, the Republic of Korea and the USA were held in New York to discuss the proposed quadripartite negotiations. Following the talks, the DPRK announced that its participation in full quadripartite negotiations was conditional upon the receipt of substantial food aid. In May representatives of the Red Cross organizations of North and South Korea (in the first such meeting for five years) reached agreement on the provision of grain to the DPRK, the distribution of which was to be monitored by South Korean Red Cross officials. Further supplies were pledged following meetings in July. Negotiations were concluded in October to allow foreign airlines, including those from South Korea, to use North Korean airspace. This was regarded as a significant breakthrough in bilateral relations.

Exploratory discussions on the proposed quadripartite negotiations were held at intervals throughout the first half of 1997. In July a military confrontation between North and South Korean troops in the DMZ jeopardized the progress of the discussions. Full quadripartite negotiations, aimed at concluding a peace treaty between North and South Korea, finally opened in Geneva, Switzerland, in December 1997. A second round of full discussions was held in March 1998, but proved unsuccessful, since the DPRK continued to insist on the inclusion on the agenda of the withdrawal of US troops from the Korean peninsula. In December 1997, meanwhile, negotiations in Beijing between the South and North Korean Red Cross organizations foundered, owing to North Korea's reluctance to allow South Korean officials access to the DPRK to monitor the distribution of food aid. At a subsequent meeting, in March 1998, the provision of additional food aid was agreed.

Following the inauguration of the new South Korean President, Kim Dae-Jung, in February 1998, the DPRK urged 'dialogue and negotiation' with the South Korean administration. Nevertheless, a ministerial-level meeting held in Beijing, People's Republic of China, in April, to discuss the provision of fertilizer to North Korea (the first such direct contact for four years), broke down amid mutual accusations of inflexibility, when the South Koreans insisted that the DPRK enter into negotiations on the reunion of families. In that month, however, as part of Kim Dae-Jung's 'sunshine' policy of co-operation with the DPRK, the South Korean Government announced measures to encourage inter-Korean economic contacts, allowing the transfer of private funds to the North and relaxing legislation on investment. In June, in an historic development, Chung Ju-Yung, the founder of the South Korean conglomerate Hyundai, was permitted to cross the DMZ to deliver a gift of cattle to his home town; proposals for several other joint ventures were also discussed, including a plan to operate tour boats to Mount Kumgang, just north of the border. This improvement in relations seemed to be in jeopardy when, during the visit, a North Korean submarine was caught in the nets of a southern fishing boat; all nine crew members were found dead inside the vessel. The UNC condemned the incursion during a meeting with North Korean army officers in Panmunjom, the first such talks to be held in seven years. A further delivery of cattle was made by Chung Ju-Yung in October 1998, when he also met with Kim Jong Il, and in November some 800 tourists from South Korea participated in the first visit to Mount Kumgang. In December, during Chung's third visit to North Korea, a proposal for the construction of an industrial complex at Haeju was approved. Following further visits in early 1999, it was announced that these would continue on a monthly basis. In December 1998, meanwhile, South Korean naval forces sank a suspected North Korean spy boat, after pursuing it into international waters.

In June 1999 a week-long confrontation between North and South Korean naval forces in the Yellow Sea resulted in a brief gun battle, during which one North Korean torpedo boat was sunk and five other vessels were damaged. Two rounds of bilateral talks in Beijing in late June and early July ended in failure, after North Korean representatives demanded an apology for the sinking of the boat, and refused to discuss the issue of reunion of families until further fertilizer aid was delivered by the South. (South Korea had recently sent 100,000 metric tons of fertilizer, and had promised a second delivery if some agreement was reached at the talks.) In September the DPRK declared invalid the Northern Limit Line (the maritime border that has separated the two Koreas since 1953), in protest at the UNC's refusal to renegotiate its demarcation. Meanwhile, no discernible progress had been achieved at sessions of the quadripartite talks held in April and August 1999. None the less, Hyundai proceeded with its plans for a number of projects in North Korea: in October the company concluded an agreement with the DPRK on the construction of the proposed industrial complex, which, it was envisaged, would comprise some 850 businesses, employing some 220,000 people, and would be capable of producing export goods worth an estimated US $3,000m. annually. In February 2000 foreign residents in South Korea were permitted to visit Mount Kumgang for the first time. In December 1999 another major South Korean company, Samsung Electronics, announced that it had signed a contract with the DPRK for the joint development of computer software and the manufacture of electronic products. In February 2000 the construction of a motor vehicle assembly plant, in a joint venture with the Pyonghwa Motor Company of South Korea, began in Nampo, south-west of Pyongyang. According to South Korean estimates, inter-Korean trade increased by 50.2% in 1999. A number of joint North-South cultural and sporting events took place in 1999. In March 2000 Kim Dae-Jung urged North Korea to develop economic contacts with the South at governmental level. In April, following a series of high-level bilateral contacts in Beijing, North and South Korea jointly announced that an historic summit meeting would take place between Kim Dae-Jung and Kim Jong Il in Pyongyang in June.

Following the presidential summit meeting on 13–15 June 2000, detailed agreements were signed pledging economic co-operation, the building of mutual trust and the resolution of reunification issues. In July ministerial-level delegations from both countries met in Seoul. This was the first visit to the South by North Korean officials since 1991. Although the two sides failed to reach an agreement on military matters, a joint communiqué was issued allowing for, *inter alia*, the reopening of liaison offices at Panmunjom, which had been closed in 1996, and the reconnection of the inter-Korean Kyongui railway line. The construction of a highway to run alongside the railway from North to South was subsequently agreed. In September Kim Dae-Jung formally inaugurated the project to remove thousands of landmines (to be undertaken by soldiers from each side respectively) and rebuild the railway line and adjacent highway. Meanwhile, benefiting from the progress made at the summit meeting in June, in August 100 North Korean families travelled to Seoul and 100 South Korean families visited Pyongyang simultaneously to meet with relatives from whom they had been separated by the Korean War. The second ministerial meeting between the two sides was held in Pyongyang later that month. Negotiations were extended for one day because of an inability to agree on terms for beginning a dialogue between the two countries' military establishments. A compromise was reached after consultation with Kim Jong Il. It was agreed to hold two more cross-border family reunions by the end of 2000 and to commence talks on economic co-operation. In a symbolic display of unity, in September the two countries marched under the same flag in the opening ceremony of the Olympic Games in Sydney, Australia. In late September the DPRK's Minister of the People's Armed Forces, Vice-Marshal Kim Il Chol, visited the South and met his counterpart, Cho Seong-Tae, the first such ministerial meeting ever held. In October Kim Dae-Jung was awarded the Nobel Peace Prize in recognition of his reunification efforts. Further rounds of inter-ministerial, military and economic talks took place during 2000 and early 2001. In an indication of the improvement in relations, in December 2000 a meeting was also held between trade union representatives from the two countries.

Despite the increased level of dialogue and co-operation between the two countries, however, in December 2000 South Korea published its annual defence policy document, which described the North as its main enemy and alleged that it had expanded its military capacity along the DMZ. The DPRK was antagonized by its continued status as South Korea's most likely adversary. International analysts, however, felt that hostility was not imminent. North Korea was also angered in that month by the approval of a resolution by the South Korean legislature to demand the repatriation of prisoners of war who, it alleged, continued to be held by the North, despite the DPRK's denial of the existence of these prisoners.

In early 2001 the uncompromising attitude displayed by the new US administration towards North Korea threatened to undermine the reconciliation process. In March the DPRK unilaterally postponed scheduled cabinet-level talks following a visit to the USA by Kim Dae-Jung, raising speculation that Pyongyang wanted time to formulate a response to US criticism of its regime (see below), and in April North Korea denounced joint US-South Korean military exercises as a betrayal of the goodwill surrounding the June 2000 summit meeting. Ministerial discussions resumed in Seoul in mid-September, the sixth round of which was concluded in mid-November (having been postponed from late October) without any agreement—the first such unsuccessful round since the presidential summit meeting. The North blamed the South, in particular the Minister of Unification, Hong Soon-Young, for the failure of the talks.

Meanwhile, during 2001 Kim Jong Il's long-awaited visit to Seoul for a second presidential summit meeting failed to materialize, and there was continued uncertainty as to when such a visit would take place. US President George W. Bush's reference in January 2002 to North Korea as part of an 'axis of evil' threatened to damage inter-Korean relations.

A stalemate in inter-Korean relations was broken in early April 2002, however, when the North received Kim Dae-Jung's special envoy, Lim Dong-Won. Following the visit, during which Lim met Kim Jong Il, the two sides agreed to further reunions for separated families (see below) and to continuing discussions on economic co-operation. The DPRK also agreed to Lim's request that it renew dialogue with the USA and Japan. In mid-May Park Geun-Hye, a South Korean legislator and the daughter of former President Park Chung-Hee, visited the North and met Kim Jong Il. The visit was remarkable because Northern agents had killed Park's mother in 1974 in a bid to assassinate her father. Despite the cordial visit, North Korea cancelled economic co-operation discussions with the South in May.

In May 2002 the increasing number of defectors from the North received international attention as several groups sought asylum at Canadian, Japanese and South Korean diplomatic buildings in China. They were eventually allowed to travel to the South, albeit via the Philippines. The South Korean Ministry of Unification reported in January 2003 that during 2002 some 1,141 North Koreans had defected to the South, compared with 583 in 2001.

At the end of June 2002 a gun battle between North and South Korean vessels in the Yellow Sea resulted in the sinking of a Southern patrol boat and the deaths of six crew members. South Korean military sources estimated that 30 Northern crewmen were also killed in the confrontation, which had started when two North Korean vessels accompanying a fishing boat reportedly crossed the Northern Limit Line. Following the incident, in July South Korea suspended rice shipments to the North and economic co-operation projects, reflecting widespread public anger there. None the less, Kim Dae-Jung maintained his 'sunshine' policy towards the North, and later expressed regret for the incident. Meanwhile, North Korean state television showed selected highlights of matches played by the South Korean football team in the 2002 football World Cup—although refrained from transmitting extensive coverage of the event, which was being co-hosted by Japan.

In mid-August 2002 North and South Korea held a seventh round of ministerial talks in Seoul, aimed at improving relations in the aftermath of the latest naval confrontation, and focusing on the issue of future family reunions, railway links (see below) and cultural exchanges. Regarding the latter, more than 300 North Korean athletes travelled to the South and participated in the Asian Games held in Busan during October. In late September the first inter-Korean military 'hotline' was inaugurated to allow for improved communications during sensitive occasions. Meanwhile, Pyongyang's revelation that it had abducted 12 Japanese citizens in the 1970s and 1980s (see below) highlighted the outstanding issue of several hundred missing South Korean citizens believed to have been abducted by the North.

The eighth round of ministerial talks was held in Pyongyang in late October 2002 and mainly focused on economic co-operation issues, despite the fact that the USA had earlier revealed the existence of a secret nuclear weapons programme in the North (see below). At the end of that month a North Korean economic delegation began a nine-day tour of the South, including several major industrial facilities in the itinerary. Noteworthy was the fact that the delegation included Jang Song Taek, Kim Jong Il's brother-in-law and reportedly one of his most trusted advisers, and also Kim Hi Taek, the first deputy head of the KWP's Central Committee. At the end of December 2002 the South Korean Ministry of National Defence published a 'white paper' which, for the first time, excluded any reference to the North as its main enemy.

By late 2002 some of the goodwill generated by the historic inter-Korean summit meeting in June 2000 had been undermined by the revelation that Kim Dae-Jung had arranged for the Korea Development Bank to give a Hyundai affiliate substantial funds to transfer to the North in order to finance the meeting. However, the election in December of Roh Moo-Hyun, the candidate of Kim's Millennium Democratic Party (MDP), as President of the Republic of Korea heralded a continuation of Kim's 'sunshine' policy. In early January 2003 representatives of Roh secretly met Northern officials in Beijing, and later in that month a ninth round of ministerial talks was held in Seoul.

North and South Korea continued their efforts to improve bilateral relations during 2003, despite a severe deterioration in relations between the North and the USA over the issue of the former's nuclear weapons programme (see below). In early 2003 Roh was exploring a long-standing idea of developing gas pipelines between Sakhalin, Russia, and North Korea that would supply the latter with energy in return for an abandonment of its nuclear programme. The DPRK hosted the 10th round of ministerial talks at the end of April. In mid-May, however, Pyongyang announced that it no longer recognized a joint declaration on the 'denuclearization' of the Korean peninsula, signed with the South in 1992 (see below). Also in May, at talks between the two Koreas on economic matters, North Korea warned that the South would risk 'unspeakable disaster' if it became too confrontational in co-operating with the USA on the nuclear issue (the threat followed a summit meeting between Roh and US President George W. Bush). Attempts to develop inter-Korean relations were also complicated by confirmation in June by South Korean investigators that former President Kim Dae-Jung had paid US $100m. to arrange the historic inter-Korean summit meeting of 2000 (see above). In August the suicide of Hyundai official Chung Mong-Hun, who had been indicted in connection with the illegal payments to the North, further undermined the credibility of the 'sunshine' policy. Meanwhile, the 50th anniversary in July of the *de facto* end of the Korean War, celebrated as a triumph in North Korea, was commemorated in a sombre fashion in South Korea. Also in July, cross-border gunfire was exchanged between North and South Korean soldiers. In October North Korean official Kim Yong Sun, an important figure in inter-Korean affairs who had attended the presidential summit meeting in 2000, died, reportedly as a result of a traffic accident. In November two well-known North Korean defectors, Hwang Jang Yop (see above) and former North Korean official Kim Dok Hong, left their posts at the South Korean Institute of National Unification Policy. There was a suggestion that their resignations might have been due to fears that their criticism of the North Korean regime might be damaging to South Korean attempts to negotiate with North Korea. The resignation in January 2004 of the South Korean Minister of Foreign Affairs, Yoon Young-Kwan, was believed to have been related to tensions within the South Korean Government over the country's co-operation with the USA on the issue of North Korean weapons.

In April 2004, following a major railway accident in North Korea at Ryongchon (see above), the DPRK accepted emergency supplies and assistance from South Korea, although the delivery of aid was delayed by the North's initial insistence that relief should be sent by sea rather than by road. At the end of the month a South Korean cargo plane arrived in Pyongyang carrying further emergency supplies, representing the first ever direct flight for humanitarian purposes. In May senior-level military discussions took place between the two sides, at which the establishment of a radio communication line between the North and South Korean navies was agreed. It was believed that the new communication line would reduce naval conflicts between the two sides; although later in the year there were none the less incidents of warning shots being fired by the South Korean navy at North Korean vessels considered to have intruded on the maritime border, amid accusations that in some instances South Korean navy officials had failed to report North Korean radio messages. In June, meanwhile, in a symbolic development, propaganda broadcasts across the DMZ were silenced for the first time in decades, with loudspeakers on both sides of the border being switched off. Also in June, a senior DPRK representative, Vice-Chairman of the Korea Asia-Pacific Peace Committee Ri Jong Hyok, made a visit to Seoul and met South Korean President Roh Moo-hyun to mark the fourth anniversary of the inter-Korean summit meeting of 2000 (see above). In July 2004 more than 450 defectors from the DPRK arrived in Seoul. Pyongyang subsequently accused South Korea of kidnapping its citizens, and suspended bilateral dialogue. Tensions were increased further in August following an admission by South Korea that it had in the past conducted secret nuclear experiments. It was believed that this disclosure would increase the DPRK's reluctance to dismantle its own nuclear programme. Also in September Song Ho Gyong, a Vice-Chairman of the Korea Asia-Pacific Peace Committee who had played an important role in arranging the 2000 meeting, died. By the end of 2004 the number of North Koreans who had defected to South Korea had reportedly exceeded 6,000.

In February 2005 the South Korean Ministry of Defence urged the resumption of senior-level military talks, apparently to ease tension following North Korean accusations that Southern naval vessels had 'infiltrated' Northern waters. In March South Korea halted all imports of poultry from the North, after it emerged that incidents of avian influenza ('bird flu') had been recorded there. In April South Korean officials travelled to Kaesong in the DPRK to discuss the provision of assistance in combating the outbreak of the virus, which had reportedly led to the cull of more than 210,000 chickens in Pyongyang. A shipment of quarantine equipment was dispatched to North Korea later that month. Also in April the highest-level meeting between the two sides for five years took place when Kim Yong Nam, the President of the Presidium of the North Korean SPA, met South Korean Prime Minister Lee Hae-Chan during the course of an Asia-Africa summit meeting in Jakarta, Indonesia; the two reportedly agreed that bilateral dialogue, suspended since July of the previous year (see above), should continue. At vice-ministerial talks in May, South Korea pledged to provide 200,000 metric tons of fertilizer to ease the DPRK's food supply problems. Three North Korean freighters reportedly docked at Ulsan in South Korea to load the fertilizer later in the month, this being the first time since 1984 that North Korean ships had docked in a South Korean port. In June South Korean Minister of Unification Chung Dong-Young visited the DPRK to mark the fifth anniversary of the inter-Korean summit of 2000, where he held an unscheduled meeting with Kim Jong Il; it was speculated that the DPRK's agreement to return to the six-party talks on its nuclear programme in the following month might have been influenced by incentives offered by Chung at this meeting, including the provision of electricity (see below). In July the 15th ministerial talks between North and South Korea, held in Seoul, concluded with a 12-point joint statement in which the two sides pledged, *inter alia*, to reopen military talks, resume reunions for separated families and hold North-South Red Cross talks to discuss the issue of 'the whereabouts of those reported missing during the Korean War' (see below). Further ministerial discussions were held in September and December. Meanwhile, a sizeable delegation from the DPRK, headed by Kim Ki Nam, a member of the KWP Politburo's Secretariat, travelled to Seoul in August to participate in celebrations commemorating the 60th anniversary of the liberation of the Korean peninsula from Japanese rule. During their stay in Seoul the North Korean officials made significant visits to the National Cemetery, where Southern casualties of the Korean War were honoured, and to the National Assembly. In November 2005 it was announced that North and South Korea would present joint teams at the 2006 Asian Games in Doha, Qatar, and at the 2008 Olympic Games in Beijing, China. In March 2006 military negotiations were held between the two Koreas in the DMZ, following a break of some two years; these were reportedly the highest-level military talks between the two sides since the 1953 armistice. In the same month, however, the Government of the DPRK postponed the scheduled 18th round of ministerial discussions between the two sides in protest at the South's conduct of joint military exercises with the USA; the annual exercises were thought to have incurred particular objection that year in consequence of the participation for the first time of a nuclear-powered aircraft carrier.

The arrangements for further family reunions came under the auspices of the North and South Korean Red Cross organizations, which held several rounds of talks on the subject and co-ordinated the exchange of lists of potential candidates for reunion. In October 2000 South Korea accepted a North Korean proposal that the second exchange of family members should take place in late November–early December. Relations between the two sides subsequently deteriorated, casting doubt on the likelihood of the meetings taking place, when North Korea accused the head of the South Korean Red Cross of defaming the former's political system. The official was replaced in January 2001. The DPRK continued to dictate terms for reunions, asking the Republic of Korea to limit the amount of money and gifts transferred during the events, which took place in November–December 2000 and at the end of February 2001. It was subsequently reported that North Korean officials had confiscated money given to delegates for use as state funds. Meanwhile, in January 2001 an historic accord between the two sides allowed 300 separated families from the North and South each to exchange letters in mid-March. A fourth round of family reunions was initially scheduled for mid-October, but was cancelled owing to the heightened security situation following the terrorist attacks in the USA on 11 September. They were subsequently held at Mount Kumgang in late April 2002. A fifth round was held in mid-September 2002, again at Mount Kumgang, where officials from the two sides planned to build a centre for such meetings. The eighth round of reunions in September 2003 involved 604 South Koreans and 365 North Koreans. In April 2004 a ninth round of reunions was delayed after a South Korean official made a joke concerning Kim Jong Il. Further rounds of reunions none the less took place during the year. As part of the reunion programme, in July 2005 the first private telephone line between North and South Korea since partition in 1945 was opened, in preparation for video conference family reunions, which took place in mid-August to coincide with the 60th anniversary of liberation from Japanese rule. Inter-Korean Red Cross talks held later that month at Mount Kumgang failed to resolve the question of South Korean soldiers and civilians 'abducted' to North Korea during and after the 1950–53 war: the Government in Seoul estimated that more than 540 prisoners of war and some 485 abducted civilians were still alive and remained in detention in the DPRK. Following the talks, an 11th round of family reunions was held at Mount Kumgang. Further reunions were held, both in person and through video conference technology, in late 2005 and early 2006. At another Red Cross conference in late February 2006, North Korea reportedly agreed to resolve the issue of South Korean prisoners of war and abductees held in the North.

As the DPRK's financial situation worsened, economic issues played an important part in inter-Korean relations from 2000. There was speculation that Pyongyang's new openness was motivated by the necessity of securing increased assistance. In January 2001, however, a South Korean vessel carrying aid was refused permission to dock in North Korea. Also in that month, it was reported that the DPRK's energy shortages had reached crisis point, and that the country was desperately researching alternative power sources. A summit meeting took place between the two Koreas in February, at which the DPRK requested immediate and substantial electricity supplies to alleviate its pressing needs. Frustration resulted from South Korean insistence on the necessity of on-site investigations prior to the commencement of deliveries. Meanwhile, in August 2000 Hyundai agreed to establish a technologically-advanced electronic industrial compound in Kaesong in the DPRK. Hyundai's financial problems, however, delayed the implementation of the project. The company was also obliged to reduce its royalty payments to Pyongyang for the Mount Kumgang tourist initiative in 2000, owing to the attraction's failure to make a profit. In March 2001 the future of the initiative was jeopardized by its lack of profitability, and Hyundai appealed to the South Korean Government for assistance; the Government subsequently pledged 90,000m. won to maintain the tourist cruises. Hyundai founder Chung Ju-Yung died in late March, meanwhile, and his funeral was attended by a delegation sent by Kim Jong Il. On May Day workers from trade unions from the North and South attended a rally at Mount Kumgang. Progress on economic co-operation in Kaesong was made from 2002, with Kaesong being declared a special industrial zone in November of that year (see also Economic Affairs). In June 2003 the DPRK announced regulations for the development of the zone, as well as plans to develop an area of 3.3 sq km in a first phase of development extending to 2007. A South Korean company, Korea Land, was to invest around US $184m. in the project. These plans were finalized at a meeting of North and South Korean economic officials in November 2003. Although inter-Korean trade increased steadily, reportedly amounting to US $700m. in 2003, South Korea shared international concerns over North Korea's suspected illicit trade in weapons and narcotics. In June 2003 South Korean customs officials in the port of Pusan seized 40 kg of methamphetamines believed to have originated in North Korea. There were also fears of very serious economic consequences for South Korea if reunification of the two Koreas were to become an imminent prospect. Further progress on the Kaesong special industrial zone was evident in 2004. It was reported that in April some 1,600 South Korean companies had applied for a lease in the zone, and in June Korea Land (see above) selected the first 15 companies that were to be permitted to conduct business in the zone. At the end of June a ceremony was held to signal the commencement of the first phase of development in Kaesong, with 350 officials from the North and the South attending the event. In March 2005 the Korea Electric Power Corporation (KEPCO), of South Korea, began to supply electricity to Kaesong, representing the first cross-border flow of electricity since the peninsula's partition. In July the South Korean Minister of Unification reportedly proposed to Kim Jong Il that South Korea compensate the North with 2,000 MW of energy assistance if the latter were to abandon its nuclear weapons programme (see below). The DPRK, however, rejected the offer. In October the first joint governmental office operated by both North and South Korea, to handle cross-border economic projects, was opened in Kaesong, and in December the first commercial telephone link between Kaesong and Seoul commenced operation.

Negotiations to re-establish the inter-Korean rail link continued during 2001. It was hoped that such a link would create a new Eurasian transport corridor that would reduce the cost and time involved in the transit of goods from North-East Asia to European markets from 25 days to about 15 days, bringing economic benefits to all participants. In February 2001 a meeting was held at the DMZ to arrange regulations for troops and workers employed to rebuild the line, and a parallel highway. However, the DPRK failed to attend a UN regional transport meeting held in Seoul in mid-November, following the failure of the sixth round of ministerial talks. A New Year's editorial in January 2002 described the upgrading of the railway as a priority during that year, and both Koreas agreed to accelerate the reconnection following bilateral talks in April 2002. Ground-breaking ceremonies for the reconnection of the railway and road links were held on both sides of the DMZ in late September 2002, and South Korea released a loan to the North to assist the funding of the work. In early February 2003 the first road reconnecting the North with the South was completed, on the eastern coast of the Korean peninsula. In June 2003 rail links between the two Koreas were officially opened, although the connections remained largely symbolic, as construction on the North Korean side to link the new railways with wider networks was yet to be completed. Following a meeting between the two sides in June 2004 it was reported that the rail links were expected to begin operating in 2005. In December 2004, meanwhile, it was reported that the road link along the eastern coast of the two Koreas had been opened to traffic. By late 2005 two major rail links between North and South Korea along the west and east coasts, with adjacent roads, were believed to be in operation. South Korea had also pledged to assist the DPRK in constructing several railway stations.

In the early 1990s there was growing international concern that the DPRK had intensified its clandestine nuclear programme at Yongbyon, north of Pyongyang, and would soon be capable of manufacturing a nuclear weapon. During 1991 pressure was increasingly applied, by the USA and Japan in particular, for the DPRK to sign the Nuclear Safeguards Agreement (NSA) with the International Atomic Energy Agency (IAEA, see p. 98). This was required by the DPRK's signature, in 1985, of the Treaty on the Non-Proliferation of Nuclear Weapons (the Non-Proliferation Treaty—NPT), in order that IAEA representatives might be permitted to inspect the country's nuclear facilities. However, the DPRK consistently refused to allow such inspections to take place unless there was to be a simultaneous inspection (or withdrawal) of US nuclear weapons sited in South Korea. Tension was eased considerably by the USA's decision, in October 1991, to remove all its tactical nuclear weapons from South Korea, and by South Korea's subsequent declaration that it would not manufacture, deploy or use nuclear, chemical or biological weapons. In December the South Korean Government stated that all US nuclear weapons had been withdrawn, and proposed that simultaneous inspections of military bases in the South and nuclear facilities in the North be conducted. Later in the month the two Korean states concluded an agreement 'to create a non-nuclear Korean peninsula', and in January 1992 the DPRK signed the NSA. In March delegates of North and South, meeting at Panmunjom, agreed to form a Joint Nuclear Control Commission (JNCC) to permit inter-Korean nuclear inspections to take place.

In May 1992 the DPRK submitted to the IAEA an unexpectedly detailed report on its nuclear facilities, describing, *inter alia*, the Yongbyon installation as a research laboratory. In the same month IAEA inspectors were permitted to visit North Korean nuclear facilities (the first in a series of official visits during that year). Despite the findings of the inspectors (who concluded that the Yongbyon plant was 'primitive' and far from completion, although potentially capable of producing plutonium), suspicions persisted regarding North Korean nuclear ambitions. Moreover, the DPRK repeatedly failed to agree to separate nuclear inspections by the JNCC, finally announcing in January 1993 its intention to boycott all future inter-Korean nuclear talks (in protest at the imminent resumption of the 'Team Spirit' manoeuvres). The situation became critical in February, when the DPRK refused to allow IAEA inspections of two 'undeclared' sites near Yongbyon, claiming that these were military installations unrelated to nuclear activities. In an unprecedented move, the DPRK announced in March that it was to withdraw from the NPT. In May the UN Security Council adopted a resolution urging the DPRK to reconsider its decision to withdraw from the NPT and calling on the country to allow an inspection by the IAEA of its nuclear facilities. Following negotiations with the USA in May and June, the DPRK agreed to suspend its withdrawal from the NPT; in return, the USA agreed to assist the DPRK in the development of its non-military nuclear programme. International concern regarding the North Korean weapons programme was, meanwhile, heightened by the successful testing of a medium-range missile, the *Rodong-1*, in May. In response to US pressure, the DPRK subsequently agreed to further negotiations with the IAEA. Talks at the organization's headquarters in Vienna, Austria, in September were, however, inconclusive, and further meetings were cancelled.

In February 1994, following further discussions between the DPRK and the USA, an agreement was reached whereby the IAEA would be allowed to visit all the country's declared nuclear facilities. In March, however, the inspectors were impeded in their efforts to remove samples from nuclear installations, and it was discovered that seals placed on nuclear materials by IAEA representatives during previous visits had been broken, leading the IAEA to conclude that the DPRK had, in all probability, produced more plutonium than had been admitted. In June the DPRK again threatened to withdraw from the NPT, and also to declare war against the Republic of Korea, if economic sanctions were imposed by the UN. In August the USA and the DPRK reached an agreement on the replacement of the latter's existing nuclear reactors by two light-water reactors, which were considered to be less easily adapted to the production of nuclear weaponry. The agreement also recommended the establishment of a restricted form of diplomatic representation between the two countries. However, the DPRK discounted the possibility of an inspection by the IAEA of the two contentious sites at Yongbyon. Further negotiations in October led to the signing of an Agreed Framework whereby the USA undertook to establish an international consortium to finance and supply the light-water reactors, while the DPRK agreed to suspend operation of its existing reactors and halt construction at two further sites. To compensate for the DPRK's consequent shortfall in energy production until the new reactors were fully operational, the USA agreed to donate to the DPRK 500,000 metric tons annually of heavy fuel oil. IAEA inspectors subsequently travelled to Pyongyang to oversee the suspension of the country's nuclear programme.

In March 1995 several countries, led by the USA, the Republic of Korea and Japan, created the Korean Peninsula Energy Development Organization (KEDO), which insisted that the DPRK accept a South Korean-designed reactor. This demand was opposed by the DPRK at renewed negotiations with the USA. However, in August the North permitted a KEDO delegation (including South Korean engineers) to visit Sinpo, on the east coast of the DPRK, in order to assess its suitability as the site of the proposed nuclear power station. Finally, in December the DPRK and KEDO reached agreement on the details of implementing the October 1994 accord; this implied acceptance by the DPRK of South Korean light-water reactors. In January 1996 the DPRK announced its willingness to permit routine inspections of its nuclear installations by the IAEA. In March KEPCO was commissioned by KEDO as the principal contractor for the construction of the light-water reactors. Discussions between KEDO and the DPRK to negotiate the terms of repayment by the latter of the construction costs of the light-water reactors were successfully concluded in April 1997, with the DPRK agreeing to reimburse KEDO over a 17-year period.

Meanwhile, US energy experts began the sealing of spent fuel rods at the DPRK's nuclear facilities. However, North Korea's continued refusal to grant IAEA inspectors access to several contentious laboratories, despite meetings to negotiate the implementation of the provisions of the NSA, again provoked concern that the DPRK was developing its nuclear programme. Preparation of the nuclear-reactor site at Sinpo formally began in August 1997: the initial project involved the construction of facilities to house the estimated 2,000 site employees. Negotiations held in early 1998 between the participants in KEDO (which the European Union—EU—had joined in mid-1997) concerning the financing of the light-water reactors (estimated at US $5,170m.) proved difficult, and were further complicated by South Korea's financial problems, raising fears that progress on the project would be hindered. In June 1998 the North Korean Government admitted to having sold nuclear missiles abroad, claiming that such exports were necessary, given ongoing US economic sanctions against the DPRK, in order to earn foreign currency. Some progress was made at talks between the USA and the DPRK in New York, USA, in September, when the DPRK agreed to resume sealing of spent fuel rods (which had been suspended earlier that year), while the USA promised to deliver the delayed shipment of heavy fuel oil. The US Congress was, however, increasingly reluctant to approve financing for the purchase of fuel oil, obliging President Clinton personally to authorize the disbursement of the necessary funds in October, in order to safeguard the 1994 nuclear accord.

Concerns regarding a suspected nuclear-related underground facility at Kumchang-ri, some 40 km north-west of Yongbyon, dominated a series of senior-level talks between the USA and the DPRK in late 1998 and early 1999. US attempts to gain access to the site, which the DPRK insisted was non-nuclear, were unsuccessful, with the USA rejecting North Korean demands for compensation in return for an inspection of the site. The North Korean authorities were angered by reports that KEDO had decided, in January 1999, to delay commencing the basic construction of the light-water reactors until mid-1999. In March, following protracted negotiations in New York, agreement was finally reached permitting US access to the suspected nuclear facility. The USA announced that it would donate substantial food aid to the DPRK, in addition to agricultural assistance, although it was emphasized that the aid was being granted on purely humanitarian grounds and did not constitute compensation. The US officials who inspected the Kumchang-ri site in May found it to be incomplete and largely empty. (The facility was reinspected in May 2000, and this finding was confirmed.) At the same time the USA announced the provision of an additional 400,000 metric tons of food aid for 1999.

In May 1999 William Perry, a former US Secretary of Defense who had been appointed to review policy towards the DPRK, visited Pyongyang, where he reportedly advised the North Korean Government to abandon its nuclear ambitions in exchange for substantial economic and political benefits. Talks held during mid-1999 between the USA and the DPRK to discuss the latter's missile development programme culminated in September in a decision by the USA to ease several long-standing economic sanctions (principally on non-military trade, travel and banking) against the DPRK. In return, the country agreed to suspend missile test-firing for the duration of negotiations with the USA. Earlier in the month Perry had presented a report recommending a comprehensive, long-term approach to the establishment of normal relations with the DPRK to the US President and Congress. Discussions aimed at improving US-North Korean relations were held in Beijing in November 1999 and January 2000. In March preparatory talks took place in New York for a proposed higher-level meeting, scheduled to be held in Washington, DC, in April. It was reported, however, that disagreement had arisen over the DPRK's insistence on its removal from the US list of countries supporting terrorism prior to the Washington talks.

Meanwhile, in November 1999 it was reported that the IAEA was supervising the final stage of the sealing of spent fuel rods at Yongbyon. After several months of delays caused by disputes over the division of the costs of the project, in December KEDO and KEPCO finally signed the contract for the construction of the two light-water reactors; in February 2000 it was reported that construction of the reactors was unlikely to be completed before 2007, some four years later than scheduled. In November 2000 North Korea, frustrated by the delay, threatened to restart missile testing unless construction of the reactors was accelerated. The DPRK refuted the IAEA's claim that delays were due to the former's refusal to allow nuclear inspections. Also in that month, the EU agreed to provide US $130m. for the construction of the reactors.

In June 2000 Pyongyang confirmed its moratorium on test flights of ballistic missiles. Various rounds of discussion on the missile issue took place throughout 2000, although no substantive progress had been achieved by the end of the year. In July the USA rejected the DPRK's demand for annual payments from the USA of US $1,000m. in return for the curtailment of weapons exports. The fundamental issues of missile development and export remained unresolved. A planned visit to Pyongyang by the outgoing US President, Bill Clinton, was cancelled in December when the DPRK rejected a US proposal that the two sides prepare a draft missile accord to form a basis for talks. In early 2001 the new administration of George W. Bush adopted a less conciliatory stance towards the DPRK, officials reportedly referring to Kim Jong Il as a 'dictator', and refusing to grant economic aid unless transparency in North Korea's missile production and export was assured and verified. Since the late 1990s elements in Bush's Republican Party had been strongly arguing in favour of a planned 'national missile defence' (NMD) system to protect the USA from long-range missile attack, and had frequently cited North Korea as a developer and exporter of such missiles. US officials feared that the DPRK had developed an intercontinental ballistic missile, the *Taepo Dong 2*, capable of striking the west coast of the USA. Bush's commitment to develop NMD was denounced by the DPRK, which responded by threatening to abandon the 1994 framework, and to resume ballistic missile testing. In March 2001 US Secretary of State Colin Powell suggested that revisions to the 1994 framework might be required. In April Charles Kartman, a former special envoy to the DPRK under the Clinton administration, was appointed as the new head of KEDO. In the following month an EU delegation travelled to North Korea, in an effort to renew diplomatic initiatives aimed at advancing the process of détente. Discussions focused on North Korea's missile programme and on humanitarian issues. Kim Jong Il reportedly agreed to maintain the moratorium on the testing of missiles until at least 2003, and declared his willingness to attend another meeting with President Kim Dae-Jung. In June 2001 President Bush sought to broaden discussions with North Korea about its missile programme to include nuclear technology and a reduction of the country's conventional forces. The North responded that discussions on the latter would take place only following the withdrawal of the 37,000 US troops from the South, and that it was also seeking financial compensation for the delay in building KEDO's two light-water reactors, which were now not expected to be completed until 2008 at the earliest. In October the North rejected suggestions by the head of the IAEA and later by US officials that inspections of its nuclear facilities were necessary; however, in December it agreed to limited international access to certain laboratories. Meanwhile, in November, a team of North Korean nuclear engineers visited power plants in the South, indicating their commitment to acquire southern-style reactors. (See relations with the USA, below, for subsequent developments on the DPRK's nuclear weapons programme.)

The DPRK's relations with Japan have long been dominated by continuing hostility towards the latter as a result of the atrocities committed in Korea during the Japanese occupation (1910–45). Pyongyang had demanded thousands of millions of dollars in compensation from Japan, before normal relations could be restored. In the 1980s, following the testimony of defectors, Japan began to suspect that North Korean agents had kidnapped a number of Japanese citizens during the late 1970s and early 1980s. Japan imposed sanctions on the DPRK after its agents were accused of attempting to assassinate the South Korean President in Burma in 1983. Following the destruction of a South Korean aircraft in 1987, allegedly by North Korean agents posing as Japanese citizens (see above), Japan reimposed sanctions during 1988; the DPRK then severed diplomatic contacts with Japan, although mutual trade continued. From late 1990 there was a significant *rapprochement* between the DPRK and Japan, and in January 1991 a Japanese government delegation visited Pyongyang for discussions concerning the possible normalization of diplomatic relations. The Japanese delegation offered apologies, on behalf of its Government, for Japanese colonial aggression on the Korean peninsula between 1910 and 1945. Moreover, the Japanese Government expressed its willingness to make reparations for Japanese abuses of human rights in Korea during this period. Subsequent negotiations in 1991 foundered, however, owing to the DPRK's demand for reparations for damage inflicted after 1945 (which the Japanese Government denied) and to Japan's insistence that North Korea's nuclear installations be opened to outside inspection; normalization talks collapsed in November 1992, as the North Korean delegation abandoned the proceedings. Relations with Japan were further strained after the DPRK's testing of the *Rodong-1* missile in the Sea of Japan in May 1993. The missile, according to US intelligence reports, would be capable of reaching most of Japan's major cities (and possibly of carrying either a conventional or a nuclear warhead). None the less, Japan, like the Republic of Korea, opposed the possible imposition of international economic sanctions on the DPRK in response to North Korea's refusal to allow inspections of its nuclear facilities. Attempts failed to resume normalization talks in 1994, but in March 1995 a Japanese parliamentary group visited the DPRK and reached an agreement for the resumption of talks later that year. In May Japan agreed to North Korea's request for emergency rice aid, and later in the year Japan provided aid to help the DPRK overcome the effects of serious flooding (see above). In early 1996 Japan provided a shipment of fuel oil to alleviate the DPRK's energy shortfall.

Relations were complicated in 1997 by Japanese allegations that North Korea had abducted several Japanese citizens during the 1970s. However, in August 1997, for the first time since 1992, negotiations opened on the restoration of normal bilateral relations. The main focus of discussions was the issue of some 1,800 Japanese women married to North Koreans, who had never been permitted to leave the DPRK. An agreement was signed whereby the women were to be allowed to visit their relatives in Japan for short periods; the first such visits took place in November 1997 and January 1998. Moreover, in October 1997 the Japanese Government resumed the provision of aid to North Korea, suspended since mid-1996, donating food and medical supplies in response to the renewed appeals issued by the UN. Relations deteriorated in mid-1998, however, when the North Korean Government cancelled a third visit of the Japanese women to their homeland, following Japan's rejection of a North Korean investigation into the alleged abduction of Japanese nationals. The testing by the DPRK of a suspected *Taepo Dong-1* missile over Japanese territory, in August, further exacerbated tensions, prompting Japan to break off normalization talks, suspend food aid and postpone its contribution to the KEDO project. The DPRK subsequently claimed that the object launched was in fact a satellite. Tension between the two countries increased in March 1999, when Japanese naval forces pursued and opened fire on suspected North Korean spy ships that had infiltrated Japanese waters. Relations improved, however, following the DPRK's agreement with the USA, in September, to suspend its reported plans to test a new long-range missile. In October unofficial talks between North Korean and Japanese government officials were held in Singapore, and two weeks later Japan decided to allow the resumption of charter flights to the DPRK. In December, following a successful visit to the DPRK by a group of Japanese parliamentarians, Japan announced an end to its ban on food aid. Later in that month intergovernmental preparatory talks on re-establishing diplomatic relations were held in Beijing, and Japanese and North Korean Red Cross officials reached some agreement on humanitarian issues. Further progress was achieved by the two countries' Red Cross Societies at a meeting in March 2000. It was reported that the DPRK had agreed to cooperate in a further investigation into the fate of some 10 missing Japanese nationals, while Japan had agreed to a search for Korean citizens who had disappeared prior to 1945. In addition, visits to their homeland by Japanese women married to North Koreans were to resume shortly, and Japan was to provide some 100,000 metric tons of rice to the DPRK through WFP. In late April Japanese charter flights to North Korea resumed. Meanwhile, following further informal contacts between the North Korean and Japanese Governments, full normalization talks commenced in April 2000; further rounds of discussions took place during the year, despite an announcement by Japan in September that relations between the two countries would not be normalized until the cases of Japanese citizens allegedly abducted by North Korean agents had been solved. In October, however, a further round of negotiations took place in Beijing, China. The two sides agreed to meet again, but no date was set. In November the DPRK rejected an offer by Japan to extend economic aid rather than grant wartime compensation. Meanwhile, in September the long-delayed third visits home by the Japanese wives of North Korean men took place. In October Japan decided, on humanitarian grounds, to provide 500,000 metric tons of rice to North Korea. Later that month meetings held with the USA and Japan focused on obtaining the extradition from the DPRK, in return for economic aid, of terrorist Japanese Red Army members, who had hijacked a Japanese aircraft and forced it to fly to Pyongyang in 1970 (later being granted political asylum in North Korea). No agreement was reached.

In December 2000 the DPRK reiterated that normal relations with Japan could be restored only after the latter delivered an apology and compensation for its earlier colonial rule. However, at the same time former Japanese Prime Minister Tomiichi Murayama led a non-governmental delegation to Pyongyang, in an attempt to improve relations. In May 2001 Japan deported Kim Jong Nam, son of Kim Jong Il, for entering the country on a false passport (see above). In June the DPRK condemned Japan's refusal to issue visas to North Koreans planning to attend a conference on Japanese compensation for Korea, held in Japan. In August the DPRK demanded compensation for Korean victims of the atomic bombs dropped on Hiroshima and Nagasaki in 1945, and also for the collision of cargo ships from the two countries in July 2001.

The DPRK was one of several Asian countries that strongly condemned Japanese Prime Minister Junichiro Koizumi's visit to the Yasukuni Shrine in August 2001. During late 2001 the DPRK denounced Japan's military support for the USA's 'war on terrorism', stating that such support was aimed entirely at expanding Japan's military sphere of activities. In November Japanese police arrested Kan Young Kwan, an executive of the pro-North Korean General Association of Korean Residents in Japan, or *Chongryon*, on charges of diverting funds through the use of local credit unions. The incident highlighted the sometimes-illegal activities of the North Korean community in Japan.

In mid-December 2001 the DPRK announced that it was abandoning efforts to locate missing Japanese nationals thought to have been abducted by North Korean agents. At the end of the month a suspected North Korean spy vessel was sunk by Japanese coastguard forces after it had been expelled from Japan's exclusive economic zone. The DPRK condemned the incident, but denied any involvement, accusing Japan of seeking to mislead world opinion. Japanese coastguard forces searched the sunken vessel in May 2002, and raised it in September of that year. In February 2002 the DPRK released a Japanese journalist who had been detained on spying charges since December 1999.

In an unexpected diplomatic move, Junichiro Koizumi visited Pyongyang in mid-September 2002, becoming the first incumbent Japanese Prime Minister to do so. His one-day visit, during which he held discussions with Kim Jong Il, was dominated by the latter's admission that North Korean agents had abducted 12 Japanese citizens in the 1970s and 1980s, of whom five were still alive. The remainder were said to have died of natural causes, although suspicions remained that they might have been executed, after Pyongyang failed to locate their graves. Kim apologized for the incidents, but attributed them to rogue elements within the security services. The admission led some sources to indicate that the total number of Japanese abductees might be as high as 100. The surviving captives were temporarily allowed to return to Japan in mid-October, although they had to leave behind any spouses or children. Among the abductees allowed to return was Hitomi Soga, the wife of Charles Jenkins, a US soldier who was believed to have defected to North Korea in 1965 and to have remained in the DPRK ever since. The couple's two daughters had never left the DPRK. The Japanese authorities refused to allow the abductees to return to the DPRK after the visit. Despite this, representatives from the two countries held the first round of resumed discussions on the restoration of normal diplomatic relations in Malaysia at the end of October, but failed to make any progress.

In October 2002 the alleged admission by North Korean officials to their visiting US counterparts that Pyongyang was pursuing a secret nuclear weapons programme, alarmed Japan. Koizumi announced that Japan would halt further economic co-operation with the DPRK until the issues of the abducted Japanese citizens and the nuclear programme were resolved. Pyongyang warned Japan that it would abandon its moratorium on missile testing if normalization talks failed to make any progress. In separate incidents in late February and early March 2003 the DPRK test-launched two short-range ground-to-ship missiles in the Sea of Japan, and in early April tested a third missile in the Yellow Sea. However, it refrained from testing longer-range ballistic missiles, which Tokyo considered a threat to its security. In late March the DPRK was angered by Japan's launching of two spy satellites, believed to be part of a programme of intelligence-gathering on the DPRK initiated following the testing of the North Korean *Taepo Dong* missile over Japan in 1998 (see above). The Director-General of Japan's Defence Agency warned the DPRK that Japan could conduct a pre-emptive strike on North Korean missile facilities if necessary.

In May 2003 a North Korean vessel which had been sunk by Japanese coastguard forces in 2001 was put on display in a Tokyo museum. Some evidence found aboard the ship suggested links between North Korean drug manufacturers and criminal gangs in Japan. In June the DPRK cancelled a voyage of the *Man Gyong Bong* passenger ferry, used by ethnic Korean residents in Japan to visit relatives in North Korea, apparently owing to more stringent inspections of North Korean ships by Japan amid speculation of illegal goods transport. In August a group of 10 North Korean refugees claimed asylum at the Japanese embassy in the Thai capital of Bangkok, in what was believed to be the first incident of this kind outside China. At the end of the month Japan was one of six nations taking part in talks on the North Korean nuclear weapons programme held in Beijing. At the talks, Japan reportedly attempted to raise the issue of Japanese citizens abducted by the DPRK (see above). In the same month, Japanese authorities seized premises owned by the General Association of Korean Residents in Japan (*Chongryon*), reportedly owing to tax evasion. Also in August, the *Man Gyong Bong* ferry arrived in the Japanese port of Niigata on its first trip to Japan in seven months. Departure of the ship from Niigata was subsequently delayed after the vessel failed safety inspections carried out by the Japanese authorities. Relatives of Japanese nationals abducted by North Korea, as well as Japanese right-wing groups, held anti-North Korean protests at the port. In October the DPRK announced that it did not wish Japan to participate in future negotiations on its nuclear weapons programme, claiming that Japan was 'an obstacle to the peaceful settlement' of the nuclear issue, and citing Japanese attempts to 'blockade' North Korea.

In January 2004 the Japanese House of Representatives approved legislation to permit the imposition of economic sanctions on the DPRK. In April legislation was approved requiring all ships entering Japanese ports from March 2005 to be insured against oil damage. This in practice amounted to a ban on entry by North Korean ships. Following a second visit by Japanese Prime Minister Koizumi to Pyongyang in May 2004, five children of the abductees who had returned to Japan in 2002 (see above) were permitted to fly to Tokyo. Their release had been secured in return for pledges of food aid and medical supplies. However, suspicions remained over the fate of other missing Japanese nationals. In July US soldier Charles Jenkins, husband of the Japanese abductee Hitomi Soga (see above), travelled to Indonesia with his two daughters and was reunited with his wife. (He subsequently received hospital treatment in Japan, and was then found guilty of desertion from the US army and sentenced to a short period of imprisonment.) In November the DPRK relinquished human remains which it claimed were those of Megumi Yokota, who had been kidnapped by North Korean agents in 1977. Pyongyang claimed that she had committed suicide. However, subsequent DNA tests indicated that the remains were not those of Megumi Yokota. North Korea refused to accept the results of the tests, claiming that these had been falsified by Japan. The Japanese Government subsequently suspended food aid to North Korea, and public pressure for the imposition of economic sanctions on the DPRK increased in Japan. In December the DPRK stated that it would regard the imposition of economic sanctions as tantamount to a declaration of war.

At the beginning of March 2005 legislation concerning insurance requirements for ships entering Japanese ports, which had been approved in early 2004 (see above), took effect, amounting to a ban on entry of all but 16 of an estimated 100 North Korean ships that were involved in trade with Japan. Whilst the majority of Japanese citizens was believed to favour the imposition of direct economic sanctions on the DPRK, the Japanese Government remained reluctant to do this, not wishing to jeopardize future negotiations concerning North Korea's nuclear weapons programme. The September 2005 six-party agreement (see above) contained a clause in which Japan and the DPRK undertook to 'take steps to normalize their relations'. Subsequently talks were held between the two countries in early February 2006 to discuss issues including the alleged abductions of Japanese citizens, the development of ballistic missiles by the DPRK and the resumption of the nuclear negotiations. However, the talks ended inconclusively, and later that month Japan's Chief Cabinet Secretary, Shinzo Abe, announced that arrest warrants had been issued for two North Korean agents suspected of abducting four Japanese nationals in 1978.

The DPRK has considered the USA to be its main enemy since the time of the Korean War and repeatedly accused the Republic of Korea of being a US 'puppet' state. Relations deteriorated after the DPRK seized a US naval vessel, the *USS Pueblo*, in 1968 and detained its crew for several months. In 1969 the DPRK shot down a US reconnaissance aircraft which had apparently violated North Korean airspace, resulting in the deaths of 31 US servicemen. In 1987, in response to alleged North Korean involvement in the bombing of a South Korean airliner, the USA placed the DPRK on its list of countries supporting terrorism, and restricted contacts between US and North Korean diplomats. Relations with the USA in the 1990s were largely dominated by the DPRK's suspected nuclear ambitions (see above). In December 1994 it was announced that agreement had been reached to establish liaison offices in Washington, DC, and Pyongyang in 1995, in preparation for an eventual resumption of full diplomatic relations. The USA insisted, however, that normal relations would be restored only when the DPRK ceased to export ballistic missiles and withdrew its troops from the border with South Korea; the DPRK, in turn, stated that liaison offices could only be opened when light-water nuclear reactors, in accordance with the October 1994 agreement between the DPRK and the USA, had been supplied. Relations faltered following the shooting-down of a US army helicopter which had apparently entered North Korean airspace; the DPRK initially refused to negotiate, but, after direct bilateral talks in December, the pilot was repatriated. In January 1995 the DPRK opened its ports to US commercial shipping and removed restrictions on the import of goods from the USA. Following the severe flooding in the DPRK in 1995 and 1996, the USA provided food aid and other flood relief.

The issue of four-way talks (see above) dominated relations between the USA and the DPRK in 1996, but parallel negotiations were conducted concerning the estimated 8,100 US soldiers who were listed as 'missing in action' following the Korean war. The USA agreed to provide funds to assist in locating the bodies, and it was reported that the DPRK had requested additional food aid in return for its co-operation. In December, following the issuing of a (US-brokered) apology by the DPRK for the submarine incursion in September, it was reported that the USA was prepared partially to revoke its economic sanctions against North Korea, and to allow the gradual expansion of bilateral trade. In early 1997 the USA responded to a renewed appeal issued by the UN for food aid and humanitarian assistance for North Korea, as a result of which the DPRK announced its intention to take part in exploratory discussions about the proposed quadripartite talks. Bilateral discussions with the USA during 1997 focused on the establishment of liaison offices, missile non-proliferation and procedures for the exhumation of the US servicemen listed as 'missing in action'. In August, however, the defection to the USA of two North Korean diplomats (the most senior officials yet to seek asylum in North America) resulted in the suspension of the third round of missile non-proliferation talks. The DPRK was unsuccessful in attempting to make its participation in full quadripartite talks conditional upon the withdrawal of US forces from the Korean peninsula and upon the provision of food aid. None the less, the USA responded positively, on humanitarian grounds, to two further UN appeals for food aid during the year. Relations with the USA were dominated by nuclear issues and other concerns regarding the DPRK's missile development programme in 1998 and 1999 (see above). The exhumation of US soldiers listed as 'missing in action' proceeded, with 22 sets of remains returned to the USA in 1998. In October 1999 US officials visited Pyongyang to receive the remains of four soldiers, in the first such transfer to take place on North Korean territory without the involvement of the UNC. A further 15 sets of remains were returned in November 2000. Trade between the USA and the DPRK increased significantly following the partial revocation of economic sanctions against the latter in September 1999 (see above); US exports to the DPRK increased massively in 1999. Meanwhile, the USA continued to provide emergency food aid to the DPRK.

Relations between the DPRK and the USA were variable during 2000. In June the USA announced the partial easing of economic sanctions against the country. In August a round of talks with the USA in Washington on the DPRK's removal from the list of terrorist sponsors ended without agreement, although the meeting was described as productive. In September, however, officials from the DPRK declined to attend the UN Millennium summit meeting in New York, following a confrontation between the delegation and US security officials, who suspected the North Koreans of terrorism, at Frankfurt airport in Germany. The USA subsequently apologized, describing the incident as an 'innocent mistake' and refuting the DPRK's claim of a 'brazen plot'. In October Kim Jong Il's special envoy, Vice-Marshal Jo Myong Rok, paid a state visit to the USA, the most senior North Korean official ever to do so. Later that month the US Secretary of State, Madeleine Albright, reciprocated the visit and in Pyongyang met Kim Jong Il, who agreed in principle to halt his country's long-range missile-testing programme. Talks were described as 'serious and constructive'. Shortly afterwards, however, tension arose when two US fighter aircraft participating in a US-South Korean joint manoeuvre briefly crossed the military demarcation line into North Korean airspace. The DPRK protested to the UN, demanding a formal apology and the implementation of measures to prevent a recurrence of the incident.

Relations between the DPRK and the USA deteriorated during 2001 following the inauguration of George W. Bush as President of the latter. Bush adopted a tougher position towards the DPRK compared with his predecessor, and this also adversely affected inter-Korean relations (see above). The DPRK condemned the joint US-South Korean military exercises held in April. In May a non-governmental delegation from the USA visited the DPRK to examine evidence of atrocities committed by US troops during the Korean War. In June Bush stated that he was willing to resume negotiations with the DPRK, albeit linking these to a reduction in North Korea's missile programme and military deployments—terms rejected by the North. In July the North Korean Minister of Foreign Affairs, Paek Nam Sun, failed to attend the Association of South East Asian Nations (ASEAN) forum in Viet Nam, also attended by the US Secretary of State. During his visit to Moscow in August, Kim Jong Il reiterated North Korea's long-standing demand for the withdrawal of US troops from the South.

Following the terrorist attacks on the USA in September 2001, the USA paid increasing attention to North Korea's biological, chemical and nuclear weapons programmes. Although the DPRK had condemned those attacks, it subsequently opposed the US bombing of Afghanistan, and failed to provide any intelligence on terrorist networks to the USA. By late 2001 the DPRK was drawing increasing criticism from the USA, and in October the US State Department released its annual report on religious freedom, which included the DPRK on a list of countries suppressing such beliefs. In November Bush warned the DPRK not to take advantage of the war in Afghanistan to increase tensions on the Korean peninsula. Despite signing two UN treaties against terrorism in November, the DPRK remained on the USA's list of states sponsoring terrorism.

In late January 2002 the DPRK's relations with the USA deteriorated further following President Bush's reference to North Korea as forming an 'axis of evil' with Iran and Iraq. Bush's comments were believed to reflect concern that the DPRK was exporting weapons technology to countries the USA considered to be 'rogue states'. (During the 1990s the DPRK had exported missiles and related technology to countries such as Egypt, Iran, Libya, Pakistan and Syria, allegedly earning up to US $1,000m. a year.) However, when Bush visited the DMZ on a visit to the South, he urged the North to open up to the outside world. Although the USA ruled out any military action against the DPRK, in March 2002 it was revealed that the DPRK was one of seven nations considered a potential target for a US nuclear first strike, in the event of emergency circumstances. The DPRK responded by threatening to withdraw from existing agreements with the USA (see above). However, in April the North accepted a South Korean request to reopen dialogue with the USA, and invited a US envoy, Jack Pritchard, to discuss outstanding issues. At the same time the USA announced that it would release US $95m. to the DPRK in order to accelerate the building of the replacement nuclear reactors—construction of which finally began in August 2002, with a view to completion in 2008. Pritchard himself attended the ground-breaking ceremony, but stated that the DPRK must accept international inspection of its nuclear facilities, a demand that Pyongyang stated was not mandatory until 2005.

Meanwhile, in July 2002 the Minister of Foreign Affairs, Paek Nam Sun, held an informal meeting with the US Secretary of State, Colin Powell, on the sidelines of the ASEAN Regional Forum (ARF) in Brunei—the highest-level contact between Pyongyang and the Bush Administration. In August the DPRK rejected US demands for a significant reduction of its conventional military forces along its border with the South. The USA had long feared that these could be used to attack the 15,000 US troops deployed between Seoul and the DMZ in the event of hostilities.

Relations between the DPRK and the USA deteriorated significantly from October 2002 after the USA announced that senior North Korean officials had admitted to the visiting US Assistant Secretary of State for East Asian and Pacific Affairs, James Kelly, that the DPRK was pursuing a secret nuclear weapons programme in violation of the 1994 agreement. The clandestine programme was allegedly based on uranium extraction, whereas the suspended programme had been based on plutonium extraction. The admission reportedly came after Kelly presented his Northern hosts with credible US intelligence reports about the programme, although Pyongyang later denied that it had made such an admission. Within days the USA declared the 1994 framework null and void and placed renewed pressure on the DPRK to halt its nuclear activities. The DPRK responded by stating that it would consider halting its nuclear programme if the USA would sign a non-aggression treaty guaranteeing the DPRK's sovereignty with Pyongyang—a demand rejected by Washington. Pyongyang subsequently warned the USA of severe military measures if it continued to reject such a treaty. In the middle of November, however, the USA finally halted petroleum shipments to North Korea, citing the latter's violation of the 1994 framework. Further confusion over Pyongyang's nuclear programme emerged on 17 November 2002 when North Korean radio reportedly admitted that the country already possessed nuclear weapons. However, the exact translation of the statement was in doubt, and most analysts concluded that the broadcast had stated that the DPRK was entitled to possess such weapons. At the same time it was widely reported that Pakistan had provided the technical expertise of North Korea's nuclear programme in exchange for ballistic missiles. Attention focused on the north-western city of Kusong, some 30 km north west of Yongbyon, as the centre of the secret programme.

The diplomatic crisis between the DPRK and the USA worsened in December 2002 when Pyongyang announced that it would restart its nuclear reactor at Yongbyon, and the USA accused the DPRK of narcotics trafficking in order to raise money to support its declining economy. Amid increasingly strong rhetoric from both sides, former US President Bill Clinton revealed that he had come close to ordering airstrikes on the DPRK's nuclear facilities in 1994, and Spanish commandos, acting on intelligence supplied by the USA, seized a North Korean cargo vessel, the *So San*, carrying Scud missiles to Yemen, in the Arabian Sea. However, the vessel was allowed to deliver its cargo after Yemen confirmed the legitimacy of the order. The incident was widely seen as a US warning to Pyongyang regarding its weapons proliferation. Later in that month the DPRK removed the IAEA's monitoring and surveillance equipment from the Yongbyon facility. The US Secretary of Defense, Donald Rumsfeld, warned Pyongyang not to take advantage of the USA's planned attack on Iraq (see the chapter on Iraq) to raise regional tensions, stating that the USA could fight against both countries simultaneously. Rumsfeld had earlier stated that the DPRK possessed nuclear weapons, and security analysts concluded that Pyongyang already possessed between two and five nuclear devices.

In late December 2002 the IAEA reported that North Korean technicians had transferred 1,000 fuel rods (out of 8,000 necessary to reactivate it) to the Yongbyon reactor, ostensibly for the production of electricity, but probably for the production of plutonium required to manufacture nuclear devices. The DPRK expelled the two remaining IAEA inspectors at the end of that year.

In early January 2003 the DPRK announced its withdrawal from the NPT, and the IAEA responded by adopting a resolution condemning Pyongyang's recent behaviour. However, President Bush indicated that the USA would resume petroleum deliveries if the DPRK abandoned its nuclear weapons programme. In February Pyongyang stated that the Yongbyon reactor was operating normally, and that any US military build-up in the region could lead the North to launch a pre-emptive strike on US forces anywhere in the world. Pyongyang also threatened to withdraw from the 1953 armistice if the USA imposed a blockade on the DPRK. Despite these threats, the USA deployed long-range bombers to its bases on the Pacific island of Guam as a precautionary measure, and warned that although it favoured a peaceful resolution of the crisis, it had not ruled out any options—including military action.

In early March 2003 the USA and South Korea began their annual joint military exercises amid condemnation by the North, which announced at the end of the month that it was severing military contacts with the USA at the liaison office in the DMZ. Also in early March four North Korean fighter aircraft intercepted a US reconnaissance aircraft in international airspace and closely pursued its flight, the first such incident in 32 years. Between late February and the beginning of April 2003 the DPRK also test-fired three short-range missiles, although refrained from testing its longer-range ballistic missiles. The commencement of the US-led campaign in Iraq in late March 2003 alarmed Pyongyang, which reportedly believed that the USA would target the DPRK at some future date. By early April the USA had imposed new sanctions on the DPRK's Government and its Changgwang Sinyong Corporation, for exporting ballistic missiles to Pakistan. However, the sanctions were largely symbolic, since the USA had minimal economic links with the DPRK. Later in the month, the seizure by Australian authorities of the *Pong Su*, a North Korean ship carrying 50 kg of heroin, confirmed US claims that the DPRK was involved in drugs trafficking. Also in April, the UN Security Council held discussions on the North Korean crisis for the first time. The DPRK stated prior to the talks that the imposition of economic sanctions through the Security Council would amount to a declaration of war.

THE DEMOCRATIC PEOPLE'S REPUBLIC OF KOREA (NORTH KOREA)

Tensions between the DPRK and the USA increased in late April 2003 after ambiguous statements by the North's official media in which it indicated it was preparing to reprocess, or was actually reprocessing, 8,000 spent fuel rods, a move that would enable it rapidly to produce nuclear weapons. Officials from North Korea, the USA and China held high-level discussions in Beijing during 23–24 April over Pyongyang's nuclear weapons programme. No agreements were reached, however, and US sources stated that the DPRK had, for the first time, admitted to possessing nuclear weapons and had threatened to carry out a nuclear test. Whilst the DPRK insisted on a guarantee of non-aggression from the USA before it would consider dismantling its nuclear programme, the latter remained adamant that North Korea should not be permitted to make demands for complying with its international obligations. In mid-May Pyongyang cited US behaviour against it as a reason for abandoning the Joint Declaration of the Denuclearization of the Korean Pensinsula, a 1992 commitment with the South on a nuclear-free peninsula.

In June 2003 the DPRK for the first time publicly defended its nuclear weapons strategy, declaring through the state news agency that the development of nuclear weapons was a 'deterrent', and that the programme 'was not aimed at threatening or blackmailing'. In July there were new indications from US and Asian intelligence sources that the DPRK was operating a second secret nuclear facility, in addition to the plant at Yongbyon. At the end of July it was announced that the DPRK had agreed to take part in multilateral talks on its nuclear weapons programme with the USA, the Republic of Korea, Japan, China and Russia. Prior to the talks, tensions were exacerbated by comments of US Under-Secretary of State John Bolton, who launched a virulent attack on Kim Jong Il in the course of a speech given in Seoul. Pyongyang responded by describing Bolton as 'human scum' and refusing to negotiate with him at the talks. Furthermore, immediately in advance of the negotiations, Jack Pritchard resigned as US special envoy to North Korea. The six-party talks duly took place in Beijing in late August, but little progress was achieved. US Assistant Secretary of State James Kelly demanded that the DPRK unconditionally abandon its nuclear weapons programme in a 'complete, verifiable and irreversible manner'. The North Korean Vice-Minister of Foreign Affairs, Kim Yong Il, however, warned that unless the USA provided a guarantee of non-aggression, Pyongyang would continue to develop its nuclear self-defence capacity.

Following the six-party talks in Beijing, it was reported in September 2003 that President George W. Bush had authorized James Kelly to abandon the USA's insistence on the full dismantling of the North Korean weapons programme before any concessions could be made. It was indicated that verifiable progress on dismantling might be sufficient. In October President Bush said in Bangkok that the USA would be prepared to offer security assurances to the DPRK in exchange for verifiable dismantling. However, he said that a bilateral non-aggression treaty, as desired by Pyongyang, was not a possibility, and that any guarantee would involve China, Russia, the Republic of Korea and Japan, as well as the USA. Also in October, the North Korean state news agency claimed that the DPRK had successfully completed the reprocessing of 8,000 spent fuel rods, thus generating sufficient plutonium to build a nuclear bomb. The USA, however, dismissed the claim. However, in November the Central Intelligence Agency (CIA) reported to the US Congress that it believed the DPRK had the technology to turn its nuclear fuel into functioning weapons. In early December KEDO (an international consortium established in 1995 following a 1994 agreement with the USA on assistance for energy development in the DPRK in return for nuclear non-proliferation, see above) announced that it would be suspending for one year its construction in the DPRK of two non-military nuclear reactors. Also in December, the USA rejected an offer from the DPRK to 'freeze' its nuclear programme in return for concessions on security and energy aid. The USA maintained that the suspension of the nuclear programme was insufficient, and that verifiable dismantling of North Korean nuclear capacity remained necessary.

In January 2004 a group of US nuclear scientists, including Siegfried Hecker, the former director of the Los Alamos nuclear research centre, was permitted to visit the Yongbyon plant in an unofficial capacity. Hecker subsequently stated that although he had seen no proof that the DPRK had produced a nuclear bomb, he had been shown radioactive plutonium metal. There was also speculation on the existence of a second nuclear programme for enriching uranium (in addition to the plutonium-reprocessing activities at Yongbyon). The DPRK continued to deny the existence of such a programme. In February a fresh round of six-party talks took place in Beijing, but no significant resolutions were reached. The DPRK continued to reject US demands for 'complete, verifiable and irreversible dismantling' of its nuclear capabilities. In April a US expert on North Korea, Selig Harrison, visited Pyongyang and was reportedly assured by the President of the Presidium of the SPA, Kim Yong Nam, that the DPRK would not transfer nuclear technology to al-Qa'ida or other 'militant' groups. Also in April, following a train accident in the DPRK at Ryongchon (see above), the DPRK accepted aid including medical supplies from the USA. At a third round of six-party talks in June little progress was achieved, with the DPRK continuing to deny the existence of a uranium enrichment programme. In July US Secretary of State Colin Powell held discussions with the North Korean Minister of Foreign Affairs, Paek Nam Sun, in Jakarta, representing the highest-level talks between the two countries since 2002. However, relations worsened after the Government of the DPRK, in response to criticism of Kim Jong Il by US President George W. Bush, issued a statement likening the US President to the Nazi leader Adolf Hitler, describing Bush as 'an idiot, an ignorant, a tyrant and a man-killer'. Also in August, it was reported that North Korea was developing a new sea-based long-range missile system, which would possibly be capable of targeting the USA. Disclosures in 2004 concerning the suspected inaccuracy of US intelligence on Iraq, which had been used to justify US military action against that country in 2003, increased uncertainty over the quality of US information on the DPRK's weapons capabilities. A fourth round of six-party talks scheduled for September 2004 was suspended when the DPRK refused to attend. Pyongyang cited US hostility towards the DPRK as the reason for this decision. Tensions in relations with the USA increased further following the re-election of George W. Bush as US President in November. Later that month the US-led organization KEDO (see above) announced its intention to suspend plans for the construction in the DPRK of two non-military nuclear reactors.

In January 2005 Pyongyang was angered by a description of the DPRK by Condoleezza Rice, the former US National Security Adviser who had recently been appointed to the position of US Secretary of State, as an 'outpost of tyranny'. Subsequently, in a state radio broadcast in February, the DPRK for the first time explicitly stated that it possessed nuclear weapons, and that it intended to postpone its participation in six-party negotiations for an indefinite period. Subsequent calls by the DPRK for bilateral talks with the USA were rejected by the latter. Early in 2005, meanwhile, Christopher Hill, hitherto the US ambassador in Seoul, replaced James Kelly as Assistant Secretary of State for East Asia and the Pacific and the USA's chief negotiator in the nuclear talks. In March Condoleezza Rice declared during a visit to Beijing that the USA would consider 'other options' if the DPRK persisted in refusing to participate in the six-party talks. In late March the DPRK issued a suggestion that any resumption of talks should focus on the wider issue of regional denuclearization; the proposal was dismissed by the USA. In April, following a visit to the DPRK, Selig Harrison reported that the Yongbyon reactor was to be shut down in order to extract 8,000 spent fuel rods, to be reprocessed into plutonium for use in warheads. In May the DPRK announced that all 8,000 rods had been unloaded from the Yongbyon reactor 'in the shortest possible time', although there was speculation that this was unlikely to have been achieved so quickly and that the announcement might be a diplomatic ploy in advance of any resumption of talks. Also in May tension was increased when the DPRK test-fired a ballistic missile into the Sea of Japan, while Mohammad el-Baradei, Director-General of the IAEA, stated that he believed the DPRK possessed enough weapons-grade plutonium for 'five of six' nuclear devices. An apparent improvement in relations in June, however, including a US pledge of 50,000 metric tons of food aid, prompted speculation that the stalled talks might resume in July. In the event, the fourth round of six-party talks began in Beijing on 26 July. On the previous day bilateral discussions were held between the representatives of the DPRK and the USA in the hope of finding a compromise between their respective opening positions. The USA continued to insist that normalization of relations, lifting of sanctions and guarantees of security could only follow the 'complete, verifiable and irreversible dismantling' of the DPRK's nuclear weapons programme, while the latter reiterated that only after the normalization of relations, including the signing of a peace treaty ending the Korean War, and the removal of US nuclear weapons from South Korea (the presence of which the US side denied) would the North agree to abandon its military nuclear aspirations. (The USA had indicated that, for the purpose of these talks, it was prepared to disregard the issue of the possible existence of a uranium enrichment programme in the DPRK.) The talks went into recess in early August; their resumption was postponed until mid-September as a mark of protest by the DPRK at the annual joint military exercises performed by South Korea and the USA in late August and early September.

On 19 September 2005 a draft joint agreement was signed by all sides in the six-party negotiations, in which the DPRK committed itself to dismantle its nuclear weapons programme, return to the NPT and permit IAEA inspectors to visit its nuclear facilities. In return, the USA declared that it maintained no nuclear weapons on the Korean peninsula and had no intention of attacking the DPRK. The DPRK's right to peaceful nuclear energy was acknowledged, and it was envisioned that the provision of a civilian light-water nuclear reactor to North Korea would be discussed 'at an appropriate time'. The other five parties also pledged to provide the DPRK with energy assistance. Described in some quarters as a major breakthrough, the agreement was nevertheless vague and was compromised almost immediately when the North Korean Government insisted that it would take no steps towards dismantling its nuclear weapons programme until provided with a light-water reactor as specified in the agreement. The USA insisted that concessions such as the reactor could be expected to come into force only after the DPRK had fulfilled its dismantlement obligations. The fifth round of talks, which began in Beijing in early November, were intended to discuss means of implementing the September agreement, but their opening was marred by North Korea's angry reaction to reported comments by President Bush during a visit to Brazil where he made reference to a 'tyrant in North Korea'. A five-point plan for dismantling its nuclear programme proposed at the talks by the DPRK was reportedly rejected by the USA; the discussions ended without agreement and without any setting of a date for the next round. Later in November KEDO (the Korean Peninsula Energy Development Organization—see above) announced that it was considering the termination of its light-water reactor construction project in the DPRK, which had been suspended since 2003. (All workers were withdrawn from KEDO's construction site in Kumho, DPRK, in January 2006.) Meanwhile, the resumption of the six-party nuclear negotiations appeared to be jeopardized by a series of attacks by the USA on the alleged financial crimes of the DPRK. In September 2005 the US Administration had ordered that all transactions with Banco Asia Delta in Macao, China, be terminated, in relation to suspected money-laundering activities conducted with the bank by the North Korean Government, and had also 'frozen' the assets of eight North Korean companies, which it accused of proliferating weapons of mass destruction. In October the US Department of Justice accused the DPRK of having forged millions of US dollars' worth of counterfeit $100 bills since 1989, and in December Alexander Vershbow, US ambassador to the Republic of Korea, publicly described the DPRK as a 'criminal regime'. Although the US Administration insisted that the sanctions were purely a legal matter and had no political connection to the nuclear issue, the North Korean Government declared that no further six-party negotiations could be held until sanctions against it were removed. In April 2006 Hill rejected North Korean overtures for bilateral discussions in Tokyo, to coincide with a regional security forum at which all six participants in the nuclear talks were present, insisting that communication between the two sides was only possible within the context of the six-party talks.

During the years of the so-called Sino-Soviet dispute the DPRK fluctuated in its allegiance to each of its powerful northern neighbours, the People's Republic of China and the USSR. Kim Il Sung made several official visits to China in the late 1980s, which were interpreted by some Western observers as an attempt to establish closer relations in view of the erosion of communist power in many Eastern European countries. However, the DPRK was aggrieved at China's establishment of full diplomatic relations with the Republic of Korea in August 1992. China appeared largely conciliatory with regard to North Korea's nuclear programme, and during 1993 and the first months of 1994 indicated that it would veto any attempt by the UN Security Council to impose economic sanctions on the DPRK. In 1997 China agreed to provide substantial food aid to the DPRK to alleviate the effects of flooding. Later in that year China accepted US and South Korean proposals for quadripartite negotiations with North Korea to conclude a new peace agreement with the South, and between December 1997 and August 1999 it participated in all six rounds of these negotiations. Relations between the DPRK and China remained close in 1998, with the latter donating grain, fertilizers and crude petroleum to Pyongyang over the course of the year. A high-level North Korean delegation visited China in June 1999. During the visit China announced that it would provide the country with 150,000 metric tons of food aid and 400,000 tons of coke over the following months. In October 1999 the Chinese Minister of Foreign Affairs, Tang Jiaxuan, participated in celebrations held in Pyongyang to commemorate the 50th anniversary of the establishment of diplomatic relations between the two countries.

In late 1999 international attention was focused on the uncertain situation of the large number of North Koreans (estimated at some 30,000 by South Korean sources and at 200,000 by the voluntary organization Médecins Sans Frontières) who had crossed the border into the People's Republic of China in recent years. In early 2000 it was reported that China had returned some 10,000 escapees to the DPRK during 1999. The number of migrants was thought to fluctuate, according to the season.

In February 2000 China permitted the DPRK to open a consulate-general in Hong Kong. In the following month Kim Jong Il attended a function at the People's Republic of China's embassy in Pyongyang. This was his first visit to the mission for 15 years. In May Kim Jong Il visited China, his first official trip abroad for 17 years, in advance of the historic inter-Korean summit meeting. In late October Kim Jong Il met the visiting Chinese Minister of Defence, Chi Haotian. In mid-January 2001 the North Korean leader paid a second visit to the People's Republic. During this visit, Kim held extensive talks with Chinese leaders in Beijing, and also toured the new business zones of Shanghai and Shenzhen, where he observed joint-venture projects with foreign multinational corporations, telecommunications projects and the Shanghai Stock Exchange. It was widely believed that he was seeking inspiration for the revival of the DPRK's crisis-ridden economy and advice from Chinese leaders on developing Pyongyang's role within the international community.

In early September 2001 Chinese President Jiang Zemin paid an official visit to North Korea, his first such visit since 1990. Jiang promised an additional 200,000 tons of food aid and 30,000 tons of diesel oil as a gesture of goodwill to alleviate North Korea's economic crisis. Jiang also reportedly urged North Korea to resume discussions with the South. By early 2002 it was thought that the DPRK was placing a renewed emphasis on relations with China in order to deflect criticism from the USA.

During 2002 the DPRK and China continued to seek the reconnection of the inter-Korean railway lines and their subsequent linking to China's own railway system. In May 2002, however, China's forcible removal of North Korean refugees from South Korean embassies in the People's Republic again brought the issue of the refugees to international attention. Several groups of North Korean refugees had, in 2002, fled to Western, Japanese and South Korean diplomatic offices in China, embarrassing the latter, since Beijing had signed a treaty with Pyongyang providing for the repatriation of refugees. In late June Beijing allowed 24 northern refugees who had been concealed in the embassy of the Republic of Korea to leave for that country. After that incident, Beijing began an operation against South Korean activists and missionaries who had been helping northerners to flee via China. It was estimated that as many as 300,000 North Korean refugees were already residing in China, with US sources stating that as many as 50,000 had fled to China in 2001 alone.

In October 2002 the DPRK appointed a Chinese entrepreneur of Dutch citizenship, Yang Bin, as the new governor of its recently created Sinuiju Special Administrative Region; however, the Beijing authorities arrested him on charges of bribery and fraud (see above). By early 2003 China was becoming increasingly concerned about the growing diplomatic crisis between the DPRK and the USA over the former's decision formally to restart its nuclear programme. In late February 2003 the President of the DPRK's SPA Presidium, Kim Yong Nam, visited Beijing and pledged to maintain strong bilateral relations. Beijing was expected to use its influence with Pyongyang to resolve the situation, albeit warning the UN Security Council not to involve itself in the matter. In March China cut its oil supply to the DPRK via a pipeline from Liaoning Province for three days, following North Korean missile tests in the Sea of Japan (see above).

In late April 2003 China hosted and participated in senior-level meetings between the DPRK and the USA over Pyongyang's nuclear weapons programme (see above). Immediately prior to the talks, Vice-Marshal Jo Myong Rok, Pyongyang's second-highest ranking official, led a military delegation to China, and held meetings with President Hu Jintao and senior military leaders. Chinese diplomatic efforts played a major role in ensuring North Korean participation in the first round of six-party talks on the nuclear issue that were held in Beijing in August 2003 (as well as in subsequent rounds—see above). In late October Wu Bangguo, Chairman of the Standing Committee of China's National People's Congress, made an official visit to Pyongyang. In April 2004 Kim Jong Il made a secretive visit to China, where he held talks with President Hu Jintao and other officials. Topics under discussion included the nuclear issue, with China reportedly urging the DPRK to modify its stance, and economic matters. During 2004 repeated instances of defectors from the DPRK seeking refuge in foreign embassies in Beijing posed a dilemma for China, which as an official ally of the DPRK continued to refuse to grant refugee status to such persons. Many defectors were none the less able to travel to Seoul via a third country. In November, however, China forcibly repatriated a group of 70 North Korean nationals. It was believed that they would be imprisoned and possibly executed upon their return to the DPRK. Meanwhile, following the DPRK's refusal to attend a fourth round of six-party talks on the nuclear issue in September, a member of the Standing Committee of the Politburo of the Chinese Communist Party, Li Changchun, headed a delegation to Pyongyang in an attempt to persuade Pyongyang to resume negotiations. As the country believed to have the most influence on the Government of the DPRK, owing to historic ties as well as to North Korean dependency on Chinese oil and food supplies, China was repeatedly urged by the USA to assist in efforts to curb the DPRK's nuclear ambitions. During a visit by US Secretary of State Condoleezza Rice to Beijing in March 2005 Chinese President Hu Jintao stated that China would be willing to co-operate with other parties in persuading the DPRK to resume negotiations. North Korean Premier Pak Pong Ju visited Beijing and Shanghai later that month. Chinese diplomacy received considerable credit for the achievement of the joint draft agreement at the end of the fourth round of six-party talks in September, although the sequence of implementation of the agreement's terms remained contentious (see above). In October Chinese President Hu Jintao made his first official visit to Pyongyang, in advance of the fifth round of nuclear talks in November. In January 2006 reports emerged that Kim Jong Il had travelled incognito to the People's Republic and was visiting the special economic zone of Shenzhen, to observe the methods and results of China's economic modernization. The visit was confirmed by North Korean media following Kim's return to the DPRK.

In the mid-1980s the DPRK placed increased emphasis on its relations with the USSR, culminating in a new arrangement for the supply of Soviet aircraft and an exchange visit by senior government officials. The DPRK's diplomatic isolation became more pronounced in the early 1990s, as former communist bloc countries moved to foster relations with the Republic of Korea. Furthermore, the USSR announced that, from January 1991, its barter trading system with the DPRK would be abolished in favour of trade in convertible currencies at world market prices. However, an agreement was reported to have been signed in May 1993 by the DPRK and the Russian Federation (which, following the dissolution of the USSR, had assumed responsibility for many of the USSR's international undertakings) on technological and scientific co-operation. Negotiations on the renewal of the 1961 bilateral treaty of friendship, co-operation and assistance, which expired in 1996 (but remained valid in the interim), opened in January 1997. Discussions on the rescheduling of the terms of repayment of North Korea's debt to Russia took place in October. In March 1999 a new bilateral treaty of friendship, good neighbourliness and co-operation was initialled in Pyongyang; a formal signing followed in February 2000, during a visit to Pyongyang by the Russian Minister of Foreign Affairs, Igor Ivanov. The treaty was ratified by the DPRK in April. In July President Vladimir Putin became the first Russian (or Soviet) leader to visit North Korea. During the trip Kim Jong Il declared himself willing to halt missile development in exchange for access to space rocket technology funded by other countries, although he subsequently seemed to renege on this offer. Following Putin's visit, co-operation between Russia and the DPRK placed a strong emphasis on connecting the latter's rail system to the Trans-Siberian railway, with a view to creating a long-awaited Eurasian transport corridor, and in March 2001 the two countries signed a railway co-operation agreement.

In late April 2001 the DPRK's Minister of the People's Armed Forces, Vice-Marshal Kim Il Chol, visited Moscow and reportedly negotiated the acquisition of defensive weapons such as SU-27 aircraft, anti-aircraft systems and intelligence-gathering equipment, in addition to signing a military co-operation protocol.

In August 2001 Kim Jong Il paid a 24-day visit across Russia to Moscow, where he and President Putin signed a new declaration of co-operation in politics, the economy, military, science and technology, and culture. However, Russia also urged the DPRK to settle the latter's outstanding bilateral debt of as much as US $5,500m. The DPRK had repaid some of this amount by sending hundreds of forced-labour woodcutters to work in Khabarovsk Krai (territory)—although such labour camps were reportedly closed down by late 2002. During his visit, Kim also toured industrial plants, including those manufacturing power equipment and tanks, a pig farm, a beer brewery and the Krunichev Space Centre, outside Moscow. Kim reaffirmed the DPRK's moratorium on missile-testing until 2003, and urged the withdrawal of US troops from South Korea. Kim's visit suggested that the DPRK was seeking closer relations with Russia, in addition to China, to strengthen its international standing. In late October 2001 the new Russian ambassador in Pyongyang, Andrei Karlov, held a banquet at which he spoke of strengthening bilateral ties. In December Kim had a meeting with Karlov.

The DPRK continued to maintain strong relations with Russia in 2002. In April two separate Russian delegations, one led by the Mayor of St Petersburg, Vladimir Yakovlev, the other by the Russian Presidential Representative in the Far Eastern Federal Okrug (district), Konstantin Pulikovskii, visited Pyongyang to discuss co-operation in all fields, particularly business. In May the Minister of Foreign Affairs, Paek Nam Sun, visited Moscow, in the first such visit in 15 years. In late July the Russian Minister of Foreign Affairs, Igor Ivanov, visited Pyongyang, and in late August Kim Jong Il visited the Russian city of Vladivostok, where he held discussions with Putin, mainly focusing on the reconnection of railway links across the Korean peninsula. At the same time the DPRK and the Russian Oblast of Amur signed a co-operation agreement on agriculture and forestry. In October 2002 two North Korean military delegations visited Russia, and in December the Mayor of Moscow, Yurii Luzhkov, visited Pyongyang.

As the diplomatic crisis over the DPRK's nuclear weapons programme deteriorated in January 2003, Russia sought to defuse the situation by sending the Deputy Minister of Foreign Affairs, Aleksandr Losyukov, to Pyongyang, where he held discussions with Kim Jong Il. Losyukov, who had earlier visited China and subsequently the USA, urged a three-stage formula whereby the international community would accept a nuclear-free Korean peninsula, guarantees for the regime's security, and a resumption of humanitarian and economic aid. Pyongyang reiterated that the crisis could be resolved only through discussions with the USA. In February Kim Jong Il again visited the Russian embassy in Pyongyang, where a banquet was held on the occasion of his 61st birthday.

In late March 2003 a hitherto unrealized Russian proposal to supply the DPRK with natural gas from the island of Sakhalin in return for Pyongyang's abandonment of its nuclear programme was raised by the South Korean Government. Russia's Deputy Minister of Foreign Affairs, Alexandr Losyukov, attended the six-party talks held in Beijing in August 2003 to discuss the North Korean nuclear weapons programme. At the talks Losyukov urged both the USA and the DPRK to show flexibility. In late 2003 Russia appeared to be expanding its economic links with the DPRK, with a team of Russian engineers inspecting a cargo port and petroleum refinery at Raijin, as well as assessing a stretch of railway linking the two countries across the Tumen river. Russia was represented at two further rounds of six-party talks on the DPRK's nuclear weapons programme in February 2004 and in June of the same year. In March 2004 Kim Jong Il sent a congratulatory message to Vladimir Putin upon his re-election as Russia's President.

The DPRK's unilateral application for UN membership, first announced in May 1991, represented a radical departure from its earlier insistence that the two Koreas should occupy a single UN seat. This development was welcomed by the Republic of Korea, and both countries were admitted separately to the UN in September of that year. In September 1999, for the first time in seven years, the North Korean Minister of Foreign Affairs attended and addressed the annual session of the UN General Assembly, in what was perceived as an attempt to end the DPRK's diplomatic isolation. Furthermore, in January 2000 Italy became the first of the G-7 group of Western industrialized nations (and the sixth member of the EU) to establish diplomatic relations with the DPRK, and in May Australia restored diplomatic ties with Pyongyang. Diplomatic relations were established with the Philippines in July and with the United Kingdom in December. During 2001 the DPRK further expanded its range of diplomatic partners, opening relations with the Netherlands, Belgium, Canada, Spain, Germany, Luxembourg, Greece, Brazil, New Zealand, Kuwait, the European Union, Bahrain, Turkey, and Liechtenstein. A number of these countries appointed chargés d'affaires to serve in Seoul prior to the foundation of embassies in Pyongyang. Relations with Timor-Leste were established in late 2002. In May 2003 the DPRK opened its first embassy in London, amid protests from human rights protesters. Relations with Ireland were established in December. In March 2004 the Australian ambassador to Beijing, Alan Thomas, was instructed to present his credentials in Pyongyang. The DPRK established diplomatic relations with San Marino in May. In September 2004 the British Parliamentary Under-Secretary of State for Foreign and Commonwealth Affairs, Bill Rammell, visited the DPRK, with the stated intention of discussing human rights issues as well as the North Korean nuclear programme. During his visit Rammell also requested that the United Kingdom's ambassador to Pyongyang be permitted to visit the location of an explosion in the DPRK, amid initial suspicion that a nuclear test had taken place at the site. The request was subsequently granted by North Korean officials.

In April 2000 the DPRK formally applied to join ASEAN (see p. 172). Following the DPRK's admittance to the ASEAN Regional Forum (ARF), a meeting in Thailand in July was attended for the first time by the North Korean Minister of Foreign Affairs, Paek Nam Sun, who held unprecedented meetings with his South Korean, Japanese and US counterparts. In November the Asia-Pacific Economic Co-operation (APEC, see p. 164) forum supported the DPRK's guest status in that organization. Full membership was expected to follow in 2007, upon the expiry of a 10-year moratorium on new members. In late July 2001 the President of the Presidium of the SPA, Kim Yong Nam, visited Viet Nam, Laos and Cambodia. In early March 2002 Kim visited Thailand and Malaysia, where he discussed mainly trade issues. Prime Minister Mahathir bin Mohamad of Malaysia accepted an invitation to visit the DPRK, and Indonesian President Megawati Sukarnoputri visited the country at the end of March 2002. Kim Yong Nam reciprocated Megawati's visit in July of that year. The President of Viet Nam, Tran Duc Luong, visited the DPRK in May 2002 and signed several economic and legal co-operation agreements. In late 2002 the DPRK and Taiwan were exploring the possibility of establishing mutual liaison offices. In 2003 there were reports that the DPRK was selling military equipment to Pakistan, and also that military relations with Myanmar were being developed. In early 2004 Pakistani nuclear scientist Abdul Qadeer Khan confessed that he had sold nuclear secrets to the DPRK. In November 2005 it was reported that the Government of Thailand was investigating claims that a Thai woman missing since 1978 had been kidnapped by North Korean agents and was now living in the DPRK.

Pyongyang maintained close links with a number of Arab and Middle Eastern countries, including Egypt, Libya, Syria and Iran. The President of the Presidium of the SPA, Kim Yong Nam, visited Libya and Syria in July 2002. The DPRK retained long-standing ties with many African nations, and reportedly had military advisers working in some 12 of that continent's countries in 2005. In January 2004 the Vice-President of the Presidium of the SPA, Yang Hyong Sop, visited Nigeria to discuss an agreement on military technology. In May 2004 it was reported that IAEA investigation of uranium delivered to the USA by Libya in late 2003 had revealed that the material had been supplied to Libya by the DPRK through an illicit nuclear technology procurement network operated by Pakistani nuclear scientist Abdul Qadeer Khan (see above). Further evidence concerning the transfer of nuclear material from the DPRK to Libya emerged in early 2005.

Government

The highest organ of state power is the unicameral Supreme People's Assembly (SPA), with 687 members, elected (unopposed) for five years by universal adult suffrage. The SPA elects, for its duration, the Chairman of the National Defence Commission, who, since the effective abolition of the presidency in September 1998, holds the most senior accessible office of state (although this is not formally stated in the Constitution). The SPA elects the Premier and, on the latter's recommendation, appoints other Ministers to form the Cabinet. The President of the SPA Presidium, whose members are elected by the SPA, represents the State in its relations with foreign countries.

Political power is held by the communist Korean Workers' Party (KWP), which is the most influential party in the Democratic Front for the Reunification of the Fatherland (comprising the KWP and two minor parties). The Front presents an approved list of candidates for elections to representative bodies. The KWP's highest authority is the Party Congress, which elects a Central Committee to supervise party work. The Committee elects a Political Bureau (Politburo) to direct policy. The Presidium of the Politburo is the KWP's most powerful policy-making body.

The DPRK comprises nine provinces and two cities, each with an elected Local People's Assembly.

Defence

Military service is selective: army five to eight years, navy five to 10 years, and air force three to four years. The estimated total strength of the armed forces in August 2005 was 1,106,000: army 950,000, air force 110,000, and navy 46,000. Security and border troops numbered 189,000, and there was a workers' and peasants' militia ('Red Guards') numbering about 3.5m. The ratio of North Korea's armed forces to total population is believed to be the highest in the world. Defence expenditure for 2004 was budgeted at 15.5% of total spending. South Korean intelligence sources estimated the real level of defence expenditure to be more than 30% of total spending in 2004.

Economic Affairs

In 2004, according to estimates by the Bank of Korea (South Korea), the DPRK's gross national income (GNI) was about US $20,800m., equivalent to some $914 per head. It was estimated that in 1998 the North Korean economy declined for the ninth successive year, with gross domestic product (GDP) contracting by 1.1%, in real terms. In 1999, however, it was estimated that GDP grew by 6.2%, and in 2000 by 1.3%. Growth was estimated at 3.7% in 2001, 1.2% in 2002 and at 1.8% in 2003. Growth in 2004 was estimated at 2.2%. During 1995–2004, according to estimates by the World Bank, the population increased by an annual average of 0.7%.

Agriculture (including forestry and fishing) contributed an estimated 26.7% of GDP in 2004, according to South Korean sources. In 2003, according to FAO estimates, 27.9% of the economically active population were employed in agriculture. The principal crops are rice, maize, potatoes, sweet potatoes and soybeans. The DPRK is not self-sufficient in food, and imports substantial amounts of wheat, rice and maize annually. Food shortages became a severe problem from the mid-1990s. By 1999 the food situation had improved to some extent, owing to fertilizer aid from international donors, agrarian reform and increased potato production, although shortages continued and were exacerbated by severe drought in 2000 and 2001, and subsequent typhoons and floods. According to the World Food Programme (WFP), cereal shortfalls of some 40,000 tons affected 2.2m. people in December 2003. In December 2000 the Government launched an intensive campaign for potato growing and double-crop farming, and in November 2001 construction began on a 7,000-ha goat farm near Pyongyang. According to South Korean estimates, grain production was 4.1m. tons in 2002 and 4.3m. tons in 2003. Potato production was 1.9m. tons in 2002 and 2.0m. tons in 2003, according to FAO. The raising of livestock (principally cattle and pigs), forestry and fishing are important. During 1995–2004, according to South Korean estimates, agricultural GDP increased by an average of 2.7% per year. In 2004, again according to South Korean estimates, agricultural GDP rose by 4.1%, following increases of 1.7% in 2003 and 4.3% in 2002.

In 2004, according to South Korean estimates, industry (including mining, manufacturing, construction and power) contributed 40.9% of GDP. In 1990 the industrial sector employed 31.6% of the labour force. During 1995–2004, according to South Korean estimates, industrial GDP decreased by an average of 0.9% per year. Industrial GDP increased by 2.8% in 2003 and by 1.3% in 2004.

Mining contributed 8.7% of GDP in 2004, according to South Korean estimates. The DPRK possesses considerable mineral wealth, with large deposits of coal, iron, lead, copper, zinc, tin, silver and gold. The country was formerly the second largest producer of magnesia products in the world, but output is believed to have declined significantly. There are unexploited offshore deposits of petroleum and natural gas. South Korean sources estimated that in 2004 output in the mining sector increased by 2.5%, compared with an increase of 3.2% in 2003 and a decline of 3.8% in 2002.

In 2004, according to South Korean estimates, the manufacturing sector contributed 18.5% of GDP. In the 1990s industrial development concentrated on heavy industry (metallurgy—notably steel production—machine-building, cement and chemicals). The textiles industry has provided significant exports. South Korean sources estimated that the GDP of the manufacturing sector increased by 0.3% in 2004, following an increase of 2.6% in 2003 and a decline of 1.9% in 2002.

In 2002 it was estimated that 70% of the DPRK's energy supply was derived from coal, followed in importance by hydroelectricity (17%) and petroleum (8%). A 30-MW nuclear reactor was believed to have been inaugurated in 1987. Light-water nuclear reactors were being constructed, for the purpose of electricity generation, in accordance with an agreement concluded with the USA in 1994. However, in December 2003 construction of the reactors was suspended for one year, following North Korea's resumption of its nuclear weapons programme. In November 2004 it was announced that construction would remain suspended for a further year, and in late 2005 there were suggestions that the project might be abandoned altogether (see Recent History). In 2004, according to South Korean sources, the DPRK's electricity generation capacity was 7.77m. kW, while the volume of actual power generation totalled 206,000m. kWh. During the 1990s the DPRK experienced increasing power shortages, as generation and transmission infrastructure deteriorated. Severe drought in the late 1990s and 2000 adversely affected the production of hydroelectric power. Electricity generation in 2004 was less than 75% of the amount generated in 1990. In 2004 the DPRK was attempting to increase its electricity output through the construction of new hydroelectric power plants in various provinces. These were believed to be smaller power plants with a generating capacity of less than 10,000 kW. Petroleum imports in 2004 amounted to only 21% of the amount imported in 1990, and less than 0.5% of the amount imported by South Korea. The USA suspended fuel oil shipments in late 2002, following Pyongyang's alleged admission that it was pursuing a secret nuclear programme. From the 1990s the DPRK sought greater foreign assistance in developing its offshore oilfields, located to the west in the Bohai Sea, and also in the north-east, near Chongjin city. A limited number of joint ventures were established with foreign oil companies. In 1999 the DPRK succeeded in producing 300,000 tons of petroleum from a well located off Sukchon County, equivalent to about half the amount of petroleum imported in that year, although falling far short of the amount needed to meet the country's acute energy needs. In September 2004 it was announced that an agreement had been signed between the North Korean Government and a British oil company for further petroleum exploration in the DPRK. In 2002, according to South Korean sources, per caput energy consumption in North Korea in 2001 was 0.70 tons of oil equivalent, more than six times less that the figure for South Korea. Until the early 1980s North Korean energy supplies had been larger than those of South Korea.

The services sector employed an estimated 30.4% of the labour force in 1990. South Korean sources estimated that in 2004 the DPRK's services sector accounted for 32.3% of GDP. In 2004 output in the sector was estimated to have increased by 1.4%, having increased by 0.6% in 2003 and decreased by 0.2% in 2002.

The trade deficit, including exchanges with South Korea, totalled US $983.1m. in 2003. In 2003 total exports, excluding trade with South Korea, reached $777.0m. and imports totalled $2,614.4m., thus giving a trade deficit of $837.4m. (compared with a deficit of $790.4m. in the previous year). The DPRK's principal source of imports in 2003 was the People's Republic of China (accounting for 30.6% of total imports), followed by the Republic of Korea (21.2%) and Thailand (9.9%). The People's Republic of China became the DPRK's principal market for exports in 2003, purchasing 37.1% of goods, surpassing the Republic of Korea, which thus became the second most important destination, purchasing 27.1% of total exports, followed by Japan (16.3%). China was a source of crude petroleum, food and vehicles, while Japan was a destination for industrial and agricultural goods. In 2002 inter-Korean trade increased by 59% to reach US $641.7m., and in 2003 the volume of trade increased by 12.9% to $724.3. Total trade (excluding exchanges with the Republic of Korea) increased by 15.1% to reach $2,270m. in 2001, but decreased slightly, by 0.4%, to $2,260.4m. in 2002, before increasing again by 5.8% to $2,391.4m in 2003. The principal exports in 2002 were live animals (35.5% of the value of total exports, excluding trade with the Republic of Korea), textiles (16.7%) and machinery and electrical equipment (11.6%). Other export commodities in the late 1990s included tobacco and silk. The principal imports in 2002 were mineral products (15.5% of the value of total imports, excluding trade with the Republic of Korea), machinery and electrical equipment (15.4%), and textiles (10.4%). Other import items included road vehicles, chemicals and groceries.

The DPRK's total external debt was estimated to be US $12,460m. in 2000. Following the introduction of market-orientated reforms in 2002, the inflation rate was said to have reached 4,000% in that year. The 2005 budget reportedly envisaged revenue and expenditure balancing at 391,310m. won, compared with revenue of 351,266m. won and expenditure of 348,870m. won in 2004.

It is difficult to present an accurate economic profile of the DPRK, owing to the lack of reliable statistical data. North Korea's economic situation deteriorated sharply in the early 1990s, following the abandonment, in 1991 and 1992, respectively, of the barter trading system between the DPRK and the USSR (then its major trading partner) and China in favour of trade conducted exclusively in convertible currencies. The USSR also substantially reduced deliveries of crude petroleum and cereals, resulting in a severe decline in industrial production. The years 1994–97 were designated 'a period of adjustment in socialist economic construction', during which emphasis was to be transferred from traditional heavy industries to agriculture, light industry and trade. From the late 1990s the DPRK slowly began to open up its economy, developing trading relations with various European and Asian countries and increasing the number of limited joint ventures with foreign firms. During 2002 there were signs of a significant change in economic policy. In July the Government abandoned rationing, allowing farmers to sell produce at market prices, and wages were raised by a factor of 10–17, to take into account the concomitant price rises caused by the reforms. State assistance was reduced, and the value of the won decreased to as little as one-fiftieth of its previous value in relation to the US dollar. From December 2002, in apparent displeasure with US policy towards the DPRK, the North Korean Government prohibited the use of the US dollar and adopted the euro as its official currency of foreign exchange. A further major reform of 2002 was the establishment of a special industrial zone at Kaesong, on the border with South Korea, and a new tourist zone at Mount Kumgang. In June 2004, following completion of a test stage, the initial phase of the Kaesong project commenced, with the first 15 companies that were to be permitted to conduct business in the zone having been selected by Korea Land, a South Korean company. The development of the Kaesong zone contributed significantly to a notable increase in inter-Korean trade, the total volume of which reportedly exceeded US $1,000m. in 2005. In April 2006, meanwhile, the Minister of Finance announced that the state budget's revenue would be 7.1% higher than in 2005, while expenditure would be 3.5% higher than in the previous year. Defence spending amounted to 15.9% of total projected expenditure. Price increases as a result of the economic reforms of 2002 were believed to have brought further hardship to some sectors of the population. This was confirmed in a UN report of November 2004, which stated that the price of rice had increased five-fold within one year, and that the price of only 1kg of rice was now around 30% of the average monthly wage. The first ever report on the DPRK's environment, meanwhile, published by the UN in co-operation with the country's National Co-ordinating Committee for Environment in August 2004, showed considerable environmental degradation in the DPRK, including depletion of forest resources by timber production as well as pollution of air, owing to widespread use of coal, and pollution of water by untreated sewage. In March 2005 legislation introduced by the Japanese Government requiring all ships entering Japanese ports to be insured took effect. This amounted to a ban on all but very few North Korean ships that were involved in trade with Japan, importing items such as sea food and mushrooms, and was thus expected to be damaging to the North Korean economy. Unofficial estimates anticipated a growth rate of 1.0% for 2005. From 2004 there were further signs of attempts to reform the economy whilst resisting any change to the DPRK's political structure, a process similar to that initiated in the People's Republic of China

THE DEMOCRATIC PEOPLE'S REPUBLIC OF KOREA (NORTH KOREA)

more than 20 years previously. In March the Government stated its desire to increase economic co-operation with foreign countries, and in May a group of North Korean officials reportedly visited Shanghai in order to study Chinese market reform. Kim Jong Il himself paid a similar research visit to the Shenzhen Special Economic Zone in January 2006 (see Recent History). In late 2005 there were reports that the Government was attempting to reverse the market-orientated reforms implemented in the agricultural sector in 2002 and reintroduce rationing for rice and other grains. This coincided with the requested termination of humanitarian food aid (see above), suggesting a deliberate policy to reimpose control of the food supply. It was also predicted that the financial sanctions imposed on the DPRK by the US Administration in the latter half of 2005, in connection with alleged money-laundering activities carried out via the Macao-based Banco Delta Asia (see Recent History), would adversely affect North Korea's already weak economy, as other lenders became reluctant to finance the DPRK's overseas transactions. Critics of the regime believed that money-laundering and counterfeiting of US currency, together with suspected state-sponsored trade in weapons and narcotics, played a crucial role in the DPRK's economy. Analysts remained doubtful about Kim Jong Il's ability to restructure the economy without destabilizing the foundations of the ruling regime. Prospects for economic development remained uncertain in the context of international tension over the DPRK's nuclear weapons programme.

Education

Universal compulsory primary and secondary education were introduced in 1956 and 1958, respectively, and are provided at state expense. Free and compulsory 11-year education in state schools was introduced in 1975. Children enter kindergarten at five years of age, and people's school at the age of six. After four years, they advance to senior middle school for six years. In 1986 there were 519 university-level institutions and colleges; in the following year 325,000 students were enrolled in such institutions. In 1988 the Government announced the creation of new educational establishments, including one university, eight colleges, three factory colleges, two farmers' colleges and five special schools. English is compulsory as a second language at the age of 14. A report submitted to UNESCO by the North Korean Government in 2000 stated that there were 27,017 nurseries for 1,575,000 pupils, 14,167 kindergartens for 748,416 pupils, 4,886 primary schools for 1,609,865 pupils, 4,772 senior middle schools for 2,181,524 pupils, and more that 300 universities and colleges with 1.89m. students and academics. The adult literacy rate was estimated by UNESCO in 2003 to be 98%.

Public Holidays

The *Juche* calendar was introduced in the DPRK in 1997; 1912, the year of the late Kim Il Sung's birth, was designated the first year of the new calendar.

2006: 1 January (New Year), 16–17 February (Kim Jong Il's Birthday), 8 March (International Women's Day), 15 April (Day of the Sun, Kim Il Sung's Birthday), 1 May (May Day), 15 August (Anniversary of Liberation), 9 September (Independence Day), 10 October (Anniversary of the foundation of the Korean Workers' Party), 27 December (Anniversary of the Constitution).

2007: 1 January (New Year), 16–17 February (Kim Jong Il's Birthday), 8 March (International Women's Day), 15 April (Day of the Sun, Kim Il Sung's Birthday), 1 May (May Day), 15 August (Anniversary of Liberation), 9 September (Independence Day), 10 October (Anniversary of the foundation of the Korean Workers' Party), 27 December (Anniversary of the Constitution).

Weights and Measures

The metric system is in force.

Statistical Survey

Area and Population

AREA, POPULATION AND DENSITY*

Area (sq km)	122,762†
Population (census results)	
31 December 1993	
Males	10,329,699
Females	10,883,679
Total	21,213,378
Population (unofficial estimates)‡	
2002	22,369,000
2003	22,522,000
2004	22,709,000
Density (per sq km) in 2004	185.0

* Excluding the demilitarized zone between North and South Korea, with an area of 1,262 sq km (487 sq miles).
† 47,399 sq miles.
‡ Source: Bank of Korea (Republic of Korea).

PRINCIPAL TOWNS
(population at 1993 census)

Pyongyang (capital)	2,741,260	Wonsan	300,148
Nampo	731,448	Pyongsong	272,934
Hamhung	709,730	Sariwon	254,146
Chongjin	582,480	Haeju	229,172
Kaesong	334,433	Kanggye	223,410
Sinuiju	326,011	Hyesan	178,020

Source: UN, *Demographic Yearbook*.

BIRTHS AND DEATHS
(UN estimates, annual averages)

	1990–95	1995–2000	2000–05
Birth rate (per 1,000)	21.0	18.9	16.4
Death rate (per 1,000)	8.9	10.1	10.7

Source: UN, *World Population Prospects: The 2004 Revision*.

Expectation of life (years at birth): 66 (males 65; females 68) in 2003 (Source: WHO, *World Health Report*).

ECONOMICALLY ACTIVE POPULATION
(ILO estimates, '000 persons at mid-1990)

	Males	Females	Total
Agriculture, etc.	2,027	1,877	3,904
Industry	2,206	1,043	3,249
Services	1,577	1,549	3,126
Total labour force	5,810	4,469	10,279

Source: ILO, *Economically Active Population: Estimates and Projections, 1950–2010*.

Mid-2003 (estimates in '000): Agriculture, etc. 3,263; Total labour force 11,676 (Source: FAO).

THE DEMOCRATIC PEOPLE'S REPUBLIC OF KOREA (NORTH KOREA)

Statistical Survey

Health and Welfare

KEY INDICATORS

Total fertility rate (children per woman, 2003)	2.0
Under-5 mortality rate (per 1,000 live births, 2004)	55
HIV/AIDS (% of persons aged 15–49, 1994)	<0.01
Health expenditure (2002): US $ per head (PPP)	57
Health expenditure (2002): % of GDP	4.6
Health expenditure (2002): public (% of total)	76.8
Access to water (% of persons, 2002)	100
Access to sanitation (% of persons, 2002)	59

For sources and definitions, see explanatory note on p. vi.

Agriculture

PRINCIPAL CROPS
('000 metric tons)

	2002	2003	2004
Wheat	145	161	175
Rice (paddy)	2,186	2,244	2,370
Barley	69	69	64
Maize	1,651	1,725	1,727
Rye	60	60	60*
Oats*	15	15	15
Millet*	65	38	38
Sorghum*	20	12	12
Potatoes	1,884	2,023	2,052
Sweet potatoes†	340	350	360
Dry beans†	300	300	310
Soybeans (Soya beans)*	360	360	360
Cottonseed†	24	24	24
Cabbages†	680	680	695
Tomatoes†	70	71	71
Pumpkins, squash and gourds†	88	89	89
Cucumbers and gherkins†	65	66	66
Aubergines (Eggplants)†	45	46	46
Chillies and green peppers†	57	59	59
Green onions and shallots†	95	96	96
Dry onions†	84	86	86
Garlic†	85	90	90
Other vegetables†	2,431	2,431	2,431
Apples†	660	660	669
Pears†	135	135	135
Peaches and nectarines†	122	122	122
Watermelons†	108	108	108
Cantaloupes and other melons†	116	116	116
Other fruits and berries†	480	485	485
Tobacco (leaves)†	64	64	64
Hemp fibre†	13	13	13
Cotton (lint)†	12	12	12

* Unofficial figure(s).
† FAO estimates.

Source: FAO.

LIVESTOCK
('000 head)

	2002	2003	2004
Horses*	48	48	48
Cattle	575	576	566
Pigs	3,152	3,178	3,194
Sheep	170	171	171
Goats	2,693	2,717	2,736
Chickens	18,506	19,958	20,309
Ducks	4,189	4,613	5,189
Rabbits	19,482	19,576	19,677

* FAO estimates.
Source: FAO.

LIVESTOCK PRODUCTS
(FAO estimates, '000 metric tons)

	2002	2003	2004
Beef and veal	21.8	21.8	21.0
Goat meat	11.0	11.1	11.2
Pig meat	162.5	162.5	165.0
Chicken meat	33.7	36.3	37.0
Cows' milk	92.0	94.0	94.0
Poultry eggs	130.0	135.0	136.0
Cattle hides (fresh)	3.0	3.0	2.9

Source: FAO.

Forestry

ROUNDWOOD REMOVALS
(FAO estimates, '000 cubic metres, excl. bark)

	2002	2003	2004
Sawlogs, veneer logs and logs for sleepers	1,000	1,000	1,000
Other industrial wood	500	500	500
Fuel wood	5,620	5,678	5,737
Total	7,120	7,178	7,237

Sawnwood production ('000 cubic metres, incl. railway sleepers): 280 (coniferous 185, broadleaved 95) per year in 1970–2004 (FAO estimates).

Source: FAO.

Fishing

(FAO estimates, '000 metric tons, live weight)

	2000	2001	2002
Capture	212.9	206.5	205.0
Freshwater fishes	8.0	4.9	5.0
Alaska pollock	60.0	60.0	60.0
Other marine fishes	112.2	109.0	107.6
Marine crustaceans	15.6	16.2	16.0
Squids	9.5	9.5	9.5
Aquaculture	66.7	63.7	63.7
Molluscs	63.0	60.0	60.0
Total catch	279.6	270.2	268.7

Note: Figures exclude aquatic plants (FAO estimates, '000 metric tons, aquaculture only): 401.0 in 2000; 391.0 in 2001; 444.3 in 2002.

2003: Figures assumed to be unchanged from 2002.

Source: FAO.

THE DEMOCRATIC PEOPLE'S REPUBLIC OF KOREA (NORTH KOREA)

Statistical Survey

Mining

(estimates, '000 metric tons, unless otherwise indicated)

	2002	2003	2004
Hard coal	24,000	22,300	22,800
Brown coal and lignite	7,000	6,300	6,500
Iron ore: gross weight	4,100	4,430	4,580
Iron ore: metal content	1,150	1,260	1,300
Copper ore*	12	12	12
Lead ore*	10	20	20
Zinc ore*	60	60	62
Tungsten concentrates (metric tons)*	600	600	600
Silver (metric tons)*	20	20	20
Gold (kg)*	6,600	6,300	6,000
Magnesite (crude)	1,000	1,000	1,200
Phosphate rock†	300	300	300
Fluorspar‡	12	12	12
Barite (Barytes)	70	70	70
Salt (unrefined)	500	500	500
Graphite (natural)	25	25	25
Talc, soapstone and pyrophyllite	50	50	50

* Figures refer to the metal content of ores and concentrates.
† Figures refer to gross weight.
‡ Metallurgical grade.

Note: No recent data are available for the production of molybdenum ore and asbestos.

Source: US Geological Survey.

Industry

SELECTED PRODUCTS
('000 metric tons, unless otherwise indicated)

	1999	2000	2001
Nitrogenous fertilizers*	72	72	n.a.
Motor spirit (petrol)	848†	902	880
Kerosene	168†	185	174
Gas-diesel (distillate fuel) oils	925†	994	940
Residual fuel oils	539†	573	585
Coke-oven coke (excl. breeze)	3,098†	3,098†	3,065
Cement‡	4,000	4,600	5,160
Pig-iron‡	800	800	800
Crude steel‡	1,000	1,000	1,000
Refined copper (primary and secondary metal)‡	16	14	14
Refined lead (primary and secondary metal)‡	75	75	75
Zinc (primary and secondary metal)	100	100	100
Electric energy (million kWh)	31,450	32,815	33,495

* Output is measured in terms of nitrogen.
† Provisional or estimated figure.
‡ Data from the US Geological Survey.

Source: mostly UN, *Industrial Commodity Statistics Yearbook*.

2002 (estimates, '000 metric tons): Cement 5,320; Pig-iron 800; Crude steel 1,030; Refined copper (primary and secondary metal) 15; Refined lead (primary and secondary metal) 6; Refined zinc (primary and secondary metal) 65 (Source: US Geological Survey).

2003 (estimates, '000 metric tons): Cement 5,540; Pig-iron 900; Crude steel 1,090; Refined copper (primary and secondary metal) 15; Refined lead (primary and secondary metal) 7; Refined zinc (primary and secondary metal) 65 (Source: US Geological Survey).

2004 (estimates, '000 metric tons): Cement 5,630; Pig-iron 900; Crude steel 1,070; Refined copper (primary and secondary metal) 15; Refined lead (primary and secondary metal) 7; Refined zinc (primary and secondary metal) 67 (Source: US Geological Survey).

Finance

CURRENCY AND EXCHANGE RATES

Monetary Units
100 chon (jun) = 1 won.

Sterling, Dollar and Euro Equivalents (30 November 2005)
£1 sterling = 244.370 won;
US $1 = 141.500 won;
€1 = 166.531 won;
1,000 won = £4.09 = $7.07 = €6.00.

Note: In August 2002 it was reported that a currency reform had been introduced, whereby the exchange rate was adjusted from US $1 = 2.15 won to $1 = 150 won: a devaluation of 98.6%.

BUDGET
(projected, million won)

	1992	1993	1994
Revenue	39,500.9	40,449.9	41,525.2
Expenditure	39,500.9	40,449.9	41,525.2
Economic development	26,675.1	27,423.8	28,164.0
Socio-cultural sector	7,730.6	7,751.5	8,218.3
Defence	4,582.1	4,692.2	4,816.9
Administration and management	513.1	582.4	326.0

1998 (estimates, million won): Total revenue 19,790.8; Total expenditure 20,015.2.

1999 (estimates, million won): Total revenue 19,801.0; Total expenditure 20,018.2.

2000 (estimates, million won): Total revenue 20,955.0; Total expenditure 20,903.0.

2001 (projected, million won): Total revenue 21,571.0; Total expenditure 21,571.0.

2002 (projected, million won): Total revenue 22,174.0; Total expenditure 22,174.0.

2003: Exact figures not made available following price reforms of August 2002.

2004 (reported, million won): Total revenue 351,266; Total expenditure 348,870.

2005 (projected, million won): Total revenue 391,310; Total expenditure 391,310.

NATIONAL ACCOUNTS

Gross Domestic Product by Economic Activity
(unofficial estimates, '000 million won)*

	2002	2003	2004
Agriculture, forestry and fishing	6,429	5,961	6,341
Mining	1,652	1,820	2,065
Manufacturing	3,825	4,043	4,388
Electricity, gas and water	939	995	1,051
Construction	1,699	1,896	2,194
Government services	4,679	5,018	5,361
Other services	2,054	2,156	2,308
Total	21,277	21,887	23,707

* Totals may not be equal to sum of component parts, owing to rounding.

Source: Bank of Korea (Republic of Korea).

External Trade

PRINCIPAL COMMODITIES
(US $ million)*

Imports	2000	2001	2002
Live animals and animal products	20.3	73.9	103.4
Vegetable products	159.0	221.0	118.4
Animal or vegetable fats and oils; prepared edible fats; animal or vegetable waxes . . . . Prepared foodstuffs; beverages, spirits and vinegar; tobacco and manufactured substitutes . .	89.1	89.9	72.3
Mineral products	171.2	231.1	235.9
Products of chemical or allied industries	108.4	123.4	122.1
Plastics, rubber and articles thereof	67.5	66.0	66.0
Textiles and textile articles	171.9	203.9	158.5
Base metals and articles thereof	85.2	100.4	88.2
Machinery and mechanical appliances; electrical equipment; sound and television apparatus	205.1	243.8	234.7
Vehicles, aircraft, vessels and associated transport equipment	146.2	88.4	76.1
Total (incl. others)	1,406.5	1,620.3	1,525.4

Exports	2000	2001	2002
Live animals and animal products	97.9	158.4	261.1
Vegetable products	30.3	42.0	27.5
Mineral products	43.2	50.5	69.8
Products of chemical or allied industries / Plastics, rubber and articles thereof	44.9	44.6	42.4
Wood, cork and articles thereof; wood charcoal; manufactures of straw, esparto, etc.	10.9	5.6	10.2
Textiles and textile articles	140.0	140.5	123.1
Natural or cultured pearls, precious or semi-precious stones, precious metals and articles thereof; imitation jewellery; coin	9.8	14.1	14.6
Base metals and articles thereof	43.9	60.2	57.4
Machinery and mechanical appliances; electrical equipment, sound and television apparatus	105.2	97.9	85.6
Total (incl. others)	565.8	650.2	735.0

* Excluding trade with the Republic of Korea (US $ million): *Imports:* 272.8 in 2000; 226.8 in 2001; 370.2 in 2002. *Exports:* 152.4 in 2000; 176.2 in 2001; 271.6 in 2002.

Source: Korea Trade-Investment Promotion Agency (KOTRA), Republic of Korea.

PRINCIPAL TRADING PARTNERS
(US $ million)*

Imports	2001	2002	2003
China, People's Republic	570.7	467.3	627.6
Germany	82.1	140.4	n.a.
Hong Kong	42.6	29.2	n.a.
India	154.8	186.6	157.9
Japan	249.1	135.1	91.5
Netherlands	9.1	27.6	n.a.
Russia	63.8	77.0	115.6
Singapore	112.3	83.0	n.a.
Spain	31.6	n.a.	n.a.
Thailand	106.0	172.0	203.6
United Kingdom	40.7	n.a.	n.a.
Total (incl. others)	1,620.3	1,525.4	1,614.4

Exports	2001	2002	2003
Bangladesh	38.0	32.3	n.a.
China, People's Republic	166.8	270.9	395.3
Germany	22.8	27.8	n.a.
Hong Kong	38.0	21.9	n.a.
India	3.1	4.8	1.6
Japan	225.6	234.4	173.8
Netherlands	10.4	6.4	n.a.
Russia	4.5	3.6	2.8
Spain	12.6	n.a.	n.a.
Thailand	24.9	44.6	50.7
Total (incl. others)	650.2	735.0	777.0

* Excluding trade with the Republic of Korea (US $ million): *Imports:* 226.8 in 2001; 370.2 in 2002; 435.0 in 2003. *Exports:* 176.2 in 2001; 271.6 in 2002; 289.3 in 2003.

2004 (US $ million): *Imports:* China, People's Republic 800; Japan 89; Korea, Republic 439; Total (incl. others) 2,280. *Exports:* China, People's Republic 586; Japan 163; Korea, Republic 258; Total (incl. others) 1,280.

Sources: Korea Trade-Investment Promotion Agency (KOTRA); Ministry of Unification, Republic of Korea.

Transport

SHIPPING

Merchant Fleet
(registered at 31 December)

	2002	2003	2004
Number of vessels	225	292	374
Total displacement ('000 grt)	870.5	959.0	1,122.8

Source: Lloyd's Register-Fairplay, *World Fleet Statistics*.

International Sea-borne Freight Traffic
(estimates, '000 metric tons)

	1988	1989	1990
Goods loaded	630	640	635
Goods unloaded	5,386	5,500	5,520

Source: UN, *Monthly Bulletin of Statistics*.

CIVIL AVIATION
(traffic on scheduled services)

	1999	2000	2001
Kilometres flown (million)	2	1	1
Passengers carried ('000)	59	83	79
Passenger-km (million)	178	37	33
Total ton-km (million)	18	5	5

Source: UN, *Statistical Yearbook*.

Tourism

	1996	1997	1998
Tourist arrivals ('000)	127	128	130

Source: World Tourism Organization, mainly *Yearbook of Tourism Statistics*.

Communications Media

	1994	1995	1996
Radio receivers ('000 in use)	2,950	3,000	3,300
Television receivers ('000 in use)	1,000	1,050	1,090
Telefax stations (number in use)	3,000*	n.a.	n.a.
Daily newspapers:			
number	11	11*	3
average circulation ('000 copies)*	5,000	5,000	4,500

* Estimate(s).

1997 ('000 in use): Radio receivers 3,360; Television receivers 1,200.

Telephones ('000 subscribers): 500 (estimate) in 2002.

Sources: UNESCO, *Statistical Yearbook*; UN, *Statistical Yearbook*.

Education

(2000)

	Institutions	Students
Kindergartens	14,167	748,416
Primary	4,886	1,609,865
Senior middle schools	4,772	2,181,524

Source: mainly Government of the Democratic People's Republic of Korea, *UNESCO Education for All Assessment Report 2000*.

Universities and Colleges: The *UNESCO Education for All Assessment Report 2000* identified more than 300 universities and colleges with 1.89m. students and academics.

Teachers (1987/88, UNESCO, *Statistical Yearbook*): Pre-primary 35,000, Primary 59,000, Secondary 111,000, Universities and colleges 23,000, Other tertiary 4,000.

Adult literacy rate (UNESCO estimates): 98.0% in 2003 (Source: UN Development Programme, *Human Development Report*).

Directory

The Constitution

A new Constitution was adopted on 27 December 1972. According to South Korean sources, several amendments were made in April 1992, including the deletion of references to Marxism-Leninism, the extension of the term of the Supreme People's Assembly from four to five years, and the promotion of limited 'economic openness'. Extensive amendments to the Constitution were approved on 5 September 1998. The main provisions of the revised Constitution are summarized below:

The Democratic People's Republic of Korea is an independent socialist state; the revolutionary traditions of the State are stressed (its ideological basis being the *juche* idea of the Korean Workers' Party), as is the desire to achieve national reunification by peaceful means on the basis of national independence. The Late President Kim Il Sung is the Eternal President of the Republic.

National sovereignty rests with the working people, who exercise power through the Supreme People's Assembly and Local People's Assemblies at lower levels, which are elected by universal, equal and direct suffrage by secret ballot.

The foundation of an independent national economy, based on socialist and *juche* principles, is stressed. The means of production are owned solely by the State and socialist co-operative organizations.

Culture and education provide the working people with knowledge to advance a socialist way of life. Education is free, universal and compulsory for 11 years.

Defence is emphasized, as well as the rights of overseas nationals, the principles of friendly relations between nations based on equality, mutual respect and non-interference, proletarian internationalism, support for national liberation struggles and due observance of law.

The basic rights and duties of citizens are laid down and guaranteed. These include the right to vote and to be elected (for citizens who are more than 17 years of age), to work (the working day being eight hours), to free medical care and material assistance for the old, infirm or disabled, and to political asylum. National defence is the supreme duty of citizens.

THE STRUCTURE OF STATE

The Supreme People's Assembly

The Supreme People's Assembly is the highest organ of state power, exercises legislative power and is elected by direct, equal, universal and secret ballot for a term of five years. Its chief functions are: (i) to adopt, amend or supplement legal or constitutional enactments; (ii) to determine state policy; (iii) to elect the Chairman of the National Defence Commission; (iv) to elect the Vice-Chairmen and other members of the National Defence Commission (on the recommendation of the Chairman of the National Defence Commission); (v) to elect the President and other members of the Presidium of the Supreme People's Assembly, the Premier of the Cabinet, the President of the Central Court and other legal officials; (vi) to appoint the Vice-Premiers and other members of the Cabinet (on the recommendation of the Premier of the Cabinet); (vii) to approve the State Plan and Budget; (viii) to receive a report on the work of the Cabinet and adopt measures, if necessary; (ix) to decide on the ratification or abrogation of treaties. It holds regular and extraordinary sessions, the former being once or twice a year, the latter as necessary at the request of at least one-third of the deputies. Legislative enactments are adopted when approved by more than one-half of those deputies present. The Constitution is amended and supplemented when approved by more than two-thirds of the total number of deputies.

The National Defence Commission

The National Defence Commission, which consists of a Chairman, first Vice-Chairman, other Vice-Chairmen and members, is the highest military organ of state power, and is accountable to the Supreme People's Assembly. The National Defence Commission directs and commands the armed forces and guides defence affairs. The Chairman of the National Defence Commission serves a five-year term of office and has the most senior post in the state hierarchy.

The Presidium of the Supreme People's Assembly

The Presidium of the Supreme People's Assembly, which consists of a President, Vice-Presidents, secretaries and members, is the highest organ of power in the intervals between sessions of the Supreme People's Assembly, to which it is accountable. It exercises the following chief functions: (i) to convene sessions of the Supreme People's Assembly; (ii) to examine and approve new legislation, the State Plan and the State Budget, when the Supreme People's Assembly is in recess; (iii) to interpret the Constitution and legislative enactments; (iv) to supervise the observance of laws of State organs; (v) to organize elections to the Supreme People's Assembly and Local People's Assemblies; (vi) to form or abolish ministries or commissions of the Cabinet; (vii) to appoint or remove Vice-Premiers and other cabinet or ministry members, on the recommendation of the Premier, when the Supreme People's Assembly is not in session; (viii) to elect or transfer judges of the Central Court; (ix) to ratify or abrogate treaties concluded with other countries; (x) to appoint or recall diplomatic envoys; (xi) to confer decorations, medals, honorary titles and diplomatic ranks; (xii) to grant general amnesties or special pardon. The President of the Presidium represents the State and receives credentials and letters of recall of diplomatic representatives accredited by a foreign state.

The Cabinet

The Cabinet is the administrative and executive body of the Supreme People's Assembly and a general state management organ. It serves a five-year term and comprises the Premier, Vice-Premiers, Chairmen of Commissions and other necessary members. Its major functions are the following: (i) to adopt measures to execute state policy; (ii) to guide the work of ministries and other organs responsible to it; (iii) to establish and remove direct organs of the Cabinet and main administrative economic organizations; (iv) to draft the State Plan and adopt measures to make it effective; (v) to compile the State Budget and to implement its provisions; (vi) to organize and execute the work of all sectors of the economy, as well as education, science, culture, health and environmental protection; (vii) to adopt measures to strengthen the monetary and banking system; (viii) to adopt measures to maintain social order, protect State interests and guarantee citizens' rights; (ix) to conclude treaties; (x) to abolish decisions and directives of economic administrative organs which run counter to those of the Cabinet. The Cabinet is accountable to the Supreme People's Assembly.

Local People's Assemblies

The Local People's Assemblies and Committees of the province (or municipality directly under central authority), city (or district) and county are local organs of power. The Local People's Assemblies consist of deputies elected by direct, equal, universal and secret ballot. The Local People's Committees consist of a Chairman, Vice-Chairmen, secretaries and members. The Local People's Assemblies and Committees serve a four-year term and exercise local budgetary functions, elect local administrative and judicial personnel and carry out the decisions at local level of higher executive and administrative organs.

THE JUDICIARY

Justice is administered by the Central Court (the highest judicial organ of the State), local courts and the Special Court. Judges and other legal officials are elected by the Supreme People's Assembly. The Central Court protects state property and constitutional rights, guarantees that all state bodies and citizens observe state laws, and executes judgments. Justice is administered by the court comprising one judge and two people's assessors. The court is independent and judicially impartial. Judicial affairs are conducted by the Central Procurator's Office, which exposes and institutes criminal proceedings against accused persons. The Office of the Central Procurator is responsible to the Chairman of the National Defence Commission, the Supreme People's Assembly and the Central People's Committee.

The Government

HEAD OF STATE

President: President KIM IL SUNG died on 8 July 1994 and was declared 'Eternal President' in September 1998.

Chairman of the National Defence Commission: Marshal KIM JONG IL.
First Vice-Chairman: Vice-Marshal JO MYONG ROK.
Vice-Chairman: Vice-Marshal RI YONG MU.
Other members: Vice-Marshal KIM YONG CHUN, KIM IL CHOL, CHOE RYONG SU, PAEK SE BONG, JON PYONG HO.

CABINET
(April 2006)

Premier: PAK PONG JU.
Vice-Premiers: RO TU CHOL, KWAK POM GI, JON SUNG HUN.
Minister of Foreign Affairs: PAEK NAM SUN.
Minister of People's Security: JU SANG SONG.
Minister of the People's Armed Forces: Vice-Marshal KIM IL CHOL.
Chairman of the State Planning Commission: KIM KWANG RIN.
Minister of Power and Coal Industry: JU TONG IL.
Minister of Extractive Industries: KANG MIN CHOL.
Minister of the Metal Industry: KIM SUNG HYON.
Minister of Machine-Building Industries: JO PYONG JU.
Minister of Construction and Building Materials Industries: TONG JONG HO.
Minister of the Electronics Industry: O SU YONG.
Minister of Railways: KIM YONG SAM.
Minister of Land and Marine Transport: KIM YONG IL.
Minister of Agriculture: RI KYONG SIK.
Minister of Chemical Industry: RI MU YONG.
Minister of Light Industry: RI JU O.
Minister of Foreign Trade: RIM KYONG MAN.
Minister of Forestry: SOK KUN SU.
Minister of Fisheries: RI SONG UNG.
Minister of City Management: CHOE JONG GON.
Minister of Land and Environmental Protection: PAK SONG NAM.
Minister of State Construction Control: PAE TAL JUN.
Minister of Commerce: RI YONG SON.
Minister of Procurement and Food Administration: CHOE NAM GYUN.
Minister of Education: KIM YONG JIN.
Minister of Post and Telecommunications: RYU YONG SOP.
Minister of Culture: KIM JIN SONG.
Minister of Finance: MUN IL BONG.
Minister of Labour: JONG YONG SU.
Minister of Public Health: KIM SU HAK.
Minister of State Inspection: KIM UI SUN.
Minister of the Crude Oil Industry: KO JONG SIK.
Chairman of the Physical Culture and Sports Guidance Committee: MUN JAE DOK.
President of the National Academy of Sciences: PYON YONG RIP.
President of the Central Bank: KIM WAN SU.
Director of the Central Statistics Bureau: KIM CHANG SU.
Chief Secretary of the Cabinet: KIM YONG HO.

MINISTRIES

All Ministries and Commissions are in Pyongyang.

Legislature

CHOE KO IN MIN HOE UI
(Supreme People's Assembly)

The 687 members of the 11th Supreme People's Assembly (SPA) were elected unopposed for a five-year term on 3 August 2003. The SPA's permanent body is the Presidium.

Chairman: CHOE TAE BOK.
President of the Presidium: KIM YONG NAM.
Vice-Presidents of the Presidium: YANG HYONG SOP, KIM YONG DAE.

Political Organizations

Democratic Front for the Reunification of the Fatherland: Pyongyang; f. 1946; a vanguard organization comprising political parties and mass working people's organizations seeking the unification of North and South Korea; Mems of Presidium PAK SONG CHOL, RYOM TAE JUN, YANG HYONG SOP, JONG TU HWAN, RI YONG SU, KIM PONG JU, PYON CHANG BOK, RYU MI YONG, RYO WON GU, KANG RYON HAK.

The component parties are:

Chondoist Chongu Party: Pyongyang; tel. (2) 334241; f. 1946; follows the guiding principle of *Innaechon* (the realization of 'heaven on earth'); satellite party of the Korean Workers' Party; Chair. RYU MI YONG.

Korean Social Democratic Party (KSDP) (Joson Sahoeminju-dang): Pyongyang; tel. (2) 5211981; fax (2) 3814410; f. 1945; advocates national independence and a democratic socialist society; satellite party of the Korean Workers' Party; Chair. KIM YONG DAE; First Vice-Chair. KANG PYONG HAK.

Korean Workers' Party (KWP): Pyongyang; f. 1945; merged with the South Korean Workers' Party in 1949; the guiding principle is the *juche* idea, based on the concept that man is the master and arbiter of all things; most significant political entity in the DPRK; 3m. mems; Gen. Sec. Marshal KIM JONG IL.

SIXTH CENTRAL COMMITTEE OF THE KWP

General Secretary: Marshal KIM JONG IL.

POLITBURO OF THE KWP

Presidium: Marshal KIM JONG IL.
Full Members: KIM YONG NAM, PAK SONG CHOL, KIM YONG JU, KYE UNG TAE, JON PYONG HO, HAN SONG RYONG.
Alternate Members: YON HYONG MUK, YANG HYONG SOP, CHOE TAE BOK, KIM CHOL MAN, CHOE YONG RIM, RI SON SIL.
Secretariat: Marshal KIM JONG IL, KYE UNG TAE, JON PYONG HO, HAN SONG RYONG, CHOE TAE BOK, KIM KI NAM, KIM KUK TAE, KIM JUNG RIN, JONG HA CHOL.

The component mass working people's organizations (see under Trade Unions) are:

General Federation of Trade Unions of Korea (GFTUK).
Kim Il Sung Socialist Youth League.
Korean Democratic Women's Union (KDWU)Union of Agricultural Working People of Korea.

THE DEMOCRATIC PEOPLE'S REPUBLIC OF KOREA (NORTH KOREA) *Directory*

Diplomatic Representation

EMBASSIES IN THE DEMOCRATIC PEOPLE'S REPUBLIC OF KOREA

Algeria: Munsudong, Taedongkang District, Pyongyang; tel. (2) 90372; Ambassador MOKHTAR REGUIEG.
Benin: Pyongyang; Ambassador BANTOLE YABA.
Bulgaria: Munsudong, Taedongkang District, Pyongyang; tel. (2) 3827343; fax (2) 3817342; Ambassador YORDAN MUTAFCHIYEV.
Cambodia: Munsudong, Taedongkang District, Pyongyang; tel. (2) 3817283; fax (2) 3817625; Ambassador CHHORN HAY.
China, People's Republic: Kinmauldong, Moranbong District, Pyongyang; tel. (2) 3823316; fax (2) 3813425; Ambassador WU DONGHE.
Cuba: Munsudong, Taedongkang District, Pyongyang; tel. (2) 3827380; fax (2) 3817703; Ambassador RUBÉN PÉREZ VALDÉS.
Czech Republic: Munsudong, Bldg 3, Apartment 39, Taedongkang District, Pyongyang; e-mail pyongyang@embassy.mzv.cz; Ambassador (vacant).
Egypt: Pyongyang; tel. (2) 3817414; fax (2) 3817611; Ambassador MOUSTAFA MUHAMMAD AHMAD EL-HATTER.
Ethiopia: POB 55, Munsudong, Taedongkang District, Pyongyang; tel. (2) 3827554; fax (2) 3827550; Chargé d'affaires FEKADE S. G. MESKEL.
Germany: Munsudong District, Pyongyang; tel. (2) 3817385; fax (2) 3817397; e-mail zreg@pjoe.auswaertiges-amt.de; Ambassador FRIEDRICH LUDWIG LOEHR.
India: Block 53, Munsudong, Taehak St, Taedongkang District, Pyongyang; tel. (2) 3817274; fax (2) 3817619; e-mail indemhoc@di.chesin.com; Ambassador N. T. KHANKHUP.
Indonesia: 5 Foreigners' Bldg, Munsudong, Taedongkang District, Pyongyang; tel. (2) 3827439; fax (2) 3817620; e-mail kbripyg@public.east.cn.net; Ambassador HENDRATI SUKENDAR MUNTHE.
Iran: Munhungdong, Monsu St, Taedongkang District, Pyongyang; tel. (2) 3817492; fax (2) 3817612; Ambassador JALALEDDIN NAMINI MIANJI.
Laos: Munhungdong, Taedongkang District, Pyongyang; tel. (2) 3827363; fax (2) 3817722; Ambassador CHANPHENG SIHAPHOM.
Libya: Munsudong, Taedongkang District, Pyongyang; tel. (2) 3827544; fax (2) 3817267; Secretary of People's Bureau BASHIR RAMADAN KHALIFA ABU JANAH.
Malaysia: Rm 1-17-05, Pyongyang Koryo Hotel, Tonghong-dong, Chaoyang District, Pyongyang; tel. (2) 3814397; fax (2) 3814422; e-mail malpygyang@kln.gov.my; Ambassador MD YUSOFF BIN MD ZAIN.
Mali: Pyongyang; Ambassador NAKOUNTE DIAKITÉ.
Mongolia: Munsudong, Taedongkang District, Pyongyang; tel. (2) 3827322; fax (2) 3817323; Ambassador JANCHIVDORJIIN LOMBO.
Nigeria: Munsudong, Taedongkang District, POB 535, Pyongyang; tel. (2) 3827558; fax (2) 3817293; Ambassador SULE BUBA.
Pakistan: Munsudong, Taedongkang District, Pyongyang; tel. (2) 3827478; fax 3817622; Ambassador NOORULLAH KHAN.
Poland: Munsudong, Taedongkang District, Pyongyang; tel. (2) 3817327; fax (2) 3817634; Ambassador ROMAN IWASZKIEWICZ.
Romania: Munhungdong, Taedongkang District, Pyongyang; tel. (2) 3827336; fax (2) 3817336; e-mail ambrophe@kcckp.net; Chargé d'affaires a.i. EUGEN POPA.
Russia: Sinyangdong, Central District, Pyongyang; tel. (2) 3823102; fax (2) 3813427; e-mail rusembdprk@yahoo.com; Ambassador ANDREI KARLOV.
Sweden: Munsudung, Taedongkang District, Pyongyang; tel. (2) 3817485; fax (2) 3817663; e-mail ambassaden.pyongyang@foreign.ministry.se; Ambassador MATS FOYER.
Syria: Munsudong, Taedongkang District, Pyongyang; tel. (2) 3827473; fax (2) 3817635; Ambassador YASSER AL-FARRA.
Thailand: Pyongyang; Ambassador NIKHOM TANTEMSAPYA.
United Kingdom: Munsudong, Taedongkang District, Pyongyang; tel. (2) 3817980; fax (2) 3817985; e-mail postmaster.PYONX@fco.gov.uk; Ambassador JOHN EVERARD.
Viet Nam: Munsudong, Taedongkang District, Pyongyang; tel. (2) 3817353; fax (2) 3817632; Ambassador PHAN TRONG THAI.

Judicial System

The judicial organs include the Central Court, the Court of the Province (or city under central authority) and the People's Court. Each court is composed of judges and people's assessors.

Procurators supervise the ordinances and regulations of all ministries and the decisions and directives of local organs of state power to ensure that they conform to the Constitution, laws and decrees, as well as to the decisions and other measures of the Cabinet. Procurators bring suits against criminals in the name of the State, and participate in civil cases to protect the interests of the State and citizens.

Central Court
Pyongyang; The highest judicial organ; supervises the work of all courts.
President: KIM PYONG RYUL.
First Vice-President: YUN MYONG GUK.

Central Procurator's Office
Supervises work of procurator's offices in provinces, cities and counties.
Procurator-General: RI KIL SONG.

Religion

The religions that are officially reported to be practised in the DPRK are Buddhism, Christianity and Chundo Kyo, a religion peculiar to Korea combining elements of Buddhism and Christianity. Religious co-ordinating bodies are believed to be under strict state control. The exact number of religious believers is unknown.

Korean Religious Believers Council: Pyongyang; f. 1989; brings together members of religious organizations in North Korea; Chair. JANG JAE ON.

BUDDHISM

In 2002 it was reported that there were an estimated 300 Buddhist temples in the DPRK; the number of believers was estimated at about 10,000.

Korean Buddhists Federation: POB 77, Pyongyang; tel. (2) 43698; fax (2) 3812100; f. 1945; Chair. Cen. Cttee PAK TAE HWA; Sec. SHIM SANG JIN.

CHRISTIANITY

In 2002 it was reported that there were approximately 14,000 Christians (including 4,000 Catholics) in the country, many of whom worshipped in house churches (of which there were said to be about 500).

Korean Catholics Association: Changchung 1-dong, Songyo District, Pyongyang; tel. (2) 23492; f. 1988; Chair. Cen. Cttee JANG JAE ON; Vice-Chair. MUN CHANG HAK.

Korean Christians Federation: Pyongyang; f. 1946; Chair. Cen. Cttee KANG YONG SOP; Sec. O KYONG U.

The Roman Catholic Church

For ecclesiastical purposes, North and South Korea are nominally under a unified jurisdiction. North Korea contains two dioceses (Hamhung and Pyongyang), both suffragan to the archdiocese of Seoul (in South Korea), and the territorial abbacy of Tokwon (Tokugen), directly responsible to the Holy See.

Diocese of Hamhung: Catholic Mission, Hamhung; 134-1 Waekwan-dong Kwan Eub, Chil kok kun, Gyeongbuk 718-800, Republic of Korea; tel. (545) 970-2000; Bishop (vacant); Apostolic Administrator of Hamhung and of the Abbacy of Tokwon Fr PLACIDUS DONG-HO RI.

Diocese of Pyongyang: Catholic Mission, Pyongyang; Bishop Rt Rev. FRANCIS HONG YONG HO (absent); Apostolic Administrator Most Rev. NICHOLAS CHEONG JIN-SUK (Archbishop of Seoul).

CHUNDO KYO

According to officials quoted in 2002, there were approximately 40,000 practitioners of Chundo Kyo in the DPRK.

Korean Chundoists Association: Pyongyang; tel. (2) 334241; f. 1946; Chair. of Central Guidance Cttee RYU MI YONG.

The Press

PRINCIPAL NEWSPAPERS

Choldo Sinmun: Pyongyang; f. 1947; every two days.
Joson Inmingun (Korean People's Army Daily): Pyongyang; f. 1948; daily; Editor-in-Chief RI TAE BONG.
Kyowon Sinmun: Pyongyang; f. 1948; publ. by the Education Commission; weekly.

THE DEMOCRATIC PEOPLE'S REPUBLIC OF KOREA (NORTH KOREA)   *Directory*

Minju Choson (Democratic Korea): Pyongyang; f. 1946; govt organ; 6 a week; Editor-in-Chief KIM JONG SUK; circ. 200,000.

Nongup Kunroja: Pyongyang; publ. of Cen. Cttee of the Union of Agricultural Working People of Korea.

Pyongyang Sinmun: Pyongyang; f. 1957; general news; 6 a week; Editor-in-Chief SONG RAK GYUN.

Rodong Chongnyon (Working Youth): Pyongyang; f. 1946; organ of the Cen. Cttee of the Kim Il Sung Socialist Youth League; 6 a week; Editor-in-Chief RI JONG GI.

Rodong Sinmun (Labour Daily): Pyongyang; f. 1946; organ of the Cen. Cttee of the Korean Workers' Party; daily; Editor-in-Chief CHOE CHIL NAM; circ. 1.5m.

Rodongja Sinmun (Workers' Newspaper): Pyongyang; f. 1945; organ of the Gen. Fed. of Trade Unions of Korea; Editor-in-Chief RI SONG JU.

Saenal (New Day): Pyongyang; f. 1971; publ. by the Kim Il Sung Socialist Youth League; 2 a week; Deputy Editor CHOE SANG IN.

Sonyon Sinmun: Pyongyang; f. 1946; publ. by the Kim Il Sung Socialist Youth League; 2 a week; circ. 120,000.

Tongil Sinbo: Kangan 1-dong, Youth Ave, Songyo District, Pyongyang; f. 1972; non-affiliated; weekly; Chief Editor PAK JIN SIK; circ. 300,000.

PRINCIPAL PERIODICALS

Chollima: Pyongyang; popular magazine; monthly.

Choson (Korea): Pyongyang; social, economic, political and cultural; bi-monthly.

Choson Minju Juuiinmin Gonghwaguk Palmyonggongbo (Official Report of Inventions in the DPRK): Pyongyang; 6 a year.

Choson Munhak (Korean Literature): Pyongyang; organ of the Cen. Cttee of the Korean Writers' Union; monthly.

Choson Yesul (Korean Arts): Pyongyang; organ of the Cen. Cttee of the Gen. Fed. of Unions of Literature and Arts of Korea; monthly.

Economics: POB 73, Pyongyang; fax (2) 3814410; quarterly.

History: POB 73, Pyongyang; fax (2) 3814410; quarterly.

Hwahakgwa Hwahakgoneop: Pyongyang; organ of the Hamhung br. of the Korean Acad. of Sciences; chemistry and chemical engineering; 6 a year.

Jokook Tongil: Kangan 1-dong, Youth Ave, Songyo District, Pyongyang; organ of the Cttee for the Peaceful Unification of Korea; f. 1961; monthly; Chief Editor LI MYONG GYU; circ. 70,000.

Korean Medicine: POB 73, Pyongyang; fax (2) 3814410; quarterly.

Kunroja (Workers): 1 Munshindong, Tongdaewon, Pyongyang; f. 1946; organ of the Cen. Cttee of the Korean Workers' Party; monthly; Editor-in-Chief RYANG KYONG BOK; circ. 300,000.

Kwahakwon Tongbo (Bulletins of the Academy of Science): POB 73, Pyongyang; fax (2) 3814410; organ of the Standing Cttee of the Korean Acad. of Sciences; 6 a year.

Mulri (Physics): POB 73, Pyongyang; fax (2) 3814410; quarterly.

Munhwao Haksup (Study of Korean Language): POB 73, Pyongyang; fax (2) 3814410; publ. by the Publishing House of the Acad. of Social Sciences; quarterly.

Philosophy: POB 73, Pyongyang; fax (2) 3814410; quarterly.

Punsok Hwahak (Analysis): POB 73, Pyongyang; fax (2) 3814410; organ of the Cen. Analytical Inst. of the Korean Acad. of Sciences; quarterly.

Ryoksagwahak (Historical Science): Pyongyang; publ. by the Acad. of Social Sciences; quarterly.

Saengmulhak (Biology): Pyongyang; fax (2) 3814410; publ. by the Korea Science and Encyclopedia Publishing House; quarterly.

Sahoekwahak (Social Science): Pyongyang; publ. by the Acad. of Social Sciences; 6 a year.

Suhakkwa Mulli: Pyongyang; organ of the Physics and Mathematics Cttee of the Korean Acad. of Sciences; quarterly.

FOREIGN LANGUAGE PUBLICATIONS

The Democratic People's Republic of Korea: Korea Pictorial, Pyongyang; f. 1956; illustrated news; Korean, Russian, Chinese, English, French, Arabic and Spanish edns; monthly; Editor-in-Chief HAN POM CHIK.

Foreign Trade of the DPRK: Foreign Trade Publishing House, Potonggang District, Pyongyang; economic developments and export promotion; English, French, Japanese, Russian and Spanish edns; monthly.

Korea: Pyongyang; f. 1956; illustrated; Korean, Arabic, Chinese, English, French, Spanish and Russian edns; monthly.

Korea Today: Foreign Languages Publishing House, Pyongyang; current affairs; Chinese, English, French, Russian and Spanish edns; monthly; Vice-Dir and Editor-in-Chief HAN PONG CHAN.

Korean Women: Pyongyang; English and French edns; quarterly.

Korean Youth and Students: Pyongyang; English and French edns; monthly.

The Pyongyang Times: Sochondong, Sosong District, Pyongyang; tel. (2) 51951; English, Spanish and French edns; weekly.

NEWS AGENCIES

Korean Central News Agency (KCNA): Potonggangdong 1, Potonggang District, Pyongyang; internet www.kcna.co.jp; f. 1946; sole distributing agency for news in the DPRK; publs daily bulletins in English, Russian, French and Spanish; Dir-Gen. KIM KI RYONG.

Foreign Bureaux

Informatsionnoye Telegrafnoye Agentstvo Rossii—Telegrafnoye Agentstvo Suverennykh Stran (ITAR—TASS) (Russia): Munsudong, Bldg 4, Flat 30, Taedongkang District, Pyongyang; tel. (2) 3817318; Correspondent ALEKSANDR VALIYEV.

The **Xinhua (New China) News Agency** (People's Republic of China) is also represented in the DPRK.

Press Association

Korean Journalists Union: Pyongyang; tel. (2) 36897; f. 1946; assists in the ideological work of the Korean Workers' Party; Chair. Cen. Cttee KIM SONG GUK.

Publishers

Academy of Sciences Publishing House: Nammundong, Central District, Pyongyang; tel. (2) 51956; f. 1953.

Academy of Social Sciences Publishing House: Pyongyang; Dir CHOE KWAN SHIK.

Agricultural Press: Pyongyang; labour, industrial relations; Pres. HO KYONG PIL.

Central Science and Technology Information Agency: Pyongyang; f. 1963; Dir JU SONG RYONG.

Education Publishing House: Pyongyang; f. 1945; Pres. KIM CHANG SON.

Foreign Language Press Group: Sochondong, Sosong District, Pyongyang; tel. (2) 841342; fax (2) 812100; f. 1949; Dir CHOE KYONG GUK.

Foreign Language Publishing House: Oesong District, Pyongyang; Dir KIM YONG MU.

Higher Educational Books Publishing House: Pyongyang; f. 1960; Pres. PAK KUN SONG.

Industrial Publishing House: Pyongyang; f. 1948; technical and economic; Dir KIM TONG SU.

Kim Il Sung University Publishing House: Pyongyang; f. 1965.

Korea Science and Encyclopedia Publishing House: POB 73, Pyongyang; tel. (2) 18111; fax (2) 3814410; publishes numerous periodicals and monographs; f. 1952; Dir Gen. KIM JUNG HYOP; Dir of International Co-operation JEAN BAHNG.

Korean People's Army Publishing House: Pyongyang; Pres. YUN MYONG DO.

Korean Social Democratic Party Publishing House: Pyongyang; tel. (2) 3818038; fax (2) 3814410; f. 1946; publishes quarterly journal Joson Sahoemingjudang (in Korean) and KSDP Says (in English); Dir KIM SOK JUN.

Korean Workers' Party Publishing House: Pyongyang; f. 1945; fiction, politics; Dir RYANG KYONG BOK.

Kumsong Youth Publishing House: Pyongyang; f. 1946; Dir HAN JONG SOP.

Literature and Art Publishing House: Pyongyang; f. by merger of Mass Culture Publishing House and Publishing House of the Gen. Fed. of Literary and Art Unions; Dir Gen. RI PHYO U.

Transportation Publishing House: Namgyodong, Hyongjaesan District, Pyongyang; f. 1952; travel; Editor PAEK JONG HAN.

Working People's Organizations Publishing House: Pyongyang; f. 1946; fiction, government, political science; Dir MIN SANG HYON.

WRITERS' UNION

Korean Writers' Union: Pyongyang; Chair. Cen. Cttee KIM PYONG HUN.

Broadcasting and Communications

North Korea established a satellite communications station in Pyongyang, through an agreement with France in 1986, which enabled North Korea to communicate by satellite with Western countries. In 1990 an agreement was reached on satellite communications for the operation of telephone, telex and telegram services between North Korea and Japan. In May the DPRK joined Intelsat (an international commercial satellite telecommunications organization). In October 2001 North Korea launched its first e-mail service provider in co-operation with China-based company Silibank.com, which was used for business and trade purposes. However, access to the internet remained severely limited, with information flow within North Korea still being conducted mainly via a closed intranet system (the Kwangmyong, meaning 'light', system). In 2002 a mobile telephone network was reportedly established in Pyongyang and surrounding areas, with mobile phone use being permitted to approximately 1,000 government officials. However, citizens were banned from using mobile phones as of mid-2004.

TELECOMMUNICATIONS

Korea Post and Telecommunications Co: Pyongyang; Dir KIM HYON JONG.

BROADCASTING

Regulatory Authorities

DPRK Radio and Television Broadcasting Committee: see Radio, below..

Pyongyang Municipal Broadcasting Committee: Pyongyang; Chair. KANG CHUN SHIK.

Radio

DPRK Radio and Television Broadcasting Committee: Jonsungdong, Moranbong District, Pyongyang; tel. (2) 3816035; fax (2) 3812100; programmes relayed nationally with local programmes supplied by local radio cttees; loudspeakers are installed in factories and in open spaces in all towns; home broadcasting 22 hours daily; foreign broadcasts in Russian, Chinese, English, French, German, Japanese, Spanish and Arabic; Chair. CHA SUNG SU.

Television

General Bureau of Television: Gen. Dir CHA SUNG SU.

DPRK Radio and Television Broadcasting Committee: see Radio..

Kaesong Television: Kaesong; broadcasts five hours on weekdays, 11 hours at weekends.

Korean Central Television Station: Ministry of Post and Telecommunications, Pyongyang; broadcasts five hours daily; satellite broadcasts commenced Oct. 1999.

Mansudae Television Station: Mansudae, Pyongyang; f. 1983; broadcasts nine hours of cultural programmes, music and dance, foreign films and news reports at weekends.

Finance

(cap. = capital; res = reserves; dep. = deposits; m. = million; brs = branches)

BANKING

During 1946–47 all banking institutions in North Korea, apart from the Central Bank and the Farmers Bank, were abolished. The Farmers Bank was merged with the Central Bank in 1959. The Foreign Trade Bank (f. 1959) conducts the international business of the Central Bank. Other banks, established in the late 1970s, are responsible for the foreign-exchange and external payment business of North Korean foreign trade enterprises.

The entry into force of the Joint-Venture Act in 1984 permitted the establishment of joint-venture banks, designed to attract investment into North Korea by Koreans resident overseas. The Foreign Investment Banking Act was approved in 1993.

Central Bank

Central Bank of the DPRK: Munsudong, Seungri St 58-1, Central District, Pyongyang; tel. (2) 3338196; fax (2) 3814624; f. 1946; bank of issue; supervisory and control bank; Pres. KIM WAN SU; 227 brs.

State Banks

Credit Bank of Korea: Chongryu 1-dong, Munsu St, Otandong, Central District, Pyongyang; tel. (2) 3818285; fax (2) 3817806; f. 1986; est. as International Credit Bank, name changed 1989; Pres. LI SUN BOK; Vice-Pres. SON YONG SUN.

Foreign Trade Bank of the DPRK: FTB Bldg, Jungsongdong, Seungri St, Central District, Pyongyang; tel. (2) 3815270; fax (2) 3814467; f. 1959; deals in international settlements and all banking business; Pres. and Chair. O KWANG CHOL; 12 brs.

International Industrial Development Bank: Jongpyong-dong, Pyongchon District, Pyongyang; tel. (2) 3818610; fax (2) 3814427; f. 2001; Pres. SHIN DOK SONG.

Korea Daesong Bank: Segoridong, Gyongheung St, Potonggang District, Pyongyang; tel. (2) 3818221; fax (2) 3814576; f. 1978; Pres. RI GYONG HA.

Koryo Bank: Ponghwadong, Potonggang District, Pyongyang; tel. (2) 3818168; fax (2) 3814033; f. 1989; est. as Koryo Finance Joint Venture Co, name changed 1994; co-operative, development, regional, savings and universal bank; Pres. PAK YONG CHIL; 10 brs.

Kumgang Bank: Jungsongdong, Central District, Pyongyang; tel. (2) 3818532; fax (2) 3814467; f. 1979; Chair. KIM JANG HO.

Private Banks

Bank of East Land: POB 32, BEL Bldg, Jonseung-dong, Moranbong District, Pyongyang; tel. (2) 3818923; fax (2) 3814410; f. 2001; commercial, investment, merchant, private and retail banking; Pres. PAK HYONG GIL.

Tanchon Commercial Bank: Saemaeul 1-dong, Pyongchon District, Pyongyang; tel. (2) 18111999; fax (2) 3814793; f. 1983; fmrly Changgwang Credit Bank, merged with Samchon-ri Bank and named as above Nov. 2003; (DPRK won) cap. 50,043.9, res 93,817.9, dep. 875,021.9 (Dec. 2003); Chair. KIM CHOL HWAN; Pres. KYE CHANG HO.

Joint-Venture Banks

Korea Commercial Bank: f. 1988; joint venture with Koreans resident in the USA.

Korea Joint Bank (KJB): Ryugyongdong, Potonggang District, Pyongyang; tel. (2) 3818151; fax (2) 3814410; e-mail kjb@silibank.com; f. 1989; est. with co-operation of the Federation of Korean Traders and Industrialists in Japan; cap. US $1,932.5m. (1994); 50% Korea International General Joint Venture Co, 50% General Asscn of Koreans in Japan; Gen. Man. O HO RYOL; 6 domestic brs, 1 br in Tokyo.

Korea Joint Financial Co: f. 1988; joint venture with Koreans resident in the USA.

Korea Nagwon Joint Financial Co: f. 1987; est. by Nagwon Trade Co and a Japanese co.

Korea Rakwon Joint Banking Co: Pyongyang; Man. Dir HO POK DOK.

Korea United Development Bank: Central District, Pyongyang; tel. (2) 3814165; fax (2) 3814497; f. 1991; 51% owned by Zhongce Investment Corpn (Hong Kong), 49% owned by Osandok General Bureau; cap. US $60m.; Pres. KIM SE HO.

Koryo Joint Finance Co: Pyongyang; Dir KIM YONG GU.

Foreign-Investment Banks

Daesong Credit Development Bank: Potonggang Hotel, 301 Ansan-dong, Pyongchon District, Pyongyang; tel. (2) 3814866; fax (2) 3814723; f. 1996; est. as Peregrine-Daesong Development Bank; fmrly jt venture between Oriental Commercial Holdings Ltd (Hong Kong) and Korea Daesong Bank; majority stake acquired by Global Group of Companies (UK) in May 2004; Man. NIGEL COWIE.

Golden Triangle Bank: Rajin-Sonbong Free Economic and Trade Zone; f. 1995.

INSURANCE

State Insurance Bureau: Central District, Pyongyang; tel. (2) 38196; handles all life, fire, accident, marine, hull insurance and reinsurance.

Korea Foreign Insurance Co (Chosunbohom): Central District, Pyongyang; tel. (2) 3818024; fax (2) 3814464; f. 1974; conducts marine, motor, aviation and fire insurance, reinsurance of all classes, and all foreign insurance; brs in Chongjin, Hungnam and Nampo, and agencies in foreign ports; overseas representative offices in Chile, France, Germany, Pakistan, Singapore; Pres. RI JANG SU.

Korea International Insurance Co: Pyongyang; Dir PAEK MYONG RON.

Korea Mannyon Insurance Co: Pyongyang; Pres. PAK IL HYONG.

Trade and Industry

GOVERNMENT AGENCIES

DPRK Committee for the Promotion of External Economic Co-operation: Jungsongdong, Central District, Pyongyang; tel. (2) 333974; fax (2) 3814498; Chair. Paek Hong Bong.

DPRK Committee for the Promotion of International Trade: Central District, Pyongyang; Pres. Ri Song Rok; Chair. Kim Jong Gi.

Economic Co-operation Management Bureau: Ministry of Foreign Trade, Pyongyang; f. 1998; Dir Kim Yong Sul.

Korea International Joint Venture Promotion Committee: Pyongyang; Chair. Chae Hui Jong.

Korean Association for the Promotion of Asian Trade: Pyongyang; Pres. Ri Song Rok.

Korean International General Joint Venture Co: Pyongyang; f. 1986; promotes joint economic ventures with foreign countries; Man. Dir Ri Kwang Gun.

INDUSTRIAL AND TRADE ASSOCIATIONS

Korea Building Materials Trading Co: Tongdaewon District, Pyongyang; tel. (2) 18111–3818085; fax (2) 3814555; chemical building materials, woods, timbers, cement, sheet glass, etc.; Dir Shin Tong Bom.

Korea Cereals Export and Import Corpn: Jungsong-dong, Central District, Pyongyang; tel. (2) 18111-3818278; fax (2) 3813451; high-quality vegetable starches, etc.

Korea Chemicals Export and Import Corpn: Central District, Pyongyang; petroleum and petroleum products, raw materials for the chemical industry, rubber and rubber products, fertilizers, etc.

Korea Daesong General Trading Corpn: Pulgungori 1-dong, Potonggang District, Pyongyang; tel. (2) 18111; fax (2) 3814432; e-mail Daesong@Silibank.com; Gen. Dir Choe Jong Son.

Korea Daesong Jei Trading Corpn: Pulgungori 1-dong, Potonggang District, Pyongyang; tel. (2) 18111-3818213; fax (2) 3814431; machinery and equipment, chemical products, textiles, agricultural products, etc.

Korea Daesong Jesam Trading Corpn: Pulgungori 1-dong, Potonggang District, Pyongyang; tel. (2) 18111-3818562; fax (2) 3814431; remedies for diabetes, tonics, etc.

Korea Ferrous Metals Export and Import Corpn: Potonggang 2-dong, Potonggang District, Pyongyang; tel. (2) 18111-3818078; fax (2) 3814581; steel products.

Korea Film Export and Import Corpn: Daedongmundong, Central District, POB 113, Pyongyang; tel. (2) 180008034; fax (2) 3814410; f. 1956; feature films, cartoons, scientific and documentary films; Dir-Gen. Choe Hyok U.

Korea First Equipment Export and Import Co: Central District, Pyongyang; tel. (2) 334825; f. 1960; export and import of ferrous and non-ferrous metallurgical plants, geological exploration and mining equipment, communication equipment, machine-building plant, etc; construction of public facilities such as airports, hotels, tourist facilities, etc; joint-venture business in similar projects; Pres. Chae Won Chol.

Korea Foodstuffs Export and Import Corpn: Kangan 2-dong, Songyo District, Pyongyang; tel. (2) 18111-3818289; fax (2) 3814417; cereals, wines, meat, canned foods, fruits, cigarettes, etc.

Korea Fruit and Vegetables Export Corpn: Central District, Pyongyang; tel. (2) 35117; vegetables, fruit and their products.

Korea General Corpn for External Construction (GENCO): Sungri St 25, Jungsong-dong, Central District, Pyongyang; tel. (2) 18111-3818090; fax (2) 3814611; e-mail gen122@co.chesin.com; f. 1961; construction of dwelling houses, public establishments, factories, hydroelectric and thermal power stations, irrigation systems, ports, bridges, and transport services, technical services; Gen. Dir Choe Bong Su.

Korea General Machine Co: Tongsin 3-dong, Tongdaewon, Pyongyang; tel. (2) 18555-3818102; fax (2) 381-4495; Dir Ra In Gyun.

Korea Hyopdong Trading Corpn: Othan-dong, Kangan St, Central District, Pyongyang; tel. (2) 18111-3818011; fax (2) 3814454; fabrics, glass products, ceramics, chemical goods, building materials, foodstuffs, machinery, etc.

Korea Industrial Technology Co: Junsongdong, Central District, Pyongyang; tel. (2) 18111-3818025; fax (2) 3814537; Pres. Kwon Yong Son.

Korea International Chemical Joint Venture Co: Pyongyang; Chair. Ryo Song Gun.

Korea Jangsu Trading Co: Kyogudong, Central District, Pyongyang; tel. (2) 18111-3818834; fax (2) 3814410; medicinal products and clinical equipment.

Korea Jeil Equipment Export and Import Corpn: Jungsong-dong, Central District, Pyongyang; tel. (2) 334825; f. 1960; ferrous and non-ferrous metallurgical plant, geological exploration and mining equipment, power plant, communications and broadcasting equipment, machine-building equipment, railway equipment, construction of public facilities; Pres. Cho Jang Dok.

Korea Koryo Trading Corpn: Jongpyongdong, Pyongchon District, Pyongyang; tel. (2) 18111-3818104; fax (2) 3814646; Dir Kim Hui Duk.

Korea Kwangmyong Trading Corpn: Jungsongdong, Central District, Pyongyang; tel. (2) 18111-3818111; fax (2) 3814410; dried herbs, dried and pickled vegetables; Dir Choe Jong Hun.

Korea Light Industry Import-Export Co: Juchetab St, Tongdaewon District, Pyongyang; tel. (2) 37661; exports silk, cigarettes, canned goods, drinking glasses, ceramics, handbags, pens, plastic flowers, musical instruments, etc; imports chemicals, dyestuffs, machinery, etc.; Dir Choe Pyong Hyon.

Korea Machine Tool Trading Corpn: Tongdaewon District, Pyongyang; tel. (2) 18555-381810; fax (2) 3814495; Dir Kim Kwang Ryop.

Korea Machinery and Equipment Export and Import Corpn: Potonggang District, Pyongyang; tel. (2) 333449; f. 1948; metallurgical machinery and equipment, electric machines, building machinery, farm machinery, diesel engines, etc.

Korea Mansu Trading Corpn: Chollima St, Central District, POB 250, Pyongyang; tel. (2) 43075; fax (2) 812100; f. 1974; antibiotics, pharmaceuticals, vitamin compounds, drugs, medicinal herbs; Dir Kim Jang Hun.

Korea Marine Products Export and Import Corpn: Central District, Pyongyang; canned, frozen, dried, salted and smoked fish, fishing equipment and supplies.

Korea Minerals Export and Import Corpn: Central District, Pyongyang; minerals, solid fuel, graphite, precious stones, etc.

Korea Namheung Trading Co: Sinri-dong, Tongdaewon District, Pyongyang; tel. (2) 18111-3818974; fax (2) 3814623; high-purity reagents, synthetic resins, vinyl films, essential oils, menthol and peppermint oil.

Korea Non-ferrous Metals Export and Import Corpn: Potonggang 2-dong, Potonggang District, Pyongyang; tel. (2) 18111-3818247; fax (2) 3814569.

Korea Okyru Trading Corpn: Kansongdong, Pyongchon District, Pyongyang; tel. (2) 18111-3818110; fax (2) 3814618; agricultural and marine products, household goods, clothing, chemical and light industrial products.

Korea Ponghwa Contractual Joint Venture Co: Pyongyang; Dir Mun Yong Ok.

Korea Ponghwa General Trading Corpn: Jungsong-dong, Central District, Pyongyang; tel. (2) 18111-3818023; fax (2) 3814444; machinery, metal products, minerals and chemicals.

Korea Publications Export and Import Corpn: Yokjondong, Yonggwang St, Central District, Pyongyang; tel. (2) 3818536; fax (2) 3814404; f. 1948; export of books, periodicals, postcards, paintings, cassettes, videos, CDs, CD-ROMs, postage stamps and records; import of books; Pres. Ri Yong.

Korea Rungra Co: Sinwondong, Potonggang District, Pyongyang; tel. (2) 18111-3818112; fax (2) 3814608; Dir Choe Heng Ung.

Korea Rungrado Trading Corpn: Segori-dong, Potonggang District, Pyongyang; tel. (2) 18111-3818022; fax (2) 3814507; food and animal products; Gen. Dir Pak Kyu Hong.

Korea Ryongaksan General Trading Corpn: Pyongyang; Gen. Dir Han Yu Ro.

Korea Samcholli General Corpn: Pyongyang; Dir Jong Un Op.

Korea Technology Corpn: Jungsongdong, Central District, Pyongyang; tel. (2) 18111-3818090; fax (2) 3814410; scientific and technical co-operation.

Korea Unha Trading Corpn: Rungra 1-dong, Taedonggang District, Pyongyang; tel. (2) 18111-3818236; fax (2) 3814506; clothing and fibres.

Korea Yonghung Trading Co: Tongan-dong, Central District, Pyongyang; tel. (2) 18111-3818223; fax (2) 3814527; e-mail greenlam@co.chesin.com; f. 1979; export of freight cars, vehicle parts, marine products, electronic goods, import of steel, chemical products; Pres. Choe Yong Dok.

Pyongsu JV Co Ltd: Pyongyang; f. 2004; pharmaceutical mfr, medical products incl. analgesics; jt venture with Interpacific/Zuellig Pharma (Switzerland).

TRADE UNIONS

General Federation of Trade Unions of Korea (GFTUK): POB 333, Dongmun-dong, Daedonggang District, Pyongyang; fax (2)

3814427; f. 1945; 1.6m. mems (2003); seven affiliated unions (2003); Pres. RYOM SUN GIL.

> **Trade Union of Construction and Forestry Workers of Korea:** Pyongyang; f. 1945; 160,000 mems (2003); Pres. WON HYONG GUK.
>
> **Trade Union of Educational and Cultural Workers:** POB 333, Dongmun-dong, Daedonggang District, Pyongyang; fax (2) 3814427; f. 1946; 89,800 mems (2003); Pres. KIM YONG DO.
>
> **Trade Union of Light and Chemical Industries of Korea:** Pyongyang; f. 1945; 372,500 mems (2003); Pres. RI JIN HAK.
>
> **Trade Union of Metal and Engineering Industries of Korea:** Pyongyang; f. 1945; 332,800 mems (2003); Pres. CHOE GWANG HYON.
>
> **Trade Union of Mining and Power Industries of Korea:** Pyongyang; f. 1945; 221,000 mems (2003); Pres. SON YONG JUN.
>
> **Trade Union of Public Employees and Service Workers of Korea:** Pyongyang; f. 1945; 305,900 mems (2003); Pres. KIM GANG HO.
>
> **Trade Union of Transport and Fisheries Workers of Korea:** Pyongyang; f. 1945; 119,800 mems (2003); Pres. CHOE RYONG SU.

General Federation of Agricultural and Forestry Technique of Korea: Chung Kuyuck Nammundong, Pyongyang; f. 1946; 523,000 mems.

General Federation of Unions of Literature and Arts of Korea: Pyongyang; f. 1946; seven br. unions; Chair. Cen. Cttee CHANG CHOL.

Kim Il Sung Socialist Youth League: Pyongyang; fmrly League of Socialist Working Youth of Korea; First Sec. KIM GYONG HO.

Korean Architects' Union: Pyongyang; f. 1954; 500 mems; Chair. Cen. Cttee PAE TAL JUN.

Korean Democratic Lawyers' Association: Ryonhwa 1, Central District, Pyongyang; fax (2) 3814644; f. 1954; Chair. HAM HAK SONG.

Korean Democratic Scientists' Association: Pyongyang; f. 1956.

Korean Democratic Women's Union: Jungsongdong, Central District, Pyongyang; fax (2) 3814416; f. 1945; Chief Officer PAK SUN HUI.

Korean General Federation of Science and Technology: Jungsongdong, Seungri St, Central District, Pyongyang; tel. (2) 3224389; fax (2) 3814410; f. 1946; 550,000 mems; Chair. Cen. Cttee CHOE HUI JONG.

Korean Medical Association: Pyongyang; f. 1970; Chair. CHOE CHANG SHIK.

Union of Agricultural Working People of Korea: Pyongyang; f. 1965; to replace fmr Korean Peasants' Union; 2.4m. mems; Chair. Cen. Cttee KANG CHANG UK.

Transport

RAILWAYS

Railways were responsible for some 62% of passenger journeys in 1991 and for some 74% of the volume of freight transported in 1997. In 2002 the total length of track was estimated at 5,235 km, of which some 70% was electrified. There are international train services to Moscow (Russia) and Beijing (People's Republic of China). Construction work on the reconnection of the Kyongui (West Coast, Sinuiju–Seoul) and East Coast Line (Wonsan–Seoul) began in September 2002. The two lines were officially opened in June 2003, but were not yet open to traffic, as construction work on the Northern side remained to be completed. The lines reportedly became fully operational in late 2005. Eventually the two would be linked to the Trans-China and Trans-Siberian railways, respectively, greatly enhancing the region's transportation links.

There is an underground railway system in Pyongyang, with two public lines. Unspecified plans to expand the system were announced in February 2002.

ROADS

In 2000, according to South Korean estimates, the road network totalled 23,407 km (of which only about 8% was paved), including 682 km of multi-lane highways. Road links between the DPRK and the Republic of Korea were believed to have opened in late 2005.

INLAND WATERWAYS

The Yalu (Amnok-gang) and Taedong, Tumen and Ryesong are the most important commercial rivers. Regular passenger and freight services: Nampo–Chosan–Supung; Chungsu–Sinuiju–Dasado; Nampo–Jeudo; Pyongyang–Nampo.

SHIPPING

The principal ports are Nampo, Wonsan, Chongjin, Rajin, Hungnam, Songnim and Haeju. In 1997 North Korean ports had a combined capacity for handling 35m. tons of cargo. At 31 December 2004 North Korea's merchant fleet comprised 374 vessels, with a combined displacement of 1,122,800 grt.

Korea Chartering Corpn: Central District, Pyongyang; arranges cargo transportation and chartering.

Korea Daehung Shipping Co: Ansan 1–dong, Pyongchon District, Pyongyang; tel. (2) 18111 ext 8695; fax (2) 3814508; f. 1994; owns 6 reefers, 3 oil tankers, 1 cargo ship.

Korea East Sea Shipping Co: Pyongyang; Dir RI TUK HYON.

Korea Foreign Transportation Corpn: Central District, Pyongyang; arranges transportation of export and import cargoes (transit goods and charters).

Korean-Polish Shipping Co Ltd: Moranbong District, Pyongyang; tel. (2) 3814384; fax (2) 3814607; f. 1967; maritime trade mainly with Polish, Far East and DPRK ports.

Korea Tonghae Shipping Co: Changgwang St, Central District, POB 120, Pyongyang; tel. (2) 345805; fax (2) 3814583; arranges transportation by Korean vessels.

Ocean Maritime Management Co Ltd: Tonghungdong, Central District, Pyongyang.

Ocean Shipping Agency of the DPRK: Moranbong District, POB 21, Pyongyang; tel. (2) 3818100; fax (2) 3814531; Pres. O JONG HO.

CIVIL AVIATION

The international airport is at Sunan, 24 km from Pyongyang. In September 2003 the first tourist flight from Seoul to Pyongyang was completed by an Air Koryo aircraft, representing the first commercial flight between North and South Korea in more than 50 years. In January 2004 plans were announced for an aviation agreement between North and South Korea, which would allow regular inter-Korean flight routes to be opened.

Chosonminhang/General Civil Aviation Bureau of the DPRK: Sunan Airport, Sunan District, Pyongyang; tel. (2) 37917; fax (2) 3814625; f. 1954; internal services and external flights by Air Koryo to Beijing and Shenyang (People's Republic of China), Bangkok (Thailand), Macao, Nagoya (Japan), Moscow, Khabarovsk and Vladivostok (Russia), Sofia (Bulgaria) and Berlin (Germany); charter services are operated to Asia, Africa and Europe; Pres. KIM YO UNG.

Tourism

The DPRK was formally admitted to the World Tourism Organization in 1987. Tourism is permitted only in officially accompanied parties. In 1999 there were more than 60 international hotels (including nine in Pyongyang) with 7,500 beds. Tourist arrivals totalled 130,000 in 1998. A feasibility study was undertaken in 1992 regarding the development of Mount Kumgang as a tourist attraction. The study proposed the construction of an international airport at Kumnan and of a number of hotels and leisure facilities in the Wonsan area. Local ports were also to be upgraded. It was hoped that the development, scheduled to cost some US $20,000m., would attract 3m. tourists to the area each year. In November 1998 some 800 South Korean tourists visited Mount Kumgang, as part of a joint venture mounted by the North Korean authorities and Hyundai, the South Korean conglomerate. By November 2000 only 350,000 South Korean tourists had visited the attraction. In November 2002, in an effort to increase profitability, Mount Kumgang was designated a special tax-free economic zone. In 1996 it was reported that proposals had been made to create a tourist resort in the Rajin-Sonbong Free Economic and Trade Zone, in the north-east of the country. It was announced that hotels to accommodate some 5,000 people were to be constructed, as well as an airport to service the area. There were reports in 1998 that a heliport had been opened in the Zone, and in 1999 the resort was completed. Mount Chilbo, Mount Kuwol, Mount Jongbang and the Ryongmum Cave were transformed into new tourist destinations in that year. In August 2000 plans were announced for the development, jointly with the People's Republic of China, of the western part of Mount Paektu, Korea's highest mountain, as a tourist resort. In September 2003 South Korean tourists were able to visit Pyongyang for the first time. In 2003 it was estimated that around 1,500 Western tourists visited North Korea annually.

Korea International Tourist Bureau: Pyongyang; Pres. HAN PYONG UN.

Korean International Youth Tourist Co: Mankyongdae District, Pyongyang; tel. (2) 73406; f. 1985; Dir HWANG CHUN YONG.

Kumgangsan International Tourist Co: Central District, Pyongyang; tel. (2) 31562; fax (2) 3812100; f. 1988.

THE DEMOCRATIC PEOPLE'S REPUBLIC OF KOREA (NORTH KOREA)

National Tourism Administration of the DPRK: Central District, Pyongyang; tel. (2) 3818901; fax (2) 3814547; e-mail nta@silibank.com; f. 1953; state-run tourism promotion organization; Dir RYO SUNG CHOL.

Ryohaengsa (Korea International Travel Company): Central District, Pyongyang; tel. (2) 3817201; fax (2) 3817607; f. 1953; has relations with more than 200 tourist companies throughout the world; Pres. CHO SONG HUN.

State General Bureau of Tourism: Pyongyang; Pres. RYO HAK SONG.

THE REPUBLIC OF KOREA

Introductory Survey

Location, Climate, Language, Religion, Flag, Capital

The Republic of Korea (South Korea) forms the southern part of the Korean peninsula, in eastern Asia. To the north, separated by a frontier which roughly follows the 38th parallel, is the country's only neighbour, the Democratic People's Republic of Korea (North Korea). To the west is the Yellow Sea, to the south is the East China Sea, and to the east is the Sea of Japan. The climate is marked by cold, dry winters, with an average temperature of −6°C (21°F), and hot, humid summers, with an average temperature of 25°C (77°F). The language is Korean. Confucianism, Mahayana Buddhism, and Chundo Kyo are the principal traditional religions. Chundo Kyo is peculiar to Korea, and combines elements of Shaman, Buddhist and Christian doctrines. There are some 17.5m. Christians, of whom about 83% are Protestants. The national flag (proportions 2 by 3) comprises, in the centre of a white field, a disc divided horizontally by an S-shaped line, red above and blue below, surrounded by four configurations of parallel, broken and unbroken black bars. The capital is Seoul.

Recent History

(For more details of the history of Korea up to 1953, including the Korean War, see the chapter on the Democratic People's Republic of Korea—DPRK.)

UN-supervised elections to a new legislature, the National Assembly (Kuk Hoe), took place in May 1948. The Assembly adopted a democratic Constitution, and South Korea became the independent Republic of Korea on 15 August 1948, with Dr Syngman Rhee, leader of the Liberal Party, as the country's first President. He remained in the post until his resignation in April 1960. Elections in July were won by the Democratic Party, led by Chang Myon, but his Government was deposed in May 1961 by a military coup, led by Gen. Park Chung-Hee. Power was assumed by the Supreme Council for National Reconstruction, which dissolved the National Assembly, suspended the Constitution and disbanded all existing political parties. In January 1963 the military leadership formed the Democratic Republican Party (DRP). Under a new Constitution, Gen. Park became President of the Third Republic in December.

Opposition to Park's regime led to the imposition of martial law in October 1972. A Constitution for the Fourth Republic, giving the President greatly increased powers, was approved by national referendum in November. A new body, the National Conference for Unification (NCU), was elected in December. The NCU re-elected President Park for a six-year term, and the DRP obtained a decisive majority in elections to the new National Assembly. In May 1975 opposition to the Government was effectively banned, and political trials followed. Elections to the NCU were held in May 1978, and the President was re-elected for a further six-year term in July. In October 1979 serious rioting erupted when Kim Young-Sam, the leader of the opposition New Democratic Party (NDP), was accused of subversive activities and expelled from the National Assembly. On 26 October Park was assassinated in an alleged coup attempt, led by the head of the Korean Central Intelligence Agency. Martial law was reintroduced (except on the island of Jeju), and in December the Prime Minister, Choi Kyu-Hah, was elected President by the NCU. Instability in the DRP and the army resulted in a military coup in December, led by the head of the Defence Security Command, Lt-Gen. Chun Doo-Hwan, who arrested the Army Chief of Staff and effectively took power. Nevertheless, President Choi was inaugurated on 21 December to complete his predecessor's term of office (to 1984).

Choi promised liberalizing reforms, but in May 1980 demonstrations by students and confrontation with the army led to the arrest of about 30 political leaders, including Kim Dae-Jung, former head of the NDP. Martial law was extended throughout the country, the National Assembly was suspended, and all political activity was banned. Almost 200 people were killed when troops stormed the southern city of Gwangju, which had been occupied by students and dissidents. In August Choi resigned, and Gen. Chun was elected President. Acting Prime Minister Nam Duck-Woo formed a new State Council (cabinet) in September. In the same month the sentencing to death of Kim Dae-Jung for plotting rebellion was condemned internationally. (This sentence was subsequently suspended.) In October a new Constitution was overwhelmingly approved by referendum.

Martial law was ended in January 1981, and new political parties were formed. In the following month President Chun was re-elected: the start of his new term, in March, inaugurated the Fifth Republic. Chun's Democratic Justice Party (DJP) became the majority party in the new National Assembly, which was elected shortly afterwards. Amid opposition demands for liberalization, Chun pledged that he would retire at the end of his term in 1988, thus becoming the country's first Head of State to transfer power constitutionally.

During 1984, following an escalation of student unrest, the Government adopted a more flexible attitude towards dissidents. Several thousand prisoners were released, and the political 'blacklist' was finally abolished in March 1985. In January 1985 the New Korea Democratic Party (NKDP) was established by supporters of Kim Young-Sam and Kim Dae-Jung. At the general election to the National Assembly held in February, the DJP retained its majority, but the NKDP emerged as the major opposition force, boosted by the return from exile of Kim Dae-Jung. The new party secured 67 of the Assembly's 276 seats, while the DJP won 148 seats. Chun appointed a new State Council, with Lho Shin-Yong as Prime Minister. Before the opening session of the new National Assembly many deputies defected to the NKDP, increasing the party's strength to 102 seats.

In April 1987 internal divisions within the NKDP led to the formation of a new opposition party, the Reunification Democratic Party (RDP); Kim Young-Sam was elected to its presidency in May. In April Chun unexpectedly announced the suspension of the process of reform until after the Olympic Games (due to be held in Seoul in September 1988). While confirming that he would leave office in February 1988, Chun indicated that his successor would be elected by the existing electoral college system, precipitating violent clashes between anti-Government demonstrators and riot police.

In June 1987 Roh Tae-Woo was nominated as the DJP's presidential candidate. However, Roh subsequently informed Chun that he would relinquish both the DJP chairmanship and his presidential candidature if the principal demands of the opposition for constitutional and electoral reform were not satisfied. Under international pressure, Chun acceded, and negotiations on constitutional amendments were announced. In August the DJP and the RDP announced that a bipartisan committee had agreed a draft Constitution. Among its provisions were the reintroduction of direct presidential elections by universal suffrage, and the restriction of the presidential mandate to a single five-year term; the President's emergency powers were also to be reduced, and serving military officers were to be prohibited from taking government office. Having been approved by the National Assembly, the amendments were endorsed in a national referendum in October, and the amended Constitution was promulgated shortly thereafter.

Kim Dae-Jung joined the RDP in August 1987; in November, however, he became President of a new Peace and Democracy Party (PDP), and declared himself a rival presidential candidate. At the election, in December, Roh Tae-Woo won some 36% of the votes, while Kim Dae-Jung and Kim Young-Sam each achieved about 27%. Roh Tae-Woo was inaugurated as President on 25 February 1988, whereupon the Sixth Republic was established. At the general election to the National Assembly, in April, the DJP failed to achieve an overall majority, securing 125 of the 299 seats. The PDP achieved 70 seats, thus becoming the main opposition party; the remainder went to the RDP and the New Democratic Republican Party (NDRP—the revived and renamed DRP), led by Kim Jong-Pil.

During 1988 the Government granted greater autonomy to universities, permitted the formation of student associations, and eased restrictions on the press. The number of trade unions increased, and greater freedom to undertake foreign travel was granted to South Korean citizens.

THE REPUBLIC OF KOREA (SOUTH KOREA)

In February 1990 the DJP merged with the RDP and the NDRP to form the Democratic Liberal Party (DLP). Roh was subsequently elected President of the DLP, while Kim Young-Sam and Kim Jong-Pil were elected as two of the party's three Chairmen. The DLP thus controlled more than two-thirds of the seats in the National Assembly. The PDP, effectively isolated as the sole opposition party, condemned the merger and demanded new elections. In March a new opposition group, the Democratic Party (DP), was formed, largely comprising members of the RDP who had opposed the merger.

In July 1990 a large rally was held in Seoul to denounce the adoption by the National Assembly of several items of controversial legislation, including proposals to restructure the military leadership and to reorganize the broadcasting media. Shortly afterwards all the opposition members of the National Assembly tendered their resignation, in protest at the legislation. Although the Assembly's Speaker refused to accept the resignations, the PDP deputies returned to the National Assembly only in November, following an agreement with the DLP that local council elections would take place in the first half of 1991, to be followed by gubernatorial and mayoral elections in 1992. The DLP also agreed to abandon plans for the transfer, by constitutional amendment, of executive powers to the State Council. The local elections (the first to be held in the Republic of Korea for 30 years) took place in March and June 1991, and resulted in a decisive victory for the DLP.

Meanwhile, in April 1991 the PDP merged with the smaller opposition Party for New Democratic Alliance to form the New Democratic Party (NDP). In September the NDP and the DP agreed to merge (under the latter's name) to form a stronger opposition front. A further opposition group, the Unification National Party (UNP), was established in January 1992 by Chung Ju-Yung, the founder and honorary chairman of the powerful Hyundai industrial conglomerate.

At elections to the National Assembly in March 1992 the DLP unexpectedly failed to secure an absolute majority, obtaining a total of 149 of the 299 seats. The remainder of the seats were won by the DP (97), the UNP (31) and independent candidates (21). In May Kim Young-Sam was chosen as the DLP's candidate for the presidential election, scheduled for December, and in August he replaced Roh as the party's President. Roh's decision to resign from the DLP altogether, in order to create a neutral government in anticipation of the election, was welcomed by opposition deputies. Serious divisions within the DLP led to defections from the party by opponents of Kim Young-Sam.

The presidential election, on 18 December 1992, was won by Kim Young-Sam, with some 42% of the votes cast. Kim (who was inaugurated on 25 February 1993) was the first South Korean President since 1960 without military connections. The defeated Kim Dae-Jung subsequently announced his retirement from political life. In February 1993 Chung Ju-Yung resigned as President of the United People's Party (UPP—as the UNP had been renamed), following allegations that he had embezzled Hyundai finances to fund his election campaign. Kim Young-Sam appointed Hwang In-Sung as Prime Minister, and a new State Council was formed.

Kim Young-Sam acted swiftly to honour his campaign pledge to eliminate corruption in business and political life; in all, during 1993, Kim's anti-corruption measures were reported to have resulted in the dismissal of, or disciplinary action against, some 3,000 business, government and military figures. One of Roh Tae-Woo's former Ministers of National Defence, Lee Jong-Koo, was sentenced in November 1993 to three years' imprisonment, after having been convicted of accepting bribes from defence contractors. At the same time the announcement of measures to restrict the activities of the country's industrial conglomerates (*chaebol*) was accompanied by corruption proceedings against several prominent business executives. In November Chung Ju-Yung was sentenced to three years' imprisonment, although the sentence was suspended on account of his age (78) and past contribution to South Korean economic development. Meanwhile, in August a presidential decree outlawed the opening of bank accounts under false names (a practice believed to have been used to conceal large-scale financial irregularities). In September the disclosure of the assets of some 1,500 public officials and the submission of these accounts for scrutiny by a government ethics committee prompted the resignation of several senior figures.

Hwang In-Sung resigned as Prime Minister in December 1993 and was succeeded by Lee Hoi-Chang, hitherto Chairman of the Board of Audit and Inspection (BAI). However, he resigned in April 1994 and was replaced by Lee Yung-Duk, latterly the Deputy Prime Minister responsible for national unification.

In July 1994 the UPP and a smaller opposition party, the New Political Reform Party, merged to form the New People's Party (NPP). In October the Government announced that its inquiry into the role played by former Presidents Chun and Roh in the 1979 coup had found that both had participated in a 'premeditated military rebellion'. Prosecution proceedings were not initiated at this stage. In December 1994 Lee Hong-Koo (hitherto the Deputy Prime Minister responsible for national unification) was appointed Prime Minister, as part of a major restructuring of the State Council.

The DLP fared badly at elections for gubernatorial, mayoral and other municipal and provincial posts in May 1995 (the first full local elections to be held in the Republic of Korea for 34 years). A contributory factor to the DLP's poor performance was the success of a new party, the United Liberal Democrats (ULD), established in March by defectors from the DLP and led by Kim Jong-Pil (who had resigned as DLP Chairman earlier in the year). In September Kim Dae-Jung returned to political life, establishing his own party, the National Congress for New Politics (NCNP). The DP was severely undermined when many of its members left to join the NCNP.

A major scandal erupted in October 1995, when Roh Tae-Woo admitted in a televised address that he had amassed a large sum of money during his term of office. He was arrested in the following month; at his trial, which opened in December, Roh confessed to having received donations from South Korean businesses, but denied that these constituted bribes. Many senior political figures and business leaders were also detained and interrogated in connection with the affair. Kim Dae-Jung, meanwhile, unexpectedly admitted that his campaign for the 1992 presidential election had been supported by a donation of money from Roh's 'slush fund'. Kim Young-Sam denied opposition allegations that he too had benefited from a similar donation. In December 1995, in an effort to distance his party from the deepening scandal, Kim Young-Sam changed the DLP's name to the New Korea Party (NKP). A major reorganization of the State Council was effected, in which Lee Hong-Koo was replaced as Prime Minister by Lee Soo-Sung, the President of Seoul National University.

In late 1995 it was announced that Roh Tae-Woo and Chun Doo-Hwan were to be prosecuted for their involvement in the 1979 coup and 1980 Gwangju massacre. Chun was arrested in December 1995, and in the following month he was additionally accused of accumulating a huge political 'slush fund'. At the opening of his trial for corruption in February 1996 Chun denied charges that the fund had been amassed as a result of bribe-taking. Legal proceedings in connection with the events of 1979 and 1980 opened in March 1996: Chun was charged with mutiny for his organization of the 1979 coup, and with sedition in connection with the Gwangju massacre, while Roh was charged with aiding Chun. Roh and Chun were convicted as charged in August. For their role in the *coup d'état* and Gwangju massacre, Chun was sentenced to death and Roh to $22\frac{1}{2}$ years' imprisonment; each was heavily fined in the corruption cases. Several others were also convicted for their part in the events of 1979 and 1980. Following an appeal, in which their contribution to the country's impressive economic growth and to the establishment of democratic government were cited as mitigating factors, Chun's sentence was commuted to one of life imprisonment, while Roh's term of imprisonment was reduced to 17 years.

Elections to the National Assembly took place in April 1996. Contrary to widespread predictions, the NKP only narrowly failed to retain its parliamentary majority, winning a total of 139 of the 299 seats. One factor contributing to the NKP's success was believed to have been the recent incursions into the demilitarized zone (DMZ) by North Korean troops, which, although apparently intended to destabilize the electoral proceedings, in fact caused many voters to favour the ruling party out of concern for national security. The NCNP performed less well than had been expected, taking 79 seats; moreover, the party's leader, Kim Dae-Jung, failed to win a seat. By the time the National Assembly convened in June, the NKP had secured a working majority with the support of several opposition and independent members.

The revision of the Republic of Korea's labour laws, with the aim of introducing greater flexibility into the labour market—a condition of the country's impending membership of the Organisation for Economic Co-operation and Development (OECD, see p. 320)—was initiated in May 1996. Reforms proposed by the Government in early December were severely criticized by trade unions and opposition parties. South Korea's principal workers' confederation, the Federation of Korean Trade Unions (FKTU), hitherto regarded as generally acquiescent to the Government, called a general strike in late December, after the Government convened a dawn session of the National Assembly, which approved the labour reform bill in the absence of opposition deputies. Many thousands of workers from key manufacturing industries, as well as public-sector employees, participated in the strike, which lasted for three weeks. Anti-Government demonstrators in Seoul and other major cities frequently clashed with riot police, and warrants were issued for the arrest of several leaders of the Korean Confederation of Trade Unions (KCTU), who were barricaded in the Roman Catholic Cathedral in Seoul. Concern was expressed that President Kim might be resorting to a more authoritarian style of leadership, particularly when it was alleged that the DPRK was lending its support to the striking workers (a tactic used by the South Korean authorities in the past to justify the suppression of domestic dissent); furthermore, foreign labour officials, including a representative of OECD, were threatened with deportation for encouraging union action. By mid-January 1997 support for the strikes was abating; the KCTU proposed weekly one-day stoppages, in order to minimize financial losses, and suggested that it might accept a modification of the labour law, having previously insisted on its complete annulment. OECD issued a severe rebuke to the Government for failing to honour its pledges on the issue of labour reform, and, in a significant concession, Kim agreed to meet the leaders of the opposition parties to discuss amendments to the law; warrants for the arrest of union leaders were also suspended. In March the National Assembly approved a revised version of the legislation, whereby the implementation of certain proposals was delayed for two years, while the KCTU was granted immediate official recognition.

Meanwhile, political and economic scandals persisted throughout 1996, particularly concerning allegations of bribery, which resulted in several government resignations. The infiltration of a North Korean submarine into South Korean waters in September (see below) resulted in the dismissal of the Minister of Defence, Lee Yang-Ho. He was subsequently charged with divulging classified information and with receiving bribes in connection with the procurement of helicopters for the army, and in December was sentenced to four years' imprisonment.

In January 1997 a further major scandal erupted when Hanbo, one of the country's largest steel and construction conglomerates, was declared bankrupt. Allegations were made that Hanbo had bribed the Government to exert pressure on banks to provide substantial loans to the conglomerate. The chief executives of several large Korean banks were arrested on charges of receiving bribes, and in February the Minister of Home Affairs, Kim Woo-Suk, resigned following allegations that he too had accepted payments from the company. President Kim issued an official apology for the loan scandal, and in March Lee Soo-Sung resigned as Prime Minister in a gesture of contrition. He was replaced by Goh Kun, hitherto President of Myongju University. In May the President's son, Kim Hyun-Chul, was arrested on charges of tax evasion and accepting bribes in return for influencing official appointments. The repercussions of the Hanbo affair widened further, implicating, among others, Kim Soo-Han, the Speaker of the National Assembly, and President Kim himself, whose 1992 election campaign was alleged to have been funded partially by the conglomerate. Kim Hyun-Chul was, however, formally cleared of any involvement. In June 1997 the former Chairman of Hanbo and several senior banking officials and politicians, including Kim Woo-Suk, were convicted on charges relating to the scandal.

In July 1997 Lee Hoi-Chang, former Prime Minister and Chairman of the NKP, was nominated as the ruling party's candidate for the presidential election, scheduled for December. Lee's candidacy was severely affected by various scandals surrounding the NKP and his family. Moreover, Rhee In-Je, the defeated challenger in the contest for the NKP nomination, decided to contest the presidency, subsequently forming his own political organization, the New Party by the People. In September Lee was elected President of the NKP, replacing Kim Young-Sam, who subsequently resigned from the party in order to ensure his neutrality in the forthcoming election. In October the NCNP and the ULD established an alliance, formulating a joint programme of proposed constitutional amendments and uniting behind the NCNP presidential nominee, Kim Dae-Jung, with the ULD to propose the Prime Minister in the event of victory. The conviction of Kim Hyun-Chul in October on charges of bribery and tax evasion was a further reverse for the NKP, which, in November, announced its merger with the DP, to form the Grand National Party (GNP).

Internal party politics were, however, overshadowed by the crisis experienced by the Korean economy in the latter half of 1997. Many of the conglomerates (*chaebol*) reported serious financial difficulties, having amassed huge debts which they were subsequently unable to service. Measures aimed at stabilizing the financial markets, announced in October, were unsuccessful. Moreover, in an unexpected reversal of its non-interventionist policy, the Government declared that part of the Kia Group, which was close to collapse, was to be nationalized, in an attempt to prevent further bankruptcies. Following the rejection by the legislature of the Government's financial liberalization measures, President Kim dismissed Kang Kyung-Shik, the Deputy Prime Minister and Minister of Finance and the Economy, in November, replacing him with Lim Chang-Yul, latterly Minister of Trade, Industry and Energy. An extensive economic stabilization programme, announced shortly afterwards, had little effect in curbing the depreciation of the national currency, the won, and the Government was forced to request the assistance of the IMF. This recourse to the IMF was condemned by opposition politicians and the media as a 'national shame'. The true extent of the country's economic crisis, described as the most serious in South Korean history, became apparent upon the conclusion of negotiations with the IMF in early December 1997. In the IMF's largest-ever rescue programme, worth US $57,000m., funds were to be allocated to prevent the Republic of Korea from defaulting on its repayments of external debt. Provision of the loans remained conditional upon the implementation of a programme of extensive financial and economic reforms.

The presidential election, held on 18 December 1997, was narrowly won by Kim Dae-Jung. Supporters of the ruling NKP were divided between Lee Hoi-Chang and Rhee In-Je, thus assuring victory for the NCNP-ULD alliance and the first peaceful transfer of power to an opposition politician in the Republic of Korea's history. Four other candidates contested the election. In a gesture to promote a sense of national unity, former Presidents Chun Doo-Hwan and Roh Tae-Woo were granted a presidential pardon and released from prison.

Legislation for financial reforms, to comply with the terms of the IMF agreement, was approved by the National Assembly in late December 1997. Discussions held throughout January 1998 with South Korea's overseas creditors to renegotiate the terms of the country's debt repayments were successfully concluded at the end of the month. An agreement was reached with labour leaders and business executives in early February to legalize redundancies (in return for which social welfare provisions would be improved); to permit unions to engage in political activities; and to allow state-employed teachers to form trade unions. Compulsory reform of the *chaebol*, which had been widely criticized for contributing to the debt-repayment crisis through their extensive borrowing, and legislation to allow foreign investors to acquire majority shareholdings in South Korean companies, were among reform measures promulgated in early 1998.

Kim Dae-Jung was formally inaugurated as President in late February 1998. Despite resistance from the opposition, Kim Dae-Jung designated Kim Jong-Pil, the leader of the ULD, as acting Prime Minister, and a Cabinet was formed in early March, with the ministries divided equally between the NCNP and the ULD. Various administrative reforms were implemented, including the abolition of the two posts of Deputy Prime Minister, the merger of the Ministries for Home Affairs and Government Administration and a reduction in the powers of the Ministry of Finance and the Economy. The number of cabinet ministers was reduced to 17 (excluding the Prime Minister).

At the beginning of May 1998 a large rally organized by the KCTU in protest at job losses ended in violent clashes with riot police. Later that month a two-day strike was called to demand that the Government fully honour its pledge to improve unemployment benefits and to reform the *chaebol*; according to the KCTU, some 120,000 workers supported the first day of the strike. The NCNP and the ULD performed well in local elections in June, although the turn-out was low. As the economic recession deepened, with the unemployment rate rising above 7%, labour unrest increased. Tens of thousands participated in strikes in July to protest against unemployment, the Government's privatization proposals and plans from Hyundai Motor and Daewoo Motor for mass redundancies.

THE REPUBLIC OF KOREA (SOUTH KOREA)

In August 1998 the National Assembly formally confirmed Kim Jong-Pil as Prime Minister, following months of legislative inactivity, during which the GNP had refused to support his nomination. The GNP, however, boycotted parliamentary sessions throughout September and into October, further delaying the consideration of urgent economic reforms, in protest at a government anti-corruption campaign, which it claimed was partisan and aimed at dividing the opposition. Several GNP members were placed under investigation on suspicion of illegally raising electoral campaign funds. In late October three former aides to Lee Hoi-Chang were charged in connection with an alleged attempt to bribe North Korean officials to organize a border incursion into the DMZ in December 1997, with the aim of aiding Lee's campaign for the presidency. The dispute escalated in December 1998, when a number of opposition deputies entered a room in the assembly buildings, which was being used by the intelligence agency, and removed confidential documents on 44 political figures. The GNP claimed that the agency had been carrying out surveillance of opposition deputies and subsequently boycotted legislative proceedings. In early January 1999, as the boycott continued, the ruling parties unilaterally passed 130 bills without debate, including legislation on banking reform and the endorsement of a controversial fishing agreement with Japan (see below). In mid-January, however, the ruling and opposition parties agreed that all issues relating to the affair be referred to the National Assembly's steering committee.

Tension arose within the ruling coalition in January 1999, when NCNP leaders proposed the postponement of plans for the introduction of a parliamentary, rather than presidential, system of government, with the Prime Minister assuming more power, as favoured by the ULD. Kim Young-Sam, who had refused to testify, was held responsible for the 1997 financial crisis in a report that was issued on the findings of parliamentary hearings held throughout February 1999. Meanwhile, the KCTU withdrew from a tripartite committee on management, labour and government (which had been established in early 1998), demanding an end to mass redundancies, a reduction in working hours and an improvement in the welfare system for the unemployed.

In late May 1999 a major reshuffle of the State Council was effected; an additional ministry was also created by the elevation to ministerial status of the Planning and Budget Commission. Kang Bong-Kyun, regarded as a strong advocate of reform, was appointed to the post of Minister of Finance and the Economy. In June, however, corruption scandals led to the replacement of the new Ministers of Justice and the Environment, and were believed to have contributed to the ruling coalition's failure to retain two parliamentary seats in by-elections held that month. In July Kim Dae-Jung and Kim Jong-Pil agreed not to seek a constitutional amendment on the adoption of a parliamentary system of government in 1999, despite protests from several senior ULD members.

Preparations for legislative elections (scheduled for April) dominated internal politics in early 2000. In January Kim Jong-Pil resigned as Prime Minister to chair the ULD, nominating Park Tae-Joon, the founder of Pohang Iron and Steel Company, as his successor. Kim Dae-Jung reshuffled the State Council, as a number of ministers resigned to concentrate on campaigning for parliamentary seats. Lee Hun-Jai, hitherto the Chairman of the Financial Supervisory Commission, was appointed as Minister of Finance and the Economy. There was speculation that by the appointments of Park and Lee, shortly before the elections, the ruling parties hoped to remind voters of the Government's relative success in overcoming the severe economic problems experienced by the Republic of Korea in 1997–98. Later in January 2000 Kim Dae-Jung established a new party, the Millennium Democratic Party (MDP), to succeed the ruling NCNP, having reportedly failed in attempts to effect a merger with the ULD. Meanwhile, civic groups exerting pressure on the main political parties to reform were receiving considerable popular support, in what was perceived as a reflection of increasing public discontent with South Korean party politics, following months of legislative inactivity. A grouping of some 470 civic organizations, styled the Citizens' Alliance for the 2000 General Elections, published a list of politicians whom it considered unfit to stand in the elections, largely on grounds of alleged corruption and incompetence. The ULD condemned the inclusion of Kim Jong-Pil on the list, accusing the MDP of involvement in its compilation. In February the National Assembly approved revisions to the election law, which reduced the number of legislative seats from 299 to 273 (227 directly elected and 46 allocated by proportional representation), and reversed a ban on campaigning by civic groups against candidates. A proposal by the MDP for the introduction of a two-ballot system was rejected by the National Assembly; the ULD was believed to have voted with the opposition GNP against its coalition partner. Lee Han-Dong, recently elected as President of the ULD, subsequently announced the party's withdrawal from the ruling coalition, claiming that the MDP had failed to fulfil its electoral pledges, although Prime Minister Park was to remain in the Government.

The elections to the National Assembly were held on 13 April 2000. The GNP, which won 133 of the 273 seats, retained its position as the largest party in the Assembly, but remained four seats short of a majority. The ruling MDP secured 115 seats, while the ULD suffered a serious reverse, taking only 17 seats (compared with 50 in the 1996 elections). Only two seats were won by the Democratic People's Party, which had been formed in February by defectors from the GNP who had failed to be nominated as parliamentary candidates by their former party. The New Korea Party of Hope won one seat, and independents five. In mid-May Park resigned as Prime Minister, amid increasing controversy over allegations of tax evasion. The designation of Lee Han-Dong as Park's successor indicated a restoration of MDP-ULD co-operation. Furthermore, the MDP's Lee Man-Sup was elected as Speaker of the National Assembly in early June, with the support of the ULD, the two smallest parliamentary parties and independents.

Amid criticism that reform of the *chaebol* was proceeding too slowly, Kim Dae-Jung effected a major government reorganization in August 2000, which primarily concerned the economic portfolios. Notably, Lee Hun-Jai was dismissed as Minister of Finance and was replaced by Jin Nyum, hitherto Minister of Planning and Budget. Later that month Song Ha resigned as Minister of Education following allegations of serious irregularities in his financial affairs.

While President Kim enjoyed increasing admiration and respect within the international community, in October 2000 being awarded the Nobel Peace Prize for his contribution to democracy and human rights (and particularly for his successful attempts at reconciliation with the Democratic People's Republic of Korea), his pursuit of reunification was criticized domestically by those who felt that the Republic of Korea, confronted by its own economic problems, could ill afford assistance to its northern neighbour, which was not perceived to be reciprocating in a magnanimous manner.

In November 2000 Kim Yong-Kap, a GNP member of the National Assembly, described the ruling MDP as a 'subsidiary of the North Korean KWP (Korean Workers' Party)'. The comments shocked and embarrassed both the MDP and the GNP, and the National Assembly was suspended. On the following day talks between the two parties were held, and it was agreed that the National Assembly would reconvene that evening, when the GNP would make a public apology for Kim's remarks and would strike them from the parliamentary record. Shortly after the legislature reconvened, however, the GNP walked out in protest at an MDP motion to dismiss Kim from his seat. A few days later there was renewed tension in the National Assembly as the GNP walked out again, this time prompted by the MDP's obstruction of a motion to impeach the Prosecutor-General, Park Soon-Yong, for alleged bias in the investigation of irregularities during the April elections. The GNP returned to the session one week later, citing the need for the Assembly to work to resolve the increasing economic difficulties and social instability. In December Kim Dae-Jung effected leadership changes in the MDP. Kim Joong-Kwon, Secretary to the President, was appointed Chairman in place of Suh Young-Hoon, who had resigned, and Park Sang-Kyu assumed the role of Secretary-General. Kim Dae-Jung rejected suggestions, both within and outside the party, that as Head of State he should relinquish the post of MDP President.

During 2000 and early 2001 dissatisfaction with the Government manifested itself on numerous occasions in the form of industrial and agricultural unrest. In late June 2000 doctors throughout the country participated in a strike to demonstrate their opposition to legislation depriving physicians of the right to prescribe drugs (which had been intended to restrict excessive prescription of medication and alleged profiteering by doctors). Several deaths were linked to the strike, which ended five days later following an offer by the Government to revise the legislation in July. Further action took place, however, in October, as a satisfactory compromise had not been reached. Mounting public anger obliged the abandonment of the renewed strike. In the following month farmers held a strike to demand that their debts be cancelled and that the Government intervene on their behalf at the World Trade Organization (WTO, see p. 370). Meanwhile, as the Daewoo Motor Company had been declared bankrupt, compounding anxieties for the future of other *chaebol*, some 15,000 workers protested in November 2000 in Seoul against government-led corporate restructuring which would result, it was feared, in large-scale retrenchment. Several more strikes in various sectors took place in late 2000, arising from fears of mass unemployment.

In January 2001 the State Council approved legislation providing for debt-relief loans to farmers and fishermen. At the end of that month a minor reorganization of the State Council was effected, when changes included Jin Nyum's elevation to the post of Deputy Prime Minister for Finance and the Economy. Simultaneously, a government organization law came into effect that conferred the status of Deputy Prime Minister on the portfolios of Finance and Economy and of Education and Human Resources. Han Wang-Sang assumed the latter position. A Ministry of Gender Equality was also created, for which Han Myeong-Sook was allocated responsibility. In late March there was a major reorganization of the State Council, following the resignation of the Minister of Foreign Affairs and Trade, Lee Joung-Binn, who had caused controversy by signing a joint statement with Russia criticizing the USA's planned 'national missile defence' (NMD) system. Han Seung-Soo, a member of the Democratic People's Party, replaced him. Lim Dong-Won, hitherto Chairman of the National Intelligence Service, was appointed Minister of Unification. The former Minister of Culture, Park Jie-Won, who had resigned in September 2000 following allegations of corruption, was appointed chief presidential policy adviser. Park had organized the historic inter-Korean summit in June 2000 (see below), and his appointment to this post reaffirmed Kim Dae-Jung's commitment to his 'sunshine' policy.

In early April 2001 the minor opposition Democratic People's Party joined the ruling MDP-led coalition, despite protests from within the MDP. Later that month the MDP suffered a defeat in local by-elections, and by May Kim Dae-Jung's popularity had fallen sharply, as voters grew disillusioned by his failure to implement political reforms. President Kim had also received criticism for his appointment of ministers and advisers from his home region of Jeolla, in the south-west, thereby antagonizing the south-eastern Gyeongsang region.

In June 2001 the KCTU organized a national strike involving 55,000 workers from 125 trade unions, who were protesting against decreasing wages and worsening working conditions. The strikes were joined by thousands of nurses and also airline pilots and ground staff, but denounced by President Kim as illegal. At the same time the country experienced its worst drought since 1904, adversely affecting agriculture and necessitating the mobilization of 130,000 troops to the most badly-stricken areas. The drought was followed by the worst floods in 37 years.

In July 2001 the Government's campaign against the alleged tax evasion and other financial dealings of the country's 23 news organizations (including major newspapers) led to accusations that President Kim was trying to stifle the media; one newspaper in particular, *Chosun Ilbo*, had been highly critical of Kim and his 'sunshine' policy. The National Tax Service had imposed fines totalling US $388m. in late June following a four-month investigation, which Kim defended as being part of ongoing anti-corruption campaigns but which opposition parties attributed to attempts by the MDP to boost its chances of winning the 2002 presidential election. Opinion polls showed the public to be generally supportive of the investigations and sceptical about the media, itself perceived as corrupt. In late August the owners of three newspapers, including *Chosun Ilbo*, were arrested for tax evasion.

Also in August 2001 the Minister of Unification, Lim Dong-Won, came under heavy criticism from the opposition after delegates from several South Korean non-governmental organizations (NGOs) travelled to the North to mark the anniversary of Korean liberation from Japanese rule, on 15 August. In early September Lim was forced to resign after the National Assembly approved a motion of no-confidence in him, organized by the GNP and supported by the MDP's coalition partner, the ULD. The latter's actions effectively dissolved the ruling coalition, and President Kim appointed four new ministers: of Labour; Agriculture and Forestry; Construction and Transportation; and Maritime Affairs and Fisheries. In addition, Hong Soon-Young, hitherto ambassador to China, was appointed Minister of Unification. Lim was immediately appointed presidential adviser on reunification, national security and foreign affairs, reaffirming Kim's confidence in him.

In late October 2001 the GNP won three by-elections, increasing its seats in the National Assembly to 136—just one short of a majority. The opposition victory created new rifts within the ruling MDP between younger reformers and party veterans, and President Kim subsequently resigned from the party presidency in early November, ostensibly in order to administer state affairs without being involved in party disputes. He was succeeded, on an interim basis, by Han Kwang-Ok. Further infighting in the MDP ensued as senior party officials sought to strengthen their positions with a view to securing the party presidential nomination for the 2002 election. At the same time Park Jie-Won, the senior secretary for policy planning and a close aide of the president, also resigned. By early December some eight presidential candidates had emerged within the MDP.

In late January 2002 President Kim again reorganized the State Council, dismissing Minister of Unification Hong Soon-Young and reallocating seven other posts, as well as the positions of six of the eight senior presidential secretaries and his chief of staff. Hong was succeeded by Jeong Se-Hyun, hitherto a special assistant to the director of the National Intelligence Service (NIS), while Jeon Yun-Churl, hitherto Minister of Planning and Budget, was appointed chief presidential secretary (chief of staff). Jeon was succeeded in his previous post by Chang Seung-Woo. Park Jie-Won returned as Kim's special aide for policy, emphasizing his close relationship with the President. The changes were intended to strengthen Kim's authority during his final year in office. Within days, the Minister of Foreign Affairs and Trade, Han Seung-Soo, was also dismissed, owing to Seoul's strained relations with the USA, and replaced by Choi Sung-Hong, hitherto Vice-Minister.

The contest for the MDP's presidential nomination intensified during February 2002 as putative reformist candidates sought to present a joint candidate, and opponents of the leading contender, Rhee In-Je, moved against him. The opposition GNP also experienced a power struggle, resulting in the party Vice-President, Park Geun-Hye (daughter of former military ruler Park Chung-Hee), leaving the party later in the month, initially with the intention of standing for the presidency as an independent candidate. In May Park established a new party, the Korean Coalition for the Future (KCF), serving as its chairwoman.

Meanwhile, in late February 2002 the country suffered another general strike, by thousands of railway and energy workers, who were protesting against privatization plans and shortened working hours. In early April the KCTU cancelled a major strike after reaching a settlement with the Government. The KCTU leadership subsequently resigned *en masse,* following criticism that it had made too many concessions to the Government. However, limited strike action continued in May.

By late April 2002 Roh Moo-Hyun had secured the MDP presidential nomination, while the GNP remained mired in internal disputes; the party's eight vice-presidents all resigned on 24 March in order to 'renew the face of the party', and were succeeded by a collective leadership. Meanwhile, Lee Hoi-Chang had secured the GNP's nomination for the national presidency. Also in mid-April President Kim replaced the Deputy Prime Minister for Finance and the Economy, Jin Nyum, with Jeon Yun-Churl, hitherto the chief of staff to the President. Jeon was succeeded by Park Jie-Won.

In early May 2002 President Kim and six of his ministers resigned from the MDP in order to focus on state affairs during the final months of Kim's presidency. By that time, Kim had become increasingly embarrassed by the corruption scandals involving his second and third sons, Kim Hong-Up and Kim Hong-Gul respectively, and he publicly apologized for their behaviour. In early June Kim Hong-Gul was charged with bribery and tax evasion, and subsequently went on trial. Kim Hong-Up was arrested later that month, accused of receiving bribes from businessmen. A nephew of the President's wife, Lee Hyung-Taek, was also sentenced for receiving bribes. The scandals adversely affected the MDP's performance in local elections held in mid-June, in which the party secured only four posts (three of which were in Jeolla, its traditional support base), while the GNP won 11 posts and the ULD one post.

In early July 2002 President Kim reorganized the cabinet, appointing Chang Sang, hitherto President of Ewha Woman's University, as the country's first female Prime Minister. At the same time, six ministers were replaced. However, at the end of that month the National Assembly rejected Chang's appointment on the grounds of questionable property dealings and the fact that her son had adopted US citizenship. In her place, President Kim nominated Chang Dae-Whan, a former newspaper proprietor, but he too was rejected by the National Assembly in late August on the grounds of questionable financial practices. In September Kim nominated Kim Suk-Soo, a former Supreme Court judge and former Head of the National Election Commission, as his candidate for the post of Prime Minister, and he was accepted by the National Assembly in early October, thus ending months of political paralysis.

Meanwhile, the popularity of Roh Moo-Hyun deteriorated so significantly after his nomination for the presidency that members of the MDP considered replacing him altogether. The MDP also suffered further set-backs in by-elections held in early August 2002 when the GNP won 11 out of 13 seats contested, giving it an overall majority in the National Assembly. In September Chung Mong-Joon (the sixth son of Hyundai founder Chung Ju-Yung, who was President of the Korean Football Association and Vice-President of FIFA (the international football federation) and also an independent legislator, announced that he was standing for the country's presidency. Chung's popularity had risen sharply following the Republic of Korea's successful co-hosting of the 2002 football World Cup and had surpassed that of Roh. In early November Chung formally launched his 'National Unity 21' party, receiving support from a broad political spectrum, including defectors from the MDP. However, later in that month Chung moved closer to Roh, and the two agreed to present a joint candidate for the presidency, namely Roh, in order to prevent Lee Hoi-Chang's election as President in December. Under the terms of the Roh-Chung partnership, there was to be a constitutional amendment whereby the powers of the presidency would be reduced in favour of those of the Prime Minister. (A similar arrangement had been agreed between Kim Dae-Jung and Kim Jong-Pil in 1997 but never implemented.)

The final months of 2002 witnessed the ruling MDP mired in further scandals. In October it emerged that President Kim and Chung Mong-Joon had arranged for a Hyundai subsidiary to transfer US $200m. to North Korea via the (Southern) state-owned Korea Development Bank prior to the historic inter-Korean summit of June 2000 (see below), effectively 'buying' the meeting. Furthermore, Kim Hong-Up was sentenced to three-and-a-half years' imprisonment in early November for accepting bribes. Kim Hong-Gul was also sentenced, separately, to two years' imprisonment (with three years' suspension) for bribery and tax evasion. Both received heavy fines, and their convictions further undermined President Kim and the MDP. In November Park Geun-Hye, who had left the opposition GNP earlier in the year to form the new KCF (see above), agreed with Lee Hoi-Chang to merge her party with the GNP, thus lending support to Lee's election campaign.

None the less, the presidential election, held on 19 December 2002, was narrowly won by Roh Moo-Hyun, who received 48.9% of the votes cast, against Lee Hoi-Chang's 46.6%. Roh's victory came despite the last-minute withdrawal of Chung Mong-Joon's support. It was generally acknowledged that Roh's victory was due to his uncompromising stance in favour of a foreign policy more independent from the USA, whereas Lee was widely seen as having very close relations with Washington, DC. The MDP in early December accused the USA of supporting Lee in the election, citing a meeting between him and the US ambassador. Relations with the USA (see below) had become a major election issue, as anti-American sentiment increased following several incidents involving US servicemen, and differences between the two countries emerged over how to resolve tensions with the North. As with past presidential elections, regionalism was manifested strongly in voting patterns, with some pro-Roh regions (Jeolla) voting 92% in his favour, while some pro-Lee regions (Gyeongsang) voted 78% in his favour. Support for the two main candidates also indicated the emergence of a generational gap, with younger voters favouring Roh, while older voters supported Lee. Kwon Young-Gil of the Democratic Labour Party came a distant third, with 3.9% of the votes cast. The level of participation was estimated at 70.8%. Following his defeat, Lee Hoi-Chang retired from politics.

In January 2003 President-elect Roh began making appointments to his new Government. Goh Kun, hitherto the president of Transparency International Korea, an anti-corruption agency, and himself a former Prime Minister, was reappointed to that post, while Moon Hee-Sang, an MDP legislator, was appointed chief of staff, and concurrently Chairman of the Civil Service Commission. Roh was inaugurated on 25 February 2003 and promptly appointed a new cabinet. Notable appointments included Kim Jin-Pyo as Deputy Prime Minister for Finance and Economy, Yoon Deok-Hong, hitherto President of Daegu University, as Deputy Prime Minister for Education and Human Resources Development, and Kang Gum-Sil as Minister of Justice. Yoon Young-Kwan, hitherto professor of International Relations at Seoul National University, was appointed Minister of Foreign Affairs and Trade, while Gen. (retd) Cho Young-Kil became Minister of National Defence. Jeong Se-Hyun was retained as Minister of National Unification, indicating continuity of Kim Dae-Jung's 'sunshine' policy towards the North. The new cabinet contained four women, a record number thus far. President Roh also reorganized the military and intelligence services, appointing Gen. Kim Jong-Hwan as Chairman of the Joint Chiefs of Staff, and Ko Young-Koo, a human rights lawyer, as director of the National Intelligence Service (NIS). The latter appointment reflected Roh's determination to depoliticize the agency, which had been responsible for surveillance of political figures even after the transition to democracy.

Roh faced immediate challenges on assuming office, most notably the diplomatic crisis between the DPRK and the USA, which had strained Seoul's relations with the latter. Other problems included the ongoing scandal surrounding Hyundai and the inter-Korean summit meeting of 2000, and a subway fire in Daegu in February 2003, which killed more than 200 people and highlighted the inadequacy of safety measures in public infrastructure. In March Roh appointed a special counsel to investigate the alleged transfer of funds by Hyundai to the DPRK in connection with the 2000 presidential summit meeting (see below). In the longer term Roh aimed to address regional imbalances and the disparity between rich and poor, to reduce corruption in business and the economy and to improve living standards and labour management.

In late April 2003 the GNP won two out of three seats in by-elections to the National Assembly, raising its total representation to 153. However, the victory of a reformist ally of the MDP, Rhyu Si-Min, was welcomed by the Government as an indication of support for the reform process. Also in April, the National Assembly voted in favour of the dispatch of South Korean troops to support US military action in Iraq in a non-combat capacity. Despite his independent stance on relations with the USA (see above), President Roh justified the deployment in terms of strengthening Korean-US relations. There was widespread public opposition to the Iraq deployment, with opinion polls showing that around 80% of the South Korean population disapproved of the US military action in Iraq. Despite this opposition, several hundred South Korean military medical and engineering personnel were sent to Iraq in May.

In June 2003 two aides of former President Kim Dae-Jung, former Minister of Unification Lim Dong-Won and former Minister of Culture and Tourism Park Jie-Won, were charged in connection with illegal payments made through the Hyundai group to the DPRK to arrange the 2000 presidential summit meeting (Lim Dong-Won received an 18-month prison sentence in September, and Park Jie-Won was sentenced to 12 years' imprisonment in December). Also implicated in the scandal was Hyundai heir Chung Mong-Hun, who committed suicide in August. In July, meanwhile, a strike by railway workers protesting against privatization in the industry was cancelled by the KCTU, representing an acknowledgement that previous strikes had not prevented the approval of legislation on privatization by the National Assembly.

In September 2003 a faction of the MDP announced its intention to form a new party owing to internal divisions over corruption and other issues within the MDP. President Roh subsequently relinquished his membership of the MDP, although he did not commit himself to joining the new organization. The new group was initially referred to as the New Party for Participatory Citizens, but in October the new name of Uri (meaning 'our') Party was adopted. A large number of MDP legislators, including MDP Chairman Chyung Dai-Chul, joined the Uri Party, thus leaving the MDP with only 62 seats in the National Assembly. The Uri Party was officially launched in November under a temporary leadership (Chung Dong-Young was elected Uri Party Chairman in early 2004). Another development in September, meanwhile, was the resignation of the Minister of Home Affairs, Kim Doo-Kwan, following an incident in which protesters had infiltrated a US base in Pocheon. The National Assembly had approved Kim Doo-Kwan's dismissal,

THE REPUBLIC OF KOREA (SOUTH KOREA)

despite President Roh's policy of increased independence in relations with the USA. In October there were renewed public protests over a proposal to send additional troops to Iraq.

President Roh's declining popularity was further undermined in October 2003 by the investigation and subsequent arrest of his former aide Choi Do-Sul, who was accused of having received illegal funds from the SK Group following the 2002 presidential election. In an attempt to restore his popularity, President Roh announced proposals for a referendum to be held on the issue of his presidency later in the year. However, the proposed referendum prompted further political instability, with Prime Minister Goh Kun and other government ministers offering their resignations (which were rejected by President Roh). Both the GNP and the MDP dismissed the referendum proposal as unconstitutional.

Official investigations into illegal campaign funding from leading *chaebol* during the 2002 presidential election, involving both the MDP and the GNP, were instigated at the end of October 2003. Initially focusing on donations from the SK Group, the investigation widened in November, with forcible searches taking place at the offices of other *chaebol*, including Hyundai, LG Group and Samsung. At the end of November President Roh vetoed a bill, already approved by the National Assembly, which urged an independent investigation into the funding allegations. GNP leader Choe Byung-Yul commenced a hunger strike in protest at the veto. In early December the National Assembly voted to rescind the veto on an independent investigation, in the country's first reversal of a presidential decision since 1954. An independent investigator was subsequently appointed. In the same month President Roh announced that he would step down if the MDP were found by the investigation to have received one-tenth of the illegal funding taken by the GNP. In a further development in December, the GNP's Lee Hoi-Chang, Roh's rival in the 2002 election, publicly admitted that his party had accepted US $42m. in illegal donations.

Meanwhile, there was further public opposition in early December 2003 to the Republic of Korea's involvement in Iraq, following the killing of two South Korean engineers engaged in reconstruction work in the country. However, the Government announced that there would be no change in its policy on Iraq as a result of the deaths.

In January 2004 the Minister of Foreign Affairs and Trade, Yoon Young-Kwan, relinquished his post, reportedly following criticism of presidential policy by his advisers. The dispute was widely reported to have been related to President Roh's policy on independence from the USA over issues such as the North Korean nuclear weapons programme. However, there was also a suggestion that Yoon Young-Kwan's departure was due to internal divisions and was only incidentally connected to the Republic of Korea's relations with the USA. Yoon Young-Kwan was replaced by Ban Ki-Moon. There were further government changes in February, following the resignation of Kim Jin-Pyo, the Deputy Prime Minister for Finance and the Economy, in order to stand as a Uri Party candidate in the legislative elections scheduled for April. Kim was replaced as Deputy Prime Minister by Lee Hun-Jai, and three further new ministers were appointed in the same month. Also in February, the National Assembly approved the deployment of an additional 3,000 non-combat troops to Iraq (the deployment was later delayed owing to security concerns—see below).

Meanwhile, investigations into political corruption continued in early 2004. In January former MDP Chairman Chyung Dai-Chul (now of the Uri Party) was arrested, amid allegations that he had accepted bribes from various business groups. The former Secretary-General of the GNP, Kim Young-Iel, was also arrested in connection with allegations of illegal fund-raising during the 2002 election. In February there was also speculation that Park Geun-Hye, who had returned to the GNP in advance of the 2002 elections (see above), had received undeclared funds from the GNP for the purposes of a merger with her Korean Coalition for the Future. In March 2004 it was reported that President Roh's MDP election campaign had received 12,500m. won in illicit funds, amounting to one-seventh of the 84,000m. allegedly received by the GNP and thus to more than the proportion of one-tenth that Roh had previously stated would prompt his resignation. At the end of March it was confirmed that Roh's former aide Choi Do-Sul (see above) had received US $530,000 in illegal funding.

As the legislative election of April 2004 approached, there were dramatic developments in mid-March with the impeachment of President Roh over the issue of his support for the pro-Government Uri Party, whereby he had allegedly violated electoral law. A total of 193 legislators, mostly from the GNP and Roh's former party, the MDP, voted in favour of the impeachment. There were vehement protests from supporters of President Roh in the National Assembly following the vote, as well as widespread public protests in support of the President, with opinion polls indicating that around 70% of the population did not support the impeachment. President Roh's position was to be reviewed by the Constitutional Court within six months, with Prime Minister Goh Kun becoming acting head of state for this period. Also in March, Park Geun-Hye, daughter of former President Park Chung-Hee, was appointed Chairwoman of the GNP following party leadership elections.

At the elections to the National Assembly on 15 April 2004, the Uri Party won a narrow majority in the legislature, securing 152 seats of the total of 299 in the newly expanded chamber. The main opposition party, the GNP, now under the leadership of Park Geun-Hye, secured 121 seats. Roh's former party, the MDP, won only nine seats. The success of the Uri Party was seen as a victory for Roh and an expression of public disapproval of his impeachment. It was believed that the Uri Party's majority might have been greater had it not been for comments made during the election campaign by the party's leader, Chung Dong-Young, who had offended older voters by suggesting that their participation in the election was unimportant. (Chung subsequently resigned as head of the Uri Party and was replaced by Shin Ki-Nam.) In May Roh was reinstated following the decision of the Constitutional Court to dismiss the case for impeachment. Roh became a formal member of the Uri Party in the same month.

Following the reinstatement of President Roh, Prime Minister Goh Kun, who had served as acting head of state during Roh's period of impeachment, resigned from his post. Deputy Prime Minister Lee Hun-Jai became acting Prime Minister for a short period. In June Lee Hae-Chan, a former education minister, was approved by the National Assembly as Prime Minister. Following the appointment of a new Prime Minister, three new ministerial appointments were made, including that of Chung Dong-Young, former head of the Uri Party, as Minister of Unification. Also in June, the Government announced that the deployment of 3,000 South Korean troops to Iraq, originally approved in February (see above), would take place in August. Public opposition to this announcement increased dramatically a few days later when a South Korean translator, Kim Sun-Il, who had been taken hostage in Iraq, was beheaded by his captors. In July the Minister of National Defence, Cho Young-Kil, resigned, taking responsibility for an incident in which a South Korean ship had fired warning shots at a North Korean vessel believed to be intruding in South Korean waters, with naval staff reportedly having failed to report radio communication with the North Korean ship. Cho was replaced by Yoon Kwang-Woong. Meanwhile, during mid-2004 there were various instances of labour unrest, including strikes by subway workers and by employees of a major oil company. In August President Roh announced that investigations were to be held into the past conduct of politicians during the period of Japanese rule and of dictatorial governments extending into the 1980s. The first political leader to be adversely affected by these investigations was Uri Party leader Shin Ki-Nam, who was forced to resign after it was found that his father had committed human rights abuses as a policeman during the period of Japanese colonization. Shin was replaced by Lee Bu-Young. During 2004 there were reports of government plans to relocate the country's capital city and to establish a new administrative capital south of Seoul, owing to Seoul's vulnerability to attack by the DPRK and to congestion in the city. However, these plans for a new capital were suspended following a ruling by the Constitutional Court in October declaring the relocation project to be unconstitutional. From September, meanwhile, controversy also arose over the anti-communist national security law, which dated back to the country's pre-democratic era. (The law had been invoked, for example, in the case of Korean-German scholar Song Doo-Yul, who had been charged under the law in 2003 in connection with his alleged links to North Korea.) Human rights groups, supported by President Roh, claimed that the law was outdated and subject to abuse. However, proposals to abolish the law were rejected by the Supreme Court. In October a number of reform bills submitted to the National Assembly by the Uri Party included a renewed attempt to abolish the national security law, amid strong opposition from the GNP. In November there were further instances of labour unrest in protest at government plans to reform labour legislation to prohibit strikes by public-sector workers and to allow employers to hire staff on a temporary basis. In December the National Assembly approved a proposal for South Korean troops in Iraq to remain there until the end of 2005, despite continuing strong public opposition to the deployment.

A number of government changes took place in January 2005, including the appointment of Kim Jin-Pyo as Deputy Prime Minister for Education and Human Resources Development, replacing Ahn Byung-Young. (Lee Ki-Jun was initially appointed to the post but resigned after only four days in office, following disclosures concerning his conduct in financial affairs as head of Seoul National University.) In March, meanwhile, the Deputy Prime Minister for Finance and the Economy, Lee Hun-Jai, resigned as a result of controversy over his wife's real-estate investments. He was replaced by Han Duck-Soo, hitherto the Minister of Government Policy Co-ordination. A new Minister of Government Policy Co-ordination, Choo Byung-Jik, was appointed in April. Further government changes took place in June, when Roh appointed Chun Jung-Bae as Minister of Justice and Lee Jae-Yong as Minister of the Environment.

In January 2005 Uri Party leader Lee Bu-Young resigned, citing his party's failure to realize its reform aims such as the abolition of the anti-communist national security law. Lim Chae-Jung became acting Chairman pending party leadership elections in April, following which Moon Hee-Sang was appointed to the post. The Uri Party had lost its majority in the National Assembly in the previous month when the Supreme Court upheld the convictions of two party legislators for malpractice in the election of April 2004, thereby depriving them of their seats and reducing the party's representation to 146. In all, six of the legislators elected in April 2004 had subsequently lost their seats as a result of malpractice convictions, temporarily reducing the National Assembly to 293 seats. At by-elections held on 29 April 2005 to fill these vacated seats, the Uri Party failed to regain its majority, while the opposition GNP took five of the six contested seats, with the sixth being won by an independent candidate. In May it was announced that the MDP was changing its name to the Democratic Party (DP). From July President Roh repeatedly proposed that a coalition government be formed between the Uri Party and the GNP, offering in turn to relinquish some of the powers of his office; Roh suggested that this could lead to changes in the electoral system that might solve the problem of 'regionalism' in South Korean politics, whereby certain regions of the country tended always to support a particular party. The proposal was comprehensively rejected by GNP Chairwoman Park Geun-Hye. Another round of by-elections was held in October to replace two legislators from the Uri Party and two from the GNP who had lost their seats, again owing to convictions for electoral malpractice. The GNP won all four contested seats, thereby further reducing the Uri Party's parliamentary representation to 144 and prompting the resignation of the party's senior leadership, including Chairman Moon. Chung Sye-Kyun was appointed acting Chairman pending a leadership election in February 2006. Former party Chairman Chung Dong-Young resigned as Minister of Unification in December 2005 in order to stand in the leadership election, as did Kim Geung-Tae, the Minister of Health and Welfare.

Consequently, in January 2006 President Roh effected a government reorganization. Notably, Rhyu Si-Min was appointed Minister of Health and Welfare, while Lee Jong-Seok became Minister of Unification and acting Uri Party Chairman Chung Sye-Kyun was appointed Minister of Commerce, Industry and Energy (his replacement as acting Chairman was Yoo Jay-Kun). At the Uri Party's national convention in February Chung Dong-Young was elected to the post of Chairman for a second time. Another series of ministerial nominations was announced in March, to replace government members who subsequently resigned in order to stand at the forthcoming mayoral and gubernatorial elections scheduled for May: the new nominees included Lee Yong-Sup as Minister of Government Administration and Home Affairs and Rho-Jun Hyong as Minister of Information and Communication. Also in March a scandal developed concerning the conduct of the Prime Minister, Lee Hae-Chan, with regard to a game of golf that he had played on 1 March, a public holiday that coincided with the first day of a national strike. Lee was criticized for choosing to play golf rather than oversee the Government's reaction to the strike. Objections were also raised to his choice of golfing partners, who reportedly included a businessman with a criminal record for fixing share prices. Lee eventually resigned on 14 March in reaction to the scandal. On 24 March Roh nominated Han Myeong-Sook as his successor; Han's nomination was approved by a vote in the National Assembly on 19 April, and she was officially appointed to the post the following day, thereby becoming the Republic of Korea's first female Prime Minister.

The country's Constitution, meanwhile, stipulates that the Republic of Korea shall seek the peaceful unification of the Korean peninsula. During the 1980s relations with the DPRK were characterized by mutual suspicion, aggravated by various incidents; these included the discovery of several pro-North Korean spy rings and the death in October 1983 of four South Korean government ministers in a bomb explosion in Burma (now Myanmar), for which President Chun held the DPRK responsible. During 1985 representatives of the two states conferred on economic and humanitarian issues, but discussions were suspended in early 1986 when Kim Il Sung denounced the annual 'Team Spirit' military manoeuvres, held jointly with US troops in South Korea. Subsequent inter-Korean negotiations were likewise regularly suspended, owing to North Korean objections to the 'Team Spirit' exercises. In November 1987 the destruction of a South Korean airliner in flight over Burma, by a bomb that had allegedly been concealed aboard the aircraft by North Korean agents, caused a new outbreak of verbal hostility between the two countries.

However, with the appointment of Roh Tae-Woo as South Korean President in 1988, there appeared to be a greater willingness by the South to foster closer relations with the DPRK. Roh's announcement in early 1990 that the forthcoming 'Team Spirit' manoeuvres would be reduced in size and duration also contributed to an improvement in inter-Korean relations. In September of that year the North Korean Premier travelled to Seoul for discussions with his South Korean counterpart. The meeting represented the most senior-level contact between the two countries since the end of the Korean War in 1953. Further talks between the two premiers took place in late 1990. The DPRK's abandonment, announced in May 1991, of its long-standing position that the two Koreas should occupy a single seat at the UN was regarded as a significant concession. Accordingly, North and South Korea were admitted separately to the UN in September.

Prime-ministerial negotiations resumed in late 1991, and resulted in the signature of an 'Agreement on Reconciliation, Non-aggression and Exchanges and Co-operation between the South and the North'. At the end of December 1991 both states pledged to ban nuclear weapons from the Korean peninsula, and in early 1992 they agreed to form a joint commission to facilitate the simultaneous inspection of nuclear installations in the North and US military bases in the South. In recognition of the recent inter-Korean *rapprochement*, the Republic of Korea cancelled the 1992 'Team Spirit' exercises, and in the latter half of the year the DPRK permitted the inspection of its nuclear facilities by the International Atomic Energy Agency (IAEA, see p. 98). This apparent progress on military and nuclear issues was, however, reversed by the North's decision, in January 1993, to boycott all future inter-Korean nuclear talks, followed in March by its threatened withdrawal from the Treaty on the Non-Proliferation of Nuclear Weapons. Inter-Korean relations deteriorated further in early 1994, following the UN's announcement that it was considering the imposition of economic sanctions on North Korea: the DPRK, in turn, threatened to declare war on South Korea. The North Korean leadership was also incensed by South Korea's decision not to send a representative to the funeral, in July, of Kim Il Sung, and by its refusal to permit public mourning within South Korea. None the less, following the signing in October of the nuclear accord between the USA and the DPRK, the South Korean Government agreed to finance, in part, the construction and supply to the DPRK of light-water nuclear reactors, which are less easily adapted to the production of nuclear weapons (a key element of the accord), provided that reactors of a South Korean design were used.

The DPRK's announcement, in April 1996, that it was abandoning the 1953 armistice agreement was followed by a series of incursions by North Korean troops into the DMZ. The USA and South Korea proposed the holding of quadripartite negotiations with the People's Republic of China and North Korea; China subsequently agreed to the proposal, but the North Korean administration refused to commit itself to discussions. In September 1996 tension increased when a North Korean submarine was found abandoned near the South Korean coast; armed crew members in South Korean military uniforms were found dead near the submarine, others were killed by South Korean troops, and one was captured and interrogated. The South Korean

Government denounced the incident and, demanding an apology, suspended all contacts with the North, including the provision of emergency food aid. In an unprecedented move, in December the DPRK issued an apology for the incident and agreed to participate in preliminary talks about the proposed negotiations.

Exploratory discussions took place in New York, USA, in March 1997. Attempts by the DPRK to link the progress of negotiations with the provision of food aid were unsuccessful. However, in May, in the first such meeting for five years, representatives of the Red Cross organizations of North and South Korea reached agreement on the provision of 50,000 metric tons of grain to the DPRK. In October negotiations to allow foreign airlines, including those from South Korea, to enter North Korean airspace reached a successful conclusion.

Despite a military confrontation between North and South Korean troops in the DMZ in July 1997, full quadripartite negotiations (with the USA and China), aimed at concluding a peace treaty between North and South Korea, opened in Geneva, Switzerland, in early December. Agreement was reached on procedural arrangements for future sessions, and a second round of full discussions was held in March 1998. A meeting held in the Chinese capital of Beijing, in April, between North and South Korean government ministers, the first such direct contact for four years, broke down following mutual accusations of inflexibility.

A further improvement in relations between North and South Korea followed Kim Dae-Jung's inauguration in February 1998. Private and business-related inter-Korean contacts increased substantially during 1998, following the South Korean Government's introduction, in April, of measures designed to facilitate such activity, as part of Kim's new 'sunshine' policy of engagement with the North. Chung Ju-Yung, the founder of the Hyundai Group, initiated a number of historic joint-ventures, including, in June and October, the delivery of cattle across the DMZ to his home town in North Korea and the organization, in November, of a visit of some 800 South Korean tourists to Mount Kumgang, just north of the border. Despite fears that this improvement in relations would be jeopardized by evidence of continued North Korean incursions, South Korea affirmed that it would continue to pursue a policy of conciliation.

Private-level economic co-operation continued throughout 1999 and early 2000, and a number of joint cultural and sporting events also took place. In October 1999 Hyundai concluded an agreement with the DPRK on the construction of an industrial complex, and in December Samsung Electronics announced it had signed a contract with the DPRK for the joint development of computer software and the manufacture of electronic products. Inter-Korean trade increased by some 50.2% in 1999. In March 2000, during a visit to Germany, Kim Dae-Jung urged the DPRK to agree to government-level talks, and proposed the development of public-sector economic co-operation in areas such as agriculture, communications and the construction of infrastructure in the North. In April, following a series of high-level contacts in Beijing between officials of both countries, North and South Korea jointly announced that an historic summit meeting would take place between Kim Dae-Jung and Kim Jong Il in June 2000, during a three-day visit by the former to Pyongyang.

Following a delay of one day requested by the DPRK for 'technical reasons', the presidential summit meeting took place on 13–15 June 2000. Detailed agreements were then signed pledging economic co-operation, the development of mutual trust and the resolution of reunification issues. In July ministerial-level delegations from both countries met in Seoul. This was the first visit to South Korea by Northern officials since 1991. Although the two sides failed to reach an agreement on military matters, a joint communiqué was issued allowing for, inter alia, the reopening of liaison offices at Panmunjom, which had been closed in 1996, and the reconnection of the inter-Korean Kyongui railway line. The construction of a highway to run alongside the railway from North to South was subsequently agreed. In September Kim Dae-Jung formally inaugurated the project to remove thousands of landmines (to be undertaken by soldiers from each side respectively) and rebuild the railway line and adjacent highway. (Final details for the restoration of the rail link were agreed in February 2001.) Meanwhile, benefiting from the progress made at the summit meeting in June, in August 100 South Korean families visited Pyongyang and 100 North Korean families travelled to Seoul simultaneously to meet with relatives from whom they had been separated by the Korean War. The second ministerial meeting between the two sides was held in Pyongyang later that month. Negotiations were extended for one day because of an inability to agree on terms for beginning a dialogue between the two countries' military establishments. A compromise was reached after consultation with Kim Jong Il. It was agreed to hold two more cross-border family reunions by the end of 2000 and to commence talks on economic co-operation. In a symbolic display of unity, in September the two countries marched under the same flag in the opening ceremony of the Olympic Games in Sydney, Australia. In late September the South Korean Minister of National Defence, Cho Seong-Tae, received his northern counterpart, Vice-Marshal Kim Il Chol, for discussions held on Jeju Island, the first such ministerial meeting ever conducted. Further rounds of inter-ministerial, military and economic talks took place during 2000 and early 2001. In an indication of the improvement in relations, in December 2000 a meeting was also held between trade union representatives from the two countries.

Despite this progress, in December 2000 the Republic of Korea published its annual defence policy document, which classified the DPRK as its main enemy, and alleged that it had expanded its military capacity along the DMZ, an accusation that angered the DPRK. International analysts, however, felt that hostility was not imminent. Also in that month a resolution was passed by the South Korean legislature to demand the repatriation of prisoners of war who it alleged continued to be held by the North, despite the DPRK's denial of the existence of these prisoners. The two incidents seemed to demonstrate the growing reluctance of many South Koreans to continue with the process of reunification as it stood, which they regarded as having become increasingly unbalanced to the detriment of the South.

In early 2001 the uncompromising attitude adopted by the new US Administration towards the DPRK threatened to undermine severely the reconciliation process. In March the DPRK unilaterally postponed scheduled cabinet-level talks following Kim Dae-Jung's visit to the USA (see below), during which the latter had criticized Pyongyang's regime. Later that month, however, a member of the North Korean football team was permitted to join a South Korean squad. In April the DPRK denounced joint US-South Korean military exercises as a betrayal of the goodwill surrounding the June 2000 summit meeting. Ministerial talks resumed in Seoul in mid-September, the sixth round of which was concluded in mid-November (having been postponed from late October) without any agreement—the first unsuccessful such round since the presidential summit meeting. North Korea blamed the South, particularly Unification Minister Hong Soon-Young, for the failure of the talks.

Meanwhile, Kim Jong Il's long-awaited visit to Seoul for a second presidential summit meeting failed to materialize during 2001, and there was continued uncertainty as to when such a visit would occur. US President George W. Bush's reference in January 2002 to North Korea as being part of an 'axis of evil' further jeopardized inter-Korean relations.

A stalemate in inter-Korean relations was broken in late March 2002, however, when the North agreed to receive Kim Dae-Jung's special envoy, Lim Dong-Won, in early April. Following the visit, during which Lim met Kim Jong Il, the two sides agreed to further reunions for separated families (see below), and to continuing talks on economic co-operation. The DPRK also agreed to Lim's request that it renew dialogue with the USA and Japan. In mid-May Park Geun-Hye visited the North and met Kim Jong Il. The visit was notable because Northern agents had killed Park's mother in 1974 in a failed bid to assassinate her father. Despite the cordial visit, North Korea cancelled economic co-operation discussions with the South in May.

In May 2002 the increasing number of defectors from the North to the South received international attention as several groups sought asylum at Canadian, Japanese and South Korean diplomatic buildings in China. They were eventually allowed to travel to the South, albeit via the Philippines. The South Korean Ministry of Unification reported in January 2003 that during 2002 some 1,141 North Koreans had defected to the South, compared with 583 in 2001.

At the end of June 2002 a gun battle between North and South Korean vessels in the Yellow Sea resulted in the sinking of a Southern patrol boat and the deaths of six crew members. South Korean military sources estimated that 30 Northern crewmen had also been killed in the confrontation, which had started when two North Korean vessels accompanying a fishing boat reportedly crossed the Northern Limit Line (the maritime border separating the two Koreas). Following the incident, in July

THE REPUBLIC OF KOREA (SOUTH KOREA)

South Korea suspended rice shipments to the North and economic co-operation projects, reflecting widespread public anger. None the less, Kim Dae-Jung maintained his 'sunshine' policy towards the North, which later expressed regret for the incident. Meanwhile, North Korean state television showed selected highlights of football matches played by the South Korean team in the 2002 World Cup, although it refrained from transmitting extensive coverage of the event, which was being co-hosted by Japan.

In mid-August 2002 North and South Korea held a seventh round of ministerial talks in Seoul, aimed at improving relations in the aftermath of the latest naval confrontation and focusing on the issue of future family reunions, railway links (see below) and cultural exchanges. Regarding the latter, more than 300 North Korean athletes travelled to the South and participated in the Asian Games held in Busan during October. In late September the first inter-Korean military 'hotline' was inaugurated to allow for improved communications during sensitive occasions. Meanwhile, Pyongyang's revelation that it had abducted 12 Japanese citizens in the 1970s and 1980s highlighted the outstanding issue of the whereabouts of several hundred missing South Korean citizens believed to have been abducted by the North.

The eighth round of ministerial talks was held in Pyongyang in late October 2002 and focused mainly on economic co-operation issues, despite the fact that the USA had earlier revealed the existence of a secret nuclear weapons programme in the North (see the chapter on the Democratic People's Republic of Korea). At the end of that month a North Korean economic delegation began a nine-day tour of the South, including several major industrial facilities. Noteworthy was the fact that the delegation included Jang Song Taek, Kim Jong Il's brother-in-law and reportedly one of his most trusted advisers, and also Kim Hi Taek, the first deputy head of the KWP's Central Committee. At the end of December 2002 the South Korean Ministry of National Defence published a 'white paper' which, for the first time, excluded any reference to the North as its main enemy.

By late 2002 some of the goodwill generated by the historic inter-Korean summit meeting in June 2000 had been undermined by the revelation that Kim Dae-Jung had arranged for the Korea Development Bank to give a Hyundai affiliate US $200m. to transfer to the North in order to arrange the summit. However, the election in December of Roh Moo-Hyun as President of the Republic of Korea heralded a continuation of Kim's 'sunshine' policy. In early January 2003 representatives of Roh secretly met Northern officials in Beijing, and later in that month a ninth round of ministerial talks was held in Seoul.

North and South Korea continued their efforts to improve bilateral relations during 2003, despite a severe deterioration in relations between the North and the USA over the issue of the North Korean nuclear weapons programme (see chapter on the Democratic People's Republic of Korea). In March 2003 Roh was exploring a long-standing idea of developing gas pipelines between Sakhalin, Russia, and the DPRK that would supply the latter with energy in return for an abandonment of its nuclear programme. The DPRK hosted the 10th round of ministerial talks at the end of April. In mid-May, however, Pyongyang announced that it no longer recognized the Joint Declaration of the Denuclearization of the Korean Peninsula, signed with the South in 1992. Also in May, at talks between the two Koreas on economic matters, North Korea warned that the South would risk 'unspeakable disaster' if it became too confrontational in co-operating with the USA on the nuclear issue (the threat followed a summit meeting between Roh and US President George W. Bush). Attempts to develop inter-Korean relations were also complicated by confirmation in June by South Korean investigators that former President Kim Dae-Jung had paid US $100m. to arrange the historic inter-Korean summit meeting of 2000 (see above). In August the suicide of Hyundai official Chung Mong-Hun, who had been indicted in connection with the illegal payments to the North, further undermined the credibility of the 'sunshine' policy. Meanwhile, the 50th anniversary in July of the *de facto* end of the Korean War, celebrated as a triumph in North Korea, was commemorated in a sombre fashion in South Korea. Also in July, cross-border gunfire was exchanged between North and South Korean soldiers. In October North Korean official Kim Yong Sun, an important figure in inter-Korean affairs who had attended the presidential summit meeting in 2000, died, reportedly as a result of a traffic accident. In November two well-known North Korean defectors, Hwang Jang Yop and Kim Dok Hong, left their posts at the South Korean Institute of National Unification Policy. There was a suggestion that their resignations might have been due to fears that their criticism of the North Korean regime might be damaging to South Korean attempts to negotiate with the North. The resignation in January 2004 of the South Korean Minister of Foreign Affairs, Yoon Young-Kwan, was believed to have been related to tensions within the Government over South Korea's co-operation with the USA on the issue of North Korean weapons (see above).

In May 2004, following a 14th round of ministerial discussions early in the month, senior-level military discussions took place between the two sides, representing a departure from the DPRK's previous insistence that military matters be discussed only with the USA. At the talks the establishment of a radio communication line between the North and South Korean navies was agreed. It was believed that the new communication line would reduce naval conflicts between the two sides; although later in the year there were none the less incidents of warning shots being fired by the South Korean navy at North Korean vessels considered to have intruded on the maritime border, amid accusations that in some instances South Korean navy officials had failed to report North Korean radio messages (one such incident in July led to the resignation of the South Korean Minister of National Defence, Cho Young-Kil—see above). In June, meanwhile, in a symbolic development, propaganda broadcasts across the DMZ were silenced for the first time in decades, with loudspeakers on both sides of the border being switched off. Also in June, a senior representative of the DPRK, Vice-Chairman of the Korea Asia-Pacific Peace Committee Ri Jong Hyok, made a visit to Seoul and met South Korean President Roh Moo-Hyun, marking the fourth anniversary of the inter-Korean summit meeting of 2000 (see above). In July 2004 more than 450 defectors from the DPRK arrived in Seoul. North Korea subsequently accused the South of kidnapping its citizens, and refused to co-operate in preparations for ministerial and economic talks that had been scheduled for August (military discussions, however, resumed in October). Tensions were increased further in August following an admission by the Republic of Korea that it had in the past conducted secret nuclear experiments (see below). It was believed that this disclosure would increase the DPRK's reluctance to dismantle its own nuclear programme. By the end of 2004 the number of North Korean refugees in South Korea had reportedly surpassed 6,000.

In February 2005 the South Korean Ministry of Defence urged that military talks be resumed at the highest level, apparently to ease tension after North Korea made accusations that South Korean naval vessels had 'infiltrated' Northern waters. In the following month South Korea suspended all imports of poultry from the North, after it emerged that outbreaks of avian influenza ('bird flu') had been recorded there. In April South Korean officials travelled to the North Korean city of Kaesong to discuss plans for providing assistance in combating the spread of the virus, and a shipment of quarantine equipment was dispatched to North Korea later that month. Also in April the highest-level bilateral meeting for five years occurred when the Prime Minister of South Korea, Lee Hae-Chan, met Kim Yong Nam, the President of the Presidium of the North Korean Supreme People's Assembly, on the periphery of an Asia-Africa summit meeting convened in the Indonesian capital of Jakarta; the two leaders were reported to have agreed that formal bilateral dialogue, suspended since mid-2004 (see above), should continue. At vice-ministerial talks held in May, South Korea agreed to provide 200,000 metric tons of fertilizer, in an effort to ease the food supply problems that continued to prevail in the DPRK. Later in the month the docking of three North Korean freighters at the South Korean port of Ulsan prior to loading the fertilizer, was reported to be the first time that North Korean ships had docked in South Korea since 1984. In June, to mark the fifth anniversary of the inter-Korean summit of 2000, the South Korean Minister of Unification, Chung Dong-Young, visited the DPRK, where he held an unscheduled meeting with Kim Jong Il. It was speculated that the incentives offered by Chung at this meeting, which included the provision of electricity (see below), might have influenced the DPRK's agreement to return to the six-party talks on its nuclear programme in the following month. The 15th ministerial talks between North and South Korea, held in July in Seoul, concluded with a 12-point joint statement, which included pledges to reopen military talks, to resume reunions for separated families and, under the auspices of the Red Cross, to hold North-South discussions on the issue of 'the whereabouts of those reported missing during the Korean War' (see below). Further ministerial talks took place in September and December. Meanwhile, celebrations held in Seoul in August to mark the 60th anniversary of the liberation of the Korean peninsula from Japanese rule were attended by a substantial delegation from the DPRK. During their stay in Seoul the North Korean officials made important visits to the National Cemetery, where Southern casualties of the Korean War were commemorated, and to the National Assembly. In November, furthermore, it was announced that North and South Korea would field joint teams at the 2006 Asian Games to be held in Doha, Qatar, and also at the 2008 Olympic Games in Beijing. In March 2006 military talks were held between the two Koreas in the DMZ, following a break of some two years; these were reportedly the highest-level military negotiations between the two sides since the 1953 armistice. Also in March, however, the DPRK postoned the scheduled 18th round of ministerial talks in protest at the South's conduct of its annual joint military exercises with the USA, which were reported to have incurred particular objections on account of the participation for the first time of a nuclear-powered aircraft carrier.

The arrangements for further family reunions came under the auspices of the North and South Korean Red Cross organizations, which held several rounds of talks on the subject and co-ordinated the exchange of lists of potential candidates for reunion. In October 2000 the Republic of Korea accepted a North Korean proposal that the second exchange of family members should take place in late November–early December. Relations between the two sides subsequently deteriorated, when North Korea accused the head of the South Korean Red Cross of defaming the former's political system. The official was replaced in January 2001. The DPRK continued to dictate terms for reunions, asking the Republic of Korea to limit the amount of money and gifts transferred during the events, which took place in November–December 2000 and at the end of February 2001. It was subsequently reported that North Korean officials had confiscated money given to delegates for use as state funds. There was a notable decline in the level of enthusiasm for the reunions, which were proceeding slowly and on a small scale, among the South Korean populace (other than those who were directly involved). Meanwhile, in January 2001 an historic accord between the two sides allowed 300 separated families from the North and South each to exchange letters in mid-March. A fourth round of family reunions was initially scheduled for mid-October, but was cancelled owing to the heightened security situation following the terrorist attacks in the USA on 11 September. They were subsequently held at Mount Kumgang in late April 2002. A fifth round was held in mid-September 2002, again at Mount Kumgang, where officials from the two sides planned to build a centre for such meetings. The eighth round of reunions in September 2003 involved 604 South Koreans and 365 North Koreans. In April 2004 a ninth round of reunions was delayed after a South Korean official made a joke concerning Kim Jong Il. Further rounds of reunions none the less took place during the year. As part of the reunion programme, in July 2005 the first private telephone line between North and South Korea since partition in 1945 was opened, in preparation for video conference family reunions. These were held in mid-August to coincide with the 60th anniversary of liberation from Japanese rule. Inter-Korean Red Cross talks held later that month at Mount Kumgang failed to resolve the question of South Korean soldiers and civilians 'abducted' to North Korea during and after the 1950–53 war: the Government in Seoul estimated that more than 540 prisoners of war and some 485 abducted civilians were still alive and detained in the DPRK. Following the talks, an 11th round of family reunions was held at Mount Kumgang. Further reunions were held, both in person and through video conference technology, in late 2005 and early 2006. At another conference held in late February 2006 under the auspices of the Red Cross, North Korea reportedly agreed to resolve the issue of South Korean prisoners of war and abductees held in the North.

Of particular concern to those South Koreans who had begun to question the wisdom of extensive aid without firm preconditions was the fact that, as the DPRK's financial situation worsened, economic issues played an increasingly important part in inter-Korean relations during 2000 and 2001. There was speculation that Pyongyang's new openness was motivated by the necessity to secure greater financial assistance. South Korea provided 52% of the total international aid to North Korea in 2000. In January 2001, however, a South Korean vessel carrying aid was refused permission to dock in the DPRK. Also in that month, it was reported that North Korea's energy shortages had reached crisis point, and that it was desperately researching alternative power sources. A summit meeting took place between the two Koreas in February, at which the DPRK requested immediate and substantial electricity supplies to alleviate its pressing needs. The Republic of Korea, however, insisted that on-site investigations be conducted prior to the commencement of deliveries. Meanwhile, in August 2000 Hyundai agreed to establish a technologically-advanced electronic industrial compound in Kaesong in the DPRK. Hyundai's financial problems, however, delayed the implementation of the project. The company was also obliged to reduce its royalty payments to Pyongyang for the Mount Kumgang tourist initiative in 2000, owing to the attraction's failure to make a profit. In March 2001 the future of the initiative was jeopardized by its lack of profitability, and Hyundai appealed to the South Korean Government for assistance; the Government subsequently pledged 90,000m. won to maintain the tourist cruises. Hyundai founder Chung Ju-Yung died in late March 2001, meanwhile, and his funeral was attended by a delegation sent by Kim Jong Il. On May Day workers from trade unions from the North and South attended a rally at Mount Kumgang. Progress on economic co-operation in Kaesong was made from 2002, with Kaesong being declared a special industrial zone in November of that year. In June 2003 the DPRK announced regulations for development of the zone, as well as plans to develop an area of 3.3 sq km in a first phase of development extending to 2007. A South Korean company, Korea Land, was to invest around US $184m. in the project. These plans were finalized at a meeting of South and North Korean economic officials in November 2003. Although inter-Korean trade increased steadily, reportedly amounting to US $700m. in 2003, South Korea shared international concerns over North Korea's suspected illicit trade in weapons and narcotics. In June 2003 South Korean customs officials in the port of Pusan seized 40 kg of methamphetamines believed to have originated in North Korea. There were also fears of very serious economic consequences for South Korea if reunification of the Koreas were to become an imminent prospect. Further progress on the Kaesong special industrial zone was evident in 2004. A round of talks between North and South Korean delegations took place in January, at which details of inter-Korean business transactions at Kaesong, including security issues, were discussed. It was reported that in April some 1,600 South Korean companies had applied for a lease in the zone, and in June Korea Land (see above) selected the first 15 companies that were to permitted to conduct business in the zone. At the end of June a ceremony was held to signal the commencement of the first phase of development in Kaesong, with 350 officials from the North and the South attending the event. In December the first South Korean company began production at Kaesong. In March 2005 the Korea Electric Power Corporation (KEPCO), of South Korea, began to supply electricity to Kaesong, representing the first cross-border flow of electricity since the peninsula's partition. In July 2005 the South Korean Minister of Unification, Chung Dong-Young, reportedly offered to provide North Korea with energy assistance totalling 2,000 MW if the country were to abandon its nuclear weapons programme (see below). The DPRK, however, rejected the offer. In October the first joint governmental office operated by both North and South Korea, to handle cross-border economic projects, was opened in Kaesong, and in December the first commercial telephone link between Kaesong and Seoul entered into service.

Negotiations to reconnect the inter-Korean rail link continued during 2001. It was hoped that such a link would create a new Eurasian transport corridor that would reduce the cost and time of the transit of goods from North-East Asia to European markets from 25 days to about 15 days, bringing economic benefits to all participants. In February 2001 a meeting was held at the DMZ to arrange regulations for troops and workers employed to rebuild the line, and a parallel highway. However, the DPRK failed to attend a UN Asian transport meeting held in Seoul in mid-November, following the breakdown of the sixth round of ministerial discussions. A New Year's editorial in the North in January 2002 described upgrading the railway as a priority during that year, and both Koreas agreed to accelerate the reconnection following bilateral talks in April 2002. Ground-breaking ceremonies for the reconnection of the railway and road links were held on both sides of the DMZ in late September 2002, and South Korea released a loan to the North to assist the funding of the work. In late 2002 South Korean officials attended the ground-breaking ceremony for the North's new industrial zone at Kaesong. In early February 2003 the first road reconnecting the North with the South was completed, on the eastern coast of the Korean peninsula. In June 2003 rail links between the two Koreas were officially opened, though the connections remained largely symbolic, as construction on the North Korean side to link the new railways with wider networks was still to be completed. Following a meeting between the two sides in June 2004 it was reported that the rail links were expected to begin operating in 2005. In December 2004, meanwhile, it was reported that the road link along the eastern coast of the two Koreas had been opened to traffic. By late 2005 two major rail links between North and South Korea along the west and east coasts, with adjacent roads, were believed to be in operation. South Korea had also pledged to assist the DPRK in constructing several railway stations.

Owing to its geographical position, Korea's foreign relations have long been dominated by its relations with the 'great powers' in the region—Russia, China, the USA and Japan. Following President Roh Tae-Woo's inauguration in 1988, relations with the communist bloc showed signs of improvement. Trade with the USSR and the People's Republic of China expanded, and in 1990 full diplomatic relations were established with the USSR. These developments were denounced by the DPRK, its diplomatic isolation being compounded by the Republic of Korea's establishment of full diplomatic relations with the People's Republic of China (hitherto the North's principal ally) in August 1992. Meanwhile, in 1991 the Republic of Korea had extended a substantial loan, of some US $1,470m., to the USSR; this debt was subsequently transferred to the Russian Federation (Russia) following the disintegration of the USSR later that year. In September 1993 it was announced that the Republic of Korea and Russia were to participate in joint naval exercises, and in 1994 it was reported that Russia was to supply 'defensive missiles' in order to repay a part of its debt to the Republic of Korea. Further arrangements were made concerning the settlement of Russia's debt, through the provision of commodities, in July 1997.

Relations were severely tested in mid-1998 by a diplomatic dispute, provoked by Russia's expulsion of a South Korean diplomat following allegations of espionage and bribery, which culminated in the resignation of the South Korean Minister of Foreign Affairs and Trade, Park Chung-Soo. During a state visit to Russia in May 1999, Kim Dae-Jung held a summit meeting with President Boris Yeltsin. Issues discussed included South Korea's engagement policy with North Korea, a proposed expansion of Moscow's role in regional affairs and bilateral economic co-operation. The Russian Minister of Defence visited Seoul in September 1999, and the two countries conducted their first joint naval exercises in April 2000. President Vladimir Putin of Russia paid a three-day state visit to the Republic of Korea in February 2001, during which the two nations confirmed their commitment to improving bilateral relations, and Putin agreed to proceed with a tripartite framework of co-operation between Russia and both Koreas. Arrangements were made for Russia to supply weapons to the Republic of Korea, which were to be partially paid for by the cancellation of some Soviet-era debt. The Republic of Korea and Russia also issued a joint statement supporting the 1972 Anti-Ballistic Missile (ABM) treaty; however, US displeasure with this led to the resignation of the Minister of Foreign Affairs and Trade, Lee Joung-Binn.

In mid-August 2001 a Russian diplomat, Valentin Moiseyev, was imprisoned for four-and-a-half years for passing secrets to South Korea; however, the incident did not adversely affect bilateral relations.

A key area of co-operation between the Republic of Korea and Russia during 2001–02 remained the reconnection of the North–South Korea rail network, and its planned connection with the Trans-Siberian railway, thereby creating a Eurasian transport corridor. This would allow South Korea to become a major trading hub, linking Europe and Asia with the Americas. Meanwhile, in December 2002 the Republic of Korea agreed to receive US $534m. worth of military equipment from Russia as part of a 1995 agreement aimed at repaying Moscow's $2,000m. debt to the Republic of Korea.

In September 2002, in response to growing labour shortages in South Korea, the Government extended working visas for ethnic Korean residents of Russia and the former Soviet Union from three months to one year. It was expected that many of the estimated 40,000 ethnic Koreans in Sakhalin, Russia, would take advantage of the changes.

There were indications that Roh Moo-Hyun would seek to improve relations with Russia during his presidency, as part of a broader policy of reducing dependency on the USA. In March 2003 Roh revived the idea of building a 4,000-km pipeline that would provide the DPRK with Russian natural gas from Sakhalin in exchange for the abandonment of its nuclear weapons programme. At a summit meeting in Bangkok in October 2003 Roh and Russian President Putin agreed to co-operate on the North Korean nuclear issue. Progress on the connection of the North–South Korea rail network to the Trans-Siberian railway (see above) was delayed in 2003 by tensions over North Korea's nuclear ambitions. However, in late 2003 a team of Russian engineers were assessing a stretch of railway linking Russia with the Korean peninsula across the Tumen river. Following President Roh's impeachment in March 2004 a planned visit by Roh to Russia was postponed. Roh eventually visited Russia in September. During the course of his visit a significant agreement between state-owned oil companies of the two countries (Korean National Oil Corporation—KNOC—and Russia's Rosneft) was signed. In April 2005 Minister of Defence Yoon Kwang-Woong visited Russia, where he met his Russian counterpart, Sergei Ivanov, to discuss the provision of Russian 'advanced weapons technology' by way of further servicing the Russian debt to the Republic of Korea.

Relations with China were strengthened in November 1998, when President Kim Dae-Jung paid an official visit to Beijing, meeting with Chinese President Jiang Zemin and Premier Zhu Rongji. Several accords were initialled during the visit. In August 1999 co-operative ties with China were further consolidated by the first visit of a South Korean defence minister to Beijing; a reciprocal visit to the Republic of Korea by the Chinese Minister of National Defence, Chi Haotian, took place in January 2000. The South Korean Government requested Chi's assistance in resolving the issue of seven North Korean defectors, who had recently been repatriated by China, despite South Korean protests. In October 2000 relations improved further when, during a visit to Seoul by Zhu Rongji, agreement was reached on the resumption of the quadripartite conference, incorporating the two Koreas, China and the USA, with the aim of establishing a peace mechanism for the Korean Peninsula. Later in the month, following strong opposition from Beijing, the Republic of Korea refused to grant a visa to the Dalai Lama, Tibet's spiritual leader, on the grounds that it would be 'inappropriate'.

During 2001 China continued to seek stability on the Korean peninsula. A diplomatic dispute arose between Seoul and Beijing in October, however, following the execution in China of a South Korean national and the alleged torture of another Korean prisoner, both convicted of drug-trafficking. In early November the ministers of economics, finance and foreign affairs from China, the Republic of Korea and Japan agreed to hold regular meetings to foster closer co-operation. In late 2001 there were concerns in South Korean business circles that China's admission to the WTO would divert investment and labour to the People's Republic and undercut the competitiveness of Korean goods. Nevertheless, the South Korean Minister of National Defence, Kim Dong-Shin, paid a week-long visit to China in December, where he sought closer military co-operation with his Chinese counterparts.

By 2002 economic and trade links were increasingly leading to closer relations between the Republic of Korea and China. During 2001 South Koreans invested more funding in China than in the USA, and in 2002 China displaced the USA as the Republic of Korea's largest trading partner. However, concern persisted among domestic manufacturers that lower labour costs in China would undermine their competitiveness, and there were occasional trade disputes between the two countries.

In January 2002 China reacted with concern following the proposal to the South Korean National Assembly of legislation that would give special rights to ethnic Koreans living in China and elsewhere. In March the two countries announced the introduction of a new extradition pact, to take effect from April, and at the same time Wang Jiarui, the deputy head of the international liaison department of the Chinese Communist Party, visited Seoul.

Tensions between South Korea and China temporarily increased in mid-2002 when the Chinese authorities sought to prevent North Korean refugees from seeking asylum in various diplomatic buildings in China, including the South Korean embassy in Beijing, where a group of 23 had hidden. The members of the group, and others like them, were later permitted to travel to South Korea, but only via a third country—often the Philippines or Singapore. In response, the Chinese authorities increased efforts to combat South Korean NGOs and religious groups that were seeking to increase the number of North Korean refugees in China. In July and September Chinese military delegations visited Seoul to discuss bilateral military co-operation, and in August the Minister of Foreign Affairs and

Trade received his Chinese counterpart in Seoul. In September Lee Hoi-Chang visited China and met President Jiang Zemin. In October the Minister of Finance proposed a three-way alliance comprising the Republic of Korea, China and Japan to manage the region's development. Also in that month the Government decided to extend working visas for ethnic Koreans in China to two years, with unlimited extensions. The move was designed to reduce the illegal trafficking of ethnic Koreans from China and its associated problems.

The growing diplomatic crisis over North Korea's nuclear programme in late 2002 and early 2003 led South Korea to seek China's assistance in persuading the North to work towards a peaceful solution. Roh made a four-day state visit to Beijing in July. Chinese diplomatic efforts played a major role in ensuring North Korean participation in talks on the DPRK's nuclear weapons programme attended by six nations, including the Republic of Korea, in Beijing in August 2003, as well as in further rounds of talks during 2004 and 2005 (see the chapter on the Democratic People's Republic of Korea). In August 2004 relations between China and the Republic of Korea were damaged by controversy over the issue of the historical kingdom of Koguryo, which had covered the area of modern North Korea and part of South Korea, as well as areas of northern China. Following the deletion of references to Koguryo from the Chinese Ministry of Foreign Affairs website, the South Korean Government feared that China was planning to claim Koguryo as part of Chinese, rather than Korean, history, and to use this historical 'distortion' as a basis for present-day expansionism. In September, however, the Chinese Ministry of Foreign Affairs issued a statement declaring that its reference to Koguryo as an ancient Chinese province had been a mistake.

Relations between the Republic of Korea and the USA were frequently strained in the late 1970s, in particular by the proposal to withdraw US ground troops from South Korea (which was abandoned in 1979) and by the trial of Kim Dae-Jung (see above). Disputes between the Republic of Korea and the USA in the late 1980s over trade issues had subsided by mid-1991. President George Bush of the USA visited the country in January 1992, and the two leaders agreed to cancel that year's 'Team Spirit' exercises. In December 1991 it had been announced that all US nuclear weapons had been withdrawn from South Korean territory. The 'Team Spirit' exercises were resumed in 1993. In July, during a visit to Seoul, President Clinton affirmed his country's continuing commitment to the defence of the Republic of Korea; he subsequently stated that an attack by the DPRK on the Republic of Korea would be tantamount to an act of aggression against the USA. In January 1994 it was announced that the USA was to deploy air-defence missiles on South Korean territory. In April 1996, during a visit to Seoul, Clinton issued a joint US-South Korean proposal for quadripartite negotiations with the DPRK and the People's Republic of China (see above). In October 1997 the US Government asked the South Korean administration to reconsider its decision to order an air-defence missile system from France. The Republic of Korea, however, was seeking to reduce its dependence on the USA for military technology. Later in that year the USA pledged financial support for the Republic of Korea, following the conclusion of the agreement with the IMF.

President Kim Dae-Jung was warmly received on a state visit to the USA in June 1998, during which he outlined his 'sunshine' policy of engagement towards North Korea. A reciprocal visit was made by Clinton to Seoul in November. In March 1999 the South Korean Government welcomed a breakthrough in negotiations between the DPRK and the USA on US access to a suspected nuclear site in North Korea (for further details, see the chapter on the DPRK). During a second visit by Kim Dae-Jung to the USA in July, the US Administration reaffirmed its support for the 'sunshine' policy. US-South Korean talks were held in late 1999 and early 2000 regarding the Republic of Korea's proposed extension of its missile range, from 180 km to 300 km for military purposes, and to 500 km for research and development. (In January 2001 a revised missile accord was signed between the Republic of Korea and the USA, permitting the former to develop missiles with greatly increased ranges and payloads.) In October 1999 the US and South Korean Governments began investigations into the alleged massacre of as many as 300 Korean refugees by US troops near Nogun-ri, in the South Korean province of North Chungcheong, shortly after the beginning of the Korean War. Revelations surrounding the use of defoliants in the DMZ in the late 1960s created further controversy in November 1999. The herbicides, which had apparently been provided by the USA but applied by South Korean troops, included Agent Orange, which had later been found to be highly toxic. The South Korean Government announced that it was prepared to compensate both soldiers and civilians adversely affected by the defoliants, but the USA reportedly refused to accept any liability. In December a lawsuit was filed against seven US chemical companies by a group of Koreans demanding compensation for damage they claimed to have suffered as a consequence of the herbicides.

In May 2000 there was further tension between the two countries when a US aircraft accidentally released several bombs close to a village south-west of Seoul, causing minor injuries and damage to property. Violent protests were held outside the US embassy in Seoul, and the USA subsequently agreed to cease using the Koon-ni range for such training missions. (Operations subsequently resumed, the USA citing a lack of suitable alternative facilities.) Following the incident, opposition politicians demanded a review of the Status of Forces Agreement (SOFA), which governed the 37,000 US troops stationed in South Korea. In August negotiations were held on the issue, and resulted in partial agreement. Further talks held in December successfully revised the agreement, which was signed in January 2001. South Korean civic groups, however, protested that the partnership between the two countries remained biased in favour of the USA. In January 2001 outgoing US President Bill Clinton made an unprecedented statement of regret for the massacre near Nogun-ri. Many South Koreans, however, were angry that no apology was forthcoming. Later, in January 2002, a British Broadcasting Corporation (BBC) investigation revealed that US commanders had repeatedly ordered troops to fire on refugees at Nogun-ri and elsewhere during the opening months of the Korean War. Some South Korean historians were, in late 2001, also investigating the USA's possible role in the massacre by South Korean troops of 30,000 people on Jeju Island in a suppression of communist elements in late 1948 and early 1949. Meanwhile, the USA welcomed the improvement in inter-Korean relations during 2000. US Secretary of State Madeleine Albright visited Seoul in June and in October of that year to discuss developments. In March 2001 Kim Dae-Jung paid a visit to the new Bush administration in Washington, DC, hoping to secure support for his 'sunshine' policy. US President George W. Bush, however, took a firmer stance than his predecessor and declared that North Korea must prove its abandonment of its missile testing and development programme prior to any improvement in relations or release of aid.

In April 2001 a Seoul court ruled that the US air force's firing and bombing ranges near the village of Maehyang-ri caused damage and duress to inhabitants, and ordered the central Government to pay them compensation. In early May the US Deputy Secretary of State, Richard Armitage, visited the Republic of Korea, seeking Seoul's support for the USA's planned NMD system and urging the continuation of negotiations between North and South.

Disagreements between South Korea and the USA on how to deal with North Korea, however, continued to strain bilateral relations during 2001. In July Seoul refused to allow Hwang Jang Yop, the highest-ranking North Korean defector, to visit the USA and testify before Congress, fearing that such a move would exacerbate the already strained inter-Korean relations.

The Republic of Korea immediately pledged support to the USA following the terrorist attacks on the latter in September 2001, and in early December the National Assembly endorsed the deployment of non-combat troops to assist the US-led campaign in Afghanistan, mainly in a logistical capacity. Meanwhile, in November the USA and the Republic of Korea agreed to a major 'land-swap' whereby existing US bases would relocate to other areas within the country, allowing a consolidation of bases and training facilities over the next 10 years.

In January 2002 the Republic of Korea reacted with concern to President Bush's reference to North Korea as being part of an 'axis of evil', a remark that further undermined Kim Dae-Jung's 'sunshine' policy. None the less the South Korean military planned to purchase US $800m. worth of surface-to-surface missiles, capable of attacking most of North Korea, from US manufacturers. At the same time GNP leader Lee Hoi-Chang visited the USA and met senior US officials, his attitude to the DPRK generally being closer to that of Bush than of Kim. Lee favoured a policy of 'strategic engagement' based on reciprocity and transparency. Bush himself visited South Korea in late February and urged the North to change its ways, while ruling out any US invasion.

THE REPUBLIC OF KOREA (SOUTH KOREA)

In March 2002 the USA announced plans to deploy a new mobile military force unit to South Korea by 2007. Some South Korean officials had previously indicated that US troops might remain in Korea even after any unification, possibly serving as peace-keepers in the North. Later in the month the USA agreed to sell a combat-radar system to the Republic of Korea, and the two countries held their biggest-ever joint military exercises, which antagonized the North. Also in that month the Republic of Korea reacted angrily to Bush's imposition of new tariffs on imported steel, since the country was a major steel exporter. At the end of the month the Ministry of National Defence announced that the Boeing Company of the USA had secured a US $4,500m. contract to supply the Republic of Korea with 40 F-15K fighter planes. The Republic of Korea hoped to develop an indigenous fighter aircraft by 2015.

Relations between the Republic of Korea and the USA deteriorated noticeably after an accident in June 2002 in which a US army vehicle killed two teenaged Korean girls. The US military charged two US soldiers with negligent homicide, and the South Korean authorities subsequently requested their submission for trial at a local court, but this was rejected by the US army. In November the two soldiers were acquitted by a US military court, leading to a significant increase in anti-US sentiment among the public. Although President Bush apologized for the incident, in mid-December hundreds of thousands of people attended anti-US rallies in Seoul and across the country, and there were several incidents of assaults on and hostility towards US troops and businesses. Although precipitated by the issue of the acquittals, the rallies became a forum of protest against the country's dependency on the USA and that country's policy towards North Korea. Meanwhile, in October a new joint base pact came into force whereby the US military would reduce the number of bases from 41 to 23 and return 50% of the land it used to South Korea. However, there had yet to be changes to the SOFA that governed the conduct of US troops in Korea—amendments to which had long been demanded by South Koreans. Public anger towards the USA was further raised by the crash of a U2 reconnaissance plane in January, causing destruction of property.

The election of Roh Moo-Hyun as President raised fears that the Republic of Korea's relations with the USA would be further undermined, since Roh had once called for the removal of US troops from South Korea (although he had subsequently rescinded such demands) and had campaigned for a foreign policy more independent from the USA. However, in January 2003 he indicated a more conciliatory stance, but nevertheless warned the USA against attacking North Korea, instead urging the USA to resume dialogue with Pyongyang. He also instructed the military to prepare contingency plans for the possible withdrawal of US troops, and the US Secretary of Defense, Donald Rumsfeld, in March stated that the troops could be reduced or withdrawn completely. The USA announced that it planned to remove its 15,000 troops stationed between Seoul and the DMZ and deploy them in the south of the country. Kim Dae-Jung had previously criticized the USA's policy of 'tailored containment' to isolate Pyongyang, warning that it would be ineffective.

In late February 2003 the commander of the United States Forces Korea, Gen. Leon LaPorte, stated that the USA and South Korea would review their 1953 Mutual Defense Treaty, with the possibility of ending provisions under the 'Combined Forces Command' for the transfer of control over South Korea's military to the USA in wartime. However, it was noted that South Korea still remained dependent on the USA for military intelligence. Despite disagreements, South Korea and the USA held their annual joint military exercises during March. In early April the US military announced that it would move its main base away from Seoul as part of a global redeployment of forces, and the two countries began major discussions on the long-term future of their alliance. The USA envisioned eventually consolidating its forces in two major hubs: the Osan-Pyeongtaek, and Daegu-Busan regions. Meanwhile, Roh arranged to send 700 non-combatant troops to Iraq in support of the USA, despite domestic protests. Roh visited President Bush in Washington, DC, in mid-May, and the two leaders agreed to work towards a peaceful solution to the crisis over North Korea's nuclear programme, although differences remained between US and South Korean policies towards Pyongyang. In July South Korea rejected US calls for UN intervention in the North Korean nuclear crisis.

In March 2003, meanwhile, US Secretary of Defense Donald Rumsfeld stated that the USA was considering withdrawing troops from the North–South Korean border, and in June plans were confirmed to withdraw US troops to locations 120 km south of the DMZ, as part of a wider reorganization of US forces in South Korea. There was some concern in South Korea that these developments were in preparation for an attack by the USA on North Korean nuclear facilities. Also in June, some 20,000 people protested at the US embassy in Seoul to mark the anniversary of the killing of two Korean girls by a US army vehicle (see above). In November Donald Rumsfeld visited the Republic of Korea to discuss the US military presence as well as the deployment of South Korean troops to Iraq.

In January 2004 the two countries agreed to relocate US troops out of Seoul. In May the USA announced its intention to transfer 3,600 US troops currently stationed in South Korea to Iraq. In June, furthermore, the USA outlined plans to reduce the number of troops in South Korea by about one-third by the end of 2005. Meanwhile, the deployment of 3,000 South Korean troops to Iraq, which had been approved by the National Assembly in February (see above), remained suspended, despite US requests for the troops to be sent. In August, during talks between South Korean and US officials, South Korea expressed its desire that the proposed withdrawal of one-third of US troops (see above) be delayed until 2006. In the same month, an admission by the South Korean Government that it had conducted secret experiments for uranium enrichment and plutonium extraction in 2000 and the early 1980s represented a serious potential threat to the country's relations with the USA (as well as to its relations with the IAEA), although the amounts of nuclear material involved were reported to have been small. Also in August, despite public outrage at the beheading of a South Korean hostage in June (see above), the Government refused to abandon its plans for the scheduled deployment of 3,000 South Korean troops to Iraq. In September it was announced that US troops would withdraw from the DMZ by the end of October (South Korean forces duly assumed responsibility for patrolling the border zone from the beginning of November). In October an agreement for the planned withdrawal of one-third of all US troops in South Korea was reached. The withdrawal was now due to take place in three phases extending to 2008.

In December 2004, following a vote in the National Assembly, it was announced that South Korean troops in Iraq (now numbering around 3,600) would remain there throughout 2005. Joint US-South Korean military exercises were held in mid-2005 and early 2006, eliciting protest on both occasions from the DPRK (see above, and the chapter on the DPRK). In late December 2005 the National Assembly voted to reduce the number of South Korean troops in Iraq to 2,300 and to extend their deployment until the end of 2006. In January 2006, meanwhile, a court in Seoul ordered two US pharmaceutical companies responsible for producing the toxic herbicide Agent Orange to pay compensation to some 6,800 South Koreans, who had been affected by the chemical while serving alongside the US military during the Viet Nam war. In February it was announced that negotiations had commenced with regard to an important free-trade agreement between the Republic of Korea and the USA.

Relations between the Republic of Korea and Japan, which had long been strained, were eased by President Chun's official visit to Japan in September 1984 (the first such visit undertaken by a South Korean Head of State), during which Emperor Hirohito and Prime Minister Nakasone formally expressed their regret for Japanese aggression in Korea in the past. In May 1990, during President Roh's visit to Japan, Emperor Akihito offered official apologies for the cruelties of Japanese colonial rule in Korea. In January 1992 the Japanese Prime Minister, Kiichi Miyazawa, visited the Republic of Korea, where he publicly expressed regret at the enslavement during the Second World War of an estimated 100,000 Korean women, who were used by the Japanese military for sexual purposes ('comfort women'), but declined to state whether the Japanese Government would consider financial compensation. In late 1994 the Japanese Government announced that it would not make compensation payments directly to individuals, but would finance a programme to construct vocational training centres for the women concerned. In August 1995, on the 50th anniversary of the end of the Second World War, the Japanese Prime Minister, Tomiichi Murayama, issued a statement expressing 'deep reflection and sincere apologies' for Japanese colonial aggression. At the end of a summit meeting with President Kim in June 1996, the Japanese Prime Minister, Ryutaro Hashimoto, issued a public apology to the 'comfort women'. However, the South Korean Government regarded Japanese proposals to provide compensation through private sources of funding, rather than government money, as amounting to a denial of moral responsibility. The conclusion of new defence co-operation guide-lines between Japan and the USA in September 1997 was of concern for the Republic of Korea, which feared an expansion in Japanese military capability. Negotiations for a new fisheries agreement, under way since mid-1996, were unilaterally terminated by Japan in January 1998, following the continuing disagreement regarding sovereignty of a group of islets in the Sea of Japan, to which both countries laid claim. In April 1998 the South Korean Government announced its intention to make payments itself to surviving 'comfort women', apparently abandoning its attempts to gain compensation for the women from the Japanese Government. Later that month, however, a Japanese district court ordered the Government to pay compensation to three former 'comfort women' from the Republic of Korea. Another group of South Korean 'comfort women' was refused the right to recompense by the Japanese High Court in November 2000, and in March 2001 the 1998 compensation ruling was overturned by a regional High Court.

Relations with Japan improved considerably in October 1998, meanwhile, during a four-day state visit to Tokyo by President Kim Dae-Jung. A joint declaration was signed, in which Japan apologized for the suffering inflicted on the Korean people during Japanese colonial rule. In addition, the Republic of Korea agreed to revoke a ban on the import of various Japanese goods, while Japan promised financial aid to the Republic of Korea in support of its efforts to stimulate economic recovery. In November the two countries concluded negotiations on the renewal of their bilateral fisheries agreement, which came into effect in January 1999, despite the objections of the main South Korean opposition party, which protested that it failed positively to affirm the Republic of Korea's claim to sovereignty over the disputed islets. Differences over the accord and its implementation continued to create tension in early 1999, however, particularly in the Republic of Korea, where protests from fishermen, who were apparently suffering heavy losses because of the revised agreement, forced the resignation of the Minister for Maritime Affairs and Fisheries. In March increasing co-operation between the two countries was highlighted during a visit to the Republic of Korea by the Japanese Prime Minister, Keizo Obuchi, despite protests against Japan's military ties with the USA and failure fully to compensate the 'comfort women'. Both countries agreed to strengthen bilateral economic relations, and Japan pledged a further US $1,000m. in aid to the Republic of Korea. The Japanese Prime Minister, Yoshiro Mori, visited Seoul in May 2000 and met with Kim Dae-Jung. In November of that year the South Korean Minister of Foreign Affairs and Trade paid a visit to Tokyo to discuss ways of improving bilateral relations.

Relations with Japan deteriorated during 2001 following the publication in February of new Japanese history textbooks which sought to justify Japan's aggression towards its Asian neighbours during the Second World War, and neglected to mention the forced prostitution of Asian (mainly Korean) 'comfort women' by the Japanese army and the forcible transfer and use of Koreans as slave labour in Japan. Large-scale protests were held in Seoul, and the Japanese ambassador was summoned to the Ministry of Foreign Affairs and Trade. In April the Republic of Korea temporarily withdrew its ambassador from Japan. President Kim Dae-Jung urged Japan to adopt 'a correct understanding of history', and the South Korean National Assembly pressed the Government to reconsider any further opening of its markets to Japanese cultural products unless the books were abandoned. The South Korean Ministry of Foreign Affairs and Trade demanded 35 major revisions to the books, but in July Japan's Ministry of Education ruled out any further significant changes, prompting Kim Dae-Jung to refuse to receive a visiting Japanese delegation and the suspension of bilateral military co-operation. Protests also took place outside the Japanese embassy in Seoul. In mid-August the Republic of Korea was further outraged by the visit of the Japanese Prime Minister, Junichiro Koizumi, to the controversial Yasukuni Shrine in Tokyo honouring Japan's war dead. Koizumi's visit was seen as a sign of resurgent Japanese nationalism and was denounced by the Republic of Korea, as well as by Japan's other Asian neighbours. Koizumi visited Seoul in mid-October and delivered an apology for the suffering of Koreans under Japanese rule, but his visit was greeted by protests and he was forced to cancel a visit to the National Assembly owing to the hostile sentiment held by some legislators. However, both sides recognized the need to improve relations prior to co-hosting the football World Cup in 2002.

Along with China and North Korea, South Korea condemned Koizumi's visits to the Yasukuni Shrine in late April 2002 and mid-January 2003. However, Koizumi and Kim Dae-Jung in late March 2002 agreed to begin discussions on a possible bilateral free-trade agreement, and at the end of May Koizumi attended the opening ceremony of the 2002 football World Cup in Seoul. Also in attendance was Prince Takamado and his wife, who were making the first official visit to the Republic of Korea by a member of the Imperial family. The football tournament, a major source of prestige for both countries, passed off without incident. Any remaining mutual hostility between the two countries was overshadowed in 2002 by the need for co-operation in engaging with the North. In December 2002 Koizumi and South Korean President-elect Roh Moo-Hyun agreed to forge a united front when dealing with the North. Koizumi subsequently attended Roh's inauguration in late February 2003. In June Roh made his first state visit to Japan and had discussions with Koizumi on the issue of North Korea's nuclear weapons programme. Although both leaders opposed any development of nuclear weapons in North Korea, Roh urged dialogue with the DPRK, whereas Koizumi favoured stricter measures towards Pyongyang. Japan and the Republic of Korea continued efforts towards reaching a free-trade agreement from 2003; however, by early 2006 no agreement had been reached. In February 2005 tensions arose over a statement by the Japanese ambassador to Seoul, Toshiyuki Takano, implying that the uninhabited Dokdo islands (or 'Takeshima' in Japanese, located in the East Sea between South Korea and Japan) belonged to Japan. The issue of the Dokdo islands aroused anger once more in March when the local legislature of Japan's Shimane Prefecture, which claimed the islands as part of its territory, voted to establish a 'Takeshima Day'. In response, the Minister of Foreign Affairs and Trade, Ban Ki-Moon, cancelled a scheduled visit to Japan, while protests were staged outside the Japanese embassy in Seoul. Further public demonstrations took place in April in reaction to the approval for use in Japanese schools of history textbooks, including one first published in 2001 (see above), which were regarded by Koreans (and Chinese) as failing to address the true nature of Japanese wartime conduct. Another visit to the Yasukuni Shrine by Prime Minister Koizumi in October provoked condemnation from the Republic of Korea, and prompted President Roh to cancel a scheduled visit to Japan in December.

In November 2000, after eight years' suspension, the 25th Joint Conference of Korea-Taiwan Business Councils took place in Seoul. It was agreed that henceforth conferences would be held annually alternately in Seoul and Taipei. In the same month a Korean passenger aircraft flew from Seoul to Taipei for the first time since 1992, when diplomatic relations had been severed. The Republic of Korea also maintained close relations with South-East Asian countries, and Minister of Defence Kim Dong-Shin and Prime Minister Lee Han-Dong visited Viet Nam in December 2001 and April 2002 respectively. Security, economic and trade issues were the main topics of discussions. Viet Nam had already become the principal recipient of South Korean aid. In early 2003 a South Korean newspaper funded the opening of a peace park in southern Viet Nam, as a gesture of atonement for atrocities committed by South Korean soldiers, some 300,000 of whom had fought on behalf of South Viet Nam during the Viet Nam war. President Roh made a state visit to the United Kingdom in December 2004, representing the first ever such visit by a South Korean head of state.

Government

Under the Constitution of the Sixth Republic (adopted in October 1987), executive power is held by the President, who is directly elected for one term of five years by universal suffrage. The President appoints and governs with the assistance of the State Council (Cabinet), led by the Prime Minister. Legislative power is vested in the unicameral National Assembly (Kuk Hoe), popularly elected for a four-year term. Following the election of 2004, the Assembly had 299 members.

Defence

Protection of the frontier separating North and South Korea is the responsibility of the UN. Military service lasts for 26 months in the South Korean army, and for 30 months in the navy and in the air force. In August 2005 the strength of the active armed forces was 687,700 (including an estimated 159,000 conscripts): army 560,000, navy 63,000, air force 64,700. Paramilitary forces included a 3.5m.-strong civilian defence corps. In August 2005 US forces stationed in South Korea comprised 25,000 army personnel, 40,360 navy, 8,900 air force and 180 marines. Expen-

THE REPUBLIC OF KOREA (SOUTH KOREA)

diture on defence was budgeted at 20,800,000m. won for 2005. In November 2004 a plan was announced to reform the armed services and to increase the defence budget between 2005 and 2008. This was in order to compensate for the withdrawal of US troops from South Korea (see Recent History). The total expenditure on military reform was to amount to around 99,000,000m. won, with a defence budget of 20,800,000m. won being projected for 2005.

Economic Affairs

In 2004, according to estimates by the World Bank, the Republic of Korea's gross national income (GNI), measured at average 2002–04 prices, was US $673,036m., equivalent to $13,980 per head (or $20,400 per head on an international purchasing-power parity basis). During 1995–2004, it was estimated, the population increased at an average annual rate of 0.7%, while gross domestic product (GDP) per head increased, in real terms, by an average of 3.7% per year. Overall GDP increased, in real terms, at an average annual rate of 4.5% in 1995–2004. GDP growth was estimated by the Asian Development Bank (ADB, see p. 169) at 4.6% in 2004 and at 4.0% in 2005.

Agriculture (including forestry and fishing) contributed 3.7% of GDP in 2004 and, according to the ADB, engaged 8.1% of the employed labour force in that year. The principal crop is rice, but maize, barley, potatoes, sweet potatoes and fruit are also important, as is the raising of livestock (principally pigs and cattle). Fishing provides food for domestic consumption, as well as a substantial surplus for export. In the early 2000s the Republic of Korea remained one of the world's leading ocean-fishing nations. During 1995–2004, according to figures from the ADB, the GDP of the agricultural sector increased by an average of 0.7% per year. Agricultural GDP increased by 7.4% in 2004 but by only 0.5% in 2005.

Industry (including mining and quarrying, manufacturing, power and construction) contributed 40.8% of GDP in 2004, and engaged 28.1% of the employed labour force in 2000. Industry is dominated by large conglomerate companies (*chaebol*), with greatly diversified interests, especially in construction and manufacturing. According to figures from the ADB, during 1995–2004 industrial GDP increased at an average annual rate of 5.6%. Industrial GDP increased by 9.0% in 2004 and by 5.6% in 2005.

South Korea is not richly endowed with natural resources, and mining and quarrying contributed only 0.3% of GDP in 2004, employing a neglible percentage of the labour force. There are deposits of coal (mainly anthracite). Other minerals include iron ore, lead, zinc, silver, gold and limestone, and sizeable offshore reserves of natural gas have been discovered.

Manufacturing contributed 28.7% of GDP in 2004 and, according to the ADB, engaged 19.0% of the employed labour force in that year. The most important branches of manufacturing include electrical machinery, transport equipment—mainly road motor vehicles and ship-building, non-electrical machinery, chemicals, food products, iron and steel, and textiles. During 1995–2004 manufacturing GDP increased by an average of 7.3% per year, according to figures from the ADB. The sector's GDP increased by 5.5% in 2003 and by 11.4% in 2004.

Energy is derived principally from nuclear power, coal and petroleum. In 2004 38.2% of total electricity output was generated by nuclear power, while thermal and hydroelectric power provided 58.8% and 1.7%, respectively. In 2000 it was announced that another eight nuclear plants were to be constructed by 2015, in addition to the four already under construction at that time. At the end of 2004 there were 20 nuclear units in operation in the country. The Republic of Korea also produces liquefied natural gas for domestic and industrial consumption. Imports of petroleum and its products comprised an estimated 19.6% of the value of merchandise imports in 2005.

The services sector contributed 55.5% of GDP in 2004, and engaged 61.0% of the employed labour force in 2000. Receipts from tourism are also significant (totalling an estimated US $6,903m. in 2003). During 1995–2004, according to figures from the ADB, the GDP of the services sector increased at an average annual rate of 4.1%. The GDP of the sector increased by 1.3% in 2004 and by 3.0% in 2005.

In 2004 the Republic of Korea recorded a visible trade surplus of US $38,161m., and there was a surplus of $27,613m. on the current account of the balance of payments. Japan and the People's Republic of China were the principal sources of imports in 2005 (accounting for, respectively, 18.5% and 14.8% of total imports in that year); another important supplier was the USA. The People's Republic of China was the principal market for

Introductory Survey

exports in 2005 (purchasing 21.8%), followed by the USA (14.5%). The main exports in 2005 were electrical machinery, basic manufactures, road vehicles, and chemical products. The principal imports in that year were machinery and transport equipment (especially electrical machinery), petroleum and petroleum products, basic manufactures and chemical products.

The Republic of Korea's budget surplus for 2005 was projected at 17,600,000m. won—the fifth consecutive year of surplus. The budget for 2005 envisaged expenditure of 182,300,000m. won (including capital expenditure of 24,400,000m. won). At the end of 2005, according to the ADB, the Republic of Korea's total external debt was US $190,010m. In that year the cost of debt-servicing was equivalent to 5.8% of the value of exports of goods and services. The average annual rate of inflation was 3.6% in 1995–2005. Consumer prices increased by an average of 3.6% in 2004 and 2.7% in 2005. The rate of unemployment was 3.7% of the labour force in 2004 and remained at the same level in 2005.

The Republic of Korea is a member of the UN Economic and Social Commission for Asia and the Pacific (ESCAP, see p. 33), the ADB, Asia-Pacific Economic Co-operation (APEC, see p. 164), the Colombo Plan (see p. 385) and the Organisation for Economic Co-operation and Development (OECD, see p. 320).

In 1997 the Republic of Korea experienced its most serious economic crisis in 50 years. Several major *chaebol* collapsed, the won depreciated substantially against the US dollar and foreign-exchange reserves were almost depleted. The country was forced to seek extensive assistance from the IMF. President Kim Dae-Jung assumed office in February 1998, promising widespread economic reform, and accepted a three-year programme formulated by the IMF, which stipulated the implementation of stringent economic and financial liberalization measures. By the end of 1999 the economy appeared to have made a remarkable recovery, and in December 2000 the IMF ended its rescue programme, which it declared to have been a success. Economic difficulties however, mainly resulting from incomplete reform of the banking sector and of the *chaebol*, persisted. In an attempt to moderate the dominance of the economy by the *chaebol*, in 2005 revised legislation was introduced that restricted to 25% the proportion of a company's net assets that could be invested in other equities. Economic difficulties in the banking sector continued from 2003, with an ongoing financial crisis at credit card lender LG Card owing to customers being unable to service their loans. In May 2004 the Government announced proposals for assisting bank customers who were not able to meet their debt obligations. A sharp decline in consumer spending during 2004, believed to be a consequence of the high levels of credit card debt, was a further cause for concern. At the end of 2004 household debt stood at the equivalent of 73.8% of GDP. Although household debt remained at similar levels in 2005, private consumption began to recover as a result of increases in real earnings. Meanwhile, from 2001 organized labour movements continued to arrange industrial action by workers fearing unemployment and seeking better working conditions. There was industrial unrest in 2003 in connection with railway privatization and lawsuits filed against union leaders, and in 2004 there were further instances of large-scale strikes. Major strikes were organized for late February and early March 2006 to protest against the introduction of legislation criticized by unions for encouraging companies to employ cheaper, temporary workers. Notably, a nation-wide rail strike from 1 March led to the resignation of the Prime Minister (see Recent History). Although the overall rate of average unemployment in 2005 was estimated at 3.7%, the rate of unemployment amongst young people was believed to be much higher. Although the economy entered recession in the first half of 2003, for the first time since 1998, the subsequent recovery was driven by strong growth in the export sector. In particular, exports to China increased by 47.8% in 2003, with China thus becoming South Korea's largest export market, surpassing the USA. Exports to China grew further by 41.7% in 2004 and by 24.4% in 2005. (In 2004 China also overtook the USA to become the Republic of Korea's second largest supplier of imports.) Export revenue increased by 31.0% in 2004, compared with the previous year, but the rate of growth decelerated to 12.0% in 2005. By early 2006 the South Korean won had reached its highest level against the dollar since the financial crisis of 1997–98, prompting concern that this might have an adverse effect on the competitiveness of South Korean exports. Foreign direct investment increased from US $100m. in 2003 to $4,588m. in 2004, with several foreign banks acquiring majority stakes in the South Korean financial sector. In 2005, however, foreign direct investment was estimated to have declined sharply, to just $26m.

THE REPUBLIC OF KOREA (SOUTH KOREA)

In December 2004 foreign ownership among all companies on the Korea Stock Exchange was reportedly some 42%. In February 2004, meanwhile, the Republic of Korea approved its first free-trade agreement, with Chile. In November 2004 a free-trade agreement with Singapore was signed. Negotiations on a free-trade agreement with Japan, initially expected to be concluded in 2005, were delayed by disagreement over liberalization of trade in agricultural products, as well as by political tensions (see Recent History). In February 2006 it was announced that negotiations had commenced on a free-trade agreement between the Republic of Korea and the USA; this was expected to be the Republic's largest trade agreement and one of the most significant such accords in the world. South Korea's expansion of its free-trade arrangements and wider incorporation of its economy into the global trading system encountered some domestic opposition, however, especially from the relatively uncompetitive agricultural sector. In November 2005 rice farmers demonstrated against the ratification by the National Assembly of a trade pact that increased foreign access to the domestic rice market; South Korean farmers were also among the most vocal and visible protesters at the WTO's ministerial meeting in Hong Kong in December. Official forecasts for 2006 envisaged a GDP growth rate of 5.0%.

Education

Education, available free of charge, is compulsory between the ages of six and 15. Primary education begins at six years of age and lasts for six years. In 2001 enrolment at primary schools included 98.2% of children in the appropriate age-group. Secondary education begins at 12 years of age and lasts for up to six years, comprising two cycles of three years each, the first of which is compulsory. Enrolment at secondary schools in 2001 included 96.7% of children in the appropriate age-group (males 98.0%; females 95.3%). In 2005 there were 173 university-level institutions, with a student enrolment of 1,859,639. In that year there were 1,051 graduate schools, with a student enrolment of 282,225. Expenditure on education by the central Government was projected at 26,384,100m. won for 2004.

Public Holidays

2006: 1 January (New Year), 28–30 January (Lunar New Year), 1 March (Sam Il Jol, Independence Movement Day), 5 April (Arbor Day), 5 May (Children's Day and Buddha's Birthday), 6 June (Memorial Day), 17 July (Constitution Day), 15 August (Liberation Day), 3 October (National Foundation Day), 5–7 October (Juseok, Korean Thanksgiving Day), 25 December (Christmas Day).

2007: 1 January (New Year), 17–19 February (Lunar New Year), 1 March (Sam Il Jol, Independence Movement Day), 5 April (Arbor Day), 5 May (Children's Day), 24 May (Buddha's Birthday), 6 June (Memorial Day), 17 July (Constitution Day), 15 August (Liberation Day), 24–26 September (Juseok, Korean Thanksgiving Day), 3 October (National Foundation Day), 25 December (Christmas Day).

Weights and Measures

The metric system is in force, although a number of traditional measures are also used.

Statistical Survey

Source (unless otherwise stated): National Statistical Office, Bldg III, Government Complex-Daejeon 920, Dunsan-dong, Seo-gu, Daejeon 302-701; tel. (42) 481-2001; fax (42) 481-2460; internet www.nso.go.kr.

Area and Population

AREA, POPULATION AND DENSITY*

Area (sq km)	99,617†
Population (census results)‡	
1 November 1995	44,608,726
1 November 2000	
Males	23,158,582
Females	22,977,519
Total	46,136,101
Population (official estimates at mid-year)	
2002	47,615,132
2003	47,849,227
2004	48,082,163
Density (per sq km) at mid-2004	482.7

* Excluding the demilitarized zone between North and South Korea, with an area of 1,262 sq km (487 sq miles).

† 38,462 sq miles. The figure indicates territory under the jurisdiction of the Republic of Korea, surveyed on the basis of land register.

‡ Excluding adjustment for underenumeration, estimated at 1.4% in 1995.

PRINCIPAL TOWNS
(population at 1995 census)

Seoul (capital)	10,231,217	Jeonju (Chonju)	563,153
Busan (Pusan)	3,814,325	Jeongju (Chongju)	531,376
Daegu (Taegu)	2,449,420	Masan	441,242
Incheon (Inchon)	2,308,188	Jinju (Chinju)	329,886
Daejeon (Taejon)	1,272,121	Kunsan	266,559
Gwangju (Kwangju)	1,257,636	Jeju (Cheju)	258,511
Ulsan	967,429	Mokpo	247,452
Seongnam		Chuncheon	
(Songnam)	869,094	(Chunchon)	234,528
Suwon	755,550		

2000 census: Seoul 9,853,972; Busan 3,655,437; Daegu 2,473,990; Incheon 2,466,338; Daejeon 1,365,961; Gwangju 1,350,948; Ulsan 1,012,110.

BIRTHS, MARRIAGES AND DEATHS*

	Registered live births		Registered marriages		Registered deaths	
	Number	Rate (per 1,000)	Number	Rate (per 1,000)	Number	Rate (per 1,000)
1997	678,402	14.8	388,591	8.4	247,938	5.3
1998	642,972	13.8	375,616	8.0	248,443	5.3
1999	616,322	13.2	362,673	7.7	246,539	5.2
2000	636,780	13.4	334,030	7.0	247,346	5.2
2001	557,228	11.6	320,063	6.7	242,730	5.1
2002	494,625	10.3	306,573	6.4	246,515	5.1
2003	493,471	10.2	304,932	6.3	245,817	5.1
2004	476,052	9.8	310,944	6.4	245,771	5.1

* Owing to late registration, figures are subject to continuous revision.

Expectation of life (WHO estimates, years at birth): 76 (males 73; females 80) in 2003 (Source: WHO, *World Health Report*).

THE REPUBLIC OF KOREA (SOUTH KOREA)

ECONOMICALLY ACTIVE POPULATION*
(annual averages, '000 persons aged 15 years and over)

	1998	1999	2000
Agriculture, forestry and fishing	2,480	2,349	2,288
Mining and quarrying	21	20	18
Manufacturing	3,898	4,006	4,244
Electricity, gas and water	61	61	63
Construction	1,578	1,476	1,583
Trade, restaurants and hotels	5,571	5,724	5,943
Transport, storage and communications	1,169	1,202	1,260
Financing, insurance, real estate and business services	1,856	1,925	2,089
Community, social and personal services	3,339	3,499	3,551
Total employed (incl. others)	19,994	20,281	21,061
Unemployed	1,461	1,353	889
Total labour force	21,456	21,634	21,950
Males	12,893	12,889	12,950
Females	8,562	8,745	9,000

2001 ('000 persons aged 15 years and over): Total employed 21,572; Unemployed 899; Total labour force 22,471 (males 13,172, females 9,299).

2002 ('000 persons aged 15 years and over): Total employed 22,169; Unemployed 752; Total labour force 22,921 (males 13,435, females 9,486).

2003 ('000 persons aged 15 years and over): Total employed 22,139; Unemployed 818; Total labour force 22,957 (males 13,539, females 9,418).

2004 ('000 persons): Total employed 22,557; Unemployed 860; Total labour force 23,417 (males 13,727, females 9,690).

2005 ('000 persons): Total employed 22,856; Unemployed 887; Total labour force 23,743 (males 13,883, females 9,860).

* Excluding armed forces.

Health and Welfare

KEY INDICATORS

Total fertility rate (children per woman, 2003)	1.4
Under-5 mortality rate (per 1,000 live births, 2004)	6
HIV/AIDS (% of persons aged 15–49, 2003)	<0.1
Physicians (per 1,000 head, 2002)	1.4
Hospital beds (per 1,000 head, 2000)	6.1
Health expenditure (2002): US $ per head (PPP)	982
Health expenditure (2002): % of GDP	5.0
Health expenditure (2002): public (% of total)	52.9
Access to water (% of persons, 2002)	92
Access to sanitation (% of persons, 2000)	63
Human Development Index (2003): ranking	28
Human Development Index (2003): value	0.901

For sources and definitions, see explanatory note on p. vi.

Agriculture

PRINCIPAL CROPS
('000 metric tons)

	2002	2003	2004
Rice (paddy)	6,687.2	6,015.0	6,945.0
Barley	304.6	249.0	277.7
Maize	73.2	70.2	78.0*
Potatoes	666.2	498.4	640.0*
Sweet potatoes	316.7	268.7	280.0†
Dry beans	10.3	8.1	9.0†
Chestnuts	72.4	60.0	55.0†
Soybeans (Soya beans)	115.0	105.1	139.0†
Sesame seed	23.8	12.0	20.9
Other oilseeds	21.5	21.6	19.3
Cabbages	2,575.8	2,959.9	3,139.4
Lettuce	179.0	190.3	204.8
Spinach	112.7	111.7	118.7
Tomatoes	226.6	269.9	394.6
Pumpkins, squash and gourds	276.5	271.8	304.3
Cucumbers and gherkins	463.7	445.0	407.5
Chillies and green peppers	381.2	350.2	410.3

—continued	2002	2003	2004
Green onions and shallots	566.8	534.9	700.2
Dry onions	933.1	745.2	947.8
Garlic	391.2	378.8	357.8
Carrots	136.1	124.5	80.0
Mushrooms	24.7	25.0	25.0†
Other vegetables*	3,498.2	3,647.1	3,681.1
Watermelons	839.6	783.3	823.7
Cantaloupes and other melons	247.2	239.4	243.1
Tangerines, mandarins, clementines and satsumas	642.5	631.9	584.4
Apples	433.2	365.4	357.2
Pears	386.3	316.6	451.9
Peaches and nectarines	187.5	189.4	200.5
Plums	75.6	77.4	72.0
Strawberries	209.9	205.4	202.5
Grapes	422.0	376.4	367.9
Persimmons	281.1	249.2	299.0
Other fruits†	87.3	83.0	90.5
Tobacco (leaves)	47.5	35.7*	35.7†

* Unofficial figure(s).
† FAO estimate(s).

Source: FAO.

LIVESTOCK
('000 head)

	2002	2003	2004
Cattle	1,954	1,999	2,163
Pigs	8,974	9,231	8,908
Goats	444	483	527
Rabbits	362	376	376*
Chickens	101,693	99,109	106,736
Ducks	7,824	9,017	8,266
Other live animals	2,071	3,109	3,106*

* FAO estimate.
Source: FAO.

LIVESTOCK PRODUCTS
('000 metric tons)

	2002	2003	2004
Beef and veal	210.8	188.0	204.0*
Pig meat	1,005.2	1,149.0*	1,100.0
Chicken meat	381.4	383.0*	386.0
Duck meat*	56.0	46.0	46.0
Other meat†	8.4	10.3	10.5
Cows' milk	2,537.0	2,366.0	2,255.0
Goats' milk†	4.6	5.0	5.2
Butter†	55.2	59.6	54.4
Hen eggs	536.6	535.0*	565.0†
Other poultry eggs†	25.0	28.0	26.0
Honey	25.5	26.0	28.0
Cattle hides (fresh)†	34.9	30.4	33.6

* Unofficial figure(s).
† FAO estimate(s).

Source: FAO.

Forestry

ROUNDWOOD REMOVALS
('000 cubic metres, excl. bark)

	2002	2003	2004
Sawlogs, veneer logs and logs for sleepers	229	289	289
Pulpwood	1,019	1,017	1,400
Other industrial wood	357	367	400*
Fuel wood*	2,458	2,461	2,463
Total	4,063	4,134	4,552

* FAO estimate(s).
Source: FAO.

THE REPUBLIC OF KOREA (SOUTH KOREA)

SAWNWOOD PRODUCTION
('000 cubic metres, incl. sleepers)

	2002	2003	2004
Coniferous (softwood)	4,209	4,200	4,200*
Broadleaved (hardwood)	201	180	166†
Total	4,410	4,380	4,366*

* FAO estimate.
† Unofficial figure.

Source: FAO.

Fishing

('000 metric tons, live weight)

	2001	2002	2003
Capture	1,990.7	1,671.3	1,647.5
Alaska (walleye) pollock	197.4	24.8	22.1
Croakers and drums	61.3	60.5	58.9
Japanese anchovy	273.9	236.3	250.1
Skipjack tuna	137.6	173.7	153.3
Chub mackerel	203.7	142.1	122.1
Largehead hairtail	79.9	60.2	62.9
Argentine shortfin squid	142.6	98.6	91.4
Japanese flying squid	225.6	226.7	233.3
Aquaculture	294.5	296.8	387.8
Pacific cupped oyster	174.1	182.2	238.3
Total catch	2,285.2	1,968.1	2,035.3

Note: Figures exclude aquatic plants ('000 metric tons): 388.5 (capture 14.9, aquaculture 373.5) in 2001; 508.0 (capture 10.4, aquaculture 497.6) in 2002 (FAO estimates); 457.2 (capture 5.2, aquaculture 452.1) in 2003 (FAO estimates). Also excluded are aquatic mammals, recorded by number rather than by weight. The number of whales caught was: 377 in 2001; 282 in 2002; 423 in 2003.

Source: FAO.

Mining

('000 metric tons, unless otherwise indicated)

	2002	2003	2004
Hard coal (Anthracite)	3,318	3,312	3,248
Iron ore: gross weight	365	289	496
Iron ore: metal content	164	125	214
Lead ore (metric tons)*	28	—	40
Zinc ore (metric tons)*	99	—	14
Kaolin	2,727	3,009	2,780
Feldspar	519.1	477.0	541.8
Salt (unrefined)†	800	800	800
Mica (metric tons)	29,870	33,645	59,238
Talc (metric tons)	37,863	47,911	79,911
Pyrophyllite	890.0	912.3	827.9

* Figures refer to the metal content of ores.
† Estimated production.

Source: US Geological Survey.

Industry

SELECTED PRODUCTS
('000 metric tons, unless otherwise indicated)

	2000	2001	2002
Wheat flour	1,871	1,843	1,814
Refined sugar	1,257	1,264	1,273
Beer (million litres)	1,654	1,777	1,822
Cigarettes (million)	94,531	94,116	94,433
Cotton yarn—pure and mixed	294.1	303.5	301.3
Plywood ('000 cu m)	817	801	886
Newsprint	1,770	1,585	1,597
Rubber tyres ('000)*	71,348	68,728	71,103
Caustic soda (metric tons)	1,203	1,309	1,340
Liquefied petroleum gas	2,997	3,379	n.a.
Naphtha	19,109	18,612	n.a.
Kerosene	11,299	9,631	n.a.
Distillate fuel oil	31,535	30,275	n.a.
Residual fuel oil	34,813	34,085	n.a.
Cement	51,417	53,062	56,823
Pig-iron	24,943	26,182	26,879
Crude steel	43,423	44,199	45,482
Television receivers ('000)	10,054	9,321	9,157
Passenger cars—produced ('000 units)	2,626	2,477	2,653
Lorries and trucks—produced (number)	265,448	254,233	288,992
Electric energy (million kWh)	295,156	313,963	n.a.
Carbon black†	454.7	438.1	460.0
Products of petroleum refineries ('000 barrels)†	911,761	930,000‡	940,000‡

* Tyres for passenger cars and commercial vehicles.
† Source: US Geological Survey.
‡ Estimate.

Shipbuilding (merchant ships launched, '000 grt): 8,977 in 1999; 11,211 in 2000; 8,385 in 2001.

Source: mostly UN, *Industrial Commodity Statistics Yearbook*.

2003 ('000 metric tons, unless otherwise indicated): Cement 59,194; Crude steel 46,310; Pig-iron 27,314; Carbon black 464.9; Products of petroleum refineries ('000 barrels) 796,000.

2004 ('000 metric tons, unless otherwise indicated): Cement 54,330; Crude steel 47,521; Pig-iron 27,556; Carbon black 473.8; Products of petroleum refineries ('000 barrels) 842,000.

Source: US Geological Survey.

Finance

CURRENCY AND EXCHANGE RATES

Monetary Units
100 chun (jeon) = 10 hwan = 1 won.

Sterling, Dollar and Euro Equivalents (30 December 2005)
£1 sterling = 1,741.87 won;
US $1 = 1,011.60 won;
€1 = 1,193.38 won;
10,000 won = £5.74 = $9.89 = €8.38.

Average Exchange Rate (won per US $)
2003   1,191.61
2004   1,145.32
2005   1,024.12

BUDGET
('000 million won)*

Revenue	2002†	2003†	2004‡
Tax revenue	104,000	114,700	122,100
Social security contributions	19,700	20,700	24,800
Non-tax and capital revenue	35,000	36,400	39,800
Total	158,700	171,700	186,600

THE REPUBLIC OF KOREA (SOUTH KOREA)

Statistical Survey

Expenditure§	2002†	2003†	2004‡
Current expenditure||	113,200	123,900	138,000
Interest	13,800	7,800	9,400
Non-interest	99,400	116,100	128,700
Capital expenditure	29,400	30,600	26,600
Total	142,500	149,300	164,700

* Figures are rounded and refer to consolidated central government operations.
† Actual figures.
‡ Projected figures.
§ Excluding net lending ('000 million won): 200 in 2002 (actual); –2,600 in 2003 (actual); 6,700 in 2004 (projection).
\|\| Excluding conversion of Korean Deposit Insurance Company (KDIC) and Korean Asset Management Company (KAMCO) bonds, amounting to 13,000,000m. won in 2003 and 12,000,000m. won in 2004.

Note: Beginning in 2003, interest payments on KDIC/KAMCO bonds worth 49,000,000m. won are excluded from consolidated budget.

2005 ('000 million won, projections): Revenue 199,900 (tax revenue 130,600, social security contributions 28,500, non-tax and capital revenue 40,800); Expenditure 182,300 (current 151,100, capital 24,400, net lending 6,800).

Sources: IMF, *Republic of Korea: 2004 Article IV Consultation—Staff Report; Staff Statement; and Public Information Notice on the Executive Board Discussion* (February 2005).

INTERNATIONAL RESERVES
(US $ million at 31 December)

	2003	2004	2005
Gold (national valuation)	70.9	72.3	73.6
IMF special drawing rights	21.1	32.8	43.7
Reserve position in IMF	754.4	788.4	305.8
Foreign exchange	154,508.8	198,175.3	209,967.7
Total	155,355.1	199,068.9	210,390.8

Source: IMF, *International Financial Statistics*.

MONEY SUPPLY
('000 million won at 31 December)

	2002	2003	2004
Currency outside banks	19,863	20,111	20,772
Demand deposits at deposit money banks	43,265	45,226	47,424
Total money (incl. others)	63,151	65,481	68,423

Source: IMF, *International Financial Statistics*.

COST OF LIVING
(Consumer Price Index; base: 2000 = 100)

	2003	2004	2005
Food	112.4	119.5	122.8
Housing	113.2	115.8	116.1
Fuel, light and water	113.1	119.4	126.6
Furniture and utensils	106.7	108.4	110.5
Clothing and footwear	110.1	110.5	111.6
Medical treatment	114.1	115.8	118.4
Education	116.8	122.9	127.9
Culture and recreation	100.0	100.3	100.4
Transport and communications	102.7	105.1	108.6
All items (incl. others)	110.7	114.7	117.8

NATIONAL ACCOUNTS
('000 million won at current prices)

National Income and Product

	2001	2002	2003
Compensation of employees	270,469.8	294,480.9	317,594.7
Operating surplus	185,661.9	210,635.9	213,593.3
Domestic factor incomes	456,131.7	505,116.8	531,188.0
Consumption of fixed capital	88,112.6	91,113.4	99,067.9
Gross domestic product (GDP) at factor cost	544,244.3	596,230.2	630,255.9
Indirect taxes, *less* subsidies	77,878.3	88,033.3	91,090.1
GDP in purchasers' values	622,122.6	684,263.5	721,346.0
Net factor income from abroad	–1,094.8	805.6	1,009.9
Gross national product	621,027.8	685,069.1	722,355.9
Less Consumption of fixed capital	88,112.6	91,113.4	99,067.9
National income in market prices	532,915.2	593,955.7	623,287.9
Other current transfers from abroad (net)	–496.2	–1,976.5	–3,345.1
National disposable income	532,419.0	591,979.1	619,942.8

Expenditure on the Gross Domestic Product

	2002	2003	2004
Government final consumption expenditure	88,512.2	96,203.2	104,960.7
Private final consumption expenditure	381,063.0	389,177.2	400,696.5
Increase in stocks	–41.5	291.9	5,544.0
Gross fixed capital formation	199,047.5	216,807.1	229,690.5
Statistical discrepancy	6,237.9	4,928.2	3,689.8
Total domestic expenditure	674,819.1	707,407.6	744,581.5
Exports of goods and services	241,209.0	274,995.1	343,229.3
Less Imports of goods and services	231,764.7	257,727.7	309,366.3
GDP in purchasers' values	684,263.5	724,675.0	778,444.6
GDP at constant 2000 prices	642,748.1	662,654.8	693,424.0

Gross Domestic Product by Economic Activity

	2002	2003	2004
Agriculture, forestry and fishing	24,654.9	24,166.1	25,587.0
Mining and quarrying	2,051.4	2,062.6	2,269.5
Manufacturing	161,952.0	169,145.4	198,863.2
Electricity, gas and water	15,929.4	17,011.2	16,676.0
Construction	51,541.7	61,329.8	64,581.5
Trade, restaurants and hotels	62,656.7	63,583.6	65,638.2
Transport, storage and communications	45,133.8	47,787.0	50,315.9
Financial intermediation	54,844.4	56,690.8	58,809.2
Real estate, renting and business activities	76,822.4	81,804.7	84,654.0
Public administration and defence, compulsory social security	35,557.2	38,700.9	41,979.2
Education	32,296.7	35,760.7	38,749.1
Health and social work	17,432.4	19,012.7	20,576.8
Other service activities	21,219.0	22,706.2	23,283.6
Gross value added at basic prices	602,091.9	639,761.9	691,983.3
Taxes, less subsidies, on products	82,171.6	84,913.1	86,461.3
Total	684,263.5	724,675.0	778,444.6

THE REPUBLIC OF KOREA (SOUTH KOREA)

BALANCE OF PAYMENTS
(US $ million)

	2002	2003	2004
Exports of goods f.o.b.	163,414	197,637	257,745
Imports of goods f.o.b.	−148,637	−175,476	−219,584
Trade balance	14,777	22,161	38,161
Exports of services	28,388	32,702	41,429
Imports of services	−36,585	−40,313	−50,198
Balance on goods and services	6,580	14,550	29,392
Other income received	6,900	7,111	8,722
Other income paid	−6,467	−6,515	−7,997
Balance on goods, services and income	7,012	15,146	30,117
Current transfers received	7,314	7,879	9,179
Current transfers paid	−8,932	−10,703	−11,683
Current balance	5,394	12,321	27,613
Capital account (net)	−1,087	−1,402	−1,773
Direct investment abroad	−2,617	−3,429	−4,792
Direct investment from abroad	2,392	3,222	8,189
Portfolio investment assets	−5,032	−4,333	−9,801
Portfolio investment liabilities	5,378	22,653	19,007
Financial derivatives assets	1,288	888	2,291
Financial derivatives liabilities	−926	−1,248	−2,228
Other investment assets	2,557	−3,496	−7,001
Other investment liabilities	4,297	274	4,427
Net errors and omissions	124	342	2,743
Overall balance	11,769	25,791	38,675

Source: IMF, *International Financial Statistics*.

External Trade

PRINCIPAL COMMODITIES
(distribution by SITC, US $ million)*

Imports c.i.f.	2003	2004	2005
Food and live animals	8,331.0	9,280.4	9,956.0
Crude materials (inedible) except fuels	10,146.5	13,535.3	15,353.8
Mineral fuels, lubricants, etc.	38,629.7	50,278.5	67,500.9
Petroleum, petroleum products, etc.	29,608.6	37,656.1	51,303.8
Crude petroleum oils, etc.	23,081.6	29,917.2	42,605.8
Gas (natural and manufactured)	6,468.7	8,184.1	10,754.2
Chemicals and related products	16,482.0	20,654.5	24,502.4
Organic chemicals	5,408.0	7,044.8	8,321.5
Basic manufactures	22,369.6	30,825.2	35,849.4
Iron and steel	7,355.0	12,181.0	15,032.8
Machinery and transport equipment	62,655.1	75,361.6	82,533.4
Machinery specialized for particular industries	5,080.6	6,812.1	7,219.2
General industrial machinery, equipment and parts	6,100.4	7,937.6	8,714.4
Office machines and automatic data-processing machines	5,433.6	5,881.9	7,047.1
Telecommunications and sound equipment	5,486.1	6,405.0	6,694.8
Other electrical machinery, apparatus, etc.	31,296.7	36,724.7	39,106.9
Thermionic valves and tubes, microprocessors, transistors, etc.	21,104.8	23,061.4	23,870.9
Digital monolithic integrated units	15,268.9	16,773.8	17,800.5
Miscellaneous manufactured articles	16,234.0	19,852.9	23,434.3
Total (incl. others)	178,826.7	224,462.7	261,238.3

Exports f.o.b.	2003	2004	2005
Mineral fuels, lubricants, etc.	6,901.6	10,531.4	15,709.4
Petroleum, petroleum products, etc.	6,799.2	10,454.4	15,622.7
Chemicals and related products	16,935.6	23,125.7	27,745.2
Organic chemicals	5,742.1	8,595.0	10,388.1
Plastics in primary forms	6,447.0	8,694.7	10,673.6
Basic manufactures	30,129.6	36,954.0	41,023.2
Textile yarn, fabrics, etc.	10,779.1	10,838.7	10,390.8
Iron and steel	7,782.6	11,632.3	14,345.9
Machinery and transport equipment	121,142.2	159,991.2	173,491.6
Office machines and automatic data-processing machines	18,069.3	21,538.9	17,756.9
Automatic data-processing machines and units, etc.	9,345.3	10,148.7	9,240.5
Parts and accessories for office machines and automatic data-processing equipment	8,404.0	11,014.1	8,141.8
Telecommunications and sound equipment	26,634.3	36,599.6	37,746.0
Transmission apparatus for radio or television	13,903.7	19,403.7	19,476.1
Other electrical machinery, apparatus, etc.	28,604.0	36,658.9	42,942.9
Thermionic valves and tubes, microprocessors, transistors, etc.	19,111.0	24,445.9	27,488.3
Digital monolithic integrated units	13,185.6	17,079.6	18,159.8
Road vehicles	22,900.5	31,959.9	37,310.9
Motor cars and other motor vehicles	17,535.7	24,632.1	27,256.1
Other transport equipment	11,645.3	15,825.1	17,616.5
Ships, boats and floating structures	11,103.9	15,321.3	17,231.5
Miscellaneous manufactured articles	12,063.4	14,765.8	20,292.0
Total (incl. others)	193,817.4	253,844.7	284,418.7

* Figures exclude trade with the Democratic People's Republic of Korea (US $ million): *Total imports:* 289.3 in 2003; n.a. in 2004 and 2005. *Total exports:* 435.0 in 2003; n.a. in 2004 and 2005 (Source: Korea Trade-Investment Promotion Agency, Republic of Korea).

Source: Korea International Trade Association.

PRINCIPAL TRADING PARTNERS
(US $ million)*

Imports c.i.f.	2003	2004	2005
Australia	5,915.7	7,437.6	9,859.1
Brazil	1,619.2	2,195.4	2,500.8
Canada	1,860.2	2,188.8	2,603.7
China, People's Republic	21,909.1	29,584.9	38,648.2
France	2,220.3	2,482.8	2,759.0
Germany	6,821.7	8,485.6	9,774.2
Hong Kong	2,735.4	3,268.2	2,043.1
Indonesia	5,212.3	6,368.1	8,184.4
Iran	1,844.7	2,435.3	3,534.9
Italy	2,382.2	2,500.2	2,777.7
Japan	36,313.1	46,144.5	48,403.2
Kuwait	3,191.1	3,832.0	5,977.0
Malaysia	4,249.1	5,678.7	6,011.6
Oman	2,322.8	2,475.0	3,705.1
Philippines	1,964.0	2,120.0	2,316.0
Qatar	3,139.8	3,649.7	5,599.3
Russia	2,521.8	3,671.5	3,936.6
Saudi Arabia	9,267.8	11,799.6	16,105.8
Singapore	4,089.8	4,460.5	5,317.7
Taiwan	5,879.6	7,312.3	8,049.6
Thailand	1,897.7	2,350.8	2,688.8
United Arab Emirates	5,756.5	7,290.1	10,018.3
United Kingdom	2,703.3	3,793.3	3,149.1
USA	24,814.1	28,782.7	30,585.9
Total (incl. others)	178,826.7	224,426.7	261,238.3

THE REPUBLIC OF KOREA (SOUTH KOREA)

Statistical Survey

Exports f.o.b.	2003	2004	2005
Australia	3,272.1	3,378.5	3,812.1
Brazil	1,137.4	1,784.6	2,410.7
Canada	2,682.1	3,383.1	3,446.2
China, People's Republic	35,109.7	49,763.2	61,915.0
France	1,755.4	2,643.6	3,172.3
Germany	5,603.3	8,334.2	10,304.0
Hong Kong	14,653.7	18,127.1	15,531.1
India	2,853.0	3,632.0	4,597.8
Indonesia	3,377.6	3,677.7	5,045.6
Iran	1,778.2	2,134.3	2,141.2
Italy	2,560.6	3,407.5	4,296.9
Japan	17,276.1	21,701.3	24,027.4
Malaysia	3,851.8	4,480.4	4,608.2
Mexico	2,455.0	2,993.9	3,789.1
Netherlands	2,535.0	3,007.2	3,646.7
Philippines	2,975.0	3,379.2	3,219.7
Russia	1,659.1	2,339.3	3,864.2
Singapore	4,636.0	5,653.5	7,406.6
Spain	2,015.8	2,808.8	2,867.1
Taiwan	7,044.6	9,844.2	10,862.9
Thailand	2,523.8	3,249.0	3,380.8
Turkey	1,374.7	2,356.2	2,782.0
United Arab Emirates	2,207.6	2,587.0	2,732.7
United Kingdom	4,094.3	5,516.0	5,338.8
USA	34,219.4	42,849.2	41,342.6
Viet Nam	2,561.2	3,255.6	3,431.7
Total (incl. others)	193,817.4	253,844.7	284,418.7

* Excluding trade with the Democratic People's Republic of Korea.

Source: Korea International Trade Association.

Transport

RAILWAYS
(traffic)

	2002	2003	2004
Passengers carried ('000)	851,715	894,620	921,223
Passenger-km (million)	27,492	27,228	28,459
Freight ('000 metric tons)	45,733	47,110	44,512
Freight ton-km (million)	10,784	11,057	10,641

ROAD TRAFFIC
(motor vehicles in use at 31 December)

	2001	2002	2003
Passenger cars	8,889,327	9,737,428	10,278,923
Goods vehicles	2,728,405	2,894,412	3,016,407
Buses and coaches	1,257,008	1,275,319	1,246,629
Motorcycles and mopeds	1,700,600	1,708,457	1,730,193

SHIPPING

Merchant Fleet
(registered at 31 December)

	2002	2003	2004
Number of vessels	2,532	2,604	2,700
Total displacement ('000 grt)	7,049.7	6,757.4	7,826.1

Source: Lloyd's Register-Fairplay, *World Fleet Statistics*.

Sea-borne Freight Traffic
('000 metric tons)*

	2002	2003	2004
Goods loaded	319,570	340,527	317,799
Goods unloaded	615,555	616,326	593,361

* Including coastwise traffic loaded and unloaded.

CIVIL AVIATION*

	2002	2003	2004
Passengers ('000)	43,965	42,839	45,824
Passenger-km (million)	92,175	82,231	96,583
Freight ('000 metric tons)	2,510	2,632	2,978
Freight ton-km (million)	12,606	n.a.	n.a.

* Domestic and international flights.

Tourism

FOREIGN VISITOR ARRIVALS*†

Country of nationality	2001	2002	2003
China, People's Republic	482,227	539,466	513,236
Hong Kong	204,959	179,299	156,373
Japan	2,377,321	2,320,837	1,802,171
Philippines	210,975	215,848	216,647
Russia	134,727	165,341	168,051
Taiwan	129,410	136,921	194,681
USA	426,817	459,362	421,709
Total (incl. others)	5,147,204	5,347,468	4,753,604

* Including same-day visitors (excursionists) and crew members from ships.
† Including Korean nationals resident abroad.

Receipts from tourism (US $ million, incl. passenger transport): 7,919 in 2001; 7,621 in 2002; 6,903 in 2003.

Source: World Tourism Organization.

Communications Media

	2002	2003	2004
Telephones ('000 main lines in use)	23,257.0	22,877.0	26,058.1
Mobile cellular telephones ('000 subscribers)	32,342.0	33,591.8	36,586.1
Personal computers ('000 in use)	23,500	26,700	26,201
Internet users ('000)	26,270	29,220	31,580
Book production:			
titles	27,126	26,290	27,527
copies ('000)	81,555	78,091	82,097
Registered daily newspapers (titles)	128	136	137

1996: Facsimile machines (estimate, '000 in use): 400.

1997: Radio receivers ('000 in use) 47,500.

2000: Television receivers ('000 in use) 17,229.

Sources: mainly UNESCO, *Statistical Yearbook*; UN, *Statistical Yearbook*; International Telecommunication Union; Korean Association of Newspapers.

Education

(2005)

	Institutions	Teachers	Pupils
Kindergarten	8,275	31,033	541,603
Primary schools	5,646	160,143	4,022,801
Middle schools	2,935	103,835	2,010,704
General high schools	1,382	79,158	1,259,792
Vocational high schools	713	503,104	37,253
Junior colleges	158	12,027	853,089
Teachers' colleges	11	798	25,141
Universities and colleges	173	49,200	1,859,639
Graduate schools	1,051	1,673	282,225

Adult literacy rate (UNESCO estimates): 97.9% (males 99.2%; females 96.6%) in 2001 (Source: UN Development Programme, *Human Development Report*).

THE REPUBLIC OF KOREA (SOUTH KOREA)

Directory

Note: from 2001 the romanization of place-names in South Korea was in the process of change. Transliteration of names of people and corporations was to remain unchanged for the time being.

The Constitution

The Constitution of the Sixth Republic (Ninth Amendment) was approved by national referendum on 29 October 1987. It came into effect on 25 February 1988. The main provisions are summarized below:

THE EXECUTIVE

The President

The President shall be elected by universal, equal, direct and secret ballot of the people for one term of five years. Re-election of the President is prohibited. In times of national emergency and under certain conditions the President may issue emergency orders and take emergency action with regard to budgetary and economic matters. The President shall notify the National Assembly of these measures and obtain its concurrence, or they shall lose effect. He may, in times of war, armed conflict or similar national emergency, declare martial law in accordance with the provisions of law. He shall lift the emergency measures and martial law when the National Assembly so requests with the concurrence of a majority of the members. The President may not dissolve the National Assembly. He is authorized to take directly to the people important issues through national referendums. The President shall appoint the Prime Minister (with the consent of the National Assembly) and other public officials.

The State Council

The State Council shall be composed of the President, the Prime Minister and no more than 30 and no fewer than 15 others appointed by the President (on the recommendation of the Prime Minister), and shall deliberate on policies that fall within the power of the executive. No member of the armed forces shall be a member of the Council, unless retired from active duty.

The Board of Audit and Inspection

The Board of Audit and Inspection shall be established under the President to inspect the closing of accounts of revenue and expenditures, the accounts of the State and other organizations as prescribed by law, and to inspect the administrative functions of the executive agencies and public officials. It shall be composed of no fewer than five and no more than 11 members, including the Chairman. The Chairman shall be appointed by the President with the consent of the National Assembly, and the members by the President on the recommendation of the Chairman. Appointments shall be for four years and members may be reappointed only once.

THE NATIONAL ASSEMBLY

Legislative power shall be vested in the National Assembly. The Assembly shall be composed of not fewer than 200 members, a number determined by law, elected for four years by universal, equal, direct and secret ballot. The constituencies of members of the Assembly, proportional representation and other matters pertaining to the Assembly elections shall be determined by law. A regular session shall be held once a year and extraordinary sessions shall be convened upon requests of the President or one-quarter of the Assembly's members. The period of regular sessions shall not exceed 100 days and of extraordinary sessions 30 days. The Assembly has the power to recommend to the President the removal of the Prime Minister or any other Minister. The Assembly shall have the authority to pass a motion for the impeachment of the President or any other public official, and may inspect or investigate state affairs, under procedures to be established by law.

THE CONSTITUTIONAL COURT

The Constitutional Court shall be composed of nine members appointed by the President, three of whom shall be appointed from persons selected by the National Assembly and three from persons nominated by the Chief Justice. The term of office shall be six years. It shall pass judgment upon the constitutionality of laws upon the request of the courts, matters of impeachment and the dissolution of political parties. In these judgments the concurrence of six members or more shall be required.

THE JUDICIARY

The courts shall be composed of the Supreme Court, which is the highest court of the State, and other courts at specified levels (for further details, see section on Judicial System). The Chief Justice and justices of the Supreme Court are appointed by the President, subject to the consent of the National Assembly. When the constitutionality of a law is a prerequisite to a trial, the Court shall request a decision of the Constitutional Court. The Supreme Court shall have the power to pass judgment upon the constitutionality or legality of administrative decrees, and shall have final appellate jurisdiction over military tribunals. No judge shall be removed from office except following impeachment or a sentence of imprisonment.

ELECTION MANAGEMENT

Election Commissions shall be established for the purpose of fair management of elections and national referendums. The National Election Commission shall be composed of three members appointed by the President, three appointed by the National Assembly and three appointed by the Chief Justice of the Supreme Court. Their term of office is six years, and they may not be expelled from office except following impeachment or a sentence of imprisonment.

POLITICAL PARTIES

The establishment of political parties shall be free and the plural party system guaranteed. However, a political party whose aims or activities are contrary to the basic democratic order may be dissolved by the Constitutional Court.

AMENDMENTS

A motion to amend the Constitution shall be proposed by the President or by a majority of the total number of members of the National Assembly. Amendments extending the President's term of office or permitting the re-election of the President shall not be effective for the President in office at the time of the proposal. Proposed amendments to the Constitution shall be put before the public by the President for 20 days or more. Within 60 days of the public announcement, the National Assembly shall decide upon the proposed amendments, which require a two-thirds' majority of the National Assembly. They shall then be submitted to a national referendum not later than 30 days after passage by the National Assembly and shall be determined by more than one-half of votes cast by more than one-half of voters eligible to vote in elections for members of the National Assembly. If these conditions are fulfilled, the proposed amendments shall be finalized and the President shall promulgate them without delay.

FUNDAMENTAL RIGHTS

Under the Constitution all citizens are equal before the law. The right of habeas corpus is guaranteed. Freedom of speech, press, assembly and association are guaranteed, as are freedom of choice of residence and occupation. No state religion is to be recognized and freedom of conscience and religion is guaranteed. Citizens are protected against retrospective legislation, and may not be punished without due process of law.

Rights and freedoms may be restricted by law when this is deemed necessary for the maintenance of national security, order or public welfare. When such restrictions are imposed, no essential aspect of the right or freedom in question may be violated.

GENERAL PROVISIONS

Peaceful unification of the Korean peninsula, on the principles of liberal democracy, is the prime national aspiration. The Constitution mandates the State to establish and implement a policy of unification. The Constitution expressly stipulates that the armed forces must maintain political neutrality at all times.

The Government

HEAD OF STATE

President: ROH MOO-HYUN (took office 25 February 2003).

STATE COUNCIL
(April 2006)

Prime Minister: HAN MYEONG-SOOK.

Deputy Prime Minister for Finance and the Economy: HAN DUCK-SOO.

Deputy Prime Minister for Education and Human Resources Development: KIM JIN-PYO.

Minister of Unification: LEE JONG-SEOK.

Minister of Foreign Affairs and Trade: BAN KI-MOON.

Minister of Justice: CHUN JUNG-BAE.

THE REPUBLIC OF KOREA (SOUTH KOREA)

Minister of National Defence: YOON KWANG-WOONG.
Minister of Government Administration and Home Affairs: LEE YONG-SUP.
Deputy Prime Minister and Minister of Science and Technology: KIM WOO-SHIK.
Minister of Culture and Tourism: KIM MYONG-GON.
Minister of Agriculture and Forestry: PARK HONG-SOO.
Minister of Commerce, Industry and Energy: CHUNG SYE-KYUN.
Minister of Information and Communication: RHO JUN-HYONG.
Minister of Health and Welfare: RHYU SI-MIN.
Minister of the Environment: LEE CHI-BEOM.
Minister of Labour: LEE SANG-SOO.
Minister of Gender Equality: JANG HA-JIN.
Minister of Construction and Transportation: CHOO BYUNG-JIK.
Minister of Maritime Affairs and Fisheries: KIM SUNG-JIN.
Minister of Planning and Budget: BYEON YANG-KYOON.

MINISTRIES

Office of the President: Chong Wa Dae (The Blue House), 1, Sejong-no, Jongno-gu, Seoul; tel. (2) 770-0055; fax (2) 770-0344; e-mail president@cwd.go.kr; internet www.bluehouse.go.kr.

Office of the Prime Minister: 77, Sejong-no, Jongno-gu, Seoul; tel. (2) 737-0094; fax (2) 739-5830; e-mail m-opm@opm.go.kr; internet www.opm.go.kr.

Ministry of Agriculture and Forestry: 3-108 Gwacheon Government Office Bldg, 1, Jungang-dong, Gwacheon City, Gyeonggi Prov.; tel. (2) 2110-4000; fax (2) 503-7238; e-mail wmaster@maf.go.kr; internet www.maf.go.kr.

Ministry of Commerce, Industry and Energy: 3, Jungang-dong, Gwacheon City, Gyeonggi Prov. 427-721; tel. (2) 2110-5291; fax (2) 503-3142; internet www.mocie.go.kr.

Ministry of Construction and Transportation: 1, Jungang-dong, Gwacheon City, Gyeonggi Prov. 427-712; tel. (2) 504-9114; fax (2) 503-7400; e-mail webmaster@moct.go.kr; internet www.moct.go.kr.

Ministry of Culture and Tourism: 82-1, Sejong-no, Jongno-gu, Seoul 110-703; tel. (2) 3704-9114; fax (2) 3704-9119; e-mail webmaster@www.mct.go.kr; internet www.mct.go.kr.

Ministry of Education and Human Resources Development: 77-6, Sejong-no, Jongno-gu, Seoul 110-760; tel. (2) 2100-6570; fax (2) 2100-6579; e-mail eduweb@moe.go.kr; internet www.moe.go.kr.

Ministry of Environment: 1, Jungang-dong, Gwacheon City, Gyeonggi Prov. 427-729; tel. (2) 2110-6546; fax (2) 504-9277; e-mail chanchan@me.go.kr; internet www.me.go.kr.

Ministry of Finance and the Economy: Government Complex II, 88 Gwanmoonro, Gwacheon City, Gyeonggi Prov. 427-725; tel. (2) 2110-2348; fax (2) 504-1335; e-mail fppr@mofe.go.kr; internet www.mofe.go.kr.

Ministry of Foreign Affairs and Trade: 95-1, Doryeom-dong, Jongno-gu, Seoul 110-787; tel. (2) 3703-2114; fax (2) 2100-7999; e-mail web@mofat.go.kr; internet www.mofat.go.kr.

Ministry of Gender Equality and Family: 55, Sejong-ro, 1-ga, Jongro-gu, Seoul 110-760; tel. (2) 2100-6600; fax (2) 2106-5145; e-mail webadmin@mogef.go.kr; internet www.moge.go.kr.

Ministry of Government Administration and Home Affairs: Central Government Complex, 77-6, Sejong-no, 1-ga, Jongno-gu, Seoul 110-760; tel. (2) 2100-6767; fax (2) 3703-5502; e-mail hdchoi@mogaha.go.kr; internet www.mogaha.go.kr.

Ministry of Health and Welfare: 1, Jungang-dong, Gwacheon City, Gyeonggi Prov. 427-721; tel. (2) 502-8272; fax (2) 2110-6453; e-mail webmaster@mohw.go.kr; internet www.mohw.go.kr.

Ministry of Information and Communication: 11–14F, Telecommunication Center Bldg, 100, Sejong-no, Jongno-gu, Seoul 100-777; tel. (2) 750-2000; fax (2) 750-2915; e-mail infor3@mic.go.kr; internet www.mic.go.kr.

Ministry of Justice: 1, Jungang-dong, Gwacheon City, Gyeonggi Prov.; tel. (2) 503-7023; fax (2) 504-3337; e-mail webmaster@moj.go.kr; internet www.moj.go.kr.

Ministry of Labour: 1, Jungang-dong, Gwacheon City, Gyeonggi Prov. 427-716; tel. (2) 503-9713; fax (2) 503-8862; e-mail m_molab@molab.go.kr; internet www.molab.go.kr.

Ministry of Maritime Affairs and Fisheries: 140-2, Gye-dong, Jongno-gu, Seoul 110-793; tel. (2) 3674-6990; fax (2) 3674-6996; internet www.momaf.go.kr.

Ministry of National Defence: 1, 3-ga, Yeongsan-dong, Yeongsan-gu, Seoul 140-701; tel. (2) 795-0071; fax (2) 703-3109; e-mail cyber@mnd.go.kr; internet www.mnd.go.kr.

Ministry of Planning and Budget: 520-3, Banpo-dong, Seocho-gu, Seoul 137-756; tel. (2) 3480-7990; fax (2) 3480-7600; e-mail nara@mpb.go.kr; internet www.mpb.go.kr.

Ministry of Science and Technology: 1, Jungang-dong, Gwacheon City, Gyeonggi Prov. 427-715; tel. (2) 503-7600; fax (2) 503-7673; e-mail webadmin@most.go.kr; internet www.most.go.kr.

Ministry of Unification: 77-6, Sejong-no, Jongno-gu, Seoul 110-760; tel. (2) 720-2424; fax (2) 720-2149; e-mail ispark@unikorea.go.kr; internet www.unikorea.go.kr.

President and Legislature

PRESIDENT

Election, 19 December 2002

Candidate	Votes	% of total
Roh Moo-Hyun	12,014,277	48.9
Lee Hoi-Chang	11,443,297	46.6
Kwon Young-Gil	957,148	3.9
Lee Han-Dong	74,027	0.3
Kim Gil-Su	51,104	0.2
Kim Yeong-Kyu	22,063	0.1
Total	**24,561,916**	**100.0**

LEGISLATURE

Kuk Hoe (National Assembly)
1 Yeouido-dong, Yeongdeungpo-gu, Seoul 150-701; tel. (2) 788-2001; fax (2) 788-3375; e-mail webmaster@assembly.go.kr; internet www.assembly.go.kr.

Speaker: KIM ONE-KI.

General Election, 15 April 2004

Party	Elected	Proportional	Total
Uri Party	129	23	152
Grand National Party	100	21	121
Democratic Labour Party	2	8	10
Millennium Democratic Party*	5	4	9
United Liberal Democrats	4	—	4
Others	3	—	3
Total	**243**	**56**	**299**

* The Millennium Democratic Party changed its name to the Democratic Party in May 2005.

Election Commission

National Election Commission: 2-3 Junggang-dong, Gwacheon-si, Gyeonggi-do 427-727; tel. (2) 504-2761; e-mail e_nec@nec.go.kr; internet www.nec.go.kr; Chair. SON JI-YOL.

Political Organizations

Democratic Labour Party (DLP): Hanyang Bldg, 14-31, Yeouido-dong, Yeongdeungpo-gu, Seoul 150-748; tel. (2) 761-1333; fax (2) 761-4115; e-mail inter@kdlp.org; internet www.kdlp.org; f. 2000; Pres. KIM HYE-KYUNG.

Democratic Party (DP): 15, Gisan Bldg, Yeongdeungpo-gu, Seoul; tel. (2) 784-7007; fax (2) 784-6070; internet www.minjoo.or.kr; f. 2000; est. as Millennium Democratic Party (MDP) following dissolution of National Congress for New Politics (f. 1995); current name adopted May 2005; Chair. CHOUGH SOON-HYUNG; Sec.-Gen. JO JAE-HWAN.

Grand National Party (GNP) (Hannara Party): 17-7, Yeouido-dong, Yeongdeungpo-gu, Seoul 150-010; tel. (2) 3786-3373; fax (2) 3786-3610; internet www.hannara.or.kr; f. 1997; est. by merger of Democratic Party and New Korea Party; Chair. PARK GEUN-HYE.

United Liberal Democrats (ULD): Insan Bldg, 103-4, Shinsu-dong, Mapo-gu, Seoul 121-110; tel. (2) 701-3355; fax (2) 707-1637; internet www.jamin.or.kr; f. 1995; est. by fmr mems of the Democratic Liberal Party; Pres. KIM HAK-WON.

Uri Party: c/o National Assembly, 1 Yeouido-dong, Yeongdeungpo-gu, Seoul 150-701; tel. (2) 784-0114; e-mail webmaster@eparty.or.kr;

THE REPUBLIC OF KOREA (SOUTH KOREA)

internet www.eparty.or.kr; f. 2003; est. by defectors from the MDP; Chair. CHUNG DONG-YOUNG.

Civic groups play an increasingly significant role in South Korean politics. These include: the People's Solidarity for Participatory Democracy (Dir Jang Hasung); the Citizens' Coalition for Economic Justice; and the Citizens' Alliance for Political Reform (Leader Kim Sok-Su).

Diplomatic Representation

EMBASSIES IN THE REPUBLIC OF KOREA

Algeria: 2-6, Itaewon 2-dong, Yeongsan-gu, Seoul 140-857; tel. (2) 794-5034; fax (2) 794-5040; e-mail sifdja01@kornet.net; internet www.algerianemb.or.kr; Ambassador RABAH HADID.

Argentina: Chun Woo Bldg, 5th Floor, 534 Itaewon-dong, Yeongsan-gu, Seoul 140-861; tel. (2) 793-4062; fax (2) 792-5820; e-mail embarcor@kornet.net; internet www.embajadaargentinaencorea.org; Ambassador RODOLFO IGNACIO RODRÍGUEZ.

Australia: Kyobo Bldg, 11th Floor, 1, 1-ga, Jongno-gu, Seoul 110-714; tel. (2) 2003-0100; fax (2) 722-9264; e-mail inform@australia.or.kr; internet www.australia.or.kr; Ambassador COLIN STUART HESELTINE.

Austria: Kyobo Bldg, Rm 1913, 1-1, 1-ga, Jongno, Jongno-gu, Seoul 110-714; tel. (2) 732-9071; fax (2) 732-9486; e-mail seoul-ob@bmaa.gv.at; internet www.austria.or.kr; Ambassador WILHELM DONKO.

Bangladesh: 7-18, Woo Sung Bldg, Dongbinggo-dong, Yeongsan-gu, Seoul; tel. (2) 796-4056; fax (2) 790-5313; Ambassador MUSTAFA KAMAL.

Belarus: 432-1636 Sindang 2-dong, Jung-gu, Seoul; tel. (2) 2237-8171; fax (2) 2237-8174; e-mail korea@belembassy.org; Ambassador ALYAKSANDR V. SYAMESHKA.

Belgium: 737-10, Hannam-dong, Yongsan-ku, Seoul 140-895; tel. (2) 749-0381; fax (2) 797-1688; e-mail seoul@diplobel.org; internet www.belgium.or.kr; Ambassador VICTOR WEI.

Brazil: Ihn Gallery Bldg, 4th and 5th Floors, 141 Palpan-dong, Jongno-gu, Seoul; tel. (2) 738-4970; fax (2) 738-4974; e-mail braseul@kornet.net; internet www.brasemb.kr; Ambassador PEDRO PAULO PINTO ASSUMPÇÃO.

Brunei: 737-11, Hannam-dong, Yongsan-gu, Seoul 140-210; tel. (2) 790-1078; fax (2) 790-1084; e-mail kbnbd_seoul@yahoo.com; Ambassador Dato' Paduka Haji HARUN BIN HJ ISMAIL.

Bulgaria: 723-42, Hannam 2-dong, Yeongsan-gu, Seoul 140-894; tel. (2) 794-8626; fax (2) 794-8627; e-mail ebdy1990@unitel.co.kr; Chargé d'affaires a.i. VALERY ARZHENTINSKI.

Cambodia: 657-162, Hannam-dong, Yeongsan-gu, Seoul 140-910; tel. (2) 3785-1041; fax (2) 3785-1040; e-mail camboemb@korea.com; Ambassador LIM SAMKOL.

Canada: POB 6299, 9/F Kolon Bldg, 45, Mugyo-dong, Jung-gu, Seoul; tel. (2) 3455-6000; fax (2) 3455-6123; e-mail canada@cec.or.kr; internet www.korea.gc.ca; Ambassador MARIUS GRINIUS.

Chile: 1801 Coryo Daeyungak Tower, 25-5 Chungmoro 1-ga, Jung-gu, Seoul 100-706; tel. (2) 779-2610; fax (2) 779-2615; e-mail echilekr@yahoo.co.kr; internet www.echilecor.or.kr; Ambassador ADOLFO CARAFÍ MELERO.

China, People's Republic: 54, Hyoja-dong, Jongno-gu, Seoul; tel. (2) 738-1038; fax (2) 738-1059; e-mail chinaemb_kr@mfa.gov.cn; internet www.chinaemb.or.kr; Ambassador NING FUKUI.

Colombia: Kyobo Bldg, 13th Floor, 1-ga, Jongno, Jongno-gu, Seoul; tel. (2) 720-1369; fax (2) 725-6959; Ambassador JORGE ENRIQUE MORA RANGEL.

Congo, Democratic Republic: 702, Daewoo Complex Bldg, 167 Naesu-dong, Jongno-gu, Seoul; tel. (2) 722-7958; fax (2) 722-7998; e-mail congokoreambassy@yahoo.com; Ambassador N. CHRISTOPHE NGWEY.

Côte d'Ivoire: Chungam Bldg, 2nd Floor, 794-4, Hannam-dong, Yeongsan-gu, Seoul; tel. (2) 3785-0561; fax (2) 3785-0564; e-mail abenikof@hotmail.com; Ambassador HONORAT ABENI KOFFI.

Czech Republic: 1-121, 2-ga, Shinmun-ro, Jongno-gu, Seoul 110-062; tel. (2) 725-6765; fax (2) 734-6452; e-mail seoul@embassy.mzv.cz; internet www.mzv.cz/seoul; Ambassador TOMÁŠ SMETÁNKA.

Denmark: Namsong Bldg, 5th Floor, 260-199, Itaewon-dong, Yeongsan-gu, Seoul 140-200; tel. (2) 795-4187; fax (2) 796-0986; e-mail selamb@um.dk; internet www.ambseoul.um.dk; Ambassador POUL O. G. HOINESS.

Dominican Republic: Taepyeong-no Bldg, 19th Floor, 2-ga, 310 Taepyeong-no, Jung-gu, Seoul; tel. (2) 756-3513; fax (2) 756-3514; e-mail embadom@kornet.net; Ambassador HÉCTOR GALUÁN.

Ecuador: Korea First Bldg, 19th Floor, 100, Gongpyeong-dong, Jongno-gu, Seoul; tel. (2) 739-2401; fax (2) 739-2355; e-mail mecuadorcor1@kornet.net; Chargé d'affaires a.i. Dr GUILLERMO LARA CALDERÓN.

Egypt: POB 3734, 46-1, Hannam-dong, Yeongsan-gu, Seoul 140-210; tel. (2) 749-0787; fax (2) 795-2588; e-mail embassyegyptkorea@yahoo.com; Ambassador MOHAMED REDA KAMEL ET-TAIFY.

El Salvador: Samsung Life Insurance Bldg, 20th Floor, Taepyeong-no 2-ga, Jung-gu, Seoul 100-716; tel. (2) 753-3432; fax (2) 753-3456; e-mail koembsal@hananet.net; Ambassador ALFREDO FRANCISCO UNGO.

Finland: POB 1518, Kyobo Bldg 15/F, Suite 1602, 1-1, 1-ga, Jongno, Jongno-gu, Seoul 110-714; tel. (2) 732-6737; fax (2) 723-4969; e-mail sanomat.seo@formin.fi; Ambassador KIM LUOTONEN.

France: 30, Hap-dong, Seodaemun-gu, Seoul 120-030; tel. (2) 3149-4300; fax (2) 3149-4328; e-mail ambafrance@korea.com; internet www.ambafrance-kr.org; Ambassador PHILIPPE THIÉBAUD.

Gabon: Yoosung Bldg, 4th Floor, 738-20, Hannam-dong, Yeongsan-gu, Seoul; tel. (2) 793-9575; fax (2) 793-9574; e-mail amgabsel@unitel.co.kr; Ambassador EMMANUEL ISSOZE-NGONDET.

Germany: 308-5, Dongbinggo-dong, Yeongsan-gu, Seoul 140-816; tel. (2) 748-4114; fax (2) 748-4161; e-mail dboseoul@kornet.net; internet www.gembassy.or.kr; Ambassador MICHAEL GEIER.

Ghana: 5-4, Hannam-dong, Yeongsan-gu, Seoul (CPOB 3887); tel. (2) 3785-1427; fax (2) 3785-1428; e-mail ghana3@kornet.net; Ambassador EDWARD OBENG KUFUOR.

Greece: Hanwha Bldg, 27th Floor, 1, Janggyo-dong, Jung-gu, Seoul 100-797; tel. (2) 729-1401; fax (2) 729-1402; e-mail greekemb@kornet.net; internet emb-greece.org; Ambassador KONSTANTINOS DRAKAKIS.

Guatemala: 614, Lotte Hotel, 1, Sogong-dong, Jung-gu, Seoul 100-635; tel. (2) 771-7582; fax (2) 771-7584; e-mail embcorea@minex.gob.gt; Ambassador RAFAEL A. SALAZAR.

Holy See: POB 393, Kwang Hwa Moon, Seoul 110-603 (Apostolic Nunciature); tel. (2) 736-5725; fax (2) 739-5738; e-mail nunseoul@kornet.net; Apostolic Nuncio Most Rev. EMIL PAUL TSCHERRIG (Titular Archbishop of Voli).

Honduras: Jongno Tower Bldg, 2nd Floor, 6, Jongno 2-ga, Jongno-gu, Seoul 110-160; tel. (2) 738-8402; fax (2) 738-8403; e-mail hondseul@kornet.net; Ambassador RENE FRANCISCO UMANA CHINCHILLA.

Hungary: 1-103, Dongbinggo-dong, Yeongsan-gu, Seoul 140-230; tel. (2) 792-2105; fax (2) 792-2109; e-mail huembsel@kornet.net; Ambassador Dr ISTVÁN TORZSA.

India: 37-3, Hannam-dong, Yeongsan-gu, CPOB 3466, Seoul 140-210; tel. (2) 798-4257; fax (2) 796-9534; e-mail eoiseoul@sinbiro.com; internet www.indembassy.or.kr; Ambassador N. PARTHASARATHI.

Indonesia: 55, Yeouido-dong, Yeongdeungpo-gu, Seoul 150-010; tel. (2) 783-5675; fax (2) 780-4280; e-mail komsel@soback.kornet.nm.kr; internet www.indonesiaseoul.org; Ambassador JAKOB TOBING.

Iran: 726-126, Hannam-dong, Yeongsan-gu, Seoul; tel. (2) 793-7751; fax (2) 792-7052; e-mail iranssy@chollian.net; internet www.mfa.gov.ir; Ambassador JAHANBAKHSH MOZAFFARI.

Ireland: Daehan Fire and Marine Insurance Bldg, 15th Floor, 51-1, Namchang-dong, Jung-gu, Seoul; tel. (2) 774-6455; fax (2) 774-6458; e-mail irelandkor@kornet.net; internet www.irelandhouse-korea.com/embassy.html; Ambassador CONOR MURPHY.

Israel: 18th Fl., Kabool Bldg, 149 Seorin-dong, Jongro-gu, Seoul 110-726; tel. (2) 739-8666; fax (2) 739-8667; e-mail seoul@israel.org; internet seoul.mfa.gov.il; Ambassador YIGAL B. CASPI.

Italy: 1-398, Hannam-dong, Yeongsan-gu, Seoul 140-210; tel. (2) 796-0491; fax (2) 797-5560; e-mail embassy.seoul@esteri.it; internet www.ambseoul.esteri.it; Ambassador FRANCESCO RAUSI.

Japan: 18-11, Junghak-dong, Jongno-gu, Seoul; tel. (2) 2170-5200; fax (2) 734-4528; e-mail info@japanem.or.kr; internet www.kr.emb-japan.go.jp; Ambassador SHOTARO OSHIMA.

Kazakhstan: 484-24, Bukak Village 11, Pyeongchang-dong, Jongno-gu, Seoul; tel. (2) 379-9714; fax (2) 395-9719; e-mail kazkor@chollian.net; Ambassador DARKHAN ALIEVICH BERDALIEV.

Kuwait: 309-15, Dongbinggo-dong, Yeongsan-gu, Seoul; tel. (2) 749-3688; fax (2) 749-3687; Ambassador ZAID ASH-SHARIDA.

Laos: 657-93, Hannam-dong, Yeongsan-gu, Seoul; tel. (2) 796-1713; fax (2) 796-1771; e-mail laoseoul@korea.com; Ambassador THONGSAVATH PRASEUTH.

Lebanon: 310-49, Dongbinggo-dong, Yongsan-ku, Seoul 140-230; tel. (2) 794-6482; fax (2) 794-6485; e-mail emleb@lebanonembassy.net; internet www.lebanonembassy.net; Ambassador HUSSEIN RAMMAL.

Libya: 4-5, Hannam-dong, Yeongsan-gu, Seoul; tel. (2) 797-6001; fax (2) 797-6007; e-mail libyaemb@kornet.net; Sec. of People's Bureau AHMAD MUHAMMAD AT-TABULI.

Malaysia: 4-1, Hannam-dong, Yeongsan-gu, Seoul 140-884; tel. (2) 795-9203; fax (2) 794-5480; e-mail mwseoul@kornet.net; internet www.malaysia.or.kr; Ambassador Dato' M. SANTHANANABAN.

Mexico: 33-6, Hannam 1-dong, Yeongsan-gu, Seoul 140-885; tel. (2) 798-1694; fax (2) 790-0939; e-mail srecor@uriel.net; internet www.sre.gob.mx/corea; Ambassador LEANDRO ARELLANO.

Mongolia: 33-5, Hannam-dong, Yeongsan-gu, Seoul 140–885; tel. (2) 794-1350; fax (2) 794-7605; e-mail mongol5@kornet.net; internet www.mongolembassy.com; Ambassador PERENLEIN URJINLKHÜNDEV.

Morocco: S-15, UN Village, 270-3, Hannam-dong, Yeongsan-gu, Seoul; tel. (2) 793-6249; fax (2) 792-8178; e-mail sifamase@kornet.net; internet www.moroccoemb.or.kr; Ambassador AHMED BOURZAIM.

Myanmar: 724-1, Hannam-dong, Yeongsan-gu, Seoul 140-210; tel. (2) 792-3341; fax (2) 796-5570; e-mail myanmare@ppp.kornet.net; Ambassador U NYO WIN.

Netherlands: Kyobo Bldg, 14th Floor, 1-ga, Jongno, Jongno-gu, Seoul 110-714; tel. (2) 737-9514; fax (2) 735-1321; e-mail seo@minbuza.nl; internet www.nlembassy.or.kr; Ambassador RADINCK J. VAN VOLLENHOVEN.

New Zealand: Kyobo Bldg, 15th Floor, 1, 1-ga, Jongno, Jongno-gu, KPO Box 2258, Seoul 110-110; tel. (2) 3701-7700; fax (2) 3701-7701; e-mail nzembsel@kornet.net; internet www.nzembassy.com/korea; Ambassador JANE COOMBS.

Nigeria: 310-19, Dongbinggo-dong, Yeongsan-gu, Seoul; tel. (2) 797-2370; fax (2) 796-1848; e-mail chancery@nigerianembassy.or.kr; Ambassador ABBA A. TIJJANI.

Norway: 258-8, Itaewon-dong Yongsan-gu, Seoul 140-200; tel. (2) 795-6850; fax (2) 798-6072; e-mail emb.seoul@mfa.no; internet www.norway.or.kr; Ambassador ARILD BRAASTAD.

Oman: 309-3, Dongbinggo-dong, Yeongsan-gu, Seoul; tel. (2) 790-2431; fax (2) 790-2430; e-mail omanembs@ppp.kornet.nm.kr; Ambassador MOUSSA HAMDAN AT-TAE.

Pakistan: 124-13, Itaewon-dong, Yeongsan-gu, Seoul 140-200; tel. (2) 796-8252; fax (2) 796-0313; e-mail heamb@pakistan-korea-trade.org; internet www.pakistan-korea-trade.org; Ambassador MASOOD KHALID.

Panama: Northgate Bldg, 6th Floor, 66, Jeokseon-dong, Jongno-gu, Seoul; tel. (2) 734-8610; fax (2) 734-8613; e-mail panaemba@kornet.net; Ambassador DANIEL E. ABREGO ECHEVERRÍA.

Papua New Guinea: 36-1, Hannam 1-dong, Yeongsan-gu, Seoul; tel. (2) 798-9854; fax (2) 798-9856; e-mail pngembsl@ppp.kornet.nm.kr; Ambassador KUMA AUA.

Paraguay: SK Bldg, 2nd Floor, 99 Seorin-dong, Jongno-gu, Seoul 110-728; tel. (2) 730-8335; fax (2) 730-8336; e-mail pyemc2@kornet.net; internet www.embaparcorea.org; Ambassador FEDERICO ALBERTO GONZÁLEZ FRANCO.

Peru: Daeyungak Bldg, Suite 2002, 25-5, 1–ga, Jungmu-ro, Jung-gu, Seoul 100-706; tel. (2) 757-1735; fax (2) 757-1738; e-mail lpruseul@uriel.net; internet www.embaperucorea.com; Ambassador JORGE BAYONA.

Philippines: 34-44, Itaewon 1-dong, Yeongsan-gu Seoul; tel. (2) 796-7387; fax (2) 796-0827; e-mail seoulpe@gmail.com; Ambassador SUSAN O. CASTRENCE.

Poland: 70, Sagan-dong, Jongno-gu, Seoul; tel. (2) 723-9681; fax (2) 723-9680; e-mail embassy@polandseoul.org; internet www.polandseoul.org; Ambassador ANDRZEJ DERLATKA.

Portugal: Wonseo Bldg, 2nd Floor, 171, Wonseo-dong, Jongno-gu, Seoul; tel. (2) 3675-2251; fax (2) 3675-2250; e-mail ambport@chollian.net; Ambassador CARLOS MANUEL LEITÃO FROTA.

Qatar: 309-5, Dongbinggo-dong, Yeongsan-gu, Seoul 140-817; tel. (2) 798-2444; fax (2) 790-1027; e-mail qatarseoul@hotmail.com; Ambassador AHMAD S. AL-MIDHADI.

Romania: 1-42, UN Village, Hannam-dong, Yeongsan-gu, Seoul 140-210; tel. (2) 797-4924; fax (2) 794-3114; e-mail romemb@uriel.net; internet www.uriel.net/~romemb; Ambassador VALERIU ARTENI.

Russia: 34-16, Jeong-dong, Jung-gu, Seoul 100-120; tel. (2) 318-2116; fax (2) 754-0417; e-mail rusemb@uriel.net; internet www.russian-embassy.org; Ambassador GLEB A. IVASHENTSOV.

Saudi Arabia: 1-112, 2-ga, Sinmun-no, Jongno-gu, Seoul; tel. (2) 739-0631; fax (2) 732-3110; Ambassador SALEH BIN MANSOUR AL-RAJHY.

Singapore: Seoul Finance Bldg, 28th Floor, 84, 1-ga, Taepyeong-no, Jung-gu, Seoul 100-102; tel. (2) 774-2464; fax (2) 773-2465; e-mail singemb@unitel.co.kr; internet www.mfa.gov.sg/seoul; Ambassador CALVIN EU MUN HOO.

Slovakia: 389-1, Hannam-dong, Yeongsan-gu, Seoul 140-210; tel. (2) 794-3981; fax (2) 794-3982; e-mail slovakemb@yahoo.com; Ambassador PAVEL HRMO.

South Africa: 1-37, Hannam-dong, Yeongsan-gu, Seoul 140-210; tel. (2) 792-4855; fax (2) 792-4856; e-mail general@southafrica-embassy.or.kr; internet www.southafrica-embassy.or.kr; Ambassador STEFANUS JOHANNES SCHOEMAN.

Spain: 726-52, Hannam-dong, Yeongsan-gu, Seoul; tel. (2) 794-3581; fax (2) 796-8207; e-mail embespkr@mail.mae.es; internet www.spainembassy.co.kr; Ambassador DELFÍN COLOMÉ.

Sri Lanka: Kyobo Bldg, Rm 2002, 1-1, 1-ga, Jongno, Jongno-gu, Seoul 110-714; tel. (2) 735-2966; fax (2) 737-9577; e-mail lankaemb@chollian.net; Ambassador G. WIJAYASIRI.

Sudan: 653-24, Hannam-dong, Yeongsan-gu, Seoul; tel. (2) 793-8692; fax (2) 793-8693; e-mail sudansol@yahoo.com; internet www.sudanseoul.net; Ambassador BABIKER ALI KHALIFA.

Sweden: Seoul Central Bldg, 12th Floor, 136, Seorin-dong, Jongno-gu, KPO Box 1154, Seoul 110-611; tel. (2) 738-0846; fax (2) 733-1317; e-mail swedemb@swedemb.or.kr; internet www.swedenabroad.com/seoul; Ambassador LARS VARGÖ.

Switzerland: 32-10, Songwol-dong, Jongno-gu, POB 2900, Seoul 110-101; tel. (2) 739-9511; fax (2) 737-9392; e-mail swissemb@elim.net; internet www.eda.admin.ch/seoul; Ambassador CHRISTIAN HAUSWIRTH.

Thailand: 653-7, Hannam-dong, Yeongsan-gu, Seoul 140-210; tel. (2) 795-3098; fax (2) 798-3448; e-mail rteseoul@kornet.net; internet www.thaiembassy.or.kr; Ambassador VASIN TEERAVECHYAN.

Tunisia: 1-17, Dongbinggo-dong, Yeongsan-gu, Seoul 140-809; tel. (2) 790-4334; fax (2) 790-4333; e-mail ambtnkor@kornet.net; Ambassador MONCEF BAATI.

Turkey: Vivien Corpn Bldg, 4th Floor, 4-52, Seobinggo-dong, Yeongsan-gu, Seoul; tel. (2) 794-0255; fax (2) 797-8546; e-mail tcseulbe@kornet.net; Ambassador SELIM KUNERALP.

Ukraine: 1-97, Dongbinggo-dong, Yeongsan-gu, Seoul; tel. (2) 790-5692; fax (2) 790-5697; e-mail secretary@ukrembrk.com; internet www.ukrembrk.com; Ambassador (vacant).

United Arab Emirates: 5-5, Hannam-dong, Yeongsan-gu, Seoul; tel. (2) 790-3235; fax (2) 790-3238; Ambassador ABDULLAH MUHAMMADD ALI ASH-SHURAFA AL-HAMMADY.

United Kingdom: Taepyeongno 40, 4, Jeong-dong, Jung-gu, Seoul 100-120; tel. (2) 3210-5500; fax (2) 725-1738; e-mail bembassy@uk.or.kr; internet www.britishembassy.or.kr; Ambassador WARWICK MORRIS.

USA: 32, Sejong-no, Jongno-gu, Seoul 110-710; tel. (2) 397-4114; fax (2) 355-3903; e-mail EmbassySeoulPA@state.gov; internet usembassy.state.gov/seoul/; Ambassador ALEXANDER R. VERSHBOW.

Uruguay: Daewoo Bldg, 1802, 541, 5-ga, Namdaemun, Jung-gu, Seoul; tel. (2) 754-0720; fax (2) 777-4129; e-mail uruseul@embrou.or.kr; Ambassador NELSON YEMIL CHABEN.

Uzbekistan: Diplomatic Center, Rm. 701, 1376-1, Seocho 2-dong, Seocho-gu, Seoul; tel. (2) 574-6554; fax (2) 578-0576; Ambassador VITALI V. FEN.

Venezuela: 16th Floor, Korea First Bank Bldg, 100 Gongpyeong-dong, Jongno-gu, 110-702 Seoul; tel. (2) 732-1546; fax (2) 732-1548; e-mail emvesel@soback.kornet.net; internet www.venezuelaemb.or.kr; Ambassador GUILLERMO QUINTERO.

Viet Nam: 28-58, Samcheong-dong, Jongno-gu, Seoul 140-210; tel. (2) 738-2318; fax (2) 739-2064; e-mail vndsq@yahoo.com; Ambassador (vacant).

Yemen: 11-444, Hannam-dong, Yeongsan-gu, Seoul 140-210; tel. (2) 792-9883; fax (2) 792-9885; internet www.gpc.org.ye; Ambassador YAHYA AHMAD AL-WAZIR.

Judicial System

SUPREME COURT

The Supreme Court is the highest court, consisting of 14 Justices, including the Chief Justice. The Chief Justice is appointed by the President, with the consent of the National Assembly, for a term of six years. Other Justices of the Supreme Court are appointed for six years by the President on the recommendation of the Chief Justice. The appointment of the Justices of the Supreme Court, however, requires the consent of the National Assembly. The Chief Justice may not be reappointed. The court is empowered to receive and decide on appeals against decisions of the High Courts, the Patent Court, and the appellate panels of the District Courts or the Family Court in civil, criminal, administrative, patent and domestic relations cases. It is also authorized to act as the final tribunal to review decisions of courts-martial and to consider cases arising from presidential and parliamentary elections.

Chief Justice: KIM YOUNG-RAN, 967, Seocho-dong, Seocho-gu, Seoul; tel. (2) 3480-1002; fax (2) 533-1911; internet www.scourt.go.kr.

THE REPUBLIC OF KOREA (SOUTH KOREA)

Justices: Koh Hyun-Chul, Kim Yong-Dam, Cho Moo-Jeh, Byun Jae-Seung, Yoo Ji-Dam, Yoon Jae-Sik, Lee Yong-Woo, Bae Ki-Won, Kang Shin-Wook, Lee Kyu-Hong, Lee Kang-Kook, Son Ji-Yol, Park Jae-Yoon.

CONSTITUTIONAL COURT

The Constitutional Court is composed of nine adjudicators appointed by the President, of whom three are chosen from among persons selected by the National Assembly and three from persons nominated by the Chief Justice. The Court adjudicates the following matters: constitutionality of a law (when requested by the other courts); impeachment; dissolution of a political party; disputes between state agencies, or between state agencies and local governments; and petitions relating to the Constitution.

President: Yun Young-Chul, 83 Jae-dong, Jongno-gu, Seoul 110-250; tel. (2) 708-3456; fax (2) 708-3566; internet www.ccourt.go.kr.

HIGH COURTS

There are five courts, situated in Seoul, Daegu, Busan, Gwangju and Daejeon, with five chief, 78 presiding and 145 other judges. The courts have appellate jurisdiction in civil and criminal cases and can also pass judgment on administrative litigation against government decisions.

PATENT COURT

The Patent Court opened in Daejeon in March 1998, to deal with cases in which the decisions of the Intellectual Property Tribunal are challenged. The examination of the case is conducted by a judge, with the assistance of technical examiners.

DISTRICT COURTS

District Courts are established in 13 major cities; there are 13 chief, 241 presiding and 966 other judges. They exercise jurisdiction over all civil and criminal cases in the first instance.

MUNICIPAL COURTS

There are 103 Municipal Courts within the District Court system, dealing with small claims, minor criminal offences, and settlement cases.

FAMILY COURT

There is one Family Court, in Seoul, with a chief judge, four presiding judges and 16 other judges. The court has jurisdiction in domestic matters and juvenile delinquency.

ADMINISTRATIVE COURT

An Administrative Court opened in Seoul in March 1998, to deal with cases that are specified in the Administrative Litigation Act. The Court has jurisdiction over cities and counties adjacent to Seoul, and deals with administrative matters, including taxes, expropriations of land, labour and other general administrative matters. District Courts will deal with administrative matters within their districts until the establishment of regional administrative courts is complete.

COURTS-MARTIAL

These exercise jurisdiction over all offences committed by armed forces personnel and civilian employees. They are also authorized to try civilians accused of military espionage or interference with the execution of military duties.

Religion

The traditional religions are Mahayana Buddhism, Confucianism and Chundo Kyo, a religion peculiar to Korea.

BUDDHISM

Korean Mahayana Buddhism has about 80 denominations. The Chogye-jong is the largest Buddhist order in Korea, having been introduced from China in AD 372. The Chogye Order accounts for almost two-thirds of all Korean Buddhists. In 1995 it had 2,426 out of 19,059 Buddhist temples and there were 12,470 monks.

Korean United Buddhist Association (KUBA): 46-19, Soosong-dong, Jongno-gu, Seoul 110-140; tel. (2) 732-4885; 28 mem. Buddhist orders; Pres. Song Wol-Joo.

Won Buddhism

Won Buddhism combines elements of Buddhism and Confucianism. In 1995 there were 404 temples, 9,815 priests, and 86,823 believers.

CHRISTIANITY

National Council of Churches in Korea: Christian Bldg, Rm 706, 136-46, Yeonchi-dong, Jongno-gu, Seoul 110-736; tel. (2) 763-8427; fax (2) 744-6189; e-mail kncc@kncc.or.kr; internet www.kncc.or.kr; f. 1924; est. as National Christian Council; present name adopted 1946; eight mem. churches; Gen. Sec. Rev. Paik Do-Woong.

The Anglican Communion

South Korea has three Anglican dioceses, collectively forming the Anglican Church of Korea (founded as a separate province in April 1993), under its own Primate, the Bishop of Seoul.

Bishop of Pusan (Busan): Rt Rev. Joseph Dae-Yong Lee, 455-2, Oncheon-1-dong, Dongnae-gu, Busan 607-061; tel. (51) 554-5742; fax (51) 553-9643; e-mail bpjoseph@hanmail.net.

Bishop of Seoul: Most Rev. Matthew Chung Chul-Bum, 3, Jeong-dong, Jung-gu, Seoul 100-120; tel. (2) 738-6597; fax (2) 723-2640; e-mail bishop100@hosanna.net.

Bishop of Taejon (Daejeon): Rt Rev. Paul Yoon Hwan, 88-1, Sonhwa 2-dong, POB 22, Daejeon 300-600; tel. (42) 256-9987; fax (42) 255-8918.

The Roman Catholic Church

For ecclesiastical purposes, North and South Korea are nominally under a unified jurisdiction. South Korea comprises three archdioceses, 12 dioceses, and one military ordinate. At 31 December 2003 some 4,363,252 people were adherents of the Roman Catholic Church.

Bishops' Conference

Catholic Bishops' Conference of Korea, 643-1, Junggok-dong, Gwangjin-gu, Seoul 143-912; tel. (2) 460-7500; fax (2) 460-7505; e-mail cbck@cbck.or.kr; internet www.cbck.or.kr; f. 1857; Pres. Most Rev. Andreas Choi Chang-Mou (Archbishop of Gwangju).

Archbishop of Kwangju (Gwangju): Most Rev. Andreas Choi Chang-Mou, Archdiocesan Office, 5-32, Im-dong, Buk-gu, Gwangju 500-868; tel. (62) 510-2838; fax (62) 525-6873; e-mail biseo@kjcatholic.or.kr.

Archbishop of Seoul: Cardinal Nicholas Cheong Jin-Suk, Archdiocesan Office, 1, 2-ga, Myeong-dong, Jung-gu, Seoul 100-022; tel. (2) 727-2114; fax (2) 773-1947; e-mail ao@seoul.catholic.or.kr.

Archbishop of Taegu (Daegu): Most Rev. Paul Ri Moon-Hi, Archdiocesan Office, 225-1, Namsan 3-dong, Jung-gu, Daegu 700-804; tel. (53) 253-7011; fax (53) 253-9441; e-mail taegu@tgcatholic.or.kr.

Protestant Churches

Korean Methodist Church: 64-8, 1-ga, Taepyeong-no, Jung-gu, Seoul 100-101; KPO Box 285, Seoul 110-602; tel. (2) 399-4300; fax (2) 399-4307; e-mail bishop@kmcweb.or.kr; internet www.kmcweb.or.kr; f. 1885; 1,417,213 mems (2003); Bishop Kim Jin Ho.

Presbyterian Church in the Republic of Korea (PROK): Academy House, San 76, Suyu 6-dong, Kangbuk-ku, Seoul 142-070; tel. (2) 3499-7600; fax (2) 3499-7630; e-mail prok3000@chollian.net; internet www.prok.org; f. 1953; 333,891 mems (2003); Gen. Sec. Rev. Yoon Kil-Soo.

Presbyterian Church of Korea (PCK): The Korean Church Centennial Memorial Bldg, 135, Yunji-dong, Jongno-gu, Seoul 110-470; tel. (2) 741-4350; fax (2) 743-7982; e-mail thepck@pck.or.kr; internet www.pck.or.kr; 2,395,323 mems (Dec. 2003); Moderator Rev. Young Rho Ahn; Gen. Sec. Rev. Seongi Cho.

There are some 160 other Protestant denominations in the country, including the Korea Baptist Convention and the Korea Evangelical Church.

CHUNDO KYO

A religion indigenous and unique to Korea, Chundo Kyo combines elements of Shaman, Buddhist, and Christian doctrines. In 1995 there were 274 temples, 5,597 priests, and 28,184 believers.

CONFUCIANISM

In 1995 there were 730 temples, 31,833 priests, and 210,927 believers.

TAEJONG GYO

Taejong Gyo is Korea's oldest religion, dating back 4,000 years, and comprising beliefs in the national foundation myth, and the triune god, Hanul. By the 15th century the religion had largely disappeared, but a revival began in the late 19th century. In 1995 there were 103 temples, 346 priests, and 7,603 believers.

THE REPUBLIC OF KOREA (SOUTH KOREA)

The Press

NATIONAL DAILIES
(In Korean, unless otherwise indicated)

Chosun Ilbo: 61, 1-ga, Taepyeong-no, Jung-gu, Seoul 100-756; tel. (2) 724-5114; fax (2) 724-5059; internet www.chosun.com; f. 1920; morning, weekly and children's edns; independent; Pres. BANG SANG-HOON; Editor-in-Chief KIM DAE-JUNG; circ. 2,470,000.

Daily Sports Seoul: 25, 1-ga, Taepyeong-no, Jung-gu, Seoul; tel. (2) 721-5114; fax (2) 721-5396; internet www.seoul.co.kr; f. 1985; morning; sports and leisure; Pres. LEE HAN-SOO; Man. Editor SON CHU-WHAN.

Dong-A Ilbo: 139-1, 3-ga, Sejong-no, Jongno-gu, Seoul 100-715; tel. (2) 2020-0114; fax (2) 2020-1239; e-mail newsroom@donga.com; internet www.donga.com; f. 1920; morning; independent; Pres. KIM HAK-JOON; Editor-in-Chief LEE HYUN-NAK; circ. 2,150,000.

Han-Joong Daily News: 91-1, 2-ga, Myeong-dong, Jung-gu, Seoul; tel. (2) 776-2801; fax (2) 778-2803; Chinese.

Hankook Ilbo: 14, Junghak-dong, Jongno-gu, Seoul; tel. (2) 724-2114; fax (2) 724-2244; internet www.hankooki.com; f. 1954; morning; independent; Pres. CHANG CHAE-KEUN; Editor-in-Chief YOON KOOK-BYUNG; circ. 2,000,000.

Hankyoreh Shinmun (One Nation): 116-25, Gongdeok-dong, Mapo-gu, Seoul 121-020; tel. (2) 710-0114; fax (2) 710-0210; internet www.hani.co.kr; f. 1988; centre-left; Chair. KIM DOO-SHIK; Editor-in-Chief SUNG HAN-PYO; circ. 500,000.

Ilgan Sports (The Daily Sports): 14, Junghak-dong, Jongno-gu, Seoul 110-792; tel. (2) 724-2114; fax (2) 724-2299; internet www.dailysports.co.kr; morning; f. 1969; Pres. CHANG CHAE-KEUN; Editor KIM JIN-DONG; circ. 600,000.

Jeil Economic Daily: 146 Ssangrin-dong, Jung-gu, Seoul; tel. (2) 6325-3114; e-mail ysk@jed.co.kr; internet www.jed.co.kr; f. 1988; morning; Pres. PARK JUNG-GU; Editor-in-Chief JANG CHANG-YONG.

JoongAng Ilbo (JoongAng Daily News): 7, Soonhwa-dong, Jung-gu, 100-759 Seoul; tel. (2) 751-9215; fax (2) 751-9219; e-mail iht@joongang.co.kr; internet www.joins.com; f. 1965; morning; Man. Dir SHIN JOONG-DON; Exec. Dir CHANG SUNG-HYO; circ. 2,300,000.

Kookmin Ilbo: 12, Yeouido-dong, Yeongdeungpo-gu, Seoul; tel. (2) 781-9114; fax (2) 781-9781; internet www.kukminilbo.co.kr; Pres. CHA IL-SUK.

Korea Daily News: 25, 1-ga, Taepyeong-no, Jung-gu, Seoul; tel. (2) 2000-9000; fax (2) 2000-9659; internet www.kdaily.com; f. 1945; morning; independent; Publr and Pres. SON CHU-HWAN; Man. Editor LEE DONG-HWA; circ. 700,000.

Korea Economic Daily: 441, Junglim-dong, Jung-gu, Seoul 100-791; tel. (2) 360-4114; fax (2) 779-4447; internet www.ked.co.kr; f. 1964; morning; Pres. PARK YONG-JUNG; Man. Dir and Editor-in-Chief CHOI KYU-YOUNG.

The Korea Herald: 1-12, 3-ga, Hoehyeon-dong, Jung-gu, Seoul; tel. (2) 727-0114; fax (2) 727-0670; internet www.koreaherald.co.kr; f. 1953; morning; English; independent; Pres. KIM CHIN-OUK; Man. Editor MIN BYUNG-IL; circ. 150,000.

The Korea Times: 14, Junghak-dong, Jongno-gu, Seoul 110-792; tel. (2) 724-2114; fax (2) 732-4125; e-mail kt@koreatimes.co.kr; internet www.koreatimes.co.kr; f. 1950; morning; English; independent; Pres. YOON KOOK-BYUNG; Man. Ed. LEE SANG-SEOK; circ. 100,000.

Kyung-hyang Shinmun: 22, Jeong-dong, Jung-gu, Seoul; tel. (2) 3701-1114; fax (2) 737-6362; internet www.khan.co.kr; f. 1946; evening; independent; Pres. HONG SUNG-MAN; Editor KIM HI-JUNG; circ. 733,000.

Maeil Business Newspaper: 51-9, 1-ga, Bil-dong, Jung-gu, Seoul 100-728; tel. (2) 2000-2114; fax (2) 2269-6200; internet www.mk.co.kr; f. 1966; evening; economics and business; Pres. CHANG DAE-WHAN; Editor JANG BYUNG-CHANG; circ. 235,000.

Munhwa Ilbo: 68, 1-ga, Chungjeong-no, Jung-gu, Seoul 110-170; tel. (2) 3701-5114; fax (2) 722-8328; internet www.munhwa.co.kr; f. 1991; evening; Pres. NAM SI-UK; Editor-in-Chief KANG SIN-KU.

Naeway Economic Daily: 1-12, 3-ga, Hoehyon-dong, Jung-gu, Seoul 100; tel. (2) 727-0114; fax (2) 727-0661; internet www.naeway.co.kr; f. 1973; morning; Pres. KIM CHIN-OUK; Man. Editor HAN DONG-HEE; circ. 300,000.

Segye Times: 63-1, 3-ga, Hangang-no, Yeongsan-gu, Seoul; tel. (2) 799-4114; fax (2) 799-4520; internet www.segyetimes.co.kr; f. 1989; morning; Pres. HWANG HWAN-CHAI; Editor MOK JUNG-GYUM.

Seoul Kyungje Shinmun: 19, Junghak-dong, Jongno-gu, Seoul 100; tel. (2) 724-2114; fax (2) 732-2140; internet www.sed.co.kr; f. 1960; morning; Pres. KIM YOUNG-LOUL; Man. Editor KIM SEO-WOONG; circ. 500,000.

Sports Chosun: 61, 1-ga, Taepyeong-no, Jung-gu, Seoul; tel. (2) 724-6114; fax (2) 724-6979; internet www.sportschosun.com; f. 1964; Publr BANG SANG-HOON; circ. 400,000.

LOCAL DAILIES

Cheju Daily News: 2324-6, Yeon-dong, Jeju; tel. (64) 740-6114; fax (64) 740-6500; internet www.chejunews.co.kr; f. 1945; evening; Pres. KIM DAE-SUNG; Man. Editor KANG BYUNG-HEE.

Chonbuk Domin Ilbo: 207-10, 2-ga, Deokjin-dong, Deokjin-gu, Jeonju, N Jeolla Prov.; tel. (63) 251-7114; fax (63) 251-7127; internet www.domin.co.kr; f. 1988; morning; Pres. LIM BYOUNG-CHAN; Man. Editor YANG CHAE-SUK.

Chonju Ilbo: 568-132, Sonosong-dong, Deokjin-dong, Jeonju, N. Jeolla Prov.; tel. (63) 285-0114; fax (63) 285-2060; f. 1991; morning; Chair. KANG DAE-SOON; Man. Editor SO CHAE-CHOL.

Chonnam Ilbo: 700-5, Jungheung-dong, Buk-gu, Gwangju, 500-758; tel. (62) 527-0015; fax (62) 510-0436; internet www.chonnamilbo.co.kr; f. 1989; morning; Pres. LIM WON-SIK; Editor-in-Chief KIM YONG-OK.

Chunbuk Ilbo: 710-5, Kumam-dong, Deokjin-dong, Jeonju, N. Jeolla Prov.; tel. (63) 250-5500; fax (63) 250-5550; f. 1950; evening; Pres. SUH JUNG-SANG; Man. Editor LEE KON-WOONG.

Chungchong Daily News: 304, Sachang-dong, Hungduk-gu, Cheongju, N. Chungcheong Prov.; tel. (43) 279-5114; fax (43) 262-2000; internet www.ccnews.co.kr; f. 1946; morning; Pres. SEO JEONG-OK; Editor IM BAIK-SOO.

Halla Ilbo: 568-1, Samdo 1-dong, Jeju; tel. (64) 750-2114; fax (64) 750-2520; internet www.hallailbo.com; f. 1989; evening; Chair. KANG YONG-SOK; Man. Editor HONG SONG-MOK.

Incheon Ilbo: 18-1, 4-ga, Hang-dong, Jung-gu, Incheon; tel. (32) 763-8811; fax (32) 763-7711; internet www.inchonnews.co.kr; f. 1988; evening; Pres. MUN PYONG-HA; Man. Editor LEE JAE-HO.

Jungdo Daily Newspaper: 274-7, Galma-dong, Seo-gu, Daejeon; tel. (42) 530-4114; fax (42) 535-5334; internet www.joongdo.com; f. 1951; morning; Chair. KI-CHANG; Man. Editor SONG HYOUNG-SOP.

Kangwon Ilbo: 53, 1-ga, Jungang-no, Chuncheon, Gangwon Prov.; tel. (33) 252-7228; fax (33) 252-5884; internet www.kwnews.co.kr; f. 1945; evening; Pres. CHO NAM-JIN; Man. Editor KIM KEUN-TAE.

Kookje Daily News: 76-2, Goje-dong, Yeonje-gu, Busan 611-702; tel. (51) 500-5114; fax (51) 500-4274; e-mail jahwang@ms.kookje.co.kr; internet www.kookje.co.kr; f. 1947; morning; Pres. LEE JONG-DEOK; Editor-in-Chief JEONG WON-YOUNG.

Kwangju Ilbo: 1, 1-ga, Geumnam-no, Dong-gu, Gwangju; tel. (62) 222-8111; fax (62) 227-9500; internet www.kwangju.co.kr; f. 1952; evening; Chair. KIM CHONG-TAE; Man. Editor CHO DONG-SU.

Kyeonggi Ilbo: 452-1, Songjuk-dong, Changan-gu, Suwon, Gyeonggi Prov.; tel. (31) 247-3333; fax (31) 247-3349; internet www.kgib.co.kr; f. 1988; evening; Chair. SHIN SON-CHOL; Man. Editor LEE CHIN-YONG.

Kyeongin Ilbo: 1121-11, Ingye-dong, Paldal-gu, Suwon, Gyeonggi Prov.; tel. (31) 231-5114; fax (31) 232-1231; internet www.kyeongin.com; f. 1960; evening; Chair. SUNG BAEK-EUNG; Man. Editor KIM HWA-YANG.

Kyungnam Shinmun: 100-5, Sinwol-dong, Changwon, S. Gyeong-sang Prov.; tel. (55) 283-2211; fax (55) 283-2227; internet www.knnews.co.kr; f. 1946; evening; Pres. KIM DONG-KYU; Editor PARK SUNG-KWAN.

Maeil Shinmun: 71, 2-ga, Gyesan-dong, Jung-gu, Daegu; tel. (53) 255-5001; fax (53) 255-8902; internet www.m2000.co.kr; f. 1946; evening; Chair. KIM BOO-KI; Editor LEE YONG-KEUN; circ. 300,000.

Pusan Daily News: 1-10, Sujeong-dong, Dong-gu, Busan 601-738; tel. (51) 461-4114; fax (51) 463-8880; internet www.pusanilbo.co.kr; f. 1946; Pres. JEONG HAN-SANG; Man. Editor AHN KI-HO; circ. 427,000.

Taegu Ilbo: 81-2, Sincheon 3-dong, Dong-gu, Daegu; tel. (53) 757-4500; fax (53) 751-8086; internet www.tgnews.go.kr; f. 1953; morning; Pres. PARK GWON-HEUM; Editor KIM KYUNG-PAL.

Taejon Ilbo: 1-135, Munhwa 1-dong, Jung-gu, Daejeon; tel. (42) 251-3311; fax (42) 253-3320; internet www.taejontimes.co.kr; f. 1950; evening; Chair. SUH CHOON-WON; Editor KWAK DAE-YEON.

Yeongnam Ilbo: 111, Sincheon-dong, Dong-gu, Daegu; tel. (53) 757-5114; fax (53) 756-9009; internet www.yeongnam.co.kr; f. 1945; morning; Chair. PARK CHANG-HO; Man. Editor KIM SANG-TAE.

SELECTED PERIODICALS

Academy News: 50, Unjung-dong, Bundang-gu, Seongnam, Gyeonggi Prov. 463-791; tel. (31) 709-8111; fax (31) 709-9945; organ of the Acad. of Korean Studies; Pres. HAN SANG-JIN.

Eumak Dong-A: 139, Sejong-no, Jongno-gu, Seoul 110-715; tel. (2) 781-0640; fax (2) 705-4547; f. 1984; monthly; music; Publr KIM BYUNG-KWAN; Editor KWON O-KIE; circ. 85,000.

THE REPUBLIC OF KOREA (SOUTH KOREA)

Han Kuk No Chong (FKTU News): Federation of Korean Trade Unions, FKTU Bldg, 168-24 Chungam-dong, Yongsan-ku, Seoul 140-050; tel. (2) 715-3954; fax (2) 715-7790; e-mail fktuintl@fktu.co.kr; internet www.fktu.or.kr; f. 1961; labour news; circ. 20,000.

Hyundae Munhak: Seoul; tel. (2) 516-3770; fax (2) 516-5433; e-mail webmaster@hdmh.co.kr; internet www.hdmh.co.kr; f. 1955; literature; Publr KIM SUNG-SIK; circ. 200,000.

Korea Business World: Yeouido, POB 720, Seoul 150-607; tel. (2) 532-1364; fax (2) 594-7663; f. 1985; monthly; English; Publr and Pres. LEE KIE-HONG; circ. 40,200.

Korea Buyers Guide: Rm 2301, Korea World Trade Center, 159, Samseong-dong, Gangnam-gu, Seoul; tel. (2) 551-2376; fax (2) 551-2377; e-mail info@buyersguide.co.kr; internet www.buykorea21.com; f. 1973; monthly, consumer goods; quarterly, hardware; Pres. YOU YOUNG-PYO; circ. 30,000.

Korea Journal: Korean National Commission for UNESCO, CPOB 64, Seoul 100-600; tel. (2) 755-6225; fax (2) 755-7478; e-mail kj@unesco.or.kr; internet www.ekoreajournal.net; organ of the UNESCO Korean Commission; Editor-in-Chief YI JEONG-HYEON.

Korea Newsreview: 1-12, 3-ga, Hoehyeon-dong, Jung-gu, Seoul 100-771; tel. (2) 756-7711; weekly; English; Publr and Editor PARK CHUNG-WOONG.

Korea and World Affairs: Rm 1723, Daewoo Center Bldg, 5-541, Namdaemun-no, Jung-gu, Seoul 100-714; tel. (2) 777-2628; fax (2) 319-9591; organ of the Research Center for Peace and Unification of Korea; Pres. CHANG DONG-HOON.

Korean Business Review: FKI Bldg, 28-1, Yeouido-dong, Yeongdeungpo-gu, Seoul 150-756; tel. (2) 3771-0114; fax (2) 3771-0138; monthly; publ. by Fed. of Korean Industries; Publr KIM KAK-CHOONG; Editor SOHN BYUNG-DOO.

Literature and Thought: Seoul; tel. (2) 738-0542; fax (2) 738-2997; f. 1972; monthly; Pres. LIM HONG-BIN; circ. 10,000.

Monthly Travel: Cross Bldg, 2nd Floor, 46-6, 2-ga, Namsan-dong, Jung-gu, Seoul 100-042; tel. (2) 757-6161; fax (2) 757-6089; e-mail kotfa@unitel.co.kr; Pres. SHIN JOONG-MOK; circ. 50,000.

News Maker: 22, Jung-dong, Jung-gu, Seoul 110-702; tel. (2) 3701-1114; fax (2) 739-6190; e-mail hudy@kyunghyang.com; internet www.kyunghyang.com/newsmaker; f. 1992; Pres. JANG JUN-BONG; Editor PARK MYUNG-HUN.

Reader's Digest: 295-15, Deoksan 1-dong, Geumcheon-gu, Seoul 153-011; tel. (2) 866-8800; fax (2) 839-4545; f. 1978; monthly; general; Pres. YANG SUNG-MO; Editor PARK SOON-HWANG; circ. 115,000.

Shin Dong-A (New East Asia): 139, Chungjeong-no, Seodaemun-gu, Seoul 120–715; tel. (2) 361-0974; fax (2) 361-0988; e-mail hans@donga.com; internet shindonga.donga.com; f. 1931; monthly; general; Publr KIM HAK-JUN; Editor LEE HYUNG-SAM; circ. 150,000.

Taekwondo: Sinmun-no Bldg, 5th Floor, 238, Sinmun-no, 1-ga, Jongno-gu, Seoul 110-061; tel. (2) 566-2505; fax (2) 553-4728; e-mail wtf@unitel.co.kr; internet www.wtf.org; f. 1973; organ of the World Taekwondo Fed; Pres. Dr KIM UN-YONG.

Vantage Point: 85-1, Susong-dong, Jongno-gu, Seoul, 110-140; tel. (2) 398-3519; fax (2) 398-3539; e-mail kseungji@yna.co.kr; internet www.yna.co.kr; f. 1978; monthly; developments in North Korea; Editor KWAK SEUNG-JI.

Weekly Chosun: 61, Taepyeong-no 1, Jung-gu, Seoul; tel. (2) 724-5114; fax (2) 724-6199; weekly; Publr BANG SANG-HOON; Editor CHOI JOON-MYONG; circ. 350,000.

The Weekly Hankook: 14, Junghak-dong, Jongno-gu, Seoul; tel. (2) 732-4151; fax (2) 724-2444; f. 1964; Publr CHANG CHAE-KUK; circ. 400,000.

Wolgan Mot: 139, Sejong-no, Jongno-gu, Seoul 110-715; tel. (2) 733-5221; f. 1984; monthly; fashion; Publr KIM SEUNG-YUL; Editor KWON O-KIE; circ. 120,000.

Women's Weekly: 14, Junghak-dong, Jongno-gu, Seoul; tel. (2) 735-9216; fax (2) 732-4125.

Yosong Dong-A (Women's Far East): 139, Sejong-no, Jongno-gu, Seoul 110-715; tel. (2) 721-7621; fax (2) 721-7676; f. 1933; monthly; women's magazine; Publr KIM BYUNG-KWAN; Editor KWON O-KIE; circ. 237,000.

NEWS AGENCIES

Yonhap News Agency: 85-1, Susong-dong, Jongno-gu, Seoul; tel. (2) 398-3114; fax (2) 398-3257; internet www.yonhapnews.co.kr; f. 1980; Pres. KIM KUN.

Foreign Bureaux

Agence France-Presse (AFP): 8/F, Dong-A Ilbo Media Center Bldg 139, Sejongno Jongno-gu 110-715 Seoul; tel. (2) 737-7353; fax (2) 737-6598; e-mail seoul@afp.com; Bureau Chief TIM WITCHER.

Associated Press (AP) (USA): Yonhap News Agency Bldg, 85-1, Susong-dong, Jongno-gu, Seoul; tel. (2) 739-0692; fax (2) 737-0650; Bureau Chief REID MILLER.

Central News Agency (Taiwan): 33-1, 2-ga, Myeong-dong, Jung-gu, Seoul; tel. (2) 753-0195; fax (2) 753-0197; Bureau Chief CHIANG YUAN-CHEN.

Deutsche Presse-Agentur (Germany): 148, Anguk-dong, Jongno-gu, Seoul; tel. (2) 738-3808; fax (2) 738-6040; Correspondent NIKOLAUS PREDE.

Informatsionnoye Telegrafnoye Agentstvo Rossii—Telegrafnoye Agentstvo Suverennykh Stran (ITAR—TASS) (Russia): 1-302, Chonghwa, 22-2, Itaewon-dong, Yeongsan-gu, Seoul; tel. (2) 796-9193; fax (2) 796-9194.

Jiji Tsushin (Jiji Press); Japan: Joong-ang Ilbo Bldg, 7, Soonhwa-dong, Jung-gu, Seoul; tel. (2) 753-4525; fax (2) 753-8067; Chief Correspondent KENJIRO TSUJITA.

Kyodo News Service (Japan): Yonhap News Agency Bldg, 85-1, Susong-dong, Jongno-gu, Seoul; tel. (2) 739-2791; fax (2) 737-1776; Bureau Chief HISASHI HIRAI.

Reuters (UK): Byuck San Bldg, 7th Floor, 12-5, Dongja-dong, Yeongsan-gu, Seoul 140-170; tel. (2) 727-5151; fax (2) 727-5666; Bureau Chief ANDREW BROWNE.

Rossiiskoye Informatsionnoye Agentstvo—Novosti (RIA—Novosti) (Russia): 14, Junghak-dong, Jongno-gu, Seoul; tel. (2) 737-2829; fax (2) 798-0010; internet www.rianovosti.com; Correspondent SERGEI KUDASOV.

United Press International (UPI) (USA): Yonhap News Agency Bldg, Rm 603, 85-1, Susong-dong, Jongno-gu, Seoul; tel. (2) 737-9054; fax (2) 738-8206; Correspondent JASON NEELY.

Xinhua News Agency (People's Republic of China): B-1, Hillside Villa, 726-111, Hannam-dong, Yeongsan-gu, Seoul; tel. (2) 795-8258; fax (2) 796-7459.

PRESS ASSOCIATIONS

Korean Association of Newspapers: Korea Press Center, 13th Floor, 25, 1-ga, Taepyeong-no, Jung-gu, Seoul 100-745; tel. (2) 733-2251; fax (2) 720-3291; e-mail iwelcome@presskorea.or.kr; internet www.presskorea.or.kr; f. 1962; 48 mems; Pres. CHANG DAE-WHAN; Sec.-Gen. PARK SU-MAN.

Korean Newspaper Editors' Association: Korea Press Center, 13th Floor, 25, 1-ga, Taepyeong-no, Jung-gu, Seoul; tel. (2) 732-1726; fax (2) 739-1985; f. 1957; 416 mems; Pres. SEONG BYONG-WUK.

Seoul Foreign Correspondents' Club: Korea Press Center, 18th Floor, 25, 1-ga, Taepyeong-no, Jung-gu, Seoul; tel. (2) 734-3272; fax (2) 734-7712; f. 1956; Pres. PARK HAN-CHUN.

Publishers

Ahn Graphics Ltd: 260-88, Seongbuk 2-dong, Seongbuk-gu, Seoul 136-012; tel. (2) 763-2320; fax (2) 743-3352; e-mail lbr@ag.co.kr; f. 1985; computer graphics; Pres. KIM OK-CHUL.

Bak-Young Publishing Co: 13-31, Pyeong-dong, Jongno-gu, Seoul; tel. (2) 733-6771; fax (2) 736-4818; f. 1952; sociology, philosophy, literature, linguistics, social science; Pres. AHN JONG-MAN.

BIR Publishing Co Ltd: 506, Sinsa-dong, Gangnam-gu, Seoul 135-120; tel. (2) 515-2000; fax (2) 514-3249.

Bobmun Sa Publishing Co: Hanchung Bldg, 4th Floor, 161-7, Yomni-dong, Mapo-gu, Seoul 121-090; tel. (2) 703-6541; fax (2) 703-6594; f. 1954; law, politics, philosophy, history; Pres. BAE HYO-SEON.

Bumwoo Publishing Co: 21-1, Kusu-dong, Mapo-gu, Seoul 121-130; tel. (2) 717-2121; fax (2) 717-0429; f. 1966; philosophy, religion, social science, technology, art, literature, history; Pres. YOON HYUNG-DOO.

Cheong Moon Gak Publishing Co Ltd: 486-9, Kirum 3-dong, Seongbuk-gu, Seoul 136-800; tel. (2) 985-1451; fax (2) 988-1456; e-mail cmgbook@cmgbook.co.kr; internet www.cmgbook.co.kr; f. 1974; science, technology, business; subsidiaries HanSeung Publishers, Lux Media; Pres. KIM HONG-SEOK; Man. Dir HANS KIM.

Design House Publishing Co: Paradise Bldg, 186-210, Jangchung-dong, 2-ga, Jung-gu, Seoul 100-392; tel. (2) 2275-6151; fax (2) 2275-7884; f. 1987; social science, art, literature, languages, children's periodicals; Pres. LEE YOUNG-HEE.

Dong-Hwa Publishing Co: 130-4, 1-ga, Wonhyoro, Yeongsan-gu, Seoul 140-111; tel. (2) 713-5411; fax (2) 701-7041; f. 1968; language, literature, fine arts, history, religion, philosophy; Pres. LIM IN-KYU.

Doosan Co-operation Publishing BG: 18-12, Ulchi-ro, 6-ga, Jeong-gu, Seoul 100-196; tel. (2) 3398-880; fax (2) 3398-2670; f. 1951; general works, school reference, social science, periodicals; Pres. CHOI TAE-KYUNG.

THE REPUBLIC OF KOREA (SOUTH KOREA)

Eulyoo Publishing Co Ltd: 46-1, Susong-dong, Jongno-gu, Seoul 110-603; tel. (2) 733-8151; fax (2) 732-9154; e-mail eulyoo@chollian.net; internet www.eulyoo.co.kr; f. 1945; linguistics, literature, social science, history, philosophy; Pres. CHUNG CHIN-SOOK.

Hainaim Publishing Co Ltd: Minjin Bldg, 5th Floor, 464-41, Seokyo-dong, Mapo-gu, Seoul 121-210; tel. (2) 326-1600; fax (2) 326-1624; e-mail hainaim@chollian.net; internet www.hainaim.com; f. 1983; philosophy, literature, children's; Pres. SONG YOUNG-SUK.

Hakwon Publishing Co Ltd: Seocho Plaza, 4th Floor, 1573-1, Seocho-dong, Seocho-gu, Seoul; tel. (2) 587-2396; fax (2) 584-9306; f. 1945; general, languages, literature, periodicals; Pres. KIM YOUNG-SU.

Hangil Publishing Co: Kangnam Publishing Center, 506 Shinsa-dong, Kangnam-ku, Seoul 135-120; tel. (2) 515-4811; fax (2) 515-4816; f. 1976; social science, history, literature; Pres. KIM EOUN-HO.

Hanul Publishing Company: 3/F Seoul Bldg, 105-90 Gongdeok-dong, Mapo Gu, Seoul 121-801; tel. (2) 336-6183; fax (2) 333-7543; internet www.hanulbooks.co.kr; f. 1980; general, philosophy, university books, periodicals; Pres. KIM CHONG-SU.

Hollym Corporation: 13-13, Gwancheol-dong, Jongno-gu, Seoul 110-111; tel. (2) 735-7551-4; fax (2) 730-5149; e-mail hollym@chollian.net; internet www.hollym.co.kr; f. 1963; academic and general books on Korea in English; Pres. HAM KI-MAN.

Hyang Mun Sa Publishing Co: 645-20, Yeoksam-dong, Gangnam-gu, Seoul 135-081; tel. (2) 538-5672; fax (2) 538-5673; f. 1950; science, agriculture, history, engineering, home economics; Pres. NAH JOONG-RYOL.

Hyonam Publishing Co Ltd: 627-5, Ahyun 3-dong, Mapo-gu, Seoul 121-013; tel. (2) 365-5056; fax (2) 365-5251; e-mail lawhyun@chollian.net; f. 1951; general, children's, literature, periodicals; Pres. CHO KEUN-TAE.

Il Ji Sa Publishing Co: 46-1, Junghak-dong, Jongno-gu, Seoul 110-150; tel. (2) 732-3980; fax (2) 722-2807; f. 1956; literature, social sciences, juvenile, fine arts, philosophy, linguistics, history; Pres. KIM SUNG-JAE.

Ilchokak Publishing Co Ltd: 9, Gongpyeong-dong, Jongno-gu, Seoul 110-160; tel. (2) 733-5430; fax (2) 738-5857; f. 1953; history, literature, sociology, linguistics, medicine, law, engineering; Pres. HAN MAN-NYUN.

Jigyungsa Publishers Ltd: 790-14, Yeoksam-dong, Gangnam-gu, Seoul 135-080; tel. (2) 557-6351; fax (2) 557-6352; e-mail jigyung@uriel.net; internet www.jigyung.co.kr; f. 1979; children's, periodicals; Pres. KIM BYUNG-JOON.

Jihak Publishing Co Ltd: 180-20, Dongkyo-dong, Mapo-gu, Seoul 121-200; tel. (2) 330-5220; fax (2) 325-5835; f. 1965; philosophy, language, literature; Pres. KWON BYONG-IL.

Jipmoondang: 95, Waryon-dong, Jongno-gu, Seoul 110-360; tel. (2) 743-3098; fax (2) 743-3192; philosophy, social science, Korean studies, history, Korean folklore; Pres. LIM KYOUNG-HWAN.

Jisik Sanup Publications Co Ltd: 35-18, Dongui-dong, Jongno-gu, Seoul 110-040; tel. (2) 738-1978; fax (2) 720-7900; f. 1969; religion, social science, art, literature, history, children's; Pres. KIM KYUNG-HEE.

Jung-Ang Publishing Co Ltd: 172-11, Yomni-dong, Mapo-gu, Seoul 121-090; tel. (2) 717-2111; fax (2) 716-1369; f. 1972; study books, children's; Pres. KIM DUCK-KI.

Kemongsa Publishing Co Ltd: 772, Yeoksam-dong, Gangnam-gu, Seoul 135-080; tel. (2) 531-5335; fax (2) 531-5520; f. 1946; picture books, juvenile, encyclopaedias, history, fiction; Pres. RHU SEUNG-HEE.

Ki Moon Dang: 286-20, Haengdang-dong, Seongdong-gu, Seoul 133-070; tel. (2) 2295-6171; fax (2) 2296-8188; f. 1976; engineering, fine arts, dictionaries; Pres. KANG HAE-JAK.

Korea Britannica Corpn: 117, 1-ga, Jungchung-dong, Seoul 100-391; tel. (2) 272-2151; fax (2) 278-9983; f. 1968; encyclopaedias, dictionaries; Pres. JANG HO-SANG, SUJAN ELEN TAPANI.

Korea University Press: 5-1, Anam-dong, 5-ga, Seongbuk-gu, Seoul 136-701; tel. (2) 3290-4231; fax (2) 923-6311; e-mail kupress@korea.ac.uk; internet www.korea.ac.kr/~kupress; f. 1956; philosophy, history, language, literature, Korean studies, education, psychology, social science, natural science, engineering, agriculture, medicine; Pres. EUH YOON-DAE.

Kum Sung Publishing Co: 242-63, Gongdeok-dong, Mapo-gu, Seoul 121-022; tel. (2) 713-9651; fax (2) 718-4362; f. 1965; literature, juvenile, social sciences, history, fine arts; Pres. KIM NAK-JOON.

Kyohak-sa Publishing Co Ltd: 105-67, Gongdeok-dong, Mapo-gu, Seoul 121-020; tel. (2) 717-4561; fax (2) 718-3976; f. 1952; dictionaries, educational, children's; Pres. YANG CHEOL-WOO.

Kyung Hee University Press: 1, Hoeki-dong, Dongdaemun-gu, Seoul 130-701; tel. (2) 961-0106; fax (2) 962-8840; f. 1960; general, social science, technology, language, literature; Pres. CHOE YOUNG-SEEK.

Kyungnam University Press: 28-42, Samchung-dong, Jongno-gu, Seoul 110-230; tel. (2) 370-0700; fax (2) 735-4359; Pres. PARK JAE-KYU.

Minumsa Publishing Co Ltd: 5/F Kangnam Publishing Culture Centre, 506, Sinsa-dong, Gangnam-gu, Seoul 135-120; tel. (2) 515-2000; fax (2) 515-2007; e-mail michellenam@minumsa.com; f. 1966; literature, philosophy, linguistics, pure science; Pres. PARK MAENG-HO.

Munhakdongne Publishing Co Ltd: 6/F Dongsomun B/D 260, Dongsomundong 4-ga, Seongbuk-gu, Seoul 136-034; tel. (2) 927-6790; fax (2) 927-6793; e-mail etepluie@hotmail.com; internet www.munhak.com; f. 1993; art, literature, science, philosophy, non-fiction, children's, periodicals; Pres. KANG BYUNG-SUN.

Panmun Book Co Ltd: 923-11, Mok 1-dong, Yangcheon-gu, Seoul 158-051; tel. (2) 653-5131; fax (2) 653-2454; e-mail skliu@panmun.co.kr; internet www.medicalplus.co.kr; f. 1955; social science, pure science, technology, medicine, linguistics; Pres. LIU SUNG-KWON.

Sakyejul Publishing Ltd: 1-181, Sinmun-no-2-ga, Jongno-gu, Seoul 110-062; tel. (2) 736-9380; fax (2) 737-8595; e-mail sakyejul@soback.kornet.nm.kr; f. 1982; social sciences, art, literature, history, children's; Pres. KANG MAR-XILL.

Sam Joong Dang Publishing Co: 261-23, Soke-dong, Yeongsan-gu, Seoul 140-140; tel. (2) 704-6816; fax (2) 704-6819; f. 1931; literature, history, philosophy, social sciences, dictionaries; Pres. LEE MIN-CHUL.

Sam Seong Dang Publishing Co: 101-14, Non Hyun-dong, Gangnam-gu, Seoul 135-010; tel. (2) 3442-6767; fax (2) 3442-6768; e-mail kyk@ssdp.co.kr; f. 1968; literature, fine arts, history, philosophy; Pres. KANG MYUNG-CHAE.

Sam Seong Publishing Co Ltd: 1516-2, Seocho-dong, Seocho-gu, Seoul 137-070; tel. (2) 3470-6900; fax (2) 597-1507; internet www.howpc.com; f. 1951; literature, history, juvenile, philosophy, arts, religion, science, encyclopaedias; Pres. KIM JIN-YONG.

Samsung Publishing Co Ltd: Seocho-dong, Seocho-gu, Seoul 137-871; tel. (2) 3470-6900; fax (2) 521-8534; e-mail lisababy@ssbooks.com; internet www.ssbooks.com; www.samsungbooks.com; children's books, comics, cooking, parenting, health, travel; f. 1951; Chief Editor BOSUNG KONG.

Segyesa Publishing Co Ltd: Dasan Bldg 102, 494-85, Yeongkan-dong, Mapo-gu, Seoul 121-070; tel. (2) 715-1542; fax (2) 715-1544; f. 1988; general, philosophy, literature, periodicals; Pres. CHOI SUN-HO.

Se-Kwang Music Publishing Co: 232-32, Seogye-dong, Yeongsan-gu, Seoul 140-140; tel. (2) 719-2652; fax (2) 719-2656; f. 1953; music, art; Pres. PARK SEI-WON; Chair. PARK SHIN-JOON.

Seong An Dang Publishing Co: 4579, Singil-6-dong, Yeongdeungpo-gu, Seoul 150-056; tel. (2) 3142-4151; fax (2) 323-5324; f. 1972; technology, text books, university books, periodicals; Pres. LEE JONG-CHOON.

Seoul National University Press: 56-1, Sinrim-dong, Gwanak-gu, Seoul 151-742; tel. (2) 889-0434; fax (2) 888-4148; e-mail snubook@chollian.net; f. 1961; philosophy, engineering, social science, art, literature; Pres. LEE KI-JUN.

Si-sa-young-o-sa, Inc: 55-1, 2-ga, Jongno, Jongno-gu, Seoul 110-122; tel. (2) 274-0509; fax (2) 271-3980; internet www.ybmsisa.co.kr; f. 1959; language, literature; Pres. CHUNG YOUNG-SAM.

Sogang University Press: 1, Sinsu-dong, Mapo-gu, Seoul 121-742; tel. (2) 705-8212; fax (2) 705-8612; f. 1978; philosophy, religion, science, art, history; Pres. LEE HAN-TAEK.

Sookmyung Women's University Press: 53-12, 2-ga, Jongpa-dong, Yeongsan-gu, Seoul 140-742; tel. (2) 710-9162; fax (2) 710-9090; f. 1968; general; Pres. LEE KYUNG-SOOK.

Tam Gu Dang Publishing Co: 158, 1-ga, Hanggangno, Yeongsan-gu, Seoul 140-011; tel. (2) 3785-2271; fax (2) 3785-2272; f. 1950; linguistics, literature, social sciences, history, fine arts; Pres. HONG SUK-WOO.

Tong Moon Gwan: 147, Gwanhoon-dong, Jongno-gu, Seoul 110-300; tel. (2) 732-4355; f. 1954; literature, art, philosophy, religion, history; Pres. LEE KYUM-NO.

Woongjin.com Co. Ltd: Woongjin Bldg, 112-2, Inui-dong, Jongno-gu, Seoul 110-340; tel. (2) 3670-1832; fax (2) 766-2722; e-mail lois.kim@email.woongjin.com; internet www.woongjin.com; children's; Pres. YOON SUCK-KEUM.

Yearimdang Publishing Co Ltd: Yearim Bldg, 153-3, Samseong-dong, Gangnam-gu, Seoul 135-090; tel. (2) 566-1004; fax (2) 567-9610; e-mail yearim@yearim.co.kr; internet www.yearim.co.kr; f. 1973; children's; Pres. NA CHOON-HO.

Yonsei University Press: 134, Sincheon-dong, Seodaemun-gu, Seoul 120-749; tel. (2) 361-3380; fax (2) 393-1421; e-mail ysup@

THE REPUBLIC OF KOREA (SOUTH KOREA)

yonsei.ac.kr; f. 1955; philosophy, religion, literature, history, art, social science, pure science; Pres. Kim Byung-Soo.

Youl Hwa Dang: Paju Bookcity, 520-10, Munbal-Li, Gyoha-Eup, Paju-Si, Gyeonggi-Do 413-832; tel. (31) 955-7000; fax (31) 955-7010; e-mail yhdp@youlhwadang.co.kr; internet www.youlhwadang.co.kr; f. 1971; art; Pres. Yi Ki-Ung.

PUBLISHERS' ASSOCIATION

Korean Publishers' Association: 105-2, Sagan-dong, Jongno-gu, Seoul 110-190; tel. (2) 735-2702; fax (2) 738-5414; e-mail kpa@kpa21.or.kr; internet www.kpa21.or.kr; f. 1947; Pres. Park Maeng-Ho; Sec.-Gen. Ko Hung-Sik.

Broadcasting and Communications

TELECOMMUNICATIONS

Dacom Corpn: Dacom Bldg, 706-1, Yeoksam-dong, Gangnam-gu, Seoul 135-610; tel. (2) 6220-0220; fax (2) 6220-0702; internet www.dacom.net; f. 1982; domestic and international long-distance telecommunications services and broadband internet services; CEO Park Un-Suh.

Daewoo Telecom Co Ltd: 14-34, Yeouido-dong, Yeongdeungpo-gu, Seoul; tel. (2) 3779-7114; fax (2) 3779-7500; internet www.dwt.co.kr; Pres. (vacant).

Hanaro Telecom: Kukje Electronics Center Bldg, 24th Floor, 1445-3, Seocho-dong, Seocho-gu, Seoul 137-728; tel. (2) 6266-4114; fax (2) 6266-4379; internet www.hanaro.com; local telecommunications and broadband internet services; Pres. and CEO Yoon Chang-Bun.

Korea Mobile Telecommunications Corpn: 267, 5-ga, Namdaemun-no, Jung-gu, Seoul; tel. (2) 3709-1114; fax (2) 3709-0499; f. 1984; Pres. Seo Jung-Uk.

Korea Telecom: 206 Jungja-dong, Bundang-gu, Seongnam-si, Gyeonggi Prov. 463-711; tel. (2) 727-0114; fax (2) 750-3994; internet www.kt.co.kr; domestic and international telecommunications services and broadband internet services; privatized in June 2002; Pres. Lee Yong-Kyung.

Korea Telecom (KT) Freetel: Seoul; internet www.ktf.co.kr; subsidiary of Korea Telecom; 10m. subscribers (2002); CEO Joong Soo-Nam.

LG Telecom: LG Gangnam Tower, 19th Floor, 679 Yeoksam-dong, Gangnam-gu, Seoul 135-985; tel. (2) 2005-7114; fax (2) 2005-7505; e-mail englishweb@lgtel.co.kr; internet www.lgtelecom.com; subsidiary of LG Corpn; mobile telecommunications and wireless internet services; commenced commercial CDMA2000 1x service in May 2001; 4m. subscribers (2002); CEO Nam Yong.

Onse Telecom: 192-2, Gumi-dong, Bundang-gu, Seongnam-si, Gyeonggi Prov. 463-500; tel. and fax (31) 738-6000; internet www.onse.net; domestic and international telecommunications services; Pres. and CEO Hwang Kee-Yeon.

SK Telecom Co Ltd: 99, Seorin-dong, Jongno-gu, Seoul 110-110; tel. (2) 2121-2114; fax (2) 2121-3999; internet www.sktelecom.com; cellular mobile telecommunications and wireless internet services; merged with Shinsegi Telecom in Jan. 2002; 16m. subscribers (2002); Pres. and CEO Shin Bae-Kim.

BROADCASTING

Regulatory Authority

Korean Broadcasting Commission: KBS Bldg, 923-5, Mok-dong, Yangcheon-gu, Seoul 158-715; tel. (2) 3219-5117; fax (2) 3219-5371; Chair. Kang Dae-In.

Radio

Korean Broadcasting System (KBS): 18, Yeouido-dong, Yeongdeungpo-gu, Seoul 150-010; tel. (2) 781-1000; fax (2) 781-4179; internet www.kbs.co.kr; f. 1926; publicly-owned corpn with 26 local broadcasting and 855 relay stations; overseas service in Korean, English, German, Indonesian, Chinese, Japanese, French, Spanish, Russian and Arabic; Pres. Jung Yun-Joo.

Buddhist Broadcasting System (BBS): 140, Mapo-dong, Mapo-gu, Seoul 121-050; tel. (2) 705-5114; fax (2) 705-5229; internet www.bbsfm.ko.kr; f. 1990; Pres. Cho Hae-Hyong.

Christian Broadcasting System (CBS): 917-1, Mok-dong, Yangcheon-gu, Seoul 158-701; tel. (2) 650-7000; fax (2) 654-2456; e-mail changsoo@cbs.co.kr; internet www.cbs.co.kr; f. 1954; independent religious network with 14 network stations, incl. Seoul, Daegu, Busan and Gwangju; also satellite, cable and digital media broadcasting; programmes in Korean; Pres. Lee Jeong-Sik.

Educational Broadcasting System (EBS): 92-6, Umyeon-dong, Seocho-gu, Seoul 137-791; tel. (2) 526-2000; fax (2) 526-2179; internet www.ebs.co.kr; f. 1990; Pres. Dr Park Heung-Soo.

Far East Broadcasting Co (FEBC): 89, Sangsu-dong, Mapo-gu, Seoul 121-707; tel. (2) 320-0114; fax (2) 320-0129; e-mail febcadm@febc.net; internet www.febc.net; Dir Dr Billy Kim.

Radio Station HLAZ: MPO Box 88, Seoul 121-707; tel. (2) 320-0114; fax (2) 320-0129; e-mail febcadm@febc.net; internet www.febc.net; f. 1973; religious, educational service operated by Far East Broadcasting Co; programmes in Korean, Chinese, Russian and Japanese; Dir Dr Billy Kim.

Radio Station HLKX: MPO Box 88, Seoul 121-707; tel. (2) 320-0114; fax (2) 320-0129; e-mail febcadm@febc.net; internet www.febc.net; f. 1956; religious, educational service operated by Far East Broadcasting Co; programmes in Korean, Chinese and English; Pres. Dr Billy Kim.

Munhwa Broadcasting Corpn (MBC): 31, Yeouido-dong, Yeongdeungpo-gu, Seoul 150-728; tel. (2) 784-2000; fax (2) 784-0880; e-mail mbcir@imbc.com; internet www.imbc.com; f. 1961; public; Pres. Kim Joong-Bae.

Pyong Hwa Broadcasting Corpn (PBC): 2-3, 1-ga, Jeo-dong, Jung-gu, Seoul 100-031; tel. (2) 270-2114; fax (2) 270-2210; internet www.pbc.co.kr; f. 1990; religious and educational programmes; Pres. Rev. Park Shin-Eon.

Seoul Broadcasting System (SBS): 10-2, Yeouido-dong, Yeongdeungpo-gu, Seoul 150-010; tel. (2) 786-0792; fax (2) 780-2530; internet www.sbs.co.kr; f. 1991; Pres. Song Do-Kyun.

US Forces Network Korea (AFN Korea): Seoul; tel. (2) 7914-6495; fax (2) 7914-5870; e-mail info@afnkorea.com; internet afnkorea.com; f. 1950; six originating stations and 19 relay stations; 24 hours a day.

Television

In late 1997 almost 40 domestic television channels were in operation.

Educational Broadcasting System (EBS): see Radio.

Inchon Television Ltd (ITV): 587-46, Hakik-dong, Nam-gu, Incheon; tel. (32) 830-1000; fax (32) 865-6300; internet www.itv.co.kr; f. 1997.

Jeonju Television Corpn (JTV): 656-3, Sonosong-dong, Deokjin-gu, Jeonju, N. Jeolla Prov.; tel. (63) 250-5231; fax (63) 250-5249; e-mail jtv@jtv.co.kr; f. 1997.

Korean Broadcasting System (KBS): 18, Yeouido-dong, Yeongdeungpo-gu, Seoul 150-790; tel. (2) 781-1000; fax (2) 781-4179; f. 1961; publicly-owned corpn with 25 local broadcasting and 770 relay stations; Pres. Jung Yun-Joo.

Munhwa Broadcasting Corpn (MBC-R/TV): 31, Yeouido-dong, Yeongdeungpo-gu, Seoul 150-728; tel. (2) 789-2851; fax (2) 782-3094; e-mail song@mbc.co.kr; internet www.imbc.com; f. 1961; public; 19 TV networks; Pres. Lee Keung-Hee.

Seoul Broadcasting System (SBS): see Radio.

US Forces Network Korea (AFN Korea): Seoul; tel. (2) 7914-2711; fax (2) 7914-5870; f. 1950; main transmitting station in Seoul; 19 rebroadcast transmitters and translators; 168 hours weekly.

Finance

(cap. = capital; res = reserves; dep. = deposits; m. = million; brs = branches; amounts in won, unless otherwise indicated)

BANKING

The modern financial system in South Korea was established in 1950 with the foundation of the central bank, the Bank of Korea. Under financial liberalization legislation, adopted in the late 1980s, banks were accorded greater freedom to engage in securities or insurance operations. In 2003 there were 59 commercial banks in South Korea, comprising eight nation-wide banks, six regional commercial banks, five specialized banks and 40 branches of foreign banks. The Financial Supervisory Service oversees the operations of commercial banks and the financial services sector.

Specialized banks were created in the 1960s to provide funds for sectors of the economy not covered by commercial banks. There are also two development banks: the Korea Development Bank and the Export-Import Bank of Korea.

In late 1997 many merchant banks were forced to cease operations, after incurring heavy losses through corporate bankruptcies. In June 1998 five commercial banks were also required to cease operations.

THE REPUBLIC OF KOREA (SOUTH KOREA)

Regulatory Authority

Financial Supervisory Service: 27, Yeouido-dong, Yeongdeungpo-gu, Seoul 150-743; tel. (2) 3771-5000; fax (2) 785-3475; internet www.fss.or.kr; Gov. YOON JEUNG-HYUN.

Central Bank

Bank of Korea: 110, 3-ga, Namdaemun-no, Jung-gu, Seoul 100-794; tel. (2) 759-4114; fax (2) 759-4139; e-mail bokdiri@bok.or.kr; internet www.bok.or.kr; f. 1950; bank of issue; res 5,750,100m., dep. 172,742,500m. (Dec. 2003); Gov. PARK SEUNG; Dep. Gov. LEE SEONG-TAE; 16 domestic brs, 7 overseas offices.

Commercial Banks

Chohung Bank: 14, 1-ga, Namdaemun-no, Jung-gu, Seoul 100-757; tel. (2) 733-2000; fax (2) 723-6473; internet www.chb.co.kr; f. 1897; merged with Chungbuk Bank in May 1999 and Kangwon Bank in Sept. 1999; 80.4% owned by Shinhan Financial Group; cap. 3,395,592m., dep. 45,125,839m. (Dec. 2002); Chair. SUNG BOK-WEE; Dir HONG CHIL-SUN; 446 domestic brs, 11 overseas brs.

Hana Bank: 101-1, 1-ga, Ulchi-no, Jung-gu, Seoul 100-191; tel. (2) 2002-1111; fax (2) 775-7472; e-mail webmaster@hanabank.com; internet www.hanabank.co.kr; f. 1991; merged with Boram Bank in Jan. 1999; merged with Seoulbank in Dec. 2002; cap. 987,161m., res 884,253m., dep. 65,520,324m. (Dec. 2003); Chair. and CEO KIM SEUNG-YU; 303 brs.

Kookmin Bank: 9-1, 2-ga, Namdaemun-no, Jung-gu, CPOB 815, Seoul 100-703; tel. (2) 317-2891; fax (2) 317-2885; e-mail corres@kookminbank.com; internet www.kookminbank.com; f. 1963; est. as Citizen's National Bank, renamed 1995; re-est. Jan. 1999, following merger with Korea Long Term Credit Bank; merged with H & CB in Nov. 2001; cap. 1,641,293m., res 6,251,573m., dep. 150,341.3m. (Dec. 2002); Chair. KIM SANG-HOON; Pres. and CEO KANG CHUNG-WON; 1,122 domestic brs, 6 overseas brs.

KorAm Bank: 39, Da-dong, Jung-gu, Seoul 100-180; tel. (2) 3455-2114; fax (2) 3455-2966; e-mail shk@goodbank.com; internet www.goodbank.com; f. 1983; acquired by Citigroup in 2004; cap. 1,054,334m., res 218,969m., dep. 29,501,138m. (Dec. 2003); CEO and Chair. HA YUNG-KU; 227 domestic brs, 4 overseas brs.

Korea Exchange Bank: 181, 2-ga, Ulchi-no, Jung-gu, Seoul 100-793; tel. (2) 729-0114; fax (2) 775-2565; internet www.keb.co.kr; f. 1967; merged with Korea International Merchant Bank in Jan. 1999; cap. 3,194,625m., res 100,674m., dep. 46,580,294m. (Dec. 2003); Pres. and CEO RICHARD F. WACKER; 269 domestic brs.

Korea First Bank: 100, Gongpyeong-dong, Jongno-gu, Seoul 110702; tel. (2) 3702-3114; fax (2) 3702-4934; e-mail master@kfb.co.kr; internet www.kfb.co.kr; f. 1929; acquired by Standard Chartered Bank in Jan. 2005; cap. 1,046,724m., res 87,645m., dep. 32,891,871m. (Dec. 2003); Pres. and CEO ROBERT COHEN; 389 domestic brs, 2 overseas brs.

Shinhan Bank: 120, 2-ga, Taepyeong-no, Jung-gu, Seoul 100-102; tel. (2) 756-0505; fax (2) 774-7013; e-mail corres@shinhan.com; internet www.shinhan.com; f. 1982; cap. 1,027,305m., res 858,703,694m., dep. 42,893,694m. (Dec. 2003); Pres. and CEO SHIN SANG-HOON; 356 domestic brs, 9 overseas brs.

Woori Bank: 203, 1-ga, Hoehyeon-dong, Jung-gu, Seoul; tel. (2) 2002-3000; fax (2) 2002-5687; internet www.wooribank.com; f. 2002; est. by merger of Hanvit Bank and Peace Bank of Korea; 78% government-owned; privatization expected by 2008; cap. 2,852,838m., res 1,852,235m., dep. 78,591,156m. (Dec. 2003); Pres. LEE DUK-HOON; 668 domestic brs.

Development Banks

Export-Import Bank of Korea: 16-1, Yeouido-dong, Yeongdeungpo-gu, Seoul 150-873; tel. (2) 3779-6114; fax (2) 3779-6732; e-mail kexim@koreaexim.go.kr; internet www.koreaexim.go.kr; f. 1976; cap. 2,725,755m., res 412,779m. (Dec. 2003); Chair. and Pres. SHIN DONG-KYU; 8 brs.

Korea Development Bank: 16-3, Yeouido-dong, Yeongdeungpo-gu, Seoul 150-973; tel. (2) 787-4000; fax (2) 787-6191; internet www.kdb.co.kr; f. 1954; cap. 8,241,861m., dep. 9,398,415m. (Sept. 2004); Gov. YOO JI-CHANG; 36 domestic brs, 5 overseas brs.

Specialized Banks

Industrial Bank of Korea: 50, 2-ga, Ulchi-no, Jung-gu, Seoul 100-758; tel. (2) 729-6114; fax (2) 729-6402; e-mail ifd@ibk.co.kr; internet www.ibk.co.kr; f. 1961; est. as the Small and Medium Industry Bank; 85.5% govt-owned; cap. 2,291,385m., res 1,180,939m., dep. 46,753,446m. (Dec. 2003); Chair. and Pres. KIM JONG-CHANG; 387 domestic brs, 6 overseas brs.

Korean-French Banking Corpn (SogeKo): 5/F Seoul Financial Center, 84 Taepyeongno 1-ga, Jung-gu, Seoul 100-768; tel. (2) 777-7711; fax (2) 318-7060; internet www.sogeko.com; f. 1977; cap. 26,000m., res 99,926m., dep. 70,380m. (March 2004); Pres. and CEO KI BUM KIM.

National Agricultural Co-operative Federation (NACF): 75, 1-ga, Chungjeong-no, Jung-gu, Seoul 100-707; tel. (2) 397-5114; fax (2) 397-5140; e-mail nacfico@nuri.net; internet www.nonghyup.com; f. 1961; merged with National Livestock Co-operatives Federation in July 2000; cap. 2,564,400m., res 1,395,800m., dep. 64,063,500m. (2002); Chair. and Pres. CHUNG DAE-KUN; 2,025 brs and member co-operatives.

National Federation of Fisheries Co-operatives: 11-6, Sincheon-dong, Songpa-gu, Seoul 138-730; tel. (2) 2240-2114; fax (2) 2240-3049; internet www.suhyup.co.kr; f. 1962; cap. 1,158,100m., res 301,900m., dep. 4,371,000m. (2002); Chair. and Pres. CHANG BYUNG-KOO; 120 brs.

Provincial Banks

Cheju Bank: 1349, Ido-1-dong, Jeju 690-021, Jeju Prov.; tel. (64) 734-1711; fax (64) 720-0183; internet www.chejubank.co.kr; f. 1969; cap. 55,500m., res. 30,700m., dep. 1,044,100m. (2002); merged with Central Banking Co in 2000; Chair. and Pres. KANG JOON-HONG; 29 brs.

Daegu Bank Ltd: 118, 2-ga, Susong-dong, Susong-gu, Daegu 706-712; tel. (53) 756-2001; fax (53) 740-6902; internet www.daegubank.co.kr; f. 1967; cap. 660,625m., res 7,262m., dep. 12,933,704m. (Dec. 2003); Chair. and Pres. KIM KUK-NYON; 183 brs.

Jeonbuk Bank Ltd: 669-2, Geumam-dong, Deokjin-gu, Jeonju 561-711, N Jeolla Prov.; tel. (63) 250-7114; fax (63) 250-7078; internet www.jbbank.co.kr; f. 1969; cap. 165,300m., res 30,200m., dep. 2,784,100m. (2002); Chair. and Pres. HONG SUNG-JOO; 68 brs.

Kwangju Bank Ltd: 7-12, Daein-dong, Dong-gu, Gwangju 501-719; tel. (62) 239-5000; fax (62) 239-5199; e-mail kbjint1@nuri.net; internet www.kjbank.com; f. 1968; cap. 170,403m., res 598m., dep. 6,277,745m. (Dec. 2002); Chair. and Pres. UM JONG-DAE; 135 brs.

Kyongnam Bank: 246-1, Sokjeon-dong, Hoewon-gu, Masan 630-010, Gyeongsang Prov.; tel. (551) 290-8000; fax (551) 294-9426; internet www.knbank.co.kr; f. 1970; est. as Gyeongnam Bank Ltd, name changed 1987; cap. 259,000m., res 22,851m., dep. 7,847,571m. (Dec. 2002); Chair. and Pres. KANG SHIN-CHUL; 110 brs.

Foreign Banks

ABN-AMRO Bank NV (Netherlands): Seoul City Tower Bldg, 11–12th Floors, 581, 5-ga, Namdaemun-no, Jung-gu, Seoul; tel. (2) 2131-6000; fax (2) 399-6554; f. 1979; Gen. Man. CHUNG DUCK-MO.

American Express Bank Ltd (USA): Gwanghwamun Bldg, 15th Floor, 64-8, 1-ga, Taepyeong-no, Jung-gu, CPOB 1390, Seoul 100-101; tel. (2) 399-2929; fax (2) 399-2966; f. 1977; Gen. Man. CHOE JAE-ICK.

Arab Bank PLC (Jordan): Daewoo Center Bldg, 22nd Floor, 541, 5-ga, Namdaemun-no, Jung-gu, CPOB 1331, Seoul 100-714; tel. (2) 317-9000; fax (2) 757-0124; Gen. Man. JO SEUNG-SHIK.

Australia and New Zealand Banking Group Ltd (Australia): Kyobo Bldg, 18th Floor, 1, 1-ga, Jongno, Jongno-gu, CPOB 1065, Seoul 110-714; tel. (2) 730-3151; fax (2) 737-6325; f. 1987; Gen. Man. PHIL MICHELL.

Bank Mellat (Iran): Bon Sol Bldg, 14th Floor, 144-27, Samseong-dong, Gangnam-gu, Seoul; tel. (2) 558-4448; fax (2) 557-4448; e-mail info@bankmellat.co.kr; internet www.bankmellat.co.kr; f. 2001; Gen. Man. ALI AFZALI.

Bank of America (USA): Hanwha Bldg, 9th Floor, 1, Janggyo-dong, Jung-gu, Seoul 100-797; tel. (2) 729-4500; fax (2) 729-4400; Gen. Man. BANG CHOON-HO.

Bank of Hawaii (USA): Daeyonkak Bldg, 14th Floor, 25-5, 1-ga, Jungmu-no, Jung-gu, Seoul 100-011; tel. (2) 757-0831; fax (2) 757-3516; Man. PARK YONG-SOO.

Bank of Nova Scotia (Canada): KCCI Bldg, 9th Floor, 45, 4-ga, Namdaemun-no, Jung-gu, Seoul 100-094; tel. (2) 757-7171; fax (2) 752-7189; e-mail bns.seoul@scotiabank.com; Gen. Man. HENRY YONG.

Bank of Tokyo-Mitsubishi UFJ Ltd (Japan): Young Poong Bldg, 4th Floor, 33, Seorin-dong, Jongno-gu, Seoul; tel. (2) 399-6474; fax (2) 735-4897; f. 1967; Gen. Man. KAZUMASA KOGA.

Bankers Trust Co (USA): Center Bldg, 10th Floor, 111-5, Sokong-dong, Jung-gu, Seoul; tel. (2) 3788-6000; fax (2) 756-2648; f. 1978; Man. Dir LEE KEUN-SAM.

BNP Paribas (France): Taepyeongno Bldg, 23/24F, 310, Taepyeongno 2-ga, Jung-gu, Seoul 100-767; tel. (2) 317-1700; fax (2) 757-2530; e-mail philippe.reynieix@asia.bnpparibas.com; internet www.bnpparibas.co.kr; f. 1976; Gen. Man. PHILIPPE REYNIEIX.

Citibank NA (USA): Citicorp Center Bldg, 89-29, 2-ga, Sinmun-no, Jongno-gu, CPOB 749, Seoul 110-062; tel. (2) 2004-1114; fax (2) 722-3644; f. 1967; Gen. Man. SAJJAD RAZVI.

THE REPUBLIC OF KOREA (SOUTH KOREA)

Crédit Agricole Indosuez (France): Kyobo Bldg, 19th Floor, 1, 1-ga, Jongno, Jongno-gu, CPOB 158, Seoul 110-714; tel. (2) 3700-9500; fax (2) 738-0325; f. 1974; Gen. Man. Patrice Couvegnes.

Crédit Lyonnais SA (France): You One Bldg, 8th–10th Floors, 75-95, Seosomun-dong, Jung-gu, Seoul 100-110; tel. (2) 772-8000; fax (2) 755-5379; f. 1978; Gen. Man. Geoffroy de Lassus.

DBS Bank Ltd (Development Bank of Singapore Ltd): Gwanghwamun Bldg, 20th Floor, 64-8, 1-ga, Taepyeong-no, Jung-gu, CPOB 9896, Seoul; tel. (2) 399-2660; fax (2) 732-7953; e-mail jeefun@dbs.com; f. 1981; Gen. Man. Low Jee Fun.

Deutsche Bank AG (Germany): Sei An Bldg, 20th–22nd Floor, 116, 1-ga, Sinmun-no, Jongno-gu, Seoul 110-700; tel. (2) 724-4500; fax (2) 724-4645; f. 1978; Gen. Man. Kim Jin-Il.

First National Bank of Chicago (USA): Oriental Chemical Bldg, 15th Floor, 50, Sokong-dong, Jung-gu, Seoul 100-070; tel. (2) 316-9700; fax (2) 753-7917; f. 1976; Vice-Pres. and Gen. Man. Michael S. Brown.

Hongkong and Shanghai Banking Corpn Ltd (Hong Kong): HSBC Bldg, 1-ga, Bongrae-dong, Jung-gu, CPOB 6910, Seoul 110-161; tel. (2) 2004-0000; fax (2) 381-9100; Gen. Man. G. P. S. Calvert.

Indian Overseas Bank: Daeyungak Bldg, 3rd Floor, 25-5, 1-ga, Jungmu-no, Jung-gu, CPOB 3332, Seoul 100-011; tel. (2) 753-0741; fax (2) 756-0279; e-mail iobseoul@chollian.net; f. 1977; Gen. Man. K. P. Munirathman.

Industrial and Commercial Bank of China (China): Taepyeong Bldg, 17th Floor, 310, 2-ga, Taepyeong-no, Seoul; tel. (2) 755-5688; fax (2) 779-2750; f. 1997; Gen. Man. Zhang Kexin.

ING Bank NV (Netherlands): Hungkuk Life Insurance Bldg, 15th Floor, 226, 1-ga, Sinmun-no, Jongno-gu, Seoul 110-061; tel. (2) 317-1800; fax (2) 317-1883; Man. Yim Sang-Kyun.

JP Morgan Chase Bank (USA): Chase Plaza, 34-35, Jeong-dong, Jung-gu, Seoul 100-120; tel. (2) 758-5114; fax (2) 758-5420; f. 1978; Gen. Man. Kim Myung-Han.

Mizuho Bank Ltd (Japan): Nae Wei Bldg, 14th Floor, 6, 2-ga, Ulchino, Jung-gu, Seoul 100-192; tel. (2) 756-8181; fax (2) 754-6844; f. 1972; Gen. Man. Tsuneo Kikuchi.

National Australia Bank Ltd: KDIC Bldg, 16th Floor, 33, Da-dong, Jung-gu, Seoul; tel. (2) 3705-4600; fax (2) 3705-4602; Gen. Man. Mark Edmonds.

National Bank of Canada: Leema Bldg, 6th Floor, 146-1, Susong-dong, Jongno-gu, Seoul 110-140; tel. (2) 733-5012; fax (2) 736-1508; Vice-Pres. and Country Man. C. N. Kim.

National Bank of Pakistan: Kyobo Bldg, 12th Floor, 1, 1-ga, Jongno, Jongno-gu, CPOB 1633, Seoul 110-121; tel. (2) 732-0277; fax (2) 734-5817; e-mail nbpseoul@kornet.net; f. 1987; Gen. Man. Abdul Ghafoor.

Royal Bank of Canada: Kyobo Bldg, 22nd Floor, 1, 1-ga, Jongno, Jongno-gu, Seoul 110-714; tel. (2) 730-7791; fax (2) 736-2995; f. 1982; Gen. Man. Thomas P. Fehlner, Jr.

Société Générale (France): Sean Bldg, 10th Floor, 1-ga, Sinmun-no, Jongno-gu, Seoul 110-700; tel. (2) 2195-7777; fax (2) 2195-7700; f. 1984; CEO Eric Berthélemy.

Standard Chartered Bank (UK): Seoul Finance Center, 22nd Floor, 84, 1-ga, Taepyeong-no, Jung-gu, Seoul; tel. (2) 750-6114; fax (2) 757-7444; Gen. Man. William Gemmel.

UBS AG (Switzerland): Young Poong Bldg, 10th Floor, 33, Seorin-dong, Jongno-gu, Seoul 110-752; tel. (2) 3702-8888; fax (2) 3708-8705; e-mail sunny.byun@ubs.com; f. 1999; Gen. Man. Sean Lee.

UFJ Bank Ltd (Japan): Lotte Bldg, 22nd Floor, 1, 1-ga, Sogong-dong, Jung-gu, Seoul; tel. (2) 752-7321; fax (2) 754-3870; Gen. Man. Hideki Yamauchi.

Union Bank of California NA (USA): Kyobo Bldg, 12th Floor, 1, 1-ga, Jongno, Jongno-gu, CPOB 329, Seoul 110; tel. (2) 721-1700; fax (2) 732-9526; Gen. Man. Kim Taek-Joong.

Union de Banques Arabes et Françaises (France): ACE Tower, 3rd Floor, 1-170, Sunhwa-dong, Jung-gu, CPOB 1224, Seoul 100-742; tel. (2) 3455-5300; fax (2) 3455-5354; f. 1979; Gen. Man. Patrick Oberreiner.

United Overseas Bank Ltd (Singapore): Suite 1508, Kyobo Bldg 1, 1-ga, Jongno, Jongno-gu, Seoul 110-714; e-mail UOB.Seoul@UOBgroup.com; tel. (2) 739-3916; fax (2) 730-9570; internet www.uobgroup.com; fmrly Overseas Union Bank; Gen. Man. Liew Chan Harn.

Banking Association

Korea Federation of Banks: 4-1, 1-ga, Myeong-dong, Jung-gu, Seoul 100-021; tel. (2) 3705-5000; fax (2) 3705-5337; internet www.kfb.or.kr; f. 1928; Chair. Shin Dong-Hyuck; Vice-Chair. Kim Kong-Jin.

STOCK EXCHANGE

Korea Exchange (KRX): 5-50 Jungang-dong, Jung-gu, Busan 600-015; tel. (51) 662-2000; internet www.krx.co.kr; f. 2005; formed by merger of Korea Stock Exchange, Korea Futures Exchange, Kosdaq Stock Market, Korea Securities Dealers Association; Chair. and CEO Young-Tak Lee.

INSURANCE
Principal Life Companies

Allianz Life Insurance Co Ltd: Allianz Tower, 45-21 Yeouido-dong, Yeongdeungpo-gu, Seoul 150-978; tel. (2) 3787-7000; e-mail webadmin@allianzlife.co.kr; internet www.allianzlife.co.kr; fmrly Allianz Jeil Life Insurance; formed in 2000 following acquisition of Jeil (First Life) by Allianz Group; renamed as above in 2002.

Choson Life Insurance Co Ltd: 111, Sincheon-dong, Dong-gu, Daegu 701-620; tel. (53) 743-3600; fax (53) 742-9263; f. 1988; cap. 12,000m.; Pres. Lee Young-Taek.

Dongbu Life Insurance Co Ltd: Dongbu Bldg, 7th Floor, 891-10, Daechi-dong, Gangnam-gu, Seoul 135-820; tel. (2) 1588-3131; fax (2) 3011-4100; internet www.dongbulife.co.kr; f. 1989; cap. 85,200m. (2002); Pres. Chang Ki-Je.

Dongyang Life Insurance Co Ltd: 185, Ulchi-no 2-ga, Jung-gu, Seoul 100-192; tel. (2) 728-9114; fax (2) 771-1347; internet www.myangel.co.kr; f. 1989; cap. 340,325m. (2002); Pres. Ku Ja-Hong.

Han Deuk Life Insurance Co Ltd: 878-1, Bumchyun 1-dong, Busanjin-gu, Busan 641-021; tel. (51) 631-8700; fax (51) 631-8809; f. 1989; cap. 10,000m.; Pres. Suh Woo-Shick.

Hanil Life Insurance Co Ltd: 118, 2-ga, Namdaemun-no, Jung-gu, Seoul 100-770; tel. (2) 2126-7777; fax (2) 2126-7631; internet www.hanillife.co.kr; f. 1993; cap. 115,000m. (2002); Pres. Lee Myung-Hyun.

Hankuk Life Insurance Co Ltd: Daehan Fire Bldg, 51-1, Namchang-dong, Jung-gu, Seoul 100-060; tel. (2) 773-3355; fax (2) 773-1778; f. 1989; cap. 10,000m.; Pres. Park Hyun-Kook.

Hansung Life Insurance Co Ltd: 3, Sujung-dong, Dong-gu, Busan 601-030; tel. (51) 461-7700; fax (51) 465-0581; f. 1988; Pres. Cho Yong-Keun.

Hungkuk Life Insurance Co Ltd: 226, Sinmun-no 1-ga, Jongno-gu, Seoul 100-061; tel. (2) 2002-7000; fax (2) 2002-7804; e-mail webmaster@hungkuk.co.kr; internet www.hungkuk.co.kr; f. 1958; cap. 12,221m. (2002); Pres. and CEO Ryu Seok-Kee.

ING Life Insurance Co Korea Ltd: Sean Bldg, 116, Sinmun-no, Jongno-gu, Seoul 110-700; tel. (2) 3703-9500; fax (2) 734-3309; f. 1991; cap. 64,820m. (2002); Pres. Joost Kenemans.

Korea Life Insurance Co Ltd: 60, Yeouido-dong, Yeongdeungpo-gu, Seoul 150-603; tel. (2) 789-5114; fax (2) 789-8173; internet www.korealife.com; f. 1946; cap. 3,550,000m. (2002); Pres. Lee Kang-Hwan.

Korean Reinsurance Company: 80, Susong-dong, Jongno-gu, Seoul 110-733; tel. (2) 3702-6000; fax (2) 739-3754; internet www.koreanre.co.kr; f. 1963; Pres. Park Jong-Won.

Kumho Life Insurance Co Ltd: 57, 1-ga, Sinmun-no, Jongno-gu, Seoul 110-061; tel. (2) 6303-5000; fax (2) 771-7561; internet www.kumholife.co.kr; f. 1988; acquired Dong-Ah Life Insurance in 2000; cap. 211,249m. (2002); Pres. Song Key-Hyuck.

Kyobo Life Insurance Co Ltd: 1, 1-ga, Jongno, Jongno-gu, Seoul 110-714; tel. (2) 721-2121; fax (2) 737-9970; internet www.kyobo.co.kr; f. 1958; cap. 92,500m.; Pres. and CEO Chang Hyung-Duk; 84 main brs.

Lucky Life Insurance Co Ltd: 3, Sujung-dong, Dong-gu, Busan 601-716; tel. (51) 461-7700; fax (51) 465-0581; internet www.luckylife.co.kr; f. 1988; cap. 139,054m. (2002); Pres. Chang Nam-Sik.

MetLife Insurance Co of Korea Ltd: Sungwon Bldg, 8th Floor, 141, Samseong-dong, Gangnam-gu, Seoul 135-716; tel. (2) 3469-9600; fax (2) 3469-9700; internet www.metlifekorea.co.kr; f. 1989; cap. 97,700m. (2002); Pres. Stuart B. Solomon.

PCA Life Insurance Co Ltd: 142, Nonhyun-dong, Gangnam-gu, Seoul 135-749; tel. (2) 515-5300; fax (2) 514-3844; f. 1990; cap. 52,100m. (2002); Pres. Mike Bishop.

Prudential Life Insurance Co of Korea Ltd: Prudential Bldg, Yeoksam-dong, Gangnam-gu, Seoul; tel. (2) 2144-2000; fax (2) 2144-2100; internet www.prudential.or.kr; f. 1989; cap. 26,400m.; Pres. James C. Spackman.

Samshin All State Life Insurance Co Ltd: Samwhan Bldg, 5th Floor, 98-5, Unni-dong, Jongno-gu, Seoul 110-742; tel. (2) 3670-5000; fax (2) 742-8197; Pres. Kim Kyung-Yop.

Samsung Life Insurance Co Ltd: 150, 2-ga, Taepyeong-no, Jung-gu, Seoul 100-716; tel. (2) 751-8000; fax (2) 751-8100; internet www.samsunglife.com; f. 1957; cap. 100,000m. (2002); Pres. Bae Jung-Choong; 1,300 brs.

THE REPUBLIC OF KOREA (SOUTH KOREA)

Shinhan Life Insurance Co Ltd: 120, 2-ga, Taepyeong-no, Jung-gu, Seoul 100-102; tel. (2) 3455-4000; fax (2) 753-9351; internet www.shinhanlife.co.kr; f. 1990; Pres. HAN DONG-WOO.

SK Life Insurance Co Ltd: 168, Gongduk-dong, Mapo-gu, Seoul 121-705; tel. (2) 3271-4114; fax (2) 3271-4400; internet www.sklife.com; f. 1988; cap. 246,275m. (2002); Pres. KANG HONG-SIN.

Non-Life Companies

Daehan Fire and Marine Insurance Co Ltd: 51-1, Namchang-dong, Jung-gu, Seoul 100-778; tel. (2) 3455-3114; fax (2) 756-9194; e-mail dhplane@daeins.co.kr; internet www.daeins.co.kr; f. 1946; cap. 19,500m.; Pres. LEE YOUNG-DONG.

Dongbu Insurance Co Ltd: Dongbu Financial Center, 891-10, Daechi-dong, Gangnam-gu, Seoul 135-840; tel. (2) 2262-3450; fax (2) 2273-6785; e-mail dongbu@dongbuinsurance.co.kr; internet www.idongbu.com; f. 1962; cap. 30,000m.; Pres. LEE SU-KWANG.

First Fire and Marine Insurance Co Ltd: 12-1, Seosomun-dong, Jung-gu, CPOB 530, Seoul 100-110; tel. (2) 316-8114; fax (2) 771-7319; internet www.insumall.co.kr; f. 1949; cap. 17,200m.; Pres. KIM WOO-HOANG.

Green Fire and Marine Insurance Co Ltd: Seoul City Tower, 581, 5-ga, Namdaemun-no, Jung-gu, Seoul 100-803; tel. (2) 1588-5959; fax (2) 773-1214; internet www.greenfire.co.kr; Pres. KIM JONG-CHEN.

Hankuk Fidelity and Surety Co Ltd: 51-1, Namchang-dong, Jung-gu, Seoul; tel. (2) 773-3355; fax (2) 773-1778; e-mail hfs025@unitel.co.kr; f. 1989; cap. 103,000m.; Pres. CHO AM-DAE.

Hyundai Marine and Fire Insurance Co Ltd: 8th Floor, 140-2, Kye-dong, Jongno-gu, Seoul 110-793; tel. (2) 3701-8000; fax (2) 732-5687; e-mail webpd@hdinsurance.co.kr; internet www.hi.co.kr; f. 1955; cap. 30,000m.; Pres. KIM HO-IL.

Korean Reinsurance Co: 80, Susong-dong, Jongno-gu, Seoul 100-733; tel. (2) 3702-6000; fax (2) 739-3754; e-mail service@koreanre.co.kr; internet www.koreanre.co.kr; f. 1963; cap. 34,030m.; Pres. PARK JONG-WON.

Kukje Hwajae Insurance Co Ltd: 120, 5-ga, Namdaemun-no, Jung-gu, Seoul 100-704; tel. (2) 753-1101; fax (2) 773-1214; internet www.directins.co.kr; f. 1947; cap. 10,784m.; Chair. LEE BONG-SUH.

Kyobo Auto Insurance Co Ltd: 76-4, Jamwon-dong, Seocho-gu, Seoul 137-909; tel. (2) 3479-4900; fax (2) 3479-4800; internet www.kyobodirect.com; Pres. SHIN YONG-KIL.

LG Insurance Co Ltd: LG Da-dong Bldg, 85, Da-dong, Jung-gu, Seoul 100-180; tel. (2) 310-2391; fax (2) 753-1002; e-mail webmaster@lginsure.com; internet www.lginsure.com; f. 1959; Pres. KOO CHA-HOON.

Oriental Fire and Marine Insurance Co Ltd: 25-1, Yeouido-dong, Yeongdeungpo-gu, Seoul 150-010; tel. (2) 3786-1910; fax (2) 3886-1940; e-mail webmaster@ofmi.co.kr; internet www.insuworld.co.kr; f. 1922; cap. 42,900m.; Pres. CHUNG KUN-SUB.

Samsung Fire and Marine Insurance Co Ltd: Samsung Insurance Bldg, 87, 1-ga, Ulchi-no, Jung-gu, Seoul 100-191; tel. (2) 758-7948; fax (2) 758-7831; internet www.samsungfire.com; f. 1952; cap. 6,566m.; Pres. LEE SOO-CHANG.

Seoul Guarantee Insurance Co: 136-74, Yeonchi-dong, Jongno-gu, Seoul 110-470; tel. (2) 3671-7459; fax (2) 3671-7480; internet www.sgic.co.kr; Pres. PARK HAE-CHOON.

Shindongah Fire and Marine Insurance Co Ltd: 43, 2-ga, Taepyeong-no, Jung-gu, Seoul; tel. (2) 6366-7000; fax (2) 755-8006; internet www.sdafire.com; f. 1946; cap. 60,220m.; Pres. JEON HWA-SOO.

Ssangyong Fire and Marine Insurance Co Ltd: 60, Doryeom-dong, Jongno-gu, Seoul 110-716; tel. (2) 724-9000; fax (2) 730-1628; e-mail sfmi@ssy.insurance.co.kr; internet www.insurance.co.kr; f. 1948; cap. 27,400m.; Pres. LEE JIN-MYUNG.

Insurance Associations

Korea Life Insurance Association: Kukdong Bldg, 16th Floor, 60-1, 3-ga, Jungmu-no, Jung-gu, Seoul 100-705; tel. (2) 2262-6600; fax (2) 2262-6580; internet www.klia.or.kr; f. 1950; Chair. BAE CHAN-BYUNG.

Korea Non-Life Insurance Association: KRIC Bldg, 6th Floor, 80, Susong-dong, Jongno-gu, Seoul; tel. (2) 3702-8539; fax (2) 3702-8549; internet www.knia.or.kr; f. 1946; 13 corporate mems; Chair. PARK JONG-IK.

Trade and Industry

GOVERNMENT AGENCIES

Fair Trade Commission: 1, Jungang-dong, Gwacheon-si, Gyeonggi Prov. 427-760; internet www.ftc.go.kr; Chair. LEE NAM-KEE.

Federation of Korean Industries: FKI Bldg, 2nd Floor, 28-1, Yeouido-dong, Yeongdeungpo-gu, Seoul 150-756; tel. (2) 3771-0114; fax (2) 3771-0110; e-mail webmaster@fki.or.kr; internet www.fki.or.kr; f. 1961; conducts research and survey work on domestic and overseas economic conditions and trends; advises the Govt and other interested parties on economic matters; exchanges economic and trade missions with other countries; sponsors business conferences; 380 corporate mems and 65 business asscns; Chair. KANG SHIN-HO.

Korea Appraisal Board: 171-2, Samseong-dong, Gangnam-gu, Seoul; tel. (2) 555-1174; Chair. KANG KIL-BOO.

Korea Asset Management Corpn (KAMCO): 814, Yeoksam-dong, Gangnam-gu, Seoul; tel. (2) 3420-5049; fax (2) 3420-5100; internet www.kamco.co.kr; f. 1963; collection and foreclosure agency; appointed following Asian financial crisis as sole institution to manage and dispose of non-performing loans for financial institutions; Pres. CHUNG JAE-RYONG.

Korea Export Industrial Corpn: 33, Seorin-dong, Jongno-gu, Seoul; tel. (2) 853-5573; f. 1964; encourages industrial exports, provides assistance and operating capital, conducts market surveys; Pres. KIM KI-BAE.

Korea Export Insurance Corpn: 136, Seorin-dong, Jongno-gu, Seoul 110-729; tel. (2) 399-6800; fax (2) 399-6679; internet www.keic.or.kr; f. 1992; official export credit agency of Korea; Pres. LIM TAE-JIN.

Korea Industrial Research Institutes: FKI Bldg, 28-1, Yeouido-dong, Yeongdeungpo-gu, Seoul; tel. (2) 780-7601; fax (2) 785-5771; f. 1979; analyses industrial and technological information from abroad; Pres. KIM CHAE-KYUM.

Korea Institute for Industrial Economics and Trade (KIET): 206-9, Cheongnyangni-dong, Dongdaemun-gu, Seoul; tel. (2) 3299-3114; fax (2) 963-8540; internet www.kiet.re.kr; f. 1976; economic and industrial research; Pres. PAI KWANG-SUN.

Korea Resources Corpn (KORES): Seoul; tel. (2) 840-5682; e-mail sbchoi@kores.or.kr; internet www.kores.or.kr; f. 1967; provides technical and financial support for the national mining industry; Pres. YANG-SOO PARK.

Korea Trade-Investment Promotion Agency (KOTRA): 300-9, Yeomgok-dong, Seocho-gu, Seoul; tel. (2) 3460-7114; fax (2) 3460-7777; e-mail digitalkotra@kotra.or.kr; internet www.kotra.or.kr; f. 1962; various trade promotion activities, market research, cross-border investment promotion, etc; 102 overseas brs; Pres. HONG KI-WHA.

Korean Intellectual Property Office: Government Complex-Daejeon, Dunsan-dong, Seo-gu, Daejeon; tel. (42) 481-5027; fax (42) 481-3455; internet www.kipo.go.kr; Commissioner KIM GWANG-LIM.

CHAMBER OF COMMERCE

Korea Chamber of Commerce and Industry: 45, 4-ga, Namdaemun-no, Jung-gu, Seoul 100-743; tel. (2) 316-3114; fax (2) 757-9475; internet www.korcham.net; f. 1884; over 80,000 mems; 63 local chambers; promotes development of the economy and of international economic co-operation; Pres. PARK YONG-SUNG.

INDUSTRIAL AND TRADE ASSOCIATIONS

Agricultural and Fishery Marketing Corpn: AGRO-TRADE & Exhibition Center, 232 Yangjae-dong, Seocho-gu, Seoul; tel. (2) 6300-1114; fax (2) 6300-1200; internet www.afmc.co.kr; f. 1967; integrated development for secondary processing and marketing distribution for agricultural products and fisheries products; Pres. AHN KYO-DUCK; Exec. Vice-Pres. KIM JIN-KYU.

Construction Association of Korea: Construction Bldg, 8th Floor, 71-2, Nonhyon-dong, Gangnam-gu, Seoul 135-701; tel. (2) 547-6101; fax (2) 542-6264; f. 1947; national licensed contractors' asscn; 2,700 mem. firms (1995); Pres. CHOI WON-SUK; Vice-Pres. PARK KU-YEOL.

Electronic Industries Association of Korea: 648, Yeoksam-dong, Gangnam-gu, CPOB 5650, Seoul 135-080; tel. (2) 553-0941; fax (2) 555-6195; e-mail eiak@soback.kornet.nm.kr; internet www.eiak.org; f. 1976; 328 mems; Chair. JOHN KOO.

Korea Automobile Manufacturers Association: 658-4. Deungchon-dong, Gangseo-gu, Seoul; tel. (2) 3660-1800; fax (2) 3660-1900; e-mail cwkim@kama.or.kr; internet www.kama.or.kr; f. 1988; Chair. KIM NOI-MYUNG.

THE REPUBLIC OF KOREA (SOUTH KOREA)

Directory

Korea Coal Association: 80-6, Susong-dong, Jongno-gu, Seoul; tel. (2) 734-8891; fax (2) 734-7959; f. 1949; 49 corporate mems; Chair. JANG BYEONG-DUCK.

Korea Consumer Goods Exporters Association: KWTC Bldg, Rm 1802, 159, Samseong-dong, Gangnam-gu, Seoul; tel. (2) 551-1865; fax (2) 551-1870; f. 1986; 230 corporate mems; Pres. YONG WOONG-SHIN.

Korea Federation of Textile Industries: Textile Center, 16/F, Daechi-dong 944-31, Kangnam-gu, Seoul 135-713; tel. (2) 528-4005; fax (2) 528-4069; e-mail kofoti@kofoti.or.kr; internet www.kofoti.or.kr; f. 1980; 50 corporate mems; Pres. PARK SANG-CHUL.

Korea Foods Industry Association: 1002-6, Bangbae-dong, Seocho-gu, Seoul; tel. (2) 585-5052; fax (2) 586-4906; internet www.kfia.or.kr; f. 1969; 104 corporate mems; Pres. CHUN MYUNG-KE.

Korea Importers Association (KOIMA): 218, Hangang-no, 2-ga, Yeongsan-gu, Seoul 140-875; tel. (2) 792-1581; fax (2) 785-4373; e-mail info@aftak.com; internet www.koima.or.kr; f. 1970; 11,903 mems; Chair. CHIN CHUL-PYUNG.

Korea International Trade Association: 159-1, Samseong-dong, Gangnam-gu, Seoul; tel. (2) 6000-5114; fax (2) 6000-5115; internet www.kita.org; f. 1946; private, non-profitmaking business org. representing all licensed traders in South Korea; provides foreign businessmen with information, contacts and advice; 80,000 corporate mems; Pres. KIM JAE-CHUL.

Korea Iron and Steel Association: 824, Yeoksam-dong, Gangnam-gu, Seoul; tel. (2) 559-3500; fax (2) 559-3508; internet www.kosa.or.kr; f. 1975; 39 corporate mems; Chair. YOO SANG-BOO.

Korea Oil Association: 28-1, Yeouido-dong, Yeongdeungpo-gu, Seoul; tel. (2) 3775-0520; fax (2) 761-9573; f. 1980; Pres. CHOI DOO-HWAN.

Korea Productivity Center: 122-1, Jeokseon-dong, Jongno-gu, Seoul 110-052; tel. (2) 724-1114; fax (2) 736-0322; internet www.kpc.or.kr; f. 1957; services to increase productivity of the industries, consulting services, education and training of specialized personnel; Chair. and CEO LEE HEE-BEOM.

Korea Sericultural Association: 17-9, Yeouido-dong, Yeongdeungpo-gu, Seoul; tel. (2) 783-6072; fax (2) 780-0706; e-mail silk@chollian.net; internet www.silktopia.or.kr; f. 1946; improvement and promotion of silk production; 50,227 corporate mems; Pres. CHOI YON-HONG.

Korea Shipbuilders' Association: 65-1, Unni-dong, Jongno-gu, Seoul; tel. (2) 766-4631; fax (2) 766-4307; internet www.koshipa.or.kr; f. 1977; 9 mems; Chair. KIM HYUNG-BYUK.

Korea Textiles Trade Association: 16/F, Textile Center, 944-31, Daechi-3dong, Kangnam-gu, Seoul; tel. (2) 528-5158; fax (2) 528-5188; e-mail webmaster@textra.or.kr; internet www.textra.or.kr; f. 1981; 947 corporate mems; Pres. KANG TAE-SEUNG.

Korean Apparel Industry Association: KWTC Bldg, Rm 801, 159, Samseong-dong, Gangnam-gu, Seoul 135-729; tel. (2) 551-1454; fax (2) 551-1467; internet www.kaia.or.kr; f. 1993; 741 corporate mems; Pres. PARK SEI-YOUNG.

Mining Association of Korea: 35-24, Dongui-dong, Jongno-gu, Seoul 110; tel. (2) 737-7748; fax (2) 720-5592; f. 1918; 128 corporate mems; Pres. KIM SANG-BONG.

Spinners and Weavers Association of Korea: 43-8, Gwancheol-dong, Jongno-gu, Seoul 110; tel. (2) 735-5741; fax (2) 735-5749; internet www.swak.org; f. 1947; 20 corporate mems; Pres. SUH MIN-SOK.

EMPLOYERS' ORGANIZATION

Korea Employers' Federation: KEF Bldg, 276-1 Daeheung-dong, Mapo-gu, Seoul 121-726; tel. (2) 3270-7310; fax (2) 706-1059; e-mail delee@kef.or.kr; internet www.kef.or.kr; f. 1970; advocates employers' interests with regard to labour and social affairs; 13 regional employers' asscns, 20 economic and trade asscns, and 4,000 major enterprises; Chair. LEE SOO-YOUNG.

UTILITIES

Electricity

Korea Electric Power Corpn (KEPCO): 167, Samseong-dong, Gangnam-gu, Seoul; tel. (2) 3456-3630; fax (2) 3456-3699; internet www.kepco.co.kr; f. 1961; transmission and distribution of electric power, and development of electric power sources; six power generation subsidiaries formed in 2001; Chair. and CEO HAN JOON-HO.

Oil and Gas

GS Caltex: 135-985, 679 Yeosksam-dong, Gangnam-gu, Seoul; tel. (2) 2005-1114; internet www.gscaltex.com; subsidiary of GS Holdings Corpn; fmrly LG Caltex Oil, renamed as above March 2005; Chair. and CEO HUR DONG-SOO.

Korea Gas Corpn: 215, Jeongja-dong, Bundang-gu, Seongnam, Gyeonggi Prov.; tel. (31) 710-0114; fax (31) 710-0117; e-mail kogasmaster@kogas.or.kr; internet www.kogas.or.kr; f. 1983; state-owned; privatization pending; Chair., Pres. and CEO OH KANG-HYUN.

Korea National Oil Corpn (KNOC): ; tel. 380-2114; fax 387-9321; e-mail webmaster@knoc.co.kr; internet www.knoc.co.kr; Pres. YI OK-SU.

Samchully Co Ltd: 35-6, Yeouido-dong, Yeongdeungpo-gu, Seoul; tel. (2) 368-3300; fax (2) 783-1206; internet www.samchully.co.kr; f. 1966; gas supply co for Seoul metropolitan area and Gyeonggi Prov; Chair. JIN JU-HWA.

Water

Korea Water Resources Corpn: 6-2, Yeonchuk-dong, Daedeok-gu, Daejeon; tel. (42) 629-3114; fax (42) 623-0963; internet www.kowaco.or.kr.

Office of Waterworks, Seoul Metropolitan Govt: 27-1 Hap-dong, Seodaemun-gu, Seoul; tel. (2) 390-7332; fax (2) 362-3653; f. 1908; responsible for water supply in Seoul; Head SON JANG-HO.

Ulsan City Water and Sewerage Board: 646-4, Sin-Jung 1-dong, Nam-gu, Ulsan; tel. (52) 743-020; fax (52) 746-928; f. 1979; responsible for water supply and sewerage in Ulsan; Dir HO KUN-SONG.

CO-OPERATIVES

Korea Computers Co-operative: 14-8, Yeouido-dong, Yeongdeungpo-gu, Seoul; tel. (2) 780-0511; fax (2) 780-7509; f. 1981; Pres. MIN KYUNG-HYUN.

Korea Federation of Knitting Industry Co-operatives: 586-1, Sinsa-dong, Gangnam-gu, Seoul; tel. (2) 548-2131; fax (2) 3444-9929; internet www.knit.or.kr; f. 1962; Chair. JOUNG MAN-SUB.

Korea Federation of Non-ferrous Metal Industry Co-operatives: Backsang Bldg, Rm 715, 35-2, Yeouido-dong, Yeongdeungpo-gu, Seoul; tel. (2) 780-8551; fax (2) 784-9473; f. 1962; Chair. PARK WON-SIK.

Korea Federation of Small and Medium Business (KFSB): 16-2, Yeouido-dong, Yeongdeungpo-gu, Seoul 150-010; tel. (2) 2124-3114; fax (2) 782-0247; f. 1962; Chair. KIM YOUNG-SOO.

Korea Mining Industry Co-operative: 35-24, Dongui-dong, Jongno-gu, Seoul; tel. (2) 735-3490; fax (2) 735-4658; f. 1966; Chair. JEON HYANG-SIK.

Korea Steel Industry Co-operative: 915-14, Bangbae-dong, Seocho-gu, Seoul; tel. (2) 587-3121; fax (2) 588-3671; internet www.kosic.or.kr; f. 1962; Pres. KIM DUK-NAM.

Korea Woollen Spinners and Weavers Co-operatives: Rm 503, Seawha Bldg, 36, 6-ga, Jongno-gu, Seoul; tel. (2) 747-3871; fax (2) 747-3874; e-mail woollen@woolspd.or.kr; internet www.woolspd.or.kr; f. 1964; Pres. KIM YOUNG-SIK.

National Agricultural Co-operative Federation (NACF): 1, 1-ga, Chungjeong-no, Jung-gu, Seoul; tel. (2) 397-5114; fax (2) 397-5380; internet www.nacf.co.kr; f. 1961; international banking, marketing, co-operative trade, utilization and processing, supply, co-operative insurance, banking and credit services, education and research; Pres. WON CHUL-HEE.

National Federation of Fisheries Co-operatives: 11-6, Sincheon-dong, Songpa-gu, Seoul; tel. (2) 2240-3114; fax (2) 2240-3024; internet www.suhyup.co.kr; f. 1962; Pres. HONG JONG-MOON.

TRADE UNIONS

Federation of Korean Trade Unions (FKTU): FKTU Bldg, 168-24, Chungam-dong, Yongsan-ku 141-050, Seoul; tel. (2) 715-3954; fax (2) 715-7790; e-mail fktuintl@fktu.or.kr; internet www.fktu.org; f. 1941; Pres. LEE YONG-DEUK; affiliated to ICFTU; 29 union federations are affiliated with a membership of some 960,000.

Federation of Foreign Organization Employees' Unions: 5-1, 3-ga, Dangsan-dong, Yeongdeungpo-gu, Seoul; tel. (2) 2068-1645; fax (2) 2068-1644; f. 1961; Pres. KANG IN-SIK; 22,450 mems.

Federation of Korean Apartment Workers' Unions: 922-1, Bangbae-dong, Seocho-gu, Seoul; tel. (2) 522-6860; fax (2) 522-4624; f. 1997; Pres. LEE DAE-HYUNG; 3,670 mems.

Federation of Korean Chemical Workers' Unions: Fiktu Bldg 802, Yeouido-dong 35, Yeongdeungpo-gu, Seoul 150-980; tel. (2) 6299-1234; fax (2) 6299-1235; e-mail fkcu@chollian.net; internet www.fkcu.or.kr; f. 1961; Pres. PARK HUN-SOO; 116,286 mems.

Federation of Korean Metalworkers' Unions: 1570-2, Sinrim-dong, Gwanak-gu, Seoul; tel. (2) 864-2901; fax (2) 864-0457; e-mail fkmtu@chollian.net; internet www.metall.or.kr; f. 1961; Pres. LEE BYUNG-KYUN; 130,000 mems.

Federation of Korean Mine Workers' Unions: Guangno Bldg, 2nd Floor, 10-4, Karak-dong, Songpa-gu, Seoul; tel. (2) 403-0973; fax (2) 400-1877; f. 1961; Pres. KIM DONG-CHUL; 6,930 mems.

THE REPUBLIC OF KOREA (SOUTH KOREA)

Federation of Korean Printing Workers' Unions: 201, 792-155, 3-ga, Guro-dong, Guro-gu, Seoul; tel. (2) 780-7969; fax (2) 780-6097; f. 1961; Pres. LEE KWANG-JOO; 5,609 mems.

Federation of Korean Public Construction Unions: 293-1, Kumdo-dong, Sujong-gu, Seongnam-si, Gyeonggi-do; tel. (2) 2304-7016; fax (2) 230-4602; f. 1998; Pres. HONG SANG-KI (acting); 9,185 mems.

Federation of Korean Public Service Unions: Sukchun Bldg, 3rd Floor, 32-100, 4-ga, Dangsan-dong, Yeongdeungpo-gu, Seoul; tel. (2) 769-1330; fax (2) 769-1332; internet www.fkpu.or.kr; f. 1997; Pres. LEE KWAN-BOO; 15,641 mems.

Federation of Korean Rubber Workers' Unions: 830-240, 2-ga, Bumil-dong, Dong-gu, Busan; tel. (51) 637-2101; fax (51) 637-2103; f. 1988; Pres. CHO YUNG-SOO; 6,600 mems.

Federation of Korean Seafarers' Unions: 544, Donhwa-dong, Mapo-gu, Seoul; tel. (2) 716-2764; fax (2) 702-2271; e-mail fksu@chollian.net; internet www.fksu.or.kr; f. 1961; Pres. PARK HEE-SUNG; 60,037 mems.

Federation of Korean State-invested Corporation Unions: Sunwoo Bldg, 501, 350-8, Yangjae-dong, Seocho-gu, Seoul; tel. (2) 529-2268; fax (2) 529-2270; internet www.publicunion.or.kr; f. 1998; Pres. JANG DAE-IK; 19,375 mems.

Federation of Korean Taxi & Transport Workers' Unions: 415-7, Janan 1-dong, Dongdaemun-gu, Seoul; tel. (2) 2210-8500; fax (2) 2247-7890; internet www.ktaxi.or.kr; f. 1988; Pres. KWAN OH-MAN; 105,118 mems.

Federation of Korean Textile Workers' Unions: 274-8, Yeomchang-dong, Gangseo-gu, Seoul; tel. (2) 3665-3117; fax (2) 3662-4373; f. 1954; Pres. OH YOUNG-BONG; 6,930 mems.

Federation of Korean United Workers' Unions: Sukchun Bldg, 32-100, 4-ga, Dangsan-dong, Yeongdeungpo-gu, Seoul; internet www.fkuwu.or.kr; f. 1961; 51,802 mems.

Federation of Korean Urban Railway Unions: Urban Railway Station, 3-ga, Yeouido-dong, Yeongdeungpo-gu, Seoul; tel. (2) 786-5163; fax (2) 786-5165; f. 1996; Pres. HA WON-JOON; 9,628 mems.

Korea Automobile & Transport Workers' Federation: 678-27, Yeoksam-dong, Gangnam-gu, Seoul; tel. (2) 554-0890; fax (2) 554-1558; f. 1963; Pres. KANG SUNG-CHUN; 84,343 mems.

Korea Federation of Bank & Financial Workers' Unions: 88, Da-dong, Jung-gu, Seoul; tel. (2) 756-2389; fax (2) 754-4893; internet www.kfiu.org; f. 1961; 113,994 mems.

Korea Federation of Communication Trade Unions: 10th Floor, 106-6, Guro 5-dong, Guro-gu, Seoul; tel. (2) 864-0055; fax (2) 864-5519; internet www.ictu.co.kr; f. 1961; Pres. OH DONG-IN; 18,810 mems.

Korea Federation of Food Industry Workers' Unions: 106-2, 1-ga, Yanpyeong-dong, Yeongdeungpo-gu, Seoul; tel. (2) 679-6441; fax (2) 679-6444; f. 2000; Pres. BAEK YOUNG-GIL; 19,146 mems.

Korea Federation of Port & Transport Workers' Unions: 19th Floor, Pyouk-San Bldg, 12-5 Dongja-dong, Yeongsan-gu, Seoul; tel. (2) 727-4741; fax (2) 727-4749; e-mail kfptwu@chollian.net; f. 1980; Pres. CHOI BONG-HONG; 33,347 mems.

Korea National Electrical Workers' Union: 167, Samseong-dong, Gangnam-gu, Seoul; tel. (2) 3456-6017; fax (2) 3456-6004; internet www.knewu.or.kr; f. 1961; Pres. KIM JU-YOUNG; 16,741 mems.

Korea Professional Artist Federation: Hanil Bldg, 43-4, Donui-dong, Jongno-gu, Seoul; tel. (2) 764-5310; fax (2) 3675-5314; f. 1999; Pres. PARK IL-NAM; 2,395 mems.

Korea Tobacco & Ginseng Workers' Unions: 100, Pyeongchon-dong, Daedeok-gu, Daejeon; tel. (42) 932-7118; fax (42) 931-1812; f. 1960; Pres. KANG TAE-HEUNG; 6,008 mems.

Korea Union of Teaching and Educational Workers: ; tel. (2) 2691-5335; fax (2) 2691-8558; e-mail leemo@korea.com; internet www.kute.or.kr; f. 1999; 18,337 mems.

Korean Postal Workers' Union: 154-1, Seorin-dong, Jongno-gu, Seoul 110-110; tel. (2) 2195-1773; fax (2) 2195-1761; e-mail cheshin@chol.com; internet www.kpwu.or.kr; f. 1958; Pres. JUNG HYUN-YOUNG; 23,500 mems.

Korean Railway Workers' Union: 40, 3-ga, Hangang-no, Yeongsan-gu, Seoul; tel. (2) 795-6174; f. 1947; Pres. KIM JONG-WOOK; 31,041 mems.

Korean Tourist Industry Workers' Federation: 749, 5-ga, Namdaemun-no, Jung-gu, Seoul 100-095; tel. (2) 779-1297; fax (2) 779-1298; f. 1970; Pres. JEONG YOUNG-KI; 27,273 mems.

National Medical Industry Workers' Federation of Korea: 134, Sincheon-dong, Seodaemun-gu, Seoul; tel. (2) 313-3900; fax (2) 393-6877; f. 1999; Pres. LEE YONG-MOO; 5,610 mems.

Korean Confederation of Trade Unions: 5th Daeyoung Bldg, 139, 2-ga, Yeouido-dong, Yeongdeungpo-gu, Seoul 150-032; tel. (2) 2636-0165; fax (2) 2635-1134; internet www.kctu.org; f. 1995; legalized 1999; Chair. CHO JUN-HO; 600,000 mems.

Transport

RAILWAYS

At the end of 2001 there were 6,819 km (including freight routes) of railways in operation. The first phase of construction of a new high-speed rail system connecting Seoul to Busan (412 km) via Cheonan, Daejeon, Daegu, and Gyungju, was completed in early 2004, with services commencing operation from April. The second phase, Daejeon–Busan, was scheduled for completion in 2010. Construction work on the reconnection of the Kyongui (West Coast, Sinuiju (North Korea)–Seoul) and East Coast Line (Wonsan (North Korea)–Seoul) began in September 2002. The two lines were officially opened in June 2003, but were not yet open to traffic, as construction work on the Northern side remained to be completed. Reconnection work was subject to disruption by the changing political situation. Eventually the two would be linked to the Trans-China and Trans-Siberian railways respectively, greatly enhancing the region's transport links.

Korean National Railroad: 920, Dunsan-dong, Seo-gu, Daejeon 302-701; tel. (42) 1544-7788; fax (42) 481-373; internet www.korail.go.kr; f. 1963; operates all railways under the supervision of the Ministry of Construction and Transportation; total track length of 6,819 km (2001); Admin. SON HAK-LAE.

City Underground Railways

Busan Subway: Busan Urban Transit Authority, 861-1, Bumchun-dong, Busan 614-021; tel. (51) 633-8783; e-mail ipsubway@buta.or.kr; internet subway.busan.kr; f. 1988; length of 71.6 km (2 lines, with a further 3rd line under construction); Pres. LEE HYANG-YEUL.

Daegu Metropolitan Subway Corpn: 1500 Sangin 1-dong, Dalseo-gu, Daegu; tel. (53) 640-2114; fax (53) 640-2229; e-mail webmaster@daegusubway.co.kr; internet www.daegusubway.co.kr; length of 28.3 km (1 line, with a further five routes totalling 125.4 km planned or under construction); Pres. YOON JIN-TAE.

Incheon Rapid Transit Corpn: 67-2, Gansok-dong, Namdong-gu, Incheon 405-233; tel. (32) 451-2114; fax (32) 451-2160; internet www.irtc.co.kr; length of 24.6 km (22 stations, 1 line), with two further lines planned; Pres. CHOUNG IN-SOUNG.

Seoul Metropolitan Rapid Transit Corporation: 133-170 Seongdong-gu, Yongdap-dong 223-3, Seoul; tel. (2) 62112000; e-mail webadmin@smrt.co.kr; internet www.smrt.co.kr; operates lines 5-8.

Seoul Metropolitan Subway Corpn: 447-7, Bangbae-dong, Seocho-gu, Seoul; tel. (2) 520-5020; fax (2) 520-5039; internet www.seoulsubway.co.kr; f. 1981; length of 134.9 km (115 stations, lines 1-4); Pres. KIM JUNG-GOOK.

Underground railways were also under construction in Daejeon and Gwangju.

ROADS

At the end of 2001 there were 91,396 km of roads, of which 76.7% were paved. A network of motorways (2,637 km) links all the principal towns, the most important being the 428-km Seoul–Busan motorway. Improvements in relations with North Korea resulted in the commencement of work on a four-lane highway to link Seoul and the North Korean capital, Pyongyang, in September 2000. In February 2003 a road link between the two countries was reportedly opened.

Korea Highway Corpn: 293-1, Kumto-dong, Sujong-gu, Seongnam, Gyeonggi Prov.; tel. (822) 2230-4114; fax (822) 2230-4308; internet www.freeway.co.kr; f. 1969; responsible for construction, maintenance and management of toll roads; Pres. OH JUM-LOCK.

SHIPPING

In December 2003 South Korea's merchant fleet (2,604 vessels) had a total displacement of 6,757,400 grt. Major ports include Busan, Incheon, Donghae, Masan, Yeosu, Gunsan, Mokpo, Pohang, Ulsan, Jeju and Gwangyang.

Busan Port Authority: c/o Ministry of Maritime Affairs and Fisheries, 50 Chungjeong-no, Seodaemun-gu, Seoul 120-715; tel. (2) 3148-6992; fax (2) 3148-6996; e-mail koo2061@momaf.go.kr; f. 2004; Contact KEE HIH-SEONG.

Korea Shipowners' Association: Sejong Bldg, 10th Floor, 100, Dangju-dong, Jongno-gu, Seoul 110-071; tel. (2) 739-1551; fax (2) 739-1565; e-mail korea@shipowners.or.kr; internet www.shipowners.co.kr; f. 1960; 40 shipping co mems; Chair. HYUN YUNG-WON.

Korea Shipping Association: 66010, Dungchon 3-dong, Gangseo-gu, Seoul 157-033; tel. (2) 6096-2024; fax (2) 6096-2029; e-mail kimny@haewoon.co.kr; internet www.haewoon.co.kr; f. 1962;

THE REPUBLIC OF KOREA (SOUTH KOREA)

management consulting and investigation, mutual insurance; 1,189 mems; Chair. PARK HONG-JIN.

Principal Companies

DooYang Line Co Ltd: 166-4, Samseong-dong, Gangnam-gu, Seoul 135-091; tel. (2) 550-1700; fax (2) 550-1777; internet www.dooyang.co.kr; f. 1984; world-wide tramping and conventional liner trade; Pres. CHO DONG-HYUN.

Hanjin Shipping Ltd: 25-11, Yeouido-dong, Yeongdeungpo-gu, Seoul; tel. (2) 3770-6114; fax (2) 3770-6740; internet www.hanjin.com; f. 1977; marine transportation, harbour service, warehousing, shipping and repair, vessel sales, harbour department and cargo service; Pres. CHOI WON-PYO.

Hyundai Merchant Marine Co Ltd: 66, Jeokseon-dong, Jongno-gu, Seoul 110-052; tel. (2) 3706-5114; fax (2) 723-2193; internet www.hmm.co.kr; f. 1976; Chair. HYUN YUNG-WON.

Korea Line Corpn: Dae Il Bldg, 43, Insa-dong, Jongno-gu, Seoul 110-290; tel. (2) 3701-0114; fax (2) 733-1610; f. 1968; world-wide transportation service and shipping agency service in Korea; Pres. JANG HAK-SE.

Pan Ocean Shipping Co Ltd: 51-1, Namchang-dong, Jung-gu, CPOB 3051, Seoul 100-060; tel. (2) 316-5114; fax (2) 316-5296; f. 1966; transportation of passenger cars and trucks, chemical and petroleum products, dry bulk cargo; Pres. CHIANG JIN-WON.

CIVIL AVIATION

There are international airports at Incheon (Seoul), Gimpo (Seoul), Busan, Cheongju, Daegu, Gwangju, Jeju and Yangyang. The main gateway into Seoul is Incheon International Airport, which opened for service in March 2001. It is used by 30m. passengers annually, and has a capacity for 240,000 aircraft movements annually. The second phase began construction in 2002, with completion due by 2008. When complete, the airport will handle 44m. passengers and 4.5m. tons of cargo annually. The airport is located 52 km from Seoul. A new airport, Yangyang International Airport, in Gangwon province, opened in April 2002.

Asiana Airlines Inc: 47, Osae-dong, Gangseo-gu, Seoul; tel. (2) 758-8114; fax (2) 758-8008; e-mail asianacr@asiana.co.kr; internet www.asiana.co.kr; f. 1988; serves 14 domestic cities and 36 destinations in 16 countries; fmrly Seoul Air International; CEO PARK SAM-KOO.

Korean Air: 1370, Gonghang-dong, Gangseo-gu, Seoul; tel. (2) 656-7092; fax (2) 656-7289; internet www.koreanair.com; f. 1962; est. by the Govt, privately owned since 1969; fmrly Korean Air Lines (KAL); operates domestic and regional services and routes to the Americas, Europe, the Far East and the Middle East, serving 73 cities in 26 countries; Chair. and CEO CHO YANG-HO.

Tourism

South Korea's mountain scenery and historic sites are the principal attractions for tourists. Jeju Island, located some 100 km off the southern coast, is a popular resort. In 2003 there were 4,753,604 visitors to South Korea, of whom some 37.9% came from Japan. Receipts from tourism in 2003 amounted to US $6,903m.

Korea National Tourism Organization: KNTO Bldg, 10, Da-dong, Jung-gu, CPOB 903, Seoul 100; tel. (2) 729-9600; fax (2) 757-5997; e-mail webmaster@mail.knto.or.kr; internet english.tour2korea.com; f. 1962; as Korea Tourist Service; Pres. LEE DEUK-RYUL.

Korea Tourism Association: Saman Bldg, 11th Floor, 945, Daechi-dong, Gangnam-gu, Seoul; tel. (2) 556-2356; fax (2) 556-3818; f. 1963; Pres. CHO HANG-KYU, KIM JAE-GI.

KUWAIT

Introductory Survey

Location, Climate, Language, Religion, Flag, Capital

The State of Kuwait lies at the north-west extreme of the Persian (Arabian) Gulf, bordered to the north-west by Iraq and to the south by Saudi Arabia. The State comprises a mainland region and nine small islands, of which the largest is Bubiyan and the most populous is Failaka. Immediately to the south of Kuwait, along the Gulf, lies a Neutral (Partitioned) Zone of 5,700 sq km, which is shared between Kuwait and Saudi Arabia. Much of Kuwait is arid desert, and the climate is generally hot and humid. Temperatures in July and August often exceed 45°C (113°F), and in the winter months are frequently above 20°C (68°F)—although there is often frost at night. Average annual rainfall is only 111 mm. The official language is Arabic, which is spoken by the majority of Kuwaiti nationals (estimated, by official definition, to have comprised 41.2% of Kuwait's population at mid-2000) and by many of the country's non-Kuwaiti residents. Apart from other Arabs, the non-Kuwaitis are mainly Iranians, Indians and Pakistanis. At the 1975 census 95.0% of the population were Muslims (of whom about 70% are now thought to belong to the Sunni sect), while 4.5% were Christians, Hindus or adherents of other faiths. The national flag (proportions 1 by 2) has three equal horizontal stripes, of green, white and red, with a superimposed black trapezoid at the hoist. The capital is Kuwait City.

Recent History

Kuwait became part of Turkey's Ottoman Empire in the 16th century. During the later years of Ottoman rule Kuwait became a semi-autonomous Arab monarchy, with local administration controlled by a Sheikh of the Sabah family, which is still the ruling dynasty. In 1899, fearing an extension of Turkish control, the ruler of Kuwait made a treaty with the United Kingdom, accepting British protection while surrendering control over external relations. Nominal Turkish suzerainty over Kuwait ended in 1918, with the dissolution of the Ottoman Empire.

Petroleum was first discovered in Kuwait in 1938, but exploration was interrupted by the Second World War. After 1945 drilling resumed on a large scale, and extensive deposits of petroleum were found. Sheikh Ahmad (ruler since 1921) was succeeded in 1950 by his cousin, Sheikh Abdullah as-Salim as-Sabah, who inaugurated a programme of public works and educational development, funded by petroleum revenues, which transformed Kuwait's infrastructure and introduced a comprehensive system of welfare services.

Kuwait became fully independent on 19 June 1961, when the United Kingdom and Kuwait agreed to terminate the 1899 treaty. The ruler took the title of Amir and assumed full executive power. Kuwait was admitted to the League of Arab States (the Arab League, see p. 306) despite opposition from Iraq, which claimed that Kuwait was historically part of Iraqi territory. Kuwait's first election took place in December 1961, when voters chose 20 members of a Constituent Assembly (the other members being cabinet ministers appointed by the Amir). The Assembly drafted a new Constitution, which was adopted in December 1962. A 50-member Majlis al-Umma (National Assembly) was elected, under a limited franchise (see Government, below), in January 1963. In the absence of formal political parties (which remain illegal), candidates contested the poll as independents, although some known opponents of the Government were elected. In the same month the Amir appointed his brother, Sheikh Sabah as-Salem as-Sabah (the heir apparent), to be Prime Minister. Iraq renounced its claim to Kuwait in October, and diplomatic relations were established.

In January 1965, following conflict between the paternalistic ruling family and the democratically inclined Majlis, the powers of the Council of Ministers were strengthened. The Amir died in November 1965, and Sheikh Sabah succeeded to the throne. He was replaced as Prime Minister by his cousin, Sheikh Jaber al-Ahmad as-Sabah, who was named heir apparent in May 1966. The Neutral (Partitioned) Zone between Kuwait and Saudi Arabia was formally divided between the two countries in 1969: revenues from oil production in the area are shared equally.

As Kuwait's petroleum sector expanded during the 1960s, the country became increasingly wealthy. The Government effected an extensive redistribution of income, through public expenditure and a land compensation scheme, but there was some popular discontent concerning corruption and official manipulation of the media and the Majlis. A more representative legislature was elected in January 1971 (again under a limited franchise). A further general election took place in January 1975, but in August 1976 the Amir dissolved the Majlis, on the grounds that it was acting against the best interests of the State. Sheikh Sabah died on 31 December 1977 and was succeeded by Crown Prince Jaber. In January 1978 the new Amir appointed Sheikh Saad al-Abdullah as-Salim as-Sabah to be his heir apparent. The new Crown Prince, hitherto Minister of Defence and the Interior, became Prime Minister in the following month. In accordance with an Amiri decree of August 1980, a new Majlis was elected in February 1981, although only one-half of the eligible 6% of the population registered to vote.

The collapse of Kuwait's unofficial stock exchange, the Souk al-Manakh, in September 1982 caused a prolonged financial crisis, and eventually led to the resignations of the Ministers of Finance (in 1983) and of Justice (in 1985). The Majlis subsequently opposed several government measures, including proposed price increases for public services, educational reforms and legislation to restrict the press, and questioned the competence of certain ministers. In July 1986 the Council of Ministers submitted its resignation to the Amir, who then dissolved the Majlis and suspended some articles of the Constitution, declaring his intention to rule by decree. The Crown Prince was immediately reappointed Prime Minister. An Amiri decree accorded the Council of Ministers greater powers of censorship, including the right to suspend publication of newspapers for up to two years.

In late 1989 the Amir refused to accept a petition, signed by more than 20,000 Kuwaiti citizens, seeking the restoration of the Majlis. In January 1990 police dispersed two pro-democracy demonstrations, although later in the month the Government agreed to relax press censorship. In June 62% of eligible voters participated in a general election for 50 members of a 'provisional' National Council; a further 25 members were appointed by the Amir. The election was boycotted by pro-democracy activists, who continued to demand the full restoration of the Majlis.

Of all the Gulf states, Kuwait has been most vulnerable to regional disruption. Immediately after independence British troops (soon replaced by an Arab League force) were dispatched to support the country against the territorial claim by Iraq. The force remained until 1963, and relations between Kuwait and Iraq were stable until 1973, when Iraqi troops occupied a Kuwaiti outpost on their joint border. Kuwait none the less supplied aid to Iraq from the outbreak of the Iran–Iraq War in 1980. As a result, Kuwaiti petroleum installations and shipping in the Persian (Arabian) Gulf were targeted intermittently by Iranian forces, and by pro-Iranian groups within Kuwait, for much of the 1980s. A large number of Iranians were among 27,000 expatriates deported in 1985–86, and in 1987 the Government initiated a five-year plan to reduce the number of expatriates in the Kuwaiti work-force. Kuwait resumed diplomatic relations with Iran following the 1988 cease-fire between Iran and Iraq.

In July 1990 the Iraqi Government implicitly criticized Kuwait (among other states) for disregarding the petroleum production quotas stipulated by the Organization of the Petroleum Exporting Countries (OPEC, see p. 344). It also declared that Kuwait should cancel Iraq's war debt and compensate it for losses of revenue incurred during the war with Iran, and as a result of Kuwait's overproduction of petroleum—to which Iraq attributed a decline in international oil prices. In addition, Iraq alleged that Kuwait had established military posts and drilled oil wells on Iraqi territory. Despite regional mediation efforts, Iraq subsequently began to deploy armed forces on the Kuwait–Iraq border. Direct negotiations in Jeddah, Saudi Arabia, at the end of the month between Kuwaiti and Iraqi officials collapsed, and on

2 August some 100,000 Iraqi troops invaded Kuwait (whose total military strength was about 20,000): Iraq stated that it had entered at the invitation of insurgents who had overthrown the Kuwaiti Government. The Amir and other government members fled to Saudi Arabia, where they established a 'Government-in-exile', while Iraq declared that a provisional Government had been formed in Kuwait comprising Iraqi-sponsored Kuwaiti dissidents. The UN Security Council immediately adopted a series of resolutions, of which the first (Resolution 660) condemned the invasion, demanded the immediate and unconditional withdrawal of Iraqi forces from Kuwait, and appealed for a negotiated settlement of the conflict. A trade embargo was then imposed on Iraq and Kuwait. Meanwhile, the USA and member states of the European Community (now European Union—EU, see p. 228) froze all Kuwait's overseas assets to prevent their repatriation. Five days after the invasion US troops and aircraft were deployed in Saudi Arabia, with the stated aim of securing that country's borders with Kuwait in the event of further Iraqi territorial expansion. A number of European Governments, together with some Arab League states, agreed to provide military support for the US forces. The Iraqi Government subsequently announced the formal annexation of Kuwait, and ordered the closure of foreign diplomatic missions there. At the end of August most of Kuwait was officially declared to be the 19th Governorate of Iraq, while a northern strip was incorporated into the Basra Governorate.

In the months following the invasion apparent attempts at demographic manipulation—by settling Iraqis and Palestinians in Kuwait and by forcing Kuwaitis to assume Iraqi citizenship—were documented. The population was estimated to have decreased from approximately 2m. prior to the invasion to some 700,000, of whom Kuwaitis constituted about 300,000, Palestinians 200,000, and the remainder comprised other Arab and Asian expatriates. Many Kuwaitis, and Arab and Asian expatriates, had fled Iraq and Kuwait into Jordan, while most European and US expatriates were detained as hostages; by the end of 1990 it was claimed that all hostages had been released.

UN Security Council Resolution 678, adopted in November 1990, authorized the multinational force by now stationed in Saudi Arabia and the Gulf region to use 'all necessary means' to liberate Kuwait. It was implied that should Iraq not begin, by 15 January 1991, to implement the terms of 10 resolutions hitherto adopted regarding the invasion, military action would ensue. Renewed international diplomatic attempts failed to avert a military confrontation. On the night of 16–17 January the US-led multinational force launched an intensive aerial bombardment of Iraq. Ground forces entered Kuwait during the night of 23–24 February, encountering relatively little effective Iraqi opposition. Within three days the Iraqi Government had agreed to comply with the terms of all Security Council resolutions concerning Kuwait, and on 28 February the USA announced a suspension of military operations. Resolutions 686 and 687, adopted by the UN Security Council in March and April respectively, dictated the terms to Iraq for a permanent cease-fire: Iraq was required to release all allied prisoners of war and Kuwaitis detained as hostages, repeal all laws and decrees concerning the annexation of Kuwait, and recognize the inviolability of the Iraq–Kuwait border. Iraq promptly announced its compliance with both resolutions. Resolution 689, adopted in April, provided for the establishment of a demilitarized zone, to be supervised by a UN Iraq-Kuwait Observation Mission (UNIKOM).

Meanwhile, in October 1990, at a conference in Jeddah of some 1,000 prominent Kuwaitis, the exiled Crown Prince Saad agreed to establish government advisory committees on political, social and financial matters, and pledged to restore the country's Constitution and legislature and to organize free elections after Kuwait's eventual liberation. In February 1991, however, the Government-in-exile excluded the possibility of early elections, maintaining that the need to rebuild and repopulate the country took precedence over that for political reform. Immediately following liberation an Amiri decree imposed martial law in Kuwait, and in March the formation of a state security committee was announced: its objectives included the investigation of individuals suspected of collaboration with the Iraqi authorities in Kuwait, the prevention of unofficial acts of reprisal and the identification of those civilians relocated to Kuwait by Iraq. Palestinians in Kuwait were a particular target of reprisals, and it was alleged by several human rights organizations that they were subject to torture by Kuwaiti security forces. Kuwait's Palestinian population, which had totalled around 400,000 prior to the Iraqi invasion, was estimated to have declined to less than 50,000 by early 1992.

The Amir, the Prime Minister and other members of the exiled regime returned to Kuwait in March 1991. The Council of Ministers resigned later that month, apparently in response to public discontent at the Government's failure to restore essential services. Although several specialists were appointed to strategic posts within the new Government named by Sheikh Saad in April (most notably to the finance, planning and oil portfolios), other important positions (including the foreign affairs, interior and defence ministries) were allocated to members of the as-Sabah family.

In May 1991 it was revealed that some 900 people were under investigation in Kuwait in connection with crimes committed during the Iraqi occupation; about 200 of these were accused of collaboration. The human rights organization Amnesty International expressed concern that trials were being conducted without the provision of adequate defence counsel, and alleged that torture had in some cases been used to extract confessions. The Government undertook to investigate such abuses. Martial law was ended in June, and 29 death sentences hitherto imposed on convicted collaborators were commuted to custodial terms. Outstanding trials relating to the occupation were to be referred to civilian courts, and in August a tribunal, said to guarantee defendants the right to greater legal protection as well as a right of appeal, was established to replace the martial law courts. Amid continuing international criticism of Kuwait's record on human rights, measures were subsequently taken to prevent clandestine deportations of alleged collaborators and to permit international supervision of the expulsion of foreign nationals. However, it was widely believed that Kuwait had been motivated to curb human rights abuses primarily in an attempt to procure international support for its efforts to secure the release of Kuwaiti nationals detained in Iraq.

It was announced in May 1991 that a US military presence would remain in Kuwait until September, by which time, it was envisaged, a regional defence force would be established. However, little progress was achieved in negotiations for such a force, and in August the USA announced that it would maintain 1,500 troops in Kuwait for several more months. In September the US and Kuwaiti Governments signed a 10-year military co-operation agreement, permitting the storage of US supplies and equipment in Kuwait, and providing for joint military training and exercises. (The agreement was renewed for a further 10 years in February 2001.) Defence accords were signed with both the United Kingdom and France in 1992.

In June 1993 the State Security Court was reported to have issued death sentences against 17 people who had been found guilty of collaborating with Iraq in 1990–91; Alaa Hussein Ali, the leader of the provisional Government installed by Iraq in August 1990, was convicted *in absentia*. In February 1994 Amnesty International again alleged serious violations of human rights in Kuwait, asserting that at least 120 alleged collaborators had been convicted by trials that failed to satisfy international minimum standards. Human rights organizations welcomed the endorsement by the Majlis, in August 1995, of government proposals to abolish the State Security Court. In January 1997 the Government announced the creation of a new human rights committee within the Ministry of the Interior.

Press censorship was partially relaxed in January 1992. Elections to the new Majlis, on 5 October, were contested by some 280 candidates, many of whom (although nominally independent) were affiliated to one of several quasi-political organizations. The franchise was again restricted, with only about 81,400 men eligible to vote. Anti-Government candidates, notably those representing Islamist groups, were unexpectedly successful, securing 31 of the Assembly's 50 seats. The Prime Minister subsequently formed a new Government, including six members of the Majlis, who were allocated, *inter alia*, the oil and justice portfolios; members of the ruling family retained control of foreign affairs, the interior and defence.

The Majlis voted in December 1992 to establish a commission of inquiry into the circumstances surrounding the 1990 invasion. The commission's report, published in May 1995, revealed profound negligence on the part of government and military officials, who had apparently ignored warnings of an imminent invasion. The report also claimed that the immediate flight of members of the royal family and the Council of Ministers had deprived the country of political leadership and military organization.

Meanwhile, in January 1993 legislation was enacted whereby the Majlis would have automatic access to the financial accounts of all state-owned companies and investment organizations, and stricter penalties would be imposed in cases of abuse of public funds. Demands for greater parliamentary scrutiny of the State's investments were largely prompted by revelations of the misappropriation of funds by the London-based Kuwait Investment Office (KIO), responsible for much of Kuwait's overseas investment portfolio (22 former KIO executives, including Sheikh Fahd Muhammad as-Sabah—its Chairman at the time of the Iraqi invasion—were reportedly implicated in the allegations), and also by emerging evidence of financial misconduct at the state-owned Kuwait Oil Tanker Co. In July 1996 three former executives received prison sentences of between 15 and 40 years, having been convicted of corruption by the criminal court; they were ordered to repay embezzled funds, together with fines totalling more than US $100m. In June 1999 the High Court in London ruled that Sheikh Fahd and two other former KIO senior executives were guilty, *in absentia*, of conspiracy and fraud involving some $460m. against the KIO's Spanish subsidiary during 1988–92.

The ruling family retained control of the foreign affairs, interior and defence portfolios following a reorganization of the Council of Ministers in April 1994. In June the Majlis approved legislation extending the franchise to sons of naturalized Kuwaitis. In July 1995 the Assembly approved a bill reducing from 30 years to 20 the minimum period after which naturalized Kuwaitis would become eligible to vote. In July 1996 the Ministry of the Interior announced that an electorate of just over 107,000 men was entitled to vote in the forthcoming elections to the Majlis, scheduled for 7 October. Pro-Government candidates were the most successful, securing the majority of the 50 seats. Sheikh Saad was reappointed Prime Minister; his new Council of Ministers included four newly elected deputies.

In March 1998 Sheikh Saad submitted his Government's resignation, after members of the Majlis proposed a motion of 'no confidence' in the Minister of Information, Sheikh Sa'ud Nasir as-Sa'ud as-Sabah, who had allowed what were deemed 'un-Islamic' publications to be exhibited at a book fair in Kuwait. The Amir immediately reappointed the Crown Prince as Prime Minister, and a new Government was named at the end of the month. The promotion of Sheikh Sa'ud to the post of Minister of Oil was controversial not only because of the recent action by the Majlis against him, but also because the oil portfolio was not customarily allocated to a member of the ruling family. An institutional crisis appeared imminent in June, when the Majlis sought to cross-examine the Minister of the Interior, Sheikh Muhammad Khalid al-Hamad as-Sabah, on issues including corruption, illicit drugs and human rights. However, the ministry in question was deemed by the Government to be 'sovereign' and therefore exempt from examination by the Majlis. Relations between the Government and the Majlis deteriorated further, necessitating intervention by the Amir to dispel rumours that the Assembly would be dissolved and a general election called. Tensions were swiftly revived in July, when the Government introduced amendments to legislation enacted in 1993 (and previously amended in 1995) regarding repayment of debts arising from the collapse of the Souk al-Manakh in 1982. Many deputies regarded new arrangements for the discharge of liabilities to be unduly favourable to debtors, many of whom were members of the ruling family, and boycotted an initial vote before reluctantly approving the amendments in August 1998.

Confrontation persisted between the Government and the Majlis, which in February 1999 refused to refer to its finance committee government proposals for economic reform. In May the Amir dissolved the legislature and called fresh elections, after deputies had in the previous month questioned the Minister of Justice and of Awqaf (Religious Endowments) and Islamic Affairs over errors that had appeared in copies of the Koran printed and distributed by his ministry. Some 80% of an eligible electorate of 113,000 Kuwaiti men voted in the election, which took place on 3 July. Pro-Government candidates recorded the greatest losses, taking only 12 seats; Islamist candidates won 20 seats, and liberals 14 seats, with the remaining four won by independents. Sheikh Saad was immediately reappointed Prime Minister, and a new Council of Ministers was inaugurated in mid-July. The ruling family retained control of the strategic foreign affairs, oil, interior and defence portfolios, although a number of liberal deputies joined the Government. Meanwhile, during the period between the dissolution of the Majlis and the election, the Government promulgated some 60 decrees (subject to legislative approval), most notably one proposing that women should be allowed to contest and to vote in elections from 2003. However, the law on female suffrage was defeated by a considerable majority when subjected to a vote in the new Majlis in November 1999, as liberal deputies, who supported women's enfranchisement, registered their protest at what they considered to be the unconstitutionality of legislation by decree by joining Islamist and conservative deputies in voting against the measure. Liberal deputies immediately submitted identical legislation regarding women's suffrage, but this was narrowly defeated in a vote at the end of the month. Kuwaiti women suffered a further reverse in their attempts to secure the right to contest and vote in elections in January 2001, when the Constitutional Court rejected a lawsuit brought by a male citizen against the State's election department for having failed to register the names of five women on electoral lists in his constituency. In March the Majlis rejected, on procedural grounds, draft legislation that would increase women's political rights.

In January 2000 Alaa Hussein Ali, leader of the provisional Government installed by Iraq in August 1990, who had been in self-imposed exile since Kuwait's liberation, returned to Kuwait in order to appeal against the death sentence pronounced in June 1993 (see above); the appeal hearing began at the Court of First Instance in February 2000. In May it was announced that Hussein had lost his appeal, and that he planned a further challenge to his sentence. The Court of Appeal upheld the previous ruling in July, but in March 2001 commuted Hussein's death sentence to one of life imprisonment.

In July 2000 unrest was reported in the Al-Jahra region, where a community of *bidoon* ('stateless' Arabs) form the majority of the population. (About 100,000 *bidoon* reside in Kuwait, but the authorities refuse to recognize their claims to Kuwaiti nationality.) The unrest followed the approval, in May, of a draft amendment to the Citizenship Law that would grant only a small number of *bidoon* the right to Kuwaiti citizenship. Some 1,000 *bidoon* obtained Kuwaiti citizenship in early 2001, leading to protests by those whose applications had been refused.

The issue of press freedom caused a renewed deterioration in relations between the Government and the Majlis in February 2000, when deputies criticized government efforts to suspend publication of two Kuwaiti newspapers, *Al-Watan* and *As-Seyassah*, for publishing reports of salary increases for the security forces. The Amir subsequently ordered that any planned action against the publications be abandoned. Later in the month a joint statement issued by several newspaper editors accused the Minister of Information of allowing actions that impeded press freedom. Amnesty International expressed concern in March that freedom of expression remained under threat in Kuwait, and urged the Government to end its practice of punishing journalists and authors for using what it deemed to be 'un-Islamic' language.

In November 2000 the Amir accepted the resignation of the Minister of Information, Dr Saad Muhammad bin Teflah al-Ajmi. Sheikh Saad tendered his Government's resignation in January 2001. The Crown Prince denied that this constituted an attempt to prevent parliamentary scrutiny of the Minister of Justice and of Awqaf and Islamic Affairs, Saad Jasem Yousuf al-Hashil, relating to allegations of inefficiency and corruption in his ministry. The Amir immediately reappointed Sheikh Saad as Prime Minister, and a new 15-member Government was named in mid-February. The new administration included five younger members of the ruling family, as well as four members of the Majlis. The outgoing Deputy Prime Minister and Minister of Defence, Sheikh Salim Sabah as-Salim as-Sabah, left the Government, although the defence, foreign affairs and interior portfolios remained in the hands of the as-Sabah family. Some controversy was caused by the allocation of the oil portfolio to Dr Adil Khalid as-Sabih, the minister previously responsible for the electricity, water and housing portfolios who had recently survived a parliamentary vote of 'no confidence' in respect of his business interests.

Meanwhile, during November 2000, as the crisis in Israeli–Palestinian relations deepened, 16 suspected Islamist militants (Kuwaitis and other Arab nationals) were arrested in Kuwait, accused of involvement in plotting bomb attacks on US military installations in the Gulf region in retaliation for perceived US support for Israel. The arrests of the alleged saboteurs followed reports that a Moroccan aide to the Saudi-born leader of the militant Islamist al-Qa'ida (Base) organization, Osama bin Laden, had entered Kuwait from Afghanistan; however, the aide subsequently fled to Iran. In June 2001 a senior Kuwaiti military official was convicted of concealing weapons to be used for terrorist purposes; he received a 10-year prison sentence, but in December this was reduced to seven years. (Eight of the suspected militants were given suspended sentences and ordered to pay fines; the remainder were acquitted.)

At the end of January 2002 four people died following a major explosion at Raudhatain, Kuwait's second largest oilfield, to the north of Kuwait City. Adil Khalid as-Sabih immediately submitted his resignation as Minister of Oil, stating that he accepted responsibility for the incident; he also ordered an investigation into the cause of the explosion. The Minister of Information, Sheikh Ahmad al-Fahd al-Ahmad as-Sabah, was subsequently named as acting Minister of Oil. However, a political crisis ensued after it proved impossible to find a permanent replacement for Dr as-Sabih, and Sheikh Ahmad was asked to remain in charge of the oil portfolio until the general election (scheduled for mid-2003). Meanwhile, several members of the increasingly assertive Majlis demanded the resignation of the entire Government, alleging that the explosion at Raudhatain was the result of state corruption and mismanagement. In January 2003 the Amir accepted the resignation of the Minister of Finance, of Planning and Minister of State for Administrative Development Affairs, Dr Yousuf Hamad al-Ibrahim, who had been the object of severe parliamentary criticism. Dr al-Ibrahim, a leading reformist, had in July 2002 survived a vote of 'no confidence' instigated by Islamist Majlis deputies who accused him of poor management of the Government's fiscal affairs.

After a campaign that was overshadowed by the US-led military intervention in Iraq (which was largely conducted from Kuwaiti territory), parliamentary elections were held, as scheduled, on 5 July 2003. Islamist candidates secured 21 of the 50 seats in the Majlis, while pro-Government candidates won 14 seats, independents (regarded as being aligned with the Government) 12 and liberals three. The rate of voter participation was reported to be only 45% of the 6% of the total population who form the electorate. The results were viewed as a major setback for those seeking political reform, and were widely interpreted as signalling popular dissatisfaction with the entire political process. In 2004 the Majlis debated proposals to reduce the number of constituencies, thereby requiring successful candidates to gain a wider appeal among voters.

Meanwhile, following the elections, in July 2003 the ailing Crown Prince relinquished the position of Prime Minister. The appointment of Sheikh Sabah as his replacement represented an unprecedented separation between the post of Prime Minister and the position of Crown Prince, and provided some encouragement to reformists after their heavy electoral losses. A new Council of Ministers, including six new appointments, was also announced in mid-July. The most significant change was the merger of the oil portfolio with the Ministry of Electricity and Water to form the Ministry of Energy, to be headed by Sheikh Ahmad al-Fahd al-Ahmad as-Sabah.

In October 2003 and May 2004 the Council of Ministers approved legislation that would permit women to vote in and contest municipal and parliamentary elections, respectively. Both pieces of legislation were subject to Majlis consent: the assembly gave provisional approval for the former in mid-April 2005, but subsequently failed to ratify the legislation at a second vote in early May. Both new laws were approved later in the month; however, this was too late to allow women to participate in the June municipal elections. By early 2006, in advance of the 2007 legislative elections, it was reported that there were already considerably more women than men registered as voters. Kuwaiti women received their first opportunity to vote and to stand in elections at a municipal by-election on 4 April 2006, where two of the eight candidates were female.

In March 2004 the Minister of Finance, Mahmud Abd al-Khaliq an-Nuri, narrowly survived a vote of 'no confidence', having been heavily criticized by the Majlis for mismanagement during the sale of state property. Citing health reasons, an-Nuri resigned shortly after the vote; however, he continued in the role of Minister of Finance until Bader al-Humaidhi, formerly Director-General of the Kuwait Fund for Arab Economic Development, was appointed as his replacement on 4 April 2005. Meanwhile, in late March 2005 Dr Anas Muhammad Ahmad ar-Rashaid was finally appointed as Minister of Information; he replaced Muhammad Abu al-Hassan, who had resigned in January, shortly before he was to be questioned in the Majlis by Islamist members over allowing 'immoral' Western-style concerts in Kuwait. The day after the appointment of al-Humaidhi, the Minister of Health, Muhammad Ahmad al-Jarallah, resigned in advance of a parliamentary vote on a motion of 'no confidence', which had been lodged on 4 April, accusing him of mismanagement. Al-Jarallah thus became the third member of the Council of Ministers to resign in connection with hostile parliamentary questioning since the elections to the Majlis in July 2003. The Prime Minister subsequently warned the Majlis that a vote of 'no confidence' in al-Jarallah, should it be carried, could 'negatively impact on our national unity', which in some quarters was interpreted as a sign that the increasingly assertive nature of the Majlis had begun to concern the ruling as-Sabah family. Al-Jarallah's resignation was accepted by the Prime Minister on 10 April 2005, and the Minister of Energy, Sheikh Ahmad al-Fahd as-Sabah, assumed the health portfolio in an acting capacity. In June the Prime Minister appointed Dr Massouma Saleh al-Mubarak as Minister of Planning and Minister of State for Administrative Development Affairs. Al-Mubarak, a human rights activist, thus became Kuwait's first female member of the Council of Ministers.

Meanwhile, in February 2005 the Majlis approved legislation giving security agencies flexible new powers to search for and seize illegal firearms, following several recent battles between government forces and armed militants. Some of the recent violence was linked to reports of hostility towards Westerners, particularly US citizens, and al-Qa'ida was believed by some to be implicated in the violence. Additionally, in early January the army announced that a number of soldiers had been detained under suspicion of plotting to attack US troops. The new legislation was to be renewed on an annual basis.

On 15 January 2006 the death was announced of the Amir, Sheikh Jaber. He was automatically succeeded by the Crown Prince, Sheikh Saad, who had, however, for some time been beset by rumours that he was too ill to accede to the role. (Sheikh Saad had frequently travelled abroad for medical treatment, especially since requiring emergency colon surgery in 1997.) In an unprecedented, but unsurprising, development, on 24 January Sheikh Saad, who had yet to take the oath of office, was removed from the position of Amir on health grounds, following a formal request from the Council of Ministers that the Majlis debate the issue. Under the Constitution, the law of succession required a two-thirds' majority of Majlis deputies in order to dismiss an Amir; in the event, the vote in favour of replacing Sheikh Saad was unanimous. Reportedly, Sheikh Saad and his close supporters had, after nine days of intense negotiation, reluctantly agreed to his removal from office prior to the Majlis debate; however, his abdication letter did not bear an official stamp and was disregarded by parliamentarians. In the absence of a nominated Crown Prince, the Prime Minister, Sheikh Sabah, who was in any case regarded as the *de facto* ruler of the emirate, assumed the powers of the Amir until the nomination of a permanent head of state by the Council of Ministers. Sheikh Sabah was duly sworn in as Amir on 29 January, after his widely predicted nomination had been unanimously approved by the Majlis. The sole controversy attached to Sheikh Sabah's accession was that, like the late Sheikh Jaber, he belonged to the al-Jaber branch of the ruling as-Sabah family that, by tradition, alternated the position of Amir with the as-Salem branch of the family, of which Sheikh Saad was a member. Pending the appointment of a new Prime Minister and a possible reorganization of the Government, on 30 January the new Amir accepted the resignation of the Council of Ministers.

On 7 February 2006 Sheikh Sabah appointed Sheikh Nasser al-Muhammad al-Ahmad as-Sabah, a former diplomat and the Amir's nephew, as the new Prime Minister and the erstwhile Deputy Prime Minister and Minister of the Interior, Sheikh Nawwaf al-Ahmad al-Jaber as-Sabah, the Amir's brother, as Crown Prince. The new appointments, which maintained the post-2003 separation between the roles, emphasized the channelling of power towards the al-Jaber branch of the ruling family, although both men were respected for their extensive political experience. On the following day the Amir approved Sheikh Nasser's first Council of Ministers. Although strategic portfolios (including those of foreign affairs, finance and energy) remained unaltered, a notable change was the addition of the interior portfolio to the responsibilities of the Minister of Defence, Sheikh Jaber Mubarak al-Hamad as-Sabah, who also became First Deputy Prime Minister. Reformers were unhappy that Faisal al-Hajji, a leading liberal politician, was removed from the position of Minister of Social Affairs and Labour.

Meanwhile, in December 2005 a Majlis committee approved a draft law repealing the official ban on the establishment of daily newspapers. If, as was widely expected, the bill gained Majlis approval, the legislation would also, inter alia, ban the imprisonment of journalists for many existing offences, reduce journalists' gaol terms for religious offences and remove the right of the Government to close newspapers without a final judicial verdict. On 9 May 2006 ar-Rashaid resigned from his position as Minister of Information in protest at draft legislation that would reduce the number of electoral constituencies from 25 to 10 and increase the number of representatives in the Majlis from 50 to 60. The former proposal was approved by the Council of Ministers on 10 May, while the latter was abandoned. Ar-Rashaid's resignation was accepted by the Amir on the same day. The reduction in the number of constituencies, which proved controversial in the Majlis, was intended to decrease opportunities for electoral corruption.

Friction between Kuwait and Iraq in the aftermath of the Gulf War was exacerbated by the issue of the demarcation of their joint border. The UN commission with responsibility for delineating the frontier formalized the land border as it had been defined by British administrators in 1932 (and officially agreed by Kuwait and Iraq in 1963). The boundary, the validity of which was now rejected by Iraq, was established some 570 m north of its pre-war position, dividing the Iraqi port of Umm Qasr, with the effect that Iraq retained the town and much of the harbour while Kuwait was awarded hinterland which included an abandoned Iraqi naval base; the border also situated several Iraqi oil wells on Kuwaiti territory. In January 1993 the USA led air attacks on Iraq, and more than 1,000 US troops were dispatched to Kuwait, in response to a series of incursions by Iraqi forces into Kuwaiti territory in the days immediately preceding the designated entry into force of the new border; its formal delineation was completed in March, when the UN commission defined the maritime border along the median line of the Khawr Abd Allah waterway. Allegations made by Kuwait of Iraqi violations of the border, and of attempts to impede construction of a trench along the land border, intensified during the second half of 1993, and there were sporadic reports of exchanges of fire in the border region. In November a 775-strong armed UNIKOM reinforcement was deployed in northern Kuwait, with authorization (under specific circumstances) to use its weapons to assist the unarmed force already in the demilitarized zone.

In October 1994 Iraq deployed some 70,000 troops and 700 tanks near the border with Kuwait, in an apparent attempt to force an easing of UN economic sanctions. Kuwait immediately mobilized its army reserves, and dispatched some 20,000 troops to the border region. The USA committed almost 40,000 land, naval and air forces to the region; France and the United Kingdom deployed naval vessels, and the United Kingdom dispatched about 1,200 troops. Following Russian mediation, Iraq announced its willingness to recognize Kuwait's sovereignty and borders, on condition that the UN ease sanctions against Iraq after six months. However, the UN Security Council adopted a resolution (No. 949) requiring Iraq's unconditional recognition of Kuwait's sovereignty and borders and restricting the movement of Iraqi troops in the border area. In November Iraq officially recognized Kuwait's sovereignty, territorial integrity and political independence, as well as its UN-defined borders. Most of the US and British reinforcements deployed in the region in October had been withdrawn by the end of the year. Kuwait's relations with Iraq deteriorated sharply in September 1996, after the Kuwaiti Government agreed to the deployment in Kuwait of US military aircraft and troops in support of a US operation to force the withdrawal of Iraqi armed forces from the Kurdish 'safe haven' in northern Iraq. In December the USA announced that some 4,200 US troops deployed in Kuwait during 1996 would be withdrawn by the end of the year, although the deployment of US F-117 *Stealth* fighter aircraft was to be extended.

Kuwait and Iraq made mutual accusations of territorial violations and attacks on shipping during 1997. Meanwhile, Kuwait continued to support the maintenance of international sanctions against Iraq, and to demand adherence by Iraq to all relevant UN resolutions adopted since the Gulf crisis. Furthermore, statements by the Iraqi Government that it was holding no Kuwaiti prisoners of war were refuted by Kuwait: the Kuwaiti authorities, asserting that some 600 Kuwaitis remained captive in Iraq, claimed in late 1997 to be in possession of documentation, passed by Iraq to the International Committee of the Red Cross (ICRC), relating to 126 Kuwaiti prisoners of war. As the crisis involving weapons inspections in Iraq by the UN Special Commission (see the Recent History of Iraq) deepened in February 1998, fears were expressed for Kuwait's security—in particular that an attack on Iraq might result in the use of chemical or other weapons of mass destruction against Kuwait. Although Kuwait was the only country in the region to announce its approval of the use of force against Iraq should diplomatic efforts fail, it emphasized that any military action would exacerbate hardship suffered by the Iraqi people and increase regional instability. The USA, supported by the United Kingdom, undertook a military deployment in the Gulf region at this time: by the end of the month, when the UN Secretary-General and the Iraqi Government reached a compromise agreement regarding weapons inspections, some 6,000 US ground troops had been dispatched to Kuwait. A series of air-strikes against targets in Iraq by US and British forces from December 1998 again increased tensions between Kuwait and Iraq. Iraq accused Kuwait of collaborating in the air attacks, and frequently reiterated claims to Kuwaiti territory. In September 1999 Kuwait lodged an official protest over changes made to the final draft of an Arab League report to which, Kuwait asserted, references to the formation of a 'mechanism' to resolve the issue of Kuwaiti and other prisoners of war in Iraq had been added; Kuwait maintained that the ICRC was the only body empowered to deal with the issue. In November the Majlis established a committee to examine future relations with Iraq, and in December the Kuwaiti Government welcomed UN Security Council Resolution 1284 (establishing a new weapons inspectorate for Iraq, q.v.), which incorporated demands for the repatriation of Kuwaiti and other prisoners from Iraq, for Iraq's co-operation with the ICRC, and for the return of Kuwaiti property seized during the occupation.

In September 2000 ministers responsible for foreign affairs of the Co-operation Council for the Arab States of the Gulf (Gulf Co-operation Council—GCC, see p. 205) expressed concerns after the Iraqi leadership had repeatedly denounced both Kuwait and Saudi Arabia for allowing US and British military aircraft to use their airspace in order to conduct military attacks on Iraq, and had vowed to launch a new invasion of Kuwait. Iraq also renewed its long-standing accusation that Kuwait was drilling oil wells on Iraqi territory, and accused Kuwait and Saudi Arabia of inflicting suffering on the Iraqi population through the maintenance of UN sanctions. In September and again in October Kuwait reinforced security along its border with Iraq, in the latter month to prevent a possible influx of *bidoon*, who had reportedly entered the demilitarized zone from Iraq and who were demanding the right of return to Kuwait (from where they had been excluded since the Gulf crisis).

In March 2001 a summit meeting of Arab League heads of state, held in Amman, Jordan, was considered as having made the most comprehensive effort hitherto in addressing divisions arising from the Gulf conflict. None the less, a draft resolution presented by the Iraqi delegation urging an end to UN sanctions and a resumption of civilian flights failed to secure adoption, owing to Iraq's unwillingness—on the grounds that it had already done sufficient to make clear its recognition of Kuwait's territorial integrity—to accede to a requirement of a specific guarantee that Iraq would not repeat the invasion of 1990. In November 2001 Kuwait issued a formal complaint to the UN following an alleged violation of its territory by Iraq. The incident occurred shortly after a senior Iraqi official had reiterated claims of sovereignty over Kuwait. In January 2002 the Kuwaiti leadership was reported to have rejected attempts by the Arab League to persuade it to accept Iraqi proposals apparently aimed at improving bilateral relations: as part of Iraq's diplomatic offensive to secure the support of the Arab world in view of the threat of US-led military action against Saddam Hussain's regime, the Iraqi leader had conveyed an appeal to Arab states to set aside their differences, referring specifically to the need to improve relations with Kuwait and Saudi Arabia. Later in the month it was reported that Iraq had announced its preparedness to allow a delegation from Kuwait to visit Iraq to verify that no Kuwaiti prisoners of war were being held. (Kuwait continued to assert that Iraq was detaining at least 90 Kuwaiti nationals.) At the Arab League summit held in Beirut, Lebanon, in late March 2002, however, it was announced that Kuwait and Iraq had reached agreement on the resolution of outstanding differences. The summit's final communiqué welcomed Iraq's assurances that it would respect the 'independence, sovereignty and security' of Kuwait, and safeguard its 'territorial integrity'; Iraq was urged to co-operate in seeking a 'definitive solution' to issues of Kuwaiti prisoners and detainees, and of the return of property, while Kuwait was called upon to 'co-operate with what Iraq offers with respect to its nationals' reported as missing through the

ICRC. Kuwait's First Deputy Prime Minister and Minister of Foreign Affairs was subsequently reported as having expressed his complete satisfaction with the agreement.

Relations with Iraq were profoundly affected by the political repercussions of the September 2001 suicide attacks against the mainland USA. Kuwait, which strongly condemned the attacks, thereafter assumed an important role in persuading other Gulf states to join the US-led 'coalition against terror'. US bases in Kuwait were subsequently used to provide logistical support to the US-led campaign against al-Qa'ida (held by the USA to be principally responsible for the attacks on New York and Washington, DC) and its Taliban hosts in Afghanistan during late 2001. Meanwhile, in October 2001 the Kuwaiti authorities revoked the citizenship of the official spokesman of al-Qa'ida, Sulayman Abu Ghaith, after remarks he had made via the Qatar-based Al-Jazeera television station. In late 2001 the Central Bank of Kuwait implemented measures designed to prevent Islamic charitable organizations from using Kuwait's financial institutions to channel funds to al-Qa'ida.

During the course of 2002 increased speculation that the US Administration of George W. Bush intended to extend the 'war on terror' to target the regime of Saddam Hussain in Iraq threatened to fuel opposition to a continued US presence in the region and exacerbate an increasingly tense political situation in Kuwait. At the end of December some 12,000 US troops were stationed in Kuwait, and in early 2003 Kuwait's Ministry of Defence declared that the entire northern half of Kuwait would be designated a closed military zone from 15 February. Several US soldiers and civilians were killed in late 2002 and early 2003 in attacks by Kuwaitis, some of whom, it was alleged, had links to al-Qa'ida. In March an emergency meeting of the Arab League, hosted by Qatar, to discuss the deepening crisis descended into a bitter exchange of insults between, primarily, a senior Iraqi official and the Kuwaiti Minister of Information. Kuwait subsequently supported a proposal made by the President of the United Arab Emirates (UAE) for Saddam Hussain to go into exile in order to prevent a US-led war to remove his regime. At the outset of military action, which commenced on 20 March, US-led troops in Kuwait, the base for the main ground assault on Iraq, numbered some 140,000. Iraqi armed forces launched several missiles at Kuwaiti territory, although little damage was caused in the emirate during the course of the conflict. In the aftermath of the most intense period of fighting, which President Bush declared to have ended by early May 2003, Kuwait renewed its financial demands against Iraq, while a number of Kuwaiti firms entered into agreements with the US-led occupying powers. In early October the demilitarized zone between Iraq and Kuwait was ended and, having fulfilled its mandate, UNIKOM's operations were terminated. The resumption of diplomatic relations between Iraq and Kuwait was announced in mid-2004; the two countries were still in the process of exchanging diplomatic staff in early 2006. Meanwhile, in August 2005 Iraqi militants reportedly fired mortar rounds into Kuwait in protest at a new 200 km steel barrier under construction along the border between the two countries.

Meanwhile, in May 1994 the governing body of the UN Compensation Commission (UNCC), responsible for considering claims for compensation arising from the 1990–91 Gulf crisis, approved the first disbursements (to 670 families or individuals in 16 countries), totalling US $2.7m. By late 1996 payments amounting to $3,000m. (to be financed partly by Iraqi petroleum revenues) had been endorsed by the UN, which had yet to consider claims for a further $190,000m. In December international arbitrators recommended that a payment of $610m. should be made to the Kuwait Oil Company (KOC), in compensation for the cost of extinguishing oil wells set alight by retreating Iraqi troops in early 1991. In March 1997 the Kuwaiti general committee responsible for evaluating war damages stated that it was to begin compensation payments, initially to some 4,500 citizens who had incurred losses valued at less than $100,000. The disbursement of a further $84m. to some 33,800 individuals was authorized by the UN in February 1999. In September 2000 the UN Security Council approved the payment to the Kuwait Petroleum Corporation (which controls the KOC) of $15,900m. in compensation for lost petroleum revenues arising from the Iraqi occupation; this was the largest claim to have been considered by the UNCC hitherto. However, the Security Council decided at the same time to reduce the share of Iraqi petroleum revenues to be paid into the compensation fund from 30% to 25%. France and Russia, which increasingly opposed the maintenance of sanctions against Iraq, had delayed a decision by the UNCC on the payment, and Russia had warned of its inclination to oppose Kuwaiti claims to reparations unless the levy on Iraqi petroleum revenues was reduced. By mid-2003 the majority of individual claimants (Kuwaitis and expatriates in Kuwait and Iraq during the Gulf war) had received compensation, with total disbursements being valued at some $17,600m. Meanwhile, the UNCC was considering a claim of $86,000m. by the Kuwait Investment Agency, principally in recompense for lost earnings during the conflict. However, in a deposition issued in June 2003, the UNCC rejected all but $1,500m. of the claim. In late May 2003 UN Security Council Resolution 1483 had reduced the share of Iraqi petroleum revenue to be used for compensation payments from 25% to 5%, which was expected to result in outstanding compensation payments believed to total more than $30,000m. remaining unpaid for several decades. In January 2004, after a meeting with US envoy James Baker and following similar announcements by the Governments of the UAE and Qatar, Sheikh Sabah stated that Kuwait was prepared to waive a 'significant proportion' of the estimated $16,000m. owed by Iraq. This did not, however, include any war reparations still claimed by the Government. In March 2005 the UN panel overseeing payments to victims of the Gulf crisis approved a further disbursement of $265m. to families of those who had died in Iraqi detention. At a final session of the UNCC governing body, held in late June, a further $367m. in compensation was awarded to successful claimants.

Relations with Jordan, which had deteriorated following that country's failure openly to denounce the Iraqi invasion, gradually eased in the mid-1990s. Flights between Kuwait and Jordan by both countries' national airlines, which had been suspended in 1990, resumed in July 1997, and the normalization of relations generally continued thereafter. In March 1999 the Jordanian embassy in Kuwait, which had been closed in 1990, was reopened. In September of that year the new King Abdullah of Jordan made his first visit to Kuwait (his father, King Hussein, had not visited after 1990), where he held talks with the Amir. Jordan and Kuwait signed a bilateral free-trade agreement in December.

In July 2000 Kuwait and Saudi Arabia signed an agreement finalizing the delineation of their maritime borders. Kuwait subsequently commenced negotiations with Iran on the demarcation of respective rights to the continental shelf, following complaints by the Kuwaiti and Saudi authorities over Iran's decision to begin drilling for gas in a disputed offshore area. Iraq asserted that, as a concerned party, it should be included in the Kuwaiti-Iranian discussions. In December a defence agreement was signed by the six member states of the GCC.

Government

Under the 1962 Constitution, executive power is vested in the Amir, the Head of State (who is chosen by and from members of the ruling family), and is exercised through the Council of Ministers. The Amir appoints the Prime Minister and, on the latter's recommendation, other ministers. Legislative power is vested in the unicameral Majlis al-Umma (National Assembly), with 50 elected members who serve for four years (subject to dissolution). Hitherto, only literate adult male Kuwaiti citizens, excluding members of the armed forces, were permitted to vote; however, in May 2005 legislation was approved allowing women to vote in forthcoming legislative and municipal elections. The country is divided administratively into six governorates.

Defence

In August 2005 Kuwait's active armed forces numbered 15,500—a land army of 11,000 (including up to 3,700 foreign personnel), an air force of an estimated 2,500 and a navy of around 2,000—and there were reserve forces of 23,700. Paramilitary forces comprised a 6,600-strong national guard and a 500-strong coastguard. Military service is voluntary. The defence budget for 2005 was estimated at KD 1,320m.

A US force numbering an estimated 19,700 (comprising army, air force, navy and marines corps personnel), a small British army force and, as part of Operation Enduring Freedom (the US-led mission in Afghanistan which commenced in late 2001), a German force of 50 were stationed in Kuwait in August 2005.

Economic Affairs

In 2003, according to estimates by the World Bank, Kuwait's gross national income (GNI), measured at average 2001–03 prices, was US $43,052m., equivalent to $17,970 per head (or $19,510 on an international purchasing-power parity basis). During 1995–2004, it was estimated, the population increased at an average annual rate of 3.5%, while gross domestic product (GDP) per head decreased, in real terms, by an average of 2.1% per year during 1995–2003. Overall GDP was estimated to have increased, in real terms, at an average annual rate of 1.5% in 1995–2003. Real GDP declined by 0.4% in 2002, before increasing by 9.9% in 2003. The IMF estimated real GDP to have grown by 7.2% in 2004.

Agriculture (including hunting, forestry and fishing) contributed 0.4% of GDP in 2004. The sector engaged 1.9% of the labour force in the same year. The principal crops are tomatoes, potatoes, cucumbers, aubergines, cauliflower and dates. Owing to scarcity of water, little grain is produced, and the bulk of food requirements is imported. (Imports of food and live animals accounted for 13.2% of merchandise imports in 2003.) Livestock, poultry and fishing are also important. Agricultural GDP increased, in real terms, by an average annual rate of 6.3% in 1995–2003.

Industry (including mining, manufacturing, construction and power) provided 57.9% of GDP in 2004, and employed 15.6% of the labour force in that year. During 1995–2003 industrial GDP increased, in real terms, at an average annual rate of 1.2%.

Mining and quarrying contributed 46.2% of GDP in 2004, although the sector engaged only 0.5% of the labour force in that year. The production of petroleum and its derivatives is the most important industry in Kuwait, providing 91.9% of export revenue in 2003. At the end of 2004 the country's proven recoverable reserves of petroleum were 99,000m. barrels, representing about 8.0% of world reserves. According to oil industry figures, Kuwait's petroleum production averaged 2.24m. barrels per day (b/d) in 2004. With effect from July 2005, Kuwait's production quota, as agreed by Organization of the Petroleum Exporting Countries (OPEC, see p. 344), was 2.25m. b/d. Kuwait aimed to increase its production capacity from 2.4m. b/d in 2005 to 4.0m. b/d by 2020. There are significant reserves of natural gas (1,570,000m. cu m at the end of 2004) associated with the petroleum deposits. During 1995–2003 the GDP of the mining sector increased, in real terms, at an average rate of 0.8% per year.

Manufacturing provided 7.8% of GDP in 2004, and employed 6.4% of the labour force in the same year. Petroleum refineries accounted for 60.5% of manufacturing activity, measured by gross value of output, in 2004. Of the other branches of manufacturing, the most important are the production of building materials (and related activities such as aluminium extrusion), fertilizer production, food processing and the extraction of salt and chlorine. During 1995–2003 manufacturing GDP increased, in real terms, at an average annual rate of 0.5%.

Electrical energy is derived from Kuwait's own resources of petroleum (providing 78.9% of total electricity production in 2002) and both local and imported natural gas (21.1%). (The value of fuel imports in 2003 was equivalent to 0.5% of the value of total merchandise imports.) Total installed electricity-generating capacity increased from 6,898 MW in 1996 to 9,298 MW in 2000, following the completion of a 2,400-MW plant at Subahiya. In 2005 the construction of a 1,000-MW gas turbine power plant at az-Zour was completed. Two further power projects were also planned: the 2,400-MW az-Zour North plant and the 1,000-MW az-Zour South II facility. Negotiations for the supply of 8,000m. cu m–15,000m. cu m per year of natural gas to Kuwait's energy industry via an offshore pipeline from Qatar were in progress in 2006.

Services contributed 41.7% of GDP in 2004, and employed 82.6% of the labour force in that year. Kuwait's second most important source of revenue is investment abroad (the total value of which was estimated to be in excess of US $45,000m. in the late 1990s), both in petroleum-related ventures and in other industries, chiefly in the USA, Western Europe and Japan; many such investments are held by the Reserve Fund for Future Generations (RFFG—to which 10% of petroleum revenues must by law be contributed each year, and which is intended to provide an income after hydrocarbon resources have been exhausted) and managed by the Kuwait Investment Authority. Prior to the Iraqi invasion the value of the RFFG was believed to have been some $100,000m. As part of its efforts to diversify the economy, the Government planned to develop the islands of Bubiyan and Failaka into major tourist resorts. In January 2004 a US company was selected as project manager for the Bubiyan island project, the first phase of which—the construction of a new port—was expected to cost about $800m. The combined GDP of the service sectors increased, in real terms, at an average rate of 3.4% per year during 1995–2003.

In 2004 Kuwait recorded a visible trade surplus of US $19,301m., and there was a surplus of $18,884m. on the current account of the balance of payments. In 2003 the principal sources of imports were the USA, Germany and Japan, which provided, respectively, 11.6%, 10.3% and 9.9% of total imports; other important suppliers in that year were Saudi Arabia, the People's Republic of China and Italy. Details concerning the destination of Kuwait's petroleum exports are not available for recent years; however, the major markets for non-petroleum exports in 2003 included Saudi Arabia (13.7%), the UAE, Indonesia and India. The principal exports are petroleum and petroleum products. The principal imports are machinery and transport equipment, which accounted for 41.8% of total imports in 2003, basic manufactures and other manufactured goods, food and live animals, and chemicals and related products.

A budget surplus of KD 2,647.2m. was recorded for the financial year ending 30 June 2005. A deficit of KD 2,625.2m. was forecast for 2005/06, although actual revenue from Kuwait's petroleum interests would undoubtedly be far greater than the projected figure. Kuwait's total external debt in 2003 was estimated at US $12,404m., equivalent to 29.7% of GDP. The average annual rate of inflation in 1998–2004 was 1.7%; consumer prices increased by an annual average of 1.0% in 2003 and 1.3% in 2004. National unemployment among Kuwaitis was estimated at 3.4% in 2003; however, underemployment was unofficially reported to be in excess of 50%.

Kuwait is a member of the GCC; the six GCC states established a unified regional customs tariff in January 2003, and it has been agreed to create a single market and currency no later than January 2010. (On 1 January 2003 Kuwait pegged the dinar to the US dollar, as part of the GCC plan.) The economic convergence criteria for the monetary union were agreed at a GCC summit in Abu Dhabi, the UAE, in December 2005. Kuwait also belongs to the Organization of Arab Petroleum Exporting Countries (OAPEC, see p. 338) and to OPEC. Kuwait is a major aid donor, disbursing loans to developing countries through the Kuwait Fund for Arab Economic Development (KFAED) and the Arab Fund for Economic and Social Development (AFESD, see p. 161).

Despite its significant, oil-based wealth, Kuwait has a number of fundamental weaknesses in its economic structure: instability in its relations with Iraq have necessitated a high level of defence expenditure; reliance on petroleum revenues has impeded diversification into other industries; and its constitutional commitment to provide employment for all Kuwaitis has resulted in a heavy burden on government spending (about 70% of the annual budget is allocated to salaries and subsidies, excluding significant expenditure on defence-sector emoluments). During the early years of this century plans by the Kuwait Petroleum Corporation to allow foreign participation in a development project (known as 'Project Kuwait'), valued at US $7,000m., for the northern oilfields made extremely slow progress; the original project aimed to increase production from 400,000 b/d to 900,000 b/d between 2000–05. However, approval by the Majlis was still required in February 2006, and, despite assurances that all reserves would remain Kuwaiti-owned, many Kuwaitis remained opposed to any foreign involvement in the petroleum sector. Nevertheless, in 2003 the Majlis passed legislation that would increase foreign investment in the economy, including the limited participation of international oil companies in the petroleum sector and measures that would permit foreign banks to operate in Kuwait. Moreover, in November of that year the legislature approved plans to deregulate the aviation sector, a decision that brought to an end the monopoly of the loss-making state-owned Kuwait Airways Corporation (KAC) and opened the industry to international competition. Two new Kuwaiti airlines had been granted licences to compete with KAC by February 2006. The recovery in world petroleum prices from late 1999 was the principal factor contributing to budget surpluses during 1999/2000–2004/05. (Projected deficits in 2005/06 and 2006/07 were expected to be more than covered by higher than predicted petroleum prices.) The main disadvantage of the huge petroleum windfalls accrued in recent years is that incentives for the Government to introduce much-needed reforms, particularly in the non-oil sector, have been further reduced. Ostensibly, the Government remained committed to its four-year action programme, which was launched in 2004 and was intended to stimulate the private sector's role in the economy and to improve the fiscal position through tax and labour market reforms and privatization; however, legislative delays hindered implementation of the proposed changes and there remained high levels of

KUWAIT

opposition to any reduction in public-sector employment and salaries. None the less, huge infrastructure and tourism projects provided some grounds for optimism that the economy could be successfully diversified. In addition, after the US-led military campaign in 2003, the removal of the threat to Kuwait from Saddam Hussain's Baathist regime in Iraq provided a special impetus to the non-hydrocarbons sector; real GDP increases of 9.9% in 2003 and some 7.2% in 2004 were recorded as, in particular, Kuwait benefited strongly from the reconstruction of its conflict-devastated neighbour. Slightly reduced, yet healthy, rates of economic growth (of an estimated 7% and 5%, respectively) were forecast for 2005 and 2006.

Education

Education is compulsory for eight years between the ages of six and 14. Although private schools exist, state education is free, and is graded into pre-primary (for children between four and six years of age), primary (for children aged six to 10), intermediate (10 to 14) and secondary (14 to 18). In 2002/03 enrolment at primary schools included 83% of children in the relevant age-group (males 82%; females 84%), while in 2001/02 secondary enrolment included 77% of children in the relevant age-group (males 75%; females 79%). There is a teacher-training college, a technical college, and a university (where some 18,000 students were enrolled in 1998/99). A KD 1,000m. project to build a new university campus and to gather the institution's dispersed facilities onto one site was in progress in early 2006. More than 4,500 Kuwaiti students receive education abroad. Expenditure on education by the central Government in 2005/06 was budgeted at KD 573.9m. (7.9% of total expenditure).

Public Holidays

2006: 1 January (New Year's Day), 10 January*† (Id al-Adha, Feast of the Sacrifice), 31 January* (Islamic New Year), 25 February (Kuwaiti National Day), 26 February (Liberation Day), 10 April* (Birth of the Prophet), 21 August* (Leilat al-Meiraj, Ascension of the Prophet), 23 October* (Id al-Fitr, end of Ramadan), 31 December*† (Id al-Adha, Feast of the Sacrifice).

2007: 1 January (New Year's Day), 20 January* (Islamic New Year), 25 February (Kuwaiti National Day), 26 February (Liberation Day), 31 March* (Birth of the Prophet), 10 August* (Leilat al-Meiraj, Ascension of the Prophet), 13 October* (Id al-Fitr, end of Ramadan), 20 December* (Id al-Adha, Feast of the Sacrifice).

* These holidays are dependent on the Islamic lunar calendar and may vary by one or two days from the dates given.

† This festival occurs twice (in the Islamic years AH 1426 and 1427) within the same Gregorian year.

Weights and Measures

The metric system is in force.

Statistical Survey

Sources (unless otherwise stated): Economic Research Department, Central Bank of Kuwait, POB 15, 13001 Safat, Kuwait City; tel. 2403257; fax 2440887; e-mail cbk@cbk.gov.kw; internet www.cbk.gov.kw; Central Statistical Office, Ministry of Planning, POB 26188, 13122 Safat, Kuwait City; tel. 2454968; fax 2430464; e-mail salah@mop.gov.kw; internet www.mop.gov.kw.

Note: Unless otherwise indicated, data refer to the State of Kuwait as constituted at 1 August 1990, prior to the Iraqi invasion and annexation of the territory and its subsequent liberation. Furthermore, no account has been taken of the increase in the area of Kuwait as a result of the adjustment to the border with Iraq that came into force on 15 January 1993.

Area and Population

AREA, POPULATION AND DENSITY

Area (sq km)	17,818*
Population (census results)†‡	
21 April 1985	1,697,301
20 April 1995	
Males	913,402
Females	662,168
Total	1,575,570
Population (official estimates at mid-year)†	
2002	2,419,900
2003	2,546,700
2004	2,753,700
Density (per sq km) at mid-2004	154.5

* 6,880 sq miles.
† Figures include Kuwaiti nationals abroad. The total population at the 1995 census comprised 653,616 Kuwaiti nationals (326,301 males, 327,315 females) and 921,954 non-Kuwaitis (587,101 males, 334,853 females).
‡ Excluding adjustment for underenumeration.

GOVERNORATES
(estimated population at mid-2001)

Governorate	Area (sq km)*	Population	Density (per sq km)
Capital	199.8	388,532	1,944.6
Hawalli	}	488,294	}
Great Mubarak	368.4	144,981	3,272.3
Farwaniya	}	572,252	}
Al-Jahra	11,230.2	282,353	25.1
Al-Ahmadi	5,119.6	364,484	71.2
Total†	16,918.0	2,243,080	132.6

* Excluding the islands of Bubiyan and Warba (combined area 900 sq km).
† Including 2,184 unallocated.

PRINCIPAL TOWNS
(population at 1995 census)

Kuwait City (capital)	28,747	Subbah as-Salem	54,608
Salmiya	129,775	Sulaibiah	53,639
Jaleeb ash-Shuyukh	102,169	Farwaniya	52,928
Hawalli	82,154	Al-Kreen	50,689
South Kheetan	62,241	Subahiya	50,644

Mid-2003 (UN estimate, incl. suburbs): Kuwait City 1,222,374 (Source: UN, *World Urbanization Prospects: The 2003 Revision*).

BIRTHS, MARRIAGES AND DEATHS

	Registered live births		Registered marriages		Registered deaths	
	Number	Rate (per 1,000)	Number	Rate (per 1,000)	Number	Rate (per 1,000)
1993	37,379	25.6	10,077	6.9	3,441	2.4
1994	38,868	24.0	9,550	5.9	3,464	2.1
1995	41,169	22.8	9,515	5.3	3,781	2.1
1996	44,620	23.6	9,022	4.8	3,812	2.0
1997	42,817	21.6	9,610	4.9	4,017	2.0
1998	41,424	20.4	10,335	5.1	4,216	2.1
1999	41,135	19.5	10,847	5.1	4,187	2.0
2000	41,843	19.1	10,785	4.9	4,227	1.9

Expectation of life (WHO estimates, years at birth): 77 (males 76; females 79) in 2003 (Source: WHO, *World Health Report*).

KUWAIT

ECONOMICALLY ACTIVE POPULATION*
('000 persons aged 15 years and over, 2004)

	Kuwaitis	Non-Kuwaitis	Total
Agriculture, hunting and fishing	0.1	26.2	26.3
Mining and quarrying	4.4	2.6	7.1
Manufacturing	8.0	82.3	90.3
Electricity, gas and water	7.0	2.5	9.5
Construction	2.0	109.2	111.2
Trade, restaurants and hotels	4.6	231.0	235.6
Transport, storage and communications	6.7	39.6	46.3
Finance, insurance, real estate and business services	9.5	57.1	66.6
Public administration	230.7	578.0	808.7
Activities not adequately defined	17.7	132.1	149.8
Total labour force	290.7	1,260.6	1,551.3
Males	n.a.	n.a.	1,160.3
Females	n.a.	n.a.	391.0

* Including 25,900 unemployed persons, categorized by their previous occupational sector.

Source: IMF, *Kuwait: Selected Issues and Statistical Appendix* (July 2005).

Health and Welfare

KEY INDICATORS

Total fertility rate (children per woman, 2003)	2.6
Under-5 mortality rate (per 1,000 live births, 2004)	12
HIV/AIDS (% of persons aged 15–49, 1994)	0.12
Physicians (per 1,000 head, 2001)	1.53
Hospital beds (per 1,000 head, 1997)	2.76
Health expenditure (2002): US $ per head (PPP)	552
Health expenditure (2002): % of GDP	3.8
Health expenditure (2002): public (% of total)	75.2
Human Development Index (2003): ranking	44
Human Development Index (2003): value	0.844

For sources and definitions, see explanatory note on p. vi.

Agriculture

PRINCIPAL CROPS
('000 metric tons)

	2002	2003*	2004*
Potatoes	32.6	33.0	33.0
Cabbages	8.9	9.0	9.0
Lettuce	6.3	6.4	6.4
Tomatoes	35.1	36.0	36.0
Cauliflower	11.4	11.5	11.5
Pumpkins, squash and gourds*	5.3	4.9	5.0
Cucumbers and gherkins	32.3	32.3	32.3
Aubergines (Eggplants)	15.9	16.0	16.0
Chillies and green peppers	6.8	6.8	6.8
Dry onions	3.7	3.8	3.8
Other vegetables (incl. melons)*	58.4	58.6	57.8
Dates	10.4	10.4	10.5

* FAO estimates.
Source: FAO.

LIVESTOCK
('000 head, year ending September)

	2002	2003*	2004*
Cattle	25	25	25
Camels	5	5	5
Sheep	800	850	900
Goats	147	148	150
Poultry*	30,000	31,000	32,000

* FAO estimates.
Source: FAO.

Statistical Survey

LIVESTOCK PRODUCTS
('000 metric tons)

	2002	2003*	2004*
Beef and veal*	2.2	1.9	2.0
Mutton and lamb*	37.0	36.9	36.9
Poultry meat	36.8	38.0	42.0
Cows' milk	40.0*	42.0	40.0
Goats' milk	4.9*	4.9	5.0
Hen eggs	26.1	25.0	25.0
Sheepskins (fresh)	13.0*	13.0	13.0

* FAO estimate(s).
Source: FAO.

Fishing

(metric tons, live weight)

	2001	2002*	2003*
Capture	5,846	5,900	5,900
Hilsa shad	337	340	340
Mullets	456	430	430
Groupers	268	265	265
Grunts and sweetlips	191	200	200
Croakers and drums	853	860	860
Yellowfin seabream	271	280	280
Indo-Pacific king mackerel	204	204	204
Carangids	242	240	240
Natantian decapods	1,977	1,980	1,980
Aquaculture	195	195	195
Total catch	6,041	6,095	6,095

* FAO estimates.
Source: FAO.

Mining*

	2002	2003	2004
Crude petroleum (million barrels)	680	817	880
Natural gas (million cu metres)†	8,700	8,800	9,600

* Estimates, including an equal share of production with Saudi Arabia from the Neutral/Partitioned Zone.
† On a dry basis.

Source: US Geological Survey.

KUWAIT

Industry

SELECTED PRODUCTS
('000 metric tons, unless otherwise stated)

	2000	2001	2002
Bran and flour*	210.0	211.2	225.1†
Sulphur (by-product)‡	512	524	634§
Chlorine*	14.8	17.7	15.8†
Caustic soda (Sodium hydroxide)*	18.5	20.0	17.8†
Salt*	36.8	37.5	35.7†
Nitrogenous fertilizers‡||	288	290	320§
Motor spirit (petrol) (million barrels)‡¶	12	10	15§
Kerosene (million barrels)‡¶	45	30	45§
Gas-diesel (Distillate fuel) oils (million barrels)‡¶	84	70	85§
Residual fuel oils (million barrels)‡¶	57	60	75§
Petroleum bitumen (asphalt)§¶	331	252	297
Liquefied petroleum gas ('000 barrels)*¶	35	35	33
Quicklime‡	40	40	40§
Cement‡	1,187	921	1,584§
Electric energy (million kWh)*¶	32,300	34,500	36,400†

2003‡§ ('000 metric tons, unless otherwise stated): Sulphur (by-product) 714; Motor spirit (petrol) (million barrels) 15¶; Kerosene 45¶; Gas-diesel (Distillate fuel) oils (million barrels) 85¶; Residual fuel oils (million barrels) 70¶; Quicklime 40; Cement 1,600.

2004‡ ('000 metric tons, unless otherwise stated): Sulphur (by-product) 730; Motor spirit (petrol) (million barrels) 15¶; Kerosene 45¶; Gas-diesel (Distillate fuel) oils (million barrels) 85¶; Residual fuel oils (million barrels) 75¶; Quicklime 40; Cement 1,600.

* Source: IMF, *Kuwait: Statistical Appendix* (July 2004).
† Figure for January–October.
‡ Source: US Geological Survey.
§ Provisional or estimated figure(s).
\|\| Production in terms of nitrogen.
¶ Including an equal share of production with Saudi Arabia from the Neutral/Partitioned Zone.

Finance

CURRENCY AND EXCHANGE RATES

Monetary Units
1,000 fils = 10 dirhams = 1 Kuwaiti dinar (KD).

Sterling, Dollar and Euro Equivalents (30 December 2005)
£1 sterling = 502.80 fils;
US $1 = 292.00 fils;
€1 = 344.47 fils;
100 Kuwaiti dinars = £198.89 = $342.47 = €290.30.

Average Exchange Rate (fils per US $)
2003 298.0
2004 294.7
2005 292.0

Since 1 January 2003 the official exchange rate has been fixed within the range of US $1 = 289 fils to $1 = 310 fils (KD 1 = $3.4602 to KD 1 = $3.2258).

GENERAL BUDGET
(KD million, year ending 30 June)

Revenue	2003/04	2004/05	2005/06*
Tax revenue	189.3	232.4	197.4
International trade and transactions	146.6	166.5	142.3
Non-tax revenue	6,748.0	8,730.0	4,409.4
Oil revenue	6,149.9	8,170.5	3,914.0
Total operating revenue of government enterprises	385.2	396.4	400.9
Total	6,937.3	8,962.4	4,606.8

Expenditure	2003/04	2004/05	2005/06*
Current expenditure	3,823.7	4,426.0	4,916.7
Defence, security and justice	1,203.9	1,320.5	1,365.7
Education	477.9	507.8	573.9
Health	338.4	352.2	381.7
Social and labour affairs	144.5	155.4	158.5
Electricity and water	459.3	651.3	796.1
Land acquisitions	48.0	147.0	—
Capital expenditure	40.5	44.5	90.0
Development expenditure	521.5	531.3	940.0
Public works	179.1	193.0	275.0
Electricity and water	240.1	234.5	260.0
Transfers to attached and public institutions	1,089.1	1,166.4	1,285.3
Total	5,522.8	6,315.2	7,232.0

* Projections.

INTERNATIONAL RESERVES
(US $ million at 31 December)

	2002	2003	2004
Gold (national valuation)	105.9	107.7	107.6
IMF special drawing rights	132.9	159.8	181.8
Reserve position in IMF	718.2	776.8	712.7
Foreign exchange	8,357.0	6,640.5	7,347.4
Total	9,314.0	7,684.8	8,349.5

Source: IMF, *International Financial Statistics*.

MONEY SUPPLY
(KD million at 31 December)

	2002	2003	2004
Currency outside banks	442.2	494.1	527.9
Demand deposits at deposit money banks	1,624.6	2,117.4	2,454.9
Total money	2,066.7	2,611.5	2,982.8

Source: IMF, *International Financial Statistics*.

COST OF LIVING
(Consumer Price Index; base: 2000 = 100)

	2002	2003	2004
Food	104.5	106.6	110.0
Beverages and tobacco	105.8	107.5	111.2
Clothing and footwear	105.9	108.0	111.0
Housing services	102.1	103.8	104.6
All items (incl. others)	102.2	103.2	104.5

NATIONAL ACCOUNTS
(KD million at current prices)

Expenditure on the Gross Domestic Product

	2002	2003	2004
Government final consumption expenditure	2,929	3,281	3,455
Private final consumption expenditure	5,747	5,960	6,205
Increase in stocks / Gross fixed capital formation	1,980	2,012	2,331
Total domestic expenditure	10,656	11,253	11,991
Exports of goods and services	5,171	7,432	9,885
Less Imports of goods and services	4,243	4,917	5,455
GDP in purchasers' values	11,584	13,768	16,420

Source: IMF, *International Financial Statistics*.

KUWAIT

Gross Domestic Product by Economic Activity

	2002	2003	2004
Agriculture, hunting, forestry and fishing	59.9	64.7	70.0
Mining and quarrying	4,423.0	5,811.3	7,837.5
Manufacturing	907.3	1,076.4	1,314.6
Electricity, gas and water	275.3	299.4	311.9
Construction	312.0	333.0	361.0
Trade	822.5	918.0	999.2
Restaurants and hotels	123.7	142.4	149.8
Transport, storage and communications	594.1	684.2	712.5
Finance, insurance, real estate and business services	1,924.5	2,118.5	2,320.7
Community, social and personal services	2,540.8	2,736.4	2,883.4
Sub-total	11,983.1	14,184.3	16,960.6
Import duties	96.9	135.1	120.8
Less Imputed bank service charges	−495.5	−551.3	−661.1
GDP in purchasers' values	11,584.5	13,768.1	16,420.3

BALANCE OF PAYMENTS
(US $ million)

	2002	2003	2004
Exports of goods f.o.b.	15,366	21,794	30,221
Imports of goods f.o.b.	−8,124	−9,882	−10,920
Trade balance	7,242	11,912	19,301
Exports of services	1,648	3,144	3,322
Imports of services	−5,837	−6,617	−7,591
Balance on goods and services	3,053	8,439	15,032
Other income received	3,708	3,725	6,844
Other income paid	−365	−369	−445
Balance on goods, services and income	6,397	11,795	21,432
Current transfers received	49	67	88
Current transfers paid	−2,195	−2,446	−2,637
Current balance	4,251	9,416	18,884
Capital account (net)	1,672	1,429	434
Direct investment abroad	155	4,983	−1,873
Direct investment from abroad	7	−67	−20
Portfolio investment assets	−3,425	−13,580	−13,784
Portfolio investment liabilities	161	336	288
Other investment assets	−3,754	−3,329	−5,036
Other investment liabilities	1,695	−285	377
Net errors and omissions	−1,733	−727	1,355
Overall balance	−973	−1,824	626

Source: IMF, *International Financial Statistics*.

External Trade

PRINCIPAL COMMODITIES
(distribution by SITC, KD million)

Imports c.i.f.	2001	2002	2003
Food and live animals	355.3	382.9	432.3
Chemicals and related products	221.9	238.6	270.6
Basic manufactures	451.9	510.5	593.3
Machinery and transport equipment	912.2	1,089.5	1,368.3
Miscellaneous manufactured articles	348.9	378.1	443.8
Total (incl. others)	2,413.3	2,735.8	3,274.1

Exports f.o.b.	2001	2002	2003
Mineral fuels, lubricants, etc.	4,594.0	4,275.8	5,683.4
Petroleum, petroleum products, etc.*	4,590.8	4,272.8	5,663.5
Chemicals and related products	246.5	248.2	264.6
Total (incl. others)*	4,969.7	4,666.2	6,162.1

* Estimates by the Central Bank of Kuwait.

PRINCIPAL TRADING PARTNERS
(KD million)*

Imports c.i.f.	2001	2002	2003
Australia	83.4	103.3	108.6
Brazil	27.2	25.0	35.1
Canada	54.3	41.3	48.9
China, People's Repub.	105.5	142.4	187.1
France (incl. Monaco)	86.7	88.0	95.2
Germany	238.8	255.1	336.4
India	90.2	106.4	122.7
Iran	39.0	43.8	56.5
Italy	141.3	153.0	168.0
Japan	230.7	292.4	322.9
Korea, Repub.	66.0	70.0	81.4
Malaysia	32.4	36.8	40.4
Netherlands	38.6	44.1	44.9
Saudi Arabia	156.0	176.5	222.1
Spain	40.2	43.3	48.3
Switzerland-Liechtenstein	37.4	39.5	41.7
Syria	16.3	27.4	17.4
Taiwan	27.9	31.2	34.9
Thailand	30.7	33.6	35.4
Turkey	41.8	56.3	66.6
United Arab Emirates	86.5	96.5	121.7
United Kingdom	120.0	122.0	146.1
USA	255.9	299.7	380.5
Total (incl. others)	2,413.3	2,735.8	3,274.1

Exports f.o.b.†	2001	2002	2003
Bahrain	8.0	7.7	12.5
Belgium-Luxembourg	6.1	5.7	3.1
China, People's Repub.	25.7	23.9	25.0
Egypt	13.1	10.6	12.0
India	19.0	25.1	29.4
Indonesia	30.0	39.5	37.3
Iran	6.6	7.8	6.8
Japan	2.8	5.8	2.4
Jordan	8.0	9.1	11.5
Korea, Repub.	6.3	0.7	1.0
Lebanon	6.0	5.5	4.7
Malaysia	10.9	7.0	5.7
Oman	6.9	6.5	5.5
Pakistan	20.7	17.6	24.0
Philippines	6.2	8.7	7.0
Qatar	6.9	11.1	9.6
Saudi Arabia	50.3	52.4	68.3
Spain	15.5	15.7	7.7
Syria	9.3	8.3	11.1
Taiwan	3.3	4.0	3.5
Turkey	3.4	8.0	4.6
United Arab Emirates	39.8	41.9	49.7
USA	6.5	2.9	27.7
Total (incl. others)	378.9	393.4	498.5

* Imports by country of production; exports by country of last consignment.
† Excluding petroleum exports.

KUWAIT

Transport

ROAD TRAFFIC
(motor vehicles in use at 31 December)

	1995	1996	1997
Passenger cars	662,946	701,172	747,042
Buses and coaches	11,937	12,322	13,094
Goods vehicles	116,813	121,753	127,386

1999: Buses and coaches 12,775; Goods vehicles 97,706.

2000: Buses and coaches 10,974; Goods vehicles 80,378.

SHIPPING

Merchant Fleet
(registered at 31 December)

	2002	2003	2004
Number of vessels	201	208	213
Displacement ('000 grt)	2,256.0	2,324.3	2,377.6

Source: Lloyd's Register-Fairplay, *World Fleet Statistics*.

International Sea-borne Freight Traffic
('000 metric tons)*

	1988	1989	1990
Goods loaded	61,778	69,097	51,400
Goods unloaded	7,123	7,015	4,522

* Including Kuwait's share of traffic in the Neutral/Partitioned Zone.

Source: UN, *Monthly Bulletin of Statistics*.

Goods loaded ('000 metric tons): 89,945 in 1997.

Goods unloaded ('000 metric tons): 746 in 1991 (July–December only); 2,537 in 1992; 4,228 in 1993; 5,120 in 1994; 5,854 in 1995; 6,497 in 1996; 6,049 in 1997.

CIVIL AVIATION
(traffic on scheduled services)

	1999	2000	2001
Kilometres flown (million)	36	37	37
Passengers carried ('000)	2,130	2,113	2,085
Passenger-km (million)	6,158	6,134	6,010
Total ton-km (million)	829	805	777

Source: UN, *Statistical Yearbook*.

Tourism

VISITOR ARRIVALS BY COUNTRY OF ORIGIN
(incl. excursionists)

	1999	2000	2001
Bahrain	49,658	50,024	61,726
Bangladesh	79,731	54,466	61,027
Egypt	226,262	219,553	238,308
India	226,629	225,642	270,619
Iran	93,801	100,328	101,604
Lebanon	48,001	48,642	50,695
Pakistan	78,206	74,429	75,854
Philippines	37,357	43,310	47,969
Saudi Arabia	574,924	641,691	660,916
Sri Lanka	54,816	54,804	56,204
Syria	146,084	143,020	165,097
Total (incl. others)	1,883,633	1,944,233	2,069,051

Tourism receipts (US $ million, incl. passenger transport): 283 in 2001; 322 in 2002; 328 in 2003.

Source: World Tourism Organization, *Yearbook of Tourism Statistics*.

Communications Media

	2002	2003	2004
Telephones ('000 main lines in use)	481.9	486.9	497.0
Mobile cellular telephones ('000 subscribers)	1,227	1,420	2,000
Personal computers ('000 in use)	285	400	450
Internet users ('000)	250	567	600

1996: Daily newspapers 8 (average circulation 635,000 copies); Non-daily newspapers 78.

1999: Radio receivers 1,200,000 in use; Television receivers 910,000 in use; Facsimile machines 60,000 in use; Book titles published 219.

2000: Television receivers 930,000 in use.

Sources: UNESCO, *Statistical Yearbook*; UN, *Statistical Yearbook*; International Telecommunication Union.

Education

(state-controlled schools, 2000/01)

	Schools	Teachers	Students Males	Females	Total
Kindergarten	153	3,379	22,142	22,128	44,270
Primary	184	8,151	48,796	49,322	98,118
Intermediate	165	9,073	47,955	47,509	95,464
Secondary	117	9,234	34,868	41,353	76,221
Religious institutes	7	351	n.a.	n.a.	2,454
Special training institutes	33	756	n.a.	n.a.	543

Private education (1996/97): 63 kindergarten schools (598 teachers, 12,172 students); 80 primary schools (2,341 teachers, 47,111 students); 82 intermediate schools (1,860 teachers, 36,254 students); 66 secondary schools (1,576 teachers, 20,932 students).

2000/01 (private education): 112 schools; 7,324 teachers; 128,204 students.

Adult literacy rate: 82.9% (males 84.7%; females 81.0%) in 2003 (Source: UN Development Programme, *Human Development Report*).

Directory

The Constitution

The principal provisions of the Constitution, promulgated on 16 November 1962, are set out below. On 29 August 1976 the Amir suspended four articles of the Constitution dealing with the National Assembly, the Majlis al-Umma. On 24 August 1980 the Amir issued a decree ordering the establishment of an elected legislature before the end of February 1981. The new Majlis was elected on 23 February 1981, and fresh legislative elections followed on 20 February 1985. The Majlis was dissolved by Amiri decree in July 1986, and some sections of the Constitution, including the stipulation that new elections should be held within two months of dissolving the legislature (see below), were suspended. A new Majlis was elected on 5 October 1992 and convened on 20 October. On 16 May 2005 the Majlis approved legislation allowing women to vote in and stand as candidates for parliamentary and local elections.

SOVEREIGNTY

Kuwait is an independent sovereign Arab State; its sovereignty may not be surrendered, and no part of its territory may be relinquished. Offensive war is prohibited by the Constitution.

Succession as Amir is restricted to heirs of the late Mubarak as-Sabah, and an Heir Apparent must be appointed within one year of the accession of a new Amir.

EXECUTIVE AUTHORITY

Executive power is vested in the Amir, who exercises it through the Council of Ministers. The Amir will appoint the Prime Minister 'after the traditional consultations', and will appoint and dismiss ministers on the recommendation of the Prime Minister. Ministers need not be members of the Majlis al-Umma, although all ministers who are not members of parliament assume membership *ex officio* in the legislature for the duration of office. The Amir also formulates laws, which shall not be effective unless published in the *Official Gazette*. The Amir establishes public institutions. All decrees issued in these respects shall be conveyed to the Majlis. No law is issued unless it is approved by the Majlis.

LEGISLATURE

A National Assembly, the Majlis al-Umma, of 50 members will be elected for a four-year term by all natural-born Kuwaitis over the age of 21 years, except servicemen and police, who may not vote. Candidates for election must possess the franchise, be over 30 years of age and literate. The Majlis will convene for at least eight months in any year, and new elections shall be held within two months of the last dissolution of the outgoing legislature.

Restrictions on the commercial activities of ministers include an injunction forbidding them to sell property to the Government.

The Amir may ask for reconsideration of a bill that has been approved by the Majlis and sent to him for ratification, but the bill would automatically become law if it were subsequently adopted by a two-thirds' majority at the next sitting, or by a simple majority at a subsequent sitting. The Amir may declare martial law, but only with the approval of the legislature.

The Majlis may adopt a vote of 'no confidence' in a minister, in which case the minister must resign. Such a vote is not permissible in the case of the Prime Minister, but the legislature may approach the Amir on the matter, and the Amir shall then either dismiss the Prime Minister or dissolve the Majlis.

CIVIL SERVICE

Entry to the civil service is confined to Kuwaiti citizens.

PUBLIC LIBERTIES

Kuwaitis are equal before the law in prestige, rights and duties. Individual freedom is guaranteed. No one shall be seized, arrested or exiled except within the rules of law.

No punishment shall be administered except for an act or abstaining from an act considered a crime in accordance with a law applicable at the time of committing it, and no penalty shall be imposed more severe than that which could have been imposed at the time of committing the crime.

Freedom of opinion is guaranteed to everyone, and each has the right to express himself through speech, writing or other means within the limits of the law.

The press is free within the limits of the law, and it should not be suppressed except in accordance with the dictates of law.

Freedom of performing religious rites is protected by the State according to prevailing customs, provided it does not violate the public order and morality.

Trade unions will be permitted and property must be respected. An owner is not banned from managing his property except within the boundaries of law. No property should be taken from anyone, except within the prerogatives of law, unless a just compensation be given.

Houses may not be entered, except in cases provided by law. Every Kuwaiti has freedom of movement and choice of place of residence within the State. This right shall not be controlled except in cases stipulated by law.

Every person has the right to education and freedom to choose his type of work. Freedom to form peaceful societies is guaranteed within the limits of law.

The Government

HEAD OF STATE

Amir of Kuwait: His Highness Sheikh SABAH AL-AHMAD AL-JABER AS-SABAH (acceded 29 January 2006).

COUNCIL OF MINISTERS
(May 2006)

Prime Minister: Sheikh NASSER AL-MUHAMMAD AL-AHMAD AS-SABAH.

First Deputy Prime Minister and Minister of the Interior and of Defence: Sheikh JABER MUBARAK AL-HAMAD AS-SABAH.

Deputy Prime Minister and Minister of Foreign Affairs: Sheikh Dr MUHAMMAD SABAH AS-SALIM AS-SABAH.

Deputy Prime Minister, Minister of State for Cabinet Affairs and for National Assembly Affairs: MUHAMMAD DHAIFALLAH SHARAR.

Minister of Health: Sheikh AHMAD ABDULLAH AL-AHMAD AS-SABAH.

Minister of Energy: Sheikh AHMAD AL-FAHD AL-AHMAD AS-SABAH.

Minister of Communications: Dr ISMAIL KHUDHUR ASH-SHATTI.

Minister of Information: (vacant).

Minister of Finance: BADER MISHARI AL-HUMAIDHI.

Minister of Public Works and Minister of State for Housing Affairs: BADER NASSER AL-HUMEIDI.

Minister of Education and Higher Education: Dr ADEL TALEB AT-TABTABA'I.

Minister of Justice and of Awqaf (Religious Endowments) and Islamic Affairs: Dr ABDULLAH ABD AR-RAHMAN AL-MA'TUQ.

Minister of State for Municipality Affairs: ABDULLAH SAUD AL-MUHAILBI.

Minister of Social Affairs and Labour: Sheikh ALI JARRAH SABAH AS-SABAH.

Minister of Planning and Minister of State for Administrative Development Affairs: Dr MASSOUMA SALEH AL-MUBARAK.

Minister of Commerce and Industry: Dr YOUSUF SAYED HASSAN AZ-ZALZALAH.

PROVINCIAL GOVERNORS

Al-Ahmadi: Sheikh ALI ABDULLAH AS-SALIM AS-SABAH.
Farwaniya: Dr IBRAHIM DUAIJ AL-IBRAHIM AS-SABAH.
Great Mubarak: MUBARAK HUMUD AL-JABER AS-SABAH.
Hawalli: IBRAHIM JASEM AL-MUDHAF.
Al-Jahra: ALI JABER AL-AHMAD AS-SABAH.
Kuwait (Capital): Dr DAUD MUSAED AS-SALIH.

MINISTRIES

Ministry of Awqaf (Religious Endowments) and Islamic Affairs: POB 13, 13001 Safat, Kuwait City; tel. 2466300; fax 2449943; internet www.awkaf.net.

Ministry of Commerce and Industry: POB 2944, 13030 Safat, Kuwait City; tel. 2463600; fax 2424411.

Ministry of Communications: POB 15, 13001 Safat, Kuwait City; internet www.mockw.net.

Ministry of Defence: POB 1170, 13012 Safat, Kuwait City; tel. 4819277; fax 4846059.

Ministry of Education and Higher Education: POB 7, 13001 Safat, Hilali St, Kuwait City; tel. 4836800; fax 2423676; e-mail webmaster@moe.edu.kw; internet www.moe.edu.kw.

Ministry of Energy: POB 12, 13001 Safat, Kuwait City; tel. 4896000; fax 4897484.

Ministry of Finance: POB 9, 13001 Safat, al-Morkab St, Ministries Complex, Kuwait City; tel. 2468200; fax 2404025; e-mail webmaster@mof.gov.kw; internet www.mof.gov.kw.

KUWAIT

Ministry of Foreign Affairs: POB 3, 13001 Safat, Gulf St, Kuwait City; tel. 2425141; fax 2430559; e-mail info@mofa.org; internet www.mofa.gov.kw.

Ministry of Health: POB 5, 13001 Safat, Arabian Gulf St, Kuwait City; tel. 4877422; fax 4865414; e-mail health@moh.gov.kw; internet www.moh.gov.kw.

Ministry of Information: POB 193, 13002 Safat, as-Sour St, Kuwait City; tel. 2415301; fax 2419642; e-mail info@media.gov.kw; internet www.media.gov.kw.

Ministry of the Interior: POB 11, 13001 Safat, Kuwait City; tel. 2524199; fax 2561268.

Ministry of Justice: POB 6, 13001 Safat, al-Morkab St, Ministries Complex, Kuwait City; tel. 2467300; fax 2466957; e-mail qht@moj.gov.kw; internet www.moj.gov.kw.

Ministry of Planning: POB 15, 13001 Safat, Kuwait City; tel. 2428100; fax 2414734; e-mail info@mop.gov.kw; internet www.mop.gov.kw.

Ministry of Public Works: POB 8, 13001 Safat, Kuwait City; tel. 5385520; fax 5380829.

Ministry of Social Affairs and Labour: POB 563, 13006 Safat, Kuwait City; tel. 2464500; fax 2419877.

Legislature

MAJLIS AL-UMMA
(National Assembly)

Speaker: JASEM AL-KHARAFI.

Elections to the 50-seat Majlis took place on 5 July 2003: 21 seats were secured by Islamist candidates, 14 were won by pro-Government candidates, three by liberals and 12 by independents.

Political Organizations

Political parties are not permitted in Kuwait. However, several quasi-political organizations are in existence. Among those that have been represented in the Majlis since 1992 are:

Constitutional Group: supported by merchants.

Islamic Constitutional Movement: Sunni Muslim.

Kuwait Democratic Forum: internet www.kuwaitdf.org/df; f. 1991; loose association of secular, liberal and Arab nationalist groups; campaigned for the extension of voting rights to women.

National Democratic Rally (NDR): f. 1997; secular, liberal; Sec.-Gen. Dr AHMAD BISHARA.

National Islamic Coalition: Shi'a Muslim.

Salafeen (Islamic Popular Movement): Sunni Muslim.

Diplomatic Representation

EMBASSIES IN KUWAIT

Afghanistan: POB 33186, 73452 Rawdah, Surra, Block 6, St 13, House 16, Kuwait City; tel. 5379211; fax 5379212; e-mail afg_emb_kuw@hotmail.com; Ambassador MUHAMMAD YOUSUF SAMAD.

Algeria: POB 578, 13006 Safat, Istiqlal St, Kuwait City; tel. 2519987; fax 2563052; Ambassador MUHAMMAD BURUBA.

Argentina: POB 3788, 40188 Mishref, Kuwait City; tel. 5379211; fax 5379212; e-mail ekuwa@mrecic.gov.ar; Ambassador RICARDO E. INSUA.

Australia: 15451 Dasmah, Le Meridien Kuwait, Bneid al-Gar, Kuwait City; tel. 2570391; fax 2570392; internet www.embassy.gov.au/kw.html; Ambassador Dr RALPH KING.

Austria: POB 15013, Daiya, 35451 Kuwait City; tel. 2552532; fax 2563052; e-mail kuwait-ob@bmaa.gv.at; Ambassador ROLAND HAUSER.

Azerbaijan: Kuwait City; Ambassador SHAHIN ABDULLAYEV.

Bahrain: POB 196, 13002 Safat, Area 6, Surra Rd, Villa 35, Kuwait City; tel. 5318530; fax 5330882; e-mail 61116@kems.net; Ambassador ABD AR-RAHMAN M. AL-FADHEL.

Bangladesh: POB 22344, 13084 Safat, Khaldya, Block 6, Ali bin Abi Taleb St, House 361, Kuwait City; tel. 5316042; fax 5316041; e-mail bdoot@ncc.moc.kw; Ambassador NAZRUL ISLAM KHAN.

Belgium: POB 3280, 13033 Safat, Baghdad St, Block 8, House 15, Kuwait City; tel. 5722014; fax 5748389; e-mail kuwait@diplobel.be; internet www.diplomatie.be/kuwait; Ambassador ROBERT VANDEMEULEBROUCKE.

Bhutan: POB 1510, 13016 Safat, Jabriya, Block 9, St 20, Villa 7, Kuwait City; tel. 5331506; fax 5338959; e-mail bhutankuwait@hotmail.com; Ambassador TSHERING WANGDI.

Bosnia and Herzegovina: POB 6131, 32036 Hawalli, Bayan, Block 3, Rd 21, St 1, House 46, Kuwait City; tel. 5392637; fax 5392106; Ambassador ŠERIF MUJKANOVIĆ.

Brazil: POB 39761, 73058 Nuzha, Block 2, St 1, Jadah 1, Villa 8, Kuwait City; tel. 5328610; fax 5328613; e-mail brasemkw@qualitynet.net; internet www.brazilianembassykw.com; Ambassador MARIO DA GRAÇA ROITER.

Bulgaria: POB 12090, 71651 Shamiya, Jabriya, Block 11, St 107, Kuwait City; tel. 5314459; fax 5321453; e-mail bgembkw@fasttelco.com; Ambassador ANGEL N. MANTCHEV.

Canada: POB 25281, 13113 Safat, Diiya, Block 4, 24 al-Motawakell St, Plot 121, Villa 24, Kuwait City; tel. 2563025; fax 2563023; e-mail kwait@dfait-maeci.gc.ca; internet www.dfait-maeci.gc.ca/kuwait/menu-en.asp; Ambassador DENIS THIBAULT.

China, People's Republic: POB 2346, 13024 Safat, Dasmah, Sheikh Ahmad al-Jaber Bldgs 4 & 5, Kuwait City; tel. 5333340; fax 5333341; e-mail chinaemb_kw@mfa.gov.cn; Ambassador WU JIUHONG.

Czech Republic: POB 1151, 13012 Safat, Kuwait City; tel. 2529018; fax 2529021; e-mail kuwait@embassy.mzv.cz; internet www.mzv.cz/kuwait; Ambassador Dr ANTONÍN BLAŽEK.

Egypt: POB 11252, 35153 Dasmah, Istiqlal St, Kuwait City; tel. 2519955; fax 2553877; Ambassador ABD ELRAHIM ISMAIL SHALABY.

Eritrea: POB 53016, 73015 Nuzha, Jabriya, Block 9, St 21, House 9, Kuwait City; tel. 5317426; fax 5317429; Ambassador MOUSA YASSIEN SHEIKH AD-DIN.

Ethiopia: POB 939, 45710 Safat, Jabriya, Block 10, St 107, Villa 30, Kuwait City; tel. 5330128; fax 5331179; e-mail ethiokuwait@yahoo.com; Ambassador KADAFOU MUHAMMAD HANFARY.

France: POB 1037, 13011 Safat, Mansouriah, Block 1, St 13, Villa 24, Kuwait City; tel. 2571061; fax 2571058; Ambassador CLAUDE LOSGUARDI.

Germany: POB 805, 13009 Safat, Dahiya Abdullah as-Salem, Area 1, Ave 14, Villa 13, Kuwait City; tel. 2520857; fax 2520763; e-mail info@kuwait.diplo.de; internet www.kuwait.diplo.de; Ambassador KLAUS ACHENBACH.

Greece: POB 23812, 13099 Safat, Khaldiya, Block 4, St 44, House 4, Kuwait City; tel. 4817101; fax 4817103; e-mail grembkw@hotmail.com; Ambassador EVANGELOS DENAXAS.

Hungary: POB 23955, 13100 Safat, Qortuba, Area 2, Al-Baha'a bin Zuheir St 776, Kuwait City; tel. 5323901; fax 5323904; e-mail huembkwi@quality.net; Ambassador JÁNOS GYURIS.

India: POB 1450, 13015 Safat, 34 Istiqlal St, Kuwait City; tel. 2530600; fax 2525811; e-mail indemb@ncc.moc.kw; Ambassador SHRI M. GANAPATHI.

Indonesia: POB 21560, 13076 Safat, Kaifan, Block 6, Al-Andalus St, House 29, Kuwait City; tel. 4839927; fax 4819250; e-mail unitkom@kbrikuwait.org; internet www.kbrikuwait.org; Ambassador HADROMI NAKIM.

Iran: POB 4686, 13047 Safat, Daiyah, Embassies Area, Block B, Kuwait City; tel. 2560694; fax 2529868; e-mail iranebassy@hotmail.com; Ambassador SAYED JAFAR MUSAVI.

Italy: POB 4453, 13045 Safat, Kuwait City; tel. 5356010; fax 5356030; e-mail ambasciata.alkuwait@esteri.it; internet www.ambalkuwait.esteri.it; Ambassador VINCENZO PRATI.

Japan: POB 2304, 13024 Safat, Jabriya, Area 9, Plot 496, Kuwait City; tel. 5312870; fax 5326168; Ambassador MASAMITSU OKI.

Jordan: POB 39891, 73059 Kuwait City; tel. 2533261; fax 2533270; e-mail kujor@qualitynet.net; Ambassador MUHAMMAD AL-QURAAN.

Korea, Republic: POB 20771, 13068 Safat, Rawda, Block 1, St 10, House 17, Kuwait City; tel. 2554206; fax 2526874; Ambassador PARK IN-KOOK.

Lebanon: POB 253, 13003 Safat, 31 Istiqlal St, Kuwait City; tel. 2562103; fax 2571682; Ambassador KHALED AL-KILANI.

Libya: POB 21460, 13075 Safat, 27 Istiqlal St, Kuwait City; tel. 2562103; fax 2571682; Chargé d'affaires IDRIS DAHMANI BU DIB.

Malaysia: POB 4105, 13042 Safat, Daiya, Diplomatic Enclave, Area 5, Istiqlal St, Plot 5, Kuwait City; tel. 2550394; fax 2550384; e-mail malkuwait@kln.gov.my; Ambassador HUSNI ZAI BIN YAACOB.

Morocco: Yarmouk, Block 2, St 2, Villa 14, Kuwait City; tel. 5312980; fax 5317423; e-mail ambkow@yahoo.fr; Ambassador MUHAMMAD BELAICH.

Netherlands: POB 21822, 13079 Safat, Jabriya, Area 9, St 1, Plot 40A, Kuwait City; tel. 5312650; fax 5326334; e-mail kwe@minbuza.nl; internet www.netherlandsembassy.gov.kw; Ambassador Dr CORNELIS VAN HONK.

Niger: POB 44451, 32059 Hawalli, Salwa, Block 12, St 6, Villa 183, Kuwait City; tel. 5652943; fax 5640478; Ambassador ASSOUMANE GUIAOURI.

Nigeria: POB 6432, 32039 Hawalli, Surra, Area 1, St 14, House 25, Kuwait City; tel. 5320794; fax 5320834; Ambassador MUHAMMAD ADAMU JUMBA.

Oman: POB 21975, 13080 Safat, Istiqlal St, Villa 3, Kuwait City; tel. 2561962; fax 2561963; Ambassador NASSER BIN KHALSAN AL-KHAROSSI.

Pakistan: POB 988, 13010 Safat, Jabriya, Police Station Rd, St 101, Plot 5, Block 11, Villa 7, Kuwait City; tel. 5327649; fax 5328013; e-mail parepkw@pakembkw.org; internet www.pakembkw.org; Ambassador KHIZER HAYAT KHAN NIAZI.

Philippines: POB 26288, 13123 Safat, Jabriya, Police Station St, Area 10, House 363, Kuwait City; tel. 5329316; fax 5329319; e-mail phembkt@ncc.moc.kw; Ambassador RICARDO ANDYA.

Poland: POB 5066, 13051 Safat, Jabriya, Plot 8, St 20, House 377, Kuwait City; tel. 5311571; fax 5311576; e-mail polamba@qualitynet.net; Ambassador WOJCIECH BOŻEK.

Qatar: POB 1825, 13019 Safat, Diiyah, Istiqlal St, Kuwait City; tel. 2513606; fax 2513604; e-mail kuwait@mofa.gov.qa; Ambassador ABD AL-AZIZ BIN SAAD AL-FEHAID.

Romania: POB 1149, 35152 Dasmah, Keifan, Area 4, Moona St, House 34, Kuwait City; tel. 4845079; fax 4848929; e-mail ambsa@qualitynet.net; Ambassador CONSTANTIN VOLODEA NISTOR.

Russia: POB 1765, Daya Diplomatic Area, Block 17, Kuwait City; tel. 2560427; fax 2524969; e-mail ruspos@qualitynet.net; Ambassador AZAMAT R. KULMUKHAMETOV.

Saudi Arabia: POB 20498, 13065 Safat, Istiqlal St, Kuwait City; tel. 2400250; fax 2426611; Ambassador AHMAD AL-HAMAD AL-YAHYA.

Senegal: POB 23892, 13099 Safat, Rawdah, Parcel 3, St 35, House 9, Kuwait City; tel. 2510823; fax 2542044; e-mail senegal_embassy@yahoo.com; Ambassador ABDOU LAHAD MBACKE.

Serbia and Montenegro: POB 20511, 13066 Safat, Jabriya, Block 7, St 12, Plot 382, Kuwait City; tel. 5327548; fax 5327568; e-mail embscgkw@qualitynet.net; Ambassador ZORAN VEJNOVIĆ.

Somalia: POB 22766, 13088 Safat, Bayan, St 1, Block 7, Villa 11, Kuwait City; tel. 5394795; fax 5394829; e-mail soamin1@hotmail.com; Ambassador ABDUL KHADIR AMIN ABUBAKER.

South Africa: POB 2262, 40173 Mishref, Kuwait City; tel. 5617988; fax 5617917; e-mail saemb@southafricaq8.com; internet www.southafricaq8.com; Chargé d'affaires DAWID DU PLESSIS.

Spain: POB 22207, 13083 Safat, Surra, Block 3, St 14, Villa 19, Kuwait City; tel. 5325827; fax 5325826; e-mail embespkw@mail.mae.es; Ambassador JESUS CARLOS RIOSALIDO GAMBOTTI.

Sri Lanka: POB 13212, 71952 Keifan, House 381, St 9, Block 5, Salwa; tel. 5612261; fax 5612264; e-mail lankemb@kuwait.net; Ambassador DARSIN SERASINGHE.

Switzerland: POB 23954, 13100 Safat, Qortuba, Block 2, St 1, Villa 122, Kuwait City; tel. 5340175; fax 5340176; e-mail vertretung@kow.rep.admin.ch; internet www.eda.admin.ch/kuwait; Ambassador JEAN-PHILIPPE TISSIÈRES.

Syria: POB 25600, 13116 Safat, Kuwait City; tel. 5396560; fax 5396509; Ambassador ALI ABD AL-KARIM.

Thailand: POB 66647, 43757 Bayan, Block 6, St 8, Villa 1, Jabiyra, Kuwait City; tel. 5317531; fax 5317532; e-mail thaiemkw@kems.net; Ambassador DUSIT CHANTASEN.

Tunisia: POB 5976, 13060 Safat, Nuzha, Plot 2, Nuzha St, Villa 45, Kuwait City; tel. 2542144; fax 2528995; e-mail tunemrku@ncc.moc.kw; Ambassador MUHAMMAD SAAD.

Turkey: POB 20627, 13067 Safat, Block 16, Plot 10, Istiqlal St, Kuwait City; tel. 2531785; fax 2560653; e-mail turkish_embassy_kuwait@hotmail.com; internet www.turkish-embassy.org.kw; Ambassador ŞAKIR FAKILI.

United Arab Emirates: POB 1828, 13019 Safat, Plot 70, Istiqlal St, Kuwait City; tel. 2528544; fax 2526382; Ambassador YOUSUF A. AL-ANSARI.

United Kingdom: POB 2, 13001 Safat, Arabian Gulf St, Kuwait City; tel. 2403336; fax 2426799; e-mail britemb@qualitynet.net; internet www.britishembassy.gov.uk/kuwait; Ambassador STUART LAING.

USA: POB 77, 13001 Safat, Bayan, Al-Masjed al-Aqsa St, Plot 14, Block 14, Kuwait City; tel. 5395307; fax 5380282; e-mail paskuwaitm@state.gov; internet kuwait.usembassy.gov; Ambassador RICHARD LEBARON.

Venezuela: POB 24440, 13105 Safat, Block 5, St 7, Area 356, Surra, Kuwait City; tel. 5324367; fax 5324368; e-mail embavene@qualitynet.net; Ambassador ELOY FERNÁNDEZ AZUAJE.

Zimbabwe: POB 36484, 24755 Salmiya, Kuwait City; tel. 5621517; fax 5621491; e-mail zimkuwait@hotmail.com; Ambassador Dr I. L. NYATHI.

Judicial System

SPECIAL JUDICIARY

Constitutional Court: Comprises five judges. Interprets the provisions of the Constitution; considers disputes regarding the constitutionality of legislation, decrees and rules; has jurisdiction in challenges relating to the election of members, or eligibility for election, to the Majlis al-Umma.

ORDINARY JUDICIARY

Court of Cassation: Comprises five judges. Is competent to consider the legality of verdicts of the Court of Appeal and State Security Court; Chief Justice MUHAMMAD YOUSUF AR-RIFA'I.

Court of Appeal: Comprises three judges. Considers verdicts of the Court of First Instance; Chief Justice RASHED AL-HAMMAD.

Court of First Instance: Comprises the following divisions: Civil and Commercial (one judge), Personal Status Affairs (one judge), Lease (three judges), Labour (one judge), Crime (three judges), Administrative Disputes (three judges), Appeal (three judges), Challenged Misdemeanours (three judges); Chief Justice MUHAMMAD AS-SAKHOBY.

Summary Courts: Each governorate has a Summary Court, comprising one or more divisions. The courts have jurisdiction in the following areas: Civil and Commercial, Urgent Cases, Lease, Misdemeanours. The verdict in each case is delivered by one judge.

There is also a **Traffic Court**, with one presiding judge.

Attorney-General: MUHAMMAD ABD AL-HAIH AL-BANNAIY.

Advocate-General: HAMED AL-UTHMAN.

Religion

ISLAM

The majority of Kuwaitis are Muslims of the Sunni or Shi'a sects. The Shi'ite community comprises about 30% of the total.

CHRISTIANITY

The Roman Catholic Church

Latin Rite

For ecclesiastical purposes, Kuwait forms an Apostolic Vicariate. At 31 December 2003 there were an estimated 158,500 adherents in the country.

Vicar Apostolic: Mgr FRANCIS ADEODATUS MICALLEF (Titular Bishop of Tinisa in Proconsulari), Bishop's House, POB 266, 13003 Safat, Kuwait City; tel. 2431561; fax 2409981; e-mail kuwaitbishop@hotmail.com; internet www.catholic-church.org/kuwait.

Melkite Rite

The Greek-Melkite Patriarch of Antioch is resident in Damascus, Syria. The Patriarchal Exarchate of Kuwait had an estimated 800 adherents at 31 December 2003.

Exarch Patriarchal: Rev. BOUTROS GHARIB, Vicariat Patriarcal Greek-Melkite, POB 1205, Salwa Block 12, St No. 6, House 58, 22013 Salmiya, Kuwait City; tel. and fax 6016691; e-mail greekcatholickuwait@yahoo.com.

Syrian Rite

The Syrian Catholic Patriarch of Antioch is resident in Beirut, Lebanon. The Patriarchal Exarchate of Basra and Kuwait, with an estimated 410 adherents at 31 December 2003, is based in Basra, Iraq.

The Anglican Communion

Within the Episcopal Church in Jerusalem and the Middle East, Kuwait forms part of the diocese of Cyprus and the Gulf. The Anglican congregation in Kuwait is entirely expatriate. The Bishop in Cyprus and the Gulf is resident in Cyprus, while the Archdeacon in the Gulf is resident in Qatar.

Other Christian Churches

National Evangelical Church in Kuwait: POB 80, 13001 Safat, Kuwait City; tel. 2407195; fax 2431087; e-mail elc@ncc.moc.kw; Rev. NABIL ATTALLAH (pastor of the Arabic-language congregation), Rev. JERRY A. ZANDSTRA (senior pastor of the English-speaking congrega-

KUWAIT

tion); an independent Protestant Church founded by the Reformed Church in America; services in Arabic, English, Korean, Malayalam and other Indian languages; combined weekly congregation of some 20,000.

The Armenian, Greek, Coptic and Syrian Orthodox Churches are also represented in Kuwait.

The Press

Freedom of the press and publishing is guaranteed in the Constitution, although press censorship was in force between mid-1986 and early 1992 (when journalists adopted a voluntary code of practice); in February 1995 a ruling by the Constitutional Court effectively endorsed the Government's right to suspend publication of newspapers (see History). The Government provides financial support to newspapers and magazines. In 1999 there were eight daily and 20 weekly newspapers, and 196 periodicals.

DAILIES

Al-Anbaa (The News): POB 23915, 13100 Safat, Kuwait City; tel. 4831168; fax 4837914; f. 1976; Arabic; general; Editor-in-Chief Bibi Khalid al-Marzooq; circ. 85,000.

Arab Times: POB 2270, Airport Road, Shuwaikh, 13023 Safat, Kuwait City; tel. 4849144; fax 4818267; e-mail arabtimes@arabtimesonline.com; internet www.arabtimesonline.com; f. 1977; English; political and financial; no Friday edition; Editor-in-Chief Ahmad Abd al-Aziz al-Jarallah; Man. Editor Mishal al-Jarallah; circ. 41,922.

Kuwait Times: POB 1301, 13014 Safat, Kuwait City; tel. 4833199; fax 4835621; e-mail info@kuwaittimes.net; internet www.kuwaittimes.net; f. 1961; weekend edition also published; English, Malayalam and Urdu; political; Publr and Editor-in-Chief Yousuf Alyyan; circ. 32,000.

Al-Qabas (Firebrand): POB 21800, 13078 Safat, Kuwait City; tel. 4812822; fax 4834355; e-mail alqabas@ncc.moc.kw; internet www.alqabas.com.kw; f. 1972; Arabic; independent; Gen. Man. Fouzan al-Fares; Editor-in-Chief Waleed Abd al-Latif an-Nisf; circ. 60,000.

Ar-Ra'i al-'Aam (Public Opinion): POB 761, 13008 Safat, Kuwait City; tel. 4817777; fax 4838352; internet www.alraialaam.com; f. 1961; Arabic; political, social and cultural; Editor-in-Chief Yousuf al-Jalahma; circ. 101,500.

As-Seyassah (Policy): POB 2270, Shuwaikh, Kuwait City; tel. 4813566; fax 4846905; e-mail alseyassah@alseyassah.com; internet www.alseyassah.com; f. 1965; Arabic; political and financial; Editor-in-Chief Ahmad Abd al-Aziz al-Jarallah; circ. 70,000.

Al-Watan (The Homeland): POB 1142, 13012 Safat, Kuwait City; tel. 4840950; fax 4818481; e-mail alwatan@alwatan.com.kw; internet www.alwatan.com.kw; f. 1962; Arabic; political; Editor-in-Chief Muhammad Abd al-Qader al-Jasem; Gen. Man. Yousuf bin Jasem; circ. 91,726.

WEEKLIES AND PERIODICALS

Al-Balagh (Communiqué): POB 4558, 13046 Safat, Kuwait City; tel. 4818606; fax 4819008; f. 1969; weekly; Arabic; general, political and Islamic; Editor-in-Chief Abd ar-Rahman Rashid al-Walayati; circ. 29,000.

Ad-Dakhiliya (The Interior): POB 71655, 12500 Shamiah, Kuwait City; tel. 2410091; fax 2410609; e-mail moipr@qualitynet.net; monthly; Arabic; official reports, transactions and proceedings; publ. by Public Relations Dept, Ministry of the Interior; Editor-in-Chief Lt-Col Ahmad A. ash-Sharqawi.

Dalal Magazine: POB 6000, 13060 Safat, Kuwait City; tel. 4832098; fax 4832039; internet www.alyaqza.com; f. 1997; monthly; Arabic; family affairs, beauty, fashion; Editor-in-Chief Ahmad Yousuf Behbehani.

Al-Hadaf (The Objective): POB 2270, 13023 Safat, Kuwait City; tel. 4813566; fax 4816042; e-mail alhadaf@alseyassah.com; internet www.alseyassah.com/alhadaf; f. 1964; weekly; Arabic; social and cultural; Editor-in-Chief Ahmad Abd al-Aziz al-Jarallah; circ. 268,904.

Hayatuna (Our Life): POB 26733, 13128 Safat, Kuwait City; tel. 2530120; fax 2530736; f. 1968; fortnightly; Arabic; medicine and hygiene; publ. by Al-Awadi Press Corpn; Editor-in-Chief Abd ar-Rahman al-Awadi; circ. 6,000.

Al-Iqtisadi al-Kuwaiti (Kuwaiti Economist): POB 775, 13008 Safat, Kuwait City; tel. 805580; fax 2412927; e-mail kcci@kcci.org.kw; internet www.kcci.org.kw; f. 1960; monthly; Arabic; commerce, trade and economics; publ. by Kuwait Chamber of Commerce and Industry; Editor Majed B. Jamaluddin; circ. 6,000.

Journal of the Gulf and Arabian Peninsula Studies: POB 17073, 72451 Khaldiya, Kuwait University, Kuwait City; tel. 4833215; fax 4833705; e-mail jotgaaps@kuc01.kuniv.edu.kw; f. 1974; quarterly; Arabic; English; Editor-in-Chief Dr Fatima Hussain al-Abdulrazzaq.

Al-Khaleej Business Magazine: POB 25725, 13118 Safat, Kuwait City; tel. 2433765; e-mail aljabriya@gulfweb.com; Editor-in-Chief Ahmad Ismail Behbehani.

Kuwait al-Youm (Kuwait Today): POB 193, 13002 Safat, Kuwait City; tel. 4842167; fax 4831044; f. 1954; weekly; Arabic; statistics, Amiri decrees, laws, govt announcements, decisions, invitations for tenders, etc; publ. by the Ministry of Information; circ. 5,000.

Al-Kuwaiti (The Kuwaiti): Information Dept, POB 9758, 61008 Ahmadi, Kuwait City; tel. 3989111; fax 3983661; e-mail kocinfo@kockw.com; f. 1961; monthly journal of the Kuwait Oil Co; Arabic; Editor-in-Chief Ali H. Murad; circ. 6,500.

The Kuwaiti Digest: Information Dept, POB 9758, 61008 Ahmadi, Kuwait City; tel. 3980651; fax 3983661; e-mail kocinfo@kockw.com; f. 1972; quarterly journal of Kuwait Oil Co; English; Editor-in-Chief Ra'ad Salem al-Jandal; circ. 7,000.

Kuwait Medical Journal (KMJ): POB 1202, 13013 Safat, Kuwait City; tel. 5317972; fax 5312630; e-mail kmj@kma.org.kw; internet www.kma.org.kw/KMJ; f. 1967; quarterly; English; publ. by the Kuwait Medical Asscn; case reports, articles, reviews; Editor-in-Chief Dr Fouad Abdullah M. Hassan; circ. 10,000.

Al-Majaless (Meetings): POB 5605, 13057 Safat, Kuwait City; tel. 4841178; fax 4847126; weekly; Arabic; current affairs; Editor-in-Chief (vacant); circ. 60,206.

Mejallat al-Kuwait (Kuwait Magazine): POB 193, 13002 Safat, Kuwait City; tel. 2415300; fax 2419642; f. 1961; monthly; Arabic; illustrated magazine; science, arts and literature; publ. by the Ministry of Information.

Mirat al-Umma (Mirror of the Nation): POB 1142, 13012 Safat, Kuwait City; tel. 4837212; fax 4838671; weekly; Arabic; Editor-in-Chief Muhammad al-Jassem; circ. 79,500.

An-Nahdha (The Renaissance): POB 695, 13007 Safat, Kuwait City; tel. 4813133; fax 4849298; f. 1967; weekly; Arabic; social and political; Editor-in-Chief Thamer as-Salah; circ. 170,000.

Osrati (My Family): POB 2995, 13030 Safat, Kuwait City; tel. 4813233; fax 4838933; f. 1978; weekly; Arabic; women's magazine; publ. by Fahad al-Marzouk Establishment; Editor Ghanima F. al-Marzouk; circ. 10,500.

Sawt al-Khaleej (Voice of the Gulf): POB 659, Safat, Kuwait City; tel. 4815590; fax 4839261; f. 1962; politics and literature; Arabic; Editor-in-Chief Christine Khraibet; Owner Baker Ali Khraibet; circ. 20,000.

At-Talia (The Ascendant): POB 1082, 13011 Safat, Kuwait City; tel. 4831200; fax 4840471; f. 1962; weekly; Arabic; politics and literature; Editor Ahmad Yousuf an-Nafisi; circ. 10,000.

Al-Yaqza (The Awakening): POB 6000, 13060 Safat, Kuwait City; tel. 4831318; fax 4832039; f. 1966; weekly; Arabic; political, economic, social and general; Editor-in-Chief Ahmad Yousuf Behbehani; circ. 91,340.

NEWS AGENCIES

Kuwait News Agency (KUNA): POB 24063, 13101 Safat, Kuwait City; tel. 4834546; fax 4813424; e-mail kuna@kuna.net.kw; internet www.kuna.net.kw; f. 1976; public corporate body; independent; also publishes research digests on topics of common and special interest; Chair. and Dir-Gen. Muhammad Ahmad al-Ajeeri.

Foreign Bureaux

Informatsionnoye Telegrafnoye Agentstvo Rossii—Telegrafnoye Agentstvo Suverennykh Stran (ITAR—TASS) (Russia): POB 1765, 13018 Safat, Kuwait City; tel. and fax 5639260; Correspondent Constantine Mathulski.

Middle East News Agency (MENA) (Egypt): POB 1927, Safat, Fahd as-Salem St, Kuwait City; Dir Reda Soliman.

Reuters Middle East Ltd (United Kingdom): POB 5616, 13057 Safat, Mubarak al-Kabir St, Kuwait Stock Exchange Bldg, 4th Floor, Kuwait City; tel. 2431920; fax 2460340; internet www.reuters.com/gulf; Country Man. Issam Makki.

Xinhua (New China) News Agency (People's Republic of China): POB 22168, Safat, Sheikh Ahmad al-Jaber Bldg, 10 Dasman St, Kuwait City; tel. 4809423; fax 4809396; Correspondent Huang Jianming.

AFP (France), Anadolu Ajansı (Turkey), AP (USA), dpa (Germany), JANA (Libya), QNA (Qatar), RIA—Novosti (Russia) and SANA (Syria) are also represented.

PRESS ASSOCIATION

Kuwait Journalist Association: POB 5454, Safat, Kuwait City; tel. 4843351; fax 4842874; Chair. Ahmad Bahbehani.

Publishers

Al-Abraj Translation and Publishing Co WLL: POB 26177, 13122 Safat, Kuwait City; tel. 2444665; fax 2436889; Man. Dir Dr TARIQ ABDULLAH.

Dar as-Seyassah Publishing, Printing and Distribution Co: POB 2270, 13023 Safat, Kuwait City; tel. 4813566; fax 4833628; internet www.contactkuwait.com/dar-alseyasa; publ. *Arab Times*, *As-Seyassah* and *Al-Hadaf*.

Gulf Centre Publishing and Publicity: POB 2722, 13028 Safat, Kuwait City; tel. 2402760; fax 2458833; Propr HAMZA ISMAIL ESSLAH.

Kuwait Publishing House: POB 29126, 13150 Safat, Kuwait City; tel. 2417810; Dir ESAM AS'AD ABU AL-FARAJ.

Kuwait United Co for Advertising, Publishing and Distribution WLL: POB 29359, 13153 Safat, Kuwait City; tel. 4817111; fax 4817797.

At-Talia Printing and Publishing Co: POB 1082, Airport Rd, Shuwaikh, 13011 Safat, Kuwait City; tel. 4840470; fax 4815611; Man. AHMAD YOUSUF AN-NAFISI.

GOVERNMENT PUBLISHING HOUSE

Ministry of Information: see Ministries.

Broadcasting and Communications

TELECOMMUNICATIONS

The privatization of the state telecommunications sector, and the reorganization of the Ministry of Communications as a company, designated the Kuwaiti Communications Corporation, were completed in 2000.

Mobile Telecommunications Co (MTC): POB 22244, 1308 Safat, Kuwait City; tel. 4842000; fax 4837755; e-mail info@mtctelecom.com; internet www.mtc.com.kw; f. 1983; Chair. ASAAD AL-BANWAN; Dep. Chair. and Man. Dir Dr SAAD AL-BARRAK.

National Mobile Telecommunications Co KSC (Wataniya Telecom): POB 613, 13007 Safat, Kuwait City; tel. 2435500; fax 2436600; e-mail info@wataniya.com; internet www.wataniya.com; f. 1998; Chair. and Man. Dir FAISAL HAMAD AL-AYYAR; CEO and Gen. Man. HARRI KOPONEN.

BROADCASTING

Radio

Radio of the State of Kuwait: POB 397, 13004 Safat, Kuwait City; tel. 2423774; fax 2456660; internet www.media.gov.kw; f. 1951; broadcasts daily in Arabic, Farsi, English and Urdu, some in stereo; Dir of Radio Dr ABD AL-AZIZ ALI MANSOUR; Dir of Radio Programmes ABD AR-RAHMAN HADI.

Television

Kuwait Television: POB 193, 13002 Safat, Kuwait City; tel. 2413501; fax 2438403; internet www.media.gov.kw; f. 1961; transmission began privately in Kuwait in 1957; transmits in Arabic; colour television service began in 1973; has a total of five channels; Head of News Broadcasting MUHAMMAD AL-KAHTANI.

Plans were announced in early 1998 for the establishment of a private satellite broadcasting television channel, with administrative offices in Kuwait and transmission facilities in Dubai, the United Arab Emirates; in October 2004 Ar-Ra'i TV was launched.

Finance

(cap. = capital; res = reserves; dep. = deposits; m. = million; brs = branches; amounts in Kuwaiti dinars unless otherwise stated)

BANKING

Central Bank

Central Bank of Kuwait: POB 526, 13006 Safat, Abdullah as-Salem St, Kuwait City; tel. 2449200; fax 2464887; e-mail cbk@cbk.gov.kw; internet www.cbk.gov.kw; f. 1969; cap. 5.0m., res 442.4m., dep. 852.8m. (March 2004); Governor Sheikh SALEM ABD AL-AZIZ SA'UD AS-SABAH.

National Banks

Al-Ahli Bank of Kuwait KSC: POB 1387, 13014 Safat, Ahmad al-Jaber St, Safat Sq., Kuwait City; tel. 2400900; fax 2424557; e-mail headoffice@abkuwait.com; internet www.abk-kuwait.com; f. 1967; wholly owned by private Kuwaiti interests; cap. 87.9m., res 101.6m., dep. 1,219.6m. (Dec. 2003); Chair. MORAD YOUSUF BEHBEHANI; Gen. Man. ABDULLAH B. AS-SUMAIT; 15 brs.

Bank of Bahrain and Kuwait: POB 24396, 13104 Safat, Ahmad al-Jaber St, Kuwait City; tel. 2417140; fax 2440937; e-mail bbkp@bbkonline.com.bh; internet www.bbkonline.com; f. 1971; owned equally by the Govts of Bahrain and Kuwait; cap. BD 56.9m., res BD 43.1m., dep. BD 1,148.3m. (Dec. 2004); Chair. MURAD ALI MURAD; CEO and Gen. Man. Dr FARID AHMAD AL MULLA AL-MULLA.

Bank of Kuwait and the Middle East KSC (BKME): POB 71, 13001 Safat, Joint Banking Centre, East Tower, Darwazat Abd ar-Razzak, Kuwait City; tel. 2459771; fax 2461430; e-mail bkmekw@bkme.com.kw; internet www.bkme.com; f. 1971; 43% owned by Ahli United Bank (Bahrain); cap. 70.4m., res 72.8m., dep. 1,247.8m. (Dec. 2003); Chair. and Man. Dir HAMAD ABD AL-MOHSEN AL-MARZOUQ; 16 brs.

Burgan Bank SAK: POB 5389, 12170 Safat, Ahmad al-Jaber St, Kuwait City; tel. 2439000; fax 2461148; e-mail mainbr@burgan.com.kw; internet www.burgan.com; f. 1975; cap. 82.0m., res 128.4m., dep. 1,559.0m. (Dec. 2003); Chair. Sheikh MUHAMMAD ABD AL-AZIZ AL-JARAH AS-SABAH; Dep. Chair., Man. Dir and Gen. Man. (acting) FAISAL AR-RAWDAN; 18 brs.

Commercial Bank of Kuwait SAK: POB 2861, 13029 Safat, Mubarak al-Kabir St, Kuwait City; tel. 2411001; fax 2450150; e-mail cbkinq@banktijari.com; internet www.cbk.com; f. 1960 by Amiri decree; cap. 106.4m., res 189.9m., dep. 1,403.3m. (Dec. 2003); Chair. and Man. Dir Sheikh ABD AL-MAJID AS-SHATTI; 28 brs.

Gulf Bank KSC: POB 3200, 13032 Safat, Mubarak al-Kabir St, Kuwait City; tel. 2449501; fax 2445212; e-mail customerservice@gulfbank.com.kw; internet www.e-gulfbank.com; f. 1960; cap. 82.1m., res 132.1m., dep. 2,093.9m. (Dec. 2003); Chair. and Man. Dir BASSAM YOUSUF ALGHANIM; CEO and Chief Gen. Man. YOUSUF ABDULLAH AL-AWADI; 29 brs.

Industrial Bank of Kuwait KSC (IBK): POB 3146, 13032 Safat, Joint Banking Centre, Commercial Area 9, Kuwait City; tel. 2457661; fax 2462057; e-mail ibk@ibkuwt.com; internet www.ibkuwt.com; 31.4% state-owned; f. 1973; cap. 20.0m., res 131.6m., dep. 36.0m. (Dec. 2003); Chair. and Man. Dir SALEH MUHAMMAD AL-YOUSUF; Gen. Man. ALI ABD AN-NABI KHAJAH.

Kuwait Finance House KSC (KFH): POB 24989, 13110 Safat, Abdullah al-Mubarak St, Kuwait City; tel. 2445050; fax 2455135; e-mail kfh@kfh.com.kw; internet www.kfh.com; f. 1977; Islamic banking and investment company; 45% state-owned; cap. 71.7m., res 212.9m., dep. 2,363.8m. (Dec. 2003); Chair. and Man. Dir BADER ABD AL-MOHSEN AL-MUKHAISEEM; Gen. Man. MUHAMMAD AL-OMAR (acting); 27 brs.

Kuwait Real Estate Bank KSC: POB 22822, 13089 Safat, West Tower, Joint Banking Centre, Mubarak al-Kabir St, Kuwait City; tel. 2458177; fax 2462516; e-mail contact@kreb.com.kw; internet www.kreb.com.kw; f. 1973; wholly owned by private Kuwaiti interests; cap. 37.9m., res 0.0m., dep. 411.8m. (Dec. 2004); Chair. TEWFIK ABDULLAH AL-GHARABALLY; Man. Dir ABDULWAHAB AL-WAZZAN; Gen. Man. SALAH M. AL-MUBARAKI (acting); 6 brs.

National Bank of Kuwait SAK (NBK): POB 95, 13001 Safat, Abdullah al-Ahmad St, Kuwait City; tel. 2422011; fax 2431888; e-mail webmaster@nbk.com; internet www.nbk.com; f. 1952; cap. 147.4m, res 248.8m., dep. 4,741.2m. (Dec. 2003); Chair. MUHAMMAD ABD AR-RAHMAN AL-BAHAR; CEO IBRAHIM S. DABDOUB; 41 brs.

Foreign Banks

Legislation permitting the entry of foreign banks to the local market was approved in December 2003.

BNP Paribas: POB 29927, 13160 Safat, Kuwait City; tel. 2997842; fax 2997800; internet www.bnpparibas.com; f. 2004.

Citigroup: Ahmad Tower, Arabian Gulf St, Kuwait City; f. 2005; Regional Man. Dir MUHAMMAD ASH-SHROOGI.

HSBC Kuwait: Qibla, Kuwait City; f. 2005; CEO NICK NICOLAOU.

National Bank of Abu Dhabi: Kuwait City; f. 2005.

INSURANCE

Al-Ahleia Insurance Co SAK: POB 1602, Ahmad al-Jaber St, 13017 Safat, Kuwait City; tel. 2240033; fax 2430308; e-mail aic@alahleia.com; internet www.alahleia.com; f. 1962; all forms of insurance; cap. 11.7m. (July 2004); Chair. and Man. Dir SULAYMAN HAMAD AD-DALALI.

Arab Commercial Enterprises WLL (Kuwait): POB 2474, 13025 Safat, Kuwait City; tel. 2425995; fax 2409450; e-mail acekwt@ace-ins.com; f. 1952; Man. SALIM ABOU HAIDER.

Gulf Insurance Co KSC: POB 1040, 13011 Safat, Ahmad al-Jaber St, Kuwait City; tel. 2423384; fax 2422320; e-mail contacts@gulfins.com.kw; internet www.gulfins.com.kw; f. 1962; cap. 11.3m. (2002); all forms of insurance; Chair. FARKAD ABDULLAH AS-SANEA; Man. Dir and CEO KHALED SAOUD AL-HASSAN.

Al-Ittihad al-Watani Insurance Co for the Near East SAL: POB 781, 13008 Safat, Kuwait City; tel. 4843988; fax 4847244; Man. JOSEPH ZACCOUR.

Kuwait Insurance Co SAK (KIC): POB 769, 13008 Safat, Abdullah as-Salem St, Kuwait City; tel. 2420135; fax 2428530; e-mail info@kic-kw.com; internet www.kic-kw.com; f. 1960; cap. US $64.6m.; all life and non-life insurance; Chair. MUHAMMAD SALEH BEHBEHANI; Gen. Man. ALI HAMAD AL-BAHAR.

Kuwait Reinsurance Company: POB 21929, Munther Tower, Salhiya, 13080 Safat, Kuwait City; tel. 2432011; fax 2427823; e-mail kuwaitre@kuwaitre.com; internet www.kuwaitre.com; f. 1972; cap. 10.0m. (Dec. 2004); Gen. Man. AMIR AL-MUHANNA.

Kuwait Technical Insurance Office: POB 25349, 13114 Safat, Kuwait City; tel. 2413986; fax 2413986.

Mohd Saleh Behbehani & Co: POB 341, 13004 Safat, Kuwait City; tel. 4721670; fax 4760070; e-mail msrybco@qualitynet.net; f. 1963; Pres. MUHAMMAD SALEH YOUSUF BEHBEHANI.

New India Assurance Co: POB 370, 13004 Safat, Kuwait City; tel. 2412085; fax 2412089.

The Northern Insurance Co Ltd: POB 579, 13006 Safat, Kuwait City; tel. 2427930; fax 2462739.

The Oriental Insurance Co Ltd: POB 22431, 13085 Safat, Kuwait City; tel. 2424016; fax 2424017; Man. JUGAL KISHORE MADAAN.

Sumitomo Marine & Fire Insurance Co (Kuwait Agency): POB 3458, 13055 Safat, Kuwait City; tel. 2433087; fax 2430853.

Warba Insurance Co SAK: POB 24282, 13103 Safat, Kuwait City; tel. 2445140; fax 2466131; e-mail warba@qualitynet.net; internet www.warbainsurance.com; f. 1976; cap. KD 7.7m. (2002); all forms of insurance; Chair. Dr HAIDER HASSAN ABD AR-RASOL AL-JUMAA; 3 brs.

STOCK EXCHANGE

Kuwait Stock Exchange: POB 22235, 13083 Safat, Mubarak al-Kabir St, Kuwait City; tel. 2992000; fax 2420779; e-mail borse@qualitynet.net; internet www.kuwaitse.com; f. 1983; 128 companies and four mutual funds listed in early 2005; Dir Dr SAFAAQ ABDULLAH AR-RUKAIBI.

Markets Association

Kuwait Financial Markets Association (KFMA): POB 25228, 13113 Safat, Kuwait City; internet www.kfma.org.kw; f. 1977; represents treasury, financial and capital markets and their members; Pres. THUNAYAN AL-GHANIM; Sec.-Gen. TAREQ M. AL-BASSAM.

Trade and Industry

GOVERNMENT AGENCY

Kuwait Investment Authority (KIA): POB 64, 13001 Safat, Kuwait City; tel. 2439595; fax 2454059; e-mail information@kia.gov.kw; internet www.kia.gov.kw; oversees the Kuwait Investment Office (London); responsible for the Kuwaiti General Reserve; Chair. BADER MISHARI AL-HUMAIDHI (Minister of Finance); Man. Dir BADER AS-SA'AD.

DEVELOPMENT ORGANIZATIONS

Arab Planning Institute (API): POB 5834, 13059 Safat, Kuwait City; tel. 4843130; fax 4842935; e-mail api@api.org.kw; internet www.arab-api.org; f. 1966; 15 mem. states; publishes annual directory, Journal of Development and Economic Policies and proceedings of seminars and discussion group meetings, offers research, training programmes and advisory services; Dir ESSA ALGHAZALI.

Industrial and Financial Investments Co (IFIC): POB 26019, 13121 Safat, Joint Banking Complex, 8th Floor, Industrial Bank Bldg, Derwaza Abdulrazak, Kuwait City; tel. 2429073; fax 2448850; e-mail info@ific.net; internet www.ific.net; f. 1983; invests directly in industry; privatized in 1996; Chair. and Man. Dir Dr TALEB AHMAD ALI.

Kuwait Fund for Arab Economic Development (KFAED): POB 2921, 13030 Safat, cnr Mubarak al-Kabir St and al-Hilali St, Kuwait City; tel. 2999000; fax 2999090; e-mail info@kuwait-fund.org; internet www.kuwait-fund.org; f. 1961; cap. KD 2,000m.; state-owned; provides and administers financial and technical assistance to the countries of the developing world; Chair. Sheikh Dr MUHAMMAD SABAH AS-SALIM AS-SABAH (Minister of Foreign Affairs); Dir-Gen. ABDULWAHAB A. AL-BADER.

Kuwait International Investment Co SAK (KIIC): POB 22792, 13088 Safat, as-Salhiya Commercial Complex, Kuwait City; tel. 2438273; fax 2454931; 30% state-owned; cap. p.u. KD 31.9m., total assets KD 146.9m. (1988); domestic real estate and share markets; Chair. and Man. Dir JASEM MUHAMMAD AL-BAHAR.

Kuwait Investment Co SAK (KIC): POB 1005, 13011 Safat, 5th Floor, al-Manakh Bldg, Mubarak al-Kabir St, Kuwait City; tel. 2438111; fax 2444896; e-mail info@kic.com.kw; internet www.kic.com.kw; f. 1981; 88% state-owned, 12% owned by private Kuwaiti interests; cap. KD 50.0m. (2002); international banking and investment; Chair. and Man. Dir BADER NASSER AS-SUBAIEE.

Kuwait Planning Board: c/o Ministry of Planning, POB 15, 13001 Safat, Kuwait City; tel. 2428200; fax 2414734; f. 1962; supervises long-term development plans; through its Central Statistical Office publishes information on Kuwait's economic activity; Dir-Gen. AHMAD ALI AD-DUAIJ.

Mega Projects Agency (MPA): c/o Ministry of Public Works, POB 8, 13001 Safat, Kuwait City; f. 2005; supervises the progress of Failaka and Bubiyan island devts; Man. Dir WALID ATH-THAQEB.

National Industries Group (Holding) SAK (NIC): POB 417, 13005 Safat, Kuwait City; tel. 4815466; fax 4839582; e-mail nigroup@nig.com.kw; internet www.nigroup.net; f. 1960; cap. KD 55.8m. (2002); has controlling interest in various construction enterprises; privatized in 1995; Chair. and Man. Dir SAUD MUHAMMAD AL-OSAIMI.

Shuaiba Area Authority SAK (SAA): POB 4690, 13047 Safat, Kuwait City; POB 10033, Shuaiba; tel. 3260903; f. 1964; an independent governmental authority to supervise and run the industrial area and Port of Shuaiba; has powers and duties to develop the area and its industries; Dir-Gen. SULAYMAN K. AL-HAMAD.

CHAMBER OF COMMERCE

Kuwait Chamber of Commerce and Industry: POB 775, 13008 Safat, Chamber's Bldg, Abdulaziz Hamad ash-Sager St, Kuwait City; tel. 805580; fax 2404110; e-mail kcci@kcci.org.kw; internet www.kcci.org.kw; f. 1959; 50,000 mems; Chair. ALI MUHAMMAD THUNAYAN AL-GHANIM; Dir-Gen. AHMAD RASHED AL-HAROUN.

STATE HYDROCARBONS COMPANIES

Kuwait Petroleum Corpn (KPC): POB 26565, 13126 Safat, as-Salhiya Commercial Complex, Fahed as-Salem St, Kuwait City; tel. 2455455; fax 2467159; e-mail info@kpc.com.kw; internet www.kpc.com.kw; f. 1980; co-ordinating organization to manage the petroleum industry; controls Kuwait Aviation Fuelling Co (KAFCO), Kuwait Foreign Petroleum Exploration Co (KUFPEC), Kuwait Gulf Oil Co (KGOC), Kuwait National Petroleum Co (KNPC), Kuwait Oil Co (KOC), Kuwait Oil Tanker Co (KOTC), Kuwait Petroleum International Ltd (Q8), Petrochemical Industries Co (PIC); Chair. Sheikh AHMAD AL-FAHD AL-AHMAD AS-SABAH (Minister of Energy); Dep. Chair. and CEO HANI ABD AL-AZIZ HUSSAIN.

Kuwait Aviation Fuelling Co KSC (KAFCO): POB 1654, 13017 Safat, Kuwait City; tel. 4330482; fax 4330475; e-mail airfuel@kafco.com.kw; internet www.kpc.com.kw/kafco.htm; f. 1963; Chair. and Gen. Man. SAAD ABD AL-WAHAB AS-SAAD; 70 employees.

Kuwait Foreign Petroleum Exploration Co KSC (KUFPEC): POB 5291, 13053 Safat, Kuwait City; tel. 2421677; fax 2420405; internet www.kufpec.com; f. 1981; state-owned; overseas oil and gas exploration and development; Chair. and Man. Dir BADER AL-KHASHTI; 169 employees.

Kuwait Gulf Oil Co KSC (KGOC): POB 9919, Ahmadi 61010; tel. 3980883; e-mail info@kgoc.com; internet www.kgoc.com; f. 2002 to take over Kuwait's interest in the Partitioned Zone's offshore operator, Khafji Joint Operations (KJO), and all of Kuwait's other offshore exploration and production activities; Chair. and Man. Dir ABD AL-HADI MARZOUK AL-AWAD.

Kuwait National Petroleum Co KSC (KNPC): POB 70, 13001 Safat, Ali as-Salem St, Kuwait City; tel. 2420121; fax 2433839; internet www.knpc.com.kw; f. 1960; oil refining, production of liquefied petroleum gas, and domestic marketing and distribution of petroleum by-products; output of 855,000 b/d of refined petroleum in 1996/97; Chair. and Man. Dir SAMI FAHD AR-RASHID; 5,611 employees.

Kuwait Oil Co KSC (KOC): POB 9758, 61008 Ahmadi; tel. 3989111; fax 3983661; e-mail kocinfo@kockw.com; internet www.kockw.com; f. 1934; state-owned; Chair. and Man. Dir FAROUK AZ-ZANKI; 4,815 employees.

Kuwait Petroleum International Ltd (Q8): POB 26565, 13126 Safat, Kuwait City; tel. 2404087; fax 2407523; e-mail info-kuwait@q8.com; internet www.q8.com; marketing division of KPC; controls 6,500 petrol retail stations in Europe, and European refineries with capacity of 235,000 b/d; Pres. KAMEL HARAMI.

UTILITIES

The Government planned to create regulatory bodies for each of Kuwait's utilities, with a view to facilitating their privatization.

Ministry of Energy: see Ministries; provides subsidized services throughout Kuwait.

TRADE UNIONS

Kuwait Trade Union Federation (KTUF): POB 5185, 13052 Safat, Kuwait City; tel. 5636389; fax 5627159; e-mail ktuf@hotmail.com; f. 1967; central authority to which all trade unions are affiliated.

KOC Workers Union: Kuwait City; f. 1964; Chair. HAMAD SAWYAN.

Federation of Petroleum and Petrochemical Workers: Kuwait City; f. 1965; Chair. JASEM ABD AL-WAHAB AT-TOURA.

Transport

RAILWAYS

There are no railways in Kuwait. However, preliminary planning of a light rail system in Kuwait City was in progress in 2006

ROADS

Roads in the towns are metalled, and the most important are motorways or dual carriageways. There are metalled roads linking Kuwait City to Ahmadi, Mina al-Ahmadi and other centres of population in Kuwait, and to the Iraqi and Saudi Arabian borders, amounting to a total road network of 4,273 km in 1989 (280 km of motorways, 1,232 km of other major roads and 2,761 km of secondary roads). The total road network was estimated at 4,450 km in 1999. A causeway linking Kuwait City with Subahiya was under consideration in 2006; the design-and-build contract was projected to be worth some US 1,500m.

Kuwait Public Transport Co SAK (KPTC): POB 375, 13004 Safat, Murghab, Safat Sq., Kuwait City; tel. 2469420; fax 2401265; e-mail info@kptc.com.kw; internet www.kptc.com.kw; f. 1962; state-owned; provides internal bus service; regular service to Mecca, Saudi Arabia; Chair. and Man. Dir MAHMOUD A. AN-NOURI.

SHIPPING

Kuwait has three commercial seaports. The largest, Shuwaikh, situated about 3 km from Kuwait City, was built in 1960. By 1987 it comprised 21 deep-water berths, with a total length of 4 km, three shallow-water berths and three basins for small craft, each with a depth of 3.35 m. In 1988 3.6m. metric tons of cargo were imported and 133,185 tons were exported through the port. A total of 1,189 vessels passed through Shuwaikh in 1988.

Shuaiba Commercial Port, 56 km south of Kuwait City, was built in 1967 to facilitate the import of primary materials and heavy equipment, necessary for the construction of the Shuaiba Industrial Area. By 1987 the port comprised a total of 20 berths, plus two docks for small wooden boats. Four of the berths constitute a station for unloading containers. Shuaiba handled a total of 3,457,871 metric tons of dry cargo, barge cargo and containers in 1988.

Doha, the smallest port, was equipped in 1981 to receive small coastal ships carrying light goods between the Gulf states. It has 20 small berths, each 100 m long. Doha handled a total of 20,283 metric tons of dry cargo, barge cargo and containers in 1988.

The oil port at Mina al-Ahmadi, 40 km south of Kuwait City, is capable of handling the largest oil tankers afloat, and the loading of over 2m. barrels of oil per day. By 1987 the port comprised 12 tanker berths, one bitumen-carrier berth, two LPG export berths and bunkering facilities.

Plans for the privatization of Kuwait's ports and for the construction of a new US $1,200m. facility at Bubiyan were under development in 2006.

At 31 December 2004 Kuwait's merchant fleet numbered 213 vessels, with a total displacement of 2,377,628 grt.

Kuwait Ports Authority: POB 3874, 13039 Safat, Kuwait City; tel. 4812622; fax 4819714; e-mail info@kpa.com.kw; internet www.kpa.com.kw; f. 1977; Dir-Gen. Dr SABER JABER AL-ALI AS-SABAH.

Principal Shipping Companies

Arab Maritime Petroleum Transport Co (AMPTC): POB 22525, 13086 Safat, Kuwait City; tel. 4844500; fax 4842996; e-mail amptc.kuwait@amptc.net; internet www.amptc.net; f. 1973; eight tankers and two LPG carriers; sponsored by OAPEC and financed by Algeria, Bahrain, Egypt, Iraq, Kuwait, Libya, Qatar, Saudi Arabia and the UAE; Gen. Man. SULAYMAN I. AL-BASSAM.

Heavy Engineering Industries and Shipbuilding CoHeisco (Heisco): POB 21998, 13080 Safat, Kuwait City; tel. 4830308; fax 4815947; e-mail commercial@heisco.com; internet www.heisco.com; f. 1974 as Kuwait Shipbuilding and Repairyard Co; name changed as above in 2003; ship repairs and engineering services, underwater services, maintenance of refineries, power stations and storage tanks; maintains floating dock for vessels up to 35,000 dwt; synchrolift for vessels up to 5,000 dwt with transfer yard; seven repair jetties up to 550 m in length and floating workshop for vessels lying at anchor; Chair. IMAD JASIM AS-SAQER; Commercial Man. MAHMOUD ASAD.

KGL Ports Int. Co (KGL PI): POB 24565, 13106 Safat, Kuwait City; tel. 4827804; fax 4827806; internet www.kglq8.com; f. 2005; subsidiary of Kuwait and Gulf Link Transport Co; port management and stevedoring; operates Shuaiba Commercial Port Container Terminal; also operations and management contracts with ports in United Arab Emirates and Saudi Arabia; Gen. Man. and Man. Dir SAID ISMAIL DASHTI.

Kuwait Maritime Transport Co KSC (KMTC): POB 22595, 13086 Safat, Nafisi and Khatrash Bldg, Jaber al-Mubarak St, Kuwait City; tel. 2449974; fax 2420513; f. 1981; Chair. YOUSUF AL-MAJID.

Kuwait Oil Tanker Co SAK (KOTC): POB 810, 13009 Safat, as-Salhiya Commercial Complex, Blocks 3, 5, 7 and 9, Kuwait City; tel. 2455455; fax 2445907; e-mail ysm@kotc.com.kw; internet www.kotc.com.kw; f. 1957; state-owned; operates eight crude oil tankers, 11 product tankers and five LPG vessels; sole tanker agents for Mina al-Ahmadi, Shuaiba and Mina Abdullah and agents for other ports; LPG filling and distribution; Chair. and Man. Dir ABDULLAH HAMAD AR-ROUMI.

United Arab Shipping Co SAG (UASC): POB 3636, 13037 Safat, Shuwaikh, Airport Rd, Kuwait City; tel. 4843150; fax 4845388; e-mail info@uasc.com.kw; internet www.uasc.com.kw; f. 1976; national shipping company of six Arabian Gulf countries; services between Europe, Far East, Mediterranean ports, Japan and east coast of USA and South America, and ports of participant states on Persian (Arabian) Gulf and Red Sea; operates 33 vessels; subsidiary cos: Kuwait Shipping Agencies, Arab Transport Co (Aratrans), United Arab Chartering Ltd (United Kingdom), Middle East Container Repair Co (Dubai), Arabian Chemicals Carriers (Saudi Arabia), United Arab Agencies Inc. (USA) and United Arab Shipping Agencies Co (Saudi Arabia); Pres. and CEO KEN SOERENSEN.

CIVIL AVIATION

Kuwait International Airport opened in 1980, and is designed to receive up to 6m. passengers per year; in 2001 3.82m. arrivals and departures were recorded. The airport is undergoing a major programme of expansion, at a cost of some US $690m.–$1,034m. The project was to expand the airport's annual capacity to 20m. passengers.

Directorate-General of Civil Aviation (DGCA): POB 17, 13001 Safat, Kuwait City; tel. 4335599; fax 4713504; Pres. Sheikh JABER AL-MUBARAK AS-SABAH; Dir-Gen. YACOUB Y. AS-SAQER.

Al-Jazeera Airways: c/o Boodai Group, POB 1287, 13013 Safat, Kuwait City; f. 2005; low-cost airline owned by Boodai Group; initially to serve nine regional destinations: Amman (Jordan); Beirut (Lebanon); Damascus (Syria); Dubai (United Arab Emirates); Chair. and CEO YACOUB Y. AS-SAQER.

Kuwait Airways Corpn (KAC): POB 394, Kuwait International Airport, 13004 Safat, Kuwait City; tel. 4345555; fax 4314118; e-mail info@kuwait-airways.com; internet www.kuwait-airways.com; f. 1954; scheduled and charter passenger and cargo services to the Arabian peninsula, Asia, Africa, the USA and Europe; scheduled for privatization; Chair. and Man. Dir Sheikh TALAL MUBARAK ABDULLAH AL-AHMAD AS-SABAH.

Kuwait National Airlines Company (KNAC): Kuwait City; f. 2006.

Tourism

Attractions for visitors include the Kuwait Towers leisure and reservoir complex, the Entertainment City theme park, the Kuwait Zoological Garden in Omariya and the Khiran Resort tourist village near the border with Saudi Arabia, as well as extensive facilities for sailing and other water sports. In early 2005 there were some 4,000 rooms available for visitors; it was intended to increase this figure to around 6,000 by 2008. Foreign tourist arrivals totalled some 2.1m. in 2001, while tourism receipts of US $328m. were recorded in 2003.

Department of Tourism: Ministry of Information, Tourism Affairs, POB 193, 18th Floor, Fahad as-Salem Tower, Fahad as-Salem St, 13002 Safat, Kuwait City; tel. 2457591; fax 2401540; e-mail tourism_kw@media.gov.kw.

Touristic Enterprises Co (TEC): POB 23310, 13094 Safat, Kuwait City; tel. 5652775; fax 5657594; e-mail info@tec.com.kw; internet www.kuwaittourism.com; f. 1976; 92% state-owned; manages 23 tourist facilities; Chair. BADER AL-BAHAR; Vice-Chair. SHAKER AL-OTHMAN.

KYRGYZSTAN

Introductory Survey

Location, Climate, Language, Religion, Flag, Capital

The Kyrgyz Republic (formerly the Kyrgyz Soviet Socialist Republic and, between December 1990 and May 1993, the Republic of Kyrgyzstan) is a small, land-locked state situated in eastern Central Asia. It borders Kazakhstan to the north, Uzbekistan to the west, Tajikistan to the south and west, and the People's Republic of China to the east. There are distinct variations in climate between low-lying and high-altitude areas. In the valleys the mean July temperature is 28°C (82°F), whereas in January it falls to an average of −18°C (−0.5°F). Annual rainfall ranges from 180 mm (7 ins) in the eastern Tien Shan mountains to 750 mm–1,000 mm (30 ins–39 ins) in the Farg'ona (Fergana) mountain range. In the settled valleys the annual average varies between 100 mm and 500 mm (4 ins–20 ins). The state language is Kyrgyz; Russian additionally has the status of an official language. The major religion is Islam, with the majority of ethnic Kyrgyz being Sunni Muslims of the Hanafi school. The national flag (proportions 3 by 5) consists of a red field, at the centre of which is a yellow sun, with 40 counter-clockwise rays surrounding a red-bordered yellow disc, on which are superimposed two intersecting sets of three red, curved, narrow bands. The capital is Bishkek (called Frunze between 1926 and 1991).

Recent History

Following the October Revolution of 1917 in Russia, Kyrgyzstan (which had been formally incorporated into the Russian Empire in 1876) experienced a period of civil war, with anti-Bolshevik forces, including the Russian White Army and local armed groups (*basmachi*), fighting against the Bolshevik Red Army. Soviet power was established in the region by 1919. In 1918 the Turkestan Autonomous Soviet Socialist Republic (ASSR) was established within the Russian Soviet Federative Socialist Republic (the Russian Federation). In 1924 the Kara-Kyrgyz Autonomous Oblast (Region) was created. (At this time the Russians used the term Kara-Kyrgyz to distinguish the Kyrgyz from the Kazakhs, then known as Kyrgyz by the Russians.) In 1925 the region was renamed the Kyrgyz Autonomous Oblast, and it became the Kyrgyz ASSR in February 1926. On 5 December 1936 the Kyrgyz Soviet Socialist Republic (SSR) was established as a full union republic of the USSR.

During the 1920s considerable economic and social developments were made in Kyrgyzstan, when land reforms resulted in the settlement of many of the nomadic Kyrgyz. The agricultural collectivization programme of the early 1930s was strongly opposed in the republic and prompted a partial revival of the *basmachi* movement. Despite the suppression of nationalism under Stalin (Iosif V. Dzhugashvili—Soviet leader in 1924–53), many aspects of Kyrgyz national culture were retained, although many so-called 'national communists' were expelled from the Kyrgyz Communist Party (KCP) and often imprisoned or exiled, particularly during the late 1930s. Tensions with the all-Union (Soviet) authorities continued following the death of Stalin in 1953.

The election of Mikhail Gorbachev as Soviet leader in 1985, and his introduction of the policies of *perestroika* (restructuring) and *glasnost* (openness), led to the resignation of Turdakan Usubaliyev as First Secretary of the KCP. His successor, Absamat Masaliyev, accused Usubaliyev of corruption and nepotism, and dismissed many of his closest allies from office. The republic's Supreme Soviet (Zhogorku Kenesh or Supreme Council—legislature) adopted Kyrgyz as the official language, although Russian was retained as a language of inter-ethnic communication. However, the conservative republican leadership opposed the development of unofficial quasi-political groups, several of which were established with the aim of alleviating the republic's acute housing shortage by seizing vacant land. One such group, Ashar, was partially tolerated by the authorities and soon developed a wider political role.

Osh Aymaghi, a similar organization to Ashar, based in Osh Duban (Oblast or Region), in the Farg'ona (Fergana) valley (which is shared between Kyrgyzstan, Tajikistan and Uzbekistan), attempted to obtain land and housing provision for ethnic Kyrgyz in the region. (Osh had been incorporated into Kyrgyzstan in 1924, although Uzbeks, who formed the majority of the population there, had recently begun to demand the establishment of an Uzbek autonomous region.) Disputes over land and homes in the crowded Farg'ona valley region precipitated violent confrontation between ethnic Kyrgyz and Uzbeks in 1990, in which, according to official reports, more than 300 people died (although other sources cited as many as 1,000 deaths). A state of emergency (which remained in force until 1995) and a curfew were introduced in the region, and the Uzbekistani–Kyrgyzstani border was closed.

Despite the growing influence of the nascent democratic movement, elections to the 350-member Kyrgyz Supreme Soviet in February 1990 were conducted along Soviet lines, with KCP candidates winning most seats unopposed. In April Masaliyev was elected to the new office of Chairman of the Supreme Soviet. He favoured the introduction of an executive presidency, election to which was to be by the Supreme Soviet. By October, when an extraordinary session of the Supreme Soviet was convened to elect the President, Masaliyev had been discredited by the conflict in Osh; moreover, the opposition, which had united as the Democratic Movement of Kyrgyzstan (DMK), had become a significant political force. In the first round of voting Masaliyev failed to achieve the requisite proportion of votes to be elected, and in a further round a compromise candidate, Askar Akayev, the President of the Kyrgyz Academy of Sciences, was elected to the executive presidency. Akayev rapidly allied himself with reformist politicians and economists, including leaders of the DMK. Plans were announced for an extensive programme of privatization. In December Masaliyev resigned as Chairman of the Supreme Soviet, and was replaced by Medetkan Sherimkulov. In that month the Supreme Soviet voted to change the name of the republic from the Kyrgyz SSR to the Republic of Kyrgyzstan. In February 1991, moreover, the capital, Frunze (named after a Red Army commander), reverted to its pre-1926 name of Bishkek. However, economic realities appeared to prevail against secession. In the referendum on the preservation of the USSR, held in nine republics in March, a majority (87.7%) of eligible voters in Kyrgyzstan approved the proposal to retain the USSR as a 'renewed federation'.

In January 1991 Akayev replaced the unwieldy Council of Ministers with a smaller cabinet, comprising mainly reformist politicians. However, his programme of political and economic reform had many opponents within the KCP and the security forces. In April Masaliyev resigned as First Secretary of the KCP; he was replaced by Jumgalbek Amanbayev, who was generally regarded as more sympathetic to Akayev's reform programme.

In August 1991, when the conservative communist State Committee for the State of Emergency (SCSE) announced that it had assumed power in the Russian and Soviet capital, Moscow, there was an attempt to depose Akayev in Kyrgyzstan. The KCP declared its support for the coup leaders, and the commander of the Turkestan Military District of the Soviet armed forces threatened to dispatch troops and tanks to the republic. Akayev dismissed the Chairman of the republican Committee of State Security (KGB) and ordered interior ministry troops to guard strategic buildings in Bishkek. He publicly denounced the coup and issued a decree prohibiting activity by any political party in government or state bodies. After the coup had collapsed in Moscow, Akayev and Vice-President German Kuznetsov renounced their membership of the Communist Party of the Soviet Union, and the entire politburo and secretariat of the KCP resigned. On 31 August the Kyrgyz Supreme Soviet voted to declare independence from the USSR. Akayev (the sole candidate) was re-elected President of Kyrgyzstan by direct popular vote on 12 October, receiving 95% of the votes cast.

In October 1991 Akayev signed, with representatives of seven other republics, a treaty to establish a new economic community, and when Russia, Belarus and Ukraine proposed the creation of the Commonwealth of Independent States (CIS, see p. 201), Akayev announced his approval. On 21 December Kyrgyzstan was among the 11 signatories to the Almaty (Alma-Ata) Declaration, which formally established the CIS.

Discussions were held throughout 1992 to draft a new constitution, during which opposition forces demanded the restriction of the President's powers and a stronger role for the legislature. The Constitution, which was finally promulgated on 5 May 1993, provided for a parliamentary system of government, with the Prime Minister as head of the executive (the Government had hitherto been subordinate to the President). Legislative power was to be vested in a smaller (105-member) Zhogorku Kenesh, following a general election, which was due to be held by 1995; in the mean time, the existing assembly continued to act as the republic's parliament. Russian was accorded the constitutional status of a language of inter-ethnic communication. None the less, the country's official name was changed from the Republic of Kyrgyzstan to the less ethnically neutral Kyrgyz Republic, and in July Akayev's attempts to encourage non-Kyrgyz to remain in the republic suffered a serious reverse when Kuznetsov, by this time the First Deputy Prime Minister and the most prominent Slav in government, announced his decision to return to Russia. At mid-1993 it was estimated that some 145,000 Russians had left the republic since 1989.

Akayev's presidency was further destabilized during 1993 by a series of corruption scandals, which his reformist supporters claimed were orchestrated by communist and nationalist forces. Two commissions of inquiry were established to investigate the business dealings of the Vice-President, Feliks Kulov, and to examine allegations that senior politicians—including the Prime Minister since February 1992, Tursunbek Chyngyshev—had been involved in unauthorized gold exports. In December 1993 Kulov resigned as Vice-President for 'ethical reasons', urging the Government to do likewise. The legislature subsequently held a vote of confidence in Chyngyshev and his Government: the motion failed to secure the required two-thirds' majority and Akayev dismissed the entire cabinet. Later in the month the legislature approved a new Government, headed by Apas Jumagulov (Chairman of the Council of Ministers in 1986–91). The Government's composition was largely ethnic Kyrgyz, although it included one representative each of the Russian, German, Uzbek and Jewish communities. Amanbayev was appointed one of the six Deputy Prime Ministers and, following a parliamentary decree that government ministers could not remain members of the legislature, he resigned his seat in the legislature, and also the leadership of the KCP. A referendum of confidence in the presidency was held (on Akayev's initiative) in January 1994, at which 96.2% of voters endorsed Akayev's leadership.

In June 1994, in an attempt to curb the rate of emigration from Kyrgyzstan, Akayev issued a decree promoting the use of Russian, simplifying the procedure of application for dual citizenship, and guaranteeing the equitable representation of ethnic Russians in the state administration. The Zhogorku Kenesh adopted a resolution based on the decree in March 1996. This measure, together with the opening of a Slavonic university in Bishkek in 1993, probably contributed to the decline in the number of Russians emigrating from the republic, estimated at 20,000 in 1996.

In September 1994 more than 180 pro-reform deputies announced their intention to boycott the next session of the Zhogorku Kenesh, in protest at the continuing obstruction by former communists of the economic reform process; they also demanded the dissolution of the Kenesh and the holding of fresh elections. The Government tendered its resignation, and Akayev announced that fresh parliamentary elections would be held. The Government was promptly reinstated by Akayev, who announced the holding of a referendum in October on constitutional amendments, at which the majority of the electorate endorsed proposals for a restructured Zhogorku Kenesh, comprising a 70-member El Okuldor Palatasy (People's Assembly—upper chamber) to represent regional interests at twice-yearly sessions and a permanent, 35-member Myizam Chygaru Palatasy (Legislative Assembly—lower chamber) representing the population as a whole.

Elections to the two chambers of the new Zhogorku Kenesh were held in two rounds on 5 and 19 February 1995. The two chambers of the Zhogorku Kenesh held their inaugural sessions on 28 March; Mukar Cholponbayev, a former Minister of Justice, was elected Chairman of the Myizam Chygaru Palatasy, and Almambet Matubraimov, a former First Deputy Prime Minister, was elected Chairman of the El Okuldor Palatasy. (Cholponbayev was replaced as Chairman of the Myizam Chygaru Palatasy by Usup Mukambayev in November 1996, however, after the Constitutional Court declared his election to have been invalid.) A new Government, again led by Jumagulov, was appointed in April.

In September 1995 the Myizam Chygaru Palatasy vetoed a proposal to hold a referendum on extending the President's term of office until 2000. (Similar votes held in 1994–95 in the Central Asian republics of Kazakhstan, Turkmenistan and Uzbekistan had enabled the respective Presidents to extend their mandates without seeking re-election.) A direct presidential election was held on 24 December 1995, at which Akayev emerged as the victor, receiving a reported 71.6% of the votes cast; Masaliyev (who had recently been reinstated as the leader of the revived KCP) won 24.4% of the votes. The rate of participation by the electorate was some 82%. Akayev was inaugurated on 30 December. Following a decree issued by Akayev, a referendum was held on 10 February 1996, at which the majority of the electorate endorsed amendments to the Constitution increasing presidential powers and decreasing those of the legislature. The Government resigned later that month; Jumagulov was reinstated as Prime Minister in March and a new Government was appointed by Akayev shortly afterwards.

In January 1998 a new criminal code was promulgated, which effectively abolished the death penalty by imposing a moratorium on its implementation. (In December 2005 Kyrgyzstan extended the moratorium, as it had every year since its inception, and announced plans to prepare legislation to proscribe capital punishment completely.) In March 1998 Jumagulov announced his retirement. The Zhogorku Kenesh endorsed the appointment of Kuvachbek Jumaliyev as the new Prime Minister, and a cabinet reorganization was effected. A further, extensive cabinet reshuffle was undertaken in early April. In July a ruling by the Constitutional Court allowed Akayev to seek a third term in the presidential election due to be held in 2000. In September 1998 Akayev announced a referendum to seek approval for several proposed constitutional amendments, prompting criticism from members of the Zhogorku Kenesh, which had not been consulted. The referendum took place on 17 October, with the participation of about 96% of the electorate, and some 90% of voters approved the following amendments: the number of deputies in the Myizam Chygaru Palatasy was to increase to 60, and representation in the El Okuldor Palatasy was to be reduced to 45; the electoral system was to be reformed; restrictions on parliamentary immunity were to be introduced; private land ownership was to be legalized; the presentation of unbalanced or unattainable budgets was to be banned; and the adoption of any legislation restricting freedom of speech or of the press was to be prohibited. The Zhogorku Kenesh and the majority of political parties declared their opposition to the constitutional changes and, in particular, to the introduction of private land ownership, which they feared would result in the transfer of land to foreign ownership.

Akayev's declared campaign to combat financial crime and corruption intensified in mid-December 1998, when a number of senior government officials, including three deputy ministers, were arrested on charges of corruption and abuse of office, bringing to 383 the number dismissed on similar grounds since 1993. In late December 1998 the President dissolved the Government for its failure to address the country's economic problems. Jumabek Ibraimov was appointed Prime Minister and a new Government was formed, in which 10 ministers from the previous administration retained their portfolios. Akayev also issued a decree extending the Prime Minister's mandate, giving him the right to appoint and dismiss ministers and heads of departments (which had previously been the exclusive right of the President). Ibraimov died in April 1999, and Amangeldy Muraliyev was appointed as his replacement.

A new electoral law was introduced at the end of May 1999 whereby, henceforth, 15 seats in the Myizam Chygaru Palatasy were to be allocated on a proportional basis for those parties that secured a minimum of 5% of the votes; the legislation also banned the use of foreign and private funds in electoral campaigns. In mid-June new legislation came into effect, which banned political organizations considered a threat to Kyrgyzstan's stability and ethnic harmony. In July two new opposition parties were established: the Dignity (Ar-Namys) Party, led by Kulov (by this time Mayor of Bishkek), and the Justice (Adilettuuluk) Party. Further opposition parties were established later in the year.

At the elections to both chambers of the Zhogorku Kenesh, held on 20 February 2000, a total of six parties passed the 5% threshold required to secure party-list seats in the Myizam Chygaru Palatasy. A number of electoral violations were reported by the Organization for Security and Co-operation in

Europe (OSCE, see p. 327). In a second round of voting on 12 March, the KCP secured 27.7% of the votes cast, the Union of Democratic Forces 18.6%, the Democratic Women's Party of Kyrgyzstan 12.7%, the Party of Veterans of the War in Afghanistan and of Participation in other Local Conflicts 8.0%, the Fatherland (Ata-Meken) Socialist Party 6.5% and the My Country Party of Action 5.0%. The Union of Democratic Forces achieved the greatest representation of any party or bloc in the combined Zhogorku Kenesh, securing a total of 12 seats, compared with the KCP's six. Independent candidates took 73 of the 105 seats in the two chambers. Kulov, who stood as an independent after Dignity was prohibited from participating, failed to win a seat, prompting opposition protests and allegations of official corruption. Later in March Kulov was arrested on charges of abuse of office during his tenure as Minister of National Security in 1997–98. Although Kulov was acquitted in August 2000, a retrial was ordered, and he was sentenced to seven years' imprisonment in January 2001. An appeal was rejected in March, prompting members of Dignity to denounce the sentence as politically motivated. (In May 2002 Kulov was also found guilty of embezzlement.)

Meanwhile, at the presidential election, held on 29 October 2000, Akayev secured 74.5% of the votes cast. Omurbek Tekebayev won 13.9% of the votes and Almazbek Atambayev 6.0%. According to the Central Commission for Elections and Referendums, 74% of the electorate participated. However, on the day of the election a criminal case opened in Bishkek following the discovery, by international observers, of several hundred ballot papers, marked in favour of Akayev, before polling had officially begun. In addition, opposition parties claimed that they had been prevented from taking part in media broadcasts during their election campaigns. The Chairman of the Central Commission for Elections and Referendums was forced to concede that electoral violations had taken place, leading to international condemnation. Mass protests took place, and demands were made for the election to be repeated. None the less, on 10 November the Constitutional Court formally endorsed the results of the election.

Akayev was inaugurated for a third term on 9 December 2000. On 21 December Kurmanbek Bakiyev, hitherto the Governor of Chui Duban, was appointed Prime Minister, and a new Government was announced at the beginning of January 2001. In April, in an apparent attempt to combat Islamist extremism, the Government banned religious education in state schools and decreed that specialist religious schools would henceforth require a licence. In the same month the leaders of nine opposition parties formally announced the establishment of an alliance known as the People's Patriotic Movement, which stated its objectives to be the safeguarding of democracy and of human and constitutional rights. The movement organized demonstrations against the erosion of the independent media and against the imprisonment of Kulov. In early November opposition parties including Dignity, the Fatherland (Ata-Meken) Socialist Party and the Liberty (Erkindik) party announced the formation of a new People's Congress, and elected the imprisoned Kulov as Chairman of the alliance. In the following month the President signed into law a constitutional amendment granting Russian the status of official language, in what was considered a further attempt to halt the emigration of ethnic Russians from Kyrgyzstan.

In January 2002 the arrest of Azimbek Beknazarov, an opposition deputy, was denounced as politically motivated (Beknazarov had publicly criticized President Akayev's signature of the 1999 Sino-Kyrgyzstani border treaty—see below). In mid-March large-scale protests took place in the southern city of Jalal-Abad against Beknazarov's trial; six people were reported to have died, following clashes with security forces, which, the Government maintained, had acted in self-defence. Although the trial was subsequently suspended and Beknazarov was temporarily released, the Government accused the opposition of instigating the riots in an attempt to stage a *coup d'état*. On 10 May the Myizam Chygaru Palatasy ratified the controversial Sino-Kyrgyzstani treaty, prompting two weeks of anti-Government demonstrations, hunger strikes and acts of civil disobedience. Protesters demanded that the Government accept responsibility for the violence of mid-March; rescind the ratification of the border treaty (which they claimed was signed illegally by President Akayev, since he had agreed to cede land to the People's Republic of China without the consent of the legislature); and close the criminal case against Beknazarov. Nevertheless, the treaty was ratified by the El Okuldor Palatasy in mid-May, and subsequently signed into law by the President. Also in mid-May a state commission established to investigate the protests in Jalal-Abad issued its report to the President, in which it criticized all levels of government and the law-enforcement bodies for failing to recognize the instability of the political situation and the rising levels of popular discontent in the region. The commission also stated that the security forces' use of weapons to control the demonstrators was illegal.

On 22 May 2002 Prime Minister Bakiyev tendered his resignation. The Chief of the Presidential Administration also resigned, together with a senior prosecutor, and several senior police-officers were dismissed. The First Deputy Prime Minister, Nikolai Tanayev, was appointed Prime Minister and a new Government was announced on 19 June. Meanwhile, in late May Beknazarov received a one-year, suspended prison sentence. Following an appeal and further large-scale demonstrations, Beknazorov's sentence was annulled (although the initial guilty verdict was upheld), enabling him to retain his parliamentary seat. In the same month Tanayev announced an amnesty (approved by the Myizam Chygaru Palatasy on 28 June) for those involved in the disturbances of mid-March. The amnesty applied to both protesters and law-enforcement officials.

In mid-January 2003 President Akayev announced that a referendum on several proposed constitutional amendments was to be held on 2 February. Despite opposition demands for the referendum's postponement, the amendments, providing, *inter alia*, for the introduction of a unicameral legislature in 2005, in which all deputies were to be elected in single-member constituencies, were duly approved by 76.6% of the electorate, and 78.7% of voters supported Akayev's remaining in office until 2005; the reported rate of participation was 86.7%. The hasty scheduling of the referendum attracted criticism from international human rights organizations, and there were also allegations of procedural violations.

A major government reorganization took place in early February 2004. In April the President introduced a new law designating Kyrgyz the state language, and stipulating measures for its promotion, apparently in order to encourage bilingualism in Kyrgyz and Russian (which remained the country's official language). In May, in advance of legislative elections, opposition parties, including Dignity, the Fatherland (Ata-Meken) Socialist Party and the Social Democratic Party of Kyrgyzstan, announced the formation of an electoral bloc, known as For Fair Elections. The bloc was led by Misir Ashyrkulov, the former Secretary of the Security Council. The formation of larger electoral bloc, known as the People's Movement of Kyrgyzstan, was announced in late September, under Bakiyev's leadership.

In late 2004 Akayev warned Kyrgyzstan's Defence Council of the potential for the parliamentary and presidential elections, scheduled for February and October 2005, respectively, to result in a severe deterioration in the social and political situation, and Tanayev announced that the Government would not allow religious extremist groups or Western organizations to interfere with the conduct of Kyrgyzstani domestic affairs. In particular, the Government emphasized the need to prevent a popular revolt from occurring in the aftermath of elections, as had happened in Georgia in late 2003, and in Ukraine in late 2004. Opposition groups denounced the Government's declared stance as an attempt to legitimatize suppression of any manifestation of dissent by appearing to combat extremism.

In January 2005 Roza Otunbayeva, a former ambassador to the United Kingdom, and the leader of the recently formed opposition Fatherland (Ata-Jurt) Party, was refused permission to register as a candidate in the parliamentary elections, on the grounds that she had not been resident in the country for the previous five years; several other former diplomatic representatives were also prohibited from contesting the elections. Campaigning for the elections officially began on 2 February. Protests against the exclusion of candidates and opposition rallies demanding free and fair parliamentary elections, or the impeachment of Akayev, continued throughout February. In the first round of legislative voting on 27 February, the rate of participation by the electorate was reported to be 60%. Some 31 candidates (each of whom had received an absolute majority of votes cast in their respective electoral districts) were elected to the restructured, single-chamber, 75-member Zhogorku Kenesh. The majority of the candidates elected were nominally independent candidates, including supporters of Akayev. Forward, Kyrgyzstan (Alga, Kyrgyzstan), established in 2003 and regarded as generally sympathetic to Akayev's administration, became the largest party faction to achieve representation, with

10 members reportedly elected. Observers from the OSCE concluded that, although the elections had been competitive, they had not fully complied with democratic standards. Opposition and independent observers, however, asserted that large-scale electoral fraud had taken place. Protests to dispute local polling results took place in various regions in advance of the second round of elections, held on 13 March, and the suppression of media outlets supportive of the opposition or critical of the authorities was reported. Following the second round of voting, at which a participation rate of 55% was reported, a further 37 candidates were reported to have been elected. According to preliminary results, only six opposition candidates obtained representation in the new legislature.

Dissatisfaction at the conduct of the elections, and at the failure of the opposition to obtain significant representation in the legislature, resulted in large-scale protests in a number of cities, initially in the south of Kyrgyzstan. From mid-March 2005 demonstrators occupied the regional governor's office in Jalal-Abad for several weeks, and later stormed a police station. Later in the month, demonstrators took control of a government building in Osh, Kyrgyzstan's second city. By mid-March the central Government had effectively lost control of the two cities. On 22 March the Central Commission for Elections and Referendums declared that the results of voting for 69 of the 75 seats were valid; investigations into the conduct of voting in the remaining six districts were to continue. (It was subsequently announced that appeals were to be launched against the results of voting in some 20 districts.) The Supreme Court, however, while emphasizing that the ruling did not constitute an annulment of the poll results, revoked the mandate of the newly elected Zhogorku Kenesh, asserting that the previous bicameral legislature continued to hold authority. On 23 March Akayev dismissed the Prosecutor-General, Myktybek Abdyldayev, and the Minister of Internal Affairs, Bakirdin Subanbekov (who had declared that he would not use force to end the protests).

By 24 March 2005 demonstrations had spread to Bishkek, and protesters stormed the presidential palace and government buildings. Akayev fled the country (although maintaining that he remained Kyrgyzstan's Head of State) and Tanayev resigned as Prime Minister, while protesters freed Kulov from gaol. On the same day, at an emergency session, the lower chamber of the legislature elected in 2000 named Bakiyev acting Prime Minister (he automatically became acting President in Akayev's absence). The upheaval was largely peaceful, but widespread looting and disorder were reported in Bishkek, and there were at least three deaths.

On 25 March 2005 Bakiyev announced the appointment of several senior officials in the interim Government, including: Otunbayeva as Minister of Foreign Affairs; Abdyldayev as Minister of Internal Affairs; Gen. Ismail Isakov as Minister of Defence; and Azimbek Beknazarov as acting Prosecutor-General. Kulov was given responsibility for overseeing the country's law-enforcement agencies and armed forces. After the Central Commission for Elections and Referendums announced that the powers of the bicameral legislature elected in 2000 were terminated, the lower and upper chambers dissolved themselves on 28 and 29 March, respectively, thereby effectively confirming the legitimacy of the recently elected legislature, and apparently overturning the ruling of the Supreme Court. Meanwhile, on 28 March the new Zhogorku Kenesh voted to confirm Bakiyev as interim Prime Minister, and to elect Tekebayev as legislative Chairman. (In late April Tekebayev was also appointed as Chairman of the Constitutional Court.) On 30 March Kulov resigned his post, reportedly owing to disagreement with Bakiyev.

On 4 April 2005 Akayev, speaking at the Kyrgyzstani embassy in Moscow, announced his resignation as President (the decision was approved by the Zhogorku Kenesh on 11 April). On 8 April Parliament voted to deprive Akayev of certain privileges associated with his status as a former president, and to remove immunity from prosecution from members of his family, allowing them to be investigated on corruption charges. The Zhogorku Kenesh subsequently scheduled a presidential election for 10 July. From mid-April around 300 people led protests outside the Supreme Court against aspects of the legislative elections, demanding, inter alia, the resignation of the Chairman of the Court, Kurmanbek Osmonov, who was regarded as an ally of Akayev. However, although Osmonov submitted his resignation in late April, it was rejected by Bakiyev. In mid-May Bakiyev reached an agreement with Kulov, whose convictions had been overturned by the Supreme Court in April and who was considered his strongest rival in the presidential contest, according to which Kulov agreed to withdraw his candidacy in return for a guarantee that Bakiyev would appoint him Prime Minister should he secure the presidency. Also in mid-May, Bakiyev dismissed acting Minister of Internal Affairs Abdyldayev and replaced him with Murat Sutalinov. Violent unrest in Bishkek was reported in June.

On 10 July 2005 Bakiyev won 88.7% of the votes cast in the presidential election, which was contested by six candidates. The OSCE reported some irregularities in the counting of votes and expressed reservations over the high official rate of participation, of 74.9%. Bakiyev was inaugurated as President on 14 August, and on 1 September the Zhogorku Kenesh confirmed Kulov's appointment as Prime Minister. In mid-September Bakiyev removed Beknazarov from his position as Prosecutor-General, together with his deputy, accusing them of negligence. Busurmankul Tabaldiyev was appointed to succeed Beknazarov on an acting basis; however, he resigned in mid-October, and was replaced by Kambaraly Kongantiyev. Meanwhile, in late September the Zhogorku Kenesh approved 10 of 16 ministers proposed by Bakiyev. Many ministers in the outgoing interim administration retained their portfolios, notably Isakov as Minister of Defence, Akylbek Zhaparov as Minister of the Economy and Finance, and Sutalinov as Minister of Internal Affairs. However, Otunbayeva's nomination as Minister of Foreign Affairs was rejected, and Alikbek Jekshenkulov was appointed to the post (Otunbayeva and Beknazarov subsequently became co-chairmen of the Banner—Asaba—Party of National Revival). Adakhan Madumarov was appointed Deputy Prime Minister and Marat Kaiypov became Minister of Justice. In early October the Office of the Prosecutor-General charged former Prime Minister Nikolai Tanayev, who was under house arrest in Bishkek, with abuse of power and corruption. (In early May 2006 it was reported that the criminal case against Tanayev had been closed.) Also in early October 2005 Bakiyev appointed Daniyar Usenov, an opponent of Kulov, to the post of acting First Deputy Prime Minister, leading to speculation that Kulov, who considered the appointment to contravene the agreement reached with Bakiyev in May, might resign to found a new opposition party. However, Usenov's nomination was rejected in November, and in early December the Zhogorku Kenesh approved the appointment of Medetbek Kerimkulov, who had been First Deputy Prime Minister in the interim administration. The Government was finally sworn in on 20 December.

Meanwhile, in late September 2005 a parliamentary deputy and businessman, who had actively participated in Akayev's removal from power and was alleged to have links to criminal groups, had been murdered; two other apparently politically motivated assassinations had taken place in April and July. Moreover, in late October a parliamentary deputy had been killed by inmates during an official visit to a gaol. Rallies had subsequently taken place to demand the dismissal of Kulov, whom the protesters accused of collaborating with prisoners to organize the murder.

In early January 2006 President Bakiyev decreed that measures be taken to organize a referendum on the division of power between the President and Parliament; Bakiyev had pledged to award Parliament increased powers following his election. Also in early January, representatives of 17 political movements and organizations agreed to establish an opposition bloc, the People's Coalition of Democratic Forces, which united those dissatisfied with the new regime. In late January Kulov demanded reform of the judicial system and the entire law-enforcement system, and criticized the Chairman of the National Security Service (SNB), Tashtemir Aitbayev, for allowing criminal elements to penetrate the organization. Although Bakiyev rejected demands by parliamentary deputies for Aitbayev's dismissal, in early February he removed the deputy head of the SNB, and accepted the resignation of the Deputy Secretary of the Security Council. Meanwhile, also in early February further tensions between the Zhogorku Kenesh and the President arose when Bakiyev accused the legislature of fomenting political instability and exceeding its mandate. The legislative Chairman, Omurbek Tekebayev, responded by describing Bakiyev as 'a disgrace', and subsequently submitted his resignation. Although the Zhogorku Kenesh initially rejected Tekebayev's resignation, leading to further strains between the legislature and the President, it was accepted in late February. Marat Sultanov was elected as the new Chairman of the Zhogorku Kenesh in early March, and pledged to attempt to resolve disagreements with the executive without recourse to confrontation. At the beginning of March

President Bakiyev signed a decree officially suspending the Chairman of the National Bank, Ulan Sarbanov, from office, during his trial on charges of having illegally transferred some US $420,000 to former President Akayev in 1999. He was replaced by Marat Alapayev at the end of March 2006. Meanwhile, in early March Bakiyev had signed a decree designating 24 March, the anniversary of Akayev's effective removal from power as a result of the so-called 'tulip revolution', a national holiday, to be known as the Day of the People's Revolution.

In 1992 the Kyrgyzstani Government participated in negotiations aimed at ending the civil conflict in neighbouring Tajikistan between forces of the Tajikistani Government and rebel Islamist and pro-democracy groups. In January 1993, however, it was reported that groups of armed Tajiks had crossed into Kyrgyzstan, seeking to incite an Islamist insurrection among the local population. The Kyrgyzstani Government subsequently intensified controls along the border with Tajikistan and contributed troops to a CIS peace-keeping mission on the Tajikistani–Afghan border. Border tensions increased in mid-1996, and requests were made by the Kyrgyzstani Government for assistance from Tajikistan in the rehabilitation of an estimated 15,000 Tajik refugees who had fled to Kyrgyzstan. The peace agreement concluded in Tajikistan in June 1997 was welcomed by the Kyrgyzstani authorities, and in late 1999 Kyrgyzstan began to withdraw its peace-keeping troops from the Tajikistani–Afghan border. The Kyrgyzstani leadership remained concerned at the increase in drugs-trafficking across the Tajikistani–Kyrgyzstani border, and a customs accord was signed by Kyrgyzstan and Tajikistan in September 1998, with the aim of combating arms- and drugs-trafficking. (However, in 2003 it was reported that drugs-trafficking from Afghanistan was increasing.) Border negotiations with Tajikistan, which had commenced in 1997, before being suspended, owing to the unstable political situation in that country, recommenced in December 2002. In late May 2004 the UN opened a drugs-control agency in Kyrgyzstan in an attempt to control the smuggling of narcotics from Afghanistan.

Kyrgyzstan has sought to establish close relations with other Turkic states, with which it shares ethnic, cultural and linguistic ties. In January 1994 Kyrgyzstan, which had introduced its own currency, the som, in May 1993, joined the economic zone newly established by Kazakhstan and Uzbekistan, and in February 1995 an Interstate Council was formed to co-ordinate economic activity in the zone. Following the admission of Tajikistan in March 1998, in May the four countries were formally constituted as the Central Asian Economic Union (known as the Central Asian Co-operation Organization from March 2002). Meanwhile, in March 1996 Kyrgyzstan signed a treaty with Russia, Belarus and Kazakhstan to create a 'community of integrated states', in an attempt to achieve closer economic, cultural and social integration, and joined a customs union established by the three other countries. In April 1998 Tajikistan joined the union, and in October 2000 it was superseded by a new economic body, the Eurasian Economic Community (EurAsEc), which announced its intention to merge with the Central Asian Co-operation Organization in October 2005.

Kyrgyzstan's campaign against Islamist extremism intensified in mid-1999, when Islamist groups believed to be based in Uzbekistan and Tajikistan took hostages in separate events in the southern region of Osh. In mid-August Kyrgyzstani and Uzbekistani forces launched airstrikes against Tajik militants in the Osh region of the Farg'ona valley, in an attempt to prevent further acts of insurgency. However, later that month a senior Kyrgyzstani military commander was among more than 25 people kidnapped by a group of rebels, which captured three villages near the Tajikistani border. The rebels appeared to be members of the Islamic Movement of Uzbekistan (IMU), which demanded the release of Islamists imprisoned in that country. The hostage crisis intensified, with Kyrgyzstani government troops engaging in a large-scale military operation in order to defeat the rebels and free the hostages; fighting continued throughout September. It was announced in late October that all of the hostages had been released. (However, it was reported in mid-November that the body of a police-officer, taken hostage in late August, had been discovered.) From mid-August Islamist militants made a further series of incursions into Kyrgyzstan from Tajikistan, leading to armed conflict with government forces. The number of insurgents amassing on the Kyrgyzstani–Tajikistani border increased, despite intensive shelling and aerial bombardment by Kyrgyzstani troops. By the end of October, however, the Government claimed that all the rebels had left Kyrgyzstan and that it had regained full control of the border regions.

In April 2001 a local government official accused the Uzbekistani authorities of laying landmines along the border with Kyrgyzstan, and demanded the removal of Uzbekistani troops, deployed in an effort to combat the incursions of Islamist militants and drugs-traffickers, from Kyrgyzstani border territories. Meanwhile, reports in May indicated that Islamist rebels were increasingly recruiting from southern Kyrgyzstan. In July 2003 it was reported that Kyrgyzstan was to commence the unilateral removal of landmines along the border with Uzbekistan. Negotiations on the final delimitation of the Kyrgyzstani–Uzbekistani border were ongoing in early 2006.

Relations with Uzbekistan were further strained in mid-2005, when the Kyrgyzstani Government refused to return a large number of refugees who had fled Uzbekistan after violence broke out in the city of Andijon in May (see the chapter on Uzbekistan). Although some refugees were repatriated, most were either given refuge in Kyrgyzstan or allowed to travel on to other countries. Apparently in response to Kyrgyzstan's refusal to co-operate with its demands, in August the Government of Uzbekistan annulled a bilateral agreement to supply natural gas to Kyrgyzstan. In September Uzbekistan issued a report accusing Kyrgyzstan of having permitted religious extremists to use bases in the south of the country to prepare to foment unrest in Andijon; Kyrgyz were among those arrested in connection with the violence there.

In May 2001 the signatories of the CIS Collective Security Treaty—Armenia, Belarus, Kazakhstan, Kyrgyzstan, Russia and Tajikistan—agreed to form a Collective Rapid Reaction Force in Bishkek to combat Islamist militancy in Central Asia; in January 2002 it was announced that the force was ready to undertake combat missions. In April 2003 a successor organization to the Collective Security Treaty was formed, with the inauguration of the Collective Security Treaty Organization (CSTO). In 2003 the Islamic Party of Turkestan and the clandestine, transnational, Islamist Hizb-ut-Tahrir al-Islami (Party of Islamic Liberation) continued to be considered threats to stability in Kyrgyzstan. The latter, which aimed to unite Muslim countries and establish Islamic law, apparently solely through peaceful means, had become the most widespread illegal movement in Kyrgyzstan, particularly in southern regions, despite government attempts to suppress it.

Kyrgyzstan endeavoured to maintain good relations with the largest and most influential CIS member, Russia, and the issue of ethnic Russians (numbering some 603,000 in 1999) has been at the centre of discussions between the two countries. In June 1992 Akayev and the Russian President, Boris Yeltsin, signed a treaty of friendship, co-operation and mutual assistance. A further declaration on friendship, alliance and partnership was signed in July 2000. Military agreements, including a treaty of non-aggression, have also been concluded. An agreement concerning the expansion of Russian-Kyrgyzstani military co-operation was concluded in October 1997, whereby Russia was to lease four military installations in Kyrgyzstan in return for training Kyrgyzstani army recruits. In October 2003 a Russian airbase became operational at Kant, some 30 km from an airbase at Manas, occupied by the US-led anti-terrorism coalition (see below); the new base was the first Russian military installation to be established outside Russia since the collapse of the USSR. In March 2005 Putin offered Akayev the opportunity to take up residence in Russia, after he fled to that country during what became known as the 'tulip revolution' (see above). In September the Russian Minister of Defence, Sergei Ivanov, declared that Russia was to provide Kyrgyzstan with several million US dollars in military aid, to be used primarily to combat terrorism. In February 2006 Russia announced its intention significantly to increase the number of servicemen and the amount of equipment at the Kant airbase; however, the proposal required the approval of the Kyrgyzstani Government.

Kyrgyzstan reached a series of bilateral co-operation agreements with the People's Republic of China during 1996, the terms of which provided for the partial demarcation of their shared border, which was undertaken from mid-2001. Another border treaty was signed in August 1999, which ceded almost 95,000 ha of disputed territory to China. Akayev signed the agreement without the consent of the legislature, prompting widespread protests upon its ratification in 2002 (see above). Meanwhile, an agreement signed in April 1997 with China, Russia, Kazakhstan and Tajikistan (which, together with Kyrgyzstan, constituted the so-called Shanghai Five, later known as the Shanghai Forum) aimed to improve joint border security. The alliance, renamed the Shanghai Co-operation Organization (SCO) upon the accession of Uzbekistan, signed the Shanghai Convention on Combating Terrorism, Separatism and Extremism in mid-2001. In August an associated anti-terrorism centre became operational in Bishkek. The Presidents of Kazakhstan and Kyrgyzstan signed a border agreement in December. In March 2002 China agreed to provide Kyrgyzstan with military assistance worth some US $1.2m. In August 2003 Kyrgyzstani forces participated in major anti-terrorist manoeuvres, hosted by China and Kazakhstan. In September 2004 Tanayev and the Chinese Prime Minister, Wen Jiabao, signed a 10-year co-operation agreement on combating terrorism, separatism and religious extremism, and a protocol on the demarcation of the border between the two countries. In addition, China announced that it would provide Kyrgyzstan with a $6m. grant as part of an agreement on technical and economic co-operation.

Following the large-scale suicide attacks on the US cities of New York and Washington, DC, on 11 September 2001, President Akayev announced that he was prepared to give US military aircraft access to Kyrgyzstani airspace for the aerial bombardment of militants of the al-Qa'ida (Base) organization (held responsible by the USA for having co-ordinated the attacks) and its Taliban hosts in Afghanistan. In late November the Government agreed to give the US-led anti-terrorism coalition access to its military bases and, later, the Khansi-Khanabad airbase at its main airport. Kyrgyzstan undertook joint exercises with US troops in February 2002, which aimed to facilitate attempts to counter insurgency in the country's mountainous regions. In September Akayev met the US President, George W. Bush, and the US Secretary of State, Colin Powell, in Washington, DC, where they discussed Kyrgyzstan's human rights record, the USA's declared 'war against terrorism' and economic issues. A US military presence remained at the Khansi-Khanabad base in 2005. Although Kyrgyzstan stated that it would permit the USA to use the airbase until the situation in Afghanistan stabilized, in early 2006 Kyrgyzstan presented the USA with new conditions for the use of the facility, apparently proposing to increase the rent paid by the USA from US $2m. to $200m.; President Bakiyev maintained that the proposed increase was in accordance with international norms.

Government

According to constitutional amendments approved at a referendum on 2 February 2003, and endorsed by the President on 18 February, supreme legislative power in the Kyrgyz Republic is vested in the unicameral, 75-member Zhogorku Kenesh (Supreme Council). The Zhogorku Kenesh is elected by universal suffrage for a term of five years. The President of the Republic, who is directly elected for a five-year term, is Head of State and Commander-in-Chief of the Armed Forces, and also holds extensive executive powers. The Prime Minister is appointed by the President, subject to the approval of the Zhogorku Kenesh; the remaining members of the Government are appointed by the President. The Prime Minister is empowered to appoint and dismiss ministers and heads of departments. For administrative purposes, Kyrgyzstan is divided into seven dubans (oblasts or regions) and the municipality of Bishkek (the capital). In August 2005 President Bakiyev announced plans to eliminate dubans by 2007, and to replace the existing administrative system with a three-tier system of government, comprising a central government, districts and villages.

Defence

Kyrgyzstan began to raise a national army in 1992. In August 2005 Kyrgyzstan's total armed forces numbered 12,500 (army 8,500, air force 4,000). There were also an estimated 5,000 personnel in paramilitary forces. Military service is compulsory and lasts for 18 months. Kyrgyzstan joined the defence structures of the Commonwealth of Independent States (CIS, see p. 201) by signing, with five other member states, a collective security agreement in May 1992; in May 2001 it was announced that the signatory countries were to form a Collective Rapid Reaction Force to combat Islamist militancy in Central Asia. In April 2003 the Collective Security Treaty Organization (CSTO) was inaugurated as the successor to the CIS collective security system, with the participation of Armenia, Belarus, Kazakhstan, Kyrgyzstan, Russia and Tajikistan. In June 1994 Kyrgyzstan joined the North Atlantic Treaty Organization's (NATO) 'Partnership for Peace' (see p. 316) programme of military co-operation. In 2005 state expenditure on defence totalled some 1,418.4m. soms (representing 7.0% of total spending).

Economic Affairs

In 2004, according to estimates by the World Bank, Kyrgyzstan's gross national product (GNI), measured at average 2002–04 prices, was US $2,050m., equivalent to $400 per head (or $1,840 per head on an international purchasing-power parity basis). During 1995–2004, it was estimated, the population increased by an annual average of 1.2%, while gross domestic product (GDP) per head increased, in real terms, at an average annual rate of 4.0%. Overall GDP increased, in real terms, at an estimated average annual rate of 5.3% in 1995–2004. Real GDP increased by 7.1% in 2004, but declined by 0.6% in 2005.

Agriculture (including forestry and fishing) contributed an estimated 36.6% of GDP in 2004, according to preliminary official figures. In 2002 52.7% of the labour force were employed in the sector. By tradition, the Kyrgyz are a pastoral nomadic people, and the majority of the population (some 65.2% in 1999) reside in rural areas. Livestock-rearing, once the mainstay of agricultural activity, is declining in importance. Only about 7% of the country's land area is arable; of this, some 70% depends on irrigation. The principal crops are grain, potatoes, vegetables and sugar beet. By 2002, according to government figures, collective farms accounted for only around 6% of agricultural production, while state farms accounted for just under 2%. The GDP of the agricultural sector increased, in real terms, by an average of 6.4% per year in 1995–2004; according to the Asian Development Bank (ADB, see p. 169), agricultural GDP increased by 4.1% in 2004, but registered a decline of 4.2% in 2005.

Industry (comprising manufacturing, mining, utilities and construction) contributed an estimated 21.1% of GDP in 2004, according to preliminary official data. The industrial sector provided 10.3% of employment in 2002. Real industrial GDP increased at an average annual rate of 5.7% in 1995–2004; according to the ADB, the GDP of the sector increased by 3.2% in 2004, but declined by 9.7% in 2005.

In 2004 the mining and quarrying sector provided 0.8% of GDP. The sector employed 0.4% of the work-force in 2002. Kyrgyzstan has considerable mineral deposits, including coal, gold, tin, mercury, antimony, zinc, tungsten and uranium. In May 2001 the Government announced the discovery of new deposits of petroleum, estimated to total 70m. barrels, in an oilfield in the west. Production of gold from the Kumtor mine, which is believed to contain the eighth largest deposit of gold in the world (over 200 metric tons), began in January 1997. As a result, by 2001 Kyrgyzstan had become the 10th largest extractor and seller of gold world-wide. The Kumtor mine reportedly produced almost 4.4m. ounces of gold between 1997 and the end of 2003. Production of gold from the Jeruy deposit, which was not expected to produce significant quantities until 2006–07, commenced in 2002. In April 2006 an agreement was signed with a Kazakhstani company on the development of the Taldy Bulak Levoberezhny gold deposit.

Manufacturing contributed 13.6% of GDP in 2004, according to preliminary official figures. The manufacturing sector employed 6.2% of the work-force in 2002. In 2005 the principal branches of manufacturing, measured by gross value of output, were metallurgy (50.6% of the total) and food products, beverages and tobacco (18.2%). Real manufacturing GDP declined by an average of 7.4% per year in 1995–2004, according to the World Bank; the GDP of the sector increased by 7.4% in 2003, but declined by 40.7% in 2004.

Kyrgyzstan's principal source of domestic energy production (and a major export) is hydroelectricity (generated by the country's mountain rivers), which provided 90.5% of the country's total energy requirements in 2002. Kyrgyzstan has insufficient petroleum and natural gas to meet its needs, and substantial imports of hydrocarbons are thus required; Kyrgyzstan exports electricity to Kazakhstan and Uzbekistan in return for coal and natural gas, respectively. Imports of mineral fuels comprised 29.0% of the value of total recorded imports in 2004. Exports of electricity contributed some 15.8% of the value of total exports in 2000.

In 2004, according to preliminary official figures, the services sector contributed an estimated 42.3% of GDP, and the sector provided 37.0% of employment in 2002. In 1995–2004 the GDP of the sector increased, in real terms, by an average of 3.4% per year; according to the ADB, services GDP increased by 11.9% in 2004 and by 8.1% in 2005.

In 2004 Kyrgyzstan recorded a visible trade deficit of US $171.3m., and there was a deficit of $100.7m. on the current account of the balance of payments. In 2004 the principal source of imports (accounting for 31.2%) was Russia; other major suppliers were Kazakhstan (21.6%), the People's Republic of China (8.5%), Germany (5.6%) and Uzbekistan (5.5%). The main market for exports in that year was the United Arab Emirates (26.3%). Other principal markets were Russia (19.2%), Switzerland (14.2%), Kazakhstan (12.1%) and China (5.5%). The main exports in 2004 were precious and semi-precious stones and metals, mineral products, textiles, and foodstuffs, beverages and tobacco. The principal imports in that year were mineral products (mostly petroleum and natural gas), chemicals, machinery and electrical equipment, foodstuffs, beverages and tobacco, vehicles and transport equipment, metals and plastics and rubber.

In 2005 Kyrgyzstan recorded an overall budgetary surplus of 224.3m. soms. Kyrgyzstan's total external debt was US $2,021m. at the end of 2003, of which $1,588m. was long-term public debt. In that year the cost of debt-servicing was equivalent to 16.0% of the value of exports of goods and services. The annual rate of inflation averaged 15.9% in 1995–2003. Consumer prices increased by 4.0% in 2004 and by 4.4% in 2005. The average rate of unemployment was 9.0% in 2005.

Kyrgyzstan participates in the economic bodies of the Commonwealth of Independent States (CIS, see p. 201), and has also joined the European Bank for Reconstruction and Development (EBRD, see p. 224), as a 'Country of Operations', the Economic Co-operation Organization (ECO, see p. 223) and the ADB. In 1998 Kyrgyzstan became the first CIS country to join the World Trade Organization (WTO, see p. 370).

Following independence in 1991, the Government embarked on an ambitious programme of economic reforms. Significant growth was recorded from 1996, although it slowed in 1998–99, apparently owing to the financial crisis in Russia. In 2001 an annual rate of inflation of less than 10% was recorded for the first time since independence. In 2002 GDP recorded negative growth for the first time since 1995, largely owing to reduced industrial output after a landslide at the Kumtor gold mine. However, growth was recorded in 2003 and 2004, partly owing to increased foreign trade and changes to fiscal regulations concerning small businesses, which had served to reduce tax evasion. In February 2005 the IMF approved a new Poverty Reduction and Growth Facility arrangement for 2005–07. In March 2005 the 'Paris Club' of official creditors announced that it was cancelling US $124m. of Kyrgyzstan's sovereign debt and rescheduling a further $431m. Planned fiscal reforms included the introduction of a uniform rate of income tax, of 10%, in order to encourage private-sector activity. A decline in gold production and the political instability resulting from the removal of President Askar Akayev and the subsequent change of government in 2005 slowed economic development, and GDP recorded negative growth in that year. The new Government declared that poverty reduction and combating corruption were among its principal aims, although by early 2006 there was little discernible progress in those areas. None the less, consumer-price inflation remained relatively low, and in early 2006 President Kurmanbek Bakiyev declared that GDP growth of 8% was attainable in that year.

However, in the medium term, growth was likely to be adversely affected by the economy's reliance on the output of the Kumtor mine (accounting for some 38.5% of industrial production in 2005), the closure of which was anticipated in 2010. In addition, the need to reduce foreign debt remained an important factor limiting growth. Ultimately, sustained economic growth, especially given the decrease in gold production, was dependent on the greater diversification of both exports and industry and increased political stability.

Education

Education is officially compulsory for nine years, comprising four years of primary school (between the ages of seven and 10), followed by five years of lower secondary school (ages 11 to 15). Pupils may then continue their studies in upper secondary schools (two years' duration), specialized secondary schools (two to four years) or technical and vocational schools (from 15 years of age). In 2000/01 total enrolment at primary schools was equivalent to 89% of the relevant age-group; enrolment at secondary-school level was equivalent to 83%. A decree signed in December 2001 abolished free schooling. In 2004/05 there 49 institutes of higher education, providing courses lasting between four and six years, and attended by 218,273 students. In 1993/94 63.6% of pupils in primary and secondary schools were taught in Kyrgyz, 23.4% were taught in Russian, 12.7% in Uzbek and 0.3% in Tajik. However, Russian was the principal language of instruction in higher educational establishments. In 2005 budgetary expenditure on education amounted to 4,917.7m. soms (24.4% of total spending).

Public Holidays

2006: 1 January (New Year's Day), 7 January (Christmas), 10 January*† (Kurban Ait, Id al-Adha or Feast of the Sacrifice), 8 March (International Women's Day), 21 March (Nooruz, Kyrgyz New Year), 24 March (Day of the People's Revolution), 1 May (International Labour Day), 5 May (Constitution Day), 9 May (Victory Day), 31 August (Independence Day), 24 October* (Orozo Ait, Id al-Fitr or end of Ramadan), 31 December*† (Kurban Ait, Id al-Adha or Feast of the Sacrifice).

2007: 1 January (New Year's Day), 7 January (Christmas), 8 March (International Women's Day), 21 March (Nooruz, Kyrgyz New Year), 24 March (Day of the People's Revolution), 1 May (International Labour Day), 5 May (Constitution Day), 9 May (Victory Day), 31 August (Independence Day), 13 October* (Orozo Ait, Id al-Fitr or end of Ramadan), 20 December* (Kurban Ait, Id al-Adha or Feast of the Sacrifice).

* These holidays are dependent on the Islamic lunar calendar and may vary by one or two days from the dates given.
† This festival occurs twice (in the Islamic years AH 1426 and 1427) within the same Gregorian year.

Weights and Measures

The metric system is in force.

KYRGYZSTAN

Statistical Survey

Source (unless otherwise stated): National Statistical Committee, 720033 Bishkek, Frunze 374; tel. (312) 22-63-63; fax (312) 22-07-59; e-mail zkudabaev@nsc.bishkek.su; internet www.stat.kg.

Area and Population

AREA, POPULATION AND DENSITY

Area (sq km)	199,900*
Population (census results)†	
12 January 1989	4,257,755
24 March 1999	
Males	2,380,465
Females	2,442,473
Total	4,822,938
Population (official estimates at 31 December)	
2002	4,984,400
2003	5,037,300
2004	5,092,802
Density (per sq km) at 31 December 2004	25.5

* 77,182 sq miles.
† The figures refer to *de jure* population. The *de facto* total was 4,290,442 at the 1989 census and 4,850,700 at the 1999 census.

PRINCIPAL ETHNIC GROUPS
(permanent inhabitants, 1999 census)

	Number	%
Kyrgyz	3,128,147	64.9
Uzbek	664,950	13.8
Russian	603,201	12.5
Dungan	51,766	1.1
Ukrainian	50,442	1.0
Uigur	46,944	1.0
Tatar	45,438	0.9
Kazakh	42,657	0.9
Tajik	42,636	0.9
Turkish	33,327	0.7
German	21,471	0.4
Korean	19,784	0.4
Others	72,175	1.5
Total	**4,822,938**	**100.0**

ADMINISTRATIVE DIVISIONS
(1999 census)

	Area (sq km)	Population	Density (per sq km)
Batken Duban	17,000	382,426	22.5
Chui Duban	20,200	770,811	38.2
Issyk-Kul Duban	43,100	413,149	9.6
Jalal-Abad Duban	33,700	869,259	25.8
Naryn Duban	45,200	249,115	5.5
Osh Duban	29,200	1,175,998	40.3
Talas Duban	11,400	199,872	17.5
Bishkek City	100	762,308	7,623.1
Total	**199,900**	**4,822,938**	**24.1**

PRINCIPAL TOWNS
(population at census of March 1999)

Bishkek (capital)*	750,327	Karakol†		64,322
Osh	208,520	Tokmok		59,409
Jalal-Abad	70,401	Kara-Balta		53,887

* Known as Frunze between 1926 and 1991.
† Formerly Przhevalsk.

Mid-2003 (UN estimate, incl. suburbs): Bishkek 805,648 (Source: UN, *World Urbanization Prospects: The 2003 Revision*).

BIRTHS, MARRIAGES AND DEATHS

	Registered live births		Registered marriages		Registered deaths	
	Number	Rate (per 1,000)	Number	Rate (per 1,000)	Number	Rate (per 1,000)
1997	102,050	21.6	26,588	5.6	34,540	7.3
1998	104,183	21.7	25,726	5.4	34,596	7.2
1999	104,068	21.4	26,033	5.4	32,850	6.8
2000	96,770	19.7	24,294	4.9	34,111	6.9
2001	98,138	19.8	27,455	5.5	32,677	6.6
2002	101,012	20.2	31,240	6.3	35,235	7.1
2003	105,490	20.9	34,266	6.8	35,941	7.1
2004	109,939	21.6	34,542	6.8	35,061	6.9

Expectation of life (WHO estimates, years at birth): 63 (males 59; females 68) in 2003 (Source: WHO, *World Health Report*).

ECONOMICALLY ACTIVE POPULATION
(annual averages, '000 persons)

	2000	2001	2002
Agriculture, hunting and forestry	938.4	944.5	950.8
Fishing	0.1	1.2	1.1
Mining and quarrying	8.5	8.4	6.5
Manufacturing	113.0	111.5	111.9
Electricity, gas and water supply	20.4	21.4	21.8
Construction	43.4	43.6	45.6
Wholesale and retail trade; repair of motor vehicles, motor cycles and personal and household goods	188.0	194.3	200.1
Hotels and restaurants	13.1	14.5	16.9
Transport, storage and communications	63.5	64.5	68.0
Financial intermediation	7.4	8.2	8.1
Real estate, renting and business activities	29.0	30.3	30.2
Public administration and defence; compulsory social security	65.2	64.2	66.3
Education	144.9	146.0	149.2
Health and social work	84.7	82.0	76.7
Other services	48.8	52.4	53.9
Total employed	**1,768.4**	**1,787.0**	**1,807.1**
Males	983.8	993.4	n.a.
Females	784.6	793.6	n.a.

Source: ILO.

Total employed (preliminary figure, '000 persons): 1,824.1 in 2003.

Total unemployed (estimates, '000 persons, incl. unregistered): 144.3 in 2000; 152.0 in 2001; 169.5 in 2002; 180.0 in 2003.

Health and Welfare

KEY INDICATORS

Total fertility rate (children per woman, 2003)	2.6
Under-5 mortality rate (per 1,000 live births, 2004)	68
HIV/AIDS (% of persons aged 15–49, 2003)	0.10
Physicians (per 1,000 head, 2002)	2.60
Hospital beds (per 1,000 head, 2002)	5.50
Health expenditure (2002): US $ per head (PPP)	117
Health expenditure (2002): % of GDP	4.3
Health expenditure (2002): public (% of total)	51.2
Access to water (% of persons, 2002)	76
Access to sanitation (% of persons, 2002)	60
Human Development Index (2003): ranking	109
Human Development Index (2003): value	0.702

For sources and definitions, see explanatory note on p. vi.

KYRGYZSTAN

Agriculture

PRINCIPAL CROPS
('000 metric tons)

	2002	2003	2004
Wheat	1,162.6	1,013.7	998.2
Rice (paddy)	20.8	18.3	18.3
Barley	149.3	197.9	233.4
Maize	373.6	398.5	452.9
Potatoes	1,244.0	1,308.2	1,362.5
Sugar beet	521.5	812.3	642.4
Pulses	44.5	42.1	44.2
Sunflower seed	60.6	59.4	67.2
Cabbages	68.6	104.1	113.2
Tomatoes	101.6	143.7	168.1
Cucumbers and gherkins	26.1	50.2	55.7
Dry onions	84.4	104.0	117.1
Garlic	10.1	19.4	25.0
Carrots	64.8	125.6	127.1
Other vegetables*	95.5	133.4	135.3
Apples*	104.0	100.0	123.0
Apricots*	15.0	12.4	15.4
Peaches and nectarines*	2.4	2.8	3.5
Grapes	17.7	12.7	14.6
Watermelons	42.2	85.3	88.0
Cotton (lint)*	43.0	42.5	48.0
Cottonseed	63.2	63.0*	70.0*
Tobacco (leaves)	6.2	8.7	13.0

* Unofficial figure(s).
Source: FAO.

LIVESTOCK
('000 head at 1 January)

	2002	2003	2004
Horses	354	361	361
Asses	45*	47*	48†
Cattle	970	988	1,003
Camels	44*	44*	43
Pigs	87	87	83
Sheep	3,104	3,104	2,884
Goats	640	661	770
Chickens	2,914†	3,279†	3,846
Turkeys	123	129	149

* FAO estimate.
† Unofficial figure.
Source: FAO.

LIVESTOCK PRODUCTS
('000 metric tons)

	2002	2003	2004
Beef and veal	104.8	94.0	94.6
Mutton and lamb	36.9	37.0	37.7
Goat meat	6.7	7.2	7.1
Pig meat	23.0	22.1	25.2
Horse meat	22.5	26.5	18.8
Poultry meat	6.2	6.5	4.9
Cows' milk	1,140.3	1,159.2	1,132.5
Cheese	4.1	4.7	4.9
Butter	1.5	1.8	1.9
Hen eggs	13.5	14.9	16.6
Honey	1.6	1.5	1.3
Wool: greasy	10.9	10.9	10.0
Wool: scoured	6.5	6.5	6.1
Cattle hides*	9.7	9.9	9.9
Sheepskins*	5.5	6.0	5.6

* FAO estimates.
Source: FAO.

Forestry

ROUNDWOOD REMOVALS
(unofficial figures, '000 cubic metres, excl. bark)

	2002	2003	2004
Sawlogs, veneer logs and logs for sleepers	6	6	5
Other industrial wood	6	6	5
Fuel wood	25	25	18
Total	37	37	28

Source: FAO.

SAWNWOOD PRODUCTION
('000 cubic metres, incl. railway sleepers)

	2001*	2002†	2003
Coniferous (softwood)	2	2	8
Broadleaved (hardwood)	4	4	7
Total	6	6	15

* Unofficial figures.
† FAO estimates.
Source: FAO.

Fishing

(metric tons, live weight)

	2001	2002	2003
Capture	57	48	14
Freshwater bream	4	3	1
Common carp	11	9	1
Silver carp	19	17	2
Other cyprinids	8	7	5
Whitefishes	12	9	3
Aquaculture	144	94	12
Common carp	27	29	7
Grass carp	43	14	1
Silver carp	74	51	4
Total catch	201	142	26

Source: FAO.

Mining

('000 metric tons, unless otherwise indicated)

	2003	2004	2005
Coal	415.3	456.3	331.6
Crude petroleum	69.5	73.8	74.4
Natural gas (million cu metres)	27.1	28.6	24.7

Gold (metric tons): 24.6 in 2001; 17.9 in 2002; 22.7 in 2003 (Source: Gold Fields Mineral Services, *Gold Survey 2004*).

Industry

SELECTED PRODUCTS
('000 metric tons, unless otherwise indicated)

	2003	2004	2005
Vegetable oil	10.7	12.3	15.2
Refined sugar	75.5	88.1	44.5
Vodka ('000 hectolitres)	24.3	21.8	16.5
Beer ('000 hectolitres)	7.7	11.6	12.3
Cigarettes (million)	3,102.4	3,169.5	3,164.7
Textile fabrics ('000 sq metres)	1,814.2	1,264.8	1,921.2
Footwear ('000 pairs)	237.8	245.7	220.5
Motor spirit (petrol)	25.0	19.7	14.0
Gas-diesel (distillate fuel) oil	21.9	26.3	31.4
Cement	757.3	870.1	975.1
Electric energy (million kWh)	14,021.1	15,091.2	14,838.7

Finance

CURRENCY AND EXCHANGE RATES

Monetary Units
100 tyiyns = 1 som.

Sterling, Dollar and Euro Equivalents (30 December 2005)
£1 sterling = 71.12 soms;
US $1 = 41.30 soms;
€1 = 48.72 soms;
1,000 soms = £14.06 = $24.21 = €20.52.

Average Exchange Rate (soms per US $)
2003   43.648
2004   42.650
2005   41.012

Note: In May 1993 Kyrgyzstan introduced its own currency, the som, replacing the Russian (former Soviet) rouble at an exchange rate of 1 som = 200 roubles.

BUDGET
(million soms)*

Revenue†	2003	2004	2005
Taxation	11,916.5	13,986.6	16,361.4
Personal income taxes	1,208.0	1,442.9	1,744.1
Profit taxes	913.1	918.6	1,283.1
Value-added tax	5,526.3	6,829.9	7,088.6
Excise taxes	1,164.0	1,245.2	1,149.7
Taxes on international trade and transactions	422.8	449.4	1,664.0
Other current revenue	3,700.2	3,418.9	3,567.9
Capital revenue	136.7	214.7	46.1
Total	15,753.4	17,620.2	19,975.4

Expenditure‡	2003	2004	2005
Government services	2,644.0	3,098.7	3,039.6
Defence	1,287.3	1,431.2	1,418.4
Internal security	1,120.7	1,256.4	1,681.4
Education	3,752.7	4,357.4	4,917.7
Health care	1,630.0	1,925.6	2,283.3
Social insurance and security	2,587.8	2,644.8	2,858.1
Housing and public utilities	1,193.4	1,060.6	1,040.6
Subsidies to economic sectors	1,840.7	1,909.7	1,911.4
Total (incl. others)	16,895.9	18,841.7	20,143.7

* Figures represent a consolidation of the budgetary transactions of the central Government and local governments. The operations of extra-budgetary accounts, including the Social Fund (formed in 1994 by an amalgamation of the Pension Fund, the Unemployment Fund and the Social Insurance Fund), are excluded.
† Excluding grants received (million soms): 461.5 in 2003; 715.8 in 2004; 392.6 in 2005.
‡ Including lending minus repayments.

INTERNATIONAL RESERVES
(US $ million at 31 December)

	2002	2003	2004
Gold	28.5	34.7	36.4
IMF special drawing rights	0.6	10.3	19.9
Foreign exchange	288.2	354.3	508.3
Total	317.3	399.3	564.6

Source: IMF, *International Financial Statistics*.

MONEY SUPPLY
(million soms at 31 December)

	2002	2003	2004
Currency outside banks	6,866	9,302	11,109
Demand deposits at banking institutions	811	1,314	1,935
Total money	7,677	10,616	13,045

Source: IMF, *International Financial Statistics*.

COST OF LIVING
(Retail price index; base: 2000 = 100)

	2002	2003	2004
Food	105.9	108.9	112.4
Fuel and light	149.7	152.0	156.7
Clothing	105.4	106.2	106.5
Rent	168.2	174.7	200.7
All items (incl. others)	109.1	112.5	117.1

NATIONAL ACCOUNTS
(million soms at current prices)

Expenditure on the Gross Domestic Product

	2002	2003	2004
Government final consumption expenditure	14,032.7	14,116.4	15,577.1
Private final consumption expenditure	50,896.7	65,344.0	74,714.3
Changes in stocks	852.1	−1,678.1	−2,329.7
Gross fixed capital formation	12,417.5	11,600.1	11,722.7
Statistical discrepancy	—	—	3,587.5
Total domestic expenditure	78,199.0	89,382.4	103,271.9
Exports of goods and services	29,831.2	32,442.4	40,288.7
Less Imports of goods and services	32,663.5	37,953.2	49,482.2
GDP in purchasers' values	75,366.7	83,871.6	94,078.4

Gross Domestic Product by Economic Activity

	2002	2003	2004*
Agriculture, forestry and fishing	25,929.8	28,199.5	30,978.9
Mining	362.9	409.5	689.6
Manufacturing	9,834.2	11,133.4	11,483.9
Electricity, gas and water supply	3,287.2	2,988.7	2,905.5
Construction	2,579.2	2,446.6	2,789.9
Trade, repair of motor vehicles, household appliances and articles of personal use	10,752.9	12,725.4	15,608.0
Hotels and restaurants	839.1	1,235.8	1,438.0
Transport and communications	3,845.4	4,514.0	5,992.2
Housing, social and personal services	801.5	904.4	1,054.5
Health care and social services	1,298.7	1,441.4	1,431.3

KYRGYZSTAN

—continued	2002	2003	2004*
Education	2,535.1	3,353.8	3,512.8
Financial activities	1,131.2	1,264.6	559.0
Real estate, rent and rendering services	2,307.3	2,353.3	2,338.9
Government administration	3,947.3	3,875.6	3,887.8
Sub-total	69,451.8	76,846.0	84,670.7
Less Imputed bank service charge	641.4	763.4	—
GDP at basic prices	68,810.4	76,082.6	84,670.7
Taxes on products / Less Subsidies on products	6,556.3	7,789.0	9,407.7
GDP in purchasers' values	75,366.7	83,871.6	94,078.4

* Preliminary data.

BALANCE OF PAYMENTS
(US $ million)

	2002	2003	2004
Exports of goods f.o.b.	498.1	590.3	733.2
Imports of goods f.o.b.	−572.1	−723.8	−904.5
Trade balance	−74.0	−133.5	−171.3
Exports of services	142.0	154.7	208.9
Imports of services	−148.4	−151.2	−231.0
Balance on goods and services	−80.5	−130.0	−193.4
Other income received	6.3	5.2	11.2
Other income paid	−63.7	−67.6	−101.4
Balance on goods, services and income	−137.8	−192.3	−283.6
Current transfers received	60.7	100.4	200.6
Current transfers paid	−2.9	−7.0	−17.6
Current balance	−80.0	−99.0	−100.7
Capital account (net)	−7.9	−0.9	−19.9
Direct investment abroad	—	—	−43.9
Direct investment from abroad	4.7	45.5	175.4
Portfolio investment assets	−2.5	1.1	−2.5
Portfolio investment liabilities	−9.5	5.0	—
Financial derivatives assets	−5.1	−20.0	−20.5
Other investment assets	21.5	−78.7	−29.6
Other investment liabilities	99.6	72.1	106.8
Net errors and omissions	−0.3	121.7	79.5
Overall balance	20.4	46.8	144.5

Source: IMF, *International Financial Statistics*.

External Trade

PRINCIPAL COMMODITIES
(US $ million)

Imports c.i.f.	2002	2003	2004
Vegetable products	21.7	16.2	23.0
Prepared foodstuffs, beverages and tobacco	47.4	59.5	83.0
Mineral products	163.4	195.6	273.3
Products of chemical or allied industries	78.4	91.7	112.9
Plastics, rubber and articles thereof	24.9	38.3	56.0
Textiles and fabrics	38.9	47.3	42.6
Metals and articles thereof	29.7	43.5	65.0
Machinery, electrical equipment and parts	89.6	89.1	107.3
Vehicles and transport equipment	32.1	51.2	70.3
Total (incl. others)	586.8	717.0	941.0

Exports f.o.b.	2002	2003	2004
Vegetable products	19.9	18.9	26.2
Prepared foodstuffs, beverages and tobacco	30.1	25.8	42.9
Mineral products	62.4	74.7	94.1
Products of chemical or allied industries	25.2	9.7	21.7
Raw hides and skins, leather, fur, travel articles and bags	24.2	11.5	9.3
Textiles and fabrics	59.8	69.9	79.5
Natural and cultured pearls, precious and semi-precious stones, precious metals and products, and coins	164.8	262.1	291.2
Metals and articles thereof	23.4	19.8	31.7
Machinery, electrical equipment and parts	26.9	28.2	35.5
Vehicles and transport equipment	21.2	14.5	14.8
Total (incl. others)	485.5	581.7	718.8

PRINCIPAL TRADING PARTNERS
(US $ million)

Imports c.i.f.	2002	2003	2004
Belarus	5.1	5.9	4.2
Belgium	1.6	3.3	2.3
Canada	9.0	8.3	12.6
China, People's Republic	59.1	77.7	80.1
Germany	31.4	38.2	52.6
Iran	4.3	5.9	7.0
Japan	6.4	11.8	11.6
Kazakhstan	123.9	170.9	202.2
Korea, Republic	7.0	11.7	25.1
Netherlands	16.1	12.3	15.7
Poland	3.9	6.1	10.3
Russia	116.7	176.1	293.7
Sweden	7.4	2.0	4.6
Turkey	17.0	26.0	33.2
Turkmenistan	1.7	0.4	1.4
Ukraine	7.8	12.6	23.3
United Arab Emirates	7.3	7.8	7.6
United Kingdom	1.1	0.6	4.2
USA	47.4	47.9	44.6
Uzbekistan	60.1	39.2	51.9
Total (incl. others)	586.8	717.0	941.0

Exports f.o.b.	2002	2003	2004
Afghanistan	4.4	6.1	8.0
Azerbaijan	5.6	2.0	1.8
China, People's Republic	41.1	23.3	39.3
France	5.6	0.2	0.3
Germany	1.8	3.0	3.1
India	6.1	0.7	0.6
Iran	4.7	2.1	3.5
Kazakhstan	36.8	57.1	87.3
Latvia	8.7	9.4	9.0
Russia	80.0	97.0	137.7
Switzerland	96.4	117.9	101.8
Tajikistan	10.2	18.9	22.1
Turkey	16.4	11.0	17.0
United Arab Emirates	68.8	144.3	189.3
United Kingdom	0.9	0.1	0.3
USA	36.1	6.5	3.2
Uzbekistan	27.8	16.3	14.7
Total (incl. others)	485.5	581.7	718.8

Transport

RAILWAYS
(traffic)

	2002	2003	2004
Passenger-km (million)	43	50	45
Freight net ton-km (million)	395	562	715

KYRGYZSTAN

ROAD TRAFFIC
(vehicles in use at 31 December)

	2001	2002	2003
Passenger cars	189,796	188,711	188,900
Motorcycles and mopeds	14,319	12,288	11,221

CIVIL AVIATION
(traffic on scheduled services)

	2002	2003	2004
Kilometres flown (million)	6	7	7
Passengers carried ('000)	185	218	258
Passenger-km (million)	342	411	459
Total ton-km (million)	39	43	46

Tourism

FOREIGN TOURIST ARRIVALS

Country of residence	2001	2002
China, People's Republic	5,240	7,495
CIS countries*	30,279	59,132
France	1,106	4,462
Germany	3,039	6,820
India	358	1,590
Iran	345	1,112
Japan	1,645	1,436
Korea, Republic	1,053	1,689
The Netherlands	628	1,102
Switzerland	1,095	1,024
Turkey	3,261	5,864
United Kingdom	1,888	2,958
USA	3,979	10,883
Total (incl. others)	98,558	139,589

* Comprising Armenia, Azerbaijan, Belarus, Georgia, Kazakhstan, Moldova, the Russian Federation, Tajikistan, Turkmenistan, Ukraine and Uzbekistan.

Tourism receipts (US $ million, incl. passenger transport): 21 in 2001; 23 in 2002; 30 in 2003.

Source: World Tourism Organization.

Communications Media

	2002	2003	2004
Television receivers ('000 in use)	7	7	7
Telephones ('000 main lines in use)	389.9	401.3	419.3
Mobile cellular telephones ('000 subscribers)	76.2	138.6	263.4
Internet users ('000)	4.7	6.4	6.2
Personal computers ('000 in use)	33	39	47
Daily newspapers:			
number	1	2	2
average circulation	35,900	65,000	21,000
Non-daily newspapers:			
number	62	77	83
average circulation	319,100	376,600	427,800
Book production:			
titles	672	642	703
copies ('000)	1,056.6	1,885.0	1,600.3

Radio receivers ('000 in use): 520 in 1997 (Source: UNESCO, *Statistical Yearbook*).

Education
(2004/05)

	Institutions	Teachers	Students
Pre-primary	440	2,333	50,935
Primary	2,104	17,729	436,159
Secondary: general	n.a.	50,526	692,724
Secondary: vocational	187	6,212	59,659
Higher (all institutions)	49	13,337	218,273

Adult literacy rate (official estimate): 98.7% in 2004.

Directory

The Constitution

A new Constitution was proclaimed on 5 May 1993. The following is a summary of its main provisions (including amendments endorsed in referendums held on 22 October 1994, 10 February 1996, 17 October 1998 and 2 February 2003, and other modifications approved by the Constitutional Court):

GENERAL PROVISIONS

The Kyrgyz Republic is a sovereign, unitary, democratic republic founded on the principle of lawful, secular government. All state power belongs to the people, who exercise this power through the state bodies, on the basis of the Constitution and laws of the republic, and through the bodies of self-governance. Matters of legislation and other issues pertaining to the state may be decided by the people by referendum. The President of the Republic, the deputies of the Zhogorku Kenesh (Supreme Council), and representatives of local administrative bodies are all elected directly by the people. Elections are held on the basis of universal, equal and direct suffrage by secret ballot. All citizens of 18 years and over are eligible to vote.

The territory of the Kyrgyz Republic is integral and inviolable. The state language is Kyrgyz, and Russian has the status of an official language. The equality and free use of other languages are guaranteed. The rights and freedoms of citizens may not be restricted on account of ignorance of the state language.

THE PRESIDENT

The President of the Kyrgyz Republic is Head of State and Commander-in-Chief of the Armed Forces, and represents Kyrgyzstan both within the country and internationally. Any citizen of the republic between the ages of 35 and 65, who has a fluent command of the state language, may stand for election. The President's term of office is five years; he/she may not serve more than two consecutive terms. The President is directly elected by the people.

The President appoints and dismisses (subject to approval by the legislature) the Prime Minister; appoints the other members of the Government, as well as heads of administrative offices and other leading state posts; presents draft legislation to the Zhogorku Kenesh on his/her own initiative; signs legislation approved by the Zhogorku Kenesh or returns it for further scrutiny; signs international agreements; may call referendums on issues of state; may dissolve the legislature (should a referendum demand this) and call fresh elections; announces a general or partial mobilization; and declares a state of war in the event of an invasion by a foreign power.

ZHOGORKU KENESH
(Supreme Council)

Supreme legislative power is vested in the Zhogorku Kenesh, which comprises one 75-member chamber. Members are elected for a term of five years on the basis of universal, equal and direct suffrage by secret ballot.

The Zhogorku Kenesh approves amendments and additions to the Constitution; enacts legislation; confirms the republican budget and

KYRGYZSTAN

supervises its execution; determines questions pertaining to the administrative and territorial structure of the republic; designates presidential elections; approves the appointment of the Prime Minister, as nominated by the President; approves the appointment of the Procurator-General, the Chairman of the Supreme Court and the Chairman of the National Bank, as nominated by the President; ratifies or abrogates international agreements, and decides questions of war and peace; and organizes referendums on issues of state.

THE GOVERNMENT

The Government of the Kyrgyz Republic is the highest organ of executive power in Kyrgyzstan. The Prime Minister heads the Government, which also comprises deputy prime ministers and ministers. The members of the Government are appointed by the President; however, the President's appointment of the Prime Minister requires approval by the Zhogorku Kenesh. The President supervises the work of the Government and has the right to chair its sessions. The Prime Minister must deliver an annual report to the Zhogorku Kenesh on the work of the Government.

The Government determines all questions of state administration, other than those ascribed to the Constitution or to the competence of the President and the Zhogorku Kenesh; drafts the republican budget and submits it to the Zhogorku Kenesh for approval; coordinates budgetary, financial, fiscal and monetary policy; administers state property; takes measures to defend the country and state security; executes foreign policy; and strives to guarantee the rights and freedoms of the citizens and to protect property and social order.

JUDICIAL SYSTEM

The judicial system comprises the Constitutional Court, the Supreme Court, the Higher Court of Arbitration and regional courts. Judges of the Constitutional Court are appointed by the Zhogorku Kenesh, on the recommendation of the President, for a term of 15 years, while those of the Supreme Court and the Higher Court of Arbitration are appointed by the Zhogorku Kenesh, on the recommendation of the President, for ten years. The Constitutional Court is the supreme judicial body protecting constitutionality. It comprises the Chairman/woman, his/her deputies and seven judges. The Supreme Court is the highest organ of judicial power in the sphere of civil, criminal and administrative justice.

The Government

HEAD OF STATE

President: Kurmanbek S. Bakiyev (elected 10 July 2005; inaugurated 14 August 2005).

GOVERNMENT
(April 2006)

Prime Minister: Feliks Kulov.
First Deputy Prime Minister: Medetbek Kerimkulov.
Deputy Prime Ministers: Adakhan K. Madumarov, Ishengul Boljurova.
Head of the Office of the Prime Minister: Turuspek Koyenaliyev.
Minister of Foreign Affairs: Alikbek Jekshenkulov.
Minister of Defence: Gen. Ismail I. Isakov.
Minister of Internal Affairs: Murat A. Sutalinov.
Minister of the Economy and Finance: Akylbek U. Zhaparov.
Minister of Agriculture, Water Resources and Processing Industry: (vacant).
Minister of Justice: Marat Kaiypov.
Minister of Industry, Commerce and Tourism: Medetbek Kerimkulov (acting).
Minister of Transport and Communications: Nurlan Sulaimanov.
Minister of Ecology and Emergency Situations: Janysh S. Rustenbekov.
Minister of Health: Shailoobek Niyazov.
Minister of Education, Science and Youth Affairs: Dosbol Nur Uulu.
Minister of Culture: Sultan Rayev.
Minister of Labour and Social Protection: Yevgenii Semenenko.

MINISTRIES

Office of the President: 720003 Bishkek, Dom Pravitelstva; tel. (312) 21-24-66; fax (312) 21-86-27; e-mail office@mail.gov.kg; internet www.president.kg.
Office of the Prime Minister: 720003 Bishkek, Dom Pravitelstva; tel. (312) 66-12-20; fax (312) 66-66-58; e-mail pmoffice@mail.gov.kg; internet www.gov.kg.
Ministry of Agriculture, Water Resources and Processing Industry: 720040 Bishkek, ul. Kievskaya 96A; tel. (312) 62-14-27; fax (312) 62-36-32; e-mail mawrpi@elcat.kg.
Ministry of Culture: 720040 Bishkek.
Ministry of Defence: 720001 Bishkek, ul. Logvinenko 26; tel. (312) 66-38-28; fax (312) 66-16-02; e-mail ud@bishkek.gov.kg; internet www.mil.kg.
Ministry of Ecology and Emergency Situations: 720055 Bishkek, ul. Ak. Toktonaliyeva 2/1; tel. (312) 54-79-86; fax (312) 54-11-79; e-mail mekdkg@exnet.kg; internet www.mecd.gov.kg.
Ministry of the Economy and Finance: 720040 Bishkek, pr. Erkindik 58; tel. (312) 66-13-50; fax (312) 66-16-45; e-mail minfin@elcat.kg; internet www.minfin.kg.
Ministry of Education, Science and Youth Affairs: 720002 Bishkek, pr. Chui 106; tel. (312) 66-19-45; fax (312) 66-18-37; e-mail postmaster@mvtp.bishkek.gov.kg.
Ministry of Foreign Affairs: 720040 Bishkek, bul. Erkindik 57; tel. (312) 62-05-45; fax (312) 66-05-01; e-mail gendep@mfa.gov.kg; internet www.mfa.kg.
Ministry of Health: 720040 Bishkek, ul. Moskovskaya 148; tel. (312) 62-26-80; fax (312) 66-07-17; e-mail minzdrav@minzdrav.bishkek.gov.kg; internet www.med.kg.
Ministry of Industry, Commerce and Tourism: 720002 Bishkek, pr. Chui 106; tel. (312) 66-19-45; fax (312) 66-18-37; e-mail postmaster@mvtp.bishkek.gov.kg.
Ministry of Internal Affairs: 720040 Bishkek, ul. Frunze 469; tel. (312) 66-24-50; fax (312) 68-20-44; e-mail mail@mvd.bishkek.gov.kg; internet www.mvd.kg.
Ministry of Justice: 720040 Bishkek, ul. M. Gandi 32; tel. (312) 65-64-90; fax (312) 65-65-02; e-mail admin@minjust.gov.kg; internet www.minjust.gov.kg.
Ministry of Labour and Social Protection: 720041 Bishkek, ul. Tynystanova 215; tel. (312) 66-34-00; fax (312) 66-57-24; e-mail mlsp@mlsp.kg; internet www.mlsp.kg.
Ministry of Transport and Communications: 720017 Bishkek, ul. Isanova 42; tel. (312) 61-04-72; fax (312) 66-47-81; e-mail mtk@mtk.bishkek.gov.kg; internet www.mtk.gov.kg.

President and Legislature

PRESIDENT

**Presidential Election, 10 July 2005*

Candidates	Votes	%
Kurmanbek S. Bakiyev	1,776,156	88.72
Tursunbai Bakir-uulu	78,701	3.93
Akbaraly Y. Aitikeyev	72,604	3.63
Zhipar Zh. Zheksheyev	18,166	0.91
Toktaiym J. Umetaliyeva	10,445	0.52
Keneshbek A. Dushebayev	10,253	0.51
Against all candidates	18,197	0.91
Total (including invalid votes)	2,001,974	100.00

* Preliminary official results.

LEGISLATURE

Zhogorku Kenesh
(Supreme Council)

720053 Bishkek, ul. Abdymomunov 207; tel. (312) 61-16-04; fax (312) 62-50-12; e-mail zs@kenesh.gov.kg; internet www.kenesh.kg.

Following legislative elections held on 27 February and 13 March 2005 the hitherto bicameral Zhogorku Kenesh was reorganized as a unicameral, 75-member body.

Following the first round of voting on 27 February 2005, 31 candidates (each of whom had received an absolute majority of votes cast in their respective electoral districts) were reported to have been elected. The majority of those candidates were nominally independent. Ten members of Forward, Kyrgyzstan (Alga, Kyrgyzstan), a party at that time regarded as generally sympathetic to the administration of President Askar Akayev, formed the largest party faction. Following the second round on 13 March, a further 37 candidates were reported to have been elected. According to preliminary results, only six opposition candidates were represented in the new legislature.

On 22 March 2005 the Central Commission for Elections and Referendums declared that the results of voting for 69 of the 75 seats

KYRGYZSTAN

were valid. (It was subsequently announced that appeals were to be launched against the results of voting in as many as 20 districts.) However, the Supreme Court, while emphasizing that the ruling did not constitute an annulment of the poll results, revoked the mandate of the newly elected Zhogorku Kenesh, asserting that the previous bicameral legislature continued to hold authority. Following an announcement from the Central Commission for Elections and Referendums terminating the powers of the bicameral legislature elected in 2000, the lower and upper chambers dissolved themselves on 28 and 29 March, respectively, thereby effectively confirming the legitimacy of the recently elected legislature, and apparently supplanting the ruling of the Supreme Court.

Akayev resigned in early April 2005, following popular protests against the results of the elections, and by-elections to appoint deputies to undecided or vacated seats in the Zhogorku Kenesh were still being conducted in early 2006.

Chairman: MARAT SULTANOV.

Election Commission

Kyrgyz Respublikasynyn Shailoo Zhana Referendum Otkoruu Boyuncha Borborduk Komissiyasy (Central Commission for Elections and Referendums of the Kyrgyz Republic): 720003 Bishkek, Dom Pravitelstva; tel. (312) 62-62-87; e-mail muhina@shailoo.gov.kg; internet www.shailoo.gov.kg; independent govt organ; the President of the Republic appoints the chair., with the agreement of the Zhogorku Kenesh, and six mems of the commission; the remaining six mems are elected by the Zhogorku Kenesh; Chair. TUIGUNAALY D. ABDRAIMOV.

Political Organizations

At December 2005 67 political organizations were registered with the Ministry of Justice.

Agrarian Party of Kyrgyzstan: Bishkek, Kievskaya 96; tel. (312) 22-68-52; f. 1993; re-registered 2001; campaigns for agrarian reform, and for the protection of the rights and interests of people working in agriculture; Chair. MEDETBEK SHAMSHIBEKOV; c. 8,000 mems. (1999).

Banner (Asaba) Party of National Revival: 720000 Bishkek, pr. Chui 26; tel. (312) 43-04-45; fax (312) 28-53-64; f. 1990; re-registered 2001; nationalist, pro-democracy; mem. of the People's Movement of Kyrgyzstan electoral alliance; critical of the progress made by the administration of Kurmanbek Bakiyev in tackling issues such as crime and corruption; Chair. AZIMBEK BEKNAZAROV, ROZA OTUNBAYEVA.

Communist Party of Kyrgyzstan (CPK): 720000 Bishkek, Panfilov 242/12; tel. (312) 22-25-80; f. 1999, following split from the Party of Communists of Kyrgyzstan; advocates state control over pricing of basic commodities and over external trade and commercial banks; participated in 2005 legislative elections as mem. of People's Movement of Kyrgyzstan electoral bloc; Co-Chair. KLARA ADZHIBEKOVA, ANARBEK USUPBAYEV; c. 8,000 mems (2004).

Democratic Movement of Kyrgyzstan (DMK): 720000 Bishkek, Abdymomunova 205; tel. (312) 27-14-95; f. 1990; registered as a political party in 1993, re-registered in 2000; campaigns for civil liberties, for democratic social and legal development; participated in 2005 legislative elections as mem. of People's Movement of Kyrgyzstan electoral bloc; Leader JYPAR JEKSHEYEV; Chair. of the Exec. Cttee EDILBEK SARYBAYEV; Chair. of the Political Council VIKTOR CHERNOMORETS.

Dignity (Ar-Namys): 720000 Bishkek, Isanova 60; e-mail info@ar-namys.org; internet www.ar-namys.org; f. 1999; pro-democracy; mem. of For Fair Elections electoral alliance; Chair. (vacant); c. 11,000 mems.

Fatherland (Ata-Jurt) Party: 720000 Bishkek; f. 2004; opposed fmr regime of President Akayev; Chair. (vacant).

Fatherland (Ata-Meken) Socialist Party: 720000 Bishkek, bulv. Erkindik 38; tel. (312) 27-17-79; f. 1992; nationalist; supports state control of the economy; participated in 2005 legislative elections as mem. of For Fair Elections electoral bloc; Leader ONURBEK TEKEBAYEV; more than 2,000 mems.

Forward, Kyrgyzstan (Alga, Kyrgyzstan): 720000 Bishkek, ul. Moskovskaya 217; tel. (312) 65-13-57; f. 2003 by merger of the Manas El Party of Spiritual Revival, New Time, New Movement and the Party of Co-operators; merged with Birimdik in 2003, and with the Unity Party of Kyrgyzstan in 2004; fmrly supportive of regime of President Akayev; Chair. BOLOT BEGALIYEV; c. 7,000 mems (2004).

Free Kyrgyzstan Progressive-Democratic Party (Erkin Kyrgyzstan—ERK): 720000 Bishkek, Abdymomunova 207; tel. (312) 22-49-57; fax (312) 22-60-35; f. 1991; registered in 1991, re-registered 1997, 2001; social-democratic; participated in 2005 legislative elections as mem. of People's Movement of Kyrgyzstan electoral alliance; Chair. BEKTUR ASANOV.

Justice (Adilet): 720000 Bishkek, Bokonbayev 109; tel. (312) 66-48-17; fax (312) 66-50-84; f. 1999; re-registered 2003; campaigns for economic reform, modernization and investment; Hon. Chair. CHINGIZ T. AITMATOV; Co-Chair. TOICHUBEK KASYMOV, KUBANYCHBEK JUMALIYEV, ALTAI BORUBAYEV; c. 15,000 mems (2003).

Liberty (Erkindik): 720000 Bishkek; f. 2000; participated in 2005 legislative elections as mem. of People's Movement of Kyrgyzstan electoral bloc; Chair. TOPCHUBEK TURGUNALIYEV; c. 3,700 mems (June 2004).

Local Communities', Peasants' and Farmers' Party of Kyrgyzstan: 720000 Bishkek, Ivanitsyn 117; f. 1999 as Socio-Political Peasants' (Farmers') Party of Kyrgyzstan; renamed as above in 2004; participated in 2005 legislative elections as mem. of People's Movement of Kyrgyzstan electoral bloc; Chair. ESENGUL ISAKOV; 38,000 mems.

My Country Party of Action (Menin olkom arakat partiyasi) (Moya strana partiya deistviya): 720040 Bishkek, Tynystanova 110; tel. (312) 62-19-51; e-mail mstrana@hotmail.com; internet www.strana.elcat.kg; f. 1998; re-registered in 2002; moderately reformist, managerial; Chair. JOOMART OTARBAYEV; 5,000 mems (2003).

New Force: 720000 Bishkek, Abdymomunova 207; tel. (312) 27-16-81; f. 1994 as the Democratic Party of Women, to encourage the participation of women in politics; membership open to both men and women; supported administration of fmr President Akayev; Chair. TOKON ASANOVNA SHAILIYEVA.

New Kyrgyzstan (Jany Kyrgyzstan): 720000 Bishkek, Kievskaya 120; tel. (312) 26-58-13; f. 1994 as Agrarian Labour Party of Kyrgyzstan; re-registered 2001; participated in 2005 legislative elections as mem. of People's Movement of Kyrgyzstan electoral bloc; Chair. DOSBOL NUR UULU.

Party of Communists of Kyrgyzstan (KCP): 720000 Bishkek, bul. Erkindik 31/6; tel. (312) 62-48-07; fax (312) 67-17-77; e-mail absamat@kenesh.gov.kg; disbanded 1991, re-established 1992, re-registered 2001; successor to the Communist Party of Kyrgyz SSR; participated in 2005 legislative elections as mem. of People's Movement of Kyrgyzstan election bloc; Chair. NIKOLAI BAILO; 25,000 mems.

Poor Nation Party (Kayran-El): 720000 Bishkek, 8 Mikroraion 29/12; registered in 1999; nationalist; contested 2005 elections as part of the People's Movement of Kyrgyzstan electoral bloc; Co-Chair. KURMANBEK TURUMBEKOV, TOKTOBAI MULKUBATOV; c. 3,000 mems.

Republican Party of Kyrgyzstan (RPK): 720000 Bishkek, ul U. Isanova 8; tel. (312) 21-14-16; registered in 1999; advocates absolute freedom of speech, full equality of all citizens before the law and environmental protection; participated in 2005 legislative elections as mem. of People's Movement of Kyrgyzstan electoral alliance; Chair. GIYAZ TOKOMBAYEV.

Social Democratic Party of Kyrgyzstan: 720000 Bishkek, Alma-Atinskaya 4B/203; tel. (312) 43-15-07; f. 1993; registered in 1994, re-registered in 2001; absorbed the El Party in 2004; participated in 2005 legislative elections as mem. of For Fair Elections electoral bloc; Chair. ALMAZ ATAMBAYEV.

Union of Democratic Forces (Soyuz demokraticheskikh sil): Bishkek; f. 2005; registered Dec. 2005; seeks constitutional, judicial and economic reform in order to combat corruption, stimulate the economy and establish a strong state; advocates creation of parliamentary republic and introduction of parliamentary elections by party lists; Leader KUBATBEK BAIBOLOV.

The following Islamist groups were banned by the Supreme Court in November 2003: **Hizb-ut-Tahrir al-Islami** (Party of Islamic Liberation), the **Islamic Party of Turkestan**, **Sharq azzat Turkestan** (East Turkestan Liberation Organization) and **Sharq Turkestan Islam Partiyasy** (East Turkestan Islamic Party).

Diplomatic Representation

EMBASSIES IN KYRGYZSTAN

Afghanistan: Bishkek, Gorkogo 210; tel. (312) 69-01-76; fax (312) 69-03-30; e-mail afghanemb_bishkek@yahoo.com; Ambassador SHAHJAHAN AHMADI.

Belarus: 720040 Bishkek, Moskovskaya 210; tel. (312) 65-13-65; fax (312) 65-11-77; e-mail kyrgyzstan@belembassy.org; Ambassador ALYAKSANDR KOZYR.

China, People's Republic: 720001 Bishkek, Toktogula 196; tel. (312) 62-19-05; fax (312) 66-30-14; e-mail chinaemb_kg@mfa.gov.cn; Ambassador ZHANG YANNIAN.

… KYRGYZSTAN

France: 720026 Bishkek, Razzakova 49; tel. (312) 66-00-53; fax (312) 66-04-41; Ambassador Gérard Perrolet (resident in Almaty, Kazakhstan).
Germany: 720040 Bishkek, Razzakova 28; tel. (312) 66-66-24; fax (312) 66-66-30; e-mail gerembi@elcat.kg; internet www.deutschebotschaft.bishkek.kg; Ambassador Dr Franz Eichinger.
India: Bishkek, pr. Chui 164A, Hotel Bishkek; tel. (312) 21-08-63; fax (312) 66-07-08; e-mail india@elcat.kg; Ambassador Appunni Ramesh.
Iran: Bishkek, Razzakova 36; tel. (312) 62-49-17; fax (312) 22-74-98; e-mail sefabish@amil.elcat.gg; Ambassador Muhammad Reza Sabouri.
Japan: 720040 Bishkek, pr. Chui 245, Demir Kyrgyz International Bank bldg, 2nd Floor; tel. (312) 61-18-75; fax (312) 61-18-82; Ambassador Tetsuo Ito.
Kazakhstan: Bishkek, Togolok Moldo 10; tel. (312) 66-04-15; fax (312) 22-54-63; e-mail kaz_emb@imfico.bishkek.su; Ambassador Umarzak Uzbekov.
Pakistan: 720040 Bishkek, Serova-Bailonova 37; tel. (312) 62-17-02; fax (312) 62-17-25; e-mail parepbishkek@elcat.kg; Ambassador (vacant).
Russia: 720000 Bishkek, ul. Razzakova 17; tel. (312) 62-47-36; fax (312) 62-18-23; e-mail rusemb@imfiko.bishkek.su; internet www.kyrgyz.mid.ru; Ambassador Yevgenii A. Shmagin.
Syria: Bishkek; Ambassador Wahib Fadel.
Tajikistan: Bishkek; tel. (312) 51-14-64.
Turkey: 720040 Bishkek, Moskovskaya 89; tel. (312) 62-23-54; fax (312) 66-05-19; e-mail biskbe@infotel.kg; Ambassador Fatma Serpil Alpman.
Ukraine: 720040 Bishkek, Panfilova 150; tel. (312) 66-13-83; fax (312) 66-20-12; e-mail embassy@ukr.gov.kg; internet www.ukraine-emb.elcat.kg; Ambassador Volodymyr Tyahlo.
USA: 720016 Bishkek, pr. Mira 171; tel. (312) 55-12-41; fax (312) 55-12-64; internet bishkek.usembassy.gov; Ambassador Marie L. Yovanovitch.
Uzbekistan: 720040 Bishkek, Tynystanova 213; tel. (312) 66-20-65; fax (312) 66-44-03; e-mail uzbembish@infotel.kg; Ambassador Alisher Salahitdinov.

Judicial System

Supreme Court
720000 Bishkek, ul. Orozbekova 37; tel. (312) 66-33-18; fax (312) 66-29-46; e-mail scourt@bishkek.gov.kg.
Chairman: Kurmanbek Osmonov.

Constitutional Court
720040 Bishkek, pr. Erkindik 39; tel. (312) 62-04-95; fax (312) 62-28-19; e-mail konsud@bishkek.gov.kg.
Chairman: Omurbek Tekebayev.
Prosecutor-General: (vacant).

Religion

State Commission for Religious Affairs: 720040 Bishkek, Kievskaya 90; e-mail mail@religion.bishkek.gov.kg; Chair. Omurzak Mamayusupov.

ISLAM
The majority of Kyrgyz are Sunni Muslims (Hanafi school), as are some other groups living in the republic, such as Uzbeks and Tajiks.
Chief Mufti Kyrgyzstan Muslims: Haji Murataly Ajy Jumanov.
International Islamic Centre of Kyrgyzstan: Osh; Pres. Haji Sadykzhan Kamaluddin.

CHRISTIANITY

Roman Catholic Church
The Church is represented in Kyrgyzstan by a Mission, established in December 1997. There were an estimated 500 adherents at 31 December 2003.
Superior: Rev. Fr Aleksandr Kan, 720072 Bishkek, Vasilyeva 203; tel. and fax (312) 21-78-32; fax (312) 21-78-32; e-mail church@freenet.kg.

Russian Orthodox Church (Moscow Patriarchate)
The Russian Orthodox Church (Moscow Patriarchate) in Kyrgyzstan comes under the jurisdiction of the Eparchy of Tashkent and Central Asia (Metropolitan of Tashkent and Central Asia, Vladimir—Ikim), resident in Uzbekistan.

JUDAISM
Chief Rabbi: Rabbi Arye Raichman, 72000 Bishkek, ul. Karpinskogo 193; tel. (312) 68-19-66; fax (312) 68-19-66; e-mail arier@mail.ru; internet www.fjc.ru.

The Press

In 2004 there were 83 non-daily newspapers, with an average circulation of 427,800 copies. Two daily newspapers were published in that year, with an average circulation of 21,000 copies.

PRINCIPAL NEWSPAPERS

Asaba (The Standard): Bishkek; tel. (312) 26-47-39; weekly; in Kyrgyz; supplement in Russian *Asaba-Bishkek*; Editors Jumabek Mederaliyev (*Asaba*), Bermet Bukasheva (*Asaba-Bishkek*); circ. 10,000.

Bishkek Observer: 720021 Bishkek, Frunze 429; tel. (312) 28-95-96; fax (312) 28-93-84; e-mail observer@elcat.kg; independent; English; Editor Avtar Singh.

Bishkek Taims (Bishkek Times): Bishkek, Pushkina 70; tel. (312) 62-15-68; e-mail b-times@yandex.ru; internet news.org.kg/bt; Editor-in-Chief Nuraly Kaparov.

Chui Baayni/Chuiskiye Izvestiya (Chui News): Bishkek, Ibraimova 24; tel. (312) 42-83-31; weekly; organ of Chui Duban administration; Kyrgyz and Russian edns; Editor (Kyrgyz edn) Kurmanbek Ramatov; Editor (Russian edn) A. Blindina.

Delo Nº. (Case Number): Bishkek; tel. (312) 62-19-80; fax (312) 66-38-66; e-mail cactus@elcat.kg; internet delo.to.kg; f. 1991; weekly; in Russian; independent; politics, crime; Editor Viktor Zapolskii; circ. 40,000.

Erkin Too (Free Mountain): 720040 Bishkek, Ibraimova 24; tel. (312) 42-03-15; fax (312) 42-22-42; f. 1991; 2 a week; organ of the Government; publishes laws, presidential, parliamentary and govt decrees, and other legal documents; Kyrgyz; Editor-in-Chief Nurlan Shakiyev; circ. 10,000.

Gazeta.kg: 720000 Bishkek; internet gazeta.kg; online only, in Russian and English; independent; politics and analysis of current affairs; culture; regional news; f. 2003.

Kyrgyz Madaniyaty (Kyrgyz Culture): 720301 Bishkek, Bokonbayeva 99; tel. (312) 26-14-58; f. 1967; weekly; organ of the Union of Writers; Editor Nuraly Kaparov; circ. 15,940.

Kyrgyz Rukhu: Bishkek, Abdymomunova 193; tel. (312) 66-45-43; fax (312) 66-45-43; f. 1991; weekly; Kyrgyz; Editor-in-Chief Bakbyrbek Alenov; circ. c. 5,000.

Kyrgyz Tuusu (Flag of Kyrgyzstan): 720040 Bishkek, Abdymomunova 193; tel. (312) 62-20-18; fax (312) 62-20-25; e-mail tuusu@infotel.kg; internet www.tuusu.kg; f. 1924; fmrly *Sovettik Kyrgyzstan*; daily; organ of the Government; Kyrgyz; Editor-in-Chief Zhediger I. Saalayev; circ. 17,000–20,000.

Kyrgyzstan Chronicle: Bishkek; tel. (312) 22-48-32; f. 1993; weekly; independent; English; Editor Bayan Sarygulov; circ. 5,000.

Limon (Lemon): Bishkek, ul. Moskovskaya 189; tel. (312) 65-03-03; fax (312) 65-02-04; e-mail limon@akipress.org; f. 1994; in Russian; youth newspaper; independent; Editor-in-Chief Venera Jamona Kulova.

MSN—Moya Stolitsa—Novosti (My Capital City—News): 720001 Bishkek, Turusbekova 47; tel. (312) 21-29-79; fax (312) 21-58-94; e-mail city@infotel.kg; internet www.msn.kg; f. 2001; independent; 3 a week; in Russian; Editor-in-Chief Alexander Kim; circ. 5,000 (Tues. and Thurs.), 50,000 (Fri.).

Res Publica (Republic): 720017 Bishkek, Isanova 8; tel. (312) 21-77-57; fax (312) 21-84-12; e-mail respub@elcat.kg; internet gazeta.respublica.kg; f. 1992; 2 a week; independent; in Russian and English; Editor Zamira Sidikova; circ. 10,000.

Slovo Kyrgyzstana (Word of Kyrgyzstan): 720004 Bishkek, Abdymomunova 193; tel. (312) 22-53-92; e-mail slovo@infotel.kg; internet www.sk.kg; f. 1925; daily; organ of the Government; in Russian; Editor Aleksandr I. Malevany.

The Times of Central Asia: 720000 Bishkek, pr. Chui 155; tel. (312) 68-05-67; fax (312) 68-07-69; e-mail edittimes@infotel.kg; internet www.times.kg; f. 1995; weekly; in English; also distributed in Kazakhstan, Turkmenistan, Uzbekistan and internationally; Editor-in-Chief Lydia Savina.

Vechernii Bishkek (Bishkek Evening News): 720021 Bishkek, ul. Usenbayeva 2; tel. (312) 68-21-21; fax (312) 68-02-68; e-mail webmaster@vb.kg; internet www.vb.kg; f. 1974; daily; independent;

KYRGYZSTAN

in Russian; Editor-in-Chief GENNADII A. KUZMIN; circ. (Mon.–Thur.) 20,000, (Fri.) 50,000.

Zaman Kyrgyzstan (Herald of Kyrgyzstan): 720040 Bishkek, Ibraimova 24; tel. (312) 42-62-35; e-mail zamantur@elcat.kg; f. 1992; weekly; independent; in Kyrgyz, Turkish and English; Editor-in-Chief A. KUSH; circ. 15,000.

PRINCIPAL PERIODICALS

Monthly, unless otherwise indicated.

Aalam (Universe): Bishkek, ul. Baitik Baatyra 73; tel. (312) 54-42-07; fax (312) 54-42-09; e-mail aalamga@hotmail.kg; f. 1991; independent; Kyrgyz; weekly; Editor-in-Chief ELNURA SHABDANBEKOVA; circ. 18,000.

Agym (Current): Bishkek, pr. Manasa 40; tel. (312) 66-56-70; fax (312) 66-55-48; e-mail agym@users.kyrnet.kg; internet www.news.org.kg/agym; f. 1992; 2 a week; in Kyrgyz; political; Editor-in-Chief MELIS ESHIMKANOV; circ. 12,000–17,000.

AKI-Press: Bishkek, ul. Moskovskaya 189; tel. (312) 61-18-23; fax (312) 65-02-04; e-mail admin@akipress.org; internet www.akipress.org; f. 1993; in Russian; two a month; independent; analysis of political and economic affairs; Editor-in-Chief ALINA SAGINBAYEVA; circ. 1,000.

Ala Too (Ala Too Mountains): Bishkek; tel. (312) 26-55-12; f. 1931; organ of the Union of Writers; politics, novels, short stories, plays, poems of Kyrgyz authors and translations into Kyrgyz; in Kyrgyz; Editor KENESH JUSUPOV; circ. 3,000.

Chalkan (Stinging Nettle): Bishkek, Ibraimova 24; tel. (312) 42-16-38; f. 1955; satirical; in Kyrgyz; Editor B. AZIZOV; circ. 7,600.

Den-sooluk (Health): Bishkek; tel. (312) 22-46-37; f. 1960; weekly; journal of the Ministry of Health; popular science; in Kyrgyz; Editor MAR ALIYEV; circ. 20,000.

Kut Bilim (Good Knowledge): Bishkek, ul. Tynystanova 257; tel. (312) 62-04-86; e-mail kutbilim@elcat.kg; internet kb.host.net.kg; f. 1953; organ of the Ministry of Education, Science and Youth Affairs; weekly; in Kyrgyz; Editor-in-Chief KUBATBEK CHEKIROV; circ. 6,000.

Kyrgyzstan Ayaldary (Women of Kyrgyzstan): Bishkek; tel. (312) 42-12-26; f. 1951; popular; in Kyrgyz; Editor S. AKMATBEKOVA; circ. 500.

Literaturnyi Kyrgyzstan (Literary Kyrgyzstan): 720301 Bishkek, Pushkina 70; tel. (312) 26-14-63; e-mail lk@users.kyrnet.kg; f. 1955; journal of the Union of Writers; fiction, literary criticism, journalism; in Russian; Editor-in-Chief A. I. IVANOV; circ. 3,000.

Zdravookhraneniye Kyrgyzstana (Healthcare of Kyrgyzstan): 720005 Bishkek, Sovetskaya 34; tel. (312) 44-41-39; f. 1938; 4 a year; publ. by the Ministry of Health; experimental medical work; in Russian; Editor-in-Chief N. K. KASIYEV; circ. 3,000.

NEWS AGENCIES

AKIpress: Bishkek, ul. Moskovskaya 189; tel. and fax (312) 61-03-96; e-mail post@akipress.org; internet www.akipress.org; f. 2000; Russian and English; independent; Dir MARAT TAZABEKOV.

Belyi Parokhod (White Steamer): 720000 Bishkek; tel. (312) 54-32-26; e-mail parohod@list.ru; internet www.parohod.kg; f. 1997; Russian; independent.

Kabar Kyrgyz News Agency: 720011 Bishkek, Sovetskaya 175; tel. (312) 62-05-74; fax (312) 66-11-68; e-mail s1@kabar.gov.kg; internet www.kabar.kg; fmrly KyrgyzTag until 1992, and Kyrgyzkabar until 1995; Dir OLEG RYABOV; Editor-in-Chief DJUMAKAN SARIYEV.

Kyrgyzinfo: 720000 Bishkek; tel. (312) 68-24-24; e-mail agency@kyrgyzinfo.kg; internet www.kyrgyzinfo.kg; f. 2003; Kyrgyz, Russian, English; independent.

Foreign Bureaux

Interfax (Russia): Bishkek, Toktogula 97, Rm 6; tel. and fax (312) 26-72-87; Bureau Chief BERMET MALIKOVA.

ITAR—TASS (Information Telegraphic Agency of Russia—Telegraphic Agency of the Sovereign Countries); Russia: Bishkek, pr. Erkindik 43/4; tel. (312) 58-24-22; fax (312) 66-09-97; Correspondent VLADIMIR NESHKUMAI.

Reuters (United Kingdom): Bishkek; tel. (312) 54-52-01.

Publishers

Akyl (Mind): 720000 Bishkek, Sovetskaya 170; tel. (312) 22-50-85; fax (312) 66-10-32; f. 1994; science, politics, economics, culture, literature; Chair. AMANBEK KARYPKULOV.

Ilim (Science): 720071 Bishkek, pr. Chui 265A; tel. (312) 65-56-88; e-mail ilimph@mail.ru; internet ilim.aknet.kg; scientific and science fiction; Dir L. V. TARASOVA.

Kyrgyz-Russian Slavic University Publishing House (Izdatelstvo Kyrgyzsko-Rossiiskogo slavyanskogo universiteta): 720000, Kiyevskaya 44; tel. (312) 25-53-60; internet www.krsu.edu.kg/Rus/EduIzd.htm; f. 1995; academic works of university staff; textbooks; Dir. LARISA V. TARASOVA.

Kyrgyzskaya Entsiklopediya (Kyrgyz Encyclopedia): 720040 Bishkek, bul. Erkindik 56; tel. (312) 22-77-57; fax (312) 62-50-03; e-mail gocst.ensk@mail.ru; dictionaries and encyclopedias; Dir BAKTYGUL KALDYBAYEVA; Editor-in-Chief USEN A. ASANOV.

Kyrgyzstan: Bishkek; tel. (312) 26-48-54; politics, science, economics, literature; Dir BERIK N. CHALAGYZOV.

Broadcasting and Communications

State Communications Agency: 720005 Bishkek, Sovetskaya 76; e-mail postmaster@nca.bishkek.gov.kg; Dir KUBAT S. KYDYRALIYEV.

TELECOMMUNICATIONS

Kyrgyztelekom: 720000 Bishkek, pr. Chui 96; tel. (312) 68-16-16; fax (312) 66-24-24; e-mail info@kt.kg; internet www.kt.kg; f. 1993, transformed into joint stock co in 1997; state telecommunications co; 77.84% state-owned; 51% scheduled for privatization; Chair. of the Bd of Dirs SALAIDIN A. AVAZOV; Mems of the Bd of Dirs MYKTARBEK JUMABAYEV, BURKAN JUMABAYEV, DUISHENBEK R. ABDYLDAYEV, MYRBEK T. BATAKANOV.

Bitel: 720011 Bishkek, pr. Chui 121; tel. (312) 58-79-15; fax (312) 58-79-07; e-mail office@bitel.kg; internet www.bitel.kg; f. 1997; mobile cellular telecommunications; indirectly owned by Tarion Ltd, in which Mobile TeleSystems (Russia) acquired a 51% stake in Dec. 2005; Dir-Gen. D. V. SHERSHNEV; over 450,000 subscribers (Jan. 2006).

BROADCASTING

Radio

State National Television and Radio Broadcasting Corpn: 720010 Bishkek, Molodoi Gvardii 59; tel. (312) 65-56-77; internet www.ktr.kg; Pres. KYYAS SATAROVICH MOLDOKASYMOV; Vice-Pres. SULTANBEK A. ABDYRAKMANOV.

Kyrgyz Radio: 720010 Bishkek, Molodoi Gvardii 59; tel. (312) 25-79-36; fax (312) 65-10-64; internet www.ktr.kg; f. 1931; broadcasts in Kyrgyz, Russian, English, German, Ukrainian, Uzbek, Dungan and Uigur; Dir BAIMA SUTENOVA.

Radio Azattyk: Bishkek; tel. (312) 66-88-17; fax (312) 66-68-14; e-mail kiyas@liberty.elcat.kg; internet www.azattyk.org; Kyrgyz language news broadcasts by Radio Free Europe/Radio Liberty (USA—based in the Czech Republic); Dir TYNTCHTYKBEK TCHOROEV; Bureau Chief KYIAS MOLDOKASYMOV.

Radio Pyramid: 720300 Bishkek, Molodoi Gvardii 59; tel. (312) 28-28-28; fax (312) 52-61-65; e-mail pyramid@mail.elcat.kg; f. 1992; privately owned; broadcasts to Bishkek and neighbouring regions; Pres. ADYLBEK T. BIINAZAROV.

Sodruzhestvo (Community): Osh; f. 1996; broadcasts to Kazakhstan, Kyrgyzstan, Tajikistan and Uzbekistan; established by ethnic Russian groups.

There are several other private radio stations operating in Kyrgyzstan.

Television

State National Television and Radio Broadcasting Corpn: see Radio.

Kyrgyz Television: 720300 Bishkek, pr. Molodoi Gvardii 63; tel. (312) 25-79-36; fax (312) 25-79-30; internet www.ktr.kg; Pres. KYYAS MOLDOKASYMOV.

Kyrgyz Public Educational Radio and Television (Kyrgyzskoe Obshchestvennoye Obrazovatelnoye Radio i Televideniye—KOORT): 720031 Bishkek, ul. Ibraimova 24; tel. (312) 54-77-27; fax (312) 54-77-15; e-mail office@koort.kg; internet www.koort.kg; f. 1997; broadcasts in Kyrgyz and Russian; family channel; educational programmes and entertainment; Gen. Dir AZIMA ABDIMAMINOVA; 103 employees.

TV Pyramid: 720005 Bishkek; tel. and fax (312) 41-01-31; e-mail pyramid@ss5-22.kyrnet.kg; f. 1991; privately owned; broadcasts to Bishkek and neighbouring regions; Pres. ADYLBEK T. BIINAZAROV.

KYRGYZSTAN   *Directory*

Finance

(cap. = capital; res = reserves; m. = million; brs = branches; amounts in soms, unless otherwise indicated)

BANKING

Central Bank

National Bank of the Kyrgyz Republic (Kyrgyz Respublikasynyn Uluttuk Banky): 720040 Bishkek, Umetaliyeva 101; tel. (312) 66-90-11; fax (312) 61-07-30; e-mail mail@nbkr.kg; internet www.nbkr.kg; f. 1991, name changed in 1992, and as above in 1993; cap. 50m., res 768.0m., dep. 1,889.1m.; Chair. MARAT ALAPAYEV.

Other Banks

In early 2001 there were 22 commercial banks in operation in Kyrgyzstan.

Amanbank: 720400 Bishkek, Tynystanova 249; tel. (312) 62-20-77; fax (312) 90-04-97; e-mail bank@amanbank.kg; internet www.amanbank.kg; f. 1995; cap. 55m., res 0.1m., dep. 72.8m. (Aug. 2004); Chair. SHATKUL I. KUDABAYEVA; 6 brs.

AsiaUniversalBank: 720001 Bishkek, Toktogula 187; tel. (312) 62-02-52; fax (312) 62-02-50; e-mail reception@aub.kg; internet www.aub.kg; f. 1997 as International Business Bank, changed name as above 2000; cap. 300.0m., dep. 2,029.8m. (Jan. 2005); CEO NURDIN ABDRAZAKOV; 2 brs.

Bank Bakai: 720001 Bishkek, Isanov 75; tel. (312) 66-06-10; fax (312) 66-06-12; e-mail bank@bakai.kg; internet www.bakai.kg; f. 1998; cap. 47.0m., dep. 181.6m. (Dec. 2003); Chair. MARAT ALAPAYEV; Pres. MUHAMMAD IBRAGIMOV; 3 brs.

Demir Kyrgyz International Bank (DKIB): 720001 Bishkek, pr. Chui 245; tel. (312) 61-06-10; fax (312) 61-04-45; e-mail dkib@demirbank.kg; internet www.demirbank.kg; f. 1997; cap. 132.5m., dep. 920.0m., net profit 88.3m. (July 2005); Chair. HALIT CINGILLIOGLU; Gen. Man. AHMET KAMIL PARMAKSIZ; 2 brs.

Ecobank: 720031 Bishkek, Geologicheskii per. 17; tel. (312) 54-35-82; fax (312) 54-35-80; e-mail office@ecobank; internet www.ecobank.kg; f. 1996 as Bank Rossiiskii Kredit; name changed 1998; joint-stock commercial bank; cap. 78.0m., dep. 181.5m. (Oct. 2003); Chair. ASKAR A. ABDYVASIYEV; Deputy Chair. GALINA V. HOHLOVA, LARISA G. CHENGIZ; 5 brs.

Energobank: 720070 Bishkek, Jibek-Jolu 493; tel. and fax (312) 67-00-47; fax (312) 67-00-47; e-mail bank@energobank.kg; internet www.energobank.kg; f. 1992 as Kyrgyzenergobank, changed name as above 2000; cap. 108.6m., res 3.9m., dep. 755.1m., total assets 599.0 (Dec. 2004); Pres. BAKIRDIN E. SARTKAZIYEV; Chair. SABIT SHAKENOV; 7 brs.

Halyk Bank: 720033 Bishkek, Frunze 390; tel. (312) 21-89-32; fax (312) 21-89-55; e-mail halyk@halykbank.kg; internet www.halykbank.kg; f. 1999 as Kairat Bank to replace Maksat Bank (f. 1991); privatized in 2004 and renamed as above; cap. 49.7m., total assets 395.9m. (July 2005); Chair. MAMYTOVA KASTORU KASYMBEKOVNA; 5 brs.

Investment Export-Import Bank (Ineximbank): 720001 Bishkek, K. Akiyev 57; tel. (312) 65-06-10; fax (312) 62-06-54; e-mail info@ineximbank.com; internet www.ineximbank.com; f. 1996 as Eridan Bank, name changed 2001; cap. 480.0m., res 3.7m., dep. 717.2m. (Aug. 2005); Chair. DANIYAR USENOV; 4 br.

Kazkommertsbank Kyrgyzstan: 720017 Bishkek, Isanova 42; tel. (312) 66-46-46; fax (312) 66-07-04; e-mail autobank@autobank.kg; internet www.kkb.kg; f. 1991, changed name as above in 2002; cap. 25.6m., dep. 101.2m. (Dec. 2001); Chair. KANAT MAMAKEYEV; 6 brs.

Kyrgyz Investment and Credit Bank: Bishkek, Bereke Business Centre, 12th floor, 8th Mikrorayon, 28A; tel. (312) 69-05-55; fax (312) 69-05-60; e-mail kicb@kicb.net; internet www.kicb.net; f. 2001; CEO KUANG YOUNG CHOI.

Kyrgyzpromstroibank: 720040 Bishkek, pr. Chui 168; tel. (312) 61-07-43; fax (312) 21-84-45; e-mail kirgpasb@transfer.kz; f. 1991; cap. 100m. (Jan. 2001), dep. 43.3m. (Jan. 2000); Pres. MURATBEK O. MUKASHEV; 26 brs.

Kyrgyzstan Bank: 720001 Bishkek, Togolok Moldo 54A; tel. (312) 21-95-98; fax (312) 61-02-20; e-mail akb@bankkg.kg; f. 1991; cap. 120.9m., res 6.7m., dep. 615.3m.; Pres. SHARIPA S. SADYBAKASOVA; 29 brs.

Tolubay Bank: 720010 Bishkek, Toktogula 247; tel. (312) 24-02-46; fax (312) 65-59-41; e-mail tolubay@infotel.kg; f. 1996; cap. 31m., res 1.4m., dep. 93.4m. (Dec. 2003); Pres. JENISHBEK S. BAIGUTTIYEV; 1 br.

COMMODITY EXCHANGE

Kyrgyzstan Commodity and Raw Materials Exchange: 720001 Bishkek, Belinskaya 40; tel. (312) 22-13-75; fax (312) 22-27-44; f. 1990; Gen. Dir TEMIR SARIYEV.

STOCK EXCHANGE

Kyrgyz Stock Exchange (Kyrgyz Fonduk Birzhasy/Kyrgyzskaya Fondovaya Birzha): 720010 Bishkek, Moskovskaya 172; tel. (312) 66-50-59; fax (312) 66-15-95; e-mail kse@kse.kg; internet www.kse.kg; Pres. ANDREI V. ZALEPO.

INSURANCE

Kyrgyzinstrakh: 72001 Bishkek, pr. Chui 219; tel. (312) 21-95-54; fax (312) 21-99-44; e-mail kinstrakh@infotel.kg; internet kyrgyzinstrakh.online.kg; f. 1996 by the Russian joint-stock insurance company Investstrakh, Kyrgyz insurance companies and the Kyrgyz Government to insure foreign investors.

Trade and Industry

GOVERNMENT AGENCIES

Drugs Control Agency of the Kyrgyz Republic: 720021 Bishkek, ul. Toktogul 80; e-mail dca@bishkek.gov.kg; internet www.dca.gov.kg; f. 2004; Dir Maj.-Gen. KURMANBEK KUBATBEKOV.

National Institute of Standards and Metrology: 720040 Bishkek, Panfilova 197; tel. (312) 62-68-70; fax (312) 66-13-67; e-mail gost@kmc.bishkek.gov.kg; internet www.kmc.bishkek.gov.kg; f. 1927; certification, control and testing of products and services; standardization, metrology, accreditation; Dir BATYRBEK DAVLESOV.

State Agency for Geology and Mineral Resources: 720739 Bishkek, pr. Erkindik 2; tel. (312) 66-49-01; fax (312) 66-03-91; e-mail mail@geoagency.bishkek.gov.kg; internet www.kgs.bishkek.gov.kg; Chair. SHEISHENALY MURZAGAZIYEV.

State Agency for Registration of Real Estate Rights: 720040 Bishkek, Orozbekova 44; e-mail gosreg@bishkek.gov.kg; Chair. KENESHBEK KARACHALOV.

State Agency for Science and Intellectual Property: 720021 Bishkek, Moskovskaya 62; tel. (312) 68-08-19; fax (312) 68-17-03; e-mail kyrgyzpatent@infotel.kg; internet www.kyrgyzpatent.kg; Dir ROMAN OMOROV.

State Committee for Management of State Property: 720017 Bishkek, ul. Moskovskaya 151; tel. (312) 62-68-52; fax (312) 66-02-36; e-mail mail@spf.bishkek.gov.kg; internet www.spf.gov.kg; f. 1991; responsible for the privatization of state-owned enterprises and deals with bankruptcies; Chair. TURSUN TURDUMAMBETOV.

State Securities Commission: 720040 Bishkek, pr. Chui 114; tel. (312) 62-44-60; fax (312) 66-26-53; e-mail nsc@nsc.kg; internet www.nsc.kg; Chair. AZAMAT SH. DIKAMBAYEV.

CHAMBER OF COMMERCE

Chamber of Commerce and Industry of the Kyrgyz Republic: 720001 Bishkek, Kievskaya 107; tel. (312) 21-05-65; fax (312) 21-05-75; e-mail cci-kr@totel.kg; f. 1959; supports foreign economic relations and the development of small and medium-sized enterprises; Pres. BORIS V. PERFILIYEV.

TRADE ASSOCIATION

Kyrgyzvneshtorg: 720033 Bishkek, Abdymomunova 276; tel. (312) 21-39-78; fax (312) 66-08-36; e-mail kvt@infotel.kg; f. 1992; export-import org.; Gen. Dir K. K. KALIYEV.

UTILITIES

Electricity

National Electric Grid of Kyrgyzstan: 720070 Bishkek, Jibek Jolu 326; tel. (312) 66-10-00; fax (312) 66-06-56; e-mail aoke@infotel.kg; divided into seven companies in 2001; privatization commenced in 2003; Gen. Dir BAKIRGIN SARATKAZIYEV.

Gas

Kyrgyzazmunayzat: 720000 Bishkek, L. Tolstogo 114; tel. (312) 24-53-80; fax (312) 24-53-93; state-owned joint-stock co; f. 1997 through merger; Dir-Gen. BAKIRDIN SUBANBEKOV.

Kyrgyzgaz: 720661 Bishkek, Gorkogo 22; tel. (312) 53-00-45; fax (312) 43-09-80; state-owned joint-stock co; scheduled for privatization; Dir-Gen. AVTANDIL SYDYKOV.

Kyrgyzneftegaz: 715622 Kochkor-Ata, Lenina 44; tel. (312) 66-12-66; fax (312) 52-60-21; internet www.kyrgysneftegaz.narod.ru; state-owned petroleum and natural gas co; scheduled for privatization; Gazprom (Russia) agreed to acquire majority shareholding in 2004; Pres. KASIM ISMANOV.

KYRGYZSTAN

TRADE UNIONS

Kyrgyzstan Federation of Trade Unions: 720032 Bishkek, Chui 207; tel. (312) 21-49-30; fax (312) 21-76-87; Chair. S. BOZBUNBAYEV.

Transport

RAILWAYS

Kyrgyzstan's railway network consists of only one main line (340 km) in northern Kyrgyzstan, which connects the republic, via Kazakhstan, with the railway system of Russia. Osh, Jalal-Abad and four other towns in regions of Kyrgyzstan bordering Uzbekistan are linked to that country by short lengths of railway track. In 2001 the Governments of Kyrgyzstan and the People's Republic of China signed a memorandum on the construction of a rail link from Kashgar (China) to Bishkek. In 2003 Kyrgyzstan and Kazakhstan announced that a 100-km railway link was to be built between Issyk-Kul and Almaty, Kazakhstan. Construction work was expected to be completed by 2008.

Kyrgyz Railway Administration: 720009 Bishkek, L. Tolstogo 83; tel. (312) 25-30-54; fax (312) 65-06-90; e-mail asoup@imfiko.bishkek.su; internet railway.aknet.kg; f. 1992; Pres. I. S. OMURKULOV.

ROADS

In 1999 Kyrgyzstan's road network totalled an estimated 18,500 km, including 140 km of motorway; in 1996 there were 3,200 km of main roads and 6,380 km of secondary roads. About 91% of roads were paved. In March 2003 it was announced that work had begun on the third and final phase of a project to reconstruct the main Bishkek—Osh highway.

CIVIL AVIATION

There are three international airports at Bishkek (Manas Airport), Osh and Tamchy (in the Issyk-Kul region—inaugurated in August 2003). At early 2001 there were 13 privately owned airlines in Kyrgyzstan.

Altyn Air: 720040 Bishkek, pr. Manasa 12 A; tel. (312) 21-85-42; e-mail altynair@altynair.kg; internet www.altynair.kg; state-owned; charter passenger services; decision to merge co with Kyrgyzstan Airlines to create new state airline announced in late 2005.

Kyrgyz Air: 720021 Bishkek, Abdrahmanova 129; tel. (312) 62-21-23; e-mail kyrgyzair@aviareps.co.ru; internet www.kyrgyzair.com; f. 2003; regional charter passenger services.

Kyrgyzstan Airlines (Kyrgyzstan Aba Zholdoru): 720044 Bishkek, 95 Mir Prospekt; tel. (312) 54-88-88; fax (312) 54-80-66; e-mail kaj@ka.kg; internet www.ka.kg; f. 1992; passenger and cargo carriers; operates scheduled and charter flights to destinations in Azerbaijan, the People's Republic of China, Germany, India, Kazakhstan, Pakistan, Russia and Uzbekistan; decision to merge co with Altyn Air to create new state airline announced late 2005; state-owned; Pres. AKYLBEK JURNABAYEV.

Tourism

There was little tourism in Kyrgyzstan during the Soviet period, and in the first years of independence. However, the Government hoped that the country's spectacular and largely unspoilt mountain scenery, as well as the great crater lake of Issyk-Kul, might attract foreign tourists and investment. By the late 1990s the number of tourists visiting Kyrgyzstan was increasing, and there were 139,589 tourist arrivals in 2003, compared with around 98,558 in 2002. Tourist receipts amounted to US $30m. in 2003. The Government's promotion strategy centred on the country's position on the ancient 'Silk Road' trade route, and its potential as a destination for nature tourism and adventure holidays.

State Committee for Tourism, Sport and Youth Policy: 720033 Bishkek, Togolok Moldo 17; tel. (312) 62-24-99; fax (312) 21-28-45; e-mail gktsm@gks.gov.kg; Chair. OKMOTBEK ALMAKUCHUKOV.

LAOS

Introductory Survey

Location, Climate, Language, Religion, Flag, Capital

The Lao People's Democratic Republic is a land-locked country in South-East Asia, bordered by the People's Republic of China to the north, by Viet Nam to the east, by Cambodia to the south, by Thailand to the west and by Myanmar (formerly Burma) to the north-west. The climate is tropical, with a rainy monsoon season lasting from May to September. The temperature in the capital ranges between 23°C and 38°C in the hottest month, April, and between 14°C and 28°C in the coolest month, January. Laos comprises 47 ethnic groups. The official language, Lao or Laotian, is spoken by about two-thirds of the population. French is also spoken, and there are numerous tribal languages, including Meo. The principal religion is Buddhism. There are also some Christians and followers of animist beliefs. The national flag (proportions 2 by 3) has three horizontal stripes, of red, blue (half the total depth) and red, with a white disc in the centre. The capital is Vientiane (Viangchan).

Recent History

Laos was formerly a part of French Indo-China and comprised the three principalities of Luang Prabang, Vientiane and Champasak. These were merged in 1946, when France recognized Sisavang Vong, ruler of Luang Prabang since 1904, as King of Laos. In May 1947 the King promulgated a democratic constitution (although women were not allowed to vote until 1957). The Kingdom of Laos became independent, within the French Union, in July 1949, and full sovereignty was recognized by France in October 1953. The leading royalist politician was Prince Souvanna Phouma, who was Prime Minister in 1951–54, 1956–58, 1960 and in 1962–75. King Sisavang Vong died in October 1959, and was succeeded by his son, Savang Vatthana.

From 1950 the Royal Government was opposed by the Neo Lao Haksat (Lao Patriotic Front—LPF), an insurgent movement formed by a group of former anti-French activists. The LPF's Chairman was Prince Souphanouvong, a half-brother of Prince Souvanna Phouma, but its dominant element was the communist People's Party of Laos (PPL), led by Kaysone Phomvihane. During the 1950s the LPF's armed forces, the Pathet Lao, gradually secured control of the north-east of the country with the assistance of the Vietnamese communists, the Viet Minh, who were engaged in war with the French (until 1954). Several agreements between the Royal Government and the LPF, attempting to end the guerrilla war and reunite the country, failed during the 1950s and early 1960s. By 1965 the *de facto* partition of Laos was established, with the LPF refusing to participate in national elections and consolidating its power over the north-eastern provinces.

During the 1960s, as the 'Ho Chi Minh Trail' (the communist supply route to South Viet Nam) ran through Pathet Lao-controlled areas, Laos remained closely involved with the war between communist forces and anti-communist troops (supported by the USA) in Viet Nam. In 1973 the Viet Nam peace negotiations included provisions for a cease-fire in Laos. A new Government was formed in April 1974 under Prince Souvanna Phouma, with royalist, neutralist and LPF participation; Prince Souphanouvong was appointed Chairman of the Joint National Political Council. However, the LPF increased its power and eventually gained effective control of the country. This was confirmed by election victories in October and November 1975. In November King Savang Vatthana abdicated, and Prince Souvanna Phouma resigned.

In December 1975 the National Congress of People's Representatives (264 delegates elected by local authorities) abolished the monarchy and elected a 45-member legislative body, the Supreme People's Council (now the Supreme People's Assembly). Souphanouvong was appointed President of the renamed Lao People's Democratic Republic and President of the Supreme People's Council. Kaysone Phomvihane, who had become Secretary-General of the Phak Pasason Pativat Lao (Lao People's Revolutionary Party—LPRP, a successor to the PPL), was appointed Prime Minister. The former King, Savang Vatthana, was designated Supreme Counsellor to the President, but he refused to co-operate with the new regime and was arrested in March 1977. (He was subsequently stated to have died in a 're-education camp'.) The LPF was replaced in February 1979 by the Lao Front for National Construction (LFNC), under the leadership of the LPRP.

In October 1986 the ailing Souphanouvong announced his resignation from his duties as President of the Republic (while retaining the title) and of the Supreme People's Assembly. Phoumi Vongvichit, formerly a Vice-Chairman in the Council of Ministers, became acting President of the Republic, while Sisomphon Lovansai, a Vice-President of the Supreme People's Assembly and a member of the LPRP Political Bureau (Politburo), became acting President of the Assembly. In November Kaysone Phomvihane was re-elected Secretary-General of the LPRP. In September 1987 it was announced that Phoumi Vongvichit had also replaced Souphanouvong as Chairman of the LFNC.

In June 1988 elections (the first since the formation of the Lao People's Democratic Republic) took place to determine the members of 113 district-level People's Councils. The LFNC approved 4,462 candidates to contest 2,410 seats. Provincial prefectural elections took place in November, when 898 candidates contested 651 seats. At the legislative election of March 1989, 121 candidates contested 79 seats in the enlarged Supreme People's Assembly. At its inaugural session in May, Nouhak Phoumsavanh (a Vice-Chairman of the Council of Ministers) was elected President of the Assembly.

Armed opposition to the Government persisted during the 1980s, particularly among hill tribes. In October 1982 Gen. Phoumi Nosavan, a 'conservative' who had been living in exile since 1965, formed the anti-communist Royal Lao Democratic Government, led by former Laotian military officers. However, many prominent exiles and resistance fighters in the United Front for the National Liberation of the Lao People (UFNLLP—formed in September 1980, and reportedly led by Gen. Phoumi since mid-1981) dissociated themselves from the Royal Government, which had established itself in southern Laos. In October 1988 the Government announced the capture of the Chief of Staff of the UFNLLP.

In December 1989 the right-wing United Lao National Liberation Front (ULNLF) proclaimed the 'Revolutionary Provisional Government' of Laos. The self-styled Government, which was headed by Outhong Souvannavong (the former President of the Royal Council of King Savang Vatthana), claimed to have used military force to 'liberate' one-third of Laotian territory. Although there were reports of attacks by insurgent guerrillas in northern Laos at this time, it was widely assumed that the ULNLF's claims were exaggerated and that its proclamation was an attempt to elicit popular support. Responsibility for defence was reportedly allocated to Gen. Vang Pao, a leader of the Hmong tribe who in the 1970s had been a commander of the Royalist army (and who had lived in exile in the USA since 1975); Somphorn Wang (also formerly a prominent Royalist) was described as secretary of state in the 'Revolutionary Provisional Government'. In late 1992 Gen. Vang Pao reportedly travelled to Singapore to direct an unsuccessful military operation from Thailand. In October Gen. Vang Pao's brother, Vang Fung, and another Hmong rebel, Moua Yee Julan (who were allegedly preparing an incursion into Laos under Gen. Vang Pao's command), were arrested in Thailand. In September 1993 Thai troops launched an offensive against Gen. Vang Pao's forces, expelling 320 rebels from Thai territory.

In June 1990 a draft constitution, enshrining free-market principles, was published in the LPRP newspaper, *Pasason*. Later in the same month the Supreme People's Assembly approved legislation that included provision for the ownership of property, for inheritance rights and contractual obligations. In October three former government officials were arrested in connection with what were termed 'activities aimed at overthrowing the regime'. It was reported in Thailand that they had formed part of a 'Social Democrat Group', which was actively seeking the introduction of multi-party democracy. In November 1992 all three were sentenced to 14 years' imprisonment.

In March 1991, at the Fifth Congress of the LPRP, Souphanouvong retired from all his party posts. Phoumi Vongvichit and Sisomphon Lovansai also retired, and the three were appointed to a newly created advisory board to the LPRP Central Committee. Kaysone Phomvihane's title was altered from General Secretary to President of the LPRP, and his power was slightly enhanced following the abolition of the party Secretariat. A new Political Bureau and (younger) Party Central Committee were elected. Gen. Sisavat Keobounphan, the military Chief of the General Staff, was not re-elected to the Political Bureau. The leadership pledged a continuance of free-market economic reforms, but denied the need for political pluralism. However, the national motto ('peace, independence, unity, socialism') was changed to 'peace, independence, democracy, unity, prosperity'.

On 14 August 1991 the Supreme People's Assembly adopted a new constitution, which provided for a National Assembly, confirmed the leading role of the LPRP, enshrined the right to private ownership, and endowed the presidency with executive powers; new electoral legislation was also promulgated. Kaysone Phomvihane was appointed President of Laos. Gen. Khamtay Siphandone, a Vice-Chairman of the Council of Ministers, Minister of National Defence and Supreme Commander of the Lao People's Army, replaced Kaysone Phomvihane as Chairman of the Council of Ministers, restyled Prime Minister.

Kaysone Phomvihane died in November 1992. He was replaced as President of the LPRP by Gen. Khamtay Siphandone, and on 25 November a specially convened meeting of the Supreme People's Assembly elected Nouhak Phoumsavanh as President of State. Elections to the new National Assembly took place on 20 December; 99.33% of eligible voters participated in the election, in which 154 LFNC-approved candidates contested 85 seats. On 22 February 1993 the new National Assembly re-elected Nouhak Phoumsavanh as President, confirmed Khamtay Siphandone as Prime Minister, and implemented the most extensive reorganization of the Council of Ministers since the LPRP's accession to power in 1975. Phoumi Vongvichit died in January 1994, and Souphanouvong in January 1995.

Although the 20th anniversary of the beginning of communist rule was celebrated in 1995, the Laotian Government was gradually attempting to replace communist ideology with Lao nationalism, as Laos developed as a market economy with increasing foreign participation. In July senior Buddhist monks were assembled in Vientiane (as Buddhism was deemed central to Laotian cultural identity) and were encouraged by the Government to lead a 'cultural renaissance'. Meanwhile, the Government urged the security forces to suppress social problems, particularly corruption and prostitution, perceived as arising from increasing external influences.

The outcome of the LPRP congress at the end of March 1996 consolidated the country's apparent progress towards a form of military-dominated authoritarian government. The armed forces gained a majority of seats on the new nine-member Political Bureau; Khamtay Siphandone was elected as its President (replacing Nouhak Phoumsavanh, who retired from this post), and the Minister of National Defence and Commander-in-Chief of the armed forces, Lt-Gen. Choummali Saignason, was promoted to third position, after the Chairman of the National Assembly, Lt-Gen. Saman Vignaket. The most significant development was the failure of Khamphoui Keoboualapha, a Deputy Prime Minister responsible for many of Laos's reforms, to be re-elected either to the Political Bureau or to the Central Committee. Lts-Gen. Choummali Saignason and Saman Vignaket were widely reported to be opposed to rapid economic and political reform.

At the opening session of the National Assembly in April 1996 Nouhak Phoumsavanh was, despite his retirement from the Political Bureau, confirmed as Head of State until the end of his term of office in February 1998. Sisavat Keobounphan (who had been restored to the Political Bureau at the previous month's elections) was elected to the new office of Vice-President, in order to relieve Nouhak Phoumsavanh of a number of presidential duties. Boungnang Volachit was approved by the National Assembly as a Deputy Prime Minister, although, contrary to expectation, Khamphoui Keoboualapha also retained his posts as Deputy Prime Minister and Chairman of the State Committee for Planning and Co-operation. However, it was expected that the latter's influence would be diminished by his exclusion from the Political Bureau and also by the establishment of a new State Planning Committee, which was to assume some of the responsibilities hitherto exercised by Khamphoui's Committee.

Elections to the National Assembly took place on 21 December 1997, at which 159 LFNC-approved candidates, including 41 members of the outgoing legislature, contested 99 seats. The three members of the LPRP Political Bureau and 10 Central Committee members who stood for election were all successful; one of the four 'independent' candidates without affiliation to the LPRP was elected. The level of participation by voters was officially registered to have been 99.37%. The first session of the new National Assembly was held on 23–26 February 1998, during which the Assembly elected Gen. Khamtay to succeed Phoumsavanh as President of State. The Assembly also endorsed the appointment of Sisavat Keobounphan as Prime Minister and of Oudom Khattigna in his place as Vice-President, re-elected Saman Vignaket as President of the National Assembly, and approved a redistribution of ministerial posts.

In March 2001 the Seventh Congress of the LPRP confirmed the military's control of the Political Bureau. In the same month, as part of another reorganization of the Council of Ministers, Oudom was replaced as the country's Vice-President by Lt-Gen. Choummali Saignason, who had relinquished his bid for the premiership owing to ill health. Prime Minister Sisavat Keobounphan was forced to resign after only three years in office, in order to take responsibility for the mismanagement of the economy in the wake of the Asian financial crisis of 1997/98. His successor, the former Deputy Prime Minister and Minister of Finance, Boungnang Volachit, provided a civilian balance to the entirely military executive branch. The appointment of Thongloun Sisolit to the post of Deputy Prime Minister further enhanced the greater civilian representation on the Council of Ministers.

From the mid-1990s uprisings against the Government became more frequent. In July 1995 an army unit based near Luang Prabang mutinied after its commander, a Hmong general, was passed over for promotion. Five members of the armed forces died in the rebellion, which was believed to be symptomatic of the resentment felt by hill tribes over the political and military dominance of the lowland Lao. About 2,000 troops were dispatched to Luang Prabang to restore order. In November several people were killed in an armed assault on a bus near Luang Prabang. The attack was attributed to disaffected Hmong tribesmen who had pledged to disrupt that year's 20th anniversary celebrations of the beginning of communist rule. In October a shipment of explosives, allegedly destined for Hmong insurgents, had been intercepted on the Mekong River. Several incidents in the Luang Prabang region during 1996 were ascribed to Hmong rebels. Meanwhile, fund-raising by the Hmong community in the USA was reportedly a cause for concern within the Laotian Government.

In October 1999 an anti-Government demonstration by students and teachers was held in Vientiane. The protest, which constituted an extremely rare overt demonstration of public dissatisfaction, was reportedly swiftly dispersed by police. The Government subsequently refuted claims that about 50 people who were involved or suspected to have been involved in the protest had been arrested, and, furthermore, denied that the demonstration had taken place; in late March 2000, however, it was reported that the whereabouts of one professor and at least five students arrested during the protest remained unknown.

Civil unrest intensified throughout 2000, with a spate of bomb attacks. The first occurred in a restaurant in March, immediately drawing international attention to the event, as several tourists were injured in the blast. Two further attacks took place in Vientiane in May, coinciding with the respective visits of the Thai Prime Minister, Chuan Leekpai, and his Minister of Foreign Affairs, Surin Pitsuwan. Two more strikes followed within a week of each other, bringing the total to five explosions within three months, more than 20 people having been injured and at least two killed. Under pressure, the Government, blaming the campaign on Hmong insurgents, claimed to have arrested two men (one Lao and one Hmong) carrying explosive devices in mid-June. Despite the arrests, the bombing operation continued unabated. A bomb was defused near the Vietnamese embassy in Vientiane at the end of July, lending credence to the suspicion that the action was part of an internal power struggle between pro-Chinese and pro-Vietnamese governmental factions. In total, at least nine bombs exploded between March 2000 and January 2001, with the penultimate detonation occurring on the eve of the meeting of the European Union and Association of South East Asian Nations (see p. 172) (EU-ASEAN summit) in December 2000.

Although no group admitted responsibility for the bombings, a pre-dawn raid in July 2000 on immigration and customs offices in Vang Tao, opposite the Chong Mek checkpoint, indicated the involvement of royalist rebels. The Government claimed that the attack was merely a robbery, but during the incursion the former royal flag was raised over the immigration office. (In October 2004, following their extradition from Thailand, 16 Lao nationals were convicted of robbery in connection with the raid and sentenced to prison terms of between two and 12 years.) In mid-November 2000 about 200 workers and students were reported to have staged a demonstration in the southern province of Champasak, calling for democracy. The protest was swiftly quelled, with 15 people being arrested. The timing of the demonstration, however, exacerbated the increasing sense of instability, as less than two weeks previously, Helen Clark, the Prime Minister of New Zealand, had confirmed that her Government had granted political asylum to Khamsay Souphanouvong, a minister attached to the Prime Minister's office and son of the first President of the Lao People's Democratic Republic.

In December 2000 Kerry and Kay Danes, an Australian couple, were arrested on suspicion of involvement in the theft of over US $6m. worth of sapphires. Following the conclusion of an investigation into the case in April 2001, a Laotian court finally convicted the couple of embezzlement, tax evasion and destruction of evidence in June. They were sentenced to prison terms of seven years each. However, the couple were provisionally released in October 2001, having spent 10 months in custody. Following protracted diplomatic negotiations, and in large part due to Laos's strong ties with Australia, the pair received a formal presidential pardon in November.

In October 2001 five European activists, including Olivier Dupuis, a Belgian member of the European Parliament, were arrested for handing out pro-democracy leaflets at a peaceful protest in Vientiane. The protest was held to commemorate the second anniversary of the disappearance of five students who had participated in the demonstration of October 1999. In November 2001, following expressions of concern at the conditions the detainees were being forced to endure, Romani Prodi, President of the European Commission, warned the Laotian authorities that the continued detention of the activists would threaten diplomatic relations with the EU. In the same month, following a swift trial, the prisoners were convicted of attempting to spread unrest and ordered to be deported. They were also fined and given two-year suspended prison terms.

On 24 February 2002 elections took place from among 166 LFNC-approved candidates for the 109 seats available in the National Assembly. Only one of the elected members was not affiliated to the LPRP, ensuring that the ruling party secured a comprehensive victory. In April, at the opening session of the National Assembly, the existing Cabinet was almost wholly re-elected. The former Minister of the Interior, Maj.-Gen. Asang Laoli, became Deputy Prime Minister and Maj.-Gen. Soudchai Thammasith subsequently assumed the interior portfolio. In January 2003 a cabinet reorganization was announced in an apparent attempt to strengthen the national economy. The former Governor of the Central Bank, Chansy Phosikham, was appointed Minister of Finance, Onneua Phommachanh became Minister of Industry and Handicrafts and Soulivong Daravong was placed in charge of the Ministry of Commerce and Tourism.

In September 2002 a bomb exploded at the Si Muang temple in Vientiane, injuring two children; it was unclear whether the attack was linked to the bombings that had occurred in 2000. In January 2003, for the first time, national celebrations were held to commemorate the anniversary of the birth of King Fa Ngoum, accredited with founding the Kingdom of Lane Xang in 1353; a statue was erected and a public holiday declared. In the following month a group of armed men ambushed a bus near the town of Vang Vieng; the attack resulted in the deaths of 13 people, including three foreign nationals, two of whom were tourists. Several arrests were later made in connection with the ambush, which was thought to have been carried out by bandits rather than terrorists. It was feared that the incident might discourage tourists from visiting the country. Such fears were intensified in April by a further attack on a bus travelling between Luang Prabang and Vientiane; at least 12 people died as a result of the incident, which was thought to have been perpetrated by Hmong rebels. In August 2003 an attack on a bus in the north of the country killed five people. In October three bombs exploded in Vientiane. A previously unknown group, the Free Democratic People's Government of Laos (FDPGL), claimed responsibility for the bombings, as well as for the spate of bomb attacks that had occurred in the capital since 2000. It was believed that the group consisted of disaffected former members of the armed forces. However, a German-based organization, the Committee for Independence and Democracy in Laos, later claimed responsibility for all the bombings, including two further attacks that occurred in early 2004, one in Savannakhet and one in Vientiane.

In June 2003 it was reported that two European journalists, together with their Lao-US interpreter, had been arrested owing to their suspected involvement in the murder of a Lao national and for reporting from the country in contravention of the terms of their tourist visas. The journalists had allegedly been researching the Hmong insurgency in the country, which they had found to be almost exhausted and desperate for assistance. Following a summary trial, the three were sentenced to 15-year prison terms. Three Hmong defendants were given 20-year prison sentences. However, following intense diplomatic pressure from their respective Governments, the three foreign nationals were released in the following month. In October Political Bureau member Bousone Boupavanh was appointed fourth Deputy Prime Minister, with responsibility for home affairs. His appointment was believed to be, in part, a governmental response to the deteriorating security situation in the country.

In early March 2004 an official from the Ministry of National Defence claimed that some 700 Hmong, including five senior commanders, had recently surrendered to the authorities, having been offered amnesty. Five bomb attacks reportedly occurred in April and May, the most serious of which killed one person and injured six others in southern Laos. In September the human rights organization Amnesty International alleged that up to 40 government troops had assaulted and murdered five Hmong children in the Xaysomboune special zone in northern Laos in May; the Government denied the accusations. Security was heightened in Vientiane in November, following two minor bomb explosions near the Thai border (for which the FDPGL claimed responsibility) and warnings of further possible attacks ahead of the ASEAN summit meeting, which was held in the capital at the end of the month. Two small bombs exploded in a village outside the capital a few days before the opening of the meeting, but no injuries were reported.

In February 2006 it was announced that a legislative election would be held at the end of April, almost a year ahead of schedule. President Khamtay Siphandone stated that the decision to hold elections before the expiry of the mandate of the current Assembly had been made in order to enable the new Council of Ministers and the incoming legislature to commence their respective terms of office within close proximity of one another, in order to facilitate the forging of a strong working relationship. In March the LPRP held its Eighth Party Congress, during which Gen. Khamtay tendered his resignation as party leader; he was replaced by Vice-President Lt-Gen. Choummali Saignason. Khamtay also resigned from the Political Bureau, to which two new members were elected: Deputy Prime Minister and Minister of Foreign Affairs Somsavat Lengsavat; and Phani Yathothu, the only female member of the Bureau. It was thought likely that Gen. Khamtay would also resign from his position as President of Laos prior to the forthcoming legislative elections; Vice-President Choummali was considered to be his probable replacement. During the Party Congress elections for a new Central Committee were also held, at which 55 members were selected. On 30 April the legislative election was duly held; an estimated 2.7m. voters cast their ballot. The counting of votes was delayed by torrential rain across parts of the country, which hindered attempts to collect ballot boxes from the affected regions. The results of polling, announced in mid-May, showed that two nominally independent candidates (of the three who had contested the election) had been elected, alongside 113 members of the LPRP. However, some 71 of the incoming deputies had not previously been members of the National Assembly, and therefore were described by some commentators as constituting a new generation of legislators. The new Assembly was expected to convene in late June.

From 1975 Laos was dependent on Vietnamese economic and military assistance, permitting the stationing of Vietnamese troops (estimated in 1987 to number between 30,000 and 50,000) on its territory. In 1977 a 25-year treaty of friendship between the two countries was signed, and Laos supported the Vietnamese-led overthrow of the Khmer Rouge regime in Kampuchea (Cambodia) in January 1979. Following the outbreak of hostilities between Viet Nam and the People's Republic of China in that year, Laos allied itself with the former. Viet Nam withdrew its military presence from Laos during 1988. The two countries signed a protocol governing military co-operation in March 1994. In July 2001 Prime Minister Boungnang Volachit visited Viet Nam on his first overseas trip since assuming office in March. In May 2002 President Gen. Khamtai Siphandone paid an official friendship visit to Viet Nam, which was reciprocated in October by the Chairman of the Vietnamese National Assembly, Nguyen Van An. The visits affirmed the strength of ties between the two countries. In February 2006 a major border crossing was opened between Sekong province in Laos and Quang Nam province in Viet Nam. It was hoped that this would facilitate economic co-operation between the two countries and would also help to control smuggling along the common border.

In February 1993 Laos, Thailand, Viet Nam and Cambodia signed a joint communiqué providing for the resumption of co-operation in the development of the Mekong River. In April 1995 in Chiang Rai, Thailand, representatives of the four countries signed an agreement on the joint exploitation and development of the lower Mekong. The accord provided for the establishment of the Mekong River Commission (see p. 387) as a successor to the Committee for Co-ordination of Investigations of the Lower Mekong Basin.

In July 1992 Laos strengthened ties with members of ASEAN by signing the ASEAN Treaty of Amity and Co-operation, which provided for wider regional co-operation and was regarded as a preliminary step to full membership of the Association. Laos attended ASEAN meetings with observer status from this time, and applied for membership of the organization in March 1996. The country was formally admitted as a full member at the organization's meeting of ministers responsible for foreign affairs in July 1997. As Chair of ASEAN for 2004/05, Laos hosted the 10th summit meeting of the Association in November 2004 and the 38th Ministerial Meeting in July 2005. Despite bomb threats made to staff at the US embassy in Vientiane, apparently by groups opposed to the Laotian Government, in the period prior to the summit meeting in November 2004, both the summit meeting itself and the ministerial conference proceeded without incident and did much to raise the international profile of Laos.

Relations with the People's Republic of China improved in December 1986, when a Chinese delegation, led by the Deputy Minister of Foreign Affairs, made the first official Chinese visit to Laos since 1978. In December 1987, after an assurance from the People's Republic of China that support would be withdrawn from Laotian resistance groups operating from within China, the two countries agreed to restore full diplomatic relations and to encourage bilateral trade. Relations between the LPRP and the Chinese Communist Party were fully restored in August 1989. In October 1991 the Laotian and Chinese Prime Ministers signed a border treaty, which established a framework for meetings of a Laotian-Chinese joint border committee. In January 1992 the committee adopted a resolution providing for the demarcation of the common border, and in June an agreement on the delineation of boundaries was signed. In November 1994 Laos and China signed a reciprocal agreement on the transport of passengers and goods on each other's sections of the Mekong River. In February 1996 Laos and China opened a section of their border to highway traffic. In October 1997 Chinese Vice-Premier Wu Bangguo made a three-day visit to Laos, and in early 1999 Prime Minister Sisavat Keobounphan made an eight-day official visit to China. The first visit ever made by a Chinese head of state to Laos was by President Jiang Zemin in November 2000.

Relations with Thailand from 1975 were characterized by mutual suspicion. Thailand intermittently closed its border to Laotian imports and exports, causing considerable hardship. Disputed sovereignty claims in border areas were a cause of friction, and led to clashes between Laotian and Thai troops in 1984. Further hostilities began in December 1987, resulting in hundreds of casualties. In February 1988 the two sides agreed to declare a cease-fire, to withdraw their troops from the combat area, and to attempt to negotiate a peaceful solution. In March 1991 (following the recent military coup in Thailand) representatives of the two countries signed an agreement providing for the immediate withdrawal of troops from disputed areas. The Thai Government also undertook to suppress the activities of Laotian insurgents operating from Thai territory. In December Thailand and Laos signed a border co-operation agreement.

In June 1992 the Thai Crown Prince, Maha Vajiralongkorn, visited Vientiane for the first time. On the following day, however, about 300 guerrillas from a Thai-based rebel group, the Free Democratic Lao National Salvation Force, attacked three Laotian government posts, killing two people and causing significant damage. In the same month Laos refuted allegations made by a senior Thai military officer that a Laotian government unit was receiving training in chemical warfare from Cuban and Vietnamese experts, and also dismissed previous accusations by Laotian resistance fighters and Western aid agencies of its use of chemical warfare to suppress the activities of rebel groups. Bilateral relations improved in July, when the Thai authorities announced the arrest of 11 Laotian citizens accused of planning subversive activities against the Government in Vientiane. The first bridge (over the Mekong River) linking Laos and Thailand was opened in April 1994. In September 1996 the countries' Joint Co-operation Commission agreed to establish a boundary commission, in an effort to resolve demarcation problems. Despite various diplomatic moves to stimulate further co-operation between the two countries, such as the signing of an extradition treaty in January 2001, the relationship was strained by the July 2000 incursion launched from Thai territory by suspected royalist rebels. (In July 2004, following a lengthy legal dispute, Thailand handed over to the Laotian authorities 16 Lao nationals who were allegedly involved in the incursion, despite an earlier ruling by a Thai court rejecting their extradition.) Meanwhile, the situation deteriorated further in August 2000 after Laotian troops occupied two islands in the Mekong River, evicting 65 Thai farming families. Laos claimed that under a 1926 treaty it had sovereignty over all the islands in the Mekong, while Thailand merely requested the withdrawal of the troops. Nevertheless, in April 2001 the Thai Minister of Foreign Affairs, Surakiart Sathirathai, visited Laos, affirming the beginning of a new era of friendly Lao-Thai relations based on shared cultural values. In June Thai Prime Minister Thaksin Shinawatra arrived in Vientiane on a two-day official visit intended further to consolidate co-operative ties between the two countries. In late 2003, following a meeting of the Joint Co-operation Commission, the two countries pledged to resolve all outstanding border demarcation issues, as well as agreeing to work together on a variety of social development initiatives. In March 2004, for the first time, the Thai and Laotian Governments held a joint cabinet meeting to discuss bilateral co-operation. The meeting ended with Prime Ministers Thaksin Shinawatra and Boungnang Volachit presiding over a ceremony to lay the foundation stone for a second Mekong Friendship Bridge, which was scheduled for completion in late 2006. In December 2004, at a meeting of the Joint Co-operation Commission, Laos and Thailand agreed to complete the demarcation of their land border in the following year to mark the 55th anniversary of the establishment of diplomatic relations between the two countries. In early 2006 tension arose between Laos and Thailand concerning 27 Hmong refugees (all but one of whom were children), who had been reported missing from a refugee camp in Phetchabun province, north-eastern Thailand, in December 2005. The group was subsequently discovered in Laos, allegedly having been forcibly repatriated by the Thai authorities. Laos and Thailand entered into negotiations regarding the possibility of reuniting the children with their parents at the Phetchabun refugee camp but by March 2006 the two countries had yet to reach an agreement.

During the 1970s and 1980s thousands of Laotian refugees fled to Thailand to escape from civil war and food shortages. In January 1989 an estimated 90,000 Laotian refugees remained in border camps in Thailand. The office of the UN High Commissioner for Refugees (UNHCR) began a programme of voluntary repatriation in 1980. By late 1990 fewer than 6,000 refugees had been repatriated under UNHCR supervision, while some 15,000 had returned independently, and others had been resettled abroad. In June 1991 UNHCR, Laos and Thailand signed an agreement guaranteeing the repatriation or resettlement in a third country of the remaining 60,000 Laotian refugees in Thailand by the end of 1994. In July 1994, however, UNHCR, Laos and Thailand revised their agreement to the effect that the repatriation programme would be completed by early 1995, and this deadline was subsequently revised on several occasions. In December 1996, according to UNHCR figures, 3,293 Laotian refugees remained in Thailand. In December 1997 UNHCR announced that a final review of the status of the last remaining refugees at Ban Napho camp in Thailand would be completed by January 1998, whereupon they would be repatriated or resettled in a third country. Among the camp's 1,344 refugees were reportedly 964 Hmong, most of whom were unwilling to return to Laos. In December 2003 the USA agreed to accept around 15,000 Laotian Hmong refugees living in refugee camps in Thailand. The first group of refugees was resettled in the USA in June 2004, under the aegis of the International Organization for Migration.

Laos's uneasy political relationship with Thailand, in conjunction with Thailand's economic superiority in the region, is widely regarded as having prompted the Laotian Government during the 1990s to forge closer links with Myanmar and, more recently, with Cambodia. In February 1992 Khamtay Siphandone was the first foreign head of government to visit Myanmar since the military coup in that country in 1988, and in June 1994 Senior Gen. Than Shwe visited Laos, his first foreign visit as Myanmar's Head of State. Bilateral contacts continued on a frequent basis. Laos signed a treaty of friendship and assistance with Cambodia in December 1995, further to which Joint Co-operation Committees were established. In November 2001 Prince Norodom Ranariddh headed a Cambodian delegation on an official goodwill visit to Laos, confirming the continued strength of bilateral ties.

From 1989 the Laotian Government sought to improve relations with non-communist countries, in order to reduce its (especially economic) dependence on the USSR and Viet Nam. Following a visit to Japan in that year by Kaysone Phomvihane (his first official visit to a non-communist country), the Japanese Government agreed to increase grant aid to Laos. In December 1995 Japan announced that it would resume the provision of official loans to Laos in 1996. In January 2000 the Japanese Prime Minister, Keizo Obuchi, made an official visit to Laos, and in August 2000 a bridge over the Mekong, built with a 5,460m.-yen grant from the Japanese Government, was officially opened in Paksé. In mid-2001 Prince Akishino of Japan made a 10-day unofficial visit to Laos and, in September, Japan agreed a further loan to fund the construction of the second Mekong Friendship Bridge.

In November 2002 the Prime Minister of India, Atal Bihari Vajpayee, paid the first visit to Laos by an Indian head of government in more than 45 years. During his stay the two countries signed agreements on co-operation in defence issues and control of drug-trafficking. The Indian Government also agreed to provide US $10m. of credit to Laos at low interest rates.

During the Viet Nam war US aircraft completed almost 600,000 bombing missions over Laos, leaving large amounts of undetonated explosives, which were estimated to cause 50–100 fatalities per year in the 1990s. The National Unexploded Ordnance Awareness and Clearance Programme was established in Laos in May 1995, with support from the UN.

In 1985 Laos agreed to co-operate with the USA in recovering the remains of US soldiers 'missing in action' in Laos since the war in Viet Nam. In August 1987 a US delegation visited Vientiane to discuss 'humanitarian co-operation' by Laos in tracing missing US soldiers, and agreed to provide Laos with aid. The first remains of US soldiers were passed to the US Government in February 1988. Laos postponed further searching for a short period in 1989, when the USA, alleging that Laos was failing to assist in the suppression of drugs-trafficking, suspended aid and preferential treatment. The USA restored aid to Laos in early 1990, following a visit to Vientiane by the Chairman of the US House of Representatives Committee on Narcotics and Drug Control. (In March 1992 Laos, Myanmar and Thailand signed a draft co-operation treaty on narcotics suppression.) In November 1991, in response to continued Laotian co-operation and the implementation of limited political and economic reforms, the US Government announced that diplomatic relations with Laos were to be upgraded to ambassadorial level. Further progress was achieved in tracing the remains of US soldiers during 1992, and in January 1993 a joint recovery operation was undertaken. In the same month, following 17 months of hearings, a special US Senate panel concluded that (despite considerable public speculation to the contrary) there was 'no compelling evidence' of the survival of US servicemen in the region. During 1993–98 Laos and the USA co-operated in further operations to locate the remains of US soldiers. In May 1995 the USA announced the ending of a 20-year embargo on aid to Laos. In November 1997 the US Deputy Secretary of State, Strobe Talbott, led the highest-level US delegation to Laos since the mid-1970s. During the visit further US support was pledged for a programme to clear unexploded ordnance from the Viet Nam war, which had been supported by the USA since 1996. In mid-1998 US officials agreed to extend financial and logistical support for the programme until September 1999. Further co-operation between the two nations occurred in March–April 2000, when a joint operation in search of US soldiers' remains was resumed. The search operation continued from 2001. In December 2004, following its adoption by Congress, President George W. Bush of the USA signed legislation according normal trade relations (NTR) status to Laos, which had been suspended in 1975. The US Senate had separately passed a resolution condemning Laos's human rights record, concerns over which had delayed the approval of NTR status. A bilateral trade agreement signed by the USA and Laos in September 2003 consequently entered into force in February 2005.

Government

Under the terms of the 1991 Constitution, executive power is vested in the President of State, while legislative power resides with the National Assembly. The President is elected for five years by the National Assembly. Members of the National Assembly are elected for a period of five years by universal adult suffrage. The Lao People's Revolutionary Party remains the sole legal political party. With the approval of the National Assembly, the President appoints the Prime Minister and members of the Council of Ministers, who conduct the government of the country. The President also appoints provincial governors and mayors of municipalities, who are responsible for local administration.

Defence

In August 2005, according to Western estimates, the strength of the armed forces was 29,100 (Lao People's Army 25,600—including an army marine section of 600—and air force 3,500). Military service is compulsory for a minimum of 18 months. There is a paramilitary self-defence force numbering more than 100,000. In 2003 defence expenditure was budgeted at an estimated 339,000m. kips.

Economic Affairs

In 2004, according to estimates by the World Bank, Laos's gross national income (GNI), measured at average 2002–04 prices, was US $2,239m., equivalent to $390 per head (or $1,850 per head on an international purchasing-power parity basis). During 1995–2004, it was estimated, the population increased by an annual average of 2.4%, while gross domestic product (GDP) per head increased, in real terms, by an average of 3.5% per year. Overall GDP increased, in real terms, at an average annual rate of 6.0% in 1995–2004. According to the Asian Development Bank (ADB), GDP increased by 6.9% in 2004 and by 7.2% in 2005.

Agriculture (including forestry and fishing) contributed an estimated 48.6% of GDP in 2003. According to FAO, an estimated 76.0% of the working population were employed in the sector in mid-2003. Rice is the staple crop. Other crops include sweet potatoes, maize, cassava, sugar cane and sesame seed. Coffee, production of which reached an estimated 23,000 metric tons in 2004, is grown for export. In 2000 forest covered about 55.4% of the country's total land area. Wood products remained a major export commodity in 2004, accounting for an estimated 18.6% of total export revenue in that year. The cultivation and illicit export of narcotic drugs has been widespread. Despite having been outlawed in 1997, the country's opium production remained substantial in 2003. According to the UN Office on Drugs and Crime (formerly the UN Office of Drug Control and Crime Prevention), Laos was the third largest source of illicit opium in the world in that year, after Afghanistan and Myanmar. However, the Government reportedly achieved considerable success in subsequent efforts to eliminate opium production. In 2004 production was reported to have declined to an estimated 43 metric tons, a dramatic reduction of 64% compared with the estimate for 2003, and the area under cultivation was also believed to be steadily decreasing. Government efforts to eradicate the drug were reported to have been so successful that by mid-2005 the authorities pronounced Laos to be an opium-free country. During 1995–2004, according to the World Bank, agricultural GDP measured at constant 2000 prices increased by an average of 4.3% per year. According to ADB estimates, compared with the previous year, the rate of sectoral growth was 3.5% in 2004 and 3.0% in 2005.

Industry (including mining, manufacturing, construction and utilities) contributed an estimated 25.9% of GDP in 2003. The sector employed about 6.3% of the working population in 1990. During 1995–2004, according to the World Bank, industrial GDP measured at constant 2000 prices increased at an average annual rate of 10.1%. According to the ADB, growth in the industrial sector was estimated at 12.5% in 2004 and at 13.0% in 2005.

Mining contributed only an estimated 1.7% of GDP in 2003, although this represented a significant increase from 0.5% in 2002. Laos has, however, considerable mineral resources: iron ore (the country's principal mineral resource), copper, coal, tin and gypsum are among the minerals that are exploited. Other mineral deposits include zinc, nickel, potash, lead, limestone, gold, silver and precious stones. In March 2005, ahead of schedule, the Sepon gold and copper project yielded its first copper cathodes, which were to be exported to various countries in the region. Copper production in 2005 was an estimated 30,480 metric tons, and this was expected to increase to 60,000 tons in 2006. During 1995–2003, according to the ADB, the GDP of the mining sector increased by an average of 37.9% per year. Growth was estimated at 367.5% in 2003, compared with a mere 1.2% in 2001 and 10.1% in 2002.

Manufacturing contributed an estimated 19.2% of GDP in 2003, although the sector employed less than 1% of the working population in the mid-1980s. It is mainly confined to the processing of raw materials (chiefly sawmilling) and agricultural produce, the production of textiles and garments (a principal export commodity), and the manufacture of handicrafts and basic consumer goods for the domestic market. According to the World Bank, manufacturing GDP increased at an average annual rate of 10.3% in 1995–2003. Manufacturing GDP increased by 13.0% in 2002 and by 6.3% in 2003.

Electrical energy is principally derived from hydroelectric power. Electricity is exported to Thailand and Viet Nam, and is one of Laos's principal sources of foreign exchange. In 2003 the country's total electricity generation reached an estimated 3,179m. kWh. Laos's total hydroelectric power potential was estimated at 25,000 MW in 2000. In 2002 the Government granted a concession to the Nam Theun 2 Power Company (NTPC), enabling it to assume control of the construction of a US $1,100m. hydroelectric dam—Nam Theun 2, which was scheduled for completion in 2009. In November 2003 the Electricity Generating Authority of Thailand signed an agreement with the NTPC to buy 995 MW of electricity over 25 years, at an estimated cost of $5,000m. In January 2005 the World Bank commenced appraisal of the scheme, which numerous critics had repeatedly argued would have a severe detrimental impact on the environment. In March the Bank announced that it had decided in favour of supporting the dam since it was confident that its benefits would outweigh any negative effects; the Bank was to provide loans and guarantees for the controversial scheme. In January 2006 the Laotian Government held talks with Thailand regarding the establishment of a joint technical committee to discuss the construction of an industrial electrical grid to receive and redistribute electricity sold by Laos to appropriate sites in Thailand. In mid-February the two countries agreed upon a renewed power-purchasing deal, to replace the existing agreement that was due to expire in mid-2006 and under the terms of which Thailand had agreed to buy 3,000 MW of electricity per year from Laos between 1996 and 2006. Under the new arrangement, the amount of electricity to be provided to Thailand (including the supply from the Nam Theun 2 project) was to increase to as much as 5,000 MW per year. In 2002 Laos also signed an agreement with Cambodia, China, Myanmar, Thailand and Viet Nam concerning the establishment of a regional power distribution system, which would form the basis for a programme of hydropower development in the Mekong region. Laos is totally dependent on imports, mainly from Thailand, for supplies of mineral fuels.

The services sector contributed an estimated 25.5% of GDP in 2003, and engaged 17.2% of the total labour force in 1980. Receipts from tourism decreased from US $113m. in 2002 to $87m. in 2003. Tourist arrivals declined from 735,662 in 2002 to 636,361 in 2003. According to the World Bank, the GDP of the services sector measured at constant 2000 prices increased at an average annual rate of 6.5% in 1995–2004. According to the ADB, the sector grew by 7.5% in 2004 and by 8.0% in 2005.

In 2004 Laos recorded a visible trade deficit of an estimated US $144.8m., and there was an estimated deficit of $18.0m. on the current account of the balance of payments. Remittances from relatives residing overseas are a significant source of income for many Lao. In 2004 Thailand was the principal source of imports, supplying an estimated 60.5% (including any goods in transit) of the total. China was also an important source of imports (9.2%) in that year, along with Viet Nam, Singapore and Germany. The principal destination of exports from Laos in 2004 was Thailand, purchasing 19.0% (including any goods in transit) of the total. Other significant purchasers in that year were Viet Nam (16.4%), France (7.9%) and Germany (5.6%). The main exports in 2003 were garments (an estimated 26.2%), wood products (23.3%) and electricity (22.7%). The principal imports in that year were consumer goods (49.2%), investment goods (37.4%), construction and electrical equipment (12.0%) and materials for the garments industry (10.6%).

In the financial year ending 30 September 2004 an overall budget deficit of 979,000m. kips was envisaged. The fiscal deficit was estimated by the ADB to have reached the equivalent of 6.0% of GDP in 2005. At the end of 2005 the country's external debt totalled US $2,212m.; in that year the cost of debt-servicing was equivalent to 12.0% of revenue from export of goods and services. Consumer prices increased by an annual average of 37.7% in 1995–2002. According to the ADB, the annual rate of inflation averaged 15.5% in 2003, before declining to 10.5% in 2004 and to 7.2% in 2005. The unemployment rate totalled 2.4% in 1995, according to the census conducted in that year.

Laos is a member of the UN Economic and Social Commission for Asia and the Pacific (ESCAP, see p. 33), of the Asian Development Bank (ADB, see p. 169), of the Association of South East Asian Nations (ASEAN, see p. 172), of the Colombo Plan (see p. 385), which promotes economic and social development in Asia and the Pacific, and of the Mekong River Commission (see p. 387).

From 1986 the Government undertook a radical programme of economic liberalization, known as the New Economic Mechanism, with the aim of transforming the hitherto centrally planned economy into a market-orientated system. Various reforms were introduced, including the enactment of a liberal foreign investment law in 1988 and the implementation of a privatization programme. Laos has remained extremely underdeveloped, however, and, as one of the poorest countries in Asia, is heavily reliant on external aid. The Fifth Five-Year Plan (2001–05), announced at the Seventh Congress of the Lao People's Revolutionary Party (LPRP) in March 2001, envisaged an average annual GDP growth rate of between 7.0% and 7.5%. The Plan emphasized the eradication of poverty, the restriction of opium cultivation and integrated rural development. Other targets included a reduction in the annual level of inflation to a single-digit rate, the maintenance of a stable exchange rate and the restriction of the budget deficit to the equivalent of 5% of GDP. International donors, however, were disappointed at the Plan's failure to incorporate development of the private sector, while corruption among Lao officials and the lack of skilled personnel to manage the financial sector remained causes for concern. Having declined sharply in value in 1997, following the regional economic crisis of that year, and fluctuated thereafter, the national currency suffered another significant depreciation in mid-2002. This weakening of the kip was accompanied by a rise in inflation, which reached a high of 18% in May 2003 (according to the IMF). However, the kip subsequently stabilized and, despite the substantial rise in global oil prices, the rate of inflation decreased during 2004–05. The investment approval process was simplified in 2003. Hitherto, much approved foreign investment had not in fact been invested in the country. Having risen from US $5m. in 2002 to $20m. in 2003, inflows of foreign direct investment declined to $17m. in 2004, before increasing to $27m. in 2005, when inflows were underpinned by continued investment in the mining sector and in the Nam Theun 2 project. An Australian mining company made a substantial investment in the Sepon gold and copper mine, after gaining full ownership of the project in 2004. In early 2005 the Laotian Government exercised its option to secure a 10% stake in Sepon, in a move that was expected to provide the country with annual revenue of as much as $15m. in taxes and royalties. Furthermore, the granting of the status of normal trade relations (NTR) to Laos by the USA, together with the US-Laos bilateral trade agreement, which came into effect in February 2005, ending the prohibitively high tariffs hitherto imposed upon Laotian products imported into the USA, augured a substantial increase in the country's exports to the USA in future years. In the first five months of 2004 tourists arrivals increased by an estimated 30% when compared with the corresponding period of the previous year, thus allaying fears that the regional outbreak of Severe Acute Respiratory Syndrome (SARS) of 2003, combined with local security concerns (see Recent History), might have continuing repercussions for the country's tourism industry. In April 2004 the Government concluded the Poverty Reduction Strategy Paper, which was to focus on reducing poverty (the incidence of which continued to exceed 30% in 2003) through economic growth, especially within the country's poorest districts, with particular emphasis on agriculture, education, health and transport. In the same month a decree relating to the promotion and development of small and medium enterprises was issued. The restructuring of a number of state-owned enterprises was also under way, in an effort to give greater encouragement to the private sector. In 2004–05 the rate of inflation was successfully contained, in sharp contrast to the annual average rate of almost 130% recorded in 1999. In 2005

LAOS

Statistical Survey

a study published by the World Bank reported that approximately 37% of educated Laotians worked abroad—a severe impediment to the country's prospects of economic development. The ADB projected GDP growth of 7.3% for 2006. It was hoped that the establishment of the Lao Business Forum in March 2005 would create a more effective reciprocal channel of dialogue between the Government and the corporate sector. In February 2006 the ADB pledged a $10m. loan-and-grant 'package' for the Laotian Government to spend on afforestation programmes; it was hoped that such programmes might lead to the creation of hundreds of new jobs. It was also hoped that the introduction of value-added tax (VAT), which the Government aimed to implement by early 2007, would raise the revenue required to promote social and economic development. Proposed reforms in the financial sector included improved access for foreign and private banking institutions. Wider reforms remained essential if an environment were to be created in which sustained economic growth might be achieved.

Education

Education was greatly disrupted by the civil war, causing a high illiteracy rate, but educational facilities subsequently improved significantly. Lao is the medium of instruction. A comprehensive education system is in force. In 1990 the Government issued a decree permitting the establishment of private schools, in an effort to accommodate the increasing number of students.

Primary education begins at six years of age and lasts for five years. In 2001 a total of 82.8% of children in the relevant age-group were enrolled in primary education. Secondary education, beginning at the age of 11, lasts for six years, comprising two three-year cycles. In 2002 enrolment in secondary education was equivalent to 44% of males and 31% of females within the relevant age-group. In 1996 the total enrolment at primary and secondary schools was equivalent to 72% of the school-age population (males 80%; females 63%). Government expenditure on education for 1997/98 was forecast at 37,400m. kips, representing 6.9% of total projected expenditure.

Public Holidays

2006: 1 January (New Year's Day), 5 January (Anniversary of Birth of King Fa Ngoum), 6 January (Pathet Lao Day), 20 January (Army Day), 8 March (Women's Day), 22 March (People's Party Day), 13–15 April (Lao New Year), 1 May (Labour Day), 1 June (Children's Day), 13 August (Free Laos Day), 23 August (Liberation Day), 12 October (Liberation from the French Day, Vientiane only), 2 December (Independence Day).

2007: 1 January (New Year's Day), 5 January (Anniversary of Birth of King Fa Ngoum), 6 January (Pathet Lao Day), 20 January (Army Day), 8 March (Women's Day), 22 March (People's Party Day), 13–15 April (Lao New Year), 1 May (Labour Day), 1 June (Children's Day), 13 August (Free Laos Day), 23 August (Liberation Day), 12 October (Liberation from the French Day, Vientiane only), 2 December (Independence Day).

Weights and Measures

The metric system is in force.

Statistical Survey

Source (unless otherwise stated): National Statistics Centre, rue Luang Prabang, Vientiane; tel. (21) 214740; fax (21) 219129; e-mail nscp@laotel.com; internet www.nsc.gov.la.

Area and Population

AREA, POPULATION AND DENSITY

Area (sq km)	236,800*
Population (census results)	
1 March 1985	3,584,803
1 March 1995	
Males	2,265,867
Females	2,315,391
Total	4,581,258
Population (official estimate at mid-year)	
2003	5,679,000
Density (per sq km) at mid-2003	24.0

*91,400 sq miles.

PROVINCES
(population at mid-2003, official estimates)

	Area (sq km)	Population ('000)	Density (per sq km)
Vientiane (municipality)	3,920	650.6	166.0
Phongsali	16,270	189.7	11.7
Luang Namtha	9,325	142.4	15.3
Oudomxay	15,370	260.9	17.0
Bokeo	6,196	141.0	22.8
Luang Prabang	16,875	452.9	26.8
Houaphanh	16,500	303.7	18.4
Sayabouri	16,389	362.2	22.1
Xiangkhouang	15,880	249.0	15.7
Vientiane	15,927	373.2	23.4
Bolikhamsai	14,863	203.1	13.7
Khammouane	16,315	338.2	20.7
Savannakhet	21,774	833.9	38.3
Saravan	10,691	318.1	29.8
Sekong	7,665	79.7	10.4
Champasak	15,415	622.4	40.4
Attopu	10,320	108.3	10.5
Xaysomboun SR	7,105	49.6	7.0
Total	236,800	5,679.0	24.0

PRINCIPAL TOWNS
(population at 1995 census)

Viangchan (Vientiane—capital)	160,000	Xam Nua (Sam Neua)	33,500
Savannakhet (Khanthaboury)	58,500	Luang Prabang	25,500
Pakxe (Paksé)	47,000	Thakek (Khammouan)	22,500

Source: Stefan Helders, *World Gazetteer* (internet www.world-gazetteer.com).

Mid-2003 (UN estimate, incl. suburbs): Vientiane 716,380 (Source: UN, *World Urbanization Prospects: The 2003 Revision*).

BIRTHS AND DEATHS
(UN estimates, annual averages)

	1990–95	1995–2000	2000–05
Birth rate (per 1,000)	41.3	38.2	35.9
Death rate (per 1,000)	15.8	14.1	12.6

Source: UN, *World Population Prospects: The 2004 Revision*.

Expectation of life (WHO estimates, years at birth): 59 (males 58; females 60) in 2003 (Source: WHO, *World Health Report*).

ECONOMICALLY ACTIVE POPULATION
('000 persons at mid-1980, ILO estimates)

	Males	Females	Total
Agriculture, etc.	717	675	1,393
Industry	79	51	130
Services	193	123	316
Total labour force	990	849	1,839

Source: ILO, *Economically Active Population Estimates and Projections, 1950–2025*.

Mid-2003 (estimates in '000): Agriculture, etc. 2,168; Total labour force 2,854 (Source: FAO).

LAOS

Health and Welfare

KEY INDICATORS

Total fertility rate (children per woman, 2003)	4.7
Under-5 mortality rate (per 1,000 live births, 2004)	83
HIV/AIDS (% of persons aged 15–49, 2003)	0.1
Physicians (per 1,000 head, 1996)	0.59
Hospital beds (per 1,000 head, 1990)	2.57
Health expenditure (2002): US $ per head (PPP)	49
Health expenditure (2002): % of GDP	2.9
Health expenditure (2002): public (% of total)	50.9
Access to adequate water (% of persons, 2002)	43
Access to adequate sanitation (% of persons, 2002)	24
Human Development Index (2003): ranking	133
Human Development Index (2003): value	0.545

For sources and definitions, see explanatory note on p. vi.

Agriculture

PRINCIPAL CROPS
('000 metric tons)

	2002	2003	2004
Rice (paddy)	2,417	2,375	2,529
Maize	124	143	204
Potatoes	35*	36*	36†
Sweet potatoes	194	150	194†
Cassava (Manioc)	83	83†	56
Sugar cane	222	308	223
Vegetables	763	663	650†
Watermelons	83	85	85†
Cantaloupes and other melons†	33	36	36
Bananas†	53	55	46
Oranges†	29	28	28
Tangerines, mandarins, clementines and satsumas†	24	23	23
Pineapples†	36	36	36
Other fruit†	68	68	68
Coffee (green)	32	22	23
Tobacco (leaves)	27	26	33

* Unofficial figure.
† FAO estimate(s).
Source: FAO.

LIVESTOCK
('000 head, year ending September)

	2002	2003	2004
Horses*	30	31	31
Cattle	1,208	1,244	1,249
Buffaloes	1,089	1,111	1,112
Pigs	1,416	1,655	1,729
Goats	128	137	139
Chickens	15,274	19,474	14,000*
Ducks*	1,700	2,600	3,000

* FAO estimate(s).
Source: FAO.

LIVESTOCK PRODUCTS
('000 metric tons)

	2002	2003	2004*
Beef and veal	20.2	21.5	21.0
Buffalo meat	17.4	18.3	18.4
Pig meat	31.6	35.5	27.2
Poultry meat	13.1	17.6	14.4
Cows' milk*	6.0	6.0	6.0
Hen eggs	12.6	12.8	12.0
Cattle and buffalo hides (fresh)*	4.4	4.6	4.6

* FAO estimates.
Source: FAO.

Forestry

ROUNDWOOD REMOVALS
('000 cubic metres, excl. bark)

	2002	2003*	2004*
Sawlogs, veneer logs and logs for sleepers	260	260	260
Other industrial wood	132	132	132
Fuel wood	5,899	5,913	5,928
Total	6,291	6,305	6,320

* FAO estimates.
Source: FAO.

SAWNWOOD PRODUCTION
('000 cubic metres, incl. railway sleepers)

	2000	2001	2002
Total (all broadleaved)	208	227	182

2003–04: Output assumed to be unchanged from 2002 (FAO estimate).
Source: FAO.

Fishing

('000 metric tons, live weight)

	2001*	2002	2003
Capture	31.0	33.4*	29.8*
Cyprinids	4.7	5.0*	4.5*
Other freshwater fishes	26.4	28.4*	25.3*
Aquaculture	50.0	59.7*	64.9*
Common carp	12.5	14.9	16.2
Roho labeo	2.1	2.5*	2.7*
Mrigal carp	2.1	2.5*	2.7*
Bighead carp	2.9	3.5*	3.8*
Silver carp	2.9	3.5*	3.8*
Nile tilapia	22.5	26.9*	29.2*
Total catch	81.0	93.2*	94.7*

* FAO estimate(s).
Source: FAO.

Mining

('000 metric tons, unless otherwise indicated)

	2001	2002	2003*
Coal (all grades)	122.9	233.8	230.0
Gemstones ('000 carats)	—	200.0*	—
Gypsum	121.2	110.3	120.0
Salt	2.6	5.4	5.0
Tin (metric tons)†	490	366	360

* Estimated production.
† Figures refer to metal content.
Source: US Geological Survey.

Industry

SELECTED PRODUCTS

	2001	2002	2003
Beer ('000 hectolitres)	577	652	702
Soft drinks ('000 hectolitres)	142	148	164
Cigarettes (million packs)	41	55	68
Garments (million pieces)	32	33	34
Wood furniture (million kips)	15,240	15,350	15,550
Plastic products (metric tons)	4,350	4,420	4,530
Detergent (metric tons)	700	700	710
Agricultural tools ('000)	4	4	4
Nails (metric tons)	740	745	760
Bricks (million)	87	89	90
Hydroelectric energy (million kWh)	3,590	3,603	3,179
Tobacco (metric tons)	358	593	947
Plywood (million sheets)	2,200	2,250	1,550

Source: IMF, *Lao People's Democratic Republic: Selected Issues and Statistical Appendix* (January 2005).

Finance

CURRENCY AND EXCHANGE RATES

Monetary Units
100 at (cents) = 1 new kip.

Sterling, Dollar and Euro Equivalents (31 May 2005)
£1 sterling = 19,353.38 new kips;
US $1 = 10,855.00 new kips;
€1 = 13,240.92 new kips;
100,000 new kips = £5.16 = $9.21 = €7.55.

Average Exchange Rate (new kips per US $)
2002   10,056.3
2003   10,569.0
2004   10,585.5

Note: In September 1995 a policy of 'floating' exchange rates was adopted, with commercial banks permitted to set their rates.

GENERAL BUDGET
('000 million new kips, year ending 30 September)*

Revenue†	2001/02	2002/03	2003/04‡
Tax revenue	1,875	1,924	2,379
Profits tax	239	221	264
Income tax	125	140	164
Turnover tax	375	466	619
Excise tax	286	293	446
Import duties	240	316	380
Timber royalties	362	218	181
Other tax revenue	248	269	326
Non-tax revenue	449	417	437
Payment for depreciation or dividend transfers	84	87	85
Overflight	187	174	175
Other revenue	177	156	177
Total	2,324	2,341	2,817

Expenditure	2001/02	2002/03	2003/04‡
Current expenditure	1,483	1,647	2,082
Wages and salaries	547	668	872
Transfers	265	341	327
Interest	138	123	249
Other recurrent expenditure	533	514	634
Capital expenditure and net lending	1,785	2,370	2,179
Domestically-financed	995	1,026	837
Foreign-financed	931	1,499	1,456
Onlending (net)	−142	−156	−114
Total (incl. others)	3,268	4,017	4,261

* Since 1992 there has been a unified budget covering the operations of the central Government, provincial administrations and state enterprises.
† Excluding grants received ('000 million new kips): 238 in 2001/02; 453 in 2002/03; 465 in 2003/04 (estimate).
‡ Estimates.

Source: IMF, *Lao People's Democratic Republic: Selected Issues and Statistical Appendix* (January 2005).

INTERNATIONAL RESERVES
(US $ million at 31 December)

	2002	2003	2004
Gold (national valuation)	2.53	4.10	4.10
IMF special drawing rights	6.07	19.13	15.37
Foreign exchange	185.51	189.46	207.87
Total	194.12	212.69	227.35

Source: IMF, *International Financial Statistics*.

MONEY SUPPLY
(million new kips at 31 December*)

	2002	2003	2004
Currency outside banks	228,810	399,100	666,420
Demand deposits at commercial banks	358,150	437,290	537,540
Total (incl. others)	587,000	836,540	1,207,290

* Figures rounded to the nearest ten million.

Source: IMF, *International Financial Statistics*.

COST OF LIVING
(Consumer Price Index for Vientiane; base: 2000 = 100)

	2002	2003	2004
All items	119.3	137.7	152.2

Source: IMF, *International Financial Statistics*.

NATIONAL ACCOUNTS

Expenditure on the Gross Domestic Product
(million new kips at current prices)

	1989	1990	1991
Government final consumption expenditure	34,929	61,754	69,499
Private final consumption expenditure	414,639	558,437	647,826
Gross capital formation*	55,560	75,572	91,435
Total domestic expenditure	505,128	695,763	808,760
Exports of goods and services	49,421	69,411	73,359
Less Imports of goods and services	128,613	150,154	156,550
GDP in purchasers' values	425,936	615,020	725,569
GDP at constant 1987 prices	213,769	228,105	237,098

* Comprising gross fixed capital formation and increase in stocks.

Source: World Bank, *Historically Planned Economies: A Guide to the Data*.

LAOS

Statistical Survey

Gross Domestic Product by Economic Activity
(million new kips at current prices)

	2001	2002	2003
Agriculture, hunting, forestry and fishing	7,974,629	9,173,517	10,828,834
Mining and quarrying	73,150	89,114	378,238
Manufacturing	2,786,838	3,483,192	4,276,550
Electricity, gas and water	450,414	536,315	619,398
Construction	376,985	389,893	508,363
Wholesale and retail trade, restaurants and hotels	1,506,869	1,792,015	2,291,722
Transport, storage and communications	929,724	1,114,964	1,408,139
Finance, insurance, real estate and business services	127,836	75,979	99,487
Public administration	517,137	633,063	804,925
Other services	820,391	930,824	1,080,569
GDP at factor cost	15,563,971	18,218,874	22,296,225
Indirect taxes *less* subsidies	140,899	171,501	239,882
GDP in purchasers' values	15,704,870	18,390,375	22,536,107

Source: Asian Development Bank, *Key Indicators of Developing Asian and Pacific Countries*.

BALANCE OF PAYMENTS
(US $ million)

	2002	2003	2004
Exports of goods f.o.b.	300.6	335.5	361.1
Imports of goods c.i.f.	−446.9	−462.1	−505.9
Trade balance	−146.3	−126.6	−144.8
Services and other income (net)	118.0	43.5	86.1
Balance on goods, services and income	−28.3	−83.1	−58.7
Current transfers received	81.6	86.0	81.3
Current transfers paid	−76.8	−71.2	−40.6
Current balance	−23.5	−68.3	−18.0
Direct investment (net)	4.5	19.5	16.9
Other investments (net)	64.4	99.1	129.8
Net errors and omissions	−9.8	−55.7	−144.8
Overall balance	35.5	−5.4	−16.1

Source: Asian Development Bank, *Key Indicators of Developing Asian and Pacific Countries*.

External Trade

PRINCIPAL COMMODITIES
(US $ million)

Imports c.i.f.	2001	2002	2003*
Investment goods	182.3	209.6	231.2
Machinery and equipment	36.2	53.0	63.0
Vehicles†	27.3	27.7	33.4
Fuel†	57.9	57.9	60.8
Construction/electrical equipment	60.9	71.0	74.0
Consumption goods	280.1	280.1	304.0
Materials for garments industry	65.6	62.6	65.4
Gold and silver‡	5.4	8.1	6.9
Electricity	6.4	7.2	8.3
Fuel purchased abroad by Lao carriers	2.4	2.5	2.4
Total	542.2	570.1	618.2

* Estimates.
† Estimates based on the assumption that 50% of total are consumption goods.
‡ Includes gold for re-export.

Exports f.o.b.	2001	2002	2003*
Wood products	92.7	93.5	93.5
Coffee	14.9	17.1	18.7
Other agricultural products	8.6	9.9	9.4
Manufactures†	11.2	10.6	24.0
Garments	98.7	104.9	104.9
Electricity	106.4	103.6	91.0
Gold (incl. re-exports)	—	—	58.7
Fuel purchases by foreign carriers	1.1	0.8	0.8
Total	333.6	340.4	401.0

* Estimates.
† Excluding garments and wood products.

Source: IMF, *Lao People's Democratic Republic: Selected Issues and Statistical Appendix* (January 2005).

2004 (US $ million): *Imports:* Total 506; *Exports:* Wood products 67; Electricity 97; Coffee 14; Garments 97; Total (incl. others) 361 (Source: Asian Development Bank, *Key Indicators of Developing Asian and Pacific Countries*).

PRINCIPAL TRADING PARTNERS
(US $ million)

Imports	2002	2003	2004
Australia	12.6	7.9	18.3
China, People's Republic	59.7	108.1	97.2
France	8.9	11.8	10.5
Germany	4.1	7.5	26.7
Hong Kong	6.1	8.1	8.0
Japan	19.6	15.0	15.4
Korea, Republic	4.9	8.7	9.2
Singapore	29.1	22.4	42.3
Thailand*	444.0	501.5	639.4
Viet Nam	71.2	86.3	91.7
Total (incl. others)	727.5	838.7	1,057.7

Exports	2002	2003	2004
Belgium	13.6	18.0	13.4
China, People's Republic	8.8	10.2	12.4
France	33.8	33.6	43.2
Germany	22.0	23.6	30.6
Italy	10.1	10.3	11.2
Japan	6.1	6.7	7.3
Netherlands	10.6	10.4	10.0
Thailand*	85.0	94.3	104.3
United Kingdom	13.4	14.1	26.8
Viet Nam	56.9	72.0	90.2
Total (incl. others)	385.8	454.1	549.9

* Trade with Thailand may be overestimated, as it may include goods in transit to and from other countries.

Source: Asian Development Bank, *Key Indicators of Developing Asian and Pacific Countries*.

Transport

ROAD TRAFFIC
(motor vehicles in use at 31 December, estimates)

	1994	1995	1996
Passenger cars	18,240	17,280	16,320
Buses and coaches	440	n.a.	n.a.
Lorries and vans	7,920	6,020	4,200
Motorcycles and mopeds	169,000	200,000	231,000

Source: International Road Federation, *World Road Statistics*.

LAOS

SHIPPING

Inland Waterways
(traffic)

	1993	1994	1995
Freight ('000 metric tons)	290	876	898
Freight ton-kilometres (million)	18.7	40.8	98.8
Passengers ('000)	703	898	652
Passenger-kilometres (million)	110.2	60.6	24.3

Source: Ministry of Communications, Transport, Post and Construction.

Merchant Fleet
(registered at 31 December)

	2002	2003	2004
Number of vessels	1	1	1
Displacement ('000 grt)	2.4	2.4	2.4

Source: Lloyd's Register-Fairplay, *World Fleet Statistics*.

CIVIL AVIATION
(traffic on scheduled services)

	1999	2000	2001
Kilometres flown (million)	2	2	2
Passengers carried ('000)	197	211	211
Passenger-kilometres (million)	78	85	86
Total ton-kilometres (million)	8	9	9

Source: UN, *Statistical Yearbook*.

Tourism

FOREIGN VISITOR ARRIVALS
(incl. excursionists)

Country of nationality	2001	2002	2003
China, People's Republic	40,644	21,724	21,232
France	21,662	26,748	23,958
Japan	15,547	19,801	17,766
Thailand	376,685	422,766	377,748
United Kingdom	15,722	21,749	22,541
USA	25,779	35,734	30,133
Viet Nam	82,411	71,001	41,594
Total (incl. others)	673,823	735,662	636,361

Tourism receipts (US $ million, excl. passenger transport): 104 in 2001; 113 in 2002; 87 in 2003.

Source: World Tourism Organization.

Communications Media

	2002	2003	2004
Telephones ('000 main lines in use)	61.9	69.8	75.0
Mobile cellular telephones ('000 subscribers)	55.2	112.3	204.2
Personal computers ('000 in use)	18	20	22
Internet users ('000)	15.0	19.0	20.9

Radio receivers ('000 in use): 730 in 1997.
Television receivers ('000 in use): 280 in 2001.
Facsimile machines (estimated number in use): 500 in 1994 (Source: UN, *Statistical Yearbook*).
Book production (1995): Titles 88; copies ('000) 995.
Daily newspapers (1996): 3 (average circulation 18,000).
Non-daily newspapers (1988, estimates): 4 (average circulation 20,000).

Sources (unless otherwise specified): International Telecommunication Union; UNESCO, *Statistical Yearbook*.

Education

(1996/97)

	Institutions	Teachers	Males	Females	Total
Pre-primary	695	2,173	18,502	19,349	37,851
Primary	7,896	25,831	438,241	348,094	786,335
Secondary:					
general	n.a.	10,717	108,996	71,164	180,160
vocational*	n.a.	808	3,731	1,928	5,659
teacher training	n.a.	197	960	780	1,740
University level	n.a.	456	3,509	1,764	5,273
Other higher	n.a.	913	5,378	2,081	7,459

* Data for 1995/96.

Source: UNESCO, *Statistical Yearbook*.

2002/03: *Primary:* Students 852,857; Teachers 28,404; Institutions 8,432. *Secondary:* Students 315,733 (Lower secondary level 213,471, Upper secondary level 102,262); Teachers 12,867; Institutions 858. *Tertiary:* Students 26,640; Teachers 1,725; Institutions 12 (Source: Ministry of Education, Vientiane).

2003/04: *Pre-primary:* Students 38,979; Teachers 2,377; Creches 820; Classrooms 1,565. *Primary:* Students 875,300; Teachers 28,571; Institutions 8,486. *Secondary:* Students 348,309 (Lower secondary level 229,023, Upper secondary level 119,286); Teachers 13,358; Institutions 879. *Tertiary:* Students 31,929; Teachers 1,740; Institutions 12 (Source: Ministry of Education, Vientiane).

Adult literacy rate (UNESCO estimates): 68.7% (males 77.0%; females 60.9%) in 2003 (Source: UN Development Programme, *Human Development Report*).

Directory

The Constitution

The new Constitution was unanimously endorsed by the Supreme People's Assembly on 14 August 1991. Its main provisions are summarized below:

POLITICAL SYSTEM

The Lao People's Democratic Republic (Lao PDR) is an independent, sovereign and united country and is indivisible.

The Lao PDR is a people's democratic state. The people's rights are exercised and ensured through the functioning of the political system, with the Lao People's Revolutionary Party as its leading organ. The people exercise power through the National Assembly, which functions in accordance with the principle of democratic centralism.

The State respects and protects all lawful activities of Buddhism and the followers of other religious faiths.

The Lao PDR pursues a foreign policy of peace, independence, friendship and co-operation. It adheres to the principles of peaceful co-existence with other countries, based on mutual respect for independence, sovereignty and territorial integrity.

SOCIO-ECONOMIC SYSTEM

The economy is market-orientated, with intervention by the State. The State encourages all economic sectors to compete and co-operate in the expansion of production and trade.

Private ownership of property and rights of inheritance are protected by the State.

The State authorizes the operation of private schools and medical services, while promoting the expansion of public education and health services.

FUNDAMENTAL RIGHTS AND OBLIGATIONS OF CITIZENS

Lao citizens, irrespective of their sex, social status, education, faith and ethnic group, are equal before the law.

Lao citizens aged 18 years and above have the right to vote, and those over 21 years to be candidates, in elections.

Lao citizens have freedom of religion, speech, press and assembly, and freedom to establish associations and to participate in demonstrations which do not contradict the law.

THE NATIONAL ASSEMBLY

The National Assembly is the legislative organ, which also oversees the activities of the administration and the judiciary. Members of the National Assembly are elected for a period of five years by universal adult suffrage. The National Assembly elects its own Standing Committee, which consists of the Chairman and Vice-Chairman of the National Assembly (and thus also of the National Assembly Standing Committee) and a number of other members. The National Assembly convenes its ordinary session twice annually. The National Assembly Standing Committee may convene an extraordinary session of the National Assembly if it deems this necessary. The National Assembly is empowered to amend the Constitution; to endorse, amend or abrogate laws; to elect or remove the President of State and Vice-Presidents of State, as proposed by the Standing Committee of the National Assembly; to adopt motions expressing 'no confidence' in the Government; to elect or remove the President of the People's Supreme Court, on the recommendation of the National Assembly Standing Committee.

THE PRESIDENT OF STATE

The President of State, who is also Head of the Armed Forces, is elected by the National Assembly for a five-year tenure. Laws adopted by the National Assembly must be promulgated by the President of State not later than 30 days after their enactment. The President is empowered to appoint or dismiss the Prime Minister and members of the Government, with the approval of the National Assembly; to appoint government officials at provincial and municipal levels; and to promote military personnel, on the recommendation of the Prime Minister.

THE GOVERNMENT

The Government is the administrative organ of the State. It is composed of the Prime Minister, Deputy Prime Ministers and Ministers or Chairmen of Committees (which are equivalent to Ministries), who are appointed by the President, with the approval of the National Assembly, for a term of five years. The Government implements the Constitution, laws and resolutions adopted by the National Assembly and state decrees and acts of the President of State. The Prime Minister is empowered to appoint Deputy Ministers and Vice-Chairmen of Committees, and lower-level government officials.

LOCAL ADMINISTRATION

The Lao PDR is divided into provinces, municipalities, districts and villages. Provincial governors and mayors of municipalities are appointed by the President of State. Deputy provincial governors, deputy mayors and district chiefs are appointed by the Prime Minister. Administration at village level is conducted by village heads.

THE JUDICIARY

The people's courts comprise the People's Supreme Court, the people's provincial and municipal courts, the people's district courts and military courts. The President of the People's Supreme Court and the Public Prosecutor-General are elected by the National Assembly, on the recommendation of the National Assembly Standing Committee. The Vice-President of the People's Supreme Court and the judges of the people's courts at all levels are appointed by the National Assembly Standing Committee.

The Government

HEAD OF STATE

President of State: Gen. KHAMTAY SIPHANDONE (took office February 1998).

Vice-President: Lt-Gen. CHOUMMALI SAIGNASON.

COUNCIL OF MINISTERS
(April 2006)

Prime Minister: BOUNGNANG VOLACHIT.

Deputy Prime Minister and President of the State Planning Committee: THONGLOUN SISOLIT.

Deputy Prime Minister and Minister of Foreign Affairs: SOMSAVAT LENGSAVAT.

Deputy Prime Ministers: Maj.-Gen. ASANG LAOLI, BOUASONE BOUPHAVANH.

Minister of National Defence: Maj.-Gen. DOUANGCHAI PHICHIT.

Minister of Finance: CHANSY PHOSIKHAM.

Minister of Security: Maj.-Gen. SOUDCHAI THAMMASITH.

Minister of Justice: KHAMOUANE BOUPHA.

Minister of Agriculture and Forestry: SIANE SAPHANTHONG.

Minister of Communications, Transport, Post and Construction: BOUATHONG VONGLOKHAM.

Minister of Industry and Handicrafts: ONNEUA PHOMMACHANH.

Minister of Commerce and Tourism: SOULIVONG DARAVONG.

Minister of Information and Culture: PHANDOUANGCHIT VONGSA.

Minister of Labour and Social Welfare: LE KAKANHYA.

Minister of Education: PHIMMASONE LEUANGKHAMMA.

Minister of Public Health: Dr PONEMEKH DARALOY.

Minister to the Office of the President: SOUBANH SRITHIRATH.

Ministers to the Office of the Prime Minister: BOUNTIEM PHITSAMAI, SOULI NANTHAVONG, SAISENGLI TENGBIACHU, SOMPHONG MONGKHONVILAY, VENTHONG LUANGVILAY.

MINISTRIES

Office of the President: rue Lane Xang, Vientiane; tel. (21) 214200; fax (21) 214208.

Office of the Prime Minister: Ban Sisavat, Vientiane; tel. (21) 213653; fax (21) 213560.

Ministry of Agriculture and Forestry: Ban Phonxay, Vientiane; tel. (21) 412359; fax (21) 412344; internet www.maf.gov.la.

Ministry of Commerce and Tourism: Ban Phonxay, Muang Saysettha, BP 4107, Vientiane; tel. (21) 911342; fax (21) 412434; e-mail citd@moc.gov.la; internet www.moc.gov.la.

Ministry of Communications, Transport, Post and Construction: ave Lane Xang, Vientiane; tel. (21) 412251; fax (21) 414123.

Ministry of Education: BP 67, Vientiane; tel. (21) 216004; fax (21) 212108.

Ministry of Finance: rue That Luang, Ban Phonxay, Vientiane; tel. (21) 412401; fax (21) 412415.

Ministry of Foreign Affairs: rue That Luang 01004, Ban Phonxay, Vientiane; tel. (21) 413148; fax (21) 414009; e-mail souknivone@mofa.gov.la; internet www.mofa.gov.la.

Ministry of Industry and Handicrafts: rue Nongbone, Ban Phai, BP 4708, Vientiane; tel. (21) 416718; fax (21) 413005; e-mail mihplan@laotel.com.

Ministry of Information and Culture: rue Sethathirath, Ban Xiengnheun, Vientiane; tel. (21) 212897; fax (21) 212408; e-mail email@mic.gov.la; internet www.mic.gov.la.

Ministry of Justice: Ban Phonxay, Vientiane; tel. (21) 414105.

Ministry of Labour and Social Welfare: rue Pangkham, Ban Sisaket, Vientiane; tel. (21) 213003.

Ministry of National Defence: rue Phone Kheng, Ban Phone Kheng, Vientiane; tel. (21) 412803.

Ministry of Public Health: Ban Simeuang, Vientiane; tel. (21) 214002; fax (21) 214001; e-mail cabinet.fr@moh.gov.la.

Ministry of Security: rue Nongbone, Ban Hatsady, Vientiane; tel. (21) 212500.

Legislature

At the election held on 30 April 2006 some 113 candidates of the Lao People's Revolutionary Party (LPRP) and two independents were elected to the National Assembly. (All but three candidates contesting the elections were members of the LPRP.)

President of the National Assembly: Lt-Gen. SAMAN VIGNAKET.

Vice-President: PANY YATHOTU.

Political Organizations

COMMUNIST PARTY

Phak Pasason Pativat Lao (Lao People's Revolutionary Party—LPRP): Vientiane; f. 1955 as the People's Party of Laos; reorg. under present name in 1972; Cen. Cttee of 55 full mems elected at Eighth Party Congress in March 2006; Gen. Sec. Lt-Gen. CHOUMMALI SAIGNASON.

Political Bureau (Politburo)

Full members: Lt-Gen. CHOUMMALI SAIGNASON, Lt-Gen. SAMAN VIGNAKET, THONGSIN THAMMAVONG, BOUNGNANG VOLACHIT, Gen. SISAVAT KEOBOUNPHAN, Maj.-Gen. ASANG LAOLI, THOUNGLONG SISOLIT, Maj.-Gen. DOUANGCHAI PHICHIT, BOUASONE BOUPHAVANH, SOMSAVAT LENGSAVAT, PHANI YATHOTHU.

OTHER POLITICAL ORGANIZATIONS

Lao Front for National Construction (LFNC): BP 1828, Vientiane; f. 1979 to replace the Lao Liberal Front and the Lao Patriotic Front; comprises representatives of various political and social groups, of which the LPRP (see above) is the dominant force; fosters national solidarity; Chair. Gen. SISAVAT KEOBOUNPHANH; Vice-Chair. SIHO BANNAVONG, KHAMPHOUI CHANTHASOUK, TONG YEUTHOR.

Numerous factions are in armed opposition to the Government. The principal groups are:

Democratic Chao Fa Party of Laos: led by Pa Kao Her until his death in Oct. 2002; Pres. SOUA HER; Vice-Pres. TENG TANG.

Free Democratic Lao National Salvation Force: based in Thailand.

United Front for the Liberation of Laos: Leader PHOUNGPHET PHANARETH.

United Front for the National Liberation of the Lao People: f. 1980; led by Gen. PHOUMI NOSAVAN until his death in 1985.

United Lao National Liberation Front: Sayabouri Province; comprises an estimated 8,000 members, mostly Hmong (Meo) tribesmen; Sec.-Gen. VANG SHUR.

Diplomatic Representation

EMBASSIES IN LAOS

Australia: rue Pandit J. Nehru, quartier Phonxay, BP 292, Vientiane; tel. (21) 413600; fax (21) 413601; internet www.laos.embassy.gov.au; Ambassador ALISTAIR CHARLES MACLEAN.

Brunei: 333 Unit 25, Ban Phonxay, Muang Xaysettha, Vientiane; tel. (21) 416114; fax (21) 416115; e-mail embdlaos@laonet.com; Ambassador Pengiran Haji HAMDAN BIN Haji ISMAIL.

Cambodia: rue Thadeua, Km 3, BP 34, Vientiane; tel. (21) 314952; fax (21) 314951; e-mail recamlao@laotel.com; Ambassador HUOT PHAL.

China, People's Republic: rue Wat Nak, Muang Sisattanak, BP 898, Vientiane; tel. (21) 315100; fax (21) 315104; e-mail embassyprc@laonet.net; Ambassador LIU YONGXING.

Cuba: Ban Saphanthong Neua 128, BP 1017, Vientiane; tel. (21) 314902; fax (21) 314901; e-mail embacuba@laonet.net; Ambassador EDUARDO VALIDO GARCÍA.

France: rue Sethathirath, BP 06, Vientiane; tel. (21) 215253; fax (21) 215250; e-mail contact@ambafrance-laos.org; internet www.ambafrance-laos.org; Ambassador MAURICE PORTICHE.

Germany: rue Sok Paluang 26, Muang Sisattanak, BP 314, Vientiane; tel. (21) 312110; fax (21) 351152; e-mail info@vien.diplo.de; Ambassador ERWIN STARNITZKY.

India: 2 Ban Wat Nak, rue Thadeua, Km 3, Sisattanak District, Vientiane; tel. (21) 352301; fax (21) 352300; e-mail indiaemb@laotel.com; internet www.indianembassylao.com; Ambassador TSEWANG TOPDEN.

Indonesia: ave Phone Keng, BP 277, Vientiane; tel. (21) 413909; fax (21) 214828; e-mail kbrivte@laotel.com; Ambassador ZAINUDDIN NASUTION.

Japan: rue Sisangvone, Vientiane; tel. (21) 414401; fax (21) 414406; Ambassador MAKOTO KATSURA.

Korea, Democratic People's Republic: quartier Wat Nak, Vientiane; tel. (21) 315261; fax (21) 315260; Ambassador PAK MYONG-GU.

Korea, Republic: rue Lao-Thai Friendship, Ban Wat Nak, Sisattanak District, BP 7567, Vientiane; tel. (21) 415833; fax (21) 415831; e-mail koramb@laotel.com; Ambassador CHANG CHUL-KYOON.

Malaysia: rue That Luang, quartier Pholnxay, BP 789, Vientiane; tel. (21) 414205; fax (21) 414201; e-mail mwvntian@laopdr.com; Ambassador AHMAD RASIDI BIN HAZIZI.

Mongolia: rue Wat Nak, Km 3, BP 370, Vientiane; tel. (21) 315220; fax (21) 315221; e-mail embmong@laotel.com; Ambassador N. ALIASUREN.

Myanmar: Ban Thong Kang, rue Sok Palaung, BP 11, Vientiane; tel. (21) 314910; fax (21) 314913; e-mail mev@loxinfo.co.th; Ambassador U TIN OO.

Philippines: Ban Phonsinuane, Sisattanak, BP 2415, Vientiane; tel. (21) 452490; fax (21) 452493; e-mail pelaopdr@laotel.com; Ambassador ELIZABETH P. BUENSUCESO.

Poland: 263 Ban Thadeua, Km 3, quartier Wat Nak, BP 1106, Vientiane; tel. (21) 312940; fax (21) 312085; e-mail polembv@yahoo.com; Chargé d'affaires Dr TOMASZ GERLACH.

Russia: Ban Thadeua, quartier Thaphalanxay, BP 490, Vientiane; tel. (21) 312222; fax (21) 312210; e-mail rusemb@laotel.com; Ambassador YURII RAIKOV.

Singapore: Unit 12, Ban Naxay, rue Nong Bong, Muang Sat Settha, Vientiane; tel. (21) 416860; fax (21) 416854; e-mail singemb_vte@sgmfa.gov.sg; internet www.mfa.gov.sg/vientiane; Ambassador KAREN TAN.

Thailand: ave Phone Keng, Vientiane; tel. (21) 214581; fax (21) 214580; e-mail thaivtn@mfa.go.th; Ambassador RATHAKIT MANATHAT.

USA: 19 rue Bartholonie, BP 114, That Dam, Vientiane; tel. (21) 267000; fax (21) 267190; e-mail khammanhpx@state.gov; internet usembassy.state.gov/laos; Ambassador PATRICIA HASLACH.

Viet Nam: 85 rue That Luang, Vientiane; tel. (21) 413409; fax (21) 413379; e-mail dsqvn@laotel.com; Ambassador HUYNH ANH DUNG.

Judicial System

President of the People's Supreme Court: KHAMMY SAYAVONG.

Vice-President: DAVON VANGVICHIT.

People's Supreme Court Judges: NOUANTHONG VONGSA, NHOTSENG LITTHIDETH, PHOUKHONG CHANTHALATH, SENGSOUVANH CHANTHALOUNNAVONG, KESON PHANLACK, KONGCHI YANGCHY, KHAMPON PHASAIGNAVONG.

Public Prosecutor-General: KHAMPANE PHILAVONG.

Religion

The 1991 Constitution guarantees freedom of religious belief. The principal religion of Laos is Buddhism.

BUDDHISM

Lao Unified Buddhists' Association: Maha Kudy, Wat That Luang, Vientiane; f. 1964; Pres. (vacant); Sec.-Gen. Rev. SIHO SIHAVONG.

CHRISTIANITY

The Roman Catholic Church

For ecclesiastical purposes, Laos comprises four Apostolic Vicariates. At 31 December 2003 an estimated 0.6% of the population were adherents.

Episcopal Conference of Laos and Cambodia

c/o Mgr Pierre Bach, Paris Foreign Missions, 254 Silom Rd, Bangkok 10500, Thailand; f. 1971; Pres. Mgr JEAN KHAMSÉ VITHAVONG (Titular Bishop of Moglaena, Vicar Apostolic of Vientiane).

Vicar Apostolic of Luang Prabang: (vacant), Evêché, BP 113, Luang Prabang.

Vicar Apostolic of Paksé: Mgr LOUIS-MARIE LING MANGKHANEKHOUN (Titular Bishop of Proconsulari), Centre Catholique, BP 77, Paksé, Champasak; tel. (31) 212879; fax (31) 251439.

Vicar Apostolic of Savannakhet: Mgr JEAN SOMMENG VORACHAK (Titular Bishop of Muzuca in Proconsulari), Centre Catholique, BP 12, Thakhek, Khammouane; tel. (51) 212184; fax (51) 213070.

Vicar Apostolic of Vientiane: Mgr JEAN KHAMSÉ VITHAVONG (Titular Bishop of Moglaena), Centre Catholique, BP 113, Vientiane; tel. (21) 216593; fax (21) 215085.

The Anglican Communion

Laos is within the jurisdiction of the Anglican Bishop of Singapore.

The Protestant Church

Lao Evangelical Church: BP 4200, Vientiane; tel. (21) 169136; Exec. Pres. Rev. KHAMPHONE KOUTHAPANYA.

LAOS   Directory

BAHÁ'Í FAITH

National Spiritual Assembly: BP 189, Vientiane; tel. and fax (21) 216996; e-mail usme@laotel.com; f. 1956; Sec. SUSADA SENCHANTHISAY.

The Press

Aloun Mai (New Dawn): Vientiane; f. 1985; quarterly; theoretical and political organ of the LPRP.

Finance: rue That Luang, Ban Phonxay, Vientiane; tel. (21) 412401; fax (21) 412415; organ of Ministry of Finance.

Heng Ngan: 87 ave Lane Xang, BP 780, Vientiane; tel. (21) 212750; fortnightly; organ of the Federation of Lao Trade Unions; Editor BOUAPHENG BOUNSOULINH.

Lao Dong (Labour): 87 ave Lane Xang, Vientiane; f. 1986; fortnightly; organ of the Federation of Lao Trade Unions; circ. 46,000.

Laos: 80 rue Setthathirath, BP 3770, Vientiane; tel. (21) 21447; fax (21) 21445; internet www.laolink.com; quarterly; published in Lao and English; illustrated; Editor V. PHOMCHANHEUANG; English Editor O. PHRAKHAMSAY.

Meying Lao: rue Manthatoarath, BP 59, Vientiane; e-mail chansoda@hotmail.com; f. 1980; monthly; women's magazine; organ of the Lao Women's Union; Editor-in-Chief VATSADY KHUTNGOTHA; Editor CHANSODA PHONETHIP; circ. 7,000.

Noum Lao (Lao Youth): Vientiane; f. 1979; fortnightly; organ of the Lao People's Revolutionary Youth Union; Editor DOUANGDY INTHAVONG; circ. 6,000.

Pasason Van Athit: Vientiane; weekly; circ. 2,000.

Pasaxon (The People): 80 rue Setthathirath, BP 110, Vientiane; tel. (21) 212466; fax (21) 212470; e-mail infonews@pasaxon.org.la; internet www.pasaxon.org.la; f. 1940; daily; Lao; organ of the Cen. Cttee of the LPRP; Editor BOUABAN VOLAKHOUN; circ. 28,000.

Pathet Lao: 80 rue Setthathirath, Vientiane; tel. (21) 215402; fax (21) 212446; f. 1979; monthly; Lao and English; organ of Khao San Pathet Lao (KPL); Dep. Dir SOUNTHONE KHANTHAVONG.

Sciences and Technics: Science, Technology and the Environment Agency (STEA), BP 2279, Vientiane; f. 1991; as Technical Science Magazine; quarterly; organ of the Dept of Science and Technology; scientific research and development.

Siang Khong Gnaovason Song Thanva (Voice of the 2nd December Youths): Vientiane; monthly; youth journal.

Sieng Khene Lao: Vientiane; monthly; organ of the Lao Writers' Association.

Suksa Mai: Vientiane; monthly; organ of the Ministry of Education.

Valasan Khosana (Propaganda Journal): Vientiane; f. 1987; organ of the Cen. Cttee of the LPRP.

Vannasinh: Vientiane; monthly; literature magazine.

Vientiane Mai (New Vientiane): 36 rue Setthathirath, BP 989, Vientiane; tel. (21) 212623; fax (21) 215989; f. 1975; morning daily; organ of the LPRP Cttee of Vientiane province and city; Editor SICHANE (acting); circ. 2,500.

Vientiane Times: rue Pangkham, BP 5723, Vientiane; tel. (21) 216364; fax (21) 216365; e-mail info@vientianetimes.gov.la; internet www.vientianetimes.org.la; f. 1994; daily; English; emphasis on investment opportunities; Editor-in-Chief SAVANKHONE RAZMOUNTRY; circ. 3,000.

Vientiane Tulakit (Vientiane Business-Social): rue Setthathirath, Vientiane; tel. (21) 2623; fax (21) 6365; weekly; circ. 2,000.

There is also a newspaper published by the Lao People's Army, and several provinces have their own newsletters.

NEWS AGENCIES

Khao San Pathet Lao (Lao News Agency—KPL): 80 rue Setthathirath, BP 3770, Vientiane; tel. (21) 215090; fax (210 212446; e-mail kplnews@yahoo.com; internet www.kplnet.net; f. 1968; organ of the Ministry of Information and Culture; news service for press, radio and television broadcasting; daily bulletins in Lao, English and French; Gen. Dir KHAMSENE PHONGSA; English Editor BOUNLERT LOUANEDOUANGCHANH.

Foreign Bureaux

Rossiiskoye Informatsionnoye Agentstvo—Novosti (RIA—Novosti) (Russia): Vientiane; tel. (21) 213510; f. 1963.

Viet Nam News Agency (VNA): Vientiane; Chief DO VAN PHUONG.

Reuters (UK) is also represented in Laos.

PRESS ASSOCIATION

The Journalists' Association of the Lao PDR: BP 122, Vientiane; tel. (21) 212420; fax (21) 212408; Pres. BOUABANE VORAKHOUNE; Sec.-Gen. KHAM KHONG KONGVONGSA.

Publishers

Khoualuang Kanphim: 2–6 Khoualuang Market, Vientiane.

Lao-phanit: Ministry of Education, Bureau des Manuels Scolaires, rue Lane Xang, Ban Sisavat, Vientiane; educational, cookery, art, music, fiction.

Pakpassak Kanphin: 9–11 quai Fa-Hguun, Vientiane.

State Printing Enterprise: 314/C rue Samsemthai, BP 2160, Vientiane; tel. (21) 213273; fax (21) 215901; Dir NOUPHAY KOUNLAVONG.

Broadcasting and Communications

TELECOMMUNICATIONS

Entreprises des Postes et Télécommunications de Laos: ave Lane Xang, 01000 Vientiane; tel. (21) 215767; fax (21) 212779; e-mail laoposts@laotel.com; state enterprise, responsible for the postal service and telecommunications; Dir-Gen. KIENG KHAMKETH.

Lao Télécommunications Co Ltd: ave Lane Xang, BP 5607, 0100 Vientiane; tel. (21) 216465; fax (21) 219690; e-mail marketin@laotel.com; internet www.laotel.com; f. 1996; a jt venture between a subsidiary of the Shinawatra Group of Thailand and Entreprises des Postes et Télécommunications de Laos; awarded a 25-year contract by the Government in 1996 to undertake all telecommunications projects in the country; Dir-Gen. HOUMPHANH INTHARATH.

BROADCASTING

Radio

In addition to the national radio service, there are several local stations.

Lao National Radio: rue Phangkham, Km 6, BP 310, Vientiane; tel. (21) 212468; fax (21) 212430; e-mail laonradio@lnr.org.la; internet www.lnr.org.la; f. 1960; state-owned; programmes in Lao, French, English, Thai, Khmer and Vietnamese; domestic and international services; Dir-Gen. BOUNTHANH INTHAXAY.

In 1990 resistance forces in Laos established an illegal radio station, broadcasting anti-Government propaganda: Satthani Vithayou Kachai Siang Latthaban Potpoi Sat Lao (Radio Station of the Government for the Liberation of the Lao Nation): programmes in Lao and Hmong languages; broadcasts four hours daily.

Television

A domestic television service began in December 1983. In May 1988 a second national television station commenced transmissions from Savannakhet. In December 1993 the Ministry of Information and Culture signed a 15-year joint-venture contract with a Thai firm on the development of broadcasting services in Laos. Under the resultant International Broadcasting Corporation Lao Co Ltd, IBC Channel 3 was inaugurated in 1994 (see below).

Lao National Television (TVNL): rue Chommany Neua, Km 6, BP 5635, Vientiane; tel. (21) 413767; fax (21) 710182; e-mail lntv@laotel.com; f. 1983; colour television service; Dir-Gen. BOUASONE PHONGPHAVANH.

Laos Television 3: BP 860, Vientiane; tel. (21) 315449; fax (21) 215628; operated by the International Broadcasting Corpn Lao Co Ltd; f. 1994 as IBC Channel 3; 30% govt-owned, 70% owned by the International Broadcasting Corpn Co Ltd of Thailand; programmes in Lao.

Finance

(cap. = capital; dep. = deposits; br.(s) = branch(es); m. = million)

BANKING

The banking system was reorganized in 1988–89, ending the state monopoly of banking. Some commercial banking functions were transferred from the central bank and the state commercial bank to a new network of autonomous banks. The establishment of joint ventures with foreign financial institutions was permitted. Foreign banks have been permitted to open branches in Laos since 1992. In 1998 there were nine private commercial banks in Laos, most of them Thai. In March 1999 the Government consolidated six state-owned

LAOS

banks into two new institutions—Lane Xang Bank Ltd and Lao May Bank Ltd; these merged in 2001.

Central Bank

Banque de la RDP Lao: rue Yonnet, BP 19, Vientiane; tel. (21) 213109; fax (21) 213108; e-mail bol@pan-laos.net.la; f. 1959 as the bank of issue; became Banque Pathetlao 1968; took over the operations of Banque Nationale du Laos 1975; known as Banque d'Etat de la RDP Lao from 1982 until adoption of present name; dep. 394,017m. kips, total assets US 361m. (Dec. 2002); Gov. PHOUMI THIPPHAVONE.

Commercial Banks

Agriculture Promotion Bank: 58 rue Hengboun, Ban Haysok, BP 5456, Vientiane; tel. (21) 212024; fax (21) 213957; e-mail apblaopdr@laonet.net; Man. Dir BOUNSONG SOMMALAVONG.

Banque pour le Commerce Extérieur Lao (BCEL): 1 rue Pangkham, BP 2925, Vientiane; tel. (21) 213200; fax (21) 213202; e-mail bcelhovt@etllao.com; internet www.bcellaos.com; f. 1975; 100% state-owned; Chair. AKSONE BOUPHAKONEKHAM; Gen. Dir SONOXAY SITHPHAXAY.

Joint Development Bank: 75/1–5 ave Lane Xang, BP 3187, Vientiane; tel. (21) 213532; fax (21) 213530; e-mail jdb@jdbbank.com; internet www.jdbbank.com; f. 1989; the first joint-venture bank between Laos and a foreign partner; 30% owned by Banque de la RDP Lao, 70% owned by Thai company, Phrom Suwan Silo and Drying Co Ltd; cap. US $4m.

Lao May Bank Ltd: 39 rue Pangkham, BP 2700, Vientiane; tel. (21) 213300; fax (21) 213340; f. 1999 as a result of the consolidation by the Government of ParkTai Bank, Lao May Bank and Nakornluang Bank; merged with Lane Xang Bank Ltd in 2001.

Lao-Viet Bank (LVB): 5 ave Lane Xang, Ban Hatsady, Chanthaboury, Vientiane; tel. (21) 216316; fax (21) 212197; e-mail lvbho@laotel.com; internet www.laovietbank.com; f. 1999; joint venture between BCEL and the Bank for Investment and Development of Vietnam.

Vientiane Commercial Bank Ltd: 33 ave Lane Xang, Ban Hatsady, Chanthaboury, Vientiane; tel. (21) 222700; fax (21) 213513; e-mail vccbank@laotel.com; f. 1993; privately-owned joint venture by Laotian, Thai, Taiwanese and Australian investors; Man. Dir SOP SISOMPHOU.

Foreign Banks

Bangkok Bank Public Co Ltd (Thailand): 38/13–15 rue Hatsady, BP 5400, Vientiane; tel. (21) 213560; fax (21) 213561; e-mail bblvte@laotel.com; f. 1993; Man. THEWAKUN CHANAKUN.

Bank of Ayudhya Public Co Ltd (Thailand): Unit 17, 79/6 ave Lane Xang, BP 5072, Vientiane; tel. (21) 213521; fax (21) 213520; e-mail baylaos@laotel.com; f. 1994; Man. SUWAT TANTIPATANASAKUL.

Krung Thai Bank Public Co Ltd (Thailand): Unit 21, 80 ave Lane Xang, Ban Xieng-yeun Thong, Chanthaboury, Vientiane; tel. (21) 213480; fax (21) 222762; e-mail ktblao@laotel.com; internet www.ktb.co.th/; f. 1993; Gen. Man. SONCHAI KANOKPETCH; COO THIRAWAT CHAROENTHAMASUK.

Public Bank Berhad (Malaysia): 100/1–4 rue Talat Sao, BP 6614, Vientiane; tel. (21) 216614; fax (21) 222743; e-mail pbbvte@laotel.com; Gen. Man. SIA KYUN MIN.

Siam Commercial Bank Public Co Ltd (Thailand): 117 ave Lane Xang-Samsenethai, BP 4809, Ban Sisaket Mouang, Chanthaboury, Vientiane; tel. (21) 213500; fax (21) 213502; Gen. Man. CHARANYA DISSAMARN.

Standard Chartered Bank ((United Kingdom)): 08/3 rue Lane Xang, Ban Hatsady, Chanthaboury, BP 6895, Vientiane; tel. (21) 222251; fax (21) 217254.

Thai Military Bank Public Co Ltd: 69 rue Khoun Boulom, Chanthaboury, BP 2423, Vientiane; tel. (21) 217174; fax (21) 216486; e-mail tmbvte@laotel.com; the first foreign bank to be represented in Laos; Man. AMNAT KOSKTPON.

INSURANCE

Assurances Générales du Laos (AGL): Vientiane Commercial Bank Bldg, ave Lane Xang, BP 4223, Vientiane; tel. (21) 215903; fax (21) 215904; e-mail agl@agl-allianz.com; internet www.agl-allianz.com; f. 1990; jt venture between Lao Govt (49%) and Assurances Générales de France (51%); sole licensed insurance co in Laos; Group Chair. Dr MICHAEL DIEKMANN; Man. Dir PHILIPPE ROBINEAU.

Trade and Industry

GOVERNMENT AGENCY

National Economic Research Institute (NERI): rue Luang Prabang, Sithanneua, Vientiane; tel. (21) 351369; fax (21) 216660; e-mail neri@pan-laos.net; govt policy development unit; Dir SOUPHAN KEOMISAY.

DEVELOPMENT ORGANIZATIONS

Department of Domestic and Foreign Investment (DDFI): rue Luang Prabang, 01001 Vientiane; tel. (21) 226290; fax (21) 215491; e-mail fimc@laotel.com; internet invest.laopdr.org; fmrly Foreign Investment Management Committee (FIMC); provides information and assistance to existing and potential investors.

Department of Livestock and Fisheries: Ministry of Agriculture and Forestry, Ban Phonxay, BP 811, Vientiane; tel. (21) 416932; fax (21) 415674; e-mail eulaodlf@laotel.com; public enterprise; imports and markets agricultural commodities; produces and distributes feed and animals; Dir-Gen. SINGKHAM PHONVISAY.

State Committee for State Planning: Office of the Prime Minister, Ban Sisavat, Vientiane; tel. (21) 213653; fax (21) 213560; Pres. THOUNGLONG SISOLIT.

CHAMBER OF COMMERCE

Lao National Chamber of Commerce and Industry (LNCCI): rue Sihom, Ban Haisok, BP 4596, Vientiane; tel. (21) 219224; fax (21) 219223; e-mail laocci@laotel.com; internet www.lncci.laotel.com; f. 1989; 789 mems; Pres. KISSANA VONGSAY; Sec.-Gen. KHAMPANH SENGTHONGKHAM.

TRADE ASSOCIATION

Société Lao Import-Export (SOLIMPEX): 43–47 ave Lane Xang, BP 278, Vientiane; tel. (21) 213818; fax (21) 217054; Dir KANHKEO SAYCOCIE; Dep. Dir PHONGSAMOUTH VONGKOT.

UTILITIES

Electricity

Electricité du Laos: rue Nongbone, BP 309, Vientiane; tel. (21) 451519; fax (21) 416381; e-mail edlgmo@laotel.com; responsible for production and distribution of electricity; Gen. Man. VIRAPHONH VIRAVONG.

Lao National Grid Co: Vientiane; responsible for Mekong hydroelectricity exports.

Water

In 1998 the Government adopted a policy of decentralization with regard to water supply and sanitation in Laos. As a result, the national water supply authority, Nam Papa Lao, was divided into Nam Papa Vientiane, with jurisdiction over the capital, and a number of provincial authorities. Activities within the sector were subsequently co-ordinated by a newly established body, the Water Supply Authority.

Nam Papa Vientiane (Lao Water Supply Authority): rue Phone Kheng, Thatluang Neue Village, Sat Settha District, Vientiane; tel. (21) 412880; fax (21) 414378; e-mail daophet@laotel.com; f. 1962; fmrly Nam Papa Lao; authority responsible for the water supply of Vientiane; Gen. Man. DAOPHET BOUAPHA.

Water Supply Authority (WASA): Dept of Housing and Urban Planning, Ministry of Communications, Transport, Post and Construction, ave Lane Xang, Vientiane; tel. and fax (21) 451826; e-mail mctpcwwa@laotel.com; internet www.wasa.gov.la; f. 1998; Dir NOUPHEUAK VIRABOUTH.

STATE ENTERPRISES

Agricultural Forestry Development Import-Export and General Service Co: trading co of the armed forces.

Bolisat Phatthana Khet Phoudoi Import-Export Co: rue Khoun Boulom, Vientiane; tel. (21) 216234; fax (21) 215046; f. 1984; trading co of the armed forces.

Dao-Heuang Import-Export Co: Ban Thaluang, Paksé, Champasak Province; tel. (31) 213805; fax (31) 212438; e-mail info@dao-heuang.com; f. 1990; imports and distributes whisky, beer, mineral water and foodstuffs.

Lao Commodities Export Co Ltd (Lacomex): Ban Wattuang, Paksé, Champasak Province; tel. (31) 212552; fax (31) 212553; e-mail sisanouk@laotel.com; f. 1994; exports coffee under the Paksong Cafe Lao brand; Man. Dir SISANOUK SISOMBAT.

Lao Houng Heuang Export-Import Co: rue Nongbone, Vientiane; tel. (21) 217344; fax (21) 212107.

Lao State Material Import-Export Co (Lasmac): 59 Ban Hatsady Tai, Chanthaboury, Vientiane; tel. (21) 216578; fax (21) 217149; e-mail lasmac@laotel.com; internet www.lasmac.laopdr.com; f. 1983; mfr of wood products and woven plastic; exports agricultural and wood products; imports construction materials.

Luen Fat Hong Lao Plywood Industry Co: BP 83, Vientiane; tel. (21) 314990; fax (21) 314992; e-mail lfhsdsj@laotel.com; internet www.luenfathongyada.laopdr.com; development and management of forests, logging and timber production.

CO-OPERATIVES

Central Leading Committee to Guide Agricultural Co-operatives: Vientiane; f. 1978; to help organize and plan regulations and policies for co-operatives; by the end of 1986 there were some 4,000 co-operatives, employing about 74% of the agricultural labour force; Chair. (vacant).

TRADE UNION ORGANIZATION

Federation of Lao Trade Unions: 87 ave Lane Xang, BP 780, Vientiane; tel. (21) 313682; e-mail kammabanlao@pan-laos.net.la; f. 1956; 21-mem. Cen. Cttee and five-mem. Control Cttee; Pres. BOSAIKHAM VONGDALA (acting); 70,000 mems.

Transport

RAILWAYS

The construction of a 30-km rail link between Vientiane and the Thai border town of Nong Khai began in January 1996 but was indefinitely postponed in February 1998 as an indirect consequence of a severe downturn in the Thai economy. In 1997 the Government announced plans to develop a comprehensive railway network, and awarded a contract to a Thai company, although no timetable for the implementation of the scheme was announced. In 2003 the Thai Government agreed to finance a 3.5-km rail link from Tha Naleng (near Vientiane) to Nong Khai, North-East Thailand; construction was scheduled to be completed by March 2007. Draft proposals to extend the track, to link Tha Naleng with Vientiane, were subsequently announced.

ROADS

The road network provides the country's main method of transport, accounting for about 90% of freight traffic and 95% of passenger traffic in 1993. In 1999 there were an estimated 21,716 km of roads, of which 9,664 km were paved. The main routes link Vientiane and Luang Prabang with Ho Chi Minh City in southern Viet Nam and with northern Viet Nam and the Cambodian border, Vientiane with Savannakhet, Phongsali to the Chinese border, Vientiane with Luang Prabang and the port of Ha Tinh (northern Viet Nam), and Savannakhet with the port of Da Nang (Viet Nam). In 2002 Laos, Thailand and China agreed to a US $45m. road project intended to link the three countries; most of the construction on the Kunming–Bangkok Highway would be carried out in Laos. The project was to be completed by 2006. In February 2004 construction of a 245-km national road (Route 9) was completed, linking Laos with Thailand and Viet Nam.

The Friendship Bridge across the Mekong River, linking Laos and Thailand between Tha Naleng and Nong Khai, was opened in April 1994. In early 1998 construction work began in Paksé on another bridge across the Mekong River. The project was granted substantial funding from the Japanese Government, and was completed in August 2000. Construction commenced in December 2003 on a second Friendship Bridge, also funded by the Japanese Government, linking Savannakhet and Mukdahan. During construction work in mid-2005, part of the bridge collapsed into the Mekong River. Nevertheless, the bridge was likely to be completed on schedule in 2006.

INLAND WATERWAYS

The Mekong River, which forms the western frontier of Laos for much of its length, is the country's greatest transport artery. However, the size of river vessels is limited by rapids, and traffic is seasonal. In April 1995 Laos, Cambodia, Thailand and Viet Nam signed an agreement regarding the joint development of the lower Mekong, and established a Mekong River Commission. There are about 4,600 km of navigable waterways.

CIVIL AVIATION

Wattai airport, Vientiane, is the principal airport. Following the signing of an agreement in 1995, the airport was to be upgraded by Japan; renovation work commenced in 1997, and a new passenger terminal was opened in 1998. The development of Luang Prabang airport by Thailand, at a cost of 50m. baht, began in May 1994 and the first phase of the development programme was completed in 1996; the second phase was completed in 1998. In April 1998 Luang Prabang airport gained formal approval for international flights. The airports at Paksé and Savannakhet were also scheduled to be upgraded to enable them to accommodate wide-bodied civilian aircraft; renovation work on the airport at Savannakhet was completed in April 2000. Construction of a new airport in Oudomxay Province was completed in the late 1990s.

In mid-2004 the Laotian Government announced that a memorandum of understanding was to be signed with Thailand by the end of 2005 providing for the development of Savannakhet Airport into an international landing strip, to be used jointly by Japan, which would partially fund the development. The plan constituted part of the east–west economic corridor project, a proposed transport network linking Laos with Myanmar, Thailand and Viet Nam.

Lao Civil Aviation Department: BP 119, Vientiane; tel. and fax (21) 512163; e-mail laodca@laotel.com; Dir-Gen. YAKUA LOPANGKAO.

Lao Airlines: National Air Transport Co, 2 rue Pangkham, BP 6441, Vientiane; tel. (21) 212057; fax (21) 212065; e-mail laoairlines@laoairlines.com; internet www.laoairlines.com; f. 1975; state airline, fmrly Lao Aviation; operates internal and international passenger and cargo transport services within South-East Asia; Gen. Man. Dir POTHONG NGONPHACHANH.

Tourism

Laos boasts spectacular scenery, ancient pagodas and abundant wildlife. However, the development of tourism remains constrained by the poor infrastructure in much of the country. Western tourists were first permitted to enter Laos in 1989. In 1994, in order to stimulate the tourist industry, Vientiane ended restrictions on the movement of foreigners in Laos. Also in 1994 Laos, Viet Nam and Thailand agreed measures for the joint development of tourism. Luang Prabang was approved by UNESCO as a World Heritage site in February 1998. The years 1999–2000 were designated as Visit Laos Years. The number of visitors reached 737,208 in 2000, when receipts from tourism totalled an estimated US $114m. By 2003, however, visitor arrivals had decreased to 636,361, and receipts had declined to $87m.

National Tourism Authority of Lao PDR: ave Lane Xang, BP 3556, Hadsady, Chanthaboury, Vientiane; tel. (21) 212251; fax (21) 212769; e-mail tmpd_lnta@yahoo.com; internet www.tourismlaos.gov.la; 18 provincial offices; Chair. SOMPHONG MONGKHONVILAY.

LATVIA

Introductory Survey

Location, Climate, Language, Religion, Flag, Capital

The Republic of Latvia is situated in north-eastern Europe, on the east coast of the Baltic Sea. The country is bounded by Estonia to the north and by Lithuania to the south and south-west. To the east it borders Russia, and to the south-east Belarus. Owing to the influence of maritime factors, the climate is relatively temperate, but changeable. Average temperatures in January range from −2.8°C (26.6°F) in the western coastal town of Liepāja to −6.6°C (20.1°F) in the inland town of Daugavpils. Mean temperatures for July range from 16.7°C (62.1°F) in Liepāja to 17.6°C (63.7°F) in Daugavpils. Average annual rainfall in Rīga is 617 mm (24 ins). The official language is Latvian. The major religion is Christianity: most ethnic Latvians are traditionally Lutherans or Roman Catholics, whereas ethnic Russians are mainly adherents of the Russian Orthodox Church or Old Believers. The national flag (proportions 1 by 2) has a maroon background, with a narrow white horizontal stripe superimposed across the central part. The capital is Rīga (Riga).

Recent History

In November 1917 representatives of Latvian nationalist groups elected a provisional national council, which informed the Russian Government of its intention to establish a sovereign, independent Latvian state. On 18 November 1918 the Latvian National Council, which had been constituted on the previous day, proclaimed the independent Republic of Latvia, with Jānis Čakste as President. Independence, under the nationalist Government of Kārlis Ulmanis, was fully achieved after the expulsion of the Bolsheviks from Rīga in May 1919, with the aid of German troops, and from the eastern province of Latgale, with Polish and Estonian assistance, in January 1920. A Latvian-Soviet peace treaty was finally signed in August 1920. Latvia's first Constitution was adopted in 1922. An electoral system based on proportional representation permitted a large number of small parties to be represented in the Saeima (Parliament). As a result, there was little administrative stability, with 18 changes of government in 1922–34. None the less, under the dominant party, the Latvian Farmers' Union (LFU, led by Ulmanis), agrarian reforms were successfully introduced and agricultural exports flourished. The world-wide economic decline of the early 1930s, together with domestic political fragmentation, prompted a (bloodless) *coup d'état* in May 1934, led by Ulmanis. Martial law was introduced, the Saeima was dissolved and all political parties, including the LFU, were banned. A Government of National Unity, with Ulmanis as Prime Minister, assumed the legislative functions of the Saeima. Ulmanis became President in 1936.

Under the Treaty of Non-Aggression (the 'Molotov-Ribbentrop Pact'), signed by Germany and the USSR in August 1939, the incorporation of Latvia into the USSR was agreed by the two powers. A Treaty of Mutual Aid between the USSR and Latvia allowed the establishment of Soviet military bases in Latvia, and in June 1940 it was occupied by Soviet forces. In common with the neighbouring Baltic states of Estonia and Lithuania, Latvia did not offer military resistance, being greatly outnumbered by the Soviet forces. A new 'puppet' administration, under Augusts Kirhenšteins, was installed, and the election to the Saeima of Soviet-approved candidates took place in July. In that month the legislature proclaimed the Latvian Soviet Socialist Republic, which was formally incorporated into the USSR as a constituent union republic in August.

In the first year of Soviet rule almost 33,000 Latvians were deported to Russia, and a further 1,350 were killed. Latvian language, traditions and culture were also suppressed. In July 1941 Soviet rule in Latvia was interrupted by German occupation. Most German troops had withdrawn by 1944, although the Kurzeme region, in south-western Latvia, was retained by Germany until the end of the Second World War. Soviet Latvia was re-established in 1944–45 and the process of 'sovietization' was resumed. There were further mass deportations of Latvians to Russia and Central Asia. Independent political activities were prohibited and exclusive political power was exercised by the Communist Party of Latvia (CPL). A process of industrialization encouraged significant and sustained Russian and other Soviet immigration into the republic. Under CPL First Secretary Arvīds Pelše (appointed in 1959) and his successor, Augusts Voss (First Secretary, 1966–84), limited autonomy gained in the 1950s was reversed.

There was a revival in traditional Latvian culture from the late 1970s. Political groups began to be established, including the Environmental Protection Club and Helsinki-86, established to monitor Soviet observance of the Helsinki Final Act adopted in 1975 by the Conference on (now Organization for) Security and Co-operation in Europe (CSCE—now OSCE, see p. 327). In June and August 1986 anti-Soviet demonstrations, organized by Helsinki-86, were suppressed by the police. In 1987 there were further demonstrations on the anniversaries of significant events in Latvian history. Such movements, fostered by the greater freedom of expression permitted under the new Soviet policy of *glasnost* (openness), were strongly opposed by the CPL. In 1988 opposition movements in Latvia began to unite, and in October representatives of the leading movements, together with CPL radicals, organized the inaugural congress of the Popular Front of Latvia (PFL), at which delegates resolved to seek sovereignty for Latvia within a renewed Soviet federation. The PFL, chaired by Dainis Īvāns, rapidly became the largest and most influential political force in Latvia, with an estimated membership of 250,000 by the end of 1988.

In September 1988 Boris Pugo was replaced as First Secretary of the CPL by Jānis Vagris. The new CPL leadership came increasingly under the influence of members of the PFL. At the end of September Latvian was designated the state language. In March 1989 candidates supported by the PFL won 26 of the 34 contested seats in elections to the USSR's Congress of People's Deputies. On 28 July, following similar measures in Lithuania and Estonia, the Latvian Supreme Soviet (Supreme Council—legislature) adopted a declaration of sovereignty and economic independence. However, there was growing support within the republic for full independence, as advocated by the Latvian National Independence Movement (LNIM), formed in 1988, particularly among ethnic Latvians (who, however, were outnumbered by ethnic Slavs in Rīga and the other large cities in the republic as a result of the Soviet policy of large-scale immigration). In December 1989, despite the establishment of political groups opposed to the PFL, candidates supported by the PFL won some 75% of seats contested in local elections.

In January 1990 the Latvian Supreme Soviet voted to abolish the constitutional provisions that guaranteed the CPL's political predominance. In the following month the Supreme Soviet adopted a declaration condemning the Latvian legislature's decision to request admission to the USSR in 1940, and the flag, state emblems and anthem of pre-1940 Latvia were restored to official use. At elections to the Supreme Soviet in March and April 1990, pro-independence candidates endorsed by the PFL won 131 of the 201 seats; the CPL and the anti-independence Interfront (International Front—dominated by members of the Russian-speaking population) together won 59 seats. The CPL subsequently split into two parties: the majority of delegates at an extraordinary congress rejected a motion to leave the Communist Party of the Soviet Union (CPSU), and elected Alfrēds Rubiks, an opponent of independence, as First Secretary.

The new Supreme Council was convened in early May 1990, and elected Anatolijs Gorbunovs of the CPL as its Chairman (*de facto* President of the Republic). On 4 May the Supreme Council adopted a resolution that declared the incorporation of Latvia into the USSR in 1940 as unlawful, and announced the beginning of a transitional period that was to lead to full political and economic independence. Four articles of the 1922 Constitution, defining Latvia as an independent democratic state and asserting the sovereignty of the Latvian people, were restored, and were to form the basis of the newly declared Republic of Latvia's legitimacy. Ivars Godmanis, the Deputy Chairman of the PFL, was elected Prime Minister in a new, PFL-dominated Government. Meanwhile, a rival body to the Supreme Soviet had been convened at the end of April 1990. This Congress of Latvia had been elected in an unofficial poll, in which some 700,000 people were reported to have participated: only citizens of the pre-1940 republic and their descendants had been entitled to vote. The Congress, in which members of the radical LNIM predominated, declared Latvia to be an occupied country and adopted resolutions on independence and the withdrawal of Soviet troops.

The Supreme Council's resolutions, although more cautious than independence declarations adopted in Lithuania and Estonia, severely strained relations with the Soviet authorities. On 14 May 1990 the Soviet President, Mikhail Gorbachev, issued a decree that annulled the Latvian declaration of independence, condemning it as a violation of the USSR Constitution. The declaration was also opposed within the republic by some ethnic Slavs, who organized protest strikes and demonstrations. In subsequent months local anti-Government movements (allied with Soviet troops stationed in Latvia) conducted a campaign of propaganda and harassment. In December the Latvian Government claimed that special units (OMON) of the Soviet Ministry of Internal Affairs had been responsible for a series of explosions in Rīga, and in January 1991 OMON troops seized the Rīga Press House, previously the property of the CPL. Later in January a 'Committee of Public Salvation', headed by Alfrēds Rubiks, declared itself as a rival Government to the Godmanis administration; on the same day five people died when OMON troops attacked the Ministry of the Interior in Rīga. (In November 1999 10 former Soviet officers were convicted of attempting to overthrow the Latvian Government in 1991; seven received suspended prison sentences of up to four years' duration.)

The attempted seizure of power by Rubiks' Committee reinforced opposition in Latvia to inclusion in the new union treaty being prepared by nine Soviet republics. Latvia refused to conduct the all-Union referendum on the future of the USSR, which was scheduled for 17 March 1991 (although some 680,000 people, mostly Russians and Ukrainians, did participate, on an unofficial basis). Instead, a referendum on Latvian independence took place on 3 March. Of those eligible to vote, 87.6% participated, of whom, according to official results, 73.7% endorsed proposals for a democratic, independent Latvian republic.

At the time of the attempted overthrow of the Gorbachev administration in the Russian and Soviet capital, Moscow, in August 1991, immediate Soviet military intervention in Latvia was widely anticipated. However, an emergency session of the Supreme Council was convened and the full independence of Latvia was proclaimed. As the coup collapsed, the Godmanis Government took prompt action to assert control in Latvia, banning the CPL and detaining Rubiks. (In July 1995 Rubiks was found guilty of the coup attempt. He was released in November 1997.) On 6 September 1991 the USSR State Council formally recognized the independent Republic of Latvia, and the country was admitted to the UN later that month. In late 1991 the Supreme Council adopted legislation guaranteeing the right of citizenship to all citizens of the pre-1940 republic (including non-ethnic Latvians) and their descendants. Remaining residents of Latvia (mainly Russians and other Slavs) were to be required to apply for naturalization after final legislation governing citizenship was determined by a restored Saeima.

The first legislative elections since the restoration of independence took place in June 1993, with the participation of about 90% of the electorate. Only citizens of pre-1940 Latvia and their descendants were entitled to vote; consequently, some 27% of the adult population (mainly ethnic Russians) were excluded from the election. A total of 23 parties, movements and alliances contested the poll, of which eight secured representation in the 100-seat Saeima. Latvian Way, a broadly-based movement established earlier in the year, emerged as the strongest party, with more than 32% of the votes and 36 seats in the assembly. Only 11 of the elected deputies were non-ethnic Latvians (six of whom were ethnic Russians). The results of the elections demonstrated strong popular support for the more moderate nationalist parties, and socialist-orientated parties (including the successor of the CPL, the Latvian Socialist Party—LSP) failed to win representation. The PFL also failed to secure any seats.

At the first session of the Saeima on 6 July 1993 Anatolijs Gorbunovs was elected Chairman (speaker). The Saeima also voted to restore the Constitution of 1922, and undertook to elect the President of the Republic from among three prominent deputies. At a third round of voting on 7 July 1993 Guntis Ulmanis (great-nephew of Kārlis Ulmanis) of the revived LFU succeeded in winning a majority, with 53 votes. He was inaugurated as President the following day, whereupon he appointed Valdis Birkavs (formerly a Deputy Chairman of the Supreme Council and a leading member of Latvian Way) as Prime Minister. Birkavs' Cabinet of Ministers represented a coalition agreement between Latvian Way (the majority partner) and the LFU.

The requirements for naturalization proposed by the Government's draft citizenship law included a minimum of 10 years' permanent residence, a knowledge of Latvian to conversational level and an oath of loyalty to the republic. In March 1994 the Saeima approved the establishment of the new post of State Minister for Human Rights, in an attempt to counter accusations of violations of minority rights. Although final legislation on citizenship and naturalization was adopted by the Saeima in June, following international criticism, and amid concern that the new law would jeopardize Latvia's application for membership of the Council of Europe (see p. 211), the Cabinet of Ministers persuaded President Ulmanis to reject it. The Saeima adopted an amended citizenship law in July. Latvia was admitted to the Council of Europe in February 1995.

Meanwhile, in July 1994 the LFU announced its withdrawal from the governing coalition, following disagreements with Latvian Way over economic and agricultural policy. A new Cabinet was appointed in September. It, too, was dominated by Latvian Way members, including the Prime Minister, Māris Gailis; Birkavs became Deputy Prime Minister and Minister of Foreign Affairs. Four opposition factions within the Saeima—including the Latvian National Conservative Party (LNCP), as the LNIM had been renamed, and the LFU—announced their union as a 'national bloc' to co-ordinate opposition activities.

A general election was held on 30 September–1 October 1995. Nine parties and coalitions succeeded in obtaining the 5% of the votes required for representation in the Saeima; as a result, the assembly was highly fragmented. Latvian Way's share of the 100 seats was reduced by more than one-half, to 17, while the largest number of seats (18) was won by the newly established, leftist Democratic Party Saimnieks (The Master—DPS). The People's Movement for Latvia (Zigerists' Party—PML), a nationalist, anti-Russian party led by Joahims Zigerists, won 16 seats. (Zigerists was linked to an extremist right-wing organization in Germany, and in 1994 had been convicted in that country for inciting racial hatred.) Negotiations among parties to form a coalition government capable of commanding a parliamentary majority proved to be protracted. In December 1995 the Saeima finally endorsed a Cabinet of Ministers led by Andris Šķēle (an entrepreneur with no party affiliation). The new Government was a broad coalition of the DPS, Latvian Way, the Union 'For Fatherland and Freedom' (UFF), the LNCP, the LFU and the Latvian Unity Party (LUP). The PML was, notably, excluded from the coalition. Former Prime Ministers Gailis and Birkavs were appointed to the new Cabinet, the former as a Deputy Prime Minister, and the latter as Minister of Foreign Affairs. In May 1996 the Deputy Prime Minister and Minister of Agriculture, Alberīs Kauls, was dismissed, after criticizing the Prime Minister's agricultural policies. The LUP (of which Kauls was the leader) temporarily withdrew its support from the coalition, but shortly afterwards rejoined the Government, having secured approval for a new candidate as Minister of Agriculture.

On 18 June 1996 the Saeima re-elected Guntis Ulmanis as President for a second three-year term. In July Šķēle conducted a cabinet reshuffle. In the same month it was announced that the LUP was to merge with the DPS, reinforcing the latter as the dominant party in the coalition. None the less, instability in both the Government and the legislature continued. In October Aivars Kreituss tendered his resignation as Minister of Finance, having in the previous month been expelled from the DPS for his perceived failure to promote the party's interests. Meanwhile, Alfrēds Čepānis was elected to the post of Chairman of the Saeima, following the removal from office of Ilga Kreituse. In the same month the Deputy Prime Minister, Ziedonis Čevers (also leader of the DPS) submitted his resignation, citing differences of opinion with Šķēle. The collapse of the coalition appeared inevitable in January 1997, when Šķēle resigned as Prime Minister, in what was interpreted as a response to criticism from President Ulmanis over Šķēle's approval of Vasilijs Melniks as the new Minister of Finance. However, Šķēle was swiftly reappointed by Ulmanis, who indicated his support for Šķēle's economic and structural reforms. A new, largely unaltered Cabinet was appointed in February; Roberts Zīle replaced Melniks as Minister of Finance. Local elections conducted in March demonstrated a considerable increase in support for the LFU.

None the less, by July 1997 the governing coalition had begun to disintegrate, not least because a series of corruption scandals had, since May, prompted the resignation of several ministers, and at the end of the month Šķēle announced the resignation of the Government. Ulmanis invited Guntars Krasts, the outgoing Minister of the Economy, to form a new administration. In early August the Saeima approved Krasts' proposals for a new, five-party coalition, comprising the Conservative Union 'For Fatherland and Freedom'/LNNK (his own party, formed in the previous month by the merger of the UFF and the Latvian National Independence Movement—LNNK), the DPS, Latvian Way, the LFU and the Christian Democratic Union of Latvia (CDUL). Krasts' leadership was tested in early 1998 following suggestions by an investigative parliamentary committee that he had been guilty of negligence with regard to a privatization proposal for the state power utility, Latvenergo, as Minister of the Economy. In March Krasts formally requested that the Saeima conduct a vote of confidence in his personal integrity, in order to confirm his mandate. The refusal of any parliamentary faction to organize such a vote was interpreted by the Prime Minister as an endorsement of his leadership. In that month Šķēle announced the formation of a new political party, later named the People's Party (Tautas partija—TP), to contest the forthcoming elections.

In April 1998 the Minister of the Economy, Atis Sausnītis, was dismissed, following a well-publicized attempt to draw attention to the possible adverse economic consequences of sustained diplomatic tensions with Russia (see below). Anticipating the collapse of Krasts' Government, the DPS announced its withdrawal from the coalition. At the end of the month, however, Krasts survived a parliamentary vote of 'no confidence' proposed by the LFU and Latvian Way. At the same session the Saeima approved appointments to a new coalition Government, with members of the Cabinet of Ministers drawn from the LFU, Latvian Way, and an alliance of the Latvian National Reform Party and the Latvian Green Party.

In April 1998 draft amendments to the strict legislation regulating rights to citizenship were adopted, in response to recommendations made by the OSCE. The amendments, which removed the age-related system of naturalization that allocated dates for application by age-group, granted citizenship to stateless children (permanently resident in Latvia) born after the 1991 declaration of independence and relaxed the citizenship requirements for Russian-speakers, were approved by the Saeima in June 1998. Although widely welcomed elsewhere in Europe, the amendments were deemed inadequate by Russia, and nationalist groups within the Latvian legislature secured sufficient support inside and outside the Saeima to force a delay to the enactment of the new legislation and the organization of a referendum on the subject. The referendum was duly conducted concurrently with the 3 October general election; 52.5% of the votes were cast in favour of the amendments, which were promulgated later in the month.

At the general election, Šķēle's TP was the most successful single party, taking 21.2% of the votes (and 24 of the 100 legislative seats), ahead of Latvian Way with 18.1% (21 seats) and the Conservative Union 'For Fatherland and Freedom'/LNNK with 14.7% (17 seats). Only six of the 21 participating political parties secured the minimum 5% of the votes necessary for representation in the Saeima. It was not until the end of November that the Saeima approved a new, three-party, minority coalition Government, to be headed by Vilis Krištopans of Latvian Way. The coalition, comprising Latvian Way, the Conservative Union 'For Fatherland and Freedom'/LNNK and the New Party (which held eight legislative seats), also drew support from the Latvian Social Democratic Alliance, which controlled 14 seats in the Saeima. In early February 1999 the Social Democrats formally joined the coalition with the appointment of one of their members to the agriculture portfolio in the Cabinet of Ministers.

On 17 June 1999 Vaira Vīķe-Freiberga was elected President at a seventh round of voting in the Saeima, with the support of 53 deputies (compared with 20 for Valdis Birkavs of Latvian Way and nine for Ingrīda Ūdre of the New Party). Born in Latvia, but resident in Canada from the end of the Second World War until 1998, Vīķe-Freiberga, a non-partisan figure who had trained as a psychologist, thus became the first female President in central or eastern Europe. At her inauguration on 8 July 1999 Vīķe-Freiberga identified as priorities for her presidency Latvia's entry into the European Union (EU, see p. 228) and the North Atlantic Treaty Organization (NATO, see p. 314). Three days before her inauguration, Krištopans announced his Government's resignation, apparently in response to the recent signing by the Conservative Union 'For Fatherland and Freedom'/LNNK of a co-operation accord with the opposition TP. President Vīķe-Freiberga subsequently asked Andris Šķēle to form a new government. Šķēle thus became Prime Minister for the third time, leading a coalition of his TP, the Conservative Union 'For Fatherland and Freedom'/LNNK and Latvian Way.

In early July 1999 the Saeima adopted controversial new language legislation, which, notably, required that all business and all state- and municipally-organized gatherings be conducted in Latvian. Russia immediately denounced the legislation as discriminatory, and it was also condemned by the OSCE, the Council of Europe, the European Commission and, within Latvia, by groups representing ethnic Slavs. Revised legislation, approved in early December, incorporated amendments urged by the OSCE, and was said by its proponents to allow the preservation and strengthening of the Latvian language, while ensuring compliance with international standards: Latvian was to be used for all business in the state sector, and for certain private-sector activities. The revised language law came into effect at the beginning of September, prompting protests from both the parliamentary opposition and the ethnic Russian community.

Šķēle resigned the premiership in April 2000, after Latvian Way withdrew from the governing coalition, owing to a dispute over the running of the Latvian Privatization Agency. President Vīķe-Freiberga asked Andris Bērziņš, hitherto the Mayor of Rīga, to form a new government; his cabinet (a coalition principally comprising the TP, Latvian Way and the Conservative Union 'For Fatherland and Freedom'/LNNK) was approved by the Saeima in early May.

In November 2001 Einārs Repše resigned as Governor of the Bank of Latvia, in order to found a new political party, New Era. The rightist party attracted immediate popular support, and Repše was elected Chairman at its founding congress in February 2002. In May the Saeima adopted amendments to national electoral legislation, abolishing the controversial requirement that candidates be fluent in the Latvian language, which had been perceived as an obstacle to NATO membership; however, the Saeima had passed legislation reinforcing Latvian as the official working language of parliament at the end of the preceding month. Also in May a new Christian democratic party, the Latvian First Party (Latvijas Pirmā Partija—LPP), was formed.

In legislative elections, held on 5 October 2002, New Era won 23.9% of the votes cast (26 seats); the leftist, pro-Russian electoral bloc For Human Rights in a United Latvia, which included the People's Harmony Party (Tautas Saskaņas Partija—TSP) and the Latvian Socialist Party, obtained 18.9% of the votes (25 seats); and the TP received 16.7% (20 seats). Other parties to achieve representation in the Saeima were the Greens' and Farmers' Union (GFU—ZZS—an alliance of the Centre Party, the Latvian Farmers' Union and the Latvian Green Party), with 12 seats, the LPP (10 seats) and the Conservative Union 'For Fatherland and Freedom'/LNNK (seven); Latvian Way failed to secure the 5% of the votes required to obtain a seat in the Saeima. The rate of participation by the electorate was some 72.5%. Following the collapse of talks with the TP, Repše formed a coalition government comprising members of New Era, the LPP, the GFU—ZZS and the Conservative Union 'For Fatherland and Freedom'/LNNK, which was approved by the Saeima on 7 November. The Minister of Defence, Ģirts Kristovskis, was the only member of the Cabinet of Ministers to have retained his previous portfolio; a new post of Deputy Prime Minister was established, to which Ainārs Šlesers was appointed. In late November Atis Slakteris replaced Šķēle as Chairman of the TP; and Šķēle subsequently announced his withdrawal from politics.

In February 2003 the TSP withdrew from the For Human Rights in a United Latvia alliance, apparently in a desire to pursue more moderate policies; in June the Latvian Socialist Party also announced its withdrawal, effectively dissolving the coalition. Meanwhile, in mid-May Jānis Naglis was elected as Chairman of Latvian Way, in succession to former Prime Minister Andris Bērziņš. In mid-June Prime Minister Repše survived a vote of 'no confidence' in the Saeima, proposed by the TP. On 20 June Vaira Vīķe-Freiberga was re-elected unopposed (by 88 votes to six) to serve a second term of office; she was inaugurated as President on 8 July. In late September tensions emerged within the Government, when its constituent parties (with the exception of New Era) issued a statement expressing a lack of confidence in the Prime Minister, accusing him of authoritarianism. A compromise agreement was reached, following inter-party discussions, and in mid-November the Chairmen of the four ruling parties signed a memorandum of understanding, which emphasized: the equality of coalition members; the importance of unanimity; the need for member parties to refrain from public criticism, in the absence of substantiating evidence; and the need for the Prime Minister to inform party leaders in a timely manner should he wish to dismiss a minister. On 26 January 2004 Repše dismissed Deputy Prime Minister Ainārs Šlesers of the LPP, apparently owing to a failure to perform his duties, although Šlesers alleged that his dismissal had been prompted by a proposal to establish a special investigative committee to examine the premier's property dealings. Two days later the LPP withdrew from the Government, and on 5 February Repše announced the resignation of his administration, declaring that a minority Government was unworkable.

Following the collapse of the Government, President Viķe-Freiberga emphasized the need to maintain a stable political course in preparation for Latvia's impending accession to full membership of NATO and the EU, and on 20 February 2004 nominated the co-Chairman of the Latvian Green Party (part of the GFU—ZZS), Indulis Emsis, as premier. Following negotiations, in early March Emsis secured the support of the GFU—ZZS, the LPP and the TP, and a new, right-of-centre, coalition Government was approved by the Saeima on 9 March, with the parliamentary support of the TSP. Šlesers was re-appointed Deputy Prime Minister.

On 1 May 2004 some 15,000–20,000 people protested against education reforms, due to be introduced in September, when Latvian was to become the sole language of instruction. On the same day Latvia formally became a full member of the EU. Sandra Kalniete, a non-partisan career diplomat and former Minister of Foreign Affairs, was appointed as Latvia's representative at the European Commission, and on 13 June elections to the European Parliament were held. The opposition Conservative Union 'For Fatherland and Freedom'/LNNK won four of the nine seats available, while its ally New Era won two, and the For Human Rights in a United Latvia alliance, the LPP and Latvian Way each won one seat. Neither of the two major parties of the ruling coalition obtained representation. The Minister of Foreign Affairs, Rihards Piks, resigned from the Cabinet in order to take up his seat in the European Parliament; he was replaced by Artis Pabriks. In mid-June the Government survived a parliamentary vote of confidence. In August Emsis announced that Kalniete was to be replaced as Latvia's representative at the European Commission by Ingrīda Ūdre, hitherto Chairman of the Saeima. Concerns were expressed at a national and European level about Ūdre's relative lack of experience, and there were allegations of irregularities in the funding of the LFU, of which Ūdre was a senior member In late October, at the request of the President-designate of the Commission, José Manuel Durão Barroso, the Latvian authorities withdrew Ūdre's nomination. Andris Piebalgs, hitherto Kalniete's *chef de cabinet*, and a former ambassador of Latvia to the EU and Minister of Education, was nominated in her place, and was appointed Commissioner for Energy, following the approval of a new Commission in November.

Meanwhile, in mid-September 2004 the Government survived another parliamentary vote of confidence. However, on 28 October the draft budget was defeated in a parliamentary vote, precipitating the collapse of the ruling coalition. President Viķe-Freiberga asked Aigars Kalvītis of the TP (which had led opposition to the proposed budget) to form a new government, and on 2 December, following prolonged negotiations, the Saeima approved the formation of a Government comprising members of the TP, New Era, the GFU—ZZS and the LPP. Several members of the outgoing administration were retained in the same posts, including Artis Pabriks and Oskars Spurdziņš (both of the TP), as Minister of Foreign Affairs and Minister of Finance, respectively. Viķe-Freiberga reportedly opposed the proposed nomination of Šķēle as Minister of Health, and consequently Gundars Bērziņš, of the TP, was appointed to that position. The new Government was able to command a majority of votes in the legislature, which approved the draft budget on 20 December.

Local elections, held on 12 March 2005, were marred by allegations of electoral malpractice in Jūrmala and Rēzekne. In July the LPP criticized plans to hold a parade in support of the homosexual community and the GFU—ZZS condemned homosexuality as a 'perverse cult'; Kalvītis also stated that the plans were unacceptable. Consequently, Rīga City Council rescinded permission for the parade to be held, but this decision was overruled by an appeal to the administrative court. In the event, protesters far outnumbered gay rights activists, necessitating a substantial police presence. The Deputy Mayor and leader of the LPP, Juris Lujāns, subsequently resigned, having assumed political responsibility for the parade. The attitude of the authorities attracted criticism from the international human rights organization Amnesty International and from the EU.

Meanwhile, in early July 2005 Jānis Jurkāns resigned as leader of the TSP, in protest at the party's intention, following electoral defeats at both European and local level, to form an alliance with the New Centre, led by Sergejs Dolgopolovs, who had been expelled from the TSP in 2003. The new union, which became known as the Harmony Centre alliance, was joined by the Latvian Socialist Party in December 2005. Jānis Urbanovičs was elected to succeed Jurkāns as leader of the TSP in November. In another example of tactical consolidation, prior to legislative elections due to take place in October 2006, Latvian Way and the LPP formed a political alliance in October 2005.

In mid-October 2005 the Minister of the Interior, Ēriks Jēkabsons, tendered his resignation, after attracting criticism for his performance in office, and for his contacts with the controversial, self-exiled Russian businessman Boris Berezovskii (which aggravated tensions with Russia, where he was charged with fraud). In early November Jēkabsons was replaced by Dzintars Jaundzeikars of the LPP. In late December Einārs Repše resigned as Minister of Defence, following the announcement of a criminal investigation into his property investments; although Repše denied any impropriety, he resigned his parliamentary seat and temporarily withdrew from the leadership of New Era. (He had been re-elected as party Chairman in the previous month, although several prominent members of New Era had resigned in response to Repše's style of leadership.) Linda Mūrniece succeeded Repše as Minister of Defence. In mid-March 2006 Kalvītis dismissed the Minister of Transport since December 2004 and founder of the LPP, Ainārs Šlesers, after evidence emerged that implicated him in electoral malpractice in Jūrmala, where a financial inducement was allegedly offered to a member of the City Council in an attempt to influence voting in the 2005 municipal elections in favour of an LPP mayoral candidate. In early April 2006 New Era withdrew its ministers from the Government, after Kalvītis (of the TP) rejected a request by New Era to decide whether to retain it or the LPP in the governing coalition. The demand had come after the economic crimes unit of the Ministry of the Interior, controlled by the LPP, launched an inquiry into the conduct of the New Era Minister of the Economy, Krišjānis Kariņš.

Latvia's post-independence relations with Russia were troubled by two issues. The first concerned the citizenship and linguistic rights of Latvia's large Russian-speaking community (see above). Of comparable importance was the issue of the 100,000 former Soviet troops still stationed in Latvia (jurisdiction over whom had been transferred, following the dissolution of the USSR, to Russia). Following negotiations, withdrawal of the troops began in early 1992. The process was hampered by a series of disagreements, in particular over the issue of a Russian military radar station at Skrunda, in western Latvia, that the Russians wished to retain. However, in April 1994 agreements were concluded on the complete withdrawal of the remaining 10,000 Russian troops by the end of August, as well as on social guarantees for the estimated 22,000 Russian military pensioners residing in Latvia. Installations at the Skrunda base were subsequently dismantled.

Negotiations regarding the demarcation of the Latvian–Russian border, and Latvia's claim to some 1,640 sq km of land transferred from Latvia to Russia during the Soviet era, commenced in April 1996. Latvia initially insisted (as Estonia had done) that any future border agreement should include a reference to the 1920 treaty in which Russia recognized Latvia's independence. However, in February 1997 the Latvian administration abandoned this demand, and agreed that claims to property in the disputed territory should be discussed separately from the main border agreement. In March a draft treaty on the demarcation of the border was agreed by the two countries, and full agreement on a border treaty was reached in October. However, the Russian Government subsequently signalled its intention to link its acceptance of the treaty to an improvement in the civil rights of ethnic Russians in Latvia.

Relations became strained in March 1998, following the use of force by the Latvian police in order to disperse a demonstration of about 1,000 protesters—mostly ethnic-Russian pensioners—who were demonstrating in Rīga against price increases. Relations deteriorated further later in the month, following the organization, in Rīga, of a rally of Latvian veterans of Nazi German *Waffen SS* units, who had fought Soviet forces during the Second World War; the participation of senior Latvian politicians and military personnel attracted particular criticism from the Russian authorities. When the rally was repeated in March 2000 government officials and serving military officers were not permitted to take part. Meanwhile, the Government had been criticized by Russia for what it perceived as anti-Soviet bias in the pursuit of criminal cases against individuals accused of war crimes. The Russian authorities asserted that Latvia's concern to expedite the prosecution of those suspected of crimes under the Soviet occupation contrasted with its apparent tardiness in investigating and bringing to justice alleged perpetrators of war crimes during the Nazi era. Tensions arising from repeated Russian threats to impose economic sanctions against Latvia, if the Government did not promptly address the perceived infringement of minority rights, were exacerbated by Latvia's new state language law (see above). The revised language law, as approved by the Saeima in December, was again denounced by Russia. The OSCE's announcement, in December 2001, that its mandate in Latvia had been fulfilled, and the subsequent closure of its office there, also prompted criticism from Russia, which maintained that insufficient measures had been taken to protect the ethnic Russian population in Latvia from discrimination. Economic issues threatened to raise further tensions between the two countries in early 2003, following Russia's decision to cease using the port of Ventspils for its petroleum exports, primarily owing to the opening of a new Russian petroleum terminal on the Baltic coast at Primorsk, Leningrad Oblast. Russia also condemned amendments to legislation on education, which took effect from September 2004, and in accordance with which 60% of lessons in minority schools were to be taught in the Latvian language; in February 2004 thousands of ethnic Russians protested in Rīga against the reforms.

On 9 May 2005 President Viķe-Freiberga travelled to Moscow to attend celebrations to commemorate the 60th anniversary of the end of the Second World War in Europe. (Notably, the Heads of State of Estonia and Lithuania declined to attend.) Three days later the Saeima adopted a declaration denouncing the Soviet occupation of Latvia and urging Russia to accept moral, legal and financial responsibility for the losses incurred by the Latvian people under Soviet rule. In late May the Saeima ratified the Council of Europe's Framework Convention for the Protection of National Minorities; however, a declaration was appended, stipulating that only Latvian citizens would be regarded as members of a national minority, thus excluding large numbers of ethnic Russians who had failed to obtain citizenship. In August a commission was established to calculate the economic damage and human loss sustained by Latvia under Soviet governance; it was estimated that the commission might take up to five years to complete its research. Latvia (together with Estonia and Lithuania) was unhappy with the signature in September of an agreement between Russia and Germany on the construction of a North European Gas Pipeline, which was to carry natural gas from Russia to Germany under the Baltic Sea, bypassing the Baltic countries.

Latvia enjoys close political, economic and cultural relations with Estonia and Lithuania, and the three countries have established institutions to promote co-operation, including the interparliamentary Baltic Assembly and the Baltic Council of Ministers (which meets twice yearly). In 1992 Latvia became a founder member, with Estonia, Lithuania and other countries of the region, of the Council of Baltic Sea States, a principal aim of which was to assist the political and economic development of its former communist member states (which included Russia). Differences arose in the mid-1990s between Latvia and its two closest Baltic neighbours, in particular concerning the demarcation of maritime borders. However, agreement on the delimitation of the sea border with Estonia was reached in May 1996, and the document was ratified by both countries' legislatures in August. A further agreement on fishing rights was concluded in early 1997. The demarcation of the land border between the two countries was completed in December 1997. Negotiations between Latvia and Lithuania on their maritime border were complicated in October 1996 by the Saeima's ratification of an agreement with two foreign petroleum companies to explore and develop offshore oilfields in disputed areas of the Baltic Sea. Although the two countries signed an agreement on the delimitation of their territorial waters in July 1999, protests from the Latvian fishing industry prevented the agreement from being ratified by the Saeima. In December 2000 a protocol was signed on the re-demarcation of the land border between the two countries. In early 2006 the leaders of all three Baltic states reached agreement on the construction of a new nuclear power plant to replace that at Ignalina, Lithuania, and various other co-operative measures aimed at reducing Russian dominance in the supply of regional energy.

A priority of Latvian foreign policy was attaining full membership of the EU. Latvia became an associate member in June 1995, and in October it applied for full membership. In May 1998, in contravention of the European Convention on Human Rights and Fundamental Freedoms, the Saeima voted to retain the death penalty for certain criminal acts, frustrating the attempts of President Ulmanis to fulfil a commitment to abolish capital punishment made by Latvia on its accession to the Council of Europe in 1995. The Saeima finally abolished the death penalty in April 1999. Formal negotiations on EU membership commenced in February 2000, and in December 2002 Latvia, together with nine other countries, was formally invited to become a full member of the EU from May 2004. A referendum on EU membership was held in Latvia on 20 September 2003. Of the 72.5% of the electorate who participated in the plebiscite, 66.8% voted in support of Latvia's accession to the EU, although in certain areas of the country, particularly in the predominately Russian-speaking, south-eastern regions around the second city of Daugavpils, a majority of votes were cast against EU membership. The country became a full member on 1 May 2004.

Latvia also sought membership of NATO, as the principal guarantor of its security. In February 2002 the Secretary-General of NATO warned the Latvian Government that its existing language requirements, which demanded that candidates standing in regional and national elections be fluent in Latvian, threatened to affect adversely the likelihood of the country being admitted to the Alliance; amendments to the electoral law were duly passed in May, mitigating the language requirements. At a summit meeting held in Prague, Czech Republic, in November, Latvia was one of seven countries (including Estonia and Lithuania) invited to join NATO in 2004. Latvia became a full member of the Alliance on 29 March 2004.

Government

Under the terms of the 1922 Constitution, which was restored in July 1993 (and amended in December 1997), Latvia is an independent democratic parliamentary republic. The supreme legislative body is the Saeima (Parliament), the 100 members of which are elected by universal adult suffrage for a four-year term. The President of the Republic, who is Head of State, is elected by a secret ballot of the Saeima, also for a period of four years. The President, who is also Head of the Armed Forces, may not serve for more than two consecutive terms. Executive power is held by the Cabinet of Ministers, which is headed by the Prime Minister. The Prime Minister is appointed by the President; the remaining members of the Cabinet are nominated by the Prime Minister. For administrative purposes, Latvia is divided into 26 districts and seven towns (including the capital, Rīga).

Defence

Until independence in August 1991, Latvia had no armed forces separate from those of the USSR. A Ministry of Defence was established in November, and in August 2005 Latvia's total armed forces numbered 5,238, comprising an army of 1,817, a navy of 685 and an air force of 255. The remainder comprised administration and command staff, central support staff and other forces. Reserve forces in the national guard numbered 11,204. Military service is compulsory from 19 years of age and lasts for 12 months. In August 1994 the withdrawal from Latvia of all former Soviet forces was completed. Latvia joined the North Atlantic Treaty Organization's (NATO) 'Partnership for Peace' (see p. 316) programme in February 1994, and became a full member of the Alliance on 29 March 2004. The budget for 2005 allocated 153m. LVL to defence.

Economic Affairs

In 2004, according to estimates by the World Bank, Latvia's gross national income (GNI), measured at average 2002–04 prices, was US $12,570m., equivalent to $5,460 per head (or $11,850 per head on an international purchasing-power parity basis). During

1995–2004, it was estimated, the population decreased by an annual average of 1.0%, while gross domestic product (GDP) per head increased at an average annual rate of 7.4%, in real terms. Overall GDP increased, in real terms, by an annual average of 6.4% in 1995–2004; according to official figures, real GDP increased by 8.5% in 2004 and by 10.2% in 2005.

Agriculture (including hunting, forestry and fishing) contributed 4.1% of GDP in 2004, and provided 13.2% of employment. The principal sectors are dairy farming and pig-breeding. Cereals, sugar beet, potatoes and fodder crops are the main crops grown. As part of the process of land reform and privatization, the dissolution of collective and state farms was undertaken in the early 1990s, and 38% of all arable land had been privatized by 1995. In 2003 Latvia approved a seven-year ban on the sale of rural land to foreign purchasers. Fishing makes an important contribution to the economy (an estimated 70% of the total annual catch is exported). There was considerable growth potential in the forestry industry (43.9% of Latvia's land area is classified as forest), and output increased from 1996. Agricultural GDP increased, in real terms, by an average of 2.0% per year in 1995–2004; the real GDP of the sector increased by 1.0% in 2003 and by 3.5% in 2004.

Industry (comprising mining and quarrying, manufacturing, construction and utilities) contributed 22.6% of GDP in 2004, and provided 27.2% of employment. According to the World Bank, industrial GDP increased, in real terms, at an average annual rate of 6.4% in 1995–2004. Official figures indicated that the GDP of the industrial sector increased, in real terms, by 6.0% in 2004 and by 5.6% in 2005.

Mining and quarrying contributed just 0.3% of GDP in 2004, and employed 0.2% of workers. Latvia has limited mineral resources, the most important being peat, dolomite, limestone, gypsum, amber, gravel and sand. Offshore and onshore petroleum reserves have been located. The GDP of the mining sector decreased at an average annual rate of 14.5% in 1990–98; however, real mining GDP increased by 5.7% in 1999, by 8.1% in 2000, by 16.7% in 2001, by 7.7% in 2002 and by 7.2% in 2003.

The manufacturing sector contributed 13.4% of GDP in 2004, and provided 16.0% of employment. In 2001 the principal branches of manufacturing, measured by value of output, were food products (31.6%), wood products, light industry and machinery and equipment. Real manufacturing GDP increased by an average of 6.5% per year in 1995–2004. The GDP of the sector increased, in real terms, by 9.1% in 2003 and by 6.0% in 2004.

Latvia is highly dependent on imported fuels to provide energy. In 2004 mineral products represented 12.7% of the total value of Latvia's imports. Electric energy is supplied primarily by Estonia and Lithuania, and petroleum products are supplied by Russia and Lithuania. In 2002 hydroelectric plants provided some 62.0% of annual domestic electricity production in Latvia; a further 33.1% was derived from natural gas, and the remainder from petroleum and coal.

The services sector has increased in importance, and by 2004 it contributed 73.3% of GDP and accounted for 59.6% of employment. The GDP of the sector increased, in real terms, by an average of 6.5% annually during 1995–2003; real services GDP increased by 5.9% in 2002 and by 6.8% in 2003. The tourism sector was expected to expand markedly in the mid-2000s, following a significant expansion in air services between Rīga and several cities in central and western Europe.

In 2004 Latvia recorded a visible trade deficit of US $2,781m., and there was a deficit of $1,766m. on the current account of the balance of payments. The principal source of imports in 2004 was Germany, which accounted for 14.6% of total imports; other major sources were Lithuania (12.5%), Russia (8.7%), Estonia (7.2%), Finland (6.5%), Sweden (6.3%) and Poland (5.6%). The main market for exports in that year was the United Kingdom, which accounted for 13.0% of the total; other significant purchasers were Germany (12.4%), Sweden (10.3%), Lithuania (9.5%), Estonia (8.4%), Russia (6.4%) and Denmark (5.7%). The principal exports in 2004 were wood and wood articles, followed by base metals and manufactures, textiles, machinery and electrical equipment, prepared foodstuffs, beverages and tobacco, chemicals and mineral products. The principal imports in that year were machinery and electrical equipment, mineral products, vehicles and transport equipment, base metals and manufactures, chemicals, prepared foodstuffs, beverages and tobacco, and textiles.

In 2004 the consolidated state budget recorded a deficit of 78.4m. LVL (equivalent to 1.1% of GDP). At the end of 2003 Latvia's external debt totalled US $8,803m., of which $1,238m. was long-term public debt. In that year the cost of debt-servicing was equivalent to 18.5% of the value of exports of goods and services. Annual consumer-price inflation averaged 5.4% in 1995–2004. Consumer prices increased by 6.2% in 2004 and by 6.7% in 2005. Some 7.7% of the population were registered as unemployed in July–October 2005, according to official figures.

Latvia is a member (as a 'country of operations') of the European Bank for Reconstruction and Development (EBRD, see p. 224). Latvia became a member of the World Trade Organization (WTO, see p. 370) in February 1999. In May 2004 Latvia acceded to the European Union (EU, see p. 228)

The Government's programme of stabilization, initiated in 1992, achieved considerable success. Latvia's external trade underwent a significant reorientation in the 1990s, away from Russia and the successor states of the USSR towards the markets of central and western Europe. Conversely, in the early 2000s, Latvia was able to reorientate its trade eastwards, to capitalize on rapid growth in the Russian economy and the concurrent slow rates of growth in several of the principal EU economies. Although growth slowed in the immediate aftermath of the Russian economic crisis of 1998, the Latvian economy demonstrated a marked recovery thereafter. A cargo port on the Baltic coast at Primorsk, Leningrad Oblast, Russia, opened in 2001, causing shipments to Latvia's main port, at Ventspils, to decline dramatically, and any eventual recovery appeared to be partially dependent on cordial relations between Latvia and Russia's state-controlled fuel transportation companies. The Government was expected to sell its remaining stake in the port in 2006, and it was anticipated that trade would resume should a Russian-owned company acquire ownership. Meanwhile, although, in terms of GDP per head, Latvia was the poorest country to accede to full membership of the EU in May 2004, its economy had enjoyed one of the highest rates of growth in the region. Strong growth had improved employment levels significantly, but it also led to price and wage inflation (consumer prices increased by 6.7% in 2005, compared with just 1.9% in 2002) and a large deficit on the current account of the balance of payments (which was estimated at some 11% of GDP in 2005); expanding international energy prices increased the severity of the situation. In contrast with Lithuania and Slovenia, Latvia's economy was not expected to be sufficiently aligned with EU requirements to permit it to adopt the common European currency, the euro, in 2008, as had been hoped. However, Latvia was admitted to the EU's exchange rate mechanism (ERM 2) in May 2005. There were plans to reduce the uniform rate of personal income tax from 25% to 22% in 2007, 19% in 2008 and 15% in 2009, but this was likely to be subject to postponement should the economic situation be deemed to be unfavourable.

Education

Primary education begins at seven years of age and lasts for four years. Secondary education, beginning at the age of 11, comprises a first cycle of five years and a second of three years. Only the first nine years of education are officially compulsory. In 2000/01 primary enrolment included 92% of children in the relevant age-group. The comparable ratio in secondary enrolment was 74%. In the 2004/05 academic year some 65% of school-age pupils were taught in Latvian-language schools and some 25% were taught in Russian-language schools; 10% were taught in schools offering instruction in both Latvian and Russian. In that year higher education was offered at 56 institutions, with a total enrolment of some 130,700 students. According to official figures, in 2004 consolidated central Government expenditure on education amounted to 429.9m. LVL (representing 16.5% of expenditure).

Public Holidays

2006: 1 January (New Year's Day), 14–17 April (Easter), 1 May (Labour Day), 23–24 June (Midsummer Festival), 18 November (National Day, proclamation of the Republic), 25–26 December (Christmas), 31 December (New Year's Eve).

2007: 1 January (New Year's Day), 6–9 April (Easter), 1 May (Labour Day), 23–24 June (Midsummer Festival), 18 November (National Day, proclamation of the Republic), 25–26 December (Christmas), 31 December (New Year's Eve).

Weights and Measures

The metric system is in force.

LATVIA

Statistical Survey

Source (unless otherwise stated): Central Statistical Bureau of Latvia, Lāčplēša iela 1, Rīga 1301; tel. 736-6850; fax 783-0137; e-mail csb@csb.lv; internet www.csb.lv.

Area and Population

AREA, POPULATION AND DENSITY

Area (sq km)	64,589*
Population (census results)†	
12 January 1989	2,666,567
31 March 2000	
Males	1,094,964
Females	1,282,419
Total	2,377,383
Population (official estimates at 1 January)	
2003	2,311,480
2004	2,319,203
2005	2,306,434
Density (per sq km) at 1 January 2005	35.7

* 24,938 sq miles.
† Figures refer to the resident population.

POPULATION BY ETHNIC GROUP
(official estimates, 1 January 2005)

	Number	%
Latvian	1,357,099	58.8
Russian	660,684	28.6
Belarusian	88,287	3.8
Ukrainian	59,011	2.6
Polish	56,511	2.5
Lithuanian	31,717	1.4
Jewish	9,883	0.4
Roma	8,491	0.4
Total (incl. others)	2,306,434	100.0

PRINCIPAL TOWNS
(population at 1 January 2005, official estimates)

Rīga (Riga, the capital)	731,762	Jūrmala	55,603
Daugavpils	110,379	Ventspils	44,017
Liepāja	86,264	Rēzekne	36,798
Jelgava	66,136		

BIRTHS, MARRIAGES AND DEATHS

	Registered live births		Registered marriages		Registered deaths	
	Number	Rate (per 1,000)	Number	Rate (per 1,000)	Number	Rate (per 1,000)
1997	18,830	7.7	9,680	4.0	33,533	13.8
1998	18,410	7.6	9,641	4.0	34,200	14.2
1999	19,396	8.1	9,399	3.9	32,844	13.7
2000	20,248	8.5	9,211	3.9	32,205	13.6
2001	19,664	8.3	9,258	3.9	32,991	14.0
2002	20,044	8.6	9,738	4.2	32,498	13.9
2003	21,006	9.0	9,989	4.3	32,437	13.9
2004	20,334	8.8	10,370	4.5	32,024	13.8

Expectation of life (WHO estimates, years at birth): 71 (males 66; females 76) in 2003 (Source: WHO, *World Health Report*).

IMMIGRATION AND EMIGRATION

	2002	2003	2004
Immigrants	1,428	1,364	1,665
Emigrants	3,262	2,210	2,744

ECONOMICALLY ACTIVE POPULATION
(annual averages, '000 persons aged 15 years and over)

	2002	2003	2004
Agriculture, hunting and forestry	147	135	132
Fishing	6	3	2
Mining and quarrying	3	2	2
Manufacturing	167	174	163
Electricity, gas and water	22	22	25
Construction	60	74	87
Wholesale and retail trade; repair of motor vehicles, motorcycles and personal and household goods	148	153	151
Hotels and restaurants	24	25	26
Transport, storage and communications	86	95	96
Financial intermediation	13	16	18
Real estate, renting and business activities	39	42	40
Public administration and defence, compulsory social security	68	67	73
Education	88	79	83
Health and social work	60	59	54
Other community, social and personal service activities	53	57	60
Total employed (incl. others)	989	1,007	1,018
Males	505	517	522
Females	484	490	496
Unemployed	135	119	119
Total labour force	1,123	1,126	1,136

Health and Welfare

KEY INDICATORS

Total fertility rate (children per woman, 2003)	1.1
Under-5 mortality rate (per 1,000 live births, 2004)	12
HIV/AIDS (% of persons aged 15–49, 2003)	0.6
Physicians (per 1,000 head, 2002)	2.91
Hospital beds (per 1,000 head, 2001)	8.20
Health expenditure (2002): US $ per head (PPP)	477
Health expenditure (2002): % of GDP	5.1
Health expenditure (2002): public (% of total)	64.1
Human Development Index (2003): ranking	48
Human Development Index (2003): value	0.836

For sources and definitions, see explanatory note on p. vi.

LATVIA

Agriculture

PRINCIPAL CROPS
('000 metric tons)

	2002	2003	2004
Wheat	519.5	468.4	499.9
Barley	252.5	240.4	283.5
Rye	101.5	87.6	96.8
Oats	79.7	78.3	107.4
Triticale (wheat-rye hybrid)	40.9	33.0	42.1
Other cereals*	39.0	24.3	37.8
Potatoes	768.4	739.0	628.4
Sugar beet	622.3	532.4	505.6
Dry peas	3.3	3.8	2.7
Other pulses*	1.4	1.6	2.1
Rapeseed	32.7	37.4	103.6
Cabbages	61.7	72.6	75.5
Cucumbers and gherkins	16.0*	17.5	12.1
Dry onions	14.1	17.5	19.8
Carrots	23.0	41.7	33.3
Other vegetables*	33.3	68.3	40.1
Apples	50.3	36.1	6.9
Currants	3.5	3.4	2.8
Cranberries*	2.0	2.2	3.4

* Unofficial figures.
Source: FAO.

LIVESTOCK
('000 head at 1 January)

	2002	2003	2004
Cattle	385	388	379
Pigs	429	453	444
Sheep	29	32	39
Goats	12	13	15
Horses	20	19	15
Chickens*	3,121	3,332	3,403

* Unofficial figures.
Source: FAO.

LIVESTOCK PRODUCTS
('000 metric tons, unless otherwise indicated)

	2002	2003	2004
Beef and veal	16.0	21.2	21.6
Pig meat	35.9	36.9	36.8
Poultry meat	10.6	12.4	14.3
Cows' milk	811.4	783.2	784.0
Cheese	12.6	15.9	18.9
Butter	7.3	7.1*	7.2
Hen eggs	30.4	30.4	31.6
Cattle hides*	2.0	2.5	2.5
Sheepskins*	11.8	12.0	11.6

* FAO estimate(s).
Source: FAO.

Forestry

ROUNDWOOD REMOVALS
('000 cubic metres, excl. bark)

	2002	2003	2004
Sawlogs, veneer logs and logs for sleepers	8,066	7,842	7,892
Pulpwood	3,655	3,525	3,292
Other industrial wood	547	558	600
Fuel wood	1,198	991	970
Total	13,466	12,916	12,754

Source: FAO.

SAWNWOOD PRODUCTION
('000 cubic metres, incl. railway sleepers)

	2002	2003	2004
Coniferous (softwood)	3,100	3,083	2,880
Broadleaved (hardwood)	848	868	1,108
Total	3,948	3,951	3,988

Source: FAO.

Fishing

('000 metric tons, live weight)

	2001	2002	2003
Capture	128.2	113.7	114.5
Atlantic cod	6.3	4.9	4.6
Jack and horse mackerels	18.5	7.8	8.7
Atlantic herring	26.6	25.3	24.2
Sardinellas	7.7	6.1	8.7
European sprat	42.8	47.5	41.7
Chub mackerel	9.9	7.1	10.4
European anchovy	9.1	6.9	n.a.
Northern prawn	3.0	1.9	3.7
Aquaculture	0.5	0.4	0.6
Total catch	128.6	114.1	115.2

Source: FAO.

Mining

('000 metric tons)

	2002	2003	2004
Peat	846.6	585.2	595.1
Gypsum	228.8	265.1	266.2
Limestone	303.0	361.8	344.0

Industry

SELECTED PRODUCTS
('000 metric tons, unless otherwise indicated)

	2001	2002	2003
Sausages	27	30	33
Preserved fish	94	88	70
Whole milk (million litres)	22.1	22.3	15.9
Yoghurt	51	51	54
Ice-cream (million litres)	10.2	12.4	14.8
Mayonnaise	6.3	7.3	7.4
Beer ('000 hectolitres)	989	1,199	1,364
Woven cotton fabrics (million sq metres)	15	22	n.a.
Leather footwear ('000 pairs)	285	99	169
Plywood ('000 cu metres)	176	189	n.a.
Paper	21	21	n.a.
Cement	500	n.a.	n.a.
Crude steel	515	520	n.a.
Electric energy (million kWh)	4,280	3,975	3,975

Source: partly UN, *Industrial Commodity Statistics Yearbook*.

LATVIA

Finance

CURRENCY AND EXCHANGE RATES

Monetary Units
100 santimi = 1 lats (LVL).

Sterling, Dollar and Euro Equivalents (30 December 2005)
£1 sterling = 102.11 santimi;
US $1 = 59.30 santimi;
€1 = 69.96 santimi;
100 LVL = £97.93 = $168.63 = €142.95.

Average Exchange Rate (LVL per US $)
2003   0.571
2004   0.540
2005   0.565

Note: Between March and June 1993 Latvia reintroduced its national currency, the lats, replacing the Latvian rouble (Latvijas rublis), at a conversion rate of 1 lats = 200 Latvian roubles. The Latvian rouble had been introduced in May 1992, replacing (and initially at par with) the Russian (formerly Soviet) rouble.

GOVERNMENT FINANCE
(general government operations, million LVL)

Summary of Balances

	2002	2003	2004
Revenue	1,874.0	2,107.4	2,522.2
Less Expense	2,022.0	2,212.5	2,599.6
Less Lending minus repayments	−17.5	−2.7	1.0
Fiscal surplus/deficit	−130.5	−102.4	−78.4

Revenue

	2002	2003	2004
Tax revenue	1,598.5	1,782.6	2,025.4
Value-added tax	383.0	459.2	486.7
Excise tax	177.5	212.1	236.9
Corporate income tax	109.7	93.9	127.8
Personal income tax	319.5	367.1	435.4
Property tax	46.4	51.7	56.7
Social security contributions	528.8	561.9	641.2
Non-tax revenue	260.3	311.7	479.1
Income of budgetary institutions from market services and self-earned income	101.3	112.1	128.0
Foreign financial aid	28.1	50.0	154.2
Receipts from other administrative bodies	3.5	4.8	7.9
Grants and gifts received	11.7	8.4	9.9
Total	1,874.0	2,107.4	2,522.2

Expense/Outlays

Expense by economic type	2002	2003	2004
Current expenditure	828.7	944.8	1,087.4
Wages and salaries	393.7	457.0	531.2
Social security contributions	103.0	106.3	123.2
Payments on services	182.8	223.3	256.8
Interest payments	46.7	51.3	55.1
Grants and subsidies	930.2	993.3	1,208.6
Capital expenditure	216.5	223.1	248.5
Total	2,022.0	2,212.5	2,599.6

Outlays by function of government	2002	2003	2004
General public services	155.3	185.2	217.6
Defence	67.4	79.5	90.2
Public order and safety	129.9	153.9	163.7
Education	369.8	387.6	430.0
Health care	187.4	207.0	245.7
Social security and social welfare	646.6	673.8	730.4
Housing and community amenities	108.8	113.3	135.3
Recreation, sport, cultural and religious affairs	78.7	88.4	95.2
Agriculture, forestry and fishing	79.7	109.1	161.2
Transport, communication	88.9	109.1	138.6
Other expenditure	92.0	102.9	192.7
Total	2,004.5	2,209.8	2,600.6

INTERNATIONAL RESERVES
(US $ million at 31 December)

	2002	2003	2004
Gold (market prices)	85.90	102.67	110.27
IMF special drawing rights	0.07	0.14	0.15
Reserve position in IMF	0.08	0.08	0.09
Foreign exchange	1,241.27	1,432.22	1,911.74
Total	1,327.32	1,535.11	2,022.25

Source: IMF, *International Financial Statistics*.

MONEY SUPPLY
(million LVL at 31 December)

	2002	2003	2004
Currency outside banks	543.13	601.05	645.41
Demand deposits at banking institutions	501.36	630.02	860.97
Total money (incl. others)	1,047.50	1,232.74	1,507.68

Source: IMF, *International Financial Statistics*.

COST OF LIVING
(Consumer Price Index; base: 2000 = 100)

	2003	2004	2005
Food and non-alcoholic beverages	111.2	119.5	130.5
Fuel and light	104.7	114.0	121.0
Clothing (incl. footwear)	103.7	106.4	106.2
Rent	104.9	112.3	126.5
All items (incl. others)	107.5	114.2	121.9

NATIONAL ACCOUNTS
(million LVL at current prices)*

Expenditure on the Gross Domestic Product

	2002	2003	2004
Final consumption expenditure	4,783.5	5,358.8	6,103.2
Households; and non-profit institutions serving households	3,575.9	3,987.6	4,623.9
General government	1,207.6	1,371.2	1,479.3
Gross capital formation	1,536.0	1,838.1	2,471.0
Gross fixed capital formation	1,370.6	1,560.1	2,041.8
Changes in inventories; and acquisitions, less disposals, of valuables	165.4	278.1	429.2
Total domestic expenditure	6,319.5	7,196.9	8,574.2
Exports of goods and services	2,353.7	2,689.3	3,268.3
Less Imports of goods and services	2,914.9	3,493.4	4,428.9
GDP in market prices	5,758.3	6,392.8	7,413.6
GDP at constant 2000 prices	5,465.1	5,858.4	6,358.7

LATVIA

Gross Domestic Product by Economic Activity

	2002	2003	2004
Agriculture, hunting and forestry	228.9	228.6	266.2
Fishing	9.9	7.4	8.3
Mining and quarrying	11.4	15.9	18.3
Manufacturing	711.0	759.8	888.4
Electricity, gas and water supply	168.8	179.2	206.0
Construction	287.4	320.9	386.5
Wholesale and retail trade; repair of motor vehicles, motorcycles and personal and household goods	922.7	1,022.9	1,214.6
Hotels and restaurants	62.4	80.4	98.3
Transport, storage and communications	785.6	876.7	1,037.9
Financial intermediation	261.1	282.6	323.2
Real estate, renting and business activities	720.5	783.3	885.7
Public administration and defence; compulsory social security	409.8	443.6	517.6
Education	256.7	321.6	346.2
Health and social work	154.5	169.3	177.8
Other community, social and personal service activities	197.9	223.4	264.4
GDP at basic prices	5,188.6	5,715.7	6,639.5
Taxes *less* subsidies on products	569.7	677.1	774.1
GDP in purchasers' values	5,758.3	6,392.8	7,413.6

* Figures revised in accordance with standard EU classification.

BALANCE OF PAYMENTS
(US $ million)

	2002	2003	2004
Exports of goods f.o.b.	2,545	3,171	4,221
Imports of goods f.o.b.	−4,024	−5,174	−7,002
Trade balance	−1,479	−2,003	−2,781
Exports of services	1,239	1,506	1,780
Imports of services	−701	−930	−1,178
Balance on goods and services	−942	−1,427	−2,179
Other income received	289	369	500
Other income paid	−235	−382	−772
Balance on goods, services and income	−888	−1,440	−2,451
Current transfers received	538	924	1,289
Current transfers paid	−275	−394	−604
Current balance	−624	−910	−1,766
Capital account (net)	21	76	144
Direct investment abroad	−3	−36	−103
Direct investment from abroad	254	292	699
Portfolio investment assets	−220	−286	−13
Portfolio investment liabilities	20	70	260
Financial derivatives assets	−7	−5	−35
Financial derivatives liabilities	20	11	−13
Other investment assets	−472	−685	−1,767
Other investment liabilities	1,095	1,528	2,929
Net errors and omissions	−71	24	69
Overall balance	12	79	403

Source: IMF, *International Financial Statistics*.

External Trade

PRINCIPAL COMMODITIES
(million LVL)

Imports c.i.f.	2002	2003	2004
Prepared foodstuffs; beverages spirits and vinegar; tobacco and manufactured substitutes	165.3	180.7	229.0
Mineral products	243.2	296.9	481.6
Products of chemical or allied industries	261.1	300.5	350.1
Plastics, rubber and articles thereof	124.0	153.4	190.2
Paper-making material; paper and paperboard and articles thereof	107.7	112.8	126.3
Textiles and textile articles	171.5	193.9	216.6
Base metals and articles thereof	210.8	277.3	388.4
Machinery and mechanical appliances; electrical equipment; sound and television apparatus	530.8	629.6	755.7
Vehicles, aircraft, vessels and associated transport equipment	244.5	313.6	413.7
Total (incl. others)	2,497.4	2,989.2	3,805.3

Exports f.o.b.	2002	2003	2004
Prepared foodstuffs; beverages spirits and vinegar; tobacco and manufactured substitutes	100.8	94.1	132.4
Mineral products	24.1	26.4	114.1
Products of chemical or allied industries	81.5	96.7	123.5
Wood, cork and articles thereof; wood charcoal; manufactures of straw, esparto, etc.	472.8	581.8	655.3
Textiles and textile articles	180.1	208.7	230.0
Base metals and artices thereof	185.4	207.4	303.3
Machinery and mechanical appliances; electrical equipment; sound and television apparatus	91.0	116.8	169.2
Miscellaneous manufactured articles	83.0	97.3	114.3
Total (incl. others)	1,408.8	1,650.6	2,150.0

PRINCIPAL TRADING PARTNERS
(million LVL)*

Imports c.i.f.	2002	2003	2004
Austria	34.8	46.6	56.6
Belarus	68.2	110.8	181.5
Belgium	48.9	52.4	60.7
China, People's Rep.	26.3	38.4	47.9
Czech Republic	34.4	41.8	58.5
Denmark	84.8	101.9	116.0
Estonia	153.9	191.8	272.3
Finland	200.2	220.9	247.1
France	65.4	84.1	91.6
Germany	429.5	479.8	556.9
Italy	104.4	130.3	131.0
Lithuania	245.8	289.7	476.6
Netherlands	84.4	92.6	131.3
Norway	31.4	38.9	38.0
Poland	125.8	152.7	213.7
Russia	218.8	260.7	332.0
Spain	30.7	36.9	36.3
Sweden	159.5	187.1	239.7
Switzerland	47.5	56.5	57.9
Ukraine	34.0	54.7	99.7
United Kingdom	57.9	67.3	80.0
USA	39.3	52.0	50.0
Total (incl. others)	2,497.4	2,989.2	3,805.3

LATVIA

Exports f.o.b.	2002	2003	2004
Belarus	21.2	23.9	45.1
Belgium	15.3	17.3	19.2
Denmark	80.4	99.0	123.0
Estonia	84.5	108.5	180.2
Finland	32.8	44.3	54.7
France	28.7	36.6	40.8
Germany	218.3	245.3	267.5
Italy	30.4	43.3	38.2
Ireland	13.3	19.7	31.3
Lithuania	117.7	135.1	203.5
Netherlands	53.8	53.7	56.9
Norway	23.3	32.1	40.7
Poland	22.0	24.6	79.6
Russia	82.5	88.8	137.5
Sweden	148.6	174.2	222.2
Ukraine	25.8	34.3	34.2
United Kingdom	205.4	256.6	278.5
USA	59.6	47.7	63.1
Total (incl. others)	1,408.8	1,650.6	2,150.0

* Imports by country of origin; exports by country of destination.

2005 (million LVL): *Imports c.i.f.*: Germany 669.3; Lithuania 662.5; Russia 413.8; Estonia 381.0; Poland 307.0; Total (incl. others) 4,834.7. *Exports f.o.b.*: Lithuania 311.5; Estonia 309.3; Germany 294.5; United Kingdom 290.3; Russia 228.3; Total (incl. others) 2,871.4.

Transport

RAILWAYS
(traffic)*

	2002	2003	2004
Passenger journeys (million)	22.0	23.0	23.9
Passenger-kilometres (million)	744	762	811
Freight transported (million metric tons)	40.1	49.4	55.9
Freight ton-kilometres (million)	15,020	17,955	18,618

* Data relating to passengers include railway personnel, and data on freight include passengers' baggage, parcel post and mail.

ROAD TRAFFIC
(motor vehicles in use at 31 December)

	2002	2003	2004
Passenger cars	619,081	648,901	686,128
Buses and coaches	11,164	10,983	10,740
Lorries and vans	102,734	104,626	107,553
Motorcycles and mopeds	22,157	22,880	n.a.

SHIPPING
Merchant Fleet
(registered at 31 December)

	2002	2003	2004
Number of vessels	158	156	162
Total displacement ('000 grt)	88.7	90.9	294.3

Source: Lloyd's Register-Fairplay, *World Fleet Statistics*.

International Sea-borne Freight Traffic
('000 metric tons)

	2002	2003	2004
Goods loaded	48,735	50,918	54,101
Goods unloaded	3,420	3,837	3,299

CIVIL AVIATION
(traffic)

	2001	2002	2003
Passengers carried ('000)	298.7	325.9	408.3
Passenger-kilometres (million)	276.0	338.1	248.6
Cargo ton-kilometres ('000)	6,544	10,491	18,000*

* Figure is rounded.
Source: Ministry of Transport, Rīga.

Tourism

FOREIGN TOURIST ARRIVALS*

Country of residence	2002	2003	2004
Estonia	35,187	39,298	50,883
Finland	55,702	61,507	65,321
Germany	48,544	62,649	87,757
Lithuania	28,382	30,830	45,193
Russia	36,403	37,238	43,545
Sweden	20,735	22,725	26,116
United Kingdom	15,657	20,910	29,090
USA	12,805	12,414	18,245
Total (incl. others)	360,927	414,924	545,366

* Figures refer to arrivals at accommodation establishments. Including excursionists, the total number of visitor arrivals (in '000) was: 2,039 in 2001; 2,273 in 2002; 2,470 in 2003; 3,033 in 2004.

Tourism receipts (€ million): 120 in 2001; 161 in 2002; n.a. in 2003; 241 in 2004.

Communications Media

	2002	2003	2004
Telephones ('000 main lines in use)*	701	662	631
Mobile cellular telephones ('000 subscribers)	917.2	1,219.6	1,526.7
Personal computers ('000 in use)	400	436	501
Internet users ('000)	310	936	810
Book production: titles	2,326	2,605	2,591
Book production: copies ('000)	4,599	5,223	4,882
Newspapers: number	219	250	252
Newspapers: average annual circulation (million copies)	192	181	201
Other periodicals: number	365	340	353
Other periodicals: average annual circulation (million copies)	27.4	28.8	32.1

* At 31 December.

Radio receivers ('000 in use): 1,760 in 1997.
Television receivers ('000 in use): 1,220 in 1997.
Facsimile machines (number in use): 900 in 1996.

Sources: partly UNESCO, *Statistical Yearbook*; UN, *Statistical Yearbook*; and International Telecommunication Union.

Education

(2004/05)

	Institutions	Students
Pre-primary	551	73,004
Schools*	993	315,633
Primary (Grades 1–4)	60	7,580
Basic (Grades 1–9)	486	74,272
Secondary (Grades 10–12)	383	209,022
Special	64	9,793
Vocational schools	103	44,651
Higher education institutions	56	130,706

* Figures are for full-time general schools.

Teachers (2002): Pre-primary 7,996 (2004); Primary (including basic schools) 9,252; Secondary 16,495; Special schools 1,837; Vocational 5,639; Higher 4,535 (2004).

Adult literacy rate (UNESCO estimates): 99.7% (males 99.8%; females 99.7%) in 2003 (Source: UN Development Programme, *Human Development Report*).

Directory

The Constitution

The Constitution of the Republic of Latvia, which had been adopted on 15 February 1922, was annulled at the time of the Soviet annexation in 1940. Latvia became a Union Republic of the USSR and a new Soviet-style Constitution became the legal basis for the governmental system of the republic. The constitutional authority for Latvian membership of the USSR, the Resolution on Latvian Entry into the USSR of 21 July 1940, was declared null and void on 4 May 1990. In the same declaration the Latvian Supreme Council announced the restoration of Articles 1, 2 and 3 of the 1922 Constitution, which describe Latvia as an independent and sovereign state, and Article 6, which states that the legislature (the Saeima) is elected by universal, equal, direct and secret vote, on the basis of proportional representation. On 6 July 1993 the 1922 Constitution was fully restored by the Saeima, following its election on 5 and 6 June. A summary of the Constitution's main provisions (including amendments adopted since its restoration) is given below.

BASIC PROVISIONS

Latvia is an independent, democratic republic, in which the sovereign power of the State belongs to the people. The territory of the Republic of Latvia comprises the provinces of Vidzeme, Latgale, Kurzeme and Zemgale, within the boundaries stipulated by international treaties.

THE SAEIMA

The Saeima (Parliament) comprises 100 representatives of the people and, according to a constitutional amendment adopted in December 1997, is elected by universal, equal, direct and secret vote, on the basis of proportional representation, for a period of four years. All Latvian citizens who have attained 18 years of age are entitled to vote and are eligible for election to the Saeima.

The Saeima elects a Board, which consists of the Chairperson, two Deputies, and Secretaries. The Board convenes the sessions of the Saeima and decrees regular and extraordinary sittings. The sessions of the Saeima are public (sittings in camera are held only by special request).

The right of legislation belongs to both the Saeima and the people. Draft laws may be presented to the Saeima by the President of the Republic, the Cabinet of Ministers, the Committees of the Saeima, no fewer than five members of the Saeima, or, in special cases, by one-tenth of the electorate. Before the commencement of each financial year, the Saeima approves the state budget, the draft of which is submitted by the Cabinet of Ministers. The Saeima decides on the strength of the armed forces during peacetime. The ratification of the Saeima is indispensable to all international agreements dealing with issues resolved by legislation.

THE PRESIDENT OF THE REPUBLIC

According to a constitutional amendment adopted by the Saeima in December 1997, the President of the Republic is elected by a secret ballot of the Saeima for a period of four years. At least 51 deputies must vote for the winning candidate. No person of less than 40 years of age may be elected President of the Republic. The office of President is not compatible with any other office, and the President may serve for no longer than two consecutive terms.

The President represents the State in an international capacity; he or she appoints Latvian representatives abroad, and receives representatives of foreign states accredited to Latvia; implements the decisions of the Saeima concerning the ratification of international treaties; is Head of the Armed Forces; appoints a Commander-in-Chief in time of war; and has the power to declare war on the basis of a decision of the Saeima.

The President has the right to pardon criminals serving penal sentences; to convene extraordinary meetings of the Cabinet of Ministers for the discussion of an agenda prepared by him or her, and to preside over such meetings; and to propose the dissolution of the Saeima. The President may be held criminally accountable if the Saeima sanctions thus with a majority vote of no fewer than two-thirds of its members.

THE CABINET OF MINISTERS

The Cabinet comprises the Prime Minister and the ministers nominated by him/her. This task is entrusted to the Prime Minister by the President of the Republic. All state administrative institutions are subordinate to the Cabinet, which, in turn, is accountable to the Saeima. If the Saeima adopts a vote expressing 'no confidence' in the Prime Minister, the entire Cabinet must resign. The Cabinet discusses all draft laws presented by the ministries as well as issues concerning the activities of the ministries. If the State is threatened by foreign invasion or if events endangering the existing order of the State arise, the Cabinet has the right to proclaim a state of emergency.

THE JUDICIARY

All citizens are equal before the law and the courts. Judges are independent and bound only by law. The appointment of judges is confirmed by the Saeima. Judges may be dismissed from office against their will only by a decision of the Supreme Court. The retiring age for judges is stipulated by law. Judgment may be passed solely by institutions that have been so empowered by law and in such a manner as specified by law. A Constitutional Court was established in 1996 to examine the legality of legislation.

The Government

HEAD OF STATE

President: VAIRA VIĶE-FREIBERGA (inaugurated 8 July 2003).

CABINET OF MINISTERS
(April 2006)

A coalition of the People's Party (TP), the Latvian First Party (LPP) and the Greens' and Farmers' Union (GFU—ZZS).

Prime Minister: AIGARS KALVĪTIS (TP).
Minister of Defence: ATIS SLAKTERIS (TP).
Minister of Foreign Affairs: ARTIS PABRIKS (TP).
Minister of Finance: OSKARS SPURDZIŅŠ (TP).
Minister of the Economy: AIGARS ŠTOKENBERGS (TP).
Minister of the Interior: DZINTARS JAUNDZEIKARS (LPP).
Minister of Education and Science: BAIBA RIVŽA (GFU—ZZS).
Minister of Agriculture: MĀRTIŅŠ ROZE (GFU—ZZS).
Minister of Culture: HELĒNA DEMAKOVA (TP).
Minister of Welfare: DAGNIJA STAĶE (GFU—ZZS).
Minister of Transport: KRIŠJĀNIS PETERS (LPP).
Minister of Justice: GUNTARS GRĪNVALDS (LPP).
Minister of the Environment: RAIMONDS VĒJONIS (GFU—ZZS).
Minister of Health: GUNDARS BĒRZIŅŠ (TP).
Minister of Regional Development and Local Governments: MĀRIS KUČINSKIS (TP).
Minister for Children and Family Affairs: AINARS BAŠTIKS (LPP).
Minister of Special Assignment on Social Integration Affairs: KARINA PĒTERSONE (LPP).
Minister of Special Assignment on Electronic Government Affairs: INA GUDELE (Independent).

MINISTRIES

Chancery of the President: Pils lauk. 3, Rīga 1900; tel. 737-7548; fax 709-2106; e-mail chancery@president.lv; internet www.president.lv.

Office of the Cabinet of Ministers: Brīvības bulv. 36, Rīga 1520; tel. 708-2800; fax 728-0469; e-mail vk@mk.gov.lv; internet www.mk.gov.lv.

Ministry of Agriculture: Republikas lauk. 2, Rīga 1981; tel. 702-7107; fax 702-7250; internet www.zm.gov.lv.

Ministry of Children and Family Affairs: Basteja bulv. 14, Rīga 1050; tel. 735-6497; fax 735-6464; e-mail pasts@bm.gov.lv; internet www.bm.gov.lv.

Ministry of Culture: K. Valdemāra iela 11A, Rīga 1364; tel. 707-8110; fax 707-8107; e-mail info@km.gov.lv; internet www.km.gov.lv.

Ministry of Defence: K. Valdemāra iela 10–12, Rīga 1473; tel. 721-0124; fax 721-2307; e-mail kanceleja@mod.gov.lv; internet www.mod.gov.lv.

Ministry of the Economy: Brīvības iela 55, Rīga 1519; tel. 701-3101; fax 728-0882; e-mail em@em.gov.lv; internet www.em.gov.lv.

Ministry of Education and Science: Vaļņu iela 2, Rīga 1050; tel. 722-2415; fax 721-3992; e-mail izm@izm.gov.lv; internet www.izm.gov.lv.

Ministry of the Environment: Peldu iela 25, Rīga 1494; tel. 702-6400; fax 782-0442; e-mail pasts@vidm.gov.lv; internet www.varam.gov.lv.

Ministry of Finance: Smilšu iela 1, Rīga 1050; tel. 722-6672; fax 709-5503; e-mail info@fm.gov.lv; internet www.fm.gov.lv.

LATVIA

Ministry of Foreign Affairs: Brīvības bulv. 36, Rīga 1395; tel. 701-6201; fax 782-8121; e-mail mfa.cha@mfa.gov.lv; internet www.mfa.gov.lv.

Ministry of Health: Brīvības iela 72, Rīga 1011; tel. 7087-6000; fax 787-6002; e-mail vm@vm.gov.lv; internet www.vm.gov.lv.

Ministry of the Interior: Raiņa bulv. 6, Rīga 1050; tel. 721-9210; fax 722-8283; e-mail pc@iem.gov.lv; internet www.iem.gov.lv.

Ministry of Justice: Brīvības bulv. 36, Rīga 1536; tel. 708-8220; fax 728-5575; e-mail info@tm.gov.lv; internet www.tm.gov.lv.

Ministry of Regional Development and Local Government: Lāčplēša iela 27, Rīga 1011; tel. 777-0401; fax 777-0479; e-mail pasts@raplm.gov.lv; internet www.raplm.gov.lv.

Ministry of Social Integration Affairs: Elizabetes iela 20, 2nd Floor, Rīga 1050; tel. 736-5332; fax 736-5335; e-mail iumsils@integracija.gov.lv; internet www.integracija.gov.lv.

Ministry of Transport: Gogoļa iela 3, Rīga 1743; tel. 722-6922; fax 721-7180; e-mail satmin@sam.gov.lv; internet www.sam.gov.lv.

Ministry of Welfare: Skolas iela 28, Rīga 1331; tel. 702-1600; fax 727-6445; e-mail lm@lm.gov.lv; internet www.lm.gov.lv.

Legislature

Saeima
(Parliament)

Jekaba iela 11, Rīga 1811; tel. 708-7111; fax 708-7100; e-mail web@saeima.lv; internet www.saeima.lv.

Chairman: INGRĪDA ŪDRE.

General Election, 5 October 2002

Parties and coalitions	Votes	%	Seats
New Era	237,452	23.98	26
For Human Rights in a United Latvia*	189,088	19.09	25
People's Party	165,246	16.69	20
Latvian First Party†	94,752	9.57	10
Greens' and Farmers' Union‡	93,759	9.47	12
Conservative Union 'For Fatherland and Freedom'/LNNK	53,396	5.39	7
Latvian Way	48,430	4.89	—
Latvian Social Democratic Workers' Party	39,837	4.02	—
Light of Latgale	15,948	1.61	—
Social Democratic Union	15,162	1.53	—
Social Democratic Welfare Party	13,234	1.34	—
Others	23,945	2.42	—
Total	**990,249**	**100.00**	**100**

* An electoral bloc composed of the Latvian Socialist Party and the People's Harmony Party.
† Including the Christian Democratic Union of Latvia.
‡ Comprising the Latvian Green Party and the Latvian Farmers' Union.

Election Commission

Central Election Commission (Centrālā vēlēšanu komisija—CVK): Smilšu ielā 4, Rīga 1050; tel. 732-2688; fax 732-5251; e-mail cvk@cvk.lv; internet web.cvk.lv; Chair. ARNIS CIMDARS.

Political Organizations

There were some 69 political organizations registered in Latvia in January 2005. The following were among the most influential in 2006:

All for Latvia (Visu Latvijai): Lugažu iela 6–33, Rīga 1045; tel. 738-3171; e-mail edgars@visulatvijai.lv; internet www.visulatvijai.lv; f. 2006 as a political party; f. 2000 as a patriotic alliance; nationalist; Chair. RAIVIS DZINTARS.

Centre Party-Latvian Farmers' Union (LFU) (Centriskā partija-Latvijas Zemnieku savienība) (LZS): Republikas lauk. 2, Rīga 1010; tel. 702-7163; fax 702-7467; e-mail lzs@latnet.lv; internet www.lzs.lv; f. 1990; re-registered 1993; rural, centrist; contested 2002 legislative elections as mem. of Greens' and Farmers' Union; Chair. INGRĪDA ŪDRE.

Christian Democratic Union of Latvia (CDUL) (Latvijas Kristīgi Demokrātiskā savienība—KDS): Jēkaba iela 26, Rīga 1811; tel. 732-3534; fax 783-0333; internet www.kds.lv; f. 1991; Chair. JURIS KOKINS; 600 mems.

Conservative Union 'For Fatherland and Freedom'/LNNK (Aprienība 'Tēvzemei un Brīvībai'/LNNK): Kalēju iela 10, Rīga 1050; tel. 708-7273; fax 708-7268; e-mail tb@tb.lv; internet www.tb.lv; f. 1997 by merger of the Union 'For Fatherland and Freedom' and the Latvian National Independence Conservative Movement; Chair. JĀNIS STRAUME.

For Human Rights in a United Latvia (Par cilvēka tiesībām vienotā Latvijā/Za prava cheloveka v yedinoi Latvii—PCTVL/ZaPChEL): Rūpniecības iela 9, Rīga 1000; tel. and fax 732-0290; e-mail pctvl@saeima.lv; internet www.pctvl.lv; f. 1998; represents interests of Russian-speaking communities in Latvia, and campaigns for the equal rights of different ethnic groups; opposed to Latvian membership of NATO; Leaders TATJANA ŽDANOKA, JAKOVS PLINERS.

Labour Party (Darba partija): Kurbada iela 2, Rīga 1009; tel. 728-8255; fax 913-8738; e-mail darbapartija@eriga.lv; internet www.darbapartija.lv; f. 1996; Chair. AIVARS KREITUSS.

Latvian First Party (Latvijas Pirmā Partija—LPP): Kungu iela 8, Rīga 1050; tel. 722-6070; fax 722-6831; e-mail lpp@lpp.lv; internet www.lpp.lv; f. 2002; absorbed New Christian Party in 2003; formed a political union with Latvian Way in 2005; Christian democratic; Chair. JURIS LUJĀNS.

Latvian Green Party (Latvijas Zaļā partija): Kalnciema iela 30, Rīga 1046; tel. and fax 761-4272; e-mail info@zp.lv; internet www.zp.lv; f. 1990; forms part of the Greens' and Farmers' Union; Co-Chair. INDULIS EMSIS, VIESTURS SILENIEKS, RAIMONDS VEJONIS.

Latvian Social Democratic Workers' Party (Latvijas Sociāldemokrātiskā strādnieku partija—LSDSP): Aldaru iela 8, Rīga 1050; tel. 735-6581; fax 761-4600; e-mail lsdsp@lis.lv; internet www.lsdsp.lv; f. 1999 as result of a merger with the Latvian Social Democratic Union; Chair. GUNTARS JIRGENSONS.

Latvian Socialist Party (Latvijas Sociālistiskā partija—LSP): Burtnieku iela 23, Rīga; tel. and fax 755-5535; internet www.latsocpartija.lv; f. 1994; mem. of the For Human Rights in a United Latvia bloc in 1998–2003; joined the Harmony Centre bloc in Dec. 2005; Chair. ALFRĒDS RUBIKS.

Latvian Way (Latvijas ceļš): Akmenu iela 15, Rīga 1000; tel. 761-8087; fax 782-1121; e-mail lc@lc.lv; internet www.lc.lv; f. 1993; formally changed status from an alliance to a political party in June 2005; formed a political union with the Latvian First Party in 2005; Chair. IVARS GODMANIS.

Light of Latgale (Latgales Gaisma): Vienības 18, Daugavpils 5401; tel. 542-4562; f. 2000; promote development and interests of Latgale region of south-eastern Latvia; Chair. RIHARDS EIGAMS.

New Centre (Jaunais Centrs): Ģertrūdes iela 20/5A, Rīga 1011; tel. 784-6114; fax 784-6115; e-mail jaunais.centrs@apollo.lv; internet www.jaunaiscentrs.lv; f. 2004; formed the Harmony Centre alliance with the People's Harmony Party in July 2005; Leader SERGEJS DOLGOPOLOVS.

New Democrats (Jaunie demokrāti): Lāčplēša iela 35/16B/6, Rīga 1011; tel. 727-9505; fax 727-9306; e-mail birojs@jauniedemokrati.lv; internet www.jauniedemokrati.lv; f. 2005 by former mems of New Era; Chair. MĀRIS GULBIS.

New Era (Jaunais laiks): Jēkaba Kazarmās, Torņa iela 4/3B, Rīga 1050; tel. 720-5472; fax 720-5473; e-mail birojs@jaunaislaiks.lv; internet www.jaunaislaiks.lv; f. 2002; right-wing; Chair. EINĀRS REPŠE; Sec.-Gen. ULDI GRAVU.

People's Harmony Party (Tautas Saskaņas Partija—TSP): Elizabetes iela 23A/15, Rīga 101; tel. 750-8552; fax 750-8553; e-mail tsp@saeima.lv; internet www.tsp.lv; f. 1993; socialist; advocates the rapid integration of non-citizens into Latvian society; mem. of the For Human Rights in a United Latvia bloc in 1998–2003; formed the Harmony Centre alliance with splinter group, the New Centre, in 2005; Chair. JĀNIS URBANOVIČS.

People's Party (Tautas partija—TP): Dzirnavu iela 68, Rīga; tel. 728-6441; fax 728-6405; e-mail arno@tautas.lv; internet www.tautaspartija.lv; f. 1998; Chair. ATIS SLAKTERIS.

Social Democratic Union (Sociāldemokrātu Savienība – SDS): Basteja bulv., Rīga 1050; tel. 722-6352; fax 722-6353; e-mail birojs@socialdemokrati.lv; internet www.socialdemokrati.lv; f. 2002; Chair. PĒTERIS SALKAZANOVS; Sec.-Gen. MĀRĪTE TEIVĀNE.

Social Democratic Welfare Party (Sociāldemokrātiskā Labklājības partija): Brīvības iela 30, Rīga 1050; tel. 770-2502; fax 728-0255; e-mail partija@socdem.lv; f. 1999; forms part of the Homeland alliance; Chair. JURIS ZURAVLOVS.

LATVIA   Directory

Diplomatic Representation

EMBASSIES IN LATVIA

Austria: Elizabetes iela 21A/11, Rīga 1010; tel. 721-6125; fax 721-4401; e-mail riga-ob@bmaa.gv.at; Ambassador Dr WERNFRIED KOEFFLER.

Azerbaijan: Alberta iela 12, 3 stāvs, Rīga 1010; tel. 733-2452; fax 733-2090; f. 2005; Ambassador TOFIG ZULFUGAROV.

Belarus: Jēzusbaznīcas iela 12, Rīga 1050; tel. 722-2560; fax 732-2891; e-mail latvia@belembassy.org; internet belembassy.org/latvia; Ambassador ALYAKSANDR HERASIMENKA (designate).

Belgium: Alberta iela 13, Rīga 1010; tel. 711-4852; fax 711-4855; e-mail riga@diplobel.be; internet www.diplomatie.be/riga; f. 2004; Ambassador CHRISTIAN VERDONCK.

Canada: Baznicas iela 20–22, Rīga 1010; tel. 781-3945; fax 781-3960; e-mail riga@dfait-maeci.gc.ca; internet www.dfait-maeci.gc.ca/dfait/missions/baltiks; Ambassador CLAIRE A. POULIN.

China, People's Republic: Ganību dambis 5, Rīga 1045; tel. 735-7023; fax 735-7025; e-mail chinaemb_lv@mfa.gov.cn; Ambassador ZHANG LIMIN.

Czech Republic: Elizabetes iela 29A, Rīga 1010; tel. 721-7814; fax 721-7821; e-mail zuczriga@parks.lv; internet www.mfa.cz/riga; Ambassador JAN FINFERLE.

Denmark: Pils iela 11, Rīga 1863; tel. 722-6210; fax 722-9218; e-mail rixamb@um.dk; internet www.ambriga.um.dk; Ambassador ARNOLD CHRISTIAN DE FINE SKIBSTED.

Estonia: Skolas iela 13, Rīga 1010; tel. 781-2020; fax 781-2029; e-mail embassy.riga@mfa.ee; internet www.estemb.lv; Ambassador TOOMAS LUKK.

Finland: Kalpaka bulv. 1, Rīga 1605; tel. 707-8800; fax 707-8814; e-mail sanomat.rii@formin.fi; internet www.finland.lv; Ambassador PEKKA WUORISTO.

France: Raiņa bulv. 9, Rīga 1050; tel. 703-6600; fax 703-6615; e-mail webmastre.ambafrance-lv@diplomatie.gouv.fr; internet www.ambafrance-lv.org; Ambassador ANDRÉ-JEAN LIBOUREL.

Germany: Raiņa blvd 13, Rīga 1050; tel. 708-5100; fax 708-5149; e-mail mailbox@deutschebotschaft-riga.lv; internet www.deutschebotschaft-riga.lv; Ambassador EBERHARD SCHUPPIUS.

Greece: Elizabetes iela 11–5, 1010 Rīga; tel. 735-6345; fax 735-6351; e-mail greekemb-riga@mfa.gr; internet www.greekembassy.se; Ambassador SPYROS ALIAGAS.

Ireland: Valdemara Centrs 632, Kr. Valdemara iela 21, Rīga 1010; tel. 703-5286; fax 703-5323; Ambassador TIM MAWE.

Israel: Elizabetes iela 2, Rīga 1010; tel. 732-0739; fax 783-0170; e-mail press@rig.mfa.gov.il; internet riga.mfa.gov.il; Ambassador GARY KOREN.

Italy: Teātra iela 9, Rīga 1050; tel. 721-6069; fax 721-6084; e-mail ambitalia.riga@apollo.lv; internet www.ambitalia.apollo.lv; Ambassador FERDINANDO ZEZZA.

Japan: Kr. Valdemāra iela 21, Rīga 1010; tel. 781-2001; fax 781-2004; e-mail eoj.001@latnet.lv; Ambassador SEIICHIRO OTSUKA.

Lithuania: Rūpniecibas iela 24, Rīga 1010; tel. 732-1519; fax 732-1589; e-mail lt@apollo.lv; internet lv.urm.lt; Ambassador OSVALDAS ČIUKŠYS.

Moldova: Basteja bulvāris 14, 1050 Rīga; tel. 735-9160; fax 735-9165; e-mail riga@moldovaembassy.lv; Chargé d'affaires a.i. ANGELA PONOMARIOV.

Netherlands: Torņu iela 4/1A, Jēkaba Kazarmas, Rīga 1050; tel. 732-6147; fax 732-6151; e-mail info@netherlandsembassy.lv; internet www.netherlandsembassy.lv; Ambassador ROBERT SCHUDDEBOOM.

Norway: Zirgu iela 14, POB 1173, Rīga 1050; tel. 781-4100; fax 781-4108; e-mail emb.riga@mfa.no; internet www.norvegija.lv; Ambassador NILS OLAV STAVA.

Poland: Mednieku iela 6B, Rīga 1010; tel. 703-1500; fax 703-1549; e-mail ambpol@apollo.lv; internet www.ambpolriga.lv; Ambassador MACIEJ KLIMCZAK.

Portugal: Grand Palaca Hotel, Pils iela 12, 1050 Rīga; tel. and fax 704-4188; Ambassador JOÃO LUIS NIZA PINHEIRO.

Russia: Antonijas iela 2, Rīga 1010; tel. 733-2151; fax 783-0209; e-mail rusembas@delfi.lv; internet www.latvia.mid.ru; Ambassador VIKTOR I. KALYUZHNYI.

Slovakia: Smilšu iela 8, Rīga 1050; tel. 781-4280; fax 781-4290; e-mail embassy@slovakia.lv; Ambassador IVAN SPILDA.

Spain: Elizabetes iela 11, 3rd Floor, 1010 Rīga; tel. 732-0281; fax 732-5005; Ambassador EMILIO LORENZO SERRA.

Sweden: A. Pumpura iela 8, Rīga 1010; tel. 768-6600; fax 768-6601; e-mail ambassaden.riga@foreign.ministry.se; internet www.swedenemb.lv; Ambassador GÖRAN HÅKANSSON.

Switzerland: Elizabetes iela 2, Rīga 1340; tel. 733-8351; fax 733-8354; e-mail vertretung@rig.rep.admin.ch; internet www.eda.admin.ch/riga; Ambassador ANNE BAUTY.

Turkey: Blaumaņa iela 5A, 1011 Rīga; tel. 782-1600; fax 732-0334; e-mail riga.be@mfa.gov.tr; Ambassador DURAY POLAT.

Ukraine: Kalpaka bulv. 3, Rīga 1010; tel. 724-3082; fax 732-5583; e-mail uaemb@neonet.lv; Ambassador RAUL CHILACHAVA.

United Kingdom: J. Alunāna iela 5, Rīga 1010; tel. 777-4700; fax 777-4707; e-mail british.embassy@apollo.lv; internet www.britain.lv; Ambassador IAN ANDREW MINTON BOND.

USA: Raiņa bulv. 7, Rīga 1510; tel. 703-6206; fax 722-2132; e-mail pas@usembassy.lv; internet www.usembassy.lv; Ambassador CATHERINE TODD BAILEY.

Uzbekistan: Elizabetes iela 11, Rīga 1010; tel. 732-2424; fax 732-2306; e-mail posoluz@apollo.lv; Ambassador KOBILJON S. NAZAROV.

Judicial System

Constitutional Court of the Republic of Latvia (Latvijas Republikas Satversmes tiesa): J. Alunāna iela 1, Rīga 1010; tel. 722-1412; fax 722-0572; e-mail aivars.e@satv.tiesa.gov.lv; internet www.satv.tiesa.gov.lv; f. 1996; comprises seven judges, appointed by the Saeima for a term of 10 years; Chair. AIVARS ENDZIŅŠ.

Supreme Court (Latvijas Republikas Augstākā tiesa): Brīvības bulv. 36, Rīga 1050; tel. 702-0350; fax 702-0351; e-mail at@at.gov.lv; internet www.at.gov.lv; Chair. ANDRIS GUĻĀNS.

Office of the Prosecutor-General: Kalpaka bulv. 6, Rīga 1801; tel. 704-4400; fax 704-4449; e-mail gen@lrp.gov.lv; internet www.lrp.gov.lv; Prosecutor-General JĀNIS MAIZĪTIS.

Religion

From the 16th century the traditional religion of the Latvians was Lutheran Christian. Russian Orthodoxy was the religion of most of the Slav immigrants. After 1940, when Latvia was annexed by the USSR, many places of religious worship were closed and clergymen were imprisoned or exiled. Following the restoration of independence in 1991, religious organizations regained their legal rights, as well as property that had been confiscated during the Soviet occupation. At 1 July 2000 the statutes of 1,095 religious organizations were registered. The total number of congregations was 1,072, of which 308 were Lutheran, 250 Roman Catholic, 118 Pentecostal, 117 Orthodox, 85 Baptist, 66 Old Believer, 45 Adventist, 11 Methodist, seven Jewish and six Muslim.

Association for Freedom of Religion (AFFOR): Ganību dambis 3–2, Rīga 1045; e-mail ringolds.balodis@apollo.lv; f. 1999; to protect religious freedom in Latvia; Vice-Pres. SINTIJA BALODE.

Board of Religious Affairs: Pils lauk. 4, Rīga 1050; tel. 722-0585; e-mail rlp@apollo.lv; f. 2000; govt agency, attached to the Ministry of Justice; Principal OLGA LEILE (acting).

CHRISTIANITY

Protestant Churches

Consistory of the Evangelical Lutheran Church of Latvia: M. Pils iela 4, Rīga 1050; tel. 722-6057; fax 782-0041; e-mail konsistorija@parks.lv; internet www.lutheran.lv; f. 1922; Archbishop JĀNIS VANAGS.

Latvian Conference of Seventh-day Adventists in Latvia: Baznīcas iela 12A, Rīga 1010; tel. and fax 724-0013; e-mail viesturs@baznica.lv; internet www.adventistu.baznica.lv; f. 1920; Pres. of Council VIESTURS REĶIS.

Latvian Pentecostal Union: J. Asara iela 8, Jelgava 3001; tel. 308-1401; fax 308-1407; e-mail lvdaddf@hotmail.com; f. 1989; Bishop JĀNIS OZOLINKEVIČS.

Union of Baptist Churches in Latvia: Lāčplēša iela 37, Rīga 1011; tel. and fax 722-3379; e-mail baptist.lbds@viva.lv; f. 1860; Bishop Dr YANIS A. SMITS.

United Methodist Church in Latvia: Klaipēdas iela 56, Liepāja 3401; tel. 343-2161; fax 346-9848; re-est. 1991; Supt ĀRIJS VĪKSNA.

The Roman Catholic Church

Latvia comprises one archdiocese and three dioceses. At 31 December 2003 there were an estimated 434,000 adherents in the country (equivalent to an estimated 18% of the population).

Bishops' Conference

M. Pils iela 2A, Rīga 1050; tel. 722-7266; fax 722-0775; Pres. Cardinal JĀNIS PUJATS.

LATVIA

Archbishop of Rīga: Cardinal JĀNIS PUJATS, M. Pils iela 2A, Rīga 1050; tel. 722-7266; fax 722-0775; e-mail curia@e-apollo.lv; internet www.catholic.lv.

The Orthodox Church

Although the Latvia Orthodox Church has close ties with the Moscow Patriarchate, it has administrative independence. The spiritual head of the Orthodox Church is elected by its Saeima (or assembly).

Latvian Orthodox Church (Moscow Patriarchate): Pils iela 14, Rīga 1050; tel. 722-5855; fax 722-4345; e-mail sinode@orthodoxy.lv; internet www.pareizticiba.lv; f. 1850; Metropolitan of Rīga and all Latvia ALEKSANDR (KUDRJASHOV).

Latvian Old Believer (Old Ritualist) Pomor Church: Krasta iela 73, Rīga 1003; tel. 711-3083; fax 714-4513; e-mail oldbel@junik.lv; f. 1760 in split from Moscow Patriarchate; Head of Central Council IVANS MIZOĻUBOVS (Fr Ioann).

JUDAISM

Jewish Religious Community of Rīga: Peitavas iela 6/8, Rīga 1050; tel. 722-4549; f. 1764; Rabbi NATAN BARKAN.

DIEVTURÎBA

Latvijas Dievturu sadraudze (LDS): Rīga; community of Dievturi, celebrating traditional Latvian animist rites; Leader ROMANS PUSSARS.

The Press

The joint-stock company Preses nams (Press House—q.v.) is the leading publisher of newspapers and magazines in Latvia. In 2002 there were eight daily newspapers, with an average circulation of 183,000. In 2004 a total of 252 daily and non-daily newspapers and 353 other periodicals were published. The publications listed below are in Latvian, unless otherwise indicated.

DAILIES

Bizness & Baltiya (Business and the Baltics): Kr. Valdemāra iela 149, Rīga 1013; tel. 703-3011; fax 703-3040; e-mail info@bb.lv; internet www.bb.lv; f. 1991; 5 a week; in Russian; Editor-in-Chief ALEKSEI SHCHERBAKOV; circ. 15,000.

Chas (Hour): Peldu iela 15, Rīga 1050; tel. 708-8712; fax 721-1067; internet www.chas-daily.com; f. 1997; in Russian; Editor-in-Chief XENIA ZAGOROVSKAYA; circ. 16,050 (weekdays); 22,000 (Saturdays).

Diena (Day): Mūkusalas iela 41, Rīga 1004; tel. 706-3100; fax 706-3190; e-mail diena@diena.lv; internet www.diena.lv; f. 1990; in Latvian; social and political issues; associated with free newspaper *5min*, launched in Sept. 2005; Editor-in-Chief SARMĪTE ĒLERTE; circ. 62,000.

Jaunā Avīze: Brīvības iela 75, Rīga 1001; tel. 724-2437; e-mail ja@parks.lv.

Neatkarīgā Rīta Avīze (Independent Morning Paper): Balasta dambis 3, Rīga 1081; tel. 706-2462; fax 706-2465; e-mail redakcija@nra.lv; internet www.nra.lv; f. 1990; Editor-in-Chief ALDIS BĒRZIŅŠ; circ. 40,000.

Rīgas Balss (RB) (Voice of Rīga): Balasta dambis 3, Rīga 1081; tel. 706-2420; fax 706-2400; e-mail balss@rb.lv; internet www.rigasbalss.lv; f. 1957; city evening newspaper; Editor-in-Chief IVETA MEDIŅA; circ. 18,100 (Mon.–Thur.), 42,700 (Fri.).

Vakara Ziņas (The Evening News): Bezdelīgas iela 12, Rīga 1007; tel. 761-7595; fax 761-2383; e-mail vakara.zinas@vz.lv; internet www.vz.lv; f. 1993; popular; Editor-in-Chief AINĀRS VLADIMIROVS; circ. 53,000.

Vesti Segodņa (News Today): Mūkusalas iela 41, Rīga 1004; tel. 706-3230; fax 706-3232; e-mail sm@fenster.lv; in Russian; Editor-in-Chief ALEKSANDRS BĻINOVS; circ. 24,000.

OTHER NEWSPAPERS

The Baltic Times: Šķūņu iela 16, Rīga 1050; tel. 722-4073; fax 722-6041; e-mail editorsdesk@baltictimes.com; internet www.baltictimes.com; f. 1996; news from Estonia, Latvia and Lithuania; in English; Man. Dir ANTRA LINARTE; Editor-in-Chief ELIZABETH CELMS; circ. 12,000.

Dienas Bizness (Daily Business): Balasta dambis 3, POB 2, Rīga 1081; tel. 706-2622; fax 706-2309; e-mail nberch@db.lv; internet www.db.lv; f. 1992; Editor-in-Chief JURIS PAIDERS; circ. 17,000.

Ieva (Eve): Stabu iela 34, Rīga 1011; tel. 700-6102; fax 700-6111; e-mail ieva@santa.lv; f. 1997; weekly; illustrated journal for women; Editor-in-Chief INGA GORBUNOVA; circ. 73,650.

Izglītība un Kultūra (Education and Culture): Palasta iela 10, Rīga 1502; tel. 735-7585; fax 735-7584; e-mail info@izglitiba-kultura.lv; internet www.izglitiba-kultura.lv; f. 1948; Editor ANITA KALMANE.

Latvijas Avīze (Latvian Newspaper): Dzirnavu iela 21, Rīga 1010; tel. 709-6600; fax 709-6645; e-mail mlredaktors@la.lv; internet www.la.lv; f. 1988; fmrly *Lauku Avīze* (Country Newspaper); present name adopted 2004; 3 a week; popular; agriculture, politics and sport; Editor-in-Chief LINDA RASA; circ. 59,500.

Latvijas Vēstnesis (Latvian Herald): Bruņinieku iela 36/2, Rīga 1001; tel. 731-2630; fax 229-9410; e-mail editor@mail.lv-laiks.lv; internet www.lv-laiks.lv; f. 1993; official newspaper of the Republic of Latvia; Editor-in-Chief OSKARS GERTS; circ. 5,200.

Privātā Dzīve (Private Life): Stabu iela 34, Rīga 1011; tel. 700-6104; fax 700-6111; e-mail pdz@santa.lv; weekly; Editor-in-Chief SANDIJA ŠĶĒLE; circ. 76,000.

Rīgas Viļņi (Riga Waves): Bruņinieku iela 49, korp. 3, Rīga 1011; tel. 784-2577; fax 784-2578; e-mail info@rigasvilni.lv; internet www.rigasvilni.lv; weekly.

PRINCIPAL PERIODICALS

Baltiskii Kurs/The Baltic Course: Balasta dambis 3, Rīga 1081; tel. 706-2560; fax 706-2664; e-mail baltkurs@baltkurs.com; internet www.baltkurs.com; f. 1996; quarterly; business; in English and Russian; International Editor EUGENE ETERIS; Editor-in-Chief OLGA PAVUK.

Cosmopolitan Latvia: A. Čaka iela 83/85–15, Rīga 1011; tel. 731-6107; e-mail andis@lilita.lv; f. 2001.

Daugava: Balasta dambis 3, Rīga 1081; tel. 728-0290; e-mail ravdin@mailbox.riga.lv; f. 1977; 6 a year; literary journal; Editor-in-Chief ZHANNA EZIT; circ. 500.

Karogs (Banner): Kuršu iela 24, Rīga 1006; tel. 755-4145; fax 755-4146; e-mail karogs@apollo.lv; f. 1940; literary monthly; Editor-in-Chief IEVA KOLMANE; circ. 1,500.

Klubs (Club): Balasta dambis 3, Rīga 1081; tel. 746-4420; fax 746-1438; e-mail klubs@santa.lv; f. 1994; monthly; politics, business, fashion; Editor-in-Chief JURIS SLEIERS; circ. 18,000.

Latvijas Ekonomists: Ieriķu ielā 67a, Rīga 1084; tel. 703-1090; e-mail birojs@ekonomists.lv; internet www.ekonomists.lv; f. 1992; monthly; in Latvian and Russian; Dir INESE LAPIŅA.

Māksla Plus (M+): Akadēmijas laukums 1, a.k. 41, Rīga 1027; tel. 722-0722; fax 782-0608; e-mail makslaplus@hotmail.com; internet www.makslaplus.lv; cultural magazine (cinema, music, theatre, photography); associated with the Ministry of Culture and the Kultūrkapitāla fonda; Editor-in-Chief MAIJA AUGSTKALNA.

Mans Mazais: Balasta dambis 3, Rīga 1081; tel. 762-8274; fax 246-5450; e-mail mansmazais@santa.lv; f. 1994; monthly; illustrated journal for young parents; Editor-in-Chief VITA BEĻAUNIECE; circ. 20,000.

Mūsmājas (Our Home): Pērnavas iela 43, Rīga 1009; tel. 727-3311; fax 729-2701; e-mail pasts@mgtops.lv; internet www.musmajas.lv; f. 1993; monthly; home and family magazine; Editor-in-Chief ILZE STRAUTIŅA; circ. 50,000.

Mūzikas Saule: Arhitektu 1–305, Rīga 1050; tel. 722-0161; fax 957-7765; e-mail saule@m-saule.lv; internet www.m-saule.lv; music; Editor-in-Chief IEVA ROZENTĀLE.

Rīgas Laiks (Rīga Times): Lāčplēša iela 25, Rīga 1011; tel. 728-7922; fax 783-0542; e-mail pasts@rigaslaiks.lv; internet www.rigaslaiks.lv; f. 1993; monthly; Editor-in-Chief INESE ZANDERE; circ. 10,000.

Santa: Balasta dambis 3, POB 32, Rīga 1081; tel. 762-8274; fax 246-5450; e-mail santa@santa.lv; f. 1991; monthly; illustrated journal for women; Editor-in-Chief SANTA ANCHA; circ. 42,000.

Zinātnes Vēstnesis (Scientific Herald): Akadēmijas lauk. 1, Rīga 1524; tel. 721-2706; fax 782-1109; e-mail lzs@ac.lza.lv; internet www.lza.lv/zv00.htm; f. 1989; publ. by the Latvian Scientific Council, the Latvian Academy of Science and the Latvian Society of Scientists; two a month; Editor-in-Chief ZAIGA KIPERE.

NEWS AGENCIES

Baltic News Service: Baznīcas iela 8, Rīga 1010; tel. 708-8600; fax 708-8601; e-mail bns@rb.bns.lv; internet bnsnews.bns.lv; f. 1990; news from Latvia, Lithuania, Estonia and the CIS; in English, Russian and the Baltic languages; Dir LIGA MENGELSONA.

LETA Latvian News Agency: Palasta iela 10, Rīga 1502; tel. 722-2509; fax 722-3850; e-mail leta.marketing@leta.lv; internet www.leta.lv; independent; Chair. MĀRTIŅŠ BARKĀNS.

FOREIGN BUREAU

Reuters (United Kingdom): Kaļķu iela 15, Rīga 1050; tel. 722-2079; fax 724-3139; e-mail reuters@reuters.lv; Bureau Chief ALAN CROSBY.

LATVIA

PRESS ASSOCIATION

Latvian Journalists' Union (Latvijas Žurnālistu savienība): Marstaļy iela 2, Rīga 1050; tel. 721-1433; fax 782-0233; e-mail reiterns@zn.apollo.lv; f. 1992; 700 mems; Pres. LIGITA AZOVSKA.

Publishers

Avots (Spring): Puskina iela 1A, Rīga 1050; tel. 721-1394; fax 722-5824; f. 1980; non-fiction, dictionaries, crafts, hobbies, etc.; Pres. JĀNIS LEJA.

Elpa (Breath): Doma lauk. 1, Rīga 1914; tel. 721-1776; fax 750-3326; f. 1990; books and newspapers; Pres. MAIRITA SOLIMA.

Jāņa sēta: Elizabetes iela 83–85, Rīga 1050; tel. 709-2290; fax 709-2292; e-mail janaseta@janaseta.lv; internet www.janaseta.lv; f. 1991; travel and culinary books; Dir AIVARS ZVIRBULIS.

Jumava: Dzirnavu iela 73, Rīga 1011; tel. and fax 728-0314; e-mail jumava@parks.lv; internet www.jumava.lv; f. 1994; translations, dictionaries, fiction, etc.; Pres. JURIS VISOCKIS.

Kontinents: Elijas iela 17, Rīga 1050; tel. 720-4130; fax 720-4129; e-mail kontinent@parks.lv; internet www.kontinent.lv; f. 1991; translated fiction, non-fiction and colour children's books; Chair. of Bd OLEG MIHALEVICH.

Nordik: Daugavgrīvas 36–9, Rīga 1048; tel. 760-2672; fax 760-2818; e-mail nordik@nordik.lv; internet www.nordik.lv; f. 1992; sister co, Tapals, at same address; Dir JĀNIS JUŠKA.

Preses nams (Press House): Balasta dambis 3, Rīga 1081; tel. 246-5732; internet www.presesnams.lv; f. 1990; newspapers, magazines, encyclopedias and scientific literature; controlling interest owned by Ventspils Nafta; Dir EGONS LAPIŅŠ.

Smaile (Peak): Brīvības iela 104, Rīga 1001; tel. 731-5137; f. 1999; fiction, poetry, fine arts; Dir ANDREJS BRIMERBERGS.

Sprīdītis: Kalēju iela 51, Rīga 1050; tel. 728-6516; fax 728-6818; f. 1989; books for children and young people; Dir ANDREJS RIJNIEKS.

Zinātne (Science): Akadēmijas lauk. 1, Rīga 1050; tel. 721-2797; fax 722-7825; e-mail zinatne@navigator.lv; f. 1951; non-fiction, text books, dictionaries, reference books; Dir IEVA JANSONE.

Zvaigzne ABC (Star ABC): K. Valdemāra iela 6, Rīga 1010; tel. 732-4518; fax 750-8798; e-mail info@zvaigzne.lv; internet www.zvaigzne.lv; f. 1966; privately owned; educational literature, manuals, dictionaries, non-fiction for children and adults, fiction; Pres. VIJA KILBLOKA.

PUBLISHERS' ASSOCIATION

Latvian Publishers' Asscn (Latvijas Grāmatizdevēju asociācija): K. Barona iela 36–4, Rīga 1011; tel. 728-2392; fax 728-0549; e-mail lga@gramatizdeveji.lv; internet www.gramatizdeveji.delfi.lv; f. 1993; 47 mems; Pres. ANITA ROŽKALNE.

Broadcasting and Communications

TELECOMMUNICATIONS

In 2004 there were 631,000 main telephone lines in use; 69% of lines were digital in 2001. In 2005 there were four providers of mobile telecommunications services.

Regulatory Organizations

Dept of Communications (Ministry of Transport): Gogoļa iela 3, Rīga 1190; tel. 724-2321; fax 782-0636; e-mail diana.ainep@sam.gov.lv; f. 1991; Dir INĀRA RUDAKA.

Public Utilities Regulatory Commission (Sabiedrisko Pakalpojumu Regulēšanas Komisija): Brīvības iela 55, Rīga 1010; tel. 709-7200; fax 709-7277; e-mail sprk@sprk.gov.lv; internet www.sprk.lv; regulates telecommunications and postal services, energy utilities and railways; Chair. INNA STEINBUKA.

Major Service Providers

Lattelekom SIA: Vaļņu iela 30, Rīga 1050; tel. 705-5222; fax 705-5001; e-mail gstrautma@exchange.telekom.lv; internet www.lattelekom.lv; f. 1992; 49% owned by TeliaSonera AB (Sweden); Pres. GUNDARS STRAUTMANIS; 6,500 employees.

Latvian Mobile Telephone Co (Latvijas Mobilais Telefons SIA—LMT): Unijas iela 39, POB 116, Rīga 1039; tel. 777-3200; fax 753-5353; e-mail info@lmt.lv; internet www.lmt.lv; f. 1992; 24.5% owned by Sonera Holding BV (Finland), 24.5% owned by TeliaSonera AB (Sweden), 23.0% owned by SIA Lattelekom, 23.0% owned by Digitālais Latvijas radio un televīzijas centrs, a/s; Gen. Man. JURIS BINDE; 150 employees.

SIA Radiokoms: Elizabetes iela 45–47, Rīga 1010; tel. 733-3355; e-mail radiokoms@radiokoms.lv; internet www.radiokoms.lv; Dir JANA BALODE.

Tele2: Kurzemes pr. 3, Rīga 1067; tel. 706-0069; fax 706-0176; internet www.tele2.lv; f. 1991; owned by Tele2 AB (Sweden); fmrly Baltkom GSM; Pres. BILL BUTLER; 110 employees.

BROADCASTING

Regulatory Organization

National Broadcasting Council of Latvia (Nacionālā Radio un Televizijas padome): Smilšu iela 1/3, Rīga 1939; tel. 722-1848; fax 722-0448; e-mail Zita.Janitena@nrtp.lv; internet www.nrtp.lv; f. 1995; Chair. AIVARS BERKIS.

Radio

Latvijas Radio (Latvian Radio): Doma lauk. 8, Rīga 1505; tel. 720-6722; fax 720-6709; e-mail radio@radio.org.lv; internet www.radio.org.lv; f. 1925; state-operated service; broadcasts in Latvian, Russian and English; supports four programme services: Latvijas Radio 1, Latvijas Radio 2, Latvijas Radio 3—Klasika and Latvijas Radio 4—Doma Square; Dir-Gen. AIGĀRS SEMEVICS (acting).

Alise Plus: Raiņa iela 28, Daugavpils 5403; e-mail alise_plus@daugavpils.apollo.lv; 24-hour transmissions in Russian and Latvian.

European Hit Radio: Elijas iela 17, Rīga 1050; tel. 957-5757; fax 720-4407; e-mail radio@superfm.lv; internet www.europeanhitradio.com; f. 1994; 24-hour transmissions in Latvian, Russian, Estonian, Lithuanian and English; Pres. UGIS POLIS; Dir RICHARD ZAKSS.

Latvijas Kristīgais Radio (Latvian Christian Radio): Lāčplēša iela 37, Rīga 1011; tel. 721-3704; fax 782-0633; e-mail lkr@lkr.lv; internet www.lkr.lv; f. 1993; 24-hour transmissions in Latvian and Russian.

Radio Ef-Ei: Atbrvōsanas aleja 98, Rēzekne 4600; e-mail efei@mailbox.riga.lv; 24-hour transmissions in Russian and Latvian.

Radio Imanta: Tērbatas iela 1, Valmiera 4201; tel. 420-7349; fax 420-7350; e-mail radio.imanta@tl.lv; internet www.radioimanta.lv; 24-hour transmissions in Russian and Latvian; Chief Editor NILS INTERBERGS.

Radio Mix FM: L. Nometņu iela 62, Rīga 1002; 24-hour transmissions in Russian.

Radio Sigulda: L. Paegles iela 3, Sigulda 2150; tel. 797-2678; fax 797-3786; e-mail mail@radiosigulda.lv; internet www.radiosigulda.lv; f. 1991; 24-hour transmissions in Latvian; music radio; Dir AIVARS PLUCIS.

Radio SWH: Skanstes iela 13, Rīga 1013; tel. 7370067; fax 7828283; e-mail radio@radioswh.lv; internet www.radioswh.lv; Pres. ZITMARS LIEPINSCH.

Radio Trīs: Vaļņu iela 5, Cēsis 4101; tel. 412-4566; fax 412-7041; e-mail radio@radio3.lv; internet www.radio3.lv; f. 1994; 24-hour transmissions in Latvian; Dir EGILS VISKRINTS.

Radio Zemgale: Grāfa lauk. 6, Lecava 3913; e-mail rz@apollo.lv; internet www.radiozemgalei.lv; f. 2000; 24-hour transmissions in Latvian; Dir DACE DUBKEVIČA.

Television

Latvijas Televīzija (Latvian Television): Zaķusalas krastmala 3, Rīga 1509; tel. 720-0315; fax 720-0025; e-mail ltv@ltv.lv; internet www.ltv.lv; f. 1954; state-operated service; two channels in Latvian (Channel II also includes programmes in Russian, Polish, Ukrainian, German, English and French); Dir EDGARS KOTS.

LNT (Latvian Independent Television): Elijas iela 17, Rīga 1050; tel. 707-0200; fax 782-1128; e-mail lnt@lnt.lv; internet www.lnt.lv; f. 1996; entertainment, news reports; Dir-Gen. ANDREJS ĒĶIS.

Finance

(cap. = capital; res = reserves; dep. = deposits; m. = million; brs = branches; amounts in LVL)

BANKING

A crisis in the banking sector in 1995 was contained by early 1996. Reorganization of the sector subsequently took place. At the end of 2004 there were 23 banks in operation.

Central Bank

Bank of Latvia (Latvijas Banka): K. Valdemāra iela 2A, Rīga 1050; tel. 702-2300; fax 702-2420; e-mail info@bank.lv; internet www.bank.lv; f. 1990; cap. 25.0m., res 66.0m., dep. 214.9m. (Dec. 2003); Gov. and Chair. of Council ILMĀRS RIMŠĒVIČS.

LATVIA

Commercial Banks

Aizkraukles Banka: Elizabetes iela 23, Rīga 1010; tel. 777-5222; fax 777-5200; e-mail bank@ab.lv; internet www.ab.lv; f. 1993; total assets 444.5m. (2004); Chair. of Bd ERNESTS BERNIS.

BTB—Baltic Trust Bank (Baltijas Tranzītu Banka): 13 Janvāra iela 3, Rīga 1050; tel. 702-4747; fax 721-1985; e-mail btb@btb.lv; internet www.btb.lv; f. 1992; joint-stock commercial bank; 49.76% owned by Finstar Baltic Investments SIA, 22.6% owned by Korowo Invest AG; cap. 8.6m., res 0.5m., dep. 144.0m. (Dec. 2003); Pres. and Chair. of Bd EDGARS DUBRA; 30 brs.

Hansabanka: Kaļķu iela 26, Rīga 1050; tel. 702-4444; fax 702-4400; e-mail info@hansabanka.lv; internet www.hansabanka.lv; f. 1992; present name adopted; 99.9% owned by Hansapank (Estonia); cap. 46.0m., res 18.9m., dep. 798.4m. (Dec. 2003); Chair. of Bd INGRĪDA BLUMA; 66 brs.

Hipotēku Banka—Latvijas Hipotēku un Zemes Banka (Latvian Mortgage and Land Bank): Doma lauk. 4, Rīga 1977; tel. 722-2945; fax 782-0143; e-mail banka@hipo.lv; internet www.hipo.lv; f. 1993; state-owned; cap. 20.1m., res 3.6m., dep. 195.6m. (Dec. 2003); Pres. and Chair. of Bd INESIS FEIFERIS; 32 brs.

HVB Bank Latvia: Elizabetes iela 63, Rīga 1050; tel. 708-5500; fax 708-5507; e-mail info@hvb.lv; internet www.hvbk.lv; f. 1997; fmrly Vereinsbank Rīga; present name adopted 2005; 100% owned by HypoVereinsbank (Germany); cap. 13.9m., res 0.6m., dep. 130.7m. (Dec. 2003); Pres. THOMAS SCHÜTZE.

Lateko Banka—Latvijas Ekonomiskā Komercbanka (Latvian Economic Commercial Bank): E. Birznieka-Upiša iela 21, Rīga 1011; tel. 704-1100; fax 704-1111; e-mail welcome@lateko.lv; internet www.lateko.lv; f. 1992; cap. 9.9m., res 0.7m., dep. 250.3m. (Dec. 2003); Pres. OSKARS GULĀNS.

Latvijas Tirdzniecības banka (Latvian Trade Bank): Grēcinieku iela 22, Rīga 1050; tel. 704-3500; fax 704-3511; e-mail info@ltblv.com; internet www.ltblv.com; f. 1991; 100% owned by MDM Holding GmbH Bank (Austria); cap. 3.0m., res 1.4m., dep. 128.6m. (Dec. 2003); Pres. and Chair. ARMANDS ŠTEINBERGS.

LBB—Latvijas Biznesa Banka (Latvian Business Bank): 3 Antonijas iela, Rīga 1010; tel. 777-5800; fax 777-5849; e-mail info@lbb.lv; internet www.lbb.lv; f. 1992; 99.81% owned by Moscow Municipal Bank—Bank of Moscow (Russian Federation); cap. 7.4m., res −0.7m., dep. 13.7m. (Dec. 2003); Chair. and Pres. GEORGIJS DRAGILEVS.

Multibanka: Elizabetes iela 57, Rīga 1772; tel. 728-9546; fax 782-8232; e-mail info@multibanka.com; internet www.multibanka.com; f. 1994; cap. 4.8m., res 0.3m., dep. 110.9m. (Dec. 2003); Pres. SVETLANA DZENE.

NORD/LB Latvija: Smilšu iela 6, Rīga 1803; tel. 701-5204; fax 732-3449; e-mail office@nordlb.lv; internet www.nordlb.lv; f. 1989; fmrly Rīgas Komercbanka PLC; present name adopted 2003; 99.47% owned by Norddeutsche Landesbank Girozentrale (Germany); cap. 20.2m., res 1.5m., dep. 118.7m. (Dec. 2002); Pres. and Chair. of Bd JÜRGEN MACHALETT; 10 brs.

Ogres Komercbanka—OK (Ogre Commercial Bank): 12 Birznieka-Upisha iela, Rīga 1050; tel. 701-6520; fax 701-6522; e-mail info@okb.lv; internet portal.okb.lv; f. 1993; 81.4% owned by Salamandra Baltik; cap. 3.3m., res 0.3m., dep. 134.1m. (Dec. 2003); Pres. and Chair. VALERIJS ROLDUGINS.

Parex Banka: Smilšu iela 3, Rīga 1522; tel. 701-0000; fax 701-0001; e-mail inquiry@parex.lv; internet www.parex.lv; f. 1992; 50.93% owned by Europe Holding Ltd; cap. 63.3m., res 13.5m., dep. 905.2m. (Dec. 2003); Pres. and Chair. of Bd VALERY KARGIN; Chair. of Council VICTOR KRASOVITSKY; 5 brs.

Sampo Banka: Lāčplēša iela, Rīga 1011; tel. 728-6661; fax 728-2788; e-mail info@sampobanka.lv; internet www.sampobanka.lv; f. 1997 as Māras bank; present name adopted March 2005; 100% owned by Sampo Bank (Finland); mortgage banking; cap. 3.5m., res 1.0m., dep. 19.4m. (Dec. 2003); Chair. of Council ROBERTAS ČIPKUS; Gen. Man. INGA GULBE.

Trasta komercbanka—TKB (Trust Commercial Bank): Miesnieku iela 9, Rīga 1050; tel. 702-7777; fax 702-7700; e-mail info@tkb.lv; internet www.tkb.lv; f. 1989; cap. 4.0m., res −0.05m., dep. 47.0m. (Dec. 2003); Pres. GUNDARS GRIEZE.

Unibanka: Pils iela 23, Rīga 1050; tel. 721-2808; fax 721-5335; e-mail sekretars@unibanka.lv; internet www.unibanka.lv; f. 1993; 98.8% owned by Skandinaviska Enskilda Banken AB (Sweden); cap. 37.1m., res 3.8m., dep. 760.40m. (Dec. 2003); Pres. and Chair. VIESTURS NEIMANIS; 68 brs.

Savings Bank

Latvijas Krājbanka (Latvian Savings Bank): Palasta iela 1, Rīga 1954; tel. 709-2001; fax 721-2083; e-mail info@lkb.lv; internet www.krajbanka.lv; f. 1924; present name adopted 1998; 83.0% owned by Snoras Bankas, Lithuania; cap. 9.1m., res 1.7m., dep. 167.4m. (Dec. 2003); Pres. ANDRIS NATRINS; 10 brs.

Regulatory Authority

Financial and Capital Markets Commission (Finanšu un kapitāla tirgus komisija—FKTK): Kungu iela 1, Rīga 1050; tel. 777-4800; fax 722-5755; e-mail fktk@fktk.lv; internet www.fktk.lv; f. 2001; Chair. ULDIS CĒRPS.

Banking Association

Association of Latvian Commercial Banks (Latvijas Komercbanku asociācija): Pērses iela 9–11, Rīga 1011; tel. 728-4528; fax 782-8170; e-mail office@bankasoc.lv; internet www.bankasoc.lv; f. 1992; 23 mems; Pres. TEODORS TVERIJONS.

INSURANCE

At September 2004 there were 18 insurance companies in Latvia, of which six were involved in life insurance and 12 in non-life insurance operations (including one mutual non-life insurance co-operative society).

Balta Insurance Co: Raunas iela 10/12, Rīga 1039; tel. 708-2333; fax 708-2345; e-mail balta@balta.lv; internet www.balta.lv; automobile, property, freight, travel, agricultural insurance; Pres. ANDRIS LAIZĀNS.

Balva: K. Valdemāra iela 36, Rīga 1010; tel. 750-6955; fax 750-6956; e-mail balva@balva.lv; internet www.balva.lv; f. 1992; non-life insurance; Pres. VASILY RAGOZIN.

ERGO Latvija: Ūnijas iela 45, Rīga 1035; tel. 708-1700; fax 784-0102; e-mail info@ergo.lv; owned by Alte Leipziger (Germany); life and non-life; Pres. of Bd ILMARS VEIDE.

Estora Reinsurance Co: Elizabetes iela 14, Rīga 1010; tel. 733-3335; fax 733-3898; e-mail estora@estora.com; internet www.estora.com; f. 1992; reinsurance; Dir-Gen. JERGENIJS TOLOČKOVS.

Ezerzeme: Raiņa iela 28, Daugavpils 5403; tel. 542-2555; fax 542-2177; f. 1992; state, private firm, personal property, long- and short-term life, domestic animals, accident, freight, travel, funeral insurance; Chair. of Bd PĒTERIS SAVOSTJANOVS.

Helga Insurance Co: Elizabetes iela 20, Rīga 1050; tel. 724-3074; fax 724-3067; e-mail helga@parks.lv.

Latva: Vaļņu iela 1, Rīga 1912; tel. 721-2341; fax 721-0134; e-mail latva@latva.lv; f. 1940; state insurance co; accident, passenger, child and adult life insurance; Chair. MARGARITA PABĒRZA.

Rīga Insurance Co: Grēcinieku iela 22–24, Rīga 1050; tel. 721-1764; fax 722-3437; general liability, professional liability, health, motor, natural disasters, fire, freight insurance; Pres. AIVARS BERGERS.

COMMODITY AND STOCK EXCHANGES

Latgale Exchange (Latgales birža): Sakņu iela 29, Daugavpils 5403; tel. 542-6044; fax 542-6351; f. 1992; Gen. Dir ANATOLII BOTUSHANSKII.

Rīga Stock Exchange (Rīgas Fondu birža): Vaļņu iela 1, Rīga 1050; tel. 721-2431; fax 722-9411; e-mail riga@omxgroup.com; internet www.omxgroup.com/riga; f. 1993; owned by HEX Helsinki Stock Exchange (Finland)—OMX ABforms Group; Pres. DAIGA AUZINA-MELALKSNE.

Trade and Industry

GOVERNMENT AGENCY

Latvian Privatization Agency (Latvijas Privatizācijas agentūra): K. Valdemāra iela 31, Rīga 1887; tel. 702-1358; fax 783-0363; e-mail lpa@mail.bkc.lv; internet www.lpa.bkc.lv; f. 1994; became state joint-stock co in 2004; Dir-Gen. ARTURS GRANTS.

DEVELOPMENT ORGANIZATIONS

Latvian Investment and Development Agency (Latvijas Investīciju un Attīstības Aģentūra—LIAA): Pērses iela 2, Rīga 1442; tel. 703-9400; fax 703-9401; e-mail invest@liaa.gov.lv; internet www.liaa.gov.lv; f. 1993; promotion of business development in Latvia and foreign markets; Dir (vacant).

CHAMBER OF COMMERCE

Latvian Chamber of Commerce and Industry (Latvijas Tirdzniecības un rūpniecības kamera): K. Valdemāra iela 35, Rīga; tel. 722-5595; fax 782-0092; e-mail info@chamber.lv; internet www.chamber.lv; f. 1934; re-est. 1990; Pres. ANDRIS LARMANIS; Dir-Gen. JĀNIS LEJA.

LATVIA

INDUSTRIAL AND TRADE ASSOCIATIONS

Latvian Employers' Confederation: Vilandes iela 12–1, Rīga 1010; tel. 722-5162; fax 722-4469; e-mail lddk@lddk.lv; internet www.lddk.lv; f. 1993 by merger of Latvian Employers' Central Assocn and Latvian Private Entrepreneurs' (Employers') Union; Pres. VITĀLIJS GAVRILOVS.

Latvian Construction Contractors' Association (LCCA) (Latvijas būvnieku asociācija—LBA): Grēcinieku ielā 22/24, kab. 201, Rīga 1050; tel. 722-8584; fax 721-0023; e-mail lba@latnet.lv; internet www.building.lv/lba; f. 1996; Pres. VIKTORS PURIŅŠ; 6 brs.

Latvian Electrical Engineering and Electronics Industry Association (LETERA): Dzirnavu iela 93, Rīga 1011; tel. and fax 728-8360; e-mail letera@latnet.lv; internet www.letera.lv; f. 1995; 50 mems (enterprises and education institutions); Pres. NORMUNDS BERGS.

Latvian Fuel Traders' Association (Latvijas Degvielas Tirgotāju Asociācija): Citadeles iela 7, korp. 43, Rīga 1010; tel. 732-0229; fax 732-0228; e-mail birojs@ldta.lv; internet www.ldta.lv; Chair. of Bd O. KARČEVSKIS; Exec. Dir U. SAKNE.

Latvian Information Technology and Telecommunications Association (LITTA): Stabu iela 47–1, Rīga 1011; tel. 731-1821; fax 731-5567; e-mail litta@dtmedia.lv; internet www.litta.lv; f. 1998; Pres. IMANTS FREIBERGS.

Latvian Timber Exporters' Association (LTEA) (Latvijas Kokmateriālu Eksportētāju Asociācija): Skaistkalnes iela 1, Rīga 1004; tel. and fax 706-7369; fax 786-0268; e-mail ltea@latvianwood.lv; internet www.latviantimber.lv; f. 1998; Pres. JANIS APSITIS.

UTILITIES

Regulatory Authority

Public Utilities Regulatory Commission (Sabiedrisko Pakalpojumu Regulēšanas Komisija): Brīvības iela 55, Rīga 1010; tel. 709-7200; fax 709-7277; e-mail sprk@sprk.gov.lv; internet www.sprk.lv; regulates telecommunications and postal services, energy utilities and railways; Chair. INNA STEINBUKA.

Electricity

Latvenergo: Pulkveža Brieža iela 12, Rīga 1230; tel. 772-8309; fax 772-8811; e-mail latvenergo@latvenergo.lv; internet www.latvenergo.lv; state-owned joint-stock co; transmits and distributes electricity and heat; seven regional subsidiary cos; Chair. of Bd KĀRLIS MIĶELSONS.

Gas

Latvian Gas (Latvijas gaze): A. Briana iela 6, Rīga 1001; tel. 736-9132; fax 782-1406; e-mail latvijas_gaze@lg.lv; internet www.lg.lv; partially privatized in 2000–01; 8% state-owned; Chair. MĀRIS GAILIS; 2,817 employees.

Water

Major suppliers include:

Aizkraukle Water Co (Aizkraukles ūdens): Torņu iela 1, Aizkraukle 5101; fax 512-2150; e-mail udens@adc.lv.

Bauska Water Co (Bauskas ūdens): Birzu iela 8A, Bauska 3901; tel. 396-0565; fax 396-0566; e-mail baude@apollo.lv.

Daugavpils Water Co (Daugavpils ūdens): Udensvada iela 3, Daugavpils 5403; tel. 544-4565; fax 542-5547; e-mail kontakti@daugavpils.udens.lv; internet www.daugavpils.udens.lv; f. 1889.

Liepāja Water Co (Liepājas ūdens): K. Valdemāra iela 12, Liepāja 3401; tel. 541-1416; fax 541-0769; e-mail dmeu@dpu.lv.

Rīga Water Co (Rīgas ūdens): Basteja bulv. 1/5, Rīga 1495; tel. 708-8555; fax 722-2660; e-mail office@ru.lv; internet www.rw.lv; water supply and sewage treatment.

TRADE UNIONS

Free Trade Union Confederation of Latvia (Latvijas Brīvo Arodbiedrību Savienība—LBAS): Bruņinieku iela 29–31, Rīga 1001; tel. 727-0351; fax 727-6649; e-mail intern@latnet.lv; internet www.lbas.lv; f. 1990; Pres. JURIS RADZEVICS.

Transport

RAILWAYS

In 2002 there were 2,270 km of railways on the territory of Latvia. In 2004 Latvian railways carried 23.9m. passengers and 51.1m. metric tons of freight.

Latvian Railways (Latvijas Dzelzceļš): Gogoļa iela 3, Rīga 1547; tel. 723-4940; fax 782-0231; e-mail info@ldz.lv; internet www.ldz.lv; f. 1993; state joint-stock co; Chair. of Bd UGIS MAGONIS.

ROADS

In 2004 Latvia's total road network was 69,532 km, of which 6,963 km were main roads.

Latvian State Roads (Latvijas Valsts Ceļi): Gogoļa iela 3, Rīga 1050; tel. 702-8169; fax 702-8171; e-mail lad@lvceli.lv; internet www.lvceli.lv; f. 2004 to replace Latvian Road Administration; state joint-stock co; manages state road network, administers State Road Fund; Chair. TĀLIS STRAUME.

SHIPPING

At 31 December 2004 the Latvian-registered merchant fleet numbered 162 vessels, with a combined total displacement of 294,300 grt. In 2004 some 54.1m. metric tons of freight were transported through the country's three main (Ventspils, Rīga and Liepāja) and seven smaller ports. Ventspils is particularly important for the shipping of petroleum and fuel exports and is included in a special economic zone; Rīga and Ventspils operate in a free port regime.

Maritime Department (Ministry of Transport): Gogoļa iela 3, Rīga 1743; tel. 702-8198; fax 733-1406; e-mail krastins@sam.gov.lv; Dir AIGARS KRASTIŅŠ.

Port Authorities

Liepāja Port Authority: Liepāja Special Economic Zone, Feniksa iela 4, Liepāja 3401; tel. 342-7605; fax 348-0252; e-mail authority@lsez.lv; internet www.lsez.lv; Man. Dir AIVARS BOJA.

Rīga Commercial Free Port SSC: Katrinas iela 5A, Rīga 1227; tel. 732-9224; fax 783-0215; e-mail rto@mail.bkc.lv; internet www.rto.lv; f. 1996.

Rīga Freeport Authority (Rīgas Brīvostas Pārvalde): Kalpaka bulv. 12, Rīga 1050; tel. 703-0800; fax 703-0835; e-mail rop@mail.rop.lv; internet www.rop.lv; f. 1994; Chief Exec. LEONIDS LOGINOVS; Chair. of Bd ANDRIS ARGALIS.

Ventspils Free Port Authority: Jāņa iela 19, Ventspils 3601; tel. 362-2586; fax 362-1297; e-mail vbparvalde@apollo.lv; f. 1991; Chief Exec. IMANTS SARMULIS.

Ventspils Commercial Port Authority (Ventspils Tirdzniecības Ostā): Dzintaru iela 22, Ventspils 3602; tel. 366-8706; fax 366-8860; e-mail vcp@vto.lv; internet www.vcp.lv; Pres. OLEGS STEPANOVS.

Shipping Company

Latvijas kugniecība (LAT) (Latvian Shipping Co): Basteja bulv. 2, Rīga 1807; tel. 702-0111; fax 782-8106; e-mail lsc@lsc.riga.lv; internet www.latshipcom.lv; f. 1991; tanker, reefer, liquid petroleum gas and dry-cargo transportation; 31.3% owned by Ventspils Nafta; Pres. IMANTS VIKMANIS.

CIVIL AVIATION

There is an international airport at Rīga, which serves direct flights to and from cities across Europe, as well as Istanbul (Turkey), Tel-Aviv (Israel) and Tashkent (Uzbekistan). The Department of Aviation of the Ministry of Transport co-ordinates the financing of air transport in Latvia, and the Civil Aviation Administration supervises the operation and safety of flights.

Civil Aviation Agency of Latvia (Latvijas Civilās Aviācijas Administrācija): Rīga Airport 1011, Rīga 1053; tel. 783-0936; fax 783-0967; internet www.caa.lv; Dir MĀRIS GORODCOVS.

Department of Aviation (Ministry of Transport): Gogoļa iela 3, Rīga 1743; tel. 702-8209; fax 721-7180; Dir ARNIS MUIŽNIEKS.

airBaltic Corpn: Rīga Airport, Rīga 1053; tel. 720-7069; fax 720-7369; e-mail info@airbaltic.lv; internet www.airbaltic.com; f. 1995; 52.6% govt-owned, 47.2% by Scandinavian Airlines System—SAS (Sweden/Denmark); operates services between Rīga and 25 international destinations in Northern, Central, Western, Southern and Eastern Europe, and domestic services between Rīga and Liepāja; also operate services between Vilnius (Lithuania) and 11 international destinations; Pres. and Chief Exec. BERTOLT FLICK.

Inversija: Rīga Airport, Rīga 1053; tel. 720-7095; fax 720-7476; e-mail inversia@latnet.lv; f. 1988; operates cargo services between Rīga and destinations in Europe and the Far East; Dir-Gen. SEFIM BROOK.

RAF-AVIA Airlines: J. Alunana iela 2A, Rīga 1010; tel. 732-4661; fax 732-4671; e-mail rafavia@mail.interfeis.lv; internet www.rafavia.com; f. 1991; scheduled and charter flights; Pres. JURIJS HMELEVSKII.

Tourism

Among Latvia's principal tourist attractions are the historic centre of Rīga, with its medieval and art nouveau buildings, the extensive beaches of the Baltic coastline, and Gauja National Park, which stretches east of the historic town of Sigulda for nearly 100 km along the Gauja river. Sigulda also offers winter sports facilities, while

LATVIA

Rīga also has an extensive cultural life. Revenue from tourism in 2004 was some €241m. Foreign tourist arrivals at accommodation establishments in 2004 numbered 545,366, of whom 16.1% were from Germany, 12.0% from Finland, 9.3% from Estonia and 8.3% from Lithuania.

Latvian Tourism Development Agency: Pils lauk. 4, Rīga 1050; tel. and fax 722-9945; e-mail tda@latviatourism.lv; internet www.latviatourism.lv; f. 1993; Dir AIVARS KALNINSCARON.

LEBANON

Introductory Survey

Location, Climate, Language, Religion, Flag, Capital

The Republic of Lebanon lies in western Asia, bordered by Syria to the north and east, and by Israel and the Palestinian Autonomous Areas to the south. The country has a coastline of about 220 km (135 miles) on the eastern shore of the Mediterranean Sea. The climate varies widely with altitude. The coastal lowlands are hot and humid in summer, becoming mild (cool and damp) in winter. In the mountains, which occupy much of Lebanon, the weather is cool in summer, with heavy snowfalls in winter. Rainfall is generally abundant. The official language is Arabic, which is spoken by almost all of the inhabitants. French is widely used as a second language, while Kurdish and Armenian are spoken by small ethnic minorities. At December 2005 there were 404,170 Palestinian refugees registered in Lebanon. The major religions are Islam and Christianity, and there is a very small Jewish community. In the early 1980s it was estimated that 57% of Lebanon's inhabitants were Muslims, with about 43% Christians. The principal Muslim sects are Shi'a and Sunni, while there is also a significant Druze community. By the 1980s it was generally considered that Shi'a Muslims, totalling an estimated 1.2m., constituted Lebanon's largest single community. Most Christians adhere to the Roman Catholic Church, principally the Maronite rite. There are also Armenian, Greek and Syrian sects (both Catholic and Eastern Orthodox) and small groups of Protestants. The national flag (proportions 2 by 3) has three horizontal stripes, of red, white (half the depth) and red, with a representation of a cedar tree (in green and brown) in the centre of the white stripe. The capital is Beirut.

Recent History

Lebanon, the homeland of the ancient Phoenicians, became part of the Turkish Ottoman Empire in the 16th century, and following the dissolution of the Ottoman Empire after the First World War (1914–18), a Greater Lebanese state was created by the Allied powers. The new state was formed in order to meet the nationalist aspirations of the area's predominantly Christian population, but it also included largely Muslim-populated territories traditionally considered to be part of Syria. Lebanon was administered by France, under a League of Nations mandate, from 1920 until independence was declared on 26 November 1941. A republic was established in 1943, and full autonomy was granted in January 1944.

Religious and cultural diversity is Lebanon's defining feature. At the time of independence Christians formed a slight majority of the population, the largest single community (nearly 30% of the total) being the Maronite Christians, who mostly inhabited the north of the country and the capital, Beirut. Other Christian groups included Greek Orthodox communities, Greek Catholics and Armenians. The Muslim groups were the Sunnis, living mainly in the coastal towns of Sur (Tyre), Saida (Sidon) and Beirut, the Shi'ites, a predominantly rural community in southern Lebanon and the northern Beka'a valley, and, in much smaller numbers, the Druzes, an ancient community in central Lebanon. The relative size of the various communities provided the basis for the unwritten 'national pact' of 1943, whereby executive and legislative posts were to be shared in the ratio of six Christians to five Muslims, and seats in the Chamber of Deputies (renamed the National Assembly in March 1979) were distributed on a religious, rather than a politico-ideological, basis. The convention according to this 'confessional' arrangement was that the President was a Maronite Christian, the Prime Minister a Sunni Muslim, and the President of the National Assembly a Shi'a Muslim.

Lebanon's first President, from 1943 until 1952, was Sheikh Bishara el-Khoury. His successor was Camille Chamoun, whose reforms included the enfranchisement of women. Following elections to the Chamber of Deputies in 1957 there was considerable unrest, mainly among Muslims who mistrusted Chamoun's pro-Western foreign policy and advocated Lebanon's closer alignment with Syria and Egypt. In July 1958 Chamoun appealed to the USA for military assistance; US forces remained in Beirut until October, by which time peace had been restored. Meanwhile, Chamoun was persuaded not to seek a further presidential term, and the Chamber elected Gen. Fouad Chehab as his successor. Chehab, who took office in September 1958, adopted a foreign policy of non-alignment, and introduced state provision of health, education and other services. In 1964 he was succeeded by Charles Hélou, who continued many of Chehab's policies but was faced by increasing controversy over the status of Palestinians in Lebanon.

After the establishment of Israel in 1948, and during the subsequent Arab–Israeli wars, thousands of Palestinians fled to Lebanon, where most were housed in refugee camps in the south of the country. Following the creation of the Palestine Liberation Organization (PLO) in 1964, military training centres for Palestinian guerrilla fighters were established in the camps. From 1968 these self-styled *fedayeen* ('martyrs') began making raids into Israel, provoking retaliatory attacks by Israeli forces. In 1969 there were clashes between Lebanese security forces and the *fedayeen*. Many Christians, particularly the Maronites, advocated strict government control over the Palestinians' activities, but the majority of Muslims strongly supported Palestinian operations against Israel.

Hélou's successor, Sulayman Franjiya, took office in 1970. During his presidency the Palestinian issue was exacerbated by an influx of Palestinian fighters expelled from Jordan in July 1971. Conflict between Israeli forces and Palestinians based in Lebanon intensified, while Christian groups began their own armed campaign against the *fedayeen*. In July 1974 Palestinian forces clashed with militia of the Phalangist Party (the Phalanges libanaises, or al-Kataeb, a militant right-wing Maronite Christian group). From April 1975 the conflict between the Palestinians and Phalangists quickly descended into full-scale civil war between the Lebanese National Movement (LNM) of left-wing Muslims (including Palestinians), led by Kamal Joumblatt of the Parti socialiste progressiste (PSP, a mainly Druze-supported group), and conservative Christian groups, mainly the Phalangist militia. Constitutional matters overtook the status of Palestinians as the main divisive issue, with the LNM advocating an end to the 'confessional' system, claiming that this unduly favoured Christians (who by now were generally accepted as no longer forming a majority of the population). Despite diplomatic efforts by Arab and Western countries, no durable cease-fire was achieved until October 1976, largely as a result of intervention in the conflict (in order to prevent an outright LNM victory) by Syrian forces in mid-1976. Under the terms of the cease-fire a 30,000-strong Arab Deterrent Force (ADF), composed mainly of Syrian troops, entered Lebanon.

President Franjiya was succeeded by Elias Sarkis in September 1976, and Prime Minister Rashid Karami by Selim al-Hoss in December. Legislative elections, due in April 1976, were postponed for an initial period of 26 months—the term of the Chamber of Deputies was subsequently extended further. Although the constitutional status quo remained intact, more than 30,000 people had died in the civil war and the militias of the various warring factions controlled most of the country. East Beirut and much of northern Lebanon was controlled by the Lebanese Forces (LF), a coalition of Maronite militias formed in September 1976; West Beirut was controlled by Muslim groups; and Palestinians dominated much of south-west Lebanon.

In March 1978 Israeli forces advanced into southern Lebanon in a counter-attack against forces of Fatah (the Palestine National Liberation Movement), the main guerrilla group within the PLO. UN Security Council Resolution 425, adopted on 17 March, demanded an Israeli withdrawal from Lebanon (thereby respecting its territorial integrity, sovereignty and independence) and also established a UN Interim Force in Lebanon (UNIFIL, see p. 74), initially of 4,000 troops. Israeli forces withdrew in June, but transferred control of a border strip to the pro-Israeli Christian militias of Maj. Saad Haddad. In October, following several months of renewed fighting in Beirut between Syrian troops of the ADF and right-wing Christian militias, the ADF states agreed on a peace plan (the Beiteddin Declaration), which aimed to restore the authority of the Lebanese Government and army. Attempts to implement the plan were unsuccessful, however, and Lebanon's fragmentation deepened.

Al-Hoss resigned the premiership in June 1980 and was replaced in October by Chafic al-Wazzan. In August 1982, in an election boycotted by most Muslim deputies, the renamed National Assembly designated Bachir Gemayel (the younger son of the founder of the Phalangist Party and commander of the LF) to succeed President Sarkis. The President-elect was assassinated in September, and his brother, Amin, was elected in his place. Following the assassination, Phalangist forces (with the apparent complicity of occupying Israeli forces) entered the Palestinian refugee camps of Sabra and Chatila, in west Beirut, killing some 2,000 refugees. Israeli forces had re-entered Lebanon in June 1982, with the declared aim of finally eliminating the PLO's military threat to Israel's northern border. Israeli troops quickly defeated Palestinian forces in south-west Lebanon and surrounded the western sector of Beirut, trapping more than 6,000 Palestinian fighters there. A US-led diplomatic initiative resulted in an agreement enabling the PLO fighters to disperse among several Arab states, and a multinational peace-keeping force was deployed in Beirut. (In September 1983 intense fighting between rival factions of Fatah resulted in a truce agreement, brokered by Saudi Arabia and Syria, which led to a second evacuation of some 4,000 Palestinian fighters, most notably of the PLO Chairman, Yasser Arafat, who was exiled to Tunisia.) Negotiations between Lebanon and Israel began in December 1982, culminating in May 1983 in an agreement to end all hostilities (including the theoretical state of war that had existed between the two countries since 1948) and to withdraw all foreign troops from Lebanon. However, Syria did not recognize the accord, leaving 40,000 of its own troops and 7,000 PLO fighters in the Beka'a valley and northern Lebanon. Israel, meanwhile, redeployed a reduced force of 10,000 troops along the Awali river, south of Beirut. Maj. Haddad's South Lebanon Army (SLA) was to police southern areas as Israel's role lessened. Meanwhile, the multinational force in Beirut (comprising some 5,800 mainly French, Italian and US personnel) was drawn increasingly into the fighting, coming under frequent attack from Muslim militias who opposed its tantamount support for the Christian-led Government. In October 241 US and 58 French marines were killed in suicide bombings by Muslim groups.

The failure to conclude a peaceful settlement, and in particular the resumption of heavy fighting in February 1984 (which the reconstituted, US-trained Lebanese army was unable to suppress), led to the resignation of Prime Minister al-Wazzan, followed shortly afterwards by the withdrawal of the USA, Italy and the United Kingdom from the peace-keeping force. French troops were withdrawn in March. By this time successive defeats had left Gemayel's forces with effective control only in the mainly Christian-populated east Beirut. In March President Gemayel abrogated the May 1983 agreement with Israel, and in April 1984, with Syrian support, he formed a Government of National Unity under former premier Rashid Karami. The Lebanese army failed to gain control of Beirut, and Gemayel's efforts to obtain approval for constitutional reform, already constrained by his fear of alienating his Christian supporters, were further undermined by divisions within the Cabinet.

The Israeli Government formed by Shimon Peres in September 1984 pledged to withdraw Israeli forces from Lebanon. However, while the Lebanese authorities demanded that UNIFIL police the Israeli–Lebanese border, by the time the Israeli withdrawal was completed, in June 1985, Israel had ensured that a narrow buffer zone, policed by the SLA (now commanded by Gen. Antoine Lahad), was in place along the border. With the Israeli presence in Lebanon reduced to a token force, Syria withdrew about one-third of its troops from the Beka'a valley in July, leaving some 25,000 in position.

Sporadic conflict persisted throughout 1985, but in December the leaders of the three main Lebanese militias (the Druze forces, Amal and the LF) signed an accord in the Syrian capital, Damascus, providing for an immediate cease-fire and for the cessation of the civil war within one year. The militias were to be disarmed and disbanded, and a new constitutional regime was to be introduced within three years. However, the militias of the Sunni Murabitoun and the Iranian-backed Shi'ite Hezbollah were not parties to the agreement, which was also opposed by influential Christian elements. Furthermore, there were clashes later in December between supporters of the agreement within the LF and those who resented the concessions made by their leader, Elie Hobeika. In January 1986 Hobeika was forced into exile and replaced as LF leader by Samir Geagea, who, in urging renegotiation of the Damascus accord, effectively ended any prospect of its implementation.

During 1986 Palestinian guerrillas resumed rocket attacks on settlements in northern Israel, provoking retaliatory air attacks by Israel on targets in the Beka'a valley and southern Lebanon. Meanwhile, Hezbollah escalated its attacks on SLA positions within the Israeli buffer zone, and also clashed with UNIFIL. Fighting between Palestinian guerrillas and Shi'ite Amal militiamen for control of the refugee camps in south Beirut escalated in May, before a cease-fire was imposed around the camps in June, as part of a Syrian-sponsored peace plan for Muslim west Beirut. The activities of the Amal, Druze and Sunni militias in west Beirut were temporarily curtailed by the deployment of Lebanese and Syrian troops, but fighting across the so-called 'Green Line', which had effectively divided the area from Christian east Beirut since early 1984, continued. By the time Amal and the PLO agreed in September 1987 to end hostilities, more than 2,500 people had died in the 'war of the camps'. Despite renewed fighting near Sidon in October, in January 1988, avowedly as a gesture of support for the *intifada* (uprising) by Palestinians in the Israeli-occupied territories, the Amal leader, Nabih Berri, announced an end to the siege of the Palestinian refugee camps in Beirut and southern Lebanon.

After Prime Minister Karami was killed in a bomb explosion in June 1987, Selim al-Hoss (Prime Minister in 1976–80) was appointed acting premier. In 1988 a political crisis developed as it proved impossible to find a successor to President Gemayal (whose term of office was due to end) that was acceptable to all the warring factions. The three leading contenders for the presidency were Gen. Michel Awn (Commander-in-Chief of the Lebanese army), Raymond Eddé (leader of the Maronite Bloc National) and Sulayman Franjiya (President in 1970–76). Franjiya was Syria's preferred candidate but was notably opposed by Geagea, who apparently ensured that the National Assembly was inquorate when it convened for the election in August 1988. In September the USA and Syria agreed to support another candidate, Mikhail ad-Daher, but Christian army and LF leaders remained opposed to the imposition of any candidate by foreign powers. Gemayel's term of office expired later in the month, when a further attempt by the National Assembly to hold an election was inquorate. The outgoing President appointed an interim military administration, comprising three Christians and three Muslims, with Awn as Prime Minister. However, there was political confusion as the three nominated Muslim officers immediately refused to serve in the new administration, while two Christian members of the al-Hoss Government resigned, signalling their recognition of the interim military administration. The constitutional crisis, with two Governments claiming legitimacy, was further complicated in November, when the Minister of Defence in the al-Hoss Government dismissed Awn as Commander-in-Chief of the Lebanese army; however, Awn retained the loyalty of large sections of the military and thus remained its *de facto* leader.

In September 1989, following six months of fighting in Beirut between Awn's Lebanese army and Syrian forces, a Tripartite Arab Committee—formed in May by an emergency session of Arab leaders, and comprising King Hassan of Morocco, King Fahd of Saudi Arabia and President Chadli of Algeria—announced a peace plan whereby, most notably, the Lebanese National Assembly would meet to discuss a draft charter of national reconciliation. The Committee's charter was approved by the Syrian Government and the leaders of Lebanon's Muslim militias. Awn initially rejected its terms, on the grounds that it did not provide for the withdrawal of Syrian forces, but he was forced to relent, in view of support for the charter by almost every Arab country, as well as the USA, the USSR, the United Kingdom and France; a cease-fire accordingly took effect. The National Assembly subsequently met in Ta'if, Saudi Arabia, to discuss the charter, which was finally approved (with some amendments) in October by 58 of the 62 attending deputies (of the 99 deputies elected in May 1972, only 73 survived); it became known as the 'Ta'if agreement'. The charter provided for the transfer of executive power from the presidency to a cabinet, with portfolios divided equally between Christian and Muslim ministers. The number of seats in the National Assembly was to be increased to 108, comprising equal numbers of Christian and Muslim deputies. Following the election of a President and the formation of a new government, all militias involved in the Lebanese conflict were to be disbanded within six months, while the internal security forces would be strengthened; the Syrian armed forces would assist the new Government in implementing the security plan for a maximum of two years.

The National Assembly elected René Mouawad, a Maronite Christian deputy and a former Minister of Education and Arts, as President in early November 1989. The Assembly also unanimously endorsed the Ta'if agreement. However, Awn, who denounced the agreement as a betrayal of Lebanese sovereignty, declared the presidential election unconstitutional and its result null and void, proclaiming himself President. Mouawad was assassinated only 17 days after his election. The National Assembly again convened and elected Elias Hrawi (who had stood against Mouawad earlier in the month) as the new President; the legislature also voted to extend its own term until 1994. A new Cabinet was formed by Selim al-Hoss in late November 1989.

The Christian communities were divided over the Ta'if agreement, and Geagea's refusal to reject the agreement precipitated violent clashes between his LF and Awn's forces in January 1990: by March more than 800 people had been killed in inter-Christian fighting. (Geagea eventually announced the LF's recognition of the al-Hoss Government, and hence the Ta'if agreement, in April.) In August the National Assembly duly approved amendments to the Constitution, in accordance with the agreement, increasing the number of seats in the National Assembly to 108, to be divided equally between Muslims and Christians. On 21 September the Second Lebanese Republic was officially inaugurated with President Hrawi formally endorsed the amendments. In October Awn and his forces (who continued to reject the Ta'if agreement) were expelled from east Beirut by Syrian forces and units of the Lebanese army loyal to Hrawi. The Lebanese army began to deploy in Beirut in December, by which time all militia forces had withdrawn from the city. In the same month al-Hoss submitted his Government's resignation, and Hrawi invited Omar Karami (Minister of Education and Arts in the outgoing administration) to form a government of national unity, as stipulated by the Ta'if agreement. By early 1991 the Lebanese army was established in most major southern Lebanese towns; by September the militias had been largely disbanded (although Hezbollah maintained armaments in southern Lebanon and the Beka'a valley). In May 1991 the National Assembly approved amendments to the electoral law, and in June the Cabinet appointed 40 deputies to fill the seats that had become vacant since the 1972 election as well as the nine new seats created under the Ta'if agreement. In August 1991 the National Assembly approved a general amnesty for crimes perpetrated during the civil war, although its terms excluded several specified crimes committed during 1975–90. Under a presidential pardon, Awn was allowed to leave the French embassy compound (where he had been sheltering since his defeat in 1990) and to depart for exile in France.

In May 1991 Lebanon and Syria signed a bilateral treaty establishing formal relations in political, military and economic affairs, and confirming the role of the Syrian army as guarantor of the security plans enshrined in the Ta'if agreement. Israel immediately condemned the treaty as a further step towards the formal transformation of Lebanon into a Syrian protectorate, while its opponents within Lebanon denounced it as a threat to the country's independence. In September Lebanon and Syria concluded a mutual security agreement. Syrian forces began to withdraw from Beirut in March 1992, in preparation for their scheduled withdrawal to eastern Lebanon by September. Israel, meanwhile, reasserted its intention of maintaining a military presence in the buffer zone, and its support for the SLA, by launching severe attacks on Palestinian bases in southern Lebanon in June 1991. Lebanese forces began to take up positions in Sidon at the beginning of July. Initial resistance from Palestinians loyal to Arafat was swiftly overcome, and an agreement was concluded with the PLO to allow the Lebanese army to assume control of the area. Israeli military activity against Hezbollah targets in southern Lebanon intensified in late 1991, and the conflict escalated further following the assassination by the Israeli air force of the Secretary-General of Hezbollah, Sheikh Abbas Moussawi, in February 1992.

The deteriorating economic situation in early 1992, combined with allegations of government corruption and incompetence, and a series of general strikes, provoked the resignation of Karami and his Cabinet in May. Subsequent talks in Damascus between President Hrawi and the Syrian leadership led to the reappointment of Rashid Solh as Prime Minister (a position that he had previously held in 1974–75). In July 1992 the National Assembly approved a new electoral law whereby the number of seats in the Assembly was raised from 108 to 128, to be divided equally between Christian and Muslim deputies. The Government's intention to conduct legislative elections in mid-1992 had prompted Christian groups to threaten a boycott of the polls, since it was not certain that Syrian forces would have withdrawn to the eastern area of the Beka'a valley by that time, in accordance with the Ta'if agreement. The Government, for its part, stated that the Lebanese army was not yet able to guarantee the country's security in the absence of Syrian troops.

Lebanon's first legislative elections for 20 years were held in three rounds, on 23 August (in the governorates of the North and the Beka'a valley), 30 August (Beirut and Mount Lebanon) and 6 September 1992 (South and An-Nabatiyah). Electoral turn-out was low (averaging 32%), especially in Maronite districts where leaders had urged a boycott. Hezbollah, contesting the elections for the first time as a political party, enjoyed considerable success in southern constituencies. The Amal leader, Nabih Berri, was appointed President of the new National Assembly in October, and Hrawi invited Rafik Hariri, a Lebanese-born Saudi Arabian business executive, to form a new government, amid hopes that he would restore some confidence in the Lebanese economy and oversee the country's reconstruction. Hariri's Cabinet was dominated by technocrats, and the system of distributing portfolios on an entirely 'confessional' basis was somewhat diluted. It emerged after the elections that Syria would only withdraw its armed forces from Lebanon once a comprehensive peace treaty had been concluded between Syria and Israel.

In December 1992 the Lebanese army took up positions in southern suburbs of Beirut for the first time in eight years, apparently meeting no resistance from Hezbollah, which had hitherto effectively controlled the areas. In mid-1993 the Lebanese Government was said to be attempting to curtail the activities of the Damascus-based Popular Front for the Liberation of Palestine—General Command (PFLP—GC), which had begun to mount guerrilla attacks on Israeli military positions from southern Lebanon. In July Israeli armed forces launched their heaviest artillery and air attacks on targets in southern Lebanon since 1982. The declared aim of 'Operation Accountability' was to eradicate the threat posed by Hezbollah and Palestinian guerrillas, and to create a flow of refugees so as to compel the Lebanese and Syrian authorities to take action against these groups. According to Lebanese sources, the week-long offensive displaced some 300,000 civilians towards the north and resulted in 128 (mainly civilian) deaths. Although a US-brokered cease-fire 'understanding' entered effect at the end of July 1993, hostilities continued in subsequent months.

In June 1994 Hezbollah reported that 26 of its fighters had been killed in an Israeli air attack on one of its training camps in the Beka'a valley; Hezbollah responded with rocket attacks into the security zone and northern Israel. In October an Israeli attack on the town of An-Nabatiyah at-Tahta (Nabatiyah), in which seven civilians died, was apparently provoked by the deaths of 22 people in a bomb attack, attributed to Palestinian militants of the Islamic Resistance Movement (Hamas), in the Israeli city of Tel-Aviv: hitherto, Israeli operations in Lebanon had tended to be in reprisal for terrorist activity in the security zone. Clashes in southern Lebanon in December reportedly resulted in the killing by Hezbollah of several members of the Israeli military and SLA, and seemingly prompted a retaliatory bomb attack on a suburb of southern Beirut, in which a senior Hezbollah official was killed. Israeli attacks south of Beirut in January 1995 targeted alleged PFLP—GC bases.

In March 1994, meanwhile, the National Assembly approved legislation instituting the death penalty for what were termed 'politically motivated' murders. Shortly afterwards the Maronite LF was proscribed (on the grounds that it had sought the country's partition) and its leader, Samir Geagea, was arrested and charged, along with several of his associates, in connection with the murder, in October 1990, of Dany Chamoun, son of former President Camille Chamoun and the leader of the right-wing Maronite Parti national libéral (PNL), and with the bombing of a Maronite church outside Beirut in January 1994. In September Geagea was reportedly relieved of the organization's leadership and his recognition of the Ta'if agreement revoked; the LF command had also reportedly countermanded Geagea's formal dissolution, under the Ta'if agreement, of the organization's militia status. (A successor political organization, the Lebanese Forces Party, had been created in September 1990.) In June 1995 Geagea and a co-defendant were convicted of instigating the murder of Chamoun, and were (together with seven others convicted *in absentia*) sentenced to death; the sentences were immediately commuted to life imprisonment with hard labour. In July 1996 Geagea was acquitted of involvement in the Maronite church bombing. However, by mid-1997, as a result of further convictions, Geagea had received another two death sentences (one for ordering the assassination of another Maronite rival in 1990, and the other for attempting to assassinate the Minister of Defence, Michel Murr, in 1991—both of which were later commuted to life imprisonment); another sentence of life imprisonment for orchestrating the death of Prime Minister Rashid Karami in 1987; and a 10-year gaol term for attempting to recruit and arm militiamen after 1991 (when all militias had been banned).

In October 1995 the National Assembly voted to amend the Constitution to extend President Hrawi's mandate for a further three years. Prime Minister Hariri had sought an extension of the presidential term in the stated interest of promoting stability in the economic reconstruction process, and the amendment had been facilitated following intervention by Syria to resolve a procedural dispute between Hariri and the President of the National Assembly, Nabih Berri.

Elections to the National Assembly took place, in five rounds, in August–September 1996. Pro-Hariri candidates enjoyed considerable success in the first three rounds of voting (in Mount Lebanon, North Lebanon and Beirut governorates), with the Prime Minister himself winning the largest number of votes at the third round; there were, however, allegations of vote-buying involving Hariri's supporters in Beirut. In the fourth and fifth rounds (in the South and An-Nabatiyah, and in the Beka'a valley) an electoral alliance led by Amal and Hezbollah was reported to have won all but one of the total 46 seats. Prior to the fifth round Syria had redeployed some 12,000 of its estimated 30,000 troops in Lebanon to the eastern part of the Beka'a valley. (Under the terms of the Ta'if agreement, the redeployment should have been completed in 1992.) The overall rate of participation averaged about 45%, suggesting that many voters had disregarded demands particularly by Awn, Gemayel and other exiled figures for a boycott of the polls. Berri was re-elected President of the National Assembly when the new legislature convened in October 1996. Hrawi invited Hariri to form a new government: the distribution of portfolios in the new Cabinet (named in early November, following consultations with Syrian leaders) among the country's various interests remained largely unchanged.

In April 1996 Israel commenced a sustained military offensive (code-named 'Operation Grapes of Wrath') in southern Lebanon and suburbs to the south of Beirut, aimed at preventing rocket attacks by Hezbollah on settlements in northern Israel—which Hezbollah claimed were in response to deliberate attacks on Lebanese civilians by Israeli armed forces or their proxies. Some 400,000 Lebanese were displaced northwards, and the shelling by Israeli forces of a UNIFIL base at Qana, which resulted in the deaths of more than 100 Lebanese civilians who had been sheltering there, and of four UNIFIL soldiers, provoked international condemnation. After more than two weeks of hostilities a cease-fire 'understanding' took effect in late April 1996. As in 1993, this was effectively a compromise confining the conflict to the area of the security zone, recognizing both Hezbollah's right to resist Israeli occupation and Israel's right to self-defence; the 'understanding' also envisaged the establishment of an Israel-Lebanon Monitoring Group (ILMG), comprising representatives of Israel, Lebanon, Syria, France and the USA, to supervise the cease-fire. According to the Israeli authorities, Operation Grapes of Wrath resulted in no Israeli deaths, while 170–200 Lebanese civilians, in addition to some 50 fighters, were killed. Hezbollah claimed to have sustained minimal casualties, and its military capacity appeared largely undiminished. A subsequent UN report on the killing of Lebanese civilians at Qana concluded that it was 'unlikely' that the shelling of the UNIFIL base had, as claimed by the Israelis, been the result of 'gross technical and/or procedural errors'. Prior to the first meeting of the ILMG, in July 1996, Israel and Hezbollah reportedly exchanged prisoners and bodies of members of their armed forces for the first time since 1991. However, despite the April 1996 cease-fire 'understanding', sporadic clashes continued during 1997–98. The extent of Israeli casualties as a result of the occupation of southern Lebanon prompted a vocal campaign within Israel for a unilateral withdrawal from the security zone. In April 1998 Israel's 'inner' Security Cabinet voted to adopt UN Security Council Resolution 425, but with the stipulation that Lebanon provide guarantees of the security of Israel's northern border. Lebanon, however, emphasized that Resolution 425 demanded an unconditional withdrawal, and stated that neither would it be able to guarantee Israel's immunity from attack, nor would it be prepared to deploy the Lebanese army in southern Lebanon for this purpose; furthermore, Lebanon could not support the continued presence there of the SLA. Concern was also expressed that a unilateral withdrawal from Lebanon in the absence of a comprehensive Middle East peace settlement might foment regional instability.

Meanwhile, in late 1996 the Government had ordered the closure of about 150 radio and 50 television stations; licences to broadcast political items had been granted to only a limited number of stations, most of which were owned by prominent political figures. In September 1997 the authorities began to close down unlicensed broadcasters, and in December the Minister of the Interior, deputy premier Michel Murr, prohibited a televised satellite broadcast, from France, by Gen. Michel Awn, on the grounds that such transmissions were undermining national security. The ban provoked a violent demonstration in Beirut, which resulted in a number of protestors being arrested and tried on charges of defying restrictions on public demonstrations imposed in 1993. (Awn's interview was eventually broadcast in January 1998 by a private terrestrial channel.)

Voting in Lebanon's first municipal elections since 1963 took place, in four rounds, in May–June 1998. At the first round (in Mount Lebanon governorate), Hezbollah won convincing victories in Beirut's southern suburbs, while right-wing organizations opposed to the Government also took control of several councils. At the second round (in North Lebanon), efforts failed to achieve an inter-community balance in Tripoli, where a council comprising 23 Muslims and only one Christian was elected; elsewhere in the governorate there was notable success for candidates loyal to Samir Geagea. However, a joint list of candidates supported by Hariri and Berri won control of the Beirut council at the third round, while Berri's Amal gained overall control in Tyre. At the final round of voting (in the Beka'a valley), Hezbollah candidates were largely defeated by their pro-Syrian secular rivals and by members of the governorate's leading families. Other than in Beirut, the rate of voter participation was high (about 70%). (Municipal elections did not take place in southern Lebanon until September 2001, following the withdrawal of Israeli troops in 2000.)

As President Hrawi's mandate neared completion in 1998, the Commander-in-Chief of the armed forces, Gen. Emile Lahoud, emerged as a suitable successor: his strong leadership, firm stance on corruption and success in having reconstructed the army following the civil war, were thought likely to assist the process of political reform and economic regeneration. Moreover, Syria, which remained a major influence on Lebanese politics, endorsed Lahoud's candidacy, despite his strong nationalist tendency. To enable Lahoud's appointment, the National Assembly overwhelmingly adopted an exceptional amendment to Article 49 of the Constitution—which requires that senior civil servants resign their post two years prior to seeking political office—and Lahoud was duly elected President on 15 October, with the approval of all 118 National Assembly deputies present (the vote was boycotted by the Druze leader, Walid Joumblatt, and his supporters). Lahoud took office on 24 November; law enforcement and the elimination of official corruption were identified as priorities for his administration. Hariri unexpectedly declined an invitation from Lahoud to form a new government, and at the beginning of December Selim al-Hoss (who had headed four administrations during the civil war) was designated Prime Minister. His new Cabinet, which was almost halved in size (to 16 members), included only two ministers from the previous administration—Michel Murr notably retained the post of deputy premier as well as the interior portfolio. Several 'reformists' were appointed to the Cabinet, which excluded representatives of the various 'confessional' blocs and former militia leaders whose rivalries had frequently undermined previous governments. Hezbollah declined to participate in the new Government. At the Cabinet's first session, held later in December, Gen. Michel Sulayman was appointed to succeed Lahoud as head of the armed forces. The al-Hoss Government's programme emphasized anti-corruption measures, economic liberalization and reduction of the public debt, as well as accelerated electoral reform. To that effect the judiciary was granted powers to investigate a number of political scandals and bring former high-ranking officials to trial. The incoming Government also revoked the five-year ban on the holding of public demonstrations.

Clashes persisted in southern Lebanon following Israel's 'adoption' of Resolution 425, amid continuing protests of violations of the April 1996 cease-fire 'understanding'. In May 1998 at least 10 people were killed in an Israeli air raid on a Fatah training camp in the central Beka'a valley; in two separate incidents in November, seven Israeli soldiers were killed as a result of attacks by Hezbollah on Israeli patrols in the occupied zone. Following further serious exchanges in December, in January 1999 Israel's Security Cabinet voted to respond to future Hezbollah offensives by targeting infrastructure in central and northern Lebanon (thereby extending the conflict beyond suspected guerrilla bases in the south). Hostilities escalated in February, when Israeli forces annexed the village of Arnoun, just outside the occupied zone; Israel also launched intensive air attacks on Hezbollah targets, following an ambush in the security zone in late February that had killed Brig.-Gen. Erez Gerstein, the commander of the Israeli army's liaison unit with the SLA.

In 1999 the Palestinian militant organizations in Lebanon were riven by factional infighting, and both the Lebanese and Syrian Governments undertook measures to seek to bring the groups to order. In May a senior official of the Fatah faction of the PLO and his wife were killed in Sidon by unidentified gunmen, believed to be PLO activists opposed to Fatah's willingness to negotiate with Israel, while a car bomb in southern Lebanon shortly afterwards seriously wounded another Fatah official, leading to fears of a renewed cycle of violence between the rival Palestinian factions. In October a senior Fatah commander, Sultan Abu al-Aynayn (a close ally of Yasser Arafat), was sentenced to death *in absentia* by a military court in Beirut, having been found guilty of leading a militia and of encouraging anti-Government rebellion. (In December 2000, again *in absentia*, al-Aynayn was convicted of weapons-trafficking and of plotting terrorist actions in southern Lebanon; he was sentenced to 15 years' imprisonment.) Two other Fatah leaders in southern Lebanon were detained by the Lebanese military in November 1999, on charges of murder and of plotting bomb attacks during the 1980s; five further officials of the organization were reportedly arrested in subsequent months. In January 2000 the Government ordered a judicial inquiry into the recent upsurge in sectarian violence.

In July 1999 the Lebanese Government was angered by an announcement made by the new Israeli Prime Minister, Ehud Barak, elected in May, that Palestinian refugees residing in Lebanon would under no circumstances be permitted to return to Israel. President Lahoud responded by demanding that any permanent peace agreement should guarantee the right of Palestinians to return home; he subsequently initiated legislation to prevent Palestinian refugees in Lebanon from being granted Lebanese citizenship.

During his election campaign Prime Minister Barak had pledged to withdraw Israeli forces from southern Lebanon by July 2000. In June 1999 the SLA completed a unilateral withdrawal from the enclave of Jezzine, in the north-east of the occupied zone. Following further Hezbollah attacks on northern Israel, in late June the outgoing administration of Binyamin Netanyahu ordered a series of air-strikes against infrastructure targets in central and southern Lebanon—the heaviest aerial bombardment since 'Operation Grapes of Wrath' in 1996. In December 1999 an 'understanding in principle' was reportedly reached between Israel and Syria in order to curb the fighting in southern Lebanon, although the informal cease-fire ended in late January 2000 when a senior SLA commander was killed; the deaths of three Israeli soldiers at the end of the month led Israel to declare that peace talks with Syria (now again postponed indefinitely) could resume only if Syria took action to restrain Hezbollah. In mid-February, after suffering further military casualties in the security zone, Israel announced that its Prime Minister would henceforth be empowered to order immediate retaliatory raids against Hezbollah without discussion with the Security Cabinet. In March the Israeli Cabinet voted unanimously to withdraw its forces from southern Lebanon by July, even if no agreement had been reached on the Israeli-Syrian track of the Middle East peace process. In April, having released 13 Lebanese prisoners held without trial for more than a decade as 'bargaining counters' for Israeli soldiers missing in Lebanon, Israel gave the UN official notification that it intended to withdraw its forces from southern Lebanon 'in one phase' by 7 July. The Lebanese Government made the unprecedented admission that it would accept a UN peace-keeping force in southern Lebanon after the Israeli withdrawal. On 23 May Israel's Security Cabinet voted to accelerate the withdrawal of its remaining troops from Lebanon, after Hezbollah had taken control of about one-third of southern Lebanon following the evacuation by the SLA of outposts transferred to its control by the Israeli army. Both the Israeli Government and the UN had expected the withdrawal to take place on 1 June; however, the rapid and chaotic withdrawal of Israeli forces from southern Lebanon was completed on 24 May, almost six weeks ahead of Barak's original deadline. In June the UN Security Council officially declared that the Israeli withdrawal had been completed. However, both the Lebanese Government and Hezbollah maintained that Israel was still required to depart from territory known as Shebaa Farms and to release all Lebanese prisoners. (The UN maintains that Shebaa Farms is part of territory captured by Israel from Syria, and as such must be considered under the Israeli-Syrian track of the peace process.) In July a limited contingent of UNIFIL troops began to redeploy close to the Lebanese border with Israel, to fill the vacuum created by the departure of Israeli forces. At the same time the UN Security Council voted to extend UNIFIL's mandate for a further six months. In August a Joint Security Force of some 1,000 Lebanese troops and Internal Security Forces reportedly deployed in southern Lebanon (other than in the border area), charged with the provision of general security in the territory. Responsibility for the border with Israel remained with UNIFIL (whose troops in Lebanon now numbered some 5,600). By January 2001 an estimated 2,041 SLA militiamen were reported to have been convicted of having collaborated with Israel during its occupation of southern Lebanon.

Elections to the National Assembly took place on 27 August (Mount Lebanon and North Lebanon) and 3 September 2000 (Beirut, the Beka'a valley, An-Nabatiyah and the South). For the first time since 1972 Lebanese citizens in the former Israeli-occupied zone of southern Lebanon participated in the elections. Voting patterns in the first round swiftly indicated a rejection of al-Hoss's premiership, as the Druze leader, Walid Joumblatt (one of former premier Rafik Hariri's staunchest allies), secured an overwhelming victory in Mount Lebanon governorate. Moreover, the election of Pierre Gemayel, son of Amin Gemayel, in the Maronite Northern Metn district was regarded as a considerable reverse for President Lahoud. Voter participation was an estimated 51%, apparently indicating that the electorate had largely ignored appeals by some Christian parties for a boycott of the poll. At the second round of voting, Hariri's Al-Karamah (Dignity) list proceeded to secure 18 of the 19 assembly seats in Beirut; al-Hoss lost his own seat in the legislature. In the south an alliance of Hezbollah and Amal candidates took all the governorate's 23 seats, while Hezbollah enjoyed similar successes in the Beka'a. Independent monitors reported numerous instances of electoral malpractice. Overall, Hariri was reported to have the support of between 92–106 of the 128 seats in the new legislature. In late October President Lahoud formally appointed Rafik Hariri to the premiership. The composition of his radically altered Cabinet (newly expanded to 30 members) was announced a few days later, with Issam Fares named as Deputy Prime Minister and Elias Murr, the son-in-law of President Lahoud and a non-parliamentarian, replacing his father, Michel Murr, as Minister of the Interior and of Municipal and Rural Affairs. (Resistance and Development, the party list including Hezbollah, had declined to join the Government.) Hariri and President Lahoud were reported to have reached an informal 'power-sharing' agreement, according to which Hariri would be responsible for economic policy and the President would take charge of defence and foreign affairs.

Divisions between pro- and anti-Syrian elements within Lebanon had become increasingly vocal in the aftermath of the Israeli withdrawal from southern Lebanon in May 2000 and the death of Syria's President Hafiz al-Assad in the following month. An unofficial visit to Beirut by his successor, Bashar al-Assad, for meetings with key Lebanese politicians shortly before the legislative elections appeared to indicate that he intended to continue his late father's role as power-broker in Lebanon. However, the decisive rejection of the Syrian-backed Government of Selim al-Hoss, combined with Joumblatt's electoral successes, appeared to suggest a redefinition of Syria's role in Lebanon. In late September Maronite bishops issued a statement urging the departure of the Syrian military from Lebanon. While the Maronite community and other Christian groups maintained that the departure of Syrian forces was necessary in order for full Lebanese sovereignty to be attained, both President Lahoud and Prime Minister Hariri continued to defend Syria's military presence. In December Syria—which had never previously confirmed that it was holding Lebanese prisoners—freed 46 Lebanese political prisoners (including many Christians who had been detained by Syrian troops during

1975–1990), apparently as a gesture of 'goodwill'. In January 2001 the Lebanese Government established a commission to examine the issue of Lebanese prisoners held in Syria. In the same month a Jordanian newspaper reported that the former Christian militia leader, Gen. Michel Awn, had declared himself ready to return to Lebanon from exile in France in order to appear before the Lebanese judiciary. In April, following student protests demanding the withdrawal of Syrian troops, the Government banned all unlicensed demonstrations against Syria.

The outbreak of the so-called 'al-Aqsa *intifada*' in the Palestinian territories of the West Bank and Gaza in September 2000 resulted in a renewed crisis in the Middle East, prompting uncertainty in Lebanon about the permanence of the Israeli withdrawal, particularly as Hezbollah had renewed its campaign against the Israeli military. In early October Hezbollah fighters captured three Israeli soldiers in Shebaa Farms, with the demand that Israel release 19 Lebanese and dozens of Palestinians from Israeli detention. The UN Secretary-General, Kofi Annan, visited Beirut for talks regarding the soldiers' release; however, in the following week a senior Israeli army reservist and businessman was kidnapped in Switzerland, apparently by Hezbollah (which claimed that the officer was working for Israeli intelligence). The killing of an Israeli soldier in Shebaa Farms at the end of November prompted Israel to launch air-strikes against suspected Hezbollah targets in southern Lebanon. In mid-November the UN Security Council had urged the Lebanese Government to comply with international law by deploying its armed forces on the Israeli border with southern Lebanon (where Hezbollah still controlled the line of withdrawal, or 'Blue Line'), but Lebanon rejected such a deployment until Israel had signed a comprehensive peace treaty with both Lebanon and Syria. At the end of January 2001 the UN Security Council voted to extend UNIFIL's mandate in Lebanon until the end of July, when its operational strength was to be reduced to about 4,500—the number of troops deployed prior to the Israeli withdrawal.

The Lebanese leadership was generally pessimistic as to the prospects for peace in the Middle East following the election, in February 2001, of Likud leader Ariel Sharon as Israeli Prime Minister. (Most Lebanese hold Sharon responsible for the deaths of 2,000 Palestinian refugees in the Sabra and Chatila camps in September 1982—at which time was Israel's Minister of Defence.) In mid-February 2001 Israel launched mortar attacks close to Shebaa Farms, in reprisal for the death of an Israeli soldier in a bomb attack there. Tensions escalated once again in mid-April: Israel responded to the killing by Hezbollah of another of its soldiers in Shebaa Farms with the first military action against Syrian troops since 1996, launching air raids on a Syrian radar base to the east of Beirut. According to Syrian sources, at least one Syrian soldier died in the attack, which Israel claimed had been provoked by Syria's sponsorship of Hezbollah.

In mid-June 2001 Syria withdrew an estimated 6,000–10,000 troops from the largely Christian eastern and southern suburbs of Beirut and from Mount Lebanon, and redeployed the majority to the Beka'a valley. However, Syria's withdrawal from the Lebanese capital was widely regarded as merely symbolic, since Syria retained 15 military bases in strategic parts of Beirut. In early August the Maronite patriarch, Cardinal Sfeir, and the Druze leader, Walid Joumblatt, held discussions, apparently to indicate a new era of 'reconciliation' between the two communities. Within days, however, the mainly pro-Syrian army intelligence service began mass arrests of Maronite Christians (mostly members of the banned LF or supporters of Awn) who were again demanding a complete Syrian withdrawal from Lebanon. Many Christian and Muslim deputies condemned the detentions as 'unconstitutional', while protesters demonstrating against the growing influence of the military clashed with police. Hariri's political standing appeared to have been weakened by the security forces' actions, which had been undertaken when he was out of the country, as in mid-August the National Assembly approved legislation granting increased powers to President Lahoud.

Israel launched a further air attack on a Syrian radar station in eastern Lebanon at the beginning of July 2001, again apparently in response to an assault by Hezbollah against the Israeli military in Shebaa Farms. At the end of July the UN Security Council voted for an extension of UNIFIL's mandate for a further six months; the peace-keeping force was to be reduced in size from 4,500 to 3,600 troops, with the possibility that its status would be downgraded to that of an observer mission (this was implemented before the expiry of the six-month mandate). In early October Hezbollah guerrillas broke what had effectively been a three-month cease-fire by launching an attack against two Israeli military positions in Shebaa Farms, to which Israeli forces responded by shelling a Hezbollah patrol in the area. Israel alleged, furthermore, that Hezbollah was directly involved in the Palestinian *intifada*, and was supplying weapons to Palestinians in the West Bank and Gaza. (Hezbollah's leadership initially denied this; however, in early March 2002 Sheikh Nasrallah admitted that two Lebanese militants detained in Jordan had been attempting to smuggle weapons into the West Bank. In April 2006 Nasrallah acknowledged for the first time that Hezbollah funded Palestinian militant groups.) In January 2002 the UN Security Council expressed concern regarding recent Israeli violations of Lebanese airspace, and criticized Hezbollah for its frequent interference with the freedom of movement of UNIFIL. The UN again urged the Lebanese Government to deploy its army along the Blue Line. The observer mission's mandate was extended for a further six months from 31 January, and for the same period from the end of July. By the end of 2002 the strength of the force had been reduced to some 2,000 troops.

Lebanon's political and religious leadership were unequivocal in their condemnation of the September 2001 suicide attacks on New York and Washington, DC. Lebanese Shi'ites feared, however, that Hezbollah might be targeted in any retaliatory campaign against militant Islamist groups deemed to be involved in terrorism. In mid-October Muslim clerics in Lebanon issued a ruling in support of the Afghan people following the commencement of US-led military action in Afghanistan against the Taliban regime and alleged bases of the al-Qa'ida (Base) organization, the militant Islamist network held by the USA to be principally responsible for September's atrocities. Three Lebanese men, believed to be members of Hezbollah involved in the 1985 hijacking of a US commercial flight, had been included on a list of 22 'most wanted' terrorist suspects, published in early October 2001 by the US Federal Bureau of Investigation. Lebanese security forces detained two men in Tripoli in mid-October, on charges of plotting terrorist actions against US targets in the Middle East. (In mid-March 2002 a military court sentenced one of the defendants to a three-year prison term, and the other to 18 months' imprisonment, both with hard labour.)

In late January 2002 Elie Hobeika, the former leader of the Christian LF militia, was killed (along with three aides and two bystanders) in a car bombing in Beirut. A previously unknown anti-Syrian group, styled the 'Lebanese for a Free and Independent Lebanon', claimed responsibility for the attack, alleging that Hobeika was a 'Syrian agent'. Israel denied in the strongest terms assertions made by some Lebanese sources that Israeli interests had instigated the killing, since Hobeika had declared his willingness to give evidence to an investigation being carried out by a Belgian court into alleged 'crimes against humanity' by Ariel Sharon, owing to his implication in the massacre of Palestinians in the Sabra and Chatila refugee camps in 1982 (see above). Hobeika was the first prominent Lebanese politician to be assassinated since the civil war ended in 1990. (A Belgian appeals court judged the case against Sharon to be inadmissible in June 2002.)

It was feared in early 2002 that rising tensions between Israel and Lebanon might escalate into a 'second front' of Arab–Israeli conflict; in February Iran denied allegations made by Israeli officials that it was supplying Hezbollah with vast consignments of *Katyusha* rockets and had sent a number of its Revolutionary Guards to Lebanon. At the end of March Hezbollah initiated cross-border mortar, missile and machine-gun attacks against Israeli military targets in Shebaa Farms, asserting that these were in retaliation for Israeli violations of Lebanese airspace. Israel responded to the escalation of Hezbollah attacks by shelling suspected militant bases in southern Lebanon. In early April Lebanese security forces arrested nine Palestinians on charges of plotting to launch rocket assaults against northern Israel. Meanwhile, the UN condemned Hezbollah for increasing the instability along the Blue Line, and also for an incident in which five members of UNIFIL allegedly came under attack by Hezbollah guerrillas near Shebaa Farms. In response to Hezbollah attacks on the Shebaa Farms in August, the Israeli Government targeted suspected Hezbollah bases in southern Lebanon, and issued a firm warning to Lebanon and Syria that they must take immediate action to end such attacks.

In early March 2002 President Bashar al-Assad of Syria undertook an historic visit to Beirut for discussions with President Lahoud. This first official visit by a Syrian leader to Beirut since 1947 was welcomed by many Lebanese as a formal recognition by Syria of Lebanese sovereignty. The talks resulted in several agreements regarding closer economic co-operation, including a pledge by Syria to reduce the cost of imported natural gas. It was reported in early April 2002 that Syrian troops were soon to redeploy from central Lebanon to the Beka'a valley, thus fulfilling one of the requirements of the 1989 Ta'if agreement. However, hundreds of Syrian intelligence officers were likely to remain in central Lebanon.

In late March 2002 Beirut hosted the annual summit meeting of the Council of the Arab League, at which the principal issue under discussion was a peace initiative for the Middle East proposed by Crown Prince Abdullah of Saudi Arabia. However, only 10 out of 22 Arab heads of state attended the summit, while President Mubarak of Egypt and King Abdullah of Jordan reportedly declined to participate in the discussions as a demonstration of solidarity with the President of the Palestinian (National) Authority (PA), Yasser Arafat, who was effectively blockaded by Israeli forces in the West Bank. At the conclusion of the summit, Arab leaders unanimously endorsed the Saudi peace initiative. Incorporated in the Beirut Declaration, this required from Israel a complete withdrawal from all Arab territories occupied in June 1967, and what were termed 'territories still occupied in southern Lebanon', a 'just solution' to the issue of Palestinian refugees, and acceptance of the establishment of a sovereign Palestinian state in the West Bank and Gaza Strip with East Jerusalem as its capital; in return, the Arab states undertook to consider the Arab–Israeli conflict at an end, to sign a peace agreement with Israel, and to establish normal relations with Israel within this comprehensive peace framework. The initiative was, however, rejected by Israel, which maintained that it would lead to the destruction of the State of Israel. During a visit to Lebanon by the US Secretary of State, Colin Powell, in mid-April 2002, the Lebanese leadership maintained its stance that its obligation to respect the Blue Line did not exclude resistance (by Hezbollah) to 'liberate' Shebaa Farms, while President al-Assad gave no indication that he would exert his influence to halt Hezbollah offensives from southern Lebanon against Israel.

Jihad Jibril, the head of the PFLP—GC's military operations and son of the group's leader, was killed by a car bomb in west Beirut in late May 2002. The Lebanese security forces blamed inter-Palestinian rivalries for the assassination, although many PFLP—GC officials held the Israeli intelligence services responsible. In August two people were killed and six others injured in the worst factional fighting at the Ain al-Hilweh Palestinian refugee camp for several years. Tensions escalated following the arrest of an Islamist militant the previous month by the Lebanese army, aided by Fatah. (In early September the Israeli daily *Ha'aretz* alleged that the violence at Ain al-Hilweh was linked to the presence there of up to 200 al-Qa'ida militants who had returned from the war in Afghanistan.) In September clashes between the Lebanese army and Palestinian militants at the normally relatively calm al-Jalil refugee camp, near Ba'albak (Ba'albek), left one soldier and three Palestinians dead.

In early September 2002 the Lebanese Government closed down a Christian opposition-controlled television station, Murr Television, and its sister radio station, Radio Mount Lebanon, claiming that they had undermined relations with Syria and violated electoral legislation banning party political broadcasts during a recent by-election in the Metn district, where one of the stations' owners, the nephew of interior minister Elias Murr, had won the seat. The ruling against Murr Television was upheld by a higher court at the end of December and a final appeal was rejected in late April 2003, resulting in the station's permanent closure.

Lebanon's economic crisis dominated the domestic political agenda in late 2002 and early 2003. In late November 2002 international donors attending a conference in Paris, France, agreed to provide Lebanon with an aid package worth some US $4,300m. to assist the country with its heavy burden of debt and to finance development projects. In mid-April 2003, following weeks of reported disagreements between members of the Cabinet over economic and other domestic policies, the Prime Minister, Rafik Hariri, tendered his resignation and that of his Government. However, after his premiership was endorsed by the Lebanese parliament, Hariri was asked by President Lahoud to form a new 30-member Cabinet. The new Lebanese Government, announced two days after Hariri's resignation, brought in 11 new ministers, including Jean Obeid, who replaced Mahmoud Hammoud as Minister of Foreign Affairs and Emigrants. Hammoud was named as the new Minister of Defence. The new Cabinet was widely considered to be the most pro-Syrian for more than a decade; it contained no members of the Christian opposition, nor of Hezbollah (who were said to have been willing to join the new administration). Syria was still believed to be exerting considerable influence over Lebanese domestic affairs, despite the decreasing Syrian military presence in the country: in mid-February 2003 Syria had commenced the redeployment of more than 4,000 troops stationed in northern Lebanon, under the terms of the Ta'if agreement; the withdrawal was reportedly carried out over several months.

It was reported in mid-May 2003 that Lebanese security forces had arrested at least nine suspected al-Qa'ida operatives in Sidon. The suspects were accused of plotting to attack the US embassy in Beirut and to kidnap members of the Lebanese Cabinet. Moreover, they were believed to be linked to the al-Qa'ida militants thought to be in hiding in the Ain al-Hilweh refugee camp. In December 27 Lebanese were found guilty, and given varying prison sentences, on charges of carrying out bomb attacks against mostly US and British businesses in Lebanon between the end of 2002 and April 2003. However, a military court in Beirut acquitted three defendants of plotting to assassinate the US ambassador to Lebanon.

The Israeli Cabinet agreed in early November 2003 to release more than 400 Palestinian, Lebanese (mostly Hezbollah) and other Arab prisoners in exchange for the remains of three soldiers kidnapped by Hezbollah in Shebaa Farms in 2000, as well as the return of the Israeli businessman, Elhanan Tannenbaum. Israel also hoped to receive information on the fate of a missing Israeli airman, Ron Arad, who had been shot down over Lebanon in 1986, and was still believed to be held in Lebanese detention. Germany, which had mediated the negotiations between Israel and Hezbollah, oversaw the exchange, and on 29 January 2004 the first 30 Lebanese and other Arab prisoners to be released by Israel were flown to the airport at Cologne, Germany, where they were exchanged for Tannenbaum and the remains of the Israeli soldiers. The remaining Palestinian prisoners, and the remains of 59 Lebanese militants held by Israel, were later released at Israeli border posts. Only a few days prior to the prisoner exchange, Israel launched an air attack against Hezbollah positions in southern Lebanon, in response to a Hezbollah rocket attack on Israeli soldiers who were using bulldozers to clear minefields in the border zone. Hezbollah carried out further attacks on Israeli troops in Shebaa Farms in late March, following the Israeli assassination of Sheikh Ahmad Yassin, the founder and spiritual leader of Hamas; in response, Israeli warplanes launched attacks against suspected Hezbollah positions in the area. There were no casualties reported in early June when Israel launched an assault on a suspected PFLP—GC base in Naameh, near Beirut, asserting that it was responding to an unsuccessful missile attack by Palestinian militants on an Israeli vessel surveying the coast. Israel's Deputy Minister of Defence demanded that the Lebanese Government take measures to ensure that its territory would not be used as a base for strikes against Israel. Allegations of repeated violations of Lebanese airspace by Israel led Hezbollah in November to send a drone over Israeli territory, and to declare that it possessed drone aircraft capable of launching attacks on targets inside that country. In early January 2005 at least one Israeli officer and two UN observers were killed when Israeli soldiers retaliated against Hezbollah guerrilla attacks on an Israeli military vehicle patrolling Shebaa Farms. Later in the month Israel responded to the bombing of an Israeli bulldozer in Shebaa Farms by attacking Hezbollah targets in Alman al-Quseir, near the border with Israel; two Lebanese civilians were wounded. UN Secretary-General Kofi Annan criticized Israel's persistent violations of Lebanese airspace and Hezbollah's launching of a drone over Israel, both of which he considered to be provocative acts; he also urged Lebanon to respect the Blue Line. On 28 January the mandate of the UNIFIL observer mission (see above), already extended four times since July 2002, was extended until 31 July 2005; the UN Security Council expressed grave concern at the persistent violence along the Blue Line. The mission's mandate was extended again in July 2005, and for a further six months in February 2006. Meanwhile, in late November 2005 Hezbollah launched what was apparently its heaviest attack on Israeli troops in the Shebaa Farms area since October 2000. Four Hezbollah militants were killed and 11 Israeli soldiers injured in the ensuing violence, in which the two sides exchanged heavy artillery fire across the border.

In early December 2004 senior Palestinian officials visited Beirut for the first time since 1983 (when the former PLO

Chairman, Yasser Arafat, was expelled after the Israeli invasion in 1982); optimism was expressed with regard to future relations between the two sides, and the Palestinian Prime Minister, Ahmad Quray, declared Palestinian interest in establishing a diplomatic presence in Lebanon. (A similar diplomatic visit by Palestinian officials to Syria earlier in the same week had also brought a positive response from both parties.)

Meanwhile, four rounds of voting took place in municipal elections held in May 2004. At the first round (in Mount Lebanon governorate), Hezbollah and other pro-Syrian groups, such as the PSP and independent Christian candidates, defeated the primarily Christian opposition, which was reportedly suffering from internal divisions. At the second round, a list of candidates supported by Hariri won in Beirut (where turn-out was reportedly only 23%) against lists connected to the Parti communiste libanais (PCL) and the opposition Christian Free Patriotic Movement; in the Beka'a valley Hezbollah took the majority of municipalities which it contested, again securing victory over its opposition, Amal. At the third round, Hezbollah again achieved success, particularly in the mostly Shi'a villages on the Israeli border, where elections took place for the first time since the withdrawal of Israeli troops. The list supported by Hariri suffered an overwhelming defeat in the region's capital and the Prime Minister's home town, Sidon, while Amal secured an unexpected victory over Hezbollah in some mainly Shi'a villages. At the final round of elections in north Lebanon, a candidate considered to be a potential rival to Hariri as Prime Minister, Najib Mikati (also the Minister of Public Works and Transport and a close friend of Syrian President al-Assad), achieved success.

In late August 2004, in advance of the expiry of President Lahoud's six-year term of office in November, the Cabinet voted to amend the Constitution, which prevented Lahoud from seeking a second term, to extend Lahoud's mandate by three years. Both Muslim and Christian politicians and Hariri protested against the decision, but Hariri eventually offered his support for the amendment after a meeting with Syrian politicians, including President al-Assad. The USA and France expressed their opposition to the move, and presented a resolution to the UN in early September in an attempt to forestall it. The UN subsequently adopted Resolution No. 1559, demanding that: Lebanon's sovereignty be respected; a 'free and fair' presidential election be held; the Government assert its power throughout the whole country; all foreign forces leave Lebanon; and all militias in the country, both Lebanese and non-Lebanese, disband and disarm. The resolution did not explicitly refer to Syria or its forces and agents, however. The Security Council gave Lebanon 30 days to comply with the resolution's demands, threatening to take measures against Lebanon if it failed to meet them. Nevertheless, the National Assembly approved the constitutional amendment by 96 votes to 29. Four ministers, including the Minister of Economy and Trade, Marwan Hamadeh, and the Minister of the Displaced, Abdullah Farhat, resigned in protest at the decision. The Syrian army responded to Resolution 1559 by redeploying about 3,000 special forces from positions to the south of Beirut, although some 14,000 Syrian troops remained in Lebanon. (Further redeployments of Syrian troops took place in December, from the northern town of Batrun and from Beirut's southern suburbs and the airport to the Beka'a valley.) In mid-October, after UN Secretary-General Kofi Annan had reported Lebanon's non-compliance with the resolution, the Security Council ordered Annan to provide a report every six months detailing steps towards its fulfilment. Hariri dissolved his Cabinet in late October, a day after the release of the statement, declaring that he would not attempt to head the next government. The following day he was replaced by Omar Karami, who revealed the composition of his Cabinet five days later (which for the first time included two women). The former Minister of Public Health, Sulayman Franjiya, assumed the post of Minister of the Interior and Municipalities, while Mahmoud Hammoud became Minister of Foreign Affairs and Emigrants; Hammoud's former National Defence portfolio was allocated to Abd ar-Rahim Mrad, previously a Minister of State without portfolio. The new Government, which received legislative approval in early November, was considered to be more favourable than its predecessor to continued Syrian influence in Lebanese affairs. The new Prime Minister criticized the recent UN Security Council resolution, asserting that: the fulfilment of its demands would lead to crises of security and stability in Lebanon; he considered the resolution to constitute external pressure on Syria and Lebanon; and the presence of Syrian troops in Lebanon was a matter only for the two countries involved. The USA exerted further pressure on Lebanon in early January 2005, when it vowed to include Lebanon among its list of states deemed to sponsor terrorism if the country did not end its support for Hezbollah.

On 22 November 2004 (Independence Day) some 3,000 students from several universities and right-wing Christian activists demonstrated in Beirut against what they perceived to be Syria's dominance in Lebanon, in defiance of a government ban. At the end of the month the Government supported a march by over 100,000 demonstrators in Beirut in praise of Syria's influence in the country and rejecting the terms of UN Resolution 1559. In mid-December parties opposed to the Lebanese Government's support of Syrian involvement in Lebanese affairs, including the main Christian opposition group, the Qornet Shehwan Gathering, Kamal Joumblatt's mainly Druze-supported PSP, and the proscribed Lebanese Forces Party, issued a joint statement demanding a cessation of foreign interference in Lebanon and calling for the release of Lebanese Forces Party leader Samir Geagea, who had been imprisoned on murder charges in 1994. They also demanded an electoral law that would allow people of all political sensibilities to participate in governing the country.

On 14 February 2005 a car bombing in Beirut killed Rafik Hariri, the former Prime Minister and business executive, and 22 other people; at least 100 were injured in the blast. The attack provoked condemnation from Syrian President Bashar al-Assad. However, the USA, emphasizing the problems caused by the Syrian military presence in Lebanon and the inability of the Syrian-dominated intelligence services to forestall the attack, removed its ambassador to Syria for consultations, and later demanded that all Syrian troops withdraw from Lebanon. Later in the month Syria announced that it would redeploy its troops in Lebanon to the Beka'a valley. On 28 February, following a general strike and mass protests (in defiance of a government ban) in Beirut advocated by opposition parties, at which protesters demanded the complete withdrawal of Syrian troops from Lebanon and an end to Syrian influence in Lebanese politics, Karami dissolved his Cabinet and resigned as premier; the move was commended by opposition legislators in the National Assembly. Nevertheless, Lahoud requested that Karami and his ministers remain in office in an interim capacity pending the appointment of a new government. Opposition to Syrian involvement continued in early March. Lebanese opposition groups demanded that all Syrian troops and security forces leave Lebanon, and that President al-Assad and the public prosecutor and senior security officials in Lebanon resign their posts in order to ensure that the investigation into Hariri's death be conducted legitimately and with integrity. They also announced their refusal to participate in any discussions on the formation of a new government until their demands were met. Also in early March US Secretary of State Condoleezza Rice reiterated demands by President Bush that Syria withdraw its troops and security forces from Lebanon. Russia, France, Spain, Germany and Saudi Arabia were also reported to have advocated an end to the Syrian military presence in Lebanon. Meanwhile, al-Assad and Lahoud agreed at a summit meeting to the withdrawal of Syrian troops to the Beka'a valley by the end of the month; Syria later pledged to withdraw all troops prior to Lebanon's general election, scheduled to begin in May, and to provide the UN with a timetable for the withdrawal. Although Rice praised the decision, she urged the two countries to complete the process more quickly. Meanwhile, protests took place in Beirut in support of the Syrian influence and military presence in Lebanon. Syria reportedly withdrew 4,000–6,000 of its troops from Lebanon to Syria in mid-March, removing Syrian soldiers and intelligence agents from their barracks and offices around Tripoli and Beirut; 8,000–10,000 troops remained in the Beka'a valley. A UN report released in late March accused Syria of allowing political tension in Lebanon to be heightened before the murder of Hariri, and criticized Lebanon's initial attempts to investigate the incident. In early April the UN Security Council approved Resolution 1595, establishing an International Independent Investigation Commission (UNIIIC) to investigate Hariri's murder. The German prosecutor appointed to head the commission, Detlev Mehlis, arrived in Lebanon in late May. Meanwhile, in early April 2005 a UN envoy reported that Syria had declared that it would completely withdraw all troops, military assets and the intelligence apparatus by the end of the month. Later in April Syria declared that it had fulfilled its promise, and in early May a UN team dispatched to Lebanon to confirm the withdrawal announced that thus far it had not found a single Syrian soldier in areas that it had inspected. However, it reported that an armed guard had blocked the road and fired shots in the air when members of the team had attempted to approach a base in Qussaya, a border village in which the PFLP—GC (which attributed the incident to a misunderstanding) has positions.

President Lahoud reappointed Karami to the post of Prime Minister on 10 March 2005. On 13 April Karami, having failed to form a new administration, tendered his resignation for a second time, and two days later Najib Mikati was appointed to the post of 'caretaker' Prime Minister. On 19 April Mikati named a new Cabinet (approved by the National Assembly on 27 April), which was to be responsible for the implementation of legislation facilitating a general election, due to be held from late May. The justice portfolio was allocated to Khalid Qabbani, Hassan as-Sab received the interior portfolio, and Mahmoud Hammoud retained that of foreign affairs and emigrants. Elias Murr was appointed Deputy Prime Minister and Minister of Defence. In late April three senior Lebanese security officials with close ties to Syria announced their resignations, and by mid-May a number of other pro-Syrian security officials, whose replacement had been demanded by the opposition, had been dismissed from their posts.

Elections to the National Assembly were held in four rounds between 29 May and 19 June 2005. The first round of voting took place in the Beirut region, where turn-out was a reported 28%. The anti-Syrian Rafik Hariri Martyr List, headed by the Future Movement (Tayar al-Mustaqbal) of Rafik Hariri's son, Saad ed-Din Hariri, and including the PSP, the Lebanese Forces Party and the Qornet Shehwan Gathering, won all 19 seats. Four days later the prominent anti-Syrian journalist Dr Samir Kassir was killed in a car bomb explosion in a Christian district of Beirut. The anti-Syrian opposition accused remaining Syrian intelligence agents of involvement in the murder, and again called on President Lahoud to resign. An estimated 45% of registered voters participated in the second round of elections conducted on 5 June in southern Lebanon; as in the first round, turn-out was reportedly lower in Christian than in Muslim districts. The Resistance and Development Bloc, consisting of the pro-Syrian Shi'a organizations Amal and Hezbollah and their allies, secured all 23 seats. The third round was held on 12 June in Mount Lebanon, where candidates contested 35 seats and turn-out was unofficially estimated at 54%, and the Beka'a Valley, where an estimated 49% of registered voters elected deputies to 23 seats. Immediately prior to the poll, Gen. Michel Awn allied himself with pro-Syrian factions as the Free Patriotic Movement (Tayar al-Watani al-Horr), declaring that he was no longer hostile to Syria now that it had withdrawn its troops from Lebanon. Awn's alliance took 21 seats, while Hariri's list secured 25. However, in the final round in north Lebanon on 19 June, at which turn-out was officially estimated at 49%, Hariri's list won all 28 seats. Consequently, according to final results, the Rafik Hariri Martyr List secured 72 of the National Assembly's 128 seats, allowing the officially prohibited Lebanese Forces Party to achieve parliamentary representation for the first time; the Resistance and Development Bloc won 35 seats; and the Free Patriotic Movement took 21. Following their victory, the various anti-Syrian factions continued to demand that President Lahoud resign, repeating their calls throughout the remainder of the year and in early 2006.

In late June 2005 George Hawi, the former Secretary-General of the PCL and an outspoken critic of Syrian interference in Lebanese politics, was killed by a car bomb in Beirut. The anti-Syrian opposition attributed the attack to Syrian agents and their allies in the Lebanese security services. Further bomb explosions took place in the capital throughout 2005, causing a number of fatalities. In mid-July two people were killed in a bomb attack that injured the pro-Syrian Deputy Prime Minister and Minister of National Defence, Elias Murr. A television journalist was seriously wounded in an explosion in late September, and in mid-December the anti-Syrian publisher of the daily newspaper *An-Nahar* (The Day), Gebran Tueni, and three others were killed in a car bombing.

Meanwhile, pro-Syrian Nabih Berri was re-elected President of the National Assembly on 28 June 2005. Two days later President Lahoud appointed Fouad Siniora of the Future Movement, a close ally of Rafik Hariri, as Prime Minister, and asked him to form a new government. On 19 July Siniora announced the composition of a new Cabinet: Elias Murr remained in post as Deputy Prime Minister and Minister of National Defence, and Hassan as-Sab as Minister of the Interior and Municipalities, while Fawzi Salloukh was appointed Minister of Foreign Affairs and Emigrants and Jihad Azour Minister of Finance. A representative of Hezbollah was to hold cabinet office for the first time, with the appointment of Muhammad Fneish as Minister of Energy and Water. Meanwhile, also in mid-July, the National Assembly passed a law pardoning Lebanese Forces Party leader Samir Geagea, as demanded by some of the opposition (see above). Almost 40 Islamist militants, some of whom were allegedly linked to al-Qa'ida, were also released by parliamentary approval. Prime Minister Siniora met Syrian President al-Assad and Prime Minister Otari in Syria in early August. The two states reportedly agreed to improve relations based on mutual respect, and Siniora emphasized Lebanon's support of Syria and its commitment to bilateral agreements.

Following reports that Syrian intelligence agents might not have completely withdrawn from Lebanon, the UN announced in early June 2005 that it was considering sending a commission to the country to investigate the claims; Syria continued to insist that it had removed all its security personnel. UNIIIC began its inquiry into Rafik Hariri's assassination in mid-June, with a three-month mandate. In late August UNIIIC arrested the three former security officials who had tendered their resignations in April (see above) for questioning regarding the assassination. A fourth security chief, who had retained his post after Hariri's murder, was also sought, and subsequently handed himself in to the organization. A former, pro-Syrian parliamentary deputy was also detained. In mid-October, shortly before the UNIIIC issued its report on the investigation, the Syrian Minister of the Interior, Maj.-Gen. Ghazi Kanaan, was found shot dead in his office. The official Syrian Arab News Agency announced that he had committed suicide. A former head of Syrian military intelligence in Lebanon, Kanaan had become Chief of Political Intelligence in Syria in 2002, and had been appointed Minister of the Interior in October 2004 (see the chapter on Syria). Shortly before his apparent suicide, he had told a Lebanese radio station that he had been questioned by UNIIIC, but had not given any evidence against Syria. According to its report, issued in late October 2005, UNIIIC had found evidence that Lebanese and Syrian intelligence and security services were directly involved in Hariri's assassination. Moreover, the report reasoned, the act was too complex and too well planned to have taken place without the approval of senior Syrian security officials and their Lebanese counterparts. UNIIIC expressed its extreme concern at the lack of co-operation of the Syrian authorities. Lebanon and Syria, which denounced the investigation's findings as politically motivated, rejected the report, and Syria announced that it had established a special judicial commission to deal with all matters relating to the UNIIIC's mission. The commission was granted an extension to its mandate to mid-December. The UN Security Council reacted to the report by adopting a resolution at the end of October 2005 establishing measures against suspects in the assassination, including prohibitions on travel and the freezing of assets, and urged Syria to co-operate fully with the investigation commission and detain suspects identified by the inquiry, threatening unspecified 'further action' should Syria not comply with the resolution's demands. The Security Council gave Syria until 15 December to comply with the resolution, which was sponsored by the USA, France and the United Kingdom. Syria reported in early November that it had arrested six government officials for questioning. Meanwhile, in late October 2005 the UN Special Envoy, Terje Roed-Larsen, issued his report on the implementation of UN Security Council Resolution 1559, in which he praised the withdrawal of Syrian troops from Lebanon, but noted that Lebanon had still not complied with the demands that Lebanese and non-Lebanese militias disarm and disband, and that government authority be extended throughout the country. Lebanon rejected the report, asserting that the Government would deal with armed groups through national dialogue.

In early December 2005 the UNIIIC began questioning five Syrian officials suspected of involvement in Hariri's assassination in Vienna, Austria. Detlev Mehlis presented his second report on the investigating body's work to the UN Security Council later in the month. While noting that Syria had presented five officials suspected of involvement in the murder to the commission for interrogation, the report again accused Syria of reluctance to co-operate with the investigating body and of hindering the investigation. It stated that the UNIIIC had found further evidence that the Lebanese and Syrian intelligence and security services had been involved in the assassination, and revealed that Mehlis had identified 19 suspects, six of whom were Syrian (of which five were those being questioned in Vienna). Mehlis resigned as the head of the UNIIIC shortly after he

LEBANON

presented the body's findings, citing personal and professional reasons; he was replaced by Serge Brammertz. The UNIIIC's mandate was extended to 15 June 2006.

In early January 2006 UNIIIC investigators declared that they wished to question Syrian President al-Assad and Minister of Foreign Affairs Farouk ash-Shara' in relation to Hariri's murder. (A few days earlier the Vice-President of Syria, Abd al-Halim Khaddam, who had been living in exile in Paris having resigned his post in June 2005, had accused al-Assad of personally threatening Hariri. He subsequently declared that, in his view, al-Assad had ordered Hariri's assassination, although he awaited the final decision of the investigating commission.) However, the following day the Syrian Minister of Information announced that Syria would not permit UNIIIC to interview al-Assad. Brammetz met ash-Shara' and other unspecified Syrian officials in late February 2006. Ash-Shara' announced in early March that he had reached an agreement with UNIIIC that provided for full Syrian co-operation with the investigation, while preserving the country's 'sovereignty and dignity'.

In early February 2006 ministers from Hezbollah and Amal announced that they were ending a boycott of cabinet meetings begun in mid-December in protest against the Government's decision to allow an international investigation into Hariri's assassination. The ministers had also demanded that the Government describe Hezbollah as a 'resistance movement' and not a militia. The announcement of the end to the boycott came shortly after Prime Minister Fouad Siniora declared to the National Assembly that the Government had always considered Hezbollah to be a movement of national resistance. Meanwhile, protests were taking place in Beirut and throughout the world against caricatures of the Prophet Muhammad (portrayal of whom is considered blasphemous in Islam), originally published in a Danish newspaper in September 2005, but subsequently reprinted in newspapers in various countries. In Beirut, the protests, which had apparently been infiltrated by Islamist extremists, culminated in early February 2006 in riots in which the Danish embassy was attacked and around 200 people were arrested. Apparently in response to this outbreak of disorder, the Minister of the Interior and Municipalities, Hassan as-Sab, resigned. The Minister of Youth and Sports, Ahmad Fatfat, assumed his responsibilities in an acting capacity.

Government

Under the 1926 Constitution (as subsequently amended), legislative power is held by the National Assembly (called the Chamber of Deputies until 1979), with 128 members elected by universal adult suffrage for four years (subject to dissolution), on the basis of proportional representation. Seats are allocated on a religious or 'confessional' basis (divided equally between Christians and Muslims). The President of the Republic (who must be a Maronite Christian) is elected for six years by the National Assembly. The President, in consultation with deputies and the President of the National Assembly, appoints the Prime Minister (a Sunni Muslim) and other ministers to form the Cabinet, in which executive power is vested. The Ta'if agreement of October 1989, which was incorporated into the Constitution in August 1990, stated that cabinet portfolios must be distributed equally between Christian and Muslim ministers.

Defence

In August 2005 the Lebanese armed forces numbered 72,100 (army 70,000, air force 1,000, navy 1,100). Paramilitary forces included an estimated 13,000 members of the Internal Security Force, which was attached to the Ministry of the Interior and Municipalities. Hezbollah's active members numbered some 2,000 in August 2005. In August 2004 there were an estimated 16,000 Syrian troops in Lebanon. However, following several Syrian redeployments, it was reported in late April 2005 that Syria had withdrawn all of its troops from Lebanon; a UN team was dispatched to the country to verify the withdrawal (for further details, see Recent History). Israeli armed forces and the Israeli-backed South Lebanon Army (SLA) withdrew from Lebanon in May 2000. Government expenditure on defence was budgeted at £L800,000m. in 2005.

The UN Interim Force in Lebanon (UNIFIL, see p. 74) observer mission numbered 1,980 troops at the end of January 2006, assisted by about 50 military observers of the UN Truce Supervision Organization (UNTSO).

Economic Affairs

In 2004, according to estimates by the World Bank, Lebanon's gross national income (GNI), measured at average 2002–04 prices, was US $22,668m., equivalent to $4,980 per head (or $5,380 per head on an international purchasing-power parity basis). During 1995–2004, it was estimated, the population increased at an average annual rate of 1.4%, while gross domestic product (GDP) per head increased, in real terms, by an average of 1.7% per year. Overall GDP increased, in real terms, at an average annual rate of 3.2% in 1995–2004, with GDP growth of some 6.3% recorded in 2004.

Agriculture (including hunting, forestry and fishing) contributed an estimated 12.9% of GDP in 2004. According to FAO data, some 3.1% of the labour force were employed in the sector in 2003. The principal crops are potatoes, citrus fruits, tomatoes, olives and cucumbers. Viticulture is also significant. Hashish is a notable, albeit illegal, export crop, although the Government is attempting to persuade growers to switch to other crops. The GDP of the agricultural sector was estimated to have increased by an average of 2.0% annually in 1995–2004; agricultural GDP grew by an estimated 6.3% in 2004.

The industrial sector (including manufacturing, construction and power) contributed an estimated 19.1% of GDP in 2004. Some 25.9% of the labour force were employed in industry in 1997. Lebanon's only mineral resources consist of small reserves of lignite and iron ore, and their contribution to GDP is insignificant. The GDP of the industrial sector decreased by an estimated average of 0.8% per year in 1995–2004; however, industrial GDP increased by an estimated 6.3% in 2004.

Manufacturing contributed an estimated 9.0% of GDP in 2004. The sector employed about 10% of the labour force in 1985. The most important branches have traditionally been food-processing, petroleum refining, textiles and furniture and woodworking. Manufacturing GDP was estimated to have increased at an average annual rate of 1.3% in 1995–2004; growth of the sector was an estimated 6.3% in 2004.

Energy is derived principally from thermal power stations, using imported petroleum (which accounted for 93.0% of total electricity production in 2002). Plans for the construction of an offshore pipeline—capable of importing 6m.–9m. cu m of natural gas per day from Syria—in order to meet Lebanon's growing energy requirements, to comply with UN regulations on climate change, and in order to reduce state and consumer expenditure on energy, were postponed indefinitely in July 2004. A second pipeline, costing an estimated US $100m., was also planned that would enable Lebanon to import an estimated 9m. cu m of natural gas per day from Egypt. The second phase of the gas pipeline project, which would also provide Syria, Jordan and Turkey with natural gas from Egypt, was initiated in January 2004. It was also expected that Lebanon would eventually be able to convert power plants in Zahrani, Hreiche, Zouk and Jieh from petroleum to natural gas, to be connected by an offshore pipeline. Moreover, there were plans to build a liquefied natural gas plant in Zahrani, which could save the Government some $80m. per year.

The services sector contributed an estimated 68.1% of GDP in 2004. In 1997 some 65.1% of the working population were employed in the sector, which has traditionally been dominated by trade and finance (accounting for an estimated 32.2% and 13.7% of GDP, respectively, in 2002). Financial services, in particular, withstood many of the disruptions inflicted on the economy by the civil conflict, although the Beirut Stock Exchange did not recommence trading until 1996. Lebanon is also becoming increasingly important as a centre for telecommunications. Recent efforts to revive the tourist industry have met with considerable success, and have been a major source of growth in the construction industry. Tourist arrivals increased by 14.3% in 2002 and by 6.2% in 2003; numbers of tourists from Gulf and other Arab states are reported to have grown in recent years. The GDP of the services sector increased at an average annual rate of some 2.8% in 1997–2004; the sector's GDP was estimated to have increased by 5.9% in 2004.

In 2004 Lebanon recorded a trade deficit of US $7,650m. The principal market for exports in 2004 was Iraq (which took 14.6% of Lebanese exports in that year); other significant purchasers included Switzerland, Syria and the United Arab Emirates. The principal supplier of imports in 2004 was Italy (9.9%); France, Germany and the People's Republic of China were also important suppliers. The principal exports in 2004 were jewellery, machinery and electrical equipment, and metals. The principal imports in that year were mineral products, machinery and electrical equipment, vehicles, and chemical products.

In 2004 Lebanon recorded an overall budget deficit of £L1,793,000m., equivalent to 20.2% of recorded expenditure. Budget forecasts for 2005 projected a deficit of £L818,000m., equivalent to 10.5% of budgeted expenditure. At the end of 2003 Lebanon's total external debt was US $18,598m., of which $15,474m. was long-term public debt. The cost of debt-servicing in that year was equivalent to 66.1% of the value of exports of goods and services. According to the Ministry of Finance, Lebanon's total domestic and external debt totalled L£50,322,000m. at the end of 2004. The annual rate of inflation averaged 23.9% in 1990–97. However, this reflected high rates of inflation in the aftermath of the civil war; consumer prices increased by 1.3% in 2001 and by 4.3% in 2002. In 1997, according to official figures, 8.5% of the labour force were unemployed (representing a significant decline from a level of 35% in 1990), although youth unemployment was reported to be much higher. In 2005 the unemployment rate was estimated to be at least 12%–13%.

Lebanon is a member of the Arab Fund for Economic and Social Development (see p. 161), the Arab Monetary Fund (see p. 163) and the Islamic Development Bank (see p. 303). A customs union with Syria entered into effect in January 1999, and in the early 2000s the creation of a free-trade zone was under discussion. Lebanon is also involved in efforts to finalize establishment of a Greater Arab Free Trade Area. A Euro-Mediterranean Association Agreement was signed with the European Union (EU, see p. 228) in June 2002. Lebanon has observer status with the World Trade Organization (see p. 370), but in early 2006 was yet to satisfy all the requirements for full membership of the organization.

By the end of the 1990s the Lebanese Government had achieved considerable success in rehabilitating and expanding basic infrastructure, as envisaged under the first phase of its Horizon 2000 investment programme, which covers the period 1995–2007; the second phase was to focus on the development of social infrastructure. The reconstruction process was undertaken with the support of the international donor community, which in late 1996 pledged grants and concessionary loans totalling some US $3,200m. However, GDP growth since 1996 has been considerably lower than the targeted annual average of 8% under Horizon 2000, principally owing to the failure to control both the budget deficit and the accumulated public debt (equivalent to an estimated 178% of GDP by the end of 2004). In early 1999 the World Bank agreed to disburse some $600m. in concessionary loans over a three-year period, and in April 2000 the EU granted its first aid programme to Lebanon (worth around $47.9m.). In early 2001 international donors agreed to provide the Lebanese authorities with $458m., and an aid package totalling an estimated $4,300m. was pledged by donors in November 2002, in order to provide further assistance with Lebanon's debt restructuring and to finance development projects. However, despite these grants and the introduction of various measures intended to stimulate growth, such as the establishment of a value-added tax of 10% in February 2002, the inability to reach a consensus on certain proposed measures prevented Rafik Hariri (who had been reappointed to the premiership in October 2000) and his administration from implementing fully their comprehensive economic reform programme. By October 2004, when Hariri was replaced as Prime Minister by Omar Karami, the Lebanese economy was beset by many of the same problems as prior to Hariri's appointment, manifested in growing levels of debt and a large budget deficit. Furthermore, the privatization of state assets saw little progress under Hariri's administrations. Between 2003 and early 2005 the planned privatization of several vital state-owned interests, notably Electricité du Liban (EdL), Middle East Airlines and the mobile telephone network, was delayed as a result of ongoing political disagreements. Nevertheless, two four-year contracts for the management of the mobile telephone network were given to the German company Detecon and Kuwait's Mobile Telecommunications Company in mid-2004. Later in the year it was announced that EdL's management would be privatized (its bill collecting having been divested in mid-2004). However, annual losses of some $800m., and the company's failure to satisfy Lebanon's electricity requirements, were considered likely to make encouraging investment difficult, and economists devising the five-year fiscal adjustment for the 'Beirut I' donor conference (see below) identified EdL as a key source of wastage of public finance. It was expected that the Government appointed in July 2005 under Fouad Siniora's premiership would oversee the privatization of the state-owned Radio Liban and Télé-Liban SAL, which were both apparently suffering from cash-flow problems; however, by early 2006 no definite measures had been announced. Also in 2005 plans were announced to establish a Telecoms Regulatory Authority to oversee the privatization of the telecommunications industry, and to implement a new telecommunications law to transfer the fixed-line operator OGERO into Liban Télécom, with plans to part-privatize Liban Télécom within two years of its establishment by selling a 40% stake in the company. It was widely considered that the Lebanese authorities handled the upheaval surrounding Rafik Hariri's assassination in February 2005 successfully, preventing devastating effects on the economy. Nevertheless, the economy reportedly showed almost no growth in 2005, although some optimism was afforded by the appointment of Siniora to the premiership in June 2005; the new Prime Minister (who had served as Minister of Finance in all five of Hariri's administrations) pledged to revitalize Hariri's failed economic reform programme. In the same month it was reported that international donors were discussing the possibility of another donors' conference, to reschedule Lebanon's debt in exchange for economic reform; further details of the meeting (expected to be called 'Beirut I') were announced later in the year. Donors were to be presented with a detailed five-year fiscal adjustment plan as the basis for aid, intended to reduce public spending and increase revenue in order to lower the overall deficit. According to the Ministry of Finance, the programme would allow Lebanon to reduce its debt to around 110% of GDP by the end of the period, providing that annual economic growth averaged 3%. Even with financial support from the international community and domestic creditors, however, such growth remained dependent on political stability, institutional reforms and the implementation of a successful privatization plan, all key elements of the proposed programme of economic reform.

Education

There are state-controlled primary and secondary schools, but private institutions provide the main facilities for secondary and higher education. Education is not compulsory, but state education is provided free of charge. Primary education begins at six years of age and lasts for five years. Secondary education, beginning at the age of 11, lasts for a further seven years, comprising a first cycle of four years and a second of three years. In 1996 the total enrolment at primary and secondary schools was equivalent to 94% of all school-age children (93% of boys; 95% of girls); enrolment at secondary schools in that year was equivalent to 81% of the appropriate age-group (males 78%; females 84%). Some 142,951 Lebanese students were enrolled in higher education in the 2001/02 academic year. In 1998 Lebanon secured a loan of US $60m. from the World Bank, in order to restructure the country's system of technical and vocational education. Lebanon has the highest literacy rate in the Arab world. Expenditure on education by the central Government in 2003 was some £L810,000m. (9.4% of total budgetary expenditure).

Public Holidays

2006: 1 January (New Year's Day), 10 January*† (Id al-Adha, Feast of the Sacrifice), 31 January* (Muharram, Islamic New Year), 9 February (Ashoura* and Feast of St Maron), 22 March (Arab League Anniversary), 10 April* (Mouloud/Yum an-Nabi, birth of Muhammad), 17 April (Easter, Western Church), 21–24 April (Greek Orthodox Easter), 25 May (Ascension Day, Western Church), 15 August (Assumption), 21 August* (Leilat al-Meiraj, ascension of Muhammad), 23 October* (Id al-Fitr, end of Ramadan), 1 November (All Saints' Day), 22 November (Independence Day), 25 December (Christmas Day), 31 December*† (Id al-Adha, Feast of the Sacrifice).

2007: 1 January (New Year's Day), 20 January* (Muharram, Islamic New Year), 29 January* (Ashoura), 9 February (Feast of St Maron), 22 March (Arab League Anniversary), 31 March* (Mouloud/Yum an-Nabi, birth of Muhammad), 6–9 April (Greek Orthodox Easter), 9 April (Easter, Western Church), 17 May (Ascension Day, Western Church), 10 August* (Leilat al-Meiraj, ascension of Muhammad), 15 August (Assumption), 13 October* (Id al-Fitr, end of Ramadan), 1 November (All Saints' Day), 22 November (Independence Day), 20 December* (Id al-Adha, Feast of the Sacrifice), 25 December (Christmas Day).

* These holidays are determined by the Islamic lunar calendar and may vary by one or two days from the dates given.

† This festival occurs twice (in the Islamic years AH 1426 and 1427) within the same Gregorian year.

Weights and Measures

The metric system is in force.

LEBANON

Statistical Survey

Sources (unless otherwise stated): Central Administration for Statistics, Beirut; internet www.cas.gov.lb; Direction Générale des Douanes, Beirut.

Area and Population

AREA, POPULATION AND DENSITY

Area (sq km)	10,452*
Population (official estimate)	
15 November 1970†	
Males	1,080,015
Females	1,046,310
Total	2,126,325
Population (UN estimates at mid-year)‡	
2002	3,469,000
2003	3,504,000
2004	3,540,000
Density (per sq km) at mid-2004	338.7

* 4,036 sq miles.
† Figures are based on the results of a sample survey, excluding Palestinian refugees in camps. The total number of registered Palestinian refugees in Lebanon was 404,170 at 31 December 2005.
‡ Source: UN, *World Population Prospects: The 2004 Revision*.

PRINCIPAL TOWNS
(population in 2003)*

Beirut (capital)	1,171,000	Jounieh	79,800
Tarabulus (Tripoli)	212,900	Zahle	76,600
Saida (Sidon)	149,000	Baabda	58,500
Sur (Tyre)	117,100	Ba'albak (Ba'albek)	29,800
An-Nabatiyah at-			
Tahta (Nabatiyah)	89,400	Alayh	26,700

*Figures are rounded.
Source: Stefan Helders, *World Gazetteer* (internet www.world-gazetteer.com).

BIRTHS, MARRIAGES AND DEATHS
(UN estimates, annual averages)

	1990–95	1995–2000	2000–05
Birth rate (per 1,000)	24.7	22.3	19.0
Death rate (per 1,000)	7.3	7.0	6.7

Source: UN, *World Population Prospects: The 2004 Revision*.

2003 (official estimates, numbers registered): Live births 71,465; Marriages 30,636; Deaths 17,187.

2004 (official estimates, numbers registered): Live births 73,900; Marriages 30,014; Deaths 17,774.

2005 (official estimates, numbers registered): Live births 73,770; Marriages 29,705; Deaths 18,012.

Expectation of life (WHO estimates, years at birth): 70 (males 68; females 72) in 2003 (Source: WHO, *World Health Report*).

EMPLOYMENT
(ISIC major divisions)

	1975	1985*
Agriculture, hunting, forestry and fishing	147,724	103,400
Manufacturing	139,471	45,000
Electricity, gas and water	6,381	10,000
Construction	47,356	25,000
Trade, restaurants and hotels	129,716	78,000
Transport, storage and communications	45,529	20,500
Other services	227,921	171,000
Total	**744,098**	**452,900**

*Estimates.

1997 (provisional estimates at mid-year): Total employed 1,246,000; Unemployed 116,000; Total labour force 1,362,000.

Source: National Employment Office.

Health and Welfare

KEY INDICATORS

Total fertility rate (children per woman, 2003)	1.3
Under-5 mortality rate (per 1,000 live births, 2004)	31
HIV/AIDS (% of persons aged 15–49, 2003)	0.1
Physicians (per 1,000 head, 2001)	3.25
Hospital beds (per 1,000 head, 1997)	2.70
Health expenditure (2002): US $ per head (PPP)	697
Health expenditure (2002): % of GDP	11.5
Health expenditure (2002): public (% of total)	30.1
Access to water (% of persons, 2002)	100
Access to sanitation (% of persons, 2002)	98
Human Development Index (2003): ranking	81
Human Development Index (2003): value	0.759

For sources and definitions, see explanatory note on p. vi.

Agriculture

PRINCIPAL CROPS
('000 metric tons)

	2002	2003	2004*
Wheat	119	116	120
Barley	17	25	20
Potatoes	397	416	350
Almonds	23	27	28
Olives	184	83	180
Cabbages	52	58	59
Lettuce	17	22	22
Tomatoes	271	217	218
Cauliflower	36	20	22
Pumpkins, squash and gourds	24	24*	24
Cucumbers and gherkins	132	150*	160
Aubergines (Eggplants)	18	19	20
Dry onions	73	63	75
Garlic	9	5	6
Green beans	29	21	21
Green broad beans	14	16	17
Carrots	25	30	30
Other vegetables	51	48	50
Watermelons	68	87	75
Cantaloupes and other melons	32	8	10
Bananas	68	72	72
Oranges	155	222	190
Tangerines, mandarins, clementines and satsumas	43	44	42
Lemons and limes	81	83	83
Grapefruit and pomelo	10	15	14
Apples	150	158	140
Pears	28	39	32
Apricots	39	31	32
Cherries	34	37	34
Peaches and nectarines	24	27	25
Plums	25	20	20
Strawberries	2	3	3
Grapes	102	119	110
Figs	9	12	10
Other fruits and berries	42	72	72

*FAO estimate(s).
Source: FAO.

LEBANON

LIVESTOCK
('000 head, year ending September)

	2002	2003	2004*
Horses*	6	6	6
Mules*	6	6	6
Asses*	25	25	25
Cattle	88	86	90
Pigs	21	14	15
Sheep	298	303	330
Goats	409	428	430
Poultry*	33,000	34,000	35,000

* FAO estimates.
Source: FAO.

LIVESTOCK PRODUCTS
('000 metric tons)

	2002	2003	2004*
Beef and veal*	54.6	52.5	52.5
Mutton and lamb*	14.3	14.3	14.7
Goat meat*	2.5	2.6	2.7
Pig meat*	1.9	1.3	1.3
Poultry meat	124.5	127.2	130.0
Cows' milk	193.5	254.4	260.0
Sheep's milk	22.1	23.4	24.0
Goats' milk	29.4	36.5	38.0
Cheese*	18.8	24.0	24.6
Hen eggs	46.2	46.5	46.8
Cattle hides*	4.7	4.5	4.5
Sheepskins*	1.9	2.0	2.0
Wool: greasy*	1.8	1.8	1.9

* FAO estimate(s).
Source: FAO.

Forestry

ROUNDWOOD REMOVALS
(FAO estimates, '000 cubic metres, excluding bark)

	2002	2003	2004
Sawlogs, veneer logs and logs for sleepers*	7.2	7.2	7.2
Fuel wood	82.0	81.8	81.6
Total	89.2	89.0	88.7

* Assumed unchanged since 1992.
Source: FAO.

SAWNWOOD PRODUCTION
(FAO estimates, '000 cubic metres, including railway sleepers)

	2002	2003	2004
Coniferous (softwood)	6.6	6.6	6.6
Broadleaved (hardwood)	2.4	2.4	2.4
Total*	9.0	9.0	9.0

* Assumed to be unchanged since 1991.
Source: FAO.

Fishing
(metric tons, live weight)

	2001	2002	2003
Capture	3,670	3,970	3,898
Groupers and seabasses	240	250	250
Porgies and seabreams	400	370	370
Surmullets (Red mullets)	200	200	200
Barracudas	250	200	250
Mullets	400	370	365
Scorpionfishes	100	125	125
Carangids	400	400	400
Clupeoids	500	650	600
Tuna-like fishes	450	400	400
Mackerel-like fishes	350	350	300
Marine crustaceans	55	60	60
Aquaculture	300	790	790
Rainbow trout	300	700	700
Total catch	3,970	4,760	4,688

Source: FAO.

Mining
(estimates, '000 metric tons)

	2002	2003	2004
Salt (unrefined)	4	4	4

Source: US Geological Survey.

Industry

SELECTED PRODUCTS
('000 metric tons, unless otherwise indicated)

	2002	2003	2004
Olive oil*†	5.3	5.3	6.5
Sunflower seed oil*‡	4.8	3.6	6.6
Wine*‡	15.0	15.0	15.0
Beer*‡	16.4	15.4	17.5
Plywood ('000 cubic metres)*‡	34	34	34
Paper*‡	42	42	42
Cement§	2,852	2,900‖	2,900‖
Sulphuric acid (gross weight)	480	485	495

* Source: FAO.
† Unofficial figures.
‡ FAO estimates.
§ Source: US Geological Survey.
‖ Estimate.

Electric energy (million kWh): 9,072 in 2002 (provisional); 10,547 in 2003.

LEBANON

Finance

CURRENCY AND EXCHANGE RATES

Monetary Units
100 piastres = 1 Lebanese pound (£L).

Sterling, Dollar and Euro Equivalents (30 December 2005)
£1 sterling = £L2,595.8;
US $1 = £L1,507.5;
€1 = £L1,778.4;
£L10,000 = £3.85 sterling = $6.63 = €5.62.

Exchange Rate: The official exchange rate has been maintained at US $1 = £L1,507.5 since September 1999.

BUDGET
(£L '000 million)*

Revenue	2002	2003	2004
Tax revenue	3,995	4,502	5,169
Taxes on income, profits and capital gains	727	783	908
Taxes on property	300	321	405
Domestic taxes on goods and services	1,162	1,537	1,971
Taxes on international trade and transactions	1,618	1,643	1,617
Other taxes	189	217	268
Other current revenue	1,390	1,717	1,907
Income from public enterprises	916	1,252	1,448
Administrative fees and charges	376	383	365
Fines and confiscations	21	6	5
Other	77	75	88
Total	**5,385**	**6,219**	**7,075**

Expenditure	2002	2003	2004
Personnel costs	3,008	3,078	3,094
Salaries and wages	1,960	2,026	2,071
Retirement and end of service compensations	857	845	810
Interest payments	4,622	4,874	4,021
Materials and supplies	130	120	116
External services	80	81	113
Various transfers	227	271	360
Other current	200	330	275
Reserves	54	66	72
Acquisitions of land, buildings, for the construction of roads, ports, airports and water networks	0	12	12
Equipment	63	57	49
Construction in progress	479	561	646
Maintenance	55	61	60
Other expenditures related to fixed capital assets	14	23	49
Total	**8,931**	**9,533**	**8,868**
Current	8,321	8,820	8,051
Capital	610	713	817

* Figures, which are rounded, represent the consolidated operations of the central Government's General Budget and the Council for Development and Reconstruction. The accounts of other central government units with individual budgets (including the general social security scheme) are excluded.

2005 (£L '000 million): *Revenue:* Tax revenue 4,867 (Customs revenue, incl. receipts from excise taxes 1,268; Valued-added tax 1,693; Other tax revenue 1,906); Non-tax revenue 2,117; Total 6,984. *Expenditure:* Debt servicing 3,534 (Domestic debt 1,533, Foreign debt 2,002); Other expenditure 4,268; Total 7,802.

Source: Ministry of Finance.

INTERNATIONAL RESERVES
(US $ million at 31 December)

	2002	2003	2004
Gold (national valuation)	3,216.3	3,833.5	4,006.0
IMF special drawing rights	27.3	30.7	32.9
Reserve position in IMF	25.6	28.0	29.2
Foreign exchange	7,190.9	12,460.8	11,672.4
Total	**10,460.1**	**16,353.0**	**15,740.5**

Source: IMF, *International Financial Statistics.*

MONEY SUPPLY
(£L '000 million at 31 December)

	2002	2003	2004
Currency outside banks	1,375.3	1,530.6	1,586.5
Demand deposits at commercial banks	1,094.3	1,277.3	1,389.3
Total money (incl. others)	**2,566.4**	**2,847.0**	**3,030.6**

Sources: IMF, *International Financial Statistics.*

COST OF LIVING
(Consumer Price Index for Beirut; base: December 1998 = 100)

	2000	2001	2002
Food and beverages	93.7	94.5	93.9
Water, electricity and gas	105.5	104.9	n.a.
Clothing and footwear	104.7	108.4	117.1
Transport and communications	109.9	111.6	133.0
All items (incl. others)	**99.8**	**101.1**	**105.4**

NATIONAL ACCOUNTS
(UN estimates, £L '000 million at current prices)

Expenditure on the Gross Domestic Product

	2000	2001	2002
Government final consumption expenditure	2,914.2	3,062.8	3,230.3
Private final consumption expenditure	26,555.1	27,372.5	28,279.8
Increase in stocks	5,434.9	5,311.4	5,211.6
Gross fixed capital formation			
Total domestic expenditure	**34,904.2**	**35,746.7**	**36,721.7**
Exports of goods and services	2,547.5	2,685.3	2,839.5
Less Imports of goods and services	12,203.8	12,426.7	12,723.7
GDP in purchasers' values	**25,247.9**	**26,005.3**	**26,837.5**
GDP at constant 1995 prices	**20,005.2**	**20,405.3**	**20,915.5**

Gross Domestic Product by Economic Activity

	2000	2001	2002
Agriculture, hunting, forestry and fishing	2,624.1	2,640.9	2,665.2
Manufacturing	2,524.7	2,570.4	2,607.1
Electricity, gas and water	1,681.3	1,722.2	1,759.8
Construction	753.1	693.4	649.6
Trade, restaurants and hotels	8,122.9	8,378.4	8,648.7
Transport, storage and communications	743.3	784.6	826.9
Finance and insurance	3,313.7	3,490.4	3,674.7
Real estate and business services	1,124.5	1,135.5	1,151.4
Government services	1,954.3	2,014.9	2,090.3
Other community, social and personal services	2,406.0	2,574.7	2,763.9
GDP in purchasers' values	**25,247.9**	**26,005.4**	**26,837.6**

Source: UN Economic and Social Commission for Western Asia, *National Accounts Studies of the ESCWA Region* (2000).

LEBANON

BALANCE OF PAYMENTS
(US $ million)

	2002	2003	2004
Exports of goods f.o.b.	1,018	1,444	1,598
Imports of goods f.o.b.	–5,979	–6,667	–8,704
Trade balance	–4,962	–5,223	–7,105
Exports of services	4,429	9,462	9,700
Imports of services	–3,367	–6,500	–8,263
Balance on goods and services	–3,899	–2,261	–5,669
Other income received	567	1,511	1,316
Other income paid	–1,131	–5,040	–2,168
Balance on goods, services and income	–4,463	–5,791	–6,521
Current transfers received	2,591	4,079	5,325
Current transfers paid	–2,513	–3,751	–3,609
Current balance	–4,385	–5,463	–4,805
Capital account (net)	13	29	50
Direct investment abroad	—	457	–385
Direct investment from abroad	1,336	2,523	1,311
Portfolio investment assets	101	–773	–614
Portfolio investment liabilities	2,881	2,475	2,843
Other investment assets	–843	–3,562	–1,140
Other investment liabilities	–125	2,885	2,802
Net errors and omissions	–1,196	–2,572	–403
Overall balance	–2,219	–4,002	–340

Source: IMF, *Government Finance Statistics*.

External Trade

PRINCIPAL COMMODITIES
(US $ million)*

Imports c.i.f.	2002	2003	2004
Live animals and animal products	381.9	418.9	452.6
Vegetable products	336.0	383.5	440.9
Prepared foodstuffs; beverages, spirits and vinegar; tobacco and manufactured substitutes	474.5	476.7	527.0
Mineral products	974.0	1,190.5	2,068.1
Products of chemical or allied industries	632.5	715.5	828.5
Plastics, rubber and articles thereof	238.9	259.2	349.3
Textiles and textile articles	423.6	433.8	507.9
Natural or cultured pearls, precious or semi-precious stones, precious metals and articles thereof; imitation jewellery; coin	299.9	302.2	526.8
Base metals and articles thereof	380.5	470.6	596.1
Machinery and mechanical appliances; electrical equipment; sound and television apparatus	862.7	872.5	1,109.1
Vehicles, aircraft, vessels and associated transport equipment	572.4	696.4	843.4
Total (incl. others)	6,444.8	7,168.2	9,397.0

Exports f.o.b.	2002	2003	2004
Vegetable products	57.2	64.5	82.5
Prepared foodstuffs; beverages, spirits and vinegar; tobacco and manufactured substitutes	102.3	149.6	148.1
Products of chemical or allied industries	108.0	114.6	149.2
Paper-making material; paper and paperboard and articles thereof	98.4	89.2	100.5
Textiles and textile articles	60.6	64.7	78.0
Natural or cultured pearls, precious or semi-precious stones, precious metals and articles thereof; imitation jewellery; coin	214.6	464.2	287.1
Base metals and articles thereof	78.7	115.4	227.9
Machinery and mechanical appliances; electrical equipment; sound and television apparatus	119.5	179.4	274.0
Total (incl. others)	1,045.5	1,523.9	1,747.0

* Figures are calculated on the basis of the official dollar rate, which is the previous month's average exchange rate of Lebanese pounds per US dollar.

Source: Ministry of Economy and Trade.

PRINCIPAL TRADING PARTNERS
(US $ million)*

Imports c.i.f.	2002	2003	2004
Belgium	207.0	156.3	170.0
China, People's Republic	435.0	530.7	717.8
Egypt	134.4	174.4	294.9
France	779.5	582.9	730.7
Germany	878.4	579.0	729.3
Greece	109.3	83.1	68.6
India	107.0	84.4	114.1
Indonesia	n.a.	40.3	52.3
Italy	1,045.2	674.3	930.5
Japan	327.8	269.1	349.2
Korea, Republic	76.9	79.0	103.0
Malaysia	n.a.	54.4	67.6
Netherlands	222.1	229.8	171.5
Russia	370.8	321.2	542.5
Saudi Arabia	138.9	219.6	413.5
Spain	263.3	198.3	189.7
Switzerland	402.8	216.2	395.8
Syria	312.5	207.2	240.0
Taiwan	63.2	54.5	75.9
Thailand	63.0	65.7	92.4
Turkey	258.7	234.1	258.2
Ukraine	102.2	166.6	145.9
United Kingdom	252.6	315.5	385.6
USA	464.5	431.5	553.2
Total (incl. others)	6,444.8	7,168.2	9,397.0

LEBANON

Statistical Survey

Exports f.o.b.	2002	2003	2004
Belgium	33.7	10.4	16.5
Canada	n.a.	7.4	7.3
Cyprus	n.a.	12.9	14.2
Egypt	27.6	28.0	39.8
France	29.7	24.0	35.0
Germany	14.1	20.2	22.8
Greece	10.9	5.4	8.4
India	14.3	13.8	27.3
Iraq	71.1	121.8	255.5
Italy	22.7	28.5	18.7
Jordan	35.3	48.4	62.8
Kuwait	32.4	50.8	67.4
Malta	18.0	14.0	7.9
Netherlands	15.6	13.4	11.1
Saudi Arabia	96.0	104.3	112.8
Spain	16.7	16.4	11.1
Switzerland	132.1	379.1	187.3
Syria	75.6	99.5	145.2
Turkey	32.1	63.3	127.3
United Arab Emirates	94.7	104.4	135.2
United Kingdom	20.7	16.1	21.3
USA	53.5	66.2	48.5
Total (incl. others)	1,045.5	1,523.9	1,747.0

* Imports by country of production; exports by country of last consignment.

Source: Ministry of Economy and Trade.

2005 (£L million): *Imports c.i.f.*: Belgium 264,100; China (People's Republic) 1,107,534; Egypt 457,532; France 1,188,504; Germany 991,224; Greece 146,910; Indonesia 71,886; Italy 1,471,306; Japan 462,877; Korea (Republic) 11,418; Netherlands 229,306; Russia 767,691; Saudi Arabia 496,140; Spain 252,891; Switzerland 636,849; Syria 296,934; Taiwan 105,136; Turkey 301,058; Ukraine 200,093; United Kingdom 487,426; USA 825,940; Total (incl. others) 1,040,896. *Exports c.i.f.*: Belgium 34,726; Canada 21,857; Cyprus 25,079; Egypt 82,298; France 48,467; Germany 27,582; Greece 20,118; Italy 25,935; Jordan 113,419; Kuwait 122,423; Netherlands 24,215; Saudi Arabia 210,805; Spain 20,606; Switzerland 188,623; Syria 282,670; Turkey 183,372; United Arab Emirates 233,703; United Kingdom 43,478; USA 86,850; Total (incl. others) 189,242.

Transport

ROAD TRAFFIC
(motor vehicles in use)

	1995	1996*	1997*
Passenger cars (incl. taxis)	1,197,521	1,217,000	1,299,398
Buses and coaches	5,514	5,640	6,833
Lorries and vans	79,222	81,000	85,242
Motorcycles and mopeds	53,317	54,450	61,471

* Estimates.

Source: International Road Federation, *World Road Statistics*.

SHIPPING

Merchant Fleet
(registered at 31 December)

	2002	2003	2004
Number of vessels	89	79	79
Total displacement ('000 grt)	229.3	193.3	184.1

Source: Lloyd's Register-Fairplay, *World Fleet Statistics*.

International Sea-borne Freight Traffic
('000 metric tons)

	1988	1989	1990
Goods loaded	148	150	152
Goods unloaded	1,120	1,140	1,150

Source: UN, *Monthly Bulletin of Statistics*.

2002 ('000 metric tons, Beirut port only): Goods loaded 393; Goods unloaded 4,827.

2003 ('000 metric tons, Beirut port only): Goods loaded 499; Goods unloaded 4,306.

2004 ('000 metric tons, Beirut port only): Goods loaded 727; Goods unloaded 4,334.

CIVIL AVIATION
(revenue traffic on scheduled services)

	1997	1998	1999
Kilometres flown (million)	21	20	20
Passengers carried ('000)	857	716	719
Passenger-km (million)	2,116	1,504	1,288
Total ton-km (million)	319	247	222

Source: UN, *Statistical Yearbook*.

Tourism

FOREIGN TOURIST ARRIVALS
('000)*

Country of nationality	2001	2002	2003
Australia	27.9	30.1	31.9
Canada	36.5	39.7	43.1
Egypt	36.4	38.6	39.0
France	66.3	70.9	76.4
Germany	35.7	36.3	37.9
Iran	51.1	65.3	70.4
Italy	13.5	12.3	13.1
Jordan	74.5	81.7	87.8
Kuwait	52.9	69.5	56.0
Saudi Arabia	116.9	114.6	162.2
Sri Lanka	18.7	16.7	17.1
United Kingdom	24.8	28.6	28.0
USA	48.0	52.6	60.1
Total (incl. others)	837.1	956.5	1,015.8

* Figures exclude arrivals of Syrian nationals, Palestinians and students.

Tourism receipts (US $ million, incl. passenger transport): 837 in 2001; 956 in 2002; 1,016 in 2003.

Source: World Tourism Organization.

Communications Media

	2002	2003	2004
Telephones ('000 main lines in use)	678.8	700.0	630.0
Mobile cellular telephones ('000 subscribers)	775.1	820.0	888.0
Personal computers ('000 in use)	300	350	400
Internet users ('000)	400	500	600

Radio receivers ('000 in use): 2,850 in 1997.

Facsimile machines (number in use): 3,000 in 1992.

Television receivers ('000 in use): 1,170 in 2000.

Daily newspapers (number of titles): 13 in 2000.

Daily newspapers (total average circulation, estimates, '000 copies): 220 in 2000.

Non-daily newspapers (number of titles): 7 in 2000.

Book production (number of titles): 289 in 1998.

Sources: UNESCO Institute for Statistics; UNESCO, *Statistical Yearbook*; UN, *Statistical Yearbook*; and International Telecommunication Union.

Education

(1996/97, unless otherwise indicated)

	Institutions	Teachers	Students
Pre-primary	1,938		164,397*
Primary	2,160	67,935†	382,309*
Secondary:			
general	n.a.		292,002*
vocational	275†	7,745	55,848*
Higher	n.a.	10,444‡	81,588‡

* Estimate.
† 1994 figure.
‡ 1995/96 figure.

Sources: UNESCO, *Statistical Yearbook*; Banque du Liban, *Annual Report*.

2001/02 (number of students): Higher 142,951 (Source: UNESCO).

Adult literacy rate (UNESCO estimates): 86.5% (males 92.4%; females 81.0%) in 2001 (Source: UN Development Programme, *Human Development Report*).

Directory

The Constitution

The Constitution was promulgated on 23 May 1926 and amended by the Constitutional Laws of 1927, 1929, 1943, 1947 and 1990.

According to the Constitution, the Republic of Lebanon is an independent and sovereign state, and no part of the territory may be alienated or ceded. Lebanon has no state religion. Arabic is the official language. Beirut is the capital.

All Lebanese are equal in the eyes of the law. Personal freedom and freedom of the press are guaranteed and protected. The religious communities are entitled to maintain their own schools, on condition that they conform to the general requirements relating to public instruction, as defined by the state. Dwellings are inviolable; rights of ownership are protected by law. Every Lebanese citizen over 21 is an elector and qualifies for the franchise.

LEGISLATIVE POWER

Legislative power is exercised by one house, the National Assembly, with 108 seats (raised, without amendment of the Constitution, to 128 in 1992), which are divided equally between Christians and Muslims. Members of the National Assembly must be over 25 years of age, in possession of their full political and civil rights, and literate. They are considered representative of the whole nation, and are not bound to follow directives from their constituencies. They can be suspended only by a two-thirds' majority of their fellow-members. Secret ballot was introduced in a new election law of April 1960.

The National Assembly holds two sessions yearly, from the first Tuesday after 15 March to the end of May, and from the first Tuesday after 15 October to the end of the year. The normal term of the National Assembly is four years; general elections take place within 60 days before the end of this period. If the Assembly is dissolved before the end of its term, elections are held within three months of dissolution.

Voting in the Assembly is public—by acclamation, or by standing and sitting. A quorum of two-thirds and a majority vote is required for constitutional issues. The only exceptions to this occur when the Assembly becomes an electoral college, and chooses the President of the Republic, or Secretaries to the National Assembly, or when the President is accused of treason or of violating the Constitution. In such cases voting is secret, and a two-thirds' majority is needed for a proposal to be adopted.

EXECUTIVE POWER

With the incorporation of the Ta'if agreement into the Lebanese Constitution in August 1990, executive power was effectively transferred from the presidency to the Cabinet. The President is elected for a term of six years and is not immediately re-eligible. He is responsible for the promulgation and execution of laws enacted by the National Assembly, but all presidential decisions (with the exception of those to appoint a Prime Minister or to accept the resignation of a government) require the co-signature of the Prime Minister, who is head of the Government, implementing its policies and speaking in its name. The President must receive the approval of the Cabinet before dismissing a minister or ratifying an international treaty. The ministers and the Prime Minister are chosen by the President of the Republic in consultation with the members and President of the National Assembly. They are not necessarily members of the National Assembly, although they are responsible to it and have access to its debates. The President of the Republic must be a Maronite Christian, and the Prime Minister a Sunni Muslim; the choice of the other ministers must reflect the level of representation of the communities in the Assembly.

Note: In October 1998 the National Assembly endorsed an exceptional amendment to Article 49 of the Constitution to enable the election of Gen. Emile Lahoud, then Commander-in-Chief of the armed forces, as President of the Republic: the Constitution requires that senior state officials relinquish their responsibilities two years prior to seeking public office. In September 2004 the National Assembly voted in favour of a constitutional amendment extending President Lahoud's term of office for a further three years.

The Government

HEAD OF STATE

President: Gen. EMILE LAHOUD (inaugurated 24 November 1998).

CABINET
(April 2006)

Prime Minister: FOUAD SINIORA.

Deputy Prime Minister and Minister of National Defence: ELIAS MURR.

Minister of Foreign Affairs and Emigrants: FAWZI SALLOUKH.

Acting Minister of the Interior and Municipalities and Minister of Youth and Sports: AHMAD FATFAT.

Minister of Justice: CHARLES RIZQ.

Minister of Industry: PIERRE GEMAYEL.

Minister of Energy and Water: MUHAMMAD FNEISH.

Minister of Public Works and Transport: MUHAMMAD AS-SAFADI.

Minister of Finance: JIHAD AZOUR.

Minister of Economy and Trade: SAMI HADAD.

Minister of Education and Higher Education: KHALID QABBANI.

Minister of Culture: TARIQ MITRI.

Minister of Information: GHAZI AL-ARIDI.

Minister of Tourism: JOSEPH SARKIS.

Minister of Telecommunications: MARWAN HAMADEH.

Minister of Labour: TARRAD HAMADEH.

Minister of Agriculture: TALAL AS-SAHILI.

Minister of the Environment: YA'COUB AS-SARRAF.

Minister of Public Health: MUHAMMAD JAWAD KHALIFAH.

Minister of Social Affairs: NAYLA MOUAWAD.

Minister of the Displaced: NEHME TOHME.

Minister of State for Administrative Development: JEAN OGHASABIAN.

LEBANON

Minister of State for Parliamentary Affairs: MICHEL FAROUN.

MINISTRIES

Office of the President: Presidential Palace, Baabda, Beirut; tel. (5) 920900; fax (5) 922400; e-mail president_office@presidency.gov.lb; internet www.presidency.gov.lb.

Office of the President of the Council of Ministers: Grand Sérail, place Riad es-Solh, Beirut; tel. (1) 746800; fax (1) 865630.

Ministry of Agriculture: blvd Camille Chamoun, Beirut; tel. (1) 455631; fax (1) 455475; e-mail ministry@agriculture.gov.lb; internet www.agriculture.gov.lb.

Ministry of Culture: Immeuble Hatab, rue Madame Curie, Verdun, Beirut; tel. (1) 756310; fax (1) 756303; internet www.culture.gov.lb.

Ministry of the Displaced: Minet el-Hosn, Starco Centre, Beirut; tel. (1) 366373; fax (1) 503040; e-mail mod@dm.net.lb; internet www.ministryofdisplaced.gov.lb.

Ministry of Economy and Trade: rue Artois, Hamra, Beirut; tel. (1) 340503; fax (1) 354640; e-mail postmaster@economy.gov.lb; internet www.economy.gov.lb.

Ministry of Education and Higher Education: Campus de l'Unesco, Beirut; tel. (1) 866430; fax (1) 645844.

Ministry of Energy and Water: Shiah, Beirut; tel. (1) 270256.

Ministry of the Environment: POB 70-1091, Antélias, Beirut; tel. (4) 522222; fax (4) 525080; e-mail webmaster@moe.gov.lb; internet www.moe.gov.lb.

Ministry of Finance: 4e étage, Immeuble MOF, place Riad es-Solh, Beirut; tel. (1) 981057; fax (1) 981059; e-mail infocenter@finance.gov.lb; internet www.finance.gov.lb.

Ministry of Foreign Affairs and Emigrants: rue Sursock, Achrafieh, Beirut; tel. (1) 333100; e-mail info@emigrants.gov.lb; internet www.emigrants.gov.lb.

    General Directorate of Emigrants: Immeuble As-Sultan, Jnah, Beirut; tel. (1) 840921; fax (1) 840924; e-mail director@emigrants.gov.lb; internet www.emigrants.gov.lb.

Ministry of Industry: Ministry of Industry and Oil Bldg, ave Sami Solh, Beirut; tel. (1) 427042; fax (1) 427112; e-mail ministry@industry.gov.lb; internet www.industry.gov.lb.

Ministry of Information: rue Hamra, Beirut; tel. (1) 345800.

Ministry of the Interior and Municipalities: Grand Sérail, place Riad es-Solh, Beirut; tel. (1) 751613; e-mail ministry@interior.gov.lb; internet www.moim.gov.lb.

Ministry of Justice: rue Sami Solh, Beirut; tel. (1) 422953; e-mail justice@ministry.gov.lb; internet www.justice.gov.lb.

Ministry of Labour: Shiah, Beirut; tel. (1) 274140.

Ministry of National Defence: Yarze, Beirut; tel. (5) 920400; fax (5) 951014; e-mail ministry@lebarmy.gov.lb; internet www.lebarmy.gov.lb.

Ministry of Public Health: place du Musée, Beirut; tel. (1) 615716; fax (1) 645099; e-mail minister@public-health.gov.lb; internet www.public-health.gov.lb.

Ministry of Public Works and Transport: Shiah, Beirut; tel. (1) 428980; internet www.public-works.gov.lb.

Ministry of State for Administrative Reform: Immeuble Starco, 5e étage, rue George Picot, Beirut; tel. (1) 371510; fax (1) 371599; e-mail newsletter@omsar.gov.lb; internet www.omsar.gov.lb.

Ministry of Telecommunications: rue Sami Solh, 3e étage, Beirut; tel. (1) 424400; fax (1) 888310; e-mail webmaster@mpt.gov.lb; internet www.mpt.gov.lb.

Ministry of Tourism: POB 11-5344, rue Banque du Liban 550, Beirut; tel. (1) 340940; fax (1) 340945; e-mail mot@lebanon-tourism.gov.lb; internet www.lebanon-tourism.gov.lb.

Ministry of Youth and Sports: Beirut.

Legislature

MAJLIS ALNWAB
(National Assembly)

The equal distribution of seats among Christians and Muslims is determined by law, and the Cabinet must reflect the level of representation achieved by the various religious denominations within that principal division. Deputies of the same religious denomination do not necessarily share the same political or party allegiances. The distribution of seats is as follows: Maronite Catholics 34; Sunni Muslims 27; Shi'a Muslims 27; Greek Orthodox 14; Druzes 8; Greek-Melkite Catholics 8; Armenian Orthodox 5; Alawites 2; Armenian Catholics 1; Protestants 1; Others 1.

President: NABIH BERRI.

Vice-President: ELIE FERZLI.

General election, 29 May–19 June 2005

Party list	Seats
Rafik Hariri Martyr List*	72
Resistance and Development Bloc†	35
Free Patriotic Movement‡	21
Total	**128**

* Electoral list comprising the Future Movement (which won 36 seats), Parti socialiste progressiste (16), Lebanese Forces Party (6), Qornet Shehwan Gathering (6), Tripoli Bloc (3), Democratic Renewal (1), Democratic Left (1) and independents (3).
† Election list comprising Amal (which won 15 seats), Hezbollah (14), the Syrian Social Nationalist Party (2) and others (4).
‡ Election list comprising the Free Patriotic Movement itself (which won 14 seats), the Skaff bloc (5) and the Murr bloc (2).

Political Organizations

Amal (Hope—Afwaj al-Muqawamah al-Lubnaniyyah—Lebanese Resistance Detachments): e-mail post@amal-movement.com; internet www.amal-movement.com; f. 1975 as a politico-military organization; Shi'ite political party; contested 2005 legislative elections with Hezbollah as Resistance and Development Bloc; Leader NABIH BERRI.

Armenian Revolutionary Federation (ARF) (Tashnag): rue Spears, Beirut; f. 1890; principal Armenian party; historically the dominant nationalist party in the independent Armenian Republic of Yerevan of 1917–21, prior to its becoming part of the USSR; socialist ideology; collective leadership.

Al-Baath (Baath Arab Socialist Party): Beirut; f. 1948; local branch of secular pro-Syrian party with policy of Arab union; Leader ASSEM QANSO.

Al-Baath (Baath Arab Socialist Party): f. 1966 following split in Syrian branch of Al-Baath; part of pro-Iraqi faction of Al-Baath; Sec.-Gen. ABD AL-MAJID RAFEI.

Bloc national libanais (National Bloc): rue Pasteur, Gemmayze, Beirut; tel. (1) 584585; fax (1) 584591; f. 1943; right-wing Lebanese party with policy of power-sharing between Christians and Muslims and the exclusion of the military from politics; Pres. CARLOS EDEH.

Free Patriotic Movement (Tayar al-Watani al-Horr): Beirut; tel. (3) 122858; e-mail info@tayyar.org; internet www.tayyar.org/tayyar/index.php; aims to recover sovereignty and complete independence for Lebanon; majority of leaders and supporters are from the Christian community; contested 2005 legislative elections in alliance with the Skaff and Murr blocs; Leader Gen. MICHEL AWN.

Future Movement (Tayar al-Mustaqbal): Beirut; opposed to Syrian influence in Lebanese affairs; contested 2005 legislative elections on the Rafik Hariri Martyr List with the Qornet Shehwan Gathering, Lebanese Forces Party and Parti socialiste progressiste; Leader SAAD ED-DIN HARIRI.

Hezbollah (Party of God): Beirut; e-mail hizbollahmedia@hizbollah.org; internet www.hizbollah.org; f. 1982 by Iranian Revolutionary Guards who were sent to Lebanon; militant Shi'ite faction, which has become the leading organization of Lebanon's Shi'a community and a recognized political party; demands the withdrawal of Israeli forces from the occupied Shebaa Farms area of southern Lebanon and the release of all Lebanese prisoners from Israeli detention; contested 2005 legislative elections with Amal as Resistance and Development Bloc; Chair. MUHAMMAD RA'D; Leader and Sec.-Gen. Sheikh HASAN NASRALLAH; Spiritual Leader Ayatollah MUHAMMED HUSSAIN FADLALLAH.

Al-Kataeb (Phalanges libanaises, Phalangist Party): POB 992, place Charles Hélou, Beirut; tel. (1) 584107; e-mail admin@kataeb.com; internet www.kataeb.com; f. 1936 by the late Pierre Gemayel; nationalist, reformist, democratic social party; largest Maronite party; mem. of the Qornet Shehwan Gathering; 100,000 mems; Pres. KARIM PAKRADOUNI.

An-Najjadé (The Helpers): c/o Sawt al-Uruba, POB 3537, Beirut; f. 1936; Arab socialist unionist party; 3,000 mems; Founder and Pres. ADNANE MOUSTAFA AL-HAKIM.

National Lebanese Front: Beirut; f. 1999; Pres. ERNEST KARAM.

Parti communiste libanais (Lebanese Communist Party—PCL): rue Al-Bahatri, Al-Watuat, Beirut; tel. and fax (1) 739615; e-mail lcparty@inco.com.lb; internet www.lcparty.org; f. 1924; officially dissolved 1948–71; Marxist, much support among intellectuals; Pres. MAURICE NOHRA; Sec.-Gen. KHALID HADDADEH.

Parti socialiste progressiste (At-Takadumi al-Ishteraki—PSP): POB 11-2893, Beirut 1107 2120; tel. (1) 303455; fax (1) 301231; e-mail secretary@psp.org.lb; internet www.psp.org.lb; f. 1949; progressive party, advocates constitutional road to socialism and democracy; over 25,000 mems; mainly Druze support; contested 2005 legislative elections as part of the Rafik Hariri Martyr List; Pres. WALID JOUMBLATT; Sec.-Gen. SHARIF FAYAD.

Qornet Shehwan Gathering: f. 2001; Christian coalition of parties of diverse political persuasions and incorporating Maronite (incl. Al-Kataeb), Orthodox and Greek Catholic mems; advocates full national sovereignty for Lebanon; supports the establishment of a Palestinian state; rejects violence as a means of solving disputes; contested 2005 legislative elections as part of the Rafik Hariri Martyr List; Maronite Christian Patriarch Cardinal NASRALLAH BOUTROS SFEIR is the group's unofficial patron.

Resistance and Development Bloc: electoral bloc consisting principally of Amal and Hezbollah; the two parties contested the 2000 and, with the Syrian Social Nationalist Party, 2005 legislative elections as this alliance; Leader NABIH BERRI.

Syrian Social Nationalist Party: internet www.ssnp.com; f. 1932 in Beirut; banned 1962–69; seeks creation of a 'Greater Syria' state, incl. Lebanon, Syria, Iraq, Jordan, Palestine, Kuwait and Cyprus; advocates separation of church and state, the redistribution of wealth, and a strong military; supports Syrian involvement in Lebanese affairs; contested 2005 legislative elections as mem. of the Resistance and Development Bloc (consisting principally of Amal and Hezbollah); Leader JIBRAN ARAIJI.

Al-Wa'ad (National Secular Democratic Party—Pledge): Beirut; f. 1986 by the late Elie Hobeika; pro-Syrian splinter group of Lebanese Forces (see below).

Other parties include the **Independent Nasserite Movement** (Murabitoun; Sunni Muslim Militia; Leader IBRAHIM QULAYAT) and the **Lebanese Popular Congress** (Pres. KAMAL SHATILA). The **Nasserite Popular Organization** and the **Arab Socialist Union** merged in January 1987, retaining the name of the former. The **Islamic Amal** is a breakaway group from Amal, based in Ba'albak (Ba'albek) (Leader HUSSEIN MOUSSAVI). **Islamic Jihad** (Islamic Holy War) is a pro-Iranian fundamentalist guerrilla group (Leader IMAAD MOUGNIEH). The **Popular Liberation Army** (f. 1985 by the late MUSTAFA SAAD) is a Sunni Muslim faction, active in the south of Lebanon. **Tawheed Islami** (the Islamic Unification Movement; f. 1982; Sunni Muslim) and the **Arab Democratic Party** (or the Red Knights; Alawites; pro-Syrian; Leader ALI EID) are based in Tripoli.

The **Lebanese Forces Party** (f. 1990; www.lebanese-forces.org), the political successor to the **Lebanese Forces (LF)** (f. 1976; coalition of Maronite militias), is still active in Lebanon, despite proscription by the Government in 1994 and the arrest, conviction and imprisonment of its leader, SAMIR GEAGEA, on murder charges.

Diplomatic Representation

EMBASSIES IN LEBANON

Algeria: POB 4794, face Hôtel Summerland, rue Jnah, Beirut; tel. (1) 826712; fax (1) 826711; Ambassador AHMAD BOUTEHRI.

Argentina: 2nd Floor, Residence des Jardins, Immeuble Moutran, 161 rue Sursock, Achrafieh, Beirut; tel. (1) 210800; fax (1) 210802; e-mail embarg@cyberia.net.lb; Ambassador JOSÉ PEDRO PICO.

Armenia: POB 70607, rue Jasmin, Mtaileb, Beirut; tel. (4) 402952; fax (4) 418860; e-mail armenia@dm.net.lb; Ambassador AREG HOVHANNISSIAN.

Australia: Embassy Complex, Semail Hill, Beirut; tel. (1) 974030; fax (1) 974029; e-mail austemle@dfat.gov.au; internet www.lebanon.embassy.gov.au; Ambassador STEPHANIE SHWABSKY.

Austria: POB 11-3942, 8th Floor, Immeuble Tabaris, 812 ave Charles Malek, Achrafieh, Beirut; tel. (1) 217360; fax (1) 217772; e-mail beirut-ob@bmaa.gv.at; Ambassador Dr GEORG MAUTNER-MARKHOF.

Bahrain: Sheikh Ahmed ath-Thani Bldg, Raoucheh, Beirut; tel. (1) 805495; Ambassador MUHAMMAD BAHLOUL.

Belgium: POB 11-1600, Riad es-Solh, Beirut; tel. (1) 976001; fax (1) 976007; e-mail beirut@diplobel.org; internet www.diplomatie.be/beirut; Ambassador STÉPHANE DE LOECKER.

Brazil: POB 40242, Baabda, Beirut; tel. (5) 921255; fax (5) 923001; e-mail braemlib@dm.net.lb; Ambassador EDUARDO AUGUSTO IBIAPINA DE SEIXAS.

Bulgaria: POB 11-6544, Immeuble Hibri, rue de l'Australie 55, Raouche, Beirut; tel. (1) 452883; fax (1) 452892; Ambassador (vacant).

Canada: POB 60163, 1e étage, Immeuble Coolrite, Autostrade Jal ed-Dib 43, Beirut; tel. (4) 713900; fax (4) 710595; e-mail berut.webmaster@dfait-maeci.gc.ca; internet www.dfait-maeci.gc.ca/beirut; Ambassador MICHEL DUVAL.

Chile: Nouvelle Naccache, 2e Bifurcation après La Belle Antique avant Carpacio, Beirut; tel. (4) 418670; fax (4) 418672; e-mail echilelb@dm.net.lb; Ambassador FELIPE DU MONCEAU DE BERGENDAL.

China, People's Republic: POB 11-8227, Beirut 1107 2260; tel. (1) 856133; fax (1) 822492; e-mail emb.prc@dm.net.lb; Ambassador LIU XIANGHUA.

Colombia: 5th Floor, Mazda Centre, Jal ed-Dib, Beirut; tel. (4) 712646; fax (4) 712656; e-mail ebeirut@minrelext.gov.co; Ambassador GEORGINE MALLAT.

Cuba: POB 116874, Immeuble Ghazzal, rue Abd as-Sabbah, rue Sakiet el-Janzir/rue de Vienne, Beirut; tel. (1) 805025; fax (1) 810339; e-mail libancub@cyberia.net.lb; internet www.embacubalebanon.com; Ambassador DARÍO DE URRA TORRIENTE.

Czech Republic: POB 40195, Baabda, Beirut; tel. (5) 468763; fax (5) 922120; e-mail beirut@embassy.mzv.cz; internet www.mzv.cz/beirut; Ambassador MAREK SKOLIL.

Denmark: POB 11-5190, Immeuble 812 Tabaris, 4e étage, ave Charles Malek, Achrafieh, Beirut; tel. (1) 335828; fax (1) 335851; e-mail dk-emb@dm.net.lb; internet www.ambbeirut.um.dk; Ambassador OLE EGBERG MIKKELSEN (resident in Damascus, Syria).

Egypt: POB 5037, rue Thomas Eddison, Er-Ramla el-Baida, Beirut; tel. (1) 862917; fax (1) 863751; Ambassador HUSSEIN ELFAROUK DERAR.

France: rue de Damas, Beirut; tel. (1) 420000; fax (1) 420013; e-mail ambafr@ciberia.net.lb; internet www.ambafrance-lb.org; Ambassador BERNARD EMIE.

Gabon: POB 11-1252, Riad es-Solh, Hadath, Beirut 1107 2080; tel. (5) 924649; fax (5) 924643; Ambassador SIMON NTOUTOUME EMANE.

Germany: POB 11-2820, Riad es-Solh, Beirut 1102-2110; tel. (4) 914444; fax (4) 914450; e-mail info@beirut.diplo.de; internet www.beirut.diplo.de; Ambassador Dr MARIUS HAAS.

Greece: POB 11-0309, Immeuble Boukhater, rue des Ambassades, Nouvelle Naccache, Beirut; tel. (4) 418772; fax (4) 418774; e-mail hellas.emb@inco.com.lb; Ambassador NIKOLAOS VAMVOUNAKIS.

Holy See: POB 1061, Jounieh (Apostolic Nunciature); tel. (9) 263102; fax (9) 264488; e-mail naliban@terra.net.lb; Apostolic Nuncio Most Rev. LUIGI GATTI (Titular Archbishop of Santa Giusta).

Hungary: POB 90618, Centre Massoud, Fanar, Beirut; tel. (1) 898840; fax (1) 873391; e-mail huembbej@inco.com.lb; Ambassador LAJOS TAMÁS.

India: POB 113-5240, Immeuble Sahmarani, rue Kantari 31, Hamra, Beirut; tel. (1) 353892; fax (1) 869806; e-mail indembei@dm.net.lb; Ambassador NANTU SARKAR.

Indonesia: Ave Palais Presidential, rue 68, Secteur 3, Baabda, Beirut; tel. (5) 924682; fax (5) 924678; e-mail indobay@cyberia.net.lb; internet www.welcome.to/indobey; Ambassador ABDULLAH SYARWANI.

Iran: POB 5030, Bear Hassan, Beirut; tel. (1) 821224; fax (1) 821230; Ambassador MASSOUD IDRISSY.

Italy: Immeuble Assicurazioni Generali, Beirut; tel. (1) 985200; fax (1) 985303; Ambassador FRANCO MISTRETTA.

Japan: POB 11-3360, Army St, Zkak al-Blat, Serail Hill, Beirut; tel. (1) 985751; fax (1) 989754; e-mail japanemb@japanemb.org.lb; internet www.lb.emb-japan.go.jp; Ambassador TOKUMITSU MURAKAMI.

Jordan: POB 109, Beirut 5113; tel. (5) 922500; fax (5) 922502; e-mail joremb@dm.net.lb; Ambassador HOSNI ABU-GHIDA.

Korea, Republic: POB 40-290, Baabda, Beirut; tel. (5) 953167; fax (5) 953170; e-mail koremadm@dm.net.lb; Ambassador YOUNG-SUN KIM.

Kuwait: Rond-point du Stade, Bir Hassan, Beirut; tel. (1) 822515; fax (1) 840613; e-mail info@kuwaitinfo.net; internet www.kuwaitinfo.net; Ambassador ALI SULEIMAN AS-SAID.

Mexico: POB 70-1150, Antélias, Beirut; tel. (4) 418871; fax (4) 418873; e-mail mail@embassyofmexicoinlebanon.org; internet www.embassyofmexicoinlebanon.org; Ambassador ARTURO PUENTE ORTEGA.

Morocco: Bir Hassan, Beirut; tel. (1) 859829; fax (1) 859839; e-mail sifmar@cyberia.net.lb.

Netherlands: POB 167190, Netherlands Tower, ave Charles Malek, Achrafieh, Beirut; tel. (1) 204663; fax (1) 204664; e-mail nlgovbei@sodetel.net.lb; internet www.netherlandsembassy.org.lb; Ambassador G. J VAN EPEN.

Norway: POB 113-7001, Immeuble Dimashki, rue Bliss, Ras Beirut, Hamra, Beirut 1103 2150; tel. (1) 365704; fax (1) 372979; e-mail noremble@cyberia.net.lb; internet www.norway-lebanon.org; Ambassador SVEIN SEVJE (resident in Damascus, Syria).

Pakistan: POB 135506, Immeuble Shell, 11e étage, Raoucheh, Beirut; tel. (1) 863041; fax (1) 864583; e-mail pakemblb@cyberia.net.lb; Ambassador KHALID M. MIR.

LEBANON   *Directory*

Philippines: POB 136631, 1er et 2e étages, Immeuble Design, rue Abdullah Machnouk, Beirut; tel. (1) 791092; fax (1) 791095; e-mail beirutpe@cyberia.net.lb; Ambassador Ramonito S. Marino.

Poland: POB 40-215, Immeuble Khalifa, ave Président Sulayman Franjiya 52, Baabda, Beirut; tel. (5) 924881; fax (5) 924882; e-mail polamb@cyberia.net.lb; Ambassador Waldemar Markiewicz.

Qatar: POB 11-6717, 1er étage, Immeuble Deebs, Shouran, Beirut; tel. (1) 865271; fax (1) 810460; e-mail beirut@mofa.gov.qa; Ambassador Jabor bin Abdullah as-Swaidi.

Romania: Route du Palais Presidentiel, Baabda, Beirut; tel. (5) 924848; fax (5) 924747; e-mail romembey@inco.com.lb; Ambassador Aurel Calin.

Russia: POB 5220, rue Mar Elias et-Tineh, Wata Mseitbeh, Beirut; tel. (1) 300041; fax (1) 303837; e-mail rusembei@cyberia.net.lb; internet www.lebanon.mid.ru; Ambassador Sergei Nikolayevich Bukin.

Saudi Arabia: POB 136144, Kuraitem, Beirut; tel. (1) 860351; fax (1) 861524; e-mail lbemb@mofa.gov.sa; Ambassador Abd al-Aziz Mahieddin al-Khoja.

Spain: POB 11-3039, Palais Chehab, Hadath Antounie, Beirut; tel. (5) 464120; fax (5) 464030; e-mail embesplb@mail.mae.es; Ambassador Miguel Benzo Perea.

Sri Lanka: POB 175, Hazmieh, Mar-Takla, Beirut; tel. (5) 924765; fax (5) 924768; e-mail slemblbn@cyberia.net.lb; Ambassador Muhammad Mohideen Amanul Faroque.

Sudan: POB 2504, Hamra, Beirut; tel. (1) 350057; fax (1) 353271; Ambassador Sayed Ahmad al-Bakhit.

Switzerland: POB 11-172, Riad es-Solh, Beirut 1107 2020; tel. (1) 324129; fax (1) 324167; e-mail vertretung@bey.rep.admin.ch; Ambassador Thomas Litscher.

Tunisia: Hazmieh, Mar-Takla, Beirut; tel. (5) 457431; fax (5) 950434; Ambassador Naziha Zarrouk.

Turkey: POB 70-666, zone II, rue 3, Rabieh, Beirut; tel. (4) 520929; fax (4) 407557; e-mail trbebeyr@intracom.net.lb; Ambassador İrfan Acar.

Ukraine: POB 431, Jardin al-Bacha, Jisr al-Bacha, Sin el-Fil, Beirut; tel. (1) 510527; fax (1) 510531; e-mail ukrembassy@inco.com.lb; Ambassador Valerii Rylach.

United Arab Emirates: Immeuble Wafic Tanbara, Jnah, Beirut; tel. (1) 857000; fax (1) 857009; Ambassador Muhammad Hamad Omran.

United Kingdom: POB 11-471, Serail Hill, Beirut Central District, Beirut; tel. (1) 990400; fax (1) 990420; e-mail chancery@cyberia.net.lb; internet www.britishembassy.gov.uk/lebanon; Ambassador James Watt.

USA: POB 70-840, Antélias, Aoucar, Beirut; tel. (4) 542600; fax (4) 544136; e-mail pas@inco.com.lb; internet lebanon.usembassy.gov; Ambassador Jeffrey D. Feltman.

Uruguay: POB 2051, Centre Stella Marris, 7e étage, rue Banque du Liban, Jounieh; tel. (9) 636529; fax (9) 636531; e-mail uruliban@dm.net.lb; Ambassador Mario Alberto Voss Rubio.

Venezuela: POB 603, Immeuble Baezevale House, 5e étage, Zalka, Beirut; tel. (1) 888701; fax (1) 900757; e-mail embavene@dm.net.lb; Ambassador Efrain Silva Méndez.

Yemen: Bir Hassan, Beirut; tel. (1) 852688; fax (1) 821610; Ambassador Ahmad Abdullah al-Basha.

Note: Lebanon and Syria have very close relations but do not exchange formal ambassadors. Libya closed its embassy in Beirut in September 2003 but still maintains diplomatic relations with Lebanon.

Judicial System

Law and justice in Lebanon are administered in accordance with the following codes, which are based upon modern theories of civil and criminal legislation:

Code de la Propriété (1930).

Code des Obligations et des Contrats (1932).

Code de Procédure Civile (1933).

Code Maritime (1947).

Code de Procédure Pénale (Code Ottoman Modifié).

Code Pénal (1943).

Code Pénal Militaire (1946).

Code d'Instruction Criminelle.

The following courts are now established:

(*a*) Fifty-six '**Single-Judge Courts**', each consisting of a single judge, and dealing in the first instance with both civil and criminal cases; there are 17 such courts in Beirut and seven in Tripoli.

(*b*) Eleven **Courts of Appeal**, each consisting of three judges, including a President and a Public Prosecutor, and dealing with civil and criminal cases; there are five such courts in Beirut.

First President of the Courts of Appeal of Beirut: Tanios el-Khoury.

(*c*) Four **Courts of Cassation**, three dealing with civil and commercial cases and the fourth with criminal cases. A Court of Cassation, to be properly constituted, must have at least three judges, one being the President and the other two Councillors. If the Court of Cassation reverses the judgment of a lower court, it does not refer the case back but retries it itself.

General Prosecutor of Cassation: Said Mirza.

(*d*) **State Consultative Council**, which deals with administrative cases.

President of the State Consultative Council: Ghaleb Ghanem.

(*e*) **The Court of Justice**, which is a special court consisting of a President and four judges, deals with matters affecting the security of the State; there is no appeal against its verdicts.

In addition to the above, the Constitutional Council considers matters pertaining to the constitutionality of legislation. Military courts are competent to try crimes and misdemeanours involving the armed and security forces. Islamic (*Shari'a*), Christian and Jewish religious courts deal with affairs of personal status (marriage, death, inheritance, etc.).

President of the Constitutional Council: Amin Faris Nasser.

Chief of the Military Court: Brig.-Gen. Maher Safi ed-Din.

Religion

Of all the regions of the Middle East, Lebanon probably presents the closest juxtaposition of sects and peoples within a small territory. Estimates for 1983 assessed the sizes of communities as: Shi'a Muslims 1.2m., Maronites 900,000, Sunni Muslims 750,000, Greek Orthodox 250,000, Druzes 250,000, Armenians 175,000. There is also a small Jewish community. In 1994 it was estimated that 29%–32% of the population of Lebanon were Shi'a Muslims, 25%–28% Maronites, 16%–20% Sunni Muslims and 3.5% Druzes. The Maronites, a uniate sect of the Roman Catholic Church, inhabited the old territory of Mount Lebanon, i.e. immediately east of Beirut. In the south, towards the Israeli frontier, Shi'a villages are most common, while between the Shi'a and the Maronites live the Druzes (divided between the Yazbakis and the Joumblatis). The Beka'a valley has many Greek Christians (both Roman Catholic and Orthodox), while the Tripoli area is mainly Sunni Muslim.

CHRISTIANITY
The Roman Catholic Church
Armenian Rite

Patriarchate of Cilicia: Patriarcat Arménien Catholique, rue de l'Hôpital orthodoxe, Jeitawi, Beirut 2078 5605; tel. (1) 570555; fax (1) 570563; e-mail teyrouzjean@terra.net.lb; f. 1742; established in Beirut since 1932; includes patriarchal diocese of Beirut, with an estimated 10,000 adherents (31 December 2003); Patriarch Most Rev. Nerses Bedros XIX Tarmouni; Protosyncellus Rt Rev. Vartan Achkarian (Titular Bishop of Tokat—Armenian Rite).

Chaldean Rite

Diocese of Beirut: Evêché Chaldéen de Beyrouth, POB 373, Hazmieh, Beirut; tel. (5) 459088; fax (5) 457731; e-mail chaldepiscopus@hotmail.com; an estimated 10,000 adherents (31 December 2003); Bishop of Beirut Michel Kassarji.

Latin Rite

Apostolic Vicariate of Beirut: Vicariat Apostolique, POB 11-4224, Riad es-Solh, Beirut 1107-2160; tel. (9) 236101; fax (9) 236102; e-mail vicariatlat@hotmail.com; an estimated 15,000 adherents (31 December 2003); Vicar Apostolic Paul Dahdah (Titular Archbishop of Arae in Numidia).

Maronite Rite

Patriarchate of Antioch and all the East: Patriarcat Maronite, Bkerké; tel. (9) 915441; fax (9) 938844; e-mail jtawk@bkerke.org.lb; includes patriarchal dioceses of Jounieh, Sarba and Jobbé; the Maronite Church in Lebanon comprises four archdioceses and six dioceses, with an estimated 1,431,983 adherents (31 December 2002); Patriarch Cardinal Nasrallah Boutros Sfeir.

LEBANON

Archbishop of Antélias: Most Rev. JOSEPH MOHSEN BÉCHARA, Archevêché Maronite, POB 70400, Antélias; tel. (4) 410020; fax (4) 921313.
Archbishop of Beirut: Most Rev. PAUL YOUSSEF MATAR, Archevêché Maronite, 10 rue Collège de la Sagesse, Achrafieh, Beirut; tel. (1) 561980; fax (1) 561931; also representative of the Holy See for Roman Catholics of the Coptic Rite in Lebanon.
Archbishop of Tripoli: Archevêché Maronite, POB 104, rue al-Moutran, Karm Sada, Tripoli; tel. (6) 624324; fax (6) 629393; e-mail rahmat@inco.com.lb.
Archbishop of Tyre: Most Rev. CHUCRALLAH-NABIL HAGE, Archevêché Maronite, Tyre; tel. (7) 740059; fax (7) 344891.

Melkite Rite

Patriarch of Antioch: Patriarcat Grec-Melkite Catholique, POB 22249, 12 ave az-Zeitoon, Bab Charki, Damascus, Syria; tel. (1) 5441030; fax (1) 5418966; e-mail pat.melk@scs-net.org; the Melkite Church in Lebanon comprises seven archdioceses, with an estimated 512,850 adherents (31 December 2003); The Patriarch of Antioch and all the East, of Alexandria and of Jerusalem Most Rev. GRÉGOIRE III LAHAM.
Archbishop of Ba'albek: Most Rev. ELIAS RAHAL, Archevêché Grec-Catholique, Ba'albek; tel. (8) 370200; fax (8) 373986.
Archbishop of Baniyas: Most Rev. ANTOINE HAYEK, Archevêché de Panéas, Jdeidet Marjeyoun; tel. (3) 814487; fax (7) 200270.
Archbishop of Beirut and Gibail: JOSEPH KALLAS, Archevêché Grec-Melkite-Catholique, POB 11-901, 655 rue de Damas, Beirut; tel. (1) 616104; fax (1) 616109; e-mail agmcb@terra.net.lb.
Archbishop of Saida (Sidon): Most Rev. GEORGES KWAÏTER, Archevêché Grec-Melkite-Catholique, POB 247, rue el-Moutran, Sidon; tel. (7) 720100; fax (7) 722055; e-mail mkwaiter@inco.com.lb.
Archbishop of Tripoli: Most Rev. GEORGE RIASHI, Archevêché Grec-Catholique, rue al-Kanaess, Tripoli; tel. (6) 435989; fax (6) 441716.
Archbishop of Tyre: Most Rev. JEAN ASSAAD HADDAD, Archevêché Grec-Melkite-Catholique, POB 257, Tyre; tel. (7) 740015; fax (7) 349180; e-mail eegc@inco.com.lb.
Archbishop of Zahleh and Furzol: Most Rev. ANDRÉ HADDAD, Archevêché Grec-Melkite-Catholique, Saidat en-Najat, Zahleh; tel. (8) 800333; fax (8) 822406; e-mail andre_haddad@hotmail.com.

Syrian Rite

Patriarchate of Antioch: Patriarcat Syrien Catholique d'Antioche, rue de Damas, POB 116/5087, Beirut 1106-2010; tel. (1) 615892; fax (1) 616573; e-mail psc_lb@yahoo.com; jurisdiction over about 150,000 Syrian Catholics in the Middle East, including (at 31 December 2002) 14,500 in the diocese of Beirut; Patriarch Most Rev. IGNACE PIERRE VIII ABDEL AHAD; Protosyncellus Mgr GEORGES MASRI.

The Anglican Communion

Within the Episcopal Church in Jerusalem and the Middle East, Lebanon forms part of the diocese of Jerusalem (see the chapter on Israel).

Other Christian Groups

Armenian Apostolic Orthodox Church: Armenian Catholicosate of Cilicia, POB 70317, Antélias, Beirut; tel. (4) 410001; fax (4) 419724; e-mail cathcil@cathcil.org; internet www.cathcil.org; f. 301 in Armenia, re-established in 1441 in Cilicia (now in Turkey), transferred to Antélias, Lebanon, 1930; Leader His Holiness ARAM KESHISHIAN I (Catholicos of Cilicia); jurisdiction over an estimated 3m. adherents in Lebanon, Syria, Cyprus, Kuwait, Greece, Iran, the United Arab Emirates, South America, the USA and Canada.
National Evangelical Synod of Syria and Lebanon: POB 70890, Antélias, Beirut; tel. (4) 525030; fax (4) 411184; e-mail nessl@synod-sl.org; f. 1959; 20,000 adherents (2006); Gen. Sec. Rev. JOSEPH KASSAB.
Patriarchate of Antioch and all the East (Greek Orthodox): Patriarcat Grec-Orthodoxe, POB 9, Damascus, Syria; tel. (11) 5424400; fax (11) 5424404; e-mail info@antiochpat.org; internet www.antiochpat.org; Patriarch His Beatitude IGNATIUS (HAZIM) IV.
Patriarcate of Antioch and all the East (Syrian Orthodox): Patriarcat Syrien Orthodoxe, Bab Toma, POB 22260, Damascus, Syria; tel. 5432401; fax 5432400; Patriarch IGNATIUS ZAKKA I IWAS.
Supreme Council of the Evangelical Community in Syria and Lebanon: POB 70/1065, rue Rabieh 34, Antélias; tel. (4) 525036; fax (4) 405490; e-mail suprcoun@minero.net; Pres. Rev. Dr SALIM SAHIOUNY.
Union of the Armenian Evangelical Churches in the Near East: POB 11-377, Beirut; tel. (1) 565628; fax (1) 565629; e-mail uaecne@cyberia.net.lb; f. 1846 in Turkey; comprises about 30 Armenian Evangelical Churches in Syria, Lebanon, Egypt, Cyprus, Greece, Iran, Turkey and Australia; 7,500 mems (1990); Pres. Rev. MEGRDICH KARAGOEZIAN; Gen. Sec. SEBOUH TERZIAN.

ISLAM

Shi'a Muslims: Leader Imam Sheikh SAYED MOUSSA AS-SADR (went missing during visit to Libya in August 1978); President of the Supreme Islamic Council of the Shi'a Community of Lebanon, ABDAL-AMIR QABALAN; Beirut.
Sunni Muslims: Grand Mufti of Lebanon, Dar el-Fatwa, rue Ilewi Rushed, Beirut; tel. (1) 422340; Leader SG Sheikh Dr MUHAMMAD RASHID QABBANI.
Druzes: Supreme Spiritual Leader of the Druze Community, Beirut; tel. (1) 341116; Supreme Spiritual Leader Sheikh al-Aql BAHJAT GHAITH; Political Leader WALID JOUMBLATT.
Alawites: a schism of Shi'ite Islam; there are an estimated 50,000 Alawites in northern Lebanon, in and around Tripoli.

JUDAISM

Jews: Leader CHAHOUD CHREIM (Beirut).

The Press

DAILIES

Al-Amal (Hope): POB 992, place Charles Hélou, Beirut; tel. (1) 382992; f. 1939; Arabic; organ of Al-Kataeb (Phalangist Party); Chief Editor ELIAS RABABI; circ. 35,000.
Al-Anwar (Lights): c/o Dar Assayad, POB 11-1038, Hazmieh, Beirut; tel. (5) 456374; fax (5) 452700; e-mail info@alanwar.com; internet www.alanwar.com; f. 1959; Arabic; independent; supplement, Sunday, cultural and social; published by Dar Assayad SAL; Editors-in-Chief MICHEL RAAD, RAFIK KHOURY; circ. 14,419.
Ararat: POB 756, Beirut 175158; tel. and fax (1) 565599; f. 1937; Armenian; communist; Editor-in-Chief SARKIS NAJARIAN; circ. 5,000.
Aztag: POB 80-860, Shaghzoyan Cultural Centre, Bourj Hammoud; tel. (1) 258526; fax (1) 258529; e-mail aztag@inco.com.lb; internet www.aztagdaily.com; f. 1927; Armenian; Editor-in-Chief SHAHANE KANDARIAN; circ. 6,500.
Al-Bairaq (The Standard): Immeuble Dimitri Trad, rue Issa Maalouf, Ashrafieh, Beirut; tel. (1) 216393; fax (1) 338928; e-mail dalwl@dm.net.lb; f. 1913; Arabic; published by Dar Alf Leila wa Leila Publishing House; politics, society; circ. 10,000.
Bairut: Beirut; f. 1952; Arabic.
Ach-Chaab (The People): POB 5140, Beirut; f. 1961; Arabic; Nationalist; Propr and Editor MUHAMMAD AMIN DUGHAN; circ. 7,000.
Ach-Chams (The Sun): Beirut; f. 1925; Arabic.
Ach-Charq (The East): POB 11-0838, rue Verdun, Riad es-Solh, Beirut; tel. (1) 810820; fax (1) 866105; e-mail info@elshark.com; f. 1926; Arabic; Gen. Dir and Editor-in-Chief AOUNI AL-KAAKI.
Daily Star: 6th Floor, Marine Tower, rue de la Sainte Famille, Achrafieh, Beirut; tel. (1) 587277; fax (1) 561333; e-mail webmaster@dailystar.com.lb; internet www.dailystar.com.lb; f. 1952; English; Publr and Editor-in-Chief JAMIL K. MROUE; circ. 10,550.
Ad-Diyar (The Homeland): an-Nahda Building, Yarze, Beirut; tel. (5) 923830; fax (5) 923773; e-mail aldiyar2002@yahoo.com; f. 1987; Arabic; Propr and Editor-in-Chief CHARLES AYYUB.
Ad-Dunya (The World): Beirut; f. 1943; Arabic; political; Chief Editor SULIMAN ABOU ZAID; circ. 25,000.
Al-Hakika (The Truth): Beirut; Arabic; published by Amal.
Al-Hayat (Life): POB 11-987, Immeuble Gargarian, rue Emil Eddé, Hamra, Beirut; tel. (1) 352674; fax (1) 866177; internet www.alhayat.com; f. 1946; Arabic; independent; circ. 196,800.
Al-Jarida (The (News) Paper): POB 220, place Tabaris, Beirut; f. 1953; Arabic; independent; Editor ABDULLAH SKAFF; circ. 22,600.
Al-Jumhuriya (The Republic): Beirut; f. 1924; Arabic.
Journal al-Haddis: POB 300, Jounieh; f. 1927; Arabic; political; Owner GEORGES ARÈGE-SAADÉ.
Al-Khatib (The Speaker): rue Georges Picot, Beirut; Arabic.
Al-Kifah al-Arabi (The Arab Struggle): POB 5158-14, Immeuble Rouche-Shams, Beirut; tel. (1) 860132; fax (1) 808281; internet www.kifaharabi.com; f. 1974; Arabic; political, socialist, Pan-Arab; Publr and Chief Editor WALID HUSSEINI.
Lisan ul-Hal (The Organ): rue Châteaubriand, Beirut; e-mail lebanon@lissan-ul-hal.com; internet www.lissan-ul-hal.com; f. 1877; Arabic; Editor GEBRAN HAYEK; circ. 33,000.

Al-Liwa' (The Standard): POB 11-2402, Beirut; tel. (1) 735749; fax (1) 735742; internet www.aliwaa.com.lb; f. 1963; Arabic; Propr ABD AL-GHANI SALAM; Editor SALAH SALAM; circ. 26,000.

Al-Mustaqbal: Beirut; tel. (1) 797770; fax (1) 797779; e-mail contactus@almustaqbal.com.lb; internet www.almustaqbal.com.lb; f. 1999; Editor HANI HAMMOUD; circ. 20,000.

An-Nahar (The Day): Immeuble An-Nahar, place des Martyrs, Marfa', Beirut 2014 5401; tel. (1) 994888; fax (1) 996777; e-mail annahar@annahar.com.lb; internet www.annahar.com; f. 1933; Arabic; independent; Editor-in-Chief GHASSAN TUENI; circ. 50,000.

An-Nass (The People): POB 4886, ave Fouad Chehab, Beirut; tel. (3) 376185; fax (8) 376610; f. 1959; Arabic; Editor-in-Chief HASSAN YAGHI; circ. 22,000.

An-Nida (The Appeal): Beirut; f. 1959; Arabic; published by the Lebanese Communist Party; Editor KARIM MROUÉ; circ. 10,000.

An-Nidal (The Struggle): Beirut; f. 1939; Arabic.

L'Orient-Le Jour: POB 11-2488, Beirut; tel. (1) 376888; fax (1) 375888; e-mail administration.lorientlejour.com; internet www.lorientlejour.com; f. 1942; French; independent; Chair. MICHEL EDDÉ; Editorial Dir NAJUIB AOUN; Editor ISSA GORAÏEB; circ. 23,000.

Rayah (Banner): POB 4101, Beirut; Arabic.

Le Réveil: Beirut; tel. (1) 890700; f. 1977; French; Editor-in-Chief JEAN SHAMI; Dir RAYMOND DAOU; circ. 10,000.

Sada Lubnan (Echo of Lebanon): Beirut; f. 1951; Arabic; Lebanese pan-Arab; Editor MUHAMMAD BAALBAKI; circ. 25,000.

As-Safir: POB 113/5015, Immeuble as-Safir, rue Monimina, Hamra, Beirut 1103-2010; tel. (1) 350005; fax (1) 743602; e-mail mail@assafir.com; internet www.assafir.com; f. 1974; Arabic; political; Publr TALAL SALMAN; Editor-in-Chief JOSEPH SAMAHA; circ. 50,000.

Sawt al-Uruba (The Voice of Europe): POB 3537, Beirut; f. 1959; Arabic; organ of the An-Najjadé Party; Editor ADNANE AL-HAKIM.

Le Soir: POB 1470, rue de Syrie, Beirut; f. 1947; French; independent; Dir DIKRAN TOSBATH; Editor ANDRÉ KECATI; circ. 16,500.

Telegraf—Bairut: rue Béchara el-Khoury, Beirut; f. 1930; Arabic; political, economic and social; Editor TOUFIC ASSAD MATNI; circ. 15,500 (5,000 outside Lebanon).

Al-Yaum (Today): Beirut; f. 1937; Arabic; Editor WAFIC MUHAMMAD CHAKER AT-TIBY.

Az-Zamane: Beirut; f. 1947; Arabic.

Zartonk: POB 11-617, rue Nahr Ibrahim, Beirut; tel. and fax (1) 566709; e-mail zartonk@dm.net.lb; f. 1937; Armenian; official organ of Armenian Liberal Democratic Party; Man. Editor BAROUYR H. AGHBASHIAN.

WEEKLIES

Achabaka (The Net): c/o Dar Assayad SAL, POB 11-1038, Hazmieh, Beirut; tel. (5) 450406; fax (5) 452700; e-mail achabaka@achabaka.com; internet www.achabaka.com; f. 1956; Arabic; society and features; Founder SAID FREIHA; Editor ELHAM FREIHA; circ. 139,775.

Al-Ahad (Sunday): Beirut; Arabic; political; organ of Hezbollah; Editor RIAD TAHA; circ. 32,000.

Al-Akhbar (The News): Beirut; f. 1954; Arabic; published by the Lebanese Communist Party; circ. 21,000.

Al-Alam al-Lubnani (The Lebanese World): POB 462, Beirut; f. 1964; Arabic, English, Spanish, French; politics, literature and social economy; Editor-in-Chief FAYEK KHOURY; Gen. Editor CHEIKH FADI GEMAYEL; circ. 45,000.

Al-Anwar Supplement: c/o Dar Assayad, POB 11-1038, Hazmieh, Beirut; tel. (5) 450406; fax (5) 452700; e-mail info@alanwar.com; internet www.alanwar.com; cultural-social; every Sunday; supplement to daily Al-Anwar; Editor ISSAM FREIHA; circ. 90,000.

Assayad (The Hunter): c/o Dar Assayad, POB 11-1038, Hazmieh, Beirut; tel. (5) 450406; fax (5) 452700; e-mail assayad@inco.com.lb; internet www.darassayad.net; f. 1943; Arabic; political and social; Editor-in-Chief MOUNIR NAJJAR; circ. 76,192.

Dabbour: place du Musée, Beirut; tel. (1) 616770; fax (1) 616771; e-mail addabbour@yahoo.com; internet www.addabbour.com; f. 1922; Arabic; Editor JOSEPH RICHARD MUKARZEL; circ. 12,000.

Ad-Dyar: Immeuble Bellevue, rue Verdun, Beirut; f. 1941; Arabic; political; circ. 46,000.

Al-Hadaf (The Target): Beirut; tel. (1) 420554; f. 1969; organ of Popular Front for the Liberation of Palestine; Arabic; Editor-in-Chief SABER MOHI ED-DIN; circ. 40,000.

Al-Hawadeth (Events): POB 1281, rue Clémenceau, Beirut; tel. (1) 216393; fax (1) 200961; e-mail info@al-hawadeth.com; internet www.al-hawadeth.com; published from London, United Kingdom (183–185 Askew Rd, W12 9AX); tel. (20) 8740-4500; fax (20) 8749-9781; f. 1911; Arabic; news; Editor-in-Chief MELHIM KARAM; circ. 120,000.

Al-Hiwar (Dialogue): Beirut; f. 2000; Arabic; Chair. FOUAD MAKHZOUMI; Editor-in-Chief SAM MOUNASSA.

Al-Hurriya (Freedom): Beirut; f. 1960; Arabic; organ of the Democratic Front for the Liberation of Palestine; Editor DAOUD TALHAME; circ. 30,000.

Al-Iza'a (Broadcasting): POB 462, rue Selim Jazaerly, Beirut; f. 1938; Arabic; politics, art, literature and broadcasting; Editor FAYEK KHOURY; circ. 11,000.

Al-Jumhur (The Public): POB 1834, Moussaitbé, Beirut; f. 1936; Arabic; illustrated weekly news magazine; Editor FARID ABU SHAHLA; circ. 45,000, of which over 20,000 outside Lebanon.

Kul Shay' (Everything): POB 3250, rue Béchara el-Khoury, Beirut; Arabic.

Magazine: POB 1404, Immeuble Sayegh, rue Sursock, Beirut; tel. (1) 202070; fax (1) 202663; e-mail info@magazine.com.lb; internet www.magazine.com.lb; f. 1956; French; political, economic and social; published by Editions Orientales SAL; Pres. CHARLES ABOU ADAL; circ. 18,000.

Massis: c/o Patriarcat Arménien Catholique, rue de l'Hôpital Libanais Jeitawi, 2400 Beirut; Armenian; Catholic; Editor Fr ANTRANIK GRANIAN; circ. 2,500.

Al-Moharrir (The Liberator): Beirut; f. 1962; Arabic; circ. 87,000; Gen. Man. WALID ABOU ZAHR.

Monday Morning: POB 165612, Immeuble Dimitri Trad, rue Issa Maalouf, Ashrafieh, Beirut; tel. (1) 200961; fax (01) 334116; e-mail info@mmorning.com; internet www.mmorning.com; f. 1971; political and social affairs; published by Dar Alf Leila wa Leila Publishing House; circ. 15,000; Editor-in-Chief MELHEM KARAM.

Al-Ousbou' al-Arabi (Arab Week): POB 1404, Immeuble Sayegh, rue Sursock, Beirut; tel. (1) 202070; fax (1) 202663; e-mail info@arabweek.com.lb; internet www.arabweek.com.lb; f. 1959; Arabic; political and social; published by Editions Orientales SAL; Pres. CHARLES ABOU ADAL; circ. 88,407 (circulates throughout the Arab world).

Phoenix: POB 113222, Beirut; tel. (1) 346800; fax (1) 346359; for women; published by Al-Hasna.

Ar-Rassed: Beirut; Arabic; Editor GEORGE RAJJI.

Revue du Liban (Lebanon Review): Immeuble Dimitri Trad, rue Issa Maalouf, Achrafieh, Beirut; tel. (1) 338930; fax (1) 335079; e-mail rdl@rdl.com.lb; internet www.rdl.com.lb; f. 1928; French; political, social, cultural; published by Dar Alf Leila wa Leila Publishing House; Publr MELHEM KARAM; Gen. Man. MICHEL MISK; circ. 22,000.

Sabah al-Khair (Good Morning): Beirut; Arabic; published by the Syrian Nationalist Party.

Samar: c/o Dar Assayad, POB 11-1038, Hazmieh, Beirut; tel. (5) 452700; fax (5) 452957; Arabic; for teenagers; published by Dar Assayad SAL.

Ash-Shira' (The Sail): POB 13-5250, Beirut; tel. (1) 70300; fax (1) 866050; internet www.alshiraa.com; Arabic; Editor HASSAN SABRA; circ. 40,000.

OTHER SELECTED PERIODICALS

Alam at-Tijarat (Business World): Immeuble Strand, rue Hamra, Beirut; f. 1965; monthly; commercial; Editor NADIM MAKDISI; international circ. 17,500.

Al Computer, Communications and Electronics: c/o Dar Assayad, POB 1038, Hazmieh, Beirut; tel. (5) 450935; fax (5) 452700; e-mail assayad@inco.com.lb; internet www.darassayad.net; f. 1984; monthly; computer technology; published by Dar Assayad International; Chief Editor ANTOINE BOUTROS; monthly average circ. 31 119 copies for the period January to June 2004..

Arab Construction World: POB 13-5121, Chouran, Beirut 1102-2802; tel. (1) 352413; fax (1) 352419; e-mail info@acwmag.com; internet www.acwmag.com; f. 1985; monthly; English and Arabic; published by Chatila Publishing House; Publr FATHI CHATILA; Editor-in-Chief MUHAMMAD RABIH CHATILA; circ. 9,900.

Arab Defense Journal: c/o Dar Assayad, POB 11-1038, Hazmieh, Beirut; tel. (5) 456374; fax (5) 450609; e-mail adj2004a@yahoo.com; internet www.darassayad.net; f. 1976; monthly; military; published by Dar Assayad International; Chief Editor FAWZI ABOU FARHAT; circ. 24,209 (Jan.–June 2004).

Arab Economist: POB 11-6068, Beirut; monthly; published by Centre for Economic, Financial and Social Research and Documentation SAL; Chair. HEKMAT KASSIR.

Arab Water World: POB 13-5121, Chouran, Beirut 1102-2802; tel. (1) 352413; fax (1) 352419; e-mail info@awwmag.com; internet www.awwmag.com; f. 1977; nine per year; English and Arabic; published by Chatila Publishing House; Editor-in-Chief FATHI CHATILA; circ. 8,443.

The Arab World: POB 567, Jounieh; tel. and fax (9) 935096; e-mail maamanculture@lynx.net.lb; internet www.biblib.com; f. 1985; 24 a year; published by Dar Naamān lith-Thaqāfa; Editor NAJI NAAMAN.

LEBANON

Argus: POB 16-5403, 6 rue Arguse Sodeco, Beirut; tel. (1) 219113; fax (1) 219955; e-mail argus@cyberia.net.lb; monthly; Arabic, French and English; economics and law; circ. 1,000.

Le Commerce du Levant: Kantari, Immeuble Kantari Corner, 11e étage, Beirut 2021-2502; tel. (1) 362361; fax (1) 360379; e-mail lecommerce@inco.com.lb; internet www.lecommercedulevant.com; f. 1929; monthly; French; commercial and financial; publ. by Société de la Presse Economique; Chief Editor NICOLAS SBIEH; circ. 15,000.

Déco: POB 11-1404, Immeuble Sayegh, rue Sursock, Beirut; tel. (1) 202070; fax (1) 202663; e-mail info@decomag.com.lb; internet www.decomag.com.lb; f. 2000; quarterly; French; architecture and interior design; published by Editions Orientales SAL; Pres. CHARLES ABOU ADAL; circ. 14,000.

Fairuz International: Dar Assayad, POB 11-1038, Hazmieh, Beirut; tel. (5) 450406; fax (5) 450609; e-mail assayad@inco.com.lb; f. 1982; monthly; Arabic; for women; published by Dar Assayad International; Chief Editor ELHAM FREIHA.

Fann at-Tasswir: POB 16-5947, Beirut; tel. (1) 498950; monthly; Arabic; photography.

Al Fares: c/o Dar Assayad, POB 11-1038, Hazmieh, Beirut; tel. (5) 450406; fax (5) 450609; e-mail assayad@inco.com.lb; internet www.darassayad.net; f. 1991; monthly; Arabic; men's interest; published by Dar Assayad International; Chief Editor ELHAM FREIHA.

Al-Idari (The Manager): c/o Dar Assayad, POB 11-1038, Hazmieh, Beirut; tel. (5) 450406; fax (5) 450609; e-mail assayad@inco.com.lb; internet www.darassayad.net; f. 1975; monthly; Arabic; business management, economics, finance and investment; published by Dar Assayad International; Pres. BASSAM FREIHA; Gen. Man. ELHAM FREIHA; circ. 31,867.

Al-Intilak (Outbreak): Al-Intilak Printing and Publishing House, POB 4958, Beirut; tel. (1) 302018; e-mail tonehnme@cyberia.net.lb; f. 1960; monthly; Arabic; literary; Chief Editor MICHEL NEHME.

Al-Jeel (The Generation): Beirut; monthly; Arabic; literary.

Al-Khalij Business Magazine: POB 11-8440, Beirut; tel. (1) 345568; fax (1) 602089; e-mail massaref@dm.net.lb; f. 1981; fmrly based in Kuwait; 6 a year; Arabic; Editor-in-Chief ZULFICAR KOBEISSI; circ. 16,325.

Lebanese and Arab Economy: POB 11-1801, Sanayeh, Beirut; tel. (1) 744160; fax (1) 353395; e-mail info@.ccib.org.lb; internet www.ccib.org.lb; f. 1951; monthly; Arabic, English and French; Publr Chamber of Commerce, Industry and Agriculture of Beirut and Mount Lebanon.

Majallat al-Iza'at al-Lubnaniat (Lebanese Broadcasting Magazine): c/o Radio Lebanon, rue des Arts et Métiers, Beirut; tel. (1) 863016; f. 1959; monthly; Arabic; broadcasting affairs.

Al-Mar'a: POB 1404, Immeuble Sayegh, rue Sursock, Beirut; tel. (1) 202070; fax (1) 202663; e-mail info@almara.com.lb; internet www.almara.com.lb; f. 2000; monthly; Arabic; for women; published by Editions Orientales SAL; Pres. CHARLES ABOU ADAL; circ. 20,000.

Middle East Food: POB 13-5121, Chouran, Beirut 1102-2802; tel. (1) 352413; fax (1) 352419; e-mail info@mefmag.com; internet www.mefmag.com; every two months; published by Chatila Publishing House; Editor-in-Chief ROULA HAMDAN; circ. 8,800.

Al-Mouktataf (The Selection): Beirut; monthly; Arabic; general.

Al-Mukhtar (Reader's Digest): Beirut; monthly; general interest.

Qitāboul A'lamil A'rabi (The Arab World Book): POB 567, Jounieh; tel. and fax (9) 935096; e-mail naaman@lynx.net.lb; internet www.biblib.com; f. 1991; 6 a year; Arabic; published by Dar Naamān lith-Thaqāfa; Editor NAJI NAAMAN.

Rijal al-Amal (Businessmen): Beirut; f. 1966; monthly; Arabic; business; Publr and Editor-in-Chief MAHIBA AL-MALKI; circ. 16,250.

Scoop: POB 165612, rue Issa Maalouf, Sioufi, Beirut; tel. (1) 482185; fax (1) 490307; weekly; general interest; published by La Régie Libanaise de Publicité; circ. 100,000.

As-Sihāfa wal I'lām (Press and Information): POB 567, Jounieh; tel. and fax (9) 935096; e-mail naamanculture@lynx.net.lb; internet www.biblib.com; f. 1987; 12 a year; Arabic; published by Dar Naaman lith-Thaqafa; Editor NAJI NAAMAN.

Siyassa was Strategia (Politics and Strategy): POB 567, Jounieh; tel. and fax (9) 935096; e-mail naamanculture@lynx.net.lb; internet www.biblib.com; f. 1981; 36 a year; Arabic; published by Dar Naaman lith-Thaqafa; Editor NAJI NAAMAN.

Tabibok (Your Doctor): POB 90434, Beirut; tel. in Syria (963-11) 3346501; fax (963-11) 3738901; e-mail tabibokmag@mail.sy; internet www.tabibokmag.com; f. 1956; monthly; Arabic; medical, social, scientific; Editor Dr SAMI KABBANI; circ. 90,000.

Takarir Wa Khalfiyat (Background Reports): c/o Dar Assayad, POB 11-1038, Hazmieh, Beirut; tel. (5) 456374; fax (5) 452700; internet www.darassayad.net; f. 1976; monthly; Arabic; political and economic bulletin; published by Dar Assayad SAL; Editor-in-Chief HASSAN EL-KHOURY.

At-Tarik (The Road): Beirut; monthly; Arabic; cultural and theoretical; published by the Parti communiste libanais; circ. 5,000.

Travaux et Jours (Works and Days): Rectorat de l'Université Saint-Joseph, rue de Damas, Beirut; tel. (1) 611172; fax (1) 423369; e-mail travauxetjours@usj.edu.lb; internet www.usj.edu.lb; f. 1961; publ. twice a year; French; political, social and cultural; Editor MOUNIR CHAMOUN.

Welcome to Lebanon and the Middle East: Beirut; f. 1959; monthly; English; entertainment, touring and travel; Editor SOUHAIL TOUFIK ABOU JAMRA; circ. 6,000.

NEWS AGENCIES

National News Agency (NNA): Hamra, Beirut; tel. (1) 754400; fax (1) 745776; e-mail nna-leb@nna-leb.gov.lb; internet www.nna-leb.gov.lb; state-owned; Dir ANDRE KASSAS.

Foreign Bureaux

Agence France-Presse (AFP): POB 11-1461, Immeuble Najjar, rue de Rome, Beirut; tel. (1) 350307; fax (1) 350318; e-mail afp_bey@inco.com.lb; internet www.afp.com; Dir PASCAL MALLET.

Agenzia Nazionale Stampa Associata (ANSA) (Italy): POB 113/6545, Sodeco Square Bldg, Block B, Achrafieh, Beirut; tel. (1) 398620; fax (1) 422003; e-mail ansa@sodetel.net.lb; f. 1945; Bureau Chief STEFANO POSCIA.

Associated Press (AP) (USA): POB 3780, Immeuble Shaker et Oueini, place Riad es-Solh, Beirut; tel. (1) 985190; fax (1) 985196; e-mail info@ap.org; internet www.ap.org; Correspondent SAM F. GHATTAS.

Kuwait News Agency (KUNA): 8th Floor, Arsku Centre, Beirut; tel. (1) 354377; fax (1) 602088; e-mail kunabt@inco.com.lb; Bureau Chief SULTAN AL-MADIRI.

Kyodo Tsushin (Japan): POB 13-5060, Immeuble Makarem, rue Makdessi, Ras Beirut, Beirut; tel. (1) 863861; Correspondent IBRAHIM KHOURY.

Middle East News Agency (MENA) (Egypt): POB 2268, rue Mneimneh, Sarolla Descent, Hamra, Beirut; tel. (1) 754142; fax (1) 754141; e-mail mena_lb@sodetel.net.lb; internet www.mena.org.eg; Chairman of the Board and Editor-in-Chief MAHFOUZ EL-ANSARI.

Reuters (United Kingdom): POB 11-1006, Immeuble Hibat al-Maarad, place Riad es-Solh, Beirut; tel. (1) 983885; fax (1) 983889; e-mail samia.nakhoul@reuters.com; internet www.reuters.com; Bureau Chief SAMIA NAKHOUL.

Rossiiskoye Informatsionnoye Agentstvo—Novosti (RIA—Novosti) (Russia): POB 11-1086, Beirut; tel. (1) 300219; fax (1) 314168; e-mail novosti@cyberia.net.lb; Dir KONSTANTIN MAXIMOV.

United Press International (UPI) (USA): Suite 302, 3rd Floor, Block D, Gefinor Centre, rue Cléemenceau, Beirut; tel. (1) 745971; fax (1) 745972; internet www.upi.com; Bureau Chief DALAL SAOUD.

Xinhua (New China) News Agency (People's Republic of China): POB 114-5075, Beirut; tel. (1) 830359.

BTA (Bulgaria), INA (Iraq), JANA (Libya), Prensa Latina (Cuba) and Saudi Press Agency (SPA) are also represented in Lebanon.

PRESS ASSOCIATION

Lebanese Press Order: POB 3084, ave Saeb Salam, Beirut; tel. (1) 865519; fax (1) 865516; e-mail mail@pressorder.org; internet www.pressorder.org; f. 1911; 18 mems; Pres. MUHAMMAD AL-BAALBAKI; Vice-Pres. GEORGES SKAFF; Sec. ABD AL-KARIM EL-KHALIL.

Publishers

Dar al-Adab: POB 11-4123, Beirut; tel. and fax (1) 861633; e-mail d_aladab@cyberia.net.lb; f. 1953; dictionaries, literary and general; Man. RANA IDRISS; Editor-in-Chief SAMAH IDRISS.

Arab Institute for Research and Publishing (Al-Mouasasah al-Arabiyah Lildirasat Walnashr): POB 11-5760, Beirut; tel. and fax (1) 751438; e-mail mkayyali@nets.com.jo; f. 1969; Dir MAHER KAYYALI; works in Arabic and English.

Arab Scientific Publishers BP: POB 13-5574, Immeuble Ein at-Tenah Reem, rue Sakiet al-Janzir, Beirut; tel. (1) 811385; fax (1) 860138; e-mail asp@asp.com.lb; internet www.asp.com.lb; computer science, biological sciences, cookery, travel, politics, fiction, children's; Pres. BASSAM CHEBARO.

Dar Assayad Group (SAL and International): POB 11-1038, Hazmieh, Beirut; tel. (5) 450406; fax (5) 452700; e-mail assayad@inco.com.lb; internet www.darassayad.net; Dar Assayad SAL founded in 1943; Dar Assayad International founded in 1983 and provides publishing, advertising and distribution services; publishes in Arabic *Al-Anwar* (daily), *Assayad* (weekly), *Achabaka* (weekly), *Background Reports*, *Arab Defense Journal* (monthly), *Fairuz*

LEBANON

(international monthly edition), *Al-Idari* (monthly), *Al Computer, Communications and Electronics* (monthly), *Al-Fares* (monthly); also publishes monthly background reports; has offices and correspondents in Arab countries and most parts of the world; CEO Bassam Freiha; Gen. Man. Elham Freiha.

Chatila Publishing House: POB 13-5121, Chouran, Beirut 1102-2802; tel. (1) 352413; fax (1) 352419; e-mail info@cph.com.lb; internet www.cph.com.lb; publishes *Arab Construction World* (monthly), *Arab Water World* (nine per year), *Middle East Food* (every two months), *Middle East and World Food Directory* (bi-annual), *Middle East and World Water Directory* (bi-annual).

Edition Française pour le Monde Arabe (EDIFRAMO): POB 113-6140, Immeuble Elissar, rue Bliss, Beirut; tel. (1) 862437; Man. Tahseen S. Khayat.

Editions Orientales SAL: POB 1404, Immeuble Sayegh, rue Sursock, Beirut; tel. (1) 202070; fax (1) 202663; e-mail info@ediori.com.lb; internet www.ediori.com.lb; political and social newspapers and magazines; Pres. and Editor-in-Chief Charles Abou Adal.

GeoProjects SARL: POB 113-5294, Immeuble Barakat, 13 rue Jeanne d'Arc, Beirut; tel. (1) 344236; fax (1) 353000; e-mail geproj@cyberia.net.lb; f. 1978; cartographers, researchers, school textbook publishers; Dir-Gen. Rida Ismail.

Dar el-Ilm Lilmalayin: POB 1085, Centre Metco, rue Mar Elias, Beirut 2045–8402; tel. (1) 306666; fax (1) 701657; e-mail malayin@malayin.com; internet www.malayin.com; f. 1945; dictionaries, encyclopaedias, reference books, textbooks, Islamic cultural books; CEO Taref Osman.

Institute for Palestine Studies, Publishing and Research Organization (IPS): POB 11-7164, rue Anis Nsouli, off Verdun, Beirut; tel. and fax (1) 868387; fax (1) 814193; e-mail ipsbrt@palestine-studies.org; internet palestine-studies.org; f. 1963; independent non-profit Arab research organization; to promote better understanding of the Palestine problem and the Arab–Israeli conflict; publishes books, reprints, research papers, etc.; Chair. Dr Hisham Nashabe; Exec. Sec. Prof. Walid Khalidi.

The International Documentary Center of Arab Manuscripts: POB 2668, Immeuble Hanna, Ras Beirut, Beirut; e-mail alafaq@cyberia.net.lb; f. 1965; publishes and reproduces ancient and rare Arabic texts; Propr Zouhair Baalbaki.

Dar al-Kashaf: POB 112091, rue Assad Malhamee, Beirut; tel. (1) 296805; f. 1930; publishers of *Al-Kashaf* (Arab Youth Magazine), maps, atlases and business books; printers and distributors; Propr M. A. Fathallah.

Khayat Book and Publishing Co SARL: 90–94 rue Bliss, Beirut; Middle East, Islam, history, medicine, social sciences, education, fiction; Man. Dir Paul Khayat.

Dar al-Kitab al-Lubnani: Beirut; tel. (1) 861563; fax (1) 351433; f. 1929; Man. Dir Hassan ez-Zein.

Librairie du Liban Publishers: POB 11-9232, Beirut; tel. (9) 217944; fax (9) 217734; e-mail psayegh@ldlp.com; internet www.ldlp.com; f. 1944; publisher of children's books, dictionaries and reference books; distributor of books in English and French; Man. Dirs Habib Sayegh, Pierre Sayegh.

Dar al-Maaref Liban SARL: Beirut; tel. (1) 931243; f. 1959; children's books and textbooks in Arabic; Man. Dir Dr Fouad Ibrahim; Gen. Man. Joseph Nachou.

Dar al-Machreq SARL: POB 11-946, Beirut 1107 2060; tel. (1) 202423; e-mail machreq@cyberia.net.lb; internet www.darelmachreq.com; f. 1848; religion, art, Arabic and Islamic literature, history, languages, science, philosophy, school books, dictionaries and periodicals; Man. Dir Camille Héchaimé.

Dar Naamān lith-Thaqāfa (Maison Naaman pour la Culture): POB 567, Jounieh; tel. and fax (9) 935096; e-mail naamanculture@lynx.net.lb; internet www.biblib.com; f. 1979; publishes *Mawsou'atul 'Alamil 'Arabiyyil Mu'asser* (Encyclopaedia of the Contemporary Arab World), *Mawsou'atul Waqa'e'il 'Arabiyya* (Encyclopaedia of Arab Events), *Qitāboul A'lamil A'rabi, Siyassa was Strategia, As-Sahafa wal I'lam* in Arabic, and *The Arab World* in English; Propr Naji Naaman; Exec. Man. Marcelle al-Ashkar.

Editions Dar an-Nahar SAL: BP 11-226, 36 rue Andraos, Immeuble Media Centre, Beirut; tel. (1) 561687; fax (1) 561693; e-mail darannahar@darannahar.com; internet www.darannahar.com; f. 1967; a pan-Arab publishing house; Pres. Ghassan Tuéni; Dir Sahia Shami.

Naufal Group SARL: POB 11-2161, Immeuble Naufal, rue Sourati, Beirut; tel. (1) 354898; fax (1) 354394; e-mail naufalgroup@terra.net.lb; f. 1970; subsidiary cos Macdonald Middle East Sarl, Les Editions Arabes; encyclopaedias, fiction, children's books, history, law and literature; Man. Dir Tony Naufal.

Publitec Publications: POB 166142, Beirut; tel. (1) 495401; fax (1) 493330; e-mail publitecpublications@hotmail.com; internet www.whoswhointhearabworld.info; f. 1965; publishes *Who's Who in Lebanon* and *Who's Who in the Arab World* (both bi-annual); Pres. Charles Gedeon; Man. Krikor Ayvazian.

Dar ar-Raed al-Lubnani: POB 93, Immeuble Kamal al-Assad, Hazmieh, Sammouri, Beirut; tel. (5) 450757; f. 1971; CEO Rayed Sammouri.

Rihani Printing and Publishing House: Beirut; f. 1963; Propr Albert Rihani; Man. Daoud Stephan.

World Book Publishing: POB 11-3176, rue Emile Eddé, Sanayeh, Beirut; tel. (1) 349370; fax (1) 351226; e-mail rafic@wbpbooks.com; internet www.wbpbooks.com; f. 1929; literature, education, philosophy, current affairs, self-help, children's books; Chair. M. Said ez-Zein; Man. Dir Rafik ez-Zein.

Broadcasting and Communications

TELECOMMUNICATIONS

Regulatory Authority

Direction Générale des Télécommunications pour l'Exploitation et la Maintenance: Ministry of Telecommunications (see above); Dir-Gen. Abdul M. Youssef.

Service Providers

OGERO (Organisme de Gestion et d'Exploitation de l'ex Radio Orient): POB 11-12226 Bir Hassan, Beirut 1107 2070; tel. (1) 840000; fax (1) 826823; internet www.ogero.gov.lb; f. 1972; 100% state-owned; fixed-line operator.

In March 2004 Mobile Telecommunications Company (MTC) of Kuwait and Detecon (Germany) were awarded the contracts to replace Cellis and LibanCell SAL as the main operators of mobile services in Lebanon.

Detecon: subsidiary of Deutsch Telecom (Germany); mobile services.

MTC Touch: POB 175051, Immeuble MTC Touch, ave Charles Helou, Beirut; tel. (1) 566111; fax (1) 564185; e-mail info@mtc.com.lb; internet www.mtctouch.com.lb; owned by Mobile Telecommunications Company (Kuwait); mobile services.

BROADCASTING

Radio

Radio Liban: rue Arts et Métiers, Beirut; tel. (1) 343217; fax (1) 347489; part of the Ministry of Information; f. 1937; scheduled for privatization; Dir-Gen. Fouad Kabalan Hamdan.

The Home Service broadcasts in Arabic on short wave, and the Foreign Service broadcasts in Portuguese, Armenian, Arabic, Spanish, French and English.

Television

Lebanese Broadcasting Corporation (LBC) Sat Ltd: POB 111, Zouk; tel. (9) 850850; fax (9) 850916; e-mail lbcsat@lbcsat.com.lb; internet www.lbcsat.com.lb; f. 1985 as Lebanese Broadcasting Corporation International SAL; name changed 1996; operates satellite channel on Arabsat 2A; programmes in Arabic, French and English; Chair. Sheikh Pierre ed-Daher.

Télé-Liban (TL) SAL: POB 11-5055, Hazmieh, 4848 Beirut; tel. (1) 793000; fax (1) 950286; e-mail tl@tele-liban.com.lb; f. 1959; commercial service; programmes in Arabic, French and English on three channels; privatization pending; Chair. and Dir-Gen. Ibrahim el-Khoury; Dep. Dir-Gen. Muhammad S. Karimeh.

Future Television (Al-Mustaqbal): White House, rue Spears, Sanayeh, Beirut; tel. (1) 355355; fax (1) 753434; e-mail future@future.com.lb; internet www.future.com.lb; commercial; privately owned; Gen. Man. Nadim al-Monla.

Al-Manar (Lighthouse): rue Abd an-Nour, Haret Hreik, Beirut; tel. (1) 540440; fax (1) 553138; e-mail info@manartv.com; internet www.manartv.com; f. 1991; television station owned by Lebanese Communication Group (LCG); broadcasts to Arab and Muslim audiences worldwide; operates satellite channel since May 2000; partially controlled by Hezbollah; Chair. of Bd Abdallah Gassir.

During 1996–98 the Government took measures to close down unlicensed private broadcasters, and to restrict the activities of those licensed to operate. In particular, the broadcasting of news and political programmes by private satellite television channels was banned.

LEBANON   *Directory*

Finance

(cap. = capital; dep. = deposits; res = reserves; m. = million; brs = branches)

BANKING

Beirut was, for many years, the leading financial and commercial centre in the Middle East, but this role was destroyed by the civil conflict. To restore the city as a regional focus for investment banking is a key element of the Government's reconstruction plans.

Central Bank

Banque du Liban: POB 11-5544, rue Masraf Loubnane, Beirut; tel. (1) 750000; fax (1) 747600; e-mail bdlit@bdl.gov.lb; internet www.bdl.gov.lb; f. 1964 as successor in Lebanon to the Banque de Syrie et du Liban; cap. £L1,914,036m. (Dec. 2003), dep. £L12,322,000m. (Dec. 2001); Gov. RIAD SALAMEH; 9 brs.

Principal Commercial Banks

Al-Ahli International Bank SAL: POB 11-5556, Immeuble International, Bab Idris, rue Omar Daouk, Beirut; tel. (1) 970921; fax (1) 970939; e-mail aibmgt@dm.net.lb; f. 1964 as Bank of Lebanon and Kuwait SAL; merged with Lebanon brs of Jordan National Bank and changed name as above 2001; subsidiary of Jordan National Bank (85.5%); Pres. and Chair. Dr RAJAJ AL-MOUASHER; 8 brs.

Allied Bank SAL: POB 113-7165, Allied House Bldg, ave Charles Malek, St Nicolas, Achrafieh, Beirut 1103-2160; tel. (1) 326757; fax (1) 200660; e-mail info@abb.com.lb; internet www.alliedbank.com .lb; f. 1962; renamed as above following takeover by Groupe Méditerranée in 2001; cap. £L15,000m., res £L13,255m., dep. £L441,139m. (Dec. 2002); Chair. and Gen. Man. Dr MUSTAFA H. RAZIAN; 14 brs.

Arab Finance House (AFH): POB 11-273, Riad es-Solh, Beirut 1107 2020; tel. (1) 329595; fax (1) 329797; e-mail info@arabfinancehouse.com; internet www.arabfinancehouse.com; f. 2003; first Islamic bank in Lebanon; commercial and investment banking; cap. US $60m.; Pres., Chair. and Gen. Man. KHALED AHMAD SOWAIDI.

Bank of Beirut SAL: POB 11-7354, Bank of Beirut SAL Bldg, Foch St, Beirut Central District, Beirut; tel. and fax (1) 983999; e-mail executive@bankofbeirut.com.lb; internet www.bankofbeirut.com.lb; f. 1973; absorbed Transorient Bank 1999, Beirut Riyad Bank 2003; cap. £L45,600m., res £L191,201m., dep. £L4,101,700m. (Dec. 2003); Chair. and Gen. Man. SALIM G. SFEIR; 41 brs.

Bank of Beirut and the Arab Countries SAL: POB 11-1536, Immeuble de la Banque, 250 rue Clémenceau, Riad es-Solh, Beirut 1107 2080; tel. (1) 366630; fax (1) 374299; e-mail marketing@bbac .com.lb; internet www.bbac.net; f. 1956; cap. £L72,000m., res £L54,142m., dep. £L2,092,817m. (Dec. 2000); Chair. and Gen. Man. GHASSAN T. ASSAF; 30 brs.

Bank of Kuwait and the Arab World SAL: POB 113-6248, Immeuble Belle Vue, Ain at-Tineh, Verdun, Beirut; tel. and fax (1) 866306; e-mail bkaw@sodetel.net.lb; f. 1959; cap. £L38,000m., res £L12,111m., dep. £L534,789m. (Dec. 2004); Chair. and Gen. Man. ABD AR-RAZZAK ACHOUR; 14 brs.

Bank Al-Madina SAL: POB 113-7221, Immeuble Bank Al-Madina, rue Commodore, Hamra, Beirut; tel. (1) 351296; fax (1) 343762; e-mail intdep@bankal-madina.com; internet www.bankal-madina .com; f. 1982; cap. £L45,540m., res £L3,017m., dep. £L868,243m. (Dec. 2001); Hon. Chair. and Gen. Man. Dr ADNAN ABOU AYYASH; Chair. and Gen. Man. Sheikh IBRAHIM ABOU AYYASH; 18 brs.

Banque Audi SAL: POB 11-2560, Riad es-Solh, Beirut 1107 2808; tel. (1) 994000; fax (1) 990555; e-mail bkaudi@audi.com.lb; internet www.audi.com.lb; f. 1962; acquired Orient Credit Bank 1997 and Banque Nasr 1998; absorbed into Audi-Saradar Group in 2004; cap. £L291,662m., dep. £L13,259,039m. (Dec. 2004); Chair. and Gen. Man. RAYMOND W. AUDI; 66 brs.

Banque de Crédit National SAL: POB 110-204, Centre Gefinor, Bloc B, 15e étage, rue Clémenceau, Beirut; tel. (1) 752777; fax (1) 752555; e-mail bcnsafra@dm.net.lb; f. 1920; cap. £L11,000m., res £L2,443m., dep. £L17,809m. (Dec. 1998); Pres., Chair. and Gen. Man. CHARLES A. JUNOD.

Banque de l'Industrie et du Travail SAL: POB 11-3948, Riad es-Solh, Beirut 1107 2150; tel. (4) 712539; fax (4) 712538; e-mail international@bitbank.com.lb; internet www.bitbank.com.lb; f. 1960; cap. £L4,000m., res £L2,207m., dep. £L400,164m. (Dec. 2003); Chair. and Gen. Man. Sheikh FOUAD JAMIL EL-KHAZEN; Dir and Gen. Man. NABIL N. KHAIRALLAH; 12 brs.

Banque Libano-Française SAL: POB 11-0808, Tour Liberty, rue de Rome, Beirut 1107-2804; tel. (1) 791332; fax (1) 340350; e-mail info@eblf.com; internet www.eblf.com; f. 1967; cap. £L100,000m., res £L214,794m., dep. £L4,584,240m. (Dec. 2002); Pres., Chair. and Gen. Man. FARID RAPHAEL; 29 brs.

Banque de la Méditerranée SAL: POB 11-348, 482 rue Clémenceau, Beirut 2022 9302; tel. (1) 373937; fax (1) 362706; f. 1944; cap. £L530,000m., res £L50,120m., dep. £L6,330,253m. (Dec. 2002); Pres., Chair. and Gen. Man. Dr MUSTAFA H. RAZIAN; 49 brs.

Banque Misr-Liban SAL: rue Riad es-Solh, Beirut 1107 2010; tel. (1) 980399; fax (1) 980604; e-mail mail@bml.com.lb; internet www .bml.com.lb; f. 1929; cap. £L27,000m., res £L23,695m., dep. £L647,668m. (31 Dec. 2004); Chair. MUHAMMAD BARAKAT; Gen. Man. MUHAMMAD ZAHRAN; 15 brs.

Banque Audi Saradar Private Bank SAL: Immeuble Clover, ave Charles Malek, Achrafieh, Beirut; tel. (1) 208400; fax (1) 205410; e-mail saradar@saradar.com; internet www.saradar.com; f. 1948; became part of Audi-Saradar Group in 2004; cap. US $26.5m., dep. $1,325.8m., total assets $1,501.1m. (Dec. 2004); Pres. and Chair. MARIO JOE SARADAR; 7 brs.

BEMO (Banque Européenne pour le Moyen-Orient) SAL: POB 16-6353, Immeuble BEMO, place Sassine, ave Elias Sarkis, Achrafieh, Beirut; tel. (1) 200505; fax (1) 330780; e-mail bemosal@dm.net .lb; internet www.bemo.com.lb; f. 1964 as Future Bank SAL; name changed as above 1994; cap. £L44,050m., res £L13,074m., dep. £L655,407m. (Dec. 2003); Pres. and Gen. Man. HENRY Y. OBEGI; 6 brs.

BLOM Bank SAL: POB 11-1912, Immeuble BLOM Bank, rue Rachid Karameh, Verdun, Beirut 1107 2807; tel. (1) 743300; fax (1) 738946; e-mail blommail@blom.com.lb; internet www.blom.com .lb; f. 1951 as Banque du Liban et d'Outre-Mer; renamed as above 2000; cap. £L192,500m., res £L509,129m., dep. £L12,027,582m. (Dec. 2003); Pres., Chair. and Gen. Man. Dr NAAMAN AZHARI; Vice-Chair. and Gen. Man. SAAD AZHARI; Gen. Man. HABIB RAHAL; 44 brs in Lebanon, 3 abroad.

Byblos Bank SAL: POB 11-5605, ave Elias Sarkis, Achrafieh, Beirut; tel. (1) 335200; fax (1) 335540; e-mail byblosbk@byblosbank.com.lb; internet www.byblosbank.com; f. 1959; merged with Banque Beyrouth pour le Commerce SAL 1997; acquired Byblos Bank Europe SA 1998, Wedge Bank Middle East SAL 2001 and ABN AMRO Bank Lebanon 2002; cap. £L246,028m., res £L175,728m., dep. £L7,069,903m. (Dec. 2002); Pres., Chair. and Gen. Man. Dr FRANÇOIS SEMAAN BASSIL; 69 brs in Lebanon, 4 abroad.

Creditbank SAL: POB 16-5795, Immeuble Crédit Bancaire SAL, 680 blvd Bachir Gemayel, Achrafieh, Beirut 1100 2802; tel. (1) 218183; fax (1) 200483; e-mail info@creditbank.com.lb; internet www.creditbank.com.lb; f. 1981 as Crédit Bancaire SAL; renamed as above following merger with Crédit Lyonnais Liban SAL 2002; cap. £L23,445m., res £L18,804m., dep. £L529,592m. (Dec. 2003); Chair. and Gen. Man. TARIK KHALIFEH; 11 brs.

Crédit Libanais SAL: POB 16-6729, Centre Sofil, ave Charles Malek, Beirut 1100 2811; tel. (1) 200028; fax (1) 325713; e-mail info@creditlibanais.com.lb; internet www.creditlibanais.com.lb; f. 1961; cap. £L80,000m., res £L182,037m., dep. £L3,489,377m. (Dec. 2003); Pres., Chair. and Gen. Man. Dr JOSEPH M. TORBEY; 52 brs in Lebanon, 2 abroad.

Federal Bank of Lebanon SAL: POB 11-2209, Immeuble Renno, ave Charles Malek, St Nicolas, Beirut; tel. (1) 212300; fax (1) 215847; e-mail federal@cyberia.net.lb; f. 1952; cap. £L20,809m. (Dec. 2002), res £L2,069m., dep. £L302,893m. (Dec. 2003); Chair. and Gen. Man. AYOUB FARID MICHEL SAAB; Vice-Chair. and Dep. Gen. Man. FADI MICHEL SAAB; 8 brs.

First National Bank SAL: POB 113-5453, Immeuble Immobilia, rue Hamra, Beirut 1103 2040; tel. (1) 738502; fax (1) 343396; e-mail info@fnb.com.lb; internet www.fnb.com.lb; f. 1996; acquired Société Bancaire du Liban SAL 2002; cap. £L47,964m., res £L2,607m., dep. £L856,008m. (Dec. 2002); Pres. and Chair. RAMI R. EN-NIMER.

Fransabank SAL: POB 11-0393, Riad es-Solh, Beirut 1107 2803; tel. (1) 340180; fax (1) 354572; e-mail fsb@fransabank.com; internet www.fransabank.com; f. 1921; acquired Banque Tohmé SAL 1993, Universal Bank SAL 1998, United Bank of Saudi and Lebanon SAL 2001 and Banque de la Beka'a SAL 2003; cap. £L315,000m., res £L89,829m., dep. £L5,775,459m., net profit £L64,418m. (Dec. 2004); Chair. and Gen. Man. ADNAN KASSAR; Vice-Chair. and Vice-Gen. Man. ADEL KASSAR; 60 brs.

Intercontinental Bank of Lebanon SAL: POB 11-5292, Immeuble Ittihadiah, ave Charles Malek, Beirut 1107 2190; tel. (1) 200350; fax (1) 204505; e-mail ibl@ibl.com.lb; internet www.ibl.com.lb; f. 1961; cap. £L30,000m., res £L19,886m., dep. £L2,127,336m. (Dec. 2004); Chair. and Gen. Man. SALIM Y. HABIB; 12 brs.

Jammal Trust Bank SAL: POB 11-5640, Immeuble Jammal, rue Verdun, Beirut; tel. (1) 805702; fax (1) 864170; e-mail services@jammalbank.com.lb; internet www.jammalbank.co.lb; f. 1963 as Investment Bank, SAL; cap. £L33,000m., res £L24,639m., dep. £L280,998m. (Dec. 2002); Pres. and Chair. ALI ABDULLAH JAMMAL; 20 brs in Lebanon, 4 in Egypt.

Lebanese Canadian Bank: POB 11-2520, Immeuble Ghantous, blvd Dora, Riad es-Solh, Beirut 1107-2110; tel. (1) 250222; fax (1) 250777; e-mail lebcan@lebcanbank.com; internet www.lebcanbank

LEBANON

Directory

.com; f. 1960; cap. £L75,225m., res £L68,906m., dep. £L2,652,794m. (Dec. 2003); Chair. and Gen. Man. Georges Zard Abou Jaoudé; 23 brs.

Lebanese Swiss Bank SAL: POB 11-9552, Immeuble Hoss, 6e étage, rue Emile Eddé, Hamra, Beirut; tel. (1) 354501; fax (1) 346242; e-mail lbs@t-net.com.lb; f. 1962; cap. £L24,000m., res £L20,571m., dep. £L476,686m. (July 2004); Pres., Chair. and Gen. Man. Dr Tanal Sabbah; 7 brs.

Lebanon and Gulf Bank SAL: POB 113-6404, Immeuble Rinno, 585 rue de Lyon, Hamra, Beirut; tel. (1) 755500; fax (1) 756500; e-mail lgbmail@lgb.com.lb; internet www.lgb.com.lb; f. 1963; as Banque de Crédit Agricole, name changed 1980; cap. £L30,000m., res £L5,593m., dep. £L1,038,039m. (Dec. 2003); Pres., Chair. and Gen. Man. Abd al-Hafiz Mahmoud Itani; 10 brs.

Middle East and Africa Bank SAL: POB 14-5958, Beirut 1105 2080; tel. (1) 826740; fax (1) 841190; e-mail meabhof@cyberia.net.lb; internet www.meabank.com; f. 1991; cap. £L24,000m., res £L1,788m., dep. £L417,808m. (Dec. 2003); Pres. Hassan Hejeij; Chair. Kassem Hejeij; Gen. Man. Mounir Karam; 5 brs.

National Bank of Kuwait (Lebanon) SAL: POB 11-5727, BAC Bldg, Sanayeh Sq., Justinien St, Riad es-Solh, Beirut 1107 2200; tel. (1) 741111; fax (1) 747866; e-mail info@nbk.com.lb; internet www.nbk.com.lb; f. 1963 as Rifbank, name changed 1996; cap. £L40,020m., res £L7,714m., dep. £L236,548m. (Dec. 2003); Chair. Ibrahim Dabdoub; Gen. Man. Hany Sherif; 10 brs.

Near East Commercial Bank SAL: POB 16-5766, 6e étage, Centre Sofil, ave Charles Malek, St Nicolas, Achrafieh, Beirut; tel. (1) 200331; e-mail necb@dm.net.lb; f. 1978; cap. £L11,500m., res £L734m., dep. £L191,911m. (Dec. 2002); Chair. and Gen. Man. Paul Caland; 5 brs.

North Africa Commercial Bank SAL: POB 11-9575, Centre Aresco, rue Justinian, Beirut; tel. (1) 346320; fax (1) 346322; e-mail nacb@sodetel.net.lb; f. 1973; cap. £L45,687m., res L£15m., dep. £L711,703m. (Dec. 2003); Pres. and Chair. Aboubaker Ali Sherif; Gen. Man. Hadi I. Engim; 2 brs.

Saudi Lebanese Bank SAL: POB 11-6765, Immeuble Ash-Shua'a, Riad es-Solh, Beirut 1107 2220; tel. (1) 868987; fax (1) 790250; e-mail slbl@inco.com.lb; f. 1979 as Lebanese Saudi Credit SAL, name changed as above 1981; cap. £L40,000m., res £L19,347m., dep. £L722,220m. (Dec. 2002); Pres., Chair. and Gen. Man. Dr Moustafa Razian; 7 brs.

Société Générale de Banque au Liban (SGBL): POB 11-2955, rond-point Salomé, Sin el-Fil, Beirut; tel. (1) 499813; fax (1) 502820; e-mail sgbl@sgbl.com.lb; internet www.sgleb.com; f. 1953 as Société Générale Libano Européenne de Banque SAL (SGLEB); absorbed Inaash Bank SAL 2000; name changed as above 2001; cap. £L117,366m., res £L67,064m., dep. £L3,160,944m. (Dec. 2002); Pres. and Chair. Maurice Sehnaoui; 43 brs in Lebanon, 18 abroad.

Société Nouvelle de la Banque de Syrie et du Liban SAL (SNBSL): POB 11-957, rue Riad es-Solh, Beirut; tel. (1) 980080; fax (1) 980091; e-mail snbsl@snbsl.com.lb; f. 1963; cap. £L36,225m., res £L13,210m., dep. £L692,965m. (June 2005); Chair. Ramsay A. El-Khoury; 17 brs.

Standard Chartered Bank SAL: POB 70216, Antélias, Beirut; tel. and fax (4) 542474; internet www.standardchartered.com/lb; f. 1979; acquired Metropolitan Bank SAL 2000; cap. £L12,000m., res £L329m., dep. £L107,000m. (Dec. 2003); Chair. Christopher Knight; CEO Aamir Hussein; 5 brs.

Syrian Lebanese Commercial Bank SAL: POB 113-5127, Immeuble Cinéma Hamra, rue Hamra, Hamra, Beirut; tel. (1) 738262; fax (1) 738228; e-mail hamra@slcbk.com; internet www.slcb.com.lb; f. 1974; cap. £L58,000m., res £L13,289m., dep. £L557,952m. (Dec. 2004); Pres. and Chair. and Gen. Man. Dr Dureid Dergham; 3 brs.

United Credit Bank SAL: POB 13-5086, 5e étage, Immeuble Al-Madina, rue Rashid Karameh, Beirut; tel. (1) 792795; fax (1) 795096; f. 1982 as Commercial Facilities Bank SAL; name changed as above 1998; cap. £L14.3m., dep. £L29.6m. (Dec. 1999); Pres., Chair. and Gen. Man. Dr Adnan M. Abou Ayyash; 4 brs.

Development Bank

Audi Investment Bank SAL: POB 16-5110, Banque Audi Plaza, Bab Idriss, Beirut; tel. (1) 994000; fax (1) 999406; e-mail info@aib.com.lb; internet www.aib.com.lb; f. 1974 as Investment and Finance Bank, present name since 1996; medium- and long-term loans, 100% from Lebanese sources; owned by Banque Audi SAL (99.3%); cap. £L25,075m., res £L13,586m., dep. £L620,014m. (Dec. 2001); Pres., Chair. and Gen. Man. Raymond Wadih Audi.

Principal Foreign Banks

Arab Bank plc (Jordan): POB 11-1015, rue Riad es-Solh, Beirut; tel. (1) 980246; fax (1) 980803; e-mail beirut@arabbank.com.lb; f. 1930; cap. £L31,700m., res £L31,100m., dep. £L2,001,400m. (Dec. 2001); Exec. Vice-Pres. and Regional Man. Dr Hisham Bsat; 12 brs.

Banque Nationale de Paris Intercontinentale SA (BNPI) (France): POB 11-1608, Tour el Ghazal/BNPI, ave Fouad Chehab, Beirut; tel. (1) 333717; fax (1) 200604; e-mail bnpi.liban@bnpi.com.lb; internet www.bnpi-liban.bnpparibas.com; f. 1944; part of the BNP Paribas group (France); total assets £L2,061,529m. (Dec. 2000); Pres. Henri Tyan; Gen. Man. Guy Lepinard; 1 br.

Citibank NA (USA): POB 113-579, Centre Gefinor, Bloc E, rue Clémenceau, Beirut; tel. (1) 738400; fax (1) 738406; cap. £L7,943m., res £L738m., dep. £L171,860m. (Dec. 2000); CEO Elia Samaha.

Habib Bank (Overseas) Ltd (Pakistan): POB 5616, Fadlallah Centre, 1st Floor, blvd esh-Shiah, Musharaffieh, Beirut; tel. (1) 558992; fax (1) 558995; e-mail habibbkbey@t-net.com.lb; Gen. Man. Muhammad Shahab Khattack.

HSBC Bank Middle East (United Kingdom): POB 11-1380, HSBC Bldg, Minet el-Hosn, Riad es-Solh, Beirut 1107-2080; tel. (1) 377477; fax (1) 372362; internet www.lebanon.hsbc.com; f. 1946; cap. £L10,750m. (Dec. 1999); CEO Kevin Smorthwaite; 5 brs.

Saudi National Commercial Bank: POB 11-2355, Riad es-Solh, Beirut 1107 2100; tel. (1) 860863; fax (1) 867728; e-mail sncb@sncb.com.lb; cap. £L10,000m., res £L7,933m., dep. £L87,470m. (Dec. 2002); Gen. Man. Hani Houssami.

Numerous other foreign banks have representative offices in Beirut.

Banking Association

Association of Banks in Lebanon: POB 976, Association of Banks in Lebanon Bldg, Gouraud St, Saifi, Beirut; tel. (1) 970500; fax (1) 970501; e-mail abl@abl.org.lb; internet www.abl.org.lb; f. 1959; serves and promotes the interests of the banking community in Lebanon; mems: 63 banks and 7 banking rep. offices; Pres. and Chair. Dr François Bassil; Gen. Sec. Dr Makram Sader.

STOCK EXCHANGE

Beirut Stock Exchange (BSE): POB 11-3552, 4e étage, Bloc A3, Immeuble Azareih, Beirut; tel. (1) 993555; fax (1) 993444; e-mail bse@bse.com.lb; internet www.bse.com.lb; f. 1920; recommenced trading in January 1996; 10 cttee mems; Cttee Pres. Dr Fadi Khalaf.

INSURANCE

About 80 insurance companies were registered in Lebanon in the late 1990s, although less than one-half of these were operational. An insurance law enacted in mid-1999 increased the required capital base for insurance firms and provided tax incentives for mergers within the sector.

Arabia Insurance Co SAL: POB 11-2172, Arabia House, rue de Phénicie, Beirut; tel. (1) 363610; fax (1) 365139; e-mail arabia@arabia-ins.com.lb; internet www.arabiainsurance.com; f. 1944; cap. £L51,000m.; Chair. Dr Hisham Bsat; Gen. Man. Fady Shammas; 20 brs.

Bankers Assurance SAL: POB 11-4293, Immeuble Capitole, rue Riad es-Solh, Beirut; tel. (1) 988777; fax (1) 984004; e-mail mail@bankers-assurance.com; internet www.bankers-assurance.com; f. 1972; Chair. Saba Nader; Gen. Man. Eugène Nader.

Commercial Insurance Co (Lebanon) SAL: POB 11-4351, Centre Starco, Beirut; POB 84, Jounieh; tel. (1) 373070; fax (1) 373071; e-mail maxzaccar@commercialinsurance.com.lb; internet www.commercialinsurance.com.lb; f. 1962; cap. £L6,000m., res £L4,000m. (March 2006); Chair. Max R. Zaccar; 2 brs.

Compagnie Libanaise d'Assurances SAL: POB 3685, rue Riad es-Solh, Beirut; tel. (1) 868988; f. 1951; cap. £L3,000m. (1991); Chair. Jean F. S. Aboujaoudé; Gen. Man. Jihad Shaker.

Al-Ittihad al-Watani: POB 11-1270, Jisr al-Wati, Immeuble Al-Ittihad al-Watani, Beirut; tel. (1) 330840; e-mail webmaster@alittihadalwatani.com.lb; internet www.alittihadalwatani.com.lb; f. 1947; cap. £L30m.; Chair. Joe I. Kairouz; Exec. Dir Tannous Feghali.

Libano-Suisse Insurance Co SAL: POB 11-3821, Commerce and Finance Bldg, Beirut 1107-2150; tel. (1) 364461; fax (1) 368724; e-mail libasuis@dm.net.lb; internet www.libano-suisse.com; f. 1959; cap. £L4,050m. (2000); Chair. Michel Pierre Pharaon; Gen. Man. Samir Nahas.

Al-Mashrek Insurance and Reinsurance SAL: POB 16-6154, Immeuble Al-Mashrek, 65 rue Aabrine, Achrafieh, Beirut 1100 2100; tel. (1) 204666; fax (1) 337625; e-mail amirco@inco.com.lb; f. 1962; cap. £L5,000m. (1999); Chair. and Gen. Man. Abraham Matossian.

'La Phénicienne' SAL: POB 11-5652, Immeuble Hanna Haddad, rue Amine Gemayel, Sioufi, Beirut; tel. (1) 425484; fax (1) 424532; f. 1964; Chair. and Gen. Man. Tannous C. Feghali.

Société Nationale d'Assurances SAL: POB 11-4805, Immeuble SNA, Hazmieh, Beirut; tel. (1) 956600; fax (1) 956624; e-mail sna@

sna.com.lb; internet www.sna.com.lb; f. 1963; Chair. ANTOINE WAKIM.

Trade and Industry

DEVELOPMENT ORGANIZATIONS

Council for Development and Reconstruction (CDR): POB 116-5351, Tallet es-Serail, Beirut; tel. (1) 643982; fax (1) 647947; e-mail general@cdr.gov.lb; internet www.cdr.gov.lb; f. 1977; an autonomous public institution reporting to the Cabinet, the CDR is charged with the co-ordination, planning and execution of Lebanon's public reconstruction programme; it plays a major role in attracting foreign funds; Pres. JAMAL ITANI; Sec.-Gen. JOSEPH HADDAD.

Investment Development Authority of Lebanon (IDAL): POB 113-7251, Cristal Bldg 1145, Hussein el-Adhab St, Nijmeh Sq., Beirut; tel. (1) 983306; fax (1) 983302; e-mail invest@idal.com.lb; internet www.idal.com.lb; f. 1994; state-owned; Chair. and Gen. Man. NABIL ITANI.

Société Libanaise pour le Développement et la Reconstruction de Beyrouth (SOLIDERE): POB 11-9493, 149 rue Saad Zagholoul, Beirut; tel. (1) 980650; fax (1) 980662; e-mail solidere@solidere.com.lb; internet www.solidere.com.lb; f. 1994; real estate co responsible for reconstruction of Beirut Central District; Chair. NASSER SHAMMA'A; Gen. Man. MOUNIR DOUAIDY.

CHAMBERS OF COMMERCE AND INDUSTRY

Federation of the Chambers of Commerce, Industry and Agriculture in Lebanon: POB 11-1801, Immeuble Elias Abd-an Nour, Achrafieh, Beirut; internet www.cci-fed.org.lb; Pres. ADNAN KASSAR; Gen. Sec. MICHEL BITAR.

Chamber of Commerce, Industry and Agriculture of Beirut and Mount Lebanon: POB 11-1801, rue Justinian, Sanayeh, Beirut; tel. (1) 744160; fax (1) 353395; e-mail info@ccib.org.lb; internet www.ccib.org.lb; f. 1898; 32,000 mems; Pres. GHAZI KRAYTEM; Dir-Gen. Dr WALID NAJA.

Chamber of Commerce, Industry and Agriculture of Tripoli and North Lebanon: rue Bechara Khoury, Tripoli; tel. (6) 425600; fax (6) 442042; e-mail abdallahg@cciat.org.lb; internet www.cciat.org.lb; Chair. ABDALLAH GHANDOUR.

Chamber of Commerce, Industry and Agriculture in Sidon and South Lebanon: POB 41, rue Maarouf Saad, Sidon; tel. (7) 720123; fax (7) 722986; e-mail chamber@ccias.org.lb; internet www.ccias.org.lb; f. 1933; Pres. MUHAMMAD ZAATARI.

Chamber of Commerce, Industry and Agriculture of Zahleh and Beka'a: POB 100, Zahleh; tel. (8) 802602; fax (8) 800050; internet www.cciaz.org.lb; f. 1939; 2,500 mems; Pres. EDMOND JREISSATI.

EMPLOYERS' ASSOCIATION

Association of Lebanese Industrialists: Chamber of Commerce and Industry Bldg, 5e étage, Sanayeh, Beirut; tel. (1) 350280; fax (1) 350282; e-mail ali@ali.org.lb; internet www.ali.org.lb; Pres. FADY ABBOUD; Gen. Man. SAAD S. OUEINI.

UTILITIES

Electricity

Electricité du Liban (EdL): POB 131, Immeuble de l'Electricité du Liban, 22 rue du Fleuve, Beirut; tel. (1) 442556; fax (1) 583084; internet www.edl.gov.lb; f. 1954; state-owned; scheduled for privatization from 2003; Chair. and Dir-Gen. KAMAL F. HAYEK.

Water

From the late 1990s the Government began a process of establishing five new regional water authorities (in the governorates of the North, South, Beka'a, Beirut and Mount Lebanon), to replace the existing water authorities and committees. Under the reorganization the new authorities were to operate under the supervision of the Ministry of Energy and Water.

Beirut Water Supply Office: Beirut; Pres. LUCIEN MOBAYAD.

North Lebanon Water Authority: Chair. and Gen. Man. JAMAL ABD AL-LATIF KARIM.

South Lebanon Water Authority: Chair. and Gen. Man. AHMAD HASSAN NIZAM.

TRADE UNION FEDERATION

Confédération Générale des Travailleurs du Liban (CGTL): POB 4381, Beirut; f. 1958; 300,000 mems; only national labour centre in Lebanon and sole rep. of working classes; comprises 18 affiliated federations including all 150 unions in Lebanon; Pres. GHASSAN GHOSN.

Transport

RAILWAYS

Office des Chemins de Fer de l'Etat Libanais et du Transport en Commun: BP 11-109, Gare St Michel, Nahr, Beirut; tel. (1) 587211; fax (1) 447007; since 1961 all railways in Lebanon have been state-owned. The original network of some 412 km is no longer functioning. However, in 2004 work began on a project to reconstruct a section of the railway network between Tripoli and the Syrian border; Dir-Gen. and Pres. RADWAN BOU NASSER ED-DIN.

ROADS

At 31 December 1996 Lebanon had an estimated 6,350 km of roads, of which 2,170 km were highways, main or national roads and 1,370 km were secondary or regional roads. The total road network was estimated at 7,300 km in 1999. The two international motorways are the north–south coastal road and the road connecting Beirut with Damascus in Syria. Among the major roads are that crossing the Beka'a and continuing south to Bent-Jbail and the Shtaura–Ba'albek road. Hard-surfaced roads connect Jezzine with Moukhtara, Bzebdine with Metn, Meyroub with Afka and Tannourine. A road construction project, costing some US $100m., was planned for Beirut in the late 1990s. A new, 8-km highway, linking around 26 villages in southern Lebanon, was inaugurated in August 2000.

SHIPPING

In the 1990s a two-phase programme to rehabilitate and expand the port of Beirut commenced, involving the construction of an industrial free zone, a fifth basin and a major container terminal, at an estimated cost of US $1,000m; the container terminal became operational in February 2005. Tripoli, the northern Mediterranean terminus of the oil pipeline from Iraq (the other is Haifa, Israel—not in use since 1948), is also a busy port, with good equipment and facilities. Jounieh, north of Beirut, is Lebanon's third most important port. A new deep-water sea port is to be constructed south of Sidon. The reconstructed port of an-Naqoura, in what was then the 'security zone' along the border with Israel, was inaugurated in June 1987.

Port Authorities

Gestion et Exploitation du Port de Beyrouth: POB 1490, Beirut; tel. (1) 580210; fax (1) 585835; e-mail info@portdebeyrouth.com; internet www.portdebeyrouth.com; Pres., Dir-Gen. and Man. Dir HASSAN KAMEL KRAYTEM; Harbour Master MAROUN KHOURY.

Service d'Exploitation du Port de Tripoli: El Mina, Tripoli; tel. (6) 601225; fax (6) 220180; e-mail tport@terra.net.lb; f. 1959; Harbour Master MARWAN BAROUDI.

Principal Shipping Companies

Youssef A Abourahal and Hanna N Tabet: POB 11-5890, Immeuble Ghantous, autostrade Dora, Beirut; tel. (1) 263872.

Ets Paul Adem: Centre Moucarri, 6e étage, autostrade Dora, Bourj Hammoud, Beirut; tel. (1) 244610; fax (1) 244612; e-mail padco@inco.com.lb; f. 1971; ship owners, operators, maritime agents, brokers, consultants; Gen. Man. PAUL ADEM.

Ademar Shipping Lines: POB 175-231, rue Shafaka, Al Medawar, Beirut; tel. and fax (1) 445093; e-mail ademar@sodetel.net.lb.

Agence Générale Maritime (AGEMAR) SARL: POB 9255, Centre Burotec, 7e étage, rue Pasteur, Beirut; tel. (1) 583885; fax (1) 583884; Dirs S. MEDLEJ, N. MEDLEJ.

Amin Kawar & Sons (Jordan): POB 4230, Beirut; tel. (1) 352525; fax (1) 353802; e-mail amkawar@inco.com.lb; internet www.kawar.com; f. 1963; Chair. and Man. Dir TAWFIQ AMIN KAWAR.

Arab Shipping and Chartering Co: POB 1084, Immeuble Ghandour, ave des Français, Beirut; tel. (1) 371044; fax (1) 373370; e-mail arabship@dm.net.lb; agents for China Ocean Shipping Co.

Associated Levant Lines SAL: POB 110371, Immeuble Mercedes, autostrade Dora, Beirut; tel. (1) 255366; fax (1) 255362; e-mail tgf-all@dm.net.lb; Dirs T. GARGOUR, N. GARGOUR, H. GARGOUR.

Wafic Begdache: Immeuble Wazi, 4e étage, rue Moussaitbé, Beirut; tel. (1) 319920; fax (1) 815002; e-mail mody@lebaneseshipping.com.

Consolidated Bulk Inc.: POB 70-152, Centre St Elie, Bloc A, 6e étage, Antélias, Beirut; tel. (4) 410724; fax (4) 402842; e-mail info@bulkgroup.net.

Continental Ship Management SARL: POB 901413, Centre Dora Moucarri, 8e étage, appt 804, Beirut; tel. (1) 583654; fax (1) 584440.

O. D. Debbas & Sons: Head Office: POB 166678, Immeuble Debbas, 530 blvd Corniche du Fleuve, Beirut; tel. (1) 585253; fax (1) 587135;

LEBANON

e-mail oddebbas@oddebbas.com; internet www.oddebbas.com; f. 1892; Man. Dir OIDIH ELIE DEBBAS.

Dery Shipping Lines Ltd: POB 5720-113, Beirut; tel. (1) 862442; fax (1) 344146.

Diana K Shipping Co: POB 113-5125, Immeuble Ajouz, rue Kenedi, Ein Mreisseh, Beirut; tel. (1) 363314; fax (1) 369712; e-mail dianak@cyberia.net.lb; Marine Dept Man. Capt. AMIN HABBAL.

Fauzi Jemil Ghandour: POB 1084, Beirut 1107 2070; tel. (1) 373376; fax (1) 360048; e-mail ali@seahorsenet.com; agents for Ecuadorian Line.

Gezairi Chartering and Shipping Co (GEZACHART): POB 11-1402, Immeuble Gezairi, place Gezairi, Ras Beirut; tel. (1) 783783; fax (1) 784784; e-mail gezachart@gezairi.com; internet www.gezairi.com; ship management, chartering, brokerage.

Gulf Agency Co (Lebanon) Ltd: POB 11 4392, Riad es-Solh, Beirut 1107 2160; tel. (1) 446189; fax (1) 446097; e-mail lebanon@gacworld.com; f. 1969; Gen. Man. SIMON G. BEJJANI.

Lebanese Navigators Co SARL: POB 11-0239, Immeuble Aleddine, blvd Ghobeiry, Beirut; tel. (1) 822664; fax (1) 603334.

Medawar Shipping Co SARL: POB 8962/11, Immeuble Kanafani, rue al-Arz, Saifi, Beirut; tel. (1) 447277; fax (1) 447662.

Mediterranean Feedering Co SARL: POB 70-1187, Immeuble Akak, autostrade Dbayeh, Beirut; tel. (1) 403056; fax (1) 406444; e-mail mfcbeirut@attmail.com; Man. Dir EMILE AKEF EL-KHOURY.

Orient Shipping and Trading Co SARL: POB 11-2561, Immeuble Moumneh, no 72, rue Ain al-Mraisseh 54, Beirut; tel. (1) 644252; fax (1) 602221; Dirs ELIE ZAROUBY, EMILE ZAROUBY.

Rassem Shipping Agency: POB 11-8460, Immeuble Agha, Raoucheh, Beirut; tel. (1) 866372; fax (1) 805593.

Riga Brothers: POB 17-5134, Immeuble Mitri Haddad, rue du Port, Beirut; tel. (1) 406882.

G. Sahyouni & Co SARL: POB 17-5452, Mar Mikhael, Beirut 1104 2040; tel. (1) 257046; fax (1) 241317; e-mail lloydsbey@inco.com.lb; f. 1989; agents for Baltic Control Lebanon Ltd., SARL, and Lloyds; Man. Dir. GEORGE SHYOUNI; Financial Man. HENRY CHIDIAC.

Sinno Trading and Navigation Agency: POB 113-6977, 4e étage, Immeuble Rebeiz, Beirut; tel. and fax (1) 446707; Chair. MUHIEDDINE F. SINNO; Man. Dir AHMED JABBOURY.

A Sleiman Co & Sons: Immeuble Saroulla, 3e étage, rue Hamra, Beirut; tel. (1) 354240; fax (1) 340262.

Union Shipping and Chartering Agency SAL: POB 2856, Immeuble Ghandour, ave des Français, Beirut 1107 2120; tel. (1) 373376; fax (1) 360048; e-mail ucsa@seahorsenet.com; agents for Jadroslobodna, Jugo Oceania, Atlanska Plovidba, Jadroplov and Maruba.

CIVIL AVIATION

Services from the country's principal airport, in Beirut, were subject to frequent disruptions after 1975; its location in predominantly Muslim west Beirut made it virtually inaccessible to non-Muslims. In 1986 a new airport, based on an existing military airfield, was opened at Halat, north of Beirut, by Christian concerns, but commercial operations from the airport were not authorized by the Government. Services to and from Beirut by Middle East Airlines (MEA) were suspended, and the airport closed, at the end of January 1987, after the Maronite Lebanese Forces (LF) militia shelled the airport and threatened to attack MEA aircraft if services from their own airport, at Halat, did not receive official authorization. Beirut airport was reopened in May, after the LF accepted government assurances that Halat would receive the necessary authorization for civil use. However, the commission concluded that Halat did not possess the facilities to cater for international air traffic. Some 3.3m. passengers used Beirut International Airport in 2004. In late 2001 a major expansion project at the airport was completed, at an estimated cost of US $600m.; facilities included a new terminal building and two new runways, increasing handling capacity to 6m. passengers a year. In May 2005 the airport was renamed Beirut Rafik Hariri International Airport in honour of the former Prime Minister who had been killed in February.

MEA (Middle East Airlines, Air Liban SAL): POB 206, Headquarters MEA, blvd de l'Aéroport, Beirut; tel. (1) 628888; fax (1) 629260; e-mail mea@mea.net.lb; internet www.mea.com.lb; f. 1945; acquired Lebanese International Airways in 1969; privatization pending; regular services throughout Europe, the Middle East, North and West Africa, and the Far East; Chair. MUHAMMAD EL-HOUT; Commercial Man. NIZAR KHOURY.

Trans-Mediterranean Airways SAL (TMA): Beirut International Airport, POB 11-3018, Beirut; tel. (1) 629210; fax (1) 629219; e-mail cargo@tma.com.lb; internet www.tma.com.lb; f. 1953; scheduled services, charter activities and aircraft lease operations covering Europe, the Middle East, Africa and the Far East; also provides handling, storage and maintenance services; Chair. and Pres. FADI N. SAAB.

Tourism

Before the civil war, Lebanon was a major tourist centre, and its scenic beauty, sunny climate and historic sites attracted some 2m. visitors annually. In 1974 tourism contributed about 20% of the country's income. Since the end of the civil conflict, tourist facilities (in particular hotels) have begun to be reconstructed, and the Government has chosen to concentrate its efforts on the promotion of cultural as well as conference and exhibition-based tourism. In 1999 UNESCO declared Beirut as the Cultural Capital of the Arab World. Lebanon is also being promoted as an 'eco-tourism' destination. Excluding Syrian visitors, the annual total of tourist arrivals increased from 177,503 in 1992 to some 1m. in 2003. Tourism receipts reached an estimated US $1,221m. in 1998; however, receipts fell to $742m. in 2000, before rising again, to $1,016m., in 2003.

National Council of Tourism in Lebanon (NCTL): POB 11-5344, rue Banque du Liban 550, Beirut; tel. (1) 343196; fax (1) 343279; e-mail tourism@cyberia.net.lb; internet www.lebanon-tourism.gov.lb; government-sponsored autonomous organization responsible for the promotion of tourism; overseas offices in Paris (France) and Cairo (Egypt); Pres. FOUAD FAWAZ; Dir-Gen. NASSER SAFI ED-DIN.

LESOTHO

Introductory Survey

Location, Climate, Language, Religion, Flag, Capital

The Kingdom of Lesotho is a land-locked country, entirely surrounded by South Africa. The climate is generally mild, although cooler in the highlands: lowland temperatures range from a maximum of 32°C (90°F) in summer (October to April) to a minimum of −7°C (20°F) in winter. Rainfall averages about 725 mm (29 ins) per year, mostly falling in summer. The official languages are English and Sesotho; other languages spoken include Zulu and Xhosa. About 90% of the population are Christians. The largest denominations are the Roman Catholic, Lesotho Evangelical and Anglican Churches. The national flag (official proportions 2 by 3) is divided diagonally from lower hoist to upper fly, with the hoist triangle of white bearing, in brown silhouette, a traditional Basotho shield with crossed knobkerrie (club), barbed assegai (spear) and a thyrsus of ostrich feathers, and the fly triangle comprising a blue diagonal stripe and a green triangle. The capital is Maseru.

Recent History

Lesotho was formerly Basutoland, a dependency of the United Kingdom. In 1868, at the request of the Basotho people's chief, the territory became a British protectorate. Basutoland was annexed to Cape Colony (now part of South Africa) in 1871, but detached in 1884. It became a separate British colony and was administered as one of the High Commission Territories in southern Africa (the others being the protectorates of Bechuanaland, now Botswana, and Swaziland). The British Act of Parliament that established the Union of South Africa in 1910 also provided for the possible inclusion in South Africa of the three High Commission Territories, subject to local consent: the native chiefs opposed requests by successive South African Governments for the transfer of the three territories.

Within Basutoland a revised Constitution, which established the colony's first Legislative Council, was introduced in 1956. A new document, granting limited powers of self-government, was adopted in September 1959. Basutoland's first general election, on the basis of universal adult suffrage, took place on 29 April 1965, and full internal self-government was achieved the following day. Moshoeshoe II, Paramount Chief since 1960, was recognized as King. The Basutoland National Party (BNP), a conservative group supporting limited co-operation with South Africa, narrowly won a majority of the seats in the new Legislative Assembly. The BNP's leader, Chief Leabua Jonathan, was appointed Prime Minister in July 1965. Basutoland became independent, as Lesotho, on 4 October 1966. The new Constitution provided for a bicameral legislature, comprising the 60-seat National Assembly and the 33-member Senate; executive power was vested in the Cabinet, which was presided over by the Prime Minister. The King was designated Head of State.

The BNP, restyled the Basotho National Party, remained in power at independence. A general election was held in January 1970, at which the opposition Basotho Congress Party (BCP), a pan-Africanist group led by Dr Ntsu Mokhehle, appeared to have won a majority of seats in the National Assembly. Chief Jonathan declared a state of emergency, suspended the Constitution and arrested several BCP organizers. The election was annulled, and the legislature prorogued. King Moshoeshoe II was placed under house arrest and subsequently exiled, although he returned in December after accepting a government order banning him from participating in politics. The country was thus effectively under the Prime Minister's personal control. An interim National Assembly, comprising the former Senate (mainly chiefs) and 60 members nominated by the Cabinet, was inaugurated in April 1973. The state of emergency was revoked in July. However, following a failed coup attempt in January 1974 by alleged supporters of the BCP, Chief Jonathan introduced stringent security laws. Mokhehle and other prominent members of the BCP went into exile abroad, and the party split into two factions, internal and external. The latter, led by Mokhehle, was supported by the Lesotho Liberation Army (LLA), which was responsible for terrorist attacks in Lesotho during the late 1970s and the 1980s. (The South African Government consistently denied allegations that it supported the LLA.)

Although Lesotho was economically dependent on South Africa, and the Government's official policy during the 1970s was one of 'dialogue' with its neighbour, Chief Jonathan repeatedly criticized the apartheid regime, and supported the then banned African National Congress of South Africa (ANC). In December 1982 South African forces launched a major assault on the homes of ANC members in Maseru, killing more than 40 people. Lesotho's persistent refusal to sign a joint non-aggression pact led South Africa to impound consignments of armaments destined for Lesotho, and again, in August 1984, to threaten economic sanctions.

The Parliament Act of May 1983 repealed the emergency order of 1970 that had suspended the Constitution. In January 1985 the National Assembly was dissolved. Legislative elections scheduled for September were cancelled in August, when no opposition candidates were nominated: the opposition parties claimed that their prospective candidates had been denied access to the voters' rolls and had therefore been prevented from securing sufficient signatures to qualify for nomination. BNP candidates in all 60 constituencies were thus returned to office unopposed.

In December 1985 South African commando troops were held responsible by the Lesotho Government for a raid in Maseru in which nine people (including several ANC members) were killed. South Africa imposed a blockade on the border with Lesotho from the beginning of 1986. Five of Lesotho's opposition leaders were arrested on their return from talks in South Africa, and there were reports of fighting between factions of the armed forces. On 20 January Chief Jonathan's Government was overthrown in a coup led by Maj.-Gen. Justin Lekhanya, the head of the armed forces. A Military Council, chaired by Lekhanya, was established. The 1983 Parliament Act was revoked, and it was announced that executive and legislative powers were to be vested in King Moshoeshoe, assisted by the Military Council and a (mainly civilian) Council of Ministers. About 60 ANC members were subsequently deported from Lesotho, and the South African blockade was ended. In March 1986 the Military Council suspended all formal political activity. In September the Council of Ministers was restructured, giving increased responsibility to Lekhanya, and the Military Council held discussions with the leaders of the five main opposition parties.

Although the South African Government denied having any part in the coup, the Lekhanya regime proved to be more amenable to South Africa's regional security policy. In March 1986 it was announced that the two countries had reached an informal agreement whereby neither would allow its territory to be used for attacks against the other. Moreover, the Lesotho Government did not join other African states in pressing for international economic sanctions against South Africa. In March 1988 Lesotho and South Africa reached final agreement on the Lesotho Highlands Water Project (LHWP), a major scheme to supply water to South Africa.

In May 1988 Mokhehle was allowed to return to Lesotho after 14 years of exile. In 1989 the LLA was said to have disbanded, and by 1990 the two factions of the BCP had apparently reunited under Mokhehle's leadership.

In February 1990 Lekhanya dismissed three members of the Military Council and one member of the Council of Ministers, accusing them of 'insubordination'. When Moshoeshoe refused to approve new appointments to the Military Council, Lekhanya suspended the monarch's executive and legislative powers, which were assumed by the Military Council in March. Moshoeshoe (who remained Head of State) was exiled in the United Kingdom. Lekhanya announced that a general election would take place during 1992; however, party political activity remained outlawed. In June 1990 a National Constituent Assembly (including Lekhanya, members of the Council of Ministers, representatives of banned political parties, traditional chiefs and business leaders) was inaugurated to draft a new constitution. In October Lekhanya invited the King to return from exile. Moshoeshoe responded that his return would be conditional upon the ending of military rule and the establishment of an interim government, pending the readoption of the 1966 Constitution. On 6 November 1990 Lekhanya promulgated an order dethroning the King with immediate effect. Lesotho's 22 principal chiefs elected Moshoeshoe's elder son, Prince David Mohato Bereng Seeiso, as the new King; on 12 November he acceded to the throne, as King Letsie III, having undertaken to remain detached from politics.

On 30 April 1991 Lekhanya was deposed in a coup organized by disaffected army officers. Col (later Maj.-Gen.) Elias Phitsoane Ramaema succeeded Lekhanya as Chairman of the Military Council. Ramaema repealed the ban on party political activity, and by July the National Constituent Assembly had completed the draft Constitution. In May 1992 Lesotho and South Africa agreed to establish diplomatic relations at ambassadorial level. Following talks in the United Kingdom with Ramaema, former King Moshoeshoe returned from exile in July.

The general election was eventually held in March 1993. The BCP secured all 65 seats in the new National Assembly, winning 54% of the votes cast. In April Mokhehle was inaugurated as Prime Minister, and King Letsie swore allegiance to the new Constitution, under the terms of which he remained Head of State with no executive or legislative powers; executive authority was vested in the Cabinet.

A mutiny in November 1993 by about 50 junior officers in the national army, the Royal Lesotho Defence Force (RLDF), was apparently precipitated by a proposal to place the military under the command of a senior member of the LLA—as part of government efforts to integrate its former armed wing with the RLDF. Four senior army officers were subsequently reported to have resigned their posts. Skirmishes near Maseru in January 1994 escalated into more serious fighting between some 600 rebel troops and a 150-strong contingent of forces loyal to the Government, reportedly resulting in the deaths of at least five soldiers and three civilians. Following mediation efforts involving representatives of Botswana, South Africa, Zimbabwe, the Commonwealth (see p. 193), the Organization of African Unity (OAU, now the African Union, see p. 153) and the UN, a truce entered force, and at the beginning of February the rival factions surrendered their weapons and returned to barracks. In April, however, the Deputy Prime Minister, Selometsi Baholo (who also held the finance portfolio), was killed during an abduction attempt by disaffected troops. In the following month police-officers demanding increased pay and allowances briefly held hostage the acting finance minister, Mpho Malie (the Minister of Information and Broadcasting). Agreement was subsequently reached on increased allowances, and the Government announced the formation of an independent commission to review salary structures in the public sector.

A commission to investigate the armed forces unrest of January and April 1994 began work in July. In that month Mokhehle appointed a commission of inquiry into the dethronement of King Moshoeshoe II. In August King Letsie petitioned the High Court to abolish the commission on the grounds of bias on the part of its members. On 17 August Letsie announced that he had dissolved the National Assembly, dismissed the Government and suspended sections of the Constitution, citing 'popular dissatisfaction' with the BCP administration. Although several thousand people gathered outside the royal palace in Maseru in support of the deposed Government, army and police support for Letsie's 'royal coup' was evident, and subsequent clashes between demonstrators and the security forces reportedly resulted in five deaths. A well-known human rights lawyer, Hae Phoofolo, was appointed Chairman of a transitional Council of Ministers, and the Secretary-General of the BNP, Evaristus Retselisitsoe Sekhonyana, was appointed Minister of Foreign Affairs. Phoofolo identified as a priority for his administration the amendment of the Constitution to facilitate the restoration of Moshoeshoe; in the mean time, King Letsie was to act as executive and legislative Head of State.

The suspension of constitutional government was widely condemned outside Lesotho. The Presidents of Botswana, South Africa and Zimbabwe led diplomatic efforts to restore the elected Government, supported by the OAU and the Commonwealth. The USA withdrew financial assistance, and several other countries threatened sanctions. Following negotiations in South Africa, in September 1994 King Letsie and Mokhehle signed an agreement, guaranteed by Botswana, South Africa and Zimbabwe, providing for the restoration of Moshoeshoe II as reigning monarch and for the restitution of the elected organs of government; the commission of inquiry into Moshoeshoe's dethronement was to be abandoned; all those involved in the 'royal coup' were to be immune from prosecution; the political neutrality of the armed forces and public service was to be guaranteed, and consultations were to be undertaken with the aim of broadening the democratic process. Moshoeshoe was restored to the throne on 25 January 1995, undertaking not to interfere in politics. Letsie took the title of Crown Prince.

Meanwhile, in October 1994 Sekhonyana was ordered to pay a substantial fine (or be sentenced to two years' imprisonment), after being convicted of sedition and the incitement to violence of army and police troops against former LLA members earlier in the year. The director and another senior officer of the National Security Service (NSS) were held hostage by junior officers (who were demanding improved terms and conditions of service, as well as the officers' enforced retirement and prosecution on charges of attempted murder, corruption and breach of security laws) for two weeks in March 1995, and were released only after intervention by the Commonwealth Secretary-General. In September the human rights organization Amnesty International urged the Mokhehle Government to act to eliminate abuses of human rights by the security forces, condemning what it alleged were arbitrary arrests and incommunicado detentions, as well as the ill-treatment of detainees.

In April 1995 government representatives and military officials from Lesotho met with their counterparts from Botswana, South Africa and Zimbabwe to discuss progress in the restoration of constitutional order in Lesotho. The conference examined the recommendations of the commission of inquiry into the army mutiny of 1994: these included a streamlining of existing forces, a clearer definition of their functions, and improved training. In August a 5,000-strong demonstration was organized in Maseru to protest against proposed legislation to debar public servants from trade union membership and Mokhehle's plans to reduce earlier salary increases that were now said to have been granted in error.

King Moshoeshoe was killed in a motor accident on 15 January 1996. The College of Chiefs subsequently elected Crown Prince David to succeed his father, and the prince was restored to the throne, resuming the title King Letsie III, on 7 February. Letsie undertook not to involve the monarchy in any aspect of political life.

In February 1996 premises of the national radio service were seized by a small group that broadcast an apparently groundless statement that the Government had been overthrown. The alleged perpetrators of the 'false coup'—Makara Sekautu, the President of the opposition United Party, together with two former members of the Lesotho Defence Force (LDF, as the RLDF had been redesignated) and a former member of the NSS—were subsequently charged with high treason; in March 1997 three of the accused, including Sekautu, were given custodial sentences.

In February 1997 the LDF was mobilized to quell a rebellion at the police headquarters in Maseru. More than 100 police-officers were arrested, and 10 alleged leaders of the rebellion were remanded in custody on charges of sedition and contravention of internal security legislation. Further individuals were subsequently indicted, and charges of high treason added. Two of the instigators of the mutiny fled to South Africa, where they were subsequently granted political asylum. In July 2000 23 police-officers were convicted of sedition, two of contravention of internal security legislation and three acquitted on both counts. All of the accused were acquitted of high treason.

Meanwhile, in April 1997 the National Assembly approved legislation for a reduction in the age of eligibility to vote (from 21 to 18 years), and for the establishment of a three-member Independent Electoral Commission (IEC). In June, following a protracted struggle between rival factions for control of the party, Mokhehle resigned from the BCP and formed the Lesotho Congress for Democracy (LCD), to which he transferred executive power. Mokhehle's opponents denounced the move as a 'political coup', declaring that he should have resigned from the premiership and sought a dissolution of the National Assembly and new elections. However, some 38 members of the National Assembly joined the LCD. In July Molapo Qhobela was elected leader of the BCP. There was further controversy in August, when the Speaker of the National Assembly designated the BCP as the official opposition party. In October members of the Senate (most of whom apparently refused to recognize the legitimacy of Mokhehle's Government) voted to suspend discussion of proposed legislation, pending the King's response to appeals for the dissolution of the National Assembly. At the first annual conference of the LCD, held in January 1998, Mokhehle resigned as leader, and was made Honorary Life President of the party. In February Deputy Prime Minister Bethuel Pakalitha Mosisili was elected to succeed him as party leader. (Mokhehle died in January 1999.)

Elections to an expanded National Assembly took place on 23 May 1998. An application by the three main opposition parties—the BCP, the BNP and the Marematlou Freedom Party (MFP)—for a postponement of the poll, on the grounds that the IEC had not allowed sufficient time for parties to examine the electoral register, had been rejected by the High Court. The LCD secured an overwhelming victory, winning 78 of the Assembly's 80 seats (with some 60.7% of the votes cast); the BNP, which took one seat (with 24.5% of the votes), was the only other party to win representation. Voting for one seat was postponed, owing to the death of a candidate. The IEC and observers representing the Southern African Development Community (SADC, see p. 358) and the Commonwealth concluded that the polls had been generally free and fair. However, the opposition protested that the outcome of the poll reflected fraud on the part of the LCD, and demonstrations in Maseru to denounce the result were reportedly attended by thousands of activists. Mosisili was elected Prime Minister by the National Assembly in late May, and a new Government was appointed in June. At the end of June the BCP, the BNP and the MFP appealed to the High Court to annul the election results; in the following month the Court ordered the IEC to permit the opposition parties to inspect election documents.

In August 1998 opposition activists began a mass vigil outside the royal palace; within one week some 2,000 people were reported to have joined the protest against the outcome of the poll. Tensions escalated as LCD militants blocked access roads to the capital, in a stated attempt to prevent supplies of weapons to the protesters, while it was reported that a government official attempting to flee the country had been stoned to death after opening fire on an opposition blockade. Following consultations involving the Lesotho Government and the main opposition parties, with mediation by the Government of South Africa, Mosisili announced the establishment of an independent commission, comprising representatives of the SADC 'troika' of Botswana, South Africa and Zimbabwe, to investigate the conduct and results of the May election. The commission was to be chaired by Pius Langa, the Deputy President of South Africa's Constitutional Court.

Meanwhile, revelations that state funds had been used to purchase farmland for the Commander of the LDF, Lt-Gen. Makhula Mosakeng, fuelled opposition allegations of the Commander's complicity in corruption and vote-rigging. (Mosakeng stated that the land had been acquired for army, rather than personal, use.) Rumours of political divisions within the army were apparently confirmed in September 1998, when Mosakeng and several of his senior colleagues were detained by junior officers (who were reported to have been angered by the recent dismissal of an officer who had countermanded orders to disperse protesters by force). Mosakeng announced his resignation and stated that 26 members of the military command had been dismissed.

By mid-September 1998 frustration was evident at delays in releasing the report of the Langa Commission. Protesters marched to the government complex in Maseru (where the South African Minister of Defence was meeting with government representatives and army officers) and subsequently to the South African High Commissioner's residence. The blockade forced the closure of government offices, and essential public services were paralysed as civil servants reportedly joined the protest. The Langa Commission's report, which was finally released on 17 September, expressed serious concerns at apparent irregularities and discrepancies in the conduct of the May general election, but the Commission was 'unable to state that the invalidity of the elections had been conclusively established'. There was considerable confusion in the days following the publication of the report. Rumours that the Mosisili Government had been overthrown were denied; however, it was confirmed that Lesotho had appealed to SADC for assistance, in view of a breakdown in security. On 22 September an SADC peace-keeping force, initially comprising 600 South African troops and 200 from Botswana, entered Lesotho. In response to criticism that he had not consulted King Letsie prior to requesting external military assistance, Mosisili stated that the monarch had, by harbouring opposition protesters in the palace grounds, contributed to the instability that had necessitated SADC intervention. (It was subsequently reported that the King had been prevented from making a broadcast to the nation.) Within Lesotho, there was widespread outrage at what was perceived as an effective 'invasion' by South Africa, and the SADC force encountered unexpectedly strong resistance. There was sustained fighting between the intervention force and rebel units of the LDF before strategic points, including military bases and the Katse Dam (part of the LHWP essential to the supply of water to South Africa), were secured, while rioting in Maseru and other towns targeted in particular South African interests and caused widespread destruction. Mosakeng and his officers, who had fled to South Africa earlier in the month, returned to resume the army command on 24 September: Mosakeng stated that his resignation had been exacted under duress and, since it had not been approved by the King, was invalid. According to figures subsequently released by the Lesotho authorities, three days of fighting resulted in the deaths of 18 members of the LDF and of 47 civilians; nine members of the South African army were killed during the operation. In addition, as many as 4,000 refugees were reported to have crossed into South Africa.

Following meetings with representatives of the SADC 'troika', in early October 1998 it was reported that the LCD and the main opposition parties had agreed in principle that fresh elections should be held within 15–18 months. In the mean time, the IEC was to be restructured, and the electoral system was to be reviewed, with the aim of ensuring wider inclusion in political affairs (many parties felt that the simple majority voting system was incompatible with the nature of Lesotho's political evolution). Tensions again escalated after shots were fired at an LCD rally east of Maseru. The opposition denied claims by the ruling party of an attempt to assassinate the Prime Minister and his deputy, who were attending the rally; further violence at the meeting reportedly resulted in the deaths of two opposition activists. None the less, inter-party talks proceeded, and in mid-October agreement was reached on a transitional structure, designated the Interim Political Authority (IPA), to comprise representatives of 12 political parties, as well as government and parliamentary delegates, to oversee preparations for fresh elections to the National Assembly.

Shortly after the conclusion of this interim settlement it was announced that some 30 members of the LDF had been arrested on suspicion of involvement in the army rebellion of September 1998. Multi-party talks took place in Pretoria, South Africa, during November, but progress towards the establishment of the IPA was impeded after warrants were issued for the arrest, on murder charges, of several opposition activists, including two leading members of the BCP and BNP youth wings. The opposition parties stated that they would not co-operate in arrangements for the IPA until outstanding security matters, including the release of all rebel soldiers, had been expedited. A court martial in October 1999 ruled against the discharge of a total of 38 members of the LDF accused of mutiny.

The BNP leader, Evaristus Sekhonyana, died in November 1998. The party elected Justin Lekhanya to succeed him in March 1999. The withdrawal of the SADC intervention force was completed in May. This force was immediately succeeded by a new SADC mission, comprising some 300 military personnel from South Africa, Botswana and (subsequently) Zimbabwe, which remained until May 2000, assisting in the retraining and restructuring of the LDF.

Meanwhile, the 24-member IPA was inaugurated on 9 December 1998. After protracted consultations, the IPA announced in September 1999 that the number of seats in the National Assembly was to be increased by 50, to 130, effective from the elections scheduled for April 2000, with seats to be allocated according to a combination of proportional representation and simple majority voting. However, arbitration was required to resolve divisions within the IPA as to the number of seats to be decided by each method, and it was not until December 1999 that a Commonwealth-brokered agreement was signed, providing for 80 seats to be allocated on the basis of simple majority in single-member constituencies, and 50 by proportional representation. The mandate of the IPA was to be extended until elections took place. In the mean time, the Presidents of South Africa, Botswana, Mozambique and Zimbabwe, together with the UN, OAU and Commonwealth Secretaries-General, were to act as guarantors to ensure the implementation of the accord.

In February 2000 the IPA accused the Government of reneging on the December 1999 accord, after the LCD-dominated National Assembly voted to submit the proposed electoral changes to a referendum. Further arbitration concluded in May 2000 that the elections should proceed within 10–12 months. In July the IEC identified 26 May 2001 as the provisional date for the elections; however, delays in enacting legislation concerning voter registration and the electoral model caused the abandonment of this date.

In April 2000 the establishment of a commission of inquiry to investigate political events during July–November 1998 was announced. The commission, comprising three senior judges and chaired by Nigel Leon, met for the first time in June 2000 and heard evidence from several public figures. However, a number of opposition politicians criticized the commission, expressing doubts as to its impartiality. In August three LDF members were convicted by a court martial of participation in the mutiny of September 1998 and sentenced to a combined 29 years' imprisonment; a further 33 LDF members were convicted in November. The Leon commission of inquiry, which submitted its report to Prime Minister Mosisili in October 2001, rejected demands for a general amnesty to be granted to perpetrators of violence during the period under review, recommending the indictment of a number of opposition politicians and members of the armed forces. The commission also proposed measures aimed at ensuring the political neutrality of the armed forces and the police, and the establishment of an informal body, comprising the King, traditional chiefs and representatives of the armed forces, the police, the NSS, churches, political organizations, and the industrial and agricultural sectors, to discuss issues affecting Basotho.

In January 2001 a congress of the LCD re-elected Mosisili as leader of the party, for a five-year term. Shakhane Mokhehle, the incumbent and brother of the party's founder, was defeated in the election to the post of Secretary-General of the LCD by the Minister in the Prime Minister's Office, Sephiri Motanyane. In a minor cabinet reshuffle in July Mokhehle, who had disputed the results of the LCD elections, was dismissed as Minister of Justice, Human Rights and Rehabilitation, Law and Constitutional Affairs. Deputy Prime Minister Kelebone Maope resigned from the Government in September and broke away from the LCD, together with Mokhehle, to form a new opposition party, the Lesotho People's Congress (LPC), to prepare for forthcoming elections. By mid-October a total of 27 deputies had defected from the LCD to join the LPC, which was declared the main opposition party. Mosisili made new cabinet appointments in October, in an effort to consolidate his position ahead of the elections.

In mid-January 2002 a protracted dispute over the leadership of the BCP, which had been ongoing since the late 1990s, also appeared to be resolved, when the High Court ruled in favour of Tseliso Makhakhe's leadership of the party. Qhobela subsequently formed a new party, known as the Basutoland African Congress (BAC), which had been the name of the BCP in 1952–59.

Meanwhile, divisions over the electoral model, notably regarding the number of seats to be allocated by proportional representation, had continued to impede progress towards the elections in 2001. In January 2002 Parliament finally approved amendments to the electoral legislation, providing for the expansion of the National Assembly to 120 members, with 80 to be elected on a constituency basis and 40 selected by proportional representation.

The LCD won a resounding victory at the general election, which took place on 25 May 2002, retaining 77 of the 78 contested constituency seats, with 54.9% of the valid votes cast. The BNP became the second largest legislative party, securing 21 of the 40 seats allocated by proportional representation (known as compensatory seats), with 22.4% of the votes cast; the LPC won one constituency seat and four compensatory seats. Voting in two constituencies was postponed, owing to the deaths of candidates. Of the remaining 15 compensatory seats, the National Independent Party secured five, the BAC and the BCP both won three, while four smaller parties each took one seat. Mosisili was re-elected Prime Minister by the National Assembly in early June and a new Cabinet was subsequently appointed.

Meanwhile, the Government declared a state of famine in April 2002, following a period of severe weather conditions, which had damaged crop production; in December the UN World Food Programme estimated that about one-quarter of the population would require emergency food aid during 2003. The rate of infection with HIV/AIDS among people aged 15–49 stood at 28.9% at the end of 2003, one of the highest in the world. In January antiretroviral drugs became available to pregnant women infected with HIV in order to reduce mother-to-child transmission. It was estimated by the IMF that expenditure on the treatment of HIV/AIDS would amount to 3% of the country's gross domestic product by 2010.

In February 2004 the Government declared a state of emergency in response to severe food shortages following a prolonged period of drought; it was estimated that some 57,000 metric tons of food aid would be required to feed 600,000–700,000 people in 2004.

In mid-October 2004 a 30-member committee was established to direct a parliamentary reform programme; the committee was chaired by the leader of the Popular Front for Democracy, Lekhetho Rakuoane, and comprised government ministers and members of the National Assembly and the Senate. In mid-November the Cabinet was reshuffled: Monyane Moleleki was appointed Minister of Foreign Affairs and was replaced as Minister of Natural Resources by Dr 'Mamphono Khaketla, while the Deputy Prime Minister, Lesao Lehohola, also assumed the home affairs portfolio; the former Minister of Home Affairs, Thomas Thabane, became Minister of Communications, Science and Technology. Other notable changes included the appointment of Mothejoa Metsing as the Minister of Justice, Human Rights and Rehabilitation, Law and Constitutional Affairs, and the appointment of Mpeo Mahase-Moiloa as Minister of Employment and Labour.

In mid-February 2005, following an amendment to the Local Government Act in September 2004, the IEC announced that elections to local councils were to be held, for the first time, on 30 April 2005; the elections had initially been scheduled for 1998. Voting took place in 1,272 electoral divisions, of which some 390 were reserved for women candidates, in accordance with SADC guidelines. Over 1,000 new councillors were elected to 129 councils replacing previous councils comprising traditional leaders and government officials. The ruling LCD won over three-quarters of the seats; the rate of voter participation, recorded by the IEC at less than 30%, was officially attributed to the fact that it was the first such election to be held.

In late January 2006 the Minister of Foreign Affairs, Monyane Moleleki, was shot and wounded at his residence by unknown assailants. The motive for the shooting was unclear and no arrests were made; however, Moleleki was believed to be a possible candidate for the presidential elections in 2007. Also in late January 2006 Khauhelo Raditapole and Kelebone Maope, the leaders of the BAC and the LPC, respectively, announced that their parties would form an alliance, following appeals by the BCP for reconciliation between political parties. In his budget speech in early February the Minister of Finance and Development Planning, Timothy Thahane, announced that M30m. had been allocated towards the construction of a new parliament building.

As exemplified by South Africa's prominent role in the resolution of the 1994 constitutional crisis and by its intervention in the political crisis of September 1998, Lesotho's internal affairs continue to be strongly influenced by South Africa. Long-standing problems of border security and, in particular, the issue of disputed land in South Africa's Free State (formerly Orange Free State) have periodically caused friction between the two countries. During a two-day state visit to Lesotho in July 1995, President Nelson Mandela of South Africa advocated the pursuit of mutually-beneficial policies of regional integration, and he and Prime Minister Mokhehle agreed that the issue of sovereignty in Free State should be discussed by 'appropriate' authorities. Relations between the two countries were strained in August 2000 when Lesotho withdrew its support shortly before the scheduled signing of an agreement with Botswana, Namibia and South Africa on the management of water resources from the Orange river. In September an official at the South African High Commission was killed in Maseru. Representatives of both countries met in Pretoria in November and recommended increased co-operation in areas including education and criminal justice. During a visit to Lesotho by President Thabo Mbeki of South Africa in April 2001, it was agreed to replace an intergovernmental liaison committee that had been established following SADC intervention in 1998 (see above) with a joint binational commission at ministerial level, with the aim of enhancing bilateral relations. Relations between Lesotho and South Africa were further enhanced in May 2002, when their ministers of foreign affairs signed the Joint Bilateral Commission of Co-operation programme, which aimed to raise Lesotho from its current status as a 'least developed country' by 2007.

Government

Lesotho is an hereditary monarchy. Under the terms of the Constitution, which came into effect following the March 1993 election, the King, who is Head of State, has no executive or legislative powers. The College of Chiefs is theoretically empowered, under traditional law, to elect and depose the King by a majority vote. Executive power is vested in the Cabinet, which is headed by the Prime Minister. Legislative power is exercised by the National Assembly, which is elected, at intervals of no more than five years, by universal adult suffrage in the context of a multi-party political system. A system of mixed member proportional representation was introduced at the general election of May 2002, when the National Assembly was expanded to 120 members (80 elected by simple majority in single-member constituencies and 40 selected from party lists). The upper house, the Senate, comprises traditional chiefs and 11 nominated members. Lesotho comprises 10 administrative districts, each with an appointed district co-ordinator.

Defence

Military service is voluntary. The Lesotho Defence Force (LDF) comprised 2,000 men in August 2005, including an air wing of 110 men. The creation of a new commando force unit, the first professional unit in the LDF, was announced in October 2001, as part of ongoing efforts to restructure the armed forces. Projected budgetary expenditure on defence for 2005 was M210m.

Economic Affairs

In 2004, according to estimates by the World Bank, Lesotho's gross national income (GNI), measured at average 2002–04 prices, was US $1,336m., equivalent to $740 per head (or $3,210 per head on an international purchasing-power parity basis). During 1995–2004, it was estimated, the population increased at an average annual rate of 1.0%, while gross domestic product (GDP) per head increased, in real terms, by an average of 2.1% per year. Overall GDP increased, in real terms, at an average annual rate of 3.0% in 1995–2004; growth in 2004 was 3.0%.

Agriculture, forestry and fishing contributed 16.6% of GDP in 2004/05, and employed some 38.6% of the labour force in 2003. The principal agricultural exports are cereals and live animals. The main subsistence crops are maize, potatoes, wheat and sorghum. Lesotho remains a net importer of staple foodstuffs, largely owing to its vulnerability to adverse climatic conditions, especially drought. According to the World Food Programme, less than 10% of land is arable and there is no irrigation. It was estimated that the country might be able to produce only 10% of its cereal requirements in 2004. During 1995–2004 agricultural GDP increased at an average annual rate of 2.5%. Agricultural GDP decreased by 1.9% in 2003, but increased by 0.7% in 2004.

Industry (including mining, manufacturing, construction and power) provided 38.8% of GDP in 2004/05, and engaged 27.9% of the labour force in 1990. During 1995–2004 industrial GDP increased by an average of 4.0% per year. Industrial GDP increased by 2.6% in 2004.

Mining contributed 0.2% of GDP in 2004/05. Lesotho has reserves of diamonds, which during the late 1970s provided more than 50% of visible export earnings, but large-scale exploitation of these ceased in 1982. The Letseng-la Terai diamond mine reopened in April 2004 and by the time of its official inauguration in November gems with an estimated value of US $28m. had been recovered. Industrial mining at other sites was also envisaged, including a second diamond mine at Liqhobong. Lesotho also possesses deposits of uranium, lead and iron ore, and is believed to have petroleum deposits. According to the IMF, the GDP of the mining sector increased by an average of 23.6% per year in 1998/99–2004/05; growth in 2003/04 was 43.8% and growth in 2004/05 was 127.3%.

Manufacturing contributed 18.5% of GDP in 2004/05. During 1995–2004 manufacturing GDP increased by an average of 4.6% per year; growth in 2004 was 3.0%.

The Lesotho Highlands Water Project (LHWP) provides hydroelectricity sufficient for all Lesotho's needs and for export to South Africa; phases 1A and 1B were inaugurated in 1998 and 2004, respectively. In late September 2005 an agreement was signed for a feasibility study concerning the location of the second phase of the project. The scheme was expected to be completed by about 2030. The R200m. (US $30m.) that Lesotho receives annually in royalties from South Africa for the LHWP represents the country's largest single source of foreign exchange. Prior to the LHWP more than 90% of Lesotho's energy requirements were imported from South Africa. Imports of mineral fuels and lubricants comprised 6.2% of the total value of imports in 2001. Legislation providing for the privatization of the Lesotho Electricity Corporation was presented to the National Assembly in January 2005.

The services sector contributed 40.5% of GDP in 2004/05. During 1995–2004 the GDP of the services sector increased at an average annual rate of 2.9%. Services GDP increased by 3.9% in 2004.

In 2004/05 Lesotho recorded a visible trade deficit of M3,802m. and a deficit of M241m. on the current account of the balance of payments. In 2003 the principal source of imports (86.1%) was the Southern African Customs Union (SACU—i.e. chiefly South Africa—see below), which was also the second largest market for exports (19.4%), behind the USA (79.5%). The principal exports in that year were basic manufactures, clothing, foodstuffs and telecommunication equipment. The principal imports in 2001 were manufactured goods, food and live animals, and machinery and transport equipment.

In the financial year ending 31 March 2005 there was an overall budgetary surplus of M318m. (equivalent to 3.7% of GDP in that year). The 2006/07 budget projected a surplus of M277.8m. Lesotho's external debt totalled US $706.5m. at the end of 2003, of which $675.9m. was long-term public debt. In that year the cost of debt-servicing was equivalent to 8.8% of revenue from exports of goods and services. The annual rate of inflation averaged 7.8% in 1997–2004; consumer prices increased by 5.0% in 2004. It was estimated that 31.4% of the labour force were unemployed in July 2002. In 2004 an estimated 58,000 Basotho were employed as miners in South Africa compared with 129,000 in 1989. The number was expected to continue to decrease in the coming years. According to the Central Bank of Lesotho, in 2004 Basotho miners' remittances amounted to M1,795.0m. and accounted for more than 70% of total earnings during the period 1997–2004. South African officials estimated that around 300,000 Basotho were employed in South Africa at any given time.

Lesotho is a member of the Common Monetary Area (with Namibia, South Africa and Swaziland), and a member of SACU (with Botswana, Namibia, South Africa and Swaziland). Lesotho also belongs to the Southern African Development Community (SADC, see p. 358).

Impediments to economic development in Lesotho include vulnerability to drought and serious land shortages, combined with the country's dependence on South Africa (the Lesotho currency, the loti, is fixed at par with the South African rand, exposing Lesotho to fluctuations within the South African economy). By the late 1990s the strong growth that had prevailed for most of the decade was being eroded, while retrenchment in the South African gold-mining sector resulted in a marked decline in remittances from Basotho working abroad. An agreement was reached with South Africa in January 2001 to restructure bilateral economic relations and to increase mutual co-operation for economic development. In March the IMF approved a three-year loan of some US $31m., under the Poverty Reduction and Growth Facility, on condition that Lesotho encouraged private economic activity, limited the role of the public sector and strengthened fiscal stability. The textile industry benefited considerably from the USA's African Growth and Opportunities Act (AGOA), for which Lesotho was first declared eligible in April 2001; under its terms, textiles and clothing made in Lesotho had unlimited access to the US market, and by early 2002 exports of these products to the USA had increased by nearly 40%. Lesotho's qualification for the benefits of the AGOA attracted interest from foreign investors in Lesotho, notably Taiwanese textile manufacturers. However, faced with increasing competition from producers in Asia, between mid-2004 and January 2005 eight textile factories closed with the loss of more than 23,000 jobs. Nevertheless, the industry remained the largest employer in the country. (It was estimated that one-quarter of all textile workers were employed by Taiwanese-owned factories; in 2004 Taiwan was the largest foreign investor in Lesotho.) In early February 2006 the Minister of Finance and Development Planning, Timothy Thahane, stated that the Government would seek to diversify Lesotho's economy, promoting agriculture and 'agroprocessing', diamond and sandstone mining and tourism as possible alternatives. The announcement was made following the recommendations of a report by the IMF the previous December. However, with a view to protecting and developing the textile industry the Government also entered into discussions with the Government of the People's Republic of China regarding future co-operation and possible joint ventures. The rates of company tax and taxes paid by manufacturers were reduced as incentives to attract investors; and the decision to exempt exporters from company tax entirely was seen as a measure favouring textile producers in particular. Meanwhile, adverse weather conditions led to severe food shortages during 2002–04, and substantial external assistance was required as agricultural productivity declined; it was estimated that almost one-quarter of the country's population urgently required emergency food aid. Furthermore, the country also faced ongoing difficulties as a result of the high level of HIV/AIDS infection among the population. In 2003 Lesotho had the third highest prevalence of HIV/AIDS in the world, affecting one in three adults in the country. Some 100,000 children had been orphaned as a result of the pandemic.

Education

As part of an initiative begun in 2000, all primary education is available free of charge, provided mainly by the three main Christian missions (Lesotho Evangelical, Roman Catholic and Anglican), under the direction of the Ministry of Education. Officially, primary education is compulsory for seven years between six and 13 years of age. Secondary education, beginning at the age of 13, lasts for up to five years, comprising a first cycle of three years and a second of two years. Of children in the relevant age-groups in 2000/01, 78% (males 75%; females 82%) were enrolled at primary schools, while only 21% (males 16%; females 26%) were enrolled at secondary schools. Some 3,266 students were enrolled at the National University of Lesotho, at Roma, in 2002. Proposed expenditure on education under the 2006/07 budget was M927.4m. (representing more than 20% of total government expenditure). In January 2006 17 new schools constructed with the assistance of the Government of Japan were opened; they were expected to accommodate some 14,000 pupils.

Public Holidays

2006: 1 January (New Year's Day), 11 March (Moshoeshoe Day), 14–17 April (Easter), 1 May (Workers' Day), 25 May (Ascension Day), 25 May (Africa Day and Heroes' Day), 17 July (King's Birthday), 4 October (National Independence Day), 25 December (Christmas Day), 26 December (Boxing Day).

2007: 1 January (New Year's Day), 11 March (Moshoeshoe Day), 6–9 April (Easter), 1 May (Workers' Day), 17 May (Ascension Day), 25 May (Africa Day and Heroes' Day), 17 July (King's Birthday), 4 October (National Independence Day), 25 December (Christmas Day), 26 December (Boxing Day).

Weights and Measures

The metric system of weights and measures is in force.

Statistical Survey

Sources (unless otherwise stated): Bureau of Statistics, POB 455, Maseru 100; tel. 22323852; fax 22310177; internet www.bos.gov.ls; Central Bank of Lesotho, POB 1184, Maseru 100; tel. 22314281; fax 22310051; e-mail cbl@centralbank.org.ls; internet www.centralbank.org.ls.

Area and Population

AREA, POPULATION AND DENSITY

Area (sq km)	30,355*
Population (census results)†	
12 April 1986 (provisional)	1,447,000
14 April 1996	1,841,967
Population (demographic survey result)	
8 April 2001	2,157,580
Density (per sq km) at demographic survey of 2001	71.1

* 11,720 sq miles.
† Excluding absentee workers in South Africa, numbering 152,627 (males 129,088, females 23,539) in 1976.

DISTRICTS

(*de jure* population at 2001 demographic survey, provisional)

District	Population
Berea	300,557
Butha-Buthe	126,907
Leribe	362,339
Mafeteng	238,946
Maseru	477,599
Mohale's Hoek	206,842
Mokhotlong	89,705
Qacha's Nek	80,323
Quthing	140,641
Thaba-Tseka	133,680
Total	**2,157,539**

PRINCIPAL TOWNS

(population at 1986 census)

Maseru (capital)	109,400	Hlotse		9,600
Maputsoa	20,000	Mohale's Hoek		8,500
Teyateyaneng	14,300	Quthing		6,000
Mafeteng	12,700			

Source: Stefan Helders, *World Gazetteer* (www.world-gazetteer.com).

Mid-2003 (UN estimate, including suburbs): Maseru, population 169,554 (Source: UN, *World Urbanization Prospects: The 2003 Revision*).

BIRTHS AND DEATHS

(UN estimates, annual averages)

	1990–95	1995–2000	2000–05
Birth rate (per 1,000)	33.2	30.2	28.5
Death rate (per 1,000)	10.9	15.1	23.6

Source: UN, *World Population Prospects: The 2004 Revision*.

Expectation of life (WHO estimates, years at birth): 38 (males 35; females 40) in 2003 (Source: WHO, *World Health Report*).

ECONOMICALLY ACTIVE POPULATION

(ILO estimates, '000 persons at mid-1990)

	Males	Females	Total
Agriculture, etc.	130	150	280
Industry	183	13	196
Manufacturing	8	7	15
Services	134	91	225
Total	**447**	**254**	**701**

1997 (household survey, '000 persons aged 15 years and over): Total employed 353.1 (males 197.3, females 155.8); Unemployed 215.9 (males 80.2, females 135.7).

Source: ILO.

Mid-2003 (estimates in '000): Agriculture, etc. 278; Total 721 (Source: FAO).

Health and Welfare

KEY INDICATORS

Total fertility rate (children per woman, 2003)	3.8
Under-5 mortality rate (per 1,000 live births, 2004)	84
HIV/AIDS (% of persons aged 15–49, 2003)	28.9
Physicians (per 1,000 head, 1995)	0.05
Health expenditure (2002): US $ per head (PPP)	119
Health expenditure (2002): % of GDP	6.2
Health expenditure (2002): public (% of total)	84.9
Access to water (% of persons, 2002)	76
Access to sanitation (% of persons, 2002)	37
Human Development Index (2003): ranking	149
Human Development Index (2003): value	0.497

For sources and definitions, see explanatory note on p. vi.

Agriculture

PRINCIPAL CROPS
('000 metric tons)

	2002	2003	2004*
Wheat	44.6	51*	51
Maize	111.1	82.1	150.0
Sorghum	38.3	46*	46
Potatoes*	90	90	90
Dry beans	6.9	8*	8
Dry peas	3	3.0	3.4
Vegetables*	18	18	18
Fruit*	13	13	13

* FAO estimate(s).
Source: FAO.

LIVESTOCK
('000 head, year ending September)

	1999	2000*	2001*
Cattle	571	560	540
Sheep	936	850	850
Goats	730	650	650
Pigs*	63	65	65
Horses*	98	100	100
Asses*	152	154	154
Mules*	1	1	1
Poultry*	1,700	1,800	1,800

* FAO estimates.
2002–04: Figures assumed to be unchanged from 2001 (FAO estimates).
Source: FAO.

LIVESTOCK PRODUCTS
(FAO estimates, '000 metric tons)

	1999	2000	2001
Cows' milk	23.0	23.8	23.8
Beef and veal	9.1	8.5	8.7
Mutton and lamb	3.3	3.1	3.1
Goat meat	2.2	1.9	1.9
Pig meat	2.7	2.8	2.8
Poultry meat	1.7	1.8	1.8
Game meat	3.8	3.9	3.9
Hen eggs	1.4	1.5	1.5
Cattle hides (fresh)	2.0	1.8	1.9
Wool (greasy)	2.4	2.6	2.6
Wool (scoured)	1.4	1.5	1.5

2002–04: Production assumed to be unchanged from 2001 (FAO estimates).
Source: FAO.

Forestry

ROUNDWOOD REMOVALS
(FAO estimates, '000 cubic metres, excluding bark)

	2002	2003	2004
Total (all fuel wood)	2,034.3	2,040.4	2,046.6

Source: FAO.

Fishing

(metric tons, live weight)

	1999*	2000*	2001
Capture	30	32	24
Common carp	18	20	8
North African catfish	2	2	2
Other freshwater fishes	10	10	14
Aquaculture	4	8	8
Common carp	4	8	8
Total catch	34	40	32

* FAO estimates.
2002–03: Figures assumed to be unchanged from 2001 (FAO estimates).
Source: FAO.

Mining

(cubic metres, unless otherwise indicated)

	2002	2003	2004*
Fire clay	42,000	14,470	15,000
Diamond (carats)	721	2,099	4,000
Gravel and crushed rock	261,037	389,695	300,000

* Estimates.
Source: US Geological Survey.

Finance

CURRENCY AND EXCHANGE RATES

Monetary Units
100 lisente (singular: sente) = 1 loti (plural: maloti).

Sterling, Dollar and Euro Equivalents (30 December 2005)

£1 sterling = 10.891 maloti;
US $1 = 6.325 maloti;
€1 = 7.462 maloti;
1,000 maloti = £91.82 = $158.10 = €134.02.

Average Exchange Rate (maloti per US $)
2003   7.5648
2004   6.4597
2005   6.3593

Note: The loti is fixed at par with the South African rand.

LESOTHO

Statistical Survey

BUDGET
(million maloti, year ending 31 March)

Revenue*	2002/03	2003/04	2004/05
Tax revenue	2,576	2,888	3,376
Customs duties	1,470	1,422	2,012
Taxes on net income and profits	1,106	1,466	1,364
Individual income tax	663	853	729
Sales tax	344	519	542
Oil levy	86	81	36
Other tax revenues	13	14	57
Non-tax revenue	459	552	480
Water royalties	213	193	195
Total	3,035	3,439	3,856

Expenditure and net lending	2002/03	2003/04	2004/05
Wages and salaries	1,082	1,123	1,177
Interest payments	220	216	156
Foreign debt	110	91	91
Goods, services and transfers	1,555	1,590	1,765
Transfers and subsidies	509	631	779
Capital expenditure (incl. lending minus repayments)	802	625	665
Total	3,659	3,555	3,762

* Excluding grants received (million maloti): 296.3 in 2002/03; 178 in 2003/04; 224 in 2004/05.

Source: partly IMF, *Kingdom of Lesotho: Selected Issues and Statistical Appendix* (December 2005).

INTERNATIONAL RESERVES
(US $ million at 31 December)

	2002	2003	2004
IMF special drawing rights	0.60	0.63	0.62
Reserve position in IMF	4.82	5.26	5.53
Foreign exchange	400.95	454.44	496.67
Total	406.37	460.33	502.82

Source: IMF, *International Financial Statistics*.

MONEY SUPPLY
(million maloti at 31 December)

	2002	2003	2004
Currency outside banks	179.68	183.52	204.54
Demand deposits at commercial banks	1,099.15	1,185.21	1,197.50
Total money (incl. others)	1,440.94	1,537.75	1,589.42

Source: IMF, *International Financial Statistics*.

COST OF LIVING
(Consumer Price Index; base: April 1997 = 100)

	2002	2003	2004
Food (incl. non-alcoholic beverages)	166.1	173.8	181.2
Alcoholic beverages and tobacco	157.6	173.3	189.3
Housing, fuel and light	142.9	155.9	164.5
Clothing (incl. footwear)	138.8	144.8	149.0
All items (incl. others)	150.1	161.3	169.4

NATIONAL ACCOUNTS
(million maloti at current prices)

National Income and Product

	2002/03	2003/04	2004/05
Gross domestic product (GDP) at factor cost	6,796.2	7,424.2	7,777.4
Indirect taxes, less subsidies	767.4	826.9	866.6
GDP in market prices	7,563.6	8,251.2	8,644.0
Net factor income from abroad	1,739.7	1,932.8	2,057.1
Gross national product (GNP)	9,303.2	10,184.0	10,701.1
Net current transfers from abroad	1,297.4	1,290.8	1,734.9
Gross national disposable income	10,600.6	11,474.8	12,436.0

Gross Domestic Product by Economic Activity

	2002/03	2003/04	2004/05
Agriculture	1,202.2	1,312.5	1,345.9
Mining and quarrying	10.4	11.9	16.0
Manufacturing and handicraft	1,372.9	1,456.9	1,499.1
Electricity and water	350.6	366.7	388.5
Construction	1,121.8	1,230.6	1,243.0
Wholesale and retail trade	670.2	784.8	838.3
Restaurants and hotels	113.3	149.1	158.3
Transport and storage	156.6	168.7	179.1
Post and telecommunications	134.0	168.5	179.4
Financial intermediation and insurance	355.2	390.6	448.8
Real estate and business services	116.8	125.6	130.0
Ownership of dwellings	258.3	264.9	276.2
Public administration	501.3	542.4	575.1
Education	540.7	573.4	616.8
Health and social work	115.7	123.8	129.7
Other services	78.9	84.5	87.6
Sub-total	7,098.9	7,754.9	8,111.8
Less Imputed bank service charge	302.5	330.7	334.5
GDP at factor cost	6,796.2	7,424.2	7,777.4
Indirect taxes, less subsidies	767.4	826.9	866.6
GDP at market prices	7,563.6	8,251.2	8,644.0

Source: partly IMF, *Kingdom of Lesotho: Selected Issues and Statistical Appendix* (December 2005).

BALANCE OF PAYMENTS
(million maloti)

	2002/03	2003/04	2004/05
Exports of goods f.o.b.	3,714	3,610	4,292
Imports of goods f.o.b.	−7,938	−7,440	−8,095
Trade balance	−4,225	−3,830	−3,802
Services (net)	−218	−281	−231
Balance on goods and services	−4,443	−4,111	−4,033
Income (net)	1,740	1,933	2,057
Balance on goods, services and income	−2,703	−2,178	−1,976
Current transfers (net)	1,297	1,291	1,735
Current balance	−1,406	−887	−241
Capital account (net)	173	118	134
Financial account (net)	2,001	1,082	9
Net errors and omissions	75	64	39
Overall balance	843	377	−59

Source: partly IMF, *Kingdom of Lesotho: Selected Issues and Statistical Appendix* (December 2005).

External Trade

PRINCIPAL COMMODITIES
(distribution by SITC, million maloti)

Imports c.i.f.*	1999	2000	2001
Food and live animals	787.8	928.7	768.7
Beverages and tobacco	33.7	115.6	386.6
Crude materials, inedible except fuels	177.7	228.6	167.7
Mineral fuels and lubricants	323.7	840.8	317.0
Animal and vegetable oils, fats and waxes	54.2	104.2	67.0
Chemicals and related products	309.4	254.6	525.1
Manufactured goods	715.6	558.7	1,026.5
Machinery and transport equipment	674.6	426.4	620.0
Miscellaneous manufactured articles	458.5	486.7	797.3
Total (incl. others)	3,888.5	4,236.2	5,119.1

* Unrevised figures.

Exports	2002	2003	2004
Foodstuffs, etc.	197.6	194.0	180.8
Cereals	75.7	71.2	55.2
Beverages and tobacco	94.9	96.5	98.5
Live animals	20.4	20.4	16.8
Livestock materials	64.6	90.3	3.3
Wool	56.1	80.6	1.8
Manufactures	3,439.8	3,238.1	4,433.3
Chemicals and petroleum	45.5	49.3	21.0
Telecommunication equipment	291.7	289.7	153.6
Machinery	50.0	53.9	55.1
Furniture and parts	37.4	33.1	2.9
Clothing, etc.	2,745.2	2,555.6	3,462.0
Footwear	135.1	130.5	128.7
Other manufactures	39.8	35.2	566.8
Total (incl. others)	3,739.9	3,557.4	4,652.2

Source: partly IMF, *Kingdom of Lesotho: Selected Issues and Statistical Appendix* (December 2005).

PRINCIPAL TRADING PARTNERS
(million maloti)

Imports c.i.f.*	2001	2002	2003
Africa	5,306.0	6,270.3	7,242.7
SACU†	5,296.6	6,261.7	7,234.1
Asia	953.3	2,021.6	1,141.7
China, People's Repub.	74.2	355.7	241.8
Hong Kong	224.3	483.8	401.3
Taiwan	527.1	913.2	367.6
European Union	44.5	82.5	8.9
North America	41.7	53.4	15.1
Canada	34.5	12.1	0.6
USA	7.2	41.3	14.5
Total (incl. others)	6,399.8	8,517.5	8,411.6

Exports f.o.b.	2001	2002	2003
Africa	899.1	856.4	695.6
SACU†	897.0	856.0	689.7
North America	1,522.5	2,874.6	2,849.1
Canada	35.0	15.9	19.7
USA	1,487.5	2,858.7	2,829.4
Total (incl. others)	2,426.0	3,739.9	3,557.3

* Valuation exclusive of import duties. Figures also exclude donated food.
† Southern African Customs Union, of which Lesotho is a member; also including Botswana, Namibia, South Africa and Swaziland.

Source: partly IMF, *Kingdom of Lesotho: Selected Issues and Statistical Appendix* (December 2005).

Transport

ROAD TRAFFIC
(estimates, motor vehicles in use at 31 December)

	1994	1995	1996
Passenger cars	9,900	11,160	12,610
Lorries and vans	20,790	22,310	25,000

Source: International Road Federation, *World Road Statistics*.

CIVIL AVIATION
(traffic on scheduled services)

	1997	1998	1999
Kilometres flown (million)	0	1	0
Passengers carried ('000)	10	28	1
Passenger-km (million)	3	9	0
Total ton-km (million)	0	1	0

Source: UN, *Statistical Yearbook*.

Tourism

FOREIGN TOURIST ARRIVALS BY COUNTRY OF RESIDENCE

	2001	2002	2003
Germany	1,289	1,256	25,991
Ireland	504	492	10,173
South Africa	280,371	273,365	225,549
UK	1,957	1,908	39,470
Total (incl. others)	294,644	287,280	360,955

Tourism receipts (US $ million, excl. passenger transport): 24 in 2000; 23 in 2001; 20 in 2002.

Source: World Tourism Organization.

Communications Media

	2002	2003	2004
Telephones ('000 main lines in use)	28.6	35.1	37.2
Mobile cellular telephones ('000 subscribers)	96.8	101.5	159.0
Internet users ('000)	21	30	43

Facsimile machines (number in use, year ending 31 March 1996): 569.
Radio receivers ('000 in use): 104 in 1997.
Television receivers ('000 in use): 70 in 2001.
Daily newspapers (1998): 2 (estimated average circulation 15,750 copies).
Non-daily newspapers (1996): 7 (average circulation 74,000 copies).

Sources: UNESCO Institute for Statistics; International Telecommunication Union.

Education

(2002)

	Institutions	Teachers	Students Males	Students Females	Total
Primary	1,333	8,908	209,024	209,644	418,668
Secondary: general	224	3,384	35,467	45,663	81,130
technical and vocational	8	172	1,040	818	1,859
teacher training	1	108	1,206	533	1,739
University	1	n.a.	1,567	1,699	3,266

Adult literacy rate (UNESCO estimates): 81.4% (males 73.7%; females 90.3%) in 2003 (Source: UN Development Programme, *Human Development Report*).

Directory

The Constitution

The Constitution of the Kingdom of Lesotho, which took effect at independence in October 1966, was suspended in January 1970. A new Constitution was promulgated following the March 1993 general election. Its main provisions, with subsequent amendments, are summarized below:

Lesotho is an hereditary monarchy. The King, who is Head of State, has no executive or legislative powers. Executive authority is vested in the Cabinet, which is headed by the Prime Minister, while legislative power is exercised by the 120-member National Assembly, which comprises 80 members elected on a single-member constituency basis and 40 selected by a system of proportional representation. The National Assembly is elected, at intervals of no more than five years, by universal adult suffrage in the context of a multi-party political system. There is also a Senate, comprising 22 traditional chiefs and 11 nominated members. The Prime Minister is the official head of the armed forces.

The Government

HEAD OF STATE

King: HM King LETSIE III (acceded to the throne 7 February 1996).

CABINET
(March 2006)

Prime Minister and Minister of Defence and National Security: BETHUEL PAKALITHA MOSISILI.
Deputy Prime Minister and Minister of Home Affairs and Public Safety: ARCHIBALD LESAO LEHOHLA.
Minister of Education and Training: MOHLABI KENNETH TSEKOA.
Minister of Local Government: Dr PONTŠO SUZAN 'MATUMELO SEKATLE.
Minister of Tourism, Environment and Culture: LEBOHANG NTŠINYI.
Minister of Natural Resources (Water, Lesotho Water Highlands Project, Energy, Mining and Technology): Dr 'MAMPHONO KHAKETLA.
Minister of Foreign Affairs: MONYANE MOLELEKI.
Minister of Trade, Industry, Co-operatives and Marketing: MPHO MALIE.
Minister of Agriculture and Food Security: Dr RAKORO PHORORO.
Minister of Forestry and Land Reclamation: LINCOLN RALECHATE 'MOKOSE.
Minister of Communications, Science and Technology: MOTSOAHAE THOMAS THABANE.
Minister of Public Works and Transport: POPANE LEBESA.
Minister of Gender, Youth, Sports and Recreation: 'MATHABISO LEPONO.
Minister of Finance and Development Planning: Dr TIMOTHY THAHANE.
Minister of Health and Social Welfare: Dr MOTLOHELOA PHOOKO.
Minister of Employment and Labour: MPEO MAHASE-MOILOA.
Minister of Justice, Human Rights and Rehabilitation, Law and Constitutional Affairs: REFILOE M. MASEMENE.
Minister in the Prime Minister's Office: RAMMOTSI LEHATA.
There were also five assistant ministers.

MINISTRIES

Office of the Prime Minister: POB 527, Maseru 100; tel. 22311000; fax 22310578; internet www.lesotho.gov.ls.
Ministry of Agriculture and Food Security: POB 24, Maseru 100; tel. 22316407; fax 22310906.
Ministry of Communications, Science and Technology: POB 36, Maseru 100; tel. 22323561; fax 22310264.
Ministry of Defence and National Security: POB 527, Maseru 100; tel. 22316570; fax 22310518.
Ministry of Education and Training: POB 47, Maseru 100; tel. 22323956; fax 22310206; e-mail kokomen@education.gov.ls.
Ministry of Employment and Labour: Private Bag A116, Maseru 100; tel. 22322602; fax 22310374.
Ministry of Finance and Development Planning: POB 395, Maseru 100; tel. 22311101; fax 22310964.
Ministry of Foreign Affairs: POB 1387, Maseru 100; tel. 22311150; fax 22310642.
Ministry of Forestry and Land Reclamation: POB 24, Maseru 100; tel. 22316407; fax 22310146.
Ministry of Gender, Youth, Sports and Recreation: POB 10993, Maseru 100; tel. 22311006; fax 22310506.
Ministry of Health and Social Welfare: POB 514, Maseru 100; tel. 22314404; fax 22310467.
Ministry of Home Affairs and Public Safety: POB 174, Maseru 100; tel. 22323771; fax 22310319.
Ministry of Justice, Human Rights and Rehabilitation, Law and Constitutional Affairs: POB 402, Maseru 100; tel. 22322683; fax 22311092; e-mail ps@justice.gov.ls.
Ministry of Local Government: POB 174, Maseru 100; tel. 22323771; fax 22310587.
Ministry of Natural Resources: POB 772, Maseru 100; tel. 22323163; fax 22310520.
Ministry of Public Service and Parliamentary Affairs: POB 527, Maseru 100; tel. 22311000.
Ministry of Public Works and Transport: POB 20, Maseru 100; tel. 22311362; fax 22310125.
Ministry of Tourism, Environment and Culture: POB 52, Maseru 100; tel. 22313034; fax 22310194; e-mail ps@tourism.gov.ls.
Ministry of Trade, Industry, Co-operatives and Marketing: POB 747, Maseru 100; tel. 22312938; fax 22310644.

Legislature

PARLIAMENT

National Assembly

POB 190, Maseru; tel. 22323035.
Speaker: NTLHOI MOTSAMAI.

General Election, 25 May 2002

Party	Constituency seats	Compensatory seats*	Total seats
Lesotho Congress for Democracy	77	—	77
Basotho National Party	—	21	21
Lesotho People's Congress	1	4	5
National Independent Party	—	5	5
Basotho Congress Party	—	3	3
Basutoland African Congress	—	3	3
Lesotho Workers' Party	—	1	1
Maremalou Freedom Party	—	1	1
National Progressive Party	—	1	1
Popular Front for Democracy	—	1	1
Total	78†	40	118†

* Allocated by proportional representation.
† Voting in two constituencies was postponed, owing to the deaths of candidates.

Senate

POB 190, Maseru; tel. 22315338.
Speaker: Chief SEMPE LEJAHA.
The Senate is an advisory chamber, comprising 22 traditional chiefs and 11 members appointed by the monarch.

Election Commission

Independent Electoral Commission (IEC): POB 12698, Maseru; tel. 314991; fax 310398; f. 1997 as successor to the Constituency Delimitation Commission; Chair. LESHELE THOHLANE.

Political Organizations

Basotho Congress Party (BCP): POB 111, Maseru 100; tel. 8737076; f. 1952; Leader NTSUKUNYANE MPHANYA.
Basotho Democratic Alliance (BDA): Maseru; f. 1984; Pres. S. C. NKOJANE.

LESOTHO

Basotho National Party (BNP): POB 124, Maseru 100; f. 1958; Leader Maj.-Gen. JUSTIN METSING LEKHANYA; Sec.-Gen. RANTHOMENG MATETE; 280,000 mems.

Basutoland African Congress (BAC): Maseru; f. 2002 following split in the BCP; Leader Dr KHAUHELO RADITAPOLE; Sec.-Gen. MAHOLELA MANDORO.

Khokanyana-Phiri Democratic Alliance: Maseru; f. 1999; alliance of opposition parties comprising:

Christian Democratic Party: Maseru.

Communist Party of Lesotho (CPL): Maseru; f. 1962; banned 1970–91; supported mainly by migrant workers employed in South Africa; Sec.-Gen. MOKHAFISI KENA.

Kopanang Basotho Party (KBP): Maseru; f. 1992; campaigns for women's rights; Leader LIMAKATSO NTAKATSANE.

National Independent Party (NIP): Maseru; f. 1984; Pres. ANTHONY CLOVIS MANYELI.

National Progressive Party (NPP): Maseru; f. 1995 following split in the BNP; Leader Chief PEETE NKOEBE PEETE.

Popular Front for Democracy (PFD): Maseru; f. 1991; left-wing; Leader LEKHETHO RAKUOANE.

Social Democratic Party: Maseru; Leader MASITISE SELESO.

Lesotho Congress for Democracy (LCD): Maseru; f. 1997 as a result of divisions within the BCP; Leader BETHUEL PAKALITHA MOSISILI; Chair. MOEKETSI MOLETSANE; Sec.-Gen. MPHO MALIE; 200,000 mems.

Lesotho Labour Party (LLP): Maseru; f. 1991; Leader MUTHUTHULEZI TYHALI.

Lesotho People's Congress (LPC): f. 2001 following split in the LCD; Leader KELEBONE ALBERT MAOPE; Sec.-Gen. SHAKHANE MOKHEHLE.

Lesotho Workers' Party (LWP): f. 2001; Leader MACAEFA BILLY.

Marematlou Freedom Party (MFP): POB 0443, Maseru 105; tel. 315804; f. 1962 following merger between the Marema Tlou Party and Basutoland Freedom Party; Leader (vacant); Dep. Leader THABO LEANYA; 300,000 mems.

Sefate Democratic Union (SDU): Maseru; Leader BOFIHLA NKUEBE.

United Democratic Party (UDP): POB 776, Maseru 100; f. 1967; Chair. BEN L. SHEA; Leader CHARLES DABENDE MOFELI; Sec.-Gen. MOLOMO NKUEBE; 26,000 mems.

United Party (UP): Maseru; Pres. MAKARA SEKAUTU.

Diplomatic Representation

EMBASSIES AND HIGH COMMISSIONS IN LESOTHO

China, People's Republic: POB 380, Maseru 100; tel. 22316521; fax 22310489; Ambassador QIU BOHUA.

Korea, Republic: Maseru; Ambassador EUN SOO KIM.

South Africa: Lesotho Bank Tower, 10th Floor, Kingsway, Private Bag A266, Maseru 100; tel. 22325758; fax 22310128; e-mail sahcmas@leo.co.ls; High Commissioner WILLIAM LESLIE.

USA: 254 Kingsway, POB 333, Maseru 100; tel. 22312666; fax 22310116; e-mail infomaseru@state.gov; internet maseru.usembassy.gov; Ambassador JUNE CARTER PERRY.

Judicial System

HIGH COURT

The High Court is a superior court of record, and in addition to any other jurisdiction conferred by statute it is vested with unlimited original jurisdiction to determine any civil or criminal matter. It also has appellate jurisdiction to hear appeals and reviews from the subordinate courts. Appeals may be made to the Court of Appeal.

POB 90, Maseru; tel. 22312188.

Chief Justice: MAHAPELA LEHOHLA.

Judges: T. NOMNGCONGO, W. C. M. MAQUTU, B. K. MOLAI, T. E. MONAPATHI, K. MAFOSO-GUNI, G. MOFOLO, S. PEETE, M. HLAJOANE, N. MAJARA.

COURT OF APPEAL

POB 90, Maseru; tel. 22312188.

President: J. H. STEYN.

Judges: M. M. RAMODIBEDI, M. E. KUMBLEBEN, H. GROSSKOPF, C. PLEWMAN, J. J. GAUNTLETT, L. S. MELUNSKY (acting).

SUBORDINATE COURTS

Each of the 10 districts possesses subordinate courts, presided over by magistrates.

Chief Magistrate: MOLEFI MAKARA.

JUDICIAL COMMISSIONERS' COURTS

These courts hear civil and criminal appeals from central and local courts. Further appeal may be made to the High Court and finally to the Court of Appeal.

CENTRAL AND LOCAL COURTS

There are 71 such courts, of which 58 are local courts and 13 are central courts which also serve as courts of appeal from the local courts. They have limited civil and criminal jurisdiction.

Religion

About 90% of the population profess Christianity.

CHRISTIANITY

African Federal Church Council (AFCC): POB 70, Peka 340; f. 1927; co-ordinating org. for 48 African independent churches.

Christian Council of Lesotho (CCL): POB 547, Maseru 100; tel. 22313639; fax 22310310; e-mail ccl@email.co.ls; f. 1833; 112 congregations; 261,350 mems (2003); Chair. Rev. M. MOKHOSI; Sec. CATHERINE RAMOKHELE.

The Anglican Communion

Anglicans in Lesotho are adherents of the Church of the Province of Southern Africa. The Metropolitan of the Province is the Archbishop of Cape Town, South Africa. Lesotho forms a single diocese, with an estimated 200,000 members.

Bishop of Lesotho: Rt Rev. JOSEPH MAHAPU TSUBELLA, Bishop's House, POB 87, Maseru 100; tel. 22311974; fax 22310161; e-mail diocese@ilesotho.com.

The Roman Catholic Church

Lesotho comprises one archdiocese and three dioceses. At 31 December 2003 there were some 973,436 adherents of the Roman Catholic Church, equivalent to an estimated 53.7% of the total population.

Lesotho Catholic Bishops' Conference
Catholic Secretariat, POB 200, Maseru 100; tel. 22312525; fax 22310294; f. 1972; Pres. Rt Rev. EVARISTUS THATHO BITSOANE (Bishop of Qacha's Nek).

Archbishop of Maseru: Most Rev. BERNARD MOHLALISI, Archbishop's House, 19 Orpen Rd, POB 267, Maseru 100; tel. 22312565; fax 22310425; e-mail archmase@lesoff.co.za.

Other Christian Churches

At mid-2000 there were an estimated 279,000 Protestants and 257,000 adherents professing other forms of Christianity.

African Methodist Episcopal Church: POB 223, Maseru 100; tel. 22311801; fax 22310416; f. 1903; Presiding Prelate Rev. DANIEL RANTLE; 11,295 mems.

Lesotho Evangelical Church: POB 260, Maseru 100; tel. 22323942; f. 1833; independent since 1964; Pres. Rev. JOHN RAPELANG MOKHAHLANE; Exec. Sec. Rev. A. M. THEBE; 230,000 mems (2003).

Other denominations active in Lesotho include the Apostolic Faith Mission, the Assemblies of God, the Dutch Reformed Church in Africa, the Full Gospel Church of God, Methodist Church of Southern Africa and the Seventh-day Adventists. There are also numerous African independent churches.

BAHÁ'Í FAITH

National Spiritual Assembly: POB 508, Maseru 100; tel. 22312346; fax 22310092; mems resident in 444 localities.

The Press

Leseli ka Sepolesa (The Police Witness): Press Dept, Police Headquarters, Maseru CBD, POB 13, Maseru 100; tel. 22317262; fax 22310045; fortnightly; Sesotho; publ. by the Lesotho Mounted Police Services.

Leselinyana la Lesotho (Light of Lesotho): Morija Printing Works, POB 190, Morija; tel. 22360244; fax 22360005; f. 1863; fortnightly; Sesotho, with occasional articles in English; publ. by Lesotho Evangelical Church; Editor MOOKHO GRACE KOBELI; circ. 10,000.

LESOTHO

Lesotho Today/Lentsoe la Basotho (Voice of the Lesotho Nation): Lesotho News Agency Complex, Lerotholi St, POB 36, Maseru 100; tel. 22323561; fax 22322764; f. 1974; weekly; Sesotho; publ. by Ministry of Communications, Science and Technology; Editor Kahliso Lesenyane; circ. 14,000.

Makatolle: POB 111, Maseru 100; tel. 22850990; f. 1963; weekly; Sesotho; Editor M. Ramangoei; circ. 2,000.

The Mirror/Setsomi sa Litaba: Mothamo House, First Floor, POB 903, Maseru 100; tel. 22323208; fax 22320941; f. 1986; weekly; English and Sesotho; Owner Tebello Pitso-Hlohlongoane; Editor Nat Molomo; circ. 4,000.

MoAfrika: CR Communications, Carlton Centre Bldg, First Floor, POB 7234, Maseru 100; tel. 22321854; fax 22321956; f. 1990; weekly; Sesotho; Editor-in-Chief Candi Ramainoane; circ. 5,000.

Moeletsi oa Basotho: Mazenod Institute, POB 18, Mazenod 160; tel. 22350465; fax 22350010; f. 1933; weekly; Sesotho; Roman Catholic; Editor Francis Khoaripe; circ. 20,000.

Mohahlaula: Allied Bldg, First Floor, Manonyane Centre, POB 14430, Maseru 100; tel. 22312777; fax 22320941; e-mail medinles@lesoff.co.za; weekly; Sesotho; publ. by Makaung Printers and Publishers; Editor Willy Mollungoa.

Moloi: Cooperatives Bldg, Main North 1 Rd, POB 9933, Maseru 100; tel. 22312287; fax 22327912; Sesotho; organ of the LCD; Monyane Moleleki.

Mopheme (The Survivor): Allied Bldg, First Floor, Manonyane Centre, POB 14184, Maseru; tel. and fax 22311670; e-mail mopheme@lesoff.co.za; weekly; English; Owner and Editor Lawrence Keketso; circ. 2,500.

Public Eye: Voice Multimedia, Victoria Hotel, Rm 206, POB 14129, Maseru; tel. 22321414; fax 22310614; e-mail voicemed@lesoff.co.za; internet publiceye.co.ls; f. 1997; weekly; 80% English, 20% Sesotho; Editor-in-Chief Bethuel Thai; circ. 18,000.

Southern Star: POB 7590, Maseru; tel. 22312269; fax 22310167; e-mail b&a-holdings@ilesotho.com; weekly; English; Editor Frank Boffoe; circ. 1,500.

PERIODICALS

Moqolotsi (The Journalist): House No. 1B, Happy Villa, Maseru 100; tel. and fax 22320941; fax 22320941; monthly newsletter; English; publ. by the Media Institute of Lesotho (MILES).

NGO Web: 544 Hoohlo Extension, Florida, Maseru 100; tel. 22325798; fax 22317205; e-mail lecongo@lecongo.org.ls; quarterly; English and Sesotho; publ. of the Lesotho Council of NGOs; circ. 2,000.

Review of Southern African Studies: Institute of Southern African Studies, National University of Lesotho, PO Roma 180; tel. 22340247; fax 22340601; e-mail t.khalanyane@nul.ls; 2 a year; arts, social and behavioural sciences; Editor Tankie Khalanyane.

Shoeshoe: POB 36, Maseru 100; tel. 22323561; fax 22310003; quarterly; women's interest; publ. by Ministry of Communications, Science and Technology.

Other publications include *Mara LDF Airwing/Airsquadron* and *The Sun/Thebe*.

NEWS AGENCIES

Lesotho News Agency (LENA): Lerotholi St, POB 36, Maseru 100; tel. 22325317; fax 22326408; e-mail l_lenanews@hotmail.com; internet www.lena.gov.ls; f. 1985; Dir Nkoe Thakali; Editor Violet Maraisane.

Foreign Bureau

Inter Press Service (IPS) (Italy): c/o Lesotho News Agency, POB 36, Maseru 100; Correspondent Lebohang Lejakane.

Publishers

Longman Lesotho (Pty) Ltd: POB 1174, 104 Christie House, Orpen Rd, Maseru 100; tel. 22314254; fax 22310118; Man. Dir Seymour R. Kikine.

Macmillan Boleswa Publishers Lesotho (Pty) Ltd: 523 Sun Cabanas, POB 7545, Maseru 100; tel. 22317340; fax 22310047; e-mail macmillan@lesoff.co.ls; Man. Dir Paul Morolong.

Mazenod Institute: POB 39, Mazenod 160; tel. 22350224; f. 1933; Roman Catholic; Man. Fr B. Mohlalisi.

Morija Sesuto Book Depot: POB 4, Morija 190; tel. and fax 22360204; f. 1862; owned by the Lesotho Evangelical Church; religious, educational and Sesotho language and literature.

St Michael's Mission: The Social Centre, POB 25, Roma; tel. 22316234; f. 1968; religious and educational; Man. Dir Fr M. Ferrange.

GOVERNMENT PUBLISHING HOUSE

Government Printer: POB 268, Maseru; tel. 22313023.

Broadcasting and Communications

TELECOMMUNICATIONS

Telecom Lesotho: POB 1037, Maseru 100; tel. 22211100; fax 22310183; internet www.telecom.co.ls; 70% holding acquired by the Mountain Kingdom Communications consortium in 2000; 30% state-owned; Chair. John Bayley; CEO Adri Van Der Veer.

VCL Communications: Development House, Kingsway Rd, POB 7387, Maseru 100; tel. 22212000; fax 22311079; f. 1996; jt venture between Telecom Lesotho and Vodacom (Pty) Ltd; operates mobile cellular telephone network; Man. Dir Mervyn Visagie.

BROADCASTING

Lesotho National Broadcasting Service: POB 552, Maseru 100; tel. 22323561; fax 22310003; programmes in Sesotho and English; radio transmissions began in 1964 and television transmissions in 1988; Lesotho Television broadcasts two hours of programmes per day; Dir of Broadcasting Dada Moqasa; Controller of Programmes Mannini Nkhereamye.

There are also five commercial radio stations: Catholic Radio FM, Joy Radio, Khotso FM, MoAfrika Radio and People's Choice Radio.

Finance

(cap. = capital; res = reserves; dep. = deposits; m. = million; brs = branches; amounts in maloti)

BANKING

Central Bank

Central Bank of Lesotho: cnr Airport and Moshoeshoe Rds, POB 1184, Maseru 100; tel. 22314281; fax 22310051; e-mail cbl@centralbank.org.ls; internet www.centralbank.org.ls; f. 1978 as the Lesotho Monetary Authority; present name adopted in 1982; bank of issue; cap. 25.0m., res 1,676.2m., dep. 1,544.7m. (Dec. 2002); Gov. and Chair. Esselen Motlatsi Matekane.

Commercial Banks

Lesotho Bank (1999) Ltd: Lesotho Bank Head Office, Kingsway Town Centre, POB 1053, Maseru 100; tel. 22315737; fax 22317321; f. 1972; transferred to majority private ownership in Aug. 1999; 70% owned by Standard Bank Lesotho Ltd; commercial bank, also carries out development banking functions; total assets 1,025.4m. (Dec. 2002); Chair. J. Chimhanda; Man. Dir D. Allan; 15 brs.

Nedbank Lesotho: Nedbank Building, 361 Kingsway, POB 1001, Maseru 100; tel. 22312696; fax 22310025; f. 1997; fmrly Standard Chartered Bank Lesotho Ltd; 100% owned by Nedcor Group (South Africa); cap. 20m., res 21.5m., dep. 704.2m. (Dec. 2002); Chair. Willem P. Frost; Man. Dir Philip D. Opperman; 3 brs and 7 agencies.

Standard Bank Lesotho Ltd: Banking Bldg, 1st Floor, Kingsway Rd, Kingsway Town Centre, POB 115, Maseru 100; tel. 22312423; fax 22310235; e-mail mokaloba@stanbic.com; internet www.stanbic.com; f. 1957 as Barclays Bank DCO; fmrly Stanbic Bank Lesotho Ltd, present name since 1997; 100% owned by Standard Bank Investment Corpn Ltd, South Africa; total assets 418.8m. (Dec. 2002); Chair. J. Chimhanda; Exec. Dir V. Kennedy; Man. Dir D. Allan; 6 brs.

INSURANCE

Alliance Insurance Co Ltd: Alliance House, 4 Bowker Rd, POB 01118, Maseru West 105; tel. 22312357; fax 22310313; e-mail alliance@alliance.co.ls; internet www.alliance.co.ls; life and short-term insurance; Man. Dir Johann Pienaar; Gen. Man. Shawn Kriedemann.

Customer Protection Insurance Co: POB 201, Maseru 100; tel. 22312643; e-mail holdings@ellerines.co.za; subsidiary of Ellerine Holdings Ltd, South Africa; Chair Jeff Dritz.

Lesotho National Insurance Group (LNIG): Lesotho Insurance House, Kingsway, Private Bag A65, Maseru 100; tel. 22313031; fax 22310008; f. 1977; 50% state-owned; part-privatized in 1995; incorporating subsidiaries specializing in life and short-term insurance; Chair. Dr M. Senaoana; CEO M. Molelekoa.

Metropolitan Lesotho Ltd: POB 645, Maseru; tel. 22323970; fax 22317126; f. 2003; subsidiary of Metropolitan Holdings Ltd, South Africa; Man. Dir Tsoane Mphahlele.

Trade and Industry

GOVERNMENT AGENCIES

Privatisation Unit: Privatisation Project, Lesotho Utilities Sector Reform Project, Ministry of Finance and Development Planning, Lesotho Bank Mortgage Division Bldg, 2nd Floor, Kingsway St, Private Bag A249, Maseru 100; tel. 22317902; fax 22317551; e-mail mntsasa@privatisation.gov.ls; internet www.privatisation.gov.ls; Dir Makalo Ntsasa (acting).

Trade Promotion Unit: c/o Ministry of Trade, Industry, Co-operatives and Marketing, POB 747, Maseru 100; tel. 322138; fax 310121.

DEVELOPMENT ORGANIZATIONS

Basotho Enterprises Development Corpn (BEDCO): POB 1216, Maseru 100; tel. 22312094; fax 22310455; e-mail admin@bedco.org.ls; f. 1980; promotes and assists in the establishment and development of Basotho-owned enterprises, with emphasis on small- and medium-scale; CEO Mpho Nthethe (acting).

Lesotho Council of Non-Governmental Organizations: House 544, Hoohlo Extension, Private Bag A445, Maseru 100; tel. 22317205; fax 22310412; e-mail seabatam@lecongo.org.ls; internet www.lecongo.org.ls; f. 1990; promotes sustainable management of natural resources, socio-economic development and social justice; Exec. Dir Seabata Motsamai.

Lesotho Highlands Development Authority (LHDA): Post Office Bldg, 3rd Floor, Kingsway, POB 7332, Maseru 100; tel. 22318573; fax 22325245; e-mail lhwp@lhda.org.ls; internet www.lhda.org.ls; f. 1986 to supervise the Lesotho Highlands Water Project, being undertaken jtly with South Africa; Chair. John J. Eager (acting); CEO Liphapang Elias Potloane.

Lesotho National Development Corpn (LNDC): Development House, Block A, Kingsway, Private Bag A96, Maseru 100; tel. 22312012; fax 22310038; e-mail info@lndc.org.ls; internet www.lndc.org.ls; f. 1967; 90% state-owned; total assets 416.2m. (March 2004); interests include candle, carpet, tyre-retreading, explosives, fertilizer, clothing, jewellery and furniture factories, potteries, two diamond prospecting operations, an abattoir, a diamond-cutting and polishing works, a housing co, a brewery and an international hotel with a gambling casino; Chair. Mohlomi Rantekoa; CEO Sophia Mohapi.

Lesotho Co-operative Handicrafts: Maseru; f. 1978; marketing and distribution of handicrafts; Gen. Man. Khotso Matla.

CHAMBER OF COMMERCE

Lesotho Chamber of Commerce and Industry: Kingsway Ave, POB 79, Maseru 100; tel. 22316937; fax 22322794; Pres. Simon Phafane.

INDUSTRIAL AND TRADE ASSOCIATIONS

Livestock Marketing Corpn: POB 800, Maseru 100; tel. 22322444; f. 1973; sole org. for marketing livestock and livestock products; liaises closely with marketing boards in South Africa; projects include an abattoir, tannery, poultry and wool and mohair scouring plants; Gen. Man. S. R. Matlanyane.

EMPLOYERS' ORGANIZATION

Association of Lesotho Employers: 8 Bowker Rd, POB 1509, Maseru 100; tel. 22315736; fax 22325384; f. 1961; represents mems in industrial relations and on govt bodies, and advises the Govt on employers' concerns; Pres. Brian McCarthy; Exec. Dir Thabo Makeka.

UTILITIES

Lesotho Electricity Corpn (LEC): POB 423, Maseru 100; tel. 22312236; fax 22310093; internet www.lec.co.ls; f. 1969; bids for transfer to the private sector were under consideration in mid-2004; Man. Dir S. L. Mhaville.

Lesotho Water and Sewerage Authority (WASA): POB 426, Maseru 100; tel. 22312449; fax 22312006; Chair. Refiloe Tlali.

TRADE UNIONS

Congress of Lesotho Trade Unions (COLETU): POB 13282, Maseru 100; tel. 22320958; fax 22310081; f. 1998; Sec.-Gen. Justice Tsiukulu; 15,587.

Construction and Allied Workers Union of Lesotho (CAWULE): Private Bag A445, Maseru 100; tel. 22333035; f. 1967; Pres. L. Putsoane; Sec. T. Tlale.

Factory Workers' Union (FAWU): Maseru; f. 2003 following split from the Lesotho Clothing and Allied Workers' Union; Pres. Khabile Tsilo; Sec.-Gen. Macaefa Billy.

Lesotho Clothing and Allied Workers' Union (LECAWU): LNDC Centre, 2nd Floor, Rm 12-14, Kingsway Rd, POB 11767, Maseru 100; tel. 22324296; fax 22320958; e-mail lecawu@lesoff.co.ls; Sec.-Gen. Danile Maraisane; 6,000 mems.

Lesotho General Workers' Union: POB 322, Maseru 100; f. 1954; Chair. J. M. Ramarothole; Sec. T. Motlohi.

Lesotho Congress of Democratic Unions (LECODU): Maseru; Sec.-Gen. E. T. Ramochela; 15,279 mems.

Lesotho Transport and Allied Workers' Union: Maseru 100; f. 1959; Pres. M. Bereng; Gen Sec. Tseko Kapa.

Lesotho University Teachers' and Researchers' Union (LUTARU): Maseru; Pres. Dr Francis Makoa.

Transport

RAILWAYS

Lesotho is linked with the South African railway system by a short line (2.6 km in length) from Maseru to Marseilles, on the Bloemfontein–Natal main line.

ROADS

In 1999 Lesotho's road network totalled 5,940 km, of which 1,084 km were main roads and 1,950 km were secondary roads. About 18.3% of roads were paved. In 1996 the International Development Association granted US $40m. towards the Government's rolling five-year road programme. From 1996/97 an extra-budgetary Road Fund was to finance road maintenance. In March 2000 a major road network was opened, linking Maseru with the Mohale Dam.

CIVIL AVIATION

King Moshoeshoe I International Airport is at Thota-Moli, some 20 km from Maseru; in January 2002 the Government announced plans for its expansion. There are 27 smaller airfields in Lesotho. International services between Maseru and Johannesburg are operated by South African Airlink. The national airline company, Lesotho Airways, was sold to a South African company in 1997 as part of the Government's ongoing privatization programme; however, after two years of losses the company was liquidated in 1999.

Tourism

Spectacular mountain scenery is the principal tourist attraction, and a new ski resort was opened in 2003. Tourist arrivals increased from 287,280 in 2002 to 360,955 in 2003. In 2002 receipts from tourism amounted to an estimated US $20m.

Lesotho Tourism Development Corporation (LTDC): cnr Linare and Parliament Rds, POB 1378, Maseru 100; tel. 22312238; fax 22310189; f. 2000; successor to the Lesotho Tourist Board; Dir of Tourism Mpho Moeketsi.

LIBERIA

Introductory Survey

Location, Climate, Language, Religion, Flag, Capital

The Republic of Liberia lies on the west coast of Africa, with Sierra Leone and Guinea to the north, and Côte d'Ivoire to the east. The climate is tropical, with temperatures ranging from 18°C (65°F) to 49°C (120°F). English is the official language but the 16 major ethnic groups speak their own languages and dialects. Liberia is officially a Christian state, although some Liberians hold traditional beliefs. There are about 670,000 Muslims. The national flag (proportions 10 by 19) has 11 horizontal stripes, alternately of red and white, with a dark blue square canton, containing a five-pointed white star, in the upper hoist. The capital is Monrovia.

Recent History

Founded by liberated black slaves from the southern USA, Liberia became an independent republic in 1847. The leader of the True Whig Party (TWP), William Tubman, who had been President of Liberia since 1944, died in July 1971 and was succeeded by his Vice-President, William R. Tolbert, who was re-elected in October 1975.

In April 1980 Tolbert was assassinated in a military coup, led by Master Sgt (later Commander-in-Chief) Samuel Doe, who assumed power as Chairman of the newly established People's Redemption Council (PRC), suspending the Constitution and proscribing all political parties. The new regime attracted international criticism for its summary execution of 13 former senior government officials who had been accused of corruption and mismanagement. In July 1981 all civilian ministers received commissions, thus installing total military rule.

A draft Constitution was approved by 78.3% of registered voters in a national referendum in July 1984. In the same month Doe dissolved the PRC and appointed a 58-member Interim National Assembly, comprising its former members and 36 civilians. The ban on political organizations was repealed in the same month, to enable parties to secure registration prior to presidential and legislative elections, which were due to take place in October 1985. In August 1984 Doe established the National Democratic Party of Liberia (NDPL) and formally announced his candidature for the presidency. By early 1985 a total of 11 political associations had been formed; however, two influential parties, the Liberian People's Party (LPP) and the United People's Party (UPP), were proscribed, and apart from the NDPL only three parties—the Liberian Action Party (LAP), the Liberia Unification Party (LUP) and the Unity Party (UP)—were eventually permitted to participate in the elections. Doe won the presidential election, receiving 50.9% of the votes. At the concurrent elections to the bicameral National Assembly, the NDPL won 22 of the 26 seats in the Senate and 51 of the 64 seats in the House of Representatives.

On 6 January 1986 Doe was inaugurated as President. He appointed a new Cabinet (which largely comprised members of the previous administration). Six members of the opposition parties continued to boycott the National Assembly, and their seats were taken by NDPL representatives at a by-election in December. In March 1988 Gabriel Kpolleh, the leader of the LUP, was among several people arrested on charges of planning to overthrow the Government. In October he and nine others were sentenced to 10 years' imprisonment for treason.

In December 1989 an armed insurrection by rebel forces began in the north-eastern border region of Nimba County. In early 1990 several hundred deaths ensued in fighting between the Liberian army (the Armed Forces of Liberia—AFL) and the rebels, who claimed to be members of a hitherto unknown opposition group, the National Patriotic Front of Liberia (NPFL), led by a former government official, Charles Taylor. The fighting swiftly degenerated into a war between Doe's ethnic group, the Krahn, and the local Gio and Mano tribes, and many thousands of people took refuge in neighbouring Guinea and Côte d'Ivoire. By April the NPFL had gained control of a large part of Nimba County. Following the advance of rebels on the capital, Monrovia, in May, most foreign residents were evacuated. NPFL forces entered Monrovia in July; Taylor's authority as self-proclaimed President of his own interim administration, known as the National Patriotic Reconstruction Assembly, was, however, challenged by a faction of the NPFL, led by Prince Yormie Johnson, which rapidly secured control of parts of Monrovia. In the subsequent conflict both government and rebel forces were responsible for numerous atrocities against civilians. The Economic Community of West African States (ECOWAS, see p. 217) repeatedly failed to negotiate a cease-fire, and in late August it dispatched a military force to restore peace in the region. Doe and Johnson accepted this Monitoring Group (ECOMOG, see p. 220), but its initial occupation of the port area of Monrovia encountered armed opposition by Taylor's forces.

On 30 August 1990 exiled representatives of Liberia's principal political parties and other influential groups met at a conference convened by ECOWAS in the Gambian capital, Banjul, where they elected Dr Amos Sawyer, the leader of the LPP, as President of an Interim Government of National Unity (IGNU). Doe was taken prisoner by Johnson's rebel Independent National Patriotic Front of Liberia (INPFL) on 9 September, and was killed on the following day. In early October, following Taylor's rejection of a proposed peace settlement, ECOMOG began an offensive aimed at establishing a neutral zone in Monrovia separating the three warring factions. By mid-October ECOMOG had gained control of central Monrovia. On 22 November Sawyer was inaugurated as Interim President, under the auspices of ECOWAS, in Monrovia. Later that month, following ECOWAS-sponsored negotiations in the Malian capital, Bamako, the AFL, the NPFL and the INPFL signed a cease-fire agreement. By January 1991 all rebel forces had withdrawn from Monrovia, and in that month Sawyer nominated ministers to the IGNU. Legislative power was vested in a 28-member Interim National Assembly, which represented the principal political factions, including the INPFL; however, the NPFL refused to participate. On 19 April a national conference re-elected Sawyer as Interim President and appointed a member of the INPFL, Peter Naigow (a former minister in Doe's administration), as Vice-President. In June Sawyer nominated a new Council of Ministers, which was subsequently approved by the Interim National Assembly. In August, however, the INPFL representatives, including Naigow, resigned from the IGNU, after Sawyer denounced the execution, apparently at Johnson's instigation, of four members of the INPFL who had reportedly complied with arrangements to relinquish weapons to ECOMOG.

In April, after members of the NPFL perpetrated several incursions into Sierra Leone, Sierra Leonean forces entered Liberian territory and launched retaliatory attacks, while the NPFL reportedly advanced within Sierra Leone. It was reported that NPFL forces were supporting a Sierra Leonean resistance movement, the Revolutionary United Front (RUF), in hostilities against government forces of that country (see the chapter on Sierra Leone). In September members of a newly emerged rebel movement, comprising former supporters of Doe, the United Liberation Movement of Liberia for Democracy (ULIMO), began attacks from Sierra Leone against NPFL forces in north-western Liberia.

At the end of October 1991 a summit meeting between Sawyer and Taylor, which took place in Yamoussoukro, Côte d'Ivoire, under the aegis of an ECOWAS five-nation committee, resulted in a peace agreement whereby the troops of all warring factions were to be disarmed and restricted to camps, while the NPFL was to relinquish the territory under its control to ECOMOG. It was also agreed that all Liberian forces would be withdrawn from Sierra Leone, and that a demilitarized zone, under the control of ECOMOG, would be created along Liberia's border with Sierra Leone. However, the NPFL failed to disarm and restrict its forces to camps within the time limit that had been stipulated in the peace agreement. In January 1992 the Interim Election Commission and Supreme Court were established, in accordance with the peace accord. At the end of April, in response to pressure from within the NPFL, Taylor agreed to withdraw NPFL troops from the border with Sierra Leone. In May ECOMOG began to disarm the rebel factions and to deploy troops in NPFL-controlled territory, and, despite continued fighting between

ULIMO and NPFL forces, established a demilitarized zone along the border with Sierra Leone.

In August 1992 ULIMO launched a renewed offensive in western Liberia, gaining control of Bomi and Grand Cape Mount Counties. In October the NPFL claimed that Nigerian aircraft under ECOMOG command had bombed its bases at Kakata and Harbel (the site of the Robertsfield International Airport and the country's principal rubber plantation), and at Buchanan, following an NPFL attack on ECOMOG forces stationed near Monrovia. The NPFL subsequently seized a number of strategic areas on the outskirts of Monrovia, causing more than 100,000 civilians to take refuge from the conflict in central Monrovia. ECOMOG forces (who were supported by members of the AFL and militia loyal to the IGNU) began retaliatory attacks against NPFL positions around the capital. In late October ECOMOG units succeeded in capturing the INPFL base at Caldwell, near Monrovia, and forcing Johnson to surrender. (The INPFL was subsequently disbanded.) In November the UN Security Council adopted a resolution imposing a mandatory embargo on the supply of armaments to Liberia, and authorized the UN Secretary-General to send a special representative to the country. In December ECOMOG announced that it had regained control of the area surrounding Monrovia, and in early 1993 began to advance in south-eastern Liberia, recapturing Harbel, while ULIMO was reported to have gained control of Lofa County in the west. In March ULIMO accepted an invitation from Sawyer to join the IGNU; ULIMO forces in Monrovia were subsequently disarmed. Following a major offensive, ECOMOG announced in April that it had gained control of Buchanan (which was reopened to shipping later that year). In June some 600 refugees were found to have been killed at the Harbel rubber plantation. Taylor denied accusations by the IGNU of NPFL involvement.

In July 1993 a conference, attended by the factions involved in the hostilities, was convened (under the auspices of the UN and ECOWAS) in Geneva, Switzerland. Following several days of negotiations, the IGNU, the NPFL and ULIMO agreed to a cease-fire (to be monitored by a joint committee of the three factions, pending the deployment of UN observers and a reconstituted peace-keeping force), and to the establishment of a transitional administration. The peace accord was formally signed in Cotonou on 25 July. Under its terms, the IGNU was to be replaced by the Liberian National Transitional Government (LNTG), with a five-member transitional Council of State and a 35-member Transitional Legislative Assembly (comprising 13 representatives of the IGNU, 13 of the NPFL and nine of ULIMO), pending elections. In response to demands by Taylor, the dominance in ECOMOG of the Nigerian contingent was to be reduced.

The cease-fire came into effect at the end of July 1993; however, ECOMOG subsequently accused the NPFL of violating the Cotonou accord by repeatedly entering territory under its control. In August the IGNU, the NPFL and ULIMO each appointed a representative to the Council of State, while a list of nine candidates, nominated by the three factions, elected the two remaining members (who were representatives of the IGNU and ULIMO respectively) from among their number. Dr Bismark Kuyon, a member of the IGNU, was subsequently elected Chairman of the Council of State. Shortly afterwards, however, Kuyon announced that the inauguration of the Council of State (originally scheduled to take place on 24 August) was to be postponed, pending the clear implementation of the process of disarmament.

In September 1993 a report by a UN mission concluded that AFL troops had perpetrated the massacre at Harbel (which had been widely attributed to the NPFL), and implied that ECOMOG had deliberately failed to identify those responsible. In the same month the UN Security Council approved the establishment of a 300-member UN Observer Mission in Liberia (UNOMIL), which was to co-operate with ECOMOG and the Organization of African Unity (now the African Union, see p. 153) in monitoring the transitional process. In October the Transitional Legislative Assembly was established, in accordance with the peace agreement. Sawyer dismissed Kuyon (who had reportedly dissociated himself from the IGNU's refusal to relinquish power prior to disarmament) and appointed Philip Banks, hitherto Minister of Justice, in his place.

Meanwhile, it was feared that renewed hostilities in several areas of the country would jeopardize the peace accord. An armed faction styling itself the Liberia Peace Council (LPC), which reportedly comprised members of the Krahn ethnic group from Grand Gedeh County, joined by a number of disaffected AFL troops, emerged in September 1993 and subsequently entered into conflict with the NPFL in south-eastern Liberia. In December fighting between ULIMO and a newly formed movement, the Lofa Defence Force (LDF), was also reported in Lofa County. The NPFL denied involvement with the LDF, which occupied territory previously controlled by ULIMO in the north-west.

In February 1994 the Council of State elected David Kpomakpor, a representative of the IGNU, as its Chairman. In early March units belonging to UNOMIL and the new ECOMOG force (which had been reinforced by contingents from Tanzania and Uganda) were deployed, and the disarmament of all factions commenced. On 7 March the Council of State was inaugurated; it was envisaged that the presidential and legislative elections (originally scheduled for February) would take place in September. However, the disarmament process was subsequently impeded by an increase in rebel activity: in addition to continuing clashes involving the LDF and the LPC, more than 200 people were killed in clashes within ULIMO between members of the Krahn and Mandingo ethnic groups, particularly in the region of Tubmanburg (in Bomi County, where the movement was officially based). The hostilities, which followed the dispute earlier that month between the leader of ULIMO, Alhaji G. V. Kromah (a Mandingo), and the Chairman of its military wing, Maj.-Gen. Roosevelt Johnson (a Krahn), were prompted by resentment among the Krahn at the predominance of the Mandingo in ULIMO's representation in the transitional institutions.

UNOMIL's mandate was renewed in April 1994. In May, following prolonged controversy over the allocation of principal portfolios, a 19-member Cabinet was installed, comprising seven representatives of the NPFL, seven of ULIMO and five of the former IGNU. In July, however, Kromah's faction (known as ULIMO—K) launched an offensive to recapture Tubmanburg, which was under the control of Roosevelt Johnson's forces (ULIMO—J). In early September (when the original mandate of the LNTG was due to expire) a meeting of the NPFL, the AFL and ULIMO—K took place in Akosombo, Ghana. On 12 September Taylor, Kromah and the Chief of Staff of the AFL, Lt-Gen. Hezekiah Bowen, signed a peace accord providing for the immediate cessation of hostilities and for the establishment later that month of a reconstituted Council of State, in which four of the five members were to be nominated, respectively, by the three factions and a civilian Liberian National Conference (LNC—which had been convened in Monrovia at the end of August). Meanwhile, following clashes between dissident members of the NPFL and troops loyal to Taylor, the dissidents' Central Revolutionary Council (CRC) announced that Taylor had been deposed and replaced by the Minister of Labour in the LNTG, Thomas Woewiyu, who indicated that he was not prepared to accept the Akosombo agreement. In mid-September disaffected members of the AFL, led by a former officer who had served in the Doe administration, Gen. Charles Julu, seized the presidential mansion, but were subsequently overpowered by ECOMOG forces. (Almost 80 members of the AFL, including Julu, were later arrested, and a further 2,000 troops were disarmed by ECOMOG.) Later that month the CRC, apparently in alliance with elements of the AFL, ULIMO, the LPC and the LDF, took control of Taylor's base at Gbarnga (in central Bong County); Taylor was reported to have fled to Côte d'Ivoire.

In October 1994 both the ECOMOG and UNOMIL contingents were reduced in size, in view of the lack of progress achieved in the peace process. In November a conference, attended by Bowen, Taylor, Woewiyu, the leader of the LPC, Dr George Boley, and the leader of the LDF, François Massaquoi, together with representatives of the LNC and the LNTG, was convened in Accra, Ghana, to discuss preparations for the installation of a reconstituted Council of State. Meanwhile, the NPFL had regained control of much of the territory, including Gbarnga, that the CRC had captured in September. On 22 December the participants of the peace conference reached agreement for a cease-fire to enter into force later that month and reaffirmed the terms of the Akosombo agreement, including provisions for the establishment of demilitarized zones throughout Liberia and for the installation of a reconstituted Council of State, to comprise a single representative of each of the NPFL, ULIMO, the 'Coalition Forces' (a loose alliance comprising the CRC, the LPC, the LDF and elements of the AFL), and the LNC, with a fifth member elected jointly by the NPFL and ULIMO from traditional rulers. Later in December 1994 the UN Security Council extended the mandate of UNOMIL (now comprising some 90 observers) until April 1995, while the Nigerian Government reduced its ECOMOG contingent to 6,000 (from about 10,000). The cease-fire entered into force on 28 December; however, factional fighting, particularly between the NPFL and LPC, continued in early

1995. The UN and ECOWAS expressed further dissatisfaction with the suspension of the peace process, and at the end of April Tanzania withdrew its 800-member ECOMOG contingent, owing to lack of funding.

Negotiations regarding the composition of the Council of State were impeded by Taylor's persistent demand to be granted its chairmanship. On 19 August 1995, following a further ECOWAS summit meeting in Abuja, the armed factions (the NPFL, ULIMO—K, the LPC, the CRC, the LDF, ULIMO—J and the AFL) finally signed a compromise agreement providing for the installation of a reconstituted Council of State, which was to remain in power, pending elections, for one year. An academic with no factional affiliations, Prof. Wilton Sankawulo, was to assume the office of Chairman, while the other seats were to be allocated to Taylor, Kromah, Boley, the LNC representative, Oscar Quiah, and a traditional ruler who had been nominated by ULIMO and the NPFL, Chief Tamba Taylor. Later that month a cease-fire entered into force, in compliance with the terms of the peace accord. The Council of State was formally installed on 1 September, and was to remain in place pending elections, scheduled for 20 August 1996. The Council of State subsequently appointed a transitional Council of Ministers, comprising members of the seven factions that had signed the Abuja agreement. Later in September the UN Security Council extended UNOMIL's mandate until the end of January 1996.

In November 1995 a demilitarized zone was established between NPFL and ULIMO—K forces in the region of St Paul River (between Bong and Lofa Counties). Deployment of ECOMOG forces commenced, in accordance with the Abuja peace terms, in December. Following continued clashes between the ULIMO factions, however, ULIMO—J attacked ECOMOG troops near Tubmanburg. ECOMOG suspended deployment of its forces, and launched a counter-offensive in an attempt to restore order. Hostilities continued in early 1996, with large numbers of civilians killed or displaced.

In February 1996 ULIMO—J officials stated that Johnson had been replaced as leader of the movement in the interests of the peace process. In March the Council of State announced his removal from the Council of Ministers. In subsequent clashes between the two factions of ULIMO—J, forces loyal to Johnson allegedly killed a supporter of the new leadership, prompting the Council of State to order that he be arrested on charges of murder. Johnson, however, refused to surrender to the authorities, and became effectively besieged in his private residence in Monrovia. In April government forces, led by Charles Taylor, engaged in hostilities with Johnson's supporters, in an effort to force him to surrender. The principal factions represented in the transitional authorities thus became involved in the conflict: elements of the LPC and AFL (which were predominantly Krahn) supported Johnson's forces, while the NPFL and ULIMO—K opposed them. Fighting rapidly intensified in central Monrovia, resulting in the displacement of large numbers of civilians, who fled the capital or took refuge in embassy compounds. ECOMOG (which had refrained from military intervention) deployed its forces in the region of Monrovia, with the aim of negotiating between the warring factions. Following a lull in the fighting, however, some of Johnson's supporters launched attacks in the residential area of Mamba Point (where embassies and offices of humanitarian organizations were situated) and seized a number of civilians as hostages. The US Government began to evacuate US citizens, and other foreign nationals, from the US embassy (where some 20,000 civilians had taken shelter). Johnson's supporters, together with their hostages, occupied former army barracks (the Barclay Training Centre) in Monrovia, which were subsequently surrounded by NPFL and ULIMO—K forces. As the evacuation of foreign nationals continued, the US Government dispatched five warships to the region, with the stated aim of ensuring the protection of US diplomatic staff in Monrovia. Later in April a further cease-fire agreement was negotiated under the aegis of the US Government, the UN and ECOWAS, allowing the deployment of ECOMOG troops throughout Monrovia, while most of the remaining hostages were released by Johnson's supporters.

In May 1996, during the absence of Johnson (who had left the country under US protection, to attend a planned ECOWAS summit meeting), the NPFL launched a further attack against the Barclay Training Centre, prompting large numbers of civilians to flee to Monrovia Freeport. At the end of May the UN Security Council renewed the mandate of UNOMIL for a further three months, but warned the armed factions that international support would be withdrawn if fighting continued;

UNOMIL was henceforth to comprise only the remaining five military and 20 civilian personnel, following the evacuation of the main mission of about 90 observers in April. In June Johnson's supporters agreed to disarm and to leave the Barclay Training Centre, while an ECOWAS arbitration mission commenced discussions with the faction leaders in an effort to restore the peace process.

In August 1996, at an ECOWAS conference in Abuja, the principal faction leaders (apart from Johnson, who remained abroad) signed a further peace agreement, whereby a reconstituted Council of State was to be installed by the end of that month, with a former senator, Ruth Perry, replacing Sankawulo as Chairman; Taylor and Boley were to remain members of the new administration. Under a revised schedule, elections were to take place at the end of May 1997, and power was to be transferred to an elected government by mid-June, following the dissolution of the armed factions by the end of January of that year. In order to implement the new timetable, ECOMOG (which then numbered 8,500) was to be reinforced by personnel from several West African states. At the end of August 1996 the mandate of UNOMIL was again extended.

Perry was inaugurated as Chairman of the Council of State in early September 1996; Johnson was again allocated a ministerial portfolio in a subsequent reorganization of the Cabinet. The faction leaders subsequently ordered their forces to disarm and to remove road-blocks in territory under their control. ECOMOG troops were deployed in strategic regions, including Kakata and Buchanan, and committees comprising ECOMOG and UNOMIL officials, together with representatives of the armed factions, visited remote areas of the country to verify the implementation of the disarmament process. Following the expiry of the deadline for the completion of the disarmament process, which had been extended to early February 1997, ECOMOG announced that about 91% of the rebel forces (who numbered 30,000–35,000, according to revised estimates) had relinquished their armaments.

In January 1997 Taylor announced that the NPFL had been officially dissolved, in accordance with the peace agreement; the movement was subsequently reconstituted as a political organization, the National Patriotic Party (NPP). In the same month Kromah declared that ULIMO—K had also ceased to exist as a military organization, and was to be reconstituted as the All Liberian Coalition Party (ALCOP). Meanwhile, political parties that had become inactive during the civil conflict were revived, and new groupings applied for official registration. In March Taylor, Kromah and Boley resigned from the Council of State, in compliance with the peace agreement, to allow their candidacy in the forthcoming elections. From March a number of West African countries began to dispatch additional contingents to reinforce ECOMOG (which was expected to be increased in size to about 16,000 personnel prior to the elections), with the USA providing logistical and financial assistance. In May, however, following a request by several political parties, the elections were postponed until 19 July to allow all the newly registered organizations sufficient time for preparation.

A 10-day voter registration process commenced at the end of June 1997. A total of 13 presidential candidates had emerged by this time, among them Ellen Johnson-Sirleaf (a former minister in the Tolbert administration and subsequently a World Bank official, who was to contest the election on behalf of the UP). Taylor conducted a large-scale electoral campaign, financed by profits accrued from unofficial exports and his private radio station, Kiss FM. Despite demands for a further postponement, the elections proceeded on 19 July. The elections commission announced on 23 July that Taylor had been elected President, with 75.3% of votes cast; Johnson-Sirleaf (who had been widely expected to be Taylor's strongest opponent) received only 9.6% of the votes. In the concurrent elections to the bicameral legislature (at which seats were allocated on a proportionate basis), the NPP secured 49 seats in the 64-member House of Representatives and 21 seats in the 26-member Senate, the UP won seven seats in the House of Representatives and three in the Senate, while ALCOP obtained three seats in the House of Representatives and two in the Senate. Kromah (who had won only 4.0% of the votes) subsequently declared that serious irregularities had occurred, but international observers declared the conduct of the elections to have been 'free and fair'. Taylor's overwhelming victory was generally ascribed to the widely held perception that he was the candidate most likely to achieve long-term stability in the country.

Taylor was inaugurated as President on 2 August 1997, and subsequently nominated a 19-member Cabinet, which was approved by the Senate. The new Government retained several members of the previous transitional administration, including Johnson and Woewiyu. A nine-member National Security Council, comprising several government ministers, the Chief of Staff of the Armed Forces and the Commander of ECOMOG, was established with the aim of ensuring the maintenance of civil order.

At an ECOWAS summit meeting, convened in Abuja, at the end of August 1997, it was agreed that ECOMOG was to be reconstituted and would henceforth assist in the process of national reconstruction, including the restructuring of the armed and security forces, and the maintenance of security; it was further envisaged that the contingent's mandate (officially due to expire on 2 February 1998) would be extended in agreement with the Liberian Government. Following the military coup in Sierra Leone in May 1997, ECOMOG was authorized to enforce international sanctions against the new junta led by Maj. Johnny Paul Koroma (see the chapter on Sierra Leone). In October, however, Taylor announced that he opposed the use of military force to oust the Koroma regime, and that ECOMOG would no longer be permitted to launch offensives against Sierra Leone from Liberian territory. Taylor ordered the closure of Liberia's border with Sierra Leone in response to civil disorder within that country. At the end of October Taylor established a National Human Rights Commission, which was empowered to investigate complaints of human rights violations.

In November 1997, following several months of rumours of the increasing strength in Guinea of Liberian rebel militia (principally members of the former ULIMO), constituting a threat to security in both countries, it was reported that some 30 members of ULIMO had been arrested in southern Guinea. The alleged presence of former Liberian factions in Guinea was discussed at a meeting between Taylor and the Guinean President, Gen. Lansana Conté, in December. Taylor subsequently appointed Kromah (who had taken up residence in Guinea following his electoral defeat in July) to the post of Chairman of a National Commission on Reconciliation.

By early 1998 the ECOMOG contingent had been reduced to about 5,000. Following Taylor's insistence that the Liberian authorities be accorded control of the restructuring of the armed forces, the Government had notified ECOWAS of its desire for ECOMOG to withdraw formally by 2 February, and had requested that Nigeria, Ghana, Burkina Faso and Niger continue to provide military assistance. Following the seizure of the Sierra Leonean capital, Freetown, by ECOMOG troops, Taylor protested that the arrest by ECOMOG of about 25 senior members of Sierra Leone's ousted junta at James Spriggs Payne Airport was an infringement of Liberian territory. The Liberian Government recalled its ambassador in Nigeria for consultations, and subsequently submitted a formal complaint to ECOWAS.

In March 1998 violent clashes erupted in Monrovia between the security forces and Johnson's supporters; Johnson subsequently claimed that members of Taylor's special security forces had attacked his private residence. ECOMOG troops were deployed to prevent further violence, and, in an attempt to ease tension in the capital, Johnson was removed from the Cabinet and appointed ambassador to India. In the same month Kromah, who had expressed concern regarding his own safety, was removed from his position as Chairman of the National Commission on Reconciliation. Later that month, following increasing tension between ECOMOG troops and Liberian security forces, the Government and ECOWAS signed an agreement revising ECOMOG's mandate in the country; the contingent was henceforth banned from intervening in civil disputes.

In September 1998 security forces attempted to arrest Johnson (who had not yet assumed his ambassadorial post), pursuing him to the US embassy compound, where he and a number of his supporters had taken refuge; some 50 people were killed in ensuing clashes between members of the security forces and Johnson's followers. The Government subsequently announced that Johnson, Kromah and 21 of their associates had been charged with treason, following an abortive coup attempt, and demanded that US embassy officials relinquish Johnson to Liberian authority. After discussions with the Liberian authorities, however, US officials transported Johnson to Sierra Leone. In response to an incursion by Liberian security forces into the US embassy compound during the fighting, the US Government temporarily closed the embassy and deployed a naval vessel near the Liberian coast to facilitate the evacuation of US nationals in the event of an escalation of violence in Monrovia. The Liberian Government subsequently issued a formal apology to the USA and announced that an investigation would be conducted into the incident, in co-operation with the US authorities. In October 32 people (several, including Johnson, *in absentia*) were formally charged with treason; their trial commenced in November. In the same month Taylor reorganized the Cabinet.

By November 1998 most of the ECOMOG forces in Liberia had been redeployed in Sierra Leone, owing to increased rebel activity in that country, and to continued tension between the Liberian Government and ECOMOG officials. In late December the Government closed Liberia's border with Sierra Leone, in response to the escalation in civil conflict in the neighbouring country, and pledged support for the administration of President Ahmed Kabbah. In January 1999 it was announced that further ECOMOG troops in Liberia were to be relocated to Sierra Leone, following a major offensive by RUF forces against Freetown. A small number of ECOMOG forces remained in Liberia to provide military assistance to the armed forces. Later that month Taylor dismissed US and British allegations that the Liberian Government was providing clandestine military support to the RUF. In April 13 of the defendants on trial for treason were convicted and sentenced to 10 years' imprisonment.

In April 1999 unidentified forces, who were believed to have entered the country from Guinea, attacked the northern town of Voinjama, in Lofa County, temporarily taking hostage several western European diplomats. AFL troops subsequently regained control of the town, and Taylor submitted a formal protest to the Guinean Government. In August members of a rebel movement reported to comprise former members of ULIMO—K, known as the Joint Forces for the Liberation of Liberia (JFLL), attacked principal towns in Lofa County from Guinea. Some 80 aid workers, including six foreign nationals, were taken hostage by the JFLL, but were released a few days later, following negotiations by humanitarian relief officials. Taylor ordered the closure of the border with Guinea and declared a temporary state of emergency in Lofa County. At an ECOWAS meeting on relations between Liberia and Guinea, which took place in Abuja in September, it was agreed that a commission would be established to address the issue of security at the border between Liberia, Guinea and Sierra Leone. The border was reopened in February 2000.

At the beginning of May 2000 the Government announced the introduction of a programme to restructure the armed forces, with the aim of reducing them substantially in size and establishing an ethnic balance. In that month Taylor assisted in negotiating the release of UN personnel taken hostage by the RUF in Sierra Leone. In June the Vice-President, Enoch Dogolea, died, apparently as a result of a deterioration in his health following a longstanding illness. He was replaced in July by a former ambassador, Moses Zeh Blah, who had been nominated by Taylor. The Government subsequently established a commission to investigate the circumstances of Dogolea's death, following rumours, strongly denied by Taylor, that he had been murdered.

Meanwhile, reports of increased activity by Liberian dissidents, both in Sierra Leone, where rebels had allied with Kamajor militia, and in Guinea, resulted in a further deterioration in relations between the Liberian authorities and the Governments of those countries. In July 2000 rebel forces again launched an offensive from Guinean territory against Voinjama. Another hitherto unknown movement, Liberians United for Reconciliation and Democracy (LURD), believed to be a grouping of former members of the armed factions (particularly ULIMO—K), claimed responsibility for the attacks. Taylor and Conté subsequently conducted further discussions, with mediation from the Malian President, Alpha Oumar Konaré. In August Johnson-Sirleaf and a further 14 prominent opposition leaders (many of whom were abroad) were charged with alleged involvement with the LURD dissidents.

In September 2000 Conté claimed that Liberian and Sierra Leonean refugees in Guinea were supporting the activity of rebels attempting to overthrow his Government (see the chapter on Guinea), and ordered them to leave the country. Following a further rebel attack on the Guinean border town of Macenta, staged from Liberian territory, government forces bombarded the Liberian town of Zorzor, 220 km north-east of Monrovia, where dissident Liberian forces were based. In January 2001 the Liberian Government withdrew its ambassador in Guinea, following further Guinean bombardment of towns in the Foya district of northern Liberia. In the same month a committee of the UN Security Council reported that the Liberian Government actively supported the RUF and proposed the imposition of UN sanctions against Liberia. In early February the authorities announced that the Commander of the RUF, Sam Bockarie, had left the country, and that the rebels' liaison office had been closed. In early March the UN Security Council renewed the embargo on the supply of armaments to Liberia and voted in favour of a 12-month ban on diamond exports from Liberia and restrictions on the foreign travel of senior government and military officials; these latter measures were, however, deferred for a period of two months to allow the Government time to comply with demands that it expel RUF members from Liberia and end financial and military aid to the rebels. (In October 2000 the US Government had announced the imposition of diplomatic sanctions against Taylor, his relatives and close associates, prohibiting them from entering the USA until Liberia withdrew support for the RUF.) In late March 2001 Taylor expelled the ambassadors of Guinea and Sierra Leone from Liberia, claiming that they had been engaged in activity incompatible with their office, and announced the closure of the border with Sierra Leone. The Sierra Leonean authorities subsequently retaliated by ordering the Liberian chargé d'affaires to leave the country.

In April 2001 François Massaquoi, the former leader of the LDF, and Minister of Youth and Sport since 1997, was killed, after LURD forces fired on the helicopter transporting him to Voinjama. The Government subsequently intensified operations to suppress the continuing insurgency in northern Lofa County, near the border with Guinea. By May, however, the LURD claimed to have gained control of that region, and to have advanced to the neighbouring newly created Gbarpolu County, prompting the displacement of several thousand civilians. Early that month, in response to Taylor's perceived failure to comply with UN demands, the embargo on exports of diamonds from Liberia, together with the travel restrictions on senior government and military officials, entered into effect. Taylor condemned the imposition of UN sanctions, claiming that he had ended all connections with the RUF, while a large demonstration was staged in Monrovia in protest at the measures.

In July 2001 Taylor offered a general amnesty to active rebel supporters and to opposition members in exile who had been charged with treason or associated crimes. In August the Government announced that its order of expulsion against the ambassadors of Guinea and Sierra Leone accredited to Liberia had been formally withdrawn, following a request by ECOWAS. In September Johnson-Sirleaf (who had been charged with supporting anti-Government activities) returned to Monrovia under the terms of the general amnesty. In October a five-member UN commission issued a report recommending the extension of the existing sanctions against Liberia. The UN report also stated that the Liberian Government continued to use revenue generated by the timber industry and maritime activities to finance illicit trade in armaments with the RUF, and proposed the imposition of additional sanctions on timber exports.

By early 2002 LURD forces had gained considerable territory from government troops, and continued to advance southwards towards Monrovia. At the end of January it was reported that the insurgents had briefly occupied the village of Sawmill, 80 km north of Monrovia, and had gained control of much of the surrounding region. Thousands of civilians took refuge in Monrovia in early February, after LURD members attacked the town of Klay, in Bomi County, 30 km north-west of the capital. In response to the continued failure of government troops to halt the rapid approach of LURD forces towards Monrovia, Taylor declared a national state of emergency on 8 February (which was subsequently ratified by the legislature, and was to be revised after three months). Later that month the Government announced that it was to establish a permanent security presence at the country's northern border with Sierra Leone and Guinea. At the beginning of March the leader of LURD, Sekou Damate Conneh, announced that his forces aimed to depose Taylor and install a transitional administration in Monrovia. The rebels declared a few days later that they were prepared to enter into dialogue with government officials, but demanded that Taylor be excluded from discussions, on the grounds that he was not the legitimate Head of State of Liberia. The Government insisted that it would not contemplate the negotiation of a power-sharing agreement with the movement. Later that month a meeting of representatives of the Liberian authorities and opposition was convened at Abuja, under the aegis of ECOWAS; however, representatives of LURD failed to attend the negotiations, purportedly owing to the logistical difficulties in travelling to Abuja. At the conclusion of the discussions delegates representing 29 political and civil society associations, including major opposition leaders, urged the Government and LURD forces to declare a cease-fire. Nevertheless, fighting continued, particularly at Liberia's northern border with Guinea. At the end of March ECOWAS imposed travel restrictions on the LURD leadership, on the grounds that the movement had renewed hostilities against the Government.

On 6 May 2002 the UN Security Council adopted a resolution extending the armaments and diamond embargoes, and the travel ban, for a further 12 months. The resolution indicated that, if an effective certification scheme were established, Liberian diamonds proven to be legally mined would be exempted from the embargo, and also urged Liberia to introduce internationally verifiable systems to ensure that revenue derived from the maritime registry and the timber industry be used only for legitimate purposes. Also in May the Liberian legislature extended for a further six months the national state of emergency, after LURD forces gained further territory, seizing control of Gbarnga, in Bong County. In July Taylor reorganized the Government. In September 12 registered political parties attended a National Peace and Reconciliation Conference to discuss preparations for forthcoming elections. In the same month Taylor ended the national state of emergency and the ban on political demonstrations, announcing that government forces had regained control of much of the territory captured by the LURD, including the significant town of Bopolu, 100 km north-west of Monrovia.

During early 2003 hostilities frequently crossed into the territory of Côte d'Ivoire, and reports emerged that Ivorian rebel groups, notably the Mouvement pour la justice et la paix (MJP) and the Mouvement populaire ivoirien du grand ouest (MPIGO), had become allied with LURD. LURD forces regained control of Bopolu in February and briefly captured Robertsport and Bo Waterside, in Grand Cape Mount County. In March LURD occupied Klay, followed by the Ricks Institute Camp for internally displaced civilians, only 20 km from Monrovia, causing large numbers of civilians to take refuge in the capital. Simultaneous heavy fighting for control of Gbarnga was reported; LURD forces had recaptured the town by April. Meanwhile, a new rebel faction, the Movement for Democracy in Liberia (MODEL), attacked and secured Zwedru in Grand Geddeh County. MODEL was believed to comprise former members of the AFL and Doe loyalists, who were mainly based in Côte d'Ivoire (and reportedly supported by the Ivorian Government). Following fierce fighting in Sinoe County in April, MODEL captured the logging port of Greenville and continued to advance towards Buchanan. By this time members of the Ivorian MJP and MPIGO had clashed with the Liberian rebel and RUF members formerly allied with them. At the end of April Taylor and President Laurent Gbagbo of Cote d'Ivoire agreed to deploy joint border patrols. On 6 May the UN Security Council renewed the existing embargoes in force against Liberia for a further year, and imposed an additional ban on timber exports (which entered into effect in early July). Also in early May the Liberian authorities announced that Bockarie (who had been indicted by the Special Court established in Sierra Leone to try suspects of war crimes committed during the 10-year conflict in the country) had been killed in Liberia during an attempt to arrest him. (It was reported that he had been leading former RUF elements involved in the conflict in Liberia.) Subsequently, however, officials at the Special Court claimed that Bockarie and his immediate family had been captured and murdered by Liberian security forces to prevent him from testifying against prominent regional leaders.

The international community repeatedly urged unconditional negotiations within the framework of a mediation process led by ECOWAS, and in March 2003 LURD finally agreed, in principle, to enter into dialogue with Taylor. LURD and MODEL halted their advances on Monrovia and Buchanan at the end of May and pledged to observe a cease-fire, provided that the Government also suspended attacks. Peace discussions, attended by Taylor and LURD, commenced in Accra on 4 June, but were disrupted by the announcement of Taylor's indictment for war crimes by the Special Court, in connection with his alleged longstanding involvement with the RUF. On the following day Taylor returned to Monrovia, where he immediately announced that the authorities had suppressed an attempted coup. On the same day LURD forces launched a major attack on Monrovia from the movement's base in Tubmanburg, and rapidly reached the capital's western outskirts, causing an exodus from refugee camps towards the city centre. On 7 June a government counter-offensive forced the rebels to withdraw back over a strategic bridge, which separated the western suburbs from the city centre. LURD's political leadership issued an ultimatum demanding Taylor's resignation, and French military forces commenced the evacuation of foreign nationals in response to the increasingly critical situation. (By that time the Liberian authorities estimated that about 400 civilians and military personnel had been killed in the fighting around Monrovia, while 50,000 civilians had become internally displaced, and humanitarian conditions had greatly deteriorated.) Following the arrival of a MODEL delegation, the peace discussions in Ghana resumed on 9 June. Repeated demands by LURD for Taylor's resignation as a precondition to the suspension of hostilities, and Taylor's insistence that his indictment by the Sierra Leone Special Court be withdrawn, impeded progress. On 17 June, however, a cease-fire agreement was signed by the LURD and MODEL leaders, and by the Minister of Defence, Daniel Chea, on behalf of the Liberian Government. Immediately beforehand, government troops recaptured Greenville, forcing LURD to withdraw to positions some 35 km from Monrovia. The cease-fire agreement required the deployment of a multinational stabilization force and a 30-day period of discussions to resolve outstanding issues, prior to the adoption of a comprehensive peace accord.

Shortly after the cease-fire agreement was signed in Accra, however, Taylor declared that he would remain in office at least until the end of his presidential term in January 2004, and rejected the Special Court indictment against him. Serious breaches of the cease-fire were reported, and on 26 June 2003, after the resumption of heavy fighting between government and rebel forces in and around Monrovia, in which about 300 civilians were killed, US President George W. Bush urged Taylor to resign. On the following day the rebel leadership declared a unilateral cease-fire (which was, however, rapidly abandoned). At the end of June the UN Secretary-General recommended to the Security Council that a multinational peace-keeping force be deployed in Liberia in response to the critical humanitarian situation, and urged US military intervention. On 6 July Taylor announced that he had accepted, in principle, an offer of asylum from the Nigerian Head of State, Olusegun Obasanjo, but stipulated that he would not leave the country until a peace-keeping operation was installed. Following continued appeals from Liberian civilians for foreign intervention to prevent the humanitarian disaster, a US mission of military observers was dispatched to Liberia. Despite increasing international support for US intervention, however, Bush indicated that he would only deploy peace-keeping troops in Liberia after Taylor had left the country and a West African mission had restored order. Later in July, after the rebel offensive to oust Taylor had reached the centre of the capital, the US embassy compound (in which some 10,000 Liberian civilians had taken refuge) was repeatedly bombarded. Some 100 US marines were flown in to defend the building, while US naval vessels were stationed off the Liberian coast. Demonstrations were staged outside the US embassy in support of demands for full-scale intervention to halt the carnage. Meanwhile, following the resumption of discussions between the government, LURD and MODEL delegations in Accra, it was announced that a peace accord, based on the terms of the failed cease-fire agreement, had been drafted.

On 22 July 2003 a summit meeting of ECOWAS Heads of State was convened in the Senegalese capital, Dakar. Following pressure from the UN Secretary-General, the West African delegates agreed on the following day to dispatch an initial 1,300 Nigerian peace-keeping troops (including a battalion redeployed from neighbouring Sierra Leone) to Liberia. On 1 August the UN Security Council officially authorized the establishment of a multinational force with a maximum strength of 3,250 troops, to be known as the ECOWAS Mission in Liberia (ECOMIL), which was to restore security to allow the distribution of emergency humanitarian assistance, and prepare for the deployment of a longer-term UN stabilization force (envisaged for October). On 11 August, following continued pressure from West African Governments and the international community, Taylor relinquished power to Vice-President Blah, before leaving Liberia for exile in the town of Calabar, in south-eastern Nigeria. Blah was inaugurated as interim Head of State, pending the installation of a government of national unity, which was the subject of continuing negotiations between the government and rebel delegations in Accra. Taylor's departure fulfilled the main demand of the rebel leadership, and was celebrated in Monrovia. Rebels ceded control of Monrovia Freeport to ECOMIL, and a further 200 US military personnel arrived in Liberia to support the peace operation. Meanwhile, an impasse at the Accra peace discussions was resolved, after the LURD delegation abandoned a demand that it be allocated the vice-presidency in the new administration. On 18 August delegates of the incumbent Government, rebel factions, political opposition and civil organizations, under the aegis of the UN, reached a comprehensive peace agreement, which provided for the establishment of a transitional power-sharing government and legislature, to comprise representatives of the participating groupings. Under the accord, Blah was to transfer power to the new administration on 14 October, all armed militia were to be disbanded, and democratic elections were to be conducted by October 2005. On 21 August 2003 the delegations elected Gyude Bryant, a prominent church figure and leader of the LAP, as Chairman of the transitional administration. Perceived as being most neutral, Bryant defeated a further two candidates for the office, Johnson-Sirleaf and Rudolph Sherman of the TWP. By the end of August a UN Joint Monitoring Committee had been dispatched to Monrovia, and ECOMIL troops (then numbering 1,500) were slowly taking control of rebel-held territory.

On 19 September 2003 the UN Security Council formally established the UN Mission in Liberia (UNMIL, see p. 76), which was mandated to support the transitional authorities and the implementation of the August peace agreement; the first contingent, of about 4,000, commenced deployment in the country (replacing ECOMIL) on 1 October. On 14 October, under the terms of the peace agreement, Bryant was officially inaugurated as Chairman of the two-year power-sharing administration, the National Transitional Government, while the leader of the UPP, Wesley Johnson, became Vice-Chairman. At the same time a 76-member unicameral legislature, the National Transitional Legislative Assembly (NTLA), comprising representatives of the groupings signatory to the August agreement and 15 deputies nominated by the counties, was installed. A prominent member of LURD, George Dweh, was subsequently elected Speaker of the new Assembly. Shortly before his inauguration, Bryant had signed an agreement for the resumption of diplomatic relations with the People's Republic of China (thereby ending links with Taiwan); the Chinese Government was expected to finance substantially reconstruction projects in the country. Later in October the former administration, LURD and MODEL (which were each allocated five ministries in the National Transitional Government) submitted ministerial nominees for approval by the legislature (although MODEL remained undecided on the selection of two representatives). Of the former Taylor loyalists, Chea retained the post of Minister of Defence, while LURD representatives were awarded the portfolios of justice and finance, and the leader of MODEL, Thomas Nimely Yaya, became Minister of Foreign Affairs. (However, the political opposition and civil society groups failed to agree on representatives for the remaining six portfolios divided between them.) In early December the International Criminal Police Organization (INTERPOL) issued an arrest notice against Taylor (who remained in Nigeria) for suspected war crimes.

On 7 December 2003, in accordance with the peace agreement, UNMIL began a programme of disarmament and demobilization, involving an estimated 40,000 former combatants; it was announced a few days later that some 11,000 had surrendered armaments. However, the process was suspended later that month, following further armed clashes in parts of the country, to allow more time for the deployment of UNMIL. On 22 December the UN Security Council adopted a resolution maintaining the embargoes on imports of armaments and on exports of timber and diamonds for a minimum of one year, but envisaged that these would be ended in response to progress in the peace process and in efforts by the National Transitional Government to prevent the illicit exploitation of resources. In January 2004 it was reported that Conneh's wife, Aisha, had ousted him from the leadership of LURD, with the support of other military commanders, resulting in the division of the movement. LURD and MODEL continued to demand Bryant's resignation from the chairmanship of the interim administration as a precondition to disarmament. UNMIL (which at the end of that month totalled about 11,500 uniformed personnel, including 500 troops contributed by the People's Republic of China) announced the establishment of three permanent garrisons in former rebel-controlled territory (where violent unrest was most prevalent). Later that month it was reported that the voluntary repatriation of refugees from Sierra Leone had commenced. On 23 March, after the remaining ministerial portfolios were finally designated, Bryant finally inaugurated the National Transitional Government. In mid-April UNMIL resumed the disarmament programme.

In May 2004 the Civil Society Organizations of Liberia, a grouping of pro-democracy and human rights organizations, presented a petition to the NTLA in support of the extradition of Taylor by the Nigerian Government. (Legal representatives of Taylor continued to plead at the Special Court in Sierra Leone that, as serving President at the time of his indictment, he was immune to prosecution.) In June, in a further struggle for leadership within LURD, the national executive council announced the removal of Sekou Conneh and his replacement by Chayee Doe (a brother of the former President). Conneh refused to acknowledge the statement, and continued to reject demands by his opponents within the movement for the replacement of the LURD Minister of Finance, Lusine Kamara. In September the International Criminal Court (ICC, see p. 291) announced that Liberia had ratified the signatory treaty, thereby allowing the Court jurisdiction to prosecute crimes committed during the civil conflict. On 17 September the UN Security Council adopted a resolution extending the mandate of UNMIL for a further year (while welcoming the progress made in the peace process).

An outbreak of rioting in Monrovia at the end of October 2004, in which 16 people were killed and a number of churches and mosques attacked, was reportedly precipitated by the reluctance of a LURD faction to relinquish armaments under the programme; order was restored, following the imposition of a curfew in the capital and deployment of additional UNMIL troops. The disarmament process, under which a total of some 96,000 former combatants had relinquished armaments, officially ended on 31 October, with a ceremony at which the three former armed factions were also officially dissolved (although operations continued after that date). In December the UN Security Council conducted a review of the sanctions in force on Liberia and concluded that, following the report of an assessment mission to the country, the National Transitional Government had not met the requisite conditions. The sanctions on armaments, timber and travel were consequently renewed for a further year, while, in view of preparations by the authorities to introduce a certification system, the embargo on the export of diamonds was extended for six months (and again extended in mid-2005).

Electoral reform legislation, which had been submitted to the NTLA at the end of August 2004, became an issue of contention, following attempts by the NTLA to add an amendment requiring a prior population census to be conducted, which would effectively prevent the elections from taking place in October 2005 (as specified in the comprehensive peace agreement). Ensuing disputes over the legislation between the NTLA and the Government were resolved only by sustained pressure from Bryant and the US Ambassador, thereby delaying the adoption of the legislation until December 2004. Nevertheless, in February 2005 the National Elections Commission (NEC) announced that the presidential and legislative elections would be conducted on 11 October. Some 40 prospective presidential candidates had emerged, notably including George Manneh Weah, a Liberian national who had gained international renown as an association footballer. In mid-March 2005 NTLA Speaker Dweh, together with the Deputy Speaker and two parliamentary deputies, were suspended from office on suspicion of corruption, following a report by a parliamentary committee that they had spent government funds without authorization. Dweh denied the charges against him, insisting that his suspension was not legitimate, and the UNMIL presence in Monrovia was reinforced, amid concerns of renewed unrest. In April Conneh also announced his intention to contest the forthcoming presidential election as the candidate of his new political grouping, the Progressive Democratic Party. Other prominent presidential candidates included Weah (who had formed his own party, the Congress of Democratic Change—CDC), a former minister in the Taylor administration, Roland Massaquoi, Johnson-Sirleaf of the UP, and long-standing opposition leaders, Winston Tubman, Togba Nah Tipoteh, and Henry Boima Fahnbulleh. (Bryant and other members of the National Transitional Government were not eligible to participate in the elections, under the terms of the comprehensive peace agreement.)

At the first round of presidential voting on 11 October 2005, which was contested by a total of 22 candidates, Weah secured 28.3% of votes cast, while Johnson-Sirleaf won 19.8% of votes and Charles Brumskine of the Liberty Party (LP) 13.9% of votes. At the elections to the 64-member lower House of Representatives the CDC won 15 seats, the LP nine seats, an alliance known as the Coalition for the Transformation of Liberia (COTOL) eight seats and the UP eight seats. At the elections to the 30-member Senate the COTOL secured seven seats, while the CDC, the UP and the LP each received three seats. Some 74.9% of the registered electorate voted in the presidential ballot and 76.5% in the legislative elections. Since no presidential candidate had secured an absolute majority, a second round was conducted on 8 November: Johnson-Sirleaf defeated Weah by 59.4% of votes cast (with 61.0% of the electorate participating). Weah immediately protested that electoral malpractice had been perpetrated and accused the NEC of bias towards Johnson-Sirleaf; a demonstration in his support was staged in Monrovia. On 23 November the NEC officially declared that Johnson-Sirleaf had won the presidential election. Nevertheless, Weah continued to claim that the election results were fraudulent, and threatened to prevent Johnson-Sirleaf's inauguration. Violent demonstrations by his supporters in Monrovia resulted in clashes with security forces and the arrest of some 40 protesters. In mid-December, following international pressure, however, Weah agreed to suspend his legal challenge to Johnson-Sirleaf's election at the Supreme Court, and subsequently announced that he would abandon his claim to the presidency in the interests of national reconciliation. Later that month the UN Security Council again extended the sanctions on armaments and travel for a further year and those on diamonds and timber for six months, and urged the establishment of a panel of experts to assess the authorities' compliance with requirements.

Johnson-Sirleaf was inaugurated as President on 16 January 2006, thereby becoming the first woman to be elected Head of State in Africa. The two legislative chambers were officially installed on the same day. The election of a close former associate of Taylor, Edwin Snowe, as Speaker of the House of Representatives attracted controversy. Johnson-Sirleaf subsequently began to nominate ministers, who, in accordance with the Constitution, were to be approved by the Senate. Opposition leaders criticized a number of presidential appointments, including that of a US officer as Johnson-Sirleaf's military adviser. In February Johnson-Sirleaf established a seven-member Truth and Reconciliation Commission, which was to investigate human rights abuses perpetrated during the civil conflict. In March 2006 Johnson-Sirleaf met US President George Bush during an official visit to Washington, DC, when the US Congress approved additional economic funding for Liberia. Johnson-Sirleaf (despite having previously indicated that national reconstruction was the greatest priority for the new Government) pledged commitment to bringing Taylor to trial. In the same month the Nigerian Government announced that it had received an official request from Liberia for Taylor's extradition. (In early November 2005 the UN Security Council had extended the mandate of UNMIL to authorize Taylor's arrest and dispatch to the Special Court in Sierra Leone, in the event that he return to Liberia.) In response to Johnson-Sirleaf's request, President Obasanjo declared that he would engage in consultations with other regional leaders. Later in March Taylor fled from his residence in Calabar, but was apprehended two days later in Borno State, near the border with Cameroon, and dispatched to Liberia, from where he was immediately extradited by UNMIL peace-keepers to the Special Court. In early April Taylor pleaded 'not guilty' to all charges at the Special Court. Tribunal officials subsequently requested that his trial be transferred to the ICC at the Hague (while remaining under the jurisdiction of the Special Court), in the interests of regional stability

Government

Under the Constitution of January 1986, legislative power is vested in the bicameral National Assembly, comprising the 64-member House of Representatives and the 30-member Senate. Members of the House of Representatives are elected by legislative constituency for a term of six years, while each county elects two members of the Senate (one for a term of nine years and one for six years). Executive power is vested in the President, who is elected to office for a six-year term (renewable only once), and who appoints the Government (subject to the approval of the Senate). Following a peace agreement in August 2003, a democratically elected administration was installed in January 2006 (replacing the power-sharing National Transitional Government). The country comprises 15 counties, which are divided into 64 districts.

Defence

The total strength of the Armed Forces of Liberia (AFL) at August 2005 was estimated at 11,000–15,000. Following a major rebel offensive against the capital in June 2003, the UN Security Council on 1 August authorized the establishment of a Economic Community of West African States (ECOWAS) peace-keeping contingent, the ECOWAS Mission in Liberia (ECOMIL), which was to restore security and prepare for the deployment of a longer-term UN stabilization force. The UN Mission in Liberia (UNMIL, see p. 76), which was officially established on 19 September and replaced ECOMIL on 1 October, was mandated to support the implementation of a comprehensive peace agreement, and a two-year transitional administration. With a total authorized strength of up to 15,000, at the end of January 2006 UNMIL numbered 14,832 troops, 205 military observers, and 1,028 civilian police, supported by 549 international civilian police and 844 local staff. Following the completion of the disarmament programme, in January 2005 a US military commission arrived in Liberia to assist in the restructuring of the armed forces. A 3,500-member police force trained by UNMIL was also to be established. In 2004 defence expenditure was estimated at US $50m. (equivalent to 10.2% of GDP).

Economic Affairs

In 2004, according to the World Bank, Liberia's gross domestic product (GDP) was US $391m., equivalent to $110 per head. During 1995–2004, it was estimated, the population increased at an average annual rate of 2.6%, while GDP per head rose by 11.5%. Overall GDP increased, in real terms, at an average annual rate of 14.5% in 1995–2004; real GDP declined by 31.0% in 2003, but increased by 2.0% in 2004.

Agriculture (including forestry and fishing) contributed an estimated 63.7% of GDP in 2004. An estimated 66.0% of the labour force were employed in the sector in 2003. The principal cash crops are rubber (which accounted for an estimated 90.0% of export earnings in 2004) and cocoa. The principal food crops are cassava, rice, bananas, plantains, yams and sweet potatoes. Timber production has traditionally represented an important source of export revenue, providing an estimated 50.1% of export earnings in 2003 (when, however, sanctions on timber exports were imposed). Agricultural GDP, according to the IMF, declined at an average annual rate of 5.5% in 1990–2002; the GDP of the agricultural sector increased by 21.5% in 2000, by 5.9% in 2001 and by an estimated 4.6% in 2002.

Industry (including mining, manufacturing, construction and power) contributed an estimated 12.5% of GDP in 2004, and employed 8% of the labour force in 1999. Industrial GDP, according to the IMF, declined at an average annual rate of 14.8% in 1988–2002; the GDP of the industrial sector increased by 61.6% in 2000, but declined by 2.8% in 2001 and by an estimated 24.4% in 2002.

Mining contributed less than 0.1% of GDP in 2004, and engaged 5.1% of the employed labour force in 1980. Gold and diamonds are mined, and Liberia possesses significant amounts of barytes and kyanite. The production and export of mineral products were severely disrupted from 1990, as a result of the civil conflict. In 1997 total mineral reserves were estimated to include more than 10m. carats of diamonds and 3m. troy oz of gold. In January 2005 the Government prohibited diamond mining in order to support the enforcement of UN sanctions on the export of diamonds (imposed in 2001—see below). The GDP of the mining sector, according to the IMF, declined at an average annual rate of 40.1% in 1988–2002; mining GDP increased by 49.8% in 2000, but declined by 74.9% in 2001 and by an estimated 69.9% in 2002.

Manufacturing provided an estimated 9.4% of GDP in 2004, and engaged about 1.2% of the employed labour force in 1980. Manufacturing GDP, according to the IMF, declined at an average annual rate of 5.6% in 1990–2002; the GDP of the manufacturing sector increased by 62.8% in 2000, but by only 0.9% in 2001, and declined by an estimated 23.7% in 2002.

Energy is derived from the consumption of fossil fuels (62.2%) and from hydroelectric power (37.8%). In 2003 the authorities announced plans to restore power throughout the country by a programme to rehabilitate a major hydroelectric power installation, which had been damaged in the civil conflict. Liberia is dependent on imports of petroleum, which comprised an estimated 26.3% of the value of total imports in 2004.

The services sector contributed an estimated 23.8% of GDP in 2004, and employed about 22% of the labour force in 1999. The GDP of the services sector, according to the IMF, declined at an average annual rate of 3.6% in 1990–2002; however, the GDP of the sector increased by 15.0% in 2000, by 3.2% in 2001 and by an estimated 7.0% in 2002.

Liberia's large open-registry ('flag of convenience') merchant shipping fleet has become an increasingly significant source of foreign exchange. In 2002 revenue from Liberia's maritime programme accounted for an estimated 18.4% of total revenue.

In 2004 Liberia recorded an estimated visible trade deficit of US $164.2m., and there was a deficit of $65.5m. on the current account of the balance of payments. In 2004 the principal source of imports (37.8%) was the Republic of Korea. The principal market for exports in that year was Germany (61.4%); other important purchasers were Belgium and China. The principal exports in 2004 were timber and rubber. The principal imports in 2004 were mineral fuels (principally petroleum), food (particularly rice) and live animals, machinery and transport equipment, miscellaneous manufactured articles and basic manufactures.

Liberia's overall budgetary deficit was US $500,000 (equivalent to 0.1% of GDP) in 2004, according to IMF estimates. The country's external debt totalled $2,567m. at the end of 2003, of which $1,127m. was long-term public debt. In that year the cost of debt-servicing was equivalent to 0.1% of the value of exports of goods and services. External public debt totalled $3,771m. (equivalent to 743.9% of GDP) in 2004. Consumer prices, according to official figures, increased by 10.4% in 2003 and by 7.8% in 2004. In 2004 unemployment was estimated at about 75.0% of the labour force.

Liberia is a member of the Economic Community of West African States (ECOWAS, see p. 217) and the Mano River Union (see p. 387), both of which aim to promote closer economic co-operation in the region.

Prior to the 1989–96 civil conflict, exports of iron ore, rubber and forestry products accounted for a significant proportion of Liberia's gross national income. Following the occupation of significant regions by rebel forces, production of these commodities was severely disrupted, although some informal exports continued. After elections in July 1997, the new Government announced that national revenue had dwindled to a negligible amount, while debt arrears had increased dramatically, and introduced measures to regain control of public expenditure. In 2000 a new tax system was introduced, currency reforms were implemented, and the financial position of the central bank was strengthened. Most significantly, however, a progressive deterioration in Liberia's relations with donors and external creditors resulted in a suspension in the disbursement of post-conflict financial assistance. In May 2001 a UN embargo on exports of diamonds from Liberia was imposed (see Recent History), and economic recovery began to slow considerably in that year, with rubber, logging and farming activity disrupted by continued rebel operations in parts of the country and failure to repair infrastructure damaged during the 1989–96 conflict. (In 2003 an additional ban on the export of timber entered into effect.) In March 2003 the IMF suspended Liberia's voting and related rights in the Fund, owing to the country's continued arrears. In August, after a major rebel offensive against the capital, Monrovia, President Charles Taylor was ousted from power and a comprehensive agreement between the Government and rebels provided for the creation of a power-sharing administration, the National Transitional Government, installed on 14 October (see Recent History). Following the deployment of the UN Mission in Liberia from October, the security situation steadily improved. In early February 2004 a UN-sponsored conference of international donors pledged some US $520m. (exceeding expectations) to support reconstruction and humanitarian efforts, and projects for infrastructural rehabilitation and employment generation. (Following the closure of private and public institutions, the level of official employment remained very low, with a high proportion of the population engaged in informal economic activities.) In March the IMF announced the resumption of assistance to Liberia, in response to improved co-operation from the new administration. Gradual economic recovery, generated by increased donor funds and some improvement in the security situation in rural areas, continued in 2005. Nevertheless, the level of exports continued to be restricted, owing, in part, to the UN sanctions in force against Liberia, including those on the export of timber and diamonds, which were again renewed by the Security Council at the end of the year. The transitional period finally ended when presidential and legislative elections were conducted successfully in October and November; Ellen Johnson-Sirleaf, a former World Bank economist, was inaugurated as President on 16 January 2006. She immediately appealed for international support for reconstruction, and announced measures to end endemic corruption, including the organization of a comprehensive financial audit of government institutions, and the introduction of restrictions on the conduct of public officials. The new Government declared that the level of external debt, in increasing arrears, had become so unsustainable that the country was unable at that time to receive new assistance from multilateral development institutions. In March an IMF mission reached agreement with the authorities on a staff-monitored programme, which was to remain in effect until the end of September, to implement urgent measures for debt and budget management. Later that month, coinciding with an official visit by Johnson-Sirleaf, the USA increased the total amount of reconstruction and development funds allocated to Liberia.

Education

Primary and secondary education are available free of charge. Education is officially compulsory for nine years, between seven and 16 years of age. Primary education begins at seven years of age and lasts for six years. Secondary education, beginning at 13 years of age, lasts for a further six years, divided into two cycles of three years each. Following elections in July 1997, the new Government aimed to rehabilitate large numbers of children who had been recruited to fight for the armed factions during the period of civil conflict. In 1999, following a programme of rehabilitation and reconstruction, the number of primary schools in the country increased to more than 4,500 (compared with 1,500 in 1998), while the number of secondary schools rose to 461 (compared with 241 in the previous year). In 1999/2000, according to UNESCO estimates, 83.4% of children in the relevant age-group (95.6% of boys; 71.2% of girls) were enrolled at primary schools, while the equivalent ratio for secondary enrolment was 20.3% of children in the appropriate age-group (23.7% of boys; 16.9% of girls). In early 2002 it was reported that only 40% of children of school age had access to educational facilities. In 1998 20,804 students were enrolled at institutes providing higher education, including the University of Monrovia, the Cuttington University College (controlled by the Protestant Episcopal Church), a college of technology and a computer science institute. The Government announced that about 10.9% of projected 1999 budget expenditure was allocated to education. A comprehensive peace agreement, signed on 18 August 2003, provided for the disbanding of all rebel groups, and the reintegration of recruited child combatants.

Public Holidays

2006: 1 January (New Year's Day), 11 February (Armed Forces Day), 12 March (Decoration Day), 15 March (J. J. Robert's Birthday), 11 April (Fast and Prayer Day), 14 April (Good Friday), 14 May (National Unification Day), 25 May (Africa Day), 26 July (Independence Day), 24 August (Flag Day), 1 November (All Saints' Day), 12 November (National Memorial Day), 29 November (President Tubman's Birthday), 25 December (Christmas Day).

2007: 1 January (New Year's Day), 11 February (Armed Forces Day), 12 March (Decoration Day), 15 March (J. J. Robert's Birthday), 6 April (Good Friday), 11 April (Fast and Prayer Day), 14 May (National Unification Day), 25 May (Africa Day), 26 July (Independence Day), 24 August (Flag Day), 1 November (All Saints' Day), 12 November (National Memorial Day), 29 November (President Tubman's Birthday), 25 December (Christmas Day).

Weights and Measures

Imperial weights and measures, modified by US usage, are in force.

Statistical Survey

Sources (unless otherwise stated): the former Ministry of Planning and Economic Affairs, POB 9016, Broad St, Monrovia.

Area and Population

AREA, POPULATION AND DENSITY

Area (sq km)	97,754*
Population (census results)	
1 February 1974	1,503,368
1 February 1984 (provisional)	
Males	1,063,127
Females	1,038,501
Total	2,101,628
Population (UN estimates at mid-year)†	
2002	3,206,000
2003	3,222,000
2004	3,241,000
Density (per sq km) at mid-2004	33.2

* 37,743 sq miles.
† Source: UN, *World Population Prospects: The 2004 Revision*.

ADMINISTRATIVE DIVISIONS
(population at 1984 census)

Counties:				
Bomi	66,420	Nimba		313,050
Bong	255,813	Rivercess		37,849
Grand Bassa	159,648	Sinoe		64,147
Grand Cape Mount	79,322	*Territories:*		
Grand Gedeh	102,810	Gibi		66,802
Lofa	247,641	Kru Coast		35,267
Maryland	85,267	Marshall		31,190
Montserrado	544,878	Sasstown		11,524
		Total		2,101,628

Note: The counties of Grand Kru and Margibi were subsequently established. Two further counties, River Gee and Gbarpolu, were created in 1998 and 2001, respectively.

PRINCIPAL TOWNS
(2003)

Monrovia (capital)	550,200	Harbel	17,700
Zwedru	35,300	Tubmanburg	16,700
Buchanan	27,300	Gbarnga	14,200
Yekepa	22,900	Greenville	13,500
Harper	20,000	Ganta	11,200
Bensonville	19,600		

Source: Stefan Helders, *World Gazetteer* (internet www.world-gazetteer.com).

BIRTHS AND DEATHS
(UN estimates, annual averages)

	1990–95	1995–2000	2000–05
Birth rate (per 1,000)	50.0	49.7	49.8
Death rate (per 1,000)	23.0	21.3	20.7

Source: UN, *World Population Prospects: The 2004 Revision*.

Expectation of life (WHO estimates, years at birth): 41 (males 40; females 43) in 2003 (Source: WHO, *World Health Report*).

LIBERIA

Statistical Survey

ECONOMICALLY ACTIVE POPULATION

	1978	1979	1980
Agriculture, forestry, hunting and fishing	355,467	366,834	392,926
Mining	25,374	26,184	28,047
Manufacturing	6,427	6,631	7,102
Construction	4,701	4,852	5,198
Electricity, gas and water	245	246	263
Commerce	18,668	19,266	20,636
Transport and communications	7,314	7,549	8,086
Services	49,567	51,154	54,783
Others	28,555	29,477	31,571
Total	**496,318**	**512,193**	**548,615**

Mid-2003 (estimates in '000): Agriculture, etc. 844; Total labour force 1,278 (Source: FAO).

Health and Welfare

KEY INDICATORS

Total fertility rate (children per woman, 2003)	6.8
Under-5 mortality rate (per 1,000 live births, 2004)	235
HIV/AIDS (% of persons aged 15–49, 2003)	5.9
Physicians (per 1,000 head, 1997)	0.02
Health expenditure (2002): US $ per head (PPP)	11
Health expenditure (2002): % of GDP	2.1
Health expenditure (2002): public (% of total)	68.0
Access to water (% of persons, 2002)	62
Access to sanitation (% of persons, 2002)	26

For sources and definitions, see explanatory note on p. vi.

Agriculture

PRINCIPAL CROPS
('000 metric tons)

	2002	2003	2004
Rice (paddy)*	110	100	110
Sweet potatoes†	18	19	19
Cassava (Manioc)†	480	490	490
Taro (Coco yam)†	26	26	26
Yams†	20	20	20
Sugar cane†	255	255	255
Oil palm fruit†	174	174	174
Vegetables and melons†	76	76	76
Bananas†	110	110	110
Plantains†	40	42	42
Other fresh fruit (excl. melons)†	17	17	17
Natural rubber (dry weight)*	109	110	117

* Unofficial figures.
† FAO estimates.
Source: FAO.

LIVESTOCK
(FAO estimates, '000 head, year ending September)

	2002	2003	2004
Cattle	36	36	36
Pigs	130	130	130
Sheep	210	210	210
Goats	220	220	220
Chickens	4,500	4,800	5,000
Ducks	200	200	200

Source: FAO.

LIVESTOCK PRODUCTS
(FAO estimates, metric tons)

	2002	2003	2004
Pig meat	4,400	4,400	4,400
Poultry meat	7,400	7,880	8,200
Other meat	8,816	8,816	8,816
Cows' milk	715	715	715
Hen eggs	4,320	4,320	4,320

Source: FAO.

Forestry

ROUNDWOOD REMOVALS
(FAO estimates, '000 cubic metres, excluding bark)

	2002	2003	2004
Sawlogs, veneer logs and logs for sleepers	157	157	157
Other industrial wood	180	180	180
Fuel wood	5,133	5,350	5,576
Total	**5,470**	**5,687**	**5,913**

Source: FAO.

SAWNWOOD PRODUCTION
('000 cubic metres, including railway sleepers)

	2002	2003*	2004*
Total (all broadleaved)	30	25	20

* Unofficial figure.
Source: FAO.

Fishing

(metric tons, live weight, capture)

	2001	2002*	2003*
Freshwater fishes	4,000	4,000	4,000
Dentex	671	680	650
Sardinellas	1,358	1,350	1,350
Sharks, rays, skates, etc.	647	650	640
Total catch (incl. others)	**11,286**	**11,500**	**11,300**

* FAO estimates.
Source: FAO.

Mining

	2002	2003	2004
Diamonds ('000 carats)*	80	40	10
Gold (kilograms)*	42	20	20

* Estimates.

Note: In addition to the commodities listed, Liberia produced significant quantities of a variety of industrial minerals and construction materials (clays, gypsum, sand and gravel, and stone), but insufficient information is available to make reliable estimates of output levels.

Source: US Geological Survey.

Industry

SELECTED PRODUCTS
('000 metric tons unless otherwise indicated)

	2001	2002	2003
Beer (metric tons)*	4,300	6,150	6,420
Palm oil†	42	42	42
Cement	63	54	25‡
Electric energy (million kWh)	540	n.a.	n.a.

* FAO estimates.
† Unofficial figures; annual output assumed to be unchanged since 1997.
‡ Estimate.

Source: FAO; US Geological Survey; UN, *Industrial Commodity Statistics Yearbook*.

Finance

CURRENCY AND EXCHANGE RATES

Monetary Units
100 cents = 1 Liberian dollar (L $).

Sterling, Dollar and Euro Equivalents (30 September 2005)
£1 sterling = L $101.56;
US $1 = L $57.50;
€1 = L $69.24;
L $1,000 = £9.85 = US $17.39 = €14.44.

Average Exchange Rate (L $ per US $)
2002 61.7542
2003 59.3788
2004 54.9058

Note: The aforementioned data are based on market-determined rates of exchange. Prior to January 1998 the exchange rate was a fixed parity with the US dollar (L $1 = US $1).

BUDGET
(US $ million)

Revenue*	2002	2003	2004
Tax revenue	70.3	42.1	62.5
Taxes on income and profits	14.4	6.4	18.0
Taxes on goods and services	3.5	4.3	6.9
Maritime revenue	13.4	11.2	13.5
Stumpage fees and land rental	13.0	2.6	0.1
Taxes on international trade	17.0	18.0	23.0
Other revenue	2.4	2.8	5.6
Total	72.7	44.9	68.2

Expenditure	2002	2003	2004
Current expenditure	26.0	24.5	59.8
Wages and salaries	13.4	11.1	24.4
Other goods and services	5.9	6.8	25.7
Subsidies and grants	0.4	0.5	5.7
Interest payments	6.3	6.0	2.6
Domestic arrears clearance	—	—	1.5
Capital expenditure†	54.1	20.4	9.8
Total	80.1	45.0	69.7

* Excluding grants received (US $ million): 3.0 in 2003; 1.0 in 2004.
† Includes expenditure related to national security.

Source: IMF, *Liberia: Selected Issues and Statistical Appendix* (May 2005).

INTERNATIONAL RESERVES
(US $ million at 31 December)

	2002	2003	2004
Reserve position in IMF	0.04	0.04	0.05
Foreign exchange	3.26	7.84	18.69
Total	3.30	7.88	18.74

Source: IMF, *International Financial Statistics*.

MONEY SUPPLY
(L $ million at 31 December)

	2002	2003	2004
Currency outside banks*	1,045.0	1,303.7	1,754.9
Demand deposits at commercial banks	1,318.2	1,391.3	1,971.9
Total money (incl. others)	2,363.5	2,755.6	3,727.5

* Figures refer only to amounts of Liberian coin in circulation. US notes and coin also circulate, but the amount of these in private holdings is unknown. The amount of Liberian coin in circulation is small in comparison to US currency.

Source: IMF, *International Financial Statistics*.

COST OF LIVING
(Consumer Price Index, annual averages; base: May 1998 = 100)

	2002	2003	2004
Food	111.0	140.9	153.8
Fuel and light	155.5	154.4	217.6
Clothing	119.1	121.2	128.7
Rent	131.2	131.8	156.1
All items (incl. others)	142.3	157.0	169.3

Source: IMF, *Liberia: Selected Issues and Statistical Appendix* (May 2005).

NATIONAL ACCOUNTS
(at current prices)

Expenditure on the Gross Domestic Product
(L $ million)

	1987	1988	1989
Government final consumption expenditure	143.9	136.3	141.6
Private final consumption expenditure	713.9	733.3	656.8
Increase in stocks*	7.0	3.5	4.0
Gross fixed capital formation	120.4	115.3	96.8
Statistical discrepancy	22.9	39.1	48.2
Total domestic expenditure	1,008.1	1,027.5	947.4
Exports of goods and services	438.2	452.3	521.4
Less Imports of goods and services	356.8	321.5	275.2
GDP in purchasers' values	1,089.5	1,158.3	1,193.6
GDP at constant 1981 prices	1,015.0	1,043.7	1,072.8

* Figures refer only to stocks of iron ore and rubber.

Source: UN, *National Accounts Statistics*.

Gross Domestic Product by Economic Activity
(US $ million, estimates)

	2002	2003	2004
Agriculture, hunting, forestry and fishing	422.4	293.9	313.6
Mining and quarrying	0.2	0.3	0.4
Manufacturing	31.8	29.9	46.3
Electricity, gas and water	2.9	3.5	4.0
Construction	10.1	9.9	10.9
Trade, restaurants and hotels	20.8	24.1	32.5
Transport, storage and communications	30.2	31.9	36.8
Finance, insurance, real estate and business services	14.3	13.1	14.1
Government services	12.6	11.6	14.3
Other services	14.0	17.1	19.2
GDP in purchasers' values	559.3	435.3	492.1

Source: IMF, *Liberia: Selected Issues and Statistical Appendix* (May 2005).

LIBERIA

BALANCE OF PAYMENTS
(US $ million, estimates)

	2002	2003	2004
Exports of goods f.o.b.	166.5	108.9	103.8
Imports of goods c.i.f.	–145.3	–140.0	–268.1
Trade balance	21.1	–31.1	–164.2
Services (net)	2.8	–17.1	–45.6
Balance on goods and services	23.9	–48.2	–209.8
Income (net)	–106.5	–77.6	–98.3
Balance on goods, services and income	–82.6	–125.8	–308.1
Current transfers (net)	63.4	46.6	242.6
Current balance	–19.2	–79.2	–65.5
Capital and financial account (net)	–14.2	–26.1	–29.4
Net errors and omissions	–47.4	36.4	22.2
Overall balance	–80.8	–68.9	–72.8

Source: IMF, *Liberia: Selected Issues and Statistical Appendix* (May 2005).

External Trade

PRINCIPAL COMMODITIES
(US $ million, estimates)

Imports c.i.f.	2002	2003	2004
Food and live animals	40.9	40.6	61.9
Rice	30.5	39.2	27.5
Beverages and tobacco	4.5	4.4	9.2
Mineral fuels and lubricants	49.7	30.7	70.6
Petroleum	48.4	29.7	66.2
Chemicals and related products	6.0	5.5	7.1
Basic manufactures	9.7	11.9	25.4
Machinery and transport equipment	11.5	11.9	50.6
Miscellaneous manufactured articles	19.2	30.3	38.3
Total (incl. others)	145.3	140.0	268.1

Exports f.o.b.	2002	2003	2004
Rubber	59.2	43.9	93.4
Timber	100.4	54.6	—
Cocoa	0.4	0.9	3.5
Total (incl. others)	166.5	108.9	103.8

Source: IMF, *Liberia: Selected Issues and Statistical Appendix* (May 2005).

PRINCIPAL TRADING PARTNERS
(US $ million)

Imports c.i.f.	1986	1987	1988
Belgium-Luxembourg	8.5	11.2	15.0
China, People's Repub.	7.1	14.7	4.8
Denmark	10.6	7.6	5.9
France (incl. Monaco)	6.5	6.4	4.7
Germany, Fed. Repub.	32.7	52.3	39.5
Italy	2.5	2.2	7.3
Japan	20.1	15.0	12.0
Netherlands	20.6	26.8	14.4
Spain	2.5	6.6	3.1
Sweden	2.4	0.6	4.6
United Kingdom	24.2	18.4	12.7
USA	42.5	58.0	57.7
Total (incl. others)	259.0	307.6	272.3

Source: UN, *International Trade Statistics Yearbook*.

Exports f.o.b.	2002	2003	2004
Belgium-Luxembourg	—	—	30.6
China, People's Repub.	—	—	5.5
France	90.0	16.3	1.7
Hong Kong	—	41.2	—
USA	52.7	34.1	63.7
Total (incl. others)	176.1	108.9	103.8

Source: Ministry of Commerce and Industry, Monrovia.

Transport

RAILWAYS
(estimated traffic)

	1991	1992	1993
Passenger-km (million)	406	417	421
Freight ton-km (million)	200	200	200

Source: UN Economic Commission for Africa, *African Statistical Yearbook*.

ROAD TRAFFIC
(estimates, vehicles in use at 31 December)

	1999	2000	2001
Passenger cars	15.3	17.1	17.1
Commercial vehicles	11.9	12.8	12.8

Source: UN, *Statistical Yearbook*.

SHIPPING

Merchant Fleet
(registered at 31 December)

	2002	2003	2004
Number of vessels	1,535	1,553	1,538
Displacement ('000 gross registered tons)	50,400.2	52,434.6	53,898.8

Source: Lloyd's Register-Fairplay, *World Fleet Statistics*.

International Sea-borne Freight Traffic
(estimates, '000 metric tons)

	1991	1992	1993
Goods loaded	16,706	17,338	21,653
Goods unloaded	1,570	1,597	1,608

Source: UN Economic Commission for Africa, *African Statistical Yearbook*.

CIVIL AVIATION
(traffic on scheduled services)

	1990	1991	1992
Passengers carried ('000)	32	32	32
Passenger-km (million)	7	7	7
Total ton-km (million)	1	1	1

Source: UN, *Statistical Yearbook*.

LIBERIA

Communications Media

	1995	1996	1997
Radio receivers ('000 in use)	675	715	790
Television receivers ('000 in use)	56	60	70
Telephones ('000 main lines in use)	5	5	6
Daily newspapers:			
number	8	6	6
average circulation ('000 copies, estimates)	35	35	36

Sources: UNESCO Institute for Statistics; UN, *Statistical Yearbook*.

Telephones ('000 main lines in use): 6.6 in 1999; 6.7 in 2000; 6.8 in 2001 (Source: International Telecommunication Union).

Mobile cellular telephones ('000 subscribers): 1.5 in 2000; 2.0 in 2001 (Source: International Telecommunication Union).

Internet users ('000): 0.3 in 1999; 0.5 in 2000; 1.0 in 2001 (Source: UN, *Statistical Yearbook*).

Daily newspapers: 6 in 1998 (estimated average circulation 36,600) (Source: UNESCO Institute for Statistics).

Education

(1999/2000)

	Teachers	Students Males	Females	Total
Pre-primary	4,322	82,215	72,908	155,123
Primary	12,966	288,227	208,026	496,253
Secondary:				
general	6,204	50,149	34,494	84,643
technical and vocational	561	26,988	18,079	45,067
Post-secondary technical and vocational	430	8,842	6,789	15,631
University	723	25,236	18,871	44,107

Source: UNESCO Institute for Statistics.

Adult literacy rate (UNESCO estimates): 55.9% (males 72.3%; females 39.3%) in 2003 (Source: UN, *Human Development Report*).

Directory

The Constitution

The Constitution of the Republic of Liberia entered into effect on 6 January 1986, following its approval by national referendum in July 1984. Its main provisions are summarized below:

PREAMBLE

The Republic of Liberia is a unitary sovereign state, which is divided into counties for administrative purposes. There are three separate branches of government: the legislative, the executive and the judiciary. No person is permitted to hold office or executive power in more than one branch of government. The fundamental human rights of the individual are guaranteed.

LEGISLATURE

Legislative power is vested in the bicameral National Assembly, comprising a Senate and a House of Representatives. Deputies of both chambers are elected by universal adult suffrage. Each county elects two members of the Senate (one for a term of nine years and one for six years), while members of the House of Representatives are elected by legislative constituency for a term of six years. Legislation requires the approval of two-thirds of the members of both chambers, and is subsequently submitted to the President for endorsement. The Constitution may be amended by two-thirds of the members of both chambers.

EXECUTIVE

Executive power is vested in the President, who is Head of State and Commander-in-Chief of the armed forces. The President is elected by universal adult suffrage for a term of six years, and is restricted to a maximum of two terms in office. A Vice-President is elected at the same time as the President. The President appoints a Cabinet, and members of the judiciary and armed forces, with the approval of the Senate. The President is empowered to declare a state of emergency.

JUDICIARY

Judicial power is vested in the Supreme Court and any subordinate courts, which apply both statutory and customary laws in accordance with standards enacted by the legislature. The judgements of the Supreme Court are final and not subject to appeal or review by any other branch of government. The Supreme Court comprises one Chief Justice and five Associate Justices. Justices are appointed by the President, with the approval of the Senate.

POLITICAL PARTIES AND ELECTIONS

Political associations are obliged to comply with the minimum registration requirements imposed by the Elections Commission. Organizations that endanger free democratic society, or that organize, train or equip groups of supporters, are to be denied registration. Prior to elections, each political party and independent candidate is required to submit statements of assets and liabilities to the Elections Commission. All elections of public officials are determined by an absolute majority of the votes cast. If no candidate obtains an absolute majority in the first ballot, a second ballot is conducted between the two candidates with the highest number of votes. Complaints by parties or candidates must be submitted to the Elections Commission within seven days of the announcement of election results. The Supreme Court has final jurisdiction over challenges to election results.

The Government

HEAD OF STATE

President: Ellen Johnson-Sirleaf (inaugurated 16 January 2006).

THE CABINET
(April 2006)

Vice-President: Joseph Nyumah Boakai.
Minister of Agriculture: J. Christopher Toe.
Minister of Commerce and Industry: Bankie King Akerele.
Minister of Defence: Brownie Samukai.
Minister of Education: Joseph Korto.
Minister of Finance: Antoinette Sayeh.
Minister of Foreign Affairs: George W. Wallace.
Minister of Gender Development: Varbah Gayflor.
Minister of Health and Social Welfare: Walter Gwenigale.
Minister of Information, Culture and Tourism: Johnny McClain.
Minister of Internal Affairs: Ambullai Johnson.
Minister of Justice: Frances Johnson-Morris.
Minister of Labour: Samuel Kofi Woods.
Minister of Lands, Mines and Energy: Eugene Shannon.
Minister of National Security: (vacant).
Minister of Planning and Economic Affairs: Toga G. McIntosh.
Minister of Posts and Telecommunications: Jackson E. Doe.
Minister of Public Works: Willie Knuckles.
Minister of Rural Development: (vacant).
Minister of Transport: Jeremiah Sulunteh.
Minister of Youth and Sport: Jamesetta Wolokollie.

MINISTRIES

Office of the Chairman: Executive Mansion, POB 10-9001, Capitol Hill, 1000 Monrovia 10; e-mail emansion@liberia.net.
Ministry of Agriculture: Tubman Blvd, POB 10-9010, 1000 Monrovia 10; tel. 226399.
Ministry of Commerce and Industry: Ashmun St, POB 10-9014, 1000 Monrovia 10; tel. 226283.
Ministry of Defence: Benson St, POB 10-9007, 1000 Monrovia 10; tel. 226077.

LIBERIA

Ministry of Education: E. G. N. King Plaza, Broad St, POB 10-1545, 1000 Monrovia 10; tel. and fax 226216.

Ministry of Finance: Broad St, POB 10-9013, 1000 Monrovia 10; tel. 47510680; internet www.finance.gov.lr.

Ministry of Foreign Affairs: Mamba Point, POB 10-9002, 1000 Monrovia 10; tel. 226763.

Ministry of Gender Development: Monrovia.

Ministry of Health and Social Welfare: Sinkor, POB 10-9004, 1000 Monrovia 10; tel. 226317.

Ministry of Information, Culture and Tourism: Capitol Hill, POB 10-9021, 1000 Monrovia 10; tel. and fax 226269.

Ministry of Internal Affairs: cnr Warren and Benson Sts, POB 10-9008, 1000 Monrovia 10; tel. 226346.

Ministry of Justice: Ashmun St, POB 10-9006, 1000 Monrovia 10; tel. 227872.

Ministry of Labour: Mechlin St, POB 10-9040, 1000 Monrovia 10; tel. 226291.

Ministry of Lands, Mines and Energy: Capitol Hill, POB 10-9024, 1000 Monrovia 10; tel. 226281.

Ministry of National Security: 1000 Monrovia 10.

Ministry of Planning and Economic Affairs: Broad St, POB 10-9016, 1000 Monrovia 10; tel. 226962.

Ministry of Posts and Telecommunications: Carey St, 1000 Monrovia 10; tel. 226079.

Ministry of Presidential Affairs: Executive Mansion, Capitol Hill, 1000 Monrovia 10; tel. 228026.

Ministry of Public Works: Lynch St, POB 10-9011, 1000 Monrovia 10; tel. 227972.

Ministry of Rural Development: POB 10-9030, 1000 Monrovia 10; tel. 227938.

Ministry of Transport: 1000 Monrovia 10.

President and Legislature

PRESIDENT

Presidential Election, First Round, 11 October 2005

	Votes	% of votes
George Manneh Weah (Congress for Democratic Change)	275,265	28.26
Ellen Johnson-Sirleaf (Unity Party)	192,326	19.75
Charles Walker Brumskine (Liberty Party)	135,093	13.87
Winston A. Tubman (National Democratic Party of Liberia)	89,623	9.20
Harry Varney Gboto-Nambi Sherman (Coalition for the Transformation of Liberia)	76,403	7.85
Roland Chris Yarkpah Massaquoi (National Patriotic Party)	40,361	4.14
Joseph D. Z. Korto (Liberia Equal Rights Party)	31,814	3.27
Alhaji G. V. Kromah (All Liberian Coalition Party)	27,141	2.79
Togba-Nah Tipoteh (Alliance for Peace and Democracy)	22,766	2.34
William Vacanarat Shadrach Tubman (Reformed United Liberia Party)	15,115	1.55
John Sembe Morlu (United Democratic Alliance)	12,068	1.24
Milton Nathaniel Barnes (Liberia Destiny Party)	9,325	0.96
Margaret J. Tor-Thompson (Freedom Alliance Party of Liberia)	8,418	0.84
Joseph Mamadee Woah-Tee (Labour Party of Liberia)	5,948	0.61
Sekou Damate Conneh (Progressive Democratic Party)	5,499	0.56
David M. Farhat (Free Democratic Party)	4,497	0.46
George Klay Kieh, Jr (New Deal Movement)	4,476	0.46
Armah Zolu Jallah (National Party of Liberia)	3,837	0.39
Robert Momo Kpoto (Union of Liberian Democrats)	3,825	0.39
George Momodu Kiadii (National Vision Party of Liberia)	3,646	0.37
Samuel Raymond Divine, Sr (Independent)	3,188	0.33
Alfred Reeves (National Reformation Party)	3,156	0.32
Total	**973,790**	**100.00**

Presidential Election, Second Round, 8 November 2005

	Votes	% of votes
Ellen Johnson-Sirleaf (Unity Party)	478,526	59.40
George Manneh Weah (Congress for Democratic Change)	327,046	40.60
Total	**805,572**	**100.00**

LEGISLATURE

House of Representatives

Speaker: EDWIN SNOWE.

General Election, 11 October 2005

Party	% of votes	Seats
Congress for Democratic Change	23.4	15
Liberty Party	14.1	9
Unity Party	12.5	8
Coalition for the Transformation of Liberia	12.5	8
Independents	10.9	7
Alliance for Peace and Democracy	7.8	5
National Patriotic Party	6.3	4
New Deal Movement	4.7	3
All Liberian Coalition Party	3.1	2
National Democratic Party of Liberia	1.6	1
United Democratic Alliance	1.6	1
National Reformation Party	1.6	1
Total	**100.0**	**64**

Senate

President: ISAAC NYENABO.

General Election, 11 October 2005

	% of votes	Seats
Coalition for the Transformation of Liberia	23.3	7
Congress for Democratic Change	10.0	3
Unity Party	10.0	3
Liberty Party	10.0	3
Alliance for Peace and Democracy	10.0	3
National Patriotic Party	10.0	3
Independents	10.0	3
National Democratic Party of Liberia	6.7	2
National Reformation Party	3.3	1
All Liberian Coalition Party	3.3	1
United Democratic Alliance	3.3	1
Total	**100.0**	**30**

Election Commission

National Elections Commission: Tubman Blvd, 16th St, Sinkor, Monrovia; internet www.necliberia.org; independent; Chair. JAMES FLOMOYAN.

Political Organizations

At the end of January 1997 the armed factions in Liberia officially ceased to exist as military organizations; a number of them were reconstituted as political parties, while long-standing political organizations re-emerged. In August 2003 the two main rebel movements in conflict with government forces, Liberians United for Reconciliation and Democracy and the Movement for Democracy in Liberia, signed a peace agreement, which provided for their inclusion in a power-sharing administration. Following the completion of the disarmament process in November 2004, these were officially dissolved. A total of 30 political parties had been granted registration prior to presidential and legislative elections in October and November 2005.

Alliance for Peace and Democracy (APD): Benson St, Monrovia; tel. (6) 547710; internet www.members.tripod.com/tipoteh12/index.html; f. 2005; Leader TOGBA-NAH TIPOTEH; Chair. DUSTY WOLOKOLIE.

Liberian People's Party (LPP): Monrovia; f. 1984 by fmr mems of the Movement for Justice in Africa; Leader DUSTY WOLOKOLLIE.

LIBERIA

United People's Party (UPP): Monrovia; f. 1984 by fmr mems of the Progressive People's Party, which led opposition prior to April 1980 coup; Leader WESLEY JOHNSON.

All Liberian Coalition Party (ALCOP): Broad St, Monrovia; tel. (6) 524735; f. 1997 from elements of fmr armed faction the United Liberation Movement of Liberia for Democracy; Leader Alhaji G. V. KROMAH; Chair. JOHNSTON P. FANNEBRDE.

Coalition for the Transformation of Liberia (COTOL): Monrovia; f. 2005; Leader HARRY VARNEY GBOTO-NAMBI SHERMAN.

Liberian Action Party (LAP): Monrovia; f. 1984; Leader GYUDE BRYANT.

Liberian Unification Party (LUP): Monrovia; f. 1984; Leader LAVELI SUPUWOOD.

People's Democratic Party of Liberia (PDPL): Monrovia; Leader FIYAH GBOLIE.

True Whig Party (TWP): Monrovia; Leader RUDOLPH SHERMAN.

Congress for Democratic Change: Bernard Beach Compound, Monrovia; tel. (6) 513469; f. 2004; Leader GEORGE MANNEH WEAH; Chair. J. BANGULA COLE.

Free Democratic Party (FDP): Center St, Monrovia; tel. (6) 582291; Leader DAVID M. FARHAT; Chair. S. CIAPHA GBOLLIE.

Liberia Equal Rights Party (LERP): Duala Gas Station, Bushrod Island, Opposite Duala Market, Monrovia; f. 2005; Leader JOSEPH D. Z. KORTO; Chair. SOLOMON KING.

Liberia Destiny Party (LDP): Congo Town Back Rd, Monrovia; tel. (6) 511531; f. 2005; Leader MILTON NATHANIEL BARNES; Sec.-Gen. BORBOR B. KROMAH.

Liberty Party (LP): Old Rd, Sinkor Opposite Haywood Mission, POB 1340, Monrovia; tel. (6) 547921; f. 2005; Leader CHARLES WALKER BRUMSKINE; Chair. LARRY P. YOUQUOI.

National Democratic Party of Liberia (NDPL): Capital Bye Pass, Monrovia; f. 1997 from the fmr armed faction the Liberia Peace Council; Leader WINSTON A. TUBMAN; Chair. NYANDEH SIEH.

National Patriotic Party (NPP): Sinkor, Tubman Bldg, Monrovia; tel. (6) 515312; f. 1997 from the fmr armed faction the National Patriotic Front of Liberia; won the majority of seats in legislative elections in July 1997; Leader ROLAND CHRIS YARKPAH MASSAQUOI; Chair. LAWRENCE A. GEORGE.

National Reformation Party (NRP): Duala Market, Monrovia; tel. (6) 511531; Leader Bishop ALFRED GARPEE REEVES; Chair. Rev. SAMUEL TORMETIEE.

New Deal Movement (NDM): Randall St, Monrovia; tel. (6) 567470; f. 2003; Leader Prof. GEORGE KLAY KIEH, Jr; Chair. T. WILSON GAYE.

Progressive Democratic Party (PRODEM): McDonald St, Monrovia; tel. (6) 521091; f. early 2005 by mems of fmr rebel movement, Liberians United for Reconciliation and Democracy (emerged 1999); Leader SEKOU DAMATE CONNEH.

Reformed United Liberia Party (RULP): 70 Ashmun St, POB 1000, Monrovia; tel. (6) 571212; f. 2005; Leader WILLIAM VACANARAT SHADRACH TUBMAN.

United Democratic Alliance (UDA): Monrovia; f. 2005 by the **Liberia National Union (LINU)**; led by HENRY MONIBA; the **Liberia Education and Development Party (LEAD)**; and the **Reformation Alliance Party (RAP)**, led by HENRY BOIMAH FAHNBULLEH; Leader JOHN SEMBE MORLU.

Unity Party (UP): 86 Broad St, Monrovia; tel. (6) 512528; e-mail info@theunityparty.org; internet www.theunityparty.org; f. 1984; Leader ELLEN JOHNSON-SIRLEAF; Chair. Dr CHARLES CLARKE.

Diplomatic Representation

EMBASSIES IN LIBERIA

Algeria: Capitol By-Pass, POB 2032, Monrovia; tel. 224311; Chargé d'affaires a.i. MUHAMMAD AZZEDINE AZZOUZ.

Cameroon: 18th St and Payne Ave, Sinkor, POB 414, Monrovia; tel. 261374; Ambassador VICTOR E. NDIBA.

China, People's Republic: Tubman Blvd, Congotown, POB 5970, Monrovia; tel. 228024; fax 226740; Ambassador LIN SONGTIAN.

Congo, Democratic Republic: Spriggs Payne Airport, Sinkor, POB 1038, Monrovia; tel. 261326; Ambassador (vacant).

Côte d'Ivoire: Tubman Blvd, Sinkor, POB 126, Monrovia; tel. 261123; Ambassador CLÉMENT KAUL MELEDJE.

Cuba: 17 Kennedy Ave, Congotown, POB 3579, Monrovia; tel. 262600; Ambassador M. GAUNEANO CARDOSO TOLEDO.

Egypt: POB 462, Monrovia; tel. 226226; fax 226122; Ambassador FATHY GUERGIS BESHARA.

Ghana: cnr 11th St and Gardiner Ave, Sinkor, POB 471, Monrovia; tel. 261477; Ambassador Maj.-Gen. FRANCIS ADU-AMANFOH.

Guinea: Monrovia; Ambassador ABDOULAYE DORÉ.

Lebanon: 12th St, Monrovia; tel. 262537; Chargé d'affaires a.i. GABRIEL GEARA.

Libya: Monrovia; Ambassador MUHAMMAD UMARAT-TABI.

Morocco: Tubman Blvd, Congotown, Monrovia; tel. 262767; Chargé d'affaires a.i. Dr MOULAY ABBES AL-KADIRI.

Nigeria: Congotown, POB 366, Monrovia; tel. 227345; fax 226135; Ambassador JOSHUA IROHA.

Russia: Payne Ave, Sinkor, POB 2010, Monrovia; tel. 261304; Ambassador VASILII S. BEBKO.

Senegal: Monrovia; Ambassador MOCTAR TRAORÉ.

Sierra Leone: Tubman Blvd, POB 575, Monrovia; tel. 261301; Ambassador KEMOH SALIA-BAO.

USA: 111 United Nations Dr., Mamba Point, POB 10-0098, Monrovia; tel. 226370; fax 226148; e-mail montgomery@state.gov; internet www.usembassy.state.gov/monrovia; Ambassador DONALD E. BOOTH.

Judicial System

In February 1982 the People's Supreme Tribunal (which had been established following the April 1980 coup) was renamed the People's Supreme Court, and its Chairman and members became the Chief Justice and Associate Justices of the People's Supreme Court. The judicial system also comprised People's Circuit and Magistrate Courts. The five-member Supreme Court was established in January 1992 to adjudicate in electoral disputes.

Chief Justice of the Supreme Court of Liberia: JOHNNIE LEWIS.

Justices: KABINNEH JANNEH, FRANCIS KORKPOR, EMMANUEL WUREH, GLADYS JOHNSON.

Religion

Liberia is officially a Christian state, although complete religious freedom is guaranteed. Christianity and Islam are the two main religions. There are numerous religious sects, and many Liberians hold traditional beliefs.

CHRISTIANITY

Liberian Council of Churches: 16 St, Sinkor, POB 10-2191, 1000 Monrovia; tel. 226630; fax 226132; f. 1982; 11 mems, two assoc. mems, one fraternal mem.; Pres. Rt Rev. Dr W. NAH DIXON; Gen. Sec. Rev. STEVEN W. MUIN.

The Anglican Communion

The diocese of Liberia forms part of the Church of the Province of West Africa, incorporating the local Protestant Episcopal Church. Anglicanism was established in Liberia in 1836, and the diocese of Liberia was admitted into full membership of the Province in 1982. In 1985 the Church had 125 congregations, 39 clergy, 26 schools and about 20,000 adherents in the country. The Metropolitan of the Province is the Bishop of Koforidua, Ghana.

Bishop of Liberia: Rt Rev. EDWARD NEUFVILLE, POB 10-0277, 1000 Monrovia 10; tel. 224760; fax 227519.

The Roman Catholic Church

Liberia comprises the archdiocese of Monrovia and the dioceses of Cape Palmas and Gbarnga. At 31 December 2003 there were an estimated 166,219 adherents in the country, equivalent to 5.8% of the total population.

Catholic Bishops' Conference of Liberia

POB 10-2078, 1000 Monrovia 10; tel. 227245; fax 226175; f. 1998; Pres. Most Rev. MICHAEL KPAKALA FRANCIS (Archbishop of Monrovia).

Archbishop of Monrovia: Most Rev. MICHAEL KPAKALA FRANCIS, Archbishop's Office, POB 10-2078, 1000 Monrovia 10; tel. 227245; fax 226411; e-mail kpakala1936@hotmail.com.

Other Christian Churches

Assemblies of God in Liberia: POB 1297, Monrovia; f. 1908; 14,578 adherents, 287 churches; Gen. Supt JIMMIE K. DUGBE, Sr.

Lutheran Church in Liberia: POB 1046, Monrovia; tel. 226633; fax 226262; e-mail lwfliberia@compuserve.com; 35,600 adherents; Pres. Bishop SUMOWARD E. HARRIS.

Providence Baptist Church: cnr Broad and Center Sts, Monrovia; f. 1821; 2,500 adherents, 300 congregations, 6 ministers, 8 schools; Pastor Rev. A. MOMOLUE DIGGS.

Liberia Baptist Missionary and Educational Convention, Inc: POB 390, Monrovia; tel. 222661; f. 1880; Pres. Rev. J. K. LEVEE

LIBERIA

MOULTON; Nat. Vice-Pres. Rev. J. GBANA HALL; Gen. Sec. CHARLES W. BLAKE.

United Methodist Church in Liberia: cnr 12th St and Tubman Blvd, POB 1010, 1000 Monrovia 10; tel. 223343; f. 1833; c. 68,300 adherents, 600 congregations, 700 ministers, 394 lay pastors, 121 schools, one university; Resident Bishop Rev. Dr JOHN G. INNIS; Sec. Rev. Dr SAMUEL J. QUIRE, Jr.

Other active denominations include the National Baptist Mission, the Pentecostal Church, the Presbyterian Church in Liberia, the Prayer Band and the Church of the Lord Aladura.

ISLAM

The total community numbers about 670,000.

National Muslim Council of Liberia: Monrovia; Leader Shaykh KAFUMBA KONNAH.

The Press

NEWSPAPERS

The Inquirer: Benson St, POB 20-4209, Monrovia; tel. and fax 227105; independent; Man. Editor PHILIP WESSEH.

Monrovia Guardian: Monrovia; independent; Editor SAM O. DEAN.

News: ACDB Bldg, POB 10-3137, Carey Warren St, Monrovia; tel. 227820; e-mail imms@afrlink.com; independent; weekly; Chair. WILSON TARPEH; Editor-in-Chief JEROME DALIEH.

PERIODICALS

The Kpelle Messenger: Kpelle Literacy Center, Lutheran Church, POB 1046, Monrovia; Kpelle-English; monthly; Editor Rev. JOHN J. MANAWU.

Liberia Orbit: Voinjama; e-mail orbit@tekmail.com; internet www.liberiaorbit.org; national current affairs; Editor LLOYD SCOTT.

Liberian Post: e-mail info@liberian.org; internet www.liberian.org; f. 1998; independent internet magazine; tourist information; Publr WILLEM TIJSSEN.

New Democrat: Monrovia; e-mail newdemnews@yahoo.com; internet www.newdemocrat.org; national news and current affairs.

Patriot: Congotown 1000, Monrovia; internet www.allaboutliberia.com/patriot.htm.

The People Magazine: Bank of Liberia Bldg, Suite 214, Carey and Warren Sts, POB 3501, Monrovia; tel. 222743; f. 1985; monthly; Editor and Publr CHARLES A. SNETTER.

PRESS ORGANIZATIONS

Liberia Institute of Journalism: Kashour Bldg, 2nd Floor, cnr Broad and Johnson Sts, POB 2314, Monrovia; tel. 227327; e-mail lij@kabissa.org; internet www.kabissa.org/lij; Dir VINICIUS HODGES.

Press Union of Liberia: Benson St, POB 20-4209, Monrovia; tel. and fax 227105; e-mail pul@kabissa.org; internet www.kabissa.org/pul; f. 1985; Pres. ELIZABETH HOFF.

NEWS AGENCIES

Liberian News Agency (LINA): POB 9021, Capitol Hill, Monrovia; tel. and fax 226269; e-mail lina@afrlink.com; Dir-Gen. ERNEST KIAZOLY (acting).

Foreign Bureaux

Agence France-Presse (AFP): Monrovia; Rep. JAMES DORBOR.

United Press International (UPI) (USA): Monrovia; Correspondent T. K. SANNAH.

Xinhua (New China) News Agency (People's Republic of China): Adams St, Old Rd, Congotown, POB 3001, Monrovia; tel. 262821; Correspondent SUN BAOYU.

Reuters (United Kingdom) is also represented in Liberia.

Broadcasting and Communications

TELECOMMUNICATIONS

Liberia Telecommunications Corpn: Monrovia; tel. 227523; Man. Dir JOE GBALAH.

BROADCASTING

Radio

Liberia Communications Network: Congotown 1000, Monrovia; govt-operated; broadcasts information, education and entertainment 24 hours daily in English, French and several African languages; short-wave service.

Liberia Rural Communications Network: POB 10-02176, 1000 Monrovia 10; tel. 271368; f. 1981; govt-operated; rural development and entertainment programmes; Dir J. RUFUS KAINE (acting).

Radio Veritas: Monrovia; Catholic; independent; nation-wide shortwave broadcasts.

Star Radio: Sekou Toure Ave, Mamba Point, Monrovia; tel. 226820; fax 227360; e-mail star@liberia.net; independent news and information station; f. July 1997 by Fondation Hirondelle, Switzerland, with funds from the US Agency for International Development; broadcasts in English, French and 14 African languages; operations suspended by the Govt March 2000; ban on transmissions ended Nov. 2003; Dir GEORGE BENNETT.

Television

Liberia Broadcasting System: POB 594, Monrovia; tel. 224984; govt-owned; Dir-Gen. CHARLES SNETTER.

Finance

(cap. = capital; res = reserves; dep. = deposits; m. = million; br. = branch; amounts in Liberian dollars, unless otherwise indicated)

BANKING

Following intensive fighting between government and rebel forces in the capital in mid-2003, it was reported that commercial banks had resumed operations at the end of August. At that time, however, only four (of a total of 18 deposit banks established since 1954) were active, the remainder having been closed as a result of poor bank management or the 1989–96 civil conflict. The Liberian Bank for Development and Investment is the only locally owned bank.

Central Bank

Central Bank of Liberia: cnr Warren and Carey Sts, POB 2048, Monrovia; tel. 226144; fax 227685; e-mail webmaster@cbl.org.lr; internet www.cbl.org.lr; f. 1974 as National Bank of Liberia; name changed March 1999; bank of issue; total assets 60,013m. (Sept. 2004); Gov. RICHARD DORLEY (acting).

Other Banks

Ecobank Liberia Ltd: Ashmun and Randall Sts, POB 4825, Monrovia; tel. 226428; fax 227029; e-mail ecobanklr@ecobank.com; internet www.ecobank.com; commenced operations Aug. 1999; cap. and res US $2.1m., total assets US $10.2m. (Dec. 2001); Chair. EUGENE H. COOPER; Man. Dir OFONG AMBAH.

Global Bank Liberia Ltd (GBLL): POB 2053, 1000 Monrovia; tel. 443804; fax 443802; e-mail rsembiante@globalbankliberia.com; f. 2005; Italian-owned; Pres. RICCARDO SEMBIANTE.

International Bank (Liberia) Ltd: 64 Broad St, POB 292, Monrovia; tel. 226279; fax 226159; e-mail tjeffrey@ib-lib.com; f. 2000 as International Trust Co of Liberia; name changed April 2000; cap. 2m. (1989), dep. 96.4m. (Dec. 1996); Pres. F. A. GUIDA; 1 br.

Liberian Bank for Development and Investment (LBDI): Ashmun and Randall Sts, POB 547, Monrovia; tel. 227140; fax 226359; e-mail lbdi@ibdi.net; internet www.lbdi.net; f. 1961; 18.6% govt-owned; cap. and res US $12.5m., total assets US $26.8m. (Dec. 2001); Chair. NATHANIEL BARNES; Pres. FRANCIS A. DENNIS.

Banking Association

Liberia Bankers' Association: POB 292, Monrovia; mems include commercial and development banks; Pres. LEN MAESTRE.

INSURANCE

American International Underwriters, Inc: Carter Bldg, 39 Broad St, POB 180, Monrovia; tel. 224921; general; Gen. Man. S. B. MENSAH.

American Life Insurance Co: Carter Bldg, 39 Broad St, POB 60, Monrovia; f. 1969; life and general; Vice-Pres. ALLEN BROWN.

Insurance Co of Africa: 64 Broad St, POB 292, Monrovia; f. 1969; life and general; Pres. SAMUEL OWAREE MINTAH.

National Insurance Corpn of Liberia (NICOL): LBDI Bldg Complex, POB 1528, Sinkor, Monrovia; tel. 262429; f. 1983; state-owned; sole insurer for Govt and parastatal bodies; also provides insurance for the Liberian-registered merchant shipping fleet; Man. Dir MIATTA EDITH SHERMAN.

Royal Exchange Assurance: Ashmun and Randall Sts, POB 666, Monrovia; all types of insurance; Man. RONALD WOODS.

LIBERIA

United Security Insurance Agencies Inc: Randall St, POB 2071, Monrovia; life, personal accident and medical; Dir EPHRAIM O. OKORO.

Trade and Industry

GOVERNMENT AGENCIES

Budget Bureau: Capitol Hill, POB 1518, Monrovia; tel. 226340; Dir-Gen. AUGUSTINE K. NGAFUAN.

General Services Agency (GSA): Sinkor, Monrovia; tel. 226745; Dir-Gen. WILLIARD RUSSELL.

DEVELOPMENT ORGANIZATIONS

Forestry Development Authority: POB 3010, 1000 Monrovia; tel. 224940; fax 226000; f. 1976; responsible for forest management and conservation; Chair. EDWIN ZELEE; Man. Dir JOHN T. WOODS.

Liberia Industrial Free Zone Authority (LIFZA): One Free Zone, Monrovia; tel. 533671; e-mail mskromah@lifza.com; internet www.lifza.com; f. 1975; 98 mems; Man. Dir MOHAMMED S. KROMAH.

National Investment Commission (NIC): Fmr Executive Mansion Bldg, POB 9043, Monrovia; tel. 226685; internet www.nic.gov.lr; f. 1979; autonomous body negotiating investment incentives agreements on behalf of Govt; promotes agro-based and industrial development; Chair. RICHARD TOLBERT.

CHAMBER OF COMMERCE

Liberia Chamber of Commerce: POB 92, Monrovia; tel. 223738; f. 1951; Pres. DAVID A. B. JALLAH; Sec.-Gen. LUESETTE S. HOWELL.

INDUSTRIAL AND TRADE ASSOCIATIONS

Liberian Produce Marketing Corpn: POB 662, Monrovia; tel. 222447; f. 1961; govt-owned; exports Liberian produce, provides industrial facilities for processing of agricultural products and participates in agricultural development programmes; Man. Dir NYAH MARTEIN.

Liberian Resources Corpn (LIBRESCO): controls Liberia's mineral resources; 60% govt-owned; 40% owned by South African co, Amalia Gold.

EMPLOYERS' ASSOCIATION

National Enterprises Corpn: POB 518, Monrovia; tel. 261370; importer, wholesaler and distributor of foodstuffs, and wire and metal products for local industries; Pres. EMMANUEL SHAW, Sr.

UTILITIES

Electricity

Liberia Electricity Corpn (LEC): Waterside, POB 165, Monrovia; tel. 226133; Chair. DUNSTAN MACAULEY; Man. Dir HARRY YUAN.

National Oil Co of Liberia (NOCL): Episcopal Church Plaza, Ashmun and Randall Sts, Monrovia; Chair. CLEMENCEAU B. UREY.

TRADE UNIONS

Congress of Industrial Organizations: 29 Ashmun St, POB 415, Monrovia; Pres. Gen. J. T. PRATT; Sec.-Gen. AMOS N. GRAY; 5 affiliated unions.

Labor Congress of Liberia: 71 Gurley St, Monrovia; Sec.-Gen. P. C. T. SONPON; 8 affiliated unions.

Liberian Federation of Labor Unions: J. B. McGill Labor Center, Gardnersville Freeway, POB 415, Monrovia; f. 1980; Sec.-Gen. AMOS GRAY; 10,000 mems (1983).

Transport

RAILWAYS

Railway operations were suspended in 1990, owing to the civil conflict. Large sections of the 480-km rail network were subsequently dismantled.

Bong Mining Co Ltd: POB 538, Monrovia; tel. 225222; fax 225770; f. 1965; Gen. Man. HANS-GEORG SCHNEIDER.

Liberian Mining Co: Monrovia; tel. 221190; govt-owned; assumed control of LAMCO JV Operating Co in 1989.

National Iron Ore Co Ltd: POB 548, Monrovia; f. 1951; Gen. Man. S. K. DATTA RAY.

ROADS

In 1999 the road network in Liberia totalled an estimated 10,600 km, of which about 657 km were paved. The main trunk road is the Monrovia–Sanniquellie motor road, extending north-east from the capital to the border with Guinea, near Ganta, and eastward through the hinterland to the border with Côte d'Ivoire. Trunk roads run through Tapita, in Nimba County, to Grand Gedeh County and from Monrovia to Buchanan. A bridge over the Mano river connects with the Sierra Leone road network, while a main road links Monrovia and Freetown (Sierra Leone). Although principal roads were officially reopened to commercial traffic in early 1997, following the 1989–96 armed conflict, much of the infrastructure remained severely damaged. In late 2003 the Liberian authorities announced plans for the extensive rehabilitation of the road network, including a highway linking Monrovia with Harper, which was to be funded by the People's Republic of China.

SHIPPING

In December 2004 Liberia's open-registry fleet (1,538 vessels), the second largest in the world (after Panama) in terms of gross tonnage, had a total displacement of 53.9m. grt. Commercial port activity in Liberia was frequently suspended from 1990, as a result of hostilities. At September 2004 only Monrovia Freeport had fully resumed operations and (compared with the corresponding period in 2003) experienced a rise in vessel traffic of 95.2%, owing to increasing commercial and humanitarian activities.

Bureau of Maritime Affairs: Tubman Blvd, POB 10-9042, 1000 Monrovia 10; tel. and fax 226069; e-mail maritime@liberia.net; internet www.maritime.gov.lr; Commissioner JOHN S. MORLU.

Liberia National Shipping Line (LNSL): Monrovia; f. 1987; jt venture by the Liberian Govt and private German interests; routes to Europe, incl. the United Kingdom and Scandinavia.

National Port Authority: POB 1849, Monrovia; tel. 226646; fax 226180; e-mail natport@liberia.net; f. 1967; administers Monrovia Freeport and the ports of Buchanan, Greenville and Harper; Chair. TOGBA NAH TIPOTEH; Man. Dir JOE T. GBALA.

CIVIL AVIATION

Liberia's principal airports are Robertsfield International Airport, at Harbel, 56 km east of Monrovia, and James Spriggs Payne Airport, at Monrovia. Following the suspension of air services in mid-2003, owing to the intensive conflict in Monrovia (see Recent History), the Belgian airline, SN Brussels Airlines, resumed flights into Robertsfield International Airport in October. However, it was reported that continued lack of regulation of civil aviation in Liberia was contributing to illicit trade. Later that year the transitional authorities planned the urgent rehabilitation of both airports in order to improve security and facilitate peace-keeping operations.

ADC Liberia Inc: Monrovia; f. 1993; services to the United Kingdom, the USA and destinations in West Africa.

Air Liberia: POB 2076, Monrovia; f. 1974; state-owned; scheduled passenger and cargo services; Man. Dir JAMES K. KOFA.

LIBYA

Introductory Survey

Location, Climate, Language, Religion, Flag, Capital

The Great Socialist People's Libyan Arab Jamahiriya extends along the Mediterranean coast of North Africa. Its neighbours are Tunisia and Algeria to the west, Niger and Chad to the south, Egypt to the east, and Sudan to the south-east. The climate is very hot and dry. Most of the country is part of the Sahara, an arid desert, but the coastal regions are cooler. Average temperatures range from 13°C (55°F) to 38°C (100°F), but a maximum of 57.3°C (135°F) has been recorded in the interior. Arabic is the official language, although English and Italian are also used in trade. Almost all of the population are Sunni Muslims. The national flag (proportions 2 by 3) is plain green. The administrative capital was formerly Tripoli (Tarabulus), but under a decentralization programme announced in September 1988 most government departments and the legislature were relocated to Sirte (Surt), while some departments were transferred to other principal towns.

Recent History

Libya, formerly an Italian colony and occupied by British and French troops in 1942, attained independence as the United Kingdom of Libya on 24 December 1951. Muhammad Idris as-Sanusi, Amir of Cyrenaica, became King Idris of Libya. British and US forces maintained bases in Libya in return for economic assistance; however, the discovery of petroleum reserves in 1959 greatly increased the country's potential for financial autonomy.

King Idris was deposed in September 1969, in a bloodless revolution led by a group of young nationalist army officers. A Revolution Command Council (RCC) was established, with Col Muammar al-Qaddafi as Chairman, and a Libyan Arab Republic was proclaimed. British and US military personnel withdrew from Libya in 1970, and in 1972 British oil interests in Libya were nationalized.

The Arab Socialist Union (ASU) was established in June 1971 as the country's sole political party. People's Congresses and Popular Committees were formed, and an undertaking was made to administer the country in accordance with Islamic principles. The General National Congress of the ASU (which comprised members of the RCC, leaders of the People's Congresses and Popular Committees and of trade unions and professional organizations) held its first session in January 1976; it was subsequently restyled the General People's Congress (GPC).

In March 1977 the GPC endorsed constitutional changes, recommended by Qaddafi, whereby the official name of the country was changed to the Socialist People's Libyan Arab Jamahiriya. Power was vested in the people through the GPC and its constituent parts. The RCC was dissolved, and a General Secretariat of the GPC (with Qaddafi as Secretary-General) was established. The GPC elected Qaddafi as Revolutionary Leader of the new state. The Council of Ministers was replaced by a General People's Committee, initially with 26 members—each a secretary of a department.

In March 1979 Qaddafi resigned from the post of Secretary-General of the General Secretariat of the GPC to devote more time to 'preserving the revolution'. The creation in early 1984 of the post of Secretary for External Security and of an office, attached to the Secretariat for Foreign Liaison, to 'combat international terrorism', combined with repressive measures to curb the activity of dissidents, apparently reflected Qaddafi's increasing sensitivity to the growth of opposition groups—principally the National Front for the Salvation of Libya (NFSL), which he accused foreign governments of fostering. In 1986 the country's official name was changed to the Great Socialist People's Libyan Arab Jamahiriya.

From 1988, in an apparent attempt to allay domestic dissatisfaction and international criticism, Qaddafi initiated a series of liberalizing economic and political reforms. In foreign policy he adopted a more pragmatic approach to his ambition of achieving Maghreb union (see below), and to his relations with other Arab and African countries. Within Libya he accused the Revolutionary Committees (young, pro-Qaddafi activists) of murdering political opponents of his regime. Qaddafi encouraged the reopening of private businesses, in recognition of the inadequacy of state-sponsored supermarkets, and declared an amnesty for all prisoners, other than those convicted of violent crimes or of conspiring with foreign powers. Libyan citizens were guaranteed freedom to travel abroad, and the powers of the Revolutionary Committees were curbed. The GPC created a People's Court and People's Prosecution Bureau to replace the revolutionary courts, and approved a charter of human rights. In August Qaddafi announced that the army was to be replaced by a force of 'Jamahiri Guards', which would be supervised by 'people's defence committees'. In September it was decided to relocate all but two of the secretariats of the GPC, mostly to the town of Sirte (Surt), 400 km east of Tripoli, and in January 1989 Qaddafi announced that all state institutions, including the state intelligence service and the official Libyan news agency, were to be abolished.

In October 1990 the GPC implemented extensive changes to the General People's Committee, creating three new secretariats and electing a new Secretary-General, Abu Sa'id Omar Durdah, as well as 11 new secretaries. Three of the five-member General Secretariat of the GPC were replaced, and Abd ar-Raziq as-Sawsa was appointed Secretary-General of the GPC. There was a further reorganization of the General People's Committee in October–November 1992. The former Secretary for Economic Planning, Omar al-Muntasir, was named Secretary for Foreign Liaison and International Co-operation. Regarded as a moderate, al-Muntasir's appointment was viewed by some observers as a sign of Libya's willingness to resume dialogue with the West over the Lockerbie issue (see below).

Western media reported in October 1993 that elements loyal to Qaddafi had suppressed an attempted military *coup d'état*, and that Libya's second-in-command, Maj. Abd as-Salam Jalloud, was among many placed under house arrest. Qaddafi denied that a coup had been attempted, but the appointment of known loyalists to senior positions in the General People's Committee was announced in January 1994. Most notably, Abd al-Majid al-Aoud, a member of Qaddafi's closest personal entourage, replaced Durdah, a close associate of Jalloud, as Secretary-General.

At its annual convention in March 1997 the GPC made changes to the composition and structure of the General People's Committee. Muhammad Ahmad al-Manqush was appointed Secretary-General of the Committee in December, as part of a further reorganization. The Secretariat for Arab Unity was abolished in a restructuring of the General People's Committee in December 1998, in accordance with Qaddafi's recently stated intention to forge closer relations with African rather than Arab countries.

In January 2000 Qaddafi unexpectedly attended the opening session of the GPC, at the end of which he demanded that the budget for 2000 be redrafted, with a view to channelling petroleum revenues into education, health and public services. Furthermore, he urged that the current administrative system, based on General People's Committees, be abandoned in favour of an alternative form of government. Accordingly, a radical decentralization of the Government was announced in March, whereby almost all of the People's Committees were dissolved and their responsibilities devolved mainly to local level: only those areas described as 'sovereign' were to remain under the control of the General People's Committee, now led by Mubarak Abdallah ash-Shamikh (hitherto responsible for housing and utilities). Most notably, Ali Abd as-Salam at-Turayki was allocated the new post of Secretary for African Unity, being replaced as Secretary for Foreign Liaison and International Co-operation by Abd ar-Rahman Muhammad Shalgam. In July it was reported that the Secretary for Finance, Muhammad Abdullah Bait al-Mal, along with the President of the Central Bank of Libya and a further 22 senior Libyan bankers, had been implicated in allegations of financial impropriety. They were suspected of having granted unsecured loans to several prominent figures, including a number of senior army officers. Al-Ujayli Abd as-Salam Burayni replaced Bait-al-Mal as Secretary for Finance in

October, when a further restructuring of the General People's Committees was announced.

In late September 2000 clashes occurred throughout the country between Libyans and nationals of several other African countries. The confrontations were believed to reflect resentment within Libya at the increasing numbers of black African migrants entering the country. A large number of Chadians and Sudanese were reportedly killed in incidents in the town of Az-Zawiyah, some 30 km west of Tripoli, and thousands more were interned in military camps. The Nigerian embassy in Tripoli was ransacked, and Libyan youths were also held responsible for an attack on a camp which was razed to the ground. The General People's Congress announced its intention formally to investigate the incidents, and in mid-October the evacuation and deportation of migrant workers from Nigeria, Chad, Niger, Sudan and Ghana commenced. It was estimated that as a result of the clashes more than 100 Africans had been killed and as many as 30,000 migrants had left Libya. Qaddafi subsequently apportioned blame for the incidents on 'foreign hostile hands' opposed to his plans to create an African Union. In May 2001 two Libyans, four Nigerians and one Ghanaian were sentenced to death for their roles in the violence. A further 12 defendants were sentenced to life imprisonment.

A minor reorganization of the General People's Committee was announced in early September 2001, including the creation of a new Secretariat for Infrastructure, Urban Planning and Environment, to be headed by Hutaywish Faraj al-Hutaywish. In November it was announced that more than 40 government and bank officials had been sentenced to varying terms of imprisonment for corruption and embezzlement; reportedly among those convicted was Secretary for Finance Burayni, who received a one-year prison sentence for negligence, although he continued to appear on official government lists. In late December Shukri Muhammad Ghanem was appointed to replace Abd es-Salem Ahmad Jouir as Secretary for the Economy and Trade.

In mid-January 2003 Libya was elected to chair the session of the UN Human Rights Commission scheduled to be held in March. For the first time since the formation of the Commission in 1947, the decision was voted upon, with Libya securing 33 of the 53 votes, with 17 countries, including the United Kingdom, abstaining; the USA, Canada and Guatemala opposed the proposal. Libya's election was widely criticized by a number of international human rights organizations.

In mid-June 2003 Qaddafi dismissed ash-Shamikh from the post of Secretary of the GPC, replacing him with Ghanem, who was succeeded as Secretary for the Economy and Trade by Abd al-Qadir Balkheir. It was also announced that the Secretariat for African Unity had been merged with the Secretariat for Foreign Liaison and International Co-operation; Shalgam assumed responsibility for both portfolios. There were reports that Qaddafi had demanded the complete privatization of leading economic sectors, including the petroleum industry, and had proposed that the Libyan economy be opened up to investment from both domestic and foreign companies. In early March 2004 Qaddafi announced a reorganization of the General People's Committee, which included the creation of four new secretariats (for national security, youth and sport, training and labour, and culture) and the restoration of the Secretariat for Energy, which had been abolished in 2000. Muhammad Ali al-Houeiz replaced Burayni as Secretary for Finance, while Ali Omar Abu Bakr was appointed Secretary of Justice.

It was announced in October 2005 that 84 members of banned opposition group the Muslim Brotherhood, originally convicted and imprisoned in 2002, were to be retried; the prisoners were subsequently released in early March 2006. An extensive reorganization of the General People's Committee was announced that same month, including the creation of seven new secretariats. Ghanem was replaced as Secretary of the GPC by the former Deputy Secretary for Production, Dr al-Baghdadi Ali al-Mahmoudi, and was handed the role of Chairman of the National Oil Corporation; al-Houeiz was promoted to Deputy Secretary and the former Governor and Chairman of the Central Bank of Libya, Dr Ahmad Munaysi Abd al-Hamid, took his former role of Secretary for Finance. The post of Secretary for National Security, which had been vacant following violent protests in Benghazi the previous month (see below), was filled by Brig. Salih Rajab al-Mismari. Ali Omar al-Hasnawi was appointed to the role of Secretary for Justice, and at-Tayib as-Safi at-Tayib was given the Economy, Trade and Investment portfolio. The Secretariat for Energy, only reinstated in March 2004, was restructured and renamed the Secretariat for Industry, Electricity and Mines; Fathi Hamad Ben Shatwan retained the revised portfolio.

Various plans for pan-Arab unity led to the formation, in January 1972, of the Federation of Arab Republics, comprising Libya, Egypt and Syria. In 1972 Libya concluded an agreement with Egypt to merge the two countries in 1973. Neither union was effective, and proposals for union with Tunisia in 1974, Syria in 1980, Chad in 1981, Morocco in 1984, Algeria in 1987 and Sudan in 1990 also proved abortive.

Relations with Egypt, already tense following the failure of the Libya-Egypt union, further deteriorated when President Anwar Sadat launched the October 1973 war against Israel without consulting Qaddafi. In common with the other members of the League of Arab States (the Arab League, see p. 306), Libya strongly objected to Sadat's peace initiative with Israel which culminated in the signing of the Camp David accords in 1978, and Libya also condemned the proposals for Middle East peace that were agreed by other Arab states in Fez, Morocco, in 1982. From the late 1980s, none the less, Egypt and Libya forged a close relationship, with Egypt acting as an intermediary between Libya and Western nations (particularly in negotiations resulting from the Lockerbie bombing—see below). Following the suspension of UN sanctions against Libya in April 1999 (see below), EgyptAir resumed regular flights to Tripoli in July 2000, and Libyan flights to Egypt recommenced later that month.

In 1973 Libyan forces occupied the 'Aozou strip', a reputedly mineral-rich region of 114,000 sq km in the extreme north of Chad, to which it laid claim on the basis of an unratified border treaty concluded by Italy and France in 1935. Thereafter, Libya became embroiled in the lengthy struggle for political control between rival forces in Chad (q.v.). During 1987 intense fighting took place for control of north-western Chad, and in August President Hissène Habré's forces advanced into the 'Aozou strip', occupying the town of Aozou. Libya responded by bombing towns in northern Chad, and recaptured Aozou. In September Chadian forces destroyed an airbase 100 km inside Libya (allegedly a base for Libyan raids on Chad). Later in September, however, the two countries agreed to observe a cease-fire sponsored by the Organization of African Unity (OAU, now African Union—AU, see p. 153), and in October 1988 Libya and Chad restored diplomatic relations. In August 1989, with Algerian mediation, Chad and Libya concluded an agreement on attempt to resolve the dispute over sovereignty of the 'Aozou strip' through a political settlement. Accordingly, the issue was submitted to the International Court of Justice in The Hague, Netherlands, which in February 1994 ruled against Libya's claim. All Libyan troops remaining in the 'Aozou strip' were withdrawn in May. In June Libya and Chad concluded a treaty of friendship, neighbourly terms and co-operation. In May 1998 Qaddafi made his first visit to Chad for 17 years, and in November the two countries officially opened two of their common border posts. Chad's President Idriss Deby (who had overthrown Habré in 1990) and members of his administration made several visits to Libya after 1997 and in January 2002 Libyan mediation resulted in the brokering of a peace agreement between the Chadian Government and the rebel Mouvement pour la démocratie et la justice au Tchad, which had been in conflict since late 1998. In February 2005 Libya hosted talks between Chad and Sudan, attended by Deby and President Omar Hassan Ahmad al-Bashir of Sudan, which aimed to reduce tensions between the two countries.

Libya's outspoken criticism of other Arab regimes, and perceived interference in the internal affairs of other countries, led to years of relative political isolation. However, in 1987 Qaddafi sought to realign Libyan policy with that of the majority of Arab states. Qaddafi was reconciled in March with Yasser Arafat's Fatah wing of the Palestine Liberation Organization (PLO—against which he had previously advocated revolt, owing to its more moderate policies) and attempted to reunite the opposing factions of the Palestinian movement. In September Libya re-established 'fraternal' links with Iraq, modifying its support for Iran in the Iran–Iraq War.

A summit meeting of North African heads of state, held in Morocco in February 1989, concluded a treaty proclaiming the Union du Maghreb arabe (UMA—Union of the Arab Maghreb, see p. 388), comprising Algeria, Libya, Mauritania, Morocco and Tunisia. The treaty envisaged the establishment of a council of heads of state; regular meetings of ministers of foreign affairs; and the eventual free movement of goods, people, services and capital throughout the countries of the region. During 1989–92 the member states formulated 15 regional co-operation conventions. In February 1993, however, it was announced that, in view of the differing economic orientations of each signatory, no convention had actually been implemented, and the UMA's activities were to be limited. UMA leaders met in April 1994 (and subsequently on an annual basis). In 1994 Libya threatened to leave the UMA unless member states ceased to comply with UN sanctions imposed on Libya (see below), and in 1995 it refused to assume the chairmanship of the organization, owing to their continuing compliance.

In February 1997, at a meeting hosted by Libya and attended by the Presidents of Sudan, Chad, Mali and Niger, and government ministers from Egypt, Burkina Faso and Tunisia, a treaty establishing the Community of Sahel-Saharan States (COMESSA, now CEN-SAD, see p. 385) was signed. CEN-SAD's general secretariat was temporarily located in Tripoli, and provisions were made for the establishment of a development bank, a council of heads of state and an executive council.

Libya's relations with the USA, which had been strained for many years, deteriorated significantly under the presidency of Ronald Reagan (1981–89), who accused the Libyan Government of sponsoring international terrorism. In January 1986 Reagan severed all economic and commercial relations with Libya, and in March Libyan forces fired missiles at US fighter aircraft which were challenging Libya's attempts to enforce recognition of the whole of the Gulf of Sirte as its territorial waters. In retaliatory attacks in April US military aircraft bombed military installations, airports and official buildings, as well as alleged terrorist training camps and communication centres, in Tripoli and Benghazi. A total of 101 people, including many civilians, were reported to have died in the raids. The US Administration claimed in justification to have irrefutable proof of Libyan involvement in terrorist attacks and plots against US targets in Europe and the Middle East (including the recent bombing of a discothèque in Berlin, Germany—see below).

In November 1991 the US and British Governments announced that they would seek to extradite two Libyan citizens, Abd al-Baset Ali Muhammad al-Megrahi (a former head of security at Libyan Arab Airlines) and Al-Amin Khalifa Fhimah (an employee of the airline), alleged to have been responsible for an explosion that destroyed a Pan American World Airways (Pan Am) passenger aircraft over Lockerbie, Scotland, in December 1988, resulting in the deaths of 270 people. The Libyan Government denied any involvement in the bombing, and recommended that the allegations be investigated by a neutral body. In January 1992 the UN Security Council adopted a resolution (No. 731) demanding Libya's compliance with requests for the extradition of its two nationals and its co-operation with a French inquiry into the bombing over Niger, in September 1989, of a UTA passenger airline, in which all 171 passengers and crew had been killed. Libya's offer to try on its own territory the two men accused of the Lockerbie bombing was rejected by the USA, the United Kingdom and France, which urged the UN to impose sanctions on Libya. On 31 March 1992 the UN Security Council adopted a resolution (No. 748) imposing economic sanctions against Libya if it refused to comply with Resolution 731, and commit itself to a renunciation of international terrorism, by 15 April. Sanctions, including the severance of international air links, the prohibition of trade in arms and the reduction of Libya's diplomatic representation abroad, were duly imposed on the specified date. In May, at Qaddafi's instigation, 1,500 People's Congresses were convened in Libya and abroad, to enable the country's citizens to decide the fate of the two Lockerbie suspects and their response to the UN sanctions. The GPC announced in the following month its decision to allow the two Lockerbie suspects to be tried abroad, provided that the proceedings were 'fair and just'.

In August 1993 the USA, the United Kingdom and France announced that they would request the UN Security Council to strengthen the sanctions in force against Libya if, by 1 October, Libya had still not complied with Resolutions 731 and 748. The Libyan Government rejected this ultimatum, but stated its willingness to commence discussions with those three countries on an appropriate venue for the trial of the two Lockerbie suspects. In October the UN Secretary-General, Dr Boutros Boutros-Ghali, met the Libyan Secretary for Foreign Liaison and International Co-operation, but failed to secure agreement on a timetable for the surrender of the two suspects to either the USA or the United Kingdom. (US and British officials remained convinced that there was sufficient evidence of Libyan involvement to continue to seek the suspects' extradition, despite various reports issued in the early 1990s which alleged that Iranian, Syrian and Palestinian agents—sometimes separately, sometimes in collaboration—had been responsible for the bombing.) In November the Security Council adopted a resolution (No. 883) providing for the strengthening of the economic sanctions in force against Libya in the event of the country's failure fully to comply with Resolutions 731 and 748 by 1 December. The sanctions, which were duly applied, included the closure of all Libyan Arab Airlines' offices abroad; a ban on the sale of equipment and services for the civil aviation sector; the sequestration of all Libyan financial resources overseas; and a ban on the sale to Libya of specified items for use in the petroleum and gas industries.

In January 1994 the Scottish lawyer representing the two Lockerbie suspects stated that they might be willing to stand trial in The Hague; this was subsequently endorsed as an appropriate venue by Qaddafi. In February, however, US President Bill Clinton recommended that an embargo should be imposed on Libya's sales of petroleum (which accounted for some 98% of its export earnings) if the country continued to defy the international community. In mid-1996, following its repeated failure to persuade the UN to agree yet more stringent sanctions against Libya, the US Congress approved unilateral 'secondary' sanctions against Libya (and Iran). The Iran-Libya Sanctions Act (ILSA) sought to penalize companies operating in US markets that were investing more than US $40m. (later amended to $20m.) in Libya's oil and gas industries.

In July 1997 the Arab League, which had been criticized by Qaddafi for its lack of support, formally proposed that the two Libyan suspects in the Lockerbie case be tried by Scottish judges under Scottish law in a neutral country. In September the members of the League urged a relaxation of the air embargo on Libya and voted to defy UN sanctions by permitting aircraft carrying Qaddafi, and other flights for religious or humanitarian purposes, to land on their territory.

In April 1998 the official spokesman for the families of the British victims of the Lockerbie bombing, together with an expert in Scottish law, held talks with Qaddafi in Libya, following which it was reported that Qaddafi had agreed to allow the two Libyan suspects to stand trial in the Netherlands under Scottish law. In August the United Kingdom and the USA proposed that the trial be held in the Netherlands under Scottish law and presided over by Scottish judges. The UN Security Council adopted a resolution (No. 1192) welcoming the initiative and providing for the suspension of sanctions upon the arrival in the Netherlands of the two suspects; additional sanctions were threatened if the Libyan authorities did not comply with the resolution.

In December 1998 the UN Secretary-General, Kofi Annan, held a meeting with Qaddafi in Libya in an attempt to expedite a trial of the Lockerbie suspects. Shortly afterwards the GPC endorsed the principle of a trial, but requested that the USA and the United Kingdom remove 'all remaining obstacles'. In a bid to break the impasse arising from Qaddafi's demand that the trial include a panel of international judges, envoys from Saudi Arabia and South Africa were dispatched to Libya in January 1999 to negotiate with Qaddafi. In February it was reported that the envoys had reached an understanding with the Libyan leader whereby UN observers would be allowed to monitor the two Libyan suspects during the trial, to ensure that they were not questioned by US and British agents, and afterwards, if they were convicted and imprisoned in Scotland. The diplomatic initiative culminated in March with a visit by President Nelson Mandela of South Africa to Libya, during which Qaddafi undertook to surrender the suspects by 6 April. The two Libyans duly arrived for trial in the Netherlands on 5 April and were transferred to Camp Zeist, a former US airbase near Utrecht designated Scottish territory for the purposes of the trial, where they were formally arrested and charged with murder, conspiracy to murder and contravention of the 1982 Aviation Security Act. The UN Security Council immediately voted to suspend sanctions against Libya indefinitely, although they were not to be permanently revoked until Libya had complied with other conditions stipulated in UN Security Council Resolution 1192 (including the payment of compensation to the families of victims of the Lockerbie bombing). The USA refused to remove 'secondary' sanctions against Libya (see above), but subsequently announced that it would permit the sale of food and medical items to Libya on a 'case-by-case' basis. In June 1999 the US and Libyan ambassadors to the UN took part in what represented the first official contact between the two countries in 18 years. During the talks the USA informed Libya that it could not support a permanent end to UN sanctions until Libya had fully complied with Resolution 1192; thus in July Kofi Annan reported to the Security Council that he was unable to secure support for the permanent revocation of sanctions against Libya.

The two Libyan suspects appeared before the Scottish court in the Netherlands for the first time in December 1999, at a pre-trial hearing to decide on the jurisdiction of the Scottish court. The presiding Scottish judge ruled that the two suspects could be tried on all three charges, and that they could be described as members of the Libyan intelligence services. (Defence lawyers had argued that to describe the Libyans as such was irrelevant and prejudicial.) The trial of al-Megrahi and Fhimah eventually commenced on 3 May 2000; both pleaded not guilty to the charges brought against them, and defence lawyers accused a number of organizations, including militant Palestinian resistance groups, of perpetrating the bombing.

In early January 2001 prosecution lawyers unexpectedly announced that they would no longer pursue charges of conspiracy to murder and contravention of the 1982 Aviation Security Act. Accordingly, the trial proceeded on the sole charge of murder. On 31 January 2001 the judges announced that they had unanimously found al-Megrahi guilty of the murder of 270 people and sentenced him to life imprisonment, with the recommendation that he serve a minimum of 20 years. The judges accepted that al-Megrahi was a member of the Libyan intelligence services, and although they acknowledged their awareness of what they termed 'uncertainties and qualifications' in the case, they concluded that the evidence against him combined to form 'a real and convincing pattern' which left them with no reasonable doubt as to his guilt. Fhimah, however, was unanimously acquitted, owing to lack of proof, and freed to return to Libya. Despite mounting pressure from Arab League states, the British Government asserted that sanctions against Libya would not be permanently revoked until Libya accepted responsibility for the bombing and paid 'substantial' compensation. The newly inaugurated US President, George W. Bush, also indicated his support for this stance, and in July 2001 ILSA was extended for a further five-year term.

Meanwhile, demands for further investigation into the bombing, and Qaddafi's role in it, were rejected by senior Scottish legal officials, who stated that there was insufficient evidence to justify any further proceedings against those alleged to have abetted al-Megrahi, despite the fact that he had apparently not acted alone. Lawyers for al-Megrahi subsequently lodged an appeal against his conviction; the hearing, before five Scottish judges, began at Camp Zeist in late January 2002. Al-Megrahi's lawyers based their case on what they termed new 'strong circumstantial evidence', which raised the possibility that the bomb had been placed on the aircraft at London, United Kingdom, and not in Malta, as the trial judges had concluded. In late February Qaddafi's eldest son, Seif al-Islam, indicated that Libya would pay compensation to the families of those killed in the Lockerbie bombing, regardless of the outcome of the appeal. In mid-March the appeal was unanimously rejected, and al-Megrahi was transferred to a prison in Scotland to begin his sentence.

In July 1999 Libya and the United Kingdom reached agreement on the full restoration of diplomatic relations after Qaddafi issued a statement in which he accepted Libya's 'general responsibility' for the death of Yvonne Fletcher, a British policewoman who was shot outside the Libyan People's Bureau in London in 1984, and agreed to co-operate with the investigation into the killing. The payment by Libya, in November 1999, of compensation to the victim's family facilitated the reopening of the British embassy in Tripoli the following month. In January 2000, however, the British Government confirmed that its customs officials had, in late 1999, seized a consignment of Scud missile parts which had arrived in the United Kingdom from Taiwan and was bound for Libya via Malta. (It subsequently transpired that the parts had been impounded in mid-1999, prior to the full restoration of diplomatic relations between the United Kingdom and Libya.) Despite this incident and the delivery of the Lockerbie trial verdict, the normalization of relations between the United Kingdom and Libya progressed and in March 2001 Libya appointed an ambassador to the United Kingdom for the first time in 17 years. In early August 2002 a minister of the British Foreign and Commonwealth Office visited Libya for talks with Qaddafi: this was the first visit by a British government minister to Libya for some 20 years.

In April 2003 it was confirmed that, following negotiations in London between senior British, US and Libyan representatives, Libya had agreed to accept civil responsibility for the actions of its officials in the Lockerbie case and would pay US $10m. in compensation to the families of the victims. Payment of the compensation was to be a three-stage process: $4m. would be paid to each family on the permanent lifting of UN sanctions; a further $4m. would follow upon the removal of unilateral US sanctions; and a final payment of $2m. would be made when Libya was removed from the list of countries that the USA deemed to support international terrorism. However, Libya would pay only an additional $1m. to each family if the USA did not complete the second and third stages.

Negotiations continued during mid-2003 and on 16 August Libya delivered a letter to the President of the UN Security Council stating that it accepted 'responsibility for the actions of its officials' in the Lockerbie bombing; agreed to pay compensation to the families of the victims; pledged co-operation in any further Lockerbie inquiry; agreed to continue its co-operation in the 'war on terror'; and to take practical measures to ensure that such co-operation was effective. Following the transfer of US $2,700m. in compensation to the International Bank of Settlements, the United Kingdom submitted a draft resolution to the Security Council requesting the formal lifting of UN sanctions against Libya. It was feared, however, that France, which had demanded a similar amount of compensation for families of victims of the UTA bombing in 1989 (see above), would veto the resolution unless Libyan officials agreed to an additional payment. The United Kingdom, France and the USA eventually agreed to postpone the vote on the draft resolution to allow more time for such an agreement to be reached. On 12 September 2003 13 of the 15 members of the UN Security Council approved the lifting of the sanctions imposed against Libya; France and the USA abstained from the vote. Later that month Libya announced its intention to commence dialogue with the USA aimed at normalizing bilateral relations. Nevertheless, the US Administration continued to insist that unilateral sanctions would remain in place until the Libyan Government addressed ongoing US concerns such as the infringement of human rights in the country and the pursuit of weapons of mass destruction.

In early September 2003, following an intervention by the French President, Jacques Chirac, the Libyan Government and the families of the UTA bombing had reached partial agreement on the payment of additional compensation to the victims' relatives. Talks between Libya and France in October aimed at reaching a final settlement regarding the issue of compensation for the UTA bombing were suspended following a number of disagreements between the two sides. However, in early January 2004 Libya agreed to pay an additional US $170m. to the relatives of the victims; the payment was to be made in four equal instalments, resulting in the families of each victim receiving an additional $1m.

Meanwhile, in October 2003 an official of the US Department of State accused Libya of having increased its efforts to purchase components for biological and chemical weapons since the lifting of UN sanctions the previous month, and warned that Libya would be added to the group of countries described by President Bush as forming an 'axis of evil' (comprising Iran, Iraq and the Democratic People's Republic of Korea). In mid-December, however, in an unexpected development, the British Prime Minister, Tony Blair, announced that Libya had agreed to disclose and dismantle its programme to develop weapons of mass destruction and long-range ballistic missiles. The statement was the culmination of nine months of clandestine negotiations between Qaddafi and British and US diplomats during which the Libyan authorities had reportedly shown evidence of a 'well advanced' nuclear weapons programme, as well as the existence of large quantities of chemical weapons and bombs designed to carry poisonous gas. Libya also agreed to adhere to the Chemical Weapons Convention and to sign an additional protocol allowing the International Atomic Energy Agency (IAEA) to carry out random inspections of its facilities. Upon visiting a number of sites in Tripoli in late December, in order to commence the process of dismantling Libya's weapons development projects, the Director-General of the IAEA, Dr Muhammad el-Baradei, insisted that these projects had been in the initial stages of development, contradicting the assessment given by the United Kingdom and the USA. In early January 2004 the US Department of State confirmed that British and US intelligence agents had, in October 2003, intercepted a shipment of centrifuges capable of developing weapons-grade uranium destined for Tripoli. It was announced in mid-January 2004 that Libya had ratified the IAEA's Comprehensive Nuclear Test Ban Treaty earlier in that month.

Further disagreements in January 2004 between the USA, the United Kingdom and the IAEA concerning their respective roles in the process of dismantling Libya's weapons facilities were finally resolved late that month: it was agreed that US and British officials would be responsible for destroying and removing the nuclear material and that the IAEA would verify that the dismantling process was complete. In early February Libyan officials held talks with the US Assistant Secretary of State in London and it was also confirmed that an American diplomat had been stationed in the US interests section of the Belgian embassy in Tripoli, providing the USA with its first permanent diplomatic presence in Libya for 25 years. Also in February the Libyan Secretary for Foreign Liaison and International Co-operation, Abd ar-Rahman Muhammad Shalgam, visited London for talks with his British counterpart and Prime Minister Blair; this represented the first meeting between cabinet-level ministers of the two countries in more than 20 years.

The Secretary of the GPC, Shukri Muhammad Ghanem, caused controversy in late February 2004 when he claimed that compensation was being paid to the families of the Lockerbie victims in order to 'buy peace' and avoid sanctions, and that the country did not accept responsibility for the Lockerbie bombing; he also denied any Libyan involvement in the murder of Yvonne Fletcher (see above). The following day, however, Shalgam issued a statement in which he announced his regret at Ghanem's comments and reiterated that Libya stood by its acceptance of responsibility for the Lockerbie bombing. The USA subsequently lifted the restrictions on its citizens travelling to Libya. In early March Libya signed an additional IAEA protocol allowing the agency to carry out random inspections of its nuclear facilities; moreover, Libya commenced the destruction of its supplies of chemical weapons and transported all of its remaining nuclear weapons-related equipment to the USA. Later that month the Organisation for the Prohibition of Chemical Weapons verified that Libya's declaration of its chemical weapons inventory (submitted to the UN in early March) had been accurate, after a series of inspections had been carried out by the agency's officials. In May it was announced that Libya would no longer conduct military trade with those countries which it believed to be involved in the proliferation of weapons of mass destruction.

Meanwhile, in late March 2004 William Burns, the US Assistant Secretary of the Bureau of Near Eastern Affairs, became the highest-ranking US official to visit Libya in more than 30 years; the principal issues under discussion were further moves towards the lifting of US sanctions on Libya and the restoration of normal bilateral relations. In late April the USA announced that it would remove the restrictions that prevented US petroleum companies and banks from conducting commercial activities in Libya and that Libyan students would be allowed to study in the USA; however, it also declared that all Libyan assets held in the USA would remain frozen. In early June it was revealed that Libya had resumed exports of petroleum to the USA. At the end of the month formal diplomatic relations were re-established between the two countries when a US liaison office was opened in Tripoli, and it was reported that Libya was preparing to establish diplomatic representation in Washington, DC. In September President Bush lifted all travel restrictions for charter and commercial flights between Libya and the USA. He also announced that the US $1,300m. of Libyan assets held in the USA or in US banks abroad would be unfrozen. In February 2005 the US authorities lifted all restrictions on Libyan diplomats travelling within the USA.

Relations between Libya and the United Kingdom continued to improve in 2004. In late March Blair visited Tripoli and held talks with Qaddafi, after which the British Prime Minister stated that there was genuine hope for a 'new relationship', while Qaddafi insisted that he was willing to join the international 'war on terror'. It was also announced that British police-officers would travel to Libya in early April to continue investigations into the murder of Fletcher. In December, with the unilateral sanctions imposed upon Libya by the USA having been lifted, Libya paid the second instalment of its compensation to the families of those killed in the Lockerbie explosion. In August 2005 the head of the Senate Foreign Relations Committee, Senator Richard Lugar, visited Libya to hold talks with Qaddafi; two months previously officials from the US State Department had praised Libya for its co-operation in the fight against international terrorism. In early May 2006 the US Secretary of State, Condoleezza Rice, announced the US Administration's intention to restore full diplomatic relations between the two countries and praised Libya for its 'excellent co-operation' in the 'war on terror'. Rice also declared the removal of Libya from the US list of countries deemed to support international terrorism. Meanwhile, in October 2005 Libya signed a memorandum of understanding with the British Government, which allowed for the deportation from the United Kingdom of Libyans suspected of involvement in terrorist activities. (The United Kingdom is legally prevented from deporting foreign nationals to countries which it suspects of using inhuman or degrading treatment.)

In January 2000 (shortly after the revelation of the seizure of missile parts by the United Kingdom) the European Union (EU, see p. 228) withdrew an invitation to Qaddafi, issued by the Commission President, Romano Prodi, to visit the European Commission headquarters in Brussels, Belgium, on the grounds that Libya had not accepted EU conditions regarding commitment to human rights, democracy, free trade and support for the Middle East peace process. Apparently in reprisal, Libya immediately announced major commercial contracts with Russia and the People's Republic of China. Qaddafi none the less attended the EU-Africa summit meeting in Cairo, Egypt, in April, at which talks with Prodi and other European officials were described as 'positive'. Relations with the EU, and particularly with France, generally improved following talks in early 1996 between Libyan and EU representatives in Belgium. In July Qaddafi granted the French authorities investigating the 1989 bombing of the UTA passenger aircraft unprecedented access to Libyan evidence. This resulted in February 1998 in a judge's decision to try *in absentia* six Libyans suspected of involvement in the attack, and in March 1999 a French court sentenced the six suspects *in absentia* to life imprisonment. The French authorities issued international arrest warrants for the Libyans, and threatened to intensify sanctions against Libya if it did not impose the verdicts on the accused. In July Libya began payment of some US $31m. in compensation to the families of those killed in the bomb attack. France stated that this represented an acknowledgement by Libya of the responsibility of its citizens for the bombing, although attempts by French lawyers on behalf of the victims' families to prosecute Qaddafi for complicity in the bombing of the aircraft were unsuccessful. Nevertheless, it was announced in January 2004 that Libya had agreed to pay an additional $170m. to the relatives of the victims (for further details, see above). During an official visit to Libya in November, French President Jacques Chirac affirmed his commitment to rebuilding diplomatic ties with Libya. In December 2005 the Libyan Government was ordered by a French court to pay an additional $4m. in compensation to families of victims of the 1989 bombing not included in the previous agreement. Despite the ongoing process of reparation, relations between the French and Libyan Governments improved in 2005 after France expressed its interest in assisting the development of civil nuclear technology in Libya. In March 2006 a deal on co-operation regarding the development of nuclear energy in Libya was signed by representatives of the two countries during a visit to Tripoli by the Director of France's Commissariat à l'Energie Atomique. It was the first such agreement since Libya had relinquished its nuclear weapons programme in 2003. Meanwhile, in late April 2004 Qaddafi, who was visiting Europe for the first time in 15 years, met with several senior EU politicians in Brussels and addressed the European Commission. The lifting of economic sanctions and an arms embargo imposed on Libya by the EU in 1986 was ratified by EU ministers in October 2004.

In October 1996, meanwhile, the German authorities announced that evidence existed to prove the Libyan Government's direct involvement in a bomb attack on a discothèque in Berlin in 1986. Arrest warrants were subsequently issued for the four Libyans suspected of carrying out the bombing, but in March 1997 a German parliamentary delegation recommended that regular contact between the German Parliament and the GPC should continue. In April 1998 Libya resolved to allow the German authorities to question the Libyan suspects. In May the two countries signed an agreement on economic co-operation. Following a lengthy trial, in mid-November 2001 a court in Berlin sentenced four people, including a Libyan national, to between 12 and 14 years' imprisonment for their involvement in the bomb attack. Although Qaddafi's personal complicity in the incident could not be proven, the presiding judge stated that there was sufficient evidence to ascertain that the bombing had been carried out by members of the Libyan secret service and employees of the Libyan People's Bureau in the former East

Germany. In August 2003 the Qaddafi International Foundation for Charitable Associations (now the Qaddafi Development Foundation), a charity run by Seif al-Islam Qaddafi, offered to compensate the relatives of the three victims of the Berlin bomb attack. While negotiations between the USA and Libya regarding this compensation continued, a new round of talks between Germany and Libya began in July 2004 to decide upon compensation payments for the non-US citizens injured in the attack. The talks were finalized in early August, and the Libyan authorities signed a deal on 3 September agreeing to pay US $35m. to compensate some 160 non-US victims. The agreement signalled the start of improved relations between Germany and Libya, and in mid-October Chancellor Gerhard Schröder paid the first ever visit of a German official to Libya. In talks with Schröder, Qaddafi requested compensation for the millions of landmines left behind by the Nazi German forces during the Second World War. While no compensation was offered, the German Chancellor agreed to provide assistance with mine detection and medical aid for victims.

In February 1998 a Spanish minister visited Tripoli, following an announcement of Spain's intention to renew political and economic ties with Libya. However, the decision by France, Spain, Italy and Portugal to create a rapid reaction force in the Mediterranean was strongly condemned by Qaddafi. In July Italy formally apologized for its colonial rule of Libya, and commitments were made to improve bilateral relations. The Italian Minister of Foreign Affairs, Lamberto Dini, visited Libya in April 1999, immediately after the suspension of international sanctions. Italy's Prime Minister, Massimo D'Alema, travelled to Libya in December, thus becoming the first EU premier to visit the country since 1992. In December 2000 officials from the two countries signed accords regarding political consultation, visas and the removal of landmines during talks in Rome. In September 2003, just days after the lifting of UN sanctions against Libya, the Spanish Prime Minister, José María Aznar López, visited Tripoli for talks with Qaddafi. In February 2004 the Italian Prime Minister, Silvio Berlusconi, became the first Western leader to meet with Qaddafi following the Libyan leader's announcement in December 2003 that his country would dismantle its nuclear weapons programme. In further talks between the two leaders in August 2004 Berlusconi exerted pressure on Qaddafi to place stricter border controls on the country's northern coastline following an influx of illegal immigrants into the Italian island of Lampedusa from Libya. In October, as a result of a sudden increase in the number of illegal immigrants arriving from North Africa (up to 1,700 a week), the Italian Government began a mass expulsion of illegal immigrants to Libya. Having agreed to assist with the immigration problem, Libya returned some 1,000 of these people to Egypt. Also in October Qaddafi agreed to lift a ban which prohibited some 20,000 Italian settlers who had been expelled from Libya in 1970 (following Qaddafi's rise to power) from visiting the country. Diplomatic relations between the two countries soured, however, in early 2006. In February the Italian consulate in Benghazi and the residence of the consul were attacked and set alight by protesters. The violence followed the publication in numerous countries, including Italy, of cartoons originally printed in a Danish newspaper depicting the Prophet Muhammad, which were deemed to be offensive towards Islam. A day prior to the protests, the Italian Minister without Portfolio for Institutional Reforms and Devolution, Roberto Calderoli, had appeared on Italian television wearing a item of clothing bearing one of the cartoons; it was claimed that Calderoli's television appearance had provoked the disturbances in Benghazi, during which 11 people were killed. Libyan Secretary for National Security Nasser al-Mabrouk was suspended and referred for investigation over the conduct of security forces during the protests; Calderoli later resigned from the Italian Council of Ministers. In the immediate aftermath of the protests, Berlusconi and Qaddafi gave assurances that bilateral relations would not be harmed. However, in early March a statement by Qaddafi appeared to contradict his previous stance. The Libyan leader was quoted by Italian newspapers as warning of further attacks against Italian interests should the issue of compensation for Italian colonial rule of Libya not be resolved.

Meanwhile, Libya came under heavy criticism from EU officials in May 2004 after five Bulgarian nurses and a Palestinian doctor were sentenced to death for deliberately infecting more than 400 children at a Benghazi hospital in 1999 with blood containing the HIV virus. The trials were also criticized by international human rights associations as being unfair, and the nurses stated that their confessions had been gained through torture. In December 2004 it was announced that Libya would review the sentences and later in the month Qaddafi's son, Seif al-Islam, reportedly stated that the medics would not be executed. By March 2005, however, the sentences remained in place and the medics launched an official appeal. The judgment regarding the medics' appeal, which was expected in May, was delayed until November. Meanwhile, Libya continued to reject calls from Bulgaria, the USA and the EU to release the medics, and demanded compensation from Bulgaria for the families affected by the case. The Bulgarian Government refused, stating that any payment would constitute an admission of the medics' guilt. In November the Supreme Court rescheduled the ruling for the end of January 2006. However, in late December 2005 the previous sentences were overturned by the Supreme Court and a retrial was ordered. The retrial began on 11 May 2006, but was adjourned until 13 June.

In mid-1998 Qaddafi announced his intention to ally Libya more closely with African rather than Arab countries; later in the year numerous African heads of state visited Tripoli, all of whom defied UN sanctions by travelling to Libya by air. In October, as further evidence of his dissatisfaction with Arab states, Qaddafi changed the name of Libya's mission to the Arab League from 'permanent' to 'resident'. In September 1999, on the occasion of the 30th anniversary of his seizure of power, Qaddafi hosted an extraordinary OAU summit in Sirte. Qaddafi presented his vision of a United States of Africa, and demanded that Africa be given veto power on the UN Security Council. The 'Sirte Declaration', a final document adopted by the 43 attending heads of state and government, called for the strengthening of the OAU, the establishment of a pan-African parliament, African monetary union and an African court of justice. At a further extraordinary summit of the OAU in Sirte in early March 2001 it was announced that the organization's member states had overwhelmingly endorsed the proposals to declare the formation of the AU. In early July 2002 Qaddafi travelled to Durban, South Africa, for the 38th and final summit of the OAU, which saw the formal creation of the new AU, chaired by South African President Thabo Mbeki. During the summit Mbeki and numerous other African heads of state attempted to persuade Qaddafi to abandon his hostility towards the New Partnership for Africa's Development, a contract between Africa and the international community under which, in exchange for aid and investment, the African states agreed to strive towards democracy and good governance. In October Libya notified the Arab League of its intention to withdraw from the organization. Although no official reason for the withdrawal was given, reports indicated that senior Libyan officials had cited the Arab League's 'inefficiency' in dealing with the crises in Iraq and the Palestinian territories as its motives. In March 2003 Libyan officials confirmed that the threat of withdrawal was 'serious and official'. Qaddafi's growing influence in Africa was also somewhat checked in January 2003 following the removal of some 300 Libyan troops from the Central African Republic, to whose Government they had been providing protection. In the previous month an agreement between Libya and Zimbabwe which would have resulted in the exchange of Libyan fuel for Zimbabwean beef, sugar and tobacco was abandoned. Attempts to revive the trade pact in mid-2003, which would have resulted in Zimbabwe mortgaging its petroleum assets to Libya, proved unsuccessful, and the abolition of the Secretariat for African Unity in mid-2003 was widely interpreted as evidence of the failure of Qaddafi's African policy. In June 2004 it was reported that in mid-2003 Qaddafi had ordered the assassination of Crown Prince Abdullah of Saudi Arabia, the kingdom's de facto leader, following a dispute between the two leaders at the Arab League summit held in March. (Libya also reportedly accused Saudi Arabia of financing Libyan opposition groups which had attempted to assassinate Qaddafi.) Libyan officials strongly refuted these allegations; however, in December 2004 Saudi Arabia recalled its ambassador from Tripoli and dismissed the Libyan ambassador in Riyadh. In the same month Libya announced that it had decided to relinquish its chairmanship of the UMA, assumed in December 2003, citing the failure of the organization to achieve regional co-operation.

Meanwhile, in early January 2004 it was reported that a senior Israeli diplomat had held talks in Paris in December 2003 with Libyan representatives, with the aim of establishing diplomatic relations between the two countries. While an Israeli official confirmed that a meeting had taken place, the Libyan Government denied that any contact had been made.

LIBYA

Introductory Survey

Government

Power is vested in the people through People's Congresses, Popular Committees, Trade Unions, Vocational Syndicates, and with the General People's Congress (GPC) and its General Secretariat. The Head of State is the Revolutionary Leader, elected by the GPC. Executive power is exercised by the General People's Committee. The country is divided into three provinces, 10 governorates and 1,500 administrative communes.

Defence

Libya's active armed forces totalled 76,000 (including an estimated 38,000 conscripts) in August 2005: army 45,000; air force 23,000; navy 8,000. Military service is by selective conscription, lasting up to two years. There was additionally a People's Militia of 40,000 reserves. Libya's defence budget for 2005 was an estimated LD 800m.

Economic Affairs

In 2004, according to estimates by the World Bank, Libya's gross national income (GNI), measured at average 2002–04 prices, was US $25,257m., equivalent to $4,450 per head. During 1995–2004, it was estimated, the population increased at an average annual rate of 2.0%, while, according to the IMF, gross domestic product (GDP) per head increased, in real terms, by an average of 1.3% per year. Overall GDP increased, in real terms, at an average annual rate of 3.3% in 1995–2004. Real GDP increased by some 9.1% in 2003 and by an estimated 4.4% in 2004.

Agriculture (including forestry and fishing) contributed an estimated 3.6% of GDP in 2004, and engaged 7.1% of the employed labour force in 2001. The principal subsistence crops are wheat and barley; other crops include watermelons, potatoes, tomatoes, onions, olives, dates and citrus fruits. Output is limited by climatic conditions and irrigation problems, although cultivable land was being significantly increased by the Great Man-made River Project, whereby water was to be carried from the south of the country to the north and thence to the east and west. In July 2005 contracts for engineering, construction and supply during the third phase of the project were awarded to a Turkish company, Tekfen, and SNC Lavalin of Canada; however, the project was not expected to be completed for more than 20 years. Agriculture is based mainly on animal husbandry; sheep are the principal livestock, but goats, cattle, camels, horses and poultry are also kept. During 1998–2004 agricultural GDP increased at an average annual rate of 1.7%; the sector's GDP increased by an estimated 2.0% in both 2003 and 2004.

Industry (including mining, manufacturing, construction and power) contributed an estimated 71.9% of GDP in 2004, and engaged 23.1% of the employed labour force in 2001. Virtually all of the industrial sector is state-controlled. During 1998–2004 the GDP of the industrial sector increased at an average annual rate of 4.7%; industrial GDP increased by an estimated 9.6% in 2003, but growth declined to some 2.8% in 2004.

Mining contributed an estimated 65.5% of GDP in 2004, but engaged only 2.0% of the employed labour force in 2001. The petroleum and natural gas sector contributed about 64.4% of GDP in 2004, and engaged 2.7% of the employed labour force in 2001. Libya's economy depends almost entirely on its petroleum and natural gas resources. The National Oil Corporation of Libya controls about three-quarters of the petroleum produced in Libya, largely through production-sharing agreements. At the end of 2004 proven recoverable reserves of petroleum were estimated at 39,126m. barrels, the largest proven reserves in Africa and sufficient to enable production to be maintained—at that year's levels, averaging 1.58m. barrels per day (b/d)—for more than 66 years. With effect from July 2005 Libya's production quota within the Organization of the Petroleum Exporting Countries (OPEC, see p. 344) was 1,500,000 b/d. Libya's natural gas reserves are extensive (estimated at 1,491,000m. cu m at the end of 2004). Libya also has reserves of iron ore, salt, limestone, clay, sulphur and gypsum. The GDP of the mining sector increased, in real terms, by an annual average of 9.6% in 1998–2004; mining GDP declined by 7.0% in 2003, but increased by an estimated 8.3% in 2004.

Manufacturing contributed some 1.9% of GDP in 2004, and engaged 11.8% of the employed labour force in 2001. The principal manufacturing activity is petroleum refining. There are five refineries, including facilities at Brega, Ras Lanouf and Az-Zawiyah. A petrochemicals site is located at Brega, and in 2005 there were plans to construct a new refinery complex at Sebha, 700 km south of Tripoli. Other important manufacturing activities were the production of iron, steel and cement, and the processing of agricultural products. The GDP of the manufacturing sector declined at an average annual rate of 2.8% during 1998–2004; the sector's GDP decreased by an estimated 5.0% in 2003 and by some 1.5% in 2004.

Energy is derived almost exclusively from oil-fired power. Libya is a net exporter of fuels (less than 10% of petroleum production is used for domestic energy requirements), with imports of energy products comprising only an estimated 0.2% of the value of merchandise imports in 1998.

Services contributed an estimated 24.5% of GDP in 2004, and engaged 69.8% of the employed labour force in 2001. In an attempt to stimulate growth in the tourism sector, the Government has invested heavily in recent years to expand and rehabilitate the country's tourism infrastructure. Visitor arrivals had declined from some 1.8m. in 1995 to 857,952 in 2002, but increased to 957,896 in 2003. Receipts from tourism in 2003 amounted to US $79m. During 1998–2004 the GDP of the services sector increased at an annual average rate of 2.9%; services GDP increased by an estimated 6.4% in 2003 and by some 4.3% in 2004.

In 2004 Libya recorded a visible trade surplus of US $8,657m., and there was a surplus of $3,705m. on the current account of the balance of payments. In 2000 the principal sources of imports were Italy (which provided 19.1% of total imports), Germany (11.8%), the Republic of Korea, the United Kingdom and France. The principal market for exports in that year was Italy (42.6%); Germany, Spain, Turkey and France were also important purchasers. The petroleum sector is overwhelmingly Libya's principal generator of exports revenue: exports of mineral fuels and lubricants accounted for 92.6% of Libya's export earnings in 1998. The principal imports were machinery and transport equipment, basic manufactures, and food and live animals.

There was a projected budgetary surplus of some LD 6,988m. in 2004. In the previous year a surplus of LD 3,218m. had been recorded. Libya's total external debt was about US $3,800m. at the end of 1999, according to estimates quoted by the *Middle East Economic Digest*. According to the Central Bank of Libya, the annual rate of inflation averaged 5.8% during 2000–04; consumer prices declined by 2.1% in 2003 and by 2.2% in 2004. The rate of unemployment was unofficially estimated to be about 30% in 2003.

Libya is a member of the Arab Monetary Fund (see p. 163), the Council of Arab Economic Unity (see p. 208), the Islamic Development Bank (see p. 303), the Organization of Arab Petroleum Exporting Countries (OAPEC, see p. 338), OPEC (see p. 344) and the Union du Maghreb arabe (UMA—Union of the Arab Maghreb, see p. 388) In July 2004 Libya was permitted to begin accession negotiations with the World Trade Organization (WTO, see p. 370), having first applied to join the WTO in 2001.

During 2003–04 prospects for the major improvement and modernization of the Libyan economy were bolstered by a number of extremely important political decisions. The appointment in mid-2003 of Shukri Muhammad Ghanem, a former Libyan representative to OPEC, as Secretary of the GPC precipitated a new phase of economic reform; Ghanem swiftly announced plans to divest more than 360 state-owned entities and to establish a stock exchange, although he emphasized that the privatization scheme would not involve companies in the hydrocarbons or chemical sectors. In September 2003 the decision to accept civil responsibility for the Lockerbie bombing facilitated the formal removal of UN sanctions, which had been imposed in 1992 and suspended in 1999 (see Recent History), and in April 2004 the USA lifted the unilateral 'secondary' sanctions which had outlawed commercial activities and financial transactions between Libyan and US companies since 1996. The devaluation of the dinar by more than 50% in early 2002 and the exchange rate reform carried out in mid-2003 were expected to increase the flow of foreign direct investment into the country. In March 2005 the Government approved plans for the privatization of the banking sector, which would allow foreign-owned banks to open branches in Libya and give greater powers over monetary policy to the Central Bank. However, the IMF's Article IV consultation published in that month criticized the slow progress of reform in the country, and reported that only 42 of the 360 companies earmarked for privatization in 2003 had been sold. Meanwhile, oil exploration licences were granted to companies from the USA, Europe and Asia, and the Libyan Government pledged to increase petroleum production capacity to more than 3m. b/d by 2015. The National Oil Corporation aims to discover a further 20,000m. barrels of reserves in the next 10 years. According to IMF estimates, overall GDP growth was 4.4%

LIBYA

in 2004, but growth in non-oil GDP was 3.0%. Despite ambitious plans to increase oil production by up to 50%, Libya's reliance on petroleum revenues remained a major concern. Libya also possesses considerable reserves of natural gas, with major potential for further discoveries. A 520-km underwater pipeline linking Libya with Italy, which was inaugurated in October 2004, exports some 8,000m. cu m of natural gas to Europe per year. In early 2006 Libya signed a deal with France to co-operate in the development of a civil nuclear energy programme (see Recent History). Attempts are under way to develop the country's largely untapped tourism potential after the enactment of a five-year investment plan, at a cost of some US $7,000m., and in February 2004 the lifting of sanctions on US citizens travelling to Libya significantly opened up the tourism market. Prospects for economic development remained high during 2005, with many foreign businesses seeking to invest in Libya. However, the replacement of Ghanem as Secretary of the GPC by Dr al-Baghdadi Ali al-Mahmoudi in March 2006 was widely interpreted as a reverse as far as prospects for further economic reforms were concerned.

Education

Education is compulsory for children between six and 15 years of age. Primary education begins at the age of six and lasts for nine years. In 1992 primary enrolment included 96% of the relevant age-group (males 97%; females 96%). Secondary education, from the age of 15, lasts for three years. In 1992 secondary enrolment was equivalent to 98% of pupils in the relevant age-group. Libya also has institutes for agricultural, technical and vocational training. There are 13 universities. In 1992 enrolment in tertiary education was equivalent to 18.4% of the relevant age-group (males 19.2%; females 17.6%).

Public Holidays

2006: 10 January*† (Id al-Adha, Feast of the Sacrifice), 31 January* (Islamic New Year), 9 February* (Ashoura), 28 March (Evacuation Day), 10 April* (Mouloud, Birth of Muhammad), 11 June (Evacuation Day), 21 August* (Leilat al-Meiraj, ascension of Muhammad), 1 September (Revolution Day), 7 October (Evacuation Day), 23 October* (Id al-Fitr, end of Ramadan), 31 December*† (Id al-Adha, Feast of the Sacrifice).

2007: 20 January* (Islamic New Year), 29 January* (Ashoura), 28 March (Evacuation Day), 31 March* (Mouloud, Birth of Muhammad), 11 June (Evacuation Day), 10 August* (Leilat al-Meiraj, ascension of Muhammad), 1 September (Revolution Day), 7 October (Evacuation Day), 13 October* (Id al-Fitr, end of Ramadan), 20 December* (Id al-Adha, Feast of the Sacrifice).

* These holidays are dependent on the Islamic lunar calendar and may vary by one or two days from the dates given.

† This festival occurs twice (in the Islamic years AH 1426 and 1427) within the same Gregorian year.

Weights and Measures

The metric system is in force.

Statistical Survey

Sources (unless otherwise stated): National Corporation for Information and Documentation; Census and Statistical Dept, Secretariat of Planning, Sharia Damascus 40, 2nd Floor, Tripoli; tel. (21) 3331731; e-mail nida@nidaly.org; internet www.nidaly.org.

Area and Population

AREA, POPULATION AND DENSITY

Area (sq km)	1,775,500*
Population (census results)	
August 1995 (provisional)	
Males	2,236,943
Females	2,168,043
Total	4,404,986†
2003 (provisional)	5,678,484
Population (UN estimates at mid-year)	
2002	5,519,000
2003	5,629,000
2004	5,740,000
Density (per sq km) at census of 2004	3.2

* 685,524 sq miles.
† Excluding 406,916 non-Libyans.

Sources: UN, *World Population Prospects: The 2004 Revision*; National Authority for Information and Authentication.

POPULATION BY REGION
(1995 census, provisional figures)

Al-Batnan	151,240	Misratah (Misurata)	488,573
Jebel Akhdar	381,165	Najghaza	244,553
Banghazi (Benghazi)	665,615	Tarabulus (Tripoli)	1,313,996
Al-Wosta	240,574	Az-Zawiyah (Zawia)	517,395
Al-Wahat	62,056	Jebel Gharbi	316,970
Al-Jufra	39,335	Fazzan (Fezzan)	314,029
Sofuljin	76,401	**Total**	4,811,902

PRINCIPAL TOWNS
(population at census of 2003)

Tarabulus (Tripoli, the capital)	1,149,957	Az-Zawiyah (Zawia)	197,177
Banghazi (Benghazi)	636,992	Al-Jabal al-Akhader	194,185
Misratah (Misurata)	360,521	Ajdabiya (Ejdabia)	165,839
Almirqeb	328,292	Garyan (Ghryan)	161,408
Turhona and Misllatah	296,092	Sirte (Surt)	156,839
Al-Jfara	289,340	Surman and Subratha	152,521
An-Niikat al-Ghames	208,954		

Source: National Authority for Information and Authentication.

BIRTHS, MARRIAGES AND DEATHS

	Registered live births		Registered marriages*		Registered deaths*	
	Number	Rate (per 1,000)	Number	Rate (per 1,000)	Number	Rate (per 1,000)
1994	98,423	20.1	19,190	3.9	14,036	2.9
1995	88,779	17.9	21,358	4.3	13,538	4.6
1996	90,428	17.8	18,743	3.7	12,281	2.4

* Registration is incomplete.

Source: UN, *Demographic Yearbook*.

2002*: Registered live births 111,053 (rate per 1,000 20.2); Registered marriages 33,323; Registered deaths 19,362 (Source: mostly UN, *Population and Vital Statistics Report*).

Expectation of life (WHO estimates, years at birth): 73 (males 71; females 76) in 2003 (Source: WHO, *World Health Report*).

LIBYA

EMPLOYMENT
('000 persons)

	1999	2000	2001
Agriculture, forestry and fishing	232.0	239.1	103.4
Oil and gas extraction	38.7	39.9	40.0
Mining and quarrying	12.0	12.5	28.9
Manufacturing	163.7	169.6	172.1
Electricity, gas and water	39.6	41.0	50.9
Construction	207.9	222.0	45.2
Trade, restaurants and hotels	66.7	69.5	161.2
Transport and communications	132.2	143.4	55.5
Financing, insurance and real estate	30.1	33.0	38.1
Other services	460.9	475.0	763.1
Total	1,383.8	1,445.0	1,458.4
Libyans	1,203.9	1,257.1	1,335.4
Non-Libyans	179.9	187.9	123.0

Source: IMF, *Socialist People's Libyan Arab Jamahiriya: Statistical Appendix* (March 2005).

Health and Welfare

KEY INDICATORS

Total fertility rate (children per woman, 2003)	3.0
Under-5 mortality rate (per 1,000 live births, 2004)	20
HIV/AIDS (% of persons aged 15–49, 2003)	0.30
Physicians (per 1,000 head, 2004)	1.29
Hospital beds (per 1,000 head, 1997)	4.3
Health expenditure (2002): US $ per head (PPP)	222
Health expenditure (2002): % of GDP	3.3
Health expenditure (2002): public (% of total)	47.2
Access to water (% of persons, 2002)	72
Access to sanitation (% of persons, 2002)	97
Human Development Index (2003): ranking	58
Human Development Index (2003): value	0.799

For sources and definitions, see explanatory note on p. vi.

Agriculture

PRINCIPAL CROPS
('000 metric tons)

	2002	2003*	2004
Wheat	125†	125	125*
Barley*	80	80	80
Potatoes	195†	195	195*
Dry broad beans*	13	13	13
Almonds	26*	26	25
Groundnuts (in shell)	22*	24	23
Olives	150	150	180*
Tomatoes	190	190	190*
Pumpkins, squash and gourds*	30	30	30
Cucumbers and gherkins	10	10	10*
Chillies and green peppers*	15	15	15
Green onions and shallots*	53	53	53
Dry onions	180	180	182
Green peas	5	5	6
Green broad beans*	15	15	15
Carrots	25*	25	25
Other vegetables*	76	76	76
Watermelons	220*	230	240
Cantaloupes and other melons	26*	26	26
Oranges	43*	43	44
Tangerines, mandarins, etc.*	10	10	10
Lemons and limes	15*	16	17
Apples	20	20	20
Apricots	17*	17	18
Peaches and nectarines	10*	10	10
Plums	33*	33	32
Grapes	30	30	30*
Figs	10	10	10*
Dates	140*	145	150

* FAO estimate(s).
† Unofficial figure.
Source: FAO.

LIVESTOCK
('000 head, year ending September)

	2002	2003*	2004*
Horses	45†	45	45
Asses	30*	30	30
Cattle	130*	130	130
Camels	46*	47	47
Sheep	4,500	4,500	4,500
Goats	1,265*	1,265	1,265
Poultry	25*	25	25

* FAO estimate(s).
† Unofficial figure.
Source: FAO.

LIVESTOCK PRODUCTS
('000 metric tons)

	2001	2002	2003
Beef and veal*	6	6	6
Mutton and lamb*	27	27	27
Goat meat*	6	6	6
Poultry meat*	99	99	99
Cows' milk*	125	130	130
Sheep's milk*	56	56	56
Goats' milk*	15	15	15
Hen eggs	60	55	60*
Wool: greasy*	9	9	9
Wool: scoured*	2	2	2
Cattle hides*	1	1	1
Sheepskins*	6	6	6

* FAO estimate(s).
2004: Figures assumed to be unchanged from 2003 (FAO estimates).
Source: FAO.

Forestry

ROUNDWOOD REMOVALS
(FAO estimates, '000 cubic metres, excl. bark)

	1997	1998	1999
Sawlogs, veneer logs and logs for sleepers*	63	63	63
Other industrial wood	51	52	53
Fuel wood*	536	536	536
Total	650	651	652

* Annual output assumed to be unchanged since 1978.
2000–04: Output assumed to be unchanged from 1999 (FAO estimates).
Source: FAO.

SAWNWOOD PRODUCTION
(FAO estimates, '000 cubic metres, incl. railway sleepers)

	1976	1977	1978
Total (all broadleaved)*	9	21	31

* Annual output assumed to be unchanged since 1978 (FAO estimates).
Source: FAO.

LIBYA

Fishing

(metric tons, live weight)

	2001	2002	2003
Capture*	33,239	33,666	33,666
Groupers*	4,000	4,000	4,000
Bogue*	2,500	2,500	2,500
Porgies and seabreams	4,000	4,000	4,000
Surmullet*	4,000	4,000	4,000
Jack and horse mackerels	3,000	3,000	3,000
Sardinellas*	7,000	7,000	7,000
Atlantic bluefin tuna	1,940	n.a.	n.a.
'Scomber' mackerels*	3,000	3,000	3,000
Aquaculture*	100	—	—
Total catch (incl. others)	33,339	33,666	33,666

* FAO estimates.

Source: FAO.

Mining

(estimates, '000 metric tons, unless otherwise indicated)

	2002	2003	2004
Crude petroleum ('000 barrels)	502,000	543,000	587,000
Natural gas (million cu m)*	11,100	10,300	11,000
Salt	40	40	40
Gypsum (crude)	150	150	175

* Figures refer to gross volume. The dry equivalent (estimates, million cubic metres) was: 6,200 in 2002; 6,400 in 2003; 7,000 in 2004.

Source: US Geological Survey.

Industry

SELECTED PRODUCTS
('000 metric tons, unless otherwise indicated)

	1999	2000	2001
Olive oil (crude)	9	7	6
Paper and paperboard	6	6	6
Jet fuels	1,352	1,453	1,477
Motor spirit (petrol)	1,991	2,030	2,059
Naphthas	2,007	2,007	2,606
Kerosene	277	297	302
Gas-diesel (distillate fuel) oil	4,319	4,662	4,721
Residual fuel oils	4,908	4,330	4,390
Liquefied petroleum gas:			
from natural gas plants	353	353	645
from petroleum refineries	238	271	267
Petroleum bitumen (asphalt)	100	111	124
Cement	3	3	n.a.
Electric energy (million kWh)	20,044	20,044*	21,470

* Provisional or estimated figure.

2002 ('000 metric tons): Olive oil (crude) 8; Paper and paperboard 6; Cement 3.

Source: UN, *Industrial Commodity Statistics Yearbook*.

Finance

CURRENCY AND EXCHANGE RATES

Monetary Units
1,000 dirhams = 1 Libyan dinar (LD).

Sterling, Dollar and Euro Equivalents (30 December 2005)
£1 sterling = 2.3280 dinars;
US $1 = 1.3520 dinars;
€1 = 1.5949 dinars;
100 Libyan dinars = £42.96 = $73.97 = €62.70.

Average Exchange Rate (Libyan dinar per US $)
2003 1.2929
2004 1.3050
2005 1.3084

Note: In March 1986 the value of the Libyan dinar was linked to the IMF's special drawing right (SDR). Between November 1994 and November 1998 the official mid-point exchange rate was SDR 1 = 525 dirhams (LD 1 = SDR 1.90476). In February 1999 a rate of LD 1 = SDR 1.577 (SDR 1 = 634.1 dirhams) was introduced, but from September 1999 to September 2000 the value of the dinar fluctuated. In September 2000 a new rate of LD 1 = SDR 1.4204 (SDR 1 = 704.03 dirhams) was established, but in June 2001 the Libyan dinar was devalued to SDR 1.224 (SDR 1 = 816.99 dirhams). The latter rate remained in effect until the end of December 2001. In January 2002 the value of the Libyan dinar was adjusted to SDR 0.608 (SDR 1 = LD 1.64474): a devaluation of 50.3%.

BUDGET
(LD million)

Revenue	2002	2003	2004*
Budgetary revenue	9,847	7,308	12,370
Hydrocarbon budget allocation	7,753	5,621	9,874
Non-hydrocarbon tax revenue	1,150	725	984
Taxes on income and profits	506	n.a.	n.a.
Taxes on international trade	379	385	602
Other tax revenue	266	—	—
Non-hydrocarbon non-tax revenue	944	962	1,512
Extrabudgetary revenue	2,725	9,307	10,692
Total	12,572	16,614	23,061

Expenditure	2002	2003	2004*
Current	6,724	10,564	10,128
Administrative budget	4,183	4,228	4,843
Expenditure on goods and services	3,684	3,499	3,607
Wages and salaries	2,546	2,812	2,935
Interest payments	—	—	60
Subsidies and other current transfers	499	728	1,176
Extrabudgetary current expenditure	2,541	6,336	5,285
Oil reserve fund	1,966	5,636	4,545
Defence	575	700	740
Capital	3,339	2,832	5,945
Development budget	2,936	2,204	5,237
Extrabudgetary capital expenditure	403	628	708
Total	10,063	13,396	16,073

* Projected figures.

Source: IMF, *Socialist People's Libyan Arab Jamahiriya: Statistical Appendix* (March 2005).

INTERNATIONAL RESERVES
(US $ million at 31 December)

	2002	2003	2004
Gold*	194	194	194
IMF special drawing rights	610	686	738
Reserve position in IMF	538	588	614
Foreign exchange	13,159	18,310	24,336
Total	14,501	19,778	25,882

* Valued at US $42 per troy ounce.

Source: IMF, *International Financial Statistics*.

LIBYA

Statistical Survey

MONEY SUPPLY
(LD million at 31 December)

	2002	2003	2004
Currency outside banks	2,630.5	2,780.1	2,612.7
Private-sector deposits at Central Bank	349.3	240.8	246.3
Demand deposits at commercial banks	4,753.6	5,209.9	6,801.6
Total money (incl. others)	7,843.4	8,340.9	10,154.0

Source: IMF, *International Financial Statistics*.

COST OF LIVING
(Consumer Price Index; base: 1999 = 100)

	2002	2003	2004
Personal services and others	81.7	80.3	78.7
Medical care	101.4	98.4	103.5
Recreation and education	85.7	83.5	82.3
Transport and communication	99.3	99.0	95.9
Clothing and shoes	65.6	60.8	60.8
Furniture	79.2	76.9	70.9
Housing	87.1	83.1	83.2
Food, beverages and tobacco	77.1	73.8	75.6
All items	79.8	78.1	76.4

Source: Central Bank of Libya.

NATIONAL ACCOUNTS
(LD million at current prices)

National Income and Product

	1983	1984	1985
Compensation of employees	2,763.1	2,865.8	2,996.2
Operating surplus	5,282.7	4,357.8	4,572.4
Domestic factor incomes	8,045.8	7,223.6	7,568.6
Consumption of fixed capital	436.1	457.5	481.6
Gross domestic product (GDP) at factor cost	8,481.9	7,681.1	8,050.2
Indirect taxes	470.0	462.2	389.0
Less Subsidies	146.7	130.0	162.2
GDP in purchasers' values	8,805.2	8,013.3	8,277.0
Factor income from abroad	200.2	142.8	122.5
Less Factor income paid abroad	989.0	727.7	397.9
Gross national product	8,016.4	7,428.4	8,001.6
Less Consumption of fixed capital	436.1	457.5	481.6
National income in market prices	7,580.3	6,970.9	7,520.0
Other current transfers from abroad	8.6	2.3	2.6
Less Other current transfers paid abroad	25.2	27.9	16.0
National disposable income	7,563.7	6,945.3	7,506.6

Source: UN, *National Accounts Statistics*.

Expenditure on the Gross Domestic Product

	2000	2001	2002
Government final consumption expenditure	3,616	3,925	4,077
Private final consumption expenditure	8,150	8,994	13,939
Increase in stocks	74	74	150
Gross fixed capital formation	2,214	2,158	3,366
Total domestic expenditure	14,054	15,151	21,532
Exports of goods and services	6,186	5,478	11,645
Less Imports of goods and services	2,690	3,433	8,868
GDP in purchasers' values	17,550	17,196	24,309

Source: IMF, *International Financial Statistics*.

Gross Domestic Product by Economic Activity*

	2002	2003	2004
Agriculture, forestry and fishing	1,348.8	1,375.8	1,439.3
Mining and quarrying	14,017.7	19,300.7	26,389.2
Petroleum and natural gas	13,630.6	18,940.5	25,958.0
Manufacturing	813.1	764.7	761.1
Electricity, gas and water	293.7	303.1	334.4
Construction	1,342.3	1,249.0	1,495.3
Trade, restaurants and hotels	2,089.5	2,193.9	2,392.1
Transport, storage and communications	1,429.2	1,515.0	1,663.6
Finance, insurance and real estate	929.9	974.0	1,070.5
Public services	3,222.3	3,606.5	4,286.0
Other services	427.5	448.9	475.5
Total	25,914.1	31,731.8	40,307.0

*Preliminary figures.

Source: Central Bank of Libya.

BALANCE OF PAYMENTS
(US $ million)

	2002	2003	2004
Exports of goods f.o.b.	9,851	14,664	17,425
Imports of goods f.o.b.	−7,408	−7,200	−8,768
Trade balance	2,443	7,464	8,657
Exports of services	401	442	437
Imports of services	−1,544	−1,597	−1,764
Balance on goods and services	1,300	6,309	7,330
Other income (net)	−404	−994	−1,301
Balance on goods, services and income	896	5,315	6,029
Current transfers (net)	−779	−1,673	−2,324
Current balance	117	3,642	3,705
Direct investment (net)	281	79	1,356
Portfolio investment (net)	72	−607	−187
Other investment (net)	−264	361	−122
Net errors and omissions	72	−459	980
Overall balance	278	3,016	5,732

Source: IMF, *International Financial Statistics*.

External Trade

PRINCIPAL COMMODITIES
(distribution by SITC, US $ million, excl. military goods)

Imports c.i.f.	1997	1998
Food and live animals	1,119.4	1,235.8
Live animals, chiefly for food	139.0	194.5
Cereals and cereal preparations	519.9	406.0
Meal and flour of wheat and meslin	185.0	175.3
Chemicals and related products	417.9	418.9
Basic manufactures	1,126.2	1,177.9
Textile yarn, fabrics, etc.	170.9	228.2
Iron and steel	398.2	236.3
Tubes, pipes and fittings	314.1	147.0
Machinery and transport equipment	2,012.4	1,892.9
Machinery specialized for particular industries	251.6	186.4
General industrial machinery, equipment and parts	554.8	511.8
Electrical machinery, apparatus, etc.	320.8	269.0
Road vehicles and parts*	562.4	537.4
Passenger motor cars (excl. buses)	314.8	292.9
Miscellaneous manufactured articles	658.5	537.1
Clothing and accessories (excl. footwear)	223.6	154.0
Total (incl. others)	5,592.9	5,691.8

*Data on parts exclude tyres, engines and electrical parts.

LIBYA

Exports f.o.b.	1997	1998
Mineral fuels, lubricants, etc.	8,557.4	5,678.4
Petroleum, petroleum products, etc.	8,386.7	5,587.5
Crude petroleum oils, etc.	6,897.5	4,524.8
Refined petroleum products	1,489.2	1,062.7
Gasoline and other light oils	282.3	226.6
Residual fuel oils	1,206.9	836.1
Chemicals and related products	294.2	258.4
Total (incl. others)	9,028.7	6,131.4

Source: UN, *International Trade Statistics Yearbook*.

PRINCIPAL TRADING PARTNERS
(US $ million)*

Imports c.i.f.	1998	1999	2000
Argentina	95.5	21.1	102.9
Australia	214.8	27.6	20.2
Austria	58.2	44.9	79.1
Belgium	n.a.	68.1	68.6
Brazil	64.8	31.0	44.0
Canada	121.5	54.5	34.3
China, People's Republic	79.1	86.5	69.4
Egypt	125.3	69.2	68.8
France (incl. Monaco)	315.7	227.6	204.1
Germany	617.3	599.3	440.5
Greece	58.8	38.3	27.4
India	62.7	24.2	22.9
Ireland	7.5	14.7	13.4
Italy	1,230.4	755.9	713.1
Japan	236.9	203.3	172.9
Korea, Republic	298.1	321.9	307.9
Malta	103.9	66.4	39.1
Morocco	99.4	115.8	67.0
Netherlands	94.4	81.8	87.0
Spain	266.6	115.9	121.6
Sweden	42.9	62.7	48.7
Switzerland-Liechtenstein	149.9	170.8	108.9
Tunisia	180.5	141.6	189.9
Turkey	78.9	27.1	36.2
United Kingdom	435.0	265.9	216.0
USA	82.5	84.0	76.7
Total (incl. others)	5,691.8	4,140.4	3,731.5

Exports f.o.b.	1998	1999	2000
Austria	125.2	87.0	18.9
Egypt	97.6	94.1	57.1
France (incl. Monaco)	236.8	509.8	574.4
Germany	1,002.9	1,507.1	1,556.2
Greece	161.6	186.1	270.7
Italy	2,449.9	2,987.0	4,343.8
Netherlands	141.0	81.8	70.0
Portugal	29.6	20.6	49.9
Spain	685.9	1,084.5	1,555.0
Switzerland-Liechtenstein	0.9	105.2	18.4
Tunisia	303.6	320.6	423.2
Turkey	394.4	5.7	769.3
United Kingdom	158.0	104.4	233.6
Total (incl. others)	6,131.4	7,905.1	10,194.9

* Imports by country of origin; exports by country of destination. Figures exclude trade in gold.

Source: UN, *International Trade Statistics Yearbook*.

Transport

ROAD TRAFFIC
(motor vehicles in use at 31 December)

	2000	2001
Passenger cars	549,600	552,700
Commercial vehicles	177,400	195,500

Buses and coaches: 1,424 in 1995; 1,490 in 1996.
Motorcycles and mopeds: 1,078 in 1995; 1,112 in 1996.
Sources: IRF, *World Road Statistics*; UN, *Statistical Yearbook*.

SHIPPING

Merchant Fleet
(registered at 31 December)

	2002	2003	2004
Number of vessels	140	138	136
Total displacement ('000 grt)	164.9	156.7	130.1

Source: Lloyd's Register-Fairplay, *World Fleet Statistics*.

International Sea-borne Freight Traffic
(estimates, '000 metric tons)

	1991	1992	1993
Goods loaded	57,243	59,894	62,491
Goods unloaded	7,630	7,710	7,808

Source: UN Economic Commission for Africa, *African Statistical Yearbook*.

CIVIL AVIATION
(traffic on scheduled services)

	1999	2000	2001
Kilometres flown (million)	4	4	4
Passengers carried ('000)	571	601	583
Passenger-km (million)	377	409	409
Total ton-km (million)	27	33	33

Source: UN, *Statistical Yearbook*.

Tourism

VISITOR ARRIVALS BY COUNTRY OF ORIGIN*

	2001	2002	2003
Algeria	82,525	70,416	71,657
Egypt	369,159	354,189	429,220
Morocco	22,835	19,076	19,120
Tunisia	386,809	329,145	346,331
Total (incl. others)	952,934	857,952	957,896

* Including same-day visitors (excursionists).

Tourism Receipts (US $ million, excl. passenger transport): 94 in 2001; 75 in 2002; 79 in 2003.

Source: World Tourism Organization.

LIBYA

Communications Media

	2002	2003	2004
Telephones ('000 main lines in use)	610	750	750*
Mobile cellular telephones ('000 subscribers)	50	100	127*
Personal computers ('000 in use)	130	n.a.	130*
Internet users ('000)	20	160	205

* Estimate.

1994: Book production (titles) 26.

1997: Radio receivers ('000 in use) 1,350; Television receivers ('000 in use) 730.

1998: Daily newspapers 4 (estimated average circulation 71,100).

Sources: UNESCO, *Statistical Yearbook*; International Telecommunication Union.

Education

(1995/96, unless otherwise indicated)

	Institutions	Teachers	Students
Primary and preparatory: general	2,733*	122,020	1,333,679
Primary and preparatory: vocational	168	n.a.	22,490
Secondary: general	n.a.	17,668	170,573
Secondary: teacher training	n.a.	2,760†	23,919
Secondary: vocational	312	n.a.	109,074
Universities	13	n.a.	126,348

* 1993/94.
† 1992/93.

Source: partly UNESCO, *Statistical Yearbook*.

1998: 1,160,315 primary school students (Source: World Bank).

Adult literacy rate (UNESCO estimates): 81.7% (males 91.8%; females 70.7%) in 2002 (Source: UN Development Programme, *Human Development Report*).

Directory

The Constitution

The Libyan Arab People, meeting in the General People's Congress in Sebha from 2–28 March 1977, proclaimed its adherence to freedom and its readiness to defend it on its own land and anywhere else in the world. It also announced: its adherence to socialism and its commitment to achieving total Arab Unity; its adherence to the moral human values; and confirmation of the march of the revolution led by Col Muammar al-Qaddafi, the Revolutionary Leader, towards complete People's Authority.

The Libyan Arab People announced the following:

(i) The official name of Libya is henceforth the Socialist People's Libyan Arab Jamahiriya.

(ii) The Holy Koran is the social code in the Socialist People's Libyan Arab Jamahiriya.

(iii) The Direct People's Authority is the basis for the political order in the Socialist People's Libyan Arab Jamahiriya. The People shall practise its authority through People's Congresses, Popular Committees, Trade Unions, Vocational Syndicates, and the General People's Congress, in the presence of the law.

(iv) The defence of our homeland is the responsibility of every citizen. The whole people shall be trained militarily and armed by general military training, the preparation of which shall be specified by the law.

The General People's Congress in its extraordinary session held in Sebha issued four decrees:

The first decree announced the establishment of the People's Authority in compliance with the resolutions and recommendations of the People's Congresses and Trade Unions.

The second decree stipulated the choice of Col Muammar al-Qaddafi, the Revolutionary Leader, as Secretary-General of the General People's Congress.

The third decree stipulated the formation of the General Secretariat of the General People's Congress (see The Government, below).

The fourth decree stipulated the formation of the General People's Committee to carry out the tasks of the various former ministries (see The Government, below).

In 1986 it was announced that the country's official name was to be the Great Socialist People's Libyan Arab Jamahiriya.

The Government

HEAD OF STATE*

Revolutionary Leader: Col MUAMMAR AL-QADDAFI (took office as Chairman of the Revolution Command Council 8 September 1969).

Second-in-Command: Maj. ABD AS-SALAM JALLOUD.

*Qaddafi himself rejects this nomenclature and all other titles.

GENERAL SECRETARIAT OF THE GENERAL PEOPLE'S CONGRESS
(April 2006)

Secretary: MUHAMMAD AZ-ZANATI.

Assistant Secretary for Popular Congresses: IBRAHIM ABD AR-RAHMAN IBJAD.

Assistant Secretary for Popular Committees: MUBARAK ABDULLAH ASH-SHAMAKH.

Secretary for Culture and Mass Mobilization: ABD AL-HAMID AS-SID ZINTANI.

Secretary for Trade Unions, Leagues and Professional Unions: ABDALLAH IDRIS IBRAHIM.

Secretary for Social Affairs: SALIMA SHAIBAN ABD AL-JABAR.

Secretary for Infrastructure, Urban Planning and Environment: Dr SALIM AHMAD FUNAYT.

Secretary for Human Resources: Dr AL-BAGHDADI ALI AL-MAHMOUDI.

Secretary for Foreign Affairs: SULEIMAN SASI ASH-SHAHUMI.

Secretary for Economy: ABD AS-SALAM AHMAD NUWEIR.

Secretary for Legal Affairs and Human Rights: HUSSEIN AL-WAHISHI AS-SADIQ.

Secretary for Security Affairs: MUFTAH ABD AS-SALAM BUKAR.

Secretary for Women's Affairs: AMAL NURI ABDULLAH AS-SAFAR.

Secretary for Union Syndicates and Vocational Association Affairs: Dr MUHAMMAD BIN HUSSEIN JABRAIL.

GENERAL PEOPLE'S COMMITTEE
(April 2006)

Secretary: Dr AL-BAGHDADI ALI AL-MAHMOUDI.

Deputy Secretary for Production: MUHAMMAD ALI AL-HOUEIZ.

Secretary for Justice: ALI OMAR AL-HASNAWI.

Secretary for Finance: Dr AHMAD MUNAYSI ABD AL-HAMID.

Secretary for Foreign Liaison and International Co-operation: ABD AR-RAHMAN MUHAMMAD SHALGAM.

Secretary for Tourism: AMMAR AT-TAEF.

Secretary for the Economy, Trade and Investment: AT-TAYIB AS-SAFI AT-TAHIB.

Secretary for Health and Environment: Dr MUHAMMAD ABU UJAYLAH RASHID.

Secretary for Industry, Electricity and Mines: FATHI HAMAD BEN SHATWAN.

Secretary for Youth and Sport: MOUSTAFA MIFTAH BEL'ID AD-DERSI.

Secretary for Culture and Information: NURI DHAW AL-HUMEIDI.

Secretary for Manpower, Training and Employment: MAATUK MUHAMMAD MAATUK.

Secretary for Planning: Dr TAHIR AL-HADI AL-JUHAYMI.

LIBYA

Secretary for Agriculture, Animals and Water Resources: Abu Bakr Mabrouk al-Mansuri.
Secretary for National Security: Brig. Salih Rajab al-Mismari.
Secretary for Social Affairs: Bakhitah Abd al-Alim ash-Shalwi.
Secretary for Transport and Communications: Ali Yousuf Zikri.
Secretary for General Education: Dr Abd al-Qadir Muhammad al-Baghdadi.
Secretary for Higher Education: Dr Ibrahim az-Zarruq ash-Sharif.

Legislature

GENERAL PEOPLE'S CONGRESS

The Senate and House of Representatives were dissolved after the *coup d'état* of September 1969, and the provisional Constitution issued in December 1969 made no mention of elections or a return to parliamentary procedure. However, in January 1971 Col Qaddafi announced that a new legislature would be appointed, not elected; no date was mentioned. All political parties other than the Arab Socialist Union were banned. In November 1975 provision was made for the creation of the 1,112-member General National Congress of the Arab Socialist Union, which met officially in January 1976. This later became the General People's Congress (GPC), which met for the first time in November 1976 and in March 1977 began introducing the wide-ranging changes outlined in the Constitution (above).

Secretary-General: Abd ar-Raziq Sawsa.

Political Organizations

In June 1971 the Arab Socialist Union (ASU) was established as the country's sole authorized political party. The General National Congress of the ASU held its first session in January 1976 and later became the General People's Congress (see Legislature, above).

The following groups are in opposition to the Government:

Ansarollah (Followers of God): f. 1996.
Fighting Islamic Group (FIG): f. 1995; seeks to establish an Islamic regime; claimed responsibility for subversive activities in early 1996, and engaged in armed clashes with security forces in mid- to late 1990s; Leader Anas Sebai.
Islamic Martyrs' Movement (IMM): seeks to establish an Islamic republic; Leader Abu Shaltilah; Spokesman Abdallah Ahmad.
Libyan Baathist Party.
Libyan Change and Reform Movement: breakaway group from NFSL.
Libyan Conservatives' Party: f. 1996.
Libyan Constitutional GroupingLibyan Democratic Authority: f. 1993.
Libyan Democratic Conference: f. 1992.
Libyan Democratic Movement: f. 1977; external group.
Libyan Movement for Change and Reform: POB 3423, London, NW6 7TZ, United Kingdom; f. 1994.
Libyan National Alliance: f. 1980 in Cairo, Egypt.
Libyan National Democratic Grouping: Leader Mahmoud Sulayman al-Maghrabi.
Movement of Patriotic Libyans: f. 1997; aims to establish a 'free Libyan state' based on a market economy.
National Front for the Salvation of Libya (NFSL): e-mail info@libya-nfsl.org; internet www.nfsl-libya.com; f. 1981 in Khartoum, Sudan; aims to replace the existing regime by a democratically elected govt; Leader Muhammad Megarief.

Diplomatic Representation

EMBASSIES IN LIBYA

Afghanistan: POB 4245, Sharia Mozhar al-Aftes, Tripoli; tel. (21) 4775192; fax (21) 609876; Ambassador (vacant).
Algeria: Sharia Kairauan 12, Tripoli; tel. (21) 4440025; fax (21) 3334631; Ambassador Muhammad Seghir Kara.
Argentina: POB 932, Gargaresh, Madina Syahia, Tripoli; tel. (21) 4834956; fax (21) 4840928; e-mail embartrip@hotmail.com; Ambassador Juan Carlos Valle Raleigh.
Austria: POB 3207, Sharia Khalid ibn al-Walid, Garden City, Tripoli; tel. (21) 4443379; fax (21) 4440838; e-mail tripolis-ob@bmaa.gv.at; Ambassador Dr Thomas Wunderbaldinger.
Bangladesh: POB 5086, Hi Damasq, Tripoli; tel. (21) 4911198; fax (21) 4906616; e-mail bdtripoli@bsisp.net.
Belarus: POB 1530, Tripoli; tel. (21) 4444708; fax (21) 3332994; e-mail libya@belembassy.org; Ambassador Derevyashko Aleksandr Nikolaevich.
Belgium: Jasmin St, Hay Andalus, Tripoli; tel. (21) 4782044; fax (21) 4782046; e-mail tripoli@diplobel.be; internet www.diplomatie.be/tripoli; Ambassador Jacques Scavée.
Benin: POB 6676, Sharia Ghout ash-Shaal, Tripoli; tel. (21) 4837663; fax (21) 834569; Ambassador Lafia Chabi.
Bosnia and Herzegovina: POB 6946, Sharia Abdul-Melik bin Kutn, Tripoli; tel. and fax (21) 4776442; fax 4774327; Ambassador Seta Ferhat.
Brazil: POB 2270, Sharia ben Ashour, Tripoli; tel. (21) 3614894; fax (21) 3614895; e-mail brcastripoli@lttnet.net; Ambassador Joaquim Palmeiro.
Bulgaria: POB 2945, Sharia Selma ben Al-Ukua, Ben Ashour Area No. 58-6, Tripoli; tel. (21) 3609988; fax (21) 3609990; e-mail tripoli@embassy.transat.bg; Ambassador Dr Zdravko Velev.
Burkina Faso: POB 81902, Route de Gargeresh, Tripoli; tel. (21) 4771221; fax (21) 4778037; Ambassador Youssouf Sangare.
Burundi: POB 2817, Sharia Ras Hassan, Tripoli; tel. (21) 608848; Ambassador Zacharie Banyiyezako.
Canada: POB 93392, Tripoli; tel. (21) 3351633; fax (21) 3351630; e-mail trpli@international.gc.ca; internet www.dfait-maeci.gc.ca/libya/menu-en.asp; Ambassador David Viveash.
Chad: POB 1078, Sharia Muhammad Mussadeq 25, Tripoli; tel. (21) 4443955; Ambassador Ibrahim Mahamat Tidei.
China, People's Republic: POB 5329, Sharia Menstir, Andalus, Gargaresh, Tripoli; tel. (21) 4832914; fax (21) 4831877; e-mail chinaemb_ly@mfa.gov.cn; Ambassador Huang Jiemen.
Croatia: Great al-Fatah Towers, Floor 12, Room 125, Tripoli; tel. (21) 3351381; fax (21) 3351386; e-mail croemb.tripoli@mvp.hr; Chargé d'affaires a.i. Mario Rožić.
Cuba: POB 83738, Sharia ibn al-Youmin, Ahmed al-Mahzumi, Tripoli; tel. (21) 4775216; fax (21) 4776294; e-mail embacuba.libia@lttnet.net; Ambassador Pablo Angél Reyes Domínguez.
Cyprus: POB 3284, Sharia adh-Dhul 60, Ben Ashour, Tripoli; tel. (21) 3601274; fax (21) 3613516; e-mail cyprusembassy@mail.lttnet.net; Ambassador Yannis Iacovou.
Czech Republic: POB 1097, Sharia Ahmad Lutfi Sayed, Sharia ben Ashour, Tripoli; tel. (21) 3615436; fax (21) 3615437; e-mail tripoli@embassy.mzv.cz; internet www.mzv.cz/tripoli; Ambassador Dušan Štrauch.
Egypt: POB 1105, The Grand Hotel, Tripoli; tel. (21) 4448909; fax (21) 4449262; e-mail egyemblib@hotmail.com; Ambassador Muhammad Fatihy Refa'a et-Tahtawi.
Equatorial Guinea: Tripoli.
Eritrea: POB 91279, Tripoli; tel. (21) 4780311; fax (21) 4780152; Ambassador Uthman Muhammad Umar.
France: POB 312, Sharia Beni al-Amar, Hay Andalus, Tripoli; tel. (21) 4774891; fax (21) 4778266; e-mail info@ambafrance-ly.org; internet www.ambafrance-ly.org; Ambassador Jean-Luc Sibiude.
Germany: POB 302, Sharia Hassan al-Mashai, Tripoli; tel. (21) 3330554; fax (21) 4440153; e-mail info@tripolis.diplo.de; internet www.tripolis.diplo.de; Ambassador Bernd Westphal.
Ghana: POB 4169, Andalus 21/A, nr Funduk Shati Gargaresh, Tripoli; tel. (21) 4772534; fax (21) 4773557; e-mail ghaemb@all-computers.com; Ambassador George Kumi.
Greece: POB 5147, Sharia Jalal Bayar 18, Tripoli; tel. (21) 3338563; fax (21) 4441907; e-mail grembtri@hotmail.com; Ambassador Chrysanthi Panagiotopoulou.
Guinea: POB 10657, Andalus, Tripoli; tel. (21) 4772793; fax (21) 4773441; e-mail magatte@lttnet.net; Ambassador Abdul Aziz Soumah.
Holy See: Tripoli; Apostolic Nuncio Most Rev. Félix del Blanco Prieto (Titular Archbishop of Vannida, resident in Malta).
Hungary: POB 4010, Sharia Talha ben Abdullah, Tripoli; tel. (21) 3618218; fax (21) 3618220; e-mail hungemtpi@lttnet.com; Ambassador Andras Szábó.
India: POB 3150, 16 Sharia Mahmud Shaltut, Tripoli; tel. (21) 4441835; fax (21) 3337560; e-mail indembtrip@hotmail.com; Ambassador D. P. Srivastava.
Indonesia: POB 5921, Tripoli; tel. (21) 4842067; fax (21) 4842069; e-mail indonesia@bsisp.net; Ambassador Achmad Nawawi Hasbi.

LIBYA

Directory

Iran: POB 6185, Tripoli; tel. (21) 3609552; fax (21) 3611674; e-mail iran_em_tripoli@hotmail.com; Ambassador MUHAMMAD MENHAJ.
Italy: POB 912, Sharia Vahran 1, Tripoli; tel. (21) 3334133; fax (21) 3331673; e-mail ambasciate.tripoli@esteri.it; Ambassador CLAUDIO PACIFICO.
Japan: POB 3265, Sharia Jamal ad-Din al-Waeli, Tripoli; tel. (21) 4781041; fax (21) 4781044; Ambassador AKIRA WATANABE.
Korea, Democratic People's Republic: Tripoli; Ambassador RI PYONG HO.
Korea, Republic: POB 4781, Gargaresh, Tripoli; tel. (21) 4831322; fax (21) 4831324; Ambassador KIM JOONG-JAE.
Kuwait: POB 2225, Beit al-Mal Beach, Tripoli; tel. (21) 4440281; fax (21) 607053; Chargé d'affaires (vacant).
Lebanon: POB 927, Sharia bin al-Arkam, Ben Achour 10, Tripoli; tel. (21) 3615744; fax (21) 3611740; e-mail emblebanon_ly@hotmail.com; Ambassador MOUNIR KHOREISH.
Lesotho: Ambassador PAUL KHOASHANE MOTHOLO.
Malaysia: POB 6309, Hay Andalus, Tripoli; tel. (21) 4830854; fax (21) 4831496; e-mail mwtripoli@lttnet.net; Ambassador Datuk SHAPII BIN ABU SAMAH.
Mali: POB 2008, Sharia Jaraba Saniet Zarrouk, Tripoli; tel. (21) 4444924; Ambassador EL BEKAYE SIDI MOCTAR KOUNTA.
Malta: POB 2534, Sharia Ubei ben Ka'ab, Tripoli; tel. (21) 3611181; fax (21) 3611180; e-mail maltaembassy.tripoli@gov.mt; Ambassador Dr JOSEPH CASSAR.
Mauritania: Sharia Eysa Wokwak, Tripoli; tel. (21) 4443223; Ambassador YAHIA MUHAMMAD EL-HADI.
Morocco: POB 908, Ave 7 Avril, Tripoli; tel. (21) 3617809; fax (21) 3614752; e-mail sifmatripo@hotmail.com; Ambassador DRISS ALAOUI.
Netherlands: POB 3801, Sharia Jalal Bayar 20, Tripoli; tel. (21) 4441549; fax (21) 4440386; e-mail tri@minbuza.nl; internet www.netherlandsembassy-libya.com; Ambassador J. WETERINGS.
Niger: POB 2251, Fachloun Area, Tripoli; tel. (21) 4443104; Ambassador AMADOU TIDJANI ALI.
Nigeria: POB 4417, Sharia Bashir al-Ibrahim, Tripoli; tel. (21) 4443038; Ambassador Prof. DANDATTI ABD AL-KADIR.
Pakistan: POB 2169, Sharia Huzayfa bin al-Yaman, Manshiya bin Ashour, Tripoli; tel. (21) 3610937; fax (21) 3600412; e-mail pareptripoli@hotmail.com; Ambassador MUHAMMAD FAROOQ QARI.
Philippines: POB 12508, Km 7 Abu Nawas, Gargaresh Rd, Hay Andalus, Gargaresh, Tripoli; tel. (21) 4833966; fax (21) 4836158; e-mail tripoli_pe76@lttnet.net; Chargé d'affaires a.i. BENITO B. VALERIANO.
Poland: POB 519, Sharia ben Ashour 61, Tripoli; tel. (21) 3608569; fax (21) 3615199; e-mail ambrp.trypolis@interia.pl; Ambassador JAKUB WOLSKI.
Qatar: POB 3506, Sharia ben Ashour, Tripoli; tel. (21) 4446660; Ambassador SAAD BEN ALI AL-MAHANDY.
Romania: POB 5085, Sharia Ahmad Lotfi Sayed, Sharia ben Ashour, Tripoli; tel. (21) 3615295; fax (21) 3607597; e-mail ambaromatrip@hotmail.com; Ambassador ILIE IONEL.
Russia: POB 4792, Sharia Mustapha Kamel, Tripoli; tel. (21) 3330545; fax (21) 4446673; Ambassador VALERYIAN V. SHUVAYEV.
Rwanda: POB 6677, Villa Ibrahim Musbah Missalati, Andalus, Tripoli; tel. (21) 72864; fax (21) 70317; Chargé d'affaires CHRISTOPHE HABIMANA.
Saudi Arabia: Sharia Kairauan 2, Tripoli; tel. (21) 30485; Chargé d'affaires MUHAMMAD HASSAN BANDAH.
Senegal: El-Arabia Gotchalle 246/5, Gargaresh, Tripoli; tel. (21) 4836090; fax (21) 4838955; Ambassador MAMADOU DIOUF.
Serbia and Montenegro: POB 1087, Sharia Turkia 14–16, Tripoli; tel. (21) 3330819; fax (21) 3334114; e-mail yuambtripoli@yahoo.com; Ambassador Dr DUSAN SIMEONOVIC.
Sierra Leone: Tripoli; Ambassador el Hadj MOHAMMED SAMURA.
Slovakia: POB 5721, Gargaresh 3 Km, Hay Andalus, Tripoli; tel. (21) 4781388; fax (21) 4781387; e-mail slovembtrp@mwc.ly; Ambassador JÁN BÓRY.
Spain: POB 2302, Sharia el-Amir Abd al-Kader al-Jazairi 36, Tripoli; tel. (21) 3336797; fax (21) 4443743; e-mail embesply@mail.mae.es; Ambassador JOAQUÍN ANTONIO PÉREZ VILLANUEVA Y TOVAR.
Sudan: POB 1076, Sharia Gargaresh, Tripoli; tel. (21) 4775387; fax (21) 4774781; e-mail sudtripoli@hotmail.com; internet www.sudtripoli.net; Ambassador OSMAN M. O. DIRAR.
Switzerland: POB 439, Sharia ben Ashour, Tripoli; tel. (21) 3614118; fax (21) 3614238; e-mail vertretung@tri.rep.admin.ch; Ambassador MARCOS PETER.
Syria: POB 4219, Sharia Muhammad Rashid Reda 4, Tripoli (Relations Office); tel. (21) 3331783; Head MUNIR BORKHAN.
Togo: POB 3420, Sharia Khaled ibn al-Walid, Tripoli; tel. (21) 4447551; fax (21) 3332423; Ambassador TCHAO SOTOU BERE.
Tunisia: POB 613, Sharia Bashir al-Ibrahim, Tripoli; tel. (21) 3331051; fax (21) 4447600; High Representative MUHAMMAD B'RAHEM.
Turkey: POB 947, Sharia Zaviya Dahmani, Tripoli; tel. (21) 3401140; fax (21) 3401146; e-mail trablusbe@yahoo.com; Ambassador RIZA ERKMENOĞLU.
Uganda: POB 80215, Sharia Jaraba, Tripoli; tel. and fax (21) 4892632; e-mail ugembatp60@hotmail.com; Ambassador NKUNDIZANA HAKIZA.
Ukraine: POB 4544, Sharia Dhil, Tripoli; tel. (21) 3608665; fax (21) 3608666; e-mail emb_ly@mfa.gov.ua; Ambassador OLEKSIY RYBAK.
United Kingdom: POB 4206, Tripoli; tel. (21) 3403644; fax (21) 3403648; e-mail tripoli.press@fco.gov.uk; internet www.britishembassy.gov.uk/libya; Ambassador Sir VINCENT FEAN.
Venezuela: POB 2584, Sharia ben Ashour, Jamaa as-Sagaa Bridge, Tripoli; tel. (21) 3600408; fax (21) 3600407; Ambassador DAVID PARAVISINI.
Viet Nam: POB 587, Sharia Gargaresh, Tripoli; tel. (21) 4835587; fax (21) 4836962; e-mail dsqvnlib@yahoo.com; Ambassador DANG SAN.
Yemen: POB 4839, Sharia Ubei ben Ka'ab 36, Tripoli; tel. (21) 607472; Ambassador HUSSEIN ALI HASSAN SABAH.

Judicial System

The judicial system is composed, in order of seniority, of the Supreme Court, Courts of Appeal, and Courts of First Instance and Summary Courts.

All courts convene in open session, unless public morals or public order require a closed session; all judgments, however, are delivered in open session. Cases are heard in Arabic, with interpreters provided for aliens.

The courts apply the Libyan codes which include all the traditional branches of law, such as civil, commercial and penal codes, etc. Committees were formed in 1971 to examine Libyan law and ensure that it coincides with the rules of Islamic *Shari'a*. The proclamation of People's Authority in the Jamahiriya provides that the Holy Koran is the law of society.

Attorney-General: SALIM MUHAMMAD SALIM.

SUPREME COURT
The judgments of the Supreme Court are final. It is composed of the President and several Justices. Its judgments are issued by circuits of at least three Justices (the quorum is three). The Court hears appeals from the Courts of Appeal in civil, penal, administrative and civil status matters.

President: ABD AR-RAHMAN MUHAMMAD ABU TOTAH.

COURTS OF APPEAL
These courts settle appeals from Courts of First Instance; the quorum is three Justices. Each court of appeal has a court of assize.

COURTS OF FIRST INSTANCE AND SUMMARY COURTS
These courts are first-stage courts in the Jamahiriya, and the cases heard in them are heard by one judge. Appeals against summary judgments are heard by the appellate court attached to the court of first instance, whose quorum is three judges.

PEOPLE'S COURT
Established by order of the General People's Congress in March 1988.
President: ABD AR-RAZIQ ABU BAKR AS-SAWSA.

PEOPLE'S PROSECUTION BUREAU
Established by order of the General People's Congress in March 1988.
Secretary: MUHAMMAD ALI AL-MISURATI.

Religion

ISLAM
The vast majority of Libyan Arabs follow Sunni Muslim rites, although Col Qaddafi has rejected the Sunnah (i.e. the practice, course, way, manner or conduct of the Prophet Muhammad, as followed by Sunnis) as a basis for legislation.

Chief Mufti of Libya: Sheikh TAHIR AHMAD AZ-ZAWI.

LIBYA

CHRISTIANITY
The Roman Catholic Church
Libya comprises three Apostolic Vicariates and one Apostolic Prefecture. At 31 December 2003 there were an estimated 74,000 adherents in the country.

Apostolic Vicariate of Benghazi: POB 248, Benghazi; tel. and fax (91) 9081599; e-mail apostvicar@yahoo.com; Vicar Apostolic Mgr SYLVESTER CARMEL MAGRO (Titular Bishop of Saldae).

Apostolic Vicariate of Derna: c/o POB 248, Benghazi; Vicar Apostolic (vacant).

Apostolic Vicariate of Tripoli: POB 365, Dahra, Tripoli; tel. (21) 3331863; fax (21) 3334696; e-mail bishoptripolibya@hotmail.com; Vicar Apostolic Mgr GIOVANNI INNOCENZO MARTINELLI (Titular Bishop of Tabuda).

The Anglican Communion
Within the Episcopal Church in Jerusalem and the Middle East, Libya forms part of the diocese of Egypt (q.v.).

Other Christian Churches
The Coptic Orthodox Church is represented in Libya.

The Press
Newspapers and periodicals are published either by the Jamahiriya News Agency (JANA), by government secretariats, by the Press Service or by trade unions.

DAILIES
Ash-Shams: POB 82331, As-Sahafa Bldg, Sharia al-Jamhouria, Tripoli; tel. (21) 4442524; fax (21) 609315; internet www.alshames.com.

Az-Zahf al-Akhdar (The Green March): POB 14273, As-Sahafa Bldg, Sharia al-Jamhouria, Tripoli; tel. (21) 4776890; fax (21) 4772502; e-mail info@azzahfalakhder.com; internet www.azzahfalakhder.com; ideological journal of the Revolutionary Committees.

PERIODICALS
Al-Amal (Hope): POB 4845, Tripoli; e-mail info@alamalmag.com; monthly; social, for children; published by the Press Service.

Ad-Daawa al-Islamia (Islamic Call): POB 2682, Sharia Sawani, km 5, Tripoli; tel. (21) 4800294; fax (21) 4800293; f. 1980; weekly (Wednesdays); Arabic, English, French; cultural; published by the World Islamic Call Society; Eds MUHAMMAD IMHEMED AL-BALOUSHI, ABDULAHI MUHAMMAD ABD AL-JALEEL.

Al-Fajr al-Jadid (The New Dawn): Press Bldg, Sharia al-Jamhariya, Tripoli; tel. (21) 3606393; fax (21) 3605728; internet www.alfajraljadeed.com; f. 1969; published by JANA; bi-monthly.

Economic Bulletin: POB 2303, Tripoli; tel. (21) 3337106; monthly; published by JANA.

Al-Jamahiriya: POB 4814, Tripoli; tel. (21) 4449294; e-mail info@aljamahiria.com; internet www.aljamahiria.com; f. 1980; weekly; Arabic; political; published by the revolutionary committees.

Al-Jarida ar-Rasmiya (The Official Newspaper): Tripoli; irregular; official state gazette.

Libyan Arab Republic Gazette: Secretariat of Justice, NA, Tripoli; weekly; English; published by the Secretariat of Justice.

Risalat al-Jihad (Holy War Letter): POB 2682, Tripoli; tel. (21) 3331021; f. 1983; monthly; Arabic, English, French; published by the World Islamic Call Society.

Scientific Bulletin: POB 2303, Tripoli; tel. (21) 3337106; monthly; published by JANA.

Ath-Thaqafa al-Arabiya (Arab Culture): POB 4587, Tripoli; f. 1973; weekly; cultural; circ. 25,000.

Al-Usbu ath-Thaqafi (The Cultural Week): POB 4845, Tripoli; weekly.

Al-Watan al-Arabi al-Kabir (The Greater Arab Homeland): Tripoli; f. 1987.

NEWS AGENCIES
Jamahiriya News Agency (JANA): POB 2303, Sharia al-Fateh, Tripoli; tel. (21) 3402606; fax (21) 3402624; e-mail mail@jamahiriyanews.com; internet www.jamahiriyanews.com; branches and correspondents throughout Libya and abroad; serves Libyan and foreign subscribers.

Foreign Bureaux
Informatsionnoye Telegrafnoye Agentstvo Rossii—Telegrafnoye Agentstvo Suverennykh Stran (ITAR—TASS) (Russia): Sharia Mustapha Kamel 10, Tripoli; Correspondent GEORG SHELENKOV.

ANSA (Italy) is also represented in Tripoli.

Publishers
Ad-Dar al-Arabia Lilkitab (Maison Arabe du Livre): POB 3185, Tripoli; tel. (21) 4447287; f. 1973 by Libya and Tunisia.

Ad-Dar al-Hikma Publishing House: Tripoli; tel. (21) 3606571; fax (21) 3606610; e-mail info@elgabooks.com; internet www.elgabooks.com.

Al-Fatah University, General Administration of Libraries, Printing and Publications: POB 13543, Tripoli; tel. (21) 621988; f. 1955; academic books.

General Co for Publishing, Advertising and Distribution: POB 921, Sirte (Surt); tel. (54) 63170; fax (54) 62100; general, educational and academic books in Arabic and other languages; makes and distributes advertisements throughout Libya.

Ghouma Publishing: POB 80092, Tripoli; tel. (21) 3630864; e-mail ghoumapub@hotmail.com; internet ghoumapublishing.homestead.com; f. 1993; book publishing, distribution and art production; Gen. Man. MOUSTAFA FETOURI.

Broadcasting and Communications
TELECOMMUNICATIONS
General Directorate of Posts and Telecommunications: POB 81686, Tripoli; tel. (21) 3604101; fax (21) 3604102; Dir-Gen. ABU ZAID JUMA AL-MANSURI.

General Post and Telecommunications Co: POB 886, Sharia Zawia, Tripoli; tel. (21) 3600777; fax (21) 3609515; f. 1985; Chair. FARAJ AMARI.

BROADCASTING
Radio
Great Socialist People's Libyan Arab Jamahiriya Broadcasting Corporation: POB 80237, Tripoli; tel. (21) 3614862; fax (21) 3403458; e-mail info@ljbc.net; internet www.ljbc.net; f. 1968; broadcasts in Arabic; additional satellite channel broadcast for 18 hours a day from 1982; Sec.-Gen. ABDULLAH MANSOUR.

Voice of Africa: POB 4677, Sharia al-Fateh, Tripoli; tel. (21) 4449209; fax (21) 4449875; f. 1973 as Voice of the Greater Arab Homeland; adopted current name in 1998; broadcasts in Arabic, French and English; transmissions in Swahili, Hausa, Fulani and Amharic scheduled to begin in 2000; Dir-Gen. ABDALLAH AL-MEGRI.

Television
People's Revolution Broadcasting TV: POB 80237, Tripoli; tel. (21) 3614862; fax (21) 3403458; e-mail info@ljbc.net; internet www.ljbc.net; f. 1957; broadcasts in Arabic; additional satellite channels broadcast for limited hours in English; Dir ABDULLAH MANSOUR.

Finance
(cap. = capital; res = reserves; dep. = deposits; LD = Libyan dinars; m. = million; brs = branches)

BANKING
Central Bank
Central Bank of Libya: POB 1103, Sharia al-Malik Seoud, Tripoli; tel. (21) 3333591; fax (21) 4441488; e-mail info@cbl.gov.ly; internet www.cbl.gov.ly; f. 1955 as National Bank of Libya, name changed to Bank of Libya 1963, to Central Bank of Libya 1977; bank of issue and central bank carrying govt accounts and operating exchange control; commercial operations transferred to National Commercial Bank 1970; cap. LD 100m., res LD 6,554.1m., dep. LD 5,466.2m. (Dec. 2003); Gov. and Chair. FARHAT OMAR EKDARA.

Other Banks
Ahli Bank: Jadu; f. 1998; private bank.

Gumhouria Bank: POB 65004, Gharyan; tel. (21) 3333553; fax (21) 3610597; e-mail edari@gumhouriabank.com; internet www.gumhouria-bank.com; f. 1969 as successor to Barclays Bank

International in Libya; known as Masraf al-Jumhuriya until March 1977, and as Jamahiriya Bank until December 2000; wholly owned subsidiary of the Central Bank; throughout Libya; cap. LD 40.0m., res LD 79.5m., dep. LD 1,714.2m. (Dec. 2001); Chair. HAMED ALARBI EL-HOUDERI; Gen. Man. MELLAD MUHAMMAD ELGHOOL; 70 brs.

Libyan Arab Foreign Bank: POB 2542, Tower 2, Dat al-Imad Complex, Tripoli; tel. (21) 3350155; fax (21) 3350164; e-mail CO@lafbank.com; internet www.lafbank.com; f. 1972; offshore bank wholly owned by Central Bank of Libya; cap. LD 222.0m., res LD 57.0m., dep. LD 8,276.1m. (Dec. 2003); Chair. and Gen. Man. MUHAMMAD H. LAYAS.

National Commercial Bank SAL: POB 543, al-Baida; tel. (21) 3612267; fax (21) 3610306; f. 1970 to take over commercial banking division of Central Bank (then Bank of Libya) and brs of Aruba Bank and Istiklal Bank; wholly owned by Central Bank of Libya; cap. LD 35m., res LD 63.4m., dep. LD 1,545.6m. (Dec. 1998); Chair. and Gen. Man. BADER A. ABU AZIZA; 49 brs.

Sahara Bank SPI: POB 70, Sharia 1 September 10, Tripoli; tel. (21) 3330724; fax (21) 3337922; e-mail sahbankgm1@lttnet.net; f. 1964 to take over br. of Banco di Sicilia; 82% owned by Central Bank of Libya; cap. and res LD 208.2m., total assets LD 1,951.8m. (March 2003); Chair. and Gen. Man. Dr SALEM MUFTAH EL-GHAMATI; 20 brs.

Umma Bank SAL: POB 685, 1 Giaddat Omar el-Mokhtar, Tripoli; tel. (21) 3334031; fax (21) 3332505; e-mail ummabank@umma-bank.com; internet www.umma-bank.com; f. 1969 to take over brs of Banco di Roma; wholly owned by Central Bank of Libya; cap. LD 23m., res LD 29.4m., dep. LD 1,425.0m. (Dec. 2002); Chair. and Gen. Man. AYAD DAHAIM; 38 brs.

Wahda Bank: POB 452, Fadiel Abu Omar Sq., El-Berkha, Benghazi; tel. (61) 24519; fax (61) 24587; f. 1970 to take over Bank of North Africa, Commercial Bank SAL, Nahda Arabia Bank, Société Africaine de Banque SAL, Kafila al-Ahly Bank; 87%-owned by Central Bank of Libya; cap. LD 36m., res LD 136.7m., dep. LD 1,505.1m. (Dec. 2003); Chair. SALIM KHALIFA AHMMOUDAH; 61 brs.

INSURANCE

Libya Insurance Co: POB 64, Sharia Jamal Abdul Nasser, Zawia; tel. (23) 629768; fax (23) 629490; f. 1964; merged with Al-Mukhtar Insurance Co in 1981; all classes of insurance; Man. BELAID ABU GHALIA.

Trade and Industry

There are state trade and industrial organizations responsible for the running of industries at all levels, which supervise production, distribution and sales. There are also central bodies responsible for the power generation industry, agriculture, land reclamation and transport.

GOVERNMENT AGENCY

Great Man-made River Water Utilization Authority (GMRA): POB 7217, Benghazi; tel. (61) 2230392; fax (61) 2230393; e-mail info@gmrwua.com; internet www.gmrwua.com; supervises construction of pipeline carrying water to the Libyan coast from beneath the Sahara desert, to provide irrigation for agricultural projects; Sec. for the Great Man-made River project ABD AL-MAJID AL-AOUD.

DEVELOPMENT ORGANIZATIONS

Arab Organization for Agricultural Development: POB 12898, Zohra, Tripoli; tel. and fax (21) 3619275; e-mail info@aoad.org; internet www.aoad.org; responsible for agricultural development projects.

General National Organization for Industrialization: Sharia San'a, Tripoli; tel. (21) 3334995; f. 1970; public org. responsible for the devt of industry.

Kufra and Sarir Authority: Council of Agricultural Development, Benghazi; f. 1972 to develop the Kufra oasis and Sarir area in southeast Libya.

CHAMBERS OF COMMERCE

Benghazi Chamber of Commerce, Trade, Industry and Agriculture: POB 208 and 1286, Benghazi; tel. (61) 95142; fax (61) 80761; f. 1956; Pres. Dr SADIQ M. BUSNAINA; Gen. Man. YOUSUF AL-JIAMI; 45,000 mems.

Tripoli Chamber of Commerce and Industry: POB 2321, Sharia Najed 6–8, Tripoli; tel. (21) 3336855; fax (21) 3332655; f. 1952; Chair. MUHAMMAD KANOON; Dir-Gen. ABDULMONEM H. BURAWI; 30,000 mems.

UTILITIES

Electricity

General Electricity Company of Libya (GECOL): POB 668, Tripoli; tel. (21) 4445068; fax (21) 4447023; e-mail gecol@gecol.ly; internet www.gecol-ly.com; Sec. of People's Cttee Eng. OMRAN IBRAHIM ABUKRAA.

STATE HYDROCARBONS COMPANIES

Until 1986 petroleum affairs in Libya were dealt with primarily by the Secretariat of the General People's Committee for Petroleum. This body was abolished in March 1986, and sole responsibility for the administration of the petroleum industry passed to the national companies that were already in existence. The Secretariat of the General People's Committee for Petroleum was re-established in March 1989 and incorporated into the new Secretariat for the General People's Committee for Energy in October 1992. This was dissolved in March 2000, and responsibility for local oil policy was transferred to the National Oil Corporation, under the supervision of the General People's Committee. Since 1973 the Libyan Government has entered into participation agreements with some of the foreign oil companies (concession holders), and nationalized others. It has concluded 85%:15% production-sharing agreements with various oil companies.

National Oil Corporation (NOC): POB 2655, Tripoli; tel. (21) 4446180; fax (21) 3331390; e-mail info@noclibya.com; internet www.noclibya.com; f. 1970 to undertake joint ventures with foreign cos; to build and operate refineries, storage tanks, petrochemical facilities, pipelines and tankers; to take part in arranging specifications for local and imported petroleum products; to participate in general planning of oil installations in Libya; to market crude and refined petroleum and petrochemical products and to establish and operate oil terminals; from 2000 responsible for deciding local oil policy, under supervision of General People's Committee; Chair. SHUKRI MUHAMMAD GHANEM.

Oilinvest International: Tripoli; wholly-owned subsidiary of the NOC; Chair. and Gen. Man. AHMAD ABD AL-KARIM AHMAD.

Agip North Africa and Middle East Ltd—Libyan Branch: POB 346, Tripoli; tel. and fax (21) 3335135; Sec. of People's Cttee OMAR AS-SWEIFI.

Arabian Gulf Oil Co (AGOCO): POB 263, Benghazi; tel. (61) 28931; fax (21) 49031; Chair. TAWSIG MESMARI.

Az-Zawiyah Oil Refining Co: POB 15715, Zawia; tel. (23) 620125; fax (23) 605948; e-mail arcp@lttnet.net; f. 1976; Gen. Man. AL-MOAMARE A. SWEDAN.

Brega Oil Marketing Co: POB 402, Sharia Bashir as-Saidawi, Tripoli; tel. (21) 4440830; f. 1971; Chair. Dr DOKALI B. AL-MEGHARIEF.

International Oil Investments Co: Tripoli; f. 1988, with initial capital of US $500m. to acquire 'downstream' facilities abroad; Chair. MUHAMMAD AL-JAWAD.

National Drilling and Workover Co: POB 1454, 208 Sharia Omar Mukhtar, Tripoli; tel. (21) 3332411; f. 1986; Chair. IBRAHIM BAHI.

Ras Lanouf Oil and Gas Processing Co (RASCO): POB 1971, Ras Lanouf, Benghazi; tel. (21) 3605177; fax (21) 607924; f. 1978; Chair. ABULKASIM M. A. ZWARY.

Sirte Oil Co: POB 385, Marsa el-Brega, Tripoli; tel. (21) 607261; fax (21) 601487; f. 1955 as Esso Standard Libya, taken over by Sirte Oil Co 1982; absorbed the National Petrochemicals Co in October 1990; exploration, production of crude oil, gas, and petrochemicals, liquefaction of natural gas; Chair. M. M. BENNIRAN.

Umm al-Jawaby Petroleum Co: POB 693, Tripoli; Chair. and Gen. Man. MUHAMMAD TENTTOUSH.

Waha Oil Co: POB 395, Tripoli; tel. (21) 3337161; fax (21) 3337169; Chair. SALEH M. KAABAR.

Zueitina Oil Co: POB 2134, Tripoli; tel. (21) 3338011; fax (21) 3339109; f. 1986; Chair. of Management Cttee BASHIR BAZAZI.

TRADE UNIONS

General Federation of Producers' Trade Unions: POB 734, Sharia Istanbul 2, Tripoli; tel. (21) 4446011; f. 1952; affiliated to ICFTU; Sec.-Gen. BASHIR IHWIJ; 17 trade unions with 700,000 mems.

General Union for Oil and Petrochemicals: Tripoli; Chair. MUHAMMAD MITHNANI.

Pan-African Federation of Petroleum Energy and Allied Workers: Tripoli; affiliated to the Organisation of African Trade Union Unity.

Transport

Department of Road Transport and Railways: POB 14527, Sharia az-Zawiyah, Secretariat of Communications and Transport Bldg, Tripoli; tel. (21) 609011; fax (21) 605605; Dir-Gen. Projects and Research MUHAMMAD ABU ZIAN.

RAILWAYS

There are, at present, no railways in Libya. In mid-1998, however, the Government invited bids for the construction of a 3,170 km-railway, comprising one branch, 2,178 km in length, running from north to south, and another, 992 km in length, running from east to west along the north coast. The railway may eventually be linked to other North African rail networks.

Railway Executive Board: Tripoli; tel. (21) 3609486; fax (21) 626734; e-mail info@libyanrailways.com; internet www.libyanrailways.com; oversees the planning and construction of railways.

ROADS

The most important road is the 1,822-km national coast road from the Tunisian to the Egyptian border, passing through Tripoli and Benghazi. It has a second link between Barce and Lamluda, 141 km long. Another national road runs from a point on the coastal road 120 km south of Misurata through Sebha to Ghat near the Algerian border (total length 1,250 km). There is a branch 247 km long running from Vaddan to Sirte (Surt). A 690-km road, connecting Tripoli and Sebha, and another 626 km long, from Ajdabiya in the north to Kufra in the south-east, were opened in 1983. The Tripoli–Ghat section (941 km) of the third, 1,352-km-long national road was opened in September 1984. There is a road crossing the desert from Sebha to the frontiers of Chad and Niger.

In addition to the national highways, the west of Libya has about 1,200 km of paved and macadamized roads and the east about 500 km. All the towns and villages of Libya, including the desert oases, are accessible by motor vehicle. In 1999 Libya had an estimated total road network of 83,200 km, of which 47,590 km was paved.

SHIPPING

The principal ports are Tripoli, Benghazi, Mersa Brega, Misurata and as-Sider. Zueitina, Ras Lanouf, Mersa Hariga, Mersa Brega and as-Sider are mainly oil ports. A pipeline connects the Zelten oilfields with Mersa Brega. Another pipeline joins the Sarir oilfield with Mersa Hariga, the port of Tobruk, and a pipeline from the Sarir field to Zueitina was opened in 1968. A port is being developed at Darnah. Libya also has the use of Tunisian port facilities at Sand Gabès, to alleviate congestion at Tripoli. At 31 December 2004 Libya's merchant fleet consisted of 136 vessels, with a combined displacement of 130,139 grt.

General National Maritime Transport Co: POB 80173, esh-Shaab Terminal, Tripoli; tel. (21) 4446972; fax (21) 3331854; e-mail tech@gnmtc.com; internet www.gnmtc.com; f. 1971 to handle all projects dealing with maritime trade; Chair. SAID MILUD AL-AHRASH.

Libya Shipping Agency: POB 4018, Tripoli; tel. (21) 3616643; fax (21) 3614954; e-mail info@libyashipping.com; internet www.libyashipping.com; provides chartering, land transportation and customs clearance services; Gen. Man. IMAD FELLAH.

CIVIL AVIATION

There are four international airports: Tripoli International Airport, situated at ben Gashir, 34 km (21 miles) from Tripoli; Benina Airport 19 km (12 miles) from Benghazi; Sebha Airport; and Misurata Airport. There are a further 10 regional airports. A US $800m. programme to improve the airport infrastructure and air traffic control network was approved in mid-2001.

Libyan Arab Airlines: POB 2555, ben Fernas Bldg, Sharia Haiti, Tripoli; tel. (21) 3617638; fax (21) 3614815; f. 1989 by merger of Jamahiriya Air Transport (which in 1983 took over operations of United African Airlines) and Libyan Arab Airlines (f. 1964 as Kingdom of Libya Airlines and renamed 1969); passenger and cargo services from Tripoli, Benghazi and Sebha to destinations in Europe, North Africa, the Middle East and Asia; domestic services throughout Libya; Chair. and Chief Exec. HUSSEIN DABNOUN.

Tourism

The principal attractions for visitors to Libya are Tripoli, with its beaches and annual International Fair, the ancient Roman towns of Sabratha, Leptis Magna and Cyrene, and historic oases. There were 957,896 visitor arrivals in 2003; in that year receipts totalled some US $79m.

Tripoli International Fair Department: POB 891, Sharia Omar Mukhtar, Tripoli; tel. (21) 3332255; fax (21) 4448385; Head of Fairs KHALIL S. AS-SENUSSI.

General Board of Tourism: POB 91871, Tripoli; tel. and fax (21) 503041; Chair. MUHAMMAD SEALNA.

LIECHTENSTEIN

Introductory Survey

Location, Climate, Language, Religion, Flag, Capital

The Principality of Liechtenstein is in central Europe. The country lies on the east bank of the Upper Rhine river, bordered by Switzerland to the west and south, and by Austria to the north and east. Liechtenstein has an Alpine climate, with mild winters. The average annual temperature is about 10°C, while average annual rainfall is about 1,000 mm. The official language is German, of which a dialect—Alemannish—is spoken. Almost all of the inhabitants profess Christianity, and about 76% are adherents of the Roman Catholic Church. The national flag (proportions 3 by 5) consists of two equal horizontal stripes, of royal blue and red, with a golden princely crown, outlined in black, in the upper hoist. The capital is Vaduz.

Recent History

Liechtenstein has been an independent state since 1719, except while under French domination briefly in the early 19th century. In 1919 Switzerland assumed responsibility for Liechtenstein's diplomatic representation, replacing Austria. In 1920 a postal union with Switzerland was agreed, and in 1924 a treaty was concluded with Switzerland whereby Liechtenstein was incorporated in a joint customs union. Franz Josef II succeeded as Reigning Prince in 1938. In 1950 Liechtenstein became a party to the Statute of the International Court of Justice, in 1973 it joined the Organization for Security and Co-operation in Europe (see p. 327) and in 1978 it was admitted to the Council of Europe (see p. 211). Liechtenstein became a member of the UN in September 1990 (hitherto the country had been a member of some UN specialized agencies). In the following year Liechtenstein became a full member of the European Free Trade Association (EFTA, see p. 386).

After 42 years as the dominant party in government, the Fortschrittliche Bürgerpartei Liechtensteins (FBP—Progressive Citizens' Party of Liechtenstein) was defeated by the Vaterländische Union (VU—Patriotic Union) at a general election to the Landtag (parliament) in February 1970. Four years later the FBP regained its majority. At the general election to the Landtag in February 1978, the VU, led by Hans Brunhart, won eight of the 15 seats, although with a minority of the votes cast, while the remaining seats were taken by the FBP, led by Dr Walter Kieber, the Head of Government since March 1974. After protracted negotiations, Brunhart replaced Kieber in April 1978. At the general election in February 1982, the distribution of seats remained unchanged, although the VU gained a majority of votes. Following a referendum in July 1984, women were granted the right to vote on a national basis. However, women were still not permitted to vote on communal affairs in three of Liechtenstein's 11 communes until April 1986, when they were finally accorded full voting rights. (An amendment to the Constitution, declaring equality between men and women, took effect in 1992.) In August 1984 Prince Franz Josef transferred executive power to his son, Prince Hans-Adam, although he remained titular Head of State until his death in November 1989, when he was succeeded by Hans-Adam (Hans-Adam II).

The composition of the Landtag remained unchanged following a general election in February 1986, when women voted for the first time in a national poll. In January 1989 the Landtag was dissolved by Prince Hans-Adam, following a dispute between the VU and the FBP regarding the construction of a new museum to accommodate the royal art collection. At the subsequent general election, which took place in March 1989, the number of seats in the Landtag was increased from 15 to 25; the VU retained its majority, securing 13 seats, while the FBP took the remaining 12 seats.

At the next general election, which took place in February 1993, the VU lost its majority, taking only 11 of the Landtag's 25 seats. The FBP again returned 12 representatives, and two seats were won by an environmentalist party, the Freie Liste (FL—Free List). Lengthy negotiations resulted in the formation of a new coalition between the FBP and the VU, in which the FBP was the dominant party, and Markus Büchel of the FBP became Head of Government. In September, however, following a unanimous vote in the Landtag expressing 'no confidence' in his leadership, Büchel was dismissed from his post, and Prince Hans-Adam dissolved the legislature. At a further general election, which was held in October, the VU regained its parliamentary majority, winning 13 seats, while the FBP took 11 seats and the FL secured one seat. The VU became the dominant party in a new coalition with the FBP, with Mario Frick of the VU as Head of Government.

In October 1992 almost 2,000 people demonstrated in Vaduz to protest against a threat by Prince Hans-Adam that he would dissolve the Landtag if deputies did not submit to his wish to hold a proposed referendum to endorse Liechtenstein's entry to the nascent European Economic Area (EEA) shortly in advance of a similar vote in Switzerland. The Prince believed that the outcome of the Swiss plebiscite might be prejudicial to that of the Liechtenstein vote, and that, in the event of voters' rejecting EEA membership at an early referendum, Liechtenstein might still be able to join other EFTA members in applying for admission to the European Community (EC—now European Union—EU, see p. 228). A compromise was reached, whereby the referendum was scheduled to take place shortly after the Swiss vote, while the Government agreed actively to promote a vote in favour of the EEA and to explore the possibility of applying to the EC should EEA membership be rejected. (The authorities subsequently decided that admission to the EU would not be beneficial to the Principality.) At the referendum in December, although Switzerland's voters had rejected accession to the EEA, Liechtenstein's membership was approved by 55.8% of those who voted (about 87% of the Principality's electorate); consequently, the two countries' joint customs union was renegotiated. In April 1995 a further national referendum was held, at which 55.9% of those who voted (around 82% of the electorate) approved the revised customs arrangements. Liechtenstein joined the EEA at the beginning of May.

In March 1996 the Landtag adopted a unanimous motion of loyalty in the hereditary monarchy, after Prince Hans-Adam offered to resign (following tension between the Prince and the legislature—see above). At the next general election, which took place in February 1997, the VU retained its majority with 13 seats, while the FBP secured 10 and the FL two seats. Frick remained Head of Government. In April the FBP withdrew from the ruling coalition, leaving a single party (the VU) to govern alone for the first time since 1938. The constitutional role of the Reigning Prince came under renewed scrutiny in 1997, when, against the wishes of the Landtag, Prince Hans-Adam refused to reappoint Dr Herbert Wille, a senior judge who had advocated that constitutional issues should be decided by the Supreme Court rather than the Monarch. Dr Wille subsequently presented a formal complaint to the European Court of Human Rights, which ruled, in November 1999, that Prince Hans-Adam had restricted Wille's right to free speech; the Prince was required to pay 100,000 Swiss francs in costs.

In December 1999 Prince Hans-Adam II requested an Austrian prosecutor, Kurt Spitzer, to investigate allegations in the German press based on an unpublished report of April 1999 by the German secret service that international criminals were using financial institutions in Liechtenstein to 'launder' the proceeds of organized crime. As a result, five people were placed under investigative arrest in May 2000, including the brothers of both the Deputy Head of Government and of one of the Principality's most senior judges; all five were later released without charge. In his final report, which was released at the end of August, Spitzer concluded that Liechtenstein was no more culpable of money-laundering than other countries in Europe. He blamed the current problems on the Principality's over-bureaucratic and inefficient banking system and the poor application of existing legislation designed to combat economic crimes; criminal proceedings were initiated against two judges for abusing their authority. Spitzer also revealed that a money-laundering investigation was under way against Herbert Batliner, a prominent lawyer who had been implicated in the party-funding scandal involving Germany's former Chancellor, Helmut Kohl, and his party, the Christian Democratic Union, and in another case involving proceeds from drugs-trafficking in Colombia. In June the Financial Action Task Force on Money Laundering (FATF), a commission of the Organisation for Economic Co-operation and Development (OECD, see p. 320), included Liechtenstein on a list of countries considered unco-operative in international attempts to combat money-laundering. In an effort to reverse some of the damage done to the country's international reputation, the Liechtenstein Bankers' Association announced in July that anonymous accounts would be abolished. In the same month the Government approved the establishment of a new financial investigative unit within the police force and measures to accelerate legal assistance to foreign countries in money-laundering investigations. Legislation was promulgated in December requiring financial institutions to maintain tighter controls over accounts and transactions, including the abolition of anonymous accounts. Liechtenstein was removed from the FATF's list of unco-operative countries in 2001, and, in October of that year, the Government appointed the former head of the Swiss anti-money-laundering authority, Daniel Thelesklaf, to administer a new financial surveillance unit, which was to enforce new regulations requiring banks and lawyers to be able to verify the identity of their clients. However, Liechtenstein was among seven jurisdictions identified on an OECD list as 'unco-operative tax havens' lacking financial transparency in April 2002, under its initiative to abolish 'harmful tax practices'. Although two jurisdictions were subsequently removed from the list, in early 2006 Liechtenstein remained one of five countries so designated. In 2004 the Government launched a publicity campaign to promote Liechtenstein and hoped to shed its reputation as a centre for improper financial transactions.

In the general election that took place on 9 and 11 February 2001 the VU lost its parliamentary majority, securing only 41.1% of the votes cast (11 of the 25 seats in the Landtag), while the FBP won 49.9% (13 seats) and the FL obtained 8.8% (one seat); voter participation was 86.7% of the electorate. The VU administration's popularity had been adversely affected by an unresolved dispute with Prince Hans-Adam over his demands for constitutional changes, notably with regard to appointments in the judiciary (the Prince advocated that judges be nominated by the reigning Monarch rather than by parliamentary deputies); the Prince claimed that these amendments would benefit the people, whilst the VU regarded them as an attempt to extend the royal prerogative. A new Government comprising solely the FBP, under the leadership of Otmar Hasler, took office on 5 April. The Prince had previously announced that if he failed to secure the support of the new Government for his proposed constitutional reforms, he would seek a national referendum; in December he also threatened to leave the Principality and take up residence in Vienna, Austria.

The issue of constitutional reform was finally resolved by a national referendum, held on 14 and 16 March 2003, in which the participation rate was 87.7% of the electorate. Following an acrimonious campaign, Prince Hans-Adam won an overwhelming majority of the votes cast, with 64.3% in favour of granting the Prince new powers. As a result of the referendum, the Prince gained the right to dismiss a government even if it retained parliamentary confidence, to appoint an interim administration pending elections, to preside over a panel to select judges, to veto laws by not signing them within a six-month period and to adopt emergency legislation. Conversely, citizens could now force a referendum on any subject (including the future of the monarchy) by collecting a minimum of 1,500 signatures. A compromise proposal put forward by a cross-party group that included the former Premier Mario Frick (the Volksinitiative für Verfassungsfrieden—People's Initiative for Constitutional Peace), which suggested that a princely veto could be overruled by a referendum and sought to limit the Prince's use of emergency legislation to times of war, received the support of only 16.5% of the voters. The overwhelming support for the Prince's proposed changes was partially attributed to widespread fear that, if fulfilled, his threat of self-imposed exile as a symbolic monarch would cause economic decline and social upheaval. Prince Hans-Adam dismissed the findings of a commission established by the Council of Europe, which stated that the constitutional amendments would constitute a retrograde step for democracy and could lead to the isolation of Liechtenstein in Europe. On 15 August 2004 Prince Hans-Adam transferred his sovereign powers to his son, Prince Alois, in accordance with an announcement that he had made the previous August. Prince Hans-Adam, however, remained Head of State.

At the general election held on 11 and 13 March 2005 the FBP failed to retain an absolute majority, winning 12 of the 25 seats, with 48.7% of the votes cast; voter participation was 86.47%. The VU won 10 seats (38.2% of the votes), while the FL increased its representation from one seat to three (with 13.0% of the votes). In April the FBP and the VU formed a coalition Government, which comprised three representatives of the FBP, including Hasler, who was once again appointed Prime Minister, while the VU were allocated the remaining two portfolios, with Dr Klaus Tschütscher being appointed Deputy Prime Minister.

In August 2005 a conservative group known as the Volksinitiative für das Leben (People's Initiative For Life) submitted 1,889 signatures to the Government in support of its demands for a national referendum to be held on constitutional revisions. The group hoped to amend Article 14 of the Constitution so that the highest responsibility of the state would be 'to protect human life from conception until natural death' and also aimed to insert a reference to the state's responsibility to protect human dignity. The initiative was intended to address the potential legalization of abortion (which was the subject of much public debate) and, indirectly, the issues of euthanasia, genetic technology and stem-cell research. Having failed to secure sufficient support in the Landtag, the proposals were to be subject to a national referendum. Considering the initiative to be too restrictive, the FBP and VU jointly drafted a counterproposal to make the protection of life and human dignity a right for Liechtenstein citizens rather than a duty of the state. A further amendment was added explicitly prohibiting the death penalty (which had already been abolished by a revision of the criminal code in 1985). Following its approval by the Landtag in September, the counterproposal was presented to the referendum concurrently with the 'For Life' initiative. At the referendum, held on 25 and 27 November, the For Life initiative, which opponents claimed would prevent abortion, birth control and assisted suicide, was rejected by 80.9% of the votes cast, while the counterproposal was adopted, with the support of 79.4% of voters.

In the latter half of the 20th century Liechtenstein's relations with the Czech Republic and Slovakia were strained. This stemmed from the expulsion of ethnic Germans from Czechoslovakia and the confiscation of their land (without compensation) following the Second World War, under the controversial Beneš Decrees. The Liechtenstein royal family lost a large part of its estates during this time—including the castles of Feldsberg and Eisgrub, now estimated to be worth some €100m. Liechtenstein, which was a sovereign, neutral state throughout both the First and Second World Wars, claimed that it was unfairly grouped together with Germany under the terms of the Decrees. Czechoslovakia, however, considered the Liechtenstein royal family to have been collaborators with the Nazi regime in Germany during the Second World War, and that its action was thus legitimate. Liechtenstein also sought damages from Germany for assets that it claimed Germany had improperly awarded to Czechoslovakia after the Second World War as reparations. The German position was that the assets were seized by the Czechs and that Germany was not responsible. In February 2005, however, the International Court of Justice (ICJ, see p. 19) ruled that it was not competent to make a decision on the claim as it dated back to 1945 and thus predated the 1980 agreement between the two countries that disputes between them should be settled by the ICJ.

At the beginning of the 21st century the Czech Republic and Slovakia still refused to recognize Liechtenstein as a sovereign state. In October 2003 Prince Hans-Adam blocked the entry of the Czech Republic and Slovakia (along with that of the eight other EU accession states) into the European Economic Area (EEA); the 10 countries were due to become members of the EU on 1 May 2004 and would, under normal circumstances, have automatically joined the EEA. Their accession to the EEA was delayed until November 2003, when Liechtenstein agreed to sign the enlargement treaty on the EEA; Slovakia subsequently agreed immediately to establish diplomatic relations with Liechtenstein. Liechtenstein reiterated its demand that the Czech Republic and Slovakia acknowledge that the Principality was a sovereign, neutral state through both World Wars. To do so, however, would expose these two countries to the possibility of legal action being brought against them by Liechtenstein for the illegal seizure of land.

Following a four-year investigation, in April 2005 an Independent Commission of Historians charged with examining Liechtenstein's role in the Second World War reported that no Jewish assets were confiscated and no forced labour was used during the War, and that while 165 refugees from Nazi-controlled Austria were turned away by Liechtenstein between 1933 and 1945, 400 others were taken in and thousands more allowed safe passage to Switzerland. The Commission was appointed by the Government in 2001 after the World Jewish Congress accused the Principality's financial institutions of having hidden plundered Jewish assets for the Nazis during the War.

Government

The Constitution of the hereditary Principality provides for a unicameral Landtag (parliament), comprising 25 members, who are elected by universal adult suffrage for a term of four years (subject to dissolution), on the basis of proportional representation. The country is divided into the two election districts of Oberland (Upper Country) and Unterland (Lower Country), in which the seats are allocated separately. The Oberland district has 15 seats, the smaller Unterland district has 10 seats. A five-member Government is nominated by the Reigning Prince, on the recommendation of the Landtag, for four years. In March 2003 constitutional changes were approved by a referendum which extended the powers of the monarch; he was empowered to dismiss governments (even if they retained parliamentary confidence), appoint an interim administration pending an election, approve judicial nominees, veto laws and invoke emergency legislation. Citizens could force a referendum on any subject, including the future of the monarchy, by collecting 1,500 signatures. On 15 August 2004 the sovereign rights pertaining to the Reigning Prince were transferred to the Hereditary (Crown) Prince, who was to exercise them as the representative of the Reigning Prince, who remained the Head of State.

Defence

Although Liechtensteiners under the age of 60 years are liable to military service in an emergency, there has been no standing army since 1868 and there is only a small police force, with approximately 60 members.

Economic Affairs

In 1997 Liechtenstein's gross national product (GNP) per head was estimated by the World Bank to be US $50,000, at average 1995–97 prices, ranking as the highest in the world at that time. During 1990–2003 the population increased at an average annual rate of 1.3%. During 1990–99, it was estimated, GDP grew at an average annual rate of 1.6%; GDP increased by 4.5% in 1998, but declined by 0.9% in 1999.

Following the Second World War, the importance of agriculture declined in favour of industry. Within the agricultural sector the emphasis is on cattle-breeding, dairy-farming and market gardening. The principal crops are maize and potatoes. In addition, wine is produced, and forestry is a significant activity. In 2004 1.3% of those employed in Liechtenstein worked in agriculture (including forestry).

In 2004 44.2% of those employed in Liechtenstein worked in industrial activity (including mining and quarrying, processing industries, energy and water supply and construction). The metal, machinery and precision instruments industry is by far the most prominent sector. Other important areas are the pharmaceutical, textiles and ceramics industries.

In 2004 some 72.5% of energy requirements were imported from other countries. In that year natural gas supplied 28.5% of energy requirements, electricity 25.8%, fuel oil 21.3%, motor fuel (petrol) 16.4% and diesel 6.2%. In 2001 79.1% of the Principality's electricity was provided by nuclear sources, 13.0% was from natural gas, 5.0% from petroleum and 2.3% from hydroelectric energy.

In 2004 54.5% of those employed in Liechtenstein worked in the services sector. Financial services are of great importance. Numerous foreign corporations, holding companies and foundations (estimated to number about 75,000) have nominal offices in Liechtenstein, benefiting from the Principality's stable political situation, tradition of bank secrecy (although stricter banking legislation was introduced in 1997 and in 2000–02, partly to increase the transparency of the sector) and low fiscal charges. Such enterprises pay no tax on profit or income, contributing instead an annual levy on capital or net worth. These levies account for about 20% of the Principality's annual direct revenue. In 1980 Liechtenstein adopted legislation to increase controls on foreign firms, many of which were thereafter subject to audit and entered in the public register. Following the Principality's accession to the European Economic Area (EEA) in 1995, the registration of foreign banks was permitted. New legislation governing insurance companies was approved in 1996, and during the late 1990s the insurance sector expanded rapidly. In December 2004 the Government and the European Union (EU, see p. 228) signed an accord on savings tax, which entered into force on 1 July 2005. Under the agreement, savings income, in the form of interest payments made in Liechtenstein to residents of the EU, became subject to a withholding tax. The building and hotel trades and other service industries are also highly developed. The Government initiated a publicity campaign in 2004 to promote Liechtenstein, with the launch of a national logo (a 'democratic crown' on an aubergine background). The objective was to increase tourism and investment and further to develop the Principality as a business centre.

With a very limited domestic market, Liechtenstein's industry is export-orientated. In 2004 total exports amounted to 3,193.1m. Swiss francs (with imports totalling 1,865.0m. Swiss francs). Switzerland is the principal trading partner, receiving 12.7% of exports in 1998. In that year members of the EU accounted for 37.8% of total exports. In 2004 Switzerland purchased 11.7% of total exports of members of the Liechtenstein Chamber of Commerce and Industry and the EEA accounted for 45.5%. Specialized machinery, artificial teeth and other materials for dentistry, and frozen food are important exports. The sale of postage stamps provided about 3.0% of the national income in 1997, when net profits were some 6m. Swiss francs. However, revenue from stamps had decreased significantly by 2005, when profits were estimated at only 350,000 Swiss francs, owing to a decline in the popularity of philately and the growing use of electronic communication. In that year responsibility for producing Liechtenstein's stamps was passed from the Government to the postal service.

In 2004 Liechtenstein's overall budget deficit was estimated at 11.7m. Swiss francs. The annual average rate of inflation decreased from 5.4% in 1990 to 1.8% in 1995, to 1.6% in 2000 and to 0.6% in 2003. Consumer prices increased by an average of 0.8% in 2004. Traditionally the unemployment rate has been negligible; in 2004 the rate of unemployment (as a percentage of those employed) was 2.5%. More than one-third of Liechtenstein's population are resident foreigners, many of whom provide the labour for industry, while in December 2004 13,911 workers crossed the borders from Austria and Switzerland each day to work in the Principality.

Liechtenstein has important economic links with neighbouring Switzerland. It is incorporated in a customs union with that country, and uses the Swiss franc as its currency. Liechtenstein became a member of the European Free Trade Association (EFTA, see p. 386) in May 1991, and the EEA in May 1995. The Principality is also a member of the European Bank for Reconstruction and Development (EBRD, see p. 224).

Education

Compulsory education begins at seven years of age. Basic instruction is given for five years at a primary school (Primarschule), after which a pupil may transfer to a lower secondary school (Oberschule) or secondary school (Realschule) for four years, or to the Liechtensteinisches Gymnasium (grammar school) for eight years. There is no university. Many Liechtensteiners continue their studies at universities in Austria and Switzerland. Liechtenstein has a further education college for the study of philosophy, a technical college (Fachhochschule), a music school, an art school, an adult education centre and a school for mentally disabled children. Government expenditure on education totalled 129.0m. Swiss francs in 2004 (16.5% of total expenditure).

Public Holidays

2006: 1 January (New Year's Day), 2 January (St Berchtold's Day), 6 January (Epiphany), 2 February (Candelmas), 28 February (Shrove Tuesday), 19 March (St Joseph's Day), 14 April (Good Friday), 17 April (Easter Monday), 1 May (Labour Day), 25 May (Ascension Day), 5 June (Whit Monday), 15 June (Corpus Christi), 15 August (Assumption and National Holiday), 8 September (Nativity of the Virgin Mary), 1 November (All Saints' Day), 8 December (Immaculate Conception), 25 December (Christmas), 26 December (St Stephen's Day).

2007: 1 January (New Year's Day), 2 January (St Berchtold's Day), 6 January (Epiphany), 2 February (Candelmas), 20 February (Shrove Tuesday), 19 March (St Joseph's Day), 6 April (Good Friday), 9 April (Easter Monday), 1 May (Labour Day), 17 May (Ascension Day), 28 May (Whit Monday), 7 June (Corpus Christi), 15 August (Assumption and National Holiday), 8 September (Nativity of the Virgin Mary), 1 November (All Saints' Day), 8 December (Immaculate Conception), 25 December (Christmas), 26 December (St Stephen's Day).

Weights and Measures

The metric system is in force.

LIECHTENSTEIN

Statistical Survey

Source: Amt für Volkswirtschaft, Gerberweg 5, 9490 Vaduz; tel. 2366111; fax 2366895; e-mail info.statistik@avw.llv.li; internet www.avw.llv.li.

AREA AND POPULATION

Area: 160.0 sq km (61.8 sq miles).

Population: 34,600 (males 17,050, females 17,550), incl. 11,852 resident aliens (males 6,064, females 5,788) at 31 December 2004 (national population register).

Density (2004): 216.3 per sq km.

Principal Towns (population at mid-2004): Schaan 5,696; Vaduz (capital) 5,014; Triesen 4,634; Balzers 4,402; Eschen 4,019; Mauren 3,614; Triesenberg 2,580.

Births, Marriages and Deaths (2004): Live births 372 (10.8 per 1,000); Marriages 164 (4.8 per 1,000); Deaths 198 (5.8 per 1,000).

Employment (2004): Agriculture and forestry 385; Industry and skilled trades 13,050 (Mining and quarrying 44, Processing industries 10,313, Energy and water supply 203, Construction 2,490); Services 16,098 (Retail, repairs, etc. 2,311, Hotels and restaurants 834, Transport and communications 1,037, Banking and insurance 2,052, Real estate, business services, etc. 2,603, Legal consultancy and trust management 2,196, Public administration 1,467, Education 907, Health and social services 1,503, Other services 1,188); *Total* 29,533.

HEALTH AND WELFARE

Key Indicators

Under-5 Mortality Rate (per 1,000 live births 2004): 5.

Physicians (per 1,000 head, 1997): 1.31 (Source: Statistik des Fürstentums Liechtenstein, *Statistisches Jahrbuch (1998)*).

For sources (unless specified) and definitions, see explanatory note on p. vi.

AGRICULTURE, ETC.

Note: Figures are for farms with a minimum of either 1 ha of arable land, 30 acres of specialized cultivation, 10 acres of protected cultivation, 8 sows, 80 porkers (or capacity for 80 porkers) or 300 head of poultry, and where livestock owners are covered by the Tierseuchenfond (insurance against epidemics).

Principal Crops (metric tons, 1987): Wheat 460; Oats 4; Barley 416; Silo-maize 27,880; Potatoes 1,040. *2004:* Grapes 150 metric tons (FAO estimate) (Source: partly FAO).

Livestock (2005): Cattle 5,564; Pigs 1,703; Horses 409; Sheep 3,603; Goats 324; Hens 10,364.

Dairy Produce (2004, metric tons): Milk delivered to dairies 13,726; Milk for consumption and pasteurization 1,027; Milk for processing 6,460; Cream 1,045; Yoghurt 154.

Forestry ('000 cubic metres, 2003): Roundwood removals (excl. bark) 22 (Sawlogs, veneer logs and logs for sleepers 18, Fuel wood 4). Source: FAO, *Yearbook of Forest Products*.

FINANCE

Currency and Exchange Rates: Swiss currency: 100 Rappen (centimes) = 1 Franken (Swiss franc). *Sterling, Dollar and Euro Equivalents* (30 December 2005): £1 sterling = 2.2631 Franken; US $1 = 1.3143 Franken; €1 = 1.5505 Franken; 100 Franken = £44.19 = $76.09 = €64.50. For average exchange rate, see chapter on Switzerland.

Budget (estimates, '000 Swiss francs, 2004): Revenue 769,027; Expenditure 780,692.

EXTERNAL TRADE

Note: Imports and exports to and from Liechtenstein presented at Swiss customs, not including trade with Switzerland and goods traffic via Switzerland.

Principal Commodities ('000 Swiss francs, 2004): *Imports:* Chemicals (excl. chemical fertilizers) 100,245; Vehicles and transport equipment 56,853; Machinery, etc. 648,553; Metal manufactures 260,702; Glass and glass or ceramic manufactures 160,515; Other finished and semi-finished products 369,109; Total (incl. others) 1,865,007. *Exports:* Animal fodder and food refuse 168,242; Chemicals (excl. chemical fertilizers) 272,329; Vehicles and transport equipment 323,921; Machinery, etc. 1,003,683; Metal manufactures 419,019; Glass and glass or ceramic manufactures 295,389; Other finished and semi-finished products 567,074; Total (incl. others) 3,193,148.

Principal Trading Partners ('000 Swiss francs, 2004): *Imports:* Austria 637,566; France 36,472; Germany 796,791; Italy 100,173; Netherlands 19,105; United Kingdom 26,161; USA 51,888; Total (incl. others) 1,865,007. *Exports:* Austria 297,576; China, People's Republic 65,594; France 355,988; Germany 748,785; Italy 232,408; Japan 64,451; Singapore 47,311; Spain 117,332; Sweden 45,963; United Kingdom 123,042; USA 531,244; Total (incl. others) 3,139,148.

TRANSPORT

Road Traffic (registered motor vehicles, December 2005): Passenger cars 24,393; Commercial vehicles 2,579; Motorcycles 3,110; Total (incl. others) 31,785.

TOURISM

Arrivals by Country of Residence (2004): Austria 2,400; France 1,201; Germany 15,772; Italy 1,778; Netherlands 1,197; Switzerland 13,760; United Kingdom 1,894; USA 2,038; Total (incl. others) 50,103.

COMMUNICATIONS MEDIA

Newspapers (1995): 3 (total circulation 10,450 copies).

Radio Receivers (1998): 12,451 in use.

Television Receivers (1998): 12,089 in use.

Telephones (2002): 19,900 main lines in use (Source: International Telecommunication Union).

Mobile Cellular Telephones (2002): 11,400 subscribers (Source: International Telecommunication Union).

Internet Users (2002): 20,000 (Source: International Telecommunication Union).

EDUCATION

(2004/05*)

Kindergarten: 53 classrooms; 88 teachers; 790 pupils.

Primary†: 138 classrooms; 260 teachers; 2,032 pupils.

Special Schools: 7 classrooms; 119 pupils.

Lower Secondary: 82 classrooms; 210 teachers; 1,112 pupils.

Optional 10th School Year: 15 teachers; 65 pupils.

Apprenticeships and Vocational Training‡: 1,076 pupils.

Grammar School: 38 classrooms(2001/02); 103 teachers; 744 pupils.

Music: 91 teachers; 2,519 pupils.

Higher Education§: 527 students.

* Excluding private institutions. In 2004/05 there were 231 pupils enrolled in private institutions (kindergarten 25, primary 79, lower secondary 127).
† Including pre-school and reception classes.
‡ Including Berufsmittelschulen (17 staff; 250 pupils) and Kunstschule Liechtenstein (19 pupils).
§ Those studying in Liechtenstein only (931 students attended institutions abroad).

Directory

The Constitution

Under the Constitution of 5 October 1921 (as amended in 1969, 1984, 2003 and 2005), the monarchy is hereditary in the male line. The Reigning Prince, who is constitutionally responsible for foreign affairs, exercises legislative power jointly with the Landtag (parliament). The Landtag comprises 25 members, who are elected for a term of four years (subject to dissolution) by universal adult suffrage, on a basis of proportional representation. Under the Constitution, all citizens of over 20 years of age are eligible to vote. The voters participate directly in legislation through referendums.

The Government is a collegial body consisting of five Ministers, including the Prime Minister. Each Minister has an Alternate who takes part in the meetings of the collegial Government if the Minister is unavailable. The Prime Minister, the other Ministers and their Alternates are appointed by the Reigning Prince on the recommendation of the Landtag. On the recommendation of the Landtag, the Reigning Prince appoints one of the Ministers as Deputy Prime Minister. Only native Liechtenstein citizens who meet the requirements for election to the Landtag are eligible for appointment to the Government. Each of the two regions of Liechtenstein, the Oberland (Upper Country) and the Unterland (Lower Country), is entitled to at least two Ministers. Their respective Alternates must come from the same region. The term of office is four years (subject to dissolution).

In a referendum on 14 and 16 March 2003 the electorate approved constitutional amendments extending the powers of the monarch. He was awarded the right to dismiss governments (even if they retained parliamentary confidence), to appoint an interim administration pending fresh elections, to veto laws by not signing them within a six-month period, to dismiss individual Ministers, subject to approval by members of the Landtag, to preside over a panel to select judges (with a casting vote) and to invoke emergency legislation. Citizens were accorded the right to force a referendum on any subject, including the future of the monarchy, by collecting 1,500 signatures.

In a referendum on 25 and 27 November 2005 the electorate approved constitutional amendments on the protection of human dignity and the right to life. The death penalty (abolished by a revision of the criminal code in 1985) was explicitly prohibited, as was the inhumane or degrading treatment of individuals.

In accordance with a treaty concluded with Switzerland in 1924, Liechtenstein is incorporated in Swiss customs territory, and uses Swiss currency, customs and postal administration.

The Government

HEAD OF STATE

Reigning Prince: Prince HANS-ADAM II (Prince of Liechtenstein, Duke of Troppau and Jägerndorf, Count of Rietberg—succeeded 13 November 1989).

On 15 August 2004 Prince Hans-Adam transferred his sovereign powers to his son, Hereditary Prince Alois.

GOVERNMENT
(April 2006)

A coalition of the Fortschrittliche Bürgerpartei Liechtensteins (FBP) and the Vaterländische Union (VU).

Prime Minister and Minister of Government Affairs, of Finance and of Construction and Public Works: OTMAR HASLER (FBP).

Deputy Prime Minister and Minister of Economic Affairs, of Justice and of Sports: Dr KLAUS TSCHÜTSCHER (VU).

Minister of Foreign Affairs, of Cultural Affairs and of Family and Equal Opportunity: RITA KIEBER-BECK (FBP).

Minister of Home Affairs, of Public Health and of Transport and Telecommunications: Dr MARTIN MEYER (FBP).

Minister of Education, of Social Affairs, of Environmental Affairs, of Land Use Planning and of Agriculture and Forestry: HUGO QUADERER (VU).

Alternate Ministers: URSULA BATLINER-ELKUCH (FBP), MAURO PEDRAZZINI (FBP), PATRICK SCHÜRMANN (FBP), HEIKE LINS-SELE (VU), RENATE MÜSSNER (VU).

GOVERNMENT OFFICES

Regierungsgebäude: 9490 Vaduz; tel. 2366111; fax 2366022; e-mail office@liechtenstein.li; internet www.liechtenstein.li.

Legislature

LANDTAG

Landtagssekretariat des Fürstentums Liechtenstein: Kirchstrasse 10, 9490 Vaduz; tel. 2366576; fax 2366580; e-mail info@landtag.li; internet www.landtag.li.

President: KLAUS WANGER (FBP).

Vice-President: IVO KLEIN (VU).

General Election, 11 and 13 March 2005

Party	Votes	% of votes	Seats
FBP	94,545	48.74	12
VU	74,162	38.23	10
FL	25,273	13.03	3
Total	193,980	100.00	25

Election Commissions

Hauptwahl- oder Hauptabstimmungskommission Oberland: c/o POB 684, 9490 Vaduz; independent; Chair. NORBERT VOGT (Vaduz).

Hauptwahl- oder Hauptabstimmungskommission Unterland: c/o POB 684, 9490 Vaduz; independent; Chair. ALOIS ALLGÄUER.

Political Organizations

Fortschrittliche Bürgerpartei Liechtensteins (FBP) (Progressive Citizens' Party of Liechtenstein): Aeulestr. 56, Postfach 1213, 9490 Vaduz; tel. 2377940; fax 2377949; e-mail marcus.vogt@fbp.li; internet www.fbp.li; f. 1918; Chair. JOHANNES MATT; Sec. MARCUS VOGT.

Freie Liste (FL) (Free List): Postfach 254, 9494 Schaan; tel. 3732042; e-mail info@freieliste.li; internet www.freieliste.li; f. 1985; progressive ecological party; Chair. KARIN JENNY.

Vaterländische Union (VU) (Patriotic Union): Bartlegrosch 19, 9490 Vaduz; tel. 2398282; fax 2398289; e-mail vu@vu-online.li; internet www.vu-online.li; f. 1936; by merger of the People's Party (f. 1918) and the Heimatdienst movement; Pres. ADOLF HEEB; Sec.-Gen. HANSJÖRG GOOP.

Diplomatic Representation

According to an arrangement concluded in 1919, Switzerland has agreed to represent Liechtenstein's interests in countries where it has diplomatic missions and where Liechtenstein is not represented in its own right. In so doing, Switzerland always acts only on the basis of mandates of a general or specific nature, which it may either refuse or accept, while Liechtenstein is free to enter into direct relations with foreign states or to establish its own additional missions. Liechtenstein has nine diplomatic missions abroad, comprising embassies in Berlin (Germany), Bern (Switzerland), Brussels (Belgium, including a permanent mission to the European Union), Washington DC (USA), Vienna (Austria, including permanent missions to the Organization for Security and Co-operation in Europe and the UN), as well as a permanent representative to the Council of Europe in Strasbourg (France), a permanent mission to the UN in New York (USA) and a permanent mission in Geneva (Switzerland). Liechtenstein also has a non-resident ambassador to the Holy See. There are 39 consular representatives accredited to Liechtenstein, of which 20 have offices in the Principality (representing Austria, the Central African Republic, Chad, Denmark, France, Germany, Hungary, Iceland, the Republic of Korea, Luxembourg, the former Yugoslav republic of Macedonia, Malta, Monaco, the Netherlands, Romania, Russia, Saint Vincent and the Grenadines, Spain, Sweden and Ukraine).

LIECHTENSTEIN

Judicial System

CIVIL AND CRIMINAL COURTS

Landgericht (County Court): Äulestr. 70, 9490 Vaduz; tel. 2366111; fax 2366539; Court of First Instance; one presiding judge, and 14 other judges; Presiding Judge Dr BENEDIKT MARXER.

Kriminalgericht (Criminal Court): bench of five judges; Presiding Judge Dr LOTHAR HAGEN.

Schöffengericht (Court of Assizes): 9490 Vaduz; for minor misdemeanours; bench of three judges; Presiding Judge Dr BENEDIKT MARXER.

Jugendgericht (Juvenile Court): 9490 Vaduz; bench of three judges; Presiding Judge Lic. Iur. UWE ÖHRI.

Obergericht (Superior Court): 9490 Vaduz; Court of Second Instance; divided into three senates, each with bench of five judges; Presiding Judge and Chair. of First Senate Lic. Iur. MAX BIZOZZERO; Chair. of Second Senate Lic. Iur. RUDOLF FEHR; Chair. of Third Senate Dr GERHARD MISLIK.

Oberster Gerichtshof (Supreme Court): 9490 Vaduz; Court of Third Instance; bench of five judges; Presiding Judge Dr HANSJÖRG RÜCK.

ADMINISTRATIVE COURTS

Verwaltungsgerichtshof (Administrative Court of Appeal): Landstr. 35, Postfach 1148, 9490 Vaduz; tel. 2381818; appeal against decrees and decisions of the Government may be made to this court; five members; Presiding Judge Lic. Iur. ANDREAS BATLINER.

Staatsgerichtshof (State Court): Geschäftsstelle, Städtle 36, Postfach 729, 9490 Vaduz; tel. 2391010; fax 2391039; e-mail kontakt@stgh.li; internet www.stgh.li; five members; exists for the protection of Public Law; Presiding Judge Lic. Iur. MARZELL BECK.

Religion

CHRISTIANITY

The Principality comprises a single archdiocese, Vaduz, created in 1997, which is directly responsible to the Holy See. At 31 December 2003 there were an estimated 25,730 adherents (some 76.0% of the population). The few Protestants (7.3%) belong to the parish of Vaduz.

Archdiocese of Vaduz: Erzbischöfliche Kanzlei, Fürst-Franz-Josef-Str. 112, Postfach 103, 9490 Vaduz; tel. 2332311; fax 2332324; e-mail ebv@supra.net; Archbishop Most Rev. WOLFGANG HAAS.

The Press

Apotheke und Marketing: A & M Verlag AG, Fürst-Johannes-Str. 70, 9494 Schaan; tel. 2332585; fax 2332586; e-mail info@am-verlag.com; internet www.am-verlag.com; Editor-in-Chief GABI KANNAMÜLLER; circ. 22,000.

Exclusiv: Aubündt 28, 9490 Vaduz; tel. 2328080; fax 2328081; e-mail info@exclusiv.li; internet www.exclusiv.li; f. 1996; monthly; Publr ALBERT MENNEL.

Liechtensteiner Vaterland: Fürst-Franz-Josef-Str. 13, 9490 Vaduz; tel. 2361616; fax 2361617; e-mail redaktion@vaterland.li; internet www.vaterland.li; f. 1913; publ. by Vaduzer Medienhaus AG; daily (Monday to Saturday); organ of the VU; Editor GÜNTHER FRITZ; circ. 10,295.

Liechtensteiner Volksblatt: Zollstr. 13, 9494 Schaan; tel. 2375151; fax 2375155; e-mail redaktion@volksblatt.li; internet www.volksblatt.li; f. 1878; daily (Monday to Saturday); organ of the FBP; Chief Editor MARTIN FROMMELT; circ. 7,503.

Liewo Sonntagszeitung: Fürst-Franz-Josef-Str. 13, 9490 Vaduz; tel. 2361616; fax 2361617; e-mail info@liewo.li; internet www.liewo.li; f. 1993 as Liechtensteiner Wochenzeitung; publ. by Vaduzer Medienhaus AG; weekly (Sunday); Editor-in-Chief NICOLE SCHÖBI-BÜCHEL; circ. 32,000.

Wirtschaft Regional: Fürst-Franz-Josef-Str. 13, 9490 Vaduz; tel. 2361616; fax 2361617; e-mail info@wirtschaft-regional.com; internet www.wirtschaft-regional.com; f. 2001; publ. by Vaduzer Medienhaus AG; weekly; Editor-in-Chief MATTHIAS HASSLER.

PRESS AGENCY

Presse- und Informationsamt (Press and Information Office): St Florinsgasse 3, 9490 Vaduz; tel. 2366721; fax 2366460; e-mail info@pia.llv.li; internet www.pia.llv.li; f. 1962; Dir DANIELA CLAVADETSCHER.

Publishers

Alpenland Verlag AG: Feldkircher Str. 13, 9494 Schaan; tel. 2395030; fax 2395031; e-mail office@alpenlandverlag.li; internet www.buchzentrum.li.

BONAFIDES Verlags-Anstalt: Pflugstr. 20, Postfach 82, 9490 Vaduz; tel. 2654680; fax 3900594; e-mail bva-fl@adon.li.

Buch und Verlagsdruckerei: Landstr. 153, 9494 Schaan; tel. 2361836; fax 2361840; e-mail bvd@bvd.li; internet www.bvd.li; Pres. KURT GÖPPEL.

DOWANI International Est.: Industriestr. 24, 9487 Bendern; tel. 3701115; fax 3701944; e-mail info@dowani.com; internet www.dowani.com; music.

van Eck Publishers: Haldenweg 8, 9495 Triesen; tel. 3923000; fax 3922277; e-mail vaneck@datacomm.ch; internet www.vaneckverlag.li; f. 1982; art, local interest, juvenile, golf, crime fiction; Man. Dirs FRANK P. VAN ECK, PETER GÖPPEL.

A. R. Gantner Verlag KG: Industriestr. 105A, Postfach 131, 9491 Ruggell; tel. 3771808; fax 3771802; e-mail bgc@adon.li; botany; Dir BRUNI GANTNER-CAPLAN.

GMG Juris Verlags-AG: Landstr. 30, 9494 Schaan; tel. 2381166; fax 2381160; e-mail verlag@gmg.li; internet www.gmg.li; f. 1990.

Lehrmittelverlag: Pflugstr. 30, 9490 Vaduz; tel. 2366390.

Liechtenstein-Verlag AG: Postfach 133, 9490 Vaduz; tel. 2322414; e-mail flbooks@verlag_ag.lol.li; f. 1947; belles-lettres and legal and scientific books; agents for international literature; Man. ALBERT SCHIKS.

Litag Anstalt—Literarische, Medien und Künstler Agentur: Industriestr. 105A, Postfach 131, 9491 Ruggell; tel. 3771808; fax 3771802; e-mail bgc@adon.li; f. 1956; Dir BRUNI GANTNER-CAPLAN.

MM-Verlag Buchhandlung Irmgard Meier: Pradafant 20, 9490 Vaduz; tel. 2329448; fax 2329449; e-mail mm.verlag@buchhandlung.li.

Neue Verlagsanstalt: In der Fina 18, Postfach 29, 9494 Schaan; tel. 2334381; fax 2334382; magazine publisher.

Sändig Reprint Verlag Wohlwend: Am Schrägen Weg 12, 9490 Vaduz; tel. 2323627; fax 2323649; e-mail saendig@adon.li; internet www.saendig.com; f. 1965; natural sciences, linguistics, freemasonry, fiction, folklore, music, history; Dir CHRISTIAN WOHLWEND.

Topos Verlag AG: Industriestr. 105A, Postfach 551, 9491 Ruggell; tel. 3771111; fax 3771119; e-mail topos@supra.net; internet www.topos.li; f. 1977; law, politics, literature, social science, periodicals; Dir GRAHAM A. P. SMITH.

Verlag der Liechtensteinischen Akademischen Gesellschaft: Bildgass 52, Postfach 829, 9494 Schaan; tel. 2323028; fax 2331449; f. 1972.

Broadcasting and Communications

TELECOMMUNICATIONS

Amt für Kommunikation: Kirchstr. 10, 9490 Vaduz; tel. 2366488; fax 2366489; e-mail office@ak.llv.li; internet www.ak.li; national regulatory authority; Dir KURT BUEHLER.

Telecom FL AG: Austr. 77, 9490 Vaduz; tel. 2377400; fax 2377401; e-mail telecom-fl@telecom-fl.com; internet www.telecom-fl.com; f. 1999.

BROADCASTING

Radio Liechtenstein: Dorfstr. 24, 9495 Triesen; tel. 3991313; fax 3991399; e-mail redaktion@radio.li; internet www.radio.li; f. 1995; Dir (vacant).

Lie-Comtel: Postfach 411, 9494 Schaan; tel. 2360111; fax 2361741; e-mail info@lie-comtel.li; internet www.lie-comtel.li; subsidiary of Liechtensteinische Kraftwerke (see Electricity); cable television operator and internet service provider.

Finance

(cap. = capital; res = reserves; dep. = deposits; m. = millions; brs = branches; amounts in Swiss francs)

BANKING

In 2003 there were 16 banks in Liechtenstein.

Bank Behring & Eberle & Co, AG: Austr. 27, Postfach 1166, 9490 Vaduz; tel. 2398889; fax 2398889; e-mail info@bbe.li; internet www.bbe.li; f. 2000; Dirs Dr HILMAR HOCH, KARL LENHERR.

Bank von Ernst (Liechtenstein) AG: POB 112, Egertastr. 10, 9490 Vaduz; tel. 2655353; fax 2655363; e-mail info@bve.li; internet www.bve.li; wholly owned by Coutts Bank von Ernst Ltd (Switzerland); cap. 25m., res 1m., dep. 149m. (Dec. 2002); Gen. Mans MAX CADERAS, ERNST WEDER.

Bank Frick & Co. AG: Landstr. 8, Postfach 43, 9496 Balzers; tel. 3882121; fax 3882122; e-mail bank@bfc.li; internet www.bfc.li; Chair. KUNO FRICK.

Centrum Bank AG: Kirchstr. 3, Postfach 1168, 9490 Vaduz; tel. 2383838; fax 2383839; e-mail info@centrumbank.li; internet www.centrumbank.li; f. 1993; cap. 20m., res 122m., dep. 926m. (Dec. 2004); Dirs Dr PETER MARXER, Dr PETER GOOP, Dr HERBERT OBERHUBER, Dr PETER MARXER, Jr.

Hypo Investment Bank (Liechtenstein) AG: POB 324, Landstr. 126A, 9494 Schaan; tel. 2350111; fax 2350102; e-mail info@hypo-alpe-adria.li; internet www.hypo-alpe-adria.li; f. 1999; 100% owned by HYPO Alpe-Adria-Bank, AG; cap. 13.8m., res −1.0m., dep. 40.9m. (Dec. 2002); Pres. DIETMAR FALSCHLEHNER.

LGT Bank in Liechtenstein Ltd: Herrengasse 12, Postfach 85, 9490 Vaduz; tel. 2351122; fax 2351522; e-mail info@lgt.com; internet www.lgt.com; f. 1920; present name adopted 1996; cap. 291m., res 897m., dep. 10.382m. (Dec. 2003); Chair. Prince PHILIPP; CEO THOMAS PISKE; 2 brs.

Liechtensteinische Landesbank AG (State Bank): Städtle 44, Postfach 384, 9490 Vaduz; tel. 2368811; fax 2368822; e-mail llb@llb.li; internet www.llb.li; f. 1861; present name adopted 1955; cap. 164m., res 597m., dep. 10,506m. (Dec. 2003); Chair. ERWIN VOGT; Exec. Dir Dr JOSEPH FEHR; brs in Schaan, Triesenberg, Eschen and Balzers.

Neue Bank AG: Marktgass 20, Postfach 1533, 9490 Vaduz; tel. 2360808; fax 2329260; e-mail info@neuebankag.com; internet www.neuebankag.li; f. 1992; cap. 40m. (Dec. 2003); Chair. GEORG VOGT.

NewCenturyBank: Städtle 17, 9490 Vaduz; tel. 2396211; fax 2396221; e-mail n-century@ncb.li; internet www.ncb.li; Chair WOLFGANG SEEGER.

Raiffeisen Bank (Liechtenstein) AG: Austr. 51, Postfach 1621, 9490 Vaduz; tel. 2370707; fax 2370777; e-mail info@raiffeisen.li; internet www.raiffeisen.li; f. 1998; total assets 651m. (Dec. 2004).

Serica Bank AG: Postfach 725, Pflugstr. 16, 9490 Vaduz; tel. 2365522; fax 2365505; e-mail bank@serica.com; internet www.serica.com; f. 1999; cap. 10.0m., res 16.2m., dep. 431.4m. (Dec. 2004); Pres. Dr PETER RITTER; Man. Dir K. HEINZ BECK.

Swissfirst Bank (Liechtenstein) AG: Austr. 61, Postfach 832, 9490 Vaduz; tel. 2393333; fax 2393300; e-mail swissfirst@swissfirst.li; internet www.swissfirst.li; Chair. RICHARD NEGELE; CEO WALTER RUPF.

Verwaltungs- und Privat-Bank AG (Private Trust Bank Corporation): Aeulestr. 6, 9490 Vaduz; tel. 2356655; fax 2356500; e-mail info@vpbank.com; internet www.vpbank.com; f. 1956; cap. 59m., res 298m., dep. 5,645m. (Dec. 2003); Chair. HANS BRUNHART; Gen. Man. ADOLF E. REAL; 4 brs.

Volksbank AG: Feldkircherstr. 2, 9494 Schaan; tel. 2390404; fax 2390405; e-mail info@volksbank.li; internet www.volksbank.li; Man. Dirs DANIEL BECK, GERHARD HAMEL.

Bankers' Association

Liechtensteinischer Bankverband: Pflugstr. 20, 9490 Vaduz; tel. 2301323; fax 2301324; e-mail info@bankenverband.li; internet www.bankenverband.li; f. 1969; Pres. THOMAS PISKE; Dir MICHAEL LAUBER; 16 mems.

INSURANCE

In 2002 insurance premiums in Liechtenstein totalled 693.5m. Swiss francs.

Alters- und Hinterlassenen-Versicherung (AHV) (Old Age and Survivors' Insurance): 9490 Vaduz; tel. 2381616; fax 2381600; e-mail postmaster@ahv.li; internet www.ahv.li; state-owned; Dir GERHARD BIEDERMANN.

AXA Lebensversicherung-AG: Neugasse 15, 9490 Vaduz; tel. 2375010; fax 2375019; e-mail kundendienst@axa-leben.li; internet www.axa-leben.li; f. 1995.

CapitalLeben Versicherung AG: Landstr. 126A, 9494 Schaan; tel. 2374837; fax 2374848; e-mail office@capitalleben.li; internet www.capitalleben.li; f. 1997; life insurance; Chair. KLAUS OSTERTAG; Man. Dirs MARKUS HETZER, ALEXANDER T. SKREINER.

Fortuna Lebens-Versicherungs-AG: Stadtle 35, 9490 Vaduz; tel. 2361545; fax 2361546; e-mail fl.service@fortuna.li; internet www.fortuna.li; f. 1996; Man. HEINER KEIL.

Swisscom Re AG: Kirchstr. 12, 9490 Vaduz; tel. 2301665; fax 2301666; Man. Dirs BERNHARD LAMPERT, URS LUGINBÜHL, MARCEL VON VIVIS, THOMAS WITTBJER.

Transmarine Insurance Co Ltd: Aeulestr. 38, 9490 Vaduz; tel. 2334488; fax 2334489; f. 1996.

Valorlife Lebensversicherungs-AG: Heiligkreuz 43, 9490 Vaduz; tel. 3992950; fax 3992959; e-mail morelli@valorlife.com; internet www.valorlife.com.

Insurance Association

Liechtensteinischer Versicherungsverbandes: (LVV): c/o CapitalLeben Versicherung AG, In der Specki 3, 9494 Schaan; tel. 3777036; fax 3707099; e-mail office@versicherungsverband.li; internet www.versicherungsverband.li; f. 1998; Pres. Dr HANS HAUMER; 25 mems.

Trade and Industry

CHAMBER OF COMMERCE

Liechtensteinische Industrie- und Handelskammer (Liechtenstein Chamber of Commerce and Industry): Altenbach 8, 9490 Vaduz; tel. 2375511; fax 2375512; e-mail info@lihk.li; internet www.lihk.li; f. 1947; Pres. MICHAEL HILTI; Gen. Man. JOSEF BECK; 40 mems.

INDUSTRIAL ASSOCIATION

Vereinigung Bäuerlicher Organisationen im Fürstentum Liechtenstein (VBO) (Agricultural Union): Postfach 351, 9493 Mauren; tel. 3759050; fax 3759051; e-mail vbo@kba.li; Pres. THOMAS BÜCHEL; Sec. KLAUS BÜCHEL.

UTILITIES

Electricity

Liechtenstein imports 75% of its electricity, mainly from Switzerland.

Liechtensteinische Kraftwerke: Im alten Riet 17, 9494 Schaan; tel. 2360111; fax 2360112; internet www.lkw.li; Pres. Dr ALEXANDER OSPELT; Gen. Man. HAGEN PÖHNERT.

Gas

Liechtensteinische Gasversorgung: Im Rietacker 4, 9494 Schaan; tel. 2361555; fax 2361566; Dir ROLAND RISCH.

Water

Wasserversorgung Liechtensteiner Unterland (WLU): Industriestr. 36, 9487 Gamprin-Bendern; tel. 3732555; fax 3735136; e-mail info@wlu.li; supplies water to Eschen, Gamprin, Mauren, Ruggell, and Schellenberg.

Gruppenwasserversorgung Liechtensteiner Oberland (GWO): supplies water to Balzers, Planken, Schaan, Triesen, Triesenberg and Vaduz.

TRADE UNIONS

Gewerbe- und Wirtschaftskammer für das Fürstentum Liechtenstein (Trades' Union): Zollstr. 23, 9494 Schaan; tel. 2377788; fax 2377789; e-mail gwk@gwk.li; internet www.gwk.li; f. 1936; aims to protect the interests of Liechtenstein artisans and tradespeople; Pres. WOLFGANG STRUNK; Sec. HARIETTE VAN DOOREN-BÜCHEL; 3,000 mems.

Liechtensteiner Arbeitnehmer-Verband (Employees' Association): 9495 Triesen; tel. 3993838; fax 3993839; e-mail lanv@supra.net; internet www.lanv.li; Pres. ALICE FEHR; Sec. ALBERT JEHLE.

Transport

RAILWAYS

Liechtenstein is traversed by some 18.5 km of railway track, which is administered by Austrian Federal Railways. There is a station at Nendeln, as well as two halts at Schaan and Schaanwald. A local service connects Feldkirch in Austria and Buchs in Switzerland via Liechtenstein, and the Arlberg express (Paris, France, to Vienna, Austria) passes through the Principality.

ROADS

Modern roads connect the capital, Vaduz, with all the towns and villages in the Principality. There are approximately 250 km of roads, all of which are paved. The Rhine and Samina valleys are connected by a tunnel 740 m long. Public transport is provided by a well-developed network of postal buses.

INLAND WATERWAYS

A canal of 26 km, irrigating the Rhine valley, was opened in 1943.

LIECHTENSTEIN

Tourism

Liechtenstein has an Alpine setting in the Upper Rhine area. The principal tourist attractions include a renowned postal museum, a National Museum and the Liechtenstein State Art Collection at Vaduz, as well as the Prince's castle (although this is closed to the public) and two ruined medieval fortresses at Schellenberg. Annually about two-fifths of foreign tourists visit the winter sports resort at Malbun, in the south-east of the Principality. For summer visitors there are some 400 km of hiking trails and an extensive network of cycling paths. In 2004 Liechtenstein received 50,103 foreign visitors.

Liechtenstein Tourismus: Postfach 139, 9490 Vaduz; tel. 2396300; fax 2396301; e-mail info@tourismus.li; internet www.tourismus.li; Dir ROLAND BÜCHEL.

LITHUANIA

Introductory Survey

Location, Climate, Language, Religion, Flag, Capital

The Republic of Lithuania (formerly the Lithuanian Soviet Socialist Republic) is situated on the eastern coast of the Baltic Sea, in north-eastern Europe. It is bounded by Latvia to the north, by Belarus to the south-east, by Poland to the south-west and by the Russian exclave, Kaliningrad Oblast, to the west. Lithuania's maritime position moderates an otherwise continental-type climate. Temperatures range from an average of −4.9°C (23.2°F) in January to a July mean of 17.0°C (62.6°F). Rainfall levels vary considerably from region to region: in the far west the annual average is 700 mm–850 mm (28 ins–33 ins), but in the central plain it is about 600 mm (24 ins). The official language is Lithuanian. The predominant religion is Christianity. Most ethnic Lithuanians are Roman Catholics by belief or tradition, but there are small communities of Lutherans and Calvinists, as well as a growing number of modern Protestant denominations. Adherents of Russian Orthodoxy are almost exclusively ethnic Slavs, while most Tatars have retained an adherence to Islam. The national flag (proportions 3 by 5) consists of three equal horizontal stripes of yellow (top), green and red (bottom). The capital is Vilnius.

Recent History

Prior to annexation by the Russian Empire in 1795, Lithuania was united in a Commonwealth with Poland. In 1915, after the outbreak of the First World War, it was occupied by German troops. A 'Lithuanian Conference' was convened in September 1917, which demanded the re-establishment of an independent Lithuanian state and elected a 'Lithuanian Council', headed by Antanas Smetona; it proceeded to declare independence on 16 February 1918. The new state survived both a Soviet attempt to create a Lithuanian-Belarusian Soviet republic and a Polish campaign aimed at reincorporating Lithuania. In October 1920 Poland annexed the region of Vilnius, but was forced to recognize the rest of Lithuania as an independent state (with its provisional capital at Kaunas). Soviet Russia had recognized Lithuanian independence in the Treaty of Moscow, signed in July. Lithuania's first Constitution, which declared Lithuania a parliamentary democracy, was adopted in August 1922. In December 1926 Smetona seized power in a military *coup d'état* and established an authoritarian regime, which endured until 1940.

According to the 'Secret Protocols' to the Treaty of Non-Aggression (the Molotov-Ribbentrop Pact), signed on 23 August 1939 by the USSR and Germany, Lithuania was to be part of the German sphere of influence. However, the Nazi-Soviet Treaty on Friendship and Existing Borders, agreed in September (following the outbreak of the Second World War), permitted the USSR to take control of Lithuania. In October Lithuania was compelled to agree to the stationing of 20,000 Soviet troops on its territory. In return, the USSR granted the city and region of Vilnius (which had been seized by Soviet troops in September) to Lithuania. In June 1940 the USSR dispatched a further 100,000 troops to Lithuania and forced the Lithuanian Government to resign. A Soviet-approved People's Government was formed. Elections to a People's Seim (parliament), which only pro-Soviet candidates were permitted to contest, took place in July. The Seim proclaimed the Lithuanian Soviet Socialist Republic on 21 July, and on 3 August Lithuania formally became a Union Republic of the USSR. The establishment of Soviet rule was followed by the arrest and imprisonment of many Lithuanian politicians and government officials.

Some 210,000 people, mainly Jews, were killed during the Nazi occupation of Lithuania (1941–44). The return of the Soviet Army, in 1944, was not welcomed by most Lithuanians, and anti-Soviet partisan warfare continued until 1952. Lithuanian agriculture was forcibly collectivized and rapid industrialization was implemented. Meanwhile, some 150,000 people were deported, many to Kazakhstan or to Russian Siberia and the Far East, and leaders and members of the Roman Catholic Church were persecuted and imprisoned. Lithuanian political parties were disbanded, and political power became the exclusive preserve of the Communist Party of Lithuania (CPL), the local branch of the Communist Party of the Soviet Union (CPSU). The leader (First Secretary) of the CPL in 1940–74 was Antanas Sniečkus.

A significant dissident movement was established during the 1960s and 1970s. With the introduction of the policy of *glasnost* (openness) by the Soviet leader, Mikhail Gorbachev, in the mid-1980s, a limited discussion of previously censored aspects of Lithuanian history appeared in the press. Dissident groups took advantage of a more tolerant attitude to political protests, organizing a demonstration in August 1987 to denounce the Nazi-Soviet Pact. However, in February 1988 security forces were deployed to prevent the public celebration of the 70th anniversary of Lithuanian independence. This, together with frustration among the intelligentsia at the slow pace of reform in the republic, led to the establishment in June of the Lithuanian Movement for Reconstruction (Sąjūdis). Sąjūdis organized mass demonstrations to protest against environmental pollution, the suppression of national culture and 'russification', and to condemn the signing of the Molotov-Ribbentrop Pact. The movement appealed to the CPL to support a declaration of independence and the recognition of Lithuanian as the state language. The latter demand was adopted by the Lithuanian Supreme Soviet (Supreme Council—legislature) in November, and traditional Lithuanian state symbols were restored. Other concessions made by the CPL during 1988 included the restoration of Independence Day as a public holiday and the return of buildings to the Roman Catholic Church.

Sąjūdis won 36 of the 42 popularly elected Lithuanian seats at elections to the all-Union Congress of People's Deputies in March 1989. Thereafter, the CPL began to adopt a more radical position, in an attempt to retain some measure of popular support. On 18 May the CPL-dominated Supreme Soviet approved a declaration of Lithuanian sovereignty, which asserted the supremacy of Lithuania's laws over all-Union legislation. Public debate concerning the legitimacy of Soviet rule in Lithuania intensified: a commission of the Lithuanian Supreme Soviet declared the establishment of Soviet power in 1940 to have been unconstitutional and, in August, on the 50th anniversary of the signing of the Pact with Nazi Germany, more than 1m. people participated in a 'human chain' extending from Tallinn in Estonia, through Latvia, to Vilnius.

Despite denunciations of Baltic nationalism by the all-Union authorities, the Lithuanian Supreme Soviet continued to adopt reformist legislation, including the establishment of freedom of religion and the legalization of a multi-party system. In December 1989 the CPL declared itself an independent party, no longer subordinate to the CPSU, adopting a new programme and declaring support for multi-party democracy and independent statehood. Shortly afterwards a group of former CPL members who were opposed to independence formed a separate movement, the Lithuanian Communist Party on the CPSU Platform (LCP). Meanwhile, Algirdas Brazauskas, First Secretary of the CPL since October 1988, was elected Chairman of the Presidium of the Lithuanian Supreme Soviet, defeating three other candidates, including Romualdas Ozolas, a leading member of Sąjūdis. None the less, Sąjūdis remained the dominant political force in the republic, and its supporters won an overall majority in the elections to the Lithuanian Supreme Soviet in February–March 1990. This new, pro-independence parliament elected Vytautas Landsbergis, the Chairman of Sąjūdis, to replace Brazauskas as its Chairman (*de facto* President of Lithuania), and on 11 March declared the restoration of Lithuanian independence: Lithuania thus became the first of the Soviet republics to make such a declaration. The Supreme Council also restored the pre-1940 name of the country (the Republic of Lithuania) and suspended the USSR Constitution on Lithuanian territory. Kazimiera Danute Prunskienė, a member of the CPL and hitherto a Deputy Chairman of the Council of Ministers, was appointed to be the first Prime Minister of the restored republic.

The Lithuanian declarations were condemned by a special session of the all-Union Congress of People's Deputies as unconstitutional, and Soviet forces occupied CPL buildings in Vilnius and took control of newspaper presses. An economic embargo was imposed on Lithuania in April 1990, and vital fuel supplies were suspended; the embargo remained in force for more than two months, until Lithuania agreed to a six-month moratorium on the independence declaration, pending formal negotiations. However, talks, which began in August, were soon terminated by the Soviet Government, and in January 1991 Landsbergis revoked the suspension of the declaration of independence, since negotiations on Lithuania's status had not resumed. Tension increased in the republic when the Soviet authorities dispatched to Vilnius troops (led by the special OMON units of the Soviet Ministry of Internal Affairs), who occupied former CPSU properties that had been nationalized by the Lithuanian Government. Landsbergis mobilized popular support to help to defend the parliament building, which he believed to be under threat. In mid-January 13 people were killed and about 500 injured, when Soviet troops seized the broadcasting centre in Vilnius. (In August 1999 six former officers of the LCP were convicted of complicity in attempts to overthrow the Lithuanian Government in January 1991, and sentenced to between three and 12 years' imprisonment.)

Meanwhile, policy differences had arisen within the Lithuanian leadership, and earlier in January 1991 Prunskienė and her Council of Ministers had resigned after the Supreme Council refused to sanction proposed price increases. Gediminas Vagnorius, a member of the Supreme Council, was appointed Prime Minister. The military intervention strengthened popular support for independence. A referendum on this issue took place on 9 February, at which 90.5% of voters expressed support for the re-establishment of an independent Lithuania and for the withdrawal of the Soviet army from the republic. In common with five other Soviet republics, Lithuania refused to conduct the all-Union referendum on the future of the USSR, which was held in March. (Voting did take place unofficially in predominantly Russian- and Polish-populated areas of Lithuania, where the majority endorsed the preservation of the USSR.)

A series of attacks by OMON forces on members of the nascent Lithuanian defence force and on the customs posts on the border with Belarus, combined with the seizure of power in Moscow by the conservative communist 'State Committee for the State of Emergency' (SCSE) in August 1991, led to fears in Lithuania that there would be a renewed attempt to overthrow the Landsbergis administration and reimpose Soviet rule. Soviet military vehicles entered Vilnius, but did not prevent the convening of an emergency session of the Supreme Council, which condemned the SCSE and issued a statement supporting Boris Yeltsin, President of the Russian Federation. As the coup collapsed, the Lithuanian Government ordered the withdrawal of Soviet forces from the republic and banned the LCP. (The successor party to the CPL, the Lithuanian Democratic Labour Party—LDLP, was not banned.) The Government also began to assume effective control of the country's borders. The failed coup prompted the recognition of Lithuanian independence by other states, and on 6 September the USSR State Council recognized the independence of Lithuania and the other Baltic republics (Estonia and Latvia), all three of which were admitted to the UN and the Conference on (now Organization for) Security and Co-operation in Europe (OSCE, see p. 327) later in the month.

During the first half of 1992 there was an increasing polarity within the Supreme Council between Sąjūdis deputies and those of the mainly left-wing opposition parties, most prominently the LDLP, led by Brazauskas. In April 10 members of the Council of Ministers criticized Vagnorius's 'dictatorial' methods, and two ministers subsequently resigned. Vagnorius tendered his resignation as Prime Minister in May, but remained in the post until July, when the legislature approved a motion of 'no confidence' in his leadership. The Seimas (Parliament—as the Supreme Council had been renamed) appointed Aleksandras Abišala, a close associate of Landsbergis, as Prime Minister; a new Council of Ministers was named shortly afterwards. Meanwhile, the growing division within the legislature had led to a boycott by pro-Sąjūdis deputies, rendering it frequently inquorate. In July, however, the Seimas approved a new electoral law, whereby Lithuania's first post-Soviet legislative elections, scheduled for late 1992, would be held under a mixed system of majority voting (for 71 seats) and proportional representation on the basis of party lists (70 seats).

The LDLP emerged as the leading party in the elections to the Seimas, which took place on 25 October and 15 November 1992, winning a total of 73 of the 141 seats. The defeat of Sąjūdis (which, in alliance with the Citizens' Charter of Lithuania, secured 30 seats) was largely attributed to popular disenchantment with its management of economic reform. The Christian Democratic Party of Lithuania (CDPL), which was closely aligned with Sąjūdis, won 16 seats. Also on 25 October a referendum approved a new Constitution, which was adopted by the Seimas on 6 November. Pending an election to the new post of President of the Republic, Brazauskas was elected by the Seimas to be its Chairman and acting Head of State. In December Brazauskas appointed Bronislovas Lubys (hitherto a Deputy Prime Minister) as Prime Minister. Lubys formed a new coalition Council of Ministers, retaining six members of the previous Government and including only three representatives of the LDLP.

The presidential election on 14 February 1993 was won by Brazauskas, with some 60% of the votes cast. His only rival was Stasys Lozoraitis, Lithuania's ambassador to the USA. Brazauskas subsequently announced his resignation from the LDLP. In March Adolfas Šleževičius replaced Lubys as Prime Minister and in April Šleževičius was appointed Chairman of the LDLP. In May a new political organization, the Conservative Party of Lithuania (CP), also known as the Homeland Union (Lithuanian Conservatives), was formed. Mainly comprising former members of Sąjūdis, and chaired by Landsbergis, the CP rapidly established itself as the principal opposition party.

The Minister of the Economy, Aleksandras Vasiliauskas, resigned in October 1995, following the collapse of several small commercial banks and in view of the slow progress achieved in the privatization programme. In November the Government survived its second vote of 'no confidence', initiated by the conservative opposition, which accused the LDLP of economic mismanagement. The banking crisis culminated in December with the suspension of the operations of the country's two largest commercial banks, owing to insolvency; senior officials of both institutions were arrested on charges of fraud. In January 1996 it was revealed that Šleževičius had withdrawn funds from the Lithuanian Joint Stock Innovation Bank (LJIB) only two days before the bank's suspension. Later in January Romasis Vaitekūnas resigned as Minister of the Interior, following intense public criticism of his handling of the crisis; it was revealed that Vaitekūnas had also withdrawn funds from the LJIB before its closure. Kazys Ratkevičius, the Chairman of the Bank of Lithuania (the central bank), also resigned. Šleževičius initially disregarded a presidential decree that he should leave office, which was upheld by the Seimas in February. He was replaced as Prime Minister by Laurynas Mindaugas Stankevičius, hitherto Minister of Government Reforms and Local Governments. Šleževičius also resigned as Chairman of the LDLP, and was succeeded by Česlovas Juršėnas, the Chairman of the Seimas. In October Šleževičius was charged with abuse of office.

A general election took place in two rounds on 20 October and 10 November 1996. The results confirmed the substantial loss of popular support for the LDLP, which retained only 12 seats in the Seimas. The CP obtained 70 seats, and the CDPL 16. The right-wing Lithuanian Centre Union won 13 seats and the Lithuanian Social Democratic Party (LSDP) 12. Some 53% of eligible voters participated in the first round, and about 40% took part in the second. Following the election, a coalition agreement was signed by the leaders of the CP and the CDPL. Landsbergis was elected Chairman of the Seimas at the assembly's first sitting in late November, and shortly afterwards the Seimas approved the appointment of Vagnorius as Prime Minister. His Government was dominated by members of the CP, with three representatives of the CDPL and two of the Centre Union. In January 1997 the Minister of Finance, Rolandas Matiliauskas, resigned, amid allegations of financial impropriety. The Prosecutor-General, Valdas Nikitinas, also resigned, following criticism of his handling of investigations into the financial crises of 1995.

Brazauskas did not contest a further term of office in the presidential election held on 21 December 1997, and in the first round of voting none of the seven candidates won the overall majority of votes required to secure the presidency. In a second round of voting on 4 January 1998 the second-placed candidate after the first round, Valdas Adamkus (a former environmental-protection executive, who had been naturalized in the USA), narrowly defeated Artūras Paulauskas (a prominent lawyer and deputy Prosecutor-General, supported by the Lithuanian Liberal Union), with 50.4% of the votes. The new President immediately endorsed the mandate of the incumbent Government, and in March Vagnorius was confirmed as Prime Minister by the Seimas. In April Paulauskas announced the formation of a new, centre-left political party, the New Union (Social Liberals), which hoped to attract the support of young voters.

A serious conflict of interests between Adamkus and Vagnorius intensified in April 1999, following the President's public criticism of what he regarded as the Government's inadequate attempts to eradicate corruption in the public sector. Although Vagnorius secured the confidence of the Seimas in a non-binding vote, at the end of the month he announced his intention to resign. In mid-May Adamkus invited the Mayor of Vilnius, Rolandas Paksas (a member of the CP), to form a new government. His Council of Ministers, announced at the beginning of June, was again formed from a coalition led by the CP and the CDPL. In October Paksas indicated that he would not endorse an agreement to sell a one-third stake in the state-owned Mažeikiai Nafta petroleum refinery to a US oil company, Williams International, under the terms of which Lithuania would be required to provide long-term financing equivalent to more than twice the price paid by the US company, in order to offset the refinery's debts. None the less, the Council of Ministers endorsed the sale, which was strongly supported by Adamkus and the majority of the CP, prompting the resignations of the Ministers of National Economy and of Finance, and, in late October, of Paksas.

At the end of October 1999 Adamkus nominated Andrius Kubilius, the First Deputy Chairman of the Seimas, as Prime Minister. Kubilius' Council of Ministers, approved by the legislature in mid-November, retained largely the same membership as the previous administration. Following the appointment of the new Government, the Lithuanian Centre Union announced that it was to become an opposition party; the party's leader, Romualdas Ozolas, had resigned as a Deputy Chairman of the Seimas after criticizing Landsbergis (who chaired both the CP and the legislature). In mid-November Paksas announced his resignation from the CP; in early December he was elected Chairman of the Lithuanian Liberal Union. Local elections in mid-March 2000 resulted in considerable successes for parties of the left, most notably the New Union (Social Liberals), which had campaigned against the sale of principal state properties to foreign interests. A lack of support for the CP apparently precipitated a split in the party, as several deputies established a 'moderate' faction in the Seimas, thus depriving the CP-CDPL coalition of an automatic majority in the legislature. In May, in advance of scheduled legislative elections the country's two largest left-wing parties, the LSDP and the LDLP, agreed to contest the election in alliance. The New Democracy Party and the Lithuanian Russians' Union subsequently joined the alliance, which was known as the A. Brazauskas Social Democratic Coalition, after the former President, who had been elected Honorary Chairman.

Some 56.2% of eligible voters participated in legislative elections held on 8 October 2000, which were contested by 28 political parties and alliances. The CP won only nine seats (compared with 70 in 1996). The A. Brazauskas Social Democratic Coalition obtained the largest representation, with 51 seats. However, the Lithuanian Liberal Union (with 34 seats) and the New Union (Social Liberals—with 29), which had formed an informal alliance prior to the elections, subsequently signed a coalition agreement and were able to form a parliamentary majority with partners that included the Lithuanian Centre Union and the Modern Christian-Democratic Union. On 26 October the legislature approved the appointment of Paksas as Prime Minister; Paulauskas was elected Chairman of the Seimas. The new Council of Ministers, in which notable appointments included that of Antanas Valionis of the New Union (Social Liberals) as Minister of Foreign Affairs, was approved at the end of the month. However, in subsequent months a number of ministers resigned from the cabinet, including the Minister of the Economy, Eugenijus Maldeikis, who was replaced by Eugenijus Gentvilas. Formalizing their electoral alliance, the LDLP merged with the LSDP at a joint congress held in late January 2001; the LSDP thereby became the single party with the greatest number of seats in the Seimas, and Brazauskas was elected its Chairman. Further political consolidation took place in May, when the CDPL merged with the Christian Democratic Union to form the Lithuanian Christian Democrats.

In mid-June 2001 the six New Union (Social Liberals) members of the Council of Ministers resigned their portfolios, following disagreements with the Lithuanian Liberal Union over privatization of the energy sector and economic reform, and criticism of the Prime Minister's style of leadership. Paksas was subsequently unable to form an alternative coalition government and, despite surviving a vote of 'no confidence', resigned on 20 June. Hopes that the previous coalition could be resurrected were short-lived; the Government had struggled for much of its brief existence, owing to the two parties' ideological differences, and the New Union sought a new alliance with the LSDP. At the end of the month President Adamkus offered the post of Prime Minister to Brazauskas, who was confirmed on 3 July. The LSDP did not, however, offer the New Union a formal coalition agreement, but instead agreed to an informal accord, which granted the New Union the same six ministerial positions from which it had withdrawn in June (including the foreign affairs portfolio). In September Paksas resigned as Chairman of the Lithuanian Liberal Union, in compliance with demands from within the party; Gentvilas was appointed acting Chairman, and was confirmed in the post in October. In late December Paksas and 10 other deputies left the parliamentary faction of the Lithuanian Liberal Union, owing, in part, to its failure to nominate Paksas as First Deputy Chairman of the Seimas, and amid indications that he would be unable to rely on the party's support were he to stand as a candidate in the presidential election due to take place in 2002. Paksas and the former Lithuanian Liberal Union deputies were formally expelled from the party in January 2002, and in March they founded the rightist Lithuanian Liberal Democratic Party (LLDP), with Paksas as its Chairman.

The results of the first round of voting in the presidential election, held on 22 December 2002, were inconclusive. A second round took place on 5 January 2003, in which Paksas obtained 54.7% of the votes cast, defeating Adamkus, with 45.3%, despite the fact that most major political parties had expressed support for the latter candidate. However, Paksas had pursued a populist campaign, and observers noted that Adamkus appeared to have lost popularity through his implementation of market economic reforms. Paksas was inaugurated as President on 26 February. On 4 March Brazauskas was re-appointed as Prime Minister; he nominated a Council of Ministers that was substantially unchanged from the outgoing administration. Following the presidential election, Paksas resigned as Chairman of the LLDP; Valentinas Mazuronis was elected as his successor. In late May Kubilius was elected as Chairman of the CP, in succession to Landsbergis. At the end of the month the Lithuanian Centre Union, the Lithuanian Liberal Union and the Modern Christian-Democratic Union merged to form the Lithuanian Liberal and Centre Union, with Artūras Zuokas as Chairman. In June a faction of the Lithuanian Centre Union that did not support the merger founded the National Centre Party, and elected Romualdas Ozolas as its Chairman. In February 2004 the CP merged with the Lithuanian Union of Political Prisoners and Deportees to form the Homeland Union—Conservatives, Political Prisoners and Deportees, Christian Democrats (HU).

Meanwhile, following the nomination by President Paksas of a new Director-General of the State Security Department, in late October 2003 a classified departmental report was disclosed, which claimed to provide evidence of links between the presidential adviser on national security, Remigijus Acas, and Yurii Borisov, an ethnic Russian with purported connections with organized crime groups, who had contributed significant funds to Paksas' presidential election campaign. It was revealed that in April Paksas had signed a presidential decree permitting Borisov to hold dual citizenship, despite warnings from the State Security Department that he was suspected of involvement in the illegal trading of weapons. In early November an emergency session of the Seimas established a special parliamentary commission to investigate Paksas' alleged links with Russian organized crime and the associated threat to national security, and the Prosecutor-General launched a criminal investigation into Borisov. Paksas subsequently dismissed a number of his senior advisers, but refused to appear before the commission. In early December the Seimas approved the commission's conclusion that the President's conduct had jeopardized national security, and the following day both Brazauskas and Paulauskas appealed for the President's resignation. On 18 December the Seimas approved a draft resolution to initiate impeachment proceedings against Paksas, and an investigative commission was subsequently established to consider the charges.

On 18 February 2004 the investigative commission endorsed six charges, which were to form the basis for the impeachment of the President: that Paksas represented a threat to national security; that he had failed to protect classified information; that he had attempted illegally to influence the operations of private companies; that he was unable to reconcile his public and private interests; that he had hindered the operations of state institutions; and that he had failed to prevent his advisers from abusing their positions. On the following day the Seimas voted to initiate formal impeachment proceedings and, in the mean time, agreed to seek a ruling from the Constitutional Court as to whether the charges technically constituted a breach of the Constitution. Paksas continued to deny the charges against him, and in late February he demanded that the Seimas initiate impeachment proceedings against the parliamentary Chairman, Paulauskas, whom he accused of the unauthorized disclosure of the confidential report that had been made public in October 2003 (the request was rejected, on the grounds that the Constitution provided only for the impeachment of deputies, and not of the parliamentary Chairman). On 24 March 2004 Paksas unexpectedly announced the nomination of Borisov as a presidential adviser, but he subsequently retracted the nomination, alleging that it had been prompted by a blackmail attempt. In response to this development, on the following day the Seimas adopted a resolution urging Paksas to resign; Borisov was placed under house arrest for having violated a pledge to avoid contact with the President. On 31 March the Constitutional Court ruled that the President had severely violated the Constitution by: granting Borisov dual citizenship in exchange for financial support; failing to protect state secrets; and using his presidential office illegally to influence the actions of a company's shareholders. The ruling was followed by a parliamentary vote on Paksas' impeachment, which took place on 6 April. Paksas was removed from office, after the necessary three-fifths' majority in the Seimas supported impeachment on the three charges confirmed by the Constitutional Court. Paulauskas immediately assumed the presidency, in an acting capacity, pending a presidential election, and subsequently suspended his membership of the New Union (Social Liberals), in compliance with the Constitution. At the end of May the Constitutional Court ruled that legislation recently passed by the Seimas, preventing an impeached head of state from seeking presidential office again, was in accordance with the Constitution, and Paksas was obliged to withdraw his candidacy from the forthcoming presidential election.

The first round of the presidential election, held on 13 June 2004 and contested by five candidates, proved inconclusive. In the second round, Adamkus was narrowly elected, receiving 52.6% of the votes cast, and defeating Prunskienė. Meanwhile, Lithuania's first elections to the European Parliament, following the accession of the country to full membership of the European Union (EU, see p. 228) on 1 May (see below), were held concurrently with the first round of presidential voting, with the participation of 46% of the electorate. The recently founded Labour Party (LP), headed by a controversial, ethnically Russian business executive, Viktor Uspaskikh, won five of the 13 mandates allocated to Lithuania; the governing LSDP, the Lithuanian Liberal and Centre Union and the HU each obtained two seats, while the LLDP and the PNDU each won one seat. Adamkus was inaugurated on 12 July, and on the following day the Seimas approved his nomination of Brazauskas as Prime Minister.

Elections to the Seimas, held in two rounds on 10 and 24 October 2004, demonstrated that the LP had further consolidated its support. It became the largest single party in the Seimas, receiving 28.4% of the votes cast on the basis of party lists, and obtaining 39 of the 141 mandates available. A coalition of the LSDP and the New Union (Social Liberals), known as Working for Lithuania, received 20.7% of the votes cast on the basis of party lists, and 31 seats. The HU obtained 25 seats, and the Liberal and Centre Union 18. The Order and Justice coalition, comprising the Liberal Democratic Party and the Lithuanian People's Union for a Free Lithuania, received 11 seats, while the PNDU obtained 10.

In late October 2004 the Vilnius District Court effectively cleared Paksas of disclosing state secrets by ruling that there was no indisputable evidence that Borisov had learnt from Paksas that his telephones were being monitored by the State Security Department. (However, this decision was overturned by the Court of Appeal in March 2005, when Paksas was ordered to pay a fine of 9,735 litai.) In December 2004 a congress of the LLDP re-elected Paksas as the party's Chairman.

Meanwhile, following prolonged negotiations, a coalition government of the LP, the LSDP, the New Union (Social Liberals) and the PNDU was presented for presidential approval at the end of November 2004. Brazauskas was to remain as Prime Minister, while several prominent members of the LSDP and the New Union (Social Liberals) were to retain the posts they had held in the outgoing administration. Uspaskikh was nominated as Minister of the Economy and Prunskienė as Minister of Agriculture. On 14 December the Seimas approved the new Government.

At the beginning of January 2005 it emerged that the Minister of Foreign Affairs, Antanas Valionis, a member of the New Union (Social Liberals), had previously served as a reservist in the Committee for State Security (KGB), the Soviet security service. However, although this revelation proved controversial, reservists were exempt from a law stating that all former KGB agents must formally declare their association with the organization. Similarly, at the end of January a Deputy Chairman of the Seimas and Chairman of the parliamentary Committee on European Affairs, Alfredas Pekeliunas, also came under investigation for membership of the KGB, a charge he denied; Pekeliunas resisted demands for his resignation. In April Algirdas Butkevičius submitted his resignation as Minister of Finance, after the governing coalition rejected a proposed tax-reform programme. He was replaced by Zigmantas Balčytis, hitherto the Minister of Transport, in May; Petras Česna assumed the transport portfolio. In mid-June Uspaskikh resigned from both the Government and the Seimas after an *ad hoc* parliamentary ethics commission concluded that he had violated the principle of the separation of public and private interests; Kęstutis Daukšys replaced him as Minister of the Economy. Meanwhile, in early June the Mayor of Vilnius, Artūras Zuokas, temporarily resigned as Chairman of the Liberal and Centre Union, pending an investigation into corruption allegations; Zuokas had been involved in a public dispute with Uspaskikh, with each accusing the other of corruption, which had led President Adamkus to appeal for their resignations. In December a parliamentary commission concluded that it was likely that Zuokas had received unauthorized financial inducements in his role as Mayor; nevertheless, in February 2006 he survived a vote of 'no confidence'.

Meanwhile, in mid-December 2005 the Supreme Court ruled that Paksas was not guilty of divulging confidential state information, and Yurii Borisov was granted permission to remain resident in the country. In January 2006 an investigation into Brazauskas' business affairs was closed, after no evidence was found to substantiate allegations of financial impropriety relating to the privatization of a Soviet-era hotel owned by his wife (the LSDP had threatened to withdraw from the governing coalition should Brazauskas be implicated in any wrongdoing).

On 11 April 2006 Artūras Paulauskas, the Chairman of the New Union (Social Liberals), was removed from his position as parliamentary speaker, following a secret ballot in the Seimas, amid accusations that he had been aware of a scandal involving the unauthorized use of official vehicles by government employees. The New Union (Social Liberals) immediately announced its intention to withdraw from the governing coalition. The remaining members of the coalition, the LSDP, the LLP and the PNDU, signed a new coalition agreement on the following day, and Viktoras Muntianas of the LLP was subsequently elected as the new Chairman of the Seimas. At the end of April Paulauskas was re-elected as Chairman of the New Union (Social Liberals), which in early May declared itself to be in opposition to the Government. The New Union (Social Liberals) Minister of Foreign Affairs, Antanas Valionis, and the Minister of Social Security and Labour, Vilija Blinkevičiūtė, were expected to be replaced in May.

Whereas Lithuania's Baltic neighbours, Estonia and Latvia, have large national minorities, ethnic Lithuanians constitute much of the republic's population: in the 2001 census ethnic Lithuanians represented some 84% of the total, while the two largest minority groups, Poles and Russians, represented 7% and 6%, respectively, of the total population. As a result, the requirements for naturalization of non-ethnic Lithuanians were less stringent than in the neighbouring Baltic republics, where national identity was perceived in some quarters as being under threat. Under citizenship laws adopted in late 1989, all residents, regardless of ethnic origin, were eligible to apply for naturalization; by early 1993 more than 90% of the country's non-ethnic Lithuanian residents had been granted citizenship. None the less, the population of Lithuania declined by some 191,000 between 1989 and 2001. In an attempt to counter emigration (in particular to the USA), in September 2002 the Seimas approved legislation permitting Lithuanian citizens to hold dual citizenship, thereby facilitating the eventual return of Lithuanian nationals to the country.

Mainly because of its citizenship laws, Lithuania's relations with Russia have been less strained than have those of Estonia and Latvia. During 1992 negotiations took place between

Lithuania and Russia for the withdrawal of the estimated 38,000 former Soviet troops remaining in Lithuania. Agreement was reached in September, and the final troops left, as scheduled, on 31 August 1993, whereupon full state sovereignty was perceived as having been restored in Lithuania.

In November 1993 Lithuania and Russia signed several agreements, including an accord on most-favoured nation status in bilateral trade, and another concerning the transportation, via Lithuania, of Russian military equipment and troops from the Russian exclave of Kaliningrad Oblast, on the Baltic coast. However, there was disagreement between the two countries during 1994, following Lithuania's decision to introduce new regulations governing military transits. A compromise appeared to have been reached in January 1995, when the Lithuanian Government extended until December the existing procedure for military transits; Russia duly indicated that the agreement on bilateral trade would enter into force immediately. In October 1997 President Brazauskas undertook the first official visit to Russia by a Baltic head of state since the disintegration of the former USSR. During the visit a state border delimitation treaty was signed by both sides, and bilateral co-operation agreements on joint economic zones, and on the Baltic continental shelf, were also concluded. The border treaty was ratified by the Seimas in October 1999, but was not ratified by the Russian side until May 2003. Lithuania expressed support for an agreement between the EU and Russia in late 2002, which proposed simplified visa arrangements for Russian citizens traversing Lithuania to reach the exclave of Kaliningrad. New transit arrangements were implemented in Lithuania at the beginning of February 2003, in advance of Lithuania's accession to the EU in the following year. However, tensions between the two countries emerged in late February 2004, when Lithuania expelled three Russian diplomats suspected of espionage; Russia reciprocated by expelling three diplomatic personnel from the Lithuanian embassy in Moscow. Further tensions were reported in the first half of 2005, following the refusal of President Adamkus to attend a commemoration held in Moscow on 9 May to mark the 60th anniversary of the end of the Second World War in Europe. All three Baltic Governments were unhappy with an agreement signed between Russia and Germany, in September 2005, on the construction of a North European Gas Pipeline, which was to carry natural gas from Russia to Germany under the Baltic Sea, bypassing the Baltic countries.

Lithuania's relations with neighbouring Poland were largely concerned with the status of the Polish minority in Lithuania. Following the failed coup attempt of August 1991 in Moscow, leaders of councils in Polish-populated regions of Lithuania were dismissed, in response to their alleged support for the coup, and direct rule was introduced. However, in January 1992 Lithuania and Poland signed a 'Declaration on Friendly Relations and Neighbourly Co-operation', which guaranteed the rights of the respective ethnic minorities and also recognized the existing border between the two countries. A full treaty of friendship and co-operation was signed by the respective Heads of State in April 1994. The treaty, notably, did not include a condemnatory reference to Poland's occupation of the region of Vilnius in 1920–39 (a provision that had originally been demanded by Lithuania). An agreement on free trade was signed by the two countries in June 1996, and during 1997 the Lithuanian and Polish Governments established regular forums for inter-presidential and inter-parliamentary discussion. In May 2005 the Chairmen of the national legislatures of Lithuania, Poland and Ukraine, meeting in Lutsk, Ukraine, signed a declaration establishing a new Inter-Parliamentary Assembly, which aimed to help fulfil Ukraine's objective of attaining membership of the EU and the North Atlantic Treaty Organization (NATO, see p. 314), by sharing the successful reform measures undertaken in Lithuania and Poland.

Lithuania enjoys close relations with Estonia and Latvia. Relations between the three states are co-ordinated through the consultative inter-parliamentary Baltic Assembly, the Council of Baltic Sea States (see p. 210) and the Baltic Council (see p. 395). However, in the mid-1990s Lithuania's relations with Latvia came under strain, as a result of disagreement over the demarcation of the countries' maritime border. In October 1995 the Lithuanian Government protested at Latvia's signature of a preliminary agreement with two foreign petroleum companies to explore oilfields in the disputed waters. Tension increased following the ratification of the agreement by the Latvian parliament in October 1996, although in July 1999 the two countries signed an agreement on the Delimitation of the Territorial Sea, Exclusive Economic Zone and Continental Shelf in the Baltic Sea. However, protests from the Latvian fishing industry prevented the agreement from being ratified by the Latvian parliament and, therefore, Lithuania's ratification was invalidated. In December 2000 a protocol was signed for the redemarcation of the land border between the two countries.

Lithuania pursued close co-operation with, and eventual integration into, the political, economic and defence systems of western Europe, notably NATO and the EU. A number of political and economic agreements concluded between the EU and the Baltic states in 1995, with the aim of facilitating their membership, came into effect on 1 February 1998. In December 1999 a summit meeting of EU Heads of State and Government in Helsinki, Finland, endorsed proposals to begin accession talks with a number of countries, including Lithuania; formal negotiations commenced in February 2000. As a concession to achieve EU membership, the Government approved a draft national energy strategy in September 1999, which provided for the decommissioning of the first unit of the Ignalina nuclear power plant by 2005. In June 2002 Lithuania agreed to decommission the plant's remaining unit in 2009, in return for a significant contribution from the EU towards the cost of the endeavour. In December 2002 Lithuania, and nine other countries, were formally invited to join the EU on 1 May 2004; at a national referendum, held on 10–11 May 2003, 89.95% of participants voted in favour of membership. Lithuania acceded to the EU as scheduled, and in November 2004 it became the first EU member state to ratify the proposed constitutional treaty of the EU (which was subsequently rejected by referendums in, notably, France and the Netherlands). Meanwhile, in November 2002 Lithuania was one of seven countries invited to join NATO in 2004. In common with Estonia and Latvia, Lithuania regarded membership of the Alliance as the principal guarantee of the country's security, and it became a full member on 29 March 2004.

Government

Under the terms of the Constitution that was approved in a national referendum on 25 October 1992, supreme legislative authority resides with the Seimas (Parliament), which has 141 members, elected by universal adult suffrage for a four-year term (71 deputies are directly elected by majority vote, with 70 being elected from party lists on the basis of proportional representation). The President of the Republic (who is Head of State) is elected by direct popular vote for a period of five years (and a maximum of two consecutive terms). Executive power is vested in the Council of Ministers. This is headed by the Prime Minister, who is appointed by the President with the approval of the Seimas. For administrative purposes, Lithuania is divided into 10 counties.

Defence

Until independence Lithuania had no armed forces separate from those of the USSR. The Department of State Defence (established in April 1990) was reorganized as the Ministry of Defence in October 1991. In August 2005 Lithuania's active armed forces totalled an estimated 13,510: army 11,600 (including 3,531 conscripts), navy 410 (including 300 conscripts) and air force 1,050 (including 150 conscripts). There was also a paramilitary force of 14,600, including a border guard of 5,000, and a total of 8,200 reserves. Military service is compulsory and lasts for 12 months. Defence expenditure in 2004 amounted to some 872m. litai. The budget for 2005 allocated 915m. litai to defence. Lithuania became a full member of the North Atlantic Treaty Organization (NATO, see p. 314) on 29 March 2004. In 2005 Lithuania contributed some 130 troops and personnel to a Provincial Reconstruction Team under the UN-mandated International Security Assistance Force in Afghanistan.

Economic Affairs

In 2004, according to estimates by the World Bank, Lithuania's gross national income (GNI), measured at average 2002–04 prices, was US $19,727m., equivalent to $5,740 per head (or $12,610 per head on an international purchasing-power parity basis). During 1995–2004 the population decreased by an annual average of 0.6%, while gross domestic product (GDP) per head increased, in real terms, by an average of 6.2% per year. Overall GDP increased, in real terms, by an average of 5.6% annually over the same period. Real GDP increased by 7.0% in 2004 and by 7.5% in 2005.

Agriculture (including hunting, forestry and fishing) contributed 5.9% of GDP in 2004, when the sector engaged 15.8% of the employed population. The principal crops are cereals, sugar beet, potatoes and vegetables. In 1991 legislation was adopted permitting the restitution of land to its former owners, and the privatization of state-owned farms and reorganization of collective farms was initiated. By the mid-1990s almost 40% of arable land was privately cultivated. Legislation approved in January 2003 authorized the sale of agricultural land to foreign owners, although its implementation was to be subject to a seven-year transition period. Real agricultural GDP increased, in real terms, by an annual average of 1.3% during 1995–2004. The GDP of the sector increased by 2.1% in 2003 and by 3.0% in 2004.

Industry (including mining, manufacturing, construction and power) contributed 32.7% of GDP in 2004, when the sector engaged 28.2% of the employed population. According to World Bank estimates, industrial GDP increased by an annual average of 6.1%, in real terms, during 1995–2004; the GDP of the sector increased by 16.0% in 2003 and by 7.0% in 2004.

In 2004 mining and quarrying contributed 0.5% of GDP, and it provided just 0.3% of employment. Lithuania has significant reserves of peat and materials used in construction (limestone, clay, dolomite, chalk, and sand and gravel), as well as small deposits of petroleum and natural gas. In terms of gross value added, the sector registered growth of 3.0% in 2004, according to official data.

The manufacturing sector provided 20.5% of GDP in 2004, when it engaged 17.7% of the employed labour force. Based on the value of sales (excluding refined petroleum products), in 2005 the principal branches of manufacturing were food products (particularly dairy products), wood products (particularly furniture), chemicals (including fertilizers) and clothing. The World Bank estimated that manufacturing GDP increased, in real terms, by an annual average of 7.4% during 1995–2004. Sectoral GDP increased by 14.1% in 2003 and by 7.0% in 2004.

In 2002 nuclear power accounted for 81.8% of gross electricity production, followed by natural gas, which accounted for 11.1%. Lithuania has substantial petroleum-refining and electricity-generating capacities, which enable it to export refined petroleum products and electricity. In 1999 Lithuania exported an estimated 55.9% of its gross electricity production. In 2005 imports of mineral products accounted for 24.6% of the total value of merchandise imports.

The services sector contributed 61.5% of GDP in 2004, and provided 55.9% of total employment. The Baltic port of Klaipėda (Memel) is a significant entrepôt for regional trade. The GDP of the services sector increased, in real terms, by an annual average of 5.7% in 1995–2004. Real services GDP increased by 7.4% in 2003 and by 5.7% in 2004.

In 2004 Lithuania recorded a visible trade deficit of US $2,382.6m., and there was a deficit of $1,724.6m. on the current account of the balance of payments. In 2005 the principal source of imports was Russia (accounting for 27.8% of the total); other major sources were Germany (15.2%) and Poland (8.3%). Russia was also the main market for exports in that year (accounting for an estimated 10.4% of the total). Other principal markets were Latvia (10.3%), Germany (9.4%), France (7.4%), Estonia (5.9%) and Poland (5.5%). In 2005 the principal exports were mineral products, machinery and electrical equipment, textiles, vehicles and transportation equipment, chemical products and miscellaneous manufactured articles. The principal imports were mineral products, machinery and electrical equipment, vehicles and transportation equipment, chemical products, base metals, textiles, and plastics and rubber.

In 2004 there was a budgetary surplus of 143.5m. litai (equivalent to 0.2% of GDP). Lithuania's total external debt was US $8,342m. at the end of 2003, of which $2,107m. was long-term public debt. In that year the cost of debt-servicing was equivalent to 67.7% of the value of exports of goods and services. Annual inflation averaged 4.4% in 1995–2004. The rate of inflation was 1.2% in 2004 and 2.7% in 2005. The average rate of unemployment was 8.3% in 2005, compared with 11.4% in 2004.

Lithuania is a member, as a 'Country of Operations', of the European Bank for Reconstruction and Development (EBRD, see p. 224), as well as of the IMF and the World Bank. In December 2000 Lithuania became a member of the World Trade Organization (WTO, see p. 370). Lithuania acceded to full membership of the European Union (EU, see p. 228) on 1 May 2004.

By the mid-1990s the Government's stabilization programme had achieved modest success: the development of the private sector was well advanced, most prices had been liberalized and progress had been achieved in restructuring the financial sector. However, the economy contracted in 1999, largely owing to the economic crisis in Russia in 1998. Major privatizations were initiated from 1999, and much was achieved in the way of recovery. The last remaining state-owned bank was privatized in 2002, and energy-sector privatization was implemented over succeeding years. In an effort to facilitate increased integration with EU economies and further reorientate foreign trade, from February 2002 the national currency's fixed rate of exchange was linked to the common European currency, the euro, instead of the US dollar. In June formal agreement was reached with the EU on the closure of the Ignalina nuclear power plant; the first of the plant's reactors was to be decommissioned in 2005 (in the event, the reactor was decommissioned in late 2004) and the second in 2009, in return for substantial financial compensation from the EU. In February 2006 the Prime Ministers of the Baltic states of Estonia, Latvia and Lithuania reached agreement on the construction of a new nuclear plant at Ignalina, which was to replace the existing plant by 2015, with equal investment from each country. Meanwhile, Lithuania was one of three new member states of the EU (along with Estonia and Slovenia) to be admitted to the EU's exchange rate mechanism (ERM 2) in June 2004, ahead of the country's adoption of the euro. In March 2006 Lithuania formally applied to become a member of the euro zone from 1 January 2007. However, increases in global energy prices and rapid economic growth had stimulated consumer-price inflation in 2005, and in mid-May 2006 the European Commission and the European Central Bank concluded that Lithuania would not be ready to adopt the euro in 2007. Growth in GDP was expected to slow slightly in 2006, to around 6.5%, compared with 7.5% in 2005.

Education

Education, beginning at six years of age, is free and compulsory until the age of 18. Pre-school education is available for children aged between one and six years. Children spend four years at primary school (Grades 1–4), followed by six years at lower secondary school (basic education, Grades 5–10) and two years at upper secondary school or gymnasium (Grades 10–12). Vocational training is available. From 2003 a uniform tuition fee was introduced for students in higher education, although there were exemptions for the highest achievers. In 2004/05 95.1% of the relevant age-group was enrolled in primary education, while enrolment in secondary education was equivalent to 95.3%. In the 2004/05 academic year 599,633 students were enrolled in 1,634 comprehensive schools (accounting for Grades 1–12). In 2004/05 there were 73 vocational schools, 38 schools of higher education and 21 universities. Total enrolment in institutions of higher education was 188,203. In 1991 the first private schools were opened; by 1999 there were 24 private schools, 11 colleges and six private universities. Lithuanian is the main language of instruction, although in 1999/2000 7.7% of students at comprehensive schools were taught in Russian and 3.8% were taught in Polish. The state budget for 2001 allocated 925.5m. litai (7.3% of total expenditure) to education. The 2003 budget allocated 5.9% of GDP to education.

Public Holidays

2006: 1 January (New Year's Day), 16 February (Day of the Restoration of the Lithuanian State), 11 March (Day of the Re-establishment of Independence), 17 April (Easter Monday), 1 May (Mothers' Day), 6 July (Anniversary of the Coronation of Grand Duke Mindaugas of Lithuania), 15 August (Assumption), 1 November (All Saints' Day), 25–26 December (Christmas).

2007: 1 January (New Year's Day), 16 February (Day of the Restoration of the Lithuanian State), 11 March (Day of the Re-establishment of Independence), 9 April (Easter Monday), 1 May (Mothers' Day), 6 July (Anniversary of the Coronation of Grand Duke Mindaugas of Lithuania), 15 August (Assumption), 1 November (All Saints' Day), 25–26 December (Christmas).

Weights and Measures

The metric system is in force.

LITHUANIA

Statistical Survey

Source (unless otherwise indicated): Department of Statistics to the Government of Lithuania (Statistics Lithuania), Gedimino pr. 29, Vilnius 01500; tel. (52) 236-4822; fax (5) 236-4845; e-mail statistika@std.lt; internet www.std.lt.

Area and Population

AREA, POPULATION AND DENSITY

Area (sq km)	65,300*
Population (census results)	
12 January 1989†	3,674,802
6 April 2001	
Males	1,629,148
Females	1,854,824
Total	3,483,972
Population (official estimates at 1 January)	
2003	3,462,553
2004	3,445,857
2005	3,425,324
Density (per sq km) at 1 January 2005	52.5

* 25,212 sq miles.
† Figure refers to the *de jure* population. The *de facto* total was 3,689,779.

POPULATION BY ETHNIC GROUP
(permanent inhabitants at 2001 census)*

	'000	%
Lithuanian	2,907.3	83.5
Polish	235.0	6.7
Russian	219.8	6.3
Belarusian	42.9	1.2
Total (incl. others)	3,484.0	100.0

* Figures are provisional.

ADMINISTRATIVE DIVISIONS
(at 1 January 2005)

County	Area (sq km)	Population	Density (per sq km)
Alytus	5,425	182,851	33.7
Kaunas	8,089	685,723	84.8
Klaipėda	5,209	382,179	73.4
Marijampolė	4,463	185,419	41.5
Panevėžys	7,881	292,376	37.1
Šiauliai	8,540	360,755	42.2
Tauragė	4,411	131,481	29.8
Telšiai	4,350	177,008	40.7
Utena	7,201	178,977	24.9
Vilnius	9,731	848,555	87.2
Total	65,300	3,425,324	52.5

PRINCIPAL TOWNS
(population at 2001 census)

Vilnius (capital)	542,287	Šiauliai	133,883
Kaunas	378,943	Panevėžys	119,749
Klaipėda	192,954	Alytus	71,491

2005 (official estimate at 1 January): Vilnius 541,278.

BIRTHS, MARRIAGES AND DEATHS

	Registered live births		Registered marriages		Registered deaths	
	Number	Rate (per 1,000)	Number	Rate (per 1,000)	Number	Rate (per 1,000)
1998	37,019	10.4	18,486	5.2	40,757	11.5
1999	36,415	10.3	17,868	5.1	40,003	11.3
2000	34,149	9.8	16,906	4.8	38,919	11.1
2001	31,546	9.1	15,764	4.5	40,399	11.6
2002	30,014	8.6	16,151	4.7	41,072	11.8
2003	30,598	8.9	16,975	4.9	40,990	11.9
2004	30,419	8.8	19,130	5.6	41,340	12.0
2005*	30,467	8.9	19,904	5.8	43,774	12.8

* Provisional figures.

Expectation of life (WHO estimates, years at birth): 72 (males 66; females 78) in 2003 (Source: WHO, *World Health Report*).

IMMIGRATION AND EMIGRATION
('000 persons)

	2003	2004	2005
Immigrants	4.7	5.5	6.8
Emigrants	11.0	15.2	15.6

ECONOMICALLY ACTIVE POPULATION
(annual averages, '000 persons)*

	2002	2003	2004
Agriculture, hunting and forestry	249.8	255.5	225.6
Fishing	0.8	1.5	1.9
Mining and quarrying	4.3	5.1	4.3
Manufacturing	260.6	264.6	254.9
Electricity, gas and water	28.4	27.8	29.5
Construction	93.2	107.1	116.2
Wholesale and retail trade; repair of motor vehicles, motorcycles and personal and household goods	211.2	214.7	228.0
Hotels and restaurants	28.0	29.4	32.7
Transport, storage and communications	87.4	92.2	93.9
Financial intermediation	14.0	16.8	15.0
Real estate, renting and business activities	54.9	53.5	55.8
Public administration and defence; compulsory social security	81.3	74.9	77.9
Education	138.9	134.8	141.0
Health and social work	94.6	98.9	98.4
Other community, social and personal service activities	53.8	54.6	55.8
Other activities not adequately defined	4.8	6.7	5.0
Total	1,405.9	1,438.0	1,436.3
Unemployed	224.4	203.9	184.4
Total labour force	1,630.3	1,641.9	1,620.6
Males	829.0	831.6	824.4
Females	801.4	810.2	796.3

* Official estimates based on results of 2001 census.

LITHUANIA

Health and Welfare

KEY INDICATORS

Total fertility rate (children per woman, 2003)	1.3
Under-5 mortality rate (per 1,000 live births, 2004)	8
HIV/AIDS (% of persons aged 15–49, 2003)	0.1
Physicians (per 1,000 head, 2001)	4.03
Hospital beds (per 1,000 head, 2001)	9.22
Health expenditure (2002): US $ per head (PPP)	549
Health expenditure (2002): % of GDP	5.9
Health expenditure (2002): public (% of total)	72.6
Human Development Index (2003): ranking	39
Human Development Index (2003): value	0.852

For sources and definitions, see explanatory note on p. vi.

Agriculture

PRINCIPAL CROPS
('000 metric tons)

	2002	2003	2004*
Wheat	1,217.6	1,204.1	1,430.2
Barley	871.3	899.6	978.0
Rye	170.2	147.1	160.0
Oats	97.5	114.6	125.0
Buckwheat	10.6	14.7	16.0
Triticale (wheat-rye hybrid)	145.3	214.2	233.0
Other cereals	18.5	28.6	31.0
Potatoes	1,531.3	1,445.2	1,432.5
Sugar beet	1,052.4	977.4	904.9
Dry peas	37.0	21.6	23.0
Other pulses*	25.9	35.8	39.1
Rapeseed	105.6	119.5	204.5
Cabbages	98.4	214.2	135.8
Tomatoes	4.4	4.1	3.0
Cucumbers and gherkins	8.3	7.3	5.0
Dry onions	22.7	28.8	18.0
Carrots	48.9	129.7	80.0
Green peas	7.0*	9.0*	6.0
Other vegetables*	100.3	156.2	98.0
Apples	80.0*	97.5	34.0
Pears	2.0*	1.5	1.3

* Unofficial figure(s).
Source: FAO.

LIVESTOCK
('000 head at 1 January)

	2002	2003	2004
Horses	64	61	64
Cattle	752	779	812
Pigs	1,011	1,061	1,057
Sheep	12	14	17
Goats	24	22	27
Chickens	6,435	6,696	7,870
Turkeys	43	46	98
Rabbits	74	75	98

Source: FAO.

LIVESTOCK PRODUCTS
('000 metric tons, unless otherwise indicated)

	2002	2003	2004
Beef and veal	44.7	51.5	60.0*
Pig meat	94.9	105.1	114.0
Poultry meat	32.8	38.8	46.0*
Cows' milk	1,764.9	1,788.7	1,863.0
Cheese	57.0	58.2	61.8†
Butter	17.5	17.6	18.0†
Eggs	51.8	48.8	52.0
Honey	1.3	1.2	1.1†
Cattle hides (fresh)†	7.1	6.3	7.6

* Unofficial figure.
† FAO estimate(s).
Source: FAO.

Forestry

ROUNDWOOD REMOVALS
('000 cubic metres, excl. bark)

	2002	2003	2004
Sawlogs, veneer logs and logs for sleepers	3,220	3,370	3,420
Pulpwood	1,580	1,570	1,430
Other industrial wood	20	15	10
Fuel wood	1,295	1,320	1,260
Total	**6,115**	**6,275**	**6,120**

Source: FAO.

SAWNWOOD PRODUCTION
('000 cubic metres, incl. railway sleepers)

	2002	2003	2004
Coniferous (softwood)	900*	950	980
Broadleaved (hardwood)	400	450	470
Total	**1,300**	**1,400**	**1,450**

* FAO estimate.
Source: FAO.

Fishing

(metric tons, live weight)

	2001	2002	2003
Capture	150,831	150,146	157,205
Atlantic redfishes	20,182	21,853	21,631
Jack and horse mackerels	57,200	46,282	32,439
Largehead hairtail	167	8,120	26,590
Sardinellas	30,800	22,205	29,517
European anchovy	9,492	14,064	n.a.
Chub mackerel	9,900	12,119	21,264
Northern prawn	5,413	6,707	5,539
Aquaculture	2,001	1,750	2,356
Total catch	**153,832**	**151,896**	**159,561**

Source: FAO.

LITHUANIA

Mining

('000 metric tons, unless otherwise indicated)

	2002	2003	2004
Crude petroleum	471	434	383
Dolomite ('000 cubic metres)	384	632	796
Limestone	894	986	960
Clay ('000 cubic metres)	171	202	200
Peat	259	491	345

Industry

SELECTED PRODUCTS
('000 metric tons, unless otherwise indicated)

	2002	2003	2004*
Sausages and smoked meat products	53.3	59.3	73.5
Flour	215.0	205.5	239.1
Refined sugar	138.3	131.5	132.9
Beer ('000 hectolitres)	268.9	264.2	269.0
Wine ('000 hectolitres)	472	355	516
Cotton fabrics (million sq m)	41.9	33.8	21.9
Woollen fabrics (million sq m)	21.1	22.0	21.5
Fabrics of man-made fibres	17.2	12.7	18.7
Footwear—excl. rubber and plastic ('000 pairs)†	1,100	900	1,200
Plywood ('000 cubic metres)	46.9	49.8	49.0
Particle board ('000 cubic metres)	230.6	314.6	423.4
Paper and paperboard	79.5	89.8	99.7
Motor spirit (petrol)	6,448	7,101	
Sulphuric acid	874	1,002	1,019
Mineral and chemical fertilizers	1,161	1,239	n.a.
Nitrogenous fertilizers	737	773	612
Cement†	600	600	800
Cast iron	17.5	15.8	18.7
Television receivers ('000)	348.3	686.8	1,201.7
Refrigerators and freezers ('000)	399.0	429.4	456.8
Bicycles ('000)	344	351	348
Electric energy (million kWh)†	17,200	19,300	19,100

* Provisional data.
† Figures are rounded.

Finance

CURRENCY AND EXCHANGE RATES

Monetary Units
100 centas = 1 litas (plural: litai).

Sterling, Dollar and Euro Equivalents (30 December 2005)
£1 sterling = 5.0141 litai;
US $1 = 2.9102 litai;
€1 = 3.4528 litai;
100 litai = £19.94 = $33.36 = €28.96.

Note: In June 1993 Lithuania reintroduced its national currency, the litas, replacing a temporary coupon currency, the talonas, at a conversion rate of 1 litas = 100 talonai. The talonas had been introduced in May 1992, initially circulating alongside (and at par with) the Russian (formerly Soviet) rouble. An official mid-point exchange rate of US $1 = 4.00 litai was in operation from 1 April 1994 until 1 February 2002. From 2 February 2002 the litas was linked to the euro, with the exchange rate set at €1 = 3.4528 litai.

BUDGET
(million litai)*

Revenue†	2002	2003	2004
Tax revenue	8,980.4	9,715.7	10,634.8
Taxes on income, profits and capital gains	2,710.7	3,294.9	3,989.5
Taxes on goods and services	6,119.1	6,254.8	6,541.8
Other taxes	150.6	166.0	103.5
Social security contributions	4,493.1	4,851.3	5,746.4
Other revenue	1,039.5	1,088.7	1,019.7
Property income	475.0	423.7	365.8
Sales of goods and services	525.4	580.6	600.3
Others	39.1	84.4	53.6
Total	14,513.0	15,655.7	17,400.9

Expenditure‡	2002	2003	2004
Compensation of employees	2,717.7	2,885.0	3,267.5
Use of goods and services	2,187.0	2,488.4	2,166.5
Consumption of fixed capital	397.0	420.5	437.4
Interest	697.9	706.2	608.3
Subsidies	102.4	141.5	401.0
Grants awarded	2,059.0	2,088.3	2,683.5
Social benefits	6,263.2	6,586.4	7,198.5
Other expenditure	417.4	761.0	1,054.7
Total	14,841.6	16,077.3	17,817.4

* Figures refer to the consolidated accounts of the central Government, comprising the operations of the central budget, the Guarantee Fund and Fund for Financial Support to Bankrupted Enterprises, Privatization Funds, the Road Fund, Social Security Funds and others.
† Excluding grants received (million litai): 333.2 in 2002; 435.0 in 2003; 560.0 in 2004.
‡ Excluding lending minus repayments.

Source: Ministry of Finance, Vilnius.

INTERNATIONAL RESERVES
(US $ million at 31 December)

	2003	2004	2005
Gold (national valuation)	77.69	81.40	95.34
IMF special drawing rights	0.06	0.09	0.08
Reserve position in IMF	0.02	0.02	0.02
Foreign exchange	3,371.89	3,512.47	3,720.07
Total	3,449.66	3,593.98	3,815.51

* National valuation.

Source: IMF, *International Financial Statistics*.

MONEY SUPPLY
(million litai at 31 December)

	2003	2004	2005
Currency outside banks	4,632.0	5,121.2	6,118.4
Demand deposits at banking institutions	5,891.9	7,334.5	10590.0
Total money (incl. others)	10,535.1	12,472.0	16,721.5

Source: IMF, *International Financial Statistics*.

COST OF LIVING
(Consumer Price Index; base: 2000 = 100)

	2002	2003	2004
Food (incl. beverages)	102.8	99.0	101.2
Fuel and light	105.2	105.4	104.9
Clothing	92.4	89.9	89.1
Rent	104.3	105.2	108.6
All items (incl. others)	101.6	100.4	101.6

Source: ILO.

LITHUANIA

Statistical Survey

NATIONAL ACCOUNTS
(million litai at current prices)

Expenditure on the Gross Domestic Product

	2003	2004	2005
Final consumption expenditure	47,087.4	51,795.8	58,490.8
Households	36,507.1	40,462.4	46,585.2
Non-profit institutions serving households	152.3	170.9	221.9
General government	10,428.1	11,162.5	11,683.6
Gross capital formation	13,003.4	15,082.6	17,663.7
Gross fixed capital formation	12,024.1	13,585.4	15,787.2
Changes in inventories	964.2	1,475.1	1,847.1
Acquisitions, less disposals, of valuables	15.1	22.1	29.5
Total domestic expenditure	60,090.8	66,878.4	76,154.5
Exports of goods and services	29,137.4	32,635.5	40,851.3
Less Imports of goods and services	32,456.3	37,073.7	46,004.4
GDP in market prices	56,772.9	62,440.2	71,001.4
GDP at constant 2000 prices	57,568	61,586	66,185

Gross Domestic Product by Economic Activity

	2002	2003	2004
Agriculture, hunting, forestry and fishing	3,247.5	3,265.9	3,283.7
Mining and quarrying	276.5	290.0	298.8
Manufacturing	8,675.8	9,828.6	11,506.4
Electricity, gas and water supply	1,876.0	2,371.8	2,486.2
Construction	2,901.6	3,603.4	4,020.0
Wholesale and retail trade; repair of motor vehicles	8,093.2	8,878.4	10,059.3
Hotels and restaurants	734.9	788.1	849.0
Transport, storage and communication	6,189.8	6,810.4	7,184.8
Financial intermediation	1,074.9	985.3	1,260.3
Real estate, renting and business activities	4,729.7	5,279.8	5,684.0
Public administration and defence	2,503.2	2,732.0	2,975.0
Education	2,806.3	2,812.4	3,024.5
Health and social work	1,473.9	1,498.4	1,684.9
Other community, social and personal service activities	1,513.7	1,576.1	1,641.9
Activities of households	56.8	73.0	74.4
Sub-total	46,153.7	50,793.6	56,033.3
Taxes on products	6,145.9	6,350.4	6,671.1
Less Subsidies on products	351.2	372.2	264.3
GDP in market prices	51,948.4	56,771.9	62,440.2

BALANCE OF PAYMENTS
(US $ million)

	2002	2003	2004
Exports of goods f.o.b.	6,028.4	7,657.8	9,306.3
Imports of goods f.o.b.	−7,343.3	−9,362.0	−11,688.9
Trade balance	−1,314.9	−1,704.2	−2,382.6
Exports of services	1,463.7	1,878.0	2,444.4
Imports of services	−915.0	−1,263.6	−1,632.1
Balance on goods and services	−766.1	−1,089.8	−1,570.2
Other income received	191.6	235.2	354.9
Other income paid	−375.0	−717.4	−967.3
Balance on goods, services and income	−949.5	−1,572.0	−2,182.5
Current transfers received	231.7	301.5	612.1
Current transfers paid	−2.9	−7.8	−154.2
Current balance	−720.7	−1,278.4	−1,724.6
Capital account (net)	56.5	67.5	287.2

—*continued*	2002	2003	2004
Direct investment abroad	−17.7	−37.2	−262.6
Direct investment from abroad	712.5	179.2	773.2
Portfolio investment assets	−124.5	29.8	−219.9
Portfolio investment liabilities	148.8	222.3	431.1
Financial derivatives assets	19.6	28.1	60.0
Financial derivatives liabilities	−22.7	−56.2	−57.4
Other investment assets	154.7	−100.9	−683.8
Other investment liabilities	177.7	1,377.2	1,100.7
Net errors and omissions	78.5	181.2	191.8
Overall balance	462.7	612.7	−104.4

External Trade

PRINCIPAL COMMODITIES
(million litai)

Imports c.i.f.	2003	2004	2005
Prepared foodstuffs; beverages, spirits and vinegar; tobacco and manufactured substitutes	1,038.2	1,303.1	1,589.4
Mineral products	5,451.6	6,786.9	10,989.0
Mineral fuels	5,098.1	6,434.1	10,564.4
Products of the chemical or allied industries	2,533.0	2,904.5	3,350.8
Plastics, rubber and articles thereof	1,510.7	1,895.5	2,403.1
Textiles and textile articles	2,283.9	2,432.4	2,408.9
Base metals and articles thereof	1,733.1	2,480.7	2,988.8
Machinery and mechanical appliances; electrical equipment; sound and television apparatus	5,463.4	6,536.8	7,688.2
Nuclear reactors, boilers, etc.	3,202.0	3,778.4	4,539.2
Electrical machinery, sound and television recorders and parts thereof	2,261.3	2,758.4	3,138.0
Vehicles, aircraft, vessels and associated transport equipment	4,580.6	4,543.2	5,011.7
Total (incl. others)	29,438.0	34,383.6	42,974.6

Exports f.o.b.	2003	2004	2005
Live animals and animal products	846.1	1,109.5	1,468.5
Vegetable products	658.4	639.6	981.7
Prepared foodstuffs; beverages, spirits and vinegar; tobacco and manufactured substitutes	1,023.1	1,147.6	1,693.0
Mineral products	4,350.9	6,509.8	9,012.4
Mineral fuels	4,308.1	6,457.8	8,931.8
Products of the chemical or allied industries	1,467.2	1,793.0	2,388.3
Fertilizers	947.1	1,132.7	1,453.3
Plastics, rubber and articles thereof	617.9	779.5	1,185.5
Wood, cork and articles thereof; wood charcoal; manufactures of straw, esparto, etc.	1,200.2	1,293.1	1,496.8
Textiles and textile articles	3,019.5	3,021.7	3,034.2
Articles of apparel and clothing accessories, not knitted	1,378.8	1,330.5	1,226.2
Base metals and articles thereof	738.1	1,137.9	1,432.2
Machinery and mechanical appliances; electrical equipment; sound and television apparatus	2,457.4	3,286.7	4,065.6
Vehicles, aircraft, vessels and associated transport equipment	3,388.6	2,339.5	2,707.3
Miscellaneous manufactured articles	1,359.9	1,651.7	1,954.4
Total (incl. others)	22,145.1	25,819.2	32,807.3

LITHUANIA

PRINCIPAL TRADING PARTNERS
(million litai)

Imports c.i.f.	2003	2004	2005
Austria	333.3	388.4	441.2
Belarus	771.6	669.0	798.4
Belgium	654.5	740.7	963.5
China, People's Republic	387.1	818.2	1,005.7
Czech Republic	422.8	527.0	643.4
Denmark	1,080.1	1,238.5	1,288.2
Estonia	1,015.4	1,109.1	1,207.9
Finland	1,176.2	1,154.9	1,279.9
France	1,012.3	1,105.0	1,197.6
Germany	5,291.7	5,770.3	6,522.2
Italy	945.2	1,109.3	1,269.5
Latvia	1,110.7	1,319.0	1,685.9
Netherlands	1,140.8	1,386.2	1,594.4
Norway	358.9	303.6	222.3
Poland	1,918.7	2,630.5	3,563.5
Russia	5,425.2	7,905.3	11,961.5
Spain	n.a.	329.8	433.8
Sweden	1,036.9	1,151.9	1,481.3
Ukraine	1,045.0	519.2	511.1
United Kingdom	913.7	806.3	950.2
USA	562.1	541.4	843.0
Total (incl. others)	29,438.0	34,383.6	42,974.6

Exports f.o.b.	2003	2004	2005
Belarus	598.1	823.5	1,063.1
Belgium	431.9	714.5	638.9
Canada	n.a.	236.1	939.5
Denmark	1,037.7	1,228.9	1,416.7
Estonia	927.3	1,291.3	1,934.3
Finland	324.6	225.6	324.6
France	1,108.6	1,629.2	2,299.0
Germany	2,169.4	2,649.8	3,076.1
Italy	455.1	539.4	629.2
Latvia	2,041.2	2,629.9	3,370.9
Netherlands	751.9	1,246.7	1,045.7
Norway	514.9	548.1	524.8
Poland	729.7	1,243.6	1,800.3
Russia	1,893.8	2,394.8	3,422.8
Singapore	n.a.	38.8	918.2
Spain	190.8	484.8	881.5
Sweden	886.8	1,305.1	1,634.5
Switzerland	2,576.4	1,179.9	198.8
Turkey	372.2	420.9	415.9
Ukraine	489.0	592.9	743.5
United Kingdom	1,396.4	1,373.8	1,535.0
USA	612.2	1,219.6	1,543.4
Total (incl. others)	21,262.6	25,819.2	32,807.3

Transport

RAILWAYS
(traffic)

	2002	2003	2004
Passenger journeys ('000)	7,217	7,005	6,983
Passenger-km (million)	498	432	443
Freight transported ('000 metric tons)	36,650	43,447	45,555
Freight ton-km (million)	9,767	11,457	11,637

ROAD TRAFFIC
(public transport and freight)

	2002	2003	2004
Passenger journeys ('000)	430,627	451,535	473,484
Passenger-km (million)	3,013	3,100	3,790
Freight transported ('000 metric tons)	45,047	52,180	51,456
Freight ton-km (million)	10,709	11,462	12,279

ROAD TRAFFIC
(motor vehicles in use at 31 December)

	2002	2003	2004
Passenger cars	1,180,945	1,256,853	1,315,914
Buses and coaches	15,376	15,543	14,377
Lorries and vans	93,508	97,454	101,284
Motorcycles and mopeds	21,017	21,873	22,861

INLAND WATERWAYS

	2002	2003	2004
Passenger journeys ('000)	2,890.2	1,993.6	1,973.9
Passenger-km (million)	3	2	2
Freight transported ('000 metric tons)	515.0	645.5	621.0
Freight ton-km (million)	1	1	1

SHIPPING

Merchant Fleet
(registered at 31 December)

	2002	2003	2004
Number of vessels	184	176	162
Total displacement ('000 grt)	435.3	442.1	453.4

Source: Lloyd's Register-Fairplay, *World Fleet Statistics*.

International Sea-borne Freight Traffic
('000 metric tons)

	1999	2000	2001
Goods loaded	12,864	18,552	18,144
Goods unloaded	2,796	4,296	4,224

Source: UN, *Monthly Bulletin of Statistics*.

CIVIL AVIATION
(traffic on scheduled services)

	2002	2003	2004
Passengers carried ('000)	376	398	592
Passenger-km (million)	524	541	896
Freight transported (million metric tons)	3.4	3.7	6.6

Kilometres flown: 10 million in 1998.

Tourism

FOREIGN VISITORS BY COUNTRY OF ORIGIN
(arrivals at accommodation establishments)

	2001	2002	2003
Belarus	19,246	23,937	21,810
Denmark	9,994	10,312	10,855
Estonia	14,127	14,659	19,067
Finland	21,429	18,756	21,300
Germany	56,174	68,090	79,182
Italy	7,659	7,324	11,548
Latvia	27,474	25,942	28,114
Norway	7,736	8,010	8,884
Poland	45,927	59,807	59,564
Russia	45,191	48,918	50,290
Sweden	14,190	13,868	14,618
United Kingdom	11,291	12,740	19,770
USA	13,494	13,608	14,111
Total (incl. others)	353,888	394,549	438,299

Source: World Tourism Organization, *Yearbook of Tourism Statistics*.

Receipts from tourism (US $ million): 227 in 2001; 333 in 2002; 476 in 2003.

Communications Media

	2002	2003	2004
Telephones ('000 main lines in use)	935.9	824.2	820.0
Mobile cellular telephones ('000 subscribers)	1,631.6	2,169.9	3,421.5
Internet users ('000)	500	695.7	968.0
Book titles (incl. brochures)	4,858	4,559	4,270
Newspapers: number	354	347	340
Newspapers: average circulation ('000 copies)	2,328	2,502	2,203
Other periodicals	529	544	536

1997: Radio receivers ('000 in use) 1,900; Facsimile machines (number in use) 6,200.

2004 ('000 in use): Personal computers 533.

Sources: International Telecommunication Union; UNESCO, *Statistical Yearbook*; UN, *Statistical Yearbook* and Ministry of Education and Science, Vilnius.

Education

(2003/04)

	Institutions	Teachers	Students*
Pre-school establishments	672	n.a.	89,500
Comprehensive schools	1,932†	49,545	583,000
Vocational schools	83	4,659	44,403
Schools of further education	42	5,238	53,000
Universities	21	9,523	130,000

* Figures are mostly rounded.

† Comprising 146 kindergartens, 448 primary schools, 24 junior schools, 644 lower secondary schools, 476 upper secondary schools, 91 gymnasiums, 72 special care schools, 3 sanatoriums and 28 evening schools.

Source: Ministry of Education and Science, Vilnius.

Adult literacy rate (UNESCO estimates): 99.6% (males 99.6%; females 99.6%) in 2003 (Source: UN Development Programme, *Human Development Report*).

Directory

The Constitution

The Constitution was approved in a national referendum on 25 October 1992 and adopted by the Seimas on 6 November. The following is a summary of its main provisions:

THE STATE

The Republic of Lithuania is an independent and democratic republic; its sovereignty is vested in the people, who exercise their supreme power either directly or through their democratically elected representatives. The powers of the State are exercised by the Seimas (Parliament), the President of the Republic, the Government and the Judiciary. The most significant issues concerning the State and the people are decided by referendum.

The territory of the republic is integral. Citizenship is acquired by birth or on other grounds determined by law. With certain exceptions established by law, no person may be a citizen of Lithuania and of another state at the same time. Lithuanian is the state language.

THE INDIVIDUAL AND THE STATE

The rights and freedoms of individuals are inviolable. Property is inviolable, and the rights of ownership are protected by law. Freedom of thought, conscience and religion are guaranteed. All persons are equal before the law. No one may be discriminated against on the basis of sex, race, nationality, language, origin, social status, religion or opinion. Citizens may choose their place of residence in Lithuania freely, and may leave the country at their own will. Citizens are guaranteed the right to form societies, political parties and associations. Citizens who belong to ethnic communities have the right to foster their language, culture and customs.

SOCIETY AND THE STATE

The family is the basis of society and the State. Education is compulsory until the age of 16. Education at state and local government institutions is free of charge at all levels. State and local government establishments of education are secular, although, at the request of parents, they may offer classes in religious instruction. The State recognizes traditional Lithuanian and other churches and religious organizations, but there is no state religion. Censorship of mass media is prohibited. Ethnic communities may independently administer the affairs of their ethnic culture, education, organizations, etc. The State supports ethnic communities.

NATIONAL ECONOMY AND LABOUR

Lithuania's economy is based on the right to private ownership and freedom of individual economic activity. Every person may freely choose an occupation, and has the right to adequate, safe and healthy working conditions, adequate compensation for work, and social security in the event of unemployment. Trade unions may be freely established and may function independently. Employees have the right to strike in order to protect their economic and social interests. The state guarantees the right of citizens to old-age and disability pensions, as well as to social assistance in the event of unemployment, sickness, widowhood, etc.

THE SEIMAS

Legislative power rests with the Seimas. It comprises 141 members, elected for a four-year term on the basis of universal, equal and direct suffrage by secret ballot. Any citizen who has attained 25 years of age may be a candidate for the Seimas. Members of the Seimas may not be found criminally responsible, may not be arrested, and may not be subjected to any other restrictions of personal freedom, without the consent of the Seimas. The Seimas convenes for two regular four-month sessions every year.

The Seimas considers and enacts amendments to the Constitution; enacts laws; adopts resolutions for the organization of referendums; announces presidential elections; approves or rejects the candidature of the Prime Minister, as proposed by the President of the Republic; establishes or abolishes government ministries, upon the recommendation of the Government; supervises the activities of the Government, with the power to express a vote of 'no confidence' in the Prime Minister or individual ministers; appoints judges to the Constitutional Court and the Supreme Court; approves the state budget and supervises the implementation thereof; establishes state taxes and other obligatory payments; ratifies or denounces international treaties whereto the republic is a party, and considers other issues of foreign policy; establishes administrative divisions of the republic; issues acts of amnesty; imposes direct administration and martial law, declares states of emergency, announces mobilization, and adopts decisions to use the armed forces.

THE PRESIDENT OF THE REPUBLIC

The President of the Republic is the Head of State. Any Lithuanian citizen by birth, who has lived in Lithuania for at least the three preceding years, who has reached 40 years of age and who is eligible for election to the Seimas, may be elected President of the Republic. The President is elected by the citizens of the republic, on the basis of universal, equal and direct suffrage by secret ballot, for a term of five years. No person may be elected to the office for more than two consecutive terms.

The President resolves basic issues of foreign policy and, in conjunction with the Government, implements foreign policy; signs international treaties and submits them to the Seimas for ratification; appoints or recalls, upon the recommendation of the Government, diplomatic representatives of Lithuania in foreign states and international organizations; appoints, upon the approval of the Seimas, the Prime Minister, and charges him or her with forming the Government, and approves its composition; removes, upon the approval of the Seimas, the Prime Minister from office; appoints or dismisses individual ministers, upon the recommendation of the Prime Minister; appoints or dismisses, upon the approval of the Seimas, the Commander-in-Chief of the armed forces and the head of the Security Service.

THE GOVERNMENT

Executive power is held by the Government of the Republic (Council of Ministers), which consists of the Prime Minister and other ministers. The Prime Minister is appointed and dismissed by the President of the Republic, with the approval of the Seimas. Ministers

LITHUANIA

are appointed by the President, on the nomination of the Prime Minister.

The Government administers the affairs of the country, protects the inviolability of the territory of Lithuania, and ensures state security and public order; implements laws and resolutions of the Seimas as well as presidential decrees; co-ordinates the activities of the ministries and other governmental institutions; prepares the draft state budget and submits it to the Seimas; executes the state budget and reports to the Seimas on its fulfilment; drafts legislative proposals and submits them to the Seimas for consideration; establishes and maintains diplomatic representation with foreign countries and international organizations.

JUDICIAL SYSTEM

The judicial system is independent of the authority of the legislative and executive branches of government. It consists of a Constitutional Court, a Supreme Court, a Court of Appeal, and district and local courts (for details, see section on Judicial System below).

The Government

HEAD OF STATE

President: VALDAS ADAMKUS (inaugurated 12 July 2004).

COUNCIL OF MINISTERS
(April 2006)

A coalition of the Lithuanian Social Democratic Party (LSDP), the Lithuanian Labour Party (LLP) and the Peasants' and New Democracy Union (PNDU).

Prime Minister: ALGIRDAS MYKOLAS BRAZAUSKAS (LSDP).
Minister of the Economy: KĘSTUTIS DAUKŠYS (LLP).
Minister of Finance: ZIGMANTAS BALČYTIS (LSDP).
Minister of National Defence: GEDIMINAS KIRKILAS (LSDP).
Minister of Culture: VLADIMIRAS PRUDNIKOVAS (LLP).
Minister of Social Security and Labour: (vacant).
Minister of Justice: GINTAUTAS BUŽINSKAS (LLP).
Minister of Transport: PETRAS ČĖSNA (LSDP).
Minister of Health Care: ŽILVINAS PADAIGA (LLP).
Minister of Foreign Affairs: (vacant).
Minister of the Interior: GINTARAS FURMANAVIČIUS (LLP).
Minister of Agriculture: KAZIMIERA DANUTĖ PRUNSKIENĖ (PNDU).
Minister of Education and Science: REMIGIJUS MOTUZAS (LSDP).
Minister of the Environment: ARŪNAS KUNDROTAS (LSDP).

MINISTRIES

Office of the President: S. Daukanto 3/8, Vilnius 01021; tel. (5) 262-8986; fax (5) 212-6210; e-mail info@president.lt; internet www.president.lt.

Office of the Prime Minister: Gedimino pr. 11, Vilnius 01103; tel. (5) 266-3874; fax (5) 216-3877; e-mail kasp@lrvk.lt; internet www.ministraspirmininkas.lt.

Ministry of Agriculture: Gedimino pr. 19, Vilnius 01103; tel. (5) 239-1032; fax (5) 239-1212; e-mail zum@zum.lt; internet www.zum.lt.

Ministry of Culture: J. Basanavičiaus 5, Vilnius 01118; tel. (5) 261-9486; fax (5) 262-3120; e-mail culture@muza.lt; internet www.muza.lt.

Ministry of the Economy: Gedimino pr. 38/2, Vilnius 01104; tel. (5) 262-2416; fax (5) 262-3974; e-mail kanc@ukmin.lt; internet www.ukmin.lt.

Ministry of Education and Science: A. Volano 2/7, Vilnius 01516; tel. (5) 274-3126; fax (5) 261-2077; e-mail smmin@smm.lt; internet www.smm.lt.

Ministry of the Environment: A. Jakšto 4/9, Vilnius 01105; tel. (5) 266-3661; fax (5) 266-3663; e-mail kanceliarija@am.lt; internet www.am.lt.

Ministry of Finance: J. Tumo-Vaižganto 8 A/2, Vilnius 01512; tel. (5) 239-0005; fax (5) 212-6387; e-mail finmin@finmin.lt; internet www.finmin.lt.

Ministry of Foreign Affairs: J. Tumo-Vaižganto 2, Vilnius 01511; tel. (5) 236-2444; fax (5) 231-3090; e-mail urm@urm.lt; internet www.urm.lt.

Ministry of Health Care: Vilniaus 33, Vilnius 01119; tel. (5) 262-1625; fax (5) 212-4601; e-mail info@sam.lt; internet www.sam.lt.

Ministry of the Interior: Šventaragio 2, Vilnius 01510; tel. (5) 271-8451; fax (5) 271-8551; e-mail atstovasspaudai@vrm.lt; internet www.vrm.lt.

Ministry of Justice: Gedimino pr. 30/1, Vilnius 01104; tel. (5) 262-4670; fax (5) 262-5940; e-mail tminfo@tic.lt; internet www.tm.lt.

Ministry of National Defence: Totorių 25/3, Vilnius 01121; tel. (5) 262-4821; fax (5) 212-6082; e-mail vis@kam.lt; internet www.kam.lt.

Ministry of Social Security and Labour: A. Vivulskio 11, Vilnius 03610; tel. (5) 266-4201; fax (5) 266-4209; e-mail post@socmin.lt; internet www.socmin.lt.

Ministry of Transport: Gedimino pr. 17, Vilnius 01505; tel. (5) 239-3911; fax (5) 212-4335; e-mail transp@transp.lt; internet www.transp.lt.

President and Legislature

PRESIDENT

Presidential Election, First Ballot, 13 June 2004

Candidates	Valid votes cast	% of valid votes cast
Valdas Adamkus	387,837	31.14
Kazimiera Danutė Prunskienė	264,681	21.25
Petras Auskevičius	240,413	19.30
Vilija Blinkevičiūtė	204,819	16.45
Česlovas Juršėnas	147,610	11.85
Total	**1,245,360**	**100.00**

Second Ballot, 27 June 2004

Candidates	Valid votes cast	% of valid votes cast
Valdas Adamkus	723,891	52.65
Kazimiera Danutė Prunskienė	651,024	47.35
Total	**1,374,915**	**100.00**

LEGISLATURE

Seimas
(Parliament)

Gedimino pr. 53, Vilnius 01109; tel. (5) 239-6212; fax (5) 239-6330; e-mail priim@lrs.lt; internet www.lrs.lt.

Chairman: VIKTORAS MUNTIANAS (LLP).

General Election, 10 and 24 October 2004

Parties and blocs	% of votes	Seats	Single-member constituency seats	Total seats
Lithuanian Labour Party	28.44	22	17	39
Working for Lithuania coalition*	20.65	16	15	31
Homeland Union (Conservatives, Political Prisoners and Deportees, Christian Democrats)	14.75	11	14	25
Order and Justice coalition†	11.36	9	2	11
Liberal and Centre Union	9.19	7	11	18
Peasants' and New Democracy Union	6.60	5	5	10
Lithuanian Poles' Electoral Action	3.79	—	2	2
Christian-Conservative Social Union	1.96	—	—	—
Lithuanian Christian Democrats	1.37	—	—	—
Others	1.89	—	—	—
Independents	—	—	5	5
Total	**100.00**	**70**	**71**	**141**

* A coalition of the Lithuanian Social Democratic Party and the New Union (Social Liberals).
† A coalition of the Liberal Democratic Party and the Lithuanian People's Union for A Free Lithuania.

LITHUANIA

Election Commission

Lietuvos Republikos Vyriausioji rinkimų komisija (Central Electoral Committee of the Republic of Lithuania): Gedimino pr. 53, Vilnius 8860715; tel. (5) 239-6969; fax (5) 239-6960; e-mail rinkim@lrs.lt; internet www.vrk.lt; Chair. ZENONAS VAIGAUSKAS.

Political Organizations

In mid-2003 37 political parties were registered with the Ministry of Justice. The following were among the most significant in 2005.

Christian-Conservative Social Union (Krikščionių Konservatorių Socialinė Sąjunga): Odminių g. 5, Vilnius 01122; tel. and fax (5) 212-6874; e-mail sekretoriatas@nks.lt; internet www.nks.lt; f. 2000; centre-right; Chair. GEDIMINAS VAGNORIUS.

Homeland Union—Conservatives, Political Prisoners and Deportees, Christian Democrats (HU) (Tėvynės Sąjunga—TS): L. Stuokos-Gucevičiaus g. 11, Vilnius 01122; tel. and fax (5) 212-1657; fax (5) 278-4722; e-mail sekretoriatas@tsajunga.lt; internet www.tslk.lt; f. 1993 as the Conservative Party of Lithuania (Homeland Union); absorbed the Lithuanian Rightist Union in Nov. 2003; merged with the Lithuanian Union of Political Prisoners and Deportees in Feb. 2004, and name changed as above; Chair. ANDRIUS KUBILIUS; 16,000 mems.

Liberal and Centre Union (Liberalų Centro Sąjunga): Vilniaus g. 22/1, Vilnius 01119; tel. (5) 231-3264; fax (5) 261-9363; e-mail info@lics.lt; internet www.lics.lt; f. 2003 by a merger of the Lithuanian Centre Union, the Lithuanian Liberal Union and the Modern Christian-Democratic Union; Chair. VYTAUTAS BOGUSIS (acting); over 5,000 mems.

Liberal Democratic Party (LDP) (Liberalų demokratų partija): Gedimino pr. 10/1, Vilnius 01103; tel. and fax (5) 269-1618; e-mail liberaldemokratai@ldp.lt; internet www.ldp.lt; f. 2002; right-wing; Chair. ROLANDAS PAKSAS; 1,500 mems.

Lithuanian Christian Democrats (Lietuvos Krikščionys Demokratai): Pylimo g. 36/2, Vilnius 01135; tel. (5) 262-6126; fax (5) 212-7387; e-mail lkdp@takas.lt; internet www.lkdp.lt; f. 2001 by merger of the Christian Democratic Party of Lithuania and the Christian Democratic Union; Chair. VALENTINAS STUNDYS; 12,000 mems.

Lithuanian Green Party (Lietuvos žalioji partija): POB 800, 01014 Vilnius 55; tel. (374) 2349693; e-mail zigmasvaisvila@lrs.lt; internet www.zalieji.lt; f. 1989; Chair. RŪTA GAJAUSKAITE; 400 mems.

Lithuanian Labour Party (LLP) (Darbo Partija): Lukiškių g. 5, Vilnius 01108; tel. (5) 210-7152; fax (5) 210-7153; e-mail darbopartija@one.lt; internet www.darbopartija.lt; f. 2003; Chair. VIKTOR USPASKIKH.

Lithuanian Liberal Movement (Lietuvos liberalų sąjūdis): A. Rotundo g. 3–4, Vilnius 01111; tel. and fax 249-6959; e-mail info@liberalusajudis.lt; internet www.liberalusajudis.lt; f. 2006; formed by a splinter group of the Liberal and Centre Union; Leader PETRAS AUŠTREVIČIUS.

Lithuanian National Union (Lietuvių Tautininkų Sąjunga): Gedimino pr. 22, Vilnius 01103; tel. (5) 262-4935; fax (5) 261-7310; e-mail lietauta@takas.lt; internet www.lts.lt; f. 1924; refounded 1989; Chair. GEDIMINAS SAKALNIKAS; 3,000 mems.

Lithuanian People's Union For A Free Lithuania (Lietuvos liaudies Sąjunga 'Už teisingą Lietuvą'): Rasų g. 56, Vilnius 11351; tel. (5) 263-0429; f. 1996; Chair. JULIUS VESELKA.

Lithuanian Polish Electoral Action (Akcji Wyborczej Polaków na Litwie—AWPL)(Lietuvos lenkų rinkimų akcija—LLRA): Didžioji g. 40, Vilnius 01128; tel. (5) 212-3388; f. 1994; Chair. WALDEMAR TOMASZEWSKI.

Lithuanian Polish People's Party (Lietuvos Lenkų Liaudies Partija/Polska Partia Ludowa): Didžioji 40, Vilnius 01128; tel. and fax (5) 212-3838; tel. lllp@mail.lt; internet www.lllp.lt; f. 2002; Chair. ANTONINA POŁTAWIEC.

Lithuanian Russians' Union (Soyuz Russkikh Litvy/Lietuvos rusų sąjunga): Pamėnkalnio g. 3–27, Vilnius 01116; tel. (5) 262-4248; e-mail sergejus.dmitrijevas@lrs.lt; internet www.sojuzrus.visiems.lt; f. 1995; Chair. SERGEJ DMITRIJEV.

Lithuanian Social Democratic Party (LSDP) (Lietuvos Socialdemokratų Partija): Barboros Radvilaites g. 1, Vilnius 01124; tel. (5) 261-3907; fax (5) 261-5420; e-mail info@lsdp.lt; internet www.lsdp.lt; absorbed the Lithuanian Democratic Labour Party in 2001; Chair. ALGIRDAS BRAZAUSKAS; 11,000 mems.

Lithuanian Socialist Party (LSP) (Lietuvos Socialistų Partija): Jasinskio g. 9/411, Vilnius 0111; tel. and fax (5) 246-0698; e-mail lsp@takas.lt; internet www.lsp.w3.lt; f. 1994; Chair. MINDAUGAS STAKVILEVIČIUS.

National Centre Party (NCP) (Nacionalinė Centro Partija): Vilnius; tel. (6) 982-2122; e-mail info@ncp.lt; internet www.ncp.lt; f. 2003 by fmr mems of the Lithuanian Centre Union unwilling to merge into the Lithuanian Liberal and Centre Union (q.v.); Chair. ROMUALDAS OZOLAS; 1,000 mems.

National Progress Party (Tautos Pažangos Partija): Vilnius; tel. (5) 239-6656; fax (5) 239-6779; e-mail egidijus.klumbys@lrs.lt; internet www.tpp.lt; active 1916–24, re-est. 1994; Chair. EGIDIJUS KLUMBYS; 1,100 mems.

New Union (Social Liberals) (Naujoji sąjunga—Socialliberalai): Gedimino pr. 10/1, Vilnius 01103; tel. (5) 260-7600; fax (5) 210-7602; e-mail centras@nsajunga.lt; internet www.nsajunga.lt; f. 1998; centre-left; Chair. ARTŪRAS PAULAUSKAS.

Peasants' and New Democracy Union (PNDU) (Valstiečių ir Naujosios Demokratijos Sąjunga—VNDS): Gedimino pr. 24, Vilnius 01103; tel. and fax (5) 212-0822; e-mail info@vnds.lt; internet www.vnds.lt; f. 2001 by the merger of the New Democracy Party and the Lithuanian Peasants' Party; Chair. KAZIMIERA DANUTĖ PRUNSKIENĖ; 1,500 mems.

Diplomatic Representation

EMBASSIES IN LITHUANIA

Austria: Gaono g. 6, Vilnius 01131; tel. (5) 266-0580; fax (5) 279-1363; e-mail wilna-ob@bmaa.gv.at; Ambassador Dr MICHAEL SCHWARZINGER.

Belarus: Mindaugo g. 13, Vilnius 03225; tel. (5) 266-2200; fax (5) 266-2212; e-mail lithuania@belembassy.org; internet www.belarus.lt; Ambassador ULADZIMIR DRAZHIN (designate).

China, People's Republic: Algirdo g. 36, Vilnius 03218; tel. (5) 216-2861; fax (5) 216-2682; e-mail chinaemb_lithuania@mfa.gov.cn; internet www.chinaembassy.lt; Ambassador YANG XIUPING.

Czech Republic: Birutės. 16, Vilnius 08117; tel. (5) 266-1040; fax (5) 266-1066; e-mail vilnius@embassy.mzv.cz; internet www.mzv.cz/vilnius; Ambassador ALOIS BUCHTA.

Denmark: T. Kosciuškos. 36, Vilnius 01100; tel. (5) 264-8760; fax (5) 231-2300; e-mail vnoamb@um.dk; internet www.ambvilnius.um.dk; Ambassador EVA JANSON.

Estonia: Mickevičiaus g. 4A, Vilnius 08119; tel. (5) 278-0200; fax (5) 278-0201; e-mail sekretar@estemb.lt; internet www.estemb.lt; Ambassador ANDRES TROPP.

Finland: Klaipėdos. g. 6, Vilnius 01117; tel. (5) 212-1621; fax (5) 212-2463; e-mail sanomat.vil@formin.fi; internet www.finland.lt; Ambassador TIMO LAHELMA.

France: Švarco g. 1, Vilnius 01131; tel. (5) 212-2979; fax (5) 212-4211; e-mail ambafrance.vilnius@diplomatie.gouv.fr; internet www.ambafrance-lt.org; Ambassador GUY YELDA.

Georgia: Poškos g. 13, Vilnius 08123; tel. (5) 273-6959; fax (5) 272-3623; e-mail cons.georgia@post.omnitel.net; Ambassador DAVIT APSIAURI.

Germany: Z. Sierakausko g. 24/8, Vilnius 03105; tel. (5) 213-1815; fax (5) 213-1812; e-mail germ.emb@takas.lt; internet www.deutschebotschaft-wilna.lt; Ambassador VOLKER HEINSBURG.

Holy See: Kosciuškos. 28, Vilnius 01100; tel. (5) 212-3696; fax (5) 212-4228; e-mail nuntiusbalt@aiva.lt; Apostolic Nuncio Most Rev. PETER STEPHAN ZURBRIGGEN (Titular Archbishop of Glastonia—Glastonbury).

Ireland: Business Centre 2000, 3rd Floor, Jogailos g. 4, Vilnius 01116; tel. (5) 269-0044; fax (5) 269-0100; e-mail ireland.vilnius@gmail.com; f. 2005; Ambassador DONAL DENHAM.

Italy: Tauro g. 12, Vilnius 01114; tel. (5) 212–0620; fax (5) 212-0405; e-mail ambasciata@ambitvilnius.lt; Ambassador GIULIO PRIGIONI.

Kazakhstan: Birutės g. 20A/35, Vilnius 08117; tel. (5) 212-2123; fax (5) 231-3580; e-mail kazemb@iti.lt; internet kazakhstan.embassy.lt; Ambassador RASHID IBRAYEV.

Latvia: M. K. Čiurlionio g. 76, Vilnius 03100; tel. (5) 213-1260; fax (5) 213-1130; e-mail embassy.lithuania@mfa.gov.lv; Ambassador HARDIJS BAUMANIS.

Netherlands: Business Centre 2000, 4th Floor, Jogailos g. 4, Vilnius 01116; tel. (5) 269-0072; fax (5) 269-0073; e-mail vil@minbuza.nk; internet www.netherlandsembassy.lt; Ambassador ANNEMUIKE RUIGROK.

Norway: Mėsinių. 5/2, Vilnius 01133; tel. (5) 261-0000; fax (5) 261-0100; e-mail emb.vilnius@mfa.no; internet www.norvegija.lt; Ambassador KÅRE HAUGE.

Poland: Smėlio g. 20A, Vilnius 10323; tel. (5) 270-9001; fax (5) 270-9007; e-mail ampol@tdd.lt; internet www.polandembassy.lt; Ambassador JANUSZ SKOLIMOWSKI.

Romania: Vivulskio g. 19, Vilnius 03115; tel. (5) 231-0527; fax (5) 231-0652; e-mail ambromania@romania.lt; internet www.romania.lt; Ambassador GHEORGHE TOKAY.

Russia: Latvių g. 53/54, Vilnius 08113; tel. (5) 272-1763; fax (5) 272-3877; e-mail post@rusemb.lt; internet www.rusemb.lt; Ambassador Boris A. Tsepov.
Sweden: Didžioji g. 16, Vilnius 01128; tel. (5) 268-5010; fax (5) 268-5030; e-mail ambassaden.vilnius@foreign.ministry.se; internet www.swedishembassy.lt; Ambassador Malin Kärre.
Turkey: Didžioji g. 37, Vilnius 01128; tel. (5) 264-9570; fax (5) 212-3277; e-mail turemvil@eunet.lt; Ambassador Kadriye Sanivar Kizildeli.
Ukraine: Teatro g. 4, Vilnius 03107; tel. (5) 212-1536; fax (5) 212-0475; e-mail emb_lt@mfa.gov.ua; Ambassador Borys P. Klymchuk.
United Kingdom: Antakalnio g. 2, Vilnius 10308; tel. (5) 246-2900; fax (5) 246-2901; e-mail be-vilnius@britain.lt; internet www.britain.lt; Ambassador Colin Roberts.
USA: Akmenų g. 6, Vilnius 03106; tel. (5) 266-5500; fax (5) 266-5510; e-mail mail@usembassy.lt; internet www.usembassy.lt; Ambassador John A. Cloud (Jr) (designate).

Judicial System

The organs of justice are the Supreme Court, the Court of Appeal, district courts, local courts of administrative areas and a special court—the Commercial Court. The Seimas (Parliament) appoints and dismisses from office the judges of the Supreme Court in response to representations made by the President of the Republic (based upon the recommendation of the chairman of the Supreme Court). Judges of the Court of Appeal are appointed by the President with the approval of the Seimas (on the recommendation of the Minister of Justice), while judges of district and local courts are appointed and dismissed by the President. The Council of Judges submits recommendations to the President of the Republic concerning the appointment of judges, as well as their promotion, transfer or dismissal from office.

The Constitutional Court decides on the constitutionality of acts of the Seimas, as well as of the President and the Government. It consists of nine judges, who are appointed by the Seimas for a single term of nine years; one-third of the Court's members are replaced every three years.

The Office of the Prosecutor-General is an autonomous institution of the judiciary, comprising the Prosecutor-General and local and district prosecutors' offices which are subordinate to him. The Prosecutor-General and his deputies are appointed for terms of seven years by the President, subject to approval by the Seimas, while the prosecutors are appointed by the Prosecutor-General. The Office of the Prosecutor-General incorporates the Department for Crime Investigation. The State Arbitration decides cases of business litigation. A six-volume Civil Code, in accordance with European Union and international law, came into effect in 2001, replacing the Soviet civil legal system, which had, hitherto, remained in operation.

Constitutional Court of the Republic of Lithuania (Lietuvos Respublikos Konstitucinis Teismas): Gedimino pr. 36, Vilnius 01104; tel. (5) 261-1466; fax (5) 212-7975; e-mail mailbox@lrkt.lt; internet www.lrkt.lt; f. 1993; Chair. Egidijus Kūris.

Court of Appeal: Gedimino pr. 40/1, Vilnius 01503; tel. (5) 266-3433; fax (5) 266-3060; Chair. Vytas Milius.

Supreme Court of Lithuania (Lietuvos Aukščiausiasis Teismas): Gynėjų g. 6, Vilnius 01109; tel. (5) 261-0560; fax (5) 262-7950; e-mail lat@tic.lt; internet www.lat.litlex.lt; Chair. Vytautas Greičius.

Office of the Prosecutor-General: A. Smetonos 4, Vilnius 01515; tel. (5) 266-2305; fax (5) 266-2317; e-mail cekelil@lrgp.lt; Prosecutor-General Algimantas Valantinas (designate).

Religion

Lithuania adopted Christianity at the end of the 14th century. However, the country's geographical position and history have long predetermined a diversity of religious communities. The restoration of independence, in 1991, stimulated the revival of religious practice, which was widely suppressed during the Soviet period. Religious communities that existed prior to Soviet rule were re-established and new ones came into existence. In 2001 there were 923 traditional and 176 non-traditional religious organizations registered in the country.

CHRISTIANITY

The Roman Catholic Church

Roman Catholicism has been the principal religious affiliation in Lithuania since its adoption by the Lithuanian State in 1387. The Roman Catholic Church in Lithuania comprises two archdioceses and five dioceses. There are seminaries at Vilnius, Kaunas and Telšiai. At 31 December 2003 the Roman Catholic Church estimated there to be 2.8m. adherents in Lithuania (equivalent to some 79% of the population).

Lithuanian Bishops' Conference
Skapo 4, Vilnius 01122; tel. (5) 212-5455; fax (5) 212-0972; e-mail lvk@lcnl.lt; internet lvk.lcn.lt; f. 2002; Pres. Cardinal Audrys Juozas Bačkis (Archbishop of Vilnius).

Archbishop of Kaunas: Most Rev. Sigitas Tamkevičius, Rotušės a. 14A, Kaunas 44279; tel. (37) 409026; fax (37) 320090; e-mail kurija@kn.lcn.lt; internet www.kaunas.lcn.lt.

Archbishop of Vilnius: Cardinal Audrys Juozas Bačkis, Šventaragio 4, Vilnius 01122; tel. (5) 262-7098; fax (5) 212-2807; e-mail curia@vilnensis.lt; internet vilnius.lcn.lt.

Byzantine Rite

Established in 1596 by the Lithuanian Brasta (Brest) Church Union, which permitted Orthodox clergymen to retain the Eastern rite, but transferred their allegiance to the Roman Pontiff, the Byzantine-rite or 'Greek' Catholic Church is headed by the Archbishop-Major of Lviv (Ukraine). At 1 January 1996 there were five communities in Lithuania, with three priests, one monastic order and one church returned to the adherents in Vilnius.

Representation of the Order of St Basil the Great in Lithuania: Aušros Vartų 7B, Vilnius 01129; tel. (5) 212-2578; Centre of the Byzantine Rite Catholics (Uniates) in Lithuania; Superior Pavlo Jachimec.

Orthodox Churches

Russian Orthodox Church (Moscow Patriarchate)

The first communities appeared during the 12th century and the first monastery was established in Vilnius in 1597. While Lithuania formed part of the Russian Empire (1795–1915), Orthodoxy was considered the state religion. At 1 January 1996 there were 41 communities. There were an estimated 180,000 adherents in 2001.

Lithuanian Orthodox Church (Moscow Patriarchate): Aušros Vartų 10/3, Vilnius 01129; tel. (5) 212-7765; e-mail lsb@takas.lt; internet www.orthodoxy.lt; Metropolitan of Vilnius and Lithuania Chryzostom (Martishkin).

Lithuanian Old Believers Pomor Church

The first communities settled in Lithuania in 1679 and the Church was established in 1709. At 1 January 1996 there were approximately 34,000 adherents (mainly ethnic Russians) in 58 communities, with 23 clergymen and 50 churches.

Supreme Council of the Old Believers Pomor Church in Lithuania: Naujininkų g. 20, Vilnius 02109; tel. (5) 269-5271; f. 1925; Chair. Mark Semionov (acting).

Protestant Churches

Lithuanian Evangelical Lutheran Church

The first parishes were established in 1539–69. In 1563 the Evangelical Church divided into Lutheran and Reformed Churches. Church attendance revived after 1990. The Lithuanian Evangelical Lutheran Church comprises one diocese. At 1 January 1998 there were approximately 30,000 adherents in 54 parishes (with 18 priests and 41 churches).

Consistory of the Lithuanian Evangelical Lutheran Church (Lietuvos Evangeliku-Liuteronu Bažnycia): Tumo-Vaižganto 50, Tauragė 72263; tel. and fax (446) 61145; e-mail konsistorya@takas.lt; internet www.liuteronai.lt; Bishop Mindaugas Sabutis.

Lithuanian Evangelical Reformed Church

The first parishes were established after 1563. At 1 January 1996 there were approximately 12,000 adherents in 11 parishes (with two pastors and nine churches).

Lithuanian Evangelical Reformed Church: POB 661, Vilnius 04008; tel. and fax (5) 245-0656; Pres. of Synodie Collegium Povilas A. Jašinskas.

Lithuanian Baptist Union and Other Churches

Parliament awarded the Baptist Union 'recognized' status in July 2001, the first religious community to be awarded this status. There has been a Baptist presence in Lithuania since the 18th century. The United Methodist Church, the New Apostolic Church, the Pentecostal Union and the Adventist Church ETH are all similarly seeking such status, beyond their status as 'registered'.

ISLAM

Sunni Islam is the religion of the ethnic Tatars of Lithuania. The first Tatar communities settled there in the 14th century. The first mosque in Vilnius was erected in 1558. At 1 January 1996 there were five Tatar religious communities (with 10 clergymen, four

LITHUANIA

mosques and one prayer house). In 2001 there were an estimated 5,000 adherents in Lithuania.

Sunni Muslim Religious Centre—Muftiate in Lithuania: A. Vivulskio g. 3, Vilnius 03220; tel. (5) 242-5124; fax (5) 260-3451; e-mail ramazanas@is.lt; f. 1998; Mufti ROMUALDAS KRINICKIS.

JUDAISM

The first Jewish communities appeared in Lithuania in the 15th century. In the 15th–17th centuries Lithuania, and particularly Vilnius, was an important centre of Jewish culture and religion. Before the Second World War approximately 200,000 Jews lived in Lithuania; an estimated 90% were murdered during the German occupation (1941–44). At 1 January 1996 there were five religious communities, with two synagogues (in Vilnius and Kaunas). There were an estimated 5,000 adherents in Lithuania in 2001.

Jewish Community of Lithuania: Pylimo g. 4, Vilnius 01117; tel. (5) 261-3003; fax (5) 212-7915; e-mail jewishcom@post.5ci.lt; internet www.litjews.org; f. 1992 to replace and expand the role of the Jewish Cultural Society; Chair. SIMONAS ALPERAVIČIUS; Chief Rabbi CHAIM BURSHTEIN.

The Press

In 2004 there were 340 newspapers and 536 periodicals published in Lithuania.

The publications listed below are in Lithuanian, except where otherwise indicated.

PRINCIPAL NEWSPAPERS

Kauno diena (Kaunas Daily): Vytauto pr. 27, Kaunas 44352; tel. (37) 341971; fax (37) 423404; e-mail redakcija@kaunodiena.lt; internet www.kaunodiena.lt; f. 1945; 6 a week; Editor-in-Chief AUŠRA LEKA; circ. 50,000.

Klaipėda: Šaulių g. 21, Klaipėda 92233; tel. (46) 397750; fax (46) 397700; e-mail office@klaipeda.daily.lt; internet www.klaipeda.daily.lt; Editor VALDEMARAS PUODŽIŪNAS.

Kurier Wileński (Vilnius Courier): Birbynių g. 4A, Vilnius 02121; tel. and fax (5) 260-8444; e-mail internet@kurierwilenski.lt; internet www.kurierwilenski.lt; f. 1953; 5 a week; in Polish; Editor-in-Chief ALEKSANDER BOROWIK; circ. 8,000.

Lietuvos aidas (Lithuanian Echo): Maironio g. 1, Vilnius 01124; tel. (52) 261-5208; fax (5) 212-4876; e-mail centr@aidas.lt; internet www.aidas.lt; f. 1917; re-est. 1990; 5 a week; Editor-in-Chief ROMA GRINIŪTĖ-GRINBERGIENĖ; circ. 20,000.

Lietuvos rytas (Lithuanian Morning): Gedimino pr. 12A, Vilnius 01103; tel. (5) 274-3600; fax (5) 274-3700; e-mail daily@lrytas.lt; internet www.lrytas.lt; f. 1990; 6 a week, with 3 supplements per week; Editor-in-Chief GEDVYDAS VAINAUSKAS; circ. 65,000 (Mon.–Fri.), 200,000 (Sat.).

Lietuvos žinios (Lithuanian News): Kęstučio g. 4, Vilnius 08117; tel. (5) 275-4904; fax (5) 275-3131; e-mail lzinios@lzinios.lt; internet www.lzinios.lt; 6 a week; Editor-in-Chief RYTAS STASELIS.

Respublika (Republic): A. Smetonos g. 2, Vilnius 01115; tel. (5) 212-3112; fax (5) 212-3538; e-mail press@respublika.lt; f. 1989; 6 a week in Lithuanian, with 5 Russian editions per week; Editor-in-Chief VITAS TOMKUS; circ. 55,000.

Šiaulių kraštas: P. Višinskio g. 26, Šiauliai 77155; tel. (41) 591555; fax (41) 524581; e-mail redakcija@skrastas.lt; internet www.skrastas.lt.

Vakaro žinios (Evening News): Jogailos g. 11/2-11, Vilnius 01116; tel. and fax (5) 261-6875; e-mail vakarozinios@takas.lt; daily; circ. 70,000.

Vakarų ekspresas (Western Express): H. Manto 2, Klaipėda 92138; tel. (46) 218074; fax (46) 310102; e-mail sek.ve@balt.net; internet www.vakaru-ekspresas.lt; f. 1990; 6 a week; Editor-in-Chief GINTARAS TOMKUS; circ. 15,000.

Verslo žinios (Business News): J. Jasinskio 16A, Vilnius 01112; tel. (5) 252-6300; fax (5) 252-6313; e-mail info@vzinios.lt; internet www.vz.lt; f. 1994; 5 a week; circ. 9,000.

PRINCIPAL PERIODICALS

Apžvalga (Review): Pylimo 36/2, Vilnius 01135; tel. (5) 261-1151; fax (5) 261-0503; f. 1990; every two weeks; publ. by Christian Democratic Party of Lithuania; Editor-in-Chief DARIUS VILIMIAS; circ. 2,000.

Artuma (Proximity): M. Daukšos g. 21, Kaunas 44282; tel. and fax (37) 209683; e-mail redakcija@artuma.lt; f. 1989; as *Caritas*; name changed as above in 1997; monthly; Catholic family magazine; Editor-in-Chief DARIUS CHMIELIAUSKAS; circ. 7,000.

Dienovidis (Midday): Pilies g. 23A, Vilnius 01123; tel. (5) 212-1911; fax (5) 212-3101; e-mail dienovidis@takas.lt; f. 1990; weekly; Editor-in-Chief ALDONA ŽEMAITYTĖ; circ. 4,500.

Kultūros barai (Domains of Culture): Latako g. 3, Vilnius 01125; tel. (5) 261-6696; fax (5) 261-0538; e-mail kulturosbarai@takas.lt; internet www.eurozine.com; f. 1965; monthly; independent cultural magazine; Editor-in-Chief BRONYS SAVUKYNAS; circ. 3,000.

Laima: K. Donelaičio g. 70–10, Kaunas 44248; tel. (5) 272-8083; fax (5) 272-1614; e-mail laima@redakcija.lt; internet www.redakcija.lt/laima; f. 1993; monthly; lifestyle and feature magazine for women; Editor-in-Chief GITANA BUKAUSKIENĖ; circ. 30,000.

Liaudies kultūra (Ethnic Culture): Barboros Radvilaitės 8, Vilnius 01124; tel. (5) 261-3412; fax (5) 212-4033; e-mail lkredaktore@lfcc.lt; internet www.lfcc.lt; f. 1988; 6 a year; Editor-in-Chief DALIA ANTANINA RASTENIENĖ; circ. 800.

Lietuvos sportas (Lithuanian Sports): Odminių g. 9, Vilnius 01122; tel. and fax (5) 261-6757; f. 1922; re-est. 1992; 3 a week; Editor-in-Chief BRONIUS ČEKANAUSKAS; circ. 18,000.

Lietuvos ūkis (Lithuanian Economy): Vilnius; tel. (5) 213-6718; f. 1921; monthly; Editor-in-Chief ALGIRDAS JASIONIS.

Literatūra ir menas (Literature and Art): Mesiniu 4, Vilnius 01133; tel. (5) 269-1977; fax (5) 212-6556; e-mail lmenas@takas.lt; internet www.culture.lt/lmenas; f. 1946; weekly; publ. by the Lithuanian Writers' Union; Editor-in-Chief KORNELIJUS PLATELIS; circ. 2,000.

Lithuania in the World: T. Vrublevskio g. 6, Vilnius 01100; tel. (5) 261-4432; fax (5) 212-5560; e-mail info@liw.lt; internet www.liw.lt; f. 1993; 6 a year; in English and Lithuanian; Exec. Editor JOLANTA LAUMENSKAITĖ; circ. 15,000.

Magazyn Wileński (Vilnius Journal): Laisvės pr. 60, Vilnius 05120; tel. (5) 242-7718; fax (5) 242-9065; e-mail magazyn@magwil.lt; internet www.magwil.lt; f. 1990; monthly; political, cultural; in Polish; Editor-in-Chief MICHAŁ MACKIEWICZ; circ. 5,000.

Metai (Year): K. Sirvydo g. 6, Vilnius 01101; tel. (5) 261-7344; e-mail metai@takas.lt; f. 1991; monthly; journal of the Lithuanian Writers' Union; Editor-in-Chief DANIELIUS MUŠINSKAS; circ. 2,000.

Mokslas ir gyvenimas (Science and Life): Antakalnio g. 36, Vilnius 10305; tel. and fax (5) 234-1572; e-mail mgredacija@takas.lt; internet ausis.gf.vu.lt/mg/; f. 1957; monthly; popular and historical science; Editor-in-Chief JUOZAS BALDAUSKAS; circ. 3,500.

Moteris (Woman): P. Smuglevičiaus g. 21, Vilnius 08311; tel. and fax (5) 247-7711; e-mail info@moteris.lt; internet www.moteris.lt; f. 1952; monthly; popular, for women; Editor-in-Chief EGLE STRIAUKIENE; circ. 20,000.

Mūsų gamta (Our Nature): Rudens g. 33B, Vilnius 01214; tel. (5) 269-6964; f. 1964; 6 a year; Editor-in-Chief VYTAUTAS KLOVAS; circ. 2,500.

Naujasis Židinys-Aidai (New Hearth–Echoes): Tilto g. 8/3–11, Vilnius 01001; tel. and fax (5) 212-2363; e-mail aidai@aidai.lt; internet www.aidai.lt/zidinys; f. 1991; monthly; religion and culture; Editor-in-Chief SAULIUS DRAZDAUSKAS; circ. 1,000.

Nemunas: Gedimino g. 45, Kaunas 44239; tel. and fax (37) 322244; e-mail nemunas.redakcija@centras.lt; f. 1967; weekly; journal of the Lithuanian Writers' Union; Editor-in-Chief VIKTORAS RUDZIANSKAS; circ. 1,500.

Panelė (Young Miss): P. Smuglevičiaus g. 23, Vilnius 08311; tel. (5) 247-7716; fax (5) 247-7715; e-mail magazine@panele.lt; internet www.panele.lt; f. 1994; monthly; popular, for ages 12–25; Editor-in-Chief JURGA BALTRUKONYTĖ; circ. 66,000.

Septynios meno dienos (7 meno dienos) (Seven Days of Art): Bernardinų g. 10, Vilnius 01124; tel. (5) 261-3039; fax (5) 261-1926; e-mail 7md@takas.lt; internet www.culture.lt/7menodienos; f. 1992; weekly; Editor-in-Chief LINAS VILDŽIŪNAS; circ. 1,500.

Švyturys (Beacon): Maironio g. 1, Vilnius 01124; tel. (5) 261-0791; fax (5) 261-4690; f. 1949; monthly; politics, economics, history, culture, fiction; Editor-in-Chief JUOZAS BAUŠYS; circ. 10,000.

Tremtinys (Deportee): Laisvės al. 39, Kaunas 44282; tel. (37) 323204; e-mail tremtinys@takas.lt; internet www.lpkts.lt; f. 1988; weekly; publ. by the Lithuanian Union of Political Prisoners and Deportees; Editor-in-Chief AUDRONĖ KAMINSKIENĖ; circ. 4,500.

Valstiečių laikraštis (Farmer's Newspaper): Laisvės pr. 60, Vilnius 05120; tel. and fax (5) 242-1281; e-mail redakcija@valstietis.lt; internet www.valstietis.lt; f. 1940; 2 a week; Editor-in-Chief JONAS ŠVOBA; circ. 68,000.

Vasario 16 (16 February): J. Gruodžio g. 9/404, Kaunas 44293; tel. (37) 225219; f. 1988; fortnightly; journal of the Lithuanian Democratic Party; Sec. PRIMAS NOREIKA; circ. 1,600.

LITHUANIA   *Directory*

NEWS AGENCIES

Baltic News Service (BNS): Jogailos g. 9/1, Vilnius 01116; tel. (5) 231-2410; fax (5) 268-1515; e-mail bns@bns.lt; f. 1991; Dir Jurgita Litviniene (acting).

ELTA Lithuanian News Agency (ELTA Lietuvos Naujienų Agentūra): Gedimino pr. 21/2, Vilnius 01103; tel. (5) 262-8864; fax (5) 261-9507; e-mail zinios@elta.lt; internet www.elta.lt; f. 1920; 18.4% owned by Ziniu Partneriai; 39.5% owned by Respublikos Investicija (both cos controlled by Respublika Gp); Dir Raimondas Kurliansksis.

Publishers

Alma littera: A. Juozapavičiaus 6/2, Vilnius 09310; tel. (5) 272-8246; e-mail post@almali.lt; internet www.almali.lt; f. 1990; fiction, children's books, textbooks; Dir-Gen. Arvydas Andrijauskas.

Baltos lankos (White Meadows): Laisvės pr. 115A/54, Vilnius 06119; tel. (5) 240-8673; fax (5) 240-7446; e-mail leidykla@baltoslankos.lt; internet www.baltoslankos.lt; f. 1992; literature, humanities, social sciences, fiction and textbooks; Dir Saulius Žukas.

Eugrimas: Šilutės 42A, Vilnius 08212; tel. and fax (5) 273-3955; e-mail info@eugrimas.lt; internet www.eugrimas.lt; f. 1995; academic and professional literature, incl. economics, education, law and politics; Dir Eugenija Petrulienė.

Katalikų pasaulio leidiniai (Editions of the Catholic World): Pylimo 27/14, Vilnius 01141; tel. (5) 212-2422; fax (5) 262-6462; e-mail leidykla@katpasaulis.lt; internet www.katalikuleidiniai.lt; f. 1990; Dir Birutė Bartasūnaite.

Lietuvos rašytojų sajungos leidykla (Lithuanian Writers' Union Publishers): K. Sirvydo 6, Vilnius 01101; tel. and fax (5) 262-8945; e-mail info@rsleidykla.lt; internet www.rsleidykla.lt; f. 1990; fiction, essays, literary heritage, children's books; Dir Giedre Soriene.

Mintis leidykla (Idea Publishing House): Z. Sierakausko g. 15, Vilnius 03105; tel. (5) 233-2943; fax (5) 216-3157; e-mail redakcija@mintis.org; internet www.mintis.org; f. 1949; philosophy, history, law, textbooks, encyclopedias, fiction; also book distributor; Editorial Dir Leonardas Armonas.

Mokslo ir enciklopedijų leidybos institutas (Science and Encyclopedia Publishing Institute): L. Asanavičiūtės 23, Vilnius 04315; tel. (5) 245-8526; fax (5) 245-8537; e-mail meli@meli.lt; internet www.meli.lt; f. 1992; encyclopedias, science and reference books, dictionaries, higher education textbooks, books for the general reader; Dir Rimantas Kareckas.

Presvika: Pamėnkalnio 25/11, Vilnius 01113; tel. (5) 262-3182; fax (5) 262-3110; e-mail presvika@vilnius.balt.net; internet www.presvika.lt; f. 1996; psychological and educational literature, textbooks and fiction; Dir Violeta Bilaišytė.

Šviesa (Light): Vytauto pr. 25, Kaunas 44352; tel. (37) 341834; fax (37) 342032; e-mail sviesa@balt.net; internet www.sviesa.lt; f. 1945; textbooks and pedagogical literature; Dir Jonas Barcys.

Tyto alba: J. Jasinskio g. 10, Vilnius 01112; tel. (5) 249-7453; fax (5) 298-8602; e-mail tytoalba@taide.lt; internet www.tytoalba.lt; f. 1993; contemporary Lithuanian literary fiction and non-fiction, fiction in translation; Dir Lolita Varanavičienė.

UAB Leidykla Vaga (Furrow Publishing House Ltd): Gedimino pr. 50, Vilnius 01110; tel. (5) 249-8121; fax (5) 249-8122; e-mail info@vaga.lt; internet www.vaga.lt; f. 1945; as Lithuanian State Publishing House of Fiction; privatized and restructured in 1994; fiction, non-fiction, art, children's books; Dir Vytas V. Petrošius.

UAB Versus Aureus leidykla: Rūdninkų g. 10, Vilnius 01135; tel. and fax (5) 265-2730; e-mail versus@versus.lt; internet www.versus.lt; f. 2003; fiction, non-fiction and educational literature.

PUBLISHERS' ASSOCIATION

Lithuanian Publishers' Association: K. Sirvydo g. 6, Vilnius 01101; tel. and fax (5) 261-7740; e-mail lla@centras.lt; f. 1989; Pres. Arvydas Andrijauskas.

Broadcasting and Communications

TELECOMMUNICATIONS

Regulatory Authority

Communications Regulatory Authority (Ryšių Reguliavimo Tarnyba): Algirdo 27, Vilnius 03219; tel. (5) 210-5633; fax (5) 216-1564; e-mail rrt@rrt.lt; internet www.rrt.lt; f. 2001; Dir Tomas Barakauskas.

SERVICE PROVIDERS

Lietuvos Telekomas AB: Savanorių pr. 28, Vilnius 03116; tel. (5) 212-7755; fax (5) 212-6655; e-mail info@telecom.lt; internet www.telecom.lt; f. 1992; privatized 1998; operates public telecommunications network, repairs telecommunications equipment; monopoly withdrawn in 2003; Gen. Man. Arūnas Šikšta; 3,200 employees.

UAB Eurocom: Naugarduko g. 99, Vilnius 03202; tel. (5) 274-4699; fax (5) 274-4612; e-mail eurocom@eurocom.lt; internet www.eurocom.lt; f. 2001; fixed line and mobile telecommunications service provider; a subsidiary of VP Market; Dir Kęstutis Skrebys.

Omnitel UAB: T. Ševčenkos 25, Vilnius 03503; tel. (698) 63333; fax (5) 274-5574; e-mail info@omnitel.net; internet www.omnnitel.lt; f. 1991; as Litcom; 90% owned by Telia Sonera (Sweden); largest mobile GSM communications provider in Lithuania; Pres. Antanas Juozas Zabulis.

UAB Tele2: POB 147, Vilnius 01003; tel. (684) 00212; fax (5) 236-6301; e-mail tele2@tele2.lt; internet www.tele2.lt; f. 1999; owned by Tele2 AB (Sweden); provider of GSM, internet and fixed-line telecommunications services; Chief Exec. Petras Masiulis.

BROADCASTING

Regulatory Authority

Lietuvos Radijo ir televizijos komisija (Radio and Television Commission of Lithuania): Vytenio 6, Vilnius 03113; tel. (5) 233-0660; fax (5) 264-7125; e-mail lrtk@rtk.lt; internet www.rtk.lt; f. 1996; licensing and licence compliance.

Radio

Lietuvos radijas ir televizija (LRT) (Lithuanian Radio and Television): S. Konarskio 49, Vilnius 03123; tel. (5) 236-3209; fax (5) 236-3208; e-mail lrt@lrt.lt; internet www.lrt.lt; f. 1926; govt-owned; non-profit public broadcasting co; operates two national radio channels and two national television channels; Chair. of Council Romas Pakalnis; Gen. Dir Kęstutis Petrauskis; 650 employees.

Lietuvos radijas (Lithuanian Radio): S. Konarskio g. 49, Vilnius 03123; tel. (5) 236-3010; fax (5) 213-5333; internet www.lrt.lt; f. 1926; broadcasts in Lithuanian, Russian, Polish, Yiddish, Belarusian and Ukrainian; Dir Rimgaudas Geleževičius.

A2 Radijo Stotis: Laisvės pr. 3, Vilnius 04215; tel. (5) 245-4922; e-mail a2@a2.lt; internet www.a2.lt; private, commercial; Dir Vydas Ivanauskas.

UAB Aukštaitijos radijas (AR): Laisvės a. 1, Panevėžys 35175; tel. and fax (45) 596969; e-mail ar@laineta.lt; private, commercial; Dir Algirdas Šatas.

Bumsas: Taikos pr. 28, Klaipėda 91220; tel. (46) 383328; e-mail info@b-91.lt; internet www.b-91.lt; private, commercial; broadcasts B-91 station; Dir Dalius Noreika.

FM 99: Rotušės a. 2, POB 119, Alytus 62141; tel. (315) 76120; fax (315) 74646; e-mail fm99@fm99.lt; internet www.fm99.lt; private, commercial; broadcast by UAB Alytaus radijas; Dir Liudas Ramanauskas.

Kapsai: P. Armino 71, Marijampolė 68127; tel. and fax (343) 54512; e-mail kapsai@mari.omnitel.net; internet www1.omnitel.net/kapsai; private, commercial; broadcast by Ventus (UAB Lamantas); Dir Raimundas Maruskevičius.

Kauno fonas 105.4: Savanorių pr. 192–802, Kaunas 44151; tel. (37) 327427; fax (37) 327447; e-mail info@kf.lt; internet www.kf.lt; private, commercial; Dir Udrys Staselka.

Labas FM: Naugarduko 91, Vilnius 2006; tel. (5) 216-3591; internet www.labasfm.lt; Dir Darius Uzkuraitis.

Laisvoji banga: Naugarduko g. 91, Vilnius 03202; tel. (5) 215-1458; fax (5) 216-3591; e-mail radio@lbanga.lt; internet www.europeanhitradio.lt; private, commercial; broadcasts European Hit Radio; Dir Vytautas Bartkus.

Laluna: Taikos pr. 81, Klaipėda 94114; tel. (46) 390808; fax (46) 390805; e-mail laluna@laluna.lt; internet www.laluna.lt; private, commercial; Dir Tadas Žemaitis.

UAB M-1: Laisvės pr. 60, Vilnius 05121; tel. (5) 236-0360; fax (5) 236-0366; e-mail m-1@m-1.fm; internet www.m-1.fm; private, commercial; Dir-Gen. Hubertas Grušnys.

Mažeikių aidas (MA): POB 17, Ventos g. 49, Mažeikiai 89103; tel. (443) 65055; fax (443) 65600; e-mail info@mazeikiuaidas.lt; internet www.mazeikiuaidas.lt; f. 1996; private, commercial; Dir Tomas Ruginis.

UAB Pūkas: Ringuvos g. 61, Kaunas 45242; tel. (37) 342424; fax (37) 342434; e-mail pukas@pukas.lt; internet www.pukas.lt; f. 1991; private, commercial; operates two radio stations and a television station; Dir Kęstutis Pūkas.

LITHUANIA

Radiocentras, UAB: Laisvės pr. 60, Vilnius 05120; tel. (5) 212-8706; fax (5) 242-9073; e-mail biuras@rc.lt; internet www.rc.lt; f. 1991; private, commercial; Gen. Man. ARTŪRAS MIRONCIKAS.

UAB Saulės radijas: Aušros al. 64, Šiauliai 76235; tel. (41) 525141; fax (41)424404; e-mail info@saulesradijas.lt; internet www.saulesradijas.lt; private, commercial; Dir RASA AKUČKIENĖ.

Tau: Draugystės g. 19–357, Kaunas 51230; tel. (37) 352790; fax (37) 352128; e-mail info@tau.lt; internet www.tau.lt; private, commercial; Dir GIEDRIUS GIPAS.

Ventus: Montuotojų g. 2, Mažeikiai 89500; tel. (443) 96225; fax (443) 96226; e-mail info@ventusradijas.lt; private, commercial; Dir-Gen. GIEDRIUS ŠTELMOKAS.

V. Mečkausko firma 'Versmės' radijas ir televizija (Versmes RTV): Pergalės 57–9, Elektrėnai 26001; tel. (528) 39543; fax (528) 39616; e-mail mesta@one.lt; Versmė radio station; Dir VYTAUTAS MEČKAUSKAS.

VšĮ Kauno radijas ir televizija: S. Daukanto 28A, Kaunas 44246; tel. (37) 321010; fax (37) 322570; e-mail kaunas@lrtv.lt; Dir P. GARNYS.

Žemaitijos radijas: Mažeikių g. 18, Telšiai 87101; tel. (444) 74433; fax (444) 75445; e-mail zemaitijos@radijas.lt; internet www.radijas.lt; private, commercial; Dir ALGIMANTAS GINČIAUSKIS.

UAB Znad Wilii radijo stotis: Laisvės pr. 60, Vilnius 05120; tel. (5) 249-0870; fax (5) 278-4446; e-mail radio@znadwilii.lt; internet www.znadwilii.lt; f. 1992; private, commercial; Dir-Gen. MIROSLAVAS JUCHNEVIČIUS.

Television

Lietuvos televizija (LTV): S. Konarskio g. 49, Vilnius 03123; tel. (5) 236-3100; fax (5) 216-3282; e-mail lrt@lrt.lt; internet www.lrt.lt; f. 1957; subsidiary of LRT (see Radio); programmes in Lithuanian, Russian, Polish, Ukrainian and Belarusian; Dir ŠARŪNAS KALINAUSKAS.

UAB Aidas (Echo): Birutės skg. 42, Trakai 21114; tel. (528) 52480; fax (528) 55656; e-mail tvaidas@uab.lt; mainly relays German programmes; private, commercial; Dir ČESLOVAS RULEVIČIUS.

Baltijos televizija (BTV): Laisvės pr. 60, Vilnius 05120; tel. (5) 278-0805; fax (5) 278-0804; e-mail info@btv.lt; internet www.btv.lt; f. 1993; broadcasts own programmes and relays German, Polish and US broadcasts; private, commercial; Dir-Gen. GINTARAS SONGAILA.

KTV plius: Nemuno g. 79, Panevėžys 37355; tel. (45) 514103; fax (45)443561; e-mail pictura@kateka.lt; internet www.ktvplius.lt; private, commercial; Pres. ROLANDAS MEILIŪNAS.

LNK TV (UAB Laisvas ir nepriklausomas kanalas): Šeškinės g. 20, Vilnius 07156; tel. (5) 212-4061; fax (5) 278-4530; e-mail info@lnk.lt; internet www.lnk.lt; private, commercial; broadcasts TV1; Dir PAULIUS KOVAS.

PAN-TV: Respublikos g. 19–8, Panevėžys 35185; tel. (45) 464267; e-mail pantv@takas.lt; private, commercial; Dir SAULIUS BUKELIS.

Raseiniu TV: Vytauto Vilniaus 1A, Raseiniai 60187; tel. (428) 54433; fax (428) 70422; e-mail office@mirkliai.lt; broadcast by VšĮ Raseinių televizijos ir radijo centras; Dir KĘSTUTIS SKAMARAKAS.

Šiaulių TV: Liejyklos g. 10, Šiauliai 78147; tel. and fax (41) 523809; e-mail info@stv.lt; internet www.stv.lt; private; Dir ANDRIUS ŠEDŽIUS.

TV3: Nemenčinės pl. 4, Vilnius 10102; tel. (5) 276-4264; fax (5) 276-4253; e-mail postmaster@tv3.lt; internet www.tv3.lt; broadcasts own programmes (20% of schedule) in Lithuanian and English, and relays international satellite channels; private, commercial; Dir RAMŪNAS ŠAUČIKOVAS.

Vilniaus TV: Vivulskio 23, Vilnius 2600; tel. (5) 213-5560; fax (5) 233-7904; e-mail vtv@iti.lt; f. 1994; private, commercial; Dir LINAS RYŠKUS.

Finance

(cap. = capital; res = reserves; dep. = deposits; m. = million; brs = branches; amounts in litai)

BANKING

During 1995 several commercial banks became bankrupt, and the crisis resulted in the eventual closure of 16 of the 28 banks in operation. As a result, the Government devised a programme, in consultation with the IMF and the World Bank, to secure and restructure the banking system. At the end of 2001 nine banks were operating under a licence from the Bank of Lithuania; there were also four branches of foreign banks, and five representative offices of foreign banks in Lithuania.

Central Bank

Bank of Lithuania (Lietuvos bankas): Gedimino pr. 6, Vilnius 01103; tel. (5) 268-0029; fax (5) 262-8124; e-mail info@lb.lt; internet www.lb.lt; f. 1922; re-est. 1990; central bank, responsible for bank supervision; cap. 100m., res 465.1m., dep. 3,811.8m. (Dec. 2003); Chair. of Bd REINOLDIJUS ŠARKINAS.

Commercial Banks

AB Bankas NORD/LB Lietuva: J. Basanavičiaus g. 26, Vilnius–6 03601; tel. (5) 239-3444; fax (5) 213-9057; e-mail info@nordlb.lt; internet www.nordlb.lt; f. 1924; registered as AB Lietuvos Žemės Ūkio Bankas in 1993; privatized in March 2002, and name changed to NORD/LB Lietuva in May 2003; 93.1% obtained by Bank DnB Nord A/S (Denmark) in Dec. 2005; cap. 213.4m., res 18.3m., dep. 1,961.6m. (Dec. 2004); Chair. of Management Bd and Pres. WERNER SCHILLI; 46 brs.

Bankas Snoras: A. Vivulskio g. 7, Vilnius 03221; tel. (5) 266-2700; fax (5) 231-0155; e-mail info@snoras.com; internet www.snoras.com; f. 1992; part of the Convers Financial Gp, 49.9% owned by Conversbank (Luxembourg) Holding Co; cap. 219m., dep. 1,420m., total assets 1,934m. (Dec. 2004); Chair. of Management Bd RAIMONDAS BARANAUSKAS.

Hansabankas: Savanorių pr. 19, Vilnius 03502; tel. (5) 268-4444; fax (52) 223-2433; e-mail info@hansa.lt; internet www.hansa.lt; 99.25% owned by Hansapank (Estonia); cap. 435.3m., res −31.5m., dep. 4,538.4m. (Dec. 2003); Chair. of Bd INDRIUS DUSEVIČIUS.

Medicinos Bankas (Medical Bank): Paménkalnio g. 40, Vilnius 01114; tel. (5) 264-4800; fax (5) 264-4801; e-mail info@medbank.lt; internet www.medbank.lt; f. 1992; cap. 34.3m., res 2.1m., dep. 121.5m. (Dec. 2003); Chair. of Bd KĘSTUTIS OLSAUSKAS; 7 brs.

Parex Bankas: K. Kalinausko g. 13, Vilnius 03107; tel. (5) 266-4600; fax (5) 266-4601; e-mail info@parex.lt; internet www.parex.lt; f. 1996; owned by Parex Group (Latvia); cap. 31.0m., res 0.9m., dep. 128.1m. (Dec. 2002); Chair. and Chief Exec. ALMA VAITKUNSKIENE; 6 brs.

Sampo Bankas: Geležinio Vilko g. 18A, Vilnius 08500; tel. (5) 210-9400; fax (5) 210-9409; e-mail bankas@sampo.lt; internet www.sampo.lt; f. 1994; fmrly Lithuanian Development Bank; present name adopted 2001; 99.99% owned by Sampo (Finland); cap. 88.0m., res 3.3m., dep. 686.5m. (Dec. 2003); Chair. of Bd GINTAUTAS GALVANAUSKAS.

Šiaulių Bankas: Tilžės g. 149, Šiauliai 76348; tel. (41) 522117; fax (41) 430774; e-mail info@sb.lt; internet www.sb.lt; f. 1992; cap. 56.0m., res 2.6m., dep. 517.1m. (Dec. 2004); Chair. ALGIRDAS BUTKUS; 43 brs and client service centres (2005).

Ūkio Bankas: Maironio g. 25, Kaunas 44250; tel. (37) 301301; fax (37) 323188; e-mail ub@ub.lt; internet www.ub.lt; f. 1989; cap. 123.5m., res 0.2m., dep. 978.8m. (Oct. 2005); Chair. of Bd EDITA KARPAVIČIENE; Chief Exec. GINTARAS UGIANSKIS; 12 brs.

SEB Vilniaus bankas (Bank of Vilnius): Gedimino pr. 12, Vilnius 01103; tel. (5) 268-2514; fax (5) 268-2333; e-mail info@vb.lt; internet www.vb.lt; f. 1990 as Spaudos Bankas; 98.9% owned by Skandinaviska Enskilda Banken AB (Sweden); cap. 154.4m., res 656.8m., dep. 6,894.7m. (Dec. 2003); Pres. and Chief Exec. AUDRIUS ZIUGZDA; 18 brs.

Property Bank

Turto Bankas AB: Kęstučio g. 45, Vilnius 08124; tel. (5) 278-0900; fax (5) 275-1155; e-mail info@turtas.lt; internet www.turtas.lt; f. 1996; cap. and res 9.7m., total assets 69.5m. (Dec. 2003); recovery of non-performing loans, administration of loans of the Ministry of Finance; Chair. of Bd JONAS BUDREVIČIUS; 6 brs.

Banking Association

Association of Lithuanian Banks (Lietuvos Bankų Asociacija): Ankštoji g. 5/3, Vilnius 01109; tel. (5) 249-6669; fax (5) 249-6139; e-mail info@lba.lt; internet www.lba.lt; f. 1991; Pres. RIMANTAS BUSILA; 9 mems.

STOCK EXCHANGE

Vilnius Stock Exchange (VSE) (Vilniaus vertybinių popierių birža): Konstitucijos pr. 7, 15A, Vilnius 08501; tel. (5) 272-3871; fax (5) 272-4894; e-mail vilnius@omxgroup.com; internet www.lt.omxgroup.com; f. 1993; 93.1% owned by HEX Helsinki Stock Exchange Ltd (Finland)—OMX ABforms Group; Chair. of Bd DALIA JASULAITYTĖ.

INSURANCE

Principal Insurance Companies

Commercial Union Lietuva Gyvybės draudimas: Jogailos g. 4, Vilnius 01116; tel. (5) 269-0169; fax (5) 269-0269; e-mail info@cu.lt; internet www.commercialunion.lt; f. 2001; owned by Commercial

LITHUANIA

Union Polska—Towarzystwo Ubezpieczeń na Zycie SA (Poland), part of the Aviva Group (United Kingdom); Dir A. UNGULAITIENĖ.

Ergo Lietuva: Geležinio vilko g. 6A, Vilnius 03507; tel. (5) 268-3000; fax (5) 268-3005; e-mail info@ergo.lt; internet www.ergo.lt; f. 1991; owned by Ergo International AG (Germany); formerly Drauda UAB; name changed as above in 2000; in 2002 merged with Preventa; Dir S. JOKUBAITIS.

Hansa Gyvybės draudimas UAB: J. Basanavičiaus g. 8/ Vingrių g. 1, Vilnius 01118; tel. (5) 266-5966; fax (5) 268-5866; e-mail draudimas@hansa.lt; internet www.hansadraudimas.lt; f. 1995; owned by Hansabankas AB (Estonia); formerly Lietuvos Draudimo Gyvybės draudimas; Lithuania's leading life insurer; Dir D. VALENTUKEVIČIUS.

Lietuvos draudimas AB (Lithuanian Insurance): J. Basanavičiaus g. 12, Vilnius 03600; tel. (5) 268-6300; fax (5) 231-4138; e-mail info@ldr.lt; internet www.lietuvosdraudimas.lt; f. 1921; privatized in 1999; owned by Codan AS (Denmark); principal non-life insurance co in Lithuania; Dir K. SERPYTIS.

PZU Lietuva UAB: Konstitucijos pr. 7, Vilnius 09308; tel. (5) 279-0007; fax (5) 279-0019; e-mail info@pzu.lt; internet www.pzu.lt; f. 1993; owned by Powszechny Zaklad Ubezpieczen (PZU) SA (Poland); Dir Z. OLBRYS.

SEB VB Gyvybės Draudimas UAB: Gedimino pr. 12, Vilnius 01103; tel. (5) 268-1555; fax (5) 268-1556; e-mail draudimas.info@vb.lt; internet www.vbgd.lt; f. 1999; owned by SEB Vilniaus bankas AB; Dir B. KAMUNTAVIČIENĖ.

Insurance Association

Association of Lithuanian Insurers: Vytenio g. 50, Vilnius 03229; tel. (5) 231-0381; e-mail asociacija@draudikai.lt; internet www.draudikai.lt; f. 1992; Pres. EDMONTAS VOLOCHOVIČIUS.

Supervisory Body

Insurance Supervisory Commission: Ukmergės g. 222, Vilnius 07157; tel. (5) 243-1370; fax (5) 272-3689; e-mail dpk@dpk.lt; internet www.dpk.lt; Chair. EDVINAS VASILIS-VASILIAUSKAS.

Trade and Industry

GOVERNMENT AGENCIES

Lithuanian Development Agency for Small and Medium-sized Enterprises (Lietuvos smulkaus ir vidutinio verslo plėtros agentūra—SMEDA/LSVVPA): Gedimino pr. 38/2, Vilnius 01104; tel. (5) 261-9219; fax (5) 261-9207; e-mail info@smeda.lt; internet www.smeda.lt; f. 1996; under the Ministry of the Economy; Dir ARVYDAS DARULIS.

State Property Fund (Valstybės Turto Fondas—VTS): Vilniaus g. 16, Vilnius 01507; tel. (5) 268-4999; fax (5) 268-4997; e-mail info@vtf.lt; internet www.vtf.lt; f. 1995; privatization and management of state-owned and municipal property; Dir POVILAS MILAŠAUSKAS.

DEVELOPMENT AGENCY

National Regional Development Agency (Nacionalinė Regionų Plėtros Agentūra): Lukiskių g. 5/502, Vilnius 01108; tel. and fax (5) 233-4151; e-mail nrda@nrda.lt; internet www.nrda.lt; f. 1999 by the Asscn of Lithuanian Chambers of Commerce, Industry and Crafts; Dir VAIDAS KAZAKEVIČIUS.

CHAMBERS OF COMMERCE

Association of Lithuanian Chambers of Commerce, Industry and Crafts (Lietuvos prekybos, pramonės ir amatų rūmų asociacija): J. Tumo-Vaižganto g. 9/1–63A, Vilnius 01108; tel. (5) 261-2102; fax (5) 261-2112; e-mail info@chambers.lt; internet www.chambers.lt; f. 1992; mem. of International Chamber of Commerce and of Asscn of European Chambers of Commerce and Industry; Dir-Gen. RIMAS VARKULEVIČIUS.

Kaunas Chamber of Commerce, Industry and Crafts: K. Donelaičio g. 8, Kaunas 44213; POB 2111, Kaunas 44010; tel. (37) 229212; fax (37) 208330; e-mail chamber@chamber.lt; internet www.chamber.lt; f. 1925; re-est. 1991; br. at Marijampolė; Pres. Prof. M. RONDOMANSKAS.

Klaipėda Chamber of Commerce, Industry and Crafts: Danės g. 17, POB 148, Klaipėda 92117; tel. (46) 390861; fax (46) 410626; e-mail klaipeda@chambers.lt; internet www.kcci.lt; Pres. SIGITAS PAULAUSKAS; Dir VIKTORAS KROLIS.

Panevėžys Chamber of Commerce, Industry and Crafts: Respublikos g. 34, Panevėžys 35173; tel. (45) 463687; fax (45) 462227; e-mail panevezys@chambers.lt; internet www.ccic.lt; f. 1991; Pres. VYTAUTAS ŠIDLAUSKAS; Gen. Dir VYTAUTAS KAZAKEVIČIUS.

Šiauliai Chamber of Commerce, Industry and Crafts: Vilniaus g. 88, Šiauliai 76285; tel. (41) 523224; fax (41) 523903; e-mail siauliai@chambers.lt; internet www.rumai.lt; f. 1993; Dir-Gen. RIMUNDAS DOMARKAS.

Vilnius Chamber of Commerce, Industry and Crafts: Algirdo g. 31, Vilnius 03219; tel. (5) 213-5550; fax (5) 213-5450; e-mail vilnius@chambers.lt; internet www.cci.lt; f. 1991; Dir-Gen. BORISAS ZAUBIDOVAS; 435 mems.

INDUSTRIAL ASSOCIATION

Lithuanian Confederation of Industrialists (Lietuvos pramonininkų konfederacija—LPK): A. Vienuolio g. 8, Vilnius 01104; tel. (5) 212-5217; fax (5) 212-5209; e-mail sekretoriatas@lpk.lt; internet www.lpk.lt; f. 1989; Pres. BRONISLOVAS LUBYS.

EMPLOYERS' ORGANIZATION

Lithuanian Business Employers' Confederation (Lietuvos verslo darbdavių konfederacija—LVDK): A. Rotundo g. 5, Vilnius 01111; tel. (5) 249-8345; fax (5) 249-6448; e-mail info@lvdk.w3.lt; internet www.ldkonfederacija.lt; f. 1999; Gen. Dir DANAS ARLAUSKAS.

UTILITIES

Energy Agency (Energetikos Agentura): Gedimino pr. 38/2, Vilnius 01104; tel. (5) 262-9731; fax (5) 262-6845; e-mail eainfo@ukmin.lt; internet www.ena.lt; f. 1993; state enterprise; attached to the Ministry of the Economy; Dir MARIJUS FRANCKEVIČIUS.

Electricity

Ignalina Nuclear Power Plant (Ignalinos Atominė Elektrinė): Karklų k., Visaginas 31500; tel. (386) 28350; fax (386) 29350; e-mail info@mail.iae.lt; internet www.iae.lt; f. 1985; largest Lithuanian state-owned enterprise; Dir VIKTOR ŠEVALDIN.

Lietuvos energija AB (Lithuanian Power): Žvejų g. 14, Vilnius 09310; tel. (5) 262-6822; fax (5) 212-6736; e-mail info@lietuvosenergija.lt; internet www.lpc.lt; f. 1995; restructured in 2000; Man. Dir RYMANTAS JUOZAITIS.

Rytų Skirstomieji Tinklai AB (RST) (Eastern Distribution Networks): P. Lukšio g. 5B, Vilnius 08221; tel. (5) 2777524; fax (5) 2777514; e-mail r@rst.lt; internet www.rst.lt; f. 2001; following the reorganization of Lietuvos Energija AB; distribution network operator and public supplier of four regions; scheduled for privatization; 156,000 customers (Dec. 2002); Dir RIMANTAS MILIŠAUSKAS.

Vakarų skirstomieji tinklai AB (VST): Jasinskio g. 16C, Vilnius 01112; tel. (5) 2781259; fax (5) 2781269; e-mail vst@vst.lt; internet www.vest.lt; f. 2001; distribution in central and western Lithuania; 96.5% of shares divested to NDX Energija in 2003–04; Chief Exec. DARIUS NEDZINSKAS; 2,000 employees.

Gas

Lietuvos Dujos AB (Lithuanian Gas): Aguonų g. 24, Vilnius 03212; tel. (5) 236-0210; fax (5) 236-0200; e-mail ld@lietuvosdujos.lt; internet www.dujos.lt; f. 1995; natural gas import, sale and transportation; 17.7% state-owned; 38.9% owned by E.ON Ruhrgas International AG (Germany); 37.1% owned by OAO Gazprom (Russia); Chair. ALEXANDER RYAZANOV; Gen. Man. VIKTORAS VALENTUKEVIČIUS; 1,900 employees.

TRADE UNIONS

Lithuanian Labour Federation (Lietuvos Darbo Federacija): Vytauto g. 14, Vilnius 03106; tel. and fax (5) 231-2029; e-mail ldforg@ldf.lt; internet www.ldf.lt; f. 1919 as a Christian trade-union org.; re-est. 1991; 20,000 mems; Chair. VYDAS PUSKEPALIS; Sec.-Gen. JANINA ŠVEDIENĖ.

Lithuanian Trade Union Confederation (LPSK): J. Jasinskio g. 9–213, Vilnius 01111; tel. (5) 249-6921; fax (5) 249-8078; e-mail lpsk@lpsk.lt; internet www.lpsk.lt; f. 2002 by merger of Lithuanian Union of Trade Unions (LPSS) and Lithuanian Trade Union Centre (LPSC); 25 branch trade unions with 120,000 mems; Pres. ARTŪRAS ČERNIAUSKAS.

Lithuanian Trade Union: Solidarumas (Lietuvos profesinė sąjunga 'Solidarumas'): V. Mykolaičio-Putino g. 5, Vilnius 03106; tel. (5) 262-1743; fax (5) 213-3295; e-mail info@solidarumasmokymai.lt; internet www.lps.lt; f. 2002; fmrly the Lithuanian Workers' Union: Labora (f. 1989); Pres. ALDONA BALSIENĖ; 52,000 mems.

Transport

RAILWAYS

In 2004 there were 1,782 km of railway track in use in Lithuania; in 2003 some 122 km of track were electrified. Main lines link Vilnius with Minsk (Belarus), Kaliningrad (Russia) and Warsaw (Poland), in the latter case via the Belarusian town of Grodno (Horadnia).

Lithuanian Railways (Lietuvos geležinkeliai): Mindaugo g. 12–14, Vilnius 03603; tel. (5) 269-3300; fax (5) 269-2028; e-mail lgkanc@litrail.lt; internet www.litrail.lt; f. 1991; Gen. Dir JONAS BIRŽIŠKIS; 11,500 employees.

ROADS

In 2004 the total length of the road network was 79,331 km. The motorway network totalled 417 km and some 88% of roads were paved.

Lithuanian Road Administration (Lietuvos automobilių kelių direkcija—LAKD): J. Basanavičiaus g. 36/2, Vilnius 03109; tel. (5) 213-1361; fax (5) 213-1362; e-mail info@lra.lt; internet www.lra.lt; Gen. Dir VIRGAUDAS PUODŽIUKAS.

SHIPPING

The main port is at Klaipėda. In 2004 there were 425 km of inland navigable waterways.

Port Authority

Klaipėda State Seaport Authority: J. Janonio g. 24, Klaipėda 92251; tel. (46) 499799; fax (46) 499777; e-mail info@port.lt; internet www.port.lt; multi-purpose, deep-water universal port; connects sea, land and rail routes from east and west; Gen. Dir SIGITAS DOBILINSKAS.

Shipowning Company

Lithuanian Shipping Company (AB Lietuvos Jūrų Laivininkystė): Malunininku g. 3, Klaipėda 92264; tel. (46) 393105; fax (46) 393119; e-mail gp@ljl.lt; internet www.ljl.lt; f. 1969 as LISCO; partially privatized and renamed as above in June 2001; 73.24% state-owned; transportation of cargo; owns 18 vessels; Gen. Dir VYTAUTAS VISMANTAS.

CIVIL AVIATION

The state airline, Lithuanian Airlines, is based at the international airports at Vilnius and Kaunas. There are also international airports at Palanga and Šiauliai.

Directorate of Civil Aviation (Oro Navigacija): Rodūnios kelias 2, Vilnius 02188; tel. (5) 273-9102; fax (5) 273-9161; e-mail info@ans.lt; internet www.ans.lt; Gen. Dir ALGIMANTAS RAŠČIUS.

Air Lithuania (Aviakompanija Lietuva): Veiverių 132, Karmėlava Airport, Kaunas 54085; tel. (37) 391420; fax (37) 226030; e-mail hdoffice@airlithuania.lt; internet www.airlithuania.lt; f. 1991; privately owned; operates passenger and cargo services to Europe; Chair. and Dir-Gen. NAGLIS VYSNIAUSKAS.

Lithuanian Airlines (Lietuvos avialinijos—LAL): A. Gustaičio g. 4, Vilnius 02512; tel. (5) 230-6017; fax (5) 216-6828; e-mail info@flylal.lt; internet www.lal.lt; f. 1991; owned by the LAL Investiciju Valdymas consortium; operates passenger and cargo flights to regional and European destinations; Dir-Gen. STASYS JARMALAVIČIUS.

Tourism

Tourist attractions in Lithuania include the historic cities of Vilnius, Kaunas, Kėdainiai, Trakai and Klaipėda, coastal resorts, such as Palanga and Kuršių Nerija, and picturesque countryside. Some 438,299 tourists visited the country in 2003; tourist receipts in that year totalled US $476.0m.

Lithuanian State Department of Tourism: A. Juozapavičiaus g. 13, Vilnius 09311; tel. (5) 210-8796; fax (5) 210-8753; e-mail vtd@tourism.lt; internet www.tourism.lt; Dir ALVITIS LUKOŠEVIČIUS.

LUXEMBOURG

Introductory Survey

Location, Climate, Language, Religion, Flag, Capital

The Grand Duchy of Luxembourg is a land-locked country in western Europe. It is bordered by Belgium to the west and north, by France to the south, and by Germany to the east. The climate is temperate, with cool summers and mild winters. In Luxembourg-Ville the average temperature ranges from 1°C (33°F) in January to 18°C (64°F) in July, while annual rainfall averages 782 mm. Letzeburgish (Luxembourgish), a German-Moselle-Frankish dialect, is the spoken language and became the official language in 1985. French is generally used for administrative purposes, while German is the principal written language of commerce and the press. Almost all of the inhabitants profess Christianity: about 87% are Roman Catholics and a small minority are Protestants. The national flag (proportions 3 by 5) consists of three equal horizontal stripes, of red, white and blue. The capital is Luxembourg-Ville (Lützelburg).

Recent History

As a founder member of the European Community (EC—now European Union—EU, see p. 228), of which Luxembourg-Ville is one of the main bases, Luxembourg has played a significant role in progress towards European integration since the Second World War. Luxembourg's commitment to such integration was exemplified by its status as one of the original signatories to the June 1990 Schengen Agreement (named after the town in Luxembourg where the accord was signed), which binds signatories to the abolition of internal border controls.

The Belgo-Luxembourg Economic Union (BLEU) has existed since 1921, except for the period from 1940–44, when the Grand Duchy was subject to wartime occupation by Germany. In 1948 the Benelux Economic Union (see p. 385) was inaugurated between Belgium, Luxembourg and the Netherlands, becoming effective in 1960, and establishing the three countries as a single customs area in 1970.

In November 1964 Grand Duchess Charlotte abdicated, after a reign of 45 years, and was succeeded by her son, Prince Jean.

Pierre Werner, leader of the Parti Chrétien Social (PCS), became Prime Minister in February 1959. After the fall of the Government in October 1968, Werner headed a coalition of the PCS and the Parti Démocratique ('Liberals') from January 1969 until May 1974. At a general election in May 1974, the PCS lost its political dominance for the first time since 1919, and in June a centre-left coalition between the Parti Ouvrier Socialiste Luxembourgeois (POSL) and the Parti Démocratique Luxembourgeois (PDL) was formed under the premiership of Gaston Thorn, the Minister of Foreign Affairs since 1969. At the next general election, which took place in June 1979, the PCS increased its strength in the 59-member Chambre des Députés from 18 to 24 seats. In July Werner again formed a coalition Government, comprising his party and the PDL, which held 15 seats.

At a general election in June 1984 the PCS again secured the largest number of seats (25) in the enlarged 64-member legislature. However, the success of the POSL, which took 21 seats (compared with 14 in the previous election), was widely attributed to general dissatisfaction with an economic austerity programme, which had been introduced during the early 1980s, and with the rising level of unemployment. A centre-left coalition was formed in July 1984 between the PCS and the POSL, with Jacques Santer of the PCS (hitherto Minister of Finance, Labour and Social Security) as Prime Minister. New elections to the Chambre des Députés (whose membership had been reduced to 60 in January 1989) took place in June 1989. The PCS, the POSL and the PDL each lost three seats (returning, respectively, 22, 18 and 11 deputies). In the following month Santer was again sworn in as the head of a coalition Government, which comprised equal numbers of representatives from the PCS and the POSL. At the next general election, in June 1994, the PCS and the POSL each lost one representative in the Chambre des Députés, winning 21 and 17 seats respectively; the PDL secured 12 seats. The PCS-POSL coalition was renewed, and Santer was reappointed Prime Minister. In January 1995 Santer took office as President of the Commission of the EU. He was succeeded as Prime Minister by Jean-Claude Juncker, hitherto Minister of the Budget, of Finance and of Labour.

In January 1998 the Minister of the Environment and of Health, Johny Lahure, resigned from his posts following the disclosure of a financial scandal within the Ministry of Health, and in May 1999 the President of the National Audit Office, Gérard Reuter, was suspended from office, pending investigation into allegations of mismanagement and fraud.

The two governing parties both recorded losses at the general election held concurrently with elections to the European Parliament on 13 June 1999, the PCS emerging with 19 seats and the POSL with 13. The PDL increased its representation from 12 to 15 seats, while the conservative Comité d'Action pour la Démocratie et la Justice took seven seats (an increase of two). The environmentalist party, Déi Gréng, retained its five seats in the Chambre des Députés. Juncker, who remained as Prime Minister, subsequently formed a new centre-right coalition of his PCS and the PDL, which took office in early August; the POSL thus returned to opposition for the first time in 15 years.

In March 1998 Grand Duke Jean conferred broad constitutional powers upon his eldest son and heir, Prince Henri, permitting him to deputize for the Grand Duke in all official capacities, including the signing of legislation, and in December 1999 Grand Duke Jean announced his intention to abdicate the following year. On 7 October 2000 Prince Henri succeeded his father as Head of State.

Luxembourg's banking secrecy laws have for many years been a cause of concern regarding the activities of banks and individual depositors benefiting from such legislation. Attempts by the EC, in the early 1990s, to impose more uniform regulations on the conduct of financial services in its member countries, in conjunction with the world-wide liquidation, in July 1991, of the Bank of Credit and Commerce International, the holding company and a subsidiary of which were incorporated in Luxembourg, focused renewed attention on Luxembourg's regulatory procedures. In April 1993 legislation was introduced which permitted the confiscation of deposits in Luxembourg banks accruing from suspected illegal drugs-related activities. Further legislation was introduced in 1997 which extended the State's powers of confiscation to include funds believed to be derived from other illegal sources, including arms-smuggling. During 1997 Luxembourg's financial sector came under renewed scrutiny when the Belgian authorities conducted an investigation into alleged widespread tax evasion by Belgian citizens and companies based in the Grand Duchy. The German authorities also launched a similar investigation. Luxembourg was further criticized for refusing, as did Switzerland, to endorse the code of conduct with respect to tax 'havens' drafted by the Organisation for Economic Co-operation and Development (OECD, see p. 320) in April 1998. During 1998 Luxembourg also opposed European Commission moves towards European taxation harmonization, which would oblige Luxembourg to impose tax on non-residents' interest and dividend income for the first time, thereby reducing the attraction of Luxembourg as a financial centre. In May 2000, however, Luxembourg for the first time endorsed reforms, proposed by a report by the OECD, aimed at limiting the use of bank secrecy laws in order to evade paying taxes; the report did, however, acknowledge the legitimacy of bank secrecy. In October the Chambre des Députés approved a relaxation of bank secrecy laws to facilitate co-operation with the US Internal Revenue Service in its attempts to halt tax evasion. Luxembourg was exempted for at least six years from a requirement for EU member states to exchange banking information from 2005 under new EU taxation rules concerning overseas investments agreed in early 2003 (see Economic Affairs).

In December 2000 the Government was very active during negotiations regarding the Treaty of Nice, which aimed to reform the institutions of the EU in light of its forthcoming enlargements. The terms of the Treaty substantially safeguarded Luxembourg's privileged position in the EU: Luxembourg was to continue to have a European Commissioner, to maintain its six seats in the European Parliament and to continue to enjoy a voting weight in the Council of the European Union out of

LUXEMBOURG

proportion to its size. In July 2001 the Chambre des Députés ratified the Treaty by a large majority. At the same time, Luxembourg continued, much to the frustration of most of its EU partners, to oppose the removal from Luxembourg-Ville of the Secretariat of the European Parliament, together with its 1,500 staff, whose continued presence in the Grand Duchy was considered by the Luxembourg Government to be vital to the local economy.

At the general election held on 13 June 2004 the PCS increased its representation from 19 to 24 seats in the 60-seat Chambre des Députés. The POSL secured 14 seats, while the PDL obtained 10, five fewer than in the previous administration. Déi Gréng won seven seats and the Comité d'Action pour la Démocratie et la Justice secured five. On 20 July Lydie Polfer of the PDL tendered her resignation as Deputy Prime Minister and Minister of Foreign Affairs and External Trade, and of the Civil Service and Administrative Reform. A new coalition Government comprising members of the PCS and the POSL was sworn in on 31 July under the leadership, once again, of Juncker. The PCS assumed nine of the 15 ministerial posts, retaining the finance and justice portfolios and gaining the Ministry of the Interior and Spatial Planning, which was now headed by Jean-Marie Halsdorf. Jean Asselborn of the POSL succeeded Polfer as Deputy Prime Minister and Minister of Foreign Affairs and Immigration.

A minor reorganization of the PCS government portfolios, which took effect in late February 2006, was designed to enable the ministers concerned to focus on the areas of employment and the budget. Jean-Louis Schiltz, hitherto Minister of Co-operation and Humanitarian Action and Minister-delegate of Communications, assumed full ministerial responsibility for communications from Juncker and was also allocated the defence portfolio, becoming Minister of Co-operation and Humanitarian Action, of Communications and of Defence. The former Minister of Defence, Luc Frieden, retained his responsibilities as Minister of Justice and of the Treasury and Budget. Furthermore, François Biltgen, the Minister of Culture, Further Education and Research, of Labour and Employment and of Religious Affairs, ceded greater control over culture, further education and research to Octavie Modert, the Secretary of State in charge of that portfolio.

Popular opposition in Luxembourg to a potential US-led military campaign in Iraq to remove the regime of Saddam Hussain culminated in nation-wide demonstrations on 15 February 2003. The Government's opposition to the military intervention (which was undertaken the following month without the support of a UN resolution), although muted, adversely affected relations with the USA. Following the swift removal of the Iraqi regime, however, the Luxembourg Government announced the allocation of €3.5m. for the financing of a humanitarian aid programme for Iraq. In March Parliament approved the secondment of 10 officers and men to the International Security and Assistance Force in Afghanistan (ISAF), and, as part of the EU's first ever military operation, that of one officer to the Union's peace-keeping mission to the former Yugoslav republic of Macedonia. Four EU countries—Luxembourg, Belgium, France and Germany—all of which had opposed the US-led military campaign in Iraq, held a special summit in April to discuss defence matters, at which it was agreed to establish an autonomous European military command headquarters near Brussels. The plan, which provoked protests from the USA and the United Kingdom, was superseded in December by a compromise agreement between France, Germany and the United Kingdom to create an EU 'planning cell' within existing defence structures.

On 1 January 2005 Juncker assumed a two-year appointment as Chairman of the Eurogroup (comprising the 12 EU member states that belong to the euro zone). In this capacity the Luxembourg Prime Minister would represent the members of the euro zone at global financial summits and would be instrumental in shaping European economic policy. Also in January Luxembourg assumed the rotating presidency of the Council of the EU for the first six months of the year. During this period the reform of the Stability and Growth Pact was successfully negotiated, the Lisbon Agenda, which aimed to create sustainable economic prosperity and full employment, was relaunched, and a new framework for relations with Russia was adopted. However, during the final European Council meeting of the presidency in June, EU leaders failed to reach agreement on a new financial strategy for 2007–13. On 10 July 2005 Luxembourg held a national referendum (the first since 1936) on the EU constitutional treaty, which had finally been approved by the EU in mid-2004. Although there were concerns that the proposed constitution was not wholly advantageous for the smaller member states of the EU, the vast majority of political parties in Luxembourg supported the document and Juncker threatened to resign if the electorate rejected the treaty. Opposition to the treaty grew when the French and Dutch, at their referendums, held in May and June respectively, voted against its ratification. None the less, the draft treaty was approved by some 56.52% of the Luxembourg electorate.

Government

Luxembourg is an hereditary and constitutional monarchy. Legislative power is exercised by the unicameral Chambre des Députés, with 60 members elected by universal adult suffrage for five years (subject to dissolution) on the basis of proportional representation. Some legislative functions are also entrusted to the advisory Conseil de l'Etat, with 21 members appointed for life by the Grand Duke, but decisions made by this body can be overruled by the legislature.

Executive power is vested in the Grand Duke, but is normally exercised by the Council of Ministers, led by the President of the Government (Prime Minister). The Grand Duke appoints ministers, but they are responsible to the legislature. Luxembourg is divided into three districts (Luxembourg, Diekirch, Grevenmacher), 12 cantons and 118 municipalities.

Defence

Luxembourg was a founder member of the North Atlantic Treaty Organization (NATO, see p. 314) in 1949. Compulsory military service was abolished in 1967, but Luxembourg maintains an army of volunteers, totalling 900, and a gendarmerie numbering 612 (in August 2005). Defence expenditure in the budget for 2005 was some €208m. In March 1987 the country became a signatory of the Benelux military convention, together with Belgium and the Netherlands, which was intended to standardize training methods and military equipment in the three countries. Luxembourg committed 100 troops to the proposed joint rapid reaction force of the European Union (EU, see p. 228), which was to be ready to be deployed by 2003. The logistics of assembling this force proved problematic, however, and in November 2004 the EU defence ministers agreed to create 13 'battle groups' (each numbering 1,000–1,500 men) by 2007, which could be deployed at short notice (within 10 days) to carry out peace-keeping activities at crisis points around the world.

Economic Affairs

In 2004, according to estimates by the World Bank, Luxembourg's gross national income (GNI), measured at average 2002–04 prices, was US $25,302m., equivalent to $56,230 per head (or $61,220 per head on an international purchasing-power parity basis). During 1995–2004, it was estimated, the population increased at an average rate of 1.1% per year, while gross domestic product (GDP) per head grew, in real terms, by an average of 3.9% per year. Overall GDP increased, in real terms, at an average annual rate of 5.0% in 1995–2004; growth was 2.1% in 2003 and 4.5% in 2004.

Agriculture (including forestry and fishing) contributed 0.5% of GDP in 2004. In the same year an estimated 1.3% of the employed labour force were engaged in the agricultural sector. The principal crops are cereals, potatoes and wine grapes. Livestock-rearing is also of some importance. Agricultural GDP decreased at an average annual rate of 2.8% in 1995–2004. Real agricultural GDP declined by 2.3% in 2003 and by 3.4% in 2004.

Industry (including mining, manufacturing, construction and power) provided 16.1% of GDP and engaged an estimated 21.1% of the employed labour force in 2004. Industrial GDP increased, in real terms, at an average annual rate of 3.4% in 1995–2004; it rose by 3.1% in 2003 and by 2.1% in 2004.

Manufacturing activities constitute the most important industrial sector, contributing 9.4% of GDP in 2003 and engaging an estimated 10.7% of the employed work-force in 2004. Although the country's deposits of iron ore are no longer exploited, the iron and steel industry remains one of the most important sectors of the Luxembourg economy; metal manufactures accounted for an estimated 31.1% of total exports in 2004. The Luxembourg steel industry is dominated by Arcelor, which was formed in June 2001 by the merger of the Luxembourg-based Aciéries Réunies de Burbach-Eich-Dudelange SA—ARBED and the steel companies Usinor, of France, and Aceralia, of Spain, to form the world's largest steel group. In January 2003 Arcelor announced that no further investment would be made in the two smelting furnaces in the Val du Fensch and that hot-phase production would gradually cease. The steelworks, which employed around 1,500 workers and contributed 85% of the Val du Fensch's annual revenue, would eventually close in 2010. In January 2006 Arcelor rejected a takeover bid by Mittal Steel, which had overtaken Arcelor as the world's largest steel group in the previous year following a number of acquisitions. Machinery and other equipment provided 18.2% of total exports in 2004. Other important branches of manufacturing are basic manufactures and chemicals and related products. Real manufacturing GDP increased by an average of 2.6% per year in 1995–2003; it grew by 1.0% in 2002 and by 2.6% in 2003.

In 2002 92.8% of electricity was derived from natural gas and 4.0% from hydroelectric installations. Imports of mineral fuels and lubricants comprised 9.7% of the value of total imports in 2004.

The services sector contributed 83.4% of GDP and engaged an estimated 77.5% of the employed labour force in 2004. Favourable laws governing banking secrecy and taxation have encouraged the development of Luxembourg as a major international financial centre. Financial services contributed 30.8% of GDP in 2003. In 2004 there were 162 banks in Luxembourg, and 22,549 people were employed in banking activities. In 2005 there were 12,444 holding companies registered in Luxembourg. Stock exchange activities (notably the 'Eurobond' market and investment portfolio management) are also prominent; at April 2000 Luxembourg's investment fund sector was the biggest in Europe, with assets of €848,000m. In 2004 there were 95 approved insurance companies in Luxembourg, as well as 271 reinsurance companies. The GDP of the services sector increased, in real terms, at an average annual rate of 5.0% in 1995–2004; it rose by 2.6% in 2003 and by 3.6% in 2004.

In 2004, according to IMF figures, Luxembourg recorded a visible trade deficit of US $3,157m.; however, there was a surplus on the current account of the balance of payments of $2,828m. Other members of the European Union (EU, see p. 228) account for much of Luxembourg's foreign trade. In 2004 the principal source of imports (35.7%) was Belgium; other major providers were Germany (27.1%), France (13.9%) and the Netherlands (5.0%). The principal market for exports in that year was Germany (26.2%); other major purchasers were France (19.8%), Belgium (12.0%) and Italy (6.7%). The principal exports in 2004 were manufactured goods, particularly metal manufactures, and machinery. The principal imports were machinery, transport equipment, manufactured articles, notably metal manufactures, and mineral fuels and lubricants.

In 2003 a small budgetary surplus, of €500,000, was recorded. Government debt was equivalent to 6.6% of GDP in 2004. The annual rate of inflation averaged 1.9% in 1995–2004; consumer prices rose by 2.0% in 2003 and by 2.2% in 2004. The rate of unemployment averaged 3.9% in 2004. However, unemployment subsequently increased and in January 2006 was recorded at 4.8%. In the same month cross-border commuters from neighbouring states totalled 122,265, constituting more than one-third of the total employed in Luxembourg.

Luxembourg was a founder member of the EU and of the Benelux Economic Union (see p. 385). Luxembourg is also a member of the European Bank for Reconstruction and Development (see p. 224), and the European System of Central Banks (ESCB), inaugurated in 1998 (see European Central Bank).

Luxembourg's economy expanded at an average annual rate of more than 5% during 1985–2000, recording increases in GDP even in the early 1990s when neighbouring countries were in recession. In January 1999 Luxembourg participated in the adoption of the euro as the single unit of currency for transactions throughout the euro zone and as an internationally traded currency in the 11 EU countries participating in Economic and Monetary Union (EMU). The country's economic success was based on its development as an international financial centre, following the decline in the importance of the country's previously dominant iron and steel industry. Rapid economic expansion in Luxembourg has attracted an increasing number of cross-border workers from neighbouring countries. These workers, who account for more than one-third of the work-force, pay social security contributions in Luxembourg but retire to their native countries to spend their pensions, which are financed by Luxembourg. The solution advanced by the Government was to eschew further job creation in favour of the development of high-technology industries (with a substantial value added), which do not require a larger work-force. This plan was also expected to help to diversify the economy away from too great a dependence on the financial sector, the future profitability of which was likely to be eroded by the effects of EU integration, including the harmonization of taxation and regulatory structures. New EU taxation rules concerning overseas investments agreed in early 2003 required most EU countries to begin exchanging account details from 2005 in an attempt to eliminate tax fraud. However, they allowed Luxembourg (as well as Austria and Belgium) to retain banking secrecy for at least the next six years. In these countries a withholding tax would be levied on non-residents' savings instead. The tax would rise incrementally from 15% in 2005 to 35% in 2011. Crucially, Switzerland would have to apply the same rate of tax, thus avoiding 'capital flight' from Luxembourg. Moreover, Luxembourg secured an agreement that it would not be forced to exchange banking information in the future without parallel action from Switzerland (which was extremely unlikely). Luxembourg also hoped to diversify into the potentially lucrative cross-border pensions fund market, and installed a flexible regulatory regime in order to take full advantage of an EU directive (incorporated into Luxembourg's national legislation in July 2005, ahead of a September deadline) allowing pension-fund providers to offer services and products to customers across the EU. The rapid economic expansion of the late 1990s declined significantly in 2000–03, when GDP growth averaged only 1.7% per year. A recovery, to 4.5%, was recorded in 2004, however, and this was sustained in 2005, according to preliminary estimates. This strong growth was largely attributed to innovation within the banking and insurance sectors, and to the expansion of international financial markets, which stimulated Luxembourg's financial intermediation and business services. However, the growth rate in the financial sector was expected to slow as the sector matured, and in 2006 the economy was forecast to expand by 4.0%. In a report published in January 2006, the IMF recommended that the Government introduce flexible working practices to combat the rising unemployment rate, which was predicted to reach 5.3% by the end of the year, and restrain expenditure, with the aim of achieving a budget surplus of 1% of GDP over the medium term, in an attempt to sustain long-term growth and support the ageing population.

Education

Education in Luxembourg is compulsory from the age of four to 15 years. Primary education begins at six years of age and lasts for six years. German is the initial language of instruction at primary level. French is added to the programme in the second year, and replaces German as the language of instruction at higher secondary level. In 2002/03 enrolment in primary education included 90.3% of children in the relevant age-group (males 90.1%; females 90.6%).

At the age of 12, children can choose between secondary school (lycée) and technical education (lycée technique). The first year of secondary school is a general orientation course on comprehensive lines, which is then followed by a choice between two sections: the Classical Section, with an emphasis on Latin, and the Modern Section, which stresses English and other modern languages. The completed secondary course lasts seven years, and leads to the Certificat de Fin d'Etudes Secondaires, which qualifies for university entrance. The technical education course (six to eight years) leads either to a vocational diploma, a technician's diploma (diplôme de technicien) or a technical baccalaureate diploma (bac technique) and is devised in three parts: an orientation and observation course, an intermediate course and an upper course. In 2002/03 enrolment in secondary education included 80.0% of children in the relevant age-group (males 77.3%; females 82.9%).

The Centre Universitaire was established in 1969, offering one-year or two-year courses in the humanities, sciences and law and economics, as well as training courses for lawyers and teachers, following which the students generally attend other European universities. The Institut Supérieur de Technologies (IST) is an institute for higher education at university level in civil engineering, electrical engineering, applied computer sciences and mechanical engineering.

Central government expenditure on national education, vocational training and sport in 2003 was projected at €662.3m. (equivalent to around 12% of total current expenditure).

Public Holidays

2006: 2 January (for New Year's Day), 27 February (Carnival), 17 April (Easter Monday), 1 May (Labour Day), 25 May (Ascension Day), 5 June (Whit Monday), 23 June (National Day), 15 August (Assumption), 4 September (Luxembourg City Fête,

LUXEMBOURG

Luxembourg City only), 1 November (All Saints' Day), 25 December (Christmas), 26 December (St Stephen's Day).
2007: 1 January (New Year's Day), 19 February (Carnival), 9 April (Easter Monday), 1 May (Labour Day), 17 May (Ascension Day), 28 May (Whit Monday), 23 June (National Day), 15 August (Assumption), 3 September (Luxembourg City Fête, Luxembourg City only), 1 November (All Saints' Day), 25 December (Christmas), 26 December (St Stephen's Day).

Weights and Measures
The metric system is in force.

Statistical Survey

Source (unless otherwise stated): Service Central de la Statistique et des Etudes Economiques (STATEC), Centre Administratif Pierre Werner, 13 rue Erasme, 1468 Luxembourg; tel. 478-42-52; fax 46-42-89; e-mail statec.post@statec.etat.lu; internet www.statec.lu.

AREA AND POPULATION

Area: 2,586 sq km (999 sq miles).

Population: 384,634 at census of 1 March 1991; 439,539 (males 216,540, females 222,999) at census of 15 February 2001; 455,000 (males 224,740, females 230,260) official estimate at 1 January 2005.

Density (January 2005): 175.9 per sq km.

Principal Towns ('000, 2004): Luxembourg-Ville (capital) 77.3; Esch-sur-Alzette 27.9; Differdange 18.9; Dudelange 17.5; Pétange 14.4; Sanem 13.7; Hesperange 11.2.

Births, Marriages and Deaths (2003): Live births 5,303 (birth rate 11.8 per 1,000); Marriages 2,001 (marriage rate 4.5 per 1,000); Deaths 4,053 (death rate 9.0 per 1,000).

Expectation of Life (WHO estimates, years at birth): 79 (males 76; females 82) in 2003. Source: WHO, *World Health Report*.

Immigration and Emigration (2003): Arrivals 12,613; Departures 10,540.

Employment (estimates, '000 persons, incl. armed forces, 2004): Agriculture, hunting, forestry and fishing 3.9; Mining and quarrying 0.3; Manufacturing 32.3; Electricity, gas and water supply 1.6; Construction 29.4; Wholesale and retail trade, repair of motor vehicles, motorcycles and personal and household goods 42.1; Hotels and restaurants 14.2; Transport, storage and communications 25.5; Financial intermediation 33.8; Real estate, renting and business activities 50.2; Public administration and defence and compulsory social security 15.8; Education 13.4; Health and social work 19.6; Other community, social and personal service activities 11.4; Private households with employed persons 7.4; *Total employed* 301.0.

HEALTH AND WELFARE
Key Indicators

Total Fertility Rate (children per woman, 2003): 1.7.
Under-5 Mortality Rate (per 1,000 live births, 2004): 6.
HIV/AIDS (% of persons aged 15–49, 2003): 0.2.
Physicians (per 1,000 head, 2002): 2.6.
Hospital Beds (per 1,000 head, 2001): 6.9.
Health Expenditure (2002): US $ per head (PPP): 3,066.
Health Expenditure (2002): % of GDP: 6.2.
Health Expenditure (2002): public (% of total): 85.4.
Access to water (% of persons, 2002): 100.
Human Development Index (2003): ranking: 4.
Human Development Index (2003): value: 0.949.

For sources and definitions, see explanatory note on p. vi.

AGRICULTURE, ETC.

Principal Crops ('000 metric tons, 2004): Wheat 80.0; Rye 8.0; Barley 53.0; Oats 11.0; Triticale (wheat-rye hybrid) 23.0; Potatoes 22.0; Rapeseed 16.0; Mushrooms 15.0 (FAO estimate); Apples 4.0 (FAO estimate); Grapes 17.0 (FAO estimate).

Livestock (2004): Cattle 185.0; Horses 3.1 (FAO estimate); Pigs 76.0; Sheep 7.0; Poultry 80.0 (FAO estimate).

Livestock Products (FAO estimates, metric tons, 2004): Beef and veal 17,500; Pigmeat 11,500; Chicken meat 15,950; Milk 265,000.

Forestry ('000 cubic metres, 2004): *Roundwood Removals* (excl. fuel wood) 264 (Sawlogs, veneer logs and logs for sleepers 136, Pulpwood 122, Other 6); *Sawnwood Production* (FAO estimates, incl. railway sleepers) 133 (Coniferous 113, Broadleaved 20).

Source: FAO.

INDUSTRY

Selected Products ('000 metric tons, 2004 unless otherwise indicated): Crude steel 2,684; Rolled steel products 4,083; Wine ('000 hl) 155.8 (2004/05); Beer ('000 hl) 390.7 (provisional figure, 2003); Electric energy (million kWh) 3,714 (2002).

FINANCE

Currency and Exchange Rates: 100 cent = 1 euro (€). *Sterling and Dollar Equivalents* (30 December 2005): £1 sterling = 1.45961 euros; US $1 = 0.84767 euros; €100 = £68.51 = $117.97. *Average Exchange Rate* (euros per US dollar): 0.8860 in 2003; 0.8054 in 2004; 0.8041 in 2005. Note: The national currency was formerly the Luxembourg franc. From the introduction of the euro, with Luxembourg's participation, on 1 January 1999, a fixed exchange rate of €1 = 40.3399 Luxembourg francs was in operation. Euro notes and coins were introduced on 1 January 2002. The euro and local currency circulated alongside each other until 28 February, after which the euro became the sole legal tender..

Budget (provisional, € million, 2003): *Revenue:* Direct taxes 3,122.4; Indirect taxes 2,877.5; Other current revenue 305.4; Capital revenue 44.4; Total 6,349.7. *Expenditure:* Ministry of Agriculture, Viticulture and Rural Development 72.1; Ministry of the Civil Service and Administrative Reform 377.7; Ministry of Culture, Further Education and Research 148.5; Ministry of the Economy 19.1; Ministry of the Environment 25.7; Ministry of Family Affairs, Social Solidarity and Youth 931.6; Ministry of Finance 185.7; Ministry of Foreign Affairs, External Trade, Co-operation, Humanitarian Action and Defence 213.1; Ministry of Health 63.1; Ministry of the Interior 451.6; Ministry of Justice 71.1; Ministry of Labour and Employment 138.4; Ministry of National Education, Vocational Training and Sport 662.3; Ministry of Public Works 113.3; Ministry of Small Business, Tourism and Housing 64.5; Ministry of Social Security 1,421.4; Ministry of State 103.6; Ministry of Transport 450.9; Ministry of Women's Affairs 7.6; Total current expenditure 5,521.4; Capital expenditure 827.8; Total 6,349.2.

International Reserves (US $ million at 31 December 2004): Gold 32.41; IMF special drawing rights 15.26, Reserve position in IMF 139.25; Foreign exchange 143.87, Total 330.78. Source: IMF, *International Financial Statistics*.

Money Supply (€ million at 31 December 2004): Currency issued 1,117*; Demand deposits at banking institutions 56,020. Source: IMF, *International Financial Statistics*.
*Currency put into circulation by the Banque Centrale du Luxembourg was €28,489m.

Cost of Living (Consumer Price Index; base: 2000 = 100): All items 104.8 in 2002; 106.9 in 2003; 109.3 in 2004. Source: IMF, *International Financial Statistics*.

National Income and Product (€ million at current prices, 2003): Compensation of employees 12,388.6; Operating surplus and mixed income (incl. consumption of fixed capital) 8,636.2; *Gross domestic product (GDP) at factor cost* 21,024.8; Taxes, *less* subsidies on production and imports 2,931.0; *GDP in market prices* 23,955.9; Primary incomes received from abroad 52,972.4; *Less* Primary incomes paid abroad 55,722.5; *Gross national income* 21,205.8; *Less* Consumption of fixed capital 3,057.5; *Net national income* 18,148.3.

Expenditure on the Gross Domestic Product (€ million at current prices, 2004): Final consumption expenditure 15,111.8 (Households 9,923.1, Non-profit institutions serving households 480.9, General government 4,707.7); Gross capital formation 4,999.0 (Gross fixed capital formation 4,959.4, Changes in inventories 97.6, Acquisitions, less disposals, of valuables –57.9); *Total domestic expenditure* 20,110.8; Exports of goods and services 37,522.3; *Less* Imports of goods and services 31,969.6; *GDP in market prices* 25,663.5.

Gross Domestic Product by Economic Activity (€ million at current prices, 2004): Agriculture, hunting, forestry and fishing

125.0; Mining and quarrying, manufacturing, electricity, gas and water supply 2,881.2; Construction 1,488.1; Wholesale and retail trade, repair of motor vehicles, motorcycles and personal and household goods, hotels and restaurants, transport and communications 5,526.3; Financial services, real estate, renting and business activities 12,684.8; Other community, social and personal service activities 4,443.5; *Sub-total* 27,148.9; *Less* Financial intermediation services indirectly measured 4,533.4; *Gross value added in basic prices* 22,615.6; Taxes on products 3,309.5; *Less* Subsidies on products 261.5; *GDP in market prices* 25,663.5.

Balance of Payments (US $ million, 2004): Exports of goods f.o.b. 13,714; Imports of goods f.o.b. −16,871; *Trade balance* −3,157; Exports of services 33,273; Imports of services −22,318; *Balance on goods and services* 7,799; Other income received 61,081; Other income paid −64,818; *Balance on goods, services and income* 4,061; Current transfers received 4,262; Current transfers paid −5,495; *Current balance* 2,828; Capital account (net) −303; Direct investment abroad −59,244; Direct investment from abroad 57,440; Portfolio investment assets −87,546; Portfolio investment liabilities 138,238; Financial derivatives liabilities −2,814; Other investment assets −117,936; Other investment liabilities 68,693; Net errors and omissions 650; *Overall balance* 8. Source: IMF, *International Financial Statistics*.

EXTERNAL TRADE

Principal Commodities (€ million, 2004): *Imports:* Food and live animals 963.9; Beverages and tobacco 460.6; Crude materials (inedible) except fuels 987.9; Mineral fuels, lubricants, etc. 1,302.1; Chemicals and related products 1,289.5; Metal manufactures 1,641.8; Other basic manufactures 1,115.9; Machinery and other equipment 2,267.9; Transport equipment 1,874.2; Miscellaneous manufactured articles 1,557.0; Total (incl. others) 13,460.8. *Exports:* Food and live animals 452.7; Chemicals and related products 673.3; Metal manufactures 3,038.2; Other basic manufactures 1,590.4; Machinery and other equipment 1,778.5; Transport equipment 594.0; Miscellaneous manufactured articles 1,228.5; Total (incl. others) 9,783.6.

Principal Trading Partners (€ million, 2004): *Imports:* Belgium 4,811.4; France 1,866.6; Germany 3,641.7; Japan 166.5; Italy 359.0; Netherlands 677.8; Switzerland 187.0; United Kingdom 220.0; USA 481.2; Total (incl. others) 13,460.8. *Exports:* Austria 234.5; Belgium 1,170.6; France 1,940.7; Germany 2,564.2; Italy 658.8; Netherlands 447.3; Spain 360.0; Sweden 126.6; United Kingdom 488.3; USA 251.7; Total (incl. others) 9,783.6.

TRANSPORT

Railways (traffic, million, 2003): Passenger-kilometres 262; Freight ton-kilometres 568.

Road Traffic (motor vehicles in use at 1 January 2004): Cars 293,398; Motorcycles 13,380; Buses and coaches 1,227; Goods vehicles 23,330; Tractors 27,164; Total 358,499.

Shipping: *River Traffic* (Port of Mertert, '000 metric tons, 2003): Goods loaded 312, Goods unloaded 1,075. *Merchant Fleet* (vessels registered at 31 December 2004): Number of vessels 56; Total displacement 689,658 grt (Source: Lloyd's Register-Fairplay, *World Fleet Statistics*).

Civil Aviation (traffic on scheduled services, 2003): Passengers carried 1,458,000; Freight (metric tons) 656,567.

TOURISM

Tourist Arrivals (at accommodation establishments): 875,845 in 2002; 923,315 in 2003; 933,359 in 2004.

Arrivals by Country (2003): Belgium 185,627; France 76,842; Germany 117,352; Italy 20,481; Netherlands 255,140; United Kingdom 49,823; USA 20,587; Total (incl. others) 923,315.

Tourism Receipts (US $ million): 1,915 in 2001; 2,186 in 2002; 2,402 in 2003.

COMMUNICATIONS MEDIA

Facsimile Machines: 20,000 in use (1998).
Mobile Cellular Telephones: 539,000 subscribers (2004).
Telephones: 360,100 main lines in use (2004).
Personal Computers ('000 in use): 296 (2004).
Internet Users ('000): 271 (2004).
Daily Newspapers: 6 (2005).
Book Production: 513 titles (1997).
Radio Receivers: 285,000 in use (1997).
Television Receivers: 260,000 in use (2000).

Sources: partly UNESCO, *Statistical Yearbook*; International Telecommunication Union.

EDUCATION

(2002/03)

Nursery: 816 teachers; 10,896 pupils.
Primary: 2,966 teachers; 32,004 pupils.
Secondary, Middle, Vocational and Technical: 3,279 teachers (state sector only); 9,963 pupils (secondary), 22,093 pupils (middle, vocational and technical).
Higher Institute of Technology: 358 students.
Teacher Training: 401 students.
Other University-level: 8,580 students, incl. 6,288 studying abroad.

Directory

The Constitution

The Constitution now in force dates back to 17 October 1868, but in 1919 a constituent assembly introduced some important changes, declaring that the sovereign power resided in the nation, that all secret treaties were denounced and that deputies were to be elected by a list system by means of proportional representation, on the basis of universal adult suffrage. Electors must be citizens of Luxembourg and must have attained 18 years of age. Candidates for election must have attained 21 years of age (this was reduced to 18 years of age by the electoral law of 18 February 2003). The Grand Duke, who is Sovereign, chooses government ministers, may intervene in legislative questions and has certain judicial powers. There is a single-chamber legislature, the Chamber of Deputies (Chambre des Députés), with 60 members elected for five years. There are four electoral districts: the North, the Centre, the South and the East. By the law of 9 October 1956 the Constitution was further revised to the effect that: 'The exercise of prerogatives granted by the Constitution to the legislative, executive and judiciary powers, can, by treaty, be temporarily vested in institutions of international law.' The Constitution was further amended on 12 December 1994, 12 July 1996 (introducing a Constitutional Court) and 12 January 1998. In addition to the Council of Ministers, which consists of the President of the Government (Prime Minister) and at least three other ministers, the State Council (Conseil d'Etat—which is the supreme administrative tribunal and which also fulfils certain legislative functions) comprises 21 members nominated by the Sovereign who serve for 15 years (not necessarily continuous) or until the age of 72.

The Government

HEAD OF STATE

Grand Duke: HRH Henri Albert Félix Marie Guillaume (succeeded to the throne 7 October 2000).
Marshal of the Court: Henri Ahlborn.

COUNCIL OF MINISTERS
(April 2006)

A coalition of the Parti Chrétien Social (PCS) and the Parti Ouvrier Socialiste Luxembourgeois (POSL).

Prime Minister and Minister of State and of Finance: Jean-Claude Juncker (PCS).
Deputy Prime Minister and Minister of Foreign Affairs and Immigration: Jean Asselborn (POSL).
Minister of Agriculture, Viticulture and Rural Development and of Small Business, Tourism and Housing: Fernand Boden (PCS).

LUXEMBOURG

Minister of Family Affairs and Integration and of Equal Opportunities: MARIE-JOSÉE JACOBS (PCS).
Minister of Culture, Further Education and Research, of Labour and Employment and of Religious Affairs: FRANÇOIS BILTGEN (PCS).
Minister of the Interior and Spatial Planning: JEAN-MARIE HALSDORF (PCS).
Minister of Justice and of the Treasury and Budget: LUC FRIEDEN (PCS).
Minister of National Education and Vocational Training: MADY DELVAUX-STEHRES (POSL).
Minister of the Economy and External Trade and of Sport: JEANNOT KRECKÉ (POSL).
Minister of Co-operation and Humanitarian Action, of Communications and of Defence: JEAN-LOUIS SCHILTZ (PCS).
Minister of Health and of Social Security: MARS DI BARTOLOMEO (POSL).
Minister of the Environment and of Transport: LUCIEN LUX (POSL).
Minister of the Civil Service and Administrative Reform and of Public Works: CLAUDE WISELER (PCS).
Minister-delegate of Foreign Affairs and Immigration: NICOLAS SCHMIT (POSL).
Secretary of State for Parliamentary Relations, for Agriculture, Viticulture and Rural Development and for Culture, Further Education and Research: OCTAVIE MODERT (PCS).

MINISTRIES

Office of the Prime Minister: Hôtel de Bourgogne, 4 rue de la Congrégation, 1352 Luxembourg; tel. 478-21-00; fax 46-17-20.

Ministry of Agriculture, Viticulture and Rural Development: 1 rue de la Congrégation, 1352 Luxembourg; tel. 478-25-00; fax 46-40-27; e-mail min.agri@ma.etat.lu; internet www.ma.etat.lu.

Ministry of the Civil Service and Administrative Reform: 63 ave de la Liberté, BP 1807, 1931 Luxembourg; tel. 478-31-01; fax 35-24-78; e-mail info@mfpra.public.lu; internet www.mfpra.public.lu.

Ministry of Culture, Higher Education and Research: 20 montée de la Pétrusse, 2273 Luxembourg; tel. 478-66-19; fax 40-24-27; e-mail info@mcesr.public.lu; internet www.ltam.lu/culture.

Ministry of the Economy and External Trade: 6 blvd Royal, 2449 Luxembourg; tel. 478-1; fax 46-04-48; e-mail info@eco.public.lu; internet www.eco.public.lu.

Ministry of the Environment: 18 montée de la Pétrusse, 2327 Luxembourg; tel. 478-68-24; fax 40-04-10; e-mail ministere_environnement@mev.etat.lu; internet www.emwelt.lu.

Ministry of Equal Opportunities: 12–14 ave Emile Reuter, 2921 Luxembourg; tel. 478-58-14; fax 24-18-86; e-mail info@mega.public.lu; internet www.mpf.lu.

Ministry of Family Affairs and Integration: 12–14 ave Emile Reuter, 2919 Luxembourg; tel. 478-65-00; fax 478-65-70.

Ministry of Finance: 3 rue de la Congrégation, L-1352 Luxembourg; tel. 478-1; fax 47-52-41; internet www.etat.lu/FI.

Ministry of Foreign Affairs and Immigration: 5 rue Notre-Dame, 2240 Luxembourg; tel. 478-1; fax 22-31-44; e-mail officielle.boite@mae.etat.lu; internet www.mae.lu.

Ministry of Health: Villa Louvigny, allée Marconi, 2120, Luxembourg; tel. 478-55-00; fax 46-79-63; e-mail ministere-sante@ms.etat.lu; internet www.etat.lu/MS.

Ministry of the Interior and Spatial Planning: 19 rue Beaumont, 1219 Luxembourg; tel. 478-46-06; fax 22-11-25; e-mail minint@mi.etat.lu; internet www.etat.lu/MI.

Ministry of Justice: 13 rue Erasme, centre administratif Pierre Werner, 1468 Luxembourg; tel. 478-45-37; fax 22-52-96; internet www.mj.public.lu.

Ministry of Labour and Employment: 26 rue Zithe, 2763 Luxembourg; tel. 478-61-22; fax 48-63-25; e-mail jean.zahlen@mt.etat.lu; internet www.etat.lu/MT.

Ministry of National Education and Vocational Training: 29 rue Aldringen, 2926 Luxembourg; tel. 478-51-00; fax 478-51-13; e-mail info@men.lu; internet www.men.lu.

Ministry of Public Works: 4 blvd F. D. Roosevelt, 2450 Luxembourg; tel. 478-33-00; fax 46-97-09; e-mail contact@tp.etat.lu; internet www.mtp.etat.lu.

Ministry of Religious Affairs: 4 rue de la Congrégation, 2910 Luxembourg; tel. 478-1; fax 46-17-20.

Ministry of Small Business, Tourism and Housing: 6 ave Emile Reuter, 2937 Luxembourg; tel. 478-47-15; fax 478-11-87; internet www.mcm.public.lu (small business), www.mdt.public.lu (tourism), www.logement.lu (housing).

Ministry of Social Security: 26 rue Zithe, L-2936 Luxembourg; tel. 478-63-11; fax 478-63-28; e-mail romain.fehr@mss.etat.lu; internet www.mss.etat.lu.

Ministry of State: 4 rue de la Congrégation, 1352 Luxembourg; tel. 478-21-00; fax 46-17-20; e-mail ministere.etat@me.etat.lu; internet www.etat.lu.

Ministry of Transport: 11 rue Notre Dame, 2938 Luxembourg; tel. 478-44-00; fax 22-85-68; e-mail transport@tr.etat.lu; internet www.tr.etat.lu.

Legislature

CHAMBRE DES DÉPUTÉS
(Chamber of Deputies)

President: LUCIEN WEILER (Parti Chrétien Social).

General Election, 13 June 2004

Party	% of votes	Seats
Parti Chrétien Social	36.11	24
Parti Ouvrier Socialiste Luxembourgeois	23.37	14
Parti Démocratique Luxembourgeois	16.09	10
Déi Gréng	11.58	7
Comité d'Action pour la Démocratie et la Justice	9.95	5
Déi Lénk	1.90	—
Parti Communiste Luxembourgeois	0.92	—
Frai Partei Lëtzebuerg	0.12	—
Total	**100.00**	**60**

Advisory Councils

Conseil Economique et Social: 13 rue Erasme, BP 1306, 1013 Luxembourg; tel. 43-58-51; fax 42-27-29; e-mail ces@ces.etat.lu; internet www.ces.etat.lu; f. 1966; consultative body on economics and social affairs; 39 mems; Pres. RAYMOND HENCKS; Sec.-Gen. MARIANNE NATI-STOFFEL.

Conseil d'Etat: 5 rue Sigefroi, 2536 Luxembourg; tel. 47-30-71; fax 46-43-22; e-mail conseil@ce.etat.lu; internet www.ce.etat.lu; 21 mems nominated by the Sovereign; Pres. PIERRE MORES; Vice-Pres JEAN-PIERRE SINNER, VICTOR ROD.

Political Organizations

Comité d'Action pour la Démocratie et la Justice (Aktiounskomitee fir Demokratie a Rentegerechtegkeet—ADR)(Action Committee for Democracy and Social Justice): 9 rue de la Loge, 1945 Luxembourg; tel. 46-37-42; fax 46-37-45; e-mail adr@chd.lu; internet www.adr.lu; f. 1989; present name adopted 1994; conservative; campaigns to secure improved pension rights for private-sector employees; Pres. GAST GIBÉRYEN; Vice-Pres. ROBERT MEHLEN.

Déi Gréng (The Greens): BP 454, 2014 Luxembourg; tel. 46-37-40-1; fax 46-37-43; e-mail greng@greng.lu; internet www.greng.lu; f. 1983; fmrly Déi Gréng Alternativ (Green Alternative Party); merged with the Gréng Lëscht Ekologesch Initiativ (Green List Ecological Initiative) in 1995; advocates 'grass-roots' democracy, environmental protection, social concern and increased aid to developing countries; Spokespersons TILLY METZ, ROBERT RINGS.

Déi Lénk (The Left): BP 817, 2018 Luxembourg; tel. 26-20-20-72; fax 26-20-20-73; e-mail sekretariat@dei-lenk.lu; internet www.dei-lenk.lu; f. 1999; individual membership; no formal leadership.

Parti Chrétien Social (Chrëschtlech Sozial Vollekspartei—PCS/CSV)(Christian Social Party): 4 rue de l'Eau, BP 826, 2018 Luxembourg; tel. 22-57-311; fax 47-27-16; e-mail csv@csv.lu; internet www.csv.lu; f. 1914; advocates political stability, sustained economic expansion, ecological and social progress; 9,500 mems; Pres. FRANÇOIS BILTGEN; Sec.-Gen. JEAN-LOUIS SCHILTZ.

Frai Partei Lëtzebuerg (FPL): Luxembourg; participated in 2004 elections.

Parti Communiste Luxembourgeois (PCL/KPL) (Communist Party): 2 rue Astrid, 1143 Luxembourg; tel. 44-60-66; e-mail info@zlv.lu; internet www.zlv.lu; f. 1921; Pres. ALI RUCKERT.

Parti Démocratique Luxembourgeois (Demokratesch Partei—PDL/DP)(Democratic Party): BP 510, 2015 Luxembourg; tel. 22-41-84-1; fax 47-10-07; e-mail groupdp@dp.lu; internet www.dp.lu; liberal; Leader CLAUDE MEISCH; Sec. ODETTE NEUMANN.

LUXEMBOURG

Parti Ouvrier Socialiste Luxembourgeois (Lëtzebuerger Sozialistesch Arbechterpartei—POSL/LSAP)(Socialist Workers' Party): 37 rue du St-Esprit, 1475 Luxembourg; tel. 45-65-73-1; fax 45-65-75; e-mail info@lsap.lu; internet www.lsap.lu; f. 1902; social democrat; 6,000 mems; Pres. ALEX BODRY; Sec.-Gen. ROMAIN SCHNEIDER.

Diplomatic Representation

EMBASSIES IN LUXEMBOURG

Austria: 3 rue des Bains, 1212 Luxembourg; tel. 47-11-88; fax 46-39-74; e-mail luxemburg-ob@bmaa.gv.at; internet www.aussenministerium.at/luxemburg; Ambassador WALTER HAGG.

Belgium: 4 rue des Girondins, 1626 Luxembourg; tel. 44-27-46-1; fax 45-42-82; e-mail luxembourg@diplobel.org; Ambassador INGEBORG KRISTOFFERSEN.

Cape Verde: 46 rue Goethe, 1637 Luxembourg; tel. 26-48-09-48; fax 26-48-09-49.

China, People's Republic: 2 rue Van der Meulen, 2152 Luxembourg; tel. 43-69-91-1; fax 42-24-23; e-mail ambchine@pt.lu; Ambassador SUN RONGMIN.

Denmark: 4 rue des Girondins, 1626 Luxembourg; tel. 22-21-22-1; fax 22-21-24; e-mail luxamb@um.dk; internet www.ambluxembourg.um.dk/da; Ambassador IB RITTO ANDREASEN.

Finland: 2 rue Heine, 1720 Luxembourg; tel. 49-55-51-1; fax 49-46-40; e-mail sanomat.lux@formin.fi; internet www.finlande.lu; Ambassador TARJA LAITIAINEN.

France: 8B blvd Joseph II, BP 359, 2013 Luxembourg; tel. 45-72-71-1; fax 45-72-71-227; Ambassador BERNARD POTTIER.

Germany: 20–22 ave Emile Reuter, BP 95, 2010 Luxembourg; tel. 45-34-45-1; fax 45-56-04; internet www.luxemburg.diplo.de; Ambassador ROLAND LOHKAMP.

Greece: 27 rue Marie-Adélaïde, L-2128 Luxembourg; tel. 44-51-93; fax 45-01-64; e-mail ambgrec@pt.lu; Ambassador NIKOLAOS KALADZIANOS.

Ireland: 28 route d'Arlon, 1140 Luxembourg; tel. 45-06-10; fax 45-88-20; e-mail luxembourg@iveagh.irlgov.ie; Ambassador MICHAEL HOEY.

Italy: 5–7 rue Marie-Adélaïde, 2128 Luxembourg; tel. 44-36-44-1; fax 45-55-23; e-mail italamb@ambitalialux.lu; internet www.amblussemburgo.esteri.it; Ambassador ERMANNO SQUADRILLI.

Japan: 62 ave de la Faïencerie, BP 92, 2010 Luxembourg; tel. 464-15-11; fax 46-41-76; internet www.lu.emb-japan.go.jp; Ambassador MITSUAKI KOJIMA.

Netherlands: 6 rue Sainte Zithe, 2763 Luxembourg; tel. 22-75-70; fax 40-30-16; e-mail lux@minbuza.nl; Ambassador G. STORM.

Poland: 2 rue de Pulvermühl, L-2356 Luxembourg; tel. 26-00-32; fax 26-68-75-54; e-mail ambapol@pt.lu; Ambassador BARBARA LABUDA.

Portugal: 24 rue Guillaume Schneider, 2522 Luxembourg; tel. 466-19-01; fax 46-51-69; e-mail embport@pt.lu; Ambassador RUI ALFREDO DE VASCONCELOS FÉLIX ALVES.

Romania 41 blvd de la Pétrusse, 2320 Luxembourg; tel. 45-51-59; fax 45-51-63; e-mail ambroum@pt.lu; Ambassador TUDOREL POSTOLACHE.

Russia: Château de Beggen, 1719 Luxembourg; tel. 42-23-33; fax 42-23-34; e-mail ambruslu@pt.lu; internet www.ruslux.mid.ru; Ambassador EDOUARD ROUBENOVITCH MALAYAN.

Spain: 4–6 blvd E. Servais, 2535 Luxembourg; tel. 46-02-55; fax 46-12-88; e-mail embesplu@pt.lu; Ambassador JULIO NUÑEZ MONTESINOS.

Sweden: 2 rue Heine, 1720 Luxembourg; tel. 26-64-61; fax 29-69-09; e-mail ambassaden.luxemburg@foreign.ministry.se; internet www.swedenabroad.com/luxembourg; Ambassador AGNETA SÖDERMAN.

Switzerland: 25A blvd Royal, BP 469, 2014 Luxembourg; tel. 22-74-74-1; fax 22-74-74-20; e-mail vertretung@lux.rep.admin.ch; Ambassador INGRID APELBAUM-PIDOUX.

Turkey: 49 rue Siggy vu Letzebuerg, 1933 Luxembourg; tel. 44-32-81; fax 44-32-81-34; e-mail ambtrlux@pt.lu.

United Kingdom: 5 blvd Joseph II, 1840 Luxembourg; tel. 22-98-64; fax 22-98-67; e-mail britemb@pt.lu; internet www.britain.lu; Ambassador JAMES CLARK.

USA: 22 blvd E. Servais, 2535 Luxembourg; tel. 46-01-23; fax 46-14-01; internet luxembourg.usembassy.gov; Ambassador ANN LOUISE WAGNER.

Judicial System

The lowest courts in Luxembourg are those of the Justices of the Peace, of which there are three, at Luxembourg-Ville, Esch-sur-Alzette and Diekirch. These are competent to deal with civil, commercial and criminal cases of minor importance. Above these are the two District Courts, Luxembourg being divided into the judicial districts of Luxembourg and Diekirch. These are competent to deal with civil, commercial and criminal cases. The Superior Court of Justice includes both a court of appeal, hearing decisions made by District Courts, and the Cour de Cassation. As the judicial system of the Grand Duchy does not employ the jury system, a defendant is acquitted if a minority of the presiding judges find him or her guilty. The highest administrative court is the Comité du Contentieux du Conseil d'Etat. Special tribunals exist to adjudicate upon various matters of social administration such as social insurance. The department of the Procureur Général (Attorney-General) is responsible for the administration of the judiciary and the supervision of judicial police investigations. In July 1996 an amendment to the Constitution introduced a Constitutional Court.

Judges are appointed for life by the Grand Duke, and are not removable except by judicial sentence.

President of the Superior Court of Justice: MARC THILL.
Attorney-General: JEAN-PIERRE KLOPP.

Religion

CHRISTIANITY

The Roman Catholic Church

For ecclesiastical purposes, Luxembourg comprises a single archdiocese, directly responsible to the Holy See. At 31 December 2003 adherents represented about 86.5% of the total population.

Archbishop of Luxembourg: Most Rev. FERNAND FRANCK, Archevêché, 4 rue Génistre, BP 419, 2014 Luxembourg; tel. 46-20-23; fax 47-53-81; e-mail archeveche@cathol.lu.

The Anglican Communion

Within the Church of England, Luxembourg forms part of the diocese of Gibraltar in Europe.

Chaplain: Rev. CHRISTOPHER LYON, 89 rue de Muhlenbach, 2168 Luxembourg; tel. and fax 43-95-93; e-mail chris.lyon@anglican.lu; internet www.anglican.lu; English-speaking church (Anglican Chaplaincy).

Protestant Church

Evangelical Church in the Grand Duchy of Luxembourg: rue de la Congrégation, 1352 Luxembourg; tel. 22-96-70; fax 46-71-88; e-mail mail@protestant.lu; internet www.protestant.lu; f. 1818; as Protestant Garnison Church, 1868 as multiconfessional community for the Grand Duchy; there are about 1,500 Evangelicals; Pres. Pasteur MICHEL FAULLIMMEL.

JUDAISM

Chief Rabbi: JOSEPH SAYAGH, 34 rue Alphouse Munchen, 2172 Luxembourg; tel. 45-23-66; fax 25-04-30.

The Press

DAILIES

Lëtzebuerger Journal: Résidence de Beauvoir, 51 rue de Strasbourg, BP 2101, 1021 Luxembourg; tel. 49-30-331; fax 49-20-65; e-mail journal@logic.lu; internet www.journal.lu; f. 1948; organ of the Democratic Party; Editor-in-Chief CLAUDE KARGER.

Luxemburger Wort: 2 rue Christophe Plantin, 2988 Luxembourg; tel. 49-93-1; fax 49-93-384; e-mail wort@wort.lu; internet www.wort.lu; f. 1848; German; Catholic; Christian Democrat; Chief Editor LÉON ZECHES; circ. 87,126 (2000).

Tageblatt/Zeitung fir Letzeburg: 44 rue du Canal, 4050 Esch-sur-Alzette; tel. 54-71-31-1; fax 54-71-30; e-mail tageblatt@tageblatt.lu; internet www.tageblatt.lu; f. 1913; French and German; Dir ALVIN SOLD.

La Voix du Luxembourg: 2 rue Christophe Plantin, 2988 Luxembourg; tel. 49-93-314; fax 49-93-773; e-mail voix@voix.lu; internet www.voix.lu; Editor LAURENT MOYSE.

Zeitung vum Lëtzeburger Vollek: BP 3008, 1030 Luxembourg; tel. 44-60-66-1; fax 44-60-66-66; internet www.zlv.lu; f. 1946; organ of the Communist Party; Editor ALI RUCKERT.

LUXEMBOURG

PERIODICALS

Carrière: BP 2535, 1025 Luxembourg; tel. 85-89-19; fax 85-89-19; e-mail carrieremag@logic.lu; internet www.logic.lu/carriere; f. 1988; women's interest; French and German; Editor MONIQUE MATHIEU; circ. 5,000.

Contacto: 2 rue Christophe Plantin, L-2988 Luxembourg; tel. 49-93-200; fax 49-93-448; e-mail contacto@saint-paul.lu; Portuguese; Editors ARMAND THILL, MARC WILLIÈRE; circ. 23,000.

Correio: 459 route de Longwy, L-1941 Bertrange; tel. 44-34-92; fax 44-34-93; e-mail correio@correio.lu; Portuguese; Editor JOSÉ DIAS; circ. 10,000.

Echo de l'Industrie: 7 rue Alcide de Gasperi, BP 1304, 1013 Luxembourg; tel. 43-53-66-1; fax 43-23-28; e-mail echo@fedil.lu; internet www.fedil.lu/Echo; f. 1920; monthly; industry, commerce; publ. by Fédération des Industriels Luxembourgeois; Dir NICOLAS SOISSON; circ. 2,100.

D'Handwierk: 2 circuit de la Foire Internationale, BP 1604, 1016 Luxembourg; tel. 42-45-11-1; fax 42-45-25; e-mail info@fda.lu; internet www.federation-des-artisans.lu; monthly; organ of the Fédération des Artisans and the Chambre des Métiers; Editor CHRISTIAN REUTER; circ. 7,000.

Horesca—Informations: 7 rue Alcide de Gasperi, BP 2524, 1025 Luxembourg; tel. 42-13-55-1; fax 42-13-55-299; e-mail info@horesca.lu; internet www.horesca.lu; monthly; hotel trade, tourism, gastronomy; Editor DAVE GIANNANDREA; circ. 6,000.

Le Jeudi: 44 rue du Canal, 4050 Esch-sur-Alzette; tel. 22-05-50; fax 22-05-44; e-mail redaction@le-jeudi.lu; internet www.lejeudi.lu; f. 1997; weekly; French; Dir DANIÈLE FONCK; circ. 10,890 (2003).

De Konsument: 55 rue des Bruyères, 1274 Howald; tel. 49-60-22-1; fax 49-49-57; e-mail ulc@pt.lu; internet www.ulc.lu; 12 a year; consumer affairs; Man. GUY GOEDERT.

De Lëtzeburger Bauer: 16 blvd d'Avranches, 2980 Luxembourg; tel. 48-81-61-1; fax 40-03-75; e-mail letzeburger.bauer@netline.lu; f. 1944; weekly; journal of Luxembourg farming; circ. 7,500.

D'Lëtzeburger Land: 59 rue Glesener, BP 2083, 1020 Luxembourg; tel. 48-57-57; fax 49-63-09; e-mail land@land.lu; internet www.land.lu; f. 1954; weekly; political, economic, cultural affairs; Editor-in-Chief MARIO HIRSCH; circ. 6,500.

Lux-Post: Editions Saphir, 23 rue des Gênets, 1621 Luxembourg; tel. 49-53-63; fax 48-53-70; local news; four regional edns; French and German.

Muselzeidung: 30 rue de Trèves, POB 36, 6701 Grevenmacher; tel. 75-87-47; fax 75-84-32; e-mail burton@pt.lu; internet www.muselzeidung.lu; f. 1981; regional magazine; monthly; German; Editor TANIA USELDINGER.

OGB-L Aktuell/Actualités: 60 blvd Kennedy, BP 149, 4002 Esch-sur-Alzette; tel. 54-05-45-1; fax 54-16-20; e-mail ogb-l@ogb-l.lu; internet www.ogb-l.lu; f. 1919; monthly; journal of the Luxembourg General Confederation of Labour; circ. 43,000.

Revue/D'Letzebuerger Illustréiert: 2 rue Dicks, BP 2755, 1027 Luxembourg; tel. 49-81-81-1; fax 48-77-22; e-mail revue@revue.lu; internet www.revue.lu; f. 1945; weekly; illustrated; Man. Dir GUY LUDIG; Editor-in-Chief CLAUDE WOLF; circ. 31,000.

Revue Technique Luxembourgeoise: 4 blvd Grande-Duchesse Charlotte, 1330 Luxembourg; tel. 45-13-54; fax 45-09-32; e-mail aliasbl@pt.lu; internet www.aliai.lu; f. 1908; quarterly; technology.

Sauerzeidung: 30 rue de Trèves, BP 36, 6701 Grevenmacher; tel. 75-87-47; fax 75-84-32; e-mail burton@pt.lu; internet www.muselzeidung.lu; f. 1988; regional newspaper; monthly; German; Publr EUGENE BURTON; circ. 10,000.

Soziale Fortschrett (LCGB): 11 rue du Commerce, BP 1208, Luxembourg; tel. 49-94-24-1; fax 49-94-24-49; internet www.lcgb.lu; f. 1921; monthly; journal of the Confederation of Christian Trade Unions of Luxembourg; Pres. ROBERT WEBER; circ. 36,000.

Télécran: 2 rue Christophe Plantin, BP 1008, 1010 Luxembourg; tel. 49-93-50-0; fax 49-93-59-0; e-mail telecran@telecran.lu; internet www.telecran.lu; f. 1978; TV and family weekly; illustrated; Editor-in-Chief ROLAND ARENS; circ. 47,630 (2003).

Transport: 13 rue du Commerce, BP 2615, 1026 Luxembourg; tel. 22-67-86-1; fax 22-67-09; e-mail syprolux@pt.lu; internet www.fcpt-syprolux.lu; fortnightly; circ. 3,800.

Woxx: 51 ave de la Liberté, BP 684, 2016 Luxembourg; tel. 29-79-99-0; fax 29-79-79; e-mail woxx@woxx.lu; internet www.woxx.lu; f. 1988; as GréngeSpoun; weekly; social, ecological, environmental and general issues; Secs ROBERT GARCIA, RICHARD GRAF, RENÉE WAGENER; circ. 3,000.

NEWS AGENCIES

Agence Europe SA: BP 428, 2014 Luxembourg; tel. 22-00-32; fax 46-22-77; e-mail info@agenceurope.com; internet www.agenceurope.com.

Reuters Ltd (United Kingdom): 25C blvd Royal, BP 915, 2449 Luxembourg; Correspondent MICHELE SINNER.

Agence France-Presse, Associated Press (USA) and United Press International (USA) are also represented in Luxembourg.

PRESS ASSOCIATIONS

Association Luxembourgeoise des Editeurs de Journaux: 2 rue Christophe Plantin, 2988 Luxembourg; tel. 49-93-200; fax 49-93-38-6; e-mail direction@saint-paul.lu; internet www.saint-paul.lu; Pres. ALVIN SOLD.

Association Luxembourgeoise des Journalistes: BP 1732, 1017 Luxembourg; tel. 44-00-44; fax 85-88-40; e-mail rinfalt@tageblatt.lu; Pres. ROGER INFALT.

Publishers

Editions Guy Binsfeld: 14 place du Parc, 2313 Luxembourg; tel. 49-68-68; fax 40-76-09; e-mail binsfeld@binsfeld.lu; internet www.editionsguybinsfeld.lu; f. 1979; Man. Dir GUY BINSFELD; Chief Editor ROB KIEFFER.

Editions Phi: BP 321, 4004 Esch-sur-Alzette; tel. 54-13-82-820; fax 54-13-87; e-mail editions.phi@editpress.lu; internet www.phi.lu; f. 1980; fmrly Editions Francis van Maele; literature, art; Dirs A. THOME, A. FIXMER.

Editions Schortgen: 43, rue Marie Muller-Tesch, BP 367, 4250 Esch-sur-Alzette; tel. 54-64-87; fax 53-05-34; e-mail editions@schortgen.lu; art, literature, factual, cuisine, comics; Dir JEAN-PAUL SCHORTGEN.

Editpress Luxembourg SA: 44 rue du Canal, BP 147, 4050 Esch-sur-Alzette; tel. 54-71-31-1; fax 54-71-30; e-mail tageblatt@tageblatt.lu; internet www.tageblatt.lu; Dir ALVIN SOLD.

Edouard Kutter: BP 319, 2013 Luxembourg; tel. 22-35-71; fax 47-18-84; e-mail kuttered@pt.lu; internet www.kutter.lu; art, photography, facsimile edns on Luxembourg.

Imprimerie Joseph Beffort: 7 rue Pletzer, 8080 Luxembourg; tel. 25-44-55-1; fax 25-44-19; e-mail jmkerschen@beffort.lu; internet www.beffort.lu; f. 1869; scientific, economic reviews; Dir JEAN-MARIE KERSCHEN.

Saint-Paul Luxembourg SA: 2 rue Christophe Plantin, 2988 Luxembourg; tel. 49-93-1; fax 49-93-38-6; e-mail direction@saint-paul.lu; internet www.saint-paul.lu; f. 1887; Dir CHARLES RUPPERT.

PUBLISHERS' ASSOCIATIONS

Fédération Luxembourgeoise des Editeurs de Livres: 31 blvd Konrad Adenauer, BP 482, 2014 Luxembourg; tel. 43-94-44; fax 43-94-50; e-mail info@clc.lu; internet www.clc.lu; Dir ALBERT DAMING; Pres. ROMAIN JEBLICK.

Fédération Luxembourgeoise des Travailleurs du Livre: 26A rue de Pulvermühl, 2356 Luxembourg; tel. 42-24-18; fax 42-24-19; e-mail fltl@pt.lu; f. 1864; Pres. GUST STEFANETTI; Sec. LOUIS PINTO.

Broadcasting and Communications

TELECOMMUNICATIONS

Regulatory Authority

Institut Luxembourgeois de Régulation (ILR): 45 allée Scheffer, 2922 Luxembourg; tel. 45-88-45-1; fax 45-88-45-88; e-mail ilr@ilr.lu; internet www.ilr.lu; Dir ODETTE WAGENER.

Major Service Providers

Cegecom SA: 3 rue Jean Piret, BP 2708, 1027 Luxembourg; tel. 26-49-91; fax 26-49-96-99; e-mail info@cegecom.net; internet www.cegecom.lu; Man. Dir FRANÇOIS THYS.

Coditel SA: route d'Arlon 283, L-8011 Strassen; tel. 34-93-93-1; fax 34-93-98; e-mail info@coditel.lu; internet www.coditel.lu; Dir CHRISTIAN DURLET.

Entreprise des Postes et Télécommunications (EPT): 8A ave Monterey, 2020 Luxembourg; tel. 47-65-1; fax 47-51-10; e-mail registry@pt.lu; internet www.ept.lu; f. 1992; post, telecommunications and internet service provider; CEO MARCEL GROSS.

Equant (Global One Communications SA): 201 route de Thionville, 5885 Howald; tel. 27-30-11; fax 27-30-13-01; e-mail info.luxembourg@equant.com; internet www.equant.com; telecommunications operator; Pres. and CEO BARBARA DALIBARD.

P&T LUXGSM: 8A ave Monterey, 2020 Luxembourg; tel. 47-65-1; fax 47-51-10; e-mail contact@ept.lu; internet www.ept.lu; f. 1993;

LUXEMBOURG

mobile cellular telephone operator; subsidiary of Entreprise des Postes et Télécommunications; Dir MARCEL GROSS.

Tango: 75 route de Longwy, 8080 Bertrange; tel. 27-77-71-01; fax 27-77-78-88; e-mail info@tango.lu; internet www.tango.lu; fmrly Millicom Luxembourg; fixed and mobile telephony, as well as data network and Internet services; owned by Tele2 AB; Dir NICO HOLZHEIMER.

3C Communications SA: 75 rte de Longwy, 8080 Bertrange; tel. 27-75-01-01; fax 27-75-02-50; e-mail info@3cint.com; internet www.ccc.lu; fmrly Télé 2 Luxembourg; operates Internet payments, credit card transactions and public telephones; owned by Tele2 AB.

BROADCASTING

Regulatory Authority

Commission Indépendante de la Radiodiffusion Luxembourgeoise: Luxembourg.

Radio

Eldoradio: 47 Mühlenweg, BP 1344, 1013 Luxembourg; tel. 40-95-09-1; fax 40-95-09-509; e-mail eldoradio@eldoradio.lu; internet www.eldoradio.lu; music station.

Radio 100,7: 45A ave Monterey, BP 1833, 2163 Luxembourg; tel. 44-00-44-1; fax 44-00-44-940; e-mail dweyler@100komma7.lu; internet www.100komma7.lu; f. 1993; non-commercial cultural broadcaster.

Radio Ara: 2 rue de la Boucherie, BP 266, 1247 Luxembourg; tel. 22-22-89; fax 22-22-66; e-mail radioara@mindless.com; internet www.ara.lu; music broadcaster.

Radio DNR: 12 rue Christophe Plantin, 2988 Luxembourg; tel. 40-70-60; fax 40-81-63; internet www.dnr.lu; e-mail dnr@dnr.lu.

Radio Latina: 3 rue du Fort Bourbon, 1249 Luxembourg; tel. 29-95-96-201; fax 40-24-76; internet ww.radiolatina.lu; programmes for foreign communities in Luxembourg; Dir LUIS BARREIRA.

Radio LRB: BP 8, 3201 Bettembourg; tel. 52-44-88; fax 52-44-88; e-mail info@lrb.lu; internet www.lrb.lu; Man. SVEN WEISEN.

Radio WAKY Power FM 107: 300D route de Thionville, BP 70, 5801 Hespérange; tel. 48-20-85; fax 48-21-13; e-mail waky@waky.lu; internet www.waky.lu; English and Letzeburgish.

RTL Group: 45 blvd Pierre Frieden, 1543 Luxembourg; tel. 42-14-21; fax 42-142-27-60; internet www.rtlgroup.com; f. 2000; by merger of CLT-UFA and Pearson TV; 90.2% owned by Bertelsmann AG (Germany); 9.8% public ownership; 37 radio stations and television channels in 8 countries; Man. Dir ALAIN BERWICK.

  RTL Radio Lëtzebuerg: tel. 42-14-2; fax 42-14-22-737; e-mail news@rtl.lu; internet www.rtl.lu; broadcasts in Luxembourgish; Station Man. FERNAND MATHES; Chief Editor MARC LINSTER.

SES Astra: Château de Betzdorf, 6815 Betzdorf; tel. 710-725-1; fax 710-725-227; e-mail yves.feltes@ses-global.com; internet www.ses-astra.com; f. 2001; owned by SES Global; operates 13 satellites (broadcasting 1,300 digital and analogue television and radio channels); Chair. ROMAIN BAUSCH; CEO FERDINAND KAYSER.

Television

RTL Télé Lëtzeburg: 45 blvd Pierre Frieden, 1543 Luxembourg; tel. 42-14-28-10; fax 42-14-27-438; e-mail online@rtl.lu; internet www.rtl.lu; subsidiary of RTL Group.

Finance

(cap. = capital; res = reserves; dep. = deposits; m. = million; brs = branches; amounts in euros unless otherwise indicated)

BANKING

In 2004 there were 162 banks in Luxembourg, most of which were subsidiaries or branches of foreign banks; a selection of the principal banks operating internationally is given below.

Central Bank

Banque centrale du Luxembourg: 2 blvd Royal, 2983 Luxembourg; tel. 47-74-1; fax 47-74-49-10; e-mail sg@bcl.lu; internet www.bcl.lu; f. 1998; represents Luxembourg within the European System of Central Banks (ESCB); cap. 25.0m., res 117.8m., dep. 5,728.4m. (Dec. 2004); Pres. YVES MERSCH; Exec. Dirs ANDRÉE BILLON, SERGE KOLB.

Principal Banks

ABN Amro Bank (Luxembourg) SA: 46 ave J. F. Kennedy, 185 Luxembourg; tel. 26-07-1; fax 26-07-29-99; internet www.abnamro.lu; f. 1991; by merger; cap. 372.0m., res 40.9m., dep. 5,818.1m. (Dec. 2002); Chair. EELCO VAN BROCKHURST; Man. Dir HUGUES DELACOURT.

Banca di Roma International SA: 26 blvd Royal, BP 692, 2449 Luxembourg; tel. 47-79-06-1; fax 47-79-06-228; e-mail info@bancaroma.lu; internet www.bancaroma.lu; f. 1992; by merger; cap. 120.0m., res 72.2m., dep. 1,915.9m. (Dec. 2002); Chair. GIANFRANCO IMPERATORI; Gen. Man. ALESSANDRO AGNOLUCCI.

Banca Nazionale del Lavoro International SA: 51 rue des Glacis, BP 286, 2012 Luxembourg; tel. 22-50-31; fax 22-36-08; e-mail info@bnli.lu; f. 1977; cap. 25.0m., res 6.4m., dep. 1,959.9m. (Dec. 2003); Pres. RODOLFO RINALDI; Gen. Man. FABIO DI VINCENZO.

Bank Sarasin Europe SA: 287–289 route d'Arlon, 1150 Luxembourg; tel. 45-78-80-1; fax 45-23-96; e-mail infolux@sarasin.com; internet www.sarasin.lu; f. 1988; cap. 16.3m., res 18.3m., dep. 926m. (Dec. 2003); Chair. GUIDO VAN BERKEL; Man. Dir THOMAS WITTLIN.

Bankgesellschaft Berlin International SA: 30 blvd Royal, 2449 Luxembourg; tel. 47-78-1; fax 47-78-20-29; e-mail contact@bankgesellschaft.lu; internet www.bankgesellschaft.lu; f. 1995; by merger; cap. 57.0m., res 128.6m., dep. 4,848.8m. (Dec. 2003); Chair. SERGE DEMOLIÈRE; Man. Dirs HORST-DIETER HOCHSTETTER, UWE JUNGERWIRTH.

Banque et Caisse d'Epargne de l'Etat, Luxembourg: 1 place de Metz, 1930 Luxembourg; tel. 40-15-1; fax 40-15-20-99; internet www.bcee.lu; f. 1856; as Caisse de l'Epargne de l'Etat du Grand-Duché de Luxembourg, name changed as above 1989; govt-owned; cap. 173.5m., res 702.6m., dep. 32,975.0m. (Dec. 2002); Chair. VICTOR ROD; Pres. and CEO JEAN-CLAUDE FINCK; 96 brs.

Banque Degroof Luxembourg SA: 12 rue E. Ruppert, 2453 Luxembourg; tel. 45-35-45-1; fax 25-07-21; e-mail investors.relationdegroof.lu; internet www.degroof.be; cap. 37.0m., res 51.7m., dep. 1,279.7m. (Sept. 2002); Chair. ALAIN PHILIPPSON; Man. Dir GEERT DE BRUYNE.

Banque LBLux SA: 3 rue Jean Monnet, BP 602, 2180 Luxembourg; tel. 42-43-41; fax 42-43-45-099; e-mail bank@lblux.lu; internet www.lblux.lu; f. 1973; cap. 300.0m., res 159.1m., dep. 12,842.5m. (Dec. 2002); Chair. Dr PETER KAHN; Man. Dirs HENRI STOFFEL, ALEX MEYER.

Banque Ippa et Associés SA: 34 ave de la Liberté, BP 1134, 1011 Luxembourg; tel. 26-29-26-29; fax 26-29-26-26; e-mail customer@bia.lu; internet www.bia.lu; f. 1989; as Banque Ippa et Associés; current name adopted in 2000 following merger with Bank Anhyp Luxembourg SA; cap. 11.0m., res 5.8m., dep. 404.0m. (2003); Chair. GÉRARD FIEVET; Man. Dir YVES LAHAYE.

Banque de Luxembourg SA: 14 blvd Royal, BP 2221, 1022 Luxembourg; tel. 26-20-26-60; fax 499-24-55-99; e-mail bllux@pt.lu; internet www.banquedeluxembourg.com; f. 1920; 71% owned by Crédit Industriel d'Alsace et de Lorraine; cap. 100.0m., res 217.9m., dep. 10,925.6m. (Dec. 2003); Chair. PIERRE AHLBORN; Pres. ROBERT RECKINGER; 4 brs.

Banque Raiffeisen SC: 46 rue Charles Martel, L-2134 Merl; tel. 24-50-1; fax 22-75-41; internet www.raiffeisen.lu; f. 1926; as Caisse Centrale Raiffeisen SC, name changed as above July 2001; res 59.2m., dep. 2,044.1m. (Dec. 2002); Pres. PAUL LAUTERBOUR; Chair. and Gen. Man. ALPHONSE SINNES.

Banque Safra Luxembourg SA: 10A blvd Joseph II, BP 887, 2018 Luxembourg; tel. 45-47-73; fax 45-47-86; internet www.safra.lu; cap. Swiss francs 24.2m., res Swiss francs 160.6m., dep. Swiss francs 2,450.8m. (Dec. 2002); Chair. JOSEPH SAFRA; Man. Dir JORGE ALBERTO KININSBERG.

BHF-BANK International SA: 283 route d'Arlon, BP 258, 2012 Luxembourg; tel. 45-76-76-1; fax 45-83-20; f. 1972; as BHF Bank, name changed as above on 1 Jan. 2005; cap. 26.0m., res 46.5m., dep. 4,098.4m. (Dec. 2003); Chair. ROLAND SCHARFF; Man. Dirs Dr HARTMUT ROTHACKER, FRANK RYBKA.

BNP Paribas Luxembourg: 10A blvd Royal, 2093 Luxembourg; tel. 46-46-1; fax 46-46-90-00; internet www.bnpparibas.lu; cap. 100.0m., res 387.6m., dep. 15,098.3m. (Dec. 2002); Chair. ALAIN PAPIASSE; Gen. Mans ERIC MARTIN, PATRICE CROCHET.

Clearstream Banking SA: 42 ave J. F. Kennedy, 1855 Luxembourg; tel. 243-0; fax 24-33-80-00; e-mail marketing@clearstream.com; internet www.clearstream.com; f. 1970; as Cedelbank, name changed as above Jan. 2000; private bank; acts as the central bank's securities depository; total assets 8,288.9m. (Dec. 2003); CEO ANDRÉ ROELANTS.

Commerzbank International SA (CISAL): 11 rue Notre Dame, BP 303, 2013 Luxembourg; tel. 47-79-11-1; fax 47-79-11-270; e-mail cisal@commerzbank.com; internet www.commerzbank.lu; f. 1969; cap. 579.8m., res 509.9m., dep. 6,536.8m. (Dec. 2003); Pres. and Chair. KLAUS-PETER MULLER; Man. Dirs BERND HOLZENTHAL, ADRIEN NEY.

Crédit Agricole Indosuez Luxembourg SA: 39 allée Scheffer, BP 1104, 1011 Luxembourg; tel. 47-67-1; fax 46-24-42; internet www.e-private.com; f. 1969; present name adopted 1997; cap. 85.0m., res

LUXEMBOURG

40.7m., dep. 6,914.4m. (Dec. 2002); Chair. Jacques Haffner; Man. Dir and Gen. Man. Charles Hamer.

Crédit Lyonnais Luxembourg SA: 26A blvd Royal, BP 32, 2094 Luxembourg; tel. 47-68-31-1; fax 42-68-31-501; e-mail info@creditlyonnais.lu; internet www.creditlyonnais.lu; cap. 55m., res 25,163.1m., dep. 2,142.5m. (Dec. 2003); Pres. Patrice Durand; Gen. Man. Pierre-Paul Cochet.

Crédit Suisse (Luxembourg) SA: 56 Grand-Rue, BP 40, 2010 Luxembourg; tel. 46-00-11-1; fax 46-32-70; internet www.credit-suisse.com; cap. Swiss francs 43.0m., res Swiss francs 16.1m., dep. Swiss francs 2,186.3m. (Dec. 2003); Chair. Walter B. Kielholz; Man. Dir Hans-Ulrich Hügli.

Danske Bank International SA: 2 rue du Fossé, 2011 Luxembourg; tel. 46-12-75-1; fax 47-30-78; e-mail information@lu.danskebank.com; internet www.danskebank.com/lu; f. 1976; cap. 146.9m., res 12.9m., dep. 563.2m. (Dec. 2002); Chair. Sven Erik Lystbøk; Man. Dir Mogens Holm.

DekaBank Deutsche Girozentrale Luxembourg SA: 38 ave J. F. Kennedy, 1855 Luxembourg; tel. 22-09-11; fax 34-09-38-09; e-mail info@dekabank.lu; internet www.dekabank.lu; f. 1971; as Deutsche Girozentrale International SA, name changed as above after merger with DekaBank Luxembourg SA in Jan. 2002; cap. 50.0m., res 106.1m., dep. 7,196.9m. (Dec. 2002); Chair. Hans-Jürgen Gutenberger; CEO and Dir Rainer Mach.

Deutsche Bank Luxembourg SA: 2 blvd Konrad Adenauer, 1115 Luxembourg; tel. 42-12-21; fax 42-12-24-49; internet www.deutsche-bank.lu; f. 1970; as Deutsche Bank Compagnie Financière Luxembourg; cap. 215.0m., res 839.1m., dep. 48,421.5m. (Dec. 2002); Chair. Dr Tessen von Heydebreck; CEO Ernst Wilhelm Contzen.

Deutsche Postbank International SA: 18–20 Parc d'Activités Sydrall, L-5365 Munsbach; tel. 34-95-31-1; fax 34-95-32-550; e-mail deutsche.postbank@postbank.lu; internet www.postbank.de; f. 1993; cap. 145.0m., res 47.0m., dep. 8,929m. (Dec. 2003); Chair. Loukas Rizos; Gen. Mans Christoph Schmitz, Jochen Begas.

Dexia Banque Internationale à Luxembourg (Dexia BIL): 69 route d'Esch, 2953 Luxembourg; tel. 45-90-1; fax 45-90-20-10; e-mail contact@dexia-bil.lu; internet www.dexia-bil.lu; f. 1856; as Banque Internationale à Luxembourg, name changed as above in 2000; 99.9% owned by Dexia SA; cap. 141.2m., res 1,350.2m., dep. 40.4m. (Dec. 2003); Chair. François Narmon; CEO Marc Hoffmann; 40 brs.

Dresdner Bank Luxembourg SA: 26 rue de Marché-aux-Herbes, 2097 Luxembourg; tel. 47-60-1; fax 47-60-33-1; e-mail info@Dresdner-Bank.lu; internet www.dresdner-bank.lu; f. 1967; cap. 125.0m., res 891.5m., dep. 16,074.6m. (Dec. 2002); Chair. Dr Herbert Walter; CEO Benedikt Buhl.

DZ Bank International SA: 4 rue Thomas Edison, BP 661, 2016 Luxembourg; tel. 44-90-31; fax 44-90-32-00-1; e-mail info@dzi.lu; internet www.dzi.lu; f. 1978; previously called DG Bank Luxembourg SA, name changed as above in November 2001 after merger with GZ Bank International SA; 70.2% owned by DG International Beteiligungsgesellschaft, 27.3% owned by Finanzverbund Beteiligungsgesellschaft; cap. 80.7m., res 225.7m., dep. 13,458.3m. (Dec. 2003); Chair. Heinz Hilgert.

EFG Private Bank (Luxembourg) SA: 5 rue Jean Monnet, BP 897, 2018 Luxembourg; tel. 42-07-24-1; fax 42-07-24-650; e-mail fund@efgbank.lu; internet www.efgnav.lu; f. 1986; cap. 70.0m., res 13.7m., dep. 1,116.6m. (Dec. 2002); Chair. Paul Munchen; Man. Dir François Ries.

Fortis Banque Luxembourg: 50 ave J. F. Kennedy, 2951 Luxembourg; tel. 42-42-1; fax 42-42-25-79; e-mail info@bgl.lu; internet www.bgl.lu; f. 1919 as Banque Générale du Luxembourg SA; merged with Fortis Bank Luxembourg SA in Nov. 2001; name changed as above in Nov. 2005; cap. 350.0m., res 949.1m., dep. 33,045.2m. (Dec. 2002); CEO Jean Meyer; Chair. Carlo Thill; 40 brs.

HSBC Private Bank (Luxembourg) SA: 32 blvd Royal, BP 733, 2017 Luxembourg; tel. 47-93-31-1; fax 47-93-31-337; e-mail hrlu@hsbcrepublic.com; internet www.hsbcpb.com; f. 1985; cap. 53.0m., res 33.9m., dep. 2,534.5m. (Dec. 2002); Chair. Michael S. Elia; Man. Dir and CEO David Levy.

HSBC Trinkaus & Burkhardt (International) SA: 1–7 rue Nina et Julien Lefèvre, BP 579, 2015 Luxembourg; tel. 47-18-47-1; fax 47-18-47-64-1; f. 1977; cap. 15.5m., res 51.8m., dep. 1,366.2m. (Dec. 2002); Pres. Dr Olaf Huth; Man. Dirs Hans-Joachim Rosteck, Jörg Meier.

HSH Nordbank International SA: 2 rue Jean Monnet, BP 612, 2016 Luxembourg; tel. 42-41-41-1; fax 42-41-97; e-mail info@hsh-nordbank.com; internet www.hsh-nordbank-int.com; f. 1977; cap. 43.0m., res 182.1m., dep. 7,350.6m. (Dec. 2003); Chair. Franz Sales Waas; CEO Constantyn Nieuwenhuis.

HVB Banque Luxembourg SA: 4 rue Alphonse Weicker, 2721 Luxembourg; tel. 42-72-1; fax 42-72-45-00; e-mail contact@hvb.lu; internet www.hypovereinsbank.lu; f. 1998; by merger of Hypobank International SA and Vereinsbank International SA Luxembourg, name changed as above in Oct. 2001; cap. 238.0m., res 635.0m., dep. 34,296.0m. (Dec. 2002); Pres. and Chair. Dr Wolfgang Sprissler; Man. Dirs Ernst-Dieter Wiesner, Gunnar Homann, Bernd Janietz.

IKB International SA: 12 rue Erasme, BP 771, 2017 Luxembourg; tel. 42-37-77; e-mail ikb.luxembourg@ikb.de; internet www.ikb.de; f. 1979; cap. 52.5m., res 77.8m., dep. 6,767.5m. (Nov. 2003); Chair. Stefan Ortseifen.

ING Luxembourg SA: 52 route d'Esch, 1470 Luxembourg; tel. 44-99-11; fax 44-99-12-31; internet www.ing.lu; f. 1960 as Crédit Européen SA, changed name as above April 2003; owned by ING Belgium SA/NV; cap. 83.4m., res 1,128.9m., dep. 8,709.7m. (Dec. 2005); Chair Jan Op de Beeck; CEO Bernard Coucke; 16 brs.

Kredietbank SA Luxembourg: 43 blvd Royal, 2955 Luxembourg; tel. 47-97-1; fax 47-26-67; internet www.kbl.lu; f. 1949; cap. 189.0m., res 883.6m., dep. 19,710.0m. (Dec. 2002); Pres. Etienne Verwilghen; 5 brs.

LRI (Landesbank Rheinland-Pfalz International SA): 10–12 blvd F.D. Roosevelt, BP 84, 2010 Luxembourg; tel. 47-59-21-1; fax 47-59-21-314; e-mail info@lri.lu; internet www.lri.lu; f. 1978; cap. 216.0m., res 148.2m., dep. 8,886.6m. (Dec. 2002); Chair. Paul K. Schminke; Man. Dirs Alain Baustert, Roby Haas.

Norddeutsche Landesbank Luxembourg SA: 26 route d'Arlon, BP 121, 2011 Luxembourg; tel. 45-22-11-1; fax 45-22-11-31-9; e-mail info@nordlb.lu; internet www.nordlb.lu; f. 1972; cap. 205.0m., res 248.5m., dep. 22,760.0m. (Dec. 2002), total assets 24,080m. (Dec. 2004); Man. Dirs Jochen Petermann, Hans Hartmann.

Nordea Bank SA: 672 rue de Neudorf-Findel, BP 562, 2015 Luxembourg; tel. 43-88-71; fax 43-93-52; e-mail nordea@nordea.lu; internet www.nordea.lu; f. 1976; as Privatbanken International (Denmark) SA, Luxembourg, changed name to Unibank SA in 1990, present name adopted Feb. 2001; cap. 25.0m., res 135.5m., dep. 2,087.5m. (Dec. 2002); Chair. Hans Dalborg; Man. Dir Lars G. Nordström.

Sanpaolo Bank SA: 12 ave de la Liberté, BP 2062, 1020 Luxembourg; tel. 40-37-60-1; fax 49-53-91; e-mail sanpaolo@sanpaolo.lu; f. 1981; as Sanpaolo-Lariano Bank SA, name changed as above 1995; acquired IMI Bank (Lux) SA in 2004; cap. 70.0m., res 7.0m., dep. 3,869.6m. (Dec. 2002); Man. Dir Doriano Demi.

SEB Private Bank SA: 6A circuit de la Foire Internationale, BP 487, 2014 Luxembourg; tel. 26-23-1; fax 26-23-20-01; internet www.sebprivatebank.com; f. 1977; as Skandinaviska Enskilda Banken (Luxembourg) SA, merged with sister bank and name changed to S-E-Banken Luxembourg SA in 1994, present name adopted in 1999; merged with BfG Bank Luxembourg SA March 2001; cap. 118.0m., res 102.4m., dep. 1,624.8m. (Dec. 2002); Chair. Ulf Peterson; Man. Dir Lars Friberg.

Société Européenne de Banque SA: 19–21 blvd du Prince Henri, BP 21, 2010 Luxembourg; tel. 46-14-11; fax 22-37-55; e-mail seb@pt.lu; internet www.seb.lu; f. 1976; cap. 45.0m., res 40.6m., dep. 2,695.0m. (Dec. 2002); Chair. Angelo Caloia; Man. Dir Clemente Benelli.

Société Générale Bank & Trust: 11 ave Emile Reuter, BP 1271, 2420 Luxembourg; tel. 47-93-111; fax 22-88-59; e-mail sgbt.lu@socgen.com; internet www.sgbt.lu; f. 1956; as International and General Finance Trust; cap. 1,179.0m., res 353.4m., dep. 17,243.7m. (Dec. 2004); Chair. Pierre Mathé; Man. Dir Albert Le Dirac'h.

UBS (Luxembourg) SA: 36–38 Grand-Rue, BP 2, 2010 Luxembourg; tel. 45-12-11; fax 45-12-12-700; internet www.ubs.com; f. 1998; by merger of Swiss Bank Corporation (Luxembourg) SA and Union de Banques Suisses (Luxembourg) SA; cap. Swiss francs 150m., res Swiss francs 168.4m., dep. Swiss francs 8,935.7m. (Dec. 2003); Chair. Arthur Decurtins; Man. Dirs Roger Hartmann, Hans-Joachim Steinbock.

WestLB International SA: 32–34 blvd Grande-Duchesse Charlotte, BP 420, 2014 Luxembourg; tel. 44-74-11; fax 44-74-12-10; e-mail info@westlb.lu; internet www.westlb.lu; f. 1972; subsidiary of WestLB AG (Germany); cap. 65.0m., res 250.4m., dep. 14,370.6m. (Dec. 2002); Man. Dirs Dr Johannes Scheel, Franz Ruf, Norbert Lersch.

Banking Association

Association des Banques et Banquiers Luxembourg (ABBL): 20 rue de la Poste, BP 13, 2010 Luxembourg; tel. 46-36-60-1; fax 46-09-21; e-mail mail@abbl.lu; internet www.abbl.lu; f. 1939; Dir Lucien Thiel.

STOCK EXCHANGE

Société de la Bourse de Luxembourg SA: 11 ave de la Porte-Neuve, BP 165, 2011 Luxembourg; tel. 47-79-36-1; fax 47-32-98; e-mail info@bourse.lu; internet www.bourse.lu; f. 1928; Chair. André Wagner; CEO Michel Maquil.

LUXEMBOURG

INSURANCE

In 2004 there were 95 approved insurance companies and, in addition, 271 reinsurance companies. A selection of insurance companies is given below:

Aon Insurance Managers (Luxembourg) SA: 19 rue de Bitbourg, BP 593, 2015 Luxembourg; tel. 22-34-221; fax 47-02-51; e-mail lambert_schroeder@aon.com; internet www.aoncaptives.com; f. 1994; Man. Dir. LAMBERT SCHROEDER.

Assurances Mutuelles d'Europe: 7 blvd Joseph II, BP 787, 1840 Luxembourg; tel. 47-46-93; fax 47-46-90; e-mail ame@ame.lu; internet www.ame.lu.

AXA Assurances Luxembourg: 7 rue de la Chapelle, 1325 Luxembourg; tel. 45-30-20-1; fax 45-83-39; e-mail info@axa.lu; internet www.axa.lu; f. 1977; all branches and life; Chair. PIERRE BULTEZ.

Fortis Luxembourg Assurances: 16 blvd Royal, 2449 Luxembourg; tel. 24-18-58-1; fax 24-18-58-905; e-mail info@fortis.lu; internet www.fortis.lu; life and non-life insurance.

Le Foyer, Groupe d'Assurances: 6 rue Albert Borschette, 1246 Luxembourg; tel. 43-74-37; fax 43-83-22; e-mail contact@lefoyer.lu; internet www.lefoyer.lu; f. 1922; all branches and life.

La Luxembourgeoise SA d'Assurances: 10 rue Aldringen, 1118 Luxembourg; tel. 47-61-1; fax 47-61-30-0; e-mail groupell@lalux.lu; internet www.lalux.lu; f. 1989; all branches of non-life; Chair. GABRIEL DEIBENER; Dir-Gen. PIT HENTGEN.

West of England Shipowners' Mutual Insurance Ascn (Luxembourg): 33 blvd du Prince Henri, BP 841, 1724 Luxembourg; tel. 47-00-67-1; fax 22-52-53; internet www.westpandi.com; f. 1970; marine mutual insurance; Gen. Man. PHILIP ASPDEN.

Trade and Industry

GOVERNMENT AGENCY

Société Nationale de Crédit et d'Investissement (SNCI): 7 rue du St Esprit, BP 1207, 1475 Luxembourg; tel. 46-19-71-1; fax 46-19-79; e-mail snci@snci.lu; internet www.snci.lu; f. 1978; cap. and res €401m. (Dec. 2000), dep. €275.5m., assets €722.8m. (1998); SNCI finances participations in certain cos, provides loans for investment and research and development projects, provides export credit; Pres. GASTON REINESCH; Sec.-Gen. EVA KREMER.

CHAMBER OF COMMERCE

Chambre de Commerce du Grand-Duché de Luxembourg: 7 rue Alcide de Gasperi, 2981 Luxembourg-Kirchberg; tel. 42-39-39-1; fax 43-83-26; e-mail chamcom@cc.lu; internet www.cc.lu; f. 1841; Pres. MICHEL WURTH; 35,000 mems.

INDUSTRIAL AND TRADE ASSOCIATIONS

Centrale Paysanne Luxembourgeoise: 44 rue de la Gare, BP 48, 7501 Mersch; tel. 64-64-480; fax 64-64-481; f. 1945; Pres. MARC FISCH; Sec. LUCIEN HALLER; groups all agricultural organizations.

Chambre d'Agriculture (Landwirtschaftskammer): 261 route d'Arlon, BP 81, 8001 Strassen; tel. 31-38-76; fax 31-38-75; e-mail info@lwk.lu; internet www.lwk.lu; Pres. MARCO GAASCH; Sec.-Gen. ROBERT LEY.

Confédération Luxembourgeoise du Commerce (CLC): 7 rue Alcide de Gasperi, BP 482, 2014 Luxembourg; tel. 43-94-44; fax 43-94-50; e-mail info@clc.lu; internet www.clc.lu; f. 1909; Pres. ERNY LAMBORELLE; Dir THIERRY NOTHUM; 50,000 mems.

Fédération des Artisans du Grand-Duché de Luxembourg: 2 circuit de la Foire Internationale, BP 1604, 1016 Luxembourg; tel. 42-45-11-1; fax 42-45-25; e-mail info@fda.lu; internet www.federation-des-artisans.lu; f. 1905; Chair. NORBERT GEISEN; Dir ROMAIN SCHMIT; 4,000 mems.

Fédération des Industriels Luxembourgeois (FEDIL): 31 blvd Konrad Adenauer, BP 1304, 1013 Luxembourg; tel. 43-53-66-1; fax 43-23-28; e-mail fedil@fedil.lu; internet www.fedil.lu; f. 1918; Pres. CHARLES KROMBACH; Administrative Dir NICOLAS SOISSON; c. 450 mems.

UTILITIES

Regulatory Authority

Service de l'Energie de l'Etat (SEE): 34 ave de la Porte-Neuve, 2227 Luxembourg, BP 10, 2010 Luxembourg; tel. 46-97-46-1; fax 22-25-24; e-mail see.direction@eg.etat.lu; internet www.see.etat.lu; f. 1967; civil service department with responsiblity for testing, standardization and certification; Dir JEAN-PAUL HOFFMANN.

Electricity

Cegedel (Compagnie Grand-Ducale d'Electricité de Luxembourg): 2089 Luxembourg; tel. 26-24-1; fax 26-24-6100; e-mail mail@cegedel.lu; internet www.cegedel.lu; f. 1928; produces and distributes electricity; 33% state-owned; Chair. ROLAND MICHEL; Dir-Gen. ROMAIN BECKER.

Cegedel Net SA: 2089 Luxembourg; tel. 2624-1; fax 2624-6100; e-mail mail@cegedel.lu; internet www.cegedelnet.lu; f. 2004; operates the Cegedel distribution grid; Chair. ROLAND MICHEL; Dir GEORGES BONIFAS.

Gas

SUDGAZ SA: BP 383, 4004 Esch-sur-Alzette; tel. 55-66-551; fax 57-20-44; e-mail contact@sudgaz.lu; internet www.sudgaz.lu; f. 1899; gas distribution co; Pres. WILL HOFFMANN; Vice-Pres. ROMAIN ROSENFELD.

TRADE UNIONS

Confédération Générale du Travail du Luxembourg (CGT)/ Onofhaengege Gewerkschaftbond-Letzeburg (OGB-L) (Luxembourg General Confederation of Labour): 60 blvd J. F. Kennedy, BP 149, 4002 Esch-sur-Alzette; tel. 54-05-45-1; fax 54-16-20; e-mail ogb-l@ogb-l.lu; internet www.ogb-l.lu; f. 1921; Pres. JEAN-CLAUDE REDING; 57,000 mems (2005).

Landesverband Luxemburger Eisenbahner, Transportarbeiter, Beamten und Angestellten (National Union of Luxembourg Railway and Transport Workers and Employees): 63 rue de Bonnevoie, 1260 Luxembourg; tel. 48-70-44-1; fax 48-85-25; e-mail info@landesverband.lu; internet www.landesverband.lu; f. 1909; affiliated to CGT and International Transport Workers' Federation; Pres. JUSTIN TURPEL; Dir JEAN REUTER; 8,000 mems.

Lëtzebuerger Chrëschtleche Gewerkschaftsbond (LCGB) (Confederation of Luxembourg Christian Trade Unions): 11 rue du Commerce, BP 1208, 1012 Luxembourg; tel. 49-94-24-1; fax 49-94-24-49; e-mail info@lcgb.lu; internet www.lcgb.lu; f. 1921; affiliated to European Trade Union Confederation and World Confederation of Labour; Pres. ROBERT WEBER; Gen. Sec. MARC SPAUTZ; 40,000 mems.

Transport

RAILWAYS

At 1 January 2005 there were 274 km of electrified railway track. A high-speed link from Luxembourg-Ville to Paris, France, was scheduled for completion in 2006.

Société Nationale des Chemins de Fer Luxembourgeois: 9 place de la Gare, BP 1803, 1018 Luxembourg; tel. 49-90-0; fax 49-90-44-70; e-mail info@cfl.lu; internet www.cfl.lu; Pres. JEANNOT WARINGO; Dir and CEO ALEX KREMER.

ROADS

At 1 January 2005 there were 2,894 km of roads, of which motorways comprised 147 km.

Ministry of Public Works: (see Ministries).

INLAND WATERWAYS AND SHIPPING

Rhine shipping has direct access to the Luxembourg inland port of Mertert as a result of the canalization of the Moselle river. An 'offshore' shipping register was established in 1991.

CIVIL AVIATION

There is an international airport near Luxembourg-Ville.

Luxair (Société Luxembourgeoise de Navigation Aérienne): Aéroport de Luxembourg, 2987 Luxembourg; tel. 47-98-42-81; fax 47-98-42-89; e-mail info@luxair.lu; internet www.luxair.lu; f. 1962; regular services to destinations in Europe and North Africa; Pres. and CEO ADRIEN NEY.

Cargolux Airlines International SA: Aéroport de Luxembourg, 2990 Luxembourg; tel. 42-11-1; fax 43-54-46; e-mail info@cargolux.com; internet www.cargolux.com; f. 1970; regular international all-freighter services; technological development; owned by Luxair, a consortium of Luxembourg banks and Swissair; Dir and CEO ULRICH OGIERMANN.

Tourism

Many tourist resorts have developed around the ruins of medieval castles such as Clerf, Esch/Sauer, Vianden and Wiltz. The Benedictine Abbey at Echternach is also much visited. There is a thermal centre at Mondorf-les-Bains, supplied by three mineralized springs.

In addition, there are numerous footpaths and hiking trails. Luxembourg-Ville, with its many cultural events and historical monuments, is an important centre for congresses. In 2004 there were 933,359 tourist arrivals at hotels and similar establishments. Receipts from tourism totalled an estimated US $2,402m. in 2003.

Office National du Tourisme (ONT): 68–70 blvd de la Pétrusse, BP 1001, 1010 Luxembourg; tel. 42-82-82-1; fax 42-82-82-38; e-mail info@ont.lu; internet www.ont.lu; f. 1931; 192 mems; Chair. M. SCHANK; Dir ROBERT L. PHILIPPART.

THE FORMER YUGOSLAV REPUBLIC OF MACEDONIA

Introductory Survey

Location, Climate, Language, Religion, Flag, Capital

The former Yugoslav republic of Macedonia (FYRM) is situated in south-eastern Europe. The FYRM is a land-locked state and is bounded by Serbia and Montenegro (Serbia, including, in the north-west, the province of Kosovo and Metohija—Kosovo) to the north, Albania to the west, Greece to the south and Bulgaria to the east. The republic is predominantly mountainous with a continental climate, although the Vardar (Axiós) river valley, which bisects the country from north-west to south-east, across the centre of the republic and into Greece, has a mild Mediterranean climate with an average summertime temperature of 27°C (80°F). The official language of the republic, under the Constitution of November 1991, was originally stipulated as Macedonian, and is most frequently written in the Cyrillic script. Constitutional amendments adopted in November 2001 accorded any minority language, such as Albanian (written in the Latin script), the status of official language in communities where its speakers constitute 20% of the population. Most of the population is nominally Christian and of the Eastern Orthodox faith. The ethnic Macedonians (who accounted for 64.2% of the total population at the 2002 census) are traditionally adherents of the Macedonian Orthodox Church, which claims autocephaly, although this is not recognized by other Orthodox churches. Most of the ethnic Albanians (officially recorded as 25.2% of the population) are Muslims, as are the majority of the remaining minority groups. The national flag (proportions 1 by 2) comprises, in the centre of a red field, a yellow disc, with eight yellow rays extending to the edges of the flag. The capital is Skopje.

Recent History

After the First World War, during which Macedonia was occupied by the Bulgarians and the Central Powers of Austria-Hungary and Germany, Vardar Macedonia, the area now known as the former Yugoslav republic of Macedonia (FYRM), became part of the new Kingdom of Serbs, Croats and Slovenes (formally named Yugoslavia in 1929), being widely referred to as 'South Serbia'. In the Second World War, however, the Bulgarian occupation of 1941–44 disillusioned many Yugoslav Macedonians. From 1943 the Partisans of Josip Broz (Tito), the General-Secretary of the banned Communist Party of Yugoslavia, began to increase their support in the region, and after the war the new Federal People's Republic of Yugoslavia and its communist rulers resolved to include a Macedonian nation as a federal partner (having rejected the idea of a united Macedonia under Bulgaria). A distinct Macedonian identity was promoted, and a linguistic policy that encouraged the establishment of a Macedonian literary language distinct from Bulgarian and Serbian, together with the consolidation of an historical and cultural tradition, increased Macedonian self-awareness. In 1967 the Orthodox Church in Macedonia declared itself autocephalous, a move strongly contested by the Serbian Orthodox Church and not recognized by other Orthodox jurisdictions.

The presence of a large ethnic Albanian minority in western Macedonia added to Macedonian insecurities. The proximity of the neighbouring Serbian province of Kosovo (officially Kosovo and Metohija from 1990), which had a majority ethnic Albanian population, and demands, from the late 1960s, for the creation of a Albanian republic within Yugoslavia alarmed the Macedonian authorities, which became particularly active against Albanian nationalism from 1981. In 1989 the communists amended the republican Constitution to allow for the introduction of a multi-party system; however, Macedonia was declared to be a 'nation-state' of the ethnic Macedonians, and mention of the 'Albanian and Turkish minorities' was excluded. Tension continued into the early 1990s (see below).

In November and December 1990 the first multi-party elections to a unicameral republican Sobranie (Assembly) were held in Macedonia. The Front for Macedonian National Unity, which principally comprised a nationalist party, the Internal Macedonian Revolutionary Organization—Democratic Party for Macedonian National Unity (IMRO—DPMNU), led by Ljubčo Georgievski, and which had previously declared its support for the return of territories within Serbia, alleged irregularities after failing to win any seats at the first round. Following two further rounds of voting, however, the IMRO—DPMNU unexpectedly emerged as the single party with the most seats (a total of 37) in the 120-member Sobranie. The League of Communists of Macedonia—Party for Democratic Reform (LCM—PDR, as the League of Communists of Macedonia had renamed itself), led by Petar Gosev, won 31 seats and the two predominantly Albanian parties (the Party for Democratic Prosperity—PDP—and the People's Democratic Party) a total of 25. The republican branch of the federal Alliance of Reform Forces (ARF, subsequently the Liberal Party of Macedonia—LPM) won 19 seats. Following lengthy negotiations to establish a parliamentary coalition, in January 1991 Kiro Gligorov of the LCM—PDR was elected President of the Republic, with Georgievski as Vice-President, and Stojan Andov of the ARF was elected President of the Sobranie. The three parties agreed to support a government largely comprising members without political affiliation. In March the Sobranie approved a new administration, headed by Nikola Kljusev. The LCM—PDR was renamed the Social Democratic Alliance of Macedonia (SDAM) in April.

On 25 January 1991 the Sobranie unanimously adopted a motion declaring the republic a sovereign territory. After June declarations of Croatian and Slovenian 'dissociation', Macedonia, wary of Serbian domination of the remaining federal institutions, declared its neutrality and emphasized its sovereign status. On 8 September a referendum (boycotted by the ethnic Albanian population) approved the sovereignty of Macedonia.

Georgievski resigned the vice-presidency in October 1991, and the IMRO—DPMNU announced that it had joined the opposition, stating that the party had been excluded from the decision-making process. The preparation of the new Constitution was delayed by the IMRO—DPMNU's proposal for an introductory nationalist statement, which was strongly opposed by the predominantly ethnic Albanian parties and was finally abandoned. On 17 November the Constitution, which declared the sovereignty of the 'Republic of Macedonia', was endorsed by 96 of the 120 Assembly members, with opposition from the majority of ethnic Albanian deputies. In January 1992 an unofficial referendum conducted among the ethnic Albanian population (declared illegal by the Macedonian authorities) reportedly resulted in 99.9% of votes being cast in favour of territorial and political autonomy for the ethnic Albanian population.

The complete withdrawal of federal troops from Macedonia in March 1992, in conjunction with the adoption in April of a new Constitution in the Federal Republic of Yugoslavia (FRY), referring only to Serbia and Montenegro, effectively signalled Yugoslav acceptance of Macedonian secession from the federation. Macedonia established diplomatic relations with Slovenia in March, and with Croatia in April.

Macedonian affairs were subsequently dominated by the question of wider international recognition. The republic, although no longer part of Yugoslavia, was unable to act as an independent nation in the international community. Bulgaria recognized the state of Macedonia (although not the existence of a distinct Macedonian nationality or language) in January 1992, closely followed by Turkey in February, provoking mass protests in Thessaloníki, the capital of the Greek region of Macedonia. The Greek authorities insisted that 'Macedonia' was a geographical term delineating an area that included a large part of northern Greece, and expressed fears that the republic's independence under the name 'Macedonia' might foster a false claim to future territorial expansion. Greece was instrumental in the formulation of an European Community (EC, now European Union, EU, see p. 228) policy, adopted in early 1992, that the republic should be awarded no formal recognition of independence until stringent constitutional requirements had been fulfilled. In May Gligorov rejected a statement by the EC that it was 'willing to recognize Macedonia as a sovereign and independent state within its existing borders under a name that can be accepted by all concerned'. Negotiations with Greece ended in failure in June. In July, after a motion expressing 'no confidence' in the Government received strong support in the Sobranie (and following large demonstrations at its failure to gain international recognition for an independent Macedonia), the Government resigned. The IMRO—DPMNU failed to form a new alliance and, eventually, in September Branko Crvenkovski, the Chairman of the SDAM, was installed as Prime Minister of a coalition Government.

The adoption of a new flag in August 1992 attracted particular opposition from Greece, which objected to the depiction outside Greece of the 'Vergina Star' (regarded as an ancient Greek symbol of Philip of Macedon and Alexander the Great). As a result of a blockade of petroleum deliveries imposed on Macedonia by Greece, reserves at the Skopje petroleum refinery were exhausted by September. In February 1993 Greece agreed to international arbitration over the issue of Macedonia's name, undertaking to abide by its final outcome. On 8 April the republic was admitted to the UN under the temporary name of 'the former Yugoslav republic of Macedonia', pending settlement of the issue of a permanent name by international mediators. However, Greece continued to assert, and the FYRM to deny, that the use of the 'Vergina Star' emblem and the name 'Macedonia' implied territorial claims on Greek territory, and in October Greece announced its withdrawal from UN-sponsored negotiations on the issue of a permanent name. In January 1994 Greece requested that the other nations of the EU prevail upon the FYRM (which was by this time recognized by all the other EU member states) to make concessions concerning its name, flag and Constitution, and threatened to ban trade with the FYRM. From February (shortly after Russia and the USA had formally recognized the FYRM) Greece blocked all non-humanitarian shipments to the FYRM from the port of Thessaloníki, and also road and rail transport links with the FYRM. In April the European Commission, which contested that the Greek embargo was in violation of EU trade legislation, initiated legal proceedings against Greece at the Court of Justice of the European Communities. In April 1995, however, the Court issued a preliminary opinion that the embargo was not in breach of Greece's obligations under the Treaty of Rome. Meanwhile, Greece agreed to resume negotiations in April with the FYRM, under the auspices of the UN; in May the Organization for Security and Co-operation in Europe (OSCE, see p. 327) announced that it was to join the mediation efforts. In September an interim accord was signed at the UN headquarters in New York, USA, by the FYRM Minister of Foreign Affairs and his Greek counterpart. The agreement provided for the mutual recognition of existing frontiers and respect for the sovereignty and political independence of each state, and for the free movement of goods and people between the two countries. Greece was to end its trade embargo and veto on the FYRM's entry into international organizations, while the FYRM undertook to abandon its use of the Vergina emblem in any form, and to amend parts of its Constitution that had been regarded by Greece as 'irredentist'. (The issue of a permanent name for the FYRM was to be the subject of further negotiations.) In early October the Sobranie approved a new state flag, depicting an eight-rayed sun in place of the Vergina emblem. The interim accord was ratified by the Sobranie on 9 October, and was formally signed in Skopje by representatives of the FYRM and Greece on 13 October. The border between the two countries was subsequently reopened.

The Albanian Government formally recognized the FYRM in April 1993. However, relations between the FYRM authorities and the country's ethnic Albanian minority continued to deteriorate. In November several ethnic Albanians were arrested in the western towns of Gostivar and Tetovo (both of which had predominantly Albanian populations) and in Skopje. The Government announced that a conspiracy to form paramilitary groups, with the eventual aim of establishing an Albanian republic in the west of the country, had been discovered. Further arrests followed, and in June 1994 Mithat Emini, the former General Secretary of the PDP, was sentenced to eight years' imprisonment, after being convicted of conspiring to engage in hostile activity; nine others received custodial sentences of between five and eight years. (In February 1995 all the sentences were reduced by two years.)

In February 1994, after months of disunity, the PDP split when a faction led by Xheladin Murati (the Deputy President of the Sobranie) and including the PDP's representatives in the Government and in the legislature, withdrew from the party's congress. The remaining grouping, led by Arben Xhaferi, made more radical demands regarding the status of ethnic Albanians in the FYRM. Organizations representing ethnic Albanians protested that inadequate preparations for a national census, conducted in mid-1994, effectively prevented the full enumeration of the ethnic Albanian community. It was reported that many ethnic Albanians boycotted the census, despite appeals by their political leaders for full participation. Following the publication of the census results, ethnic Albanian groups continued to assert that their community was considerably larger than officially indicated. The sentencing of Emini and his co-defendants prompted ethnic Albanian deputies to boycott the Sobranie in July (although they resumed their seats to defeat a motion, proposed by the IMRO—DPMNU, expressing 'no confidence' in the Government). Murati resigned from the leadership of his PDP faction (and from his role at the Sobranie) later in July, reportedly in protest at the sentences; he was succeeded as party leader by Abdurahman Aliti.

Gligorov, representing the Alliance for Macedonia (an electoral coalition of the SDAM, the LPM and the Socialist Party of Macedonia—SPM) was re-elected to the presidency on 16 October 1994, winning 78.4% of the valid votes cast; his only challenger was Georgievski of the IMRO—DPMNU. A first round of voting to the new Sobranie took place on the same day. The IMRO—DPMNU, which failed to secure any seats, alleged widespread electoral fraud in both elections, and boycotted the second round of legislative voting, which took place on 30 October (a third round was necessary in 10 constituencies on 13 November, owing to irregularities in earlier rounds). The final results confirmed that the Alliance for Macedonia had won the majority of seats in the Sobranie (with the SDAM taking 58 seats, the LPM 29 and the SPM eight). Aliti's 'moderate' PDP, which had been legally recognized as the successor to the original party, secured 10 seats; members of the 'radical' PDP had been obliged to stand as independent candidates (Xhaferi was among the independent candidates to be elected). Gligorov subsequently requested that Crvenkovski form a new government, and the SDAM-led administration, which also included members of the LPM, Aliti's PDP and the SPM, was approved by the Sobranie in December.

Tensions were exacerbated by efforts by the ethnic Albanian community to establish an Albanian-language university in Tetovo, following continued claims by ethnic Albanian groups that the education system of the FYRM disadvantaged ethnic minorities. Despite government objections that to establish such an institution would be unconstitutional, the university was formally established in December 1994. In February 1995 the opening of the university provoked considerable unrest; an ethnic Albanian was killed in clashes with security forces, and several people were arrested, including the university's rector. Following negotiations with the PDP, the authorities agreed to withdraw police reinforcements from Tetovo (while continuing to assert that the university was illegal). In July 1996 five of the university's founders, including its rector, received custodial sentences for inciting the riots, prompting protests by ethnic Albanians in Tetovo and other parts of the country. (In May 2000 the Sobranie approved legislation granting the university at Tetovo legal status as a private foundation, and in January 2004 further legislation was passed, transforming it into a state university.)

In October 1995 Gligorov was injured in a car-bomb attack in Skopje; he resumed full presidential duties in January 1996. Meanwhile, divisions had emerged within the governing Alliance for Macedonia, which collapsed in February, prompting the LPM to be excluded from the Government. Andov resigned as President of the Sobranie in early March, stating that Crvenkovski had acted unconstitutionally in expelling the LPM from the Government. A new penal code, under which the death penalty was abolished, entered into force in November.

In September 1996, prior to local elections scheduled for 17 November, the Sobranie approved legislation reorganizing the territorial division of the FYRM into 123 municipalities. In October three opposition parties, the IMRO—DPMNU, the PDP and the newly established Movement for All-Macedonian Action—Conservative Party, formed a coalition to contest the elections. Xhaferi's faction, which had been reconstituted as the Party of Democratic Prosperity of Albanians in Macedonia (PDPAM), and the (also ethnic Albanian) National Democratic Party (NDP) agreed to present joint candidates in some constituencies. Following the first round of the local elections, opposition parties claimed that the electoral lists had been falsified by the Government to ensure favourable results for the SDAM. The SDAM received the greatest number of votes, followed by the coalition led by the IMRO—DPMNU, and the PDP. Observers from the Council of Europe (see p. 211) declared that, overall, the elections had been conducted fairly.

In January 1997, following a campaign by ethnic Albanian students, legislation was adopted to permit Albanian to become the language of instruction at the teacher-training faculty of the university at Skopje. This provoked outrage among ethnic Macedonian students at the faculty, and a series of protests by university and secondary-school students ensued. Ethnic tensions were further compounded by the civil conflict in Albania in early 1997. A financial scandal emerged in the FYRM in March, involving the embezzlement of funds invested in 'pyramid' savings schemes. Crvenkovski pledged an investigation to identify those responsible for the losses sustained by large numbers of investors, and several senior officials were subsequently arrested on suspicion of involvement. Although the Government won a vote of confidence in its management of the affair, the LPM deputies withdrew from the parliamentary chamber to register their disapproval of the measures undertaken. In April the Government announced plans to reimburse losses incurred by investors, following the failure of a major savings institution in the south-western town of Bitola; in May the Sobranie approved the replacement of the Governor of the central bank, who was believed to have been involved in the failure of the investment scheme. Following an IMRO—DPMNU demonstration in Skopje to demand the resignation of the Government, a reorganized administration was approved by the Sobranie at the end of May.

In May 1997 ethnic Albanians in Gostivar took part in protests against a ruling by the Constitutional Court that prohibited the use of the Albanian flag in the FYRM. In June the President of the Constitutional Court issued a statement demanding that the Government enforce the ruling. In early July the Sobranie adopted legislation stipulating that the use of the Albanian flag, and flags of other ethnic minorities, would only be permitted on national holidays, with the Macedonian flag being displayed at the same time. None the less, the mayors of Gostivar and Tetovo continued to refuse to comply with the order of the Constitutional Court, and government officials forcibly removed Albanian flags that had been displayed at municipal buildings. Ensuing protests in Gostivar resulted in violent clashes between security forces and demonstrators, as a result of which three ethnic Albanians were killed; some 500 protesters were arrested. A report on the violence submitted to the Sobranie by the Ministry of Internal Affairs was rejected by ethnic Albanian deputies, who condemned the actions of the security forces. In September the mayor of Gostivar, Rufi Osmani, received a custodial sentence of some 13 years (reduced to seven years in February 1998), after being convicted on charges of inciting ethnic tension and rebellion, while the Chairman of the municipal council was sentenced to three years' imprisonment for failing to adopt the ruling of the Constitutional Court. In April 1998 the Democratic Party of Albanians (DPA—which had been formed in July 1997 by the amalgamation of the PDPAM and the NDP) announced that it was to withdraw its representatives from all government bodies, in protest at Osmani's imprisonment.

In August 1998 the PDP and the DPA established an alliance to contest forthcoming legislative elections. In early September the IMRO—DPMNU and the newly formed Democratic Alternative (DA) formed an electoral coalition, For Changes. The legislative elections were conducted in two rounds on 18 October and 1 November 1998; the For Changes coalition secured an absolute majority in the Sobranie, with 58 seats, while the SDAM obtained 29 seats, and the alliance of the PDP and the DPA 24. Owing to irregularities, a further round of voting took place in two electoral districts, at which one seat was won by the For Changes alliance, and the other by the PDP–DPA alliance. Later in November Georgievski was nominated as Prime Minister. The DPA was subsequently invited to join the governing coalition of the IMRO—DPMNU and the DA. In early December a new Government, comprising 14 representatives of the IMRO—DPMNU, eight of the DA and five of the DPA, was formed. At the end of December the Sobranie approved legislation (supported by the new Government) providing for the release of some 8,000 prisoners, among them Osmani. In January 1999, however, Gligorov refused to approve the amnesty, which he claimed to be unconstitutional. In February the amnesty legislation was resubmitted to the Sobranie (in accordance with the Constitution) and subsequently adopted.

The first round of the presidential election on 31 October 1999 was contested by six candidates: Tito Petkovski, representing the SDAM, secured 33.2% of the votes cast, and Boris Trajkovski, the IMRO—DPMNU candidate, won 20.6%; Vasil Tupurkovski, the DA leader, took 16.0%, and Muharem Nexipi, the DPA candidate, 14.8%. Since no candidate had secured an outright majority of the votes, Petkovski and Trajkovski progressed to a second round, held on 14 November; Trajkovski was elected to the presidency with 52.8% of the votes cast (after DPA and DA voters transferred support to his candidacy). The SDAM disputed the results of the election, alleging widespread malpractice. In late November the Supreme Court upheld a legal appeal by the SDAM against the results, and ruled that a further ballot take place in some western regions. A partial round, affecting about 10% of the total electorate, consequently took place on 5 December. However, the overall results were almost unchanged after the ballot, with Trajkovski receiving 52.9% of the votes cast. Although the SDAM again claimed that irregularities had taken place, Petkovski finally accepted Trajkovski's election to the presidency. Trajkovski was formally inaugurated as President on 15 December. Following negotiations between the two leaders of the For Changes coalition, Georgievski and Tupurkovski, the IMRO—DPMNU, DA and DPA reached agreement on the formation of a new Government. The coalition administration, which contained seven new ministers (including Tupurkovski, as a Deputy Prime Minister), was formally approved by the Sobranie on 27 December.

In January 2000 the Government announced that amendments to the Constitution, which would allow higher education to be conducted in the language of ethnic minorities, would be submitted for approval by the Sobranie. In April legislation was adopted, obliging the authorities to return property expropriated under the communist regime. In the same month disaffected members of the IMRO—DPMNU, headed by a former Minister of Finance, Boris Zmejkovski, established a breakaway faction, which became known as the IMRO—True Macedonian Reform Option (IMRO—TMRO). In May the SDAM, the Liberal-Democratic Party (LDP) and the Democratic League—Liberal Party established an electoral alliance. In July Georgievski reorganized the Government, reducing the number of ministries from 21 to 14. Local government elections took place in two rounds on 10 and 24 September, amid reports of numerous violent incidents. After a further round of voting took place, owing to electoral irregularities, it was announced at the end of the month that the parties of the governing coalition had secured 75 of the 123 municipalities. Following prolonged dissent between Georgievski and Tupurkovski, the DA withdrew from the coalition Government and from the Sobranie at the end of November. Georgievski subsequently formed a new administration, which, for the first time, included members of the LDP.

In early 2001 ethnic Albanian militants, members of the self-styled National Liberation Army (NLA—which had emerged as the successor movement to the KLA), began to infiltrate northern parts of the FYRM from Kosovo, clashing with FYRM security forces. In early March NLA forces seized the border village of Tanusevci, north of Skopje, prompting counter-attacks from government troops. The border with Kosovo was officially closed, after senior government officials visiting the border region were attacked and temporarily besieged by the NLA. Although the authorities succeeded in regaining control of Tanusevci, in mid-March some 200 NLA forces attempted to occupy Tetovo, precipitating the imposition of curfew regulations in the city. Following an appeal by the Government to the international community for military assistance, the North Atlantic Treaty Organization (NATO, see p. 314) reinforced its military presence at the border with Kosovo to prevent the NLA from receiving supplies from the province. On 21 March the UN Security Council adopted Resolution 1345, condemning the violence by ethnic Albanian nationalists in the FYRM as constituting a threat to the stability of the region. Despite reports that the ethnic Albanian rebels aimed to establish a 'greater Albania' (to include some northern and western regions of the FYRM), the NLA insisted that the conflict had been initiated to pressurize the FYRM Government to institute constitutional changes guaranteeing equal rights for ethnic Albanians. The prolonged bombardment of rebel positions by government forces resulted in a withdrawal by the NLA from the Tetovo region, and hostilities temporarily subsided in early April. However, at the end of the month eight members of the state security forces were killed in an NLA attack near the border with Kosovo. Their funeral precipitated rioting and attacks by Macedonians on Albanian-owned property in the southern town of Bitola. Government troops subsequently launched an offensive against rebel ethnic Albanian positions near Kumanovo, after two further members of the armed forces were killed.

Meanwhile, in early April 2001, following the temporary suppression of the insurgency, inter-party discussions regarding the ethnic Albanian demands commenced. After signing a Stabilization and Association Agreement with the EU, the Government pledged to initiate political, social and economic reforms by mid-2001. Ethnic Albanian proposals included: the postponement of the national census, due to take place in May, until October, to allow the return of refugees who had fled the conflict; state funding for the university at Tetovo; and the conversion of the state television's third service into an Albanian-language channel. However, the Government continued to oppose principal demands that the Constitution be amended to grant the ethnic Albanian population (hitherto officially categorized as a minority) equal rights with the Macedonian population, and Albanian the status of a second official language.

In early May 2001, following the resumption of intensive hostilities in the north of the country, the Government announced that the declaration of a state of war (which would allow the authorities to adopt emergency powers and Trajkovski to rule by decree) was under debate; the declaration, which required the approval of a two-thirds' majority in the Sobranie, was strongly opposed by ethnic Albanian deputies. Intensive discussions ensued between the principal political parties, with EU and NATO mediation, and it was agreed that the SDAM, the DPA and the PDP would join a government of national unity, and the parliamentary debate on the declaration of a state of war was suspended. The PDP subsequently demanded that the Government declare a cease-fire in the conflict in the north, as a precondition to the ethnic Albanian party's participation in the new administration. After the government offensive against the rebels was temporarily suspended, the Government of national unity (which was again headed by Georgievski) was approved by the Sobranie on 13 May. NLA leaders stated that the rebel movement (which still held several villages) would continue hostilities until the Government agreed to enter into negotiations.

On 8 June 2001 Trajkovski announced proposals for a comprehensive peace plan, which provided for the proportional representation of ethnic Albanians at all levels of government, the increased official use of the Albanian language, and a partial amnesty for NLA combatants. Despite EU support for the plan, the NLA demanded that the Government end hostilities and enter into negotiations on constitutional reforms, and rebel forces seized the town of Aracinovo, some 6 km east of Skopje. Later in June the Government announced the suspension of its offensive against the NLA, following pressure from international envoys. However, violent protests were staged by Macedonian nationalists at the parliament building in Skopje, in response to the NATO-mediated cease-fire arrangement at Aracinovo, which was perceived to be lenient towards the ethnic Albanian rebels. On 29 June NATO formally approved an operation to deploy a 3,500-member multinational force in the FYRM to assist in the disarmament of the NLA, which was, however, conditional on the imposition of a lasting cease-fire. On 5 July the Government announced that an official cease-fire agreement had been signed by both sides, and negotiations resumed between leaders of the principal Macedonian and ethnic Albanian parties regarding a permanent peace settlement. However, Georgievski and his nationalist cabinet supporters strongly opposed proposals, detailed by the EU and US special envoys, for the extension of the use of the Albanian language, and accused them of bias towards the rebels. After minor violations, the cease-fire collapsed after 17 days, when the NLA launched further attacks on government forces deployed near Tetovo. (By that time some 60,000 ethnic Albanians had fled to Kosovo, while a further 30,000 had become internally displaced.) International diplomatic efforts subsequently intensified, following renewed fears of widespread civil conflict. On 26 July it was announced that an accord had been reached to restore the cease-fire between government forces and the ethnic Albanian rebels, who had agreed to withdraw from newly captured territory near Tetovo. At the end of July further negotiations on the peace proposals, between government and ethnic Albanian representatives, commenced at the western town of Ohrid. Progress in the discussions was reported, following the resolution of the two main issues of contention (the extension of the official use of the Albanian language and the right to proportional representation of the ethnic Albanian community in the security forces). In response to increasing pressure from the EU and the USA, the Government announced a unilateral cease-fire, and on 13 August the Government and ethnic Albanian leaders at Ohrid signed a framework peace agreement, providing for the amendment of the Constitution to grant greater rights to the ethnic Albanian community. On the following day the NLA leader, Ali Ahmeti, agreed that the NLA, numbering an estimated 2,500–3,000, would relinquish its armaments to NATO troops. Following an assessment of the security situation, NATO announced that the cease-fire was generally being observed, and on 22 August the activation order for a NATO mission, Operation Essential Harvest, was released. The force, which finally comprised 4,500 troops (of which the United Kingdom contributed about 1,900), had a mandate to disarm the ethnic Albanian combatants and destroy their weapons within 30 days of its deployment. Contention ensued, after the Ministry of Internal Affairs claimed the NLA to be in possession of some 85,000 armaments; however, NATO estimated the number of weapons to be collected at 3,000–4,000.

In early September 2001 parliamentary debate on constitutional reform was delayed by mass nationalist protests against the peace plan. Macedonian nationalist parties in the legislature continued to dispute the details of a number of the proposed amendments, while ethnic Albanian representatives insisted that attempts to limit the reforms would provoke renewed conflict. Meanwhile, investigators from the International Criminal Tribunal for the former Yugoslavia (ICTY, see p. 17) at the Hague, Netherlands, had been dispatched to the FYRM to conduct preliminary inquiries into the killing of six ethnic Albanian civilians in the village of Ljuboten in early August; the nationalist Minister of Internal Affairs, Ljube Boskovski, was suspected of responsibility for the operation. On 26 September NATO's 30-day disarmament programme was declared to have been successful, with the collection of some 3,875 armaments. On the same day the establishment of a further, reduced NATO mission, Operation Amber Fox, was authorized. (In response to international pressure, the Government had invited NATO to retain a military presence in the country, despite domestic opposition.) The new mission, comprising 700 troops, together with 300 forces already stationed in the FYRM, was deployed under German leadership, with a three-month renewable mandate to protect EU and OSCE monitors supervising the implementation of the peace agreement. On 27 September Ahmeti announced that the NLA had been formally dissolved, following the completion of the disarmament process. In early October the EU criticized delays in implementing constitutional reforms, after Macedonian parties announced that the legislative process would be suspended pending the release of 14 Macedonian civilians allegedly seized by the NLA earlier that year. Following pressure from Trajkovski, and the international community, which urged acceptance of the plan, discussion on the measures resumed in the Sobranie. Later that month Trajkovski approved plans for the deployment of ethnically-mixed security units in regions formerly held by the NLA.

On 16 November 2001 the Sobranie finally adopted 15 main amendments to the existing Constitution (although the extent of some provisions had been reduced at the insistence of the Macedonian parties). The principal reforms were: the revision of the Constitution's preamble to include a reference to members of non-ethnic Macedonian communities as citizens of the country; the introduction in the Sobranie of a 'double majority' system, whereby certain legislation would require the approval of a minority group; the establishment of Albanian as the second official language in communities where ethnic Albanians comprised more than 20% of the population; and the right to proportional representation for ethnic Albanians in the Constitutional Court, all areas of government administration and the security forces. The adoption of the reforms was received with approval by the international community. Later in November the SDAM and the LDP withdrew from the coalition Government (which was subsequently reorganized), on the grounds that their participation was no longer necessary.

In early December 2001 NATO extended the mandate of Operation Amber Fox until 26 March 2002, and it was subsequently extended until 26 June. An EU-sponsored international donor conference on economic assistance for the FYRM, originally scheduled to take place in October 2001, was further postponed in December, pending the implementation of additional reforms. In January 2002 new legislation providing for the devolution of greater authority to local government (thereby granting a measure of self-rule to predominantly ethnic Albanian regions) was approved by the Sobranie, and the donor conference duly took place in March. Also in January a Deputy Prime Minister, Dosta Dimovska (who was considered to be a moderate), resigned from the Government, following disagreement with Georgievski over issues relating to the deployment of security units in previously NLA-controlled villages. In February the three principal ethnic Albanian political parties (the DPA, the PDP and the NDP) and the former NLA leadership officially established a co-ordinating council. In March the Sobranie adopted legislation granting immunity from prosecution to several thousand former NLA insurgents (excluding those indictable by the ICTY), in accordance with the peace settlement. In May the mandate of Operation Amber Fox was further extended, to 26 October. In accordance with the peace agreement, the Sobranie was dissolved on 18 July, prior to legislative elections, which were scheduled for 15 September and were to be monitored by the OSCE.

In May 2002 Ahmeti established a new political party, the Democratic Union for Integration (DUI), which was believed to comprise mainly former NLA combatants. Later that month two ministers belonging to the IMRO—TMRO resigned from the Government, on the grounds that former NLA members had become dominant within the principal ethnic Albanian parties. In the same month the Sobranie approved legislation whereby Albanian became an official language, in accordance with the Ohrid peace accord. At the end of August fears of a resurgence in violence emerged, after ethnic Albanians took hostage five Macedonian civilians at Gostivar; security forces surrounded an ethnic Albanian base and killed two of the kidnappers. However, the elections to the legislature took place peacefully on 15 September, attracting commendation from the international community, after OSCE observers declared them to have been conducted democratically. Georgievski's Government was removed from power by a 10-party alliance (led by the SDAM and the LDP), known as Together for Macedonia, which secured 60 of the 120 seats in the Sobranie. The IMRO—DPMNU won 33 seats and the DUI 16 seats. The Together for Macedonia alliance and the DUI subsequently signed an agreement for the establishment of a coalition Government (which was, however, to exclude former NLA combatants). The new administration, comprising members of the SDAM, the LDP and the DUI, and headed by Crvenkovski, was officially approved by the Sobranie on 1 November.

In October 2002 NATO agreed to extend the mandate of Operation Amber Fox until December. On 14 December Operation Amber Fox was succeeded by a 450-member mission, Allied Harmony, with a mandate to protect international monitors and advise FYRM security forces. On 31 March 2003 this contingent was, in turn, replaced by an EU-led mission, known as Operation Concordia, comprising 350 military personnel; 13 EU member states and 14 non-EU nations were to participate in the force. The purpose of the operation, which was deployed at the official request of Trajkovski, was to maintain security in order to facilitate the implementation of the Ohrid peace agreement. Meanwhile, in early 2003 a newly emerged ethnic Albanian extremist group, the Albanian National Army (ANA), threatened to launch a military offensive against the Government. The ANA, which favoured the creation of a 'greater Albania', had claimed responsibility for a number of bomb attacks. In September, after ethnic Albanian militants clashed with a security patrol at the border with Kosovo, the authorities dispatched security forces to the region in an operation to suppress dissident activity (a measure that was criticized by the DUI).

In April 2003 Georgievski announced his resignation from the leadership of the IMRO—DPMNU; he was replaced in late May by Nikola Gruevski. In early November Ljuben Paunovski, a member of the IMRO—DPMNU and a former Minister of Defence, was sentenced to over five years' imprisonment, on charges of the embezzlement of public funds during his time in office. In the same month Crvenkovski replaced four ministers. Notably, Nikola Popovski (a member of the SDAM and hitherto President of the Sobranie) replaced the leader of the LDP, Petar Gosev, as Deputy Prime Minister and Minister of Finance. Later that month Ljupco Jordanovski, also of the SDAM, was elected as the new parliamentary President. In early December the DA, the SPM and the Democratic Alliance (led by Pavle Trajanov, a former Minister of Internal Affairs) established a new opposition alliance, known as Third Path. In mid-December Operation Concordia was replaced by a 200-member EU mission, Operation Proxima, which, in addition to maintaining security and combating organized crime in the country, was to advise the FYRM police forces (the mandate of Operation Proxima expired in December 2005). In early 2004 the Government announced plans to redemarcate municipal boundaries, as part of a process of administrative decentralization included in the provisions of the Ohrid agreement. However, approval of the draft legislation in the Sobranie was expected to be problematic, owing to widespread popular opposition to the proposals.

On 26 February 2004 President Trajkovski, together with eight government officials, was killed, when an aircraft transporting him to a international investment conference in Bosnia and Herzegovina crashed in a southern, mountainous region of that country. Jordanovski, as speaker of the Sobranie, assumed the presidency in an acting capacity, pending an election, which, under the terms of the Constitution, was to take place within 40 days. At the presidential election, held on 14 April, Crvenkovski, representing the SDAM, won 42.5% of the votes cast; since he failed to secure the 50% of the votes necessary to be elected outright, he progressed to a second round with Sasko Kedev, hitherto a parliamentary deputy and a member of the IMRO—DPMNU (who had won 34.1% of the votes). Two former NLA commanders, the DUI Secretary-General, Gzim Ostreni, and Zudi Xhelili of the DPA, also contested the election, obtaining 14.8% and 8.7% of the votes cast, respectively. On 28 April Crvenkovski was elected to the presidency with 62.7% of the votes. Kedev immediately claimed that widespread malpractice had been perpetrated and appealed against the election results, which were, however, described as legitimate by OSCE monitors. Crvenkovski was inaugurated on 12 May.

Meanwhile, at the end of April 2004 an arrest warrant was issued for the former Minister of Internal Affairs, Ljube Boskovski, who, together with four security officers, was charged in connection with the killing of seven South Asian migrants (then purported to be Islamist militants) in March 2002; the FYRM authorities conceded that the incident had been staged to attract the approval of the international community for their efforts in combating militant Islamist groups. Boskovski, who possessed joint dual Croatian–FYRM citizenship, fled to Croatia, where he was arrested, at the request of the FYRM authorities, in late August 2004.

On 2 June 2004 the Sobranie approved the formation of a coalition administration, with Hari Kostov of the SDAM as Prime Minister, and comprising members of that party, the DUI and the LDP. The only new ministerial appointment was that of Siljan Avramovski as Minister of Internal Affairs, replacing Kostov. In July, after lengthy negotiations, the parties of the governing coalition reached an agreement on the redemarcation of the country's municipal boundaries. Concern that the local government elections would be suspended completely should the discussions end in failure, together with pressure from the international community, finally resulted in a decision to integrate two predominantly Albanian municipalities with Skopje, as well as three surrounding rural municipalities with the municipality of Struga. The total number of administrative districts was to be reduced from 123 to 85, with the ethnic balance of 26 districts becoming predominantly Albanian, and the adoption of Albanian as a second official language in a number of these, including Skopje and Struga. The agreement prompted immediate strong public criticism. Protests in Struga escalated into violence; it was reported that 15 protesters and 24 members of the security forces had been injured. On 26 July a large demonstration was staged in Skopje, in protest at the draft agreement on decentralization, which was submitted for approval to the Sobranie

On 7 November 2004, following a petition presented by Macedonian nationalist parties, a referendum on the proposed redemarcation of administrative districts was conducted. However, the governing coalition, together with representatives of the international community, urged a boycott and voter participation in the referendum was estimated at only 26%, thereby invalidating the results and allowing the local government reforms to proceed. In mid-November Kostov tendered his resignation as Prime Minister, claiming that the DUI had obstructed the parliamentary approval of reforms essential to attract foreign investment and that the DUI Minister of Transport and Communications, in particular, had been involved in corrupt practices. Later that month Crvenkovski nominated Vlado Buckovski, hitherto the Minister of Defence, as Prime Minister, shortly after his election as Chairman of the SDAM. On 17 December the Sobranie approved a new Government, formed by Buckovski, who pledged his commitment to the implementation of economic reforms, and again comprising members of the SDAM, the LDP and the DUI. In mid-March 2005 the ICTY issued indictments against Boskovski and a former head of security, John Tarculovski, in connection with the August 2001 killings in Ljuboten. At the beginning of April Boskovski pleaded 'not guilty' to all charges before the Tribunal.

The first round of local government elections, which were to effect the significant devolution of powers to 85 municipal authorities (including the City of Skopje), took place, with some reported irregularities, on 13 March 2005. A second round of voting for 47 of the 85 municipalities was conducted on 27 March. After upholding claims of irregularities in the first round, the Supreme Court had ordered polls to be repeated in several constituencies, and an OSCE observer mission announced that the second round of the elections again failed to meet OSCE and Council of Europe standards in some municipalities. (Buckovski insisted, however, that irregularities had been recorded in only a small proportion of constituencies.) The DPA and the PDP, which had urged a boycott of the vote, refused to recognize the results. Supporters of the IMRO—DPMNU staged protests in Ohrid to demand that the second round be repeated in that municipality on grounds of malpractice. On 10 April further ballots were conducted in 19 municipalities and the City of Skopje, where electoral irregularities had occurred. According to official results, 36 of the mayoral contests were won by the Together for Macedonia governing coalition, and 15 by the DUI, with the IMRO—DPMNU securing 21 mayoralties. In mid-July, in accordance with the Ohrid Agreement, the Sobranie adopted legislation enabling any ethnic minority community to display its flag, together with the Macedonian flag, in regions where it constituted at least 50% of the population (in effect, in 19 municipalities, of which 16 were predominantly ethnic Albanian, two ethnic Turkish and one Roma).

In September 2005 the Government survived a motion of 'no confidence' in the Sobranie, which had been proposed by opposition parties alleging economic mismanagement and demanding early elections. In December the Sobranie approved a series of constitutional amendments providing for extensive reform of the judicial system; the process of ensuring the complete independence of the judiciary, regarded as important to the country's application for EU membership (see below), was to be implemented over several years. In early 2006 the planned privatization of the state electricity utility, Elektrostopanstvo na Makedonija (ESM), prompted considerable domestic tension. In February up to 30 opposition parties signed a declaration against the planned sale, and civic groups staged a series of protests, owing to environmental concerns and fears of increased electricity prices. In late March the Secretary-General of NATO, which the FYRM hoped to be invited to join in 2008, welcomed the progress achieved by the FYRM Government, particularly with regard to reform of the police force and the increased representation of ethnic minorities in the state administration. Later in March the Sobranie adopted a series of amendments to electoral regulations, in preparation for the legislative elections due to be held in July 2006.

Both the September 1995 interim agreement with Greece and the November Dayton peace accord (for further details, see the chapter on Bosnia and Herzegovina) were of great significance for the FYRM, despite the unresolved issue of a permanent name for the country. The FYRM was admitted to the Council of Europe in late September, and to the OSCE in mid-October; in the following month the FYRM joined NATO's 'Partnership for Peace' (see p. 316) programme. The agreement with Greece facilitated the establishment of full diplomatic relations with the EU from January 1996, and negotiations subsequently began for a co-operation accord; a declaration on co-operation was, furthermore, signed with the European Free Trade Association (see p. 386) in early April. By the end of 1996 more than 75 countries had recognized the FYRM, with about two-thirds using the country's constitutional name, the Republic of Macedonia. The FYRM Government signed a Stabilization and Association Agreement with the EU in April 2001, which came into effect on 1 April 2004. A formal application for membership of the EU was submitted on 22 March 2004 (having been postponed from February, following the death of President Trajkovski—see above). In November 2005 the European Commission recommended that the FYRM be granted the status of candidate country. The FYRM was officially declared to have candidate status at an EU summit meeting in Brussels, Belgium, in mid-December, prompting public celebrations in Skopje. (No date for the opening of membership negotiations was announced, and initiation of the process was conditional on the Government's compliance with EU recommendations.) In March 2006 both EU and NATO officials declared that the organization of forthcoming legislative elections in the FYRM in accordance with international standards was crucial to the progress of the country's application for membership.

In July 1995 the FYRM and Turkey signed a 20-year co-operation agreement and a mutual security accord. Turkey, together with Albania, Bulgaria and Italy, was involved (between February 1994 and October 1995) in providing trading routes to permit the FYRM to bypass the Greek blockade. None the less, the issue of ethnic Albanian rights in the FYRM was a frequent source of tension with Albania, and relations with Bulgaria continued to be impeded, specifically by the question of its recognition of a distinct Macedonian language and nationality.

Regular trade with Greece and the FRY resumed in late 1995, and discussions continued between FYRM, Greek and UN officials regarding the issue of a permanent name for the FYRM. By 1999 the FYRM's relations with Greece had improved significantly, and the principal border crossing between the FYRM and Greece was reopened at the end of 2000. Meanwhile, work on the construction of a 214-km pipeline to transport petroleum from the FYRM's capital, Skopje, to Thessaloníki was officially completed in July 2002. Greece strongly opposed a decision by the USA, announced in November 2004, that it would henceforth recognize the FYRM by its constitutional name of 'Republic of Macedonia'; UN-mediated negotiations on the issue continued in 2005. In April the UN proposed the adoption of the name 'Republic of Macedonia-Skopje'; however, the compromise arrangement was rejected by both countries, although Greece indicated that it might provide a basis for further dialogue.

Although the FYRM formally supported the UN embargo on the FRY, there was frequent evidence that the FYRM Government permitted violations of the blockade. An agreement signed by the FYRM and the FRY in early April 1996, regulating bilateral relations and promoting mutual co-operation, was regarded as particularly significant in formalizing the FRY's recognition of the FYRM as a sovereign state, although it was criticized by most opposition groups within the FYRM. Meanwhile, the FYRM, Bosnia and Herzegovina, Croatia and Slovenia co-operated in efforts to secure international recognition for all the former republics as successor states to the SFRY, and thereby win access to a share of the assets of the former Yugoslavia. In September the FRY Prime Minister, Radoje Kontić, on his first official visit to the FYRM, signed several bilateral agreements. The Governments of the FYRM and Serbia and Montenegro (as the FRY was renamed in February 2003) increased bilateral co-operation in a number of areas, particularly measures to combat organized crime and promote regional stability.

In late 1992 the UN Security Council approved the deployment of members of the UN Protection Force (UNPROFOR) along the FYRM's border with the FRY and Albania, in an effort to protect the FYRM from any external threat to its security; in March 1995 the operation in the FYRM was renamed the UN Preventive Deployment Force (UNPREDEP). Following a reduction in UNPREDEP's authorized strength by the Security Council, the US contingent of military personnel was placed under direct US administration. In April 1997 the mandate of UNPREDEP was extended to the end of May, in view of the civil disorder in Albania (q.v.); it was further extended in June and December. Following the civil unrest in Albania, a number of border incursions by armed groups of Albanian rebels were reported. In October the Ministers of Defence of the FYRM and Albania signed an agreement providing for increased security along the joint border between the two countries.

In early 1998 increasing clashes were reported in Kosovo between members of the Serbian security forces and the ethnic Albanian KLA. In late July the UN Security Council extended the mandate of UNPREDEP until 28 February 1999 and agreed to increase the size of the contingent from 750 to about 1,100, with the aim of reinforcing border control. In early December 1998, following discussions between President Gligorov and NATO officials, it was announced that a NATO 'extraction force' was to be deployed in the FYRM to effect the evacuation of OSCE monitors in Kosovo in the event of large-scale conflict. In late February 1999 the People's Republic of China vetoed a UN Security Council resolution to extend the mandate of UNPREDEP for a further six months, following a decision by the FYRM

THE FORMER YUGOSLAV REPUBLIC OF MACEDONIA

Introductory Survey

Government to extend diplomatic recognition to Taiwan, which also prompted the People's Republic of China to suspend diplomatic relations with the FYRM. Following the commencement by NATO forces of an intensive aerial bombardment of strategic targets in the FRY in late March (see the chapter on Serbia and Montenegro), by early April some 140,000 refugees had fled to the FYRM. By mid-April about 14,000 NATO troops were deployed near the FYRM border with Kosovo, and were involved in assisting the refugees. Owing to concern over internal destabilization, the FYRM authorities repeatedly closed the border with Kosovo to prevent the continued arrival of large numbers of ethnic Albanians, and demanded that the international community fulfil pledges to accept a proportion of the refugees. By late May some 60,000 refugees had been transported from the FYRM for provisional resettlement abroad, while an estimated 250,000 remained in the country. In early June the strength of NATO forces stationed in the FYRM was increased to 16,000. Shortly afterwards the Yugoslav Government accepted a peace plan, which provided for the withdrawal of Serbian forces from Kosovo, the return of ethnic Albanian refugees and the deployment of a NATO-led Kosovo Force (KFOR). NATO troops, which were to be deployed under the KFOR mandate, entered Kosovo from the FYRM. On 20 June NATO announced that the air campaign had officially ended, and large numbers of ethnic Albanian refugees subsequently began to return to the province from the FYRM.

In June 2001 the FYRM and the People's Republic of China agreed to restore diplomatic relations, thereby ensuring Chinese support in the UN Security Council for the deployment of a NATO peace-keeping operation from August (following an ethnic Albanian insurgency—see above); Taiwan subsequently severed relations with the FYRM. In March 2004 the FYRM Minister of Foreign Affairs met the Head of the UN Interim Administration Mission in Kosovo (UNMIK) and NATO and US envoys for emergency discussions on Kosovo, following an outbreak of ethnic Albanian violence in the province, amid concern that the clashes would result in further destabilization in the FYRM. In March 2005 Prime Minister Buckovski urged a resolution on demarcation of the border between the FYRM and Kosovo (contested since a 2001 agreement between the Governments of the FYRM and Serbia and Montenegro, owing to the continued unresolved status of Kosovo). Negotiations on the status of Kosovo commenced in February 2006. In March the FYRM Minister of Foreign Affairs protested to his Albanian counterpart, who had declared that Albania would be unable to guarantee the inviolability of its borders if Kosovo underwent division. (The Prime Minister of Kosovo subsequently assured the FYRM Government of the continued inviolability of the common border.)

Government

According to the 1991 Constitution, which was amended in November 2001, legislative power is vested in the Sobranie (Assembly), with 120 members, elected for a four-year term by universal adult suffrage (85 in single-seat constituencies and 35 members by proportional representation). The President is directly elected for a five-year term, and appoints a Prime Minister to head the Government. The Ministers are elected by the Sobranie. For the purposes of local government, the FYRM is divided into 85 municipalities (including the City of Skopje).

Defence

In August 2005 the armed forces of the FYRM totalled 10,890 in active service: army 9,760, air force 1,130. Paramilitary forces comprised a police force of 7,600. Conscription was introduced in April 1992, and military service lasts for six months. On 31 March 2003 the North Atlantic Treaty Organization (NATO, see p. 314) contingent in the FYRM was replaced by a European Union (EU, see p. 228) mission, known as Operation Concordia, which was, in turn, replaced on 15 December by a 200-member EU police mission, Operation Proxima. The mandate of Operation Proxima, which had been renewed for one year, expired at the end of 2005. The EU subsequently provided support and assistance for the FYRM police force. The budget for 2005 allocated US $129m. to defence.

Economic Affairs

In 2004, according to World Bank estimates, the FYRM's gross national income (GNI), measured at average 2002–04 prices, was US $4,855m., equivalent to $2,350 per head (or $6,480 per head on an international purchasing-power parity basis). During 1995–2004, it was estimated, the population increased by an average of 0.5% per year, while gross domestic product (GDP) per head rose, in real terms, at an average annual rate of 1.3%. Overall GDP increased, in real terms, at an average annual rate of 1.8% in 1995–2004; real GDP increased by 2.8% in 2003 and by an estimated 4.1% in 2004.

Agriculture (including hunting, forestry and fishing) contributed 12.9% of GDP in 2004, according to preliminary figures, and engaged 16.8% of the employed labour force. Dairy farming is significant, and the principal agricultural exports are tobacco, vegetables and fruit. The wine industry is of considerable importance, and the FYRM is also a producer of wheat, maize and barley. During 1995–2004, according to the World Bank, the GDP of the agricultural sector declined by 0.4%; however, real agricultural GDP increased by 2.2% in 2003 and by 2.0% in 2004.

Industry contributed an estimated 28.6% of GDP in 2004, when it engaged 32.8% of the employed labour force. During 1995–2004, according to the World Bank, the GDP of the industrial sector increased, in real terms, at an average annual rate of 2.6%; real industrial GDP increased by 3.7% in 2003 and by 3.0% in 2004.

Mining contributed an estimated 0.4% of GDP and engaged 0.5% of the employed labour force in 2004. The only major mining activity is the production of lignite (brown coal), although there are also deposits of iron, zinc, lead, copper, chromium, manganese, antimony, silver, gold and nickel. Production in the mining and quarrying sector increased at an average annual rate of 5.9% in 1996–2000.

The manufacturing sector contributed an estimated 17.0% of GDP and engaged 22.2% of the employed labour force in 2004. In 1996 the principal branches of the sector, measured by gross value of output, were food products (accounting for 19.1% of the total), textiles and clothing (11.9%), machinery (11.0%), chemicals, and iron and steel. The GDP of the manufacturing sector increased, in real terms, at an average annual rate of 1.8% in 1995–2004; real manufacturing GDP rose by 6.0% in 2003 and by 3.0% in 2004.

Energy is derived principally from coal and lignite, which provided 79.8% of the electricity generated in 2000. The first stage of a pipeline from the Bulgarian border to carry natural gas to the FYRM from Russia became operational in 1995. A 214-km pipeline to transport petroleum from the Greek port of Thessaloníki to Skopje was inaugurated in July 2002. Mineral fuels accounted for 19.2% of the value of total imports in 2005.

Services accounted for an estimated 58.5% of GDP in 2004, when the sector engaged 50.4% of the employed labour force. Regional instability, notably ethnic hostilities in the north of the FYRM in 2001, had an adverse impact on tourist activity, although tourist receipts increased thereafter. During 1995–2004, according to the World Bank, the GDP of the services sector increased, in real terms, at an average annual rate of 2.0%; services GDP rose by 3.0% in 2003 and by 2.3% in 2004.

In 2004 the FYRM recorded a visible trade deficit of US $1,112.1m., and there was a deficit of $414.8m. on the current account of the balance of payments. In 2005 the principal source of imports was Russia (accounting for 13.2%); other major sources were Germany (10.4%), Greece (9.2%), Serbia and Montenegro (8.2%), Bulgaria (7.3%) and Italy (6.0%). The principal market for exports in that year was Serbia and Montenegro (22.5%); other important purchasers were Germany (17.8%), Greece (15.3%) and Italy (8.3%). The principal exports in 2005 were miscellaneous basic manufactures, miscellaneous manufactured articles, food and live animals, mineral fuels and lubricants, beverages and tobacco, and machinery and transport equipment. The main imports in that year were basic manufactures, mineral fuels and lubricants (notably petroleum and petroleum products), machinery and transport equipment, food and live animals, chemical products and miscellaneous manufactured articles.

The FYRM recorded an overall budgetary surplus of 577m. new denars in 2005. At the end of 2003 the FYRM's external debt totalled US $1,837m., of which $1,438m. was long-term public debt. In that year the cost of debt-servicing was equivalent to 12.9% of the value of exports of goods and services. The annual rate of inflation averaged 2.0% in 1995–2004. Consumer prices declined by 0.5% in 2004 and increased by only 0.04% in 2005. The rate of unemployment was 36.5% in the third quarter of 2005.

The FYRM is a member of the IMF and the European Bank for Reconstruction and Development (EBRD, see p. 224). It become a member of the World Trade Organization (WTO, see p. 370) in

2003. The FYRM joined the Central European Free Trade Association (CEFTA) in February 2006.

The FYRM's economic prospects were significantly improved by the removal, in late 1995, of the Greek embargo on trade with the FYRM and the UN sanctions against the FRY, which had severely disrupted the FYRM's trading links. Progress was achieved through mass privatization, and a stock exchange was opened in Skopje in 1996. A subsequent improvement in relations between Greece and the FYRM allowed substantial Greek investment. Value-added tax was successfully introduced in 2000, and in November the IMF agreed new lending to support the Government's economic reforms. A Stabilization and Association Agreement was signed with the European Union (EU, see p. 228) in April 2001. However, ethnic hostilities in the north of the country in early 2001 (see Recent History) prompted renewed fears of widespread civil conflict, and a substantial deterioration of the fiscal position. A peace agreement was negotiated in August, and in March 2002 a donor aid conference, sponsored by the EU and the World Bank, resulted in considerable pledges to support reconstruction. In September the Government, which had been widely regarded as responsible for mismanagement and corruption, was replaced. Measures to investigate suspected embezzlement in public institutions and to combat further malpractice were immediately introduced. A new stand-by credit agreement with the IMF was signed in early 2003; the Government's success in adhering to conditions of fiscal restraint and macroeconomic targets was commended, despite delays in implementing investment projects, and in introducing measures to privatize or close loss-making enterprises. In March 2004 the FYRM submitted a formal application for membership of the EU. A new Government, established in December, appeared to make some progress in attracting major investment projects (regarded as essential in addressing the critically high rate of unemployment). In August 2005 the IMF finally approved a further three-year stand-by arrangement (the previous agreement had expired in August 2004) to finance the Government's economic programme. The IMF-supported policies were to give priority to structural reforms of the state pension and health-care funds, judiciary and state administration, and the labour market, with the aim of improving the unfavourable business conditions. In December 2005 the EU formally granted the FYRM candidate status, although no date for the opening of membership negotiations was announced; initiation of the process was regarded as conditional on the Government's compliance with EU recommendations. The Government was to submit a pre-accession programme annually in order to detail its reform strategy for meeting EU economic criteria (which included the full development of a market economy). Continuing police and judicial reforms and the organization of forthcoming legislative elections in accordance with international standards were regarded as essential to the success of the FYRM's application for membership. In March 2006 the state electricity utility was purchased by an Austrian company, as part of efforts to attract increased foreign investment; plans for its sale had prompted public protests (see Recent History).

Education

Elementary education is provided free of charge, and is officially compulsory for all children between the ages of seven and 15 years. Various types of secondary education, beginning at 15 years of age and lasting for four years, are available to those who qualify. In 2002/03 some 91% of children in the relevant age-group (males 91%, females 91%) were enrolled in primary education, while in 2001/02 the comparable ratio for secondary education was equivalent to 81% (males 82%; females 80%). The Constitution guarantees nationals the right to elementary and secondary education in their mother tongue. In 2001/02 Albanian was the language of education in 275 primary schools and 24 secondary schools, Turkish in 55 primary schools and five secondary schools, and Serbian in 13 primary schools. In 2003/04 some 46,637 students were enrolled at the universities at Skopje and at Bitola. In July 2000 new legislation permitted the use of Albanian and other languages in private tertiary institutions, and an Albanian-language university (the South-East Europe University) at Tetovo opened as a private institution, with funding from the international community, in November 2001. In 2004, under further amendments to legislation on higher education, the Albanian-language Tetovo University (previously declared illegal) became the third state-funded university. Expenditure on education by the central Government in 2002 was budgeted at 7,591m. denars (11.4% of total expenditure).

Public Holidays

2006: 1 January (New Year), 6–7 January (Orthodox Christmas), 10 January*† (Great Bayram, Feast of the Sacrifice), 14–15 January (Orthodox New Year), 8 March (International Women's Day), 23–24 April (Orthodox Easter), 1 May (Labour Day), 24 May (Day of the Apostles SS Methodius), 2 August (National Day), 8 September (Independence Day), 11 October (Anti-Fascism Day), 24 October* (Small Bayram, end of Ramadan), 31 December*† (Great Bayram, Feast of the Sacrifice).

2007: 1 January (New Year), 6–7 January (Orthodox Christmas), 14–15 January (Orthodox New Year), 8 March (International Women's Day), 8–9 April (Orthodox Easter), 1 May (Labour Day), 24 May (Day of the Apostles SS Cyril and Methodius), 2 August (National Day), 8 September (Independence Day), 11 October (Anti-Fascism Day), 13 October* (Small Bayram, end of Ramadan), 20 December* (Great Bayram, Feast of the Sacrifice).

* These holidays are dependent on the Islamic lunar calendar and may vary by one or two days from the dates given.

† This festival occurs twice (in the Islamic years AH 1426 and 1427) within the same Gregorian year.

Weights and Measures

The metric system is in force.

THE FORMER YUGOSLAV REPUBLIC OF MACEDONIA

Statistical Survey

Source (unless otherwise indicated): State Statistical Office of the Republic of Macedonia, 91000 Skopje, Dame Gruev 4, POB 506; tel. (2) 114904; fax (2) 111336; e-mail info@stat.gov.mk; internet www.stat.gov.mk.

Area and Population

AREA, POPULATION AND DENSITY

Area (sq km)	25,713*
Population (census results)†	
20 June 1994	1,945,932
31 October 2002	
Males	1,015,377
Females	1,007,170
Total	2,022,547
Density (per sq km) at 31 October 2002	78.6

* 9,928 sq miles.

† Comprising persons with an official place of residence in the country (including those temporarily abroad for less than a year), persons from other countries who have been granted a residence permit in the FYRM and have been present there for at least a year and foreigners with refugee status; excluding foreign diplomatic and military personnel.

PRINCIPAL ETHNIC GROUPS
(census results)

	1991	1994	2002
Macedonian	1,328,187	1,295,964	1,297,981
Albanian	441,987	441,104	509,083
Turkish	77,080	78,019	77,959
Roma (Gypsy)	52,103	43,707	53,879
Serbian	42,775	40,228	35,939
Muslim	31,356	15,418	17,018
Vlach	7,764	8,601	9,695
Total (incl. others)	2,033,964	1,945,932	2,022,547

PRINCIPAL TOWNS
(official estimates, 2004)*

Skopje (capital)	515,419	Prilep	76,768
Kumanovo	105,484	Struga	63,376
Bitola	95,385	Ohrid	55,749
Tetovo	86,580	Velec	55,108
Gostivar	81,042	Strumica	54,676

* Population by municipality, except for Skopje, which comprises 10 municipalities.

Source: Ministry of Local Self-Government, Skopje.

BIRTHS, MARRIAGES AND DEATHS

	Registered live births Number	Rate (per 1,000)	Registered marriages Number	Rate (per 1,000)	Registered deaths Number	Rate (per 1,000)
1997	29,478	14.8	14,072	7.0	16,596	8.3
1998	29,244	14.6	13,993	7.0	16,870	8.4
1999	27,309	13.5	14,172	7.0	16,789	8.3
2000	29,308	14.5	14,255	7.0	17,253	8.5
2001	27,010	13.3	13,267	6.5	16,919	8.3
2002	27,761	13.7	14,522	7.2	17,962	8.9
2003	27,011	n.a.	14,402	n.a.	18,006	n.a.
2004	26,883	n.a.	14,073	n.a.	18,265	n.a.

Expectation of life (WHO estimates, years at birth): 72 (males 69; females 75) in 2003 (Source: WHO, *World Health Report*).

ECONOMICALLY ACTIVE POPULATION
(sample surveys, '000 persons aged 15 years and over, at April)

	2002	2003	2004
Agriculture, hunting and forestry	133.6	120.0	87.6
Fishing	0.7	0.2	0.4
Mining and quarrying	6.9	2.5	2.8
Manufacturing	132.4	131.3	116.3
Electricity, gas and water	14.8	15.2	15.8
Construction	32.8	35.9	36.5
Wholesale and retail trade, repair of motor vehicles, motorcycles and articles for personal use and for households	64.3	62.5	74.2
Hotels and restaurants	11.2	12.8	12.7
Transport, storage and communications	32.6	30.6	30.8
Financial intermediation	8.4	7.1	7.7
Real estate, renting and business activities	12.0	10.8	13.5
Public administration and defence, compulsory social security	33.0	34.7	39.7
Education	33.7	32.0	33.6
Health and social work	26.2	30.2	29.9
Other community, social and personal services	17.5	17.8	19.7
Private households with employed persons	0.3	—	0.2
Extra-territorial organizations and bodies	0.9	1.5	1.6
Total employed	561.3	545.1	523.0
Unemployed	263.5	315.9	309.3
Total labour force	824.8	861.0	832.3
Males	501.9	519.1	506.9
Females	322.9	341.8	325.4

Source: ILO.

Health and Welfare

KEY INDICATORS

Total fertility rate (children per woman, 2003)	1.9
Under-5 mortality rate (per 1,000 live births, 2004)	14
HIV/AIDS (% of persons aged 15–49, 2003)	<0.1
Physicians (per 1,000 head, 2001)	2.19
Hospital beds (per 1,000 head, 2002)	4.83
Health expenditure (2002): US $ per head (PPP)	341
Health expenditure (2002): % of GDP	6.8
Health expenditure (2002): public (% of total)	84.7
Human Development Index (2003): ranking	59
Human Development Index (2003): value	0.797

For sources and definitions, see explanatory note on p. vi.

Agriculture

PRINCIPAL CROPS
('000 metric tons)

	2002	2003	2004
Wheat	267.2	225.5	358.4
Rice (paddy)	8.9	13.0	14.7
Barley	128.4	83.2	150.0
Maize	140.2	141.4	146.1
Rye	7.1	6.1	10.3
Potatoes	183.1	174.5	199.0
Sugar beet	43.8	38.9	52.2
Dry beans	13.8	15.2	14.6
Olives*	13.0	16.0	14.0
Cabbages	71.0	70.0	68.3

THE FORMER YUGOSLAV REPUBLIC OF MACEDONIA

—continued

	2002	2003	2004
Tomatoes	109.5	113.2	116.8
Cucumbers and gherkins	22.0*	28.9*	35.7
Chillies and green peppers	108.1	111.4	110.0*
Dry onions	34.6	30.8	34.2
Green beans	13.8	13.8*	13.8*
Watermelons	152.4	136.8	125.4
Apples	63.3	61.9	82.4
Peaches and nectarines	6.3	7.3	11.6
Plums	23.8	15.3	26.0
Grapes	119.0	237.3	247.7
Tobacco (leaves)	22.0	21.6	21.1

* FAO estimate(s).

Source: FAO.

LIVESTOCK
('000 head, year ending September)

	2002	2003	2004
Horses*	57	57	57
Cattle	259	260	255
Pigs	196	179	158
Sheep	1,234	1,239	1,432
Poultry	2,900	2,417	2,725

* FAO estimates.

Source: FAO.

LIVESTOCK PRODUCTS
('000 metric tons)

	2002	2003	2004
Beef and veal	6.7	8.7	8.8
Mutton and lamb	4.6	5.9	7.0
Pig meat	10.6	9.6	9.4
Poultry meat	4.0	4.1	3.2
Cows' milk	198.4	191.5	212.9
Sheep's milk	51.6	52.5	47.9
Butter*	9.5	9.5	9.5
Cheese	3.7	3.8	4.3
Poultry eggs	19.4	15.5	18.7
Honey	0.9	1.0	0.9
Wool: greasy	1.9	2.0	3.2
Wool: scoured	1.0	1.0	1.6
Cattle hides*	1.3	1.9	1.3
Sheepskins*	1.1	1.1	1.1

* FAO estimates.

Source: FAO.

Forestry

ROUNDWOOD REMOVALS
('000 cubic metres, excl. bark)

	2002	2003	2004
Sawlogs, veneer logs and logs for sleepers	104	118	126
Other industrial wood	8	6	6
Fuel wood	603	688	699
Total	715	812	831

Source: FAO.

SAWNWOOD PRODUCTION
('000 cubic metres, incl. railway sleepers)

	2002	2003	2004
Coniferous (softwood)	6	5	8
Broadleaved (hardwood)	15	16	20
Total	21	21	28

Source: FAO.

Fishing
(metric tons, live weight)

	2001	2002	2003
Capture	128	148	162
Trouts	115	120	130
Aquaculture	1,053	1,215	1,486
Common carp	153	173	280
Bleak	70	98	89
Other freshwater fishes	221	214	56
Trouts	454	560	880
Huchen	110	120	125
Total catch	1,181	1,363	1,648

Source: FAO.

Mining
('000 metric tons, unless otherwise indicated)

	2001	2002	2003
Lignite	8,106	8,640	8,360
Copper concentrates*	9†	6†	4
Lead concentrates*	20†	15†	5
Zinc concentrates*	20†	10†	4
Gold (kilograms)†	500	500	400
Silver (kilograms)†	15,000	12,000	10,000
Gypsum (crude)†	20	20	20

* Figures refer to the metal content of concentrates.
† Estimate(s).

Source: US Geological Survey.

Industry

SELECTED PRODUCTS
('000 metric tons, unless otherwise indicated)

	2000	2001	2002
Vegetable oils: refined	11	15	14
Flour	129	119	114
Refined sugar	32	18	37
Wine ('000 hectolitres)	931	736	254
Beer ('000 hectolitres)	661	618	657
Soft drinks ('000 hectolitres)	860	882	1,020
Cigars (million)	8,883	7,766	6,567
Wool yarn: pure and mixed	2.9	2.2	0.5
Cotton yarn: pure and mixed	2.6	2.1	2.8
Footwear, excl. rubber ('000 pairs)	2,059	1,246	1,654
Wrapping and packaging paper and paperboard	13	15	18
Sulphuric acid	109	101	95
Motor spirit (petrol)	131	104	n.a.
Naphthas	161	127	n.a.
Gas-diesel (distillate fuel) oil	259	224	n.a.
Residual fuel oils	377	282	n.a.
Cement	801	630	777
Ferro-alloys*†	65	70	77
Crude steel*	296.3	261.9	305.1
Lead: refined*†	22.9	19.7	19.8
Zinc: refined*†	62.8	52.0	38.0
Electric energy (million kWh)	6,811	6,361	n.a.

* Data from US Geological Survey.
† Estimates.

Source (unless otherwise indicated): UN, *Industrial Commodity Statistics Yearbook*.

THE FORMER YUGOSLAV REPUBLIC OF MACEDONIA

Finance

CURRENCY AND EXCHANGE RATES

Monetary Units
100 deni = 1 new Macedonian denar.

Sterling, Dollar and Euro Equivalents (30 November 2005)
£1 sterling = 89.617 new denars;
US $1 = 51.891 new denars;
€1 = 61.071 new denars;
1,000 new denars = £11.16 = $19.27 = €16.37.

Average Exchange Rate (new denars per US $)
2002   64.350
2003   54.322
2004   49.410

Note: The Macedonian denar was introduced in April 1992, replacing (initially at par) the Yugoslav dinar. In May 1993 a new Macedonian denar, equivalent to 100 of the former units, was established as the sole legal tender.

BUDGET
(million new denars)*

Revenue	2003	2004	2005
Tax revenue	49,840	53,188	55,681
Personal income tax	7,502	7,707	8,097
Profit tax	3,271	2,361	2,837
Value-added tax	21,175	25,757	27,082
Excises	11,241	10,996	11,748
Import duties	6,140	5,815	5,266
Social contributions	27,215	28,072	28,595
Pension insurance	17,574	18,040	18,300
Unemployment contributions	1,224	1,270	1,313
Health insurance	8,417	8,762	8,982
Non-tax revenue	6,331	6,306	7,596
Capital revenue	576	600	933
Grants	2	—	—
Repayment of loans	123	11	—
Total	84,087	88,176	92,805

Expenditure	2003	2004	2005
Current expenditure	81,125	82,136	83,965
Wage, salaries and allowances	20,881	21,440	22,159
Other purchases of goods and services	8,708	8,200	8,545
Transfers	48,518	50,125	50,684
Pensions	24,008	25,121	24,969
Unemployment benefits	2,438	3,289	2,940
Social benefits	3,986	3,993	4,138
Health care	14,028	14,428	14,823
Interest payments	2,730	2,312	2,577
Guarantees	288	58	—
Capital expenditure	5,623	6,033	8,263
Total	86,748	88,169	92,228

* Figures refer to the consolidated accounts of the general Government, comprising the transactions of the central Government and the operations of extrabudgetary funds.

Source: Ministry of Finance, Skopje.

INTERNATIONAL RESERVES
(US $ million at 31 December)

	2003	2004	2005
Gold (national valuation)	37.1	86.5	112.0
IMF special drawing rights	0.3	0.8	0.8
Foreign exchange	897.4	904.2	1,227.7
Total	934.8	991.5	1,340.5

Source: IMF, *International Financial Statistics*.

MONEY SUPPLY
(million new denars at 31 December)

	2003	2004	2005
Currency outside banks	14,177	14,162	14,439
Demand deposits at deposit money banks	12,800	13,154	15,206
Total (incl. others)	28,291	28,884	31,219

Source: IMF, *International Financial Statistics*.

COST OF LIVING
(Consumer Price Index; base: 2000 = 100)

	2002	2003	2004
Food	108.8	107.3	104.0
Fuel and light	104.9	109.6	112.8
Clothing (incl. footwear)	108.2	110.5	111.6
Housing	115.9	120.4	120.0
All items (incl. others)	107.4	108.7	108.2

Source: ILO.

NATIONAL ACCOUNTS
(million new denars at current prices)

National Income and Product

Expenditure on the Gross Domestic Product

	2002	2003	2004*
Government final consumption expenditure	54,616	51,980	55,112
Private final consumption expenditure	188,179	191,873	206,612
Changes in inventories	9,991	8,151	9,916
Gross fixed capital formation	40,448	42,110	47,286
Total domestic expenditure	293,234	294,114	318,925
Exports of goods and services	92,791	95,254	106,758
Less Imports of goods and services	142,055	137,882	160,425
GDP in purchasers' values	243,970	251,486	265,257
GDP at constant 1995 prices	188,941	194,263	202,189

* Preliminary figures.

Gross Domestic Product by Economic Activity

	2002	2003	2004*
Agriculture, hunting and forestry	24,509	28,672	30,073
Fishing	48	27	21
Mining and quarrying	960	989	1,042
Manufacturing	37,925	39,651	39,663
Electricity, gas and water supply	9,146	11,778	11,080
Construction	11,893	13,537	14,736
Wholesale and retail trade	27,438	28,282	36,000
Hotels and restaurants	4,088	4,653	4,172
Transport and communications	20,610	21,062	20,642
Financial services	7,427	6,110	7,510
Real estate and business services†	18,960	22,185	24,515
Public administration and defence	16,145	16,984	17,874
Education	8,688	9,436	9,913
Health care and social work	9,361	9,897	9,650
Other community, social and personal services	5,553	5,503	5,984
Sub-total	202,751	218,767	232,876
Less Imputed bank service charge	4,160	3,797	4,720
Gross value added at basic prices	198,592	214,970	228,156
Value-added tax	38,874	30,229	31,290
Import duties	6,504	6,291	5,815
Less Subsidies on products	—	4	4
GDP in purchasers' values	243,970	251,486	265,257

* Preliminary figures.
† Including imputed rents of owner-occupied dwellings.

THE FORMER YUGOSLAV REPUBLIC OF MACEDONIA

BALANCE OF PAYMENTS
(US $ million)

	2002	2003	2004
Exports of goods f.o.b.	1,112.1	1,362.7	1,672.4
Imports of goods f.o.b.	−1,916.5	−2,210.6	−2,784.5
Trade balance	−804.3	−847.9	−1,112.1
Exports of services	253.0	326.9	407.9
Imports of services	−275.3	−337.0	−462.3
Balance on goods and services	−826.6	−858.1	−1,166.4
Other income received	51.0	60.4	84.6
Other income paid	−80.8	−91.9	−123.8
Balance on goods, services and income	−856.4	−889.6	−1,205.7
Current transfers received	535.7	778.9	836.9
Current transfers paid	−37.2	−38.2	−46.0
Current balance	−357.9	−149.0	−414.8
Capital account (net)	8.3	−6.7	−4.6
Direct investment abroad	−0.1	−0.3	−1.2
Direct investment from abroad	77.8	96.3	157.0
Portfolio investment assets	1.2	0.3	−0.9
Portfolio investment liabilities	0.1	3.3	14.7
Other investment assets	246.2	−3.8	6.6
Other investment liabilities	−67.9	141.2	263.4
Net errors and omissions	−29.7	−26.0	7.8
Overall balance	−122.1	55.4	28.0

Source: IMF, *International Financial Statistics*.

External Trade

PRINCIPAL COMMODITIES
(distribution by SITC, US $ million)

Imports c.i.f.	2001	2002	2003
Food and live animals	194.1	246.5	270.5
Meat and meat preparations	61.8	70.9	70.2
Mineral fuels, lubricants, etc.	234.7	264.5	323.5
Petroleum, petroleum products etc.	193.2	207.0	259.4
Crude petroleum and bituminous oils	118.1	96.2	192.0
Refined petroleum products	65.1	101.7	56.6
Chemicals and related products	168.3	207.3	248.8
Basic manufactures	214.8	270.6	335.3
Iron and steel	37.7	47.1	78.1
Machinery and transport equipment	281.9	406.5	433.0
Telecommunications, sound recording and reproducing equipment	36.2	50.6	89.4
Electrical machinery, apparatus etc. (excl. telecommunications and sound equipment)	46.9	69.7	75.8
Road vehicles and parts*	62.1	130.9	101.9
Passenger motor vehicles (excl. buses)	30.4	91.3	59.2
Miscellaneous manufactured articles	101.3	113.1	130.3
Total (incl. others)	1,687.6	1,995.2	2,299.9

* Data on parts exclude tyres, engines and electrical parts.

Source: UN, *International Trade Statistics Yearbook*.

2004 (US $ million): Food and live animals 337.5 Crude materials (inedible) except fuels 77.3; Mineral fuels, lubricants, etc. 397.8; Chemicals and related products 303.9; Basic manufactures 698.2; Machinery and transport equipment 547.0; Miscellaneous manufactured articles 171.8; Total (incl. others) 2,931.6.

2005 (US $ million): Food and live animals 343.1; Crude materials (inedible) except fuels 106.7; Mineral fuels, lubricants, etc. 618.4; Chemicals and related products 333.9; Basic manufactures 947.6; Machinery and transport equipment 563.0; Miscellaneous manufactured articles 252.0; Total (incl. others) 3,228.0.

Exports f.o.b.	2001	2002	2003
Food and live animals	65.3	74.7	91.1
Vegetables and fruit	30.1	36.0	42.5
Beverages and tobacco	121.5	124.9	136.7
Beverages	46.5	48.7	55.4
Tobacco and tobacco manufactures	75.0	76.2	81.3
Crude materials (inedible) except fuels	37.3	35.4	39.6
Mineral fuels, lubricants, etc.	43.4	25.1	73.8
Refined petroleum products	40.4	22.5	68.6
Chemicals and related products	57.4	67.1	66.2
Basic manufactures	379.5	323.8	411.3
Textile yarn, fabrics, etc.	37.3	35.8	42.5
Iron and steel	196.0	156.7	251.6
Ferro-alloys	28.2	32.7	75.0
Sheets and plates	84.9	68.3	89.7
Non-ferrous metals	73.4	62.0	40.7
Zinc	51.0	40.1	20.4
Machinery and transport equipment	76.0	74.4	80.6
Electrical machinery, apparatus etc. (excl. telecommunications and sound equipment)	46.4	42.0	44.4
Miscellaneous manufactured articles	370.0	383.7	460.4
Clothing and accessories (excl. footwear)	319.4	334.1	409.3
Total (incl. others)	1,155.5	1,115.5	1,363.3

Source: UN, *International Trade Statistics Yearbook*.

2004 (US $ million): Food and live animals 125.6; Beverages and tobacco 127.8; Crude materials (inedible) except fuels 44.1; Mineral fuels, lubricants, etc. 78.3; Chemicals and related products 79.6; Basic manufactures 546.3; Machinery and transport equipment 99.0; Miscellaneous manufactured articles 570.8; Total (incl. others) 1,675.9.

2005 (US $ million): Food and live animals 167.2; Beverages and tobacco 163.1; Crude materials (inedible) except fuels 67.8; Mineral fuels, lubricants, etc. 163.6; Chemicals and related products 90.7; Basic manufactures 682.5; Machinery and transport equipment 109.9; Miscellaneous manufactured articles 589.9; Total (incl. others) 2,041.3.

PRINCIPAL TRADING PARTNERS
(US $ million)

Imports c.i.f.	2004	2005
Austria	68.9	69.2
Bulgaria	209.7	234.3
China, People's Republic	82.0	115.0
Croatia	65.8	75.2
France	67.5	61.0
Germany	368.2	334.9
Greece	282.6	296.8
Italy	168.8	193.7
Netherlands	57.1	53.2
Poland	78.3	94.6
Romania	113.1	n.a.
Russia	271.0	424.5
Serbia and Montenegro	243.7	264.2
Slovenia	140.3	128.0
Spain	31.0	n.a.
Switzerland-Liechtenstein	45.7	63.7
Turkey	94.9	113.6
Ukraine	74.1	72.0
United Kingdom	54.7	44.0
USA	47.9	45.2
Total (incl. others)	2,931.6	3,228.0

THE FORMER YUGOSLAV REPUBLIC OF MACEDONIA

Exports f.o.b.	2004	2005
Bosnia and Herzegovina	n.a.	50.5
British Virgin Islands	n.a.	83.6
Bulgaria	51.5	76.1
Croatia	80.2	81.1
France	77.3	19.9
Germany	315.6	364.0
Greece	228.8	312.9
Italy	134.6	169.6
Netherlands	47.3	44.6
Russia	19.7	21.4
Serbia and Montenegro	347.6	459.5
Slovenia	27.2	31.8
Spain	23.0	n.a.
Turkey	54.0	46.3
United Kingdom	42.5	42.9
USA	72.1	44.3
Total (incl. others)	1,675.9	2,041.3

Transport

RAILWAYS
(traffic)

	2003	2004	2005
Passenger journeys ('000)	902	917	903
Passenger-km (million)	92	94	94
Freight carried ('000 metric tons)	2,388	2,610	3,129
Freight ton-km (million)	373	423	531

ROAD TRAFFIC
(motor vehicles in use at 31 December)

	2000	2001	2002
Motorcycles	3,729	4,483	2,918
Passenger cars	299,588	309,562	307,581
Buses	2,498	2,620	2,497
Commercial vehicles	20,763	21,727	20,213
Special vehicles	8,552	9,554	10,292
Tractors and working vehicles	1,417	1,560	918

INLAND WATERS
(lake transport)

	2000	2001	2002
Passengers carried ('000)	10	3	6
Passenger-km ('000)	321	117	389

CIVIL AVIATION
(traffic on scheduled services)

	1999	2000	2001
Kilometres flown (million)	7	10	5
Passengers carried ('000)	488	599	315
Passenger-kilometres (million)	599	740	377
Total ton-kilometres (million)	57	70	36

Source: UN, *Statistical Yearbook*.

Tourism

TOURISTS BY COUNTRY OF ORIGIN*

	2001	2002	2003
Albania	6,419	9,086	12,088
Austria	1,300	1,919	2,564
Bosnia and Herzegovina	1,377	1,885	2,687
Bulgaria	8,484	11,703	14,147
Croatia	2,609	4,097	5,467
France	2,313	2,542	3,513
Germany	4,860	6,084	6,317
Greece	10,637	14,677	27,042
Hungary	2,130	1,985	2,173
Italy	2,511	3,076	3,626
Netherlands	1,564	2,016	2,470
Serbia and Montenegro	16,429	23,239	27,325
Slovenia	2,658	3,837	4,579
Turkey	3,101	5,180	5,755
United Kingdom	4,357	3,916	4,517
USA	7,099	6,997	7,403
Total (incl. others)	98,946	122,861	157,692

* Figures refer to arrivals from abroad at all accommodation establishments.

Tourism receipts (US $ million, incl. passenger transport): 49 in 2001; 55 in 2002; 65 in 2003.

Source: World Tourism Organization.

Communications Media

	2000	2001	2002
Television receivers ('000 in use)	570	n.a.	n.a.
Telephones ('000 main lines in use)	507.3	538.5	578.3
Mobile cellular telephones ('000 subscribers)	99.9	221.3	365.3
Internet users ('000)	50	70	100
Book production: titles*	727	737	1,102
Book production: copies ('000)*	968	1,061	1,899
Daily newspapers: titles	6	8	9
Daily newspapers: average circulation ('000 copies)	32,640	43,689	45,536
Non-daily newspapers: titles	33	29	30
Non-daily newspapers: average circulation ('000 copies)	2,619	2,961	2,618

* Including pamphlets.

Radio receivers ('000 in use): 410 in 1997.
Facsimile machines (number in use): 3,000 in 1997.
Telephones ('000 main lines in use): 525.0 in 2003.
Mobile cellular telephones ('000 subscribers): 776.0 in 2003.
Personal computers ('000 in use): 140 in 2004.
Internet users ('000): 159 in 2004.

Sources: mainly International Telecommunication Union; UNESCO, *Statistical Yearbook*; and UN, *Statistical Yearbook*.

Education

(2004/05, unless otherwise indicated)

	Institutions	Teachers	Students
Primary and lower secondary	1,012	13,972	227,254
Upper secondary	96	5,876	95,268
University level*	29	1,487	44,731
Other higher*	1	32	893

* 2002/03 figures.

Adult literacy rate (UNESCO estimates): 96.1% (males 98.2%; females 94.1%) in 2003 (Source: UN Development Programme, *Human Development Report*).

THE FORMER YUGOSLAV REPUBLIC OF MACEDONIA

Directory

The Constitution

The Constitution of the former Yugoslav republic of Macedonia was promulgated on 17 November 1991. The September 1995 interim agreement with Greece required guarantees that the Macedonian Constitution enshrined or implied no claim to territory beyond the country's existing borders. Some amendment of the 1991 document was thus necessitated. Following the framework agreement between the principal Macedonian and ethnic Albanian parties, reached in August 2001 (see Recent History), the Constitution was revised on 16 November to include 15 principal amendments. The following is a summary of the main provisions of the Constitution, which describes the country as the Republic of Macedonia:

GENERAL PROVISIONS

The Republic of Macedonia is a sovereign, independent, democratic state, where sovereignty derives from democratically elected citizens, referendums and other forms of expression. The citizens of the Republic of Macedonia are defined as the Macedonian people, as well as citizens living within its borders who are, *inter alia*, ethnic Albanians, ethnic Turks, ethnic Serbs and Vlach. The fundamental values defined by the Constitution are: basic human rights, free expression of nationality, the rule of law, a policy of pluralism and the free market, local self-government, entrepreneurship, social justice and solidarity, and respect for international law. State power is divided into legislative, executive and judicial power.

BASIC RIGHTS

The following rights and freedoms are guaranteed and protected in the Republic: the right to life, the inviolability of each person's physical and moral integrity, the right to freedom of speech, public appearance, public information, belief, conscience and religion, and the freedom to organize and belong to a trade union or a political party. All forms of communication and personal data are secret, and the home is inviolable.

The Macedonian language is the official language in use throughout the Republic of Macedonia. Any other language spoken by at least 20% of the population is also an official language. The official personal documentation of citizens speaking an official language other than Macedonian will also be issued in that language.

Military and semi-military associations, which do not belong to the Armed Forces of the Republic, are prohibited.

Any citizen who has reached the age of 18 years has the right to vote and to be elected to organs of government. The right to vote is equal, general and direct, and is realized in free elections by secret ballot. The proportional representation of each community must be assured in the public services and in all areas of public life. Citizens enjoy equal freedoms and rights without distinction as to sex, race, colour, national and social origin, political and religious conviction, material and social position. All religious creeds are separate from the State and are equal under the law. They are identified, *inter alia*, as the Macedonian Orthodox Church, the Islamic Community of Macedonia, the Roman Catholic Church, the Evangelical Methodist Church and the Jewish Community. The members of all such communities are free to establish schools and other charitable institutions in the fields of culture, art and education.

GOVERNMENT

Legislature

Legislative power resides with the Sobranie (assembly), which consists of between 120 and 140 deputies elected for four years. The Sobranie adopts and amends the Constitution, enacts laws and gives interpretations thereof, adopts the budget of the Republic, decides on war and peace, chooses the Government, elects judges and releases them from duty. The Sobranie may decide, by a majority vote, to call a referendum on issues within its competence. A decision is adopted at a referendum if the majority of voters taking part in the ballot votes in favour of it and if more than one-half of the electorate participates in the vote. The Sobranie forms a Council for Inter-Ethnic Relations, comprising seven representatives from each of the ethnic Macedonian and Albanian communities, and five representatives of other nationalities living in the state. Parliamentary legislation on issues of culture and identity, particularly in the areas of language and education, can only be adopted if a majority of the deputies representing these communities votes in favour, in addition to the overall majority. Three of the nine judges of the Constitutional Court and three of the seven members of the Republican Judicial Council must also be elected by a double majority vote.

President

The President of the Republic represents the country and is responsible for ensuring respect for the Constitution and laws. He is Commander of the Armed Forces and appoints the Prime Minister. He appoints three members of the Security Council of the Republic (of which he is President) and ensures that the Council reflects the composition of the country's population.

Ministers

Executive power in the Republic resides with the Prime Minister and Ministers, who are not permitted concurrently to be deputies in the Sobranie. The Ministers are elected by the majority vote of all the deputies in the Sobranie. The Ministers implement laws and the state budget, and are responsible for foreign and diplomatic relations.

Judiciary

Judicial power is vested in the courts, and is autonomous and independent. The Supreme Court is the highest court. The election and dismissal of judges is proposed by the Republican Judicial Council.

Local Government

Legislation at local and municipal level is adopted by a two-thirds' majority vote of the total number of representatives. Legislation regulating such areas as local finance, elections and municipal boundaries must be adopted by a majority of the representatives representing the minority communities, as well as by an overall majority. In units of local self-government, citizens participate in decision-making on issues of local relevance directly, and through representatives.

OTHER PROVISIONS

The Sobranie elects an Ombudsman to ensure that constitutional rights are upheld, particularly the principles of non-discrimination and fair representation of the respective communities in public life. Revision of the Constitution must be approved by a two-thirds' majority in the Sobranie. Certain articles, such as the Preamble and those relating to local councils and minority rights, also require a majority of the vote by deputies from the minority communities.

The Government

HEAD OF STATE

President of the Republic: BRANKO CRVENKOVSKI (elected 28 April 2004; inaugurated 12 May 2004).

GOVERNMENT
(April 2006)

A coalition of the Social Democratic Alliance of Macedonia (SDAM), the Liberal-Democratic Party (LDP) and the Democratic Union for Integration (DUI).

Prime Minister: VLADO BUCKOVSKI (SDAM).

Deputy Prime Ministers: RADMILA SHEKERINSKA (SDAM), MINCO JORDANOV (SDAM), MUSA XHAFERI (DUI).

Deputy Prime Minister and Minister of Defence: JOVAN MANASIEVSKI (LDP).

Minister of Finance: NIKOLA POPOVSKI (SDAM).

Minister of Foreign Affairs: ILINKA MITREVA (SDAM).

Minister of Internal Affairs: LJUBOMIR MIHAJLOVSKI (SDAM).

Minister of Labour and Social Welfare: STEVCO JAKIMOVSKI (LDP).

Minister of Justice: MERI MLADENOVSKA-GORGIEVSKA (SDAM).

Minister of the Economy: FATMIR BESIMI (DUI).

Minister of Transport and Communications: DZEMAIL MEHAZI (DUI).

Minister of Agriculture, Forestry and Water Resources: SADULA DURAKU (DUI).

Minister of Education and Science: AZIZ POLOZHANI (DUI).

Minister of Culture: BLAGOJA STEFANOVSKI (SDAM).

Minister of Health: VLADIMIR DIMOV (SDAM).

Minister of Local Self-Government: RIZVAN SULEJMANI (DUI).

Minister of the Environment and Urban Planning: ZORAN SAPURIK (SDAM).

Minister without Portfolio: VLADO POPOVSKI (LDP).

THE FORMER YUGOSLAV REPUBLIC OF MACEDONIA

MINISTRIES

Office of the President: 1000 Skopje, 11 Oktomvri bb; tel. (2) 3113318; fax (2) 3112147; internet www.president.gov.mk.

Office of the Prime Minister: 1000 Skopje, Ilindenska bb; tel. (2) 3115455; fax (2) 3112561; e-mail office@primeminister.gov.mk; internet www.vlada.mk.

Ministry of Agriculture, Forestry and Water Resources: 1000 Skopje, Leninova 2; tel. (2) 3134477; fax (2) 3239429; internet www.mzsv.gov.mk.

Ministry of Culture: 1000 Skopje, Ilindenska bb; tel. (2) 3118022; fax (2) 3127112; internet www.gov.mk/kultura.

Ministry of Defence: 1000 Skopje, Orce Nikolov bb; tel. and fax (2) 3119577; fax (2) 3227835; e-mail info@morm.gov.mk; internet www.morm.gov.mk.

Ministry of the Economy: 1000 Skopje, Bote Bocevski 9; tel. (2) 384470; fax (2) 384472; e-mail ms@mt.net.mk; internet www.ms.gov.mk.

Ministry of Education and Science: 1000 Skopje, Dimitrija Čupovski 9; tel. (2) 3117896; fax (2) 3118414; e-mail mofk@mofk.gov.mk; internet www.mofk.gov.mk.

Ministry of the Environment and Urban Planning: 1000 Skopje, ul. Drezdenska 52; tel. (2) 3366930; fax (2) 3366931; e-mail info@moe.gov.mk; internet www.moe.gov.mk.

Ministry of Finance: 1000 Skopje, Dame Gruev 14; tel. (2) 3117288; fax (2) 3117280; internet www.finance.gov.mk.

Ministry of Foreign Affairs: 1000 Skopje, Dame Gruev 6; tel. (2) 3115266; fax (2) 3115790; e-mail mailmnr@mfa.gov.mk; internet www.mfa.gov.mk.

Ministry of Health: 1000 Skopje, Vodnjanska bb; tel. (2) 3147147; fax (2) 3113014; internet www.zdravstvo.com.mk.

Ministry of Internal Affairs: 1000 Skopje, Dimitar Mirchev bb; tel. (2) 3117222; fax (2) 3112468; internet www.mvr.gov.mk.

Ministry of Justice: 1000 Skopje, Dimitrija Čupovski 9; tel. (2) 3117277; fax (2) 3226975; internet www.covekovi-prava.gov.mk.

Ministry of Labour and Social Welfare: 1000 Skopje, Dame Gruev 14; tel. (2) 3117787; fax (2) 3118242; e-mail mtsp@mt.net.mk; internet www.mtsp.gov.mk.

Ministry of Local Self-Government: 1000 Skopje, Dimitrija Čupovski 9; tel. (2) 3106302; fax (2) 3106303; internet www.mls.gov.mk.

Ministry of Transport and Communications: 1000 Skopje, pl. Crvena skopska opstina 4; tel. (2) 3126228; fax (2) 3123292; internet www.mtc.gov.mk.

President and Legislature

PRESIDENT

Presidential Election, First Ballot, 14 April 2004

Candidate	Votes	% of votes
Branko Crvenkovski (SDAM)	385,347	42.47
Sasko Kedev (IMRO—DPMNU)	309,132	34.07
Gzim Ostreni (DUI)	134,208	14.79
Zidi Xhelili (DPA)	78,714	8.67
Total	**907,401**	**100.00**

Second Ballot, 28 April 2004

Candidate	Votes	% of votes
Branko Crvenkovski (SDAM)	553,522	62.70
Sasko Kedev (IMRO—DPMNU)	329,271	37.30
Total	**882,793**	**100.00**

Sobranie (Assembly)

1000 Skopje, 11 Oktomvri bb; tel. (2) 3112255; fax (2) 3237947; e-mail sobranie@sobranie.mk; internet www.sobranie.mk.

President: Dr LJUBCO JORDANOVSKI.

General Election, 15 September 2002*

Party	Votes	% of votes	Seats
Together for Macedonia†	494,744	40.46	60
Internal Macedonian Revolutionary Organization—Democratic Party for Macedonian National Unity-Liberal Party of Macedonia alliance	298,404	24.41	33
Democratic Union for Integration	114,913	11.85	16
Democratic Party of Albanians	63,695	5.21	7
Party for Democratic Prosperity	28,397	2.32	2
National Democratic Party	26,237	2.15	1
Socialist Party of Macedonia	25,976	2.12	1
Others	140,345	11.48	—
Total	**1,222,711**	**100.00**	**120**

* 85 members of the Sobranie were elected in single-member constituencies. The remaining 35 were elected by proportional representation on the basis of national party lists.

† Electoral coalition of 10 parties, led by the Social Democratic Alliance of Macedonia and the Liberal-Democratic Party.

Election Commission

State Election Commission: 1000 Skopje, 11 Oktomvri bb; tel. (2) 3112439; fax (2) 3112643; e-mail info_dik@zic.gov.mk; internet www.dik.mk; Chair. STEVO PENDAROVSKI.

Political Organizations

Democratic Alliance: Skopje; f. 2000; Chair. PAVLE TRAJANOV.

Democratic Alliance of Serbs in Macedonia (Demokratski Savez Srba u Makedoniji—DSSM): Skopje; f. 1994; Chair. BORIVOJE RISTIĆ.

Democratic Alternative (DA) (Demokratska Alternativa): 1000 Skopje, ul. Dame Gruev 1; tel. (2) 3212361; fax (2) 3227810; f. 1998; formed an electoral alliance with the IMRO—DPMNU; Chair. VASIL TUPURKOVSKI.

Democratic League—Liberal Party: Skopje, Gale Hristov k. 3-6; tel. (2) 3263523; Leader XHEMIL IDRIZI.

Democratic Muslim Party: Skopje; f. 2001; Leader TEFIK KADRI.

Democratic Party of Albanians (DPA) (Partia Demokratike Shqiptare) (PDSh): Tetovo, Maršal Tito 2; tel. and fax (44) 7332572; e-mail webmaster@pdsh.org; internet www.pdsh.org; f. July 1997; by a merger of the Party of Democratic Prosperity of Albanians in Macedonia (f. 1994) and the National Democratic Party (f. 1990); officially registered in July 2002; absorbed the National Democratic Party (f. 2001) and the Republican Party of Albanians (f. 2002) in June 2003; Chair. ARBEN XHAFERI.

Democratic Party of Serbs in Macedonia (DPSM): Skopje, 27 Mart 11; tel. (2) 3254274; f. 1996; Pres. DRAGISA MILETIĆ.

Democratic Party of Turks in Macedonia (DPTM) (Demokratska Partija na Turcite na Makedonija): 1000 Skopje, bul. Krste Misirkova 67; tel. (2) 3114696; Leader ERDOĞAN SARACH.

Democratic Party of Yugoslavs of Macedonia (DPYM) (Demokratska Partija Jugoslovena Makedonije—DPJM): Skopje; f. 1993; Chair. ZIVKO LEKOSKI; Gen. Sec. BOGDAN MICKOSKI.

Democratic Union for Integration (DUI) (Bashkimi Demokratik për Integrim/Demokratska Unija za Integracija) (BDI): 1200 Tetovo, RR 170 Nr 2, Reçicë e Vogël; tel. (4) 4334398; fax (4) 4334397; e-mail bdi@bdi.org.mk; internet www.bdi.org.mk; f. 2002; ethnic Albanian, dominated by former mems of rebel National Liberation Army; Chair. ALI AHMETI; Sec.-Gen. GZIM OSTRENI.

Internal Macedonian Revolutionary Organization—Democratic Party for Macedonian National Unity (IMRO—DPMNU) (Vnatrešno-Makedonska Revolucionerna Organizacija—Demokratska Partija za Makedonsko Nacionalno Edinstvo—VMRO—DPMNE): 1000 Skopje, Petar Drapshin br. 36; tel. (2) 3111441; fax (2) 3211586; e-mail info@vmro-dpmne.org.mk; internet www.vmro-dpmne.org.mk; nationalist; formed an electoral alliance with the Democratic Alternative; Pres. NIKOLA GRUEVSKI; Sec. DEN DONCEV.

Internal Macedonian Revolutionary Organization—People's Party (IMRO—People's Party) (Vnatrešno Makedonska Revolucionerna Organizacija—Narodna Partija—VMRO—NP): Skopje; f. July 2004; by fmr Prime Minister Ljubčo Georgievski as breakaway party of IMRO—DPMNU; Chair. VESNA JANEVSKA.

THE FORMER YUGOSLAV REPUBLIC OF MACEDONIA

Liberal-Democratic Party (LDP) (Liberalno-Demokratska Partija): 1000 Skopje, Partizanski odredi 89; tel. (2) 3063675; e-mail contact@ldp.org.mk; internet www.ldp.org.mk; f. 1996; by a merger of the Liberal Party and the Democratic Party; Chair. RISTO PENOV; Sec.-Gen. ROZA TOPUZOVA-KAREVSKA.

Liberal Party of Macedonia (LPM) (Liberalna Partija na Makedonija): 1000 Skopje, ul. Vasko Karangeleski 66; tel. (2) 464955; fax (2) 464956; e-mail lpm@mt.net.mk; internet www.liberalna.org.mk; Chair. STOJAN ANDOV.

Macedonian Democratic Party: Tetovo, Bazaar 3; tel. (44) 20826; fax (44) 24860; Leader TOMISLAV STOJANOVSKI.

Movement for all-Macedonian Action (MAAK)—Conservative Party: Skopje, Maksim Gorki 18/111; tel. (2) 116540; f. 1996; right-wing nationalist; Leader STRASO ANGELOVSKI.

Party of Democratic Action—Islamic Way (Stranka Demokratske Akcije—Islamski Put): Tetovo, Ilindenska 191; tel. (44) 32113; Leader MAZLAM KENAN.

Party for Democratic Future (PAD): Tetovo; f. 2005; Chair. ALAIDIN DEMIRI; Sec.-Gen. XHEMAL ABDIU.

Party for Democratic Prosperity (PDP) (Partija za Demokratski Prosperitet): Tetovo, Karaorman 62; tel. (44) 25709; f. 1990; split 1994; predominantly ethnic Albanian and Muslim party; Chair. ABDULADI VEJSELI; Sec.-Gen. NASER ZYBERI.

Party for the Full Emancipation of Romanies in Macedonia (Demokratska Progresivna Partija na Romite od Makedonija): Skopje, Shuto Orizari bb; tel. (2) 3612726; Leader FAIK ABDIĆ.

Social Democratic Alliance of Macedonia (SDAM) (Socijaldemokratski Sojuz na Makedonija—SDSM): 1000 Skopje, Bihačka 8; tel. (2) 3135380; fax (2) 3120462; e-mail contact@sdsm.org.mk; internet www.sdsm.org.mk; f. 1943; name changed from League of Communists of Macedonia—Party of Democratic Reform in 1991; led alliance, Together for Macedonia, which was elected to govt in Sept. 2002; Chair. VLADO BUČKOVSKI; Gen. Sec. GEORGI SPASOV.

Social Democratic Party of Macedonia (Socijaldemokratska Partija na Makedonija): 1000 Skopje, bul. Kliment Ohridski 54; tel. and fax (2) 3134077; Leader BRANKO JANEVSKI.

Socialist Party of Macedonia (SPM) (Socijalistiska Partija na Makedonija): 1000 Skopje, 11 Oktomvri 17; tel. (2) 3228015; fax (2) 3220025; e-mail spm@mol.com.mk; f. 1990; left-wing; Chair. LJUBISAV IVANOV.

Diplomatic Representation

EMBASSIES IN THE FORMER YUGOSLAV REPUBLIC OF MACEDONIA

Albania: 1000 Skopje, Hristijan Todorovski-Karposh 94; tel. (2) 2614636; fax (2) 2614200; e-mail ambshquip@lotus.mpt.com.mk; Ambassador VLADIMIR PRELJA.

Austria: 1000 Skopje, Vasil Stefanovski 7; tel. (2) 3109550; fax (2) 3130237; e-mail austramb@unet.com.mk; Ambassador PHILIP HOYOS.

Bosnia and Herzegovina: 1000 Skopje, Mile Pop-Jordanov 56; tel. (2) 3086216; fax (2) 3086221; Ambassador Dr SAVA ČEKLIČ.

Bulgaria: 1000 Skopje, Zlatko Shnaider 3; tel. (2) 3229444; fax (2) 3116139; e-mail bgemb@unet.com.mk; Ambassador MIHO MIHOV.

China, People's Republic: 1000 Skopje, 474 No 20; tel. (2) 3213163; fax (2) 3212500; Ambassador ZHANG WANXUE.

Croatia: 1000 Skopje, Mitropolit Teodosij Gologanov 59; tel. (2) 3127350; fax (2) 3127417; e-mail velhrskp@mpt.com.mk; Ambassador IVAN KUJUNDŽIĆ.

France: 1000 Skopje, Salvador Aljende 73; tel. (2) 3118749; fax (2) 3117760; e-mail framamba@nic.mpt.com.mk; internet www.ambafrance-mk.org; Ambassador VÉRONIQUE BUJON-BARRÉ.

Germany: 1000 Skopje, Leninska 59; tel. (2) 3093900; fax (2) 3093899; e-mail dtboskop@unet.com.mk; internet www.deutschebotschaft-skopje.com.mk; Ambassador RALF ANDREAS BRETH.

Hungary: 1000 Skopje, Mirka Ginova 27; tel. (2) 3063423; fax (2) 3063070; e-mail hungemb@mt.net.mk; Ambassador Dr FERENC PÓKA.

Italy: 1000 Skopje, 8 Udarna brig. 22; tel. (2) 3117430; fax (2) 3117087; e-mail segreteria@ambasciata.org.mk; internet www.ambasciata.org.mk; Ambassador Dr GIORGIO MARINI.

Netherlands: 1000 Skopje, Leninova 69–71; tel. (2) 3129319; fax (2) 3129309; e-mail nethemb@mt.com.mk; internet www.nlembassy.org.mk; Ambassador FRÉDÉRIQUE DE MAN.

Norway: 1000 Skopje, Mitropolit Teodosie Gologanov 59/2 A; tel. (2) 3129165; fax (2) 3111138; e-mail embskp@mfa.no; Ambassador CARL SCHIØTZ WIBYE.

Poland: 1000 Skopje, Djuro Djakovic 50; tel. and fax (2) 3119744; e-mail ambpol@unet.com.mk; Ambassador ANDRZEJ DOBRZYŃSKI.

Romania: 1000 Skopje, Rajko Zinzifov 42; tel. (2) 3228055; fax (2) 3228036; e-mail romanamb@on.net.mk; Ambasssador (vacant).

Russia: 1000 Skopje, Pirinska 44; tel. (2) 3117160; fax (2) 3117808; e-mail rusembas@mol.com.mk; internet www.macedonia.mid.ru; f. 1994; Ambassador AGARON N. ASATUR.

Serbia and Montenegro: 1000 Skopje, Pitu Guli 8; tel. (2) 3129298; fax (2) 3129427; e-mail yuamb@unet.com.mk; Ambassador ZORAN POPOVIĆ.

Slovenia: 1000 Skopje, Vodnjanska 42; tel. (2) 3178730; fax (2) 3176631; e-mail vsk@mzz-dkp.gov.si; Ambassador MARJAN SIFTAR.

Sweden: 1000 Skopje, Nikola Vapcarov 2/4; tel. (2) 3297880; fax (2) 3112065; e-mail swedembsk@mt.net.mk; Ambassador ULRIKA CRONENBERG-MOSSBERG.

Switzerland: 1000 Skopje, Maksim Gorki 19; tel. (2) 3128300; fax (2) 3116205; e-mail vertretung@sko.rep.admin.ch; internet www.eda.admin.ch/skopje; Ambassador THOMAS FÜGLISTER.

Turkey: 1000 Skopje, Slavej Planina bb; tel. (2) 3113270; fax (2) 3117024; e-mail turkish@mol.com.mk; Ambassador TANER KARAKAŞ.

Ukraine: 1000 Skopje, Pitu Guli 3; tel. (2) 3178120; fax (2) 3179259; e-mail amukr@on.net.mk; Ambassador VITALIJ MOSKALENKO.

United Kingdom: 1000 Skopje, Dimitrija Čupovski 26, 4th Floor; tel. (2) 3299299; fax (2) 3117555; e-mail britishembassyskopje@fco.gov.uk; internet www.britishembassy.gov.uk/macedonia; Ambassador ROBERT CHATTERTON DICKSON.

USA: 1000 Skopje, Ilindenska bb; tel. (2) 3116180; fax (2) 3117103; internet skopje.usembassy.gov; Ambassador GILLIAN ARLETTE MILOVANOVIĆ.

Judicial System

The FYRM has 27 Courts of First Instance and three Courts of Appeal. The Republican Judicial Council, which comprises seven members elected by the Sobranie for a term of six years, proposes the election or dismissal of judges to the Sobranie. The Constitutional Court, comprising nine judges elected by the Sobranie with a mandate of nine years, is responsible for the protection of constitutional and legal rights, and ensures that there is no conflict in the exercise of legislative, executive and judicial powers. The Supreme Court is the highest court in the country, and guarantees the equal administration of legislation by all courts. In December 2005 the Sobranie approved a series of constitutional amendments providing for extensive reform of the judicial system; as part of the reform, the Sobranie was no longer to be responsible for the appointment of judges.

Constitutional Court of the Republic of Macedonia (Ustaven Sud na Republika Makedonija): 1000 Skopje, 12 Udarna brig. 2; tel. (2) 3165153; fax (2) 3119355; e-mail usud@usud.gov.mk; internet www.usud.gov.mk; Pres. Dr TODOR DŽUNOV.

Supreme Court: 1000 Skopje, Krste Misirkova bb; tel. (2) 3234064; fax (2) 3237538; Pres. SIMEON GELEVSKI.

Republican Judicial Council: 1000 Skopje, Veljko Vlahovik bb; tel. (2) 3218130; fax (2) 3218131; Pres. LENČE SOFRONIEVSKA.

Office of the Public Prosecutor: 1000 Skopje, Krste Misirkova bb; tel. (2) 3229314; Public Prosecutor ALEKSANDR PRCEVSKI.

Religion

Most ethnic Macedonians are adherents of the Eastern Orthodox Church, and since 1967 there has been an autocephalous Macedonian Orthodox Church. However, the Serbian Orthodox Church (of which the Macedonian Church formed a part) does not recognize the autocephalous church, and nor do the Ecumenical Patriarchate (based in Istanbul, Turkey) and other Orthodox Churches. There are some adherents of other Orthodox jurisdictions in the country. Those Macedonian (and Bulgarian) Slavs who converted to Islam during the Ottoman era are known as Pomaks or as ethnic Muslims. The substantial Albanian population is mostly Muslim (mainly Sunni, but some adherents of a Dervish sect); there are a few Roman Catholic Christians and a small Jewish community.

CHRISTIANITY

Macedonian Orthodox Church: Skopje, Partizanski Odredi 12, POB 69; tel. (2) 3230697; fax (2) 3230685; internet www.mpc.org.mk; Metropolitan See of Ohrid revived in 1958; autocephaly declared 1967; 1.5m. mems; comprises seven bishoprics in Macedonia and three abroad; Head of Church and Archbishop of Ohrid and Macedonia Metropolitan Archbishop STEFAN VELJANOVSKI (of Skopje).

THE FORMER YUGOSLAV REPUBLIC OF MACEDONIA

Evangelical Methodist Church of Macedonia: Strumica; 14 congregations; mem. of the Methodist Conference of Central and Southern Europe, based in Geneva (Switzerland); Superintendent WILHELM NAUSNER (based in Linz, Austria); Pastor MIHAIL CEKOV.

The Roman Catholic Church

The diocese of Skopje, suffragan to the archdiocese of Vrhbosna (based in Sarajevo, Bosnia and Herzegovina), covers most of the FYRM. The Bishop is also Apostolic Exarch for Catholics of the Byzantine Rite in the FYRM. At 31 December 2003 there were an estimated 3,572 adherents of the Latin Rite in the diocese, and the country had 11,398 adherents of the Byzantine Rite.

Bishop of Skopje: Rt Rev. KIRO STOJANOV (Biskupski Ordinarijat), 1000 Skopje, Risto Siškov 31; tel. and fax (2) 3164123; e-mail katbiskupija@mt.net.mk.

ISLAM

Islamic Community of Macedonia (Bashkësia Fetare Islame e Republikës së Maqedonisë): Skopje, Çairska 52; tel. (2) 3117530; fax (2) 3117883; e-mail bim@bim.org.mk; internet www.bim.org.mk; formerly headquarters of the Skopje Region, one of the four administrative divisions of the Yugoslav Muslims; Leader Haji ARIF EMINI.

JUDAISM

Jewish Community: 1000 Skopje, Borka Taleski 24.

The Press

In 2002 a total of 39 newspapers and 178 magazines were published in the FYRM.

PRINCIPAL DAILY NEWSPAPERS

Denes (Today): 1000 Skopje, M. H. Jasmin 50; tel. (2) 3110239; fax (2) 3110150; e-mail denes@unet.com.mk; Editor NIK DENES.

Dnevnik (Daily): 1000 Skopje, Teodosij Gologanov 28; tel. (2) 3297555; fax (2) 3297554; e-mail dnevnik@dnevnik.com.mk; internet www.dnevnik.com.mk; independent; Editor-in-Chief BRANKO GEROSKI.

Flaka e vëllazërimit (Flame of Brotherhood): 1000 Skopje, Mito Hadživasilev bb; tel. (2) 3112025; fax (2) 3224829; f. 1945; relaunched 1994; in Albanian; Editor-in-Chief ABDULHAĐI ZULFIQARI; circ. 4,000.

Nova Makedonija (New Macedonia): 1000 Skopje, Mito Hadživasilev Jasmin bb; tel. and fax (2) 3233500; e-mail contact@novamakedonija.com.mk; internet www.novamakedonija.com.mk; f. 1944; morning; in Macedonian; Editor-in-Chief MIRCHE ADAMCHEVSKI; circ. 25,000.

Utrinski Vesnik (Morning Herald): 1000 Skopje, Dame Gruev 5; tel. (2) 3117377; fax (2) 3118638; e-mail vesnik@utrinski.com.mk; internet int.utrinskivesnik.com.mk; Dir EROL RIZAOV; Editor-in-Chief BRANKO TRICKOVSKI.

Večer (The Evening): 1000 Skopje, Mito Hadživasilev bb; tel. (2) 3111537; fax (2) 3238327; f. 1963; evening; Editor-in-Chief STOJAN NASEV; circ. 29,200.

Vest (News): Skopje; internet www.vest.com.mk; popular.

PERIODICALS

Delo: Skopje, Petar Drapshin 26; tel. (2) 3231949; fax (2) 3115748; f. 1993; weekly; nationalist; Editor-in-Chief BRATISLAV TASKOVSKI.

Fokus: Skopje, Zheležnička 53; tel. (2) 3111327; fax (2) 3111685; weekly; independent; Editor-in-Chief NIKOLA MLADENOV.

Makedonsko Vreme/Macedonian Times: 1000 Skopje, Vasil Gorgov 39; tel. and fax (2) 3121182; e-mail mian@mian.com.mk; internet www.unet.com.mk/mian; f. 1994; monthly; politics and current affairs; in Macedonian and English; Editor-in-Chief JOVAN PAVLOSKI.

Puls (Pulse): 1000 Skopje, Mito Hadživasilev bb; tel. (2) 3117124; fax (2) 3118024; internet www.puls.com.mk; weekly; business and technology; Editor-in-Chief MIRCE TOMOVSKI.

Roma Times: Skopje; e-mail mail@dostae.net.mk; internet www.dostae.net.mk/mk/press_mk_roma.htm; f. 2001; 3 a week; circ. 3,000.

Sport Magazine: 1000 Skopje, Mito Hadživasilev Jasmin bb; tel. and fax (2) 3116254; e-mail lav@unet.com.mk; f. 1991; weekly; circ. 6,000.

Trudbenik (Worker): 1000 Skopje, Udarna brigada 12; weekly; organ of Macedonian Trade Unions; Editor SIMO IVANOVSKI.

NEWS AGENCIES

Agency for Information (Agencija za Informacii): 1000 Skopje, Veljko Vlahonik 11; tel. (2) 3127453; fax (2) 3118038; e-mail sinf@sinf.gov.mk; internet www.sinf.gov.mk; govt press agency; f. 2000; Dir VELE MITANOSKI.

Macedonian Information Agency (Makedonska Informativna Agencija—MIA): 1000 Skopje, Bojmija 2; tel. (2) 2461600; fax (2) 2464048; e-mail mia@mia.com.mk; internet www.mia.com.mk; f. 1992; news service in Macedonian, Albanian and English; Exec. Dir ZIVKO GEORGIEVSKI.

Makfax: 1000 Skopje, Goce Delčev bb, POB 738; tel. (2) 3110125; fax (2) 3110184; e-mail makfax@makfax.com.mk; internet www.makfax.com.mk; f. 1993; independent; provides daily regional news service; Macedonian, Albanian and English.

PRESS ASSOCIATION

Journalists' Association of Macedonia: 1000 Skopje, Gradskizid 13, POB 498; tel. and fax (2) 3116447; Pres. STOJAN NASEV.

Publishers

Detska radost/Nova Makedonija (Children's Happiness/New Macedonia) Publishing House: 1000 Skopje, Mito Hadživasilev Jasmin bb; tel. (2) 3213059; fax (2) 3225830; f. 1944; children's books; Dir KIRIL DONEV.

Kultura: 1000 Skopje, Sv. Kliment Ohridski 68A; tel. (2) 3111332; fax (2) 3228608; e-mail ipkultura@simt.com.mk; f. 1945; history, philosophy, art, poetry, children's literature and fiction; in Macedonian; Dir DIMITAR BAŠEVSKI.

Kulturen Život (Cultural Life) Publishing House: 1000 Skopje, Ruzveltova 6; tel. (2) 3239134; f. 1971; Editor LJUBICA ARSOVSKA.

Makedonska kniga (Macedonian Book) Publishing House: 1000 Skopje, 11 Oktomvri; tel. (2) 3224055; fax (2) 3236951; f. 1947; arts, non-fiction, novels, children's books; Dir SANDE STOJČEVSKI.

Matica Makedonska: 1000 Skopje, ul. Maršal Tito br. 43/1-6; tel. (2) 3230358; fax (2) 3229244; f. 1991; Dir RADE SILJAN.

Metaforum: 1000 Skopje, Goce Delčev 6; tel. (2) 3114890; fax (2) 3115634; f. 1993; Dir RUŽICA BILKO.

Misla (Thought) Publishing House: 1000 Skopje, Partizanski odredi 1; tel. (2) 3221844; fax (2) 3118439; f. 1966; modern and classic Macedonian and translated literature; Pres. ZLATA BUNTESLEA.

Naša kniga (Our Book) Publishing House: 1000 Skopje, M. Gorki 21, POB 132; tel. (2) 3228066; fax (2) 3116872; f. 1948; Dir STOJAN LEKOVSKI.

Prosvetno delo (Educational) Publishing House: 1000 Skopje, Dimitrija Čupovski 15; tel. (2) 3117255; fax (2) 3225434; f. 1945; works of domestic writers and textbooks in Macedonian for elementary, professional and high schools; fiction and scientific works; Dir Dr KRSTE ANGELOVSKI.

Tabernakul: 1000 Skopje, POB 251, Mihail Cokov bb; tel. (2) 3127073; fax (2) 3115329; e-mail contact@tabernakul.com.mk; internet www.tabernakul.com.mk; f. 1989; religion, history, literature, philosophy, popular science; Dir CVETAN VRAŽIVIRSKI.

Broadcasting and Communications

TELECOMMUNICATIONS

Makedonski Telekomunikacii (MT): 1000 Skopje, Direkcija, Orce Nikolov bb; tel. (2) 3141141; fax (2) 3126244; e-mail info@mpt.com.mk; internet www.mt.com.mk; 51% owned by Matáv (Hungary); Chief Exec. DAN DONCEV.

Cosmofon: 1000 Skopje, Orce Nikolov bb; internet www.cosmofon.com.mk; f. 2003; owned by Organismos Telepikoinonion tis Elladas (Greece); mobile cellular telecommunications; 140,000 subscribers (June 2004).

Mobimak: 1000 Skopje, Orce Nikolov bb; e-mail kontakt@mobimak.com.mk; internet www.mobimak.com.mk; f. 1996; mobile cellular telecommunications; 450,000 subscribers (Aug. 2003).

BROADCASTING

Radio

Makedonska Radio-Televizija (MRT): 1000 Skopje, Goce Delčev bb; tel. (2) 3236839; fax (2) 3111821; e-mail mkrtvcor@mt.com.mk; internet www.mkrtv.com.mk; f. 1944; fmrly Radiotelevizija Skopje, name changed 1991; 3 radio channels; broadcasts in Macedonian, Albanian, Turkish, Serb, Roma and Vlach; Dir-Gen. GORDANA STOSIĆ; Dir of Radio GRIGORI POPOVSKI.

THE FORMER YUGOSLAV REPUBLIC OF MACEDONIA

Antenna 5 Radio: 1000 Skopje, Tetovska 35; tel. (2) 3111911; fax (2) 3113281; e-mail mail@antenna5.com.mk; internet www.antenna5.com.mk; 12 transmitters broadcast to 80% of the country.

Television

Makedonska Radio-Televizija (MRT): 1000 Skopje, Goce Delčev bb; tel. (2) 3112200; fax (2) 3111821; e-mail gstosic@unet.com.mk; internet www.mkrtv.com.mk; f. 1964; fmrly Radiotelevizija Skopje, name changed 1991; state broadcasting co; 3 television services; broadcasts in Macedonian, Albanian, Turkish, Serb, Roma and Vlach; Dir-Gen. GORDANA STOSIĆ; Dir of Television LJUBCO TOZIJA.

A1 Television: 1000 Skopje, Pero Nakov bb; tel. (2) 2550350; fax (2) 2551970; e-mail altv@a1.com.mk; internet www.a1.com.mk; Gen. Man. DARKO PERUSEVSKI.

SITEL Television: Skopje; tel. (2) 3116566; fax (2) 3114898; e-mail sitel@unet.com.mk; internet www.sitel.com.mk; Gen. Man. GOVAN IVANOVSKI.

Finance

(cap. = capital; res = reserves; dep. = deposits; m. = million; amounts in new Macedonian denars, unless otherwise indicated; brs = branches)

BANKS

A programme to privatize the banking sector was completed in early 2000. In early 2005 there were 21 commercial banks and 15 savings houses in the FYRM. Eight of the 21 banks were majority foreign-owned, and only one was state-owned; foreign capital accounted for 48.6% of total banking capital.

National Bank

National Bank of the Republic of Macedonia (Narodna Banka na Makedonija): 1000 Skopje, POB 401, Kompleks banki bb; tel. (2) 3108108; fax (2) 3113481; e-mail governorsoffice@nbrm.gov.mk; internet www.nbrm.gov.mk; central bank and bank of issue; cap. and res 8,267.0m., dep. 18,886.1m. (Dec. 2002); Gov. PETAR GOSHEV.

Selected Banks

Alpha Banka a.d.—Skopje: 1000 Skopje, Dame Gruev 1, POB 564; tel. (2) 3116433; fax (2) 3116830; e-mail kreditnabank@mt.net.mk; f. 1993 as Kreditna Banka a.d.; name changed as above in 2002; cap. 185.8m., res 601.6m., dep. 1,747.8m. (Dec. 2003); Chair. SPYROS FILARETOS; 3 brs.

Eksport-Import Banka a.d. Skopje: 91000 Skopje, DTC Paloma Bjanka, Dame Gruev 16; tel. (2) 3133411; fax (2) 3112744; f. 1994; cap. 601.4m., res 162.6m., dep. 1,645.3m. (Dec. 2001); Pres. METODIJA SMILENSKI.

Eurostandard Banka: 1000 Skopje, Vasil Glavinov St, TCC Plaza; tel. (2) 3228444; fax (2) 3224095; e-mail info@eurostandard.com.mk; internet esbnovosti.eurostandard.com.mk; f. 2001; cap. 548.6m., res 4.5m., dep. 646.9m. (Dec. 2003); Pres. RODOLFO PIZZOCHERI.

InvestBanka a.d.—Skopje: 1000 Skopje, Makedonija 9/11; tel. (2) 3114166; fax (2) 3135367; internet www.investbanka.com.mk; f. 1992; cap. 575.0m., res 3.6m., dep. 1,218.8m. (Dec. 2002); Pres. SVETLANA PENDAROVSKA.

IK Banka—Izvozna i Kreditna Banka (Export and Credit Bank): 1000 Skopje, Partizanski odredi 3, POB 421; tel. (2) 3129147; fax (2) 3122393; e-mail ikbanka@ikbanka.com.mk; internet www.ikbanka.com.mk; f. 1993; cap. 132.0m., res 19.9m., dep. 576.7m. (Dec. 2003); Pres. RUDO MIKULIĆ.

Komercijalna Banka a.d.—Skopje: 1000 Skopje, Kej Dimitar Vlahov 4; tel. (2) 3107107; fax (2) 3124064; e-mail contact@kbnet.com.mk; internet www.kb.com.mk; f. 1955; as Komunalna Banka; name changed as above in 1991; cap. 2,014.1m., res 1,086.5m., dep. 25,010.6m. (Dec. 2003); Pres. TRAJKO DAVITKOVSKI; 33 brs.

Makedonska Banka a.d.—Skopje: 1000 Skopje, bul. VMRO 3, POB 505; tel. (2) 3117111; fax (2) 3117191; e-mail info@makbanka.com.mk; internet www.makbanka.com; f. 1972; present name adopted 1994; cap. 239.6m., res 515.2m., dep. 1,813.2m. (Dec. 2000); Pres. ALEKSANDAR NIKOLOVSKI.

Ohridska Banka (Ohrid Bank): 6000 Ohrid, Makedonski Prosvetiteli 19; tel. (46) 206600; fax (46) 254130; e-mail obinfo@ob.com.mk; internet www.ob.com.mk; cap. 652.4m., res 179.0m., dep. 4,083.6m. (Dec. 2003); Pres. NAUM HADZILEGA; Chair. VANGEL NIKOLOSKI; 5 brs.

ProCredit Bank Macedonia: 1000 Skopje, Marks i Engels 3; tel. (2) 3219900; fax (2) 3219901; e-mail info@procreditbank.com.mk; internet www.procreditbank.com.mk; f. 2003; cap. 306.5m., dep. 115.3m. (Dec. 2003); Chair. HELEN ALEXANDER.

Radobank: 1000 Skopje, J. Gagarin 17; tel. (2) 3093300; fax (2) 3080453; e-mail radobank@radobank.com.mk; internet www.radobank.com.mk; f. 1993; Chair. RUBIN GRADOVSKI.

Stopanska Banka a.d.—Bitola: 7000 Bitola, Dobrivoe Radosavljević 21; tel. (47) 207500; fax (47) 207541; e-mail stbbt@mt.net.mk; f. 1948; as Komunalna Banka Bitola; present name adopted 1995; cap. 896.9m., res 180.2m., dep. 2,433.1m. (Dec. 2002); Pres. NAUM SIMJANOVSKI.

Stopanska Banka a.d.—Skopje: 1000 Skopje, 11 Oktomvri 7; tel. (2) 3295295; fax (2) 3114503; e-mail sbank@stb.com.mk; internet www.stb.com.mk; f. 1944; cap. 3,602.2m., res 1.1m., dep. 24,640.3m. (Dec. 2003); 73.0% owned by National Bank of Greece, 10.8% by European Bank for Reconstruction and Development (United Kingdom), 10.8% by International Finance Corpn (World Bank); Chair. TAKIS ARAPOGLOU; 23 brs.

Teteks-Kreditna Banka a.d. Skopje: 1000 Skopje, POB 198, ul. Naroden Front 19A; tel. (2) 3236401; fax (2) 3236444; e-mail contact@tkb.com.mk; internet www.tkb.com.mk; f. 2001 by merger of Teteks Banka and Kreditna Banka; merger with Tetovska Bank a.d.—Tetovo scheduled for April 2006; cap. 12.2m., res 2.2m., dep. 7.4m. (Dec. 2004); CEO NIKOLA PETKOSKI; 10 brs.

Tetovska Banka a.d.—Tetovo: Tetovo, Marshal Tito 14; tel. (44) 335280; fax (44) 335274; e-mail tbtb@mt.net.mk; f. 1995; merger with Teteks-Kreditna Banka a.d. Skopje scheduled for April 2006; cap. 518.0m., res 14.5m., dep. 804.3m. (Dec. 2003); Dir ATANAS SPIROSKI.

Tutunska Banka: 1000 Skopje, 12-ta Udarna brigada bb, POB 702; tel. (2) 3105601; fax (2) 3105681; e-mail tbanka1@tb.com.mk; internet www.tb.com.mk; f. 1985; cap. 693.9m., res 1,510.1m., dep. 6,328.6m. (Dec. 2003); Pres. BORIS ZAKRAJSEK.

UniBanka—Universalna Investiciona Banka a.d. Skopje (Universal Investment Bank): 1000 Skopje, M. Gorki 6; tel. (2) 3286100; fax (2) 3132186; e-mail info@unibank.com.mk; internet www.unibank.com.mk; f. 1993 as Balkanska Banka a.d. Skopje; present name adopted Feb. 2004; cap. 308.2m., res 311.4m., dep. 896.3m. (Dec. 2002); Gen. Man. STOJAN KRALCEV.

STOCK EXCHANGE

Macedonian Stock Exchange (Makedonska Berza a.d. Skopje): 1000 Skopje, Mito Hadživasilev 20; tel. (2) 3122055; fax (2) 3122069; e-mail mse@mse.org.mk; internet www.mse.org.mk; f. 1995; Chair. ZVONKO STANKOVSKI.

INSURANCE

QBE Makedonija: 1000 Skopje, 11 Oktomvri 25; tel. (2) 3115188; fax (2) 3115374; subsidiary of QBE Insurance Group (Australia); stock company for insurance and reinsurance.

Trade and Industry

CHAMBERS OF COMMERCE

Economic Chamber of Macedonia (Stopanska Komora na Makedonija): 1000 Skopje, Dimitrija Čupovski 13; tel. (2) 3118088; fax (2) 3116210; e-mail ic@ic.mchamber.org.mk; internet www.mchamber.org.mk; f. 1962; Pres. BRANKO AZESKI.

Regional Chamber of Commerce of Skopje: 1000 Skopje, Partizanski odredi 2, POB 509; tel. (2) 3112511; fax (2) 3116419; e-mail regkomsk@regkom.org.mk; Pres. BORIS DIMOVSKI.

UTILITIES

Electricity

Elektrostopanstvo na Makedonija (ESM) (Electric Power Co of Macedonia): 1000 Skopje, Bate Bacevski br. 9; tel. (2) 3111077; fax (2) 3227827; e-mail contact@esmak.com.mk; internet www.esmak.com.mk; production, transfer and distribution of electric power; sale of 90% share to Energie-Versorgung-Niederösterreich AG (Austria) announced in March 2006; Dir-Gen. PANDE LAZAROV.

TRADE UNIONS

Federation of Trade Unions of Macedonia: 1000 Skopje; tel. (2) 3231374; fax (2) 3115787; Pres. VANCO MURATOVSKI; 320,000 mems.

Transport

RAILWAYS

In 2002 the rail network totalled 699 km, of which 233 km were electrified. From 2000 the European Investment Bank made a series of loans to finance the modernization of the railways. Train services

THE FORMER YUGOSLAV REPUBLIC OF MACEDONIA

between Skopje and the capital of the Serbian province of Kosovo, Priština, suspended since 1999, resumed in February 2006.

Makedonski Železnici (MZ) (Macedonian Railways): 1000 Skopje, Železnička 50; tel. (2) 3227903; fax (2) 3462330; e-mail mz65dir@mt.net.mk; internet www.mz.com.mk; f. 1992; Chair. TIKHOMIR NIKOLOVSKI; Dir-Gen. STOJAN NAUMOV.

ROADS

The FYRM's road network totalled 12,974 km in 2002, of which about 6,806 km were paved. The principal road links Tabanovtse, at the border with Serbia and Montenegro, and Bogoroditsa, at the border with Greece. In July 2003 the European Bank for Reconstruction and Development (EBRD) granted the FYRM a US $45m. loan in support of two major road construction projects.

Fund for National and Regional Roads: 1000 Skopje, Dame Gruev 14; tel. (2) 3118044; fax (2) 3220535; e-mail tanjam@mpt.net.mk.

CIVIL AVIATION

The FYRM has two international airports, at Petrovets, 25 km from Skopje, and at Ohrid.

Avioimpex: 1000 Skopje, 11 Oktomvri 32; tel. (2) 3239933; fax (2) 3119348; f. 1992; flights within Europe; Pres. ILIJA SMILEV.

Macedonian Airlines (MAT): 1000 Skopje, Vasil Glavinov 3; tel. (2) 3292333; fax (2) 3229576; e-mail mathq@mat.com.mk; internet www.mat.com.mk; f. 1994; domestic services and flights within Europe; Man. Dir DUSKO GRUEVSKI.

Palair Macedonian Airlines: 1000 Skopje, Kuzman Jusifovski Pitu bb; tel. (2) 3115868; fax (2) 3238238; f. 1991; domestic services and flights within Europe and to the USA, Canada and Australia; Chair. BITOLJANA VANJA.

Tourism

Following independence in 1991, the FYRM's tourist industry (formerly a major source of foreign exchange) experienced a decline, largely owing to the country's proximity to the conflict in other republics of the former Yugoslavia, domestic instability and the sanctions imposed by Greece. Fighting in the north of the FYRM further adversely affected tourism in 2001, when there were 98,946 tourist arrivals and receipts amounted to US $49m. Tourist arrivals increased to 122,861 in 2002 and to 157,692 in 2003 (when receipts totalled $65m.).

Tourist Association of Macedonia: 1000 Skopje, Dame Gruev 28/5; tel. (2) 3290862; e-mail tarm@mt.net.mk.

MADAGASCAR

Introductory Survey

Location, Climate, Language, Religion, Flag, Capital

The Republic of Madagascar comprises the island of Madagascar, the fourth largest in the world, and several much smaller offshore islands, in the western Indian Ocean, about 500 km (300 miles) east of Mozambique, in southern Africa. The inland climate is temperate; in Antananarivo temperatures are generally between 8°C (48°F) and 27°C (81°F), with cooler, dryer weather between May and October. The coastal region is tropical, with an average daily maximum temperature of 32°C (90°F). The rainy season extends from November to April in the highlands (average annual rainfall is 1,000 mm–1,500 mm) but is more prolonged on the coast, where average annual rainfall can reach 3,500 mm. The official language is Malagasy, and government acts are published in both Malagasy and French. Hova and other dialects are also widely spoken. More than 50% of the population follow animist beliefs, while about 41% are Christians and the remainder are Muslims. The national flag (proportions 2 by 3) has a vertical white stripe (one-third of the length) at the hoist and two equal horizontal stripes, of red and green, in the fly. The capital is Antananarivo.

Recent History

A French possession since 1896, Madagascar became an autonomous state within the French Community in October 1958, as the Malagasy Republic. In May 1959 Philibert Tsiranana, leader of the Parti social démocrate (PSD), was elected President. The country achieved full independence on 26 June 1960. Prior to independence France supported the PSD, which was identified with the majority coastal tribes (*côtiers*), as an alternative to the more nationalistic highland people, the Merina, who were the traditional ruling group in the island.

After 1967 the economy deteriorated, and there was growing opposition to the Government's alleged authoritarianism and subservience to French interests. In May 1972, following civil unrest, President Tsiranana transferred full powers to the Army Chief of Staff, Gen. Gabriel Ramanantsoa. In October 1973 pro-Government parties secured a decisive victory in legislative elections. A prolonged crisis followed an attempted military coup in December 1974, and in early February 1975 Ramanantsoa transferred power to Col Richard Ratsimandrava, hitherto Minister of the Interior; however, Ratsimandrava was assassinated shortly afterwards. On 12 February Brig.-Gen. Gilles Andriamahazo assumed power and imposed martial law. All political parties were suspended. In June Andriamahazo was succeeded as Head of State by Lt-Commdr (later Adm.) Didier Ratsiraka, a *côtier* and a former Minister of Foreign Affairs, who became Chairman of the Supreme Revolutionary Council (SRC).

In a referendum in December 1975 more than 94% of voters approved a new Constitution, which provided for radical administrative and agrarian reforms, and the appointment of Ratsiraka as President of the Republic for a term of seven years. The country's name was changed to the Democratic Republic of Madagascar, and a 'Second Republic' was proclaimed. In March the Avant-garde de la révolution malgache (AREMA—Antoky Ny Revolosiona Malagasy) was founded as the nucleus of the Front national pour la défense de la révolution socialiste malgache (FNDR), the only political organization permitted by the Constitution.

At local government elections in March–June 1977 AREMA secured the majority of votes, resulting in division within the FNDR. The left-wing Mouvement national pour l'indépendance de Madagascar (Monima Ka Miviombio, known as Monima), led by Monja Jaona, withdrew from the FNDR and was subsequently proscribed. At legislative elections in June AREMA secured 112 of the 137 seats in the National People's Assembly. A new Council of Ministers was formed in August, and the membership of the SRC was extended to include leaders of the former political parties and additional *côtiers*, in an effort to restore political equilibrium.

In November 1982 Ratsiraka was re-elected President, receiving 80.2% of the votes cast. At elections to the National People's Assembly in August 1983 AREMA won 117 of the 137 seats. Open dissatisfaction with the Government's policies persisted, however.

In February 1988 the Prime Minister, Col Désiré Rakotoarijaona, resigned, owing to poor health, and was replaced by Lt-Col Victor Ramahatra, formerly Minister of Public Works. Ratsiraka was re-elected to the presidency in March 1989 for a further seven-year term, with 62.7% of the total votes cast. In April rioting followed opposition allegations of electoral irregularities. At legislative elections in May AREMA won 120 seats. The Mouvement pour le pouvoir prolétarien (Mpitolona ho amin'ny Fonjakan'ny Madinika—MFM), which obtained only seven seats, rejected the official results, alleging electoral misconduct. The Elan populaire pour l'unité nationale (Vonjy Iray Tsy Mivaky, known as Vonjy) secured four seats, AKFM/Fanavaozana (a newly formed group, comprising former members of the Parti du congrès de l'indépendance de Madagascar—AKFM), won three seats, the original AKFM two seats, and Monima only one seat.

In August 1989 Ratsiraka assented to opposition demands for discussions about the future role and structure of the FNDR. In September AREMA secured the majority of votes in local government elections. In December the National People's Assembly adopted a constitutional amendment abolishing the requirement for political parties to be members of the FNDR (thereby effectively dissolving the FNDR), despite opposition from MFM deputies.

In March 1990 the Government formally permitted the resumption of multi-party politics. Numerous new organizations emerged, while other parties that had hitherto operated within the FNDR became official opposition movements. Several pro-Government political associations joined AREMA to form a new coalition, the Mouvement militant pour le socialisme malgasy (MMSM). The principal opposition movements included the Union nationale pour le développement et la démocratie (UNDD) and the MFM (restyled the Mouvement pour le progrès de Madagascar, or Mpitolona ho amin'ny Fandrosoan'ny Madagasikara). An informal alliance, the Comité des forces vives—subsequently known as Forces vives (FV, Hery Velona)—was formed by 16 opposition factions, and trade unions and other groups.

In May 1991 legislation providing for extensive constitutional amendments was submitted to the National People's Assembly. Opposition parties criticized the proposals, on the grounds that the revised Constitution would retain references to socialism. In June opposition leaders applied to the Constitutional High Court to effect Ratsiraka's removal from office, while the FV organized demonstrations in support of its demands for the resignation of the President and the convening of a national conference to draft a new constitution. Ratsiraka refused to resign. Later in June the FV formed a 'parallel' administration, which it termed the 'Provisional Government'.

In July 1991 the FV organized a general strike, warning that it would continue until the Government acceded to its demands for constitutional reform. Subsequent negotiations between the MMSM and the FV achieved little. The FV appointed Jean Rakotoharison, a retired army general, as President of the 'Provisional Government', and Albert Zafy, the leader of the UNDD, as its Prime Minister. However, Manandafy Rakotonirina, the leader of the MFM, rejected the formation of the 'Provisional Government', favouring further negotiations, and withdrew his party from the FV. Members of the 'Provisional Government' subsequently occupied the premises of six official government ministries. Later in July Ratsiraka ordered the detention of several members of the 'Provisional Government' and imposed a state of emergency in Antananarivo. The FV withdrew from negotiations with the MMSM, in protest against the arrests, while the French Government appealed to Ratsiraka to release the opposition leaders. In response to increasing public pressure, Ratsiraka dissolved the Council of Ministers and pledged to organize a constitutional referendum before the end of 1991. Members of the 'Provisional Government' were released from custody, and Ratsiraka repealed legislation that authorized the detention of opponents of the Government.

In August 1991 Ratsiraka appointed Guy Razanamasy, the mayor of Antananarivo, as Prime Minister. Later that month Ratsiraka declared Madagascar to be a federation of six states, with himself as President, and claimed to command the support of five provinces where AREMA continued to hold the majority of seats in regional councils. However, the FV disregarded the proclamation and continued to demand that Ratsiraka relinquish the presidency. At the end of August Razanamasy formed an interim Government, which did not include any members of the FV or the MFM.

On 31 October 1991 representatives of the Government, the FV, the MFM, church leaders and the armed forces signed an agreement providing for the suspension of the Constitution and the creation of a transitional Government, which was to remain in office for a maximum period of 18 months, pending presidential and legislative elections. The SRC and the National People's Assembly were to be replaced by interim bodies, respectively the High State Authority for Transition to the Third Republic and the National Committee for Economic and Social Regeneration. On an interim basis, Ratsiraka was to remain as President of the Republic and Razanamasy as Prime Minister. Zafy was designated President of the High State Authority, which was to comprise 18 representatives of the FV, seven of the MFM and six of the MMSM. Rakotonirina and Pastor Richard Andriamanjato, the leader of AKFM/Fanavaozana, were appointed as joint Presidents of the 131-member National Committee for Economic and Social Regeneration. The power to appoint or to dismiss government ministers, hitherto vested in the President, was granted to Razanamasy. A new constitution was to be submitted to a national referendum by the end of 1991. Zafy subsequently rejected the agreement, on the grounds that Ratsiraka was to retain the nominal post of Commander-in-Chief of the Armed Forces. In November Razanamasy formed a new interim Government, which included three representatives of the MFM and one MMSM member. Francisque Ravony, of the MFM, was appointed to the new post of Deputy Prime Minister. Owing to Zafy's refusal to participate in the Government, 10 portfolios that had been allocated to the FV remained vacant. Later in November, however, Zafy agreed to accept the presidency of the High State Authority.

In December 1991 Razanamasy announced that the formation of the coalition Government had proved unsuccessful, and 11 ministers, including Ravony, resigned. Razanamasy appointed a larger Government of national consensus, in which 14 (of 36) portfolios were allocated to the FV. In January 1992 it was announced that all political factions had now accepted the terms of the October 1991 agreement. The institutions that had been established by the accord were to prepare for the constitutional referendum, now scheduled for June 1992, and for local, presidential and legislative elections, which were to take place by the end of the year. In February the High State Authority for Transition to the Third Republic announced the dissolution of the SRC and the National People's Assembly, in accordance with the October 1991 agreement, and indicated that a new body was to be created to supervise local elections, replacing the existing system of government, based on village assemblies (*fokontany*). However, the MMSM claimed that the High State Authority was not empowered to dissolve the local government structure. The Government subsequently announced that control of local government was to be transferred from elected councils to special delegations, and that security commissions were to be established to organize the *fokontany*.

The draft Constitution of the Third Republic, as submitted to the Government in April 1992, envisaged a unitary state and provided for a bicameral legislature, comprising a Senate and a National Assembly. Two-thirds of the members of the Senate were to be selected by an electoral college, with the remaining one-third to be appointed by the President, while the 184-member National Assembly was to be elected by universal suffrage, under a system of proportional representation, for a four-year term. The authority of the President was reduced, and executive power was vested in the Prime Minister, who was to be appointed by the National Assembly. Ratsiraka reiterated his intention to contest the presidential election and demanded that a draft providing for a federal system of government also be submitted to the forthcoming referendum.

In August 1992 supporters of a federal system of government took control of the airport and the radio and television stations at Antsiranana, and announced the establishment of a federal directorate in the town; similar incidents followed at Toamasina, in the east, and Toliary, in the south-west of the country. The new Constitution was approved by 72.2% of votes cast in a national referendum on 19 August. Federalists forcibly prevented the electorate from voting in a number of regions, and several people were killed in clashes between supporters of the MMSM and members of the FV at Toamasina. Later that month the armed forces regained control of the towns that had been occupied by the federalists.

In September 1992 several prominent political figures, including Zafy and Rakotonirina, announced that they were to contest the forthcoming presidential election. Divisions emerged within the FV after a number of constituent parties presented alternative candidates to Zafy, the alliance's official candidate. Later in September a committee of government officials and church leaders proposed that a stipulation restricting the President to two terms of office be incorporated in the electoral code. Shortly afterwards MMSM supporters unilaterally declared Antsiranana, Toliary, Toamasina and Fianarantsoa (in central Madagascar) to be federal states, and suspended infrastructural links between these provinces and Antananarivo. In October federalists in Antsiranana, apparently supported by members of the presidential guard, took hostage members of the FV and seized control of the radio and television stations. Razanamasy declared the unilateral proclamation of independence of the four provinces to be illegal, but initiated negotiations with the federalists, in an effort to prevent disruption of the presidential election. Later that month there were further clashes in Toliary between supporters of the FV and federalists, led by Monja Jaona, who had declared himself to be Governor of the province. At the end of October, however, the federalists agreed to participate in the presidential election, although the MMSM continued officially to reject the new Constitution.

The presidential election took place on 25 November 1992, contested by eight candidates. Zafy secured 45.1% of votes cast, and Ratsiraka 29.2%. Prior to a second round of voting, on 10 February 1993, the remaining six candidates withdrew in favour of Zafy, who thus secured 66.7% of the votes cast. Zafy's inauguration, on 27 March, was accompanied by violent clashes between security forces and federalists in the north. In accordance with the Constitution, Zafy resigned as President of the UNDD at a party congress in May; Emmanuel Rakotovahiny, the Minister of State for Agriculture and Rural Development, was elected as his successor.

Several constituent parties of the FV that had not supported Zafy in the first round of the presidential election subsequently presented independent lists of candidates for the forthcoming legislative elections; the remaining parties in the alliance became known as Forces vives Rasalama (Hery Velona Rasalama—HVR). Violence intensified prior to polling: two people were killed, and 40 (including Jaona) arrested, after security forces attacked federalists who had occupied the prefecture at Toliary. The elections, to a reduced 138-member National Assembly, took place on 16 June 1993, and were contested by 121 political associations. The HVR secured 46 seats, the MFM 15, and a new alliance of pro-Ratsiraka parties 11 seats. The official results indicated that parties supporting Zafy had won 75 seats in the National Assembly. In August Francisque Ravony was elected Prime Minister and formed a new Council of Ministers. Richard Andriamanjato was elected President of the National Assembly.

By early 1994, owing to frequent party realignments, Ravony no longer commanded a majority in the legislature. In June government proposals for economic reforms were rejected by the National Assembly. Nevertheless, in July a motion of censure against Ravony's Government was rejected. In the same month scheduled elections to establish new regional authorities were delayed, owing to lack of agreement regarding proposals for decentralization. In August 1994, following negotiations with the HVR, Ravony formed a new Council of Ministers.

In October 1994 controversy over a local subsidiary enterprise, Flamco Madagascar, which had failed to reimburse funds advanced by the Government, prompted increased division between Ravony and Andriamanjato regarding economic policy. Meanwhile, opposition leaders demanded the removal of Zafy, Ravony and Andriamanjato, amid general resentment towards the Government, which had been precipitated by an increase in the rate of inflation resulting from the flotation of the Malagasy franc. At a regional congress of AREMA, which took place at the end of October, Ratsiraka urged the resignation of Ravony and dissolution of the Government. In January 1995 Ravony dismissed the Governor of the central bank, who had approved the financial transaction with Flamco Madagascar, at the insistence of the IMF and World Bank, and (apparently as a concession to Andriamanjato) also dismissed Raserijaona, assuming the finance and budget portfolio himself.

In July 1995, apparently at Zafy's instigation, deputies belonging to the HVR, the UNDD and AKFM/Fanavaozana proposed a motion of censure against Ravony in the National Assembly (which was, however, rejected by a large majority). Zafy subsequently announced that he was unable to co-operate with Ravony and decreed that a constitutional amendment empowering the President, rather than the National Assembly, to select the Prime Minister, be submitted for approval in a national referendum. Ravony indicated that he would resign after the referendum, regardless of the outcome. In August Ravony formed a new Council of Ministers, comprising representatives of the parliamentary majority that had supported him in the previous month. The referendum proceeded in September, at which the constitutional amendment was approved by 63.6% of votes cast. Ravony duly resigned in October, and Zafy appointed Rakotovahiny as Prime Minister. Rakotovahiny's Council of Ministers included several members of the outgoing administration, although the leader of the HVR, Alain Ramaroson (the only member of the HVR to be allocated a portfolio), refused to join the Government. In accordance with government plans to restructure local government, elections to 1,400 new communes took place on 5 November. An abstention rate of 60% was recorded, and a decline in support for the HVR was apparent.

Following the installation of the new Government, disagreement between Rakotovahiny and the Minister of the Budget, Finance and Planning, Jean Claude Raherimanjato, delayed the adoption of the budget for 1996. In addition, dissension emerged between the parties that supported Zafy over the composition of the Council of Ministers; in December 1995 associates of Andriamanjato demanded that an alternative cabinet be appointed. In April 1996 an attempt by Raherimanjato to dismiss senior ministry officials (which Rakotovahiny refused to endorse) prompted industrial action by civil servants at the Ministry of the Budget, Finance and Planning. In May a motion of censure against Rakotovahiny's Government, apparently instigated by Raherimanjato, was approved by a large majority in the National Assembly. Rakotovahiny submitted his administration's resignation, and Zafy appointed Norbert Ratsirahonana, hitherto President of the Constitutional High Court, as Prime Minister.

Zafy refused to approve the new Government initially proposed by Ratsirahonana, insisting on the inclusion of five UNDD members who had served in the previous Council of Ministers. In protest, most of the opposition deputies consequently left the legislative chamber when the Prime Minister presented the new Government to the National Assembly in June 1996. Ratsirahonana, however, won a vote of confidence in the legislature in July, by associating the vote with legislation providing for the implementation of economic reforms stipulated by the IMF and the World Bank. On 26 July a motion in the National Assembly to remove Zafy from office for numerous contraventions of the Constitution was supported by 99 of 131 votes cast. (Meanwhile, local elections, which had been scheduled for August, and were to replace the existing six provinces with 28 regions, were postponed as a result of the presidential crisis.) The Constitutional High Court endorsed the President's impeachment in September, upholding the majority of the charges against him; Zafy maintained that his impeachment was illegal, but resigned the same day. Ratsirahonana was appointed interim President by the Constitutional High Court, pending an election; he formed a new interim Government that represented the majority in the National Assembly and excluded members of the UNDD. Zafy announced his intention to contest the forthcoming election, as did Ratsiraka, Ratsirahonana and Ravony. In October Ravony withdrew from the presidential election and, unexpectedly, declared his support for Zafy.

In all, 15 candidates stood in the first round of the presidential election, which proceeded peacefully on 3 November 1996; Ratsiraka (with 36.6% of the votes cast) and Zafy (with 23.4%) qualified to contest the second round. The head of Libéralisme économique et action démocratique pour la reconstruction nationale (LEADER/Fanilo), Herizo Razafimahaleo, obtained 15.1%, and Ratsirahonana 10.1%, of the votes. Razafimahaleo urged his supporters to vote for Ratsiraka. None of the unsuccessful candidates chose to support Zafy, who declared his intention, if elected, to retain Ratsirahonana (who had successfully concluded an agreement with the IMF in August) as Prime Minister; Ratsirahonana, however, refused to endorse either candidate. At the second round, which took place on 29 December, Ratsiraka narrowly won, with 50.71% of the valid votes cast, although more than 50% of the registered electorate abstained from voting. Ratsiraka was inaugurated as President on 9 February. He appointed Pascal Rakotomavo (a former Minister of Finance) as Prime Minister. Rakotomavo's Government included Razafimahaleo as Deputy Prime Minister, responsible for Foreign Affairs.

In May 1997 legislative elections, which had been scheduled for August, were postponed, officially to allow time for identity cards to be issued to voters. The opposition, led by Zafy, denounced the delay as a violation of the Constitution and, in early August, demanded the resignation of the Government and of the Constitutional High Court (which had endorsed the extension of the existing legislature's mandate), as well as the dissolution of the National Assembly. In August a commission that had been appointed by the Prime Minister to draft constitutional amendments presented its proposals. However, apparently following intervention from Andriamanjato, who was said to have insisted that the National Assembly alone was responsible for constitutional revision, regional forums, attended by local officials and representatives of non-governmental organizations, were held in September to put forward proposals for one constitutional project. (Ratsiraka had originally favoured submitting two alternatives to a referendum, one for a federal state, the other for a decentralized but unitary state.) A new constitution was then to be drafted by a 15-member National Consultative Commission, nominated by Ratsiraka, Rakotomavo and Andriamanjato.

In January 1998 Ratsiraka invited political leaders to attend discussions on constitutional reform, although Hery Miara-dia, an opposition grouping led by Zafy, and members of the Panorama Group, a more moderate alliance led by Ravony and Ratsirahonana, refused to participate. None the less, Ratsiraka subsequently announced that a constitutional referendum would take place on 15 March 1998, to be followed by legislative elections. The draft amendments to the Constitution envisaged a 'federal-style' state, composed of six autonomous provinces, and also provided for increased presidential powers.

In February 1998 a motion of impeachment against Ratsiraka failed to gain the requisite two-thirds' majority in the National Assembly. Later that month the principal opposition parties urged voters to boycott the forthcoming referendum, claiming that the Government had ignored the views presented at the regional forums and the proposals of the National Consultative Commission, and had deliberately delayed discussion on legislation proposed by Rakotonirina (who had chaired the Commission) whereby any draft constitution would require the approval of more than 50% of all registered voters in order to become law. The referendum proceeded on 15 March 1998, when extensive revisions to the Constitution were narrowly endorsed by 50.96% of votes cast. Rakotonirina's proposed legislation was approved by the National Assembly later that month. However, Ratsiraka referred the legislation back to the National Assembly, and in April it was rejected after further deliberation.

Elections to an expanded National Assembly followed on 17 May 1998, under a new electoral law. Of the 150 seats, 82 were to be filled from single-member constituencies, with the remaining deputies to be elected by a system of proportional representation in 34 two-member constituencies. Ratsiraka's party, AREMA, performed well in the elections, winning 63 seats, while the pro-presidential LEADER/Fanilo and the Rassemblement pour le socialisme et la démocratie (RPSD) secured 16 and 11 seats, respectively. Ratsirahonana's party, Ny asa vita no ifampitsara (AVI), emerged as the strongest opposition party, with 14 seats, while Zafy's new party—Asa, Faharaminana, Fampandrosoana, Arinda (AFFA)—won six seats; independent candidates took 32 seats. The AVI and 24 independent deputies were subsequently reported to have joined the AREMA majority, leaving the AFFA and the remaining independents as the only significant parliamentary opposition. In July Tantely Andrianarivo, hitherto Deputy Prime Minister, was appointed as Prime Minister, retaining responsibility for finance and the economy. The 31-member Council of Ministers was dominated by AREMA, with the key portfolios largely unchanged; 12 new ministers were appointed.

The first local government elections—communal voting for 20,000 councillors and 1,392 mayors—since the reintroduction of the three-tier system of local government (provinces, regions and communes), under the amended Constitution of 1998, took place on 14 November 1999. The greatest successes were recorded by nominally independent candidates. Most notably, Marc Ravalomanana, the head of the country's largest agro-industrial processor, Tiko, was elected mayor of Antananarivo; Ravalomanana had been a principal donor of electoral funds to the AVI, but had stood as an independent. Roland Ratsiraka, a nephew of the President, was elected independent mayor of Toamasina.

Provincial elections took place on 3 December 2000 to elect 336 councillors, as a preliminary step to the decentralization of certain powers to six autonomous provinces (legislation on the organization of which had been approved by the National Assembly in August). Voter participation in the capital was reported to have been very low, at about 30%, following calls by various organizations, including opposition parties and the Christian Council of Churches in Madagascar, for a boycott of the elections. It was reported that AREMA had secured control of most of the major towns, although the AVI won a majority of seats in Antananarivo.

On 18 March 2001 a 1,727-member electoral college, which included mayors and local councillors, elected 60 members of the new Senate. AREMA won 49 of the 60 seats, while LEADER/Fanilo secured five seats and opposition parties a total of six, including two for the AVI. President Ratsiraka subsequently named the remaining 30 senators who would constitute the 90-seat upper house.

A presidential election took place on 16 December 2001, contested by six candidates, including Ratsiraka, Zafy, Razafimahaleo and Ravalomanana. According to the official results, Ravalomanana, whose candidacy was supported by a number of opposition parties, most notably the AVI, the RPSD and the MFM, secured 46.21% of the votes cast and Didier Ratsiraka 40.89%, thereby necessitating a second round of voting. However, Ravalomanana's own electoral observers disputed this result, claiming that he had won an outright victory, with 52.15% of the votes, and demanded a public comparison of voting records. The opposition was supported in these demands by international electoral observers. A re-count was subsequently conducted, and on 25 January 2002 the Constitutional High Court endorsed the official results and ruled that a second round of voting should take place within 30 days. Ravalomanana rejected this verdict and called for a national strike in protest. Some 500,000 people responded by gathering in Antananarivo; government offices, public utilities and banks ceased operations, and air traffic was suspended. Ravalomanana's supporters also closed the central bank in order to prevent Ratsiraka from withdrawing special funds from the treasury. Strike action continued, in varying forms, for eight weeks. Following a meeting between Ravalomanana and Ratsiraka in mid-February, negotiations were conducted between their representatives, with mediation by the Organization of African Unity (OAU); Ratsiraka's delegates rejected Ravalomanana's proposals for the formation of an interim government and new appointments to the Constitutional High Court and electoral committee. Meanwhile, the Minister of the Armed Forces, Gen. Marcel Ranjeva, declared that the army would remain neutral in the electoral dispute.

On 22 February 2002 Ravalomanana accelerated events by unilaterally declaring himself President in an inaugural ceremony in Antananarivo attended by 100,000 supporters. The President of the Senate immediately declared Ravalomanana's proclamation to be illegal, and it was widely condemned by the international community. In response, President Ratsiraka declared a three-month 'state of national necessity', according himself broad powers, including the right to pass laws by decree. On 26 February Ravalomanana named Jacques Sylla, a former Minister of Foreign Affairs under Zafy's presidency, as his Prime Minister. On the following day Ratsiraka's Minister of Foreign Affairs and Minister of Post and Telecommunications both resigned. Meanwhile, after weeks of largely peaceful protests, violent clashes erupted between supporters of Ratsiraka and Ravalomanana in Antananarivo, prompting Ratsiraka to decree martial law and appoint a military governor, Gen. Léon-Claude Raveloarison, in the capital. None the less, Ravalomanana proceeded with the formation of his rival Government in early March, while opposition supporters erected barricades against the army and set fire to the military headquarters; 17 of those appointed to Ravalomanana's administration were successfully installed in government offices, accompanied by large crowds of supporters and unopposed by the military. On the same day the governors of the five remaining provinces of the country declared their allegiance to Ratsiraka, recognizing his hometown, Toamasina (where Ratsiraka and his ministers had relocated) as a temporary 'alternative capital'. A few days later Gen. Ranjeva resigned as Minister of the Armed Forces, shortly after Ravalomanana's rival Government had taken control of his offices in Antananarivo. Gen. Raveloarison resigned as military governor of Antananarivo some three weeks after his appointment, having failed to apply martial law and order troops to end protests, on the grounds that this would have incurred deaths. Later in March 58 of Madagascar's 150 deputies attended a parliamentary session called by Ravalomanana and elected an interim President of the National Assembly.

An OAU mission held talks with Ravalomanana and Ratsiraka in March 2002, in an attempt to resolve the ongoing political crisis, but its proposal for a 'government of national reconciliation' was rejected by both sides. In late March four supporters of Ravalomanana were killed, and a further 28 injured, during clashes with the security forces in Fianarantsoa, bringing the estimated number of deaths in the protests since January to 25. At the beginning of April, supporters of Ratsiraka, who had erected roadblocks to isolate Antananarivo in February, destroyed two of the bridges located on its supply routes to the rest of the island, in an effort to intensify the effective siege of the capital, which was already suffering from severe fuel shortages. The situation fostered fears of ethnic conflict, with Ravalomanana supported by the predominantly Merina population of Antananarivo and the central highlands, and Ratsiraka by the *côtiers*. This concern was exacerbated by Ravalomanana's appeal for his supporters to overthrow the roadblocks around the capital, declaring the country to be in a state of war and listing the names of those considered to be enemies. The OAU condemned Ravalomanana's statements as incitement to violence.

On 10 April 2002 the Supreme Court ruled that there had been irregularities in the appointment, shortly before the presidential election, of six of the nine judges of the Constitutional High Court, which had endorsed the official results; one week later the Supreme Court annulled the disputed results and ordered a recount of the votes. On the following day Ratsiraka and Ravalomanana signed a peace accord in Dakar, Senegal, where they had been holding talks under the auspices of the OAU and the UN, and with mediation by the Presidents of Senegal, Benin, Côte d'Ivoire and Mozambique. Following the completion of the recount, in late April, the Constitutional High Court ruled that Ravalomanana had secured the presidency, with 51.46% of the votes cast, while Ratsiraka had won 35.90%. Ratsiraka, who had failed to remove the blockade of Antananarivo (in contravention of the Dakar accord), refused to accept the Court's decision. Nevertheless, Ravalomanana was inaugurated as President on 6 May, largely without international recognition, and appointed a new Council of Ministers later that month. Four of the country's six provincial governors, who were loyal to Ratsiraka, subsequently threatened to secede. Ravalomanana and Ratsiraka failed to reach agreement at further talks in Dakar in early June. Heavy fighting ensued, as troops loyal to Ravalomanana conducted a military offensive against areas controlled by Ratsiraka, securing two provincial capitals, Mahajanga and Toliary, in mid-June.

In mid-June 2002 Ravalomanana dissolved the Government that he had formed in May, immediately reappointing Sylla as Prime Minister; however, despite nominating six new members of the Council of Ministers, he failed to appoint a government of national unity. At the end of June the USA recognized Ravalomanana as the legitimate leader of Madagascar; endorsement soon followed from France and, in contravention of the policy of the OAU, Senegal. Meanwhile, the OAU suspended Madagascar from its meetings, pending the staging of free and fair elections leading to the establishment of a legitimate government; this decision was upheld by the African Union (AU, see p. 153), which replaced the OAU in July. In early July Ravalomanana's government troops took control of Antsiranana and Toamasina, and Ratsiraka sought exile in France; this apparent admission of defeat allowed for an international conference to take place in Paris, France, on the donation of aid for the reconstruction of Madagascar. The new Government was in full control of the island by the middle of the month. Ravalomanana replaced the 30 presidentially appointed members of the Senate, with the approval of the Constitutional High Court, despite the fact that those appointed by Ratsiraka had been appointed for a tenure of six years. In August six of the nine members of the Constitutional High Court were also replaced. In early October Ravalomanana dismissed Narisoa Rajaonarivony as Deputy Prime Minister and Minister of Finance and Development and altered the portfolio of Benjamin Andriamparany Radavidson from Minister of the

MADAGASCAR

Economy and Planning to that of Minister of the Economy, Finance and the Budget.

In mid-October 2002 the National Assembly was dissolved in preparation for legislative elections, brought forward from May 2003, in response to pressure from aid donors, in order to finalize the legitimacy of Ravalomanana's mandate. At the elections, which took place on 15 December 2002, Ravalomanana's party, Tiako i Madagasikara (TIM—I Love Madagascar), won 104 of the 160 seats and the pro-Ravalomanana Firaisankinam-Pirenena, an alliance of the AVI and elements of the RPSD, secured a further 22 seats; notably, 23 independent deputies were elected, and the formerly incumbent AREMA party won only three seats. (Foreign observers were permitted to be present at the elections for the first time in Malagasy electoral history.) In mid-January 2003 a new Government was appointed, which included 10 new ministers and was reduced in overall size from 30 to 20 ministers; the former Minister of Public Works, Jean Lahiniriako, was elected President of the National Assembly. Madagascar's suspension from meetings of the AU—hitherto the only remaining significant authority not to have recognized the new Government—was formally revoked at the organization's General Assembly in July of that year; the legitimacy of the Ravalomanana administration was thus considered finally to have been established. Meanwhile, various members of the former Ratsiraka administration were arrested and tried in court, including the former Governors of Fianarantsoa and Toamasina. In August former President Ratsiraka was sentenced, *in absentia*, to 10 years' hard labour for the embezzlement of public funds and declared unfit for public office.

In December 2003 former Prime Minister Andrianarivo was sentenced to 12 years' hard labour and fined 42,000m. francs MG for embezzling public funds and endangering state security; however, in the following month he was authorized to seek medical treatment abroad. In January 2004 Ravalomanana restructured and reshuffled the Council of Ministers, reducing its membership to 17 ministers and two secretaries of state. Several former supporters of Ratsiraka were appointed in order to diversify the ethnic composition of the Government, which had hitherto been dominated by the Merina. In March the President granted pardons to those sentenced to less than three years' imprisonment for involvement with the pro-Ratsiraka resistance; those with more serious sentences would have the right to apply individually for an amnesty.

Civil unrest was evident from January 2004, initially among army reservists protesting at the non-payment of their demobilization bonuses. More generalized public demonstrations subsequently took place, in response to economic hardship, caused by high global petroleum prices and the suspension of import taxes and tariffs on a range of goods from August 2003 which had led to a large increase in imports, thus undermining the national currency and inflating consumer prices. This atmosphere culminated in a series of grenade attacks on associates of President Ravalomanana in June, July and November. There were also concerns regarding the respect of the new regime for human rights: some individuals arrested following the conflict in 2002, regarded as political prisoners by the international community, remained under detention without trial in early 2005 and certain private radio stations were forced to close in 2004.

In December 2004 the TIM held its first national congress, at which Jaques Sylla resigned as Secretary-General. A reshuffle of the Council of Ministers was effected early in the same month, with the replacement of the Minister of Energy and Mines, the Minister of Telecommunications, Post and Communications and the Secretary of State for Decentralization and National and Regional Development. President Ravalomanana increased the accountability of the Government with ministerial performances being graded, financial bonuses awarded for the attainment of performance targets and the introduction of possible dismissal from office as the result of failure to reach such targets.

In March 2005 Zaza Ramandimbiarisona resigned as Deputy Prime Minister in charge of Economic Programmes and the post was subsequently abolished, although a successor was appointed to his secondary role as Minister of Transport and Public Works. As part of the same process of reorganization the office of Secretary of State for Decentralization and National and Regional Development was redesignated as a ministerial portfolio. In October a further minor reshuffle was effected, with the appointment of Roger-Marie Rafanomezantsoa as Minister of Industry, Trade and the Development of the Private Sector and of Tombo Ramandimbisoa to the Ministry of Youth and Sports. Furthermore, the Minister of the Interior and Administrative Reform,

Gen. Soja, was unexpectedly dismissed in November, following an alleged attempt on the President's life; he was replaced by Lt-Gen. Charles Rabemananjara. Meanwhile, in October the Government forcibly closed the Fiangonana Protestanta Vaovao eto Madagasikara protestant church, for illegally occupying churches of the Fiangonan' i Jesoa Kristy eto Madagasikara, of which President Ravalomanana was a senior official, and posing a threat to public order. Some observers feared a threat to the secular status of the country, with the President declaring that he hoped for a Christian nation. Although, according to the Constitution, a presidential election was scheduled to be held by the end of 2006, it was announced that this would not take place until 2007, when legislative elections were also due to be held.

Madagascar's foreign policy is officially non-aligned: while it formerly maintained close links with communist countries (particularly the People's Republic of China, the Democratic People's Republic of Korea and the former USSR), the Zafy Government established relations with Israel, South Africa and the Republic of Korea. Relations with France have been affected by disputes over compensation for nationalized French assets and over the continuing French claim to the Iles Glorieuses, north of Madagascar, and three other islets in the Mozambique Channel. In 1980 the UN voted in favour of restoring all the disputed islets to Madagascar. In early 1986 the Government announced the extension of Madagascar's exclusive economic zone to include the Iles Glorieuses and the three islets. In 1997 government announcements regarding future privatization plans in Madagascar prompted renewed appeals from France for compensation for nationalized French assets. In response, the Government allocated some 50,000m. francs MG as initial compensation in the budget for 1998. In February 2000 it was agreed that the Iles Glorieuses would be co-administered by France, Madagascar and Mauritius, without prejudice to the question of sovereignty. In April 2004, during a state visit to Madagascar by Prime Minister Paul Bérenger of Mauritius, political and economic co-operation agreements between the two countries were signed.

Relations with the People's Republic of China were strengthened in January 1999, during a visit by Vice-President Hu Jintao; agreements were signed on the expansion of bilateral economic relations and China's provision of preferential loans to Madagascar. In September 2000 the representative office for Taiwan in Madagascar was closed down, following an official visit by the Malagasy Minister of Foreign Affairs to China. (It was claimed that this was carried out by the Government in support of the 'one China' policy; however, the Taiwanese claimed that the office had never functioned effectively.) In 2005 Prime Minister Sylla denounced the Taiwanese authorities' decision to terminate the National Unification Council, which had been established in 1990 to oversee the island's eventual unification with China.

Government

The Constitution of the Third Republic was endorsed by national referendum on 19 August 1992, but was extensively revised by amendments that were endorsed by national referendum on 15 March 1998. The amended Constitution enshrined a 'federal-style' state, composed of six autonomous provinces (faritany), each with a provincial council (holding legislative power) elected by universal suffrage for a term of five years. Each provincial council elected a governor; however, these officials were replaced on an interim basis by presidentially-appointed representatives following the governmental crisis in 2002 (see above). Legislation was passed subsequently whereby local administration was restructured into 22 regions and in September 2004 each region was nominated a regional chief responsible for decentralizing operations. The first local elections (for communal councillors and mayors) under the restored three-tier system of provinces, regions and communes, as envisaged in the Constitution, took place in November 1999. Provincial elections were held in December 2000 and in November 2003. The Constitution provides for a bicameral legislature, comprising a Senate (established in March 2001) and a National Assembly. Two-thirds of the members of the Senate are elected by the autonomous provinces, and the remaining one-third of the members are appointed by the President, while the National Assembly is elected by universal suffrage for a five-year term of office. The constitutional Head of State is the President, who is elected for a term of five years, and can be re-elected for two further terms. The President appoints the Prime Minister and, on the latter's recommendation, the other members of the Council of Ministers.

Defence

At 1 August 2005 total armed forces numbered about 13,500 men: army 12,500, navy 500 and air force 500. There is a paramilitary gendarmerie of 8,100. The defence budget for 2004 was estimated at 101,800m. ariary.

Economic Affairs

In 2004, according to estimates by the World Bank, Madagascar's gross national income (GNI), measured at average 2002–04 prices, was US $5,181m., equivalent to about $300 per head (or $830 per head on an international purchasing-power parity basis). During 1995–2004, it was estimated, the population increased at an average annual rate of 3.0%, while gross domestic product (GDP) per head decreased, in real terms, by an average of 0.1% per year. Overall GDP increased, in real terms, at an average annual rate of 2.9% in 1995–2004; GDP increased by 5.3% in 2004.

In 2004 the agricultural sector (including forestry and fishing) accounted for an estimated 28.6% of GDP and employed an estimated 72.9% of the economically active population in 2003. Rice, the staple food crop, is produced on some 50% of cultivated land. Since 1972, however, imports of rice have been necessary to supplement domestic production. The most important cash crops are vanilla (which accounted for an estimated 24.6% of total export revenue in 2003), cloves and coffee. Following a long drought in 2003, vanilla production was estimated to have halved in that year, leading to a dramatic escalation in world prices and the development of the crop in other countries, as well as an increase in synthetic alternatives; however, prices had declined significantly at the beginning of 2005, having a negative impact on producers, for whom crop yields were expected to improve in that year. Sugar, coconuts, tropical fruits, cotton and sisal are also cultivated. Cattle-farming is important. Sea fishing by coastal fishermen (particularly for crustaceans) is being expanded, while vessels from the European Union fish for tuna and prawns in Madagascar's exclusive maritime zone, within 200 nautical miles (370 km) of the coast, in return for compensation. According to the World Bank, agricultural GDP increased by an average of 1.9% per year in 1995–2004; the sector's GDP by 3.1% in 2004.

Industry (including mining, manufacturing, construction and power) contributed an estimated 18.1% of Madagascar's GDP in 2004, and employed about 6.7% of the employed labour force in 2002. According to the World Bank, industrial GDP increased at an average annual rate of 2.8% in 1995–2004; the sector's GDP increased by 6.6% in 2004.

The mining sector contributed only 0.3% of GDP in 1991 and engaged 0.2% of the employed labour force in 2002. However, Madagascar has sizeable deposits of a wide range of minerals, principally chromite (chromium ore), which, with graphite and mica, is exported, together with small quantities of semi-precious stones. A major project to resume the mining of ilmenite (titanium ore) in south-eastern Madagascar, which would generate US $550m. over a 30-year period but which had prompted considerable controversy on environmental grounds, received approval from the Government in 2001, on the basis that QIT Madagascar Minerals would pursue simultaneously a strong environmental conservation programme. Construction of the mining facilities and rehabilitation of a deep-sea multi-purpose port at Ehoala, near Fort Dauphin (Tolagnaro) commenced in 2006, with an estimated budget of $585m. The operation was expected to commence production in late 2008, with an initial capacity of 750,000 metric tons. Other potential mineral projects included the exploitation of an estimated 100m. tons of bauxite in the south-east of the country, and of nickel and cobalt deposits in Ambatovy, central Madagascar. The presence of significant grades of the platinum group of metals were confirmed, as well as copper and nickel, in 2004. Renewed interest was also shown in that year in reviving the country's long-inactive uranium mines. An agreement with the People's Republic of China in 2005 for the export of chrome ore held significant potential for the development of that sector. Following exploratory drilling for petroleum at three offshore areas in the early 1990s, it was announced that only non-commercial deposits of petroleum and gas had been discovered, although contracts for further exploration were granted in 1997 and 1999. The mining of sapphires commenced in southern Madagascar in 1998, but in March 1999 the Government ordered the suspension of sapphire mining pending the results of studies into the effects of exploitation on the environment; however, unauthorized mining continued on a wide scale.

According to the World Bank, manufacturing contributed 14.7% of GDP in 2004 and engaged some 5.5% of the employed labour force in 2002. The petroleum refinery at Toamasina, using imported petroleum, provides a significant share of export revenue. Other important branches of manufacturing are textiles and clothing, food products, beverages and chemical products. The introduction of a new investment code in 1990 and the creation of a number of export-processing zones achieved some success in attracting foreign private investment, particularly in the manufacturing branches of textiles, cement, fertilizers and pharmaceuticals. According to the World Bank, manufacturing GDP increased at an average annual rate of 3.4% in 1995–2004; the GDP of the sector increased by 6.1% in 2004.

Energy generation depends on imports of crude petroleum (which accounted for an estimated 13.6% of the value of total imports in 2004) to fuel thermal installations, although hydroelectric resources have also been developed, and accounted for an estimated 67.6% of electricity production in 2001. In 2005 the Government finally awarded a two-year management contract for the national electricity and water utility, Jiro sy rano Malagasy (JIRAMA), to the German company Lahmeyer International; however, the company experienced severe problems in that year.

The services sector accounted for an estimated 53.3% of GDP in 2004, and engaged some 15.2% of the employed labour force in 2002. An information communication technologies business park was under development in Antananarivo as part of an effort to diversify Madagascar's economic growth. According to the World Bank, the GDP of the services sector increased by an average of 3.2% per year in 1995–2004; services GDP increased by 6.0% in 2004.

In 2003 Madagascar recorded a visible trade deficit of US $254m., and there was a deficit of $439m. on the current account of the balance of payments. The principal source of imports in 2003 was the People's Republic of China (17.6%); other major suppliers were France (16.3%) and South Africa (7.1%). France was the principal market for exports (accounting for 39.1% of exports in that year); the USA (28.5%) was also an important purchaser. The principal exports in 2003 were vanilla, crustaceans and cloves; food and live animals constituted 55.4% of the value of total exports. The principal imports in that year were basic manufactures, machinery and transport equipment, food and live animals and mineral fuels.

Madagascar's overall budget deficit for 2004 (excluding grants) was estimated at 1,071,700m. ariary (equivalent to 13.1% of GDP). Madagascar's external debt totalled US $4,958m. at the end of 2003, of which $4,622m. was long-term public debt. In the same year the cost of debt-servicing was estimated to be equivalent to 6.1% of the value of exports of goods and services. The annual rate of inflation averaged 0.9% in 1992–2002; consumer prices increased by 15.9% in 2002 but decreased by 1.2% in 2003. About 4.5% of the labour force was unemployed in 2002.

Madagascar is a member of the Indian Ocean Commission (see p. 386) and of the Common Market for Eastern and Southern Africa (COMESA, see p. 191). In August 2005 Madagascar joined the Southern African Development Community (SADC, see p. 358).

Madagascar's dominant agricultural sector is vulnerable to adverse climatic conditions, including cyclones, and to fluctuations in the market prices of the country's principal exports. In March 2001 Madagascar was declared eligible to benefit from the USA's African Growth and Opportunity Act (AGOA), allowing duty-free access to the US market, and both exports to the USA and foreign investment in Madagascar increased dramatically as a result. Economic activity was paralysed from the beginning of 2002—amid political uncertainty caused by the disputed presidential election (see Recent History)—by the strikes called by Marc Ravalomanana and the blockades ordered by Didier Ratsiraka. In February the World Bank estimated that the strike was costing Madagascar up to $14m. per day (the entire annual savings from debt-relief) and that 50,000 jobs were threatened. The closure of the central bank from the end of January also resulted in the freezing of the nation's assets, rendering Madagascar unable to service its debts and at risk of default; real GDP for the year declined by 11.9%. Companies in the export-processing zone (EPZ) and in the agricultural sector were severely affected by the political crisis, being highly dependent on foreign purchasers and the transportation network; tourism also was drastically curtailed. In July international donors pledged some US $2,300m. (one-half of which was to be supplied by the Bretton

MADAGASCAR

Woods institutions) over a period of four years towards the reconstruction and development of the country; this subsequently enabled the authorities to repay the arrears on all external payments. In October the IMF fully disbursed a structural adjustment credit of $100m., and in November it approved an Emergency Economic Recovery Credit and other loans aimed at public-sector management and private-sector development. In December the Fund granted $15m. under the Poverty Reduction and Growth Facility (PRGF) and extended the arrangement (initiated in 2001) until November 2004, in addition to allotting $4m. in interim assistance under the Heavily Indebted Poor Countries (HIPC) initiative. The economy recovered significantly in 2003, and a Poverty Reduction Strategy Paper was adopted in July. Madagascar's new currency, the ariary (which had been reintroduced in July to replace the franc MG), depreciated considerably in 2004, prompting significant increases in food and fuel prices, but some optimism with regard to potential foreign investment. The budget for 2005 increased expenditure levels by some 33% in comparison with the previous year, with a large proportion of the increased funds being allocated to health and education in conformity with the poverty-reduction strategy agreed with the IMF. In November 2004, following Madagascar's completion of its obligations under the HIPC initiative, the 'Paris Club' of international creditors once more restructured the country's debt; many participants, including France and, subsequently, Japan and the USA, cancelled the entire amount owed to them, reaching a total reduction of some $836m. Madagascar was also one of the first countries to negotiate a compact with the USA under its Millennium Challenge Account foreign-aid programme; this constituted some $110m. to be disbursed over four years as part of a poverty-reduction project which was to: expand property rights for citizens, strengthen the financial sector and promote investment in agriculture. All sectors (particularly agriculture, construction, textile exports and tourism) demonstrated further growth and recovery in 2005, although the economy remained vulnerable to external shocks and the effect of the expiry of the favourable Multi-Fibre Agreement and AGOA at the end of 2004. In July 2005 Madagascar qualified as a candidate for debt cancellation, owing to its success under the HIPC initiative; in the same month the World Bank announced $129.8m. of funding under an 'integrated growth poles' project, aimed at broadening the base of the country's growth and employment beyond the narrow sector of textiles in the EPZ. ($35m. of this amount was allocated for the reconstruction of the deep-sea port at Ehoala–see above.) However, during 2005 JIRAMA experienced severe difficulties when it failed to realign its tariffs with escalated international petroleum prices, in spite of a strong dependence on diesel for the generation of much of the country's energy supply. Rationing of electricity was introduced as a consequence, with a detrimental effect on economic growth. The renewal of the PRGF was postponed (in November), dependent upon a demonstrable improvement in revenue collection and the resolution of a recovery plan for JIRAMA. In January 2006 a $125m. support plan for the restructuring of the company was announced by donors; it was hoped that Madagascar would eventually become more reliant on hydroelectric power. Meanwhile, the authorities also announced a major road improvement project for 2006, which was intended to provide employment in the medium term and improve trade in the long term.

Education

Six years' education, to be undertaken usually between six and 13 years of age, is officially compulsory. Madagascar has both public and private schools, although legislation that was enacted in 1978 envisaged the progressive elimination of private education. In 2002 primary school fees were abolished. Primary education generally begins at the age of six and lasts for five years. Secondary education, beginning at 11 years of age, lasts for a further seven years, comprising a first cycle of four years and a second of three years. In 2002/03 primary net enrolment included 82% of children in the relevant age-group, while, according to UNESCO estimates, in 1998/99 secondary enrolment included 11% of children in the relevant age-group (males 11%; females 12%). In 1998/99 31,013 students attended institutions providing tertiary education. In 1999 the OPEC Fund granted a loan worth US $10m. to support a government programme to improve literacy standards and to increase access to education. In 2001 the Arab Bank for Economic Development in Africa granted a loan of $8m. to finance a project in support of general education. The budget for 2004 allocated 205,400m. ariary (22.9% of budgetary expenditure) to education.

Public Holidays

2006: 1 January (New Year), 29 March (Martyr's Day, Commemoration of 1947 Rebellion), 17 April (Easter Monday), 1 May (Labour Day), 25 May (Ascension Day), 25 May (Organization of African Unity Day), 4 June (Whitsun), 26 June (Independence Day), 15 August (Assumption), 1 November (All Saints' Day), 25 December (Christmas).

2005: 1 January (New Year), 29 March (Martyr's Day, Commemoration of 1947 Rebellion), 9 April (Easter Monday), 1 May (Labour Day), 17 May (Ascension Day), 25 May (Organization of African Unity Day), 27 May (Whitsun), 26 June (Independence Day), 15 August (Assumption), 1 November (All Saints' Day), 25 December (Christmas).

Weights and Measures

The metric system is in force.

Statistical Survey

Source (unless otherwise stated): Institut National de la Statistique Malagache, BP 485, Anosy Tana, 101 Antananarivo; tel. (20) 2227418; e-mail dridnstat@wanadoo.mg; internet www.instat.mg.

Area and Population

AREA, POPULATION AND DENSITY

Area (sq km)	587,041*
Population (census results)	
1974–75†	7,603,790
1–19 August 1993	
Males	5,991,171
Females	6,100,986
Total	12,092,157
Population (official estimates at mid-year)	
2002	15,981,000
2003	16,441,000
2004	16,908,000
Density (per sq km) at mid-2004	28.8

* 226,658 sq miles.

† The census took place in three stages: in provincial capitals on 1 December 1974; in Antananarivo and remaining urban areas on 17 February 1975; and in rural areas on 1 June 1975.

PRINCIPAL ETHNIC GROUPS
(estimated population, 1974)

Merina (Hova)	1,993,000		Sakalava	470,156*
Betsimisaraka	1,134,000		Antandroy	412,500
Betsileo	920,600		Antaisaka	406,468*
Tsimihety	558,100			

* 1972 figure.

PRINCIPAL TOWNS
(population at 1993 census)

Antananarivo (capital)	1,103,304		Mahajanga (Majunga)	106,780
Toamasina (Tamatave)	137,782		Toliary (Tuléar)	80,826
Antsirabé	126,062		Antsiranana (Diégo-Suarez)	59,040
Fianarantsoa	109,248			

2001 (estimated population, incl. Renivohitra and Avaradrano): Antananarivo 1,111,392.

MADAGASCAR

BIRTHS AND DEATHS

	2001	2002	2003
Birth rate (per 1,000)	42.1	41.6	41.1
Death rate (per 1,000)	13.5	13.2	12.9

Source: African Development Bank.

Expectation of life (WHO estimates, years at birth): 57 (males 55; females 59) in 2003 (Source: WHO, *World Health Report*).

ECONOMICALLY ACTIVE POPULATION
(labour force survey, '000 persons)

	2002
Agriculture, hunting and forestry	6,228.5
Fishing	87.5
Mining and quarrying	14.2
Manufacturing	449.3
Electricity, gas and water	18.6
Construction	60.6
Wholesale and retail trade; repair of motor vehicles, motor cycles and personal and household goods	420.5
Hotels and restaurants	47.7
Transport, storage and communications	117.1
Financial intermediation; real estate, renting and business activities	5.7
Public administration and defence; compulsory social security	205.7
Education	66.2
Health and social work	14.4
Other community, social and personal service activities	362.6
Total employed	**8,098.5**
Unemployed	382.9
Total labour force	**8,481.5**

Source: ILO.

Health and Welfare

KEY INDICATORS

Total fertility rate (children per woman, 2003)	5.7
Under-5 mortality rate (per 1,000 live births, 2004)	123
HIV/AIDS (% of persons aged 15–49, 2003)	1.7
Physicians (per 1,000 head, 2002)	0.14
Hospital beds (per 1,000 head, 2002)	0.42
Health expenditure (2002): US $ per head (PPP)	18.0
Health expenditure (2002): % of GDP	2.1
Health expenditure (2002): public (% of total)	55.0
Access to water (% of persons, 2002)	45
Access to sanitation (% of persons, 2002)	33
Human Development Index (2003): ranking	146
Human Development Index (2003): value	0.499

For sources and definitions, see explanatory note on p. vi.

Agriculture

PRINCIPAL CROPS
('000 metric tons)

	2002	2003	2004
Rice (paddy)	2,604	2,800	3,030
Maize	172	318	350
Potatoes	296	255	281
Sweet potatoes	493	493	542
Cassava (Manioc)	2,366	1,992	2,191
Taro (Coco yam)*	200	200	200
Sugar cane	2,223	2,460	2,460
Dry beans	70	75	83
Other pulses*	19	19	19
Groundnuts (in shell)	35	36	39
Coconuts*	85	85	85
Oil palm fruit*	21	21	21
Cottonseed*	4	5	5
Tomatoes*	22	22	22
Other vegetables*	322	322	322
Bananas*	290	290	290

—continued	2002	2003	2004
Oranges*	83	83	83
Mangoes*	210	210	210
Avocados*	23	23	23
Pineapples*	51	51	51
Cashewapple*	68	68	68
Other fruits*	166	166	166
Coffee (green)	61	70	65
Vanilla	2	2*	3*
Cinnamon (Canella)*	2	2	2
Cloves*	16	16	16
Cotton (lint)	4†	6*	11*
Sisal	17	17	17
Tobacco (leaves)	1	1	1

* FAO estimate(s).
† Unofficial figure.

Source: FAO.

LIVESTOCK
('000 head, year ending September)

	2002	2003	2004
Cattle	7,887	8,020	10,500
Pigs*	1,600	1,600	1,600
Sheep	654	843	650*
Goats	1,220	1,252	1,200*
Chickens	24,000	24,000*	24,000*
Ducks*	3,800	3,800	3,800
Geese*	3,000	3,000	3,000
Turkeys*	2,000	2,000	2,000

* FAO estimate(s).

Source: FAO.

LIVESTOCK PRODUCTS
(FAO estimates, '000 metric tons)

	2002	2003	2004
Beef and veal	111.6	114.8	146.6
Mutton and lamb	2.5	3.2	2.5
Goat meat	6.1	6.1	6.1
Pig meat	70	70	70
Chicken meat	35.5	35.5	35.5
Duck meat	10.6	10.6	10.6
Goose meat	12.6	12.6	12.6
Turkey meat	8.4	8.4	8.4
Cows' milk	535	535	535
Hen eggs	14.9	14.9	14.9
Other eggs	4.5	4.5	4.5
Honey	3.9	3.9	3.9
Cattle hides	15.8	16.2	20.7

Source: FAO.

Forestry

ROUNDWOOD REMOVALS
('000 cubic metres, excl. bark)

	2002	2003	2004
Sawlogs, veneer logs and logs for sleepers	103	185	160
Pulpwood	23	23	23
Fuel wood*	10,202	10,486	10,770
Total	**10,328**	**10,694**	**10,953**

* FAO estimates.

Source: FAO.

MADAGASCAR

SAWNWOOD PRODUCTION
('000 cubic metres, incl. railway sleepers)

	2002	2003	2004
Coniferous (softwood)	4*	8	8
Broadleaved (hardwood)	91	485	886
Total	95	493	894

* FAO estimate.

Source: FAO.

Fishing
('000 metric tons, live weight)

	2001	2002	2003
Capture	135.6	141.3	140.8
Cichlids	21.5	21.5	21.5
Other freshwater fishes	4.5	4.5	4.5
Narrow-barred Spanish mackerel	12.0	12.0	12.0
Other marine fishes	77.6	82.7	82.1
Shrimps and prawns	11.8	13.2	13.3
Aquaculture	7.7	9.7	9.5
Giant tiger prawn	5.4	7.3	7.0
Total catch	143.3	150.0	150.3

Note: Figures exclude aquatic plants ('000 metric tons, capture only): 5.0 in 2001; 2.9 in 2002; 1.7 in 2003. Also excluded are crocodiles, recorded by number rather than weight, and shells. The number of Nile crocodiles caught was: 9,408 in 2001; 6,936 in 2002; 7,300 in 2003. The catch of marine shells (in metric tons) was: 32 in 2001; 26 in 2002; 194 in 2003.

Source: FAO.

Mining
(metric tons)

	1999	2000	2001
Chromite*	144	131,293	23,637
Salt	26,131	25,530	25,928
Graphite (natural)	16,137	40,328	2,013
Mica	54	66	90

* Figures refer to gross weight. The estimated chromium content is 27%.

Industry

SELECTED PRODUCTS
(metric tons, unless otherwise indicated)

	1999	2000	2001
Raw sugar	61,370	62,487	67,917
Beer ('000 hectolitres)	610.1	645.5	691.7
Cigarettes	3,839	4,139	4,441
Woven cotton fabrics (million metres)	20.4	23.3	29.6
Leather footwear ('000 pairs)	460	570	568
Plastic footwear ('000 pairs)	375	303	291
Paints	1,918	1,487	1,554
Soap	15,884	15,385	15,915
Motor spirit—petrol ('000 cu metres)	98.0	122.6	128.3
Kerosene ('000 cu metres)	65.0	65.2	75.1
Gas-diesel (distillate fuel) oil ('000 cu metres)	119.0	150.4	150.2
Residual fuel oils ('000 cu metres)	198.8	225.7	247.2
Cement	45,701	50,938	51,882
Electric energy (million kWh)*	721.3	779.8	833.9

* Production by the state-owned utility only, excluding electricity generated by industries for their own use.

Finance

CURRENCY AND EXCHANGE RATES

Monetary Units
5 iraimbilanja = 1 ariary.

Sterling, Dollar and Euro Equivalents (30 December 2005)
£1 sterling = 3,718.99 ariary;
US $1 = 2,159.82 ariary;
€1 = 2,547.94 ariary;
100,000 ariary = £2.69 = $4.63 = €3.92.

Average Exchange Rate (ariary per US $)
2003 1,238.3
2004 1,868.9
2005 2,003.0

Note: A new currency, the ariary, was introduced on 31 July 2003 to replace the franc malgache (franc MG). The old currency was to remain legal tender until 30 November. Some figures in this survey are still given in terms of francs MG.

BUDGET
('000 million francs MG, central government operations)*

Revenue†	2002	2003‡	2004§
Tax revenue	2,304.2	3,389.3	4,210.0
Non-tax revenue	98.8	108.0	281.6
Total	2,403.0	3,497.3	4,491.6

Expenditure‖	2002	2003‡	2004§
Current expenditure	3,109.4	4,047.9	4,302.3
Budgetary expenditure	2,781.2	3,916.9	4,140.2
Wages and salaries	1,380.0	1,887.9	1,931.3
Other non-interest expenditure	741.7	1,235.3	1,330.6
Interest payments	659.5	793.7	878.3
Treasury operations (net)	202.0	91.9	156.3
Emergency expenditure	122.2	35.0	—
Counterpart funds-financed operations	3.9	4.1	5.8
Capital expenditure	1,445.8	1,968.9	3,075.7
Total	4,555.2	6,016.8	7,377.9

* Figures exclude the net cost of structural reforms ('000 million francs MG): 5.8 in 2002; –20.0 in 2003 (estimate); –42.7 in 2004 (forecast).
† Excluding grants received ('000 million francs MG): 650.1 in 2002; 1,369.6 in 2003 (estimate); 1,890.0 in 2004 (forecast).
‡ Estimates.
§ Forecasts.
‖ Excluding lending minus repayments ('000 million francs MG): 154.4 in 2002; 146.1 in 2003 (estimate); nil in 2004 (forecast). Also excluded is adjustment for changes in payment arrears ('000 million francs MG): 212.6 in 2002; 256.6 in 2003 (estimate); 347.3 in 2004 (forecast).

Source: Ministry of the Economy, Finance and Budget.

INTERNATIONAL RESERVES
(US $ million at 31 December)

	2002	2003	2004
IMF special drawing rights	0.0	0.0	0.2
Foreign exchange	363.2	414.2	503.3
Total	363.2	414.2	503.5

Source: IMF, *International Financial Statistics*.

MONEY SUPPLY
('000 million ariary at 31 December)

	2002	2003	2004
Currency outside banks	466.02	514.00	591.38
Demand deposits at deposit money banks	659.56	658.46	808.05
Total money	1,125.58	1,172.46	1,399.43

Source: IMF, *International Financial Statistics*.

MADAGASCAR

Statistical Survey

COST OF LIVING

(Consumer Price Index for Madagascans in Antananarivo; base: 2000 = 100)

	2001	2002	2003
Food	101.9	117.2	112.9
Clothing*	107.7	111.7†	115.4
Rent	111.9	129.4†	132.0
All items (incl. others)	107.4	125.1	123.0

* Including household linen.
† Average for 11 months.

2004: All items 140.0.

Source: ILO.

NATIONAL ACCOUNTS

('000 million francs MG at current prices)

Expenditure on the Gross Domestic Product

	2002	2003	2004
Government final consumption expenditure	2,450	3,254	3,424
Private final consumption expenditure	25,280	27,866	30,141
Increase in stocks			
Gross fixed capital formation	4,285	5,419	7,295
Total domestic expenditure	32,014	36,539	40,860
Exports of goods and services	4,809	6,932	8,026
Less Imports of goods and services	6,782	9,607	11,235
GDP in purchasers' values	30,042	33,863	37,651
GDP at constant 1984 prices	2,158.2	2,366.4	2,508.3

Source: IMF, *International Financial Statistics*.

Gross Domestic Product by Economic Activity

	2002	2003	2004
Agriculture, hunting, forestry and fishing	8,963	9,073	9,857
Mining and quarrying			
Manufacturing	4,078	4,777	5,456
Electricity, gas and water			
Construction	552	652	794
Trade, restaurants and hotels	3,555	3,909	4,316
Transport, storage and communications	4,817	5,154	5,796
Financial intermediation	246	293	324
Administration	1,641	2,140	2,281
Other services	4,610	5,289	5,644
Sub-total	28,462	31,287	34,468
Less imputed bank charges	196	226	251
GDP at factor cost	28,265	31,061	34,217
Indirect taxes, less subsidies	1,777	2,803	3,435
GDP in purchasers' values	30,042	33,863	37,651

Source: Ministry of the Economy, Finance and Budget.

BALANCE OF PAYMENTS

(US $ million)

	2001	2002	2003
Exports of goods f.o.b.	928	486	856
Imports of goods f.o.b.	−955	−603	−1,109
Trade balance	−27	−117	−254
Exports of services	351	224	270
Imports of services	−511	−398	−545
Balance on goods and services	−187	−291	−529
Other income received	24	26	16
Other income paid	−106	−101	−95
Balance on goods, services and income	−270	−366	−607
Current transfers received	114	88	349
Current transfers paid	−15	−21	−180
Current balance	−170	−298	−439
Capital account (net)	113	58	140
Direct investment from abroad	93	8	13
Other investment assets	−128	42	−27
Other investment liabilities	−103	−104	−104
Net errors and omissions	−57	11	52
Overall balance	−253	−283	−365

Source: IMF, *International Financial Statistics*.

External Trade

PRINCIPAL COMMODITIES

(US $ million)

Imports c.i.f.	2001	2002	2003
Food and live animals	88.2	60.3	131.2
Cereals and cereal preparations	51.5	23.7	77.7
Rice	35.0	10.3	49.2
Mineral fuels, lubricants and related materials	203.1	219.2	111.8
Petroleum, petroleum products and related materials	200.6	216.9	110.1
Crude petroleum and oils obtained from bituminous materials	77.5	77.8	0.0
Petroleum products, refined	119.8	136.7	106.8
Gas oils	119.6	136.6	106.6
Chemicals and related products	82.1	60.9	104.8
Medicinal and pharmaceutical products	28.3	27.0	35.1
Basic manufactures	186.9	72.9	352.7
Textile yarn and related products	86.2	11.6	213.5
Woven cotton fabrics	20.9	2.7	54.0
Machinery and transport equipment	190.6	92.8	222.7
Electric machinery, apparatus and appliances	30.0	17.1	37.6
Road vehicles	58.2	28.8	67.5
Miscellaneous manufactures	65.3	34.8	107.9
Total (incl. others)	858.3	566.1	1,091.1

MADAGASCAR

Exports f.o.b.	2001	2002	2003
Food and live animals	417.9	390.2	424.5
Fish, crustaceans and molluscs and preparations thereof	138.6	162.3	169.6
Crustaceans and molluscs	104.5	130.5	125.9
Vegetables and fruit	21.2	22.5	20.2
Coffee, tea, cocoa, spices	248.2	203.6	230.6
Spices	239.2	191.1	219.7
Vanilla	145.6	165.5	188.7
Cloves	91.3	23.2	28.8
Crude materials, inedible, except fuels	42.3	35.4	387.7
Basic manufactures	41.4	34.4	31.0
Miscellaneous manufactures	318.7	145.1	253.3
Articles of apparel and clothing accessories	280.3	113.2	236.1
Men's and boys' outerwear	56.5	25.4	34.2
Women's, girls' and infants' outerwear	42.9	17.2	59.9
Knitted or crocheted outerwear	102.5	40.2	95.3
Total (incl. others)	860.0	639.7	766.0

Source: UN, *International Trade Statistics Yearbook*.

PRINCIPAL TRADING PARTNERS
(US $ million)

Imports	2001	2002	2003
Bahrain	51.2	57.2	11.5
Belgium	10.9	8.8	20.5
China, People's Repub.	79.4	33.2	191.9
France	133.8	85.6	177.5
Germany	26.9	14.9	37.2
Hong Kong	14.3	1.3	23.7
India	18.2	21.0	50.5
Indonesia	18.7	12.3	23.8
Italy	19.9	8.8	36.1
Japan	33.1	10.3	29.3
Korea, Republic	10.8	6.4	14.3
Malaysia	10.9	8.4	17.0
Mauritius	36.8	18.0	37.9
Pakistan	22.2	3.5	24.7
Qatar	28.7	17.6	0.5
Singapore	7.2	3.6	12.1
South Africa	42.2	29.7	77.5
Spain	8.2	5.4	11.4
Thailand	4.7	2.9	13.4
United Arab Emirates	61.1	79.1	17.4
United Kingdom	11.1	4.2	11.9
USA	28.1	14.3	29.9
Total (incl. others)	858.3	566.1	1,091.1

Exports	2001	2002	2003
Belgium	10.4	8.6	6.3
Canada	6.3	13.8	9.6
France	309.9	267.4	299.7
Germany	32.6	31.0	39.5
Hong Kong	9.1	7.4	8.2
Italy	19.0	19.4	13.8
Japan	21.1	23.9	13.1
Mauritius	23.6	19.9	10.6
Netherlands	22.8	8.4	10.4
Singapore	66.9	20.9	24.8
South Africa	2.5	1.2	16.2
Spain	15.8	13.7	7.1
Thailand	5.6	6.8	9.0
United Kingdom	29.2	21.7	15.8
USA	202.3	128.9	218.5
Total (incl. others)	860.0	639.7	766.0

Source: UN, *International Trade Statistics Yearbook*.

Transport

RAILWAYS
(traffic)

	1997	1998	1999
Passengers carried ('000)	359	293	273
Passenger-km (millions)	37	35	31
Freight carried ('000 metric tons)	227	213	141
Ton-km (millions)	81	71	46

Source: Réseau National des Chemins de Fer Malagasy.

ROAD TRAFFIC
(vehicles in use)

	1994	1995	1996*
Passenger cars	54,821	58,097	60,480
Buses and coaches	3,797	4,332	4,850
Lorries and vans	35,931	37,232	37,972
Road tractors	488	560	619

* Estimates.

Source: IRF, *World Road Statistics*.

SHIPPING

Merchant Fleet
(registered at 31 December)

	2002	2003	2004
Number of vessels	103	103	103
Displacement ('000 gross registered tons)	34.8	34.8	32.9

Source: Lloyd's Register-Fairplay, *World Fleet Statistics*.

International Sea-borne Freight Traffic
('000 metric tons)

	1987	1988	1989
Goods loaded:			
Mahajanga	17	18	29.4
Toamasina	252	350	360.6
other ports	79	100	137.4
Total	348	468	527.4
Goods unloaded:			
Mahajanga	37	32	30.8
Toamasina	748	778	708.9
other ports	48	53	52.0
Total	833	863	791.7

1990 ('000 metric tons): Goods loaded 540; Goods unloaded 984 (Source: UN, *Monthly Bulletin of Statistics*).

CIVIL AVIATION
(traffic on scheduled services)

	1996	1997	1998
Kilometres flown (million)	8	9	9
Passengers carried ('000)	542	575	318
Passenger-km (million)	659	758	718
Total ton-km (million)	85	98	94

Source: UN, *Statistical Yearbook*.

Tourism

TOURIST ARRIVALS BY NATIONALITY

	2000	2001	2002
Canada and USA	6,402	6,808	1,880
France	88,039	95,316	32,070
Germany	6,403	6,808	3,084
Italy	8,004	8,510	3,084
Japan	2,055	3,404	617
Mauritius	4,526	8,510	3,134
Réunion	14,406	17,021	3,084
Switzerland	3,201	3,404	2,467
United Kingdom	4,802	5,106	2,467
Total (incl. others)	160,071	170,208	61,674

2003: Total arrivals 139,000.

Tourism receipts (US $ million, incl. passenger transport): 149 in 2001; 61 in 2002; 118 in 2003.

Source: World Tourism Organization.

Communications Media

	2002	2003	2004
Telephones ('000 main lines in use)	59.5	59.6	n.a.
Mobile cellular telephones ('000 subscribers)	163.0	283.7	333.9
Personal computers ('000 in use)	70	80	91
Internet users ('000)	55	71	90.0

Source: International Telecommunication Union.

1995: Radio receivers ('000 in use) 2,850; Book production (incl. pamphlets): titles 131, copies ('000) 292; Daily newspapers: number 6, circulation ('000 copies) 59 (Source: UNESCO, *Statistical Yearbook*).

1996: Radio receivers ('000 in use) 2,950; Book production (incl. pamphlets): titles 119, copies ('000) 296; Daily newspapers: number 5, circulation ('000 copies) 66 (Source: UNESCO, *Statistical Yearbook*).

1997: Radio receivers ('000 in use) 3,050 (Source: UNESCO, *Statistical Yearbook*).

2000: Television receivers ('000 in use) 375.

Education

(1998, unless otherwise indicated)

	Institutions	Teachers	Males	Females	Total
Pre-primary*	n.a.	n.a.	28.7	29.2	57.8
Primary	14,438	42,678	1,024.3	988.1	2,012.4
Secondary:					
general	n.a.	18,987†	168.6	165.6	334.3
teacher training‡	n.a.	58	0.2	0.1	0.3
vocational§	n.a.	1,092	5.7	2.4	8.1
Tertiary	6	1,471	16.8	14.2	31.0

Pupils ('000)

* 1994/95 figures.
† UNESCO estimate.
‡ 1993/94 figures.
§ 1995/96 figures, public education only.

Source: UNESCO, Institute for Statistics.

2003/04: Primary schools 19,961 (3,556,042 pupils) (Source: IMF, *Republic of Madagascar: Poverty Reduction Strategy Paper Progress Report* (December 2004)).

Adult literacy rate (UNESCO estimates): 70.6% (males 76.4%; females 65.2%) in 2003 (Source: UN Development Programme, *Human Development Report*).

Directory

The Constitution

The Constitution of the Third Republic of Madagascar was endorsed by national referendum on 19 August 1992, but was substantially altered by amendments that were endorsed in a national referendum on 15 March 1998. The amended Constitution enshrines a 'federal-style' state, composed of six autonomous provinces—each with a governor and up to 12 general commissioners (holding executive power) and a provincial council (holding legislative power). It provides for a government delegate to each province, who is charged with supervising the division of functions between the state and the province. The bicameral legislature consists of the National Assembly (the lower house), which is elected by universal adult suffrage in single-seat constituencies for a five-year term of office. The Constitution also provides for a Senate (the upper house), of which one-third of the members are presidential nominees and two-thirds are elected in equal numbers by the provincial councillors and mayors of each of the six autonomous provinces, for a term of six years. The constitutional Head of State is the President. If no candidate obtains an overall majority in the presidential election, a second round of voting is to take place a maximum of 30 days after the publication of the results of the first ballot. Any one candidate can be elected for a maximum of three five-year terms. The powers of the President were greatly increased by constitutional amendments of March 1998: he has the power to determine general state policy in the Council of Ministers, to call referendums on all matters of national importance, and to dissolve the National Assembly not less than one year after a general election. Executive power is vested in a Prime Minister, who is appointed by the President. The President appoints the Council of Ministers, on the recommendation of the Prime Minister.

The Government

HEAD OF STATE

President: MARC RAVALOMANANA (inaugurated 6 May 2002).

COUNCIL OF MINISTERS
(April 2006)

Prime Minister: JACQUES SYLLA.

Minister of the Economy, Finance and the Budget: BENJAMIN ANDRIAMPARANY RADAVIDSON.

Minister of Justice and Keeper of the Seals: LALA HENRIETTE RATSIHAROVALA.

Minister of Foreign Affairs: Gen. MARCEL RANJEVA.

Minister of the Interior and Administrative Reform: Gen. CHARLES RABEMANANJARA.

Minister of Defence: Maj.-Gen. PETERA BEHAJAINA.

Minister of National Education and Scientific Research: HAJA NIRINA RAZAFINJATOVO.

Minister of Health and Family Planning: JEAN-LOUIS ROBINSON.

Minister of the Population, Social Protection and Leisure: ZAFILAZA.

Minister of Industry, Trade and the Development of the Private Sector: ROGER-MARIE RAFANOMEZANTSOA.

Minister of the Civil Service, Labour and Social Legislation: JEAN THÉODORE RANJIVASON.

MADAGASCAR

Minister of the Environment, Water and Forests: Gen. CHARLES SYLVAIN RABOTOARISON.

Minister of Energy and Mining: OLIVIER DONAT ANDRIAMAHEFAPARANY.

Minister of Agriculture, Livestock and Fisheries: HARISON EDMOND RANDRIAIMANANA.

Minister of Telecommunications, Post and Communications: BRUNO RAMAROSON ANDRIANTAVISON.

Minister of Transport and Public Works: ROLAND RANDRIAMAMPIONONA.

Minister of Youth and Sports: TOMBO RAMANDIMBISOA.

Minister of Culture and Tourism: JEAN-JACQUES RABENIRINA.

Minister of Decentralization and National and Regional Development: JEAN ANGELIN RANDRIANARISON.

Secretary of State for Public Security at the Ministry of the Interior and Administrative Reform: LUCIEN VICTOR RAZAKANIRINA.

MINISTRIES

Office of the Prime Minister: BP 248, Mahazoarivo, 101 Antananarivo; tel. (20) 2225258; fax (20) 2235258.

Ministry of Agriculture, Livestock and Fisheries: BP 301, Ampandrianomby, 101 Antananarivo; tel. (20) 2261002; fax (20) 2226561; e-mail ifo@maep.gov.mg; internet www.maep.gov.mg.

Ministry of the Civil Service, Labour and Social Legislation: BP 207, Cité des 67 Hectares, 101 Antananarivo; tel. (20) 2224209; fax (20) 2233856; e-mail ministre@mfptls.gov.mg; internet www.mfptls.gov.mg.

Ministry of Culture and Tourism: BP 610, rue Fernand Kasanga Tsimbazaza, 101 Antananarivo; tel. (20) 2266805; fax (20) 2235410; e-mail mct@tourisme.gov.mg; internet www.tourisme.gov.mg.

Ministry of Decentralization and National and Regional Development: BP 24 bis, 101 Antananarivo; tel. (20) 2235881; fax (20) 2237516.

Ministry of Defence: BP 08, Ampahibe, 101 Antananarivo; tel. (20) 2222211; fax (20) 2235420; e-mail mdn@wanadoo.mg.

Ministry of the Economy, Finance and the Budget: BP 61, Antaninarenina, 101 Antananarivo; tel. (20) 2264681; fax (22) 2234530; e-mail cabmefb@wanadoo.mg; internet www.mefb.gov.mg.

Ministry of Energy and Mining: BP 527, Immeuble de l'Industrie, Antaninarenina, 101 Antananarivo; tel. (20) 2228928; fax (20) 2232554; internet www.cite.mg/mine.

Ministry of the Environment, Water and Forests: rue Farafaty, BP 571 Ampandrianomby, 101 Antananarivo; tel. (20) 2240908; fax (20) 2241919.

Ministry of Foreign Affairs: BP 836, Anosy, 101 Antananarivo; tel. (20) 2221198; fax (20) 2234484.

Ministry of Health and Family Planning: BP 88, Ambohidahy, 101 Antananarivo; tel. (20) 2263121; fax (20) 2264228; e-mail cabminsan@wanadoo.mg; internet www.sante.gov.mg.

Ministry of Industry, Trade and the Development of the Private Sector: Nouvel Immeuble Aro, Ampefiloha, 101 Antananarivo; tel. (20) 2230512; fax (20) 2228024; e-mail infos@industrie.gov.mg; internet www.micdsp.gov.mg.

Ministry of the Interior and Administrative Reform: BP 833, Anosy, 101 Antananarivo; tel. (20) 2223084; fax (20) 2235579.

Ministry of Justice: rue Joel Rakotomalala, BP 231, Faravohitra, 101 Antananarivo; tel. (20) 2237684; fax (20) 2264458; e-mail minjust.roger@simicro.mg; internet www.justice.gov.mg.

Ministry of National Education and Scientific Research: BP 4163, Tsimbazaza, 101 Antananarivo; tel. (20) 2229423; fax (20) 2234508; internet www.refer.mg/edu/minesup.

Ministry of the Population, Social Protection and Leisure: BP 723, Ambohijatovo, 101 Antananarivo; tel. (20) 2223075; fax (20) 2264823; e-mail minpopcgp@blueline.mg; internet www.population.gov.mg.

Ministry of Telecommunications, Post and Communications: Antaninarenina, 101 Antananarivo; tel. (20) 2223267; fax (20) 2235894; internet www.mtpc.gov.mg.

Ministry of Transport and Public Works: BP 4139, 101 Antananarivo; tel. (20) 2223215; fax (20) 2220890; e-mail viceprimature@mttpat.gov.mg.

Ministry of Youth and Sports: Ambohijatovo, Place Goulette, BP 681, 101 Antananarivo; tel. (20) 2227780; fax (20) 2234275.

Secretariat for Public Security: BP 23 bis, 101 Antananarivo; tel. (20) 2221029; fax (20) 2231861.

President and Legislature

PRESIDENT

Presidential Election, 16 December 2001

Candidate	% of votes
Marc Ravalomanana	51.46
Adm. (retd) Didier Ratsiraka	35.90
Others	12.64
Total	100.00

LEGISLATURE

Senate

President: GUY RAJEMISON RAKOTOMAHARO.

Senatorial Election, 18 March 2001

Party	Seats
AREMA	49
LEADER/Fanilo	5
Independents	3
AVI	2
AFFA	1
Total	60*

*Elected by a 1,727-member electoral college of provincial councillors and mayors. An additional 30 seats were appointed by the President.

National Assembly

President: JEAN LAHINIRIKO.

General Election, 15 December 2002

Party	Seats
TIM	104
Front Patriotique	22
AVI	20
RPSD	2
RPSD	5
AREMA	3
MFM	2
LEADER/Fanilo	1
Independents	23
Total	160

Election Commission

Conseil national électoral (CNE): Immeuble Microréalisation, 4 étage, 67 ha, 101 Antananarivo; tel. (20) 2225179; fax (20) 2225881; e-mail cnelecmadagascar@hotmail.com; internet www.cne.mg; Pres. THÉODORE RANDREZASON.

Political Organizations

Following the restoration of multi-party politics in March 1990, more than 120 political associations emerged, of which six secured representation in the National Assembly in 2002. The following were among the more influential political organizations in 2006:

Association pour la renaissance de Madagascar (Andry sy riana enti-manavotra an'i Madigasikara) (AREMA): f. 1975 as Avant-garde de la révolution malgache; adopted present name 1997; party of fmr Pres. Adm. (retd) Ratsiraka (now in exile); control disputed between two factions, headed by Gen. Sec. PIERROT RAJAONARIVELO (in exile), and Asst. Gen. Sec. PIERRE RAHARIJAONA.

Comité pour la Réconciliation Nationale (CRN): Antananarivo; f. 2002 by fmr President Zafy; radical opposition; does not recognize the presidency of Marc Ravalomanana; Leader ALBERT ZAFY.

Herim-Bahoaka Mitambatra (HBM) (Union of Popular Forces): formed part of the coalition supporting Pres. Ravalomanana prior to the presidential election; Leader TOVONANAHARY RABETSITONTA.

Libéralisme économique et action démocratique pour la reconstruction nationale (LEADER/Fanilo) (Torch): f. 1993 by Herizo Razafimahaleo; Leader Prof. MANASSE ESOAVELOMANDROSO.

MADAGASCAR

Mouvement pour le progrès de Madagascar (Mpitolona ho amin'ny fandrosoan'ny Madagasikara) (MFM): 101 Antananarivo; f. 1972 as Mouvement pour le pouvoir prolétarien (MFM); adopted present name in 1990; advocates liberal and market-orientated policies; Leader MANANDAFY RAKOTONIRINA; Sec.-Gen. GERMAIN RAKOTONIRAINY.

Ny asa vita no ifampitsara (AVI—People are judged by the work they do): f. 1997 to promote human rights, hard work and development; Leader NORBERT RATSIRAHONANA.

Rassemblement pour le socialisme et la démocratie (RPSD): f. 1993 by fmr mems of PSD; also known as Renaissance du parti social-démocratique; Jean-Eugène Voninahitsy formed a breakaway party known as the RPSD Nouveau in 2003; Leader EVARISTE MARSON.

Tiako i Madagasikara (TIM—I Love Madagascar): internet www.tim-madagascar.org; f. 2002; supports Pres. Ravalomanana; Pres. RAZOHARIMIHAJA SOLOFONANTENAINA.

Diplomatic Representation

EMBASSIES IN MADAGASCAR

China, People's Republic: Ancien Hôtel Panorama, BP 1658, 101 Antananarivo; tel. (20) 2240129; fax (20) 2240215; Ambassador LI SHULI.

Egypt: Lot MD 378 Ambalatokana Mandrosoa Ivato, BP 4082, 101 Antananarivo; tel. (20) 2245497; fax (20) 2245379; Ambassador AZZAH ABD AL-FATAH NASSIR.

France: 3 rue Jean Jaurès, BP 204, 101 Antananarivo; tel. (20) 2239898; fax (20) 2239927; e-mail ambatana@wanadoo.mg; Ambassador ALAIN LE ROY.

Germany: 101 rue du Pasteur Rabeony Hans, BP 516, Ambodirotra, 101 Antananarivo; tel. (20) 2223802; fax (20) 2226627; e-mail amballem@wanadoo.mg; internet www.antananarivo.diplo.de; Ambassador Dr DIETER HUBERTUS ZEISLER.

Holy See: Amboniloha Ivandry, BP 650, 101 Antananarivo; tel. (20) 2242376; fax (20) 2242384; e-mail nuntiusantana@wanadoo.mg; Apostolic Nuncio Most Rev. AUGUSTINE KASUJJA (Titular Archbishop of Caesarea de Numidia).

India: 4 Làlana Emile Rajaonson, Tsaralalana, BP 1787, 101 Antananarivo; tel. (20) 2223334; fax (20) 2233790; e-mail indembmd@wanadoo.mg; Ambassador DILJIT SINGH PANNUN.

Indonesia: 26–28 rue Patrice Lumumba, BP 3969, 101 Antananarivo; tel. (20) 2224915; fax (20) 2232857; Chargé d'affaires a.i. SLAMET SUYATA SASTRAMIHARDZA.

Iran: route Circulaire, Lot II L43 ter, Ankadivato, 101 Antananarivo; tel. (20) 2228639; fax (20) 2222298; Ambassador ABDOL RAHIM HOMATASH.

Italy: 22 rue Pasteur Rabary, BP 16, Ankadivato, 101 Antananarivo; tel. (20) 2221217; fax (20) 2223814; e-mail ambanta@simicro.mg; Ambassador RENATO VOLPINI.

Japan: 8 rue du Dr Villette, BP 3863, Isoraka, 101 Antananarivo; tel. (20) 2226102; fax (20) 2221769; Ambassador OSAMU YOSHIHARA.

Korea, Democratic People's Republic: 101 Antananarivo; tel. (20) 2244442; Ambassador RI YONG HAK.

Libya: Lot IIB, 37A route Circulaire Ampandrana-Ouest, 101 Antananarivo; tel. (20) 2221892; Chargé d'affaires a.i. Dr MOHAMED ALI SHARFEDIN AL-FITURI.

Mauritius: Anjaharay, route Circulaire, BP 6040, Ambanidia, 101 Antananarivo; tel. (20) 2221864; fax (20) 2221939; Ambassador (vacant).

Norway: Hilton Hotel, Antananarivo; e-mail emb.antananarivo@mfa.no; f. 2004; Ambassador HANS FREDERIK LEHNE.

Russia: BP 4006, Ivandry-Ambohijatovo, 101 Antananarivo; tel. (20) 2242827; fax (20) 2242642; e-mail ambrusmad@wanadoo.mg; Ambassador YURII A. ROMANOV.

South Africa: Villa Chandella, Lot Bonnet 38, Ivandry, BP 12101-05, 101 Antananarivo; tel. (20) 2243350; fax (20) 2243386; e-mail antananarivo@foreign.gov.za; Ambassador WALTER THEMBA THABETHE.

Switzerland: BP 118, 101 Antananarivo; tel. (20) 2262997; fax (20) 2228940; e-mail swiemant@wanadoo.mg; Chargé d'affaires a.i. ROSMARIE SCHELLING.

USA: 14–16 rue Rainitovo, Antsahavola, BP 620, 101 Antananarivo; tel. (20) 2221257; fax (20) 2234539; internet www.usmission.mg; Ambassador JAMES D. MCGEE.

Judicial System

HIGH CONSTITUTIONAL COURT

Haute Cour Constitutionnelle: POB 835, Ambohidahy, 101 Antananarivo; tel. (20) 2266061; e-mail hcc@simicro.mg; internet www.simicro.mg/hcc; interprets the Constitution and rules on constitutional issues; nine mems; Pres. JEAN-MICHEL RAJAONARIVONY.

HIGH COURT OF JUSTICE

Haute Cour de Justice: 101 Antananarivo; nine mems.

SUPREME COURT

Cour Suprême: Palais de Justice, Anosy, 101 Antananarivo; Pres. ALICE RAJAONAH (acting); Attorney-General COLOMBE RAMANANTSOA (acting); Chamber Pres YOLANDE RAMANGASOAVINA, FRANÇOIS RAMANANDRAIBE.

COURT OF APPEAL

Cour d'Appel: Palais de Justice, Anosy, 101 Antananarivo; Pres. AIMÉE RAKOTONIRINA; Pres of Chamber CHARLES RABETOKOTANY, PÉTRONILLE ANDRIAMIHAJA, BAKOLALAO RANAIVOHARIVONY, BERTHOLIER RAVELONTSALAMA, LUCIEN RABARIJHON, NELLY RAKOTOBE, ARLETTE RAMAROSON, CLÉMENTINE RAVANDISON, GISÈLE RABOTOVAO, JEAN-JACQUES RAJAONA.

OTHER COURTS

Tribunaux de Première Instance: at Antananarivo, Toamasina, Antsiranana, Mahajanga, Fianarantsoa, Toliary, Antsirabé, Ambatondrazaka, Antalaha, Farafangana and Maintirano; for civil, commercial and social matters, and for registration.

Cours Criminelles Ordinaires: tries crimes of common law; attached to the Cour d'Appel in Antananarivo but may sit in any other large town. There are also 31 Cours Criminelles Spéciales dealing with cases concerning cattle.

Tribunaux Spéciaux Economiques: at Antananarivo, Toamasina, Mahajanga, Fianarantsoa, Antsiranana and Toliary; tries crimes specifically relating to economic matters.

Tribunaux Criminels Spéciaux: judges cases of banditry and looting; 31 courts.

Religion

It is estimated that more than 50% of the population follow traditional animist beliefs, some 41% are Christians (about one-half of whom are Roman Catholics) and some 7% are Muslims.

CHRISTIANITY

Fiombonan'ny Fiangonana Kristiana eto Madagasikara (FFKM)/Conseil Chrétien des Eglises de Madagascar (Christian Council of Churches in Madagascar): Vohipiraisama, Ambohijatovo-Atsimo, BP 798, 101 Antananarivo; tel. (20) 2229052; f. 1980; four mems and one assoc. mem.; Pres. Pastor EDMOND RAZAFIMAHALEO; Gen. Sec. Rev. RÉMY RALIBERA.

Fiombonan'ny Fiangonana Protestanta eto Madagasikara (FFPM)/Fédération des Eglises Protestantes à Madagascar (Federation of the Protestant Churches in Madagascar): VK 3 Vohipiraisana, Ambohijatovo-Atsimo, BP 4226, 101 Antananarivo; tel. (20) 2220144; f. 1958; two mem churches; Pres. Pastor EDMOND RAZAFIMAHEFA; Gen. Sec. Rev. Dr ROGER ANDRIATSIRATAHINA.

The Anglican Communion

Anglicans are adherents of the Church of the Province of the Indian Ocean, comprising six dioceses (four in Madagascar, one in Mauritius and one in Seychelles). The Archbishop of the Province is the Bishop of Antananarivo. The Church has about 160,000 adherents in Madagascar, including the membership of the Eklesia Episkopaly Malagasy (Malagasy Episcopal Church), founded in 1874.

Bishop of Antananarivo (also Archbishop of the Province of the Indian Ocean): Most Rev. RÉMI JOSEPH RABENIRINA, Evêché anglican, Lot VK57 ter, Ambohimanoro, 101 Antananarivo; tel. (20) 2220827; fax (20) 2261331; e-mail eemdanta@wanadoo.mg.

Bishop of Antsiranana: Rt Rev. ROGER CHUNG PO CHEN, Evêché anglican, 4 rue Grandidier, BP 278, 201 Antsiranana; tel. (20) 8222650; e-mail eemdants@wanadoo.mg.

Bishop of Fianarantsoa: Rt Rev. GILBERT RATELOSON RAKOTONDRAVELO, Evêché anglican, BP 1418, 531 Fianarantsoa.

Bishop of Mahajanga: Rt Rev. JEAN-CLAUDE ANDRIANJAFIMANANA, Evêché anglican, BP 169, 401 Mahajanga; e-mail eemdmaha@wanadoo.mg.

MADAGASCAR

Bishop of Toamasina: Rt Rev. JEAN PAUL SOLO, Evêché anglican, rue James Seth, BP 531, 501 Toamasina; tel. (20) 5332163; fax (20) 5331689.

The Roman Catholic Church

Madagascar comprises four archdioceses and 16 dioceses. At 31 December 2003 the number of adherents in the country represented about 23.5% of the total population.

Bishops' Conference

Conférence episcopale de Madagascar, 102 bis, rue Cardinal Jerôme Rakotomalala, BP 667, 101 Antananarivo; tel. (20) 2220478; fax (20) 2224854; e-mail ecar@vitelcom.mg; f. 1969; Pres. Most Rev. FULGENCE RABEONY (Archbishop of Toliary).

Archbishop of Antananarivo: ODON ARSÈNE RAZANAKOLONA, Archevêché, Andohalo, BP 3030, 101 Antananarivo; tel. (20) 2220726; fax (20) 2264181; e-mail didih@simicro.org.

Archbishop of Antsiranana: Most Rev. MICHEL MALO, Archevêché, BP 415, 201 Antsiranana; tel. (82) 21605; e-mail archevediego@blueline.mg.

Archbishop of Fianarantsoa: Most Rev. FULGENCE RABEMAHAFALY, Archevêché, place Mgr Givelet, BP 1440, Ambozontany, 301 Fianarantsoa; tel. (20) 7550027; fax (20) 7551436; e-mail ecarfianar@vitelcom.mg.

Archbishop of Toliary: Most Rev. FULGENCE RABEONY, Archevêché, Maison Saint Jean, BP 30, 601 Toliary; tel. (20) 9442416; e-mail diocesetulear@wanadoo.mg.

Other Christian Churches

Fiangonan'i Jesoa Kristy eto Madagasikara/Eglise de Jésus-Christ à Madagascar (FJKM): Lot 11 B18, Tohatohabato Ranavalona 1, Trano 'Ifanomezantsoa', BP 623, 101 Antananarivo; tel. (20) 2226845; fax (20) 2226372; e-mail fjkm@dts.mg; f. 1968; Pres. LALA HAJA RASENDRAHASINA; Gen. Sec. Rev. RÉMY RALIBERA; 2m. mems.

Fiangonana Loterana Malagasy (Malagasy Lutheran Church): BP 1741, 101 Antananarivo; tel. (20) 3212107; fax (20) 2233767; e-mail flm@wanadoo.mg; Pres. Rev. ENDOR MODESTE RAKOTO; 600,000 mems.

The Press

In December 1990 the National People's Assembly adopted legislation guaranteeing the freedom of the press and the right of newspapers to be established without prior authorization.

PRINCIPAL DAILIES

Bulletin de l'Agence Nationale d'Information 'TARATRA' (ANTA): 8/10 Làlana Rainizanabololona, Antanimena, BP 194, 101 Antananarivo; tel. (20) 2234308; e-mail administration@taratramada.com; internet www.taratramada.com; f. 1977; Malagasy; Man. Dir CHARLES ANDRIANTSITOHAINA.

L'Express de Madagascar: BP 3893, 101 Antananarivo; tel. (20) 2221934; fax (20) 2262894; e-mail lexpress@malagasy.com; internet www.lexpressmada.com; f. 1995; French and Malagasy; Editor (vacant); circ. 10,000.

Gazetiko: BP 1414 Ankorondrano, 101 Antananarivo; tel. (20) 2269779; fax (20) 2227351; e-mail gazetikom@yahoo.fr; Malagasy; circ. 50,000.

La Gazette de la Grande Ile: Lot II, W 23 L Ankorahotra, route de l'Université, Antananarivo; tel. (20) 2261377; fax (20) 2265188; e-mail admin@lagazette-dgi.com; internet www.lagazette-dgi.com; French; 24 pages; Pres. LOLA RASOAMAHARO; circ. 15,000–30,000.

Imongo Vaovao: 11K 4 bis Andravoahangy, BP 7014, 101 Antananarivo; tel. (20) 2221053; f. 1955; Malagasy; Dir CLÉMENT RAMAMONJISOA; circ. 10,000.

Madagascar Tribune: Immeuble SME, rue Ravoninahitriniarivo, BP 659, Ankorondrano, 101 Antananarivo; tel. (20) 2222635; fax (20) 2222254; e-mail tribune@wanadoo.mg; internet www.madagascar-tribune.com; f. 1988; independent; French and Malagasy; Editor RAHAGA RAMAHOLIMIHASO; circ. 12,000.

Maresaka: 12 Làlana Ratsimba John, Isotry, 101 Antananarivo; tel. (20) 2223568; f. 1953; independent; Malagasy; Editor M. RALAIARIJAONA; circ. 5,000.

Midi Madagasikara: Làlana Ravoninahitriniarivo, BP 1414, Ankorondrano, 101 Antananarivo; tel. (20) 2269779; fax (20) 2227351; e-mail infos@midi-madagasikara.mg; internet www.midi-madagasikara.mg; f. 1983; French and Malagasy; Dir MAMY RAKOTOARIVELO; circ. 21,000 (Mon.–Fri.), 35,000 (Sat.).

Les Nouvelles: BP 194, 101 Antananarivo; tel. (20) 2235433; fax (20) 2229993; e-mail administration@les-nouvelles.com; internet www.les-nouvelles.com; in French and Taratra; f. 2003; Editor-in-Chief CHRISTIAN CHADEFAUX.

Ny Vaovaontsika: BP 11137, MBS Anosipatrana; tel. (20) 2227717; e-mail nyvaovaontsika@mbs.mg; f. 2004; re-estd as a daily; Malagasy; Malagasy Broadcasting System; Editor-in-Chief ROLAND ANDRIAMAHENINA; circ. 10,000.

Le Quotidien: BP 11 097, 101 Antananarivo; tel. (20) 2227717; fax (20) 2265447; e-mail lequotidien@mbs.mg; internet www.lequotidien.mg; f. 2003; owned by the Tiko Group plc ; French.

PRINCIPAL PERIODICALS

Basy Vava: Lot III E 96, Mahamasina Atsimo, 101 Antananarivo; tel. (20) 2220448; f. 1959; Malagasy; Dir GABRIEL RAMANANJATO; circ. 3,000.

Bulletin de la Société du Corps Médical Malgache: Imprimerie Volamahitsy, 101 Antananarivo; Malagasy; monthly; Dir Dr RAKOTOMALALA.

Dans les Médias Demain (DMD): Immeuble Jeune Afrique, 58 rue Tsiombikibo, BP 1734, Ambatovinaky, 101 Antananarivo; tel. (20) 2230755; fax (20) 2230754; e-mail dmd@wanadoo.mg; internet www.dmd.mg; f. 1986; independent; economic information and analysis; weekly; Editorial Dir JEAN ERIC RAKOTOARISOA; circ. 4,000.

Feon'ny Mpiasa: Lot M8, Isotry, 101 Antananarivo; trade union affairs; Malagasy; monthly; Dir M. RAZAKANAIVO; circ. 2,000.

Fiaraha-Miasa: BP 1216, 101 Antananarivo; Malagasy; weekly; Dir SOLO NORBERT ANDRIAMORASATA; circ. 5,000.

Gazetinao: Lot IPA 37, BP 1758, Anosimasina, 101 Antananarivo; tel. (33) 1198161; e-mail jamesdigne@caramail.com; f. 1976; French and Malagasy; monthly; Editors-in-Chief ANDRIANIAINA RAKOTOMAHANINA, JAMES FRANKLIN; circ. 3,000.

L'Hebdo: BP 3893, 101 Antananarivo; tel. (20) 2221934; f. 2005; French and Malagasy; weekly; Editor-in-Chief NASOLO VALIAVO ANDRIAMIHAJA.

Isika Mianakavy: Ambatomena, 301 Fianarantsoa; f. 1958; Roman Catholic; Malagasy; monthly; Dir J. RANAIVOMANANA; circ. 21,000.

Journal Officiel de la République de Madagascar/Gazetim-Panjakan' Ny Repoblika Malagasy: BP 248, 101 Antananarivo; tel. (20) 2265010; fax (20) 2225319; e-mail segma.gvt@wanadoo.mg; f. 1883; official announcements; Malagasy and French; weekly; Dir HONORÉE ELIANNE RALALAHARISON; circ. 1,545.

Journal Scientifique de Madagascar: BP 3855, Antananarivo; f. 1985; Dir Prof. MANAMBELONA; circ. 3,000.

Jureco: BP 6318, Lot IVD 48 bis, rue Razanamaniraka, Behoririka, 101 Antananarivo; tel. (20) 2255271; e-mail jureco@malagasy.com; internet www.jureco.com; law and economics; monthly; French; Dir MBOARA ANDRIANARIMANANA.

Lakroan'i Madagasikara/La Croix de Madagascar: BP 7524, CNPC Antanimena, 101 Antananarivo; tel. (20) 2266128; fax (20) 2224020; e-mail info@lakroa.orgg; internet www.geocities.com/lakroam; f. 1927; Roman Catholic; French and Malagasy; weekly; Dir Fr VINCENT RABEMAHAFALY; circ. 25,000.

La Lettre de Madagascar (LLM): Antananarivo; f. 2003; 2 a month; in French and English; economic; Editor-in-Chief DANIEL LAMY.

Mada—Economie: 15 rue Ratsimilaho, BP 3464, 101 Antananarivo; tel. (20) 2225634; f. 1977; reports events in south-east Africa; monthly; Editor RICHARD-CLAUDE RATOVONARIVO; circ. 5,000.

Mpanolotsaina: BP 623, 101 Antananarivo; tel. (20) 2226845; fax (20) 2226372; e-mail fjkm@wanadoo.mg; religious, educational; Malagasy; quarterly; Dir RAYMOND RAJOELISOL.

New Magazine: BP 7581, Newprint, Route des Hydrocarbures, 101 Antananarivo; tel. (20) 2233335; fax (20) 2236471; e-mail newmag@wanadoo.mg; internet www.newmagazine.mg; monthly; in French; Dir CLARA RAVOAVAHY.

Ny Mpamangy-FLM: 9 rue Grandidier Isoraka, BP 538, Antsahamanitra, 101 Antananarivo; tel. (20) 2232446; f. 1882; monthly; Dir Pastor JEAN RABENANDRASANA; circ. 3,000.

Ny Sakaizan'ny Tanora: BP 538, Antsahaminitra, 101 Antananarivo; tel. (20) 2232446; f. 1878; monthly; Editor-in-Chief DANIEL PROSPER ANDRIAMANJAKA; circ. 5,000.

PME Madagascar: rue Hugues Rabesahala, BP 953, Antsakaviro, 101 Antananarivo; tel. (20) 2222536; fax (20) 2234534; f. 1989; French; monthly; economic review; Dir ROMAIN ANDRIANARISOA; circ. 3,500.

Recherche et Culture: BP 907, 101 Antananarivo; tel. (20) 2226600; f. 1985; publ. by French dept of the University of Antananarivo; 2 a year; Dir GINETTE RAMAROSON; circ. 1,000.

Revue Ita: BP 681, 101 Antananarivo; tel. (20) 2230507; f. 1985; controlled by the Ministry of Population, Social Protection and Leisure; monthly; Dir FILS RAMALANJAONA; circ. 1,000.

MADAGASCAR

Revue de l'Océan Indien: Communication et Médias Océan Indien, rue H. Rabesahala, BP 46, Antsakaviro, 101 Antananarivo; tel. (20) 2222536; fax (20) 2234534; e-mail roi@dts.mg; internet www.madatours.com/roi; f. 1980; monthly; French; Man. Dir GEORGES RANAIVOSOA; Sec.-Gen. HERY M. A. RANAIVOSOA; circ. 5,000.
Sahy: Lot VD 42, Ambanidia, 101 Antananarivo; tel. (20) 2222715; f. 1957; political; Malagasy; weekly; Editor ALINE RAKOTO; circ. 9,000.
Sosialisma Mpiasa: BP 1128, 101 Antananarivo; tel. (20) 2221989; f. 1979; trade union affairs; Malagasy; monthly; Dir PAUL RABEMANANJARA; circ. 5,000.
Vaovao: BP 271, 101 Antananarivo; tel. (20) 2221193; f. 1985; French and Malagasy; weekly; Dir MARC RAKOTONOELY; circ. 5,000.

NEWS AGENCIES

Agence Nationale d'Information 'TARATRA' (ANTA): 7 rue Jean Ralaimongo, Ambohiday, BP 386, 101 Antananarivo; tel. and fax (20) 2236047; e-mail taratra.mtpc@mtpc.gov.mg; f. 1977; Man. Dir JOË ANACLET RAKOTOARISON.
Mada: Villa Joëlle, Lot II J 161 R, Ivandry, 101 Antananarivo; tel. (20) 2242428; e-mail communication@mada.mg; internet www.mada.mg; f. 2003; independent information agency; Dir RICHARD CLAUDE RATOVONARIVO.

Foreign Bureaux

Associated Press (AP) (USA): BP 73, 101 Antananarivo; tel. (20) 2241944; e-mail zadefo@malagasy.com; Correspondent (vacant).
Korean Central News Agency (KCNA) (Democratic People's Republic of Korea): 101 Antananarivo; tel. (20) 2244795; Dir KIM YEUNG KYEUN.
Xinhua (New China) News Agency (People's Republic of China): BP 1656, 101 Antananarivo; tel. (20) 2229927; Chief of Bureau WU HAIYUN.
Reuters (United Kingdom) is also represented in Madagascar.

Publishers

Edisiona Salohy: BP 4226, 101 Antananarivo; Dir MIRANA VOLOLOARISOA RANDRIANARISON.
Editions Ambozontany Analamalintsy: BP 7553, 101 Antananarivo; tel. (20) 2243111; e-mail editionsj@wanadoo.mg; f. 1962; religious, educational, historical, cultural and technical textbooks; Dir Fr GUILLAUME DE SAINT PIERRE RAKOTONANDRATONIARIVO.
Foibe Filankevitry Ny Mpampianatra (FOFIPA): BP 202, 101 Antananarivo; tel. (20) 2227500; f. 1971; textbooks; Dir Frère RAZAFINDRAKOTO.
Imprimerie Nouvelle: PK 2, Andranomahery, route de Majunga, BP 4330, 101 Antananarivo; tel. (20) 2221036; fax (20) 2269225; e-mail nouvelle@wanadoo.mg; Dir EUGÈNE RAHARIFIDY.
Imprimerie Takariva: 4 rue Radley, BP 1029, Antanimena, 101 Antananarivo; tel. (20) 2222128; f. 1933; fiction, languages, school textbooks; Man. Dir PAUL RAPATSALAHY.
Madagascar Print and Press Co (MADPRINT): rue Rabesahala, Antananarivo, BP 953, 101 Antananarivo; tel. (20) 2222536; fax (20) 2234534; f. 1969; literary, technical and historical; Dir GEORGES RANAIVOSOA.
Maison d'Edition Protestante Antso: 19 rue Venance Manifatra, Imarivolanitra, BP 660, 101 Antananarivo; tel. (20) 2220886; fax (20) 2226372; e-mail fjkm@dts.mg; f. 1972; religious, school, social, political and general; Dir HANS ANDRIAMAMPIANINA.
Nouvelle Société de Presse et d'Edition (NSPE): Immeuble Jeune Afrique, 58 rue Tsiombikibo, BP 1734, Ambatorinaky, 101 Antananarivo; tel. (20) 2227788; fax (20) 2230629.
Office du Livre Malgache: Lot 111 H29, Andrefan' Ambohijanahary, BP 617, 101 Antananarivo; tel. (20) 2224449; f. 1970; children's and general; Sec.-Gen. JULIETTE RATSIMANDRAVA.
Société Malgache d'Edition (SME): BP 659, Ankorondrano, 101 Antananarivo; tel. (20) 2222635; fax (20) 2222254; e-mail tribune@wanadoo.mg; f. 1943; general fiction, university and secondary textbooks; Man. Dir RAHAGA RAMAHOLIMIHASO.
Société Nouvelle de l'Imprimerie Centrale (SNIC): Làlana Ravoninahitriniarivo, BP 1414, 101 Antananarivo; tel. (20) 2221118; e-mail mrakotoa@wanadoo.mg; f. 1959; science, school textbooks; Man. Dir MAMY RAKOTOARIVELO.
Société de Presse et d'Edition de Madagascar: Antananarivo; non-fiction, reference, science, university textbooks; Man. Dir RAJAOFERA ANDRIAMBELO.
Trano Printy Fiangonana Loterana Malagasy (TPFLM): BP 538, 9 ave Général Gabriel Ramanantsoa, 101 Antananarivo; tel. (20) 2223340; fax (20) 2262643; e-mail impluth@wanadoo.mg; f. 1877; religious, educational and fiction; Man. RAYMOND RANDRIANATOANDRO.

GOVERNMENT PUBLISHING HOUSE

Imprimerie Nationale: BP 38, 101 Antananarivo; tel. (20) 2223675; e-mail dinm@wanadoo.mg; all official pubs; Dir JEAN DENIS RANDRIANIRINA.

Broadcasting and Communications

TELECOMMUNICATIONS

Mobile cellular telephone networks are operated by Antaris, Sacel and Telecel.

Office Malagasy d'Etudes et de Régulation des Télécommunications (OMERT): BP 99991, Route des Hydrocarbures-Alarobia, 101 Antananarivo; tel. (20) 2242119; fax (20) 2321516; e-mail omert@wanadoo.mg; internet www.omert.mg; f. 1997; Gen. Man. GILBERT ANDRIANIRINA RAJAONASY.
Madacom SA: BP 763, Bâtiments B1-B2, Explorer Business Park, Ankorondrano, 101 Antananarivo; tel. (22) 66055; fax (20) 66056; e-mail madacom@madacom.mg; internet www.madacom.com; f. 1997; mobile telecommunications GSM network provider; partly owned by Celtel International B. V. (Netherlands).
Orange Madagascar: Antananarivo; internet www.orange.mg; f. 1998; fmrly Antaris, la Société Malgache de Mobiles, name changed as above 2003; mobile telecommunication GSM network provider; market leader; Dir-Gen. PATRICE PEZAT.
Télécom Malagasy SA (TELMA): BP 763, 101 Antananarivo; tel. (20) 2242705; fax (20) 2242654; e-mail telmacorporate@telma.mg; internet www.telma.mg; 68% owned by Distacom (Hong Kong); owns DTS Wanadoo internet service provider; Chair. DAVID WHITE; Dir-Gen. EUGENE BECKERS.

BROADCASTING

Radio

In 2001 there were an estimated 127 radio stations.
Radio MBS (Malagasy Broadcasting System): BP 11137, Anosipatrana, Antananarivo; tel. (20) 2266702; fax (20) 2268941; e-mail marketing@mbs.mg; internet www.mbs.mg; broadcasts by satellite; Man. SARAH RAVALOMANANA.
Radio Nationale Malagasy: BP 442, Anosy, 101 Antananarivo; tel. (20) 2221745; fax (20) 2232715; e-mail radmad@wanadoo.mg; internet www.takelaka.dts/radmad; state-controlled; broadcasts in French and Malagasy; Dir ALAIN RAJAONA.
Le Messager Radio Evangélique: BP 1374, 101 Antananarivo; tel. (20) 2234495; broadcasts in French, English and Malagasy; Dir JOCELYN RANJARISON.
Radio Antsiva: Lot VA, BP 6323, 21 Ambohitantely, 101 Antananarivo; tel. (20) 2265789; internet www.antsiva.mg; broadcasts in French, English and Malagasy; Dir ISMAËL RAZAFINARIVO.
Radio Don Bosco: BP 60, 105 Ivato; tel. (20) 2244387; fax (20) 2244511; e-mail rdb@wanadoo.mg; internet www.radiodonbosco.mg; f. 1996; Catholic, educational and cultural; Chair. Fr GIUSEPPE MIELE.
Radio Feon'ny Vahoaka (RFV): 103 Immeuble Ramaroson, 8e étage, 101 Antananarivo; tel. (20) 2233820; broadcasts in French and Malagasy; Dir ALAIN RAMAROSON.
Radio Lazan'iarivo (RLI): Lot V A49, Andafiavaratra, 101 Antananarivo; tel. (20) 2229016; fax (20) 2267559; e-mail rli@simicro.mg; broadcasts in French, English and Malagasy; privately owned; specializes in jazz music; Dir IHOBY RABARIJOHN.
Radio Tsioka Vao (RTV): Tana; tel. (20) 2221749; f. 1992; broadcasts in French, English and Malagasy; Dir DETKOU DEDONNAIS.

Television

In 2001 there were an estimated 13 television stations.
MA TV: BP 1414 Ankorondrano, 101 Antananarivo; tel. (20) 2220897; fax (20) 2234421; e-mail matv@wanadoo.mg; internet www.matvonline.tv.
MBS Television (Malagasy Broadcasting System): BP 11137, Anosipatrana, Antananarivo; tel. (20) 2266702; fax (20) 2268941; e-mail journaltv@mbs.mg; internet www.mbs.mg; broadcasts in French and Malagasy.
Radio Télévision Analamanga (RTA): Immeuble Fiaro, 101 Antananarivo; e-mail rta@rta.mg; internet www.rta.mg; including four provincial radio stations; Dir-Gen. J. C. AUCHAN.
Télévision Nasionaly Malagasy: BP 1202, 101 Antananarivo; tel. (20) 2222381; state-controlled; broadcasts in French and Malagasy; Dir-Gen. RAZAFIMAHEFA HERININIRINA LALA.

MADAGASCAR

Finance

(cap. = capital; res = reserves; dep. = deposits; m. = million; brs = branches; amounts in Malagasy francs)

BANKING

Central Bank

Banque Centrale de Madagascar: ave de la Révolution Socialiste Malgache, BP 550, 101 Antananarivo; tel. (20) 2221751; fax (20) 2234532; e-mail banque-centrale@banque-centrale.mg; internet www.banque-centrale.mg; f. 1973; bank of issue; cap. 1,000m., res 113,997.3m., dep. 2,680,504.6m. (Dec. 2002); Gov. GASTON RAVELOJAONA.

Other Banks

Bank of Africa (BOA)—Madagascar: 2 pl. de l'Indépendance, BP 183, 101 Antananarivo; tel. (20) 2239100; fax (20) 2229408; e-mail boamg.dg@bkofafrica.com; internet www.bkofafrica.net; f. 1976 as Bankin'ny Tantsaha Mpamokatra; name changed as above 1999; 35.1% owned by African Financial Holding, 15% state-owned; commercial bank, specializes in micro-finance; cap. 40.0m., res 17.4m., dep. 2,075.7m. (Dec. 2004); Pres. PAUL DERREUMAUX; Gen. Man. ALAIN LEPATRE LAMONTAGNE; 51 brs.

Banque Internationale Chine Madagascar (BICM): 2 rue du Dr Raseta Andraharo, BP 889, 101 Antananarivo; tel. (20) 2356568; fax (20) 2356656; e-mail bicm@bicm.mg; internet www.cmb.mg; f. 2002; successor of the Compagnie Malgache de Banque; cap. 7,116.7m. (2006), res 708m., dep. 780.7m. (Dec. 2002); Dir Gen. GUY VAN ASS.

Banque Malgache de l'Océan Indien (BMOI) (Indian Ocean Malagasy Bank): pl. de l'Indépendance, BP 25 bis, Antaninarenina, 101 Antananarivo; tel. (20) 2234609; fax (20) 2234610; e-mail bmoi.st@simicro.mg; internet www.bmoi.mg; f. 1990; 75% owned by BNP Paribas SA (France); cap. 30,000m., res 105,700m., dep. 1,389,200m. (Dec. 2003); Pres. GASTON RAMENASON; Dir-Gen. JEAN-CLAUDE HERIDE; 8 brs.

Banque de Solidarité Malgache (SBM): rue Andrianary Ratianarivo Antsahavola 1, 101 Antananarivo; tel. (20) 2266607; fax (20) 2266608; e-mail sbmm@wanadoo.mg; f. 1996; 79.99% owned by SBM Global Investments Ltd, 20.01% owned by Nedbank Africa Investments Ltd (South Africa); cap. and res 20,873.4m., dep. 186,682.8m. (Dec. 2002); Chair. CHAITLALL GUNNESS; Gen. Man. KRISHNADUTT RAMBOJUN.

BFV—Société Générale: 14 Làlana Jeneraly Rabetevitra, BP 196, Antananarivo 101; tel. (20) 2220691; fax (20) 2234554; internet www.bfvsg.mg; f. 1977 as Banky Fampandrosoana ny Varotra; changed name in 1998; 70% owned by Société Générale (France) and 30% state-owned; cap. 70,000m., res 12,012.4m., dep. 938,877.3m. (Dec. 2003); Chief Exec. JEAN-PIERRE DUCROQUET; 26 brs.

BNI—Crédit Lyonnais Madagascar: 74 rue du 26 Juin 1960, BP 174, 101 Antananarivo; tel. (20) 2223951; fax (20) 2233749; e-mail info@bni.mg; internet www.bni.mg; f. 1976 as Bankin 'ny Indostria; 51% owned by Crédit Lyonnais Global Banking (France), 32.58% state-owned; cap. 13,500m., res 129,638.1m., dep. 1,800,471.3m. (Dec. 2003); Pres. and Chair. EVARISTO MARSON; Dir-Gen. DOMINIQUE TISSIER; 22 brs.

Union Commercial Bank SA (UCB): 77 rue Solombavambahoaka Frantsay, Antsahavola, BP 197, 101 Antananarivo; tel. (20) 2227262; fax (20) 2228740; e-mail ucb.int@wanadoo.mg; f. 1992; 70% owned by Mauritius Commercial Bank Ltd; cap. 6,000m., res 60,087.6m., dep. 327,141.9m. (Dec. 2002); Pres. RAYMOND HEIN; Gen. Man. MARC MARIE JOSEPH DE BOLLIVIER; 3 brs.

INSURANCE

ARO (Assurances Réassurances Omnibranches): Antsahavola, BP 42, 101 Antananarivo; tel. (20) 2220154; fax (20) 2234464; e-mail arol@wanadoo.mg; Pres. GUY ROLLAND RASOANAIVO; Dir-Gen. JIMMY RAMIANDRISON.

Assurance France-Madagascar: 7 rue Rainitovo, BP 710, 101 Antananarivo; tel. (20) 2223024; fax (20) 2269201; e-mail l.afm@wanadoo.mg; f. 1951; Dir RAKOUTH ZAFIARISOA.

Compagnie Malgache d'Assurances et de Réassurances 'Ny Havana': Immeuble 'Ny Havana', Zone des 67 Ha, BP 3881, 101 Antananarivo; tel. (20) 2226760; fax (20) 2224303; e-mail nyhavana@wanadoo.mg; f. 1968; cap. 16,050m. (1996); Dir-Gen. BERA RAZANAKOLONA.

Mutuelle d'Assurances Malagasy (MAMA): Lot 1F, 12 bis, rue Rainibetsimisaraka, Ambalavao-Isotry, BP 185, 101 Antananarivo; tel. (20) 2261882; fax (20) 2261883; f. 1965; Pres. FRÉDÉRIC RABARISON.

Société Malgache d'Assurances (SMA—ASCOMA): 13 rue Patrice Lumumba, BP 673, 101 Antananarivo; tel. (20) 2223162; fax (20) 2222785; e-mail ascoma@simicro.mg; f. 1952; Dir VIVIANE RAMANITRA.

Directory

Trade and Industry

DEVELOPMENT ORGANIZATIONS

Bureau d'Information pour les Entreprises (BIPE): Nouvel Immeuble ARO, Ampefiloha, 101 Antananarivo; tel. (20) 2230512; e-mail micdsp@wanadoo.mg; internet www.bipe.mg; part of the Ministry of Industry, Trade and the Development of the Private Sector.

Office des Mines Nationales et des Industries Stratégiques (OMNIS): 21 Làlana Razanakombana, BP 1 bis, 101 Antananarivo; tel. (20) 2224439; fax (20) 2222985; e-mail omnis@simicro.mg; f. 1976; promotes the exploration and exploitation of mining resources, in particular oil resources; Dir-Gen. ELISE ALITERA RAZAKA.

Société d'Etude et de Réalisation pour le Développement Industriel (SERDI): BP 3180, 101 Antananarivo; tel. (20) 2225204; fax (20) 2229669; e-mail serdi@wanadoo.mg; f. 1966; Dir-Gen. RAOILISON RAJAONARY.

CHAMBER OF COMMERCE

Fédération des Chambres de Commerce, d'Industrie et d'Agriculture de Madagascar: 20 rue Paul Dussac, BP 166, 101 Antananarivo; tel. (20) 2221567; 12 mem. chambers; Pres. JEAN RAMAROMISA; Chair. HENRI RAZANATSEHENO; Sec.-Gen. HUBERT RATSIANDAVANA.

Chambre de Commerce, d'Industrie, d'Artisanat et d'Agriculture—Antananarivo (CCIAA): BP 166, 20 rue Henri Razanatseheno, Antaninarenina, 101 Antananarivo; tel. (20) 2220211; fax (20) 2220213; e-mail cciaa@tana-cciaa.org; internet www.tana-cciaa.org; f. 1993.

TRADE ASSOCIATION

Société d'Intérêt National des Produits Agricoles (SINPA): BP 754, rue Fernand-Kasanga, Tsimbazaza, Antananarivo; tel. (20) 2220558; fax (20) 2220665; f. 1973; monopoly purchaser and distributor of agricultural produce; Chair. GUALBERT RAZANAJATOVO; Gen. Man. JEAN CLOVIS RALIJESY.

EMPLOYERS' ORGANIZATIONS

Groupement des Entreprises de Madagascar (GEM): Kianja MDRM sy Tia Tanindrazana, Ambohijatovo, BP 1338, 101 Antananarivo; tel. (20) 2223841; fax (20) 2221965; e-mail gem@simicro.mg; internet www.gem-madagascar.com; f. 1976; 10 nat. syndicates and five regional syndicates comprising 700 cos and 47 directly affiliated cos; Pres. NAINA ANDRIANTSITOHAINA; Sec.-Gen. ZINAH RASAMUEL RAVALOSON.

Groupement National des Exportateurs de Vanille de Madagascar (GNEV): BP 21, Antalaha; tel. (13) 20714532; fax (13) 20816017; e-mail rama.anta@sat.blueline.mg; 18 mems; Pres. JEAN GEORGES RANDRIAMIHARISOA.

Malagasy Entrepreneurs' Association (FIV.MPA.MA): Lot II, 2e étage, Immeuble Santa Antaninarenina; tel. (20) 2229292; fax (20) 2229290; e-mail fivmpama@simicro.mg; comprises 10 trade assocs, representing 200 mems, and 250 direct business mems; Chair. HERINTSALAMA RAJAONARIVELO.

Syndicat Professionel des Producteurs d'eExtraits Aromatiques, Alimentaires et Medicinaux de Madagascar (SYPEAM): Lot II M 80 bis, Antsakaviro, BP 8530, 101 Antananarivo; tel. (20) 2226934; fax (20) 2261317.

Syndicat des Industries de Madagascar (SIM): Immeuble Holcim, Lot 1 bis, Tsaralalàna; BP 1695, 101 Antananarivo; tel. (20) 2224007; fax (20) 2222518; e-mail syndusmad@wanadoo.mg; internet www.syndusmad.com; f. 1958; Chair. SAMUEL RAVELOSON; 82 mems (2006).

Syndicat des Planteurs de Café: 37 Làlana Razafimahandry, BP 173, 101 Antananarivo.

Syndicat Professionnel des Agents Généraux d'Assurances: Antananarivo; f. 1949; Pres. SOLO RATSIMBAZAFY; Sec. IHANTA RANDRIAMANDRANTO.

UTILITIES

Electricity and Water

Office de Regulation de l'Électricité (ORE): Antananarivo; f. 2004; Dir MAMY RAKOTOMIZAO.

Jiro sy Rano Malagasy (JIRAMA): BP 200, 149 rue Rainandriamampandry, Faravohitra, 101 Antananarivo; tel. (20) 2220031; fax (20) 2233806; e-mail dgjirama@wanadoo.mg; f. 1975; controls production and distribution of electricity and water; managed by Lahmeyer International (Germany) from April 2005; Chair. PATRICK RAMIARAMANANA; Dir-Gen. LAURENT CUPANI.

TRADE UNIONS

Cartel National des Organisations Syndicales de Madagascar (CARNOSYMA): BP 1035, 101 Antananarivo.

Confédération des Travailleurs Malagasy Révolutionnaires (FISEMARE): Lot IV N 76-A, Ankadifotsy, BP 1128, Befelatanana-Antananarivo 101; tel. (20) 2221989; fax (20) 2267712; f. 1985; Pres. PAUL RABEMANANJARA.

Confédération des Travailleurs Malgaches (Fivomdronamben'ny Mpiasa Malagasy—FMM): Lot IVM 133 A Antetezanafovoany I, BP 846, 101 Antananarivo; tel. (20) 2224565; f. 1957; Sec.-Gen. JEANNOT RAMANARIVO; 30,000 mems.

Fédération des Syndicats des Travailleurs de Madagascar (Firaisan'ny Sendika eran'i Madagaskara—FISEMA): Lot III, rue Pasteur Isotry, 101 Antananarivo; f. 1956; Pres. DESIRÉ RALAMBOTAHINA; Sec.-Gen. M. RAZAKANAIVO; 8 affiliated unions representing 60,000 mems.

Sendika Kristianina Malagasy (SEKRIMA) (Christian Confederation of Malagasy Trade Unions): Soarano, route de Mahajanga, BP 1035, 101 Antananarivo; tel. (20) 2223174; f. 1937; Pres. MARIE RAKOTOANOSY; Gen. Sec. RAYMOND RAKOTOARISAONA; 158 affiliated unions representing 40,000 mems.

Union des Syndicats Autonomes de Madagascar (USAM): Ampasadratsarahoby, Lot 11 H67, Faravohitra, BP 1038, 101 Antananarivo; tel. (20) 2227485; fax (20) 2222203; e-mail usam@wanadoo.mg; Pres. NORBERT RAKOTOMANANA; Sec.-Gen. VICTOR RAHAGA; 46 affiliated unions representing 30,000 mems.

Transport

RAILWAYS

In 2001 there were 893 km of railway, including four railway lines, all 1-m gauge track. The northern system, which comprised 720 km of track, links the east coast with Antsirabé, in the interior, via Moramanga and Antananarivo, with a branch line from Moramanga to Lake Alaotra and was privatized in 2001. The southern system, which comprised 163 km of track, links Manakara, on the east coast, with Fianarantsoa.

Réseau National des Chemins de Fer Malagasy (RNCFM): 1 ave de l'Indépendance, BP 259, Soarano, 101 Antananarivo; tel. (20) 2220521; fax (20) 2222288; f. 1909; in the process of transfer to private sector; Administrator DANIEL RAZAFINDRABE.

Fianarantsoa-Côte Est (FCE): FCE Gare, Fianarantsoa; tel. (20) 7551354; e-mail fce@blueline.mg; internet www.fce-madagascar.com; f. 1936; southern network, 163 km.

Madarail: Gare de Soarano, 1 ave de l'Indépendance, BP 1175, 101 Antananarivo; tel. (20) 2234599; fax (20) 2221883; e-mail madarail@wanadoo.mg; internet www.comazar.com/madarail.htm; f. 2001; joint venture, operated by Comazar, South Africa; 45% of Comazar is owned by Sheltam Locomotive and Rail Services, South Africa; 31.6% is owned by Spoornet, South Africa; operates the northern network of the Madagascan railway (650 km); Chair. ERIC PEIFFER; Gen. Dir PATRICK CLAES; 878 employees.

ROADS

In 2001 there were an estimated 49,837 km of classified roads; about 11.6% of the road network was paved. In 1987 there were 39,500 km of unclassified roads, used only in favourable weather. A road and motorway redevelopment programme, funded by the World Bank (€300m.) and the European Union (EU—€61m.), began in June 2000. In August 2002 the EU undertook to disburse US $10m. for the reconstruction of 11 bridges destroyed during the political crisis in that year. In 2003 Japan pledged $28m. to build several bridges and a 15-km bypass. The Government planned to have restored and upgraded 14,000 km of highways and 8,000 km of rural roads to an operational status by 2008.

INLAND WATERWAYS

The Pangalanes Canal runs for 600 km near the east coast from Toamasina to Farafangana. In 1990 432 km of the canal between Toamasina and Mananjary were navigable.

SHIPPING

There are 18 ports, the largest being at Toamasina, which handles about 70% of total traffic, and Mahajanga; several of the smaller ports are prone to silting problems. In 1987 Madagascar received foreign loans totalling US $34.8m., including a credit of $16m. from the World Bank, to finance a project to rehabilitate 10 ports. A new deep-sea port was to be constructed at Ehoala, near Fort Dauphin, in order to accommodate the activity of an ilmenite mining development by 2008.

CMA—CGM: BP 12042, Village des jeux, Bat. C1 Ankorondrano, 101 Antananarivo; tel. (20) 2235949; fax (20) 2266120; e-mail tnr@cma-cgm.mg; maritime transport; Gen. Man. PHILIPPE MURCIA.

Compagnie Générale Maritime Sud (CGM): BP 1185, lot II U 31 bis, Ampahibe, 101 Antananarivo; tel. (20) 2220113; fax (20) 2226530.

Compagnie Malgache de Navigation (CMN): rue Rabearivelo, BP 1621, 101 Antananarivo; tel. (20) 2225516; fax (20) 2230358; f. 1960; coasters; 13,784 grt; 97.5% state-owned; privatization pending; Pres. ELINAH BAKOLY RAJAONSON; Dir-Gen. ARISTIDE EMMANUEL.

SCAC-SDV Shipping Madagascar: rue Rabearivelo Antsahavola, BP 514, 102 Antananarivo; tel. (20) 2220631; fax (20) 2247862; operates the harbour in Antananarivo Port.

Société Malgache des Transports Maritimes (SMTM): 6 rue Indira Gandhi, BP 4077, 101 Antananarivo; tel. (20) 2227342; fax (20) 2233327; f. 1963; 59% state-owned; privatization pending; services to Europe; Chair. ALEXIS RAZAFINDRATSIRA; Dir-Gen. JEAN RANJEVA.

CIVIL AVIATION

The Ivato international airport is at Antananarivo, while the airports at Mahajanga, Toamasina and Nossi-Bé can also accommodate large jet aircraft. There are 211 airfields, two-thirds of which are privately owned. In 1996 the Government invited tenders for a rehabilitation project, which was to include nine of the major airports. Later that year the Government authorized private French airlines to operate scheduled and charter flights between Madagascar and Western Europe.

Aviation Civile de Madagascar (ACM): BP 4414, 101 Tsimbazaza-Antananarivo; tel. (20) 2222162; fax (20) 2224726; e-mail acm@acm.mg; Pres. NARIFERA RAOBANITRA; Dir-Gen. FRANÇOIS XAVIER RANDRIAMAHANDRY.

Société Nationale Malgache des Transports Aériens (Air Madagascar): 31 ave de l'Indépendance, Analakely, BP 437, 101 Antananarivo; tel. (20) 2222222; fax (20) 2225728; e-mail commercial@airmadagascar.com; internet www.airmadagascar.mg; f. 1962; 89.58% state-owned; transfer to the private sector pending; managed by Lufthansa Consulting since 2002; extensive internal routes connecting all the principal towns; external services to France, Italy, the Comoros, Kenya, Mauritius, Réunion, South Africa and Thailand; Pres. HERINIAINA RAZAFIMAHEFA; Chief Exec. BEREND BRUNS.

Transports et Travaux Aériens de Madagascar (TAM): 17 ave de l'Indépendance, Analakely, Antananarivo; tel. (20) 2222222; fax (20) 2224340; e-mail tamdg@wanadoo.mg; f. 1951; provides airline services; Administrators LALA RAZAFINDRAKOTO, FRANÇOIS DANE.

Tourism

Madagascar's attractions include unspoiled scenery, many unusual varieties of flora and fauna, and the rich cultural diversity of Malagasy life. In 2003 some 139,000 tourists visited Madagascar. Revenue from tourism in that year was estimated at US $118m. The number of hotel rooms increased from some 3,040 in 1991 to an estimated 8,435 in 2001.

Direction d'Appui aux Investissements Publiques: Ministry of Culture and Tourism, BP 610, rue Fernand Kasanga Tsimbazaza, 101 Antananarivo; tel. (20) 2262816; fax (20) 2235410; e-mail mintourdati@wandaoo.mg; internet www.tourisme.gov.mg.

La Maison du Tourisme de Madagascar: place de l'Indépendance, BP 3224, 101 Antananarivo; tel. (20) 2235178; fax (20) 2269522; e-mail mtm@simicro.mg; internet www.tourisme.madagascar.com; Exec. Dir ANDRÉ ANDRIAMBOAVONJY.

MALAWI

Introductory Survey

Location, Climate, Language, Religion, Flag, Capital

The Republic of Malawi is a land-locked country in southern central Africa, with Zambia to the west, Mozambique to the south and east, and Tanzania to the north. Lake Malawi forms most of the eastern boundary. The climate is tropical, but much of the country is sufficiently high above sea-level to modify the heat. Temperatures range from 14°C (57°F) to 18°C (64°F) in mountain areas, but can reach 38°C (100°F) in low-lying regions. There is a rainy season between November and April. The official language is English, although Chichewa is being promoted as the basis for a 'Malawi Language'. Chitumbuka, a national language, and Yao are also widely spoken. More than 70% of the population profess Christianity, while a further 20%, largely Asians, are Muslims. Most of the remaining Malawians follow traditional beliefs, although there is also a Hindu minority. The national flag (proportions 2 by 3) has three equal horizontal stripes, of black, red and green, with a rising sun, in red, in the centre of the black stripe. The capital is Lilongwe.

Recent History

Malawi was formerly the British protectorate of Nyasaland. In 1953 it was linked with two other British dependencies, Northern and Southern Rhodesia (now Zambia and Zimbabwe), to form the Federation of Rhodesia and Nyasaland. Elections in August 1961 gave the Malawi Congress Party (MCP), led by Dr Hastings Kamuzu Banda, a majority of seats in the Legislative Council. Dr Banda became Prime Minister in February 1963, and the Federation was dissolved in December. Nyasaland gained independence, as Malawi, on 6 July 1964. The country became a republic and a one-party state, with Banda as its first President, on 6 July 1966. Malawi created a major controversy among African states in 1967 by officially recognizing the Republic of South Africa. In 1971 Banda, named Life President in that year, became the first African head of state to visit South Africa. In 1976, however, Malawi recognized the communist-backed Government in Angola in preference to the South African-supported forces. Malawi did not recognize the 'independence' granted by South Africa to four of its African 'homelands'.

Until 1993 all Malawian citizens were obliged to be members of the MCP; no political opposition was tolerated, and only candidates who had been approved by Banda were allowed to contest elections to the National Assembly.

Frequent reorganizations of the Cabinet effectively prevented the emergence of any political rival to Banda. However, it was reported in 1983 that a conflict had developed between Dick Matenje, the Minister without Portfolio in the Cabinet and Secretary-General of the MCP, and John Tembo, the Governor of the Reserve Bank of Malawi, concerning the eventual succession to Banda. In May the authorities reported that Matenje and three other senior politicians had died in a road accident; Malawian exiles claimed that the four men had been shot while attempting to flee the country.

Opposition to the Government intensified during 1992: in March Malawi's Roman Catholic bishops published an open letter criticizing the Government's alleged abuses of human rights. In April Chakufwa Chihana, a prominent trade union leader who had demanded multi-party elections, was arrested. In July Chihana was charged with sedition, and in August the police detained 11 church leaders and prohibited a planned rally by pro-democracy supporters. In September opposition activists formed the Alliance for Democracy (AFORD), a pressure group operating within Malawi, under the chairmanship of Chihana, which aimed to campaign for democratic political reform. Another opposition grouping, the United Democratic Front (UDF), was formed in October. In that month Banda conceded that a referendum on the introduction of a multi-party system would take place. However, in November the Government banned AFORD. In the following month Chihana was found guilty of sedition and sentenced to two years' hard labour (reduced to nine months' in March 1993).

At the referendum on the introduction of a multi-party system, held on 14 June 1993, 63.2% of those who participated (some 63.5% of the electorate) voted for an end to single-party rule.

Banda rejected opposition demands for the immediate installation of an interim government of national unity. He agreed, however, to the establishment of a National Executive Council to oversee the transition to a multi-party system and the holding of free elections, and of a National Consultative Council to implement the necessary amendments to the Constitution. Both councils were to include members of the Government and the opposition. Banda announced an amnesty for thousands of political exiles, and stated that a general election would be held, on a multi-party basis, within a year. In late June the Constitution was amended to allow the registration of political parties other than the MCP: by mid-August five organizations, including AFORD and the UDF, had been accorded official status.

In September 1993 Banda carried out an extensive cabinet reshuffle, relinquishing the post of Minister of External Affairs, which he had held since 1964. In October 1993 Banda underwent neurological surgery in South Africa. Interim executive power was assumed by a three-member Presidential Council, chaired by the new Secretary-General of the MCP, Gwandaguluwe Chakuamba. The two other members, Tembo and the Minister of Transport and Communications, Robson Chirwa, were also senior MCP officials. In November 1993 a further cabinet reshuffle relieved Banda of all ministerial responsibilities. Later in November the National Assembly approved a Constitutional Amendment Bill, which, *inter alia*, abolished the institution of life presidency, ended the requirement that election candidates be members of the MCP, repealed the right of the President to nominate members of the legislature exclusively from the MCP, and lowered the minimum voting age from 21 to 18 years.

Having made a rapid and unexpected recovery, Banda resumed full presidential powers in December 1993. Shortly afterwards, in response to increasing pressure from the opposition, the Government amended the Constitution to provide for the appointment of an acting President in the event of the incumbent's being incapacitated. In February 1994 the MCP announced that Banda was to be the party's presidential candidate in the forthcoming general election (scheduled for May); Chakuamba was named as the MCP's candidate for the vice-presidency. Also in February the National Assembly approved an increase in the number of elective seats in the legislature from 141 to 177.

Meanwhile, the MCP announced in September 1993 that members of the Malawi Young Pioneers (MYP), a notorious paramilitary section of the ruling party, were to be gradually disarmed. In December, following the murder of three soldiers by MYP members, the regular army acted to close MYP offices and camps. In the ensuing violence, exacerbated by long-standing tensions between the army and the MYP, 32 people were reported to have been killed. Banda appointed a Minister of Defence (having hitherto held personal responsibility for defence) to oversee the MYP disarmament process and investigate army grievances. By early 1994 the authorities stated that the disarmament had been satisfactorily completed; it was known, however, that several thousand MYP members had crossed the border into Mozambique to take refuge in rebel bases. In January the Governments of Malawi and Mozambique agreed to a programme for the repatriation of MYP members. In the following month the MYP was officially disbanded, although it was subsequently reported that many armed MYP members remained in hiding in Mozambique (see below).

On 16 May 1994 the National Assembly adopted a provisional Constitution, which provided for the appointment of a Constitutional Committee and of a human rights commission, and abolished the system of 'traditional' courts. Malawi's first multi-party parliamentary and presidential elections took place on 17 May. In the presidential election the Secretary-General of the UDF, (Elson) Bakili Muluzi (a former government minister and MCP Secretary-General), took 47.3% of the votes cast, defeating Banda (who won 33.6% of the votes). Eight parties contested the legislative elections: of these, the UDF won 85 seats in the National Assembly, the MCP 56 and AFORD 36. The distribution of seats was strongly influenced by regional affiliations, with

AFORD winning all of the Northern Region's seats, and the MCP and UDF particularly successful in the Central and Southern Regions, respectively. The Constitution was introduced for a one-year period on 18 May; it was to be subject to further review prior to official ratification one year later.

President Muluzi and his Vice-President, Justin Malewezi, were inaugurated on 21 May 1994. The new UDF-dominated Government proclaimed an amnesty for the country's remaining political prisoners, and commuted all death sentences to terms of life imprisonment. Attempts to recruit members of AFORD into a coalition administration failed, owing to disagreements regarding the allocation of senior portfolios, and in June AFORD and the MCP agreed to function as an opposition front. The Muluzi Government was thus deprived of a majority in the National Assembly, which was inaugurated at the end of June. In August it was announced that Banda, while remaining honorary Life President of the MCP, was to retire from active involvement in politics. Chakuamba, as Vice-President of the party, effectively became the leader of the MCP.

In September 1994 a number of AFORD members were appointed to the Government, including Chihana as Second Vice-President and Minister of Irrigation and Water Development. In January 1995 AFORD announced an end to its co-operation with the MCP. Meanwhile, the creation of the post of Second Vice-President had necessitated a constitutional amendment, and provoked severe criticism from the MCP. Moreover, the National Constitutional Conference recommended that the post be abolished. In March, however, the National Assembly (in the absence of MCP deputies, who boycotted the vote) approved the retention of the second vice-presidency; the Assembly also endorsed recommendations for the establishment—although not before May 1999—of a second chamber of parliament. The Constitution took effect on 18 May 1995.

In June 1994 Muluzi established an independent commission of inquiry to investigate the deaths of Matenje and his associates in May 1983. In January 1995, in accordance with the findings of the commission, Banda was placed under house arrest and Tembo and two former police-officers were detained; the four were charged with murder and conspiracy to murder. A former inspector-general of police was charged later in the month. In April Cecilia Kadzamira, Tembo's niece and the former President's 'Official Hostess', was charged with conspiracy to murder and was subsequently released on bail. The trial opened later that month, but was immediately adjourned, owing to Banda's failure to appear in court (his defence counsel asserted that he was too ill to stand trial) and to the failure of the state prosecution to submit certain evidence to the defence. Hearings resumed, in Banda's absence, in July. In September Tembo and the two former police-officers were granted bail, and most restrictions on Banda's movements were ended. The case against Kadzamira was abandoned in December, owing to lack of evidence, and later that month Banda, Tembo and the other defendants were found not guilty of conspiracy to murder and conspiracy to defeat justice. In January 1996 an MCP-owned newspaper printed a statement by Banda in which he admitted that he might unknowingly have been responsible for brutalities perpetrated under his regime and apologized to Malawians for 'pain and suffering' inflicted during his presidency.

In July 1995 lawyers acting for Banda demanded that Muluzi explain the apparent payment of a substantial sum to a witness in the trial of Banda and his associates. Meanwhile, there were further allegations that the Muluzi administration had been involved in dubious financial transactions. It emerged, in mid-1995, that the President had authorized the payment of some 6.2m. kwacha from the state poverty alleviation account to UDF deputies (to enable the payment of loans to their constituents); there was also evidence of the involvement of government ministers in the smuggling of maize to neighbouring countries. An investigation of Banda's financial interests was initiated in September. In February 1996 Muluzi announced that an independent Anti-Corruption Bureau (ACB) was to be established to investigate allegations of corruption.

In July 1995 the UDF and AFORD signed a formal co-operation agreement. In December, however, Chihana warned that AFORD might withdraw from the coalition Government, alleging that the UDF was using public funds to secure political influence, and complaining of a lack of openness in the Muluzi administration. Chihana resigned from the Government in May 1996, expressing his intention to devote himself more fully to the work of his party. The post of Second Vice-President remained vacant following a subsequent reorganization of the Cabinet. In June AFORD withdrew from its coalition with the UDF, declared that remaining AFORD ministers should resign, and appointed a 'shadow cabinet'. Five members were dismissed from AFORD's National Executive, and another was suspended, having refused to relinquish their ministerial posts. AFORD and the MCP insisted that AFORD ministers should be regarded as members of the UDF. The rejection of this demand resulted in a parliamentary boycott by both opposition parties. At the beginning of December the AFORD ministers remaining in the Cabinet asserted that they were independent and had not joined the UDF. In March 1997 AFORD stated that the party would continue its boycott until the ministers resigned both their government posts and parliamentary seats. In April the MCP and AFORD ended their parliamentary boycott, following a meeting with Muluzi at which he had allegedly promised to amend the Constitution to prevent parliamentary delegates from changing their political affiliation without standing for re-election.

In January 1997 it was announced that Banda was to be charged with embezzling state funds for the establishment of a private school; however, in May he was discharged as unfit to attend court and in July Muluzi reportedly requested that all criminal cases against Banda be discontinued. Also in July Banda announced his intention to resign as President of the MCP. In November Banda died in South Africa, where he had been undergoing emergency medical treatment. He was accorded a state funeral, with full military honours.

In June 1998 the National Assembly approved legislation providing for the introduction of a single-ballot electoral system to replace the existing multiple-ballot system and for a strengthening of the authority and independence of the Malawi Electoral Commission (MEC). In November legislation was adopted to allow presidential and parliamentary elections to run concurrently (as Muluzi's term was due to end several weeks earlier than that of the National Assembly), and the elections were subsequently scheduled for 18 May 1999. An electoral alliance between the MCP and AFORD, which was officially announced in February 1999, created serious divisions within the MCP, when the party's leader and presidential candidate, Chakuamba, chose Chihana, the leader of AFORD, as the candidate for the vice-presidency, in preference to Tembo. Thousands of Tembo's supporters were reported to have mounted protests to demand Chakuamba's resignation. The Chakuamba-Chihana partnership also provoked a wider dispute with the UDF and the MEC, which claimed that the arrangement was unconstitutional. In February the National Assembly adopted a controversial report by the MEC that recommended the creation of a further 72 parliamentary seats, including an additional 42 in the Southern Region, a UDF stronghold. In response to widespread opposition to the proposals, however, only 16 of the 72 seats were approved.

Having been postponed twice, the presidential and legislative elections were held on 15 June 1999. Muluzi was re-elected to the presidency, securing 51.37% of the votes cast, while Chakuamba obtained 43.30%. Turn-out was high, with some 93.8% of registered voters reported to have participated. At the elections to the expanded National Assembly the ruling UDF won 94 seats, while the MCP secured 66 seats, AFORD 29 and independent candidates four. Despite declarations from international observers that the elections were largely free and fair, the MCP-AFORD alliance filed two petitions with the High Court, challenging Muluzi's victory and the results in 16 districts. The opposition alleged irregularities in the voter registration process and claimed that Muluzi's victory was unconstitutional, as he had failed to gain the support of 50% of all registered voters. None the less, Muluzi was inaugurated later in June, and a new Cabinet was appointed. In mid-August the UDF regained a parliamentary majority when the four independent deputies decided to ally themselves with the UDF, of which they had previously been members.

Chakuamba, who had maintained a boycott of the new parliament pending the result of his party's challenge to the outcome of the elections, was suspended from the chamber in June 2000. Tembo assumed the leadership of the opposition and appointed his supporters to prominent posts within the MCP. Chakuamba was reinstated in September, and a dispute between the two factions ensued. In October the opposition's petitions against the election results were dismissed by the High Court.

Muluzi reorganized the Cabinet in March 2000 and again in August, following the resignation of a deputy minister who had been charged with manslaughter. In November, following these and other allegations of corruption made against several ministers, Muluzi dismissed the entire Cabinet and announced direct presidential rule, before appointing a new administration some days later.

The country's first multi-party local elections were held in November 2000. The MCP was disqualified from contesting a number of wards where both factions of the party had submitted nominations. Amid allegations of electoral malpractice, the UDF secured victory in 610 of the 860 contested wards, AFORD winning 120 seats and the MCP 84.

In January 2001 deputies from the Tembo faction of the MCP ensured the approval by the National Assembly of a UDF proposal to abandon plans (ostensibly for financial reasons) for the creation of a second legislative chamber, the Senate, which would have had powers to impeach the President; AFORD boycotted the vote. In March 2001 six people were arrested and charged with treason for allegedly planning a coup against Muluzi; the leader of the plot was said to be Sudi Sulaimana, a political activist who had previously been arrested in 1993 for attempting to overthrow Banda. However, Chakuamba claimed that the Government had fabricated the plot in order to curb the activities of its political opponents. In October the leader of the opposition National Democratic Alliance (NDA), Brown Mpinganjira, was arrested and charged with treason for alleged involvement in the March coup attempt, but was released after a court ruled that his detention was unconstitutional. Meanwhile, in June, at a rally in Lilongwe, 37 of the 41 MCP district chairmen publicly endorsed Tembo as their new leader, declaring that they had lost confidence in Chakuamba; however, the latter dismissed the significance of the endorsement. In November seven deputies who had joined the NDA were excluded from the National Assembly for abandoning the political parties for which they had been elected, an action proscribed by law since May, when the UDF acted to prevent defections to the NDA; Sam Mpasu, the Speaker, defied an order of the High Court restraining him from expelling the deputies.

In January 2002 Muluzi effected a minor cabinet reshuffle. In the meantime, negotiations between Chihana and Muluzi on the possible formation of a government of national unity had created divisions within AFORD. The minister responsible for poverty alleviation, Leonard Mangulama, was dismissed in August after a report was published implicating him in the sale of emergency maize reserves to Kenya when Minister of Agriculture and Irrigation Development. A minor reorganization of ministerial portfolios took place in September. In the same month it was reported that Mpinganjira had fled the country following the murder of a supporter of the UDF in late August.

Proposed legislation to change the Constitution to allow Muluzi to seek a third presidential term failed to gain the requisite support of two-thirds of the members of the National Assembly in July 2002. A further attempt to introduce a constitutional amendment also failed in January 2003, when the bill was withdrawn. The UDF declared that it would hold a referendum on the issue later in the year. However, in late March Muluzi declared that he would not seek a third presidential term, and proposed Dr Bingu wa Mutharika, recently appointed Minister of Economic Planning and Development, as his successor, to contest the presidential election scheduled for May 2004. (Mutharika had represented the United Party at the 1999 presidential election, but subsequently defected to the UDF.) In early April 2003 Muluzi dismissed his entire Cabinet, apparently without explanation. However, several ministers reported that Muluzi had imposed the appointment of Mutharika on the party without sufficient consultation, and suggested that they had been dismissed for expressing opposition to the President's decision; Muluzi appointed a new administration later that month.

In May 2003, at a party convention in Blantyre that was disrupted by violent incidents, Tembo and Chakuamba, were elected, respectively, as President and Vice-President of the MCP. Tembo was subsequently named as the MCP's candidate to contest the 2004 presidential election. Chakuamba subsequently resigned from the MCP and formed the Republican Party (RP). On 1 January 2004 Justin Malewezi, Malawi's First Vice-President and Minister responsible for Privatization, announced his resignation from the UDF for 'personal reasons'. He did not, however, relinquish his position in the Government, stating that he would remain in office, but on leave, until after the presidential election had taken place. One week after leaving the UDF Malewezi joined the People's Progressive Movement (PPM), an opposition party founded in April 2003. Later in January 2004 Aleke Banda, who had resigned from the UDF in May 2003, was elected as President of the PPM, while Malewezi was chosen as its Vice-President.

In February 2004 the Government initiated legal proceedings aimed at having Malewezi's position within the Cabinet declared vacant on the grounds that he had resigned as Vice-President 'by implication or by his own conduct'. Meanwhile, in late January several opposition parties, including the PPM and the RP, announced their formation of the Mgwirizano Coalition to contest the forthcoming presidential election; Chakuamba was elected as the coalition's presidential candidate in February. Malewezi subsequently announced that he would contest the election as an independent. A minor cabinet reshuffle was effected in late February, and Muluzi appointed Hetherwick Ntaba, the leader of the New Congress for Democracy (NCD), as Minister of Energy and Mining at the end of March, following the NCD's decision to join the UDF-AFORD electoral alliance. Presidential and legislative elections were to take place on 18 May, but were subsequently postponed, in compliance with a judicial ruling, until 20 May after the opposition lodged complaints of irregularities in the voters' register.

At the presidential election held on 20 May 2004 Mutharika, representing the ruling UDF, secured 35.9% of the valid votes cast, according to official results. Tembo, of the MCP, and Chakuamba, representing the Mgwirizano Coalition, took 27.1% and 25.7% of the vote, respectively. Cassim Chilumpha, of the UDF, was elected as Vice-President. At concurrent elections to the National Assembly, however, the MCP emerged as the largest party, winning 56 of the 193 seats in the legislature, while the UDF gained 49 seats and the Mgwirizano Coalition 25; 39 of the remaining seats were taken by independent candidates, while voting in six constituencies was not conducted owing to irregularities. International observers criticized the conduct of the polls and opposition parties disputed the results. Mutharika was sworn in as President on 24 May amid rioting by opposition supporters. The Mgwirizano Coalition lodged a court appeal challenging the result of the presidential election, however, in February 2005 the group withdrew the appeal. The new Cabinet, appointed in mid-June 2004, comprised 21 ministers, compared with 32 under the previous administration. Mutharika, in defiance of critics who believed he would merely serve to act as Muluzi's 'puppet', pledged to take measures to combat corruption and to effect wide-ranging economic reforms. In late October the former Minister of Finance, Friday Jumbe, was arrested in connection with illegal sales of maize during 2001–02 (see above) when he held the position of General Manager of the Agriculture Development and Marketing Corporation; he was subsequently charged with four counts of corruption. The Director of Public Prosecutions, Ishmael Wadi, also announced in October 2004 that at least ten former senior ministers were under investigation by the ACB following the disappearance of more than 10,000m. kwacha during the Muluzi presidency. The investigation was ongoing in early 2006.

In early January 2005 three members of the UDF were arrested for attempting to enter the presidential palace carrying handguns, prior to a scheduled meeting with Mutharika. The three were suspected of being part of an assassination plot and were charged with treason; however, the men were later pardoned by Mutharika and released. (Ministers were legally permitted to carry weapons for protection.) Mutharika subsequently ordered the dissolution of the National Intelligence Bureau (NIB), according to official explanations, for restructuring. It was believed that the NIB remained sympathetic to Muluzi and thus undermined the new President.

In early February 2005 Mutharika resigned from the leadership of the UDF—of which Muluzi was Chairman—claiming that the party was opposing his campaign against corruption. Prior to the announcement, Mutharika dismissed three members of the Government loyal to Muluzi, including the Minister of Labour, Lilian Patel, and Chihana, who was replaced as Minister of Agriculture, Irrigation and Food Security by Chakuamba. Later that month Mutharika announced his intention to form a new political party, the Democratic Progressive Party (DPP), which was formally registered in mid-March. In late May the Minister of Education and Human Resources, Yusuf Mwawa, was arrested on charges of corruption, fraud and misuse of public funds. He was replaced by the former Secretary-General of the MCP, Kate Kainja Kaluluma. (In February 2006 Mwawa was sentenced to five years' imprisonment.) Meanwhile, in late June 2005 the UDF introduced before the National Assembly a motion of impeachment against Mutharika, alleging statutory violations of the Constitution and misuse of public funds. The session was suspended following the collapse of the Speaker, Rodwell Munyenyembe, who died several days later. Louis Chimango of the MCP was elected as Speaker in early July and the impeachment debate resumed later that month.

In late July 2005 Mutharika faced criticism for increasing the size of the Cabinet from 27 members to 33. A new Ministry of Irrigation and Water Development was created, headed by Chakuamba, while the streamlined agriculture and food security portfolio was awarded to Uladi Mussa, who was replaced as Minister of Home Affairs and Internal Security by Anna Kachikho. In early September Sidik Mia replaced Chakuamba at the Ministry of Irrigation and Water Development. Chakuamba was dismissed in advance of an investigation by the ACB over misuse of World Bank funds; he was arrested later that month for allegedly slandering the President at a rally for the RP.

In October 2005 Muluzi was summoned to appear before the ACB, which was investigating the misappropriation of 1,400m. kwacha in foreign aid during his presidency. It was alleged that much of this money had been diverted to personal bank accounts and had also been used to finance the 2004 presidential campaign. Muluzi was able to obtain an injunction from the High Court against answering the ACB's questions. However, later that month police and ACB officers raided three properties belonging to Muluzi, confiscating computer equipment and banking documents. In November Vice-President Chilumpha was arrested in connection with the alleged embezzlement of 187m. kwacha during his tenure as Minister of Education. However, Chilumpha obtained an injunction against criminal proceedings being initiated against him on the grounds that as the incumbent Vice-President he was immune from prosecution.

Following an agreement between the UDF and Tembo, in mid-October 2005 the National Assembly voted in favour of beginning proceedings to impeach Mutharika. Envoys from several donor countries (including the United Kingdom, the USA and South Africa) were signatories to a letter to the opposition requesting them to reconsider their decision in the interests of the country at large. Despite their appeal Mutharika was summoned to face indictment before the National Assembly later that month. However, the impeachment process was halted by the High Court after concern was expressed over the constitutionality of the process. At by-elections in December (following the deaths of five UDF members of the National Assembly and the conviction of a sixth) the DPP won all six seats suggesting that there was general support for Mutharika among the populace. Later that month, in South Africa, former regional heads of state—Nelson Mandela of South Africa, Joachim Chissano of Mozambique and Sir Ketumile Masire of Botswana—brokered talks between Mutharika, Muluzi and Tembo in an attempt to halt the impeachment proceedings, however they ended without success.

The impeachment motion was eventually withdrawn in late January 2006 prompting the resignation of seven UDF members, five of whom subsequently joined the DPP. The next session of Parliament, scheduled for February, was postponed owing to the continuing food crisis (see below) as it was believed that the allocated budget would be more beneficial to ongoing relief efforts. (Expenditure on the previous four-week session had amounted to 56m. kwacha and had been largely occupied with the failed impeachment proceedings.) In early February it was announced that Mutharika had accepted Chilumpha's 'constructive resignation'. In a letter to Chilumpha the President asserted that Chilumpha had abandoned his duties as Vice-President, leading the Cabinet to conclude that he had resigned. Chilumpha refuted the allegations made against him—inter alia, that he had only attended 16 out of 48 cabinet meetings and had left the country without informing Mutharika—and brought the matter before the High Court on the grounds that his dismissal was unconstitutional: as an elected minister he could only be dismissed by Parliament, not by the President. In March the High Court apparently ordered Chilumpha's full restitution; however, the Supreme Court ruled later that month that although Chilumpha was confirmed in his position as Vice-President the Government was permitted to strip him of all benefits and entitlements. In late April Chilumpha was arrested and charged with treason and conspiring to murder the President.

Despite being the only African country to have maintained full diplomatic relations with South Africa during the apartheid era, Malawi joined the Southern African Development Co-ordination Conference (subsequently the Southern African Development Community, see p. 358—SADC), which originally aimed to reduce the dependence of southern African countries on South Africa.

Relations with Mozambique were frequently strained during the early and mid-1980s by the widely held belief that the Banda regime was supporting the Resistência Nacional Moçambicana (Renamo—see the chapter on Mozambique). Following the death of President Machel of Mozambique in an air crash in South Africa in October 1986, the South African Government claimed that documents discovered in the wreckage revealed a plot by Mozambique and Zimbabwe to overthrow the Banda Government. Angry protests from Malawi were answered by denials of the accusations from the Mozambican and Zimbabwean Governments. In December, however, Malawi and Mozambique signed an agreement on defence and security matters, which was believed to include co-operation in eliminating Renamo operations. In July 1988, during an official visit to Malawi, President Chissano of Mozambique stated that he did not believe Malawi to be supporting Renamo. In December of that year Malawi, Mozambique and the office of the UN High Commissioner for Refugees (UNHCR) signed an agreement to promote the voluntary repatriation of an estimated 650,000 Mozambican refugees who had fled into Malawi during the previous two years. However, by mid-1992 the number of Mozambican refugees in Malawi had reportedly reached 1m. Large numbers of refugees returned to Mozambique in 1993–94, but in May 1995 Malawi demanded the repatriation of the remainder—estimated to total some 39,000—stating that food aid and other assistance to those who failed to leave would be reduced. The programme of the Malawi-Mozambique-UNHCR commission officially ended in November: it was estimated that a total of 1m. refugees had been repatriated. None the less, the continued presence of more than 2,000 MYP members in Mozambique (many of whom were said to have been harboured in Renamo bases) remained a cause of concern. In October it was announced that the two countries were to establish a commission to locate renegade MYP members and persuade them to return to Malawi.

Government

The Head of State is the President, who is elected by universal adult suffrage, in the context of a multi-party political system, for a term of five years. Executive power is vested in the President, and legislative power in the National Assembly, which has 193 elective seats. Members of the Assembly are elected for five years, by universal adult suffrage, in the context of a multi-party system. Cabinet ministers are appointed by the President. The country is divided into three administrative regions (Northern, Central and Southern), sub-divided into 24 districts.

Defence

Malawi's active defence forces in August 2005 comprised a land army of 5,300, a marine force of 220 and an air force of 200; all form part of the army. There was also a paramilitary police force of 1,500. Projected budgetary expenditure on defence was 1,500m. kwacha in 2005.

Economic Affairs

In 2004, according to estimates by the World Bank, Malawi's gross national income (GNI), measured at average 2002–04 prices, was US $1,922m., equivalent to $170 per head (or $620 per head on an international purchasing-power parity basis). During 1995–2004, it was estimated, the population increased at an average annual rate of 2.2%, while gross domestic product (GDP) per head increased, in real terms, by an average of 0.6% per year. Overall GDP increased, in real terms, at an average annual rate of 2.8% in 1995–2004; real GDP increased by 3.8% in 2004.

Measured at constant 1994 prices, agriculture (including forestry and fishing) contributed 37.7% of GDP in 2004, and engaged an estimated 81.7% of the labour force in 2003. The principal cash crops are tobacco (which accounted for 42.4% of total export earnings in 2004), tea and sugar cane. The principal food crops are cassava, potatoes, maize, pulses, bananas and groundnuts. Periods of severe drought and flooding have necessitated imports of basic foods in recent years (see below). During 1995–2004, according to the World Bank, agricultural GDP increased at an average annual rate of 6.3%; growth in agricultural GDP was 4.0% in 2004.

Industry (including manufacturing, mining, construction and power) contributed 16.1% of GDP in 2004 at constant 1994 prices, and engaged 4.5% of the employed labour force in 1998. During 1995–2004, according to the World Bank, industrial GDP increased by an average of 0.7% per year. Industrial GDP increased by 5.1% in 2004.

Mining and quarrying contributed 0.9% of GDP in 2004, at constant 1994 prices, and engaged less than 0.1% of the employed labour force in 1998. Limestone, coal and gemstones are mined, and there are plans to develop deposits of bauxite, high-calcium marble and graphite. There are also reserves of phosphates, uranium, glass sands, asbestos and vermiculite. In August 2000 an Australian company announced its intention to establish a uranium mine in northern Malawi, near the border with Tanzania; it was anticipated that production would commence in 2005. Environmental and financial concerns have delayed plans to exploit an estimated 30m. metric tons of bauxite deposits at Mount Mulanje. The GDP of the mining sector increased at an average annual rate of 15.1% in 1994–2003, according to official figures; mining GDP increased by 18.6% in 2003, but decreased by 12.1% in 2004.

Measured at constant 1994 prices, manufacturing contributed 11.07% of GDP in 2004, and engaged 2.7% of the employed labour force in 1998. During 1995–2004, according to the World Bank, manufacturing GDP decreased by an average of 1.1% per year. However, manufacturing GDP increased by 0.7% in 2003 and by 4.1% in 2004.

Production of electrical energy is by hydroelectric (principally) and thermal installations. Some 90% of energy for domestic use is derived from fuel wood. In October 1997 an agreement was signed to link Malawi's electricity system to the Cahora Bassa hydroelectric dam in Mozambique, but completion of the project was not expected until 2006. In October 2000 a hydroelectric power plant, with a generation capacity of 64 MW, was opened at Kapichira. In 2003 full capacity of Malawi's hydroelectric power plants was 240 MW. However, as a result of flooding at the Nkula plant in March overall capacity was reduced to 140 MW and power was rationed until June. In January 2001 the Government introduced a campaign to widen access to electricity, especially in rural areas; in 2005 it was reported that only 4% of Malawians had access to electricity. By October 2004 five coalfields had been identified in Malawi with estimated reserves of 20m. metric tons and probable reserves of up to 750m. tons; at that time there was only one coal producer in Malawi, which mainly supplied domestic manufacturers. Imports of fuel comprised an estimated 11.9% of the value of total imports in 2003.

The services sector contributed 46.2% of GDP in 2004, at constant 1994 prices, and engaged 11.0% of the employed labour force in 1998. The GDP of the services sector increased by an average of 1.5% per year in 1995–2004, according to the World Bank. Services GDP increased by 3.3% in 2004.

According to provisional figures, in 2004 Malawi recorded a visible trade deficit of 37,669.8m. kwacha, while there was a deficit of 58,713m. kwacha on the current account of the balance of payments. In 2004 the principal source of imports was South Africa (31.7%); Mozambique (13.5%) and the United Kingdom were also notable suppliers. South Africa was also the principal market for exports (14.6%) in that year; other important markets were the USA, the United Kingdom, Germany and Mozambique. The principal imports in 2001 were machinery and transport equipment (particularly road vehicles), basic manufactures, mineral fuels and lubricants, mineral fuels, chemicals and related products and food and live animals. The principal exports in that year were tobacco and food and live animals.

In the financial year ending 30 June 2004 Malawi's overall budget surplus was an estimated 20,898m. kwacha. The country's external debt totalled US $3,134m. at the end of 2003, of which $2,960m. was long-term public debt. In that year the cost of debt-servicing was equivalent to 7.7% of the value of exports of goods and services. The annual rate of inflation averaged 28.8% in 1990–2002; consumer prices increased by an average of 11.5% in 2004. Some 1.1% of the labour force were unemployed in 1998.

Malawi is a member of the Southern African Development Community (see p. 358) and the Common Market for Eastern and Southern Africa (COMESA, see p. 191). Nine members of COMESA, including Malawi, became inaugural members of the COMESA Free Trade Area in October 2000. The country belongs to the International Tea Promotion Association (see p. 383) and to the International Tobacco Growers' Association (see p. 383) and is also a signatory to the Cotonou Agreement with the European Union (EU).

Malawi's natural impediments to growth (including its landlocked position, the vulnerability of the dominant agricultural sector to drought, and a high rate of population growth), were compounded by the severe mismanagement of economic affairs by the Banda regime. The Muluzi Government continued policies of economic liberalization and diversification initiated in the last years under Banda. In November 2000 Malawi was granted debt relief equating to US $1,000m. under the World Bank's initiative for heavily indebted poor countries (HIPCs), and in December the IMF approved a loan of some $65m. under its Poverty Reduction and Growth Facility (PRGF), disbursing $9m. immediately. However, unsatisfactory progress in the implementation of the IMF-supported economic programme repeatedly delayed the first review of performance under the PRGF arrangement, and thus further disbursements. Moreover, in late 2001 and early 2002 the EU, the USA and other donors suspended aid to Malawi, in response to concerns regarding corruption and economic mismanagement. In April 2002 Malawi was suspended from the HIPC initiative over allegations of corruption concerning the sale of its grain reserves, although in October 2003 the IMF finally completed the first review of Malawi's economic performance under the PRGF arrangement approved in December 2000, authorizing the disbursement of some $9m. The Fund extended the arrangement until December 2004, and agreed to resume interim assistance under the HIPC initiative. The EU and other donors also agreed conditionally to resume lending to Malawi. Upon his accession to the presidency in May, Dr Bingu wa Mutharika pledged to take steps to combat corruption and these measures precipitated further improvements in relations with donor institutions. An IMF team visiting in March had praised the Government for the efforts it had made to address the issues that had led to the country's suspension from the HIPC initiative, however, it was not until August 2005 that approval was finally given for a three-year PRGF programme worth $55m. The report on the first review of the PRGF programme, published in March 2006, concluded that it was still possible for Malawi to reach the HIPC initiative completion point later that year whereupon the country would qualify for debt relief equivalent to $37m. The report commended the Government for its ongoing efforts to reduce public expenditure and observe budget limits, while acknowledging that spending on food security remained a priority. Based on the report's findings, in late February the IMF approved the disbursement of a further $7.1m. Also that month the EU provided assistance in launching a $27m. income-generating public works programme, as an extension of a four-year programme which had ended the previous year. In the short term the programme would provide rural employment in road construction and rehabilitation, forestry, irrigation and aquaculture, with the long-term aim of improving food security. The Malawi Economic Growth Strategy sought to address poverty by promoting the industrialization of Malawi's largely rural economy, which it was hoped would increase annual GDP growth to 6%. During 2005/06 planned projects included investment in the clothing and textiles industry; construction of a sugar refinery and a fertilizer plant in Nkhata Bay and Kanengo, respectively; and the promotion of high value-added 'agro-processing', including a food fortification programme. Meanwhile, the UN World Food Programme (WFP) declared the 2005 harvest the worst in a decade and the price of maize increased by some 90% at local markets. Maize supplies amounted to just over one-half of the 2.3m. metric tons that were required to feed the population and in October Mutharika declared a 'state of disaster'. The following month, in conjunction with aid agencies, the Government commenced a campaign to encourage people to reduce their reliance on maize (the basis for the staple food nsima, a type of porridge) and to cultivate other crops—such as millet, cassava, bananas and sweet potatoes—which were better suited to the climate. The forecast for the April 2006 maize harvest was for 2.4m. tons, almost double the previous year's total, owing to good rains and a wider availability of fertilizer. Nevertheless, the Government and WFP were still preparing to deliver food relief to some 4.9m. people.

Education

Primary education is officially compulsory, beginning at six years of age and lasting for eight years. Secondary education, which begins at 14 years of age, lasts for four years, comprising two cycles of two years. According to UNESCO estimates, in 1999/2000 primary enrolment included 69% of children in the relevant age-group (males 66%; females 71%), while in 2000/01 secondary enrolment included 25% of children in the relevant age-group (males 27%; females 23%). A programme to expand education at all levels has been undertaken; however, the introduction of free primary education in September 1994 led to the influx of more than 1m. additional pupils, resulting in severe overcrowding in schools. In January 1996 the International

MALAWI

Development Association granted US $22.5m. for the training of 20,000 newly recruited teachers, appointed in response to the influx. In mid-1997 additional funding was provided by the African Development Bank for the construction of primary and secondary schools. There were 4,757 university students in 2003. Some students attend institutions in the United Kingdom and the USA. Expenditure on education in 2003/04 was estimated at 8,714m. kwacha (equivalent to 19.6% of total expenditure).

Public Holidays

2006: 1 January (New Year's Day), 15 January (John Chilembwe Day), 3 March (Martyrs' Day), 14–17 April (Easter), 1 May (Labour Day), 14 June (Freedom Day), 6 July (Republic Day), 9 October (Mothers' Day), 25–26 December (Christmas).

2007: 1 January (New Year's Day), 15 January (John Chilembwe Day), 3 March (Martyrs' Day), 6–9 April (Easter), 1 May (Labour Day), 14 June (Freedom Day), 6 July (Republic Day), 8 October (Mothers' Day), 25–26 December (Christmas).

Weights and Measures

The metric system is in use.

Statistical Survey

Sources (unless otherwise indicated): National Statistical Office of Malawi, POB 333, Zomba; tel. 1524377; fax 1525130; e-mail enquiries@statistics.gov.mw; internet www.nso.malawi.net; Reserve Bank of Malawi, POB 30063, Capital City, Lilongwe 3; tel. 1770600; fax 1772752; e-mail webmaster@rbm.mw; internet www.rbm.mw.

Area and Population

AREA, POPULATION AND DENSITY

Area (sq km)	118,484*
Population (census results)	
1–21 September 1987	7,988,507
1–21 September 1998	
Males	4,867,563
Females	5,066,305
Total	9,933,868
Population (UN estimates at mid-year)†	
2002	12,070,000
2003	12,339,000
2004	12,608,000
Density (per sq km) at mid-2004	106.4

* 45,747 sq miles. The area includes 24,208 sq km (9,347 sq miles) of inland water.
† Source: UN, *World Population Prospects: The 2004 Revision*.

REGIONS
(census of September 1998)

Region	Area (sq km)*	Population	Density (per sq km)	Regional capital
Southern	31,753	4,633,968	145.9	Blantyre
Central	35,592	4,066,340	114.2	Lilongwe
Northern	26,931	1,233,560	45.8	Mzuzu
Total	94,276	9,933,868	105.4	

* Excluding inland waters, totalling 24,208 sq km.

PRINCIPAL TOWNS
(population at census of September 1998)

Blantyre	502,053*	Karonga	27,811
Lilongwe (capital)	440,471	Kasungu	27,754
Mzuzu	86,890	Mangochi	26,570
Zomba	65,915	Salima	20,355

* Including Limbe.

BIRTHS AND DEATHS
(UN estimates, annual averages)

	1990–95	1995–2000	2000–05
Birth rate (per 1,000)	50.0	48.1	44.6
Death rate (per 1,000)	19.6	21.2	21.8

Source: UN, *World Population Prospects: The 2004 Revision*.

Expectation of Life (WHO estimates, years at birth): 42 (males 41; females 42) in 2003 (Source: WHO, *World Health Report*).

ECONOMICALLY ACTIVE POPULATION*
(persons aged 10 years and over, 1998 census)

	Males	Females	Total
Agriculture, hunting, forestry and fishing	1,683,006	2,082,821	3,765,827
Mining and quarrying	2,206	293	2,499
Manufacturing	94,545	23,938	118,483
Electricity, gas and water	6,656	663	7,319
Construction	70,196	3,206	73,402
Trade, restaurants and hotels	176,466	80,923	257,389
Transport, storage and communications	29,438	3,185	32,623
Financing, insurance, real estate and business services	10,473	3,484	13,957
Public administration	82,973	18,460	101,433
Community, social and personal services	52,980	33,016	85,996
Total employed	2,208,940	2,249,989	4,458,929
Unemployed	34,697	15,664	50,361
Total labour force	2,243,637	2,265,653	4,509,290

* Excluding armed forces.

Mid-2003 (estimates in '000): Agriculture, etc. 4,733; Total 5,791 (Source: FAO).

Health and Welfare

KEY INDICATORS

Total fertility rate (children per woman, 2003)	6.1
Under-5 mortality rate (per 1,000 live births, 2004)	175
HIV/AIDS (% of persons aged 15–49, 2003)	14.2
Physicians (per 1,000 head, 1993)	0.03
Hospital beds (per 1,000 head, 1998)	1.34
Health expenditure (2002): US $ per head (PPP)	48
Health expenditure (2002): % of GDP	9.8
Health expenditure (2002): public (% of total)	41.1
Access to water (% of persons, 2002)	67
Access to sanitation (% of persons, 2002)	46
Human Development Index (2003): ranking	165
Human Development Index (2003): value	0.404

For sources and definitions, see explanatory note on p. vi.

MALAWI

Agriculture

PRINCIPAL CROPS
('000 metric tons)

	2002	2003	2004
Rice (paddy)	92.0	88.2	49.7
Maize	1,557.0	1,983.4	1,733.1
Millet	20.9	24.6	17.3
Sorghum	39.2	45.0*	40.9
Potatoes	1,061.4	1,100.0†	1,784.7
Cassava (Manioc)	1,540.2	1,735.1	2,559.3
Dry beans	94.0	109.8	79.4
Chick-peas†	35	35	35
Cow peas (dry)†	54	54	54
Pigeon peas†	79	79	79
Groundnuts (in shell)	157.9	190.1	161.2
Cottonseed	40.0	40.4	53.6
Cabbages	28†	28†	50
Tomatoes†	35	35	35
Onions (dry)	30†	35†	50
Other vegetables†	174	174	174
Mangoes	50†	60	33†
Bananas	150†	200†	360
Plantains	200†	200†	300
Other fruits†	182	182	182
Sugar cane	1,900†	2,100	2,100
Coffee (green)	3.0	2.6	1.6
Tea	39.2	41.7	50.1
Tobacco (leaves)	69.4	69.5†	69.5†
Cotton (lint)	14	14	18.8

* Unofficial figure.
† FAO estimate(s).

Source: FAO.

LIVESTOCK
('000 head, year ending September)

	2002	2003	2004
Cattle	750*	750*	765
Pigs	456.3	456.3*	456.3*
Sheep*	115	115	115
Goats	1,700*	1,700*	1,900
Poultry*	15,200	15,200	15,200

* FAO estimate(s).

Source: FAO.

LIVESTOCK PRODUCTS
(FAO estimates, '000 metric tons)

	2002	2003	2004
Beef and veal	16.0	16.0	16.0
Goat meat	6.0	6.0	6.6
Pig meat	21	21	21
Poultry meat	15.3	15.3	15.3
Cows' milk	35	35	35
Hen eggs	19.5	19.5	19.5

Source: FAO.

Forestry

ROUNDWOOD REMOVALS
(FAO estimates, '000 cubic metres, excluding bark)

	2002	2003	2004
Sawlogs, veneer logs and logs for sleepers*	130	130	130
Other industrial wood†	390	390	390
Fuel wood	5,029	5,064	5,102
Total	5,549	5,584	5,622

* Production assumed to be unchanged since 1993.
† Production assumed unchanged since 1999.

Source: FAO.

SAWNWOOD PRODUCTION
('000 cubic metres, including railway sleepers)

	1991*	1992†	1993
Coniferous (softwood)	28	28	30
Broadleaved (hardwood)	15	15	15†
Total	43	43	45

* Unofficial figures.
† FAO estimate(s).

1994–2004: Annual production as in 1993 (FAO estimates).

Source: FAO.

Fishing

('000 metric tons, live weight)

	2001	2002	2003
Capture	40.6	41.3	53.5
Cyprinids	6.3	6.4	6.7
Tilapias	5.2	5.2	5.7
Cichlids	20.5	20.9	29.8
Torpedo-shaped catfishes	6.4	6.5	8.2
Other freshwater fishes	2.3	2.3	3.1
Aquaculture	0.6	0.6	0.7
Total catch	41.2	42.0	54.2

Note: Figures exclude aquatic mammals, recorded by number rather than weight. The number of Nile crocodiles caught was: 1,256 in 2001; 60 in 2002; 301 in 2003.

Source: FAO.

Mining

('000 metric tons, unless otherwise indicated)

	2002	2003	2004
Bituminous coal	43.4	47.0	40.1
Lime	6.8	18.9	23.1
Gemstones (kilograms)	2,305	2,297	1,820
Aggregate ('000 cubic metres)	114.0	160.0	168.6
Limestone	86.2	24.0	21.2

Source: US Geological Survey.

Industry

SELECTED PRODUCTS
('000 metric tons, unless otherwise indicated)

	2000	2001	2002
Raw sugar	96	107	260
Beer ('000 hectolitres)	739	1,033	n.a.
Blankets ('000)	574	281	n.a.
Cement	198	111	174

Source (unless otherwise indicated): UN, *Industrial Commodity Statistics Yearbook*.

Cement (estimates, '000 metric tons): 190 in 2003; 190 in 2004 (Source: US Geological Survey).

Electric energy (million kWh): 1,127.5 in 2001; 1,177.5 in 2002; 1,203.0 in 2003 (Source: partly Electricity Supply Commission of Malawi and National Electricity Council).

MALAWI
Statistical Survey

Finance

CURRENCY AND EXCHANGE RATES

Monetary Units
100 tambala = 1 Malawi kwacha (K).

Sterling, Dollar and Euro Equivalents (30 November 2005)
£1 sterling = 213.8 kwacha;
US $1 = 123.8 kwacha;
€1 = 145.7 kwacha;
1,000 Malawi kwacha = £4.68 = $8.08 = €6.86.

Average Exchange Rate (kwacha per US $)
2002   76.687
2003   97.433
2004   108.898

BUDGET
(K million, year ending 30 June)

Revenue*	2001/02	2002/03†	2003/04†
Tax revenue	20,382	27,251	36,902
Taxes on income and profits	9,458	12,146	15,839
Companies	2,914	3,678	4,589
Individuals	4,174	5,708	7,954
Taxes on goods and services	8,935	12,379	16,634
Surtax	6,684	9,322	11,778
Excise duties	2,251	3,056	4,856
Taxes on international trade	2,423	3,136	5,082
Other‡	−435	−410	−653
Non-tax revenue	2,471	4,758	5,852
Departmental receipts	1,141	1,614	2,237
Total	22,853	32,009	42,754

Expenditure	2001/02	2002/03†	2003/04†
General public services	13,553	14,798	17,200
General administration	10,830	11,252	13,588
Defence	988	1,185	1,306
Public order and safety	1,734	2,360	2,307
Social and community services	18,552	16,565	17,582
Education	6,045	7,128	8,714
Health	5,303	4,532	5,559
Social security and welfare	4,363	1,466	2,149
Housing and community amenities	2,611	3,283	963
Recreational, cultural and other social services	101	59	87
Broadcasting and publishing	128	96	109
Economic affairs and services	6,950	5,143	9,685
Energy and mining	25	47	1,830
Agriculture and natural resources	3,187	2,630	2,131
Tourism	32	154	257
Physical planning and development	55	126	3,304
Transport and communications	3,004	1,813	1,613
Industry and commerce	253	120	296
Labour relations and employment	46	237	235
Environmental protection and conservation	296	—	—
Scientific and technological services	36	—	—
Other economic services	15	15	18
Unallocable expenditure	6,821	1,005	—
Total	45,875	37,510	44,467

* Excluding grants received (K million): 9,144 in 2001/02; 10,675 in 2002/03; 22,611 in 2003/04.
† Estimates.
‡ Including deduction for tax refunds (K million): −320 in 2001/02; −652 in 2002/03; −820 in 2003/04.

Source: IMF, *Malawi: Selected Issues and Statistical Appendix* (December 2004).

INTERNATIONAL RESERVES
(US $ million at 31 December)

	2002	2003	2004
Gold (national valuation)	0.51	0.54	0.54
IMF special drawing rights	0.09	0.47	1.20
Reserve position in IMF	3.11	3.40	3.56
Foreign exchange	161.98	122.58	128.59
Total	165.68	127.00	133.89

Source: IMF, *International Financial Statistics*.

MONEY SUPPLY
(K million at 31 December)

	2002	2003	2004
Currency outside banks	5,964.0	7,838.1	10,992.8
Demand deposits at commercial banks	7,929.3	9,925.2	14,730.2
Total money (incl. others)	13,979.0	17,763.4	25,723.0

Source: IMF, *International Financial Statistics*.

COST OF LIVING
(Consumer Price Index; base: 2000 = 100)

	2002	2003	2004
Food (incl. beverages)	136.4	143.6	154.4
Clothing (incl. footwear)	152.7	166.8	179.5
Rent	156.6	180.0	211.7
All items (incl. others)	140.8	154.3	172.0

Source: ILO.

NATIONAL ACCOUNTS

Expenditure on the Gross Domestic Product
(K million at current prices)

	2001	2002	2003*
Government final consumption expenditure	19,591	21,858	28,025
Private final consumption expenditure	100,182	131,898	145,942
Increase in stocks	1,360	1,417	1,559
Gross fixed capital formation	15,741	14,110	17,058
Total domestic expenditure	136,874	169,283	192,584
Exports of goods and services	34,753	36,171	42,753
Less Imports of goods and services	48,547	62,527	69,587
GDP in purchasers' values	123,080	142,928	165,751
GDP at constant 1994 prices	13,999	14,265	14,893

* Provisional figures.

Source: IMF, *Malawi: Selected Issues and Statistical Appendix* (December 2004).

Gross Domestic Product by Economic Activity
(K million at constant 1994 prices)

	2002	2003	2004
Agriculture, forestry and fishing	5,025.9	5,323.0	5,460.5
Mining and quarrying	123.7	146.7	128.9
Manufacturing	1,453.5	1,500.0	1,592.4
Electricity and water	185.9	190.2	204.1
Construction	311.2	352.6	402.5
Distribution	2,826.0	2,804.7	2,944.8
Transport and communications	640.9	694.4	740.5
Finance, insurance and business services	1,088.9	1,155.4	1,269.5
Ownership of dwellings	195.0	200.4	205.9
Private social services	287.1	295.4	303.7
Government services	1,182.7	1,202.9	1,227.9
Sub-total	13,320.8	13,865.7	14,480.6
Less Imputed bank service charges	438.0	480.2	528.6
GDP at factor cost	12,882.8	13,385.5	13,952.0

MALAWI

BALANCE OF PAYMENTS
(K million)

	2002	2003	2004*
Exports of goods f.o.b.	31,713.1	42,252.0	50,638.6
Imports of goods f.o.b.	−45,608.4	−66,652.2	−88,308.4
Trade balance	−13,895.3	−24,400.2	−37,669.8
Exports of services	3,815.2	3,899.0	4,421.6
Imports of services	−16,494.9	−18,444.2	−22,040.3
Balance on goods and services	−26,575.0	−38,945.4	−55,288.5
Other income received	933.8	1,187.3	504.4
Other income paid	−3,728.0	−4,455.1	−5,171.6
Balance on goods, services and income	−29,369.2	−42,213.2	−59,955.7
Current transfers received	1,652.9	2,101.5	2,349.3
Current transfers paid	−1,029.7	−1,490.9	−1,106.9
Current balance	−28,746.0	−41,602.5	−58,713.3
Government transfers (net)	9,185.3	11,779.6	19,057.1
Government drawings on loans	4,194.1	2,125.9	2,616.4
Public enterprises (net)	669.6	1,060.0	1,173.1
Private sector (net)	275.7	350.6	391.9
Short-term capital (net)	826.4	−1,304.0	65.0
Errors and omissions	19,498.4	22,216.5	28,799.3
Overall balance†	5,903.5	−5,374.1	−6,610.5

* Provisional figures.
† Excluding debt relief (K million): 2,244.0 in 2002; 4,634.2 in 2003; 5,125.2 in 2004.

External Trade

PRINCIPAL COMMODITIES
(distribution by SITC, US $ million)

Imports c.i.f.	2000	2001
Food and live animals	30.3	30.2
Cereals and cereal preparations	14.4	16.4
Beverages and tobacco	12.5	20.8
Tobacco and tobacco products	10.9	19.4
Mineral fuels, lubricants, etc.	83.2	91.8
Petroleum, petroleum products, etc.	82.6	91.2
Refined petroleum products	80.8	87.8
Chemicals and related products	68.4	72.2
Medicinal and pharmaceutical products	14.6	23.5
Manufactured fertilizers	17.1	4.1
Basic manufactures	97.6	108.9
Paper, paperboard, etc.	18.9	20.8
Textile yarn, fabrics, etc.	27.8	32.0
Iron and steel	15.6	18.3
Machinery and transport equipment	173.6	154.6
Machinery specialized for particular industries	29.4	16.2
General industrial machinery, equipment and parts	17.9	17.9
Office machinery and automatic data processing equipment	8.3	18.0
Electrical machinery, apparatus, etc.	16.7	22.1
Telecommunications and sound equipment	12.9	17.4
Road vehicles	81.5	57.5
Passenger motor vehicles (excl. buses)	21.7	17.7
Goods vehicles (lorries and trucks)	33.6	17.3
Miscellaneous manufactured articles	52.3	41.8
Total (incl. others)	544.0	545.9

Exports f.o.b.	2000	2001
Food and live animals	98.5	168.0
Sugar and honey	37.5	113.2
Raw beet and cane sugars	29.6	101.7
Coffee, tea, cocoa and spices	43.3	42.7
Tea	36.1	35.1
Beverages and tobacco	229.2	262.4
Tobacco and tobacco products	227.7	262.2
Unmanufactured tobacco, tobacco refuse	227.4	258.8
Unstripped tobacco	174.1	181.0
Stripped or partly stripped tobacco	36.4	50.1
Basic manufactures	15.2	35.4
Clothing and accessories	13.0	31.7
Total (incl. others)	368.6	489.4

Source: UN, *International Trade Statistics Yearbook*.

2002 (K million): *Imports c.i.f.*: Motor spirit (petrol) 1,828; Gas-diesel oil 2,574; Fertilizers 3,710; Total (incl. others) 53,657. *Exports f.o.b.* (incl. re-exports): Tobacco 17,893; Tea 2,828; Sugar 2,684; Total (incl. others) 31,416.

2003 (K million): *Imports c.i.f.*: Motor spirit (petrol) 2,761; Gas-diesel oil 4,211; Fertilizers 4,556; Total (incl. others) 76,650. *Exports f.o.b.* (incl. re-exports): Tobacco 24,191; Tea 3,482; Sugar 10,571; Total (incl. others) 51,672.

2004 (K million): *Imports c.i.f.*: Motor spirit (petrol) 3,500; Gas-diesel oil 5,954; Fertilizers 6,980; Total (incl. others) 101,554. *Exports f.o.b.* (incl. re-exports): Tobacco 22,304; Tea 5,132; Sugar 2,224; Total (incl. others) 52,627.

PRINCIPAL TRADING PARTNERS
(K million)

Imports	2002	2003	2004
France	1,379	530	2,680
Germany	504	1,099	1,116
Japan	1,597	3,202	3,924
Mozambique	1,576	4,061	13,705
Netherlands	431	429	579
South Africa	22,272	30,621	32,221
United Kingdom	2,806	4,079	5,193
USA	2,264	2,874	2,795
Zambia	968	2,172	3,915
Zimbabwe	3,118	4,996	4,800
Total (incl. others)	53,657	76,650	101,554

Exports	2002	2003	2004
France	451	1,726	385
Germany	3,321	3,655	3,974
Japan	1,238	2,681	1,052
Mozambique	548	1,873	3,050
Netherlands	863	3,174	2,319
South Africa	4,246	7,865	7,706
United Kingdom	2,905	3,822	5,197
USA	4,659	6,394	5,934
Zambia	255	884	1,114
Zimbabwe	485	851	1,002
Total (incl. others)	31,416	51,672	52,627

Transport

RAILWAYS
(traffic)

	2002	2003	2004
Passengers carried ('000)	402	488	394
Passenger-kilometres ('000)	23,845	30,311	29,523
Net freight ton-kilometres ('000)	86,018	26,009	26,055

MALAWI

ROAD TRAFFIC
(estimates, motor vehicles in use at 31 December)

	1994	1995	1996
Passenger cars	23,520	25,480	27,000
Lorries and vans	26,000	29,000	29,700

Source: International Road Federation, *World Road Statistics*.

SHIPPING

Inland Waterways
(lake transport)

	2002	2003	2004
Passengers carried ('000)	78	68	55
Passenger-km ('000)	6,955	5,659	4,299
Net freight-ton km	392	1,438	316

CIVIL AVIATION
(traffic on scheduled services)

	1999	2000	2001
Kilometres flown (million)	2	3	3
Passengers carried ('000)	112	116	113
Passenger-km (million)	224	210	221
Total ton-km (million)	21	22	23

Source: UN, *Statistical Yearbook*.

Freight carried (metric tons): 3,468 in 2002; 2,768 in 2003; 4,011 in 2004.

Passengers carried ('000): 431 in 2002; 239 in 2003; 335 in 2004.

Tourism

FOREIGN TOURIST ARRIVALS BY COUNTRY OF RESIDENCE

	2001*	2002	2003†
Mozambique	36,500	83,064	91,370
North America	14,500	14,885	16,371
Southern Africa‡	28,500	46,755	51,431
United Kingdom and Ireland	27,500	20,693	22,762
Zambia	39,600	39,189	43,108
Zimbabwe	28,500	54,075	59,483
Total (incl. others)	266,300	382,647	420,911

* Rounded figures.
† Provisional data.
‡ Comprising South Africa, Botswana, Lesotho and Swaziland.

Tourism receipts (US $ million, incl. passenger transport): 40 in 2001; 45 in 2002; 43 in 2003.

Source: World Tourism Organization.

Communications Media

	2002	2003	2004
Telephones ('000 main lines in use)	73.1	85.0	93.0
Mobile cellular telephones ('000 subscribers)	86.0	135.1	222.1
Personal computers ('000 in use)	14	16	20
Internet users ('000)	27.0	36.0	46.1

Radio receivers ('000 in use): 4,929 in 1998.
Television receivers ('000 in use): 40 in 2001.
Facsimile machines (number in use): 1,250 in 1997.
Book production (first editions only): 120 titles in 1996.
Daily newspapers: 5 in 1998 (estimated average circulation 26,000 copies).
Non-daily newspapers: 4 in 1996 (estimated average circulation 120,000 copies).

Sources: UNESCO Institute for Statistics; UN, *Statistical Yearbook*; International Telecommunication Union.

Education
(2003)

	Institutions	Teachers	Students
Primary	3,160*	45,100	3,112,513
Secondary	n.a.	7,076	131,100
Universities	6	654	4,757

* 1997 figure. Source: UNESCO Institute for Statistics.

Primary education (2004): Schools 5,103; Students 3,166,786; Teachers 43,952 (Source: partly Ministry of Education, Science and Technology).

Adult literacy rate (UNESCO estimates): 64.1% (males 74.9%; females 54.0%) in 1995–99 (Source: UN Development Programme, *Human Development Report*).

Directory

The Constitution

A new Constitution, replacing the (amended) 1966 Constitution, was approved by the National Assembly on 16 May 1994, and took provisional effect for one year from 18 May. During this time the Constitution was to be subject to review, and the final document was promulgated on 18 May 1995. The main provisions (with subsequent amendments) are summarized below:

THE PRESIDENT

The President is both Head of State and Head of Government. The President is elected for five years, by universal adult suffrage, in the context of a multi-party political system. The Constitution provides for up to two Vice-Presidents.

PARLIAMENT

Parliament comprises the President, the Vice-President(s) and the National Assembly. The National Assembly has 193 elective seats, elections being by universal adult suffrage, in the context of a multi-party system. Cabinet ministers who are not elected members of parliament also sit in the National Assembly. The Speaker is appointed from among the ordinary members of the Assembly. The parliamentary term is normally five years. The President has power to prorogue or dissolve Parliament.

In 1995 the National Assembly approved proposals for the establishment of a second chamber, the Senate, to be implemented in 1999. The chamber was not established by that date, however, and in January 2001 the National Assembly approved a proposal to abandon plans for its creation.

MALAWI

EXECUTIVE POWER

Executive power is exercised by the President, who appoints members of the Cabinet.

The Government

HEAD OF STATE

President: Dr BINGU WA MUTHARIKA (took office 24 May 2004).
Vice-President: Dr CASSIM CHILUMPHA.

CABINET
(March 2006)

President and Commander-in-Chief of the Malawi Defence Force and Police Service and Minister Responsible for Defence, the Civil Service, Statutory Corporations and Privatization: Dr BINGU WA MUTHARIKA.
Vice-President: Dr CASSIM CHILUMPHA.
Minister of Irrigation and Water Development: SIDIK MIA.
Minister of Agriculture and Food Security: ULADI MUSSA.
Minister of Finance: Dr GOODALL E. GONDWE.
Minister of Economic Planning and Development: DAVID FAITI.
Minister of Foreign Affairs: DAVIS KATSONGA.
Minister of Justice and Constitutional Affairs: HENRY PHOYA.
Attorney-General: RALPH KASAMBARA.
Minister of Industry, Science and Technology: JOHN B. KHUMBO CHIRWA.
Minister of Home Affairs and Internal Security: ANNA KACHIKHO.
Minister of Trade and Private-Sector Development: Dr MARTIN KANSICHI.
Minister of Education and Human Resources: KATE KAINJA KALULUMA.
Minister of Transport and Public Works: HENRY MUSSA.
Minister of Lands, Housing and Surveys: BAZUKA MHANGO.
Minister of Local Government and Rural Development: Dr GEORGE CHAPONDA.
Minister of Information and Tourism: PATRICIA KALYATI.
Minister of Labour and Vocational Training: Dr KENNETH LIPENGA.
Minister of Health: HETHERWICK NTABA.
Minister of Mines, Natural Resources and Environment: HENRY CHIMUNTHU BANDA.
Minister of Youth, Sports and Culture: JAFFALIE MUSSA.
Minister of Gender, Child Welfare and Community Services: JOYCE BANDA.
Minister of Social Development and Persons with Disabilities: (vacant).
There were also 12 Deputy Ministers.

MINISTRIES

Office of the President and Cabinet: Private Bag 301, Capital City, Lilongwe 3; tel. 1789311; fax 1788456; internet www.malawi.gov.mw/opc/opc.htm.
Ministry of Agriculture, Irrigation and Food Security: POB 30134, Capital City, Lilongwe 3; tel. 1789033; fax 1789218; internet www.malawi.gov.mw/agric/agric.htm.
Ministry of Defence: Private Bag 339, Lilongwe 3; tel. 1789600; fax 1789176; e-mail defence@malawi.gov.mw; internet www.malawi.gov.mw/defence/defence.htm.
Ministry of Economic Planning and Development: POB 30136, Capital City, Lilongwe 3; tel. 1788390; fax 1788131; e-mail epd@malawi.net; internet www.malawi.gov.mw/nec/nec.htm.
Ministry of Education and Human Resources: Private Bag 328, Capital City, Lilongwe 3; tel. 1789422; fax 1788064; e-mail secretaryforeducation@sdnp.org.mw; internet www.malawi.gov.mw/educ/educ.htm.
Ministry of Finance and Economic Planning: Capital Hill, POB 30049, Lilongwe 3; tel. 1789355; fax 1789173; internet www.finance.malawi.gov.mw.
Ministry of Foreign Affairs and International Co-operation: POB 30315, Capital City, Lilongwe 3; tel. 1789010; fax 1788482; e-mail foreign@malawi.net; internet www.malawi.gov.mw/foreign/foreign.htm.

Ministry of Gender, Child Welfare and Community Services: Private Bag 330, Capital City, Lilongwe 3; tel. 1770411; fax 1770826; internet www.malawi.gov.mw/gender/gender.htm.
Ministry of Health and Population: POB 30377, Capital City, Lilongwe 3; tel. 1789400; fax 1789431; e-mail doccentre@malawi.net; internet www.malawi.gov.mw/health/health.htm.
Ministry of Home Affairs and Internal Security: Private Bag 331, Lilongwe 3; tel. 1789177; fax 1789509; internet www.malawi.gov.mw/homeaff/homeaffairs.htm; comprises the Immigration Dept, Prison and Police Services.
Ministry of Industry, Science and Technology: Magetsi House, Private Bag B303, Capital City, Lilongwe 3; tel. 1776077; fax 1774778; e-mail mist@globemw.net; internet www.malawi.gov.mw/mist/misthome.htm.
Ministry of Information and Tourism: Private Bag 326, Capital City, Lilongwe 3; tel. 1775499; fax 1770650; e-mail psinfo@sdnp.org.mw; internet www.information.gov.mw.
Ministry of Justice and Constitutional Affairs: Private Bag 333, Capital City, Lilongwe 3; tel. 1788411; fax 1788332; e-mail justice@malawi.gov.mw; internet www.malawi.gov.mw/mojca/mojca.htm; comprises the Attorney-General's Chambers and the Directorate of Public Prosecutions.
Ministry of Labour and Vocational Training: Private Bag 344, Capital City, Lilongwe 3; tel. 1783277; fax 1783805; e-mail labour@eo.wn.apc.org.
Ministry of Lands, Housing and Surveys: POB 30548, Lilongwe 3; tel. 1774766; fax 1773990; internet www.malawi.gov.mw/lands/lands.htm.
Ministry of Local Government and Rural Development: POB 30312, Lilongwe 3; tel. 1784500; fax 1782130.
Ministry of Mines, Natural Resources and Environment: Private Bag 350, Lilongwe 3; tel. 1789488; fax 1773379; internet www.malawi.gov.mw/natres/natres.htm.
Ministry of Social Development and Persons with Disabilities: Lilongwe.
Ministry of Statutory Corporations: Gemini House, 7th Floor, City Centre, POB 30061, Lilongwe 3; tel. 1774266; fax 1774110; e-mail dsc@malawi.net; internet www.malawi.gov.mw/statcoorp/statcohome.htm; manages parastatal cos.
Ministry of Trade and Private-Sector Development: POB 30366, Capital City, Lilongwe 3; tel. 1770244; fax 1770680; internet www.malawi.gov.mw/commerce/commerce.htm.
Ministry of Transport and Public Works: Private Bag 322, Capital City, Lilongwe 3; tel. 1789377; fax 1789328; internet www.malawi.gov.mw/transport/transhq.htm.
Ministry of Water Development: Tikwere House, Private Bag 390, Capital City, Lilongwe 3; tel. 1770238; fax 1773737; e-mail wrd@eomw.net; internet www.malawi.gov.mw/water/water.htm.
Ministry of Youth, Sports and Culture: Lingadzi House, Private Bag 384, Lilongwe 3; tel. 1774999; fax 1771018; internet www.malawi.gov.mw/sports/sports.htm.

President and Legislature

PRESIDENT

Presidential Election, 20 May 2004

Candidate	Votes	% of votes
Bingu wa Mutharika (UDF)	1,119,738	35.89
John Tembo (MCP)	846,457	27.13
Gwandaguluwe Chakuamba (Mgwirizano Coalition*)	802,386	25.72
Brown Mpinganjira (NDA)	272,172	8.72
Justin Malewezi (Independent)	78,892	2.53
Total	**3,119,645**	**100.00**

* Comprising the Malawi Democratic Party, the Malawi Forum for Unity and Development, the Movement for Genuine Democratic Change (MGODE), the National Unity Party, the People's Progressive Movement, the People's Transformation Party and Chakuamba's Republican Party (RP); in early June 2004 the MGODE and the RP signed a memorandum of understanding on co-operation with the UDF.

NATIONAL ASSEMBLY

National Assembly: Parliament Bldg, Private Bag B362, Lilongwe 3; tel. 1773566; fax 1774196; internet www.malawi.gov.mw/parliament/parliament.htm.
Speaker: LOUIS JOSEPH CHIMANGO.

MALAWI

General Election, 20 May 2004*

Party	Seats
Malawi Congress Party (MCP)	56
United Democratic Front (UDF)	49
Republican Party (RP)†	15
National Democratic Alliance (NDA)	8
Alliance for Democracy (AFORD)	6
People's Progressive Movement (PPM)†	6
Movement for Genuine Democratic Change (MGODE)†	3
Congress for National Unity (CONU)	1
People's Transformation Party (PETRA)†	1
Independents	39
Total	**193‡**

* Provisional results.

† Contested the election as part of the Mgwirizano Coalition, which also comprised the Malawi Democratic Party, the Malawi Forum for Unity and Development and the National Unity Party; in early June 2004 the MGODE and the RP signed a memorandum of understanding on co-operation with the UDF.

‡ Disputed results in three constituencies remained under investigation in early June 2004, while voting in a further six constituencies was not conducted owing to irregularities.

Election Commission

Malawi Electoral Commission (MEC): Development House, Private Bag 113, Blantyre; tel. 1623960; internet www.sdnp.org.mw/~solomon/mec/index.htm; f. 1998; Chair. JAMES KALAILE; Chief Elections Officer ANTHONY MASANZA.

Political Organizations

Alliance for Democracy (AFORD): Private Bag 28, Lilongwe; f. 1992; in March 1993 absorbed membership of fmr Malawi Freedom Movement; Pres. CHAKUFWA CHIHANA; First Vice-Pres. KALUNDI CHIRWA; Sec.-Gen. WALLACE CHIUME.

Congress for National Unity (CONU): Lilongwe; f. 1999; Pres. Bishop DANIEL KAMFOSI NKHUMBWA.

Democratic Progressive Party (DPP): Lilongwe 3; f. 2005 following Bingu wa Mutharika's resignation from the UDF; ; Leader Dr BINGU WA MUTHARIKA; Sec.-Gen. JOYCE BANDA.

Malawi Congress Party (MCP): Private Bag 388, Lilongwe 3; tel. 1730388; f. 1959; sole legal party 1966–93; Pres. JOHN TEMBO.

Malawi Democratic Party (MDP): Pres. KAMLEPO KALUA.

Malawi Forum for Unity and Development (MAFUNDE): f. 2002; aims to combat corruption and food shortages; Pres. GEORGE MNESA.

Movement for Genuine Democratic Change (MGODE): Lilongwe; f. 2003 by fmr mems of AFORD; Pres. SAM KANDODO BANDA; Nat. Chair. GREENE LULILO MWAMONDWE; Sec.-Gen. ROGERS NKHWAZI.

National Democratic Alliance (NDA): POB 994, Blantyre; tel. 1842593; internet www.geocities.com/nda_mw; f. 2001 by fmr mems of the UDF; officially merged with the UDF in June 2004 but maintained independent structure; Pres. BROWN JAMES MPINGANJIRA; Nat. Chair. JAMES MAKHUMULA NKHOMA.

National Solidarity Movement: Leader NGWAZI KAZUNI KUMWENDA.

National Unity Party (NUP): Blantyre; Pres. HARRY CHIUME; Sec.-Gen. HARRY MUYENZA.

New Congress for Democracy (NCD): Lilongwe; f. 2004 by fmr mems of the MCP; Pres. HETHERWICK NTABA.

New Dawn for Africa (NDA): Lilongwe; f. 2003; associated with the UDF; Pres. THOM CHIUMIA; Sec.-Gen. CHIKUMBUTSO MTUMODZI.

Pamodzi Freedom Party (PFP): Lilongwe; f. 2002; Pres. RAINSFORD CHIGADULA NDIWO.

People's Progressive Movement (PPM): f. 2003 by fmr mems of the UDF; Pres. ALEKE KADONAPHANI BANDA; Sec.-Gen. KNOX VARELA.

People's Transformation Party (PETRA): POB 31964, Chichiri, Blantyre 3; tel. 1671577; fax 1671573; e-mail president@petra.mw; internet www.petra.mw; f. 2002; Pres. KAMUZU CHIBAMBO.

Republican Party (RP): f. 2004; Leader (vacant).

Social Democratic Party (SDP): Pres. ISON KAKOME.

United Democratic Front (UDF): POB 5446, Limbe; internet www.udf.malawi.net; f. 1992; officially merged with the NDA in June 2004 but maintained independent structure; Nat. Chair. Dr BAKILI MULUZI; Sec.-Gen. KENNEDY MAKWANGWALA.

United Front for Multi-party Democracy (UFMD): f. 1992 by three exiled political groups: the Socialist League of Malawi, the Malawi Freedom Party and the Malawi Democratic Union; Pres. EDMOND JIKA.

United Party (UP): f. 1997.

The Movement for the Restoration of Democracy in Malawi (f. 1996) is based in Mozambique and consists of fmr Malawi Young Pioneers; it conducts occasional acts of insurgency.

Diplomatic Representation

EMBASSIES AND HIGH COMMISSIONS IN MALAWI

China (Taiwan): Area 40, Plot No. 9, POB 30221, Capital City, Lilongwe 3; tel. 1773611; fax 1774812; e-mail rocemml@malawi.net; Ambassador JAMES CHEUNG.

Egypt: 10/247 Tsoka Rd, POB 30451, Lilongwe 3; tel. 1780668; fax 1780691; Ambassador ADEL EL-HAMID AHMED MARZOUK.

Germany: Convention Dr., POB 30046, Lilongwe 3; tel. 1772555; fax 1770250; e-mail info@lilongwe.diplo.de; internet www.lilongwe.diplo.de; Ambassador ALBERT JOSEF GISY.

Mozambique: POB 30579, Lilongwe 3; tel. 1784100; fax 1781342; High Commissioner JORGE DE SOUSA MATEUS.

Norway: Plot 13–14 Arwa House, City Centre, Private Bag B323, Lilongwe 3; tel. 1774211; fax 1772845; e-mail emb.lilongwe@mfa.no; Ambassador GUNNAR FØRELAND.

South Africa: Kang'ombe House, 3rd Floor, City Centre, POB 30043, Lilongwe 3; tel. 1773722; fax 1772571; e-mail sahc@malawi.net; High Commissioner N. M. TSHEOLE.

United Kingdom: British High Commission Bldg, Capital Hill, POB 30042, Lilongwe 3; tel. 1772400; fax 1772657; e-mail bhclilongwe@fco.gov.uk; High Commissioner RICHARD WILDASH.

USA: Area 40, Plot 18, POB 30016, Lilongwe 3; tel. 1773166; fax 1770471; internet usembassy.state.gov/malawi; Ambassador ALAN W. EASTHAM.

Zambia: POB 30138, Lilongwe 3; tel. 1782635; fax 1784349; High Commissioner IAN SIKAZWE.

Zimbabwe: Gemini House, 7th Floor, POB 30187, Lilongwe 3; tel. 1784988; fax 1782382; e-mail zimhighcomllw@malawi.net; High Commissioner (vacant).

Judicial System

The courts administering justice are the Supreme Court of Appeal, High Court and Magistrates' Courts.

The High Court, which has unlimited jurisdiction in civil and criminal matters, consists of the Chief Justice and five puisne judges. Traditional Courts were abolished under the 1994 Constitution. Appeals from the High Court are heard by the Supreme Court of Appeal in Blantyre.

High Court of Malawi

POB 30244, Chichiri, Blantyre 3; tel. 1670255; fax 1670213; e-mail highcourt@sdnp.org.mw; internet www.judiciary.mw; Registrar SYLVESTER KALEMBERA.

Chief Justice: LEONARD E. UNYOLO.

Justices of Appeal: J. B. KALAILE, D. G. TAMBALA, H. M. MTEGHA, A. S. E. MSOSA, I. J. MTAMBO, A. K. TEMBO.

High Court Judges: D. F. MWAUNGULU, A. K. C. NYIRENDA, G. M. CHIMASULA PHIRI, B. S. CHIUDZA BANDA, E. B. TWEA, R. R. MZIKAMANDA, Dr J. M. ANSAH, R. R. CHINANGWA, A. C. CHIPETA, F. E. KAPANDA, L. P. CHIKOPA, H. S. B. POTANI, E. CHOMBO, J. N. KATSALA, J. S. MANYUNGWA, M. L. KAMWAMBE, M. C. C. MKANDAWIRE, I. C. KAMANGA.

Religion

More than 70% of the population profess Christianity. Islam, the fastest growing religion, is practised by about 20% of the population. Traditional beliefs are followed by about 10% of the population. The Asian community includes Hindus.

CHRISTIANITY

Malawi Council of Churches (MCC): POB 30068, Capital City, Lilongwe 3; tel. 1783499; fax 1783106; f. 1939; Chair. Rev. HOWARD MATIYA NKHOMA; Gen. Sec. Rev. Dr A. C. MUSOPOLE; 22 mem. churches.

MALAWI

The Anglican Communion

Anglicans are adherents of the Church of the Province of Central Africa, covering Botswana, Malawi, Zambia and Zimbabwe. The Church comprises 12 dioceses, including three in Malawi. The Archbishop of the Province is the Bishop of Botswana. There were about 230,000 adherents in Malawi at mid-2000.

Bishop of Lake Malawi: (vacant), POB 30349, Capital City, Lilongwe 3; tel. 1797858; fax 1797548.

Bishop of North Malawi: Rt Rev. CHRISTOPHER JOHN BOYLE, POB 120, Mzuzu; tel. 1331486; fax 1333805; e-mail bishopboyle@sdnp.org.mw.

Bishop of Southern Malawi: Rt Rev. JAMES TENGATENGA, POB 30220, Chichiri, Blantyre 3; tel. 1641218; fax 1641235.

Protestant Churches

At mid-2001 there were an estimated 2.1m. Protestants in Malawi.

Assemblies of God in Malawi: POB 1220, Lilongwe; tel. 1761057; fax 1762056; 639,088 mems in 3,114 churches (2005).

Baptist Convention of Malawi (BACOMA): POB 51083, Limbe; tel. 1643224; Gen. Sec. Rev. FLETCHER KAIYA.

Church of Central Africa (Presbyterian) (CCAP): Blantyre Synod: POB 413, Blantyre; tel. and fax 1633942; comprises three synods in Malawi (Blantyre, Livingstonia and Nkhoma); Co-ordinator Rev. J. J. MPHATSE; Gen. Sec. DANIEL GUNYA; Exec. Dir ROBSON CHITENGO; more than 1m. adherents in Malawi.

Evangelical Association of Malawi: Lilongwe; tel. and fax 1730373; Chair. Rev. Dr LAZARUS CHAKWERA; Gen. Sec. FRANCIS MKANDAWIRE.

Lutheran Church of Central Africa—Malawi Conference: POB 748, Blantyre; tel. 1630821; fax 1630821; e-mail pwegner@africa-online.net; f. 1963; evangelical and medical work; Pres. FRACKSON B. CHINYAMA; Co-ordinator PAUL WENGER; 30,000 mems.

Seventh-day Adventists: Robins Rd, Kabula Hill, POB 951, Blantyre; tel. 1620264; fax 1620528; e-mail musda@malawi.net; Pres. SAUSTIN K. MFUNE; Exec. Sec. BAXTER D. CHILUNGA; 200,000 mems.

The African Methodist Episcopal Church, the Churches of Christ, the Free Methodist Church, the New Apostolic Church and the United Evangelical Church in Malawi are also active. At mid-2000 there were an estimated 2m. adherents professing other forms of Christianity.

The Roman Catholic Church

Malawi comprises one archdiocese and six dioceses. At 31 December 2003 there were some 3.3m. adherents of the Roman Catholic Church (equivalent to approximately 21.8% of the total population).

Episcopal Conference of Malawi

Catholic Secretariat of Malawi, Chimutu Rd, POB 30384, Capital City, Lilongwe 3; tel. 1772066; fax 1782019; e-mail ecm@malawi.net; f. 1969; Pres. Most Rev. TARCISIUS GERVAZIO ZIYAYE (Archbishop of Blantyre).

Archbishop of Blantyre: Most Rev. TARCISIUS GERVAZIO ZIYAYE, Archbishop House, POB 385, Blantyre; tel. and fax 1637905.

ISLAM

Muslim Association of Malawi (MAM): POB 497, Blantyre; tel. 1622060; fax 1623581; f. 1946 as the Nyasaland Muslim Asscn; umbrella body for Muslim orgs; provides secular and Islamic education; Sec.-Gen. MOHAMMED IMRAN SHAREEF.

BAHÁ'Í FAITH

National Spiritual Assembly: POB 30922, Lilongwe 3; tel. 1771713; e-mail bahaimalawi@africa-online.net; f. 1970; mems resident in over 1,500 localities.

The Press

Boma Lathu: POB 494, Blantyre; tel. 1620266; fax 1620039; internet www.maform.com/bomalathu.htm; f. 1973; monthly; Chichewa; publ. by the Ministry of Information; circ. 100,000.

Business Monthly: POB 906646, Blantyre 9; tel. 16301114; fax 1620039; f. 1995; 6 a year; English; economic, financial and business news; Editor ANTHONY LIVUZA; circ. 10,000.

The Chronicle: Private Bag 77, Lilongwe; tel. 1756530; e-mail thechronicle@africa-online.net; f. 1993; Mon. and Thurs.; English; independent; Owner and Editor-in-Chief ROBERT JAMIESON; circ. 5,000.

The Daily Times: Private Bag 39, Blantyre; tel. 1670115; fax 1671114; e-mail bnl@sdnp.org.mw; f. 1895; fmrly the *Nyasaland Times*; Mon.–Fri., Sun.; English; publ. by Blantyre Print and Publishing; affiliated to the MCP; Editor-in-Chief JIKA NKOLOKOSA; circ. 11,500.

The Dispatch: The Dispatch Publications Ltd, POB 30353, Capital City, Lilongwe 3; tel. 1751639; fax 9510120; e-mail thedispatchmw@sdnp.org.mw; Thurs. and Sun; Man. Editor MARTINES NAMINGAH; circ. Thurs. 5,000, Sun. 7,000.

The Enquirer: POB 1745, Blantyre; tel. 1670022; e-mail pillycolette@yahoo.co.uk; English and Nyanja; affiliated to the UDF; Owner LUCIOUS CHIKUNI.

Kuunika (The Light): POB 17, Nkhoma, Lilongwe; tel. 1722807; e-mail nkhomasynod@globemw.net; f. 1909; monthly; Chichewa; publ. by the Church of Central Africa (Presbyterian) Nkhoma Synod; Presbyterian; Editor Rev. M. C. NKHALAMBAYAUSI; circ. 6,000.

Malawi Government Gazette: Government Printer, POB 37, Zomba; tel. 1523155; f. 1894; weekly.

Malawi Medical Journal: College of Medicine and the Medical Assen of Malawi, POB 360, Chichiri, Blantyre; f. 1980; quarterly; English; journal of the Medical Assen of Malawi; replaced *Medical Quarterly*; Chair. J. J. WIRIMA; Editor-in-Chief M. E. MOLYNEUX.

Malawi News: Private Bag 39, Blantyre; tel. 1671679; fax 1671233; e-mail malawinews@globemw.net; f. 1959; weekly; English and Chichewa; publ. by Blantyre Newspapers Ltd; Gen. Man. JIKA NKOLOKOSA; Man. Editor EDWARD CHISAMBO; Editor FREDERICK NDALA JR; circ. 30,000.

The Malawi Standard: POB 31781, Blantyre 3; tel. 1674013.

The Mirror: POB 30721, Blantyre; tel. 1675043; f. 1994; weekly; English and Nyanja; affiliated to the UDF; Owner and Publr BROWN MPINGANJIRA; circ. 10,000.

The Nation: POB 30408, Chichiri, Blantyre 3; tel. 1673611; fax 1674343; e-mail nation@nationmalawi.com; internet www.nationmalawi.com; f. 1993; daily; weekly edn of *The Weekend Nation*; English and Nyanja; Owner ALEKE BANDA; Editor-in-Chief ALFRED NTONGA; circ. 10,000.

Odini: POB 133, Lilongwe; tel. 1721135; fax 1721141; f. 1949; fortnightly; Chichewa and English; Roman Catholic; Dir P. I. AKOMENJI; circ. 12,000.

This is Malawi: POB 494, Blantyre; tel. 1620266; fax 1620807; e-mail alivuza@malawi.net; f. 1964; monthly; English and Chichewa edns; publ. by the Dept of Information; Editor ANTHONY LIVUZA; circ. 12,000.

UDF News: POB 3052, Blantyre; tel. 1645314; fax 1645725; e-mail echapusa@yahoo.co.uk; organ of the UDF; fortnightly; English and Nyanja.

The Weekly News: Dept of Information, POB 494, Blantyre; tel. 1642600; fax 1642364; f. 1996; English and Nyanja; publ. by the Ministry of Information; Editor-in-Chief GEORGE TUKHUWA.

PERIODICALS

Journal of Humanities: Faculty of Humanities, Univ. of Malawi, Chancellor College, POB 280, Zomba; tel. (1) 522622; fax (1) 524046; e-mail publications@chanco.unima.mw; annually; focus on east, central and southern Africa; Chief Editor PASCAL KASHINDO; circ. 250.

The Lamp: Montfort Media, POB 280, Balaka, Zomba; tel. 1545267; e-mail montfortmedia@malawi.net; f. 1995; fortnightly; Roman Catholic and ecumenical; Editor Fr GAMBA PIERGIORGIO; circ. 5,500.

Malawi Journal of Science and Technology: The Research Co-ordinator, University Office, POB 278, Zomba; tel. (1) 522622; fax (1) 522760; e-mail publications@chanco.unima.mw; annually; applied and natural sciences; Editor Dr M. W. MFITILODZE.

Malawi Medical Journal: College of Medicine and Medical Assen of Malawi, c/o Ms Mirriam Chilongo, POB 30096, Blantyre 3; e-mail mchilongo@mlw.medcol.mw; quarterly; Editor-in-Chief Prof. MALCOLM E. MOLYNEUX.

Moni Magazine: POB 5592, Limbe; tel. 1651833; fax 1651171; f. 1964; monthly; Chichewa and English; Editor PRINCE SHONGA; circ. 40,000.

Moyo Magazine: Health Education Unit, POB 30377, Lilongwe 3; 6 a year; English; publ. by the Ministry of Health and Population; Editor-in-Chief JONATHAN NKHOMA.

Pride: POB 51668, Limbe; tel. 1640569; f. 1999; quarterly; Publr JOHN SAINI.

Together: Montfort Media, POB 280, Balaka, Zomba; tel. 1545267; e-mail together@sdnp.org.mw; f. 1995; quarterly; Roman Catholic and ecumenical, youth; Editor LUIGI GRITTI; circ. 6,000.

NEWS AGENCIES

Malawi News Agency (MANA): POB 20284 Luwinga, Mzuzu 2; tel. 1332390; fax 1332063; f. 1966.

MALAWI   Directory

Foreign Bureau

Newslink Africa (United Kingdom): POB 2688, Blantyre; Correspondent HOBBS GAMA.

Publishers

Christian Literature Association in Malawi (CLAIM): POB 503, Blantyre; tel. 1620839; f. 1968; Chichewa and English; general and religious; Gen. Man. J. T. MATENJE.

Likuni Press and Publishing House: POB 133, Lilongwe; tel. 1721388; fax 1721141; f. 1949; English and Chichewa; general and religious.

Macmillan Malawi Ltd: Private Bag 140, Kenyatta Dr., Chitawira, Blantyre; tel. 1676499; fax 1675751; e-mail macmillan@macmillanmw.net; Gen. Man. HASTINGS MATEWERE.

Montfort Press and Popular Publications: POB 5592, Limbe; tel. 1651833; fax 1641126; e-mail mpp@cloom.net; f. 1961; general and religious; Gen. Man. VALES MACHILA.

GOVERNMENT PUBLISHING HOUSE

Government Press: Government Printer, POB 37, Zomba; tel. 1525515; fax 1525175.

Broadcasting and Communications

TELECOMMUNICATIONS

Celtel Malawi: Celtel House, Raynor Ave, Limbe, Blantyre; tel. 1644022; internet www.mw.celtel.com; f. 1999; 80% owned by Mobile Systems International Cellular Investments Holding B.V., 10% owned each by Malawi Devt Corpn and Investment and Devt Bank of Malawi Ltd; Man. Dir TIM BAHRANI.

Malawi Telecommunications Ltd (MTL): Lamya House, Masauko Chipembere Highway, POB 537, Blantyre; tel. 1620977; fax 1624445; e-mail mtlceo@malawi.net; f. 2000 following division of Malawi Posts and Telecommunications Corpn into two separate entities; privatized in Dec. 2005; 65.4% owned by Press Corpn Ltd, 25.1% owned by Old Mutual Malawi, 20% state-owned; CEO EMMANUEL MAHUKA.

Telekom Networks Malawi (TNM): POB 3039, Munif House, Livingstone Ave, Limbe, Blantyre; tel. 1641088; fax 1642805; e-mail nasirbah@malawi.net; internet www.telekom.co.mw; f. 1995; 60% owned by Telekom Malaysia Berhad; operates mobile cellular telephone network; CEO GHAZALI HASHIM.

BROADCASTING

Radio

Capital Radio 102.5 FM: Plot 475, cnr Victoria Ave and Juachim Chissano Rd, SunnysidePrivate Bag 437, Chichiri, Blantyre 3; tel. 1620858; fax 1623282; e-mail stationmanager@capitalradiomalawi.com; internet www.capitalradiomalawi.com; f. 1999; commercial; music and entertainment; broadcasts 18 hours daily; Man. Dir and Editor-in-Chief ALAUDIN OSMAN.

Malawi Broadcasting Corpn: POB 30133, Chichiri, Blantyre 3; tel. 1671222; fax 1671257; e-mail dgmbc@malawi.net; internet www.mbcradios.com; f. 1964; statutory body; semi-commercial, partly state-financed; two channels: MBC 1 and Radio 2 (MBC 2); programmes in English, Chichewa, Chitonga, Chitumbuka, Kyangonde, Lomwe, Sena and Yao; Chair. LEONARD NAMWERA; Dir-Gen. OWEN MAUNDE.

Power 101 FM: POB 761, Blantyre; tel. 1644101; e-mail fm101@malawi.net; f. 1998; commercial; music and entertainment; broadcasts in English, 24 hours daily; Dir and Station Man. OSCAR THOMSON.

Zodiac Broadcasting Station (ZBS): Blantyre; f. 2005; programmes in Chichewa and English; Man. Dir GOSPEL KAZAKO.

Other radio stations include Dzimwe Radio and MIJ Radio. There are also several religious stations including ABC (Africa Bible College) Radio, Calvary Family Church Radio, Radio Islam and Transworld Radio Blantyre FM.

Television

Television Malawi (TVM): Private Bag 268, Blantyre; tel. 1675033; fax 1762627; e-mail tvmalawi@sdnp.org.mw; f. 1999; broadcasts 55 hours per week, of which 10 hours are produced locally; relays programmes from France, Germany, South Africa and the United Kingdom; Chair. MOHAMMED KULESI; Dir-Gen. RODRICK MULONYA.

Finance

(cap. = capital; res = reserves; dep. = deposits; m. = million; brs = branches; amounts in kwacha)

BANKING

Central Bank

Reserve Bank of Malawi: Convention Dr., POB 30063, Capital City, Lilongwe 3; tel. 1770600; fax 1772752; e-mail reserve-bank@rbm.malawi.net; internet www.rbm.malawi.net; f. 1965; bank of issue; cap. 306.0m., res 3,627.3m., dep. 14,267.9m. (Dec. 2001); Gov. and Chair. VICTOR MBEWE; br. in Blantyre.

Commercial Banks

Finance Bank Malawi Ltd: Finance House, Victoria Ave, POB 421, Blantyre; tel. 1624232; fax 1622957; e-mail finbank@malawi.net; internet www.financebank.co.mw; f. 1995; 93.6% owned by Finance Holdings Corpn Ltd (International); 6.4% owned by Finance Bank Zambia Ltd; cap. and res 439.2m., total assets 4,152m. (Dec. 2003); Chair. Dr RAJAN L. MAHTANI; CEO A. S. PILLAI; 5 brs, 1 agency.

Loita Investment Bank Ltd: Loita House, cnr Victoria Ave and Henderson St, Private Bag 389, Chichiri, Blantyre 3; tel. 1620099; fax 1622683; internet www.loita.com; total assets 3,100.3m. (Dec. 2003); 100% owned by Loita Capital Partners International; Chair. N. JUSTIN CHIMYANTA; CEO AUBERY CHALERA (acting); 2 brs.

National Bank of Malawi: Victoria Ave, POB 945, Blantyre; tel. 1620622; fax 1620321; e-mail natbank@malawi.net; internet www.natbank.mw.com; f. 1971; 50.1% owned by Press Corpn Ltd, 20.7% owned by ADMARC (Investments Holding Co), 11.2% owned by Old Mutual Life Assurance; total assets 18,395.2m. (Dec. 2003); Chair. Dr M. A. P. CHIKAONDA; CEO ISAAC K. NSAMALA; 13 brs; 9 agencies.

NBS Bank Ltd: Ginnery Cnr, Chipembere Highway, off Masajico, POB 32251 Chichiri, Blantyre; tel. 1676222; fax 1675041; e-mail nbs@nbsmw.com; f. 2001; fmrly New Building Society; total assets 5,229.5m. (Jan. 2004); Chair. FELIX L. MLUSU; Gen. Man. JOHN S. BIZIWICK.

Nedbank (Malawi) Ltd: Development House, cnr Henderson St and Victoria Ave, POB 750, Blantyre; tel. 1620477; fax 1620102; e-mail office@mw.nedcor.com; f. 1999; fmrly Fincom Bank of Malawi Ltd; 68.8% owned by Nedbank Africa Investments Ltd, 28.4% owned by SBM Nedcor Holdings Ltd; 1,426.9m. (Dec. 2003); Chair. C. DREW; Man. Dir PAUL TUBB.

Stanbic Bank Ltd: Kaomba Centre, cnr Sir Glyn Jones Rd and Victoria Ave, POB 1111, Blantyre; tel. 1620144; fax 1620360; e-mail malawi@stanbic.com; internet www.stanbic.com; f. 1970 as Commercial Bank of Malawi; present name adopted June 2003; 60% owned by Stanbic Africa Holdings Ltd, 20% owned by National Insurance Co; total assets 15,548m. (Dec. 2003); Chair. DAVE ALLEN; Man. Dir VICTOR MBEWE; 19 brs.

Development Bank

IndeBank Ltd: Indebank House, Kaushong Rd, Top Mandala, POB 358, Blantyre; tel. 1620055; fax 1623353; e-mail enquiries@indebank.com; f. 1972 as Investment and Devt Bank of Malawi Ltd; total assets 2,162.6m. (Dec. 2003); 25.5% owned by ADMARC (Investments Holding Co), 22.1% owned each by Commonwealth Devt Corpn, DEG, and FMO; provides loans to statutory corpns and to private enterprises in the agricultural, industrial, tourism, transport and commercial sectors; Chair. S. G. MALATA; CEO MAKWEMBA MALONJE (acting).

Opportunity International Bank of Malawi Ltd (OIBM): Amina House, Second Floor, Chilambula Rd, Private Bag A71, Lilongwe; tel. 1758403; fax 1758400; e-mail uwct@sdnp.org.mw; internet www.oibm.mw; f. 2003; 57.1% owned by Opportunity Micro Investments (UK) Ltd, 30.5% owned by Opportunity Transformation Investments (USA), 12.4% owned by Opportunity International-Usiwa Watha Credit Trust (MW); total assets 269.5m. (Dec. 2003); Chair. and CEO FRANCIS PELEKAMOYO.

Discount Houses

Continental Discount House: Unit House, 5th Floor, Victoria Ave, POB 1444, Blantyre; tel. 1621300; fax 1622826; e-mail discount@cdh-malawi.com; internet www.cdh-malawi.com; f. 1998; 81% owned by Trans-Africa Holdings; total assets 3,370.6m. (Dec. 2002); Chair. ROBERT SEKOH ABBEY; CEO JOSEPH MWANAMVEKHA.

First Discount House Ltd: Umoyo House, Upper Ground Floor, 8 Victoria Ave North, POB 512, Blantyre; tel. 1620219; fax 1623044; e-mail fdh@fdh.co.mw; internet www.fdh.co.mw; f. 2000; 30% owned by Press Corpn Ltd, 25.1% owned by Kingdom Financial Holdings Ltd, 24.9% owned by Thomson F. Mpinganjira Trust, 20% owned by Old Mutual Life Assurance Co (Malawi) Ltd; total assets 3,030.4m. (Dec. 2003); CEO THOMSON FRANK MPINGANJIRA; Chair. NIGEL CHAKANIRA.

MALAWI

Merchant Banks

First Merchant Bank Ltd: First House, Glyn Jones Rd, Private Bag 122, Blantyre; tel. 1621955; fax 1621978; e-mail fmb.headoffice@fmbmalawi.com; internet www.fmbmalawi.com; f. 1994; cap. and res 895m., total assets 7,685.7 (Dec. 2004); 50% owned by Zambezi Investments Ltd, 25% owned by Simsbury Holdings Ltd, 12.5% owned each by Prime Capital and Credit Ltd, Kenya, and Prime Bank Ltd, Kenya; Chair. Rasikbhai C. Kantaria; CEO Kashinath N. Chaturvedi; Gen. Man. Seetharaman S. Srinivasan; 7 brs.

Leasing and Finance Co of Malawi Ltd: cnr Michiru and Sharpe Rd, POB 1963, Blantyre; tel. 1620233; fax 1620275; e-mail lfc@malawi.net; f. 1986; subsidiary of First Merchant Bank Ltd since June 2002; total assets 663.1m. (Dec. 2003); Chair. Hitesh Anadkat; Gen. Man. Mbachazwa Lungu.

National Finance Co Ltd: Plantation House, POB 821, Blantyre; tel. 1623670; fax 1620549; e-mail natfin@malawi.net; internet www.natbank.mw.com; f. 1958; 69.8% owned by National Bank of Malawi, 12% owned by each Lincoln Investments and Mbabzi Estates; cap. and res 148.0m., total assets 475.0m. (Dec. 2004); Chair. I. K. Nsamala; Gen. Man. M. T. Bamford.

Savings Bank

Malawi Savings Bank: Umoyo House, Victoria Ave, POB 521, Blantyre; tel. 1625111; fax 1621929; e-mail msb@msb.malawi.net; 99.9% state-owned; total assets 1,191.7m. (Dec. 2003); Sec.-Treas. P. E. Chilambe; Gen. Man. Ian C. Bonongwe.

STOCK EXCHANGE

Malawi Stock Exchange: Old Reserve Bank Bldg, 17 Victoria Ave, Private Bag 270, Blantyre; tel. 1624233; fax 1623636; e-mail mse@mse-mw.com; internet www.mse.co.mw; f. 1996; Chair. Krishna Savjani; CEO Symon W. Msefula.

INSURANCE

NICO Holdings Limited: NICO House, 3 Stewart St, POB 501, Blantyre; tel. 1622699; fax 1622364; e-mail info@nicomw.com; internet www.nicomw.com; f. 1970; fmrly National Insurance Co Ltd; transferred to private sector in 1996; incorporates NICO General Insurance Co Ltd, NICO Life Insurance Co Ltd and NICO Technologies Ltd; cap. and res 104.7m. (Sept. 1997); offices at Blantyre, Lilongwe, Mzuzu and Zomba; agencies country-wide; CEO and Man. Dir Felix L. Mlusu.

Old Mutual Malawi: Trust Finance Ltd, Michiru House, Ground Floor, Victoria Ave, POB 1396, Blantyre; tel. 0623856; f. 1845; subsidiary of Old Mutual plc, United Kingdom; Chair. Mike Levett; Man. Dir Jean du Plessis.

Royal Insurance Co of Malawi Ltd: Hannover House, Independence Dr., POB 442, Blantyre; tel. 1624044; fax 1623862; e-mail royalinsurance@malawi.net; internet www.royalinsure.com/malawi.htm; associate of Royal and SunAlliance plc, United Kingdom; Man. Dir Robert G. Ndungu; Gen. Man. Elton Nkumba.

United General Insurance Co Ltd (UGI): Michiru House, Victoria Ave, POB 383, Blantyre; tel. 1621770; fax 1621980; e-mail ugi@malawi.net; internet www.ugimalawi.com; f. 1986 as Pearl Assurance Co Ltd; latterly Property and Gen. Insurance Co Ltd; present name adopted following merger with Fide Insurance Co Ltd in July 1998; subsidiary of ZimRE Holdings, Zimbabwe; Chair. Albert Nduna; Man. Dir Ian K. Kumwenda.

Vanguard Life Assurance Co (Pvt) Ltd: MDC House, 2nd Floor, Sir Glyn Jones Rd, POB 1625, Blantyre; tel. 1623356; fax 1623506; f. 1999; 90% owned by Fidelity Life Assurance Ltd, Zimbabwe; Man. Dir Themba Mpala.

Trade and Industry

GOVERNMENT AGENCIES

Agricultural Development and Marketing Corpn (ADMARC): POB 5052, Limbe; tel. 1640500; fax 1640486; f. 1971; manages the national strategic grain reserves; involved in cultivation, processing, marketing and export of tobacco, grain and other crops; privatization pending; Chair. Prof. Kanyama Phiri.

Malawi Export Promotion Council (MEPC): Kanabar House, 2nd Floor, Victoria Ave, POB 1299, Blantyre; tel. 1620499; fax 1635429; e-mail mepco@malawi.net; internet www.malawiepc.com; f. 1971; promotes and facilitates export and investment, and provides technical assistance and training to exporters; Gen. Man. Lawrence M. Chaluluka.

Malawi Investment Promotion Agency (MIPA): Aquarius House, Private Bag 302, Lilongwe 3; tel. 1770800; fax 1771781;

Directory

e-mail mipall@malawi.net; f. 1993; promotes and facilitates local and foreign investment; CEO James R. Kaphweleza Banda.

Petroleum Control Commission: POB 2827, Blantyre; responsible for importing and distributing approx. 20% of petroleum products; Chair. Rev Dr Lazarus Chakwera.

Privatisation Commission of Malawi: Livingstone Towers, 2nd Floor, Glyn Jones Rd, POB 937, Blantyre; tel. 1623655; fax 1621248; e-mail info@privatisationmalawi.org; internet www.privatisationmalawi.org; f. 1996; has sole authority to oversee divestiture of Govt interests in public enterprises; Chair. Edward Sawerengera; Exec. Dir Maziko Sauti-Phiri; 65 privatizations completed by July 2005.

Tobacco Control Commission: POB 40045, Kanengo, Lilongwe 4, Malawi; tel. 1712777; fax 1712632; regulates tobacco production and marketing; Chair Dr Andrew Mzumacharo IV; Gen. Man. Dr Godfrey M. Chapola; brs in Mzuzu and Limbe.

DEVELOPMENT ORGANIZATIONS

Council for Non-Governmental Organizations in Malawi (CONGOMA): Chitawira, Waya Bldg, POB 480, Blantyre; tel. 1676459; fax 1677908; e-mail info@congoma.org; internet www.congoma.org; f. 1992; promotes social and economic development; Chair. Tadeyo Shaba; Exec. Dir Emmanuel Ted Nandolo; 86 mem orgs (2004).

Human Rights Consultative Committee (HRCC): c/o Centre for Human Rights and Rehabilitation, POB 2340 Lilongwe; tel. 1761700; fax 1761122; e-mail chrr@sdnp.org.mw; f. 1995; umbrella body comprising 40 mem orgs; promotes human rights and the rule of law; Chair. Rogers Newa.

Small Enterprise Development Organization of Malawi (SEDOM): POB 525, Blantyre; tel. 1622555; fax 1622781; e-mail sedom@sdnp.org.mw; f. 1982; financial services and accommodation for indigenous small- and medium-scale businesses; Chair. Stella Ndau.

CHAMBER OF COMMERCE

Malawi Confederation of Chambers of Commerce and Industry (MCCCI): Masauko Chipembere Highway, Chichiri Trade Fair Grounds, POB 258, Blantyre; tel. 1671988; fax 1671147; e-mail ckaferapanjira@mccci.org; internet www.mccci.org; f. 1892; promotes trade and encourages competition in the economy; Pres. Martin Kansichi; CEO Chancellor L. Kaferapanjira; 400 mems.

INDUSTRIAL AND TRADE ASSOCIATIONS

Dwangwa Cane Growers Trust (DCGT): POB 156, Dwangwa; tel. 1295111; fax 1295164; e-mail dcgt@malawi.net; f. 1999; fmrly Smallholder Sugar Authority; Chair M. R. Mbendera.

National Hawkers and Informal Business Association (NAHIBA): POB 60544, Ndirande, Blantyre; tel. 1935415; Exec. Dir Eva Joachim.

Smallholder Coffee Farmers Trust: POB 20133, Luwinga, Mzuzu 2; tel. 1332899; fax 1333902; e-mail mzuzucoffee@malawi.net; f. 1971; successor to the Small Holder Coffee Authority, disbanded in 1999; producers and exporters of arabica coffee; Gen. Man. Harrison Karua; 4,000 mems.

Smallholder Tea Company (STECO): POB 135, Mulanje; f. 2002 by the merger of the Smallholder Tea Authority and Malawi Tea Factory Co Ltd.

Tea Association of Malawi Ltd (TAML): Kidney Cres., POB 930, Blantyre; tel. 1671182; fax 1671427; f. 1936; Exec. Dir G. T. Banda; 20 mems.

Tobacco Association of Malawi (TAMA): TAMA House, POB 31360, Lilongwe 3; tel. 1773099; fax 1773493; e-mail tama@eomw.net; f. 1929; Pres. Albert W. Kamulaga; Exec. Sec. Felix Mkumba; brs in Mzuzu and Limbe; 60,000 mems.

Tobacco Exporters' Association of Malawi Ltd (TEAM): Private Bag 403, Kanengo, Lilongwe 4; tel. 1775839; fax 1774069; f. 1930; Chair. Charles A. M. Graham; Gen. Man. H. M. Mbale; 9 mems.

EMPLOYERS' ORGANIZATIONS

Employers' Consultative Association of Malawi (ECAM): POB 2134, Blantyre; tel. 1670007; fax 1671337; e-mail ecam@malawi.net; f. 1963; Pres. Dickens Chaula; Exec. Dir Dr Vincent Sinjani; 250 mem. asscns and six affiliates representing 80,000 employees.

Master Printers' Association of Malawi: POB 2460, Blantyre; tel. 1632948; fax 1632220; f. 1963; Chair. Paul Frederick; 21 mems.

Motor Traders' Association: POB 311, Blantyre; tel. and fax 1624754; f. 1954; Chair. A. R. Osman; 24 mems (2003).

UTILITY

Electricity

Electricity Supply Commission of Malawi (ESCOM): ESCOM House, Haile Selassie Rd, POB 2047, Blantyre; tel. and fax 1622008; f. 1966; controls electricity distribution; Chair. ABDUL WAHAB MIA; CEO Dr ALLEXON CHIWAYA.

TRADE UNIONS

According to the Ministry of Information, in 2005 less than 10% of the workforce was unionized.

Congress of Malawi Trade Unions (COMATU): POB 1443 Lilongwe; tel. 1757255; fax 1770885; affiliated to the World Confederation of Labour; Pres. THOMAS L. BANDA; Gen. Sec. PHILLMON E. CHIMBALU.

Malawi Congress of Trade Unions (MCTU): POB 1271, Lilongwe; tel. 1754581; fax 1755614; e-mail mctu@malawi.net; f. 1964; affiliated to the International Confederation of Free Trade Unions; Pres. BERNARD MANDA; Gen. Sec. AUSTIN KALIMANJIRA; 82,456 mems (2005); the MCTU comprises 16 affiliated unions:

Building Construction, Civil Engineering and Allied Workers' Union: c/o POB 5094, Limbe; tel. 1620381; f. 1961; Pres. LAWRENCE KAFERE; Gen. Sec. JOHN O. MWAFULIRWA; 6,000 mems.

Commercial Industrial and Allied Workers' Union: c/o MCTU, POB 5094, Limbe; tel. 1756099; Gen. Sec. J. KANKHWANGWA.

Communications Workers' Union: POB 186, Blantyre; tel. 1620716; Pres. B. KULEMERO; Gen. Sec. R. D. MKWEZALAMBA.

Electronic Media Workers' Union: POB 30133, Chichiri, Blantyre; tel. 1671343; Pres. L. KUNKEYANI.

ESCOM Workers' Union: POB 2047, Bantyre; tel. 1622000; Gen. Sec. M. CHIPHWANYA.

Hotels, Food and Catering Service Union: c/o MCTU 5094, Limbe; tel. 8865408; Pres. AUSTIN KALIMANJIRA; Pres. DOROTHEA MAKHASU.

Malawi Housing Co-operation Workers' Union: c/o MHC, POB 84, Mzuzu; tel. 1332655; Pres. GREY SADIKI; Gen. Sec. R. MSISKA.

Plantation and Agriculture Workers' Union: Nchima Tea Estate, POB 52, Thyolo; tel. 1473211; Pres. M. KABANGO; Gen. Sec. DENNIS BANDA (acting).

Private Schools Employees' Union: c/o MCTU, POB 5094, Limbe; tel. 1755614; Pres. (vacant); Gen. Sec. H. S. BANDA.

Railway Workers' Union of Malawi: POB 5393, Limbe; tel. 1640844; f. 1954; Pres. Mr MTALIMANJA; Gen. Sec. LUTHER MAMBALA; 3,000 mems.

Sugar Plantation and Allied Workers' Union: Nchalo; tel. 1425200; Pres. K. GUMBO; Gen. Sec. S. MKWAPATIRA.

Teachers' Union of Malawi: Private Bag 11, Lilongwe; tel. 1727006; Pres. B. MANDA; Gen. Sec. L. CHIKADZA.

Textiles, Garments, Leather and Security Services' Union: David Whitehead and Sons Ltd, POB 30070, Blantyre 3; tel. 1641244; Pres. EMMANUEL CHAVULA; Gen. Sec. GRACE NYIRENDA.

Tobacco Tenants Workers' Union: POB 477, Nkhotakota; tel. 1292288; Pres. JOHN SIMITI; Gen. Sec. R. SANDRAM.

Transport and General Workers' Union: POB 2778, Blantyre; tel. 1756226; Pres. F. ANTONIO; Gen. Sec. RONALD MBEWE.

Water Employees' Trade Union of Malawi: c/o Lilongwe Water Board, POB 96, Lilongwe; tel. 1752162; Pres. M. CHIMPHEPO; Gen. Sec. P. MDOLO.

Transport

RAILWAYS

The Central East African Railways Co (fmrly Malawi Railways) operates between Nsanje (near the southern border with Mozambique) and Mchinji (near the border with Zambia) via Blantyre, Salima and Lilongwe, and between Nkaya and Nayuchi on the eastern border with Mozambique, covering a total of 797 km. The Central East African Railways Co and Mozambique State Railways connect Malawi with the Mozambican ports of Beira and Nacala. These links, which traditionally form Malawi's principal trade routes, were effectively closed during 1983–85, owing to insurgent activity in Mozambique. The rail link to Nacala was reopened in October 1989; however, continued unrest and flooding in Mozambique prevented full use of the route until the completion of a programme of improvements in September 2000; the service was temporarily suspended in 2002 while safety was improved. There is a rail/lake interchange station at Chipoka on Lake Malawi, from where vessels operate services to other lake ports in Malawi.

Central East African Railways Co Ltd (CEAR): Station Rd, POB 5144, Limbe; tel. 1640844; fax 1643496; f. 1994 as Malawi Railways Ltd; sold to a consortium owned by Mozambique's Empresa Nacional dos Portos e Caminhos de Ferro de Moçambique and the USA's Railroad Corpn in mid-1999 and subsequently renamed as above; ceased passenger services in Oct. 2005; Dir RUSSELL NEELY.

ROADS

In 2004 Malawi had a total road network of some 15,500 km, of which 3,600 km was paved. In addition, unclassified community roads total an estimated 10,000 km. All main roads, and most secondary roads, are all-weather roads. Major routes link Lilongwe and Blantyre with Harare (Zimbabwe), Lusaka (Zambia) and Mbeya and Dar es Salaam (Tanzania). A 480-km highway along the western shore of Lake Malawi links the remote Northern Region with the Central and Southern Regions. A project to create a new trade route, or 'Northern Corridor', through Tanzania, involving road construction and improvements in Malawi, was completed in 1992.

Department of Road Traffic: c/o Ministry of Transport and Public Works, Private Bag 257, Capital City, Lilongwe 3; tel. 1756138; fax 1752592; comprises the National Road Authority.

Road Transport Operators' Association: Chitawira Light Industrial Site, POB 30740, Chichiri, Blantyre 3; tel. 1670422; fax 1671423; e-mail rtoa@sdnp.org.mw; f. 1956; Chair. P. CHAKHUMBIRA; Exec. Dir SHADRECK MATSIMBE; 200 mems (2004).

Shire Bus Lines Ltd: POB 176, Blantyre; tel. 1671388; fax 1670038; 100% state-owned; operates local and long-distance bus services between Mzuzu, Lilongwe, and Blantyre; services to Harare in Zimbabwe and Johannesburg in South Africa; Chair. Al-haj Sheik ALIDI LIKONDE.

SHIPPING

There are 23 ports and landing points on Lake Malawi. The four main ports are at Chilumba, Nkhata Bay, Chipoka and Monkey Bay. In 2004/05 a weekly service carried some 64,244 passengers. In that year some 4,167 tons of cargo were also transported, the principal cargoes being sugar, dried fish and maize. The amount of cargo transported was expected to rise from August 2005 with the inclusion of a new landing point at Dwangwa to carry sugar to Chipoka. Smaller vessels are registered for other activities including fishing and tourism. Lake Malawi is at the centre of the Mtwara Development Corridor transport initiative agreed between Zambia, Malawi, Tanzania and Mozambique in mid-December 2004.

Department of Marine Services: c/o Department of Transport and Public Works, Private Bag A-81; tel. 1751531; fax 1756290; e-mail marinedepartment@malawi.net; responsible for vessel safety and control, ports services, and maritime pollution control.

Malawi Lake Services (MLS): POB 15, Monkey Bay; tel. 1587311; fax 1587203; e-mail ilala@malawi.net; f. 1994; privatized in 2001; 20-year operating concession granted to Glens Waterways Ltd; operates services between Malawi, Tanzania and Mozambique; Gen. Man. ANTON BOTES; 5 vessels.

CIVIL AVIATION

Kamuzu (formerly Lilongwe) International Airport was opened in 1982. There is another main airport, Chileka, at Blantyre, which serves a number of regional airlines, and three domestic airports.

Department of Civil Aviation: c/o Ministry of Transport and Public Works, Private Bag B311, Lilongwe 3; tel. 1770577; fax 1774986; e-mail aviationhq@malawi.net; Dir B. W. CHISAMILE.

Air Malawi Ltd: 4 Robins Rd, POB 84, Blantyre; tel. 1620811; fax 1620042; e-mail cd@airmalawi.net; internet www.airmalawi.net; f. 1967; privatization, begun in 1999, was postponed in 2003; scheduled domestic and regional services; Chair. JIMMY KOREIA-MPATSA; CEO FRANCIS PELEKAMOYO.

Tourism

Fine scenery, beaches on Lake Malawi, big game and an excellent climate form the basis of the country's tourist potential. The number of foreign visitor arrivals declined from 254,352 in 1999 to 228,100 in 2000, but rose to an estimated 420,911 in 2003; receipts from tourism totalled US $43m. in that year.

Department of Tourism: POB 402, Blantyre; tel. 1620300; fax 1620947; f. 1969; responsible for tourist policy; inspects and licenses tourist facilities, sponsors training of hotel staff and publishes tourist literature; Dir of Tourism Services F. MASIMBE.

Malawi Tourism Association (MTA): POB 1044, Lilongwe; tel. 1770010; fax 1770131; e-mail mta@malawi.net; internet www.malawi-tourism-association.org.mw; f. 1998; Exec. Dir SAM BOTOMANI.

MALAYSIA

Introductory Survey

Location, Climate, Language, Religion, Flag, Capital

The Federation of Malaysia, situated in South-East Asia, consists of 13 states. Eleven of these are in Peninsular Malaysia, in the southern part of the Kra peninsula (with Thailand to the north and the island of Singapore to the south), and two, Sabah and Sarawak, are on the north coast of the island of Borneo, two-thirds of which comprises the Indonesian territory of Kalimantan. Sarawak also borders Brunei, a coastal enclave in the north-east of the state. The climate is tropical, there is rain in all seasons and temperatures are generally between 22°C (72°F) and 33°C (92°F), with little variation throughout the year. The official language is Bahasa Malaysia, based on Malay, but English is also widely used. Chinese, Tamil and Iban are spoken by minorities. Islam is the established religion, practised by about 53% of the population (including virtually all Malays), while about 19%, including most of the Chinese community, follow Buddhism. The Indians are predominantly Hindus. There is a minority of Christians among all races, and traditional beliefs are practised, particularly in Sabah and Sarawak. Malaysia's national flag (proportions 1 by 2) has 14 horizontal stripes, alternating red and white, with a blue rectangular canton, containing a yellow crescent and a 14-pointed yellow star, in the upper hoist. The capital is Kuala Lumpur. A new administrative capital, Putrajaya, has been developed south of Kuala Lumpur.

Recent History

The 11 states of Malaya, under British protection, were united as the Malayan Union in April 1946 and became the Federation of Malaya in February 1948. An armed communist offensive began in 1948, and was not effectively suppressed until the mid-1950s. After 1960 the remainder of the banned Communist Party of Malaya (CPM) took refuge in southern Thailand. Meanwhile, Malaya was granted independence, within the Commonwealth, on 31 August 1957.

Malaysia was established on 16 September 1963, through the union of the independent Federation of Malaya (renamed the States of Malaya), the internally self-governing state of Singapore, and the former British colonies of Sarawak and Sabah (North Borneo). Singapore left the federation in August 1965, reducing the number of Malaysia's component states from 14 to 13. The States of Malaya were designated West Malaysia in 1966 and later styled Peninsular Malaysia.

In 1970 serious inter-communal rioting, engendered by Malay resentment of the Chinese community's economic dominance and of certain pro-Chinese electoral results, precipitated the resignation of Tunku Abdul Rahman, who had been Prime Minister of Malaya (and subsequently of Malaysia) since independence. The new Prime Minister, Tun Abdul Razak, widened the government coalition, dominated by the United Malays National Organization (UMNO), to create a national front, Barisan Nasional (BN). The BN originally comprised 10 parties, absorbing most of the former opposition parties. In January 1976 the Prime Minister died and was succeeded by the Deputy Prime Minister, Dato' Hussein bin Onn.

Political stability was subsequently threatened by the resurgence of the communist guerrilla movement, which conducted a series of terrorist attacks in Peninsular Malaysia during 1976–78. However, CPM activity subsequently declined, owing to co-operation between Malaysia and Thailand in military operations along their common border. In 1987, in a Thai-sponsored amnesty, about 700 Malaysian communists surrendered to the Thai authorities. In December 1989, following a year of negotiations with the Thai Government, the remaining 1,188 rebels (including recruits from Thailand and Singapore) agreed to terminate all armed activities. The peace agreements, signed by the leader of the CPM and representatives of the Malaysian and Thai Governments, made provision for the resettlement of the insurgents in either Malaysia or Thailand and their eventual participation in legitimate political activity in Malaysia.

In October 1977 the expulsion of the Chief Minister (Menteri Besar) of Kelantan from the dominant Parti Islam se Malaysia (PAS—Islamic Party of Malaysia) resulted in violent political disturbances in Kelantan and the declaration of a state of emergency by the federal Government. Direct rule was imposed in Kelantan, and the PAS was expelled from the BN coalition in December. In the federal and state elections of July 1978 Hussein consolidated the position of the BN, while the PAS, in opposition, suffered a serious reversal. In 1978, following the federal Government's rejection of proposals for a Chinese university, racial and religious tensions re-emerged.

In July 1981 Hussein was succeeded as Prime Minister by Dato' Seri Dr Mahathir Mohamad, Deputy Prime Minister since 1976. Mahathir called a general election in April 1982; the BN coalition won convincingly in all states and increased its overall strength in the House of Representatives.

At an election for the Sabah State Legislative Assembly in April 1985, a new political party, the Parti Bersatu Sabah (PBS—Sabah United Party) obtained more than one-half of the seats; Sabah thus became the only state that was not controlled by the BN. The legality of the new PBS Government was challenged by Muslim opponents, and in February 1986 the Chief Minister (Ketua Menteri) called a further election. In the May election the PBS won an increased majority of seats in the Assembly, and in June the BN agreed to admit the PBS into its ruling coalition, together with the United Sabah National Organization (USNO), which had been expelled in 1984.

In February 1986 Mahathir's leadership of the federal Government and of UMNO was challenged when Datuk Musa Hitam, the Deputy Prime Minister, resigned from the Government, owing to 'irreconcilable differences' with Mahathir. However, Musa retained his position as Deputy President of UMNO. During the following months Musa's supporters became increasingly critical of Mahathir, and divisions within the party widened. At an early general election in August, the BN coalition took 148 of the 177 seats in an enlarged House of Representatives: UMNO secured 83 seats, while the Malaysian Chinese Association (MCA) won 17. Of the opposition parties, the Democratic Action Party (DAP) won 24 seats, having gained support from ethnic Chinese voters who were disillusioned with the MCA. In state elections held simultaneously, the BN retained control of all the State Legislative Assemblies in Peninsular Malaysia. Several ministers who had supported Musa were subsequently demoted or removed from the Government.

In early 1987 there was a serious challenge for the presidency of UMNO from Tengku Razaleigh Hamzah, the Minister of Trade and Industry. At the UMNO General Assembly in April, none the less, Mahathir was elected UMNO President for the third time (and thus retained the position of Prime Minister at the head of the BN coalition), albeit with a greatly reduced majority. The General Assembly also narrowly elected Abdul Ghafar Baba (who had replaced Musa as Deputy Prime Minister in February 1986) as UMNO Deputy President. Mahathir subsequently announced the resignation of Razaleigh and of Datuk Rais Yatim, the Minister of Foreign Affairs, from the Cabinet, and the dismissal of several other pro-Razaleigh ministers.

Criticism of Mahathir's leadership persisted during 1987, both from within UMNO and from other political parties. At the same time, racial tensions intensified in various parts of the country over Chinese-language education, religion and other issues. In October–November, allegedly to prevent violent racially-motivated riots between Chinese and Malays over politically sensitive issues, 106 people were detained under the provisions of the Internal Security Act (ISA), which allows detention without trial on grounds of national security. Those detained included politicians from all parties (most notably the leader of the DAP, Lim Kit Siang), lawyers, journalists and leaders of pressure groups. Three newspapers were closed by the Government, and political rallies were prohibited. In November the Government introduced legislation to impose stringent penalties on editors and publishers disseminating what the Government regarded as 'false' news. From December the Minister of Information was empowered to monitor all radio and television broadcasts, and to revoke the licence of any private broadcasting company not conforming with 'Malaysian values'. By April 1989 all the detainees under the ISA had been released (although often under restrictive conditions).

In February 1988 the High Court gave a ruling on a suit filed by dissatisfied members of UMNO, who claimed that, since some of the delegations taking part in the UMNO elections of April 1987 had not been legally registered, the elections should be declared null and void. On account of the irregularities, the Court ruled that UMNO was an 'unlawful society' and that there had been 'no election at all'. Mahathir maintained that the ruling did not affect the legal status of the Government, and the Head of State, Tunku Mahmood Iskandar, expressed support for Mahathir. Later in February 1988 Mahathir announced that UMNO Baru (New UMNO) had been formed and that members of the original party would have to re-register in order to join. In March it was stated that Razaleigh and his supporters were to be excluded from the new party. The assets of UMNO Baru (hereafter referred to as UMNO) were 'frozen' and placed under judicial control until the party's legal status had been resolved; they were finally returned in September 1994.

Tension between the executive and the judiciary was intensified by Parliament's approval in March 1988 of constitutional amendments limiting the power of the judiciary to interpret laws. The Lord President of the Supreme Court, Tun Mohammed Salleh bin Abas, wrote to the Head of State to complain about government attempts to reduce the independence of the judiciary, and was subsequently dismissed from office. In June 1989 the Government further limited the powers of the judiciary when it introduced a security law, removing the right of persons being detained under provisions of the ISA to have recourse to the courts.

In September 1988 Razaleigh and 12 others followed two earlier dissidents and left the BN coalition to join the opposition in the House of Representatives as independents. They were joined in October by Musa. In December Musa and his supporters drafted a six-point resolution (the Johore Declaration), specifying the terms under which they would consent to join UMNO. These terms were accepted by UMNO in January 1989 but were binding only in the state of Johore. Following the defeat at a by-election in that month of an opposition representative by an MCA candidate with UMNO support, Musa announced his membership of UMNO, prompting a further eight dissident representatives in Johore to join the party.

In March 1989 Razaleigh's movement established an alliance with the fundamentalist PAS. In May Razaleigh's party registered as Semangat '46 (Spirit of 1946, a reference to the year of foundation of the original UMNO). The DAP, whose followers were largely urban Chinese, agreed to co-operate with Semangat '46 and the PAS, but refused to join a formal alliance, owing to their opposition to the PAS's proclaimed policy of forming an Islamic state in Malaysia. In June a former breakaway faction from the PAS, Barisan Jama'ah Islamiah Sa-Malaysia, left the BN coalition to join Semangat '46, the PAS and the Parti Hisbul Muslimin Malaysia in an opposition coalition, Angkatan Perpaduan Ummah (APU—Muslim Unity Movement). APU subsequently won a by-election by a small margin in Trengganu. In May and August, however, the BN won three by-elections. In December Mahathir held a cordial but unproductive meeting with Razaleigh, in an attempt to heal the rift in the ethnic Malay community.

A general election took place in October 1990. The opposition parties formed an informal electoral alliance, Gagasan Rakyat (People's Might). (Gagasan Rakyat was formally registered in April 1992, and Razaleigh was elected as Chairman in July.) Prior to the election the PBS withdrew from the BN and aligned itself with the opposition. Despite the defection of the PBS (which won the 14 seats that it contested), the BN controlled 127 of the 180 seats in the enlarged House of Representatives, thus retaining the two-thirds' majority necessary to amend the Constitution. The opposition's share of the seats increased from 37 to 53. However, Semangat '46 won only eight seats (compared with the 12 that it had held previously) of a total of 61 that it contested. Elections to 11 of the 13 State Legislative Assemblies (excluding Sabah and Sarawak) took place simultaneously. The BN obtained a majority of seats in every state except Kelantan, where APU won every seat in both the federal and state elections.

In November 1990, at a meeting of the UMNO General Assembly, Mahathir and Abdul Ghafar Baba were unanimously re-elected as President and Deputy President of the party. Two incumbent Vice-Presidents of UMNO, Dato' Anwar Ibrahim, the Minister of Education, and Datuk Abdullah Ahmad Badawi, a former Minister of Defence (who had been dismissed in 1987 for supporting Razaleigh's leadership challenge), were re-elected; Datuk Seri Sanusi Junid, the Minister of Agriculture, was also elected a Vice-President. In February 1991 Mahathir announced cabinet changes, appointing Anwar, widely regarded as the probable future leader of UMNO, as Minister of Finance and Badawi, his long-standing rival, as Minister of Foreign Affairs.

In January 1991 the Chief Minister of Sabah and President of the PBS, Datuk Seri Joseph Pairin Kitingan, was arrested and charged with corruption. It was widely conjectured that his arrest and his press adviser's detention, under the ISA, were politically motivated. In May UMNO secured its first seat in Sabah, in a by-election necessitated by the defection to UMNO of USNO's founder and President, Tun Mustapha Harun. Shortly afterwards Jeffrey Kitingan (the brother of the Chief Minister) was detained under the ISA, accused of plotting Sabah's secession from Malaysia.

At the UMNO General Assembly in November 1991, Mahathir made reference to the nine hereditary rulers' supposed abuse of privilege for personal gain. In February 1992 a delegation of senior UMNO representatives (excluding Mahathir) presented the Sultans with a memorandum that alleged interference by the rulers in both political and commercial spheres. UMNO criticism of the Sultans was widely suspected to be due, in part, to the Sultan of Kelantan's open support for Razaleigh (a prince of Kelantan) in the 1990 general election. In July 1992 four of the nine Sultans approved a Proclamation of Constitutional Principles, drafted in consultation with UMNO, establishing a code of conduct for the Sultans. Mahathir, who in 1983 had successfully forced the Sultans to surrender their right to refuse assent to laws passed by Parliament, proposed to remove the rulers' constitutional immunity from prosecution. In January 1993 Parliament approved amendments ending the Sultans' legal immunity, curtailing their power to pardon the offences of family members, and allowing parliamentary criticism of their misdeeds. Under the terms of the Constitution, however, the Sultans' privileges could not be restricted without the consent of the Conference of Rulers, comprising the nine Sultans. The Sultans indicated initially that they would approve the amendments, but, two hours before Parliament met, the rulers rejected the changes entirely. Mahathir responded by withdrawing from the Sultans various customary royal privileges (many of them financial) not stipulated in the Constitution. A constitutional crisis was averted when, in February, the Conference of Rulers agreed to the amendments with the inclusion of slight modifications; they were thus finally adopted with royal consent in March.

In August 1993, despite earlier assertions that he would not challenge the incumbent Ghafar, Anwar announced his decision to contest the post of UMNO Deputy President in the party's divisional elections, which Mahathir had postponed until November. The post was particularly significant as the Deputy President of UMNO was traditionally also accorded the position of Deputy Prime Minister and would be regarded as Mahathir's probable successor. In October Mahathir was returned unopposed as President of UMNO. Ghafar submitted his resignation as Deputy Prime Minister, seemingly in protest against Mahathir's failure actively to support his candidacy for the party post. By November Anwar, representing the *Malayu baru* (new Malays—younger, urban, mainly professional Malays who had prospered as a result of economic expansion), had secured overwhelming support for his candidacy, prompting the more traditional Ghafar to withdraw from the contest and also resign from UMNO. Anwar was duly elected Deputy President of UMNO, and all three vice-presidential posts were won by his self-styled 'Vision Team', which comprised Tan Sri Haji Muhyiddin Yassim (the Chief Minister—Menteri Besar—of Johore), Datuk Seri Najib Razak (the Minister of Defence) and Tan Sri Dato' Mohammed Haji Mohammed Taib (the Chief Minister—Menteri Besar—of Selangor). Anwar was appointed Deputy Prime Minister in December.

In April 1993 USNO, now led by Tun Mustapha Amirkahar (the son of Tun Mustapha Harun), left the opposition in the Sabah State Legislative Assembly to form a coalition with the ruling PBS. Prior to the announcement six of the 11 elected representatives of USNO joined UMNO. USNO's defection prompted the federal Government successfully to seek the party's deregistration in August, on the grounds that it had breached its own statutes. In the same month Tun Mustapha Harun was appointed to the federal post of Minister of Sabah Affairs.

In January 1994 Pairin Kitingan dissolved the Sabah State Legislative Assembly in preparation for elections, although the Assembly's mandate did not expire until 1995. Shortly afterwards Pairin Kitingan was convicted on charges of corruption by the High Court. (Hearings had begun in January 1992.) He was, however, fined less than the minimum RM 2,000 that was required to disqualify him from office. Although Pairin Kitingan gained popular sympathy owing both to his perceived victimization in the corruption case and to his resistance to federal encroachment on Sabahan authority, a faction emerged in the PBS that favoured more harmonious relations with the federal Government. Former members of the deregistered USNO joined the PBS for the election, and the party also gained the support of Tun Mustapha Harun, who had resigned as Minister of Sabah Affairs and as a member of UMNO in January. (Tun Mustapha Harun died in January 1995.) At the election, which took place on 18–19 February 1994, the PBS won a narrow majority, securing 25 of the 48 elective seats. Pairin Kitingan was sworn in as Chief Minister. In March, however, several PBS members defected to the opposition; among these was Jeffrey Kitingan, who had been released from detention under the ISA in December 1993. Although he was initially confined to Seremban town in Negeri Sembilan for two years, all restrictions on him were swiftly revoked, encouraging suspicions of an agreement with the federal authorities. On 17 March 1994 Pairin Kitingan resigned as Chief Minister, and on the following day Tan Sri Sakaran Dandai, a leader of the Sabah wing of UMNO, was sworn in at the head of a new administration.

In June 1994 the BN coalition agreed to admit two breakaway parties from the PBS, the Parti Demokratik Sabah (Sabah Democratic Party), led by Datuk Bernard Dompok, and the Parti Bersatu Rakyat Sabah (PBRS—United Sabah People's Party), led by Joseph Kurup. In August Dompok was appointed as Minister in the Prime Minister's Department and Jeffrey Kitingan became Deputy Minister for Housing and Local Government. Also in June Jeffrey Kitingan was cleared of corruption in the High Court.

In May 1994 the House of Representatives approved the 1994 Constitution (Amendment) Act, which further restricted the powers of the monarchy and provided for the restructuring of the judiciary. Hitherto the Yang di-Pertuan Agong (Head of State) had been competent to withhold assent from and return legislation, within 30 days, to Parliament for further consideration. The amendment required the Yang di-Pertuan Agong to give his assent to a bill within 30 days; if he failed to do so, the bill would, none the less, become law. The changes to the judiciary in the amendment included the creation of a Court of Appeal, the restyling of the Supreme Court as the Federal Court and of the Lord President as the Chief Justice.

From June 1994 the Government took action to suppress the activities of Al-Arqam, an Islamic sect that had been founded by Ashaari Muhammad in 1968. Al-Arqam was believed to have about 10,000 members in Malaysia, many of whom were public servants, and was alleged to control considerable assets. Although Al-Arqam had traditionally eschewed politics, the Government asserted that the group was a threat to national security and denounced its Islamic teachings as 'deviationist'; moreover, the Malaysian authorities accused it of training a military force in Thailand, although this was denied by both Al-Arqam and the Thai Government. In July UMNO threatened to expel party members who refused to leave Al-Arqam, and in early August the National Fatwa (Islamic Advisory) Council banned the sect on the grounds that its doctrine contravened Islamic principles.

A general election took place on 24–25 April 1995. Following an often acrimonious campaign, the BN won an overwhelming majority, taking 162 of the 192 seats in the House of Representatives (with some 64% of the total votes cast). The PBS won eight of Sabah's federal seats, including those held by Jeffrey Kitingan and Dompok. Although this constituted a loss of six seats, it was an indication that, despite the BN's assumption of power at state level through the defection of former PBS members of the legislature, the PBS remained a significant political force in Sabah. The BN also retained control of 10 of the 11 State Legislative Assemblies for which voting took place, in most cases securing a two-thirds' majority. In Kelantan, which remained the only state under opposition control, a coalition of the PAS and Semangat '46 took 35 of the 43 state seats.

Despite his overwhelming election victory, Mahathir's position appeared vulnerable during the divisional elections of UMNO in 1995. The defeat of several Mahathir supporters was widely attributed to the influence of Anwar's associates, and prompted speculation that Anwar might challenge Mahathir for the leadership. In November, however, UMNO's General Assembly adopted an unprecedented resolution to avoid any contest for the two senior party positions in 1996; Anwar finally declared that he would not challenge Mahathir, and Mahathir for the first time said that he would retire in the near future and again named Anwar as his successor.

Semangat '46 was formally dissolved in October 1996, and its members were admitted to UMNO. At that month's UMNO General Assembly Mahathir and Anwar were, as anticipated, returned unopposed to their posts. In contrast to the 1993 party elections, in which Anwar's supporters had been particularly successful, a large proportion of Mahathir loyalists were now elected. Notably, in the elections for the vice-presidencies, Muhyiddin Yassim, the only member of Anwar's 'Vision Team' who had remained loyal to the Deputy President, was defeated by Dato' Abdullah Ahmad Badawi (the Minister of Foreign Affairs, who had been a vice-president prior to 1993); Najib Razak and Mohammad Taib were re-elected. However, the Minister of International Trade and Industry, Dato' Seri Paduka Rafidah Aziz, a Mahathir loyalist, who had been investigated in 1994 by the Anti-Corruption Agency for corrupt share-dealing, was defeated as head of the women's wing by an Anwar-backed candidate, while Rahim was ousted from the youth-wing leadership by another supporter of Anwar. No former member of Semangat '46, including Razaleigh, secured a position on the UMNO Supreme Council.

In October 1996 the PAS announced that it was to abandon its attempt (of some six years' standing) to replace secular criminal laws with *hudud*, the Islamic criminal code, in Kelantan, unless this was approved by the federal Government: Mahathir was known to be strongly opposed to such a policy. The PAS won a by-election for the State Legislative Assembly in Kelantan in January 1997. Although the PAS took the seat by only a narrow margin (the seat had been won convincingly at the previous election by a Semangat '46 candidate), the results were nevertheless indicative of Razaleigh's weakened position in the state.

In May 1997 Mahathir appointed Anwar as Acting Prime Minister while he took two months' leave of absence from the post. On his return, Mahathir's response to the currency crisis affecting the region, following Thailand's effective devaluation of the baht in early July, was widely perceived to have exacerbated Malaysia's economic position. His criticism of international investors resulted in further losses to the value of both the currency and shares on the stock exchange. Meanwhile, Anwar benefited politically from the situation, appearing to act responsibly in reassuring investors and rescinding the newly imposed financial restrictions. Political opponents, however, attempted to undermine Anwar through the circulation of a series of letters accusing him of sexual indiscretions. International criticism of Mahathir's outspokenness prompted popular demonstrations of support for the premier within Malaysia and near unanimous support for a vote of confidence in his leadership, which was held in the House of Representatives during November. In the same month Mahathir announced the formation of an executive authority to address the economic crisis, the National Economic Action Council. The composition of the Council, including the appointment of the former Minister of Finance, Dato' Paduka Daim Zainuddin, as Executive Director of the Council, was approved by the Cabinet in January 1998. At the UMNO annual convention in September 1997 Mahathir criticized the increasing tendency of Malaysian Muslims to attach excessive importance to external symbols of Islam (such as beards and headscarves) and warned of the dangers of extremism. Mahathir's speech, which was resented by many Muslims, followed the widely publicized arrest, in June, of three Muslim women for taking part in a beauty contest in Selangor. The arrests prompted debate concerning the position of women in Malaysian society and resulted in demands for the reform of the Islamic Syariah (Shariah) courts; a *fatwa* (religious edict) had the force of law in the state in which it was issued, which arguably violated the liberties of Malaysians as guaranteed under the federal Constitution. In November 10 men were detained under the ISA for disseminating Shia Muslim teachings (Malaysian Muslims belong predominantly to the Sunni sect) that were perceived as militant and a threat to national security. Many non-governmental organizations and political parties called for the detainees to be released or allowed to stand trial under the Sedition Act.

MALAYSIA

Introductory Survey

At internal elections for divisional committee members in UMNO, which took place in March 1998, most of Mahathir's supporters retained their positions. However, evidence of a growing divide between Mahathir and Anwar became apparent at the UMNO annual party congress held in June, where Ahmad Zahid Hamidi, the head of the youth wing of UMNO and one of Anwar's supporters, made a speech attacking what he termed the debilitating impact of corruption in the party. Zahid's speech, which was reminiscent of Anwar's recent condemnation of corruption and political restrictions, was perceived as an attack on the party's leadership; Mahathir responded by publishing a list of hundreds of people and companies who had received privatization contracts in recent years, which included close associates of Anwar and members of his family. During the following weeks Mahathir acted to counter the influence of Anwar. He promoted Daim Zainuddin (a close personal ally) to the position of Minister of Special Functions in charge of economic development, thus undermining Anwar's position as Minister of Finance. It was suggested that the rift between Mahathir and Anwar was a result of economic policy divisions. (Mahathir's solution to the economic crisis lay in protectionism and continued expansion, in contrast to Anwar's support for austerity measures.) These allegations were, however, formally denied by Mahathir. Mahathir also dismissed newspaper editors close to Anwar and ordered the arrest of an associate of Anwar on firearms charges, which carried the death penalty under Malaysian law. The resignation in August of the Governor (a close ally of Anwar) and Deputy Governor of the central bank, reportedly owing to a disagreement over policy with Mahathir, served as an indication of the intensification of the rift within the Government. Supporters loyal to the Prime Minister responded to the perceived threat to Mahathir's leadership by circulating a brochure entitled *Fifty Reasons Why Anwar Cannot Become Prime Minister*, in which Anwar was accused of sexual offences and corruption.

Allegations of Anwar's supposed sexual misconduct increased throughout the months following the UMNO congress, and, following Anwar's refusal to resign, culminated in Mahathir's dismissal of Anwar as Deputy Prime Minister and Minister of Finance on 2 September 1998, on the grounds that he was morally unfit to hold office. On the following day Anwar was expelled from UMNO, and affidavits accusing him of sexual impropriety were filed with the High Court. The allegations were denied by Anwar, who asserted that they constituted part of a high-level political conspiracy to discredit him. Anwar began a tour of the country, drawing extensive support for his calls for the wide-ranging reform of the political system from the many thousands who attended his public appearances. His supporters adopted the slogan '*reformasi*' (reform), which had united the popular forces that ousted President Suharto in Indonesia. In mid-September Anwar's adoptive brother, Sukma Darmawan Samitaat Madja, and a former speech-writer for Anwar, Munawar Ahmad Anees, were each sentenced to six months' imprisonment after they confessed to illegal homosexual activity with Anwar. The following day, at a meeting attended by at least 40,000 people in Kuala Lumpur, Anwar called directly for Mahathir's resignation; he was arrested shortly afterwards and detained under the ISA. A further 17 people, including a number of close associates of Anwar, were also detained under the same act. Anwar's arrest provoked demonstrations of protest, which erupted into violence when demonstrations involving up to 60,000 people were violently dispersed by the security forces; 132 people were arrested.

Following Anwar's arrest, his wife, Wan Azizah Wan Ismail, emerged as the *de facto* leader of the opposition movement. Despite a restriction order issued against Wan Azizah, barring her from holding rallies at her residence, demonstrations in protest at Anwar's detention were held throughout September 1998 and became the forum for demands for widespread political reform and the removal of the restrictions on freedom of speech and assembly imposed under the ISA. Anwar finally appeared in court in Petaling Jaya at the end of September, where he pleaded not guilty to five charges of corruption and five charges of sexual impropriety. Allegations made by Anwar, who appeared in court with visible bruising to his face, that he had been severely beaten while in police custody and had subsequently been denied medical attention for a number of days, provoked expressions of extreme concern from foreign Governments—in particular from the Presidents of the Philippines and Indonesia—and prompted the UN Secretary-General, Kofi Annan, to urge the Malaysian Government to ensure humane treatment for Anwar.

The Malaysian Government initially dismissed Anwar's claims of assault; however, it was subsequently announced that a special investigation would be established. In December the Inspector-General of the Malaysian police force, Tan Sri Abdul Rahim Noor, resigned after an initial inquiry blamed the police for the injuries Anwar had received. Malaysia's Attorney-General publicly admitted in January 1999 that Anwar had been assaulted by the police while in custody, and a Royal Commission of Inquiry into Anwar's injuries, which was completed in March, found Rahim Noor to be personally responsible for the beating. In accordance with the recommendations of the inquiry, in April Rahim Noor was charged with assaulting Anwar. In March 2000 Rahim Noor was sentenced to two months' imprisonment and fined RM 2,000 after pleading guilty to a lesser charge of assault against Anwar.

Anwar's trial on four charges of corruption (which related to efforts allegedly made by him in 1997 to obtain through the police written denials that he was guilty of sexual misconduct and sodomy) began in November 1998. The presiding judge ruled that official foreign observers were not to be allowed at the trial. The credibility of the prosecution was undermined by the professed willingness of a principal witness to lie under oath, the withdrawal by a witness for the prosecution of his claims to have engaged in illegal homosexual activity with Anwar and the retraction by Anwar's adoptive brother and his speech-writer of their confessions, which they claimed had been obtained through police coercion. The defence suffered a number of reverses during the trial: in November the judge sentenced one of Anwar's lawyers to three months' imprisonment for contempt of court, because of a motion he had filed on behalf of Anwar to have two of the prosecutors dismissed from the case; the charges against Anwar were unexpectedly amended in January 1999, with the emphasis being shifted from sexual misconduct to abuse of power (the amendment meant that the prosecution would no longer have to prove that Anwar had committed sexual offences, but only that he had attempted to use his position to influence the police to quash the investigation into the allegations, effectively making it far easier for the prosecution to obtain a conviction). In addition, the judge ruled that all evidence given by several witnesses was inadmissible, despite requests from Anwar's lawyers that some parts of the testimony be retained as evidence for the defence. Following a disagreement between the defence and the presiding judge over the judge's refusal to hear a motion tabled by the defence that he be dismissed, the defence team refused to sum up its case, and the trial was ended abruptly in late March. In mid-April Anwar was found guilty on each of the four charges of corruption and a sentence of six years' imprisonment was imposed (under Malaysian law, this would be followed by a five-year period of disqualification from political office). Following the delivery of the verdict, supporters of the former Deputy Prime Minister clashed with security forces outside the court. Violent protests continued for the next three days, resulting in the arrest of 18 demonstrators. Following the trial, the three prosecution witnesses who had withdrawn their testimony against Anwar were charged with perjury. In late April Anwar was further charged with one count of illegal homosexual activity, to which he pleaded not guilty; it was announced that four other similar charges and one additional corruption charge against him had been suspended.

On the first day of Anwar's second trial in early June 1999 the prosecution amended the wording of its charge, changing the month and year (for the second time) in which the alleged crimes were supposedly committed. The trial was adjourned in September and Anwar was sent for medical examination following claims by the defence that Anwar had proven high levels of arsenic in his blood and was quite possibly the victim of deliberate poisoning. In the same month some 10,000 Anwar supporters gathered to demonstrate against the Government's treatment of the former Deputy Prime Minister and Minister of Finance; following the protests, several prominent allies of Anwar were reported to have been arrested. Anwar's trial resumed in late September, however, after medical tests found that he showed no clinical signs of arsenic poisoning, although concerns over his health continued to be expressed in October. In his testimony in court in October and November, Anwar made potentially damaging allegations of corruption against members of the Government (including the Minister of Finance, Daim, and the Minister of Domestic Trade and Consumer Affairs, Dato' Seri Megat Junid bin Megat Ayob) who, he alleged, had conspired to remove him from office. In mid-November the trial of Anwar was adjourned indefinitely without explanation; supporters of

Anwar claimed that the adjournment was a government attempt to silence him in the approach to the general election, which was to be held in late November. The trial resumed on 25 January 2000, but was adjourned again in late February at the request of the defence. Meanwhile, in April 2000 the Court of Appeal upheld Anwar's conviction on four charges of corruption.

Anwar suffered a further set-back in early June 2000, after the Court of Appeal rejected his plea for a stay of proceedings, ordering the trial on charges of sodomy to continue. In July the presiding judge ordered Anwar's defence lawyers to conclude their case, although they protested that they had intended to call further witnesses. Despite an indefinite postponement of the verdict, initially scheduled for early August, by the judge, and several police warnings, some 200 protesters gathered outside the High Court in a pro-Anwar rally. The High Court found Anwar guilty of sodomy, sentencing him to a further nine years' imprisonment, thus bringing his term to a total of 15 years. His adopted brother, Sukma Darmawan, was sentenced to six years' imprisonment and four strokes of the cane for the same offence. Although the verdict of guilty had been widely expected, observers were surprised by the severity of the sentence and by the judge's ruling that the punishments should be served consecutively rather than concurrently.

Although Anwar had been effectively removed from public office for 15 years, the affair continued to receive prominence in the media. Anwar was hospitalized in November, suffering from an acute back problem that required critical surgery. The Government refused a request for Anwar to travel abroad for surgery and, after becoming exasperated at Anwar's indecision, in April 2001 issued an ultimatum to Anwar either to accept treatment in a state hospital or return to his cell. He returned to his cell in May. In the same month public prosecutors announced that the remaining charges of corruption and sodomy against him were to be abandoned and, in July, Anwar lodged an appeal against his sodomy conviction. Meanwhile, in June 2001 the contempt verdict passed against one of Anwar's lawyers was overturned after the High Court ruled that the lawyer had been acting only in the interests of his client. In July 2002 Anwar lost his final appeal against his corruption conviction. In October of the same year Mahathir launched bankruptcy proceedings against Anwar, following his refusal to pay the costs of a defamation lawsuit he had brought against the Prime Minister in 1999. In April 2003 Anwar's appeal against his final conviction for sodomy was rejected by the Court of Appeal. A few days earlier he had completed his sentence for corruption, the last two years of his six-year sentence having been remitted for good behaviour. Despite speculation that the accession of Abdullah Badawi to the premiership in October 2003 (see below) would bring about a change in the Government's stance towards Anwar, in January 2004 a court denied his application for bail pending the result of a further appeal against his sodomy conviction.

In early September 2004 Anwar was released from prison after his appeal against his conviction for sodomy was upheld by the Federal Court, which found the evidence against Anwar unreliable. Shortly afterwards Anwar travelled to Germany for surgery on the back condition that he claimed had resulted from the severe beatings he had received in police custody in 1998, returning to Malaysia at the end of October 2004. Although he remained disqualified from holding political office until April 2008 owing to his corruption conviction, against which the Federal Court refused to allow a new appeal, Anwar announced his intention to resume his campaign for political reform.

In January 1999, meanwhile, prior to the closure of the first trial of Anwar, Mahathir effected a major cabinet reorganization, in which Abdullah Badawi was appointed as Deputy Prime Minister and Minister for Home Affairs (a post relinquished by Mahathir) and Daim Zainuddin was allocated the finance portfolio, which had been assumed by Mahathir following the dismissal of Anwar in September 1998. Also in January 1999 the UMNO Supreme Council announced its decision to postpone for 18 months elections for senior posts within the party, previously scheduled to be held in June, effectively preventing any potential challenge to Mahathir's leadership from within the party. The BN won a significant victory in the elections to the State Legislative Assembly in Sabah on 12–13 March, securing 31 of the 48 seats; Mahathir indicated, however, that the result would not induce him to call an early general election. In early April a new opposition party, the Parti Keadilan Nasional (PKN—National Justice Party), was launched by Wan Azizah in anticipation of the general election; the new party reportedly aimed to establish itself as a multi-ethnic and multi-religious party and declared that its first act, should it come to power, would be to seek a royal pardon for Anwar. Anwar himself, however, did not join the new party. Despite its stated aspirations to multi-ethnicity, the initial membership of the party appeared to be predominantly Muslim.

In November 1999 the Government unexpectedly announced that a general election was to be held later the same month. The opposition expressed dissatisfaction at the limited period of time allowed for campaigning. At the election, which was held on 29 November, a decisive victory was won by the governing BN coalition, which gained 148 of a total of 193 seats in the House of Representatives, thereby retaining the two-thirds' majority required to allow the Government to amend the Constitution. The opposition coalition, the Barisan Alternatif (Alternative Front—which had been formed by the PAS, the PKN, the DAP and the Parti Rakyat Malaysia (PRM—Malaysian People's Party) in June 1999 and which subsequently selected Anwar as its prime ministerial candidate) won a total of 42 seats, while the opposition PBS (which remained outside the Barisan Alternatif) secured three seats. Despite the BN's victory, UMNO experienced a significant decline in support amongst Malay voters (mainly to the PAS, which secured 27 seats) and lost 23 seats, including those of four cabinet ministers. The party also performed poorly in the assembly elections held simultaneously in 11 Malaysian states: the PAS secured control of the state legislature in Trengganu, retained power in Kelantan and made significant gains in Mahathir's home state of Kedah. This erosion of confidence in UMNO was widely believed to be a result of the Government's treatment of Anwar and the concomitant decline of public confidence in the country's institutions, including the police and the judicial system. While there were a number of new appointments to the Cabinet, which was announced in early December, many of the key portfolios remained unchanged. In an unexpected move, however, Mahathir promoted the unelected academic, Musa Mohamad, neither an existing government minister nor a member of UMNO, to the influential post of Minister of Education; Musa replaced Dato' Seri Najib Abdul Razak, a former potential successor to Mahathir, who was transferred to the less powerful Ministry of Defence in what was perceived by many as an effective demotion. Also in December Mahathir announced that he intended this (his fifth) term of office to be his last, and for the first time formally identified the Deputy Prime Minister, Abdullah Ahmad Badawi, as his preferred successor. In the same month the Barisan Alternatif nominated Fadzil Nor, President of the PAS, as the new parliamentary leader of the opposition. He replaced Lim Kit Siang, who had lost his seat in the general election and who in early December resigned as the Secretary-General of the DAP.

In May 2000, at the UMNO party elections, Mahathir and Badawi were formally elected President and Deputy President of the party, respectively. Recognizing the need for change in order to improve the increasingly unfavourable public image of the Government, in November the Prime Minister appointed Mohamed Dzaiddin Abdullah as the new Chief Justice, in a bid to enhance the credibility of the judiciary, tarnished by the Anwar trials. Later that month UMNO held a special general assembly, at which measures were approved to revitalize the image of the party and to attract more young professionals, including women. These developments failed to prevent the opposition PKN from taking a seat from the BN coalition at a by-election in the Lunas constituency of Kedah. The loss, thought to be due to the thousands of ethnic Chinese and young voters who had joined the electorate since the 1999 election, was unexpected, as the BN had held the Lunas seat since independence in 1957.

In April 2001 the Minister of Finance, Daim Zainuddin, took a two-month leave of absence. The leave was seen as having been enforced by Mahathir, who wanted to distance himself from criticism arising from two controversial nationalization agreements involving the heavily-indebted Malaysia Airlines and Time dotCom (the telecommunications unit of the Renong Group) in late 2000, both companies being connected to protégés of Daim. In June 2001 Daim formally resigned from his post, following widespread allegations that he had taken advantage of public funds to help business associates. Mahathir assumed the finance portfolio on an interim basis.

Possibly fearing a split in the Malay vote over the Anwar affair, Mahathir attempted to strengthen support by using the race issue in August 2000, when he criticized Suqiu, the Malaysian Chinese Organizations' Election Appeals Committee, branding some of its members extremists and likening them to communists for urging the abolition of the New Vision Policy. The policy had for 30 years ensured favouritism for the Malay majority in education and commerce, in an attempt to reduce the inequality of wealth between Malays and Chinese. The effect of the criticism may have been merely to alienate Chinese supporters, integral to the BN's 1999 victory, although Suqiu did withdraw its demands after a series of meetings with UMNO in January 2001. In early March Mahathir confirmed that the New Vision Policy, due to end in 2001, was to be extended for a further 10 years.

In January 2000, meanwhile, government suppression of dissent increased significantly. Three prominent members of the opposition were arrested; the deputy leader of the DAP and Anwar's legal representative, Karpal Singh, and the Vice-President of the PKN, Marina Yusoff, were charged under the Sedition Act, while Mohamad Ezam Mohamad Noor was charged under the Official Secrets Act. In the same month the editor and the printer of the popular PAS newspaper, *Harakah*, were also charged with sedition in connection with an article concerning the trial of Anwar that reportedly included a quote accusing the authorities of conspiring against him. The arrests were perceived by observers to constitute an attempt by the Government to curb the influence of the PAS following the party's strong performance in the general election. In early March 2000 the Government ordered that *Harakah* be published just twice a month instead of twice weekly and restricted sales of the publication to members of the PAS only. In an apparent further attempt by the Government to stifle dissent, the group editor of the *New Straits Times*, Kadir Jasin, was forced to resign in January following the publication of an editorial that questioned the decision by the UMNO Supreme Council to reject demands that the party's two most senior positions be contested from within the party in the forthcoming UMNO internal elections (the Supreme Council proposed instead that Mahathir and Abdullah Ahmad Badawi be renominated for the party presidency and vice-presidency unopposed). In January 2002 public prosecutors abandoned the sedition charges against Karpal Singh. No explanation was given for the decision.

The Anwar issue continued to incite public unrest, and in April 2000 a protest to mark the anniversary of Anwar's conviction for corruption was broken up by riot police, 48 PKN activists being arrested. Public criticism of the Government, and subsequent detentions, became more frequent after Anwar's second conviction, as confidence in Mahathir's leadership continued to decline. Mohamad Ezam Mohamad Noor was arrested in March 2001 as a result of allegedly seditious comments, despite already being on trial for releasing a secret report on corruption. A month later he was detained again, along with six other opposition leaders, including the PKN Vice-President, Tian Chua, and the PKN youth Vice-Chairman, N. Gobala Krishnan, under the ISA (which allows for detention without trial for up to two years). The aim of these arrests seemed to be to dissuade protesters from gathering for the second anniversary of Anwar's conviction. The effect was significant as only 2,000 demonstrators defied the authorities' ban to attend the peaceful 'Black 14' rally, named after and coinciding with the date of Anwar's first conviction, 14 April. The seven detainees were not immediately released after the rally, however, and three more arrests were made under the ISA. During late April the PKN youth leaders, Dr Badrul Amin Baharom and Lokman Noor Adam, were arrested, as was the human rights activist, Badarudiin Ismail, thus bringing the total of recent detainees under the provisions of the ISA to 10. In August 2002 Mohamad Ezam Mohamad Noor was sentenced to a two-year prison term, having been convicted of 'leaking' state secrets. In June 2003 he was freed on bail, pending an appeal; his conviction was overturned by the High Court in April 2004.

In early August 2001 an extraordinary session of the Court of Final Appeal heard arguments against the detention of five people under the ISA. Significantly, the judges ruled that the onus was on the State to produce evidence that those arrested posed a real threat to national security. Meanwhile, Nik Adli Nik Abdul Aziz, son of PAS spiritual leader Datuk Haji Nik Abdul Aziz Nik Mat, was one of 10 men detained under the Act on suspicion of membership of the Kumpulan Mujahidin Malaysia (KMM), an Islamist fundamentalist group believed to be engaged in a long-term plot to overthrow the Government. Seven of those taken into custody were also members of the PAS. Soon afterwards 25 supporters of Anwar Ibrahim were freed from prison and promptly rearrested on new charges, before being granted bail. In September the Government announced that Nik Adli Nik Abdul Aziz was to be detained for two years without trial under the provisions of the ISA. Eight of the nine men arrested with him were also imprisoned. Human rights activists accused the Government of exploiting the aftermath of the terrorist attacks on the USA in the same month (see the chapter on the USA) to suppress national opposition groups. Further arrests continued to be made under the ISA, as the Government tightened its control of national security.

In September 2001 the opposition was destabilized by the withdrawal of the DAP from the Barisan Alternatif. The party accused the PAS of alienating Chinese voters through its support for an Islamic state. In the same month an election in Malaysia's largest state, Sarawak, confirmed the strength of the ruling coalition. The BN won 60 out of 62 available seats in the state legislature. The DAP secured one seat; an independent candidate the other. In November the PBS decided to rejoin the Government following more than a decade of absence from power; the party was formally readmitted to the BN in January 2002. Also in January, at a by-election in the Perlis district of Indera Kayangan, the PKN was heavily defeated by the BN. The PAS accused the Government of using devious methods to exploit popular fear of Islamist militancy in the aftermath of the September terrorist attacks and thus secure a resounding victory in the election.

On 21 November 2001 Sultan Salahuddin Abdul Aziz Shah Al-Haj ibni Al-Marhum Sultan Hisamuddin Alam Shah Al-Haj died at the age of 75. On 13 December the Raja of Perlis, Tuanku Syed Sirajuddin Syed Putra Jamalullail, was sworn in as the new monarch, following his election by secret ballot from amongst the remaining eight Malay rulers. The Sultan of Trengganu continued as his deputy.

In December 2001 a court convicted 19 members of the Islamist cult al-Ma'unah of treason for plotting to overthrow the Government. The men had been arrested following the murder of two hostages during a confrontation with security forces after a weapons robbery in July 2000. Ten other cult members had pleaded guilty to lesser charges and received 10-year prison terms. Three of the sect's ringleaders were sentenced to death for their part in the armed rebellion. The remaining men were given life terms. (In November 2003 15 members of the cult, who had played only minor roles in the robbery and who later expressed remorse for their actions, were released, having been held under the ISA.) In the same month *The Sun* published a story claiming the existence of a plot to assassinate Prime Minister Mahathir. The story was later proved to be false and more than one-half of the editorial staff were dismissed, leading to allegations that the authorities had plotted to discredit the newspaper and thus more easily subject it to Malaysia's rigorous censorship laws. In January 2002 the Government announced further measures intended to stifle potential sources of dissent, stating that, with effect from May 2002, students and staff at public universities would be required to sign a pledge declaring allegiance to their king, country and government. Students had played a leading role in the protests that had followed the dismissal of Anwar Ibrahim in 1998.

In June 2002, during a speech to the annual congress of UMNO, Prime Minister Mahathir made the dramatic announcement that he intended to resign from the Government, with immediate effect. However, he was persuaded to withdraw his resignation shortly afterwards and, following some discussion, it was decided that he would remain in power until October 2003, when he would be succeeded by the Deputy Prime Minister, Abdullah Ahmad Badawi. During the transition period Badawi would assume increased responsibility for the running of the Government. Meanwhile, Fadzil Nor, President of the PAS, died following complications arising from heart surgery; Abdul Hadi Awang assumed the party leadership on an interim basis.

In July 2002 Abdul Hadi Awang announced the imposition of Islamic law in Terengganu state, of which he was the Chief Minister. The Government continued to oppose efforts to enforce the new law code, however. In the same month, at a by-election to the Kedah seat of Pendang, which had become vacant upon the death of Fadzil Nor, the BN secured a narrow victory.

In October 2002 police arrested five men, believed to be members of the regional terrorist organization Jemaah Islamiah, under the ISA. The arrests brought the total number of ISA detainees to approximately 70. Members of Jemaah Islamiah were believed to be responsible for the recent terrorist attack on the Indonesian island of Bali (see the chapter on Indonesia), which had resulted in the deaths of 202 people, including many tourists. In November the ISA attracted renewed criticism when a court ordered the release of Nasharuddin Nasir, who had been detained under its provisions since April of that year, on the grounds that no evidence had been provided to substantiate claims that he had engaged in terrorist activities. The Government, in contravention of the judicial order, rearrested him almost immediately after his release. It was announced subsequently that the ISA was to be strengthened in order to prevent further challenges by the courts. Meanwhile, Prime Minister Mahathir announced the appointment of Datuk Dr Jamaluddin Jarjis as Minister of Finance II; Mahathir himself continued to hold the other finance portfolio.

In May 2003 Minister of Transport Ling Liong Sik announced his resignation. In the following month it was announced that three members of the PKN who had been imprisoned under the ISA for more than two years were to be released. In August the PKN merged with the smaller PRM, forming the Parti Keadilan Rakyat Malaysia (PKR), in advance of the general election scheduled to be held in 2004. It was hoped that the merger would strengthen opposition to the BN and promote Anwar's cause. The President of the PKN, Wan Azizah, continued as President of the new party. In September it was announced that nine suspected members of the KMM who had been detained under the ISA in August 2001, including Nik Adli Nik Abdul Aziz, would be imprisoned for a further two years.

On 31 October 2003 Prime Minister Mahathir Mohamad retired, having spent 22 years in power; his designated successor, Deputy Prime Minister Abdullah Ahmad Badawi, was then sworn in as Prime Minister. Badawi retained the home affairs portfolio and, in addition, assumed Mahathir's role as Minister of Finance. In November Badawi was also endorsed as the new Chairman of the BN. Meanwhile, the PAS announced plans to transform Malaysia fully into an Islamic state should it come to power, attracting criticism not only from non-Muslim members of the BN but also from political allies of the PAS, including the PKR. In January 2004 the new Prime Minister effected his first cabinet reorganization, nominating Minister of Defence Najib Razak as Deputy Prime Minister. Amongst other changes, the economist Nor Mohamed Yakcop became Minister of Finance II, replacing Jamaluddin Jarjis, who was allocated the domestic trade and consumer affairs portfolio.

In February 2004, as a result of an ongoing anti-corruption campaign initiated by the new Prime Minister, both the Minister of Land and Co-operative Development, Tan Sri Datuk Kasitah bin Gaddam, and the former head of the national steel company Perwaja Steel Bhd, Eric Chia Eng Hock, were arrested and charged with corruption. Kasitah announced his resignation shortly afterwards. In the same month a national service programme was introduced with the intention of promoting national unity; conscripts were to perform military service for three months. A Royal Commission into the police force was also appointed in February. The Commission's preliminary report, presented in August, included numerous allegations of corruption and evidence that excessive force had been used against detainees. The Commission's final report, published in May 2005; called for the swift establishment of an Independent Police Complaints and Misconduct Commission, in order to render the police more accountable to the public; the report noted that the incidence of corruption within the police force was higher than in other government agencies. Meanwhile, in early March 2004 Badawi announced that Parliament was to be dissolved and a general election held later in that month, several months before the constitutional deadline of November. Later in March it was reported that six suspected Indonesian members of Jemaah Islamiah had been captured in Malaysia and were being held under the ISA, bringing the total number of suspected militants detained under the ISA to 96.

On 21 March 2004, following a brief campaign period, elections took place to an enlarged 219-member House of Representatives and to 12 of the 13 State Legislative Assemblies (Sarawak was exempted, having held elections to its legislature in September 2001). The BN secured a commanding victory, winning 198 of the 219 seats in the House of Representatives and taking control of 11 of the 12 State Legislative Assemblies, including that of Terengganu, which had previously been governed by the PAS. The PAS retained control of Kelantan by a narrow margin. The DAP secured 12 seats in the House of Representatives, followed by the PAS, which won seven (compared with 27 at the election of 1999) and the PKR, which retained only one seat, that held by Wan Azizah. Having been sworn in again as head of government, Abdullah Badawi announced a major reorganization of his Cabinet, which was enlarged through the creation of two new ministries—the Ministry of Federal Territories and the Ministry of Natural Resources and the Environment—and the division of three existing ministries, those of Home Affairs, Education and Culture, Arts and Tourism. Badawi retained the finance portfolio and that of internal security, created following the division of the Ministry of Home Affairs. Najib Razak continued as Deputy Prime Minister and Minister of Defence.

Prime Minister Badawi launched a National Integrity Plan in April 2004, aimed at reducing corruption and abuse of power. In late May the Government allowed journalists to visit a detention centre for those held under the ISA, in an attempt to dispel recent allegations, made by the US-based organization Human Rights Watch, that detainees had been tortured. In August the BN succeeded in retaining its seat at a state assembly by-election in Kuala Berang in Terengganu, increasing its majority in the constituency.

Badawi's control over UMNO was questioned in September 2004, when three members of his Cabinet failed to secure re-election to the party's Supreme Council at its General Assembly; some observers attributed their defeat to a reaction by party members against the Prime Minister's anti-corruption campaign. In addition, only one of those elected to the three posts of Vice-President was regarded as being a close ally of the Prime Minister: incumbent Tan Sri Dato' Muhyiddin Mohd Yassin, the Minister of Agriculture and Agro-based Industry. Tan Sri Mohamed Isa Abdul Samad, the Minister of Federal Territories, and Datuk Wira Mohamed Ali Rustam, the Chief Minister (Ketua Menteri) of Melaka (Malacca), were also elected as Vice-Presidents. Allegations of vote-buying emerged after the announcement of the results. None the less, Badawi and Najib Razak were formally endorsed as the party's President and Deputy President. UMNO leaders ruled out a return to the party for Anwar Ibrahim, who had been freed from prison earlier in September (see above). Anwar's release was widely regarded as evidence that Badawi was fulfilling a pledge to respect the independence of the judiciary. In December Anwar launched a nation-wide campaign against the ISA.

In January 2005 religious police conducted a raid on a nightclub in Kuala Lumpur, arresting about 100 Muslims, including many women, on charges of public indecency and other 'anti-Islamic' crimes. Amid the ensuing public outcry, the legitimacy of these arrests was questioned, as the application of Islamic law in federal territories was restricted to marriage and related matters. In the following month the Government instructed the Federal Territories Islamic Department to abandon the charges. In July 21 members of the religious group Sky Kingdom, one of 22 organizations deemed by the Government earlier that month to be 'deviant sects of Islam', were arrested at the group's compound in Terengganu and charged with propagating teachings that 'humiliated' Islam. One of those arrested pleaded guilty and was sentenced to a one-year period of religious 'rehabilitation' under the supervision of local Islamic officials. Two of the detainees applied for a hearing at the Federal Court; when the hearing opened in August, they pleaded not guilty on the grounds that they had previously renounced Islam and therefore could no longer be held accountable to the laws of that religion, citing Article 11 of the Constitution (which prescribes religious freedom for all) in their defence. The remaining 18 detainees pleaded not guilty and opted for trial before an Islamic Court. The forthcoming verdicts, regarded as being of considerable significance in the continuing debate about the issue of religious tolerance within Malaysia, were awaited with great interest by the international community. Also in August Anwar Ibrahim was awarded RM 4.5m. in damages by the High Court for the false allegations contained within the pamphlet *Fifty Reasons Why Anwar Ibrahim Cannot Become Prime Minister*, published in 1998.

In October 2005 Tan Sri Mohamed Isa Abdul Samad resigned from the position of Minister of Federal Territories, having been found guilty by the ruling party of vote-buying and political corruption pertaining to the UMNO party elections of September 2004. The UMNO Supreme Council subsequently rejected Isa's appeal against his three-year suspension from the party. In November a new Malaysian coastguard agency was launched, with operations initially focused on the Strait of Melaka, where piracy remained a serious problem. The Government was to disburse an estimated RM 578m. by the end of 2007 to finance the agency's operations, which were to be expanded gradually to cover Malaysia's other territorial waters. Malaysia, Indonesia and Singapore agreed to improve co-operation in their efforts to protect vessels traversing the busy maritime trade route. In the same month Azahari Husin, the notorious Malaysian bombmaker thought to be responsible for many of Jemaah Islamiah's operations, was killed in Indonesia during a police raid on a property in Batu, near Malang, East Java (see the chapter on Indonesia). In January 2006 another prominent Malaysian Islamist militant, Noordin Mohammad Top, released a message in which he claimed responsibility for the bombings on the Indonesian island of Bali in 2005 (see the chapter on Indonesia) and declared himself to be the head of a new South-East Asian Islamist militant organization, namely Tanzam Qaedat al Jihad (Organization of the Basis of Jihad). The statement served to remind Malaysia of the threat posed by its own nationals to regional security. Later that month Anwar Ibrahim filed a lawsuit against former Prime Minister Mahathir Mohamad for falsely having depicted him as a homosexual and causing 'irreparable damage' to his reputation. (In September 2005 Mahathir had controversially admitted to reporters that he had dismissed Anwar in order to avert the prospect of the appointment of a homosexual prime minister.)

In February 2006 Prime Minister Badawi effected a reorganization of the Cabinet. Datuk Paduka Abdul Kadir Shiekh Fadzir had previously announced his resignation from the position of Minister of Information and was replaced by Datuk Zainuddin Maidin. Other notable changes included the appointment of Datuk Seri Radzi Sheikh as Minister of Home Affairs, in place of Datuk Azmi Khalid, and the appointment of Dato' Haji Zulhasnan Rafique as Minister of Federal Territories. In the same month the Malaysian Government suspended indefinitely the licence of the *Sarawak Tribune*, in response to the newspaper's decision to reprint controversial cartoons depicting the Prophet Muhammad, which had first been published in a Danish newspaper and had provoked outrage from the international Muslim community. This was the first time in almost two decades that a Malaysian publication had had its licence revoked, and the episode renewed concerns about the status of religious freedom and freedom of expression. Shortly afterwards the licences of *Guang Ming Daily* and *Berita Petang Sarawak* were also revoked, for a two-week period, after they too reprinted the cartoons. Also in February, the Government announced plans to slaughter all poultry in four villages, following official confirmation of the first outbreak of avian influenza ('bird flu') in the country for more than a year: 40 chickens on a farm near Kuala Lumpur had been diagnosed with the deadly H5N1 strain of the virus earlier that month, prompting the Singapore Government to ban all imports from the affected region. Further cases followed.

Malaysia's foreign policy was dominated by its membership of the regional grouping, the Association of South East Asian Nations (ASEAN, see p. 172), founded in 1967. Mahathir was instrumental in bringing Myanmar into ASEAN in 1997 under the Policy of Constructive Engagement. Malaysia also played an integral role in bringing together the military junta and Aung San Suu Kyi for negotiations in late 2000, although it was thought that financial considerations might have been significant, with a promise of direct investment in Myanmar by Malaysia's national petroleum corporation, PETRONAS, in return for a semblance of progress on the part of the junta. Mahathir's visit to Myanmar in January 2001 confirmed Malaysia's interest in Myanmar, a possible alternative source of natural gas. In September 2001 the Myanma leader, Gen. Than Shwe, paid an official visit to Malaysia during which a number of bilateral agreements were signed. In August 2002 Mahathir visited Myanmar again; during his visit he met with Aung San Suu Kyi and, it was thought, attempted to encourage the junta to engage in further dialogue with the opposition.

Relations with Singapore had always been characterized by mistrust, after the city-state left the Federation of Malaya in 1965. Resentment increased as Singapore advanced more swiftly than Malaysia economically, creating a certain acrimonious competition between the two countries. As Malaysia also developed, however, bilateral relations became more cordial, and co-operation increased. The visit in August 2000 by Singapore's Senior Minister and figurehead, Lee Kuan Yew, to Mahathir in Kuala Lumpur demonstrated the growing convergence of the two countries' viewpoints. In September 2001 Lee Kuan Yew travelled to Kuala Lumpur again, on a visit intended to further enhance ties between the two countries. Relations were threatened from early 2002, however, as tensions arose over the renegotiation of a 1961 agreement by which Malaysia supplied Singapore with water. Negotiations took place in July and October 2002 in an attempt to resolve the problems arising from the water dispute, but without success. In February 2003 Prime Minister Mahathir stated that, while Malaysia would cease to supply Singapore with untreated water in 2011, it would continue to supply filtered water, at a reasonable price, for as long as necessary. Following the retirement of Mahathir in October 2003, bilateral relations showed signs of improvement under new Prime Minister Abdullah Badawi. In January 2004 Badawi and his Singaporean counterpart, Goh Chok Tong, reciprocated visits and discussed the tensions in the relationship. In October, on his first official visit to Malaysia, the new Prime Minister of Singapore, Lee Hsien Loong, announced that his predecessor, Goh, now Senior Minister in the Prime Minster's Office, would lead his country's efforts to resolve outstanding bilateral issues. Badawi and Goh held talks in Kuala Lumpur in mid-December. Issues discussed included the dispute over the sale of water to Singapore; the use of Malaysian airspace by Singapore's air force; the joint development of unused railway land in Singapore; the release of pension funds owed to Malaysians who had worked in Singapore; and the proposed construction of a bridge between the two countries. In early January 2005 Malaysia and Singapore appeared to have resolved a dispute over the latter's land reclamation project in the Straits of Johor, which separate the two countries. Malaysia accepted that the reclamation work could proceed, while Singapore agreed to co-operate with Malaysia to ensure navigational safety and environmental protection of the waterway.

In January 1993 Gen. Fidel Ramos visited Malaysia, the first Philippine President to do so since 1968, owing to strained relations over the Philippines' claim to Sabah. Mahathir and Ramos agreed to establish a joint commission to address bilateral problems. In February 1994 Mahathir made the first official visit by a Malaysian head of government to the Philippines. Relations with the Philippines, however, were strained in April 2000, when Muslim separatists from the southern Philippines abducted a group of tourists from the Malaysian resort of Sipadan, off the coast of Sabah. Following a similar kidnapping incident in September, the Malaysian Government dispatched an additional 600 troops to the region.

Relations with Indonesia generally improved from the mid-1990s. In June 1996 the two countries agreed on joint measures to limit the flow of illegal workers into Malaysia. Wide-ranging amendments to the Immigration Act in Malaysia in October 1996 failed to halt the flow of illegal immigrants, which was blamed for rising social tensions. The regional economic crisis, which began in mid-1997, led to an increase in illegal immigrants arriving in Malaysia and prompted Malaysia to begin a repatriation programme to Indonesia and elsewhere. Violent protests against deportation took place in detention centres in March 1998. In addition, groups of illegal Indonesian immigrants entered the compounds of several foreign embassies and the office of the UN High Commissioner for Refugees in March and April and requested political asylum to prevent their repatriation to the Indonesian province of Aceh, where they claimed that, as members of secessionist groupings, they would be subject to persecution. Some of the immigrants were subsequently granted asylum by Denmark and Norway. In November 2000 Malaysia and Indonesia agreed to intensify border patrols, after four Malaysians were detained by Indonesian police in June of that year for allegedly stealing logs.

Relations with both Indonesia and the Philippines, meanwhile, were strained in 1998 following the arrest in September of the former Malaysian Deputy Prime Minister and Minister of Finance, Anwar Ibrahim: both the President of Indonesia and the President of the Philippines made explicit criticisms of the Malaysian Government regarding its treatment of Anwar. Although the controversy surrounding Anwar's treatment receded as an international issue in 1999, bilateral relations with the Philippines were adversely affected by President Estrada's granting of an audience to Anwar's wife, Wan Azizah Wan Ismail, when she visited the Philippines in April. The new President of Indonesia, Abdurrahman Wahid, demonstrated the close relations between Indonesia and Malaysia by visiting Kuala Lumpur immediately after his election in October 1999.

In August 2001 President Wahid's successor, Megawati Sukarnoputri, visited Malaysia on the final stage of her tour of ASEAN nations. In the same month the new President of the Philippines, Gloria Macapagal Arroyo, also paid her first official visit to the country. However, relations with Indonesia soon threatened to deteriorate again. In 2001 the Government announced that it would deport 10,000 Indonesian illegal immigrants each month in an attempt to tighten controls on foreign labour in the country at a time of economic slowdown. In December 2001 and January 2002 a series of riots by Indonesian labourers led Prime Minister Mahathir to comment that Malaysia might give workers of different nationalities preference in the labour market owing to the problems caused by the illegal immigrants. In late January a temporary ban was imposed on new workers arriving from Indonesia. Soon afterwards the Indonesian Government issued a formal apology for the behaviour of its workers and stated that it hoped that the trouble caused would not affect an otherwise harmonious relationship. Relations with the Philippines were also threatened in November 2001 when the authorities arrested the fugitive Philippine rebel leader, Nur Misuari, on charges of attempting to enter Malaysia illegally. After much indecision, he was finally deported in January 2002 to face trial in Manila (see the chapter on the Philippines). In May 2002 Malaysia, Indonesia and the Philippines signed an anti-terrorism pact enabling them to exchange intelligence and to launch joint police operations, in an effort to combat regional terrorist organizations; Thailand and Cambodia also acceded to the pact later in the year. In August the implementation of new legislation requiring that all illegal immigrants leave the country, or face penalties including fines, imprisonment and caning, strained relations with both the Philippines and Indonesia, as the majority of the workers affected were citizens of those countries. In September the Malaysian Government announced that, owing to diplomatic pressure, exacerbated by public protests being held in Indonesia and the Philippines over the apparently inhumane nature of the expulsions, deportations were being temporarily halted. In early 2004 relations with Indonesia were threatened again when the Indonesian Government called for a global boycott of Malaysian timber, following the release of a report alleging that protected trees from Indonesia were being smuggled across the joint border, 'laundered' and re-exported. The Government denied the claims. At the end of October a 17-day amnesty began for illegal migrant workers to leave Malaysia voluntarily without penalty. Thousands of Indonesians had fled to Malaysia since the Indonesian authorities had commenced military operations against separatists in the province of Aceh in May 2003. In November 2004 Malaysia agreed to extend the amnesty until the end of the year in response to disquiet expressed by the Indonesian Government. The amnesty was subsequently further extended following a written request from President Susilo Bambang Yudhoyono of Indonesia, who was concerned at the prospect of an influx of migrants, at a time when the country was still struggling to recover from the devastation caused by a series of tsunamis in late December (which had killed at least 111,000 people in Indonesia and some 68 in Malaysia). None the less, it was reported that around 380,000 of an estimated 1.2m. illegal foreign workers had left Malaysia by the end of January 2005. In mid-February, following talks with President Yudhoyono in Kuala Lumpur, Badawi announced that the amnesty would expire at the end of the month, and in March the forced repatriation of illegal immigrants recommenced. However, in early 2006 it was estimated that hundreds of thousands of illegal immigrants still remained in Malaysia. Human rights organizations, including Amnesty International, expressed serious misgivings about the standard of training and supervision given to officers of the Malaysian Immigration Department, amidst allegations of widespread physical abuse of immigrants. In August the Malaysian Government expressed frustration at the Indonesian authorities' apparent failure adequately to address the recurrent issue of the heavy smoke emanating from forest fires on the Indonesian island of Sumatra. Originating in the fires lit by farmers to clear land for crop plantations, the haze had become an annual problem, but in 2005 the resultant smog was more severe than in any year since 1998. Owing to the dangerously high levels of air pollution, the Government declared a state of emergency in western and central regions of the country, including Kuala Lumpur.

In 1994 Malaysian and Indonesian officials commenced discussions to resolve their conflicting claims to the sovereignty of Sipadan and Ligitan, two small islands off the coast of Borneo. In October 1996 an agreement was reached by both countries to refer the issue to the International Court of Justice (ICJ, see p. 19). In December 2002 the ICJ ruled that Malaysia would be awarded sovereignty of the islands, thus bringing an end to the dispute. Another territorial claim being pursued through negotiations was the dispute with Singapore over the island of Batu Putih (Pedra Branca). In February 2003 the two countries finally signed a formal agreement referring the dispute to the ICJ. Malaysia is also involved with Brunei, Viet Nam, the People's Republic of China, the Philippines and Taiwan in disputed sovereignty claims over the Spratly Islands in the South China Sea. In November 2002 the ASEAN member states approved a Code of Conduct for the islands; the agreement was also sanctioned by China.

Relations with Thailand were strained at the end of 1995 following the killing by the Malaysian navy of two Thai citizens fishing illegally in Malaysian waters. In December the two countries agreed to establish a committee to resolve a long-standing dispute over fishing rights. In February 1996 relations deteriorated, owing to Thailand's opposition to Malaysia's construction of a 27-km wall (completed in 1997) along its border with Thailand, intended to deter illegal immigration from that country. However, in January 1997 the two countries agreed to co-operate in preventing Bangladeshi migrant workers from entering Malaysia and in expediting the return of illegal Thai workers from Malaysia. The arrest in January 1998 of three Thai Muslim separatists by the Malaysian authorities and their deportation to Thailand demonstrated continued co-operation between the two countries since Malaysia was often regarded as a place of sanctuary for Muslim separatists in southern Thailand. Relations between Malaysia and Thailand were further enhanced in April, when the two countries signed an agreement to share equally the natural gas produced in an offshore area to which both countries had made territorial claims. However, the Thai Minister of Foreign Affairs, Surin Pitsuwan, was amongst a number of international political figures who expressed concern at the arrest and detention of the former Deputy Prime Minister and Minister of Finance, Anwar Ibrahim, in September. In April 2001 the Thai Prime Minister, Thaksin Shinawatra, made his first official visit to the country on a trip intended to enhance co-operative ties. Bilateral talks were also held in January 2002 in an attempt to resolve problems arising from a planned project to build a gas pipeline between the two countries. In January 2004 new Prime Minister Abdullah Badawi visited Thailand for security discussions, following several attacks believed to have been perpetrated by separatists along the Thai side of the joint border. The two countries agreed to co-operate in efforts to bring an end to the violence and began joint border patrols. The Thai Government subsequently announced that it intended to fence off parts of the border, owing to speculation that Muslim separatists thought to be responsible for the violence might be inside Malaysia. Malaysia rejected such suggestions by the Thai Prime Minister. Amid continuing unrest in southern Thailand, Thaksin Shinawatra visited Malaysia in mid-April for further talks with Badawi on improving security along the border. In late April Malaysia increased its border security after militants launched a series of attacks on police posts in southern Thailand; the attacks were violently suppressed by the Thai security forces. Security at the border was heightened again in October following renewed clashes in southern Thailand between government troops and Muslim protesters in which 85 people died, many of whom suffocated after being forced into army trucks. Hundreds of Malaysians demonstrated outside the Thai embassy in Kuala Lumpur in protest at the deaths. Bilateral relations were further strained in December, when the Thai Government claimed to have photographic evidence that militants in southern Thailand had received training in the Malaysian state of Kelantan. In January 2005 the Malaysian authorities arrested Abdul Rahman Ahmad, whom Thailand held responsible for organizing the separatist violence in the south. A diplomatic dispute arose between the two countries in October 2005, concerning the fate of 131 Muslim villagers who had fled from the violence-stricken province of Narathiwat, in southern Thailand, to neighbouring Malaysia. The Malaysian authorities insisted that they would not sanction the return of the asylum-seekers to Thailand unless they received a guarantee of their safety from the Thai authorities. One of the villagers, suspected of involvement in a raid on a Thai military camp in January 2004, was subsequently relinquished to the Thai authorities, while the other 130 refugees remained in a Malaysian detention centre in Terengganu. Discussions aimed at resolving the dispute were held in November between former Prime Minister Mahathir Mohamad and Thai Prime Minister Thaksin Shinawatra; negotiations were also held between Shinawatra and Prime Minister Badawi in the same month, during the course of the APEC summit meeting in Busan, the Republic of Korea. The ongoing dispute took relations between the two countries to their lowest point in recent years. In February 2006 the Thai Government indicated that it was prepared to cease its attempts to repatriate the villagers and was to allow them to remain in Malaysia.

Malaysia's relations with the People's Republic of China remained extremely cordial, with Malaysia frequently offering public support to China, particularly in response to US criticism. Mahathir paid another of a long series of official visits to China in November 2000, and the Chinese Premier, Zhu Rongji, made an official visit to Malaysia in November 1999. In May 2001 the Yang di-Pertuan Agong paid an official state visit to China at the invitation of the Chinese President, Jiang Zemin.

Malaysia forged closer ties with Japan in December 2005 with the signing of a bilateral free-trade agreement, which was expected to take effect in late 2006. Under the terms of the accord, the two countries were to eliminate tariffs on all industrial goods and on most agricultural, forestry and fishery products within a 10-year period. The agreement also covered intellectual property-rights protection, investment rules, competition policies, business facilitation and personnel training. In keeping with the spirit of invigorated relations, the Emperor and Empress of Japan were scheduled to pay a state visit to Malaysia in June 2006, their first official trip to the country since 1991.

Mahathir's proposal to establish an East Asian Economic Caucus (EAEC), a trade group intended to exclude the USA, met with considerable resistance from the US Government (which continued to promote the US-dominated Asia-Pacific Economic Co-operation forum—APEC, see p. 164) and Australia. In July 1993 ASEAN agreed, despite the continuing reluctance of Japan to participate, that the EAEC should operate as an East Asian interest group within APEC. In November 1999 (although Mahathir was absent owing to the Malaysian general election) the third informal summit meeting of the 10 ASEAN countries and the People's Republic of China, Japan and the Republic of Korea (collectively known as 'ASEAN + 3') took place. At the meeting it was agreed to hold annual East Asian summits of all 13 nations and to strengthen present economic co-operation with the distant aim of forming an East Asian bloc with a common market and monetary union. This ambition was brought closer in April 2001 when, at a meeting of the ASEAN + 3 group, plans were agreed for a network of currency 'swap' arrangements to prevent a repetition of the regional financial crisis of 1997. At the annual ASEAN summit meeting held in Laos in November 2004 it was agreed to transform the ASEAN + 3 summit meeting, which was first held in 1997, into the East Asia summit, with the long-term objective of establishing an East Asian Community. In December 2005 Kuala Lumpur hosted the inaugural East Asia Summit, held during the course of the ASEAN summit meeting. At the first East Asia Summit, which was chaired by Malaysian Prime Minister Badawi, representatives from the participating nations held discussions on a wide range of issues, including international terrorism, maritime security, the threat of avian influenza, trade and development and the promotion of human rights and democracy. It was agreed that the Summit should convene annually, with the second meeting scheduled to be held in Cebu, the Philippines, in December 2006.

In 1999 Mahathir objected to Australia's leadership of the UN-mandated peace-keeping mission in East Timor (now Timor-Leste, following the territory's accession to independence in May 2002), the UN Transitional Administration in East Timor (UNTAET), claiming that an ASEAN-led mission would be more appropriate. Other ASEAN members were, however, reluctant to assume responsibility for the peace-keeping body and Australia and East Timor both objected to the notion of Malaysia leading transitional arrangements, owing to its close relations with Indonesia. Only after the intervention of the UN Secretary-General did Malaysia finally contribute limited personnel to UNTAET. In February 2001 Malaysia announced that it would open a liaison office in Dili, East Timor, which became an embassy upon the declaration of East Timor as a fully independent state in May 2002.

Malaysia's relations with Australia, which were often strained under Mahathir, appeared to improve following the succession of Abdullah Ahmad Badawi to the premiership in October 2003. In June 2004, during a visit to Malaysia by the Australian Minister for Foreign Affairs, Alexander Downer, agreement was reached to hold formal annual talks between the two countries' foreign ministers and separate regular consultations between senior security officials. At the same time Prime Minister Badawi accepted an invitation to make a state visit to Australia. This took place in April 2005 and was the first by a Malaysian leader in more than 20 years. However, the Malaysian Government had dismissed a plan announced by the Australian Prime Minister, John Howard, in September 2004 to establish specialist counter-terrorist centres in South-East Asia and Australia, complaining that it had not been consulted about the proposal. None the less, formal negotiations on a free-trade agreement between Malaysia and Australia commenced in mid-2005, following the completion of a preliminary study undertaken by both countries; in August the Australian Deputy Prime Minister and Minister for Trade, Mark Vaile, announced that negotiations had progressed well and were expected to be concluded by mid-2006.

In July 1997 Mahathir (who was often regarded as the international spokesperson for developing countries) indicated that he might submit a proposal to the UN to review its 1948 Universal Declaration of Human Rights, with regard to the specific priorities of less-developed countries. While this sentiment was supported by many Asian countries, the USA reacted angrily to any suggestion of compromise on the issue of human rights. Relations with the USA were also strained by the involvement of PETRONAS in a consortium that signed an agreement during September to invest in Iran, in contravention of US sanctions against Iran. In October Mahathir paid a formal visit to Cuba, the first such visit by a Malaysian leader, and urged Malaysian firms to invest in the country, in defiance of US legislation that threatened reprisals against firms conducting business with Cuba. Bilateral relations deteriorated further in the same month following Mahathir's suggestion that the economic crisis in the South-East Asian region was due to hostile Jewish currency speculation aimed at preventing progress among Muslim nations. A resolution tabled by 34 members of the US Congress calling for the withdrawal of the remarks or Mahathir's resignation was condemned by Mahathir and the Malaysian press. Relations with the USA were further strained in 1998 following US condemnation of the detention and treatment of the former Deputy Prime Minister and Minister of Finance, Anwar Ibrahim; the Malaysian Government was particularly angered by a speech delivered at the APEC summit meeting in Kuala Lumpur in November by the US Vice-President, Albert Gore, in which Gore expressed support for the movement for political reform in Malaysia. During a speech to UMNO members in June 1999, Mahathir criticized the influence on the country of non-Malaysians (and, in particular, ethnic Europeans), who Mahathir claimed were attempting to 're-colonize' Malaysia. Relations with the USA were improved following a visit by Adm. Dennis Blair, the Commander-in-Chief of the US Pacific Command, to Kuala Lumpur in January 2001. At his meeting with Mahathir, the first between the Prime Minister and a US Pacific commander, the two countries agreed to extend military co-operation. However, the new US President, George W. Bush, insisted that any further improvement in relations would depend on better treatment for Anwar Ibrahim and other detained members of the Malaysian opposition.

In September 2001 bilateral ties with the USA were greatly strengthened when Mahathir moved quickly to condemn attacks on the US mainland thought to have been carried out by the al-Qa'ida terrorist network. However, during a meeting with the US President at an APEC summit meeting in Shanghai in October, Mahathir refused to lend his Government's support to the US-led retaliatory attacks on Afghanistan that had begun earlier that month, voicing his concerns at the large numbers of civilian casualties resulting from the raids. At a meeting of ASEAN leaders in November, Malaysia agreed to co-operate with other member nations in the fight against terrorism. In January 2002 the USA congratulated the Malaysian Government on its demonstration of support for the international coalition against terrorism, following the detention of at least 15 suspected terrorists. However, it demanded assurances that the suspects would receive a fair trial under the ISA. In October it was reported that the US Government had requested that Malaysia be the host for a regional anti-terrorism training centre.

While Mahathir made clear his opposition to the US-led campaign to remove the regime of Saddam Hussain in Iraq in 2003, relations with the USA remained generally stable, owing largely to the Government's ongoing operation against suspected domestic terrorists, which was in line with the global anti-terrorism campaign being pursued by the Bush Administration. However, in October 2003, at a summit meeting of the Organization of the Islamic Conference (OIC, see p. 340) held in Putrajaya, Prime Minister Mahathir attracted criticism from the USA, Israel and several European countries when he attacked what he described as Jewish subjugation of Islamic countries during his opening address to the meeting. The Government later issued an apology for the comments. In early 2004 relations with the USA were threatened when new Prime Minister Abdullah Badawi accused the USA of using unreliable intelligence to implicate Malaysia in a global nuclear smuggling network. (The US Government had alleged that a company owned by Badawi's son had supplied components to the network.) In May the USA welcomed the arrest, under the ISA, of Buhary Syed Abu Tahir, a Sri Lankan businessman resident in Malaysia, for his alleged involvement in the network. Meanwhile, in April the Deputy Prime Minister and Minister of Defence, Najib Razak, rejected a proposal by the Commander-in-Chief of the US Pacific Command, Adm. Thomas Fargo, that US warships should patrol the Strait of Melaka between Malaysia and Indonesia to deter terrorism. In July Malaysia, Indonesia and Singapore commenced co-ordinated patrols of the Strait, a critical maritime trade route through which 50% of the world's oil passes, in an attempt to curb piracy. On his first official visit to the USA as Prime Minister in the same month, Badawi offered to consider dispatching a medical team to Iraq.

In June 1997 the inauguration took place of a group that aimed to foster economic co-operation among Muslim developing countries, the Developing-Eight (D-8), comprising Malaysia, Bangladesh, Egypt, Indonesia, Iran, Nigeria, Pakistan and Turkey. Malaysia continued to express its close relationship with Arab countries after it denounced US and British air strikes against Iraq in February 2001, while demanding the removal of UN sanctions.

Government

Malaysia is a federation of 13 states. The capital, Kuala Lumpur, is a separate Federal Territory, as is the island of Labuan and the newly developed administrative capital of Putrajaya. The Head of State, or Supreme Head of Malaysia, is a monarch (Yang di-Pertuan Agong), elected for a five-year term (with a Deputy Head of State) by and from the hereditary rulers of nine of the states. The monarch acts on the advice of Parliament and the Cabinet. Parliament consists of the Dewan Negara (Senate) and the Dewan Rakyat (House of Representatives). The Senate has 70 members, including 44 appointed by the Head of State, four of which are from the Federal Territories, and 26 elected members, two chosen by each of the 13 State Legislative Assemblies. The House of Representatives consists of 219 members (increased from 193 at the March 2004 general election), elected for five years by universal adult suffrage: 165 from Peninsular Malaysia (including 11 from Kuala Lumpur and one from Putrajaya), 28 from Sarawak and 26 from Sabah (including one from Labuan). The Head of State appoints the Prime Minister and, on the latter's recommendation, other ministers. The Cabinet is responsible to Parliament. The country is divided into 137 administrative districts.

Defence

Malaysia participates in the Five-Power Defence Arrangements with Australia, New Zealand, Singapore and the United Kingdom. In August 2005 the active armed forces totalled 110,000 men: army 80,000 (although it was planned to reduce this to 60,000–70,000), navy 15,000 and air force 15,000. In February 2004 a programme of national service was introduced, initially on an experimental basis, requiring conscripts to perform three months of military service. Reserve forces numbered 51,600 (army 50,000, navy 1,000, air force 600). Paramilitary forces in 2005 included a General Operations Force (formerly the Police Field Force) of 18,000 men and a People's Volunteer Corps with about 240,000 members. Federal budget plans for 2005 allocated RM 9,390m. to defence.

Economic Affairs

In 2004, according to estimates by the World Bank, Malaysia's gross national income (GNI), measured at average 2002–04 prices, was US $117,132m., equivalent to $4,650 per head (or $9,630 per head on an international purchasing-power parity basis). During 1995–2004, it was estimated, the population increased at an annual average of 2.3%, while gross domestic product (GDP) per head increased, in real terms, by an average of 2.2% per year. Overall GDP increased, in real terms, at an average annual rate of 4.5% in 1995–2004. According to the Bank Negara Malaysia (BNM), GDP increased by 7.1% in 2004 and by 5.3% in 2005.

Agriculture (including forestry and fishing) contributed 8.4% of GDP in 2005. The sector engaged 14.3% of the employed labour force in 2003. Malaysia is the world's leading producer of palm oil, exports of which contributed an estimated 4.4% of the value of total merchandise exports in 2005. Other important crops include rice, rubber (although this accounted for just 1.3% of total exports in 2005), cocoa, coconuts, bananas, tea and pineapples. The production of sawlogs declined during the 1990s, owing to a government policy of sustainable management that led to the imposition of restrictions on exports of logs in 1993. During 1995–2004, according to the Asian Development Bank (ADB), agricultural GDP increased, in real terms, at an average annual rate of 2.4%. According to the BNM, agricultural GDP increased by 5.0% in 2004 and by 2.1% in 2005.

Industry (including mining, manufacturing, construction and utilities) contributed 49.8% of GDP in 2005. The sector engaged 32.0% of the employed labour force in 2003. During 1995–2004, according to the ADB, industrial GDP increased, in real terms, at an average annual rate of 5.2%. According to the BNM, industrial GDP grew by 7.9% in 2004 and by 3.9% in 2005.

Mining contributed 14.7% of GDP in 2005. However, it engaged only 0.3% of the employed labour force in 2003. At the end of 2004 estimated proven gas reserves stood at 2,460,000m. cu m, and petroleum reserves at 4,300m. barrels. Petroleum production in 2004 averaged 912,000 barrels per day from Malaysia's 33 oilfields, enough to sustain production for less than 13 years. At that year's level, natural gas production could be sustained for 46 years. Exports of crude petroleum and condensates provided an estimated 5.4% of total export earnings in 2005. Malaysia is one of the world's leading producers of tin, although in 2005 sales of this commodity accounted for only 0.2% of total export revenue. Bauxite, copper, iron, gold and coal are also mined. The GDP of the mining sector increased at an average annual rate of 2.7% in 1995–2004, according to the ADB. Mining GDP increased by 3.9% in 2004 and by 0.8% in 2005, according to the BNM.

Manufacturing (the largest export sector) contributed 29.4% of GDP in 2005. The manufacturing sector engaged 21.6% of the employed labour force in 2003. The most important branches of manufacturing include electrical machinery and appliances, food products, metals and metal products, non-electrical machinery, transport equipment, rubber and plastic products, chemical products, wood products and furniture. According to the ADB, during 1995–2004 manufacturing GDP increased, in real terms, at an average annual rate of 6.3%. Manufacturing GDP increased by 9.8% in 2004 and by 4.9% in 2005, according to the BNM.

Energy is derived principally from Malaysia's own reserves of hydrocarbons. The country's dependence on petroleum as a source of electric energy declined from 55.9% in 1990 to 9.3% in 2002. The share contributed by natural gas increased from 22.0% to 77.5% over the same period. In 2002 hydropower and coal accounted for 7.1% and 6.0%, respectively, of the country's electricity output. Production of electricity rose from 84,022m. kWh in 2003 to 90,663 kWh in 2004. Construction of a controversial 2,400-MW hydroelectric dam at Bakun, in Sarawak, was postponed in 1997, owing to the financial crisis. In August 2002 responsibility for the project was assumed by a seven-member consortium that included Kuala Lumpur-based Sime Darby Bhd. However, in March 2005 the Malaysian Government announced that it did not expect construction to be completed on schedule in 2007. Imports of mineral products comprised 6.8% of the value of merchandise imports in 2004.

The services sector contributed 41.8% of GDP in 2005. It engaged 53.7% of the employed labour force in 2003. Tourism makes a significant contribution to the economy. In the aftermath of the terrorist attack on Bali in October 2002 (see the chapter on Indonesia), tourist arrivals in Malaysia declined to 10.6m. in 2003, while tourist receipts decreased to RM 21,291.1m. In 2004, however, tourist arrivals rose to 15.7m. and revenue increased to almost RM 29.7m. Preliminary indications suggested that the tsunami disaster of December 2004 would not have as severe an effect as was initially feared in the tourism sector. In January 2005 Malaysia received 1,394,032 visitors, a modest decline of 1.0% on the figure for the corresponding period of the previous year. In 2005 the financial and real estate sector, along with business services, contributed 10.5% of GDP. The banking system in Malaysia was severely damaged by the regional financial crisis in 1997; a series of mergers subsequently took place as part of plans to consolidate the sector. The GDP of the services sector increased by an average of 5.8% per year in 1995–2004, according to the ADB. According to the BNM, services GDP grew by 6.7% in 2004 and by 6.6% in 2005.

MALAYSIA

In 2003 Malaysia recorded a visible trade surplus of US $25,711m., with a surplus of $13,381m. on the current account of the balance of payments. In 2005 the principal source of imports (providing 14.5% of the total) was Japan; other major suppliers were the USA (12.9%), Singapore (11.7%), the People's Republic of China, Taiwan and Thailand. The principal market for exports (purchasing 19.7%) was the USA; other significant purchasers were Singapore (15.6%) and Japan (9.4%). The principal imports in 2003 were machinery and transport equipment, basic manufactures and mineral products. The principal exports in 2005 were electrical machinery and parts (particularly electronic equipment and semiconductors), chemicals, crude petroleum and condensates and liquefied natural gas.

The 2005 budget envisaged expenditure of RM 117,400m., resulting in a projected deficit of 17,700m., equivalent to 3.8% of GDP; the 2006 budget predicted that the budgetary deficit would decline to 3.5% of GDP. According to the ADB, at the end of 2005 Malaysia's external debt totalled US $51,719m.; the cost of debt-servicing in that year was equivalent to 4.0% of the value of exports of goods and services. The annual rate of inflation averaged 2.4% in 1995–2004. Consumer prices increased by an average of 1.4% in 2004 and by 3.0% in 2005. At September 2005 3.8% of the labour force were unemployed.

Malaysia is a member of the UN Economic and Social Commission for Asia and the Pacific (ESCAP, see p. 33), the Asian Development Bank (ADB, see p. 169), the Association of South East Asian Nations (ASEAN, see p. 172), the Colombo Plan (see p. 385) and Asia-Pacific Economic Co-operation (APEC, see p. 164), all of which aim to accelerate economic progress in the region. In January 1992 the member states of ASEAN agreed to establish a free-trade zone, the ASEAN Free Trade Area (AFTA). The original target for the reduction of tariffs to between 0% and 5% was 2008, but this was subsequently advanced to 2003 and then 2002, when AFTA was formally established. Malaysia itself, however, was granted a three-year delay in January 2001 for the opening of its politically-sensitive automotive industry to the free-trade agreements, fearing competition from Thailand; this was subsequently extended until 2008.

The Malaysian economy made a rapid recovery from the regional economic crisis of 1997/98. The ringgit 'peg' of 3.80 to the US dollar, however, remained in place. Despite increasing pressure during the course of 2004 for a review of the viability of the 'peg', owing to a decline in the value of the US dollar from late 2003, the arrangement remained unchanged. At October 2004 the ringgit was deemed by foreign investors to be undervalued by approximately 15%, an undervaluation that had served to improve Malaysia's competitiveness in the export market, as well as to encourage capital inflows. Compared with the previous year, the value of exports of manufactured goods increased by 19.7% in 2004; transport equipment registered the strongest growth, rising by 65%. In July 2005 it was unexpectedly announced that the ringgit 'peg' was to be removed, with immediate effect, in favour of a managed 'float' system; the BNM was to monitor the exchange rate against a basket of currencies in order to ensure that it remained at a fair value. It was hoped that the ringgit would appreciate significantly, thereby lowering the cost of imports, alleviating the impact of increased oil prices and helping to reduce the Government's debt burden as more than 50% of its external debt was US dollar-denominated. However, by December 2005 the ringgit had appreciated only modestly, to RM 3.780 to the dollar, although it was forecast to appreciate more considerably during the course of 2006. Despite the economic recovery of 1999–2000, foreign investment in Malaysia decreased sharply in 2001, partly owing to the increasing attractiveness of the People's Republic of China as an alternative destination for investment, before recovering in 2002. Foreign direct investment rose from US $1,104m. in 2003 to $2,563m. in 2004, but suffered a significant decline in the following year, decreasing to just $713m. Following the retirement of Prime Minister Mahathir Mohamad in October 2003, his successor, Abdullah Ahmad Badawi, deferred several large-scale infrastructure projects and launched an anti-corruption campaign in an attempt to reduce public spending. He also announced his intention to focus on developing the country's agricultural sector and to prioritize educational reforms. In September 2004 it was announced that a new goods-and-services tax (GST) was to be implemented on 1 January 2007, replacing the existing consumption tax. In February 2006, however, the Government announced that implementation of GST was to be delayed so as to allow more time to refine the tax model and to ensure that businesses were fully prepared for the changes. It was hoped that the new tax scheme would be more readily comprehensible to tourists than the extant system, with its two separate consumer taxes on sales and service. Introduction of GST was also expected to improve revenue collection, on account of its greater transparency. The Government predicted a GDP growth rate of 5.5% for 2006, thought likely to be largely driven by strong expansion in the transport, storage and communications, trade and utilities sectors. However, reforms to the country's education and health sectors would continue to be necessary in the long term, in order to reduce Malaysia's reliance on foreign direct investment and exports to drive economic growth.

Education

Under the Malaysian education system, free schooling is provided at government-assisted schools for children between the ages of six and 18 years. There are also private schools, which receive no government financial aid. Education is compulsory for 11 years between the ages of six and 16 years. Bahasa Malaysia is the main medium of instruction, while English is taught as a second language; Chinese and Tamil are used for instruction only in primary institutions. In January 2003 new legislation came into effect, requiring that all mathematics and science classes in schools be taught in English. Primary education begins at six years of age and lasts for six years. In 2001 95.2% of all children in the relevant age-group were enrolled in primary schools. Secondary education, beginning at the age of 12, lasts for seven years, comprising a first cycle of three years and a second of four. Pupils may attend vocational and technical secondary schools instead of the final four years of academic education. In 2002 the total enrolment at secondary schools was equivalent to 67% of males and 74% of females within the relevant age-group. In 1997 Malaysia had 11 state universities and three private universities; in 1995 total enrolment at tertiary level was equivalent to 12% of the relevant age-group. In October 1994 the Government introduced a bill that would allow foreign universities to establish branch campuses in Malaysia. From the end of that year the Government permitted the use of English as a medium of instruction in science and engineering subjects at tertiary level. At the seventh ASEAN summit meeting in November 2001 it was decided that the town of Bandar Nusajaya in Johor would be the location for the first ASEAN university. It would be Malaysia's second international university.

Federal budget expenditure for 2005 allocated RM 21,577m. (24.2% of total expenditure) to education.

Public Holidays

Each state has its own public holidays, and the following federal holidays are also observed:

2006: 10 January* (Hari Raya Haji, Feast of the Sacrifice), 29–30 January† (Chinese New Year), 31 January* (Muharram, Islamic New Year), 10 April* (Mouloud, Prophet Muhammad's Birthday), 1 May (Labour Day), 12 May (Vesak Day), 5 June (Official Birthday of HM the Yang di-Pertuan Agong), 31 August (National Day), 21 October‡ (Deepavali), 23 October* (Hari Raya Puasa, end of Ramadan), 20 December* (Hari Raya Haji, Feast of the Sacrifice), 25 December (Christmas Day).

2007: 20 January* (Islamic New Year), 18–19 February (Chinese New Year), 31 March* (Mouloud, Prophet Muhammad's Birthday), 1 May (Labour Day), 31 May (Vesak Day), 5 June (Official Birthday of HM the Yang-di Pertuan Agong), 31 August (National Day), 13 October* (Hari Raya Puasa, end of Ramadan), 9 November‡ (Deepavali), 20 December* (Hari Raya Haji, Feast of the Sacrifice), 25 December (Christmas Day).

* These holidays are dependent on the Islamic lunar calendar and may vary by one or two days from the dates given.

† The first two days of the first moon of the lunar calendar.

‡ Except Sabah and Sarawak.

Weights and Measures

The metric system is in force. There is also a local system of weights and measures:

1 cupak = 1 quart (1.1365 litres)
1 gantang = 1 gallon (4.5461 litres)
1 tahil = 11/3 ounces (37.8 grams)
16 tahils = 1 kati = 11/3 lb (604.8 grams)
100 katis = 1 picul = 1331/3 lb (60.48 kg)
40 piculs = 1 koyan = 5,3331/3 lb (2,419.2 kg)

MALAYSIA

Statistical Survey

Sources (unless otherwise stated): Department of Statistics, Blok C6, Parcel C, Pusat Pentadbiran Kerajaan Persekutuan, 62514 Putrajaya; tel. (3) 88857000; fax (3) 88889248; e-mail jpbpo@stats.gov.my; internet www.statistics.gov.my; Bank Negara Malaysia (Central Bank of Malaysia), Jalan Dato' Onn, PO Box 10922, 50929 Kuala Lumpur; tel. (3) 26988044; fax (3) 26912990; e-mail info@bnm.gov.my; internet www.bnm.gov.my; Departments of Statistics, Kuching and Kota Kinabalu.

Note: Unless otherwise indicated, statistics refer to all states of Malaysia.

Area and Population

AREA, POPULATION AND DENSITY

Area (sq km)	
Peninsular Malaysia	131,686
Sabah (incl. Labuan)	73,711
Sarawak	124,450
Total	329,847*
Population (census results)	
14 August 1991	18,379,655
5–20 July 2000	
Males	11,853,432
Females	11,421,258
Total	23,274,690
Population (official estimate at mid-year)	
2003	25,050,000
2004	25,580,000
2005	26,130,000
Density (per sq km) at mid-2005	79.2

* 127,355 sq miles.

PRINCIPAL ETHNIC GROUPS
(at census of August 1991)*

	Peninsular Malaysia	Sabah†	Sarawak	Total
Malays and other indigenous groups	8,433,826	1,003,540	1,209,118	10,646,484
Chinese	4,250,969	218,233	475,752	4,944,954
Indians	1,380,048	9,310	4,608	1,393,966
Others	410,544	167,790	10,541	588,875
Non-Malaysians	322,229	464,786	18,361	805,376
Total	14,797,616	1,863,659	1,718,380	18,379,655

* Including adjustment for underenumeration.
† Including the Federal Territory of Labuan.

Mid-1997 (estimates, '000 persons): Malays 10,233.2; Other indigenous groups 2,290.9; Chinese 5,445.1; Indian 1,541.7; Others 685.7; Non-Malaysians 1,468.9; Total 21,665.5.

STATES
(census of 5–20 July 2000)

	Area (sq km)	Population*	Density (per sq km)	Capital
Johor (Johore)	18,987	2,740,625	144.3	Johor Bahru
Kedah	9,425	1,649,756	175.0	Alor Star
Kelantan	15,024	1,313,014	87.4	Kota Baharu
Melaka (Malacca)	1,652	635,791	384.9	Melaka
Negeri Sembilan (Negri Sembilan)	6,644	859,924	129.4	Seremban
Pahang	35,965	1,288,376	35.8	Kuantan
Perak	21,005	2,051,236	97.7	Ipoh
Perlis	795	204,450	257.2	Kangar
Pulau Pinang (Penang)	1,031	1,313,449	1,274.0	George Town
Sabah	73,619	2,603,485	35.4	Kota Kinabalu
Sarawak	124,450	2,071,506	16.6	Kuching
Selangor	7,960	4,188,876	526.2	Shah Alam
Terengganu (Trengganu)	12,955	898,825	69.4	Kuala Terengganu
Federal Territory of Kuala Lumpur	243	1,379,310	5,676.2	—
Federal Territory of Labuan	92	76,067	826.8	Victoria
Total	329,847	23,274,690	70.6	

* Including adjustment for underenumeration.

PRINCIPAL TOWNS
(population at 2000 census)

Kuala Lumpur (capital)*	1,297,526	Kuala Terengganu (Kuala Trengganu)	250,528
Ipoh	566,211	Seremban	246,441
Kelang (Klang)	563,173	Kota Baharu (Kota Bahru)	233,673
Petaling Jaya	438,084	Sandakan	220,000†
Shah Alam	319,612	Taiping‡	183,320
Kuantan	283,041	George Town (Penang)	180,573

* The new town of Putrajaya is now the administrative capital.
† Provisional.
‡ Excluding a part of Pondok Tanjong, which is in the District of Kerian.

Source: Thomas Brinkhoff, *City Population* (internet www.citypopulation.de).

Mid-2003 (UN estimate, incl. suburbs): Kuala Lumpur 1,352,057 (Source: UN, *World Urbanization Prospects: The 2003 Revision*).

MALAYSIA

BIRTHS AND DEATHS

	Registered live births		Registered deaths	
	Number	Rate (per 1,000)	Number	Rate (per 1,000)
1997	540,486	24.9	97,432	4.5
1998	524,696	23.7	98,219	4.4
1999	554,200	24.4	100,900*	4.4*
2000	569,500	24.5	102,100*	4.4*
2001	n.a.	22.3	n.a.	4.4
2002	n.a.	21.7	n.a.	4.5
2003*	533,600	21.3	113,900	4.5

* Provisional figures.

Sources: Ministry of Health, Kuala Lumpur; UN, *Demographic Yearbook* and *Population and Vital Statistics Report*.

2004 (provisional): Birth rate 20.1 per 1,000; Death rate 4.5 per 1,000.
2005 (provisional): Birth rate 19.6 per 1,000; Death rate 4.4 per 1,000.

Expectation of life (WHO estimates, years at birth): 72 (males 70; females 75) in 2003 (Source: WHO, *World Health Report*).

EMPLOYMENT*
(sample surveys, ISIC major divisions, '000 persons aged 15 to 64 years)

	2001	2002	2003
Agriculture, hunting and forestry	1,288.2	1,316.8	1,301.2
Fishing	127.7	107.7	107.0
Mining and quarrying	26.7	27.5	29.5
Manufacturing	2,184.1	2,068.9	2,131.0
Electricity, gas and water	57.3	50.6	57.6
Construction	829.8	905.1	942.5
Wholesale and retail trade; repair of motor vehicles, motorcycles and personal and household goods	1,458.1	1,497.0	1,592.2
Hotels and restaurants	585.1	616.1	644.2
Transport, storage and communications	468.3	496.8	481.6
Financial intermediation	225.3	240.5	223.4
Real estate, renting and business activities	348.6	397.1	404.2
Public administration and defence; compulsory social security	664.6	663.6	666.5
Education	508.6	508.6	594.3
Health and social work	173.3	189.3	217.3
Other community, social and personal service activities	190.4	192.5	216.1
Private households with employed persons	219.9	262.7	258.0
Extra-territorial organizations and bodies	1.2	2.0	3.2
Total employed	**9,357.0**	**9,542.6**	**9,869.7**

* Excluding members of the armed forces.

Source: ILO.

Health and Welfare

KEY INDICATORS

Total fertility rate (children per woman, 2003)	2.9
Under-5 mortality rate (per 1,000 live births, 2004)	12
HIV/AIDS (% of persons aged 15–49, 2003)	0.4
Physicians (per 1,000 head, 2000)	0.70
Hospital beds (per 1,000 head, 1996)	2.01
Health expenditure (2002): US $ per head (PPP)	349
Health expenditure (2002): % of GDP	3.8
Health expenditure (2002): public (% of total)	53.8
Access to water (% of persons, 2002)	95
Access to sanitation (% of persons, 1990)	96
Human Development Index (2003): ranking	61
Human Development Index (2003): value	0.796

For sources and definitions, see explanatory note on p. vi.

Agriculture

PRINCIPAL CROPS
('000 metric tons)

	2002	2003	2004
Rice (paddy)	2,197	2,259	2,184
Maize*	70	72	75
Sweet potatoes	41	27	27
Cassava (Manioc)†	380	400	430
Other roots and tubers†	44	44	45
Sugar cane†	1,500	1,300	1,200
Coconuts	693*	580*	580†
Oil palm fruit†	59,546	66,775	69,881
Other oilseeds†	120	120	120
Cabbages	24	29	35
Tomatoes	22	32	34
Cucumbers and gherkins†	45	45	45
Other vegetables†	254	264	264
Watermelons	91	130†	132†
Bananas†	500	530	530
Pineapples†	310	320	320
Papayas†	65	71	72
Other fruit†	335	375	375
Coffee (green)*	39	40	39
Cocoa beans	48	36	33
Pepper	24	22	22†
Natural rubber	890	986	1,190

* Unofficial figure(s).
† FAO estimate(s).

Source: FAO.

LIVESTOCK
('000 head, year ending September)

	2002	2003	2004
Cattle	748	723	750*
Buffaloes	154	160*	163*
Goats	233	227	227
Sheep	126	122	120*
Pigs	2,047	2,052	2,100*
Chickens	160,843	165,000*	180,000*
Ducks*	15,000	16,000	16,000

* FAO estimate(s).

Source: FAO.

LIVESTOCK PRODUCTS
('000 metric tons)

	2002	2003	2004
Beef and veal*	18.5	19.7	21.3
Buffalo meat*	3.7	4.3	4.7
Pig meat	192.9	198.1	203.5
Chicken meat	761.3	765.0	825.5
Duck meat	52.7	81.6†	102.0
Cows' milk	34.9	35.5	37.7
Buffaloes' milk*	7.4	7.5	7.5
Hen eggs	411.8	421.3	431.0
Other poultry eggs	10.5	10.7	11.0
Cattle and buffalo hides*	3.4	3.7	4.0

* FAO estimates.
† Unofficial figure.

Source: FAO.

Forestry

ROUNDWOOD REMOVALS
('000 cubic metres, excl. bark)

	2002	2003	2004
Sawlogs, veneer logs and logs for sleepers	17,913	21,531*	22,000*
Fuel wood†	3,228	3,172	3,119
Total	21,141	24,703	25,119

* Unofficial figure.
† FAO estimates.
Source: FAO.

SAWNWOOD PRODUCTION
('000 cubic metres, incl. railway sleepers)

	2002	2003	2004
Total (all broadleaved)	4,643	4,769	5,598*

* Unofficial figure.
Source: FAO.

Fishing

('000 metric tons, live weight)

	2001	2002	2003
Capture	1,234.7	1,275.6	1,287.1
Indian scad	77.4	90.3	79.1
Kawakawa	53.2	59.4	21.1
Yellowstripe scad	39.9	41.0	33.5
Indian mackerels	99.5	87.9	124.9
Prawns and shrimps	77.5	76.0	73.2
Squids	45.3	52.5	49.9
Aquaculture	158.2	165.1	167.2
Blood cockle	70.8	78.7	71.1
Total catch	1,392.9	1,440.7	1,454.2

Note: Figures exclude crocodiles, recorded by number rather than by weight. The number of estuarine crocodiles caught was: 375 in 2001; 122 in 2002; 307 in 2003. Also excluded are shells and corals. Catches of turban shells (FAO estimates, metric tons) were: 80 in 2001; 80 in 2002; 80 in 2003. Catches of hard corals (FAO estimates, metric tons) were: 4,000 in 2001; 4,000 in 2002; 4,000 in 2003.

Source: FAO.

Mining

PRODUCTION
(metric tons, unless otherwise indicated)

	2001	2002	2003*
Tin-in-concentrates	4,972	4,215	3,359
Bauxite ('000 metric tons)	64	40	6
Iron ore ('000 metric tons)†	376	404	597
Kaolin	364,458	323,916	376,958
Gold (kg)	3,965	4,289	4,739
Barytes	649	3,082	—
Hard coal	497,733	352,513	172,820
Crude petroleum ('000 barrels)	243,696	254,770	269,370
Natural gas (million cu m)‡	58,751	60,791	65,173
Ilmenite†	129,750	106,046	95,148
Zirconium†	3,768	5,292	3,456

* Data are preliminary.
† Figures refer to the gross weight of ores and concentrates.
‡ Including amount reinjected, flared and lost.
Sources: US Geological Survey.

Industry

SELECTED PRODUCTS
('000 metric tons, unless otherwise indicated)

	2002	2003	2004
Canned fish, frozen shrimps/prawns	42.2	47.7	45.8
Palm oil (crude)	11,909	13,355	13,976
Refined sugar	1,408.8	1,424.1	1,447.7
Soft drinks ('000 litres)	440.2	524.7	517.7
Cigarettes (metric tons)	23,079	23,971	24,602
Woven cotton fabrics (million metres)	166.4	163.3	175.8
Veneer sheets ('000 cu metres)	1,089.6	956.8	835.4
Plywood ('000 cu metres)	3,972.3	4,171.1	5,104.5
Kerosene and jet fuel	3,170.7	3,056.5	3,165.5
Liquefied petroleum gas	2,945.4	3,277.5	3,191.0
Inner tubes and pneumatic tyres ('000)	27,107	27,851	27,824
Rubber gloves (million pairs)	12,207.7	15,059.7	18,153.1
Earthen brick and cement roofing tiles (million)	1,315.6	1,579.1	1,439.8
Cement	14,336	17,243	17,326
Iron and steel bars and rods	3,221.5	3,347.1	3,016.0
Refrigerators for household use ('000)	172.1	186.9	80.4
Television receivers ('000)	10,409.7	9,915.2	9,748.8
Radio receivers ('000)	21,735	27,634	28,605
Semiconductors (million)	15,036	15,958	18,228
Electronic transistors (million)	20,401	24,189	28,236
Integrated circuits (million)	19,916	23,424	30,247
Passenger motor cars ('000)*	418.8	348.1	384.3
Commercial vehicles ('000)*	72.3	81.3	78.1
Motorcycles and scooters ('000)	242.4	257.5	385.8
Electric energy (million kWh)†	75,328	84,022	90,663

* Vehicles assembled from imported parts.
† Source: Asian Development Bank.

Tin (smelter production of primary metal, metric tons): 30,417 in 2001; 30,887 in 2002; 18,250 (preliminary figure) in 2003 (Source: US Geological Survey).

Finance

CURRENCY AND EXCHANGE RATES

Monetary Units
100 sen = 1 ringgit Malaysia (RM—also formerly Malaysian dollar).

Sterling, US Dollar and Euro Equivalents (30 December 2005)
£1 sterling = RM 6.5088;
US $1 = RM 3.7800;
€1 = RM 4.4593;
RM 100 = £15.36 = US $26.46 = €22.43.

Exchange Rate
A fixed exchange rate of US $1 = RM 3.8000 was in effect between September 1998 and July 2005.

FEDERAL BUDGET
(RM million)

Revenue	2003	2004	2005
Tax revenue	64,891	72,050	80,594
Taxes on income and profits	43,016	48,703	53,543
Companies (excl. petroleum)	23,990	24,388	26,381
Individuals	7,984	8,977	8,649
Petroleum	8,466	11,479	14,566
Export duties	1,156	1,600	2,085
Import duties	3,919	3,874	3,385
Excises on goods	5,031	6,427	8,641
Sales tax	7,965	6,816	7,709
Service tax	2,038	2,350	2,582
Others	1,766	2,280	2,648
Other revenue	27,717	27,347	25,709
Total	92,608	99,397	106,304

MALAYSIA

Statistical Survey

Expenditure	2003	2004	2005
Emoluments	21,721	23,779	25,587
Pensions and gratuities	5,870	6,060	6,809
Debt service charges	10,546	10,920	11,604
Domestic	8,663	9,161	9,875
External	1,883	1,758	1,729
Supplies and services	13,968	16,633	17,984
Subsidies	2,679	5,796	12,831
Asset acquisition	1,409	1,764	1,603
Other grants and transfers	16,323	21,264	20,982
Other expenditure	2,706	5,082	344
Total	75,224	91,298	97,744

FEDERAL DEVELOPMENT EXPENDITURE
(RM million)

	2003	2004	2005
Defence and security	6,029	4,133	4,803
Social services	17,707	10,260	7,450
Education	10,193	4,316	3,736
Health	2,681	2,352	1,220
Housing	1,928	1,593	1,082
Economic services	13,793	11,851	14,957
Agriculture and rural development	1,620	2,881	2,482
Public utilities	920	945	1,481
Trade and industry	3,456	1,201	3,221
Transport	7,354	6,630	7,660
General administration	1,824	2,620	3,325
Sub-total	39,353	28,864	30,534
Less Loan recoveries	1,041	1,346	3,250
Total	38,312	27,518	27,284

INTERNATIONAL RESERVES
(US $ million at 31 December)

	2002	2003	2004
Gold*	56	61	64
IMF special drawing rights	151	178	199
Reserve position in IMF	790	871	776
Foreign exchange	33,280	43,466	65,409
Total	34,277	44,576	66,448

*Valued at SDR 35 per troy ounce.

Source: IMF, *International Financial Statistics*.

MONEY SUPPLY
(RM million at 31 December)

	2002	2003	2004
Currency outside banks	23,897	26,101	28,617
Demand deposits at commercial banks	62,124	73,387	81,515
Total money (incl. others)	90,163	103,907	112,690

Source: IMF, *International Financial Statistics*.

COST OF LIVING
(Consumer Price Index; base 2000 = 100)

	2002	2003	2004
Food	101.4	102.7	105.0
Beverages and tobacco	109.2	111.0	119.7
Clothing and footwear	95.2	93.3	91.6
Rent and other housing costs, heating and lighting	102.1	103.1	104.0
Furniture, domestic appliances, tools and maintenance	99.7	99.1	99.5
Medical care	105.4	107.2	108.7
Transport and communications	110.4	112.3	113.1
Education and leisure	100.1	100.7	100.6
Other goods and services	101.8	103.1	105.0
All items	103.2	104.4	105.9

NATIONAL ACCOUNTS
(RM million at current prices)

Expenditure on the Gross Domestic Product

	2003	2004	2005
Government final consumption expenditure	54,913	59,317	64,592
Private final consumption expenditure	172,366	192,771	215,876
Change in stocks	−1,814	10,009	−1,059
Gross fixed capital formation	87,089	91,818	98,930
Total domestic expenditure	312,554	353,915	378,339
Exports of goods and services	447,846	544,956	609,133
Less Imports of goods and services	365,383	449,262	492,928
GDP in purchasers' values	395,017	449,609	494,544
GDP at constant 1987 prices	232,359	248,954	262,029

Gross Domestic Product by Economic Activity

	2003	2004	2005
Agriculture, forestry and fishing	37,987	42,665	42,882
Mining and quarrying	41,071	56,679	75,177
Manufacturing	122,706	141,172	150,693
Electricity, gas and water	12,680	13,696	14,434
Construction	15,071	15,199	15,205
Trade, restaurants and hotels	52,654	58,557	65,183
Transport, storage and communications	26,919	29,847	32,351
Finance, insurance, real estate and business services	47,208	49,806	52,050
Government services	29,643	32,109	35,043
Other services	26,293	27,840	29,539
Sub-total	412,232	467,570	512,557
Import duties	6,507	6,396	6,595
Less Imputed bank service charges	23,720	24,356	24,609
GDP in purchasers' values	395,017	449,609	494,544

BALANCE OF PAYMENTS
(US $ million)

	2001	2002	2003
Exports of goods f.o.b.	87,981	93,383	104,999
Imports of goods f.o.b.	−69,597	−75,248	−79,289
Trade balance	18,383	18,135	25,711
Exports of services	14,455	14,878	13,578
Imports of services	−16,657	−16,448	−17,532
Balance on goods and services	16,182	16,565	21,757
Other income received	1,847	2,139	3,448
Other income paid	−8,590	−8,734	−9,376
Balance on goods, services and income	9,439	9,970	15,829
Current transfers received	537	661	508
Current transfers paid	−2,689	−3,442	−2,955
Current balance	7,287	7,190	13,381
Direct investment abroad	−267	−1,905	−1,369
Direct investment from abroad	554	3,203	2,473
Portfolio investment assets	254	−563	−196
Portfolio investment liabilities	−666	−836	1,174
Financial derivatives assets	−2,702	−4,597	−4,502
Financial derivatives liabilities	−829	1,868	−895
Other investment assets	−234	−174	−24
Other investment liabilities	−3	−139	142
Net errors and omissions	−2,394	−391	−4
Overall balance	1,000	3,657	10,181

Source: IMF, *International Financial Statistics*.

MALAYSIA

External Trade

PRINCIPAL COMMODITIES
(RM million)

Imports c.i.f.	2003	2004	2005
Capital goods*	40,799	55,487	59,743
Intermediate goods	235,448	287,717	309,330
Miscellaneous industrial supplies, processed	59,164	82,381	87,726
Parts and accessories of capital goods (excl. transportation equipment)	143,724	159,344	163,544
Consumption goods	18,721	23,226	24,613
Total (incl. others)†	316,538	400,077	434,030

Exports f.o.b.	2003	2004	2005
Palm oil	20,192	20,107	19,062
Crude oil and condensates	15,659	21,318	28,573
Liquefied natural gas	13,358	17,079	20,759
Semi-conductors	85,140	89,298	89,967
Electronic components	82,240	99,307	118,266
Consumer electrical products	19,712	22,170	22,639
Industrial and commercial electrical products	20,285	25,769	28,601
Electrical industrial machinery and equipment	13,598	17,783	20,480
Chemicals and chemical products	21,200	27,767	29,734
Metal manufactures	11,242	16,140	17,157
Total (incl. others)	397,884	480,722	533,790

* Figures net of re-exports.
† Including re-exports.

PRINCIPAL TRADING PARTNERS
(RM million)

Imports c.i.f.	2003	2004	2005
Australia	4,803	6,793	8,171
China, People's Republic	27,739	39,279	49,879
France	4,563	5,543	5,660
Germany	14,787	17,798	19,265
Hong Kong	8,580	10,850	10,797
India	2,555	4,897	4,164
Indonesia	11,168	15,936	16,566
Japan	54,273	63,693	63,000
Korea, Republic	17,308	19,843	21,604
Philippines	11,835	10,667	12,192
Singapore	37,283	44,437	50,831
Taiwan	15,698	21,630	23,973
Thailand	14,549	21,992	22,889
United Kingdom	5,991	6,640	6,522
USA	48,757	57,752	55,918
Total (incl. others)	316,538	399,648	434,030

Exports f.o.b.	2003	2004	2005
Australia	9,932	15,783	18,042
China, People's Republic	25,878	32,143	35,224
France	6,688	7,081	6,913
Germany	9,145	10,485	11,258
Hong Kong	25,778	28,686	31,205
India	9,629	11,411	14,972
Indonesia	8,091	11,677	12,580
Japan	42,643	48,553	49,918
Korea, Republic	11,550	16,839	17,945
Netherlands	13,036	15,752	17,452
Philippines	5,459	7,362	7,476
Singapore	62,786	72,176	83,333
Taiwan	14,351	15,763	14,813
Thailand	17,538	22,954	28,723
United Kingdom	8,872	10,556	9,470
USA	78,005	90,182	105,033
Total (incl. others)	397,884	480,722	533,790

Transport

RAILWAYS
(traffic, Peninsular Malaysia only)

	1999	2000	2001
Passenger-km (million)	1,313	1,220	1,181
Freight ton-km (million)	908	917	1,094

Source: UN, *Statistical Yearbook*.

ROAD TRAFFIC
(registered motor vehicles at 31 December)

	2000	2001	2002
Passenger cars	4,212,567	4,624,557	5,069,412
Buses and coaches	48,662	49,771	51,158
Lorries and vans	665,284	689,668	713,148
Road tractors	315,687	329,198	345,604
Motorcycles and mopeds	5,356,604	5,609,351	5,842,617

Source: International Road Federation, *World Road Statistics*.

SHIPPING

Merchant Fleet
(registered at 31 December)

	2002	2003	2004
Number of vessels	915	972	1,013
Total displacement ('000 grt)	5,394.4	5,745.8	6,056.6

Source: Lloyd's Register-Fairplay, *World Fleet Statistics*.

Sea-borne Freight Traffic*
(Peninsular Malaysia, international and coastwise, '000 metric tons)

	2001	2002	2003
Goods loaded	70,092	81,648	87,960
Goods unloaded	68,184	74,460	73,416

* Including transhipments.

Source: UN, *Monthly Bulletin of Statistics*.

CIVIL AVIATION
(traffic on scheduled services)

	1999	2000	2001
Kilometres flown (million)	207	220	217
Passengers carried ('000)	14,985	16,561	16,107
Passenger-km (million)	33,708	37,939	35,658
Total ton-km (million)	4,431	5,346	5,233

Source: UN, *Statistical Yearbook*.

Tourism

TOURIST ARRIVALS BY COUNTRY OF RESIDENCE*

	2002	2003	2004
Brunei	256,952	215,634	453,664
China, People's Republic	557,647	350,597	550,241
Indonesia	769,128	621,651	789,925
Japan	354,563	213,527	301,429
Singapore	7,547,761	5,922,306	9,520,306
Thailand	1,166,937	1,152,296	1,518,452
Total (incl. others)	13,292,010	10,576,915	15,703,406

* Including Singapore residents crossing the frontier by road through the Johore Causeway.

Tourism receipts (RM million): 25,781.1 in 2002; 21,291.1 in 2003; 29,651.4 in 2004.

Source: Malaysia Tourism Promotion Board.

MALAYSIA

Communications Media

	2002	2003	2004
Telephones ('000 main lines in use)	4,669.9	4,571.6	4,446.3
Mobile cellular telephones ('000 subscribers)	9,253.4	11,124.1	14,611.9
Personal computers ('000 in use)	3,600	4,200	4,900
Internet users ('000)	7,840.6	8,661.0	9,878.2

Radio receivers ('000 in use, 1997): 9,100.

Television receivers ('000 in use, 2001): 4,773.

Facsimile machines ('000 in use): 175.0* in 1998.

Book production (1999): 5,084 titles (29,040,000 copies in 1996)†.

Daily newspapers (2000): 31 (average circulation 2,191,000 copies).

Non-daily newspapers (1997): 3 (average circulation 312,000 copies).

Periodicals (1992): 25 titles (average circulation 996,000 copies).

* Estimate(s).
† Including pamphlets (106 titles and 646,000 copies in 1994).

Sources: International Telecommunication Union; UNESCO, *Statistical Yearbook*; UN, *Statistical Yearbook*.

Education

(January 2004, unless otherwise indicated)

	Institutions	Teachers	Students
Primary	7,557	179,622	3,044,797
Secondary	1,962	130,372	2,093,645
Regular	1,751	116,006	1,979,526
Fully residential	53	3,135	29,813
Technical	88	7,224	34,710
Religious	55	3,053	37,732
Special	3	140	884
Special Model	10	688	10,437
Sports*	2	142	912
Tertiary†	48	14,960	210,724
Universities	9	7,823	97,103
Teacher training	31	3,220	46,019
MARA Institute of Technology	1	2,574	42,174

* 2003 figures.
† 1995 figures.

Source: Ministry of Education.

Pre-primary: 9,743 schools (1994); 20,352 teachers (1994); 459,015 pupils (1995) (Source: UNESCO, *Statistical Yearbook*).

Adult literacy rate (UNESCO estimates): 88.7% (males 92.0%; females 85.4%) in 2003 (Source: UN Development Programme, *Human Development Report*).

Directory

The Constitution

The Constitution of the Federation of Malaya became effective at independence on 31 August 1957. As subsequently amended, it is now the Constitution of Malaysia. The main provisions are summarized below.

SUPREME HEAD OF STATE

The Yang di-Pertuan Agong (King or Supreme Sovereign) is the Supreme Head of Malaysia.

Every act of government is derived from his authority, although he acts on the advice of Parliament and the Cabinet. The appointment of a Prime Minister lies within his discretion, and he has the right to refuse to dissolve Parliament even against the advice of the Prime Minister. He appoints the Judges of the Federal Court and the High Courts on the advice of the Prime Minister. He is the Supreme Commander of the Armed Forces. The Yang di-Pertuan Agong is elected by the Conference of Rulers, and to qualify for election he must be one of the nine hereditary Rulers. He holds office for five years or until his earlier resignation or death. Election is by secret ballot on each Ruler in turn, starting with the Ruler next in precedence after the late or former Yang di-Pertuan Agong. The first Ruler to obtain not fewer than five votes is declared elected. The Deputy Supreme Head of State (the Timbalan Yang di-Pertuan Agong) is elected by a similar process. On election the Yang di-Pertuan Agong relinquishes, for his tenure of office, all his functions as Ruler of his own state and may appoint a Regent. The Timbalan Yang di-Pertuan Agong exercises no powers in the ordinary course, but is immediately available to fill the post of Yang di-Pertuan Agong and carry out his functions in the latter's absence or disability. In the event of the Yang di-Pertuan Agong's death or resignation he takes over the exercise of sovereignty until the Conference of Rulers has elected a successor.

CONFERENCE OF RULERS

The Conference of Rulers consists of the Rulers and the heads of the other states. Its prime duty is the election by the Rulers only of the Yang di-Pertuan Agong and his deputy. The Conference must be consulted in the appointment of judges, the Auditor-General, the Election Commission and the Services Commissions. It must also be consulted and concur in the alteration of state boundaries, the extension to the federation as a whole, of Islamic religious acts and observances, and in any bill to amend the Constitution. Consultation is mandatory in matters affecting public policy or the special position of the Malays and natives of Sabah and Sarawak. The Conference also considers matters affecting the rights, prerogatives and privileges of the Rulers themselves.

FEDERAL PARLIAMENT

Parliament has two Houses—the Dewan Negara (Senate) and the Dewan Rakyat (House of Representatives). The Senate has a membership of 70, comprising 26 elected and 44 appointed members. Each state legislature, acting as an electoral college, elects two Senators; these may be members of the State Legislative Assembly or otherwise. The Yang di-Pertuan Agong appoints the other 44 members of the Senate; these include four Senators representing the three Federal Territories—Kuala Lumpur, Labuan and Putrajaya. Members of the Senate must be at least 30 years old. The Senate elects its President and Deputy President from among its members. It may initiate legislation, but all proposed legislation for the granting of funds must be introduced in the first instance in the House of Representatives. All legislative measures require approval by both Houses of Parliament before being presented to the Yang di-Pertuan Agong for the Royal Assent in order to become law. A bill originating in the Senate cannot receive Royal Assent until it has been approved by the House of Representatives, but the Senate has delaying powers only over a bill originating from and approved by the House of Representatives. Senators serve for a period of three years, but the Senate is not subject to dissolution. Parliament can, by statute, increase the number of Senators elected from each state to three. The House of Representatives consists of 219 elected members (see Amendments). Of these, 165 are from Peninsular Malaysia (including 11 from Kuala Lumpur and one from Putrajaya), 28 from Sarawak and 26 from Sabah (including one from Labuan). Members are returned from single-member constituencies on the basis of universal adult franchise. The term of the House of Representatives is limited to five years, after which time a fresh general election must be held. The Yang di-Pertuan Agong may dissolve Parliament before then if the Prime Minister so advises.

THE CABINET

To advise him in the exercise of his functions, the Yang di-Pertuan Agong appoints the Cabinet, consisting of the Prime Minister and an unspecified number of Ministers (who must all be Members of Parliament). The Prime Minister must be a citizen born in Malaysia and a member of the House of Representatives who, in the opinion of the Yang di-Pertuan Agong, commands the confidence of that House. Ministers are appointed on the advice of the Prime Minister. A number of Deputy Ministers (who are not members of the Cabinet) are also appointed from among Members of Parliament. The Cabinet meets regularly under the chairmanship of the Prime Minister to formulate policy.

PUBLIC SERVICES

The Public Services, civilian and military, are non-political and owe their loyalty not to the party in power but to the Yang di-Pertuan

MALAYSIA

Agong and the Rulers. They serve whichever government may be in power, irrespective of the latter's political affiliation. To ensure the impartiality of the service, and its protection from political interference, the Constitution provides for a number of Services Commissions to select and appoint officers, to place them on the pensionable establishment, to determine promotion and to maintain discipline.

THE STATES

The heads of nine of the 13 states are hereditary Rulers. The Ruler of Perlis has the title of Raja, and the Ruler of Negeri Sembilan that of Yang di-Pertuan Besar. The rest of the Rulers are Sultans. The heads of the States of Melaka (Malacca), Pinang (Penang), Sabah and Sarawak are each designated Yang di-Pertua Negeri and do not participate in the election of the Yang di-Pertuan Agong. Each of the 13 states has its own written Constitution and a single Legislative Assembly. Every state legislature has powers to legislate on matters not reserved for the Federal Parliament. Each State Legislative Assembly has the right to order its own procedure, and the members enjoy parliamentary privilege. All members of the Legislative Assemblies are directly elected from single-member constituencies. The head of the state acts on the advice of the State Government. This advice is tendered by the State Executive Council or Cabinet in precisely the same manner in which the Federal Cabinet tenders advice to the Yang di-Pertuan Agong.

The legislative authority of the state is vested in the head of the state in the State Legislative Assembly. The executive authority of the state is vested in the head of the state, but executive functions may be conferred on other persons by law. Every state has its own Executive Council or Cabinet to advise the head of the state, headed by its Chief Minister (Ketua Menteri in Melaka, Pinang, Sabah and Sarawak and Menteri Besar in other states), and collectively responsible to the state legislature. Each state in Peninsular Malaysia is divided into administrative districts, each with its District Officer. Sabah is divided into four residencies: West Coast, Interior, Sandakan and Tawau, with headquarters at Kota Kinabalu, Keningua, Sandakan and Tawau, respectively. Sarawak is divided into five Divisions, each in charge of a Resident—the First Division, with headquarters at Kuching; the Second Division, with headquarters at Simanggang; the Third Division, with headquarters at Sibu; the Fourth Division, with headquarters at Miri; the Fifth Division, with headquarters at Limbang.

AMENDMENTS

From 1 February 1974, the city of Kuala Lumpur, formerly the seat of the Federal Government and capital of Selangor State, is designated the Federal Territory of Kuala Lumpur. It is administered directly by the Federal Government and returns five members to the House of Representatives.

In April 1981 the legislature approved an amendment empowering the Yang di-Pertuan Agong to declare a state of emergency on the grounds of imminent danger of a breakdown in law and order or a threat to national security.

In August 1983 the legislature approved an amendment empowering the Prime Minister, instead of the Yang di-Pertuan Agong, to declare a state of emergency.

The island of Labuan, formerly part of Sabah State, was designated a Federal Territory as from 16 April 1984.

The legislature approved an amendment increasing the number of parliamentary constituencies in Sarawak from 24 to 27. The amendment took effect at the general election of 20–21 October 1990. The total number of seats in the House of Representatives, which had increased to 177 following an amendment in August 1983, was thus expanded to 180.

In March 1988 the legislature approved two amendments relating to the judiciary (see Judicial System).

In October 1992 the legislature adopted an amendment increasing the number of parliamentary constituencies from 180 to 192. The Kuala Lumpur Federal Territory and Selangor each gained three seats, Johor two, and Perlis, Kedah, Kelantan and Pahang one. The amendment took effect at the next general election (in April 1995).

In March 1993 an amendment was approved which removed the immunity from prosecution of the hereditary Rulers.

In May 1994 the House of Representatives approved an amendment which ended the right of the Yang di-Pertuan Agong to delay legislation by withholding his assent from legislation and returning it to Parliament for further consideration. Under the amendment, the Yang di-Pertuan Agong was obliged to give his assent to a bill within 30 days; if he failed to do so, the bill would, none the less, become law. An amendment was simultaneously approved restructuring the judiciary and introducing a mandatory code of ethics for judges, to be drawn up by the Government.

In 1996 an amendment was approved, increasing the number of parliamentary constituencies from 192 to 193.

In July 2001 an amendment was approved banning all discrimination on grounds of gender.

From 1 February 2001 the city of Putrajaya, formerly part of Selangor State, was designated a Federal Territory.

In 2003 the legislature approved an amendment increasing the number of parliamentary constituencies from 193 to 219. The amendments took effect at the next general election (held in March 2004).

The Government

SUPREME HEAD OF STATE

HM Yang di-Pertuan Agong: HM Tuanku SYED SIRAJUDDIN IBNI AL-MARHUM SYED PUTRA JAMALULLAIL (Raja of Perlis) (took office 13 December 2001).

Deputy Supreme Head of State

Timbalan Yang di-Pertuan Agong: HRH Sultan MIZAN ZAINAL ABIDIN (Sultan of Terengganu).

THE CABINET
(April 2006)

Prime Minister and Minister of Finance and of Internal Security: Dato' Seri ABDULLAH BIN Haji AHMAD BADAWI.

Deputy Prime Minister and Minister of Defence: Dato' Seri NAJIB BIN Tun Haji ABDUL RAZAK.

Minister of Housing and Local Government: Dato' ONG KAH TING.

Minister of Foreign Affairs: Datuk Seri SYED HAMID BIN SYED JAAFAR ALBAR.

Minister of Home Affairs: Datuk Seri RADZI SHEIKH.

Minister of International Trade and Industry: Dato' Seri Paduka RAFIDAH BINTI AZIZ.

Minister of Domestic Trade and Consumer Affairs: Datuk SHAFIE APDAL.

Minister of Transport: Dato' CHAN KONG CHOY.

Minister of Energy, Water and Communications: Datuk Seri Dr LIM KENG YAIK.

Minister of Works: Dato' Seri S. SAMY VELLU.

Minister of Youth and Sports: Datuk AZALINA OTHMAN SAID.

Minister of Education: Datuk HISHAMMUDDIN Tun HUSSEIN.

Minister of Higher Education: Datuk MUSTAPHA MOHAMED.

Minister of Information: Datuk ZAINUDDIN MAIDIN.

Minister of Human Resources: Datuk Dr FONG CHAN ONN.

Minister of Natural Resources and the Environment: Datuk Seri AZMI KHALID.

Minister of Plantation Industries and Commodities: Datuk PETER CHIN FAH KUI.

Minister of Arts, Culture and Heritage: Datuk Seri Dr RAIS YATIM.

Minister of Tourism: Datuk Tengku ADNAN Tengku MANSOR.

Minister of Science, Technology and Innovations: Datuk Dr JAMALUDDIN JARJIS.

Minister of Health: Datuk Dr CHUA SOI LEK.

Minister of Agriculture and Agro-Based Industry: Tan Sri Dato' Haji MUHYIDDIN BIN Haji MOHD YASSIN.

Minister of Rural and Regional Development: Datuk ABDUL AZIZ SHAMSUDDIN.

Minister of Federal Territories: Datuk ZULHASNAN RAFIQUE.

Minister of Entrepreneur and Co-operative Development: Datuk MOHAMED KHALED NORDIN.

Minister of Women, Family and Community Development: Datuk SHAHRIZAT bte ABDUL JALIL.

Minister of Finance II: NOR MOHAMED YAKCOP.

Ministers in the Prime Minister's Department: Tan Sri BERNARD GILUK DOMPOK, Dato' Seri MOHAMAD NAZRI BIN ABDUL AZIZ, Datuk MUSTAPA BIN MOHAMED, Datuk Seri MOHD RADZI BIN Sheikh AHMAD, Prof. Datuk Dr ABDULLAH BIN MOHAMED ZIN, Datuk Dr MAXIMUS JOHNITY ONGKILI, Datuk Seri Dr MOHAMAD EFFENDI NORWAWI.

MINISTRIES

Prime Minister's Office (Jabatan Perdana Menteri): Blok Utama, Tingkat 1–5, Pusat Pentadbiran Kerajaan Persekutuan, 62502 Putrajaya; tel. (3) 88888000; fax (3) 88883424; e-mail ppm@pmo.gov.my; internet www.pmo.gov.my.

Ministry of Agriculture and Agro-Based Industry: Wisma Tani, Lot 4G1, Pusat Pentadbiran Kerajaan Persekutuan, 62624

Putrajaya; tel. (3) 88701000; fax (3) 88701467; e-mail muhyiddin@agri.moa.my; internet agrolink.moa.my.

Ministry of Arts, Culture and Heritage: 26th, 27th, 30th, 34th & 35th Floors, TH Perdana Tower, Maju Junction, 1001 Jalan Sultan Ismail, 50694 Kuala Lumpur; tel. (3) 26127600; fax (3) 26935114; e-mail info@heritage.gov.my; internet www.heritage.gov.my.

Ministry of Defence (Kementerian Pertahanan): Wisma Pertahanan, Jalan Padang Tembak, 50634 Kuala Lumpur; tel. (3) 26921333; fax (3) 26914163; e-mail cpa@mod.gov.my; internet www.mod.gov.my.

Ministry of Domestic Trade and Consumer Affairs (Kementerian Perdagangan Dalam Negeri Dan Hal Ehwal Pengguna): Lot 2G3, Presint 2, Pusat Pentadbiran Kerajaan Persekutuan, 62623 Putrajaya; tel. (3) 88825500; fax (3) 88825762; e-mail aduan@kpdnhep.gov.my; internet www.kpdnhep.gov.my.

Ministry of Education (Kementerian Pendidikan): Kompleks Kerajaan Persekutuan, Parcel E, Pusat Pentadbiran Kerajaan Persekutuan, 62604 Putrajaya; tel. (3) 888460000; fax (3) 88895235; e-mail webmaster@moe.gov.my; internet www.moe.gov.my.

Ministry of Energy, Water and Communications (Kementerian Tenaga, Air dan Komunikasi): Block E4–5, Parcel E, Pusat Pentadbiran Kerajaan Persekutuan, 62668 Putrajaya; tel. (3) 88836000; fax (3) 88893712; e-mail webmaster@ktak.gov.my; internet www.ktak.gov.my.

Ministry of Entrepreneur and Co-operative Development (Kementerian Pembangunan Usahawan Dan Koperasi): Lot 2G6, Presint 2, Pusat Pentadbiran Kerajaan Persekutuan, 62100 Putrajaya; tel. (3) 88805000; fax (3) 88805106; e-mail webmaster@mecd.gov.my; internet www.mecd.gov.my.

Ministry of Federal Territories (Kementerian Wilayah Persekutuan): Aras 1-4, Blok 2, Menara PJH, Presint 2, 62100 Putrajaya; tel. (3) 88897888; fax (3) 88889140; e-mail admin@kwp.gov.my; internet www.kwp.gov.my.

Ministry of Finance (Kementerian Kewangan): Kompleks Kementerian Kewangan, Presint 2, Pusat Pentadbiran Kerajaan Persekutuan, 62592 Putrajaya; tel. (3) 88823000; fax (3) 88823893; e-mail pertanyaan@treasury.gov.my; internet www.treasury.gov.my.

Ministry of Foreign Affairs (Kementerian Luar Negeri): Wisma Putra, 1 Jalan Wisma Putra, Presint 2, 62602 Putrajaya; tel. (3) 88874000; fax (3) 88891717; e-mail webmaster@kln.gov.my; internet www.kln.gov.my.

Ministry of Health (Kementerian Kesihatan): Blok E1, Parcel E, Pusat Pentadbiran Kerajaan Persekutuan, 62590 Putrajaya; tel. (3) 26985077; fax (3) 26985964; e-mail wmmoh@moh.gov.my; internet www.moh.gov.my.

Ministry of Higher Education (Kementerian Pengajian Tinggi): Blok E3, Parcel E, Pusat Perbadanan Kerajaan Persekutuan, Putrajaya; tel. (3) 88835000; fax (3) 88893921; e-mail webmasterkpt@mohe.gov.my; internet www.mohe.gov.my.

Ministry of Home Affairs (Kementerian Hal Ehwal Dalam Negeri): Blok D1, Parcel D, Pusat Pentadbiran Kerajaan Persekutuan, 62546 Putrajaya; tel. (3) 88863000; fax (3) 88891613; e-mail azmi@mofa.gov.my; internet www.moha.gov.my.

Ministry of Housing and Local Government (Kementerian Perumahan dan Kerajaan Tempatan): Paras 3–7, Blok K, Pusat Bandar Damansara, 50782 Kuala Lumpur; tel. (3) 20947033; fax (3) 20949720; e-mail menteri@kpkt.gov.my; internet www.kpkt.gov.my.

Ministry of Human Resources (Kementerian Sumber Manusia): Level 6–9, Blok D3, Parcel D, Pusat Pentadbiran Kerajaan Persekutuan, 62502 Putrajaya; tel. (3) 88865000; fax (3) 88892381; e-mail ksm@mohr.gov.my; internet www.mohr.gov.my.

Ministry of Information (Kementerian Penerangan): 5th Floor, Wisma TV, Angkasapuri, Bukit Putra, 50610 Kuala Lumpur; tel. (3) 22825333; fax (3) 22821255; e-mail webmaster@kempen.gov.my; internet www.kempen.gov.my.

Ministry of Internal Security (Kementerian Keselamatan Dalam Negeri): Blok D1, Parcel D, Pusat Pentadbiran Kerajaan Persekutuan, 62546 Putrajaya; tel. (3) 88868000; e-mail abdullah@mois.gov.my; internet www.mois.gov.my.

Ministry of International Trade and Industry (Kementerian Perdagangan Antarabangsa dan Industri): Blok 10, Kompleks Pejabat Kerajaan, Jalan Duta, 50622 Kuala Lumpur; tel. (3) 62033022; fax (3) 62032337; e-mail webmiti@miti.gov.my; internet www.miti.gov.my.

Ministry of Natural Resources and the Environment (Kementerian Sumber Asli dan Alam Sekitar): Aras 14, Blok Menara 4G3, Presint 4, Pusat Pentadbiran Kerajaan Persekutuan, 62574 Putrajaya; tel. (3) 88861111; fax (3) 88861512; e-mail adenan@nre.gov.my; internet www.nre.gov.my.

Ministry of Plantation Industries and Commodities (Kementerian Perusahaan Perladangan dan Komoditi): Aras 6–13, Lot 2G4, Presint 2, Pusat Pentadbiran Kerajaan Persekutuan, 62654 Putrajaya; tel. (3) 88803300; fax (3) 88803422; e-mail pybm@kppk.gov.my; internet www.kppk.gov.my.

Ministry of Rural and Regional Development (Kementerian Kemajuan Luar Bandar dan Wilayah): Aras 5–9, Blok D9, Parcel D, Pusat Pentadbiran Kerajaan Persekutuan, 62606 Putrajaya; tel. (3) 88863500; fax (3) 88892104; e-mail info@kplb.gov.my; internet www.kplb.gov.my.

Ministry of Science, Technology and Innovations: Aras 1-7, Blok C5, Pusat Pentadbiran Kerajaan Persekutuan, 62662 Putrajaya; tel. (3) 88858000; fax (3) 88886070; e-mail pro@mosti.gov.my; internet www.mosti.gov.my.

Ministry of Tourism (Kementerian Pelancongan): Tingkat 32–36, Menara Dato' Onn, Pusat Dagangan Dunia Putra, 45 Jalan Tun Ismail, 50695 Kuala Lumpur; tel. (3) 26937111; fax (3) 26941146; e-mail info@motour.gov.my; internet www.motour.gov.my.

Ministry of Transport (Kementerian Pengangkutan): Aras 4–7, Blok D5, Parcel D, Pusat Pentadbiran Kerajaan Persekutuan, 62616 Putrajaya; tel. (3) 88866000; fax (3) 88892537; e-mail saptuyah@mot.gov.my; internet www.mot.gov.my.

Ministry of Women, Family and Community Development (Kementerian Pembangunan Wanita, Keluarga dan Masyarakat): Aras 1–6, Blok E, Kompleks Petabat, Kerajaan Bukit Perdana, Jalan Dato' Onn, 50515 Kuala Lumpur; tel. (3) 26930095; fax (3) 26934982; e-mail info@kpwkm.gov.my; internet www.kpwkm.gov.my.

Ministry of Works (Kementerian Kerja Raya): Tingkat 4, Blok B, Kompleks Kerja Raya, Jalan Sultan Salahuddin, 50580 Kuala Lumpur; tel. (3) 27111100; fax (3) 27112591; e-mail pro@kkr.gov.my; internet www.kkr.gov.my.

Ministry of Youth and Sports (Kementerian Belia dan Sukan): Lot G4, Presint 4, Pusat Pentadbiran Kerajaan Persekutuan, 62570 Putrajaya; tel. (3) 88713333; fax (3) 88888767; e-mail pejabatmenteri@kbs.gov.my; internet www.kbs.gov.my.

Legislature

PARLIAMENT

Dewan Negara
(Senate)

The Senate has 70 members, of whom 26 are elected. Each State Legislative Assembly elects two members. The Supreme Head of State appoints the remaining 44 members, including four from the three Federal Territories.

President: Dr ABDUL HAMID PAWANTEH.

Dewan Rakyat
(House of Representatives)

The House of Representatives has a total of 219 members: 165 from Peninsular Malaysia (including 11 from Kuala Lumpur and one from the Federal Territory of Putrajaya), 28 from Sarawak and 26 from Sabah (including one from the Federal Territory of Labuan).

Speaker: DiRaja RAMLI BIN NGAH TALIB.
Deputy Speaker: Dr YUSOF YACOB.

General Election, 21 March 2004

Party	Seats
Barisan Nasional (National Front)	198
United Malays National Organization	109
Malaysian Chinese Association	31
Parti Pesaka Bumiputera Bersatu	11
Parti Gerakan Rakyat Malaysia	10
Malaysian Indian Congress	9
Parti Bansa Dayak Sarawak	6
Sarawak United People's Party	6
Parti Bersatu Sabah	4
Sabah Progressive Democratic Party	4
United Kadazan People's Organization	4
Sabah Progressive Party	2
Parti Bersatu Rakyat Sabah	1
Parti Progresif Pendukuk Malaysia	1
Democratic Action Party	12
Parti Islam se Malaysia	7
Parti Keadilan Rakyat	1
Independents	1
Total	**219**

MALAYSIA

The States

JOHOR
(Capital: Johor Bahru)

Sultan: HRH Tuanku Mahmood Iskandar ibni Al-Marhum Sultan Ismail.
Menteri Besar: Datuk Haji Abdul Ghani Othman.
State Legislative Assembly: 56 seats: Barisan Nasional 55; Parti Islam se Malaysia 1; elected March 2004.

KEDAH
(Capital: Alor Star)

Sultan: HRH Tuanku Haji Abdul Halim Mu'adzam Shah ibni Al-Marhum Sultan Badlishah.
Menteri Besar: Datuk Syed Razak Syed Zain Barakbah.
State Legislative Assembly: 36 seats: Barisan Nasional 31; Parti Islam se Malaysia 5; elected March 2004.

KELANTAN
(Capital: Kota Baharu)

Sultan: HRH Tuanku Ismail Petra ibni Al-Marhum Sultan Yahaya Petra.
Menteri Besar: Tuan Guru Haji Nik Abdul Aziz bin Nik Mat.
State Legislative Assembly: 45 seats: Parti Islam se Malaysia 24; Barisan Nasional 21; elected March 2004.

MELAKA (MALACCA)
(Capital: Melaka)

Yang di-Pertua Negeri: Tan Sri Khalil Yaakob.
Ketua Menteri: Datuk Wira Mohamed Ali Rustam.
State Legislative Assembly: 28 seats: Barisan Nasional 26; Democratic Action Party 2; elected March 2004.

NEGERI SEMBILAN
(Capital: Seremban)

Yang di-Pertuan Besar: Tuanku Ja'afar ibni Al-Marhum Tuanku Abdul Rahman.
Menteri Besar: Datuk Mohamad Hasan.
State Legislative Assembly: 36 seats: Barisan Nasional 34; Democratic Action Party 2; elected March 2004.

PAHANG
(Capital: Kuantan)

Sultan: HRH Haji Ahmad Shah Al-Musta'in Billah ibni Al-Marhum Sultan Abu Bakar Ri'ayatuddin Al-Mu'adzam Shah.
Menteri Besar: Dato' Adnan bin Yaakob.
State Legislative Assembly: 41 seats: Barisan Nasional 40; Democratic Action Party 1; elected March 2004.

PERAK
(Capital: Ipoh)

Sultan: HRH Sultan Tuanku Azlan Muhibuddin Shah ibni Al-Marhum Sultan Yusuf Izuddin Ghafarullah Shah.
Menteri Besar: Dato' Seri DiRaja Mohamad Tajol Rosli.
State Legislative Assembly: Pejabat Setiausaha Kerajaan Negeri, Perak Darul Ridzuan, Bahagian Majlis, Jalan Panglima Bukit Gantang Wahab, 30000 Ipoh; tel. (5) 2410451; fax (5) 2552890; e-mail master@perak.gov.my; internet www.perak.gov.my; 59 seats: Barisan Nasional 52; Democratic Action Party 7; elected March 2004.

PERLIS
(Capital: Kangar)

Regent: Tuanku Syed Faizuddin Putra ibni Tuanku Syed Sirajuddin Putra Jamalulail.
Menteri Besar: Dato' Seri Shahidan Kassim.
State Legislative Assembly: internet www.perlis.gov.my; 15 seats: Barisan Nasional 14; Parti Islam se Malaysia 1; elected March 2004.

PULAU PINANG (PENANG)
(Capital: George Town)

Yang di-Pertua Negeri: HE Datuk Abdul Rahman Haji Abbas.
Ketua Menteri: Tan Sri Dr Koh Tsu Koon.
State Legislative Assembly: 40 seats: Barisan Nasional 38; Democratic Action Party 1; Parti Islam se Malaysia 1; elected March 2004.

SABAH
(Capital: Kota Kinabalu)

Yang di-Pertua Negeri: HE Datuk Ahmadshah Abdullah.
Ketua Menteri: Datuk Seri Musa Aman.
State Legislative Assembly: Dewan Undangan Negeri Sabah, Aras 4, Bangunan Dewan Undangan Negeri Sabah, Peti Surat 11247, 88813 Kota Kinabalu; tel. (88) 427533; fax (88) 427333; e-mail pejduns@sabah.gov.my; internet www.sabah.gov.my; 60 seats: Barisan Nasional 59; Independents 1; elected March 2004.

SARAWAK
(Capital: Kuching)

Yang di-Pertua Negeri: HE Tun Datuk Patinggi Abang Haji Muhammed Salahuddin.
Ketua Menteri: Datuk Patinggi Tan Sri Haji Abdul Taib bin Mahmud.
State Legislative Assembly: Bangunan Dewan Undangan Negeri, 93502 Petra Jaya, Kuching, Sarawak; tel. (82) 441955; fax (82) 440790; e-mail mastapaj@sarawaknet.gov.my; internet www.dun.sarawak.gov.my; 62 seats: Barisan Nasional 60; Democratic Action Party 1; Independents 1; elected September 2001.

SELANGOR
(Capital: Shah Alam)

Sultan: Tuanku Idris Salahuddin Abdul Aziz Shah.
Menteri Besar: Mohamad Khir Toyo.
State Legislative Assembly: 56 seats: Barisan Nasional 54; Democratic Action Party 2; elected March 2004.

TERENGGANU
(Capital: Kuala Terengganu)

Sultan: HRH Sultan Tuanku Mizan Zainal Abidin ibni al-Marhum Sultan Mahmud.
Menteri Besar: Datuk Idris Jusoh.
State Legislative Assembly: 32 seats: Barisan Nasional 28; Parti Islam se Malaysia 4; elected March 2004.

Election Commission

Suruhanjaya Pilihan Raya (SPR): Aras 4–5, Blok C7, Parcel C, Pusat Pentadbiran Kerajaan Persekutuan, 62690 Putrajaya; tel. (3) 88856500; fax (3) 88889117; e-mail spr@spr.gov.my; internet www.spr.gov.my; f. 1957; Chair. Tan Sri Datuk Rashid bin Rahman.

Political Organizations

Barisan Nasional (BN) (National Front): Suites 1–2, 8th Floor, Menara Dato' Onn, Pusat Dagangan Dunia Putra, Jalan Tun Ismail, 50480 Kuala Lumpur; tel. (3) 26920384; fax (3) 26934743; e-mail info@bn.org.my; internet www.bn.org.my; f. 1973; the governing multiracial coalition of 14 parties; Chair. Dato' Seri Abdullah bin Haji Ahmad Badawi; Sec.-Gen. Dato' Datuk Sri Mohammed Rahmat; comprises:

  Liberal Democratic Party: Tingkat 1, No. 33, Karamunsing Warehouse, POB 16033, 88868 Kota Kinabalu, Sabah; tel. (88) 218985; fax (88) 240598; e-mail ldpkk@tm.net.my; Chinese-dominated; Pres. Datuk Chong Kah Kiat; Sec.-Gen. Liew Vui Keong.

  Malaysian Chinese Association (MCA): Wisma MCA, 8th Floor, 163 Jalan Ampang, POB 10626, 50450 Kuala Lumpur; tel. (3) 21618044; fax (3) 21619772; e-mail info@mca.org.my; internet www.mca.org.my; f. 1949; 1,072,556 mems; Pres. Dato' Seri Ong Ka Ting; Sec.-Gen. Dato' Ong Ka Chuan.

  Malaysian Indian Congress (MIC): Menara Manickavasagam, 6th Floor, 1 Jalan Rahmat, 50350 Kuala Lumpur; tel. (3) 40424377; fax (3) 40427236; e-mail michq@mic.org.my; internet www.mic.org.my; f. 1946; 401,000 mems (1992); Pres. Dato' Seri S. Samy Vellu; Sec.-Gen. Dato' S. Sothinathan.

  Parti Bansa Dayak Sarawak (PBDS) (Sarawak Native People's Party): 622 Jalan Kedandi, Tabuan Jaya, POB 2148, Kuching, Sarawak; tel. (82) 365240; fax (82) 363734; f. 1983 by fmr mems of Sarawak National Party; Pres. Datuk Daniel Tajem.

  Parti Bersatu Rakyat Sabah (PBRS) (United Sabah People's Party): POB 20148, Luyang, Kota Kinabalu, 88761 Sabah; tel. and fax (88) 269282; f. 1994; breakaway faction of PBS; mostly Christian Kadazans; Leader Datuk Joseph Kurup.

  Parti Bersatu Sabah (PBS) (Sabah United Party): Block M, Lot 4, 2nd and 3rd Floors, Donggongon New Township, 89500 Penam-

MALAYSIA

pang, Sabah; tel. (88) 702111; fax (88) 718067; e-mail pbshq@pbs-sabah.org; internet www.pbs-sabah.org; f. 1985; multiracial party, left the BN in 1990 and rejoined in Jan. 2002; Pres. Datuk Seri JOSEPH PAIRIN KITINGAN; Sec.-Gen. Datuk RADIN MALLEH.

Parti Gerakan Rakyat Malaysia (GERAKAN) (Malaysian People's Movement): Tingkat 5, Menara PGRM, 8 Jalan Pudu Ulu, Cheras, 56100 Kuala Lumpur; tel. (3) 92876868; fax (3) 92878866; e-mail gerakan@gerakan.org.my; internet www.gerakan.org.my; f. 1968; 300,000 mems; Pres. Dato' Seri Dr LIM KENG YAIK; Sec.-Gen. CHIA KWANG CHYE.

Parti Pesaka Bumiputera Bersatu (PBB) (United Traditional Bumiputra Party): Lot 401, Jalan Bako, POB 1953, 93400 Kuching, Sarawak; tel. (82) 448299; fax (82) 448294; f. 1983; Pres. Tan Sri Datuk Patinggi Amar Haji ABDUL TAIB MAHMUD; Dep. Pres. Datuk ALFRED JABU AK NUMPANG.

Parti Progresif Penduduk Malaysia (PPP) (People's Progressive Party): 27–29A Jalan Maharajalela, 50150 Kuala Lumpur; tel. (3) 2441922; fax (3) 2442041; e-mail info@ppp.com.my; f. 1953; as Perak Progressive Party; joined the BN in 1972; Pres. Datuk M. KAYVEAS.

Sabah Progressive Party (SAPP) (Parti Maju Sabah): Lot 23, 2nd Floor, Bornion Centre, 88300 Kota Kinabalu, Sabah; tel. (88) 242107; fax (88) 249188; e-mail sapp@po.jaring.my; internet www.sapp.org.my; f. 1994; non-racial; Pres. Datuk YONG TECK LEE; Sec.-Gen. RICHARD YONG WE KONG.

Sarawak Progressive Democratic Party (SPDP): Lot 4319–4320, Jalan Stapok, Sungai Maong, 93250 Kuching, Sarawak; tel. (82) 311180; fax (82) 311190; f. 2003 by breakaway faction of Sarawak National Party; Pres. Datuk WILLIAM MAWAN ANAK IKOM; Sec.-Gen. Agung Dr JUDSON SAKAI TAGAL.

Sarawak United People's Party (SUPP): 7 Jalan Tan Sri Ong Kee Hui, POB 454, 93710 Kuching, Sarawak; tel. (82) 246999; fax (82) 256510; e-mail supphq@hotmail.com; internet www.supp.org.my; f. 1959; Sarawak Chinese minority party; Pres. Datuk Dr GEORGE CHAN HONG NAM; Sec.-Gen. SIM KHENG HUI.

United Kadazan People's Organization (UPKO): Penampang Service Centre, Km 11, Jalan Tambunan, Peti Surat 420, 89507 Penampang, Sabah; tel. (88) 718182; fax (88) 718180; e-mail n4upko@yahoo.com; internet www.upko.org.my; f. 1994 as the Parti Demokratik Sabah (PDS—Sabah Democratic Party); formed after collapse of PBS Govt by fmr leaders of the party, represents mostly Kadazandusun, Rungus and Murut communities; Pres. Tan Sri BERNARD GILUK DOMPOK.

United Malays National Organization (Pertubuhan Kebangsaan Melayu Bersatu—UMNO Baru)(New UMNO): Menara Dato' Onn, 38th Floor, Jalan Tun Ismail, 50480 Kuala Lumpur; tel. (3) 40429511; fax (3) 40412358; e-mail email@umno.net.my; internet www.umno-online.com; f. 1988; replaced the original UMNO (f. 1946), which had been declared an illegal organization, owing to the participation of unregistered branches in party elections in April 1987; Supreme Council of 45 mems; 2.5m. mems; Pres. Dato' Seri ABDULLAH BIN Haji AHMAD BADAWI; Sec.-Gen. Datuk Seri MOHD RADZI BIN Sheikh AHMAD.

Angkatan Keadilan Insan Malaysia (AKIM) (Malaysian Justice Movement): f. 1994 by fmr members of PAS and Semangat '46; Pres. HAMBALI YAZID.

Barisan Alternatif (Alternative Front): Kuala Lumpur; f. June 1999 to contest the general election; opposition electoral alliance originally comprising the PAS, the DAP, the PKN and the PRM; the DAP left in Sept. 2001.

Barisan Jama'ah Islamiah Sa-Malaysia (Berjasa) (Front Malaysian Islamic Council—FMIC): Kelantan; f. 1977; pro-Islamic; 50,000 mems; Pres. Dato' Haji WAN HASHIM BIN Haji WAN ACHMED; Sec.-Gen. MAHMUD ZUHDI BIN Haji ABDUL MAJID.

Bersatu Rakyat Jelata Sabah (Berjaya) (Sabah People's Union): Natikar Bldg, 1st Floor, POB 2130, Kota Kinabalu, Sabah; f. 1975; 400,000 mems; Pres. Haji MOHAMMED NOOR MANSOOR.

Democratic Action Party (DAP): 24 Jalan 20/9, 46300 Petaling Jaya, Selangor; tel. (3) 79578022; fax (3) 79575718; e-mail dap.Malaysia@pobox.com; internet www.dapmalaysia.org; f. 1966; main opposition party; advocates multiracial society based on democratic socialism; 12,000 mems; Chair. KARPAL SINGH; Sec.-Gen. LIM GUAN ENG.

Democratic Malaysia Indian Party (DMIP): f. 1985; Leader V. GOVINDARAJ.

Kongres Indian Muslim Malaysia (KIMMA): Kuala Lumpur; tel. (3) 2324759; f. 1977; aims to unite Malaysian Indian Muslims politically; 25,000 mems; Pres. AHAMED ELIAS; Sec.-Gen. MOHAMMED ALI BIN Haji NAINA MOHAMMED.

Malaysian Solidarity Party: Kuala Lumpur.

Parti Hisbul Muslimin Malaysia (Hamim) (Islamic Front of Malaysia): Kota Bahru, Kelantan; f. 1983 as an alternative party to PAS; Pres. Datuk ASRI MUDA.

Parti Ikatan Masyarakat Islam (Islamic Alliance Party): Terengganu.

Parti Islam se Malaysia (PAS) (Islamic Party of Malaysia): Pejabat Agung PAS, Pusat Lorong Haji Hassan, off Jalan Batu Geliga, Taman Melewar, 68100 Batu Caves, Selangor Darul Ehsan; tel. (3) 61895612; fax (3) 61889520; e-mail editor@parti-pas.org; internet www.parti-pas.org; f. 1951; seeks to establish an Islamic state; 700,000 mems; Pres. ABDUL HADI AWANG; Sec.-Gen. KAMARUDDIN JAAFAR.

Parti Keadilan Masyarakat (PEKEMAS) (Social Justice Party): Kuala Lumpur; f. 1971; by fmr mems of GERAKAN; Chair. SHAHARYDDIN DAHALAN.

Parti Keadilan Rakyat (PKR) (People's Justice Party): 110–3 Jalan Tun Sambanthan, 50470 Kuala Lumpur; tel. (3) 22723220; fax (3) 22721220; e-mail contact@partikeadilanrakyat.org; internet www.keadilanrakyat.org; f. Aug. 2003 following merger between Parti Keadilan Nasional (PKN) and Parti Rakyat Malaysia (PRM); Pres. Datin Seri Dr WAN AZIZAH WAN ISMAIL; Sec.-Gen. Datuk KAMARUL BAHRIN ABAS.

Parti Nasionalis Malaysia (NasMa): f. 1985; multiracial; Leader ZAINAB YANG.

Parti Rakyat Jati Sarawak (PAJAR) (Sarawak Native People's Party): 22A Jalan Bampeylde, 93200 Kuching, Sarawak; f. 1978; Leader ALI KAWI.

Persatuan Rakyat Malaysian Sarawak (PERMAS) (Malaysian Sarawak Party): Kuching, Sarawak; f. March 1987; by fmr mems of PBB; Leader Haji BUJANG ULIS.

Pertubuhan Bumiputera Bersatu Sarawak (PBBS) (United Sarawak National Association): Kuala Lumpur; f. 1986; Chair. Haji WAN HABIB SYED MAHMUD.

Pertubuhan Rakyat Sabah Bersatu (United Sabah People's Organization—USPO): Kota Kinabalu, Sabah.

Sabah Chinese Consolidated Party (SCCP): POB 704, Kota Kinabalu, Sabah; f. 1964; 14,000 mems; Pres. JOHNNY SOON; Sec.-Gen. CHAN TET ON.

Sabah Chinese Party (PCS): Kota Kinabalu, Sabah; f. 1986; Pres. Encik FRANCIS LEONG.

Sarawak National Party (SNAP): 304–305 Bangunan Mei Jun, 1 Jalan Rubber, POB 2960, 93758 Kuching, Sarawak; tel. (82) 254244; fax (82) 253562; f. 1961; deregistered Nov. 2002 but deregistration deferred indefinitely in April 2003 following appeal; Pres. EDWIN DUNDANG BUGAK; Sec.-Gen. STANLEY JUGOL.

Setia (Sabah People's United Democratic Party): Sabah; f. 1994.

Diplomatic Representation

EMBASSIES AND HIGH COMMISSIONS IN MALAYSIA

Afghanistan: 2nd Floor, Wisma Chinese Chamber, 258 Jalan Ampang, 50450 Kuala Lumpur; tel. (3) 42569400; fax (3) 42566400; e-mail consular@afghanembassykl.org; internet www.afghanembassykl.org; Ambassador MOHAMMAD YUNOS FARMAN.

Albania: 2952 Jalan Bukit Ledang, off Jalan Duta, 50480 Kuala Lumpur; tel. (3) 20937808; fax (3) 20937359; e-mail albania@streamyx.com; Chargé d'affaires a.i. HAJDAR MUNEKA.

Algeria: 5 Jalan Mesra, off Jalan Damai, 55000 Kuala Lumpur; tel. (3) 21488159; fax (3) 21488154; e-mail enquiries@algerianembassy.org.my; internet www.algerianembassy.org.my; Ambassador AMAR BELANI.

Argentina: 3 Jalan Semantan Dua, Damansara Heights, 50490 Kuala Lumpur; tel. (3) 20950176; fax (3) 20952706; e-mail emsia@pd.jaring.my; Ambassador ALFREDO MORELLI.

Australia: 6 Jalan Yap Kwan Seng, 50450 Kuala Lumpur; tel. (3) 21465555; fax (3) 21415773; e-mail Public-Affairs-KLPR@dfat.gov.au; internet www.australia.org.my; High Commissioner JAMES WISE.

Austria: Suite 10.01-02, Level 10, Wisma Goldhill 67, Jalan Raja Chulan, 50200 Kuala Lumpur; tel. (3) 23817160; fax (3) 23817168; e-mail kuala-lumpur-ob@bmaa.gv.at; Ambassador Dr DONATUS KOECK.

Bangladesh: Block 1, Lorong Damai 7, Jalan Damai, 55000 Kuala Lumpur; tel. (3) 21487490; fax (3) 21413381; e-mail bddoot@po.jaring.my; High Commissioner SHAFIE U. AHMAD.

Belgium: Suite 10-02, 10th Floor, Menara Tan & Tan, 207 Jalan Tun Razak, 50400 Kuala Lumpur; tel. (3) 21620025; fax (3) 21620023; e-mail kualalumpur@diplobel.org; internet www.diplomatie.be/kualalumpur; Ambassador ROLAND VAN REMOORTELE.

MALAYSIA

Bosnia and Herzegovina: JKR 854, Jalan Bellamy, 50460 Kuala Lumpur; tel. (3) 21440353; fax (3) 21426025; e-mail hsomun@hotmail.com; Ambassador Mustafa Mujezinović.

Brazil: Suite 20-01, 20th Floor, Menara Tan & Tan, 207 Jalan Tun Razak, 50400 Kuala Lumpur; tel. (3) 21711420; fax (3) 21711427; e-mail brazil@po.jaring.my; Ambassador Marcos Caramuru De Paiva.

Brunei: Suite 19-01, 19th Floor, Menara Tan & Tan, 207 Jalan Tun Razak, 50400 Kuala Lumpur; tel. (3) 21612800; fax (3) 2631302; e-mail bhckl@brucomkul.com.my; High Commissioner Dato' Paduka Haji Abdullah bin Haji Mohammad Jaafar.

Cambodia: 46 Jalan U Thant, 55000 Kuala Lumpur; tel. (3) 42573711; fax (3) 42571157; e-mail reckl@tm.net.my; Ambassador HRH Samdech Preah Anoch Norodom Arunrasmy.

Canada: POB 10990, 50732 Kuala Lumpur; tel. (3) 27183333; fax (3) 27183399; e-mail klmpr-gr@international.gc.ca; internet www.dfait-maeci.gc.ca/kualalumpur; High Commissioner David Summers.

Chile: 8th Floor, West Block, Wisma Selangor Dredging, 142-C Jalan Ampang, Peti Surat 27, 50450 Kuala Lumpur; tel. (3) 21616203; fax (3) 21622219; e-mail eochile@ppp.nasionet.net; Ambassador Patricio Torres.

China, People's Republic: 229 Jalan Ampang, 50450 Kuala Lumpur; tel. (3) 21428495; fax (3) 21414552; e-mail cn@tm.net.my; internet my.china-embassy.org/eng; Ambassador Wang Chungui.

Colombia: Level 28, UOA Centre, 19 Jalan Pinang, 50450 Kuala Lumpur; tel. (3) 21645488; fax (3) 21645487; e-mail emcomal@streamyx.com; Ambassador Sergio G. Naranjo Pérez.

Croatia: 3 Jalan Menkuang, off Jalan Ru Ampang, 55000 Kuala Lumpur; tel. (3) 42535340; fax (3) 42535217; e-mail croemb@tm.net.my; Ambassador Zeljko Cimbur.

Cuba: 10 Lorong Gurney, 54100 Kuala Lumpur; tel. (3) 26911066; fax (3) 26911141; e-mail admin@cubemb.com.my; internet www.cubaemb.com.my; Ambassador Pedro Monzón Barata.

Czech Republic: 32 Jalan Mesra, off Jalan Damai, 55000 Kuala Lumpur; tel. (3) 21427185; fax (3) 21412727; e-mail kualalumpur@embassy.mzv.cz; internet www.mzv.cz/kualalumpur; Ambassador Dana Hunátová.

Denmark: Wisma Denmark, 22nd Floor, 86 Jalan Ampang, 50450 Kuala Lumpur; tel. (3) 20322001; fax (3) 20322012; e-mail kulamb@um.dk; internet www.ambkualalumpur.um.dk; Ambassador Børge Petersen.

Ecuador: 10th Floor, West Block, Wisma Selangor Dredging, 142-C Jalan Ampang, 50450 Kuala Lumpur; tel. (3) 21635078; fax (3) 21635096; e-mail embecua@po.jaring.my; Ambassador Manuel Pesantes.

Egypt: 12 Jalan Rhu, off Jalan Ampang, 55000 Kuala Lumpur; tel. (3) 42568184; fax (3) 42573515; e-mail egyembkl@tm.net.my; Ambassador Muhammad Ali Afifi.

Fiji: Level 2, Menara Chan, 138 Jalan Ampang, 50450 Kuala Lumpur; tel. (3) 27323335; fax (3) 27327555; e-mail fhckl@pd.jaring.my; High Commissioner Adi Samanunu Q. Talakuli Cakobau.

Finland: Wisma Chinese Chamber, 5th Floor, 258 Jalan Ampang, 50450 Kuala Lumpur; tel. (3) 42577746; fax (3) 42577793; e-mail sanomat.kul@formin.fi; Ambassador Lauri Korpinen.

France: 192–6 Jalan Ampang, 50450 Kuala Lumpur; tel. (3) 20535500; fax (3) 20535501; e-mail ambassade.kuala-lumpur-amba@diplomatie.gouv.fr; internet www.ambafrance-my.org; Ambassador Alain du Boispean.

Germany: 26th Floor, Menara Tan & Tan, 207 Jalan Tun Razak, 50400 Kuala Lumpur; tel. (3) 21709666; fax (3) 21619800; e-mail contact@german-embassy.org.my; internet www.german-embassy.org.my; Ambassador Herbert D. Jess.

Ghana: 14 Ampang Hilir, off Jalan Ampang, 55000 Kuala Lumpur; tel. (3) 42526995; fax (3) 42578698; e-mail ghcomkl@tm.net.my; High Commissioner Nana Kwadwo Seinti.

Guinea: 5 Jalan Kedondong, off Jalan Ampang Hilir, 55000 Kuala Lumpur; tel. (3) 42576500; fax (3) 42511500; e-mail mwcnakry@sotelgui.net.gn; Ambassador Mohamed Sampil.

Hungary: City Square Centre, 30th Floor, Empire Tower, Jalan Tun Razak, 50400 Kuala Lumpur; tel. (3) 21637914; fax (3) 21637918; e-mail huembkl@tm.net.my; Ambassador Tamás Tóth.

India: 2 Jalan Taman Duta, off Jalan Duta, 50480 Kuala Lumpur; tel. (3) 20933510; fax (3) 20933507; e-mail highcomm@po.jaring.my; High Commissioner Rajamani Lakshmi Narayan.

Indonesia: 233 Jalan Tun Razak, POB 10889, 50400 Kuala Lumpur; tel. (3) 21452011; fax (3) 21417908; e-mail dubresi_kul@kbrikl.org.my; internet www.kbrikl.org.my; Ambassador K. P. H. Rusdihardjo.

Iran: 1 Lorong U Thant Satu, off Jalan U Thant, 55000 Kuala Lumpur; tel. (3) 42514824; fax (3) 42562904; e-mail emb@iranembassy.com.my; internet www.iranembassy.com.my; Ambassador Zamani Nia.

Iraq: 2 Jalan Langgak Golf, off Jalan Tun Razak, 55000 Kuala Lumpur; tel. (3) 21480555; fax (3) 21414331.

Ireland: Ireland House, The Amp Walk, 218 Jalan Ampang, POB 10372, 50450 Kuala Lumpur; tel. (3) 21612963; fax (3) 21613427; e-mail info@ireland-embassy.com.my; internet www.ireland-embassy.com.my; Ambassador Eugene Hutchinson.

Italy: 99 Jalan U Thant, 55000 Kuala Lumpur; tel. (3) 42565122; fax (3) 42573199; e-mail embassyit@italy-embassy.org.my; internet www.ambkualalumpur.esteri.it; Ambassador Anacleto Felicani.

Japan: 11 Pesiaran Stonor, off Jalan Tun Razak, 50450 Kuala Lumpur; tel. (3) 21427044; fax (3) 21672314; internet www.my.emb-japan.go.jp; Ambassador Masaki Konishi.

Jordan: 2 Jalan Kedondong, off Jalan Ampang Hilir, 55000 Kuala Lumpur; tel. (3) 42521268; fax (3) 42528610; e-mail jordanembassy@po.jaring.my; Ambassador Mazen Juma.

Kazakhstan: 115 Jalan Ampang Hilir, 55000 Kuala Lumpur; tel. (3) 42522999; fax (3) 42523999; e-mail kuala-lumpur@kazaembassy.org.my; Ambassador Mukhtar Tileuberdi.

Kenya: Kuala Lumpur Empire Tower, Unit 38c, 38th Floor, 182 Jalan Tun Razak, 50400 Kuala Lumpur; tel. (3) 21645015; fax (3) 21645017; e-mail kenya@po.jaring.my; High Commissioner David Gachoki Njoka.

Korea, Democratic People's Republic: 4 Jalan Persiaran Madge, off Jalan U Thant, 55000 Kuala Lumpur; tel. (3) 42569913; fax (3) 42569933; Ambassador Kim Won Ho.

Korea, Republic: Lot 9 and 11, Jalan Nipah, off Jalan Ampang, 55000 Kuala Lumpur; tel. (3) 42512336; fax (3) 42521425; e-mail korem-my@mofat.go.kr; Ambassador Lee Young-Joon.

Kuwait: 229 Jalan Tun Razak, 50400 Kuala Lumpur; tel. (3) 21410033; fax (3) 21456121; e-mail kuwait@streamyx.com; Ambassador Abdulhamid Al-Failakawi.

Kyrgyzstan: 10 Lorong Damai 9, 55000 Kuala Lumpur; tel. (3) 21649862; fax (3) 21632024; e-mail kyrgyz@tm.net.my; Ambassador Akhbar Ryskulov.

Laos: 25 Jalan Damai, 55000 Kuala Lumpur; tel. (3) 21487059; fax (3) 21450080; Ambassador Chaleune Warinthrasak.

Lebanon: 56 Jalan Ampang Hilir, 55000 Kuala Lumpur; tel. (3) 42516690; fax (3) 42603426; e-mail lebanon@streamyx.com; Ambassador Khaled Al Kilani.

Libya: 6 Jalan Madge, off Jalan U Thant, 55000 Kuala Lumpur; tel. (3) 21411293; fax (3) 21413549; Ambassador Dr Ahmad Muhammad Ali al-Hanesh.

Luxembourg: Menara Keck Seng Bldg, 16th Floor, 203 Jalan Bukit Bintang, 55100 Kuala Lumpur; tel. (3) 21433134; fax (3) 21433157; e-mail kualalumpur.amb@mae.etat.lu; Chargé d'affaires a.i. Charles Schmit.

Mauritius: Lot W17-B1 and C1, 17th Floor, West Block, Wisma Selangor Dredging, 142-C Jalan Ampang, 50450 Kuala Lumpur; tel. (3) 21636306; fax (3) 21636294; e-mail maur@tm.net.my; High Commissioner Prithiviraj Fookerah (acting).

Mexico: Suite 22-05, 22nd Floor, Menara Tan & Tan, 207 Jalan Tun Razak, 50400 Kuala Lumpur; tel. (3) 21646362; fax (3) 21640964; e-mail contact@embamex.org.my; internet www.embamex.org.my; Ambassador Alfredo Pérez Bravo.

Morocco: Unit 9, 3rd Floor, East Block, Wisma Selangor Dredging, 142b Jalan Ampang, 50450 Kuala Lumpur; tel. (3) 21610701; fax (3) 21623081; e-mail sifmakl@po.jaring.my; Chargé d'affaires a.i. Mohamed Meskaouni.

Myanmar: 1 Lorong Ru Kedua, off Jalan Ampang Hilir, 55000 Kuala Lumpur; tel. (3) 42560280; fax (3) 42568320; e-mail mekl@tm.net.my; Ambassador U Myint Aung.

Namibia: Suite 15-01, Level 15, Menara HLA, 3 Jalan Kia Peng, 50450 Kuala Lumpur; tel. (3) 21646520; fax (3) 21688790; e-mail namhckl@streamyx.com; High Commissioner Neville Melvin Gertze.

Nepal: Suite 13A-01, 13th Floor, Wisma MCA, 163 Jalan Ampang, 50450 Kuala Lumpur; tel. (3) 21645934; fax (3) 21648659; e-mail mekl_88@streamyx.com; Chargé d'affaires a.i. Deepak Dhital.

Netherlands: The Amp Walk, 7th Floor, South Block, 218 Jalan Ampang, POB 10543, 50450 Kuala Lumpur; tel. (3) 21686200; fax (3) 21686240; e-mail kll@minbuza.nl; internet www.netherlands.org.my; Ambassador J. C. F. von Mühlen.

New Zealand: Menara IMC, 21st Floor, 8 Jalan Sultan Ismail, 50250 Kuala Lumpur; tel. (3) 20782533; fax (3) 20780387; e-mail nzhckl@po.jaring.my; High Commissioner Geoff Randal.

MALAYSIA

Nigeria: 85 Jalan Ampang Hilir, 55000 Kuala Lumpur; tel. (3) 42517843; fax (3) 42524302; e-mail nighcomm@tm.net.my; High Commissioner Dr WAHAB OLASEINDE DOSUNMU.

Norway: Suite CD, 53rd Floor, Empire Tower, Jalan Tun Razak, 50400 Kuala Lumpur; tel. (3) 21750300; fax (3) 21750308; e-mail emb.kualalumpur@mfa.no; Ambassador ARILD EIK.

Oman: 109 Jalan U Thant, 55000 Kuala Lumpur; tel. (3) 42577378; fax (3) 42571400; e-mail omanemb@po.jaring.my; Ambassador Sheikh GHAZI BIN SAID BIN ABDULLAH AL BAHR AR-RAWAS.

Pakistan: 132 Jalan Ampang, 50450 Kuala Lumpur; tel. (3) 21618877; fax (3) 21645958; e-mail pakistan@streamyx.com; High Commissioner Maj.-Gen. (retd) TALAT MUNIR.

Papua New Guinea: 11 Lingkungan U Thant, off Jalan U Thant, 55000 Kuala Lumpur; tel. (3) 42575405; fax (3) 42576203; High Commissioner PETER P. MAGINDE.

Peru: Wisma Selangor Dredging, 6th Floor, South Block, 142A Jalan Ampang, 50450 Kuala Lumpur; tel. (3) 21633034; fax (3) 21633039; e-mail info@embperu.com.my; internet www.embperu.com.my; Ambassador ALEJANDRO GORDILLO FERNÁNDEZ.

Philippines: 1 Changkat Kia Peng, 50450 Kuala Lumpur; tel. (3) 21484233; fax (3) 21483576; e-mail consular@philembassykl.org.my; internet www.philembassykl.org.my; Ambassador VICTORIANO M. LECAROS.

Poland: 495 Bt 4½ Jalan Ampang, 68000 Ampang, Selangor; tel. (3) 42576733; fax (3) 42570123; e-mail polamba@tm.net.my; Ambassador EUGENIOSZ SAWICKI.

Qatar: 113 Jalan Ampang Hilir, POB 13118, 55000 Kuala Lumpur; tel. (3) 42565552; fax (3) 42565553; Ambassador ABDULHAMEED MUBARAK AL-KUBAISI.

Romania: 114 Jalan Damai, off Jalan Ampang, 55000 Kuala Lumpur; tel. (3) 21423172; fax (3) 21448713; e-mail roemb@streamyx.com; Ambassador GABRIEL GAFITA.

Russia: 263 Jalan Ampang, 50450 Kuala Lumpur; tel. (3) 42567252; fax (3) 42576091; e-mail ruemvvl@tm.net.my; Ambassador VLADIMIR NIKOLAEVICH MOROZOV.

Saudi Arabia: Level 4, Wisma Chinese Chamber, 258 Jalan Ampang, 50450 Kuala Lumpur; tel. (3) 42579433; fax (3) 42578751; e-mail saembssy@tm.net.my; Ambassador HAMID MUHAMMAD YAHYA.

Senegal: 5 Persiaran Ampang, 55000 Kuala Lumpur; tel. (3) 42567343; fax (3) 42563205; e-mail senamb_mal@yahoo.fr; Ambassador ABDEL KADER PIERRE FALL.

Seychelles: 12th Floor, West Block, Wisma Selangor Dredging, POB 24, 142C Jalan Ampang, 50450 Kuala Lumpur; tel. (3) 21635726; fax (3) 21635727; e-mail seyhicom@po.jaring.my; High Commissioner LOUIS SYLVESTRE RADEGONDE.

Singapore: 209 Jalan Tun Razak, 50400 Kuala Lumpur; tel. (3) 21616277; fax (3) 21616343; e-mail singhc_kul@sgmfa.gov.sg; internet www.mfa.gov.sg/kl; High Commissioner ASHOK KUMAR MIRPURI.

Slovakia: 11 Jalan U Thant, 55000 Kuala Lumpur; tel. (3) 21150016; fax (3) 21150014; e-mail slovemb@tm.net.my; Ambassador MILAN LAJCIAK.

South Africa: Menara HLA, Suite 22.01, 3 Jalan Kia Peng, 50450 Kuala Lumpur; tel. (3) 21688663; fax (3) 21643742; e-mail sahcpol@streamyx.com; internet www.afrikaselatan.com; High Commissioner Dr ABRAHAM SOKHAYA NKOMO.

Spain: 200 Jalan Ampang, 50450 Kuala Lumpur; tel. (3) 21484868; fax (3) 21424582; e-mail embespmy@mail.mae.es; Ambassador GERMÁN BEJARANO GARCÍA.

Sri Lanka: 12 Jalan Keranji Dua, off Jalan Kedondong, Ampang Hilir, 55000 Kuala Lumpur; tel. (3) 42568987; fax (3) 42532497; e-mail slhicom@streamyx.com; internet www.slhc.com.my; High Commissioner CHRISTOPHER DANESHAN CASSIE CHETTY.

Sudan: 2A Persiaran Ampang, off Jalan Ru, 55000 Kuala Lumpur; tel. (3) 42569104; fax (3) 42568107; e-mail assalamiz@hotmail.com; Ambassador ABDEL RAHMAN HAMZAH ELRAYA.

Swaziland: Suite 22-03 and 03 (A), Menara Citibank, 165 Jalan Ampang, 50450 Kuala Lumpur; tel. (3) 21632511; fax (3) 21633326; e-mail swazi@tm.net.my; High Commissioner NEWMAN SIZWE NTSHANGASE (acting).

Sweden: Wisma Angkasa Raya, 6th Floor, 123 Jalan Ampang, POB 10239, 50708 Kuala Lumpur; tel. (3) 20522550; fax (3) 21486325; e-mail ambassaden.kuala-lumpur@foreign.ministry.se; internet www.swedenabroad.com/pages/start____16351.asp; Ambassador HELENA SÅNGELAND.

Switzerland: 16 Persiaran Madge, 55000 Kuala Lumpur; tel. (3) 21480622; fax (3) 21480935; e-mail vertretung@kua.rep.admin.ch; Ambassador Dr PETER A. SCHWEIZER.

Syria: Suite 23-03, 23rd Floor, Menara Tan & Tan, 207 Jalan Tun Razak, 50400 Kuala Lumpur; tel. (3) 21634110; fax (3) 21634199; Ambassador LAMIA MERIE ASSI.

Thailand: 206 Jalan Ampang, 50450 Kuala Lumpur; tel. (3) 21488222; fax (3) 21486527; e-mail thaikl@pop1.jaring.my; Ambassador OUM MAOLANON.

Timor-Leste: 62 Jalan Ampang Hilir, 55000 Kuala Lumpur; tel. (3) 42562046; fax (3) 42562016; e-mail embaixada_tl_kl@yahoo.com; Ambassador DJAFAR AMUDE BIN ALCATIRI.

Turkey: 118 Jalan U Thant, 55000 Kuala Lumpur; tel. (3) 42572225; fax (3) 42572227; e-mail turkbe@tm.net.my; Ambassador BARLAS OZENER.

Ukraine: Suite 22-02, 22nd Floor, Menara Tan & Tan, 207 Jalan Tun Razak, 50400 Kuala Lumpur; tel. (3) 21669552; fax (3) 21664371; e-mail emb_my@mfa.gov.ua; Ambassador OLEKSANDR SHEVCHENKO.

United Arab Emirates: 1 Gerbang Ampang Hilir, off Persiaran Ampang Hilir, 55000 Kuala Lumpur; tel. (3) 42535221; fax (3) 42535220; e-mail uaemal@tm.net.my; Ambassador NASSER SALMAN ALABOODI.

United Kingdom: 185 Jalan Ampang, 50450 Kuala Lumpur; tel. (3) 21702200; fax (3) 21702303; e-mail political.kualalumpur@fco.gov.uk; internet www.britain.org.my; High Commissioner BOYD MCCLEARY (designate).

USA: 376 Jalan Tun Razak, POB 10035, 50700 Kuala Lumpur; tel. (3) 21685000; fax (3) 21422207; e-mail lrckl@po.jaring.my; internet www.usembassymalaysia.org.my; Ambassador CHRISTOPHER J. LAFLEUR.

Uruguay: 6 Jalan 3, Taman Tun Abdul Razak, 68000 Ampang, Selangor Darul Bhsan; tel. (3) 42518831; fax (3) 42517878; e-mail urukual@po.jaring.my; Ambassador ROBERTO PABLO TOURINO TURNES.

Uzbekistan: 2 Jalan 12, Taman Tun Abdul Razak, 68000 Ampang, Selangor; tel. (3) 42532406; fax (3) 42535400; e-mail uzbekemb@streamyx.com; Ambassador AYBEK KHASANOV.

Venezuela: Suite 20-05, 20th Floor, Menara Tan & Tan, 207 Jalan Tun Razak, 50400 Kuala Lumpur; tel. (3) 21633444; fax (3) 21636819; e-mail venezuela@po.jaring.my; Ambassador Maj.-Gen. (retd) NOEL ENRIQUE MARTÍNEZ OCHOA.

Viet Nam: 4 Jalan Persiaran Stonor, 50450 Kuala Lumpur; tel. (3) 21484036; fax (3) 21483270; e-mail daisevn@putra.net.my; Ambassador NGUYEN QUOC DUNG.

Yemen: 7 Jalan Kedondong, off Jalan Ampang Hilir, 55000 Kuala Lumpur; tel. (3) 42511793; fax (3) 42511794; e-mail yemenkl@tm.net.my; Ambassador Dr ABDUL NASSER ALI ABDO MUNIBARI.

Zimbabwe: 124 Jalan Sembilan, Taman Ampang Utama, 68000 Ampang, Selangor Darul Ehsan; tel. (3) 42516779; fax (3) 42517252; e-mail zhck@tm.net.my; Ambassador LUCAS PANDE TAVAYA.

Judicial System

The two High Courts, one in Peninsular Malaysia and the other in Sabah and Sarawak, have original, appellate and revisional jurisdiction as the federal law provides. Above these two High Courts is the Court of Appeal, which was established in 1994; it is an intermediary court between the Federal Court and the High Court. When appeals to the Privy Council in the United Kingdom were abolished in 1985 the former Supreme Court became the final court of appeal. Therefore, at that stage only one appeal was available to a party aggrieved by the decision of the High Court. Hence, the establishment of the Court of Appeal. The Federal Court (formerly the Supreme Court) has, to the exclusion of any other court, jurisdiction in any dispute between states or between the Federation and any state; and has special jurisdiction as to the interpretation of the Constitution. The Federal Court is headed by the Chief Justice (formerly the Lord President); the other members of the Federal Court are the President of the Court of Appeal, the two Chief Judges of the High Courts and the Federal Court Judges. Members of the Court of Appeal are the President and the Court of Appeal judges, and members of the High Courts are the two Chief Judges and their respective High Court judges. All judges are appointed by the Yang di-Pertuan Agong on the advice of the Prime Minister, after consulting the Conference of Rulers. In 1993 a Special Court was established to hear cases brought by or against the Yang di-Pertuan Agong or a Ruler of State (Sultans).

The Sessions Courts, which are situated in the principal urban and rural centres, are presided over by a Sessions Judge, who is a member of the Judicial and Legal Service of the Federation and is a qualified barrister or a Bachelor of Law from any of the recognized universities. Their criminal jurisdiction covers the less serious indictable offences, excluding those that carry the death penalty. Civil jurisdic-

MALAYSIA

tion of a Sessions Court is up to RM 250,000. The Sessions Judges are appointed by the Yang di-Pertuan Agong.

The Magistrates' Courts are also found in the main urban and rural centres and have both civil and criminal jurisdiction, although of a more restricted nature than that of the Sessions Courts. The Magistrates consist of officers from the Judicial and Legal Service of the Federation. They are appointed by the State Authority in which they officiate on the recommendation of the Chief Judge.

There are also Syariah (Shariah) courts for rulings under Islamic law. In July 1996 the Cabinet announced that the Syariah courts were to be restructured with the appointment of a Syariah Chief Judge and four Court of Appeal justices, whose rulings would set precedents for the whole country.

Prior to February 1995 trials for murder and kidnapping in the High Courts were heard with jury and assessors, respectively. The amendment to the Criminal Procedure Code abolished both the jury and the assessors systems, and all criminal trials in the High Courts are heard by a judge sitting alone. In 1988 an amendment to the Constitution empowered any federal lawyer to confer with the Attorney-General to determine the courts in which any proceedings, excluding those before a Syariah court, a native court or a court martial, be instituted, or to which such proceedings be transferred.

Federal Court of Malaysia

Palace of Justice, Presint 3, 62506 Putrajaya; tel. (3) 88803500; internet www.kehakiman.gov.my.

Chief Justice of the Federal Court: Tan Sri Dato' Sri AHMAD FAIRUZ BIN Dato' Sheikh ABDUL HALIM.

President of the Court of Appeal: Dato' Haji ABDUL MALEK BIN Haji AHMAD.

Chief Judge of the High Court in Peninsular Malaysia: Dato' SITI NORMA BINTI YAAKOB.

Chief Judge of the High Court in Sabah and Sarawak: Datuk STEVE SHIP LIM KIONG.

Attorney-General: ABDUL GANI PATAIL.

Religion

Islam is the established religion. Whilst freedom of religious practice is enshrined in the Constitution, Malaysia's parallel Islamic judicial system holds great sway over the Muslim majority on religious issues. In May 2005 21 members of the controversial sect known as 'Sky Kingdom' were arrested for propagating 'devious' teachings said to humiliate Islam. Almost all ethnic Malays are Muslims, representing 60.4% of the total population in 2000. In that year 19.2% of the population followed Buddhism, 9.1% followed Christianity and 6.3% followed Hinduism.

Malaysian Consultative Council of Buddhism, Christianity, Hinduism and Sikhism (MCCBCHS): 8 Jalan Duku, off Jalan Kasipillai, 51200 Kuala Lumpur; tel. (3) 40414669; fax (3) 40444304; e-mail hsangam@po.jaring.my; f. 1981; a non-Muslim group.

ISLAM

President of the Majlis Islam: Datuk Haji MOHD FAUZI BIN Haji ABDUL HAMID (Kuching, Sarawak).

Istitut Kefahaman Islam Malaysia (IKIM) (Institute of Islamic Understanding Malaysia): 2 Langgak Tunku, off Jalan Duta, 50480 Kuala Lumpur; tel. (3) 62010889; fax (3) 62014189; internet www.ikim.gov.my.

Jabatan Kemajuan Islam Malaysia (JAKIM) (Department of Islamic Development Malaysia): Aras 4–9, Block D7, Pusat Pentadbiran Kerajaan Persekutuan, 62519 Putrajaya; tel. (3) 88864000; e-mail faizal@islam.gov.my; internet www.islam.gov.my.

BUDDHISM

Malaysian Buddhist Association (MBA): MBA Bldg, 182 Jalan Burmah, 10050 Pinang; tel. (4) 2262690; fax (4) 2263024; e-mail email@mba.net.my; internet www.mba.net.my; f. 1959; the national body for Chinese-speaking monks and nuns and temples from the Mahayana tradition; 9 state brs and 23 other brs nation-wide; 27,115 mems; Pres. Venerable CHEK HUANG.

Young Buddhist Association of Malaysia (YBAM): 9 Jalan SS25/24, 47301 Petaling Jaya, Selangor; tel. (3) 78049154; fax (3) 78049021; e-mail ybam@streamyx.com; internet www.ybam.org.my; f. 1970; Pres. GOH TAY HOCK.

Buddhist Missionary Society Malaysia (BMSM): 123 Jalan Berhala, off Jalan Tun Sambanthan, 50470 Kuala Lumpur; tel. (3) 22730150; fax (3) 22740245; e-mail president@bmsm.org.my; internet www.bmsm.org.my; f. 1962 as Buddhist Missionary Society; Pres. ANG CHOO HONG.

Directory

Buddhist Tzu-Chi Merit Society (Malaysia): 24 Jesselton Ave, 10450 Pinang; e-mail mtzuchi@po.jaring.my; internet www.tzuchi.org.my.

Malaysian Fo Kuang Buddhist Association: 2 Jalan SS3/33, Taman University, 47300 Petaling Jaya, Selangor; tel. (3) 78776512; fax (3) 78776511; e-mail myfoguang@yahoo.com.

Sasana Abhiwurdhi Wardhana Society: 123 Jalan Berhala, off Jalan Tun Sambanthan, 50490 Kuala Lumpur; f. 1894; the national body for Sri Lankan Buddhists belonging to the Theravada tradition.

CHRISTIANITY

Majlis Gereja-Gereja Malaysia (Council of Churches of Malaysia): 26 Jalan Universiti, 46200 Petaling Jaya, Selangor; tel. (3) 7567092; fax (3) 7560353; e-mail cchurchm@tm.net.my; internet www.ccmalaysia.org; f. 1947; 15 mem. churches; 10 associate mems; Pres. Right Rev. Tan Sri Dr LIM CHENG EAN (Anglican Bishop of West Malaysia); Gen. Sec. Rev. Dr HERMEN SHASTRI.

The Anglican Communion

Malaysia comprises three Anglican dioceses, within the Church of the Province of South East Asia.

Primate: Most Rev. Datuk YONG PING CHUNG (Bishop of Sabah).

Bishop of Kuching: Rt Rev. MADE KATIB, Bishop's House, POB 347, 93704 Kuching, Sarawak; tel. (82) 240187; fax (82) 426488; e-mail bkg@pc.jaring.my; has jurisdiction over Sarawak, Brunei and part of Indonesian Kalimantan (Borneo).

Bishop of Sabah: Most Rev. Datuk YONG PING CHUNG, Rumah Bishop, Jalan Tangki, POB 10811, 88809 Kota Kinabalu, Sabah; tel. (88) 247008; fax (88) 245942; e-mail pcyong@pc.jaring.my.

Bishop of West Malaysia: Rt. Rev. Tan Sri Dr LIM CHENG EAN, Bishop's House, 16 Jalan Pudu Lama, 50200 Kuala Lumpur; tel. (3) 20312728; fax (3) 20313213; e-mail diocese@tm.net.my.

The Baptist Church

Malaysia Baptist Convention: 2 Jalan 2/38, 46000 Petaling Jaya, Selangor; tel. (3) 77823564; fax (3) 77833603; e-mail mbcpj@tm.net.my; Chair. Dr TAN ENG LEE.

The Methodist Church

Methodist Church in Malaysia: 69 Jalan 5/31, 46000 Petaling Jaya, Selangor; tel. (3) 79541811; fax (3) 79541787; e-mail ace@methodistchurch.org.my; 140,000 mems; Bishop Dr HWA YUNG.

The Presbyterian Church

Presbyterian Church in Malaysia: Joyful Grace Church, Jalan Alsagoff, 82000 Pontian, Johor; tel. (7) 711390; fax (7) 324384; Pastor TITUS KIM KAH TECK.

The Roman Catholic Church

Malaysia comprises two archdioceses and six dioceses. At 31 December 2003 approximately 3.2% of the population were adherents.

Catholic Bishops' Conference of Malaysia, Singapore and Brunei

Xavier Hall, 133 Jalan Gasing, 46000 Petaling Jaya, Selangor Darul Ehsan; tel. and fax (3) 79581371; e-mail cbcmsb@pc.jaring.my; Pres. Most Rev. NICHOLAS CHIA (Archbishop of Singapore).

Archbishop of Kuala Lumpur: Most Rev. MURPHY NICHOLAS XAVIER PAKIAM, Archbishop's House, 528 Jalan Bukit Nanas, 50250 Kuala Lumpur; tel. (3) 20788828; fax (3) 20313815; e-mail mpakiam@pd.jaring.my.

Archbishop of Kuching: Most Rev. JOHN HA TIONG HOCK, Archbishop's Office, 118 Jalan Tun Abang Haji Openg, POB 940, 93718 Kuching, Sarawak; tel. (82) 242634; fax (82) 425724; e-mail johnha@pd.jaring.my.

BAHÁ'Í FAITH

Spiritual Assembly of the Bahá'ís of Malaysia: 4 Lorong Titiwangsa 5, off Jalan Pahang, 53200 Kuala Lumpur; tel. (3) 40233000; fax (3) 40226277; e-mail nsa-sec@bahai.org.my; internet www.bahai.org.my; f. 1964; mems resident in 800 localities.

The Press

PENINSULAR MALAYSIA DAILIES

English Language

Business Times: Balai Berita 31, Jalan Riong, 59100 Kuala Lumpur; tel. (3) 22822628; fax (3) 22825424; e-mail bt@nstp.com.my;

MALAYSIA

internet www.btimes.com.my; f. 1976; morning; Editor ZAINUL ARIFIN; circ. 15,000.

Malay Mail: Balai Berita 31, Jalan Riong, 59100 Kuala Lumpur; tel. (3) 22822829; fax (3) 22849133; e-mail malaymail@nstp.com.my; internet www.mmail.com.my; f. 1896; afternoon; Editor AHIRUDIN ATTAN; circ. 75,000.

Malaysiakini: 48 Jalan Kemuja, Bangsar Utama, 59000 Kuala Lumpur; tel. (3) 22835567; fax (3) 22892579; e-mail enquiries@malaysiakini.com; internet www.malaysiakini.com; f. 1999; Malaysia's first online newspaper; English and Malay; Editor STEVEN GAN.

New Straits Times: Balai Berita 31, Jalan Riong, 59100 Kuala Lumpur; tel. (3) 22823322; fax (3) 22821434; e-mail mailed@nstp.com.my; internet www.nst.com.my; f. 1845; morning; Group Editor-in-Chief Datuk HISHAMUDDIN AUN; circ. 190,000.

The Edge: G501–G801, Levels 5–8, Block G, Phileo Damansara I, Jalan 16/11, off Jalan Damansara, 46350 Petaling Jaya, Selangor; tel. (3) 76603838; fax (3) 76608638; e-mail eeditor@bizedge.com; internet www.theedgedaily.com; f. 1996; weekly, with daily internet edition; business and investment news; Editor-in-Chief HO KAY TAT.

The Star: 13 Jalan 13/6, 46200 Petaling Jaya, POB 12474, Selangor; tel. (3) 7581188; fax (3) 7551280; e-mail msd@thestar.com.my; internet www.thestar.com.my; f. 1971; morning; Group Chief Editor NG POH TIP; circ. 192,059.

The Sun: Sun Media Corpn Sdn Bhd, Lot 6, Jalan 51/217, Section 51, 46050 Petaling Jaya, Selangor Darul Ehsan; tel. (3) 77846688; fax (3) 77835871; e-mail editor@thesundaily.com; internet www.thesundaily.com; f. 1993; free tabloid newspaper in print and online formats; Group Editor-in-Chief HO KAY TAT; Editor CHONG CHENG HAI; circ. 82,474.

Chinese Language

China Press: 80 Jalan Riong, 59100 Kuala Lumpur; tel. (3) 2828208; fax (3) 2825327; circ. 206,000.

Chung Kuo Pao (China Press): 80 Jalan Riong, 59100 Kuala Lumpur; tel. (3) 2828208; fax (3) 2825327; f. 1946; Editor POON CHAU HUAY; Gen. Man. NG BENG LYE; circ. 210,000.

Guang Ming Daily: 19 Jalan Semangat, 46200 Petaling Jaya, Selangor; tel. (3) 7582888; fax (3) 7575135; licence suspended for two weeks in Feb. 2006 following the publication's decision to reprint controversial cartoons depicting the Prophet Muhammad; Editor-in-Chief YE NING; circ. 87,144.

Kwong Wah Yit Poh: 19 Jalan Presgrave, 11300 Pinang; tel. (4) 2612312; fax (4) 2610510; e-mail editor@kwongwah.com.my; internet www.kwongwah.com.my; f. 1910; morning; Chief Editor WONG KWAN CHEUNG; circ. 100,000.

Nanyang Siang Pau (Malaysia): 1st Floor, 1 Jalan SS7/2, 47301 Petaling Jaya, Selangor; tel. (3) 78726888; fax (3) 78726800; e-mail info@nanyang.com.my; internet www.nanyang.com.my; f. 1923; morning and evening; Editor-in-Chief CHENG KHEE CHIEN; circ. 180,000 (daily), 220,000 (Sunday).

Shin Min Daily News: 31 Jalan Riong, Bangsar, 59100 Kuala Lumpur; tel. (3) 2826363; fax (3) 2821812; f. 1966; morning; Editor-in-Chief CHENG SONG HUAT; circ. 82,000.

Sin Chew Jit Poh (Malaysia): 19 Jalan Semangat, POB 367, Jalan Sultan, 46200 Petaling Jaya, Selangor; tel. (3) 7582888; fax (3) 7570527; internet www.sinchew-i.com; f. 1929; morning; Chief Editor LIEW CHEN CHUAN; circ. 227,067 (daily), 230,000 (Sunday).

Malay Language

Berita Harian: Balai Berita 31, Jalan Riong, 59100 Kuala Lumpur; tel. (3) 22822323; fax (3) 22822425; e-mail bh@bharian.com.my; internet www.bharian.com.my; f. 1957; morning; Group Editor Datuk HISHAMUDDIN AUN; circ. 350,000.

Mingguan Perdana: 48 Jalan Siput Akek, Taman Billion, Kuala Lumpur; tel. (3) 619133; Group Chief Editor KHALID JAFRI.

Utusan Malaysia: 46M Jalan Lima, off Jalan Chan Sow Lin, 55200 Kuala Lumpur; tel. (3) 2217055; fax (3) 2220911; e-mail corpcomm@utusan.com.my; internet www.utusan.com.my; Editor ABDUL AZIZ ISHAK; circ. 239,385.

Watan: 23–1 Jalan 9A/55A, Taman Setiawangsa, 54200 Kuala Lumpur; tel. (3) 4523040; fax (3) 4523043; circ. 80,000.

Tamil Language

Malaysia Nanban: 11 Jalan Murai Dua, Batu Kompleks, off Jalan Ipoh, 51200 Kuala Lumpur; tel. (3) 6212251; fax (3) 6235981; circ. 45,000.

Tamil Nesan: 28 Jalan Yew, Pudu, 55100 Kuala Lumpur; tel. (3) 2216411; fax (3) 2210448; f. 1924; morning; Editor V. VIVEKANANTHAN; circ. 35,000 (daily), 60,000 (Sunday).

Tamil Osai: 19 Jalan Murai Dua, Batu Kompleks, off Jalan Ipoh, Kuala Lumpur; tel. (3) 671644; circ. 21,000 (daily), 40,000 (Sunday).

Tamil Thinamani: 9 Jalan Murai Dua, Batu Kompleks, off Jalan Ipoh, Kuala Lumpur; tel. (3) 66719; Editor S. NACHIAPPAN; circ. 18,000 (daily), 39,000 (Sunday).

SUNDAY NEWSPAPERS

English Language

New Sunday Times: Balai Berita 31, Jalan Riong, 59100 Kuala Lumpur; tel. (3) 2822328; fax (3) 2824482; e-mail news@nstp.com.my; f. 1931; morning; Group Editor Datuk HISHAMUDDIN AUN; circ. 191,562.

Sunday Mail: Balai Berita 31, Jalan Riong, 59100 Kuala Lumpur; tel. (3) 2822328; fax (3) 2824482; e-mail smail@nstp.com.my; f. 1896; morning; Editor JOACHIM S. P. NG; circ. 75,641.

Sunday Star: 13 Jalan 13/6, 46200 Petaling Jaya, POB 12474, Selangor Darul Ehsan; tel. (3) 7581188; fax (3) 7551280; f. 1971; Editor DAVID YEOH; circ. 232,790.

Malay Language

Berita Minggu: Balai Berita 31, Jalan Riong, 59100 Kuala Lumpur; tel. (3) 2822328; fax (3) 2824482; e-mail bharian@bharian.com.my; f. 1957; morning; Editor Dato' AHMAD NAZRI ABDULLAH; circ. 421,127.

Metro Ahad: Balai Berita 31, Jalan Riong, 59100 Kuala Lumpur; tel. (3) 22822328; fax (3) 22821482; e-mail metahad@nstp.com.my; internet www.nstp.com.my/Corporate/nstp/products/productMetroAhd.htm; f. 1995; morning; circ. 136,974.

Mingguan Malaysia: 11A The Right Angle, Jalan 14/22, 46100 Petaling Jaya; tel. (3) 7563355; fax (3) 7577755; f. 1964; Editor MOHD HASSAN MOHD NOOR; circ. 543,232.

Utusan Zaman: 11A The Right Angle, Jalan 14/22, 46100 Petaling Jaya; tel. (3) 7563355; fax (3) 7577755; f. 1939; Editor MUSTAFA FADULA SUHAIMI; circ. 11,782.

Tamil Language

Makkal Osai: 11 Jalan Murai Dua, Batu Kompleks, off Jalan Ipoh, 51200 Kuala Lumpur; tel. (3) 6212251; fax (3) 6235981; circ. 28,000.

PENINSULAR MALAYSIA PERIODICALS

English Language

Her World: Berita Publishing Sdn Bhd, Balai Berita 31, Jalan Riong, 59100 Kuala Lumpur; tel. (3) 2824322; fax (3) 2828489; monthly; Editor ALICE CHEE LAN NEO; circ. 35,000.

Malaysia Warta Kerajaan Seri Paduka Baginda (HM Government Gazette): Percetakan Nasional Malaysia Berhad, Jalan Chan Sow Lin, 50554 Kuala Lumpur; tel. (3) 92212022; fax (3) 92220690; e-mail pnmb@po.jaring.my; fortnightly.

Malaysian Agricultural Journal: Ministry of Agriculture, Publications Unit, Wisma Tani, Jalan Sultan Salahuddin, 50624 Kuala Lumpur; tel. (3) 2982011; fax (3) 2913758; f. 1901; 2 a year.

Malaysian Forester: Forestry Department Headquarters, Jalan Sultan Salahuddin, 50660 Kuala Lumpur; tel. (3) 26988244; fax (3) 26925657; e-mail skthai@forestry.gov.my; f. 1931; quarterly; Editor THAI SEE KIAM.

The Planter: Wisma ISP, 29–33 Jalan Taman U Thant, POB 10262, 50708 Kuala Lumpur; tel. (3) 21425561; fax (3) 21426898; e-mail isphq@tm.net.my; internet www.isp.org.my/index.php?id=4; f. 1919; publ. by Isp Management (M); monthly; Editor Tuan Haji DAUD Haji AMATZIN; circ. 4,000.

Young Generation: 11A The Right Angle, Jalan 14/22, 46100 Petaling Jaya, Selangor; tel. (3) 7563355; fax (3) 7577755; monthly; circ. 50,000.

Chinese Language

Mister Weekly: 2A Jalan 19/1, 46300 Petaling Jaya, Selangor; tel. (3) 7562400; fax (3) 7553826; f. 1976; weekly; Editor WONG AH TAI; circ. 25,000.

Mun Sang Poh: 472 Jalan Pasir Puteh, 31650 Ipoh; tel. (5) 3212919; fax (5) 3214006; bi-weekly; circ. 77,958.

New Life Post: 80M Jalan SS21/39, Damansara Utama, 47400 Petaling Jaya, Selangor; tel. (3) 7571833; fax (3) 7181809; f. 1972; bi-weekly; Editor LOW BENG CHEE; circ. 231,000.

New Tide Magazine: Nanyang Siang Pau Bldg, 2nd Floor, Jalan 7/2, 47301 Petaling Jaya, Selangor; tel. (3) 76202118; fax (3) 76202131; e-mail newtidemag@hotmail.com; f. 1974; monthly; Editor NELLIE OOI; circ. 39,000.

Malay Language

Dewan Masyarakat: Dewan Bahasa dan Pustaka, Jalan Wisma Putra, POB 10803, 50926 Kuala Lumpur; tel. (3) 2481011; fax (3)

MALAYSIA

2484211; f. 1963; monthly; current affairs; Editor ZULKIFLI SALLEH; circ. 48,500.

Dewan Pelajar: Dewan Bahasa dan Pustaka, Jalan Wisma Putra, POB 10803, 50926 Kuala Lumpur; tel. (3) 2481011; fax (3) 2484211; f. 1967; monthly; children's; Editor ZALEHA HASHIM; circ. 100,000.

Dewan Siswa: POB 10803, 50926 Kuala Lumpur; tel. (3) 2481011; fax (3) 2484208; monthly; circ. 140,000.

Gila-Gila: 38-1, Jalan Bangsar Utama Satu, Bangsar Utama, 59000 Kuala Lumpur; tel. (3) 22824970; fax (3) 22824967; fortnightly; circ. 70,000.

Harakah: Jabatan Penerangan dan Penyelidikan PAS, 28A Jalan Pahang Barat, Off Jalan Pahang, 53000 Kuala Lumpur; tel. (3) 40213343; fax (3) 40212422; e-mail hrkh@pc.jaring.my; internet www.harakahdaily.net; two a month; organ of the Parti Islam se Malaysia (PAS—Islamic Party of Malaysia); Editor ZULKIFLI SULONG.

Jelita: Berita Publishing Sdn Bhd, 16–20 Jalan 4/109E, Desa Business Park, Taman Desa, off Jalan Klang Lama, 58100 Kuala Lumpur; tel. (3) 76208111; fax (3) 76208114; e-mail jelita@beritapub.com.my; internet www.beritapublishing.com.my; monthly; fashion and beauty magazine; Editor ROHANI PA' WAN CHIK; circ. 80,000.

Mangga: 11A The Right Angle, Jalan 14/22, 46100 Petaling Jaya, Selangor; tel. (3) 7563355; fax (3) 7577755; monthly; circ. 205,000.

Mastika: 11A The Right Angle, Jalan 14/22, 46100 Petaling Jaya, Selangor; tel. (3) 7563355; fax (3) 7577755; monthly; illustrated magazine; Editor AZIZAH ALI; circ. 15,000.

Utusan Radio dan TV: 11A The Right Angle, Jalan 14/22, 46100 Petaling Jaya, Selangor; tel. (3) 7563355; fax (3) 7577755; fortnightly; Editor NORSHAH TAMBY; circ. 115,000.

Wanita: 11A The Right Angle, Jalan 14/22, 46100 Petaling Jaya, Selangor; tel. (3) 7563355; fax (3) 7577755; monthly; women; Editor NIK RAHIMAH HASSAN; circ. 85,000.

Punjabi Language

Navjiwan Punjabi News: 52 Jalan 8/18, Jalan Toman, 46050 Petaling Jaya, Selangor; tel. (3) 7565725; f. 1950; weekly; Assoc. Editor TARA SINGH; circ. 9,000.

SABAH DAILIES

Api Siang Pau (Kota Kinabalu Commercial Press): 24 Lorong Dewan, POB 170, Kota Kinabalu; f. 1954; morning; Chinese; Editor Datuk LO KWOCK CHUEN; circ. 3,000.

Borneo Mail (Nountan Press Sdn Bhd): 1 Jalan Bakau, 1st Floor, off Jalan Gaya, 88999 Kota Kinabulu; tel. (88) 238001; fax (88) 238002; English; circ. 14,610.

Daily Express: News House, 16 Jalan Pasar Baru, POB 10139, 88801 Kota Kinabalu; tel. (88) 256422; fax (88) 238611; e-mail sph@tm.net.my; internet www.dailyexpress.com.my; f. 1963; morning; English, Bahasa Malaysia and Kadazan; Editor-in-Chief SARDATHISA JAMES; circ. 30,000.

Hwa Chiaw Jit Pao (Overseas Chinese Daily News): News House, 16 Jalan Pasar Baru, POB 10139, 88801 Kota Kinabalu; tel. (88) 256422; e-mail sph@tm.net.my; internet www.dailyexpress.com.my; f. 1936; morning; Chinese; Editor HII YUK SENG; circ. 30,000.

Merdeka Daily News: Lot 56, BDC Estate, Mile 1½ North Road, POB 332, 90703 Sandakan; tel. (89) 214517; fax (89) 275537; e-mail merkk@tm.net.my; f. 1968; morning; Chinese; Editor-in-Chief FUNG KON SHING; circ. 8,000.

New Sabah Times: Jalan Pusat Pembangunan Masyarakat, off Jalan Mat Salleh, 88100 Kota Kinabalu; POB 20119, 88758 Kota Kinabalu; tel. (88) 230055; fax (88) 231155; internet www.newsabahtimes.com.my; English, Malay and Kadazan; Editor-in-Chief EDDY LOK; circ. 30,000.

Syarikat Sabah Times: Kota Kinabalu; tel. (88) 52217; f. 1952; English, Malay and Kadazan; circ. 25,000.

Tawau Jih Pao: POB 464, 1072 Jalan Kuhara, Tawau; tel. (89) 72576; Chinese; Editor-in-Chief STEPHEN LAI KIM YEAN.

SARAWAK DAILIES

Berita Petang Sarawak: Lot 8322, Lorong 7, Jalan Tun Abdul Razak, 93450 Kuching; POB 1315, 93726 Kuching; tel. (82) 480771; fax (82) 489006; f. 1972; evening; Chinese; licence suspended for two weeks in Feb. 2006 following the publication's decision to reprint controversial cartoons depicting the Prophet Muhammad; Chief Editor HWANG YU CHAI; circ. 12,000.

Borneo Post: 40 Jalan Tuanku Osman, POB 20, 96000 Sibu; tel. (84) 332055; fax (84) 321255; internet www.borneopost.com.my; morning; English; Man. Dir LAU HUI SIONG; Editor NGUOI HOW YIENG; circ. 60,000.

International Times: Lot 2215, Jalan Bengkel, Pending Industrial Estate, POB 1158, 93724 Kuching; tel. (82) 482215; fax (82) 480996; e-mail news@intimes.com; internet www.intimes.com.my; f. 1968; morning; Chinese; Editor LEE FOOK ONN; circ. 37,000.

Malaysia Daily News: 7 Island Rd, POB 237, 96009 Sibu; tel. (84) 330211; tel. (84) 320540; f. 1968; morning; Chinese; Editor WONG SENG KWONG; circ. 22,735.

Sarawak Tribune and Sunday Tribune: Lot 231, Jalan Abell Utara, 93100 Kuching; tel. (82) 424411; fax (82) 415024; internet www.sarawaktribune.com.my; f. 1945; English; licence suspended indefinitely in Feb. 2006 following the publication's decision to reprint controversial cartoons depicting the Prophet Muhammad; Editor (vacant); circ. 29,598.

See Hua Daily News: 40 Jalan Tuanku Osman, POB 20, 96000 Sibu; tel. (84) 332055; fax (84) 321255; f. 1952; morning; Chinese; Man. Editor LAU HUI SIONG; circ. 80,000.

United Daily News: internet www.uniteddaily.com.my; f. 2004 following merger between Chinese Daily News and Miri Daily News; morning; Chinese; Dep. Publr WONG KEH HUONG; circ. 35,000.

SARAWAK PERIODICALS

Pedoman Rakyat: Malaysian Information Dept, Mosque Rd, 93612 Kuching; tel. (82) 240141; f. 1956; monthly; Malay; Editor SAIT BIN HAJI YAMAN; circ. 30,000.

Pembrita: Malaysian Information Services, Mosque Rd, 93612 Kuching; tel. (82) 247231; f. 1950; monthly; Iban; Editor ALBAN JAWA; circ. 20,000.

Sarawak Gazette: Sarawak Museum, Jalan Tun Abang Haji Openg, 93566 Kuching; tel. (82) 244232; fax (82) 246680; e-mail museum@po.jaring.my; f. 1870; 2 a year; English; Chief Editor Datu Haji SALLEH SULAIMAN.

Utusan Sarawak: Lot 231, Jalan Nipah, off Jalan Abell, POB 138, 93100 Kuching; tel. (82) 424411; fax (82) 420358; internet www.utusansarawak.com.my; f. 1949; Malay; Editor Haji ABDUL AZIZ Haji MALIM; circ. 32,292.

NEWS AGENCIES

Bernama (Malaysian National News Agency): Wisma Bernama, 28 Jalan 1/65A, off Jalan Tun Razak, POB 10024, 50700 Kuala Lumpur; tel. (3) 26939933; fax (3) 2941020; e-mail sjamil@bernama.com; internet www.bernama.com; f. 1968; general and foreign news, economic features and photo services, public relations wire, screen information and data services, stock market on-line equities service, real-time commodity and monetary information services; daily output in Malay and English; in June 1990 Bernama was given the exclusive right to receive and distribute news in Malaysia; Gen. Man. SYED JAMIL JAAFAR.

Foreign Bureaux

Agence France-Presse (AFP): 26 Hotel Equatorial, 1st Floor, Jalan Sultan Ismail, 50250 Kuala Lumpur; tel. (3) 26911906; fax (3) 21615606; Correspondent MERVIN NAMBIAR.

Associated Press (AP) (USA): Wisma Bernama, 28 Jalan 1/65A, off Jalan Tun Razak, POB 12219, Kuala Lumpur; tel. (3) 2926155; Correspondent HARI SUBRAMANIAM.

Inter Press Service (IPS) (Italy): 32 Jalan Mudah Barat, Taman Midah, 56000 Kuala Lumpur; tel. (3) 9716830; fax (3) 2612872; Correspondent (vacant).

Press Trust of India: 114 Jalan Limau Manis, Bangsar Park, Kuala Lumpur; tel. (3) 940673; Correspondent T. V. VENKITACHALAM.

United Press International (UPI) (USA): Room 1, Ground Floor, Wisma Bernama, Jalan 1/65A, 50400 Kuala Lumpur; tel. (3) 2933393; fax (3) 2913876; Rep. MARY LEIGH.

Reuters (United Kingdom) and Xinhua (People's Republic of China) are also represented in Malaysia.

PRESS ASSOCIATION

Persatuan Penerbit-Penerbit Akhbar Malaysia (Malaysian Newspaper Publishers' Asscn): Unit 706, Block B, Phileo Damansara 1, 9 Jalan 16/11, off Jalan Damansara, 46350 Petaling Jaya; tel. (3) 76608535; fax (3) 76608532; e-mail mnpa@macomm.com.my; Chair. ROSELINA JOHARI.

Publishers

KUALA LUMPUR

Arus Intelek Sdn Bhd: Plaza Mont Kiara, Suite E-06-06, Mont Kiara, 50480 Kuala Lumpur; tel. (3) 62011558; fax (3) 62018698; e-mail arusintelek@po.jaring.my; Man. Datin AZIZAH MOKHZANI.

Berita Publishing Sdn Bhd: 16–20 Jalan 4/109E, Desa Business Park, Taman Desa, Off Jalan Klang Lama, 58100 Kuala Lumpur; tel.

(3) 76208111; fax (3) 76208018; e-mail mbeditor@beritapub.com; internet www.beritapublishing.com.my; education, business, fiction, cookery; Chair. A. KADIR JASIN.

Dewan Bahasa dan Pustaka (DBP) (Institute of Language and Literature): Jalan Dewan Bahasa, 50460 Kuala Lumpur; tel. (3) 21481011; fax (3) 21447248; e-mail aziz@dbp.gov.my; internet www.dbp.gov.my; f. 1956; textbooks, magazines and general; Chair. Tan Sri KAMARUL ARIFFIN MOHAMED YASSIN; Dir-Gen. Dato' Haji A. AZIZ DERAMAN.

Jabatan Penerbitan Universiti Malaya (University of Malaya Press): University of Malaya, Lembah Pantai, 50603 Kuala Lumpur; tel. (3) 79574361; fax (3) 79574473; e-mail terbit@um.edu.my; internet umweb.um.edu.my/umpress; f. 1954; general fiction, literature, economics, history, medicine, politics, science, social science, law, Islam, engineering, dictionaries; Chief Editor Dr HAMEDI MOHD ADNAN.

Malaya Press Sdn Bhd: Kuala Lumpur; tel. (3) 5754650; fax (3) 5751464; f. 1958; education; Man. Dir LAI WING CHUN.

Pustaka Antara Sdn Bhd: Lot UG 07 and 09, Upper Ground Floor, Kompleks Wilayah, 2 Jalan Munshi Abdullah, 50100 Kuala Lumpur; tel. (3) 26980044; fax (3) 26917997; e-mail pantara4@streamyx.com; textbooks, children's, languages, fiction; Man. Dir Datuk ABDUL AZIZ BIN AHMAD.

Utusan Publications and Distributors Sdn Bhd: 1 and 3 Jalan 3/91A, Taman Shamelin Perkasa, Cheras, 56100 Kuala Lumpur; tel. (3) 9856577; fax (3) 9846554; e-mail rose@utusan.com.my; internet www.upnd.com.my; school textbooks, children's, languages, fiction, general; Exec. Dir ROSELINA JOHARI.

JOHOR

Penerbitan Pelangi Sdn Bhd: 66 Jalan Pingai, Taman Pelangi, 80400 Johor Bahru; tel. (7) 89269553; fax (7) 3329201; e-mail info@pelangibooks.com; internet www.pelangibooks.com; f. 1979; children's books, guidebooks and reference; Man. Dir SAMUEL SUM KOWN CHEEK.

Textbooks Malaysia Sdn Bhd: 49 Jalan Tengku Ahmad, POB 30, 85000 Segamat, Johor; tel. (7) 9318323; fax (7) 9313323; school textbooks, children's fiction, guidebooks and reference; Man. Dir FREDDIE KHOO.

NEGERI SEMBILAN

Bharathi Press: 166 Taman AST, POB 74, 70700 Seremban, Negeri Sembilan Darul Khusus; tel. (6) 7622911; f. 1939; Mans M. SUBRAMANIA BHARATHI, BHARATHI THASAN.

PULAU PINANG

Syarikat United Book Sdn Bhd: 187–189 Lebuh Carnarvon, 10100 Pulau Pinang; tel. (4) 2626891; fax (4) 2626892; textbooks, children's, reference, fiction, guidebooks; Man. Dir CHEW SING GUAN.

SELANGOR

Federal Publications Sdn Bhd: Lot 46, Subang Hi-Tech Industrial Park, Batu Tiga, 40000 Shah Alam, Selangor; tel. (3) 56286888; fax (3) 56364620; e-mail fpsb@tpg.com.my; f. 1957; computer, children's magazines; Gen. Man. STEPHEN K. S. LIM.

FEP International Sdn Bhd: 6 Jalan SS 4C/5, POB 1091, 47301 Petaling Jaya, Selangor; tel. (3) 7036150; fax (3) 7036989; f. 1969; children's, languages, fiction, dictionaries, textbooks and reference; Man. Dir LIM MOK HAI.

International Law Book Services: 10 Jalan PJU 8/5 G, Perdana Business Centre, Bandar Damansara Perdana, 47820 Petaling Jaya, Selangor Darul Ehsan; tel. (3) 77274121; fax (3) 77273884; e-mail gbc@pc.jaring.my; internet www.malaysialawbooks.com; Man. Dr SYED IBRAHIM.

Mahir Publications Sdn Bhd: 39 Jalan Nilam 1/2, Subang Sq., Subang Hi-Tech Industrial Park, Batu Tiga, 40000 Shah Alam, Selangor; tel. (3) 7379044; fax (3) 7379043; e-mail mahirpub@tm.net.my; Gen. Man. ZAINORA BINTI MUHAMAD.

Minerva Publications (NS) Sdn Bhd: 51 Jalan SG 3/1, Tan Sri Gombak, Batu Caves, 68100 Selangor; tel. (3) 61882876; fax (3) 61883876; e-mail minerva@streamyx.com; internet www.minervaa.com; f. 1974; general, children's, reference, medical, law; Dir and Chief Editor SUJAUDEEN; Man. Dir THANJUDEEN.

Pearson Education Malaysia Sdn Bhd: Lot 2, Jalan 215, off Jalan Templer, 46050 Petaling Jaya, Selangor; tel. (3) 77820466; fax (3) 77818005; e-mail inquiry@pearsoned.com.my; internet www.pearsoned.com.my; textbooks, mathematics, physics, science, general, educational materials; Dir WONG WEE WOON; Man. WONG MEI MEI.

Pelanduk Publications (M) Sdn Bhd: 12 Jalan SS 13/3E, Subang Jaya Industrial Estate, 47500 Subang Jaya, Selangor; tel. (3) 56386885; fax (3) 56386575; e-mail pelpub@tm.net.my; internet www.pelanduk.com; f. 1984; Man. JACKSON TAN.

Penerbit Fajar Bakti Sdn Bhd: 4 Jalan U1/15, Sekseyen U1, Hicom-Glenmarie Industrial Park, 40150 Shah Alam, Selangor; tel. (3) 7047011; fax (3) 7047024; e-mail edes@pfb.po.my; school, college and university textbooks, children's, fiction, general; Man. Dir EDDA DE SILVA.

Penerbit Pan Earth Sdn Bhd: 11 Jalan SS 26/6, Taman Mayang Jaya, 47301 Petaling Jaya, Selangor; tel. (3) 7031258; fax (3) 7031262; Man. STEPHEN CHENG.

Penerbit Universiti Kebangsaan Malaysia: Universiti Kebangsaan Malaysia, 43600 UKM, Selangor; tel. (3) 8292840; fax (3) 8254375; Man. HASROM BIN HARON.

Pustaka Delta Pelajaran Sdn Bhd: Wisma Delta, Lot 18, Jalan 51A/22A, 46100 Petaling Jaya, Selangor; tel. (3) 7570000; fax (3) 7576688; e-mail dpsb@po.jaring.my; economics, language, environment, geography, geology, history, religion, science; Man. Dir LIM KIM WAH.

Pustaka Sistem Pelajaran Sdn Bhd: Lot 17–22 and 17–23, Jalan Satu, Bersatu Industrial Park, Cheras Jaya, 43200 Cheras, Selangor; tel. (3) 9047558; fax (3) 9047573; Man. T. THIRU.

Sasbadi Sdn Bhd: Lot 12, Jalan Teknologi 3/4, Taman Sains Selangor 1, Kota Damansara, 47810 Petaling Jaya, Selangor; tel. (3) 61577720; fax (3) 61569080; Man. LAW KING HUI.

SNP Panpac (Malaysia) Sdn Bhd: Lot 3, Jalan Saham 23/3, Kawasan MIEL Phase 8, Section 23, 40300 Shah Alam, Selangor Darul Ehsam; tel. (3) 55481088; fax (3) 55481080; e-mail eastview@snpo.com.my; f. 1980; fmrly SNP Eastview Publications Sdn Bhd; school textbooks, children's, fiction, reference, general; Dir CHIA YAN HENG.

Times Educational Co Sdn Bhd: 22 Jalan 19/3, 46300 Petaling Jaya, Selangor; tel. (3) 79571766; fax (3) 79573607; e-mail presco@po.jaring.my; general and reference; Man. FOONG CHUI LIN.

GOVERNMENT PUBLISHING HOUSE

Percetakan Nasional Malaysia Bhd (Malaysia National Printing Ltd): Jalan Chan Sow Lin, 50554 Kuala Lumpur; tel. (3) 2212022; fax (3) 2220690; fmrly the National Printing Department, incorporated as a company under govt control in January 1993.

PUBLISHERS' ASSOCIATION

Malaysian Book Publishers' Association: 306 Block C, Glomac Business Centre, 10 Jalan SS 6/1 Kelana Jaya, 47301 Petaling Jaya, Selangor; tel. (3) 7046628; fax (3) 7046629; e-mail mabopa@po.jaring.my; internet www.mabopa.com.my; f. 1968; Pres. NG TIEH CHUAN; Hon. Sec. ZAINORA MUHAMAD; 95 mems.

Broadcasting and Communications

TELECOMMUNICATIONS

Celcom (Malaysia) Sdn Bhd: Menara Celcom, 82 Jalan Raja Muda Abdul Aziz, 50300 Kuala Lumpur; tel. (3) 26883939; e-mail cpr@celcom.com.my; internet www.celcom.com.my; f. 1988; private co licensed to operate mobile cellular telephone service; merged with TM Cellular Sdn Bhd in 2003; Chair. Tan Sri Dato' Ir MUHAMMAD RADZI BIN Haji MANSOR; CEO Dato' SHAZALLI RAMLY.

DiGi Telecommunications Sdn Bhd: Lot 30, Jalan Delima 1/3, Subang Hi-Tech Industrial Park, 40000 Shah Alam, Selangor; tel. (3) 57211800; fax (3) 57211857; internet www.digi.com.my; private co licensed to operate mobile telephone service; Chair. Tan Sri Dato' Seri VINCENT TAN CHEE YIOUN; CEO TORE JOHNSEN.

Jabatan Telekomunikasi Malaysia (JTM) (Department of Telecommunications): c/o Ministry of Energy, Water and Communications, Block E4–5, Parcel E, Pusat Pentadbiran Kerajaan Persekutuan, 62668 Putrajaya; tel. (3) 88836000; fax (3) 88893712; internet www.ktkm.gov.my; regulatory body for telecommunications industry.

Maxis Communications Bhd: Menara Maxis, Aras 18, Kuala Lumpur City Centre, 50088 Kuala Lumpur; tel. (3) 23307000; fax (3) 23300008; internet www.maxis.com.my; f. 1995; provides mobile, fixed line and multimedia services; approx. 3.25m. subscribers in 2003; CEO JAMALUDIN IBRAHIM; Chair. Datuk MEGAT ZAHARUDDIN BIN MEGAT MOHAMED NOOR.

Technology Resources Industries Bhd (TRI): Menara TR, 23rd Floor, 161B Jalan Ampang, 50450 Kuala Lumpur; tel. (3) 2619555; fax (3) 2632018; operates mobile cellular telephone service; Chair. and Chief Exec. Tan Sri Dato' TAJUDIN RAMLI.

Telekom Malaysia Bhd: Level 51, North Wing, Menara Telekom, off Jalan Pantai Baru, 50672 Kuala Lumpur; tel. (3) 22401221; fax (3) 22832415; internet www.telekom.com.my; f. 1984; public listed co

MALAYSIA

responsible for operation of basic telecommunications services; 74% govt-owned; 4.22m. fixed lines (95% of total); Chair. Haji MUHAMMAD RADZI BIN Haji MANSOR; Chief Exec. Dato' ABDUL WAHID BIN OMAR.

Time dotCom Bhd: Wisma Time, 1st Floor, 249 Jalan Tun Razak, 50400 Kuala Lumpur; tel. (3) 27208000; fax (3) 27200199; internet www.time.com.my; f. 1996; as Time Telecommunications Holdings Bhd; name changed as above in Jan. 2000; state-controlled co licensed to operate trunk network and mobile cellular telephone service; Chair. Dato' WAN MUHAMAD WAN IBRAHIM; Man. Dir TAN SEE YIN.

BROADCASTING

Regulatory Authority

Under the Broadcasting Act (approved in December 1987), the Minister of Information is empowered to control and monitor all radio and television broadcasting, and to revoke the licence of any private company violating the Act by broadcasting material 'conflicting with Malaysian values'.

Radio Televisyen Malaysia (RTM): Dept of Broadcasting, Angkasapuri, Bukit Putra, 50614 Kuala Lumpur; tel. (3) 22825333; fax (3) 2824735; e-mail helpdesk@rtm.net.my; internet www.rtm.net.my; f. 1946; television introduced 1963; supervises radio and television broadcasting; Dir-Gen. JAAFAR KAMIN; Dep. Dir-Gen. TAMIMUDDIN ABDUL KARIM.

Radio

Radio Malaysia: Radio Televisyen Malaysia (see Regulatory Authority), POB 11272, 50740 Kuala Lumpur; tel. (3) 2823991; fax (3) 2825859; f. 1946; domestic service; operates six networks; broadcasts in Bahasa Malaysia, English, Chinese (Mandarin and other dialects), Tamil and Aborigine (Temiar and Semai dialects); Dir of Radio MADZHI JOHARI.

Radio Televisyen Malaysia—Sabah: Jalan Tuaran, 88614 Kota Kinabalu; tel. (88) 213444; fax (88) 223493; f. 1955; television introduced 1971; a dept of RTM; broadcasts programmes over two networks for 280 hours a week in Bahasa Malaysia, English, Chinese (two dialects), Kadazan, Murut, Dusun and Bajau; Dir of Broadcasting JUMAT ENGSON.

Radio Televisyen Malaysia—Sarawak: Broadcasting House, Jalan P. Ramlee, 93614 Kuching; tel. (82) 248422; fax (82) 241914; e-mail pvgrtmsw@tm.net.my; f. 1954; a dept of RTM; broadcasts 445 hours per week in Bahasa Malaysia, English, Chinese, Iban, Bidayuh, Melanau, Kayan/Kenyah, Bisayah and Murut; Dir of Broadcasting NORHYATI ISMAIL.

Rediffusion Sdn Bhd: Rediffusion House, 17 Jalan Pahang, 53000 Kuala Lumpur; tel. (3) 4424544; fax (3) 4424614; f. 1949; two programmes; 44,720 subscribers in Kuala Lumpur; 11,405 subscribers in Pinang; 6,006 subscribers in Province Wellesley; 20,471 subscribers in Ipoh; Gen. Man. ROSNI B. RAHMAT.

Suara Islam (Voice of Islam): Islamic Affairs Division, Prime Minister's Department, Blok Utama, Tingkat 1–5, Pusat Pentadbiran Kerajaan Persekutuan, 62502 Putrajaya; f. 1995; Asia-Pacific region; broadcasts in Bahasa Malaysia on Islam.

Suara Malaysia (Voice of Malaysia): Wisma Radio, Angkasapuri, POB 11272, 50740 Kuala Lumpur; tel. (3) 22887824; fax (3) 22847594; f. 1963; overseas service in Bahasa Malaysia, Arabic, Myanmar (Burmese), English, Bahasa Indonesia, Chinese (Mandarin/Cantonese), Tagalog and Thai; Controller of Overseas Service STEPHEN SIPAUN.

Time Highway Radio: All Asia Broadcast Centre, Technology Park Malaysia, Bukit Jalil, 57000 Kuala Lumpur; tel. (3) 95438888; fax (3) 95433888; e-mail feedback@thr.fm; internet www.thr.fm; f. 1994; serves Kuala Lumpur region; broadcasts in English; CEO ABDUL AZIZ HAMDAN.

Television

Measat Broadcast Network Systems Sdn Bhd: All Asia Broadcast Centre, Technology Park Malaysia, Lebuhraya Puchong, Simpang Besi, Bukit Jalil, 57000 Kuala Lumpur; tel. (3) 95434188; fax (3) 95437333; e-mail custcare@astro.com.my; internet www.astro.com .my; nation-wide subscription service; Malaysia's first satellite, Measat 1, was launched in January 1996; a second satellite was launched in October of that year; Chair. T. ANANDA KRISHNAN.

Metropolitan Television Sdn Bhd (8TV): 3 Persiaran Bandar Utama, 47800 Petaling Jaya, Selangor; tel. (3) 77288282; fax (3) 77268282; e-mail izham@8tv.com.my; internet www.8tv.com.my; began broadcasting in July 1995; commercial station; operates only in Klang Valley; 44%-owned by Senandung Sesuria Sdn Bhd, 56%-owned by Metropolitan Media Sdn Bhd; COO AHMAD ISHAM OMAR.

Radio Televisyen Malaysia—Sabah: see Radio.

Radio Televisyen Malaysia—Sarawak: see Radio.

Directory

Sistem Televisyen Malaysia Bhd (TV 3): 3 Persiaran Bandar Utama, Bandar Utama, 47800 Petaling, Selangor Darul Ehsan; tel. (3) 77266333; fax (3) 77278455; e-mail enquiries@tv3.com.my; internet www.tv3.com.my; f. 1983; Malaysia's first private television network, began broadcasting in 1984; Chair. Dato' ABDUL MUTALIB BIN Datuk Seri MOHAMED RAZAK; Man. Dir Hisham Dato' ABDULLAH RAHMAN.

Televisyen Malaysia: Radio Televisyen Malaysia (see Regulatory Authority); f. 1963; operates two national networks, TV1 and TV2; Controller of Programmes ISMAIL MOHAMED JAH.

Under a regulatory framework devised by the Government, the ban on privately owned satellite dishes was ended in 1996.

Finance

(cap. = capital; auth. = authorized; res = reserves; dep. = deposits; m. = million; brs = branches; amounts in ringgit Malaysia)

BANKING

In January 2004 there were 46 domestic commercial banks, merchant banks and finance companies. In February 2000 the Government announced that it had approved plans for the creation of up to 10 banking groups to be formed through the merger of existing institutions. By August 2001 51 banks had merged under the terms of these plans. In February 2004 53 banks held offshore licences in Labuan.

Central Bank

Bank Negara Malaysia: Jalan Dato' Onn, POB 10922, 50929 Kuala Lumpur; tel. (3) 26988044; fax (3) 26912990; e-mail info@bnm.gov .my; internet www.bnm.gov.my; f. 1959; bank of issue; financial regulatory authority; cap. 100.0m., res 42,307.2m., dep. 123,101.0m. (Dec. 2003); Gov. Tan Sri Dato' Sri ZETI AKHTAR AZIZ; 6 brs.

Regulatory Authority

Labuan Offshore Financial Services Authority (LOFSA): Level 17, Main Office Tower, Financial Park Labuan, Jalan Merdeka, 87000 Labuan; tel. (87) 591200; fax (87) 413328; e-mail communication@lofsa.gov.my; internet www.lofsa.gov.my; regulatory body for the International Offshore Financial Centre of Labuan established in October 1990; Chair. Datuk ZETI AKHTAR AZIZ (Gov. of Bank Negara Malaysia); Dir-Gen. Dato' AZIZAN ABDUL RAHMAN.

Commercial Banks

Peninsular Malaysia

ABN Amro Bank Bhd: Levels 25–27, MNI Twins, Tower II, 11 Jalan Pinang, POB 10094, 50704 Kuala Lumpur; tel. (3) 21627888; fax (3) 21625692; e-mail info@abnamro.com.my; internet www .abnamromalaysia.com; f. 1963.

Affin Bank Bhd: Menara AFFIN, 17th Floor, 80 Jalan Raja Chulan, 50200 Kuala Lumpur; tel. (3) 20559000; fax (3) 20261415; e-mail head.ccd@affinbank.com.my; internet www.affinbank.com.my; f. 1975 as Perwira Habib Bank Malaysia Bhd; name changed to Perwira Affin Bank Bhd 1994; merged with BSN Commercial Bank (Malaysia) Bhd Jan. 2001, and name changed as above; cap. 1,017.3m., res 368.2m., dep. 17,523.0m. (Dec. 2003); Chair. Gen. Tan Sri Dato' Seri ISMAIL Haji OMAR; Pres. and CEO Dato' ABDUL HAMIDY ABDUL HAFIZ; 106 brs.

Alliance Bank Malaysia Bhd: Menara Multi-Purpose, Ground Floor, Capital Sq., 8 Jalan Munshi Abdullah, 50100 Kuala Lumpur; POB 10069, 50704 Kuala Lumpur; tel. (3) 26948800; fax (3) 26946727; e-mail multilink@alliancebg.com.my; internet www .alliancebank.com.my; f. 1982 as Malaysian French Bank Berhad; name changed to Multi-Purpose Bank Bhd 1996; name changed as above Jan. 2001, following acquisition of six merger partners; cap. 596.5m., res 584.9m., dep. 16,225.6m. (March 2004); Chair. LUTFIAH BINTI ISMAIL; CEO BRIDGET ANNE LAI HUNG YEE; 80 brs.

AmBank Bhd: 22nd Floor, Bangunan AmBank Group, 55 Jalan Raja Chulan, 50200 Kuala Lumpur; tel. (3) 20782633; fax (3) 20316453; e-mail customercare@ambg.com.my; internet www .ambg.com.my; f. 1994; fmrly Arab-Malaysian Bank Bhd; name changed as above 2002; cap. 505.5m., res −72.0m., dep. 9,036.3m. (March 2003); Chair. Tan Sri Dato' AZMAN HASHIM; Man. Dir KUNG BENG HONG.

Bangkok Bank Bhd (Thailand): 105 Jalan Tun H. S. Lee, 50000 Kuala Lumpur; tel. (3) 20724555; fax (3) 20788569; e-mail bbb@tm .net.my; f. 1958; cap. 265m. (Dec. 2003), res 82m., dep. 612m. (Dec. 2004); Chair. ALBERT CHEOK SAYCHUAN; CEO SAKSITH TEJASAKULSIN; 1 br.

Bank of America Malaysia Bhd: Wisma Goldhill, Jalan Raja Chulan, 50200 Kuala Lumpur; tel. (3) 20321133; fax (3) 20319087;

MALAYSIA

internet www.bankofamerica.com.my; cap. 135.8m., res 177.2m., dep. 546.7m. (Dec. 2002); Chair. RICHARD LINEBAUGH.

Bank of Nova Scotia Bhd: POB 11056, Menara Boustead, 69 Jalan Raja Chulan, 50200 Kuala Lumpur; tel. (3) 21410766; fax (3) 21412160; e-mail bns.kualalumpur@scotiabank.com; internet www.scotiabank.com.my; f. 1973; cap. 122.4m., res 239.7m., dep. 1,354.7m. (Oct. 2003); Man. Dir RASOOL KHAN.

Bank of Tokyo-Mitsubishi (Malaysia) Bhd (Japan): 1 Leboh Ampang, 50100 Kuala Lumpur; tel. (3) 20789100; fax (3) 20708340; e-mail edpbtm@tm.net.my; f. 1996 following merger of the Bank of Tokyo and Mitsubishi Bank; cap. 200m., res 516.1m., dep. 1,832.5m. (Dec. 2002); Chair. YOSHIHIRO WATANABE; Pres. and CEO HIROYUKI KUDO.

Bumiputra Commerce Bank Bhd: 6 Jalan Tun Perak, 50050 Kuala Lumpur; tel. (3) 26931722; fax (3) 26986628; internet www.bcb.com.my; f. 1999 following merger of Bank Bumiputra Malaysia Bhd with Bank of Commerce Bhd; cap. 2,064.0m., res 2,570.3m., dep. 54,230.8m. (Dec. 2003); Chair. Tan Sri HAIDAR MOHAMED NOOR; Group CEO Dato' MOHAMED NAZIR ABDUL RAZAK ALI; 230 brs.

Citibank Bhd (USA): 165 Jalan Ampang, POB 10112, 50450 Kuala Lumpur; tel. (3) 23830000; fax (3) 2328763; internet www.citibank.com.my; f. 1959; cap. 121.7m., res 1,577.4m., dep. 17,132.8m. (Dec. 2002); Country Officer PIYUSH GUPTA; 3 brs.

Deutsche Bank (Malaysia) Bhd (Germany): 18–20 Menara IMC, 8 Jalan Sultan Ismail, 50250 Kuala Lumpur; tel. (3) 20536788; fax (3) 20319822; f. 1994; cap. 125.0m., res 226.9m., dep. 1,980.7m. (Dec. 2002); Man. Dir KUAH HUN LIANG.

EON Bank Bhd: Menara EON Bank, 12th Floor, 288 Jalan Raja Laut, 50350 Kuala Lumpur; tel. (3) 26941188; fax (3) 26949588; e-mail caf@eonbank.com.my; internet www.eonbank.com.my; f. 1963; fmrly Kong Ming Bank Bhd; merged with Oriental Bank Bhd, Jan. 2001; cap. 1,329.8m., res 621.9m., dep. 20,910.2m. (Dec. 2003); Chair. Datin Dr UMIKALSUM BINTI MOHAMED NOH; CEO and Exec. Dir Albert Lau YIONG; 95 brs.

Hong Leong Bank Bhd: Wisma Hong Leong, Level 3, 18 Jalan Perak, 50450 Kuala Lumpur; tel. (3) 21642828; fax (3) 27156365; internet www.hlb.com.my; f. 1905; fmrly MUI Bank Bhd; merged with Wah Tat Bank Bhd, Jan. 2001; cap. 1,435.0m., res 1,899.1m., dep. 23,746.3m. (June 2003); Chair. Tan Sri QUEK LENG CHAN; Man. Dir YVONNE CHIA; 167 local brs, 2 overseas brs.

HSBC Bank Malaysia Bhd (Hong Kong): 2 Leboh Ampang, POB 10244, 50912 Kuala Lumpur; tel. (3) 20700744; fax (3) 20702678; e-mail manager.public.affairs@hsbc.com.my; internet www.hsbc.com.my; f. 1860; fmrly Hongkong Bank Malaysia Bhd; adopted present name in 1999; cap. 114.5m., res 1,779.5m., dep. 25,423.9m. (Dec. 2003); Chair. MICHAEL SMITH; CEO ZARIR J. CAMA.

Malayan Banking Bhd (Maybank): Menara Maybank, 14th Floor, 100 Jalan Tun Perak, 50050 Kuala Lumpur; tel. (3) 20747037; fax (3) 20789761; e-mail publicaffairs@maybank.com.my; internet www.maybank2u.com; f. 1960; acquired Pacific Bank Bhd, Jan. 2001; merged with PhileoAllied Bank (Malaysia) Bhd, March 2001; cap. and res 12,099m., dep. 111,046m. (June 2004); Chair. Tan Sri MOHAMED BASIR BIN AHMAD; Pres. and CEO Datuk AMIRSHAM A. AZIZ; 327 domestic brs, 30 overseas brs.

OCBC Bank (Malaysia) Bhd: Menara OCBC, 18 Jalan Tun Perak, 50050 Kuala Lumpur; tel. (3) 83175000; fax (3) 26984363; internet www.ocbc.com.my; f. 1932; cap. 287.5m., res 1,465.2m., dep. 20,737.9m. (Dec. 2003); Group Chair. Dr CHEONG CHOONG KONG; CEO ALBERT YEOH BEOW TIT; 25 brs.

Public Bank Bhd: Menara Public Bank, 146 Jalan Ampang, 50450 Kuala Lumpur; tel. (3) 21638888; fax (3) 21639917; e-mail customerservice@publicbank.com.my; internet www.publicbank.com.my; f. 1965; merged with Hock Hua Bank Bhd, March 2001; cap. 3,206.6m., res 4,320.3m., dep. 48,201.3m. (Dec. 2003); Chair. Tan Sri Dato' Dr TEH HONG PIOW; 216 domestic brs, 3 overseas brs.

RHB Bank Bhd: Towers Two and Three, Menara AA, 426 Jalan Tun Razak, 50400 Kuala Lumpur; tel. (3) 92068118; fax (3) 92068088; e-mail md_ceo@rhbbank.com.my; internet www.rhbbank.com.my; f. 1997 as a result of merger between DCB Bank Bhd and Kwong Yik Bank Bhd; acquired Sime Bank Bhd in mid-1999; merged with Bank Utama (Malaysia) Bhd, May 2003; cap. 3,318.1m., res 1,420.8m., dep. 38,994.4m. (June 2002); Chair. Dato' ALI BIN HASSAN; 148 brs.

Southern Bank Bhd: Level 3, Menara Southern Bank, 83 Medan Setia Satu, Plaza Damansara, Bukit Damansara, 50490 Kuala Lumpur; tel. (3) 20873000; fax (3) 20933157; e-mail info@sbbgroup.com.my; internet www.sbbgroup.com.my; f. 1963; merged with Ban Hin Lee Bank Bhd, July 2000; cap. 1,122.8m., res 1,342.4m., dep. 23,447.0m. (Dec. 2003); Chair. Dato' NIK IBRAHIM KAMIL; CEO Tan Sri Dato' TAN TEONG HEAN; 105 domestic brs, 1 overseas br.

Standard Chartered Bank Malaysia Bhd: 1st Floor, 2 Jalan Ampang, 50450 Kuala Lumpur; tel. (3) 20726555; fax (3) 2010621; internet www.standardchartered.com.my; 31 brs.

Directory

United Overseas Bank (Malaysia) Bhd: Menara UOB, Jalan Raja Laut, POB 11212, 50738 Kuala Lumpur; tel. (3) 26924511; fax (3) 26913110; e-mail uob121@uob.com.my; internet www.uob.com.my; f. 1920; merged with Chung Khiaw Bank (Malaysia) Bhd in 1997 and with Overseas Union Bank (Malaysia) Bhd in 2002; cap. 470m., res 1,166.9m., dep. 19,889.2m. (Dec. 2003); Chair. WEE CHO YAW; CEO CHAN KOK SEONG; 37 brs.

Merchant Banks

Affin Merchant Bank Bhd: Menara Boustead, 27th Floor, 69 Jalan Raja Chulan, POB 11424, 50744 Kuala Lumpur; tel. (3) 21423700; fax (3) 21423799; e-mail general@affinmerchantbank.com.my; internet www.affinmerchantbank.com.my; f. 1970 as Permata Chartered Merchant Bank Bhd; name changed as above March 2001; cap. 187.5m., res 166.3m., dep. 2,974.6m. (Dec. 2003); Chair. Tan Sri YAACOB MOHAMED ZAIN; Pres. and CEO Dato' Dr Sheikh AWAB BIN Sheikh ABOD.

Alliance Merchant Bank Bhd: Menara Multi-Purpose, 20th Floor, Capital Sq., 8 Jalan Munshi Abdullah, 50100 Kuala Lumpur; tel. (3) 26927788; fax (3) 26928787; e-mail ambb@alliancemerchant.my; internet www.alliancemerchantbank.com.my; f. 1974 as Amanah-Chase Merchant Bank Bhd; name changed as above Jan. 2001, following merger with Bumiputra Merchant Bankers Bhd; cap. 365.0m., res 74.1m., dep. 1,694.1m. (March 2004). Chair. LUTFIAH BINTI ISMAIL; CEO FOO KOK SIEW.

AmMerchant Bank Bhd: 22nd Floor, Bangunan Arab-Malaysian, 55 Jalan Raja Chulan, 50200 Kuala Lumpur; tel. (3) 20782655; fax (3) 20782842; e-mail customercare@ambg.com.my; internet www.ambg.com.my; f. 1975; fmrly Arab-Malaysian Merchant Bank Bhd; name changed as above 2002; cap. 300.0m., res 480.3m., dep. 13,871.2m. (March 2003); Chair. Tan Sri Dato' AZMAN HASHIM; Man. Dir CHEAH TEK KUANG; 4 brs.

Aseambankers Malaysia Bhd: Menara Maybank, 33rd Floor, 100 Jalan Tun Perak, 50050 Kuala Lumpur; tel. (3) 20591888; fax (3) 20784194; e-mail faudziah@aseam.com.my; internet www.aseam.com.my; f. 1973; cap. 50.1m., res 246.0m., dep. 2,791.1m. (June 2003); Chair. Dato' MOHAMED BASIR AHMAD; CEO AGIL NATT; 2 brs.

Commerce International Merchant Bankers Bhd: Bangunan CIMB, 10th Floor, Jalan Semantan, Damansara Heights, 50490 Kuala Lumpur; tel. (3) 2536688; fax (3) 2535522; e-mail info@cimb.com.my; f. 1974; cap. 319.2m., res 876.7m., dep. 6,774.6m. (Dec. 2002); Chair. Dato' MOHAMED NOR BIN MOHAMED YOUSOF.

Malaysian International Merchant Bankers Bhd: Menara EON Bank, 21st Floor, 288 Jalan Raja Laut, 50350 Kuala Lumpur; tel. (3) 26910200; fax (3) 26985388; internet www.mimb.com.my; f. 1970; cap. 75m., res 190.3m. (Dec. 2003), dep. 196.6m. (Dec. 2002); Chair. Tan Sri Dato' MOHAMMED SALEH BIN SULONG; 1 br.

Public Merchant Bank Bhd: 25th Floor, Menara Public Bank, 146 Jalan Ampang, 50450 Kuala Lumpur; tel. (3) 21669382; fax (3) 21669362; e-mail merchantbank@publicbank.com.my; f. 1973 as Asian International Merchant Bankers Bhd; became Sime Merchant Bankers Bhd 1996; name changed as above 2000; cap. 165.0m., res −28.9m., dep. 1,086.6m. (Dec. 2002); Chair. Tan Sri Dato' THONG YAW HONG.

RHB Sakura Merchant Bankers Bhd: Tower Three, 9th Floor, RHB Centre, 426 Jalan Tun Razak, 50400 Kuala Lumpur; tel. (3) 92805475; fax (3) 27118501; e-mail publicaffairs@rhb.com.my; internet www.rhb.com.my; f. 1974; cap. 338.6m., res 438.5m., dep. 3,070.6m. (June 2003); Chair. Datuk AZLAN ZAINOL.

Southern Investment Bank Bhd: 11th Floor, Wisma Genting, Jalan Sultan Ismail, 50250 Kuala Lumpur; tel. (3) 20594188; fax (3) 20722964; e-mail sibb@sibb.com.my; internet www.southernbank.com.my; f. 1988; fmrly Perdana Merchant Bankers Bhd; cap. 77.9m., res −3.5m., dep. 572.7m. (Dec. 2003); Chair. Dato' Nik IBRAHIM KAMIL; CEO Tan Sri Dato' TAN TEONG HEAN.

Utama Merchant Bank Bhd: Menara Maxis, Level 33, Suite A, 50088 Kuala Lumpur; tel. (3) 20789133; fax (3) 20725511; e-mail umbb@umbb.po.my; internet www.cmsb.com.my/ubg; f. 1975 as Utama Wardley Bhd; name changed as above in 1996; cap. 223.0m., res 63.6m., dep. 992.6m. (Dec. 1999); Chair. Nik HASHIM BIN Nik YUSOFF; CEO DONNY KWA SOO CHUAN; 1 br.

Co-operative Bank

Bank Kerjasama Rakyat Malaysia Berhad: Bangunan Bank Rakyat, Jalan Tangsi, Peti Surat 11024, 50732 Kuala Lumpur; tel. (3) 2985011; fax (3) 2985981; f. 1954; 83,095 mems. of which 823 were co-operatives (Dec. 1996); Chair. Dr YUSUF YACOB; Man. Dir Dato' ANUAR JAAFAR; 67 brs.

Development Banks

Bank Pembangunan Malaysia Bhd: Menara Bank Pembangunan, POB 12352, Jalan Sultan Ismail, 50774 Kuala Lumpur; tel. (3) 26113888; fax (3) 26928520; e-mail enq_y@bpmb.com.my; internet www.bpmb.com.my; f. 1973; govt-owned; fmrly known as Bank Pembangunana & Infrastruktur Malaysia Bhd; name changed as above following merger with Bank Industri & Teknologi Malaysia Bhd in 2005; specializes in infrastructure, maritime and high-technology sectors; cap. 1,200m., res 731.5m., dep. 4,534.7m. (Dec. 2002); Pres. and Man. Dir Datuk ABDUL RAHIM MOHAMED ZIN; Chair. Tan Sri Dr ZAINUL ARIF HUSSAIN; 14 brs.

Bank Perusahaan Kecil & Sederhana Malaysia Bhd (SME Bank): Menara SME Bank, Jalan Sultan Ismail, Peti Surat 12352, 50774 Kuala Lumpur; tel. (3) 26152020; fax (3) 26928520; e-mail enq_y@smebank.com.my; internet www.smebank.com.my; f. 2005; wholly-owned subsidiary of Bank Pembangunana Malaysia Bhd; provides both financial and non-financial assistance to SMEs; Chair. Dato' GUMURI HUSSIN; Man. Dir Dato' AZMI ABDULLAH.

Sabah Development Bank Bhd: SDB Tower, Wisma Tun Fuad Stephens, POB 12172, 88824 Kota Kinabalu, Sabah; tel. (88) 232177; fax (88) 261852; e-mail info@sabahdevbank.com; internet www.sabahdevbank.com; f. 1977; wholly owned by State Government of Sabah; cap. 350m., res –121.1m., dep. 890.6m. (Dec. 2003); Chair. PETER SIAU; Man. Dir and CEO PETER LIM.

Islamic Banks

Bank Islam Malaysia Bhd: Darul Takaful, 11th Floor, Jalan Sultan Ismail, 50250 Kuala Lumpur; tel. (3) 26168000; fax (3) 26980587; e-mail communications@bankislam.com.my; internet www.bankislam.com.my; f. 1983; cap. 500m., res 613.1m., dep. 12,397.1m. (June 2003); Chair. Dato' MOHAMED YUSOFF BIN MOHAMED NASIR; Man. Dir Dato' NOORAZMAN A. AZIZ; 76 brs.

Bank Muamalat Malaysia Bhd: Menara Bumiputra, 21 Jalan Melaka, 50100 Kuala Lumpur; tel. (3) 26988787; fax (3) 20325997; e-mail webmaster@muamalat.com.my; internet www.muamalat.com.my; f. 1999; CEO Tuan Haji MOHD SHUKRI HUSSIN; 40 brs.

'Offshore' Banks

ABN Amro Bank, Labuan Branch: Level 9 (A), Main Office Tower, Financial Park Labuan, Jalan Merdeka, 87000 Labuan; tel. (87) 423008; fax (87) 421078; Man. ANTHONY RAJAN.

Al-Hidayah Investment Bank (Labuan) Ltd: Level 7 (C), Main Office Tower, Financial Park Labuan, Jalan Merdeka, 87000 Labuan; tel. (87) 451660; fax (87) 583088.

AMInternational (L) Ltd: Level 12 (B), Block 4, Office Tower, Financial Park Labuan, Jalan Merdeka, 87000 Labuan; tel. (87) 413133; fax (87) 425211; e-mail felix-leong@ambg.com.my; internet www.ambg.com.my; CEO PAUL ONG WHEE SEN.

AmMerchant Bank Bhd, Labuan Branch: Level 12 (B), Block 4, Main Office Tower, Financial Park Labuan, Jalan Merdeka, 87000 Labuan; tel. (87) 413133; fax (87) 425211; Gen. Man. PAUL ONG WHEE SEN.

Bank of America, National Trust and Savings Association, Labuan Branch: Level 13 (D), Main Office Tower, Financial Park Labuan, Jalan Merdeka, 87000 Labuan; tel. (87) 411778; fax (87) 424778; Gen. Man. Pengiran NUR FARHAH OOI ABDULLAH.

Bank of East Asia Ltd, Labuan Offshore Branch: Level 10 (C), Main Office Tower, Financial Park Labuan, Jalan Merdeka, 87000 Labuan; tel. (87) 451145; fax (87) 451148; e-mail wongtwy@hkbea.com; Gen. Man. THOMAS WAI YIP WONG.

Bank Islam (L) Ltd: Level 15A, Main Office Tower, Financial Park, Jalan Merdeka, 87000 Labuan; tel. (87) 451802; fax (87) 453077; e-mail engkuafandi@bankislam.com.my; Branch Man. ENGKU AFANDI TAIB.

Bank Muamalat Malaysia Bhd, Labuan Branch: Level 15 (A1), Main Office Tower, Financial Park Labuan, Jalan Merdeka, 87000 Labuan; tel. (87) 412898; fax (87) 451164; e-mail fuad@muamalat.com.my; Gen. Man. ZAINOL RASHID KHAIRUDDIN.

Bank of Nova Scotia, Labuan Branch: Level 10 (C2), Main Office Tower, Financial Park Labuan, Jalan Merdeka, 87000 Labuan; tel. (87) 451101; fax (87) 451099; Man. KWAN SING HUNG.

Bank of Tokyo-Mitsubishi UFJ Ltd, Labuan Branch: Level 12 (A & F), Main Office Tower, Financial Park Labuan, Jalan Merdeka, 87000 Labuan; tel. (87) 410487; fax (87) 410476; e-mail pulaubtm@tm.net.my; Gen. Man. WATURU TANAKA.

Barclays Bank PLC: Level 5(A), Main Office Tower, Financial Park Labuan, Jalan Merdeka, 87000 Labuan; tel. (87) 425571; fax (87) 425575; e-mail barclay@tm.net.my; Man. MIAW SIAW LOONG.

Bayerische Landesbank Girozentrale, Labuan Branch: Level 14 (C), Block 4, Office Tower, Financial Park Labuan, Jalan Merdeka, 87000 Labuan; tel. (87) 422170; fax (87) 422175; e-mail blblab@tm.net.my; Exec. Vice-Pres., CEO and Gen. Man. LOUISE PAUL.

BNP Paribas, Labuan Branch: Level 9 (E), Main Office Tower, Financial Park Labuan, Jalan Merdeka, 87000 Labuan; tel. (87) 422328; fax (87) 419328; e-mail bnpkul@tm.net.my; Gen. Man. YAP SIEW YING.

Bumiputra Commerce Bank (L) Ltd: Level 14 (B), Main Office Tower, Financial Park Labuan, Jalan Merdeka, 87000 Labuan; tel. (87) 410302; fax (87) 410313; e-mail bumitrst@tm.net.my; Gen. Man. ASARAF ABU BAKAR.

Cathay United Bank, Labuan Branch: Level 3 (C), Main Office Tower, Financial Park Labuan, Jalan Merdeka, 87000 Labuan; tel. (87) 452168; fax (87) 453678; Gen. Man. YEH PIN HUNG.

CIMB (L) Ltd: Unit 11 (B1), Level 11, Main Office Tower, Financial Park Labuan, Jalan Merdeka, 87000 Labuan; tel. (87) 451608; fax (87) 451610; CEO ADHA AMIR ABDULLAH.

Citibank Malaysia (L) Ltd: Level 11 (F), Main Office Tower, Financial Park Labuan, Jalan Merdeka, 87000 Labuan; tel. (87) 421181; fax (87) 419671; Gen. Man. CLARA LIM AI CHENG.

City Credit Investment Bank Ltd: Level 11 (D1), Main Office Tower, Financial Park Labuan, Jalan Merdeka, 87000 Labuan; tel. (87) 582268; fax (87) 581268; Dir ABDUL RAHMAN ABDULLAH.

Commercial IBT Bank, Labuan Branch: 02-01, 2nd Floor, Wisma Lucas Kong Bldg, U0185 Jalan Merdeka, 87000 Labuan; tel. (87) 411868; fax (87) 416818; e-mail aong@cibtbank.com; Pres. Dir Dr ADRIAN ONG CHEE BENG.

Commerzbank AG, Labuan Branch: Level 6 (E), Main Office Tower, Financial Park Labuan, Jalan Merdeka, 87000 Labuan; tel. (87) 416953; fax (87) 413542; Prin. Officer HO KAH HENG.

Crédit Agricole Indosuez, Labuan Branch: Level 11 (C), Main Office Tower, Financial Park Labuan, Jalan Merdeka, 87000 Labuan; tel. (87) 425118; fax (87) 424998; Gen. Man. BOON EONG TAN.

Crédit Industriel et Commercial: Level 11 (C2), Main Office Tower, Financial Park Labuan, Jalan Merdeka, 87000 Labuan; tel. (87) 452008; fax (87) 452009; Gen. Man. YEOW TIANG HUI.

Crédit Lyonnais, Labuan Branch: Level 6 (B), Main Office Tower, Financial Park Labuan, Jalan Merdeka, 87000 Labuan; tel. (87) 408531; fax (87) 439133; Man. CLEMENT WONG.

Crédit Suisse First Boston, Labuan Branch: Level 10 (B), Main Office Tower, Financial Park Labuan, Jalan Merdeka, 87000 Labuan; tel. (87) 425381; fax (87) 425384; Gen. Man. RUDOLF ZAUGG.

Danaharta Managers (L) Ltd: Tingkat 10, Bangunan Setia 1, 15 Lorong Dungun, Bukit Damansara, 50490 Kuala Lumpur; tel. (3) 2531122; fax (3) 2534375; Gen. Man. (vacant).

Deutsche Bank AG, Labuan Branch: Level 9 (G2), Main Office Tower, Financial Park Labuan, Jalan Merdeka, 87000 Labuan; tel. (87) 439811; fax (87) 439866; Man. Dir KUAH HUN LIANG.

Development Bank of Singapore (DBS Bank) Ltd, Labuan Branch: Level 12 (E), Main Office Tower, Financial Park Labuan, Jalan Merdeka, 87000 Labuan; tel. (87) 423375; fax (87) 423376; Gen. Man. KEVIN WONG.

Dresdner Bank AG, Labuan Branch: Level 13 (C), Main Office Tower, Financial Park Labuan, Jalan Merdeka, 87000 Labuan; tel. (87) 419271; fax (87) 419272; Gen. Man. JAMALUDIN NASIR.

ECM Libra Investment Bank Ltd: Level 3 (I1), Main Office Tower, Financial Park Complex, Jalan Merdeka, 87000 Labuan; tel. (87) 408525; fax (87) 408527.

Hongkong & Shanghai Banking Corporation, Offshore Banking Unit: Level 11 (D), Main Office Tower, Financial Park Labuan, Jalan Merdeka, 87000 Labuan; tel. (87) 417168; fax (87) 417169; Man. PREM KUMAR.

ING Bank NV: Level 8 (B2), Main Office Tower, Financial Park Labuan, Jalan Merdeka, 87000 Labuan; tel. (87) 425733; fax (87) 425734; Gen. Man. MILLY TAN.

International Commercial Bank of China: Level 7 (E2), Main Office Tower, Financial Park Labuan, Jalan Merdeka, 87000 Labuan; tel. (87) 581688; fax (87) 581668; Gen. Man. TAI CHI-HSIEN.

J. P. Morgan Chase Bank, Labuan Branch: Level 5 (F), Main Office Tower, Financial Park Labuan, Jalan Merdeka, 87000 Labuan; tel. (87) 424384; fax (87) 424390; e-mail fauziah.hisham@chase.com; Gen. Man. LEONG KET TI.

J. P. Morgan Malaysia Ltd: Unit 5 (F), Level 5, Main Office Tower, Financial Park Labuan, Jalan Merdeka, 87000 Labuan; tel. (87) 459000; fax (87) 451328; Gen. Man. LEONG KET TI.

KBC Bank NV, Labuan Branch: Level 3 (B), Main Office Tower, Financial Park Labuan, Jalan Merdeka, 87000 Labuan; tel. (87) 581778; fax (87) 583787; Gen. Man. KONG KOK CHEE.

Lloyds TSB Bank PLC: Lot B, 11th Floor, Wisma Oceanic, Jalan OKK Awang Besar, 87007 Labuan; tel. (87) 418918; fax (87) 411928; e-mail labuan@lloydstsb.com.my; Dir and Gen. Man. BARRY FRANCIS LEA.

Macquarie Bank Ltd, Labuan Branch: Level 3 (A), Main Office Tower, Financial Park Labuan, Jalan Merdeka, 87000 Labuan; tel. (87) 583080; fax (87) 583088; Division Dir DARREN WOODWARD.

Maybank International (L) Ltd: Level 16 (B), Main Office Tower, Financial Park Labuan, Jalan Merdeka, 87000 Labuan; tel. (87)

MALAYSIA

Directory

414406; fax (87) 414806; e-mail millmit@tm.net.my; Gen. Man. LAM HEE.

Mizuho Corporate Bank Ltd, Labuan Branch: Level 9 (B and C), Main Office Tower, Financial Park Labuan, Jalan Merdeka, 87000 Labuan; tel. (87) 417766; fax (87) 419766; Gen. Man. ISAKU TANIMURA.

Natexis Banque Populaires: Level 9 (G), Main Office Tower, Financial Park Labuan, Jalan Merdeka, 87000 Labuan; tel. (87) 581009; fax (87) 583009; Gen. Man. RIZAL ABDULLAH.

National Australia Bank, Labuan Branch: Level 12 (C2), Main Office Tower, Financial Park Complex, Jalan Merdeka, 87008 Labuan; tel. (87) 426386; fax (87) 428387; e-mail natausm@po.jariq.my; Gen. Man. LIONEL LIM.

OSK Investment Bank (Labuan) Ltd: Lot 3B, Level 5, Wisma Lazenda, Jalan Kemajuan, Labuan; tel. (87) 581885; fax (87) 582885; Prin. Officer ONG LEONG HUAT.

Oversea-Chinese Banking Corporation Ltd, Labuan Branch: Level 8 (C), Main Office Tower, Financial Park Labuan, Jalan Merdeka, 87000 Labuan; tel. (87) 423381; fax (87) 423390; Gen. Man. BERNARD FERNANDO.

Public Bank (L) Ltd: Level 8 (A and B), Main Office Tower, Financial Park Labuan, Jalan Merdeka, 87000 Labuan; tel. (87) 411898; fax (87) 413220; Man. ALEXANDER WONG.

RHB Bank (L) Ltd: Level 15 (B), Main Office Tower, Financial Park Labuan, Jalan Merdeka, 87000 Labuan; tel. (87) 417480; fax (87) 417484; Gen. Man. TOH AY LENG.

RUSD Investment Bank, Inc.: Level 4–A1, Main Office Tower, Financial Park Labuan, Jalan Merdeka, 87000 Labuan; tel. (87) 452100; fax (87) 543100; Man. Dir NASEERUDDIN A. KHAN.

Société Générale, Labuan Branch: Level 11 (B), Main Office Tower, Financial Park Labuan, Jalan Merdeka, 87000 Labuan; tel. (87) 421676; fax (87) 421669; Gen. Man. RAMZAN ABU TAHIR.

Standard Chartered Bank Offshore Labuan: Level 10 (F), Main Office Tower, Financial Park Labuan, Jalan Merdeka, 87000 Labuan; tel. (87) 417200; fax (87) 417202; Gen. Man. EDWARD NG.

Sumitomo Mitsui Banking Corpn, Labuan Branch: Level 12 (B and C), Main Office Tower, Financial Park Labuan, Jalan Merdeka, 87000 Labuan; tel. (87) 410955; fax (87) 410959; Gen. Man. JUNICHI IKENO.

UBS AG, Labuan Branch: Level 5 (E), Main Office Tower, Financial Park Labuan, Jalan Merdeka, 87000 Labuan; tel. (87) 421743; fax (87) 421746; Man. ZELIE HO SWEE LUM.

UFJ Bank Ltd, Labuan Branch: Level 10 (D), Main Office Tower, Financial Park Labuan, Jalan Merdeka, 87000 Labuan; tel. (87) 419200; fax (87) 419202; Gen. Man. MASAYUKI KUNISHIGE.

United Overseas Bank Ltd, Labuan Branch: Level 6 (A), Main Office Tower, Financial Park Labuan, Jalan Merdeka, 87000 Labuan; tel. (87) 424388; fax (87) 424389; Gen. Man. HO FONG KUN.

United World Chinese Commercial Bank: Level 3 (C), Main Office Tower, Financial Park Labuan, Jalan Merdeka, 87000 Labuan; tel. (87) 452168; fax (87) 453678; Gen. Man. PIN HUNG YEH.

Banking Associations

Association of Banks in Malaysia (ABM): UBN Tower, 34th Floor, 10 Jalan P. Ramlee, 50250 Kuala Lumpur; tel. (3) 20788041; fax (3) 20788004; e-mail banks@abm.org.my; internet www.abm.org.my; f. 1973; Chair. Dr ROZALI BIN MOHAMED ALI; Exec. Dir WONG SUAN LYE.

Institute of Bankers Malaysia: Wisma IBI, 5 Jalan Semantan, Damansara Heights, 50490 Kuala Lumpur; tel. (3) 20956833; fax (3) 20952322; e-mail ibbm@ibbm.org.my; internet www.ibbm.org.my; f. 1977; professional and educational body for the banking and finance industry; Chair. Tan Sri Dato' Sri Dr ZETI AKHTAR AZIZ.

Malayan Commercial Banks' Association: POB 12001, 50764 Kuala Lumpur; tel. (3) 2983991.

Persatuan Institusi Perbankan Tanpa Faedah Malaysia (Association of Islamic Banking Institutions Malaysia—AIBIM): Tingkat 9, Wisma Kraftangan, Jalan Tun Perak, 50050 Kuala Lumpur; tel. (3) 26112096; fax (3) 26112097; e-mail admin@aibim.com; internet www.aibim.com.

STOCK EXCHANGES

Bursa Malaysia: Exchange Sq., 10th Floor, Bukit Kewangan, 50200 Kuala Lumpur; tel. (3) 20347000; fax (3) 27320069; e-mail enquiries@bursamalaysia.com; internet www.bursamalaysia.com; f. 1973; fmrly known as Kuala Lumpur Stock Exchange (KLSE); name changed as above in 2004; in 1988 KLSE authorized the ownership of up to 49% of Malaysian stockbroking companies by foreign interests; 283 mems (April 2003); 921 listed cos (March 2004); merged with Malaysian Exchange for Securities Dealing and Automated Quotation Bhd (MESDAQ) in March 2002; Chair. TUN MOHAMED DZAIDDIN HAJI ABDULLAH; CEO YUSLI MOHAMED YUSOFF.

Malaysia Derivatives Exchange Bhd (MDEX): 10th Floor, Exchange Sq., Bukit Kewangan, 50200 Kuala Lumpur; tel. (3) 20708199; fax (3) 20702376; e-mail info@mdex.com.my; internet www.mdex.com.my; f. 2001 as a result of the merger of the Kuala Lumpur Options and Financial Futures Exchange Bhd (KLOFFE) and the Commodity and Monetary Exchange of Malaysia; multi-product futures exchange; Exec. Chair. Dato' ABDUL JABBAR BIN ABDUL MAJID; Gen. Man. RAGHBIR SINGH BHART.

Regulatory Authority

Securities Commission (SC): 3 Persiaran Bukit Kiara, Bukit Kiara, 50490 Kuala Lumpur; tel. (3) 62048000; fax (3) 62015078; e-mail cau@seccom.com.my; internet www.sc.com.my; f. 1993; Chair. Tan Sri MOHAMED NOR MOHAMED YUSOF.

INSURANCE

From 1988 onwards, all insurance companies were placed under the authority of the Central Bank, Bank Negara Malaysia. In 1997 there were 69 insurance companies operating in Malaysia, including; nine reinsurance companies, 11 composite, 40 general and life and two takaful insurance companies.

Principal Insurance Companies

Allianz General Insurance Malaysia Bhd: Wisma UOA II, Floors 23 and 23A, 21 Jalan Pinang, 50450 Kuala Lumpur; tel. (3) 21623388; fax (3) 21626387; e-mail partner@allianz.com.my; internet www.allianz.com.my/general; f. 2001; CEO WILLIAM MEI YORK LIANG; Chair. Tan Sri RAZALI ISMAIL.

Allianz Life Insurance Malaysia Bhd: Wisma UOA II, Floors 23 and 23A, 21 Jalan Pinang, 50450 Kuala Lumpur; tel. (3) 21616001; fax (3) 21626387; e-mail partner@allianz.com.my; internet life.allianz.com.my; fmrly MBA Life Assurance Sdn Bhd; CEO CHRIS JAMES; Chief Financial Officer CHARLES ONG ENG CHOW.

Asia Insurance Co Ltd: Bangunan Asia Insurance, 2 Jalan Raja Chulan, 50200 Kuala Lumpur; tel. (3) 2302511; fax (3) 2323606; f. 1923; general.

Commerce Life Assurance Bhd: 338 Jalan Tunku Abdul Rahman, 50100 Kuala Lumpur; tel. (3) 26123600; fax (3) 26987035; internet www.xlife.com.my; f. 1992 as AMAL Assurance Bhd; name changed as above in 1999.

Great Eastern Life Assurance (Malaysia) Bhd: Menara Great Eastern, 303 Jalan Ampang, 50450 Kuala Lumpur; tel. (3) 42598888; fax (3) 42590500; e-mail wecare@lifeisgreat.com.my; internet www.lifeisgreat.com.my; Dir and CEO ALEX FOONG SOO HAH.

Manulife Insurance (Malaysia) Bhd: Menara Manulife RB, 12th Floor, 6 Jalan Gelenggang, Damansara Heights, 50490 Kuala Lumpur; tel. (3) 20948055; fax (3) 20935487; internet www.manulife.com.my; f. 1963; life and non-life insurance; fmrly British American Life and General Insurance Bhd; name then changed to John Hancock Life Insurance (Malaysia) Bhd; name changed as above in 2005, following 2004 merger between John Hancock Financial Services, Inc. and Manulife Financial Corpn; Chair. Tan Sri Dato' MOHAMED SHERIFF BIN MOHAMED KASSIM.

Hong Leong Assurance Sdn Bhd: Menara HLA, 26th Floor, 3 Jalan Kia Peng, 50450 Kuala Lumpur; tel. (3) 27199228; fax (3) 27101735; internet www.hla.com.my; Chair. Tan Sri QUEK LENG CHAN; Man. Dir and CEO LOW TEIK LEONG.

ING Insurance Bhd: Menara ING, 84 Jalan Raja Chulan, POB 10846, 50927 Kuala Lumpur; tel. (3) 21617255; fax (3) 21610549; internet www.ing.com.my; f. 1987; fmrly Aetna Universal Insurance Bhd; Chair. Tengku ABDULLAH IBNI AL-MARHUM Sultan ABU BAKAR.

Jerneh Insurance Corpn Sdn Bhd: Wisma Jerneh, 12th Floor, 38 Jalan Sultan Ismail, POB 12420, 50788 Kuala Lumpur; tel. (3) 2427066; fax (3) 2426672; f. 1970; general; Gen. Man. GOH CHIN ENG.

Malaysia National Insurance Sdn Bhd: Tower 1, 26th Floor, MNI Twins, 11 Jalan Pinang, 50450 Kuala Lumpur; tel. (3) 21769000; fax (3) 21769090; internet www.mni.com.my; f. 1970; life and general; CEO MOHAMED NAJIB ABDULLAH.

Malaysian Co-operative Insurance Society Ltd: Wisma MCIS, Jalan Barat, 46200 Petaling Jaya, Selangor; tel. (3) 7552577; fax (3) 7571563; e-mail info@mcis.po.my; internet www.mcis.com.my/mcis; f. 1954; CEO L. MEYYAPPAN.

Mayban Assurance Bhd: Mayban Assurance Tower, Dataran Maybank, 1 Jalan Maarof, 50000 Kuala Lumpur; tel. (3) 22972888; fax (3) 22972828; e-mail mayassur@tm.net.my; internet www.maybank2u.com.my; Chair. Tan Sri MOHAMED BASIR AHMAD.

MBf Insurans Sdn Bhd: Plaza MBf, 5th Floor, Jalan Ampang, POB 10345, 50710 Kuala Lumpur; tel. and fax (3) 2613466; Man. MARC HOOI TUCK KOK.

MCIS Zürich Insurance Bhd: Wisma MCIS Zürich, Jalan Barat, 46200 Petaling Jaya, Selangor; tel. (3) 79552577; fax (3) 79574780; e-mail info@mciszurich.com.my; internet www.mciszurich.com.my;

CEO Datuk L. MEYYAPPAN; Chair. Dato' MOHAMAD WAHIDUDDIN BIN ABDUL WAHAB.

Multi-Purpose Insurans Bhd: Menara Multi-Purpose, 9th Floor, Capital Square, 8 Jalan Munshi Abdullah, 50100 Kuala Lumpur; tel. (3) 26919888; fax (3) 26945758; e-mail info@mpib.com.my; fmrly Kompas Insurans Bhd; Senior Gen. Mans WONG FOOK WAH, VISWANATH A. L. KANDASAMY.

Oriental Capital Assurance Bhd: 36 Jalan Ampang, 50450 Kuala Lumpur; tel. (3) 20702828; fax (3) 20724150; e-mail oricap@oricap.net; internet www.oricap.net; f. 2002 as a result of the merger of Capital Insurance Bhd and United Oriental Assurance Sdn Bhd; Chair. Datuk Dr K. AMPIKAIPAKAN; Exec. Dir MOHD YUSOF BIN IDRIS.

Overseas Assurance Corpn Ltd: Wisma Lee Rubber, 21st Floor, Jalan Melata, 50100 Kuala Lumpur; tel. (3) 2022939; fax (3) 2912288; Gen. Man. A. K. WONG.

Progressive Insurance Sdn Bhd: Plaza Berjaya, 9th, 10th and 15th Floors, 12 Jalan Imbi, POB 10028, 50700 Kuala Lumpur; tel. (3) 2410044; fax (3) 2418257; Man. JERRY PAUT.

RHB Insurance Bhd: Tower 1, 4th Floor, RHB Centre, Jalan Tun Razak, 50450 Kuala Lumpur; tel. (3) 9812731; fax (3) 9812729; Man. MOHAMMAD ABDULLAH.

Sime AXA Assurance Bhd: Wisma Sime Darby, 15th Floor, Jalan Raja Laut, 50350 Kuala Lumpur; tel. (3) 2937888; fax (3) 2914672; e-mail hkkang@simenet.com; Gen. Man. HAK KOON KANG.

South-East Asia Insurance Bhd: Tingkat 9, Menara SEA Insurance, 1008 Jalan Sultan Ismail, 50250 Kuala Lumpur; POB 6120 Pudu, 55916 Kuala Lumpur; tel. (3) 2938111; fax (3) 2930111; CEO HASHIM HARUN.

UMBC Insurans Sdn Bhd: Bangunan Sime Bank, 16th Floor, Jalan Sultan Sulaiman, 50000 Kuala Lumpur; tel. (3) 2328733; fax (3) 2322181; f. 1961; CEO ABDULLAH ABDUL SAMAD.

Trade and Industry

GOVERNMENT AGENCIES

Danamodal Nasional Bhd (Danamodal): 10th Floor, Bangunan Sime Bank, Jalan Sultan Sulaiman, 50000 Kuala Lumpur; tel. (3) 20312255; fax (3) 20310786; e-mail info@danamodal.com.my; internet www.bnm.gov.my/danamodal; f. 1998 to recapitalize banks and restructure financial institutions, incl. arranging mergers and consolidations; ; Chair. Raja Datuk ARSHAD Raja Tun UDA; Man. Dir MARIANUS VONG SHIN TZOI.

Federal Agricultural Marketing Authority (FAMA): Bangunan Fama Point, Lot 17304, Jalan Persiaran 1, Bandar Baru Selayang, 68100 Batu Caves, Selangor Darul Ehsan; tel. (3) 61389622; fax (3) 61365597; internet www.famaxchange.com; f. 1965 to supervise, co-ordinate and improve marketing of agricultural produce, and to seek and promote new markets and outlets for agricultural produce; Chair. AZIZI MEOR NGAH; Dir-Gen. HARON A. RAHIM.

Federal Land Development Authority (FELDA): Jalan Maktab, 54000 Kuala Lumpur; tel. (3) 2935066; fax (3) 2920087; f. 1956; govt statutory body formed to develop land into agricultural smallholdings to eradicate rural poverty; 893,150 ha of land developed (1994); involved in rubber, oil palm and sugar-cane cultivation; Chair. Raja Tan Sri MUHAMMAD ALIAS; Dir-Gen. MOHAMED FADZIL YUNUS.

Khazanah Nasional: 21 Putra Place 100, Ilu Putra, 50350 Kuala Lumpur; e-mail knb@po.jaring.my; f. 1994; state-controlled investment co; assumed responsibility for certain assets fmrly under control of the Minister of Finance Inc; holds 40% of Telekom Malaysia Bhd, 40% of Tenaga Nasional Bhd, 6.6% of HICOM Bhd and 17.8% of PROTON; Chair. Datuk Seri Dr MAHATHIR MOHAMAD.

Malaysia Export Credit Insurance Bhd (MECIB): Bangunan Bank Industri, 17th Floor, Bandar Wawasan, 1016 Jalan Sultan Ismail, POB 11048, 50734 Kuala Lumpur; tel. (3) 26910677; fax (3) 26910353; e-mail mecib@mecib.com.my; internet www.mecib.com.my; f. 1977; wholly owned subsidiary of Bank Industri & Teknologi Malaysia Bhd; provides insurance, financial guarantee and other trade-related services for exporters of locally manufactured products and for banking community; cap. RM 150m., exports declared RM 1,478m. (2004); Chair. Tan Sri Dato' OTHMAN BIN MOHAMED RIJAL; Gen. Man. AMINURRASHID BIN ZULKIFFY; 63 employees.

Malaysia External Trade Development Corpn (MATRADE): Wisma Sime Darby, 7th Floor, Jalan Raja Laut, 50350 Kuala Lumpur; tel. (3) 26163333; fax (3) 26947363; e-mail info@matrade.gov.my; internet www.matrade.gov.my; f. 1993; responsible for external trade development and promotion; CEO MERLYN KASIMIR.

Malaysian Institute of Economic Research: Menara Dayabumi, 9th Floor, Jalan Sultan Hishamuddin, POB 12160, 50768 Kuala Lumpur; tel. (3) 22725897; fax (3) 22730197; e-mail Admin@mier.po.my; internet www.mier.org.my; f. 1986; Exec. Dir Dr MOHAMED ARIFF; Chair. Tan Sri Dato' MOHAMED SHERIFF MOHAMED KASSIM.

Malaysian Palm Oil Board (MPOB): 6 Persiaran Institusi, Bandar Baru Bangi, 43000 Kajang, Selangor; tel. (3) 89259155; fax (3) 89259446; e-mail webmaster@pmob.gov.my; internet www.mpob.gov.my; f. 2000 by merger of Palm Oil Registration and Licensing Authority and Palm Oil Research Institute of Malaysia; Chair. Tan Sri Dato' Haji BASIR ISMAIL.

Malaysian Timber Industry Board (Lembaga Perindustrian Kayu Malaysia): 13–17 Menara PGRM, 8 Jalan Pudu Ulu, 56100 Cheras, Kuala Lumpur; tel. (3) 92822235; fax (3) 92851477; e-mail info@mtib.gov.my; internet www.mtib.gov.my; f. 1973 to promote and regulate the export of timber and timber products from Malaysia; Chair. Dr MICHAEL DOSIM LUNJEW; Dir-Gen. MOHD NAZURI BIN HASHIM SHAH.

Muda Agricultural Development Authority (MADA): MADA HQ, Ampang Jajar, 05990 Alor Setar, Kedah; tel. (4) 7728255; fax (4) 7722667; internet www.mada.gov.my; Chair. Dato' Seri SYED RAZAK BIN SYED ZAIN.

National Economic Action Council: NEAC-MTEN, Prime Minister's Office, Blok Utama, Tingkat 1–5, Pusat Pentadbiran Kerajaan Persekutuan, 62502 Putrajaya; tel. (3) 88882903; fax (3) 88882902; e-mail effendi@epu.jpm.my; internet www.neac.gov.my; Exec. Dir Datuk Seri MOHAMED EFFENDI NORWAWI.

National Information Technology Council (NITC): Kuala Lumpur; Sec. Datuk Tengku Dr MOHD AZZMAN SHARIFFADEEN.

National Timber Certification Council: Kuala Lumpur; Chair. CHEW LYE TENG.

Pengurusan Danaharta Nasional Bhd (Danaharta): Tingkat 10, Bangunan Setia 1, 15 Lorong Dungun, Bukit Damansara, 50490 Kuala Lumpur; tel. (3) 20931122; fax (3) 20937482; e-mail info@danaharta.com.my; internet www.danaharta.com.my; f. 1998 to acquire non-performing loans from the banking sector and to maximize the recovery value of those assets; Man. Dir ZUKRI SAMAT.

Perbadanan Nasional Bhd (PERNAS): Kuala Lumpur; tel. (3) 2935177; internet www.pns.com.my; f. 1969; govt-sponsored; promotes trade, banking, property and plantation development, construction, mineral exploration, steel manufacturing, inland container transportation, mining, insurance, industrial development, engineering services, telecommunication equipment, hotels and shipping; cap. p.u. RM 116.25m.; 10 wholly owned subsidiaries, over 60 jointly owned subsidiaries and 18 assoc. cos; Chair. Tunku Dato' SHAHRIMAN BIN Tunku SULAIMAN; Man. Dir Dato' A. RAHMAN BIN HAMIDON.

DEVELOPMENT ORGANIZATIONS

Fisheries Development Authority of Malaysia: 7th–11th Floors, Wisma PKNS, Jalan Raja Laut, 50784 Kuala Lumpur; tel. (3) 26177000; fax (3) 26911931; e-mail info@kim.moa.my; internet agrolink.moa.my/lkim; Dir-Gen. Dato' Sheikh AHMAD BIN Sheikh LONG.

Johor Corporation: 13th Floor, Menara Johor Corporation, Kotaraya, 80000 Johor Bahru; tel. (7) 2232692; fax (7) 2233175; e-mail pdnjohor@jcorp.com.my; internet www.jcorp.com.my; development agency of the Johor state govt; Chair. Dato' Haji ABDUL GHANI BIN OTHMAN; Chief Exec. Dato' MUHAMMAD ALI HASHIM.

Kumpulan FIMA Bhd (Food Industries of Malaysia): Kompleks FIMA, International Airport, Subang, Selangor; tel. (3) 7462199; f. 1972; fmrly govt corpn, transferred to private sector in 1991; promotes food and related industry through investment on its own or by co-ventures with local or foreign entrepreneurs; oil palm, cocoa and fruit plantation developments; manufacturing and packaging, trading, supermarkets and restaurants; Man. Dir Dato' MOHD NOOR BIN ISMAIL; 1,189 employees.

Majlis Amanah Rakyat (MARA) (Trust Council for the People): Bangunan Medan MARA, 13th Floor, 21 Jalan Raja Laut, 50609 Kuala Lumpur; tel. (3) 26915111; fax (3) 26913620; e-mail webmaster@mara.gov.my; internet www.mara.gov.my; f. 1966 to promote, stimulate, facilitate and undertake economic and social development; to participate in industrial and commercial undertakings and jt ventures; Chair. Tan Sri NAZRI AZIZ.

Malaysian Agricultural Research and Development Institute (MARDI): POB 12301, General Post Office, 50774 Kuala Lumpur; tel. (3) 89437111; fax (3) 89483664; e-mail saharan@mardi.my; internet www.mardi.my; f. 1969; research and development in food and tropical agriculture; Dir-Gen. Dr SAHARAN BIN Haji ANANG.

Malaysian Industrial Development Authority (MIDA): Plaza Sentral, Block 4, 5 Jalan Stesen Sentral, 50470 Kuala Lumpur; tel. (3) 22673633; fax (3) 22734211; e-mail library@mida.gov.my; internet www.mida.gov.my; f. 1967; Chair. Tan Sri Datuk ZAINAL ABIDIN BIN SULONG; Dir-Gen. Datuk R. KARUNAKARAN.

Malaysian Industrial Development Finance Bhd: Bangunan Amanah Capital, 21st Floor, 82 Jalan Raja Chulan, 50200 Kuala Lumpur; tel. (3) 21619011; fax (3) 21617580; e-mail inquiry@midf.com.my; internet www.midf.com.my; f. 1960 by the Govt; banks, insurance cos, industrial financing, advisory services, project development, merchant and commercial banking services; Chair. Tan Sri Dato' MAHMOOD TAIB; Man. Dir Dato' MOHAMED SALLEHUDDIN BIN OTHMAN.

Malaysian Pepper Marketing Board: Lot 115, Jalan Utama, 93916 Kuching, Sarawak; tel. (82) 331811; fax (82) 336877; e-mail pmb@pepper.po.my; internet www.sarawakpepper.gov.my; f. 1972; responsible for the statutory grading of all Sarawak pepper for export, licensing of pepper dealers and exporters, trading and the development and promotion of pepper grading, storage and processing facilities; Chair. Dr JERIP SUSIL; Gen. Man. GRUNSIN AYOM.

Pinang Development Corporation: 1 Pesiaran Mahsuri, Bandar Bayan Baru, 11909 Bayan Lepas, Pinang; tel. (4) 6340111; fax (4) 6432405; e-mail enquiry@pdc.gov.my; internet www.pdc.gov.my; f. 1969; development agency of the Pinang state government; Chair. Tan Sri Dr KOH TSU KOON.

Sarawak Economic Development Corpn: Menara SEDC, 6th–11th Floors, Sarawak Plaza, Jalan Tunku Abdul Rahman, POB 400, 93902 Kuching; tel. (82) 416777; fax (82) 424330; e-mail ssedc@pop1.jaring.my; internet www.sedc.com.my; f. 1972; statutory org. responsible for commercial and industrial development in Sarawak either solely or jtly with foreign and local entrepreneurs; responsible for the development of tourism infrastructure; Chair. Datuk Haji TALIB ZULPILIP.

Selangor State Development Corporation (PKNS): Persiaran Barat, off Jalan Barat, 46505 Petaling Jaya, Selangor; tel. (3) 79572955; fax (3) 79575250; e-mail general@pkns.gov.my; internet www.pkns.gov.my; f. 1964; partially govt-owned; Corporate Man. YUSOF OTHMAN.

CHAMBERS OF COMMERCE

The Associated Chinese Chamber of Commerce: Wisma Chamber, 4th Floor, Lot 214, Jalan Bukit Mata, 93100 Kuching; tel. (82) 428815; fax (82) 429950; e-mail kcjong@pc.jaring.my; f. 1965; Pres. TIONG SU KOUK; Sec. Gen. LEE KHIM SIN.

Associated Chinese Chambers of Commerce and Industry of Malaysia: Lot 6.05, Menara Promet, 6th Floor, Jalan Sultan Ismail, 50250 Kuala Lumpur; tel. (3) 21452503; fax (3) 21452562; e-mail acccim@acccim.org.my; internet www.acccim.org.my; Pres. Tan Sri WILLIAM CHENG; Sec.-Gen. Tan Sri Dato' SOONG SIEW HOONG.

Malay Chamber of Commerce Malaysia: Plaza Pekeliling, 17th Floor, Jalan Tun Razak, 50400 Kuala Lumpur; tel. (3) 4418522; fax (3) 4414502; f. 1957 as Associated Malay Chambers of Commerce of Malaya; name changed as above 1992; Pres. Tan Sri Dato' TAJUDIN RAMLI; Sec.-Gen. ZAKI SAID.

Malaysian Associated Indian Chambers of Commerce and Industry: 116 Jalan Tuanku Abdul Rahman, 2nd Floor, 50100 Kuala Lumpur; tel. (3) 26931033; fax (3) 26911670; e-mail info@maicci.org.my; internet www.maicci.org.my; f. 1950; Pres. PARDIP KUMAR KUKREJA; Hon. Sec.-Gen. VENKITESWARAN SANKAR; 8 brs.

Malaysian International Chamber of Commerce and Industry (MICCI) (Dewan Perniagaan dan Perindustrian Antarabangsa Malaysia): C-8-8, 8th Floor, Block C, Plaza Mont' Kiara, 50480 Kuala Lumpur; tel. (3) 62017708; fax (3) 62017705; e-mail micci@micci.com; internet www.micci.com; f. 1837; brs in Pinang, Perak, Johor, Melaka and Sabah; 1,100 corporate mems; Pres. Datuk JON CHADWICK; Exec. Dir STEWART J. FORBES.

National Chamber of Commerce and Industry of Malaysia: 37 Jalan Kia Peng, 50450 Kuala Lumpur; tel. (3) 2419600; fax (3) 2413775; e-mail nccim@po.jaring.my; internet www.nccim.org.my; f. 1962; Pres. Dato' Seri ABDUL RAHMAN MAIDIN; Sec.-Gen. HARITH SIDDIK.

Sabah Chamber of Commerce and Industry: Jalan Tiga, Sandakan; tel. (89) 2141; Pres. T. H. WONG.

Sarawak Chamber of Commerce and Industry (SCCI): POB A-841, Kenyalang Park Post Office, 93806 Kuching; tel. (82) 237148; fax (82) 237186; e-mail phtay@pc.jaring.my; internet www.cmsb.com.my/scci; f. 1950; Chair. Datuk Haji MOHAMED AMIN Haji SATEM; Dep. Chair. Datuk Abang Haji ABDUL KARIM Tun Abang Haji OPENG.

South Indian Chamber of Commerce of Sarawak: 37C India St, Kuching; f. 1952; Pres. HAJA NAZIMUDDIN BIN ABDUL MAJID; Vice-Pres. SYED AHMAD.

INDUSTRIAL AND TRADE ASSOCIATIONS

Federation of Malaysian Manufacturers: Wisma FMM, 3 Persiaran Dagang, PJU 9 Bandar Sri Damansara, 52200 Kuala Lumpur; tel. (3) 62761211; fax (3) 62741266; e-mail webmaster@fmm.org.my; internet www.fmm.org.my; f. 1968; offers guidance and advice relating to trade and industry; presents problems and concerns to the Govt; 2,117 mems (Jan. 2005); Pres. Datuk YONG POH KON; CEO LEE CHENG SUAN.

Federation of Rubber Trade Associations of Malaysia: 138 Jalan Bandar, 50000 Kuala Lumpur; tel. (3) 2384006.

Malayan Agricultural Producers' Association: Kuala Lumpur; tel. (3) 42573988; fax (3) 42573113; e-mail mapa@myjaring.net; f. 1997; 406 mem. estates and 108 factories/mills; Pres. Dato' Dr MOHD NOOR BIN ISMAIL; Dir MOHAMAD BIN AUDONG.

Malaysian Iron and Steel Industry Federation: 28E, 30E, 5th Floor, Block 2, Worldwide Business Park, Jalan Tinju 13/50, Section 13, 40675 Shah Alam, Selangor; tel. (3) 55133970; fax (3) 55133891; e-mail misif@po.jaring.my; Chair. Tan Sri Dato' SOONG SIEW HOONG; 150 mems.

Malaysian Palm Oil Association (MPOA): Bangunan Getah Asli I, 12th Floor, 148 Jalan Ampang, 50450 Kuala Lumpur; tel. (3) 27105680; fax (3) 27105679; e-mail kay@mpoa.org.my; internet www.mpoa.org.my; f. 1999 as result of rationalization of plantation industry; secretariat for producers of palm oil; Chief. Exec. M. R. CHANDRAN.

Malaysian Pineapple Industry Board: Wisma Nanas, 5 Jalan Padi Mahsuri, Bandar Baru UDA, 81200 Johor Bahru; tel. (7) 2361211; fax (7) 2365694; e-mail mpib@tm.net.my; Dir-Gen. Tuan Haji ISMAIL BIN ABD JAMAL.

Malaysian Rubber Board: Bangunan Getah Asli, Tingkat 17 and 18, 148 Jalan Ampang, 50450 Kuala Lumpur; tel. (3) 92062000; fax (3) 21634492; e-mail general@lgm.gov.my; internet www.lgm.gov.my; f. 1998; implements policies and development programmes to ensure the viability of the Malaysian rubber industry; regulates the industry (in particular, the packing, grading, shipping and export of rubber); Dir-Gen. Dr KAMARUL BAHARAIN BIN BASIR.

Malaysian Rubber Products Manufacturers' Association: 1 Jalan USJ 11/1J, Subang Jaya, 47620 Petaling Jaya, Selangor; tel. (3) 56316150; fax (3) 56316152; e-mail mrpma@po.jaring.my; internet www.mrpma.com; f. 1952; Pres. Tan Sri Datuk ARSHAD AYUB; 144 mems.

Malaysian Timber Certification Council (MTCC): 19th Floor, Menara PGRM, 8 Jalan Pudu Ulu, Cheras, 56100 Kuala Lumpur; tel. (3) 92005008; fax (3) 92006008; e-mail mtcc@tm.net.my; internet www.mtcc.com.my; f. 1999; operates a voluntary national timber certification scheme to encourage sustainable forest management; CEO CHEW LYE TENG.

Malaysian Wood Industries Association: 19B, 19th Floor, Menara PGRM, 8 Jalan Pudu Ulu, Cheras, 56100 Kuala Lumpur; tel. (3) 92821789; fax (3) 92821779; e-mail mwia@tm.net.my; f. 1957; Exec. Officer PANG SUET KUM.

National Tobacco Board Malaysia (Ibu Pejabat Lembaga Tembakau Negara): Kubang Kerian, POB 198, 15720 Kota Bharu, Kelantan; tel. (9) 7652212; fax (9) 7655640; e-mail teo@ltn.gov.my; internet www.ltn.gov.my; Dir-Gen. TEO HUI BEK.

Northern Malaya Rubber Millers and Packers Association: 22 Pitt St, 3rd Floor, Suites 301–303, 10200 Pinang; tel. (4) 620037; f. 1919; 153 mems; Pres. HWANG SING LUE; Hon. Sec. LEE SENG KEOK.

Palm Oil Refiners' Association of Malaysia (PORAM): 801C/802A Blok B, Executive Suites, Kelana Business Centre, 97 Jalan SS7/2, 47301 Kelana Jaya, Selangor; tel. (3) 74920006; fax (3) 74920128; e-mail poram@poram.org.my; internet www.poram.org.my; f. 1975 to promote the palm oil refining industry; Chair. RICHARD CHEANG KWAN CHOW; 27 mems.

Rubber Industry Smallholders' Development Authority (RISDA): 4½ Miles, Jalan Ampang, 50450 Kuala Lumpur; tel. (3) 4564022; Dir-Gen. MOHD ZAIN BIN Haji YAHYA.

Tin Industry Research and Development Board: West Block, 8th Floor, Wisma Selangor Dredging, Jalan Ampang, POB 12560, 50782 Kuala Lumpur; tel. (3) 21616171; fax (3) 21616179; e-mail mcom@mcom.com.my; Chair. MOHAMED AJIB ANUAR; Sec. MUHAMAD NOR MUHAMAD.

EMPLOYERS' ORGANIZATIONS

Malaysian Employers' Federation: 3A06–3A07, Block A, Pusat Dagangan Phileo Damansara II, 15 Jalan 16/11, off Jalan Damansara, 46350 Petaling Jaya, Selangor; tel. (3) 79557778; fax (3) 79559008; e-mail mef-hq@mef.org.my; internet www.mef.org.my; f. 1959; Pres. JAFAR ABDUL CARRIM; Sec. SHAMSUDDIN BARDAN; private-sector org. incorporating 13 employer organizations and 3,745 individual enterprises, including:

Association of Insurance Employers: c/o Royal Insurance (M) Sdn Bhd, Menara Boustead, 5th Floor, 69 Jalan Raja Chulan, 50200 Kuala Lumpur; tel. (3) 2410233; fax (3) 2442762; Pres. NG KIM HOONG.

Commercial Employers' Association of Peninsular Malaysia: c/o The East Asiatic Co (M) Bhd, 1 Jalan 205, 46050 Petaling Jaya, Selangor; tel. (3) 7913322; fax (3) 7913561; Pres. HAMZAH Haji GHULAM.

MALAYSIA

Malayan Commercial Banks' Association: see Banking Associations, above.

Malaysian Chamber of Mines: West Block, Wisma Selangor Dredging, 8th Floor, 142c Jalan Ampang, 50450 Kuala Lumpur; tel. (3) 21616171; fax (3) 21616179; e-mail mcom@mcom.com.my; internet www.mcom.com.my; f. 1914; promotes and protects interests of Malaysian mining industry; Pres. MOHAMED AJIB ANUAR; Exec. Dir MUHAMAD NOR MUHAMAD.

Malaysian Textile Manufacturers' Association: West Block, Wisma Selangor Dredging, 9th Floor, 142c Jalan Ampang, 50450 Kuala Lumpur; tel. (3) 21621587; fax (3) 21623953; e-mail textile@po.jaring.my; internet www.fashion-asia.com; Pres. BAHAR AHMAD; Exec. Dir CHOY MING BIL; 230 mems.

Pan Malaysian Bus Operators' Association: 88 Jalan Sultan Idris Shah, 30300 Ipoh, Perak; tel. (5) 2549421; fax (5) 2550858; Sec. Datin TEOH PHAIK LEAN.

Sabah Employers' Consultative Association: Dewan SECA, No. 4, Block A, 1st Floor, Bandar Ramai-Ramai, 90000 Sandakan, Sabah; tel. and fax (89) 272846; Pres. E. M. KHOO.

Stevedore Employers' Association: 5 Pengkalan Weld, POB 288, 10300 Pinang; tel. (4) 2615091; Pres. ABDUL RAHMAN MAIDIN.

UTILITIES

Electricity

Energy Commission of Malaysia: Levels 15, 19 and 20, Menara Dato' Onn, Putra World Centre, Jalan Tun Ismail, Kuala Lumpur; internet www.st.gov.my; f. 2002; regulatory body supervising electricity and gas supply.

Tenaga Nasional Bhd: 129 Jalan Bangsar, POB 11003, 50732 Kuala Lumpur; tel. (3) 2825566; fax (3) 2823274; e-mail webadmin@tnb.com.my; internet www.tnb.com.my; f. 1990 through the corporatization and privatization of the National Electricity Board; 53% govt-controlled; generation, transmission and distribution of electricity in Peninsular Malaysia; generating capacity of 7,621 MW (63% of total power generation); also purchases power from 12 licensed independent power producers; Chair. Tan Sri Dato' AMAR LEO MOGGIE; Pres. and CEO Dato' KHALIB BIN MOHAMAD NOH.

Sabah Electricity Board (SEB): Wisma Lembaga Letrik Sabah, 88673 Kota Kinabalu; tel. (88) 211699; generation, transmission and distribution of electricity in Sabah.

Syarikat Sesco Bhd (SESCO): POB 149, 93700 Kuching, Sarawak; tel. (82) 441188; fax (82) 444433; e-mail public_enquiry@sesoc.com.my; internet www.sesco.com.my; fmrly known as Sarawak Electricity Supply Corpn; generation, transmission and distribution of electricity in Sarawak; Chair. Datuk Haji Awang TENGAH ALI HASAN.

Gas

Energy Commission of Malaysia: see above.

Gas Malaysia Sdn Bhd: 5 Jalan Serendah 26/17, Seksyen 26, Peti Surat 7901, 40732 Shah Alam, Selangor Darul Ehsan; tel. (3) 51923000; e-mail ccu@gasmalaysia.com; internet www.gasmalaysia.com; f. 1992; Chair. Tan Sri Datuk Dr AHMAD TAJUDDIN ALI; CEO MUHAMAD NOOR HAMID.

Water

Under the federal Constitution, water supply is the responsibility of the state Governments. In 1998, owing to water shortages, the National Water Resources Council was established to co-ordinate management of water resources at national level. Malaysia's sewerage system is operated by Indah Water Konsortium, owned by Prime Utilities.

National Water Resources Council: c/o Ministry of Works, Jalan Sultan Salahuddin, 50580 Kuala Lumpur; tel. (3) 2919011; fax (3) 2986612; f. 1998 to co-ordinate management of water resources at national level through co-operation with state water boards; Chair. Dato' Seri Dr MAHATHIR BIN MOHAMAD.

Regulatory Authorities

Johor State Regulatory Body: c/o Pejabat Setiausaha Kerajaan Negeri Johor, Aras 1, Bangunan Sultan Ibrahim, Jalan Bukit Timbalan, 80000 Johor Bahru; tel. (7) 223850; Dir Tuan Haji OMAR BIN AWAB.

Kelantan Water Department: Tingkat Bawah Blok 6, Kota Darul Naim, 15503 Kota Bahru, Kelantan; tel. (9) 7475240; e-mail hjabaziz@yahoo.com.my; Dir Tuan Haji ABDUL AZIZ BIN Haji ABDUL RAHMAN.

Water Supply Authorities

Kedah Public Works Department: Bangunan Sultan Abdul Halim, Jalan Sultan Badlishah, 05582 Alor Setar, Kedah; tel. (4) 7334041; fax (4) 7341616; Dir Dr NORDIN BIN YUNUS.

Kelantan Water Sdn Bhd: 14 Beg Berkunci, Jalan Kuala Krai, 15990 Kota Bahru, Kelantan; tel. (10) 9022222; fax (10) 9022236; Dir PETER NEW BERKLEY.

Kuching Water Board: Jalan Batu Lintang, 93200 Kuching, Sarawak; tel. (82) 240371; fax (82) 244546; Dir DAVID YEU BIN TONG.

Labuan Public Works Department: Jalan Kg. Jawa, POB 2, 87008 Labuan; tel. (87) 414040; fax (87) 412370; Dir Ir ZULKIFLY BIN MADON.

LAKU Management Sdn Bhd: Soon Hup Tower, 6th Floor, Lot 907, Jalan Merbau, 98000 Miri; tel. (85) 442000; fax (85) 442005; e-mail chuilin@pd.jaring.my; serves Miri, Limbang and Bintulu; CEO YONG CHIONG VAN.

Melaka Water Corpn: Tingkat Bawah, 1 10–13, Graha Maju, Jalan Graha Maju, 75300 Melaka; tel. (6) 2825233; fax (6) 2837266; Dir Ir ABDUL RAHIM SHAMSUDI.

Negeri Sembilan Water Department: Wisma Negeri, 70990 Seremban; tel. (6) 7622314; fax (6) 7620753; Dir Ir Dr MOHD AKBAR.

Pahang Water Supply Department (Jabatan Bekalan Air Pahang): 9–10 Kompleks Tun Razak, Bandar Indera Mahkota, 25582 Kuantan, Pahang; tel. (9) 5721222; fax (9) 5721221; e-mail p-jba@pahang.gov.my; Dir Ir Haji ISMAIL BIN Haji MAT NOOR.

Perak Water Board: Jalan St John, Peti Surat 589, 30760 Ipoh, Perak; tel. (5) 2551155; fax (5) 2556397; Dir Ir SANI BIN SIDIK.

Pinang Water Supply Department: Level 29, KOMTAR, 10000 Pinang; tel. (4) 6505462; fax (4) 2645282; e-mail lyc@sukpp.gov.my; f. 1973; Gen. Man. Datuk Ir LEE YOW CHING.

Sabah Water Department: Wisma MUIS, Blok A, Tingkat 6, Beg Berkunci 210, 88825 Kota Kinabalu; tel. (88) 232364; fax (88) 232396; Man. Ir BENNY WANG.

SAJ Holdings Sdn Bhd: Bangunan Ibu Pejabat SAJ Holdings, Jalan Garuda, Larkin, POB 262, 80350 Johor Bahru; tel. (7) 2244040; fax (7) 2236155; e-mail support@saj.com.my; internet www.saj.com.my; f. 1999; Exec. Chair. Dir Dato' Haji HAMDAN BIN MOHAMED.

Sarawak Public Works Department: Wisma Seberkas, Jalan Tun Haji Openg, 93582 Kuching; tel. (82) 244041; fax (82) 429679; Dir MICHAEL TING KUOK NG.

Selangor Water Department: POB 5001, Jalan Pantai Baru, 59990 Kuala Lumpur; tel. (3) 2826244; fax (3) 2827535; f. 1972; Dir Ir LIEW WAI KIAT.

Sibu Water Board: Km 5, Jalan Salim, POB 405, 96007 Sibu, Sarawak; tel. (84) 211001; fax (84) 211543; e-mail swbs@swb.gov.my; Man. DANIEL WONG PARK ING.

Terengganu Water Department: Tkt 3, Wisma Negeri, Jalan Pejabat, 20200 Kuala Terengganu; tel. (9) 6222444; fax (9) 6221510; Dir Ir Haji WAN NGAH BIN WAN.

TRADE UNIONS

In 1995 there were 502 trade unions, 56% of which were from the private sector. About 8.2% of the Malaysian work-force of 7.9m. belonged to unions.

Congress of Unions of Employees in the Public Administrative and Civil Services (CUEPACS): a nat. fed. with 53 affiliates, representing 120,150 govt workers (1994).

Malaysian Trades Union Congress: Wisma MTUC, 10–5, Jalan USJ 9/5T, 47620 Subang Jaya, Selangor; POB 3073, 46000 Petaling Jaya, Selangor; tel. (3) 80242953; fax (3) 80243224; e-mail mtuc@tm.net.my; internet www.mtuc.org.my; f. 1949; 247 affiliated unions, representing approx. 500,000 workers; Pres. SYED SHAHIR BIN SYED MOHAMUD; Sec.-Gen. G. RAJASEKARAN.

Principal affiliated unions:

All Malayan Estates Staff Union: POB 12, 46700 Petaling Jaya, Selangor Darul Ehsan; tel. (3) 7249533; e-mail mes@po.jaring.my; 2,654 mems; Pres. TITUS GLADWIN; Gen. Sec. D. P. S. THAMOTHARAM.

Amalgamated Union of Employees in Government Clerical and Allied Services: 32A Jalan Gajah, off Jalan Yew, Pudu, 55100 Kuala Lumpur; tel. (3) 9859613; fax (3) 9838632; 6,703 mems; Pres. IBRAHIM BIN ABDUL WAHAB; Gen. Sec. MOHAMED IBRAHIM BIN ABDUL WAHAB.

Chemical Workers' Union: Petaling Jaya, Selangor; 1,886 mems; Pres. RUSIAN HITAM; Gen. Sec. JOHN MATHEWS.

Electricity Industry Workers' Union: 55-2 Jalan SS 15/8A, Subang Jaya, 47500 Petaling Jaya, Selangor; tel. (3) 7335243; 22,000 mems; Pres. ABDUL RASHID; Gen. Sec. P. ARUNASALAM.

Federation of Unions in the Textile, Garment and Leather Industry: c/o Selangor Textile and Garment Manufacturing Employees Union, 9D Jalan Travers, 50470 Kuala Lumpur; tel. (3)

MALAYSIA

2742578; f. 1989; four affiliates; Pres. ABDUL RAZAK HAMID; Gen. Sec. ABU BAKAR IBRAHIM.

Harbour Workers' Union, Port Kelang: 106 Persiaran Raja Muda Musa, Port Kelang; 2,426 mems; Pres. MOHAMED SHARIFF BIN YAMIN; Gen. Sec. MOHAMED HAYAT BIN AWANG.

Kesatuan Pekerja Tenaga Nasional Bhd: 30 Jalan Liku Bangsar, POB 10400, 59100 Kuala Lumpur; tel. (3) 2745657; 10,456 mems; Pres. MOHAMED ABU BAKAR; Gen. Sec. IDRIS BIN ISMAIL.

Kesatuan Pekerja-Pekerja FELDA: 2 Jalan Maktab Enam, Melalui Jalan Perumahan Gurney, 54000 Kuala Lumpur; tel. (3) 26929972; fax (3) 26913409; 2,900 mems; Pres. INDERA PUTRA Haji ISMAIL; Gen. Sec. MOHAMAD BIN ABDUL RAHMAN.

Kesatuan Pekerja-Pekerja Perusahaan Membuat Tekstil dan Pakaian Pulau Pinang dan Seberang Prai: 23 Lorong Talang Satu, Prai Gardens, 13600 Prai; tel. (4) 301397; 3,900 mems; Pres. ABDUL RAZAK HAMID; Gen. Sec. KENNETH STEPHEN PERKINS.

Malayan Technical Services Union: 3A Jalan Menteri, off Jalan Cochrane, 55100 Kuala Lumpur; tel. (3) 92851778; fax (3) 92811875; 6,500 mems; Pres. Haji MOHAMED YUSOP Haji HARMAIN SHAH; Gen. Sec. SAMUEL DEVADASAN.

Malaysian Rubber Board Staff Union: POB 10150, 50908 Kuala Lumpur; tel. (3) 42565102; 850 mems; Pres. HASNAH GANI; Gen. Sec. SUBRAMANIAM SINNASAMY.

Metal Industry Employees' Union: Metalworkers' House, 5 Lorong Utara Kecil, 46200 Petaling Jaya, Selangor; tel. (3) 79567214; fax (3) 79550854; e-mail mieum@tm.net.my; 15,491 mems; Pres. SAMUSUDDIN USOP; Gen. Sec. JACOB ENGKATESU.

National Union of Bank Employees: NUBE Bldg, 61 Jalan Ampang, POB 12488, 50780 Kuala Lumpur; tel. (3) 20789800; fax (3) 20703800; e-mail nubehq@pd.jaring.my; internet www.nube.org.my; 27,000 mems; Gen. Sec. J. SOLOMON.

National Union of Commercial Workers: Bangunan NUCW, 98A–D Jalan Masjid India, 50100 Kuala Lumpur; POB 12059, 50780 Kuala Lumpur; tel. (3) 26927385; fax (3) 26925930; f. 1959; 11,937 mems; Pres. TAIB SHARIF; Gen. Sec. C. KRISHNAN.

National Union of Plantation Workers: 428 A–B, Jalan 5/46, Gasing Indah, POB 73, 46700 Petaling Jaya, Selangor; tel. (3) 77827622; fax (3) 77815321; e-mail sangkara@tm.net.my; f. 1946; 34,338 mems; Pres. SELVARAJOO A/L KUPPUSAMY; Gen. Sec. Dato' G. SANKARAN.

National Union of PWD Employees: 32B Jalan Gajah, off Jalan Yew, 55100 Kuala Lumpur; tel. (3) 9850149; 5,869 mems; Pres. KULOP IBRAHIM; Gen. Sec. S. SANTHANASAMY.

National Union of Telecoms Employees: Wisma NUTE, 17A Jalan Bangsar, 59200 Kuala Lumpur; tel. (3) 2821599; fax (3) 2821015; 15,874 mems; Pres. MOHAMED SHAFIE B. P. MAMMAL; Gen. Sec. MOHD JAFAR BIN ABDUL MAJID.

Non-Metallic Mineral Products Manufacturing Employees' Union: 99A Jalan SS 14/1, Subang Jaya, 47500 Petaling Jaya, Selangor; tel. (3) 56339006; fax (3) 56333863; e-mail nonmet@tm.net.my; 10,000 mems; Pres. ABDULLAH ABU BAKAR; Sec. S. SOMAHSUNDRAM.

Railwaymen's Union of Malaya: Bangunan Tong Nam, 1st Floor, Jalan Tun Sambathan (Travers), 50470 Kuala Lumpur; tel. (3) 2741107; fax (3) 2731805; 5,500 mems; Pres. ABDUL GAFFOR BIN IBRAHIM; Gen. Sec. S. VEERASINGAM.

Technical Services Union—Tenaga Nasional Bhd: Bangunan Keselamatan, POB 11003, Bangsar, Kuala Lumpur; tel. (3) 2823581; 3,690 mems; Pres. RAMLY YATIM; Gen. Sec. CLIFFORD SEN.

Timber Employees' Union: 10 Jalan AU 5c/14, Ampang, Ulu Kelang, Selangor; 7,174 mems; Pres. ABDULLAH METON; Gen. Sec. MINHAT SULAIMAN.

Transport Workers' Union: 21 Jalan Barat, Petaling Jaya, 46200 Selangor; tel. (3) 7566567; 10,447 mems; Pres. NORASHIKIN; Gen. Sec. ZAINAL RAMPAK.

Independent Federations and Unions

Kongres Kesatuan Guru-Guru Dalam Perkhidmatan Pelajaran (Congress of Unions of Employees in the Teaching Services): Johor; seven affiliates; Pres. RAMLI BIN MOHD JOHAN; Sec.-Gen. KASSIM BIN Haji HARON.

Malaysian Medical Association: MMA House, 4th Floor, 124 Jalan Pahang, 53000 Kuala Lumpur; tel. (3) 40420617; fax (3) 40418187; e-mail info@mma.org.my; internet www.mma.org.my; 10 affiliates; Pres. Datuk Dr TEOH SIANG CHIN.

National Union of Journalists: 30B Jalan Padang Belia, 50470 Kuala Lumpur; tel. (3) 2742867; fax (3) 2744776; f. 1962; 1,700 mems; Gen. Sec. ONN EE SENG.

National Union of Newspaper Workers: 11B Jalan 20/14, Paramount Garden, 46300 Petaling Jaya, Selangor; tel. (3) 78768118; fax (3) 78751490; e-mail nunwl@tm.net.my; 3,000 mems; Pres. GAN HOE JIAN; Gen. Sec. R. CHANDRASEKARAN.

Sabah

Sabah Banking Employees' Union: POB 11649, 88818 Kota Kinabalu; internet sbeukk@tm.net.my; 729 mems; Gen. Sec. LEE CHI HONG.

Sabah Civil Service Union: Kota Kinabalu; f. 1952; 1,356 mems; Pres. J. K. K. VOON; Sec. STEPHEN WONG.

Sabah Commercial Employees' Union: Sinsuran Shopping Complex, Lot 3, Block N, 2nd Floor, POB 10357, 88803 Kota Kinabalu; tel. (88) 225971; fax (88) 213815; e-mail sceu-kk@tm.net.my; f. 1957; 980 mems; Gen. Sec. REBECCA CHIN.

Sabah Medical Services Union: POB 11257, 88813 Kota Kinabalu; tel. (88) 242126; fax (88) 242127; e-mail smsu65@hotmail.com; 4,000 mems; Pres. KATHY LO NYUK CHIN; Gen. Sec. LAURENCE VUN.

Sabah Petroleum Industry Workers' Union: POB 1087, Kota Kinabalu; tel. (88) 720737; e-mail victor.yb.sang@exxonmobil.com; internet www.sabah.org.my/spiwu; f. 1966; 168 mems; Pres. ABDULLAH JAMIL AHMAD.

Sabah Teachers' Union: POB 10912, 88810 Kota Kinabalu; tel. (88) 420034; fax (88) 431633; f. 1962; 3,001 mems; Pres. KWAN PING SIN; Sec.-Gen. PATRICK Y. C. CHOK.

Sarawak

Kepak Sarawak (Kesatuan Pegawai-Pegawai Bank, Sarawak): POB 62, Bukit Permata, 93100 Kuching, Sarawak; tel. (19) 8549372; e-mail kepaksar@tm.net.my; bank officers' union; 1,430 mems; Gen. Sec. DOMINIC CH'NG YUNG TED.

Sarawak Commercial Employees' Union: POB 807, Kuching; 1,636 mems; Gen. Sec. SONG SWEE LIAP.

Sarawak Teachers' Union: 139A Jalan Rock, 1st Floor, 93200 Kuching; tel. (82) 245727; fax (82) 245757; e-mail swktu@po.jaring.my; internet www.geocities.com/swktu; f. 1965; 12,832 mems; Pres. WILLIAM GHANI BINA; Sec.-Gen. THOMAS HUO KOK SEN.

Transport

RAILWAYS

Peninsular Malaysia

The state-owned Malayan Railways had a total length of 1,672 km in Peninsular Malaysia in 1996. The main railway line follows the west coast and extends 782 km from Singapore, south of Peninsular Malaysia, to Butterworth (opposite Pinang Island) in the north. From Bukit Mertajam, close to Butterworth, the Kedah line runs north to the Thai border at Padang Besar where connection is made with the State Railway of Thailand. The East Coast Line, 526 km long, runs from Gemas to Tumpat (in Kelantan). A 21-km branch line from Pasir Mas (27 km south of Tumpat) connects with the State Railway of Thailand at the border station of Sungei Golok. Branch lines serve railway-operated ports at Port Dickson and Telok Anson as well as Port Klang and Jurong (Singapore). An express rail link connecting central Kuala Lumpur and the new Kuala Lumpur International Airport (KLIA) opened in 2001.

Keretapi Tanah Melayu Bhd (KTMB) (Malayan Railways): KTMB Corporate Headquarters, Jalan Sultan Hishamuddin, 50621 Kuala Lumpur; tel. (3) 22631111; fax (3) 27105706; e-mail pro@ktmb.com.my; internet www.ktmb.com.my; f. 1885; incorporated as a co under govt control in Aug. 1992; privatized in Aug. 1997; managed by the consortium Marak Unggal (Renong, DRB and Bolton); Chair. Tan Sri Dato' LIM AH LEK.

Sabah

Sabah State Railway: Karung Berkunci 2047, 88999 Kota Kinabalu; tel. (88) 254611; fax (88) 236395; 134 track-km of 1-m gauge (1995); goods and passenger services from Tanjong Aru to Tenom, serving part of the west coast and the interior; diesel trains are used; Gen. Man. Ir BENNY WANG.

ROADS

Peninsular Malaysia

Peninsular Malaysia's road system is extensive, in contrast to those of Sabah and Sarawak. In 1999 the road network in Malaysia totalled an estimated 65,877 km, of which 16,206 km were highways and 31,777 km secondary roads; 75.8% of the network was paved.

Sabah

Jabatan Kerja Raya Sabah (Sabah Public Works Department): Jalan Sembulan, 88582 Kota Kinabalu, Sabah; tel. (88) 244333; fax

MALAYSIA — Directory

(88) 237234; e-mail pos@jkr.sabah.gov.my; internet www.jkr.sabah.gov.my; f. 1881; implements and maintains public infrastructures such as roads, bridges, buildings and sewerage systems throughout Sabah; maintains a network totalling 12,106 km, of which 3,908 km were sealed roads; Dir ANGIN Haji AJIK.

Sarawak

Jabatan Kerja Raya Sarawak (Sarawak Public Works Department): Tingkat 11–18, Wisma Saberkas, Jalan Tun Abg Haji Openg, 93582 Kuching, Sarawak; tel. (82) 203100; fax (82) 429679; e-mail limkh@sarawaknet.gov.my; internet www.jkr.sarawak.gov.my; implements and maintains public infrastructures in Sarawak; road network totalling 10,979 km, of which 3,986 km were sealed roads; Dir HUBERT THIAN CHONG HUI.

SHIPPING

The ports in Malaysia are classified as federal ports, under the jurisdiction of the federal Ministry of Transport, or state ports, responsible to the state ministries of Sabah and Sarawak.

Peninsular Malaysia

The federal ports in Peninsular Malaysia are Klang (the principal port), Pinang, Johor and Kuantan.

Johor Port Authority: 6A1–8A1 Pusat Perdagangan Pasir Gudang, Jalan Bandar, 81700 Pasir Gudang, Johor; tel. (7) 2534000; fax (7) 2517684; e-mail admin@lpj.gov.my; internet www.lpj.gov.my; f. 1973; Gen. Man. MOHD ROZALI BIN MOHD ALI.

Johor Port Bhd: POB 151, 81707 Pasir Gudang, Johor; tel. (7) 2535888; fax (7) 2510980; e-mail jpb@johorport.com.my; internet www.johorport.com.my; Exec. Chair. Dato' MOHD TAUFIK ABDULLAH.

Klang Port Authority: POB 202, Jalan Pelabuhan, 42005 Port Klang, Selangor; tel. (3) 31688211; fax (3) 31670211; e-mail onestopagency@pka.gov.my; internet www.pka.gov.my; f. 1963; Gen. Man. Datin Paduka O. C. PHANG.

Kuantan Port Authority: Tanjung Gelang, POB 161, 25720 Kuantan, Pahang; tel. (9) 5858000; fax (9) 5833866; e-mail lpktn@lpktn.gov.my; internet www.lpktn.gov.my; f. 1974; Gen. Man. KHAIRUL ANUAR BIN ABDUL RAHMAN.

Penang Port Commission: 3A-6 Sri Weld Bldg, Weld Quay, Pinang; tel. (4) 2633211; fax (4) 2626211; e-mail sppp@po.jaring.my; internet www.penangport.gov.my; f. 1956; Gen. Man. Dato' Capt. Haji ADBUL RAHIM ABDUL AZIZ.

Sabah

The chief ports are Kota Kinabalu, Sandakan, Tawau, Lahad Datu, Kudat, Semporna and Kunak and are administered by the Sabah Ports Authority. Many international shipping lines serve Sabah. Local services are operated by smaller vessels. The Sapangar Bay oil terminal, 25 km from Kota Kinabalu wharf, can accommodate oil tankers of up to 30,000 dwt.

Sabah Ports Authority: Bangunan SPA, Jalan Tun Fuad, Tanjung Lipat, Locked Bag 2005, 88617 Kota Kinabalu, Sabah; tel. (88) 538400; fax (88) 223036; e-mail sabport@po.jaring.my; internet www.infosabah.com.my/spa; f. 1968; Gen. Man. MAYONG OMAR.

Sarawak

There are four port authorities in Sarawak: Kuching, Rajang, Miri and Bintulu. Kuching, Rajang and Miri are statutory ports, while Bintulu is a federal port. Kuching port serves the southern region of Sarawak, Rajang port the central region, and Miri port the northern region.

Kuching Port Authority: Jalan Pelabuhan, Pending, POB 530, 93450 Kuching, Sarawak; tel. (82) 482144; fax (82) 481696; e-mail hq@kuport.com.my; internet www.kpa.gov.my; f. 1961; Gen. Man. LIU MOI FONG.

Rajang Port Authority: 96000 Sibu, Sarawak; tel. (84) 319004; fax (84) 318754; e-mail rajang@po.jaring.my; f. 1970; Gen. Man. Haji BAHRIN Haji ADENG.

Principal Shipping Companies

Achipelego Shipping (Sarawak) Sdn Bhd: Lot 267/270, Jalan Chan Chin Ann, POB 2998, 93758 Kuching; tel. (82) 412581; fax (82) 416249; Gen. Man. MICHAEL M. AMAN.

Malaysia Shipping Corpn Sdn Bhd: Office Tower, Plaza Berjaya, Suite 14C, 14th Floor, 12 Jalan Imbi, 55100 Kuala Lumpur; tel. (3) 21418788; fax (3) 21429214; Chair. Y. C. CHANG.

Malaysian International Shipping Corpn Bhd (National Shipping Line of Malaysia): Menara Dayabumi, Level 25, Jalan Sultan Hishamuddin, 50050 Kuala Lumpur; tel. (3) 22738088; fax (3) 22736602; e-mail asmadput@miscbhd.com; internet www.misc.com.my; f. 1968; regular sailings between the Far East, South-East Asia, Australia, Japan and Europe; also operates chartering, tanker, haulage and warehousing and agency services; major shareholder, Petroliam Nasional Bhd (PETRONAS); Chair. Tan Sri Dato' MOHD HASSAN BIN MARICAN; Pres. and CEO Dato' SHAMSUL AZHAR BIN ABBAS.

Perbadanan Nasional Shipping Line Bhd (PNSL): Kuala Lumpur; tel. (3) 2932211; fax (3) 2930493; f. 1982; specializes in bulk cargoes; Chair. Tunku Dato' SHAHRIMAN BIN Tunku SULAIMAN; Exec. Dep. Chair. Dato' SULAIMAN ABDULLAH.

Persha Shipping Agencies Sdn Bhd: Bangunan Mayban Trust, Penthouse Suite, Jalan Pinang, 10200 Pinang; tel. (4) 2612400; fax (4) 2623122; Man. Dir MOHD NOOR MOHD KAMALUDIN.

Syarikat Perkapalan Kris Sdn Bhd (The Kris Shipping Co Ltd): 3AO7 Block A, Kelana Centre Point, 3 Jalan SS7/19, Kelana Jaya; POB 8428, 46789 Petaling Jaya, Selangor; tel. (3) 7046477; fax (3) 7048007; domestic services; Chair. Dato' Seri SYED NAHAR SHAHABUDIN; Gen. Man. ROHANY TALIB; Dep. Gen. Man. THO TEIT CHANG.

Trans-Asia Shipping Corpn Sdn Bhd: Unit 715–718, Block A, Kelana Business Centre, 97 Jalan SS7/2, Kelana Jaya, 47301 Petaling Jaya, Selangor; tel. (3) 78802020; fax (4) 78802200; e-mail bernard@tasco.com.my; internet www.tasco.com.my; Exec. Dir BERNARD TAN.

CIVIL AVIATION

The new Kuala Lumpur International Airport (KLIA), situated in Sepang, Selangor (50 km south of Kuala Lumpur) began operations in June 1998, with an initial capacity of 25m.–30m. passengers a year, rising to 45m. by 2020. It replaced Subang Airport in Kuala Lumpur (which was renamed the Sultan Abdul Aziz Shah Airport in 1996). An express rail link between central Kuala Lumpur and KLIA opened in early 2001. There are regional airports at Kota Kinabalu, Pinang, Johor Bahru, Kuching and Pulau Langkawi. In addition, there are airports catering for domestic services at Alor Star, Ipoh, Kota Bahru, Kuala Terengganu, Kuantan and Melaka in Peninsular Malaysia, Sibu, Bintulu and Miri in Sarawak and Sandakan, Tawau, Lahad Datu and Labuan in Sabah. There are also numerous smaller airstrips.

Department of Civil Aviation (Jabatan Penerbangan Awam Malaysia): Aras 1–4, Lot 4G4, Presint 4, Pusat Pentadbiran Kerajaan Persekutuan, 62570 Putrajaya; tel. (3) 88714000; fax (3) 88714331; e-mail webmaster@dca.gov.my; internet www.dca.gov.my; Dir-Gen. Dato' KOK SOO CHON.

Air Asia Sdn Bhd: Asia Pacific Auction Center, 1st Floor, Sultan Abdul Aziz Shah Airport, 47200 Subang, Selangor; tel. (3) 78445555; fax (3) 78445400; e-mail tellus@airasia.com; internet www.airasia.com; f. 1993; a second national airline, budget carrier with a licence to operate domestic, regional and international flights; 85%-owned by HICOM; Chair. PAHAMIN A. RAJAB; Chief Exec. TONY FERNANDES.

Berjaya Air: Apprentice Training Bldg, 1st Floor, Mas Complex B (Hangar 1), Lapangan Terbang Sultan Abdul Aziz Shah, Shah Alam, Selangor, 47200 Kuala Lumpur; tel. (3) 7476828; fax (3) 7476228; e-mail berjayaa@tm.net.my; f. 1989; scheduled and charter domestic services; Pres. Dato TENGKU ADNAN MANSOR.

Malaysia Airlines: 31st Floor, Bangunan MAS, Jalan Sultan Ismail, 50250 Kuala Lumpur; tel. (3) 21655140; fax (3) 21633178; e-mail corpcomm@mas.com.my; internet www.malaysiaairlines.com.my; f. 1971 as the Malaysian successor to the Malaysia Singapore Airlines (MSA); known as Malaysian Airline System (MAS) until Oct. 1987; 114 international routes and 118 domestic routes; Chair. Dato' Dr MOHAMED MUNIR BIN ABDUL MAJID; Man. Dir and CEO IDRIS JALA.

Pelangi Airways Sdn Bhd: Technology Resource Tower, 18th Floor, 161B Jalan Ampang, 50450 Kuala Lumpur; tel. (3) 5532294; fax (3) 5532292; f. 1988; domestic scheduled passenger services; Chair. Tan Sri SAW HWAT LYE.

Transmile Air Sdn Bhd: Wisma Semantan, Mezzanine 2, Block B, 12 Jalan Gelenggang, Bukit Damansara, 50490 Kuala Lumpur; tel. (3) 2537718; fax (3) 2537719; f. 1992; scheduled and charter regional and domestic services for pasengers and cargo; Chair. Tan Sri ZAINOL MAHMOOD.

Tourism

Malaysia has a rapidly-growing tourist industry, and tourism remains an important source of foreign-exchange earnings. In 2004 some 15.7m. tourists visited Malaysia, an increase of 48.5% compared with the previous year. In 2004 tourist receipts totalled RM 29,651.4m.

Malaysia Tourism Promotion Board: Menara Dato' Onn, 15th–18th, 24th–27th, 29th–30th Floors, Putra World Trade Centre, 45 Jalan Tun Ismail, 50480 Kuala Lumpur; tel. (3) 26158188; fax (3) 26935884; e-mail enquiries@tourism.gov.my; internet www.tourismmalaysia.gov.my; f. 1972 to co-ordinate and promote

MALAYSIA

activities relating to tourism in Malaysia; ; Chair. Datuk ABDULLAH JONID; Dep. Chair. Dato' KEE PHAIK CHEEN.

Sabah Tourist Association: POB 12181, 88824 Kota Kinabalu; tel. (88) 221234; fax (88) 218909; e-mail willie@tm.net.my; f. 1963; 55 mems; parastatal promotional org.; Chair. THOMAS MORE WILLIE.

Sarawak Tourism Board: Levels 6 and 7, Bangunan Yayasan Sarawak, Jalan Masjid, 93400 Kuching; tel. (82) 423600; fax (82) 416700; e-mail stb@sarawaktourism.com; internet www.sarawaktourism.com; f. 1995; CEO GRACIE GEIKIE.

THE MALDIVES

Introductory Survey

Location, Climate, Language, Religion, Flag, Capital

The Republic of Maldives (commonly referred to as 'the Maldives') is in southern Asia. The country, lying about 675 km (420 miles) south-west of Sri Lanka, consists of 1,192 small coral islands (of which 197 are inhabited), grouped in 26 natural atolls (but divided, for administrative purposes, into 20 atolls), in the Indian Ocean. The climate is hot and humid. The average annual temperature is 27°C (80°F), with little daily or seasonal variation, while annual rainfall is generally between 2,540 mm and 3,800 mm (100 ins to 150 ins). The national language is Dhivehi (Maldivian), which is related to Sinhala. Islam is the state religion, and most Maldivians are Sunni Muslims. The national flag (proportions 2 by 3) is red, with a green rectangle, containing a white crescent, in the centre. The capital is Malé.

Recent History

The Maldives, called the Maldive Islands until April 1969, formerly had an elected Sultan as head of state. The islands were placed under British protection, with internal self-government, in 1887. They became a republic in January 1953, but the sultanate was restored in February 1954. The Maldives became fully independent, outside the Commonwealth, on 26 July 1965. Following a referendum, the country became a republic again in November 1968, with Amir Ibrahim Nasir, Prime Minister since 1957, as President.

In 1956 the Maldivian and British Governments agreed to the establishment of a Royal Air Force staging post on Gan, an island in the southernmost atoll, Addu. In 1975 the British Government's decision to close the base and to evacuate British forces created a large commercial and military vacuum. In October 1977 President Nasir rejected an offer of an annual payment of US $1m. from the USSR to lease the former base on Gan, announcing that he would not lease the island for military purposes, nor lease it to a superpower. In 1981 the President announced plans to establish an industrial zone on Gan. By 1990 there were two factories (producing ready-made garments) operating on Gan. The airport on Gan, which links the capital, Malé, with the south, is now fully operational and became an international airport in late 2005.

A new Constitution, promulgated in 1968, vested considerable powers in the President, including the right to appoint and dismiss the Prime Minister and the Cabinet of Ministers.

In March 1975, following rumours of a coup conspiracy, President Nasir dismissed the Prime Minister, Ahmed Zaki, and the premiership was abolished. Unexpectedly, President Nasir announced that he would not seek re-election at the end of his second term in 1978. To succeed him, the Majlis (legislature) chose Maumoon Abdul Gayoom, Minister of Transport under Nasir, who was approved by referendum in July 1978 and took office in November. President Gayoom announced that his main priority would be the development of the poor rural regions, while in foreign affairs the existing policy of non-alignment would be continued.

Ex-President Nasir left the country after his resignation, but the authorities subsequently sought his return to the Maldives, where he was required to answer charges of misappropriating government funds. In 1980 President Gayoom confirmed an attempted coup against the Government and implicated Nasir in the alleged plot. Nasir was to stand trial, in his absence, on these and other charges. In April 1981 Ahmed Naseem, former Deputy Minister of Fisheries and brother-in-law of Nasir, was sentenced to life imprisonment for plotting to overthrow President Gayoom. Nasir himself denied any involvement in the coup, and attempts to extradite him from Singapore were unsuccessful. (In July 1990, however, President Gayoom officially pardoned Nasir *in absentia*, in recognition of the role that he had played in winning national independence.) In September Gayoom was re-elected as President, for a further five years, by a national referendum (with 95.6% of the popular vote). In September 1988 he was again re-elected unopposed, for a third five-year term, obtaining a record 96.4% of the popular vote.

Another attempt to depose President Gayoom took place in November 1988, when a sea-borne mercenary force, which was composed of around 80 alleged Sri Lankan Tamil separatists (led by a disaffected Maldivian businessman, Abdullah Luthufi), landed in Malé and endeavoured to seize control of important government installations. At the request of President Gayoom, however, the Indian Government dispatched an emergency contingent of 1,600 troops, which rapidly and successfully suppressed the attempted coup. Nineteen people were reported to have been killed in the fighting. In September 1989 the President commuted to life imprisonment the death sentences imposed on 12 Sri Lankans and four Maldivians, who took part in the aborted coup.

In February 1990, despite alleged opposition from powerful members of the privileged élite, President Gayoom announced that, as part of proposals for a broad new policy of liberalization and democratic reform, he was planning to introduce legislation, in the near future, enabling him to distribute powers, currently enjoyed by the President alone, amongst other official bodies. A further sign of growing democratization in the Maldives was the holding of discussions by the President's Consultative Council, in early 1990, concerning freedom of speech (particularly in the local press). In April, however, it became apparent that some Maldivians opposed political change, when three pro-reform members of the Majlis received anonymous death threats. A few months later, following the emergence of several politically outspoken magazines, including *Sangu* (The Conchshell), there was an abrupt reversal of the Government's policy regarding the liberalization of the press. All publications not sanctioned by the Government were banned, and a number of leading writers and publishers were arrested.

As part of a major cabinet reshuffle in May 1990, President Gayoom dismissed the Minister of State for Defence and National Security, Ilyas Ibrahim (who also held the Trade and Industries portfolio and headed the State Trading Corporation), from his post, following the latter's abrupt and unannounced departure from the country. The Government later disclosed that Ibrahim (Gayoom's brother-in-law) was to have appeared before a presidential special commission investigating alleged embezzlement and misappropriation of government funds. On his return to the Maldives in August, Ibrahim was placed under house arrest. In March 1991, however, the special commission concluded that there was no evidence of involvement, either direct or indirect, by Ibrahim in the alleged financial misdeeds; in the same month the President appointed Ibrahim as Minister of Atolls Administration. In April the President established an anti-corruption board, which was to investigate allegations of corruption, bribery, fraud, misappropriation of government funds and property, and misuse of government office.

In early August 1993, a few weeks before the Majlis vote on the presidential candidate, Gayoom was informed that Ibrahim, whose position as Minister of Atolls Administration had afforded him the opportunity to build a political base outside Malé (where he already enjoyed considerable popularity), was seeking the presidency and attempting to influence members of the Majlis (at that time, the Majlis nominated and elected by secret ballot a single candidate, who was presented to the country in a referendum). In the Majlis vote, held in late August, the incumbent President, who had previously been unanimously nominated for the presidency by the legislature, obtained 28 votes, against 18 for his brother-in-law. For his allegedly unconstitutional behaviour, however, Ibrahim was charged with attempting to 'influence the members of the Majlis' and he promptly left the country. Ibrahim was subsequently tried *in absentia* and sentenced to 15 years' imprisonment. In addition, his brother, Abbas Ibrahim, was removed from his post as Minister of Fisheries and Agriculture. (Ibrahim returned to the Maldives in 1996 when he was placed under house arrest; this restriction was lifted in 1997.) In October 1993 Gayoom's re-election as President for a further five years was endorsed by a national referendum, in which he obtained 92.8% of the popular vote.

In November 1994, at an official ceremony marking Republic Day, President Gayoom outlined various measures intended to strengthen the political system and to advance the process of democratization. These included the granting of greater autonomy and responsibilities to members of the Cabinet of Ministers, the introduction of regulations governing the conduct of civil servants (in order to increase their accountability), the introduction of democratic elections to island development committees and atoll committees, and the establishment of a Law Commission to carry out reforms to the judicial system.

In November 1996 President Gayoom effected an extensive cabinet reshuffle and a reorganization of government bodies, including the establishment of a Supreme Council for Islamic Affairs, which was to be under direct presidential control and was to advise the Government on matters relating to Islam. In early 1997 President Gayoom announced that the Citizens' Special Majlis (which was established in 1980 with the specific task of amending the Constitution) had resolved to complete the revision of the Constitution during that year and to implement the amended version by 1 January 1998. The Citizens' Special Majlis finished its 17-year-long task in early November 1997. The revised Constitution was ratified by the President on 27 November and came into effect, as planned, on 1 January 1998. Under the new 156-article Constitution, a formal, multi-candidate contest was permitted for the legislature's nomination for the presidency; no restriction was placed on the number of terms a president may serve; for administrative purposes, the number of atolls was increased from 19 to 20; the Majlis, which was henceforth known as the People's Majlis, was enlarged from 48 to 50 seats; the Citizens' Special Majlis was renamed the People's Special Majlis; the rights of the people were expanded; parliamentary immunity was introduced; the office of auditor-general was created; the post of commissioner of elections was constitutionalized; ministers were afforded greater power; public officers were made more accountable; parliamentary questions were allowed; and judges and magistrates were obliged to take special oaths of loyalty.

In September 1998 five individuals declared their candidacy for the presidency; the People's Majlis unanimously voted by secret ballot for the incumbent President Gayoom to go forward to the national referendum. In the referendum, which was held in mid-October, Gayoom was re-elected as President for a fifth term in office, obtaining 90.9% of the popular vote. Following his re-election, the President carried out a cabinet reorganization. In an unexpected move, Ilyas Ibrahim was appointed to hold the new portfolio of transport and civil aviation.

In November 1999 elections for 42 members of the 50-seat People's Majlis were conducted (on a non-partisan basis). In September 2000 the Comprehensive Nuclear Test Ban Treaty was ratified by the Maldives. As part of a government initiative to promote the advancement of women in public life, President Gayoom appointed a woman as the new Island Chief of Himmafushi in June 2001. In December a woman was appointed as Atoll Chief of Vaavu Atoll (the first woman to be assigned a senior executive position of an atoll).

Meanwhile, in early 2001 an attempt by 42 prominent Maldivians, including members of the People's Majlis, former cabinet ministers and businessmen, to register the newly formed Maldivian Democratic Party (MDP) was blocked by the People's Majlis on the grounds that the existence of political parties would encourage divisions among the public and, therefore, be counter-productive. It was believed by some, however, that President Gayoom had enforced the decision and, in doing so, had acted unconstitutionally.

In July 2002 three journalists were charged with defamation and inciting violence and sentenced to life imprisonment (their assistant was sentenced to a term of 10 years) for writing articles criticizing the President and the Government. In early 2003 international activists demanded the release of the detainees, claiming that the journalists had not advocated violent opposition to President Gayoom or the Government, and that they had only been exercising their right to freedom of speech. In July a businessman was sentenced to life imprisonment for publishing an article via the internet urging that the Government be overthrown. Later that month the human rights organization Amnesty International issued a report citing frequent cases of arbitrary detentions, unfair trials and long-term imprisonment and torture of political opponents in the Maldives. The human rights group urged the Government to release political prisoners, investigate allegations of torture and reform the criminal justice system. The Maldives authorities strongly rejected the allegations.

In September 2003 detainees at a prison in Malé held protests in response to the death of a fellow prisoner. Reports of the violent suppression of the rioting by the country's National Security Service (NSS), and the death of another two detainees, prompted major anti-Government protests in the capital (the first ever during President Gayoom's tenure). Large numbers of alleged demonstrators were subsequently arrested, and a curfew was imposed on the city. Gayoom appealed for calm and announced an investigation into the death of the prisoners (the number of fatalities later increased to four, after one died in prison). Eleven members of the NSS were arrested for their involvement, and the Deputy Chief of the NSS and Police Commissioner, Brig. Adam Zahir, was removed (he was appointed executive director of the Ministry of Information, Arts and Culture until his reinstatement as Police Commissioner in mid-February 2004, after the inquiry cleared him of any misconduct). Amnesty International reiterated demands for an end to widespread political repression and to the violation of human rights and for reform of the judicial system.

On 25 September 2003, nevertheless, Gayoom was re-elected unanimously by secret ballot in the People's Majlis for a sixth presidential term, defeating three other candidates. His re-election was ratified at a public referendum on 17 October, where he secured 90.3% of the votes cast. One day after his new term began President Gayoom effected a cabinet reorganization, in which Dr Mohamed Munavvar, the Attorney-General, and Ibrahim Hussain Zaki, the Minister of Planning and National Development, were dismissed. Gayoom gave no reason for the changes, although it was alleged that the two had been removed for supporting reformers attempting to register a political party. Gayoom also announced that the judicial system, executive and legislature would be reformed over the next five years (without specifying what the changes would be) and that a human rights commission would be established in Malé. In the same month political activists decided to establish the MDP (which had been prevented from registering as a political party in the Maldives in 2001—see above) in exile in Sri Lanka, in response to the rise in discontent with the Maldives Government. In mid-February 2004 members of the MDP claimed that more than 15 of its supporters had been arrested in Malé in an alleged attempt to disrupt a planned protest march; however, the Government asserted that the raids were aimed at criminal offenders and that only eight people had been detained.

In December 2003 a Human Rights Commission was established. At the end of that month a report by the Presidential Commission investigating the death of four prisoners in September 2003 (see above) was submitted to President Gayoom. In his speech on the findings of the Commission to the People's Majlis in January 2004, Gayoom stated that the security personnel involved in the prisoners' deaths had acted illegally and would be prosecuted. The President also announced that a programme of penal reform was under way. However, Mohamed Latheef, the exiled leader of the MDP, criticized the report, claiming that the names of those responsible for the deaths had been omitted from the report, and demanded the President's resignation.

In May 2004 the election, by universal suffrage, of a People's Special Majlis took place. Voters chose 42 members out of 121 independent candidates. The President appointed another eight people to serve on the council; the People's Special Majlis also included members of the People's Majlis and the Council of Ministers. The People's Special Majlis was empowered to amend the Constitution. At the same time Gayoom invited members of the public to send him proposals for constitutional reform. In early June Gayoom himself proposed a number of radical constitutional reforms. He suggested that a President's tenure should be limited to two five-year terms and that women should be allowed to stand for the presidency. According to the reforms, the President would also lose the right to appoint eight members of the People's Majlis. The People's Majlis would become independent of the executive and the post of Prime Minister would be created. The judiciary would be restructured: a Supreme Court would be created as the highest court of appeal, which the President would appoint, on the advice of the People's Majlis. Furthermore, the formation and functioning of political parties would be allowed. The People's Special Majlis, which was sworn in on 15 June, convened in July to discuss the proposals.

In mid-August 2004 President Gayoom declared an indefinite state of emergency after a pro-democracy protest in the capital became violent. Four police officers were reportedly stabbed and about 185 people were arrested during the protests. The Government called the demonstration a coup attempt, a charge denied by the opposition MDP. The exiled opposition leader Latheef accused the Government of 'ruthlessly suppressing dissent'. The

Government invited a European Union (EU) fact-finding team to Malé. The EU envoys, however, were denied access to the detainees and expressed concern about the continuing detention without charge of the alleged protesters and the ongoing state of emergency. By early September 122 people had been released, while about 60 people remained in detention, including the former Attorney-General, Dr Mohamed Munavvar, and members of the People's Special Majlis. On 1 September, meanwhile, Gayoom relinquished the defence and finance portfolios, as part of a cabinet reorganization, in a move towards government reform. Ismail Shafeeu and Mohamed Jaleel were appointed as the new Ministers of Defence and National Security and of Finance and Treasury, respectively. Gayoom's announcement was made amid international criticism of the Government's suppression of the August demonstration.

In October 2004 the state of emergency that had been declared in August was revoked. While a curfew was still in place, the lifting of the state of emergency meant that the opposition members indefinitely detained following the August pro-democracy protest would either have to be charged or released from prison. In December four of the detained opposition members were charged with treason. However, later in that month President Gayoom announced that all charges of treason and public order offences against those taken into custody following the August protest were to be suspended.

On 26 December 2004 a tsunami generated by a massive earthquake in the Indian Ocean, off the coast of Indonesia, devastated many of the low-lying Maldive islands. While the resultant death toll was not as high as might have been expected, several of the islands were rendered uninhabitable and an estimated 15,000 people were left homeless by the disaster. The economic consequences of the catastrophe on the Maldives were extensive, owing in large part to the significant contribution made by the tourism industry to the economy. The process of reconstruction continued in 2006.

On 22 January 2005 149 independent candidates contested elections to the People's Majlis. The elections had been postponed from the previous month owing to the December tsunami. Candidates supported by the opposition MDP reportedly succeeded in winning 18 of the 42 available legislative seats. However, the Government stated that only 12 opposition candidates had done so, claiming that the results were a sign of widespread popular support for its reform policies. President Gayoom insisted after the election that he intended to establish a multi-party democracy in the Maldives within one year.

In May 2005 Fathimath Nisreen, who had been sentenced to 10 years' imprisonment in July 2002 for allegedly having participated in subversive activities, was freed, having received a presidential pardon. In June the People's Majlis unanimously approved a constitutional amendment permitting the registration of political parties in the Maldives, reversing its 2001 decision opposing the establishment of a multi-party democracy. The MDP was subsequently officially registered in the Maldives as a political party, together with several others, including the Dhivehi Raiyyithunge Party established by President Gayoom. In mid-July Gayoom instigated a major reorganization of his Cabinet in which, most notably, the long-serving Minister of Foreign Affairs, Fathulla Jameel, was dismissed and replaced by Dr Ahmed Shaheed. Jameel later resigned from his seat in the People's Majlis. In the following month Qasim Ibrahim was sworn in as Minister of Finance and Treasury, replacing Mohamed Jaleel.

In August 2005 a protest took place in Malé calling for the release of all political prisoners. Shortly afterwards the Chairman of the MDP, Mohamed Nasheed, was arrested, provoking several days of unrest in the capital and on various other atolls. Nasheed was subsequently charged with terrorism and attempting to perpetrate anti-Government actions; his trial began in October. Also in October Jennifer Latheef, daughter of the exiled Mohamed Latheef, was convicted of having incited a riot in Malé in September 2003 (see above) and sentenced to a 10-year prison term. Amnesty International condemned the trial, describing Jennifer Latheef as a 'prisoner of conscience'. In February 2006 two dissidents who had been sentenced to lengthy prison terms in 2002 were released, having received presidential pardons.

Meanwhile, in early 2006 meetings of the People's Special Majlis, which had been convened in order that it could begin work upon amending the Constitution, were obstructed by President Gayoom's refusal to permit the removal of presidential appointees from the body. The opposition MDP condemned the continued presence of representatives who had not been elected, stressing that they should be withdrawn in advance of the redrafting of the Constitution, and also proposed that the President's power to assent to the Constitution should be removed. Tensions were heightened in late February when the Speaker of the Special Majlis, Abbas Ibrahim, removed a scheduled debate on the matter from the legislative agenda. The MDP boycotted the opening of the People's Majlis in that month in protest at what it alleged to be the President's obstruction of the constitutional amendment process.

In November 1989, meanwhile, the Maldives hosted an international conference, with delegates from other small island nations, to discuss the threat posed to low-lying island countries by the predicted rise in sea-level caused by heating of the earth's atmosphere as a result of pollution (the 'greenhouse effect'). In June 1990 an Environmental Research Unit, which was to operate under the Ministry of Planning and the Environment, was established in the Maldives. The Maldives again expressed its serious concern with regard to problems of world-wide environmental pollution when it hosted the 13th conference of the UN's Intergovernmental Panel on Climate Change (IPCC, see p. 148) in September 1997. In September 1999 a special session of the UN General Assembly was convened in New York to address the specific problems faced by the 43-member Alliance of Small Island States (see p. 395) (including the Maldives), notably climate change, rising sea levels and globalization. At the UN Millennium Summit meeting in September 2000 the President of the Maldives again took the opportunity to urge leaders to address environmental issues. The Government expressed its grave disappointment and concern at the USA's decision in April 2001 to reject the Kyoto Protocol to the UN's Framework Convention on Climate Change. The rest of the international community adopted the protocol in July after many of the targets had been reduced. The USA proposed an alternative initiative in February 2002; however, most states dismissed it as ineffective. In early March the Maldives, Kiribati and Tuvalu announced their decision to take legal action against the USA for refusing to sign the Kyoto Protocol (thus contributing to global warming, which has produced the rising sea levels that threaten to submerge the islands). President Gayoom attended the South Asian Regional Conference on Ecotourism in India in January 2002. At the World Summit on Sustainable Development held in September 2002 in Johannesburg, South Africa, President Gayoom warned the international community that low-lying islands were at greater risk than ever before. He called for urgent action, including the universal ratification and implementation of the Kyoto Protocol, to prevent a global environmental catastrophe. On his return to the Maldives, the President stated that some progress had been made in certain areas, although the decisions were not as far-reaching as desired by small island nations. The President again urged the international community to enforce the Kyoto Protocol during a television interview in August 2004.

The Maldives is a founder member of the South Asian Association for Regional Co-operation (SAARC, see p. 356), which was formally constituted in December 1985, and the country became a full member of the Commonwealth in June 1985. The Maldives' international standing was enhanced in November 1990, when it successfully hosted the fifth SAARC summit meeting, which was held in Malé. In November 2004 the Maldives opened its fourth resident diplomatic mission (in addition to those in Sri Lanka, at the UN headquarters in New York and in London, United Kingdom) in New Delhi, India. The 11th SAARC Summit Conference of heads of state and government took place in early January 2002 in Kathmandu, Nepal, despite rising tensions between India and Pakistan. The member countries signed two conventions on the promotion of child welfare in South Asia (proposed by President Gayoom) and the prevention and combat of the trafficking of women and children for prostitution. At the 12th SAARC Summit Conference in early January 2004, held in the Pakistani capital of Islamabad, the members agreed to form a South Asia Free Trade Area (SAFTA); this came into effect on 1 January 2006. The leaders also signed the Social Charter and agreed on the Additional Protocol on Terrorism. In April 2003 the number of countries with which the Maldives had established diplomatic relations stood at 136.

Government

Legislative power is held by the unicameral People's Majlis, with 50 members, including 42 elected for five years by universal adult suffrage (two by the National Capital Island and two from each of the 20 atolls) and eight appointed by the President. Executive power is vested in the President, who is elected by secret ballot by the People's Majlis (under the 1998 constitutional revisions, more than one candidate may be nominated for election) and endorsed in office for five years by a national referendum. He governs with the assistance of an appointed Cabinet of Ministers, which is responsible to the People's Majlis. The country has 21 administrative districts: the capital is under direct central administration while the 20 atolls are each under an atoll chief (verin) who is appointed by the President, under the general guidance of the Minister of Atolls Administration.

Economic Affairs

In 2004, according to estimates by the World Bank, the Maldives' gross national income (GNI), measured at average 2002–04 prices, was US $752m., equivalent to $2,510 per head. During 1995–2004, it was estimated, the population increased at an average annual rate of 2.4%, while gross domestic product (GDP) per head increased, in real terms, by an average of 5.1% per year. Overall GDP increased, in real terms, at an average annual rate of 7.6% in 1995–2004. According to the IMF, GDP growth increased to 8.5% in 2003, and rose to 8.8% in 2004. However, GDP contracted by an estimated 3.6% in 2005.

Agriculture and fishing contributed an estimated 8.6% of GDP (at constant 1995 prices) in 2004. About 14% of the total working population were employed in the sector (more than 10% in fishing) in 2000. In 2004 revenue from exports of marine products totalled 1,155.3m. rufiyaa, thus accounting for 73.5% of total export earnings. The fisheries sector suffered significant damage as a result of the December 2004 tsunami disaster, with the destruction of boats and equipment contributing to the loss of many livelihoods. Small quantities of various fruits, vegetables and cereals are produced, but virtually all of the principal staple foods have to be imported. As a result of salt-water intrusion caused by the tsunami, a significant amount of cultivable land was ruined. The dominant agricultural activity (not including fishing) in the Maldives is coconut production. The GDP of the agriculture and fisheries sector increased, in real terms, by an annual average of 4.3% in 1995–2004. Real agricultural GDP grew by 1.6% in 2003 and by 2.6% in 2004.

Industry (including mining, manufacturing, construction and utilities) employed about 19% of the working population in 2000, and, according to the Asian Development Bank (ADB, see p. 169), provided 16.2% of GDP in 2004. Sectoral GDP increased, in real terms, by an annual average of 9.8% in 1995–2004. Industrial GDP grew by 7.4% in 2003 and by 9.8% in 2004.

Mining and quarrying contributed 0.6% of GDP in 2004, and employed 0.5% of the working population in 2000. No reserves of petroleum or natural gas have, as yet, been discovered in Maldivian waters. According to the ADB, mining GDP increased, in real terms, by an annual average of 4.8% in 1995–2004. The GDP of the mining sector increased by 6.3% in 2003 and by 7.0% in 2004.

The manufacturing sector employed 13% of the working population in 2000, and contributed 7.7% of GDP in 2004. There are only a small number of 'modern' manufacturing enterprises in the Maldives, including fish-canning, garment-making and soft-drink bottling. Although cottage industries (such as the weaving of coir yarn and boat-building) employ nearly one-quarter of the total labour force, there is little scope for expansion, owing to the limited size of the domestic market. Because of its lack of manufacturing industries, the Maldives has to import most essential consumer and capital goods. In the late 1980s and 1990s traditional handicrafts, such as lacquer work and shell craft, revived as a result of the expansion of the tourism sector. Manufacturing GDP increased, in real terms, by an annual average of 7.4% in 1995–2004. Real manufacturing GDP grew by 15.5% in 2002, but by only 2.0% in 2003 and 1.7% in 2004.

Energy is derived principally from petroleum, imports of which comprised 11.8% of the cost of imports in 2001. Owing to a surge in commercial activities and a significant increase in construction projects in Malé, demand for electricity in the capital grew rapidly in the late 1980s and early 1990s. Accordingly, plans were formulated in late 1991 to augment the generating capacity of the power station in Malé and to improve the distribution network. By 2004 21 inhabited islands had been provided with electricity. In 2001 the third phase of the Malé power project, further to increase the capital's power supply, was under way. In December the ADB agreed to provide a loan to improve the supply of electricity to some 40 outer islands. In 2006 the ADB was to supply a further loan, of US $8m., to enable the electrification of those outer islands not included in the first project.

Following the decline of the shipping industry in the 1980s, tourism gained in importance as an economic sector, and by 1989 it had overtaken the fishing industry as the Maldives' largest source of foreign exchange. In 1999 the tourism sector provided 18.5% of GDP. In 2003 tourist arrivals increased by 16.3%, compared with the previous year, to reach 563,593. In that year receipts from tourism totalled an estimated 896.2m. rufiyaa. In 2004 tourist arrivals increased by a further 9.4%, to 616,716, and receipts grew to an estimated 1,044.9m. rufiyaa. In March 2004 the Government announced that nine more atolls would be opened for tourism and that 11 further islands would be converted into resorts. The devastating impact upon the Maldives of the massive tsunami in the Indian Ocean in December 2004 significantly affected the performance of the tourism sector in 2005, with several tourist resorts damaged and adverse publicity surrounding the disaster further discouraging prospective tourists. However, all the affected resorts had reopened by the end of that year and tourist arrivals were expected to have returned to pre-tsunami levels by the end of 2006. The services sector contributed 75.2% of GDP in 2004. The GDP of the sector increased, in real terms, by an annual average of 7.6% in 1995–2004. Compared with the previous year, sectoral GDP expanded by 9.5% in 2003 and by 9.4% in 2004.

In 2005 the Maldives recorded a visible trade deficit of an estimated US $517.2m., and there was a deficit of approximately $297.9m. on the current account of the balance of payments. In 2004 the principal source of imports was Singapore (accounting for 25.1% of the total); other major sources were Sri Lanka, the United Arab Emirates and India. The principal market for exports was the USA (accounting for 26.5% of the total); other major purchasers were Thailand, Sri Lanka and Japan. The principal exports were marine products (tuna being the largest export commodity) and clothing. The principal imports were machinery and mechanical appliances and electrical equipment, mineral products and textile and textile articles.

Foreign grant aid in 2000 totalled an estimated US $17.7m. Japan has traditionally been the Maldives' largest aid donor (disbursing $11.9m. in 1997). The 2005 budget envisaged expenditure of 4,742.9m. rufiyaa and revenue of 4,207.3m., including grants of 82.6m. rufiyaa. The budgetary deficit was equivalent to approximately 1.7% of GDP in 2004 but increased significantly, to the equivalent of 12.3% of GDP, in 2005. The Maldives' total external debt was $281.0m. at the end of 2003, of which $255.1m. was long-term public debt. In that year the cost of debt-servicing was equivalent to 3.6% of revenue from exports of goods and services. During 1995–2004 the average annual rate of inflation was 2.1%. According to the IMF, consumer prices increased by 6.4% in 2004 and 5.7% in 2005. According to the ADB, 2.0% of the labour force were unemployed in 2001.

The Maldives is a member of the UN Economic and Social Commission for Asia and the Pacific (ESCAP, see p. 33), the ADB, the Colombo Plan (see p. 385) and the South Asian Association for Regional Co-operation (SAARC, see p. 356).

One result of the rapid growth and increasing importance of the tourism sector in the Maldives from the late 1990s onwards was the Government's efforts to improve the infrastructure (including development of communication systems, sanitation and water supply). By 1999 the Maldivian telecommunications company, DHIRAAGU, had provided telephone facilities to all of the inhabited islands and, by February 2004, more than 72,000 inhabitants had also subscribed to mobile cellular telephones, with coverage reaching more than 70% of the population. However, despite a recovery in fish exports and buoyant tourism receipts in the latter half of the 1990s, the current-account deficit persisted and the trade deficit continued to grow. In early 2001 the Government opened up the export of fresh and canned fish to the private sector, and in that year the Maldives Industrial Fisheries Company recorded a 13% increase in sales of fish, compared with the previous year. In 2002 the fisheries sector continued to expand and tourism gradually began to recover. The current-account deficit, however, remained high and the fiscal deficit continued to grow, largely owing to an increase in government expenditure. Furthermore, the islands continued to experience a shortage of domestic labour: in 2003 about 33,765 expatriate workers (mainly from India, Sri Lanka and Bangladesh) were employed in the Maldives, and it was estimated that in 1999 almost 20% of the country's GDP went to non-Maldivians. In 2004 earnings from exports of fish increased by a further 18%, compared with the previous year. The Government had also commenced the introduction of necessary reforms for the development of the financial market. In December 2004 the tsunami generated by a massive earthquake in the Indian Ocean had a devastating effect on the Maldives, leading to widespread destruction of infrastructure and housing. An estimated 14 of the 200 inhabited islands were completely destroyed by the huge waves, which also damaged approximately 8% of the country's fishing fleet and several tourist resorts. The economic consequences of the disaster were profound; the cost of reconstruction was estimated at US $375m., the equivalent of approximately 50% of GDP. The Government was believed to have lost an estimated $40m. in revenue in 2005. In conjunction with a large increase in government expenditure, this contributed to a significant increase in both the fiscal and current-account deficits. As a direct result of the tsunami, the IMF estimated that GDP had contracted by 3.6% in 2005, compared with the 6.5% growth forecast before the disaster. The reconstruction effort was ongoing in early 2006, largely funded by international donors, although the Government continued to seek further international aid in order to overcome a budgetary shortfall. It was hoped that a significant increase in tourist arrivals towards the end of 2005 would contribute to a recovery in GDP in 2006. Extensive regulatory and structural reforms continued to be necessary if the economy was to attract the private investment needed to ensure continued growth and diversification and to reduce its vulnerability to external events. The high average annual rate of population growth (estimated at 2.7% in 1990–95), which has placed a heavy burden on the economy in general and on the congested capital island of Malé in particular, is an issue that is effectively being addressed (according to the results of the March 2000 census, the rate of population increase had fallen to 1.9% in 1995–2000). From 1997, in an attempt to solve the problem of overcrowding in Malé, the artificially constructed island of Hulhumalé was developed as a suburb to relieve congestion in the capital. The first group of people was appointed to move to the island in early 2004. The demand for local construction and transport generated by this project and other regional development programmes was beneficial to the economy.

Education

Education is not compulsory. There are three types of formal education: traditional Koranic schools (Makthab), Dhivehi-language primary schools (Madhrasa) and English-language primary and secondary schools. Schools of the third category are the only ones equipped to teach a standard curriculum. In 1984 a national curriculum was introduced in all schools. In 1989 the Government established a National Council on Education to oversee the development of education in the Maldives. Primary education begins at six years of age and lasts for five years. Secondary education, beginning at the age of 11, lasts for up to seven years, comprising a first cycle of five years and a second of two years. In 2000/01 the total enrolment at primary and secondary schools was equivalent to 101% of the school-age population. In that year primary enrolment was equivalent to 131% of children in the relevant age-group (boys 131%; girls 131%); the comparable ratio for secondary enrolment was 55% (boys 53%; girls 57%). The construction of the first secondary school outside Malé was completed, on Hithadoo Island in Addu atoll, in 1992. By late 2003 there were 22 schools in Malé and 293 schools in the rest of the Maldives. There is a full-time vocational training centre, a teacher-training institute, an institute of hotel and catering services, an Institute of Management and Administration, a Science Education Centre, an Islamic education centre, and a Non-formal Education Centre (renamed as Centre for Continuing Education in October 2002). The Maldives Institute of Technical Education, which was completed in late 1996, was expected to alleviate the problem of the lack of local skilled labour. The Maldives College of Higher Education, which was established to provide a uniform framework and policies for post-secondary education institutes, was opened in late 1998. At least 116 of the country's schools were affected by the December 2004 tsunami. In the aftermath of the disaster, eight schools required complete reconstruction. A large quantity of school equipment was also lost. Projected budgetary expenditure on education by the central Government in 2005 was 970.0m. rufiyaa, representing 20.5% of total spending.

Public Holidays

2006: 10 January* (Id al-Adha, feast of the Sacrifice), 31 January* (Islamic New Year), 1 April* (National Day), 11 April* (Birth of the Prophet Muhammad), 26–27 July (Independence Days), 24 September* (Ramadan begins), 24 October* (Id al-Fitr, end of Ramadan), 3 November (Victory Day), 11–12 November (Republic Days), 10 December (Fishermen's Day), 31 December* (Id al-Adha, feast of the Sacrifice).

2007: 20 January* (Islamic New Year), 20 March* (National Day), 31 March* (Birth of the Prophet Muhammad), 26–27 July (Independence Days), 13 September* (Ramadan begins), 13 October* (Id al-Fitr, end of Ramadan), 3 November (Victory Day), 11–12 November (Republic Days), 10 December (Fishermen's Day), 20 December* (Id al-Adha, feast of the Sacrifice).

* These holidays are dependent on the Islamic lunar calendar and may vary by one or two days from the dates given.

Statistical Survey

Source (unless otherwise stated): Ministry of Planning and National Development, Ghaazee Bldg, 4th Floor, Ameer Ahmed Magu, Malé 20-05; tel. 3322919; fax 3327351; internet www.planning.gov.mv.

AREA AND POPULATION

Area: 298 sq km (115 sq miles).

Population: 244,814 at census of 25 March 1995; 270,101 (males 137,200, females 132,901) at census of 31 March–7 April 2000; 289,480 (official estimate) at mid-2004.

Density (mid-2004): 971 per sq km.

Administrative Divisions (population, 2000 census): *Capital City* Malé 74,069. *Atolls*: North Thiladhunmathi 14,161, South Thiladhunmathi 16,956, North Miladhunmadulu 11,406, South Miladhunmadulu 14,486, North Maalhosmadulu 14,486, South Maalhosmadulu 9,612, Faadhippolhu 9,385, Malé 13,474, North Ari 5,518, South Ari 7,803, Felidhu 1,753, Mulakatholhu 5,084, North Nilandhe 3,827, South Nilandhe 5,067, Kolhumadulu 9,305, Hadhdhunmathi 11,588, North Huvadhu 8,249, South Huvadhu 11,886, Fuvahmulah 7,528, Addu 18,515.

Births and Deaths (2004): Registered live births 5,198 (birth rate 18.0 per 1,000); Registered deaths 1,007 (death rate 3.5 per 1,000).

Expectation of Life (WHO estimates, years at birth): 65 (males 66; females 64) in 2003. Source: WHO, *World Health Report*.

Economically Active Population (persons aged 12 years and over, census of April 2000): Agriculture, hunting and forestry 2,495; Fishing 9,294; Mining and quarrying 473; Manufacturing 11,081; Electricity, gas and water 1,132; Construction 3,691; Trade, restaurants and hotels 15,606; Transport, storage and communications 7,873; Financing, insurance, real estate and business services 1,690; Community, social and personal services 18,089; Activities not adequately defined 14,821; *Total employed* 86,245 (males 57,351, females 28,894); Unemployed 1,742 (males 928, females 814); *Total labour force* 87,987 (males 58,279, females 29,708).

HEALTH AND WELFARE

Key Indicators

Total Fertility Rate (children per woman, 2003): 5.3.

Under-5 Mortality Rate (per 1,000 live births, 2004): 46.

HIV/AIDS (% of persons aged 15–49, 2001): 0.06.

Physicians (per 1,000 head, 2000): 0.78.

Hospital Beds (per 1,000 head, 1990): 0.76.

Health Expenditure (2002): US $ per head (PPP): 307.

Health Expenditure (2002): % of GDP: 5.8.

Health Expenditure (2002): public (% of total): 87.7.

Access to Water (% of persons, 2002): 84.

Access to Sanitation (% of persons, 2002): 58.

Human Development Index (2003): ranking: 96.

Human Development Index (2003): value: 0.745.

For sources and definitions, see explanatory note on p. vi.

AGRICULTURE, ETC.

Principal Crops (production in long-term leased islands*, metric tons, 2004): Coconuts 127.1; Tender coconuts 28.6; Brinjal 62.6; Cucumbers 71.0; Pumpkins 29.0; Bitter gourds 3.4; Ridged peppers 7.6; Papaya 292.5; Watermelons 371.0; Bananas 60.1.
* Comprising the atolls of North Thiladhunmathi, South Thiladhunmathi, North Miladhunmadulu, South Ari, Mulakatholhu, North Nilandhe, Kolhumadulu and Hadhdhunmathi.

Coconuts (number): 43.5m. in 2002; 73.4m. in 2003; 40.6m. in 2004.

Sea Fishing ('000 metric tons, 2003): Total catch 155.4 (Skipjack tuna—Oceanic skipjack 108.3; Yellowfin tuna 22.9; Sharks, rays, skates, etc. 11.5. Source: FAO.

INDUSTRY

Selected Products (metric tons, 2003): Frozen tuna 47,546; Salted, dried or smoked fish 9.2; Canned fish 7,094. Source: FAO.

Electric Energy (million kWh): 130.3 in 2001; 140.8 in 2002; 156.7 in 2003.

FINANCE

Currency and Exchange Rates: 100 laari (larees) = 1 rufiyaa (Maldivian rupee). *Sterling, Dollar and Euro Equivalents* (30 December 2005): £1 sterling = 22.040 rufiyaa; US $1 = 12.800 rufiyaa; €1 = 15.100 rufiyaa; 1,000 rufiyaa = £45.37 = $78.13 = €66.22. *Average Exchange Rate* (rufiyaa per US dollar): 12.800 in 2003; 12.800 in 2004; 12.800 in 2005. Note: Between October 1994 and July 2001 the mid-point rate of exchange was maintained at US $1 = 11.77 rufiyaa. In July 2001 a new rate of $1 = 12.80 rufiyaa was introduced.

Budget (forecasts, million rufiyaa, 2005): *Revenue*: Tax revenue 1,877.5; Other current revenue 2,221.2; Capital revenue 26.0; Total 4,124.7, excl. grants received (82.6). *Expenditure*: General public services 1,029.4; Public order and internal security 726.1; Environmental protection 43.6; Education 970.0; Health 533.4; Social security and welfare 168.7; Community programmes 313.2; Economic services 818.5 (Agriculture and fishing 94.0, Trade and industry 49.9, Electricity, gas and water 31.7, Transport and communications 526.3, Tourism 116.6); Interest on public debt 140.0; Total 4,742.9 (Current 3,475.1, Capital 1,267.8), excl. net lending (−106.7).

International Reserves (US $ million at 31 December 2004): IMF special drawing rights 0.50; Reserve position in IMF 2.41; Foreign exchange 200.66; Total 203.57. Source: IMF, *International Financial Statistics*.

Money Supply (million rufiyaa at 31 December 2004): Currency outside banks 762.54; Demand deposits at commercial banks 1,662.46; Total money (incl. others) 2,520.12. Source: IMF, *International Financial Statistics*.

Cost of Living (Consumer Price Index; base: June 1995 = 100): All items 116.4 in 2002 (Food, excl. fish, 125.4; Fish 143.6; Clothing and footwear 97.7; Housing 106.8); 113.1 in 2003 (Food, excl. fish, 118.3; Fish 132.3; Clothing and footwear 97.5; Housing 105.9); 120.3 in 2004 (Food, excl. fish, 131.2; Fish 184.3; Clothing and footwear 95.5; Housing 103.7).

Gross Domestic Product by Economic Activity (million rufiyaa at constant 1995 prices, 2004): Agriculture and fishing 712.3; Coral and sand mining 47.2; Manufacturing 638.2; Electricity, gas and water supply 303.4; Construction 348.1; Wholesale and retail trade 325.1; Transport and communications 1,216.4; Finance, real estate and business services 730.9; Public administration 1,014.6; Other services (incl. tourism) 2,912.6; Sub-total 8,248.8; Indirect taxes *less* subsidies 1,034.7; *GDP in purchasers' values* 9,283.5. Source: Asian Development Bank, *Key Indicators of Developing Asian and Pacific Countries*.

Balance of Payments (US $ million, 2004): Exports of goods f.o.b. 181.0; Imports of goods f.o.b. −567.3; *Trade balance* −386.4; Exports of services 507.2; Imports of services −157.8; *Balance on goods and services* −36.9; Other income received 8.3; Other income paid −51.1; *Balance on goods, services and income* −79.7; Current transfers received 6.9; Current transfers paid −61.1; *Current balance* −133.9; Direct investment from abroad 14.7; Other investment assets 107.0; Other investment liabilities 30.8; Net errors and omissions 25.4; *Overall balance* 44.1. Source: IMF, *International Financial Statistics*.

Official Development Assistance (US $ million, 2000): Bilateral 12.1; Multilateral 7.2; *Total* 19.3 (Grants 17.7, Loans 1.6); *Per Caput Assistance* (US $): 71.4. Source: UN, *Statistical Yearbook for Asia and the Pacific*.

EXTERNAL TRADE

Principal Commodities (million rufiyaa, 2004): *Imports*: Live animals and animal products 385.9 (Dairy produce, eggs, honey and edible products 206.2); Vegetable products 485.1; Prepared food, beverages, spirits and tobacco 579.2; Mineral products 1,408.8 (Mineral fuels, oils, waxes, bituminous substances 1,161.4); Chemicals and allied industries 406.4; Wood, wood charcoal, cork, straw, plaiting materials and articles thereof 428.8 (Wood and articles of wood, and wood charcoal 425.0); Textiles and textile articles 684.4 (Cotton incl. yarns and woven fabrics thereof 192.8); Base metal and articles of base metal 564.4; Machinery and mechanical appliances and electrical equipment, parts and accessories 1,713.5 (Nuclear reactors, boilers, machinery and mechanical appliances, computers 927.1; Electrical machinery and equipment and parts thereof, telecommunications equipment, sound recorders, television recorders 786.4); Vehicles, aircraft, vessels and associated transport equipment 354.4 (Ships, boats and floating structures 261.2); Miscellaneous manufactured articles 331.6; Total (incl. others) 8,215.3. *Exports*: Marine products 1,155.3 (Fresh or chilled tuna 271.1; Frozen fish 449.7; Dried tuna 121.5; Canned fish 176.1); Apparel and clothing accessories 409.0; Total (incl. others) 1,572.3.

Principal Trading Partners (million rufiyaa, 2004): *Imports*: Australia 221.7; Bahrain 409.7; Canada 112.6; China, People's Republic 101.9; France 158.1; Germany 137.7; Hong Kong 133.3; India 842.7; Indonesia 163.8; Italy 153.7; Japan 154.5; Malaysia 623.8; New Zealand 107.3; Singapore 2,058.8; Sri Lanka 876.3; Thailand 313.4; United Arab Emirates 852.4; United Kingdom 175.3; USA 107.6; Total (incl. others) 8,215.3. *Exports*: France 36.3; Germany 77.2; Italy 27.0; Japan 184.1; Singapore 61.9; Sri Lanka 193.5; Thailand 368.9; United Kingdom 153.7; USA 416.7; Total (incl. others) 1,572.3.

TRANSPORT

Road Traffic (registered motor vehicles, 2004): Passenger cars 1,757; Buses, pick-ups and vans 1,178; Lorries and tractors 527; Motorcycles and mopeds 14,448; Total (incl. others) 18,715.

Merchant Shipping Fleet (displacement, '000 gross registered tons at 31 December): 58.1 in 2002; 63.7 in 2003; 78.1 in 2004. Source: Lloyd's Register-Fairplay, *World Fleet Statistics*.

International Shipping (freight traffic, '000 metric tons, 1990): Goods loaded 27; Goods unloaded 78. Source: UN, *Monthly Bulletin of Statistics*.

Civil Aviation (traffic at Malé International Airport, 2004): *International Flights*: Arrivals 711,388; Departures 721,508. *Domestic Flights*: Arrivals 321,022; Departures 307,322.

TOURISM

Foreign Visitors by Country of Nationality (2004): Austria 13,059; People's Republic of China (incl. Taiwan and Hong Kong) 20,599; France 46,156; Germany 72,967; Italy 131,044; Japan 46,939; Russia 18,075; Switzerland 29,252; United Kingdom 113,991; Total (incl. others) 616,716.

Tourism Receipts (million rufiyaa): 883.1 in 2002; 896.2 in 2003 (provisional figure); 1,044.9 in 2004 (estimate). Source: Ministry of Tourism and Civil Aviation, Malé.

COMMUNICATIONS MEDIA

Radio Receivers (July 2000): 29,724 registered.

Television Receivers (July 2000): 10,701 registered.

Telephones (main lines in use): 28,651 in 2002; 30,056 in 2003; 31,503 in 2004.

Mobile Cellular Telephones: 41,899 in 2002; 66,466 in 2003; 113,246 in 2004.

Personal Computers (2004): 36,000 in use.

Internet Users (registered): 1,067 in 2002; 1,155 in 2003; 1,260 in 2004.

Sources: Telecommunications Authority of Maldives, Malé; International Telecommunication Union.

EDUCATION

Schools (2003): 315.

Teachers (2003): Pre-primary 499; Primary 3,644; Lower secondary 1,760; Upper secondary 101.

Pupils (2003): Pre-primary 11,206; Primary 66,169; Lower secondary 25,486; Upper secondary 1,481; Special needs 66.

Maldives College of Higher Education (2003): Academic staff 138; Students 6,898. Source: Maldives College of Higher Education.

Adult Literacy Rate (UNESCO estimates): 97.2% (males 97.3%; females 97.2%) in 2002. Source: UN Development Programme, *Human Development Report*.

Directory

The Constitution

Following a referendum in March 1968, the Maldive Islands (renamed the Maldives in April 1969) became a republic on 11 November 1968. On 27 November 1997 the President ratified a new 156-article Constitution, which was to replace the 1968 Constitution; the new Constitution came into effect on 1 January 1998. The main constitutional provisions are summarized below:

STATE, SOVEREIGNTY AND CITIZENS

The Maldives shall be a sovereign, independent, democratic republic based on the principles of Islam, and shall be a unitary State, to be known as the Republic of Maldives. In this Constitution, the Republic of Maldives shall hereinafter be referred to as 'the Maldives'.

The powers of the State of the Maldives shall be vested in the citizens. Executive power shall be vested in the President and the Cabinet of Ministers, legislative power shall be vested in the People's Majlis (People's Council) and the People's Special Majlis, and the power of administering justice shall be vested in the President and the courts of the Maldives.

The religion of the State of the Maldives shall be Islam. The national language of the Maldives shall be Dhivehi.

FUNDAMENTAL RIGHTS AND DUTIES OF CITIZENS

Maldivian citizens are equal before and under the law and are entitled to the equal protection of the law. No Maldivian shall be deprived of citizenship, except as may be provided by law. No person shall be arrested or detained, except as provided by law. Any Maldivian citizen subjected to oppressive treatment shall have the right to appeal against such treatment to the concerned authorities and to the President.

The following are guaranteed: inviolability of residential dwellings and premises; freedom of education; inviolability of letters, messages and other means of communication; freedom of movement; the right to acquire and hold property; protection of property rights; the right to work; and freedom of expression, assembly and association.

Loyalty to the State and obedience to the Constitution and to the law of the Maldives shall be the duty of every Maldivian citizen, irrespective of where he may be.

THE PRESIDENT

The President shall be the Head of State, Head of Government and the Commander-in-Chief of the Armed Forces and of the Police.

The President shall be elected by secret ballot by the People's Majlis (more than one candidate may be nominated for election) and endorsed in office for five years by a national referendum.

In addition to the powers and functions expressly conferred on or assigned to the President by the Constitution and law, the President shall have the power to execute the following: appointment to and removal from office of the Vice-President, Chief Justice, Speaker and Deputy Speaker of the People's Majlis, Ministers, Attorney-General, Atoll Chiefs, judges, Auditor-General and Commissioner of Elections; appointment and dissolution of the Cabinet of Ministers; presiding over meetings of the Cabinet of Ministers; making a statement declaring the policies of the Government at the opening session of the People's Majlis every year; promulgating decrees, directives and regulations, as may be required from time to time for the purposes of ensuring propriety of the affairs of the Government and compliance with the provisions of the Constitution and law; holding public referendums on major issues; the declaration of war and peace.

While any person holds office as President, no proceedings shall be instituted or continued against him in any court or tribunal in respect of anything done or omitted to be done by him either in his official or private capacity.

A motion to remove the President from office may be considered in the People's Majlis only when one-third of the members of the Majlis have proposed it and two-thirds of the Majlis have resolved to consider it.

In the event that the presidency becomes vacant by reason of death, resignation or removal from office, the Speaker of the People's Majlis shall discharge the functions as Acting President from the time of occurrence of such vacancy. He shall continue to discharge these functions until a three-member Council is elected by a secret ballot of the People's Majlis to administer the State.

The President shall have the right to appoint at his discretion a Vice-President to discharge the duties and responsibilities assigned by the President.

THE CABINET OF MINISTERS

There shall be a Cabinet of Ministers appointed by the President, and the Cabinet shall be presided over by the President. The Cabinet of Ministers shall consist of the Vice-President (if any), Ministers charged with responsibility for Ministries and the Attorney-General.

The Cabinet of Ministers shall discharge the functions assigned to it by the President. The following shall be included in the said functions: to assist the President in formulating government policy on important national and international matters and issues; to advise the President on developing the Maldives economically and socially; to assist the President in the formulation of the annual state budget and government bills to be submitted to the People's Majlis; and to advise the President on the ratification of international treaties and agreements signed by the Maldivian Government with foreign administrations that require ratification by the State.

The President may, at his discretion, remove any Minister or the Attorney-General from office.

In the event of a vote of no confidence by the People's Majlis in a member of the Cabinet of Ministers, such member shall resign from office.

The President may dissolve the Cabinet of Ministers if, in his opinion, the Cabinet of Ministers is unable effectively to discharge its functions. Upon dissolution of the Cabinet of Ministers, the President shall inform the People's Majlis of the fact, specifying the reasons thereof, and shall appoint a new Cabinet of Ministers as soon as expedient.

THE PEOPLE'S MAJLIS

Legislative power, except the enactment of the Constitution, shall be vested in the People's Majlis. The People's Majlis shall consist of 50 members, of whom eight members shall be appointed by the President, two members elected from Malé and two members elected from each of the atolls. The duration of the People's Majlis shall be five years from the date on which the first meeting of the People's Majlis is held after its election. The Speaker and Deputy Speaker of the People's Majlis shall be appointed to and removed from office by the President. The Speaker shall not be a member of the People's Majlis, whereas the Deputy Speaker shall be appointed from among the members of the People's Majlis.

There shall be three regular sessions of the People's Majlis every year. The dates for the commencement and conclusion of these sessions shall be determined by the Speaker. An extraordinary sitting of the People's Majlis shall only be held when directed by the President. With the exception of the matters that, in accordance with the Constitution, require a two-thirds' majority for passage in the People's Majlis, all matters proposed for passage in the People's Majlis shall be passed by a simple majority.

Prior to the commencement of each financial year, the Minister of Finance shall submit the proposed state budget for approval by the People's Majlis.

A bill passed by the People's Majlis shall become law and enter into force upon being assented to by the President.

A motion expressing want of confidence in a member of the Cabinet of Ministers may be moved in the People's Majlis.

THE PEOPLE'S SPECIAL MAJLIS

The power to draw up and amend the Constitution of the Maldives shall be vested in the People's Special Majlis. The People's Special Majlis shall consist of: members of the Cabinet of Ministers, members of the People's Majlis, 42 members elected from Malé and the atolls, and eight members appointed by the President.

Any article or provision of the Constitution may be amended only by a law passed by a majority of votes in the People's Special Majlis and assented to by the President.

THE JUDICIARY

The High Court shall consist of the Chief Justice and such number of Judges as may be determined by the President. The Chief Justice and the Judges of the High Court shall be appointed by the President.

All appeals from the courts of the Maldives shall, in accordance with regulations promulgated by the President, be heard by the High Court. The High Court shall hear cases determined by the President to be filed with the High Court from among the proceedings instituted by the State.

There shall be in the Maldives such number of courts at such places as may be determined by the President. The judges of the courts shall be appointed by the President.

PROCLAMATION OF EMERGENCY

Where the President has determined that the security of the Maldives or part thereof is threatened by war, foreign aggression or civil unrest, the President shall have the right to issue a Proclamation of Emergency. While the Proclamation is in force, the President shall have the power to take and order all measures expedient to protect national security and public order. Such measures may include the suspension of fundamental rights and laws. A Proclamation of Emergency shall initially be valid for a period of three months. The Proclamation may be extended, if approved by the People's Majlis, for a period determined by the People's Majlis.

GENERAL PROVISIONS

No bilateral agreement between the Government of the Maldives and the government of a foreign country and no multilateral agreement shall be signed or accepted by the Government of the Maldives unless the President has authorized in writing such signature or acceptance. In the event that such agreement requires ratification by the Maldives, such agreement shall not come into effect unless the President has ratified the same on the advice of the Cabinet of Ministers.

The Government

HEAD OF STATE

President: MAUMOON ABDUL GAYOOM (took office 11 November 1978; re-elected 30 September 1983, 26 September 1988, 1 October 1993, 16 October 1998 and 17 October 2003).

THE CABINET OF MINISTERS
(April 2006)

Minister of Defence and National Security: ISMAIL SHAFEEU.
Minister of Finance and Treasury: QASIM IBRAHIM.
Minister of Environment, Energy and Water: AHMED ABDULLA.
Minister of Higher Education, Employment and Social Security: ABDULLA YAMEEN.
Minister of Fisheries, Agriculture and Marine Resources: ABDULLA KAMALUDDEEN.
Minister of Foreign Affairs: Dr AHMED SHAHEED.
Minister of Gender and Family: AISHATH MOHAMED DIDI.
Minister of Education: ZAHIYA ZAREER.
Minister of Justice: MOHAMED JAMEEL AHMED.
Minister of Construction and Public Works: MOHAMED MAUROOF JAMEEL.
Minister of Health: ILYAS IBRAHIM.
Minister of Tourism and Civil Aviation: Dr MAHMOOD SHAUGEE.
Minister of Transport and Communication: MOHAMED SAEED.
Minister of Planning and National Development: HAMDOON HAMEED.
Minister of Home Affairs: AHMED THASMEEN ALI.
Minister of Atolls Development: MOHAMED WAHEED DEEN.
Minister of Youth Development and Sports: HUSSAIN HILMY.
Minister of Information, Arts and Culture: MOHAMED NASHEED.
Minister of Economic Development and Trade: MOHAMED JALEEL.
Minister of Housing and Urban Development: IBRAHIM RAFEEQ.
Minister of the President's Office: ANEESA AHMED.
Minister of Presidential Affairs: MOHAMED HUSSAIN.
Minister of State for Foreign Affairs: ABDULLA SHAHID.
Minister of State for Finance and Treasury: ABDULLA JIHAD.
Minister of State for Higher Education, Employment and Social Security: AHMED NAZIM.
Minister of State for the Arts: HUSSAIN SHIHAB.
Minister of State and Auditor-General: ISMAIL FATHY.
Minister of State and Principal Collector of Customs: IBRAHIM RASHAD.
Attorney-General: Dr HASSAN SAEED.

MINISTRIES

President's Office: Boduthakurufaanu Magu, Malé 20-05; tel. 3323701; fax 3325500; internet www.presidencymaldives.gov.mv.
Attorney-General's Office: Huravee Bldg, Malé 20-05; tel. 3323809; fax 3314109; e-mail info@agoffice.gov.mv; internet www.agoffice.gov.mv.
Ministry of Atolls Development: Faashana Bldg, Boduthakurufaanu Magu, Malé 20-05; tel. 3323070; fax 3327750; e-mail info@atolls.gov.mv; internet www.atolls.gov.mv.
Ministry of Communication, Science and Technology: Aa-ge, 4th Floor, 12 Boduthakurufaanu Magu, Malé 20-094; tel. 3331695; fax 3331694; e-mail secretariat@mcst.gov.mv; internet www.mcst.gov.mv.
Ministry of Construction and Public Works: Izzuddeen Magu, Malé 20-01; tel. 3323234; fax 3328300; e-mail mcpw@dhivehinet.net.mv.
Ministry of Defence and National Security: Bandaara Koshi, Ameer Ahmed Magu, Malé 20-05; tel. 3322607; fax 3332689; e-mail admin@defence.gov.mv; internet www.defence.gov.mv.
Ministry of Economic Development and Trade: Ghaazee Bldg, Ameer Ahmed Magu, Malé 20-05; tel. 3323668; fax 3323840; e-mail contact@trademin.gov.mv; internet www.trademin.gov.mv.
Ministry of Education: Ghaazee Bldg, 2nd Floor, Ameer Ahmed Magu, Malé 20-05; tel. 3323262; fax 3321201; e-mail educator@dhivehinet.net.mv; internet www.moe.gov.mv.
Ministry of Employment and Labour: Ghaazee Bldg, 3rd Floor, Ameer Ahmed Magu, Malé 20-125; tel. 3317172; fax 3331578; e-mail admin@employment.gov.mv; internet www.employment.gov.mv.
Ministry of Environment, Energy and Water: Huravee Bldg, Ameer Ahmed Magu, Malé 20-05; tel. 3324861; fax 3322286; e-mail env@environment.gov.mv; internet www.environment.gov.mv.
Ministry of Finance and Treasury: Block 379, Ameenee Magu, Malé 20-03; tel. 3317590; fax 3324432; e-mail minfin@dhivehinet.net.mv.
Ministry of Fisheries, Agriculture and Marine Resources: Ghaazee Bldg, 1st Floor, Ameer Ahmed Magu, Malé 20-05; tel. 3322625; fax 3326558; e-mail it@fishagri.gov.mv; internet www.fishagri.gov.mv.
Ministry of Foreign Affairs: PA Complex, 5th Floor, Hilaalee Magu, Maafannu, Malé 10-307; tel. 3323400; fax 3323841; e-mail admin@foreign.gov.mv.
Ministry of Gender and Family: Umar Shopping Arcade, 2nd and 4th Floors, Chaandhanee Magu, Malé 20-02; tel. 3323687; fax 3316237; internet www.urcmaldives.gov.mv.
Ministry of Health: Ameenee Magu, Malé 20-04; tel. 3328887; fax 3328889; e-mail moh@health.gov.mv; internet www.health.gov.mv.
Ministry of Home Affairs: Huravee Bldg, 3rd Floor, Ameer Ahmed Magu, Malé 20-05; tel. 3324861; fax 3322286; e-mail env@environment.gov.mv; internet www.homeaffairs.gov.mv.
Ministry of Housing and Urban Development: MTCC Tower, 7th Floor, Boduthakurufaanu Magu, Malé 20-05; tel. 3323949; fax 3328999.
Ministry of Information, Arts and Culture: Buruzu Magu, Malé 20-04; tel. 3323836; fax 3326211; e-mail informat@dhivehinet.net.mv; internet www.maldivesinfo.gov.mv.
Ministry of Justice: Justice Bldg, Orchid Magu, Malé 20-05; tel. 3322303; fax 3325447; e-mail maljust@dhivehinet.net.mv; internet www.justice.gov.mv.
Ministry of Planning and National Development: Ghaazee Bldg, 4th Floor, Ameer Ahmed Magu, Malé 20-05; tel. 3322919; fax 3327351; e-mail admin@planning.gov.mv; internet www.planning.gov.mv.
Ministry of Tourism and Civil Aviation: Ghazee Bldg, 1st Floor, Ameer Ahmed Magu, Malé 20-05; tel. 3323224; fax 3322512; e-mail info@maldivestourism.gov.mv; internet www.maldivestourism.gov.mv.
Ministry of Transport and Communication: Huravee Bldg, Ameer Ahmed Magu, Malé 20-05; tel. 3323992; fax 3323994; e-mail admin@transport.gov.mv; internet www.transport.gov.mv.
Ministry of Youth Development and Sports: Ghaazee Bldg, Ameeruahmed Magu, Malé 20-02; tel. 3326986; fax 3327162; e-mail youthspo@dhivehinet.net.mv; internet www.youthsports.gov.mv.

Legislature

PEOPLE'S MAJLIS

The People's Majlis (People's Council) comprises 50 members, of whom eight are appointed by the President, two elected by the people of Malé and two elected from each of the 20 atolls (for a five-year term). The most recent election was held on 22 January 2005.

Speaker: AHMED ZAHIR.
Deputy Speaker: AHMED THASMEEN ALI.

Election Commission

Election Commission of Maldives: Malé; f. 1998; independent; appointed by the President; Commr of Elections K. D. AHMED MANIK.

Political Organizations

In June 2005 legislation was approved permitting the establishment of political parties in the Maldives for the first time since 1952. The following parties subsequently registered with the Ministry of Home Affairs:

Adhaalaath Party (Justice Party): Malé; f. 2005; Leader SHEIKH HUSSAIN RASHEED AHAMED.

Dhivehi Raiyyithunge Party (DRP) (Maldivian People's Party): Malé; f. 2005; Leader MAUMOON ABDUL GAYOOM.

Islamic Democratic Party: Malé; f. 2005; Leader OMAR NASEER.

Maldivian Democratic Party (MDP): 1st Floor, M. Glorype, Fareedhee Magu, Malé; tel. 3340044; fax 3322960; e-mail secretariat@maldiviandemocraticparty.org; internet www.maldiviandemocraticparty.org; f. 2001; fmrly based in Colombo, Sri Lanka; official registration in Maldives permitted June 2005; Leader MOHAMED NASHEED.

Maldives Labour Party: Malé; f. 2005; Leader AHMED NASHEED.

Diplomatic Representation

HIGH COMMISSIONS IN THE MALDIVES

Bangladesh: H. High Grove, 6 Hithafinivaa Magu, Malé; tel. 3315541; fax 3315543; e-mail bdootmal@dhivehinet.net.mv; High Commissioner MOHAMED MIJARUL QUAYES.

India: H. Athireege-Aage, Ameeru Ahmed Magu, Malé; tel. 3323015; fax 3324778; High Commissioner A. K. PANDEY.

Pakistan: G. Penta Green, Majeedhee Magu, Malé; tel. 3322024; fax 3321832; e-mail pakistan@dhivehinet.net.mv; High Commissioner AMANULLAH GICHKEE.

Sri Lanka: H. Sakeena Manzil, Medhuziyaaraiyh Magu, Malé 20-05; tel. 3322845; fax 3321652; e-mail highcom@dhivehinet.net.mv; High Commissioner MOHAMED ALI FAROOK.

Judicial System

The administration of justice is undertaken in accordance with Islamic (*Shari'a*) law. In 1980 the Maldives High Court was established. There are four courts in Malé, and one island court in every inhabited island. All courts, with the exception of the High Court, are under the control of the Ministry of Justice.

In January 1999 the Government declared that the island court of each atoll capital would thenceforth oversee the administration of justice in that atoll. At the same time it was announced that arrangements were being made to appoint a senior magistrate in each atoll capital.

HIGH COURT

Chief Justice: MOHAMED RASHEED IBRAHIM.

Judges: ABDUL GHANEE MOHAMED, AHMED HAMEED FAHMY, ALI HAMEED MOHAMED.

In February 1995 the President established a five-member Advisory Council on Judicial Affairs. The Council was to function under the President's Office (equivalent, in this respect, to a Supreme Court) and was to study and offer counsel to the President on appeals made to the President by either the appellant or the respondent in cases adjudicated by the High Court. The Council was also to offer such counsel as and when requested by the President on other judicial matters.

ADVISORY COUNCIL ON JUDICIAL AFFAIRS

Members: MOOSA FATHY, ABDULLA HAMEED, DR MOHAMED MUNAVVAR, Prof. MOHAMED RASHEED IBRAHIM, AL-SHEIKH HASSAN YOOSUF.

Religion

Islam is the state religion, and the Maldivians are Sunni Muslims. In mid-1991 there were 724 mosques and 266 women's mosques throughout the country.

In late 1996 a Supreme Council for Islamic Affairs was established, under the authority of the President's Office. The new body was to authorize state policies with regard to Islam and to advise the Government on Islamic affairs.

Musthashaaru of the Supreme Council for Islamic Affairs: MOOSA FATHY.

President of the Supreme Council for Islamic Affairs: MOHAMED RASHEED IBRAHIM.

Deputy President of the Supreme Council for Islamic Affairs: AHMED FAROOG MOHAMED.

The Press

In 1993 the Government established a National Press Council to review, monitor and further develop journalism in the Maldives.

DAILIES

Aafathis Daily News: Feeroaz Magu, Maafannu, Malé 20-02; tel. 3318609; fax 3312425; e-mail aafathis@dhivehinet.net.mv; internet www.aafathisnews.com.mv; f. 1979; daily; Dhivehi and English; Editor AHMED ZAHIR; circ. 3,000.

Haveeru Daily: Ameenee Magu, POB 20103, Malé; tel. 3325671; fax 3323103; e-mail haveeru@haveeru.com.mv; internet www.haveeru.com.mv; f. 1979; Dhivehi and English; Chair. MOHAMED ZAHIR HUSSAIN; Editor ALI RAFEEQ; circ. 4,500.

Miadhu News: G. Mascot, Koimalaa Hingun, Malé 20-02; tel. 3320700; fax 3320500; e-mail miadhu@dhivehinet.net.mv; internet www.miadhu.com; Propr IBRAHIM RASHEED MOOSA; Chair. AHMED ABDULLA.

Minivan News: Malé; e-mail minivan.news@gmail.com; internet www.minivannews.com; f. 2005; independent; predominantly Dhivehi, with English section; Editor AMINATH NAJEEB.

PERIODICALS

Adduvas: Malé; f. 2000; weekly; news, entertainment, health issues and social affairs; Editor AISHATH VELEZINEE.

Dheenuge Magu (The Path of Religion): The President's Office, Boduthakurufaanu Magu, Malé 20-05; tel. 3323701; fax 3325500; e-mail info@presidencymaldives.gov.mv; f. 1986; weekly; Dhivehi; religious; publ. by the President's Office; Editor President MAUMOON ABDUL GAYOOM; Dep. Editor MOHAMED RASHEED IBRAHIM; circ. 7,500.

Dhivehingetharika (Maldivian Heritage): National Centre for Linguistic and Historical Research, Soasun Magu, Malé 20-05; tel. 3323206; fax 3326796; e-mail nclhr@dhivehinet.net.mv; internet www.qaumiyyath.gov.mv; f. 1998; Dhivehi; Maldivian archaeology, history and language.

The Evening Weekly: Ameenee Magu, POB 20103, Malé; tel. 3325671; fax 3323103; e-mail info@eveningweekly.com.mv; internet www.eveningweekly.com.mv; weekly; English; Chair. MOHAMED ZAHIR HUSSAIN.

Faiythoora: National Centre for Linguistic and Historical Research, Soasun Magu, Malé 20-05; tel. 3323206; fax 3326796; e-mail nclhr@dhivehinet.net.mv; internet www.qaumiyyath.gov.mv; f. 1979; monthly magazine; Dhivehi; Maldivian history, culture and language; Editor UZ ABDULLA HAMEED; circ. 800.

Furadhaana: Ministry of Information, Arts and Culture, Buruzu Magu, Malé 20-04; tel. 3321749; fax 3326211; e-mail informat@dhivehinet.net.mv; internet www.maldives-info.com; f. 1990; monthly; Dhivehi; Editor IBRAHIM MANIK; circ. 1,000.

Huvaas: Ameenee Magu, POB 20103, Malé; tel. 3325671; fax 3323103; e-mail huvaas@haveeru.com.mv; internet www.haveeru.com.mv/huvaas; fortnightly; Chair. MOHAMED ZAHIR HUSSAIN.

Jamaathuge Khabaru (Community News): Centre for Continuing Education, Salahudeen Bldg, Malé 20-04; tel. 3328772; fax 3322223; monthly; Dhivehi; Editor AHMED ZAHIR; circ. 1,500.

Maldives News Bulletin: Maldives News Bureau, Ministry of Information, Arts and Culture, Buruzu Magu, Malé 20-04; tel. 3323838; fax 3326211; e-mail informat@dhivehinet.net.mv; internet www.maldives-info.com; f. 1980; weekly; English; Editor ALI SHAREEF; circ. 350.

Marine Research Centre Bulletin: Marine Research Centre, Ministry of Fisheries, Agriculture and Marine Resources, H. White Waves, Malé 20-06; tel. 3322242; fax 3322509; e-mail info@mrc.gov.mv; f. 1984; biannual; fisheries and marine research; Exec. Dir Dr MOHAMED SHIHAM ADAM.

Monday Times: H. Neel Villa, Boduthakunufaanu Magu, Malé; tel. and fax 3315084; e-mail editor@mondaytimes.com; internet www.mondaytimes.com; f. 2000; banned 2002; restarted 2004; weekly.

Our Environment: Forum of Writers on the Environment, c/o Ministry of Planning and National Development, Ghaazee Bldg, Ameer Ahmed Magu, Malé 20-05; tel. 3324861; fax 3327351; f. 1990; monthly; Dhivehi; Editor FAROUQ AHMED.

Rasain: Ministry of Fisheries, Agriculture and Marine Resources, Ghaazee Bldg, Ameer Ahmed Magu, Malé 20-05; tel. 3322625; fax 3326558; e-mail fishagri@dhivehinet.net.mv; f. 1980; annual; fisheries development.

Samugaa: Malé; f. 1995; publ. by the Government Employees' Club.

NEWS AGENCIES

Haveeru News Service (HNS): POB 20103, Malé; tel. 3313825; fax 3323103; e-mail haveeru@dhivehinet.net.mv; internet www.haveeru.com.mv; f. 1979; Chair. MOHAMED ZAHIR HUSSAIN; Man. Editor AHMED ZAHIR.

Hiyama News Agency: H. Navaagan, Malé 20-05; tel. 3322588.

Maldives News Bureau (MNB): Ministry of Information, Arts and Culture, Buruzu Magu, Malé 20-04; tel. 3323836; fax 3326211; e-mail informat@dhivehinet.net.mv; internet www.maldives-info.com.

Publishers

Corona Press: Feeroaz Magu, Maafannu, Malé; tel. 3310052; fax 3314741.

Cyprea Print: 25 Boduthakurufaanu Magu, Malé; tel. 3333883; fax 3323523; e-mail cyprea@dhivehinet.net.mv; f. 1984; Man. Dir ABDULLA SAEED.

Loamaafaanu Print: Alkariyya Bldg, Ground Dloor, Ameenee Magu, Malé 20-354; tel. 3317209; fax 3313815; e-mail haveeru@netlink.net.mv.

Novelty Printers and Publishers: Malé 20-340; tel. 3318844; fax 3327039; e-mail novelty@dhivehinet.net.mv; general and reference books; Man. Dir ASAD ALI.

Ummeedhee Press: M. Aasthaanaa Javaahirumagu, Malé 20-02; tel. 3325110; fax 3326412; e-mail ummpress@dhivehinet.net.mv; f. 1986; printing and publishing; Principal Officers ABDUL SHAKOOR ALI, MOHAMED SHAKOOR.

Broadcasting and Communications

TELECOMMUNICATIONS

Ministry of Communication, Science and Technology (Post and Telecommunication Section): Telecom Bldg, Husnuheena Magu, Malé 20-04; tel. 3323344; fax 3320000; e-mail telecom@dhivehinet.net.mv; internet www.mcst.gov.mv; policy-making authority; Dir-Gen. (Post and Telecommunication Section) HUSSAIN SHAREEF.

Telecommunications Authority of Maldives: Telecom Bldg, Malé; tel. 3323344; fax 3320000; e-mail secretariat@tam.gov.mv; internet www.tam.gov.mv; f. 2003; regulatory authority; Chair. Dr HASSAN HAMEED; Exec. Dir MOHAMED AMIR.

Dhivehi Raajjeyge Gulhun Ltd (DHIRAAGU): 19 Medhuziyaaraiy Magu, POB 2082, Malé 20-03; tel. 3322802; fax 3322800; e-mail info@dhiraagu.com.mv; internet www.dhiraagu.com.mv; f. 1988; jointly owned by the Maldivian Govt (55%) and by Cable and Wireless PLC of the United Kingdom (45%); functions under Ministry of Communication, Science and Technology; operates all national and international telecommunications services in the Maldives (incl. internet service–Dhivehinet); Chair. MAUROOF JAMEEL; CEO ISMAIL WAHEED.

Wataniya Telecom Maldives Pvt Ltd: 2nd Floor, Urban Development Bldg, Hulhumalé; tel. 9621111; fax 3350519; internet www.wataniya.mv; f. 2005; provides advanced cellular mobile telephone services throughout the Maldives; Chair. SOLAH FAHUD SULTAN; CEO MARK HANNA.

RADIO

Radio Eke: Malé.

Voice of Islam: Malé.

Voice of Maldives (VOM) (Dhivehi Raajjeyge Adu): Voice of Maldives Bldg, Maafaanu, Malé; tel. 3325577; fax 3328357; internet www.vom.gov.mv; radio broadcasting began in 1962 under name of Malé Radio; name changed as above in 1980; three channels; home service in Dhivehi and English; began broadcasting 24 hrs daily from Jan. 2005; Dir-Gen. IBRAHIM MANIK.

TELEVISION

Television Maldives: Buruzu Magu, Malé 20-04; tel. 3323105; fax 3325083; e-mail comments@tvm.gov.mv; internet www.tvm.gov.mv; television broadcasting began in 1978; two channels: TVM broadcasts for an average of 18 hrs daily and TVM Plus (f. 1994) broadcasts for 10 hrs daily; covers a 40-km radius around Malé; Exec. Dir HUSSAIN MOHAMED; Asst Dir-Gens MOHAMED ASIF, THOYYIB MOHAMED.

Finance

(cap. = capital; brs = branches; amounts in US dollars unless otherwise stated)

BANKING

Central Bank

Maldives Monetary Authority (MMA): Umar Shopping Arcade, 3rd Floor, Chandhanee Magu, Maafannu, Malé 20-156; tel. 3323783; fax 3323862; e-mail mail@mma.gov.mv; internet www.mma.gov.mv; f. 1981; bank of issue; supervises and regulates commercial bank and foreign-exchange dealings and advises the Govt on banking and monetary matters; authorized cap. 1m. rufiyaa, res 75.6m. rufiyaa, dep. 2,405.1m. rufiyaa (Dec. 2004); Gov. QASIM IBRAHIM; Man. Dir KHADEEJA HASSAN.

Commercial Bank

Bank of Maldives (PLC) Ltd (BML): 11 Boduthakurufaanu Magu, Malé 20-094; tel. 3330100; fax 3328233; e-mail info@bml.com.mv; internet www.bankofmaldives.com.mv; f. 1982; 75% state-owned, 25% privately-owned; cap. 36.5m., res 156m., dep. 1,677m. (2002); Chair. ABDULLA SAEED; Gen. Man. and CEO SERENE HO OI KHUEN; 18 brs.

Foreign Banks

Bank of Ceylon (Sri Lanka): Aage Bldg, Boduthakurufaanu Magu, Malé; tel. 3323045; fax 3320575; e-mail bcmale@dhivehinet.net.mv; internet www.bankofceylon.net; Country Man. ROY JAYASUNDARA; 1 br.

Habib Bank Ltd (Pakistan): Ship Plaza, Ground Floor, 1/6 Orchid Magu, POB 20121, Malé; tel. 3322051; fax 3326791; e-mail hblmale@dhivehinet.net.mv; Vice-Pres. and Chief Man. MUHAMMAD JAMIL ANJUM.

The Hongkong and Shanghai Banking Corpn Ltd (Hong Kong): MTCC Bldg, 1st Floor, Boduthakurufaanu Magu, Malé 20-05; tel. 3330770; fax 3312072; e-mail sarathweerakoon@hsbc.com.lk; Country Man. SARATH WEERAKOON.

State Bank of India: Boduthakurufaanu Magu, Malé 20-05; tel. 3320860; fax 3323053; e-mail sbimale@dhivehinet.net.mv; CEO R. GHOSE.

DEVELOPMENT FINANCE ORGANIZATION

Housing Development Finance Corpn: H. Fulidhooge, 5th Floor, Kalaafaanu Hingun, Malé; tel. 3338810; fax 3315138; f. 2004 to provide public housing loans; 100% state-owned; Chair. IBRAHIM NAEEM.

INSURANCE

Allied Insurance Co of the Maldives (Pte) Ltd: 04–06 STO Trade Centre, Orchid Magu, Malé; tel. 3324612; fax 3325035; e-mail allied@dhivehinet.net.mv; internet www.alliedmaldives.com; f. 1985; all classes of non-life insurance; operated by State Trading Organization (see below); Chief Exec. MOHAMED MANIKU; Man. Dir ISMAIL RIZA.

Trade and Industry

GOVERNMENT AGENCY

Foreign Investment Services Bureau (FISB): Ministry of Economic Development and Trade, Ghazee Bldg, 1st Floor, Ameer Ahmed Magu, Malé; tel. 3323890; fax 3323756; e-mail contact@trademin.gov.mv; internet www.trademin.gov.mv; under administration of Ministry of Economic Development and Trade; Dir-Gen. AHMED NASEEM.

CHAMBER OF COMMERCE AND INDUSTRY

Maldives National Chamber of Commerce and Industry (MNCCI): G. Viyafaari Hiya, Ameenee Magu, Malé 20-04; tel. 3326634; fax 3310233; e-mail mncci@dhivehinet.net.mv; f. 1978; merged with the Maldivian Traders' Association in 2000; Pres. MOHAMED SOLIH; Sec.-Gen. ABDULLAH FAIZ.

INDUSTRIAL AND TRADE ASSOCIATIONS

Maldives Association of Construction Industry (MACI): PA Complex Magu, Malé; tel. 3318660; fax 3318796; e-mail maci@avasmail.com.mv; f. 2003; Chair. ABDULLA MOHAMED; Sec.-Gen. AMIN IBRAHIM.

Sri Lanka Trade Centre: Girithereyege Bldg, 3rd Floor, Hithaffinivaa Magu, Malé; tel. 3315183; fax 3315184; e-mail dirsltc@avasmail.com.mv; f. 1993; to facilitate and promote trade, tourism, investment and services between Sri Lanka and the Maldives; Dir M. I. SUFIYAN.

State Trading Organization PLC (STO): Boduthakurufaanu Magu, Maafannu, Malé 20-345; tel. 3344333; fax 3344334; e-mail info@stomaldives.net; internet www.stomaldives.com; f. 1964 as Athirimaafannuge Trading Account, renamed as above in 1976; became public limited company in 2001; state-controlled commercial organization; under administration of independent Board of Directors; imports and distributes staple foods, fuels, pharmaceuticals and general consumer items; acts as purchaser for govt requirements; undertakes long-term development projects; Man. Dir MOHAMED MANIKU; Chair. AHMED MOHAMED.

UTILITIES

Electricity

Maldives Energy Authority: Malé; f. 2006 to replace Maldives Electricity Bureau; under administration of Ministry of Environment, Energy and Water; regulatory authority.

State Electric Co (STELCO) Ltd: Ameenee Magu, Malé; tel. 3320982; fax 3327036; e-mail admin@stelco.com.mv; internet www.stelco.com.mv; f. 1997 to replace Maldives Electricity Board; under administration of Ministry of Trade and Industries; provides electricity, consultancy services, electrical spare parts service, etc.; operates 22 power stations; installed capacity 32,921 kW (Dec. 2000); Chair. Dr ABDUL MUHSIN MOHAMED; Man. Dir ABDUL SHAKOOR.

Gas

Maldive Gas Pvt Ltd: 1st Floor, STO Trade Centre, Orchid Magu, Malé; tel. 3335614; fax 3335615; e-mail info@maldivegas.com; internet www.maldivegas.com; f. 1999 as a jt venture between State Trading Organization and Champa Gas and Oil Co; Chair. MOHAMED MANIK.

Water

Maldives Water and Sanitation Authority (MWSA): Ameenee Magu, Malé; tel. 3317562; fax 3317569; f. 1973; Dir FAROOQ MOHAMED HASSAN.

Malé Water and Sewerage Co: Ameenee Magu, Machangolhi, POB 2148, Malé 20-375; tel. 3323209; fax 3324306; e-mail mwsc@dhivehinet.net.mv; f. 1995; 70% govt-owned; produces approximately 6,000 metric tons of fresh, desalinated water daily, using seven plants; provides water and sewerage services to the islands of Malé, Hulhumalé and Villingili; provides water services to the island of Maafushi; Chair. Dr ABDULLA NASEER; Gen. Man. MOHAMED AHMED DIDI.

Transport

Maldives Transport and Contracting Co Ltd (MTCC): MTCC Bldg, 5th Floor, Boduthakurufaanu Magu, POB 263, Malé 20-181; tel. 3326822; fax 3323221; e-mail info@mtcc.com.mv; internet www.mtcc.com.mv; f. 1980; 60% state-owned, 40% privately owned; marine transport, civil and technical contracting, harbour development, shipping agents for general cargo, passenger liners and oil tankers; Man. Dir IBRAHIM ATHIF SHAKOOR; Chair. Dr FATHIN HAMEED.

SHIPPING

Vessels operate from the Maldives to Sri Lanka and Singapore at frequent intervals, also calling at points in India, Pakistan, Myanmar (formerly Burma), Malaysia, Bangladesh, Thailand, Indonesia and the Middle East. In December 2004 the merchant shipping fleet of the Maldives numbered 69 vessels, with a combined displacement of 78,129 grt. Smaller vessels provide services between the islands on an irregular basis. Malé is the only port handling international traffic. In 1986 a new commercial harbour was opened in Malé. The Malé Harbour Development Project was implemented during 1991–97, and improved and increased the capacity and efficiency of Malé Port. In July 2003 a new harbour was opened in Fuvah Mulah, on Gnaviyani atoll.

Maldives Ports Authority (MPA): Boduthakurufaanu Magu, Maafaanu, Malé 20-250; tel. 3329339; fax 3325293; e-mail info@maldport.com.mv; internet www.maldport.com.mv; f. 1986; under administration of Ministry of Transport and Civil Aviation; Man. Dir MAHUDY IMAD; Harbour Master AHMED RASHEED.

Island Enterprises Pvt Ltd: Maaram, 1st Floor, Ameeru Ahmed Magu, Henveiru, POB 20169, Malé 20-05; tel. 3323531; fax 3325645; e-mail info@ielmaldives.com; internet www.ielmaldives.com; f. 1978; fleet of eight vessels; exporters of frozen fish, owners of processing plant, shipping agents, chandlers, cruising agents, surveyors and repairs; Man. Dir OMAR MANIK.

Precision Marine Pvt Ltd: Maaram, 1st Floor, Ameeru Ahmed Magu, Henveiru, POB 20169, Malé 20-05; tel. 3323531; fax 3325645; e-mail fiberbot@dhivehinet.net.mv; internet www.pmlboatyard.com.mv; subsidiary of Island Enterprises Pvt Ltd; mfrs and repairers of fibreglass boats, launches, yachts, marine sports equipment, etc.; Dir OMAR MANIK.

Madihaa Co (Pvt) Ltd: 1/40 Shaheed Ali Higun, Malé; tel. 3327812; fax 3322251; e-mail madicom@dhivehinet.net.mv; f. 1985; imports and exports fresh fruit and vegetables, construction raw materials, confectionery items and soft drinks; Man. Dir MOOSA AHMED.

Maldives National Shipping Ltd: Ship Plaza, 2nd Floor, 1/6 Orchid Magu, POB 2022, Malé 20-02; tel. 3323871; fax 3324323; e-mail mns@dhivehinet.net.mv; f. 1965; 100% state-owned; fleet of three container vessels; br. in Singapore; Gen. Man. AIMON JAMEEL.

Matrana Enterprises (Pvt) Ltd: 97 Majeedhee Magu, Malé; tel. 3321733; fax 3322832; Sr Exec. MOHAMED ABDULLA.

Villa Shipping and Trading Co (Pvt) Ltd: Villa Bldg, POB 2073, Malé 20-02; tel. 3325195; fax 3325177; e-mail villa@dhivehinet.net.mv; Man. Dir QASIM IBRAHIM.

CIVIL AVIATION

The existing airport on Hululé Island near Malé, which was first opened in 1966, was expanded and improved to international standard with financial assistance from abroad and, as Malé International Airport, was officially opened in 1981. Charter flights from Europe subsequently began. In addition, there are four domestic airports covering different regions of the country: one on Gan Island, Addu atoll, another on Kadhdhoo Island, Hadhdhummathi atoll, another on Hanimaadhoo Island, South Thiladhummathi atoll, and another on Kaadedhdhoo Island, South Huvadhu atoll. The airport on Gan Island began servicing international flights in 2005. In early 1995 there were 10 helipads in use in the Maldives.

Maldives Airport Co Ltd: Malé International Airport, Hululé; tel. 3338800; fax 3331515; e-mail info@maclnet.net; internet www.airports.com.mv; f. 2000; 100% govt-owned; under administration of Ministry of Tourism and Civil Aviation; Man. Dir AHMED ALI MANIKU.

Air Maldives Ltd: 26 Ameer Ahmed Magu, Henveiru, POB 2049, Malé 20-05; tel. 3328454; fax 3318757; e-mail airmldvs@dhivehinet.net.mv; f. 1974; 51% govt-owned, 49% owned by Naluri Bhd (Malaysia); under administration of Ministry of Transport and Civil Aviation; domestic flights; operated international flights until March 2000; national carrier.

Island Aviation Services Ltd: 1st Floor, STO Aifaanu Bldg, Boduthakurufaanu Magu, Henveiru, Malé; tel. 3335544; fax 3315661; e-mail info@island.com.mv; internet www.island.com.mv; f. 2000; 100% govt-owned; operates domestic flights; Chair. MOHAMED UMAR MANIK; Man. Dir BANDHU IBRAHIM SALEEM.

Maldivian Air Taxi: Kaafu Hulhulé, POB 2023, Malé; tel. 3315201; fax 3315203; e-mail mat@mat.com.mv; internet www.mataxi.com; f. 1993; seaplane services between Malé and outer islands; operates 15 aircraft; Chair. LARS ERIK NIELSEN; Gen. Man. AUM FAWZY.

Trans Maldivian Airways (Pvt) Ltd: POB 2079, Malé; tel. 3325708; fax 3323161; e-mail service@tma.com.mv; internet www.tma.com.mv; f. 1989 as Hummingbird Island Airways Pvt Ltd, name changed as above in 2000; operates 12 floatplanes; Man. Dir BRAM STELLER.

Tourism

The tourism industry brings considerable foreign exchange to the Maldives. The islands' attractions include white sandy beaches, excellent diving conditions and multi-coloured coral formations. At the end of 2004 there were 87 island resorts in operation, and some 16,858 hotel beds were available. The annual total of foreign visitors increased from only 29,325 in 1978 to 616,716 in 2004. Revenue from tourism was estimated at 1,044.9m. rufiyaa in the latter year. The Government announced in March 2004 that nine more atolls would be opened for tourism and that 11 islands would be converted into resorts. It was feared that the devastating effect on the Maldives of the tsunami in the Indian Ocean in December 2004 would severely affect the country's tourism industry. By the end of 2005 all the resorts affected by the tsunami had reopened. However, tourist arrivals in that year totalled only 395,320, a decline of 35.9% compared with the previous year. Arrivals were expected to have completely recovered by the end of 2006.

Maldives Association of Tourism Industry (MATI): Gadhamoo Bldg, 3rd Floor, Boduthakurufaanu Magu, Malé; tel. 3326640; fax 3326641; e-mail mati@dhivehinet.net.mv; internet www.maldivestourism.org.mv; f. 1984; promotes and develops tourism; Chair. MOHAMED UMAR MANIKU; Sec.-Gen. S. I. MOHAMED.

Maldives Tourism Promotion Board: H. Aage, 3rd Floor, 12 Boduthakurufaanu Magu, Malé 20-05; tel. 3323228; fax 3323229; e-mail mtpb@visitmaldives.com; internet www.visitmaldives.com; f. 1998; Dir Dr ABDULLA MAUSOOM.

Air Maldives Travel Bureau/Tourist Information: Aifaan Bldg, Boduthakurufaanu Magu, Malé; tel. 3310917; fax 3318757; e-mail airmldvs@dhivehinet.net.mv; f. 1997.

MALI

Introductory Survey

Location, Climate, Language, Religion, Flag, Capital

The Republic of Mali is a land-locked country in West Africa, with Algeria to the north, Mauritania and Senegal to the west, Guinea and Côte d'Ivoire to the south, and Burkina Faso and Niger to the east. The climate is hot throughout the country. The northern region of Mali is part of the Sahara, an arid desert. It is wetter in the south, where the rainy season is from June to October. Temperatures in Bamako are generally between 16°C (61°F) and 39°C (103°F). The official language is French but a number of other languages, including Bambara, Fulfulde, Sonrai, Tamashek, Soninke and Dogon, are widely spoken. It is estimated that about 80% of the population are Muslims and 18% follow traditional animist beliefs; under 2% are Christians. The national flag (proportions 2 by 3) has three equal vertical stripes, of green, gold and red. The capital is Bamako.

Recent History

Mali, as the former French West African colony of Soudan, merged in April 1959 with Senegal to form the Federation of Mali, which became independent on 20 June 1960. Senegal seceded two months later, and the remnant of the Federation was proclaimed the Republic of Mali on 22 September 1960. Its first President was Modibo Keita, the leader of the Union soudanaise—Rassemblement démocratique africain (US—RDA), who pursued authoritarian socialist policies. Mali withdrew from the Franc Zone (see p. 282) in 1962, and developed close relations with the communist bloc. Economic difficulties caused Mali to return to the Franc Zone in 1968, although the country was not fully reintegrated into the Zone's monetary union until 1984.

Keita dissolved the elected legislature in January 1968. Following a series of purges of US—RDA and public officials, Keita was overthrown in November of that year by a group of junior officers, who assumed power as the Comité militaire pour la libération nationale (CMLN). The Constitution was abrogated, and all political activity was banned. Lt (later Gen.) Moussa Traoré became Head of State and President of the CMLN, while Capt. Yoro Diakité became President of the Government (Prime Minister). In September 1969 Traoré assumed the presidency of the Government, demoting Diakité to a lesser ministerial post.

A draft Constitution, providing for the establishment of a one-party state at the end of a five-year transitional period of military rule, was approved by a national referendum in June 1974. Keita died in custody in 1977, prompting anti-Government demonstrations. The single political party, the Union démocratique du peuple malien (UDPM), was officially constituted in March 1979, and presidential and legislative elections took place in June. Traoré, the sole candidate for the presidency, was elected for a five-year term; a single list of UDPM candidates for the 82-member Assemblée nationale was elected for a four-year term.

A constitutional amendment in September 1981 increased the presidential term of office to six years and reduced that of the legislature to three years. Elections to the Assemblée nationale were thus held in June 1982 and June 1985, with UDPM candidates being elected unopposed on both occasions. In June 1985 Traoré was re-elected President, reportedly obtaining 99.9% of the votes cast. At legislative elections in June 1998 only about one-half of the incumbent deputies were returned to office, after provision was made for as many as three UDPM-nominated candidates to contest each seat.

In March 1990 Traoré initiated a nation-wide series of conferences to consider the exercise of democracy within and by the UDPM. Mali's first cohesive opposition movements began to emerge in that year, among them the Comité national d'initiative démocratique (CNID) and the Alliance pour la démocratie au Mali (ADEMA), which together organized mass pro-democracy demonstrations in December.

The security forces harshly repressed violent pro-democracy demonstrations in Bamako in March 1991: official figures later revealed that 106 people were killed, and 708 injured, in three days of unrest. On 26 March it was announced that Traoré had been arrested. A military Conseil national de réconciliation (CNR), led by Lt-Col (later Gen.) Amadou Toumani Touré, the commander of the army's parachute regiment, assumed power, and the Constitution and its institutions were abrogated. The CNR was succeeded by a 25-member Comité de transition pour le salut du peuple (CTSP), chaired by Touré. It was announced that a national conference would be convened, and that the armed forces would relinquish power to democratic institutions in January 1992. Soumana Sacko (who had briefly been Minister of Finance and Trade in 1987) returned to Mali from the Central African Republic to head a transitional, civilian-dominated government.

The transitional regime affirmed its commitment to the economic adjustment efforts of recent years, and undertook the reform of Malian political life. Among those arrested in subsequent months were Gen. Sékou Ly, Brig-Gen. Mamadou Coulibaly (respectively, Minister of the Interior and Basic Development and Minister of Defence at the time of the violently repressed demonstrations in early 1991) and the former army Chief of Staff, Ousmane Coulibaly. In July 1991 an amnesty for most political prisoners detained under Traoré was proclaimed, and provision made for the legalization of political parties. The CNID was registered as the Congrès national d'initiative démocratique, and ADEMA adopted the additional title of Parti panafricain pour la liberté, la solidarité et la justice. Pre-independence parties, banned for many years, re-emerged, most notably the US—RDA.

The National Conference began in July 1991. Over a period of two weeks its 1,800 delegates adopted a draft Constitution, an electoral code and a charter governing the activities of political parties. In November the period of transition to democratic rule was extended until March 1992. The delay was attributed principally to the CTSP's desire to conclude a peace agreement with Tuareg rebels in the north of the country (see below). The draft Constitution was submitted to a national referendum on 12 January 1992, when it was endorsed by 99.8% of those who voted (about 43% of the registered electorate).

At municipal elections, held on 19 January 1992, and at which 23 of the 48 authorized parties presented candidates, ADEMA enjoyed the greatest success, winning 214 of 751 seats. At the elections to the Assemblée nationale, on 23 February and 8 March, ADEMA won 76 of the 129 seats, the CNID took nine seats, and the US—RDA eight. The date for the transition to civilian rule was again postponed, and the first round of the presidential election eventually proceeded on 12 April, contested by nine candidates. The leader of ADEMA, Alpha Oumar Konaré, won the largest share of the votes cast (some 45%). He and his nearest rival, Tiéoulé Mamadou Konaté (of the US—RDA), proceeded to a second round, on 26 April, at which Konaré secured 69% of the votes. Overall, only about 20% of the electorate were reported to have voted in the presidential election; a similar turn-out was reported in the legislative polls. Konaré was inaugurated as President on 8 June. He appointed Younoussi Touré (hitherto the national director of the Banque centrale des états de l'Afrique de l'ouest) as Prime Minister. Touré's first Council of Ministers was dominated by members of ADEMA, although a small number of portfolios were allocated to representatives of the US—RDA and of the Parti pour la démocratie et le progrès (PDP).

The trial of Traoré and his associates began in November 1992. In February 1993 Traoré, Ly, Mamadou Coulibaly and Ousmane Coulibaly were sentenced to death, having been convicted, inter alia, of premeditated murder at the time of the March 1991 unrest. The Supreme Court rejected appeal proceedings in May 1993; however, Konaré subsequently indicated that no death penalty would be exacted under his presidency. Charges remained against Traoré, his wife and several others in connection with the 'economic crimes' of the former administration.

Touré resigned in April 1993, following violent disturbances in Bamako, involving students and school pupils disaffected by the adverse effects of economic austerity measures. The new Prime Minister, Abdoulaye Sekou Sow (hitherto Minister of State, responsible for Defence, and who was not a member of any political party), implemented an extensive reorganization of the

Government. The Council of Ministers remained dominated by ADEMA, but also included representatives of other parties, including the CNID. Following the resignation of ADEMA's Vice-President, Mohamed Lamine Traoré, from a senior government post, a major reorganization of the Council of Ministers was effected in November.

Meanwhile, a programme of austerity measures, announced in September 1993, provoked considerable political controversy and failed to prevent the suspension of assistance by the IMF and the World Bank. The 50% devaluation of the CFA franc, in January 1994, exacerbated differences regarding economic policy within the Government. Sow resigned in February, and was replaced by Ibrahim Boubacar Keita, a member of ADEMA's 'radical' wing, which was opposed to Sow's economic policies. The withdrawal from the coalition of the CNID and the Rassemblement pour la démocratie et le progrès (RDP) prompted the appointment of a new Government, again dominated by ADEMA; the PDP in turn withdrew.

Mali's first national forum took place in December 1994; the Prime Minister and other government members answered questions submitted by members of the public on any matter of national concern. The forum was broadcast nationally, and was held on an annual basis thereafter.

Following the election of Keita as President of ADEMA in September 1994, Mohamed Lamine Traoré and other prominent figures resigned from the party and subsequently formed the Mouvement pour l'indépendance, la renaissance et l'intégration africaine (MIRIA). In January 1995 a party established by supporters of the UDPM, the Mouvement patriotique pour le renouveau (MPR), was granted official status. In October the Parti pour la renaissance nationale (PARENA), comprising several leading members of the CNID, who alleged excessive dominance by the party Chairman, Mountaga Tall, was registered. PARENA and ADEMA established a political alliance in February 1996, and PARENA's leaders, Yoro Diakité and Tiébilé Dramé, were appointed to the Government in July. In October it was announced that a prominent member of the MPR and former minister under Traoré, Mady Diallo, had been arrested, together with several armed forces officers, following the discovery of a plot to assassinate Konaré, Keita and other government ministers. Diallo was later released, but was rearrested in April 1997. The trial of Diallo and six army officers accused of plotting to overthrow President Konaré began in March 1998, and in March 1999 the seven were sentenced to prison terms of 15–18 months.

In early 1997 the first round of legislative elections was postponed from 9 March until 13 April. More than 1,500 candidates, mainly representing 36 of the country's 61 registered political parties, sought election to the enlarged (147-seat) Assemblée nationale. As early results indicated that ADEMA was the only party to have won seats outright at this round, the main opposition parties denounced the results as fraudulent and announced their intention to withdraw from the second round. The opposition parties also withdrew their candidates from the forthcoming presidential and municipal elections. On 24 April the Constitutional Court invalidated the results of the first round of voting, citing irregularities in the conduct of the poll.

The presidential election was postponed, by one week, until 11 May 1997. Konaré stated that he did not wish to be the sole candidate and appealed to the opposition to participate. In early May the leader of the Parti pour l'unité, la démocratie et le progrès, Mamadou Maribatou Diaby, announced that he was prepared to contest the presidency. The Constitutional Court rejected an opposition petition for the cancellation of the poll. According to the final results, Konaré was re-elected to the presidency, securing 95.9% of the valid votes cast. Although members of the radical opposition, which had campaigned for a boycott by voters, stated that the low rate of participation (28.4% of the registered electorate) effectively invalidated Konaré's victory, the turn-out was higher than that recorded at the 1992 presidential election. At the end of the month the municipal elections were postponed indefinitely.

Violent protests occurred in Bamako in June 1997, as Konaré was sworn in for a second term of office. Five opposition leaders, among them Tall (the CNID Chairman), Almamy Sylla (the RDP President and leader of the radical opposition collective) and Sogal Maïga (the MPR Secretary-General), were subsequently arrested and charged with various offences, including incitement to violence. They were released on bail in mid-June, shortly after the first round of the legislative elections (due on 6 July) had been postponed by two weeks. Meanwhile, several opposition activists had been sentenced to three months' imprisonment for their part in recent disturbances.

A small number of opposition parties announced their intention to present candidates for the Assemblée nationale, but the radical collective, known as the Collectif des partis politiques de l'opposition (COPPO), at this time numbering 18 parties of varying political tendencies, reiterated its refusal to re-enter the electoral process. Violent disturbances, in which two deaths were reported, preceded the first round of voting on 20 July 1997, which was contested by 17 parties (including five 'moderate' opposition parties) and a number of independent candidates. COPPO again asserted that its appeal for a boycott had been heeded, and that the low rate of participation by voters (at about 12% of the registered electorate in Bamako, and 22% outside the capital) would render the new parliament illegitimate. A second round of voting was necessary for eight seats on 3 August. The final results allocated 130 of the 147 seats to ADEMA, eight to PARENA, four to the Convention démocratique et sociale (CDS), three to the Union pour la démocratie et le développement (UDD) and two to the PDP.

In September 1997 Konaré held a meeting with some 20 opposition leaders, including representatives of COPPO, at which he presented proposals for a broadly based coalition government. A new Council of Ministers, under Keita, was appointed in mid-September. The new administration included, in addition to members of ADEMA and its allies, a small number of representatives of the moderate opposition parties (among them the UDD and PDP). Further measures intended to promote national reconciliation were implemented, and in December Konaré commuted some 21 death sentences, including those imposed on ex-President Traoré and his associates. Although several parties had withdrawn from COPPO, little progress was made towards a full political reconciliation.

In April 1998 former US President Jimmy Carter visited Bamako to mediate between the Government and opposition. He recommended that the opposition recognize Konaré's legitimacy as elected President, that a new electoral commission be formed, and that new electoral lists be prepared prior to municipal elections. The radical opposition accepted the principle of mediation, but reiterated their demands for Konaré's resignation. The cohesion of the opposition was undermined in July, Daba Diawara, who had recently announced his willingness to recognize Konaré as President was elected as Chairman of the US—RDA, and members who opposed political reconciliation were expelled.

The municipal elections finally commenced on 21 June 1998, with voting in 19 communes, amid sporadic violence, in which one death was reported, while several members of the CNID were arrested on attempted sabotage charges. The remaining COPPO parties boycotted the elections. Elections in the majority of communes (some 682) were scheduled to take place in November 1998; however, in September it was announced that voting was to be postponed until April 1999, to allow for the resolution of outstanding administrative problems and, furthermore, for negotiations on participation by all political tendencies.

In October 1998 the trial for 'economic crimes' began in Bamako of ex-President Traoré, his wife Mariam, her brother, Abraham Douah Cissoko (the former head of customs), a former Minister of Finance and Trade, Tiénan Coulibaly, and the former representative in France of the Banque de développement du Mali, Moussa Koné. In January 1999 Traoré, his wife and brother-in-law were sentenced to death, having been convicted of 'economic crimes' to the value of some US $350,000 (the original charges had cited embezzled funds amounting to $4m.). Coulibaly and Koné were acquitted. In September Konaré commuted the death sentences to terms of life imprisonment.

Clashes were reported in July 1999 in Gao and Kidal between members of the Arab and Kounta communities. Ten people were reportedly killed in the violence, and security forces were deployed in the area. Meanwhile, ethnic violence was also reported in the Kayes region, where eight people were killed in a dispute between Soninké farmers and Fulani (Peul) herders. Numerous disputes between the two groups had been reported in the area since early 1999, but at the end of July a peace agreement was signed by representatives of both communities and by the President of the Assemblée nationale. In August further clashes between the Arab and Kounta communities resulted in nine deaths. The Minister of the Interior subsequently visited the area in an attempt to restore order; in October, however, renewed clashes between the two groups were reported to have killed up to 40 people.

In February 2000 Keita submitted his Government's resignation. An extensively reorganized Council of Ministers was subsequently appointed. The new Prime Minister, Mandé Sidibé, was widely regarded as a supporter of economic reform. In June Choguel Kokala Maïga, the leader of the MPR, was among opposition leaders who announced their intention to participate fully in the presidential and parliamentary elections to be held in 2002, stating that conditions for electoral fairness and transparency seemed likely to be achieved.

In July 2000 the Assemblée nationale approved legislation providing for state funding of political parties. The Assemblée also adopted a revision of the Constitution proposed by Konaré, according to which some 50 articles of the 1992 document would be amended, subject to approval by referendum. Notably, people of dual nationality were to be permitted to contest presidential elections, while the Supreme Court was to be abolished. Also in July COPPO, which now comprised 15 parties and was led by Almamy Sylla of the RDP, announced that it would henceforth participate in the electoral process.

Keita resigned from the leadership of ADEMA in October 2000, following the announcement that his opponents within the party had succeeded in calling an extraordinary congress of the party, to be held in late November. At the congress, several new members were appointed to the ADEMA's executive committee, and Dioncounda Traoré was elected as the new Chairman of the party. A minor ministerial reshuffle was effected in June 2001. In July a new party led by Keita, the Rassemblement pour le Mali (RPM), was officially registered.

In November 2001 Konaré indefinitely postponed a referendum, which had been due to take place in December, on the constitutional amendments adopted by the legislature in July 2000, following pressure from opposition parties and the judiciary. In January 2002 Soumaïla Cissé was elected as ADEMA's candidate for the forthcoming presidential election. In March Modibo Keita, hitherto Secretary-General at the presidency, was appointed as Prime Minister, following Sidibé's resignation to contest the presidency as an independent candidate. In early April 16 opposition parties, including the CNID, the RPM and the MPR, formed an electoral alliance, Espoir 2002, agreeing to support a single opposition candidate (generally expected to be Ibrahim Boubacar Keita, who was to contest the election on behalf of the RPM) in the event of a second round of voting. Meanwhile, an alliance of 23 political parties, including MIRIA, PARENA and the US—RDA declared their support for the candidacy of Gen. (retd) Amadou Toumani Touré.

At the first round of the presidential election, which was held on 28 April 2002, contested by 24 candidates, Touré secured the largest share of the votes cast, with 28.7%, followed by Cissé, with 21.3%, and Keita, with 21.0%. As no candidate had secured an overall majority, Touré and Cissé progressed to a second round of voting, held on 12 May. Touré, was elected to the presidency, with 65.0% of the votes cast, having obtained the support of support of more than 40 parties, including those of Espoir 2002. The electoral process was marred by allegations of fraud and incompetence, which led the Constitutional Court to annul 25% of the votes cast in the first ballot. None the less, international observers described the elections as generally free, fair and open. Touré was inaugurated as President on 8 June, and subsequently formed an interim Government, comprising 21 ministers. The new Prime Minister and Minister of African Integration, Ahmed Mohamed Ag Hamani, was regarded as a technocrat; in addition to having previously held various ministerial posts under Traoré, he had, more recently, served as ambassador to Belgium and to Morocco and as High Commissioner of the Organisation pour la mise en valeur du fleuve Sénégal (see p. 386). President Touré emphasized that he was not affiliated to any particular political party, and would be prepared to govern with any future parliamentary majority. Meanwhile, in late May, in the stated interests of national reconciliation, Konaré announced that Traoré and his wife were to be pardoned. However, Traoré denounced the gesture as politically motivated, and only left prison in mid-July, after Konaré's term of office had ended.

The elections to the Assemblée nationale in July 2002 further demonstrated the lack of any one dominant political grouping in Mali, while the rate of participation, at 25.7% nation-wide, in the second round, was low. The first round of polls was largely inconclusive. According to provisional results, ADEMA won the largest number of seats (57) in the new Assemblée, although remaining short of the overall majority that the party had held in the outgoing legislature. However, as a result of various irregularities in the conduct of the polls, several thousand votes were invalidated; following the publication, in early August, of revised results by the Constitutional Court, the RPM emerged as the single largest party, with 46 of the 147 seats (although 20 of its seats had been won in local electoral alliances with other parties of the Espoir 2002 grouping), while other parties of Espoir 2002 obtained a further 21 seats, giving a total of 67 to allies of the RPM. ADEMA secured 45 seats, while the pro-ADEMA Alliance pour la République et la démocratie won an additional six seats, giving a total of 51. The CNID received 13 seats, while parties belonging to an informal alliance supportive of President Touré, the Alliance pour l'alternance et le changement (ACC), including PARENA and the US—RDA, won a total of 10 seats. The Constitutional Court declared void the results of voting in eight constituencies in Sikasso, in the south, and Tin-Essako, in the north, owing to administrative flaws; by-elections were scheduled to be held in October. In early September 19 deputies, comprising those of the ACC parties, several independent deputies and other declared supporters of Touré, formed a grouping within the legislature, with the declared intention of forming a stable presidential majority. Later in the month Ibrahim Boubakar Keita was elected President of the Assemblée nationale.

In mid-October 2002 Touré announced the formation of a Government of National Unity. Although many of the principal posts remained unchanged from the interim administration appointed in June, one notable appointment was that of Bassari Touré, a former official of the World Bank, as Minister of the Economy and Finance, who was expected to institute an expedited process of reform. The new Government stated that improvements to the health and education systems were among its priorities, as was the introduction of measures to alleviate the consequences of recent price rises in foodstuffs, electricity and water. Meanwhile, ADEMA increased its representation in the Assemblée nationale to 53 deputies, becoming the largest party grouping, following its victory in by-elections in all eight constituencies where elections were rerun on 20 October. A minor government reorganization was announced in mid-November.

In mid-2003 a split in ADEMA resulted in the formation, by Cissé, of a new party, the Union pour la République et la démocratie, which held its inaugural conference in early June. However, as Cissé's responsibilities as a commissioner of the Union économique et monétaire ouest-africaine meant that he was prohibited from political activity, former Prime Minister Younoussi Touré was elected as the interim Chairman of the party. In late August clashes between adherents of rival Islamic groups, apparently provoked by a dispute over land, resulted in 13 deaths in the west of the country. (In April 2005 some 84 people were found guilty of participating in the violence; five of the defendants were sentenced to death.)

In November 2003 the Council of Ministers proposed legislation that, subject to its approval by the Assemblée nationale, would provide for political parties to receive state funding, subject to certain conditions. Some 54 parties were stated to qualify for funding at this time.

In late April 2004 Ag Hamani tendered his resignation as Prime Minister, apparently in response to a request by President Touré. A new administration, headed by Prime Minister Ousmane Issoufi Maïga, hitherto Minister of Equipment and Transport (and not affiliated to any political party), was formed in early May. Moktar Ouane was appointed Minister of Foreign Affairs and International Co-operation, and Aboubacar Traoré became Minister of the Economy and Finance. ADEMA was the most successful party at municipal elections held on 23 May (postponed from the previous month), winning 28% of the seats contested, followed by the URD, which secured 14%, and the RPM, with 13%; the rate of participation by the electorate was relatively high, at 43.6%. ADEMA and the RPM subsequently formed an alliance, which, with ADEMA holding 44 seats and the RPM 35, gave the new grouping a majority in the 147-seat Assemblée nationale (although still short of the two-thirds majority needed to enact a motion of 'no confidence' against the head of the Government).

The death of a student in clashes between two rival student groups provoked violent unrest at the University of Bamako in December 2004, during which a further two students were killed. In late March 2005 rioting and looting erupted in Bamako following the defeat of the national association football team in a match against Togo. The security forces were widely criticized for failing to suppress the disturbances, which were attributed to by the media to youths angered by high unemployment, poverty and a lack of prospects. In June cotton workers held a two-day strike in support of demands for social assistance, following the privatization of a cottonseed oil plant, and the payment of salary arrears.

From mid-2004 there was considerable speculation regarding potential realignments of political organizations ahead of the presidential and legislative elections due in 2007. In February and March 2005 the President held a series of consultations with the leaders of various political organizations. However, there were signs that the political consensus that had existed since Touré's election in 2002 was likely to come to an end before the elections, as parties began to distance themselves from the President. Notably, in April 2005 the RPM, the URD and a faction of ADEMA refused to attend a meeting of support for the President, which was organized in response to the rioting of late March. In late June Touré effected a minor government reshuffle, dismissing the Minister of Youth and Sports, Moussa Balla Diakité, and the Minister for the Promotion of Women, Children and the Family, Berthé Aïssata Bengaly; a new Minister of Employment and Professional Training was also appointed. In early November the RPM announced that it would henceforth oppose the Government, stating that it had been increasingly marginalized within the ruling coalition; moreover, the party alleged that the death of one of its parliamentary deputies (who also held the post of a vice-president of the party), in an automobile collision in that month, constituted a planned political assassination. The victory of an RPM candidate in a legislative by-election, in mid-November, was interpreted by some observers as reflecting a decline in support for the ruling coalition, and it was subsequently reported that the RMP and URD were considering forming a common political programme. In February 2006 the executive committee of ADEMA announced that the party would support the candidacy of Touré at the presidential election due in 2007 and that it would not, consequently, present its own candidate in the election. Also in February the Government amended various clauses in the electoral law, including increasing two-fold the deposit required to be paid by presidential candidates.

A predominant concern in the first half of the 1990s was the rebellion in the north of Mali, which began as large numbers of Tuareg nomads, who had migrated to Algeria and Libya at times of drought, began to return to West Africa (see also the chapter on Niger). A Tuareg attack in June 1990 on Menaka (near the border with Niger) precipitated a state of emergency in the Gao and Tombouctou regions, and the armed forces began a campaign against the nomads. A peace accord signed in January 1991 in Tamanrasset, Algeria, by representatives of the Traoré Government and delegates from two Tuareg groups, the Mouvement populaire de l'Azaouad (MPA) and the Front islamique-arabe de l'Azaouad (FIAA), failed to provide a lasting solution to the conflict. Following the overthrow of the Traoré regime, the transitional administration affirmed its commitment to the Tamanrasset accord, and Tuareg groups were represented in the CTSP. However, unrest continued. At the time of the National Conference it was reported that at least 150 members of the armed forces had been killed since 1990; meanwhile, thousands of Tuaregs, Moors and Bella (the descendants of the Tuaregs' black slaves, some of whom remained with the nomads) had fled to neighbouring countries.

In February 1992, following negotiations between representatives of the Malian Government and of the Mouvements et fronts unifiés de l'Azaouad (MFUA), comprising the MPA, the FIAA and the Armée révolutionnaire de l'Azaouad (ARLA), with Algerian mediation, a truce entered into force, and a commission of inquiry was inaugurated to examine acts of violence perpetrated and losses suffered during the conflict; the more militant Front populaire de libération de l'Azaouad (FPLA) was not reported to have attended the talks. Following further discussions, the Malian authorities and the MFUA signed a draft 'National Pact' in April. Although sporadic attacks continued, particularly against members of the northern majority Songhaï, provisions of the National Pact were implemented: joint patrols were established, and in November President Konaré visited the north to inaugurate new administrative structures. In February 1993 the Malian Government and the MFUA signed an accord facilitating the integration of an initial 600 Tuaregs into the national army. In May Rhissa Ag Sidi Mohamed, the leader of the FPLA, expressed satisfaction at the success of early efforts to repatriate refugees, and he and his supporters returned from their base in Burkina to Mali. In that month it was announced that the office of the UN High Commissioner for Refugees (UNHCR) was to oversee a two-year voluntary repatriation programme, whereby 12,000 refugees would be resettled from southern Algeria to Mali by the end of 1993. However, the assassination, in February 1994, of the MPA's military leader—now, in accordance with the Pact, a senior officer in the Malian army—resulted in several weeks of clashes between the MPA and the ARLA, which was blamed for his death.

In May 1994 the Malian authorities and Tuareg leaders reached agreement regarding the integration of 1,500 former rebels into the Malian army and of a further 4,860 Tuaregs into civilian sectors. The success of the agreement was, however, undermined by an intensification of disorder in northern Mali. Meanwhile, a Songhaï-dominated black resistance movement, the Mouvement patriotique malien Ghanda Koy ('Masters of the Land'), emerged, amid rumours of official complicity in its offensives against the Tuaregs. In June one of the leaders of the FIAA died as a result of a clash with members of the armed forces. Meeting in Tamanrasset shortly afterwards, the Malian authorities and the MFUA endorsed a reinforcement of the army presence in areas affected by the violence, and agreed procedures for the more effective integration of Tuareg fighters. Despite a serious escalation of violence in July, the ministers responsible for foreign affairs of Mali, Algeria, Burkina Faso, Libya, Mauritania and Niger met in Bamako in August to discuss the Tuareg issue, and a new agreement for the voluntary repatriation from Algeria of Malian refugees was reached. Although MFUA leaders welcomed the agreement, pledged the reconciliation of the Tuareg movements, and reiterated their commitment to the National Pact, sporadic hostilities continued.

In October 1994 both the Government and the MFUA appealed for an end to the violence, following an attack on Gao (for which the FIAA claimed responsibility) and retaliatory action, as a result of which 66 deaths were officially reported. A new Minister of the Armed Forces and Veterans was appointed shortly afterwards, and the authorities subsequently appeared to adopt a less conciliatory approach to the dissident rebel groups, with the FIAA becoming increasingly marginalized in the peace process. In January 1995 representatives of the FPLA and Ghanda Koy issued a joint statement appealing for an end to hostilities, and for the implementation of the Pact. Further discussions involving Tuareg groups, Ghanda Koy and representatives of local communities resulted in the signing, in April, of an agreement providing for co-operation in resolving hitherto contentious issues. In June the FIAA announced an end to its armed struggle, and expressed its willingness to join national reconciliation efforts. In July a meeting of representatives of the Government and of Mali's creditors agreed development strategies for the northern regions, incorporating the restoration of civilian local government, education and health-care facilities and basic utilities. A programme for the encampment of former rebels, in preparation for their eventual integration into the national army or civilian structures, began in November and ended in February 1996, by which time some 3,000 MFUA fighters and Ghanda Koy militiamen had registered and surrendered their weapons. The MFUA and Ghanda Koy subsequently issued a joint statement affirming their adherence to Mali's Constitution, national unity and territorial integrity, urging the full implementation of the National Pact and associated accords and proclaiming the 'irreversible dissolution' of their respective movements.

In September 1997 the graduation of MFUA and Ghanda Koy contingents in the gendarmerie was reported as marking the accomplishment of the integration of all fighters within the national armed and security forces. In October the former FPLA leader, Rhissa Ag Sidi Mohamed, who had not previously been regarded as a party to the peace process, returned to Mali and expressed willingness to join efforts to consolidate peace and promote the development of the north. None the less the Ministers of Justice and of the Armed Forces and Veterans expressed concern that the continued proliferation of weapons, as well as the inadequacy of military and administrative structures in the north, could result in renewed clashes. In November 2000 it was reported that Malian government forces had been dispatched to end widespread banditry by an armed group, led by Ibrahim Bahanga, a former Tuareg rebel, in the Kidal area, near to the border with Algeria. In September 2001 Bahanga reportedly announced that his forces were to cease hostilities, following talks with a state official.

The presence of large numbers of refugees from the conflict in northern Mali dominated Mali's relations with its neighbours during the 1990s, and even after the completion of the process of repatriation in mid-1998 (and the conclusion of a UNHCR programme in June 1999) the north of the country remained vulnerable to cross-border banditry. In May 1998 the ministers responsible for the interior of Mali, Mauritania and Senegal met with a view to strengthening co-operation and border controls, and in December Mali and Senegal agreed to improve border security. In February 1999 Mali and Algeria agreed to revive their joint border committee to promote development and stability in the region. In March Konaré visited Mauritania to discuss border stability; however, in June a dispute over watering rights escalated into an armed conflict between neighbouring Malian and Mauritanian communities, in which 13 people were killed. The two Governments responded to the disturbances by increasing border controls and by sending a joint delegation to the villages involved. In August 1999 at a meeting in Dakar, Senegal, the Malian, Mauritanian and Senegalese ministers responsible for the interior agreed to establish an operational unit drawn from the police forces of the three countries in order to ensure security in the area of their joint border. Bilateral relations between Mali and Mauritania were further strengthened by a military co-operation agreement regarding border security signed by the countries' respective Presidents in Nouakchott in January 2005.

Concerns about insecurity in the region re-emerged in mid-2003, following reports, in late July, that some 15 German, Swiss and Dutch tourists, said to have been kidnapped in February by Islamist militants allegedly associated with the Groupe salafiste pour la prédication et le combat in southern Algeria, had been smuggled into Mali. Following negotiations with the kidnappers, conducted by a former rebel Tuareg leader, Iyad Ag Agaly, 14 hostages were released in mid-August (the remaining hostage had reportedly died earlier from heatstroke). In late October the Malian Minister of the Armed Forces and War Veterans, Mahamane Kalil Maïga, visited Algeria and met the Chief of Staff of the Algerian Army, Lt-Gen. Muhammad Lamari, to discuss security in the region. In March 2004 Mali announced that it was to increase anti-terrorism co-operation with the authorities in Algeria, Chad and Niger.

France remains an important trading partner and the principal donor of bilateral aid. From mid-1996 a series of expulsions from France of illegal immigrants, including many Malians, was generally criticized in Mali. The issue of immigration was a principal focus of discussions during a visit by the French Prime Minister, Lionel Jospin, in December 1997. Progress was achieved in September 1998, with the establishment of a Franco-Malian joint committee on immigration, intended to promote co-operation on the repatriation of migrants and their reintegration into Malian society. The new Government formed in October 2002 included a Minister-delegate for Malians Abroad and African Integration, and the issue of immigration was, again, a principal topic of discussion when the French Minister of the Interior, Internal Security and Local Freedoms, Nicolas Sarkozy, visited Mali later that month. During a visit to Mali in October 2003, the French President, Jacques Chirac, held talks with officials on the country's economic development, as well as illegal immigration.

In February 1999 some 488 Malian troops joined ECOMOG (see p. 220) forces in Sierra Leone, although the Malian authorities emphasized that these troops would take on a purely peace-keeping role. However, following widespread demands in Mali for a withdrawal, during August the majority of the force departed Sierra Leone; it was later announced that seven Malian soldiers had been killed and 10 seriously injured while serving in Sierra Leone. As Chairman of ECOWAS, in March 2001 Konaré hosted a mini-summit, attended by the leaders of the three countries of the Mano River Union (see p. 387), Sierra Leone, Liberia and Guinea, in Bamako on the subject of the peace process in Sierra Leone. Konaré sought to emphasize the role of Mali in ECOWAS, and in November 2000 a 120-member ECOWAS parliament, which was to promote regional co-operation, was inaugurated in Bamako.

Mali has in recent years forged closer relations with Libya, and was a founder member of the Community of Sahel-Saharan States (see p. 385), established in Tripoli in 1997.

In early 2004 some 30 US military instructors were dispatched to Mali to train troops in techniques to combat banditry and international terrorism.

Government

The Constitution of the Third Republic, which was approved in a national referendum on 12 January 1992, provides for the separation of the powers of the executive, legislative and judicial organs of state. Executive power is vested in the President of the Republic, who is elected for five years by universal suffrage. The President appoints a Prime Minister, who, in turn, appoints a Council of Ministers. Legislative power is vested in the 147-seat unicameral Assemblée nationale, elected for five years by universal suffrage. Elections take place in the context of a multi-party political system.

Mali has eight administrative regions, each presided over by a governor, and a district government in Bamako. Following a significant revision of local government structures in 1999, and a further minor revision in 2001, the number of elected mayors across Mali increased from 19 to 703. The Constitution makes provision for the establishment of a High Council of Local Communities.

Defence

In August 2005 the active Malian army numbered about 7,350 men, including a naval force of about 50 men (with patrol boats on the River Niger) and an air force of 400. Paramilitary forces comprised the gendarmerie (1,800), republican guard (2,000), militia (3,000) and national police (1,000). Military service is by selective conscription and lasts for two years. The defence budget for 2005 was estimated at 53,000m. francs CFA.

Economic Affairs

In 2004, according to estimates by the World Bank, Mali's gross national income (GNI), measured at average 2002–04 prices, was US $4,335m., equivalent to $360 per head (or $980 on an international purchasing-power parity basis). During 1995–2004, it was estimated, the population increased at an average annual rate of 2.4%, while gross domestic product (GDP) per head increased, in real terms, by an average of 3.2% per year. Overall GDP increased, in real terms, at an average annual rate of 5.7% in 1995–2004. According to the World Bank, real GDP increased by 2.2% in 2004.

Agriculture (including livestock-rearing, forestry and fishing) contributed 40.7% of GDP in 2003. An estimated 79.3% of the labour force were employed in the sector in that year. Mali is among Africa's foremost producers and exporters of cotton (exports of which contributed an estimated 38.0% of the value of merchandise exports in 2004). Cotton production increased significantly in 2001, to a record 571,335 metric tons, reflecting a marked expansion in the area of land cultivated for the crop in that year; output declined to 439,722 tons in 2002. According to unofficial figures, output increased to a record level of 635,000 tons in 2003, before declining to 600,000 tons in 2004. Shea-nuts (karité nuts), groundnuts, vegetables and mangoes are also cultivated for export. The principal subsistence crops are millet, rice, sorghum, maize and fonio. Cereal imports remain necessary in most years, and although a successful harvest in 2003 raised overall crop production by some 32%, according to official figures, the agricultural sector was badly damaged by the large locust swarms that affected the countries of the Sahel region in mid-2004. The livestock-rearing and fishing sectors make an important contribution to the domestic food supply and (in the case of the former) to export revenue, providing an estimated 4.7% of total exports in 2004, although both are highly vulnerable to drought. According to the World Bank, agricultural GDP increased by an average of 3.0% per year in 1995–2004; it increased by 17.7% in 2003, but declined by 4.7% in 2004, chiefly as a result of the locust invasion.

Industry (including mining, manufacturing, construction and power) contributed 22.8% of GDP in 2003. According to the World Bank, industrial GDP increased at an average annual rate of 7.4% in 1995–2004. However, industrial GDP declined by 9.4% in 2003 and by 0.2% in 2004.

Mining contributed 8.6% of GDP in 2003. The importance of the sector has increased with the successful exploitation of the country's gold reserves: exports of gold contributed an estimated 55.8% of the value of total exports in 2004. Output of gold increased significantly in the second half of the 1990s, as new mining facilities commenced operations, and by 2001 Mali had become the third largest gold producer in Africa. In 2002 exports of gold amounted to some 66.1 metric tons, yielding 400,000m. francs CFA, although exports of gold subsequently declined, to 44.5 tons, yielding 270,400m. francs CFA in 2004. Two new open-pit mines, at Yalea and Loulo, operated by Randgold Resources (of South Africa), commenced operations in late 2005; underground development at the same sites was expected, in due course, to produce 1.8m. oz of gold in total over a 10-year period. Salt, diamonds, marble and phosphate rock are also mined. The future exploitation of deposits of iron ore and uranium is envisaged. According to the IMF, the GDP of the mining sector increased at an average annual rate of 46.8% in 1996–2002;

growth in mining GDP reached 181.3% in 1997, before slowing to an estimated 23.1% by 2002.

The manufacturing sector, including electricity and water, contributed 7.0% of GDP in 2003. The main areas of activity are agro-industrial (chiefly the processing of cotton, sugar and rice). Brewing and tobacco industries are represented, and some construction materials are produced for the domestic market. According to the World Bank, manufacturing GDP declined at an average annual rate of 1.2% in 1995–2004. Manufacturing GDP declined by 5.5% in 2003, but increased by 20.8% in 2004.

Of total electric energy generated in 1995, about 80% was derived from hydroelectric installations. Mali began to receive power supplies from the Manantali hydroelectric project (constructed and operated under the auspices of the Organisation pour la mise en valeur du fleuve Sénégal—OMVS) from December 2001, and there were also plans to link the Malian network with those of Côte d'Ivoire, Burkina Faso and Ghana. An agreement on energy supply was also reached with Algeria in February 1998. In July 2000 Belgium provided a loan of 2,600m. francs CFA for the construction of two high-voltage power stations in Bamako. Imports of petroleum products comprised an estimated 27.2% of the value of merchandise imports in 2004.

The services sector contributed 35.5% of GDP in 2003. According to the World Bank, the GDP of the services sector increased at an average annual rate of 5.5% in 1995–2004. Services GDP increased by 9.1% in 2004.

In 2002 Mali recorded a visible trade deficit of US $60.5m., while there was a deficit of $271.0m. on the current account of the balance of payments. In 2004 the principal sources of imports were France, Senegal and Côte d'Ivoire (which supplied, respectively, 14.5%, 9.8% and 7.6% of total imports). The largest market for exports were the People's Republic of China (which accounted for 31.6% of total exports), Thailand (6.9%), Italy (6.9%) and Germany (5.1%). The principal exports in 2004 were gold and cotton, comprising, respectively, 55.8% and 38.0% of total exports. The principal imports in that year were petroleum products (accounting for 27.2% of total imports), chemical products (14.2%), foodstuffs (13.9%) and construction materials (12.3%).

In 2004, according to the IMF, Mali recorded an overall budget deficit of 75,600m. francs CFA. Mali's total external debt was US $3,129m. at the end of 2003, of which $2,910m. was long-term public debt. In 2002 the cost of debt-servicing was equivalent to 6.9% of the value of exports of goods and services. The annual rate of inflation averaged 0.9% in 1996–2004. Consumer prices declined by 1.3% in 2003, and further declined by 3.1% in 2004.

Mali is a member of numerous international and regional organizations, including the Economic Community of West African States (ECOWAS, see p. 217), the West African organs of the Franc Zone (see p. 282), the African Groundnut Council (see p. 381), the Liptako-Gourma Integrated Development Authority (see p. 386), the Niger Basin Authority (see p. 387) and the OMVS (see p. 386).

Mali's economic development is hindered by its vulnerability to drought, its dependence on imports and its narrow range of exports. The country also lacks facilities for the processing of its important cotton crop; it was reported in 2002 that only 1% of Mali's cotton crop was processed in the country. In August 1999 the IMF approved a loan for Mali under the Enhanced Structural Adjustment Facility (ESAF), equivalent to about US $633m.; the facility was subsequently extended for a further year, and in June 2004 the IMF approved a three-year arrangement with Mali under the Poverty Reduction and Growth Facility (PRGF—the successor to the ESAF) equivalent to $13.7m. Mali's external debt remains at a high level, despite the granting of some $870m. in debt-service relief under the initiative of the IMF and the World Bank for heavily indebted poor countries (HIPCs) in 2000, and the cancellation by France, in September 2002, of €80m. of bilateral debt. In March 2003 the Bretton Woods institutions announced that Mali had reached completion point under the terms of the HIPC initiative, thus becoming eligible for additional debt-relief, and in February 2005 the United Kingdom pledged to meet $45.4m. of Mali's debt to the World Bank and the African Development Bank. In July 2005 Mali was among 18 countries to be granted 100% debt relief on multilateral debt agreed by the Group of Eight leading industrialized nations (G-8), subject to the approval of the lenders. In the first half of the 2000s the Government pursued a programme of privatization, notably transferring the railway from Bamako to Dakar, Senegal, to private management in 2003. In addition, the cotton sector was undergoing restructuring and a partial transfer to private ownership, having been adversely affected by a decline in international prices during the late 1990s, and a controlling stake in the state oilseed-processing plant, the Huilerie Cotonnière du Mali (HUICOMA) was transferred to private ownership in 2005. The privatization of a majority share of the cotton ginning company, the Compagnie Malienne pour le Développement des Textiles (CMDT) was, however, postponed from 2006 until 2008. Moreover, the state electricity company, Energie du Mali, which had been privatized in 2000, returned to majority state control in late 2005, following the withdrawal of the majority private stakeholder, Saur International (of France) from the company, following several policy disputes with the Government. The Malian economy recorded high rates of growth in 2001 and 2002, largely attributable to a series of successful cotton and cereal harvests aided by favourable climactic conditions; despite another successful harvest, the economy slowed in 2003, partly due to the political crisis in Côte d'Ivoire, which functions as the major transit country for Mali's external trade. The rate of growth in 2004 was further reduced by the locust swarms which affected the Sahel region from mid-year; The Government appealed for international assistance to alleviate the consequences of the infestation of locusts and announced that ministers would each donate one month's salary to a special fund. In November it was estimated that some 900,000 people were suffering severe food shortages. Food scarcity (and a consequent short-term increase in food prices) continued to be of concern throughout the first half of 2005 as a result of drought, as well as the damage caused by the locusts. In March 2005 the Government announced a 12,000m. francs CFA spending programme intended to protect the agricultural sector from future locust attacks. It was predicted that the rate of growth would increase again in 2005 and 2006. None the less, in the absence of a more diversified economic base, Mali's economy remained vulnerable both to external shocks and to fluctuations in the terms of trade of its principal import and export commodities, particularly with regard to the global prices of gold and cotton.

Education

Education is provided free of charge and is officially compulsory for nine years between seven and 16 years of age. Primary education begins at the age of seven and lasts for six years. Secondary education, from 13 years of age, lasts for a further six years, generally comprising two cycles of three years. The rate of school enrolment in Mali is among the lowest in the world: in 1997 total enrolment at primary and secondary schools excluding Medersas (Islamic schools) was equivalent to only 32% of the school-age population (males 39%; females 25%). In 2000/01 primary enrolment was equivalent to 61% of the appropriate age-group (males 71%; females 51%), while in 1998/99 secondary enrolment was equivalent to only 15% (males 20%; females 10%). Tertiary education facilities include the national university, developed in the mid-1990s. Hitherto many students have received higher education abroad, mainly in France and Senegal. Estimated budgetary expenditure on education in 2000 was 64,930m. francs CFA, equivalent to 15.6% of total government expenditure in that year.

Public Holidays

2006: 1 January (New Year's Day), 10 January*† (Tabaski, Feast of the Sacrifice), 20 January (Armed Forces Day), 25 March (Commemoration of the overthrow of Moussa Traoré), 10 April* (Mouloud, Birth of the Prophet), 17 April (Easter Monday), 1 May (Labour Day), 9 May* (Baptism of the Prophet), 25 May (Africa Day, anniversary of the OAU's foundation), 22 September (Independence Day), 23 October* (Korité, end of Ramadan), 25 December (Christmas Day), 31 December*† (Tabaski, Feast of the Sacrifice).

2007: 1 January (New Year's Day), 20 January (Armed Forces Day), 25 March (Commemoration of the overthrow of Moussa Traoré), 31 March* (Mouloud, Birth of the Prophet), 9 April (Easter Monday), 30 April* (Baptism of the Prophet), 1 May (Labour Day), 25 May (Africa Day, anniversary of the OAU's foundation), 22 September (Independence Day), 13 October* (Korité, end of Ramadan), 20 December* (Tabaski, Feast of the Sacrifice), 25 December (Christmas Day).

* These holidays are determined by the Islamic lunar calendar and may vary by one or two days from the dates given.

† This festival occurs twice (in the Islamic years AH 1426 and 1427) within the same Gregorian year.

Weights and Measures

The metric system is in force.

Statistical Survey

Source (unless otherwise stated): Direction Nationale de la Statistique et de l'Informatique, BP 12, Bamako; tel. 22-24-55; fax 22-71-45.

Area and Population

AREA, POPULATION AND DENSITY

Area (sq km)	1,240,192*
Population (census results)†	
1–30 April 1987	7,696,348
17 April 1998	
Males	4,847,436
Females	4,943,056
Total	9,790,492
Population (UN estimates at mid-year)‡	
2002	12,358,000
2003	12,736,000
2004	13,124,000
Density (per sq km) at mid-2004	10.6

* 478,841 sq miles.
† Figures are provisional and refer to the *de jure* population.
‡ Source: UN, *World Population Prospects: The 2004 Revision*; Figures have not been revised to take account of the 1998 census result.

Ethnic Groups (percentage of total, 1995): Bambara 36.5; Peul 13.9; Sénoufo 9.0; Soninké 8.8; Dogon 8.0; Songhaï 7.2; Malinké 6.6; Diola 2.9; Bobo and Oulé 2.4; Tuareg 1.7; Moor 1.2; Others 1.8 (Source: La Francophonie).

ADMINISTRATIVE DIVISIONS
(*de jure* population at 1998 census, provisional figures)

District		Mopti	1,475,274
Bamako	1,016,167	Kayes	1,372,019
Regions		Tombouctou	461,956
Sikasso	1,780,042	Gao	397,516
Ségou	1,679,201	Kidal	42,479
Koulikoro	1,565,838		

PRINCIPAL TOWNS*
(*de jure* population at 1998 census, provisional figures)

Bamako (capital)	1,016,167	Koutiala	74,153
Sikasso	113,813	Kayes	67,262
Ségou	90,898	Gao	54,903
Mopti	79,840	Kati	49,756

* With the exception of Bamako, figures refer to the population of communes (municipalities).

BIRTHS AND DEATHS
(UN estimates, annual averages)

	1990–95	1995–2000	2000–05
Birth rate (per 1,000)	50.8	51.2	49.7
Death rate (per 1,000)	19.0	18.4	17.8

Source: UN, *World Population Prospects: The 2004 Revision*.

Expectation of life (WHO estimates, years at birth): 45 (males 44; females 46) in 2003 (Source: WHO, *World Health Report*).

ECONOMICALLY ACTIVE POPULATION
('000 persons, ILO estimates, 1990)

	Males	Females	Total
Agriculture, hunting, forestry and fishing	1,990	1,846	3,837
Industry	55	33	88
Manufacturing	40	32	72
Services	352	195	547
Total	2,437	2,106	4,544

Source: ILO.

Mid-2003 ('000 persons, estimates): Agriculture, etc. 4,826; Total labour force 6,088 (Source: FAO).

Health and Welfare

KEY INDICATORS

Total fertility rate (children per woman, 2003)	7.0
Under-5 mortality rate (per 1,000 live births, 2004)	219
HIV/AIDS (% of persons aged 15–49, 2003)	1.9
Physicians (per 1,000 head, 2000)	0.04
Hospital beds (per 1,000 head, 1998)	0.24
Health expenditure (2002): US $ per head (PPP)	33
Health expenditure (2002): % of GDP	4.5
Health expenditure (2002): public (% of total)	50.8
Access to water (% of persons, 2002)	48
Access to sanitation (% of persons, 2002)	45
Human Development Index (2003): ranking	174
Human Development Index (2003): value	0.333

For sources and definitions, see explanatory note on p. vi.

Agriculture

PRINCIPAL CROPS
('000 metric tons)

	2002	2003	2004
Wheat	4.6	6.0	7.0
Rice (paddy)	710.4	938.0	877.0
Maize	363.6	365.2	365.2*
Millet	795.1	815.0†	815.0*
Sorghum	641.7	650.0†	650.0*
Fonio	16.3	14.0†	14.0*
Sweet potatoes	74.5	74.5*	74.5*
Cassava (Manioc)	24.2	24.2*	24.2*
Yams	47.8	47.8*	47.8*
Sugar cane	333.3	350.0*	350.0*
Pulses	92.3	108.3*	108.3*
Groundnuts (in shell)	120.8	156.0†	156.0*
Karité nuts (Sheanuts)*	85	85	85
Cottonseed*	170	185	175
Tomatoes	49.7	50.0*	50.0*
Dry onions	28.5	29.0*	30.0*
Other vegetables*	252.8	252.8	252.8
Mangoes	29.1	30.0*	31.0*
Cotton (lint)†	181.0	261.0	239.5

* FAO estimate(s).
† Unofficial figure(s).

Source: FAO.

LIVESTOCK
('000 head, year ending September)

	2002	2003	2004
Cattle	6,893	7,312	7,500
Sheep*	7,226	7,967	8,364
Goats*	10,398	11,464	12,036
Pigs	67	68	68
Horses†	170	170	172
Asses†	700	700	720
Camels†	470	470	472
Chickens	28,000	29,000	30,000

* Unofficial figures.
† FAO estimates.

Source: FAO.

MALI

LIVESTOCK PRODUCTS
(FAO estimates, '000 metric tons)

	2002	2003	2004
Beef and veal	103.5	113.0	97.8
Mutton and lamb	30.6	33.8	36.0
Goat meat	41.6	46.0	48.5
Chicken meat	32.5	33.6	34.8
Game meat	18.0	18.0	18.0
Other meat	12.3	12.3	12.4
Cows' milk	169.1	179.3	183.8
Sheeps' milk	108.0	117.0	124.5
Goats' milk	205.9	227.0	238.3
Camels' milk	54.9	54.9	55.2
Cattle hides (fresh)	15.9	17.4	15.0
Sheepskins (fresh)	7.1	7.8	8.4
Goatskins (fresh)	5.9	6.6	6.9

Source: FAO.

Forestry

ROUNDWOOD REMOVALS
(FAO estimates, '000 cubic metres, excl. bark)

	2002	2003	2004
Sawlogs, veneer logs and logs for sleepers	4	4	4
Other industrial wood	409	409	409
Fuel wood	4,846	4,905	4,965
Total	5,258	5,318	5,378

Source: FAO.

SAWNWOOD PRODUCTION
('000 cubic metres, incl. railway sleepers)

	1987	1988	1989
Total (all broadleaved)	11	13	13*

* FAO estimate.

1990–2004: Annual production as in 1989 (FAO estimates).
Source: FAO.

Fishing

('000 metric tons, live weight)

	2000	2001*	2002*
Capture	109.9	100.0	100.0
Nile tilapia	33.0	30.0	30.0
Elephantsnout fishes	7.7	7.0	7.0
Characins	5.5	5.0	5.0
Black catfishes	4.4	4.0	4.0
North African catfish	27.5	25.0	25.0
Nile perch	6.6	6.0	6.0
Other freshwater fishes	25.3	23.0	23.0
Aquaculture	0.0	0.5	1.0
Total catch	109.9	100.5	101.0

* FAO estimates.

Source: FAO.

2003 (FAO estimates): Data assumed to be unchanged from 2002.

Mining

(metric tons, unless otherwise indicated)

	2001	2002	2003
Gold (kg)*	42,288	56,043	45,535†
Gypsum‡	500	500	500
Salt‡	6,000	6,000	6,000

* Excluding artisanal output, estimated at 2,000 kg per year.
† Reported figure.
‡ Estimates.

Source: US Geological Survey.

Industry

SELECTED PRODUCTS
('000 metric tons, unless otherwise indicated)

	1999	2000	2001
Raw sugar*	31.2†	29.1	28.0
Salted, dried or smoked fish*	6.4	8.0	7.9
Cigarettes ('000 packets)	51.4	n.a.	n.a.
Cement‡	10	10	n.a.
Electric energy (million kWh)§	404	412	415

* Data from FAO.
† Unofficial figure.
‡ Data from the US Geological Survey.
§ Provisional or estimated figures.

2002: Raw sugar ('000 metric tons) 32.0 (Data from FAO).

Source: mainly UN, *Industrial Commodity Statistics Yearbook*.

Finance

CURRENCY AND EXCHANGE RATES

Monetary Units
  100 centimes = 1 franc de la Communauté financière africaine (CFA).

Sterling, Dollar and Euro Equivalents (30 December 2005)
  £1 sterling = 957.440 francs CFA;
  US $1 = 556.037 francs CFA;
  €1 = 655.957 francs CFA;
  10,000 francs CFA = £10.44 = $17.98 = €15.24.

Average Exchange Rate (francs CFA per US $)
  2003   581.20
  2004   528.29
  2005   527.47

Note: An exchange rate of 1 French franc = 50 francs CFA, established in 1948, remained in force until January 1994, when the CFA franc was devalued by 50%, with the exchange rate adjusted to 1 French franc = 100 francs CFA. This relationship to French currency remained in effect with the introduction of the euro on 1 January 1999. From that date, accordingly, a fixed exchange rate of €1 = 655.957 francs CFA has been in operation.

MALI

BUDGET
('000 million francs CFA)*

Revenue†	2002	2003	2004
Budgetary revenue	354.7	397.6	422.3
Tax revenue	323.5	362.4	403.6
Taxes on net income and profits	45.1	63.0	68.6
Enterprises	13.8	31.9	32.2
Individuals	28.4	29.3	34.5
Payroll tax	6.5	9.7	7.9
Taxes on goods and services	72.0	70.0	89.3
Value-added tax	42.9	48.1	66.8
Taxes on international trade	180.4	194.1	218.2
Customs duties	42.8	45.0	51.5
Value-added tax on imports	83.8	91.3	111.5
Petroleum import duties	30.2	33.7	30.3
Other tax revenue	19.3	25.0	19.4
Stamp duties	9.9	11.9	12.4
Other current revenue	31.2	35.2	18.7
Special funds and annexed budgets	33.7	37.4	42.6
Total	388.4	435.0	464.9

Expenditure‡	2002	2003	2004
Budgetary expenditure	511.7	535.5	592.2
Current expenditure	308.7	316.3	350.0
Wages and salaries	93.5	106.2	121.7
Goods and services	109.0	107.6	136.5
Transfers and subsidies	87.8	83.8	74.5
Interest payments (scheduled)	18.4	18.8	17.2
Capital expenditure	203.1	219.2	242.2
Externally financed	140.3	140.9	152.8
Special funds and annexed budgets	33.7	37.4	42.6
Total	545.4	572.9	634.8

* Figures represent a consolidation of the central government budget, special funds and annexed budgets.
† Excluding grants received ('000 million francs CFA): 85.8 in 2002; 114.8 in 2003; 103.3 in 2004.
‡ Excluding net lending ('000 million francs CFA): −4.9 in 2002; −3.9 in 2003; −9.0 in 2004.

Source: IMF, *Mali: Statistical Appendix* (March 2006).

INTERNATIONAL RESERVES
(excluding gold, US $ million at 31 December)

	2002	2003	2004
IMF special drawing rights	0.0	0.9	0.6
Reserve position in IMF	12.0	13.2	13.9
Foreign exchange	582.4	938.4	846.2
Total	594.5	952.5	860.7

Source: IMF, *International Financial Statistics*.

MONEY SUPPLY
('000 million francs CFA at 31 December)

	2002	2003	2004
Currency outside banks	247.5	340.9	275.4
Demand deposits	238.2	272.8	294.1
Total money (incl. others)	486.1	614.2	569.7

Source: IMF, *International Financial Statistics*.

COST OF LIVING
(Consumer Price Index for Bamako: base: 1996 = 100)

	2002	2003	2004
Food, beverages and tobacco	110.9	106.3	98.9
Clothing	109.3	111.7	103.9
Housing, water, electricity and gas	117.5	117.3	115.4
All items (incl. others)	112.0	110.5	107.1

Source: Banque centrale des états de l'Afrique de l'ouest.

NATIONAL ACCOUNTS
('000 million francs CFA at current prices)

Expenditure on the Gross Domestic Product

	2001	2002	2003
Final consumption expenditure	1,876.9	1,904.3	2,022.2
Households	} 1,530.6	} 1,536.2	} 1,638.2
Non-profit institutions serving households			
General government	346.3	368.1	384.0
Gross capital formation	540.2	431.5	631.0
Gross fixed capital formation	420.6	439.5	446.0
Changes in inventories	} 119.6	} −8.0	} 185.0
Acquisitions, less disposals, of valuables			
Total domestic expenditure	2,417.1	2,335.8	2,653.2
Exports of goods and services	642.4	728.0	674.8
Less Imports of goods and services	847.5	766.3	833.6
GDP in market prices	2,212.0	2,297.5	2,494.4

Gross Domestic Product by Economic Activity

	2001	2002	2003
Agriculture, livestock-rearing, forestry and fishing	774.1	740.3	924.9
Mining	206.4	238.8	196.1
Manufacturing	127.3	171.0	158.1
Electricity, gas and water	30.2	36.6	42.8
Construction and public works	110.8	118.5	119.7
Trade	92.4	96.6	111.0
Transport, storage and communications	153.8	161.8	168.0
Non-market services	232.4	249.1	259.6
Other services	301.6	273.6	290.5
Sub-total	2,029.0	2,086.3	2,270.7
Import duties	183.0	211.2	223.7
GDP in purchasers' values	2,212.0	2,297.5	2,494.4

Source: Banque centrale des états de l'Afrique de l'ouest.

BALANCE OF PAYMENTS
(US $ million)

	2001	2002	2003
Exports of goods f.o.b.	725.2	875.1	927.8
Imports of goods f.o.b.	−734.7	−712.5	−988.3
Trade balance	−9.6	162.7	−60.5
Exports of services	151.2	169.4	224.3
Imports of services	−421.4	−387.0	−482.2
Balance on goods and services	−279.8	−54.9	−318.5
Other income received	22.1	36.1	21.3
Other income paid	−188.2	−276.3	−181.2
Balance on goods, services and income	−445.8	−295.1	−478.4
Current transfers received	160.7	182.1	265.5
Current transfers paid	−25.0	−35.7	−58.1
Current balance	−310.0	−148.8	−271.0
Capital account (net)	107.4	104.2	113.7
Direct investment abroad	−17.3	−1.6	−1.4
Direct investment from abroad	121.7	243.8	132.3
Portfolio investment assets	−0.8	−0.5	−27.1
Portfolio investment liabilities	12.4	54.1	27.6
Other investment assets	−87.7	−248.4	3.7
Other investment liabilities	117.8	141.1	155.1
Net errors and omissions	9.4	−6.1	4.6
Overall balance	−47.0	137.8	137.4

Source: IMF, *International Financial Statistics*.

MALI

External Trade

PRINCIPAL COMMODITIES
('000 million francs CFA)

Imports c.i.f.	2002	2003	2004*
Foodstuffs	82.7	86.8	114.6
Cereals	27.1	28.7	17.1
Sugar	19.9	20.7	10.2
Petroleum products	112.9	108.6	224.2
Construction materials	79.7	85.5	101.2
Chemical products	129.2	122.2	116.7
Textiles and leather	19.3	20.2	12.1
Total (incl. others)	640.0	564.3	823.8

Exports f.o.b.	2002	2003	2004*
Cotton	158.0	144.3	184.2
Cotton fibre	155.4	140.9	181.4
Livestock	27.3	24.0	22.9
Gold	400.0	326.8	270.4
Total (incl. others)	596.5	503.8	484.7

* Estimates.

Source: IMF, *Mali: Statistical Appendix* (March 2006).

SELECTED TRADING PARTNERS
(US $ million)

Imports	2002	2003	2004
Belgium	32.4	32.0	49.2
China, People's Repub.	37.1	31.6	34.5
Côte d'Ivoire	197.5	107.6	141.3
France	192.1	234.1	268.8
Germany	54.4	54.9	73.7
India	27.7	42.4	29.6
Senegal	92.5	117.8	182.4
South Africa	19.3	25.6	63.0
USA	12.2	34.3	47.4
Total (incl. others)	1,382.7	1,523.1	1,857.6

Exports	2002	2003	2004
Belgium	5.1	n.a.	n.a.
China, People's Repub.	1.7	25.8	103.3
Côte d'Ivoire	1.8	0.1	0.1
France (incl. Monaco)	6.5	7.7	7.4
Germany	8.5	7.3	16.5
India	14.0	25.8	15.5
Indonesia	3.8	4.1	7.3
Italy	16.9	16.1	22.4
Korea, Repub.	3.6	2.2	1.2
Spain	8.4	n.a.	n.a.
Thailand	23.9	30.0	22.7
Tunisia	3.2	4.8	2.3
United Kingdom	4.8	n.a.	n.a.
Total (incl. others)	162.3	214.5	326.7

Source: mostly IMF, *Mali: Statistical Appendix* (March 2006).

Transport

RAILWAYS
(traffic)

	1997	1998	1999
Passengers ('000)	862	790	778
Freight carried ('000 metric tons)	565	566	536
Passenger-km (million)	223	218	210
Freight ton-km (million)	258	256	241

ROAD TRAFFIC
(estimates, motor vehicles in use)

	1994	1995	1996
Passenger cars	24,250	24,750	26,190
Lorries and vans	16,000	17,100	18,240

Source: IRF, *World Road Statistics*.

CIVIL AVIATION
(traffic on scheduled services)*

	1997	1998	1999
Kilometres flown (million)	3	3	3
Passengers carried ('000)	86	91	84
Passenger-km (million)	242	258	235
Total ton-km (million)	38	38	36

* Including an apportionment of the traffic of Air Afrique.

Source: UN, *Statistical Yearbook*.

Communications Media

	2002	2003	2004
Telephones ('000 main lines in use)	56.6	n.a.	74.9
Mobile cellular telephones ('000 subscribers)	52.6	244.9	400.0
Personal computers ('000 in use)	15	n.a.	42
Internet users ('000)	25.0	n.a.	50.0

Source: International Telecommunication Union.

Television receivers ('000 in use): 160 in 2000 (Source: UNESCO, *Statistical Yearbook*).

Book production (first editions, excluding pamphlets): 14 titles (28,000 copies) in 1995 (first editions only, excluding pamphlets); 33 in 1998 (Sources: UNESCO, *Statistical Yearbook*, UNESCO Institute for Statistics).

Daily newspapers (national estimates): 3 (total circulation 12,350 copies) in 1997; 3 (total circulation 12,600) in 1998 (Source: UNESCO Institute for Statistics).

Radio receivers ('000 in use): 570 in 1997 (Source: UNESCO, *Statistical Yearbook*).

Tourism

FOREIGN VISITORS BY COUNTRY OF RESIDENCE*

	2001	2002	2003
Belgium, Luxembourg and the Netherlands	8,193	8,971	3,262
Canada	2,512	3,217	1,562
France	20,418	22,325	22,539
Germany	2,821	3,103	2,412
Italy	9,852	10,676	3,476
Spain	3,089	3,559	2,637
United Kingdom	1,269	1,395	1,460
USA	5,881	6,015	1,817
West African states	16,478	18,125	14,232
Total (incl. others)	88,639	95,851	69,691

* Arrivals at hotels and similar establishments.

Receipts from tourism (US $ million, incl. passenger transport): 47 in 2000; 91 in 2001; 105 in 2002.

Source: World Tourism Organization.

Education

(2002/03, unless otherwise indicated)

	Institutions*	Teachers	Students Males	Females	Total
Pre-primary	212	984	10,559	10,268	20,827
Primary	2,871	22,577	742,087	552,585	1,294,672
Secondary	n.a.	8,274†	229,141	122,330	351,471
Tertiary	n.a.	960‡	n.a.	n.a.	28,332

* 1998/99.
† 1999/2000.
‡ 1998/99.

Source: mainly UNESCO Institute for Statistics.

2005/06 (unless otherwise indicated): *Pre-primary*: 412 institutions; 1,510 teachers; 51,071 students; *Primary and Secondary (lower)*: 8,079 institutions; 39,109 teachers; 1,990,765 students (1,137,787 males, 852,978 females); *Secondary (higher)*: 121 institutions; 1,904 teachers; 47,279 students (31,724 males, 15,555 females—estimates); *Secondary (technical and vocational)*: 119 institutions; 41,137 students); *Secondary (teacher training)*: 10,467 students; *University of Bamako*: 32,609 students (2004/05) (Source: Office of the Secretary-General of the Government, Bamako).

Adult literacy rate (UNESCO estimates): 19.0% (males 26.7%; females 11.9%) in 1995–99 (Source: UN Development Programme, *Human Development Report*).

Directory

The Constitution

The Constitution of the Third Republic of Mali was approved in a national referendum on 12 January 1992. The document upholds the principles of national sovereignty and the rule of law in a secular, multi-party state, and provides for the separation of the powers of the executive, legislative and judicial organs of state.

Executive power is vested in the President of the Republic, who is Head of State and is elected for five years by universal adult suffrage. The President appoints the Prime Minister, who, in turn, appoints other members of the Council of Ministers.

Legislative authority is exercised by the unicameral 147-member Assemblée nationale, which is elected for five years by universal adult suffrage.

The Constitution guarantees the independence of the judiciary. Final jurisdiction in constitutional matters is vested in a Constitutional Court.

The rights, freedoms and obligations of Malian citizens are enshrined in the Constitution. Freedom of the press and of association are guaranteed.

The Government

HEAD OF STATE

President: Gen. (retd) AMADOU TOUMANI TOURÉ (took office 8 June 2002).

COUNCIL OF MINISTERS
(April 2006)

Prime Minister: OUSMANE ISSOUFI MAÏGA.
Minister of the Environment and Decontamination: NANCOUMA KÉITA.
Minister of Planning and Territorial Development: MARIMATIA DIARRA.
Minister of Stockbreeding and Fisheries: OUMAR IBRAHIMA TOURÉ.
Minister of Crafts and Tourism: BAH N'DIAYE.
Minister of National Education: MAMADOU LAMINE TRAORÉ.
Minister of Industry and Trade: CHOGUEL KOKALA MAÏGA.
Minister of Territorial Administration and Local Communities: Gen. KAFOUGOUNA KONÉ.
Minister of Foreign Affairs and International Co-operation: MOKTAR OUANE.
Minister of Malians Abroad and African Integration: OUMAR HAMADOUN DICKO.
Minister of Agriculture: SEYDOU TRAORÉ.
Minister of Communication and New Information Technologies: GAOUSSOU DRABO.
Minister of Mining, Energy and Water Resources: AHMED DIANE SEMEGA.
Minister of Culture: CHEICK OUMAR SISSOKO.
Minister of Social Development, Solidarity and the Elderly: DJIBRIL TANGARA.
Minister of the Economy and Finance: ABOUBACAR TRAORÉ.
Minister of the Civil Service, the Reform of the State and Relations with the Institutions: BADI OULD GANFOUD.
Minister of Employment and Professional Training: BÂ AWA KÉÏTA.
Minister of the Promotion of Investment and of Small- and Medium-sized Enterprises, Government Spokesperson: OUSMANE THIAM.
Minister for the Promotion of Women, Children and the Family: DIALLO M'BODJI SÈNE.
Minister of Defence and Veterans: MAMADOU CLAZIÉ SISSOUMA.
Minister of Justice, Keeper of the Seals: FANTA SYLLA.
Minister of State-Administered Estates and Housing Affairs: SOUMARÉ AMINATA SIDIBÉ.
Minister of Health: MAÏGA ZEINAB MINT YOUBA.
Minister of Capital Works and Transport: ABDOULAYE KOÏTA.
Minister of Internal Security and Civil Protection: Col SADJO GASSAMA.
Minister of Youth and Sports: NATHIÉ PLÉA.
Minister of Housing and Town Planning: MODIBO SYLLA.
Minister, Secretary-General of the Government: FOUSSEYNI SAMAKE.

MINISTRIES

Office of the President: BP 1463, Koulouba, Bamako; tel. 222-25-72; fax 223-00-26; e-mail presidence@koulouba.pr.ml; internet www.koulouba.pr.ml.
Office of the Prime Minister: quartier du Fleuve, BP 790, Bamako; tel. 223-06-80; fax 222-85-83.
Office of the Secretary-General of the Government: BP 14, Koulouba, Bamako; tel. 222-25-52; fax 222-70-50; e-mail sgg@sgg.gov.ml; internet www.sgg.gov.ml.
Ministry of Agriculture: BP 1676, Bamako; tel. 222-27-85.

MALI

Ministry of Capital Works and Transport: Bamako; tel. 222-39-37.

Ministry of the Civil Service, the Reform of the State and Relations with the Institutions: Bamako; tel. 222-31-80.

Ministry of Communication and New Information Technologies: quartier du Fleuve, BP 116, Bamako; tel. 222-26-47; fax 223-20-54.

Ministry of Crafts and Tourism: Badalabougou, Semagesco, BP 2211, Bamako; tel. 223-64-50; fax 223-82-01; e-mail malitourisme@afribone.net.ml; internet www.malitourisme.com.

Ministry of Culture: Korofina, BP 4075, Bamako; tel. 224-66-63; fax 224-57-27; e-mail info@culture.gov.ml; internet w3.culture.gov.ml.

Ministry of Defence and Veterans: route de Koulouba, BP 2083, Bamako; tel. 222-50-21; fax 223-23-18.

Ministry of the Economy and Finance: BP 234, Koulouba, Bamako; tel. 222-51-56; fax 222-01-92.

Ministry of Employment and Professional Training: Bamako; tel. 222-34-31.

Ministry of the Environment and Decontamination: Bamako; tel. 223-05-39.

Ministry of Foreign Affairs and International Co-operation: Koulouba, Bamako; tel. 222-83-14; fax 222-52-26.

Ministry of Health: BP 232, Koulouba, Bamako; tel. 222-53-02; fax 223-02-03.

Ministry of Housing and Town Planning: Bamako; tel. 223-05-39.

Ministry of Industry and Trade: quartier du Fleuve, BP 234, Koulouba, Bamako; tel. 222-43-87; fax 222-88-53.

Ministry of Internal Security and Civil Protection: BP E4771, Bamako; tel. 222-00-82.

Ministry of Justice: quartier du Fleuve, BP 97, Bamako; tel. 222-26-42; fax 223-00-63; e-mail ucprodej@afribone.net.ml; internet www.justicemali.org.

Ministry of Malians Abroad and African Integration: Bamako; e-mail info@maliensdelexterieur.gov.ml; internet www.maliensdelexterieur.gov.ml.

Ministry of Mining, Energy and Water Resources: BP 238, Bamako; tel. 222-41-84; fax 222-21-60.

Ministry of National Education: BP 71, Bamako; tel. 222-57-80; fax 222-21-26; e-mail info@education.gov.ml; internet www.education.gov.ml.

Ministry of Planning and Territorial Development: Bamako; tel. 223-20-02.

Ministry of the Promotion of Investment and of Small- and Medium-sized Enterprises: Bamako.

Ministry for the Promotion of Women, Children and the Family: Porte G9, rue 109, Badalabougou, BP 2688, Bamako-; tel. 222-66-59; fax 223-66-60; e-mail mpfef@mpfef.gov.ml; internet www.mpfef.gov.ml.

Ministry of Social Development, Solidarity and the Elderly: Bamako; tel. 223-23-01.

Ministry of State-Administered Estates and Housing Affairs: Bamako; tel. 223-63-44.

Ministry of Stockbreeding and Fisheries: Bamako; tel. 223-36-96.

Ministry of Territorial Administration and Local Communities: face Direction de la RCFM, BP 78, Bamako; tel. 222-42-12; fax 223-02-47; internet www.matcl.gov.ml.

Ministry of Youth and Sports: route de Koulouba, BP 91, Bamako; tel. 222-31-53; fax 223-90-67; e-mail mjsports@mjsports.gov.ml; internet www.mjsports.gov.ml.

President and Legislature

PRESIDENT

Presidential Election, First Ballot, 28 April 2002

Candidates	Votes	% of votes
Gen. (retd) Amadou Toumani Touré (Independent)	449,176	28.71
Soumaïla Cissé (ADEMA)	333,525	21.31
Ibrahim Boubacar Keita (RPM)	329,143	21.03
Tiébilé Dramé (PARENA)	62,493	3.99
Mountaga Tall (CNID)	58,695	3.75
Moussa Balla Coulibaly (UDD)	50,211	3.21
Choguel Kokala Maïga (MPR)	42,469	2.71
Mamadou Bakary Sangaré (CDS)	34,603	2.21
Mandé Sidibé (Independent)	31,389	2.01
Others	173,072	11.06
Total	**1,564,776**	**100.00**

Second Ballot, 12 May 2002

Candidates	Votes	% of votes
Gen. (retd) Amadou Toumani Touré (Independent)	926,243	65.01
Soumaïla Cissé (ADEMA)	498,503	34.99
Total	**1,424,746**	**100.00**

LEGISLATURE

Assemblée nationale

BP 284, Bamako; tel. 221-57-24; fax 221-03-74; e-mail mamou@blonba.malinet.ml.

President: IBRAHIM BOUBACAR KEITA.

General Election, 14 and 28 July 2002*

Parties and alliances	Seats
Alliance pour la démocratie au Mali—Parti panafricain pour la liberté, la solidarité et la justice (ADEMA)	53
Rassemblement pour le Mali (RPM)	46†
Congrès national d'initiative démocratique—Faso Yiriwa Ton (CNID)	13
Rassemblement pour la démocratie et le travail (RDT)	7
Parti de la solidarité africaine pour la démocratie et l'indépendance (SADI)	6
Convention démocratique et sociale (CDS)	4
Bloc pour la démocratie et l'intégration africaine—Faso Jigi (BDIA)	3
Union soudanaise—Rassemblement démocratique africaine (US—RDA)/Rassemblement national pour la démocratie (RND)	3
Mouvement patriotique pour le renouveau (MPR)	2
Rassemblement malien pour le travail (RAMAT)	2
Parti pour la démocratie et le renouveau—Dounkafa Ton (PDR)	1
Parti pour la renaissance nationale (PARENA)	1
Independents	6
Total	**147**

* These figures include the results of voting in eight constituencies where the elections were rerun on 20 October 2002.
† Including 20 seats won in coalitions with other parties.

Election Commission

Commission électorale nationale indépendante (CENI): Bamako.

Advisory Councils

Economic, Social and Cultural Council: Koulouba, Bamako; tel. 222-43-68; fax 222-84-52; e-mail cesc@cefib.com; f. 1987; Pres. MOUSSA BALLA COULIBALY.

High Council of Communities: Bamako; compulsorily advises the Govt on issues relating to local and regional development; comprises national councillors, elected indirectly for a term of five years; Sec-Gen. MAMANI NASSIRE.

MALI

Political Organizations

In 2004 there were some 96 political parties officially registered in Mali, of which 51 received funding from the state authorities. In early 2006 the most active parties and political groupings included:

Alliance pour la démocratie au Mali—Parti pan-africain pour la liberté, la solidarité et la justice (ADEMA): rue Fankélé, porte 145, BP 1791, Bamako-Coura; tel. 222-03-68; f. 1990 as Alliance pour la démocratie au Mali; Pres. DIONCOUNDA TRAORÉ; Sec.-Gen. MARIMATIA DIARRA.

Bloc pour la démocratie et l'intégration africaine—Faso Jigi (BDIA): Bolibana, rue 376, porte 83, BP E 2833, Bamako-Coura; tel. 223-82-02; f. 1993; liberal, democratic; Leader SOULEYMANE MAKAMBA DOUMBIA.

Congrès national d'initiative démocratique—Faso Yiriwa Ton (CNID): rue 426, porte 58, Niarela, BP 2572, Bamako; tel. 221-42-75; fax 222-83-21; e-mail cnid@cefib.com; f. 1991; Chair. Me MOUNTAGA TALL; Sec.-Gen. N'DIAYE BA.

Convention démocratique et sociale (CDS): Ouolofobougou-Bolibana, rue 417, porte 46, Bamako; tel. 229-26-25; f. 1996; Chair. MAMADOU BAKARY SANGARÉ.

Convention parti du peuple (COPP): Korofina nord, BP 9012, Bamako; fax 221-35-91; e-mail lawyergakou@datatech.toolnet.org; f. 1996; Pres. Me MAMADOU GACKOU.

Mouvement patriotique pour le renouveau (MPR): Quinzambougou, BP E1108, Bamako; tel. 221-55-46; fax 221-55-43; f. 1995; Pres. Dr CHOGUEL KOKALA MAÏGA.

Mouvement pour l'indépendance, la renaissance et l'intégration africaine (MIRIA): Dravéla, Bolibana, rue 417, porte 66, Bamako; tel. 229-29-81; fax 229-29-79; e-mail miria12002@yahoo.fr; f. 1994 following split in ADEMA; Pres. MOHAMED LAMINE TRAORÉ.

Parti citoyen pour le renouveau (PCR): Bamako; f. 2005; supports administration of Pres. Touré; Pres. OUSMANE BEN FANA TRAORÉ.

Parti de la solidarité africaine pour la démocratie et l'indépendance (SADI): Djélibougou, rue 246, porte 559, BP 3140, Bamako; tel. 224-10-04; f. 2002; Leader CHEICK OUMAR SISSOKO.

Parti malien pour le développement et le renouveau (PMDR): Sema I, rue 76, porte 62, BP 553, Badalabougou, Bamako; tel. 222-25-58; f. 1991; social democratic; Pres. Me ABDOUL WAHAB BERTHE.

Parti pour la démocratie et le progrès (PDP): Korofina sud, rue 96, porte 437, Bamako; tel. 224-16-75; fax 220-23-14; f. 1991; Leader MADY KONATÉ.

Parti pour la démocratie et le renouveau—Dounkafa Ton (PDR): Bamako; f. 1998; Pres. ADAMA KONÉ; Leader KALILOU SAMAKE.

Parti pour la renaissance nationale (PARENA): rue Soundiata, porte 1397, BP E2235, Ouolofobougou, Bamako; tel. 223-49-54; fax 222-29-08; e-mail info@parena.org.ml; internet www.parena.org.ml; f. 1995 following split in CNID; Pres. TIÉBILÉ DRAMÉ; Sec.-Gen. AMIDOU DIABATÉ.

Parti pour l'indépendance, la démocratie et la solidarité (PIDS): Hippodrome, rue 250, porte 1183, BP E1515, Bamako; tel. 277-45-75; f. 2001 by dissidents from US—RDA; Pres. DABA DIAWARA.

Rassemblement malien pour le travail (RAMAT): Marché, Hippodrome, rue 224, porte 1393, BP E2281, Bamako; tel. 674-46-03; f. 1991; Leader ABDOULAYE MACKO.

Rassemblement national pour la démocratie (RND): Niaréla, route Sotuba, porte 1892, Hamdallaye, Bamako; tel. 229-18-49; fax 229-09-39; f. 1997 by 'moderate' breakaway group from RDP; Pres. ABDOULAYE GARBA TAPO.

Rassemblement pour la démocratie et le progrès (RDP): Niarela, rue 485, porte 11, BP 2110, Bamako; tel. 221-30-92; fax 224-67-95; f. 1991; Sec.-Gen. IBRAHIM DIAKITE (acting).

Rassemblement pour la démocratie et le travail (RDT): Bamako; tel. 222-25-58; f. 1991; Leader AMADOU ALI NIANGADOU.

Rassemblement pour le Mali (RPM): Hippodrome, rue 232, porte 130, BP 9057, Bamako; tel. 221-14-33; fax 221-13-36; e-mail siegerpmbko@yahoo.fr; internet www.rpm.org.ml; f. 2001; Pres. IBRAHIM BOUBACAR KEITA; Sec.-Gen. Dr BOCARY TRETA.

Union des forces démocratiques pour le progrès—Sama-ton (UFDP): quartier Mali, BP E37, Bamako; tel. 223-17-66; f. 1991; Sec.-Gen. Col YOUSSOUF TRAORÉ.

Union pour la démocratie et le développement (UDD): ave OUA, porte 3626, Sogoniko, BP 2969, Bamako; tel. 220-39-71; f. 1991 by supporters of ex-Pres. Traoré; Leader Me HASSANE BARRY.

Union pour la République et la démocratie (URD): Niaréla, rue 268, porte 41, Bamako; tel. 221-86-40; e-mail urd@timbagga.com.ml; f. 2003 by fmr mems of ADEMA (q.v.) allied to 2002 presidential candidate Soumaïla Cissé; Pres. YOUNOUSSI TOURÉ.

Union soudanaise—Rassemblement démocratique africain (US—RDA): Hippodrome, porte 41, BP E 1413, Bamako; tel. and fax 221-45-22; f. 1946; sole party 1960–68, banned 1968–1991; 'moderate' faction split from party in 1998; Leader Dr BADARA ALIOU MACALOU.

Diplomatic Representation

EMBASSIES IN MALI

Algeria: Sogoninko, BP 02, Bamako; tel. 220-51-76; fax 222-93-74; Ambassador ABDELKREM GHRAIEB.

Burkina Faso: ACI 2000, Commune III, BP 9022, Bamako; tel. 223-31-71; fax 221-92-66; e-mail ambafaso@experco.net; Ambassador Prof. SANNÉ MOHAMED TOPAN.

Canada: route de Koulikoro, Immeuble Séméga, BP 198, Hippodrome, Bamako; tel. 221-22-36; fax 221-43-62; e-mail bmako@international.gc.ca; internet www.dfait-maeci.gc.ca/world/embassies/mali; Ambassador LOUISE OUIMET.

China, People's Republic: route de Koulikoro, Hippodrome, BP 112, Bamako; tel. 221-35-97; fax 222-34-43; e-mail Chinaemb_ml@mfa.gov.cn; Ambassador WEI WENHUA.

Côte d'Ivoire: square Patrice Lumumba, Immeuble CNAR, BP E 3644, Bamako; tel. 222-03-89; fax 222-13-76; Ambassador ABOUBACAR SIRIKI DIABATÉ.

Cuba: porte 31, rue 328, Niarela, Bamako; tel. 221-02-89; fax 221-02-93; e-mail emcuba.mali@malinet.ml; Ambassador ALBERTO MIGUEL OTERO LÓPEZ.

Egypt: Badalabougou-est, BP44, Bamako; tel. 222-35-65; fax 222-08-91; e-mail mostafa@datatech.net.ml; Ambassador MOSTAFA ABDEL HAMID GENDY.

France: square Patrice Lumumba, BP 17, Bamako; tel. 222-29-51; fax 222-31-36; e-mail ambassade@france-mali.org.ml; Ambassador NICOLAS NORMAND.

Germany: Badalabougou-est, rue 14, porte 334, BP 100, Bamako; tel. 222-32-99; fax 222-96-50; e-mail allemagne.presse@afribone.net.ml; Ambassador Dr REINHARD SCHWARZER.

Ghana: Bamako; Ambassador Maj.-Gen. C. B. YAACHIE.

Guinea: Immeuble Saybou Maïga, quartier du Fleuve, BP 118, Bamako; tel. 222-30-07; fax 221-08-06; Ambassador MAMADOUBA DIABATÉ.

Iran: Hippodrome, ave al-Quds, BP 2136, Bamako; tel. 221-76-38; fax 221-07-31; Ambassador MOHAMMED SOLEIMANI.

Korea, Democratic People's Republic: Bamako; Ambassador KIM PONG HUI.

Libya: Badala Ouest, face Palais de la Culture, BP 1670, Bamako; tel. 222-34-96; fax 222-66-97; Ambassador Dr SALAHEDDIN AHMED ZAREM.

Mauritania: route de Koulikoro, Hippodrome, BP 135, Bamako; tel. 221-48-15; fax 222-49-08; Ambassador SIDAMINE OULD AHMED CHALLA.

Morocco: rue 25, porte 80, BP 2013, Badalabougou-est, Bamako; tel. 222-21-23; fax 222-77-87; e-mail sifamali@afribone.net.ml; Ambassador MOHAMED RCHOUK.

Netherlands: rue 437, BP 2220, Hippodrome, Bamako; tel. 221-56-11; fax 221-36-17; e-mail bam@minbuza.nl; Ambassador Dr R. HARRY BUIKEMA.

Nigeria: BP 57, Badala-est; tel. 221-53-28; fax 222-39-74; e-mail ngrbko@malinet.ml; Ambassador MOHAMMED SANI KANGIWA.

Russia: BP 300, Niarela, Bamako; tel. 221-55-92; fax 221-99-26; e-mail ambrusse_mali@datatech.toolnet.org; Ambassador ANATOLII I. KLIMENKO.

Saudi Arabia: Villa Bal Harbour, 28 Cité du Niger, BP 81, Bamako; tel. 221-25-28; fax 221-50-64; e-mail mlemb@mofa.gov.sa; Chargé d'affaires a.i. KHALED OMAR ABDRABUH.

Senegal: porte 341, rue 287, angle ave Nelson Mandela, BP 42, Bamako; tel. 221-08-59; fax 216-92-68; Ambassador AMADOU DEME.

South Africa: Bâtiment Diarra, Hamdallaye, ACI-2000, BP 2015, Bamako; tel. 229-29-25; fax 229-29-26; e-mail bamako@foreign.gov.za; internet www.samali.info; Ambassador Dr P. T. MATHOMA.

Tunisia: quartier du Fleuve, Bamako; tel. 223-28-91; fax 222-17-55; Ambassador FARHAT CHEOUR.

USA: rue Rochester NY, angle ave Mohamed V, BP 34, Bamako; tel. 222-54-70; fax 222-37-12; e-mail webmaster@usa.org.ml; internet w3.usa.org.ml; Ambassador TERENCE PATRICK MCCULLEY.

MALI

Judicial System

The 1992 Constitution guarantees the independence of the judiciary.

High Court of Justice: Bamako; competent to try the President of the Republic and ministers of the Government for high treason and for crimes committed in the course of their duties, and their accomplices in any case where state security is threatened; mems designated by the mems of the Assemblée nationale, and renewed annually.

Supreme Court: BP 7, Bamako; tel. 222-24-06; e-mail csupreme@afribone.net.ml; f. 1969; comprises judicial, administrative and auditing sections; judicial section comprises five chambers, administrative section comprises two chambers, auditing section comprises three chambers; Pres. ASKIA M'BARAKOU TOURÉ; Sec.-Gen. ALKAÏDY SANIBIÉ TOURÉ.

President of the Bar: Me MAGATTÉ SÈYE.

Constitutional Court: BP E213, Bamako; tel. 222-56-09; fax 223-42-41; e-mail tawatybouba@yahoo.fr; f. 1994; Pres. SALIF KANOUTÉ; Sec.-Gen. BOUBACAR TAWATY.

There are three Courts of Appeal, seven Tribunaux de première instance (Magistrates' Courts) and also courts for labour disputes.

Religion

According to the UN Development Programme's *Human Development Report*, around 80% of the population are Muslims, while 18% follow traditional animist beliefs and under 2% are Christians.

ISLAM

Association Malienne pour l'Unité et le Progrès de l'Islam (AMUPI): Bamako; state-endorsed Islamic governing body.

Chief Mosque: place de la République, Bagadadji, Bamako; tel. 221-21-90.

Haut Conseil Islamique: Bamako; f. 2002; responsible for management of relations between the Muslim communities and the State; Pres. MODY SYLLA (acting).

CHRISTIANITY

The Roman Catholic Church

Mali comprises one archdiocese and five dioceses. At 31 December 2003 there were an estimated 228,883 Roman Catholics, comprising about 2.0% of the total population.

Bishops' Conference
Conférence Episcopale du Mali, Archevêché, BP 298, Bamako; tel. 222-67-84; fax 222-67-00; e-mail cemali@afribone.net.ml; f. 1973; Pres. Most Rev. JEAN-GABRIEL DIARRA (Bishop of San).

Archbishop of Bamako: JEAN ZERBO, Archevêché, BP 298, Bamako; tel. 222-54-99; fax 222-52-14; e-mail mgrjeanzerbo@afribone.net.ml.

Other Christian Churches

There are several Protestant mission centres, mainly administered by US societies.

BAHÁ'Í FAITH

National Spiritual Assembly: BP 1657, Bamako; e-mail ntirandaz@aol.com.

The Press

The 1992 Constitution guarantees the freedom of the press. In 2000 there were six daily newspapers, 18 weekly or twice-weekly publications and six monthly or twice-monthly publications.

DAILY NEWSPAPERS

Les Echos: Hamdallaye, ave Cheick Zayed, porte 2694, BP 2043, Bamako; tel. 229-62-89; fax 226-76-39; e-mail jamana@malinet.ml; f. 1989; publ. by Jamana cultural co-operative; circ. 30,000; Dir ALEXIS KALAMBRY; Editor-in-Chief ABOUBACAR SALIPH DIARRA.

L'Essor: square Patrice Lumumba, BP 141, Bamako; tel. 222-36-83; fax 222-47-74; e-mail info@essor.gov.ml; internet www.essor.gov.ml; f. 1949; pro-Govt newspaper; Editor SOULEYMANE DRABO; circ. 3,500.

Info Matin: rue 56/350, Bamako Coura, BP E 4020, Bamako; tel. 223-82-09; fax 223-82-27; e-mail redaction@info-matin.com; internet www.info-matin.com; independent; Dir SAMBI TOURÉ; Editor-in-Chief MOHAMED SACKO.

Le Républicain: 116 rue 400, Dravéla-Bolibana, BP 1484, Bamako; tel. 229-09-00; fax 229-09-33; e-mail republicain@cefib.com; f. 1992; independent; Dir SALIF KONÉ.

PERIODICALS

26 Mars: Badalabougou-Sema Gesco, Lot S13, BP MA 174, Bamako; tel. 229-04-59; f. 1998; weekly; independent; Dir BOUBACAR SANGARÉ.

L'Aurore: Niarela 298, rue 438, BP 3150, Bamako; tel. and fax 221-69-22; e-mail aurore@timbagga.com.ml; f. 1990; 2 a week; independent; Dir KARAMOKO N'DIAYE.

Le Canard Enchanté: Immeuble Koumara, bloc 104, Centre Commercial, Bamako; tel. 673-47-59; f. 2002; weekly; satirical; Dir OUMAR BABI.

Le Carrefour: ave Cheick Zayed, Hamdallaye, Bamako; tel. 223-98-08; e-mail journalcarrefour@yahoo.fr; f. 1997; Dir MAHAMANE IMRANE COULIBALY.

Citoyen: Bamako; f. 1992; fortnightly; independent.

Le Continent: AA 16, Banankabougou, BP E 4338, Bamako; tel. and fax 229-57-39; e-mail le_continent@yahoo.fr; f. 2000; weekly; Dir IBRAHIMA TRAORÉ.

Le Courrier: 230 ave Cheick Zayed, Lafiabougou Marché, BP 1258, Bamako; tel. and fax 229-18-62; e-mail journalcourrier@webmails.com; f. 1996; weekly; Dir SADOU A. YATTARA; also *Le Courrier Magazine*, monthly.

L'Indépendant: Immeuble ABK, Hamdallaye ACI, BP E 1040, Bamako; tel. and fax 223-27-27; e-mail independant@cefib.com; 2 a week; Dir SAOUTI HAÏDARA.

L'Inspecteur: Immeuble Nimagala, bloc 262, BP E 4534, Bamako; tel. 672-47-11; e-mail inspecteurmali@yahoo.fr; f. 1992; weekly; Dir ALY DIARRA.

Jamana—Revue Culturelle Malienne: BP 2043, Bamako; BP E 1040; e-mail jamana@malinet.ml; f. 1983; quarterly; organ of Jamana cultural co-operative.

Journal Officiel de la République du Mali: Koulouba, BP 14, Bamako; tel. 222-59-86; fax 222-70-50; official gazette.

Kabaaru: Village Kibaru, Bozola, Bamako; f. 1983; state-owned; monthly; Fulbé (Peul) language; rural interest; Editor BADAMA DOUCOURÉ; circ. 5,000.

Kabako: Bamako; tel. 221-29-12; f. 1991; weekly; general; Dir DIABY MACORO CAMARA.

Kibaru: Village Kibaru, Bozola, BP 1463, Bamako; f. 1972; monthly; state-owned; Bambara and three other languages; rural interest; Editor NIANZÉ SAMAKÉ; circ. 5,000.

Liberté: Immeuble Sanago, Hamdallaye Marché, BP E 24, Bamako; tel. 228-18-98; e-mail ladji.guindo@cefib.com; f. 1999; weekly; Dir ABDOULAYE LADJI GUINDO.

Le Malien: rue 497, porte 277, Badialan III, BP E 1558, Bamako; tel. 223-57-29; fax 229-13-39; e-mail lemalien2000@yahoo.fr; f. 1993; weekly; Dir SIDI KEITA.

Match: 97 rue 498, Lafiabougou, BP E 3776, Bamako; tel. 229-18-82; e-mail bcissouma@yahoo.fr; f. 1997; 2 a month; sports; Dir BABA CISSOUMA.

Musow: Bamako; e-mail musow@musow.com; internet www.musow.com; women's interest.

Nyéléni Magazine: Niarela 298, rue 348, BP 13150, Bamako; tel. 229-24-01; f. 1991; monthly; women's interest; Dir MAÏMOUNA TRAORÉ.

L'Observateur: Galérie Djigué, rue du 18 juin, BP E 1002, Bamako; tel. and fax 223-06-89; e-mail belcotamboura@hotmail.com; f. 1992; 2 a week; Dir BELCO TAMBOURA.

Le Reflet: Immeuble Kanadjigui, Route de Koulikoro, Boulkassoumbougou, BP E 1688, Bamako; tel. 224-39-52; fax 223-23-08; e-mail lereflet@afribone.malinet.ml; weekly; fmrly Le Carcan; present name adopted Jan. 2001; Dir ABDOUL KARIM DRAMÉ.

Le Scorpion: 230 ave Cheick Zayed, Lafiabougou Marché, BP 1258, Bamako; tel. and fax 229-18-62; f. 1991; weekly; Dir MAHAMANE HAMÈYE CISSÉ.

Le Tambour: rue 497, porte 295, Badialan III, BP E 289, Bamako; tel. and fax 222-75-68; e-mail tambourj@yahoo.fr; f. 1994; 2 a week; Dir YÉRO DIALLO.

Royal Sports: BP 98, Sikasso; tel. 672-49-88; weekly; also *Tatou Sports*, published monthly; Pres. and Dir-Gen. ALY TOURÉ.

NEWS AGENCIES

Agence Malienne de Presse et Publicité (AMAP): square Patrice Lumumba, BP 141, Bamako; tel. 222-36-83; fax 222-47-74; e-mail amap@afribone.net.ml; f. 1977; Dir SOULEYMANE DRABO.

MALI   Directory

Foreign Bureau

Agence France-Presse (AFP): BP 778, Bamako; tel. 222-07-77.
IPS (Italy) and Xinhua (New China) News Agency (People's Republic of China) are also represented in Mali.

PRESS ASSOCIATIONS

Association des Editeurs de la Presse Privée (ASSEP): BP E 1002, Bamako; tel. 671-31-33; e-mail belcotamboura@hotmail.com; Pres. BELCO TAMBOURA.

Association des Femmes de la Presse Privée: Porte 474, rue 428, BP E 731, Bamako; tel. 221-29-12; Pres. FANTA DIALLO.

Association des Journalistes Professionels des Médias Privés du Mali (AJPM): BP E 2456, Bamako; tel. 222-19-15; fax 223-54-78; Pres. MOMADOU FOFANA.

Association des Professionnelles Africaines de la Communication (APAC MALI): Porte 474, rue 428, BP E 731, Bamako; tel. 221-29-12; Pres. MASSIRÉ YATTASSAYE.

Maison de la Presse de Mali: 17 rue 619, Darsalam, BP E 2456, Bamako; tel. 222-19-15; fax 223-54-78; e-mail maison.presse@afribone.net.ml; internet www.mediamali.org; independent media association; Pres. SADOU A. YATTARA.

Union Interprofessionnelle des Journalistes et de la Presse de Langue Française (UIJPLF): rue 42, Hamdallaye Marché, BP 1258, Bamako; tel. 229-98-35; Pres. MAHAMANE HAMÉYE CISSÉ.

Union Nationale des Journalistes Maliens (UNAJOM): BP 141, Bamako; tel. 222-36-83; fax 223-43-13; e-mail amap@afribone.net.ml; Pres. OUSMANE MAÏGA.

Publishers

EDIM SA: ave Kassé Keïta, BP 21, Bamako; tel. 222-40-41; f. 1972 as Editions Imprimeries du Mali; general fiction and non-fiction, textbooks; Chair. and Man. Dir ALOU TOMOTA.

Editions Donniya: Cité du Niger, BP 1273, Bamako; tel. 221-46-46; fax 221-90-31; e-mail imprimcolor@cefib.com; internet www.imprimcolor.cefib.com; f. 1996; general fiction, history, reference and children's books in French and Bambara.

Le Figuier: 151 rue 56, Semal, BP 2605, Bamako; tel. and fax 223-32-11; e-mail lefiguier@afribone.net.ml; f. 1997; fiction and non-fiction.

Editions Jamana: BP 2043, Bamako; tel. 229-62-89; fax 229-76-39; e-mail jamana@timbagga.com.ml; f. 1988; literary fiction, poetry, reference; Dir BA MAÏRA SOW.

Editions Teriya: BP 1677, Bamako; tel. 224-11-42; theatre, literary fiction; Dir GAOUSSOU DIAWARA.

Broadcasting and Communications

TELECOMMUNICATIONS

Ikatel: Immeuble SONAVIE ACI-2000, BP E3991, Bamako; tel. 499-90-00; fax 499-90-01; internet www.ikatel.net; f. 2002; fixed-line and mobile cellular telecommunications; jtly owned by France Télécom and Société Nationale des Télécommunications du Sénégal; Dir-Gen. ALIOUNE N'DIAYE; 100,000 subscribers (2003).

Société des Télécommunications du Mali—Malitel (SOTELMA): route de Koulikoro, Hippodrome, BP 740, Bamako; tel. 221-52-80; fax 221-30-22; e-mail segal@sotelma.ml; internet www.sotelma.ml; f. 1990; state-owned; 49% privatization proposed; operates fixed-line telephone services, also mobile and cellular telecommunications in Bamako, Kayes, Mopti, Ségou and Sikasso; 47,000 subscribers to mobile cellular telecommunications services (2003); Pres. and Dir-Gen. SIDIKI KONATE.

BROADCASTING

Radio

Office de Radiodiffusion-Télévision Malienne (ORTM): BP 171, Bamako; tel. 221-20-19; fax 221-42-05; e-mail ortm@afribone.net.ml; internet www.ortm.net; Dir-Gen. SIDIKI KONATÉ; Dir of Radio OUMAR TOURÉ.

Radio Mali–Chaîne Nationale: BP 171, Bamako; tel. 221-20-19; fax 221-42-05; e-mail ortm@spider.toolnet.org; f. 1957; state-owned; radio programmes in French, Bambara, Peulh, Sarakolé, Tamachek, Sonrai, Moorish, Wolof, English.

Chaîne 2: Bamako; f. 1993; radio broadcasts to Bamako.

In late 2003 there were an estimated 130 community, commercial and religious radio stations broadcasting in Mali.

Fréquence 3: Bamako; f. 1992; commercial.

Radio Balanzan: BP 419, Ségou; tel. 232-02-88; commercial.

Radio Bamakan: Marché de Médine, BP E 100, Bamako; tel. and fax 221-27-60; e-mail radio.bamakan@ifrance.com; f. 1991; community station; 104 hours of FM broadcasts weekly; Man. MODIBO DIALLO.

Radio Espoir—La Voix du Salut: Sogoniko, rue 130, porte 71, BP E 1399, Bamako; tel. 220-67-08; e-mail accm@mali.maf.net; f. 1998; broadcasts 16 hours of radio programming daily on topics including Christianity, development and culture; Dir DAOUDA COULIBALY.

Radio Foko de Ségou Jamana: BP 2043, Bamako; tel. 232-00-48; fax 222-76-39; e-mail radiofoko@cefib.com.

Radio Guintan: Magnambougou, BP 2546, Bamako; tel. 220-09-38; f. 1994; community radio station; Dir RAMATA DIA.

Radio Jamana: BP 2043, Bamako; tel. 229-62-89; fax 229-76-39; e-mail jamana@malinet.net.

Radio Kayira: Djélibougou Doumanzana, BP 3140, Bamako; tel. 224-87-82; fax 222-75-68; f. 1992; community station; Dir OUMAR MARIKO.

Radio Klédu: Cité du Niger, BP 2322, Bamako; tel. 221-00-18; f. 1992; commercial; Dir FADIALA DEMBÉLÉ.

Radio Liberté: BP 5015, Bamako; tel. 223-05-81; f. 1991; commercial station broadcasting 24 hours daily; Dir ALMANY TOURÉ.

Radio Patriote: Korofina-Sud, BP E 1406, Bamako; tel. 224-22-92; f. 1995; commercial station; Dir MOUSSA KEÏTA.

Radio Rurale: Plateau, BP 94, Kayes; tel. 253-14-76; e-mail rrk@afribone.net.ml; f. 1988; community stations established by the Agence de coopération culturelle et technique (ACTT); transmitters in Niono, Kadiolo, Bandiagara and Kidal; Dir FILY KEÏTA.

Radio Sahel: BP 394, Kayes; tel. 252-21-87; f. 1991; commercial; Dir ALMAMY S. TOURÉ.

Radio Tabalé: Bamako-Coura, BP 697, Bamako; tel. and fax 222-78-70; f. 1992; independent public-service station; broadcasting 57 hours weekly; Dir TIÉMOKO KONÉ.

La Voix du Coran et du Hadit: Grande Mosquée, BP 2531, Bamako; tel. 221-63-44; f. 1993; Islamic station broadcasting on FM in Bamako; Dir El Hadj MAHMOUD DICKO.

Radio Wassoulou: BP 24, Yanfolila; tel. 265-10-97; commercial.

Radio France International, the Voix de l'Islam and the Gabonese-based Africa No. 1 began FM broadcasts in Mali in 1993; broadcasts by Voice of America and the World Service of the British Broadcasting Corpn are also transmitted via private radio stations.

Television

Office de Radiodiffusion-Télévision Malienne (ORTM): see Radio; Dir of Television BALY IDRISSA SISSOKO.

Multicanal SA: Quinzambougou, BP E 1506, Bamako; tel. 221-49-64; e-mail sandrine@multi-canal.com; internet www.multi-canal.com; private subscription broadcaster; relays international broadcasts; Pres. ISMAÏLA SIDIBÉ.

TV Klédu: 600 ave Modibo Keïta, BP E 1172, Bamako; tel. 223-90-00; fax 223-70-50; e-mail info@tvkledu.com; private cable TV operator; relays international broadcasts; Pres. MAMADOU COULIBALY.

Finance

(cap. = capital; res = reserves; dep. = deposits; m. = million; brs = branches; amounts in francs CFA)

BANKING

Central Bank

Banque Centrale des Etats de l'Afrique de l'Ouest (BCEAO): BP 206, Bamako; tel. 222-37-56; fax 222-47-86; internet www.bceao.int; f. 1962; HQ in Dakar, Senegal; bank of issue for the mem. states of Union économique et monétaire ouest-africaine (UEMOA, comprising Benin, Burkina Faso, Côte d'Ivoire, Guinea-Bissau, Mali, Niger, Senegal and Togo); cap. and res 859,313m., total assets 5,671,675m. (Dec. 2002); Gov. CHARLES KONAN BANNY; Dir in Mali IDRISSA TRAORÉ; brs at Mopti and Sikasso.

Commercial Banks

Bank of Africa—Mali (BOA-MALI): 418 ave de la Marné, Bozola, BP 2249, Bamako; tel. 221-47-61; fax 221-65-67; e-mail boadg@boamali.net; internet www.bkofafrica.net/mali.htm; f. 1983; cap. 2,500m., res 1,652m., dep. 74,042m. (March 2005); Pres. BOUREIMA SYLLA; Dir-Gen. CHRISTOPHE LASSUS-LALANNE; 7 brs.

Banque Commerciale du Sahel (BCS–SA): ave Kassé Keïta, BP 2372, Bamako; tel. 221-01-95; fax 221-97-82; e-mail bcs@cefib.com; f. 1980; fmrly Banque Arabe Libyo-Malienne pour le Commerce Extérieur et le Développement; 50% owned by Libyan-Arab Foreign

MALI

Bank, 49.5% state owned; cap. 1,100m., total assets. 22,555m. (Dec. 2000); Pres. FANGATIGUI DOUMBIA; Dir-Gen. MOHAMED SAED EL ATRACH; 1 br.

Banque de l'Habitat du Mali (BHM): ACI 2000, ave Kwamé N'Krumah, BP 2614, Bamako; tel. 222-91-90; fax 222-93-50; e-mail bhm@bhm.malinet.ml; f. 1990; present name adopted 1996; 37.1% owned by Institut National de Prévoyance Social, 25.9% by Agence Cession Immobilière; cap. and res 5,414.7m., total assets 98,237.5m. (Dec. 2003); Pres. and Dir-Gen. MAMADOU BABA DIAWARA; 1 br.

Banque International pour le Commerce et l'Industrie au Mali (BICI–Mali): Immeuble Nimagala, blvd du Peuple, BP 72, Bamako; tel. 223-33-70; fax 223-33-71; e-mail secretariatdirection@bicim.com; f. 1998; 50% owned by SFOM Interafrica (Switzerland), 35% by BNP Paribas BDDI Participations (France); cap. and res 3,678m., total assets 40,076m. (Dec. 2003); Pres. and Dir-Gen. LUC-MARIE VIDAL; 1 br.

Banque Internationale pour le Mali (BIM): ave de l'Indépendance, BP 15, Bamako; tel. 222-51-11; fax 222-45-66; e-mail bim@bim.com.ml; f. 1980; present name adopted 1995; 61.5% state-owned; privatization pending; cap. 4,255m., res 1,099m., dep. 78,806m. (Dec. 2002); total assets 91,725m. (Dec. 2003); Pres. and Dir-Gen. DIAKARIDIA KEITA; 7 brs.

Banque Malienne de Crédit et de Dépôts: ave Mobido Keita, BP 45, Bamako; tel. 222-53-36; fax 222-79-50; e-mail bmcd@malinet.ml; 100% state-owned; transfer to private-sector ownership proposed.

Ecobank Mali: place de la Nation, quartier du Fleuve, BP E 1272, Bamako; tel. 223-33-00; fax 223-33-05; e-mail ecobank@cefib.com; f. 1998; 49.5% owned by Ecobank Transnational Inc., 17.8% by Ecobank Bénin, 14.9% by Ecobank Togo, 9.9% by Ecobank Burkina; cap. and res 2,973.9m., total assets 46,222.7m. (Dec. 2003); Pres. SEYDOU DJIM SYLLA; Dir-Gen. KASSIM ABOU KABASSI; 2 brs.

Development Banks

Banque de Développement du Mali (BDM-SA): ave Modibo Keita, quartier du Fleuve, BP 94, Bamako; tel. 222-20-50; fax 222-50-85; e-mail info@bdm-sa.com; internet www.bdm-sa.com; f. 1968; absorbed Banque Malienne de Crédit et de Dépôts in 2001; 22.1% state-owned, 20.7% owned by Banque Marocaine du Commerce Extérieur (Morocco), 16.0% by by BCEAO, 16% by Banque ouest-africaine de développement; cap. and res 15,658m., total assets 276,148m. (Dec. 2002); Pres. and Dir-Gen. ABDOULAYE DAFFÉ; 14 brs.

Banque Malienne de Solidarité (BMS): ave du Fleuve, Immeuble Dette Publique, 2e étage, BP 1280, Bamako; tel. and fax 223-50-43; e-mail bms-sa@bms-sa.com; f. 2002; cap. 2.4m.; 1 br.

Banque Nationale de Développement Agricole—Mali (BNDA–Mali): Immeuble BNDA, blvd du Mali, ACI 2000, BP 2424, Bamako; tel. 229-64-64; fax 229-25-75; e-mail bnda@bndamali.com; f. 1981; 40.6% state-owned, 21.2% owned by Agence française de développement (France), 20.0% owned by Deutsche Entwicklangs Gesellschaft (Germany), 18.2% owned by BCEAO; cap. 10,510m., res 1,551m., dep. 72,623m. (Dec. 2002); Chair., Pres. and Gen. Man. MOUSSA KALIFA TRAORÉ; Dir-Gen. YVES PICARD; 22 brs.

Financial Institutions

Direction Générale de la Dette Publique: Immeuble ex-Caisse Autonome d'Amortissement, quartier du Fleuve, BP 1617, Bamako; tel. 222-29-35; fax 222-07-93; management of the public debt; Dir NAMALA KONÉ.

Equibail Mali: rue 376, porte 1319, Niarela, BP E 566, Bamako; tel. 21-37-77; fax 21-37-78; e-mail equip.ma@bkofafrica.com; internet www.bkofafrica.net/jeux_de_cadres/equibail/equibail_mali/equibail_mali.htm; f. 1999; 50.2% owned by African Financial Holding, 17.5% by Bank of Africa—Benin; cap. 300m. (Dec. 2002); Mems of Administrative Council RAMATOULAYE TRAORÉ, PAUL DERREUMAUX, LÉON NAKA.

Société Malienne de Financement (SOMAFI): Immeuble Air Afrique, blvd du 22 octobre 1946, BP E 3643, Bamako; tel. 222-18-66; fax 222-18-69; e-mail somafi@malinet.ml; f. 1997; cap. and res 96.9m., total assets 3,844.9m. (Dec. 2002); Pres. PHILIPPE DE; Man. Dir ERIC LECLÈRE.

STOCK EXCHANGE

Bourse Régionale des Valeurs Mobilières (BRVM): Chambre de Commerce et de l'Industrie du Mali, place de la Liberté, BP E 1398, Bamako; tel. 223-23-54; fax 223-23-59; e-mail abocoum@brvm.org; f. 1998; national branch of BRVM (regional stock exchange based in Abidjan, Côte d'Ivoire, serving the mem. states of UEMOA); Man. AMADOU DJÉRI BOCOUM.

INSURANCE

Les Assurances Générales de France (AGF): ave du Fleuve, BP 190, Bamako; tel. 222-58-18.

Directory

Assurance Colina Mali SA: BP E 154, Bamako; tel. 222-57-75; fax 223-24-23; e-mail c-mali@colina-sa.com; f. 1990; cap. 1,000m.; Dir-Gen. MARYUONNE SIDIRE.

Caisse Nationale d'Assurance et de Réassurance du Mali (CNAR): BP 568, Bamako; tel. 222-64-54; fax 222-23-29; f. 1969; state-owned; cap. 50m.; Dir-Gen. F. KEITA; 10 brs.

Compagnie d'Assurance Privée—La Soutra: BP 52, Bamako; tel. 222-36-81; fax 222-55-23; f. 1979; cap. 150m.; Chair. AMADOU NIONO.

Compagnie d'Assurance et de Réassurance de Mali: BP 1822, Bamako; tel. 222-60-29.

Compagnie d'Assurance Sabu Nyuman: Bamako Coura 135–136, BP 1822, Bamako; tel. 222-60-29; fax 222-57-50; f. 1984; cap. 250m.; Dir-Gen. MOMADOU SANOGO.

Gras Savoye Mali: ave Amílcar Cabral, angle rue 224, porte 1052, Hippodrome, BP 9032, Bamako; tel. 221-41-93; fax 221-42-71; e-mail grassavoye.mali@afribone.net.ml; affiliated to Gras Savoye (France); Man. ALASSANE TOURÉ.

Lafía Assurances: ave de la Nation, BP 1542, Bamako; tel. 222-35-51; fax 222-52-24; f. 1983; cap. 50m.; Dir-Gen. ABDOULAYE TOURÉ.

Trade and Industry

GOVERNMENT AGENCIES

Centre d'Etudes et de Promotion Industrielle (CEPI): BP 1980, Bamako; tel. 222-22-79; fax 222-80-85.

Direction Nationale des Affaires Economiques (DNAE): Bamako; tel. 222-23-14; fax 222-22-56; involved in economic and social affairs.

Direction Nationale des Travaux Publics (DNTP): ave de la Liberté, BP 1758, Bamako; tel. and fax 222-29-02; administers public works.

Guichet Unique–Direction Nationale des Industries: rue Titi Niare, Quinzambougou, BP 96, Bamako; tel. and fax 222-31-66.

Office National des Produits Pétroliers (ONAP): quartier du Fleuve, rue 315, porte 141, BP 2070, Bamako; tel. 222-28-27; fax 222-44-83; e-mail onap@datatech.toolnet.org; Dir-Gen. TAPA NOUGA NADIO.

Office du Niger: BP 106, Ségou; tel. 232-02-92; fax 232-01-43; f. 1932; taken over from the French authorities in 1958; restructured in mid-1990s; cap. 7,139m. francs CFA; principally involved in cultivation of food crops, particularly rice; Pres. and Man. Dir NANCOMA KEÏTA.

Office des Produits Agricoles du Mali (OPAM): BP 132, Bamako; tel. 222-37-55; fax 221-04-06; e-mail opam@datatech.toolnet.org; f. 1965; state-owned; manages National (Cereals) Security Stock, administers food aid, responsible for sales of cereals and distribution to deficit areas; cap. 5,800m. francs CFA; Pres. and Dir-Gen. YOUSSOUF MAHAMANE TOURÉ.

DEVELOPMENT ORGANIZATIONS

Agence Française de Développement (AFD): Quinzambougou, Route de Sotuba, BP 32, Bamako; tel. 221-28-42; fax 221-86-46; e-mail afdbamako@ml.groupe-afd.org; internet www.afd.fr; Country Dir JEAN-FRANÇOIS VAVASSEUR.

Agence pour le Développement du Nord-Mali (ADN): Gao; f. 2005 to replace l'Autorité pour le Développement Intégré du Nord-Mali (ADIN); govt agency with financial autonomy; promotes development of regions of Tombouctou, Gao and Kidal; br. in Bamako.

Office de Développement Intégré du Mali-Ouest (ODIMO): square Patrice Lumumba, Bamako; tel. 222-57-59; f. 1991 to succeed Office de Développement Intégré des Productions Arachidières et Céréalières; development of diversified forms of agricultural production; Man. Dir ZANA SANOGO.

Service de Coopération et d'Action Culturelle: square Patrice Lumumba, BP 84, Bamako; tel. 221-83-38; fax 221-83-39; administers bilateral aid from France; Dir BERTRAND COMMELIN.

CHAMBER OF COMMERCE

Chambre de Commerce et d'Industrie du Mali (CCIM): place de la Liberté, BP 46, Bamako; tel. 222-50-36; fax 222-21-20; e-mail ccim@cefip.com; f. 1906; Pres. JEAMILLE BITTAR; Sec.-Gen. DABA TRAORÉ.

EMPLOYERS' ASSOCIATIONS

Association Malienne des Exportateurs de Légumes (AME-LEF): Bamako; f. 1984; Pres. BADARA FAGANDA TRAORÉ; Sec.-Gen. BIRAMA TRAORÉ.

MALI

Directory

Association Malienne des Exportateurs de Ressources Animales (AMERA): Bamako; tel. 222-56-83; f. 1985; Pres. AMBARKÉ YERMANGORE; Admin. Sec. ALI HACKO.

Fédération Nationale des Employeurs du Mali (FNEM): BP 2445, Bamako; tel. 221-63-11; fax 221-90-77; f. 1980; Pres. MOUSSA MARY BALLA COULIBALY; Permanent Sec. LASSINA TRAORÉ.

UTILITIES

Electricity

Energie du Mali (EDM): square Patrice Lumumba, BP 69, Bamako; tel. 222-30-20; fax 222-84-30; e-mail sekou.edm@cefib.com; f. 1960; 66% state-owned, 34% owned by Industrial Promotion Services (West-Africa); planning, construction and operation of power-sector facilities; cap. 7,880m. francs CFA.

Enertech GSA: marché de Lafiabougou, BP 1949, Bamako; tel. 222-37-63; fax 222-51-36; f. 1994; cap. 20m. francs CFA; solar energy producer; Dir MOCTAR DIAKITÉ.

Société de Gestion de l'Energie de Manantali (SOGEM): Immeuble 790, Hippodrome, rue 335 x 336, BP 4015, Bamako; tel. 221-03-92; fax 221-11-22; to generate and distribute electricity from the Manantali HEP project, under the auspices of the Organisation pour la mise en valeur du fleuve Sénégal.

Gas

Maligaz: route de Sotuba, BP 5, Bamako; tel. 222-23-94; gas distribution.

TRADE UNION FEDERATION

Union nationale des travailleurs du Mali (UNTM): Bourse du Travail, blvd de l'Indépendance, BP 169, Bamako; tel. 222-36-99; fax 223-59-45; f. 1963; 13 national and 8 regional unions, and 52 local organizations; Sec.-Gen. SIAKA DIAKITÉ.

There are, in addition, several non-affiliated trade unions.

Transport

RAILWAYS

Mali's only railway runs from Koulikoro, via Bamako, to the Senegal border. The line continues to Dakar, a total distance of 1,286 km, of which 729 km is in Mali. The track is in very poor condition, and is frequently closed during the rainy season. In 1995 the Governments of Mali and Senegal agreed to establish a joint company to operate the Bamako–Dakar line, and the line passed fully into private ownership in 2003. Some 536,000 metric tons of freight were handled on the Malian railway in 1999. Plans exist for the construction of a new rail line linking Bamako with Kouroussa and Kankan, in Guinea.

Transrail: BP 260, Bamako; tel. 222-59-68; fax 222-83-88; f. 2003 on transfer to private management of fmr Régie du Chemin de Fer du Mali; jt venture of Canac (Canada) and Getma (France); Pres. REJEAN BELANGER.

ROADS

The Malian road network in 1999 comprised 17,107 km, of which about 1,500 km were main roads. About 2,760 km of the network were paved. A bituminized road between Bamako and Abidjan (Côte d'Ivoire) provides Mali's main economic link to the coast; construction of a road linking Bamako and Dakar (Senegal) is to be financed by the European Development Fund. The African Development Bank also awarded a US $31.66m. loan to fund the Kankan–Kouremale–Bamako road between Mali and Guinea. A road across the Sahara to link Mali with Algeria is also planned.

Compagnie Malienne de Transports Routiers (CMTR): BP 208, Bamako; tel. 222-33-64; f. 1970; state-owned; Man. Dir MAMADOU TOURÉ.

INLAND WATERWAYS

The River Niger is navigable in parts of its course through Mali (1,693 km) during the rainy season from July to late December. The River Senegal was, until the early 1990s, navigable from Kayes to Saint-Louis (Senegal) only between August and November, but its navigability was expected to improve following the inauguration, in 1992, of the Manantali dam, and the completion of works to deepen the river-bed.

Compagnie Malienne de Navigation (COMANAV): BP 10, Koulikoro; tel. 226-20-94; fax 226-20-09; f. 1968; 100% state-owned; river transport; Pres. and Man. Dir YACOUBA DIALLO.

Conseil Malien des Chargeurs (CMC): Dar-salam, Bamako; f. 1999; Pres. AMADOU DJIGUÉ.

Société Navale Malienne (SONAM): Bamako; tel. 222-60-52; fax 222-60-66; f. 1981; transferred to private ownership in 1986; Chair. ALIOUNE KEÏTA.

Société Ouest-Africaine d'Entreprise Maritime (SOAEM): rue Mohamed V, BP 2428, Bamako; tel. 222-58-32; fax 222-40-24; maritime transport co.

CIVIL AVIATION

The principal airport is at Bamako-Senou. The other major airports are at Bourem, Gao, Goundam, Kayes, Kita, Mopti, Nioro, Ségou, Tessalit and Tombouctou. There are about 40 small airfields. Mali's airports are being modernized with external financial assistance. In early 2005 the Malian Government announced its intention to establish a new national airline, in partnership with the Aga Khan Fund for Economic Development and Industrial Promotion Services.

Agence Nationale de l'Aéronautique Civile (ANAC): Ministère de l'Equipement et des Transports, BP 227, Bamako; tel. 229-55-24; fax 228-61-77; e-mail anacmali@hotmail.com; f. 2005 to replace Direction Nationale de l'Aéronautique Civile (f. 1990); National Dir KHALILOU BOUGONNO SANOGHO.

Air Affaires Mali: BP E 3759, Badalabougou, Bamako; tel. 222-61-36.

Compagnie Aérienne du Mali (CAM): Bamako; f. 2005; 51% owned by Fonds Aga Khan pour le Développement Economique (AKAFED), 20% state-owned; domestic and international flights.

STA Trans African Airlines: quartier du Fleuve, BP 775, Bamako; tel. 222-44-44; fax 221-09-81; e-mail sta-airlines@sta-airlines.com; internet www.sta-airlines.com; f. 1984 as Société des Transports Aériens; privately-owned; local, regional and international services; Man. Dir MELHEM ELIE SABBAGUE.

Tourism

Mali's rich cultural heritage is promoted as a tourist attraction. In 1999 the Government launched a three-year cultural and tourism development programme centred on Tombouctou, Gao and Kidal. 69,691 tourists visited Mali in 2003, while receipts from tourism totalled some US $105m. in 2002.

Ministry of Crafts and Tourism: see section on The Government.

MALTA

Introductory Survey

Location, Climate, Language, Religion, Flag, Capital

The Republic of Malta is in southern Europe. The country comprises an archipelago in the central Mediterranean Sea, consisting of the inhabited islands of Malta, Gozo and Comino, and the uninhabited islets of Cominotto, Filfla and St Paul's. The main island, Malta, lies 93 km (58 miles) south of the Italian island of Sicily and 288 km (179 miles) east of the Tunisian coast, the nearest point on the North African mainland. The climate is warm, with average temperatures of 22.6°C (72.7°F) in summer and 13.7°C (56.6°F) in winter. Average annual rainfall is 578 mm (22.8 ins). Maltese and English are the official languages, although Italian is widely spoken. About 95% of the inhabitants are Christians belonging to the Roman Catholic Church. The national flag (proportions 2 by 3) consists of two equal vertical stripes, white at the hoist and red at the fly, with a representation of the George Cross, edged with red, in the upper hoist. The capital is Valletta, on the island of Malta.

Recent History

Malta, which had been a Crown Colony of the United Kingdom since 1814, became an independent sovereign state, within the Commonwealth, on 21 September 1964. The Government, led by Dr Giorgio Borg-Olivier of the Nationalist Party (Partit Nazzjonalista—PN), negotiated defence and financial aid agreements, effective over a 10-year period, with the United Kingdom.

In June 1971 the Malta Labour Party (Partit Laburista—MLP), led by Dom Mintoff, assumed power after winning a general election. Pursuing a policy of non-alignment, the Government concluded agreements for cultural, economic and commercial co-operation with Italy, Libya, Tunisia, the USSR, several East European countries, the USA, the People's Republic of China and others, and received technical assistance, notably from Libya. The MLP Government abrogated the 1964 Mutual Defence and Assistance Agreement with the United Kingdom. This agreement was replaced in 1972 by a new seven-year agreement, under which Malta was to receive substantially increased rental payments for the use of military facilities by the United Kingdom and other members of the North Atlantic Treaty Organization (NATO, see p. 314). British troops were finally withdrawn in March 1979.

Malta became a republic in December 1974. The MLP retained power at general elections held in September 1976 and in December 1981, when it secured a majority of three seats in the House of Representatives, although obtaining only 49.1% of the votes cast. The PN, which had received 50.9% of the votes cast, contested the result, refused to take its seats in the House of Representatives, and organized a campaign of civil disobedience. In March 1983 the PN terminated its legislative boycott, but immediately withdrew again, in protest against a government resolution to loosen ties with the European Community (EC, now the European Union—EU, see p. 228). Although Mintoff promised constitutional amendments and weekly consultations with the opposition, these arrangements collapsed in June, when the Government blamed the PN for a bomb attack on government offices. In November a police raid on the PN headquarters was alleged to have discovered a cache of arms and ammunition.

In June 1983 the House of Representatives approved controversial legislation, under which about 75% of church property was to be expropriated to provide finance for a programme of universal free education and the abolition of fee-paying church schools. Opponents of the measure denounced it as both unconstitutional and a violation of religious liberty, and in September 1984 the courts disallowed the legislation. In April 1984 the House approved legislation forbidding any school to accept fees (including voluntary gifts and donations). The Roman Catholic Archbishop of Malta rejected the government conditions and closed all church schools, in response to growing tensions and public unrest. A strike by state school teachers in October and November further polarized opinion, but an agreement was reached in November, when the schools were re-opened.

Mintoff retired in December 1984 and was replaced as Prime Minister by the new leader of the MLP, Dr Carmelo Mifsud Bonnici. In April 1985 the Government reached agreement with the Roman Catholic Church, providing for the phased introduction of free education in church secondary schools, and guaranteeing the autonomy of church schools. However, in July 1988 the enforced introduction of new licensing procedures for church schools led to demands by the Roman Catholic Church that the State should reduce its supervisory powers over church education.

At a general election held in May 1987 the PN obtained 50.9% of the votes cast, but won only 31 of the 65 seats in the House of Representatives, while the MLP, with 48.9% of the votes cast, won the remaining 34 seats. However, in accordance with a constitutional amendment that had been adopted in January (see Government, below), the PN was allocated four additional seats, giving it a majority of one in the legislature, thus ending the MLP's 16-year tenure in office. The leader of the PN, Dr Eddie Fenech Adami, became Prime Minister. The PN secured an increased majority of three seats over the MLP at a general election held in February 1992. This result was widely interpreted as an endorsement of the PN's pro-EC policies.

Malta has maintained a policy of non-alignment in its international relations, and has negotiated economic co-operation agreements with many countries. In 1984 the Governments of Malta and Libya signed a five-year treaty of co-operation, which included an undertaking by Libya to provide military training. The treaty signified a return to the previously close relations between the two countries, which had deteriorated in 1980, owing to a dispute over a maritime boundary (eventually resolved by the International Court of Justice in 1985). Malta also has an association agreement with the EU, originally signed in 1970 and periodically renewed until Malta's accession to the EU in 2004. On becoming Prime Minister in May 1987, Fenech Adami declared that the Government, while retaining Malta's non-aligned status and its links with Libya, would seek closer relations with the USA and other Western countries, and would apply for full membership of the EC.

A formal application for full membership of the EC was submitted by the Maltese Government in July 1990. In June 1993 the EC Commission recommended that, subject to the Government of Malta's satisfying EC requirements for regulatory reforms in financial services, competition and consumer protection, favourable consideration should be given to the future accession of Malta to the EU. In June 1994 the Council of the EU affirmed that the next phase of enlargement, following the (then) expected accession to the EU in January 1995 of Austria, Finland, Norway and Sweden, would involve Malta and Cyprus. In June 1995 the EU affirmed that full negotiations on Malta's accession were to begin six months after the conclusion of the 1996 Intergovernmental Conference.

Domestic opposition to Maltese accession to the EU had been led by the MLP, on the grounds that EU agricultural policies would increase the cost of living, and that integration into the EU would conflict with the Republic's traditional neutrality in its foreign relations. In September 1996 the PN Government, seeking to confirm its mandate to pursue the goal of full membership of the EU, called a general election for the following month. Although the PN contested the election on its record of economic success, the Government's introduction of value-added tax (VAT), as a precondition of Malta's admission to the EU, had proved unpopular with the electorate, and its proposed abolition by the MLP (which would concurrently disqualify Malta from EU membership) was widely regarded as the decisive factor in the election. With a participation rate of 97.1% of eligible voters, the MLP secured 50.7% of the votes cast, as against 47.8% for the PN. The MLP obtained 35 seats in the House of Representatives, with the PN receiving 34 seats. (As the MLP actually won three seats less than the PN in the election, four seats were added to its final total, giving it a one-seat majority in the House.) Dr Alfred Sant, the leader of the MLP, formed a new Government with the declared intention of replacing the 1970 association agreement (see above) with new arrangements providing for an eventual 'free-trade zone' between Malta and the EU. The MLP also emphasized its commitment to the advancement of Malta's financial services sector.

In February 1997 the Government announced the initiation of a 'national discussion' of proposals to legalize divorce. However, the imposition of tax increases and levies on public utilities substantially diminished the Government's popularity. Sant called a general election for September, three years earlier than constitutionally required, and in the poll, for which there was a participation rate of 95.4%, the PN, led by Fenech Adami, obtained a five-seat majority, having obtained 51.8% of votes cast, with the MLP receiving 48.0%. Immediately following the election, Fenech Adami reactivated Malta's application for full membership of the EU. In December 1999 the European Commission agreed that accession negotiations could begin in February 2000, and in the following month the President of the Commission paid an official visit to the island. In November 2000 the Commission published a report which stated that Malta was among the best-equipped economically of those countries seeking to join the EU. Further action was required in Malta to reduce state aid (notably the politically sensitive LM 15m. annual subsidy to the island's dry docks), to implement privatization plans and to strengthen tax and customs administrations. There were also some environmental issues that required attention, notably the inadequate sewerage system.

Accession talks for the EU were formally concluded on 13 December 2002 in Copenhagen. Malta had obtained 77 exemptions in the discussions aimed largely at protecting its industrial and agricultural sectors but also including cultural issues, such as the right to maintain the predominantly Roman Catholic country's ban on divorce. A non-binding referendum was called for 8 March 2003 to determine whether the country would join the EU. Support for membership of the EU was led by the ruling PN of Fenech Adami and opposition to it by Sant's MLP, which told voters to abstain, vote against the motion to join or spoil their ballots. Following an acrimonious campaign, 53.65% of the votes cast were in favour of joining, with 46.35% against. Sant refused to concede defeat, however, arguing that since the turn-out had been only 91% of the electorate the vote in support of membership of the EU did not represent an absolute majority. In accordance with the Constitution, Fenech Adami, whose mandate expired in 2004, called a general election for 12 April 2003 to confirm the referendum result, four days before the proposed signing of the EU accession treaty by 10 applicant countries, including Malta.

At the general election that took place on 12 April 2003 96.95% of the electorate participated; the PN won an absolute majority of 35 seats with 51.8% of the votes, while the MLP won 30 seats (47.5%) and the environmentalist Alternattiva Demokratika (Green Party) none (0.7%). Fenech Adami was sworn in as Prime Minister on 14 April, announced the new Cabinet the following day (which included two new ministries with responsibility for rural affairs and the environment and for youth and the arts) and signed the EU accession treaty in Athens, Greece, on 16 April. The House of Representatives eventually ratified the treaty on 14 July by 34 votes to 25 (with six members boycotting the vote), and the President signed it on 16 July. Malta thus became a full member of the EU on 1 May 2004.

Malta's accession to the EU marked the beginning of a change in the country's politics. Since independence Malta's politics had been deeply partisan and bitterly polarized over who could best govern the archipelago, or more recently over whether to join the EU. Following the 2003 general election, however, the parties moved towards unity and consensus in order to obtain the maximum benefits for Malta from its EU membership. The MLP, which had previously been opposed outright to accession, accepted the result of the general election as a final arbiter of Maltese opinion on the question. Accordingly, following the MLP's defeat at the polls, the party leadership decided to embrace majority public opinion and work within the reality of EU membership. This decision proved divisive, and was resisted by a 'fundamentalist wing' of the MLP led by Carmelo Mifsud Bonnici, the former MLP leader and Prime Minister. However, delegates at a subsequent party conference agreed that the MLP would not withdraw Malta from the EU if the party came to power. Moreover, it was agreed that the incumbent Government would henceforth be able to rely on the MLP's support in its efforts to defend Malta's influence within the EU, particularly with regard to negotiations relating to the draft EU constitutional treaty. In January 2004 the Minister of Foreign Affairs, Dr Joe Borg, was named as Malta's first member of the European Commission.

On 7 February 2004 Fenech Adami used the occasion of his 70th birthday to announce his intention to resign as leader of the PN. He had always maintained that he would relinquish this post, and that of Prime Minister, when he reached 70 years of age, and he indicated that he would step down as Prime Minister once the party had appointed his successor. At a party conference on 29 February the Deputy Prime Minister and Minister for Social Policy, Dr Lawrence Gonzi, was elected as the PN's new leader. Gonzi won 59.3% of the delegates' votes in the first round. His nearest rival, John Dalli, the Minister for Finance and Economic Affairs, withdrew from the contest, thereby obviating the need for a second round of voting. (None the less, a second round was held as a formality; Gonzi won 94% of the votes cast.) Fenech Adami duly resigned from his seat in the House of Representatives and from his post as Prime Minister, and Gonzi was sworn in on 23 March 2004. On his assumption of the premiership he stated that his main priorities in the post would be full participation in the EU, the creation of jobs and the improvement of the economy. When naming his Cabinet, Gonzi assumed responsibility for the finance portfolio and appointed Dalli as Minister of Foreign Affairs.

On 29 March 2004 Fenech Adami was elected President by the House of Representatives, by 33 votes to 29, following his nomination by Gonzi. His appointment was controversial, as party leaders had not traditionally stood for the post, and it was bitterly opposed by the MLP. Fenech Adami was sworn in as Malta's seventh President on 4 April 2004.

On 12 June 2004 Malta participated for the first time in elections to the European Parliament. The participation rate, at 82.4%, was the third highest among the member states, surpassed only by Belgium and Luxembourg (where voting is mandatory). The MLP won three seats and the PN two.

On 3 July 2004 Dalli resigned his post as Minister of Foreign Affairs, claiming he was unable to continue amid attacks from 'different sides', which was thought to be a reference to criticism from within the PN. There were also allegations, which Dalli denied, of irregularities involving a large shipping deal and the handling of ministry travel expenses. He was replaced by his junior minister, Michael Frendo.

The Treaty establishing a Constitution for Europe was signed by the EU Heads of State and of Government on 29 October 2004, but adoption remained dependent on ratification by all 25 member states, either through a referendum or by approval of the legislature. Gonzi had confirmed in June, when the final text of the constitution was agreed, that there was no need for a referendum on the issue in Malta. On 6 July 2005 the House of Representatives unanimously ratified the constitutional treaty. However, the future of the treaty was uncertain, following its rejection at public referendums in France and the Netherlands, and the ratification process came to a halt later in July.

Following its accession to the EU, illegal immigration became an increasing problem for Malta, partly owing to its proximity to North Africa. In the first half of 2005 the number of asylum applications submitted in Malta increased by 103% compared to the same period in 2004. According to the Office of the UN High Commissioner for Refugees (UNHCR, see p. 62), of all EU states Malta received the second largest number of asylum-seekers per 1,000 inhabitants in 2005 (after Cyprus). Given Malta's extremely high population density (1,236 per sq km at 31 December 2004), the European Commission supported the Government's request in July 2005 that a proportion of the migrants arriving there be transferred to other EU states. Malta received offers of assistance from the Czech Republic, Ireland, the Netherlands and the United Kingdom. The Commission also proposed that the detention period for illegal immigrants and asylum-seekers be reduced from one year to six months. The detention centres reached capacity in September, with new arrivals housed in tents. An investigation was launched in that month to determine whether the recent influx of illegal immigrants was the result of human trafficking. In October the House of Representatives adopted amendments to refugee legislation aimed at facilitating the repatriation of failed asylum-seekers. Also in that month the European Commission proposed the establishment of a fund, initially of €20m., to assist countries such as Malta in dealing with illegal immigration. It was intended that the first payments from the fund would be made in mid-2006. In December 2005 a first group of migrants granted refugee status was transferred to the Netherlands. The USA also pledged to accept a small group in 2006. Malta also sought an agreement with Libya on the repatriation of illegal immigrants to that country. In February 2006 immigrants housed in detention centres across Malta protested, claiming that they were poorly fed and kept in insanitary conditions. Malta had been criticized by UNHCR over its treatment of asylum-seekers in January 2005.

Malta is a member of the Council of Europe (see p. 211) and the Organization for Security and Co-operation in Europe (see p. 327). Participation by Malta in the NATO 'Partnership for Peace' programme formally commenced in 1995, but was suspended by the MLP Government during 1996–98. In September 2005 Malta applied for full membership of the Organisation for Economic Co-operation and Development (OECD, see p. 320).

In November 2005 Malta hosted the Commonwealth Heads of Government Meeting, at which leaders discussed improving co-operation in development, mass migration and combating terrorism. The British Prime Minister, Tony Blair, attended the meeting and later held talks with Gonzi on a number of issues, including illegal immigration. It was the first visit in some 60 years by a British Prime Minister.

In July 2005 Malta extended its maritime jurisdiction and established exclusive fisheries zones in response to similar measures adopted by Libya and Tunisia. Malta also requested permission from Libya for 15 vessels to operate within its unilaterally declared fisheries conservation zone at any one time during the year. In early 2006 Malta and Libya discussed reviving their 1984 co-operation agreement and agreed to consider a number of options with regard to petroleum, not limited to exploration. Also in February Malta and Tunisia signed an agreement on joint petroleum exploration and exploitation in zones of the continental shelf located between the two countries.

Government

Under the 1974 Constitution, legislative power is held by the unicameral House of Representatives, whose 65 members are elected by universal adult suffrage for five years (subject to dissolution) on the basis of proportional representation. The Constitution was amended in January 1987 to ensure that a party that received more than 50% of the total votes cast in a general election would obtain a majority of seats in the legislature (by the allocation—if necessary—of extra seats to that party). The President is the constitutional Head of State, elected for a five-year term by the House, and executive power is exercised by the Cabinet. The President appoints the Prime Minister and, on the latter's recommendation, other Ministers. The Cabinet is responsible to the House.

Defence

In August 2005 the armed forces of Malta comprised a regular army of 2,149. Military service is voluntary. Budgetary expenditure on defence in 2005 was LM 16.4m.

Economic Affairs

In 2004, according to estimates by the World Bank, Malta's gross national income (GNI), measured at average 2002–2004 prices, was US $4,913.2m., equivalent to $12,250 per head (or $18,720 per head on an international purchasing-power parity basis). During 1995–2004, it was estimated, the population increased at an average annual rate of 0.7%, while gross domestic product (GDP) per head increased, in real terms, at an average annual rate of 1.8%. Overall GDP increased, in real terms, at an average annual rate of 2.5% in 1995–2004; GDP declined by 1.7% in 2003, but increased by 1.4% in 2004.

Agriculture (including hunting, forestry and fishing) contributed 2.4% of GDP and engaged 2.5% of the working population in 2005. The principal export crop is potatoes. Tomatoes and other vegetables, cereals (principally wheat and barley) and fruit are also cultivated. Livestock and livestock products are also important, and efforts are being made to develop the fishing industry. Exports of food and live animals accounted for 3.3% of total exports in 2005 (excluding re-exports). According to FAO figures, Malta's agricultural production increased at an average rate of 0.7% per year in 1995–2004. Output increased by 5.3% in 2003 and by 4.4% in 2004.

Industry (including mining, manufacturing and construction) provided 23.2% of GDP and engaged 28.6% of the employed labour force in 2005. Industrial production (including electricity and water, but excluding construction) increased at an average rate of 12.2% per year in 1990–96. It rose by 11.0% in 1995, but declined by 4.7% in 1996.

Mining and quarrying contributed 0.4% of GDP and engaged 0.4% of the employed labour force in 2005. The mining sector's output expanded at an average annual rate of 18.3% in 1990–96. Production rose by 26.6% in 1995 and by 11.0% in 1996. The principal activities are stone and sand quarrying. There are reserves of petroleum in Maltese offshore waters, and petroleum and gas exploration is proceeding.

Manufacturing contributed 17.3% of GDP and engaged 17.9% of the working population in 2005. Based on the gross value of output, the principal branches of manufacturing, excluding ship-repairing, in 1999 were transport equipment and machinery (accounting for 54.7% of the total), food products and beverages (12.4%) and textiles, footwear and clothing (8.4%). Manufacturing production increased at an average rate of 7.6% per year in 1990–96. It advanced by 8.1% in 1995, but declined by 6.2% in 1996.

Energy is derived principally from imports of crude petroleum (the majority of which is purchased, at preferential rates, from Libya) and coal. Imports of mineral fuels comprised 11.0% of the value of total imports in 2005.

Services provided 74.4% of GDP and engaged 68.8% of the employed labour force in 2005. Tourism is a major source of foreign exchange earnings. In 2003 Malta received 1,126,601 foreign visitors, and revenue from the sector was US $856m. In 2005 6.2% of the employed labour force were engaged in hotels and restaurants.

In 2004 Malta recorded a visible trade deficit of US $841.9m., and there was a deficit of $548.6m. on the current account of the balance of payments. More than two-thirds of Malta's trade is with the countries of the European Union (EU, see p. 228). In 2001 the principal source of imports (accounting for 19.9% of the total) was Italy (including San Marino); other major suppliers were France (15.0%), the USA (11.6%) and the United Kingdom (10.0%). The USA was the principal market for exports (taking 19.8% of the total); other significant purchasers of exports were Germany (13.1%), Singapore (11.8%) and France (9.3%). The principal domestic exports in 2005 were machinery and transport equipment, accounting for 63.5% of the total, and miscellaneous manufactured articles (20.3%). The principal imports were machinery and transport equipment, accounting for 43.6% of the total, miscellaneous manufactured articles (12.5%) and basic manufactures (11.1%).

In 2004 Malta recorded a budgetary deficit of LM 94.0m. (equivalent to 5.1% of GDP in that year). At the end of 1997 Malta's external debt totalled US $1,034m., of which $125m. was long-term public debt. In that year the cost of debt-servicing was equivalent to 2.1% of the value of exports of goods and services. The annual rate of inflation averaged 2.1% in 1995–2004; consumer prices increased by 1.3% in 2003 and by 2.7% in 2004. In 2005 5.0% of the labour force were unemployed.

Malta is a member of the World Trade Organization (WTO, see p. 370) and of the European Bank for Reconstruction and Development (EBRD, see p. 224). Malta joined the EU, with nine other countries, on 1 May 2004.

Following the closure, in 1979, of the British military base and naval docks, on which Malta's economy had been largely dependent, successive governments have pursued a policy of restructuring and diversification. The domestic market is limited, owing to the small population. There are few natural resources, and almost all raw materials have to be imported. Malta's development has therefore been based on the promotion of the island as an international financial centre and on manufacturing for export (notably in non-traditional fields, such as electronics, information technology and pharmaceuticals), together with the continuing development of tourism. From 2004 Malta's EU membership entailed a commitment on the part of the Government to reduce Malta's budgetary deficit below 3.0% of GDP in order to comply with the convergence criteria for participation in Economic and Monetary Union (EMU). The convergence criteria also required conditions to be met in the areas of inflation, debt and interest-rate and exchange-rate stability, including a requirement to spend at least two years in the successor to the original Exchange Rate Mechanism (ERM), known as ERM II. Although the Government's stated objective was to adopt the euro as soon as possible, its aim to reduce the budgetary deficit to the required level by 2006 was regarded as ambitious. In 2004 Malta had the third highest deficit in the EU, at 5.1% of GDP, despite having halved it from the previous year. It was the country's best performance since 1995, when the deficit had stood at 3.9%. Compliance with the convergence criteria necessitated radical reforms, which were expected to adversely affect both government and household consumption. Moreover, the difficulty of implementing these reforms was expected to be considerable, as relations between the Government and trade unions were deteriorating. In May 2005 Malta entered ERM-II, with the aim of joining the euro area on 1 January 2008. None the less, the EU expressed some concerns about Malta's ability to achieve this, urging the Government to accelerate its preparations. In November 2005 the European Commission reported that Malta had met only three of the 38 prerequisites for adopting the common currency. Another significant challenge to Malta's economy was the female employment rate, which was the lowest in the EU. In 2004 only 30% of Maltese women aged between 15 and 64 years were employed; the EU average was 55.7%. In other respects, Malta faced the same challenges as the other EU member states: restraining government expenditure, modernizing the welfare state, improving flexibility in the labour market, increasing international competitiveness, and generating stronger economic growth. Pensions reform was a priority: expenditure on old-age pensions was expected to more than double during 2004–24, to about the equivalent of 11% of GDP, according to the IMF. Moreover, in line with present trends, the number of workers supporting one pensioner was forecast to decrease from four to two over the same period. Nevertheless, an EU report published in early 2006 concluded that the impact of demographic change would not be as severe in Malta as was expected in other EU countries. In November 2005 the Government presented a three-year national reform programme, in the context of the EU's renewed Lisbon Agenda (a programme of reforms initially agreed in 2000 at a summit in the Portuguese capital). The programme, which entailed an investment of €228m., to be financed both nationally and with EU funds, was intended to promote the country's competitiveness, economic growth and job creation.

Education

Education is compulsory between the ages of five and 16 years, and is available free of charge in government schools and institutions, from kindergarten to university. Kindergarten education is provided for three- and four-year-old children. In 2002/03 enrolment at pre-primary level included 86% of children in the relevant age-group (males 85%; females 87%). Primary education begins at five years of age and lasts for six years. In 2002/03 enrolment at primary level included 96% of children in the relevant age-group (males 96%; females 96%). Secondary education, beginning at 11 years of age, lasts for a maximum of seven years, but this period is extended in the case of technology and vocational courses. Enrolment at secondary level in 2002/03 included 87% of children in the relevant age-group (males 86%; females 88%). After completing five years of secondary-level education, students having the necessary qualifications may opt to follow a higher academic or technical or vocational course. The junior college, administrated by the University, prepares students specifically for a university course. About 30% of the student population attend schools administered by the Roman Catholic Church, from kindergarten to higher secondary level. The Government subsidizes the provision of free education for students in church schools. Higher education is available at the University of Malta. There are also a number of technical institutes, specialist schools and an extended skill-training scheme for trade-school leavers. Enrolment at tertiary level was equivalent to 30% of those in the relevant age-group in 2002/03 (males 25%; females 35%). The Government also provides adult education courses. Of total recurrent budgetary expenditure in 2004 LM 50.2m. (6.9%) was allocated to education. In July 2005 the Government announced its intention to reform the education system. From September state primary schools, area secondary schools and junior colleges were to be grouped together into autonomous regional colleges. The Government also proposed establishing a national commission on higher education, and the inclusion of a scholarship fund in the 2006 budget.

Public Holidays

2006: 1 January (New Year's Day), 10 February (St Paul's Shipwreck), 19 March (St Joseph), 14 April (Good Friday), 31 March (Freedom Day), 1 May (St Joseph the Worker), 7 June (Memorial of 1919 Riot), 29 June (St Peter and St Paul), 15 August (Assumption), 8 September (Our Lady of Victories), 21 September (Independence Day), 8 December (Immaculate Conception), 14 December (Republic Day), 25 December (Christmas).

2007: 1 January (New Year's Day), 10 February (St Paul's Shipwreck), 19 March (St Joseph), 6 April (Good Friday), 31 March (Freedom Day), 1 May (St Joseph the Worker), 7 June (Memorial of 1919 Riot), 29 June (St Peter and St Paul), 15 August (Assumption), 8 September (Our Lady of Victories), 21 September (Independence Day), 8 December (Immaculate Conception), 14 December (Republic Day), 25 December (Christmas).

Weights and Measures

The metric system is in force.

Statistical Survey

Source (unless otherwise stated): National Statistics Office, Lascaris, Valletta; tel. 21223221; fax 21249841; e-mail nso@magnet.mt; internet www.nso.gov.mt.

AREA AND POPULATION

Area: 316 sq km (122 sq miles).

Population: 378,132 (males 186,836, females 191,296) at census of 26 November 1995 (figures refer to *de jure* population); 402,668 (males 199,580, females 203,088) at 31 December 2004 (incl. 11,999 non-Maltese residents).

Density (Maltese only, 31 December 2004): 1,236.3 per sq km.

Principal Towns (estimated total population at 31 December 2004): Birkirkara 22,568; Qormi 18,589; Mosta 18,172; Zabbar 15,217; San Gwann 12,967; Sliema 12,742; Valletta (capital) 7,111.

Births, Marriages and Deaths (2004): Registered live births 3,887 (birth rate 9.6 per 1,000); Marriages 2,402 (marriage rate 6.0 per 1,000); Registered deaths 2,999 (death rate 7.4 per 1,000).

Expectation of Life (WHO estimates, years at birth): 79 (males 76; females 81) in 2003. Source: WHO, *World Health Report*.

Migration (2004, unless otherwise indicated): Emigrants 70 (all to United Kingdom); Returning emigrants 459; Non-Maltese nationals settling in the islands 533 (in 2002).

Economically Active Population (September 2005): Agriculture and hunting 3,089; Fishing 427; Crude petroleum and natural gas extraction 177; Mining and quarrying 326; Manufacturing 24,780; Recycling 43; Electricity, gas and water supply 3,375; Construction 10,818; Wholesale and retail trade and repair of motor vehicles, motorcycles and personal and household goods 21,147; Hotels and restaurants 8,613; Transport, storage and communications 11,121; Financial intermediation 5,110; Real estate, renting and business activities 10,682; Public administration and defence and compulsory social security 10,869; Education 12,109; Health and social work 9,164; Other community, social and personal service activities 6,107; Extra-territorial organizations and bodies 171; *Total employed* 138,128; Unemployed 7,210; *Total labour force* 145,338. Note: figures exclude apprentices, trainees and students engaged in holiday work.

HEALTH AND WELFARE

Key Indicators

Total Fertility Rate (children per woman, 2003): 1.8.

Under-5 Mortality Rate (per 1,000 live births, 2004): 6.

HIV/AIDS (% of persons aged 15–49, 2003): 0.2.

Physicians (per 1,000 head, 2001): 2.93.

Hospital Beds (per 1,000 head, 2001): 4.96.

Health Expenditure (2002): US $ per head (PPP): 965.

Health Expenditure (2002): % of GDP: 9.7.

Health Expenditure (2002): public (% of total): 71.8.

Access to Water (% of persons, 2002): 100.

Access to Sanitation (% of persons, 2000): 100.

Human Development Index (2003): ranking: 32.

Human Development Index (2003): value: 0.867.

For sources and definitions, see explanatory note on p. vi.

MALTA

Statistical Survey

AGRICULTURE, ETC.

Principal Crops ('000 metric tons, 2004, unofficial figures unless otherwise indicated): Wheat 9.5*; Barley 2.2*; Potatoes 28.6; Cabbages 3.0; Tomatoes 15.4; Cauliflowers 2.8*; Pumpkins, squash and gourds 5.5; Dry onions 7.0; Garlic 0.7; Green broad beans 1.1; Other vegetables 7.4*; Melons 12.8*; Citrus fruit 1.0*; Grapes 2.7; Other fruits and berries 3.5*.

* FAO estimate.

Livestock ('000 head, year ending September 2004, FAO estimates unless otherwise indicated): Cattle 19.4*; Pigs 76.9*; Sheep 14.2*; Goats 5.4; Rabbits 0.2; Chickens 1,000; Turkeys 10; Horses 1.0; Asses 0.5; Mules 0.3.

* Unofficial figure.

Livestock Products ('000 metric tons, 2004, FAO estimates unless otherwise indicated): Beef and veal 1.3; Pig meat 8.5*; Rabbit meat 1.4; Poultry meat 7.5; Cows' milk 41.3; Sheep's milk 3.7; Poultry eggs 6.1.

* Unofficial figure.

Fishing (metric tons, live weight 2003): Capture 1,138 (Atlantic bluefin tuna 255, Common dolphinfish 507, Swordfish 163); Aquaculture 881 (European seabass 93, Gilthead seabream 788); *Total catch* 2,019.

Source: FAO.

INDUSTRY

Production ('000 metric tons, 2001, unless otherwise indicated): Limestone flux and calcareous stones 2,000 (Limestone only); Cigarettes (1992, million) 1,475; Washing powders and detergents 9.7; Quicklime (1992, incl. other types of lime) 5; Tankers, launched (1996, number, completions) 5; Other sea-going merchant vessels launched (number) 1 (5 grt); Electricity (2000, million kWh, by public utilities, provisional) 1,875. Source mainly UN, *Industrial Commodity Statistics Yearbook*; UN Economic Commission for Europe; US Geological Survey; US Dept of Agriculture; Lloyd's Register of Shipping.

FINANCE

Currency and Exchange Rates: 1,000 mils = 100 cents = 1 Maltese lira (LM; plural: liri). *Sterling, Dollar and Euro Equivalents* (30 December 2005): £1 sterling = 624.6 mils; US $1 = 362.7 mils; €1 = 427.9 mils; LM 100 = £160.11 = $275.70 = €233.70. *Average Exchange Rate* (Maltese lira per US $): 0.3772 in 2003; 0.3447 in 2004; 0.3458 in 2005.

Budget (LM million, 2004): *Revenue:* Income tax 211.2; Customs and excise 62.3; Value-added tax 141.6; Social security 189.7; Grants and loans 130.3; Total (incl. others) 921.9. *Expenditure:* Recurrent expenditure 732.8 (Social security 207.5, Education 50.2); Public debt servicing 96.4; Capital expenditure 104.6; Total 933.9.

International Reserves (US $ million at 31 December 2005): Gold 1.9; IMF special drawing rights 45.9; Reserve position in IMF 57.5; Foreign exchange 2,473.0; Total 2,578.3. Source: IMF, *International Financial Statistics*.

Money Supply (LM million at 31 December 2004): Currency outside banks 485.99; Demand deposits at commercial banks 894.61; Total money 1,380.60. Source: IMF, *International Financial Statistics*.

Cost of Living (Consumer Price Index; base: 2000 = 100): All items 105.2 in 2002; 106.6 in 2003; 109.5 in 2004. Source: IMF, *International Financial Statistics*.

Gross Domestic Product (LM '000 at current prices): 1,829,068 in 2003; 1,830,406 in 2004; 1,927,093 in 2005.

Expenditure on Gross Domestic Product (LM '000 at current prices, 2005): Final consumption expenditure 1,683,355 (General government final consumption expenditure 417,800, Households 1,232,475, Non-profit institutes serving households 33,080); Gross capital formation 445,437 (Changes in stocks 28,966, Gross fixed capital formation 410,471, Acquisitions, less disposals, of valuables 6,000); *Total domestic expenditure* 2,128,792; Exports of goods and services 1,372,525; *Less* Imports of goods and services 1,574,224; *GDP in purchasers' values* 1,927,093.

Gross Domestic Product by Economic Activity (LM '000 at current prices, 2005): Agriculture, hunting and forestry 36,069; Fishing 3,897; Mining and quarrying 5,959; Manufacturing 284,784; Electricity, gas and water supply 12,438; Construction 78,146; Wholesale and retail trade, repair of motor vehicles, motorcycles and household goods 198,000; Hotels and restaurants 104,768; Transport, storage and communication 164,554; Financial intermediation 73,361; Real estate, renting and business activities 235,651; Public administration and defence, compulsory social security 130,288; Education 119,107; Health and social work 101,475; Other community, social and personal services 98,035; *Gross value added at basic prices* 1,646,530; Indirect taxes 294,456; *Less* Subsidies 13,894; *GDP in purchasers' values* 1,927,093.

Balance of Payments (US $ million, 2004): Exports of goods f.o.b. 2,654.3; Imports of goods f.o.b. −3,496.2; *Trade balance* −841.9; Exports of services 1,367.4; Imports of services −931.6; *Balance on goods and services* −406.1; Other income received 948.7; Other income paid −1,015.5; *Balance on goods, services and income* −473.0; Current transfers received 221.3; Current transfers paid −296.9; *Current balance* −548.6; Capital account (net) 84.1; Direct investment abroad −79.9; Direct investment from abroad 507.5; Portfolio investment assets −1,643.6; Portfolio investment liabilities −8.2; Financial derivatives assets −761.6; Financial derivatives liabilities 764.3; Other investment assets −1,080.9; Other investment liabilities 2,350.8; Net errors and omissions 209.4; *Overall balance* −206.6. Source: IMF, *International Financial Statistics*.

EXTERNAL TRADE

Principal Commodities (LM million, provisional, 2005): *Imports c.i.f.:* Food and live animals 128.1; Mineral fuels, lubricants, etc. 143.4; Chemicals 113.9; Basic manufactures 145.2; Machinery and transport equipment 569.0; Miscellaneous manufactured articles 163.6; Total (incl. others) 1,304.7. *Exports (excl. re-exports) f.o.b.:* Food and live animals 26.3; Chemicals 28.4; Basic manufactures 54.1; Machinery and transport equipment 509.1; Miscellaneous manufactured articles 162.6; Total (incl. others) 802.0.

Selected Trading Partners (US $ million, 2001): *Imports:* France (incl. Monaco) 409.3; Germany 238.9; Italy (incl. San Marino) 543.8; Singapore 182.3; United Kingdom 273.5; USA 315.3; Total (incl. others) 2,726.8. *Exports:* France (incl. Monaco) 182.8; Germany 255.8; Singapore 230.9; Switzerland (incl. Liechtenstein) 132.4; United Kingdom 169.5; USA 388.0; Total (incl. others) 1,958.8. Source: UN, *International Trade Statistics Yearbook*.

TRANSPORT

Road Traffic (motor vehicles in use, December 2005): Private cars 206,148; Commercial vehicles 44,371; Minibuses 422; Coaches and buses 721; Motorcycles 11,905; Total (incl. others) 271,338.

Shipping: *Merchant Fleet* (31 December 2004): Vessels 1,181; Total displacement 22,352,570 grt (Source: Lloyds Register-Fairplay, *World Fleet Statistics*). International Freight Traffic (metric tons, 2001): Goods loaded 319,972; Goods unloaded 1,453,574.

Civil Aviation (traffic on scheduled services, 2001): Kilometres flown (million) 25; Passengers carried ('000) 1,340; Passenger-km (million) 2,359; Total ton-km (million) 227. Source: UN, *Statistical Yearbook*.

TOURISM

Tourist Arrivals: 1,180,145 in 2001; 1,133,814 in 2002; 1,126,601 in 2003.

Arrivals by Country of Origin (provisional, 2003): Austria 28,416; Belgium 23,724; France 76,384; Germany 125,811; Italy 94,175; Netherlands 44,395; United Kingdom 459,565; Total (incl. cruise passengers and others) 1,126,601.

Tourism Receipts (US $ million, incl. passenger transport): 721 in 2001; 714 in 2002; 856 in 2003. Source: World Tourism Organization.

COMMUNICATIONS MEDIA

Radio Receivers (1997): 255,000 in use*.

Television Receivers (1999): 212,000 in use*.

Telephones (main lines, 2005): 209,305 in use.

Facsimile Machines (1996): 6,000 in use (estimate)†.

Mobile Cellular Telephones (2005): 324,787 subscribers.

Personal Computers (2004): 126,000 in use‡.

Internet Users (2005): 88,771.

Book Production (1998): 237 titles*.

Daily Newspapers (1999): 4 titles (combined average circulation 54,000 copies per issue).

Non-daily Newspapers (1999): 10 titles.

Other Periodicals (1992): 359 titles*.

* Source: UN, *Statistical Yearbook*.
† Source: UNESCO, *Statistical Yearbook*.
‡ Source: International Telecommunication Union.

MALTA

EDUCATION

Pre-primary (2002/03, unless otherwise stated): 131 schools (1999/2000); 1,144 teachers; 9,368 students. Source: UNESCO.

Primary (2002/03, unless otherwise stated): 126 schools (1999/2000); 1,745 teachers; 31,710 students. Source: UNESCO.

Secondary (2002/03, unless otherwise stated): *General:* 75 schools (1999/2000); 3,289 teachers; 35,229 students. *Vocational:* 23 schools (1999/2000); 551 teachers; 2,327 students. *Junior College* (1995/96): 1 school; 1,800 students. Source: UNESCO, partly *Statistical Yearbook*.

Universities, etc. (2002/03): 579 teachers; 8,946 students. Source: UNESCO.

Adult Literacy Rate (UNESCO estimates): 87.9% (males 86.4%; females 89.2%) in 1995–99. Source: UN Development Programme, *Human Development Report*.

Directory

The Constitution

On 13 December 1974 the Independence Constitution of 1964 was substantially amended to bring into effect a Republican Constitution, under the terms of which Malta became a democratic republic within the Commonwealth, founded on work and on respect for the fundamental rights and freedoms of the individual. The new Constitution provided for the creation of the office of President of Malta to replace that of Governor-General.

The religion of the Maltese people is recognized to be the Roman Catholic Apostolic Religion, and the Church Authorities have the constitutional right and duty to teach according to its principles. The religious teaching of the Roman Catholic Church is provided in all state schools as part of compulsory education.

The Constitution provides that the national language and the language of the Courts is Maltese but that both Maltese and English are official languages.

An independent Public Services Commission, consisting of three to five members, is appointed by the President, on the advice of the Prime Minister, to make recommendations to the Prime Minister concerning appointments to public office and the dismissal and disciplinary control of persons holding public office.

The Constitution also provides for an Employment Commission, consisting of a chairman and four other members, the function of which is to ensure that, in respect of employment, no distinction, exclusion or preference that is not justifiable is made or given in favour of or against any person by reason of his or her political opinion.

The Judicature is independent.

Radio and television broadcasting is controlled by an independent authority.

DECLARATION OF PRINCIPLES

The Constitution upholds the right to work and to reasonable hours of work, the safeguarding of rights of women workers, the encouragement of private economic enterprise, the encouragement of co-operatives, the provision of free and compulsory primary education, and the provision of social assistance and insurance.

FUNDAMENTAL RIGHTS AND FREEDOMS OF THE INDIVIDUAL

The Constitution provides for the protection of the right to life, freedom from arbitrary arrest or detention, protection of freedom of conscience, protection from discrimination on the grounds of race, etc.

THE PRESIDENT

Under the Constitution, the office of President becomes vacant after five years from the date of appointment made by resolution of the House of Representatives. The President appoints the Prime Minister, choosing the member of the House of Representatives who is judged to be ablest to command the confidence of a majority of the members. On the advice of the Prime Minister, the President appoints the other ministers, the Chief Justice, the Judges and the Attorney-General.

THE CABINET

The Cabinet consists of the Prime Minister and such number of other ministers as recommended by the Prime Minister.

PARLIAMENT

The House of Representatives consists of such number of members, being an odd number and divisible by the number of divisions, as Parliament by law determines from time to time. In future the electoral divisions are not to be fewer than nine and not more than 15, as Parliament may from time to time determine. The normal life of the House of Representatives is five years, after which a general election is held. Election is by universal adult suffrage on the basis of proportional representation. The age of majority is 18 years. Under a constitutional amendment adopted in January 1987, it was ensured that a party receiving more than 50% of the total votes cast in a general election would obtain a majority of seats in the House of Representatives, by the allocation (if necessary) of extra seats to that party.

NEUTRALITY AND NON-ALIGNMENT

In January 1987 a constitutional amendment was adopted, aiming to entrench in the Constitution Malta's status of neutrality and adherence to a policy of non-alignment, and stipulating that no foreign military base was to be permitted on Maltese territory.

The Government

HEAD OF STATE

President: Dr EDWARD (EDDIE) FENECH ADAMI (took office 4 April 2004).

THE CABINET
(April 2006)

Prime Minister and Minister of Finance: Dr LAWRENCE GONZI.

Deputy Prime Minister and Minister for Justice and Home Affairs: Dr TONIO BORG.

Minister of Education, Youth and Employment: Dr LOUIS GALEA.

Minister for Tourism and Culture: Dr FRANCIS ZAMMIT DIMECH.

Minister for Competitiveness and Communications: CENSU GALEA.

Minister for Resources and Infrastructure: NINU ZAMMIT.

Minister for Gozo: GIOVANNA DEBONO.

Minister of Health, the Elderly and Community Care: Dr LOUIS DEGUARA.

Minister for Investment, Industry and Information Technology: Dr AUSTIN GATT.

Minister for Rural Affairs and the Environment: GEORGE PULLICINO.

Minister for Urban Development and Roads: JESMOND MUGLIETT.

Minister for the Family and Social Solidarity: DOLORES CRISTINA.

Minister of Foreign Affairs: MICHAEL FRENDO.

PARLIAMENTARY SECRETARIES (ATTACHED TO MINISTRIES)

Parliamentary Secretary in the Office of the Prime Minister: ANTHONY ABELA.

Parliamentary Secretary in the Ministry for Justice and Home Affairs: CARMELO MIFSUD BONNICI.

Parliamentary Secretary in the Ministry of Finance: TONIO FENECH.

Parliamentary Secretary for Small Business and the Self-Employed in the Ministry for Competitiveness and Communications: EDWIN VASSALLO.

Parliamentary Secretary for the Elderly and Community Care in the Ministry of Health, the Elderly and Community Care: HELEN D'AMATO.

Parliamentary Secretary for Agriculture and Fisheries in the Ministry for Rural Affairs and the Environment: FRANCIS AGIUS.

MALTA

MINISTRIES

Office of the President: The Palace, Valletta CMR 02; tel. 21221221; fax 21241241; e-mail president@gov.mt; internet president.gov.mt.

Office of the Prime Minister: Auberge de Castille, Valletta CMR 02; tel. 22001400; fax 22001467; internet www.opm.gov.mt.

Ministry for Competitiveness and Communications: Casa Leoni, St Joseph High Rd, St Venera CMR 02; tel. 21485100; fax 23886116; e-mail info.mcmp@gov.mt; internet www.mcmp.gov.mt.

Ministry of Education, Youth and Employment: Great Siege Rd, Floriana CMR 02; tel. 21223622; fax 21242759; e-mail communications.moed@gov.mt; internet www.education.gov.mt.

Ministry for the Family and Social Solidarity: Palazzo Ferreria, 310 Republic St, Valletta CMR 02; tel. 25903100; fax 25903121; e-mail info.mfss@gov.mt; internet mfss.gov.mt.

Ministry of Finance: Maison Demandols, 30 South St, Valletta CMR 02; tel. 25998285; fax 21251712; e-mail info.mfin@gov.mt; internet www.mfin.gov.mt.

Ministry of Foreign Affairs: Palazzo Parisio, Merchants St, Valletta CMR 02; tel. 21242853; fax 21237822; e-mail info.mfa@gov.mt; internet www.foreign.gov.mt.

Ministry for Gozo: St Francis Sq., Victoria VCT 112, Gozo; tel. 21561482; fax 21561755; internet www.gozo.gov.mt.

Ministry of Health, the Elderly and Community Care: Palazzo Castellania, 15 Merchants St, Valletta CMR 02; tel. 21224071; fax 22992655; internet www.health.gov.mt.

Ministry for Investment, Industry and Information Technology: 168 Triq id-Dejqa, Valletta CMR 02; tel. 22951310; fax 21250700; e-mail miti@gov.mt; internet www.miti.gov.mt.

Ministry for Justice and Home Affairs: Auberge d'Aragon, Independence Sq., Valletta CMR 02; tel. 22957000; fax 22957348; internet www.mjha.gov.mt.

Ministry for Resources and Infrastructure: Block B, Floriana CMR 02; tel. 21222378; fax 21243306; internet www.mri.gov.mt.

Ministry for Rural Affairs and the Environment: Barriera Wharf, Valletta CMR 02; tel. 22952000; fax 22952212; e-mail info.mrae@gov.mt; internet www.mrae.gov.mt.

Ministry for Tourism and Culture: Auberge d'Italie, Merchants St., Valletta CMR 02; tel. 21225111; fax 22981301; e-mail marisa.delorenzo@gov.mt; internet www.tourism.gov.mt.

Ministry for Urban Development and Roads: House of Four Winds, Hastings Gdns, Valletta CMR 02; tel. 22985000; fax 22985125; internet www.mudr.gov.mt.

Legislature

HOUSE OF REPRESENTATIVES

Speaker: ANTON TABONE.

General Election, 12 April 2003

Party	Votes	% of votes	Seats
Partit Nazzjonalista (Nationalist Party)	146,172	51.79	35
Malta Labour Party (Partit Laburista)	134,092	47.51	30
Alternattiva Demokratika (Green Party)	1,929	0.68	—
Others	20	0.01	—
Total	282,213	100.00	65

Election Commission

Kummissjoni Elettorali: Electoral Office, Evans Bldg, St Elmo Pl., Valletta; tel. 21245086; fax 21248457; independent; Chair. and Chief Electoral Officer EDWARD R. GATT; Sec. JOE CALLEJA.

Political Organizations

Alternattiva Demokratika (AD) (Green Party): 10 Manwel Dimech St, Sliema; tel. 21314040; fax 21314046; e-mail info@alternattiva.org.mt; internet www.alternattiva.org.mt; f. 1989; emphasizes social and environmental issues; Chair. Dr HARRY VASSALLO; Sec.-Gen. MARIO MALLIA.

Malta Labour Party (MLP) (Partit Laburista): National Labour Centre, Mile End Rd, Hamrun HMR 02; tel. 21249900; fax 21244204; e-mail mlp@mlp.org.mt; internet www.mlp.org.mt; f. 1921; democratic socialist; Leader Dr ALFRED SANT; Pres. STEFAN ZRINZO AZZOPARDI; Gen. Sec. JASON MICALLEF; 39,000 mems.

Partit Nazzjonalista (Nationalist Party—PN): Herbert Ganado St, Pietà HMR 08; tel. 21243641; fax 21243640; e-mail pn@pn.org.mt; internet www.pn.org.mt; f. 1880; Christian democratic; Leader Dr LAWRENCE GONZI; Sec.-Gen. JOE SALIBA; 33,000 mems.

Diplomatic Representation

EMBASSIES AND HIGH COMMISSIONS IN MALTA

Australia: Villa Fiorentina, Ta'Xbiex Terrace, Ta'Xbiex MSD 11; tel. 21338201; fax 21344059; e-mail aushicom@vol.net.mt; High Commissioner RICHARD PALK.

Austria: Whitehall Mansions, 3rd Floor, Ta'Xbiex Seafront, Ta'Xbiex MSD 11; tel. 23279000; fax 21317430; Ambassador Dr ELISABETH KEHRER.

Belgium: Europa Office Block, 8–9 John Lopez St., Floriana VLT 14; tel. 21230893; fax 21237606; e-mail valletta@diplobel.be; Ambassador THOMAS BAEKELANDT.

China, People's Republic: Karmnu Court, Lapsi St, St Julian's STJ 09; tel. 21384889; fax 21344730; e-mail ceim@keyworld.net; internet www.chinaembassy.org.mt; Ambassador LIU ZHENGXIU.

Egypt: Villa Mon Rêve, 10 Sir Temi Zammit St, Ta'Xbiex MSD 11; tel. 21314158; fax 21319230; e-mail embegmlt@onvol.net; Ambassador ABDELKARIM MAHMOUD SOLIMAN.

France: POB 408, Valletta CMR 01; 130 Melita St, Valletta CMR 01; tel. 21233430; fax 21233528; e-mail france@global.net.mt; internet www.ambafrance.org.mt; Ambassador JEAN-MARC RIVES.

Germany: 'Il-Piazzetta', Entrance B, 1st Floor, Tower Rd, Sliema SLM 16; tel. 21336520; fax 21341271; e-mail germanembassy@kemmunet.net.mt; Ambassador GEORG MERTEN.

Greece: Vilino Fondgalland, 6 Ir-Rampa Ta'Xbiex, T'Xbiex MSD 11; tel. 21320998; fax 21320788; e-mail embassy.malta@mfa.gr; Ambassador DOROTHEA TSIMBOUKELI-DOUVUS.

Holy See: V20/22 Pietru Caxaru St, Tal-Virtù, Rabat RBT 09; tel. 21453422; fax 21453423; e-mail apost@keyworld.net; Apostolic Nuncio Most Rev. FÉLIX DEL BLANCO PRIETO (Titular Archbishop of Vannida).

Italy: 5 Vilhena St, Floriana VLT 14; tel. 21233157; fax 21235339; e-mail ambasciata.lavalletta@esteri.it; internet www.amblavalletta.esteri.it; Ambassador Dr ALVISE MEMMO.

Libya: Dar Jamahariya, Notabile Rd, Balzan BZN 01; tel. 21486347; fax 21483939; e-mail libyanpeople@waldonet.net.mt; Sec. of the People's Bureau Dr SAAD A. F. ELSHLMANI.

Portugal: Whitehall Mansions, 3rd Floor, Ta'Xbiex Seafront, Ta'Xbiex, MSD 11; tel. 21322924; fax 21322927; Ambassador ANTÓNIO AUGUSTO RUSSO DIAS.

Netherlands: Whitehall Mansions, 3rd Floor, Ta'Xbiex Seafront, Ta'Xbiex MSD 11; tel. 21313980; fax 21313990; e-mail val@minbuza.nl; internet www.netherlandsembassy.org.mt; Ambassador JAN HEIDSMA.

Russia: Ariel House, 25 Anthony Schembri St, Kappara, San Gwann; tel. 21371905; fax 21372131; e-mail rusemb@keyworld.net; internet www.malta.mid.ru; Ambassador VALENTIN S. VLASOV.

Spain: Whitehall Mansions, Ta'Xbiex Seafront, Ta'Xbiex MSD 11; tel. 21317382; fax 21317362; e-mail emb.valletta@mae.es; Ambassador MARÍA ROSA BOCETA OSTOS.

Tunisia: Valletta Rd, Attard BZN 03; tel. 21417070; fax 21413414; e-mail at.lavalette@maltanet.net; Ambassador MUHAMMAD MEZGHENI.

United Kingdom: Whitehall Mansions, Ta'Xbiex Seafront, Ta'Xbiex MSD 11; tel. 23230000; fax 23232216; e-mail bhcvalletta@fco.gov.uk; internet www.britishhighcommission.gov.uk/malta; High Commissioner NICHOLAS ARCHER.

USA: Development House, 3rd Floor, St Anne St, Floriana VLT 14; tel. 25614000; fax 21243229; e-mail usembmalta@state.gov; internet malta.usembassy.gov; Ambassador MOLLY HERING BORDONARO.

Judicial System

The legal system consists of enactments of the Parliament of Malta, and those of the British Parliament not repealed or replaced by enactments of the Maltese legislature. Maltese Civil Law derives largely from Roman Law, while British Law has significantly influenced Maltese public law.

The Constitutional Court, composed of three judges, is appellate in cases involving alleged violations of human rights, the interpretation of the Constitution and the invalidity of laws. It has jurisdiction to decide questions as to membership of the House of Representatives and any reference made to it relating to voting for election of members of the House of Representatives.

The Court of Appeal is composed of three judges, when it hears appeals from the judgments of the Civil Court, and of one judge, when it hears appeals from the Court of Magistrates in its civil jurisdiction. An appeal also lies to the Court of Appeal from the decisions of a number of administrative tribunals, mostly on points of law.

The Court of Criminal Appeal consists of three judges and hears appeals from persons convicted by the Criminal Court. A person convicted on indictment may appeal against his conviction in all cases or against the sentence passed on his conviction, unless the sentence is one fixed by law. An appeal can never result in a sentence of greater severity. An accused person may also appeal against a verdict of not guilty on the grounds of insanity. In certain cases the Court may also order a retrial. The Attorney-General, who is the prosecutor before the Criminal Court, cannot appeal from a verdict of acquittal or, in certain cases, against the sentence passed. This Court, when formed of one judge, hears appeals from judgments delivered by the Court of Magistrates in its criminal jurisdiction.

The Criminal Court is formed by one judge, who sits with a jury of nine persons to try, on indictment, offences exceeding the competence of the Court of Magistrates. This court may, in certain exceptional cases, sit without a jury.

The Civil Court is divided in two Halls. The First Hall takes cognisance of all causes of a civil and a commercial nature, exceeding the jurisdiction of the Courts of Magistrates. The Second Hall is a Court of voluntary jurisdiction in matters of a civil nature, such as authority to proceed the tutorship of minors, adoption, the interdiction and incapacitation of persons, the opening of successions and the confirmation of testamentary executors. One Judge presides in both Halls.

The Magistrates' Court, which is composed of one Magistrate, exercises both a civil and a criminal jurisdiction. The Court of Magistrates, in civil matters, has an inferior jurisdiction of first instance, limited to claims exceeding LM 1,500 but not exceeding LM 5,000. In criminal matters, the Court has a two-fold jurisdiction, namely, as a court of criminal judicature for the trial of offences which fall within its jurisdiction, and as a court of inquiry in respect of offences which fall within the jurisdiction of a higher tribunal.

The Court of Magistrates for Gozo, in civil matters, has a two-fold Jurisdiction—an inferior jurisdiction comparable to that exercised by its counterpart Court in Malta, and a superior jurisdiction, both civil and commercial, in respect of causes which in Malta are cognisable by the First Hall of the Civil Court. Within the limits of its territorial jurisdiction, this Court has also the powers of a Court of voluntary jurisdiction.

The Small Claims Tribunal is presided over by an adjudicator who decides cases on principles of equity, according to law. Adjudicators are appointed from amongst advocates for a term of five years, and decide cases brought before them without delay. The aim is to have claims not exceeding the sum of LM 1,500 decided summarily. Sittings of this Tribunal are held in Malta or Gozo. An appeal from the decision of the Tribunal lies to the Court of Appeal on specific cases listed in the Act establishing the Tribunal.

The Juvenile Court consists of a Magistrate, as Chairman, and two members. Sittings are held outside Valletta, namely in Santa Venera. The Court hears charges against, and holds other proceedings relating to, minors under the age of 16 years, and may also issue Care Orders in their regard. Given the confidential nature of such sittings, attendance to hearings is restricted to persons mentioned in the law establishing the Court.

Chief Justice and President of the Court of Appeal and the Constitutional Court: Dr VINCENT A. DE GAETANO.

Judges: CARMEL A. AGIUS, JOSEPH D. CAMILLERI, JOSEPH A. FILLETTI, ANTON DEPASQUALE, ALBERTO J. MAGRI, GEOFFREY VALENZIA, GIANNINO CARUANA DEMAJO, GINO CAMILLERI, CARMELO FARRUGIA SACCO, RAYMOND PACE, DAVID P. SCICLUNA, JOSEPH R. MICALLEF, JOSEPH GALEA DEBONO, TONIO MALLIA, PHILIP SCIBERRAS, NOEL CUSCHIERI, JOSEPH AZZOPARDI.

Attorney-General: ANTHONY BORG BARTHET.

Religion

CHRISTIANITY

The Roman Catholic Church

Malta comprises one archdiocese and one diocese. At 31 December 2003 about 95.4% of the total population were adherents of the Roman Catholic Church.

Bishops' Conference

Conferenza Episcopale Maltese, Archbishop's Curia, Floriana; tel. 21234317; fax 21223307; e-mail info@maltachurch.org.mt; f. 1971; Pres. Most Rev. JOSEPH MERCIECA (Archbishop of Malta).

Archbishop of Malta: Most Rev. JOSEPH MERCIECA, Archbishop's Curia, Floriana; POB 29, Valletta; tel. 21234317; fax 21223307; e-mail info@maltachurch.org.mt.

Bishop of Gozo: Rt Rev. MARIO GRECH, Chancery Office, POB 1, Republic St, Victoria VCT 103, Gozo; tel. 21556661; fax 21551278; e-mail diocese@gozodiocese.org.

The Anglican Communion

Malta forms part of the diocese of Gibraltar in Europe.

Church of England: Pro-Cathedral of St Paul, Independence Sq., Valletta VLT 12; tel. 21225714; fax 21225867; e-mail anglican@onvol.net; internet www.vol.net.mt/anglicansmalta; Bishop of Gibraltar in Europe Rt Rev. GEOFFREY ROWELL (resident in England); Suffragan Bishop, Archdeacon of Italy and Malta Rt Rev. DAVID HAMID (resident in England); Senior Chaplain and Chancellor of the Pro-Cathedral Rev. Canon TOM MENDEL.

Other Christian Churches

In 2004 there were approximately 680 Jehovah's Witnesses and 148 members of the Church of Jesus Christ of Latter-day Saints (Mormons). The Bible Baptist Church had 30 members and the Fellowship of Evangelical Churches had about 100 affiliates.

OTHER RELIGIONS

There is one Jewish congregation. Zen Buddhism and the Bahá'í Faith have about 30 members each. There is one Muslim mosque and a Muslim primary school. There are an estimated 3,000 Muslims in the country.

The Press

DAILY NEWSPAPERS

The Malta Independent: Standard House, Birkirkara Hill, St Julian's STJ 09; tel. 21345888; fax 21344860; e-mail tmid@independent.com.mt; internet www.independent.com.mt; English; Editor STEPHEN CALLEJA.

In-Nazzjon (The Nation): Herbert Ganado St, POB 37, Pietà HMR 08; tel. 21243641; fax 21242886; e-mail news@media.link.com.mt; internet www.media.link.com.mt; f. 1970; Maltese; publ. by Media.link Communications; Editor JOHN ZAMMIT; circ. 20,000.

L-Orizzont (The Horizon): Union Print Co, A-41 Industrial Estate, Valletta Rd, Marsa HMR 15; tel. 21244557; fax 21238484; e-mail unionprint@kemmunet.net.mt; f. 1962; Maltese; Editor FRANS GHIRXI; circ. 25,000.

The Times: Allied Newspapers Ltd, 341 St Paul St, Valletta VLT 07; tel. 25594100; fax 25594116; e-mail daily@timesofmalta.com; internet www.timesofmalta.com; f. 1935; English; Editor RAY BUGEJA; circ. 23,000.

WEEKLY NEWSPAPERS

Il-Gens (The People): Media Centre, National Rd, Blata il-Bajda HMR 02; tel. 25699119; fax 25699123; e-mail gens@mediacentre.org.mt; internet www.mediacentre.org.mt; f. 1988; Maltese; Editor NICHOLAS BALDACCHINO; circ. 13,000.

Kulhadd: Centru Nazzjonali Laburista, Mile End Rd, Hamrun, HMR 02; tel. 21235313; fax 21240717; e-mail kulhadd@keyworld.net; f. 1993; Maltese; Editor FELIX AGIUS.

Lehen is-Sewwa: Catholic Institute, Floriana VLT 16; tel. and fax 21225847; e-mail lehenissewwa@vol.net.mt; internet www.lehenissewwa.com.mt; f. 1928; Roman Catholic; Editor Rev. Fr JOHN CIARLÓ; circ. 10,000.

The Malta Business Weekly: Standard House, Birkirkara Hill, St Julian's STJ 09; tel. 21345888; fax 21344860; e-mail tmbw@independent.com.mt; internet www.maltabusinessweekly.com; f. 1994; English; Editor CHRISTOPHER SULTANA.

The Malta Financial and Business Times: Newsworks Ltd, Vjal ir-Rihan, San Gwann SGN 07; tel. 21382741; fax 21385075; e-mail businesstimes@newsworksltd.com; internet www.businesstimes.com.mt; f. 1999; Editor SAVIOUR BALZAN.

The Malta Independent on Sunday: Standard House, Birkirkara Hill, St Julian's STJ 09; tel. 21345888; fax 21344884; e-mail amanduca@independent.com.mt; internet www.independent.com.mt; English; Editor ANTHONY MANDUCA.

Malta Today: Vjal ir-Rihan, San Gwann SGN 02; tel. 21382741; fax 21385075; e-mail maltatoday@mediatoday.com.mt; internet www.maltatoday.com.mt; Sundays; English; Editor KURT SANSONE.

MALTA

Il-Mument (The Moment): Herbert Ganado St, POB 37, Pietà HMR 08; tel. 21243641; fax 21240839; e-mail nazzjon@mbox.vol.net.mt; f. 1972; Maltese; Editor VICTOR CAMILLERI; circ. 25,000.

The Sunday Times: Allied Newspapers Ltd, POB 328, Valletta CMR 01; tel. 25594500; fax 25594510; e-mail sunday@timesofmalta.com; internet www.timesofmalta.com; f. 1922; English; Editor LAURENCE GRECH; circ. 40,000.

It-Tórca (The Torch): Union Press, A 41, Marsa Industrial Estate, Marsa HMR 15; tel. 21244557; fax 21238484; e-mail unionprint@kemmunet.net.mt; f. 1944; Maltese; Editor ALFRED BRIFFA; circ. 30,000.

SELECTED PERIODICALS

Business Today: Vjal ir-Rihan, San Gwann SGN 07; tel. 21382741; fax 21385075; internet www.businesstoday.com.mt; Editor KURT SANSONE.

Commercial Courier: Malta Chamber of Commerce and Enterprise, Exchange Bldgs, Republic St, Valletta VLT 05; tel. 21247233; fax 21245223; e-mail admin@chamber.org.mt; monthly; Editor KEVIN J. BORG; circ. 1,500.

The Employer: Malta Employers' Asscn, 35/1 South St, Valletta VLT 11; tel. 21222992; fax 21230227; e-mail mea@maltanet.net; internet www.maltaemployers.com; quarterly; Editor JOSEPH FARRUGIA.

Industry Today: Casa Leone, Robert Samut Sq., Floriana VLT 15; tel. 21234428; fax 21240702; e-mail info@foi.org.mt; internet www.foi.org.mt; f. 1946; journal of the Malta Fed. of Industry; quarterly; Editor WILFRED KENELY; circ. 1,000.

Malta Government Gazette: Department of Information, 3 Castille Pl., Valletta CMR 02; tel. 22001770; fax 22001775; e-mail info.doi@gov.mt; internet www.doi.gov.mt; f. 1813; official notices; Maltese and English; 2 a week; circ. 3,000.

Malta In Figures: National Statistics Office, Lascaris, Valetta CMR 02; tel. 25997000; fax 25997205; e-mail nso@gov.mt; internet www.nso.gov.mt; official statistics; annual.

Malta This Month: Advantage Advertising Ltd, 118 St John's St, Valletta VLT 07; tel. 21249924; fax 21249927; e-mail advantage@onvol.net; publ. by Air Malta; monthly; Editor PETER DARMANIN.

The Retailer: Association of General Retailers and Traders, Exchange Bldgs, Republic St, Valletta VLT 05; tel. 21230459; fax 21246925; monthly; Editor VINCENT FARRUGIA.

The Teacher: Teachers' Institute, 213 Republic St, Valletta VLT 03; tel. 21237815; fax 21244074; e-mail info@mut.org.mt; internet www.mut.org.mt; journal of the Malta Union of Teachers; 2 a year; Editor JOSEPH P. DEGIOVANNI.

Xpress: 149 Archbishop St, Valletta; tel. 21240334; fax 21224745; publ. of the Alternattiva Demokratika; Maltese; monthly; Editor NEIL SPITERI.

NEWS AGENCIES

Agence France-Presse (AFP): 428 Zabbar Rd, Fgura PLA 16; tel. 79478680; e-mail jinguanez@waldonet.net.mt; Correspondent JOHN INGUANEZ.

Agenzia Nazionale Stampa Associata (ANSA) (Italy): c/o The Sunday Times, Allied Newspapers Ltd, 341 St Paul St, POB 328, Valletta CMR 01; tel. 21224406; fax 25594510; e-mail lgrech@timesofmalta.com; Correspondent LAURENCE GRECH.

Associated Press (AP) (USA): c/o The Times, Allied Newspapers Ltd, 341 St Paul St, Valletta VLT 07; tel. 21241464; fax 21247901; e-mail gcini@timesofmalta.com; Correspondents VICTOR AQUILINA, GEORGE CINI.

Jamahiriya News Agency (JANA) (Libya): 239 St Paul's St, POB 270, Valletta; tel. 21239392; fax 21239405; Correspondent F. M. HEWAT.

Reuters (United Kingdom): 119 Censu Busuttil St, Iklin BZN 11; tel. 79415171; fax 21247901; e-mail cscicluna@timesofmalta.com; Correspondent CRISTOPHER SCICLUNA.

United Press International (USA): 1 The Elms, Dahlet Ic-Cipress, Attard; tel. 21423068; fax 21247901; Correspondent VICTOR AQUILINA.

Publishers

Malta University Publishers Ltd: University Campus, Msida MSD 06; tel. 21313416; fax 21344879; e-mail mupl@mus.com.mt; internet www.mus.com.mt; f. 1953; owned by University of Malta; Maltese folklore, history, law, bibliography and language; Admin. Officer TITA BONNICI.

Publishers Enterprises Group (PEG) Ltd: PEG Bldg, UB7 Industrial Estate, San Gwann SGN 09; tel. 21440083; fax 21488908; e-mail contact@peg.com.mt; internet www.peg.com.mt; f. 1983; educational, children's, cookery, technical, tourism, leisure; Man. Dir EMANUEL DEBATTISTA.

Broadcasting and Communications

TELECOMMUNICATIONS

Regulatory Authority

Malta Communications Authority (MCA): Il-Piazzetta, Suite 43/44, Tower Rd, Sliema SLM 16; tel. 21336840; fax 21336846; e-mail mca@mca.org.mt; internet www.mca.org.mt; national agency responsible for regulating telecommunications; f. 2001; Chair. and Dir-Gen. JOSEPH V. TABONE.

Service Providers

Maltacom PLC: POB 40, Marsa CMR 01; tel. 21212121; fax 25945895; e-mail info@maltacom.com; internet www.maltacom.com; f. 1975; operates all telecommunications services; 60% govt-owned, 40% held by private-sector investors, privatization pending; Chair. SONNY PORTELLI.

Go Mobile: Fra Diego St, Marsa HMR 12; tel. 21246200; fax 21234314; mobile cellular subsidiary; CEO Prof. JUANITO CAMILLERI.

BROADCASTING

Regulatory Authority

Malta Broadcasting Authority: Mile End Rd, Hamrun HMR 02; tel. 21247908; fax 21240855; e-mail info@ba-malta.org; internet www.ba-malta.org; f. 1961; statutory body responsible for the supervision and regulation of radio and television broadcasting; Chair. Chief Justice Emeritus Dr JOSEPH SAID PULLICINO; CEO Dr KEVIN AQUILINA.

Radio and Television

Bay Radio: St George's Bay, St Julian's STJ 02; tel. 21373813; fax 21376113; e-mail 897@bay.com.mt; Station Man. TERRY FARRUGIA.

Campus FM: Old Humanities Bldg, University of Malta, Msida MSD 06; tel. 21333313; fax 21314485; e-mail campusfm@um.edu.mt; internet www.campusfm.um.edu.mt; Man. VICKY SPITERI.

Capital Radio: Media Co-op Ltd, 87 Ursula St, Valletta; tel. 21233078; fax 21239701; e-mail capital@maltanet.net; internet www.capitalradio.com.mt; Station Man. JOHN MALLIA.

Island Sound Radio: 46 Robert Samut Sq., Floriana VLT 14; tel. 21249141; fax 21249785; News Co-ordinator BERNIE LYNCH.

Media.link Communications Co Ltd: Dar Centrali, Herbert Ganado St, Pietà HMR 08; tel. 21243641; fax 21243640; e-mail antona@vol.net.mt; internet www.media.link.com.mt.

Net TV: Dar Centrali, Herbert Ganado St, Pietà HMR 08; tel. 21243641; fax 21226645; CEO ANTON ATTARD.

Radio 101: Independence Point, Herbert Ganado St, Pietà HMR 08; tel. 21241164; fax 21564111; Head of News PIERRE PORTELLI.

Melita Cable PLC: Gason Centre, Mrichel Bypass, Mrichel BKR 14; tel. 21490006; fax 22745050; e-mail admin@melitacable.com; internet www.melitacable.com; CEO JOSEPH R. AQUILINA.

Multi Media Education and Broadcasting Centre: Maria Regina School, Mile End Rd, Hamrun HMR 02; tel. 21239274; fax 21240701; operates television channel Education 22.

One Productions Ltd: A28B, Industrial Estate, Marsa LQA 06; tel. 21226634; fax 21248249; e-mail livetv@super1.com; internet www.super1.com; f. 1999; owned by Malta Labour Party; Chair. RENALD DALLI; CEO ALBERT MARSHALL.

Super One Radio: tel. 21244905; fax 21231472; e-mail radio@super1.com; broadcasts 24 hours daily.

Super One Television: A28B Industrial Estate, Marsa LQA 06; tel. 25682568; fax 21231472; e-mail kullhadd@keyworld.net; broadcasts 126 hours weekly; CEO RENALD DALLI.

Public Broadcasting Services Ltd: St Luke's Rd, G'Mangia MSD 09; tel. 21225051; fax 21244601; e-mail info@pbs.com.mt; internet www.pbs.com.mt; f. 1991; govt-owned; operates national radio and television services: Radio 'Radju Malta' and 'Radju Parlament'; Television Malta; Chair. ANDREW AGIUS MUSCAT; CEO ALBERT DEBONO.

Radio Calypso: Oasis, Mons. P. Pace St, Victoria VCT 111, Gozo; tel. 21563000; fax 21563565; e-mail info@calypso102.com; internet www.calypso102.com; News Editor PIERRE MEYLAK.

Radju MAS: 15 Old Mint St, Valletta VLT 12; tel. 21237755; fax 21247246; Editor Mgr FORTUNATO MIZZI.

RTK Radio: Media Centre, National Rd, Blata il-Bajda HMR 02; tel. 25699100; fax 25699151; e-mail vformosa@mediacentre.org.mt;

MALTA

internet www.rtk.org.mt; f. 1992; radio station of the Catholic Church of Malta; Exec. Chair. VICTOR FORMOSA.

Smash TV and Radio: Smash Communications, Thistle Lane, Paola PLA 19; tel. 21697829; fax 21697830; f. 1992; Man. Dir JOSEPH BALDACCHINO.

Finance

(cap. = capital; res = reserves; dep. = deposits; m. = million; brs = branches; amounts in Maltese liri, unless otherwise stated)

BANKING

Central Bank

Central Bank of Malta: Pjazza Kastilja, Valletta CMR 01; tel. 25500000; fax 25502500; e-mail info@centralbankmalta.com; internet www.centralbankmalta.com; f. 1968; bank of issue; cap. 5m., res 80m., dep. 293m. (Dec. 2004); Gov. MICHAEL C. BONELLO.

Commercial Banks

APS Bank Ltd: APS House, 24 St Anne Sq., Floriana VLT 16; tel. 21226644; fax 21226202; e-mail headoffice@apsbank.com.mt; internet www.apsbank.com.mt; f. 1910; cap. 5m., res 2m., dep. 177m. (Dec. 2003); Chair. Prof. EMMANUEL P. DELIA; CEO EDWARD CACHIA; 5 brs.

Bank of Valletta PLC: 58 Zachary St, Valletta VLT 04; tel. 21255638; fax 21255639; e-mail customercare@bov.com; internet www.bov.com; f. 1974; cap. 13.8m., res 119.3m., dep. 1,452.0m. (March 2005); merged with Valletta Investment Bank Ltd in Oct. 2000; Chair. RODERICK CHALMERS; CEO TONIO DEPASQUALE; 41 brs.

Dişbank Malta Ltd: 114/5 The Strand, Gzira GZR 03; tel. 21323571; fax 21323576; e-mail malta@disbank.com.tr; internet www.disbankmalta.com.mt; owned by Türk Dis Bankasi AS; cap. US $45m., res US $3m., dep. US $298m. (Dec. 2003); Chair. TAYFUN BAYAZIT; Gen. Man. VEDAT KORAN.

HSBC Bank Malta PLC: 233 Republic St, Valletta VLT 05; tel. 21245281; fax 21485857; e-mail info@hsbcmalta.com; internet www.hsbcmalta.com; f. 1975 as Mid-Med Bank; 70.03% owned by HSBC Europe BV; cap. 9m., res 21m., dep. 1,308m. (Dec. 2003); Chair. ALBERT MIZZI; Dir and CEO CHRISTOPHER HOTHERSALL; 43 brs.

Lombard Bank Malta PLC: 67 Republic St, Valletta VLT 05; tel. 21240442; fax 21247442; e-mail mail@lombardmalta.com; internet www.lombardmalta.com; f. 1969; cap. 2m., res 5m., dep. 168m. (Dec. 2003); Chair. CHRISTIAN LEMMERICH; Dir and CEO JOSEPH SAID; 6 brs.

Principal 'Offshore' Bank

First International Merchant Bank PLC: Plaza Commercial Centre, 7th Floor, Bisazza St, Sliema SLM 15; tel. 21322100; fax 21322122; e-mail info@fimbank.com; internet www.fimbank.com; f. 1994; cap. US $33m., res US $12m., dep. US $119m. (Dec. 2003); Chair. NAJEEB H. M. AL-SALEH; Pres. CLAUDE L. ROY.

STOCK EXCHANGE

Malta Stock Exchange: Garrison Chapel, Castille Pl., Valletta CMR 01; tel. 21244051; fax 25696316; e-mail borza@maltanet.net; internet www.borzamalta.com.mt; f. 1992; Chair. ALFRED MALLIA.

INSURANCE

Aon Malta Ltd: 53 Mediterranean Bldg, Abate Rigord St, Ta'Xbiex MSD 12; tel. 23433234; fax 21341597; e-mail info@aon.com.mt; internet www.aon.com.mt; f. 1976; Chair. ALFREDO SCOTTI; Man. Dir JOSEPH CUTAJAR.

Middle Sea Insurance PLC: Middle Sea House, Floriana VLT 16; tel. 21246262; fax 21248195; e-mail middlesea@middlesea.com; internet www.middlesea.com; f. 1981; Chair. MARIO C. GRECH; Gen. Man. JOSEPH M. RIZZO.

Numerous foreign insurance companies, principally British, Canadian and Italian, are represented in Malta by local agents.

Insurance Association

Malta Insurance Association: 43A/2, St Paul's Bldgs, West St, Valletta VLT 12; tel. 21232640; fax 21248388; e-mail mia@maltainsurance.org; internet www.maltainsurance.org; Pres. MARIO C. GRECH; Dir-Gen. Dr ANTON FELICE.

Directory

Trade and Industry

GOVERNMENT AGENCIES

Malta Enterprise: POB 8, San Gwann SGN 01; tel. 25420000; fax 25423401; e-mail info@maltaenterprise.com; internet www.maltaenterprise.com; f. 2003 by merger of Malta External Trade Corpn Ltd (METCO), Malta Development Corpn (MDC) and Institute for the Promotion of Small Enterprise (IPSE); national agency for the promotion of inward investment and trade and the support of enterprises; Chair. ALEC MIZZI.

Malta Financial Services Authority: Notabile Rd, Attard BKR 14; tel. 21441155; fax 21441189; e-mail communications@mfsa.com.mt; internet www.mfsa.com.mt; f. 1994; supervises the financial services sector, incl. banking, insurance and investments; regulates activities of Malta Stock Exchange; houses Malta's Companies Registry; Chair. Prof. JOSEPH V. BANNISTER; COO JOSEPH DEMANUELE.

Malta Freeport Terminals Ltd: Freeport Centre, Port of Marsaxlokk, Kalafrana BBG 05; tel. 21650200; fax 22251900; e-mail marketing@maltafreeport.com.mt; internet www.maltafreeport.com.mt; f. 1988; two container terminals and distribution centre; also operates petroleum products terminal and general warehousing facilities; Man. Dir UWE MALEZKI.

Malta Investment Management Co Ltd (MIMCOL): Trade Centre, San Gwann Industrial Estate, B'Kara SGN 09; tel. 21497970; fax 21499568; e-mail info@mimcol.com; internet www.mimcol.com; f. 1988; manages govt investments in domestic commercial enterprises and encourages their transfer to private-sector ownership; Chair. IVAN FALZON.

CHAMBER OF COMMERCE

Malta Chamber of Commerce and Enterprise: Exchange Bldgs, Republic St, Valletta VLT 05; tel. 21233873; fax 21245223; e-mail admin@chamber.org.mt; internet www.chamber.org.mt; f. 1848; Pres. VICTOR A. GALEA; 900 mems.

EMPLOYERS' ORGANIZATIONS

Malta Employers' Association: 35/1 South St, Valletta VLT 11; tel. 21222992; fax 21230227; e-mail mea@maltanet.net; internet www.maltaemployers.com; f. 1965; Pres. PIERRE FAVA; Dir-Gen. JOSEPH FARRUGIA.

Malta Federation of Industry: Casa Leone, Robert Samut Sq., Floriana VLT 15; tel. 21234428; fax 21240702; e-mail info@foi.org.mt; internet www.foi.org.mt; f. 1946; nat. org. for industry; 300 corporate mems; Pres. ADRIAN BAJADA; Dir-Gen. WILFRED KENELY.

UTILITIES
Electricity

Enemalta Corporation: Church Wharf, Marsa HMR 01; POB 6, Hamrun HMR 01; tel. 21223601; fax 21243055; e-mail info@enemalta.com.mt; internet www.enemalta.com.mt; f. 1977; state energy corpn; purchases and distributes petroleum products and operates two petroleum-fired power stations for electricity generation; distributes electricity, petroleum products and LPG; Chair. Ing. ALEXANDER J. TRANTER; CEO ANTHONY RIZZO.

Water

Water Services Corporation: Qormi Rd, Luqa LQA 05; tel. 21249851; fax 21223016; e-mail customercare@wsc.com.mt; internet www.wsc.com.mt; f. 1992; govt agency responsible for the production and distribution of drinking water and the local sewerage system; Chair. MICHAEL FALZON; CEO ANTOINE GALEA (acting).

TRADE UNIONS

Confederation of Malta Trade Unions (CMTU): 9C M. A. Vassalli St, Valletta VLT 13; tel. 21237313; fax 21250146; e-mail info@cmtu.org.mt; internet www.cmtu.org.mt; f. 1958; affiliated to the World Confed. of Labour, to the Commonwealth Trade Union Council and to the European Trade Union Confed; Pres. WILLIAM PORTELLI; Gen. Sec. ANTHONY MICALLEF DEBONO; 28,000 mems.

The principal affiliated unions include:

Association of General Retailers & Traders Union (GRTU): Exchange Bldgs, Republic St, Valletta VLT 05; tel. 21230459; fax 21246925; f. 1948; Pres. CHARLES J. BUSUTTIL; Sec. PHILIP FRENCH; 6,400 mems.

Malta Union of Teachers: Teachers' Institute, 213 Republic St, Valletta VLT 03; tel. 21237815; fax 21244074; e-mail info@mut.org.mt; internet www.mut.org.mt; f. 1919; Pres. J. BENCINI; Gen. Sec. JOSEPH P. DEGIOVANNI; 6,074 mems.

Union Haddiema Maghqudin (UHM): 'Dar Reggie Miller', St Thomas St, Floriana VLT 15; tel. 21220847; fax 21246091; e-mail uhm@maltanet.net; internet www.uhm.org.mt; f. 1966; Pres. G. TANTI; Sec.-Gen. G. VELLA; 25,793 mems.

The General Workers' Union (GWU): Workers' Memorial Bldg, South St, Valletta VLT 11; tel. 21244300; fax 21242975; e-mail info@gwu.org.mt; internet www.gwu.org.mt; f. 1943; affiliated to the Int. Confed. of Free Trade Unions, to the European Trade Union Confed. and to the Commonwealth Trade Union Confed; Pres. SALV SAMMUT; CEO and Gen. Sec. TONY ZARB; 48,758 mems.

Transport

RAILWAYS

There are no railways in Malta.

ROADS

In 2002 there were 2,222 km of roads, of which 183 km were highways and 2,039 km were secondary roads. About 90.0% of roads are paved. Bus services serve all parts of the main island and most parts of Gozo.

Malta Transport Authority: Sa Maison Rd, Floriana CMR 02; tel. 25608000; fax 21255740; e-mail info@maltatransport.com; internet www.maltatransport.com; regulatory body for all land transport in Malta; Chair. MARK PORTELLI.

    Public Transport Directorate: Sa Maison Rd, Pietà MSD 08; tel. 21255165; fax 21255175; e-mail pta@maltanet.net; internet www.maltatransport.com; f. 1989; regulatory body for public transport in Malta, part of Malta Transport Authority.

Roads Department: Cannon Rd, St Venera CMR 02; tel. 21483609; fax 21243753; e-mail carmel.zammit@magnet.mt; Chair. C. DEMICOLI; CEO M. FALZON.

SHIPPING

Malta's national shipping register is open to ships of all countries. At 31 December 2004 Malta's merchant fleet comprised 1,181 vessels, with a total displacement of 22,352,570 gross registered tons. The island's dry dock facilities are also an important source of revenue.

Malta Maritime Authority: Corporate Office, Marina Pinto, Valletta VLT 01; tel. 21222203; fax 21250365; e-mail info@mma.gov.mt; internet www.mma.gov.mt; f. 1991; govt agency supervising the administration and operation of ports and yachting centres, and of vessel registrations under the Maltese flag; Chair. Dr MARC BONELLO.

Bianchi & Co (1916) Ltd: Palazzo Marina, 143 St Christopher St, Valletta VLT 02; tel. 21232241; fax 21232991; e-mail info@bianchi.com.mt; Man. Dir R. BIANCHI.

Cassar & Cooper Ltd: Valletta Bldgs, 54 South St, POB 311, Valletta VLT 11; tel. 21232221; fax 21237864; e-mail info@cassar-cooper.com; internet www.cassar-cooper.com; Dir MICHAEL COOPER.

O. F. Gollcher & Sons Ltd: 19 Zachary St, POB 268, Valletta VLT 10; tel. 25691100; fax 21234195; e-mail contact@gollcher.com; internet www.gollcher.com; Dir MARK GOLLCHER.

Medserv Ltd: Malta Freeport, Port of Marsaxlokk, Birzebbugia BBG 07; tel. 22202302; fax 22202328; e-mail info@medservmalta.com; internet www.medservmalta.com; logistic and supply base for petroleum and gas extraction industry; Dirs ANTHONY S. DIACONO, ANTHONY J. DUNCAN.

Mifsud Brothers Ltd: 27 South St, Valletta VLT 11; tel. 21232157; fax 21221331; e-mail info@mbl.com.mt; internet www.mbl.com.mt; f. 1860; shipping and travel agents; Man. Dir IVAN MIFSUD.

S. Mifsud & Sons Ltd (SMS): 131 East St, Valletta VLT 06; tel. 21233127; fax 21234180; cargo and ferry services between Malta/Catania, Reggio di Calabria; Dir ADRIAN S. MIFSUD.

Ripard, Larvan & Ripard Ltd: 156 Ta'Xbiex Seafront, Gzira GZR 03; tel. 21335591; fax 21343419; e-mail chandlery@rlryachting.com; Man. Dir CHRISTIAN RIPARD.

Sea Malta Co Ltd: Flagstone Wharf, Marsa HMR 12; tel. 21232230; fax 21225776; e-mail info@seamalta.com.mt; internet www.seamalta.com.mt; f. 1973; govt-owned national shipping line, privatization pending; operates roll-on/roll-off services between Malta, France, Italy, Northern Europe, Sicily, Spain and Tunisia; represents shipping line that operates passenger service between Malta and Libya; agency and insurance services, ship management, freight forwarding, ship-broking, bunkering, warehouse and passenger services; Chair. MARLENE MIZZI; Gen. Man. JOSEPH BUJEGA.

Sullivan Shipping Agencies Ltd: Exchange Bldgs, Republic St, Valletta VLT 05; tel. 21245127; fax 21233417; e-mail info@sullivanshipping.com.mt; Dir JOHN E. SULLIVAN.

Thomas Smith & Co Ltd: 12 St Christopher St, Valletta VLT 06; tel. 21245071; fax 21220078; e-mail info@tcsmith.com; internet www.tcsmith.com; Man. Dir JOE GERADA.

Virtu Steamship Co Ltd: 3 Princess Elizabeth Terrace, Ta'Xbiex MSD 11; tel. 21345220; fax 21314533; f. 1945; ship-owners; ship agents; shipbrokers; Malta–Sicily express passenger ferry service; Man. Dir F. A. PORTELLI.

CIVIL AVIATION

Malta International Airport is situated at Gudja (8 km from Valletta).

Air Malta PLC: Luqa LQA 01; tel. 21690890; fax 21673241; e-mail info@airmalta.com.mt; internet www.airmalta.com; f. 1973; national airline with a 96.4% state shareholding; scheduled passenger and cargo services to mainland Europe, the United Kingdom, Sicily, North Africa and the Middle East; charter services to the United Kingdom and mainland Europe; CEO ERNST FUNK.

Tourism

Malta offers climatic, scenic and historical attractions, including fine beaches. Tourism forms a major sector of Malta's economy, generating foreign-exchange earnings of US $856m. in 2003; in that year tourist arrivals totalled 1,126,601.

Malta Tourism Authority: Auberge d'Italie, Merchants St, Valletta CMR 02; tel. 22915000; fax 22915893; e-mail info@visitmalta.com; internet www.mta.com.mt; Chair. ROMWALD LUNGARO-MIFSUD; CEO LESLIE VELLA.

THE MARSHALL ISLANDS

Introductory Survey

Location, Climate, Language, Religion, Flag, Capital

The Republic of the Marshall Islands consists of two groups of islands, the Ratak ('sunrise') and Ralik ('sunset') chains, comprising 29 atolls (some 1,225 islets) and five islands, and covering about 180 sq km (70 sq miles) of land. The territory lies within the area of the Pacific Ocean known as Micronesia (which includes Kiribati, Tuvalu and other territories). The islands lie about 3,200 km (2,000 miles) south-west of Hawaii and about 2,100 km (1,300 miles) south-east of Guam. Rainfall decreases from south to north, with January, February and March being the driest months, although seasonal variations in rainfall and temperature are generally small. The native population comprises various ethno-linguistic groups, but English is widely understood. The principal religion is Christianity. The national flag (proportions 100 by 190) is dark blue, with a representation of a white star (with 20 short and four long rays) in the upper hoist; superimposed across the field are two progressively-wider stripes (orange above white), running from near the lower hoist corner to near the upper fly corner. The capital is the Dalap-Uliga-Darrit Municipality, on Majuro Atoll.

Recent History

The first European contact with the Marshall and Caroline Islands was by Spanish expeditions in the 16th century, including those led by Alvaro de Saavedra and Fernão de Magalhães (Ferdinand Magellan), the Portuguese navigator. The islands received their name from the British explorer, John Marshall, who visited them at the end of the 18th century. Spanish sovereignty over the Marshall Islands was recognized in 1886 by the Papal Bull of Pope Leo XIII, which also gave Germany trading rights there (German trading companies had been active in the islands from the 1850s). In 1899 Germany bought from Spain the Caroline Islands and the Northern Mariana Islands (except Guam, which had been ceded to the USA after the Spanish–American War of 1898). In 1914, at the beginning of the First World War, Japan occupied the islands, and received a mandate for its administration from the League of Nations in 1920. After the capture of the islands by US military forces in 1944 and 1945, most of the Japanese settlers were repatriated, and in 1947 the UN established the Trust Territory of the Pacific Islands (comprising the Caroline Islands, the Marshall Islands and the Northern Mariana Islands), to allow the USA to administer the region. The territory was governed by the US Navy from 1947 until 1951, when control passed to a civil administration—although the Northern Mariana Islands remained under military control until 1962.

From 1965 onwards there were increasing demands for local autonomy. In that year the Congress of Micronesia was formed; in 1967 a commission was established to examine the future political status of the islands. In 1970 it declared Micronesians' rights to sovereignty over their own lands, of self-determination, to their own constitution and to revoke any form of free association with the USA. In 1977, after eight years of negotiations, US President Jimmy Carter announced that his Administration intended to adopt measures to terminate the trusteeship agreement by 1981.

On 9 January 1978 the Marianas District achieved separate status as the Commonwealth of the Northern Mariana Islands (q.v.), but remained legally a part of the Trusteeship until 1986. The Marshall Islands District drafted its own Constitution, which came into effect on 1 May 1979, and the four districts of Yap, Truk (now Chuuk), Ponape (now Pohnpei) and Kosrae ratified a new Constitution, to become the Federated States of Micronesia (q.v.), on 10 May 1979. In the Palau District a referendum in July 1979 approved a proposed local constitution, which came into effect on 1 January 1981, when the district became the Republic of Palau (q.v.).

The USA signed a Compact of Free Association with the Republic of Palau in August 1982, and with the Marshall Islands and the Federated States of Micronesia in October of that year. The trusteeship of the islands was due to end after the principle and terms of the Compacts had been approved by the respective peoples and legislatures of the new countries, by the US Congress and by the UN Security Council. Under the Compacts, the four countries (including the Northern Mariana Islands) would be independent of each other and would manage their internal and foreign affairs separately, while the USA would be responsible for defence and security. Moreover, Marshallese citizens were granted the right to live and work in the USA. The Compacts with the Federated States of Micronesia and the Marshall Islands were approved in plebiscites in June and September 1983, respectively. The Congress of the Federated States of Micronesia ratified the country's decision in September. Under the Compact with the Marshall Islands, the USA was to retain its military bases in the Marshall Islands for at least 15 years and, over the same period, was to provide annual aid of US $30m.

The Compact between the Marshall Islands and the USA came into effect on 21 October 1986, following its approval by the islands' Government. In November President Ronald Reagan issued a proclamation formally ending US administration of Micronesia. The first President of the Republic of the Marshall Islands was Iroijlaplap (paramount chief) Amata Kabua, who was re-elected in 1984, 1988, 1992 and 1995. In December 1990 the UN Security Council finally ratified the termination of the trusteeship agreement; the Marshall Islands became a member of the UN in 1991. Prior to their scheduled expiry in 2001, the terms of Compact were extended for a further two year period, pending negotiation of new arrangements (see below).

The Marshall Islands' atolls of Bikini and Enewetak were used by the USA for experiments with nuclear weapons: Bikini in 1946–58 and Enewetak in 1948–58. A total of 67 such tests were carried out during this period. The native inhabitants of Enewetak were evacuated before tests began, and were allowed to return to the atoll in 1980, after much of the contaminated area had supposedly been rendered safe. The inhabitants of Bikini Atoll campaigned for similar treatment, and in 1985 the US Administration agreed to decontaminate Bikini Atoll over a period of 10–15 years. In 1985 the entire population of Rongelap Atoll, which had been engulfed by radioactive fall-out from the tests at Bikini in 1954, was forced to resettle on Mejato Atoll, after surveys suggested that levels of radiation there remained dangerous. In April 2001, following the adoption by the USA of a new standard of radioactivity considered to be acceptable, some six times lower than the previous level, the Tribunal announced that Ailuk Atoll was to be evacuated and environmental studies conducted.

Under the terms of the Compact, the US Government consented to establish a US $150m. Nuclear Claims Fund to settle claims against the USA resulting from nuclear testing in the Marshall Islands during the 1940s and 1950s. Accordingly, the Marshall Islands Nuclear Claims Tribunal was established in 1988, with jurisdiction to 'render final determination upon all claims past, present and future, of the Government, citizens and nationals of the Marshall Islands' in respect of the nuclear testing programme. A compensation programme was implemented in 1991 for personal injuries deemed to have resulted from the testing programme. Following an approach defined in legislation adopted by the US Congress in 1990, which established a 'presumptive' programme of compensation for specified diseases contracted by US civilian and military personnel who had been physically present in what was termed the 'affected area' during periods of atmospheric testing in Nevada, the Marshall Islands Nuclear Claims Tribunal initially identified 25 diseases for which credible evidence demonstrated a significant statistical relationship between exposure to radiation and subsequent development of a disease; in response to the findings of later studies, the Tribunal's list had by 2003 been extended to include 11 further conditions. Compensation awards totalling $83m. had by the end of 2003 been made to, or on behalf of, 1,865, individuals who had contracted one or more of these conditions. Additionally, an award of some $578m. had been ordered in May 2000 in respect of a class action brought by the people of Enewetak for loss of and damage to property; and an award of $563m. had been made in March 2002 in settlement of a class action brought by the peoples of Bikini Atoll; settlements of similar class actions by the peoples of Rongelap and Utrik Atolls were being finalized, while a new class action had been submitted by the people of Ailuk Atoll. However, only $45.8m. had been made available for actual payment of awards decided by the Tribunal; furthermore, less than $6m. remained of the original value of the Fund. In view of the inadequacy of the Fund to meet the compensation awards made by the Tribunal, in September 2000 the Marshall Islands Government formally petitioned the US Congress for a renegotiation of the settlement agreed under the Compact; the basis of the petition, which sought additional compensation amounting to some $3,000m., was an article of the agreement providing for what were termed 'Changed Circumstances'. In early August 2004 the Tribunal declared a deadline for islanders' compensation claims of the end of that month (subsequently extended to 31 December). The reason given for the deadline was that the Tribunal's funds had diminished to some $5m., a level that not only jeopardized future compensation payments but also the very existence of the Tribunal itself. In January 2005, following the publication of a report by the US State Department's Bureau of East Asian and Pacific Affairs, the Bush Administration recommended that Congress reject the Marshall Islands' request for additional compensation payments, citing a lack of a scientific or legal basis for the request. In late February delegates from Bikini, Rongelap, Enewetak and Utrik met in Seattle, Washington, with officials of the US Senate Committee on Energy and Natural Resources in preparation for a congressional hearing on the Marshall Islands' request for additional payments. At the hearing, held in May, the Bush Administration's rejection of the appeal was reiterated, although several committee members expressed support for further consideration of the matter. At a Small Islands Summit meeting held in October in the Papua New Guinean capital of Port Moresby, the Marshall Islands' delegation demanded a further $3,000m. in compensation from the US Government. In November, during a visit to Israel, President Note appealed to the Israeli President, Moshe Katsav, for his country's support for the Marshall Islands' claim for additional compensation from the USA.

In January 1994, meanwhile, several senior members of the Marshall Islands' legislature, the Nitijela, demanded that the US authorities release detailed information on the effects of its nuclear-testing programme in the islands. In July documentation released by the US Department of Energy gave conclusive evidence that Marshall Islanders had been deliberately exposed to high levels of radiation in order that its effects on their health could be studied by US medical researchers. Further evidence emerged during 1995 that the USA had withheld the medical records of islanders involved in radiation experiments (which included tritium and chromium-51 injections and genetic and bone-marrow transplant experiments).

Despite the publication of a study conducted by US scientists (in 1992) into contamination levels on Bikini atoll, which suggested that radiation levels there remained dangerous, in February 1997 a group of Bikini Islanders returned for the first time since 1946 to assist in the rehabilitation of the atoll for resettlement. The operation was to involve the removal of radioactive topsoil (although the matter of its disposal presented a serious problem) and the saturation of the remaining soil with potassium, which was believed to inhibit the absorption of radioactive material by root crops. In early 1999 the Nuclear Claims Tribunal demanded the adoption of US Environmental Protection Agency standards in the rehabilitation of contaminated islands, claiming that Marshall Islanders deserved to receive the same treatment as US citizens would in similar circumstances. The US Department of Energy, however, expressed strong resistance to the suggestion. In February 2001 a report published by an eminent Japanese scientist stated that radiation levels on Rongelap Island, according to research conducted in 1999, had now declined to such a level that human habitation of the island was again possible. In early 2004 the Marshall Islands protested that a reduction, decided upon by the US Department of Energy without consultation with Island representatives, of some US $740,000 in congressional funding allocated to nuclear test-related studies would result in the closure of a centre on Bikini Atoll used to support scientific studies at the former test site.

Another atoll in the Marshall Islands, Kwajalein, has been used since 1947 as a target for the testing of missiles fired from California, USA. The Compact as ratified in 1986 committed the US Government to provide an estimated US $170m. in rent over a period of 30 years for land used as the site of a missile-tracking station, and a further $80m. for development projects. The inhabitants of Kwajalein Atoll were concentrated on the small island of Ebeye, adjacent to the US base on Kwajalein Island, before a new programme of weapons-testing began in 1961. Consequent overcrowding reportedly led to numerous social problems on Ebeye. In 1989 the Marshall Islands Government agreed that the USA could lease a further four islands in the atoll, for five years, for the purpose of military tests. A further lease agreement was signed in 1995 for the use of Biken Island (in Aur Atoll) and Wake Island in the missile-testing programme. The issue of the Kwajalein lease proved to be one of the most controversial aspects of the renegotiated terms of the Compact, as signed in 2003 (see below). In January 2003 it was announced that the Marshall Islands Government and the USA had reached agreement on new terms extending the lease of the Kwajalein site, previously scheduled to end in 2016, until 2066 (with the USA retaining the right to extend the lease by a further 20 years). The renegotiated terms envisaged that payments for use of the site would be increased from $13.5m. annually to $16.9m. (including continued provision of $1.9m. annually in social funding for the residents of Ebeye), with a further increase, to more than $19.9m. per year, to enter into effect from 2014. However, Kwajalein landowners, who deemed the new terms unacceptable, asserted that the new arrangement was invalid, since they had not consented, as constitutionally required, to its terms.

Following legislative elections in November 1995, at which eight incumbent members of the 33-seat Nitijela were defeated, Kabua was re-elected for a fifth term. The President died in December 1996. Iroijlaplap Imata Kabua, a cousin of the late President, was elected as his successor on 13 January 1997.

In 1996 the Nitijela approved legislation allowing for the introduction of gambling in the islands, in order to provide an additional source of revenue. However, income earned from the venture did not fulfil expectations. Moreover, a vociferous campaign by local church leaders to revoke the legislation led to fierce debate in the Nitijela in early 1998. Divisions within the Cabinet ensued, with three members supporting the President's pro-gambling stance and four others opposing. In April the Nitijela voted to repeal the law legalizing gambling: several influential politicians (including Imata Kabua) known to have major gambling interests were disqualified from voting. A second bill containing further measures to ensure the prohibition of all gambling activity in the islands was narrowly approved. Three ministers who had supported the anti-gambling legislation were dismissed in a cabinet reorganization in August. In the following month one of the dismissed ministers proposed a motion of 'no confidence' in Kabua. The President and his supporters boycotted subsequent sessions of the Nitijela, thereby rendering the legislature inquorate and effectively precluding the vote, as well as delaying the approval of the budget for the impending financial year. Despite opposition claims that Kabua's continued absence from the Nitijela violated the terms of the Constitution, the motion of 'no confidence' in Kabua was eventually defeated by a margin of one vote in October.

At legislative elections held in November 1999 the opposition United Democratic Party (UDP) secured a convincing victory over the incumbent administration, winning 18 of the 33 seats in the Nitijela. Five senior members of the outgoing Government were defeated, including the Ministers of Finance and of Foreign Affairs and Trade—both of whom had played a prominent role in the establishment of diplomatic relations with Taiwan in 1998 (see below). The former Nitijela Speaker, Kessai Note, was elected President on 3 January 2000 (the islands' first non-traditional leader to assume the post). The UDP Chairman, Litokwa Tomeing, became Speaker of the legislature. Note subsequently appointed a 10-member Cabinet, and reiterated his administration's intention to pursue anti-corruption policies. In May a task-force was established by the Government for the purposes of investigating misconduct and corruption; it was hoped that the task-force would help to render government more accountable.

In November 2000 it was reported that finance officials had discovered that Imata Kabua had used funds granted to the Marshall Islands under the terms of the Compact of Free Association to pay off a personal loan, although the former President denied any wrongdoing. In mid-January 2001 Imata Kabua and former ministers in his Government, including the former Minister of Education, Justin DeBrum, presented a 'no confidence' motion against President Note to the Nitijela. Although it was suggested that the vote had been intended to delay the publication of a report into mismanagement and corruption on the part of the former Government, DeBrum stated that the motion resulted from a number of failings by the Note Government, including its unwillingness to renegotiate land rental payments with the USA for the use of the military base on Kwajalein Atoll and also the development of an economic relationship between the Note Government and Rev. Sun Myung Moon, the founder of the Unification Church (known as the 'Moonies'). However, the Government was successful in defeating the vote by a margin of 19 to 14.

In September 2000 the Nitijela approved legislation to ensure the closer regulation of the banking and financial sector. In May of that year the Group of Seven industrialized nations (G-7) had expressed its view that the Marshall Islands had become a significant centre for the 'laundering' of money generated by international criminal activity, and, in June the Marshall Islands was one of more than 30 countries and territories criticized by the Organisation for Economic Co-operation and Development (OECD, see p. 320) for the provision of inappropriate offshore financial establishments. OECD threatened to implement sanctions against 'unco-operative tax havens' unless reforms were introduced before July 2001. Following a commendation from the IMF on a series of new measures to combat fraud, including specific legislation and the establishment of a Domestic Financial Intelligence Unit, in October 2002 the Financial Action Task Force on Money Laundering (see p. 389) removed the Marshall Islands from its list of countries judged to be unhelpful in the combating of international financial crime.

Negotiations began between the US and Marshall Islands Governments in July 2001 to renew the provisions of the Compact of Free Association ratified in 1986, which was due to expire at the end of September 2001. A two-year extension was permitted while negotiations were under way, during which time annual assistance to the Marshall Islands was to increase by some US $5.5m. An agreement was originally scheduled for early 2002 in order to allow adequate time for the US Congress to review it and to approve the requisite legislation (by 1 October 2003), but the procedure was postponed until early May 2002 after the Marshall Islands Government submitted a proposal seeking financing of more than $1,000m. over 15 years. The Government had also objected to being allocated 25%–30% less in US grant assistance per caput than that apportioned to the Federated States of Micronesia since the year 2000. In a further attempt to increase the national income, the Government sought to raise significantly the level of taxes levied on the Kawajalein base (see above). In early November 2002 the USA and the Marshall Islands announced a programme of direct funding of $822m., to be disbursed over 20 years, in addition to the expansion of many US government services in the islands. It was envisaged that the Marshall Islands would receive some $30.5m. a year; furthermore, a trust fund would be established, to which the USA would contribute $7m. annually in order to provide a means of income after the termination of direct US assistance in 2023. The amended Compact of Free Association was signed by the Governments of the Marshall Islands and the USA in May 2003. Under the new Compact, Marshall Islanders would for the first time require passports in order to enter the USA. They would, however, retain the right to enter the USA to live, work and study, and would no longer be required to obtain work authorization documentation before taking up employment in the USA. Other than the issue of the Kwajalein lease, a principal obstacle to the negotiation of Compact amendments had been that of immigration: the USA, increasingly preoccupied by issues of homeland security, had been notably concerned to prevent future sales of Marshallese passports (a controversial programme of which had been implemented in the 1990s, although this had officially been suspended in 1997). Final terms, including the restoration of some rights of access to US health care and education programmes, were approved by the US Congress in November 2003, and ratified by President George W. Bush in December.

At a general election held on 17 November 2003 the UDP returned 20 Senators to the 33-member Nitijela. The opposition grouping Ailin Kein Ad (Our Islands), which had campaigned against the terms of the renewed Compact and which received particularly strong support from Marshall Islanders resident in the USA, secured 10 seats (the re-election of the incumbent Ailin Kein Ad Senator for Ailinglaplap Atoll was decided following a recount of votes conducted in late January 2004). Note was re-elected for a second presidential term in a vote held in the Nitijela on 4 January 2004, defeating Justin DeBrum, the candidate of Ailin Kein Ad, by 20 votes to nine. He and his new Cabinet were sworn in on 12 January.

In late March 2005 the Nitijela considered a bill providing for the establishment of a constitutional convention, to be made up of 43 representatives representing every district. Proposals for the direct election of the country's President and for the clear separation of the executive branch of government from the legislature were among the constitutional amendments to be considered. However, in February 2006 a spokesperson for Ailin Kein Ad argued that the establishment of the constitutional convention should be deferred at least until after the next legislative election, scheduled for November 2007. In April 2006, therefore, having failed to secure the requisite parliamentary majority enabling it to proceed with its programme, the ruling United Democratic Party announced that its proposals for a constitutional convention were to be submitted to the electorate in a national referendum. Voters were to be asked if they wished a constitutional convention to consider a total of 22 amendments to the country's Constitution.

In 1989 a UN report on the 'greenhouse effect' (heating of the earth's atmosphere) predicted a possible resultant rise in sea-level of some 3.7 m by 2030, which would completely submerge the Marshall Islands. The islands' Government strongly criticized the Australian Government's refusal, at the conference on climate change in Kyoto, Japan, in December 1997, to reduce its emission of pollutant gases known to contribute to the 'greenhouse effect'. Furthermore, in early 2002 the Intergovernmental Panel on Climate Change (IPCC) projected that during the 21st century global sea-level rises would submerge over 80% of Majuro atoll. However, the Marshall Islands Government has itself caused regional concerns regarding pollution, notably with regard to the possible establishment of large-scale facilities for the storage of nuclear waste. Criticism by the US Government of the plans, announced in 1994, was strongly denounced by the Marshall Islands authorities, which claimed that the project constituted the only opportunity for the country to generate sufficient income for the rehabilitation of contaminated islands and the provision of treatment for illnesses caused by the US nuclear-test programme. In mid-1997 President Imata Kabua announced the indefinite suspension of the project (despite the initiation of a feasibility study into the development of a nuclear waste storage facility). None the less, the Government approved plans for a new feasibility study on the subject in April 1998.

In November 1998 the Marshall Islands established full diplomatic relations with Taiwan. The action was immediately condemned by the People's Republic of China, which in December severed diplomatic ties with the islands, closing its embassy in Majuro and suspending all intergovernmental agreements. The Marshall Islands Government insisted that it wished to maintain cordial relations with both governments. The Note administration, which took office in January 2000, emphasized its commitment to the maintenance of diplomatic relations with Taiwan. In February 2001 a proposed visit by a flotilla of Taiwanese naval vessels to the Marshall Islands was vetoed by the USA, on the grounds that the defence protocol of the Compact of Free Association prohibited such a visit. In August 2004 the Chinese Vice-Minister of Foreign Affairs, Zhou Wenzhong, expressed his country's willingness to restore normal relations, on condition that the Marshall Islands withdraw its diplomatic recognition of Taiwan. In April 2005 it was alleged that members of the ruling UDP had accepted bribes from Chinese officials hoping to expedite a return to normal diplomatic relations and the end of Marshallese recognition of Taiwan; the Government denied the allegations. Meanwhile, in September 2004 it was announced that Taiwan was to contribute more than US $40m. over a 20-year period to the Marshall Islands trust fund established in May.

Government

The Constitution of the Republic of the Marshall Islands, which became effective on 1 May 1979, provides for a parliamentary form of government, with legislative authority vested in the 33-member Nitijela. The Nitijela (members of which are elected, by popular vote, for a four-year term) elects the President of the Marshall Islands (also a four-year mandate) from among its own members. Under the terms of the Compact of Free Association, the Republic of the Marshall Islands is a sovereign, self-governing state. The first Compact was signed by the Governments of the Marshall Islands and the USA on 25 June 1983, and was effectively ratified by the US Congress on 14 January 1986. A revised Compact was signed by the Governments of the two countries on 1 May 2003; it was ratified by the US Congress in

THE MARSHALL ISLANDS

November 2003, and signed by US President George W. Bush in December of that year. Amendments to the compact were signed in May 2004.

Local governmental units are the municipalities and villages. Elected Magistrates and Councils govern the municipalities. Village government is largely traditional.

Defence

Under the terms of the Compact of Free Association as ratified in 1986 and amended in 2003, the defence of the Marshall Islands is the responsibility of the USA, which maintains a military presence on Kwajalein Atoll.

Economic Affairs

In 2004, according to estimates by the World Bank, the Marshall Islands' gross national income (GNI), measured at average 2002–04 prices, was US $142.1m., equivalent to $2,370 per head. During 1995–2004, it was estimated, the population increased at an average annual rate of 3.4%; gross domestic product (GDP) per head declined, in real terms, at an average rate of 1.9% per year during 1999–2004. Overall GDP decreased, in real terms, at an average annual rate of 1.9% in 1995–2004. According to the Asian Development Bank (ADB), GDP increased by 0.4% in 2004 and by 3.5% in 2005.

Agriculture is mainly on a subsistence level. The sector (including fishing and livestock-rearing) contributed an estimated 14.2% of GDP in the year ending September 2002. According to FAO, the sector engaged 6,000 people in 2003. The principal crops are coconuts, cassava and sweet potatoes. Copra production suffered a severe decline in the late 1990s, following sustained low prices, an ageing tree stock and a reduction in the number of government-owned vessels used for transport purposes. In 2003, however, some 4,283 short tons of copra were produced, compared with 2,653 tons in the previous year. By 2004 the sector was reportedly making a good recovery, with the volume of copra exports having risen by 14% compared with the previous year. In 2004/05 exports of coconut oil and copra accounted for 15.9% of the total value of exports. The fishing sector incorporates a commercial tuna-fishing industry, including a tuna-canning factory and transhipment base on Majuro. In August 2004 a tuna-loining factory, which employed more than 500 people and from which the yearly exports had been valued at US $3.4m., was closed down, owing to financial difficulties. The cultivation of seaweed was developed extensively in 1992, and in 1994 a project to cultivate blacklip pearl oysters on Arno Atoll was undertaken with US funding. The sale of fishing licences is an important source of revenue and earned the islands an estimated US $1.5m. in 2004/05. The Marshall Islands expected to receive annual revenues of some $21m. following the renewal of a treaty between the USA and the Forum Fisheries Agency (FFA) group of Pacific island nations in 2003. In 2001 the Japanese Government funded the construction of a commercial fishing base at Jaluit Atoll. All shark-fishing licences, however, were revoked in August 2004, owing to low stocks. In June 2005 the Forum Fisheries Committee (an agency of the Pacific Islands Forum) convened in Majuro to discuss how best to increase the Pacific islands' share of revenue from fishing, an industry dominated by foreign companies. In mid-2005 an agreement signed in late 2004 to establish a Tuna Commission to oversee the protection of Pacific tuna stocks had yet to be implemented. The GDP of the agricultural sector increased by 8.3% in 2000, by 9.7% in 2001 and by 10.3% in 2002, according to the ADB.

Industrial activities (including mining, manufacturing, construction and power) contributed an estimated 14.2% of GDP in 2002. Construction and manufacturing engaged 10.1% of the private-sector work-force in 2003/04. Between 1990 and 1999 industrial GDP declined at an average annual rate of 1.5%. The islands have few mineral resources, although there are high-grade phosphate deposits on Ailinglaplap Atoll. The GDP of the industrial sector increased by 16.4% in 2000, by 18.6% in 2001 and by 19.5% in 2002, according to the ADB.

Manufacturing activity, which provided 1.9% of GDP in 2002, consists mainly of the processing of coconuts (to produce copra and coconut oil) and other agricultural products and of fish (see above). According to the ADB, the manufacturing sector engaged a total of 800 workers in 2000.

The services sector (comprising trade, transport, storage, communications and other activities) provided an estimated 72.6% of GDP in 2002. Retail businesses provided employment for 28.8% of the private-sector work-force in 2003/04. The international shipping registry experienced considerable expansion following the political troubles in Panama in 1989, and subsequently continued to expand (largely as a result of US ships' reflagging in the islands). The number of vessels registered rose from 515 in December 2003 to 632 in December of the following year. The shipping industry also benefited from the construction of a floating dry-dock on Majuro in 1995. Tourist receipts reached US $4m. in 2002. The number of tourist arrivals rose from 6,002 in 2002 to 7,195 in 2003. According to the ADB, the GDP of the services sector grew by 69.5% in 2000, by 68.9% in 2001 and by 68.5% in 2002.

In 2004/05 the Marshall Islands recorded an estimated trade deficit of US $69.3m., but a surplus of $0.4m. on the current account of the balance of payments. The latter surplus was estimated to be the equivalent to 0.3% of GDP in that year. The only significant domestic exports in 2005 were coconut products. Re-exports of diesel fuel totalled $13.3m., their value greatly exceeding that of domestic exports. The principal imports in 2000 included mineral fuels and lubricants (which accounted for 37.3% of total expenditure on merchandise imports), food and live animals, and machinery and transport equipment. In 2003 the principal sources of imports were the USA (which provided 68.0% of total imports) and Australia (14.0%). In 2000 the USA was also the principal export destination (providing 57.1% of total exports).

Financial assistance from the USA, in accordance with the terms stipulated in the Compact of Free Association, contributes a large part of the islands' revenue. Central government current expenditure in 2003/04 totalled some $70.1m., according to the IMF. It was envisaged that US grants, trust-fund contributions and US military payments for use of the missile-testing site on Kwajalein would provide about two-thirds of government revenue, while Taiwan was to provide some $10m. Government expenditure was an estimated $86.9m. in 2004/05. Although it had been anticipated that the country's fiscal surplus would strengthen in 2004/05, in August 2005 the Ministry of Finance announced that all non-payroll spending by government departments would be 'frozen', owing to a shortfall in revenues. The islands' external debt was estimated at $100.8m. in 2004/05, equivalent to some 69.8% of GDP. In that year the Marshall Islands spent $6.2m. on debt-servicing. The Marshall Islands received $551 of aid per caput in 2003. In 2004/05 budgeted aid from the USA amounted to $71m. ($64.3m. of which was to be provided under the Compact agreement). Aid is also provided by Japan and Taiwan. Annual inflation in Majuro averaged 2.4% in 1995–2004. According to the IMF, consumer prices increased by 2.2% in 2004 and by 4.5% in 2005. It was reported that some 40% of the work-force were unemployed in 2004.

The Marshall Islands is a member of the Pacific Community (see p. 350), the Pacific Islands Forum (see p. 352), the South Pacific Regional Trade and Economic Co-operation Agreement (SPARTECA, see p. 354), the UN Economic and Social Commission for Asia and the Pacific (ESCAP, see p. 33) and the Asian Development Bank (ADB, see p. 169). In early 1996 the Marshall Islands and other countries and territories of Micronesia established the Council of Micronesian Government Executives. The new body aimed to facilitate discussion of economic developments in the region, and to examine possibilities for reducing the considerable cost of shipping essential goods between the islands.

The introduction, from the mid-1990s, of retrenchment measures in the public sector was welcomed by several international financial organizations and supported by the ADB. However, it was subsequently observed that reform of the public sector, which until the recession of the mid-1990s had employed up to one-half of the economically-active population, had been accompanied by a decline in employment in the private sector, leading to a very high rate of unemployment (according to US assessments, the highest of any US-affiliated state in the Pacific) and emigration. In 1999 the Kabua Government reduced import duties by more than 50% on many items, in an attempt to revitalize the local economy. Reforms to promote the private sector were also announced. The Marshall Islands has since 1998 notably benefited from numerous economic agreements with Taiwan, worth an estimated US $20m., which have financed many projects including the construction of roads, the acquisition of boats and the development of the agricultural sector. However, in 1999 concern was expressed by the ADB, a major creditor of the Marshalls, that reliance on external aid was hampering economic reform in the Marshall Islands. Some have considered that reforms of the public sector in the mid-1990s, combined with low world prices for Marshallese products, have

THE MARSHALL ISLANDS

contributed directly to the islands' economic decline. The lack of internationally marketable natural resources and the remote location of the islands also present major difficulties for the Marshall Islands Government in its efforts to revitalize and expand the economy. Attempts to overcome these obstacles, including the introduction of passport sales and efforts to promote gambling and offshore financial services (see Recent History) have generated political controversy, both domestically and internationally. None the less, in October 2002 the Marshall Islands was removed from the Financial Action Task Force (FATF) list of Non Co-operative Countries and Territories following the successful implementation of a series of regulatory measures (see above). The Government has also been able to obtain a further source of income by expanding ship registrations, to the effect that by 2002 the Marshallese merchant fleet was reportedly the sixth largest in the world. A notable feature of the amended Compact of Free Association, which was signed by the Governments of the Marshall Islands and the USA in May 2003 (see Recent History), was the planned gradual decrement in grant assistance over the 20-year period of the renewed Compact. In September it was announced that the Taiwanese Government had agreed to make a substantial contribution to the Marshall Islands' government trust fund (see Recent History), which had been established in May with an initial investment of $25m. and a deposit of $7m. from the USA. Taiwan planned to transfer a total of $1m. to the fund each year until 2009 and thereafter, until 2023, an annual sum of $2.4m. The assets of the Intergenerational Trust Fund were estimated at more than $30m. in September 2004. In February 2006 the USA proposed a budget for 2006/07 that provided $63.7m. of Compact funding to the Marshall Islands. Meanwhile, in April 2005 it was announced that the Government would seek to negotiate a free-trade agreement with the European Union (EU), in order to stimulate foreign investment and expand the islands' market for tuna exports. Opposition groups expressed concern, however, that the removal of import duties would cause a reduction in government revenues exceeding the increase in revenues accruing from increased investment and exports. In October concern was expressed over reports that while public-sector wages had risen sharply in 1997–2004, in real terms private-sector wages had declined over the same period. In February 2006 it was reported that, owing to a shortfall in budgeted government revenues, the Marshall Islands had defaulted on two loan payments to the ADB and that further spending from the Government's general fund would cease. The 2006/07 budget included measures to make income tax more progressive and to simplify the import-tax system. GDP growth of 4.0% was predicted for 2005/06, with growth in 2006/07 forecast at 3.5%.

Education

Education is compulsory between the ages of six and 14. In 2000/01 a total of 8,530 children attended primary schools in the Marshall Islands. A total of 6,353 pupils were enrolled at secondary schools in that year. The College of the Marshall Islands (which became independent from the College of Micronesia in 1993) is based on Majuro and had 903 students enrolled in 2000/01. In 1995 the University of the South Pacific opened an extension centre on Majuro. The Fisheries and Nautical Center offers vocational courses for Marshall islanders seeking employment in the fishing industry or on passenger liners, cargo ships and tankers. Government expenditure on education in 2004/05 was US $7.4m., equivalent to 10.6% of total recurrent budgetary spending.

Public Holidays

2006 (provisional): 1–2 January (New Year), 1 March (Nuclear Victims' Remembrance Day), 14 April (Good Friday), 1 May (Constitution Day), 4 July (Fishermen's Day), 4 September (Dri-Jerbal), 30 September (Manit—Culture Day), 18 November (Presidents' Day), 1 December (Kamolol—Gospel Day), 25 December (Christmas).

2007 (provisional): 1–2 January (New Year), 1 March (Nuclear Victims' Remembrance Day), 6 April (Good Friday), 1 May (Constitution Day), 4 July (Fishermen's Day), 5 September (Dri-Jerbal), 30 September (Manit—Culture Day), 18 November (Presidents' Day), 2 December (Kamolol—Gospel Day), 25 December (Christmas).

Weights and Measures

With certain exceptions, the imperial system is in force. One US cwt equals 100 lb; one long ton equals 2,240 lb; one short ton equals 2,000 lb. A policy of gradual voluntary conversion to the metric system is being undertaken.

Statistical Survey

AREA AND POPULATION

Area: 181.4 sq km (70.0 sq miles) (land only); two island groups, the Ratak Chain (88.1 sq km) and the Ralik Chain (93.3 sq km).

Population: 43,380 at census of 13 November 1988; 50,848 (males 26,034, females 24,814) at census of June 1999. *Mid-2004:* 61,200 (estimated figure from Asian Development Bank, *Key Indicators of Developing Asian and Pacific Countries*). *By Island Group* (1999): Ratak Chain 30,932 (Majuro Atoll 23,682); Ralik Chain 19,916 (Kwajalein Atoll 10,903).

Density (mid-2004, land area only): 337.4 per sq km.

Births and Deaths (estimates, 2001): Live births 1,511 (birth rate 29.6 per 1,000); Deaths 271 (death rate 5.2 per 1,000). Sources: UN, *Population and Vital Statistics Report* and UN Economic and Social Commission for Asia and the Pacific, *Statistical Yearbook for Asia and the Pacific*.

Expectation of Life (WHO estimates, years at birth): 61 (males 61; females 63) in 2003. Source: WHO, *World Health Report*.

Economically Active Population (year ending September 2004): Private sector 5,366 (Agriculture 42; Manufacturing 43; Construction 499; Retail 1,545); Public sector 3,795; *Total labour force* 9,161. Source: IMF, *Selected Issues and Statistical Appendix* (March 2006).

HEALTH AND WELFARE

Key Indicators

Total Fertility Rate (children per woman, 2003): 5.4.

Under-5 Mortality Rate (per 1,000 live births, 2003): 61.

Physicians (per 1,000 head, 1996): 0.42.

Health Expenditure (2002): US $ per head (PPP): 415.

Health Expenditure (2002): % of GDP: 10.6.

Health Expenditure (2002): public (% of total): 67.3.

Access to Water (% of persons, 2002): 85.

Access to Sanitation (% of persons, 2002): 82.

For sources and definitions, see explanatory note on p. vi.

AGRICULTURE, ETC.

Principal Crops, Livestock and Livestock Products (FAO estimate, '000 metric tons, 2004): Coconuts 15.

Fishing (metric tons, live weight): Total catch 38,375 in 2003.

Source: FAO.

INDUSTRY

Electric Energy (million kWh, Majuro only): 74 in 2001; 80 in 2002; 81 in 2003. Source: Asian Development Bank, *Key Indicators of Developing Asian and Pacific Countries*.

FINANCE

Currency and Exchange Rates: United States currency is used: 100 cents = 1 United States dollar (US $). Sterling and Euro Equivalents (30 December 2005): £1 sterling = US $1.7219; €1 = US $1.1797; US $100 = £58.08 = €84.77.

Budget (estimates, US $ million, year ending 30 September 2005): *Revenue:* Recurrent 30.3 (Tax 22.1, Non-tax 8.1); Grants 53.6; Total 83.9. *Expenditure:* Recurrent 69.7; Capital (incl. net lending) 17.2; Total 86.9. Source: IMF, *Selected Issues and Statistical Appendix* (March 2006).

Cost of Living (Consumer Price Index for Majuro; base: Jan.–March 2003 = 100): All items 100.9 in 2003; 103.1 in 2004; 107.7 in

THE MARSHALL ISLANDS

2005. Source: IMF, *Selected Issues and Statistical Appendix* (March 2006).

Gross Domestic Product by Economic Activity (US $ million at current prices, 2002): Agriculture 15; Mining, manufacturing, electricity, gas and water 5; Construction 10; Trade 19; Transport, storage and communications 7; Other activities 51; *Total* 106. Source: UN, *Statistical Yearbook for Asia and the Pacific*.

Balance of Payments (estimates, US $ million, year ending 30 September 2005): Merchandise exports f.o.b. 16.5; Merchandise imports c.i.f. −85.8; *Trade balance* −69.3; Services (net) −6.9; *Balance on goods and services* −76.2; Other income 35.6; *Balance on goods, services and income* −40.6; Private unrequited transfers (net) −12.6; Official unrequited transfers (net) 53.6; *Current balance* 0.4; Capital and financial account (net) −7.5; Net errors and omissions 1.2; *Overall balance* −5.9. Source: IMF, *Selected Issues and Statistical Appendix* (March 2006).

EXTERNAL TRADE

Principal Commodities (US $ million, 2000, estimates): *Imports*: Food and live animals 5.0, Beverages and tobacco 6.0; Crude materials, inedible, except fuels 2.6; Mineral fuels, lubricants and related materials 20.4; Animal and vegetable oils and fats 2.4; Chemicals 0.1; Basic manufactures 3.0; Machinery and transport equipment 8.2; Miscellaneous manufactured articles 1.4; Goods not classified by kind 5.8; Total 54.7. *Exports* (year ending September 2005): Coconut oil (crude) 2.5; Copra cake 0.1; Total (incl. others) 16.4. Sources: Asian Development Bank, *Key Indicators of Developing Asian and Pacific Countries* and IMF, *Selected Issues and Statistical Appendix* (March 2006).

Principal Trading Partners (US $ million, estimates): *Imports* (2003): Australia 10.1; Hong Kong 2.5; Japan 3.7; New Zealand 2.5; USA 49.2; Total (incl. others) 72.3. *Exports* (2000): USA 5.2; Total (incl. others) 9.1. Source: mainly Asian Development Bank, *Key Indicators of Developing Asian and Pacific Countries*.

TRANSPORT

Road Traffic (vehicles registered, 1999): Trucks 64; Pick-ups 587; Sedans 1,404; Jeeps 79; Buses 75; Vans 66; Scooters 47; Other motor vehicles 253.

Shipping: *Merchant Fleet* (at 31 December 2004): Vessels 632; Displacement ('000 grt) 22,495 (Source: Lloyd's Register-Fairplay, *World Fleet Statistics*). *International Sea-borne Freight Traffic* (estimates, '000 metric tons, 1990):* Goods loaded 29; Goods unloaded 123 (Source: UN, *Monthly Bulletin of Statistics*).
* Including the Northern Mariana Islands, the Federated States of Micronesia and Palau.

Civil Aviation (traffic on scheduled services, 2001): Kilometres flown 1 million; Passengers carried 19,000; Passenger-km 25 million; Total ton-km 2 million. Source: UN, *Statistical Yearbook*.

TOURISM

Tourist Arrivals: 5,444 in 2001; 6,002 in 2002; 7,195 in 2003.

Arrivals by Country (2003): Japan 1,024; Other Asia 1,704; USA 2,193; Total (incl. others) 7,195.

Tourism Receipts (US $ million, incl. passenger transport): 4 in 2000; 4 in 2001; 4 in 2002.

Sources: World Tourism Organization, Marshall Islands Visitor Authority and IMF, *Federated States of Micronesia: Selected Issues and Statistical Appendix* (March 2005).

COMMUNICATIONS MEDIA

Telephones (main lines in use): 4,500 in 2004*.

Mobile Cellular Telephones (subscriptions): 600 in 2004*.

Facsimile Machines (number): 160 in 1996†.

Personal Computers: 5,000 in 2004*.

Internet Users: 2,000 in 2004*.

Non-daily Newspaper: 1 (average circulation 10,000 copies) in 1996‡.
* Source: International Telecommunication Union.
† Source: UN, *Statistical Yearbook*.
‡ Source: UNESCO, *Statistical Yearbook*.

EDUCATION

Primary (2000/01, unless otherwise indicated): 103 schools (1998); 517 teachers; 8,530 pupils enrolled.

Secondary (2000/01, unless otherwise indicated): 16 schools (1998); 381 teachers; 6,353 pupils enrolled.

Higher (2000/01, unless otherwise indicated): 1 college (1994); 48 teachers; 903 students enrolled.

Source: UNESCO Institute for Statistics.

Directory

The Constitution

On 1 May 1979 the locally drafted Constitution of the Republic of the Marshall Islands became effective. The Constitution provides for a parliamentary form of government, with legislative authority vested in the 33-member Nitijela. Members of the Nitijela are elected by a popular vote, from 25 districts, for a four-year term. There is an advisory council of 12 high chiefs, or Iroij. The Nitijela elects the President of the Marshall Islands (who also has a four-year mandate) from among its own members. The President then selects members of the Cabinet from among the members of the Nitijela. On 25 June 1983 the final draft of a Compact of Free Association was signed by the Governments of the Marshall Islands and the USA, and the Compact was effectively ratified by the US Congress on 14 January 1986. An amended Compact was signed by the Governments of the two countries on 1 May 2003; final terms were ratified by the US Congress in November, and signed by the US President in December of that year. By the terms of the Compact, free association recognizes the Republic of the Marshall Islands as an internally sovereign, self-governing state, whose policy concerning foreign affairs must be consistent with guide-lines laid down in the Compact. Full responsibility for defence lies with the USA, which undertakes to provide regular economic assistance. The economic and defence provisions of the Compact are renewable after 15 years, but the status of free association continues indefinitely.

The Government

HEAD OF STATE

President: KESSAI H. NOTE (took office 10 January 2000; re-elected by the Nitijela 4 January 2004).

THE CABINET
(April 2006)

Minister in Assistance to the President: WITTEN T. PHILIPPO.
Minister of Education: WILFRED I. KENDALL.
Minister of Finance: BRENSON S. WASE.
Minister of Transportation and Communication: MICHAEL M. KONELIOS.
Minister of Health and Environment: ALVIN T. JACKLICK.
Minister of Public Works: MATTLAN ZACKHRAS.
Minister of Internal Affairs: REIN MORRIS.
Minister of Justice: DONALD CAPELLE.
Minister of Resources and Development: JOHN M. SILK.
Minister of Foreign Affairs and Trade: GERALD ZACKIOS.

MINISTRIES

Office of the President: Govt of the Republic of the Marshall Islands, POB 2, Majuro, MH 96960; tel. (625) 3213; fax (625) 4021; e-mail presoff@ntamar.net.

Ministry of Education: POB 3, Majuro, MH 96960; tel. (625) 5262; fax (625) 3861; e-mail secmoe@ntamar.net.

Ministry of Finance: POB D, Majuro, MH 96960; tel. (625) 8320; fax (625) 3607; e-mail secfin@ntamar.net.

Ministry of Foreign Affairs and Trade: POB 1349, Majuro, MH 96960; tel. (625) 3181; fax (623) 4979; e-mail mofatadm@ntamar.net.

Ministry of Health and Environment: POB 16, Majuro, MH 96960; tel. (625) 3355; fax (625) 3432; e-mail mipamohe@ntamar.net.

Ministry of Internal Affairs: POB 18, Majuro, MH 96960; tel. (625) 8240; fax (625) 5353; e-mail rmihpo@ntamar.net.

Ministry of Justice: c/o Office of the Attorney General, Majuro, MH 96960; tel. (625) 3244; fax (625) 5218; e-mail agoffice@ntamar.net.

Ministry of Public Works: POB 1727, Majuro, MH 96960; tel. (625) 8911; fax (625) 3005; e-mail mpwmin@ntamar.net.

Ministry of Resources and Development: POB 1727, Majuro, MH 96960; tel. (625) 3206; fax (625) 7471; e-mail rmitisd@ntamar.net.

Ministry of Transportation and Communication: POB 1079, Majuro, MH 96960; tel. (625) 8869; fax (625) 3486; e-mail rmimotc@ntamar.net.

STATE TRIBUNAL

Nuclear Claims Tribunal: POB 702, Majuro, MH 96960; tel. (625) 3396; fax (625) 3389; e-mail nctmaj@ntamar.net; internet www.nuclearclaimstribunal.com; f. 1988; authorized under Section 177 of the first Compact of Free Association between the Government of the Marshall Islands and the Government of the USA to decide all claims arising from the nuclear-testing programme conducted by the USA in the Marshall Islands in 1946–58; Chair. JAMES H. PLASMAN; Defender of the Fund PHILIP A. OKNEY; Public Advocate BILL GRAHAM.

Legislature

THE NITIJELA

The Nitijela (lower house) consists of 33 elected Senators. The most recent national election was held on 17 November 2003, as a result of which the United Democratic Party held 20 seats and Ailin Kein Ad 10.

Speaker: Sen. LITOKWA TOMEING.

THE COUNCIL OF IROIJ

The Council of Iroij is the upper house of the bicameral legislature, comprising 12 tribal chiefs who advise the Presidential Cabinet and review legislation affecting customary law, land tenure or any traditional practice.

Chairman: Iroij KOTAK LOEAK.

Election Commission

Electoral Commission: POB 18, Majuro, MH 96900; Chief Election Officer HEMLEY BENJAMIN.

Political Organizations

Ailin Kein Ad (Our Islands): Majuro; f. 2002; opposed to President Note; Leader TONY DEBRUM.

United Democratic Party: Majuro; Chair. LITOKWA TOMEING.

Diplomatic Representation

EMBASSIES IN THE MARSHALL ISLANDS

China (Taiwan): A5-6, Lojkar Village, Long Island, POB 1229, Majuro, MH 96960; tel. (247) 4141; fax (247) 4143; e-mail eoroc@ntamar.net; Ambassador LIEN-GENE CHEN.

Japan: A-1 Lojkar Village, POB 300, Majuro, MH 96960; tel. (247) 7463; fax (247) 7493; Ambassador KENRO IINO.

USA: POB 1379, Majuro, MH 96960; tel. (247) 4011; fax (247) 4012; e-mail publicmajuro@state.gov; internet usembassy.state.gov/majuro; Ambassador GRETA N. MORRIS.

Judicial System

The judicial system consists of the Supreme Court and the High Court, which preside over District and Community Courts, and the Traditional Rights Court.

Supreme Court of the Republic of the Marshall Islands: POB 378, Majuro, MH 96960; tel. (625) 3201; fax (625) 3323; e-mail jutrep@ntamar.com; Chief Justice DANIEL CADRA.

High Court of the Republic of the Marshall Islands: Majuro; e-mail judrep@ntamar.net; Chief Justice CARL INGRAM.

District Court of the Republic of the Marshall Islands: Majuro, MH 96960; tel. (625) 3201; fax (625) 3323; Presiding Judge BOKEPOK HELAI.

Traditional Rights Court of the Marshall Islands: Majuro, MH 96960; customary law only; Chief Judge RAILEY ALBERILTAR.

Religion

The population is predominantly Christian, mainly belonging to the Protestant United Church of Christ. The Roman Catholic Church, Assembly of God, Bukot Nan Jesus, Seventh-day Adventists, the Church of Jesus Christ of Latter-day Saints (Mormons), the Full Gospel and the Bahá'í Faith are also represented.

CHRISTIANITY

The Roman Catholic Church

The Apostolic Prefecture of the Marshall Islands included 4,601 adherents at 31 December 2003.

Prefect Apostolic of the Marshall Islands: Rev. Fr JAMES C. GOULD, POB 8, Majuro, MH 96960; tel. (625) 6675; fax (625) 5520; e-mail catholic@ntamar.com.

Protestant Churches

The Marshall Islands come under the auspices of the United Church Board for World Ministries (475 Riverside Drive, New York, NY 10115, USA); Sec. for Latin America, Caribbean and Oceania Dr PATRICIA RUMER.

BAHÁ'Í FAITH

National Spiritual Assembly: POB 1017, Majuro, MH 96960; tel. (247) 3512; fax (247) 7180; e-mail nsamarshallislands@yahoo.com; internet www.mh.bahai.org; mems resident in 50 localities; Sec. Dr IRENE J. TAAFAKI.

The Press

Kwajalein Hourglass: POB 23, Kwajalein, MH 96555; tel. (355) 3539; e-mail jbennett@kls.usaka.smdc.army.mil; internet www.smdc.army.mil/KWAJ/Hourglass/Hourglass.html; f. 1954; 2 a week; Editor JIM BENNETT; circ. 2,300.

Marshall Islands Gazette: monthly; government publ.

Marshall Islands Journal: POB 14, Majuro, MH 96960; tel. (625) 8143; fax (625) 3136; e-mail journal@ntamar.net; f. 1970; weekly; Editor GIFF JOHNSON; circ. 3,700.

Broadcasting and Communications

TELECOMMUNICATIONS

National Telecommunications Authority (NTA): POB 1169, Majuro, MH 96960; tel. (625) 3852; fax (625) 3952; internet www.ntamar.com; privatized in 1991; sole provider of local and long-distance telephone services and internet communications in the Marshall Islands; Pres. and Gen. Man. TONY MULLER.

BROADCASTING

Radio

Radio Marshalls V7AB: POB 3250, Majuro, MH 96960; tel. (625) 8411; fax (625) 5353; govt-owned; commercial; programmes in English and Marshallese; Station Man. ANTARI ELBON.

Marshall Islands Broadcasting Co: POB 19, Majuro, MH 96960; tel. (625) 3250; fax (625) 3505; privately-owned; Chief Information Officer PETER FUCHS.

Television

Alele Museum Foundation: POB 629, Majuro, MH 96960; tel. and fax (625) 3226; broadcasts educational programmes.

Marshalls Broadcasting Co Television: POB 19, Majuro, MH 96960; tel. (625) 3413; privately-owned; Chief Information Officer PETER FUCHS.

The US Department of Defense operates the American Forces Radio and Television Service for the Bucholz Army Airfield on Kwajalein Atoll.

THE MARSHALL ISLANDS

Finance

(cap. = capital; res = reserves; dep. = deposits; amounts in US dollars)

BANKING

Bank of Guam (USA): POB C, Majuro, MH 96960; tel. (625) 3322; fax (625) 3444; internet www.bankofguam.com; Man. ROMY A. ANGEL; brs in Ebeye, Kwajalein and Majuro.

Bank of the Marshall Islands: POB J, Majuro, MH 96960; tel. (625) 3636; fax (625) 3661; e-mail bankmar@ntamar.net; internet www.angelfire.com/ms/bankofMI; f. 1982; 40% govt-owned; dep. 47.5m., total assets 61.8m. (Dec. 2003); Chair. GRANT LABAUN; Pres. and Gen. Man. PATRICK CHEN; brs in Majuro, Ebeye and Santo.

Marshall Islands Development Bank: POB 1048, Majuro, MH 96960; tel. (625) 3230; fax (625) 3309; f. 1989; total assets 19.5m. (Dec. 1992); lending suspended in 2003; Man. Dir AMON TIBON.

INSURANCE

Majuro Insurance Company: POB 60, Majuro, MH 96960; tel. (625) 8885; fax (625) 8188; Man. LUCY RUBEN.

Marshalls Insurance Agency: POB 113, Majuro, MH 96960; tel. (625) 3366; fax (625) 3189; Man. TOM LIKOVICH.

Moylan's Insurance Underwriters (Marshall) Inc: POB 727, Majuro, MH 96960; tel. (625) 3220; fax (625) 3361; e-mail marshalls@moylansinsurance.com; internet www.moylansinsurance.com; Pres. JOEL PHILLIP.

Trade and Industry

DEVELOPMENT ORGANIZATIONS AND STATE AUTHORITIES

Marshall Islands Development Authority: Majuro, MH 96960; Gen. Man. DAVID KABUA.

Marshall Islands Environmental Protection Authority: POB 1322, Majuro, MH 96960; tel. (625) 3035; fax (625) 5202; e-mail eparmi@ntamar.net; Dir ABRAHAM HICKIN (acting).

Marshall Islands Marine Resources Authority: Majuro, MH 96960; Dir DANNY WASE.

Kwajalein Atoll Development Authority (KADA): POB 5159, Ebeye Island, Kwajalein, MH 96970; Dir JEBAN RIKLON.

Tobolar Copra Processing Authority: POB G, Majuro, MH 96960; tel. (625) 3494; fax (625) 7206; e-mail tobolar@ntamar.com; Gen. Man. MIKE SLINGER.

CHAMBER OF COMMERCE

Majuro Chamber of Commerce: POB 1226, Majuro, MH 96960; tel. (625) 3177; fax (625) 2500; e-mail commerce@ntamar.net; internet www.majurochamber.net/index.html; Pres. JACK NIEDENTHAL; Sec. JIM MCLEAN.

UTILITIES

Electricity

Marshalls Energy Company: POB 1439, Majuro, MH 96960; tel. (625) 3829; fax (625) 3397; e-mail meccorp@ntamar.net; Chair. Minister of Public Works MATTLAN ZACKHRAS; Gen. Man. WILLIAM F. ROBERTS.

Kwajalein Atoll Joint Utility Resource (KAJUR): POB 5819, Ebeye Island, Kwajalein, MH 96970; tel. (329) 3799; fax (329) 3722.

Water

Majuro Water and Sewage Services: POB 1751, Majuro, MH 96960; tel. (625) 8934; fax (625) 3837; e-mail mwsc@ntamar.net; internet www.omip.org/majuro.html; Man. TERRY MELLAN.

CO-OPERATIVES

These include the Ebeye Co-op, Farmers' Market Co-operative, Kwajalein Employees' Credit Union, Marshall Is Credit Union, Marshall Is Fishermen's Co-operative, and the Marshall Is Handicraft Co-operative.

Transport

ROADS

Macadam and concrete roads are found in the more important islands. In 1996 there were 152 km of paved roads in the Marshall Islands, mostly on Majuro and Ebeye. Other islands have stone and coral-surfaced roads and tracks. In 1997 the Marshall Islands received a grant of some US $0.5m. from Japan for a road-improvement project on Majuro. The project was to form part of an extensive programme costing US $15m., and was completed in 1999.

SHIPPING

The Marshall Islands operates an 'offshore' shipping register. At the end of 2004 the merchant fleet comprised 632 vessels, with a combined displacement of some 22.5m. grt.

Vessel Registry:

Marshall Islands Maritime and Corporate Administrators Inc: 11495 Commerce Park Drive, Reston, VA 20191-1507, USA; tel. (703) 620-4880; fax (703) 476-8522; e-mail info@register-iri.com; internet www.register-iri.com; Pres. WILLIAM R. GALLAGHER; Vice-Pres. MELISSA A. HURST.

The Trust Company of the Marshall Islands Inc: Trust Company Complex, Ajeltake Island, POB 1405, Majuro, MH 96960; tel. (247) 3018; fax (247) 3017; e-mail tcmi@ntamar.net; Pres. GUY EDISON CLAY MAITLAND.

Marshall Islands Ports Authority (MIPA): Majuro; tel. 625-8269; fax 625-4269; responsible for seaports and airports; Dir JACK CHONG GUM.

Micronesian Shipping Agencies Inc: 3396 Lagoon Rd, Majuro; tel. 625-2021; fax 625-2020; e-mail msaiship@ntamar.net.

CIVIL AVIATION

In 1995 the Marshall Islands, Kiribati, Nauru and Tuvalu agreed to begin discussions on the establishment of a joint regional airline. In 1997 the Marshall Islands signed a bilateral agreement on international air transport with the Federated States of Micronesia. Continental Micronesia operates three flights a week from Honolulu and Guam; Air Marshall Islands provides a daily domestic service; and Aloha Airlines provides a weekly service from Honolulu to Kwajalein and to Majuro.

Air Marshall Islands (AMI): POB 1319, Majuro, MH 96960; tel. (247) 3113; fax (247) 3888; e-mail amisales@ntamar.net; internet www.airmarshallislands.com; f. 1980; internal services for the Marshall Islands; international operations ceased in early 1999; also charter, air ambulance and maritime surveillance operations; agency for Aloha airlines; Chair. KUNIO LAMARI; CFO NEIL ESCHERRA.

Continental Air Micronesia: POB 156, Majuro; tel. (625) 3209; fax (625) 3730; e-mail cmimaj@ntamar.net; international flights between Majuro, the Federated States of Micronesia, Guam and Honolulu; also internal services between Majuro and Kwajalein; based in Hagåtña, Guam; Man. LEO SION.

Tourism

Tourism, which has been hindered by the difficulty of gaining access to the islands and a lack of transport facilities, was expected to develop significantly from the late 1990s, owing to the establishment of major resort complexes on Majuro and on Mili Atoll, funded at an estimated cost of US $1,000m. by South Korean investors. Tourism receipts totalled some $4m. in 2002. There were 7,195 tourist arrivals in 2003. In that year some 30.5% of visitors came from the USA and 14.2% from Japan. The islands' attractions include excellent opportunities for diving, game-fishing and the exploration of sites and relics of Second World War battles. The Marshall Islands Visitor Authority has implemented a short-term tourism development programme focusing on special-interest tourism markets. In the longer term the Visitor Authority planned to promote the development of small-island resorts throughout the country.

Marshall Islands Visitor Authority: POB 5, Majuro, MH 96960; tel. (625) 6482; fax (625) 6771; e-mail tourism@ntamar.net; internet www.visitmarshallislands.com; f. 1997; Chair. KIRT PINHO.

MAURITANIA
Introductory Survey

Location, Climate, Language, Religion, Flag, Capital

The Islamic Republic of Mauritania lies in north-west Africa, with the Atlantic Ocean to the west, Algeria and the disputed territory of Western Sahara (occupied by Morocco) to the north, Mali to the east and south, and Senegal to the south. The climate is hot and dry, particularly in the north, which is mainly desert. Average annual rainfall in the capital in the 1990s was 131 mm (5.1 ins). The 1991 Constitution designates Arabic (which is spoken by the Moorish majority) as the official language, and Arabic, Poular, Wolof and Solinke as the national languages. The black population in the south is largely French-speaking, and French is widely used in commercial and business circles. Islam is the state religion, and the inhabitants are almost all Muslims. The national flag (proportions 2 by 3) comprises a green field, bearing, on the vertical median, a yellow five-pointed star between the upward-pointing horns of a yellow crescent. The capital is Nouakchott.

Recent History

Mauritania, formerly part of French West Africa, achieved full independence on 28 November 1960 (having become a self-governing member of the French Community two years earlier). Moktar Ould Daddah, leader of the Mauritanian Assembly Party (MAP) and Prime Minister since June 1959, became Head of State, and was elected President in August 1961. All parties subsequently merged with the MAP to form the Mauritanian People's Party (MPP), with Ould Daddah as Secretary-General, and Mauritania became a one-party state in 1964. In 1973 Mauritania joined the League of Arab States (see p. 306), and withdrew from the Franc Zone in the following year.

Under a tripartite agreement of November 1975, Spain ceded Spanish (now Western) Sahara to Mauritania and Morocco, to be apportioned between them. The agreement took effect in February 1976, when Mauritania occupied the southern portion of the territory. Fighting ensued between Moroccan and Mauritanian troops and the guerrilla forces of the Frente Popular para la Liberación de Saguia el-Hamra y Río de Oro (the Polisario Front), which sought independence for Western Sahara. Attacks within Mauritania by Polisario forces proved highly damaging to the economy. Diplomatic links with Algeria, which supported Polisario bases within its borders, were severed in March 1976. Meanwhile, relations with Morocco improved, following that country's renunciation of territorial claims that included Mauritania, and in mid-1977 a joint defence pact was formed.

By 1977 Mauritania was spending two-thirds of its budget on defending territory that promised no economic benefits. In July 1978 Ould Daddah was deposed in a bloodless coup, led by the armed forces Chief of Staff, Lt-Col (later Col) Moustapha Ould Mohamed Salek, who took power as Chairman of a Military Committee for National Recovery (MCNR). Polisario immediately declared a cease-fire with Mauritania, but the continuing presence of several thousand Moroccan troops in Mauritania impeded a full settlement. In April 1979 the MCNR was replaced by a Military Committee for National Salvation (MCNS). Salek continued to head the MCNS, but appointed Lt-Col Ahmed Ould Bouceif as Prime Minister. Ould Bouceif died in an air crash in May, and the MCNS appointed Lt-Col Mohamed Khouna Ould Haidalla as premier. Salek resigned in June, and was replaced as Head of State by Lt-Col Mohamed Mahmoud Ould Ahmed Louly. In July Polisario announced a resumption of hostilities against Mauritania. Later that month the Organization of African Unity (OAU, now the African Union—AU, see p. 153) recommended that a referendum be held to determine the future of the disputed region. These events provided the impetus for Mauritania's withdrawal from the war: Ould Haidalla renounced Mauritania's territorial claims in Western Sahara, and a peace treaty was signed with Polisario in August. Morocco announced its annexation of the entire territory, and diplomatic relations between Mauritania and Algeria were re-established.

Ould Haidalla succeeded Louly as Head of State in January 1980; he retained the posts of Prime Minister and Minister of Defence until December, when Sid'Ahmed Ould Bneijara was appointed premier in a largely civilian Council of Ministers. Although a draft Constitution, envisaging a multi-party system, was prepared, an attempted coup in March 1981 prompted Ould Haidalla to end civilian participation in the Government. The new Prime Minister, Lt-Col (later Col) Maaouiya Ould Sid'Ahmed Taya (a prominent member of the MCNS and the army Chief of Staff) assumed the defence portfolio in April, and the draft Constitution was abandoned.

In March 1984 widespread student unrest was denounced by the Government as a Libyan-backed 'destabilization plot'. Ould Haidalla again assumed the positions of Prime Minister and Minister of Defence, reappointing Col Taya as army Chief of Staff. On 12 December, while Ould Haidalla was temporarily absent from the country, Taya assumed the presidency in a bloodless coup and also took the defence portfolio in the new Government. An amnesty was proclaimed for all political prisoners and exiles. Ould Haidalla was detained upon his return to Mauritania, but was released, with five of his associates, in December 1988.

In late 1986 the conviction of 20 prominent black activists, on charges of 'undermining national unity', was followed by civil disturbances and increased activity by organizations opposed to what they claimed to be the oppression of black Mauritanians by the light-skinned Moorish community. Following the discovery of a coup plot in October 1987, three military officers of the black Toucouleur ethnic group were sentenced to death, and 41 others were imprisoned. In January 1988 it was reported that more than 500 black personnel had been expelled from the armed forces, as a result of disturbances following the executions of the convicted officers.

At a national referendum on 12 July 1991, a draft Constitution, which accorded extensive powers to the presidency and provided for the introduction of a multi-party political system, was supported by 97.9% of those who voted (85.3% of the registered electorate), according to official reports. Meanwhile, legislation permitting the registration of political parties was promulgated: among the first organizations to be accorded official status was the Democratic and Social Republican Party (DSRP), which was closely linked with Taya.

Taya was elected President on 17 January 1992, with 62.7% of the votes cast, defeating three other candidates; his nearest rival was Ahmed Ould Daddah, with 32.8%. The rate of voter participation was 51.7%.

Six opposition parties withdrew their candidates prior to legislative elections, which were held on 6 and 13 March 1992, protesting that certain electoral procedures were unduly favourable to the DSRP. Taya's party took 67 of the 79 seats in the National Assembly, and independent candidates won 10 of the remaining twelve seats; a low rate of participation by voters was reported. Following indirect elections to the Senate, on 3 and 10 April, the new, 56-member upper house (which was elected by municipal leaders) included 36 DSRP members and 17 independents (one other party had, unsuccessfully, presented candidates for election); three seats were reserved for representatives of Mauritanians resident abroad. Taya was inaugurated as President on 18 April. He named the hitherto Minister of Finance, Sidi Mohamed Ould Boubacar, as Prime Minister, to lead a Government that included three black ministers, one opposition representative, and only one member of the military.

The DSRP secured control of 172 of Mauritania's 208 administrative districts at Mauritania's first multi-party municipal elections, held in January and February 1994. Ahmed Ould Daddah's Union of Democratic Forces—New Era (UDF—NE) won control of 17 districts, the remainder being taken by independent candidates.

In early 1995 internal tensions within the UDF—NE, including a faction that left to join the DSRP, threatened to undermine the influence of the party. In July several UDF—NE members were reported to have defected to another opposition party, the Union for Democracy and Progress—UDP. In mid-1995 six opposition parties (including the UDF—NE and the UDP) announced that they had agreed a series of joint demands regarding future elections, including the compilation of an

MAURITANIA

accurate voters' register, the formulation of a new electoral code, and guarantees of judicial independence.

In October 1995 the Taya administration declared the Iraqi ambassador *persona non grata* and demanded his departure from Mauritania. The expulsion coincided with reports of a foiled coup in Mauritania, allegedly sponsored by the Iraqi Government, and a series of arrests ensued; among those detained were two parliamentarians (one from the DSRP, the other from the UDP), the Secretary-General of the National Assembly and army officers. In December 52 defendants stood trial on charges of forming an illegal organization; all 52 were discharged on appeal in January 1996.

In January 1996 Taya appointed Cheikh el Avia Ould Mohamed Khouna as Prime Minister, to head a new Council of Ministers. At legislative elections held on 11 and 18 October, the DSRP won 71 of the 79 seats in the National Assembly. The Rally for Democracy and Unity (RDU), closely allied with the administration, also secured a seat. Action for Change (AC), which sought to represent the interests of Harratin (mainly dark-skinned Moors who had formerly been slaves), was the only opposition party to obtain representation in the Assembly; six independent candidates also secured election. Later in October the Prime Minister named a new Council of Ministers.

In January 1997 several opposition leaders, including Messaoud Ould Boulkheir, the AC Chairman, were arrested on charges of maintaining 'suspicious relations' with Libya. Although Ould Boulkheir and several others had been freed by February, five other opposition activists received prison sentences for conspiring to break the law; in April four of the five convicted were acquitted on appeal. In February five prominent opposition parties, including the AC and the UDF—NE, formed a coalition, the Forum of Opposition Parties (FOP).

At the presidential election, held on 12 December 1997, contested by four candidates and boycotted by the member parties of the FOP, Taya was returned to office with 90.9% of the valid votes cast; his nearest rival, Mohamed Lemine Ch'Bih Ould Cheikh Melainine, won 7.0% of the vote. Opposition parties alleged that there had been widespread electoral fraud and disputed the official rate of voter participation, of 73.8%. Taya subsequently appointed Mohamed Lemine Ould Guig, a university academic, as Prime Minister, and a new Council of Ministers was installed. In November 1998 Khouna was again appointed Prime Minister.

Meanwhile, in March 1998 internal divisions in the UDF—NE resulted in a split in the party into two rival factions, led by Ahmed Ould Daddah and Moustapha Ould Bedreddine. In December Ould Daddah and two other members of his faction were placed under house arrest after they demanded that a public inquiry be held into allegations that Mauritania had agreed to allow Israeli nuclear waste to be stored underground in its territory. They were acquitted in March 1999 of charges of threatening public order. In November the Government banned the pro-Iraqi Baathist National Vanguard Party (Taliaa), a constituent member of the FOP, following its criticism of the Mauritanian Government's decision to establish full diplomatic relations with Israel in the previous month. In April 2000 Ould Daddah was detained two days prior to a meeting of the UDF—NE, at which he was expected to address the acquisition of wealth by associates of President Taya. Ould Daddah was released after five days, although a ban on public gatherings implemented following his arrest remained in force.

From October 2000, following the onset of the second *intifada* (uprising) in the Palestinian Autonomous Areas, the Mauritanian Government experienced increasing pressure from opposition groups, including the UDF—NE, to break off diplomatic relations with Israel. In October several pro-Palestinian demonstrations in Nouakchott and Nouadhibou led to violent anti-Israeli protests. Arrests of members of clandestine Islamist groups and of UDF—NE activists were reported. In late October the Council of Ministers officially dissolved the UDF—NE, on the grounds that the party had incited violence and sought to damage Mauritanian national interests. Several members of the party's executive committee were detained in November. A demonstration in Nouadhibou by supporters of the UDF—NE reportedly attracted 15,000 protesters. Ould Daddah refused to recognize the dissolution of the party, and the UDF—NE's partners in the FOP condemned the Government's action as unconstitutional. Six detained officials of the party began a hunger strike, although four of these were released by the end of November. Meanwhile, the faction of the UDF—NE led by Moustapha Ould Bedreddine, which remained authorized, restyled itself as the Union of Progressive Forces (UPF).

In December 2000 President Taya announced that an element of proportional representation would be introduced in subsequent elections to the National Assembly, and that the State would seek to facilitate funding and equal access to the media for all parties, although independent candidacies were to be prohibited. The National Assembly approved these measures in January 2001, although they were rejected as insufficient by the radical opposition, including the FOP. Also in January, a government reshuffle included the appointment of a new Minister of Foreign Affairs and Co-operation, Dah Ould Abdi. In April it was announced that six new political groupings had been officially recognized, including a breakaway group from the AC, the Alliance for Justice and Democracy. Meanwhile, in early April Melainine, now the leader of the Popular Front (PF—a constituent party of the FOP), was arrested on charges of conspiring with Libya to commit acts of sabotage and terrorism. In June Melainine was sentenced to five years' imprisonment; in protest at this decision, the Mauritanian Renewal Party, one of the new parties officially registered in April, announced its withdrawal from the governing coalition.

Some 15 political parties contested legislative and municipal elections held on 19 and 26 October 2001, at which an electoral turn-out of some 55% was reported. The DSRP won 64 of the 81 seats in the enlarged National Assembly, and the RDU and the UDP, which were now both allied with the ruling party, each secured three seats. The AC was the most successful of the opposition parties, winning four seats, while the UPF and the newly formed Rally of Democratic Forces (RDF), which replaced the banned UDF—NE, also each took three seats, and the PF secured the remaining seat. In November President Taya reappointed Khouna as Prime Minister, and a reshuffled Council of Ministers was appointed.

In January 2002 Ould Daddah was elected President of the RDF; four former vice-presidents of the UDF—NE were also appointed to the 12-member executive committee of the RDF. In that month the Government officially dissolved the AC, on the grounds that the party promoted racism and extremism, as well as attempting to undermine national unity and good relations with Senegal. At partial senatorial elections, held in April, the RDF won one seat, the first time that part of the radical opposition had secured representation in the Senate, in which the DSRP enjoyed a large majority. In August the Convention for Change (CC), an organization including many former members of the AC, and led by Ould Boulkheir, was denied the right to register as a political party.

In October 2002 the UFP announced that it was to organize a series of meetings intended to promote a 'national dialogue' between the authorities and the opposition parties. However, later that month seven other opposition parties, including the CC (which remained banned), the PF and the RDF, formed a new grouping, the United Opposition Framework (UOF), which also stated as its purpose the co-ordination of dialogue between the opposition and the Government pertaining to democratic reform; the UFP was, notably, excluded from the UOF. Consequently, the initial meeting was postponed indefinitely, and, expressing discontent at the situation, in mid-November the UFP announced its withdrawal from the National Assembly. As a result of the withdrawal of the three UFP deputies from the Assembly, the group of opposition deputies was dissolved, as it was now reduced to eight members, less than the 10 required for the formation of a parliamentary group. On 27 October a government reorganization was effected. Notably, Dah Ould Abdi was replaced as Minister of Foreign Affairs and Co-operation by Mohamed Ould Tobar.

In March 2003 US-led military action in Iraq, aimed at ousting the Baathist regime of Saddam Hussain, prompted protests in Mauritania, with widespread demonstrations held to demand that the Government break off diplomatic relations with the two principal nations involved in the conflict, the United Kingdom and the USA, and also with Israel. As opposition to the Government's broadly pro-US stance intensified in early May, police raided the headquarters of a tolerated—although not officially authorized—Baathist party, the National Renaissance Party (NRP—Nouhoudh). Three leaders of the NRP, including its Secretary-General, Mohamed Ould Abdellahi Ould Eyye, were arrested on unspecified charges; 13 other Baathists were also arrested over a period of four days, including the former Secretary-General of the Taliaa party. (Ten of those arrested were later charged with attempting to re-establish Taliaa.) The

MAURITANIA

Government's increasing intolerance of radical opposition movements targeted not only secularist Arab nationalist groupings, but also Islamist activists: a senior member of the RDF, Mohamed Jemil Ould Mansour was one of several prominent Islamists and religious leaders arrested. The Government also stated that it would close any mosques that were being used for political purposes or that incited hatred against Jews.

In early May 2003 Taya effected a minor government reorganization, dismissing Cheyakh Ould Ely, the Minister of Communication and Relations with Parliament, who was considered a pan-Arab nationalist. The appointment of Abdellahi Ould Souleimane Ould Cheikh Sidya, reportedly a close relation of Ahmed Ould Daddah, as Minister of Economic and Development Affairs was apparently aimed at attracting supporters of the RDF to the Government, while the appointment of Lembrabott Ould Mohamed Lemine as Minister of Culture and Islamic Affairs was regarded as an attempt to reduce tensions between the Government and Islamic communities. However, at the end of May the publication of a pro-Islamist weekly journal, Ar-Rayah, was suspended, and nine Baathists were convicted by a Nouakchott court of engaging in illegal political activity. In early June four Islamic cultural associations were closed down, and, according to opposition reports, more than 100 alleged Islamists were detained, 36 of whom were charged with plotting against the constitutional order.

The tensions that had been escalating throughout the first half of 2003 culminated in an attempted *coup d'état*, which commenced on 8 June. Exchanges of fire were reported near the presidential palace and at other strategic locations in Nouakchott. According to official reports, 15 people (including six civilians) died in ensuing clashes between the insurgents and the security forces including the Chief of Staff of the Armed Forces, Col Mohamed Lamine Ould Ndiayane, with a further 68 people injured. Government forces regained control of the city on 9 June. Although the exact identity and motives of the rebels were unclear, reports named the leaders of the coup as Saleh Ould Hnana, a former colonel and Baathist sympathizer, who had been expelled from the Mauritanian armed forces in 2002, and Mohammed Ould Sheikhna, a squadron leader in the national air force; Taya subsequently stated, however, that Islamists had been responsible for the rebellion. (Other sources claimed that the attempted coup had been prompted by tribal rivalries.)

In the days following the restoration of order at least 12 alleged rebel leaders were arrested, including Ould Sheikhna, although the whereabouts of Ould Hnana remained unknown. Ould Mansour fled to Senegal before later being granted political asylum in Belgium. Meanwhile, more than 30 detained Islamists, who had been freed during the disorder, were reported to have surrendered themselves to the authorities. In mid-June 2003 several senior officials, including the Chief of Staff of the National Gendarmerie, the President of the High Court of Justice and the Mayor of Nouakchott, were replaced by new appointees regarded as loyal to the President. In July another suspected coup leader, Lt Didi Ould M'Hamed, who had fled to Senegal, was extradited to Mauritania; it was subsequently announced that he would face a civil trial.

In early July 2003 Taya appointed a new Prime Minister: Sghaïr Ould M'Barek, a Harratin, was regarded as a close ally of the President. A new Government was subsequently formed. Although several of the high-ranking officials who had been arrested in mid-June had been released from custody by mid-July, it was reported that the former Prime Minister, Khouna, had been detained after having sought political asylum in Spain. Further arrests of Islamists were reported throughout the month. In early August more than 80 members of the military who had been arrested following the attempted coup were released, although many more remained in detention. At the end of the month Melainine was freed, having been granted a presidential pardon. Some 41 Islamists had also been released from detention by the end of the month, although others continued to face charges. In early September it was announced that some 30 members of the military, including 20 senior officers, were to be tried in connection with the coup attempt.

In October 2003 the Constitutional Council approved the nominations of six candidates, including Taya, Ould Daddah, Ould Boulkheir and former President Ould Haidalla, for the forthcoming presidential election. Ould Haidalla was widely regarded as the most credible challenger to Taya; the former President's campaign attracted the support of several prominent Islamists and secular Arab nationalists, as well as a number of proponents of liberal reform. On 3 November Ould Haidalla's home was raided by police, apparently in response to reports that illicit weapons were being stored at the property. On 5 November police used tear gas to disperse a demonstration in Nouakchott organized by supporters of Ould Haidalla, Ould Daddah and Ould Boulkheir in protest at the raid. On 6 November Ould Haidalla and four of his close associates were detained; the State Prosecutor announced that all five were to be charged with planning a *coup d'état* and endangering national security, although they were released without charge later that day. According to official results of the election, held, as scheduled, on 7 November, Taya won 66.7% of the votes cast, followed by Ould Haidalla, with 18.7%, Ould Daddah, with 6.9%, and Ould Boulkheir, with 5.0%. Some 60.8% of the electorate participated in the election. Opposition candidates accused the Government of perpetrating fraud at the election, which international observers had not been permitted to monitor. On 13 November Taya announced the formation of a new Government, which included eight new appointees, among them Mohamed Vall Ould Bellal as Minister of Foreign Affairs and Co-operation, although most of the other principal posts remained unchanged.

In mid-November 2003 the trial of Ould Haidalla (who had again been arrested on 9 November) and 14 of his supporters, on charges of seeking to obtain power by force and by threatening the strategic interests of Mauritania, commenced. In late December the Government claimed that the Libyan authorities had provided significant financial support for Ould Haidalla's election campaign. The trial concluded at the end of December, when Ould Haidalla and four of his co-defendants, including one of his sons, were convicted of plotting to overthrow the Head of State; they received five-year suspended sentences, during which time they were forbidden to engage in political activity, and were fined the equivalent of US $1,600 each. Four others received lesser sentences and fines. Ould Haidalla's conviction and sentence were upheld on appeal in April 2004.

In January 2004 the Constitutional Council rejected an appeal by Ould Haidalla that the results of the presidential election be annulled. In early April supporters of Ould Haidalla attempted to register a new political party, the Party for Democratic Convergence, with the Ministry of the Interior, Posts and Telecommunications. However, the party's President subsequently announced that the authorities had refused to consider the application on the grounds that the party leadership comprised Islamist radicals, a number of individuals who were being sought by the courts, and others who had recently received suspended prison sentences.

The DSRP won 15 of the 18 seats contested at partial elections to the Senate, held on 9 and 16 April 2004, while its ally, the RDU, secured its first senatorial representation. The opposition Popular Progressive Alliance also obtained legislative representation for the first time, winning two seats. In July Taya effected a major government reshuffle, notably replacing the ministers responsible for finance, economic affairs and trade, following a sharp rise in consumer prices and a decline in the value of the national currency, the ouguiya.

In August 2004 some 31 army officers were arrested after the security forces discovered a plot to overthrow Taya. The Mauritanian authorities accused the Governments of Libya and Burkina Faso of providing assistance to the alleged conspirators, however, both states strongly refuted the allegations. In September, the Government announced that it had averted another attempted *coup d'état*, seizing a large quantity of weapons and making a number of arrests; among those detained was Capt. Abderahmane Ould Mini, who, it was reported, had also participated in the failed *coup d'état* in June 2003, while Ould Hnana and Ould Sheikhna were also sought by the authorities in connection with the alleged conspiracy.

In October 2004 the Government announced that Ould Hnana had been arrested at the town of Rosso on the Senegalese border. In November the trial of more than 190 soldiers and civilians, accused of participation in the attempted *coup d'état* in June 2003 and in subsequent conspiracies to overthrow the Head of State, commenced at an army barracks near Ouad Naga, some 50 km east of Nouakchott. The defendants included the alleged leaders of the group, Ould Hnana, Ould Mini and Ould Sheikhna, the latter being one of 19 people tried *in absentia* (also among this number was Sidi Mohamed Mustapha Ould Limam Chavi, an advisor to Burkinabè President Blaise Compaoré); the civilians on trial, meanwhile, included opposition leaders Ould Haidalla, Ould Daddah and Cheikh Ould Horma. The prosecution alleged that the army officers, who had reportedly organized themselves into a grouping called the Knights of Change following the failed *coup d'état* in June 2003, had received funding from the Islamist opposition and had been granted refuge in Burkina Faso, while also receiving funding and equipment from that country and Libya. However, Ould Hnana denied that Burkina Faso, Libya and the accused opposition politicians had provided assistance to the conspirators but pleaded guilty to the charge of conspiring to overthrow President Taya, stating that he had acted in response to the 'tribalism, clientism, discrimination against black Mauritanians and economic mismanagement' of the incumbent regime. Ould Mini also admitted conspiring to overthrow the President; the remaining accused military personnel entered pleas of not guilty. In February 2005 Ould Hnana, Ould Mini, Ould Sheikhna and a fourth officer, Capt. Mohammed Ould Salek, were sentenced to life imprisonment with hard labour, while 79 others received lesser jail sentences; Ould Haidalla, Ould Daddah and Ould Horma were among the 111 acquitted. Following his release, Ould Daddah urged the Government to initiate dialogue with the opposition. In mid-February the three Islamist leaders arrested in November were released pending trial, shortly after two of them commenced a hunger strike in protest against their continued detention.

Taya effected a government reshuffle in March 2005, notably creating a new Ministry of Petroleum and Energy, headed by Zeidane Ould H'Maeyda, hitherto Minister of Mines and Industry. Other changes included the appointment of Lemrabott Sidi Mahmoud Ould Cheikh Ahmed as Minister of the Interior, Posts and Telecommunications. One day earlier it had emerged that, in an attempt to combat high-level corruption, the salaries of government ministers had been increased more than six-fold.

In April 2005 police arrested some 20 prominent Islamists on charges of preparing acts of terrorism. At the same time the Government announced that seven Mauritanians had recently been intercepted on their return from Algeria, where they had allegedly received military training from the radical Islamist militant group, the Groupe salafiste pour la prédication et le combat (GSPC). The seven men were reportedly charged with establishing a criminal association in May. Security was increased ahead of the visit of the Israeli Deputy Prime Minister and Minister of Foreign Affairs, Silvan Shalom to Nouakchott in May, during which tear gas was used to disperse protesters. In that month several people were arrested during police raids on mosques in Nouakchott. The Government stated that weapons, in addition to plans to carry out acts of subversion and terrorism, had been discovered in the mosques. At the end of the month 40 Islamists appeared in court, variously charged with membership of an unauthorized group and fomenting unrest; 14 others were released without charge.

In June 2005 some 15 soldiers were killed, and a further 17 injured, in an attack by some 150 assailants on a military post in north-eastern Mauritania, for which the GSPC subsequently claimed responsibility. Later in June it was reported that the existence of a radical Islamist group based in Mauritania with links to the GSPC, the Mauritanian Group for Preaching and Jihad, had been uncovered, as had details of proposed targets of attack in the country. At the end of the month the Senate adopted legislation aimed at countering terrorism and money-laundering.

On 3 August 2005, while President Taya was absent from Mauritania, attending the funeral of the late King Fahd ibn Abd al-Aziz as-Sa'ud of Saudi Arabia, a group of army officers seized control of state broadcasting services and the presidential palace in a bloodless *coup d'état*. A 16-member Military Council for Justice and Democracy (MCJD) under the leadership of Col Ely Ould Mohamed Vall, hitherto the Director of National Security, who had hitherto been regarded as a close ally of Taya, announced that it had assumed power. The Council stated that it would preside over the country for a transitional period of up to two years, at the end of which democratic elections, in which members of the MCJD and the Government would be prohibited from participating, would be held; although the National Assembly elected in 2001 was dissolved, the 1991 Constitution and most of its institutions (including the Constitutional Council and judicial bodies) were to be retained, as supplemented and amended by the charter of the MCJD. Taya was prevented from re-entering the country and was flown initially to Niamey, Niger; he subsequently took up residence in The Gambia.

On 7 August 2005 Vall appointed Sidi Mohamed Ould Boubacar, hitherto Ambassador to France, as Prime Minister, a position that he had previously held in 1992–96; a new, civilian, government was named on 10 August, and Vall announced the intention of holding a constitutional referendum within the period of one year. None of the ministers in the outgoing Government were re-appointed, although, notably, Ahmed Ould Sid'Ahmed, who, in his former capacity as Minister of Foreign Affairs and Co-operation, had been largely responsible for Mauritania's rapprochement with Israel in 1999, was re-appointed to that position. In the immediate aftermath of the coup, which was initially widely condemned internationally, the AU announced the immediate suspension of Mauritania's membership. However, the overthrow of Taya's regime was reported to have widespread domestic support. In mid-August a delegation from the AU met members of the MCJD, subsequently announcing the willingness of the Union to co-operate with the new leadership of Mauritania, although the country was to remain suspended from the organization pending democratic elections, in accordance with the Constitutive Act of the AU.

In early September 2005 the new administration announced that it was to offer a general amnesty for political prisoners; 32 such detainees, principally from among those imprisoned in February 2005 for their role in attempted *coups d'état* in 2003 and 2004, were among the first to benefit from the amnesty. However, some Islamist detainees were not freed, prompting 19 such prisoners to commence a hunger strike demanding their release later in September. In mid-October, moreover, the authorities refused to recognize a recently formed Islamist political party, the Party for Democratic Convergence, on the grounds that its programme violated Mauritanian law. Indeed, Ould Vall announced that no Islamist party would be legalized. Meanwhile, Vall dismissed all 13 regional governors appointed by Taya. Later in the month the CMJD announced a schedule for the transition to democratic rule: firstly, a referendum on certain provisions of the 1991 Constitution (principally concerned with the duration and renewability of the presidential mandate) was to be held in June 2006, to be followed in October by municipal elections. Elections to the National Assembly were to be scheduled for April 2007, for the Senate one month later, with Presidential elections to be held in June, marking the end of the transitional period. The CMJD announced its intention of consulting widely with the Government, political actors and civil society concerning the schedule, and emphasized that these dates were provisional and subject to change. (By the end of 2005, the proposed date of the Presidential election had been brought forward to March 2007, and that of elections to the National Assembly to November 2006.) In late November 2005 a 15-member National Independent Electoral Commission was inaugurated. In late 2005 reformist elements of the DSRP joined with the leadership of the Knights of Change movement to form a new political party, the Party for Reconstruction and Rebirth. In January 2006 Ould Hnana and Ould Mini were appointed as the party's President and Secretary-General, respectively.

A long-standing border dispute with Senegal was exacerbated by the deaths, in April 1989, of two Senegalese farmers, who had been involved in a dispute regarding grazing rights with Mauritanian livestock-breeders. Mauritanian nationals resident in Senegal were attacked, and their businesses (primarily those of the retail trade) looted, while Senegalese nationals in Mauritania and black Mauritanians suffered similar aggression. By early May it was believed that several hundred people, mostly Senegalese, had been killed. Operations to repatriate nationals of both countries commenced, with international assistance. Amid allegations that the Mauritanian authorities had begun to instigate expulsions of the indigenous black population to Senegal or to Mali, a prominent human rights organization, Amnesty International, expressed concern at the reported violation of black Mauritanians' rights. Mauritania and Senegal suspended diplomatic relations in August 1989, and sporadic outbreaks of violence were reported later that year. In late 1990 the Senegalese Government denied accusations made by the Mauritanian authorities that it was implicated in an alleged attempt to overthrow Taya. In December the arrests of large numbers of black Mauritanians were reported. In early 1991 Mauritanian naval vessels were reported to have opened fire on Senegalese fishing boats, apparently in Senegal's territorial waters; in March several deaths were reported to have resulted from a military engagement on Senegalese territory, following an incursion by Senegalese troops into Mauritania.

Following renewed diplomatic activity, diplomatic relations with Senegal were resumed in April 1992, and the process of reopening the border began in May. However, Mauritanian refugees in Senegal insisted that, as long as the Taya Government refused to recognize their national identity (*mauritanité*) and land and property rights, they would not return to Mauritania. In June 2000 relations between Mauritania and Senegal deteriorated after Mauritania accused the new Senegalese administration of relaunching an irrigation project, which involved the use of joint waters from the Senegal river, in contravention of the Organisation pour la mise en valeur du fleuve Sénégal project (see p. 387). The dispute escalated when the Mauritanian authorities requested that all of its citizens living in Senegal return home and issued the estimated 100,000 Senegalese nationals living in Mauritania with a 15-day deadline by which to leave the country. In mid-June, following mediation by King Muhammad VI of Morocco and the Presidents of The Gambia and Mali, the Mauritanian Minister of the Interior announced that the decision to expel Senegalese citizens had been withdrawn and that Mauritanians living in Senegal could remain there. President Abdoulaye Wade of Senegal visited Mauritania later that month and announced that the irrigation project had been abandoned. By late 2000 the number of Mauritanian refugees in Senegal had declined to 19,800 (compared with 65,500 in mid-1995). In April 2001 President Taya's presence as guest of honour at a ceremony in Dakar to commemorate the 41st anniversary of the independence of Senegal demonstrated an improvement in relations between the countries. At the end of 2004 some 19,778 Mauritanian refugees still remained in Senegal, according to provisional figures.

Meanwhile, in April 1994 Mauritania, Mali and Senegal agreed to strengthen military co-operation in order to improve joint border security. In mid-1996, at the conclusion of a meeting in Nouakchott of their ministers responsible for the interior, the three countries established joint security measures on their common borders. In August 1999 representatives of the Malian, Senegalese and Mauritanian Governments signed an agreement, which provided for the establishment of a special operational unit drawn from the police forces of the three countries to combat border crime. In January 2005 the Presidents of Mali and Mauritania signed an agreement on military co-operation intended to strengthen border security. In response to a request from the Mauritanian authorities following an attack on the military post at Lemgheity, in north-eastern Mauritania (see above), Mali dispatched troops to the common border in June. Meanwhile, both countries joined seven other North and West African countries in participating in US-led military exercises aimed at increasing co-operation in combating cross-border banditry and terrorism in the region. In July the army chiefs of Mauritania, Mali, Niger and Algeria discussed security issues with a US military delegation at a meeting in Nouakchott.

Diplomatic relations between Mauritania and Morocco were severed in 1981, following accusations, denied by both countries, of involvement in mutual destabilization attempts. In 1983 Mauritania sought to improve relations between the Maghreb countries (Algeria, Morocco, Mauritania, Tunisia and Libya) and was a signatory of the Maghreb Fraternity and Co-operation Treaty, drafted by Algeria and Tunisia. Relations with Morocco again deteriorated from February 1984, when Mauritania announced its recognition of the Sahrawi Arab Democratic Republic (the Western Saharan state proclaimed by Polisario in 1976), although Taya restored diplomatic relations with Morocco in April 1985. In February 1989 Mauritania was a founder member, with Algeria, Libya, Morocco and Tunisia, of the Union of the Arab Maghreb (UMA, see p. 388), although relations with Libya were reported to have deteriorated from the mid-1990s; Libya was a particularly vehement critic of Mauritania's decision to establish and maintain full diplomatic relations with Israel. Diplomatic relations with Libya, severed in 1995, were none the less restored in 1997. In September 2001 King Muhammad VI of Morocco paid a three-day official visit to Mauritania, aimed at improving bilateral relations between the two countries. In March 2004 President Taya led an official delegation to Morocco, and again met with King Muhammad. King Muhammad returned to Mauritania in March 2005 as part of a tour of West Africa. There was speculation that, during his visits to both Mauritania and Burkina Faso, the King had attempted to mediate informally between the two countries' Presidents (whose relations remained strained following Mauritania's accusation that Burkina Faso and Libya had supported an attempt to overthrow Taya), but without apparent success.

Relations with both Libya and Burkina Faso were severely strained in the wake of allegations by the Mauritanian Government that those two countries had provided support to rebel elements in the Mauritanian military, accused of participating in the failed *coup d'état* of June 2003 and of subsequently conspiring to overthrow President Taya (see above). It was alleged that Ould Hnana and Ould Sheikhna, who were held responsible by the Mauritanian authorities of leading the 2003 *coup d'état*, had been granted refuge in Burkina Faso and received weapons, money and training, while the Libyan Government was accused of supplying the rebels with weapons, vehicles and other equipment. Libya and Burkina Faso, meanwhile, strenuously denied the accusations. In March 2005 a ministerial commission appointed by the UMA to investigate the Mauritanian allegations against Libya concluded that the Libyan Revolutionary Leader Col Muammar al-Qaddafi had 'no connection' to the events in Mauritania, which it described as a 'purely Mauritanian affair'.

In November 1995 Mauritania signed an agreement to recognize and establish relations with Israel. In October 1998 Mauritania's Minister of Foreign Affairs and Co-operation visited Israel, where he held talks with the Prime Minister, Binyamin Netanyahu. The Arab League strongly criticized the visit, claiming that it contravened the League's resolutions on the suspension of the normalization of relations with Israel, and threatened to impose sanctions on Mauritania. Widespread controversy was provoked both domestically, and in Arab countries, by the establishment of full diplomatic relations between Mauritania and Israel in October 1999. (Of Arab countries, only Egypt and Jordan had taken such a step, under the terms of their respective peace treaties with Israel.) Following the resumption of the Palestinian uprising in September 2000, the Mauritanian Government came under renewed pressure to suspend diplomatic relations with Israel. A visit by the Mauritanian Minister of Foreign Affairs and Co-operation, Dah Ould Abdi, to Israel in May 2001, when he met Israeli Prime Minister Ariel Sharon and President Moshe Katsav, and entered into negotiations with the Minister of Foreign Affairs, Shimon Peres, provoked further controversy, particularly as a result of an appeal by the Arab League, issued earlier that month, for all member countries to cease political contacts with Israel. A further meeting between Peres, Taya and Ould Abdi, in Nouakchott, in October 2002, provoked further controversy. A visit to Mauritania by the Israeli Deputy Prime Minister and Minister of Foreign Affairs, Silvan Shalom, in early May 2005 was preceded, and followed, by the detention of several Islamists (see above), although the Government denied that the arrests were linked to Shalom's presence. His visit was accompanied by a number of anti-Israeli protests in Nouakchott. Although some concern was initially expressed, following the *coup d'état* of August 2005, that diplomatic relations between the two countries might be terminated, the appointment, later in the month, of Ahmed Ould Sid'Ahmed as Minister of Foreign Affairs and Co-operation (who had held that position when Mauritania re-established full diplomatic relations with Israel in 1999) appeared to indicate that the new regime intended to maintain amicable relations with Israel.

Despite widespread public opposition to the US-led military campaign against Iraq, which intensified in March 2003, the authorities in Nouakchott refused to support the regime of Saddam Hussain (which Mauritania had, however, expressed support for during the conflict in the region of the Persian—Arabian Gulf in 1990–91).

Mauritania withdrew from the Economic Community of West African States (see p. 217), with effect from 31 December 2000, owing to decisions adopted by the organization at its summit in December 1999, including the integration of the armed forces of member states and the removal of internal border controls and tariffs.

Government

The Constitution that was approved in a national referendum on 12 July 1991 vests executive power in the President of the Republic (who is elected by universal adult suffrage for a period of six years). The bicameral legislature comprises an 81-member National Assembly (elected by universal suffrage for five years, with 20% of its membership being elected by a form of proportional representation, with effect from the elections held in October 2001) and a 56-member Senate (elected by municipal leaders with a six-year mandate—part of its membership being elected every two years). All elections are conducted in the context of a multi-party political system. The President of the Republic is empowered to appoint a Prime Minister, who is designated Head of Government. Following the *coup d'état* of 3 August 2005, a 16-member Military Council for Justice and Democracy (MCJD) assumed power. The Council stated that it

MAURITANIA

would preside over the country for a transitional period of up to two years, following which democratic elections would be held. The 1991 Constitution and most of its institutions, including judicial bodies, and the Constitutional Council, were to be retained, as supplemented and amended by the charter of the MCJD, although the existing legislative organs were dissolved. The MCJD announced the intention of holding a referendum on various aspects of the 1991 Constitution (in particular those relating to the Presidency), prior to municipal, legislative and presidential elections.

For the purpose of local administration, Mauritania is divided into 13 wilayat (regions), comprising a total of 53 moughataa (counties), which are subdivided into 216 communes (districts).

Defence

In August 2005 the total armed forces were estimated to number 15,870 men: army 15,000, navy 620, air force 250. Full-time membership of paramilitary forces totalled about 5,000. Military service is by authorized conscription, and lasts for two years. The defence budget for 2005 was estimated at UM 5,400m.

Economic Affairs

In 2004, according to estimates by the World Bank, Mauritania's gross national income (GNI), measured at average 2002–04 prices, was US $1,210.3m., equivalent to $420 per head (or $2,050 on an international purchasing-power parity basis). During 1995–2004, it was estimated, the population increased at an average annual rate of 2.6%, while gross domestic product (GDP) per head increased, in real terms, by an average of 1.9% per year. According to the World Bank, overall GDP increased, in real terms, at an average annual rate of 4.6% in 1995–2004; GDP increased by 6.6% in 2004.

Agriculture (including forestry and fishing) contributed 19.1% of GDP in 2004. In 2003 about 52.1% of the labour force were employed in the sector. Owing to the unsuitability of much of the land for crop cultivation, output of staple foods (millet, sorghum, rice and pulses) is insufficient for the country's needs. Livestock-rearing is the principal occupation of the rural population. Fishing, which in 2002 provided 43.4% of export earnings, supplies 5%–10% of annual GDP and up to 30% of budgetary revenue, and also makes a significant contribution to domestic food requirements. During 1995–2004, according to the World Bank, agricultural GDP increased by an average of 1.5% per year. Agricultural GDP increased by 3.7% in 2004.

Industry (including mining, manufacturing, construction and power) provided 30.1% of GDP in 2004. An estimated 11.6% of the labour force were employed in the industrial sector in 1994. During 1995–2001, according to the World Bank, industrial GDP increased at an average annual rate of 0.4%. Industrial GDP increased by 1.1% in 2001.

Mining contributed 12.2% of GDP in 2002. The principal activity in this sector is the extraction of iron ore, exports of which contributed 55.6% of total merchandise export earnings in 2002. Gypsum, salt, gold and copper are also mined. Other exploitable mineral resources include diamonds, phosphates, sulphur, peat, manganese and uranium. In October 1999 highly valuable blue granite deposits were discovered in the north of the country. Many international companies were involved in offshore petroleum exploration in Mauritania in the early 2000s, with reserves at the offshore Shafr el Khanjar and Chinguetti fields estimated at 450m.–1,000m. barrels; production commenced at Chinguetti in February 2006. In September 2000 a five-year programme intended to accelerate the growth of the mining sector commenced, with a US $16.5m. loan from the World Bank. The GDP of the mining sector declined by an average of 4.3% per year in 1998–2002, according to the IMF. Mining GDP declined by 9.2% in 2001 and by 7.3% in 2002.

The manufacturing sector contributed 8.7% of GDP in 2004. Fish processing (which contributed 3.9% of GDP in 2002) is the most important activity. The processing of minerals (including imported petroleum) is also of some significance. According to the World Bank, manufacturing GDP declined at an average annual rate of 1.9% in 1995–2001; however, it increased by 5.9% in 2001.

Mauritania began to utilize electricity generated at hydroelectric installations constructed under the auspices of the Organisation pour la mise en valeur du fleuve Sénégal (OMVS) in late 2002, thus reducing the country's dependence on power generated at thermal stations. Imports of petroleum products comprised 8.8% of the value of merchandise imports in 2001.

The services sector contributed 50.8% of GDP in 2004, and engaged an estimated 25.8% of the labour force in 1994. According to the World Bank, the combined GDP of the services sector increased by an average rate of 7.7% per year during 1995–2001. Services GDP increased by 7.4% in 2001.

In 2002 Mauritania recorded a visible trade deficit of an estimated US $87.7m. and a deficit of an estimated $51.2m. on the current account of the balance of payments. In 2002 the principal source of imports (20.8%) was France; other major suppliers were the Belgo-Luxembourg Economic Union, Spain and Germany. The principal markets for exports in that year were Italy (14.8%), France (14.4%), Spain and the Belgo-Luxembourg Economic Union. The principal exports in 2002 were iron ore and fish, crustaceans and molluscs. The principal imports in that year were petroleum products.

Mauritania's overall budget surplus for 2002 was UM 20,900m., equivalent to 7.8% of GDP. Mauritania's total external debt was US $2,360m. at the end of 2003, of which $2,084m. was long-term public debt. In 1998 the cost of debt-servicing was equivalent to 27.7% of the value of exports of goods and services. The annual rate of inflation averaged 5.7% in 1990–2002; consumer prices increased by an average of 5.1% in 2003. The overall rate of unemployment in 2000 was 28.9%.

Mauritania is a member of the Islamic Development Bank (see p. 303), of the OMVS (see p. 387) and of the Union of the Arab Maghreb (see p. 388).

Mauritania has undertaken a series of economic adjustment programmes since the late 1980s. In July 1999 the IMF approved a three-year loan worth US $56.5m. under its Enhanced Structural Adjustment Facility (ESAF) to support the Government's 1999–2002 economic programme, and in June 2002 Mauritania became the sixth country to reach 'completion point' under the joint IMF/World Bank initiative for heavily indebted poor countries, which would amount to a reduction of Mauritania's debt by $622m. In July 2003 a further arrangement, worth some $8.8m., was agreed with the IMF for 2003–05, under the Poverty Reduction and Growth Facility (PRGF—the successor of the ESAF). A substantial reorganization and simplification of the taxation system was implemented in 2003, although the proposed transfer of the state electricity company to the private sector was suspended in mid-2004, owing to a global recession in the electricity sector. However, the PRGF arrangement was cancelled in November 2004, after it had emerged that the Mauritanian authorities had supplied incorrect information to the IMF, in particular failing to report substantial extrabudgetary spending. The exploitation, from the mid-2000s, of previously untapped petroleum reserves, principally at offshore locations, was expected to have a significant impact on Mauritania's export revenues, hitherto largely dependent on fishing and on the extraction of iron ore. The first major offshore field, at Chinguetti began production, operated by Woodside Petroleum (of Australia) at a rate of around 75,000 barrels per day (b/d) in February 2006; it was estimated that output could reach 165,000 b/d by 2009, while revenue from petroleum exports was predicted to increase the Mauritanian Government's overall income by an estimated 25% by 2008. In recent years government revenue has also been bolstered by the sale of fishing licences to foreign fleets. In 2001 the European Union (EU) renewed its fishing agreement with Mauritania. In return for increased financial aid (of some €430m. during 2001–06), EU vessels were granted improved fishing rights in Mauritania's waters. The services sector showed strong growth in the early 2000s, and a series of road-building projects undertaken from 2002, most notably the completion in 2004 of a road linking the administrative capital, Nouakchott, with the chief commercial port, Nouadhibou, was expected to contribute to the continuing expansion of the services sector, particularly with regard to external trade and the underdeveloped tourism industry. The agricultural sector, meanwhile, already negatively affected by a drought in late 2002, was severely damaged by the swarms of locusts that affected the Sahel region from mid-2004. The swarms impacted heavily upon the agricultural southern regions of Mauritania; in January 2005 the United Nations World Food Programme appealed for $31m. to assist in providing food to 400,000 victims of drought and locust damage in southern Mauritania over three years. The bloodless *coup d'état* of August 2005 and the subsequent installation of a transitional Government was not expected to have any substantial detrimental impact on the Mauritanian economy, the future development of which was expected to depend on the successful exploitation of revenue from petroleum exports and the continued expansion of the country's production base and services sector.

MAURITANIA

Education

Primary education, which is officially compulsory, begins at six years of age and lasts for six years. In 2000/01 total enrolment at primary schools included 64% of children in the relevant age-group (66% of boys; 62% of girls), according to UNESCO estimates. Secondary education begins at 12 years of age and lasts for six years, comprising two cycles of three years each. Total enrolment at public secondary schools in 2000/01 included only 14% of children in the appropriate age-group (16% of boys; 13% of girls), according to UNESCO estimates. In 1998/99 a total of 12,912 students were enrolled at Mauritania's four higher education institutions (including the Université de Nouakchott, which was opened in 1983). In 2001 a UN project was initiated to address sexual inequality in the Mauritanian education system, which was particularly evident at higher education institutions, where only 16.6% of students were female in 1998. Total expenditure on education in 1998 was UM 6,197.8m. (equivalent to 27.5% of total government expenditure). In 1999 total expenditure on education amounted to UM 6,557.6m.

Public Holidays

2006: 1 January (New Year's Day), 10 January*† (Tabaski—Id al-Adha, Feast of the Sacrifice), 31 January* (Islamic New Year), 10 April* (Mouloud, Birth of Muhammad), 1 May (Labour Day), 25 May (African Liberation Day, anniversary of the OAU's foundation), 10 July (Armed Forces Day), 21 August* (Leilat al-Meiraj, Ascension of Muhammad), 23 October* (Korité—Id al-Fitr, end of Ramadan), 28 November (Independence Day), 31 December*† (Tabaski—Id al-Adha, Feast of the Sacrifice).

2007: 1 January (New Year's Day), 20 January* (Islamic New Year), 31 March* (Mouloud, Birth of Muhammad), 1 May (Labour Day), 25 May (African Liberation Day, anniversary of the OAU's foundation), 10 July (Armed Forces Day), 10 August* (Leilat al-Meiraj, Ascension of Muhammad), 13 October* (Korité—Id al-Fitr, end of Ramadan), 28 November (Independence Day), 20 December* (Tabaski—Id al-Adha, Feast of the Sacrifice).

* These holidays are determined by the Islamic lunar calendar and may vary by one or two days from the dates given.

† This festival occurs twice (in the Islamic years AH 1426 and 1427) within the same Gregorian year.

Weights and Measures

The metric system is in force.

Statistical Survey

Source (unless otherwise stated): Office National de la Statistique, BP 240, Nouakchott; tel. 525-28-80; fax 525-51-70; e-mail webmaster@ons.mr; internet www.ons.mr.

Area and Population

AREA, POPULATION AND DENSITY

Area (sq km)	1,030,700*
Population (census results)	
5–20 April 1988	1,864,236†
1–15 November 2000‡	
Males	1,241,712
Females	1,266,447
Total	2,508,159
Population (UN estimates at mid-year)§	
2002	2,807,000
2003	2,893,000
2004	2,980,000
Density (per sq km) at mid-2004	2.9

* 397,950 sq miles.
† Including an estimate of 224,095 for the nomad population.
‡ Figures include nomads, totalling 128,163 (males 66,007, females 62,156), enumerated during 10 March–20 April 2001.
§ Source: UN, *World Population Prospects: The 2004 Revision*.

Ethnic Groups (percentage of total, 1995): Moor 81.5; Wolof 6.8; Toucouleur 5.3; Sarakholé 2.8; Peul 1.1; Others 2.5 (Source: La Francophonie).

REGIONS
(census of November 2000)

Region	Area ('000 sq km)	Population*	Chief town
Hodh Ech Chargui	183	281,600	Néma
Hodh el Gharbi	53	212,156	Aïoun el Atrous
Assaba	37	242,265	Kiffa
Gorgol	14	242,711	Kaédi
Brakna	33	247,006	Aleg
Trarza	68	268,220	Rosso
Adrar	215	69,542	Atâr
Dakhlet-Nouadhibou	22	79,516	Nouadhibou
Tagant	95	76,620	Tidjikja
Guidimagha	10	177,707	Sélibaby
Tiris Zemmour	253	41,121	Zouïrât
Inchiri	47	11,500	Akjoujt
Nouakchott (district)	1	558,195	Nouakchott
Total	**1,030**	**2,580,159**	

* Including nomad population, enumerated during 10 March–20 April 2001.

PRINCIPAL TOWNS
(population at census of 2000*)

Nouakchott (capital)	588,195	Kiffa	32,716
Nouadhibou	72,337	Bougadoum	29,045
Rosso	48,922	Atâr	24,021
Boghé	37,531	Boutilimit	22,257
Adel Bagrou	36,007	Theiekane	22,041
Kaédi	34,227	Ghabou	21,700
Zouïrât	33,929	Mal	20,488

* With the exception of Nouakchott, figures refer to the population of communes (municipalities), and include nomads.

BIRTHS AND DEATHS
(UN estimates, annual averages)

	1990–95	1995–2000	2000–05
Birth rate (per 1,000)	42.4	42.6	41.8
Death rate (per 1,000)	16.2	15.5	14.2

Source: UN, *World Population Prospects: The 2004 Revision*.

Expectation of life (WHO estimates, years at birth): 51 (males 48; females 53) in 2003 (Source: WHO, *World Health Report*).

ECONOMICALLY ACTIVE POPULATION
(census of 2000, persons aged 10 years and over, including nomads)

	Males	Females	Total
Agriculture, hunting, forestry and fishing	219,771	94,535	314,306
Mining and quarrying	5,520	249	5,769
Manufacturing	18,301	11,855	30,156
Electricity, gas and water	2,655	182	2,837
Construction	15,251	311	15,562
Trade, restaurants and hotels	83,733	24,799	108,532
Transport, storage and communications	17,225	691	17,916
Financing, insurance, real estate and business services	1,557	454	2,011
Community, social and personal services	72,137	26,583	98,720
Other and unspecified	33,350	22,608	55,958
Total	**469,500**	**182,267**	**651,767**

Mid-2003 ('000 persons, estimates): Agriculture, etc. 673; Total labour force 1,291 (Source: FAO).

MAURITANIA

Health and Welfare

KEY INDICATORS

Total fertility rate (children per woman, 2003)	5.8
Under-5 mortality rate (per 1,000 live births, 2004)	125
HIV/AIDS (% of persons aged 15–49, 2003)	0.6
Physicians (per 1,000 head, 1995)	0.14
Hospital beds (per 1,000 head, 1990)	0.67
Health expenditure (2002): US $ per head (PPP)	54
Health expenditure (2002): % of GDP	3.9
Health expenditure (2002): public (% of total)	74.2
Access to water (% of persons, 2002)	56
Access to sanitation (% of persons, 2002)	42
Human Development Index (2003): ranking	152
Human Development Index (2003): value	0.477

For sources and definitions, see explanatory note on p. vi.

Agriculture

PRINCIPAL CROPS
('000 metric tons)

	2002	2003*	2004*
Rice (paddy)	77.4	77.0	77.0
Maize	4.8	6.0	6.0
Sorghum	28.7	68.0	68.0
Roots and tubers	6.5*	6.7	6.7
Peas, dry	10*	10	10
Cow peas	7.3	7.5	7.5
Beans, dry	10.0	10.0	10.0
Other pulses	17*	17	17
Vegetables	3.9*	3.9	3.9
Dates	24	24	24
Other fruit	3.3*	3.3	3.4

* FAO estimate(s).

Source: FAO.

LIVESTOCK
('000 head, year ending September)

	2002	2003*	2004*
Cattle	1,564	1,600	1,600
Goats	5,555	5,600	5,600
Sheep	8,774	8,800	8,850
Asses	158*	158	158
Horses	20*	20	20
Camels	1,297	1,300	1,300
Chickens	4,200*	4,200	4,200

* FAO estimate(s).

Source: FAO.

LIVESTOCK PRODUCTS
(FAO estimates, '000 metric tons)

	2002	2003	2004
Beef and veal	22.0	23.0	23.0
Mutton and lamb	24.0	24.0	24.8
Goat meat	13.7	13.8	13.8
Camel meat	22.0	22.0	22.0
Chicken meat	4.2	4.3	4.3
Camel milk	21.5	22.0	22.0
Cows' milk	120.4	120.8	120.8
Sheep's milk	96.0	96.0	96.0
Goats' milk	110.4	109.8	109.8
Cheese	2.2	2.2	2.2
Hen eggs	5.3	5.3	5.3
Cattle hides	3.3	3.4	3.4
Sheepskins	3.2	3.2	3.3
Goatskins	1.6	1.7	1.7

Source: FAO.

Forestry

ROUNDWOOD REMOVALS
(FAO estimates, '000 cubic metres, excl. bark)

	2002	2003	2004
Sawlogs, veneer logs and logs for sleepers	1	1	1
Other industrial wood	5	5	5
Fuel wood	1,502	1,541	1,581
Total	1,508	1,547	1,587

Source: FAO.

Fishing

(FAO estimates, '000 metric tons, live weight)

	2001	2002	2003
Freshwater fishes	5.0	5.0	5.0
Sardinellas	4.0	4.0	4.0
Cuttlefishes and bobtail squids	5.0	2.3	2.5
Other squids	2.2	1.2	1.2
Octopuses	13.6	12.2	12.2
Total catch (incl. others)	84.9	78.9	80.0

Source: FAO.

Mining

('000 metric tons)

	2001	2002	2003
Gypsum*	100	100	100
Iron ore: gross weight	10,302	9,553	10,600
Iron ore: metal content	6,700	6,200	6,890
Salt*	5.5	5.5	5.5

* Estimated production.

Source: US Geological Survey.

Industry

SELECTED PRODUCTS
('000 metric tons, unless otherwise indicated)

	1999	2000	2001
Frozen fish*	23.2	24.2	26.2
Salted, dried and smoked fish*	0.9	1.0	0.9
Electric energy (million kWh)	156	163	165

* Data from FAO.

Source: UN, *Industrial Commodity Statistics Yearbook*.

2002: Frozen fish ('000 metric tons): 20.1 (data from FAO).

MAURITANIA

Finance

CURRENCY AND EXCHANGE RATES

Monetary Units
5 khoums = 1 ouguiya (UM).

Sterling, Dollar and Euro Equivalents (30 April 2004)
£1 sterling = 476.46 ouguiyas;
US $1 = 268.70 ouguiyas;
€1 = 321.02 ouguiyas;
1,000 ouguiyas = £2.10 = $3.72 = €3.12..

Average Exchange Rate (ouguiyas per US $)
2001 255.629
2002 271.739
2003 263.030

BUDGET
('000 million ouguiyas)

Revenue*	2000	2001	2002
Budgetary revenue	57.9	51.8	101.1
Tax revenue	33.3	36.4	38.7
Taxes on income and profits	10.6	11.3	12.1
Taxes on goods and services	16.5	18.2	19.5
Value-added tax	7.8	9.3	10.4
Turnover taxes	4.8	4.3	4.3
Tax on petroleum products	2.1	2.6	2.6
Taxes on international trade	5.5	6.1	6.3
Other current revenue	23.0	13.0	62.5
Fishing royalties and penalties	16.4	5.3	51.8
Revenue from public enterprises	4.1	3.6	4.9
Capital revenue	1.6	2.4	2.3
Special accounts	0.1	0.0	0.0
Statistical discrepancy	—	—	-2.4
Total	58.0	51.8	101.1

Expenditure	2000	2001	2002
Current expenditure	39.4	42.6	52.4
Wages and salaries	11.0	12.2	13.0
Goods and services	13.0	14.3	21.6
Transfers and subsidies	3.9	4.4	4.6
Military expenditure	4.2	4.4	4.9
Interest on public debt	7.4	7.2	8.3
Capital expenditure and net lending	28.7	23.1	32.0
Fixed capital formation	16.9	20.5	29.0
Restructuring and net lending	11.8	2.6	2.9
Total	68.1	65.6	84.4

* Excluding grants received ('000 million ouguiyas): 2.7 in 2000; 4.0 in 2001; 4.2 in 2002.

Source: IMF, *Islamic Republic of Mauritania: Statistical Appendix* (October 2003).

INTERNATIONAL RESERVES
(US $ million at 31 December)

	2001	2002	2003
Gold*	3.1	3.1	4.0
IMF special drawing rights	0.2	0.2	0.1
Foreign exchange	284.3	396.0	415.2
Total	287.6	399.3	419.3

* Valued at market-related prices.

Source: IMF, *International Financial Statistics*.

MONEY SUPPLY
(million ouguiyas at 31 December)

	2001	2002	2003
Currency outside banks	6,688	6,282	6,412
Demand deposits at deposit money banks	21,033	22,628	25,790
Total money (incl. others)	27,721	28,910	32,202

Source: IMF, *International Financial Statistics*.

COST OF LIVING
(Consumer Price Index in Nouakchott; base: July 1985 = 100)

	2000	2001	2002
Food (incl. beverages)	271.1	288.8	301.6
Clothing (incl. footwear)	220.1	225.0	226.4
Rent	262.5	271.0	285.1
All items (incl. others)	254.0	265.9	276.4

Source: IMF, *Islamic Republic of Mauritania: Statistical Appendix* (October 2003).

NATIONAL ACCOUNTS

Expenditure on the Gross Domestic Product
(million ouguiyas at current prices)

	2000	2001	2002
Government final consumption expenditure	38,696	38,408	49,674
Private final consumption expenditure*	151,605	178,611	206,890
Increase in stocks / Gross fixed capital formation	73,616	86,766	88,899
Total domestic expenditure	263,917	303,785	345,463
Exports of goods and services	90,945	96,967	103,684
Less Imports of goods and services	125,423	149,434	180,091
GDP in purchasers' values	229,439	251,318	269,056
GDP at constant 1985 prices	89,350	92,930	96,031

* Including public enterprises.

Source: IMF, *Islamic Republic of Mauritania: Statistical Appendix* (October 2003).

Gross Domestic Product by Economic Activity
(million ouguiyas at current prices)

	2000	2001	2002
Agriculture, hunting, forestry and fishing	45,536	47,188	50,436
Mining and quarrying	31,224	31,741	29,521
Manufacturing	19,018	21,121	21,491
Electricity, gas and water / Construction	14,343	17,242	20,253
Trade, restaurants and hotels	41,030	44,512	47,965
Transport and communications	20,786	25,508	29,233
Public administration	23,371	26,378	29,465
Other services	12,150	13,175	14,340
GDP at factor cost	207,458	226,865	242,703
Indirect taxes, *less* subsidies	21,981	24,453	26,353
GDP in purchasers' values	229,439	251,318	269,056

Source: IMF, *Islamic Republic of Mauritania: Statistical Appendix* (October 2003).

BALANCE OF PAYMENTS
(US $ million)

	2000	2001	2002*
Exports of goods f.o.b.	344.7	338.6	330.3
Imports of goods f.o.b.	-336.2	-372.3	-418.0
Trade balance	8.5	-33.7	-87.7
Services (net)	-133.3	-194.4	-59.0
Balance on goods and services	-124.8	-228.1	-146.7
Private unrequited transfers (net)	35.4	47.9	30.4
Official transfers	63.4	75.6	65.1
Current balance	-26.0	-104.5	-51.2
Direct investment	40.1	92.2	117.6
Official medium- and long-term loans	-28.0	-30.0	-31.9
Other capital and errors and omissions	6.7	-22.5	21.1
Overall balance	-7.2	-64.8	55.6

* Estimates.

Source: IMF, *Islamic Republic of Mauritania: Statistical Appendix* (October 2003).

MAURITANIA

External Trade

PRINCIPAL COMMODITIES
(distribution by SITC, US $ million)

Imports c.i.f.	1999	2000	2001
Food and live animals	160.3	112.1	77.6
Live animals chiefly for food	80.2	56.1	38.8
Cereals and cereal preparations	39.8	32.2	20.6
Sugar and honey	30.1	17.3	12.6
Mineral fuels, lubricants, etc.	41.5	35.4	94.7
Petroleum products, refined	41.5	35.4	94.7
Animal and vegetable oils, fats and waxes	18.7	8.0	5.9
Animal oils and fats	18.6	7.9	5.9
Basic manufactures	14.6	17.2	35.1
Non-metallic mineral manufactures	13.4	15.6	34.4
Machinery and transport equipment	34.9	33.0	34.9
Road vehicles	34.9	33.0	34.9
Total (incl. others)*	342.8	310.2	353.0

Exports f.o.b.	1999	2000	2001
Food and live animals	154.6	148.2	142.2
Fish, fresh, chilled or frozen	154.6	148.2	142.2
Basic manufactures	217.5	209.0	204.5
Iron and steel	217.5	209.0	204.5
Total (incl. others)	373.5	358.6	347.9

* Including commodities not classified according to kind (US $ million): 62.8 in 1999, 95.1 in 2000, 97.2 in 2001.

Source: UN, *International Trade Statistics Yearbook*.

2002 (US $ million): *Imports c.i.f.:* Petroleum products 107.6; Total imports (incl. others) 418.0. *Exports f.o.b.:* Iron ore 183.8, Fish, crustaceans and molluscs 143.5; Total exports (incl. others) 330.3 (Source: IMF, *Islamic Republic of Mauritania: Statistical Appendix*—October 2003).

PRINCIPAL TRADING PARTNERS
(US $ million)*

Imports c.i.f.	2000	2001	2002
Belgium-Luxembourg	32.9	31.4	36.8
France	94.5	89.2	86.9
Germany	17.2	21.3	23.2
Italy	21.9	22.1	17.6
Japan	9.2	9.8	16.2
Netherlands	10.0	10.7	14.0
Spain	21.8	21.5	27.9
United Kingdom	8.5	7.2	14.0
USA	9.6	16.0	14.4
Total (incl. others)	336.2	372.3	418.0

Exports c.i.f.	2000	2001	2002
Belgium-Luxembourg	30.8	28.9	33.9
France	63.5	50.7	47.6
Germany	13.2	20.8	35.7
Italy	47.4	51.0	48.8
Japan	53.0	27.1	21.0
Portugal	7.6	7.0	7.8
Spain	38.1	42.2	39.9
United Kingdom	5.4	5.4	1.5
Total (incl. others)	344.7	338.6	330.3

* Data are compiled on the basis of reporting by Mauritania's trading partners. Data detailing imports and exports of trade with developing and emerging countries were not available.

Source: IMF, *Islamic Republic of Mauritania: Statistical Appendix* (October 2003).

Transport

RAILWAYS

1984: Passengers carried 19,353; Passenger-km 7m.; Freight carried 9.1m. metric tons; Freight ton-km 6,142m.

Freight ton-km (million): 6,365 in 1985; 6,411 in 1986; 6,473 in 1987; 6,535 in 1988; 6,610 in 1989; 6,690 in 1990; 6,720 in 1991; 6,810 in 1992; 6,890 in 1993 (figures for 1988–93 are estimates) (Source: UN Economic Commission for Africa, *African Statistical Yearbook*).

ROAD TRAFFIC
('000 motor vehicles in use)

	1996	1997	1998
Passenger cars	5.2	5.3	5.4
Commercial vehicles	6.0	6.3	6.6

Source: UN, *Statistical Yearbook*.

SHIPPING

Merchant Fleet
(registered at 31 December)

	2002	2003	2004
Number of vessels	142	142	146
Total displacement ('000 grt)	47.6	47.6	49.3

Source: Lloyd's Register-Fairplay, *World Fleet Statistics*.

International Sea-borne Freight Traffic
(Port of Nouadhibou, '000 metric tons)

	1996	1997	1998
Goods loaded	11,623	11,906	11,450
Goods unloaded	139	119	119

Source: Port Autonome de Nouadhibou.

CIVIL AVIATION
(traffic on scheduled services)*

	1999	2000	2001
Kilometres flown (million)	4	4	2
Passengers carried ('000)	187	185	156
Passenger-km (million)	290	275	174
Total ton-km (million)	41	37	23

* Including an apportionment of the traffic of Air Afrique.

Source: UN, *Statistical Yearbook*.

Tourism

Tourist arrivals (estimates, '000): 24 in 1999.

Receipts from tourism (US $ million, excl. passenger transport): 28 in 1999 (Source: World Tourism Organization).

Communications Media

	2002	2003	2004
Telephones ('000 main lines in use)	31.5	38.2	n.a.
Mobile cellular telephones ('000 subscribers)	247.2	350.9	522.4
Personal computers ('000 in use)*	29	n.a.	42
Internet users ('000)*	10.0	12.0	14.0

* Estimates.

Television receivers ('000 in use, 1999): 247.

Facsimile machines (number in use, 1999): 3,300.

Daily newspapers (1996): Number 2; Estimated average circulation ('000 copies) 12.

Radio receivers ('000 in use, 1997): 570.

Sources: UNESCO, *Statistical Yearbook*; UN, *Statistical Yearbook*; International Telecommunication Union.

Education

(2002/03, unless otherwise indicated)

	Institutions	Teachers	Males	Females	Total
Pre-primary	n.a.	n.a.	n.a.	n.a.	5,040
Primary	2,676*	9,606	200,484	193,917	394,401
Secondary:	n.a.	3,237	47,198	37,209	84,407
Tertiary	4†	353	7,223	1,975	9,198

* 1998/99.
† 1995/96.

Adult literacy rate (UNESCO estimates): 51.2% (males 59.5%; females 43.4%) in 2003 (Source: UN Development Programme, *Human Development Report*).

Sources: mainly UNESCO Institute for Statistics and Ministry of National Education, Nouakchott.

Directory

While no longer an official language under the terms of the 1991 Constitution (see below), French is still widely used in Mauritania, especially in the commercial sector. Many organizations are therefore listed under their French names, by which they are generally known.

The Constitution

Following the *coup d'état* of 3 August 2005, the self-styled Military Council for Justice and Democracy (MCJD) introduced a Constitutional Charter that was intended to supplement and partially replace the Constitution approved by referendum in 1991 for a transitional period for up to two years, following which time democratic elections were to be held. Those provisions of the Constitution pertaining to the role of Islam, individual and collective freedoms and the prerogatives of the State were to remain in force, while certain judicial organs (namely: the High Council of Magistrates; courts and tribunals; the High Council of Islam; the Audit Court; and the Constitutional Council) were to continue to function. A number of the legislative powers previously held by a bicameral legislature (which was abolished) were transferred to the MCJD, which was also to assume executive powers. The President of the MCJD was empowered to appoint a Prime Minister and other Ministers, who were to be responsible to the MCJD and its President. The MCJD was permitted to consult with the Constitutional Council with regard to any constitutional question.

The Constitution states that the official language is Arabic, and that the national languages are Arabic, Pular, Wolof and Solinké.

The Government

The administration headed by President Col MAAWIYA OULD SID'AHMED TAYA (who took office in 1984, before being elected to that position in 1992, 1997 and 2003) was overthrown in a *coup d'état* on 3 August 2005. Leadership of a self-styled Military Council for Justice and Democracy (MCJD) was assumed by Col ELY OULD MOHAMED VALL. Vall subsequently appointed SIDI MOHAMED OULD BOUBACAR as Prime Minister, and a new Government was formed on 10 August. The MCJD announced the intention of holding democratic elections within the period of two years from its assumption of power.

HEAD OF STATE

President of the Military Council for Justice and Democracy: Col ELY OULD MOHAMED VALL (took office 3 August 2005).

MEMBERS OF THE MILITARY COUNCIL FOR JUSTICE AND DEMOCRACY

Col ABDERRAHMANE OULD BOUBACAR, Col MOHAMED ABDEL AZIZ, Col MOHAMED OULD CHEIKH MOHAMED AHMED, Col AHMED OULD BEKRINE, Col SOGHO ALASSANE, Col GHOULAM OULD MOHAMED, Col SIDI MOHAMED OULD CHEIKH EL ALEM, Col NEGRI FELIX, Col MOHAMED OULD MEGUETT, Col MOHAMED OULD MOHAMED ZNAGUI, Col KANE HAMEDINE, Col MOHAMED OULD ABDI, Col AHMED OULD AMEINE, Col TALEB MOUSTAPHA OULD CHEIKH, Col MOHAMED CHEIKH OULD MOHAMED LEMINE, Capt ISSELKOU OULD CHEIKH EL OUELY.

COUNCIL OF MINISTERS
(April 2006)

Prime Minister: SIDI MOHAMED OULD BOUBACAR.
Minister of Foreign Affairs and Co-operation: AHMED OULD SID'AHMED.
Minister of Justice: MAHFOUDH OULD BETTAH.
Minister of the Interior, Posts and Telecommunications: MOHAMED AHMED OULD MOHAMED LEMINE.
Minister of Finance: ABDELLAHI OULD SOULEYMANE OULD CHEIKH SIDIYA.
Minister of Economic Affairs and Development: MOHAMED OULD AHMED.
Minister of Fisheries and the Maritime Economy: SIDI MOHAMED OULD SIDINA.
Minister of Capital Works and Transport: BÂ IBRAHIMA DEMBA.
Minister of Culture, Youth and Sports: MEHLA MINT AHMED.
Minister of Trade, Crafts and Tourism: BÂ ABDERRAHMANE.
Minister of Energy and Petroleum: MOHAMED ALI OULD SIDI MOHAMED.
Minister of Water Resources: ELY OULD AHMEDOU.
Minister of Mines and Industry: MOHAMED OULD ISMAËL OULD ABEIDNA.
Minister of Rural Development and the Environment: GANDEGA SILLY.
Minister of Higher Education and Scientific Research: NAJI OULD MOHAMED MAHMOUD.
Minister of Fundamental and Secondary Education: CHEIKH AHMED OULD SID'AHMED.
Minister of the Civil Service and Employment: MOHAMED OULD AHMED OULD JEK.
Minister of Health and Social Affairs: SAADNA OULD BEHAIDE.
Minister, responsible for Literacy, Islamic Orientation and Elementary Education: YAHYA OULD SID'EL MOUSTAPH.
Minister of Communication: CHEIKH OULD EBBE.
Secretary of State, responsible for the Status of Women: NEBGHOUHA MINT TLAMID.
Secretary of State to the Prime Minister, responsible for New Technologies: MANIANA SOW MOHAMED DEYNA.
Secretary of State, responsible for Civil Status: ABDI OULD HORMA.
Secretary of State, responsible for the Union of the Arab Maghreb: BISMILLAH ELIH OULD AHMED.
Secretary-General of the Government: BÂ SEYDOU MOUSSA.

MAURITANIA

MINISTRIES

Office of the President of the Military Council for Justice and Democracy: BP 184, Nouakchott; tel. and fax 525-26-36; internet www.ami.mr/fr/Conseil_Militaire/Conseil_militaire.htm.

Office of the Prime Minister: BP 237, Nouakchott; tel. 525-33-37.

Ministry of Capital Works and Transport: BP 237, Nouakchott; tel. 525-33-37.

Ministry of the Civil Service and Employment: BP 193, Nouakchott; tel. and fax 525-84-10.

Ministry of Communication: Nouakchott.

Ministry of Culture, Youth and Sports: BP 223, Nouakchott; tel. 525-11-30.

Ministry of Economic Affairs and Development: 303 Ilot C, BP 5150, Nouakchott; tel. 525-16-12; fax 525-51-10; e-mail nfomaed@mauritania.mr; internet www.maed.gov.mr.

Ministry of Energy and Petroleum: Nouakchott; tel. 525-71-40.

Ministry of Finance: BP 181, Nouakchott; tel. 525-20-20.

Ministry of Fisheries and the Maritime Economy: BP 137, Nouakchott; tel. 525-46-07; fax 525-31-46; e-mail ministre@mpem.mr; internet www.mpem.mr.

Ministry of Foreign Affairs and Co-operation: BP 230, Nouakchott; tel. 525-26-82; fax 525-28-60.

Ministry of Fundamental and Secondary Education: BP 387, Nouakchott; tel. 525-12-37; fax 525-12-22.

Ministry of Health and Social Affairs: BP 177, Nouakchott; tel. 525-20-52; fax 525-22-68.

Ministry of Higher Education and Scientific Research: Nouakchott.

Ministry of the Interior, Posts and Telecommunications: BP 195, Nouakchott; tel. 525-36-61; fax 525-36-40; e-mail paddec@mauritania.mr.

Ministry of Justice: BP 350, Nouakchott; tel. 525-10-83; fax 525-70-02.

Ministry of Mines and Industry: BP 199, Nouakchott; tel. 525-30-83; fax 525-69-37; e-mail mmi@mauritania.mr.

Ministry of Rural Development and the Environment: BP 366, Nouakchott; tel. 525-15-00; fax 525-74-75.

Ministry of Trade, Crafts and Tourism: BP 182, Nouakchott; tel. 525-35-72; fax 525-76-71.

Ministry of Water Resources: BP 4913, Nouakchott; tel. 525-71-44; fax 529-42-87; e-mail saadouebih@yahoo.fr.

Office of the Secretary-General of the Government: BP 184, Nouakchott.

Office of the Secretary of State to the Prime Minister, responsible for New Technologies: Immeuble du Gouvernement, BP 184, Nouakchott; tel. 529-37-43; e-mail aziz@mauritania.mr; internet www.setn.mr.

President and Legislature

Following the *coup d'état* of 3 August 2005, the legislative and executive organs provided for by the 1991 Constitution were abolished, and their powers were transferred to the self-styled ruling Military Council for Justice and Democracy. New presidential and legislative elections were to take place within a period of two years.

Election Commission

National Independent Electoral Commission: Nouakchott; 15 mems; Pres. Col (retd) CHEIKH SID'AHMED OULD BABAMINE.

Advisory Council

Economic and Social Council: Nouakchott.

Political Organizations

Following the *coup d'état* of August 2005, and in advance of the election of a new legislature and president, scheduled for November 2006 and March 2007 respectively, several new political parties were formed, and several politicians hitherto in exile returned to Mauritania. The organizations listed below were among the most significant believed to operate in early 2006.

Alliance for Democracy in Mauritania (ADEMA): Nouakchott; f. 2003; registration refused by regime of fmr Pres. Taya; Leader ZEIN EL ABIDINE SY.

Alliance for Justice and Democracy: Nouakchott; f. 2000 as breakaway group from fmr Action for Change (which was subsequently prohibited); seeks to represent the interests of Harratins; fmrly mem. of United Opposition Framework, opposed to regime of fmr Pres Taya; Leader KABEH ABDOULAYE.

Alliance for Youth and Democracy (AYD): Nouakchott; Leader CISSE AMADOU CHIEKHOU.

Convention for Change (CC): Nouakchott; f. 2002 to replace the banned Action for Change, to represent the interests of Harratin (black Moors who had fmrly been slaves); refused registration by Govt in Aug. 2002; fmrly mem. of United Opposition Framework, opposed to regime of fmr Pres Taya; Chair. MESSAOUD OULD BOULKHEIR; Sec.-Gen. IBRAHIM ASSAR.

Democratic Alliance: Nouakchott; f. 2001; Leader MOHAMED OULD TALEB OTHMAN.

Democratic and Social Republican Party (DSRP): Nouakchott; tel. 525-58-55; f. 1991; fmr ruling party, prior to *coup d'état* of August 2005; Sec.-Gen. Dr BOULLAHA OULD MEGUEYA; 451,333 mems (2000).

Mauritanian Labour Party: Nouakchott; f. 2001; Leader MOHAMED HAFID OULD DENNA.

Mauritanian Liberal Democrats: Nouakchott; f. 2001; Leader MUSTAPHA OULD LEMRABET.

Mauritanian Party for Renewal and Construction: Nouakchott; f. 2001; Leader MOULAY EL-HASSEN OULD JIYED.

National Renaissance Party (NRP—Nouhoudh) (El Nouhoudh El Watani): Nouakchott; f. 2001; Baathist; although not officially recognized, the party's existence was tolerated by authorities prior to May 2003, when several senior leaders of the party were arrested, and its headquarters closed by police; Sec.-Gen MOHAMED OULD ABDELLAHI OULD EYYE.

National Union for Democracy and Development (NUDD): f. 1997; Leader TIDJANE KOITA.

Party for Reconstruction and Rebirth: Nouakchott; f. 2005 by leadership of the fmr prohibited Knights of Change militia and reformist elements of the fmr ruling Democratic and Social Republican Party; Pres. SALEH OULD HNANA; Sec.-Gen. ABDERAHMANE OULD MINI.

Popular Front (PF): Nouakchott; f. 1998; social-liberal; fmrly mem. of United Opposition Framework, opposed to regime of fmr Pres Taya; Leader MOHAMED LEMINE CH'BIH OULD CHEIKH MELAININE.

Popular Progressive Alliance (APP): Nouakchott; f. 1991; fmrly mem. of United Opposition Framework, opposed to regime of fmr Pres Taya; Sec.-Gen. MESSAOUD OULD BOULKHAR.

Rally for Democracy and Unity (RDU): f. 1991; supported regime of fmr Pres. Taya; Chair. AHMED OULD SIDI BABA.

Rally of Democratic Forces (RDF): f. 2001 by fmr mems of the officially dissolved Union of Democratic Forces—New Era (f. 1991); fmrly mem. of United Opposition Framework, opposed to regime of fmr Pres Taya; Sec.-Gen. AHMED OULD DADDAH.

Reward (Sawab): Nouakchott; internet www.sawab.info; f. 2004; social democratic; Chair. of Central Council MOHAMED MAHMOUD OULD GHOULMA; Pres. Dr CHEIKH OULD SIDI OULD HANNENA; Sec.-Gen. MOHAMED SALEM OULD BABE.

Social Democrat Union: Nouakchott; Pres. ISSELMOU OULD HANNEFI.

Third Generation: Nouakchott; f. 2001; Leader LEBAT OULD JEH.

Union for Democracy and Progress (UDP): Ilot V, no. 70, Tevragh Zeina, BP 816, Nouakchott; tel. 525-52-89; fax 525-29-95; e-mail www.udp.mr; f. 1993; Pres. NAHA HAMDI MOUKNASS; Sec.-Gen. AHMED AHMED BEDDA.

Union of Progressive Forces (UPF) (Ittihad Quwa al-Taqaddum): Nouakchott; e-mail ufpweb2@yahoo.fr; internet www.ufpweb.org; f. 2000, following the enforced dissolution of the fmr Union of Democratic Forces—New Era, which it had existed as a faction thereof since 1998; Pres. MOHAMED OULD MAOULOUD; Sec-Gen. MOHAMED EL MOUSTAPHA OULD BEDREDDINE.

Unauthorized, but influential, is the Islamic **Ummah Party** (the Constitution prohibits the operation of religious political organizations), founded in 1991 and led by Imam SIDI YAHYA, and the Baathist **National Vanguard Party (Taliaa)**, which was officially dissolved by the Government in 1999 and is led by AHMEDOU OULD BABANA. The clandestine **Mauritanian African Liberation Forces (MALF)** was founded in 1983 in Senegal to represent Afro-Mauritanians (internet members.lycos.co.uk/flamnet; Pres. SAMBA THIAM). A further group based in exile is the **Arab-African Salvation Front Against Slavery, Racism and Tribalism—AASF** (e-mail faas@caramail.com; internet membres.lycos.fr/faas). In mid-2003 the

MAURITANIA

Directory

Mauritanian Forum for Reform and Democracy, based in Brussels, Belgium, was formed by opponents of the Taya regime in exile; it stated as its principal aims the promotion of peaceful change in Mauritania and the reinforcement of Islamic principles (Pres. MOHAMED JEMIL MANSOUR, Sec.-Gen. ABOU BAKR BENELMARWANI).

Diplomatic Representation

EMBASSIES IN MAURITANIA

Algeria: Tevragh Zeina, BP 625, Nouakchott; tel. 525-35-69; fax 525-47-77; Ambassador ABDELKRIM BEN HOCINE.

China, People's Republic: Tevragh Zeina, BP 257, Nouakchott; tel. 525-20-70; fax 525-24-62; e-mail chinaemb_mr@mfa.gov.cn; internet mr.china-embassy.org; Ambassador LI GUOXUE.

Congo, Democratic Republic: Tevragh Zeina, BP 5714, Nouakchott; tel. 525-46-12; fax 525-50-53; e-mail ambardc.rim@caramail.com; Chargé d'affaires a.i. TSHIBASU MFUAD.

Egypt: Villa no. 468, Tevragh Zeina, BP 176, Nouakchott; tel. 525-21-92; fax 525-33-84; Ambassador MOHAMED EZZ EL-DIN FOUDA.

France: rue Ahmed Ould M'Hamed, Tevragh Zeina, BP 231, Nouakchott; tel. 529-96-99; fax 525-69-38; e-mail ambafrance.nouakchott-amba@diplomatie.gouv.fr; internet www.france-mauritanie.mr; Ambassador PATRICK NICOLOSO.

Germany: Tevragh Zeina, BP 372, Nouakchott; tel. 525-17-29; fax 525-17-22; e-mail amb-allemagne@toptechnology.mr; Ambassador ERNST-JOACHIM DÖRING.

Israel: Ilot A516, Tevragh Zeina, BP 5714, Nouakchott; tel. 525-82-35; fax 525-46-12; e-mail info@nouakchott.mfa.gov.il; Ambassador BOAZ BESMUTH BISMUTH.

Korea, Democratic People's Republic: Nouakchott; Ambassador PAK HO IL.

Kuwait: Tevragh Zeina, BP 345, Nouakchott; tel. 525-33-05; fax 525-41-45.

Libya: BP 673, Nouakchott; tel. 525-52-02; fax 525-50-53.

Mali: Tevragh Zeina, BP 5371, Nouakchott; tel. 525-40-81; fax 525-40-83; e-mail ambmali@hotmail.com; Ambassador MOUSSA KALILOU COULIBALY.

Morocco: 569 ave de Gaulle, Tevragh Zeina, BP 621, Nouakchott; tel. 525-14-11; fax 529-72-80; e-mail sifmanktt@mauritel.mr; Ambassador ABDERRAHMANE BENOMAR.

Nigeria: Ilot P9, BP 367, Nouakchott; tel. 525-23-04; fax 525-23-14; Ambassador Alhaji BALA MOHAMED SANI.

Qatar: BP 609, Nouakchott; tel. 525-23-99; fax 525-68-87; e-mail nouakchoti@mofa.gov.qa; Ambassador MAJED AWAD AL-SUWAIDI.

Russia: rue Abu Bakr, BP 221, Nouakchott; tel. 525-19-73; fax 525-52-96; e-mail ambruss@opt.mr; Ambassador LEONID V. ROGOV.

Saudi Arabia: Las Balmas, Zinat, BP 498, Nouakchott; tel. 525-26-33; fax 525-29-49; e-mail mremb@mofa.gov.sa; Ambassador MOHAMED AL FADH EL ISSA.

Senegal: Villa 500, Tevragh Zeina, BP 2511, Nouakchott; tel. 525-72-90; fax 525-72-91; Ambassador MAHMOUDOU CHEIKH KANE.

Spain: BP 232, Nouakchott; tel. 525-20-80; fax 525-40-88; e-mail ambespmr@correo.mae.es; Ambassador ALEJANDRO POLANCO MATA.

Syria: Tevragh Zeina, BP 288, Nouakchott; tel. 525-27-54; fax 525-45-00.

Tunisia: BP 681, Nouakchott; tel. 525-28-71; fax 525-18-27; Ambassador ABDEL WEHAB JEMAL.

United Arab Emirates: BP 6824, Nouakchott; tel. 525-10-98; fax 525-09-92.

USA: rue Abdallaye, BP 222, Nouakchott; tel. 525-26-60; fax 525-15-92; e-mail Mauritania@foreignservice.net; internet mauritania.usembassy.gov; Ambassador JOSEPH LEBARON.

Yemen: Tevragh Zeina, BP 4689, Nouakchott; tel. 525-55-91; fax 525-56-39.

Judicial System

The Code of Law was promulgated in 1961 and subsequently modified to incorporate Islamic institutions and practices. The main courts comprise three courts of appeal, 10 regional tribunals, two labour tribunals and 53 departmental civil courts. A revenue court has jurisdiction in financial matters. The members of the High Court of Justice are elected by the National Assembly and the Senate.

Shari'a (Islamic) law was introduced in February 1980. A special Islamic court was established in March of that year, presided over by a magistrate of Islamic law, assisted by two counsellors and two *ulemas* (Muslim jurists and interpreters of the Koran). A five-member High Council of Islam, appointed by the President, advises upon the conformity of national legislation to religious precepts, at the request of the President.

Audit Court (Cour des Comptes): Nouakchott; audits all govt institutions; Pres. SOW ADAMA SAMBA.

Constitutional Council: f. 1992; includes six mems, three nominated by the Head of State and three designated by the Presidents of the Senate and National Assembly; Pres. ABDOULLAH OULD ELY SALEM; Sec.-Gen. MOHAMED OULD M'REIZIG.

High Council of Islam (al-Majlis al-Islamiya al-A'la'): Nouakchott; f. 1992; Pres. AHMED OULD NEINI.

High Court of Justice: Nouakchott; f. 1961; comprises an equal number of appointees elected from their membership by the National Assembly and the Senate, following each partial or general renewal of those legislative bodies; competent to try the President of the Republic in case of high treason, and the Prime Minister and members of the Government in case of conspiracy against the state.

Supreme Court: BP 201, Palais de Justice, Nouakchott; tel. 525-21-63; f. 1961; comprises an administrative chamber, a civil and commercial chamber, a social and employment chamber and a criminal chamber; also functions as the highest court of appeal; Pres. KABR OULD ELEWA.

Religion

ISLAM

Islam is the official religion, and the population are almost entirely Muslims of the Malekite rite. The major religious groups are the Tijaniya and the Qadiriya. Chinguetti, in the region of Adrar, is the seventh Holy Place in Islam. A High Council of Islam supervises the conformity of legislation to Muslim orthodoxy.

CHRISTIANITY

Roman Catholic Church

Mauritania comprises the single diocese of Nouakchott, directly responsible to the Holy See. The Bishop participates in the Bishops' Conference of Senegal, Mauritania, Cape Verde and Guinea-Bissau, based in Dakar, Senegal. At 31 December 2003 there were an estimated 4,500 adherents, mainly non-nationals, in the country.

Bishop of Nouakchott: Most Rev. MARTIN ALBERT HAPPE, Evêché, BP 5377, Nouakchott; tel. 525-04-27; fax 525-37-51; e-mail mgr-martin-happe@mauritel.mr.

The Press

Of some 400 journals officially registered in Mauritania in mid-2004, some 30 were regular, widely available publications, of which the following were among the most important:

Al-Akhbar: BP 5346, Nouakchott; tel. 525-08-94; fax 525-37-57; f. 1995; weekly; Arabic.

Al-Qalam/Le Calame: BP 1059, Nouakchott; tel. 529-02-34; fax 525-75-55; e-mail calame@compunet.mr; internet www.calame.8k.com; f. 1994; weekly; Arabic and French; independent; Editors-in-Chief RIYAD OULD AHMED EL-HADI (Arabic edn), HINDOU MINT AININA (French edn).

Le Carrefour: Nouakchott; Dir MOUSSA OULD SAMBA SY.

Châab: BP 371, Nouakchott; tel. 525-29-40; fax 525-85-47; daily; Arabic; also publ. in French *Horizons*; publ. by Agence Mauritanienne de l'Information; Dir-Gen. MOHAMED EL-HAFED OULD MAHAM.

Challenge: BP 1346, Nouakchott; tel. and fax 529-06-26.

Ech-tary: BP 1059, Nouakchott; tel. 525-50-65; fortnightly; Arabic; satirical.

L'Essor: BP 5310, Nouakchott; tel. 529-19-83; fax 525-04-07; e-mail sidiel2000@yahoo.fr; monthly; economics; Dir SIDI EL-MOCTAR CHEÏGUER; circ. 2,500.

El-Anba: BP 3901, Nouakchott; tel. and fax 525-99-27.

L'Eveil-Hebdo: BP 587, Nouakchott; tel. 525-67-14; fax 525-87-54; e-mail symoudou@yahoo.fr; f. 1991; weekly; independent; Dir of Publication SY MAMADOU.

Inimich al-Watan: Nouakchott; independent; Arabic; Dir of Publication MOHAMED OULD ELKORY.

Journal Officel: BP 188, Nouakchott; tel. 525-33-37; fax 525-34-74; fortnightly.

Maghreb Hebdo: BP 5266, Nouakchott; tel. 525-98-10; fax 525-98-11; f. 1994; weekly; Dir KHATTRI OULD DIE.

Nouakchott-Info: Immeuble Abbas, Tevragh Zeina, BP 1905, Nouakchott; tel. 525-02-71; fax 525-54-84; e-mail jedna@mapeci.com; internet www.akhbarnouakchott.com; f. 1995; daily; indepen-

MAURITANIA

dent; Arabic and French; Dir of Publication and Editor-in-Chief CHEIKHNA OULD NENNI.

L'Opinion Libre: Nouakchott; weekly; Editor ELY OULD NAFA.

Rajoul Echarée: Nouakchott; e-mail rajoul_echaree@toptechnology.mr; weekly; independent; Arabic; Dir SIDI MOHAMED OULD YOUNÈS.

Ar-Rayah (The Banner): Nouakchott; e-mail team@rayah.info; internet www.rayah.info; f. 1997; independent; weekly; pro-Islamist; publication prohibited in May 2003; Editor AHMED OULD WEDIAA.

Le Rénovateur: Nouakchott; every 2 months; f. 2001; Editor Chiekh TIDIANE DIA.

La Tribune: BP 6227, Nouakchott; tel. 525-44-92; fax 525-02-09; Editor-in-Chief MOHAMMED FALL OULD OUMÈRE.

NEWS AGENCIES

Agence Mauritanienne de l'Information (AMI): BP 371, Nouakchott; tel. 525-29-40; fax 525-45-87; e-mail ami@mauritania.mr; internet www.ami.mr; fmrly Agence Mauritanienne de Presse; state-controlled; news and information services in Arabic and French; Dir MOHAMED CHEIKH OULD SIDI MOHAMED.

Foreign Bureaux

Foreign bureaux represented in Mauritania include Agence France-Presse, Reuters (UK) and Xinhua (New China) News Agency (People's Republic of China).

Publishers

Imprimerie Commerciale et Administrative de Mauritanie: BP 164, Nouakchott; textbooks, educational.

Imprimerie Nationale: BP 618, Nouakchott; tel. 525-44-38; fax 525-44-37; f. 1978; state-owned; Pres. RACHID OULD SALEH; Man. Dir ISSIMOU MAHJOUB.

GOVERNMENT PUBLISHING HOUSE

Société Nationale d'Impression: BP 618, Nouakchott; Pres. MOUSTAPHA SALECK OULD AHMED BRIHIM.

Broadcasting and Communications

TELECOMMUNICATIONS

Mauritel: BP 7000, Nouakchott; tel. 525-23-40; fax 525-17-00; e-mail webmaster@mauritel.mr; internet www.mauritel.mr; fmrly Société Mauritanienne des Télécommunications; 46% state-owned, 34% owned by Maroc Télécom (Morocco), 20% owned by Abdallahi Ould Noueigued group; Dir Col AHMEDOUL OULD MOHAMED EL KORY

El-Jawel Mauritel Mobiles: ave du Roi Fayçal, Nouakchott; tel. 29-63-36; fax 29-53-16; e-mail infos@mauritelmobiles.mr; internet www.mauritel.mr; f. 2000; operates a mobile cellular telephone network (El Jawal) in Nouakchott and more than 20 other locations nation-wide.

Société Mauritano-Tunisienne de Télécommunications (Mattel): Nouakchott; f. 2000; privately owned Mauritanian-Tunisian co; operates mobile cellular communications network in Nouakchott and more than 10 other locations nation-wide.

BROADCASTING

Radio

Radio de Mauritanie (RM): ave Nasser, BP 200, Nouakchott; tel. and fax 525-21-64; e-mail rm@mauritania.mr; f. 1958; state-controlled; five transmitters; radio broadcasts in Arabic, French, Sarakolé, Toucouleur and Wolof; Dir SID BRAHIM OULD HAMDINOU.

Television

Télévision de Mauritanie (TVM): BP 5522, Nouakchott; tel. 525-40-67; fax 525-40-69; Dir-Gen. HAMOUD OULD M'HAMED.

Finance

(cap. = capital; res = reserves; dep. = deposits; m. = million; brs= branches; amounts in ouguiyas, unless otherwise stated)

BANKING

Central Bank

Banque Centrale de Mauritanie (BCM): ave de l'Indépendance, BP 623, Nouakchott; tel. 525-22-06; fax 525-27-59; e-mail anima@bnm.mr; f. 1973; bank of issue; total assets 200m. (2001); Gov. AHMED OULD ZEÏN; Dir MOHAMMED OULD NANY; 4 brs.

Commercial Banks

Banque El Amana pour le développement et l'Habitat (BADH): BP 5559, Nouakchott; tel. 525-34-90; fax 525-34-95; e-mail badh@opt.mr; f. 1996; 50% privately owned; cap. and res 1,297.4m., total assets 7,248.4m. (Dec. 2001); Pres. AHAMED SALEM OULD BOUNA MOKHTAR; Dir-Gen. MOHAMMED OULD OUMAROU; 4 brs.

Banque pour le Commerce et l'Industrie (BCI): ave Nasser, BP 5050, Nouakchott; tel. 529-28-76; fax 529-28-79; e-mail bci@mauritel.mr; f. 1999; cap. 1,000m. (Dec. 1999); Pres. and Dir-Gen. ISSELMOU OULD DIDI OULD TAJEDINE; 5 brs.

Banque pour le Commerce et l'Investissement en Mauritanie (Bacim-Bank): BP 1268, Nouakchott; tel. 529-19-00; fax 529-13-60; e-mail bacim-bank@mauritel.mr; f. 2002; privately owned; cap. US $4m. (Feb. 2002); Pres. and Dir-Gen. AHMED OULD EL WAFI.

Banque Mauritanienne pour le Commerce International (BMCI): Immeuble Afarco, ave Nasser, BP 622, Nouakchott; tel. 525-28-26; fax 525-20-45; e-mail info@bmci.mr; internet www.bmci.mr; f. 1974; privately owned; cap. and res 4,233.5m., total assets 28,080.5m. (Dec. 2003); Pres. and Dir-Gen. MOULAY SIDI OULD HACEN OULD ABASS; 10 brs.

Banque Nationale de Mauritanie (BNM): ave Nasser, BP 614, Nouakchott; tel. 525-26-02; fax 525-33-97; e-mail bnm10@bnm.mr; f. 1989; privately owned; cap. 2,500m., res 2,485m., dep. 20,030m. (Dec. 2003); Pres. and Dir-Gen. MOHAMED OULD NOUEIGUED; 11 brs.

Chinguitty Bank: ave Nasser, BP 626, Nouakchott; tel. 525-21-42; fax 525-23-82; e-mail chinguittybank@mauritel.mr; f. 1972; 51% owned by Libyan Arab Foreign Bank, 49% state-owned; cap. and res 2,434.3m., total assets 13,832.4m. (Dec. 2002); Pres. M. EL HASSEN OULD SALEH; Gen. Man. DAW AMAR ABDALLA; 2 brs.

Générale de Banque de Mauritanie pour l'Investissement et le Commerce SA (GBM): ave de l'Indépendance, BP 5558, Nouakchott; tel. 525-36-36; fax 525-46-47; e-mail gbm@gbm.mr; f. 1995; 70% privately owned, 30% owned by Banque Belgolaise (Belgium); cap. 5,100m, res. 2,941.6., dep. 12,989.1m. (Dec. 2003); Pres. and Dir-Gen. MOHAMED HMAYEN OULD BOUAMATOU; 1 br.

Islamic Bank

Banque al-Wava Mauritanienne Islamique (BAMIS): 758, rue 22–018 ave du Roi Fayçal, BP 650, Nouakchott; tel. 525-14-24; fax 525-16-21; e-mail bamis@bamis.mr; internet www.bamis.mr; f. 1985; fmrly Banque al-Baraka Mauritannienne Islamique; majority share privately owned; cap. 2,000m., res 2,821m., dep. 13,778m. (Dec. 2005); Pres. MOHAMED ABDELLAHI OULD ABDELLAHI; Dir-Gen. MOHAMED ABDELLAHI OULD SIDI; Exec. Dir MOHAMED OULD TAYA; 4 brs.

INSURANCE

Assurances Générales de Mauritanie: BP 2141, ave de Gaulle, TZA Ilot A 667, Nouakchott; tel. 529-29-00; fax 529-29-11; Man. MOULAYE ELY BOUAMATOU.

Cie Nationale d'Assurance et de Réassurance (NASR): 12 ave Nasser, BP 163, Nouakchott; tel. 525-26-50; fax 525-18-18; e-mail nasr@nasr.mr; internet www.nasr.mr; f. 1994; state-owned; Pres. MOHAMED ABDALLAHI OULD SIDI; Dir-Gen. AHMED OULD SIDI BABA.

Société Anonyme d'Assurance et de Réassurance (SAAR): ave J. F. Kennedy, Immeuble El-Mamy, BP 2841, Nouakchott; tel. 525-30-56; fax 525-25-36; e-mail saar@infotel.mr; f. 1999; Pres. and Dir-Gen. AHMED BEZEID OULD MED LEMINE.

TAAMIN: BP 5164, Nouakchott; tel. 529-40-00; fax 529-40-02; e-mail taamin@toptechnology.mr; Pres. and Dir-Gen. MOULAYE EL HASSEN OULD MOCTAR EL HASSEN.

Trade and Industry

DEVELOPMENT ORGANIZATIONS

Agence Française de Développement (AFD): rue Mamadou Kouaté prolongée, BP 5211, Nouakchott; tel. 525-25-25; fax 525-49-10; e-mail afdnouakchott@groupe-afd.org; internet www.afd.fr; Country Dir GILLES CHAUSSE.

Mission Française de Coopération et d'Action Culturelle: BP 203, Nouakchott; tel. 525-21-21; fax 525-20-50; e-mail mcap.coop.france@opt.mr; administers bilateral aid from France; Dir MAURICE DADOUCHE.

Société Nationale pour le Développement Rural (SONADER): BP 321, Nouakchott; tel. 521-18-00; fax 525-32-86; e-mail sonader@toptechnology.mr; f. 1975; Dir AHMED OULD BAH OULD CHEIKH SIDIA.

MAURITANIA

CHAMBER OF COMMERCE

Chambre de Commerce, d'Industrie et d'Agriculture de Mauritanie: BP 215, Nouakchott; tel. 525-22-14; fax 525-38-95; f. 1954; Pres. Mahmoud Ould Ahmedou; Dir Habib Ould Ely.

EMPLOYERS' ORGANIZATION

National Confederation of Mauritanian Employers (CNPM) (Confédération Nationale du patronat de Mauritanie): 824 ave de Roi Fayçal, Ksar, BP 383, Nouakchott; tel. 525-33-01; fax 525-91-08; e-mail germe@opt.mr; f. 1960; professional asscn for all employers active in Mauritania; Pres. Mohamed Ould Bouamatou; Sec.-Gen. Seyid Ould Abdallahi.

UTILITIES

Electricity

Société Mauritanienne d'Electricité (SOMELEC): BP 355, Nouakchott; tel. 525-23-08; fax 525-39-95; f. 2001; state-owned; transfer to majority private-sector ownership planned for 2005; production and distribution of electricity; Dir-Gen. Col Ahmedou Ould Mohamed el-Kori.

Gas

Société Mauritanienne des Gaz (SOMAGAZ): POB 5089, Nouakchott; tel. 525-18-71; fax 529-47-86; e-mail somagaz@compunet.mr; production and distribution of butane gas; Dir-Gen. Mohamed Yahya Ould Mohamed el-Moctar.

Water

Société Nationale d'Eau (SNDE): ave 42-096, no. 106, Tevragh Zeina, BP 796, Nouakchott; tel. 525-52-73; fax 525-19-52; e-mail mfoudail@infotel.mr; f. 2001; Dir-Gen. Thiam Samba.

TRADE UNIONS

Confédération Générale des Travailleurs de Mauritanie: Nouakchott; f. 1992; obtained official recognition in 1994.

Confédération Libre des Travailleurs de Mauritanie: Nouakchott; f. 1995; Sec.-Gen. Samori Ould Beyi.

Union des Travailleurs de Mauritanie (UTM): Bourse du Travail, BP 630, Nouakchott; f. 1961; Sec.-Gen. Abderahmane Ould Boubou; 45,000 mems.

Transport

RAILWAYS

A 670-km railway connects the iron-ore deposits at Zouérate with Nouadhibou; a 40-km extension services the reserves at El Rhein, and a 30-km extension those at M'Haoudat. Motive power is diesel-electric. The Société Nationale Industrielle et Minière (SNIM) operates one of the longest (2.4 km) and heaviest (22,000 metric tons) trains in the world.

SNIM—Direction du Chemin de Fer et du Port: BP 42, Nouadhibou; tel. 574-51-74; fax 574-53-96; e-mail m.khalifa.beyah@zrt.snim.com; internet www.snim.com; f. 1963; Gen. Man. Mohamed Saleck Ould Heyine; Dir Khalifa Ould Beyah.

ROADS

In 1999 there were about 7,891 km of roads and tracks, of which only 2,090 km were paved. The 1,100-km Trans-Mauritania highway, completed in 1985, links Nouakchott with Néma in the east of the country. Plans exist for the construction of a 7,400-km highway, linking Nouakchott with the Libyan port of Tubruq (Tobruk). In August 1999 the Islamic Development Bank granted Mauritania a loan worth US $9.4m. to help finance the rebuilding of the Chouk–Kiffa road. The construction of a 470-km highway between Nouakchott and Nouadhibou was completed in 2004.

Société Mauritanienne des Transports (SOMATRA): Nouakchott; tel. 525-29-53; f. 1975; Pres. Cheikh Malainine Robert; Dir-Gen. Mamadou Souleymane Kane.

INLAND WATERWAYS

The River Senegal is navigable in the wet season by small coastal vessels as far as Kayes (Mali) and by river vessels as far as Kaédi; in the dry season as far as Rosso and Boghé, respectively. The major river ports are at Rosso, Kaédi and Gouraye.

SHIPPING

The principal port, at Point-Central, 10 km south of Nouadhibou, is almost wholly occupied with mineral exports. In 1998 the port handled 11.6m. metric tons of cargo, and cleared 3,804 vessels. There is also a commercial and fishing port at Nouadhibou. The deep-water Port de l'Amitié at Nouakchott, built and maintained with assistance from the People's Republic of China, was inaugurated in 1986. The port, which has a total capacity of about 1.5m. tons annually, handled 843,000 tons in 1998 (compared with 479,791 tons in 1990); the port cleared 453 vessels in 1998 (compared with 244 in 1990). In 2004 Mauritania's merchant fleet consisted of 146 vessels and had a total displacement of 497,296 grt.

Port Autonome de Nouakchott (Port de l'Amitié): BP 267/5103, El Mina, Nouakchott; tel. 525-14-53; fax 525-16-15; f. 1986; deep-water port; Dir-Gen. Col Wallad Ould Haimdoune.

Port Autonome de Nouadhibou: BP 236, Nouadhibou; tel. 574-51-34; f. 1973; state-owned; Pres. Bal Mohameded El Habib; Dir-Gen. Bébaha Ould Ahmed Youra.

Shipping Companies

Cie Mauritanienne de Navigation Maritime (COMAUNAM): 119 ave Nasser, BP 799, Nouakchott; tel. 525-36-34; fax 525-25-04; f. 1973; 51% state-owned, 49% owned by Govt of Algeria; nat. shipping co; forwarding agent, stevedoring; Chair. Mohand Tighilt; Dir-Gen. Kamil Abdelkader.

Société d'Acconage et de Manutention en Mauritanie (SAMMA): BP 258, Nouadhibou; tel. 574-52-63; fax 574-52-37; f. 1960; freight and handling, shipping agent, forwarding agent, stevedoring; Dir-Gen. Didi Ould Biha.

Société Générale de Consignation et d'Entreprises Maritimes (SOGECO): 1765 rue 22-002, Commune du Ksar, BP 351, Nouakchott; tel. 525-22-02; fax 525-39-03; e-mail sogeco@sogeco.sa.mr; internet www.sogecosa.com; f. 1973; shipping agent, forwarding, stevedoring; Man. Dir Sid' Ahmed Abeidna.

Société Mauritanienne pour la Pêche et la Navigation (SMPN): BP 40254, Nouakchott; tel. 525-36-38; fax 525-37-87; e-mail smpn@toptechnology.mr; Dir-Gen. Abdallahi Ould Ismail.

VOTRA: Route de l'Aéroport, BP 454, Nouakchott; tel. 525-24-10; fax 525-31-41; e-mail votra@mauritel.mr; internet www.votra.net; Dir-Gen. Mohamed Mahmoud Ould Maye.

CIVIL AVIATION

There are international airports at Nouakchott, Nouadhibou and at Néma, and 23 smaller airstrips. Facilities at Nouakchott were expanded considerably in the 1980s and early 1990s.

Air Mauritanie (Société Mixte Air Mauritanie): BP 41, Nouakchott; tel. 525-22-11; fax 525-38-15; e-mail reservation@airmauritanie.mr; internet www.airmauritanie.mr; f. 1974; 11% state-owned; domestic, regional and international passenger and cargo services; Dir-Gen. Sidi Zein.

Tourism

Mauritania's principal tourist attractions are its historical sites, several of which have been listed by UNESCO under its World Heritage Programme, and its game reserves and national parks. Some 24,000 tourists visited Mauritania in 1999. Receipts from tourism in 1999 totalled an estimated US $28m.

Office National du Tourisme: BP 246, Nouakchott; tel. 525-35-72; f. 2002; Dir Khadijétou Mint Boubou.

SOMASERT: BP 42, Nouadhibou; tel. 574-29-91; fax 574-90-43; e-mail somasert@snim.com; subsidiary of SNIM; responsible for promoting tourism, managing hotels and organizing tours; Dir-Gen. Mohamed Ould Biyah.

MAURITIUS

Introductory Survey

Location, Climate, Language, Religion, Flag, Capital

The Republic of Mauritius lies in the Indian Ocean. The principal island, from which the country takes its name, lies about 800 km (500 miles) east of Madagascar. The other main islands are Rodrigues, the Agalega Islands and the Cargados Carajos Shoals (St Brandon Islands). The climate is maritime sub-tropical and generally humid. The average annual temperature is 23°C (73°F) at sea-level, falling to 19°C (66°F) at an altitude of 600 m (about 2,000 ft). Average annual rainfall varies from 890 mm (35 ins) at sea-level to 5,080 mm (200 ins) on the highest parts. Tropical cyclones, which may be severe, occur between September and May. Most of the population are of Indian descent. The most widely spoken languages in 2000 were Creole (38.6%) and Bhojpuri (30.6%). English is the country's official language, and Creole (derived from French) the lingua franca. The principal religious group are Hindus, who comprise more than 50% of the population. About 30% are Christians and 17% are Muslims. The national flag (proportions 2 by 3) has four equal horizontal stripes, of red, blue, yellow and green. The capital is Port Louis.

Recent History

The islands of Mauritius and Rodrigues, formerly French possessions, passed into British control in 1810. Subsequent settlement came mainly from East Africa and India, and the European population has remained largely French-speaking.

A ministerial form of government was introduced in 1957. The first elections under universal adult suffrage, held in 1959, were won by the Mauritius Labour Party (MLP), led by Dr (later Sir) Seewoosagur Ramgoolam. Mauritius became independent, within the Commonwealth, on 12 March 1968, with Ramgoolam as Prime Minister.

In November 1965 the United Kingdom transferred the Chagos Archipelago (including the atoll of Diego Garcia), a Mauritian dependency about 2,000 km (1,250 miles) north-east of the main island, to the newly created British Indian Ocean Territory (BIOT, q.v.). Mauritius has subsequently campaigned for the return of the islands, which have been developed as a major US military base. Mauritius also claims sovereignty of the French-held island of Tromelin, about 550 km (340 miles) to the north-west.

During the 1970s political opposition to successive coalition governments formed by Ramgoolam was led by a radical left-wing group, the Mouvement Militant Mauricien (MMM), founded by Paul Bérenger. Although the MMM became the largest single party in the Legislative Assembly following a general election in December 1976, Ramgoolam was able to form a new coalition Government with the support of the Parti Mauricien Social Démocrate (PMSD). However, social unrest and rising unemployment undermined popular support for the Government, and at a general election in June 1982 the MMM, in alliance with the Parti Socialiste Mauricien (PSM), won all 60 contested seats on the main island. Aneerood (later Sir Aneerood) Jugnauth, the leader of the MMM, became Prime Minister, and Bérenger Minister of Finance.

The MMM/PSM coalition collapsed in March 1983, when Bérenger and his supporters resigned, following differences concerning economic policy. Jugnauth formed a new Government and a new party, the Mouvement Socialiste Militant (MSM), which subsequently merged with the PSM. A general election took place in August, at which an electoral alliance of the MSM, the MLP and the PMSD, led by Sir Gaëtan Duval, gained a legislative majority. Jugnauth formed a new coalition Government, in which Duval became Deputy Prime Minister. The MLP, however, withdrew from the coalition in February 1984.

Following a general election in August, the MSM again formed an electoral alliance with the PMSD and the MLP; the three parties obtained 39 of the 62 elective seats. Bérenger, who failed to secure a seat, transferred his functions as leader of the opposition in the Legislative Assembly to Dr Paramhansa Nababsingh (while Bérenger himself replaced Nababsingh as Secretary-General of the MMM). A new coalition, led by Jugnauth, took office in September, and the Government subsequently announced plans to make Mauritius a republic within the Commonwealth. In August 1988, following a disagreement over employment policies, the PMSD withdrew from the coalition.

In July 1990 the MSM and the MMM agreed to form an alliance to contest the next general election, and to promote constitutional measures allowing Mauritius to become a republic within the Commonwealth. This proposal, however, was jointly opposed by the MLP and the PMSD, prompting Jugnauth to dismiss the MLP leader, Sir Satcam Boolell, from the Government, together with two dissident ministers from the MSM. A further three ministers representing the MLP resigned, leaving only one MLP member in the Government. Boolell subsequently relinquished the leadership of the MLP to Dr Navinchandra Ramgoolam (the son of the late Sir Seewoosagur Ramgoolam). In September Jugnauth formed a new coalition Government.

Jugnauth dissolved the Legislative Assembly in August 1991. At the subsequent general election, which took place on 15 September, an alliance of the MSM, the MMM and the small Mouvement des Travaillistes Démocrates (MTD), won 57 of the 62 directly elected seats, while the MLP/PMSD alliance obtained three seats. The two remaining seats were secured by the Organisation du Peuple Rodriguais (OPR). Four 'additional' seats were subsequently allocated to members of the MLP/PMSD alliance. Jugnauth formed a new government coalition, to which nine representatives of the MMM (including Bérenger, who became Minister of External Affairs) and one representative of the MTD were appointed. Shortly afterwards Duval resigned from the Legislative Assembly.

In December 1991 the Legislative Assembly approved the constitutional framework for the country's transition to a republic within the Commonwealth. Following the proclamation of the Republic of Mauritius on 12 March 1992, the Legislative Assembly was redesignated as the National Assembly, and the incumbent Governor-General, Sir Veerasamy Ringadoo, became interim President. Later in March the Government announced its choice of Cassam Uteem, the Minister of Industry and Industrial Technology and a member of the MMM, to assume the presidency in June. Uteem was duly elected President by the National Assembly; Sir Rabindrah Ghurburrun, a member of the MMM, took office as Vice-President.

The government coalition came under increasing pressure during 1993, amid intensifying disputes between the MSM and the MMM. In August, following an unexpected success by the PMSD in municipal by-elections in a constituency that traditionally supported the MMM, a meeting between Bérenger and Ramgoolam prompted speculation that an MMM/MLP alliance was contemplated. Shortly afterwards Jugnauth dismissed Bérenger from the Council of Ministers, on the grounds that he had repeatedly criticized government policy.

The removal of Bérenger precipitated a serious crisis within the MMM, whose political bureau decided that the other nine members of the party who held ministerial portfolios should remain in the coalition Government. Led by Nababsingh, the Deputy Prime Minister, and Jean-Claude de l'Estrac, the Minister of Industry and Industrial Technology, supporters of the pro-coalition faction announced in October 1993 that Bérenger had been suspended as Secretary-General of the MMM. Bérenger and his supporters responded by expelling 11 MMM officials from the party, and seeking a legal ban on Nababsingh and de l'Estrac from using the party name. The split in the MMM led in November to a government reshuffle, in which the remaining two MMM ministers supporting Bérenger were replaced by members of the party's pro-coalition faction.

In April 1994 the MLP and the MMM announced that they had agreed terms for an alliance to contest the next general elections. Under its provisions, Ramgoolam was to be Prime Minister and Bérenger the Deputy Prime Minister, with ministerial portfolios allocated on the basis of 12 ministries to the MLP and nine to the MMM. In the same month, three deputies from the MSM, who had been close associates of a former Minister of Agriculture dismissed two months earlier, withdrew their support from the Government.

Nababsingh and the dissident faction of the MMM, having lost Bérenger's legal challenge for the use of the party name, formed a new party, the Renouveau Militant Mauricien (RMM), which formally commenced political activity in June 1994. In the same month Jugnauth declared that the Government, which retained a cohesive parliamentary majority, would remain in office to the conclusion of its mandate in September 1996.

During the course of a parliamentary debate in November 1994, Bérenger and de l'Estrac accepted a mutual challenge to resign their seats in the National Assembly and to contest by-elections. In the following month the MSM indicated that it would not oppose RMM candidates in the two polls. In January 1995, however, Jugnauth unsuccessfully sought to undermine the MLP/MMM alliance by offering electoral support to the MLP. The by-elections, held in February, were both won by MLP/MMM candidates, and Bérenger was returned to the National Assembly. Following these results, Jugnauth opened political negotiations with the PMSD, whose leader, Charles Gaëtan Xavier-Luc Duval (the son of Sir Gaëtan Duval), entered the coalition as Minister of Industry and Industrial Technology and Minister of Tourism. The post of Attorney-General and Minister of Justice was also allocated to the PMSD, and Sir Gaëtan Duval agreed to act as an economic adviser to the Prime Minister. As a result, however, of widespread opposition within the PMSD to participation in the coalition, Xavier-Luc Duval left the Government in October, and Sir Gaëtan Duval subsequently resumed the leadership of the party. The Minister for Rodrigues, representing the OPR, also left the Government.

In November 1995 the Government was defeated in a parliamentary vote, requiring a two-thirds' majority, to introduce a constitutional requirement for instruction in oriental languages to be provided in primary schools. Jugnauth dissolved the National Assembly, and at the subsequent general election in December the MLP/MMM alliance won a decisive victory: of the 62 elected seats, the MLP secured 35 seats, the MMM obtained 25 seats and the OPR two seats. Under constitutional arrangements providing representation for unsuccessful candidates attracting the largest number of votes, Sir Gaëtan Duval re-entered the National Assembly, together with two members of the Mouvement Rodriguais and one representative of Hizbullah, an Islamist fundamentalist group. Ramgoolam became Prime Minister of the new MLP/MMM coalition, with Bérenger as Deputy Prime Minister with responsibility for foreign and regional relations. Sir Gaëtan Duval died in May 1996 and was succeeded in the National Assembly and as leader of the PMSD by his brother, Hervé Duval, although Xavier-Luc Duval continued to command a significant following within the party.

Serious divisions began to emerge within the coalition Government in late 1996, when differences were reported between Ramgoolam and Bérenger over the allocation of ministerial responsibilities and the perception by the MMM of delays in the implementation of social and economic reforms. In January 1997 rumours had begun to circulate of a possible political alliance between the MMM and the MSM, and in March it was reported that Ramgoolam intended to seek support from certain members of the PMSD should the MMM decide to withdraw from the Government. Bérenger's criticism of the coalition's performance intensified in the following months, and culminated in June in his dismissal from the Government and the consequent withdrawal of the MMM from the coalition. Following unsuccessful efforts by Ramgoolam to draw the PMSD into a new administration, an MLP Council of Ministers was formed by Ramgoolam, who additionally assumed Bérenger's former responsibilities for foreign affairs. Ramgoolam emphasized his determination to remain in office for the full legislative term to December 2000. On 28 June 1997 the National Assembly re-elected Cassam Uteem to a second five-year term as President. A prominent supporter of the MLP, Angidi Verriah Chettiar, was elected Vice-President.

Following the dissolution of the MLP/MMM alliance, Bérenger sought to assume the leadership of a consolidated political opposition to the Government. In August 1997 two small parties, the Mouvement Militant Socialiste Mauricien (MMSM) and the Rassemblement pour la Réforme (RPR), agreed to support Bérenger in this aim. The alliance was extended to include a breakaway faction of the PMSD, known as the 'Vrais Bleus', under the leadership of Hervé Duval, who had been replaced as party leader by his nephew, Xavier-Luc Duval, an opponent of co-operation with the MMM.

In April 1998 the MMM, the MMSM, the RPR and the 'Vrais Bleus' formed an electoral coalition, the Alliance Nationale, to contest a by-election for a vacant seat in the National Assembly. The seat, which was retained by the MLP, had also been sought by Jugnauth on behalf of the MSM, which remained unrepresented in the National Assembly. Jugnauth, seeking to revitalize his party's prospects in preparation for the next general election (which was constitutionally required to take place by December 2000), subsequently entered negotiations with Bérenger for an electoral alliance, and in December 1998 both parties agreed terms for a joint list of candidates. Ramgoolam, following a reshuffle of the Council of Ministers in October, announced proposals in the following month for an all-party review of the electoral system, with a view to considering the adoption of proportional representation.

The MLP announced in mid-1999 its endorsement of the candidature of Xavier-Luc Duval for a legislative by-election to be held in September. Xavier-Luc Duval, after obtaining the vacant seat, joined the Government as Minister of Industry, Commerce, Corporate Affairs and Financial Services, following an extensive government reshuffle completed at the end of the month. The selection in October of Pravind Jugnauth, the son of Sir Anerood Jugnauth, as Deputy Leader of the MSM gave rise to speculation that Sir Anerood was contemplating retirement from politics and intended his son to be his successor. It also provoked divisions within the informal alliance that had been formed between the MMM and the MSM in February 1999.

None the less, in August 2000 the MSM/MMM alliance was made official, in advance of the imminent general election, on the basis that Jugnauth would lead as Prime Minister for three years in the event of victory, before assuming the more honorary role of President, thus allowing Bérenger to become Prime Minister for the remaining two years. In the same month both the Minister of Social Security and National Unity, Prakash Bundhun, and the Minister of Health, Nundhkeshwarsingh Deerpalsingh, resigned, following separate allegations of fraud and investigations by the Economic Crime Office; Deerpalsingh was subsequently arrested.

A general election was held on 11 September 2000. There was a high rate of participation, with 81% of the 790,000 registered electors casting their ballots. The MSM/MMM alliance achieved an overwhelming victory, winning 54 of the 62 directly elected seats in the National Assembly, while the MLP/PMSD alliance gained only six seats and the OPR two seats. As agreed, Sir Anerood Jugnauth became Prime Minister again, while Paul Bérenger was appointed Deputy Prime Minister and Minister of Finance. A new Council of Ministers was appointed one week later.

In November 2000 the British High Court of Justice ruled that the eviction of several thousand inhabitants of the Chagos Archipelago between 1967 and 1973, to allow the construction of a US military base on the atoll of Diego Garcia, had been unlawful, and overturned a 1971 ordinance preventing the islanders from returning to the Archipelago. (The majority of the displaced islanders had been resettled in Mauritius, which had administered the Chagos Archipelago until its transfer to BIOT in 1965.) Following the ruling, the Mauritian Government declared its right to sovereignty over the islands to be indisputable and sought international recognition as such. Jugnauth stated that he would be prepared to negotiate with the USA over the continued presence of the military base. The United Kingdom responded that it would return the islands if, as had been maintained for many years, the USA was prepared to move out of the base on Diego Garcia. India declared its support for the Mauritian Government's claim to sovereignty, as part of the close relationship being encouraged between the two countries.

In November 2001 exiled Chagos islanders demonstrated outside the British High Commission in Port Louis, in support of their demands for compensation from the British Government. In February 2002 legislation allowing the displaced islanders to apply for British citizenship received royal assent in the United Kingdom. At that time the British Government was also examining the feasibility of a return to the Chagos Archipelago for the islanders, who continued to seek compensation.

In January 2002 a commission on constitutional and electoral reform presented its proposals at a series of public forums, before submitting them to the Government for consideration. Recommendations included the introduction of a system of proportional representation in legislative elections and a reinforcement of presidential powers. In mid-February controversial legislation on the prevention of terrorism was finally promulgated by the Chief Justice of the Supreme Court, Arianga Pillay, acting as interim President, following the resignations of both President

Uteem and his successor, Vice-President Chettiar, over the issue. The legislation had been rejected by opposition parties and proved unpopular with many sections of society for arrogating excessive powers to the authorities and infringing on citizens' rights. On 25 February Karl Offman was elected as President by an extraordinary session of the National Assembly, which was boycotted by opposition deputies. Although formally elected for five years, Offman was to relinquish the presidency to Jugnauth in October 2003; in preparation for this, in April 2003 Jugnauth announced his resignation from the leadership of the MSM, to be succeeded by his son, Pravind.

In August 2003, in preparation for the transfer of governing roles, a constitutional amendment was approved by the National Assembly to increase the powers of the President, giving the incumbent the right to refuse a request from the Prime Minister to dissolve the legislature following a vote of 'no confidence'. As agreed, on 1 October Offman resigned as President and was replaced, in an acting capacity, by the Vice-President, Raouf Bundhun, pending the election by the National Assembly of Sir Aneerood Jugnauth as his successor one week later. Jugnauth had resigned as Prime Minister on 30 September and was immediately replaced by Paul Bérenger, who appointed a new Council of Ministers. On 23 December Bérenger effected a government reshuffle, notably appointing Jaya Krishna Cuttaree as Minister of Foreign Affairs, International Trade and Regional Co-operation. During his first months in office Bérenger conducted a premiership active in international diplomacy, visiting two of the country's principal trading partners, India and France, and signing co-operation agreements with Madagascar. In early 2004 he also renewed the campaign to reclaim sovereignty of the Chagos Archipelago from the United Kingdom, on the basis that international law does not allow the dismemberment of a country before independence, and of Tromelin from France. It was established in 2004 that Mauritius had the right to pursue the case of the Chagos islands at the International Court of Justice, in spite of British objections on the basis of restrictions imposed by membership of the Commonwealth. In mid-December a minor reorganization of the Cabinet of Ministers took place.

In early February 2005 the Minister of Public Infrastructure, Land Transport and Shipping, Anil Bachoo, resigned, to be replaced by Govindranath Gunness; the Minister of Local Government and Solid Waste Management, Mookhesswur Choonee, also left office the following week and was succeeded by Prithvirajsing Roopun. The two erstwhile ministers formed a new opposition party the following month, the Mouvement Sociale Démocrate (MSD), having also resigned from the MSM alleging poor leadership of that party by Pravind Jugnauth. Bachoo and Choonee reportedly disapproved of an apparent pre-electoral agreement between the parties of the ruling coalition, whereby, should they successfully be re-elected to office, Bérenger would relinquish the premiership in mid-term in favour of Pravind Jugnauth, just as the incumbent President (Pravind Jugnauth's father) had in September 2003. The MSD announced the formation of an electoral alliance with the MLP, known as the Social Alliance, thus creating a credible rival political force to the governing parties for the forthcoming legislative elections.

At the elections, which were held on 3 July 2005, the Social Alliance bloc defeated the incumbent coalition, winning 38 of the 62 directly elected mandates. The MSM/MMM alliance took 22 seats while the OPR secured two. The rate of voter participation was 81.5%. Ramgoolam was appointed as Prime Minister and a new 19-member Council of Ministers was sworn into office on later that month. At local elections held in early October the Social Alliance won 122 of the 126 seats contested, including many long-term MSM/MMM strongholds. Following the elections the PMSD withdrew from the opposition alliance in which it had participated with the MSM and MMM. Tensions between the politically opposed premier and President initially proved somewhat obstructive to the functioning of the Government, however, they subsequently eased.

Government

Constitutional amendments, which were approved by the Legislative Assembly (henceforth known as the National Assembly) in December 1991 and came into effect on 12 March 1992, provided for the establishment of a republic. The constitutional Head of State is the President of the Republic, who is elected by a simple majority of the National Assembly for a five-year term of office. Legislative power is vested in the unicameral National Assembly, which comprises the Speaker, 62 members elected by universal adult suffrage for a term of five years, up to eight 'additional' members (unsuccessful candidates who receive the largest number of votes at a legislative election, to whom seats are allocated by the Electoral Supervisory Commission to ensure a balance in representation of the different ethnic groups), and the Attorney-General (if not an elected member). Executive power is vested in the Prime Minister, who is appointed by the President and is the member of the National Assembly best able to command a majority in the Assembly. The President appoints other ministers, on the recommendation of the Prime Minister.

Defence

The country has no standing defence forces, although at 1 August 2005 paramilitary forces were estimated to number 2,000, comprising a special mobile force of 1,500, to ensure internal security, and a coastguard of 500. Projected budgetary expenditure on defence for 2005 was Rs 622m.

Economic Affairs

In 2004, according to estimates by the World Bank, Mauritius' gross national income (GNI), measured at average 2002–04 prices, was US $5,730m., equivalent to $4,640 per head (or $11,870 per head on an international purchasing-power parity basis). During 1995–2004, it was estimated, the population increased at an average annual rate of 1.1%, while gross domestic product (GDP) per head increased, in real terms, by an average of 3.9% per year. Overall GDP increased, in real terms, at an average annual rate of 5.0% in 1995–2004; growth in 2004 was 4.2%.

Agriculture (including hunting, forestry and fishing) contributed 5.4% of GDP in 2005, according to provisional estimates, and engaged 9.7% of the employed labour force in 2004. The principal cash crops are sugar cane (sugar accounted for 24.2% of export earnings in 2005, according to provisional figures), tea and tobacco. Food crops include potatoes and vegetables. Poultry farming is also practised. During 1995–2004, according to the World Bank, the GDP of the agricultural sector increased, in real terms, at an average rate of 1.2% per year; it declined by 12.2% in 2003, but increased by 2.3% in 2004.

Industry (including mining, manufacturing, construction and utilities) contributed 26.0% of GDP in 2005, according to provisional estimates, and engaged 35.2% of the employed labour force in 2004. During 1995–2004, according to the World Bank, industrial GDP increased, in real terms, at an average annual rate of 4.4%; growth in 2004 was 1.2%. Mining is negligible, accounting for only 0.1% of employment in 2004 and a provisional 0.1% of GDP in 2005.

Manufacturing contributed 18.7% of GDP in 2005, according to provisional estimates, and engaged 24.8% of the employed labour force in 2004. The principal branches of manufacturing are clothing and food products, mainly sugar. Clothing (excluding footwear) provided 46.8% of export earnings in 2005, according to provisional figures. Factories in the Export Processing Zone (EPZ) import raw materials to produce goods for the export market. Clothing and apparel firms accounted for 75.8% of total EPZ employment in September 2005. Other important products include fish preparations, textiles, and precious stones. Export receipts from EPZ products provisionally represented 46.1% of total export earnings (and 16.6% of import earnings) in 2005. During 1995–2004, according to the World Bank, the GDP of the manufacturing sector, increased, in real terms, at an average annual rate of 4.0%; manufacturing GDP declined by 1.1% in 2003, but grew by 0.9% in 2004.

Electric energy is derived principally from thermal (oil-fired) and hydroelectric power stations. Bagasse (a by-product of sugar cane) is also used as fuel for generating electricity and in 2004 it accounted for 21.7% of electricity produced (93% of indigenous production; 22% of electricity was locally produced). Imports of refined petroleum products comprised 14.3% of the value of merchandise imports in 2005, according to provisional figures. Thermal energy accounted for 96.5% of electricity generated in 2004.

The services sector contributed 68.6% of GDP in 2005, according to provisional estimates, and engaged 55.1% of the employed labour force in 2004. Tourism is the third most important source of revenue, after manufacturing and agriculture. The number of foreign tourist arrivals increased to 761,063 in 2005 from 422,000 in 1995. Gross receipts from tourism were estimated to total Rs 25,704m. in 2005. An 'offshore' banking sector and a stock exchange have operated since 1989. According to the World Bank, the real GDP of the services sector increased at an average annual rate of 5.9% in 1995–2004; growth in 2004 was also 5.9%.

In 2004 Mauritius recorded a visible trade deficit of US $575.0m., and a deficit of $107.5m. on the current account of the balance of payments. In 2005 the principal source of imports (9.8%) was the People's Republic of China; other major suppliers were South Africa (8.6%), France, India and Bahrain. The principal market for exports in that year (32.0%) was the United Kingdom; other significant purchasers were France, the USA, the United Arab Emirates, Madagascar and Italy. The principal exports in 2005 were clothing, sugar, basic manufactures and fish and fish preparations. The principal imports in that year were machinery and transport equipment (28.1%), basic manufactures, refined petroleum products and food and live animals.

In 2004/05 there was an estimated budgetary deficit of Rs 9,028.7m. (equivalent to 4.8% of GDP). Mauritius' external debt totalled US $2,550m. at the end of 2003, of which $927m. was long-term public debt. In that year the cost of debt-servicing was equivalent to 7.2% of the value of exports of goods and services. The annual rate of inflation averaged 7.2% in 1990–2004. Consumer prices increased by an average of 4.9% in 2005. About 8.2% of the labour force were unemployed in 2004.

Mauritius is a member of the Common Market for Eastern and Southern Africa (COMESA, see p. 191), the Southern African Development Community (SADC, see p. 358) and the Indian Ocean Commission (IOC, see p. 386), which aims to promote regional economic co-operation. Mauritius was among the founder members of the Indian Ocean Rim Association for Regional Co-operation (IOR—ARC, see p. 386) in 1997.

Mauritius' economy was traditionally dependent on sugar production, and economic growth was therefore vulnerable to adverse climatic conditions and changes in international prices for sugar. However, from the 1980s the Government pursued a successful policy of diversification, encouraging labour-intensive manufacturing (particularly of clothing) in the EPZ, and implemented extensive reforms with IMF support. Port Louis has been established as a free port and the Government has promoted further measures to achieve economic diversification and liberalization, aimed at encouraging foreign investment and increasing export revenue. The geographical location of Mauritius, as well as a number of incentive measures implemented by the Government, has contributed to its successful establishment as an international financial centre. By the late 1990s the island had become a significant provider of 'offshore' banking and investment services for a number of south Asian countries (particularly India), as well as for members of SADC and IOR—ARC groupings. By positioning itself as a conduit for capital and encouraging foreign companies to register there, attracted by beneficial double-taxation treaties agreed with many countries, Mauritius has become the largest foreign investor in India. Mauritius has also been promoted as a future hub of communications and information technology (IT), with the aim of encouraging the next stage of economic development and transferring the emphasis towards services. The construction of a free zone 'cybercity' was initiated, with an investment of US $110m. from India, and in 2000 a South Africa–Far East underwater fibre optic cable was laid, linking Port Louis to both regions. The expiry of the preferential Multi-Fibre Arrangement (subsequently known as the Agreement on Textiles and Clothing) with the European Union (EU, see p. 228) in December 2004 posed a further threat to the already beleaguered textiles industry, exposing it to direct competition from countries with lower labour costs, particularly those in Asia; many Hong Kong companies withdrew from the country. The Government was also in negotiations with the EU over compensation arrangements for the reduction of preferential trade terms for countries of the African, Caribbean and Pacific from July 2005 (although this was to decrease sugar prices by some 36%, the effects were expected to be evident over the longer term). The Government was reluctant to close down the sugar sector altogether, as sugar cane is one of the few crops resilient to the extreme weather conditions, is strongly resistant to soil erosion and covers more than one-third of the land. (It was hoped that the remaining consolidated companies could develop more specialized, high-value products and the further production of bagasse.) In light of the inevitable decline in the mainstays of the economy—sugar and textiles—the country sought further to diversify its strengths. The authorities also focused on the development of the high-end tourist sector, the most important result of which was the liberalization of international air routes, and the introduction of favourable terms for those wishing to purchase holiday homes. A major obstacle to the expansion of the country's IT and communications industry was a shortage of skilled workers, and efforts were being made to eliminate obstructive bureaucracy that inhibited the employment of skilled foreign migrants. A third sector for expansion and optimization was that of seafood; Mauritius has the advantage of a well established infrastructure for processing, storage and transport, as well as access to prime fishing areas. Plans were also under way to transform the island into a duty-free shopping hub for tourists as part of a four-year programme. The budgetary deficit in 2005/06 remained a concern, as did the high level of unemployment, while the Government was warned by international institutions to balance its social spending with economic rigour. In 2005 the external current account developed a deficit owing to a decline in exports and a sharp increase in the prices of petroleum imports; Mauritius is obliged to import petroleum and is thus vulnerable to the high price rises, which the authorities have been reluctant to pass on to the public. A contraction in sugar production of some 9% in 2005 had a negative effect on GDP growth. Growth was forecast to remain subdued in 2006 and 2007.

Education

Education is officially compulsory for seven years between the ages of five and 12. Primary education begins at five years of age and lasts for six years. Secondary education, beginning at the age of 11, lasts for up to seven years, comprising a first cycle of three years and a second of four years. Primary and secondary education are available free of charge and became compulsory in 2005. In 2005 the number of children attending primary schools included 102% of the appropriate age-group, while the comparable ratio for secondary schools was 67%. The education system provides for instruction in seven Asian languages (71% of primary school children and 30% of secondary school children were studying at least one of these in 2005). The Government exercises indirect control of the large private sector in secondary education (in 2005 only 70 of 188 schools were state administered). The University of Mauritius had 6,602 students in 2005/06 (35% of whom were part-time students); in addition, many students receive further education abroad. Of total expenditure by the central Government in 2004/05, Rs 6,743m. (15.2%) was for education, according to provisional figures.

Public Holidays

2006: 1–2 January (New Year), 29 January (Chinese New Year), 1 February (Abolition of Slavery Commemoration), 26 February (Maha Shivaratree), 12 March (National Day), 30 March (Ougadi), 1 May (Labour Day), 15 August (Assumption), 27 August (Ganesh Chathurti), 2 November (Arrival of Indentured Labourers), 21 October (Divali), 23 October* (Id al-Fitr, end of Ramadan), 25 December (Christmas Day).

2007: 1–3 January (New Year), 1 February (Abolition of Slavery Commemoration), 16 February (Maha Shivaratree), 18 February (Chinese New Year), 12 March (National Day), 20 March (Ougadi), 1 May (Labour Day), 15 August (Assumption), 15 September (Ganesh Chathurti), 13 October* (Id al-Fitr, end of Ramadan), 2 November (Arrival of Indentured Labourers), 9 November (Divali), 25 December (Christmas Day).

Thaipoosam Cavadee is also celebrated in late January or early February. However, the exact date is dependent on the appearance of a full moon.

*This holiday is dependent on the Islamic lunar calendar and may vary by one or two days from the dates given.

Weights and Measures

The metric system is in standard use.

MAURITIUS

Statistical Survey

Source (unless otherwise stated): Central Statistics Office, LIC Bldg, President John F. Kennedy St, Port Louis; tel. 212-2316; fax 211-4150; e-mail cso@mail.gov.mu; internet statsmauritius.gov.mu.

Area and Population

AREA, POPULATION AND DENSITY

Area (sq km)	2,040*
Population (census results)	
1 July 1990	1,058,942†
2 July 2000‡	
Males	583,949
Females	595,188
Total	1,179,137
Population (official estimates at 31 December)	
2003	1,228,128
2004	1,238,061
2005	1,248,592
Density (per sq km) at 31 December 2005	612.0

* 788 sq miles.
† Including an adjustment of 2,115 for underenumeration.
‡ Excluding an adjustment for underenumeration.

ISLANDS

		Population	
			Official estimates
	Area (sq km)	2000 census	31 December 2005
Mauritius	1,865	1,143,069	1,211,308
Rodrigues	104	35,779	36,995
Other islands	71	289	289

Ethnic Groups: Island of Mauritius, mid-1982: 664,480 Indo-Mauritians (507,985 Hindus, 156,495 Muslims), 264,537 general population (incl. Creole and Franco-Mauritian communities), 20,669 Chinese.

LANGUAGE GROUPS
(census of 2 July 2000)*

Arabic	806	Marathi	16,587
Bhojpuri	361,250	Tamil	44,731
Chinese	16,972	Telegu	18,802
Creole	454,763	Urdu	34,120
English	1,075	Other languages	169,619
French	21,171	Not stated	3,170
Hindi	35,782	**Total**	**1,178,848**

* Figures refer to the languages of cultural origin of the population of the islands of Mauritius and Rodrigues only. The data exclude an adjustment for underenumeration.

POPULATION BY DISTRICT
(mid–2004, provisional figures)

Plaine Wilhems	372,700	Riv du Rempart	104,200
Flacq	133,800	Moka	78,600
Port Louis	130,500	Savanne	68,700
Pamplemousses	129,600	Black River	67,200
Grand Port	111,400	Rodrigues	36,700

PRINCIPAL TOWNS
(census of 2 July 2000)

Port Louis (capital)	144,303	Curepipe	78,920
Beau Bassin/Rose Hill	103,872	Quatre Bornes	75,884
Vacoas/Phoenix	100,066		

Source: Thomas Brinkhoff, *City Population* (internet www.citypopulation.de).

Mid-2003 (UN estimate, incl. suburbs): Port Louis 143,447 (Source: UN, *World Urbanization Prospects: The 2003 Revision*).

BIRTHS, MARRIAGES AND DEATHS*

	Registered live births		Registered marriages		Registered deaths	
	Number	Rate (per 1,000)	Number	Rate (per 1,000)	Number	Rate (per 1,000)
1998	19,434	16.7	10,898	9.4	7,839	6.8
1999	20,311	17.3	11,295	9.6	7,944	6.8
2000	20,205	17.0	10,963	9.2	7,982	6.7
2001	19,696	16.4	10,635	8.9	7,983	6.7
2002	19,983	16.5	10,484	8.6	8,310	6.9
2003	19,343	15.8	10,812	8.8	8,520	7.0
2004	19,230	15.5	11,385	9.2	8,475	6.8
2005†	18,829	15.1	11,294	9.0	8,648	7.0

* Figures refer to the islands of Mauritius and Rodrigues only. The data are tabulated by year of registration, rather than by year of occurrence.
† Provisional figures.

Expectation of life (WHO estimates, years at birth): 72 (males 69; females 76) in 2003 (Source: WHO, *World Health Report*).

ECONOMICALLY ACTIVE POPULATION
('000 persons aged 15 years and over, incl. foreign workers)

	2002	2003	2004
Agriculture, forestry and fishing	50.1	49.5	49.0
Sugar cane	21.6	19.9	19.1
Mining and quarrying	1.3	0.3	0.3
Manufacturing	136.8	132.0	125.2
EPZ	85.7	80.0	71.6
Electricity and water	3.1	3.0	3.0
Construction	46.3	48.0	49.1
Wholesale and retail trade, repair of motor vehicles and household goods	67.4	71.3	74.8
Hotels and restaurants	26.3	27.4	28.4
Transport, storage and communications	34.1	34.9	35.9
Financial intermediation	7.4	7.8	7.9
Real estate, renting and business activities	15.7	16.6	18.1
Public administration and defence	38.2	39.2	39.2
Education	23.6	25.1	26.2
Health and social work	13.4	14.0	14.5
Other services	30.1	31.3	33.1
Total employed	**493.8**	**500.4**	**504.5**
Males	328.6	332.4	336.9
Females	165.2	168.0	167.6
Unemployed	37.4	40.5	45.1
Total labour force	**531.2**	**540.9**	**549.6**

* From 2004, figures are based on a quarterly continuous multi-purpose household survey with a minimum qualification age of 15 years; figures for the years prior to 2004 have been recalculated on the basis of the 2004 data and criteria.

MAURITIUS   Statistical Survey

Health and Welfare

KEY INDICATORS

Total fertility rate (children per woman, 2003)	1.9
Under-5 mortality rate (per 1,000 live births, 2004)	15
HIV/AIDS (% of persons aged 15–49, 2001)	0.10
Physicians (per 1,000 head, 1995)	0.85
Hospital beds (per 1,000 head, 1994)	3.07
Health expenditure (2002): US $ per head (PPP)	317
Health expenditure (2002): % of GDP	2.9
Health expenditure (2002): public (% of total)	76.9
Access to water (% of persons, 2002)	100
Access to sanitation (% of persons, 2002)	99
Human Development Index (2003): ranking	65
Human Development Index (2003): value	0.791

For sources and definitions, see explanatory note on p. vi.

Agriculture

PRINCIPAL CROPS
('000 metric tons)

	2002	2003	2004*
Potatoes	13.3	12.3	12.3
Sugar cane	4,873.9	5,198.7	5,200.0
Coconuts	1.9*	1.9*	1.9
Cabbages	8.2	6.2	6.2
Lettuce	2.2	2.0	2.0
Tomatoes	11.7	13.2	13.2
Cauliflower	1.8	1.7	1.7
Pumpkins, squash and gourds	8.0*	8.0*	8.0
Cucumbers and gherkins*	9.0	9.0	9.0
Aubergines (Eggplants)*	1.6	1.6	1.6
Dry onions	7.1	3.9	4.0
Carrots	8.6	4.9	5.0
Other vegetables*	21.7	21.9	22.0
Bananas	7.2	12.1	12.1
Pineapples	1.9	4.6	4.6
Other fruit*	1.2	1.2	1.2
Tea (made)	1.4	1.4	1.4
Tobacco (leaves)	0.5	0.4	0.5

* FAO estimate(s).
Source: FAO.

LIVESTOCK
('000 head, year ending September)

	2001	2002	2003
Cattle*	28	28	28
Pigs	14*	12*	13
Sheep*	12	12	12
Goats*	95	93	93
Poultry*	8,900	9,800	9,800

* FAO estimate(s).
2004: Production as in 2003 (FAO estimates).
Source: FAO.

LIVESTOCK PRODUCTS
('000 metric tons)

	2002	2003	2004*
Beef and veal	2	3	5
Poultry meat	29	28	28
Cows' milk	4	4	4
Hen eggs*	5	5	5

* FAO estimates.
Source: FAO.

Forestry

ROUNDWOOD REMOVALS
('000 cubic metres, excl. bark)

	2002	2003	2004
Sawlogs, veneer logs and logs for sleepers	4	5	5
Other industrial wood	2	3	3
Fuel wood	9	6	6
Total	15	14	14

SAWNWOOD PRODUCTION
('000 cubic metres, incl. railway sleepers)

	2002*	2003	2004
Coniferous (softwood)	2	2	2
Broadleaved (hardwood)	1	1	1
Total	3	3	3

* FAO estimates.
Source: FAO.

Fishing

(metric tons, live weight)

	2001	2002	2003
Capture	10,985	10,706	11,136
Unicorn cod	340	271	295
Groupers and seabasses	938	885	879
Snappers and jobfishes	2,184	2,113	1,806
Emperors (Scavengers)	4,008	4,078	3,955
Goatfishes	556	501	537
Spinefeet (Rabbitfishes)	450	365	404
Swordfish	37	189	602
Tuna-like fishes	745	745	745
Octopuses	347	335	327
Aquaculture	59	56	33
Total catch	11,044	10,762	11,169

Source: FAO.

Industry

SELECTED PRODUCTS
('000 metric tons, unless otherwise indicated)

	2002	2003	2004*
Raw sugar	520.7	537.2	572.4
Molasses	140.8	160.0	155.8
Beer and stout (hectolitres)	348.4	400.8	430.5
Iron bars and steel tubes	52.4	58.7	65.0
Fertilizers	86.1	82.0	89.4
Electric energy (million kWh)	1,715	2,058	2,117

* Provisional figures.
Frozen fish (metric tons): 4,700 in 2000.
Canned fish (metric tons): 20,173 in 2000.
Cigarettes (million): 976 in 2000.

MAURITIUS

Finance

CURRENCY AND EXCHANGE RATES

Monetary Units
100 cents = 1 Mauritian rupee.

Sterling, Dollar and Euro Equivalents (30 December 2005)
£1 sterling = 52.80 rupees;
US $1 = 30.67 rupees;
€1 = 36.18 rupees;
1,000 Mauritian rupees = £18.94 = $32.61 = €27.64.

Average Exchange Rate (Mauritian rupees per US $)
2003   27.901
2004   29.498
2005   29.496

BUDGET
(million rupees, year ending 30 June)

Revenue*	2002/03	2003/04	2004/05†
Tax revenue	25,879.2	29,067.9	32,718.6
Taxes on income, profits and capital gains	4,013.5	4,669.3	5,829.0
Individual income tax	1,859.0	2,264.6	2,553.2
Corporate tax	2,154.5	2,404.7	3,275.8
Taxes on property	1,374.6	1,469.0	1,680.2
Financial transactions	1,068.3	1,130.1	1,270.8
Domestic taxes on goods and services	13,957.0	15,531.3	17,464.7
Excise duties	2,332.2	2,407.9	2,838.4
Taxes on services	1,069.0	1,097.2	1,235.1
Value-added tax	9,811.5	11,189.1	12,528.5
Taxes on international trade	6,522.6	7,385.3	7,730.5
Stamp duty	11.5	13.0	14.2
Non-tax revenue	4,033.2	3,919.9	2,473.8
Property income	2,860.9	2,688.6	1,234.7
Other non-tax revenue	1,172.3	1,231.3	1,538.8
Capital revenue	23.0	69.7	413.8
Total	29,935.4	33,057.5	35,606.2

Expenditure‡	2002/03	2003/04	2004/05†
General public services	3,077.8	3,315.9	3,535.4
Public order and safety	2,905.1	3,562.6	3,608.0
Education	5,587.9	6,132.8	6,742.8
Health	3,151.2	3,764.9	3,948.1
Social security and welfare	7,011.6	7,886.6	8,720.0
Housing and community amenities	3,322.5	2,982.0	3,209.0
Recreational, cultural and religious services	819.8	773.4	541.1
Agriculture, forestry, fishing and hunting	1,275.3	1,571.4	1,554.8
Transportation and communications	1,122.7	1,090.0	695.5
Other economic services	2,131.8	1,913.4	2,118.1
Other expenditure	8,146.9	8,968.4	9,714.3
Public debt interest	6,390.4	6,585.8	7,184.0
Total expenditure	38,552.6	41,963.4	44,387.1
Current	31,538.1	34,885.4	38,042.3
Capital	7,014.5	7,078.0	6,344.8

* Excluding grants received (million rupees): 362.7 in 2002/03; 618.3 in 2003/04; 444.0 in 2004/05.
† Provisional figures.
‡ Excluding lending minus repayments (million rupees): 980.2 in 2002/03; 603.9 in 2003/04; 687.8 in 2004/05.

Source: Ministry of Finance.

INTERNATIONAL RESERVES
(US $ million at 31 December)

	2003	2004	2005
Gold (market prices)	21.1	23.9	25.9
IMF special drawing rights	25.6	27.2	25.7
Reserve position in IMF	32.5	34.0	25.0
Foreign exchange	1,519.2	1,544.7	1,298.2
Total	1,598.4	1,629.8	1,374.8

Source: IMF, *International Financial Statistics*.

MONEY SUPPLY
(million rupees at 31 December)

	2003	2004	2005
Currency outside banks	9,347.0	10,731.2	11,743.7
Demand deposits at deposit money banks	10,940.5	12,682.7	14,104.5
Total money (incl. others)	20,401.1	23,616.5	26,265.2

Source: IMF, *International Financial Statistics*.

COST OF LIVING
(Consumer Price Index; base: July 2001–June 2002 = 100)

	2002	2003	2004
Food and non-alcoholic beverages	103.5	105.9	112.5
Alcoholic beverages and tobacco	104.8	109.7	119.8
Clothing and footwear	102.2	103.3	105.0
Housing, fuel and electricity	103.4	105.0	107.1
Household operations	103.9	105.5	107.6
All items (incl. others)	104.2	107.0	112.1

NATIONAL ACCOUNTS
(million rupees in current prices, revised estimates)

National Income and Product

	2003	2004	2005*
Compensation of employees	58,658	63,821	68,880
Operating surplus / Consumption of fixed capital	76,742	86,565	93,968
Gross domestic product (GDP) at factor cost	135,400	150,386	162,848
Taxes on production and imports / Less Subsidies	21,239	24,733	24,395
GDP in purchasers' values	156,639	175,119	187,243
Primary incomes received from abroad / Less Primary incomes paid abroad	−833	−389	−1,219
Gross national income	155,806	174,730	186,024
Current transfers from abroad / Less Current transfers paid abroad	1,471	−1,374	1,773
Gross national disposable income	157,277	173,356	187,797

* Provisional figures.

Expenditure on the Gross Domestic Product

	2003	2004	2005
Private final consumption expenditure	96,153	111,326	128,949
Government final consumption expenditure	22,272	25,043	27,265
Gross fixed capital formation	35,554	38,003	39,814
Increase in stocks	640	4,913	2,313
Total domestic expenditure	154,619	179,285	198,341
Exports of goods and services	88,714	94,859	112,856
Less Imports of goods and services	86,694	99,025	124,224
GDP in purchasers' values	156,639	175,119	186,973

MAURITIUS

Gross Domestic Product by Economic Activity

	2003	2004	2005
Agriculture, hunting, forestry, and fishing	8,727	9,647	9,357
Mining and quarrying	84	87	93
Manufacturing	29,581	31,799	32,333
Electricity, gas and water	3,409	3,663	3,408
Construction	8,269	8,835	9,078
Wholesale and retail trade, repair of motor vehicles and personal goods	15,166	17,337	19,640
Hotels and restaurants	9,427	11,302	12,426
Transport, storage and communications	18,496	19,964	22,476
Financial intermediation	13,072	14,429	16,175
Real estate, renting and business activities	13,026	14,604	16,569
Public administration and defence; compulsory social security	9,408	10,580	11,504
Education	6,280	7,088	7,809
Health and social work	4,423	5,107	5,693
Other services	4,839	5,390	6,166
Sub-total	**144,207**	**159,832**	**172,727**
Less Financial intermediation services indirectly measured	7,374	7,885	8,600
Gross value added in basic prices	**136,833**	**151,947**	**164,127**
Taxes, less subsidies, on products	19,806	23,172	22,846
GDP in market prices	**156,639**	**175,119**	**186,973**

BALANCE OF PAYMENTS
(US $ million)

	2002	2003	2004
Exports of goods f.o.b.	1,801.3	1,898.1	2,004.3
Imports of goods f.o.b.	−2,012.6	−2,201.1	−2,579.4
Trade balance	**−211.3**	**−303.0**	**−575.0**
Exports of services	1,148.7	1,280.1	1,455.6
Imports of services	−792.7	−906.3	−1,023.5
Balance on goods and services	**144.7**	**70.8**	**−142.9**
Other income received	79.9	47.0	51.8
Other income paid	−66.7	−77.1	−65.7
Balance on goods, services and income	**157.9**	**40.8**	**−156.8**
Current transfers received	195.3	163.0	168.1
Current transfers paid	−103.8	−110.6	−118.7
Current balance	**249.4**	**93.2**	**−107.5**
Capital account (net)	−1.9	−0.9	−1.6
Direct investment abroad	−8.7	6.0	−31.8
Direct investment from abroad	32.1	62.6	13.9
Portfolio investment assets	−18.3	−27.1	−52.4
Portfolio investment liabilities	0.9	8.9	15.3
Other investment assets	−106.7	−22.8	−49.4
Other investment liabilities	184.9	62.0	113.2
Net errors and omissions	9.4	40.4	72.7
Overall balance	**341.1**	**222.4**	**−27.5**

Source: IMF, *International Financial Statistics*.

External Trade

PRINCIPAL COMMODITIES
(million rupees)

Imports c.i.f.	2003	2004	2005*
Food and live animals	10,308	11,947	13,828
Fish and fish preparations	2,542	3,170	4,261
Mineral fuels, lubricants, etc.	7,290	10,020	15,327
Refined petroleum products	6,391	8,791	13,403
Chemicals	5,770	6,412	7,389
Basic manufactures	18,863	19,806	19,300
Textile yarn, fabrics, etc	4,283	4,189	3,167
Cotton fabrics	2,325	2,210	1,751
Machinery and transport equipment	14,241	17,916	26,250
Machinery specialized for particular industries	2,237	3,451	3,048
General industrial machinery, equipment and parts	1,982	2,368	2,798
Telecommunications and sound equipment	1,576	2,666	9,739
Other electrical machinery, apparatus, etc.	2,246	2,796	2,996
Road motor vehicles	2,805	4,028	4,217
Miscellaneous manufactured articles	6,521	6,624	7,260
Total (incl. others)	**65,942**	**76,387**	**93,371**

Exports f.o.b.†	2003	2004	2005*
Food and live animals	11,959	13,277	15,141
Sugar	8,775	9,631	10,181
Fish and fish preparations	2,019	2,250	3,225
Basic manufactures	2,622	3,371	3,450
Textile yarn, fabrics, etc.	1,051	1,453	1,334
Pearls, precious and semi-precious stones	1,109	1,252	1,379
Miscellaneous manufactured articles	26,687	26,136	22,494
Clothing and accessories (excl. footwear)	24,427	23,386	19,677
Total (incl. others)	**42,138**	**43,676**	**42,017**

* Provisional figures.
† Excl. re-exports (million rupees): 8,840 in 2003; 9,028 in 2004; 17,230 in 2005 (provisional). Also excluded are stores and bunkers for ships and aircraft (million rupees): 2,044 in 2003; 2,201 in 2004 4,123 in 2005 (provisional).

PRINCIPAL TRADING PARTNERS
(million rupees)*

Imports c.i.f.	2003	2004	2005†
Argentina	732	910	1,137
Australia	2,153	2,845	2,698
Bahrain	2,571	4,021	4,874
Belgium	945	1,368	1,487
China, People's Repub.	5,539	7,068	9,167
Denmark	281	196	1,010
Finland	158	822	4,485
France	7,841	6,818	7,017
Germany	2,148	2,852	3,799
Hong Kong	1,049	771	652
Hungary	n.a.	226	2,140
India	5,438	6,989	6,461
Indonesia	1,137	1,558	2,112
Italy	2,109	2,431	2,403
Japan	2,326	3,083	3,341
Korea, Repub.	693	797	906
Madagascar	1,407	932	436
Malaysia	2,026	2,285	2,670
Pakistan	1,022	1,182	1,024
Saudi Arabia	1,638	1,418	3,619

MAURITIUS

Imports c.i.f.—continued	2003	2004	2005†
Singapore	1,684	1,175	1,586
South Africa	8,068	8,562	8,001
Spain	1,104	1,475	2,089
Switzerland	925	1,444	1,121
Taiwan	1,163	1,246	1,718
Thailand	969	1,168	1,531
United Arab Emirates	485	1,737	3,588
United Kingdom	2,175	2,377	2,593
USA	1,734	1,651	2,037
Total (incl. others)	65,942	76,387	93,371

Exports f.o.b.	2003	2004	2005†
Belgium	925	1,363	1,554
France	9,403	9,084	8,446
Germany	1,525	1,268	1,066
Italy	1,900	2,156	3,348
Madagascar	3,184	2,689	3,381
Netherlands	820	914	724
Portugal	648	732	540
Réunion	1,489	1,485	1,566
South Africa	773	775	796
Spain	651	860	1,651
Switzerland	525	640	644
United Arab Emirates	60	778	5,096
United Kingdom	15,915	17,356	18,933
USA	8,772	7,768	5,716
Total (incl. others)	50,978	52,704	59,247

* Imports by country of origin; exports by country of destination (including re-exports, excluding ships' stores and bunkers).
† Provisional figures.

Transport

ROAD TRAFFIC
(motor vehicles registered at 31 December)

	2002	2003	2004
Private vehicles: cars	95,635	101,928	111,527
Private vehicles: motorcycles and mopeds	122,801	125,602	129,500
Commercial vehicles: buses	2,450	2,460	2,457
Commercial vehicles: taxis	5,801	5,979	6,482
Commercial vehicles: goods vehicles	32,986	33,997	35,100

SHIPPING
Merchant Fleet
(registered at 31 December)

	2002	2003	2004
Number of vessels	45	49	50
Total displacement ('000 grt)	62.7	67.6	79.0

Source: Lloyd's Register-Fairplay, *World Fleet Statistics*.

Sea-borne Freight Traffic
('000 metric tons)

	2001	2002	2003
Goods unloaded	4,362	3,961	4,076
Goods loaded*	1,365	947	1,165

* Excluding ships' bunkers.

CIVIL AVIATION
(traffic)

	2002	2003	2004
Aircraft landings*	9,172	9,455	9,316
Freight unloaded (metric tons)†	19,100	20,000	22,400
Freight loaded (metric tons)†	25,700	24,300	26,000

* Commercial aircraft only.
† Figures are rounded.

Tourism

FOREIGN TOURIST ARRIVALS

Country of residence	2003	2004	2005*
France	200,229	210,411	220,421
Germany	53,970	52,277	55,983
India	25,367	24,716	29,755
Italy	39,774	41,277	43,458
Réunion	95,679	96,510	99,036
South Africa	45,756	52,609	58,446
Switzerland	17,929	16,110	15,773
United Kingdom	91,210	92,652	95,407
Total (incl. others)	702,018	718,861	761,063

* Provisional figures.

Tourism earnings (gross, million rupees): 19,415 in 2003; 23,448 in 2004; 25,704 in 2005.

Communications Media

	2002	2003	2004
Telephones ('000 main lines in use)	327.2	348.2	353.8
Mobile cellular telephones ('000 subscribers)	348	326	510
Personal computers ('000 in use)	180	n.a.	344
Internet users ('000)	125	150	180
Television sets licensed ('000)	241.4	259.4	260.3
Daily newspapers	6	7	7
Non-daily newspapers	34	35	35

1996: Book production: titles 80, copies ('000) 163.
1997: Facsimile machines (number in use) 28,000.

Sources: partly UNESCO, *Statistical Yearbook*; UN, *Statistical Yearbook*; International Telecommunication Union.

Education

(March 2005)

	Institutions	Teachers	Students*
Pre-primary	1,072	2,501	37,356
Primary	291	5,531	123,562
Secondary	188	6,785	110,287
Technical and vocational	147	648	9,845

* By enrolment.

Adult literacy rate (official estimates): 84.3% (males 88.2%; females 80.5%) in 2003 (Source: UN Development Programme, *Human Development Report*).

Directory

The Constitution

The Mauritius Independence Order, which established a self-governing state, came into force on 12 March 1968, and was subsequently amended. Constitutional amendments providing for the adoption of republican status were approved by the Legislative Assembly (henceforth known as the National Assembly) on 10 December 1991, and came into effect on 12 March 1992. The main provisions of the revised Constitution are listed below:

HEAD OF STATE

The Head of State is the President of the Republic, who is elected by a simple majority of the National Assembly for a five-year term of office. The President appoints the Prime Minister (in whom executive power is vested) and, on the latter's recommendation, other ministers.

COUNCIL OF MINISTERS

The Council of Ministers, which is headed by the Prime Minister, is appointed by the President and is responsible to the National Assembly.

THE NATIONAL ASSEMBLY

The National Assembly, which has a term of five years, comprises the Speaker, 62 members elected by universal adult suffrage, a maximum of eight additional members and the Attorney-General (if not an elected member). The island of Mauritius is divided into 20 three-member constituencies for legislative elections. Rodrigues returns two members to the National Assembly. The official language of the National Assembly is English, but any member may address the Speaker in French.

The Government

HEAD OF STATE

President: Sir ANEROOD JUGNAUTH (took office 7 October 2003).
Vice-President: RAOUF BUNDHUN.

COUNCIL OF MINISTERS
(April 2006)

Prime Minister and Minister of Defence and Home Affairs, Civil Service and Administrative Reforms and Rodrigues and Outer Islands: NAVINCHANDRA RAMGOOLAM.
Deputy Prime Minister and Minister of Public Infrastructure, Land Transport and Shipping: AHMED RASHID BEEBEEJAUN.
Deputy Prime Minister and Minister of Tourism, Leisure and External Communications: CHARLES GAËTAN XAVIER-LUC DUVAL.
Deputy Prime Minister and Minister of Finance and Economic Development: RAMA KRISHNA SITHANEN.
Minister of Foreign Affairs, International Trade and Co-operation: MADAN MURLIDHAR DULLOO.
Minister of the Environment and the National Development Unit: ANIL KUMAR BACHOO.
Minister of Education and Human Resources: DHARAMBEER GOKHOOL.
Minister of Public Utilities: ABU TWALIB KASENALLY.
Minister of Local Government: JAMES BURTY DAVID.
Minister of Agro-industry and Fisheries: ARVIN BOOLELL.
Minister of Labour, Industrial Relations and Employment: VASANT KUMAR BUNWAREE.
Minister of Social Security, National Solidarity and Senior Citizens' Welfare and Reform Institutions: SHEILABAI BAPPOO.
Minister of Women's Rights, Child Development, Family Welfare and Consumer Protection: INDRANEE SEEBUN.
Attorney-General and Minister of Justice and Human Rights: JAYARAMA VALAYDEN.
Minister of Health and Quality of Life: SATYA VEYASH FAUGOO.
Minister of Industry, Small and Medium Enterprises, Commerce and Co-operatives: RAJESHWAR JEETAH.
Minister of Arts and Culture: MAHENDRA GOWRESSOO.
Minister of Housing and Land: MOHAMMED ASRAF ALLY DULULL.
Minister of Information Technology and Telecommunications: JOSEPH NOËL-ETIENNE GHISLAIN SINATAMBOU.
Minister of Youth and Sports: SYLVIO HOCK SHEEN TANG WAH HING.

MINISTRIES

President's Office: State House, Le Réduit, Port Louis; tel. 454-3021; fax 464-5370; e-mail statehouse@mail.gov.mu; internet president.gov.mu.
Prime Minister's Office: New Treasury Bldg, Port Louis; tel. 201-1003; fax 208-8619; e-mail primeminister@mail.gov.mu; internet pmo.gov.mu.
Ministry of Agro-industry and Fisheries: Renganaden Seeneevassen Bldg, 8th and 9th Floor, cnr Jules Koenig and Maillard Sts, Port Louis; tel. 212-2335; fax 212-4427; e-mail moa-headoffice@mail.gov.mu; internet agriculture.gov.mu.
Ministry of Arts and Culture: Renganaden Seeneevassen Bldg, 7th Floor, cnr Pope Hennessy and Maillard Sts, Port Louis; tel. 212-9993; fax 208-0315; e-mail minoac@intnet.mu; internet culture.gov.mu.
Ministry of Civil Service Affairs and Administrative Reform: New Government Centre, 7th Floor, Port Louis; tel. 201-1886; fax 212-9528; e-mail civser@intnet.mu; internet civilservice.gov.mu.
Ministry of Defence and Home Affairs: New Government Centre, 4th Floor, Port Louis; e-mail pmo@mail.gov.mu; internet pmo.gov.mu/dha.
Ministry of Education and Human Resources: IVTB House, Pont Fer, Phoenix; tel. 601-5200; fax 698-2550; e-mail moeps@mail.gov.mu; internet ministry-education.gov.mu.
Ministry of the Environment and the National Development Unit: Ken Lee Tower, Barracks St, Port Louis; tel. 212-3363; fax 212-8324; e-mail admenv@intnet.mu; internet environment.gov.mu.
Ministry of Finance and Economic Development: Government House, Ground Floor, Port Louis; tel. 201-2557; fax 208-9823; e-mail mof@bow.intnet.mu; internet mof.gov.mu.
Ministry of Foreign Affairs, International Trade and Co-operation: New Government Centre, 5th Floor, Port Louis; tel. 201-1648; fax 208-8087; e-mail mfa@mail.gov.mu; internet foreign.gov.mu.
Ministry of Health and Quality of Life: Emmanuel Anquetil Bldg, Sir Seewoosagur Ramgoolam St, Port Louis; tel. 201-1912; fax 208-0376; e-mail mohql@intnet.mu; internet health.gov.mu.
Ministry of Housing and Land: Moorgate House, Port Louis; tel. 212-6022; fax 212-7482; internet housing.gov.mu.
Ministry of Industry, Small and Medium Enterprises, Commerce and Co-operatives: Air Mauritius Centre, 7th Floor, John F. Kennedy St, Port Louis; tel. 210-7100; fax 212-8201; e-mail mind@mail.gov.mu; internet industry.gov.mu.
Ministry of Information Technology and Telecommunications: Air Mauritius Centre, Level 9, John F. Kennedy St, Port Louis; tel. 210-0201; fax 212-1673; e-mail mtel@mail.gov.mu; internet telecomit.gov.mu.
Ministry of Justice and Human Rights: Renganaden Seeneevassen Bldg, 2nd Floor, Port Louis; tel. 212-2139; fax 212-6742; e-mail ago@intnet.mu; internet attorneygeneral.gov.mu.
Ministry of Labour, Industrial Relations and Employment: Victoria House, cnr St Louis and Barracks Sts, Port Louis; tel. 207-2600; fax 212-3070; e-mail mol@mail.gov.mu; internet labour.gov.mu.
Ministry of Local Government: Emmanuel Anquetil Bldg, 3rd Floor, cnr Sir Seewoosagur Ramgoolam and Jules Koenig Sts, Port Louis; tel. 201-1216; fax 208-9729; e-mail mlg@mail.gov.mu; internet localgovernment.gov.mu.
Ministry of Public Infrastructure, Land Transport and Shipping: Moorgate House, 9th Floor, Sir William Newton St, Port Louis; tel. 210-7270; fax 212-8373; internet publicinfrastructure.gov.mu.
Ministry of Public Utilities: Medcor Bldg, 10th Floor, John F. Kennedy St, Port Louis; tel. 210-3994; fax 208-6497; e-mail minpuuti@intnet.mu; internet publicutilities.gov.mu.
Ministry of Rodrigues and Outer Islands: Fon Sing Bldg, 1st floor, Edith Cavell St, Port Louis; tel. 208-8472; fax 212-6329; internet shipping.gov.mu.
Ministry of Social Security, National Solidarity and Senior Citizens' Welfare and Reform Institutions: Renganaden Seeneevassen Bldg, Jules Koenig St, Port Louis; tel. 212-9813; fax 212-8190; e-mail mssns@intnet.mu; internet socialsecurity.gov.mu.
Ministry of Tourism, Leisure and External Communications: Air Mauritius Centre, Level 12, John F. Kennedy St, Port Louis; tel. 211-7930; fax 208-6776; e-mail mot@intnet.mu; internet tourism.gov.mu.
Ministry of Women's Rights, Child Development, Family Welfare and Consumer Protection: CSK Bldg, cnr Remy Ollier

MAURITIUS

and Emmanuel Anquetil Sts, Port Louis; tel. 240-1377; fax 240-7717; e-mail mwfwcd@bow.intnet.mu; internet women.gov.mu.
Ministry of Youth and Sports: Emmanuel Anquetil Bldg, 3rd Floor, Sir Seewoosagur Ramgoolam St, Port Louis; tel. 201-2543; fax 211-2986; e-mail mys@mail.gov.mu; internet youthsport.gov.mu.

Legislature

National Assembly
Port Louis; tel. 201-1414; fax 212-8364; e-mail themace@intnet.mu; internet mauritiusassembly.gov.mu.
Speaker: KAILASH PURRYAG.

General Election, 3 July 2005

	Seats		
Party	Directly elected	Additional*	Total
Social Alliance†	38	4	42
Mouvement Socialiste Militant (MSM)/Mouvement Militant Mauricien (MMM)	22	2	24
Organisation du Peuple Rodriguais (OPR)	2	2	4
Total	62	8	70

* Awarded to those among the unsuccessful candidates who attracted the largest number of votes, in order to ensure that a balance of ethnic groups are represented in the Assembly.
† Alliance primarily comprising the Mauritius Labour Party, the Parti Mauricien Xavier-Luc Duval, the Mouvement Républicain and the Mouvement Militant Socialiste Mauricien.

Election Commission

Electoral Commissioner's Office (ECO): 4th Floor, Max City Bldg, cnr Louis Pasteur and Remy Ollier Sts, Port Louis; tel. 241-7000; fax 241-9409; e-mail elec@mail.gov.mu; internet www.gov.mu/portal/site/eco; under the aegis of the Prime Minister's office; Commissioner appointed by the Judicial and Legal Service Commission; Electoral Commissioner M. I. ABDOOL RAHMAN.

Political Organizations

Mauritius Labour Party (MLP) (Parti Travailliste): 7 Guy Rozemont Sq., Port Louis; tel. 212-6691; e-mail labour@intnet.mu; internet labour.intnet.mu; f. 1936; formed part of the Social Alliance for the 2005 election and subsequently a govt; Leader Dr NAVINCHANDRA RAMGOOLAM; Chair. JEAN-FRANÇOIS CHAUMIÈRE; Sec.-Gen. SARAT DUTT LALLAH.

Mouvement Militant Mauricien (MMM): 21 Poudrière St, Port Louis; tel. 212-6553; fax 208-9939; internet mmm.mmmonline.org; f. 1969; socialist; formed an alliance with the Mouvement Socialiste Militant for both the 2000 and the 2005 elections; Pres. SAM LAUTHAN; Leader PAUL BÉRENGER; Sec.-Gen. STEVEN OBEEGADOO, RAJESH BHAGWAN.

Mouvement Militant Socialiste Mauricien (MMSM): Port Louis; forms part of the incumbent Social Alliance, elected in 2005; Leader MADUN DULLOO.

Mouvement Rodriguais: Port Mathurin, Rodrigues; tel. 831-1876 (Port Mathurin); tel. and fax 686-8859 (Port Louis); f. 1992; represents the interests of Rodrigues; Leader JOSEPH (NICHOLAS) VON-MALLY.

Mouvement Sociale Démocrate (MSD) (Social Democratic Movement): Port Louis; f. 2005; Leader ANIL BACHOO.

Mouvement Socialiste Militant (MSM): Sun Trust Bldg, 31 Edith Cavell St, Port Louis; tel. 212-8787; fax 208-9517; e-mail request@msmsun.com; internet www.msmsun.com; f. 1983; by fmr mems of the MMM; dominant party in subsequent coalition govts until Dec. 1995 and again from 2000–05; Leader PRAVIND JUGNAUTH; Chair. JOE LESJONGARD; Sec.-Gen. VISHWANATH SAJADAH.

Organisation du Peuple Rodriguais (OPR): Port Mathurin, Rodrigues; represents the interests of Rodrigues; Leader LOUIS SERGE CLAIR.

Parti Mauricien Social Démocrate (PMSD): Melville, Grand Gaube; centre-right; participated in an alliance with the MSM and MMM for the 2005 legislative and municipal elections; Leader MAURICE ALLET; Sec.-Gen. JACQUES PANGLOSE.

Directory

Parti Mauricien Xavier-Luc Duval (PMXD): Port Louis; f. 1998; forms part of the Social Alliance; Leader CHARLES GAËTAN XAVIER-LUC DUVAL.

Some of the blocs and parties that participated in the 2005 election include the **Front Solidarité Mauricienne (FSM)**, **Les Verts Fraternels/The Greens** (Leader SYLVIO MICHEL), the **Mouvement Républicain** (Leader RAMA VALAYDEV), the **Parti du Peuple Mauricien (PPM)**, the **Front Populaire Musulman (FPM)**, the **Mouvement Démocratique National Raj Dayal (MDN Raj Dayal)**, the **Rezistans ek Alternativ** (Secretary ASHOK SUBRON), **Lalit** (lalitmauritius.com) and the **Tamil Council**.

Diplomatic Representation

EMBASSIES AND HIGH COMMISSIONS IN MAURITIUS

Australia: Rogers House, 2nd Floor, John F. Kennedy St, POB 541, Port Louis; tel. 208-1700; fax 208-8878; e-mail austhc@intnet.mu; internet www.mauritius.embassy.gov.au; High Commissioner IAN MCCONVILLE.

China, People's Republic: Royal Rd, Belle Rose, Rose Hill; tel. 454-9111; fax 464-6012; e-mail chinaemb_mu@mfa.gov.cn; internet www.ambchine.mu; Ambassador GAO YUCHEN.

Egypt: Sun Trust Bldg, 2nd floor, Edith Cavell St, Port Louis; tel. 213-1765; fax 213-1768; e-mail egyemb@intnet.mu; Ambassador MAGDA HOSNI NASR AHMED.

France: 14 St George St, Port Louis; tel. 202-0100; fax 202-0110; e-mail ambafr@intnet.mu; internet www.ambafrance-mu.org; Ambassador DOMINIQUE RENAUX.

India: Life Insurance Corpn of India Bldg, 6th Floor, John F. Kennedy St, POB 162, Port Louis; tel. 208-3775; fax 208-6859; e-mail hicom.ss@intnet.mu; internet indiahighcom.intnet.mu; High Commissioner PRIPURAN SINGH HAER.

Madagascar: Guiot Pasceau St, Floreal, POB 3, Port Louis; tel. 686-5015; fax 686-7040; e-mail madmail@intnet.mu; Ambassador BRUNO RANARIVELO.

Pakistan: 9A Queen Mary Ave, Floreal, Port Louis; tel. 698-8501; fax 698-8405; e-mail pareportlouis@hotmail.com; High Commissioner SYED HASAN JAVED.

Russia: Queen Mary Ave, POB 10, Floreal, Port Louis; tel. 696-1545; fax 696-5027; e-mail rusemb.mu@intnet.mu; Ambassador OLGA IVANOVA.

South Africa: BAI Bldg, 4th Floor, 25 Pope Hennessy St, POB 908, Port Louis; tel. 212-6925; fax 212-6936; e-mail sahc@intnet.mu; High Commissioner AJAY KUMAR BRAMDEO.

United Kingdom: Les Cascades Bldg, 7th Floor, Edith Cavell St, POB 1063, Port Louis; tel. 202-9400; fax 202-9408; e-mail bhc@intnet.mu; High Commissioner ANTHONY GODSON.

USA: Rogers House, 4th Floor, John F. Kennedy St, Port Louis; tel. 208-4400; fax 208-9534; e-mail usembass@intnet.mu; internet mauritius.usembassy.gov; Chargé d'affaires a.i. STEPHEN M. SCHWARTZ.

Judicial System

The laws of Mauritius are derived both from the French Code Napoléon and from English Law. The Judicial Department consists of the Supreme Court, presided over by the Chief Justice and such number of Puisne Judges as may be prescribed by Parliament (currently nine), who are also Judges of the Court of Criminal Appeal and the Court of Civil Appeal. These courts hear appeals from the Intermediate Court, the Industrial Court and 10 District Courts (including that of Rodrigues). The Industrial Court has special jurisdiction to protect the constitutional rights of the citizen. There is a right of appeal in certain cases from the Supreme Court to the Judicial Committee of the Privy Council in the United Kingdom.

Supreme Court: Jules Koenig St, Port Louis; tel. 212-0275; tel. 212-9946; internet supremecourt.intnet.mu.

Chief Justice: ARIANGA PILLAY.
Senior Puisne Judge: B. YEUNG SIK YUEN.
Puisne Judges: B. DOMAH, K. P. MATADEEN, N. MATADEEN, A. F. CHUI YEW CHEONG, M. F. E. BALANCY, P. LAM SHANG LEEN, P. BALGOBIN, S. PEEROO, A. A. CAUNHYE.

Religion

Hindus are estimated to comprise more than 50% of the population, with Christians accounting for some 30% and Muslims 17%. There is also a small Buddhist community.

CHRISTIANITY

The Anglican Communion

Anglicans in Mauritius are within the Church of the Province of the Indian Ocean, comprising six dioceses (four in Madagascar, one in Mauritius and one in Seychelles). The Archbishop of the Province is the Bishop of Antananarivo, Madagascar. In 1983 the Church had 5,438 members in Mauritius.

Bishop of Mauritius: Rt Rev. IAN ERNEST, Bishop's House, Phoenix; tel. 686-5158; fax 697-1096; e-mail dioang@intnet.mu.

The Presbyterian Church of Mauritius

Minister: Pasteur ANDRÉ DE RÉLAND, cnr Farquhar and Royal Rds, Coignet, Rose Hill; tel. 464-5265; fax 395-2068; e-mail embrau@bow.intnet.mu; f. 1814.

The Roman Catholic Church

Mauritius comprises a single diocese, directly responsible to the Holy See, and an apostolic vicariate on Rodrigues. At 31 December 2003 there were an estimated 310,863 adherents in the country, representing about 26.4% of the total population.

Bishop of Port Louis: Rt Rev. MAURICE PIAT, Evêché, 13 Mgr Gonin St, Port Louis; tel. 208-3068; fax 208-6607; e-mail eveche@intnet.mu.

BAHÁ'Í FAITH

National Spiritual Assembly: Port Louis; tel. 212-2179; mems resident in 190 localities.

ISLAM

Mauritius Islamic Mission: Noor-e-Islam Mosque, Port Louis; Imam S. M. BEEHARRY.

The Press

DAILIES

China Times: 24 Emmanuel Anquetil St, POB 325, Port Louis; tel. 240-3067; f. 1953; Chinese; Editor-in-Chief LONG SIONG AH KENG; circ. 3,000.

Chinese Daily News: 32 Rémy Ollier St, POB 316, Port Louis; tel. 240-0472; f. 1932; Chinese; Editor-in-Chief WONG YUEN MOY; circ. 5,000.

L'Express: 3 Brown Sequard St, POB 247, Port Louis; tel. 202-8200; fax 208-8174; e-mail sentinelle@bow.intnet.mu; internet www.lexpress-net.com; f. 1963; owned by La Sentinelle Ltd; English and French; Editor-in-Chief RAJ MEETARBHAN; circ. 35,000.

Maurice Soir: Port Louis; f. 1996; Editor SYDNEY SELVON; circ. 2,000.

Le Matinal: AAPCA House, 6 La Poudrière St, Port Louis; tel. 207-0909; fax 213-4069; e-mail editorial@lematinal.com; internet www.lematinal.com; f. 2003; in French and English; AAPCA (Mauritius) Ltd; Dir SIDHARTH BHATIA.

Le Mauricien: 8 St George St, POB 7, Port Louis; tel. 208-3251; fax 208-7059; e-mail redaction@lemauricien.com; internet www.lemauricien.com; f. 1907; English and French; Editor-in-Chief GILBERT AHNEE; circ. 35,000.

Le Quotidien: Pearl House, 4th Floor, 16 Sir Virgile Naz St, Port Louis; tel. 208-2631; fax 211-7479; e-mail quotidien@bow.intnet.mu; f. 1996; English and French; Dirs JACQUES DAVID, PATRICK MICHEL; circ. 30,000.

Le Socialiste: Manilall Bldg, 3rd Floor, Brabant St, Port Louis; tel. 208-8003; fax 211-3890; English and French; Editor-in-Chief VEDI BALLAH; circ. 7,000.

The Tribune: Port Louis; f. 1999; Publr HARISH CHUNDUNSING.

WEEKLIES AND FORTNIGHTLIES

5-Plus Dimanche: 3 Brown Sequard St, Port Louis; tel. 213-5500; fax 213-5551; e-mail comments@5plusltd.com; internet www.5plusltd.com; f. 1994; English and French; Editor-in-Chief FINLAY SALESSE; circ. 30,000.

5-Plus Magazine: 3 Brown Sequard St, Port Louis; tel. 213-5500; fax 213-5551; e-mail comments@5plusltd.com; f. 1990; English and French; Editor-in-Chief PIERRE BENOÎT; circ. 10,000.

Business Magazine: TN Tower, 2nd Floor, 13 St George St, Port Louis; tel. 211-1925; fax 211-1926; e-mail businessmag@intnet.mu; internet www.businessmag.mu; f. 1993; owned by La Sentinelle Ltd; English and French; Editor-in-Chief LINDSAY RIVIÈRE; circ. 6,000.

Le Croissant: cnr Velore and Noor Essan Mosque Sts, Port Louis; tel. 240-7105; English and French; Editor-in-Chief RAYMOND RICHARD NAUVEL; circ. 25,000.

Le Défi-Plus: Sun Trust Bldg, 31 Edith Cavell St, Port Louis; tel. 211-7766; Saturdays.

Le Dimanche: 5 Jemmapes St, Port Louis; tel. 212-5887; fax 212-1177; e-mail ledmer@intnet.mu; f. 1961; English and French; Editor RAYMOND RICHARD NAUVEL; circ. 25,000.

Impact News: 10 Dr Yves Cantin St, Port Louis; tel. 211-5284; fax 211-7821; e-mail farhadr@wanadoo.mu; internet www.impactnews.info; English and French; Editor-in-Chief FARHAD RAMJAUN.

Lalit de Klas: 153B Royal Rd, G.R.N.W., Port Louis; tel. 208-2132; e-mail lalitmail@intnet.mu; internet www.lalitmauritius.org; English, French and Mauritian Creole; Editor RADA KISTNASAMY.

Le Mag: Industrial Zone, Tombeay Bay; tel. 247-1005; fax 247-1061; f. 1993; English and French; Editor (vacant); circ. 8,000.

Mauritius Times: 23 Bourbon St, Port Louis; tel. and fax 212-1313; e-mail mtimes@intnet.mu; internet mauritiustimes.com; f. 1954; English and French; Editor-in-Chief MADHUKAR RAMLALLAH; circ. 15,000.

Mirror: 39 Emmanuel Anquetil St, Port Louis; tel. 240-3298; Chinese; Editor-in-Chief NG KEE SIONG; circ. 4,000.

News on Sunday: Dr Eugen Laurent St, POB 230, Port Louis; tel. 211-5902; fax 211-7302; e-mail newsonsunday@news.intnet.mu; internet newsonsunday.150m.com; f. 1996; owned by Le Défi Group; weekly; in English; Editor NAGUIB LALLMAHOMED; circ. 10,000.

Le Nouveau Militant: 21 Poudrière St, Port Louis; tel. 212-6553; fax 208-2291; f. 1979; publ. by the Mouvement Militant Mauricien; English and French; Editor-in-Chief J. RAUMIAH.

Le Rodriguais: Saint Gabriel, Rodrigues; tel. 831-1613; fax 831-1484; f. 1989; Creole, English and French; Editor JACQUES EDOUARD; circ. 2,000.

Star: 38 Labourdonnais St, Port Louis; tel. 212-2736; fax 211-7781; e-mail starpress@intnet.mu; internet www.mauriweb.com/star; English and French; Editor-in-Chief REZA ISSACK.

Sunday: Port Louis; tel. 208-9516; fax 208-7059; f. 1966; English and French; Editor-in-Chief SUBASH GOBIN.

Turf Magazine: 8 George St, POB 7, Port Louis; tel. 207-8200; fax 208-7059; e-mail bdlm@intnet.mu; internet www.lemauricien.com/turfmag; owned by Le Mauricien Ltd.

La Vie Catholique: 28 Nicolay Rd, Port Louis; tel. 242-0975; fax 242-3114; e-mail viecatho@intnet.mu; internet pages.intnet.mu/lavie; f. 1930; weekly; English, French and Creole; Editor-in-Chief Fr GEORGES CHEUNG; circ. 8,000.

Week-End: 8 St George St, POB 7, Port Louis; tel. 207-8200; fax 208-3248; e-mail redaction@lemauricien.com; internet www.lemauricien.com/weekend; f. 1966; owned by Le Mauricien Ltd; French and English; Editor-in-Chief GÉRARD CATEAUX; circ. 80,000.

Week-End Scope: 8 St George St, POB 7, Port Louis; tel. 207-8200; fax 208-7059; e-mail wes@lemauricien.com; internet www.lemauricien.com/wes; owned by Le Mauricien Ltd; English and French; Editor-in-Chief JACQUES ACHILLE.

OTHER SELECTED PERIODICALS

CCI-INFO: 3 Royal St, Port Louis; tel. 208-3301; fax 208-0076; e-mail mcci@intnet.mu; internet www.mcci.org; English and French; f. 1995; publ. of the Mauritius Chamber of Commerce and Industry.

Ciné Star Magazine: 64 Sir Seewoosagur Ramgoolam St, Port Louis; tel. 240-1447; English and French; Editor-in-Chief ABDOOL RAWOOF SOOBRATTY.

Education News: Edith Cavell St, Port Louis; tel. 212-1303; English and French; monthly; Editor-in-Chief GIAN AUBEELUCK.

Le Message de L'Ahmadiyyat: c/o Ahmadiyya Muslim Asscn, POB 6, Rose Hill; tel. 464-1747; fax 454-2223; e-mail darussalaam@intnet.mu; French; monthly; Editor-in-Chief MOHAMMAD AMEEN JOWAHIR; circ. 3,000.

Le Progrès Islamique: 51B Solferino St, Rose Hill; tel. 467-1697; fax 467-1696; f. 1948; English and French; monthly; Editor DEVINA SOOKIA.

La Voix d'Islam: Parisot Rd, Mesnil, Phoenix; f. 1951; English and French; monthly.

NEWS AGENCIES

The following foreign bureaux are represented in Mauritius: Agence France Presse, Associated Press (United Kingdom), International News Service (USA), Reuters (United Kingdom).

Publishers

Boukié Banané (The Flame Tree): 5 Edwin Ythier St, Rose Hill; tel. 454-2327; fax 465-4312; e-mail limem@intnet.mu; internet pages

MAURITIUS

Directory

.intnet.mu/develog; f. 1979; Morisien literature, poetry and drama; Man. Dir Dev Virahsawmy.

Business Publications Ltd: TN Tower, 1st Floor, St George St, Port Louis; tel. 211-1925; fax 211-1926; f. 1993; English and French; Dir Lyndsay Rivière.

Editions du Dattier: 82 Goyavier Ave, Quatre Bornes; tel. 466-4854; fax 446-3105; e-mail dattier@intnet.mu; English and French; Dir Jean-Philippe Lagesse.

Editions de l'Océan Indien: Stanley, Rose Hill; tel. 464-6761; fax 464-3445; e-mail eoibooks@intnet.mu; f. 1977; textbooks, literature; English, French and Asian languages; Gen. Man. (vacant).

Editions Le Printemps: 4 Club Rd, Vacoas; tel. 696-1017; fax 686-7302; e-mail elp@bow.intnet.mu; Man. Dir A. I. Sulliman.

Editions Vizavi: 9 St George St, Port Louis; tel. 211-3047; e-mail vizavi@intnet.mu; Dir Pascale Siew.

Broadcasting and Communications

TELECOMMUNICATIONS

Information and Communication Technologies Authority (ICTA): Jade House, 1st floor, cnr Rémy Ollier and Jumman Mosque Sts, Port Louis; tel. 217-222; fax 217-777; e-mail icta@intnet.mu; internet www.icta.mu; f. 1999; regulatory authority; Chair. Ashok Radhakissoon.

Mauritius Telecom Ltd: Telecom Tower, Edith Cavell St, Port Louis; tel. 203-7000; fax 208-1070; e-mail ceo@mauritiustelecom.com.mu; internet www.mauritiustelecom.com; f. 1992; 40% owned by France Telecom; privatized in 2000; provides all telecommunications services, including internet and digital mobile cellular services; Chair. Appalsamy (Dass) Thomas; Dir Gen. Sarat Lallah.

Cellplus Mobile Communications Ltd: Telecom Tower, 9th Floor, Edith Cavell St, Port Louis; tel. 203-7500; fax 211-6996; e-mail cellplus@intnet.mu; internet www.cellplus.mu; f. 1996; introduced the first GSM cellular network in Mauritius and recently in Rodrigues (Cell-Oh); a wholly-owned subsidiary of Mauritius Telecom.

BROADCASTING

In 1997 the Supreme Court invalidated the broadcasting monopoly held by the Mauritius Broadcasting Corporation.

Independent Broadcasting Authority: 5 de Courson St, Curepipe Rd, Curepipe; tel. 670-4621; fax 670-2335; e-mail iba@intnet.mu; internet iba.gov.mu; Dir Pierre Ah-Fat.

Radio

Mauritius Broadcasting Corpn: Broadcasting House, Louis Pasteur St, Forest Side; tel. 675-5001; fax 676-7332; e-mail mbc@intnet.mu; internet mbc.intnet.mu; f. 1964; independent corpn operating five national radio services and three television channels; Chair. Fareed Jangeerkhan; Dir-Gen. Bijaye Madhou.

Radio One: Port Louis; tel. 211-4555; fax 211-4142; e-mail sales@r1.mu; internet www.r1.mu; f. 2002; owned by Sentinelle media group; news and entertainment; Dir-Gen. Jean-Michel Fontaine.

Top FM: Harbour Front, 6th Floor, cnr Queen Elizabeth and John F. Kennedy Sts, Port Louis; tel. 213-2121; fax 213-2222; e-mail topfm@intnet.mu; internet www.topfmradio.com; f. 2003; part of the International Broadcasting Group, in partnership with the Sunrise Group; Chair. Balkrishna Kaunhye.

A further two private stations, Radio Plus and Sunrise Radio, were issued licences in early 2002.

Television

Independent television stations were to commence broadcasting from 2002, as part of the liberalization of the sector.

Mauritius Broadcasting Corpn: see Radio..

Finance

(cap. = capital; res = reserves; dep. = deposits; m. = million; brs = branches; amounts in Mauritian rupees, unless otherwise stated)

BANKING

Central Bank

Bank of Mauritius: Sir William Newton St, POB 29, Port Louis; tel. 208-4164; fax 208-9204; e-mail bomrd@bow.intnet.mu; internet bom.intnet.mu; f. 1966; bank of issue; cap. 10.0m., res 14,415.6m., dep. 17,275.9m. (June 2003); Gov. Rameswurlall Basant Roi; Man. Dir Baboo Rajendranathsing Gujadhur.

Principal Commercial Banks

Bank of Baroda: 32 Sir William Newton St, POB 553, Port Louis; tel. 208-1504; fax 208-3892; e-mail info@bankofbaroda-mu.com; internet www.bankofbaroda-mu.com; f. 1962; total assets 130.3m. (March 2003); Chair. P. S. Shenoy; 7 brs.

Barclays Bank PLC, Mauritius: Harbour Front Bldg, 8th Floor, John F. Kennedy St, POB 284, Port Louis; tel. 208-2685; fax 208-2720; e-mail barclays.mauritius@barclays.com; f. 1919; absorbed Banque Nationale de Paris Intercontinentale in 2002; cap. 100.0m., res 616.1m., dep. 6,886.7m. (Dec. 2001); Dir Jacques de Navacelle; 16 brs.

First City Bank Ltd: 16 Sir William Newton St, POB 485, Port Louis; tel. 208-5061; fax 208-5388; e-mail info@firstcitybank-mauritius.com; internet www.firstcitybank-mauritius.com; f. 1991 as the Delphis Bank Ltd; merged with Union International Bank in 1997; private bank; taken over by consortium in 2002; 51.6% owned by the Development Bank of Mauritius; cap. 420.1m., res 34.2, dep. 4,530.5m. (June 2002); Chair. Eric Ng Ping Cheun; Chief Exec. Ranapartad Tacouri.

Hongkong and Shanghai Banking Corpn Ltd (HSBC): place d'Armes, POB 50, Port Louis; tel. 208-1801; fax 210-0400; e-mail hsbcmauritius@hsbc.co.mu; internet www.hsbc.co.mu; f. 1916; CEO Phillip Dawe.

Indian Ocean International Bank Ltd (IOIB): 34 Sir William Newton St, POB 863, Port Louis; tel. 208-0121; fax 208-0127; e-mail ioibltd@intnet.mu; f. 1978; 51% purchased by the State Bank of India in 2005; cap. 100.5m., res 270.1m., dep. 2,791.5.9m. (June 2004); Pres. Viswanathen Valaydon; Chief Exec. V. Rajagopalan; 8 brs.

Mauritius Commercial Bank Ltd: MCB Centre, 9–15 Sir William Newton St, POB 52, Port Louis; tel. 202-5000; fax 208-7054; e-mail mcb@mcb.mu; internet www.mcb.mu; f. 1838; cap. and res 9,355m., dep. 65,622m. (June 2004); Chief Exec. Pierre-Guy Noël; Gen. Man. Joseph Alain Sauzier; 41 brs.

South East Asian Bank Ltd: Max City Bldg, 2nd Floor, cnr Rémy Ollier and Louis Pasteur Sts, POB 13, Port Louis; tel. 208-8826; fax 211-4900; e-mail seab@intnet.mu; internet www.seabmu.com; f. 1989; cap. 200.0m., res 3.8m., dep. 1,578.6m. (Dec. 2004); Chief Exec. Vincent Lee; Chair. Tan Sri Dato' Abdul Khalid Bin Sahan; 5 brs.

Standard Chartered Bank (Mauritius) Ltd: Happy World House, Level 8, 37 Sir William Newton St, Port Louis; tel. 213-9000; fax 208-5992; e-mail scbmauritius@intnet.mu; internet www.standardchartered.com/mu; wholly owned subsidiary of Standard Chartered Bank Plc; offshore banking unit.

State Bank of Mauritius Ltd: State Bank Tower, 1 Queen Elizabeth II Ave, POB 152, Port Louis; tel. 202-1111; fax 202-1234; e-mail sbm@sbm.intnet.mu; internet www.sbm-online.com; f. 1973; cap. 336.2m., res 4,273.9m., dep. 27,044.9m. (June 2003); Chief Exec. Chaitlall Gunness; Chair. Muni Krishna T. Reddy; 43 brs.

Development Bank

Development Bank of Mauritius Ltd: La Chaussée, POB 157, Port Louis; tel. 208-0241; fax 208-8498; e-mail dbm@intnet.mu; internet www.dbm-ltd.com; f. 1964; name changed as above in 1991; 65% govt-owned; cap. 125m., res 1,796.2m., dep. 2,942.8m. (June 2003); Chair. Chandan Kheswar Jankee; Man. Dir B. Chooramun; 6 brs.

Principal 'Offshore' Banks

Mascareignes International Bank Ltd: 1 Cathedral Square, Level 8, 16 Jules Koenig St, POB 489, Port Louis; tel. 207-8700; fax 212-4983; e-mail mib@mib.mu; internet www.mib.mu; f. 1991; name changed as above 2004; jt venture of Banque de la Réunion (50.5%), Mauritius Commercial Bank Ltd (35%) and Crédit Lyonnais Global Banking, France (14.5%); cap. US $6.0m., res $4.0m. (Mar. 2004); Chair. Jean-Claude Clarac; Chief. Exec. Philippe Sirand.

SBI International (Mauritius) Ltd: Harbour Front Bldg, 7th Floor, John F. Kennedy St, POB 376, Port Louis; tel. 212-2054; fax 212-2050; e-mail sbilmaur@intnet.mu; f. 1989; 98% owned by the State Bank of India; cap. US $10.0m., res $9.0m., dep. $93.9m. (Mar. 2003); Chair. A. K. Purwar; Man. Dir M. C. Mulay.

Bank of Baroda, Barclays Bank PLC, African Asian Bank, PT Bank International Indonesia, Investec Bank (Mauritius) and HSBC Bank PLC also operate 'offshore' banking units.

STOCK EXCHANGE

Financial Services Commission: Harbour Front Bldg, 4th Floor, John F. Kennedy St, Port Louis; tel. 210-7000; fax 208-7172; e-mail fscmauritius@intnet.mu; internet www.fscmauritius.org; f. 2001; regulatory authority for securities, insurance and global business activities; Chief Exec. MILAN MEETARBHAN.

Stock Exchange of Mauritius Ltd: 1 Cathedral Sq. Bldg, 4th Floor, 16 Jules Koenig St, Port Louis; tel. 212-9541; fax 208-8409; e-mail stockex@intnet.mu; internet www.semdex.com; f. 1989; 11 mems; Chair. JEAN DE FONDAUMIÈRE; CEO SUNIL BENIMADHU.

INSURANCE

Albatross Insurance Co Ltd: 22 St George St, POB 116, Port Louis; tel. 207-9007; fax 208-4800; e-mail headoffice@albatross.mu; internet www.albatross-insurance.com; f. 1975; Chair. TIMOTHY TAYLOR; Man. Dir JEAN DE LA HOGUE.

Anglo-Mauritius Assurance Society Ltd: Swan Group Centre, 10 Intendance St, POB 837, Port Louis; tel. 202-8600; fax 208-8956; e-mail anglomtius@intnet.mu; internet www.groupswan.com; f. 1951; Chair. J. CYRIL LAGESSE; CEO JEAN DE FONDAUMIÈRE.

British American Insurance Co (Mauritius) Ltd: BAI Bldg, 25 Pope Hennessy St, POB 331, Port Louis; tel. 202-3600; fax 208-3713; e-mail bai@intnet.mu; f. 1920; Chair. DAWOOD RAWAT; Man. Dir HEINRICH K. DE KOCK.

Ceylinco Stella Insurance Co Ltd: 36 Sir Seewoosagur Ramgoolam St, POB 852, Port Louis; tel. 208-0056; fax 208-1639; e-mail stellain@intnet.mu; internet www.stellain.com; f. 1977; Chair. and Man. Dir R. KRESHAN JHOBOO.

Indian Ocean General Assurance Ltd: 35 Corderie St, POB 865, Port Louis; tel. 212-4125; fax 212-5850; e-mail iogaltd@intnet.mu; f. 1971; Chair. SAM M. CUNDEN; Man. Dir SHRIVANA CUNDEN.

Island Insurance Co Ltd: Labourdonnais Court, 5th Floor, cnr Labourdonnais and St George Sts, Port Louis; tel. 212-4860; fax 208-8762; e-mail island.ins@intnet.mu; f. 1998; Chair. CARRIM A. CURRIMJEE; Man. Dir OLIVIER LAGESSE.

Jubilee Insurance (Mauritius) Ltd: PCL Bldg, 4th Floor, 43 Sir William Newton St, POB 301, Port Louis; tel. 210-3678; fax 212-7970; e-mail jubilee@intnet.mu; f. 1998; Chair. and CEO AUGUSTINE J. HATCH.

Lamco International Insurance Ltd: 12 Barracks St, Port Louis; tel. 212-4494; fax 208-0630; e-mail lamco@intnet.mu; internet www.lamcoinsurance.com; f. 1978; Chair. A. B. ATCHIA.

Life Insurance Corpn of India: LIC Centre, John F. Kennedy St, Port Louis; tel. 212-5316; fax 208-6392; e-mail liccmm@intnet.mu; f. 1956; Chief Man. HEMANT BHARGAVA.

Mauritian Eagle Insurance Co Ltd: 1st Floor, IBL House, Caudan Waterfront, POB 854, Port Louis; tel. 203-2200; fax 208-8608; e-mail meagle@meagle.intnet.mu; internet www.iblgroup.com/mauritianeagle; f. 1973; Chair. P. D'HOTMAN DE VILLIERS; Exec. Dir G. LAN HUN KUEN.

Mauritius Union Assurance Co Ltd: 4 Léoville L'Homme St, POB 233, Port Louis; tel. 208-4185; fax 212-2962; e-mail mua@mua.mu; internet www.muaco.com; f. 1948; Chair. Sir MAURICE LATOUR-ADRIEN; Gen. Man. JEAN-NÖEL LAM CHUN.

The New India Assurance Co Ltd: Bank of Baroda Bldg, 3rd Floor, 15 Sir William Newton St, POB 398, Port Louis; tel. 208-1442; fax 208-2160; e-mail niasurance@intnet.mu; internet www.niacl.com; f. 1935; general insurance; Chief Man. A. K. JAIN.

La Prudence Mauricienne Assurances Ltée: Le Caudan Waterfront, 2nd Floor, Barkly Wharf, POB 882, Port Louis; tel. 207-2500; fax 208-8936; e-mail prudence@intnet.mu; Chair. ROBERT DE FROBERVILLE; Man. Dir FÉLIX MAUREL.

Rainbow Insurance Co Ltd: 23 Edith Cavell St, POB 389, Port Louis; tel. 212-5767; fax 208-8750; f. 1976; Chair. B. GOKULSING; Man. Dir PREVIN RENBURG.

State Insurance Co of Mauritius Ltd (SICOM): SICOM Bldg, Sir Célicourt Antelme St, Port Louis; tel. 203-8400; fax 208-7662; e-mail email@sicom.intnet.mu; internet www.sicom.mu; f. 1975; Chair. A. F. HO CHAN FONG; Man. Dir K. BHOOJEDHUR-OBEEGADOO.

Sun Insurance Co Ltd: 2 St George St, Port Louis; tel. 208-0769; fax 208-2052; f. 1981; Chair. Sir KAILASH RAMDANEE; Man. Dir A. MUSBALLY.

Swan Insurance Co Ltd: Swan Group Centre, 10 Intendance St, POB 364, Port Louis; tel. 211-2001; fax 208-6898; e-mail swan@intnet.mu; f. 1955; Chair. J. M. ANTOINE HAREL; CEO JEAN DE FONDAUMIÈRE.

L. and H. Vigier de Latour Ltd: Les Jamalacs Bldg, Old Council St, Port Louis; tel. 212-2034; fax 212-6056; Chair. and Man. Dir L. J. D. HENRI VIGIER DE LATOUR.

Trade and Industry

GOVERNMENT AGENCIES

Agricultural Marketing Board (AMB): Dr G. Leclézio Ave, Moka; tel. 433-4025; fax 433-4837; e-mail agbd@intnet.mu; markets certain locally produced and imported food products (such as potatoes, onions, garlic, spices and seeds); also collects raw milk and distributes pasteurized milk; provides storage facilities to importers and exporters; Chair. SHEKAR DEEWOO.

Mauritius Meat Authority: Abattoir Rd, Roche Bois, POB 612, Port Louis; tel. 242-5884; fax 217-1077; e-mail mauritiusmeat@intnet.mu; licensing authority; controls and regulates sale of meat and meat products; also purchases and imports livestock and markets meat products; Gen. Man. A. BALGOBIN.

Mauritius Sugar Authority: Ken Lee Bldg, 2nd Floor, Edith Cavell St, Port Louis; tel. 208-7466; fax 208-7470; e-mail msa@bow.intnet.mu; internet www.mns.intnet.mu/msa.htm; Chair. S. HANOOMANJEE; Exec. Dir Dr G. RAJPATI.

Mauritius Tea Board: Wooton St, Curepipe Rd, Curepipe; POB 28, Eau Coolée; tel. 675-3497; fax 676-1445; e-mail teaboard@intnet.mu; internet www.gov.mu/portal/site/teaboard; f. 1975; regulates and controls the activities of the tea industry; Gen. Man. A. SEEPERGAUTH.

Mauritius Tobacco Board: Plaine Lauzun, Port Louis; tel. 212-2323; fax 208-6426; e-mail tobacco@intnet.mu; internet agriculture.gov.mu/tobacco; Chair. A. L. JADOO.

DEVELOPMENT ORGANIZATIONS

Board of Investment—Mauritius (BOI): Cathedral Square Bldg 1, 10th Floor, 16 Jules Koenig St, Port Louis; tel. 211-4190; fax 208-2924; e-mail invest@boi.intnet.mu; internet www.boimauritius.com; f. 2001; to promote international investment, business and services; Chair. of Bd MAURICE LAM; Gen. Man. RAJU JADDOO.

Enterprise Mauritius: BAI Bldg, 3rd floor, 25 Pope Hennessy St, Port Louis; tel. 212-9760; fax 212-9767; e-mail info@em.intnet.mu; f. 2004 from parts of the Mauritius Industrial Development Authority, the Export Processing Zones Development Authority and the Sub-contracting and Partnership Exchange—Mauritius; comprises a Corporate Services Unit, a Strategic Direction Unit, a Business Development Unit, a Client-Services Unit and a Special Support Unit (estd from the former Clothing and Textile Centre); Chair. AMÉDÉE DARGA.

Joint Economic Council (JEC): Plantation House, 3rd Floor, Place d'Armes, Port Louis; tel. 211-2980; fax 211-3141; e-mail jec@intnet.mu; internet www.jec-mauritius.org; f. 1970; the co-ordinating body of the private sector of Mauritius, including the main business organisations of the country; Pres. ARIF CURRIMJEE; Dir RAJ MAKOOND.

Mauritius Freeport Authority (MFA): Trade and Marketing Centre, 1st Floor, Freeport Zone 6, Mer Rouge; tel. 206-2500; fax 206-2600; e-mail mfa@freeport.gov.mu; internet www.efreeport.com; f. 1990; Chair. KAVYDASS RAMANO; Dir-Gen. RAJAKRISHNA CHELLAPERMAL.

National Productivity and Competitiveness Council (NPCC): St James' Court, 7th Floor, St Denis St, Port Louis; tel. 211-8118; fax 211-8056; e-mail natpro@intnet.mu; internet www.npccmauritius.com; f. 1999; represents the Government, the private sector and trade unions; Exec. Dir NIKHIL TREEBHOOHUN.

Small and Medium Industries Development Organization (SMIDO): Industrial Zone Coromandel; tel. 233-0500; fax 233-5545; e-mail smido@intnet.mu; internet smido.gov.mu; f. 1993.

State Investment Corpn Ltd (SIC): Air Mauritius Centre, 15th Floor, John F. Kennedy St, Port Louis; tel. 202-8900; fax 208-8948; e-mail contactsic@stateinvestment.com; internet www.stateinvestment.com; f. 1984; provides support for new investment and transfer of technology, in agriculture, industry and tourism; Man. Dir SEILENDRA GOKHOOL; Chair. RAJ RINGADOO.

CHAMBERS OF COMMERCE

Chinese Chamber of Commerce: Port Louis; tel. 208-0946; fax 242-1193; Pres. JEAN KOK SHUN.

Mauritius Chamber of Commerce and Industry: 3 Royal St, Port Louis; tel. 208-3301; fax 208-0076; e-mail mcci@intnet.mu; internet www.mcci.org; f. 1850; 416 mems; Pres. Prof. DONALD AH CHUEN; Sec.-Gen. MAHMOOD CHEEROO.

INDUSTRIAL ASSOCIATIONS

Association of Mauritian Manufacturers (AMM): c/o The Mauritius Chamber of Commerce and Insdustry, 3 Royal St, Port Louis; tel. 208-3301; e-mail mcci@intnet.mu; f. ; Dir JACQUES LI WAN PO.

Mauritius Export Processing Zone Association (MEPZA): Unicorn House, 6th Floor, 5 Royal St, Port Louis; tel. 208-5216;

MAURITIUS

fax 212-1853; internet www.mepza.org; f. 1976; consultative and advisory body; Chair. LOUIS LAI FAT FUR.

Mauritius Sugar Producers' Association (MSPA): Plantation House, 2nd Floor, Place d'Armes, Port Louis; tel. 212-0295; fax 212-5727; e-mail mspa@intnet.mu; Chair. ARNAUD LAGESSE; Dir PATRICE LEGRIS.

EMPLOYERS' ORGANIZATION

Mauritius Employers' Federation: Cernée House, 1st Floor, Chaussée St, Port Louis; tel. 212-1599; fax 212-6725; e-mail info@mef-online.org; internet www.mef-online.org; f. 1962; Chair. MOOKHESHWARSING GOPAL; Dir Dr AZAD JEETUN.

UTILITIES
Electricity

Central Electricity Board: Royal Rd, POB 40, Curepipe; tel. 675-5010; fax 675-7958; e-mail ceb@intnet.mu; internet ceb.intnet.mu; f. 1952; state-operated; scheduled for privatization; Chair. PATRICK ASSIRVADEN; Gen. Man. RAVIN DAJEE.

Water

Central Water Authority: Royal Rd, St Paul-Phoenix; tel. 601-5000; fax 686-6264; e-mail cwa@intnet.mu; internet ncb.intnet.mu/putil/cwa; corporate body; scheduled for privatization; f. 1971; Gen. Man. ROBIN SOONARANE; Chair. Dr ANWAN HUSSEIN SUBRATTY.

TRADE UNIONS
Federations

Federation of Civil Service and Other Unions (FCSOU): Jade Court, Rm 308, 3rd Floor, 33 Jummah Mosque St, Port Louis; tel. 216-1977; fax 216-1475; e-mail f.c.s.u@intnet.mu; internet www.fcsu.org; f. 1957; 72 affiliated unions with 30,000 mems (2005); Pres. TOOLSYRAJ BENYDIN; Sec. SOONDRESS SAWMYNADEN.

General Workers' Federation: 13 Brabant St, Port Louis; tel. 212-3338; Pres. FAROOK AUCHOYBUR; Sec.-Gen. DEVANAND RAMJUTTUN.

Mauritius Federation of Trade Unions: Arc Bldg, 3rd Floor, cnr Sir William Newton and Sir Seewoosagur Ramgoolam Sts, Port Louis; tel. 208-9426; f. 1958; four affiliated unions; Pres. FAROOK HOSSENBUX; Sec.-Gen. R. MAREEMOOTOO.

Mauritius Labour Congress (MLC): 8 Louis Victor de la Faye St, Port Louis; tel. 212-4343; fax 208-8945; e-mail mlcongress@intnet.mu; f. 1963; 55 affiliated unions with 70,000 mems (1992); Pres. NURDEO LUCHMUN ROY; Gen. Sec. JUGDISH LOLLBEEHARRY.

Mauritius Trade Union Congress (MTUC): Emmanuel Anquetil Labour Centre, James Smith St, Port Louis; internet www.mtucmauritius.org; f. 1946.

Trade Union Trust Fund: Richard House, 2nd Floor, cnr Jummah Mosque and Remy Ollier Sts, Port Louis; tel. and fax 217-2073; internet www.gov.mu/portal/site/tradeuniontf; f. 1997 to receive and manage funds and other property obtained from the Government and other sources; to promote workers' education and provide assistance to workers' organizations; Chair. RADHAKRISNA SADIEN.

Principal Unions

Government Servants' Association: 107A Royal Rd, Beau Bassin; tel. 464-4242; fax 465-3220; e-mail gsa@intnet.mu; internet www.gsa.mauritius.org; f. 1945; Pres. R. SADIEN; Sec.-Gen. P. RAMJUG.

Government Teachers' Union: 3 Mgr Gonin St, POB 1111, Port Louis; tel. 208-0047; fax 208-4943; f. 1945; Pres. JUGDISH LOLLBEEHARRY; Sec. SHEIKH NASHIR RAMJAN; 4,358 mems (1998).

Nursing Association: Royal Rd, Beau Bassin; tel. 464-5850; f. 1955; Pres. CASSAM KUREEMAN; Sec.-Gen. FRANCIS SUPPARAYEN.

Organization of Artisans' Unity: 42 Sir William Newton St, Port Louis; tel. 212-4557; fax 212-4557; f. 1973; Pres. AUGUSTE FOLLET; Sec. ROY RAMCHURN; 2,874 mems (1994).

Plantation Workers' Union: 8 Louis Victor de la Faye St, Port Louis; tel. 212-1735; f. 1955; Pres. C. BHAGIRUTTY; Sec. N. L. ROY; 13,726 mems (1990).

Port Louis Harbour and Docks Workers' Union: Port Louis; tel. 208-2276; Pres. M. VEERABADREN; Sec.-Gen. GERARD BERTRAND.

Sugar Industry Staff Employees' Association: 1 Rémy Ollier St, Port Louis; tel. 212-1947; f. 1947; Chair. T. BELLEROSE; Sec.-Gen. G. CHUNG KWAN FANG; 1,450 mems (1997).

Textile, Clothes and Other Manufactures Workers' Union: Thomy d'Arifat St, Curepipe; tel. 676-5280; Pres. PADMATEE TEELUCK; Sec.-Gen. DÉSIRÉ GUILDAREE.

Union of Bus Industry Workers: Port Louis; tel. 212-3338; f. 1970; Pres. M. BABOOA; Sec.-Gen. F. AUCHOYBUR.

Union of Employees of the Ministry of Agriculture and other Ministries: 28 Hennessy Ave, Quatre-Bornes; tel. 465-1935; e-mail bruno5@intnet.mu; f. 1989; Sec. BRUNEAU DORASAMI; 2,500 mems (Dec. 2003).

Union of Labourers of the Sugar and Tea Industry: Royal Rd, Curepipe; f. 1969; Sec. P. RAMCHURN.

Transport

RAILWAYS
There are no operational railways in Mauritius.

ROADS
In 2002 there were 2,000 km of classified roads, of which 60 km were motorways, 950 km were other main roads, and 592 km were secondary roads. About 98% of the road network is paved. An urban highway links the motorways approaching Port Louis. A motorway connects Port Louis with Plaisance airport.

SHIPPING
Mauritius is served by numerous foreign shipping lines. In 1990 Port Louis was established as a free port to expedite the development of Mauritius as an entrepôt centre. In 1995 the World Bank approved a loan of US $30.5m. for a programme to develop the port. At 31 December 2004 Mauritius had a merchant fleet of 50 vessels, with a combined displacement of 79.0 grt.

Mauritius Ports Authority: Port Administration Bldg, POB 379, Mer Rouge, Port Louis; tel. 206-5400; fax 240-0856; e-mail mauport@intnet.mu; internet www.mauport.com; f. 1976; Chair. EDDY BOISSÉZON; Dir-Gen. Capt. JEAN WONG CHUNG TOI.

Ireland Blyth Ltd: IBL House, Caudan, Port Louis; tel. 203-2000; fax 203-2001; e-mail iblinfo@iblgroup.com; internet www.iblgroup.com; Chair. THIERRY LAGESSE; CEO P. D'HOTMAN DE VILLIERS; 2 vessels.

Islands Services Ltd: Rogers House, 5 John F. Kennedy St, POB 60, Port Louis; tel. 208-6801; fax 208-5045; services to Indian Ocean islands; Chair. Sir RENÉ MAINGARD; Exec. Dir Capt. RENÉ SANSON.

Mauritius Shipping Corpn Ltd: St James Court, Suite 417/418, St Denis St, Port Louis; tel. 210-6120; fax 210-5176; e-mail info@msc.intnet.mu; internet www.mauritiusshipping.intnet.mu; f. 1985; state-owned; Pres. B. P. DAUMOO.

Société Mauricienne de Navigation Ltée: 1 rue de la Reine, POB 53, Port Louis; tel. 208-3241; fax 208-8931; e-mail iblsh@bow.intnet.mu; Man. Dir Capt. FRANÇOIS DE GERSIGNY.

CIVIL AVIATION
Sir Seewoosagur Ramgoolam International Airport is at Plaisance, 4 km from Mahébourg. From 2006 air routes with France and the United Kingdom were to be liberalized, allowing new carriers to operate on the routes.

Civil Aviation Department: Sir Seewoosagur Ramgoolam International Airport, Plaine Magnien; tel. 603-2000; fax 637-3164; e-mail civa@mail.gov.mu; internet civil-aviation.gov.mu; overseen by the Ministry of Training, Skills Development, Productivity and External Communications; Dir SARUPANAND KINNOO.

Air Mauritius: Air Mauritius Centre, John F. Kennedy St, POB 441, Port Louis; tel. 207-7070; fax 208-8331; e-mail mkcare@airmauritius.intnet.mu; internet www.airmauritius.com; f. 1967; 51% state-owned; services to 28 destinations in Europe, Asia, Australia and Africa; Chair. SANJAY BUCKHORY; Man. Dir NIRVAN VEERASAMY.

Tourism

Tourists are attracted to Mauritius by its scenery and beaches, the pleasant climate and the blend of cultures. Accommodation capacity totalled 21,072 beds in 2005. The number of visitors increased from 300,670 in 1990 to 761,063 in 2005, when the greatest numbers of visitors were from France (29.0%), Réunion (13.0%) and the United Kingdom (12.5%). Gross revenue from tourism in 2005 was estimated at Rs 25,704m. The Government sought to increase the volume of tourists visiting the country (to some 2m. people by 2015) by improving the jetty facilities in the port in order to welcome cruise ships and by liberalizing air transit routes.

Mauritius Tourism Promotion Authority: Air Mauritius Centre, 11th Floor, John F. Kennedy St, Port Louis; tel. 210-1545; fax 212-5142; e-mail info@mtpa.mauritius.net; internet www.mauritius.net; Chair. SURESH SEEGOBIN; Dir ROBERT DESVAUX.

MEXICO

Introductory Survey

Location, Climate, Language, Religion, Flag, Capital

The United Mexican States is bordered to the north by the USA, and to the south by Guatemala and Belize. The Gulf of Mexico and the Caribbean Sea lie to the east, and the Pacific Ocean and Gulf of California to the west. The climate varies with altitude. The tropical southern region and the coastal lowlands are hot and wet, with an average annual temperature of 18°C (64°F), while the highlands of the central plateau are temperate. Much of the north and west is arid desert. In Mexico City, which lies at about 2,250 m (nearly 7,400 ft) above sea-level, temperatures are generally between 5°C (42°F) and 25°C (78°F). The country's highest recorded temperature is 58°C (136°F). The principal language is Spanish, spoken by more than 90% of the population, while about 8% speak indigenous languages, of which Náhuatl is the most widely spoken. Almost all of Mexico's inhabitants profess Christianity, and about 90% are adherents of the Roman Catholic Church. The national flag (proportions 4 by 7) has three equal vertical stripes from hoist to fly, of green, white and red, with the state emblem (a brown eagle, holding a snake in its beak, on a green cactus, with a wreath of oak and laurel beneath) in the centre of the white stripe. The capital is Mexico City.

Recent History

Conquered by Hernán Cortés in the 16th century, Mexico was ruled by Spain until the wars of independence of 1810–21. After the war of 1846, Mexico ceded about one-half of its territory to the USA. Attempts at political and social reform by the anti-clerical Benito Juárez precipitated civil war in 1857–60, and the repudiation of Mexico's external debts by Juárez in 1860 led to war with the United Kingdom, the USA and France. The Austrian Archduke Maximilian, whom France tried to install as Emperor of Mexico, was executed, on the orders of Juárez, in 1867. Order was restored during the dictatorship of Porfirio Díaz, which lasted from 1876 until the Revolution of 1910. The Constitution of 1917 embodied the aims of the Revolution by revising land ownership, drafting a labour code and curtailing the power of the Roman Catholic Church. From 1929–2000 the country was dominated by the Partido Revolucionario Institucional (PRI), for much of that time in an effective one-party system, although a democratic form of election was maintained. However, allegations of widespread electoral malpractice persistently arose in connection with PRI victories.

In a presidential election held in July 1976 the PRI candidate, José López Portillo, was elected with almost 95% of the votes cast. In 1977 López Portillo initiated reforms to increase minority party representation in the legislature and to widen democratic participation. The high level of political participation in the presidential election of July 1982 (held amid a financial crisis) was without precedent, with left-wing groups taking part for the first time; however, the PRI's candidate, Miguel de la Madrid Hurtado, was successful. The concurrent elections to the Cámara Federal de Diputados (Federal Chamber of Deputies) resulted in another overwhelming victory for the PRI. On taking office in December, the new President embarked on a programme of major economic reform, giving precedence to the repayment of Mexico's debts, a policy which imposed severe financial constraints upon the middle and lower classes and which led to growing disaffection among traditional PRI supporters. Notably, the Partido Acción Nacional (PAN), an opposition party, made important gains at municipal elections in two state capitals in mid-1983. The PRI's effective response ensured success at the remaining elections, but provoked opposition allegations of widespread electoral fraud. Contrary to expectations, at gubernatorial and congressional elections conducted in July 1985, the PRI secured all seven of the available state governorships and won 288 of the 300 directly elective seats in the Cámara Federal de Diputados.

The formation of a major left-wing alliance, the Partido Mexicano Socialista—PMS (comprising six parties), in 1987 and, in particular, the emergence of a dissident faction, the Corriente Democrática (CD), within the PRI in 1986 were disturbing political developments for the ruling party. In early 1988 the CD and four left-wing parties (including the PMS coalition) formed an electoral alliance, the Frente Democrático Nacional (FDN), headed by CD leader Cuauhtémoc Cárdenas Solórzano. The legitimacy of the PRI victory at the presidential and congressional elections, conducted in July, was fiercely challenged by the opposition groups, following a delay in the publication of official results, reports of widespread electoral fraud and the failure of the Federal Electoral Commission to release details of results from almost 50% of polling stations. Moreover, Cárdenas claimed victory on behalf of the broad-left coalition; for the first time ever, the opposition secured seats in the Senado (Senate), while the PRI suffered defeats in the Distrito Federal and at least three other states.

In August 1988 the new Congreso de la Unión (Congress) was installed and immediately assumed the function of an electoral college, in order to investigate the claims of both sides. In September the allocation of 200 seats in the Cámara Federal de Diputados by proportional representation afforded the PRI a congressional majority and effective control of the electoral college. Opposition members withdrew from the Cámara in protest at the PRI's obstruction of the investigation, enabling the ruling party to ratify Carlos Salinas de Gortari as the new President with 51% of the votes cast. Cárdenas was credited with 31% of the ballot. The results, although widely regarded as having been manipulated by the PRI, revealed a considerable erosion in support for the party, particularly among the traditional bastions of the trade unions, peasant groups and bureaucracy.

Agreements on rescheduling Mexico's vast foreign debts were reached with the 'Paris Club' of official creditors in 1989, and with some 450 commercial banks in early 1990. Success for the Government in financial negotiations with creditors was largely dependent upon its ability to provide evidence of a stable and developing domestic economy. In January 1989 a Pact for Economic Stability and Growth was implemented, with the agreement of employers' organizations and trade unions, and was subsequently extended until the end of 1994. None the less, the country experienced severe labour unrest in 1989 in support of greater pay increases and in protest at the Government's divestment programme.

During 1989 political opposition to the PRI was strengthened by success in gubernatorial and municipal elections, and by further accusations against the PRI of electoral fraud. In October proposed constitutional amendments were approved with the unexpected support of the PAN. A 'governability clause', whereby an absolute majority of seats in the Cámara Federal de Diputados would be awarded to the leading party, should it receive at least 35% of the votes at a general election, was criticized by the Partido de la Revolución Democrática (PRD), the successor party to the FDN.

In July 1991 the Federal Electoral Code was approved by the Cámara Federal de Diputados with support from all represented parties, except the PRD. The legislation contained provisions for the compilation of a new electoral roll, the issue of more detailed identification cards for voters, the modification of the Instituto Federal Electoral (IFE—Federal Electoral Institute), and the creation of a Tribunal Federal Electoral (Federal Electoral Tribunal, which, in 1996, became the Tribunal Electoral del Poder Judicial de la Federación). The PRD was highly critical of many of the provisions, including alleged procedural obstacles to the formation of political alliances, and the power given to the President to appoint the head of the IFE (the Secretary of the Interior) and to nominate six 'independent' lawyers to its executive. Further constitutional reform, with regard to agriculture, education and religion, were adopted in 1992.

Meanwhile, in June 1990, in response to continuing allegations of federal police complicity in abuses of human rights, President Salinas announced the creation of the Comisión Nacional de los Derechos Humanos (CNDH—National Commission for Human Rights). Opposition groups and independent human rights organizations were critical of the Government's stipulation that the Commission should be excluded from addressing cases relating to political campaigns or electoral processes. In October the Government proposed legislation transferring responsibility for the interrogation of suspected criminals from the federal judicial police to the public magistrate's office. The proposed legislation also sought to undermine the validity of confession alone (often allegedly extracted under torture) as sufficient grounds for conviction.

The PRI continued to secure disputed electoral success at municipal and state level in 1991. At mid-term congressional elections in August, the party won almost all of the 300 directly elective seats in the Cámara Federal de Diputados (plus 30 of the 200 seats awarded by proportional representation) and 31 of the 32 contested seats in the Senado. The return to the level of support that the PRI had enjoyed prior to the 1988 elections was largely attributed to the success of the Government's programme of economic reform. The election results were less encouraging for the opposition; the PAN secured 10 directly elective seats in the Cámara and its first seat in the Senado, but the PRD failed to win a directly elective seat in either congressional house.

PRI victories at gubernatorial and legislative elections in several states during 1993 were denounced by the opposition as fraudulent. In September the Congreso approved electoral reforms that included provisions for greater access to the media for all parties, restrictions on party funding, and improved impartiality of supervision. Other measures sought to increase the representation of minority parties in the Senado, and to end over-representation of larger parties in the Cámara Federal de Diputados. The 'governability clause' introduced in 1989 was to be removed. Divisions within the PRI emerged in November, following the selection of Luis Donaldo Colosio, the Secretary of Social Development, as the party's candidate in the presidential elections. Additional electoral reforms, which claimed to end PRI control of the IFE, received congressional approval in March 1994, but failed to appease PRD leaders, who demanded that the incumbent head of the IFE should be replaced by an impartial president elected by the IFE's newly created six-member commission.

In March 1994 Colosio was assassinated at a campaign rally. Mario Aburto Martínez, arrested at the scene of the murder, was later identified as the apparently motiveless assassin. However, speculation that Colosio had been the victim of a conspiracy within the PRI establishment increased following the arrest, in connection with the incident, of a number of party members associated with police and intelligence agencies. The PRI subsequently named Ernesto Zedillo Ponce de León, a former cabinet minister who had most recently been acting as Colosio's campaign manager, as the party's presidential candidate. Zedillo was elected President on 21 August, with 49% of the votes, ahead of the PAN candidate, Diego Fernández de Cevallos (26%), and the PRD candidate, Cuauhtémoc Cárdenas (17%). The PRI also achieved considerable success at the concurrent congressional elections. Despite the participation of some 70,000 impartial monitors and the attendance of a UN advisory technical team, numerous incidents of electoral malpractice were reported.

Zedillo identified the immediate aims of his administration as the promotion of the independence of the judiciary, the separation of party political activity from the functions of federal government and the further reform of the electoral system. Public confidence in the impartiality and ability of the judiciary had been seriously undermined by the inconsistency and confusion surrounding recent investigations into the deaths of Colosio and José Francisco Ruiz Massieu (see below). Zedillo's appointment of a senior member of the PAN to the post of Attorney-General in a new Cabinet announced in November 1994, together with the disclosure, in December, of more detailed plans for judicial reform, sought to restore the prestige of the judiciary.

The report of a special investigation into Colosio's murder, published in July 1994, concluded that Aburto Martínez had acted alone in the assassination, reversing the findings of a preliminary investigation which had suggested the existence of a number of conspirators. The report provoked incredulity, and President Salinas commissioned a further independent investigation. Speculation that Colosio had been the first victim of a politically motivated campaign of violence, conducted by a cabal of senior PRI traditionalists in order to check the advance of the party's reformist wing, intensified following the murder, in September, of the PRI Secretary-General, José Francisco Ruiz Massieu. In February 1995, however, a report issued by the Attorney-General was highly critical of all previous investigations of the Colosio assasination, concluding that the assassination had involved at least two gunmen. (An alleged second gunman was acquitted in August 1996.) Meanwhile, in November 1994 Ruiz Massieu's brother, Mario, resigned his post as Deputy Attorney-General, claiming that senior PRI officials, including the party's President and Secretary-General, had impeded his investigation into his brother's death, in an attempt to protect the identities of those responsible for the assassination. In February 1995 Raúl Salinas de Gortari, brother of former President Salinas, was arrested on charges of complicity in Ruiz Massieu's murder, and in April Fernando Rodríguez González (a former employee at the Cámara Federal de Diputados, who was charged with hiring the assassins) implicated several new conspirators, including five state Governors. Mario Ruiz Massieu was subsequently detained in the USA. In October two men were each sentenced to 18 years' imprisonment for perpetrating the murder of the PRI Secretary-General. In October 1996 the case against Raúl Salinas was prejudiced further by the discovery of a body buried in the grounds of his property in Mexico City.

In March 1995, following the arrest of his brother, former President Salinas began a public campaign to discredit the new administration and to defend himself from accusations of responsibility for the country's economic crisis and from allegations that he had obstructed attempts to bring to justice those responsible for Colosio's death. Salinas's efforts culminated in a highly publicized but brief hunger strike which prompted the Attorney-General to issue a statement confirming that there was no evidence that Salinas had impeded the Colosio murder inquiry. Raúl Salinas was convicted of murder and, in January 1999, sentenced to 50 years' imprisonment (later reduced to almost 28 years); in August 2002 he was additionally charged with the embezzlement of up to 209m. new pesos from a secret presidential fund under his brother's control. In September 1999 Mario Ruiz Massieu committed suicide in the USA while awaiting trial on charges of 'laundering' money gained from drugs-trafficking; he left a note repeating his earlier accusations against the PRI and blaming Zedillo and other senior officials for his own death and the assassination of Colosio.

The Government's ongoing attempts to effect political reform were reactivated in January 1996 at a meeting of some 50 civil and political groups. In July the PRI, the PAN, the PRD and the Partido del Trabajo (PT, a labour party) reached consensus on reforms that would include introducing a directly elected governor of the Distrito Federal, increasing and regulating public financing for political parties, employing proportional representation in elections to the Senado, granting a right of vote to Mexican citizens resident abroad, and allowing the IFE greater independence. The reforms received congressional approval in August. However, in November, in apparent response to their diminishing share of the vote in recent municipal elections, PRI traditionalists secured the adoption by the Cámara Federal de Diputados of a series of amendments to the electoral reform bill, increasing public funding in 1997 for political parties by some 476%, pronouncing that to exceed campaign finance limits would no longer be a criminal or electoral offence, expanding the Government's access to the media, and restricting the right of opposition parties to form coalitions. Internal tensions in the PRI became increasingly apparent during 1996. At the party's National Assembly, PRI traditionalists retaliated against the progressive faction by voting to alter the prerequisites for senior government positions. The new conditions would have prevented the selection of President Zedillo and of most of his Cabinet.

In May 1996 President Zedillo dismissed Mexico City's chief of police following public outcry at the violent tactics employed by his officers to disperse a group of striking teachers in the capital. In the following months hundreds of police employees throughout the country were dismissed for incompetence or corruption, while army officers were increasingly appointed to positions within the police force. In March 1997 some 2,500 members of Mexico City's police force were replaced by army personnel, and in October an élite police unit was disbanded after accusations that as many as 35 of its members were implicated in the torture and murder of three youths in September. Several officers at the anti-abduction unit in the state of Morelos were also accused of torture and murder in early 1998, precipitating the resignation of the state's PRI Governor in May.

At elections held on 6 July 1997 for all 500 members of the Cámara Federal de Diputados the PRI lost its overall majority for the first time, while the PRD and the PAN made substantial gains. At concurrent elections held for one-quarter of the seats in the Senado the PRI retained its overall majority, albeit significantly reduced, while the PAN and the PRD increased their representation. An informal congressional alliance between the

PAN, the PRD, the Partido Verde Ecologista de México (PVEM) and the PT meant that opposition parties were able to take control of important legislative committees. In addition to the poor legislative electoral performance, the PRI was defeated by the PAN in two of six gubernatorial elections conducted at the same time. Most significant, however, was the election of Cárdenas, the PRD candidate, as Head of Government of the Distrito Federal. The electoral defeats suffered by the PRI exacerbated tensions within the party and several party members defected to the PRD, some of whom were selected as candidates in gubernatorial elections.

In mid-1998 the PRI encountered strong opposition in the Congreso to its proposals to convert into public debt liabilities to the value of some US $65,000m. assumed by the bank rescue agency, the Fondo Bancario de Protección al Ahorro (FOBAPROA), after the financial crisis of late 1994. In December revised legislation establishing a successor to the FOBAPROA was approved by the Cámara Federal de Diputados, and the Government was forced to concede that FOBAPROA's liabilities would not automatically become public debt. FOBAPROA's successor, the Instituto de Protección al Ahorro Bancario, was created in May 1999.

A presidential election was held on 2 July 2000. The PRI's candidate was the former Secretary of the Interior, Francisco Labastida Ochoa, while the former Governor of Guanajuato state, Vicente Fox Quesada, represented a PAN-PVEM alliance known as the Alianza por el Cambio—AC, and Cárdenas was once again the PRD's nominee (officially he stood for the PRD-dominated Alianza por México—AM). Fox secured 43.5% of the votes cast, while Labastida attracted 36.9% and Cárdenas 17.0%. Fox was thus elected President, ending the PRI's 71-year hegemony in Mexican government. In the concurrent elections to the Congreso the AC secured 223 of the 500 seats (208 of them won by the PAN, 15 by the PVEM), compared with 209 won by the PRI and 68 by the parties of the AM. The PRI remained the largest grouping in the Senado, however, with 60 seats, compared with 51 held by the AC and 17 by the AM. The election for Head of Government of the Distrito Federal, contested on the same day as the federal elections, was won by Andrés Manuel López Obrador of the PRD, who secured some 34.5% of the votes cast, compared with his nearest rival, Santiago Creel Miranda of the PAN, who obtained some 33.4% of the ballot. Fox took office as President on 1 December, stating that his priorities were a reduction in poverty, improved relations with the USA and peace and reconciliation within Mexico. His first Cabinet contained members of the PAN, PRI and other parties, in addition to a number of prominent figures from commerce and academia. The PRD declined an offer of three cabinet portfolios.

In October 2001 the Government announced that eight parties, including the PRI and the PRD, had signed the Acuerdo Político para el Desarrollo Nacional (Political Agreement for National Development), designed to facilitate law-making. Under the terms of the Agreement, the parties promised to support government measures to improve public finances and to deregulate the energy and telecommunications sectors. Nevertheless, the Government continued to encounter congressional opposition to its proposed fiscal reforms.

In January 2002 the Government announced that an investigation was to be held into allegations that the state petroleum company, PEMEX, had covertly funded the election campaign of the PRI presidential candidate, Francisco Labastida Ochoa, in 2000. The affair centred on the alleged diversion of 1,580m. new pesos in PEMEX funds into PRI accounts by two leaders of the petroleum workers' union, the Sindicato de Trabajadores Petroleros de la República Mexicana. In May a former director of PEMEX, Manuel Gómez-Peralta, was detained in connection with the allegations; furthermore, a former PEMEX President, Rogelio Montemayor, was arrested in Houston, Texas (USA) in October. In that month opposition parties demanded that President Fox allow the re-opening of investigations into allegations that the PAN organization Amigos de Fox, responsible for Fox's presidential campaign, had received substantial illegal foreign funding. (The investigation had been suspended on grounds of banking secrecy, but had been ordered to recommence by the electoral tribunal in May.) The PRI threatened to initiate a congressional investigation unless the Amigos de Fox's accounts were made public. In October 2003 the IFE fined both the PAN and the PVEM for receiving illegal campaign funding from Amigos de Fox.

In May 2002 27 Zapotec Indians were killed in suspicious circumstances at Agua Fría, in Santiago Textitlán, Oaxaca; state authorities arrested 17 villagers, but local Indian organizations claimed that paramilitary groups had been involved in the attacks. Following the incident, an official from the human rights organization Amnesty International denounced the state Attorney-General's office for abuses. In July protests by farmers and Zapatistas (see below) over the proposed construction of a new international airport for Mexico City descended into violence; in subsequent clashes with the police one person was killed and 31 injured. In response, the protestors, who were opposed to proposed legislation expropriating their land, threatened to kill 12 hostages (a further three hostages were later taken). The Government subsequently reversed its policy on the project.

In his annual 'Informe' address in September 2002, President Fox urged the Congreso to support legislation for structural reform, particularly of the electricity sector, and stressed the need for partnership between President and legislature. This, however, proved difficult to achieve, particularly in the midst of allegations and counter-allegations of electoral financial malpractice between the PRI and the PAN. In November there was conflict over both a proposed delay in the extension of value-added tax (VAT), and the introduction of a so-called 'luxuries tax', proposed by the PRD. Furthermore, in December the PRD obstructed legislation proposing the reduction in the number of lower-house seats elected by proportional representation (from 200 to 100).

In January 2003 the Secretary of Foreign Affairs, Jorge Castañeda, resigned, prompting President Fox to carry out a cabinet reshuffle. Castañeda was replaced by the Secretary of the Economy, Luis Ernesto Derbez Bautista, who in turn was succeeded by Fernando Canales Barragán, the Governor of Nuevo León. In February conflicts within the PRD had led to the cancellation of internal elections for candidates for the July elections. Instead, candidates were picked by the national committee, and included a number of recent PRI converts who had left the party following the electoral funding scandal of 2002.

Municipal elections, held in the state of México in March 2003, saw the PAN lose its majority in the state legislature to the PRI, which contested the ballot in conjunction with the PVEM. President Fox's negative reaction to the US-led military campaign in Iraq in 2003 (see below), as well as the consequent deterioration in relations with the USA, resulted in an increase in public support for his Government; nevertheless, in the mid-term congressional elections on 6 July, the PAN's representation in the Cámara Federal de Diputados was reduced from 205 to 153 seats. In contrast, the PRI increased its lower-house representation to 224 seats (from 209), as did the PRD, securing 95 seats (compared with 52 seats in the previous legislature). The opposition's gains, however, were marred by an electoral turn-out of only 42%. In the concurrently held gubernatorial elections, the PRI and its allies won three of the six states contested, while PAN candidates were successful in two states.

In early November 2003 the Supreme Court ruled that prosecution for murder could proceed even in cases where no body had been found. The ruling enabled prosecutions to proceed for human rights abuses committed during the 'guerra sucia' ('dirty war') of the late 1970s; in February 2004 Miguel Nazar Haro, former director of the covert Dirección General de Seguridad, was arrested in connection with the disappearance of left-wing activist Jesús Piedra Ibarra in 1975. In mid-2004 the Supreme Court made a further ruling that cases concerning disappearance could be brought in connection with the suppression of dissent in the 1970s and 1980s. Meanwhile, a special prosecutor, Ignacio Carrillo, was appointed to investigate the role of, among others, the former President Luis Echeverría in the 'guerra sucia'; however, Carrillo's request that Echeverría be arrested was rejected. In February 2005 the Supreme Court ruled that the Vienna Convention on genocide, which came into force in 2002, could not be applied retrospectively, while in July 2005 the case against Echeverría was dismissed on the grounds that there was no evidence of genocide.

In November 2003 the Government's budget proposals were rejected by the Cámara Federal de Diputados. The PRI, the largest congressional party, subsequently presented its own budget proposals to the legislature. However, divisions appeared within that party, ostensibly over the alternative proposals. In December 118 PRI deputies voted to replace Elba Esther Gordillo Morales as leader of the PRI legislative bloc. Gordillo, who had originally supported the Government's proposed budget, initially refused to accept her dismissal and continued to rely on the support of 104 PRI deputies. It was widely believed that the underlying reason for the split was an ongoing feud between

Gordillo and party president, Roberto Madrazo Pintado, over who would secure the PRI nomination for the presidential election due in 2006. To this end, in January 2005 Gordillo and the powerful teachers' union, the Sindicato Nacional de Trabajadores de la Educación, launched the Nueva Alianza (NA), in order to consolidate support for her candidacy. Further discord appeared within the PRI in March, when senior members of the party asked Madrazo to resign prior to campaigning for the PRI's nomination.

In March 2004 a scandal emerged surrounding the PRD Head of Government of the Distrito Federal, Andrés Manuel López Obrador, who was a popular and likely candidate in the 2006 presidential election. A videotape appeared to show López Obrador's finance chief, Gustavo Ponce Meléndez, gambling large amounts at a casino in Las Vegas, USA (Ponce was arrested in October). A further video recording came to light that apparently showed the Head of Government's former private secretary, René Bejarano, accepting money from a prominent Argentine businessman, Carlos Ahumada, who was accused of corruption. López Obrador denied any knowledge of either incident and claimed that a 'dirty tricks' campaign was being waged against him. In June 2004 the Attorney-General's office announced it was to prosecute López Obrador for allegedly ignoring an injunction against a compulsory purchase order and disregarding a federal ruling to re-employ numerous dismissed city officials; as a result, a formal request was made to the Congreso to rescind López Obrador's immunity from prosecution. In an indication of his popularity in Mexico City, however, in early August thousands of supporters attended a march in the capital against the move to impeach him. Following much deliberation, on 1 April 2005 a four-member committee of the Cámara Federal de Diputados voted to recommend that López Obrador be stripped of his immunity; on 7 April the lower house concurred with the committee's recomendation, in order that charges might be brought against López Obrador. Following the vote López Obrador took a leave of absence from office, although the Distrito Federal assembly approved a motion confirming him in office. Furthermore, on 24 April as many as 1.2m. people participated in a demonstration in Mexico City in support of their mayor, who returned to his post the following day. On 27 April the federal Attorney-General, Rafael Macedo de la Concha, was sacked. His dismissal was widely interpreted as an admission by the Government that its plan to prevent López Obrador from contesting the forthcoming presidential election had failed (people facing criminal charges were prohibited from running for office); indeed, in early May Macedo de la Concha's successor dismissed all charges against López Obrador.

In May 2004 Felipe Calderón, the Secretary of State for Energy, resigned following a disagreement with President Fox over his intention to stand as the PAN candidate in the 2006 presidential election. He was replaced by Fernando Elizondo. In June a group of PRI senators asserted that there were financial irregularities in the running of Vamos México, a charity set up by the President's wife, Marta Sahagún. An investigation was subsequently launched into money received by the foundation from the national lottery, and, as a consequence, the director of the lottery was sacked. Fox's supporters dismissed the inquiry as an opposition attempt to discredit the President. However, in early July Alfonso Durazo, President's Fox's spokesman, resigned, citing Sahagún's influence and her plans to run for President as the reasons for his departure. Sahagún subsequently denied that she would be contesting the election.

In August 2004 the Senado approved legislation on social security reform which, it was hoped, would allow money previously spent on pensions to be reallocated to health care. On 1 September Fox gave his annual 'Informe' address, in which he called for more co-operation between the legislature and the Government; however, he was heckled by opposition deputies and the event attracted protests outside the Congreso building. In the same month the Government submitted to the Congreso its 2005 budget, which aimed to reduce federal spending by 12%. An amended budget finally received legislative approval in mid-November; however, President Fox then returned the budget to the Congreso with a number of changes. The Cámara Federal de Diputados interpreted this as an attempt to veto the chamber, something prohibited by the Constitution, and rejected Fox's proposals. In response, the President appealed to the Supreme Court to rule on the matter. The Court subsequently froze spending on contested funds while it considered the case.

Preparations for the 2006 presidential and legislative elections intensified from mid-2005. In June the Congreso approved legislation granting the right to vote to Mexicans living abroad (although by January 2006 only 25,145 Mexicans abroad had registered to vote in that year's elections). In June 2005 the Secretary of the Interior, Santiago Creel, resigned in order to campaign for the PAN's nomination in the presidential ballot. Carlos Abascal Carranza, one of the more conservative members of Fox's Cabinet, was given the interior portfolio. In July the PRI comfortably won the gubernatorial election in the Estado de México; great significance was placed on the result of the ballot, as it was seen as a precursor to the presidential election due 12 months later. At the end of July López Obrador resigned as Head of Government of the Distrito Federal and, in the following month, secured the PRD's presidential nomination. He was succeeded, in an interim capacity, by Alejandro Encinas, hitherto López Obrador's deputy.

Meanwhile, discord continued within the PRI. Roberto Madrazo, president of the party, had been due to resign in mid-2005 to contest the party's primary election for the presidential nomination. Traditionally, he would have been succeeded as party president by the secretary-general, Elba Esther Gordillo; however, the ongoing rivalry between the two meant that Madrazo delayed his resignation until August. At the end of that month the party's national political council elected Mariano Palacios Alcocer, who had previously served as party president, as Madrazo's successor. Gordillo had announced that she would not be attending the meeting of the council; subsequent legal action undertaken by her supporters to prove that Palacios Alcocer's election had been illegal was unsuccessful. Gordillo stepped down as Secretary-General in September. Divisions within between the three main factions of the party—those supporting Madrazo, supporters of Gordillo and a third grouping, Unidad Democrática, more commonly known as Todos Unidos Contra Madrazo (TUCOM—Everyone United against Madrazo), were such that there was speculation that the PRI might split. Madrazo's past was particularly divisive: in 1994 he was alleged to have seriously exceeded campaign spending regulations in the gubernatorial election in Tabasco (in which he defeated López Obrador), while it was also alleged that the ballot by which he became party president in 2002 was rigged.

In early August 2005 TUCOM elected Arturo Montiel, the outgoing Governor of the Estado de México, as that faction's nominee to be the PRI's presidential candidate. However, in October allegations of corruption emerged regarding Montiel's use of public money during his time as Governor. Relations between Madrazo and Montiel worsened before, on 20 October, Montiel suddenly withdrew from the primary contest. It was widely assumed that Madrazo had been behind the allegations. A series of defections in late 2005 by prominent members of the PRI opposed to Madrazo further highlighted the divisions within the party. None the less, in mid-November, Madrazo won an overwhelming victory in the election for the PRI's presidential nomination, although turn-out was reportedly only 3.2m., less than one-half the anticipated number.

In September 2005 President Fox gave his fifth 'Informe' address, in which he called for more co-operation between the Government and the Congreso. In the same month the Government presented legislation to the Congreso concerning the state budget for 2006 and providing for a series of reforms of the energy sector. The President also vetoed a congressional decree to reduce PEMEX's tax burden. On 21 September the Secretary for Public Security, Ramón Martín Huerta, was killed in a helicopter crash. He was replaced by Eduardo Medina Mora. Further changes to the Government took place at the end of the month as the energy and agriculture ministers resigned in order to contest gubernatorial and senatorial elections due in 2006. As a result, Fernando Canales moved from the economy secretariat to the key position of Secretary of Energy, while Sergio García became Secretary of the Economy. Francisco Mayorga Castañeda was given responsibility for agriculture. In early November the revenue section of the 2006 budget, which anticipated a 0.2% surplus, was approved by the Cámara Federal de Diputados.

In October 2005 the former Secretary of Energy, Felipe Calderón, from the traditional, clericist wing of the PAN, unexpectedly won the election to decide that party's 2006 presidential nomination, defeating Santiago Creel, who had enjoyed the support of President Fox.

In municipal elections in mid-November 2005 in Hidalgo, traditionally a PRI stronghold, the PRI won only 37 of the 84 municipalities, 12 fewer than it had previously held; the PRD, however, increased its representation in the state. In December the PRI and the PVEM announced an alliance, Alianza por el

México, in advance of the 2006 elections. The PRD also formed an alliance, named Por el Bien de Todos (For the Good of Everyone), with two smaller left-wing parties, Convergencia and the PT, to contest the elections.

The presidential election campaign officially began on 19 January 2006. There were five main candidates: López Obrador for the PRD, Madrazo, representing the PRI, Calderón of the PAN, Roberto Campa (who had left the PRI in late 2005 and received the backing of Gordillo's new party, the NA) and Patricia Mercado Castro, the candidate of the newly formed Partido Alternativa Socialdemócrata y Campesina. In early 2006, according to opinion polls, López Obrador remained the most likely to secure the presidency.

Mexico's poor human rights record was highlighted in late 2001 by the assassination in October of the leading civil liberties lawyer, Digna Ochoa, and by the publication, in December, of an Amnesty International report alleging that Mexican security forces were involved in widespread human rights violations. In response, President Fox, whose electoral campaign had prioritized the elimination of corruption and an improvement in human rights, announced an official inquiry into the 'disappearance' of 532 people detained by security forces in the 1970s and 1980s. In February 2002 Fox ordered the immediate release of Gen. José Francisco Gallardo, who had been sentenced to 28 years' imprisonment in 1993 after being convicted of misappropriating military property. Human rights groups and supporters of Gallardo had maintained that the charges were fabricated and that he had been incarcerated after demanding a reform of the military justice system. However, in August 2003 Amnesty International published a report that accused the Government of inefficiency and negligence in investigating the rape and murder of an estimated 307 women (and the disappearance of a further 500) in Ciudad Juárez over the previous 10 years. In 2004 some 130 government officials were investigated for negligence in the ongoing murder investigations. In mid-2004 a further Amnesty International report asserted that widespread abuse of human rights persisted. The report alleged that the police and military routinely abused peasants, and that torture was commonly used by police and in the justice system. According to official figures, 531 kidnappings occurred in Mexico in 2003; however, other sources estimated that the real figure was 3,000. In December 2004 President Fox unveiled a National Plan for Human Rights, aimed at eliminating torture and abuse and, in the following month, announced a restructuring of federal security.

The Fox administration had pledged to address the problem of drugs-trafficking. The subsequent anti-narcotics effort led to an increased number of arrests in 2002–04, including the leaders of the Tijuana and Golfo cocaine cartels. However, the anti-drugs programme was itself the subject of an anti-corruption drive in 2002, leading to a number of specialized army units being dismantled. Meanwhile, in November the investigation into the 'guerra sucia' of the late 1970s resulted in the conviction of Brig.-Gen. Mario Acosta and Gen. Francisco Quirós on charges of protecting the operations of the Juárez cartel; they also faced charges over the disappearance of 143 activists. In July 2004 President Fox admitted that his Government had not, thus far, effectively addressed the crime problem, and announced a new anti-crime policy. Drugs-related crime continued to escalate, however, as the amount of drugs crossing the Mexican–US border increased. It appeared that an internecine war between the Tijuana, Golfo and Sinaloa cartels was taking place in the north of Mexico, and in June 2005 President Fox announced a further security operation, México Seguro, to combat drugs-related violence in the three northern states of Baja California, Sinaloa and Tamaulipas. By December more than 180 people, including police-officers, had been killed in 2005 in Nuevo Laredo, Tamaulipas, in what appeared to be an ongoing conflict between two drugs cartels. In November Ricardo García Urquiza, alleged to be the leader of the Juárez cartel, was arrested in Mexico City.

On 1 January 1994 armed Indian groups numbering 1,000–3,000 took control of four municipalities of the southern state of Chiapas. The rebels issued the Declaration of the Lacandona Jungle, identifying themselves as the Ejército Zapatista de Liberación Nacional—EZLN (after Emiliano Zapata, who championed the land rights of Mexican peasants during the 1910–17 Revolution), and detailed a series of demands for economic and social change in the region, culminating in a declaration of war against the Government and a statement of intent to depose the 'dictator', President Salinas. A charismatic rebel spokesman, identified as 'subcomandante Marcos' (later tentatively identified as Rafael Sebastián Guillén Vicente, a former professor at the Universidad Autónoma Metropolitana), stated that the insurgency had been timed to coincide with the implementation of the North American Free Trade Agreement (NAFTA—see below), which the rebels considered to be the latest in a series of segregative government initiatives adopted at the expense of indigenous groups. Negotiations between the Zapatistas and government representatives concluded with the publication of a document detailing 34 demands of the EZLN, and the Government's response to them. A preliminary accord was reached following the Government's broad acceptance of many of the rebels' stipulations, including an acceleration of the wide-ranging anti-poverty programme in the region, the incorporation of traditional Indian structures of justice and political organization, and a commitment from the Government to investigate the impact of NAFTA and recent land reform legislation on Indian communities. Official figures suggested that 100–150 guerrillas, soldiers and civilians had been killed during the conflict, while the Roman Catholic Church estimated that there had been as many as 400 casualties. In June the EZLN announced that the Government's peace proposal had been rejected by an overwhelming majority of the movement's supporters. However, a similar majority had rejected the resumption of hostilities with the security forces, and had endorsed the extension of the cease-fire pending renewed bilateral discussions. Tensions, however, continued over the following years, and attempts to reach an accord between the Zapatistas and the Government proved unsuccessful, and the Government sanctioned a series of counter-insurgency measures. In February 1996 the ELZN and the Government signed an agreement in San Andrés Larraínzar on the guarantee of cultural, linguistic and local government rights for indigenous groups. However the ELZN announced its withdrawal from negotiations in September on the grounds that the agreement had not been implemented. In September 1997 several thousand Zapatistas and their sympathizers staged a peaceful demonstration in Mexico City, during which the EZLN inaugurated the Frente Zapatista de Liberación Nacional, a political movement that embodied the Zapatistas' ideology. In December there was widespread disquiet at the killing of 45 Indians in a church in the village of Acteal, in the municipality of Chenalhó, Chiapas. Emilio Chuayffet, the Secretary of the Interior, and Julio César Ruiz Ferro, the Governor of Chiapas, were forced to resign, following criticism of their roles in the events leading to the Acteal massacre. In April 1998 Gen. Julio César Santiago Díaz, who had been acting chief of staff of Chiapas state police at the time of the massacre, was arrested and charged with failing to intervene to prevent the bloodshed. In September 1999 Jacinto Arias, mayor of Chenalhó at the time of the massacre, was convicted on charges of supplying the weapons used in the massacre and sentenced to 35 years' imprisonment. In November 2002 18 people were each sentenced to 36 years' imprisonment for their involvement in the deaths as part of a paramilitary group with links to the PRI; they joined 70 others previously convicted.

In February 2001 subcomandante Marcos, other Zapatista leaders and numerous other campaigners for indigenous rights began a tour of Mexico, which culminated in Mexico City in early March, where a rally in the capital's main square, attended by an estimated 150,000 people, was held in support of congressional approval of the proposed indigenous rights legislation. Following a congressional vote four EZLN leaders were permitted to address both legislative chambers and, on 28 March, the EZLN announced that formal dialogue with the Government would recommence, although its other demands had not been met. Subcomandante Marcos successfully negotiated the dismantling of the remaining three garrisons in Chiapas, and in April the Congreso approved amendments to six articles of the Constitution, which recognized and guaranteed indigenous political, legal, social and economic rights, and prohibited discrimination against Indians based on race and tribal affiliation. However, the legislation fell short of granting indigenous peoples the right to autonomy over land and natural resources; in response, the EZLN suspended all contact with the Government. On 10 August 2003 the EZLN declared that 30 municipalities in Chiapas, hitherto under Zapatista control, were to be granted autonomy. Juntas de Buen Gobierno would oversee the transition from military to civilian control in these areas. The transformation of the EZLN into a political force was underlined in August 2005, when subcomandante Marcos announced his plans to create a left-wing alliance of peasants' organizations. In early

2006 the Zapatistas began an alternative presidential election campaign, although by April it failed to gather significant support.

Mexico's foreign policy has been determined largely by relations with the USA. The rapid expansion of petroleum production from the mid-1970s onwards gave Mexico a new independence, empowering it to favour the left-wing regimes in Cuba and Nicaragua, opposed by the USA, during the 1980s. In February 1985 relations between Mexico and the USA deteriorated following the murder of an agent of the US Drug Enforcement Administration (DEA) by Mexican drugs-traffickers. The situation worsened in April 1990, when a Mexican physician was abducted, in Mexico, by agents employed by the DEA, and transported to the USA to be arrested on charges relating to the murder. Meanwhile, relations between Mexico and the USA remained tense, largely because of disagreement over the problem of illegal immigration from Mexico into the USA and Mexico's failure to take effective action against the illegal drugs trade. This situation improved following the deportation to the USA in 1996 of Juan García Abrego, the alleged head of the Golfo drugs cartel. In February 1997 Mexico's credibility in combating drugs-trafficking was seriously undermined when Gen. Jesús Gutiérrez Rebollo, the head of the counter-narcotics agency, was dismissed and charged with receiving payment from Amado Carrillo Fuentes, the head of the Juárez drugs cartel. (He was later sentenced to more than 30 years' detention.) Nevertheless, in March the USA 'certified' Mexico as a country co-operating in its campaign against drugs-trafficking. In May Mexico's discredited counter-narcotics agency was disbanded and replaced with a specially trained) anti-drugs unit. Bilateral relations were strained in May 1998, when a major US counter-narcotics operation was conducted in Mexico, without Mexican authorization. None the less, additional co-operation agreements were signed by the two countries in early 1999, and Mexico continued to be 'certified' by the USA. Although President Fox advocated abolition of the certification practice, it was reaffirmed in March 2001. Following a modification of the certification process in 2002, in September 2003 and 2004 Mexico appeared in a list of countries deemed to be major illicit drugs-producing or -trafficking countries by the USA. It was estimated that 70% of cocaine destined for the USA passed through Mexico.

NAFTA, comprising Mexico, the USA and Canada, took effect from 1 January 1994. Among the Agreement's provisions are the gradual reduction of tariffs on 50% of products over a period of 10–15 years (some 57% of tariffs on agricultural trade between the USA and Mexico was removed immediately), and the establishment, by Mexico and the USA, of a North American Development Bank (NADBank) charged with the funding of initiatives for the rehabilitation of the two countries' common border. From January 2003 tariffs on a number of agricultural products were reduced or removed entirely, provoking widespread discontent among Mexico's 25m.-strong rural community. In particular, they pointed to the greater subsidies received by US farmers and to a poor transport infrastructure, which resulted in higher costs. A pledge by President Fox in May 2002 to repay Mexico's 'water debt' to the USA had also angered Mexican farmers. Following the collapse, in September 2003, of the fifth Ministerial Conference of the World Trade Organization (WTO) in Cancún, Mexico joined the group of developing countries led by Brazil that opposed US-EU subsidies of agricultural products. At a summit meeting in March 2005 between President Fox, US President George W. Bush and Canadian Prime Minister Paul Martin, the three leaders announced an accord to increase regional co-operation on economic and security issues.

The Fox Government sought to persuade the US Administration of George W. Bush (2001–) to adopt a more liberal position on Mexican immigrants to the USA. However, progress on immigration policy was suspended following the terrorist attacks in the USA on 11 September 2001, and proposals to tighten security on the US-Mexican border were approved by the US Congress in 2002. In March of that year, nevertheless, following a summit meeting in Monterrey, the two Presidents announced a 'smart border' partnership agreement, intended to facilitate the legal entry of Mexican people and goods into the USA while, at the same time, securing the frontier against possible acts of terrorism. Attempts to regularize the status of illegal Mexican immigrants in the USA led to the preliminary introduction of identity cards in Texas in May. In September, however, Fox requested that the emphasis in US-Mexican relations be shifted back to bilateral issues, which had been neglected in favour of border security. Also in September, Mexico unilaterally withdrew from the Inter-American Treaty of Reciprocal Assistance (the Rio Treaty), the defence pact linking Mexico to the USA, resulting in a downturn in relations with the USA.

In March 2003, with Mexican public opinion strongly against armed intervention to remove the regime of Saddam Hussain in Iraq, President Fox risked a deterioration of relations with both the USA and Spain by stating his opposition to war. His opposition was all the more significant owing to Mexico's place as one of the five non-permanent members of the UN Security Council. In January 2004 the announcement of a revised US immigration initiative, which offered significantly less to Mexican immigrants in the USA than had been hoped, was met with disappointment by the Mexican Government, which had hoped to increase freedom of movement between the two countries. In the same month US officials began managing the security arrangements for US bound flights leaving Mexico City's airport. In March, following a summit with the President Bush in Texas, President Fox announced that the USA had agreed to relax certain immigration restrictions for Mexicans. Following his re-election in November 2004, President Bush announced that an accord on immigration would be signed during his second term.

Throughout 2005 tensions remained high between Mexico and the USA over border security, specifically regarding illegal immigration from Mexico to the USA, and also escalating drugs-related violence in Mexico (see above). The US ambassador to Mexico was outspoken in his criticism of the Mexican Government's attempts to control the violence, and temporarily closed the US consulate in Nuevo Laredo in mid-2005. However, in October a Mexican-US joint effort to reduce lawlessness in the border area was announced: a bilateral agreement was signed in March 2006. The Mexican Government, however, was unhappy with the US plan, announced in late 2005, to build fences along the border in order to deter illegal immigrants.

In April 2004 Mexico's relations with Cuba were strained after Mexico voted in favour of a UN motion to censure Cuba for human rights abuses. In early May the Cuban leader, Fidel Castro Ruz, criticized Mexico's stance and accused the Fox Government of interference in the island's affairs. In response, President Fox expelled the Cuban ambassador from the country and recalled the Mexican ambassador in Havana; the ambassadors returned to their posts in July. In late 2005 Mexico and Venezuela recalled their ambassdors, after left-wing President Lt-Col (retd) Hugo Chávez Frías of Venezuela criticized President Fox for being subservient to the USA.

In January 1991 a preliminary free trade agreement was signed with Honduras, Guatemala, El Salvador, Nicaragua and Costa Rica, in order to facilitate the negotiation of bilateral agreements between Mexico and each of the five countries, leading to free trade in an increasing range of products over a six-year period. During the 1990s Mexico concluded agreements for greater economic co-operation and increased bilateral trade with Colombia and Venezuela as the Group of Three (G-3, see p. 386), with Bolivia, Costa Rica and with the European Union (EU, see p. 228). A free trade accord with Nicaragua came into force in 1998; a similar accord with Chile was signed in 1998 and came into force in the following year. A further trade agreement with Guatemala, Honduras and El Salvador (the Northern Triangle) was concluded in 2000. In March 2000 Mexico and the EU signed a free trade agreement, the first to be signed between the EU and a Latin American country. The accord provided for the gradual elimination of tariffs on industrial and agricultural products, the progressive liberalization of trade in services, and preferential access to public procurement; it also obliged the signatories to respect democratic principles and human rights. In October 2003 Mexico signed an Organization of American States agreement on regional security, which was also aimed at increasing co-operation on social and environmental issues. In a series of meetings held in late 2003, Mexico supported the Brazilian Government in demanding revisions to the proposed Free Trade Area of the Americas, due to come into force in 2005. In April 2004 the Secretary of State for Foreign Affairs, Luis Ernesto Derbez, announced Mexico's aim of becoming a full member of Mercosur (Mercado Común del Sur, or Southern Common Market, see p. 363), and in late 2004 he declared Mexico's intention of seeking permanent representation on the UN Security Council (see p. 14).

Government

Mexico is a federal republic comprising 31 states and a Distrito Federal—Federal District (around the capital). Under the 1917 Constitution, legislative power is vested in the bicameral Congreso de la Unión, elected by universal adult suffrage. The

MEXICO

Senado has 128 members (four from each state and the Distrito Federal), serving a six-year term. The Cámara Federal de Diputados, directly elected for three years, has 500 seats, of which 300 are filled from single-member constituencies. The remaining 200 seats, allocated so as to achieve proportional representation, are filled from parties' lists of candidates. Executive power is held by the President, directly elected for six years at the same time as the Senado. He governs with the assistance of an appointed Cabinet. Each state has its own constitution and is administered by a Governor (elected for six years) and an elected chamber of deputies. The Distrito Federal is administered by a Head of Government.

Defence

Military service, on a part-time basis (four hours per week), is compulsory for conscripts selected by lottery, for one year. In August 2005 the active armed forces totalled 192,770: 144,000 in the army (including some 60,000 conscripts), 37,000 in the navy (including naval air force—1,100—and marines—8,700) and 11,770 in the air force. There is a rural defence militia numbering 11,000. The reserve numbered 300,000. Defence expenditure for 2005 was budgeted at 33,700m. new pesos.

Economic Affairs

In 2003, according to estimates by the World Bank, Mexico's gross national income (GNI), measured at average 2002–04 prices, was US $703,080.1m., equivalent to $6,770 per head (or $9,590 per head on an international purchasing-power parity basis). During 1995–2004, it was estimated, the population increased at an average annual rate of 1.5%, while gross domestic product (GDP) per head increased, in real terms, by an average of 2.2% per year. Overall GDP increased, in real terms, at an average annual rate of 3.7% in 1995–2004; GDP increased by 4.2% in 2004.

Agriculture (including forestry and fishing) contributed an estimated 4.0% of GDP in 2004 and engaged about 15.1% of the employed labour force in 2005. The staple food crops are maize, wheat, sorghum, barley, rice, beans and potatoes. The principal cash crops are coffee, cotton, sugar cane, and fruit and vegetables (particularly tomatoes). Livestock-raising and fisheries are also important. During 1995–2004, according to World Bank estimates, agricultural GDP increased at an average annual rate of 2.2%; agricultural GDP rose by 3.5% in 2003 and by 4.0% in 2004. The reduction and eventual removal of import tariffs proposed under the North American Free Trade Agreement (NAFTA) was a significant blow to Mexico's agriculture sector, which had lower subsidies and higher overhead costs than in the USA. In late 2004 the Congreso approved a law regulating the use of genetically modified seeds.

Industry (including mining, manufacturing, construction and power) engaged an estimated 25.6% of the employed labour force in 2005, and provided an estimated 26.1% of GDP in 2004. During 1995–2004 industrial GDP increased by an average of 4.0% per year; industrial GDP decreased by 0.2% in 2003, but rose by 3.8% in 2004.

Mining contributed an estimated 1.3% of GDP in 2004, and, together with electricity production and distribution, engaged an estimated 0.9% of the employed labour force in 2005. During 1990–2001 the GDP of the mining sector increased by an average of 1.9% per year; mining GDP increased by 3.8% in 2000 and by 0.8% in 2001. Mexico has large reserves of petroleum and natural gas (mineral products accounted for an estimated 15.5% of total export earnings in 2005). Zinc, salt, silver, copper, celestite and fluorite are also major mineral exports. In addition, mercury, bismuth, antimony, cadmium, manganese and phosphates are mined, and there are significant reserves of uranium.

Manufacturing provided an estimated 17.9% of GDP in 2004, and engaged an estimated 15.5% of the employed labour force in 2005. Manufacturing GDP increased by an annual average of 4.0% in 1995–2004; the sector decreased by 1.3% in 2003, but increased by 3.7% in 2004. In the 1990s the *maquila* sector (where intermediate materials produced on US territory are processed or assembled on the Mexican side of the border) grew in importance. By December 2000 Mexico had 3,703 *maquila* export plants, providing an estimated 1.3m. jobs and making a significant contribution to the manufacturing sector, however, the sector suffered a downturn in the early 2000s, and the number of plants fell to 2,821 in 2004, before increasing again in 2005. *Maquila* exports were valued at an estimated 214,430.2m. new pesos in 2005, an increase of 4.5% from 2004 and equivalent to 45.3% of total revenue from manufacturing exports. In 2005 an estimated 1.2m. people were employed in the *maquila* sector.

Energy is derived principally from mineral fuels and lubricants and hydroelectric power. In 2002, according to the World Bank, some 36.9% of total output of electricity production was derived from petroleum, 32.1% came from natural gas, 11.6% was derived from hydroelectric plants, and 12.1% came from coal-powered plants. The Fox Government's planned liberalization of the energy sector, including the troubled state-run Petróleos Mexicanos (PEMEX), ran into difficulties owing to congressional opposition. In late 2004 the IMF recommended that Mexico further open its energy sector to private investment. In 2005, according to PEMEX, oil production was an estimated 3,333,000 barrels per day, while production of natural gas was 4,818m. cu ft per day. In 2005 mineral imports were estimated at 5.5% of total merchandise imports, while exports of petroleum accounted for an estimated 14.9% of the total export value. In late 2001 the Governments of Mexico and Guatemala reached agreement, under the regional 'Plan Puebla-Panamá' (a series of joint transport, industry and tourism projects intended to integrate the Central American region), to link their electricity grids.

The services sector contributed an estimated 70.0% of GDP in 2004, and engaged an estimated 58.8% of the employed labour force in 2005. According to World Bank figures, the GDP of the sector increased by an average of 3.8% per year in 1995–2004; the sector experienced growth of 1.2% in 2003 and of 4.6% in 2004. Tourism is one of Mexico's principal sources of foreign exchange. 'Hurricane Wilma' in October 2005 inflicted heavy damage on some tourist areas, notably Cancún. In 2005 there were an estimated 22.0m. foreign visitors to Mexico (mostly from the USA and Canada), providing revenue of US $9,186m.

In 2004 Mexico recorded a visible trade deficit of an estimated US $8,811m., and there was a deficit of $7,286m. on the current account of the balance of payments. In 2004 the principal source of imports (56.5%) was the USA, which was also the principal market for exports (87.7%). The principal exports in 2003 were electric and electronic products, parts for road vehicles, and industrial machinery and the principal imports were electric and electronic products, industrial machinery and transport equipment.

In 2005 there was an estimated budgetary deficit of 540,497m. new pesos. Mexico's external debt totalled US $140,004m. at the end of 2003, of which $130,826m. was long-term public debt. In that year the cost of debt-servicing was equivalent to 20.9% of the value of exports of goods and services. The average annual rate of inflation was 12.7% in 1995–2004. Consumer prices increased by an average of 4.7% in 2004 and 3.3% in 2005. An estimated 3.6% of the total labour force were officially recorded as unemployed in 2005. In 2005 remittances from Mexicans in the USA totalled an estimated US $20,034.8m., a 20.6% increase on 2004. It was estimated that remittances were Mexico's second largest source of foreign income, after petroleum exports.

Mexico is a member of the Inter-American Development Bank (IDB, see p. 284), and of the Latin American Integration Association (see p. 305). Mexico was admitted to the Asia-Pacific Economic Co-operation group (APEC, see p. 164) in 1993, and joined the Organisation for Economic Co-operation and Development (OECD, see p. 320) in 1994. Mexico is also a signatory nation to NAFTA (see p. 312). In September 2004 Mexico concluded a free trade agreement with Japan.

Mexico's economic development, centred on the expansion of the petroleum industry, was impeded from the mid-1980s by the decrease in international petroleum prices, in addition to the persistent problems of the flight of capital, the depreciation of the peso, a shortage of foreign exchange and vast foreign debt. A programme of tax reform and economic liberalization was undertaken from the late 1980s, but in late 1994 and early 1995 a sharp devaluation of the peso provoked a financial crisis, necessitating a stringent policy of economic adjustment and the procurement of substantial international credit facilities. Strong export performance in the latter half of the decade, particularly in the *maquila* industries, prompted an economic recovery, and annual economic growth reached 6.6% in 2000. An economic slowdown occurred in the early 2000s, caused by the sluggish economy of Mexico's largest trading partner, the USA, particularly in the *maquila* sector. This area expanded in 2004, assuaging fears that jobs in the sector were moving to the People's Republic of China; nevertheless, in 2005 Mexico's manufacturing sector faced increasingly fierce competition from that country. There was also increasing dissatisfaction that membership of NAFTA had not brought many advantages: it was claimed that although

MEXICO

Mexican agricultural exports had doubled during the 10 years that NAFTA had been in place, 1.3m. jobs had been lost in the farming sector. Mexico was also one of the developing countries opposed to the agricultural subsidies of the developed world, particularly the USA. Another major factor inhibiting growth in 2005 was the continuing conflict between President Fox and Congreso over the Government's economic reform programme, particularly plans to liberalize the energy sector. In 2005 the rate of economic growth slowed to an estimated 2.7%. Inflation remained relatively low (at 3.3%), although the annual rate of increase was forecast to rise in 2006 to 4%. GDP growth was also expected to be higher in 2006, however, at around 3.7%.

Education

Education in state schools is provided free of charge and is officially compulsory. It covers six years of primary education, beginning at six years of age, and three years of secondary education, either general or technical, from the age of 12. This can then be followed by another three-year cycle of higher or specialized secondary education. In 2002/03 99% of children in the relevant age-group were enrolled in primary education (males 99%; females 100%), while 63% of children in the relevant age-group were enrolled in secondary schools (males 61%; females 64%). In 2005 there were an estimated 4,876 institutes of higher education, while in 2003 attendance was 2,250,461 students. In 2002 there were 56 universities in Mexico. In 2001/02 nursery schools for the indigenous population numbered 8,487, while there were 9,065 primary schools for the indigenous population. However, in spite of the existence of more than 80 indigenous languages in Mexico, there were few bilingual secondary schools. Total enrolment at primary school was 14,781,327 students in 2003; in that year 5,780,437 students were enrolled at all levels of secondary education. The National Agreement for the Modernization of Basic Education of 1992 envisaged the future devolution of federal responsibility for education, to state and municipal bodies. Federal expenditure on education in 2003 was an estimated 265,238.1m. new pesos (equivalent to 21.4% of total central government expenditure).

Public Holidays

2006: 1 January (New Year's Day), 5 February (Constitution Day), 21 March (Birthday of Benito Juárez), 13 April (Maundy Thursday)*, 14 April (Good Friday)*, 1 May (Labour Day), 5 May (Anniversary of the Battle of Puebla)*, 16 September (Independence Day), 12 October (Discovery of America), 1 November (All Saints' Day)*, 2 November (All Souls' Day), 20 November (Anniversary of the Revolution), 12 December (Day of Our Lady of Guadalupe)*, 25 December (Christmas), 31 December (New Year's Eve).

2007: 1 January (New Year's Day), 5 February (Constitution Day), 21 March (Birthday of Benito Juárez), 5 April (Maundy Thursday)*, 6 April (Good Friday)*, 1 May (Labour Day), 5 May (Anniversary of the Battle of Puebla)*, 16 September (Independence Day), 12 October (Discovery of America), 1 November (All Saints' Day)*, 2 November (All Souls' Day), 20 November (Anniversary of the Revolution), 12 December (Day of Our Lady of Guadalupe)*, 25 December (Christmas), 31 December (New Year's Eve).

* Widely celebrated unofficial holidays.

Weights and Measures

The metric system is in force.

Statistical Survey

Sources (unless otherwise stated): Dirección General de Estadística, Instituto Nacional de Estadística, Geografía e Informática (INEGI), Edif. Sede, Avda Prolongación Héroe de Nacozari 2301 Sur, 20270 Aguascalientes, Ags; tel. (14) 918-1948; fax (14) 918-0739; e-mail webmaster@inegi.gob.mx; internet www.inegi.gob.mx; Banco de México, Avda 5 de Mayo 1, Col. Centro, Del. Cuauhtémoc, 06059 México, DF; tel. (55) 5237-2000; fax (55) 5237-2370; internet www.banxico.org.mx

Area and Population

AREA, POPULATION AND DENSITY

Area (sq km)	
Continental	1,959,248
Islands	5,127
Total	1,964,375*
Population (census results)†	
5 November 1995	91,158,290
14 February 2000	
Males	47,592,253
Females	49,891,159
Total	97,483,412
Population (official estimates at mid-year)‡	
2003	104,213,503
2004	105,349,837
2005§	103,088,021
Density (per sq km) at mid-2005§	52.5

* 758,449 sq miles.
† Including adjustment for underenumeration (90,855 in 1995 and 1,730,016 in 2000).
‡ Source: Presidencia de la República, *Cuarto Informe de Gobierno*.
§ Preliminary figure.

ADMINISTRATIVE DIVISIONS
(at census of 14 February 2000)

States	Area (sq km)*	Population	Density (per sq km)	Capital
Aguascalientes (Ags)	5,623	944,285	167.9	Aguascalientes
Baja California (BC)	71,540	2,487,367	34.8	Mexicali
Baja California Sur (BCS)	73,937	424,041	5.7	La Paz
Campeche (Camp.)	57,718	690,689	12.0	Campeche
Chiapas (Chis)	73,680	3,920,892	53.2	Tuxtla Gutiérrez
Chihuahua (Chih.)	247,490	3,052,907	12.3	Chihuahua
Coahuila (de Zaragoza) (Coah.)	151,447	2,298,070	15.2	Saltillo
Colima (Col.)	5,629	542,627	96.4	Colima
Distrito Federal (DF)	1,485	8,605,239	5,794.8	Mexico City
Durango (Dgo)	123,364	1,448,661	11.7	Victoria de Durango
Guanajuato (Gto)	30,617	4,663,032	152.3	Guanajuato
Guerrero (Gro)	63,618	3,079,649	48.4	Chilpancingo de los Bravos
Hidalgo (Hgo)	20,855	2,235,591	107.2	Pachuca de Soto
Jalisco (Jal.)	78,624	6,322,002	80.4	Guadalajara
México (Méx.)	22,332	13,096,686	586.5	Toluca de Lerdo
Michoacán (de Ocampo) (Mich.)	58,672	3,985,667	67.9	Morelia
Morelos (Mor.)	4,894	1,555,296	317.8	Cuernavaca
Nayarit (Nay.)	27,861	920,185	33.0	Tepic
Nuevo León (NL)	64,206	3,834,141	59.7	Monterrey
Oaxaca (Oax.)	93,348	3,438,765	36.8	Oaxaca de Juárez

MEXICO

Statistical Survey

States— continued	Area (sq km)*	Population	Density (per sq km)	Capital
Puebla (Pue.)	34,246	5,076,686	148.2	Heroica Puebla de Zaragoza
Querétaro (de Arteaga) (Qro)	11,659	1,404,306	120.4	Querétaro
Quintana Roo (Q.Roo)	42,544	874,963	20.6	Ciudad Chetumal
San Luis Potosí (SLP)	61,165	2,299,360	37.6	San Luis Potosí
Sinaloa (Sin.)	57,334	2,536,844	44.2	Culiacán Rosales
Sonora (Son.)	179,527	2,216,969	12.3	Hermosillo
Tabasco (Tab.)	24,747	1,891,829	76.4	Villahermosa
Tamaulipas (Tam.)	80,155	2,753,222	34.3	Ciudad Victoria
Tlaxcala (Tlax.)	3,988	962,646	241.4	Tlaxcala de Xicohténcatl
Veracruz-Llave (Ver.)	71,856	6,908,975	96.2	Jalapa Enríquez
Yucatán (Yuc.)	39,675	1,658,210	41.8	Mérida
Zacatecas (Zac.)	75,412	1,353,610	17.9	Zacatecas
Total	1,959,248	97,483,412	49.8	—

* Excluding islands.

PRINCIPAL TOWNS
(population at census of 14 February 2000)

Town	Population	Town	Population
Ciudad de México (Mexico City, capital)	8,605,239	Querétaro	536,463
Guadalajara	1,646,183	Torreón	502,964
Ecatepec de Morelos (Ecatepec)	1,621,827	San Nicolás de los Garzas	496,879
Heroica Puebla de Zaragoza (Puebla)	1,271,673	Santa María Chimalhuacán (Chimalhuacán)	482,530
Nezahualcóyotl	1,225,083	Atizapán de Zaragoza	467,544
Ciudad Juárez	1,187,275	Tlaquepaque	458,674
Tijuana	1,148,681	Toluca de Lerdo (Toluca)	435,125
Monterrey	1,110,909	Cuautitlán Izcalli	433,830
León	1,020,818	Victoria de Durango (Durango)	427,135
Zapopan	910,690	Tuxtla Gutiérrez	424,579
Naucalpan de Juárez (Naucalpan)	835,053	Veracruz Llave (Veracruz)	411,582
Tlalnepantla de Baz (Tlalnepantla)	714,735	Reynosa	403,718
Guadalupe	669,842	Benito Juárez (Cancún)	397,191
Mérida	662,530	Matamoros	376,279
Chihuahua	657,876	Jalapa Enríquez (Xalapa)	373,076
San Luis Potosí	629,208	Villahermosa	330,846
Acapulco de Juárez (Acapulco)	620,656	Mazatlán	327,989
Aguascalientes	594,092	Cuernavaca	327,162
Saltillo	562,587	Valle de Chalco (Xico)	322,784
Morelia	549,996	Irapuato	319,148
Mexicali	549,873	Tonalá	315,278
Hermosillo	545,928	Nuevo Laredo	308,828
Culiacán Rosales (Culiacán)	540,823		

2003 (UN estimate, including suburbs): Ciudad de México 18,660,221 (Source: UN, *World Urbanization Prospects: The 2003 Revision*).

BIRTHS, MARRIAGES AND DEATHS

	Registered live births		Registered marriages		Registered deaths	
	Number	Rate (per 1,000)	Number	Rate (per 1,000)	Number	Rate (per 1,000)
1997	2,698,425	23.7	707,840	7.5	440,437	4.4
1998	2,668,428	23.0	n.a.	n.a.	444,665	4.4
1999	2,769,089	22.3	743,856	n.a.	443,950	4.3
2000	2,798,339	21.1	707,422	7.0	437,667	4.5
2001	2,767,610	20.5	665,434	6.5	443,127	4.5
2002	2,699,084	19.9	n.a.	6.0	459,687	4.5
2003	2,655,894	19.3	n.a.	5.6	472,140	4.5
2004	2,625,056	18.8	n.a.	5.7	473,417	4.5

Expectation of life (UN estimates, years at birth): 74 (males 72; females 77) in 2003 (Source: WHO *World Health Report*).

ECONOMICALLY ACTIVE POPULATION
(sample surveys, '000 persons aged 12 years and over, April–June)

	2003	2004	2005
Agriculture, hunting, forestry and fishing	6,813.6	6,937.9	6,249.8
Mining, quarrying and electricity	352.2	409.2	383.3
Manufacturing	6,991.5	7,350.7	6,935.5
Construction	2,748.4	2,741.8	3,255.7
Trade	7,688.3	8,147.7	8,126.2
Services	12,197.0	12,851.5	12,217.1
Transport and communications	1,865.5	1,888.7	2,043.7
Public sector	1,829.8	1,816.2	1,900.3
Activities not adequately defined	147.0	162.5	209.2
Total employed	40,633.2	42,306.1	41,320.8
Unemployed	882.5	1,092.7	1,497.8
Total labour force	41,515.7	43,398.8	42,818.6
Males	27,277.0	28,013.5	n.a.
Females	14,238.6	15,385.2	n.a.

Health and Welfare

KEY INDICATORS

Total fertility rate (children per woman, 2003)	2.5
Under-5 mortality rate (per 1,000 live births, 2004)	28
HIV/AIDS (% of persons aged 15–49, 2003)	0.3
Physicians (per 1,000 head, 2002)	1.5
Hospital beds (per 1,000 head, 2001)	1.1
Health expenditure (2002): US $ per head (PPP)	550
Health expenditure (2002): % of GDP	6.1
Health expenditure (2002): public (% of total)	44.9
Access to water (% of persons, 2002)	91
Access to sanitation (% of persons, 2002)	77
Human Development Index (2003): ranking	53
Human Development Index (2003): value	0.814

For sources and definitions, see explanatory note on p. vi.

Agriculture

PRINCIPAL CROPS
('000 metric tons)

	2002	2003	2004
Wheat	3,236	2,750	2,900*
Rice (paddy)	227	191	191*
Barley	737	1,109	1,109*
Maize	19,299	19,652	22,000*
Oats	64	147	147*
Sorghum	5,206	6,462	6,400*
Potatoes	1,483	1,735	1,735*
Sugar cane	45,635	45,126	45,126*
Dry beans	1,549	1,400	1,400*
Chick-peas	235	240*	240*
Soybeans (Soya beans)	87	76	76*

MEXICO

—continued	2002	2003	2004
Groundnuts (in shell)	75	75*	75*
Coconuts*	1,105	1,015	959
Safflower seed	53	213	213*
Cottonseed	68	102	200*
Cabbages	197	197*	197*
Lettuce	228	243	243*
Tomatoes	1,990	2,148	2,148*
Cauliflower*	200	210	215
Pumpkins, squash and gourds*	470	470	560
Cucumbers and gherkins*	433	472	475
Chillies and green peppers	1,784	1,854	1,854*
Green onions and shallots	1,131	1,131*	1,131*
Dry onions*	100	100	100
Carrots	378	378*	378*
Green corn*	186	186	186
Bananas	1,886	2,027	2,027*
Oranges	3,844	3,970†	3,970*
Tangerines, mandarins, clementines and satsumas*	360	360	360
Lemons and limes	1,725	1,825	1,825*
Grapefruit and pomelos	269	258†	258*
Apples	428	488†	503*
Peaches and nectarines	198	224	224*
Strawberries	142	150	150*
Grapes	363	457	457*
Watermelons	858	970	970*
Cantaloupes and other melons*	510	510	510
Mangoes	1,523	1,503	1,503*
Avocados	901	1,040	1,040*
Pineapples	660	721	721*
Papayas	876	956	956*
Coffee (green)	313	311	311*
Cocoa beans	46	48	48*
Pimento and allspice*	55	55	55
Cotton (lint)	43	65	120*
Tobacco (leaves)	22	22	22*

* FAO estimate(s).
† Unofficial figure.

Source: FAO.

LIVESTOCK
('000 head, year ending September)

	2002	2003	2004
Horses*	6,255	6,260	6,260
Mules*	3,280	3,280	3,280
Asses*	3,260	3,260	3,260
Cattle	31,390	31,477	31,477*
Pigs	15,123	14,625	14,625*
Sheep	6,417	6,820	6,820*
Goats	9,130	8,992	8,992*
Chickens	402,459	413,915	425,000*
Ducks*	8,100	8,100	8,100
Turkeys	4,928	4,806	4,806*

* FAO estimate(s).

Source: FAO.

LIVESTOCK PRODUCTS
('000 metric tons)

	2002	2003	2004
Beef and veal	1,468	1,504	1,543
Mutton and lamb	38	42	42
Goat meat	42	42	42
Pig meat	1,070	1,035	1,058
Horse meat*	79	79	79
Poultry meat	2,123	2,163	2,272
Cows' milk	9,658	9,784	9,874
Goats' milk	146	152	154
Butter	14	16	18
Cheese	152	140	146
Evaporated and condensed milk*	158	158	158
Hen eggs	1,901	1,872	1,906
Cattle hides*	176	176	176
Honey	59	57	57

* FAO estimates.

Source: FAO.

Forestry

ROUNDWOOD REMOVALS
('000 cubic metres, excl. bark)

	2002	2003	2004
Sawlogs, veneer logs and logs for sleepers	5,022	5,255	5,737
Pulpwood	801	845	954
Other industrial wood	231	180	222
Fuel wood*	37,913	38,090	38,269
Total	45,967	44,370	45,182

* FAO estimates.

Source: FAO.

SAWNWOOD PRODUCTION
('000 cubic metres, incl. railway sleepers)

	2002	2003	2004
Coniferous (softwood)	2,430	2,454	2,716
Broadleaved (hardwood)	261	286	246
Total	2,691	2,740	2,962

Source: FAO.

Fishing

('000 metric tons, live weight)

	2001	2002	2003*
Capture	1,398.6	1,450.6	1,450.0
Tilapias	60.3	54.9	54.5
California pilchard (sardine)	609.8	624.8	620.0
Yellowfin tuna	135.5	148.6	165.8
Marine shrimps and prawns	57.5	54.6	54.6
American cupped oyster	48.6	47.6	47.6
Jumbo flying squid	73.7	115.9	100.0
Aquaculture	76.1	73.7	73.7
Whiteleg shrimp	48.0	45.9	45.9
Total catch (incl. others)	1,474.7	1,524.3	1,523.7

* FAO estimates.

Note: Figures exclude aquatic plants ('000 metric tons, capture only): 46.9 in 2001; 30.1 in 2002; 30.0 in 2003 (FAO estimate). Also excluded are aquatic mammals and crocodiles (recorded by number rather than by weight), shells and corals. The number of Morelet's crocodiles caught was: 3,643 in 2001; 1,588 in 2002; 1,037 in 2003. The catch of marine shells (metric tons) was: 363 in 2001 (FAO estimate); 265 in 2002; 249.7 in 2003 (FAO estimate).

Source: FAO.

Mining

(metric tons, unless otherwise indicated)

	2002	2003	2004
Antimony*	153	434	503
Arsenic*	1,946	1,729	1,828
Barytes	163,621	287,451	306,668
Bismuth*	1,126	1,064	1,014
Cadmium*	1,389	1,639	1,618
Coal	6,370,874	6,648,257	6,450,594
Coke	1,451,094	1,462,106	1,445,052
Copper*	314,820	303,765	352,286
Crude petroleum ('000 barrels per day)	3,177	3,371	3,383
Celestite	94,016	130,329	87,610
Diatomite	48,029	53,395	59,818
Dolomite	457,665	565,896	1,158,929
Feldspar	332,101	346,315	364,166
Flourite	622,478	756,258	842,698
Gas (million cu ft per day)	4,423	4,498	4,573
Gold (kg)*	23,596	22,177	24,496
Graphite	13,885	8,730	14,769

MEXICO

—continued	2002	2003	2004
Gypsum	3,549,550	3,779,659	4,840,099
Iron*	5,965,427	6,759,198	6,889,538
Lead*	138,749	144,297	141,578
Manganese*	88,358	114,550	135,893
Molybdenum*	3,427	3,524	3,731
Silica	1,778,714	1,689,042	2,055,940
Silver*	3,146,257	2,945,710	3,093,366
Sulphur	887,035	1,051,968	1,121,546
Wollastonite	29,197	31,234	28,224
Zinc*	431,663	412,255	384,338

* Figures for metallic minerals refer to metal content of ores.

Industry

SELECTED PRODUCTS
('000 metric tons, unless otherwise indicated)

	2000	2001	2002
Wheat flour	2,538	2,611	2,619
Other cereal flour	1,179	1,678	1,614
Raw sugar	2,531	3,018	2,736
Beer ('000 hectolitres)	59,851	61,632	63,530
Soft drinks ('000 hectolitres)	126,460	130,050	127,530
Cigarettes (million units)	56,383	56,057	54,704
Cotton yarn (pure and mixed)	21	19	17
Tyres ('000 units)*	16,780	13,533	11,628
Cement	33,429	32,239	33,478
Gas stoves—household ('000 units)	3,973	4,021	4,510
Refrigerators—household ('000 units)	2,049	2,071	2,222
Washing machines—household ('000 units)	1,720	1,636	1,657
Lorries, buses, tractors, etc. ('000 units)	554	529	504
Passenger cars ('000 units)	1,294	1,273	1,247
Electric energy (million kWh)	228,873	226,686	n.a.

* Tyres for road motor vehicles.

Source: UN, *Industrial Commodity Statistics Yearbook*.

Finance

CURRENCY AND EXCHANGE RATES

Monetary Units
100 centavos = 1 Mexican nuevo peso.

Sterling, Dollar and Euro Equivalents (30 December 2005)
£1 sterling = 18.558 nuevos pesos;
US $1 = 10.778 nuevos pesos;
€1 = 12.714 nuevos pesos;
1,000 Mexican nuevos pesos = £53.88 = $92.78 = €78.65.

Average Exchange Rate (nuevos pesos per US $)
2003   10.7890
2004   11.2860
2005   10.8979

Note: Figures are given in terms of the nuevo (new) peso, introduced on 1 January 1993 and equivalent to 1,000 former pesos.

BUDGET*
(million new pesos)

Revenue	2003	2004	2005†
Taxation	766,582	770,120	808,210
Income taxes	337,015	345,217	384,496
Value-added tax	254,433	285,022	318,659
Excise tax	117,758	85,245	49,436
Import duties	26,898	29,521	26,823
Other tax revenue	30,477	25,113	28,795
Other revenue	366,403	500,091	604,977
Total revenue	1,132,985	1,270,211	1,413,188

Expenditure	2003	2004	2005†
Programmable expenditure	1,216,023	1,317,011	1,451,472
Current expenditure	1,016,428	1,044,632	1,169,614
Personal services	506,355	517,897	557,518
Transfers, subsidies and aid	170,696	178,462	202,606
Other current expenditure	339,376	348,273	409,491
Capital expenditure	199,596	272,379	281,858
Non-programmable expenditure	432,220	475,286	502,213
Interest and fees	190,863	206,830	210,377
Revenue sharing	225,228	239,890	278,843
Other	16,129	28,565	12,994
Total expenditure	1,648,243	1,792,297	1,953,685

* Figures refer to the consolidated accounts of the central Government, including government agencies and the national social security system. The budgets of state and local governments are excluded.
† Provisional figures.

INTERNATIONAL RESERVES*
(US $ million at 31 December)

	2002	2003	2004
IMF special drawing rights	392	433	465
Reserve position in the Fund	308	782	898
Foreign exchange	49,895	57,740	62,778
Total	50,594	58,956	64,141

* Excluding gold reserves ($357m. at 30 September 1989).

Source: IMF, *International Financial Statistics*.

MONEY SUPPLY
(million new pesos at 31 December)

	2002	2003	2004
Currency outside banks	232,082	263,387	300,977
Demand deposits at deposit money banks	364,664	415,909	435,392
Total money	596,746	679,296	736,369

Source: IMF, *International Financial Statistics*.

COST OF LIVING
(Consumer Price Index; base: 2000 = 100)

	2002	2003	2004
Food, beverages and tobacco	109.6	115.1	122.9
Clothing and footwear	108.9	109.8	110.9
Electricity, gas and other fuel	117.2	135.8	149.1
Rent	114.3	120.6	125.2
All items (incl. others)	111.7	116.8	122.3

Source: ILO.

NATIONAL ACCOUNTS

National Income and Product
(million new pesos at current prices)

	2000	2001	2002
Compensation of employees	1,719,560	1,890,992	2,038,916
Operating surplus	2,737,411	2,811,796	3,071,658
Domestic factor incomes	4,456,971	4,702,789	5,110,573
Consumption of fixed capital	525,596	568,522	617,368
Gross domestic product at factor cost	4,982,567	5,271,311	5,727,942
Indirect taxes	525,808	561,612	548,710
Less Subsidies	17,617	21,577	20,271
GDP in purchasers' values	5,490,757	5,811,346	6,256,382

Source: ECLAC, *Statistical Yearbook for Latin America and the Caribbean*.

MEXICO

Expenditure on the Gross Domestic Product
('000 million new pesos at current prices)*

	2002	2003	2004
Government final consumption expenditure	759.87	855.75	890.46
Private final consumption expenditure	4,326.51	4,731.20	5,227.00
Increase in stocks	87.39	111.39	119.56
Gross fixed capital formation	1,205.94	1,304.89	1,541.00
Total domestic expenditure	6,379.71	7,003.23	7,778.02
Exports of goods and services	1,678.38	1,919.36	2,295.73
Less Imports of goods and services	1,794.95	2,031.15	2,438.82
GDP in purchasers' values	6,263.14	6,891.43	7,634.93
GDP at constant 1993 prices	1,616.99	1,640.26	1,709.78

* Quarterly data seasonally adjusted at annual rates; figures are rounded to the nearest 10 million new pesos.

Source: IMF, *International Financial Statistics*.

Gross Domestic Product by Economic Activity
(provisional figures, million new pesos at current prices)

	2002	2003	2004
Agriculture, forestry and fishing	226,397	243,080	281,392
Mining and quarrying	77,207	82,512	91,523
Manufacturing	1,068,603	1,123,213	1,253,500
Electricity, gas and water	81,881	79,687	93,144
Construction	292,180	326,319	388,947
Trade, restaurants and hotels	1,148,997	1,270,197	1,418,090
Transport, storage and communications	611,602	645,750	724,264
Finance, insurance, real estate and business services	769,222	824,536	895,732
Community, social and personal services	1,547,672	1,728,288	1,848,760
Sub-total	5,823,761	6,323,582	6,995,352
Less Imputed bank service charge	84,778	75,036	84,778
GDP at factor cost	5,738,983	6,248,545	6,910,904
Indirect taxes, *less* subsidies	528,491	646,448	724,002
GDP in purchasers' values	6,267,474	6,894,993	7,634,926

BALANCE OF PAYMENTS
(US $ million)

	2002	2003	2004
Exports of goods f.o.b.	161,046	164,766	187,999
Imports of goods f.o.b.	−168,679	−170,546	−196,810
Trade balance	−7,633	−5,780	−8,811
Exports of services	12,740	12,617	14,004
Imports of services	−17,660	−18,141	−19,779
Balance on goods and services	−12,553	−11,304	−14,586
Other income received	4,051	3,858	5,049
Other income paid	−15,270	−15,028	−14,778
Balance on goods, services and income	−23,772	−22,474	−24,314
Current transfers received	10,287	13,880	17,108
Current transfers paid	−35	−37	−80
Current balance	−13,520	−8,631	−7,286
Direct investment abroad	−930	−1,784	−3,490
Direct investment from abroad	17,122	12,751	17,910
Portfolio investment assets	1,134	91	1,718
Portfolio investment liabilities	−632	3,864	6,126
Other investment assets	11,601	8,627	−4,066
Other investment liabilities	−3,535	−4,419	−4,581
Net errors and omissions	−3,880	−680	−2,227
Overall balance	7,359	9,817	4,104

Source: IMF, *International Financial Statistics*.

External Trade

PRINCIPAL COMMODITIES
(distribution by SITC, US $ million)

Imports f.o.b.	2001	2002	2003
Food and live animals	7,886.0	8,131.8	8,705.1
Crude materials (inedible) except fuels	4,440.5	4,666.7	5,172.2
Mineral fuels, lubricants and related materials	5,395.3	4,563.5	5,819.9
Chemicals and related products	14,420.8	15,341.9	16,973.7
Artificial resins, plastics, cellulose esters, etc.	4,226.3	4,707.9	5,147.2
Basic manufactures	27,232.7	27,359.6	27,410.7
Textile yarn, fabrics, etc.	5,407.8	5,602.7	5,504.6
Machinery and transport equipment	87,804.8	86,094.2	84,202.7
Power-generating machinery and equipment	6,298.2	6,919.2	6,909.4
General industrial machinery and equipment and parts	9,116.5	8,691.2	9,025.7
Office machines and automatic data-processing equipment	8,053.7	8,944.2	10,181.6
Telecommunications and sound equipment	9,249.1	7,829.4	8,032.5
Other electrical machinery, apparatus, etc.	31,273.7	29,288.2	26,916.3
Switchgear, resistors, printed circuits, switchboards, etc.	7,438.2	7,230.1	7,117.8
Thermionic valves, tubes, etc.	12,503.9	11,531.5	9,808.8
Electronic microcircuits	7,939.6	7,529.3	6,693.0
Road vehicles and parts*	17,044.4	18,364.6	17,221.2
Passenger vehicles (excl. buses)	5,093.5	6,072.2	5,749.5
Parts and accessories for cars, buses, lorries, etc.*	10,068.5	9,813.1	9,187.2
Miscellaneous manufactured articles	19,176.1	20,138.2	20,714.3
Articles of plastic materials, etc.	5,472.7	5,812.8	6,429.4
Total (incl. others)	168,376.9	168,650.6	171,290.8

* Data on parts exclude tyres, engines and electrical parts.

Exports f.o.b.	2001	2002	2003
Food and live animals	6,145.3	6,015.1	7,025.9
Mineral fuels, lubricants, etc.	12,632.1	14,318.1	18,522.9
Petroleum, petroleum products, etc.	12,486.2	14,266.1	18,416.6
Crude petroleum oils, etc.	11,590.8	13,110.2	16,826.5
Chemicals and related products	5,324.5	5,512.1	5,710.5
Basic manufactures	12,807.5	13,229.7	12,761.5
Machinery and transport equipment	95,507.2	94,740.0	94,243.8
Power-generating machinery and equipment	6,022.7	6,286.3	6,827.9
General industrial machinery equipment and parts	5,073.2	5,910.4	5,894.8
Office machines and automatic data-processing equipment	13,215.8	12,192.3	13,369.7
Automatic data-processing machines and units	9,694.0	9,261.5	10,065.1
Telecommunications and sound equipment	19,147.1	18,165.3	15,817.2
Colour television receivers	6,244.8	6,694.3	6,440.5

MEXICO

Statistical Survey

Exports f.o.b.—continued	2001	2002	2003
Other electrical machinery apparatus, etc.	22,288.2	22,561.6	23,475.0
Equipment for distributing electricity	4,546.1	5,221.3	5,181.1
Insulated electric wire, cable etc.	5,952.0	5,886.8	6,082.9
Road vehicles and parts*	27,875.9	27,843.4	27,263.2
Passenger motor cars (excl. buses)	15,297.6	13,948.1	12,546.2
Goods vehicles (lorries and trucks)	6,453.0	6,356.3	6,642.8
Parts and accessories for cars, buses, lorries, etc.*	5,579.8	6,698.5	7,009.2
Miscellaneous manufactured articles	22,4555.7	23,058.4	23,063.0
Clothing and accessories (excl. footwear)	8,012.5	7,751.8	7,343.1
Total (incl. others)	158,423.5	160,669.9	165,394.6

* Data on parts exclude tyres, engines and electrical parts.

Source: UN, *International Trade Statistics Yearbook*.

2004 (US $ million, preliminary figures): *Imports f.o.b.*: Chemical products 12,803.4; Mineral products 7,541.8; Transport equipment 22,886.0; Total (incl. others) 196,809.6; *Exports f.o.b.*: Agricultural products 5,683.9; Petroleum 23,666.6; Manufactured goods 157,747.3; Total (incl. others) 187,998.6.

2005 (US $ million, preliminary figures): *Imports f.o.b.*: Chemical products 14,199.0; Mineral products 12,167.1; Transport equipment 19,340.4; Total (incl. others) 221,269.8; *Exports f.o.b.*: Agricultural products 6,127.1; Petroleum 31,895.2; Manufactured goods 174,521.2; Total (incl. others) 213,771.2.

PRINCIPAL TRADING PARTNERS*
(US $ million)

Imports c.i.f.	2002	2003	2004
Argentina	687.3	867.1	1,109.8
Brazil	2,565.0	3,267.4	4,343.8
Canada	4,480.3	4,120.5	5,334.1
Chile	1,010.2	1,081.9	1,463.8
China, People's Republic	6,274.4	9,400.6	14,459.4
China (Taiwan)	4,250.1	2,509.1	3,502.1
France	1,806.8	2,015.4	2,397.6
Germany	6,065.8	6,218.2	7,154.1
Italy	2,171.1	2,473.9	2,820.9
Japan	9,348.6	7,595.1	10,624.1
Korea, Republic	3,910.0	4,112.9	5,262.7
Malaysia	1,993.2	2,760.6	3,399.9
Singapore	1,555.0	1,337.8	2,225.5
Spain	2,223.9	2,288.0	2,853.3
Thailand	838.8	987.4	1,270.0
United Kingdom	1,349.8	1,242.2	1,460.5
USA	106,921.9	105,724.0	111,319.0
Total (incl. others)	168,678.9	170,545.8	197,156.5

Exports f.o.b.	2002	2003	2004
Aruba†	166.1	780.5	1,443.8
Canada	2,991.3	3,041.8	3,298.7
Germany	1,159.1	1,715.2	1,609.3
Spain	1,393.7	1,512.4	2,000.3
USA	142,167.3	144,557.2	165,423.2
Total (incl. others)	161,046.0	164,766.4	188,626.5

* Imports by country of origin; exports by country of destination.
† Estimates.

Transport

RAILWAYS
(traffic)

	2002	2003	2004
Passengers carried ('000)	237	270	253
Passenger-kilometres (million)	69	78	74
Freight carried ('000 tons)	80,451	85,168	88,097
Freight ton-kilometres (million)	51,616	54,132	54,387

Source: Dirección General de Planeación, Secretaría de Comunicaciones y Transportes.

ROAD TRAFFIC
(estimates, vehicles in use at 31 December)

	1998	1999	2000
Passenger cars	9,378,587	9,842,006	10,443,489
Buses and coaches	108,690	109,929	111,756
Lorries and vans	4,403,953	4,639,860	7,931,590

Source: IRF, *World Road Statistics*.

SHIPPING

Merchant Fleet
(registered at 31 December)

	2002	2003	2004
Number of vessels	658	654	687
Total displacement ('000 grt)	937.2	972.7	1,008.0

Source: Lloyd's Register-Fairplay, *World Fleet Statistics*.

Sea-borne Shipping
(domestic and international freight traffic, '000 metric tons)

	2002	2003	2004
Goods loaded	160,894	175,923	177,915
Goods unloaded	87,203	88,816	88,093

Source: Coordinación General de Puertos y Marina Mercante.

CIVIL AVIATION
(traffic on scheduled services)

	2002	2003	2004
Passengers carried ('000)	33,190	35,287	39,422
Freight carried ('000 tons)	389.0	410.0	466.7

Sources: Dirección General de Planeación, Secretaría de Comunicaciones y Transportes.

Tourism

	2003	2004	2005
Tourist arrivals ('000)	18,665	20,618	21,959
Border tourists ('000)	8,312	9,605	9,381
Total expenditure (US $ million)	7,252	8,382	9,186

Source: Secretaría de Turismo de México.

MEXICO

Communications Media

	2002	2003	2004
Telephone ('000 main lines in use)	14,941.6	16,311.1	18,073.2
Mobile cellular telephones ('000 subscribers)	25,928.3	30,097.7	38,451.1
Personal computers ('000 in use)	8,353	n.a.	11,210
Internet users ('000)	10,032.7	12,250.3	14,036.5

Radio receivers ('000 in use): 31,000 in 1997.

Television receivers ('000 in use): 28,000 in 2000.

Facsimile machines ('000 in use): 285 in 1997.

Daily newspapers (2000): Number 311; Average circulation 9,251,000.

Non-daily newspapers (2000): Number 26; Average circulation 614,000.

Books published (titles): 6,952 in 1998.

Sources: International Telecommunication Union; UNESCO Institute for Statistics; UNESCO, *Statistical Yearbook*; UN, *Statistical Yearbook*.

Education

(2004/05 estimates, unless otherwise indicated)

	Institutions	Teachers	Students*
Pre-primary	87,182	197,065	3,742.6
Primary	97,135	557,001	14,781.3
Secondary (incl. technical)	31,859	346,301	5,780.4
Intermediate: professional/technical	1,584	31,617	359.9
Intermediate: Baccalaureate	11,268	224,635	3,083.8
Higher (incl. post-graduate)	4,876	260,152	2,322.9

* Figures (in '000) are for 2003/04.

Adult literacy rate (UNESCO estimates): 90.3% (males 92.0%; females 88.7%) in 2003 (Source: UN Development Programme, *Human Development Report*).

Directory

The Constitution

The present Mexican Constitution was proclaimed on 5 February 1917, at the end of the revolution, which began in 1910, against the regime of Porfirio Díaz. Its provisions regarding religion, education and the ownership and exploitation of mineral wealth reflect the long revolutionary struggle against the concentration of power in the hands of the Roman Catholic Church and the large landowners, and the struggle which culminated, in the 1930s, in the expropriation of the properties of the foreign petroleum companies. It has been amended from time to time.

GOVERNMENT

The President and Congress

The President of the Republic, in agreement with the Cabinet and with the approval of the Congreso de la Unión (Congress) or of the Permanent Committee when the Congreso is not in session, may suspend constitutional guarantees in case of foreign invasion, serious disturbance, or any other emergency endangering the people.

The exercise of supreme executive authority is vested in the President, who is elected for six years and enters office on 1 December of the year of election. The presidential powers include the right to appoint and remove members of the Cabinet and the Attorney-General; to appoint, with the approval of the Senado (Senate), diplomatic officials, the higher officers of the army, and ministers of the supreme and higher courts of justice. The President is also empowered to dispose of the Armed Forces for the internal and external security of the federation.

The Congreso is composed of the Cámara Federal de Diputados (Federal Chamber of Deputies) elected every three years, and the Senado whose members hold office for six years. There is one deputy for every 250,000 people and for every fraction of over 125,000 people. The Senado is composed of two members for each state and two for the Distrito Federal. Regular sessions of the Congreso begin on 1 September and may not continue beyond 31 December of the same year. Extraordinary sessions may be convened by the Permanent Committee.

The powers of the Congreso include the right to: pass laws and regulations; impose taxes; specify the criteria on which the Executive may negotiate loans; declare war; raise, maintain and regulate the organization of the Armed Forces; establish and maintain schools of various types throughout the country; approve or reject the budget; sanction appointments submitted by the President of the Supreme Court and magistrates of the superior court of the Distrito Federal; approve or reject treaties and conventions made with foreign powers; and ratify diplomatic appointments.

The Permanent Committee, consisting of 29 members of the Congreso (15 of whom are deputies and 14 senators), officiates when the Congreso is in recess, and is responsible for the convening of extraordinary sessions of the Congreso.

The States

Governors are elected by popular vote in a general election every six years. The local legislature is formed by deputies, who are changed every three years. The judicature is specially appointed under the Constitution by the competent authority (it is never subject to the popular vote).

Each state is a separate unit, with the right to levy taxes and to legislate in certain matters. The states are not allowed to levy inter-state customs duties.

The Federal District

The Distrito Federal (DF) consists of Mexico City and several neighbouring small towns and villages. The first direct elections for the Head of Government of the Distrito Federal were held in July 1997; hitherto a Regent had been appointed by the President.

EDUCATION

According to the Constitution, the provision of educational facilities is the joint responsibility of the federation, the states and the municipalities. Education shall be democratic, and shall be directed to developing all the faculties of the individual students, while imbuing them with love of their country and a consciousness of international solidarity and justice. Religious bodies may not provide education, except training for the priesthood. Private educational institutions must conform to the requirements of the Constitution with regard to the nature of the teaching given. The education provided by the states shall be free of charge.

RELIGION

Religious bodies of whatever denomination shall not have the capacity to possess or administer real estate or capital invested therein. Churches are the property of the nation; the headquarters of bishops, seminaries, convents and other property used for the propagation of a religious creed shall pass into the hands of the state, to be dedicated to the public service of the federation or of the respective state. Institutions of charity, provided they are not connected with a religious body, may hold real property. The establishment of monastic orders is prohibited. Ministers of religion must be Mexican; they may not criticize the fundamental laws of the country in a public or private meeting; they may not vote or form associations for political purposes. Political meetings may not be held in places of worship.

A reform proposal, whereby constitutional restrictions on the Catholic Church were formally ended, received congressional approval in December 1991 and was promulgated as law in January 1992.

LAND AND MINERAL OWNERSHIP

Article 27 of the Constitution vests direct ownership of minerals and other products of the subsoil, including petroleum and water, in the nation, and reserves to the Federal Government alone the right to grant concessions in accordance with the laws to individuals and companies, on the condition that they establish regular work for the exploitation of the materials. At the same time, the right to acquire ownership of lands and waters belonging to the nation, or concessions for their exploitation, is limited to Mexican individuals and companies, although the State may concede similar rights to foreigners who agree not to invoke the protection of their governments to enforce such rights.

The same article declares null all alienations of lands, waters and forests belonging to towns or communities made by political chiefs or other local authorities in violation of the provisions of the law of 25 June 1856*, and all concessions or sales of communally-held lands, waters and forests made by the federal authorities after 1 December 1876. The population settlements which lack ejidos (state-owned smallholdings), or cannot obtain restitution of lands previously held, shall be granted lands in proportion to the needs of the population. The area of land granted to the individual may not be less than 10 hectares of irrigated or watered land, or the equivalent in other kinds of land.

The owners affected by decisions to divide and redistribute land (with the exception of the owners of farming or cattle-rearing properties) shall not have any right of redress, nor may they invoke the right of amparo† in protection of their interests. They may, however, apply to the Government for indemnification. Small properties, the areas of which are defined in the Constitution, will not be subject to expropriation. The Constitution leaves to the Congreso the duty of determining the maximum size of rural properties.

In March 1992 an agrarian reform amendment, whereby the programme of land-distribution established by the 1917 Constitution was abolished and the terms of the ejido system of tenant farmers were relaxed, was formally adopted.

Monopolies and measures to restrict competition in industry, commerce or public services are prohibited.

A section of the Constitution deals with work and social security. On 30 December 1977 a Federal Law on Political Organizations and Electoral Procedure was promulgated. It includes the following provisions:

Legislative power is vested in the Congreso de la Unión which comprises the Cámara Federal de Diputados and the Senado. The Cámara shall comprise 300 deputies elected by majority vote within single-member electoral districts and up to 100 deputies (increased to 200 from July 1988) elected by a system of proportional representation from regional lists within multi-member constituencies. The Senado comprises two members for each state and two for the Distrito Federal, elected by majority vote.

Executive power is exercised by the President of the Republic of the United Mexican States, elected by majority vote.

Ordinary elections will be held every three years for the federal deputies and every six years for the senators and the President of the Republic on the first Sunday of July of the year in question. When a vacancy occurs among members of the Congreso elected by majority vote, the house in question shall call extraordinary elections, and when a vacancy occurs among members of the Cámara elected by proportional representation it shall be filled by the candidate of the same party who received the next highest number of votes at the last ordinary election.

Voting is the right and duty of every citizen, male or female, over the age of 18 years.

A political party shall be registered if it has at least 3,000 members in each one of at least half the states in Mexico or at least 300 members in each one of at least half of the single-member constituencies. In either case the total number of members must be no less than 65,000. A party can also obtain conditional registration if it has been active for at least four years. Registration is confirmed if the party obtains at least 1.5% of the popular vote. All political parties shall have free access to the media.

In September 1993 an amendment to the Law on Electoral Procedure provided for the expansion of the Senado to 128 seats, representing four members for each state and the Distrito Federal, three to be elected by majority vote and one by proportional representation.

* The Lerdo Law against ecclesiastical privilege, which became the basis of the Liberal Constitution of 1857.

† The Constitution provides for the procedure known as *juicio de amparo*, a wider form of habeas corpus, which the individual may invoke in protection of his constitutional rights.

The Government

HEAD OF STATE

President: Vicente Fox Quesada (took office 1 December 2000).

CABINET
(April 2006)

Secretary of the Interior: Carlos María Abascal Carranza.
Secretary of Foreign Affairs: Dr Luis Ernesto Derbez Bautista.
Secretary of Finance and Public Credit: Francisco Gil Díaz.
Secretary of National Defence: Gen. Gerardo Clemente Ricardo Vega García.
Secretary of the Navy: Adm. Marco Antonio Peyrot González.
Secretary of the Economy: Sergio Alejandro García de Alba.
Secretary of Social Development: Ana Teresa Aranda Orozoco.
Secretary of Public Security: Eduardo Medina Mora Icaza.
Secretary of Public Function: Eduardo Romero Ramos.
Secretary of Communications and Transport: Pedro Cerisola y Weber.
Secretary of Labour and Social Welfare: Francisco Javier Salazar Sáenz.
Secretary of the Environment and Natural Resources: José Luis Luege Tamargo.
Secretary of Energy: Fernando Canales Clariond.
Secretary of Agriculture, Livestock, Rural Development, Fisheries and Food: Francisco Javier Mayorga Castañeda.
Secretary of Public Education: Dr Reyes S. Tamez Guerra.
Secretary of Health: Dr Julio José Frenk Mora.
Secretary of Tourism: Rodolfo Elizondo Torres.
Secretary of Agrarian Reform: Abelardo Escobar Prieto.
Attorney-General: Daniel Francisco Cabeza de Vaca Hernández.

SECRETARIATS OF STATE

Office of the President: Los Pinos, Col. San Miguel Chapultepec, 11850 México, DF; tel. (55) 5091-1100; fax (55) 5277-2376; e-mail vicente.fox.quesada@presidencia.gob.mx; internet www.presidencia.gob.mx.

Secretariat of State for Agrarian Reform: Edif. de Avda Heroica, 1°, Escuela Naval Militar 701, Col. Presidentes Ejidales, 04470 México, DF; tel. (55) 5695-6776; fax (55) 5695-6368; e-mail sra@sra.gob.mx; internet www.sra.gob.mx.

Secretariat of State for Agriculture, Livestock, Rural Development, Fisheries and Food: Avda Municipio Libre 377, A°, Col. Santa Cruz Atoyac, Del. Benito Juárez, 03310 México, DF; tel. (55) 9183-1000; fax (55) 9183-1018; e-mail ofsec@sagarpa.gob.mx; internet www.sagarpa.gob.mx.

Secretariat of State for Communications and Transport: Avda Xola y Universidad, Col. Narvarte, Del. Benito Juárez, 03020 México, DF; tel. (55) 5723-9300; fax (55) 5530-0093; e-mail lruizmar@sct.gob.mx; internet www.sct.gob.mx.

Secretariat of State for the Economy: Alfonso Reyes 30, Col. Hipódromo Condesa, 06170 México, DF; tel. (55) 5729-9100; fax (55) 5729-9320; e-mail fcanales@economia.gob.mx; internet www.economia.gob.mx.

Secretariat of State for Energy: Insurgentes Sur 890, 17°, Col. del Valle, 03100 México, DF; tel. (55) 5000-6000; fax (55) 5000-6222; e-mail felizondo@energia.gob.mx; internet www.energia.gob.mx.

Secretariat of State for the Environment and Natural Resources: Blvd Adolfo Ruíz Cortines 4209, Col. Jardines en la Montaña, Tlalpan, 14210 México, DF; tel. (55) 5628-0602; fax (55) 5628-0643; e-mail contactodgeia@semarnat.gob.mx; internet www.semarnat.gob.mx.

Secretariat of State for Finance and Public Credit: Palacio Nacional, Primer Patio Mariano, 3°, Of. 3045, Col. Centro, Del. Cuauhtémoc, 06000 México, DF; tel. (55) 9158-2000; fax (55) 9158-1142; e-mail secretario@hacienda.gob.mx; internet www.shcp.gob.mx.

Secretariat of State for Foreign Affairs: Avda Ricardo Flores Magón 2, Col. Guerrero, Del. Cuauhtémoc, 06995 México, DF; tel. (55) 5063-3000; fax (55) 5063-3195; e-mail comentario@sre.gob.mx; internet www.sre.gob.mx.

Secretariat of State for Health: Lieja 7, 1°, Col. Juárez, Del. Cuauhtémoc, 06600 México, DF; tel. (55) 5286-2383; fax (55) 5553-7917; e-mail jfrenk@salud.gob.mx; internet www.salud.gob.mx.

Secretariat of State for the Interior: Bucareli 99, 1°, Col. Juárez, 06069 México, DF; tel. (55) 5592-1141; fax (55) 5546-5350; internet www.gobernacion.gob.mx.

Secretariat of State for Labour and Social Welfare: Edif. A, 4°, Anillo Periférico Sur 4271, 4°, Col. Fuentes del Pedregal, 14149 México, DF; tel. (55) 5645-3965; fax (55) 5645-5594; e-mail correo@stps.gob.mx; internet www.stps.gob.mx.

Secretariat of State for National Defence: Blvd Manuel Avila Camacho, esq. Avda Industria Militar, 3°, Col. Lomas de Sotelo, Del. Miguel Hidalgo, 11640 México, DF; tel. (55) 5557-5571; fax (55) 5395-2935; e-mail secretariaparticular2@prodigy.net.mx; internet www.sedena.gob.mx.

Secretariat of State for the Navy: Eje 2 Oeste, Tramo Heroica, Escuela Naval Militar 861, Col. Los Cipreses, Del. Coyoacán, 04830 México, DF; tel. (55) 5624-6500; e-mail srio@semar.gob.mx; internet www.semar.gob.mx.

MEXICO

Secretariat of State for Public Education: Dinamarca 84, 5°, Col. Juárez, 06600 México, DF; tel. (55) 5510-2557; fax (55) 5329-6873; e-mail educa@sep.gob.mx; internet www.sep.gob.mx.

Secretariat of State for Public Function: Insurgentes Sur 1735, 10°, Col. Guadalupe Inn, Del. Alvaro Obregón, 01020 México, DF; tel. (55) 1454-3000; e-mail sactel@funcionpublica.gob.mx; internet www.secodam.gob.mx.

Secretariat of State for Public Security: Londres 102, 7°, Col. Juaréz, 06600 México, DF; e-mail webmaster@ssp.gob.mx; internet www.ssp.gob.mx.

Secretariat of State for Social Development: Avda Reforma 116, Col. Juárez, Del. Cuauhtémoc, 06600 México, DF; tel. (55) 5328-5000; e-mail secretariadelramo@sedesol.gob.mx; internet www.sedesol.gob.mx.

Secretariat of State for Tourism: Presidente Masaryk 172, Col. Chapultepec Morales, 11587 México, DF; tel. (55) 3002-6300; fax (55) 1036-0789; e-mail relizondo@sectur.gob.mx; internet www.sectur.gob.mx.

Office of the Attorney-General: Avda Paseo de la Reforma 211–213, Col. Cuauhtémoc, Del. Cuauhtémoc, 06500 México, DF; tel. (55) 5346-0114; fax (55) 5346-0908; e-mail ofproc@pgr.gob.mx; internet www.pgr.gob.mx.

State Governors
(April 2006)

Aguascalientes: Luís Armando Reynoso (PAN).

Baja California: Eugenio Elorduy Walther (PAN).

Baja California Sur: Narciso Agúndez (PRD).

Campeche: Jorge Carlos Hurtado Valdez (PRI).

Chiapas: Pablo Salazar Mendiguchía (Ind.).

Chihuahua: José Reyes Baeza (PRI).

Coahuila (de Zaragoza): Humberto Moreira Valdes (PRI).

Colima: Jesús Silverio Cavazos Ceballos (PRI-PT-PVEM).

Durango: Ismael Hernández (PRI).

Guanajuato: Juan Carlos Romero Hicks (PAN).

Guerrero: Zeferino Torreblanco (PRD).

Hidalgo: Miguel Angel Osorio Chong (PRI).

Jalisco: Lic. Francisco Ramirez Acuña (PAN).

México: Enrique Peña Nieto (PRI).

Michoacán (de Ocampo): Lazaro Cárdenas Batel (PRD).

Morelos: Lic. Sergio Estrada Cajigal Ramírez (PAN).

Nayarit: Ney González Sánchez (PRI).

Nuevo León: Lic. José Natividad González Parás (PRI-PVEM-PLM-Fuerza Ciudadana).

Oaxaca: Ulises Ruíz (PRI).

Puebla: Mario Marín Torres (PRI).

Querétaro (de Arteaga): Francisco Garrido Patrón (PAN).

Quintana Roo: Félix González Canto (PRI).

San Luis Potosí: Marcelo de los Santos Fraga (PAN).

Sinaloa: Jesús Aguilar Padilla (PRI).

Sonora: José Eduardo Robinson Bours Castelo (PRI-PVEM).

Tabasco: Manuel Andrade Díaz (PRI).

Tamaulipas: Eugenio Hernández Flores (PRI).

Tlaxcala: Mariano González Zarur (PRI).

Veracruz-Llave: Fidel Herrera (PRI).

Yucatán: Patricio Patrón Laviada (PAN-PRD-PT-PVEM).

Zacatecas: Amalia García (PRD).

Head of Government of the Distrito Federal: Alejandro Encinas (acting—PRD).

President and Legislature
PRESIDENT

Election, 2 July 2000

Candidate	Number of votes	% of votes
Vicente Fox Quesada (Alianza por el Cambio*)	15,988,740	43.47
Francisco Labastida Ochoa (PRI)	13,576,385	36.91
Cuauhtémoc Cárdenas Solórzano (Alianza por México)	6,259,048	17.02
Others	957,455	2.60
Total	36,781,628	100.00

* An alliance of the PAN and the PVEM.

CONGRESO DE LA UNIÓN
Senado

Senate: Xicoténcatl 9, Centro Histórico, 06010 México, DF; tel. (55) 5130-2200; internet www.senado.gob.mx.

President: Enrique Jackson Ramírez.

Elections, 2 July 2000

Party	Seats
Partido Revolucionario Institucional (PRI)	60
Partido Acción Nacional (PAN)*	46
Partido de la Revolución Democrática (PRD)†	15
Partido Verde Ecologista de México (PVEM)*	5
Convergencia por la Democracia (CD)†	1
Partido del Trabajo (PT)†	1
Total	128

* Contested the elections jointly as the Alianza por el Cambio.
† Contested the elections as part of the Alianza por México.

Cámara Federal de Diputados

Federal Chamber of Deputies: Avda Congreso de la Unión 66, Col. El Parque, Del. Venustiano Carranza, 15969 México, DF; tel. (55) 5628-1300; internet www.cddhcu.gob.mx.

President: Maria Marcela González Salas y Petricioli.

Elections, 6 July 2003

Party	Seats
Partido Revolucionario Institucional (PRI)	224
Partido Acción Nacional (PAN)	153
Partido de la Revolución Democrática (PRD)	95
Partido Verde Ecologista de México (PVEM)	17
Partido del Trabajo (PT)	6
Convergencia por la Democracia (CD)	5
Total	500

Election Commission

Instituto Federal Electoral (IFE): Viaducto Tlalpan 100, Col. Arenal Tepepan, Del. Tlalpan, 14610 México, DF; e-mail info@ife.org.mx; internet www.ife.org.mx; f. 1990; independent; Pres. Dr Luis Carlos Ugalde Ramírez.

Political Organizations

To retain legal political registration, parties must secure at least 1.5% of total votes at two consecutive federal elections. In early 2006 eight national political parties were registered. Several of the parties listed below are no longer officially registered but continue to be politically active.

Convergencia: Louisiana 113, Col. Nápoles, Del. Benito Juárez, 03810 México, DF; tel. (55) 5543-8517; e-mail convergencia@prodigy.net.mx; internet www.convergencia.org.mx; f. 1995 as Convergencia por la Democracia; part of the Por el Bien de Todos alliance formed to contest 2006 presidential election; Pres. Dante Delgado Rannauro; Sec.-Gen. Pedro Jiménez León.

Nueva Alianza: Río Volga 77, Col. Cuauhtémoc, Del. Cuauhtémoc, 06500 México, DF; tel. (55) 5207-4464; e-mail secretariageneral@nueva-alianza.org.mx; internet www.nueva-alianza.org.mx; f. 2005; by dissident faction of the PRI, mems of the Sindicato Nacional de

MEXICO

Trabajadores de la Educación (SNTE, see Trade Unions); Pres. MIGUEL ANGEL JIMÉNEZ GODÍNEZ; Sec.-Gen. JUAN DÍAZ DE LA TORRE.

Partido Acción Nacional (PAN): Avda Coyoacán 1546, Col. del Valle, Del. Benito Juárez, 03100 México, DF; tel. (55) 5200-4000; e-mail correo@cen.pan.org.mx; internet www.pan.org.mx; f. 1939; democratic party; 150,000 mems; Pres. MANUEL ESPINO BARRIENTOS; Sec.-Gen. JOSÉ ESPINA VON ROERICH.

Partido Alternativa Socialdemócrata y Campesina (PASC): Puebla 262, Col. Roma, 06700 México, DF; tel. (55) 5208-8360; e-mail info@alternativa.org.mx; internet www.alternativa.org.mx; f. 2005; progressive and peasants' rights; Pres. ALBERTO BEGNÉ GUERRA.

Partido Liberal México (PLM): México, DF; f. 2002; Pres. C. SALVADOR ORDAZ MONTES DE OCA.

Partido Popular Socialista de México (PPS): Avda Alvaro Obregón 185, Col. Roma, Del. Cuauhtémoc, 06797 México, DF; tel. (55) 5511-0184; fax (55) 5514-9498; e-mail info@ppsdemexico.org.mx; internet www.ppsdemexico.org.mx; f. 1948; left-wing party; Sec.-Gen. CUAUHTÉMOC AMEZCUA DROMUNDO.

Partido de la Revolución Democrática (PRD): Avda Benjamín Franklin 84, Col. Escandón, 11800 México, DF; tel. (55) 1085-8000; fax (55) 1085-8144; e-mail comunicacion@prd.org.mx; internet www.prd.org.mx; f. 1989; centre-left; leading mem. of the Por el Bien de Todos alliance formed to contest 2006 presidential election; Pres. LEONEL COTA MONTAÑO; Sec.-Gen. GUADALUPE ACOSTA NARANJO.

Partido Revolucionario Institucional (PRI): Edif. 2, Insurgentes Norte 59, Col. Buenavista, Del. Cuauhtémoc, 06359 México, DF; tel. (55) 5729-9600; internet www.pri.org.mx; f. 1929 as the Partido Nacional Revolucionario; regarded as the natural successor to the victorious parties of the revolutionary period; broadly based and centre govt party; formed Alianza por el México alliance with PVEM to contest 2006 presidential election; Pres. MARIANO PALACIOS ALCOCER; Sec.-Gen. ROSARIO GREEN MACIAS; groups within the PRI include: the Corriente Crítica Progresista, the Corriente Crítica del Partido, the Corriente Constitucionalista Democratizadora, Corriente Nuevo PRI XIV Asamblea, Democracia 2000, México Nuevo, Galileo and Unidad Democrática (more commonly known as Todos Unidos contra Madrazo—TUCOM).

Partido del Trabajo (PT): Avda Cuauhtémoc 47, Col. Roma Norte, 06700 México, DF; tel. and fax (55) 5525-6287; internet www.partidodeltrabajo.org.mx; f. 1990; labour party; part of the Por el Bien de Todos alliance formed to contest 2006 presidential election; Leader ALBERTO ANAYA GUTIÉRREZ.

Partido Verde Ecologista de México (PVEM): Loma Bonita 18, Col. Lomas Altas, 11950 México, DF; tel. and fax (55) 5257-0188; internet www.pvem.org.mx; f. 1987; ecologist party; formed Alianza por el México alliance with PRI to contest 2006 presidential election; Pres. JORGE EMILIO GONZÁLEZ MARTÍNEZ; Sec.-Gen. NATALIA ESCUDERO BARRERA.

The following parties are not legally recognized:

Fuerza Ciudadana: Rochester 94, Col. Nápoles, 03810 México, DF; tel. (55) 5534-4628; e-mail info@fuerzaciudadana.org.mx; internet www.fuerzaciudadana.org.mx; f. 2002; citizens' asscn; Pres. JORGE ALCOCER VILLANUEVA; Dir-Gen. KARYNA GARCÍA CASTILLOURDIALES.

Partido Auténtico de la Revolución Mexicana (PARM): Pueblo 286, 1°, Col. Roma, 06700 México, DF; tel. (55) 5514-9676; f. 1954; to sustain the ideology of the Mexican Political Constitution of 1917; 191,500 mems; Pres. CARLOS GUZMÁN PÉREZ.

Partido de Centro Democrático (PCD): Amores 923, Col. del Valle, Del. Benito Juárez, 03100 México, DF; tel. (55) 5575-3101; fax (55) 5575-8888; e-mail pcdcen@pcd2000.org.mx; centrist party; f. 1997; Leader MANUEL CAMACHO SOLÍS.

Partido Popular Revolucionario Democrático: f. 1996; political grouping representing the causes of 14 armed peasant orgs, including the EPR and the PROCUP.

Partido Revolucionario Obrerista y Clandestino de Unión Popular (PROCUP): peasant org.

Partido de la Sociedad Nacionalista (PSN): Magdalena 117, Col. del Valle, 03100 México, DF; tel. (55) 5682-5960; e-mail psn@psn.org.mx; Pres. GUSTAVO RIOJAS SANTANA.

Illegal organizations active in Mexico include the following:

Ejército Popular Revolucionario (EPR): e-mail pdprepr@hotmail.com; internet www.pengo.it/PDPR-EPR/; f. 1994; left-wing guerrilla group active in southern states, linked to the Partido Popular Revolucionario Democrático (q.v.).

Ejército Revolucionario Popular Insurgente (ERPI): f. 1996; left-wing guerrilla group active in Guerrero, Morelos and Oaxaca; Leader JACOBO SILVA NOGALES.

Ejército Zapatista de Liberación Nacional (EZLN): internet www.ezln.org; f. 1993; left-wing guerrilla group active in the Chiapas region; Leader 'Subcomandante MARCOS'.

Frente Democrático Oriental de México Emiliano Zapata (FDOMEZ): peasant org.

Other armed groups include the Tendencia Democrática Revolucionaria-Ejército del Pueblo and the Comando Popular Revolucionario—La Patria es Primero.

Diplomatic Representation

EMBASSIES IN MEXICO

Algeria: Sierra Madre 540, Col. Lomas de Chapultepec, Del. Miguel Hidalgo, 11000 México, DF; tel. (55) 5520-6950; fax (55) 5540-7579; e-mail embjargl@iwm.com.mx; Ambassador MERZAK BELHIMEUR.

Angola: Gaspar de Zúñiga 226, Col. Lomas de Chapultepec, Sección Virreyes, Del. Miguel Hidalgo, 11000 México, DF; tel. (55) 5202-4421; fax (55) 5540-5928; e-mail info@embangolamex.org; Ambassador JOSÉ JAIME FURTADO GONCALVEZ.

Argentina: Blvd Manuel Avila Camacho 1, 7°, Plaza Comermex, Col. Lomas de Chapultepec, Del. Miguel Hidalgo, 11009 México, DF; tel. (55) 5520-9430; fax (55) 5540-5011; e-mail embajadaargentina@prodigy.net.mx; Chargé d'affaires a.i. MÓNICA ELISABET DEREGIBUS.

Australia: Rubén Darío 55, Col. Polanco, Del. Miguel Hidalgo, 11580 México, DF; tel. (55) 1101-2200; fax (55) 1101-2201; e-mail dima-mexico.city@dfat.gov.au; internet www.mexico.embassy.gov.au; Ambassador NEIL ALLAN MULLES.

Austria: Sierra Tarahumara 420, Col. Lomas de Chapultepec, Del. Miguel Hidalgo, 11000 México, DF; tel. (55) 5251-1606; fax (55) 5245-0198; e-mail mexiko-ob@bmaa.gv.at; internet www.embajadadeaustria.com.mx; Ambassador Dr WERNER DRUML.

Belgium: Alfredo Musset 41, Col. Polanco, Del. Miguel Hidalgo, 11550 México, DF; tel. (55) 5280-0758; fax (55) 5280-0208; e-mail mexico@diplobel.org; internet www.diplobel.org/mexico; Ambassador MICHEL DELFOSSE.

Belize: Bernardo de Gálvez 215, Col. Lomas de Chapultepec, Del. Miguel Hidalgo, 11000 México, DF; tel. (55) 5520-1274; fax (55) 5520-6089; e-mail embelize@prodigy.net.mx; Ambassador SALVADOR AMÍN FIGUEROA.

Bolivia: Paseo de la Reforma 45, 4°, Col. Tabacalera, Del. Cuauhtémoc, 06030 México, DF; tel. (55) 5703-0983; fax (55) 5703-0994; e-mail embajada@embol.org.mx; internet www.embol.org.mx; Chargé d'affaires a.i. GONZALO RAMIRO ERICK CHACÓN CAMACHO.

Brazil: Lope de Armendáriz 130, Col. Lomas Virreyes, Del. Miguel Hidalgo, 11000 México, DF; tel. (55) 5201-4531; fax (55) 5520-4929; e-mail embrasil@brasil.org.mx; internet www.brasil.org.mx; Ambassador IVÁN OLIVEIRA CANNABRAVA.

Bulgaria: Paseo de la Reforma 1990, Col. Lomas de Chapultepec, Del. Miguel Hidalgo, 11000 México, DF; tel. (55) 5596-3283; fax (55) 5596-1012; e-mail ebulgaria@yahoo.com; Ambassador VALENTIN PETROV MODEV.

Canada: Schiller 529, Col. Polanco, Del. Miguel Hidalgo, 11560 México, DF; tel. (55) 5724-7900; fax (55) 5724-7980; e-mail embajada@canada.org.mx; internet www.canada.org.mx; Ambassador GAËTAN LAVERTU.

Chile: Andrés Bello 10, 18°, Col. Polanco, Del. Miguel Hidalgo, 11560 México, DF; tel. (55) 5280-9681; fax (55) 5280-9703; e-mail echilmex@prodigy.net.mx; internet www.embajadadechile.com.mx; Ambassador EURARDO ANINAT URETA.

China, People's Republic: Avda San Jerónimo 217B, Del. Álvaro Obregón, 01090 México, DF; tel. (55) 5616-0609; fax (55) 5616-0460; e-mail embchina@data.net.mx; internet www.embajadachina.org.mx; Ambassador REN JINGYU.

Colombia: Paseo de la Reforma 379, 1°, 5° y 6°, Col. Cuauhtémoc, Del. Cuauhtémoc, 06500 México, DF; tel. (55) 5525-0277; fax (55) 5208-2876; e-mail emcolmex@prodigy.net.mx; internet www.colombiaenmexico.org; Ambassador LUIS GUILLERMO GIRALDO HURTADO.

Costa Rica: Río Po 113, Col. Cuauhtémoc, Del. Cuauhtémoc, 06500 México, DF; tel. (55) 5525-7764; fax (55) 5511-9240; e-mail embcrica@ri.redint.com; Ambassador RONALD GURDIÁN MARCHENA.

Côte d'Ivoire: Tennyson 67, Col. Polanco, Del. Miguel Hidalgo, 11560 México, DF; tel. 5280-8573; fax 5282-2954; Ambassador YAO CHARLES KOFFI.

Cuba: Presidente Masaryk 554, Col. Polanco, Del. Miguel Hidalgo, 11560 México, DF; tel. and fax (55) 5280-8039; e-mail cancilleria@embacuba.com.mx; internet www.embacuba.com.mx; Ambassador JORGE ALBERTO BOLAÑOS SUÁREZ.

Cyprus: Sierra Gorda 370, Col. Lomas de Chapultepec, Del. Miguel Hidalgo, 11000 México, DF; tel. (55) 5202-7600; fax (55) 5520-2693; e-mail chipre@att.net.mx; Ambassador ANTONIS GRIVAS.

Czech Republic: Cuvier 22, Col. Nueva Anzures, Del. Miguel Hidalgo, 11590 México, DF; tel. (55) 5531-2777; fax (55) 5531-1837; e-mail mexico@embassy.mzv.cz; internet www.czechembassy.org; Ambassador VLADIMIRE EISENBRUCK.

Denmark: Tres Picos 43, Col. Chapultepec Morales, Del. Miguel Hidalgo, 11580 México, DF; tel. (55) 5255-3405; fax (55) 5545-5797; e-mail mexamb@um.dk; internet www.danmex.org; Ambassador SØREN HASLUND.

Dominican Republic: República de Guatemala 84, Centro Histórico, Del. Cuauhtémoc, 06020 México, DF; tel. (55) 5542-3553; fax (55) 5522-7409; e-mail embadomi@data.net.mx; internet www.embadom.org.mx; Ambassador PABLO A. MARIÑEZ ALVAREZ.

Ecuador: Tennyson 217, Col. Polanco, Del. Miguel Hidalgo, 11560 México, DF; tel. (55) 5545-3141; fax (55) 5254-2442; e-mail mecuamex@prodigy.net.mx; Ambassador REYNALDO EDUARDO HUERTA ORTEGA.

Egypt: Alejandro Dumas 131, Col. Polanco, Del. Miguel Hidalgo, 11560 México, DF; tel. (55) 5281-0823; fax (55) 5282-1294; e-mail embofegypt@prodigy.net.mx; Ambassador MAMDOUH SHAWKY MOUSTAFA KAMEL.

El Salvador: Temístocles 88, Col. Polanco, Del. Miguel Hidalgo, 11560 México, DF; tel. (55) 5281-5725; fax (55) 5280-0657; e-mail embesmex@webtelmex.net.mx; Ambassador HUGO ROBERTO CARRILLO CORLETO.

Finland: Monte Pelvoux 111, 4°, Col. Lomas de Chapultepec, Del. Miguel Hidalgo, 11000 México, DF; tel. (55) 5540-6036; fax (55) 5540-0114; e-mail finmex@prodigy.net.mx; internet www.finlandia.org.mx; Ambassador ILKKA HEISKANEN.

France: Campos Elíseos 339, Col. Polanco, Del. Miguel Hidalgo, 11560 México, DF; tel. (55) 9171-9700; fax (55) 9171-9703; e-mail info@francia.org.mx; internet www.francia.org.mx; Ambassador ALAIN LE GOURRIÉREC.

Germany: Lord Byron 737, Col. Polanco, Del. Miguel Hidalgo, 11560 México, DF; tel. (55) 5283-2200; fax (55) 5281-2588; e-mail info@embajada-alemana.org.mx; internet www.embajada-alemana.org.mx; Ambassador EBERHARD KOLSCH.

Greece: Sierra Gorda 505, Col. Lomas de Chapultepec, Del. Miguel Hidalgo, 11010 México, DF; tel. (55) 5520-2070; fax (55) 5202-4080; e-mail grecemb@prodigy.net.mx; Ambassador ALEXANDER MIGLIARESSIS.

Guatemala: Explanada 1025, Col. Lomas de Chapultepec, Del. Miguel Hidalgo, 11000 México, DF; tel. (55) 5540-7520; fax (55) 5202-1142; e-mail embaguate@mexis.com; Ambassador MANUEL ARTURO SOTO AGUIRRE.

Haiti: Presa Don Martín 53, Col. Irrigación, Del. Miguel Hidalgo, 11500 México, DF; tel. (55) 5557-2065; fax (55) 5395-1654; e-mail ambadh@mail.internet.com.mx; Ambassador IDALBERT PIERRE-JEAN.

Holy See: Juan Pablo II 118, Col. Guadalupe Inn, Del. Alvaro Obregón, 01020 México, DF; tel. (55) 5663-3999; fax (55) 5663-5308; e-mail nuntiusmex@infosel.net.mx; Apostolic Nuncio Most Rev. GIUSEPPE BERTELLO (Titular Archbishop of Urbisaglia).

Honduras: Alfonso Reyes 220, Col. Condesa, Del. Cuauhtémoc, 06170 México, DF; tel. (55) 5211-5747; fax (55) 5211-5425; e-mail emhonmex@mail.internet.com.mx; Ambassador FRANCISCO RAMÓN ZEPEDA ANDINO.

Hungary: Paseo de las Palmas 2005, Col. Lomas de Chapultepec, Del. Miguel Hidalgo, 11000 México, DF; tel. (55) 5596-0523; fax (55) 5596-2378; e-mail secretaria@embajadahungria.com.mx; internet www.embajadadehungria.com.mx; Ambassador GYÖRGY TIBOR HERCZSG.

India: Musset 325, Col. Polanco, Del. Miguel Hidalgo, 11550 México, DF; tel. (55) 5531-1050; fax (55) 5254-2349; e-mail indembmx@prodigy.net.mx; internet www.indembassy.org; Ambassador RAJIV KUMAR BHATIA.

Indonesia: Julio Verne 27, Col. Polanco, Del. Miguel Hidalgo, 11560 México, DF; tel. (55) 5280-6363; fax (55) 5280-7062; e-mail kbrimex@prodigy.net.mx; Chargé d'affaires a.i. HENDRAR PRAMUDYO.

Iran: Paseo de la Reforma 2350, Col. Lomas Altas, Del. Miguel Hidalgo, 11950 México, DF; tel. (55) 9172-2691; fax (55) 9172-2694; e-mail iranembmex@hotmail.com; Ambassador MOHAMMAD ROOHI SEFAT.

Iraq: Paseo de la Reforma 1875, Col. Lomas de Chapultepec, Del. Miguel Hidalgo, 11000 México, DF; tel. (55) 5596-0933; fax (55) 5596-0254.

Ireland: Cerrada Blvd Manuel Avila Camacho 76, 3°, Col. Lomas de Chapultepec, Del. Miguel Hidalgo, 11000 México, DF; tel. (55) 5520-5803; fax (55) 5520-5892; e-mail embajada@irlanda.org.mx; Ambassador DERMOT BRANGAN.

Israel: Sierra Madre 215, Col. Lomas de Chapultepec, Del. Miguel Hidalgo, 11000 México, DF; tel. (55) 5201-1500; fax (55) 5201-1555; e-mail embisrael@prodigy.net.mx; Ambassador DAVID DADONN.

Italy: Paseo de las Palmas 1994, Col. Lomas de Chapultepec, Del. Miguel Hidalgo, 11000 México, DF; tel. (55) 5596-3655; fax (55) 5596-2472; e-mail info@embitalia.org.mx; internet www.embitalia.org.mx; Ambassador FELICE SCAUSO.

Jamaica: Schiller 326, 8°, Col. Chapultepec Morales, Del. Miguel Hidalgo, 11570 México, DF; tel. (55) 5250-6804; fax (55) 5250-6160; e-mail embjamaicamex@infosel.net.mx; Ambassador SHEILA IVOLINE SEALY-MONTEITH.

Japan: Paseo de la Reforma 395, Apdo 5-101, Col. Cuauhtémoc, Del. Cuauhtémoc, 06500 México, DF; tel. (55) 5211-0028; fax (55) 5207-7743; e-mail embjapmx@mail.internet.com.mx; internet www.mx.emb-japan.go.jp; Ambassador YUBUN NARITA.

Korea, Democratic People's Republic: Eugenio Sue 332, Col. Polanco, Del. Miguel Hidalgo, 11550 México, DF; tel. (55) 5545-1871; fax (55) 5203-0019; e-mail dpkoreaemb@prodigy.net.mx; Ambassador SO JAE MYONG.

Korea, Republic: Lope de Armendáriz 110, Col. Lomas Virreyes, Del. Miguel Hidalgo, 11000 México, DF; tel. (55) 5202-9866; fax (55) 5540-7446; e-mail coremex@prodigy.net.mx; Chargé d'affaires a.i. DUCK BO SIM.

Lebanon: Julio Verne 8, Col. Polanco, Del. Miguel Hidalgo, 11560 México, DF; tel. (55) 5280-5614; fax (55) 5280-8870; e-mail embalib@prodigy.net.mx; Ambassador NOUHAD MAHMOUD.

Malaysia: Calderón de la Barca 215, Col. Polanco, 11550 México, DF; tel. (55) 5254-1118; fax (55) 5254-1295; e-mail mwmexico@infosel.net.mx; Ambassador SHAMSUDIN BIN ABDULLAH.

Morocco: Paseo de las Palmas 2020, Col. Lomas de Chapultepec, Del. Miguel Hidalgo, 11000 México, DF; tel. (55) 5245-1786; fax (55) 5245-1791; e-mail sifamex@infosel.net.mx; internet www.marruecos.org.mx; Ambassador MAHMOUD RMIKI.

Netherlands: Edif. Calakmul 7°, Avda Vasco de Quiroga 3000, Col. Santa Fe, Del. Alvaro Obregón, 01210 México, DF; tel. (55) 5258-9921; fax (55) 5258-8138; e-mail nlgovmex@nlgovmex.com; internet www.paisesbajos.com.mx; Ambassador JAN-JAAP VAN DE VELDE.

New Zealand: Edif. Corporativo Polanco 4°, Jaime Balmes 8, Col. Polanco, Del. Miguel Hidalgo, 11510 México, DF; tel. (55) 5283-9460; fax (55) 5283-9480; e-mail kiwimexico@compuserve.com.mx; Ambassador GEORGE ROBERT FURNESS TROUP.

Nicaragua: Prado Norte 470, Col. Lomas de Chapultepec, Del. Miguel Hidalgo, 11000 México, DF; tel. (55) 5540-5625; fax (55) 5520-6961; e-mail embanic@prodigy.net.mx; Ambassador LEOPOLDO RAMÍREZ EVA.

Nigeria: Paseo de las Palmas 1880, Col. Lomas de Chapultepec, Del. Miguel Hidalgo, 11000 México, DF; tel. (55) 5251-0966; fax (55) 5245-0105; e-mail nigembmx@att.net.mx; Ambassador IYORWUESE HAGHER.

Norway: Avda de los Virreyes 1460, Col. Lomas Virreyes, Del. Miguel Hidalgo, 11000 México, DF; tel. (55) 5540-3486; fax (55) 5202-3019; e-mail emb.mexico@mfa.no; internet www.noruega.org.mx; Ambassador KNUT SOLEM.

Pakistan: Hegel 512, Col. Chapultepec Morales, Del. Miguel Hidalgo, 11570 México, DF; tel. (55) 5203-3636; fax (55) 5203-9907; Ambassador KHALID AZIZ BABAR.

Panama: Sócrates 339, Col. Polanco, Del. Miguel Hidalgo, 11560 México, DF; tel. (55) 5280-7857; fax (55) 5280-7586; e-mail embanmx@prodigy.net.mx; internet www.embpanamamexico.com; Ambassador RICARDO JOSÉ ALEMAN ALFARO.

Paraguay: Homero 415, 1°, esq. Hegel, Col. Polanco, Del. Miguel Hidalgo, 11570 México, DF; tel. (55) 5545-0405; fax (55) 5531-9905; e-mail embapar@prodigy.net.mx; Ambassador JOSÉ FÉLIX FERNÁNDEZ ESTIGARRIBIA.

Peru: Paseo de la Reforma 2601, Col. Lomas Reforma, Del. Miguel Hidalgo, 11000 México, DF; tel. (55) 5570-2443; fax (55) 5259-0530; e-mail embaperu@prodigy.net.mx; Ambassador ALFREDO AROSEMENA FERREYROS.

Philippines: Sierra Gorda 175, Col. Lomas de Chapultepec, Del. Miguel Hidalgo, 11000 México, DF; tel. (55) 5202-8456; fax (55) 5202-8403; e-mail ambamexi@mail.internet.com.mx; Ambassador JUSTO O. ORROS, Jr.

Poland: Cracovia 40, Col. San Angel, Del. Alvaro Obregón, 01000 México, DF; tel. (55) 5550-4700; fax (55) 5616-0822; e-mail embajadadepolonia@prodigy.net.mx; internet www.polonia.org.mx; Ambassador WOJCIECH TOMASZEWSKI.

Portugal: Avda Alpes 1370, Lomas de Chapultepec, Del. Miguel Hidalgo, 11000 México, DF; tel. (55) 5520-7897; fax (55) 5520-4688; e-mail embpomex@prodigy.net.mx; internet www.portugalenmexico.com.mx; Ambassador FRANCISCO HENRIQUES DA SILVA.

Romania: Sófocles 311, Col. Polanco, Del. Miguel Hidalgo, 11560 México, DF; tel. (55) 5280-0197; fax (55) 5280-0343; e-mail ambromaniei@prodigy.net.mx; Ambassador VASILE DAN.

Russia: José Vasconcelos 204, Col. Hipódromo Condesa, Del. Cuauhtémoc, 06140 México, DF; tel. (55) 5273-1305; fax (55) 5273-1545; e-mail embrumex@mail.internet.com.mx; Ambassador VALERY IVANOVICH MOROZOV.

MEXICO
Directory

Saudi Arabia: Paseo de las Palmas 2075, Col. Lomas de Chapultepec, Del. Miguel Hidalgo, 11000 México, DF; tel. (55) 5596-0173; fax (55) 5020-3160; e-mail saudiemb@prodigy.net.mx; Chargé d'affaires a.i. ALI AHMAD ALGHAMDI.

Serbia and Montenegro: Montañas Rocallosas Oeste 515, Col. Lomas de Chapultepec, Del. Miguel Hidalgo, 11000 México, DF; tel. (55) 5520-0524; fax (55) 5520-9927; e-mail ambayumex@att.met.mx; Ambassador MILISAV PAIC.

Slovakia: Julio Verne 35, Col. Polanco, Del. Miguel Hidalgo, 11560 México, DF; tel. (55) 5280-6669; fax (55) 5280-6294; e-mail eslovaquia@prodigy.net.mx; Ambassador JOZEF ADAMEC.

South Africa: Andrés Bello 10, Edif. Forum, Col. Polanco 9°, Del. Miguel Hidalgo, 11560 México, DF; tel. and fax (55) 5282-9260; fax (55) 5282-9259; e-mail safrica@prodigy.net.mx; Ambassador MALCOLM GRANT FERGUSON.

Spain: Galileo 114, esq. Horacio, Col. Polanco, Del. Miguel Hidalgo, 11550 México, DF; tel. (55) 5282-2271; fax (55) 5282-1520; e-mail embaes@prodigy.net.mx; Ambassador MARÍA CRISTINA BARRIOS Y ALMAZOR.

Sweden: Paseo de las Palmas 1375, Col. Lomas de Chapultepec, Del. Miguel Hidalgo, 11000 México, DF; tel. (55) 9178-5010; fax (55) 5540-3253; e-mail info@suecia.com.mx; internet www.suecia.com.mx; Ambassador EWA POLANO.

Switzerland: Paseo de las Palmas 405, 11°, Torre Óptima, Col. Lomas de Chapultepec, Del. Miguel Hidalgo, 11000 México, DF; tel. (55) 5520-3003; fax (55) 5520-8685; e-mail vertretung@mex.rep.admin.ch; internet www.eda.admin.ch/mexico_emb/s/home.html; Ambassador GIAN FEDERICO PEDOTTI.

Thailand: Paseo de la Reforma 930, Col. Lomas de Chapultepec, Del. Miguel Hidalgo, 11000 México, DF; tel. (55) 5540-4551; fax (55) 5540-4817; e-mail thaimex@prodigy.net.mx; Ambassador RAVEE HONGSAPRABHAS.

Turkey: Monte Libano 885, Col. Lomas de Chapultepec, Del. Miguel Hidalgo, 11000 México, DF; tel. (55) 5282-5446; fax (55) 5282-4894; e-mail turkem@mail.internet.com.mx; Ambassador AHMET SEDAT BANGUOGLU.

Ukraine: Paseo de la Reforma 730, Col. Lomas de Chapultepec, Del. Miguel Hidalgo, 11000 México, DF; tel. and fax (55) 5282-4085; e-mail ukrainembasy@mexis.com; Ambassador OLEXANDER TARANENKO.

United Kingdom: Río Lerma 71, Col. Cuauhtémoc, Del. Cuauhtémoc, 06500 México, DF; tel. (55) 5242-8500; fax (55) 5242-8517; e-mail ukinmex@att.net.mx; internet www.embajadabritanica.com.mx; Ambassador GILES PAXMAN.

USA: Paseo de la Reforma 305, Del. Cuauhtémoc, 06500 México, DF; tel. (55) 5080-2000; fax (55) 5080-2150; internet www.usembassy-mexico.gov; Ambassador ANTONIO O. GARZA, Jr.

Uruguay: Hegel 149, 1°, Col. Chapultepec Morales, Del. Miguel Hidalgo, 11570 México, DF; tel. (55) 5531-4029; fax (55) 5545-3342; e-mail uruazte@ort.org.mx; Ambassador JOSÉ IGNACIO KORZENIAK PASTORINO.

Venezuela: Schiller 326, Col. Chapultepec Morales, Del. Miguel Hidalgo, 11570 México, DF; tel. (55) 5203-4233; fax (55) 5203-5072; e-mail venez-mex@embajadadevenezuela.com.mx; Ambassador HELY VLADIMIR VILLEGAS POLJAK (recalled in Nov. 2005); Chargé d'affaires a.i. NESTOR ALEXANDER GONZÁLEZ PACHECO.

Viet Nam: Sierra Ventana 255, Col. Lomas de Chapultepec, Del. Miguel Hidalgo, 11000 México, DF; tel. (55) 5540-1632; fax (55) 5540-1612; e-mail dsqvn@terra.com.mx; Ambassador LE VAN THINH.

Judicial System

The principle of the separation of the judiciary from the legislative and executive powers is embodied in the 1917 Constitution. The judicial system is divided into two areas: the federal, dealing with federal law, and the local, dealing only with state law within each state.

The federal judicial system has both ordinary and constitutional jurisdiction and judicial power is exercised by the Supreme Court of Justice, the Electoral Court, Collegiate and Unitary Circuit Courts and District Courts. The Supreme Court comprises two separate chambers: Civil and Criminal Affairs, and Administrative and Labour Affairs. The Federal Judicature Council is responsible for the administration, surveillance and discipline of the federal judiciary, except for the Supreme Court of Justice.

In 2005 there were 172 Collegiate Circuit Courts (Tribunales Colegiados), 62 Unitary Circuit Courts (Tribunales Unitarios) and 285 District Courts (Juzgados de Distrito). Mexico is divided into 29 judicial circuits. The Circuit Courts may be collegiate, when dealing with the derecho de amparo (protection of constitutional rights of an individual), or unitary, when dealing with appeal cases. The Collegiate Circuit Courts comprise three magistrates with residence in the cities of México, Toluca, Naucalpan, Guadalajara, Monterrey, Hermosillo, Puebla, Boca del Río, Xalapa, Torreón, Saltillo, San Luis Potosí, Villahermosa, Morelia, Mazatlán, Oaxaca, Mérida, Mexicali, Guanajuato, León, Chihuahua, Ciudad Juárez, Cuernavaca, Ciudad Victoria, Ciudad Reynosa, Tuxtla Gutiérrez, Tapachula, Acapulco, Chilpancingo, Querétaro, Zacatecas, Aguascalientes, Tepic, Durango, La Paz, Cancún, Tlaxcala and Pachuca. The Unitary Circuit Courts comprise one magistrate with residence mostly in the same cities as given above.

SUPREME COURT OF JUSTICE

Suprema Corte de Justicia de la Nación: Pino Suárez 2, Col. Centro, 06065 México, DF; tel. (55) 5522-0096; fax (55) 5522-0152; e-mail administrator@mail.scjn.gob.mx; internet www.scjn.gob.mx.
Chief Justice: MARIANO AZUELA GÜITRÓN.

First Chamber—Civil and Criminal Affairs
President: JOSÉ DE JESÚS GUDIÑO PELAYO.

Second Chamber—Administrative and Labour Affairs
President: GUILLERMO I. ORTIZ MAYAGOITIA.

Religion

CHRISTIANITY

The Roman Catholic Church

The prevailing religion is Roman Catholicism, but the Church, disestablished in 1857, was for many years, under the Constitution of 1917, subject to state control. A constitutional amendment, promulgated in January 1992, officially removed all restrictions on the Church. For ecclesiastical purposes, Mexico comprises 14 archdioceses, 67 dioceses, five territorial prelatures and two eparchates (both directly subject to the Holy See). An estimated 90% of the population are adherents.

Bishops' Conference
Conferencia del Episcopado Mexicano (CEM), Edif. S. S. Juan Pablo II, Prolongación Ministerios 24, Col. Tepeyac Insurgentes, Apdo 118-055, 07020 México, DF; tel. (55) 5781-8462; e-mail segcem@cem.org.mx; internet www.cem.org.mx; Pres. JOSÉ GUADALUPE MARTÍN RÁBAGO (Bishop of León).

Archbishop of Acapulco: FELIPE AGUIRRE FRANCO, Arzobispado, Quebrada 16, Apdo 201, Centro, 39300 Acapulco, Gro; tel. and fax (744) 482-0763; e-mail arzobispadoaca@aca.cableonline.com.mx; internet www.arquidiocesisacapulco.org.mx.

Archbishop of Antequera/Oaxaca: JOSÉ LUIS CHÁVEZ BOTELLO, García Virgil 600, Anexos de Catedral, Col. Centro, 68000 Oaxaca, Oax.; tel. (951) 516-4822; fax (951) 514-1348; e-mail arzobispadoaxaca@hotmail.com; internet arquidiocesisoaxaca.org.mx.

Archbishop of Chihuahua: JOSÉ FERNÁNDEZ ARTEAGA, Arzobispado, Avda Cuauhtémoc 1828, Col. Cuauhtémoc, 31000 Chihuahua, Chih.; tel. (614) 410-3202; fax (614) 410-5621; e-mail ferar@megalink.com.mx.

Archbishop of Durango: HÉCTOR GONZÁLEZ MARTÍNEZ, Arzobispado, 20 de Noviembre 306, Poniente Centro, 34000 Durango, Dgo; tel. (618) 811-4242; fax (618) 812-8881; e-mail arqdgo@prodigy.net.mx.

Archbishop of Guadalajara: Cardinal JUAN SANDOVAL IÑIGUEZ, Arzobispado, Liceo 17, Apdo 1-331, Col. Centro, 44100 Guadalajara, Jal.; tel. (33) 3614-5504; fax (33) 3658-2300; e-mail arzgdl@arquinet.com.mx; internet www.arquidiocesisgdl.org.mx.

Archbishop of Hermosillo/Sonora: JOSÉ ULISES MACÍAS SALCEDO, Arzobispado, Dr Paliza y Ocampo, Ala Sur de la Catedral, Col. Centenario, 83260 Hermosillo, Son.; tel. (662) 213-2138; fax (662) 213-1327; e-mail obispo@rtn.uson.mx; internet www.iglesiahermosillo.com.mx.

Archbishop of Jalapa: SERGIO OBESO RIVERA, Arzobispado, Avda Manuel Avila Camacho 73, Apdo 359, Col. Centro, 91000 Jalapa, Ver.; tel. (228) 812-0579; fax (228) 817-5578; e-mail arzobispadoalxal@prodigy.net.mx.

Archbishop of Mexico City: Cardinal NORBERTO RIVERA CARRERA, Curia del Arzobispado de México, Durango 90, 5°, Col. Roma, Apdo 24433, 06700 México, DF; tel. (55) 5208-3200; fax (55) 5208-5350; e-mail arzobisp@arzobispadomexico.org.mx; internet www.arzobispadomexico.org.mx.

Archbishop of Monterrey: FRANCISCO ROBLES ORTEGA, Zuazua 1100 Sur con Ocampo Centro, Apdo 7, 64000 Monterrey, NL; tel. (81) 1158-2450; fax (81) 1158-2488; e-mail cancilleria@arquidiocesismty.org; internet www.arquidiocesismty.org.mx.

MEXICO

Archbishop of Morelia: ALBERTO SUÁREZ INDA, Arzobispado, Costado Catedral, Frente Avda Madero, Apdo 17, 58000 Morelia, Mich; tel. (443) 313-2493; fax (443) 312-0919; e-mail asuarexi@prodigy.net.mx; tel. www.arquimorelia.com.

Archbishop of Puebla de los Angeles: ROSENDO HUESCA PACHECO, Avda 2 Sur 305, Apdo 235, Col. Centro, 72000 Puebla, Pue.; tel. (222) 232-4591; fax (222) 246-2277; e-mail rhuesca@mail.cem.org.mx.

Archbishop of San Luis Potosí: LUIS MORALES REYES, Arzobispado, Francisco Madero 300, Apdo 1, Col. Centro, 78000 San Luis Potosí, SLP; tel. (444) 812-4555; fax (444) 812-7979; e-mail arqsanluis@iglesiapotosina.org; internet www.iglesiapotosina.org.

Archbishop of Tlalnepantla: RICARDO GUÍZAR DÍAZ, Arzobispado, Avda Juárez 42, Apdo 268, Col. Centro, 54000 Tlalnepantla, Méx.; tel. (55) 5565-3944; fax (55) 5565-2751; e-mail curia@arqtlalnepantla.org; internet www.arqtlalnepantla.org.

Archbishop of Yucatán: EMILIO CARLOS BERLIE BELAUNZARÁN, Arzobispado, Calle 58 501, Col. Centro, 97000 Mérida, Yuc.; tel. (999) 924-7777; fax (999) 923-7983; e-mail aryu@prodigy.net.mx; internet www.arquidiocesisdeyucatan.org.

The Anglican Communion

Mexico is divided into five dioceses, which form the Province of the Anglican Church in Mexico, established in 1995.

Bishop of Cuernavaca: MARTINIANO GARCÍA MONTIEL, Minerva 1, Col. Las Delicias, 62330 Cuernavaca, Mor.; tel. and fax (777) 315-2870; e-mail diovca@edsa.net.mx.

Bishop of Mexico City and Primate of the Anglican Church in Mexico: CARLOS TOUCHE-PORTER, La Otra Banda 46, Avda San Jerónimo 117, Col. San Ángel, 01000 México, DF; tel. (55) 5616-2205; fax (55) 5616-2205; e-mail diomex@adetel.net.mx.

Bishop of Northern Mexico: MARCELINO RIVERA, Simón Bolívar 2005 Nte, Col. Mitras Centro, 64460 Monterrey, NL; tel. (81) 333-0922; fax (81) 348-73625; e-mail diocesisdelnorte@att.net.mx.

Bishop of South-Eastern Mexico: BENITO JUÁREZ MARTÍNEZ, Avda de las Américas 73, Col. Aguacatl, 91130 Jalapa, Ver.; tel. and fax (228) 814-4387; e-mail dioste99@aol.com; internet diosemexico.org.

Bishop of Western Mexico: LINO RODRÍGUEZ-AMARO, Javier J. Gamboa 255, Col. Sector Juárez, 44100 Guadalajara, Jal; tel. (33) 615-5070; fax (33) 615-4413; e-mail diocte@vianet.com.mx.

Protestant Churches

Iglesia Evangélica Luterana de México: POB 1-1034, 44100 Guadalajara, Jal.; tel. (52) 3639-7253; e-mail dtrejocoria@hotmail.com; Pres. ENCARNACIÓN ESTRADA; Pres. DANIEL TREJO CORIA; 1,500 mems.

Iglesia Metodista de México, Asociación Religiosa: Miravelle 209, Col. Albert, 03570 México, DF; tel. (55) 5539-3674; e-mail prenapro@iglesia-metodista.org.mx; internet www.iglesia-metodista.org.mx; f. 1930; 55,000 mems; Pres. Bishop RAÚL ROSAS GONZÁLEZ; 370 congregations; comprises six episcopal areas; Bishop (México) MOISÉS VALDERRAMA GÓMEZ; Bishop (North-West) JAIME VÁSQUEZ OLMEDA; Bishop (North-Central) JUAN MILTON VELASCO LEGORRETA, Bishop (East) RAÚL ROSAS GONZÁLEZ; Bishop (South) BASILIO HERRERA LÓPEZ, Bishop (South-East) PEDRO MORENO CANO.

National Baptist Convention of Mexico: Tlalpan 1035-A, Col. Américas Unidas, 03610 México, DF; tel. and fax (55) 5539-7720; e-mail webmaster@cnbm.org.mx; internet www.cnbm.org.mx; f. 1903; Pres. GILBERTO GUTIÉRREZ LUCERO.

BAHÁ'Í FAITH

National Spiritual Assembly of the Bahá'ís of Mexico: Emerson 421, Col. Chapultepec Morales, 11570 México, DF; tel. (55) 5545-2155; fax (55) 5255-5972; e-mail bahaimex@mx.inter.net; internet www.bahaimex.org; mems resident in 978 localities.

JUDAISM

The Jewish community numbered some 40,000 in 2004.

Comité Central de la Comunidad Judía de México: Cofre de Perote 115, Lomas Barrilaco, 11010 México, DF; tel. (55) 5520-9393; fax (55) 5540-3050; Pres. BENJAMÍN SPECKMAN BORG.

The Press

DAILY NEWSPAPERS

México, DF

La Afición: Ignacio Mariscal 23, Apdo 64 bis, Col. Tabacalera, 06030 México, DF; tel. (55) 5546-4780; fax (55) 5546-5852; internet www.mileniodiario.com/mexico/laaficion; f. 1930; sport; Pres. FRANCISCO A. GONZÁLEZ; circ. 85,000.

La Crónica de Hoy: Grupo Editorial Convergencia, SA de CV, Balderas 33, 6°, Col. Centro, 06040 México, DF; tel. and fax (52) 5512-3429; e-mail suscripciones@cronica.com.mx; internet www.cronica.com.mx; Pres. JORGE KAHWAGI GASTINE; Editorial Dir PABLO HIRIART LE BERT.

Cuestión: Laguna de Mayrán 410, Col. Anáhuac, 11320 México, DF; tel. (55) 5260-0499; fax (55) 5260-3645; e-mail contacto@cuestion.com.mx; internet www.cuestion.com.mx; f. 1980; midday; Dir-Gen. Lic. ALBERTO GONZÁLEZ PARRA; circ. 48,000.

Diario de México: Chimalpopoca 38, Col. Obrera, 06800 México, DF; tel. (55) 5442-6501; fax (55) 5588-4289; e-mail dirgral@diariodemexico.com.mx; internet www.diariodemexico.com.mx; f. 1948; morning; Dir-Gen. FEDERICO BRACAMONTES GÁLVEZ; Dir ABRAHAM SHEIMBERG; circ. 76,000.

El Economista: Avda Coyoacán 515, Col. del Valle, 03100 México, DF; tel. (55) 5326-5454; fax (55) 5687-3821; e-mail jppadilla@eleconomista.com.mx; internet www.economista.com.mx; f. 1988; financial; Pres. JOSÉ GÓMEZ CAÑIBE; Editor-in-Chief DAVID CUEN; circ. 37,448.

Esto: Guillermo Prieto 7, 1°, Col. San Rafael, Del. Cuauhtémoc, 06470 México, DF; tel. and fax (55) 5566-1511; e-mail esto@oem.com.mx; internet www.esto.com.mx; f. 1941; published by Organización Editorial Mexicana; morning; sport; Dir CARLOS TRAPAGA BARRIENTOS; circ. 400,000, Mondays 450,000.

Excélsior: Paseo de la Reforma 18 y Bucareli 1, Apdo 120 bis, Col. Centro, 06600 México, DF; tel. (55) 5705-4444; fax (55) 5566-0223; e-mail foro@excelsior.com.mx; internet www.excelsior.com.mx; f. 1917; morning; independent; Dir DANIEL MORENO; Gen. Man. JUVENTINO OLIVERA LÓPEZ; circ. 200,000.

El Financiero: Lago Bolsena 176, Col. Anáhuac entre Lago Peypus y Lago Onega, 11320 México, DF; tel. (55) 5227-7600; fax (55) 5254-6427; e-mail pilar@elfinanciero.com.mx; internet www.elfinanciero.com.mx; f. 1981; financial; Dir-Gen. PILAR ESTANDÍA DE CÁRDENAS; circ. 119,000.

El Heraldo de México: Dr Lucio, esq. Dr Velasco, Col. Doctores, 06720 México, DF; tel. (55) 5578-7022; fax (55) 5578-9824; e-mail heraldo@iwm.com.mx; internet www.heraldo.com.mx; f. 1965; morning; Dir-Gen. GABRIEL ALARCÓN VELÁZQUEZ; circ. 209,600.

La Jornada: Avda Cuauhtémoc 1236, Col. Santa Cruz Atoyac, Del. Benito Juárez, 03310 México, DF; tel. (55) 9183-0300; internet www.jornada.unam.mx; f. 1984; morning; Dir-Gen. Lic. CARMEN LIRA SAADE; Gen. Man. Lic. JORGE MARTÍNEZ JIMÉNEZ; circ. 86,275.

Milenio Diario: México, DF; internet www.mileniodiario.com.mx; publishes México, DF, and regional editions, and a weekly news magazine, Milenio Semanal (www.milenio.com/semanal); Pres. FRANCISCO A. GONZÁLEZ; Dir-Gen. CARLOS MARÍN.

Novedades: Balderas 87, esq. Morelos, Col. Centro, 06040 México, DF; tel. (55) 5518-5481; fax (55) 5521-4505; internet www.novedades.com.mx; f. 1936; morning; independent; Pres. and Editor-in-Chief ROMULO O'FARRILL, Jr; Vice-Pres. JOSÉ ANTONIO O'FARRILL AVILA; circ. 42,990, Sundays 43,536.

Ovaciones: Lago Zirahuén 279, 20°, Col. Anáhuac, 11320 México, DF; tel. (55) 5328-0700; fax (55) 5260-2219; e-mail ovaciones@ova.com.mx; internet www.ovaciones.com; f. 1947; morning and evening editions; Pres. and Dir-Gen. MAURICIO VAZQUEZ RAMOS; circ. 130,000, evening circ. 100,000.

La Prensa: Basilio Badillo 40, Col. Tabacalera, 06030 México, DF; tel. (55) 5228-8981; fax (55) 5521-8209; e-mail bmedina@la-prensa.com.mx; internet www.la-prensa.com.mx; f. 1928; published by Organización Editorial Mexicana; morning; Pres. and Dir-Gen. Lic. MARIO VÁZQUEZ RAÑA; Dir MAURICIO ORTEGA CAMBEROS; circ. 270,000.

Reforma: Avda México Coyoacán 40, Col. Santa Cruz Atoyac, 03310 México, DF; tel. (55) 5628-7777; fax (55) 5628-7188; internet www.reforma.com; f. 1993; morning; Pres. and Dir-Gen. ALEJANDRO JUNCO DE LA VEGA ELIZONDO; circ. 94,000.

El Sol de México: Guillermo Prieto 7, 20°, Col. San Rafael, 06470 México, DF; tel. (55) 5566-1511; fax (55) 5535-5560; e-mail enlinea@elsoldemexico.com.mx; internet www.elsoldemexico.com.mx; f. 1965; published by Organización Editorial Mexicana; morning and midday; Pres. and Dir-Gen. Lic. MARIO VÁZQUEZ RAÑA; Dir ISABEL ZAMORANO RAMOS; circ. 76,000.

El Universal: Bucareli 8, Apdo 909, Col. Centro, Del. Cuauhtémoc, 06040 México, DF; tel. (55) 5709-1313; fax (55) 5510-1269; e-mail redaccio@servidor.unam.mx; internet www.el-universal.com.mx; f. 1916; morning; independent; centre-left; Pres. and Dir-Gen. Lic. JUAN FRANCISCO EALY ORTIZ; circ. 165,629, Sundays 181,615.

Unomásuno: Gabino Barreda 86, Col. San Rafael, México, DF; tel. (55) 1055-5500; fax (55) 5598-8821; e-mail cduran@servidor.unam.mx; internet www.unomasuno.com.mx; f. 1977; morning; left-wing; Pres. NAIM LIBIEN KAUI; Dir JOSÉ LUIS ROJAS RAMÍREZ; circ. 40,000.

MEXICO   Directory

PROVINCIAL DAILY NEWSPAPERS

Baja California

El Sol de Tijuana: Rufino Tamayo 4, Zona del Río, 22320 Tijuana, BC; tel. (664) 634-3232; fax (664) 634-2234; e-mail soltij@oem.com.mx; internet www.oem.com.mx/elsoldetijuana; f. 1989; published by Organización Editorial Mexicana; morning; Dir ARTURO GONZÁLEZ PÉREZ; circ. 50,000.

La Voz de la Frontera: Avda Madero 1545, Col. Nueva, Apdo 946, 21100 Mexicali, BC; tel. (686) 562-4545; fax (686) 562-6912; e-mail ramondiaz@lavozdelafrontera.com.mx; internet www.oem.com.mx/lavozdelafrontera; f. 1964; morning; published by Organización Editorial Mexicana; Dir FELIPE DE JESÚS LÓPEZ RODRÍGUEZ; Gen. Man. Lic. MARIO VALDÉS HERNÁNDEZ; circ. 65,000.

Chihuahua

El Diario: Publicaciones Paso del Norte, Avda Paseo Triunfo de la República 2505, Zona Pronaf, 32310 Ciudad Juárez, Chih.; tel. (656) 629-6900; internet www.diario.com.mx; f. 1976; Pres. OSVALDO RODRÍGUEZ BORUNDA.

El Heraldo de Chihuahua: Avda Universidad 2507, Apdo 1515, 31240 Chihuahua, Chih.; tel. (614) 413-9339; fax (614) 413-5625; e-mail elheraldo@buzon.online.com.mx; internet www.oem.com.mx/elheraldodechihuahua; f. 1927; published by Organización Editorial Mexicana; morning; Dir Lic. JAVIER H. CONTRERAS; circ. 27,520, Sundays 31,223.

El Mexicano de Ciudad Juárez: Ciudad Juárez, Chih.; e-mail director@pesquisasenlinea.org; internet www.pesquisasenlinea.org/elmexicano; f. 1959; published by Organización Editorial Mexicana; morning; Dir RAFAEL NAVARRO; Editor-in-Chief JAIME NÚÑEZ; circ. 80,000.

Coahuila

La Opinión: Blvd Independencia 1492 Oeste, Apdo 86, 27010 Torreón, Coah.; tel. (871) 559-8777; fax (871) 759-8164; internet www.opinion.com.mx; f. 1924; morning; Dir-Gen. OSCAR LÓPEZ MORALES; circ. 40,000.

El Siglo de Torreón: Avda Matamoros 1056 Pte, Col. Centro, 27000 Torreón, Coah.; tel. (871) 759-1200; e-mail internet@elsiglodetorreon.com.mx; internet www.elsiglodetorreon.com.mx; f. 1922; morning; Pres. OLGA DE JUAMBELZ Y HORCASITAS; Dir-Gen. ANTONIO IRAZOQUI Y DE JUAMBELZ; circ. 38,611, Sundays 38,526.

Vanguardia: Blvd Venustiano Carranza 1918, esq. con Chiapas, República Oriente, 25280 Saltillo, Coah.; tel. (844) 450-1000; e-mail hola@vanguardia.com.mx; internet www.vanguardia.com.mx; Dir-Gen. DIANA MARÍA GALINDO DE CASTILLA.

Colima

Diario de Colima: Avda 20 de Noviembre 380, 28060 Colima, Col.; tel. (312) 312-5688; internet www.diariodecolima.com; f. 1953; Dir-Gen. HÉCTOR SÁNCHEZ DE LA MADRID; Man. Dir ENRIQUE ZÁRATE CANSECO.

Guanajuato

Correo: Carr. Guanajuato—Juventino Rosas Km 9.5, 36260 Guanajuato, Gto; tel. (477) 733-1263; fax (477) 733-0057; e-mail magana@correo-gto.com.mx; internet www.correo-gto.com.mx; Dir-Gen. ARNALDO CUÉLLAR.

El Sol de Salamanca: Faro de Oro 800, 36700 Salamanca, Gto; tel. (464) 647-0144; e-mail aherrera@elsoldeirapuato.com.mx; internet www.elsoldesalamanca.com.mx; published by Organización Editorial Mexicana; Dir-Gen. Lic. ALEJANDRO HERRERA SÁNCHEZ.

Jalisco

El Informador: Independencia 300, Apdo 3 bis, 44100 Guadalajara, Jal.; tel. (33) 614-6340; fax (33) 614-4653; e-mail webmanager@informador.com.mx; internet www.informador.com.mx; f. 1917; morning; Editor JORGE ÁLVAREZ DEL CASTILLO; circ. 50,000.

El Occidental: Calzada Independencia Sur 324, Apdo 1-699, 44100 Guadalajara, Jal.; tel. (33) 613-0690; fax (33) 613-6796; internet www.eloccidental.com.mx; f. 1942; published by Organización Editorial Mexicana; morning; Dir Lic. RICARDO DEL VALLE DEL PERAL; circ. 49,400.

México

ABC: Avda Hidalgo Oriente 1339, Centro Comercial, Col. Ferrocarriles Nacionales, 50070 Toluca, Méx.; tel. (722) 217-9880; fax (722) 217-8402; e-mail miled1@mail.miled.com; internet www.miled.com; f. 1984; morning; Pres. and Editor MILED LIBIEN KAUI; circ. 65,000.

Diario de Toluca: Allende Sur 209, 50000 Toluca, Méx.; tel. (722) 215-9105; fax (722) 214-1523; e-mail eldiario@netspace.com.mx; f. 1980; also publishes Siete Dias and El Noticiero; morning; Pres. ANUAR MACCISE DIB; circ. 22,200.

El Heraldo de Toluca: Salvador Díaz Mirón 700, Col. Sánchez Colín, 50150 Toluca, Méx.; tel. (722) 217-3542; fax (722) 212-2535; e-mail editotol@prodigy.net.mx; f. 1955; morning; Editor ALBERTO BARRAZA SÁNCHEZ; circ. 90,000.

El Sol de Toluca: Santos Degollado 105, Apdo 54, Col. Centro, 50050 Toluca, Méx.; tel. (722) 214-7077; fax (722) 215-2564; internet www.oem.com.mx/elsoldetoluca; f. 1947; published by Organización Editorial Mexicana; morning; Dir RAFAEL VILCHIS GIL DE ARÉVALO; circ. 42,000.

Michoacán

La Voz de Michoacán: Blvd del Periodismo 1270, Col. Arriaga Rivera, Apdo 121, 58190 Morelia, Mich.; tel. (443) 327-3712; fax (443) 327-3728; e-mail jcgonzalez@voznet.com.mx; internet www.voznet.com.mx; f. 1948; morning; Dir-Gen. Lic. MIGUEL MEDINA ROBLES; circ. 50,000.

Morelos

El Diario de Morelos: Morelos Sur 132, Col. Las Palmas, 62050 Cuernavaca, Mor.; tel. and fax (777) 362-0220; e-mail mbracs@yahoo.com; internet www.diariodemorelos.com; f. 1978; morning; Dir-Gen. MIGUEL ANGEL BRACAMONTES BAZ; circ. 30,000.

Nayarit

Meridiano de Nayarit: E. Zapata 73 Pte, Apdo 65, 63000 Tepic, Nay.; internet www.meridiano.com.mx; f. 1942; morning; Dir Dr DAVID ALFARO; circ. 60,000.

Nuevo León

ABC: Platón Sánchez Sur 411, 64000 Monterrey, NL; tel. (81) 8344-4480; fax (81) 8344-5990; e-mail abc2000@mexis.com; f. 1985; morning; Pres. GONZALO ESTRADA CRUZ; Dir-Gen. GONZALO ESTRADO TORRES; circ. 40,000, Sundays 45,000.

El Norte: Washington 629 Oeste, Apdo 186, 64000 Monterrey, NL; tel. (81) 8345-3388; fax (81) 8343-2476; internet www.elnorte.com.mx; f. 1938; morning; Man. Dir Lic. ALEJANDRO JUNCO DE LA VEGA; circ. 133,872, Sundays 154,951.

El Porvenir: Galeana Sur 344, Apdo 218, 64000 Monterrey, NL; tel. (81) 8345-4080; fax (81) 8345-7795; internet www.elporvenir.com.mx; f. 1919; morning; Dir-Gen. JOSÉ GERARDO CANTÚ ESCALANTE; circ. 75,000.

Oaxaca

El Imparcial: Armenta y López 312, Apdo 322, 68000 Oaxaca, Oax.; tel. (951) 516-2812; fax (951) 514-7020; e-mail el_imparcial@infosel.net.mx; internet www.imparoax.com.mx; f. 1951; morning; Dir-Gen. Lic. BENJAMÍN FERNÁNDEZ PICHARDO; circ. 17,000, Sundays 20,000.

Puebla

El Sol de Puebla: Avda 3 Oeste 201, Apdo 190, 72000 Puebla, Pue.; tel. (222) 242-4560; fax (222) 246-0869; e-mail elsoldepuebla@elsoldepuebla.com.mx; internet www.oem.com.mx/elsoldepuebla; f. 1944; published by Organización Editorial Mexicana; morning; Dir MARCO A. PONCE DE LEÓN; circ. 67,000.

San Luis Potosí

El Heraldo: Villerías 305, 78000 San Luis Potosí, SLP; tel. (444) 812-3312; fax (444) 812-2081; e-mail redaccion@elheraldoslp.com.mx; internet www.elheraldoslp.com.mx; f. 1954; morning; Dir-Gen. ALEJANDRO VILLASANA MENA; circ. 60,620.

Pulso: Galeana 485, Centro, 78000 San Luis Potosí, SLP; tel. (444) 812-7575; fax (444) 812-3525; internet www.pulsoslp.com.mx; morning; Dir-Gen. PABLO VALLADARES GARCÍA; circ. 60,000.

El Sol de San Luis: Avda Universidad 565, Apdo 342, 78000 San Luis Potosí, SLP; tel. and fax (444) 812-4412; internet www.elsoldesanluis.com.mx; f. 1952; published by Organización Editorial Mexicana; morning; Dir JOSÉ ANGEL MARTÍNEZ LIMÓN; circ. 60,000.

Sinaloa

El Debate de Culiacán: Madero 556 Pte, 80000 Culiacán, Sin.; tel. (667) 716-6353; fax (667) 715-7131; e-mail redaccion@debate.com.mx; internet www.debate.com.mx; f. 1972; morning; Dir ROSARIO I. OROPEZA; circ. 23,603, Sundays 23,838.

Noroeste Culiacán: Grupo Periodicos Noroeste, Angel Flores 282 Oeste, Apdo 90, 80000 Culiacán, Sin.; tel. (667) 713-2100; fax (667) 712-8006; e-mail cschmidt@noroeste.com.mx; internet www.noroeste.com.mx; f. 1973; morning; Pres. MANUEL J. CLOUTHIER; Editor RODOLFO DIAZ; circ. 35,000.

MEXICO

El Sol de Sinaloa: Blvd G. Leyva Lozano y Corona 320, Apdo 412, 80000 Culiacán, Sin.; tel. (667) 713-1621; fax (667) 713-1800; internet www.elsoldesinaloa.com.mx; f. 1956; published by Organización Editorial Mexicana; morning; Dir JORGE LUIS TÉLLEZ SALAZAR; circ. 30,000.

Sonora

Expreso: Hermosillo, Son.; tel. (662) 108-3000; e-mail holguin@expreso.com.mx; internet www.expreso.com.mx; Dir-Gen. MARTÍN HOLGUÍN ALATORRE; circ. 17,000; 18,000 on Sundays.

El Imparcial: Sufragio Efectivo y Mina 71, Col. Centro, Apdo 66, 83000 Hermosillo, Son.; tel. (662) 259-4700; fax (662) 217-4483; e-mail lector@elimparcial.com.; internet www.imparcial.com.mx; f. 1937; morning; Pres. and Dir-Gen. JUAN HEALY; circ. 32,083, Sundays 32,444.

Tabasco

Tabasco Hoy: Avda de los Ríos 206, Col. Tabasco 2000, 86035 Villahermosa, Tab.; tel. (993) 310-0229; internet www.tabascohoy.com.mx; f. 1987; morning; Dir-Gen. MIGUEL CANTÓN ZETINA; circ. 50,000.

Tamaulipas

El Bravo: Morelos y Primera 129, Apdo 483, 87300 Matamoros, Tamps; tel. (871) 816-0100; fax (871) 816-2007; e-mail comenta@elbravo.com.mx; internet www.elbravo.com.mx; f. 1951; morning; Pres. and Dir-Gen. JOSÉ CARRETERO BALBOA; circ. 60,000.

El Diario de Nuevo Laredo: González 2409, Apdo 101, 88000 Nuevo Laredo, Tamps; tel. (867) 712-8444; fax (867) 712-8221; internet www.diario.net; f. 1948; morning; Editor RUPERTO VILLARREAL MONTEMAYOR; circ. 68,130, Sundays 73,495.

Expresión: Calle 3 y Novedades 3, Col. Periodistas, 87457 Matamoros, Tamps; tel. (868) 817-9555; fax (868) 817-3307; e-mail xpresion@prodigy.net.mx; morning; Dir-Gen. MIGUEL GARAY AVILA; circ. 50,000.

El Mañana: Juárez y Perú, Col. Juárez, Nuevo Laredo, Tamps; tel. (867) 711-9900; fax (867) 715-0405; e-mail ramon.cantu@elmanana.com.mx; internet www.elmanana.com.mx; f. 1932; morning; Pres. NINFA DEÁNDAR MARTÍNEZ; Editor RAMÓN CANTÚ DEANDAR; circ. 16,473, Sundays 20,957.

El Mañana de Reynosa: Prof. Lauro Aguirre con Matías Canales, Apdo 14, Col. Ribereña, 88620 Ciudad Reynosa, Tamps; tel. (899) 921-9950; fax (899) 924-9348; internet www.elmananarey.com.mx; f. 1949; morning; Dir-Gen. HERIBERTO DEANDAR MARTÍNEZ; circ. 52,000.

Prensa de Reynosa: Matamoros y González Ortega, Zona Centro, 88500 Reynosa, Tamps; tel. (899) 922-0299; fax (899) 922-2412; e-mail prensa_88500@yahoo.com; internet www.prensadereynosa.com; f. 1963; morning; Dir-Gen. FÉLIX GARZA ELIZONDO; circ. 60,000.

El Sol de Tampico: Altamira 311 Pte, Apdo 434, 89000 Tampico, Tamps; tel. (833) 212-3566; fax (833) 212-6986; internet www.elsoldetampico.com.mx; f. 1950; published by Organización Editorial Mexicana; morning; Dir-Gen. Lic. RUBÉN DÍAZ DE LA GARZA; circ. 77,000.

Veracruz

Diario del Istmo: Avda Hidalgo 1115, Col. Centro, 96400 Coatzacoalcos, Ver.; tel. (921) 211-8000; e-mail info@istmo.com.mx; internet www.diariodelistmo.com; f. 1979; morning; Dir-Gen. HÉCTOR ROBLES BARAJAS; circ. 64,600.

El Dictamen: 16 de Septiembre y Arista, 91700 Veracruz, Ver.; tel. (229) 931-1745; fax (229) 931-5804; internet www.eldictamen.com.mx; f. 1898; morning; Pres. CARLOS ANTONIO MALPICA MARTÍNEZ; circ. 38,000, Sundays 39,000.

La Opinión: Poza Rica de Hidalgo, Ver.; e-mail publicidad@laopinion.com.mx; internet www.laopinion.com.mx; Dir ABEL ANDRADE LICONA.

Yucatán

Diario de Yucatán: Calle 60 521, 97000 Mérida, Yuc.; tel. (999) 942-2222; fax (999) 942-2204; internet www.yucatan.com.mx; f. 1925; morning; Dir-Gen. CARLOS R. MENÉNDEZ NAVARRETE; circ. 54,639, Sundays 65,399.

El Mundo al Día: Calle 62 514A, 97000 Mérida, Yuc.; tel. (999) 23-9933; fax (999) 24-9629; e-mail nmerida@cancun.novenet.com.mx; f. 1964; morning; Pres. ROMULO O'FARRILL, Jr; Gen. Man. Lic. GERARDO GARCÍA GAMBOA; circ. 25,000.

Por Esto!: Calle 60, No 576 entre 73 y 71, 97000 Mérida, Yuc.; tel. (999) 24-7613; fax (999) 28-6514; e-mail redaccion@poresto.net; internet www.poresto.net; f. 1991; morning; Dir-Gen. MARIO RENATO MENÉNDEZ RODRÍGUEZ; circ. 26,985, Sundays 28,727.

Zacatecas

Imagen: Calzada Revolución 24, Col. Tierra y Libertad, Guadalupe, Zac.; tel. and fax (492) 923-8898; e-mail buzon@imagenzac.com.mx; internet www.imagenzac.com.mx; Dir-Gen. EUGENIO MERCADO.

SELECTED WEEKLY NEWSPAPERS

Bolsa de Trabajo: San Francisco 657, 9A, Col. del Valle, 03100 México, DF; tel. (55) 5536-8387; f. 1988; employment; Pres. and Dir-Gen. MÓNICA ELÍAS CALLES; circ. 30,000.

El Heraldo Bajio: Hermanos Aldama 222, Apdo 299, Zona Centro, 37000 León, Gto; tel. (477) 719-8800; e-mail heraldo@el-heraldo-bajio.com.mx; internet www.el-heraldo-bajio.com.mx; f. 1957; Pres. and Dir-Gen. MAURICIO BERCÚN LÓPEZ; circ. 85,000.

Segundamano: Insurgentes Sur 619, Col. Nápoles, Del. Benito Juárez, 03810 México, DF; tel. (55) 5350-7070; e-mail soporte@segundamano.com.mx; internet www.segundamano.com.mx; f. 1986; Dir-Gen. LUIS MAGAÑA MAGAÑA; circ. 105,000.

Zeta: Avda las Américas 4633, Fraccionamiento El Paraíso, Tijuana, BC; e-mail zeta@zetatijuana.com; internet www.zetatijuana.com; f. 1980; news magazine; Dir JESÚS BLANCORNELOS.

PERIODICALS

Boletín Industrial: Goldsmith 37-403, Col. Polanco, 11550 México, DF; tel. (55) 5280-6463; fax (55) 5280-3194; e-mail bolind@viernes.iwm.com.mx; internet www.bolind.com.mx; f. 1983; monthly; Dir-Gen. HUMBERTO VALADÉS DÍAZ; circ. 22,000.

Car and Driver: Alabama 123, Col. Nápoles, 03810 México, DF; tel. (55) 5523-5201; fax (55) 5536-6399; f. 1999; monthly; Pres. PEDRO VARGAS G.; circ. 80,000.

Casas & Gente: Amsterdam 112, Col. Hipódromo Condesa, 06100 México, DF; tel. (55) 5286-7794; fax (55) 5211-7112; e-mail informac@casasgente.com; internet www.casasgente.com; 10 a year; interior design; Dir-Gen. IGNACIO DÍAZ SÁNCHEZ.

Comercio: Río Tíber 87, 06500 México, DF; tel. (55) 5514-0873; fax (55) 5514-1008; f. 1960; monthly; business review; Dir RAÚL HORTA; circ. 40,000.

Conozca Más: Vasco de Quiroga 2000, Col. Santa Fe, Del. Alvaro Obregón, 01210 México, DF; tel. (55) 5261-2000; fax (55) 5261-2704; internet www.esmas.com.conozcamas; f. 1990; monthly; scientific; Dir EUGENIO MENDOZA; circ. 90,000.

Contenido: Darwin 101, Col. Anzures, 11590 México, DF; tel. (55) 5531-3162; fax (55) 5545-7478; e-mail contenido@contenido.com.mx; internet www.contenido.com.mx; f. 1963; monthly; popular appeal; Dir ARMANDO AYALA ANGUIANO; circ. 124,190.

Cosmopolitan México: Vasco de Quiroga 2000, Col. Santa Fe, Del. Alvaro Obregón, 01210 México, DF; tel. (55) 5261-2600; fax (55) 5261-2704; internet www.esmas.com/editorialtelevisa; f. 1973; fortnightly; women's magazine; Dir SARA MARÍA CASTANY; circ. 260,000.

Expansión: Avda Constituyentes 956, Col. Lomas Altas, 11950 México, DF; tel. and fax (55) 9177-4100; e-mail quien@expansion.com.mx; internet www.expansion.com.mx; fortnightly; business and financial; Editor ALBERTO BELLO.

Fama: Avda Eugenio Garza Sada 2245 Sur, Col. Roma, Apdo 3128, 64700 Monterrey, NL; tel. (81) 8359-2525; fortnightly; show business; Pres. JESÚS D. GONZÁLEZ; Dir RAÚL MARTÍNEZ; circ. 350,000.

Gaceta Médica de México: Academia Nacional de Medicina, Unidad de Congresos del Centro Médico Nacional Siglo XXI, Bloque B, Avda Cuauhtémoc 330, Col. Doctores, 06725 México, DF; tel. (55) 5578-2044; fax (55) 5578-4271; e-mail gaceta@medigraphic.com; internet www.medigraphic.com; f. 1864; every 2 months; journal of the Academia Nacional de Medicina de México; Editor ALFREDO ULLOA AGUIRRE; circ. 20,000.

Impacto: Avda Ceylán 517, Col. Industrial Vallejo, Apdo 2986, 02300 México, DF; tel. (55) 5587-3855; fax (55) 5567-7781; f. 1949; weekly; politics; Man. and Dir-Gen. JUAN BUSTILLOS OROZCO; circ. 115,000.

Kena Mensual: Río Balsas 101, Col. Cuauhtémoc, 06500 México, DF; tel. (55) 5442-9600; e-mail corporativo@grupoarmonia.com.mx; f. 1977; fortnightly; women's interest; Editor GINA URETA; circ. 100,000.

Letras Libres: Presidente Carranza 210, Col. Coyoacán, 04000 México, DF; tel. (55) 5554-8810; fax (55) 5658-0074; e-mail suscripciones@letraslibres.com; internet www.letraslibres.com; monthly; culture; Editor-in-Chief JULIO TRUJILLO.

Manufactura: Avda Constituyentes 956, esq. Rosaleda, Col. Lomas Altas, 11950 México, DF; tel. (55) 9177-4100; e-mail dluna@expansion.com.mx; internet www.manufacturaweb.com; f. 1994; monthly; industrial; Dir-Gen. DAVID LUNA ARELLANO; circ. 25,000.

Marie Claire: Vasco de Quiroga 2000, Col. Santa Fe, Del. Alvaro Obregón, 01210 México, DF; tel. (55) 5261-2600; fax (55) 5261-2704;

MEXICO

f. 1990; monthly; women's interest; Editor Louise Mereles Gras; circ. 70,000.

Mecánica Popular (Popular Mechanics en Español): Vasco de Quiroga 2000, Col. Santa Fe, Del. Alvaro Obregón, 01210 Mexico, DF; tel. (55) 5447-4711; fax (55) 5261-2705; internet www.mimecanicapopular.com; f. 1947; monthly; crafts and home improvements; Dir Andrés Jorge; circ. 55,000.

Men's Health: Vasco de Quiroga 2000, Col. Santa Fe, Del. Alvaro Obregón, 01210 México, DF; tel. (55) 5261-2645; fax (55) 5261-2733; e-mail mens.health@editorial.televisa.com.mx; internet www.esmas.com/editorialtelevisa; f. 1994; monthly; health; Editor Juan Antonio Sempere; circ. 130,000.

Muy Interesante: Vasco de Quiroga 2000, Col. Santa Fe, Del. Alvaro Obregón, 01210 México, DF; tel. (55) 5261-2600; fax (55) 5261-2704; internet www.esmas.com/editorialtelevisa; f. 1984; monthly; scientific devt; Dir Pilar S. Hoyos; circ. 250,000.

Negocios y Bancos: Bolívar 8-103, Apdo 1907, Col. Centro, 06000 México, DF; tel. (55) 5510-1884; fax (55) 5512-9411; e-mail nego_bancos@mexico.com; f. 1951; fortnightly; business, economics; Dir Alfredo Farrugia Reed; circ. 10,000.

Proceso: Fresas 7, Col. del Valle, 03100 México, DF; tel. (55) 5636-2028; internet www.proceso.com.mx; f. 1976; weekly; news analysis; Pres. Julio Scherer García; circ. 98,784.

La Revista Peninsular: Calle 35, 489 x 52 y 54, Zona Centro, Mérida, Yuc.; tel. and fax (999) 926-3014; e-mail direccion@larevista.com.mx; internet www.larevista.com.mx; weekly; news and politics; Dir-Gen. Rodrigo Menéndez Cámara.

Selecciones del Reader's Digest: Avda Prolongación Paseo de la Reforma 1236, 10°, Col. Santa Fe, Del. Alvaro Obregón, 05348 México, DF; tel. (55) 5351-2200; internet www.selecciones.com.mx; f. 1940; monthly; Editor Audón Coria; circ. 611,660.

Siempre!: Vallarta 20, Col. Tabacalera, 06030 México, DF; tel. and fax (55) 5566-1804; e-mail suscripciones@siempre.com.mx; internet www.siempre.com.mx; f. 1953; weekly; left of centre; Dir Lic. Beatriz Pagés Rebollar de Nuño; circ. 100,000.

Tele-Guía: Vasco de Quiroga 2000, Col. Santa Fe, Del. Alvaro Obregón, 01210 México, DF; tel. (55) 5261-2600; fax (55) 5261-2704; internet www.esmas.com/editorialtelevisa; f. 1952; weekly; television guide; Editor María Eugenia Hernández; circ. 375,000.

Tiempo Libre: Holbein 75 bis, Col. Nochebuena Mixcoac, Del. Benito Juárez, 03720 México, DF; tel. (55) 5611-2884; fax (55) 5611-3982; e-mail buzon@tiempolibre.com.mx; internet www.tiempolibre.com.mx; f. 1980; weekly; entertainment guide; Dir-Gen. Angeles Aguilar Zinser; circ. 95,000.

Tú: Vasco de Quiroga 2000, Col. Santa Fe, Del. Alvaro Obregón, 01210 México, DF; tel. (55) 5261-2600; fax (55) 5261-2730; internet www.esmas.com/editorialtelevisa; f. 1980; monthly; teenage; Editor María Antonieta Salamanca; circ. 250,000.

TV y Novelas: Vasco de Quiroga 2000, Col. Santa Fe, Del. Alvaro Obregón, 01210 México, DF; tel. (55) 5261-2600; fax (55) 5261-2704; f. 1982; weekly; television guide and short stories; Dir Jesús Gallegos; circ. 460,000.

Ultima Moda: Morelos 16, 6°, Col. Centro, 06040 México, DF; tel. (55) 5518-5481; fax (55) 5512-8902; f. 1966; monthly; fashion; Pres. Romulo O'Farrill, Jr; Gen. Man. Lic. Samuel Podolsky Rapoport; circ. 110,548.

Vanidades: Vasco de Quiroga 2000, Col. Santa Fe, Del. Alvaro Obregón, 01210 México, DF; tel. (55) 5261-2600; fax (55) 5261-2704; e-mail vanidades@editorialtelevisa.com; internet www.esmas.com/vanidades; f. 1961; fortnightly; women's magazine; Dir Jaqueline Blanco; circ. 290,000.

Visión: Homero 411, 5°, Col. Polanco, 11570 México, DF; tel. (55) 5531-4914; fax (55) 5531-4915; e-mail 74174.3111@compuserve.com; offices in Bogotá, Buenos Aires and Santiago de Chile; f. 1950; fortnightly; politics and economics; Gen. Man. Roberto Bello; circ. 27,215.

Vogue (México): Condé Nast México, México, DF; tel. (55) 5095-8076; fax (55) 5245-7109; e-mail suscrip@condenast.com.mx; internet www.vogue.com.mx; f. 1999; monthly; women's fashion; circ. 208,180.

ASSOCIATIONS

Asociación Nacional de Periodistas y Comunicadores, A.C.: Luis G. Obregón 17, Of. 209, Col. Centro, 06020 México, DF; tel. (55) 5341-1523; Pres. Moisés Huerta.

Federación de Asociaciones de Periodistas Mexicanos (Fapermex): Humboldt 5, Col. Centro, 06030 México, DF; tel. (55) 5510-2679; e-mail fapermex@fapermex.com; internet www.fapermex.com; Pres. José Antonio Calcáneo Collado; Sec.-Gen. Aurora Sansores Serrano; 88 mem. asscns; c. 9,000 mems.

Federación Latinoamericana de Periodistas (FELAP): Nuevo Leon 144, 1°, Col. Hipódromo Condesa, 06170 México, DF; tel. (55) 5286-6055; fax (55) 5286-6085; Pres. Juan Carlos Camaño; Sec.-Gen. José Rafael Vargas.

Fraternidad de Reporteros de México (FREMAC): Avda Juárez 88, Col. Centro, Del. Cuauhtémoc, México, DF; e-mail info@fremac.org.mx; internet www.fremac.org.mx; f. 1995; Sec.-Gen. Marcela Yarce Viveros.

NEWS AGENCIES

Agencia de Información Integral Periodística, SA (AIIP): Tabasco 263, Col. Roma, Del. Cuauhtémoc, 06700 México, DF; tel. (55) 8596-9643; fax (55) 5235-3468; e-mail aiipsa@axtel.net; internet www.aiip.com.mx; f. 1987; Dir-Gen. Miguel Herrera López.

Agencia Mexicana de Información (AMI): Avda Cuauhtémoc 16, Col. Doctores, 06720 México, DF; tel. (55) 5761-9933; e-mail info@red-ami.com; internet www.ami.com.mx; f. 1971; Dir-Gen. José Luis Becerra López; Gen. Man. Eva Vázquez López.

Notimex, SA de CV: Morena 110, 3°, Col. del Valle, 03100 México, DF; tel. (55) 5420-1172; fax (55) 5420-1188; e-mail ventas@notimex.com.mx; internet www.notimex.com.mx; f. 1968; services to press, radio and television in Mexico and throughout the world; Dir-Gen. Dr Jorge Medina Viedas.

Foreign Bureaux

Agence France-Presse (AFP): Torre Latinoamericana, 15°, Eje Central y Madero 1, Col. Centro, 06007 México, DF; tel. (55) 5518-5494; fax (55) 5510-4564; e-mail redaccion.mexico@afp.com; Bureau Chief Bertrand Jaques Rosenthal.

Agencia EFE (Spain): Lafayette 69 esq. Gutenberg, Col. Anzures, 11590 México, DF; tel. (55) 5545-8256; fax (55) 5254-1412; e-mail directora@efe.com.mx; Bureau Chief Patricia Vázquez Orbegozo.

Agenzia Nazionale Stampa Associata (ANSA) (Italy): Emerson 150, 2°, Col. Chapultepec Morales, 11570 México, DF; tel. (55) 5255-3696; fax (55) 5255-3018; e-mail ansamexico@prodigy.net.mx; internet www.ansa.it/ansalatina; Bureau Chief Marcos Romero Martínez.

Associated Press (AP) (USA): Paseo de la Reforma 350, Col. Juárez, 06600 México, DF; tel. (55) 5080-3400; fax (55) 5208-2684; e-mail apmexico@ap.org; Bureau Chief Eloy O. Aguilar.

Deutsche Presse-Agentur (dpa) (Germany): Avda Cuauhtémoc 16-303, Col. Doctores, Del. Cuauhtémoc, 06720 México, DF; tel. (55) 5578-4829; fax (55) 7561-0762; e-mail info@dpa.com.mx; Bureau Chief Franz Johannes Smets.

Informatsionnoye Telegrafnoye Agentstvo Rossii—Telegrafnoye Agentsvo Suverennykh Stran (ITAR—TASS) (Russia): Monte Líbano 965, Col. Lomas de Chapultepec, 11000 México DF; tel. (55) 5202-4831; fax (55) 5202-4879; e-mail itartass@prodigy.net; Bureau Chief Igor Varlamov.

Inter Press Service (IPS) (Italy): Avda Cuauhtémoc 16-403, Col. Doctores, Del. Cuauhtémoc, 06720 México, DF; tel. (55) 5578-0417; fax (55) 5578-0099; e-mail mex@ipslatam.net; Chief Correspondent Diego Cevallos Rojas.

Kyodo Tsushin (Japan): Cerro Dios de Hacha 66, Col. Romero de Terreros, 04310 México, DF; tel. (55) 5554-7199; fax (55) 5658-2957; e-mail kyodonews@prodigy.net.mx; Bureau Chief Daisuke Konishi.

Maghreb Arabe Presse (Morocco): Miguel de Cervantes Saavedra 448, 4°, Col. Irrigación, 11500 México, DF; tel. (55) 3093-3760; fax (55) 3093-3761; e-mail mohammedtanji@hotmail.com; Correspondent Mohammed Tanji.

Prensa Latina (Cuba): Edif. B 504, Insurgentes Centro 125, Col. San Rafael, Del. Cuauhtémoc, 06470 México, DF; tel. (55) 5546-6015; fax (55) 5592-0570; e-mail plmexico@prensalatina.com.mx; internet www.prensalatina.com.mx; Bureau Chief Raimundo López Medina.

Reuters Ltd (United Kingdom): Edif. Torre Esmeralda 11, 19°, Blvd Manuel Avila Camacho 36, Col. Lomas de Chapultepec, 11000 México, DF; tel. (55) 5282-7000; fax (55) 5540-3001; e-mail mexicocity.newsroom@reuters.com; Bureau Chief Kieran Michael Murray.

Viet Nam News Agency (VNA) (Viet Nam): Río Pánuco 180, Col. Cuauhtémoc, 06500 México, DF; tel. (55) 5514-9013; fax (55) 5514-1015; e-mail hop@vnamex.com.mx; Bureau Chief Do Van Hop.

Xinhua (New China) News Agency (People's Republic of China): Francisco I. Madero 17, Col. Tlacopac San Angel, 01040 México, DF; tel. (55) 5662-8548; fax (55) 5662-9028; e-mail xinhuamx@xinhuanet.com; Bureau Chief Huang Yongxian.

Other foreign news agencies include Agencia Getty (USA), Agencia Novosti (Russia), Bloomberg Business News (USA), Dow Jones Newswires (USA), Europa Press (Spain), Market News International (USA), United Press International (USA), Voller Ernst International Press (Germany) and Yonhap News Agency (Republic of Korea).

FOREIGN CORRESPONDENTS' ASSOCIATION

Asociación de Corresponsales Extranjeros en México (ACEM): Avda Cuauhtémoc 16, 1°, Col. Doctores, Del. Cuauhtémoc, 06720 México, DF; tel. (55) 5588-3241; fax (55) 5588-6382.

Publishers

MÉXICO, DF

Aguilar, Altea, Taurus, Alfaguara, SA de CV: Avda Universidad 767, Col. del Valle, 03100 México, DF; tel. (55) 5688-8966; fax (55) 5604-2304; e-mail sealtiel@santillana.com.mx; f. 1965; general literature; Dir SEALTIEL ALATRISTE.

Arbol Editorial, SA de CV: Avda Cuauhtémoc 1430, Col. Santa Cruz Atoyac, 03310 México, DF; tel. (55) 5688-4828; fax (55) 5605-7600; e-mail editorialpax@maxis.com; f. 1979; health, philosophy, theatre; Man. Dir GERARDO GALLY TEOMONFORD.

Artes de México y del Mundo, SA de CV: Plaza Río de Janeiro, Col. Roma, 06700 México, DF; tel. (55) 5525-5905; fax (55) 5525-5925; e-mail artesdemexico@artesdemexico.com; internet www.artesdemexico.com; f. 1988; art, design, poetry.

Editorial Avante, SA de CV: Luis G. Obregón 9, 1°, Apdo 45-796, Col. Centro, 06020 México, DF; tel. (55) 5510-8804; fax (55) 5521-5245; e-mail editorialavante@editorialavante.com.mx; internet www.editorialavante.com.mx; f. 1948; educational, drama, linguistics; Man. Dir Lic. MARIO A. HINOJOSA SAENZ.

Editorial Azteca, SA: Calle de la Luna 225–227, Col. Guerrero, 06300 México, DF; tel. (55) 5526-1157; fax (55) 5526-2557; f. 1956; religion, literature and technical; Man. Dir ALFONSO ALEMÓN JALOMO.

Cía Editorial Continental, SA de CV (CECSA): Renacimiento 180, Col. San Juan Tlihuaca, Azcapotzalco, 02400 México, DF; tel. (55) 5561-8333; fax (55) 5561-5231; e-mail info@patriacultural.com.mx; f. 1954; business, technology, general textbooks; Pres. CARLOS FRIGOLET LERMA.

Ediciones de Cultura Popular, SA: Odontología 76, Copilco Universidad, México, DF; f. 1969; history, politics, social sciences; Man. Dir URIEL JARQUÍN GALVEZ.

Editorial Diana, SA de CV: Arenal Nº 24, Edif. Norte, Ex-Hacienda Guadalupe, Chimalistac, Del. Alvaro Obregón, 01050 México, DF; tel. (55) 5089-1220; fax (55) 5089-1230; e-mail jlr@diana.com.mx; internet www.editorialdiana.com.mx; f. 1946; general trade and technical books; Pres. and CEO JOSÉ LUIS RAMÍREZ.

Edamex, SA de CV: Heriberto Frias 1104, Col. del Valle, 03100 México, DF; tel. (55) 5559-8588; fax (55) 5575-0555; e-mail info@edamex.com; internet www.edamex.com; arts and literature, sport, journalism, education, philosophy, food, history, children's, health, sociology; Dir-Gen. MONICA COLMENARES.

Ediciones Era, SA de CV: Calle del Trabajo 31, Col. La Fama, Tlalpan, 14269 México, DF; tel. (55) 5528-1221; fax (55) 5606-2904; e-mail edicionesera@laneta.apc.org; internet www.edicionesera.com.mx; f. 1960; general and social science, art and literature; Gen. Man. NIEVES ESPRESATE XIRAU.

Editorial Everest Mexicana, SA: Calzada Ermita Iztapalapa 1631, Col. Barrio San Miguel del Iztapalapa, 09360 México, DF; tel. (55) 5685-1966; fax (55) 5685-3433; f. 1980; general textbooks; Gen. Man. JOSÉ LUIS HUIDOBRO LEÓN.

Espasa Calpe Mexicana, SA: Pitágoras 1139, Col. del Valle, 03100 México, DF; tel. (55) 5575-5022; f. 1948; literature, music, economics, philosophy, encyclopaedia; Man. FRANCISCO CRUZ RUBIO.

Fernández Editores, SA de CV: Eje 1 Pte México-Coyoacán 321, Col. Xoco, 03330 México, DF; tel. (55) 5605-6557; fax (55) 5688-9173; f. 1943; children's literature, textbooks, educational toys; Man. Dir LUIS GERARDO FERNÁNDEZ PÉREZ.

Editorial Fondo de Cultura Económica, SA de CV: Carretera Picacho-Ajusco 227, Col. Bosques del Pedregal, 14200 México, DF; tel. (55) 5227-4672; fax (55) 5227-4640; e-mail editorial@fce.com.mx; f. 1934; economics, history, philosophy, children's books, science, politics, psychology, sociology, literature; Dir Lic. MIGUEL DE LA MADRID.

Editorial Grijalbo, SA de CV: Calzada San Bartolo-Naucalpan 282, Col. Argentina, Apdo 17-568, 11230 México, DF; tel. (55) 5358-4355; fax (55) 5576-3586; e-mail diredit@grijalbo.com.mx; internet www.randomhousemondadori.com.mx; f. 1954; owned by Mondadori (Italy); general fiction, history, sciences, philosophy, children's books; Man. Dir AGUSTÍN CENTENO RÍOS.

Nueva Editorial Interamericana, SA de CV: Cedro 512, Col. Atlampa, Apdo 4-140, 06450 México, DF; tel. (55) 5541-6789; fax (55) 5541-1603; f. 1944; medical publishing; Man. Dir RAFAEL SÁINZ.

Distribuidora Intermex, SA de CV: Lucio Blanco 435, Azcapotzalco, 02400 México, DF; tel. (55) 5230-9500; fax (55) 5230-9516; e-mail pmuhechi@televisa.com.mx; f. 1969; romantic fiction; Gen. Dir Lic. ALEJANDRO PAILLÉS.

McGraw-Hill Interamericana de México, SA de CV: Cedro 512, Col. Atlampa Cuauhtémoc, 06450 México, DF; tel. (55) 5576-7304; fax (55) 5628-5367; e-mail mcgraw-hill@infosel.net.mx; internet www.mcgraw-hill.com.mx; education, business, science; Man. Dir CARLOS RIOS.

Editorial Joaquín Mortiz, SA de CV: Insurgentes Sur 1162, 3°, Col. del Valle, 03100 México, DF; tel. (55) 5575-8585; fax (55) 5559-3483; f. 1962; general literature; Man. Dir Ing. HOMERO GAYOSO ANIMAS.

Editorial Jus, SA de CV: Plaza de Abasolo 14, Col. Guerrero, 06300 México, DF; tel. (55) 5526-0616; fax (55) 5529-0951; f. 1938; history of Mexico, law, philosophy, economy, religion; Man. Dir TOMÁS G. REYNOSO.

Ediciones Larousse, SA de CV: Londres 247, Col. Juárez, Del. Cuauhtémoc, 06600 México, DF; tel. (55) 1102-1300; fax (55) 5208-6225; e-mail larousse@larousse.com.mx; internet www.larousse.com.mx; f. 1965; Dir-Gen. FAROUD AOURAGH.

Editora Latino Americana, SA: Guatemala 10-220, México, DF; popular literature; Dir JORGE H. YÉPEZ.

Editorial Limusa, SA de CV: Balderas 95, 1°, Col. Centro, 06040 México, DF; tel. (55) 5521-2105; fax (55) 5512-2903; e-mail limusa@noriega.com.mx; internet www.noriega.com.mx; f. 1962; science, general, textbooks; Pres. CARLOS NORIEGA MILERA.

Editorial Nuestro Tiempo, SA: Avda Universidad 771, Despachos 103–104, Col. del Valle, 03100 México, DF; tel. (55) 5688-8768; fax (55) 5688-6868; f. 1966; social sciences; Man. Dir ESPERANZA NACIF BARQUET.

Editorial Oasis, SA: Avda Oaxaca 28, 06700 México, DF; tel. (55) 5528-8293; f. 1954; literature, pedagogy, poetry; Man. MARÍA TERESA ESTRADA DE FERNÁNDEZ DEL BUSTO.

Editorial Orión: Sierra Mojada 325, 11000 México, DF; tel. (55) 5520-0224; f. 1942; archaeology, philosophy, psychology, literature, fiction; Man. Dir SILVIA HERNÁNDEZ BALTAZAR.

Editorial Patria, SA de CV: Renacimiento 180, Col. San Juan Tlihuaca, Azcapotzalco, 02400 México, DF; tel. (55) 5561-6042; fax (55) 5561-5231; e-mail info@patriacultural.com; f. 1933; fiction, general trade, children's books; Pres. CARLOS FRIGOLET LERMA.

Editorial Planeta Mexicana, SA de CV: Clavijero 70, Col. Esperanza, México DF; tel. (55) 5533-1250; internet www.editorialplaneta.com.mx; general literature, non-fiction; part of Grupo Planeta (Spain); Man. Dir JOAQUIN DIEZ-CANEDO.

Editorial Porrúa Hnos, SA: Argentina 15, 5°, 06020 México, DF; tel. (55) 5702-4574; fax (55) 5702-6529; e-mail servicios@porrua.com; internet www.porrua.com; f. 1944; general literature; Dir JOSÉ ANTONIO PÉREZ PORRÚA.

Editorial Posada, SA de CV: Eugenia 13, Despacho 501, Col. Nápoles, 03510 México, DF; tel. (55) 5682-0660; f. 1968; general; Dir-Gen. CARLOS VIGIL ZUBIETA.

Editorial Quetzacoatl, SA: Medicina 37, Local 1 y 2, México, DF; tel. (55) 5548-6180; Man. Dir ALBERTO RODRÍGUEZ VALDÉS.

Medios Publicitarios Mexicanos, SA de CV: Eugenia 811, Eje 5 Sur, Col. del Valle, 03100 México, DF; tel. (55) 5523-3342; fax (55) 5523-3379; e-mail editorial@mpm.com.mx; internet www.mpm.com.mx; f. 1958; advertising media rates and data; Man. FERNANDO VILLAMIL AVILA.

Reverté Ediciones, SA de CV: Río Pánuco 141A, 06500 México, DF; tel. (55) 5533-5658; fax (55) 5514-6799; e-mail 101545.2361@compuserve.com; f. 1955; science, technical, architecture; Man. RAMÓN REVERTÉ MASCÓ.

Salvat Mexicana de Ediciones, SA de CV: Presidente Masaryk 101, 5°, 11570 México, DF; tel. (55) 5250-6041; fax (55) 5250-6861; medicine, encyclopaedic works; Dir GUILLERMO HERNÁNDEZ PÉREZ.

Siglo XXI Editores, SA de CV: Avda Cerro del Agua 248, Col. Romero de Terreros, Del. Coyoacán, 04310 México, DF; tel. (55) 5658-7999; fax (55) 5658-7599; e-mail informes@sigloxxieditores.com.mx; internet www.sigloxxieditores.com.mx; f. 1966; art, economics, education, history, social sciences, literature, philology and linguistics, philosophy and political science; Dir-Gen. Lic. JAIME LABASTIDA OCHOA; Gen. Man. Ing. JOSÉ MARÍA CASTRO MUSSOT.

Editorial Trillas, SA: Avda Río Churubusco 385 Pte, Col. Xoco, Apdo 10534, 03330 México, DF; tel. (55) 5688-4233; fax (55) 5601-1858; e-mail trillas@ovinet.com.mx; internet www.trillas.mx; f. 1954; science, technical, textbooks, children's books; Man. Dir FRANCISCO TRILLAS MERCADER.

Universidad Nacional Autónoma de México: Dirección General de Fomento Editorial, Avda del Iman 5, Ciudad Universitaria, 04510 México, DF; tel. (55) 5622-6581; fax (55) 5665-2778; f. 1935; publications in all fields; Dir-Gen. ARTURO VELÁZQUEZ JIMÉNEZ.

MEXICO   Directory

ESTADO DE MÉXICO

Pearson Educación de México, SA de CV: Calle 4, 25, Fraccionamiento Industrial Alce Blanco, 53370 Naucalpan de Juárez, Méx.; tel. (55) 5387-0700; fax (55) 5358-6445; internet www.pearson.com.mx; f. 1984; educational books under the imprints Addison-Wesley, Prentice Hall, Allyn and Bacon, Longman and Scott Foresman; Pres. STEVE MARBAN.

ASSOCIATIONS

Cámara Nacional de la Industria Editorial Mexicana: Holanda 13, Col. San Diego Churubusco, 04120 México, DF; tel. (55) 5688-2011; fax (55) 5604-3147; e-mail cepromex@caniem.com; internet www.caniem.com; f. 1964; Pres. JOSÉ ANGEL QUINTANILLA; Gen. Man. GUILLERMO COCHRAN.

Instituto Mexicano del Libro, AC: México, DF; tel. (55) 5535-2061; Pres. KLAUS THIELE; Sec.-Gen. ISABEL RUIZ GONZÁLEZ.

Prensa Nacional Asociada, SA (PRENASA): Insurgentes Centro 114-411, 06030 México, DF; tel. (55) 5546-7389.

Broadcasting and Communications

TELECOMMUNICATIONS

Regulatory Authorities

Comisión Federal de Telecomunicaciones (Cofetel): Bosque de Radiatas 44, 4°, Col. Bosques de las Lomas, Del. Cuajimalpa, 05120 México, DF; tel. and fax (55) 5261-4000; e-mail nuevaimagen@cft.gob.mx; internet www.cofetel.gob.mx; Pres. JORGE ARREDONDO MARTÍNEZ.

Dirección General de Politica de Telecomunicaciones: Eje Central Lazaro Cardeñas 567, Torre Telecomunicaciones, 15° Ala Sur, Col. Narvarte, Del. Benito Juárez, 03028 México, DF; tel. (55) 5519-1993; fax (55) 5530-1816; e-mail buzon_dgpt@sct.gob.mx; Dir Ing. LEONEL LÓPEZ CELAYA.

Dirección General de Telecomunicaciones: Lázaro Cárdenas 567, 11°, Ala Norte, Col. Narvarte, 03020 México, DF; tel. (55) 5519-9161; Dir-Gen. Ing. ENRIQUE LUENGAS H.

Principal Operators

Alestra: Paseo de las Palmas 405, Col. Lomas de Chapulţepec, 11000 México, DF; internet www.alestra.com.mx; 49% owned by AT&T; Dir-Gen. ROLANDO ZUBIRÁN SHETLER.

America Movil, SA de CV (Telcel): Lago Alberto, 366 Col. Anáhuac, 11320 México, DF; internet www.telcel.com; CEO DANIEL HAJJ.

Avantel: Liverpool 88, Col. Juárez, 06600 México, DF; e-mail webmaster@avantel.com.mx; internet www.avantel.net.mx; f. 1994; Dir-Gen. OSCAR RODRÍGUEZ MARTÍNEZ.

Carso Global Telecom, SA de CV: Insurgentientes Sur 3500, Col. Peña Pobre, 14060 México DF; tel. (55) 5726-3686; fax (55) 5238-0601; internet www.cgtelecom.com.mx; Chair. CARLOS SLIM DOMIT.

Grupo Iusacell, SA de CV: Avda Prolongación Paseo de la Reforma 1236, Col. Santa Fe, 05438 México, DF; e-mail webmaster@iusacell.com.mx; internet www.iusacell.com.mx; f. 1992; operates mobile cellular telephone network; 74% owned by Móvil Access; Dir-Gen. GUSTAVO GUZMÁN SEPÚLVEDA.

Telecomunicaciones de México (TELECOMM): Torre Central de Telecomunicaciones, Eje Central Lázaro Cárdenas 567, 11°, Ala Norte, Col. Narvarte, 03020 México, DF; tel. (55) 5629-1166; fax (55) 5559-9812; internet www.sct.gob.mx; govt-owned; Dir-Gen. ANDRÉS FIGUEROA COBIÁN.

Telefónica México: Prolongación Paseo de la Reforma 1200, Lote B-2, Col. Santa Fe, Cruz Manca, 05348 México, DF; tel. (55) 1616-5000; internet www.telefonicamoviles.com.mx; operates mobile telephone service Telefónica Móviles (MoviStar), telecommunications co Telefónica Data; controls Pegaso, Cedetel, Norcel, Movitel and Baja Celular; owned by Telefónica, SA (Spain).

Teléfonos de México, SA de CV (Telmex): Parque Via 198, Of. 701, Col. Cuauhtémoc, 06599 México, DF; tel. (55) 5222-5462; fax (55) 5545-5500; internet www.telmex.com.mx; Dir-Gen. CARLOS SLIM DOMIT.

BROADCASTING

Regulatory Authorities

Cámara Nacional de la Industria de Radio y Televisión (CIRT): Horacio 1013, Col. Polanco Reforma, Del. Miguel Hidalgo, 11550 México, DF; tel. (55) 5726-9909; fax (55) 5545-6767; e-mail cirt@cirt.com.mx; internet www.cirt.com.mx; f. 1942; Pres. ALEJANDRO GARCÍA GAMBOA; Dir CESAR HERNÁNDEZ ESPEJO.

Dirección General de Radio, Televisión y Cine (RTC): Secretaría de Gobernación, Bucareli 99, Col. Juaréz, Del. Cuahtémoc, 06600 México, DF; internet www.rtc.gob.mx; tel. (55) 5566-0262.

Dirección de Normas de Radiodifusión: Eugenia 197, 1°, Col. Narvarte, 03020 México, DF; tel. (55) 5590-4372; e-mail amilpg@sct.gob.mx; internet www.sct.gob.mx; licence-issuing authority; Dir Dr ALFONSO AMILPAS.

Instituto Mexicano de Televisión: Anillo Periférico Sur 4121, Col. Fuentes del Pedregal, 14141 México, DF; tel. (55) 5568-5684; Dir-Gen. Lic. JOSÉ ANTONIO ALVAREZ LIMA.

Radio

There were 1,423 radio stations in Mexico in 2004. Among the most important commercial networks are:

ARTSA: Avda de Los Virreyes 1030, Col. Lomas de Chapultepec, 11000 México, DF; tel. (55) 5202-3344; fax (55) 5202-6940; Dir-Gen. Lic. GUSTAVO ECHEVARRÍA ARCE.

Corporación Mexicana de Radiodifusión: Tetitla 23, esq. Calle Coapa, Col. Toriello Guerra, 14050 México, DF; tel. (55) 5424-6380; fax (55) 5666-5422; e-mail comentarios@cmr.com.mx; internet www.cmr.com.mx; Pres. ENRIQUE BERNAL SERVÍN; Dir-Gen. OSCAR BELTRÁN.

Firme, SA: Gauss 10, Col. Nueva Anzures, 11590 México, DF; tel. (55) 55250-7788; fax (55) 5250-7788; Dir-Gen. LUIS IGNACIO SANTIBÁÑEZ.

Grupo Acir, SA: Monte Pirineos 770, Col. Lomas de Chapultepec, 11000 México, DF; tel. (55) 5540-4291; fax (55) 5540-4106; f. 1965; comprises 140 stations; Pres. FRANCISCO IBARRA LÓPEZ.

Grupo Radio Centro, SA de CV: Constituyentes 1154, Col. Lomas Atlas, Del. Miguel Hidalgo, 11950 México, DF; tel. (55) 5728-4947; fax (55) 5259-2915; f. 1965; comprises 100 radio stations; Pres. ADRIÁN AGUIRRE GÓMEZ; Dir-Gen. Ing. GILBERTO SOLIS SILVA.

Grupo Siete Comunicácion: Montecito 38, 31°, Of. 33, México, DF; tel. (55) 5488-0887; e-mail jch@gruposiete.com.mx; internet www.gruposiete.com.mx; f. 1997; Pres. Lic. FRANCISCO JAVIER SÁNCHEZ CAMPUZANO.

Instituto Mexicano de la Radio (IMER): Mayorazgo 83, 2°, Col. Xoco, 03330 México, DF; tel. (55) 5628-1730; f. 1983; Dir-Gen. CARLOS LARA SUMANO.

MVS Radio Stereorey y FM Globo: Mariano Escobedo 532, Col. Anzures, 11590 México, DF; tel. (55) 5203-4574; fax (55) 5255-1425; e-mail vargas@data.net.mx; f. 1968; Pres. Lic. JOAQUÍN VARGAS G; Vice-Pres. Lic. ADRIÁN VARGAS G.

Núcleo Radio Mil: Prolongación Paseo de la Reforma 115, Col. Paseo de las Lomas, Santa Fe, 01330 México, DF; tel. (55) 5258-1200; e-mail radiomil@rnm.com.mx; internet www.nrm.com.mx; f. 1942; comprises seven radio stations; Pres. and Dir-Gen. Lic. E. GUILLERMO SALAS PEYRÓ.

Organización Radio Centro: Artículo 123, No 90, Col. Centro, 06050 México, DF; tel. (55) 5709-2220; fax (55) 512-8588; nine stations in Mexico City; Pres. MARÍA ESTHER GÓMEZ DE AGUIRRE.

Organización Radiofónica de México, SA: Tuxpan 39, 8°, Col. Roma Sur, 06760 México, DF; tel. (55) 5264-2025; fax (55) 5264-5720; Pres. JAIME FERNÁNDEZ ARMENDÁRIZ.

Radio Cadena Nacional, SA (RCN): Lago Victoria 78, Col. Granada, 11520 México, DF; tel. (55) 2624-0401; e-mail loregonzalez@rcn.com.mx; internet www.rcn.com.mx; f. 1948; Pres. RAFAEL C. NAVARRO ARRONTE; Dir-Gen. SERGIO FAJARDO ORTIZ.

Radio Comerciales, SA de CV: Avda México y López Mateos, 44680 Guadalajara, Jal.; tel. (33) 615-0852; fax (33) 630-3487; 7 major commercial stations.

Radio Educación: Angel Urraza 622, Col. del Valle, 03100 México, DF; tel. (55) 1500-1015; fax (55) 1500-1053; e-mail direccion@radioeducacion.edu.mx; internet www.radioeducacion.edu.mx; f. 1968; Dir-Gen. LIDIA CAMACHO.

Radio Fórmula, SA: Privada de Horacio 10, Col. Polanco, 11560 México, DF; tel. (55) 282-1016; Dir Lic. ROGERIO AZCARRAGA.

Radiodifusoras Asociadas, SA de CV (RASA): Durango 331, 2°, Col. Roma, 06700 México, DF; tel. (55) 5553-6620; fax (55) 5286-2774; f. 1956; Pres. JOSÉ LARIS ITURBIDE; Dir-Gen. JOSÉ LARIS RODRÍGUEZ.

Radiodifusores Asociados de Innovación y Organización, SA: Emerson 408, Col. Chapultepec Morales, 11570 México, DF; tel. (55) 5203-5577; fax (55) 5545-2078; Dir-Gen. Lic. CARLOS QUIÑONES ARMENDÁRIZ.

Radiópolis, SA de CV: owned by Grupo Televisa and Grupo Prisa; owns 5 radio stations; affiliated to Radiorama, SA de CV (q.v.) in 2004; Dir-Gen. RAÚL RODRÍGUEZ GONZÁLEZ.

Radiorama, SA de CV: Reforma 56, 5°, 06600 México, DF; tel. (55) 5566-1515; fax (55) 5566-1454; Dir JOSÉ LUIS C. RESÉNDIZ.

Representaciones Comerciales Integrales: Avda Chapultepec 431, Col. Juárez, 06600 México, DF; tel. (55) 5533-6185; Dir-Gen. ALFONSO PALMA V.

Sistema Radio Juventud: Pablo Casals 567, Prados Providencia, 44670 Guadalajara, Jal.; tel. (33) 641-6677; fax (33) 641-3413; f. 1975; network of several stations including Estereo Soul 89.9 FM; Dirs ALBERTO LEAL A., J. JESÚS OROZCO G., GABRIEL ARREGUI V.

Sistema Radiofónico Nacional, SA: Baja California 163, Of. 602, 06760 México, DF; tel. (55) 5574-0298; f. 1971; represents commercial radio networks; Dir-Gen. RENÉ C. DE LA ROSA.

Sociedad Mexicana de Radio, SA de CV (SOMER): Gutenberg 89, Col. Anzures, 11590 México, DF; tel. (55) 5255-5297; fax (55) 5545-0310; Dir-Gen. EDILBERTO HUESCA PERROTIN.

Radio Insurgente, the underground radio station of the Ejército Zapatista de Liberación Nacional (EZLN—Zapatistas), is broadcast from south-eastern Mexico. Programmes can be found on www.radioinsurgente.org.

Television

There were 658 television stations in 2004. Among the most important are:

Asesoramiento y Servicios Técnicos Industriales, SA (ASTISA): México, DF; tel. (55) 5585-3333; commercial; Dir ROBERTO CHÁVEZ TINAJERO.

MVS (Multivisión): Blvd Puerto Aéreo 486, Col. Moctezuma, 15500 México, DF; tel. (55) 5764-8100; internet www.mvs.com; subscriber-funded.

Once TV: Carpio 475, Col. Casco de Santo Tomás, 11340 México, DF; tel. (55) 5356-1111; fax (55) 5396-8001; e-mail canal11@vmredipn.ipn.mx; f. 1959; Dir-Gen. ALEJANDRA LAJOUS VARGAS.

Tele Cadena Mexicana, SA: Avda Chapultepec 18, 06724 México, DF; tel. (55) 5535-1679; commercial, comprises about 80 stations; Dir Lic. JORGE ARMANDO PIÑA MEDINA.

Televisa, SA de CV: Edif. Televicentro, Avda Chapultepec 28, Col. Doctores, 06724 México, DF; tel. (55) 5709-3333; fax (55) 5709-3021; e-mail webmaster@televisa.com.mx; internet www.televisa.com; f. 1973; commercial; began broadcasts to Europe via satellite in Dec. 1988 through its subsidiary, Galavisión; 406 affiliated stations; Chair. and CEO EMILIO AZCÁRRAGA JEAN; Vice-Pres. ALEJANDRO BURILLO AZCÁRRAGA.

Televisión Azteca, SA de CV: Anillo Periférico Sur 4121, Col. Fuentes del Pedregal, 14141 México, DF; tel. (55) 5420-1313; fax (55) 5645-4258; e-mail webtva@tvazteca.com; internet tvazteca.todito.com; f. 1992; assumed responsibility for fmr state-owned channels 7 and 13; Pres. RICARDO B. SALINAS PLIEGO; CEO PEDRO PADILLA LONGORIA.

Televisión de la República Mexicana: Mina 24, Col. Guerrero, México, DF; tel. (55) 5510-8590; cultural; Dir EDUARDO LIZALDE.

As a member of the Intelsat international consortium, Mexico has received communications via satellite since the 1960s. The launch of the Morelos I and Morelos II satellites, in 1985, provided Mexico with its own satellite communications system. The Morelos satellites were superseded by a new satellite network, Solidaridad, which was inaugurated in early 1994. In late 1997 Mexico's three satellites (grouped in a newly formed company, SatMex) were transferred to private ownership.

Finance

(cap. = capital; res = reserves; dep. = deposits; m. = million; amounts in new pesos unless otherwise stated)

BANKING

The Mexican banking system is comprised of the Banco de México (the central bank of issue), multiple or commercial banking institutions and development banking institutions. Banking activity is regulated by the Federal Government.

Commercial banking institutions are constituted as *Sociedades Anónimas*, with wholly private social capital. Development banking institutions exist as *Sociedades Nacionales de Crédito*, participation in their capital is exclusive to the Federal Government, notwithstanding the possibility of accepting limited amounts of private capital. In 2005 there were 34 commercial and development banks operating in Mexico and 71 foreign banks maintained offices.

All private banks were nationalized in September 1982. By July 1992, however, the banking system had been completely returned to the private sector. Legislation removing all restrictions on foreign ownership of banks received congressional approval in 1999.

Supervisory Authority

Comisión Nacional Bancaria y de Valores (CNBV) (National Banking and Securities Commission): Avda Insurgentes Sur 1971, Torre Norte, Sur y III, Col. Guadalupe Inn, Del. Alvaro Obregón, 01020 México, DF; tel. and fax (55) 5724-6000; e-mail info@cnbv.gob.mx; internet www.cnbv.gob.mx; f. 1924; govt commission controlling all credit institutions in Mexico; Pres. JONATHAN DAVIS ARZAC.

Central Bank

Banco de México (BANXICO): Avda 5 de Mayo 1, Col. Centro, Del. Cuauhtémoc, 06059 México, DF; tel. (55) 5237-2000; fax (55) 5237-2070; e-mail comsoc@banxico.org.mx; internet www.banxico.org.mx; f. 1925; currency issuing authority; became autonomous on 1 April 1994; cap. 4,869.0m., res 15,000.0m., dep. 526,808.0m. (Dec. 2003); Gov. Dr GUILLERMO ORTIZ MARTÍNEZ; 6 brs.

Commercial Banks

Banca Serfín, SA: Mod 409, 4°, Prolongación Paseo de la Reforma 500, Col. Lomas de Santa Fe, 01219 México, DF; tel. (55) 5259-8860; fax (55) 5257-8387; internet www.serfin.com.mx; f. 1864; merged with Banco Continental Ganadero in 1985; transferred to private ownership in Jan. 1992; acquired by Banco Santander Central Hispano (Spain) in Dec. 2000; cap. 6,874.9m., res 2,982.7m., dep. 96,919.7m. (Dec. 2003); Chair. and Pres. CARLOS GÓMEZ; CEO and Gen. Man. ADOLFO LAGOS ESPINOSA; 554 brs.

Banco del Bajío, SA: Avda Manuel J. Clouthier 508, Col. Jardines del Campestre, 37128 León, Gto; tel. (477) 710-4600; fax (477) 710-4693; e-mail internacional@bancobajio.com.mx; internet www.bancobajio.com.mx; f. 1994; cap. 1,285.1m., res −17.0m., dep. 10,995.4m. (Dec. 2003); Pres. SALVADOR OÑATE; Gen. Man. CARLOS DE LA CERDA SERRANO.

Banco Mercantil del Norte, SA (BANORTE): Avda Morones Prieto 2312 Pte, 2°, Col Lomas de San Francisco, 64710 Monterrey, NL; tel. (81) 3319-7200; fax (81) 3319-5216; internet www.banorte.com; f. 1899; merged with Banco Regional del Norte in 1985; cap. 5,351.8m., res 1,332.8m., dep. 179,725.6m. (Dec. 2002); Chair. ROBERTO GONZÁLEZ BARRERA; CEO LUIS PEÑA KEGEL; 457 brs.

Banco Nacional de México, SA (Banamex): Roberto Medellín 800, Col. Santa Fe, 01210 México, DF; tel. (55) 5720-7091; fax (55) 5920-7323; internet www.banamex.com; f. 1884; transferred to private ownership in 1991; merged with Citibank México, SA in 2001; cap. 25,551.0m., res 22,922.0m., dep. 305,063.0m. (Dec. 2003); CEO MANUEL MEDINA MORA; 1,260 brs.

BBVA Bancomer, SA: Centro Bancomer, Avda Universidad 1200, Col. Xoco, 03339 México, DF; tel. (55) 5621-3434; fax (55) 5621-3230; internet www.bancomer.com.mx; f. 2000 by merger of Bancomer (f. 1864) and Mexican operations of Banco Bilbao Vizcaya Argentaria (Spain); privatized in 2002; cap. 67,283.2m., res −22,306.5m., dep. 358,537.3m. (Dec. 2002); Chair. RICARDO GUAJARDO TOUCHÉ.

HSBC México: Paseo de la Reforma 156, Col. Juárez, Del. Cuauhtémoc, 06600 México, DF; tel. (55) 5721-2222; fax (55) 5721-2393; internet www.hsbc.com.mx; f. 1941; bought by HSBC (UK) in 2002; name changed from Banco Internacional, SA (BITAL) in 2004; cap. 14,962.0m., res 662.1m., dep. 141,533.3m. (Dec. 2002); Gen. Man. and CEO ALEXANDER FLOCKHART; 1,400 brs.

Scotiabank Inverlat, SA: Blvd Miguel Avila Camacho 1, 18°, Col. Polanco, Del. Miguel Hidalgo, 11009 México, DF; tel. (55) 5728-1000; fax (55) 5229-2157; internet www.inverlat.com.mx; f. 1977 as Multibanco Comermex, SA; changed name to Banco Inverlat, SA 1995; 55% holding acquired by Scotiabank Group (Canada) and name changed as above 2001; cap. 2,957.8m., res 1,240.1m., dep. 73,860.3m. (Dec. 2002); CEO ANATOL VON HANN; 371 brs.

Development Banks

Banco Nacional de Comercio Exterior, SNC (BANCOMEXT): Camino a Santa Teresa 1679, Jardines de Pedegral, Del. Álvaro Obregón, 14210 México, DF; tel. (55) 5481-6000; fax (55) 5449-9030; internet www.bancomext.com; f. 1937; cap. 19,324.0m., res −12,152.0m., dep. 44,544.0m. (Dec. 2003); Man. Dir ENRIQUE VILATELA RIBA.

Banco Nacional del Ejército, Fuerza Aérea y Armada, SNC (BANJERCITO): Avda Industria Militar 1055, Col. Lomas de Sotelo, 11200 México, DF; tel. and fax (55) 5626-6290; internet www.banjercito.com.mx; f. 1947; Dir-Gen. Brig.-Gen. FERNANDO MILLÁN VILLEGAS; 51 brs.

Banco Nacional de Obras y Servicios Públicos, SNC (BANOBRAS): Avda Javier Barros Sierra 515, Col. Lomas de Santa Fe, México, DF; tel. (55) 5270-1200; fax (55) 5723-6108; e-mail bneumann@banobras.gob.mx; internet www.banobras.gob.mx; f. 1933; govt-owned; cap. 8,176.4m., res 1,743.1m., dep. 118,041.0m. (Dec. 2001); Chair. Dr GUILLERMO ORTIZ MARTÍNEZ.

Nacional Financiera, SNC: Insurgentes Sur 1971, Torre IV, 13°, Col. Guadalupe Inn, 01020 México, DF; tel. (55) 5325-6700; fax (55) 5661-8418; e-mail info@nafin.gob.mx; internet www.nafin.com; f. 1934; cap. 6,777.2m, res 253.9m., dep. 253,542.4m. (Dec. 2003);

MEXICO

Chair. JOSÉ ANGEL GURRIA TREVINO; Pres. CARLOS SALES GUTIÉRREZ; 32 brs.

Foreign Bank

Dresdner Bank Mexico, SA: Bosque de Alisos 47A, 4°, Col. Bosques de las Lomas, 05120 México, DF; tel. (55) 5258-3170; fax (55) 5258-3199; e-mail mexico@dbla.com; f. 1995; Man. Dir LUIS NIÑO DE RIVERA.

BANKERS' ASSOCIATION

Asociación de Banqueros de México: 16 de Setiembre 27, Col. Centro Histórico, 06000 México, DF; tel. (55) 5722-4305; internet www.abm.org.mx; f. 1928; fmrly Asociación Mexicano de Bancos; Pres. MARCOS MARTÍNEZ; Dir-Gen. Lic. ADOLFO RIVAS MARTIN DEL CAMPO; 52 mems.

STOCK EXCHANGE

Bolsa Mexicana de Valores, SA de CV: Paseo de la Reforma 255, Col. Cuauhtémoc, 06500 México, DF; tel. (55) 5726-6794; fax (55) 5726-6836; e-mail cinforma@bmv.com.mx; internet www.bmv.com.mx; f. 1894; Pres. GUILLERMO PRIETO DE CASTILLA; Dir-Gen. Ing. GERARDO FLORES DEUCHLER.

INSURANCE
México, DF

ACE Seguros: Bosques de Alisos, 47A, 1°, Col. Bosques de las Lomas, 5120 México, DF; tel. (5) 258-5800; fax (5) 258-5899; e-mail info@acelatinamerica.com; f. 1990; fmrly Seguros Cigna.

Aseguradora Cuauhtémoc, SA: Manuel Avila Camacho 164, 11570 México, DF; tel. (55) 5250-9800; fax (55) 5540-3204; f. 1944; general; Exec. Pres. JUAN B. RIVEROLL; Dir-Gen. JAVIER COMPEÁN AMEZCUA.

Aseguradora Hidalgo, SA: Presidente Masaryk 111, Col. Polanco, Del. Miguel Hidalgo, 11570 México, DF; f. 1931; life; Dir-Gen. JOSÉ GÓMEZ GORDOA; Man. Dir HUMBERTO ROQUE VILLANUEVA.

ING Comercial América—Seguros: Insurgentes Sur 3900, Col. Tlalpan, 14000 México, DF; tel. (55) 5169-2500; internet www.comercialamerica.com.mx; f. 1936 as La Comercial; acquired by ING Group in 2000; life, etc.; Pres. GLENN HILLIARS; Dir-Gen. Ing. ADRIÁN PÁEZ.

La Nacional, Cía de Seguros, SA: México, DF; f. 1901; life, etc.; Pres. CLEMENTE CABELLO; Chair. Lic. ALBERTO BAILLERES.

Pan American de México, Cía de Seguros, SA: México, DF; f. 1940; Pres. Lic. JESS N. DALTON; Dir-Gen. GILBERTO ESCOBEDA PAZ.

Royal & SunAlliance Mexico: Blvd Adolfo López Mateos 2448, Col. Altavista, 01060 México, DF; tel. (55) 5723-7999; fax (55) 5723-7941; e-mail omar.antonio@mx.royalsun.com; internet www.royalsun.com.mx; f. 1941; acquired Seguros BBV-Probursa in 2001; general, except life.

Seguros Azteca, SA: Insurgentes 102, México, DF; f. 1933; general including life; Pres. JUAN CAMPO RODRÍGUEZ.

Seguros Banamex, SA: Isabel la Católica 44, Col Centro Histórico, Del. Cuauhtémoc, 06000 México, DF; e-mail sbainternet@banamex.com; internet www.segurosbanamex.com; f. 1994; life, accident and health; Pres. AGUSTÍN F. LEGORRETA; Dir-Gen. JUAN OROZCO GÓMEZ PORTUGAL.

Seguros Constitución, SA: Avda Revolución 2042, Col. La Otra Banda, 01090 México, DF; tel. (55) 5550-7910; f. 1937; life, accident; Pres. ISIDORO RODRÍGUEZ RUIZ; Dir-Gen. ALFONSO DE ORDUÑA Y PÉREZ.

Seguros el Fénix, SA: México, DF; f. 1937; Pres. VICTORIANO OLAZÁBAL E.; Dir-Gen. JAIME MATUTE LABRADOR.

Seguros Internacional, SA: Abraham González 67, México, DF; f. 1945; general; Pres. Lic. GUSTAVO ROMERO KOLBECK.

Seguros de México, SA: Insurgentes Sur 3496, Col. Peña Pobre, 14060 México, DF; tel. (55) 5679-3855; f. 1957; life, etc.; Dir-Gen. Lic. ANTONIO MIJARES RICCI.

Seguros La Provincial, SA: México, DF; f. 1936; general; Pres. CLEMENTE CABELLO; Chair. ALBERTO BAILLERES.

Seguros La República, SA: Paseo de la Reforma 383, México, DF; f. 1966; general; 43% owned by Commercial Union (United Kingdom); Pres. LUCIANO ARECHEDERRA QUINTANA; Gen. Man. JUAN ANTONIO DE ARRIETA MENDIZÁBAL.

Guadalajara, Jal.

Nueva Galicia, Compañía de Seguros Generales, SA: Guadalajara, Jal.; f. 1946; fire; Pres. SALVADOR VEYTIA Y VEYTIA.

Monterrey, NL

Seguros Monterrey Aetna, SA: Avda Diagonal Santa Engracia 221 Oeste, Col. Lomas de San Francisco, 64710 Monterrey, NL; tel.

Directory

(81) 319-1111; fax (81) 363-0428; f. 1940; casualty, life, etc.; Dir-Gen. FEDERICO REYES GARCÍA.

Seguros Monterrey del Círculo Mercantil, SA, Sociedad General de Seguros: Padre Mier Pte 276, Monterrey, NL; f. 1941; life; Gen. Man. CARMEN G. MASSO DE NAVARRO.

Insurance Association

Asociación Mexicana de Instituciones de Seguros, AC (AMIS): Fco I Madero 21, Col. Tlacopac, San Angel, 01040 México, DF; tel. (55) 5662-6161; e-mail amis@mail.internet.com.mx; internet www.amis.com.mx; f. 1946; all insurance cos operating in Mexico are mems; Pres. ROLANDO VEGA SAÉNZ; Dir-Gen. RECAREDO ARIAS JIMÉNEZ.

Trade and Industry
GOVERNMENT AGENCIES

Comisión Federal de Protección Contra Riesgos Sanitarios (COFEPRIS): Monterrey 33, Esq. Oaxaca, Col. Roma, Del. Cuauhtémoc, 06700 Mexico, DF; tel. (55) 5280-5200; e-mail contacto_cofepris@salud.gob.mx; internet www.cofepris.gob.mx; f. 2003; pharmaceutical regulatory authority; Sec.-Gen. ALEJANDRA OLGUÍN RAMÍREZ.

Comisión Nacional Forestal (CONAFOR): Carretera a Nogales s/n, Esq. Periférico Pte. 5°, San Juan de Ocotán, 45019 Zapopan, Jal.; tel. (33) 3777-7077; fax (33) 3770-7078; e-mail transparencia@conafor.gob.mx; internet www.conafor.gob.mx; f. 2001; Dir-Gen. Ing. MANUEL AGUSTÍN REED SEGOVIA.

Comisión Nacional de Precios: Avda Juárez 101, 17°, México 1, DF; tel. (55) 5510-0436; f. 1977; national prices commission; Dir-Gen. JESÚS SÁNCHEZ JIMÉNEZ.

Comisión Nacional de los Salarios Mínimos (CNSM): Avda Cuauhtémoc 14, 2°, Col. Doctores, 06720 México 7, DF; tel. (55) 5761-5778; fax (55) 5578-5775; f. 1962, in accordance with Section VI of Article 123 of the Constitution; national commission on minimum salaries; Pres. Lic. BASILIO GONZÁLEZ-NUÑEZ; Tech. Dir ALIDA BERNAL COSIO.

Consejo Mexicano de Comercio Exterior (CONCE): Lancaster 15, Col. Juárez, 06600 México, DF; tel. (52) 5231-7100; fax (55) 5321-7109; e-mail comce@comce.org.mx; internet www.comce.org.mx; f. 1999 to promote international trade; Chair. FEDERICO SADA GONZÁLEZ.

Consejo Nacional de Comercio Exterior, AC (CONACEX): Avda Parque Fundidora 501, Of. 95E, Edif. CINTERMEX, Col. Obrera, 64010 Monterrey, NL; tel. (81) 369-0284; fax (81) 369-0293; e-mail conacex@technet.net.mx; f. 1962 to promote national exports; Chair. Ing. JAVIER PRIETO DE LA FUENTE; Pres. Lic. JUAN MANUEL QUIROGA LAM.

Instituto Nacional de Investigaciones Nucleares (ININ): Centro Nuclear de México, Carretera México–Toluca km 36.5, 52045 Ocoyoacac, Méx.; tel. (55) 5329-7200; fax (55) 5329-7298; e-mail webmaster@nuclear.inin.mx; internet www.inin.mx; f. 1979 to plan research and devt of nuclear science and technology; also researches the peaceful uses of nuclear energy, for the social, scientific and technological devt of the country; administers the Secondary Standard Dosimetry Laboratory, the Nuclear Information and Documentation Centre, which serves Mexico's entire scientific community; operates a tissue culture laboratory for medical treatment; the 1 MW research reactor which came into operation, in 1967, supplies part of Mexico's requirements for radioactive isotopes; also operates a 12 MV Tandem van de Graaff. Mexico has two nuclear reactors, each with a generating capacity of 654 MW; the first, at Laguna Verde, became operational in 1989 and is administered by the Comisión Federal de Electricidad (CFE); Dir-Gen. JOSÉ RAÚL ORTÍZ MAGAÑA.

Instituto Nacional de Pesca (National Fishery Institute): Pitágoras 1320, Col. Santa Cruz Atoyac, Del. Juárez, 03310 México, DF; tel. (55) 5688-1469; fax (55) 5604-9169; e-mail compean@inp.sagarpa.gob.mx; internet inp.sagarpa.gob.mx; f. 1962; Dir GUILLERMO COMPEAN JIMÉNEZ.

Procuraduría Federal del Consumidor (Profeco): Dr Carmona y Valle 11, Col. Doctores, 06720 México, DF; tel. (55) 5761-3021; internet www.profeco.gob.mx; f. 1975; consumer protection; Procurator CARLOS ARCE MACÍAS.

Servicio Geológico Mexicano: Blvd Felipe Angeles, Carretera México–Pachuca, km 93.5, Col. Venta Prieta, 42080 Pachuca, HI; tel. (771) 771-4016; fax (771) 771-3938; e-mail dirgeneral@coremisgm.gob.mx; internet www.coremisgm.gob.mx; f. 1957; govt agency for the devt of mineral resources; Dir-Gen. Ing. FRANCISCO JOSÉ ESCANDÓN VALLE.

MEXICO

DEVELOPMENT ORGANIZATIONS

Centro de Investigación para el Desarollo, AC (CIDAC) (Centre of Research for Development): Jaime Balmes 11, Edif. D-2, Col. Los Morales Polanco, 11510 México, DF; tel. (55) 5985-1010; fax (55) 5985-1030; e-mail info@cidac.org.mx; internet www.cidac.org; f. 1984; researches economic and political development.

Comisión Nacional de las Zonas Aridas: Blvd Venustiano Carranza 1623, Col. República, 25280 Saltillo, Coah.; e-mail uenlace@conaza.gob.mx; internet www.conaza.gob.mx; f. 1970; commission to co-ordinate the devt and use of arid areas; Dir-Gen. Lic. EDUARDO TERRAZAS RAMOS.

Fideicomiso de Fomento Mineiro (Fifomi): Puente de Tecamachalco 26, 2°, Col. Lomas de Chapultepec, Del. Miguel Hidalgo, 11000 México, DF; tel. (55) 5202-0968; e-mail pguerra@fifomi.gob.mx; internet www.fifomi.gob.mx; trust for the devt of the mineral industries; Dir-Gen. PEDRO GUERRA MENÉNDEZ.

Fideicomisos Instituídos en Relación con la Agricultura (FIRA): Km 8, Antigua Carretera Pátzucuaro, 58341 Morelia, Mich.; tel. (443) 322-2390; fax (443) 327-7860; e-mail webmaster@correo.fira.gob.mx; internet www.fira.gob.mx; Dir FRANCISCO MERÉ PALAFOX; a group of devt funds to aid agricultural financing, under the Banco de México, comprising:

Fondo de Garantía y Fomento para la Agricultura, Ganadería y Avicultura (FOGAGA): f. 1954.

Fondo Especial para Financiamientos Agropecuarios (FEFA): f. 1965.

Fondo Especial de Asistencia Técnica y Garantía para Créditos Agropecuarios (FEGA): f. 1972.

Fondo de Garantía y Fomento para las Actividades Pesqueras (FOPESCA).

Fondo de Operación y Financiamiento Bancario a la Vivienda (FOVI): Ejército Nacional 180, Col. Anzures, 11590 México, DF; tel. (55) 5263-4500; fax (55) 5263-4541; e-mail jmartinez@fovi.gob.mx; internet www.fovi.gob.mx; f. 1963 to promote the construction of low-cost housing through savings and credit schemes; devt fund under the Banco de México; Dir-Gen. Lic. MANUEL ZEPEDA PAYERAS.

Instituto Mexicano del Petróleo (IMP): Eje Central Lázaro Cárdenas 152, Col. Bernardo Atepehuacan, Del. Gustavo A. Madero, 07730 México, DF; tel. (55) 9175-6000; fax (55) 9175-8000; e-mail sabugalp@imp.mx; internet www.imp.mx; f. 1965 to foster devt of the petroleum, chemical and petrochemical industries; Dir GUSTAVO A. CHAPELA CASTAÑARES.

CHAMBERS OF COMMERCE

American Chamber of Commerce of Mexico (Amcham): Lucerna 78, Col Juárez, 06600 México, DF; tel. (55) 5141-3800; fax (55) 5703-3908; e-mail amchammx@amcham.com.mx; internet www.amcham.com.mx; f. 1917; brs in Guadalajara and Monterrey; Exec. Vice-Pres. and CEO LARRY D. RUBIN.

Confederación de Cámaras Nacionales de Comercio, Servicios y Turismo (CONCANACO-SERVYTUR) (Confederation of National Chambers of Commerce, Services and Tourism): Balderas 144, 3°, Col. Centro, 06079 México, DF; tel. (55) 5772-9300; fax (55) 5709-1152; e-mail gerardo@concanacored.com; internet www.concanacored.com; f. 1917; Pres. RAÚL ALEJANDRO PADILLA OROZCO; Dir-Gen. Lic. ANA MARÍA AMEZCUA RÍOS; comprises 283 regional Chambers.

Cámara de Comercio, Servicios y Turismo Ciudad de México (CANACO) (Chamber of Commerce, Services and Tourism of Mexico City): Paseo de la Reforma 42, 3°, Col. Centro, Apdo 32005, 06048 México, DF; tel. (55) 5592-2677; fax (55) 5592-2279; internet www.ccmexico.com.mx; f. 1874; 50,000 mems; Pres. MANUEL TRON CAMPOS; Dir-Gen. Lic. EDUARDO GARCÍA VILLASEÑOR.

Cámara Nacional de la Industria de Transformación (CANACINTRA): Avda San Antonio 256, Col. Ampliación Nápoles, Del. Juárez, México, DF; tel. (55) 5482-3000; internet contacto@canacintra-digital.com.mx; internet www.canacintra.org.mx; represents majority of smaller manufacturing businesses; Pres. CUAUHTÉMOC MARTÍNEZ GARCÍA; Dir-Gen. ANGÉLICA RUBÍ RUBÍ.

Chambers of Commerce exist in the chief town of each state as well as in the larger centres of commercial activity. There are also other international Chambers of Commerce.

CHAMBERS OF INDUSTRY

The 46 National Chambers, 19 Regional Chambers, 3 General Chambers and 40 Associations, many of which are located in the Federal District, are representative of the major industries of the country.

Central Confederation

Confederación de Cámaras Industriales de los Estados Unidos Mexicanos (CONCAMIN) (Confed. of Industrial Chambers): Manuel María Contreras 133, 7°, Col. Cuauhtémoc, 06500 México, DF; tel. (55) 5140-7800; fax (55) 5140-7831; e-mail webmaster@concamin.org.mx; internet www.concamin.org.mx; f. 1918; represents and promotes the activities of the entire industrial sector; Pres. LÉON HALKIN BIDER; Dir-Gen. GERARDO BARRIOS ESPINOSA; 108 mem. orgs.

INDUSTRIAL AND TRADE ASSOCIATIONS

Asociación Nacional de Importadores y Exportadores de la República Mexicana (ANIERM) (National Association of Importers and Exporters): Monterrey 130, Col. Roma, Del. Cuauhtémoc, 06700 México, DF; tel. (55) 5584-9522; fax (55) 5584-5317; e-mail anierm@anierm.org.mx; internet www.anierm.org.mx; f. 1944; Pres. RODRIGO GUERRA B.; Vice-Pres. Lic. HUMBERTO SIMONEEN ARDILA.

Comisión de Fomento Minero (COFOMI): Puente de Tecamachalco 26, Lomas de Chapultepec, 11000 México, DF; tel. (55) 5540-3400; fax (55) 5202-0342; f. 1934 to promote the devt of the mining sector; Dir Lic. LUIS DE PABLO SERNA.

Comisión Nacional de Inversiones Extranjeras (CNIE): Blvd Avila Camacho 1, 11°, 11000 México, DF; tel. (55) 5540-1426; fax (55) 5286-1551; f. 1973; commission to co-ordinate foreign investment; Exec. Sec. Dr CARLOS CAMACHO GAOS.

Comisión Nacional de Seguridad Nuclear y Salvaguardias (CNSNS): Dr Barragán 779, Col. Narvarte, Del. Juárez, 03020 México, DF; tel. (55) 5095-3200; fax (55) 5095-3295; e-mail swaller@cnsns.gob.mx; f. 1979; nuclear regulatory agency; Dir-Gen. JUAN EIBENSCHUTZ HARTMAN.

Comisión Petroquímica Mexicana: México, DF; promotes the devt of the petrochemical industry; Tech. Sec. Ing. JUAN ANTONIO BARGÉS MESTRES.

Consejo Empresarial Mexicano para Asuntos Internacionales (CEMAI): Homero 527, 7°, Col. Polanco, 11570 México, DF; tel. (55) 5250-7033; fax (55) 5531-1590.

Consejo Mexicano del Café (CMCAFE): José María Ibarrarán 84, 1°, Col. San José Insurgentes, Del. Juárez, 03900 México, DF; tel. and fax (55) 5611-9075; e-mail cmc@sagar.gob.mx; internet www.cmcafe.org.mx; f. 1993; devt of coffee sector.

Consejo Nacional de la Industria Maquiladora de Exportación (CNIME): Ejército Nacional 418, 12°, Of. 1204, Col. Chapultepec Morales, Del. Miguel Hidalgo, 11570 México, DF; tel. and fax (55) 5250-6093; internet www.cnime.org.mx; f. 1975; Pres. ENRIQUE CASTRO SEPTIEN; Sec. ENRIQUE HURTADO.

Instituto Nacional de Investigaciones Forestales y Agropecuarios (INIFAP) (National Forestry and Agricultural Research Institute): Serapio Rendón 83, Col. San Rafael, Del. Cuauhtémoc, 06470 México, DF; tel. (55) 5140-1674; fax (55) 5566-3799; internet www.inifap.gob.mx; f. 1985; conducts research into plant genetics, management of species and conservation; Dir-Gen. PEDRO BRAJCICH GALLEGOS.

EMPLOYERS' ORGANIZATIONS

Consejo Coordinador Empresarial (CCE): Lancaster 15, Col. Juárez, 06600 México, DF; tel. (55) 5229-1100; fax (55) 5592-3857; e-mail sistemas@cce.org.mx; internet www.cce.org.mx; f. 1974; co-ordinating body of private sector; Pres. JOSÉ LUIS BARRAZA; Dir FRANCISCO CALDERÓN.

Consejo Mexicano de Hombres de Negocios (CMHN): México, DF; f. 1963; represents leading businesspeople; affiliated to CCE; Pres. ANTONIO DEL VALLE RUIZ.

STATE HYDROCARBONS COMPANY

Petróleos Mexicanos (PEMEX): Avda Marina Nacional 329, Col. Huasteca, 11311 México, DF; tel. (55) 1944-2500; fax (55) 5531-6354; internet www.pemex.com; f. 1938; govt agency for the exploitation of Mexico's petroleum and natural gas resources; Dir-Gen. LUIS RAMÍREZ CORZO; 106,900 employees.

UTILITIES

Regulatory Authorities

Comisión Nacional del Agua (CNA): Avda Insurgentes Sur 2146, Col. Copilco el Bajo, Del. Coyoacán, 04340 México, DF; tel. (55) 5550-7607; fax (55) 5550-6721; e-mail direccion@cna.gob.mx; internet www.cna.gob.mx; commission to administer national water resources; Dir-Gen. CRISTOBAL JAIME JAQUEZ.

Comisión Reguladora de Energía (CRE): Horacio 1750, Col. Polanco, Del. Miguel Hidalgo, 11510 México, DF; tel. (55) 5283-1500; internet www.cre.gob.mx; f. 1994; commission to control energy

MEXICO

policy and planning; Pres. DIONISIO PÉREZ-JÁCOME; Exec. Sec. FRANCISCO J. VALDES LÓPEZ.

Secretariat of State for Energy: see section on The Government (Secretariats of State).

Electricity

Comisión Federal de Electricidad (CFE): 2 Sec. del Bosque de Chapultepec, Museo Tecnológico, Del. Miguel Hidalgo, México, DF; tel. (55) 5229-4400; fax (55) 5553-5321; e-mail alfredo.elias@cfe.gob.mx; internet www.cfe.gob.mx; state-owned power utility; Dir-Gen. ALFREDO ELÍAS AYUB.

Luz y Fuerza del Centro: Melchor Ocampo 171, Col. Tlaxpana, Del. Miguel Hidalgo, 11379 México, DF; tel. (55) 5140-0040; fax (55) 5140-0300; e-mail ldpablo@inter01.lfc.gob.mx; internet www.lfc.gob.mx; operates electricity network in the centre of the country; Dir-Gen. LUIS DE PABLO SERNA.

Gas

Gas Natural México (GNM): Jaime Blames 8-703, Col. Los Morales, Del. Polanco, 11510 México, DF; e-mail sugerencias@gnm.com.mx; internet www.gasnaturalmexico.com.mx; f. 1994 in Mexico; distributes natural gas in the states of Tamaulipas, Aguascalientes, Coahuila, San Luis Potosí, Guanajuato, Nuevo León and México and the in Distrito Federal; subsidiary of Gas Natural (Spain).

Petróleos Mexicanos (PEMEX): see State Hydrocarbons Company; distributes natural gas.

TRADE UNIONS

Congreso del Trabajo (CT): Avda Ricardo Flores Magón 44, Col. Guerrero, 06300 México 37, DF; tel. (55) 5583-3817; f. 1966; trade union congress comprising trade union federations, confederations, etc.; Pres. Lic. HÉCTOR VALDÉS ROMO.

Confederación Regional Obrera Mexicana (CROM) (Regional Confederation of Mexican Workers): República de Cuba 60, México, DF; f. 1918; Sec.-Gen. IGNACIO CUAUHTÉMOC PALETA; 120,000 mems, 900 affiliated syndicates.

Confederación Revolucionaria de Obreros y Campesinos de México (CROC) (Revolutionary Confederation of Workers and Farmers): Hamburgo 250, Col. Juárez, Del. Cuauhtémoc, 06600 México, DF; tel. (55) 5208-5449; e-mail crocmodel@hotmail.com; internet www.croc.org.mx; f. 1952; Sec.-Gen. ISIAS GONZÁLEZ CUEVAS; 4.5m. mems in 32 state federations and 17 national unions.

Confederación Revolucionaria de Trabajadores (CRT) (Revolutionary Confederation of Workers): Dr Jiménez 218, Col. Doctores, México, DF; f. 1954; Sec.-Gen. MARIO SUÁREZ GARCÍA; 10,000 mems, 10 federations and 192 syndicates.

Confederación de Trabajadores de México (CTM) (Confederation of Mexican Workers): Insurgente Norte 59, Edif. 2, 2°, Col. Buena Vista, México, DF; tel. (55) 5703-3137; fax (55) 5705-0966; f. 1936; admitted to ICFTU; Sec.-Gen. JOAQUÍN GAMBOA; 5.5m. mems.

Federación Obrera de Organizaciones Femeniles (FOOF) (Workers' Federation of Women's Organizations): Vallarta 8, México, DF; f. 1950; women workers' union within CTM; Sec.-Gen. HILDA ANDERSON NEVÁREZ; 400,000 mems.

Federación Nacional de Sindicatos Independientes (National Federation of Independent Trade Unions): Isaac Garza 311 Oeste, 64000 Monterrey, NL; tel. (81) 8375-6677; e-mail fnsi@prodigy.net.mx; internet www.fnsi.org.mx; f. 1936; Sec.-Gen. JACINTO PADILLA VALDEZ; 230,000 mems.

Federación de Sindicatos de Trabajadores al Servicio del Estado (FSTSE) (Federation of Unions of Government Workers): Gómez Farías 40, Col. San Rafael, 06470 México, DF; f. 1938; Sec.-Gen. Lic. JOEL AYALA; 2.5m. mems; 80 unions.

Frente Unida Sindical por la Defensa de los Trabajadores y la Constitución (United Union Front in Defence of the Workers and the Constitution): f. 1990 by more than 120 trade orgs to support the implementation of workers' constitutional rights.

Unión General de Obreros y Campesinos de México, Jacinto López (UGOCM-JL) (General Union of Workers and Farmers of Mexico, Jacinto López): José María Marroquí 8, 2°, 06050 México, DF; tel. (55) 5518-3015; f. 1949; admitted to WFTU/CSTAL; Sec.-Gen. JOSÉ LUIS GONZÁLEZ AGUILERA; 7,500 mems, over 2,500 syndicates.

Unión Nacional de Trabajadores (UNT) (National Union of Workers): Villalongen 50, Col. Cuauhtémoc, México, DF; tel. (55) 5140-1425; fax (55) 5703-2583; e-mail secretariageneral@strm.org.mx; internet www.unt.org.mx; f. 1998; Sec.-Gen. FRANCISCO HERNÁNDEZ JUÁREZ.

A number of major unions are non-affiliated; they include:

Federación Democrática de Sindicatos de Servidores Públicos (Democratic Federation of Public Servants): México, DF; f. 2005.

Frente Auténtico de los Trabajadores (FAT).

Pacto de Unidad Sindical Solidaridad (PAUSS): comprises 10 independent trade unions.

Sindicato Nacional de Trabajadores Mineros, Metalúrgicos y Similares de la República Mexicana (SNTMM) (Industrial Union of Mine, Metallurgical and Related Workers of the Republic of Mexico): Avda Dr Vertiz 668, Col. Narvarte, 03020 México, DF; tel. (55) 5519-5690; f. 1933; Sec.-Gen. ELÍAS MORALES HERNÁNDEZ; 86,000 mems.

Sindicato Nacional de Trabajadores de la Educación (SNTE): Venezuela 44, Col. Centro, México, DF; tel. (55) 5702-0005; fax (55) 5702-6303; f. 1943; teachers' union; Pres. ELBA ESTHER GORDILLO MORALES; Sec.-Gen. TOMÁS VÁZQUEZ VIGIL; 1.3m. mems.

Coordinadora Nacional de Trabajadores de la Educación (CNTE): dissident faction; Leader TEODORO PALOMINO.

Sindicato de Trabajadores Petroleros de la República Mexicana (STPRM) (Union of Petroleum Workers of the Republic of Mexico): Zaragoza 15, Col. Guerrero, 06300 México, DF; tel. (55) 5546-0912; close links with PEMEX; Sec.-Gen. CARLOS ROMERO DESCHAMPS; 110,000 mems; includes:

Movimiento Nacional Petrolero: reformist faction; Leader HEBRAÍCAZ VÁSQUEZ.

Sindicato de Trabajadores Ferrocarrileros de la República Mexicana (STFRM) (Union of Railroad Workers of the Republic of Mexico): Avda Ricardo Flores Magón 206, Col. Guerrero, México 3, DF; tel. (55) 5597-1011; f. 1933; Sec.-Gen. VÍCTOR F. FLORES MORALES; 100,000 mems.

Sindicato Unico de Trabajadores Electricistas de la República Mexicana (SUTERM) (Sole Union of Electricity Workers of the Republic of Mexico): Río Guadalquivir 106, Col. Cuauhtémoc, 06500 México, DF; tel. (55) 5207-0578; Sec.-Gen. LEONARDO RODRÍGUEZ ALCAINE.

Sindicato Unico de Trabajadores de la Industria Nuclear (SUTIN): Viaducto Río Becerra 139, Col. Nápoles, 03810 México, DF; tel. (55) 5523-8048; fax (55) 5687-6353; e-mail sutin@nuclear.inin.mx; internet www.prodigyweb.net.mx/sutin; Sec.-Gen. RICARDO FLORES BELLO.

Unión Obrera Independiente (UOI): non-aligned.

The major agricultural unions are:

Central Campesina Independiente (CCI): México, DF; e-mail cencci@prodigy.net.mx; Dir RAFAEL GALINDO JAIME.

Confederación Nacional Campesina (CNC): Mariano Azuela 121, Col. Santa María de la Ribera, México, DF; Sec.-Gen. Lic. BEATRIZ PAREDES RANGEL.

Confederación Nacional Ganadera: Calzada Mariano Escobedo 714, Col. Anzures, México, DF; tel. (55) 5203-3506; Pres. Ing. CÉSAR GONZÁLEZ QUIROGA; 300,000 mems.

Consejo Agrarista Mexicano: 09760 Iztapalapa, México, DF; Sec.-Gen. HUMBERTO SERRANO.

Unión Nacional de Trabajadores Agriculturas (UNTA).

Transport

Road transport accounts for about 98% of all public passenger traffic and for about 80% of freight traffic. Mexico's terrain is difficult for overland travel. As a result, there has been an expansion of air transport and there were 61 international and national airports in 2004. In 2002 plans to build a new airport in the capital were postponed after conflict over the proposed site. International flights are provided by a large number of national and foreign airlines. Mexico has 140 seaports, 29 river docks and a further 29 lake shelters. More than 85% of Mexico's foreign trade is conducted through maritime transport. In the 1980s the Government developed the main industrial ports of Tampico, Coatzacoalcos, Lázaro Cárdenas, Altamira, Laguna de Ostión and Salina Cruz in an attempt to redirect growth and to facilitate exports. The port at Dos Bocas, on the Gulf of Mexico, was one of the largest in Latin America when it opened in 1999. A 300-km railway link across the isthmus of Tehuantepec connects the Caribbean port of Coatzacoalcos with the Pacific port of Salina Cruz.

In 1992, as part of an ambitious divestment programme, the Government announced that concessions would be offered for sale to the private sector, in 1993, to operate nine ports and 61 of the country's airports. The national ports authority was to be disbanded, responsibility for each port being transferred to Administraciones Portuarias Integrales (APIs). In 1998 plans were announced for public share offerings in 35 airports. From 1997 the national railway system underwent privatization granted under 50-year concessions.

MEXICO

By early 2006 two of the four airport operating companies had been privatized.

Secretariat of State for Communications and Transport: see section on The Government (Secretariats of State).

Aeropuertos y Servicios Auxiliares (ASA): Avda 602 161, Col. San Juan de Aragón, Del. V. Carranza, 15620 México, DF; tel. (55) 5786-9526; fax (55) 5786-9709; internet www.asa.gob.mx; Dir-Gen. ERNESTO VALESCO LEÓN.

Caminos y Puentes Federales (CAPUFE): e-mail contacto@capufe.gob.mx; internet www.capufe.gob.mx; Dir-Gen. MANUEL ZUBIRIA MAQUEO.

STATE RAILWAYS

In 2004 there were 26,662 km of main line track. In 2004 the railway system carried an estimated 253,000 passengers and 54,387m. freight ton-km. Ferrocarriles Nacionales de México (FNM), government-owned since 1937, was liquidated in 2001 following a process of restructuring and privatization. A suburban train system for the Valle de México was due to be operational by October 2006.

Ferrocarril del Noreste: Avda Manuel L. Barragán 4850, Col. Hidalgo, 64281 Monterrey, NL; tel. (81) 8305-7931; fax (81) 8305-7766; e-mail tfm@tfm.com.mx; internet www.tfm.com.mx; concession awarded to Transportación Ferroviaria Mexicana (TFM) in 1997; 4,251 km of line, linking Mexico City with the ports of Lázaro Cárdenas, Veracruz, Tampico, Altamira and Matamoros and the US border at Nuevo Laredo; Dir-Gen. M. MOHAR.

Ferrocarril Pacifico-Norte: Avda Baja California 200, Col. Roma Sur, 06760 México, DF; internet www.ferromex.com.mx; 50-year concession awarded to Grupo Ferroviario Mexicano, SA, (GFM) commencing in 1998; owned by Grupo México, SA de CV; operates through wholly-owned subsidiary Ferrocarril Mexicano, SA de CV (FERROMEX); 7,500 km of track and Mexico's largest rail fleet; Dir of Operations Ing. LORENZO REYES RETANA.

Ferrocarril del Sureste (Ferrosur): Jaime Balmes 11, 4°, Col. Los Morales Polanco, 11510 México, DF; tel. (55) 5387-6500; fax (55) 5387-6533; 50-year concession awarded to Grupo Tribasa in 1998; 66.7% sold to Empresas Frisco, SA de CV, in 1999, owned by Grupos Carso, SA de CV; Dir GUILLERMO MUÑOZ LARA.

Servicio de Transportes Eléctricos del Distrito Federal (STE): Avda Municipio Libre 402, Col. San Andrés Tetepilco, México, DF; tel. (55) 5539-6500; fax (55) 5672-4758; e-mail infoste@df.gob.mx; internet www.ste.df.gob.mx; suburban tram route with 17 stops upgraded to light rail standard to act as a feeder to the metro; also operates bus and trolleybus networks; Dir-Gen. Dra FLORENCIA SERRANIA SOTO.

Sistema de Transporte Colectivo (Metro): Delicias 67, 06070 México, DF; tel. (55) 5709-1133; fax (55) 5512-3601; internet www.metro.df.gob.mx; f. 1967; the first stage of a combined underground and surface railway system in Mexico City was opened in 1969; 10 lines, covering 158 km, were operating, in 1998, and five new lines, bringing the total distance to 315 km, are to be completed by 2010; the system is wholly state-owned and the fares are partially subsidized; Dir-Gen. Dr JAVIER GONZÁLEZ GARZA.

ROADS

In 2003 there were 352,072 km of roads, of which 34.5% were paved.

Long-distance buses form one of the principal methods of transport in Mexico, and there are some 600 lines operating services throughout the country.

Dirección General de Autotransporte Federal: Calzada de las Bombas 411, 11°, Col. San Bartolo Coapa, 04800 México, DF; tel. (55) 5684-0757; co-ordinates long distance bus services.

SHIPPING

At the end of 2004 Mexico's registered merchant fleet numbered 687 vessels, with a total displacement of 1,007,998 grt. The Government operates the facilities of seaports. In 1989–94 US $700m. was spent on port development, much of it from the private sector. In 1994–95 management of several ports were transferred to the private sector.

Coordinación General de Puertos y Marina Mercante (CGPMM): Avda Nuevo León 210, Col. Hipódromo, 06100 México, DF03310 México, DF; tel. (55) 5723-9300; e-mail cgpmmweb@sct.gob.mx; Dir CÉSAR PATRICIO REYES ROEL.

Port of Acapulco: Puertos Mexicanos, Malecón Fiscal s/n, Acapulco, Gro; tel. (744) 22067; fax (744) 31648; Harbour Master Capt. RENÉ F. NOVALES BETANZOS.

Port of Coatzacoalcos: Administración Portuaria Integral de Coatzacoalcos, SA de CV, Interior recinto portuario s/n Coatzacoalcos, 96400 Ver.; tel. (921) 214-6744; fax (921) 214-6758; e-mail apicoa@apicoatza.com; internet www.apicoatza.com; Dir-Gen. Ing. GILBERTO ANTÓNIO RIOS RUÍZ.

Port of Dos Bocas: Administración Portuaria Integral de Dos Bocas, SA de CV, Carretera Federal Puerto Ceiba–Paraíso 414, Col. Quintín Arzuz Paraíso, 86600 Tabasco, Tab.; tel. (933) 353-2744; e-mail dosbocas@apidosbocas.com; internet www.apidosbocas.com.

Port of Manzanillo: Administración Portuaria Integral de Manzanillo, SA de CV, Avda Tte Azueta 9, Col. Burócrata, 28250 Manzanillo, Col.; tel. (314) 331-1400; fax (314) 332-1005; e-mail comercializacion@apimanzanillo.com.mx; internet www.apimanzanillo.com.mx; Dir-Gen. Capt. HÉCTOR MORA GÓMEZ.

Port of Tampico: Administración Portuaria Integral de Tampico, SA de CV, Edif. API de Tampico, 1°, Recinto Portuario, 89000 Tampico, Tamps; tel. (833) 212-4660; fax (833) 212-5744; e-mail apitam@puertodetampico.com.mx; internet www.puertodetampico.com.mx; Gen. Dir Ing. RAFAEL MESEGUER LIMA.

Port of Veracruz: Administración Porturia Integral de Veracruz, SA de CV, Avda Marina Mercante 210, 7°, Col. Centro, 91700 Veracruz, Ver.; tel. (229) 932-2170; fax (229) 932-3040; e-mail mfernandez@apiver.com; internet apiver.com; privatized in 1994; Dir-Gen. JORGE ALEJANDRO GONZÁLEZ OLIVIERI.

Petróleos Mexicanos (PEMEX): Edif. 1917, 2°, Avda Marina Nacional 329, 44°, Col. Anáhuac, 11300 México, DF; tel. (55) 5531-6053; Dir-Gen. J. R. MOCTEZUMA.

Transportación Marítima Mexicana, SA de CV: Avda de la Cúspide 4755, Col. Parques del Pedregal, Del. Tlalpan, 14010 México, DF; tel. (55) 5652-4111; fax (55) 5665-3566; internet www.tmm.com.mx; f. 1955; cargo services to Europe, the Mediterranean, Scandinavia, the USA, South and Central America, the Caribbean and the Far East; Pres. JUAN CARLOS MERODIO; Dir-Gen. JAVIER SEGOVIA.

CIVIL AVIATION

There were 61 airports in Mexico in 2004, of which 47 were international. Of these, México, Cancún, Guadalajara, Monterrey and Tijuana registered the highest number of operations.

Aeropuertos y Servicios Auxiliares (ASA): Edif. B, Avda 602 161, Col. San Juan de Aragón, Del. Venustiano Carranza, 15620 México, DF; tel. (55) 5133-1000; fax (55) 5133-2985; e-mail evelasco@asa.gob.mx; internet www.asa.gob.mx; oversees airport management and development; Dir-Gen. ERNESTO VELASCO LEÓN.

Dirección General de Aeronáutica Civil (DGAC): Avda Xola y Universidad, Col. Narvarte, Del. Benito Juárez, 03020 México, DF; tel. (55) 5723-9300; fax (55) 5530-0093; internet dgac.sct.gob.mx; subdivision of Secretariat of State for Communications and Transport; regulates civil aviation; Dir-Gen. GILBERTO LÓPEZ MEYER.

Aerocalifornia: Aquiles Serdán 1955, 23000 La Paz, BCS; e-mail aeroll@aerocalifornia.uabcs.mx; f. 1960; regional carrier with scheduled passenger and cargo services in Mexico and the USA; Chair. PAUL A. ARECHIGA.

Aerocancún: Edif. Oasis 29, Avda Kukulcan, esq. Cenzontle, Zona Hotelera, 77500 Cancún, Q. Roo; charter services to the USA, South America, the Caribbean and Europe; Dir-Gen. JAVIER MARANÓN.

Aeroliteral: e-mail comentarios@aerolitoral.com; internet www.aerolitoral.com.mx; owned by state holding co Consorcio Aeroméxico, SA (formerly Cintra, SA); operates internal flights, and flights to the USA.

Aeromar, Transportes Aeromar: Hotel Maria Isabel Sheraton, Paseo de la Reforma 325, Local 10, México, DF; tel. (55) 5514-2248; e-mail web.aeromar@aeromar.com.mx; internet www.aeromar.com.mx; f. 1987; scheduled domestic passenger and cargo services; Dir-Gen. JUAN I. STETA.

Aerovías de México (Aeroméxico): Paseo de la Reforma 445, 3°, Torre B, Col. Cuauhtémoc, 06500 México, DF; tel. (55) 5133-4000; fax (55) 5133-4619; internet www.aeromexico.com; f. 1934 as Aeronaves de México, nationalized 1959; owned by state holding co Consorcio Aeroméxico, SA (fmrly Cintra, SA); due to be privatized by mid-2006; services between most principal cities of Mexico and the USA, Brazil, Peru, France and Spain; Dir-Gen. GILBERTO PEREZALONSO; Pres. ANDRES CONSESA.

Aviacsa: Aeropuerto Internacional, Zona C, Hangar 1, Col. Aviación General, 15520 México, DF; tel. (55) 5716-9005; fax (55) 5758-3823; internet www.aviacsa.com; f. 1990; operates internal flights, and flights to the USA.

Azteca Lineas Aéreas: e-mail info@aazteca.com; internet www.aazteca.com.mx; f. 2000; domestic flights.

Click Mexicana: Avda Xola 535, Col. Del Valle, 03100 México, DF; tel. (55) 5284-3132; internet www.clickmx.com; f. 2005; owned by Grupo Posadas; budget airline operating internal flights; CEO ISAAC VOLIN BOLOK.

Mexicana (Compañía Mexicana de Aviación, SA de CV): Avda Xola 535, Col. del Valle, 03100 México, DF; tel. (55) 5448-3000; fax (55) 5448-3129; e-mail dirgenmx@mexicana.com.mx; internet www.mexicana.com; f. 1921; fmrly state-owned; sold to Grupo Posadas in late 2005; international services between Mexico City and the USA,

Central America and the Caribbean; domestic services; CEO EMILIO ROMANO MUSSALI.

Volaris: Aeropuerto Internacional de la Ciudad de Toluca, 50500 Toluca, DF; tel. (55) 1102-8000; e-mail comentarios@volaris.com.mx; internet www.volaris.com.mx; f. 2006; operated by Vuela Compañia de Aviación; budget airline operating internal flights; Pres. PEDRO ASPE ARMELLA; Dir-Gen. ENRIQUE BELTRANENA.

Tourism

Tourism remains one of Mexico's principal sources of foreign exchange. Mexico received an estimated 22.0m. foreign visitors in 2005, and receipts from tourism in that year were estimated at US $9,186m. More than 90% of visitors come from the USA and Canada. The country is famous for volcanoes, coastal scenery and the great Sierra Nevada (Sierra Madre) mountain range. The relics of the Mayan and Aztec civilizations and of Spanish Colonial Mexico are of historic and artistic interest. Zihuatanejo, on the Pacific coast, and Cancún, on the Caribbean, were developed as tourist resorts by the Government. In 2004 an estimated 1.8m. people were employed in the tourism sector. In October 2005 'Hurricane Wilma' inflicted heavy damage on some tourist areas, notably Cancún. The government tourism agency, FONATUR, encourages the renovation and expansion of old hotels and provides attractive incentives for the industry. FONATUR is also the main developer of major resorts in Mexico.

Secretariat of State for Tourism: see section on The Government (Secretariats of State).

Asociación Mexicana de Agencias de Viajes (AMAV): Guanajuato 128, México, DF; tel. (55) 5584-9300; e-mail amav@prodigy.net.mx; internet www.amavnacional.com; f. 1945; asscn of travel agencies; Pres. JORGE HERNÁNDEZ DELGADO.

Fondo Nacional de Fomento al Turismo (FONATUR): Tecoyotitla 100, Col. Florida, 01030 México, DF; tel. (55) 5090-4200; fax (55) 5090-4469; e-mail jmccarthy@fonatur.gob.mx; internet www.fonatur.gob.mx; f. 1956 to finance and promote the devt of tourism; Dir Lic. JOHN MCCARTHY.

THE FEDERATED STATES OF MICRONESIA

Introductory Survey

Location, Climate, Language, Religion, Flag, Capital

The Federated States of Micronesia forms (with Palau, q.v.) the archipelago of the Caroline Islands, about 800 km east of the Philippines. The Federated States of Micronesia comprises 607 islands and includes (from west to east) the states of Yap, Chuuk (formerly Truk), Pohnpei (formerly Ponape) and Kosrae. The islands are subject to heavy rainfall, although precipitation decreases from east to west. January, February and March are the driest months, although seasonal variations in rainfall and temperature are generally small. Average annual temperature is 27°C (81°F). The native population consists of various ethno-linguistic groups, but English is widely understood. The principal religion is Christianity, much of the population being Roman Catholic. The national flag (proportions 10 by 19) consists of four five-pointed white stars, arranged as a circle, situated centrally on a light blue field. The capital is Kolonia, on Pohnpei.

Recent History

The Federated States of Micronesia was formerly part of the US-administered Trust Territory of the Pacific Islands (for history up to 1965, see the chapter on the Marshall Islands).

From 1965 there were increasing demands for local autonomy within the Trust Territory of the Pacific Islands. In that year the Congress of Micronesia was formed, and in 1967 a commission was established to examine the future political status of the islands. In 1970 it declared Micronesians' rights to sovereignty over their own lands, to self-determination, to devise their own constitution and to revoke any form of free association with the USA. In May 1977, after eight years of negotiations, US President Jimmy Carter announced that his administration intended to adopt measures to terminate the trusteeship agreement by 1981. Until 1979 the four districts of Yap, Truk (Chuuk since 1990), Ponape (Pohnpei since 1984) and Kosrae were governed by a local Administrator, appointed by the President of the USA. However, on 10 May 1979 the four districts ratified a new Constitution to become the Federated States of Micronesia. The Constitution was promulgated in 1980.

The USA signed the Compact of Free Association with the Republic of Palau in August 1982, and with the Marshall Islands and the Federated States of Micronesia in October. Under the Compacts, the four countries (including the Northern Mariana Islands) became independent of each other and took charge of both their internal and foreign affairs separately, while the USA remained responsible for defence and security. The Compact was approved by plebiscite in the Federated States of Micronesia in June 1983, and was ratified by the islands' Congress in September.

In May 1986 the UN Trusteeship Council endorsed the US Government's request for the termination of the existing trusteeship agreement with the islands. US administration of the Federated States of Micronesia was formally ended in November of that year. The UN Security Council ratified the termination of the trusteeship agreement in December 1990. Ponape was renamed Pohnpei in November 1984, when its Constitution came into effect. Truk was renamed Chuuk in January 1990, when its new Constitution was proposed (being later adopted). The Federated States of Micronesia was admitted to the UN in September 1991.

The incumbent President (since 1987), John Haglelgam, was replaced by Bailey Olter, a former Vice-President, in May 1991. At congressional elections in March 1995 Olter was re-elected to the Pohnpei Senator-at-Large seat, and in early May he was re-elected to the presidency unopposed. Similarly, Jacob Nena was re-elected as Vice-President. Allegations that financial mismanagement by the Governor of Chuuk, Sasao Gouland, had resulted in state debts of some US $20m. led to his resignation in June 1996, in order to avoid impeachment proceedings. In July Olter suffered a stroke. Jacob Nena served as acting President during Olter's absence from office, and in May 1997 was sworn in as President of the country. (Olter died in February 1999.)

Congressional elections took place in early March 1997 for the 10 Senators elected on a two-yearly basis, at which all of the incumbents were returned to office. A referendum held concurrently on a proposed amendment to the Constitution (which envisaged increasing the allocation of national revenue to the state legislatures from 50% to 80% of the total budget) was approved in Chuuk and Yap, but rejected in Pohnpei and Kosrae.

Allegations of government interference in the media became widespread when the editor of the country's principal newspaper, *FSM News*, was refused permission to re-enter the islands in June 1997. The Government had sought to deport the editor (who was a Canadian national) following publication in the periodical of reports on government spending, which the authorities claimed were false and malicious. It was also thought that by enforcing the exclusion order, the Government hoped to suppress the publication in the newspaper of information relating to alleged corruption among public officials. The newspaper ceased publication in late 1997.

In February 1998 Congress approved proposals to restructure and reorganize the Cabinet. Several ministerial portfolios were consequently merged or abolished, with the aim of reducing government expenditure. Congressional elections took place on 2 March 1999, at which President Nena was re-elected to the Kosrae Senator-at-Large seat and Vice-President Leo Falcam to the Pohnpei Senator-at-Large seat. On 11 May Congress elected Falcam as President and the Chuuk Senator-at-Large, Redley Killion, as Vice-President.

A first round of renegotiations of the Compact of Free Association (certain terms of which were due to expire in 2001) was completed in late 1999. The USA and the Federated States of Micronesia pledged to maintain defence and security relations. It was also agreed that the USA would continue to provide economic aid to the islands and assist in the development of the private sector, as well as in promoting greater economic self-sufficiency. In July 2001 the USA offered annual assistance of US $61m. and a trust fund of $13m., and expressed concern that the $2,600m. it had given to Micronesia and the Marshall Islands since 1986 had been mismanaged. The Compact's funding terms for Micronesia were originally due to expire on 3 November 2001, but negotiations regarding a new Compact were not completed by this time. Funding was, nevertheless, continued at the Compact's 15-year average level while negotiations remained in progress. Following a proposal by the USA in April 2002 to extend economic assistance for a period of 20 years, a new draft funding structure was agreed, and in March the US budget projections for 2004 granted Micronesian citizens access to private health care resources in the USA as part of the Federated States' continued entitlement to US federal programmes. On 1 May 2003 the amended Compact of Free Association was signed by representatives of the two countries in Pohnpei. The new Compact envisaged direct annual grants of $76.2m. in 2004, in addition to a further $16m. annually, which was to be paid into a Trust Fund for Micronesia. From 2007, direct grants were to decrease by some $800,000, with this amount being transferred to the trust fund. (The total amount to be paid prior to the expected termination of US assistance in 2023 amounted, in 2004 terms, to some $1,760m.) Furthermore, the Micronesian Government also undertook to provide frequent, strictly monitored audit information on all US funding in order to ensure greater accountability. In October 2003 final agreement was reached on some outstanding security and immigration issues, and the US Congress approved the amended Compact in November. President George W. Bush signed the pact in December, and representatives of both Governments signed a document of implementation in June 2004. Nevertheless, there remained widespread concern in the Federated States of Micronesia that the new Compact represented a substantial overall reduction in annual income over the long term. Moreover, the formula for the distribution of Compact funds to each of Micronesia's states and the removal of certain US subsidies remained the subject of considerable controversy. In August representatives of Micronesia and the USA met to review the management of Compact funds in the first session of the Joint Economic Management Committee.

In September 2002 unrest occurred on the Faichuk islands, part of Chuuk, where the Faichuk Commission for Statehood continued its campaign to secede from Chuuk and gain equal status within the Federation. The secessionists believed that independence would bring more goods, services, medical treatment and capital improvement projects. Local dissatisfaction worsened in September following allegations of electoral manipulation against the village mayor of Udot island, with a large crowd appearing to support attempts by local security forces to prevent the mayor's arrest. In March 2005 Congressman Twiter Aritos introduced to the national Congress legislation to grant Faichuk the status of the Federation's fifth state. Congressional approval of the legislation was pending in early 2006.

Also in September 2002 a referendum was held on a number of proposed amendments to the Constitution. The prospective changes included a provision for the direct election of presidential candidates, the extension of the right of islanders to hold dual citizenship and changes to the distribution formula for Compact of Free Association funds. However, the measures did not receive the required three-quarters' majority of votes and were thus rejected.

At the congressional elections of 6 March 2003 President Leo Falcam unexpectedly failed to achieve re-election to a further four-year term as Senator-at-Large for Pohnpei. In mid-May Congress appointed the Senator-at-Large for Yap, Joseph J. Urusemal, to the presidency. The elections were the subject of some controversy, as it appeared that elected officials had disbursed a portion of the 2002 US funding for Micronesia in order to enhance their electoral prospects. The alleged misallocation of funds was reportedly a significant factor in the worsening fiscal positions of Chuuk, Pohnpei and Kosrae. Moreover, perceptions of official accountability continued to deteriorate in 2003; in November three serving Congressmen were indicted for their role in an alleged fraud involving some $1.2m. in public funds. In January 2004 the national Congress approved a resolution to dismiss the judge assigned to the case. President Urusemal lodged a petition against the dismissal on the grounds that it infringed the constitutionally guaranteed separation of powers. In August the Supreme Court ruled in favour of the petition and overturned the judge's dismissal. Also in January 2004, members of the national Congress attempted to introduce legislation effectively absolving public officials from corruption allegations relating to Compact of Free Association funds. The proposals aroused widespread public hostility, and several representatives of state legislatures threatened to secede from the federation unless the measure were withdrawn. In March the so-called 'amnesty bill' was returned to a congressional subcommittee for further discussion.

At congressional elections held on 7 March 2005 all but one of the incumbent Senators-at-Large were re-elected, with results from Chuuk awaiting confirmation in early April. At congressional elections held on the following day eight of the 10 incumbent Senators with two-year mandates were re-elected. (Results from Chuuk were annulled, owing to alleged voting irregularities, and in late April a new round of voting was held in this state, at which, amid further allegations of electoral malpractice, Peter S. Sitan was elected.) Concurrent to the second round of congressional elections, a referendum was held over three proposed amendments to the Constitution, including the question of whether each state should recognize and uphold the laws and judicial rulings of other states, and whether to allow dual citizenship. Although a majority of voters favoured the proposed amendments, these could not be implemented because the majority of 75% or more of the votes, as required by the Constitution, had not been obtained.

Periodic extreme weather formations have caused loss of life and severe damage to crops, property and infrastructure in Micronesia. Following a severe typhoon in December 2002, President George W. Bush of the USA declared Micronesia a federal disaster area and ordered emergency US funding and resources to be allocated to the relief effort. A further typhoon which struck Yap in April 2004 left 1,200 people homeless; the US Government offered to assume 75% of the cost of the recovery effort.

In late 2000 marine biologists issued a warning regarding the erosion of the islands' coastlines, caused by the destruction of the coral reefs by pollution, overfishing and increasing sea temperatures. Furthermore, in late 2003 concerns over environmental pollution increased, due to environmental damage caused by former US and Japanese military equipment submerged in Micronesian waters. A former US Navy oil tanker submerged off the remote Ulithi Atoll was reported at this time to be leaking. Meanwhile, in September 2003 President Urusemal urged the UN General Assembly to work towards halting climate change and its consequent effects on sea-levels and weather systems.

In May 2000 a state of emergency was declared on Pohnpei, following an outbreak of cholera. In August the Government announced a vaccination scheme for the entire population over two years of age. Import restrictions were introduced on the surrounding islands. Pohnpei was officially declared free of cholera on 16 February 2001. During the epidemic some 20 people had died and a further 3,525 were estimated to have been infected.

In February 2003 Pohnpei hosted the first Summit of Micronesian Leaders. At the second summit, held in Koror, Palau, in March 2004, President Urusemal and the leaders of Palau, the Northern Mariana Islands and Guam undertook to increase co-operation among the Pacific island states in the areas of tourism and the environment.

Government

On 10 May 1979 the locally drafted Constitution of the Federated States of Micronesia, incorporating the four states of Kosrae, Yap, Ponape (later Pohnpei) and Truk (later Chuuk), became effective. The federal legislature, the Congress, comprises 14 members (Senators). The four states each elect one 'Senator-at-Large', for a four-year term. The remaining 10 Senators are elected for two-year terms: their seats are distributed in proportion to the population of each state. Each of the four states also has its own Constitution, Governor and legislature. The federal President and Vice-President are elected by the Congress from among the four Senators-at-Large; the offices rotate among the four states. (By-elections are then held for the seats to which the President and Vice-President had been elected.) In November 1986 the Compact of Free Association was signed by the Governments of the Federated States of Micronesia and the USA. Certain of its terms, due to expire in 2001, were renegotiated in late 1999, and an amended Compact was signed by the Governments of both countries on 1 May 2003. By the terms of the Compact, the Federated States of Micronesia is a sovereign, self-governing state.

Local government units are the municipalities and villages. Elected Magistrates and Councils govern the municipalities. Village government is largely traditional.

Defence

The USA is responsible for the defence of the Federated States of Micronesia.

Economic Affairs

In 2004, according to estimates by the World Bank, gross national income (GNI) in the Federated States of Micronesia, measured at average 2002–04 prices, was US $251.9m., equivalent to $1,990 per head. During 1995–2004, it was estimated, the population increased at an average annual rate of 1.9%, while gross domestic product (GDP) per head decreased, in real terms, at an average of 2.2% per year. Overall GDP decreased, in real terms, at an average annual rate of 0.4% in 1995–2004; in 2004 GDP decreased by 3.8%.

Agriculture is mainly on a subsistence level, although its importance is diminishing. The principal crops are coconuts (from which some 500 short tons of copra were produced in 2001), bananas, betel-nuts, cassava and sweet potatoes. White peppercorns are produced on Pohnpei. The sector (including forestry and fishing) contributed 27.6% of the GDP of defined activities in 2002 and engaged 26.1% of the employed labour force in 2003. Exports of betel nuts accounted for 6.1% of export earnings in 2002, while copra exports accounted for 1.5%. In 2001/02 fishing access fees, mainly from Japanese fleets, totalled US $10.6m. (some $3.4m. less than budgeted).

Industry (including mining, manufacturing, utilities and construction) provided 21.1% of the GDP of defined activities in 2002. There is little manufacturing, other than garment production (in Yap) and the manufacture of buttons using trochus shells. The sector provided 1.4% of GDP in 1996 and engaged 3.5% of the employed labour force in 1994. The islands are dependent on imported fuels, with imports of mineral products accounting for 15.8% of the value of total imports in 2002.

The services sector provided an estimated 51.2% of the GDP of defined activities in 2002. A total of 6,015 people were employed by the national and state Governments in 1996/97. Tourism is an increasingly important industry; it was hoped that several projects to improve communications would further stimulate tourism, hitherto hindered by the territory's remote situation. The industry was identified in a report by the Asian Development Bank (ADB) in mid-1995 as having the greatest potential for development and thus contribution to the islands' economic growth. A total of 18,496 tourists arrived on the islands in the year ending September 2003, and full-year tourism receipts for 2003 totalled some US $17m. However, it was reported that tourist arrivals in 2004 had decreased by some 10%, compared with the previous year. Remittances from overseas emigrants are a significant source of income support.

In the financial year ending September 2004 there was a visible trade deficit of an estimated US $113.8m., with a deficit of $24.5m. on the current account of the balance of payments. The principal sources of imports in 2002, according to ADB estimates, were the USA (which supplied 61.9% of the total), Japan (10.6%) and Australia (8.3%). The USA was the principal market for exports in that year, purchasing 33.4% of the total, while Japan accounted for 18.7%. The principal imports in 2002 were prepared foodstuffs (21.3% of the total), machinery, mechanical appliances, electrical equipment and transport equipment (16.8%), and mineral products (15.8%). Fish is the major export commodity, mainly in the form of re-exports to Japan. Other significant exports in that year were garments and buttons (24.9%) and betel nuts.

In 2002/03 there was an estimated budget surplus of US $9.7m., with grants totalling $116.2m. There was a reported budget deficit equivalent to 9.5% of GDP in 2004, decreasing to 6.1% in 2005. The Federated States of Micronesia relies heavily on financial assistance, particularly from the USA which, according to the IMF, provided an estimated $97.7m. (equivalent to 42.1% of GDP) in 2002 and an estimated $92.7m. in Compact funding in 2004. At the end of the 2003/04 financial year, according to the ADB, the islands' total external debt was $59m., and in that year the cost of debt-servicing was equivalent to 6.1% of the value of exports of goods and services. According to the ADB, the inflation rate steadily decreased from an annual average of 6.0% in 1993 to 0.5% in 2001. A deflation rate of 0.1% was recorded in 2002, mainly owing to the decline in food prices. Inflation was reached 0.1% in 2003 and was estimated at 2.5% in 2004, remaining at a similar level in 2005. According to the ADB, some 2.6% of the labour force were unemployed in 2000.

The Federated States of Micronesia is a member of the Pacific Community (see p. 350), the Pacific Islands Forum (see p. 352), the South Pacific Regional Trade and Economic Co-operation Agreement (SPARTECA, see p. 354), the UN Economic and Social Commission for Asia and the Pacific (ESCAP, see p. 33) and the Asian Development Bank (ADB, see p. 169). In November 2002 the Federated States of Micronesia was announced as the location of the headquarters for the Tuna Commission, a new multilateral agency to manage migratory fish stocks in the central and western Pacific region. The organization's remit included the management of waters outside each nation's 200-mile exclusive economic zone, in accordance with the framework established under the 1995 UN Fish Stocks Agreement. The Council of Micronesian Government Executives, of which the Federated States of Micronesia was a founder member in 1996, aims to facilitate discussion of economic developments in the region and to examine possibilities for reducing the considerable cost of shipping essential goods between the islands.

The islands are vulnerable to adverse climatic conditions, as was illustrated in late 1997 and early 1998, when a prolonged drought caused problems throughout the islands, and following a series of tropical storms in 2002–05. The country's prospects for economic development are, furthermore, constrained by the islands' remote position and lack of marketable commodities. An extremely high rate of natural increase in the population has exacerbated certain economic problems, but is, however, partially offset by an annual emigration rate of more than 2%. In December 2000 the ADB approved a US $8m. loan to fund a six-year reform programme of the health and education sectors, and followed this in December 2001 with a further loan of $13m., targeted at job creation, increasing production for both domestic and export markets, and the development of a competitive services sector. No further ADB loans were approved in 2003, although three technical assistance projects, totalling $1.2m., received approval. Cumulative ADB lending to the Federated States of Micronesia, as of 31 December 2004, was $75.1m. The private sector continued to be constrained by the disproportionately high cost of domestic labour, rates of pay in the public sector having risen substantially in recent years as a result of the large external inflows (although public-sector salaries were 'frozen' under the 2004 budget). Moreover, an IMF report released in February 2003 noted that infrastructure for the private sector remained underdeveloped, notwithstanding the authorities' largely positive oversight of the banking sector. Further criticism was attached to the private sector's role as an effective provider of services to the public sector, and the public sector's tendency to operate in unequal competition with private-sector interests. Concerns also continued as to the relative lack of progress in restructuring the economy in preparation for the potentially dramatic impact of the decline and eventual withdrawal of direct US aid in 2023, upon the expiry of the Compact as amended in 2003. (According to the UN, bilateral and multilateral aid to Micronesia totalled $111.7m. in 2002, the latter accounting for only $1.6m. of the total.) The trust fund for Micronesia established to alleviate such pressures upon expiry of the Compact was expected to remain vulnerable to international economic performance, the majority of this capital being invested in US stock markets. Moreover, it was considered in some quarters that the amended Compact of Free Association represented a substantial real reduction in Micronesia's grant income. Under the terms of the amended Compact of Free Association (signed in May 2003), gross US financial contributions were to be $104.9m. annually from September 2005. In February 2006 the USA's proposed budget for 2006/07 provided $97.6m. of Compact funding to Micronesia. It was hoped that Micronesia would have achieved financial self-sufficiency by the year 2023. Under the amended Compact, instead of general budgetary grants, US aid was to be targeted more towards specific projects and government departments. Also, aid was to be conditional upon the efficiency of its management and use, and to be reviewed annually by the Joint Economic Management and Financial Accountability Committee (JEMFAC). This committee first convened in August 2004, in Honolulu, Hawaii. At the third Federated States of Micronesia Economic Summit, which began in late March 2004 in Palikir, a consensus was reached to work towards self-sufficiency by the end of the term of the Compact. This goal was to be achieved by improving infrastructure and sustaining growth in agriculture, fishing and tourism. At a meeting of JEMFAC in March 2005 an Infrastructure Development Plan was approved. In July a Preliminary Strategic Development Plan for Micronesia was drafted. According to ADB estimates, government tax revenues declined by some 2.3% in the year ending September 2004. In early 2005 the Government was considering an adjustment of existing taxes and the introduction of value-added tax (VAT), in order to increase its revenues. In September 2005 the Economic Policy Implementation Council (EPIC), established in 1999, convened in Palikir and approved a radical programme of tax reform in order to increase government revenues. The ADB estimated that GDP expanded by about 1.0% in 2005, partly owing to an expansion of the public-works programme and improvement in receipts from the tourism sector. A similar rate of growth was forecast for 2006.

Education

Primary education, which begins at six years of age and lasts for eight years, is compulsory. Secondary education, beginning at 14 years of age, comprises two cycles, each of two years. The Micronesia Maritime and Fisheries Academy, which was opened in Yap in 1990, provides education and training in fisheries technology at secondary and tertiary levels. The College of Micronesia offers two- and three-year programmes leading to a degree qualification. A summit meeting was held in September 2000 to discuss the improvement and reform of the education sector. In 1997 Micronesia had a student-teacher ratio of 17. An average of 37% of students remained in education from first grade to graduation.

Public Holidays

2006: 1 January (New Year's Day), 14 April (Good Friday, Pohnpei only), 10 May (Constitution Day), 24 October (United Nations Day), 3 November (Independence Day), 25 December (Christmas Day).

2007: 1 January (New Year's Day), 6 April (Good Friday, Pohnpei only), 10 May (Constitution Day), 24 October (United Nations Day), 3 November (Independence Day), 25 December (Christmas Day).

Weights and Measures

With certain exceptions, the imperial system is in force. One US cwt equals 100 lb; one long ton equals 2,240 lb; one short ton equals 2,000 lb. A policy of gradual voluntary conversion to the metric system is being undertaken.

THE FEDERATED STATES OF MICRONESIA

Statistical Survey

AREA AND POPULATION

Area: 700 sq km (270.3 sq miles): Chuuk (294 islands) 127 sq km; Kosrae (5 islands) 110 sq km; Pohnpei (163 islands) 344 sq km; Yap (145 islands) 119 sq km.

Population: 105,506 (53,923 males, 51,583 females) at census of 18 September 1994; 107,008 (males 54,191, females 52,817) at 2000 census (provisional). *By State* (2000): Chuuk 53,595; Kosrae 7,686; Pohnpei 34,486; Yap 11,241. *2004:* (estimate at 30 September): 108,000 (Source: Asian Development Bank, *Key Indicators of Developing Asian and Pacific Countries*).

Density (September 2004): 154.3 per sq km.

Births and Deaths (2000, official estimates): Birth rate 27.1 per 1,000; Death rate 6.0 per 1,000. *1997:* Live births 2,575; Deaths 464 (Source: UN, *Population and Vital Statistics Report*).

Expectation of Life (WHO estimates, years at birth): 70 (males 68; females 71) in 2003. Source: WHO, *World Health Report*.

Economically Active Population ('000 persons, 2000): Agriculture, forestry and fishing 17.25; Total employed (incl. others) 31.21; Unemployed 0.82; Total labour force 32.02 (Source: Asian Development Bank, *Key Indicators of Developing Asian and Pacific Countries*). *Mid-2003* (estimates in '000): Agriculture, etc. 12; Total labour force 46 (Source FAO).

HEALTH AND WELFARE
Key Indicators

Total Fertility Rate (children per woman, 2003): 3.8.

Under-5 Mortality Rate (per 1,000 live births, 2004): 23.

Physicians (per 1,000 head, 1999): 0.57.

Hospital Beds (per 1,000 head, 1989): 3.47.

Health Expenditure (2002): US $ per head (PPP): 311.

Health Expenditure (2002): % of GDP: 6.5.

Health Expenditure (2002): public (% of total): 88.2.

Access to Water (% of persons, 2002): 94.

Access to Sanitation (% of persons, 2002): 28.

For sources and definitions, see explanatory note on p. vi.

AGRICULTURE, ETC.

Principal Crops (FAO estimates, '000 metric tons, 2004): Coconuts 140; Cassava 12; Bananas 2; Sweet potatoes 3.

Livestock (FAO estimates, '000 head, year ending September 2004): Pigs 32; Cattle 14; Goats 4; Poultry 185.

Livestock Products ('000 metric tons, 2004): Beef and veal 245; Pig meat 873; Poultry meat 135; Hen eggs 175; Cattle hides 45.

Fishing ('000 metric tons, live weight, 2003): Skipjack tuna 23.8; Yellowfin tuna 5.7; Bigeye tuna 1.0; Total capture (incl. others) 32.0. Source: FAO.

FINANCE

Currency and Exchange Rates: United States currency is used: 100 cents = 1 United States dollar (US $). *Sterling and Euro Equivalents* (30 December 2005): £1 sterling = US $1.7219; €1 = US $1.1797; US $100 = £58.08 = €84.77.

Budget (estimates, US $ million, year ending 30 September 2003): *Revenue:* Current 44.0 (Tax 25.9, Non-tax 18.1); Grants 116.2; Total 160.2. *Expenditure:* Current 126.4; Capital 24.1; Total 150.5. Source: IMF, *Federated States of Micronesia: Selected Issues and Statistical Appendix* (March 2005).

Gross Domestic Product at Current Prices (US $ million, year ending 30 September): 221.1 in 2002; 221.8 in 2003 (estimate); 214.5 in 2004 (estimate). Source: Asian Development Bank, *Key Indicators of Developing Asian and Pacific Countries*.

Gross Domestic Product at Constant 1998 Prices (US $ million, year ending 30 September): 211.2 in 2002; 211.4 in 2003 (estimate); 204.5 in 2004 (estimate). Source: Asian Development Bank, *Key Indicators of Developing Asian and Pacific Countries*.

Gross Domestic Product by Economic Activity (US $ million at current prices, 2002): Agriculture, hunting, forestry and fishing 34; Manufacturing 2; Mining, electricity, gas and water 3; Construction 21; Wholesale and retail trade, hotels and restaurants 34; Transport, storage and communications 29; Other activities 117; *GDP in purchasers' values* 240. Source: UN, *Statistical Yearbook for Asia and the Pacific*.

Balance of Payments (estimates, US $ million, year ending 30 September 2004): Merchandise exports (incl. re-exports) f.o.b. 19.6; Merchandise imports f.o.b. –133.4; *Trade balance* –113.8; Exports of services 19.9; Imports of services –50.8; *Balance on goods and services* –144.7; Other income received 20.1; Other income paid –6.6; *Balance on goods, services and income* 131.2; Private unrequited transfers 2.4; Official unrequited transfers 104.3; *Current balance* –24.5; Capital and financial account 0.1; *Overall balance* –24.3. Source: IMF, *Federated States of Micronesia: Selected Issues and Statistical Appendix* (March 2005).

EXTERNAL TRADE

Principal Commodities (US $'000, 2002, estimates): *Imports:* Prepared foodstuffs 22,227; Mineral products 16,446; Machinery, mechanical appliances and electrical equipment 12,335; Animals and animal products 7,657; Vegetable products 6,284; Chemicals 6,071; Textiles and textile articles 6,043; Transportation equipment 5,151; Base metals and articles thereof 4,783; Total (incl. others) 104,290. *Exports:* Garments 3,591; Betel nuts 888; Kava 241; Copra 211; Crabs and lobsters 206; Total (incl. others) 14,441. Source: Asian Development Bank, *Key Indicators of Developing Asian and Pacific Countries*.

Principal Trading Partners (US $'000, 2002, estimates): *Imports:* Australia 8,621; Japan 11,100; USA 64,588; Total (incl. others) 104,290. *Exports:* Japan 2,706; USA 4,825; Total (incl. others) 14,441. Source: Asian Development Bank, *Key Indicators of Developing Asian and Pacific Countries*.

TRANSPORT

Shipping: Merchant Fleet (registered at 31 December 2004): Vessels 21; Total displacement ('000 grt) 18.3. Source: Lloyd's Register-Fairplay, *World Fleet Statistics*.

TOURISM

Foreign Tourist Arrivals: 15,265 in 2001; 19,046 in 2002; 18,496 in year ending September 2003. Sources: World Tourism Organization, *Yearbook of Tourism Statistics* and IMF, *Federated States of Micronesia: Selected Issues and Statistical Appendix* (March 2005).

Tourist Arrivals by Country of Residence (year ending September 2003): Japan 3,984; Other Asia 1,842; USA 7,736; Total (incl. others) 18,496. Source: IMF, *Federated States of Micronesia: Selected Issues and Statistical Appendix* (March 2005).

Tourism Receipts (US $ million, incl. passenger transport): 15 in 2001; 17 in 2002; 17 in 2003. Source: World Tourism Organization.

COMMUNICATIONS MEDIA

Telephones ('000 main lines in use, 2001): 10.0*.

Facsimile Machines (number in use, 1998): 539*.

Radio Receivers (1996): 22,000 in use.

Internet Users ('000, 2000): 4.0*.

Television Receivers (1996): 19,800 in use.

*Source: International Telecommunication Union.

EDUCATION

Primary (1995): 174 schools; 1,051 teachers (1984); 27,281 pupils.

Secondary (1995): 24 schools; 314 teachers (1984); 6,898 pupils.

Tertiary (1998/99): 1,510 students.

Sources: UN, *Statistical Yearbook for Asia and the Pacific* and UNESCO Institute for Statistics.

THE FEDERATED STATES OF MICRONESIA

Directory

The Constitution

On 10 May 1979 the locally drafted Constitution of the Federated States of Micronesia, incorporating the four states of Kosrae, Yap, Ponape (formally renamed Pohnpei in November 1984) and Truk (renamed Chuuk in January 1990), became effective. Each of the four states has its own Constitution, elected legislature and Governor. The Constitution guarantees fundamental human rights and establishes a separation of the judicial, executive and legislative powers. The federal legislature, the Congress of the Federated States of Micronesia, is a unicameral parliament with 14 members, popularly elected. The executive consists of the President, elected by the Congress, and a Cabinet. The Constitution provides for a review of the governmental and federal system every 10 years.

In November 1986 the Compact of Free Association was signed by the Governments of the Federated States of Micronesia and the USA. By the terms of the Compact, the Federated States of Micronesia is an internally sovereign, self-governing state, whose policy concerning foreign affairs must be consistent with guide-lines laid down in the Compact. Full responsibility for defence lies with the USA, and the security arrangements may be terminated only by mutual agreement. Furthermore, the Compact guaranteed exclusivity to US military forces in Micronesia's waters. The Governments of the Federated States of Micronesia and the USA signed an amended Compact on 1 May 2003, whereby its terms were renewed until 2023. The agreement was approved by the US Congress in November 2003 and ratified by President George W. Bush in December. The amended Compact came into force in June 2004 and was due to expire in 2023.

The Government

HEAD OF STATE

President: JOSEPH J. URUSEMAL (took office 14 July 2003).
Vice-President: REDLEY KILLION.

THE CABINET
(April 2006)

Secretary of the Department of Finance and Administration: NICK L. ANDON.
Secretary of the Department of Foreign Affairs: SEBASTIAN L. ANEFAL.
Secretary of the Department of Economic Affairs: AKILLINO H. SUSAIA.
Secretary of the Department of Health, Education and Social Services: NENA S. NENA.
Secretary of the Department of Justice: MARSTELLA E. JACK.
Secretary of the Department of Transportation, Communications and Infrastructure: ANDREW R. YATILMAN.
Public Defender: BEAULEEN CARL-WORSWICK.
Postmaster-General: BETHWEL HENRY.

GOVERNMENT OFFICES

Office of the President: POB PS-53, Palikir, Pohnpei, FM 96941; tel. 320-2228; fax 320-2785; internet www.fsmpio.fm.
Department of Economic Affairs: POB PS-12, Palikir, Pohnpei, FM 96941; tel. 320-2646; fax 320-5854; e-mail fsmdea@mail.fm; e-mail invest@fsminvest.fm; internet www.fsminvest.fm.
Department of Finance and Administration: POB PS-158, Palikir, Pohnpei, FM 96941; tel. 320-2640; fax 320-2380; e-mail fsmsofa@mail.fm.
Department of Foreign Affairs: POB PS-123, Palikir, Pohnpei, FM 96941; tel. 320-2614; fax 320-2933; e-mail foreignaffairs@mail.fm.
Department of Health, Education and Social Services: POB PS-70, Palikir, Pohnpei, FM 96941; tel. 320-2872; fax 320-5263; e-mail fsmhesa@mail.fm.
Department of Justice: POB PS-105, Palikir, Pohnpei, FM 96941; tel. 320-2644; fax 320-2234; e-mail doj@mail.fm.
Department of Transportation, Communications and Infrastructure: POB PS 2 Palikir, Pohnpei, FM 96941; tel. 320-2892; fax 320-5383; e-mail transfsm@mail.fm.
Office of the Public Defender: POB PS-174, Palikir, Pohnpei, FM 96941; tel. 320-2648; fax 320-5775.
Public Information Office: POB PS-34, Palikir, Pohnpei, FM 96941; tel. 320-2548; fax 320-4356; e-mail fsmpio@mail.fm; internet www.fsmpio.fm.

The Legislature

CONGRESS OF THE FEDERATED STATES OF MICRONESIA

The Congress comprises 14 members (Senators), of whom four are elected for a four-year term and 10 for a two-year term. The most recent election, for the 10 two-year seats, was held on 8 March 2005, elections for the other seats having been conducted on the previous day.
Speaker: PETER M. CHRISTIAN.

STATE LEGISLATURES

Chuuk State Legislature: POB 189, Weno, Chuuk, FM 96942; tel. 330-2234; fax 330-2233; Senate of 10 mems and House of Representatives of 28 mems elected for four years; Gov. WESLEY W. SIMINA.
Kosrae State Legislature: POB 187, Tofol, Kosrae, FM 96944; tel. 370-3002; fax 370-3162; e-mail kosraelc@mail.fm; unicameral body of 14 mems serving for four years; Gov. RENSLEY A. SIGRAH.
Pohnpei State Legislature: POB 39, Kolonia, Pohnpei, FM 96941; tel. 320-2235; fax 320-2505; internet www.fm/pohnpeileg; 27 representatives elected for four years (terms staggered); Gov. JOHNNY P. DAVID.
Yap State Legislature: POB 39, Colonia, Yap, FM 96943; tel. 350-2108; fax 350-4113; 10 mems, six elected from the Yap Islands proper and four elected from the Outer Islands of Ulithi and Woleai, for a four-year term; Gov. ROBERT A. RUECHO.

Election Commission

National Election Commission: POB PS-355, Palikir, Pohnpei 96941; tel. 320-4283; fax 320-7534; e-mail ned@mail.fm; Dir BERNELL EDWARDS.

Diplomatic Representation

EMBASSIES IN MICRONESIA

Australia: POB S, Kolonia, Pohnpei, FM 96941; tel. 320-5448; fax 320-5449; e-mail australia@mail.fm; internet www.australianembassy.fm; Ambassador CORRINE TOMPKINSON.
China, People's Republic: POB 530, Kolonia, Pohnpei, FM 96941; tel. 320-5575; fax 320-5578; e-mail chinaemb@mail.fm; Ambassador YANG QIANG.
Japan: Pami Bldg, 3rd Floor, POB 1847, Kolonia, Pohnpei, FM 96941; tel. 320-5465; fax 320-5470; Chargé d'affaires a.i. TOSHIO OMURA.
USA: POB 1286, Kolonia, Pohnpei, FM 96941; tel. 320-2187; fax 320-2186; e-mail usembassy@mail.fm; internet www.fm/usembassy; Ambassador SUZANNE K. HALE.

Judicial System

Supreme Court of the Federated States of Micronesia: POB PS-J, Palikir Station, Pohnpei, FM 96941; tel. 350-2159; fax 320-2756; internet www.fsmlaw.org; Chief Justice ANDON L. AMARAICH.

State Courts and Appellate Courts have been established in Yap, Chuuk, Kosrae and Pohnpei.

Religion

The population is predominantly Christian, mainly Roman Catholic. The Assembly of God, Jehovah's Witnesses, Seventh-day Adventists, the Church of Jesus Christ of Latter-day Saints (Mormons), the United Church of Christ, Baptists and the Bahá'í Faith are also represented.

CHRISTIANITY

The Roman Catholic Church

The Federated States of Micronesia forms a part of the diocese of the Caroline Islands, suffragan to the archdiocese of Agaña (Guam). The Bishop participates in the Catholic Bishops' Conference of the Pacific, based in Fiji. At 31 December 2003 there were 77,733 adherents in the diocese.

THE FEDERATED STATES OF MICRONESIA

Bishop of the Caroline Islands: Most Rev. AMANDO SAMO, Bishop's House, POB 939, Weno, Chuuk, FM 96942; tel. 330-2399; fax 330-4585; e-mail diocese@mail.fm; internet www.dioceseofthecarolines.org.

Other Churches

Calvary Baptist Church: Kolonia, Pohnpei, POB H, FM 96941; Pastor RICKSON KIHLENGS.

Liebenzell Mission: Rev. Roland Rauchholz, POB 9, Weno, Chuuk, FM 96942; tel. 330-3869; e-mail missions@liebenzellusa.org; internet www.liebenzellusa.org/mcrnesia.htm.

Truth Independent Baptist Church: Kolonia, Pohnpei, POB 65, FM 969410065; tel. 320-3643; fax 320-6769; Pastor RICARDO P. VERACRUZ.

United Church of Christ in Pohnpei: Kolonia, Pohnpei, POB 864, FM 96941; tel. 320-2271; fax 320-4404; Pres. BERNELL EDWARD.

The Press

The Island Tribune: Pohnpei, FM 96941; internet www.islandtribune.com; f. 1997; fortnightly.

Micronesia Focus: Pohnpei, POB 627, FM 96941; tel. 320-4672; f. 1993; Editor KETSON JOHNSON.

The National Union: FSM Public Information Office, POB 490, Kolonia, Pohnpei, FM 96941; tel. 320-2548; fax 320-2785; f. 1979; 2 a month; Public Information Officer KETSON JOHNSON; circ. 500.

Yap State Bulletin: Dept of Youth and Civic Affairs, POB 430, Colonia, Yap 96943; tel. 350-2168; fax 350-3898; e-mail bigj@mail.fm; f. 1989; fortnightly; circ. 500.

Broadcasting and Communications

TELECOMMUNICATIONS

FSM Telecommunication Corporation: POB 1210, Kolonia, Pohnpei, FM 96941; tel. 320-2740; fax 320-2745; e-mail customerservice@telecom.fm; internet www.telecom.fm; provides domestic and international services; Gen. Man. TAKURO AKINAGA.

BROADCASTING

Radio

Federated States of Micronesia Public Information Office: POB PS-34, Palikir, Pohnpei, FM 96941; tel. 320-2548; fax 320-4356; e-mail fsmpio@mail.fm; internet www.fsmpio.fm; govt-operated; four regional stations, each broadcasting 18 hours daily; Information Officer KESTER JAMES.

Station V6AH: POB 1086, Kolonia, Pohnpei, FM 96941; programmes in English and Pohnpeian; Man. JOSEPH C. P. ALANNZO.

Station V6AI: POB 117, Colonia, Yap, FM 96943; tel. 350-2174; fax 350-4426; programmes in English, Yapese, Ulithian and Satawalese; Man. PETER GARAMFEL.

Station V6AJ: POB 147, Tofol, Kosrae, FM 96944; tel. 370-3040; fax 370-3880; e-mail v6aj@.mail.fm; programmes in English and Kosraean; Man. MCDONALD ITTU.

Station V6AK: Wenn, Chuuk, FM 96942; tel. 330-2596; programmes in Chuukese and English; Man. JOE COMMOR.

WSZA Yap: Dept of Youth and Civic Affairs, POB 30, Colonia, Yap 96943; tel. 350-2174; Media Dir PETER GARAMFEL.

WSZD Pohnpei: POB 1086, Kolonia, Pohnpei 96941; tel. 320-2296; programmes in English and Pohnpeian; Man. JOSEPH C. P. ALANNZO.

Television

Island Cable TV—Pohnpei: POB 1628, Pohnpei, FM 96941; tel. 320-2671; fax 320-2670; e-mail ictv@mail.fm; f. 1991; Pres. BERNARD HELGENBERGER; Gen. Man. DAVID O. CLIFFE.

TV Station Chuuk (TTKK): Wenn, Chuuk, FM 96942; commercial.

TV Station Pohnpei (KPON): Central Micronesia Communications, POB 460, Kolonia, Pohnpei, FM 96941; f. 1977; commercial; Pres. BERNARD HELGENBERGER; Tech. Dir DAVID CLIFFE.

TV Station Yap (WAAB): Colonia, Yap, FM 96943; tel. 350-2160; fax 350-4113; govt-owned; Man. LOU DEFNGIN.

Finance

BANKING

Regulatory Authority

Federated States of Micronesia Banking Board: POB 1887, Kolonia, Pohnpei, FM 96941; tel. 320-2015; fax 320-5433; e-mail fsmbb@mail.fm; e-mail wfwbb_gov@mail.fm; f. 1980; Chair. LARRY RAIGETAL; Commissioner WILSON F. WAGUK.

Banks are also supervised by the US Federal Deposit Insurance Corporation.

Commercial Banks

Bank of the Federated States of Micronesia: POB BF, Tofol, Kosrae, FM 96944; tel. 370-3225; e-mail bofsmhq@mail.fm; brs in Kosrae, Yap, Pohnpei and Chuuk.

Bank of Guam (USA): POB 367, Kolonia, Pohnpei, FM 96941; tel. 320-2550; fax 320-2562; e-mail bogpohn@mail.fm; internet www.bankofguam.com; Man. VIDA B. RICAFRENTE; Pres. ANTHONY A. LEON GUERRERO; brs in Chuuk and Pohnpei.

Yap Credit Union: POB 610, Colonia, Yap; tel. 350-2142.

Development Bank

Federated States of Micronesia Development Bank: POB M, Kolonia, Pohnpei, FM 96941; tel. 320-2840; fax 320-2842; e-mail fsmdb@mail.fm; f. 1979; total assets US $31.7m. (2004); Chair. IHLEN JOSEPH; Pres. ANNA MENDIOLA; 4 brs.

Banking services for the rest of the islands are available in Guam, Hawaii and on the US mainland.

INSURANCE

Actouka Executive Insurance: POB 55, Kolonia, Pohnpei; tel. 320-5331; fax 320-2331; e-mail mlamar@mail.fm.

Caroline Insurance Underwriters: POB 37, Chuuk; tel. 330-2705; fax 330-2207.

FSM Insurance Group: Kosrae; tel. 370-3788; fax 370-2120.

Islands Insurance: POB K, Kolonia, Pohnpei; tel. 320-3422; fax 320-3424.

Moylan's Insurance Underwriters: POB 1448, Kolonia, Pohnpei; tel. 320-2118; fax 320-2519; e-mail pohnpei@moylansinsurance.com; Pres. and Gen. Man. LOREN PETERSON.

Oceania Insurance Co: POB 1202, Weno, Chuuk, FM 96942; tel. 330-3036; fax 330-2334; e-mail oceanpac@mail.fm; also owns and manages Pacific Basin Insurance.

Pacific Islands Insurance Underwriters: POB 386, Colonia, Yap; tel. 350-2340; fax 350-2341.

Transpacific Insurance: POB 510, Kolonia, Pohnpei; tel. 320-5525; fax 320-5524.

Yap Insurance Agency: POB 386, Colonia, Yap; tel. 350-2340; fax 350-2341; e-mail tachelioyap@mail.fm.

Trade and Industry

GOVERNMENT AGENCIES

Coconut Development Authority: POB 297, Kolonia, Pohnpei, FM 96941; tel. 320-2892; fax 320-5383; e-mail fsmcda@mail.fm; responsible for all purchasing, processing and exporting of copra and copra by-products in the islands; Gen. Man. NAMIO NANPEI.

Pohnpei Economic Development Authority: POB 738, Kolonia, Pohnpei, FM 96941; tel. 320-2298; fax 320-2775; e-mail eda@mail.fm; Chair. President JOSEPH J. URUSEMAL (ex officio); Exec. Dir SHELTEN NETH.

FSM National Fisheries Corporation: POB R, Kolonia, Pohnpei, FM 96941; tel. 320-2529; fax 320-2239; e-mail nfcairfreight@mail.fm; internet www.fsmgov.org/nfc/; f. 1984; established in 1990, with the Economic Devt Authority and an Australian co, the Caroline Fishing Corpn (three vessels); promotes fisheries development; Pres. PETER SITAN.

Micronesian Fisheries Authority: PS122, Palikir, Pohnpei State, FM 96941; tel. 320-2700; fax 320-2383; e-mail fsmfish@mail.fm; name changed as above from Micronesian Maritime Authority in 2000.

National Oceanic Resource Management Authority (NORMA): POB PS-122, Palikir, Pohnpei, FM 96941; tel. 320-2700; fax 320-2383; e-mail norma@mail.fm; fmrly Micronesian Fisheries Authority; name changed 2002; responsible for conservation, management and development of tuna resources and for issue of fishing licences; Exec. Dir BERNARD THOULAG; Deputy Dir EUGENE PANGELINAN.

THE FEDERATED STATES OF MICRONESIA

CHAMBERS OF COMMERCE

Chuuk Chamber of Commerce: POB 700, Weno, Chuuk, FM 96941; tel. 330-2318; fax 330-2314; e-mail larry.bruton@mail.fm; Pres. LARRY J. BRUTON.

Kosrae Chamber of Commerce: POB 1075, Tofol, Kosrae, FM 96944; tel. 370-2044; fax 370-2066; e-mail kosraeci@mail.fm; Chair. GEOFF RASCHOU.

Pohnpei Chamber of Commerce: POB 405, Kolonia, Pohnpei, FM 96941; tel. 320-2452; fax 320-5277; e-mail amc@mail.fm; Pres. AMBROS SENDA.

Yap Chamber of Commerce: Colonia, Yap, FM 96943; tel. 350-2298.

UTILITIES

Chuuk Public Works (CPW): POB 248, Weno, Chuuk, FM 96942; tel. 330-2242; fax 320-4815; e-mail chkpublicworks@mail.fm.

Kosrae Utility Authority: POB 277, Tofol, Kosrae, FM 96944; tel. 370-3799; fax 370-3798; e-mail kua@mail.fm; corporatized in 1994; Gen. Man. ROBERT NELSON.

Pohnpei Utility Corporation: POB C, Kolonia, Pohnpei, FM 96941; tel. 320-5606; fax 320-2505; f. 1992; provides electricity, water and sewerage services.

Yap Public Services Corporation: POB 621, Colonia, Yap, FM 96943; tel. 350-2175; fax 350-2331; f. 1996; provides electricity, water and sewerage services.

CO-OPERATIVES

Chuuk: Chuuk Co-operative, Faichuk Cacao and Copra Co-operative Asscn, Pis Fishermen's Co-operative, Fefan Women's Co-operative.

Pohnpei: Pohnpei Federation of Co-operative Asscns (POB 100, Pohnpei, FM 96941), Pohnpei Handicraft Co-operative, Pohnpei Fishermen's Co-operative, Uh Soumwet Co-operative Asscn, Kolonia Consumers' and Producers' Co-operative Asscn, Kitti Minimum Co-operative Asscn, Kapingamarangi Copra Producers' Asscn, Metalanim Copra Co-operative Asscn, PICS Co-operative Asscn, Mokil Island Co-operative Asscn, Ngatik Island Co-operative Asscn, Nukuoro Island Co-operative Asscn, Kosrae Island Co-operative Asscn, Pingelap Consumers' Co-operative Asscn.

Yap: Yap Co-operative Asscn, POB 159, Colonia, Yap, FM 96943; tel. 350-2209; fax 350-4114; e-mail yca@mail.fm; f. 1952; Pres. FAUSTINO YANGMOG; Gen. Man. TONY GANNGIYAN; 1,832 mems.

Transport

ROADS

Macadam and concrete roads are found in the more important islands. Other islands have stone and coral-surfaced roads and tracks.

SHIPPING

Pohnpei, Chuuk, Yap and Kosrae have deep-draught harbours for commercial shipping. The ports provide warehousing and transhipment facilities.

Caroline Fisheries Corporation (CFC): POB 7, Kolonia, Pohnpei, FM 96941; tel. 320-3926; fax 320-4733; e-mail cfc@mail.fm; Gen. Man. MILAN KAMBER.

Pacific Shipping Agency: POB 154, Lelu, Kosrae FM 96944; tel. 350-2475; Gen. Man. THEODORE SIGRAH.

Pohnpei Transfer & Storage, Inc: POB 340, Kolonia, Pohnpei FM 96941; tel. 320-2552; fax 320-2389; e-mail fsmlinejv@mail.fm; Gen. Man. JOE VITT.

Truk Transportation Company (TRANSCO): POB 99, Weno, Chuuk FM 96942; tel. 330-2143; fax 330-2726; e-mail transco@mail.fm; Pres. NYRON HACHIGUCHI; Gen. Man. SEREMEA ARNOLD.

Waab Transportation Company: POB 177, Colonia, Yap FM 96943; tel. 350-2301; fax 350-4110; e-mail waabtrans@mail.fm; agents for PM & O Lines (USA); Gen. Man. CYRIL CHUGRAD.

CIVIL AVIATION

The Federated States of Micronesia is served by Continental Micronesia, Air Nauru and Continental Airlines (USA). Pacific Missionary Aviation, based in Pohnpei and Yap, provides domestic air services. There are international airports on Pohnpei, Chuuk, Yap and Kosrae, and airstrips on the outer islands of Onoun and Ta in Chuuk.

Tourism

The tourist industry is a significant source of revenue, although it has been hampered by the lack of infrastructure. Visitor attractions include excellent conditions for scuba-diving (notably in Chuuk Lagoon), Second World War battle sites and relics (many underwater) and the ancient ruined city of Nan Madol on Pohnpei. In 1990 there was a total of 362 hotel rooms. The number of tourist arrivals totalled 18,496 in the year ending September 2003. Tourist receipts totalled some US $13m. in 2001.

Federated States of Micronesia Visitors Board: Dept of Economic Affairs, National Government, PO Box PS-12, Palikir, Pohnpei, FM 96941; tel. 320-5133; fax 320-3251; e-mail fsminfo@visit-fsm.org; internet www.visit-fsm.org.

Chuuk Visitors Bureau: POB FQ, Weno, Chuuk FM 96942; tel. 330-4133; fax 330-4194; e-mail cvb@mail.fm.

Kosrae Visitors Bureau: POB 659, Tofol, Kosrae, FM 96944; tel. 370-2228; fax 370-3000; e-mail kosrae@mail.fm; internet www.kosrae.com.

Pohnpei Department of Tourism and Parks: POB 66, Kolonia, Pohnpei, FM 96941; tel. 320-2421; fax 320-6019; e-mail tourismparks@mail.fm; Deputy Chief BUMIO SILBANUZ.

Pohnpei Visitors Bureau: POB 1949, Kolonia, Pohnpei, FM 96941; tel. 320-4851; fax 320-4868; e-mail pohnpeiVB@mail.fm; internet www.visit-pohnpei.fm.

Yap Visitors Bureau: POB 36, Colonia, Yap, FM 96943; tel. 350-2298; fax 350-2571; e-mail lngaden@yahoo.com; internet www.visityap.com; Chair. ALPHONSO GANANG; Asst Gen. Man. ALBERT J. FALRUW.

MOLDOVA

Introductory Survey

Location, Climate, Language, Religion, Flag, Capital

The Republic of Moldova is a small, land-locked country situated in south-eastern Europe. It includes only a small proportion of the historical territories of Moldova (Moldavia), most of which are in Romania, while others (southern Bessarabia and northern Bucovina) are in Ukraine. The republic is bounded to the north, east and south by Ukraine. To the west it borders Romania. The climate is very favourable for agriculture, with long, warm summers and relatively mild winters. Average temperatures in Chişinău range from 21°C (70°F) in July to −4°C (24°F) in January. The Constitution of July 1994 describes the official language as Moldovan (although this is widely considered to be identical to Romanian). Most of the inhabitants of Moldova profess Christianity, the largest denomination being the Eastern Orthodox Church. The national flag (proportions 1 by 2) consists of three equal vertical stripes, of light blue, yellow and red; the yellow stripe has at its centre the arms of Moldova (a shield bearing a stylized bull's head in yellow, set between an eight-pointed yellow star, a five-petalled yellow flower, and a yellow crescent, the shield being set on the breast of an eagle, in gold and red, which holds a green olive branch in its dexter talons, a yellow sceptre in its sinister talons, and a yellow cross in its beak). The capital is Chişinău.

Recent History

The area of the present-day Republic of Moldova corresponds to only part of the medieval principality of Moldova (Moldavia), which emerged as an important regional power in the 15th century. In the following century, however, the principality came under Ottoman domination. Following a period of conflict between the Ottoman and Russian Empires in the late 18th century, Moldova was divided into two parts under the Treaty of Bucharest of 1812: the eastern territory of Bessarabia, situated between the Prut and Dniester (Dnestr or Nistru) rivers (which roughly corresponds to modern Moldova), was ceded to Russia, while the Ottomans retained control of western Moldova. A Romanian nationalist movement evolved in western Moldova and the neighbouring region of Wallachia during the 19th century, culminating in the proclamation of a sovereign Romanian state in 1877, independent of the Ottoman Empire. In 1881 Romania became a kingdom. In June 1918, after the collapse of the Russian Empire, Bessarabia was proclaimed an independent republic, although in November it voted to become part of Romania. This union was recognized in the Treaty of Paris (1920). However, the USSR (established in 1922) refused to recognize Romania's claims to the territory, and in October 1924 formed a Moldovan Autonomous Soviet Socialist Republic (ASSR) on the eastern side of the Dniester, in the Ukrainian Soviet Socialist Republic (SSR). In June 1940 Romania was forced to cede Bessarabia and northern Bucovina to the USSR, under the terms of the Treaty of Non-Aggression (the 'Molotov-Ribbentrop Pact'), concluded with Nazi Germany in August 1939. Northern Bucovina, southern Bessarabia and the Kotovsk-Balţa region of the Moldovan ASSR were incorporated into the Ukrainian SSR. The remaining parts of the Moldovan ASSR and of Bessarabia were merged to form the Moldovan SSR, which formally joined the USSR on 2 August 1940. Political power in the republic was vested in the Communist Party of Moldova (CPM), a subsidiary of the Communist Party of the Soviet Union (CPSU).

Between July 1941 and August 1944 the Moldovan SSR was reunited with Romania. However, the Soviet Army reannexed the region in 1944, and the Moldovan SSR was re-established. Soviet policy in Moldova concentrated on isolating the region from its historical links with Romania: cross-border traffic virtually ceased, the Cyrillic script was imposed on the Romanian language (which was referred to as Moldovan) and Russian and Ukrainian immigration was encouraged. In the 1950s thousands of ethnic Romanians were deported to Central Asia. Moldova remained among the more conservative republics of the USSR. Two future Soviet leaders, Leonid Brezhnev and Konstantin Chernenko, held prominent positions in the CPM during their early years of CPSU service: Brezhnev as First Secretary (leader) of the CPM in 1950–52, and Chernenko as head of party propaganda in 1948–56.

The policy of *glasnost* (openness), introduced by Soviet leader Mikhail Gorbachev in 1986, allowed the expression within Moldova of opposition to the process of 'russification'. In May 1989 a number of independent cultural and political groups, which had recently emerged, but were denied legal status by the authorities, allied to form the Popular Front (PF). In June some 70,000 people attended a protest demonstration, organized by the PF, on the anniversary of the Soviet annexation of Bessarabia in 1940. This was followed, in August 1989, by mass demonstrations in the capital, Chişinău, in support of proposals by the Moldovan Supreme Soviet (Supreme Council—legislature) to declare Romanian the official language of the republic. Following protests by non-ethnic Romanians, the proposals were amended: legislation was enacted providing for Russian to be retained as a language of inter-ethnic communication, but the official language was to be Romanian, written in the Latin script. Following disturbances and riots in Chişinău, during the celebrations of the anniversary of the Bolshevik Revolution on 7 November, the First Secretary of the CPM, Semion Grossu, was dismissed. He was replaced by Petru Lucinschi, an ethnic Romanian considered to be more supportive of Gorbachev's reforms.

The increasing influence of the Romanian-speaking population was strongly opposed by other inhabitants of the republic (who, at the 1989 census, comprised some 35% of the total population). In the areas east of the Dniester, where Russians and Ukrainians predominated, the local authorities refused to implement the language law. Opposition to growing Moldovan nationalism was led by the Yedinstvo (Unity) Movement, dominated by leading CPM members, and the United Work Collectives, a Slav-dominated organization based among the towns east of the Dniester. Both organizations had strong links with Gagauz Halky (Gagauz People), the most prominent of the political groups representing the 150,000-strong Gagauz minority (a Turkic, Orthodox Christian people, resident mostly in southern regions of Moldova). In January 1990 a referendum took place in the eastern town of Tiraspol, in which the predominantly Russian-speaking population voted to seek greater autonomy for the region beyond the Dniester (Transnistria or Transdnestria).

None of the independent political groups was officially allowed to endorse candidates in elections to the Moldovan Supreme Soviet in February 1990, but individual candidates made clear where their sympathies lay. About 80% of the 380 deputies elected were members of the CPM, but many were also sympathetic to the aims of the PF. The new Supreme Soviet convened in April, whereupon Mircea Snegur, a CPM member supported by the PF, was elected Chairman. In the following month the Government resigned after losing a vote of 'no confidence'. A new Council of Ministers, chaired by an economist, Mircea Druc, implemented far-reaching political changes. The CPM's constitutional right to power was revoked, and media organizations belonging to the CPM were transferred to state control. On 23 June the Supreme Soviet adopted a declaration of sovereignty asserting the supremacy of Moldova's Constitution and laws throughout the republic, which was to be known as the Soviet Socialist Republic of Moldova (as opposed to the russified 'Moldaviya'). The Supreme Soviet also declared the 1940 annexation of Bessarabia to have been illegal. In September Snegur was elected to the newly instituted post of President of the Republic, and the role of Chairman of the Supreme Soviet became that of a parliamentary speaker.

The actions of the increasingly radical Romanian majority in the legislature provoked further anxiety among the country's ethnic minorities during 1990. In August the Gagauz proclaimed a separate 'Gagauz SSR' in the southern region around Comrat (Komrat). In the following month east-bank Slavs proclaimed their secession from Moldova and the establishment of the 'Transdnestrian SSR', comprising Moldovan territory east of the Dniester, with its self-styled capital at Tiraspol. Both declarations were immediately annulled by the Moldovan

Supreme Soviet. In October Moldovan nationalists sought to thwart elections to a Gagauz Supreme Soviet by sending some 50,000 armed volunteers to the area. Violence was prevented only by the dispatch of Soviet troops to the region. The new Gagauz Supreme Soviet convened in Comrat and elected Stepan Topal as its President. Further inter-ethnic violence occurred east of the Dniester in November, when elections were announced to a Transnistrian Supreme Soviet. Negotiations in Moscow, the Russian and Soviet capital, involving the Moldovan Government, the east-bank Slavs and the Gagauz, failed to resolve the crisis, but the elections proceeded without further violence.

In mid-December 1990 an estimated 800,000 people, attending a 'Grand National Assembly', voted to reject any new union treaty (which was being negotiated by other Soviet republics), and in February 1991 the Moldovan Supreme Soviet resolved not to participate in the all-Union referendum on the future of the USSR. Despite the official boycott, in March some 650,000 people (mostly ethnic Russians, Ukrainians and Gagauz) did take part, voting almost unanimously for the preservation of the USSR. Nevertheless, the ethnic-Romanian-dominated Government and legislature continued the process of *de facto* secession. All-Union enterprises were placed under republican jurisdiction, a Moldovan state bank was established, the CPM was prohibited from activities in state and government organs, and conscription to the USSR armed forces was not implemented. In May the designation 'Soviet Socialist' was removed from the republic's name and the Supreme Soviet was renamed Parlamentul (the Parliament). In the same month, following a vote of 'no confidence' by the legislature, Mircea Druc was removed as Prime Minister.

Following the coup attempt by conservative communists in Moscow in August 1991, the commanders of the USSR's South-Western Military District sought to impose a state of emergency in Moldova. However, the republican leadership immediately announced its support for the Russian President, Boris Yeltsin, in his opposition to the coup, and demanded the reinstatement of Gorbachev as President of the USSR. On 27 August, after the coup had collapsed, Parlamentul and the 'Grand National Assembly' proclaimed Moldova's independence from the USSR. The Government asserted its jurisdiction over the border with Romania and introduced customs posts on the border with Ukraine. In September President Snegur ordered the creation of national armed forces, and assumed control of the republican KGB (state security service), transforming it into a Ministry of National Security. The Government announced that it would no longer participate in any Soviet structures or in negotiations for a new political union.

At the election to the republican presidency on 8 December 1991 Snegur, the sole candidate, received 98.2% of the votes cast. On 21 December Moldova was among the 11 signatories to the Alma-Ata (Almaty) Declaration establishing the Commonwealth of Independent States (CIS, see p. 201). The establishment of the CIS led to wider international recognition of Moldova's independence, which had been delayed by concerns at inter-ethnic tension within the republic. Moldovan affairs during the first half of 1992 were, none the less, dominated by the armed conflict in Transnistria (see below) and by the question of possible unification with Romania, strongly advocated by the ruling PF (which in February was re-formed as the Christian Democratic Popular Front—CDPF). Moreover, a National Council for Reintegration had been established in December 1991, comprising legislators from both Moldova and Romania who were committed to the idea of a unified Romanian state. Within Moldova, however, popular support for unification remained insubstantial. In June 1992 the CDPF-dominated Government announced its resignation. Andrei Sangheli, a Deputy Prime Minister in the outgoing administration, was appointed Prime Minister, and a new Government 'of national accord' was formed, led by the Agrarian Democratic Party (ADP), which largely comprised members of the former communist leadership—in particular, collective farm managers. Several portfolios that had been reserved for representatives from Transnistria and Gagauz-Yeri (Gagauzia, as the Gagauz-majority area around Comrat was known) were refused. The CDPF became the main opposition party. The ADP declared its commitment to consolidating Moldovan statehood, rejecting any future union with Romania in favour of a closer alignment with Russia and the CIS. The ADP's anti-unification policies were strongly supported by President Snegur, who in January 1993 proposed that the issue be resolved in a referendum. Snegur's proposal was narrowly rejected by Parlamentul, but the ensuing political crisis led to several resignations, including that of the pro-unification Chairman of Parlamentul, Alexandru Moșanu. Moșanu was replaced in February by Petru Lucinschi, the former leader of the CPM (which had been banned following the attempted coup in Moscow in 1991).

During 1993 the ADP made substantial progress with the drafting of a new Moldovan constitution, which was to be ratified following the election of a new Parlamentul. The draft constitution provided, *inter alia*, for a reduced, 104-member legislature. Moldova's first multi-party elections were held on 27 February 1994, with the participation of more than 73% of the electorate. On the eve of the elections, the authorities in Gagauz-Yeri rescinded their decision to boycott the poll, and the rate of participation in the region was reported to be high. In Transnistria the local leadership did not open polling stations, although residents were able to vote on the left bank of the Dniester. In all, 13 parties and blocs contested the elections, the results of which demonstrated popular support for parties advocating continued Moldovan independence. The ADP obtained an overall majority in Parlamentul (56 seats). The successor party to the CPM, the Socialist Party (SP), in alliance with the Yedinstvo Movement, won 28 seats. Two pro-unification groups shared the remaining 20 seats: the Peasants' Party of Moldova/Congress of Intelligentsia alliance (11) and the CDPF alliance (nine). The relative lack of support for the pro-unification parties was confirmed in a national referendum on Moldova's statehood on 6 March. More than 95% of the votes cast by some 75% of the electorate were in favour of continued independence. In late March Andrei Sangheli was re-elected Prime Minister, and Petru Lucinschi was re-elected Chairman of Parlamentul. A new, smaller Council of Ministers, solely comprising members of the ADP, was appointed in April. In May the CPM was permitted to re-form, as the Party of Communists of the Republic of Moldova (Partidul Comuniștilor din Republica Moldova—PCRM).

The new Constitution was adopted by Parlamentul in July 1994 and entered into force in August. As well as establishing the country's permanent neutrality, the Constitution provided for a 'special autonomous status' for Transnistria and Gagauz-Yeri within Moldova (the exact terms of which were to be determined at a later date). The official state language was specified as Moldovan (rather than Romanian), although the two languages were acknowledged to be identical. In March–April 1995 thousands of students participated in rallies in Chișinău, demanding that Romanian be redesignated the official state language. In response, Snegur decreed a six-month moratorium on the language issue; meanwhile, a special committee was to examine the matter. In June, following the rejection by the ADP and its allies in Parlamentul of the proposal that Romanian replace Moldovan in the Constitution as the state language, Snegur resigned his membership of the ADP (which he had joined in 1994). In August 1995 he established the Party of Rebirth and Conciliation (PRC), with the support of several disaffected ADP deputies and a Deputy Chairman of the legislature, Nicolae Andronic (who was removed from his post). In February 1996 Parlamentul again rejected the proposed redesignation of the state language.

Some 68% of the registered electorate participated in the presidential election held on 17 November 1996, which was contested by nine candidates. Although Snegur received the largest share of the votes cast (39%), his failure to win an absolute majority necessitated a second round of voting, contested by the incumbent and his closest rival, the ADP-supported Petru Lucinschi (who had secured 28%). The rate of participation was slightly higher (72%) in the second round, held on 1 December, when Lucinschi emerged with 54% of the votes. The authorities in Transnistria again boycotted the poll, and there were reports that residents were prevented from leaving the region to vote on the left bank of the Dniester. Lucinschi was inaugurated as President on 15 January 1997, and a new Government was announced later that month. It retained approximately one-half of the members of the outgoing administration, and was headed by Ion Ciubuc, a non-party economist. In March the leader of the ADP, Dumitru Moțpan, was elected as Lucinschi's successor as Chairman of Parlamentul (he had hitherto served as a Deputy Chairman).

Relations between Lucinschi and Parlamentul were strained during 1997, in particular over the progress of economic reforms. Parliamentary elections took place on 22 March 1998. In an apparent rejection of Lucinschi's economic reform programme, the elections were won by the PCRM, led by Vladimir Voronin, which took 30.1% of the votes cast (40 seats). The Democratic

Convention of Moldova (CDM), an alliance of right-wing parties that included the PRC, under the leadership of Snegur, won 19.2% (26 seats), while the Movement for a Democratic and Prosperous Moldova (MDPM) received 18.2% (24 seats) and the Moldovan Party of Democratic Forces 8.8% (11 seats). The remaining 11 parties (including the ADP) failed to secure the 4% of the votes required for representation. Three independent candidates won seats; the rate of participation was 67%, according to preliminary results. The elections were, once again, boycotted in Transnistria, but voters were permitted to cross the Dniester to vote.

At the first session of the new legislature, convened in late April 1998, Dumitru Diacov was elected Chairman. The Government resigned shortly afterwards. Since none of the political parties had secured an overall parliamentary majority, the new Government, appointed in late May (with Ciubuc retaining his post as Prime Minister), was a coalition of the MDPM, the CDM and the Moldovan Party of Democratic Forces. Within Parlamentul, the coalition (known as the Alliance for Democracy and Reforms) was led by Snegur. The efficacy of the new Government was swiftly undermined by differences between coalition members, although a motion of 'no confidence' was defeated in November.

Ciubuc resigned as Prime Minister in February 1999. Snegur resigned as parliamentary leader of the government coalition one day later, after his nominee for the premiership, Deputy Prime Minister Nicolae Andronic, was rejected. Shortly afterwards Lucinschi nominated the Mayor of Chişinău, Serafim Urecheanu, as Prime Minister. However, Urecheanu resigned in mid-February, having failed to reach agreement with the parliamentary majority, notably on the issue of strengthening executive powers. Lucinschi had, in the mean time, submitted a presidential bill to Parlamentul providing for a substantial expansion of the executive's authority over the next two years, which, he maintained, was essential in order to address the economic crisis. Following Urecheanu's resignation, Lucinschi nominated Ion Sturza, the Deputy Prime Minister and Minister of the Economy and Reforms, as Prime Minister. Although Parlamentul twice failed to endorse his proposed government, Lucinschi nominated Sturza a third time. Confronted with a choice between acceptance or an early general election (the Constitution permits the President to dissolve the legislature if a candidate for the premiership is twice rejected), Parlamentul narrowly approved Sturza's Government in mid-March.

Local elections were held on 23 May 1999, after which the country was reorganized into nine provinces and two autonomous entities (Gagauz-Yeri and Transnistria). A referendum was held on the same day, to approve increased presidential powers. Although initially invalidated because of the low rate of electoral participation, in June the Constitutional Court ruled the referendum to be valid; however, it was to have no judicial effect. In August a draft law on amending the Constitution was published, whereby the President would appoint the prime minister and members of the government and adopt their programme of activity; it was also proposed that the presidential term of office be extended from four to five years and that the number of deputies be reduced from 101 to 70, elected solely on the basis of single-mandate constituencies. In September Lucinschi announced his willingness to cancel a proposed referendum on the issue if parliamentary representatives, together with experts from the Council of Europe (see p. 211), succeeded in proposing revisions to the draft legislation. In the following month a group of deputies advanced a reform plan for debate in Parlamentul, which included a proposal that the President be appointed by the legislature. In November the Constitutional Court ruled the May referendum to have been illegal, as it had not been announced and prepared by Parlamentul; in future the President would not have the right to organize plebiscites.

In October 1999 the creation of a new, independent political bloc, by members of the MDPM and a former deputy of the Moldovan Party of Democratic Forces, weakened the Government's support in Parlamentul. In the following month Sturza lost a vote of confidence in the legislature, after the defeat of a controversial bill on the privatization of the wine and tobacco industries; the IMF and the World Bank subsequently suspended credits to Moldova (the bill was finally approved in October 2000). In mid-November 1999 Lucinschi nominated the former ambassador to Russia, Valeriu Bobutac, as Prime Minister. However, he failed to secure the necessary support in the legislature and, following the failure of a second candidate, Voronin, the President decided to propose a third, rather than dissolve the legislature. The President finally nominated Dumitru Braghiş, hitherto Deputy Minister of Economy and Reform, who was approved as Prime Minister in late December.

In early July 2000 Parlamentul voted, by 92 votes to five, in favour of amending the Constitution to permit the legislature to elect the Head of State. Although President Lucinschi vetoed the proposed constitutional change, Parlamentul swiftly overturned his decision, and legislation was enacted in late July; the President declared the new law to be in contravention of the (non-binding) referendum of May 1999. In September 2000 Parlamentul approved a further amendment to the law on presidential electoral procedure and an alteration to the electoral code, and in mid-October it announced that a presidential election would be held at the beginning of December. Lucinschi, who insisted that the public should retain the right to elect the president, announced that he would not contest the election. In November the PCRM selected Voronin as its presidential candidate. Also contesting the election was the Chairman of the Constitutional Court, Pavel Barbalat, who had been proposed by a coalition of the Democratic Party of Moldova (Partidul Democrat din Moldova—PDM, as the MDPM had been renamed in April), the CDM, the People's Christian Democratic Party (Partidul Popular Creştin Democrat—PPCD, formerly the CDPF) and the Moldovan Party of Democratic Forces.

Three rounds of voting in the presidential election proved inconclusive in early December 2000, with neither candidate obtaining the requisite number of votes to secure an overall victory. After Voronin refused to withdraw his candidacy, the PDM, the CDM, the PPCD and the Moldovan Party of Democratic Forces boycotted a fourth round of voting on 21 December, preventing it from taking place, thereby permitting the President to dissolve the legislature and schedule early parliamentary elections; Lucinschi emphasized the right of the new Parlamentul to overturn measures introduced by the previous legislature. Parlamentul was duly dissolved on 12 January 2001.

At the legislative elections, held on 25 February 2001, the PCRM won an overall majority in Parlamentul, securing 49.9% of the votes cast and 71 seats. The Braghiş Alliance, formed by the incumbent Prime Minister, obtained 19 seats, while the PPCD obtained 11 seats. The elections were described as free and fair by Organization for Security and Co-operation in Europe (OSCE, see p. 327) observers. The rate of voter participation was some 70%. In early March the PCRM, which pledged to maintain a multi-party system, again nominated Voronin as its presidential candidate. In the election, which took place on 4 April, Voronin secured 71 votes, Braghiş obtained 15 and another communist candidate, Valerian Cristea, won three; the 11 PPCD deputies abstained from voting. Following his inauguration as President on 7 April, Voronin nominated Vasile Tarlev, a former businessman without party affiliation, to head a new government.

Proposals by the Minister of Education, Ilie Vancea, for the introduction of the compulsory teaching of Russian language and history to the national curriculum from 2002, were confirmed in December 2001. A demonstration, organized by the PPCD and involving an estimated 3,000 people, took place in Chişinău in early January 2002 to protest against these measures; large-scale, daily protests continued throughout the month, prompting fears of destabilization and demands for PPCD members to be deprived of their parliamentary immunity. In late January the Ministry of Justice suspended the PPCD from participation in political activities for a period of one month, thus preventing it from organizing further protests. However, in February, following intervention by the Council of Europe, the PPCD's suspension was annulled in order to allow the party to campaign for local elections, due to be held in April. In mid-February, however, the Constitutional Court ruled that the scheduling of early local elections for April, before the expiry of the four-year mandate of the local government officials elected in 1999, was unconstitutional.

Meanwhile, in early February 2002 the Deputy Prime Minister and Minister of the Economy, Andrei Cucu, and the reformist Minister of Finance, Mihai Manole, tendered their resignations, prompting concern internationally that the withdrawal of the only two non-PCRM members of the Council of Ministers might hinder the implementation of economic reforms. Protests against the proposed reform of the education system intensified throughout February, eventually prompting Vancea to announce that the controversial legislation would be retracted. Vancea was dismissed on 26 February. The following day Vasile Draganel resigned as Minister of the Interior, amid reports that he had been unwilling to dispel protesters by force. Draganel was replaced by Gheorghe Papuc, a long-serving member of the security forces. Despite a ruling by the Supreme Court declaring the ongoing protests to be illegal and demanding that they be halted, in late February 2002 demonstrators began to protest outside the headquarters of the national television company against state censorship and misinformation. In late March the Deputy Chairman of the PPCD, Vlad Cubreacov, who had been involved in organizing the anti-Government protests, was declared missing; thousands of demonstrators subsequently gathered to protest against Cubreacov's disappearance, which members of the PPCD attributed to the Government. At the end of the month the PPCD announced that it had discontinued its anti-Government protests, in compliance with Council of Europe recommendations, but declared that they would resume should the Government fail to comply with Council resolutions on, *inter alia*, granting independence to the state-owned media and the judiciary. In late May Cubreacov was discovered alive, although his kidnappers remained unidentified. In June judicial proceedings against members of the opposition involved in the organization of public protests (including Cubreacov) were suspended indefinitely.

In early June 2002 Parlamentul approved a new Civil Code. A number of government changes were made in late 2002, including the creation of the new post of Minister of Reintegration, with responsibility for the resolution of the issue of Transnistria and the co-ordination of government structures. Also in December the Social Liberal Party absorbed the Moldovan Party of Democratic Forces. Local elections took place on 25 May and 8 June 2003, in which the PCRM won the majority of seats, followed by the newly formed 'Our Moldova' alliance, comprising the Alliance of Independents of Moldova, the Moldovan Liberal Party and the Social Democratic Alliance of Moldova. Following the elections, new legislation on administrative reform, approved by the Government in January, came into effect, according to which the nine provinces and two autonomous regions introduced in 1999 were replaced with a structure comprising 33 districts and two municipalities (Balți and Chișinău). In July 2003 the parties of the 'Our Moldova' bloc formally merged, together with the Popular Democratic Party of Moldova, to form the 'Our Moldova' Alliance, led by Dumitru Braghiș, Serafim Urecheanu and Veaceslav Untilă.

Thousands of protesters took part in opposition demonstrations in November 2003, against the Government's initial support for a Russian proposal for the federalization of Moldova as a solution to the unresolved status of Transnistria (see below). The proposals, rejected in late November, had envisaged the installation of a popularly elected president and new, bicameral legislature, with an upper house comprising nine representatives elected from Transnistria, four from Gagauz-Yeri and 13 from the remainder of Moldova; Transnistria and Gagauz-Yeri were to have been represented at federal level by deputy prime ministers. In early December the Prosecutor-General, Vasile Rusu, resigned, following criticism of his response to the protests; he was replaced by Valeriu Balaban. Further protests took place in December against legislation on nationalities policy, which was submitted to Parlamentul by Voronin. The new law, which was approved on 19 December, intended to promote the use of Russian as a language of inter-ethnic communication, although Moldovan was to remain the official language.

In February 2004 Andrei Strătan replaced Nicolae Dudău as Minister of Foreign Affairs. In the same month Parlamentul withdrew the immunity from prosecution of three members of the PPCD, including the party's Chairman, Iurie Roșca, at the request of the Prosecutor-General, to permit their prosecution on charges of organizing and participating in unauthorized protests. From April the PDM and the Social Liberal Party agreed to co-operate with the 'Our Moldova' Alliance, as the Democratic Moldova bloc, in preparation for parliamentary elections scheduled to be held in 2005. In October the Minister of Defence, Victor Gaicuc, was dismissed from office following the large-scale theft of military ordnance from army depots in the previous month. In December Andrei Strătan was appointed as Deputy Prime Minister, retaining the foreign affairs portfolio.

In the legislative elections, held on 6 March 2005, the PCRM won 46.0% of the votes cast and 56 seats, the Democratic Moldova bloc obtained 28.5% (34 seats) and the PPCD received 9.1% (11 seats). No other party or grouping obtained legislative representation. Although the PCRM held an absolute majority of seats in Parlamentul, it did not hold the quorum of 61 mandates necessary for the election of a president. At the inaugural session of Parlamentul the PDM withdrew from the Democratic Moldova bloc, forming its own eight-member faction, and three members of the Social Liberal Party subsequently also left the bloc, which was renamed the 'Our Moldova' Alliance faction in the legislature. Despite declarations that opposition deputies would boycott the presidential vote, in the event only the 'Our Moldova' Alliance did so. The election was held on 4 April, contested by the incumbent, Voronin, and another PCRM-nominated candidate, Gheorghe Duca, the President of the Moldovan Academy of Sciences (in order to comply with the constitutional requirement that presidential elections be contested). Voronin secured 75 of the 101 votes available (some 95 legislators were present); Duca received only one vote. Voronin was inaugurated as President on 7 April, and on 19 April Parlamentul approved a new Government, again led by Tarlev and retaining many members of the previous Council of Ministers. The elections were generally regarded to have been conducted in a free and fair fashion, although there was criticism of some aspects of media coverage.

In April 2005 Serafim Urecheanu resigned as Mayor of Chișinău, announcing that the role was incompatible with his leadership of the 'Our Moldova' Alliance. In October members of the PCRM voted in Parlamentul to remove the parliamentary immunity of Urecheanu and two other deputies, following allegations of abuse of office. In early November Dumitru Braghiș left the 'Our Moldova' Alliance, of which Urecheanu remained the sole leader, in order to form a new party. Meanwhile, in October Mihai Pop had been appointed as Minister of Finance, in succession to Zinaida Grecianîi, who had become First Deputy Prime Minister. In November the Minister of Health and Social Protection, Valerian Revenco, was dismissed and replaced by Ion Ababii. In the same month the Unionist Movement of Moldova was founded, with the objective of pursuing closer relations with Romania. In December mayoral elections in Chișinău failed for a fourth time, owing to a low rate of participation by the electorate (of less than 20%).

In January 2006 a former Minister of Defence, Valeriu Pasat, was sentenced to 10 years' imprisonment, after being convicted of defrauding the state when selling redundant fighter aircraft to the USA in 1997. The Government denied claims that the case had been politically motivated. In February 2006 the US embassy reportedly asserted that the Moldovan Government had acted appropriately in selling the aircraft to the USA, since had it accepted a higher bid from a country associated with international terrorism, its relations with the international community would have been adversely affected. In February 2006 Pasat was indicted on further, unrelated charges of having organized protests during the 2005 legislative elections in an attempt to overthrow Voronin and of conspiring to murder PPCD leader Iurie Roșca.

Following the proclamation of Transnistria's secession in September 1990, relations with the central Government in Chișinău remained tense. Armed conflict broke out in December 1991, as the leadership of the self-proclaimed republic, opposed to the Government's objective of reunification with Romania, launched a campaign to gain control of Transnistria (with the ultimate aim of unity with Russia). More than six months of military conflict ensued, as Moldovan government troops were dispatched to combat the local Slav militia. The Moldovan Government claimed that the east-bank forces were actively supported by the Russian Government, while the Moldovans were, in turn, accused of receiving military and other assistance from Romania. The situation was complicated by the presence (and alleged involvement in support of the east-bank Slavs) of the former Soviet 14th Army, which was still stationed in the region and jurisdiction over which had been transferred to Russia. Peace negotiations were held at regular intervals, with the participation of Moldova, Russia, Ukraine and Romania; however, none of the agreed cease-fires was observed. By June 1992 some 700 people were believed to have been killed in the conflict, with an estimated 50,000 people forced to take refuge in neighbouring Ukraine. On 21 July, however, a peace agreement was finally negotiated by Presidents Snegur and Yeltsin, whereby Transnistria was accorded 'special status' within Moldova (the terms of which were to be formulated later). Later in July Russian, Moldovan and Transnistrian peace-keeping troops were deployed in the region to monitor the cease-fire.

Transnistria continued to demand full statehood, and in January 1994 the Moldovan Government accepted proposals by the Conference on Security and Co-operation in Europe (CSCE—later OSCE) for greater autonomy for Transnistria, within a Moldovan confederation. The Transnistrian leadership expressed approval of the proposals, and the result of the Moldovan parliamentary elections of the following month (which eliminated the possibility of Moldova's future unification with Romania) further enhanced the prospects for peace in the region. In April President Snegur and the Transnistrian leader, Igor Smirnov, pledged their commitment to holding negotiations for a peaceful resolution of the conflict, based on the CSCE recommendations.

In July 1994, following the adoption of the new Moldovan Constitution, which provided for a 'special autonomous status' for Transnistria, negotiations commenced on the details of the region's future status within Moldova. Progress was obstructed, in particular, by disagreement over the future of the 15,000-strong 14th Army, since the Transnistrian leadership demanded the continued presence of the Army in the region as a guarantor of security. In October, however, the Moldovan and Russian Governments reached an agreement, under which Russia was gradually to withdraw the 14th Army, whereupon Transnistria's negotiated 'special autonomous status' would take effect. A referendum (declared illegal by President Snegur) was held in Transnistria in March 1995, in which some 91% of participants voted against the withdrawal of the 14th Army. In late June, however, the withdrawal of weapons and ammunition of the 14th Army was begun. In December 2005 two further referendums were held in Transnistria: 82.7% of the electorate endorsed a new constitution (which proclaimed the region's independence), while 89.7% voted for Transnistria to join the CIS as a sovereign state. In February 1996, however, the CIS rejected admittance for Transnistria on such terms.

In July 1996 the executive and legislative authorities of Moldova and Transnistria initialled a memorandum, drafted with the aid of Russian, Ukrainian and OSCE mediators, on normalizing relations; this was viewed as an important stage towards defining the 'special status' of Transnistria within a future Moldovan confederation. Smirnov was re-elected as 'President' of Transnistria in December. In May 1997 the memorandum was signed in Moscow by the new Moldovan President, Petru Lucinschi, and Smirnov, with Russia and Ukraine acting as guarantors of the document. Representatives of the Moldovan and Transnistrian sides, meeting in Moscow in October, subsequently reached agreement on a number of 'confidence-building measures'. On 20 March 1998 a further agreement was signed in Odesa, Ukraine, by Lucinschi, Smirnov, Russian Prime Minister Viktor Chernomyrdin and President Leonid Kuchma of Ukraine, which envisaged a reduction in Moldovan and Transnistrian peace-keeping forces, while Russian troops were to remain in Transnistria until a final political settlement was reached.

In June 1998 Russian and Moldovan delegations to the joint commission monitoring the Odesa Accords agreed proposals for the composition of peace-keeping forces in the Transnistrian security zone, and Moldova's peace-keeping troops were gradually reduced in number. From late May 1999, following local elections in Moldova (in which the region refused to participate), Transnistria was designated an autonomous entity. In July Lucinschi met Smirnov, along with Russian Prime Minister Sergei Stepashin and an OSCE representative in Kyiv, Ukraine, and a joint declaration on the normalization of relations between Moldova and Transnistria was signed; however, Smirnov declared that differences remained. At an OSCE summit in Istanbul, Turkey, in November, Russia agreed to withdraw from Transnistria in three stages, with all hardware to be removed by the end of 2001, and all troops by the end of 2002.

In June 2000 the 'Transdnestrian Supreme Soviet' was converted to a reduced, unicameral legislature and in July Smirnov introduced a form of presidential rule. The Moldovan President elected in April 2001, Vladimir Voronin, declared the pursuit of a final political settlement for Transnistria to be a priority but no substantive progress was made. A deterioration in Transnistria's relations with the Moldovan Government took place in September, following the Government's introduction of new customs procedures, in accordance with World Trade Organization specifications, leading to claims by Transnistria that the Moldovan Government was attempting to impose an 'economic blockade' on the region. Smirnov was re-elected as 'President' of the region in December, although the election result was recognized by neither the Moldovan Government nor the international community. In December 2002 the OSCE amended the deadline agreed in 1999 for the removal of Russian forces from Moldova, extending it for a further year, until 31 December 2003; however, Russia indicated that some troops might remain, with a possible mandate for maintaining peace and stability in the event of a final settlement.

In July 2002 mediators from Russia, Ukraine and the OSCE submitted a new draft agreement (the 'Kyiv agreement'), according to which Moldova would become a federal state, in which the autonomous territories would maintain their own legislature and constitution; however, Smirnov insisted that recognition of Transnistria's 'independence' was a fundamental prerequisite. On 27 February 2003 the European Union (EU, see p. 228) and the USA, and subsequently other countries, imposed a travel ban on those Transnistrian officials considered to be 'primarily responsible for a lack of co-operation in promoting a political settlement' (in response, in March certain Moldovan officials were temporarily deemed *personae non gratae* in Transnistria). The travel ban remained in place in 2006. In mid-November 2003 the Russian President, Vladimir Putin, announced new proposals for a political settlement. Drafted by the deputy head of the presidential administration, Dmitrii Kozak, the plan envisaged the establishment of an 'asymmetrical federation', comprising Moldova and Transnistria, with unified defence, customs and finance systems. The leaders of both Transnistria and Moldova initially responded positively to the proposals, but Voronin withdrew his support in late November, following opposition protests and reservations expressed by the OSCE. The 'Kozak memorandum' had also attracted criticism from those who considered it to serve Russian interests. Although new proposals for Moldova's federalization were submitted to OSCE mediators in February 2004, the Transnistrian authorities considered them to offer the region insufficient autonomy, and representatives of the Moldovan Government also criticized the draft for its failure to clarify the issue of the continued presence of Russian troops and military equipment in Transnistria. In mid-2004 controversy arose over the closure by the Transnistrian authorities of Moldovan-language schools teaching a Moldovan syllabus, in the Latin script. The Moldovan Government responded by withdrawing from the OSCE-mediated negotiation process and imposing economic sanctions on the separatist region, which retaliated in kind. The EU, the USA and other international parties condemned the closure of the schools as an infringement of human rights, adding a further 10 Transnistrian officials to the list of those prohibited from travelling to their countries, and a case was submitted to the European Court of Human Rights.

In December 2004, at an OSCE meeting held in Sofia, Bulgaria, the Russian delegation obstructed the adoption of a final statement containing a reference to the Russian commitment to withdraw troops and ammunition from Moldova (first made in 1999). Russian representatives also refused to sign a Moldovan-drafted Declaration of Stability and Security for the Republic of Moldova, which proposed the inclusion of the EU and the USA in talks for the resolution of the Transnistrian conflict and acknowledged the failure of the existing five-party panel (comprising Moldova, Transnistria, Russia, Ukraine and the OSCE). In January 2005 Moldova banned foreign diplomats and representatives from visiting Transnistria, although the decision was rescinded the following month in order to allow for the free movement of international election monitors. In response, the Russian State Duma (Gosudarstvennaya Duma) approved a resolution in March, recommending punitive sanctions against Moldova, such as prohibitive taxation on exports and restrictive visa regulations.

In April 2005 President Viktor Yushchenko of Ukraine presented a plan for the resolution of the Transnistrian conflict (which became known as the Yushchenko Plan or the Kyiv Plan) during a summit meeting in Chișinău. The plan: envisaged that Transnistria would be awarded 'special status', as an autonomous entity within the Republic of Moldova; would provide for a Transnistrian constitution (to comply with the Moldovan Constitution) and symbols; and would permit Transnistria to participate in foreign-policy decisions affecting its interests. In June Parlamentul endorsed the Yushchenko Plan, while noting that it made no mention of either the withdrawal of Russian troops or the establishment of border controls along the Transnistrian section of the border with Ukraine. At the end of July the Moldovan Government removed the trade sanctions imposed against Transnistria in the previous year. In late September all five parties to the negotiations on the status of Transnistria agreed to invite the EU and the USA (but not Romania) to participate in the process as observers, as suggested in the Yushchenko plan; however, talks in late 2005 failed to record any substantive progress. Legislative elections (recognized by neither the Moldovan Government nor the international community) were held in Transnistria in December. Notably, the reformist, pro-western Obnovleniye (Renewal) bloc won the most seats in the region's Supreme Soviet.

At the end of November 2005 the EU launched a Border Assistance Mission to help secure the Transnistrian–Ukrainian border, following appeals from Presidents Voronin and Yushchenko. As part of the same initiative, at the end of December the Prime Ministers of Moldova and Ukraine signed a joint declaration on external trade, whereby Ukraine agreed not to recognize Transnistria's customs regime and to deal only in goods processed through the Moldovan customs system, in an attempt to combat smuggling. The new measures came into force in March 2006. In response, the Transnistrian authorities, which interpreted the new regulations as an economic blockade, withdrew from the internationally mediated negotiations. The Transnistrian authorities subsequently introduced legislation banning all foreign-financed non-governmental organizations, and Smirnov appealed to Russia to dispatch more troops to the region. (In February Russia had reportedly confirmed that it did not intend to complete the withdrawal of its troops from Transnistria before a final settlement on the region's status had been reached.) In late March Moldova recalled its ambassador to Russia for consultations, after the Russian ambassador to Moldova reportedly alleged that Moldova and Ukraine were attempting to destabilize the region. In late March Russia halted the import of Moldovan wine, ostensibly owing to safety concerns. At the end of March, following the initiation in February of formal negotiations to agree the final status of the Serbian province of Kosovo (see the chapter on Serbia and Montenegro), Transnistrian officials declared their intention to schedule a referendum on future relations with Moldova.

During the Transnistrian conflict in 1991–92, the situation in Gagauz-Yeri remained peaceful, although the region continued to demand full statehood. The new Moldovan Constitution, adopted in July 1994, provided for a 'special autonomous status' for Gagauz-Yeri, as for Transnistria, and negotiations duly commenced on the details of this status. Agreement was quickly reached between the Government and the Gagauz authorities, and in December Parlamentul adopted legislation on the 'special status of Gagauz-Yeri'. The regions of southern Moldova populated by the Gagauz were to enjoy broad self-administrative powers, and Gagauz was to be one of three official languages (with Moldovan and Russian). Legislative power was to be vested in a regional assembly, and a directly elected başkan was to hold a quasi-presidential position. The law on the status of Gagauz-Yeri entered into force in February 1995, and in the following month a referendum was held in the region to determine which settlements would form part of the region. Elections to the 35-seat Halk Toplusu (Popular Assembly) took place in May–June. Elections, held simultaneously, to the post of başkan were won by Gheorghe Tabunscic, the First Secretary of the Comrat branch of the PCRM. Under the new Constitution, Tabunscic, as Gagauz leader, became a member of the Council of Ministers of Moldova. At the first session of the assembly, the self-proclaimed 'Gagauz SSR' was declared defunct. Following local elections in Moldova in late May 1999, Gagauz-Yeri, like Transnistria, was designated an autonomous entity. Elections to the Halk Toplusu and to the post of başkan were held in late August. Following a second round of voting in early September, Dumitru Croitor was elected as başkan, with 61.5% of the votes cast. In mid-February 2002 the Halk Toplusu passed a vote of 'no confidence' in Croitor, and scheduled a referendum in the hope of securing his dismissal. On 24 February, the date that the referendum was scheduled to take place, the regional security forces reportedly seized the offices of the regional Election Commission, declaring its mandate to have expired and the plebiscite to be illegal. President Voronin subsequently visited the region and demanded the resignations of both Croitor and the Chairman of the Halk Toplusu. Croitor finally resigned at the end of June. At a second round of voting in an election held on 11 October, Tabunscic secured the highest proportion of the votes cast and regained the position of başkan; a new Government was subsequently approved. On 25 July 2003 Parlamentul officially recognized the autonomous status of Gagauz-Yeri through an amendment to the national Constitution, which awarded the Halk Toplusu the right to self-determination and to propose its own legislation. Legislative elections were held in the region in November and December, in which the PCRM and independent candidates each won almost one-half of the seats contested.

Owing to the changing domestic situation, Moldova's membership of the CIS was equivocal from its signature of the Alma-Ata Declaration in December 1991 until early 1994. In August 1993 Parlamentul failed by four votes to ratify the Alma-Ata Declaration, largely owing to the influence of deputies favouring unification with Romania, thus technically removing Moldova from the CIS. However, it was increasingly recognized that Moldova's economic survival depended on the CIS, and in September President Snegur signed a treaty to join the new CIS economic union. Following Moldova's parliamentary elections of February 1994 and the referendum in March, which strongly endorsed continued independence, Parlamentul reversed its earlier decision, and in late April it finally ratified membership of the CIS. However, the legislature indicated that Moldova would participate neither in CIS military structures nor in monetary union.

The communist Government elected in 2001 initially undertook a policy of *rapprochement* with Russia, and in late December Parlamentul ratified a treaty on friendship and co-operation, which had been signed by the two countries' respective Presidents in the previous month. The treaty was ratified by the Russian State Duma in April 2002. However, in 2004 relations deteriorated, largely owing to developments associated with Transnistria (see above). Speculation that Russia might seek to become involved in and influence the outcome of the legislative elections in Moldova in 2005 further heightened tensions: in February 2005 five Russian citizens were expelled from Moldova as a result of their suspected illegal involvement with the elections, and both Russian and Belarusian election monitors were either expelled from or prevented from entering the country, apparently for having failed to obtain the appropriate authorization. The discord largely stemmed from the distancing of the ruling PCRM from Russian associations, as the party was widely believed to have been supported by the Russian authorities at the previous elections. From the beginning of 2006 Russia attempted to increase two-fold the price charged to Moldova for supplies of natural gas (from US $80 to $160 per 1,000 cu m). Gas supplies from Russia temporarily ceased in January, after Moldova refused to sign a new contract with the Russian gas supplier, Gazprom, and accused Russia of adopting punitive measures in response to the country's new western orientation. In mid-January a compromise agreement was reached, covering the first three months of the year; in return for agreeing to relinquish the Transnistrian assets of the joint-venture company Moldovagaz to Gazprom (which already held a majority stake in the company), Moldova was be charged $110 per cu m for its gas supplies from Russia. Moldova was expected to be required to surrender further control of its gas-delivery system in order to achieve a long-term solution to the dispute with Russia.

Since gaining independence Moldova has sought to develop good relations with the neighbouring countries of Ukraine and Romania. Agreement on the delimitation of the Moldovan–Ukrainian border, apart from the Transnistrian section, was reached in November 1997, and the two countries finally defined their border in May 1999. In November 2004 Moldova dissociated itself from the countries in Russia's sphere of influence by condemning suspected electoral malpractice in Ukraine during the presidential election there. The Moldovan Government subsequently established cordial relations with the new administration of President Viktor Yushchenko in Ukraine, which supported Moldovan appeals for the involvement of the USA and the EU in negotiations on Transnistria and responded positively to efforts to co-ordinate border control and curb illegal trade with Transnistria (see above). Moldova had also established good relations with the new, western-orientated Government in Georgia, under President Mikheil Saakashvili, who was inaugurated in early 2004. In December 2005 Moldova attended a meeting in Kyiv, Ukraine, to launch the new Community of Democratic Choice, originally conceived by Ukraine and Georgia. The nine-member alliance aimed to remove divisions and resolve conflicts in the Baltic, Black Sea and Caspian regions, and observers in Russia expressed concern that the grouping might serve to weaken its influence.

Relations with Romania were subject to tensions. A basic political treaty, in preparation for six years, was agreed in May 1999 and initialled in April 2000; however, it was not signed, and in late 2003 the Romanian Prime Minister, Adrian Năstase, indicated that the country no longer considered the treaty to be relevant to the political situation. Meanwhile, in February 2000 many Moldovans had applied to obtain Romanian citizenship as formal negotiations on Romania's accession to the EU commenced. The Romanian Government subsequently introduced measures to simplify the application process, angering the

Moldovan authorities, since the Constitution did not permit dual citizenship. The situation was resolved when President Lucinschi drafted a new law, allowing Moldovans to hold dual citizenship with Israel, Romania and Russia, which was enacted in August. From August Romania expressed concern at the apparent 'russification' of Moldova, in particular following a decision to introduce compulsory Russian-language teaching from 2002 (see above). In March 2002 a Romanian diplomat was expelled from Moldova, after having reportedly met organizers of opposition protests; Romania responded by expelling a Moldovan diplomat. None the less, following a meeting in September between the Presidents of the two countries, held in Beirut, Lebanon, it was agreed to establish working groups to resolve problems in diplomatic relations. From April 2003 ministerial co-operation between Moldova and Romania was resumed, together with discussions on the initiation of negotiations regarding a border agreement; it was confirmed that Romania would not require Moldovan citizens to possess entry visas until its accession to the EU, anticipated by 2008. None the less, in October 2003 the Moldovan Government appealed to the Council of Europe for assistance with its deteriorating relations with Romania, after that country failed to sign a bilateral treaty confirming Moldova's borders. In 2004 the apparent realignment of Moldovan foreign policy towards the West provided a greater convergence of interests. In January 2005 the new President of Romania, Traian Băsescu, visited Moldova and declared his support for the country's desire to achieve eventual membership of the EU, which had begun to formulate an official policy towards Moldova.

Government

Under the Constitution of 1994, supreme legislative power is held by the unicameral Parlamentul (Parliament), which is directly elected every four years. Parlamentul comprises 101 members. The President is Head of State and holds executive power in conjunction with the Council of Ministers, led by the Prime Minister. According to constitutional amendments introduced in July 2000, the President is elected by the legislature for a four-year term. Following local elections in May 1999 the country was reorganized into nine provinces and two autonomous entities—Gagauz-Yeri and Transnistria. However, in January 2003 the Government approved new legislation on administrative reform, replacing the structure introduced in 1999 with one based upon 33 districts (rayons) and two municipalities, although the two autonomous entities retained that status.

Defence

Following independence from the USSR in 1991, the Moldovan Government initiated the creation of national armed forces. By August 2005 these numbered 6,750, including an army of 5,710 and an air force of 1,040. There were an estimated 2,379 paramilitary forces, attached to the Ministry of Internal Affairs. Military service is compulsory (with exemptions for students) and lasts for one year. Under an agreement concluded by the Moldovan and Russian Governments in late 1994, the former Soviet 14th Army (under Russian jurisdiction) was to have been withdrawn from Transnistria within three years. In July 2000 Russia agreed to withdraw from Transnistria in three stages, with all hardware to be removed by the end of 2001 and all troops by the end of 2002; the deadline was subsequently extended until December 2003, but both troops and equipment remained in Transnistria at 2006. In early 1994 Moldova joined the North Atlantic Treaty Organization's (NATO) 'Partnership for Peace' (see p. 316) programme. In 2004 defence expenditure amounted to 175m. Moldovan lei. The 2005 budget allocated 115m. lei to defence.

Economic Affairs

In 2004, according to estimates by the World Bank, Moldova's gross national income (GNI), measured at average 2002–04 prices, was US $2,563m., equivalent to $710 per head (or $1,930 per head on an international purchasing-power parity basis). During 1995–2004, it was estimated, the population decreased by an annual average of 0.3%, while gross domestic product (GDP) per head increased, in real terms, at an average rate of 1.9% per year. Overall GDP increased, in real terms, at an average annual rate of 1.6% in 1995–2004; GDP increased by 6.3% in 2003 and by 7.3% in 2004.

As a result of its extremely fertile land and temperate climate, Moldova's economy is dominated by agriculture and related industries. Some 85% of the country's terrain is cultivated. In 2004 agriculture (including hunting, forestry and fishing) contributed some 20.8% of GDP, and the sector provided 40.7% of employment in 2005. Principal crops include wine grapes and other fruit, tobacco, vegetables and grain. The wine industry has traditionally occupied a central role in the economy. The private ownership of land was legalized in 1991, although the sale of agricultural land was permitted until 2001. In 2004 some 73.1% of agricultural land was privately owned and the private sector accounted for some 99% of production. According to the World Bank, the GDP of the agricultural sector declined, in real terms, at an average rate of 1.0% per year during 1995–2004. Agricultural GDP declined by 9.9% in 2003, but increased by 3.2% in 2004.

In 2004 industry (including mining, manufacturing, power and construction) contributed 23.3% of GDP. The sector provided 16.0% of employment in 2005. In 1995–2004, according to the World Bank, industrial GDP increased at an average rate of 1.0% per year. Real industrial GDP increased by 13.4% in 2003 and by 5.0% in 2004.

Mining and quarrying employed just 0.1% of the working population in 2004, when it contributed 0.4% of GDP. Moldova has extremely limited mineral resources, and there is no domestic production of fuel or non-ferrous metals. Activity is focused primarily on the extraction and processing of industrial minerals such as gypsum, limestone, sand and gravel. Deposits of petroleum and natural gas were discovered in southern Moldova in the early 1990s; total reserves of natural gas have been estimated at 22,000m. cu m.

The manufacturing sector provided 10.3% of employment in 2004, when it contributed 16.4% of GDP. The sector is dominated by food-processing, wine and tobacco production, machine-building and metal-working, and light industry. In 2005 the principal branches, measured by gross value of output, were food-processing and beverages (62.6%), non-metallic mineral products (11.6%) and clothing and furs (3.3%). According to the World Bank, manufacturing GDP increased, in real terms, by an annual average of 0.7% in 1995–2003. Manufacturing GDP increased by 2.6% in 2002 and by 12.8% in 2003.

Moldova relies heavily on imported energy—primarily natural gas and petroleum products—from Russia, Romania and Ukraine (such imports accounted for 76.7% of consumption in 2004). The Russian supplier Gazprom increased gas prices from 2006 (see Recent History), and Moldova announced its intention to diversify its gas suppliers and develop closer relations with neighbouring Romania. Moldova also hoped to participate in the Nabucco project, which aimed to construct a natural gas pipeline under the Black Sea, to supply gas to Europe from Central Asia. Moldova planned to increase domestic energy production three-fold by 2010; domestic production represented 23.3% of consumption in 2004. A large proportion of natural gas imports supply the Moldoveneasca power station, located in Transnistria, which contributes much of the country's electricity generating capacity; supplies were disrupted in 2005. In February 2005 an Azerbaijani company purchased the unfinished Giurgiulesti petroleum terminal in southern Moldova, with plans for its further development; completion was scheduled for 2006. In 2002 natural gas accounted for 91.8% of electricity production, and coal accounted for just 3.8% (compared with 43.8% in 1994). Mineral products comprised an estimated 21.9% of the value of total imports in 2005.

Services accounted for 55.9% of GDP in 2004, and the sector provided 43.3% of total employment in 2005. The GDP of the services sector increased, in real terms, by an annual average of 3.2% in 1995–2004. Services GDP increased by 6.5% in 2003 and by 11.1% in 2004.

In 2004 Moldova recorded a visible trade deficit of US $754.2m., while there was a deficit of $70.2m. on the current account of the balance of payments. In 2005 the principal source of imports was Ukraine (accounting for 21.3% of the value of total imports). Other major suppliers were Russia (11.8%), Romania (11.1%), Germany (8.3%) and Italy (6.6%). The main market for exports in that year was Russia (accounting for 31.8% of the value of total exports). Other important purchasers were Italy (12.2%), Romania (10.2%), Ukraine (9.1%) and Belarus (6.5%). In 2005 the principal imports were mineral products, machinery and mechanical appliances, chemicals and related products, textiles, base metals, foodstuff, beverages and tobacco, plastics and rubbers, and vehicles and transport equipment. The main exports in that year were food products, beverages and tobacco, textiles, vegetable products and raw hides, skins and leather.

MOLDOVA

In 2004 the state budget recorded a surplus of 131.4m. Moldovan lei (equivalent to 0.4% of GDP). At the end of 2003 Moldova's total external debt totalled US $1,901m., of which $848m. was long-term public debt. In that year the cost of debt-servicing was equivalent to 10.4% of the value of exports of goods and services. Consumer prices increased by an annual average of 16.5% during 1995–2004. The average rate of inflation was 11.8% in 2003 and 12.5% in 2004. The average rate of unemployment was 7.3% in 2005.

Moldova became a member of the IMF and the World Bank in 1992. It also joined the European Bank for Reconstruction and Development (EBRD, see p. 224), as a 'Country of Operations'. Moldova subsequently became a member of the Organization of the Black Sea Economic Co-operation (see p. 339), and it joined the World Trade Organization (see p. 370) in 2001.

After independence, economic performance was adversely affected by disruptions in inter-republican trade, as well as the armed conflict in Transnistria (the main industrial centre) in the first half of 1992 and the region's subsequent attempts to secede from Moldova (see Recent History). After 1998 the reform process stalled, and from 1999 the IMF repeatedly suspended lending. The communist Government elected in 2001 cancelled several privatization agreements, and concerns over possible renationalization resulted in reduced investment. A communist Government was again elected in early 2005, but it intended to reinvigorate the privatization process and increasingly sought to reorient itself towards the West, seeking eventual membership of the European Union (EU, see p. 228); in late 2005 the EU initiated a programme to combat smuggling and arms-trading along the Transnistrian–Ukrainian border. Although the economy had recorded continued growth since 2000, the country remained the poorest in Europe, and remittances from workers seeking employment abroad accounted for some 30% of GDP in 2005. The IMF had suspended lending under its Poverty Reduction and Growth Facility (PRGF) in mid-2003, but agreement was expected to be reached in mid-2006 on a new, three-year PRGF, to be followed by the resumption of lending by the World Bank. Economic growth remained strong in 2005, at an estimated 7%, and the rate of inflation was reduced to some 10%, despite increased global energy prices. However, the deficit on the current account of the balance of payments widened in 2005, and was expected to increase further in 2006, owing to Russian restrictions on exports (particularly wine) and the increased price of natural gas imports. Growth was expected to slow slightly from 2006, partly owing to the higher energy prices, and in December 2005 the IMF advised that increased private-sector investment would be required in order to avoid a more rapid deceleration. The IMF also urged the Government to implement a cautious fiscal policy in 2006, reducing government expenditure, in order to constrain inflation and to avoid obstructing private-sector investment. Meanwhile, Moldova's dependence on the Russian market, and increasing tensions with Russia, placed it in a vulnerable position, and the economy continued to be adversely affected by the unresolved issue of Transnistria.

Education

Education is officially compulsory in Moldova between seven and 16 years of age. Primary education begins at seven years of age and lasts for four years. Secondary education, beginning at 11, lasts for a maximum of seven years, comprising a first cycle of five years and a second of two years. Primary enrolment in 2002 was equivalent to 95% of children in the relevant age-group, and the comparable ratio for secondary enrolment was 88%. In 1997 total enrolment at primary, secondary and tertiary levels was equivalent to 71% of females and 69% of males. In 2004 consolidated budgetary expenditure on education was 1,727m. lei (equivalent to 6.1% of GDP).

Public Holidays

2006: 1 January (New Year's Day), 7–8 January (Orthodox Christmas), 8 March (International Women's Day), 23–24 April (Orthodox Easter), 1 May (Labour Day), 9 May (Victory and Commemoration Day), 27 August (Independence Day), 31 August ('Limbă Noastră', National Language Day).

2007: 1 January (New Year's Day), 7–8 January (Orthodox Christmas), 8 March (International Women's Day), 8–9 April (Orthodox Easter), 1 May (Labour Day), 9 May (Victory and Commemoration Day), 27 August (Independence Day), 31 August ('Limbă Noastră', National Language Day).

Weights and Measures

The metric system is in force.

Statistical Survey

Principal sources (unless otherwise indicated): State Department for Statistics and Sociology, 2028 Chişinău, şos. Hînceşti 53D; tel. (22) 73-37-74; fax (22) 22-61-46; e-mail dass@statistica.md; internet www.statistica.md.

Note: Most of the figures for 1993–2006 exclude the Transnistria (Transdnestr) region of eastern Moldova, which remained outside central government control.

Area and Population

AREA, POPULATION AND DENSITY

Area (sq km)	33,800*
Population (census results)†	
12 January 1989	4,335,360
5–12 October 2004 (preliminary)	
Males	1,632,519
Females	1,755,552
Total	3,388,071
Population (official estimates at 1 January)‡§	
2004	3,606,800
2005	3,386,000
2006	3,391,700
Density (per sq km) at January 2006‡	100.3

* 13,050 sq miles.
† Figures refer to the *de jure* population. The *de facto* total at the 1989 census was 4,337,592 (males 2,058,160, females 2,279,432).
‡ Excluding Transnistria.
§ Rounded figures calculated on the basis of preliminary census data.

POPULATION BY ETHNIC GROUP*
(permanent inhabitants, 1989 census)

	Number	%
Moldovan	2,794,749	64.5
Ukrainian	600,366	13.8
Russian	562,069	13.0
Gagauz	153,458	3.5
Bulgarian	88,419	2.0
Jewish	65,672	1.5
Others and unknown	70,627	1.7
Total	**4,335,360**	**100.0**

* According to official declaration of nationality.

MOLDOVA

ADMINISTRATIVE DIVISIONS
(preliminary estimates of population at 1 January 2005)

Bălți (municipality)	127,600	Hîncești	119,800
Chișinău (municipality)	716,700	Ialoveni	97,800
Anenii Noi	81,700	Leova	51,100
Basarabeasca	29,000	Nisporeni	65,000
Briceni	77,800	Ocnița	56,600
Cahul	119,200	Orhei	116,200
Cantemir	60,000	Rezina	48,000
Călărași	75,100	Rîșcani	69,300
Căușeni	90,600	Sîngerei	87,100
Cimișlia	60,900	Soroca	94,800
Criuleni	72,200	Strășeni	88,900
Dondușeni	46,300	Șoldănești	42,200
Drochia	86,900	Ștefan Vodă	70,600
Dubăsari	34,000	Taraclia	43,100
Edineț	81,200	Telenești	70,000
Fălești	89,800	Ungheni	110,800
		Autonomous Territory of	
Florești	89,200	*Gagauz-Yeri*	155,700
Glodeni	60,800	**Total**	**3,386,000**

Population of Transnistria (estimated figure obtained as residual from total country population estimates at 1 January 2003): 601,088.

Note: In January 2003 the Government approved legislation in accordance with which the existing 10 regions were to be replaced by 33 districts (raions) and two municipalities (the capital city, Chișinău, and Bălți). Gagauz-Yeri was to retain its autonomous status. These new administrative divisions took effect later in the year.

PRINCIPAL TOWNS
(estimated population at 1 January 1996)

Chișinău (Kishinev) (capital)	655,000	Tighina (Bender)	128,000
Tiraspol	187,000	Râbnita (Rybnitsa)	62,900
Bălți (Beltsy)	153,500		

2005 (estimate, 1 January): Chișinău 592,600; Bălți 122,700.

BIRTHS, MARRIAGES AND DEATHS

	Registered live births		Registered marriages		Registered deaths	
	Number	Rate (per 1,000)	Number	Rate (per 1,000)	Number	Rate (per 1,000)
1997	51,286	11.9	26,305	6.1*	51,138	11.9
1998	46,755	10.9	25,793	6.0*	47,691	11.1
1999†	38,501	9.0	23,524	5.5	41,315	9.6
2000†	36,939	8.7	21,684	5.1	41,224	9.7
2001	36,448	10.0	21,200‡	5.8	40,100‡	11.0
2002	35,705	9.9	21,700‡	6.0	41,900‡	11.6
2003	36,471	10.1	n.a.	n.a.	43,079	11.9
2004	38,272	11.3	n.a.	n.a.	41,700‡	12.3

* Estimate.
† Numbers exclude, but rates include, Transnistria.
‡ Rounded figures.
Sources: partly UN, *Population and Vital Statistics Report*.

Expectation of life (WHO estimates, years at birth): 67 (males 63; females 71) in 2003 (Source: WHO, *World Health Report*).

ECONOMICALLY ACTIVE POPULATION
('000 persons aged 15 years and over)

	2002	2003	2004
Agriculture, hunting and forestry	745.2	581.6	531.9
Fishing	1.9	1.6	1.0
Mining and quarrying	2.6	1.4	0.8
Manufacturing	142.3	136.7	135.4
Electricity, gas and water supply	26.5	26.4	25.6
Construction	46.0	53.2	52.0
Wholesale and retail trade; repair of motor vehicles, motorcycles and personal and household goods	155.1	158.2	159.6
Hotels and restaurants	19.7	17.5	19.1
Transport, storage and communications	61.7	67.6	73.4
Financial intermediation	9.2	10.5	13.6
Real estate, renting and business activities	20.2	25.8	28.9
Public administration and defence; compulsory social security	65.8	65.6	64.1
Education	105.3	109.5	107.9
Health and social work	72.2	68.9	68.7
Other community, social and personal service activities	27.7	26.9	30.3
Private households with employed persons	3.5	4.4	3.3
Extra-territorial organizations and bodies	0.1	0.5	0.4
Total employed	**1,505.1**	**1,356.5**	**1,316.0**
Unemployed	110.0	117.1	116.5
Total labour force	**1,615.1**	**1,473.6**	**1,432.5**
Males	795.3	731.2	701.6
Females	819.6	742.4	731.0

Source: ILO.

2005 ('000 persons): Agriculture, hunting, forestry and fishing 536.5; Industry 159.3; Construction 51.6; Commerce, hotels and restaurants 182.9; Transport and communications 71.0; Public administration, education, health and social work 239.2; Other services 78.1; *Total employed* 1,318.7; Unemployed 103.7; *Total labour force* 1,422.3.

Health and Welfare

KEY INDICATORS

Total fertility rate (children per woman, 2003)	1.4
Under-5 mortality rate (per 1,000 live births, 2004)	28
HIV/AIDS (% of persons aged 15–49, 2003)	0.2
Physicians (per 1,000 head, 2001)	2.71
Hospital beds (per 1,000 head, 2001)	5.89
Health expenditure (2002): US $ per head (PPP)	151
Health expenditure (2002): % of GDP	7.0
Health expenditure (2002): public (% of total)	58.2
Access to water (% of persons, 2000)	100
Human Development Index (2003): ranking	115
Human Development Index (2003): value	0.671

For sources and definitions, see explanatory note on p. vi.

Agriculture

PRINCIPAL CROPS
('000 metric tons)

	2002	2003	2004
Wheat	1,116.2	102.4	690.0*
Barley	220.5	56.6	260.0*
Maize	1,193.6	1,413.6	1,840.0*
Potatoes	325.2	302.8	318.0*
Sugar beet	1,129.4	656.8	907.0*
Dry beans	21.7	19.1	80.0*
Dry peas	24.6	9.6	67.0*
Sunflower seed	317.5	390.0	331.0*
Cabbages	48.8	54.1	50.0*
Tomatoes	99.9	105.6	95.0*
Cucumbers and gherkins	36.5	33.1	25.0*

MOLDOVA

—continued

	2002	2003	2004
Chillies and green peppers	22.1	20.2	18.0*
Aubergines (Eggplants)	9.7	6.2	7.0*
Dry onions	58.0	32.0	30.0*
Carrots	21.2	14.0	10.0*
Watermelons	25.1	67.8	56.0*
Other vegetables*	100.7	96.0	85.6*
Apples	224.0	494.3	338.0*
Plums	31.6	50.8	29.0*
Grapes	641.2	677.2	600.0†
Other fruits*	62.5	69.1	61.9*
Tobacco (leaves)	11.8	6.7	10.2*

* Unofficial figure.
† FAO estimate.
Source: FAO.

LIVESTOCK
('000 head at 1 January)

	2002	2003	2004
Horses	77	78	78
Cattle	405	410	373
Pigs	449	508	446
Sheep	835	830	817
Goats	112	126	121
Chickens*	14,077	14,900	15,686

* Unofficial figures.
Source: FAO.

LIVESTOCK PRODUCTS
('000 metric tons)

	2002	2003	2004
Beef and veal	16.1	16.3	23.0*
Mutton and lamb	2.7	2.6	2.5*
Pig meat	44.9	43.2	38.0*
Poultry meat	21.1	21.7	22.2*
Cows' milk	582.5	570.2	600.0*
Sheep's milk	16.3	17.4	20.0*
Goats' milk	5.5	5.5	8.0*
Butter	2.6	2.7	3.2†
Cheese†	5.2	5.4	6.1
Hen eggs*	37.4	34.6	37.3
Honey	2.3	2.2	2.2†
Wool: greasy	2.1	2.1	2.1†
Cattle hides (fresh)†	2.3	2.4	3.3

* Unofficial estimate(s).
† FAO estimate(s).
Source: FAO.

Forestry

ROUNDWOOD REMOVALS
('000 cubic metres, excl. bark)

	1999	2000	2001
Sawlogs, veneer logs and logs for sleepers	3	5	3
Other industrial wood	9	24	24*
Fuel wood	36	30	30*
Total	48	59	57

* FAO estimate.
2002–04: Annual production as in 2001 (FAO estimates).
Source: FAO.

SAWNWOOD PRODUCTION
('000 cubic metres, incl. railway sleepers)

	1998	1999	2000
Coniferous (softwood)	25	—	—
Broadleaved (hardwood)	5	6	5
Total	30	6	5

2001–2004: Annual production as in 2000 (FAO estimates).
Source: FAO.

Fishing

(metric tons, live weight)

	2001	2002	2003
Capture	387	565	343
Common carp	212	274	125
Crucian carp	127	183	139
Aquaculture	1,189	1,765	2,638
Common carp	105	205	197
Crucian carp	23	24	35
Grass carp (White amur)	63	101	115
Silver carp	998	1,435	2,291
Total catch	1,576	2,330	2,981

Source: FAO.

Mining

('000 metric tons)

	2000	2001	2002
Gypsum	32.1	32.0	32.0*
Peat*	475	475	475

* Estimated production.
Source: US Geological Survey.

Industry

SELECTED PRODUCTS
('000 metric tons, unless otherwise indicated)

	2002	2003	2004
Vegetable oil	51.7	72.8	85.3
Flour	151.4	116.7	45.3
Raw sugar	165.5*	107.1	112.0
Wine ('000 hectolitres)†	1,480	1,900	3,060
Mineral water ('000 hectolitres)	535	n.a.	n.a.
Soft drinks ('000 hectolitres)†	420	600	550
Cigarettes (million)	6,310	7,126	7,300
Carpets ('000 sq m)	2,444	3,537	4,467
Footwear ('000 pairs, excl. rubber)	1,925	2,738	2,877
Cement	279.0	255.4	439.7
Washing machines ('000 units)	40.1	47.7	53.8
Television receivers ('000 units)	7.6	10.3	0.5
Electric energy (million kWh)	1,180	1,046	1,022

* Including Transnistria region.
† Rounded figures.

MOLDOVA   Statistical Survey

Finance

CURRENCY AND EXCHANGE RATES

Monetary Units
100 bani (singular: ban) = 1 Moldovan leu (plural: lei).

Sterling, Dollar and Euro Equivalents (30 December 2005)
£1 sterling = 22.095 lei;
US $1 = 12.832 lei;
€1 = 15.138 lei;
1,000 Moldovan lei = £45.26= $77.93= €66.06.

Average Exchange Rate (Moldovan lei per US$)
2003   13.945
2004   12.330
2005   12.600

Note: The Moldovan leu was introduced (except in Transnistria) on 29 November 1993, replacing the Moldovan rouble at a rate of 1 leu = 1,000 roubles. The Moldovan rouble had been introduced in June 1992, as a temporary coupon currency, and was initially at par with the Russian (formerly Soviet) rouble.

STATE BUDGET
(million lei)*

Revenue†	2001	2002	2003
Tax revenue	4,645	5,827	7,596
Taxes on profits	350	428	577
Taxes on personal incomes	348	468	623
Value-added tax	1,498	2,034	2,792
Excises	681	658	888
Taxes on international trade	234	333	477
Social Fund contributions	1,304	1,644	1,978
Other taxes	231	263	259
Non-tax revenue	749	710	731
Total	5,394	6,537	8,327

Expenditure‡	2001	2002	2003
Current budgetary expenditure	2,890	3,392	5,082
National economy	298	417	999
Social sphere	1,795	2,489	3,503
Education	923	1,240	1,841
Health care	542	792	1,068
Interest payments	797	486	580
Capital budgetary expenditure	206	258	0
Social Fund expenditure	1,373	1,900	2,261
Project loan spending	190	334	338
Other expenditure	926	1,251	1,898
Total	5,585	7,135	9,579

* Figures refer to a consolidation of the operations of central (republican) and local governments, including the Social Fund.
† Excluding grants received (million lei): 147 in 2001; 73 in 2002; 1 in 2003.
‡ Excluding net lending (million lei): −17 in 2001; −78 in 2002; −52 in 2003.

Source: IMF, *Republic of Moldova: Statistical Appendix* (February 2005).

Consolidated Budget (excl. Social Fund) (million lei, revised figures): *Revenue:* 5,084.4 in 2002; 6,619.9 in 2003; 7,521.5 in 2004. *Expenditure:* 5,194.1 in 2002; 6,177.5 in 2003; 7,390.1 in 2004.

INTERNATIONAL RESERVES
(US $ million at 31 December)

	2003	2004	2005
IMF special drawing rights	0.04	0.07	0.01
Reserve position in IMF	0.01	0.01	0.01
Foreign exchange	302.22	470.18	597.43
Total (excl. gold)	302.27	470.26	597.45

Source: IMF, *International Financial Statistics*.

MONEY SUPPLY
(million lei at 31 December)

	2002	2003	2004
Currency outside banks	2,288.56	2,740.52	3,699.91
Demand deposits at commercial banks	1,271.14	1,674.28	2,401.62
Total money (incl. others)	3,559.80	4,415.07	6,106.45

Source: IMF, *International Financial Statistics*.

COST OF LIVING
(Consumer Price Index; base: 2000 = 100)

	2002	2003	2004
Food	115.5	131.2	147.9
All items (incl. others)	115.6	129.2	145.3

Source: ILO.

NATIONAL ACCOUNTS
(million lei at current prices, excl. Transnistria)

Expenditure on the Gross Domestic Product

	2002	2003	2004
Final consumption expenditure	23,289	30,451	33,832
Gross capital formation	4,886	6,401	8,097
Total domestic expenditure	28,175	36,852	41,929
Balance on goods and services*	−5,619	−9,233	−9,937
GDP in market prices	22,556	27,619	31,992

* Figure obtained as a residual.

Gross Domestic Product by Economic Activity

	2002	2003	2004
Agriculture, hunting, forestry and fishing	4,742	5,062	5,833
Mining	50	71	105
Manufacturing	3,352	4,265	4,602
Electricity, gas and water supply	499	524	524
Construction	665	812	1,314
Wholesale and retail trade, and repairs of vehicles and personal and household goods	2,488	2,967	3,392
Transport, storage and communications	2,254	2,977	3,692
Other services	6,102	7,492	8,609
Sub-total	20,152	24,170	28,071
Less Financial intermediation services indirectly measured	463	647	718
Gross value added in basic prices	19,689	23,523	27,353
Taxes, less subsidies, on products and imports	2,867	4,096	4,639
GDP in market prices	22,556	27,619	31,992

BALANCE OF PAYMENTS
(US $ million)

	2002	2003	2004
Exports of goods f.o.b.	659.7	805.9	994.1
Imports of goods f.o.b.	−1,037.5	−1,428.1	−1,748.2
Trade balance	−377.8	−622.2	−754.2
Exports of services	217.5	254.4	337.1
Imports of services	−257.0	−299.8	−373.8
Balance on goods and services	−417.3	−667.6	−790.8
Other income received	229.4	340.7	490.0
Other income paid	−120.0	−111.6	−133.3
Balance on goods, services and income	−307.9	−438.5	−434.1
Current transfers received	255.6	331.7	399.0
Current transfers paid	−19.3	−27.5	−35.2
Current balance	−71.6	−134.3	−70.2
Capital account (net)	−15.3	−12.8	−10.9

MOLDOVA

—continued

	2002	2003	2004
Direct investment abroad	−0.5	−0.1	−3.3
Direct investment from abroad	132.7	78.3	80.6
Portfolio investment assets	−1.5	0.4	−1.5
Portfolio investment liabilities	−25.9	−24.2	−8.3
Financial derivatives assets	—	—	−0.5
Financial derivatives liabilities	—	0.1	1.0
Other investment assets	−43.9	−17.0	−52.9
Other investment liabilities	2.1	24.6	88.7
Net errors and omissions	−23.3	69.3	121.3
Overall balance	−47.1	−15.7	144.1

Source: IMF, *International Financial Statistics*.

External Trade

PRINCIPAL COMMODITIES
(US $ million)

Imports c.i.f.	2003	2004	2005
Vegetable products	82.3	73.5	67.1
Foodstuffs, beverages and tobacco	92.0	105.3	150.6
Mineral products	297.7	384.9	505.2
Mineral fuels, mineral oils and related materials	287.2	370.6	n.a.
Chemicals and related products	132.7	161.8	232.6
Medicinal and pharmaceutical products	51.0	48.2	n.a.
Plastics, rubber and articles thereof	69.3	101.1	140.2
Plastics	53.3	79.4	n.a.
Raw hides, skins, leather and articles thereof	36.3	72.5	n.a.
Pulp of wood, paper and paperboard and articles thereof	56.4	63.4	69.6
Textiles and textile articles	118.4	150.6	180.0
Articles of stone, plaster, cement, ceramic or glass	52.7	64.4	69.1
Base metals and articles of base metals	70.3	111.9	161.1
Machinery and mechanical appliances	214.0	239.7	322.2
Vehicles and associated transport equipment	75.2	96.0	130.2
Total (incl. others)	1,402.3	1,768.5	2,311.8

Exports f.o.b.	2003	2004	2005
Live animals and animal products	28.6	20.2	17.2
Vegetable products	91.2	120.0	131.9
Edible fruit	54.5	64.7	n.a.
Animal or vegetable fats	28.9	41.2	37.8
Foodstuffs, beverages and tobacco	314.3	345.9	396.2
Preparations of vegetables or fruits	38.4	40.3	n.a.
Mineral products	20.6	30.3	20.1
Raw hides, skins and leather	44.8	77.9	71.6
Textiles and textile articles	129.7	170.1	193.9
Articles of apparel and clothing accessories, not knitted	70.6	89.6	n.a.
Base metals and articles of base metals	19.4	29.9	48.8
Machinery and mechanical appliances	30.3	39.3	46.3
Total (incl. others)	789.9	985.2	1,091.3

PRINCIPAL TRADING PARTNERS
(US $ million)

Imports c.i.f.	2003	2004	2005
Belarus	50.6	64.3	84.5
Belgium	18.4	21.7	30.1
Bulgaria	30.1	29.6	29.0
China, People's Repub.	21.5	37.7	74.0
Czech Republic	19.0	21.5	28.8
France	35.2	52.7	64.5
Germany	135.6	150.2	190.9
Hungary	19.6	22.9	33.8
Italy	116.6	131.6	152.3
Kazakhstan	48.3	50.3	59.8
Netherlands	13.2	17.5	31.0
Poland	39.5	44.8	65.1
Romania	97.9	164.1	257.4
Russia	182.9	212.3	273.6
Turkey	48.2	69.1	93.0
Ukraine	309.2	436.3	491.4
USA	34.5	29.4	40.7
Total (incl. others)	1,402.3	1,768.5	2,311.8

Exports f.o.b.	2003	2004	2005
Austria	11.3	10.0	n.a.
Belarus	41.1	58.7	71.2
Belgium	7.2	11.8	14.6
France	9.3	11.4	16.5
Germany	56.2	71.2	47.4
Hungary	8.0	14.5	14.7
Italy	82.4	136.4	133.6
Kazakhstan	9.2	15.4	17.3
Poland	4.5	6.6	25.3
Romania	90.2	98.9	111.7
Russia	308.4	353.3	347.5
Turkey	7.2	12.3	24.7
Ukraine	56.1	64.7	99.7
USA	33.6	42.7	37.5
Total (incl. others)	789.9	985.2	1,091.3

Transport

RAILWAYS
(traffic, incl. Transnistria)

	2002	2003	2004
Passenger journeys (million)	5.1	5.3	5.1
Passenger-km (million)	355	352	346
Freight transported (million metric tons)	12.6	14.7	13.3
Freight ton-km (million)	2,748	3,019	3,006

ROAD TRAFFIC
(motor vehicles in use)

	1997	1998	1999
Passenger cars	205,973	222,769	232,278
Buses and coaches	11,169	12,917	13,582
Lorries and vans	56,924	57,404	52,430

2002 (motor vehicles in use): Passenger cars 268,882; Buses and coaches 15,777; Lorries and vans 46,277; Motorcycles and mopeds 78,814.
Source: IRF, *World Road Statistics*.

INLAND WATERWAYS
(traffic)

	2002	2003	2004
Freight transported ('000 metric tons)	107.5	120.0	119.7

MOLDOVA

CIVIL AVIATION
(traffic)

	2002	2003	2004
Passengers carried ('000)	240	250	310
Passenger-km (million)	324	304	365
Freight transported ('000 metric tons)	0.9	0.75	0.72
Freight ton-km (million)	1.3	0.9	1.0

Tourism

FOREIGN VISITOR ARRIVALS
(incl. excursionists)

Country of origin	2002	2003	2004
Belarus	720	750	1,072
Bulgaria	326	625	471
Germany	560	717	632
Italy	491	702	1,019
Netherlands	161	529	223
Poland	486	320	428
Romania	1,929	2,381	2,350
Russia	3,758	3,270	3,952
Turkey	2,869	3,965	3,521
Ukraine	2,947	3,283	3,173
United Kingdom	190	219	3,054
USA	1,707	2,494	2,494
Total (incl. others)	20,161	23,598	26,045

Receipts from tourism (US $ million): 85 in 2001; 99 in 2002; 116 in 2003.

Source: World Tourism Organization.

Communications Media

	2002	2003	2004
Telephones ('000 main lines in use)	719.3	791.1	863.4
Mobile cellular telephones ('000 subscribers)	338.2	475.9	787.0
Personal computers ('000 in use)	77	n.a.	112
Internet users ('000)	150	288	406

Television receivers ('000 in use): 1,300 in 2000.

Radio receivers ('000 in use): 3,220 in 1997.

Book production (including pamphlets): 921 titles (2,779,000 copies) in 1996.

Facsimile machines ('000 in use): 716 in 1999.

Daily newspapers: 4 (average circulation 261,000) in 1996.

Non-daily newspapers: 206 (estimated average circulation 1,350,000) in 1996.

Other periodicals: 76 (average circulation 196,000) in 1994.

Sources: UNESCO, *Statistical Yearbook*; International Telecommunication Union.

Education

(2004/05)

	Institutions	Teachers	Students
Primary	116	41,100	15,800
Secondary: general	1,454		530,800
Secondary: vocational	81	2,200	22,696
Higher: colleges	56	1,898	23,618
Higher: universities	35	5,909	114,552

Adult literacy rate (UNESCO estimates): 96.2% (males 97.5%; females 95.0%) in 2003 (Source: UN Development Programme, *Human Development Report*).

Directory

The Constitution

The Constitution of the Republic of Moldova, summarized below, was adopted by the Moldovan Parliament on 28 July 1994 and entered into force on 27 August. On 28 July 2000 amendments to the Constitution were enacted, which transformed Moldova into a parliamentary republic. Following alterations to the law on presidential election procedure, approved on 22 September, the President of the Republic was, henceforth, to be elected by the legislature, rather than directly. The Constitution was further amended, to recognize the autonomous status of Gagauz-Yeri (Gagauzia) in July 2003.

GENERAL PRINCIPLES

The Republic of Moldova is a sovereign, independent, unitary and indivisible state. The rule of law, the dignity, rights and freedoms of the people, and the development of human personality, justice and political pluralism are guaranteed. The Constitution is the supreme law. The Constitution upholds principles such as human rights and freedoms, democracy and political pluralism, the separation and co-operation of the legislative, executive and judicial powers of the State, respect for international law and treaties, fundamental principles regarding property, free economic initiative and the right to national identity. The national language of the republic is Moldovan and its writing is based on the Latin alphabet, although the State acknowledges the right to use other languages spoken within the country.

FUNDAMENTAL RIGHTS, FREEDOMS AND DUTIES

The Constitution grants Moldovan citizens their rights and freedoms and lays down their duties. All citizens are equal before the law; they should have free access to justice, are presumed innocent until proven guilty and have a right to an acknowledged legal status.

The State guarantees fundamental human rights, such as the right to life and to physical and mental integrity, the freedoms of movement, conscience, expression, assembly and political association, and the enfranchisement of Moldovan citizens aged over 18 years. Moldovan citizens have the right of access to information and education, of health security, of establishing and joining a trade union, of working and of striking. The family, orphaned children and the disabled enjoy the protection of the State. Obligations of the citizenry include the payment of taxes and the defence of the motherland.

PARLAMENTUL

Parlamentul (The Parliament) is the supreme legislative body and sole legislative authority of Moldova. It consists of 101 members, directly elected for a four-year term. The Chairman of Parlamentul is elected by members, also for a four-year term. Parlamentul holds two ordinary sessions per year. Parlamentul's basic powers include: the enactment of laws, the holding of referendums, the provision of legislative unity throughout the country, the approval of state policy, the approval or suspension of international treaties, the election of state officials, the mobilization of the armed forces and the declaration of the states of national emergency, martial law and war.

THE PRESIDENT OF THE REPUBLIC

The President of the Republic is the Head of State and is elected by the legislature for a four-year term. A candidate must be aged no less than 40 years, be a Moldovan citizen and a speaker of the official language. The candidate must be in good health and, with his or her application, must submit the written support of a minimum of 15 parliamentarians. A decision on the holding of a presidential election

MOLDOVA

is taken by parliamentary resolution, and the election must be held no fewer than 45 days before the expiry of the outgoing President's term of office. To be elected President, a candidate must obtain the support of three-fifths of the parliamentary quorum. If necessary, further ballots must then be conducted, contested by the two candidates who received the most votes. The candidate who receives more votes becomes President. The post of President may be held by the same person for not more than two consecutive terms.

The President's main responsibilities include the promulgation of laws, the issue of decrees, the scheduling of referendums, the conclusion of international treaties and the dissolution of Parlamentul. The President is allowed to participate in parliamentary proceedings. The President, after consultation with the parliamentary majority, is responsible for nominating a Prime Minister-designate and a Government. The President can preside over government meetings and can consult the Government on matters of special importance and urgency. On proposals submitted by the Prime Minister, the President may revoke or renominate members of the Government in cases of vacancies or the reallocation of portfolios. The President is Commander-in-Chief of the armed forces.

If the President has committed a criminal or constitutional offence, the votes of two-thirds of the members of Parlamentul are required to remove the President from office; the removal must be confirmed by the Supreme Court of Justice, for a criminal offence, and by a national referendum, for a constitutional offence.

THE COUNCIL OF MINISTERS

The principal organ of executive government is the Council of Ministers, which supervises state policy and public administration of the country. The Council of Ministers is headed by a Prime Minister, who co-ordinates the activities of the Government. The Council of Ministers must resign if Parlamentul votes in favour of a motion of 'no confidence' in the Council.

LOCAL ADMINISTRATION

For administrative purposes, the Republic of Moldova is divided into districts, towns and villages, in which local self-government is practised. At village and town level, elected local councils and mayors operate as autonomous administrative authorities. At district level, an elected council co-ordinates the activities of village and town councils.

The area on the left bank of the Dniester (Dnestr or Nistru) river, as well as certain other places in the south of the republic (i.e. Gagauz-Yeri) may be granted special autonomous status, according to special statutory provisions of organic law.

JUDICIAL AUTHORITY

Every citizen has the right to free access to justice. Justice shall be administered by the Supreme Court of Justice, the Court of Appeal, tribunals and the courts of law. Judges sitting in the courts of law and the Supreme Court of Justice are appointed by the President following proposals by the Higher Magistrates' Council. They are elected for a five-year term, and subsequently for a 10-year term, after which their term of office expires on reaching the age limit. The Higher Magistrates' Council is composed of 11 magistrates, who are appointed for a five-year term. It is responsible for the appointment, transfer and promotion of judges, as well as disciplinary action against them.

The Prosecutor-General, who is appointed by Parlamentul, exercises control over the enactment of law, as well as defending the legal order and the rights and freedoms of citizens.

THE CONSTITUTIONAL COURT

The Constitutional Court is the sole authority of constitutional judicature in Moldova. It is composed of six judges, who are appointed for a six-year term. The Constitutional Court's powers include: the enforcement of constitutionality control over laws, decrees and governmental decisions, as well as international treaties endorsed by the republic; the confirmation of the results of elections and referendums; the explanation and clarification of the Constitution; and decisions over matters of the constitutionality of parties. The decisions of the Constitutional Court are final and are not subject to appeal.

CONSTITUTIONAL REVISIONS

A revision of the Constitution may be initiated by one of the following: a petition signed by at least 200,000 citizens from at least one-half of the country's districts and municipalities; no less than one-third of the members of Parlamentul; the President of the Republic; the Government. Provisions regarding the sovereignty, independence, unity and neutrality of the State may be revised only by referendum.

The Government

HEAD OF STATE

President: VLADIMIR VORONIN (indirectly elected 4 April 2001; indirectly re-elected 4 April 2005).

COUNCIL OF MINISTERS
(April 2006)

Prime Minister: VASILE TARLEV.
First Deputy Prime Minister: ZINAIDA GRECIANÎI.
Deputy Prime Minister: VALERIAN CRISTEA.
Deputy Prime Minister and Minister of Foreign Affairs and European Integration: ANDREI STRĂTAN.
Minister of Agriculture and the Food Industry: ANATOLIE GORODENCO.
Minister of the Economy and Trade: VALERIU LAZĂR.
Minister of Finance: MIHAI POP.
Minister of Industry and Infrastructure: VALADIMIR ANTOSII.
Minister of Information Development: VLADIMIR MOLOJEN.
Minister of Transport and Road Management: MIRON GAGAUZ.
Minister of Ecology and Natural Resources: CONSTANTIN MIHAILESCU.
Minister of Education, Youth and Sport: VICTOR ȚVIRCUN.
Minister of Health and Social Protection: ION ABABII.
Minister of Culture and Tourism: ARTUR COZMA.
Minister of Justice: VICTORIA IFTODI.
Minister of Internal Affairs: GHEORGHE PAPUC.
Minister of Defence: VALERIU PLEȘCA.
Minister of Reintegration: VASILI ȘOVA.

Note: the President of the Moldovan Academy of Sciences, GHEORGHE DUCA, and the Başkan (leader) of the Autonomous Territory of Gagauz-Yeri (Gagauzia) are also members of the Government. GHEORGHE TABUNSCIC was elected to this position in October 2002.

MINISTRIES

Office of the President: 2073 Chişinău, bd Ştefan cel Mare 154; tel. (22) 23-47-93; e-mail president@prm.md; internet www.president.md.

Office of the Council of Ministers: 2033 Chişinău, Piaţa Marii Adunări Naţionale 1; tel. (22) 23-30-92; internet www.gov.md.

Ministry of Agriculture and the Food Industry: 2012 Chişinău, bd Ştefan cel Mare 162; tel. (22) 23-34-27; fax (22) 23-23-68; e-mail adm_maia@moldova.md; internet www.maia.gov.md.

Ministry of Culture and Tourism: 2033 Chişinău, Piaţa Marii Adunări Naţionale 1, Of. 326; tel. (22) 22-76-20; fax (22) 23-23-88; e-mail dept@turism.md; internet www.turism.md.

Ministry of Defence: 2021 Chişinău, şos. Hînceşti 84; tel. (22) 79-98-44; fax (22) 23-45-35; e-mail valeriusu@army.md; internet www.army.md.

Ministry of Ecology and Natural Resources: 2005 Chişinău, str. Cosmonauţilor 9; tel. (22) 22-16-68; fax (22) 22-07-48; e-mail capcelea@moldova.md; internet www.cim.moldova.md.

Ministry of the Economy and Trade: 2033 Chişinău, Piaţa Marii Adunări Naţionale 1; tel. (22) 23-74-48; fax (22) 23-40-64; e-mail minecon@moldova.md; internet www.mec.md.

Ministry of Education, Youth and Sport: 2033 Chişinău, Piaţa Marii Adunări Naţionale 1; tel. (22) 23-35-15; fax (22) 23-35-15; e-mail consilier@edu.md; internet www.edu.md.

Ministry of Finance: 2005 Chişinău, str. Cosmonauţilor 7; tel. (22) 23-35-75; fax (22) 22-13-07; e-mail protocol@minfin.moldova.md; internet www.moldova.md.

Ministry of Foreign Affairs and European Integration: 2012 Chişinău, str. 31 August 80; tel. (22) 57-82-07; fax (22) 23-23-02; e-mail secdep@mfa.md; internet www.mfa.md.

Ministry of Health and Social Protection: 2009 Chişinău, str. V. Alecsandri 1; tel. (22) 72-98-60; fax (22) 73-87-81; e-mail sdomente@mednet.md; internet www.ms.md.

Ministry of Industry and Infrastructure: 2012 Chişinău, bd Ştefan cel Mare 69; tel. (22) 27-80-59; fax (22) 27-80-00.

Ministry of Information Development: Chişinău, str. Puşkin 42; tel. (22) 22-91-23; fax (22) 22-80-20; e-mail mdi@registru.md; internet www.mdi.gov.md.

Ministry of Internal Affairs: 2012 Chişinău, bd Ştefan cel Mare 75; tel. (22) 22-45-47; fax (22) 22-27-43; e-mail mai@mai.md; internet www.mai.md.

MOLDOVA

Ministry of Justice: 2012 Chișinău, str. 31 August 1989 82; tel. (22) 23-47-95; fax (22) 23-47-97; e-mail iftodi@justice.gov.md; internet www.justice.gov.md.

Ministry of Reintegration: Chișinău, str. A. Mateevici 109/1; tel. (22) 21-40-80.

Ministry of Transport and Road Management: 2012 Chișinău, bd Ștefan cel Mare 134; tel. (22) 22-10-01; fax (22) 24-15-53; e-mail secretary@mci.gov.md; internet mci.gov.md.

President and Legislature

PRESIDENT

The President of the Republic is elected by parliamentary deputies, and is required to receive the support of at least 61 of the 101 members of Parlamentul. VLADIMIR VORONIN was re-elected President on 4 April 2005, receiving 75 votes. His sole opponent, GHEORGHE DUCA, obtained one vote.

LEGISLATURE

Parlamentul
(The Parliament)

2073 Chișinău, bd Ștefan cel Mare 105; tel. (22) 23-33-52; fax (22) 23-30-12; e-mail info@parlament.md; internet www.parliament.md.

Chairman: MARIAN LUPU.

General Election, 6 March 2005

Parties and alliances	Votes	%	Seats
Party of Communists of the Republic of Moldova	716,336	45.98	56
Democratic Moldova*	444,377	28.53	34
People's Christian Democratic Party	141,341	9.07	11
Fatherland-Motherland (Patria-Rodina)†	77,490	4.97	—
Social Democratic Party of Moldova	45,551	2.92	—
Equal Rights (Ravnopravie) Republican Socio-Political Movement	44,129	2.83	—
Other parties, alliances and independents	88,604	5.69	—
Total	1,557,828	100.00	101

* An electoral bloc, comprising: the Democratic Party of Moldova; the 'Our Moldova' Alliance; and the Social Liberal Party.
† An electoral bloc, led by the Socialist Party of Moldova.

Election Commission

Comisia Electorală Centrală a Republicii Moldova (Central Electoral Commission of the Republic of Moldova): Chișinău, str. Vasile Alecsandri 119; tel. (22) 25-14-51; fax (22) 25-14-70; e-mail cec@molddata.md; internet www.cec.md; Pres. EUGENIU ȘTIRBU.

Political Organizations

In March 2003 26 political parties were registered with the Ministry of Justice. The following were among the most important in existence in early 2006.

Agrarian Party of Moldova (APM) (Partidul Agrar din Moldova): Chișinău, str. Teatrului 15; tel. (22) 22-22-74; fax (22) 22-60-50; f. 1991 by moderates from both the Popular Front of Moldova and the Communist Party of Moldova; supports economic and agricultural reform; Chair. ANATOL POPUȘOI.

Centrist Union of Moldova (Uniunea Centristă din Moldova): Chișinău, str. Tricolorului 35; tel. (22) 21-13-26; fax (22) 22-46-71; internet www.ucm.md; f. 2000; splinter group of fmr Movement for a Democratic and Prosperous Moldova; Chair. MIHAI PETRACHE.

Democratic Party of Moldova (Partidul Democrat din Moldova—PDM): 2001 Chișinău, str. Tighina 32; tel. (22) 27-82-29; fax (22) 27-82-30; e-mail pdm@mtc.md; internet www.pdm.md; f. 1997; centrist; fmrly Movement for a Democratic and Prosperous Moldova, name changed in April 2000; contested 2005 legislative elections as mem. of the Democratic Moldova bloc; Chair. DUMITRU DIACOV.

Equal Rights (Ravnopravie) Socio-political Republican Movement (Mișcarea social-politică Republicană 'Ravnopravie'—RSPMR): Chișinău, str. Sarmisegetuza 90/2/201; tel. (22) 27-12-71; f. 1998; formed an alliance with the Patria Rodina party in Oct. 2005; Chair. VALERIU CLIMENCO.

Directory

'Green Alliance' Ecological Party of Moldova (Alianța Verde—PEM–AVE): 2012 Chișinău, str. Șciusev 63; tel. and fax (22) 72-16-43; e-mail iondediu@yahoo.com; f. 1992; Pres. Prof. ION DEDIU; 10,000 mems.

'Our Moldova' Alliance (Alianța Moldova Noastra—AMN): Chișinău, str. Pușkin 62A; tel. (22) 54-85-38; e-mail alianta@amn.md; internet www.amn.md; f. 2003 by merger of the Alliance of Independents of Moldova, the Moldovan Liberal Party, the Social Democratic Alliance of Moldova and the Popular Democratic Party of Moldova; supports Moldova's integration into Europe, a market economy and inter-ethnic harmony; contested 2005 legislative elections as mem. of the Democratic Moldova bloc; Chair. SERAFIM URECHEANU; c. 100,000 mems.

Party of Communists of the Republic of Moldova (Partidul Comuniștilor din Republica Moldova—PCRM): 2012 Chișinău, str. N. Iorga 11; tel. (22) 23-46-14; fax (22) 23-36-73; e-mail sava_valeriuion@yahoo.com; internet www.pcrm.md; fmrly the Communist Party of Moldova (banned Aug. 1991); revived as above 1994; First Sec. VLADIMIR VORONIN.

People's Christian Democratic Party (Partidul Popular Creștin Democrat—PPCD): 2009 Chișinău, str. N. Iorga 5; tel. (22) 23-33-56; fax (22) 23-86-66; e-mail magic@ppcd.md; internet www.ppcd.md; f. 1989 as the People's Front of Moldova, renamed 1992, and as above 1999; advocates Moldova's entry into the European Union and North Atlantic Treaty Organization; Chair. IURIE ROȘCA.

Reform Party of Moldova (Partidul Reformei din Moldova—PRM): Chișinău, str. București 87; tel. (22) 23-26-89; fax (22) 22-80-97; f. 1993; Christian-democratic; Leader MIHAI GIMPU; Chair. ȘTEFAN GORDA; 12,000 mems.

Republican Party of Moldova (Partidul Republican din Moldova—PRM): 2005 Chișinău, str. A. Vlahuță 11/4; tel. and fax (22) 21-09-51; e-mail pr.md@rambler.ru; f. 1993; Pres. VALERIU EFREMOV.

Social Democratic Party of Moldova (Partidul Social Democrat din Moldova—PSDM): 2071 Chișinău, str. Alba Iulia 75; tel. (22) 58-03-46; fax (22) 58-94-45; e-mail info@psdm.md; internet www.psdm.md; f. 1990; Pres. ION MUȘUC; Chair. of National Council OAZU NANTOI.

Social Liberal Party (Partidul Social-Liberal): Chișinău, str. Bulgară 24B; tel. (22) 27-66-20; fax (22) 22-25-03; e-mail secretariat@psl.md; internet www.psl.md; f. 1999; contested 2005 legislative elections as mem. of the Democratic Moldova bloc; Leader OLEG SEREBREAN.

Socialist Party of Moldova (Partidul Socialist din Moldova): Chișinău, str. Calea Ieșilor 61/1/15; tel. (22) 75-87-62; successor to the fmr Communist Party of Moldova; favours socialist economic and social policies, defends the rights of Russian and other minorities and advocates continued CIS membership; contested 2005 legislative election as mem. of the Fatherland-Motherland (Patria-Rodina) electoral bloc; Pres. VICTOR MOREV.

Unionist Movement of Moldova (UMM): Chișinău; f. 2005; aims to pursue closer relations with Romania; Pres. ILIE BRATU.

Parties and organizations in Transnistria include: **Obnovleniye** (Renewal—Leader YEVGENII SHEVCHUK) and **Respublica** (Republic—Leader YURII SUHOV).

Parties and organizations in Gagauz-Yeri include: the **Vatan (Fatherland) Party** (Comrat; Leader ANDREI CHESHMEJI) and **Gagauz Halky—Gagauz People** (Comrat; Leader KONSTANTIN TAUSHANDJI).

Diplomatic Representation

EMBASSIES IN MOLDOVA

Azerbaijan: 2012 Chișinău, bd Ștefan cel Mare 127; tel. (22) 21-42-09; fax (22) 23-22-77; e-mail azembassy@moldnet.md; Ambassador ISFENDIYAR VAHABZADEH.

Belarus: 2012 Chișinău, str. Mateevici 35; tel. (22) 23-83-02; fax (22) 23-83-00; internet www.belembassy.org/moldova; Ambassador VASILIY A. SAKOVICH.

Bulgaria: 2012 Chișinău, str. București 92; tel. (22) 23-79-83; fax (22) 23-79-08; e-mail ambasada-bulgara@meganet.md; Ambassador NIKOLAI ILIYEV.

China, People's Republic: Chișinău, str. Mitropolit Dosoftei 124; tel. (22) 24-85-51; fax (22) 24-75-46; e-mail chinaemb@mtc.md; internet md.china-embassy.org; Ambassador GONG JIANWEI.

Czech Republic: 2004 Chișinău, Str. Sfatul Tarii 59; tel. (22) 296215; fax (22) 234884; f. 2005; Chargé d'affaires a.i. OLDŘICH WACHTL.

France: Chișinău, str. Vlaicu Pîrcălab 6; tel. (22) 20-04-00; fax (22) 20-04-01; e-mail amb-fr@cni.md; internet www.ambafrance.md; Ambassador EDMOND PAMBOUKJIAN.

MOLDOVA

Germany: 2012 Chişinău, str. Maria Cibotari 35, Hotel Jolly Alon; tel. (22) 20-06-00; fax (22) 23-46-80; e-mail info@chisinau.diplo.de; internet www.chisinau.diplo.de; Ambassador WOLFGANG LERKE.

Hungary: 2004 Chişinău, bd Ştefan cel Mare 131; tel. (22) 22-34-04; fax (22) 22-45-13; e-mail hu.emb@cni.md; Ambassador Dr SÁNDOR RÓBEL.

Poland: Chişinău, str. Plămădeală 3; tel. (22) 23-85-51; fax (22) 23-85-53; e-mail ambpolsk@ch.moldpac.md; Ambassador KRZYSZTOF SUPROWICZ.

Romania: Chişinău, str. Bucureşti 66/1; tel. (22) 21-30-37; fax (22) 22-81-29; e-mail ambrom@moldnet.md; internet chisinau.mae.ro; Ambassador FILIP TEODORESCU.

Russia: 2004 Chişinău, bd Ştefan cel Mare 153; tel. (22) 23-49-43; fax (22) 23-51-07; e-mail domino@mdl.net; internet www.moldova.mid .ru; Ambassador NIKOLAI T. RYABOV.

Turkey: Chişinău, str. Valeriau Cupcea 60; tel. (22) 50-91-00; fax (22) 22-55-28; e-mail tremb@moldova.md; Ambassador FATMA FIRAT TOPÇUOĞLU.

Ukraine: 2008 Chişinău, str. Vasile Lupu 17; tel. (22) 58-21-51; fax (22) 58-51-08; e-mail emb_md@mfa.gov.ua; Ambassador PETRO F. CHALYI.

United Kingdom: 2012 Chişinău, str. N. Iorga 18; tel. (22) 22-59-02; fax (22) 24-25-00; e-mail enquiries.chisinau@fco.gov.uk; internet www.britishembassy.md; Ambassador BERNARD WHITESIDE.

USA: 2009 Chişinău, str. Mateevici 103; tel. (22) 23-37-72; fax (22) 23-30-44; e-mail woodwarda@state.gov; internet www.usembassy .md; Ambassador HEATHER M. HODGES.

Judicial System

Supreme Court of the Republic of Moldova
(Curtea Supremă de Justiţie a Republicii Moldova)
2009 Chişinău, str. M. Kogălniceanu 70; tel. and fax (22) 22-15-47.
Chairman: VALERIA ŞTERBEŢ.

Constitutional Court of the Republic of Moldova
(Curtea Constitutionala a Republicii Moldova)
2004 Chişinău, str. A. Lapuşneanu 28; tel. (22) 25-37-08; fax (22) 25-37-46; e-mail curtea@constcourt.md; internet www.constcourt.md; f. 1994
Chairman: VICTOR PUSCAS.
Prosecutor-General: VALERIU BALABAN.

Religion

The majority of the inhabitants of Moldova profess Christianity, the largest denomination being the Eastern Orthodox Church. The Gagauz, although of Turkic descent, are also adherents of Orthodox Christianity. The Russian Orthodox Church (Moscow Patriarchate) claims jurisdiction in Moldova, but there are Romanian and Turkish liturgies.

CHRISTIANITY

Eastern Orthodox Church

In December 1992 the Patriarch of Moscow and All Russia issued a decree altering the status of the Eparchy of Chişinău and Moldova to that of a Metropolitan See. The Government accepted this decree, thus tacitly rejecting the claims of the Metropolitan of Bessarabia (based in Romania). However, at the end of July 2002 the Government agreed to register the Bessarabian Metropolitan Church, following international pressure.

Russian Orthodox Church (Moscow Patriarchate): 2004 Chişinău, str. Bucuresti 119; tel. (22) 23-78-78; e-mail sec@mitropolia .md; internet www.mitropolia.md; 1,520 parishes, 25 monasteries and 24 convents (2004); Metropolitan of Chişinău and Moldova VLADIMIR.

Roman Catholic Church

In October 2001 the diocese of Chişinău, covering the whole country, was established. At 31 December 2003 there were an estimated 20,000 Roman Catholics in Moldova.

Bishop of Chişinău: Rt Rev. ANTON COŞA, 2012 Chişinău, str. Mitropolit Dosoftei 85; tel. (22) 22-34-70; fax (22) 22-52-10; e-mail administ@apost.moldpac.md.

The Press

In 1996 there were four daily newspapers published in Moldova (with a combined circulation averaging 261,000 copies). In that year 206 non-daily newspapers were published (with an estimated circulation of 1,350,000). In 1994 there were 76 other periodicals (31 for the general public and 45 for specific readership, with a total circulation of 196,000).

The publications listed below are in Moldovan, except where otherwise indicated.

PRINCIPAL NEWSPAPERS

Accente Libere: Chişinău, str. Renasterii 22/1, bir. 48; tel. (22) 23-86-28; e-mail accente@rambler.ru; internet accente.com.md; weekly; Editor-in-Chief SERGIU AFANASIU.

Dnestrovskaya Pravda (Dnestr Truth): Tiraspol, str. 25 October 101; tel. and fax (284) 3-46-86; f. 1941; 3 a week; in Russian; Editor TATYANA M. RUDENKO; circ. 7,000.

Ekonomicheskoye Obozreniye (Economic Review): Chişinău, bd Ştefan cel Mare 180; tel. (22) 24-69-52; fax (22) 24-69-50; e-mail red@ logos.press.md; internet logos.press.md; f. 1990; weekly; in Russian; Editor-in-Chief SERGEI MIŞIN.

Glasul Naţiunii (The Voice of the Nation): Chişinău, str. 31 August 15; tel. and fax (22) 54-31-37; e-mail glasul_natiunii@hotmail.com; 4 a month; Editors VASILE NĂSTASE, EMANUELA JORGA.

GP Flux: Chişinău, str. Corobceanu 17; tel. (22) 23-22-14; fax (22) 24-75-29; e-mail secretar@flux.press.md; internet flux.press.md; daily; Editor-in-Chief IGOR BURCIU.

Jurnal de Chişinău: 2012 Chişinău, str. Puşkin 22/446; tel. (22) 23-40-41; fax (22) 23-42-30; e-mail cotidian@jurnal.md; internet www .jurnal.md; f. 1999; daily; Editor-in-Chief (vacant); circ. 13,400.

Kishinevskii Obozrevatel (Chişinău Correspondent): Chişinău, bd Ştefan cel Mare 162/604/7; tel. (22) 21-02-34; fax (22) 21-02-64; e-mail oboz@molodvacc.md; internet www.ko.md; weekly; in Russian; Editor-in-Chief IRINA ASTAKHOVA.

Kishinevskiye Novosti (Chişinău News): Chişinău, str. Puşkin 22; tel. (22) 23-39-18; fax (22) 23-42-40; e-mail kn@mdl.net; internet www.kn.md; weekly; in Russian; Editor-in-Chief MAIA FILILOVNA IONKO.

Kommersant Moldovy (Businessman of Moldova): 2012 Chişinău, str. Puşkin 22/601; tel. (22) 23-36-94; fax (22) 23-33-31; e-mail vartem@commert.press.md; internet www.km.press.md; weekly; in Russian; also known as *Kommersant Plus*; Editor-in-Chief ARTEM VARENIŢA.

Komsomolskaya Pravda—v Moldove (Young Communist League Truth—in Moldova): Chişinău, str. Vlaicu Pîrcălab 45; tel. (22) 22-96-62; fax (22) 22-12-74; e-mail ser@kp.md; internet www.kp.md; daily; owned by Komsomolskaya Pravda (Basarabia), a subsidiary of Komsomolskaya Pravda (Russia); in Russian; Editor-in-Chief SERGEI CIURICOV.

Moldavskiye Vedomosti (Moldovan Gazette): 2012 Chişinău, str. Bănulescu-Bodoni 21; tel. and fax (22) 23-86-18; e-mail editor@mv .net.md; internet vedomosti.md; f. 1995; weekly; in Russian; Editor-in-Chief DMITRII A. CIUBASENKO; circ. 5,100 (2004).

Moldova Suverană (Sovereign Moldova): 2012 Chişinău, str. Puşkin 22, 3rd Floor; tel. (22) 23-35-38; fax (22) 23-31-96; e-mail cotidian@suverana.press.md; internet www.moldova-suverana.md; f. 1924; daily; fmrly organ of the Govt; Editor ION BERLINSCHI; circ. 105,000.

Nezavisimaya Moldova (Independent Moldova): 2012 Chişinău, str. Puşkin 22, 303; tel. (22) 23-36-05; fax (22) 23-31-41; e-mail admin@nm.mldnet.com; internet www.nm.md; f. 1991; daily; fmrly organ of the Govt; in Russian; Editor IURII TISCENCO; circ. 60,692.

Tinerimya Moldovei/Molodezh Moldovy (Youth of Moldova): Chişinău; f. 1928; 3 a week; editions in Romanian (circ. 12,212) and Russian (circ. 4,274); Editor V. BOTNARU.

Trudovoi Tiraspol (Working Tiraspol): Tiraspol, str. 25 October 101; tel. (284) 3-04-12; f. 1989; in Russian; Editor DIMA KONDRATOVICH.

Viaţă Satului (Life of the Village): 2612 Chişinău, str. Puşkin 22, Casa presei, 4th Floor; tel. (22) 23-03-68; f. 1945; weekly; govt publ; Editor V. S. SPINEY.

Vremya (Time): 2068 Chişinău, str. Alecu Russo 1, 166; tel. (22) 44-09-41; fax (22) 44-73-33; e-mail nata@vremea.md; internet www .vremea.net; f. 1999; daily; in Russian; Editor NATALIA UZUN.

PRINCIPAL PERIODICALS

Basarabia (Bessarabia): 2004 Chişinău, str. 31 August 98, 401; tel. (22) 21-05-13; e-mail libr@mnc.md; f. 1931; fmrly *Nistru*; monthly; journal of the Union of Writers of Moldova; fiction; Editor-in-Chief D. MATKOVSKY.

MOLDOVA

Chipăruș (Peppercorn): 2612 Chișinău, str. Pușkin 22; tel. (22) 23-38-16; f. 1958; fortnightly; satirical; Editor-in-Chief Ion Vikol.

Democratia (Democracy): 2012 Chișinău, str. Pușkin 22, 516–518; tel. (22) 24-32-53; fax (22) 24-35-85; e-mail democratia@cfem.md; internet www.democratia.cfem.md; f. 2001; weekly; political; Editor-in-Chief Cornel Ciurea.

Femeia Moldovei (Moldovan Woman): 2470 Chișinău, str. 28 June 45; tel. (22) 23-31-64; f. 1951; monthly; popular, for women.

Lanterna Magică (Magic Lantern): Chișinău, str. Pușkin 24, 49; tel. (22) 74-86-43; fax (22) 23-23-88; e-mail lung_ro@yahoo.com; internet www.iatp.md/lanternamagica; f. 1990; publ. by the Ministry of Culture and Tourism; 6 a year; art, culture.

Literatură și Artă: 2009 Chișinău, str. Sfatul Țării 2; tel. (22) 23-82-12; fax (22) 23-82-17; e-mail literatura@moldnet.md; f. 1954; weekly; organ of the Union of Writers of Moldova; literary; Editor Nicolae Dabija.

Moldova si Lumea (Moldova and the World): 2012 Chișinău, str. Pușkin 22, 510; tel. (22) 23-75-81; fax (22) 23-40-32; f. 1991; monthly; state-owned; international socio-political review; Editor Boris Stratulat.

Noi (Us): Chișinău; tel. (22) 23-31-91; f. 1930; fmrly Scînteia Leninista (Leninist Sparks); monthly; fiction; for 12–18-year-olds; Man. Valeriu Volontir; circ. 5,000.

Politica: 2033 Chișinău, bd Ștefan cel Mare 105; tel. (22) 23-74-03; fax (22) 23-32-10; e-mail vppm@cni.md; f. 1991; monthly; political issues.

Săptămína (The Week): Chișinău, str. 31 August 107; tel. (22) 22-44-61; fax (22) 21-37-07; e-mail saptamin@mom.mldnet.com; internet www.net.md/saptamina; weekly magazine; Editor-in-Chief Viorel Mihail.

Sud-Est Cultural (South-East Cultural): Chișinău, str. 31 August 78; tel. (22) 234-11-01; fax 76-55-80; e-mail vtazlauanu@dnt.md; internet www.sud-est.md; f. 2004; quarterly; art, culture; Editor-in-Chief Valentina Tazlauanu.

Timpul de Dimineata (The Morning Times): Chișinău, str. Mitropolitul Dosoftei 95; tel. (22) 29-40-45; fax (22) 29-24-28; e-mail timpul@mdl.net; internet www.timpul.md; weekly; independent; Editor-in-Chief Constantin Tanase.

NEWS AGENCIES

AP Flux Press Agency: Chișinău, str. Corobceanu 17; tel. (22) 24-92-72; fax (22) 24-91-51; e-mail flux@cni.md; internet flux.press.md; f. 1995; Dir Nadine Gogu.

BASA-press—Moldovan Information and Advertising Agency: 2012 Chișinău, str. Vasile Alecsandri 72; tel. (22) 22-03-90; fax (22) 22-13-96; e-mail basa@basa.md; internet www.basa.md; f. 1992; independent; co-operates with Deutsche Presse-Agentur (Germany); Gen. Dir Valeriu Renita.

DECA Press Agency: Bălți, str. Independenței 33; tel. (231) 61-385; fax (231) 607-44; e-mail info@deca-press.net; internet www.deca-press.net; f. 1996; local news; non-profit; Dir Vitalie Cazacu.

InfoMarket.MD (Denimax Grup): Chișinău; tel. (22) 27-76-26; e-mail editor@infomarket.md; internet www.infomarket.md; on-line business news; Editor Alecsandru Burdeinii.

Infotag News Agency: 2014 Chișinău, str. Kogâlniceanu 76; tel. (22) 23-49-30; fax (22) 23-49-33; e-mail office@infotag.md; internet www.infotag.md; f. 1993; leading private news agency; Dir Alexandru Tanas.

Interlic News Agency: 2012 Chișinău, str. M. Cibotari 37, bir. 306; tel. and fax (22) 25-16-49; fax (22) 23-20-67; e-mail red@interlic.md; internet www.interlic.md; f. 1995; independent; Dir Ivan Sveatcenko.

Olvia-Press: 3300 Tiraspol, str. Pravda 31; tel. (3022) 8-24-97; fax (3022) 8-20-04; e-mail olvia@idknet.com; internet www.olvia.idknet.com; f. 1992; sole press agency of the 'Transnistrian Moldovan Republic'; reports political, economic and cultural developments in the region; Editor-in-Chief Oleg A. Yelkov.

Reporter.md: 2001 Chișinău, bd Ștefan cel Mare 65; tel. (22) 27-12-94; fax (22) 54-77-39; e-mail info@reporter.md; internet www.reporter.md; f. 2000 as an online journal; began operating as an independent news agency from 2002.

State Information Agency—Moldpres: 2012 Chișinău, str. Pușkin 22; tel. (22) 23-26-69; fax (22) 23-26-98; e-mail director@moldpres.md; internet www.moldpres.md; f. 1940 as ATEM, reorganized 1990 and 1994; Dir Valeriu Renita.

PRESS ASSOCIATIONS

Independent Journalism Centre (IJC): 2012 Chișinău, str. Șciusev 53; tel. (22) 21-36-52; fax (22) 22-66-81; e-mail editor@ijc.md; internet ijc.iatp.md; f. 1994; non-governmental org..

Independent Press Association (API): Chișinău, str. Corobceanu 15; tel. (22) 21-06-02; fax (22) 20-36-86; e-mail api@moldtelecom.md; internet api.iatp.md; f. 1997; Pres. Ion Ciumeica.

Union of Journalists of Moldova: 2012 Chișinău, str. Pușkin 22; tel. and fax (22) 23-34-19; e-mail ujm@moldnet.md; internet www.iatp.md/ujm; f. 1957; Chair. Valeriu Saharneanu.

Publishers

Editura Cartea Moldovei: 2004 Chișinău, bd Ștefan cel Mare 180; tel. (22) 24-65-10; fax (22) 24-64-11; f. 1977; fiction, non-fiction, poetry, art books; Dir Dumitru Furdui; Editor-in-Chief Raisa Suveica.

Editura Hyperion: 2004 Chișinău, bd Ștefan cel Mare 180; tel. (22) 24-40-22; f. 1976; fiction, literature, arts; Dir Valeriu Matei.

Editura Lumina (Light): 2004 Chișinău, bd Ștefan cel Mare 180; tel. (22) 24-63-95; f. 1966; educational textbooks; Dir Victor Stratan; Editor-in-Chief Anatol Malev.

Editura Științța (Science): 2028 Chișinău, str. Academiei 3; tel. (22) 73-96-16; fax (22) 73-96-27; e-mail prini@stiinta.asm.md; f. 1959; textbooks, encyclopedias, dictionaries, children's books and fiction in various languages; Dir Gheorghe Prini.

Broadcasting and Communications

TELECOMMUNICATIONS

National Regulatory Agency in Telecommunications and Informatics (ANRTI): 2012 Chișinău, bd Ștefan cel Mare 134; tel. (22) 25-13-17; fax (22) 22-28-85; e-mail office@anrti.md; internet www.anrti.md; f. 2000; Dir Iurie Tabirța.

Moldcell SA: 2060 Chișinău, str. Belgrad 3; tel. (22) 20-62-06; fax (22) 20-62-07; e-mail moldcell@moldcell.md; internet www.moldcell.md; f. 1999; mobile telecommunications; owned by Fintur Holdings b.v. (Netherlands).

Moldtelecom SA: 2001 Chișinău, bd Ștefan cel Mare 10; tel. (22) 54-87-97; fax (22) 54-64-19; e-mail office@moldtelecom.md; internet www.moldtelecom.md; f. 1993; telephone communication and internet service provider; scheduled for partial privatization; Gen. Dir Stela Școla.

VoxTel SA: 2071 Chișinău, str. Alba-Iulia 75; tel. (22) 57-50-10; e-mail corporate@voxtel.md; internet www.voxtel.md; f. 1998; mobile cellular telecommunications; 51% owned by France Telecom Mobiles.

BROADCASTING

Regulatory Authorities

Radio and Television Co-ordinating Council (Consiliul Coordonator al Audiovizualului): 2012 Chișinău, str. Mihai Eminescu 28; tel. (22) 27-74-70; fax (22) 27-74-71; e-mail cca_moldova@tmg.md; internet www.cca.telemedia.md; f. 1995; state owned; regulatory and licensing body; Chair. Ion Mihailo.

State Communication Inspectorate (Inspectoratul de Stat al Comunicatiilor): 2021 Chișinău, str. Drumul Viilor 28-2; tel. (22) 73-53-64; fax (22) 73-39-41; e-mail ciclicci@isc.net.md; f. 1993; responsible for frequency allocations and monitoring, certification of post and communications equipment and services; Dir Teodor Ciclicci.

Radio

State Radio and Television Company of Moldova (Teleradio) (Televiziunea de Stat a Republicii Moldova): 2028 Chișinău, str. Miorița 1; tel. (22) 72-10-77; fax (22) 72-33-52; e-mail info@trm.md; internet www.trm.md; f. 1994; Dir Ilie Telescu; Exec. Dir (Radio) Sergiu Patoc.

Radio Moldova: 2028 Chișinău, str. Miorița 1; tel. (22) 72-13-88; fax (22) 72-35-37; f. 1930; broadcasts in Romanian, Russian, Ukrainian, Gagauz and Yiddish; Exec. Dir Victor Tabarta.

Television

State Radio and Television Company of Moldova (Teleradio) (Televiziunea de Stat a Republicii Moldova): 2028 Chișinău, str. Miorița 1; tel. (22) 72-10-77; fax (22) 72-33-52; e-mail info@trm.md; internet www.trm.md; f. 1994; Dir Ilie Telescu.

TV Moldova (Televiziunea Nationala Moldova): f. 1958; Exec. Dir Adela Raileanu.

Chișinău Television: 2028 Chișinău, str. Hîncești 64; tel. (22) 73-91-94; fax (22) 72-35-37; f. 1958; Dir-Gen. Arcadie Gherasim.

MOLDOVA

Association

Electronic Media Association (APEL): 2012 Chişinău, str. Şciusev 73; tel. and fax (22) 21-12-54; e-mail info@apel.md; internet www.apel.md; represents 29 radio and television stations; Dir ALEXANDRU DOROGAN.

Finance

(cap. = capital; res = reserves; dep. = deposits; m. = million; brs = branches; amounts in Moldovan lei, unless otherwise stated)

BANKING

The National Bank of Moldova (NBM), established in 1991, is independent of the Government (but responsible to Parlamentul) and has the power to regulate monetary policy and the financial system. At February 2006 there were 16 commercial banks in operation.

Central Bank

National Bank of Moldova (Banca Naţională a Moldovei): 2006 Chişinău, bd Renaşterii 7; tel. (22) 40-90-06; fax (22) 22-05-91; e-mail official@bnm.org; internet www.bnm.org; f. 1991; cap. 200.0m., res 352.4m., dep. 2,515.3m. (Dec. 2004); Gov. LEONID TALMACI; First Deputy Gov. DUMITRU URSU.

Commercial Banks

Banca de Finanţe şi Comerţ SA (FinComBank SA—Finance and Trade Bank JSC): 2012 Chişinău, str. Puşkin 26; tel. (22) 22-74-35; fax (22) 23-73-08; e-mail fincom@fincombank.com; internet www.fincombank.com; f. 1993; cap 122.7m., dep. 554.8m., total assets 772.3m. (June 2005); Chair. VICTOR KHVOROSTOVSKY; 13 brs.

Banca Socială SA: 2005 Chişinău, str. Bănulescu-Bodoni 61; tel. (22) 22-14-94; fax (22) 22-42-30; e-mail office@socbank.md; internet www.socbank.md; f. 1991; joint-stock commercial bank; cap. 57.6m., res 19.5m., dep. 873.9m. (Jan. 2005); Pres. VLADIMIR SUETNOV; Chair. VALENTIN CUNEV; 20 brs.

Businessbank SA: 2012 Chişinău, str. Alecsandru cel Bun 97; tel. (22) 20-56-10; fax (22) 22-23-70; e-mail bank@busbank.mldnet.com; internet www.businessbank.md; f. 1997; cap. 72.1m., res 1.1m., dep. 81.1m. (Jan. 2003); Chair. of Bd SERGIU N. BRINZILA.

Comerţbank (Commercebank): 2001 Chişinău, str. Hînceşti 38A; tel. (22) 73-99-91; fax (22) 73-99-81; e-mail comertbank@mdl.net; internet www.comertbank.md; f. 1991; cap. 96.0m., total assets 149.9m. (Jan. 2003); Chair. NATALIA ULIYANOVA.

Energbank: 2012 Chişinău, str. Vasile Alecsandri 78; tel. (22) 54-43-77; fax (22) 25-34-09; e-mail office@energbank.com; internet www.energbank.com; f. 1997; cap. 80.0m., dep. 263.9m., total assets 390.3m. (June 2005); Chair. MIHAIL OGORODNICOV; 48 brs.

EuroCreditBank SA: 2001 Chişinău, str. Ismail 33; tel. (22) 50-01-01; fax (22) 54-88-27; e-mail info@ecb.md; internet www.ecb.md; f. 2002 to replace Petrolbank; jt-stock co; commercial investment bank; cap. 92.0m., res 8.4m., dep. 35.2m. (June 2005); Pres. of Bd of Dirs ANDREI CUCU; Pres. and Gen. Man. AURELIU CINCILEI; 3 brs.

Eximbank SA (Eximbank Jt-Stock Commercial Bank): 2001 Chişinău, bd Ştefan cel Mare 6; tel. (22) 27-25-83; fax (22) 54-62-34; e-mail info@eximbank.com; internet www.eximbank.com; Chair. MARCEL CHIRCĂ.

Guinea: 2068 Chişinău, str. Alecu Russo 1; tel. (22) 43-05-11; fax (22) 44-41-40; cap. 10.4m., total assets 59.1m. (Jan. 1998); Chair. IURII STASIEV.

IBID-MB (International Bank for Investment and Development): 2067 Chişinău, bd Moscow 21; tel. (22) 34-62-49; fax (22) 34-62-31; cap. 9.6m., total assets 24.7m. (Jan. 1998); Chair. GHEORGHE NECHIT.

Investprivatbank SA: 2001 Chişinău, str. Şciusev 34; tel. (22) 27-43-86; fax (22) 54-05-10; e-mail ipb@ipb.md; internet www.ipb.md; f. 1994; cap. 70m., dep. 92.8m., total assets 186.3m. (31 July 2004); Chair. IVAN CHIRPALOV; 3 brs.

Mobiasbanca SA: 2012 Chişinău, bd Ştefan cel Mare şi Sfânt 81A; tel. (22) 25-64-56; fax (22) 25-63-36; e-mail office@mobiasbanca.md; internet www.mobiasbanca.md; f. 1990; acquired Bancoop in 2001; commercial bank; cap. US $15.5m., res $0.9m., dep. $49.1m. (June 2005); Chair. of Bd VICTOR POPUSOI; Chair. of Administrative Bd NICOLAE DORIN; 11 brs.

Moldindconbank SA (Moldovan Bank for Industry and Construction): 2012 Chişinău, str. Armeneasca 38; tel. (22) 57-67-82; fax (22) 27-91-95; e-mail info@moldinconbank.com; internet www.moldindconbank.com; f. 1991; joint-stock commercial bank; cap. 29.8m., res 6.4m., dep. 870.7m. (Dec. 2003); Chair. of Bd VALERIAN MIRZAC; 21 brs.

Moldova Agroindbank SA: 2005 Chişinău, str. Cosmonauţilor 9; tel. (22) 21-28-28; fax (22) 22-80-58; e-mail aib@maib.md; internet www.maib.md; f. 1991; joint-stock commercial bank; cap. 51.9m., res 116.0m., dep. 1,453.5m. (Dec. 2003); Chair. of Bd VICTOR MICULEŢ; Chair. NATALIA VRABIE; 45 brs.

Unibank SA: 2012 Chişinău, str. Mitropolit G. Bănulescu-Bodoni 45; tel. (22) 22-55-86; fax (22) 22-05-30; e-mail welcome@unibank.md; internet www.unibank.md; f. 1993; jt-stock commercial bank; cap. 95.0m., res 8.5m., dep. 240.6m. (June 2005); Pres. CLAUDIA MELNIK; 5 brs.

Universalbank SA: 2004 Chişinău, bd Ştefan cel Mare 180, et. 4; tel. (22) 29-59-00; fax (22) 29-59-06; e-mail ub@mail.universalbank.md; internet www.universalbank.md; f. 1994; cap. 74.2m., res 8.0m., dep. 110.5m., total assets 229.4m. (Aug. 2005); Chair. of Bd DIANA MOTOLOGA; 5 brs.

Vias: 2002 Chişinău; tel. (22) 54-14-10; fax (22) 54-14-20; cap. 10.3m., total assets 18.1m. (Jan. 1998); Chair. NICOLAE DEDE.

Victoriabank: 2004 Chişinău, str. 31 August 141; tel. (22) 23-30-65; fax (22) 23-39-33; e-mail mail@victoriabank.md; internet www.victoriabank.md; f. 1989; cap. 146.0m., total assets 767.5m. (Dec. 2001); Chair. VICTOR ŢURCANU; 12 brs.

Savings Bank

Banca de Economii a Moldovei SA: 2012 Chişinău, str. Columna 115; tel. (22) 24-47-22; fax (22) 24-47-31; e-mail bem@bem.md; internet www.bem.md; f. 1992; cap. 29.3m., res 4.4m., dep. 862.4m. (Dec. 2002); Pres. GRIGORE GACIKEVICI; 37 brs.

STOCK EXCHANGE

Moldovan Stock Exchange (Bursa de Valori a Moldovei SA): 2001 Chişinău, bd Ştefan cel Mare 73; tel. (22) 27-75-94; fax (22) 27-73-56; e-mail dodu@moldse.md; internet www.moldse.md; f. 1994; Chair. Dr CORNELIU DODU.

INSURANCE

QBE Asito SA: 2005 Chişinău, str. Bănulescu-Bodoni 57/1; tel. and fax (22) 22-62-12; fax (22) 22-11-79; e-mail asito@qbe-asito.com; internet www.qbe-asito.com; f. 1991; 74% owned by QBE Insurance Group (Australia); Gen. Man. EUGEN SHLOPAK; 1,100 employees.

Trade and Industry

GOVERNMENT AGENCIES

State Department for Privatization (Departamentul Privatizarii al Republicii Moldova): 2012 Chişinău, str. Puşkin 26; tel. (22) 23-43-50; fax (22) 23-43-36; e-mail dep.priv@moldtelecom.md; internet www.privatization.md; Dir-Gen. ALEXANDR BANNICOV.

Moldovan Export Promotion Organization (MEPO) (Organizaţia de Promovare a Exportului din Moldova): 2009 Chişinău, str. Mateevici 65; tel. (22) 27-36-54; fax (22) 22-43-10; e-mail mepo@mepo.net; internet www.mepo.net; f. 1999; assists enterprises in increasing exports and improving business environment; Dir-Gen. VALERIU CANNA.

CHAMBER OF COMMERCE

Chamber of Commerce and Industry of the Republic of Moldova (Camera de Comerţ şi Industrie a Republicii Moldova): 2012 Chişinău, str. M. Eminescu 28; tel. (22) 22-15-52; fax (22) 24-14-53; e-mail inform@chamber.md; internet www.chamber.md; f. 1969; Chair. GHEORGHE CUCU.

UTILITIES

Regulatory Authority

National Energy Regulatory Agency (ANRE): 2012 Chişinău, str. Columna 90; tel. (22) 54-13-84; fax (22) 22-46-98; e-mail anre@anre.md; internet www.anre.md; f. 1997; autonomous public institution; Dir ANATOL BURLACOB; Gen. Dir NICOLAE TRIBOI.

Electricity

The sector comprises one transmission company, five distribution companies and four power-generation plants.

MoldElectrica IS: 2012 Chişinău, str. V. Alecsandri 78; tel. (22) 22-22-70; fax (22) 25-31-42; f. 2001 to assume the transmission and distribution functions of Moldtranselectro; Dir VASILE PLESAN.

Reţelele Electrice de Distribuţie Centru SA (RED Centru): 2055 Vatra, str. Luceafarul 13; tel. and fax (22) 50-13-37; e-mail uf@moldova.com; privatized in 2000; wholly owned by Unión Eléctrica Fenosa (Spain); distribution co.

Reţelele Electrice (mun. Chişinău) SA: 2024 Chişinău, str. A. Doga 4; tel. (22) 42-16-55; privatized in 2000; wholly owned by Unión Eléctrica Fenosa (Spain); distribution co.

Reţelele Electrice de Distribuţie Nord SA (RED Nord): 3121 Bălţi, bd Ştefan cel Mare 180A; tel. (231) 2-20-00; fax (231) 2-33-12; e-mail red-nord@mdl.net; f. 1997; owns nine regional distribution divisions; Dir GHEORGHE I. PELIN.

Reţelele Electrice de Distribuţie Nord-Vest (RED Nord-Vest): Donduşeni; owns six regional distribution divisions.

Reţelele Electrice de Distribuţie Sud SA (RED Sud): 3901 Cahul, str. Tineretului 2; tel. (299) 43-16-55; e-mail uf@moldova.com; f. 1997; privatized in 2000; wholly owned by Unión Eléctrica Fenosa (Spain); distribution co.

Gas

MoldovaGaz SA: 2005 Chişinău, str. Albişoara 38; tel. (22) 57-80-02; fax (22) 22-00-02; e-mail office@moldovagaz.md; f. May 1999; national gas pipeline and distribution networks; purchases, sells and transports natural gas; comprises two transmission companies and 18 distribution companies; 51.0% owned by Gazprom (Russia), 35.3% owned by Moldova and 13.4% held by Transnistria (pending transfer to Gazprom); Gen. Dir GHENADII ABASCIN (acting).

Moldovatransgas SRL: 5233 Drochia, şos. Ţarigrad, POB 24; tel. (52) 24-452; fax (52) 26-238; f. 1986; natural gas transportation, supply and equipment service.

TRADE UNIONS

Confederation of Trade Unions of the Republic of Moldova (Confederaţia Sindecatelor din Republica Moldova): 2012 Chişinău, str. 31 August 129; tel. (22) 23-76-74; fax (22) 23-76-98; e-mail cfsind@cni.md; internet www.csrm.md; f. 1990; Pres. PETRU CHIRIAC.

CONSUMER ORGANIZATION

Central Union of Consumers' Co-operatives of Moldova (Uniunea Centrală a Cooperativelor de Consum din Republica Moldova—MOLDCOOP): 2001 Chişinău, bd Ştefan cel Mare 67; tel. (22) 27-15-95; fax (22) 27-41-50; e-mail moldcoop@moldova.md; internet www.moldcoop.md; f. 1925; Chair. VASILE I. CARAUŞ.

Transport

RAILWAYS

Plans for the construction of a new rail link, connecting Chişinău wth Iaşi, Romania, were announced in mid-2002.

Moldovan Railways: 2012 Chişinău, str. Vlaicu Pîrcălab 48; tel. (22) 25-44-08; fax (22) 22-13-80; e-mail secr@railway.md; internet www.railway.md; f. 1992; total network 1,075 km; Dir-Gen. MIRON GAGAUZ.

ROADS

In 2000 Moldova's network of roads totalled 12,691 km (86.1% of which was hard-surfaced), including 3,328 km of main roads and 6,105 km of regional roads.

INLAND WATERWAYS

In 1997 the total length of navigable waterways in Moldova was 424 km. The main river ports are at Tighina (Bender, Bendery), Rîbniţa and Reni. The construction of a maritime port (petroleum terminal) on the River Danube was under way.

SHIPPING

Neptun-M SA: 2064 Chişinău, str. V. Belinski 101; tel. (22) 74-95-51; fax (22) 74-09-01; f. 1992; Gen. Dir VICTOR ANDRUŞCA.

CIVIL AVIATION

The refurbishment of Chişinău International Airport, funded by the European Bank for Reconstruction and Development (EBRD—based in the United Kingdom) was completed in 2000. Moldova has three civilian airports, in Chişinău, Tiraspol and Bălţi. In 2004 the country's only military airbase, at Marculesti, became a fourth civilian international airport.

Civil Aviation Administration (Administraţia de stat a Aviaţiei Civile): 2026 Chişinău, Aeroportul Chişinău; tel. (22) 52-40-64; fax (22) 52-91-18; e-mail info@caa.md; internet www.caa.md; f. 1993; Gen. Dir IURIE ZIDU (acting).

Air Moldova (Compania Aeriana Moldova): 2026 Chişinău, bd Dacia 80/2, Aeroportul Chişinău; tel. (22) 52-55-02; fax (22) 52-44-49; e-mail info@airmoldova.md; internet www.airmoldova.md; f. 1993; 51% state-owned, 49% owned by Unistar Ventures GmbH (Germany); scheduled and charter passenger and cargo flights to destinations in Europe and the CIS; Dir-Gen. VASILE BOTNARI.

Air Moldova International: 2026 Chişinău, Aeroportul Chişinău, 4th Floor; tel. (22) 52-97-91; fax (22) 52-64-14; e-mail info@ami.md; internet www.ami.md; scheduled and charter flights to destinations in Europe and the CIS; Dir-Gen. DORIN TIMCIUC.

Moldavian Airlines SA: 2026 Chişinău, Aeroportul Chişinău; tel. (22) 52-93-56; fax (22) 52-50-64; e-mail sales@mdv.md; internet www.mdv.md; f. 1994; scheduled and charter passenger and cargo flights to destinations in Europe, the Middle East and North Africa; Pres. and Chief Exec. NICOLAE PETROV.

Moldtransavia SRL: 2026 Chişinău, Aeroportul Chişinău; tel. (22) 52-59-71; fax (22) 52-63-99; e-mail mold@travia.mldnet.com; air freight and passenger transportation.

Tourism

There were 26,045 tourist arrivals in 2004, compared with 18,964 in 2000. Tourist receipts totalled US $116m. in 2003.

Department of Tourism Development: 2004 Chişinău, bd Ştefan cel Mare si Sfânt 180, bir. 901; tel. (22) 21-07-74; fax (22) 23-26-26; e-mail dept@turism.md; internet www.turism.md.

Federation of Sport and Tourism of the Republic of Moldova: Chişinău; tel. (22) 44-51-81; e-mail ftsmd@narod.ru; internet www.ftsmd.narod.ru; Pres. IVAN D. ZABUNOV.

MONACO

Introductory Survey

Location, Climate, Language, Religion, Flag

The Principality of Monaco lies in western Europe. The country is a small enclave in south-eastern France, about 15 km east of Nice. It has a coastline on the Mediterranean Sea but is otherwise surrounded by French territory. The climate is Mediterranean, with warm summers and very mild winters. The official language is French, but Monégasque (a mixture of the French Provençal and Italian Ligurian dialects), Italian and English are also spoken. Most of the population profess Christianity, with about 91% belonging to the Roman Catholic Church. The national flag (proportions 4 by 5) has two equal horizontal stripes, of red and white. The state flag (proportions 4 by 5) displays the princely arms of Monaco (a white shield, held by two monks and superimposed on a pavilion of ermine) on a white background.

History

The Principality of Monaco is an hereditary monarchy, which has been ruled by the Grimaldi dynasty since 1297. It was abolished during the French Revolution but re-established in 1814. In 1861 Monaco became an independent state under the protection of France. The Constitution, promulgated in January 1911, vested legislative power jointly in the Prince and an 18-member Conseil national, selected for a term of five years by a panel comprising nine delegates of the municipality and 21 members elected by universal suffrage. Agreements in 1918 and 1919 between France and Monaco provided for Monaco's incorporation into France should the reigning prince die without leaving a male heir. Prince Louis II, the ruler of Monaco since 1922, died in May 1949, and was succeeded by his grandson, Prince Rainier III. A new Constitution, introduced in December 1962, abolished the formerly held principle of the divine right of the ruler, and stipulated that the Conseil national be elected by universal adult suffrage.

Supporters of Prince Rainier, grouped in the Union nationale et démocratique (UND), dominated at five-yearly elections in 1963–88, on all but two occasions taking all 18 seats on the Conseil national. In January 1993, however, two lists of candidates, the Liste Campora (led by Jean-Louis Campora, the President of the football team, AS Monaco) and the Liste Médecin, secured 15 and two seats, respectively, while an independent candidate won the remaining seat. At legislative elections in February 1998 UND candidates secured all 18 seats.

Controversy surrounding the use of Monaco's financial sector for the transfer of funds derived from criminal activities intensified in 1998 with the culmination of an investigation into the deposit of US $5.5m. in cash, suspected of originating from the illegal drugs trade, at a bank in Monaco in 1995. The affair led to a crisis in relations between France and the Principality, with the French Government overruling Prince Rainier by refusing to extend the mandate of Monaco's Chief Prosecutor, whom it suspected of not conducting a sufficiently thorough investigation of the scandal. Following further criticisms of Monégasque banking practice in a report by the Organisation for Economic Co-operation and Development (OECD, see p. 320) in 2000, the French Government recommended a rapid revision of the bilateral treaties between Monaco and France, proposing that Monégasque institutions be brought into greater conformity with French excise, fiscal and banking regulations. In a list published in April 2002, OECD defined Monaco as an 'unco-operative tax haven'. According to a progress report on harmful tax practices issued by OECD in March 2004, Monaco was one of five jurisdictions still refusing to co-operate with the Organisation. In December 2004 the EU signed an agreement with Monaco on the taxation of savings income. Under the agreement, savings income, in the form of interest payments made in Monaco to residents of the EU, was to be subject to a withholding tax from 1 July 2005. Monaco also agreed to exchange information on request with EU member states in criminal or civil cases of tax fraud or comparable offences.

In March 2002 the electoral law was amended, and in April the Conseil national approved a number of significant constitutional amendments. Both measures were in part intended to expedite Monaco's application for full membership of the Council of Europe (see p. 211), which had been submitted in October 1998. The age of majority was lowered from 21 years to 18 years, and several executive powers of the Prince were transferred to the Conseil national, the size of which was to be increased to 24 members following the elections in 2003. Additionally, the law of succession was modified, to permit succession through the female line.

In late 2002 discontent was reported at a proposal, supported by Campora, to sell AS Monaco to a Ukrainian investment company, Fedcominvest, which was also the football club's principal sponsor. Following a report in *Le Monde*, in December 2002, which alleged that Fedcominvest was involved in 'money laundering', Prince Rainier, who, on behalf of the Principality, retained ultimate control over the club, prohibited the proposed sale. The ensuing scandal appeared to be a significant factor in appreciably reducing support for Campora's UND at the legislative elections, held on 9 February 2003, when the UND secured only three seats on the enlarged Conseil national; the remaining 21 seats were awarded to the Union pour Monaco list, led by a former member of the UND, Stéphane Valéri.

In April 2004 the Parliamentary Assembly of the Council of Europe (PACE) ruled that Monaco was entitled to receive special 'guest status' at PACE but that further reforms were required before the Principality could be considered for full membership of the Council; among the principal requirements were the extension of eligibility for several senior government positions, including the Minister of State (who, under the terms of a 1930 treaty, was required to be a French civil servant), to Monégasque citizens, and an enhancement of fiscal regulation. Following the decision of the Joint Committee of the Council of Europe (comprising representatives of the Parliamentary Assembly and the Committee of Ministers) that talks between France and Monaco had demonstrated significant progress towards the eventual reform of the 1930 convention, Monaco was admitted as the 46th member of the Council of Europe on 5 October.

In early 2005 a reorganization of the Council of Government took place. The number of Government Councillors was increased from three to five, with the creation of Government Councillors for Social Affairs and Health and for External Relations, and it was announced that Jean-Paul Proust was to replace Patrick Leclercq as Minister of State from the beginning of May. On 6 April, following a protracted period of ill health, Prince Rainier died at the age of 81. He was succeeded by his son, Prince Albert II, who had acted as Regent of the Principality since 31 March. In early July, several days before his formal inauguration as Head of State, it was confirmed that Prince Albert, who was unmarried and had no legal heir, had fathered an illegitimate child in 2003. It was announced, however, that the Prince's son would neither bear the name Grimaldi nor be eligible to inherit the throne. Albert II was formally enthroned in mid-November, marking the conclusion of the formal transfer of power.

Monaco participates in the work of a number of international organizations, and in 1993 became a member of the UN. In January 2006 France upgraded the status of its diplomatic representation in Monaco from consular to ambassadorial level, becoming the first country to operate an embassy in the Principality.

Government

Legislative power is vested jointly in the Prince, an hereditary ruler, and the 24-member Conseil national, which is elected by universal adult suffrage, partly under a system of proportional representation, for a term of five years. The electorate comprises only Monégasque citizens aged 18 years or over. Executive power is exercised, under the authority of the Prince, by the five-member Council of Government, headed by the Minister of State (a French civil servant selected by the Prince from a list of three candidates presented by the French Government). The Prince represents the Principality in its relations with foreign powers,

MONACO

and signs and ratifies treaties. There is, additionally, a consultative Conseil communal, elected for a term of four years, headed by a mayor.

Economic Affairs

In 2001, according to World Bank estimates, Monaco's gross national income (GNI), measured at average 1999–2001 prices, was equivalent to approximately US $24,700 per head. In 2000, according to World Bank estimates, GNI, measured at average 1998–2000 prices, was equivalent to approximately $25,200 per head, or approximately $25,700 on an international purchasing-power parity basis. According to UN estimates, Monaco's gross domestic product (GDP) was $847m. in 1995 (equivalent to $26,470 per head). During 1990–95 GDP increased, in real terms, at an average annual rate of 1.1%. GDP grew by 2.2% in 1995. The annual rate of population increase averaged 0.6% in 1990–2000. Monaco has the highest population density of all the independent states in the world.

There is no agricultural land in Monaco. In 1990 a Belgian enterprise established an offshore fish farm for sea bass and sea bream.

Industry (including construction and public works) contributed 17.2% of revenue in 2004. Excluding construction and public works, the sector engaged 16.9% of those employed in the private sector in 2003 and provided employment for 9.2% of the total labour force in 2004; construction and public works employed a further 31.8% of the labour force in the latter year. Industry is mainly light in Monaco. The principal sectors, measured by gross value of output, are chemicals, pharmaceuticals and cosmetics (which together accounted for 43.4% of all industrial revenue in 2004), plastics (29.1%), electrical and electronic goods, paper and textile production.

Service industries represent the most significant sector of the economy in Monaco, contributing 82.8% of total revenue in 2004, and providing employment for 83.1% of those working in the private sector in 2003. Banking and finance accounted for more than 38% of the services sector and employed some 1,400 people in the late 1990s. At the end of 2004 the total value of deposits in Monaco's private banking sector was estimated at €16,900m. Trade accounted for 39.1% of national revenue in 2004, while banking and financial activities accounted for 14.5%.

Tourism is also an important source of income, providing an estimated 25% of total government revenue in 1991 and engaging some 20% of the employed labour force in the late 1990s, while the hotel business alone employed 11.8% of the total labour force in 2003. In 2004 some 250,159 tourists (excluding excursionists) visited Monaco. The greatest number of visitors (excluding excursionists) in 2004 were from Italy (23.1%), France (16.1%), the United Kingdom (14.4%) and the USA (7.9%).

Monaco's external trade is included in the figures for France. Revenue is derived principally from real estate, light and medium industry, indirect taxation and tourism.

In 2004 there was a budgetary deficit of €58.6m.; expenditure amounted to €694.8m. In 2000 value-added tax (VAT) contributed 52.8% of total government revenue. In the late 1990s it was estimated that less than 3% of the population were unemployed in the Principality.

Monaco is largely dependent on imports from France, owing to its lack of natural resources. There is a severe labour shortage in the Principality, and the economy is reliant on migrant workers (many of whom remain resident in France and Italy). Following the establishment of a casino in the 1860s, tourism became the dominant sector in the economy. In particular, the Principality has sought to establish itself as a major centre of the conference industry; about one-quarter of the nights spent at Monaco's hotels in 2004 were connected with this sector, compared with one-10th in the early 1970s. From the 1980s, however, the industry and real estate sectors expanded, as a series of land reclamation projects increased Monaco's area by 20%. A number of foreign companies and banks are registered in Monaco in order to take advantage of the low rates of taxation on company profits. Since the removal of French restrictions on foreign exchange in 1987, Monaco's banking industry (which includes an 'offshore' sector) has expanded. The role of tourism in the economy was expected to grow further, following the construction of a new pier for luxury vessels, completed in August 2002. Further measures, which aimed to create an additional 350 berthing spaces for leisure yachts in Monaco (in addition to the 350 already extant), were announced in 2003. A new state-owned company, the Société d'Exploitation des Ports de Monaco was formed in that year, to oversee the operations and future development of Monaco's two principal ports, at La Condamine (Port Hercule) and Fontvieille. The shipping sector is also significant, contributing some 4% of business revenue and providing employment for around 1,300 people. The telecommunications sector was also a focus of expansion in the Principality in the first half of the 2000s.

Education

Education follows the French system, and is compulsory for 10 years for children aged six to 16 years. Primary education begins at six years of age and lasts for five years. Secondary education begins at 11 years of age and lasts for seven years. Total expenditure on education amounted to 221m. French francs in 1996, equivalent to 6.3% of total budgetary expenditure.

Public Holidays

2006: 1 January (New Year's Day), 27 January (Feast of St Dévote, Patron Saint of the Principality), 17 April (Easter Monday), 1 May (Labour Day), 25 May (Ascension Day), 5 June (Whit Monday), 15 August (Assumption), 1 November (All Saints' Day), 19 November (National Day/Fête du Prince), 8 December (Immaculate Conception), 25–26 December (Christmas).

2007: 1 January (New Year's Day), 27 January (Feast of St Dévote, Patron Saint of the Principality), 9 April (Easter Monday), 1 May (Labour Day), 17 May (Ascension Day), 28 May (Whit Monday), 15 August (Assumption), 1 November (All Saints' Day), 19 November (National Day/Fête du Prince), 8 December (Immaculate Conception), 25–26 December (Christmas).

Weights and Measures

The metric system is in force.

Statistical Survey

Source: (unless otherwise stated): Direction de l'expansion économique, division des statistiques et des études économiques, 9 rue du Gabian, MC 98000; tel. 93-15-41-59; fax 93-15-87-59.

AREA AND POPULATION

Area: 1.95 sq km.

Population: 29,972 at census of 23 July 1990; 32,020 (males 15,544, females 16,476) at census of July 2000.

Density (July 2000): 16,435 per sq km.

Population by Nationality (2000): French 10,229; Italian 6,410; Monégasque 6,089; Other 9,292. *2004* (official estimate at 4 February): Monégasque 7,600 (males 3,264, females 4,336). Source: Monaco—La Mairie.

Districts (population at 2000 census): Monte-Carlo 15,507; Condamine 12,187; Fontvieille 3,292; Monaco-Ville (capital) 1,034.

Births, Marriages and Deaths (2003): Live births 842; Marriages 183; Deaths 617. Source: Monaco—La Mairie.

Expectation of Life (WHO estimates, years at birth): 81 (males 78; females 85) in 2003. Source: WHO, *World Health Report*.

Economically Active Population (incl. non-residents, December 2004): 41,110.

HEALTH AND WELFARE

Key Indicators

Total Fertility Rate (children per woman, 2003): 1.8.

Under-5 Mortality Rate (per 1,000 live births, 2004): 5.

Physicians (per 1,000 head, 1998): 6.64.

Health Expenditure (2002): US $ per head (PPP): 4,258.

Health Expenditure (2002): % of GDP: 11.0.

MONACO — *Directory*

Health Expenditure (2002): public (% of total): 79.6.
Access to Water (% of persons, 2000): 100.
Access to Sanitation (% of persons, 2000): 100.
For sources and definitions, see explanatory note on p. vi.

FINANCE

Currency and Exchange Rates: French currency: 100 cent = 1 euro (€). *Sterling and Dollar Equivalents* (30 December 2005): £1 sterling = 1.4596 euros; US $1 = 0.8477 euros; €100 = £68.51 = $117.97. *Average Exchange Rate* (euros per US dollar): 0.8860 in 2003; 0.8054 in 2004; 0.8041 in 2005. *Note:* The local currency was formerly the French franc, although some Monégasque currency, at par with the French franc, also circulated. From the introduction of the euro, with French participation, on 1 January 1999, a fixed exchange rate of €1 = 6.55957 French francs was in operation. Euro notes and coins were introduced on 1 January 2002. The euro and local currency circulated alongside each other until 17 February, after which the euro became the sole legal tender.

Budget (€ million, 2004): Revenue 636.2; Expenditure 694.8 (Current expenditure 467.2, Capital expenditure 227.7).

EXTERNAL TRADE

Monaco's imports and exports are included in the figures for France.

TRANSPORT

Road Traffic (vehicles in use at 31 December 1996, estimates): Passenger cars 21,120; Buses and coaches 70; Lorries and vans 2,700; Road tractors 80; Motorcycles and mopeds 5,400. Source: IRF, *World Road Statistics*.

TOURISM

Tourist Arrivals (excluding excursionists): 262,520 in 2002; 234,638 in 2003; 250,159 in 2004. Figures refer to arrivals of foreign visitors at hotels and similar establishments.

Tourist Arrivals by Country (2004): Belgium 3,891; France 40,158; Germany 9,479; Italy 57,708; Japan 8,884; Netherlands 4,203; Russia 4,478; Spain 6,886; Switzerland 6,749; United Kingdom 36,147; USA 19,861; Total (incl. others) 250,159.

COMMUNICATIONS MEDIA

Radio Receivers (1997): 34,000 in use.
Television Receivers (1997): 25,000 in use.
Daily Newspapers (1996): 1 title (estimated circulation 8,000 copies—1995).
Non-daily Newspapers (1996): 5 titles (estimated circulation 50,000 copies).
Telephones (2000): 30,000 main lines in use.
Facsimile Machines (1992): 1,880 in use.
Book production (1999): 72 titles.
Mobile Cellular Telephones (2000): 18,700 subscribers. (Sources: International Telecommunication Union; UN, *Statistical Yearbook*; UNESCO Institute for Statistics).

EDUCATION

(2004/05)

Pre-primary: 40 teachers (33 public, 7 private); 903 pupils (736 public, 167 private).
Elementary: 133 teachers (108 public, 25 private); 1,827 pupils (1,365 public, 462 private).
Secondary: 330 teachers (277 public, 53 private); 3,095 pupils (2,399 public, 696 private).

Note: Educational establishments in Monaco in 2004/05 comprised the following: three public pre-primary schools; four primary schools (three public, one private), which integrate pre-primary and elementary age groups; one public elementary school; three public secondary schools, comprising one lower secondary school, one general upper secondary school, and one vocational secondary school; and one private school integrating primary and secondary age groups. There was also one private higher educational establishment, the International University of Monaco, a business school where instruction is conducted in English.

Source: Direction de l'éducation nationale, de la jeunesse et des sports.

Directory

The Constitution

The Constitution of 17 December 1962, as amended on 2 April 2002, vests legislative power jointly in the Prince and the 24-member Conseil national (National Council), which is elected by universal adult suffrage, partly under a system of proportional representation, for a term of five years. Executive power is exercised, under the authority of the Prince, by the five-member Council of Government, headed by the Minister of State. The Constitution maintains the traditional hereditary monarchy, although the principle of the divine right of the ruler is renounced. The law of succession was modified to permit succession through the female line in April 2002. The right of association, trade union freedom and the right to strike are guaranteed. The Supreme Tribunal safeguards fundamental liberties. Constitutional amendments have to be submitted for approval by the Conseil national. Several executive powers of the Prince were transferred to the Conseil national in April 2002.

The Government

HEAD OF STATE

Ruling Prince: HSH Prince ALBERT II (succeeded 6 April 2005).

COUNCIL OF GOVERNMENT
(April 2006)

Minister of State: JEAN-PAUL PROUST.
Government Councillor for the Interior: PAUL MASSERON.
Government Councillor for Finance and Economic Affairs: FRANCK BIANCHERI.
Government Councillor for Social Affairs and Health: DENIS RAVERA.
Government Councillor for Capital Works, the Environment and Town Planning: GILLES TONELLI.
Government Councillor for External Relations: RAINIER IMPERTI.

There is also a Chef de Cabinet (MARIE-NOËLLE ALBERTINI).

MINISTRIES

The postal address for all ministries is: BP 522, MC 98015; tel. 93-15-80-00; fax 93-15-82-17; e-mail centre-info@gouv.mc; internet www.gouv.mc.

Ministry of State: place de la Visitation, MC 98000; tel. 93-15-82-43; fax 93-15-80-12; e-mail cabminetat@gouv.mc.

Legislature

Conseil national

12 rue Col Bellando de Castro, MC; tel. 93-30-41-15; fax 93-25-31-90; internet www.conseilnational.mc.

The Conseil national (National Council) has 24 members. At the most recent elections, which took place on 9 February 2003, the Union pour Monaco (UPM) list secured 21 seats, with the Union nationale et démocratique (UND) controlling the remaining three.

President: STÉPHANE VALÉRI.
Vice-President: CLAUDE BOISSON.

Advisory Councils

Conseil d'état: Palais de Justice, Monte-Carlo; advises on proposed laws or ordinances submitted for its approval by the Ruling Prince or by the Government, or on any other matter; seven mems, appointed by the Ruling Prince, following the advice of the Director of Judicial Services; Pres. PHILIPPE NARMINO; Vice-Pres. NORBERT FRANÇOIS; Sec. BRIGITTE GRINDA-GAMBARINI.

Conseil de la Couronne: Monte-Carlo; f. 1942; advises the Ruling Prince on matters of state, and must be consulted by the Ruling Prince prior to the implementation of certain constitutional matters, including the signature or ratification of treaties, the dissolution of the Conseil national, questions of naturalization or reintegration, the issuing of pardons or amnesties; seven mems, appointed for renewable terms of three years; Pres. and three mems are appointed by free choice of the Ruling Prince, the remaining three mems are named by the Ruling Prince and approved by the Conseil national; all mems must hold Monégasque nationality; Pres. CHARLES BALLERIO; Sec. ROBERT PROJETTI.

Conseil économique et social: Centre Administratif, 8 rue Louis-Notari, MC; tel. 93-30-20-82; fax 93-50-05-96; f. 1945; advises on economic matters; 33 mems, appointed for a term of three years; 11 mems directly appointed by Govt, 11 appointed by Govt from list prepared by Union des Syndicats de Monaco, 11 appointed by Govt from list prepared by the Fédération Patronale Monégasque; the Ruling Prince appoints Pres. and two Vice-Pres from among the mems; Pres. ANDRÉ GARINO; Vice-Pres ANDRÉ THIBAULT, JACQUES WOLZOK.

Political Organizations

There are no political parties as such in Monaco; however, candidates are generally grouped into lists to contest elections to the Conseil national. Between 1963 and 1992, and 1998 and 2003 the Conseil national was dominated by representatives of the Union nationale et démocratique (UND). At the 1993 elections, however, the two main groupings were the Liste Campora, led by Jean-Louis Campora, and the Liste Médecin, led by Jean-Louis Médecin. The majority of seats at the 2003 elections were secured by the Union pour Monaco list.

Diplomatic Representation

In January 2006 France opened an embassy in Monaco, becoming the first country to institute ambassadorial-level diplomatic relations with the Principality. In March 2006 career or honorary consulates representing some 70 countries were accredited to Monaco.

France: Le Roc fleuri, 1 rue du Tenao, BP 45, MC 98000 Cedex; tel. 92-16-54-60; fax 92-16-54-64; internet www.consulatfrance.mc; Ambassador SERGE TELLE.

Judicial System

The organization of the legal system is similar to that of France. There is one Justice of the Peace, a Tribunal de Première Instance (Court of First Instance), a Cour d'Appel (Court of Appeal), a Cour de Révision judiciaire (High Court of Appeal), a Tribunal Criminel (Crown Court) and finally the Tribunal Suprême (Supreme Tribunal), which deals with infringements of the rights and liberties provided by the Constitution, and also with legal actions aiming at the annulment of administrative decisions for abusive exercise of power.

Palais de Justice
5 rue Col Bellando de Castro, MC 98000; tel. 93-15-81-28; fax 93-15-85-89.

Director of Judicial Services: PHILIPPE NARMINO.
President of the Supreme Tribunal: ROLAND DRAGO.
President of the High Court of Appeal: YVES JOUHAUD.
First President of the Court of Appeal: MONIQUE FRANÇOIS.
President of the Court of First Instance: BRIGITTE GRINDA-GAMBARINI.

Religion

CHRISTIANITY

The Roman Catholic Church

Monaco comprises a single archdiocese, directly responsible to the Holy See. At 31 December 2003 there were an estimated 29,000 adherents in the Principality, representing about 90.6% of the total population.

Archbishop of Monaco: Most Rev. BERNARD BARSI, Archevêché, 1 rue de l'Abbaye, BP 517, MC 98015 Cedex; tel. 93-30-88-10; fax 92-16-73-88; e-mail contact@eglise-catholique.mc; internet www.eglise-catholique.mc.

The Anglican Communion

Within the Church of England, Monaco forms part of the diocese of Gibraltar in Europe.

Chaplain: JAN JOUSTRA, St Paul's Church House, 22 ave de Grande Bretagne, MC 98000; tel. 93-30-71-06; fax 93-30-50-39; e-mail stpauls@monaco.mc; internet www.stpauls.monaco.mc.

The Principality also has two Protestant churches and a synagogue.

The Press

Gazette Monaco-Côte d'Azur: 1 ave Princesse Alice, MC 98000; tel. 97-97-61-20; fax 93-50-68-27; e-mail lagazette@aip.mc; f. 1976; monthly; regional information; Dir-Gen. MAX POGGI; Chief Editor NOËLLE BINE-MULLER; circ. 10,000.

Journal de Monaco: Ministère d'Etat, BP 522, MC 98015; tel. 93-15-83-15; fax 93-15-82-17; internet www.gouv.mc/DataWeb/jourmon.nsf; f. 1858; edited at the Ministry of State; official weekly; contains texts of laws and decrees; Editor ROBERT COLLE.

Monaco Actualité: 2 rue du Gabian, MC 98000; tel. 92-05-75-36; fax 92-05-75-34; e-mail actualite@monaco.mc; Dir-Gen. MAURICE RICCOBONO; circ. 15,000.

Monaco Hebdo: 27 blvd d'Italie, MC 98000; tel. 93-50-56-52; fax 93-50-19-22; Man. Editor ROBERTO TESTA.

Monte-Carlo Méditerranée: tel. 92-05-67-67; fax 92-05-37-01; Dir-Gen. GÉRARD COMMAN; Chief Editor CAROLE CHABRIER.

French newspapers are widely read, and a special Monaco edition of *Nice-Matin* is published in Nice, France.

NEWS AGENCIES

Monte-Carlo Press: Monte-Carlo; e-mail mcpress@monaco.net; internet www.mcpress.mc; f. 1987.

Sportel/Monaco Mediax: Villa Le Mas, 4 blvd du Jardin Exotique, MC 98000; tel. 93-30-20-32; fax 93-30-20-33; e-mail info@sportelmonaco.com; internet www.sportelmonaco.com; f. 1990; sport; Exec. Vice-Pres. DAVID TOMATIS.

Publishers

EDIPROM: Monte-Carlo; tel. 92-05-67-67; fax 92-05-37-01; advertising material, official publications; Pres. GÉRARD COMMAN.

Editions Alphée: 28 rue Comte Félix Gastaldi, MC 98015 Cedex; tel. 99-99-67-17; fax 99-99-67-18.

Editions EGC: 9 ave du Prince Héréditaire Albert, BP 438, MC 98011 Cedex; e-mail multiprint@multiprintmc.com; economics, history, literature; Gen. Man. GÉRARD COMMAN.

Editions Victor Gadoury: 57 rue Grimaldi, MC 98000; tel. 93-25-12-96; fax 93-50-13-39; e-mail contact@gadoury.com; internet www.gadoury.com; f. 1967; numismatics.

Editions de l'Oiseau-Lyre SAM: Les Remparts, BP 515, MC 98015 Cedex; tel. 93-30-09-44; fax 93-30-19-15; e-mail oiseaulyre@monaco377.com; internet www.oiseaulyre.com; f. 1932; music publishers; Dir KENNETH GILBERT.

Editions de Radio Monte Carlo SAM: Monte-Carlo; tel. 93-15-17-57; general; Pres. JEAN PASTORELLI.

Editions Regain S.N.C. Boy et Cie: Monte-Carlo; tel. 93-50-62-04; f. 1946; fiction, essays, autobiography, travel, religion, philosophy, poetry; Dir-Gen. MICHÈLE G. BOY.

Editions du Rocher: 28 rue Comte Félix Gastaldi, MC 98015; tel. 93-30-33-41; fax 93-50-73-71; f. 1943; scientific, medical, detective and general; Dir JEAN PAUL BERTRAND.

Editions André Sauret SAM: Monte-Carlo; tel. 93-50-67-94; fax 93-30-71-04; art, fiction; Dir RAYMOND LEVY.

Marsu Productions: 9 ave des Castelans, MC 98000; tel. 92-05-61-11; fax 92-05-76-60; e-mail info@marsupilami.com; internet www.marsupilami.com; comic-strips, children's entertainment.

Broadcasting and Communications

TELECOMMUNICATIONS

Direction du Controle des Concessions et des Télécommunications: 23 ave Prince Héréditaire Albert, MC 98000; tel. 93-15-88-00; fax 97-98-56-57; Dir RAOUL VIORA.

MONACO

Monaco Telecom: 25 blvd de Suisse, MC 98000 Cedex; tel. 99-66-63-00; fax 99-66-63-01; e-mail communication@monaco-telecom.mc; internet www.monaco-telecom.mc; f. 1997; 49% owned by Cable & Wireless (United Kingdom), 45% by the Société Nationale de Financement (wholly owned by Govt of Monaco); incorporates the wholly owned subsidiaries Monaco Telecom International, Monaco Interactive, Société Monégasque de Services de Telecoms (SMST), Société Monégasque de Télédistribution (SMT) and Divona; Chief Exec. ANTOINE VERAN.

BROADCASTING

Radio

Radio Monte Carlo SAM (RMC): Monte-Carlo; tel. 93-15-16-17; fax 93-15-16-30; 83% owned by the French Government (Société financière de la radiodiffusion); Pres. C. C. SOLAMITO; Dir-Gen. JEAN NOEL TASSEZ.

Riviera Radio: 10 quai Antoine 1er, MC 98000; tel. 97-97-94-94; fax 97-97-94-95; e-mail info@rivieraradio.mc; internet www.rivieraradio.mc; broadcasts in English; Man. Dir PAUL KAVANAGH.

Société Monégasque d'Exploitation et d'Études de Radiodiffusion (SOMERA): Monte-Carlo; tel. 93-15-16-17; fax 93-15-16-60; fmr subsidiary of RMC, transferred to Radio-France Internationale in 1996; in French and Arabic; Pres. JEAN-PAUL CLUZEL; Dir-Gen. CHRISTIAN CHARPY.

Trans World Radio SC: BP 349, MC 98007; tel. 92-16-56-00; fax 92-16-56-01; internet www.twr.org; f. 1955; evangelical Christian broadcaster; Pres. DAVID TUCKER.

Television

TVI Monte-Carlo: 8 quai Antoine 1er, MC 98000; tel. 92-16-88-20; fax 93-25-46-39; e-mail tvimc@frateschi.mc; programmes in Italian; CEO LUIGI FRATESCHI.

Société Spéciale d'Entreprises Télé Monte-Carlo: 16 blvd Princesse Charlotte, BP 279, MC 98090; tel. 93-50-59-40; fax 93-25-01-09; f. 1954; Pres. JEAN-LOUIS MÉDECIN.

Finance

(cap. = capital, res = reserves, dep. = deposits, brs = branches, m. = million, amounts in euros—€)

BANKING

In 2004 a total of 43 banks, including major British, French, Italian and US banks, were represented in the Principality.

Banque Centrale Monégasque de Crédit: Monte-Carlo; tel. 92-16-52-00; fax 93-30-91-93; f. 1969; Pres. JEAN DEFLASSIEUX; Gen. Man. MARC LANZERINI.

Banque de Gestion Edmond de Rothschild: BP 317, Les Terrasses, 2 ave de Monte-Carlo, MC 98000; tel. 93-10-47-47; fax 93-25-75-57; e-mail banque@lcf-rothschild.mc; internet www.lcf-rothschild.com; f. 1986; present name adopted 1993; cap. 12.0m., res 11.4m., dep. 433.6m. (Dec. 2003); Chair. LEONARDO P. A. POGGI; Gen. Man. GIAMPAOLO BERNINI.

Banque du Gothard/Banca del Gottardo (Monaco): La Belle Epoque, 15–17 bis ave d'Ostende, MC 98000; tel. 93-10-66-66; fax 93-50-60-71; e-mail bdg_monaco@gottardo.com; internet www.gottardo.com; f. 1994; 100% owned by Banca del Gottardo (Switzerland); cap. 40.0m., res 21.0m., dep. 799.8m. (Dec. 2003); Chair of Bd PHILIPPE TRON LOZAI; Exec. Dir YVES BRACCALENTI.

Banque Sudameris: 47–49 blvd d'Italie, MC 98000; tel. 92-16-51-00; fax 92-16-51-13; e-mail monaco@sudameris.fr; Man. MICHEL DE GIRONDE.

Barclays Bank: 31 ave de la Costa, BP 339, MC 98007; tel. 93-15-35-35; fax 93-25-15-68; Gen. Man. J. B. BUISSON; 3 brs.

BNP Paribas Private Bank Monaco: 15–17 ave d'Ostende, MC 98000; tel. 93-15-68-00; fax 93-15-68-01; f. 2003 by merger of United European Bank—Monaco and BNP Paribas Private Bank Monaco; acquired Société Monégasque de Banque Privée and Bank Von Ernst (Monaco) in 2004; private banking; Dir-Gen. ERIC GEORGES.

Compagnie Monégasque de Banque: 23 ave de la Costa, BP 149, MC 98007; tel. 93-15-77-77; fax 93-25-08-69; e-mail cmb@cmb.mc; internet www.cmb.mc; f. 1976; 61.6% owned by Mediobanca—Banca di Credito Finanziario SpA (Italy), 33.9% by Intesa Holding International SA (Luxembourg); cap. 111.1m., res 58.9m., dep. 1,226.3m. (Dec. 2003); Chair. ENRICO BRAGGIOTTI; Gen. Man. ETIENNE FRANZI.

Crédit Foncier de Monaco (CFM Monaco): 11 blvd Albert 1er, BP 499, MC 98012; tel. 93-10-20-00; fax 93-10-23-50; e-mail info@cfm.mc; internet www.cfm.mc; f. 1922; 77.1% owned by Calyon (France); cap. 35.0.m., res 85.5m., dep. 1,800.2m. (Dec. 2003); Chair. YVES BARSALOU; Gen. Man. HERVÉ CATALA.

Crédit Suisse (Monaco): 27 ave de la Costa, BP 155, MC 98003; tel. 93-15-27-27; fax 93-25-27-99; e-mail arthur.jayloyan@cspb.com; f. 1987; cap. 12.0m., res 2.4m., dep. 468.5m. (Dec. 2003); Chair. ARTHUR JAYLOYAN.

EFG Eurofinancière d'Investissements: Ville Les Aigles, 15 ave d'Ostende, MC 98000; tel. 93-15-11-11; fax 93-15-11-12; e-mail enquiries_mco@efgbank.com; internet www.efggroup.com; f. 1990; 100% owned by Private Financial Investments Holding Limited (Switzerland); private banking; cap. 16.0m., res 1.7m., dep. 318.9m. (Dec. 2002); Dir-Gen. GEORGE CATSIAPIS.

HSBC Private Bank (Monaco): 17 ave d'Ostende, MC 98000; tel. 93-15-25-25; fax 93-15-25-00; internet www.hsbcprivatebank.com; f. 1997; as Republic National Bank of New York (Monaco) SA, present name adopted 2004; owned by HSBC Private Banking Holdings (Suisse—Switzerland); private banking; cap. 86.0m., dep. 2,171.3m., total assets 2,362.3m. (Dec. 2003); Chief Exec. and Dir-Gen. GÉRARD COHEN.

KB Luxembourg (Monaco): 8 ave de Grande Bretagne, BP 262, MC 98005; tel. 92-16-55-55; fax 92-16-55-99; e-mail foreigndept@kblmonaco.com; f. 1996; 100% owned by Kredietbank SA Luxembourgeoise (Luxembourg); cap. 7.2m., res 1.7m., dep. 250.8m. (Dec. 2004); Chair. of Bd JEAN-PAUL LOOS; Man.-Dir PAUL-MARIE JACQUES.

UBS (Monaco): 2 ave de Grande Bretagne, BP 189, MC 98007; tel. 93-15-58-15; fax 93-15-58-00; e-mail rolf.meier@ubs.com; internet www.ubs.com/monaco; f. 1956; present name adopted 1998; 100% owned by UBS AG (Switzerland); cap. 9.2m., res 24.4m., dep. 3,148.0m. (Dec. 2004); Chair. DIETER KIEFER; Chief Exec. CHRISTIAN GRÜTTER.

INSURANCE

Assurances J.P. et C. Sassi AXA: Le Suffren, 7 rue Suffren-Reymond, BP 25, MC 98001; tel. 93-30-45-88; fax 93-25-86-07; e-mail agence.sassi@axa.fr; f. 1968; Dir JEAN-PIERRE SASSI.

Eric Blair Network Insurance: 33 blvd Princesse Charlotte, BP 265, MC 98005 Cedex; tel. 93-50-99-66; fax 97-70-72-00; e-mail eric@insure.monaco.mc; internet www.ericblairnet.com; Chief Exec. ERIC BLAIR.

Gramaglia Assurances: 14 blvd des Moulins, BP 153, MC 98003 Cedex; tel. 92-16-59-00; fax 92-16-59-16; e-mail info@gramaglia.mc; internet www.gramaglia.mc; Dir ANTOINE GRAMAGLIA.

Monaco Insurance Services: 9 rue de Millo, MC 98000; tel. 97-97-39-39; fax 93-25-74-37; e-mail maoun@monaco377.com; Dir PIERRE AOUN.

Mourenon et Giannotti: 22 blvd Princesse Charlotte, MC 98000; tel. 97-97-08-88; fax 97-97-08-80; f. 1975; Dirs JEAN-PHILIPPE MOURENON, JOSÉ GIANNOTTI.

Silvain Assurances: 33 blvd Princesse Charlotte, BP 267, MC 98005; tel. 93-25-54-45; fax 93-50-39-05; Dir FRANÇOIS SILVAIN.

Société Française de Recours Cie d'Assurances: 28 blvd Princesse Charlotte, MC 98000; tel. 93-50-52-63; fax 93-50-54-49; Dir FLORIANO CONTE.

Trade and Industry

GOVERNMENT AGENCIES

Direction de l'Action Sanitaire et Sociale: 46–48 blvd d'Italie, MC 98000; tel. 93-15-84-20; fax 93-15-81-59; Dir Dr ANNE NEGRE.

Direction des Affaires Culturelles: 4 blvd des Moulins; tel. 93-15-85-15; fax 93-50-66-94; Dir RAINIER ROCCHI.

Direction des Affaires Juridiques: Stade Louis II, 1 ave des Castelans, MC 98013; Dir LAURENT ANSELMI.

Direction des Affaires Maritimes: La Capitainerie, quai Jean-Charles Rey, MC 98000; tel. 93-15-86-78; fax 93-15-37-15; Dir PHILIPPE REMY.

Direction du Budget et du Trésor: 12 quai Antoine 1er, BP 512, 98000 MC Cedex; tel. 93-15-87-73; fax 93-15-84-26; Dir ISABELLE ROSABRUNETTO.

Direction du Contrôle des Concessions et des Télécommunications: 23 ave Prince Héréditaire Albert, MC 98000; tel. 93-15-88-00; fax 97-98-56-57; Dir RAOUL VIORA.

Direction de l'Education Nationale, de la Jeunesse et des Sports: Lycée Technique, ave de l'Annonciade, MC 98000; tel. 93-15-83-99; fax 93-15-85-74; e-mail denjs@gouv.mc; internet www.monaco.gouv.mc; Dir YVETTE LAMBIN-BERTI.

Direction de l'Environnement, de l'Urbanisme et de la Construction: 23 ave Prince Héréditaire Albert; tel. 93-15-22-99; fax 93-15-88-02; Dir MAUD COLLE-GAMERDINGER.

MONACO

Direction de l'Expansion Economique: 9 rue du Gabian, MC 98000; tel. 93-15-40-63; fax 92-05-75-20; Dir CATHERINE ORECCHIA-MATTHYSSENS.

Direction de la Fonction Publique et des Ressources Humaines: Stade Louis II, entrée H, 1 ave des Castelans; tel. 93-15-81-13; fax 93-15-42-91; Dir CLAUDE COTTALORDA.

Direction de l'Habitat: 10 bis, quai Antoine 1er; tel. 93-15-80-08; fax 93-15-20-06; Dir MARIE-JOSÉ CALENCO.

Direction de la Prospective et des Etudes d'Urbanisme: 3 ave de Fontvieille; tel. 93-15-80-00; fax 93-15-46-60; e-mail prospective@gouv.mc; Dir PATRICE CELLARIO.

Direction des Services Fiscaux: 57 rue Grimaldi, BP 475, MC 98000 Cedex; tel. 93-15-84-35; fax 93-15-81-55; Dir GÉRARD EMMEL.

Direction de la Sûreté Publique: 3–4 rue Louis Notari, BP 465, MC 98012; tel. 93-15-30-15; fax 93-50-65-47; Dir JEAN-FRANÇOIS SAUTIER.

Direction du Travail et Service de l'Emploi: 2 rue Princesse Antoinette, BP 281, MC 98000; tel. 93-15-88-14; Head of Service PATRICIA NOVARETTI.

Trésorerie Générale des Finances: Cour de la Trésorie, Palais de Monaco; tel. 93-15-88-19; fax 93-15-85-75; Treas. YVON BERTRAND.

CHAMBER OF COMMERCE

Jeune Chambre Economique de Monaco: MC 98000; tel. 92-05-20-19; fax 92-05-31-29; e-mail jcemonaco@jcemonaco.mc; internet www.jcemonaco.mc; f. 1963; 102 mems; Pres. CARLO PICOZZI.

EMPLOYERS' ASSOCIATION

Fédération Patronale Monégasque (FPM) (Employers' Federation of Monaco): 'Le Coronado', 20 ave de Fontvieille, MC 98000; tel. 92-05-38-92; fax 92-05-20-04; e-mail info@federation-patronale.mc; internet www.federation-patronale.mc; f. 1944; Pres. FRANCIS E. GRIFFIN; Sec.-Gen. PHILLIPE ORTELLI; 23 member orgs, with 1,500 individual mems.

UTILITIES

Electricity and Gas

Société Monégasque de l'Electricité et du Gaz (SMEG): 10 ave de Fontvieille, BP 633, MC 98013 Cedex; tel. 92-05-05-00; fax 92-05-05-92; e-mail smeg@smeg.mc; internet www.smeg.mc; f. 1890; 64% owned by Groupe Suez; 20% owned by the State.

Water

Société Monégasque des Eaux (SME): 29 ave Princesse Grace, MC 98000; tel. 93-30-83-67; fax 92-05-05-00.

TRADE UNION FEDERATION

Union des Syndicats de Monaco (USM): 28 blvd Rainier III, MC 98000; tel. 93-30-19-30; fax 93-25-06-73; e-mail usm@usm.mc; internet www.usm.mc; f. 1944; Sec.-Gen. ANGÈLE BRAQUETTI; 35 mem. unions with 2,500 individual mems.

Transport

RAILWAYS

The 1.7 km of railway track in Monaco, running from France to Monte-Carlo, is operated by the French state railway, the Société Nationale des Chemins de fer Français (SNCF). As part of the Government's policy of land reclamation, an underground railway station was opened in 1999, at a cost of 1,930m. francs.

ROADS

In 2005 there were an estimated 50 km of major roads in the Principality.

SHIPPING

Monaco has an estimated docking capacity of 100 cruise ships.

Service de la Marine: 7 ave J. F. Kennedy; tel. 93-15-80-00.

Société d'Exploitation des Ports de Monaco: Siège social, 6 quai Antoine 1er, BP 453, MC 98011 Cedex; tel. 97-77-30-00; e-mail info@ports-monaco.com; f. 2003; 100% state-owned; responsible for management and development of the two principal ports in Monaco, at La Condamine (Port Hercule) and Fontvieille; Pres. ALECO KEUSSEOGLOU.

Shipping Companies

Compagnie pour la Géstion des Affaires Maritimes et Industrielles SAM (COGEMA SAM): 20 blvd de Suisse, MC 98000 Cedex; tel. 93-10-52-70; fax 93-50-03-81; e-mail hq.mc@damicoint.com; internet www.cogema-sam.com; CEO MARCO FIORI.

MC Shipping Inc.: Aigue Marine, 24 ave de Fontvieille, BP 658, MC 98000 Cedex; tel. 92-05-94-04; fax 92-05-94-16; e-mail contact@mcshipping.com; internet www.mcshipping.com; f. 1989; Chair. of Bd CHARLES LONGBOTTOM; Pres. and CEO TONY CRAWFORD.

Société Anonyme Monégasque d'Administration Maritime et Aérienne (SAMAMA): L'Estoril, Bloc B, 1er étage, 31 ave Princesse Grace, MC 98000; tel. 99-99-51-00; fax 99-99-51-09; e-mail general@samama-monaco.com; Pres. FRANK O. WALTERS; Dir-Gen. J. F. MEGGINSON.

V. Ships Inc: Aigue Marine, 24 ave de Fontvieille, BP 639, MC 98013 Cedex; tel. 92-05-10-10; fax 92-05-94-10; e-mail mark.stokes@vships.com; internet www.vships.com; Pres. TULLIO BIGGI; Man. Dir LORENZO MALVAROSA.

CIVIL AVIATION

There is a helicopter shuttle service between the international airport at Nice, France, and Monaco's heliport at Fontvieille.

Heli-Air Monaco SAM: Héliport de Monaco, MC 98000; tel. 92-05-00-50; fax 92-05-00-51; e-mail helico@heliairmonaco.com; internet www.heliairmonaco.com; Pres. JACQUES CROVETTO.

Tourism

Tourists are attracted to Monaco by the Mediterranean climate, dramatic scenery and numerous entertainment facilities, including a casino. In 2004 250,159 tourists (excluding excursionists) visited Monaco. There were 2,249 hotel rooms available in that year.

Direction du Tourisme et des Congrès: 2A blvd des Moulins, MC 98030 Cedex; tel. 92-16-61-16; fax 92-16-60-00; e-mail dtc@monaco-tourisme.com; internet www.monaco-tourisme.com; there are also international conference centres in Monte-Carlo at Grimaldi Forum, ave Princesse Grace; Dir-Gen. MICHEL BOUQUIER.

Société des Bains de Mer (SBM): place du Casino, BP 139, MC 98007; tel. 92-16-25-25; fax 92-16-26-26; e-mail resort@sbm.mc; internet www.montecarloresort.com; f. 1863; corpn in which the Government holds a 69.6% interest; controls the entertainment facilities of Monaco, including the casino and numerous hotels, clubs, restaurants and sporting facilities; Chair. JEAN-LUC BIAMONTI; Gen. Man. MICHEL NOVATIN.

MONGOLIA

Introductory Survey

Location, Climate, Language, Religion, Flag, Capital

Mongolia is a land-locked country in central Asia, with the Russian Federation to the north and the People's Republic of China to the south, east and west. The climate is dry, with generally mild summers but very cold winters. Temperatures in Ulan Bator range between −32°C (−26°F) and 22°C (71°F). The principal language is Khalkha Mongolian. Kazakh is spoken in the province of Bayan-Ölgii. There is no state religion, but Buddhist Lamaism is being encouraged once again. The national flag (proportions 1 by 2) has three equal vertical stripes, of red, blue and red, with the 'soyombo' symbol (a combination of abstract devices) in gold on the red stripe at the hoist. The capital is Ulan Bator (traditional spelling; Ulaanbaatar in transcription from Mongolian Cyrillic).

Recent History

The country was formerly the Manchu province of Outer Mongolia. In 1911, following the republican revolution in China, Mongolian princes declared the province's independence. With support from Tsarist Russia, Outer Mongolia gained autonomy, as a feudal Buddhist monarchy, but Russia accepted Chinese suzerainty over the province in 1915. Following the Russian revolution of 1917, China began to re-establish control in Mongolia in 1919. In 1920 Mongol nationalists appealed to the new Soviet regime for assistance, and in March 1921 they met on Soviet territory to found the Mongolian People's Party (called the Mongolian People's Revolutionary Party—MPRP—from 1924) and established a Provisional People's Government. After nationalist forces, with Soviet help, drove anti-Bolshevik troops from the Mongolian capital, independence was proclaimed on 11 July 1921. Soviet Russia recognized the People's Government in November of that year. In November 1924, after the death of Bogd Khan (King) Javzandamba Khutagt VIII, the Mongolian People's Republic was proclaimed.

The Mongolian People's Republic became increasingly dependent on the USSR's support. The Government conducted campaigns to collectivize the economy and to destroy the power of the nobility and Buddhist priests. In 1932 an armed uprising was suppressed with Soviet assistance. Following a purge of the MPRP and army leadership in 1936–39, power was held by Marshal Khorloogiin Choibalsan as Prime Minister and MPRP leader. The dictatorship of Choibalsan closely followed the pattern of Stalin's regime in the USSR, and its thousands of victims included eminent politicians, military officers, religious leaders and intellectuals. In 1939 a Japanese invasion from Manchuria was repelled by Soviet and Mongolian forces at Khalkhyn Gol (Nomonhan). In keeping with the Yalta agreement to preserve the status quo in Mongolia, war was declared on Japan in August 1945, four days before the Japanese surrender, and northern China was invaded. In a Mongolian plebiscite in October 1945, it was reported that 100% of the votes were cast in favour of independence, and this was recognized by China in January 1946.

Choibalsan died in January 1952 and was succeeded as Prime Minister by Yumjaagiin Tsedenbal, who had been the MPRP's First Secretary since 1940. Dashiin Damba became First Secretary of the MPRP in April 1954. In 1955 India became the first non-communist country to recognize Mongolia. Tsedenbal replaced Damba as First Secretary of the MPRP in November 1958, and a new Constitution was adopted in July 1960. Mongolia became a member of the UN in October 1961 and was subsequently accorded diplomatic recognition by the United Kingdom (1963), other Western European and developing countries. By January 1987, when Mongolia was finally granted diplomatic recognition by the USA, it maintained diplomatic relations with more than 100 states.

Jamsrangiin Sambuu, Head of State since July 1954, died in May 1972. He was replaced in June 1974 by Tsedenbal, who remained First Secretary of the MPRP (restyled General Secretary in 1981) but relinquished the post of Chairman of the Council of Ministers to Jambyn Batmönkh. In August 1984 Tsedenbal was removed from the party leadership and state presidency, apparently owing to ill health, and Batmönkh replaced him as General Secretary of the MPRP. In December Batmönkh also became Head of State, while Dumaagiin Sodnom, hitherto a Deputy Chairman of the Council of Ministers and the Chairman of the State Planning Commission, was appointed Chairman of the Council of Ministers.

By the end of 1988 the MPRP Political Bureau was obliged to admit that economic renewal was not succeeding because of the need for social reforms. Batmönkh advocated greater openness and offered the prospect of multi-candidate elections. He criticized Tsedenbal for the country's 'stagnation', also stating that the former leader had belittled collective leadership.

Between December 1989 and March 1990 there was a great upsurge in public political activity, as several newly formed opposition movements organized a series of peaceful demonstrations in Ulan Bator, demanding political and economic reforms. The most prominent of the new opposition groups was the Mongolian Democratic Union (MDU), founded in December 1989. In January 1990 dialogue was initiated between MPRP officials and representatives of the MDU, including its chief co-ordinator, Sanjaasürengiin Zorig (a lecturer at the Mongolian State University). The emergence of further opposition groups, together with escalating public demonstrations (involving as many as 20,000 people), led to a crisis of confidence within the MPRP. At a party plenum in mid-March 1990 Batmönkh announced the resignation of the entire Political Bureau as well as of the Secretariat of the Central Committee. Gombojavyn Ochirbat, a former head of the Ideological Department of the Central Committee and a former Chairman of the Central Council of Mongolian Trade Unions, was elected the new General Secretary of the party, replacing Batmönkh. A new five-member Political Bureau was formed. The plenum voted to expel the former MPRP General Secretary, Yumjaagiin Tsedenbal, from the party and to rehabilitate several prominent victims of Tsedenbal's purges of the 1960s.

At a session of the People's Great Khural (legislature), held shortly after the MPRP plenum, Punsalmaagiin Ochirbat, hitherto the Minister of Foreign Economic Relations and Supply, was elected Chairman of the Presidium (Head of State), replacing Batmönkh, and other senior positions in the Presidium were reorganized. Dumaagiin Sodnom was dismissed from his post as Chairman of the Council of Ministers and was replaced by Sharavyn Gungaadorj, a Deputy Chairman and Minister of Agriculture and the Food Industry. The Khural also adopted amendments to the Constitution, including the deletion of references to the MPRP as the 'guiding force' in Mongolian society, and approved a new electoral law. It was decided that the next elections to the Khural would be held in mid-1990, and not in 1991 as originally planned. Meanwhile, all limits on personal livestock holdings were removed, and new regulations were introduced to encourage foreign investment in Mongolia. However, in late March 1990 an estimated 13,000 people, dissatisfied with the results of the Khural's session, demonstrated in Ulan Bator to demand the dissolution of the Khural. Opposition leaders declared that the changes introduced by the legislature were insufficient, and demanded the introduction of a multi-party electoral law.

In April 1990 the MPRP held an extraordinary congress, at which more than three-quarters of the membership of the Central Committee was renewed. General Secretary Gombojavyn Ochirbat was elected to the restyled post of Chairman of the party. The Political Bureau was renamed the Presidium, and a new, four-member Secretariat of the Central Committee was appointed. In May the People's Great Khural adopted a law on political parties, which legalized the new 'informal' parties through official registration, and also adopted further amendments to the Constitution, introducing a presidential system with a standing legislature called the State Little Khural, elected by proportional representation of parties.

At the July 1990 legislative election and consequent re-elections, 430 deputies were elected to serve a five-year term: 357 from the MPRP (in some instances unopposed), 16 from the Mongolian Democratic Party (MDP, the political wing of the MDU), 19 shared among the Mongolian Revolutionary Youth

League, the Mongolian National Progress Party (MNPP), and the Mongolian Social-Democratic Party (MSDP), and 39 without party affiliation. Under constitutional amendments adopted in May, the People's Great Khural was required to convene at least four times in the five years of its term.

In September 1990 the People's Great Khural elected Punsalmaagiin Ochirbat to be the country's first President, with a five-year term of office; the post of Chairman of the Presidium was abolished. Dashiin Byambasüren was appointed Prime Minister (equivalent to the former post of Chairman of the Council of Ministers) and began consultations on the formation of a multi-party government. The newly restyled Cabinet was elected by the State Little Khural in September and October. Under the amended Constitution, the President, Vice-President and Ministers were not permitted to remain concurrently deputies of the People's Great Khural; therefore, re-elections of deputies to the legislature were held in November.

The 20th Congress of the MPRP, held in February 1991, elected a new 99-member Central Committee, which, in turn, appointed a new Presidium. The Central Committee also elected a new Chairman, Büdragchaagiin Dash-Yondon, the Chairman of the Ulan Bator City Party Committee, who had become a Presidium member in November 1990.

A new Constitution was adopted by an almost unanimous vote of the Great Khural in January 1992, and entered into force in the following month. It provided for a unicameral Mongolian Great Khural, comprising 76 members, to replace the People's Great Khural, following elections to be held in June. (The State Little Khural was abolished.) The country's official name was changed from the Mongolian People's Republic to Mongolia, and the communist gold star was removed from the national flag.

At the elections to the Mongolian Great Khural in June 1992, contested by the MPRP, an alliance of the MDP, the MNPP and the United Party (UP), the MSDP, and six other parties and another alliance, a total of 293 candidates stood for 76 seats in 26 constituencies, comprising the 18 *aimag* (provinces), the towns of Darkhan and Erdenet, and Ulan Bator City (six). A total of 95.6% of the electorate participated in the elections. Candidates were elected by a simple majority, provided that they obtained the support of at least 50% of the electorate in their constituency. The MPRP candidates received some 57% of the total votes, while the candidates of the other parties (excluding independents) achieved a combined total of 40%. The outcome of the election was disproportionate, however, with the MPRP taking 70 seats (71 including a pro-MPRP independent). The remaining seats went to the MDP (two, including an independent), the MSDP, MNPP and UP (one each).

The first session of the Mongolian Great Khural opened in July 1992 with the election of officers, the nomination of Puntsagiin Jasrai (who had served as a Deputy Chairman of the Council of Ministers in the late 1980s) to the post of Prime Minister, and the approval of his Cabinet. Natsagiin Bagabandi, a Vice-Chairman of the MPRP Central Committee, was elected Chairman of the Great Khural. Jambyn Gombojav (Chairman of the People's Great Khural from late 1990 to late 1991) was elected Vice-Chairman of the new Khural. Meanwhile, a National Security Council was established, with the country's President as its Chairman, and the Prime Minister and Chairman of the Great Khural as its members.

In October 1992 the MDP, MNPP, UP and the Mongolian Renewal Party amalgamated to form the Mongolian National Democratic Party (MNDP), with a General Council headed by the MNPP leader, Davaadorjiin Ganbold, and including Sanjaasürengiin Zorig and other prominent opposition politicians. In the same month the MPRP Central Committee was renamed the MPRP Little Khural, and its membership was increased to 169 (and subsequently to 198). The Presidium was replaced by a nine-member Party Leadership Council, headed by Büdragchaagiin Dash-Yondon as its General Secretary.

The Great Khural adopted a Presidential Election Law in March 1993, and direct elections to the presidency were scheduled for 6 June. Lodongiin Tüdev, a member of the Party Leadership Council and Editor-in-Chief of the MPRP organ, *Ünen*, was chosen as the MPRP's candidate, while President Ochirbat was nominated by a coalition of the MNDP and the MSDP. The result of the election was a convincing popular victory for Ochirbat: he received 57.8% of the votes cast, compared with 38.7% for Tüdev.

The MPRP in early 1996 forced through the Great Khural amendments that increased the number of constituencies from 26 to 76, making them all single-seat constituencies, while preserving the majority vote system. To be declared elected, a candidate would have to receive only 25% of the constituency votes. In response, opposition parties formed an election coalition, the Democratic Alliance, which received support from the Mongolian Green Party and the MDU.

At the legislative election, held on 30 June 1996, a resounding victory was achieved by the Democratic Alliance, which won 50 of the 76 seats in the Great Khural, receiving some 46.7% of the total votes cast. The MPRP took only 25 seats (40.6%), while one seat went to a candidate of the United Heritage Party (UHP). Electoral turn-out was 92.2%. At the legislature's inaugural session, in mid-July, the leader of the MSDP, Radnaasümbereliin Gonchigdorj, was elected to the post of Chairman of the Great Khural. Mendsaikhany Enkhsaikhan, the leader of the Democratic Alliance and the group's choice for Prime Minister, was nominated by President Ochirbat and voted into office. Following the rejection of MPRP demands concerning the allocation of positions in the Great Khural, MPRP members staged a three-day boycott of the legislature, leaving it inquorate and unable to function. After the boycott ended, the MNDP leader, Tsakhiagiin Elbegdorj, was elected Vice-Chairman of the Great Khural; a new Government was formed at the end of July.

Following their election defeat, and amid growing evidence of a rift between supporters of tradition and advocates of the reform process, in July 1996 the MPRP Little Khural elected a new Leadership Council and General Secretary of the party, Nambaryn Enkhbayar. Indications of a split in the party increased in February 1997, when the leaders of the MPRP sought to enforce their uncompromising policies on the party congress. Several prominent dissenting members resigned from the party, and Natsagiin Bagabandi, who had been Chairman of the Great Khural in 1992–96, was elected Chairman of the party.

With 18 May 1997 set by the Great Khural as the date for the presidential election, the MNDP and the MSDP proposed a joint candidate for the post of President—the incumbent, Ochirbat. The MPRP nominated the party Chairman, Bagabandi, while the UHP adopted Jambyn Gombojav, a former Vice-Chairman of the Great Khural. The election was won convincingly by Bagabandi, with some 60.8% of the total votes cast. In a severe setback to the democratic movement, Ochirbat received only 29.8%, a reflection of popular dissatisfaction at the rigorous economic reform policies implemented by the ruling Democratic Alliance. Gombojav obtained 6.6% of the votes. Following Bagabandi's success in the presidential election, Enkhbayar was elected Chairman of the MPRP in his place. In August 1997 he won a by-election for Bagabandi's former seat in the Great Khural.

In April 1998 the Democratic Alliance decided that, henceforth, the Cabinet was to comprise members of the Great Khural, headed by the leader of the Alliance. Tsakhiagiin Elbegdorj, leader of the MNDP, was thus appointed Prime Minister, and a new Cabinet was formed in May. The Government became embroiled in a dispute over the amalgamation of the state-owned Reconstruction Bank, declared bankrupt after over-extending its credit, with the private Golomt Bank. Amid accusations that Democratic Alliance leaders had obtained loans from the bank shortly before its failure, the MPRP effected a boycott of the Great Khural. The party rejected the Government's reinstatement of Reconstruction Bank and returned to the Great Khural in late July to pursue a vote of 'no confidence' in the Government. The vote was carried by 42 votes to 33, with the support of 15 members of the Democratic Alliance.

In August 1998 the Democratic Alliance nominated as its candidate for Prime Minister Davaadorjiin Ganbold, Chairman of the Economic Standing Committee of the Great Khural (who had been chief Deputy Prime Minister in 1990–92 and President of the MNDP in 1992–96). President Bagabandi rejected Ganbold's nomination, on the grounds of his failure to act to resolve the bank merger crisis in his capacity as Chairman of the Committee. Ganbold was nominated a second time, and again rejected by Bagabandi, who proposed Great Khural member Dogsomyn Ganbold. The Democratic Alliance persisted, and by the end of the month Davaadorjiin Ganbold had been nominated and rejected five times. The Democratic Alliance then proposed Rinchinnyamyn Amarjargal, acting Minister of External Relations and a member of the MNDP General Council. President Bagabandi accepted the nomination, but it was rejected by one vote in the Great Khural in September. Two other candidates were subsequently rejected by Bagabandi.

In October 1998 Sanjaasürengiin Zorig, the Minister of Infrastructure Development, was murdered. Zorig, the founder of the Mongolian Democratic Movement, had not been nominated, but was widely seen as a potential prime ministerial candidate. Following Zorig's state funeral, Bagabandi named six more candidates of his own, including Dogsomyn Ganbold and the Mayor of Ulan Bator, Janlavyn Narantsatsralt. The Democratic Alliance disregarded the presidential list and for the sixth time nominated Davaadorjiin Ganbold. Although the nomination was supported by all 48 Democratic Alliance members of the Great Khural, Bagabandi once again rejected him. The political crisis was then deepened by a new Constitutional Court ruling that members of the Great Khural could not serve concurrently in the Government. Two months later the Democratic Alliance finally nominated Bagabandi's candidate, Janlavyn Narantsatsralt, who was appointed Prime Minister in December. The formation of his Government was completed with the appointment of the last four ministers in January 1999.

Narantsatsralt's Government remained in power for just over six months. In July 1999 the Prime Minister was challenged in the Great Khural over a letter that he had written in January to Yurii Maslyukov, First Deputy Chairman of the Russian Government, in which he seemingly acknowledged Russia's right to privatize its share in the Erdenet joint venture without reference to the Mongolians. Unable to offer a satisfactory explanation, in late July Narantsatsralt lost a vote of confidence, in which MSDP members of the Great Khural voted with the opposition MPRP. The Democratic Alliance nominated Rinchinnyamyn Amarjargal for the post of Prime Minister, but the proposal was immediately challenged by Bagabandi. The President insisted that, following the Constitutional Court ruling of late 1998, he could consider Amarjargal's suitability for nomination in the Great Khural only after the candidate had resigned his seat. After several days of arguments, representatives of the Democratic Alliance and the President adopted a formula that allowed the Great Khural's approval of the prime ministerial nomination and the nominee's resignation of his Great Khural seat to take place simultaneously. Amarjargal was elected Prime Minister at the end of July. The ministers of Narantsatsralt's Government remained in office in an acting capacity until early September, when all but one (the Minister of Law) were reappointed. The formation of the Government was completed in late October with the appointment of Dashpuntsagiin Ganbold as Minister of Law. In November 1999 Amarjargal assumed the presidency of the MNDP, replacing Narantsatsralt.

The 1992 Constitution was amended for the first time in December 1999 by a Great Khural decree supported by all three parliamentary parties, which simplified the procedure for the appointment of the Prime Minister and allowed members of the Great Khural to serve as government ministers while retaining their seats in the legislature. An attempt by the President to veto the decree was defeated by the Great Khural in January 2000, but the Constitutional Court ruled in March that the decree had been illegal. When the Great Khural opened its spring session in April, members rejected the ruling and refused to discuss it. The Constitutional Court's demand for a statement on the issue was disregarded by the Great Khural.

As the legislative election approached, party political activity increased dramatically. A breakaway grouping of the MNDP reformed the Mongolian Democratic Party, and a faction of the MSDP founded the Mongolian New Social Democratic Party. Sanjaasürengiin Oyuun, the sister of the murdered minister, Zorig, established the Civil Courage Party (CCP, or Irgenii Zorig Nam), drawing away from the MNDP several more members of the Great Khural, and formed an electoral alliance with the Green Party. The MNDP, unable to reconstitute the previously-successful Democratic Alliance with the MSDP, therefore formed a new Democratic Alliance with the Mongolian Believers' Democratic Party.

At the election, held on 2 July 2000, three coalitions and 13 parties were represented by a total of 603 candidates, including 27 independents. The MPRP took 72 of the 76 seats in the Great Khural. Prime Minister Rinchinnyamyn Amarjargal and his entire Cabinet lost their seats. The MPRP received 50.2% of the votes cast. The level of participation was 82.4% of the electorate. The MPRP's main support lay in rural constituencies, where it was widely seen as willing and able to halt the economic and social stagnation of the countryside. The Democratic Alliance won 13% of the votes cast, while the Mongolian Democratic New Socialist Party (MDNSP, which had amalgamated with the Mongolian Workers' Party in 1999) received 10.7% of the votes; each of them won one seat. The MSDP received 8.9% of the votes cast but won no seats.

When the Great Khural opened, Lkhamsürengiin Enebish, the MPRP General Secretary, was elected Chairman (Speaker) of the chamber. The nomination of the MPRP Chairman, Nambaryn Enkhbayar, for the post of Prime Minister was, however, rejected by President Bagabandi, on the grounds that priority be given to the constitutional amendments. After a week of discussions a compromise was reached whereby Enkhbayar's nomination was presented to the Great Khural, while the amendments remained in force pending a Great Khural debate and a full nine-member session of the Constitutional Court. In July 2000 the Great Khural approved Enkhbayar's appointment as Prime Minister by 67 MPRP members' votes to three. Enkhbayar's Cabinet was approved in August.

At a conference on 6 December 2000 five parties—the MNDP, the MSDP, the Mongolian Democratic Party, the Believers' Democratic Party and the Democratic Renewal Party—resolved to dissolve themselves and form a new Democratic Party (DP). Dambyn Dorligjav, a former Minister of Defence and director of the Erdenet copper enterprise, was elected Chairman, while Janlavyn Narantsatsralt and the former Minister of the Environment, Sonomtserengiin Mendsaikhan, were elected as Vice-Chairmen. At its registration in late December the DP claimed a membership of 160,000. The party's National Advisory Committee was formed in February 2001 and comprised two members from each of the Great Khural's 76 constituencies.

In mid-December 2000 the Great Khural readopted, unchanged and for immediate implementation, the decree of December 1999 amending the 1992 Constitution. The decree was vetoed by the President, and this veto was rejected. The Constitutional Court, however, was unable to meet in full session because the election of replacements for time-expired members was delayed in the Great Khural. President Bagabandi finally set his seal to the amendments in May 2001.

In February 2001 the 23rd Congress of the ruling MPRP re-elected Prime Minister Nambaryn Enkhbayar as its Chairman, approved the establishment of a new Little Khural of 244 members and enlarged the Party Leadership Council from 11 to 15 members. At the end of September Lkhamsürengiin Enebish, Chairman of the Great Khural and recently re-elected as General Secretary of the MPRP, died; he was succeeded in the latter post by Doloonjingiin Idevkhten and as Chairman of the Great Khural by Sanjbegziin Tömör-Ochir, Secretary of the MPRP.

The presidential election of 20 May 2001 was won by the MPRP's candidate, Natsagiin Bagabandi, who received 57.95% of the votes cast. Radnaasümbereliin Gonchigdorj of the Democratic Party won 36.58% of votes, and Luvsandambyn Dashnyam of the Civil Courage Party received 3.54%.

In January 2001, meanwhile, during one of Mongolia's most severe winters ever, a helicopter carrying 23 people, who were investigating the zud (livestock starvation owing to frozen fodder) in the Uvs aimag in western Mongolia, crashed, killing eight. The dead included several UN staff and Shagdaryn Otgonbileg, a member of the Great Khural and former director of the Erdenet copper enterprise, who was given a state funeral. Later that month the UN appealed for humanitarian aid to help Mongolian herders, whose animals were dying in huge numbers. In May Otgonbileg's widow Tuyaa was elected Great Khural MPRP member for his Zavkhan 22 constituency unopposed.

In March 2002 Sanjaasürengiin Oyuun's Civil Courage Party merged with Bazarsadyn Jargalsaikhan's Mongolian Republican Party (MRP) to form the Civil Courage Republican Party, under Oyuun's leadership. However, in June 2003 the MRP leader Bazarsadyn Jargalsaikhan withdrew from the merger after disagreement about the formation of a coalition with the DP. Attempts in December to oust Oyuun from the party leadership failed, and in March 2004 she agreed to join the Motherland Democracy (MD) coalition comprising Erdenebat's MDNSP and the DP (see below).

In June 2002, meanwhile, the Great Khural approved the Law on Land and the Law on Land Privatization. Although less than 1% of the country's total territory was to be available for privatization, the laws generated much controversy. From November there were several demonstrations by tractor-driving farmers who were arrested for parking their vehicles on Sükhbaatar Square in Ulan Bator. The demonstrators, led by DP leader Erdeniin Bat-Üül, protested that the poor would be denied land by the 'oligarchy'. The privatization law duly entered into force in May 2003.

Meanwhile, an effective protest against the Government's silencing of the opposition was made by Lamjavyn Gündalai, a

DP member of the Great Khural, who interrupted the Prime Minister's televised address and disrupted the opening ceremony of the autumn 2002 session of the Great Khural by displaying to television cameras a series of placards on which he demanded the right to speak, condemned the imprisonment of journalists and criticized the land privatization programme. When the 2003 spring session opened at the beginning of April Gündalai again displayed a range of slogans; the President and the Prime Minister were unable to deliver their speeches, and the televised session was suspended.

At the end of May 2003 Gündalai made a public allegation that there was 'top secret' information that the Minister of Justice and Home Affairs, Tsendiin Nyamdorj, had links with the special services of a foreign country. Nyamdorj denied the allegations. In July Gündalai was removed from an aircraft at Ulan Bator airport while on his way via the Republic of Korea to a conference in Singapore and arrested by plain-clothes policemen for 'violation of the border'. This provoked an uproar regarding the breaching of Gündalai's parliamentary immunity, and the DP sought an investigation by the human rights committee of the Inter-Parliamentary Union (a non-governmental organization based in Geneva, Switzerland). In late July, on the same day as the newspaper Önöödör published extracts from the 'top secret' material relating to Nyamdorj, Gündalai was released. In August the charges against Gündalai were abandoned on the instructions of the Deputy Chief Prosecutor. In October Gündalai succeeded, for a third time, in disrupting the opening of the Great Khural's autumn session, with the result that the Prime Minister was once again unable to deliver his report to the cameras.

The National Human Rights Commission's 2003 annual report was highly critical of bureaucracy, corruption and cronyism. The police were accused of numerous cases of brutality; the right of detainees to contact a lawyer was widely abused, the report stated. The National Human Rights Programme was adopted in December. Also in 2003, Damirangiin Enkhbat, who had been suspected of the murder of the Minister of Infrastructure Development, Sanjaasürengiin Zorig, in 1998 and had since been resident in France, was reported to have been abducted by Mongolian secret agents and subsequently imprisoned in Mongolia. In early 2004 reports from Amnesty International, the human rights organization, suggested that he had been tortured during interrogation. (Enkhbat was released from prison in February 2006 on the grounds of ill health, and subsequently died.)

In the spring of 2004 political campaigning began for the election to the Mongolian Great Khural, which was held in late June. Huge placards went up all over Ulan Bator, praising the achievements and plans of the ruling MPRP. The new General Election Committee (GEC) incorporated many MPRP nominees. The electorate was calculated to total nearly 1.3m. persons, but there was no provision for the 70,000 people who were resident abroad to vote. The opposition 'Motherland-Democracy' (MD) election pact, formed by Mendsaikhany Enkhsaikhan's DP and Badarchiin Erdenebat's 'Motherland' Mongolian Democratic New Socialist Party, was joined by Sanjaasürengiin Oyuun's Civil Courage Republican Party, minus the followers of Bazarsadyn Jargalsaikhan, who left to re-form the Republican Party.

After the registration of participating political parties and coalitions, the GEC examined the official lists, rejecting all Mongolian Youth Party candidates. Before polling day three candidates withdrew, leaving the final number at 241: 76 each for the MPRP and the MD coalition, 33 for the Republican Party, 23 for the National Solidarity Party, nine for the Mongolian Traditional United Party (also known as the United Heritage Party), five for the Green Party, four for the Liberal Party and 15 Independents.

The initial results of the election of 27 June 2004 (compiled as percentages of the total ballot in each constituency) left the political scene in disarray: the MPRP and the MD coalition had each won about one-half of the seats, leaving neither with the necessary majority of 39 (one-half of the Great Khural seats plus one seat). The three Independents elected, although all DP members, were ruled as not counting in this process. The Republican Party won one seat. The rate of participation was 82.2% of registered voters. In 25 constituencies there was a straight contest between the MPRP and the MD coalition. Amid mutual accusations of bribery and electoral fraud in a number of constituencies, efforts to form a government soon became embroiled in disputes at the GEC and the recently established City Administrative Court.

The GEC submitted the results in 74 of the 76 constituencies to President Bagabandi on 9 July 2004, at the first session of the newly elected Great Khural, which was boycotted by the MPRP. The President stated that it was right to convene the first session, even if two results had yet to be confirmed, because of the need to discuss the many issues that the legislature should address. The MD members, however, were not allowed to take the oath. Meeting separately, 70 of the MPRP members elected in 2000 filed a lawsuit against the President on the grounds that he had contravened the Constitution and allowed the Great Khural to meet without a quorum (57 members being present) before the final session of the Great Khural elected in 2000 had taken place.

The closing session of the previous Great Khural was held on 22 July 2004. Among other decisions, it released the Great Khural's Deputy Chairman Jamsrangiin Byambadorj (who had lost his parliamentary seat in the recent election) to take up a vacant seat in the Constitutional Court and accused the President of acting unconstitutionally in convening the 9 July session. All these decisions were vetoed by President Bagabandi in late July as unconstitutional. (Byambadorj was elected a member, then the Chairman, of the Constitutional Court in January 2005.)

Postponed from 23 July after another MPRP boycott, the first plenary session of the 2004 Great Khural was held three days later, when 74 members were sworn in. The meeting was chaired by the senior member present, Damdingiin Demberel. The first business was the election of the new Chairman of the chamber. The MPRP group supported the candidature of the MPRP leader and acting Prime Minister, Nambaryn Enkhbayar, but protracted discussion of this proposal with the MD members of the Khural continued for days without resolution. In late July the MPRP members of the Great Khural proposed that the MD members should nominate the next Prime Minister, while the MD members proposed the formation of a joint working group to draw up a programme for a government of 'national accord'.

Eventually, at the end of August 2004, former Prime Minister Nambaryn Enkhbayar of the MPRP was appointed Chairman of the Great Khural, and Tsakhiagiin Elbegdorj of the MD coalition was appointed Prime Minister. Although the newly elected members of the Mongolian Great Khural agreed on the formation, chairmanship and membership of the Khural's standing committees and sub-committees, discussion of the basic principles for the establishment of a coalition government were protracted. In mid-September Prime Minister Elbegdorj forwarded to President Bagabandi proprosals for the composition of a new Cabinet, and on 28 September the new Government was appointed. The deputy ministers, one-half nominated by the MD coalition and one-half by the MPRP, were appointed in November and December respectively. The Government Action Programme 2004–2008, approved by the Great Khural in November 2004, included provision for a monthly grant of 3,000 tögrög from 1 January 2005 to each child under the age of 18 in families with more than three children and a per caput income below the national minimum—a compromise of MPRP and MD election pledges.

The National Human Rights Commission's annual report for 2004 noted the need for the rights of vulnerable groups and the human rights activities of legal organizations to remain the 'centre of attention'. The report also noted that torture and severe punishment, both violations of human rights, were still common activities and that many police officers equated punishment with physical torture. Provisions of the Convention against Torture and other Cruel, Inhumane or Degrading Treatment or Punishment, which Mongolia joined in 2000, were not widely known, and effective measures were not being taken to curb illegal acts, the report said.

At the end of December 2004 Radnaasümberellin Gonchigdorj took the chairmanship of the DP at a meeting of the executive of its National Consultative Committee (NCC) and installed his supporters in other senior posts. His predecessor, Mendsaikhany Enkhsaikhan, who seemed to retain the support of the DP's National Assembly, referred the issue to court. The court ruled that the leadership change was contrary to the party's rules, but would not intervene. Badarchiin Erdenebat, the Minister of Defence and leader of the Mongolian Democratic New Socialist Party, then withdrew from the MD coalition, which collapsed. The Civil Courage Republican Party leader, Sanjaasürengiin Oyuun, was obliged to relinquish her post of Deputy Chairwoman of the Great Khural in January. Prime Minister Elbegdorj took over the defence portfolio from Erdenebat in February 2005, and a new Minister of Defence, Tserenkhüügiin Sharavdorj, was appointed in March. The MD coalition's parliamentary group in the Great Khural disbanded, and many DP members, including Gonchigdorj (but not Enkhsaikhan), joined the Khural's MPRP group members to form a parliamentary 'combined group', of which Gonchigdorj was elected Deputy Chairman. Meanwhile, Doloonjingiin Idevkhten was replaced as General Secretary of the MPRP by Sanjaagiin Bayar, the Mongolian ambassador to Russia. In February Jügderdemidiin Gürragchaa (MPRP) and in September Zandaakhüügiin Enkhbold (MD) were declared the winners in the two constituencies where the results of the 2004 election to the Great Khural election had been contested. Gürragchaa was duly sworn in, but Enkhbold had already accepted the post of Chairman of the State Property Committee in the previous December.

In March 2005, in the fourth demonstration since January by the Healthy Society Citizens' Movement, protesters broke through a police cordon to enter Ulan Bator's central Sükhbaatar Square and forced their way onto the Sükhbaatar-Choibalsan mausoleum on the south side of the Government Palace. The demonstrators demanded the resignations of the Great Khural Chairman and MPRP leader Nambaryn Enkhbayar, of Prime Minister Elbegdorj and of the DP 'turncoats' in the Great Khural who had joined the MPRP's parliamentary group. Four of the five parliamentary political parties presented candidates for the forthcoming presidential election, scheduled for late May, and they were registered in early April. The candidates were Nambaryn Enkhbayar (of the MPRP), Bazarsadyn Jargalsaikhan (Republican Party), Badarchiin Erdenebat ('Motherland' Party, the recently renamed Mongolian Democratic New Socialist Party); and Mendsaikhany Enkhsaikhan (DP). The election, held on 22 May, was won by Enkhbayar, who secured more than 53% of the votes cast, thereby receiving more votes than the other three candidates combined.

Enkhbayar's victory led to personnel changes in the MPRP and in the Great Khural. At the MPRP's congress in June 2005 the Mayor of Ulan Bator, Miyeegombyn Enkhbold, was chosen to replace Enkhbayar as the new party Chairman. The party's Leadership Council was enlarged to 21 members: nine re-elected (with four failing to secure re-election) and 10 new members, including Party Secretary Yondongiin Otgonbayar, the Ministers of Foreign Affairs, of Food and Agriculture, and of Health, and six MPRP Great Khural members. Two vacancies were held open, including one for a new head of the Presidential Secretariat. Enkhbayar was inaugurated as President of Mongolia on 24 June. At the beginning of July the Great Khural elected the Minister of Justice and Home Affairs, Tsendiin Nyamdorj (of the MPRP), to replace Enkhbayar as Chairman of the Great Khural, but Nyamdorj's ministerial portfolio was not immediately reallocated.

After an attempt by the MPRP to force the Prime Minister to resign, including the expulsion of DP members from the 'combined' MPRP parliamentary group (the 'group of 62'), just before the closing of its spring 2005 session the Great Khural voted in favour of the formation of a DP parliamentary group, which 25 party members (headed by Gonchigdorj) joined. The date of 28 August was set for the by-election in Enkhbayar's former constituency. The MPRP chose its Chairman, Miyeegombyn Enkhbold, as its candidate, and the DP nominated Prime Minister Tsakhiagiin Elbegdorj. However, Elbegdorj's nomination was withdrawn at the beginning of August, a coalition accord having been signed by the DP and the MPRP to 'respect the results of the 2004 election and maintain the stability of the coalition government', and the by-election was subsequently won by Miyeegombyn Enkhbold.

Rebuilding of the south front of the State Palace, which houses the Great Khural and government offices, to accommodate a Genghis Khan Memorial, Ceremony and Worship Complex, began in August 2005. The work was carried out in keeping with presidential and government decrees adopted in May 2001 with a view to celebrating, in August 2006, the 800th anniversary of the founding of the Mongolian state by Genghis Khan. Plans drawn up in March 2003 provided for the demolition of the mausoleum of revolutionary leaders Sükhbaatar and Choibalsan, which stood where the complex was being built, and the removal of their remains for burial at the main Altan-Ölgii cemetery in Ulan Bator. When details and pictures of a model of the complex were released in October 2004, the Government claimed that it had the consent of the relatives to transfer the remains of Sükhbaatar and Choibalsan. On the night of 23–24 August 2005 the remains were secretly removed from the mausoleum and cremated. When this was announced a day later, there was widespread public dissatisfaction that they had been disposed of in such an 'undignified' manner. (The relatives had wanted the remains placed in stupas, to be built at Altan-Ölgii cemetery and at the revolutionaries' birth places in Sükhbaatar and Dornod provinces.) Meanwhile, construction of the complex (by Chinese builders) continued, with completion due in May 2006.

In January 2006 a Motherland Party deputy defected to the MPRP, thereby giving the latter its 38th seat in the Great Khural. Following calls by the MPRP for Prime Minister Elbegdorj's resignation, the 10 MPRP ministers in his Cabinet resigned and on 13 January the 'grand coalition' Government was voted out of office. On 25 January MPRP Chairman Miyeegombyn Enkhbold was elected Prime Minister. He formed a new 'national solidarity' Government that included the Motherland and Republican Party leaders Erdenebat and Jargalsaikhan, ex-DP member Gündalai, who had recently established a new party, the Party of the People, and three DP members—Enkhsaikhan, Narantsatsralt and Sonompil—who were subsequently expelled from the rump DP, now excluded from the MPRP's new coalition. One newspaper described these politicians as 'unscrupulous'; another claimed that the MPRP's abandonment of its coalition with the DP was intended to halt the progress of a new anti-corruption bill that would focus on corruption within its ranks. The upheaval was also likely to delay a decision on amendments to the 1997 Minerals Law, which caused disquiet amongst foreign investors in Mongolia's mining industry.

Two important documents outlining Mongolian foreign policy objectives were published in July 1994. Advocating 'political realism', *The Mongolian National Security Concept* emphasized the importance of maintaining a 'balanced relationship' with Russia and China, while 'strengthening trust and developing all-round good-neighbourly relations and mutually beneficial co-operation with both'. *The Mongolian Foreign Policy Concept* also described as the 'foremost objective' of the country's foreign policy the pursuit of 'friendly relations with Russia and China, and without favouring one or the other to develop co-operation with them in complete equality'. Traditional features and specific aspects of economic co-operation were to be safeguarded. Other priorities listed were: good relations with the USA, Japan, Germany and other highly developed nations of West and East; consolidation of political and economic integration in the Asian region; co-operation with the UN and its various bodies; and sound relations with the newly independent states of eastern Europe and the CIS, as well as with developing countries.

Following the dissolution of the USSR in 1991, co-operation with the Russian Federation, the largest of the successor states, continued. During an official visit to Russia in January 1993, President Ochirbat and the Russian President, Boris Yeltsin, issued a joint statement expressing regret at the execution and imprisonment of Mongolian citizens in the USSR during the Stalinist purges. Ochirbat and Yeltsin also signed a new 20-year Mongolian-Russian Treaty of Friendship and Co-operation to replace the defunct Mongolian-Soviet treaty of 1986. A similar treaty had been signed with Ukraine in November 1992, during the official visit to Mongolia by Ukrainian President Leonid Kravchuk. In November 2000 the Russian President, Vladimir Putin, stayed overnight in Ulan Bator en route to an Asia-Pacific Economic Co-operation (APEC) conference in Brunei. He was the most senior Russian or Soviet visitor to Mongolia since 1974. Presidents Bagabandi and Putin issued a joint declaration on bilateral co-operation and the protection of each other's national interests. Russia affirmed its commitment to guaranteeing Mongolia's security in connection with its nuclear weapons-free status. In March Russia sent food aid to relieve starvation resulting from the severe Mongolian winter, during which much livestock had perished (see above). Russian Prime Minister Mikhail Kasyanov officially visited Mongolia in late March 2002, to discuss economic and military co-operation, and also the issue of the latter's outstanding debt of 11,400m. transferable roubles that Moscow claimed it was owed for Soviet aid granted to Mongolia during 1947–91, which the Mongolians referred to as the 'big debt'. The two countries had been unable to agree terms for the previous 10 years. Mongolia disagreed with Russia's position that the debt should be paid in full at par value with the US dollar, and there was also Mongolian opposition pressure to offset the cost of damage done to the environment by Soviet military activity. The disagreement disrupted Mongolian-Russian discussions in early 2003 on a new contract for the Erdenet copper-mining joint venture.

However, when the two Prime Ministers did eventually meet in Moscow in July 2003, a new five-year agreement on the operation of the Erdenet copper enterprise was reached, preserving Mongolia's 51% ownership of stock. Russia agreed that Mongolia had already repaid the cost of building the Erdenet plant. Otherwise, Mongolia's main concern was to reduce Russian taxes on imports of Mongolian goods. At the end of December Russia announced that it had received Mongolia's payment in settlement of the 'big debt'. Russia had waived 98% of the total debt and accepted US $250m. Prime Minister Nambaryn Enkhbayar celebrated a political and diplomatic victory for the MPRP Government, but the details of the settlement remained unclear. DP leader and ex-Prime Minister Enkhsaikhan pointed out that under the Constitution international agreements were supposed to be approved by the Great Khural. Former Prime Minister Byambasüren revived charges of Soviet price-fixing, stating that from 1976 Mongolia had been paid only 0.39 roubles for every one rouble of the value of its exports to the USSR but had been charged 1.5 roubles for its imports of Soviet goods. In March 2005 the Great Khural established a parliamentary working group to investigate the circumstances of the repayment of the 'big debt'.

Relations with the People's Republic of China were good until the onset of the Sino-Soviet dispute in the 1960s. In 1986, however, Sino-Mongolian relations improved significantly when the Chinese Vice-Minister of Foreign Affairs visited Ulan Bator, and the two countries signed agreements on consular relations and trade. In June 1987 a delegation from the Chinese National People's Congress visited Ulan Bator, and in the same month a treaty concerning the resolution of border disputes was initialled by representatives of the two Governments.

A new Treaty of Friendship and Co-operation was concluded during a visit to Ulan Bator by Premier Li Peng in April 1994. An agreement on cultural, economic and technical co-operation was also signed. Mongolia continued to protest in 1995 at the ongoing series of nuclear tests being carried out in China (in the Xinjiang Autonomous Region). Mongolian human rights groups and the Ulan Bator press supported protests in Inner Mongolia against the arrest by the Chinese authorities of Inner Mongolian human rights activists in December. Prime Minister Jasrai's official visit to China in March 1996, focusing on trade and co-operation, appeared not to have been affected by these events. Relations with China were further consolidated in 1997 by the visits to Ulan Bator of Qiao Shi, the Chairman of the National People's Congress Standing Committee, in April, and of Qian Qichen, the Chinese Deputy Premier and Minister of Foreign Affairs, in August.

In June 2003 Chinese President Hu Jintao visited Ulan Bator, where he held talks with President Bagabandi and Prime Minister Enkhbayar and addressed the Great Khural on the subject of 'neighbourly partnership of mutual trust' which, besides reiterating respect for each other's independence, sovereignty and territorial integrity, embodied in the handling of bilateral relations 'a spirit of consultation, co-operation and friendship'. China granted Mongolia 50m. yuan for the purposes of building of a road across their border from Zamyn-Üüd to Erlian.

Mongolia received three important foreign visitors in mid-1999: President Kim Dae-Jung of the Republic of Korea visited in May, and in July official visits were paid by Prime Minister Keizo Obuchi of Japan and President Jiang Zemin of China. In November Prime Minister Amarjargal visited both North and South Korea and also China. In March 2000 he paid an official visit to the United Kingdom. Nambaryn Enkhbayar's first overseas trip as Prime Minister was to the World Economic Forum in Davos, Switzerland, in January 2001. He subsequently travelled to Japan.

During an official visit to the USA in November 2001, Prime Minister Enkhbayar addressed the UN General Assembly in New York and also had a meeting with President George W. Bush. Enkhbayar reaffirmed the strategic partnership with the USA and urged greater investment in Mongolia. Having condemned the terrorist attacks of 11 September against the USA, he informed President Bush of Mongolia's readiness to allow the use of its air space to help combat terrorism. Following US military action in Iraq in March 2003, soldiers of the Mongolian army's élite battalion were sent to Iraq for tours of duty with the Polish contingent stationed north of Baghdad.

The Secretary-General of the United Nations, Kofi Annan, paid a brief visit to Mongolia in October 2002. The Dalai Lama visited Ulan Bator in November 2002, travelling via Japan after Russia refused him a visa and Korean Air, the national carrier of South Korea, banned him on the grounds that he posed a security threat. Although his visit was at the invitation of Mongolia's Buddhist leaders rather than of the Government, the Chinese authorities indicated their displeasure by halting rail traffic on their mutual border for 36 hours. In September 2003 Mongolia hosted the fifth International Conference of New and Restored Democracies (ICNRD), attended by representatives of 119 states. The conference issued a declaration of key principles for democratic societies and initiated a parallel parliamentary forum. Meanwhile, the MPRP was accepted as a member of Socialist International at the grouping's 22nd congress in São Paolo, Brazil, in October 2003. Prime Minister Enkhbayar (the MPRP leader) declared that this signified Mongolia's international acceptance as a 'democratic country with a leftist-centrist ideology'.

President Natsagiin Bagabandi paid a state visit to China in July 2004, visiting Hainan and the Special Administrative Region of Macao, and discussing economic co-operation with President Hu Jintao. Later in the same month Bagabandi visited the USA, where he had talks with President George W. Bush and signed a Trade and Investment Framework Agreement. US Assistant Secretary of State James Kelly and the Japanese Minister of Foreign Affairs Yoriko Kawaguchi visited Ulan Bator in August. Also in October, President Bagabandi paid a state visit to Canada, after a brief stop in the South Korean capital of Seoul. At the invitation of the Chairman of the Presidium of the Supreme People's Assembly, Kim Yong Nam, President Bagabandi visited North Korea in December to promote bilateral co-operation, but his Pyongyang meetings also touched upon hopes for North Korea's return to the six-party talks (see the chapter on the Democratic People's Republic of Korea). In January 2005 President Bagabandi visited Viet Nam and Laos. Meanwhile, Great Khural Chairman Nambaryn Enkhbayar was received by Queen Elizabeth and Prince Philip of the United Kingdom in November 2004 during his visit to London for a conference of the Alliance of Religion and Conservation, of which he was President. He also met Michael Martin, the Speaker of the House of Commons, and Bill Rammell, Parliamentary Under-Secretary of State at the Foreign and Commonwealth Office. After visits to Austria and Moscow in January 2005, Enkhbayar participated in the World Leaders on Faith and Development Conference in Dublin, Ireland. The eighth British-Mongolian 'Round-Table' Conference, held in London in March 2005, was attended by the new Minister of Industry and Trade, Sükhbaataryn Batbold. (The seventh had been held in Ulan Bator in September 2002.)

The US Secretary of Defense, Donald Rumsfeld, visited Ulan Bator briefly in October 2005. Standing in front of a large statue of Genghis Khan, Rumsfeld told Minister of Defence Sharavdorj that the USA was 'anxious and willing' to help Mongolia enhance its peace-keeping capabilities. In 2005 the USA provided Mongolia with US $18m. in military assistance, including regular training exchanges and bilateral peace-keeping exercises.

Nambaryn Enkhbayar's first official foreign travel after his inauguration as President of Mongolia was in July 2005 to Astana, the capital of Kazakhstan, where he attended a meeting of the Shanghai Co-operation Organization with Russian President Vladimir Putin, Chinese President Hu Jintao and other leaders (Mongolia had observer status). Shortly afterwards he welcomed Turkish Prime Minister Reçep Erdoğan to Ulan Bator. Mongolia's relations with Turkey had been developing on the basis of a co-operation agreement concluded in 1995, which incorporated investment in Mongolia's mining sector. The Turkish Government had also agreed to refurbish the ancient Turkish monuments at Khöshöö Tsaidam, the heart of the Turkish sixth-century state, and to build a road there from Karakorum. During Erdoğan's visit the Turkish Exim Bank facilitated a loan of US $20m. for industrial and housing development in Mongolia.

On the first visit to Mongolia by a sitting US President, George W. Bush spent four hours in Ulan Bator on 21 November 2005 and held talks with President Enkhbayar. In an address President Bush declared that both nations had built successful free societies. A joint statement issued by the two Presidents noted that President Bush welcomed Mongolia's progress towards becoming a mature and stable democracy and the country's development of a free market economy, led by the private sector. The two Presidents also emphasized their commitment to combating terrorism.

In February 2006, following a closed meeting in Ulan Bator with foreign donors (specifically the World Bank, the Asian

Development Bank (ADB), the IMF, the UN, Japan, the USA and Germany), which called for greater accountability, the US Administration issued a statement noting that the US Agency for International Development had found that corruption in Mongolia was increasing at all levels. The Mongolian Government was to be required to draw up lists of specific actions to combat corruption and to detail all the changes needed within existing law in order that Mongolia might comply with the UN Convention Against Corruption (UNCAC).

Government

Supreme legislative power is vested in the 76-member Mongolian Great Khural (Assembly), elected by universal adult suffrage for four years. The Great Khural recognizes the President on his election and appoints the Prime Minister and members of the Cabinet, which is the highest executive body. The President, who is directly elected for a term of four years, is Head of State and Commander-in-Chief of the Armed Forces.

In August 2002 the Great Khural approved the reorganization of government agencies, reducing the number of regulatory agencies to eight and executive agencies to 33. Those subordinated to the Prime Minister included the Chief Directorate of Intelligence, State Property Committee, National Radio and Television, and the Montsame News Agency. The coalition Government formed in 2004 increased the number of ministries to 13 and began restructuring the agencies.

Mongolia is divided into 21 provinces (*aimag*) and one municipality (Ulan Bator), with appointed governors and elected local assemblies. However, plans to reduce the number of *aimag* to four (the original pre-revolutionary divisions) and to develop the town of Kharkhorin (the ancient Karakorum) as the future capital were under consideration in 2005.

Defence

Under the 1992 Constitution, the President of Mongolia is, *ex officio*, Commander-in-Chief of the Armed Forces. The defence roles of the President, the Mongolian Great Khural, the Government and local administrations are defined by the Mongolian Law on Defence (November 1993). Mongolia's *Military Doctrine*, a summary of which was issued by the Great Khural in July 1994, defines the armed forces as comprising general purpose troops, air defence troops, construction troops and civil defence troops. The border troops and internal troops, which are not part of the armed forces, are responsible for protection of the borders and of strategic installations, respectively. In August 2005, according to the International Institute for Strategic Studies, Mongolia's defence forces numbered 8,600, comprising an army of 7,500 (of whom 3,300 were thought to be conscripts), 800 air defence personnel and 300 construction troops. There was a paramilitary force of about 7,200, comprising 1,200 internal security troops and 6,000 border guards. Military service is for 12 months (for males aged 18–25 years), but a system of alternative service is being introduced. In September 2003 the first contingent of Mongolian soldiers was dispatched to serve with coalition forces in Iraq. Defence spending for 2006 was projected at 24,571.9m. tögrög, some 3.6% of total expenditure.

Economic Affairs

In 2004, according to estimates by the World Bank, Mongolia's gross national income (GNI), measured at average 2002–04 prices, was US $1,484m., equivalent to $590 per head (or $2,020 per head on an international purchasing-power parity basis). During 1995–2004, it was estimated, the population increased at an average annual rate of 1.1%, while gross domestic product (GDP) per head decreased, in real terms, at an average of 2.7% per year. Overall GDP increased, in real terms, at an average annual rate of 3.9% in 1995–2004. GDP growth in was estimated at 10.6% in 2004 and at 6.2% in 2005.

Agriculture (including forestry) contributed 20.7% of GDP in 2004. The sector engaged 40.2% of the employed labour force in that year. Animal herding is the main economic activity and is practised throughout the country. By mid-1995 more than 90% of all livestock was privately owned. Following exceptionally severe weather, livestock numbers (sheep, goats, horses, cattle and camels) declined sharply in 2002, to fewer than 23.7m., before recovering to almost 26.2m. in 2003. The total number of livestock was almost 28.0m. at the year-end census in 2004, and by the end of 2005 had exceeded 30m. The principal crops are cereals, potatoes and vegetables. Annual grain production decreased by 90,000 metric tons, to 75,200 tons, between 2003 and 2005. During 1995–2004, according to figures from the World Bank, the GDP of the agricultural sector declined, in real terms, at an average annual rate of 0.7%. According to the Asian Development Bank (ADB), agricultural GDP increased by 17.7% in 2004 and by 7.7% in 2005.

Industry (comprising manufacturing, mining, construction and utilities) provided 27.3% of GDP in 2004 and engaged 16.1% of the employed labour force in the same year. According to the World Bank, during 1995–2004 industrial GDP increased, in real terms, at an average rate of 4.2% per year. According to the ADB, the industrial sector's GDP increased by 4.8% in 2003 and by 15.0% in 2004. Industrial GDP increased by 4.2% in 2005, according to the Mongolian Statistical Directorate.

Mining contributed 16.8% of GDP in 2004. Mongolia has significant, largely unexplored, mineral resources and is a leading producer and exporter of copper, gold, molybdenum and fluorspar concentrates. Exports of copper concentrate in 2004 were worth an estimated US $284.3m. The copper-molybdenum works at Erdenet, a Mongolian-Russian joint venture, is the most important mining operation in the country. A Canadian company continued to upgrade the Oyuu Tolgoi (Turquoise Hill) mineral deposits at Khanbogd, South Gobi, not only raising its estimates of copper and gold content but also finding plentiful supplies of underground water in 2003. Copper production was provisionally scheduled to begin in 2006. Other mineral resources include coal, tungsten, tin, uranium and lead. In May 2000 Mongolia's coal reserves were estimated at 150,000m. metric tons. Output of coal reached 6.9m. metric tons in 2004, and rose by 21.5% in 2005, according to the Mongolian Statistical Directorate. Gold production rose from 11.1m. metric tons in 2003 to 19.4m. tons in 2004. Petroleum reserves were discovered in 1994. Extraction of crude petroleum, from the Tamsag basin, commenced in 1997. According to the Mongolian Statistical Directorate, the GDP of the mining sector increased by 4.2% in 2005.

The manufacturing sector accounted for 5.2% of GDP in 2004. Manufacturing industries are based largely on the products of the agricultural and animal husbandry sector. The principal branches of manufacturing include food products, textiles and non-metallic mineral products. Mongolia is one of the world's foremost producers of cashmere, and also manufactures garments, leather goods and carpets. According to figures from the World Bank, manufacturing GDP increased by 2.1% in 2003 and by 1.5% in 2004.

Energy is derived principally from thermal power stations, fuelled by coal. Most provincial centres have thermal power stations or diesel generators, while minor rural centres generally rely on small diesel generators. In more isolated areas wood, roots, bushes and dried animal dung are used for domestic fuel. The Ulan Bator No. 4 power station, the largest in the country, went into operation in 1985. Its capacity of 380 MW doubled Mongolia's generating capacity. Mongolia's production of crude petroleum increased sharply, from 183,047 barrels in 2003 to 215,700 barrels in 2004. Mongolia imports from Russia electricity and petroleum products, including liquid petroleum gas. In 2004 the cost of Mongolia's imports of petroleum products (90% of which were purchased from Russia) reached US $200.9m., accounting for 19.7% of the total cost of merchandise imports.

The services sector contributed 52.0% of GDP in 2004 and engaged an estimated 33.6% of the employed labour force in the same year. During 1995–2004, according to figures from the World Bank, the GDP of the sector increased, in real terms, by an average of 7.4% annually. According to the ADB, the GDP of the services sector increased by 6.3% in 2004 and by 9.1% in 2005. Receipts from tourism were estimated at US $154m. in 2003. The number of visitor arrivals rose from 204,845 in 2003 to 305,117 in 2004.

In 2005 Mongolia's visible trade deficit reached US $95m., and there was an estimated deficit of $151m. on the current account of the balance of payments, according to the ADB. In 2005 the principal source of imports was Russia, supplying 34.8% of the total. Another major supplier was the People's Republic of China (7.7%). China was the principal market for exports in that year, purchasing 48.1% of the total. Another important purchaser was the USA (14.2%). The principal imports in 2004 were mineral products (20.6%) and machinery (13.5%). The principal exports in 2004 were copper concentrate (33.3% of the total, the world copper price having risen by 75% year-on-year), and gold (28.1%).

According to the ADB, Mongolia's fiscal deficit increased from the equivalent of 2.0% of GDP in 2004 to 2.3% in 2005. The budget for 2005, despite having originally envisaged a deficit of 66,900.0m. tögrög, achieved a surplus of 60,400m. tögrög, largely in consequence of rising international prices for gold and copper.

MONGOLIA

Mongolia's total external debt was US $1,472.4m. at the end of 2003, of which $1,137.7m. was long-term public debt. In that year the cost of debt-servicing was equivalent to 32.3% of the value of exports of goods and services. The annual rate of inflation averaged 10.3% during 1995–2004. Annual inflation reached 11.0% in 2004 and was estimated by the ADB at 12.7% in 2005. The number of registered unemployed persons increased from 33,300 (3.5% of the labour force) in 2003 to 35,600 in 2004, but declined to 32,900 in 2005. The number of unregistered unemployed persons, however, was believed to be far greater, with unemployment reportedly reaching some 17% of the labour force in 2002.

In 1989 Mongolia joined the Group of 77 (an organization of developing countries, founded under the auspices of UNCTAD, see p. 51, to promote economic co-operation). In February 1991 Mongolia became a member of the Asian Development Bank (ADB, see p. 169) as well as of the IMF and World Bank. In 1994 the European Union (EU, see p. 228) announced the inclusion of Mongolia in TACIS, the EU's programme of technical assistance to the Commonwealth of Independent States. In 1997 Mongolia became a member of the World Trade Organization (WTO, see p. 370). In July 1998 Mongolia was admitted to the ASEAN Regional Forum (ARF, see p. 176), and in May 2000 the country became a member of the European Bank for Reconstruction and Development (EBRD, see p. 224). Mongolia is also a member of the UN Economic and Social Commission for Asia and the Pacific (ESCAP, see p. 33).

The Democratic Alliance coalition Government, elected in June 1996, initiated a wide-ranging programme of economic reforms, which included plans for the transfer of state assets to the private sector. By 2000, however, the privatization programme had made little progress. Concerned about the capacity of the nomadic herding economy to meet the growing needs of large towns, especially Ulan Bator, Prime Minister Enkhbayar advocated a gradual replacement of traditional nomadic family herding by livestock farming settlements, with adequate provision of winter care for animals and community facilities for herders. Numbers of livestock, which had decreased in the four years to 2002, subsequently increased in 2003, 2004 and 2005 (see above). The national development plan announced in 2001, meanwhile, aimed to end Mongolia's traditional dependency on nomadic herding and envisaged the building of new towns and urbanizing 90% of the population during the next 30 years. These towns would be linked by a 2,400-km east–west highway ('the Millennium Road'), which would serve as a development corridor across the country as well as foster new trade zones on the Russian and Chinese borders. Legislation allowing for the privatization of various state industries was also approved. In May 2002 a stake of 76% in the Trade and Development Bank of Mongolia was purchased by Swiss and US interests. The Agricultural Bank was sold to a Japanese-financed company in February 2003, and the State's 80% share in Neft Import Kontsern (NIK), the oil import company, was purchased by the Mongolian rival distribution company, Petrovis, in February 2004. In June 2002, meanwhile, the Great Khural approved a land privatization law (see Recent History), which entered into force in May 2003. Mongolia remained dependent on external aid. Between 1991 and 2002 Mongolia received a total of US $2,500m. in aid: of this, 52.5% was in the form of grants (of which 46% was allocated for technical assistance) and 47.5% as loans. At a meeting of the Mongolia Consultative Group (formerly the Mongolia Assistance Group) in Tokyo, Japan, in November 2003 (involving 16 donor countries and 14 international organizations), an aid programme of $335m. in grants and loans was agreed. From 2002 there were signs of an improvement in the economy. There was renewed interest in Mongolia's copper, zinc and gold resources, as well as in opportunities for coal mining and petroleum exploration, especially from China. Foreign direct investment was estimated by the ADB to have increased from US $93m. in 2004 to $110m. in 2005. Higher tax revenues, particularly receipts from mining companies, enabled a continued improvement in the Government's fiscal balance. The strong economic performance of 2004 resulted largely from the improvement in the agricultural sector and the expansion in the mining sector, the latter being aided in particular by the increase in international copper prices. Although high gold and copper prices sustained the performance of the mining sector in 2005, the overall rate of GDP growth decelerated in that year, partly owing to major reductions in textile output: following the expiry of the WTO's Multi-Fibre Arrangement (MFA) in January, the clothing industry's production declined by more than 66% in 2005 according to the Mongolian Statistical Directorate, a trend largely attributable to the relocation of Chinese-owned firms in Mongolia to the People's Republic. In the latter part of 2005, meanwhile, several pressure groups held a series of demonstrations in Ulan Bator to demand changes to Mongolian mining legislation, which they claimed did not protect the right of ordinary citizens to benefit from the profits made by foreign mining companies. In response to this public pressure, in December the Minerals and Petroleum Directorate submitted to the Great Khural draft amendments to the 1997 Minerals Law. The amendments included a proposal for state ownership of 30% of the shares in existing and new large mineral deposits. The international mining community and investors sent teams of negotiators to Ulan Bator in an attempt to liberalize the terms. However, following the collapse of the 'grand coalition' Government in January 2006 (see Recent History), the new Minister of Industry and Trade proposed state ownership of 51% of three large mineral deposits. Foreign investors and the Mongolian business community continued to express concern that state control might seriously damage investment in the country's mining industry. The ADB envisaged GDP growth of 6.0% in 2006. Nevertheless, in the longer term the continued development of the private sector, along with the implementation of sound monetary and fiscal policies, remained essential if high levels of growth were to be sustained, thus permitting a reduction in unemployment and progress in the alleviation of poverty.

Education

Ten-year general education is compulsory, beginning at six years of age, and 11-year schooling was being introduced as of early 2005. Pupils may attend vocational-technical schools from the ages of 16 to 18 years. In 2005/06 724 general education schools, with a total enrolment of 556,876 pupils, employed 22,627 teachers. The 44 vocational training schools (some of them private) had a total enrolment of 23,249 in that year. In higher education, in 2004/05 there were 46 state-owned universities and colleges with 84,041 students, and 137 private universities and colleges with 39,405 students. Many Mongolian students continue their academic careers at universities and technical schools in Russia, Germany the United Kingdom and the USA. Government expenditure on education in 2004 amounted to 131,719.5m. tögrög (18.4% of budgetary expenditure). The state budget allocation to the Ministry of Education, Culture and Science for 2006 was 183,798.7m. tögrög (19.6% of planned budgetary expenditure).

Public Holidays

2006: 1 January (New Year), 30–31 January (Tsagaan Sar, lunar new year), 8 March (International Women's Day), 1 June (Children's Day), 11–13 July (National Days), 26 November (Republic Day).

2007: 1 January (New Year), 18–19 February (Tsagaan Sar, lunar new year), 8 March (International Women's Day), 1 June (Children's Day), 11–13 July (National Days), 26 November (Republic Day).

Weights and Measures

The metric system is in force.

MONGOLIA

Statistical Survey

Unless otherwise indicated, revised by Alan J. K. Sanders

Area and Population

AREA, POPULATION AND DENSITY

Area (sq km)	1,564,116*
Population (census results)	
5 January 1989	2,043,400
5 January 2000	
Males	1,177,981
Females	1,195,512
Total	2,373,493
Population (official estimates at 31 December)	
2003	2,504,000
2004	2,533,100
2005	2,562,800
Density (per sq km) at 31 December 2005	1.6

* 603,909 sq miles.

ADMINISTRATIVE DIVISIONS
(estimates at 31 December 2004)

Province (Aimag)	Area ('000 sq km)	Estimated population ('000)	Provincial centre
Arkhangai	55.3	94.9	Tsetserleg
Bayankhongor	116.0	83.8	Bayankhongor
Bayan-Ölgii	45.7	101.2	Ölgii
Bulgan	48.7	60.8	Bulgan
Darkhan-Uul	3.3	87.8	Darkhan
Dornod (Eastern)	123.6	73.7	Choibalsan
Dornogobi (East Gobi)	109.5	52.5	Sainshand
Dundgobi (Central Gobi)	74.7	49.9	Mandalgobi
Gobi-Altai	141.4	60.9	Altai
Gobi-Sümber	5.5	12.3	Choir
Khentii	80.3	71.2	Öndörkhaan
Khovd	76.1	87.8	Khovd
Khövsgöl	100.6	121.4	Mörön
Orkhon	0.8	78.4	Erdenet
Ömnögobi (South Gobi)	165.4	46.8	Dalanzadgad
Övörkhangai	62.9	113.2	Arvaikheer
Selenge	41.2	100.8	Sükhbaatar
Sükhbaatar	82.3	56.6	Baruun Urt
Töv (Central)	74.0	88.9	Zuun mod
Ulan Bator (Ulaanbaatar)*	4.7	928.5	(capital city)
Uvs	69.6	81.0	Ulaangom
Zavkhan	82.5	80.7	Uliastai
Total	**1,564.1**	**2,533.1**	

* Ulan Bator, including Nalaikh, and Bagakhangai and Baganuur districts beyond the urban boundary, has special status as the capital city.

ETHNIC GROUPS
(January 2000 census)

	Number	%
Khalh (Khalkha)	1,934,700	81.5
Kazakh (Khasag)	103,000	4.3
Dörvöd (Durbet)	66,700	2.8
Bayad (Bayat)	50,800	2.1
Buryat (Buriat)	40,600	1.7
Dariganga	31,900	1.3
Zakhchin	29,800	1.3
Uriankhai	25,200	1.1
Other ethnic groups	82,600	3.5
Foreign citizens	8,100	0.3
Total	**2,373,500**	**100.0**

PRINCIPAL TOWNS
(estimated population, December 1999 unless otherwise indicated)

Ulan Bator (capital)	942,747*	Erdenet	65,700
Darkhan	72,600	Choibalsan	40,900†

* January 2005.
† January 2000 census.

BIRTHS, MARRIAGES AND DEATHS

	Registered live births		Registered marriages*		Registered deaths	
	Number	Rate (per 1,000)	Number	Rate (per 1,000)	Number	Rate (per 1,000)
1998	49,256	21.2	13,908	10.3	15,799	6.8
1999	49,461	21.0	13,722	10.1	16,105	6.8
2000	48,721	20.4	12,601	9.0	15,472	6.5
2001	49,658	20.5	12,393	8.6	15,999	6.6
2002	46,922	19.1	13,514	9.2	15,857	6.4
2003	45,723	18.4	14,572	9.6	16,006	6.4
2004	45,501	18.1	11,242	7.2	16,404	6.5
2005	45,200	17.6	n.a.	n.a.	n.a.	6.0

* Persons aged 18 years and over.

Expectation of life (years at birth): 64.58 (males 61.64; females 67.77) in 2004.

Source: *Mongolian Statistical Yearbook*.

EMPLOYMENT
('000 employees at 31 December)

	2002	2003	2004
Agriculture and forestry	391.4	387.5	381.8
Industry*	99.2	109.5	114.2
Transport and communications	38.8	39.5	42.2
Construction	25.5	35.1	39.2
Trade	104.5	129.7	133.7
Public administration	43.9	44.8	46.2
Education			
Science, research and development	59.3	55.3	57.8
Health	34.5	36.8	39.4
Total (incl. others)	**870.8**	**926.5**	**950.5**

* Comprising manufacturing (except printing and publishing), mining and quarrying, electricity, water, logging and fishing.

Source: *Mongolian Statistical Yearbook*.

Unemployed ('000 registered at 31 December): 30.9 in 2002; 33.3 in 2003; 35.6 in 2004; 32.9 in 2005 (Source: Asian Development Bank, *Key Indicators of Developing Asian and Pacific Countries*, Mongolian Statistical Directorate).

Health and Welfare

KEY INDICATORS

Total fertility rate (children per woman, 2003)	2.4
Under-5 mortality rate (per 1,000 live births, 2004)	52
HIV/AIDS (% of persons aged 15–49, 2003)	<0.1
Physicians (per 1,000 head, 2003)	2.7
Hospital beds (per 1,000 head, 2003)	7.3
Health expenditure (2002): US $ per head (PPP)	128
Health expenditure (2002): % of GDP	6.6
Health expenditure (2002): public (% of total)	70.4
Access to water (% of persons, 2002)	62
Access to sanitation (% of persons, 2002)	59
Human Development Index (2003): ranking	114
Human Development Index (2003): value	0.679

For sources and definitions, see explanatory note on p. vi.

MONGOLIA

Agriculture

PRINCIPAL CROPS
(metric tons)

	2003	2004	2005
Cereals*	165,046	138,500	75,200
Potatoes	78,673	80,200	82,700
Other vegetables	59,610	49,200	64,000
Hay	840,700	850,500	830,700

* Mostly wheat, but also small quantities of barley and oats.

LIVESTOCK
(at 31 December)

	2003	2004	2005
Sheep	10,756,400	11,686,400	12,900,000
Goats	10,652,900	12,238,000	13,300,000
Horses	1,968,900	2,005,300	2,000,000
Cattle	1,792,800	1,841,600	1,900,000
Camels	256,700	256,600	254,200
Pigs	13,733	17,180	n.a.
Poultry	90,591	177,395	n.a.

LIVESTOCK PRODUCTS
('000 metric tons, unless otherwise indicated)

	2002	2003	2004
Meat	204.4	153.4	199.3
Beef	60.7	43.6	52.3
Mutton and goat meat	94.9	80.9	98.1
Sheep's wool	17.0	15.2	15.3
Cashmere	2.9	2.7	3.2
Milk	276.6	292.4	328.6
Eggs (million)	4.2	7.1	16.0

Source: *Mongolian Statistical Yearbook*.

Forestry

ROUNDWOOD REMOVALS
('000 cubic metres)

	2001	2002	2003
Total	609.9	568.3	576.5

Source: *Mongolian Statistical Yearbook*.

SAWNWOOD PRODUCTION
('000 cubic metres, incl. railway sleepers)

	2002	2003	2004
Total	28.3	55.0	38.7

Source: *Mongolian Statistical Yearbook*.

Fishing

(metric tons, live weight)

	2001	2002	2003*
Total catch (freshwater fishes)	117	129	130

* FAO estimate.
Source: FAO.

Mining

(metric tons, unless otherwise indicated)

	2002	2003	2004
Salt	680	281	258
Coal	5,544,400	5,666,100	6,865,000
Fluorspar concentrate	159,800	198,400	148,200
Copper concentrate*	376,300	372,200	371,400
Molybdenum concentrate*	3,384	3,836	2,428
Gold (kilograms)	12,097	11,118	19,418
Crude petroleum (barrels)	139,205	183,047	215,700

* Figures refer to the gross weight of concentrates. Copper concentrate has an estimated copper content of 35%, while the metal content of molybdenum concentrate is 47%.

Source: *Mongolian Statistical Yearbook*.

Industry

SELECTED PRODUCTS

	2002	2003	2004
Flour ('000 metric tons)	49.6	54.1	57.8
Bread ('000 metric tons)	21.7	22.1	23.4
Confectionery ('000 metric tons)	5.9	6.5	7.1
Sheep's guts ('000 bunches)	456.9	437.8	385.4
Vodka ('000 litres)	9,436.2	8,873.1	9,161.0
Beer ('000 litres)	3,375.3	3,027.6	7,980.7
Soft drinks ('000 litres)	12,907.3	24,561.1	34,032.7
Cashmere (combed) (metric tons)	622.1	396.9	357.0
Wool, scoured (metric tons)	1,179.6	507.8	1,782.1
Felt ('000 metres)	112.9	303.0	67.8
Camelhair blankets ('000)	38.2	27.4	36.8
Spun thread (metric tons)	55.9	55.1	57.4
Knitwear ('000 garments)	5,563.6	5,148.1	7,989.9
Carpets ('000 sq metres)	533.9	633.1	690.4
Leather footwear ('000)	9.5	4.6	3.0
Felt footwear ('000 pairs)	16.1	9.0	4.9
Surgical syringes (million)	22.8	25.3	24.4
Bricks (million)	13.2	22.9	12.5
Petrol (metric tons)	6,442.2	5,215.0	n.a.
Diesel (metric tons)	3,232.6	3,014.7	n.a.
Fuel oil (metric tons)	748.2	246.8	n.a.
Lime ('000 metric tons)	42.5	42.1	30.0
Cement ('000 metric tons)	147.6	162.3	61.9
Ferroconcrete ('000 cu metres)	11.9	6.9	2.4
Steel sheet and blanks ('000 metric tons)	26.3	60.0	84.4
Copper (metric tons)	1,500.0	1,341.1	2,376.1
Electricity (million kWh)	3,111.7	3,137.7	3,303.4

Sources: *Mongolian Statistical Yearbook*; Ministry of Industry and Trade (Ulan Bator).

Finance

CURRENCY AND EXCHANGE RATES

Monetary Units
100 möngö = 1 tögrög (tughrik).

Sterling, Dollar and Euro Equivalents (31 October 2005)
£1 sterling = 2,170.327 tögrög;
US $1 = 1,221.000 tögrög;
€1 = 1,468.009 tögrög;
10,000 tögrög = £4.61 = $8.19 = €6.81.

Average Exchange Rate (tögrög per US $)
2003   1,146.54
2004   1,185.28
2005   1,205.27

MONGOLIA

BUDGET
(million tögrög)

Revenue	2002	2003	2004
Tax revenue	359,179.2	420,969.2	578,800.9
Income tax	72,433.9	97,584.7	143,349.9
Customs duty	51,321.3	58,575.3	70,230.1
Taxes on goods and services	178,605.1	190,132.6	243,807.8
Value-added tax	118,688.2	121,870.6	162,691.6
Other current revenue	110,569.4	124,257.9	111,680.0
Social insurance	54,397.6	65,205.2	79,625.9
Foreign aid (grants)	6,841.7	8,662.2	6,096.4
Capital revenue (privatization)	458.6	759.0	801.7
Total	477,049.0	554,648.3	697,378.9

Expenditure	2002	2003	2004
Goods and services	283,957.2	291,816.7	345,103.5
Wages and salaries	105,034.1	116,945.9	129,360.5
Interest payments	19,581.9	17,649.4	22,069.6
Subsidies and transfers	109,928.0	125,365.7	158,705.1
Capital expenditure	68,100.3	90,465.1	101,981.2
Lending (net)	67,071.9	90,474.5	85,979.5
Total (incl. others)	548,639.2	615,771.3	713,838.8

Source: *Mongolian Statistical Yearbook*.

2004 (revised figures, million tögrög): Total revenue 671,908.3; Total expenditure 711,245.5 (Source: *Töriin Medeelel*—State Information).

2005 (provisional, million tögrög): Total revenue 833,300.0; Total expenditure 772,900.0 (Source: *Zuuny Medee*—Century's News).

2006 (forecasts, million tögrög): Total revenue 851,199.0; Total expenditure 935,006.0 (Source: *Zuuny Medee*—Century's News).

INTERNATIONAL RESERVES
(US $ million at 31 December)

	2002	2003	2004
Gold (national valuation)	49.79	6.65	14.06
IMF special drawing rights	0.04	0.04	0.04
Reserve position in IMF	0.12	0.14	0.19
Foreign exchange	349.50	235.90	236.10
Total	399.44	242.73	250.40

Source: IMF, *International Financial Statistics*.

MONEY SUPPLY
(million tögrög at 31 December)

	2002	2003	2004
Currency outside banks	120,755	131,482	143,513
Demand deposits at deposit money banks	66,944	81,337	78,572
Total money	187,699	212,819	222,085

Source: IMF, *International Financial Statistics*.

COST OF LIVING
(Consumer Price Index at December; base: December 2000 = 100)

	2002	2003	2004
Foods	107.0	115.2	132.7
Clothing and footwear	110.4	110.3	111.7
Rent and utilities	127.6	125.3	130.2
All items (incl. others)	109.8	114.9	127.5

Source: *Mongolian Statistical Yearbook*.

NATIONAL ACCOUNTS
(million tögrög at current prices, unless otherwise indicated)

Expenditure on the Gross Domestic Product

	2001	2002	2003
Government final consumption expenditure	217,491.3	236,658.8	259,587.7
Private final consumption expenditure	834,662.4	957,789.8	1,072,724.6
Increase in stocks	50,614.5	38,689.6	48,077.2
Gross fixed capital formation	351,594.1	360,918.0	375,354.7
Total domestic expenditure	1,454,362.3	1,594,056.2	1,755,744.2
Exports of goods and services / *Less* Imports of goods and services	−211,310.0	−264,596.4	−291,170.6
Sub-total	1,243,052.3	1,329,459.8	1,464,573.6
Statistical discrepancy*	−127,410.9	−88,673.0	−3,404.4
GDP in purchasers' values	1,115,641.4	1,240,786.8	1,461,169.2
GDP at constant 1995 prices	639,013.0	664,868.3	702,421.7

* Referring to the difference between the sum of the expenditure components and official estimates of GDP, compiled from the production approach.

Source: Asian Development Bank, *Key Indicators of Developing Asian and Pacific Countries*.

Gross Domestic Product by Economic Activity

	2002	2003	2004
Agriculture	256,623.5	293,377.9	385,690.5
Mining	125,896.3	185,788.5	312,780.5
Manufacturing	77,974.9	90,463.5	96,444.4
Electricity, heating and water supply	46,812.1	49,212.0	53,561.6
Construction	29,013.7	44,765.9	47,004.2
Trade	344,010.5	387,086.4	445,488.4
Hotels and restaurants	15,413.4	16,394.8	18,189.3
Transport and communications	182,765.1	202,754.4	229,075.7
Finance	39,510.8	55,415.7	71,733.2
Real estate	14,717.5	21,490.9	23,669.6
Public administration, defence and social security	55,959.4	61,658.5	68,162.9
Education and health, other services	87,580.1	100,384.4	113,334.3
Sub-total	1,276,277.3	1,508,792.9	1,865,134.6
Less Financial intermediation services indirectly measured	35,490.5	47,624.0	57,148.8
GDP in purchasers' values	1,240,786.8	1,461,169.2	1,807,985.9

Source: *Mongolian Statistical Yearbook*.

BALANCE OF PAYMENTS
(US $ million)

	2000	2001	2002
Exports of goods f.o.b.	535.8	523.2	524.0
Imports of goods f.o.b.	−608.4	−623.8	−680.2
Trade balance	−72.6	−100.6	−156.2
Exports of services	77.7	113.5	183.9
Imports of services	−162.8	−205.4	−265.8
Balance on goods and services	−157.7	−192.5	−238.1
Other income received	13.0	14.8	14.1
Other income paid	−19.5	−16.8	−18.6
Balance on goods, services and income	−164.2	−194.5	−242.6
Current transfers received	25.0	40.3	126.9
Current transfers paid	−16.9	—	−42.3
Current balance	−156.1	−154.2	−158.0
Direct investment from abroad	53.7	43.0	77.8
Other investment assets	−44.3	−5.2	−32.1
Other investment liabilities	80.5	69.2	111.7
Net errors and omissions	−19.3	−32.2	14.1
Overall balance	−85.5	−79.4	−13.4

Source: IMF, *International Financial Statistics*.

MONGOLIA

External Trade

PRINCIPAL COMMODITIES
(US $ million)

Imports c.i.f.	2002	2003	2004
Foodstuffs	70.4	69.2	81.7
Mineral products	112.1	143.4	208.1
Petroleum products	108.4	137.7	200.9
Chemical products	21.4	25.6	27.6
Textiles	59.3	59.6	79.5
Metals	19.5	26.9	42.7
Machinery	90.7	96.9	136.1
Vehicles	55.4	73.6	88.8
Household electrical goods	7.2	6.7	10.0
Electricity	3.4	5.5	6.4
Total (incl. others)	690.8	801.0	1,021.1

Exports f.o.b.	2002	2003	2004
Beef	14.0	9.3	4.9
Sheepskin	26.3	33.9	11.7
Copper concentrate	140.2	163.7	284.3
Cathode copper	2.3	2.2	6.8
Fluorite concentrate	16.9	20.5	11.4
Molybdenum concentrate	10.1	15.3	20.0
Petroleum	3.1	4.5	5.7
Gold	119.3	139.8	239.8
Textiles	59.3	61.8	61.1
Knitwear	29.2	37.6	75.8
Cashmere	31.3	26.0	44.1
Wool	5.1	5.3	6.2
Total (incl. others)	524.0	615.8	869.7

Source: Ministry of Industry and Trade (Ulan Bator).

PRINCIPAL TRADING PARTNERS
(US $ million)

Imports c.i.f.	2003	2004	2005
China, People's Republic	196.3	257.2	318.2
Japan	63.4	75.0	68.9
Korea, Republic	67.7	61.2	60.8
Russia	265.4	341.9	399.7
USA	23.5	46.5	35.6
Total (incl. others)	801.0	1,021.1	1,148.7

Exports f.o.b.	2003	2004	2005
Canada	0.7	14.7	122.2
China, People's Republic	287.0	413.9	506.8
Korea, Republic	7.5	9.7	65.3
United Kingdom	26.1	137.4	87.5
USA	142.9	156.3	149.6
Total (incl. others)	615.8	869.7	1,053.7

Sources: *Mongolian Statistical Yearbook*; Ministry of Industry and Trade (Ulan Bator).

Transport

FREIGHT CARRIED
('000 metric tons)

	2003	2004	2005
Rail	12,284.7	14,031.8	15,600.0
Road	5,335.9	7,561.9	9,600.0
Air	2.2	1.9	2.0
Total	17,622.8	21,595.6	25,200.0

Water ('000 metric tons): 1.8 in 2002.

Source: Mongolian Statistical Directorate.

PASSENGERS CARRIED
(million)

	2003	2004	2005
Rail	3.9	4.3	4.2
Road	163.7	189.6	188.2
Air*	0.3	0.3	0.3
Total	167.9	194.2	192.7

* MIAT only.

Source: *Mongolian Statistical Yearbook*.

RAILWAYS
(traffic)

	2003	2004	2005
Passengers carried ('000)	3,947.8	4,326.1	4,200.0
Freight carried ('000 metric tons)	12,284.7	14,031.8	15,600.0
Freight ton-km (million)	7,253.3	8,878.1	n.a.

Source: Mongolian Statistical Directorate.

ROAD TRAFFIC
(motor vehicles in use)

	2003	2004	2005
Passenger cars	68,458	79,691	87,773
Buses and coaches	9,834	10,645	11,021
Lorries, special vehicles and tankers	27,483	30,082	32,406

Source: Mongolian Statistical Directorate.

CIVIL AVIATION
(traffic on scheduled services)

	2003	2004	2005
Passengers carried ('000)	251.9	254.2	318.1
Freight carried (tons)	2,230.7	1,877.3	2,000.0

Source: Mongolian Statistical Directorate.

Tourism

FOREIGN ARRIVALS BY NATIONALITY

Country	2002	2003	2004
China, People's Republic	92,657	91,934	141,473
France	2,891	2,751	5,567
Germany	6,856	4,999	8,826
Japan	13,708	7,757	13,196
Korea, Republic	14,536	17,205	26,754
Russia	71,368	53,330	55,563
United Kingdom	3,537	2,859	4,970
USA	6,860	5,570	9,549
Total (incl. others)	235,165	204,845	305,117

Source: *Mongolian Statistical Yearbook*.

Tourism receipts (US $ million, incl. passenger transport): 49 in 2001; 143 in 2002; 154 in 2003 (Source: World Tourism Organization).

Communications Media

	2002	2003	2004
Television receivers ('000 in use)	200.0	220.0	290.0
Telephones ('000 main lines in use)	126.7	135.5	152.6
Mobile cellular telephones ('000 subscribers)	256.8	319.4	445.1
Internet users ('000)	10.0	11.2	20.4
Books (million printers' sheets)	24.6	31.8	34.8
Newspapers (million printers' sheets)	52.9	71.9	68.7

2005: Telephones ('000 main lines in use) 159.3; Mobile cellular telephones ('000 subscribers) 570.9.

Book production (1994): 128 titles; 640,000 copies.

Newspapers (titles): 170 in 2004 (daily 6, non-daily 164).

Periodicals (titles): 60 in 2004.

Sources: mainly *Mongolian Statistical Yearbook*.

Education

(2004/05)

	Institutions	Teachers	Students
General education schools:*			
Primary (grades 1–3)	75		
Incomplete secondary (grades 4–8)	189	21,458†	537,581‡
Complete secondary (grades 9–10)	446		
Vocational schools (incl. private)	32	1,160	22,024
Higher education:			
Universities and colleges¶			
State-owned	46	6,337	84,041
Private	137		39,405

* Including 124 private schools.
† Including 1,400 teachers in private schools.
‡ Including 19,477 students in private schools.
¶ Excluding 378 students studying abroad.

2005/06: *General education schools:* 724 institutions, 22,627 teachers, 556,876 students. *Vocational schools:* 44 institutions, 1,141 teachers, 23,249 students. *Higher education:* 177 institutions, 6,399 teachers, 130,930 students (excl. 682 students studying abroad).

Pre-school institutions (2005): 687 kindergartens (of which 637 state-owned) staffed by 3,424 teachers and attended by 82,674 infants.
Source: Ministry of Education, Culture and Science (Ulan Bator).

Adult literacy rate (estimates based on census data): 97.8% (males 98.0%; females 97.5%) in 2003 (Source: UN Development Programme, *Human Development Report*).

Directory

The Constitution

The Constitution was adopted on 13 January 1992 and came into force on 12 February of that year. It proclaims Mongolia (*Mongol Uls*), with its capital at Ulan Bator (Ulaanbaatar), to be an independent sovereign republic which ensures for its people democracy, justice, freedom, equality and national unity. It recognizes all forms of ownership of property, including land, and affirms that a 'multi-structured economy' will take account of 'universal trends of world economic development and national conditions'.

The 'citizen's right to life' is qualified by the death penalty for serious crimes, and the law provides for the imposition of forced labour. Freedom of residence and travel within the country and abroad may be limited for security reasons. The citizens' duties are to respect the Constitution and the rights and interests of others, pay taxes, and serve in the armed forces, as well as the 'sacred duty' to work, safeguard one's health, bring up one's children and protect the environment.

Supreme legislative power is vested in the Mongolian Great Khural (Assembly), a single chamber with 76 members elected by universal adult suffrage for a four-year term, with a Chairman and Vice-Chairman elected from amongst the members. The Great Khural recognizes the President on his election and appoints the Prime Minister and members of the Cabinet. A presidential veto of a decision of the Great Khural can be overruled by a two-thirds majority of the Khural. Decisions are taken by a simple majority.

The President is Head of State and Commander-in-Chief of the Armed Forces. He must be an indigenous citizen at least 45 years old who has resided continuously in Mongolia for the five years before election. Presidential candidates are nominated by parties with seats in the Great Khural; the winning candidate in general presidential elections is President for a four-year term.

The Cabinet is the highest executive body and drafts economic, social and financial policy, takes environmental protection measures, strengthens defence and security, protects human rights and implements foreign policy for a four-year term.

The Supreme Court, headed by the Chief Justice, is the highest judicial organ. Judicial independence is protected by the General Council of Courts. The Procurator General, nominated by the President, serves a six-year term.

Local administration in the 21 *aimag* (provinces) and Ulan Bator is effected on the basis of 'self-government and central guidance', comprising local khurals of representatives elected by citizens and governors (*zasag darga*), nominated by the Prime Minister to serve four-year terms.

The Constitutional Court, which guarantees 'strict observance' of the Constitution, consists of nine members nominated for a six-year term, three each by the Great Khural, the President and the Supreme Court.

The first amendments to the Constitution, adopted by the Mongolian Great Khural in December 2000, despite opposition over procedure from the Constitutional Court, were finally approved by President Bagabandi in May 2001. The main effects of the amendments were to clarify the method of appointment of Prime Ministers, enable decision-making by a simple majority vote, and shorten the minimum length of sessions of the Khural from 75 days to 50.

The Government

PRESIDENCY

President and Commander-in-Chief of the Armed Forces: NAMBARYN ENKHBAYAR (elected 22 May 2005; inaugurated 24 June 2005).

Head of Presidential Secretariat: TÜDEVIIN BILEGT.

NATIONAL SECURITY COUNCIL

The President heads the National Security Council; the Prime Minister and the Chairman of the Mongolian Great Khural are its members. The Secretary is the President's national security adviser.

Chairman: NAMBARYN ENKHBAYAR.
Members: TSENDIIN NYAMDORJ, MIYEEGOMBYN ENKHBOLD.
Secretary: (vacant).

CABINET
(May 2006)

Prime Minister: MIYEEGOMBYN ENKHBOLD.
Deputy Prime Minister: MENDSAIKHANY ENKHSAIKHAN.

General Ministries

Minister of Foreign Affairs: NYAMAAGIIN ENKHBOLD.
Minister of Finance: NADMIDYN BAYARTSAIKHAN.
Minister of Justice and Home Affairs: DORJIIN ODBAYAR.

MONGOLIA

Sectoral Ministries

Minister of Nature and the Environment: ICHINKHORLOOGIIN ERDENEBAATAR.

Minister of Defence: MISHIGIIN SONOMPIL.

Minister of Education, Culture and Science: ÖLZIISAIKHANY ENKHTÜVSHIN.

Minister of Construction and Urban Development: JANLAVYN NARANTSATSRALT.

Minister of Roads, Transport and Tourism: TSEGMEDIIN TSENGEL.

Minister of Social Welfare and Labour: LUVSANGIIN ODONCHIMED.

Minister of Industry and Trade: BAZARYN JARGALSAIKHAN.

Minister of Fuel and Power: BADARCHIIN ERDENEBAT.

Minister of Food and Agriculture: DENDEVIIN TERBISHDAGVA.

Minister of Health: LAMJAVYN GÜNDALAI.

Head of Government Affairs Directorate: SUNDUIN BATBOLD.

Minister in charge of Professional Qualifications Control: UNKHNAAGIIN KHÜRELSÜKH.

Minister in charge of Disaster Reduction: SAINBUYANGIIN OTGONBAYAR.

MINISTRIES AND GOVERNMENT DEPARTMENTS

All Ministries and Government Departments are in Ulan Bator.

Prime Minister's Office: State Palace, Sükhbaataryn Talbai 1, Ulan Bator; fax (11) 328329; internet www.pmis.gov.mn/primeminister.

Ministry of Construction and Urban Development: Barilgachdyn Talbai 3, Chingeltei District, Ulan Bator; tel. and fax (11) 322904; e-mail webmaster@mcud.pmis.gov.mn; internet www.gate1.pmis.gov.mn/mcud.

Ministry of Defence: Government Bldg 7, Dandaryn Gudamj, Bayanzürkh District, Ulan Bator; tel. (11) 458495; fax (11) 451727; e-mail mdef@mongol.net; internet www.pmis.gov.mn/mdef.

Ministry of Education, Culture and Science: Government Bldg 3, Baga Toiruu 44, Sükhbaatar District, Ulan Bator; tel. (11) 322480; fax (11) 323158; internet www.mecs.pmis.gov.mn.

Ministry of Finance: Government Bldg 2, Negdsen Ündestnii Gudamj 5/1, Chingeltei District, Ulan Bator; tel. and fax (11) 320247; internet www.mof.pmis.gov.mn.

Ministry of Food and Agriculture: Government Bldg 9, Enkh Taivny Örgön Chölöö 16A, Bayanzürkh District, Ulan Bator; tel. (11) 450258; fax (11) 452554; e-mail mofa@mofa.pmis.gov.mn; internet www.pmis.gov.mn/food&agriculture.

Ministry of Foreign Affairs: Enkh Taivny Örgön Chölöö 7A, Sükhbaatar District, Ulan Bator; tel. (11) 311311; fax (11) 322127; e-mail mongmer@magicnet.mn; internet www.mongolia-foreign-policy.net.

Ministry of Fuel and Power: Ulan Bator.

Ministry of Health: Government Bldg 8, Olimpiin Gudamj 2, Sükhbaatar District, Ulan Bator; tel. (11) 323381; fax (11) 320916; e-mail moh@moh.mng.net; internet www.pmis.gov.mn/health/index.

Ministry of Industry and Trade: Block A, Government Bldg 2, Negdsen Ündestnii Gudamj 5/1, Chingeltei District, Ulan Bator; tel. (11) 329222; fax (11) 322595; e-mail mit@mit.pmis.gov.mn; internet www.mit.pmis.gov.mn.

Ministry of Justice and Home Affairs: Government Bldg 5, Khudaldaany Gudamj 61A, Chingeltei District, Ulan Bator; tel. and fax (11) 325225; e-mail forel@moj.pmis.gov.mn; internet www.monjustice.url.mn.

Ministry of Nature and the Environment: Government Bldg 3, Baga Toiruu 44, Sükhbaatar District, Ulan Bator; tel. (11) 264627; fax (11) 321401; e-mail mne@mongol.net; internet www.mne.mn.

Ministry of Roads, Transport and Tourism: Negdsen Ündestnii Gudamj 5/2, Chingeltei District, Ulan Bator; tel. (11) 330971; fax (11) 310612; e-mail info@mrtt.pmis.gov.mn; internet www.mrtt.pmis.gov.mn.

Ministry of Social Welfare and Labour: Government Bldg 2, Negdsen Ündestnii Gudamj 5, Chingeltei District, Ulan Bator; tel. (11) 324918; fax (11) 328634; e-mail mswl@mongolnet.mn; internet www.mswl.gov.mn.

Government Affairs Directorate (Cabinet Secretariat): State Palace, Sükhbaataryn Talbai 1, Ulan Bator; tel. (11) 323501; fax (11) 310011; internet www.pmis.gov.mn/cabinet.

Main Directorate of Intelligence: Chingeltei District, Ulan Bator (POB 46/74); fmrly State Security Directorate, renamed in 2000; directorates of state communications and state special protection, special archives, museum and higher training school; Head NAVAANSÜRENGIIN GANBOLD.

National Audit Office: Government Bldg 4, Baga Toiruu 6, Ulan Bator; tel. (11) 261745; fax (11) 323266; internet www.mnao.pmis.gov.mn; Chief Auditor LKHAMSÜRENGIIN JAVZMAA.

National Statistical Office: Government Bldg 3, Baga Toiruu 44, Sükhbaatar District, Ulan Bator; tel. (11) 322424; fax (11) 324518; e-mail info@nso.mn; internet www.nso.mn; Head PANDIIN BYAMBAATSEREN.

President and Legislature

PRESIDENT

Office of the President: Ulan Bator; fax (11) 311121; internet www.president.mn.

Election, 22 May 2005

Candidate	Votes	%
Nambaryn Enkhbayar (MPRP)	495,975	53.46
Mendsaikhany Enkhsaikhan (Democratic Party)	182,990	19.73
Bazarsadyn Jargalsaikhan (Republican Party)	129,278	13.94
Badarchiin Erdenebat (Motherland Party)	106,762	11.51

MONGOLIAN GREAT KHURAL

Under the fourth Constitution, which came into force in February 1992, the single-chamber Mongolian Great Khural is the State's supreme legislative body. With 76 members elected for a four-year term, the Great Khural must meet for at least 50 working days in every six months. Its Chairman may act as President of Mongolia when the President is indisposed.

Chairman: TSENDIIN NYAMDORJ.
Vice-Chairman: DANZANGIIN LÜNDEEJANTSAN.
General Secretary: NAMSRAIJAVYN LUVSANJAV.

General Election, 27 June 2004

Party	Seats
Mongolian People's Revolutionary Party (MPRP)	36
Motherland Democracy (MD) coalition*	34
Mongolian Republican Party	1
Independents†	3
Undeclared‡	2
Total	**76**

* Comprising the Democratic Party (DP), the 'Motherland' Mongolian Democratic New Socialist Party (MDNSP) and the Civil Courage Republican Party.
† All three candidates were DP members who stood independently.
‡ In two constituencies the declaration of the final results of voting was delayed. The result in one constituency was declared in February 2005, the seat being awarded to the MPRP; the final result in the other seat was confirmed in favour of the MD at the end of September 2005.

Election Commission

Central Election Organization: Government Bldg 11, Sambuugiin Gudamj 11, Ulan Bator 38; tel. (11) 328383; internet www.gec.gov.mn; f. 1992; Chair. BATAAGIIN BATTULGA.

Political Organizations

Civil Courage (Citizens' Will) Party (CCP): Rm 1, Altai College, Sükhbaatar District, Ulan Bator (CPOB 37); tel. and fax (11) 319006; e-mail oyun@mail.parl.gov.mn; f. 2002; est. by merger of the Civil Courage Party and Mongolian Republican Party; Chair. SANJAASÜRENGIIN OYUUN; Sec.-Gen. MÖNKHCHULUUNY ZORIGT.

Democratic Party (DP): Chingisiin Örgön Chölöö 1, Ulan Bator; f. 2000; est. by amalgamation of the Mongolian National Democratic Party, Mongolian Social-Democratic Party, Mongolian Democratic Party, Mongolian Democratic Renewal Party and the Mongolian Believers' Democratic Party; Mongolian Social-Democratic Party re-established as an independent party in Dec. 2004; c. 170,000 mems.

(May 2002); Chair. TSAKHIAGIIN ELBEGDORJ; Sec.-Gen. SHARAVDORJIIN TUVDENDORJ.

Mongolian Democratic Party (MDP): Ulan Bator; f. 1990; merged in Oct. 1992 with other parties to form the Mongolian National Democratic Party (MNDP); reconstituted in Jan. 2000, the party won no seats in the 2000 elections, and in Dec. 2000 most members merged with the MDNP and other parties to form the Democratic Party; a splinter group opposed to the merger tried unsuccessfully to challenge the legal status of the DP and then elected a new MDP leadership; Chair. DAMDINDORJIIN NINJ.

Mongolian Green Party: Erkh Chölöönii Gudamj 11, Ulan Bator (POB 38/51); tel. (11) 323871; fax (11) 458859; f. 1990; political wing of the Alliance of Greens; 5,000 mems (March 1997); Chair. DAVAAGIIN BASANDORJ.

Mongolian Liberal Democratic Party: Ulan Bator (POB 44/470); tel. (11) 315555; fax (11) 310076; e-mail mldp@magicnet.mn; internet www.mldp.mn; f. 1998; as Mongolian Socialist Democratic (Labour) Party; ruling body is Political Council; 848 mems (1998); Chair. (vacant).

Mongolian Liberal Party: f. 1999 as Mongolian Civil Democratic New Liberal Party, renamed 2004; ruling body Little Khural of 90 mems with Leadership Council of nine; Chair. D. BANZRAGCH.

Mongolian National Solidarity Party: 'Ikh Zasag' Institute Bldg, 4th Sub-District, Tusgaar Togtnolyn Örgön Chölöö, Bayanzürkh District, Ulan Bator; e-mail lawyer_sux@yahoo.com; tel. (11) 457826; fax (11) 455736; f. 1994; est. as Mongolian Solidarity Party; 16,800 mems (March 2004); Chair. NAMSRAIN NYAM-OSOR.

Mongolian People's Party (MPP): Ulan Bator; tel. (11) 311083; f. 1991; forestalled any MPRP plans to revert to its original name, MPP; 2,000 mems (June 1995); in March 2000 some mems (led by Chairman Dembereliin Ölziibaatar) claimed to have merged the MPP with the MPRP; others reaffirmed the MPP's independence at a party congress in April; in Feb. 2006 the merged MPP members declared their separation from the MPRP and named Sükhbaatar as MPP Sec.-Gen; Sec.-Gen. O. SÜKHBAATAR; Chair. Lama DORLIGJAVYN BAASAN.

Mongolian People's Revolutionary Party (MPRP): Baga Toiruu 37/1, Ulan Bator; tel. (11) 320432; fax (11) 323503; e-mail contact@mprp.mn; internet www.mprp.mn; f. 1921; est. as Mongolian People's Party; c. 156,000 mems (Dec. 2004); ruling body Party Little Khural (240 mems), which elects the Leadership Council; Chair. MIYEEGOMBYN ENKHBOLD; Gen. Sec. SANJAAGIIN BAYAR.

Mongolian Republican Party: c/o The Mongolian Great Khural, Ulan Bator; this party was re-registered in 2004 after the split in the leadership of the Civil Courage Party (see above); Chair. BAZARSADYN JARGALSAIKHAN.

Mongolian Rural Development Party: f. 1995; est. as the Mongolian Countryside Development Party, reorganized in December 1999; Pres. L. CHULUUNBAATAR.

Mongolian Social-Democratic Party (MSDP): Ulan Bator; re-formed and registered January 2005; Chair. ARYAAGIIN GANBAATAR; Gen. Sec. TS. SAINBAYAR.

Mongolian Traditional United Party: Huvisgalchdyn Örgön Chölöö 26, Ulan Bator; tel. (11) 325745; fax (11) 342692; also known as the United Heritage (conservative) Party; f. 1993; est. as an amalgamation of the United Private Owners' Party and the Independence Party; 14,000 mems (1998); ruling body General Political Council; Chair. ÜRJINGIIN KHÜRELBAATAR.

Motherland Party: Erel Co, Bayanzürkh District, Ulan Bator; f. 1998; fmrly Mongolian Democratic New Socialist Party, name changed as above Jan. 2005; amalgamated with Mongolian Workers' Party 1999; 110,000 mems (May 2002); Chair. BADARCHIIN ERDENEBAT.

Party of the People: c/o The Mongolian Great Khural, Ulan Bator; f. Dec. 2005 by fmr member of DP; 3,000 mems; Pres. LAMJAVYN GÜNDALAI.

Diplomatic Representation

EMBASSIES IN MONGOLIA

Bulgaria: Olimpiin Gudamj 8, Ulan Bator (CPOB 702); tel. and fax (11) 322841; e-mail posolstvobg@magicnet.mn; Ambassador MIRCHO IVANOV.

China, People's Republic: Zaluuchuudyn Örgön Chölöö 5, Ulan Bator (CPOB 672); tel. (11) 320955; fax (11) 311943; Ambassador GAO SHUMAO.

Cuba: Negdsen Ündestnii Gudamj 18, Ulan Bator (CPOB 710); tel. (11) 323778; fax (11) 327709; e-mail embacuba@mongol.net; Ambassador EDUARDO CASTELLANOS SOTO.

Czech Republic: Olimpiin Gudamj 14, Ulan Bator (CPOB 665); tel. (11) 321886; fax (11) 323791; e-mail czechemb@mongol.net; internet www.mzv.cz/ulaanbaatar; Ambassador JIŘI NEKVASIL.

France: Diplomatic Corps Bldg, Apartment 48, Ulan Bator (CPOB 687); tel. (11) 324519; fax (11) 329633; e-mail ambafrance@magicnet.mn; internet www.ambafrance-mn.org; Ambassador PATRICK CHRISMANT.

Germany: Negdsen Ündestnii Gudamj 7, Ulan Bator (CPOB 708); tel. (11) 323325; fax (11) 323905; e-mail germanemb_ulanbator@mongol.net; Ambassador ULRICH DREESEN.

Hungary: Enkh Taivny Gudamj 1, Ulan Bator (CPOB 668); tel. (11) 323973; fax (11) 311793; e-mail huembuln@mongol.net; Ambassador MIHÁLY ILLÉS.

India: Zaluuchuudyn Örgön Chölöö 10, Ulan Bator (CPOB 691); tel. (11) 329522; fax (11) 329532; e-mail indembmongolia@magicnet.mn; Ambassador S. SWAMINATAN.

Japan: Zaluuchuudyn Gudamj 12, Ulan Bator (CPOB 1011); tel. (11) 320777; fax (11) 313332; e-mail eojmongol@magicnet.mn; internet www.eojmongolia.mn; Ambassador YASUYOSHI ICHIHASHI.

Kazakhstan: Diplomatic Corps Bldg, Apartment 11, Chingeltei District, Ulan Bator (CPOB 291); tel. (11) 312240; fax (11) 312204; e-mail kzemby@magicnet.mn; Ambassador ZH. S. KARYBDZHANOV.

Korea, Democratic People's Republic: Ulan Bator; Ambassador PAK JONG DO.

Korea, Republic: Olimpiin Gudamj 10, Ulan Bator (CPOB 1039); tel. (11) 321548; fax (11) 311157; Ambassador PARK JIN-HO.

Laos: Ikh Toiruu 59, Ulan Bator (CPOB 1030); tel. (11) 322834; fax (11) 321048; e-mail laoemb@mongol.net; Ambassador (vacant).

Poland: Diplomatic Corps Bldg, 95, Apartment 66–67, Ulan Bator; tel. (11) 320641; fax (11) 320576; e-mail polkonsulat@magicnet.mn; Ambassador ZBIGNIEW JERZY KULAK.

Russia: Enkh Taivny Gudamj A-6, Ulan Bator (CPOB 661); tel. (11) 327851; fax (11) 327018; e-mail embassy_ru@mongol.net; Ambassador BORIS ALEKSANDROVICH GOVORIN.

Turkey: Enkh Taivny Örgön Chölöö 5, Ulan Bator (CPOB 1009); tel. (11) 313992; fax (11) 313992; e-mail turkemb@mongol.net; Ambassador ÖMÜR ŞÖLENDIL.

United Kingdom: Enkh Taivny Gudamj 30, Ulan Bator 13 (CPOB 703); tel. (11) 458133; fax (11) 458036; e-mail britemb@magicnet.mn; Ambassador CHRISTOPHER OSBORNE.

USA: Ikh Toiruu 59/1, Ulan Bator (CPOB 1021); tel. (11) 329606; fax (11) 320776; e-mail webmaster@us-mongolia.com; Ambassador PAMELA JO SLUTZ.

Viet Nam: Enkh Taivny Örgön Chölöö 47, Ulan Bator (CPOB 670); tel. (11) 458917; fax (11) 458923; Ambassador (vacant).

Judicial System

Under the fourth Constitution, judicial independence is protected by the General Council of Courts, consisting of the Chief Justice (Chairman of the Supreme Court), the Chairman of the Constitutional Court, the Procurator General, the Minister of Justice and Home Affairs and others. The Council nominates the members of the Supreme Court for approval by the Great Khural. The Chief Justice is chosen from among the members of the Supreme Court and approved by the President for a six-year term. Routine civil, criminal and administrative cases are handled by 30 rural district and inter-district courts and eight urban district courts. There are 22 appellate courts at provincial and capital city level. Some legal cases are required by law to be dealt with by the Supreme Court, appellate courts or special courts (military, railway etc.). The Procurator General and his deputies, who play an investigatory role, are nominated by the President and approved by the Great Khural for six-year terms. The Constitutional Court safeguards the constitutional legality of legislation. It consists of nine members, three nominated each by the President, Great Khural and Supreme Court, and elects a Chairman from among its number.

Chief Justice: SODNOMDARJAAGIIN BATDELGER.

Procurator General: MONGOLYN ALTANKHUYAG.

Chairman of Constitutional Court: JAMSRANGIIN BYAMBADORJ.

Religion

The 1992 Constitution maintains the separation of Church and State but forbids any discrimination, declaring that 'the State shall respect religion and religion shall honour the State'. During the early years of communist rule Mongolia's traditional Mahayana Buddhism was virtually destroyed, then exploited as a 'show-piece' for visiting dignitaries (although the Dalai Lama himself was not permitted to

MONGOLIA

visit Mongolia until the early 1980s). The national Buddhist centre is Gandantegchinlen Khiid (monastery) in Ulan Bator, with about 100 lamas and a seminary; it is the headquarters of the Asian Buddhist Conference for Peace. In the early 1990s some 2,000 lamas established small communities at the sites of 120 former monasteries, temples and religious schools, some of which were being restored. These included two other important monasteries, Erdene Zuu and Amarbayasgalant. The Kazakhs of western Mongolia are nominally Sunni Muslims, but their mosques, also destroyed in the 1930s or closed subsequently, are only now being rebuilt or reopened. Traces of shamanism from the pre-Buddhist period still survive. In recent years there has been a new upsurge in Christian missionary activity in Mongolia. However, the Law on State-Church Relations (of November 1993) sought to make Buddhism the predominant religion and restricted the dissemination of beliefs other than Buddhism, Islam and shamanism. The law was challenged by human rights campaigners and Mongolian Christians as unconstitutional.

BUDDHISM

At the end of 2003 there were 214 Buddhist temples and monasteries in Mongolia (including 53 in Ulan Bator) with 2,091 lamas (monks) and 4,465 apprentices in religious schools, of whom 1,021 were under 16 years of age. It is estimated that about 70% of the adult population (975,600) are Buddhists, that is, some 39% of the total population.

Living Buddha: The Ninth Javzandamba Khutagt (Ninth Bogd), Jambalnamdolchoijinjaltsan (resident in Dharamsala, India).

Gandantegchinlen Monastery: Ulan Bator; tel. (11) 360023; Centre of Mongolian Buddhists; Khamba Lama (Abbot) DEMBERELIIN CHOIJAMTS.

Mongolian Buddhist Association: Pres. G. ENKHSAIKHAN.

Pethub Buddhist Institute: Ulan Bator (POB 38/105); tel. (11) 322366; fax (11) 320676; e-mail pethubmongolia@magicnet.mn; internet www.pethubmonastery.com; f. 2001 by Ven. Kushok Bakula Rinpoche (Indian Ambassador to Mongolia 1990–2000).

CHRISTIANITY

Roman Catholic Church

The Church is represented in Mongolia by a single mission. At April 2004 there were 187 Catholics in the country.

Catholic Mission: Ulan Bator (CPOB 694); tel. (11) 458825; fax (11) 458027; e-mail ccmvatican@magicnet.mn; f. 1992; Apostolic Prefect Bishop WENCESLAO PADILLA.

Cathedral of St. Peter and St. Paul: Bayanzürkh District, Ulan Bator.

Protestant Church

Association of Mongolian Protestants: f. 1990; Pastor M. BOLD-BAATAR.

Mongolian Evangelical Alliance: Kseni Bldg, Baga Toiruu, Chingeltei District, Ulan Bator; tel. (11) 312771; e-mail mea@magicnet.mn; f. 1998; a branch of the World Evangelical Alliance.

Russian Orthodox Church

Holy Trinity Church: Jukovyn Gudamj 55, Ulan Bator; opened in 1870, closed in 1930; services recommenced 1997 for Russian community; Head Father ANATOLII FESECHKO.

ISLAM

It is assumed that the majority of Mongolia's ethnic Kazakh population (numbering 103,000 at the January 2000 census) are Muslim. It was stated in March 2005 that Mongolia had 32 mosques in Bayan-Ölgii and Khovd provinces and in the towns of Darkhan and Nalaikh.

Chief Imam (Ölgii): KH. BATYRBEK.

Imam of Gümyr shrine (Ölgii): DÖITENGIIN SHERKHAN.

Muslim Society: f. 1990; Hon. Pres. K. SAIRAAN; Chair. of Central Council M. AZATKHAN; Exec. Dir KH. BATYRBEK.

BAHÁ'Í FAITH

Bahá'í Community: Ulan Bator; tel. (11) 321867; f. 1989; Leader A. ARIUNAA.

SHAMANISM

Darkhad Shamanist Study Centre: Ulan Bator; Leader CH. TSERENBAAVAI.

Tengeriin Süld Shamanist Union: Ulan Bator; Pres. CH. CHINBAT.

The Press

PRINCIPAL NATIONAL NEWSPAPERS

State-owned publications in Mongolia were denationalized with effect from 1 January 1999, although full privatization could not proceed immediately. The number of newspapers published annually decreased from 134.1m. copies in 1990 to 18.5m. copies in 2003.

Ardyn Erkh (People's Power): Ulan Bator; f. 2004; original title ceased publication in 1999 (see *Ödriin Sonin*, below); subsequently assumed by new publr; 256 a year.

MN-Önöödör (Today): Mongol News Co, Ikh Toiruu 20, Ulan Bator; tel. (11) 352504; fax (11) 352501; e-mail mntoday@mobinet.mn; internet www.mongolnews.mn; f. 1996; 304 a year; Editor-in-Chief TS. BALDORJ; circ. 5,500.

Mongolyn Medee (Mongolian News): Tsetseg Centre, Baga Toiruu 1, Ulan Bator; tel. (11) 318720; fax (11) 318718; e-mail news-of-mon@mongolnet.mn; internet www.mongolmedia.com; 256 a year; Editor-in-Chief DENDEVIIN SANDAGSÜREN; circ. 2,900.

Ödriin Sonin (Daily News): Mongol News Co Bldg, Ikh Toiruu 20, Ulan Bator; tel. (11) 354165; fax (11) 353897; e-mail daily_news@mbox.mn; internet www.dn.mongolmedia.com; f. 1924; restored 1990; fmrly Ardyn Erkh, Ardyn Ündesnii Erkh, Ündesnii Erkh and Ödriin Toli; 312 a year; Editor-in-Chief JAMBALYN MYAGMARSÜREN; circ. 14,200.

Ünen (Truth): Baga Toiruu 11, Ulan Bator; tel. (11) 320482; fax (11) 323223; e-mail unen@mongol.net; internet www.unen.mongolmedia.com; f. 1920; publ. by MPRP; 256 a year; Editor-in-Chief TSERENSODNOMYN GANBAT; circ. 8,330.

Zuuny Medee (Century's News): Amaryn Gudamj 1, Ulan Bator; tel. (11) 320940; fax (11) 321279; e-mail zuunii_medee@yahoo.com; internet www.zuuniimedee.mn; f. 1991; as Zasgiin Gazryn Medee; 312 a year; Editor-in-Chief TSERENDORJIIN TSETSEGCHULUUN; circ 8,000.

OTHER NEWSPAPERS AND PERIODICALS

4 dekh Zasaglal (Fourth Estate): Mongol Sonin Co, Gazar Holding Bldg, Variete Centre, Ulan Bator (POB 46A/81); tel. 99188125; e-mail dorovdekhzasaglal@yahoo.com; internet www.mongolmedia.com/4thEstate; monthly; Editor A. ENKHBAYAR.

81-r Suvag (Channel 81): Ulan Bator Administration Bldg 2, Rm 504, Ulan Bator (CPOB 367); fax (11) 460718; e-mail channel81@mongolmedia.com; internet www.channel81.mongolmedia.com; publishes views of the Mongolian Newspaper Asscn; 36 a year; Editor-in-Chief JAMSRANGIIN BAYARJARGAL.

Anagaakh Arga Bilig (The Healthy Way of Yin and Yang): Ulan Bator (CPOB 1053); tel. (11) 321367; e-mail arslny7144@magicnet.mn; twice monthly; Editor YA. ARSLAN.

Ardchilal (Democracy): Democratic Party, Chingisiin Örgön Chölöö 1, Ulan Bator; political journal; 48 a year.

Bagsh (Teacher): Rm 106, Teachers' College, Ulan Bator; tel. 99183398; f. 1989; by Ministry of Education; 24 a year.

Biznes Medee (Business News): Democratic Party Bldg, Sükhbaatar District, Ulan Bator (POB 20/335); tel. (11) 350541; fax (11) 350548; e-mail info@businessnews.mn; internet www.businessnews.mn; 48 a year; Editor-in-Chief S. KHÜREL.

Biznes Toim (Business Review): Ulan Bator; tel. (11) 321312; f. 2006; monthly.

Business Times: Chamber of Commerce and Industry, Government Bldg 11, Rm 712, Erkh Chölöönii Talbai, Ulan Bator; tel. (11) 325374; fax (11) 324620; e-mail biztimes@mongolchamber.mn; 48 a year; Editor B. SARANTUYAA.

Deed Shuukhiin Medeelel (Supreme Court Information): Mongolian Supreme Court, Ulan Bator; quarterly journal.

Deedsiin Amidral (Elite's Life): Bldg 4, Rm 514, A. Amaryn Gudamj, Ulan Bator (POB 356); tel. 95155295; fax (11) 323847; e-mail deedsiinamidral@mongol.mn; internet www.elitslife.mongolmedia.com; 36 issues a year; Editor-in-Chief B. OTGONBAYAR.

Deedsiin Khüreelen (Elite's Forum): Ulan Bator (CPOB 1114); tel. (11) 325687; fax (11) 326480; e-mail deedhuree@yahoo.com; 36 a year; Editor G. DASHRENTSEN; circ. 12,000.

Erüül Mend (Health): Super Zuun Co, Ulan Bator (POB 20/412); tel. 99192239; fax (11) 321278; e-mail dr_jargal_d@yahoo.com; internet www.erul_mend.net; publ. by Ministry of Health; monthly; Editor D. JARGALSAIKHAN; circ. 5,600.

Khani (Spouse): National Agricultural Co-operative Members' Association Bldg, Rm 103, Enkh Taivny Gudamj 18A-1, Bayanzürkh District, Ulan Bator (POB 49/600); tel. (11) 460698; fax (11) 458550; e-mail khanisonin@yahoo.com; women and family issues; 36 a year; Editor-in-Chief D. BATSÜKH; circ. 64,920.

MONGOLIA

Khödölmör (Labour): Sükhbaataryn Talbai 3, Ulan Bator; tel. (11) 323026; f. 1928; publ. by the Confederation of Mongolian Trade Unions; 36 a year; Editor-in-Chief TSOODOLYN KHULAN; circ. 64,920.

Khökh Tolbo (Blue Spot): Mon-Azi Co Bldg, Ulan Bator (POB 24/306); tel. and fax (11) 313405; 48 a year; Editor-in-Chief BATYN ERDENEBAATAR; circ. 3,500.

Khöröngiin Zakh Zeel (Capital Market): Mongolian Stock Exchange, Sükhbaataryn Talbai 2, Ulan Bator; tel. (11) 313511; fax (11) 325170; e-mail info@mse.mn; monthly; Editor RENTSENGIIN SODKHÜÜ.

Khuuli Züin Medee (Legal News): Ministry of Justice and Home Affairs, Ulan Bator; f. 1990; 24 a year.

Khuviin Soyol (Personal Culture): Rm 2, Block 39, behind No. 5 School, Baga Toiruu, Ulan Bator (CPOB 1254); 24 a year; Editor BEKHBAZARYN BEKHSÜREN.

Khümüün Bichig (People and Script): Montsame News Agency, Jigjidjavyn Gudamj 8, Ulan Bator (CPOB 1514); tel. (11) 329486; fax (11) 327857; e-mail khumuun@montsame.mn; current affairs in Mongolian classical script; 48 a year; Editor T. GALDAN; circ. 15,000.

Khümüüs (People): Central Palace of Culture South Bldg, Rm 206, Ulan Bator (POB 46/411); tel. and fax (11) 318363; e-mail khumuus@magicnet.mn; 48 a year; Editor R. KHADBAATAR; circ. 21,500.

Khümüüsiin Amidral (People's Life): Central Palace of Culture South Bldg, Rm 206, Ulan Bator (CPOB 2348); tel. and fax (11) 314147; e-mail peopleslife@hotmail.com; internet www.peopleslife.mongolmedia.co; 48 a year; Editor B. AMGALAN.

Mash Nuuts (Top Secret): Mongol Shaazan Bldg, Ulan Bator (POB 49/113); tel. (11) 330690; fax (11) 648109; e-mail tsecret@mongolnet.mn; 36 a year; Editor-in-Chief ONONGIIN CHINZORIG.

Mongoljin Goo (Mongolian Beauty): Mongolian Women's Federation, Ulan Bator (POB 44/717); tel. (11) 320790; fax (11) 367406; e-mail monwofed@magicnet.mn; f. 1990; monthly; Editor J. ERDENECHIMEG; circ. 3,000.

Mongolyn Anagaakh Ukhaan (Mongolian Medicine): Ulan Bator (CPOB 696); tel. (11) 112306; fax (11) 451807; e-mail nymadawa@hotmail.com; publ. by Scientific Society of Mongolian Physicians, Sub-assembly of Medical Sciences and Mongolian Academy of Sciences; quarterly; Editor-in-Chief Prof. PAGVAJAVYN NYAMDAVAA.

Mongolyn Khödöö (Mongolian Countryside): Agricultural University, Zaisan, Ulan Bator; tel. (11) 345211; e-mail haaint@magicnet.mn; publ. by Mongolian State University of Agriculture and Academy of Agricultural Sciences; 24 a year; Editor-in-Chief Prof. BEGZIIN DORJ.

Montsame-giin Medee (Montsame News): Montsame News Agency, Jigjidjavyn Gudamj 8, Ulan Bator (CPOB 1514); tel. (11) 266904; fax (11) 327857; e-mail montsame@pop.magicnet.mn; daily news digest primarily for government departments; 252 a year; Editor BAYANBATYN BAYASGALAN.

Notstoi Medee (Important News): Maximus Press Co, Ulan Bator (POB 20/359); tel. (11) 316953; 36 a year; Editor T. TSOGT-ERDENE.

Sankhüügiin Medee (Financial News): Ulan Bator; 36 a year; Editor L. DONDOG.

Serüüleg (Alarm Clock): Amryn Gudamj, Ulan Bator (CPOB 1094); tel. (11) 329059; fax (11) 318006; e-mail seruuleg@mongolmedia.com; 40 a year; Editor-in-Chief TSERENNADMIDYN BULGANZAYAA; circ. 28,600.

Setgüülch (Journalist): Ulan Bator (POB 46/600); tel. (11) 325388; fax (11) 313912; f. 1982; publ. by Union of Journalists; journalism, politics, literature, art, economy; quarterly; Editor TSENDIIN ENKHBAT.

Shar Sonin (Yellow Newspaper): Ulan Bator (POB 46A/225); tel. (11) 313984; e-mail thesharsonin@yahoo.com; 36 a year; Editor B. NAMUUN.

Shinjlekh Ukhaany Akademiin Medee (Academy of Sciences News): Yörönkhii Said Amaryn Gudamj 1, Ulan Bator; tel. (11) 321993; fax (11) 261993; e-mail mas@mas.ac.mn; internet www.mas.ac.mn; f. 1961; publ. by Academy of Sciences; quarterly; Editor-in-Chief L. TSEDENDAMBA.

Shuurkhai Zar (Quick Advertisement): Ulan Bator Bank Bldg, Rm 104, 1st Floor, Ulan Bator (POB 46A/151); tel. (11) 313778; e-mail shirevger@mobinet.mn; 100 a year; Editor E. TSEYENKHORLOO.

Strategi Sudlal (Strategic Studies): Institute of Strategic Studies, Ulan Bator (CPOB 870); f. 1991; 4 a year; Editor L. MOLOMJAMTS.

Tavan Tsagarig (Five Rings): National Olympic Committee, Ikh Toiruu 20, Ulan Bator; tel. (11) 352487; fax (11) 343541; e-mail t_ts_sport@yahoo.com; noc@olympic.mn; weekly; Editor-in-Chief SODNOMDARJAAGIIN BATBAATAR.

Tonshuul (Woodpecker): Enkhtaivny Örgön Chölöö 4, Rm 148, Bayanzürkh District (CPOB 322), Ulan Bator; tel. (11) 459265; e-mail ariun_tonshuul@yahoo.com; internet www.tonshuul.mongolmedia.com; fortnightly magazine of cartoons, humour and satire; Editor TS. ARIUNAA.

Töriin Medeelel (State Information): Secretariat of the Mongolian Great Khural, State Palace, Ulan Bator; tel. (11) 265958; fax (11) 322866; e-mail luvsanjav@mail.parl.gov.mn; internet www.parl.gov.mn; f. 1990; presidential and governmental decrees, state laws; 48 a year; circ. 5,000.

Tsenkher Delgets (Light Blue Screen): Ulan Bator; tel. (11) 312010; fax (11) 311850; e-mail bsnews@magicnet.mn; weekly guide to TV and radio programmes; Editor-in-Chief GALIGAAGIIN BAYARSAIKHAN.

Tsonkh (Window): Chingisiin Örgön Chölöö 1, Ulan Bator (CPOB 1085); tel. (11) 310717; publ. by the Democratic Party's Political Department; monthly.

Tsog (Ember): Mongolian Writers' Association, Ulan Bator; literary quarterly.

Ulaanbaatar Taims (Ulan Bator Times): A. Amaryn Gudamj 1, Ulan Bator; tel. and fax (11) 311187; f. 1990; est. as Ulaanbaatar; publ. by Ulan Bator City Govt; 264 a year; Editor-in-Chief (vacant); circ. 2,000.

Uls Töriin Sonin (Political Newspaper): Delta Centre, Juulchny Gudamj, Chingeltei District, Ulan Bator; tel. 99830184; fax (11) 312608; e-mail political newspaper@yahoo.com; f. 2005 following closure of the *Mongol Times*; 48 a year; Owner CHONOIN KULANDA; Editor GANTÖMÖRIIN UYANGA.

Utga Zokhiol Urlag (Literature and Art): Union of Writers, Sükhbaataryn Gudamj 11, Ulan Bator; tel. (11) 321863; f. 1955; 36 a year; Editor-in-Chief Ü. KHÜRELBAATAR; circ. 3,000.

Üg-Il Tovchoo (Word-Openness): est. through the merger of the fmr Mongolian Social Democratic Party's journal *Üg* with the current affairs magazine *Il Tovchoo*; 36 a year; Editor-in-Chief G. AKIM.

Zar Medee (Advertisement News): Government Bldg 5, 1st Floor, Rm 130, Juulchny Gudamj, Chingeltei District, Ulan Bator; tel. and fax (11) 312379; e-mail advertisement-news@yahoo.com; personal and company advertisements; 100 a year; Editor D. BAYASGALAN.

Zindaa (Ranking): Room 305, former Ardyn Erkh Bldg., Sükhbaatar District, Ulan Bator; tel. and fax (11) 354545; internet www.zindaa.mongolmedia.com; wrestling news; 48 a year; Editor-in-Chief KH. MANDAKHBAYAR.

FOREIGN LANGUAGE PUBLICATIONS

Inspiring Mongolia: Mongolian National Chamber of Commerce and Industry, Government Bldg 11, Ulan Bator; tel. (11) 325374; fax (11) 324620; e-mail marketing@mongolchamber.mn; internet www.mongolchamber.mn; quarterly magazine in English; Editor-in-Chief S. DEMBEREL.

Menggu Xiaoxi Bao (News of Mongolia): Montsame News Agency, Ulan Bator (CPOB 1514); tel. (11) 320077; e-mail mgxxbao@chinggis.com; f. 1929; closed 1991, reopened 1998; weekly; in Chinese; Sec. P. OYUUNTSETSEG.

Mongolian Magazine: Interpress Publishers, Ulan Bator; f. 2004; English-language monthly illustrated magazine about Mongolian history, culture, nature, life and customs.

Mongolia This Week: Ulan Bator; tel. and fax (11) 318339; e-mail mongoliathisweek@mobinet.mn; internet www.mongoliathisweek.mn; weekly in English, online daily; Editor-in-Chief D. NARANTUYAA; English Editor ERIC MUSTAFA.

Mongoliya Segodnya (Mongolia Today): Ulan Bator (POB 46/609); tel. and fax (11) 324141; e-mail MNSegodnia@mongol.net; weekly; in Russian; Editor-in-Chief DÜNGER-YAICHILIIN SOLONGO.

The Mongol Messenger: Montsame News Agency, Jigjidjavyn Gudamj 8, Ulan Bator (CPOB 1514); tel. (11) 325512; fax (11) 325512; e-mail monmessenger@magicnet.mn; internet www.mongolmessenger.mn; f. 1991; weekly newspaper in English; Editor-in-Chief B. INDRA; circ. 2,000.

Mongoru Tsushin (Mongolia News): Montsame News Agency, Jigjidjavyn Gudamj 8, Ulan Bator (CPOB 1514); 36 a year; in Japanese.

Montsame Daily News: Montsame News Agency, Jigjidjavyn Gudamj 8, Ulan Bator (CPOB 1514); tel. (11) 314574; fax (11) 327857; e-mail montsame@magicnet.mn; daily English news digest for embassies, etc.; Editor-in-Chief BAYANBATYN BAYASGALAN.

Novosti Mongolii (News of Mongolia): Montsame News Agency, Jigjidjavyn Gudamj 8, Ulan Bator (CPOB 1514); tel. (11) 310157; fax (11) 314511; e-mail novosty_mongolii@yahoo.com; f. 1942; weekly; in Russian; Editor-in-Chief D. ARIUNBOLD.

The UB Post: Mongol News Co, Ikh Toiruu 20, Ulan Bator; tel. (11) 352487; fax (11) 352495; e-mail ubpost@yahoo.com; internet ubpost.mongolnews.mn; f. 1996; weekly; in English; Editor-in-Chief NAMSRAIN OYUUNBAYAR; circ. 4,000.

MONGOLIA

NEWS AGENCIES

Montsame (Mongol Tsakhilgaan Medeenii Agentlag) (Mongolian News Agency): Jigjidjavyn Gudamj 8, Ulan Bator (CPOB 1514); tel. (11) 266904; fax (11) 327857; e-mail montsame@magicnet.mn; internet www.montsame.mn; f. 1921; govt-controlled; Gen. Dir D. Ariunbold; Editor-in-Chief Bayanbatyn Bayasgalan.

Mongolyn Medee (Mongolian News): Public Radio and Television, Khuvisgalyn Zam, Ulan Bator; Dir O. Otgonbaatar.

Foreign Bureaux

Informatsionnoye Telegrafnoye Agentstvo Rossii—Telegrafnoye Agentstvo Suverennykh Stran (ITAR—TASS) (Russia): Khudaldaany Gudamj 4, Rm 323, Ulan Bator; Bureau Chief V. B. Ionov; Correspondent N. A. Kerzhentsev.

Rossiiskoye Informatsionnoye Agentstvo—Novosti (RIA—Novosti) (Russia): Ulan Bator (CPOB 686); tel. (11) 327384; Correspondent Aleksandr Altman.

Xinhua (New China) News Agency (People's Republic of China): Ulan Bator; tel. (11) 322718; Correspondent Li Ren.

PRESS ASSOCIATIONS

Mongolian Newspaper Association: Ulan Bator; Pres. R. Khadbaatar; Vice-Pres. D. Batsükh.

Publishers

The Government remains the largest publisher, but the ending of the state monopoly has led to the establishment of several small commercial publishers, including Shuvuun Saaral (Ministry of Defence), Mongol Khevlel and Soyombo Co, Mongolpress (Montsame), Erdem (Academy of Sciences), Süülenkhüü children's publishers, Sudaryn Chuulgan, Interpress, Sükhbaatar Co, Öngöt Khevlel, Admon, Odsar, Khee Khas Co, etc. The two main press, periodical and book subscription agencies are Mongol Shuudan and Gurvan Badrakh Co.

Admon Co: Amaryn Gudamj 2, Sükhbaatar District, Ulan Bator (CPOB 92); tel. (11) 329253; fax (11) 327251; e-mail admon@magicnet.mn; Dir R. Enkhbat.

Darkhan Sergelen Co: Naadamchdyn Gudamj, Darkhan; tel. (372) 23049; fax (372) 24741; internet www.munkhiin-useg.mn.

Chölööt Khevlel San (Free Press Foundation): Newspaper Printing House, Ikh Toiruu 116, Ulan Bator; tel. (11) 353551; e-mail freepress@mongol.net; f. 1996; the country's largest printer of newspapers; Exec. Dir B. Galsandorj.

Khevleliin Khüreelen (Press Institute NGO): Ikh Toiruu 11, Sükhbaatar District, Ulan Bator; tel. and fax (11) 350012; e-mail ts_byambaa12@yahoo.com; internet www.owc.org.mn/pressinstitute; Chair. Ts. Enkhbat.

Mongol News Group: Mongol News Group Bldg, Juulchny Gudamj, Ulan Bator; tel. (11) 330797; fax (11) 330798; e-mail mntoday@mobinet.mn; f. 1996; owns newspapers *MN-Önöödör*, *Tavan Tsagarig*, *Nyam Garig* and *The UB Post*, TV Channel 25 and ABM Co printers; Pres. Ts. Baldorj.

Mönkhiin Üseg Group: Teeverchdiin Gudamj, Songinokhairkhan District, Ulan Bator; tel. (11) 320807; fax (11) 321318; e-mail munuseg@mbox.mn; internet www.munkhiin-useg.mn; Chair. G. Batmönkh.

Novum Co: Migma Bldg, Ulan Bator; tel. (11) 319140; fax (11) 319319; e-mail print@mynovum.com; internet www.mynovum.com.

Öngöt Khevlel Co: Amaryn Gudamj 2, Sükhbaatar District, Ulan Bator; tel. (11) 323121; fax (11) 329519; e-mail ungut_khevlel@mongolnet.mn.

Soyombo Printing Co: Natsagdorjiin Gudamj, Sükhbaatar District, Ulan Bator; tel. (11) 325052.

Sükhbaatarprint Co: Amaryn Gudamj 2, Sükhbaatar District, Ulan Bator; tel. and fax (11) 320504; e-mail sukhprint@magicnet.mn.

Zurag Züi Co (Cartography): Ikh Toiruu 15, Ulan Bator; tel. (11) 322164; e-mail cart@magicnet.mn; publisher and retailer of maps and atlases.

PUBLISHERS' ASSOCIATIONS

Local Press and Information Association: Ulan Bator; f. 2006; Pres. S. Sharavdorj.

Mongolian Book Publishers' Association: Ulan Bator; Exec. Dir S. Tserendorj.

Mongolian Free Press Publishers' Association: POB 306, Ulan Bator 24; tel. and fax (11) 313405; Pres. Batyn Erdenebaatar.

Broadcasting and Communications

TELECOMMUNICATIONS

Digital exchanges have been installed in Ulan Bator, Darkhan, Erdenet, Sükhbaatar, Bulgan and Arvaikheer, while radio-relay lines have been digitalized between: Ulan Bator–Darkhan–Sükhbaatar; Ulan Bator–Darkhan–Erdenet; and Dashinchilen–Arvaikheer. Mobile telephone companies operate in Ulan Bator and other central towns, in addition to Arvaikheer, Sainshand and Zamyn-Üüd. By May 2005 a total of 1,776 km of fibre optic cable had been installed in Mongolia, with plans to lay another 1,400 km by the end of the year. The Ulan Bator–Bulgan cable was under construction.

Bodicom: Ulan Bator; tel. (11) 325144; fax (11) 318486; e-mail bodicom@mongolnet.mn; internet www.bodicom.mn.

Datakom: Negdsen Ündestnii Gudamj 49, Ulan Bator; tel. (11) 315544; fax (11) 320210; e-mail sales@datacom.mn; internet www.web.mn; service provider for Magicnet connection to internet; Dir Dangaasürengiin Enkhbat.

MagicNet Co: Rm 104, Ground Fl., Science and Technology Information Centre, Ulan Bator; tel. (11) 312061; fax (11) 315668; e-mail support@magicnet.mn; internet www.magicnet.mn; internet service provider.

MCSCom: MCS Plaza, 3rd Fl., Ulan Bator; tel. (11) 327854; fax (11) 311323; e-mail mcscom@mcs.mn; internet www.mcscom.mn; internet service provider.

Micom: Mongol Tsakhilgaan Kholboo Co Bldg, 3rd Floor, Sükhbaataryn Talbai 1, Ulan Bator; tel. (11) 313229; fax (11) 322473; e-mail info@micom.mng.net; internet www.micom.mng.net; Dir Ch. Narantungalag.

MobiCom: Mobicom Corp. Bldg, Enkhtayvyny Örgön Chölöö 3/1, Ulan Bator; tel. (11) 312222; fax (11) 324017; e-mail mobicom@mobicom-corp.com; internet www.mobicom.mn; mobile telephone service provider; Dir G. Battör.

Moncom: Ulan Bator (POB 51/207); tel. (11) 329409; e-mail ch.enkhmend@hotmail.com; pager services.

Mongolia Telecom: Sükhbaataryn Talbai 1, Ulan Bator (CPOB 1166); tel. (11) 320597; fax (11) 325412; e-mail mt@mtcone.net; internet www.mongol.net; 54.6% state-owned, 40.0% owned by Korea Telecom; Pres. and CEO Oonoigiin Shaaluu.

Railcom: Mongolian Railways (MTZ), Ulan Bator; tel. and fax (21) 942600; e-mail zorigt.mrc@mtz.mn; internet www.railcom.mn; telephone, TV and internet service provider.

Skytel: Skytel Plaza Centre, Chingisiin Örgön Chölöö, Ulan Bator; tel. (11) 319191; fax (11) 318487; e-mail skytel@mtcone.net; mobile telephone and voice mail service provider; Mongolia-Republic of Korea jt venture; Dir-Gen. D. Erdenebat; Marketing Man. G. Tüvshintögs.

Unitel: Ulan Bator; f. 2005 by MBSB Telecom, Uangel Corpn (Republic of Korea) and Dream Choice Co (Canada); mobile telephone service provider.

BROADCASTING

A 1,900-km radio relay line from Ulan Bator to Altai and Ölgii provides direct-dialling telephone links as well as television services for western Mongolia. New radio relay lines have been built from Ulan Bator to Choibalsan, and from Ulan Bator to Sükhbaatar and Sainshand. Most of the population is in the zone of television reception, following the inauguration of relays via satellites operated by the International Telecommunications Satellite Organization (INTELSAT). In 2004 Mongolia had 30 radio stations and 35 television stations.

All provincial centres receive two channels of Mongolian national television; and all district centres can receive television, although only one-third can receive Mongolian television. At the beginning of 2005 the first legislative measures were taken to end state control, with the passing of the Law on Public Broadcasting, the provisions of which entered into force on 1 July 2005, creating an independent public service broadcaster to be known as Public Radio and Television. Also in 2005 it was planned to extend television coverage (UBS, TV-5, TV-9 and Channel 25) to outlying areas of Ulan Bator, including Partizan, Songino and Gachuurt, by installing additional local transmitters.

Public Radio and Television (ONRT): Khuvisgalyn Zam 3, Ulan Bator; f. 2006; replaced the government-run Directorate of Radio and Television Affairs; Chair. of National Council Khaidavyn Chilaajav; Dir-Gen. Sodnompilyn Myagmar; Dir of Public Radio Baarangiin Pürevdash; Dir of Public Television L. Ariunbat.

Radio

Mongolradio: Khuvisgalyn Zam 3, Ulan Bator; tel. (11) 323096; f. 1934; operates for 17 hours daily on three long-wave and one medium-wave frequency, and VHF; programmes in Mongolian (two)

MONGOLIA
Directory

and Kazakh; part of Public Radio and Television; Dir Baarangiin Pürevdash.

Voice of Mongolia: Ulan Bator; e-mail radiomongolia@magicnet.mn; external service of Mongolradio; broadcasts in Russian, Chinese, English and Japanese on short wave; Dir B. Narantuyaa.

AE and JAAG Studio: Amryn Gudamj 2, Ulan Bator (POB 20/126); tel. (11) 310631; fax (11) 326545; e-mail aejaag@magicnet.mn; f. 1996; broadcasts for 4.5–5 hours daily; CEO Z. Altai.

FM 98.9 Hi Fi (Hit First): Ulan Bator.

FM 99.3 Ineemseglel (Smile): Ulan Bator; Dir Kh. Ikhbayar.

FM 100.1 Elgen Nutag (Native Place): Orkhun Centre (East Entrance), 3 Ger District, Ulan Bator; tel. (11) 305388.

FM 100.5 Minii Mongol (My Mongolia): Central Palace of Culture, Sükhbaatar District, Ulan Bator; tel. (11) 323599.

FM 100.9 Khökh Tenger (Blue Sky Radio): Mongolian National Television Bldg, Chingeltei District, Ulan Bator; tel. (11) 320522; broadcasts for 12 hours Mon. to Sat. and shorter hours on Sun; short-wave transmitter on 4,850 kHz; Dir L. Amarzayaa.

FM 101.7 Radio Ulan Bator: Ulan Bator Bank Bldg, Baga Toiruu, Chingeltei District, Ulan Bator; tel. (11) 322503; fax (11) 322472; Dir U. Bulgan.

FM 102.1 Ekh Oron (Homeland): MPRP Bldg, Sükhbaatar District, Ulan Bator (POB 20A/65); tel. (11) 322503; fax (11) 322472; operated by the Open Information Foundation.

FM 102.5 Puls-Misheel (Pulse-Laugh): Central Palace of Culture, Ulan Bator; tel. 310485; f. 2001; est. by Mongolradio and Buryat Puls radio; 24 hour broadcasts in Russian; hourly news in Russian and Mongolian.

FM 103.1: Ulan Bator; BBC World Service Relay.

FM 103.6: Mongol Machine Concern Bldg, Khan-Uul District, Ulan Bator; TV-9's radio station.

FM 104: Enebishiin Örgön Chölöö 17, Bayangol District, Ulan Bator; tel. (11) 369081.

FM 104.5 Salkhi (Wind): Wind Entertainment Co, Mamba Datsan, Bayanzürkh District, Ulan Bator (CPOB 1042); tel. (11) 461212; fax (11) 458927; e-mail windfm@mongol.net.

FM 105 Dijital (Digital): Central Palace of Culture, Sükhbaatar District, Ulan Bator; tel. (11) 319589.

FM 105.5 Info Radio: Youth Palace, Ulan Bator; tel. (11) 329353; e-mail inforadio@mongol.net.

FM 106.6: Democratic Party Bldg, Chingisiin Örgön Chölöö, Ulan Bator; tel. (11) 329353; Voice of America news and information in Mongolian, English lessons and music.

FM 107: Central Palace of Culture, Sükhbaatar District, Ulan Bator; tel. (11) 312011.

FM 107.5 Shine Dolgion (New Wave): Namyanjugiin Gudamj 40, Bayanzürkh District, Ulan Bator; tel. and fax (11) 452444; e-mail fm107_5@yahoo.com; relays of Voice of America broadcasts in English and Russian, entertainment programmes.

There are seven long- and short-wave radio transmitters and 49 FM stations in 23 towns.

Television

Channel 25: AE and JAAG Studio, Mongol News Group, Ulan Bator; broadcasts entertainment in the evening from Tue. to Sun; 50 hours a week; Gen. Man. Ayuushiin Avirmed.

Khiimori Co: Bldg 3A, No. 2 Combined Clinical General Hospital, Ulan Bator; tel. (11) 458531; fax (11) 458569; e-mail khiimore@mongol.net; f. 1995; cable TV service provider.

Mongolteleviz (MNTV): Khuvisgalyn Zam 3, Ulan Bator (CPOB 365); tel. (11) 365774; fax (11) 326939; e-mail mrtv@magicnet.mn; f. 1967; daily morning and evening transmissions of locally-originated material relayed by land-line and via INTELSAT satellites; short news bulletins in English Mon., Wed. and Fri; state-owned; part of Public Radio and Television; Dir L. Ariunbat.

Sansar (STV): Ikh Toiruu 46, Ulan Bator; tel. (11) 313752; fax (11) 313770; e-mail sansarl@magicnet.mn; cable television equipment and services, reaches 220,000 households; f. 1994; Dir-Gen. A. Enkhbat.

TV-5: evening broadcasts from 6 p.m., repeated the following morning.

TV-9: f. 2003; broadcaster for the Ulan Bator area, general entertainment, with 20% religious content; Dir Ts. Enkhbat.

UBS (Ulan Bator Broadcasting System): Khuvsgalchdyn Gudamj 3, Ulan Bator (POB 24/983); tel. (11) 326429; fax (11) 368108; e-mail inter@ubs.mn; internet www.ubs.mn; f. 1992; operated by Ulan Bator City Government; evening broadcasts repeated the following morning except Mondays; Dir-Gen. L. Balkhjav.

Cable television companies (29 in total) operate in 19 towns. There are local television stations in Ulan Bator (three), Darkhan, Sükhbaatar and Baganuur. Chinese, Kazakh, Russian, German and French television services are among those that can also be received.

Finance

(cap. = capital; res = reserves; dep. = deposits; m. = million; brs = branches; amounts in tögrög, unless otherwise stated)

BANKING

Before 1990 the State Bank was the only bank in Mongolia, responsible for issuing currency, controlling foreign exchange and allocating credit. With the inauguration of market reforms in Mongolia in the early 1990s, the central and commercial functions of the State Bank were transferred to the newly created specialized commercial banks: the Bank of Capital Investment and Technological Innovation and the State Bank International. In May 1991 the State Bank became an independent central bank, and the operation of private, commercial banks was permitted. By the end of 1996 there were 15 commercial banks. The performance of these banks was poor, owing to high levels of non-performing loans, inexperienced management and weak supervision. Loss of confidence in the sector resulted in the implementation of extensive restructuring: in November 1996 amendments were made to banking legislation to improve the regulation and supervision of commercial banks, and two major insolvent banks were liquidated. Restructuring continued in the late 1990s and beyond.

Central Bank

Bank of Mongolia (Mongolbank): Baga Toiruu 9, Ulan Bator; tel. (11) 322169; fax (11) 311471; e-mail ad@mongolbank.mn; internet www.mongolbank.mn; f. 1924; est. as the State Bank of the Mongolian People's Republic; gross int. res US $251.4m. (June 2005); Gov. Ochirbatyn Chuluunbat.

Other Banks

Anod Bank: Juulchny Gudamj 18, Chingeltei District, Ulan Bator (CPOB 361); tel. (11) 315315; fax (11) 315431; e-mail info@anod.mn; internet www.anod.mn; cap. 12,247m., dep. 139,985m. (June 2005); Dir-Gen. D. Enkhtör; Exec. Dir E. Gür-Aranz.

Avtozam Bank (Motor Roads Bank): Bridge-Building Office, Ulan Bator; tel. (11) 381744; fax (11) 368094; f. 1990; cap. 95m.; Dir-Gen. Ts. Sangidorj.

Aziin Khöröngö Oruulaltyn Bank (Asian Capital Investment Bank): Khölög Group Bldg, Eastern entrance, 2nd Floor, Bayangol District, Ulan Bator; tel. (11) 367386; Dir-Gen. Tsedengiin Batbold.

Chinggis Khaan Bank: Chinggis Khaan Bank Bldg, 5th Sub-District, Bayangol District, Ulan Bator; tel. (11) 633105; fax (11) 633185; e-mail chkhbank@magicnet.mn; f. 2001; est. by Millennium Securities Management Ltd and Coral Sea Holdings Ltd (British Virgin Islands); cap. 39,372.m, dep. 73,051m. (Dec. 2004).

Erel Bank: Erel Co No 2 Bldg, Chingisiin Örgön Chölöö, Khan-Uul District, Ulan Bator (POB 36/500); tel. (11) 325650; fax (11) 343567; e-mail info@erelbank.mn; internet www.erelbank.mn; f. 1997; cap. 3,000m., res 243.6m., dep. 1636.9m. (Oct. 2003); Owner Badarchiin Erdenebat; CEO Gombojavyn Dorj.

Golomt Bank of Mongolia: Bodi Tower, Sükhbaataryn Talbai 3, 4th Floor, Ulan Bator; tel. (11) 311530; fax (11) 312307; e-mail mail@golomtbank.com; internet www.golomtbank.com; f. 1995; est. by Mongolian-Portuguese IBH Bodi International Co Ltd; cap.,805m., dep. 205,166m. (June 2005); Chair. Luvsanvandangiin Bold; Pres. and CEO Danzandorjiin Bayasgalan; 14 brs.

Interbank of Mongolia: Interbank Bldg, Usny Gudamj 4, Sükhbaatar District, Ulan Bator (CPOB 1130); tel. (11) 327403; fax (11) 328372; e-mail interbank@mongolnet.mn; internet www.interbank.mn; f. 2001; cap. 4,004., dep. 73,051m. (Dec. 2004); Gen. Dir Khorolsürengiin Chinbat.

Kapital Bank (Capital Bank): Sambugiin Gudamj 48, Chingeltei District, Ulan Bator; tel. (11) 312531; fax (11) 310833; e-mail center@capitalbank.mn; internet www.capitalbank.mn; cap. 4,000m., res 400m., dep 8,024m. (June 2004); Chair. Agvaanjamtsyn Ariunbold; Exec. Dir Enkhbazaryn Amgalan; 10 brs.

Kapitron Bank: Enkh Taivny Örgön Chölöö 11A, Ulan Bator; tel. (11) 327550; fax (11) 315635; e-mail info@capitronbank.mn; internet www.capitronbank.mn; f. 2001; cap. 4,223m., dep 34,726m. (Dec. 2004); Exec. Dir A. Mönkhbat.

Khadgalamjiin Bank (Savings Bank): Khudaldaany Gudamj 6, Ulan Bator; tel. (11) 310835; fax (11) 312049; e-mail savbank@magicnet.mn; internet www.savingsbank.mn; f. 1996; est. as Ardyn Bank; cap. 4,000.0m, res 1,243.7m., dep. 51,364.0m. (Dec. 2004); Dir G. Tserenpürev; 39 brs.

MONGOLIA

Khan Bank (KhAAN or Agricultural Bank): Enkhtaivny Örgön Chölöö, Ulan Bator; tel. (11) 457880; fax (11) 458670; e-mail info@khanbank.mn; internet www.khanbank.mn; f. 1991; purchased by H and S Securities (Japan) in Feb. 2003; cap. 14,307m., dep. 179,098m. (June 2005); CEO J. Peter Morrow; 380 brs.

Kredit Bank (Credit Bank): State Palace Bldg (east side), Sükhbaataryn Talbai, Sükhbaatar District, Ulan Bator; tel. (11) 319038; fax (11) 310853; e-mail creditbk@creditbank.mn; internet www.creditbank.mn; f. 1997; cap. 4,292m., res. 1,293m., dep. 2,828m. (June 2004); Exec. Dir B. Tsengel.

Mongol Shuudan Bank (Post Bank): Kholboochdyn Gudamj 4, Ulan Bator (CPOB 874); tel. (11) 310103; fax (11) 328501; e-mail post_bank@mongol.net; internet www.postbank.mn; f. 1993; cap. 7,469m., res 10,363m.dep. 46,964m. (June 2005); 100% in private ownership; Pres. and CEO D. Oyuunjargal.

Trade and Development Bank of Mongolia (Khudaldaa Khögjliin Bank): Khudaldaany Gudamj 6, Ulan Bator; tel. (11) 326289; fax (11) 311618; e-mail tdbank@tdbm.mn; internet www.tdbm.mn; f. 1991; carries out Mongolbank's foreign operations; cap. 15,876m., res. 8,383m., dep. 38,064m. (June 2004); 76% equity bought by Banca Commerciale (Lugano) and Gerald Metals (Stanford, CT), May 2002; CEO Chris Teunissen; Exec. Dir Siilegmaagiin Mönkhbat.

Ulaanbaatar City Bank: Sükhbaataryn Gudamj 16, Ulan Bator (POB 46/370); tel. (11) 319041; fax (11) 330508; e-mail center@ubcbank.mn; internet www.ubcbank.mn; f. 1998; est. by Capital City with assistance from the Bank of Taipei (Taiwan); cap. 5,349m., dep. 50,064m. (June 2005); Exec. Dir Dashdorjiin Badraa.

XacBank: Yörönkhii said Amaryn Gudamj, Sükhbaatar District, Ulan Bator (POB 46/721); tel. (11) 318185; fax (11) 328701; e-mail bank@xacbank.mn; internet www.xacbank.mn; f. 2001; cap. 5,391m., dep. 45,579m. (June 2005); Dir-Gen. Magvany Bold; Chair. Chuluuny Ganbold.

Zoos Bank: Baga Toiruu 7/1, Ulan Bator (POB 44/304); tel. (11) 312107; fax (11) 329537; e-mail secretary@zoosbank.mn; internet www.zoosbank.mn; f. 1999; cap. 5,612m., dep. 64,803m. (March 2005); Exec. Dir Sharavyn Chudanjii.

Banking Associations

Mongolian Banks Association: Ulan Bator; e-mail monba@mongolnet.mn; Exec. Dir Gotovyn Tserenpürev.

STOCK EXCHANGE

In mid-2005 there were 391 listed companies, of which 65 were wholly or partly state-owned. At the end of 2005 there were 363 listed companies valued at 55,700m. tögrög, almost double the 2004 figure. In 2005 25.9m. shares, worth 2,650m. tögrög, were traded. The largest number of shares traded was 336,000, in the machinery importer Tekhnikimport. The biggest growth in share value was 850 tögrög, in the distillers Spirt Bal Buram.

Stock Exchange: Sükhbaataryn Talbai 2, Ulan Bator; tel. (11) 310501; fax (11) 325170; e-mail mse@mongol.net; internet www.mse.mn; f. 1991; Dir Rentsengiin Sodkhüü.

INSURANCE

Ard Daatgal: Tavan Bogd Plaza, Amaryn Gudamj 1, Ulan Bator; tel. (11) 456103; fax (11) 330083; est. with Omni Whittington Guernsey.

Bodi Daatgal Co: Bodi Tower, Sükhbaataryn Talbai, Ulan Bator; tel. (11) 323444; fax (11) 326535; e-mail enbodi@bodiinsurance.mn; internet www.bodiinsurance.mn; Dir L. Boldkhuyag.

Ganzam Insurance: Mongolian Railways (MTZ), Ulan Bator; tel. and fax (21) 942631; e-mail gzd@mtz.mn.

Mongol Ündesnii Daatgal (National Insurance and Reinsurance Co): Sööliin Gudamj 15, Ulan Bator; tel. (11) 313697; fax (11) 310347; e-mail insurance@mongoldaatgal.mn; internet www.mongoldaatgal.mn; f. 1934; sold Dec. 2003 to consortium formed by Angara-SKB and Chinggis Khan Bank; Chair. and CEO Badarchiin Enkhbat; Snr Vice-Pres. Chimidyn Battsogt.

Mongolyn Daatgal Grupp (Mongolian Insurance Group): Royal Centre, Chingisiin Örgön Chölöö 5, Sükhbaatar District, Ulan Bator; tel. (11) 330130; fax (11) 330132; e-mail mig@magicnet.mn; internet www.mig.mn.

Ochir Undraa Daatgal: Skytel Co Bldg, Chingisiin Örgön Chölöö 5, Sükhbaatar District, Ulan Bator; tel. (11) 324248; fax (11) 326466; e-mail insurance@ochir-undraa.com; internet www.ochir-undraa.com.

Trade and Industry

GOVERNMENT AGENCIES

Labour Co-ordination Directorate: Khuvisgalchdyn Gudamj 14, Ulan Bator; tel. and fax (11) 327906; Dir D. Jantsan.

Minerals and Petroleum Directorate: Üildverchnii Gudamj, Ulan Bator (POB 37/8); tel. (11) 631208; e-mail petromon@magicnet.mn; fmrly Mongol Gazryn Tos (Petroleum Authority of Mongolia) and Mineral Resources Authority—amalgamated Dec. 2004; Dir Lu. Bold.

State Industry and Trade Control Service: Barilgachdyn Talbai, Ulan Bator (POB 38/66); tel. and fax (11) 328049; e-mail chalkhaajavd@mongolnet.mn; f. 2000; enforces laws and regulations relating to trade and industry, services, consumer rights, and geology and mining; Dir Dambadarjaagiin Chalkhaajav.

State Property Committee: Government Bldg 4, Ulan Bator; tel. (11) 312460; fax (11) 312798; internet odmaa@spc.gov.mn; supervision and privatization of state property; Chair. Dulamyn Sugar.

DEVELOPMENT ORGANIZATIONS

Economics and Market Research Center: Government Bldg 1, J. Sambuugiin Gudamj 11, Ulan Bator; tel. (11) 324258; fax (11) 324620; e-mail emrc@mongolchamber.mn; internet www.mongolchamber.mn; Dir J. Bozkhüükhen.

Foreign Investment and Foreign Trade Agency (FIFTA): Government Bldg 1, J. Sambuugiin Gudamj 11, Ulan Bator; tel. (11) 326040; fax (11) 324076; e-mail fifta@investnet.mn; internet www.investmongolia.com; Chair. Baasankhüügiin Ganzorig.

Mongolian Business Development Agency: Yörönkhii Said Amaryn Gudamj, Ulan Bator (CPOB 458); tel. (11) 311094; fax (11) 311092; e-mail mbda@mongol.net; internet www.mbda-mongolia.org; f. 1994; Gen. Man. D. Bayarbat.

Mongolian Development Research Centre: Rm 50, Baga Toiruu 13, Chingeltei District, Ulan Bator (POB 20A/63); tel. and fax (11) 315686; internet www.mdrc.mn; f. 1998; Chair. Tsedendambyn Batbayar.

CHAMBERS OF COMMERCE

Central Asian Chamber of Commerce: Ulan Bator (POB 44/470); tel. (11) 38970; fax (11) 311757; Chair. G. Tömörmönkh.

Junior Chamber of Commerce: Youth Union Bldg, Ulan Bator; tel. (11) 328694; Chair Natsagdorj.

Mongolian National Chamber of Commerce and Industry: Sambuugiin Gudamj 11, Ulan Bator; tel. (11) 325374; fax (11) 324620; e-mail chamber@mongolchamber.mn; internet www.mongolchamber.mn; f. 1960; responsible for establishing economic and trading relations, contacts between trade and industrial organizations, both at home and abroad, and for generating foreign trade; organizes commodity inspection, press information, and international exhbns and fairs at home and abroad; registration of trademarks and patents; issues certificates of origin and of quality; Sec. Gen. Enebishiin Oyuuntegsh; Chair. and CEO Sambuugiin Demberel.

INDUSTRIAL AND TRADE ASSOCIATIONS

Association of Exporters of Livestock Raw Materials and Semi-Processed Products: Ulan Bator; Exec. Dir B. Törmönkh.

Association of Mongolian Sewn Goods and Knitwear Products Manufacturers: Ulan Bator; Pres. N. Dash-Ölzii.

Mongolian Association of Container and Packaging Makers and Users: Ulan Bator; Pres. Dembereliin Otgonbaatar.

Mongolian Farmers and Flour Producers' Association: Agro-Pro Business Centre, 19th Sub-District, Bayangol District, Ulan Bator; tel. (11) 300114; fax (11) 362875; e-mail agropro@magicnet.mn; f. 1997; research and quality inspection services in domestic farming and flour industry; Pres. Sharavyn Gungaadorj.

Mongolian Foodstuffs Traders' Association: Ulan Bator; Exec. Dir L. Damdinsüren.

Mongolian Franchising Council of the Mongolian National Chamber of Commerce and Industry: Ulan Bator; tel. (11) 327178; fax (11) 324620; e-mail tecd@mongolchamber.mn; Pres. Baataryn Chadraa.

Mongolian Institute of Internal Auditors: Ulan Bator; tel. (11) 312773; e-mail miia@bizcon.mn; internet www.bizcon.mn/miia; Pres. L. Otgonbayar.

Mongolian Marketing Association: Ulan Bator; Pres. D. Dagvadorj.

Mongolian National Industrialists' Association: Ulan Bator; Pres. Namjaagiin Dashzeveg.

MONGOLIA

Mongolian National Mining Association: Sky Plaza Centre, Olimpiin Gudamj 14, Ulan Bator (POB 46/910); tel. (11) 314877; fax (11) 314877; e-mail mongma@mobinet.mn; internet www.owc.org.mn/monnma; f. 1994; provides members of the mining sector with legal protection, and reflects their views in Government mining policy and mineral sector development; Pres. DUGARYN JARGALSAIKHAN; Exec. Dir NAMGARYN ALGAA.

Mongolian PR Association: Ulan Bator; Chair. D. BOLDKHUYAG.

Mongolian Printing Works Association: Ulan Bator; Pres. G. KHAVCHUUR.

Mongolian Wool and Cashmere Association: Ulan Bator; Pres. D. GANKHUYAG.

Mongolian Wool and Cashmere Federation: Khan-Uul District, Ulan Bator; tel. (11) 341871; fax (11) 342814; Pres. G. YONDONSAMBUU.

Petroleum Gas Association: Ulan Bator; f. 2005; Pres. SH. GUNGAADORJ.

EMPLOYERS' ORGANIZATIONS

Employers' and Owners' United Association: Rm 401, 4th Fl., Mongolian Youth Association 'B' Bldg, Ulan Bator; tel. (11) 326513; Exec. Dir. B. SEMBEEJAV.

Federation of Professional Business Women of Mongolia: Ulan Bator; tel. and fax (11) 315638; e-mail mbpw@mongolnet.mn; f. 1992; provides education, training, and opportunities for women to achieve economic independence, and the running of businesses; Pres. OCHIRBATYN ZAYAA; 7,000 mems, 14 brs.

Immovable Property (Real Estate) Business Managers' Association: Ulan Bator; Pres. J. BYAMBADORJ.

Mongolian Management Association: Ulan Bator; Chair. Exec. Council DAGVADORJIIN TSERENDORJ.

Mongolian United Employers' Association: Ulan Bator; f. 1990; fmrly Private Industry Owners' Association; 39 mems; Pres. LUVSANBALDANGIIN NYAMSAMBUU.

Private Business Owners' Association: Ulan Bator; Pres. T. NYAMDORJ.

Private Employers' Association: Ulan Bator; Pres. O. NATSAGDORJ.

UTILITIES

Electricity

TsTS: Ulan Bator; tel. (11) 41294; supervision of electric power network in Ulan Bator; Exec. Dir D. BYAMBA-OCHIR.

Water

Dulaany Süljee Co: Ulan Bator; tel. (11) 343047; e-mail engineer@dhc.mn; internet www.dhc.mn; supervision of hot water district heating network in Ulan Bator; Dir D. BYAMBA-OCHIR.

USAG: Khökh Tengeriin Gudamj 5, Ulan Bator; tel. (11) 455055; fax (11) 450120; e-mail usag@magicnet.mn; supervision of water supply network in Ulan Bator; Chair. OSORYN ERDENEBAATAR.

IMPORT AND EXPORT ORGANIZATIONS

Agrotekhimpeks: Ulan Bator; imports agricultural machinery and implements, seed, fertilizer, veterinary medicines and irrigation equipment.

Altjin: Ulan Bator; company importing and distributing oil and oil products and also running distilleries, a spin-off from APU; Dir G. ALTAN.

Arisimpex: Ulan Bator; tel. (11) 343007; fax (11) 343008; exports hides and skins, fur and leather goods; imports machinery, chemicals and accessories for leather, fur and shoe industries; Pres. A. TSERENBALJID.

Avtoimpeks: Ulan Bator; f. 1934; state-owned; international trader in motor vehicles; Exec. Dir S. CHULUUNBAT.

Barter and Border: Khuvisgalchdyn Örgön Chölöö, Ulan Bator; tel. (11) 324848; barter and border trade operations.

Böönii Khudaldaa: Songinokhairkhan District, Ulan Bator; wholesale trader; privately-owned; Dir-Gen. OCHBADRAKHYN BALJINNYAM.

Khorshoololimpeks: Tolgoit, Ulan Bator (CPOB 262); tel. (11) 332926; fax (11) 331128; f. 1964; exports sub-standard skins, hides, wool and furs, handicrafts and finished products; imports equipment and materials for housing, and for clothing and leather goods; Dir L. ÖLZIIBUYAN.

Kompleksimport: Enkh Taivny Gudamj 7, Ulan Bator; tel. and fax (11) 382718; f. 1963; imports consumer goods, foodstuffs, sets of equipment and turnkey projects; training of Mongolians abroad; state-owned pending planned privatization; cap. 3,500m. tögrög.

Makhimpeks: 4th Sub-District, Songinokhairkhan District, Ulan Bator; tel. (11) 63247; fax (11) 632517; e-mail makhimpex@mongol.net; f. 1946; abattoir, meat processing, canning, meat imports and exports; 51% share privatized in 1999; cap. 7,800m. tögrög; Dir H. BATTULGA.

Materialimpex: Teeverchdiin Gudamj, Ulan Bator; tel. (11) 365143; fax (11) 367904; e-mail matimpex@magicnet.mn; f. 1957; exports cashmere, wool products, animal skins; imports glass, roofing material, dyes, sanitary ware, metals and metalware, wallpaper, bitumen, wall and floor tiles; partially privatized Feb. 1999, but most shares still state-owned; Gen. Dir B. ZORIG; 126 employees.

Metallimpeks (Metalimpex): Ulan Bator; Dir D. GANBAT.

Mongoleksport Co Ltd: Government Bldg 7, 8th Floor, Erkh Chölöönii Talbai, Ulan Bator; tel. (11) 329234; fax (11) 324848; exports wool, hair, cashmere, mining products, antler, skins and hides; Dir-Gen. D. CHIMEDDAMBAA.

Mongolemimpex: Ikh Toiruu 39, Ulan Bator; tel. (11) 323961; fax (11) 323877; e-mail moemim@magicnet.mn; internet www.mongolemimpex.mon; procurement and distribution to hospitals and pharmacies of drugs and surgical appliances; Dir-Gen. CHOIJAMTSYN GOTOV.

Mongolimpeks: Khuvisgalchdyn Örgön Chölöö, Ulan Bator; tel. (11) 326081; exports cashmere, camels' wool, hair, fur, casings, powdered blood and horn, antler, wheat gluten, alcoholic drinks, cashmere and camels' wool knitwear, blankets, copper concentrate, souvenirs, stamps and coins; imports light and mining industry machinery, scientific instruments, chemicals, pharmaceuticals and consumer goods; state-owned; Dir-Gen. DORJPALAMYN DÖKHÖMBAYAR.

Mongol Safari Co: Ulan Bator; tel. (11) 360267; fax (11) 360067; e-mail monsafari@magicnet.mn; exports hunting products; imports hunting equipment and technology; organizes hunting and trekking tours; Dir-Gen. U. BUYANDELGER.

Monnoos: Ulan Bator (POB 36/450); tel. (11) 343201; fax (11) 342591; e-mail monnoos@mongolnet.mn; wool trade enterprise; Dir SANJIIN BAT-OYUUN.

Monos Cosmetics: Sonsgolongiin Toiruu 5, 20th Sub-District, Songinokhairkhan District, Ulan Bator (POB 37/62); tel. and fax (11) 633257; e-mail info@monoscosmetics.mn; internet www.monoscosmetics.mn; f. 1990; production, export and import of cosmetics; Chair. and CEO BALDANDORJIIN ERDENEKHISHIG; 90 employees.

Monospharma Co Ltd: Chingünjavyn gudamj 9, 2nd Sub-District, Bayangol District, Ulan Bator; tel. and fax (11) 361419; e-mail monospharma@mongol.net; f. 1990; production, export and import of medicine, medical equipment and health food; Dir-Gen. LUVSANGIIN KHÜRELBAATAR; 280 employees.

Noosimpeks: Ulan Bator; tel. (11) 342611; fax (11) 343057; exports scoured sheep's wool, yarn, carpets, fabrics, blankets, mohair and felt boots; imports machinery and chemicals for wool industry.

Nüürs: Ulan Bator; tel. (11) 327428; exports and imports in coal-mining field; Man. D. DÜGERJAV.

Packaging: Tolgoit, Ulan Bator; tel. (11) 31053; exports raw materials of agricultural origin, sawn timber, consumer goods, unused spare parts and equipment, and non-ferrous scrap; imports machinery and materials for packaging industry, and consumer goods.

Petrovis: Ulan Bator; oil products importer and distributor; in February 2004 acquired the 80% state-owned shares in the country's biggest distributor NIK (Neft Import Kontsern) for $8.5m; Exec. Dir J. OYUUNGEREL.

Raznoimpeks: 3rd Sub-District, Bayangol District, Ulan Bator; tel. (11) 329465; fax (11) 329901; f. 1933; exports wool, cashmere, hides, canned meat, powdered bone, alcoholic drinks, macaroni and confectionery; imports cotton and woollen fabrics, silk, knitwear, shoes, fresh and canned fruit, vegetables, tea, milk powder, acids, paints, safety equipment, protective clothing, printing and packaging paper; state-owned pending planned privatization; cap. 6,100m. tögrög; Exec. Dir TS. BAT-ENKH.

TAS Petroleum: Ulan Bator; distribution division of TAS Group; Dir R. PÜREVSÜREN.

Tekhnikimport: Ulan Bator; tel. (11) 32336; imports machinery, instruments and spare parts for light, food, wood, building, power and mining industries, road-building and communications; state-owned; Dir-Gen. G. GANTULGA.

Tüshig Trade Co Ltd: Enkh Taivny Örgön Chölöö, Ulan Bator (POB 44/481); tel. (11) 314062; fax (11) 314052; e-mail d.ganbaatar@mongol.net; exports sheep and camel wool, and cashmere goods; imports machinery for small enterprises, foodstuffs and consumer goods; Dir-Gen. D. GANBAATAR.

MONGOLIA   *Directory*

CO-OPERATIVES

Association of Private Herders' Co-operatives: Ulan Bator (POB 21/787); tel. (11) 633601; fax (11) 325935; e-mail mongolherder@magicnet.mn; f. 1991; Pres. R. ERDENE; Exec. Dir Ts. MYAGMAR-OCHIR.

Central Association of Consumer Co-operatives: Ulan Bator; tel. and fax (11) 329025; f. 1990; wholesale and retail trade; exports animal raw materials; imports foodstuffs and consumer goods; Chair. G. MYANGANBAYAR.

Mongolian United Association of Savings and Credit Co-operatives: Ulan Bator; Pres. YO. TSOOMOO.

Mongolian Co-operatives Development Centre: Ulan Bator; Dir DANZANGIIN RADNAARAGCHAA.

National Association of Mongolian Agricultural Co-operative Members: Enkhtayvny Örgön Chölöö, 18 A/1, Ulan Bator; tel. (11) 453535; fax (11) 458899; e-mail namac63@mongol.net; f. 1992.

Union of Mongolian Production and Services Co-operatives: Bldg 16, II-40,000, 3rd Sub-District, Chingeltei District, Ulan Bator (POB 46/470); tel. (11) 327583; fax (11) 328446; e-mail umpscoop@hotmail.com; f. 1990; Pres. SAMDANY ENKHTUYAA.

TRADE UNIONS

Confederation of Mongolian Trade Unions: Sükhbaataryn Talbai 3, Ulan Bator; tel. (11) 327253; fax (11) 322128; brs throughout the country; Chair. NYAMJAVYN SODNOMDORJ; International Relations Adviser Ts. NATSAGDORJ.

Transport

MTT (Mongol Transport Team): Ulan Bator (POB 21/582); tel. (11) 689000; fax (11) 684953; e-mail mtt@mtteam.mn; internet www.mtteam.mn; international freight forwarding by air, sea, rail and road; offices in Beijing, Berlin, Moscow and Prague.

Tuushin Co Ltd: Yörönkhii Said Amaryn Gudamj 2, Ulan Bator; tel. and fax (11) 325909; e-mail tuushin@magicnet.mn; f. 1990; international freight forwarders; transport and forwarding policy and services, warehousing, customs agent; tourism; offices in Beijing, Moscow and Prague; Dir-Gen. N. ZORIGT.

RAILWAYS

In 2004 the total track length was 2,083km, of which 1,815km was the main-line track. In 1990 the system carried 2.6m. passengers and 14.5m. tons of freight (about 70% of total freight traffic). However, traffic by rail later declined, owing to fuel shortages; in 1991 rail freight carriage was 10.3m. tons, falling to 8.6m. tons in 1992. In 2003 the railways carried 3.9m. passengers and 12.4m. tons of freight (about 70% of all freight carriage). Freight turnover in 2003 was 7,253.3m. ton/km, of which 5,470.7m. ton/km was international traffic, including 4,041.7 ton/km of transit freight traffic. Passengers carried on international routes totalled 141,100, while 3.8m. passengers were carried on local routes.

Ulan Bator Railway: Ulan Bator (CPOB 376); tel. (21) 944409; fax (11) 328360; e-mail noms@mtz.mn; internet www.mtz.mn; f. 1949; joint-stock co with Russian Federation; Dir VASILII VASILYEVICH MAGDEI; Chair. DAVAAGIIN GANBOLD.

External Lines: from the Russian frontier at Naushki/Sükhbaatar (connecting with the Trans-Siberian Railway) to Ulan Bator and on to the Chinese frontier at Zamyn-Üüd/Erenhot, connecting with Beijing (total length 1,110 km).

Branches: from Darkhan to Sharyn Gol coalfield (length 63 km); branch from Salkhit near Darkhan, westwards to Erdenet (Erdenet-iin-ovoo open-cast copper mine) in Bulgan Province (164 km); from Bagakhangai to Baganuur coal-mine, south-east of Ulan Bator (96 km); from Khar Airag to Bor-Öndör fluorspar mines (60 km); from Sainshand to Züünbayan oilfield (63 km).

Eastern Railway, linking Mongolia with the Trans-Siberian and Chita via Borzya; from the Russian frontier at Solovyevsk to Choibalsan (238 km), with branch from Chingis Dalan to Mardai uranium mine near Dashbalbar (110 km), possibly inactive.

IFFC (International Freight-forwarding Centre of Mongolian Railways): Mongolian Railway Headquarters, Zamchyn Gudamj 1, Bayangol District, Ulan Bator (CPOB 376); tel. (11) 312509; fax (11) 313165; e-mail iffc@railcom.mn; internet www.iffc.mn; international freight forwarding.

Mongolian Express Co: Khos Jürj Bldg, Chingisiin Örgön Chölöö, Ulan Bator; tel. (11) 318329; fax (11) 318125; e-mail info@monex.mn; internet www.monex.mn; international dispatching agency; Dir Gen. D. ENKHBAT.

Mongoltrans: Khan-Uul District, Ulan Bator (POB 21/373); tel. (11) 682100; fax (11) 687517; e-mail mtc@mongoltrans.mn; internet www.mongoltrans.mn; rail freight forwarding; offices in Beijing and Moscow; Dir-Gen. B. NOROLKHOOSUREN.

Progresstrans: Ulan Bator (POB 26/345); tel. (11) 633992; fax (11) 631924; e-mail ptrans@magicnet.mn; internet www.progresstrans.com; international despatch and freight forwarding.

ROADS

Main roads link Ulan Bator with the Chinese frontier at Zamyn üüd/Erenhot and with the Russian frontier at Altanbulag/Kyakhta. A road from Chita in Russia crosses the frontier in the east at Mangut/Onon (Ölzii) and branches for Choibalsan and Öndörkhaan. In the west and north-west, roads from Biisk and Irkutsk in Russia go to Tsagaannuur, Bayan-Ölgii aimag, and Khankh, on Lake Khövsgöl, respectively. The total length of the road network was 45,000 km in 2005, of which asphalted roads comprised 1,500 km (incl. 400 km in Ulan Bator), gravel roads comprised 1,400 km, and improved earth roads comprised 1,300 km. The first section of a hard-surfaced road between Ulan Bator and Bayankhongor was completed in 1975. The road from Darkhan to Erdenet was also surfaced. Construction has been focused on the routes from Ulan Bator southwards to Choir and Sainshand and eastward to Öndörkhaan. In 2005 a further 389 km of hard-topped road was built, and 747 km of gravel road. There was concern that the asphalted surfaces of some new hard-topped roads were not thick enough to take the weight of heavy lorry traffic. Mongolia divides its road system into state-grade and country-grade roads. State-grade roads (of which there were 11,000 km in 2005) run from Ulan Bator to provincial centres and from provincial centres to the border. Country-grade roads account for the remaining roads, but they are mostly rough cross-country tracks.

To mark the millennium, the Government decided to construct a new east–west road, linking the Chinese and Russian border regions via Ölgii, Lake Khar Us, Zavkhan and Arkhangai provinces, Dashinchilen, Lün, Ulan Bator, Nalaikh, Baganuur, Öndörkhaan and Sümber. Construction was expected to take about 10 years, but because of the cost, the road was not expected to be surfaced for the whole length.

There are bus services in Ulan Bator and other large towns, and road haulage services throughout the country on the basis of motor transport depots, mostly situated in provincial centres. However, in some years services have been truncated, owing to fuel shortages.

Tav Co: 20th Sub-District, Songinokhairkhan District, Ulan Bator; tel. (11) 632741; fax (11) 632737; e-mail avtotav@mongol.net; road freight transport from Ulan Bator to the Mongolian provinces.

CIVIL AVIATION

Civil aviation in Mongolia, including the provision of air traffic control and airport management, is the responsibility of the Main Directorate of Civil Aviation, which provides air traffic and airport management services. It also supervises the Mongolian national airline (MIAT) and smaller operators such as Khangarid and Tengeriin Ulaach, which operate local flights. There are scheduled services to Ulan Bator (Buyant-Ukhaa) by Aeroflot (Russia) and Air China. In 2005 Mongolian airlines carried 318,100 passengers on international routes and internal routes. Ulan Bator's Buyant-Ukhaa Airport was renamed Chingis Khan International in December 2005.

Director-General of Civil Aviation: MANJIIN DAGVA.

Aero Mongolia Co Ltd: Buyant-Ukhaa Airport, Ulan Bator (POB 34/105); tel. 95154188; fax (11) 379616; e-mail management@aeromongolia.mn; internet www.aeromongolia.mn; f. 2001; began operations June 2003, scheduled international flights to Irkutsk and Hohhot and scheduled internal flights to five provincial centres and Juulchin's South Gobi tourist camp by Fokker-50 aircraft; twice-weekly flights by Fokker-100 to the Republic of Korea inaugurated in Feb. 2006; Dir Ts. LKHAGVAA.

Blue Sky Aviation: Door 2, Apt S-61, 1st Sub-District, Sukhbaatar District, Ulan Bator; tel. (11) 312085; fax (11) 322857; e-mail bsa@maf-europe.org; internet www.blueskyaviation.mn; jt venture of Mission Aviation Fellowship and Exodus International; operates charter flights and medical emergency services; f. 1999; Dir NIRI LID; Operations Man. JAN TORE FOLDØY.

Central Mongolia Airways: Ulan Bator (POB 46/202); tel. and fax (11) 318480; e-mail cma@jetmongol.com; internet www.cma.mn; 3 Mi-8 helicopters for tourist travel.

Eznis (Easiness) Airways: Newcom Group, Ulan Bator; f. 2006; operates two SAAB 340B aircraft on internal routes.

Khangarid: Room 210, MPRP Bldg, Baga Toiruu 37/1, Ulan Bator; tel. (11) 320138; fax (11) 311333; e-mail hangard_air_co@magicnet.mn; domestic and international passenger and freight services; Dir L. SERGELEN.

Mongolian Civil Air Transport (MIAT): MIAT Bldg, Buyant-Ukhaa, Ulan Bator; tel. (11) 379935; fax (11) 379919; e-mail contact@

miat.com; internet www.miat.com; f. 1956; scheduled services to Moscow, Irkutsk, Beijing, Seoul, Osaka, Berlin, Hohhot, and to some Mongolian provincial centres; carried 303,500 passengers in 2004; Pres. LUTYN SANDAG; Exec. Dir BALTAVYN TSOGOO.

Tengeriin Ulaach (Sky Horse Aviation): Buyant-Ukhaa, Khan-Uul District, Ulan Bator (POB 34/17); tel. (11) 983043; fax (11) 379765; e-mail skyhorsenew@mbox.mn; internal transport for tourists and businesspeople; Dir L. TÖMÖR.

Trans-Ölgii: Ölgii, Bayan-Ölgii Province; f. 2006; operates one leased An-24 on Ölgii–Ulan Bator route twice a week.

Tourism

A foreign tourist service bureau was established in 1954, but tourism is not very developed. In 2003 Mongolia had 132 tourist camps with 6,400 beds and 260 hotels with 7,000 beds. By 2005 the numbers of camps and hotels had increased to around 160 and 300 respectively. Of the 30 or more hotels in Ulan Bator, all but four are relatively small, and in the peak summer season there is a shortage of rooms. The outlying tourist centres (Terelj, South Gobi, Öndör-Dov and Khujirt) have basic facilities. The country's main attractions are its scenery, wildlife and historical relics. According to the Soros Foundation, there were 344,635 foreign visitors to Mongolia in 2005, of whom 234,352 described the purpose of their visit as leisure or holiday. Tourism revenue in 2004 reportedly amounted to US $181m.

Juulchin Tourism Corporation of Mongolia: Chingis Khaany Örgön Chölöö 5B, Ulan Bator; tel. (11) 328428; fax (11) 320246; e-mail juulchin@mongol.net; internet www.mongoljuulchin.mn; f. 1954; offices in Berlin, New Jersey, Beijing, Tokyo, Osaka and Seoul; tours, trekking, safaris, jeep tours, expeditions; Exec. Dir S. NERGÜI.

Mongolian Tourism Association: 3/F, Rm 318, Building of the Mongolian Trade Unions Confederation, Sükhbaataryn Talbai, Ulan Bator; tel. (11) 327820; fax (11) 323026; e-mail info@travelmongolia.org; internet www.travelmongolia.org; Pres. BAYARSAIKHANY TSEVELMAA.

MOROCCO

Introductory Survey

Location, Climate, Language, Religion, Flag, Capital

The Kingdom of Morocco is situated in the extreme north-west of Africa. It has a long coastline on the shores of the Atlantic Ocean and, east of the Strait of Gibraltar, on the Mediterranean Sea, facing southern Spain. Morocco's eastern frontier is with Algeria, while to the south lies the disputed territory of Western Sahara (under Moroccan occupation), which has a lengthy Atlantic coastline and borders Mauritania to the east and south. Morocco's climate is semi-tropical. It is warm and sunny on the coast, while the plains of the interior are intensely hot in summer. Average temperatures are 27°C (81°F) in summer and 7°C (45°F) in winter for Rabat, and 38°C (101°F) and 4°C (40°F), respectively, for Marrakesh. The rainy season in the north is from November to April. The official language is Arabic, but a large minority speak Berber. Spanish is widely spoken in the northern regions, and French in the rest of Morocco. The established religion is Islam, and most of the country's inhabitants are Muslims. There are small minorities of Christians and Jews. The national flag (proportions 2 by 3) is red, with a green pentagram (intersecting lines in the form of a five-pointed star), known as 'Solomon's Seal', in the centre. The capital is Rabat.

Recent History

In 1912, under the terms of the Treaty of Fez, most of Morocco became a French protectorate, while a smaller Spanish protectorate was instituted in the north and far south of the country. Spain also retained control of Spanish Sahara (now Western Sahara), and Tangier became an international zone in 1923. A nationalist movement developed in Morocco during the 1930s and 1940s, led by the Istiqlal (Independence) grouping, and on 2 March 1956 the French protectorate achieved independence as the Sultanate of Morocco. Sultan Muhammad V, who had reigned since 1927 (although he had been temporarily removed from office by the French authorities between 1953 and 1955), became the first Head of State. The northern zone of the Spanish protectorate joined the new state in April 1956, and Tangier's international status was abolished in October. The southern zone of the Spanish protectorate was ceded to Morocco in 1958, but no agreement was reached on the enclaves of Ceuta and Melilla, in the north, the Ifni region in the south, or the Saharan territories to the south of Morocco, which all remained under Spanish control. The Sultan was restyled King of Morocco in August 1957, and became Prime Minister in May 1960. He died in February 1961, and was succeeded by his son, Moulay Hassan, who took the title of Hassan II.

Elections to Morocco's first House of Representatives took place in May 1963, and six months later King Hassan relinquished the post of Prime Minister. In June 1965, however, increasing political fragmentation prompted Hassan to declare a 'state of exception', and to resume full legislative and executive powers. The emergency provisions remained in force until July 1970, when a new Constitution was approved. Elections in the following month resulted in a pro-Government majority in the new Majlis an-Nuab (Chamber of Representatives).

In July 1971 an attempted *coup d'état* was suppressed by forces loyal to the King. Among those subsequently arrested were numerous members of the left-wing Union nationale des forces populaires (UNFP), five of whom were sentenced to death. Although a revised Constitution was approved in March 1972 by popular referendum, a general election did not take place until June 1977. Two-thirds of the deputies in the Chamber of Representatives were directly elected, the remainder being elected by local government councils, professional associations and labour organizations. Supporters of the King's policies won a majority of seats in the new legislature. A Government of national unity was formed, including opposition representatives from Istiqlal and the Mouvement populaire (MP) in addition to the pro-monarchist independents.

In October 1981, when it was announced that the term of office of the Chamber of Representatives was to be extended from four to six years, all 14 deputies belonging to the Union socialiste des forces populaires (USFP) withdrew from the assembly. Elections to the legislature were postponed and an interim Government of national unity was appointed, headed by Muhammad Karim Lamrani (Prime Minister in 1971–72). The new Government included members of the six main political parties: Istiqlal, the MP, the Parti national démocrate (PND), the Rassemblement national des indépendants (RNI), the Union constitutionnelle (UC) and the USFP. The postponed legislative elections took place in September and October 1984. Despite significant gains by the USFP, the Chamber of Representatives was again dominated by the centre-right parties. A new Cabinet, appointed in April 1985, included members of the MP, the PND, the RNI and the UC. Lamrani resigned in September 1986, on the grounds of ill health, and was replaced by Az ad-Dine Laraki (hitherto Deputy Prime Minister and Minister of National Education).

In March 1992 King Hassan announced that the Constitution was to be revised and submitted for approval in a national referendum, in preparation for legislative elections (which had been postponed since 1990, pending settlement of the Western Sahara dispute). The King indicated in July that the elections would take place in November, and that voting would be extended to include Western Sahara—irrespective of the UN's progress in organizing a referendum on the territory's status (see below). In August the King dissolved the Government, and named Lamrani as Prime Minister in an interim, non-partisan Government. According to official results, the revised Constitution was overwhelmingly endorsed by 99.96% of voters in the national referendum, which was held in September; approval was officially reported to be unanimous in the major cities and in three of the four provinces of Western Sahara. Under the terms of the new Constitution, the King would retain strong executive powers, including the right to appoint the Prime Minister, although government members would henceforth be nominated by the premier. The Government would be required to reflect the composition of the Chamber of Representatives, and was obliged to submit its legislative programme for the Chamber's approval; new legislation would automatically be promulgated one month after having been endorsed by parliament, regardless of whether royal assent had been received. Provision was also made for the establishment of a Constitutional Council and of an Economic and Social Council, and guarantees of human rights were enshrined in the document.

Legislative elections eventually took place on 25 June 1993. Parties of the Bloc démocratique—grouping Istiqlal, the USFP, the Parti du progrès et du socialisme (PPS), the Organisation de l'action démocratique et populaire (OADP) and the UNFP—won a combined total of 99 of the 222 directly elective seats in the enlarged chamber. (Within the Bloc, the USFP won 48 seats and Istiqlal 43.) The MP won 33 seats, the RNI 28 and the UC 27. The indirect election (by an electoral college) of the remaining 111 members of the Chamber, which followed on 17 September, was less favourable to the Bloc démocratique, which won only 21 further seats. Of the 333 seats in the Chamber, the USFP now controlled 56, the UC 54, Istiqlal 52, the MP 51 and the RNI 41. In November the King reappointed Lamrani as premier. The new Government comprised technocrats and independents, and did not include any representatives of the parties that had contested the legislative elections. (By-elections took place in April 1994 in 14 constituencies—in all but one of which the Constitutional Council had annulled results of the previous year's legislative elections.)

In May 1994 Hassan replaced Lamrani with Abd al-Latif Filali, hitherto Minister of State for Foreign Affairs and Co-operation. Although the new Prime Minister held consultations with the political groupings represented in parliament, the composition of the new Government (in which he retained the foreign affairs portfolio) was effectively unchanged. In July the King appealed to all political parties to participate in a government of national unity, and in October he announced his intention to select a premier from the ranks of the opposition. However, negotiations on the formation of a coalition government failed, apparently owing to the Bloc démocratique's refusal to join an administration in which Driss Basri (a long-serving government member and close associate of the King) remained as Minister of the Interior and Information, and in January 1995

Hassan instructed Filali to form a new cabinet. The interior and information portfolios, were, notably, separated in the new Government: Basri remained Minister of the Interior, while Driss Alaoui M'Daghri took responsibility for the restyled Ministry of Communications.

Muhammad Basri, a prominent opposition figure (sentenced to death *in absentia* in 1974) and founder member of both the UNFP and the USFP, returned to Morocco from France in June 1995, after 28 years in exile. It was widely believed that his rehabilitation had been precipitated by the royal amnesty of July 1994 and by the return to Morocco (also from France) in May 1995 of the First Secretary of the USFP, Abd ar-Rahman el-Youssoufi, both of which seemed to indicate a greater level of political tolerance on the part of the Moroccan authorities. In December Abd as-Salam Yassin, the leader of the proscribed Islamist movement Al Adl wa-'l Ihsan (Justice and Charity), was briefly released after six years of house arrest, but restrictions on his movement were reinstated after Yassin criticized the Government. Despite the King's assertion that there were no longer any political detainees in Morocco, a report published by the Association marocaine des droits de l'homme (AMDH) in February 1996 claimed that 58 political prisoners (primarily radical Islamists, supporters of independence for Western Sahara and left-wing activists) remained in detention.

In August 1996 the King presented further constitutional amendments, including the creation of an indirectly elected second parliamentary assembly, the Majlis al-Mustasharin (Chamber of Advisers), and the introduction of direct elections for all members of the Chamber of Representatives. Most political parties supported the reforms; however, an appeal by the OADP leadership for a boycott of a planned referendum on the amendments led to a split in the party and the subsequent creation of the Parti socialiste démocratique (PSD). According to official results of the referendum, held in September, the reforms were approved by 99.6% of voters. Legislation regarding the new bicameral parliament was promulgated in August 1997: the Chamber of Representatives was to comprise 325 members, directly elected for a five-year term; the 270 members of the Chamber of Advisers would be indirectly elected, for a nine-year term, by local councils (which would chose 162 members), chambers of commerce (81) and trade unions (27).

At elections to the Chamber of Representatives, held on 14 November 1997, the Bloc démocratique won a combined total of 102 seats (of which the USFP took 57 and Istiqlal 32); the centre-right Entente nationale took 100 (50 secured by the UC, 40 by the MP), and centrist parties 97 (including 46 obtained by the RNI). The Mouvement populaire constitutionnel et démocratique (MPCD), which earlier in the year had formally absorbed members of the Islamist Al Islah wa Attajdid, won nine seats, securing parliamentary representation for the first time. (In October 1998 the MPCD changed its name to the Parti de la justice et du développement—PJD.) According to official results, 58.3% of the eligible electorate participated in the poll. At indirect elections to the Chamber of Advisers, which followed on 5 December, centrist parties won 90 of the seats (42 secured by the RNI, 33 by the Mouvement démocratique et social), the Entente nationale 76 (28 obtained by the UC, 27 by the MP) and the Bloc démocratique 44 (21 won by Istiqlal). In February 1998 the King appointed el-Youssoufi as the new Prime Minister, in an apparent attempt to appease opposition parties dissatisfied with the outcome of the legislative elections. This was the first time since independence that a socialist had been appointed to the Moroccan premiership. In March a new Cabinet was formed, including members of the USFP, the RNI, Istiqlal, the PPS, the Mouvement national populaire (MNP), the Front des forces démocratiques and the PSD.

King Hassan died on 23 July 1999, after several years of ill health. His eldest son, Crown Prince Sidi Muhammad, succeeded as King Muhammad VI. At the end of July the new King decreed an amnesty whereby some 8,000 prisoners were freed and more than 38,000 had their sentences reduced. In August the King ordered the creation within the Conseil Consultatif des Droits de l'Homme (CCDH)—established by King Hassan in April 1990—of an independent commission to determine levels of compensation for families of missing political activists and for those subjected to arbitrary detention. In April 1999 the CCDH had announced that it had been agreed to compensate the families of 112 people who were now officially acknowledged as having 'disappeared' between 1960 and 1990. Independent Moroccan human rights organizations asserted that the number of missing people amounted to almost 600.

In September 1999 King Muhammad approved the return to Morocco of Abraham Serfaty, a left-wing dissident who had been deported to France in 1991; Serfaty had been granted a passport by the el-Youssoufi administration in 1998, but his return had not been authorized. The family of former opposition leader Mehdi Ben Barka, who had been abducted and subsequently murdered in Paris, France, in 1965, was also permitted to return to Morocco in November. In January 2000 the location was apparently revealed of Ben Barka's burial site, beneath the Courcouronnes mosque in Paris—which was constructed in the mid-1980s with finance from King Hassan II. The French Prime Minister, Lionel Jospin, announced an end to the ban on access to archives where documents relating to the abduction and murder were kept, and later that month a French judge reopened an inquiry into the disappearance of four men who had been convicted *in absentia* in 1967 of the kidnap of Ben Barka and were believed to have fled to Morocco.

Meanwhile, in November 1999 King Muhammad dismissed the long-serving Minister of State for the Interior, Driss Basri. Basri's removal from office, apparently in response to the violent suppression of protests in Western Sahara in September (see below) was interpreted as a particularly important step towards the modernization of Moroccan society. The new Minister of the Interior, Ahmed Midaoui (a former Director of National Security), immediately pledged to work towards the strengthening of democracy and the reconciliation of the administration and the people of Morocco. Victims of repression and their families, together with left-wing political parties and non-governmental organizations, subsequently formed a 'Justice and Trust' organization, which aimed to investigate human rights abuses in Morocco since independence. In April 2000 the Government commenced payments, reportedly totalling 40m. dirhams, in respect of the cases of an initial 40 victims of arbitrary detention, from the fund established in the previous year. Abd as-Salam Yassin was released from house arrest in May.

In September 2000 King Muhammad effected a cabinet reorganization, reducing the number of ministerial portfolios from 43 to 33. Notably, the Secretary-General of Istiqlal, Abbas el-Fassi, was appointed Minister of Social Development, Solidarity, Employment and Vocational Training. Shortly afterwards indirect elections were held to renew one-third of the seats in the Chamber of Advisers. The RNI won 14 of the 90 seats available, the MNP 12 and the PND 10, with the remaining 54 seats divided among smaller parties.

In March 2001 King Muhammad announced the establishment of a royal commission to revise the country's laws on personal rights and responsibilities; the commission was to be chaired by the First President of the Supreme Court, Driss Dahak, and included leading Islamic scholars and jurists. Meanwhile, the King demonstrated a commitment to greater rights for Moroccan women by appointing women to posts of royal advisers, ambassadors and other senior public offices. In September King Muhammad appointed Driss Jettou, a former Minister of Finance and Industry, as Minister of the Interior; Ahmed Midaoui became an adviser to the King. In October Muhammad established a royal institute charged with preserving the language and culture of the country's Berber population, which would also work towards the integration of the Berber language into the education system.

In June 2001 the Moroccan authorities granted Jean-Baptiste Parlos, the French judge leading the inquiry into the Ben Barka affair (see above), permission to visit Morocco as part of his investigation. Later that month Ahmed Boukhari, a former member of the Moroccan special services, alleged in an article published in *Le Journal* and in the French daily *Le Monde* that Ben Barka had been kidnapped in Paris by French police-officers in the employ of the Moroccan secret service and taken to a chateau in the south of the city where he died after being tortured by Morocco's then Minister of the Interior, Gen. Muhammad Oufkir; Ben Barka's body was subsequently smuggled out of France in a Moroccan military aircraft and was dissolved in a tank of acid at a torture and detention centre in Rabat. According to Boukhari, the bodies of many opponents of King Hassan's regime had been disposed of in this way during the 1960s. (In a statement to a Moroccan newspaper in March 2004, Boukhari claimed to have compiled a list of 123 alleged torturers.) The USFP's political bureau demanded that legal proceedings be commenced against Boukhari and the other special services operatives named in his confession, while the Organisation marocaine des droits de l'homme and the AMDH demanded that the Moroccan Government establish an inquiry into the affair. In mid-July 2001 Boukhari received a summons to appear before the French investigation into Ben Barka's disappearance; however, the Moroccan authorities refused to grant Boukhari a passport, and in the following month he was arrested on charges of cashing cheques for which he had insufficient funds. Boukhari's detention was condemned by human rights organizations, which claimed that the Moroccan Government was attempting to prevent Boukhari from testifying at the Parlos inquiry. In late August Boukhari was sentenced to one year's imprisonment, although in mid-October the sentence was reduced on appeal to three months and he was released the following month. Three former Moroccan secret service agents cited in Boukhari's revelations announced their intention to sue him for defamation, and in mid-December, after he was found guilty of the charges by a court in Casablanca, he was again imprisoned for three months and ordered to pay compensation of 300,000 dirhams. In December 2002 the Moroccan authorities announced that they would co-operate fully with the French investigation into the Ben Barka affair, and in January 2003 a French judge travelled to Rabat where he interviewed Boukhari about the disappearance of Ben Barka.

Meanwhile, in late January 2002 el-Youssoufi stated that he would stand down as Prime Minister after the legislative elections scheduled for September, but would remain as First Secretary of the USFP. In March the Government agreed a number of changes to the electoral system, including the abandonment of the simple majority system in favour of proportional representation. The Government insisted that the new system would reduce fraudulent practices and increase public confidence in the electoral process; at least 10% of the 325 seats in the lower house were to be reserved for women. The general election took place on 27 September 2002. According to official figures, the USFP won the largest number of seats, although its representation in the Chamber of Representatives was reduced from 57 to 50 seats. Istiqlal increased its parliamentary representation to 48 members, while the PJD took 42 seats, the RNI 41, the MP 27, the MNP 18 and the UC 16. The rate of voter participation was recorded at just 51.6% of the electorate. In early October King Muhammad appointed Jettou as the new Prime Minister, and a new Government was announced in the following month. Despite securing the third highest number of seats in the Chamber of Representatives, the PJD was not allocated any ministerial portfolios. The new Cabinet comprised members of the USFD, Istiqlal, the RNI, the MNP, the MP and the PPS, as well as a number of non-affiliated technocrats—one of whom, Al Mustapha Sahel, replaced Jettou as Minister of the Interior. Three women were appointed to the Government.

In early May 2003 King Muhammad marked the occasion of the birth of a son and heir to the throne, Prince Moulay Hassan, by ordering the release of an estimated 9,000 prisoners and reducing the gaol terms of a further 38,000. Later that month Ali Lamrabet, the editor of two satirical magazines, was sentenced to four years' imprisonment for 'insulting the King' and 'undermining the monarchy'. Lamrabet had commenced a hunger strike earlier in May, and his case had been closely followed by a number of international human rights groups. Lamrabet's sentence was subsequently commuted, on appeal, to a term of three years, and in late June he ended his hunger strike. In January 2004 Lamrabet was granted a royal pardon and released from prison.

Meanwhile, in mid-May 2003 45 people died and more than 100 others were injured in a series of suicide bomb attacks in central Casablanca, which targeted the Belgian consulate, a Spanish restaurant and a Jewish cultural centre. Among those killed were reported to be 12 suicide bombers, and two other suspected attackers were detained by the security forces along with some 30 others thought to have been involved in the bombings. The Moroccan authorities believed that the bombers were linked to a small Moroccan-based militant Islamist group, al-Assirat al-Moustaquim (Righteous Path), but that the attacks had been orchestrated by an international terrorist network operating in Europe, possibly the al-Qa'ida (Base) organization of the fugitive Saudi Arabian-born Islamist Osama bin Laden. In late May the suspected co-ordinator of the attacks, who had been arrested in Fez, died in police custody as a result of ill health. Days earlier Jettou had led an anti-terrorism march through Casablanca attended by an estimated 1m. people. Later in May stricter anti-terrorism measures were approved by the legislature, which broadened the definition of terrorism to 'any premeditated act, by an individual or a group, that aims to breach public order through terror and violence', and increased the number of offences punishable by the death sentence.

In mid-July 2003 10 of the alleged 31 members of the radical Islamist group Salafia Jihadia, who had been arrested during police operations against Islamist networks in mid-2002, were sentenced to death by a court in Casablanca, having been convicted of murder and attempted murder. Eight of the accused received sentences of life imprisonment, and the remainder were given custodial terms of 10–20 years. Later in July 2003 it was announced that more than 700 people would be tried in connection with the bomb attacks; 52 defendants subsequently appeared before Casablanca's criminal court, charged with 'forming a criminal band, acting against the security of the state, and sabotage and homicide'. In mid-August four men, including the two suspected surviving suicide bombers, received the death sentence for their roles in the violence; 39 others were sentenced to life imprisonment for plotting further attacks in Essaouira, Agadir and Marrakesh. Some 50 Islamists received various prison sentences during September for their alleged roles in attempting to carry out further bomb attacks within Morocco, and in February 2005 10 men were imprisoned for eight years for membership of Salafia Jihadia. Two members of Salafia Jihadia were sentenced to death in July, having been convicted of the murders in Casablanca of five people, including an official of the Ministry of the Interior.

Despite the clampdown on Islamist activity in the wake of the Casablanca bombings, King Muhammad continued to pursue his policies of reform and modernization of Moroccan society. In June 2003 it was announced that teaching of the Berber language in primary schools would commence in the 2003/04 academic year, and that 1,000 Berber teachers had been appointed. It was planned eventually to extend the subject to all levels of the school system. In October King Muhammad announced major revisions to the *mudawana* (family code), which he claimed would promote female equality and protect children's rights. The reforms (originally outlined in 2000) would raise the legal age of marriage for women from 15 to 18 and simplify the procedure for women seeking a divorce from their husband. Although polygamy was not to be outlawed under the new legislation, women would be able to prevent their husbands from taking a second wife and would also be provided with equal authority and property rights within the marriage. In January 2004 the changes to the *mudawana* were approved by the legislature.

In late February 2004 an earthquake measuring 6.4 on the Richter scale hit the province of Al-Hoceima in the north of the country, killing more than 600 people and leaving thousands more homeless. While international aid organizations were quick to respond to the disaster, relief efforts were hampered by a reported lack of organization on the part of the Moroccan authorities, leading to angry demonstrations by hundreds of people demanding food, medical assistance and tents.

At the PJD party conference in April 2004, Saâdeddine Othmani was elected to the position of Secretary-General. The party reiterated its commitment to democracy and its rejection of any form of terrorism or violence. In May, under ongoing plans to reform and modernize the Moroccan judicial system which had been announced by King Muhammad in January, the Special Court of Justice was dismantled. The court had presided over crimes and felonies allegedly committed by government officials or judges involving 25,000 dirhams or more, and it was reported that its responsibilities would be transferred to the Courts of Appeal. It was also announced that a new High Court of Justice would be created in which government officials could be tried in the case of allegations being made against them. In early June, in a government reshuffle implemented by King Muhammad, the number of cabinet posts was reduced from 37 to 34 and the Ministry in charge of Human Rights was dismantled, with human rights issues henceforth to be dealt with under the auspices of the Ministry of Justice.

In June 2005 Nadia Yassine, the daughter of Abd as-Salam Yassin and spokesperson for Al Adl wa'l Ihsan, was charged with attacking the monarchy following the publication of an interview in which she stated that the monarchy was no longer relevant for Morocco. Along with Abdelaziz Koukas, the editor of the magazine in which the interview appeared, Yassine faced up to five years' imprisonment if found guilty. However, the trial was immediately postponed. In late September and early October a series of attempts by large organized groups of African migrants to scale fences along the border between Morocco and the Spanish enclaves of Ceuta and Melilla resulted in the deaths of at least 11 people. Moroccan troops later admitted to shooting dead four of the victims and seven others were reported to have been crushed. In mid-October the Government denied allegations that groups of migrants sent back to Morocco from Spain had been transported to the country's southern desert region and abandoned without food or water. Later the same month the Moroccan authorities repatriated more than 1,000 migrants by air to various sub-Saharan African countries. In February 2006 King Muhammad appointed Chakib Benmoussa, a non-affiliate, as Minister of the Interior to replace Sahel, who became Morocco's ambassador to the UN. In late February the criminal proceedings against Yassine and Koukas resumed.

Following the cession of the Spanish enclave of Ifni to Morocco in 1969, political opinion in Morocco was united in opposing the continued occupation by Spain of areas considered to be historically parts of Moroccan territory: namely Spanish Sahara and Spanish North Africa (q.v.)—a number of small enclaves on Morocco's Mediterranean coast. A campaign to annex Spanish Sahara, initiated in 1974, received active support from all Moroccan political parties. In October 1975 King Hassan ordered a 'Green March' by more than 300,000 unarmed Moroccans to occupy the territory. The marchers were stopped by the Spanish authorities when they had barely crossed the border, but in November Spain agreed to cede the territory to Morocco and Mauritania, to be apportioned equally between them. Spain formally relinquished sovereignty of Spanish Sahara in February 1976. Moroccan troops moved into the territory to confront a guerrilla uprising led by the Frente Popular para la Liberación de Saguia el-Hamra y Río de Oro (the Polisario Front), a national liberation movement supported by Algeria and (later) Libya which aimed to achieve an independent Western Saharan state. On 27 February the Polisario Front declared the 'Sahrawi Arab Democratic Republic' (SADR), and shortly afterwards established a 'Government-in-exile' in Algeria. In protest, Morocco severed diplomatic relations with Algeria.

Moroccan troops inflicted heavy casualties on the insurgents, and ensured the security of Western Sahara's main population centres, but they failed to prevent constant infiltration, harassment and sabotage by Polisario forces. Moreover, Polisario had considerable success against Mauritanian troops, and in August 1979 Mauritania renounced its claim to Saharan territory and signed a peace treaty with the Polisario Front. Morocco immediately asserted its claim to the whole of Western Sahara and annexed the region.

In July 1980 the SADR applied to join the Organization of African Unity (OAU—now African Union, see p. 153) as a sovereign state. Although 26 of the 50 members then recognized the Polisario Front as the rightful government of Western Sahara, Morocco insisted that a two-thirds' majority was needed to confer membership. Morocco rejected an OAU proposal for a cease-fire and a referendum on the territory, and in 1981 heavy fighting resumed in the region. The SADR was accepted as the OAU's 51st member in early 1982, but a threat by 18 members to leave the organization in protest necessitated a compromise whereby the SADR, while remaining a member, agreed not to attend OAU meetings. In late 1984 a SADR delegation did attend a summit meeting of the OAU with little opposition from other states, causing Morocco to resign from the organization. Meanwhile, fighting continued in Western Sahara; decisive victories for Polisario proved impossible, however, as Morocco constructed a 2,500-km defensive wall of sand, equipped with electronic detectors, to surround Western Sahara.

In October 1985 Morocco announced a unilateral cease-fire in Western Sahara, and invited the UN to supervise a referendum to be held there the following January. A series of indirect talks between the two sides, arranged by the UN and the OAU in 1986–87, failed to achieve a solution, and in January 1988 Polisario forces renewed their offensive against Moroccan positions in Western Sahara. In August, however, it was announced that the Polisario Front and Morocco had provisionally accepted a peace plan proposed by the UN Secretary-General, Javier Pérez de Cuéllar, which envisaged the conclusion of a formal cease-fire, a reduction in Moroccan military forces in Western Sahara and the withdrawal of Polisario forces to their bases, to be followed by a referendum on self-determination in Western Sahara. A list of eligible voters was to be based on the Spanish census of 1974. A meeting in Marrakesh in January 1989 between King Hassan and officials of the Polisario Front and the SADR—the first direct contact for 13 years—was apparently limited to exchanges of goodwill, but was followed, in February, by the announcement of a unilateral cease-fire by Polisario. A further meeting was postponed by Hassan, who in September rejected the possibility of official negotiations with the SADR; later that month Polisario renewed its military attacks on Moroccan positions.

UN Security Council Resolution No. 690 of April 1991 established a peace-keeping force, the UN Mission for the Referendum in Western Sahara (MINURSO, see p. 74), which was to implement the 1988 plan for a referendum on self-determination. In June 1991 Polisario agreed to a formal cease-fire, with effect from 6 September, from which date the 2,000-strong MINURSO delegation would undertake its duties in the region. The cease-fire came into effect as scheduled, and the MINURSO deployment began. Reports at this time suggested that some 30,000 people had entered Western Sahara from Morocco, prompting claims that the Moroccan authorities were attempting to alter the region's demography in advance of the referendum. It was also reported that more than 170,000 Sahrawi who had fled the region since 1976 were being repatriated in order that they might participate in the referendum. By November 1991 only 200 MINURSO personnel had been deployed in Western Sahara, and the peace process was undermined further by Morocco's failure to withdraw any of its forces from the region (under the terms of the cease-fire agreement, Morocco was to have withdrawn one-half of its 130,000 troops from Western Sahara by mid-September). In May 1992 Pérez de Cuéllar's successor as UN Secretary-General, Dr Boutros Boutros-Ghali, announced that Morocco and Polisario representatives were to begin indirect talks under his auspices. In the same month, however, Morocco appeared to prejudge the result of the proposed referendum by including the population of Western Sahara in the voting lists for its own regional and local elections. In June the SADR Government, which by this time was recognized by 75 countries, appealed to the international community and the UN to condemn alleged Moroccan violations of the cease-fire and to exert pressure for the implementation of the UN peace plan. UN-sponsored negotiations in the USA in September failed to formulate acceptable criteria for the drafting of lists of eligible voters at an eventual referendum.

In March 1993 the UN Security Council approved plans for the holding of the referendum on Western Sahara by the end of the year. In July the first direct negotiations took place between the Moroccan Government and Polisario, although little progress was achieved. In March 1994 Boutros-Ghali submitted a report to the UN Security Council detailing possible procedures for overcoming the impasse on the Western Saharan issue, including the effective withdrawal of the UN from the peace process. (It had been reported in September 1993 that only 360 of the proposed 2,000 UN military personnel were in place.) The Security Council subsequently agreed to a continuation of negotiations for a further three months, and undertook to review the future of MINURSO if a referendum was not organized before the end of the year. In April Polisario accepted the UN programme for the registration of voters. However, the work of a UN voter identification commission, which had been due to commence in June, was delayed by the Moroccan Government's objection to the inclusion of OAU observers in the process.

In mid-1995 Polisario withdrew from the voter identification process, in protest at the severity of sentences placed upon pro-independence Sahrawi protesters by the Moroccan authorities and at alleged Moroccan violations of the cease-fire. In September the SADR announced the formation of a new 14-member Government, headed by Mahfoud Ali Beïba, and in October the first elected Sahrawi National Assembly was inaugurated in a refugee camp in Tindouf, Algeria.

The UN Security Council voted periodically to extend MINURSO's mandate on a short-term basis, noting in January 1996 that it was improbable that the referendum would take place during that year. In May the Security Council voted to suspend the registration of voters in Western Sahara until 'convincing proof' was offered by the Moroccan Government and the Sahrawi leadership that they would not further obstruct preparations for the referendum. The mandate of MINURSO was extended, but its personnel was to be reduced by 20%.

In March 1997 the new UN Secretary-General, Kofi Annan, appointed James Baker (a former US Secretary of State) as his Personal Envoy to Western Sahara. Baker visited the region in April, and in June he mediated in talks in Portugal between representatives of Morocco and the SADR. The process of voter identification resumed in December for a referendum scheduled to be held one year later. However, disagreement between Morocco and Polisario regarding the eligibility of voters delayed the identification process and led the UN to revise the proposed date for the referendum on several occasions. By September 1998 a total of 147,350 voters had been identified since the commencement of the process in August 1994, but the issue of the disputed tribes remained unresolved. In June 1998, meanwhile, as Morocco intensified its efforts to rejoin the OAU, several OAU member states debated the expulsion from the organization of the SADR; only a minority of member countries continued to recognize its independent status.

During talks with Moroccan and SADR officials in November 1998, the UN Secretary-General warned that the UN would withdraw from Western Sahara if the two parties failed to show political will towards resolving the conflict. Annan presented proposals regarding the disputed tribes, the publication of a list of voters not contested by either party, and the repatriation of refugees under the auspices of the UN High Commissioner for Refugees. Although the proposals were accepted by Polisario, the Moroccan authorities expressed reservations. Morocco delayed the signing of a technical agreement with the UN (defining the legal status of MINURSO troops in Western Sahara) until February 1999: Algeria and Mauritania had signed similar accords with the UN in November 1998. In July 1999 MINURSO published a list of 84,251 people provisionally entitled to vote in the referendum, which was scheduled to be held on 31 July 2000.

In February 1999, meanwhile, the SADR announced the formation of a new Government, led by Beïba's predecessor, Bouchraya Hammoudi Bayoune. In September the Polisario Front congress re-elected the President of the SADR, Muhammad Abd al-Aziz, as Secretary-General of the organization. Abd al-Aziz subsequently effected a reshuffle of the SADR Government; Bayoune retained the premiership and also assumed the interior portfolio. In October a delegation comprising several ministers of the Moroccan Government was dispatched to el-Aaiún for consultations with the Sahrawi population at the behest of King Muhammad—who had in September established a royal commission to monitor affairs in Western Sahara.

UN officials indicated in November 1999 that the referendum was likely to be subject to a further postponement; Polisario responded by stating that it could not rule out a return to an armed struggle. Nevertheless, in late November Polisario released 191 Moroccan prisoners. In December the mandate of MINURSO was once again extended to enable it to complete its work on the identification of possible voters in the referendum. However, the UN Secretary-General subsequently announced that it would be impossible to organize the referendum before 2002, owing to the large number of appeals lodged by those deemed ineligible to vote. In January 2000 it was announced that 86,381 out of a total of 198,481 people identified in Western Sahara would be eligible to vote in the referendum. In February, however, Annan postponed the referendum indefinitely, and warned, furthermore, of the possibility that it might never take place, owing to the persistent differences regarding criteria for eligibility to vote. The mandate of MINURSO was further extended in February. By March the number of appeals lodged had reached over 130,000, and Abd al-Aziz reiterated the threat of the resumption of armed hostilities if Morocco continued to obstruct the UN peace plan.

In April 2000 Baker toured Morocco and Western Sahara, and in London, United Kingdom, in May he chaired the first direct talks between representatives of Morocco and Polisario for three years. Algeria and Mauritania also sent delegations, but the meeting failed to make any substantive progress. In October Annan urged Morocco partially to devolve authority in Western Sahara, stating that if no such concessions were granted, the UN would reactivate plans to hold a referendum in the territory. Concurrently, MINURSO's mandate was extended until the end of February 2001.

In December 2000, to mark the beginning of Ramadan, Polisario released 201 Moroccan prisoners, urging Morocco to release some 150 Sahrawi from detention in Morocco. The Moroccan authorities denied the detention of any Sahrawi in Morocco, and in turn demanded the release of a further 1,500 Moroccans whom they claimed were being held by Polisario. In late February 2001, on the 25th anniversary of the beginning of the Polisario Front's struggle for independence, the Moroccan Minister of the Interior, Ahmed Midaoui, asserted that there remained only one solution to the dispute—that Morocco retain control over its entire territory. At the end of February, as MINURSO's mandate was extended for a further two months, Annan announced that if Morocco failed to offer or support some devolution of governmental authority, MINURSO would be directed to begin the process of hearing appeals regarding eligibility to vote in the referendum. A further two-month extension was approved by the UN Security Council in late April, in accordance with recommendations made by the Secretary-General: although Annan had been unable, in his latest report, to report progress towards overcoming the obstacles to implementation of the settlement plan, he expressed his view that 'substantial progress' had been made towards determining whether the Government of Morocco was 'prepared to offer or support some devolution of authority for all the inhabitants and former inhabitants of the Territory'.

In late June 2001 the UN Security Council unanimously approved a compromise resolution (No. 1359), formulated by Baker, which encouraged Polisario and Morocco to discuss an autonomy plan for Western Sahara without abandoning the delayed referendum. The resolution also extended MINURSO's mandate until the end of November. Under the terms of the autonomy proposal the inhabitants of Western Sahara would have the right to elect their own legislative and executive bodies and have control over most areas of local government for a period of at least five years, during which Morocco would retain control over defence and foreign affairs. A referendum on the final status of the territory would take place within this five-year period. In late August Baker hosted three days of talks in Wyoming, USA, attended by representatives from Polisario, Mauritania and Algeria; however, Polisario subsequently accused the UN of bowing to Moroccan pressure and in mid-September Polisario announced its formal rejection of Baker's proposal. In late October King Muhammad visited Western Sahara for the first time since his accession to the throne, and in early November he granted an amnesty to 56 prisoners in Western Sahara. Later that month MINURSO's mandate was extended until February 2002, and in early December 2001 William Lacy Swing, a former US ambassador, was appointed as the UN Secretary-General's Special Representative for Western Sahara.

In early February 2002 UN legal counsel advised the Secretary-General that the Moroccan Government could not issue exploration licences for petroleum in Western Sahara without the consent of the Sahrawi people; the advice followed a request made by the SADR in late 2001 for clarification on the legality of reconnaissance licences signed by Morocco and two oil companies. In February 2002 Annan outlined four possible measures to be considered by the UN Security Council in order to attempt to resolve the continuing impasse over Western Sahara: to resume attempts to implement the 1988 settlement plan, with or without the agreement of Polisario and the Moroccan Government; to charge Baker with revising his earlier draft framework agreement; to commence discussions regarding the division of the territory; or to terminate MINURSO's mandate. Later that month the UN Security Council approved an extension of its mandate until the end of April. Meanwhile, in early March King Muhammad again visited Western Sahara, vowing not to relinquish any part of the disputed territory. Upon its expiry at the end of April, MINURSO's mandate was renewed for a further three months.

The UN Security Council admitted in July 2002 that it had been unable to agree on the resolution of the Western Sahara issue (as none of the four proposals had secured the required support), but had voted unanimously to allow Baker to pursue efforts to find a political solution which would provide for self-determination. MINURSO's mandate was extended until the end of January 2003. In that month Baker visited government officials in Mauritania and Algeria, as well as Abd al-Aziz and King Muhammad, to present them with the UN's most recent proposal for the settlement of the ongoing dispute. Although no details of the plan were officially disclosed, Baker asked all parties to present their comments on the proposal to him by early March. Just days later, however, it was reported that Polisario had rejected the plan. In an attempt to give the parties more time in which to consider Baker's proposals, the UN Security Council extended MINURSO's mandate until the end of March; it was subsequently extended for a further two months in order to give Baker sufficient time to evaluate the parties' responses to his proposal. In February Polisario had released another 100 Moroccan prisoners of war, although more than 1,100 reportedly remained in detention.

In late May 2003 Annan formally released details of a new peace plan aimed at ending the Western Sahara dispute and urged Morocco, Polisario and Algeria to accept the proposals. The new plan, known as 'Baker Plan II', proposed immediate self-government for Western Sahara for a period of four to five years, after which time a referendum would be held in order to give all bona fide residents the opportunity to decide the long-term future of the territory. Annan suggested an extension of MINURSO's mandate for a further two months to enable the Security Council to consider the proposals thoroughly. The Security Council approved Annan's proposals at the beginning of June. At the end of June Polisario, under strong pressure from Algeria, accepted the Baker plan as a basis for negotiation. Morocco, however, refused to accept any 'imposed decision' on Western Sahara.

On 31 July 2003 the UN Security Council unanimously adopted Resolution 1495, which supported Baker Plan II, and called on parties and states of the region to co-operate fully with the Secretary-General and his special envoy in working towards the implementation of the peace plan. MINURSO's mandate was extended until 31 October. Following strong opposition from France (which lends Morocco considerable support on the Western Sahara issue), Resolution 1495 did not demand that Morocco and Polisario comply with the plan. Nevertheless, the Spanish permanent representative to the UN, chairing the Security Council, insisted that the resolution provided the two parties with sufficient 'political room' to reach a definite solution to the dispute on the basis of Baker Plan II: this had not imposed a solution on the parties but urged them to resume sustained discussions. The resolution also called on Polisario to release without further delay all remaining Moroccan prisoners of war, and for Morocco and Polisario to co-operate with the International Committee of the Red Cross (ICRC) to resolve the fate of persons unaccounted for since the beginning of the conflict.

In early August 2003 Annan announced that a former Peruvian diplomat, Alvaro de Soto, would replace Swing as the UN Secretary-General's Special Representative for Western Sahara. In September Polisario released 243 Moroccan prisoners of war, although the ICRC maintained that a further 914 Moroccans were still being held captive. In late October Annan again urged Morocco to accept and implement Baker Plan II; concurrently, MINURSO's mandate was extended until January 2004. In November 2003 Polisario released a further 300 Moroccan prisoners of war. In January 2004 MINURSO's mandate was again extended until April, by which time Annan stated that he required a 'final response' from Morocco with regard to Baker Plan II. In late February 100 Moroccans were released from detention by Polisario.

In late April 2004 the UN Security Council unanimously adopted Resolution 1541, which urged the two sides to accept the UN plan to grant Western Sahara immediate self-government and which extended MINURSO's mandate until October. Morocco, however, continued to reject this proposal and remained insistent on granting the territory 'autonomy within the framework of Moroccan sovereignty'. In mid-June James Baker resigned as the UN special envoy to the region; at the request of Annan, Alvaro de Soto took over the role. In early September de Soto commenced talks with the Moroccan authorities and Polisario to attempt to resolve the impasse, and a resolution (No. 1570) adopted by the Security Council in late October calling for an end to the deadlock and an advancement towards a political solution, while extending MINURSO's mandate until the end of April 2005, was welcomed by the Moroccan authorities. Protests against Moroccan policy towards the region took place in several cities in Western Sahara towards the end of 2004, and in early December King Muhammad expressed his country's readiness to find a suitable political solution, while emphasizing that he was not prepared to jeopardize Morocco's sovereignty. In April 2005 Resolution 1598, which reiterated previous calls for a political solution and extended MINURSO's mandate until October, was unanimously adopted by the Security Council. In early May 2005 de Soto left his role of Special Representative and immediately assumed the position of UN Special Co-ordinator for the Middle East Peace Process. Following the transfer of a Sahrawi prisoner from el-Aaiún to a gaol in Morocco, pro-independence demonstrations took place in el-Aaiún in late May, during which Moroccan flags were burned and 50 people were reportedly injured. More than 30 youths were subsequently arrested by Moroccan police and charged with participating in the demonstrations; 12 people were later convicted of crimes relating to the unrest, each receiving sentences of between five and 20 years' imprisonment. Meanwhile, in July Annan appointed Peter van Walsum of the Netherlands as his new Personal Envoy for Western Sahara, and in August it was announced that Francesco Bastagli of Italy would replace de Soto as Special Representative of the Secretary-General and MINURSO Chief of Mission. Later the same month the Polisario Front released the remaining 408 Moroccan prisoners of war, some of whom had been held in Tindouf for more than 20 years, one month after Abd al-Aziz had urged Morocco to release 150 Sahrawis he claimed were still in detention. The UN Security Council adopted Resolution 1634 in late October, reaffirming its commitment to achieving an acceptable political solution and extending MINURSO's mandate for a further six months. In November one person was killed during further violent confrontations in el-Aaiún, which preceded celebrations to mark the 30th anniversary of the Green March, between protesters demanding independence and Moroccan security forces. In a televised address on the anniversary, King Muhammad announced his intention to consult with Morocco's political parties on the issue of autonomy for Western Sahara 'within the sovereignty of the kingdom'. However, Polisario immediately rejected the plan and stated that a referendum was the only viable solution. In March 2006 King Muhammad visited Western Sahara for the third time since his accession to the throne in 1999, and royal pardons were granted to 216 Sahrawi prisoners. During the visit the King also announced the appointment of a revised Royal Advisory Council for Saharan Affairs (CORCAS), which included the former Minister in charge of Saharan Affairs, Khali Hanna Ould ar-Rachid, as Chairman; CORCAS had been originally established in 1981 by King Hassan II. The 140 newly appointed members were handed the task of assisting the formulation of draft proposals for Sahrawi autonomy, scheduled for presentation to the UN in April 2006.

Relations with other North African states improved significantly in the late 1980s. In May 1988 Algeria and Morocco agreed to re-establish diplomatic relations. (Relations with Mauritania had been suspended in 1981 and resumed in April 1985.) In February 1989 North African heads of state, meeting in Marrakesh, signed a treaty establishing the Union du Maghreb arabe (UMA—Union of the Arab Maghreb, see p. 388). The new body, grouping Morocco, Algeria, Libya, Mauritania and Tunisia, aimed to promote trade by allowing the free movement of goods, services and workers. During 1990 bilateral agreements on economic co-operation were concluded by Morocco with Algeria and Libya, and there were further discussions within the UMA on the formation of a North African free-trade area. However, there were political disagreements particularly concerning Algeria's continued support for the Polisario Front, and over Moroccan condemnation of Iraq's invasion of Kuwait in August 1990. In early 1993 it was announced that the five UMA members had decided there should be a 'pause' in the development of a closer union; of 15 conventions signed since the inauguration of the UMA, none had as yet been fully applied. However, the organization continued to hold meetings on an annual basis. In December 1995 King Hassan expressed disapproval at Algeria's continued support for the independence of Western Sahara, and demanded that UMA activities be suspended. An impending UMA summit was subsequently postponed. In March 1999 President Ben Ali of Tunisia made his first official visit to Morocco, during which he pledged to improve bilateral relations and to reactivate the UMA. At bilateral meetings during 2000 with other Maghreb heads of state King Muhammad pledged to take measures to revive the UMA. A summit meeting of ministers responsible for foreign affairs of the five UMA states proceeded in the Algerian capital in March 2001. However, the meeting, which was to have made preparations for the first summit meeting of UMA heads of state since 1995, quickly broke down following disagreements between Moroccan and Algerian representatives. Libya assumed the chairmanship of the UMA in December 2003, and Libyan leader Col Muammar al-Qaddafi pledged to host a summit meeting of the UMA heads of state following the presidential election in Algeria, due to be held in April of the following year. The meeting was subsequently scheduled to take place in Tripoli, Libya, in May 2005. However, a statement of renewed support for the Polisario Front by the Algerian President, Abdelaziz Bouteflika, provoked a fresh dispute between Morocco and Algeria days before the summit meeting was due to begin and King Muhammad declined to attend. The summit meeting was subsequently postponed and, by early 2006, had yet to be rescheduled.

Relations with Algeria had been further undermined in mid-1994 by the murder, apparently by radical Islamists, of two Spanish tourists in Marrakesh, which the Moroccan authorities attributed in part to Algerian nationals. The imposition by Morocco of entry restrictions on Algerian citizens prompted the Algerian Government to introduce reciprocal visa restrictions and to close its border with Morocco. Tensions eased somewhat in September, when Algeria announced the appointment of a new ambassador to Morocco, and in October a Moroccan minister attended ceremonies in Algeria to mark the commencement of work on a Maghreb–Europe gas pipeline. In January 1995 three people, including one Algerian, were sentenced to death for their part in acts of terrorism, including the murders in Marrakesh; three others were sentenced to life imprisonment. The French security forces made further arrests in connection with the murder of the two Spaniards during 1995–96, and in early 1997 a French court sentenced another 29 alleged conspirators (two Moroccans, the remainder French citizens of Maghreb origin) to terms of imprisonment ranging from one to eight years. The Western Sahara issue remained a source of tension between Morocco and Algeria, but in mid-1998 the Moroccan authorities indicated their desire to normalize relations with Algeria and to reopen the common border. In September 1999, however, Algeria's new President, Abdelaziz Bouteflika, claimed that radical Islamist rebels were launching attacks on Algeria from Morocco, and accused Morocco of ignoring the increasing trade in illicit drugs between the two countries. Bouteflika also criticized Morocco for negotiating a separate trade agreement with the European Union (EU, see p. 228), claiming that this was not in the interests of the UMA. Both Morocco and Algeria none the less subsequently reiterated their commitment to reviving the activities of the UMA. Although relations remained generally co-operative, Bouteflika was vocal in opposing the UN proposals for Western Sahara in mid-2001, which he claimed favoured Morocco. In late February 2002, furthermore, Morocco asserted that Algerian support for the partition of Western Sahara risked destabilizing the region; for its part, Algeria accused Morocco of blocking a UN-sponsored solution to the Western Sahara issue. During a visit to Algiers by the Moroccan Minister of Foreign Affairs and Co-operation in mid-June 2003, it was agreed to establish three bilateral commissions to consider political, economic and social matters. Following talks in July 2004 between the Moroccan Minister of the Interior, Al Mustapha Sahel, and his Algerian counterpart, Noureddine Yazid Zerhouni, the two countries signalled their desire to improve diplomatic relations. In May 2005, however, Bouteflika issued a statement renewing Algeria's support for the Polisario Front, and in October allegations by Polisario that Morocco had abandoned African migrants in the Western Saharan desert further increased tensions between the two countries. Jettou accused Algeria of instigating the allegations, and claimed that Algeria had exacerbated the problem by allowing some illegal immigrants to establish camps close to their joint border.

From the late 1990s Morocco was actively involved in wider regional integration efforts, as a member of the Community of Sahel-Saharan States (CEN-SAD, see p. 385), and also through bilateral and multilateral free-trade arrangements; in May 2001, notably, the Governments of Morocco, Iraq, Jordan and Tunisia agreed, at a meeting in Agadir, to establish a free-trade zone. In October Morocco and Mauritania took steps to improve bilateral relations after King Muhammad visited that country.

A visit to Rabat by the Israeli Prime Minister, Itzhak Rabin, in September 1993 was regarded as an indication of improved relations between Morocco and Israel, and of the role played by King Hassan in the Middle East peace process. In September 1994 Morocco became only the second Arab country (after Egypt) to establish direct links with Israel; liaison offices were subsequently opened in Rabat and Tel-Aviv. In March 1997, however, in condemnation of recent Israeli settlement policy, ministers of foreign affairs of the League of Arab States (the Arab League, see p. 306) recommended a number of sanctions against Israel, including the closure of representative missions. In January 2000 Morocco and Israel agreed in principle to upgrade diplomatic relations to ambassadorial level, although no indication was given as to when embassies would be established. In October, however, as the crisis in Israeli–Palestinian relations deepened, Morocco announced that it had closed down Israel's liaison office in Rabat and its own representative office in Tel-Aviv. There was widespread outrage in Morocco in response to the Israeli military offensive in Palestinian-controlled areas of the West Bank from the end of March 2002. A national march in solidarity with the Palestinian people took place in Rabat in early April, attracting more than 1m. people—the biggest demonstration in the Arab world.

Morocco has generally maintained close relations with France. However, the French Government expressed considerable concern following the imposition of death sentences on three defendants in January 1995 (see above), all of whom had been resident in France prior to their arrest. As the development of a Maghreb union slowed, Morocco attempted to improve relations with the EU, which had been critical of Morocco's human rights record. In February 1996, after two years of negotiations, Morocco signed an association agreement with the EU, which provided for greater political and economic co-operation, financial aid and the eventual establishment of a free-trade zone. In March 2000 King Muhammad made his first state visit abroad since acceding to the throne when he attended talks with President Chirac in France. During the visit Muhammad expressed his hope that Morocco would be accorded partnership status with the EU and, ultimately, full membership of the union.

In February 1995, following the approval by the Spanish parliament of statutes of autonomy for the enclaves of Ceuta and Melilla, Morocco intensified its diplomatic campaign to obtain sovereignty over the territories. Relations between Morocco and Spain deteriorated further in April, when responsibility for two bomb explosions in Ceuta was claimed by a guerrilla group suspected by the Spanish authorities of receiving clandestine support from Morocco. Prime Minister Filali made an official visit to Spain in mid-1997, and in January 1998 the two countries established a joint commission to examine security issues including illegal immigration (to Spain) and drugs-trafficking. In August 1999 Prime Minister el-Youssoufi urged a review of the statutes of Ceuta and Melilla; however, Spain's ruling Partido Popular asserted that no Moroccan sovereignty claims with regard to this issue would be considered. The Spanish premier, José María Aznar López, visited Morocco in May 2000, and in September, during King Muhammad's first visit to Spain since his accession, two economic co-operation agreements were signed. Nevertheless, relations remained strained owing to lack of progress in negotiations with the EU regarding a new fisheries accord and attacks by Spanish fishermen on lorries carrying Moroccan products through Spanish ports.

In July 2001, in an attempt to limit the increasing number of Moroccans entering Spain illegally, the two countries signed an agreement that would allow as many as 20,000 Moroccans to enter Spain each year in search of employment. In September, however, Spain refuted allegations made by King Muhammad that Spanish criminal associations were responsible for the large increase in numbers of Moroccan economic migrants attempting illegally to cross the Straits of Gibraltar, asserting that collusion between Moroccan police and the smugglers was ongoing. Relations between the two countries deteriorated further later that month after Morocco recalled its ambassador from Spain. The Moroccan Government was critical of border controls introduced by the Spanish authorities for Moroccans entering the Spanish enclaves of Ceuta and Melilla, and the breakdown, in April 2002, of talks on renewing the EU fisheries accord also contributed to strained bilateral relations. Moroccan–Spanish relations were further strained in mid-July 2002 when a small detachment of Moroccan troops occupied the uninhabited rocky islet of Perejil (known as Leila to Morocco), west of the Spanish enclave of Ceuta and close to the Moroccan coastline. Morocco claimed that it was establishing a surveillance post on the island as part of its campaign against illegal emigration and drugs-smuggling. However, Spain insisted that there had been since 1990 an agreement that neither Morocco nor Spain would occupy Perejil, and, with the support of the EU and NATO, demanded the immediate evacuation of Moroccan troops from the island. A few days later Spain's ambassador to Morocco was recalled, and Spanish special forces intervened and forcibly removed Moroccan troops from Perejil. Spanish officials insisted that their troops would be withdrawn if King Muhammad gave assurances that Moroccan forces would not reoccupy the island, and the Spanish Minister of Foreign Affairs, Ana Palacio, stated that Spain had no interest in maintaining a permanent military presence on the island. Both sides emphasized their desire to end the dispute through diplomatic means, and, following mediation by the US Secretary of State, Colin Powell, Spanish forces withdrew from the island. Talks held later in July 2002 in Rabat between Palacio and her Moroccan counterpart Muhammad Benaïssa resulted in an accord whereby both states agreed to return to the *status quo ante*. By early 2003 relations had improved somewhat: in January Muhammad temporarily allowed Spanish boats to fish in Moroccan waters, and in the following month the two countries agreed to the return of their respective ambassadors. In December Morocco and Spain announced plans to construct a 39-km underwater rail tunnel between the two countries.

In March 2004 a series of bomb attacks on commuter trains in the Spanish capital, Madrid, killed 191 people. A number of Moroccans from the Groupe islamique combattant marocain (GICM), who had also been linked with the Casablanca bombings of 2003, were among a group of suspected militant Islamists detained by the Spanish authorities in connection with the attacks, and in December 2004 a Moroccan man, Hassan al-Haski, was charged with having planned the bombings. The Moroccan authorities were quick to show their commitment to fighting terrorism, and in late April 2004, following an official visit to Morocco by the new Spanish Prime Minister, José Luís Rodriguez Zapatero, the two countries announced renewed diplomatic ties. In May the two Governments revealed plans to establish a joint task force to tackle terrorism and organized crime. Diplomatic relations between Morocco and Spain remained stable into early 2005, following a visit by King Juan Carlos of Spain to Morocco in mid-January. However, during June–July six delegations of Spanish politicians and journalists, seeking to conduct investigations following demonstrations in Western Sahara, were accused by Morocco of supporting Sahrawi independence and were refused permission to enter the disputed territory (see above). In late September and early October at least 11 African migrants were reported to have died while attempting to enter Ceuta and Melilla illegally. Four were shot dead by Moroccan troops as the migrants scaled fences constructed to protect the borders between Morocco and the Spanish enclaves. The Spanish Government urged its Moroccan counterpart to increase its efforts to prevent illegal border crossings but later ended the practice of returning unsuccessful migrants to Morocco, amid claims by human rights organizations that migrants had been taken to the southern Moroccan desert and abandoned by the authorities. At the end of January 2006 Zapatero visited Ceuta and Melilla in an apparent show of support for the enclaves. The visit was the first by an incumbent Spanish premier for 25 years.

The Moroccan Government was swift to condemn the September 2001 attacks on New York and Washington, DC, for which the al-Qa'ida network was believed to be responsible. In early June 2002 the Moroccan authorities announced that they had arrested three Saudi nationals who were alleged to be members of an Islamist cell linked to al-Qa'ida that was preparing terrorist attacks on US and British warships in the Strait of Gibraltar. Seven Moroccans, including two of the suspects' wives, had also been arrested for allegedly acting as couriers between the Saudis in Morocco and al-Qa'ida, which had provided them with funds and logistical support. In February 2003 the three Saudis were sentenced to 10 years' imprisonment by a court in Casablanca; six of the Moroccans received sentences ranging from four months to one year for their roles in the plot. Also in February a Moroccan student, Mounir al-Motassadek, who was alleged to have been a member of the cell that had planned and executed the September 2001 attacks, was convicted by a court in Hamburg, Germany, of belonging to a terrorist group and of aiding and abetting the murder of 3,066 people. He was sentenced to 15 years' imprisonment. In mid-August 2003 the trial commenced in Hamburg of a second Moroccan student charged with identical offences; however, he was acquitted of all charges in February 2004. In March al-Motassadek's conviction was quashed by the German Federal Criminal Court and he was released from detention in April. A retrial began in August, and al-Motassadek was acquitted in August 2005 of involvement in the September 2001 attacks; he was nevertheless convicted of belonging to a terrorist organization and sentenced to seven years' imprisonment.

In mid-June 2004 Morocco became only the second Arab country (after Jordan in 2001) to sign a free-trade agreement with the USA. Both the Moroccan Chamber of Representatives and Chamber of Advisers ratified the accord in mid-January 2005.

Government

The 1992 Constitution (amended by referendum in 1996) provides for a modified constitutional monarchy, with an hereditary King as Head of State. Legislative power is vested in the Majlis an-Nuab (Chamber of Representatives), with 325 members directly elected, on the basis of universal adult suffrage, for five years, and in the Majlis al-Mustasharin (Chamber of Advisers), with 270 members chosen by electoral colleges (representing mainly local councils, with the remainder selected from professional associations and trade unions) for a nine-year term. Executive power is vested in the King, who appoints (and may dismiss) the Prime Minister and (on the latter's recommendation) other members of the Cabinet. The King may also dissolve the legislature.

Defence

In August 2005 Morocco's active armed forces numbered 200,800, consisting of an army of 180,000 (including an estimated 100,000 conscripts), a navy of 7,800 and an air force of 13,000. In addition, there was a paramilitary 'gendarmerie royale' of 20,000, and a paramilitary 'force auxiliaire' of 30,000 men (including a mobile intervention corps of 5,000). Army reserve forces totalled 150,000. Military service of 18 months is by authorized conscription. Under the 2005 budget, government expenditure on defence was projected at 18,100m. dirhams.

Economic Affairs

In 2004, according to estimates by the World Bank, Morocco's gross national income (GNI), measured at average 2002–04 prices, was US $46,518m., equivalent to $1,520 per head (or $4,100 per head on an international purchasing-power parity basis). During 1995–2004, it was estimated, the population increased at an average annual rate of 1.7%, while gross domestic product (GDP) per head increased, in real terms, by an average of 2.3% per year. Overall GDP increased, in real terms, at an average annual rate of 4.0% in 1995–2004; it increased by 5.5% in 2003 and by 4.2% in 2004.

Agriculture (including forestry and fishing) contributed an estimated 17.1% of GDP and engaged 45.8% of the employed labour force in 2004. The principal crops are cereals (mainly wheat and barley), sugar beet, potatoes, citrus fruit, tomatoes and sugar cane. Almost all of Morocco's meat requirements are produced within the country. The sale of licences to foreign fishing fleets is an important source of revenue. In 2004 seafoods and seafood products accounted for 6.4% of total exports. During 1995–2004 agricultural GDP increased at an average annual rate of 7.6%. Agricultural GDP increased by an estimated 18.8% in 2003 and by about 1.9% in 2004.

Industry (including mining, manufacturing, construction and power) provided some 32.7% of GDP and engaged 19.5% of the employed labour force in 2004. During 1995–2004 industrial GDP increased by an average of 3.7% per year. Industrial GDP rose by about 2.6% in 2003 and 4.9% in 2004.

Mining and quarrying contributed an estimated 1.8% of GDP in 2004; the sector engaged 0.6% of the employed labour force in 2000. The major mineral exports are phosphate rock and phosphoric acid, which together earned 12.2% of export revenues in 2004. Morocco is the world's largest exporter of phosphate rock. Petroleum exploration activity was revived at the end of the 1990s, and in August 2000 the discovery of major oil and natural gas reserves in the Talsinnt region of eastern Morocco was announced. Coal, salt, iron ore, barytes, lead, copper, zinc, silver, gold and manganese are mined. Deposits of nickel, cobalt and bauxite have been discovered. During 1990–2002 mining GDP increased at an average annual rate of 1.3%. According to official estimates, mining GDP decreased by 5.7% in 2003 but rose by 9.5% in 2004.

Manufacturing contributed about 17.8% of GDP in 2004, and employed 12.3% of the employed labour force in 2000. The most important branches, measured by gross value of output, are food-processing, textiles, and chemicals. In 2004 manufactured garments accounted for 21.6% of export revenues. During 1995–2004 manufacturing GDP was estimated to have increased at an average annual rate of 3.3%. Manufacturing GDP was estimated to have risen by 3.7% in 2003 and 3.0% in 2004.

Electric energy is derived principally from thermal power stations (which accounted for an estimated 94.5% of production in 2001) using coal and imported petroleum and gas. Facilities for generating hydroelectric and wind power have also been developed. Imports of fuel and energy products comprised an estimated 16.7% of the value of total merchandise imports in 2004.

The services sector contributed an estimated 50.2% of GDP and engaged 34.7% of the employed labour force in 2004. The tourist industry is generally a major source of revenue, and tourist arrivals totalled some 2.7m. in 2004. The GDP of the services sector increased by an estimated average of 3.3% per year during 1995–2004. The GDP of the sector rose by about 3.1% in 2003 and 5.3% in 2004.

In 2004 Morocco recorded a visible trade deficit of US $6,487m., but there was a surplus of $922m. on the current account of the balance of payments. In 2004 the principal source of imports was France (which provided an estimated 17.9% of merchandise imports); other major suppliers in that year included Spain, Italy, Germany and Russia. France was also the principal market for exports (33.1%) in 2004; Spain, the United Kingdom and Italy were also important purchasers of Moroccan exports. The principal exports in 2004 were manufactured garments, phosphates and phosphoric acid, hosiery and electronic components. The principal imports in that year were crude petroleum and textiles.

In 2004 there was a budget deficit of 15,318m. dirhams, equivalent to an estimated 3.5% of GDP. Morocco's total external debt in 2003 was US $18,795m., of which $17,542m. was long-term public debt. The cost of debt-servicing in that year was equivalent to 23.9% of exports of goods and services. The annual rate of inflation averaged 3.3% in 1989–2005. Annual inflation slowed from 1.5% in 2004 to 1.0% in 2005. Some 10.8% of the labour force were recorded as unemployed in 2004, although certain sources reported the rate to be closer to 20%.

Morocco is a member of the African Development Bank (see p. 151), the Islamic Development Bank (see p. 303) and of the Arab Fund for Economic and Social Development (see p. 161). It is a founder member of the Union du Maghreb arabe (Union of the Arab Maghreb, see p. 388).

Since 1980 the Moroccan authorities have undertaken a series of economic reforms (under the auspices of the IMF), including the reduction of taxes, tariffs and subsidies, and the introduction of a more efficient tax system. Efforts to stimulate foreign investment have had considerable success, while a programme of privatization has bolstered government revenue. In March 2000 a trade and co-operation agreement with the European Union (EU) came into effect, which provided for the establishment of a free-trade zone with the EU within 10 years. The Government was able to compensate for the loss of revenue from the fisheries accord with the EU, which expired in 2001, with the sale, for US $1,100m., of Morocco's second mobile cellular telephone operating licence and the partial privatization of Maroc Télécom—35% of which was sold to the French telecommunications company Vivendi Universal for $2,330m. A free-trade agreement was also signed between Morocco and the USA in June 2004, making 95% of trade between the two countries duty-free. The tourism sector was adversely affected by the volatile situation in the Middle East from 2002 and the suicide bombings launched against Western targets in Casablanca in May 2003. Nevertheless, the Government continued with ambitious plans to raise the number of tourist visitors to Morocco to 10m., and to significantly increase tourism revenues from an estimated 8% of GDP per year to nearer 20%, by 2010. Reasonable economic growth occurred in Morocco every year during 2000–04, with official figures estimating GDP growth of 4.2% in 2004. However, high international petroleum prices, a decline in agricultural output and the abolition of the WTO quota system in the textile industry were expected to contribute to slower growth in both 2005 and 2006. There were, nevertheless, a number of positive macroeconomic developments in 2004–05: the rate of inflation remained low, a balance-of-payments surplus was recorded and foreign-exchange reserves increased. Furthermore, a number of high-profile privatizations took place in 2004, including the sale in November of a further 16% stake in Maroc Télécom to Vivendi Universal. Pressure on the Government to devalue the dirham subsided in 2005, despite a significant rise in the trade deficit during the previous year. However, according to analysts, devaluation remained a likely prospect in the long term.

Education

Morocco has state-controlled primary, secondary and technical schools, and there are also private schools. Education (at the primary level) is compulsory for seven years, to be undertaken between the ages of six and 13 years. Secondary education, beginning at the age of 13, lasts for up to six years (comprising two cycles of three years). Primary enrolment in 2002/03 included 90% of children in the relevant age-group (92% of boys; 87% of girls), while, according to UNESCO estimates, secondary enrolment included 36% of the relevant age-group (boys 38%; girls 33%). The Government has recently taken steps to expand the teaching of the Berber language in primary schools (see Recent History). There were 277,442 students enrolled at state universities and equivalent-level institutions in 2003/04. Under the 2004 budget, expenditure on education by the central Government was 28,485m. dirhams (20.8% of total spending).

Public Holidays

2006: 1 January (New Year), 10 January (Independence Manifesto), (Eid el-Kebir—Id al-Adha, Feast of the Sacrifice*†), 31 January* (Islamic New Year), 9 February* (Ashoura), 10 April* (Mouloud, Birth of the Prophet), 1 May (Labour Day), 23 May (National Day), 30 July (Festival of the Throne, anniversary of King Muhammad's accession), 14 August (Oued ed-Dahab Day, anniversary of 1979 annexation), 24 September (Beginning of Ramadan), 23 October* (Eid es-Seghir—Id al-Fitr, end of Ramadan), 6 November (Anniversary of the Green March*), 18 November (Independence Day), 31 December (Eid el-Kebir—Id al-Adha, Feast of the Sacrifice*†).

2007: 1 January (New Year), 11 January (Independence Manifesto), 20 January* (Islamic New Year), 29 January* (Ashoura), 31 March* (Mouloud, Birth of the Prophet), 1 May (Labour Day), 23 May (National Day), 30 July (Festival of the Throne, anniversary of King Muhammad's accession), 14 August (Oued ed-Dahab Day, anniversary of 1979 annexation), 13 September* (Beginning of Ramadan), 13 October* (Eid es-Seghir—Id al-Fitr, end of Ramadan), 6 November (Anniversary of the Green March), 18 November (Independence Day), 20 December* (Eid el-Kebir—Id al-Adha, Feast of the Sacrifice).

* These holidays are dependent on the Islamic lunar calendar and may vary by one or two days from the dates given.

† This festival occurs twice (in the Islamic years AH 1426 and 1427) within the same Gregorian year.

Weights and Measures

The metric system is in force.

MOROCCO

Statistical Survey

Sources (unless otherwise stated): Haut Commissariat au Plan, Direction de la Statistique, rue Muhammad Belhassan el-Ouazzani, BP 178, Rabat 10001; tel. (3) 7773606; fax (3) 7773217; e-mail statguichet@statistic.gov.ma; internet www.statistic-hcp.ma; Bank Al-Maghrib, 277 ave Muhammad V, BP 445, Rabat; tel. (3) 7702626; fax (3) 7706677; e-mail dai@bkam.gov.ma; internet www.bkam.ma.

Note: Unless otherwise indicated, the data exclude Western (formerly Spanish) Sahara, a disputed territory under Moroccan occupation.

Area and Population

AREA, POPULATION AND DENSITY

Area (sq km)	710,850*
Population (census results)†	
2 September 1994	
Males	12,944,517
Females	13,074,763
Total	26,019,280
2 September 2004	29,891,708
Density (per sq km) at 2 September 2004	42.1

* 274,461 sq miles. This area includes the disputed territory of Western Sahara, which covers 252,120 sq km (97,344 sq miles).
† Including Western Sahara, with an estimated population of 417,000 at the 2004 census.

REGIONS
(population at 2004 census)

	Population
Oued ed-Dahab Lagouira*	99,367
El-Aaiún Boujdour*	256,152
Guelmim es-Semara†	462,410
Souss Massa-Draa	3,113,653
Gharb Chrarda Beni-Hsen	1,859,540
Chaouia Ouardigha	1,655,660
Marrakech Tensift al-Haou	3,102,652
Oriental	1,918,094
Grand Casablanca	3,631,061
Rabat Salé Zemmour Zaer	2,366,494
Doukkala Abda	1,984,039
Tadla Azilal	1,450,519
Meknès Tafilalet	2,141,527
Fès Boulemane	1,573,055
Taza al-Hoceima Taounate	1,807,113
Tanger Tétouan	2,470,372
Total	**29,891,708**

* Regions situated in Western Sahara.
† Region partly situated in Western Sahara.

PRINCIPAL TOWNS
(population at 2004 census)

Casablanca	2,933,684	Tétouan	320,539
Rabat (capital)*	1,622,860	Safi	284,750
Fès (Fez)	946,815	Mohammedia	188,619
Marrakech (Marrakesh)	823,154	El-Aaiún†	183,691
Agadir	678,596	Khouribga	166,397
Tanger (Tangier)	669,685	Beni-Mellal	163,286
Meknès	536,232	El-Jadida	144,440
Oujda	400,738	Taza	139,686
Kénitra	359,142		

* Including Salé and Temara.
† Town situated in Western Sahara.

Source: Thomas Brinkhoff, *City Population* (internet www.citypopulation.de).

BIRTHS AND DEATHS
(UN estimates, annual averages)

	1990–95	1995–2000	2000–05
Birth rate (per 1,000)	27.3	24.2	23.3
Death rate (per 1,000)	7.1	6.2	5.8

Source: UN, *World Population Prospects: The 2004 Revision*.

Expectation of life (WHO estimates, years at birth): 71 (males 69; females 73) in 2003 (Source: WHO, *World Health Report*).

ECONOMICALLY ACTIVE POPULATION
(sample surveys, '000 persons aged 15 years and over)

	2002	2003	2004
Agriculture, hunting, forestry and fishing	3,951	4,380	4,498
Mining and quarrying; manufacturing; electricity, gas and water	1,231	1,218	1,250
Construction	646	627	662
Wholesale and retail trade	1,180	1,166	1,247
Transport, storage and communications	332	325	347
General administration and community services	976	905	916
Other services	856	855	895
Activities not adequately defined	4	7	7
Total employed	**9,176**	**9,484**	**9,822**
Unemployed	1,203	1,223	1,193
Total labour force	**10,379**	**10,707**	**11,015**

Health and Welfare

KEY INDICATORS

Total fertility rate (children per woman, 2003)	2.7
Under-5 mortality rate (per 1,000 live births, 2004)	43
HIV/AIDS (% of persons aged 15–49, 2003)	0.1
Physicians (per 1,000 head, 2004)	0.48
Hospital beds (per 1,000 head, 1997)	0.98
Health expenditure (2002): US $ per head (PPP)	186
Health expenditure (2002): % of GDP	4.6
Health expenditure (2002): public (% of total)	32.8
Access to water (% of persons, 2002)	80
Access to sanitation (% of persons, 2002)	61
Human Development Index (2003): ranking	124
Human Development Index (2003): value	0.631

For sources and definitions, see explanatory note on p. vi.

Agriculture

PRINCIPAL CROPS
('000 metric tons)

	2002	2003	2004
Wheat	3,359	5,147	5,540
Rice (paddy)	27	17	17*
Barley	1,669	2,620	2,760
Maize	199	139	224
Other cereals*	40	50	49
Potatoes	1,334	1,435	1,440*
Sugar cane	938	947	992†
Sugar beet	2,987	3,429	4,560†
Dry broad beans	89	103	103*
Dry peas	22	23	26
Chick-peas	51	43	42
Lentils	42	34	36
Other pulses*	59	63	63
Almonds	82	71	70*
Groundnuts (in shell)	40	29†	49
Olives	455	470*	470*
Sunflower seed	16	56	56*
Cabbages	33	45	45*
Artichokes	44	50	54
Tomatoes	991	1,004	1,201
Cauliflowers	48	135	82

MOROCCO

—continued

	2002	2003	2004
Pumpkins, squash and gourds	114	110*	184
Cucumbers and gherkins	45	45*	41
Aubergines (Eggplants)	31	30*	39
Chillies and green peppers	156	168	182
Dry onions	610	684	789
Green beans	64	60*	129
Green peas	69	116	145
Green broad beans	104	141	141*
String beans	53	55*	55*
Carrots	233	332	311
Carobs*	24	26	26
Other vegetables*	471	465	472
Watermelons	370	492	684
Cantaloupes and other melons	574	500*	665
Figs	98	67	60
Grapes	276	281	267
Dates	33	54	69
Apples	373	275	393
Pears	46	39	45
Quinces	28	28*	28*
Peaches and nectarines	55	55	54
Plums	43	54	48
Strawberries	90*	91	106
Oranges	723	822	719
Tangerines, mandarins, clementines and satsumas	406	479	530†
Apricots	86	98	85
Bananas	162	173	189
Other fruits and berries*	80	84	83
Anise*	23	23	23
Peppermint	53	53*	53*

* FAO estimate(s).
† Unofficial figure.
Source: FAO.

LIVESTOCK
('000 head, year ending September)

	2002	2003	2004
Cattle	2,670	2,689	2,729
Sheep	16,336	16,743	17,026
Goats	5,090	5,208	5,359
Camels*	36	36	36
Horses	148	148*	148*
Mules	511	510*	510*
Asses	982	980*	980*
Poultry	137,000	137,000*	137*

* FAO estimate(s).
Source: FAO.

LIVESTOCK PRODUCTS
('000 metric tons)

	2002	2003	2004
Beef and veal	170	150	148
Mutton and lamb	110	100	103
Goat meat*	20	21	21
Poultry meat	280	280*	280*
Other meat*	38	38	38
Cows' milk	1,236	1,250	1,300
Sheep's milk*	27	27	27
Goats' milk*	34	34	34
Butter*	19	19	20
Cheese*	28	29	29
Hen eggs	235	230	230*
Honey	3	3	3*
Wool: greasy*	40	40	40
Wool: scoured*	17	17	17
Cattle hides (fresh)*	21	20	20
Sheepskins (fresh)*	12	12	13
Goatskins (fresh)*	3	3	3

* FAO estimate(s).
Source: FAO.

Forestry

ROUNDWOOD REMOVALS
('000 cubic metres, excl. bark)

	2002	2003	2004
Sawlogs, veneer logs and logs for sleepers	253	160	185
Pulpwood	273	351	378
Fuel wood	400	374	298
Total	926	885	861

Source: FAO.

SAWNWOOD PRODUCTION
('000 cubic metres, incl. railway sleepers)

	1987*	1988	1989
Coniferous (softwood)	40	26*	43*
Broadleaved (hardwood)	40	27	40
Total	80	53	83

* FAO estimate(s).
1990–2004: Annual production as in 1989 (FAO estimates).
Source: FAO.

Fishing

('000 metric tons, live weight)

	2001	2002	2003
Capture	1,084.0	895.0	885.1
European pilchard (sardine)	763.2	685.0	659.0
European anchovy	47.4	21.0	17.2
Chub mackerel	26.0	24.3	40.7
Cuttlefish, bobtails and squids	17.6	2.5	7.8
Octopuses	112.6	38.7	28.9
Aquaculture	1.4	1.7	1.5
Total catch (incl. others)	1,085.4	896.6	886.7

Note: Figures exclude aquatic plants ('000 metric tons, capture only): 10.0 in 2001; 7.9 in 2002; n.a. in 2003.

Mining

('000 metric tons)

	2002	2003	2004*
Crude petroleum	6.5	11.8	32.3
Iron ore†	1.6	6.3	9.9
Copper concentrates†	17.8	17.5	14.2
Lead concentrates†	87.4	54.8	44.7
Manganese ore†	17.5	—	9.0
Zinc concentrates†	178.4	136.4	146.2
Phosphate rock‡	23,041.0	22,877.0	25,369.0
Fluorspar (acid grade)	94.9	81.2	112.1
Barytes	469.9	358.5	355.8
Salt (unrefined)	266.1	236.7	253.8
Bentonite	65.8	67.7	85.4

* Preliminary figures.
† Figures refer to the gross weight of ores and concentrates.
‡ Including production in Western Sahara.

MOROCCO

Industry

SELECTED PRODUCTS*
('000 metric tons, unless otherwise indicated)

	2001	2002	2003
Cement	8,058	8,486	9,277
Electric energy (million kWh)	14,804	15,539	16,779†
Phosphate fertilizers‡	550	432	n.a.
Carpets and rugs ('000 sq m)	546	407	384†
Wine§	28	33	34
Olive oil (crude)	39	68	n.a.
Motor spirit—petrol	344	377	132
Naphthas	532	527	553
Kerosene	114	80	52
Distillate fuel oils	2,415	2,323	1,535
Residual fuel oils	2,401	2,000	1,748
Jet fuel	271	137	108
Petroleum bitumen—asphalt	127	131	57
Liquefied petroleum gas ('000 barrels)‖	2,710	2,690	1,000†

* Major industrial establishments only.
† Provisional figure.
‡ Estimated production in terms of phosphoric acid.
§ Source: FAO.
‖ Source: US Geological Survey.

Source: partly UN, *Industrial Commodity Statistics Yearbook*.

Finance

CURRENCY AND EXCHANGE RATES

Monetary Units
100 centimes (santimat) = 1 Moroccan dirham.

Sterling, Dollar and Euro Equivalents (30 December 2005)
£1 sterling = 15.93 dirhams;
US $1 = 9.25 dirhams;
€1 = 10.91 dirhams;
1,000 Moroccan dirhams = £62.79 = $108.12 = €91.65.

Average Exchange Rate (dirhams per US $)
2003 9.574
2004 8.868
2005 8.865

GENERAL BUDGET
(million dirhams)

Revenue*	2002	2003	2004
Tax revenue	91,020	94,229	100,762
Taxes on income and profits	30,378	33,145	36,467
Individual	16,353	17,783	19,583
Corporate	12,917	14,536	15,857
Taxes on international trade	14,231	12,578	13,292
Indirect taxes	40,056	41,890	43,901
Value-added tax	23,951	26,010	29,070
Excises	16,105	15,880	14,831
Registration and stamps	4,999	5,296	5,505
Revenue accruing to the road fund	1,356	1,320	1,597
Non-tax revenue	7,241	8,631	10,553
Dividend and licence income	4,244	5,038	7,132
Total	98,261	102,860	111,315

Expenditure	2002	2003	2004
General public services	6,885	6,870	7,136
Defence	16,994	17,476	17,632
Public order	10,096	9,199	10,026
Education	25,894	27,810	28,485
Health, social security and welfare	5,183	5,189	5,495
Housing	969	791	784
Recreation, culture, etc.	930	579	591
Agriculture, mines and energy	5,107	4,505	4,173
Transport and communications	3,604	2,193	1,685
General expenditure	11,355	12,540	13,253
Transfers to local governments	6,989	7,185	7,803
Other	24,793	32,635	39,986
Total	118,799	126,973	137,049

* Excluding receipts from privatization 621 in 2002; 11,957 in 2003; 10,416 in 2004.

Source: IMF, *Morocco, Statistical Appendix* (November 2005).

INTERNATIONAL RESERVES
(US $ million at 31 December)

	2003	2004	2005
Gold*	224	239	280
IMF special drawing rights	112	120	79
Reserve position in IMF	105	109	101
Foreign exchange	13,634	16,107	15,864
Total	14,075	16,575	16,324

* National valuation US $316 per troy oz at 31 December 2003; US $338 per troy oz at 31 December 2004; US $396 per troy oz at 31 December 2005.

Source: IMF, *International Financial Statistics*.

MONEY SUPPLY
(million dirhams at 31 December)

	2003	2004	2005
Currency outside banks	74,893	79,715	89,246
Demand deposits at deposit money banks	222,896	247,310	283,123
Total money (incl. others)	298,983	328,689	374,737

Source: IMF, *International Financial Statistics*.

COST OF LIVING
(Consumer Price Index for urban areas; base: 1989 = 100)

	2003	2004	2005
Food	166.4	169.0	169.5
Clothing	167.6	169.2	170.4
Shelter	167.0	169.8	172.0
Household equipment	139.8	140.6	142.0
All items (incl. others)	164.6	167.1	168.7

NATIONAL ACCOUNTS
(million dirhams at current prices)

Expenditure on the Gross Domestic Product

	2002	2003*	2004*
Government final consumption expenditure	79,962	88,113	93,050
Private final consumption expenditure	240,608	247,714	267,952
Change in inventories	−825	584	2,033
Gross fixed capital formation	91,142	100,498	109,083
Total domestic expenditure	410,887	436,910	472,118
Exports of goods and services	115,148	117,023	127,328
Less Imports of goods and services	128,253	134,447	155,774
GDP in purchasers' values	397,782	419,486	443,672
GDP at constant 1980 prices	147,969	156,139	162,767

* Provisional figures.

MOROCCO

Gross Domestic Product by Economic Activity

	2002	2003*	2004*
Agriculture, hunting, forestry and fishing	64,141	69,978	70,398
Mining and quarrying	7,314	6,437	7,228
Energy	27,129	27,985	32,043
Manufacturing	66,864	70,074	73,227
Construction	19,314	20,724	22,299
Commerce	47,149	49,789	53,075
Transport and communications	28,673	29,619	31,456
Public administration	59,972	66,569	70,808
Other services	48,666	50,026	51,812
Sub-total	369,223	391,201	412,346
Taxes, less subsidies, on imports	28,559	28,285	31,326
GDP in purchasers' values	397,782	419,486	443,672

* Provisional figures.

BALANCE OF PAYMENTS
(US $ million)

	2002	2003	2004
Exports of goods f.o.b.	7,839	8,771	9,922
Imports of goods f.o.b.	−10,900	−13,117	−16,408
Trade balance	−3,061	−4,345	−6,487
Exports of services	4,360	5,478	6,710
Imports of services	−2,413	−2,861	−3,451
Balance on goods and services	−1,115	−1,728	−3,228
Other income received	377	370	505
Other income paid	−1,115	−1,162	−1,176
Balance on goods, services and income	−1,853	−2,520	−3,898
Current transfers received	3,441	4,214	4,974
Current transfers paid	−115	−141	−154
Current balance	1,472	1,552	922
Capital account (net)	−6	−10	−8
Direct investment abroad	−28	−13	−20
Direct investment from abroad	79	2,313	769
Portfolio investment liabilities	−8	8	572
Other investment assets	—	−869	−454
Other investment liabilities	−1,380	−2,529	−797
Net errors and omissions	−182	−297	−247
Overall balance	−52	154	736

Source: IMF, *International Financial Statistics*.

External Trade

PRINCIPAL COMMODITIES
(million dirhams)

Imports c.i.f.	2002	2003	2004
Foodstuffs, beverages and tobacco	15,144	11,430	13,604
Wheat	5,820	3,674	4,944
Energy and lubricants	20,182	21,181	26,058
Crude petroleum	12,861	9,222	14,539
Gas oils and fuel oils	1,546	4,375	3,092
Crude animal and vegetable products	6,646	7,325	7,624
Semi-finished products	28,498	30,815	36,262
Chemical products	3,852	4,215	4,678
Finished industrial capital goods	25,215	28,971	33,186
Finished consumer products	31,211	32,214	35,264
Synthetic and artificial fabrics	3,990	3,819	3,344
Cotton fabrics	4,382	4,400	4,239
Total (incl. others)	130,409	136,070	156,296

Exports f.o.b.	2002	2003	2004
Foodstuffs, beverages and tobacco	18,164	17,472	13,587
Crustaceans and molluscs	5,926	4,260	2,365
Prepared and preserved fish	2,798	3,229	3,151
Energy and lubricants	2,426	889	1,763
Crude mineral products	5,772	4,994	6,299
Phosphates	4,006	3,468	4,003
Semi-finished products	19,724	19,564	23,426
Phosphoric acid	5,128	4,856	6,523
Natural and chemical fertilizers	3,650	3,554	3,888
Electronic components (transistors)	5,487	5,697	5,546
Finished industrial capital goods	5,603	6,461	6,581
Electric wire and cable	3,369	3,835	3,486
Finished consumer products	32,679	32,295	31,947
Manufactured garments	18,451	18,549	18,644
Hosiery	7,936	8,109	7,641
Total (incl. others)	86,389	83,887	86,365

Source: Office des Changes, Rabat.

PRINCIPAL TRADING PARTNERS
(million dirhams)*

Imports c.i.f.	2002	2003	2004
Algeria	1,758.7	1,671.8	1,414.7
Argentina	1,370.6	2,022.5	2,233.8
Belgium-Luxembourg	2,653.2	2,659.6	2,890.0
Brazil	3,341.0	2,564.1	3,961.0
Canada	1,765.4	1,323.8	1,401.9
China, People's Republic	3,753.2	4,655.8	6,612.9
France	26,760.9	27,985.2	27,999.5
Germany	6,917.4	7,075.8	9,330.3
India	956.6	1,568.5	1,091.9
Iran	3,190.6	433.5	2,453.6
Iraq	3,008.4	—	591.4
Ireland	612.8	1,357.7	1,519.2
Italy	7,566.5	9,693.0	10,282.9
Japan	2,281.0	2,833.7	3,174.9
Korea, Republic	1,346.7	1,537.6	1,998.2
Netherlands	2,136.2	3,239.0	2,609.9
Portugal	1,112.3	1,550.0	1,836.6
Russia	3,928.0	6,721.8	8,835.7
Saudi Arabia	7,642.0	6,861.0	8,400.6
South Africa	1,676.6	1,334.9	1,277.0
Spain	15,159.4	16,873.0	18,833.2
Sweden	2,195.7	1,907.8	1,691.2
Switzerland	1,560.3	2,037.3	2,588.7
Turkey	1,652.7	2,009.2	3,226.8
Ukraine	1,685.5	1,005.9	2,222.3
United Kingdom	6,415.3	5,356.0	5,219.3
USA	5,614.7	5,512.8	6,472.4
Total (incl. others)	130,408.9	136,070.1	156,296.4

Exports f.o.b.	2002	2003	2004
Belgium-Luxembourg	1,769.0	1,847.5	2,023.9
Brazil	1,565.6	1,738.7	2,430.1
France	29,084.1	28,679.5	28,590.0
Germany	3,604.2	3,299.9	2,648.4
India	2,851.0	2,611.9	2,991.6
Italy	4,676.8	4,321.4	4,067.2
Japan	3,079.8	1,652.0	587.3
Netherlands	1,856.3	2,119.2	2,368.5
Portugal	683.6	923.6	875.6
Spain	13,520.5	14,967.2	15,020.0
United Kingdom	6,834.0	6,109.9	6,637.1
USA	2,656.6	2,346.6	3,514.2
Total (incl. others)	86,389.2	83,887.4	86,365.2

* Imports by country of production; exports by country of last consignment.

Source: Office des Changes, Rabat.

MOROCCO

Transport

RAILWAYS
(traffic)*

	2002	2003	2004†
Passengers carried ('000)	14,685	16,516	18,429
Passenger-km (million)	2,145	2,374	n.a.
Freight ('000 metric tons)	29,945	30,552	32,899
Freight ton-km (million)	4,974	4,146	n.a.

* Figures refer to principal railways only.
† Provisional figures.

ROAD TRAFFIC
('000 motor vehicles in use at 31 December)

	1999	2000	2001
Passenger cars	1,161.9	1,211.1	1,253.0
Commercial vehicles	400.3	415.7	431.0

Motorcycles and scooters: 20,388 in 2000; 20,569 in 2001.

2003: 1,326,108 passenger cars in use.

Sources: IRF, *World Road Statistics*; UN, *Statistical Yearbook*.

SHIPPING

Merchant Fleet
(registered at 31 December)

	2002	2003	2004
Number of vessels	483	483	497
Total displacement ('000 grt)	501.7	503.8	522.6

Source: Lloyd's Register-Fairplay, *World Fleet Statistics*.

International Sea-borne Freight Traffic
('000 metric tons)

	2002	2003	2004*
Goods loaded	24,891	24,355	27,355
Goods unloaded	32,097	31,785	34,149

* Provisional figures.

CIVIL AVIATION
(traffic on Royal Air Maroc scheduled services)

	2001	2002	2003*
Kilometres flown (million)	62.8	61.6	63.6
Passengers carried ('000)	3,677	3,517	3,457
Passenger-km (million)	6,642	6,605	6,547

* Estimates.

Total ton-km (million): 718.5 in 2000.

Tourism

FOREIGN TOURIST ARRIVALS BY COUNTRY OF NATIONALITY*

	2002	2003	2004
France	877,465	916,147	1,167,088
Germany	172,860	129,391	146,269
Italy	112,518	100,001	112,807
Spain	201,258	231,156	333,028
United Kingdom	146,511	134,009	169,152
Other European countries	90,037	103,171	112,564
Maghreb countries	67,279	73,225	81,969
USA	72,845	64,445	76,889
Total (incl. others)	2,222,267	2,223,875	2,747,347

* Excluding Moroccans resident abroad (2,081,179 in 2002; 2,327,809 in 2003; 2,769,132 in 2004).
† Provisional figures.

Cruise-ship passengers: 255,305 in 2002; 259,937 in 2003; 255,663 in 2004.

Receipts from tourism (US $ million, incl. passenger transport): 2,980 in 2001; 3,157 in 2002; 3,369 in 2003.

Communications Media

	2002	2003	2004
Telephones ('000 main lines in use)	1,127.4	1,219.2	1,308.6
Mobile cellular telephones ('000 subscribers)	6,198.7	7,332.8	9,336.9
Personal computers ('000 in use)	400	600	620
Internet users ('000)	500	800	3,500

1997: Radio receivers ('000 in use) 6,640; Telefax stations (number in use) 18,000 (estimate).

1999: Book production (titles) 386.

2000: Television receivers ('000 in use) 4,700; Daily newspapers 23 (average circulation 846,000 copies); Other newspapers 507 (average circulation 4,108,000 copies); Periodicals 364 (average circulation 4,956,000 copies).

Sources: UNESCO, *Statistical Yearbook*; UN, *Statistical Yearbook*; and International Telecommunication Union.

Education

(1999/2000, unless otherwise indicated)

	Institutions	Teachers	Males	Females	Total
Pre-primary	33,577*	43,952	532,076	284,978	817,054
Primary:					
public	5,940	121,763	1,932,806	1,565,120	3,497,926
private	625	5,819	92,595	79,084	171,679
Secondary:					
general (public)	1,446	84,024†	785,550	610,346	1,393,896
general (private)	218	4,277	26,834	18,258	45,092
vocational	69	n.a.	12,810	9,981	22,791
University level*‡	68	9,667	154,314	112,193	266,507

* 1997/98 figure(s).
† Including vocational teachers.
‡ Provisional; state institutions only.

2001/02 (pupils/students): Primary 4,029,112 (public 3,832,356; private 196,756); Secondary 1,610,753 (public 1,561,686; private 49,067); University level 266,621.

2002/03 (pupils/students): Primary 4,101,157 (public 3,884,638; private 216,519); Secondary 1,679,077 (public 1,628,490; private 50,587); University level 280,599.

2003/04 (pupils/students): Primary 4,070,182 (public 3,846,950; private 223,232); Secondary 1,764,787 (public 1,707,871; private 56,916); University 277,442.

2004/05 (pupils/students, estimates): Primary 4,023,000; Secondary 1,865,000.

Source: mainly Ministère de l'Education Nationale.

Adult literacy rate (UNESCO estimates): 50.7% (males 63.3%; females 38.3%) in 2002 (Source: UN Development Programme, *Human Development Report*).

Directory

The Constitution

The following is a summary of the main provisions of the Constitution, as approved in a national referendum on 4 September 1992, and as amended by referendum on 13 September 1996.

PREAMBLE

The Kingdom of Morocco, a sovereign Islamic State whose official language is Arabic, constitutes a part of the Great Arab Maghreb. As an African State, one of its aims is the realization of African unity. It adheres to the principles, rights and obligations of those international organizations of which it is a member and works for the preservation of peace and security in the world.

GENERAL PRINCIPLES

Morocco is a constitutional, democratic and social monarchy. Sovereignty pertains to the nation and is exercised directly by means of the referendum and indirectly by the constitutional institutions. All Moroccans are equal before the law, and all adults enjoy equal political rights including the franchise. Freedoms of movement, opinion and speech and the right of assembly are guaranteed. Islam is the state religion. All Moroccans have equal rights in seeking education and employment. The right to strike, and to private property, is guaranteed. All Moroccans contribute to the defence of the Kingdom and to public costs. There shall be no one-party system.

THE MONARCHY

The Crown of Morocco and its attendant constitutional rights shall be hereditary in the line of HM King Hassan II, and shall be transmitted to the oldest son, unless during his lifetime the King has appointed as his successor another of his sons. The King is the symbol of unity, guarantees the continuity of the state, and safeguards respect for Islam and the Constitution. The King appoints, and may dismiss, the Prime Minister and other Cabinet Ministers (appointed upon the Prime Minister's recommendation), and presides over the Cabinet. He shall promulgate adopted legislation within a 30-day period, and has the power to dissolve the Chamber of Representatives and/or the Chamber of Advisers. The Sovereign is the Commander-in-Chief of the Armed Forces; makes appointments to civil and military posts; appoints Ambassadors; signs and ratifies treaties; presides over the Supreme Council of the Magistracy, the Supreme Council of Education and the Supreme Council for National Reconstruction and Planning; and exercises the right of pardon. In cases of threat to the national territory or to the action of constitutional institutions, the King, having consulted the President of the Chamber of Representatives, the President of the Chamber of Advisers and the Chairman of the Constitutional Council, and after addressing the nation, has the right to declare a State of Emergency by royal decree. The State of Emergency shall not entail the dissolution of Parliament and shall be terminated by the same procedure followed in its proclamation.

LEGISLATURE

This consists of a bicameral parliament: the Chamber of Representatives and the Chamber of Advisers. Members of the Chamber of Representatives are elected by direct universal suffrage for a five-year term. Three-fifths of the members of the Chamber of Advisers are elected by electoral colleges of local councils; the remainder are elected by electoral colleges representing chambers of commerce and trade unions. Members of the Chamber of Advisers are elected for a nine-year term, with one-third renewable every three years. Deputies in both chambers enjoy parliamentary immunity. Parliament shall adopt legislation, which may be initiated by members of either chamber or by the Prime Minister. Draft legislation shall be examined consecutively by both parliamentary chambers. If the two chambers fail to agree on the draft legislation the Government may request that a bilateral commission propose a final draft for approval by the chambers. If the chambers do not then adopt the draft, the Government may submit the draft (modified, if need be) to the Chamber of Representatives. Henceforth the draft submitted can be definitively adopted only by absolute majority of the members of the Chamber of Representatives. Parliament holds its meetings during two sessions each year, commencing on the second Friday in October and the second Friday in April.

GOVERNMENT

The Government, composed of the Prime Minister and his Ministers, is responsible to the King and Parliament and ensures the execution of laws. The Prime Minister is empowered to initiate legislation and to exercise statutory powers except where these are reserved to the King. He presents to both parliamentary chambers the Government's intended programme and is responsible for co-ordinating ministerial work.

RELATIONS BETWEEN THE AUTHORITIES

The King may request a second reading, by both Chambers of Parliament, of any draft bill or proposed law. In addition, he may submit proposed legislation to a referendum by decree; and dissolve either Chamber or both if a proposal that has been rejected is approved by referendum. He may also dissolve either Chamber by decree after consulting the Chairman of the Constitutional Council, and addressing the nation, but the succeeding Chamber may not be dissolved within a year of its election. The Chamber of Representatives may force the collective resignation of the Government either by refusing a vote of confidence or by adopting a censure motion. The election of the new Parliament or Chamber shall take place within three months of its dissolution. In the interim period the King shall exercise the legislative powers of Parliament, in addition to those conferred upon him by the Constitution. A censure motion must be signed by at least one-quarter of the Chamber's members, and shall be approved by the Chamber only by an absolute majority vote of its members. The Chamber of Advisers is competent to issue 'warning' motions to the Government and, by a two-thirds' majority, force its resignation.

THE CONSTITUTIONAL COUNCIL

The Constitutional Council consists of six members appointed by the King (including the Chairman) for a period of nine years, and six members appointed for the same period—three selected by the President of the Chamber of Representatives and three by the President of the Chamber of Advisers. One-third of each category of the Council are renewed every three years. The Council is empowered to judge the validity of legislative elections and referendums, as well as that of organic laws and the rules of procedure of both parliamentary chambers, submitted to it.

JUDICIARY

The Judiciary is independent. Judges are appointed on the recommendation of the Supreme Council of the Magistracy presided over by the King.

THE ECONOMIC AND SOCIAL COUNCIL

An Economic and Social Council shall be established to give its opinion on all matters of an economic or social nature. Its constitution, organization, prerogatives and rules of procedure shall be determined by an organic law.

THE HIGH AUDIT COUNCIL

The High Audit Council exercises the general supervision of the implementation of fiscal laws. It ensures the regularity of revenues and expenditure operations of the departments legally under its jurisdiction, as it assesses the management of the affairs thereof. It is competent to penalize any breach of the rules governing such operations. Regional audit councils exercise the supervision of the accounts of local assemblies and bodies, and the management of the affairs thereof.

LOCAL GOVERNMENT

Local government in the Kingdom consists of establishing regions, governorships, provinces and communes.

REVISING THE CONSTITUTION

The King, the Chamber of Representatives and the Chamber of Advisers are competent to initiate a revision of the Constitution. The King has the right to submit the revision project he initiates to a national referendum. A proposal for a revision by either parliamentary chamber shall be adopted only if it receives a two-thirds' majority vote by the chamber's members. Revision projects and proposals shall be submitted to the nation for referendum by royal decree; a revision of the Constitution shall be definitive after approval by referendum. Neither the state, system of monarchy nor the prescriptions related to the religion of Islam may be subject to a constitutional revision.

The Government

HEAD OF STATE

Monarch: HM King MUHAMMAD VI (acceded 23 July 1999).

MOROCCO

CABINET
(April 2006)

A coalition of the Union socialiste des forces populaires (USFP); Istiqlal; Rassemblement national des indépendants (RNI); Mouvement populaire (MP); Parti du progrès et du socialisme (PPS); Mouvement national populaire (MNP); Union démocratique (UD); and non-affiliates.

Prime Minister: DRISS JETTOU.
Minister of State: ABBAS EL-FASSI (Istiqlal).
Minister of Foreign Affairs and Cooperation: MUHAMMAD BENAÏSSA (RNI).
Minister of the Interior: CHAKIB BENMOUSSA.
Minister of Justice: MUHAMMAD BOUZOUBAÂ (USFP).
Minister of Habous (Religious Endowments) and Islamic Affairs: AHMED TAOUFIQ.
Minister of Territorial Administration, Water Resources and the Environment: MUHAMMAD EL-YAZGHI (USFP).
Minister of Finance and Privatization: FATHALLAH OUALALOU (USFP).
Secretary-General of the Government: ABDESSADEK RABIAÂ.
Minister of Agriculture, Rural Development and Maritime Fisheries: MOHAND LAENSER (MP).
Minister of Employment and Vocational Training: MUSTAPHA MANSOURI.
Minister of National Education, Higher Education, Training and Scientific Research: HABIB EL-MALKI (USFP).
Minister in charge of the Modernization of the Public Sector: MUHAMMAD BOUSSAID (RNI).
Minister of Cultural Affairs: MUHAMMAD ACHAÂRI (USFP).
Minister of Tourism: ADIL DOUIRI (Istiqlal).
Minister of Equipment and Transport: KARIM GHELLAB (Istiqlal).
Minister of Industry, Commerce and Economic Development: SALAHEDDINE MEZOUAR.
Minister of Health: MUHAMMAD CHEIKH BIADILLAH.
Minister in charge of Relations with Parliament: MUHAMMAD SAÂD EL-ALAMI (Istiqlal).
Minister of Energy and Mining: MUHAMMAD BOUTALEB (RNI).
Minister of Communication and Government Spokesperson: MUHAMMAD NABIL BENABDALLAH (PPS).
Minister of Foreign Trade: MUSTAPHA MECHAHOURI (MP).
Minister of Social Development, Families and Solidarity: ABDERRAHIM HAROUCHI.
Minister-delegate to the Prime Minister, in charge of Economic and General Affairs: RACHID TALBI ALAMI (RNI).
Minister-delegate to the Prime Minister, in charge of the Administration of National Defence: ABD AR-RAHMAN SBAI.
Minister-delegate to the Minister of Foreign Affairs and Co-operation: TAIEB FASSI FIHRI.
Minister-delegate to the Minister of Foreign Affairs and Co-operation, in charge of Moroccans Resident Abroad: NEZHA CHEKROUNI (USFP).
Minister-delegate to the Minister of the Interior: FOUAD ALI EL-HIMMA.
Minister-delegate to the Prime Minister, in charge of Housing and Town Planning: AHMED TAOUFIQ HEJIRA (Istiqlal).

There are also six Secretaries of State.

MINISTRIES

Office of the Prime Minister: Palais Royal, Touarga, Rabat; tel. (3) 7219400; fax (3) 7769995; e-mail courrier@pm.gov.ma; internet www.pm.gov.ma.

Ministry of Agriculture, Rural Development and Maritime Fisheries: Quartier Administratif, Place Abdellah Chefchaouni, BP 607, Rabat; tel. (3) 7760933; fax (3) 7763378; e-mail webmaster@mardrpm.gov.ma.

Ministry of Communication: ave Allal al-Fassi, Madinat al-Irfane Souissi, 10000 Rabat; tel. (3) 7772412; fax (3) 7767815; e-mail webmaster@mincom.gov.ma; internet www.mincom.gov.ma.

Ministry of Culture: 1 rue Ghandi, Rabat; tel. (3) 7209494; fax (3) 7209401; e-mail webmaster@minculture.gov.ma; internet www.minculture.gov.ma.

Ministry of Economic Planning: ave Al Haj Ahmed Cherkaoui, BP 826, 10004 Rabat; e-mail idoubba@cnd.mpep.gov.ma.

Ministry of Employment and Vocational Training: Route Akrach, Hay Ennahda 2, Takadoum, BP 5015, Souissi, Rabat; tel. (3) 7750266; fax (3) 7750192; e-mail communication@emploi.gov.ma; internet www.emploi.gov.ma.

Ministry of Energy and Mining: rue Abou Marouane Essaadi, BP 6208, Agdal, Rabat; tel. (3) 7688830; fax (3) 7688831; e-mail webmaster@mem.gov.ma; internet www.mem.gov.ma.

Ministry of Equipment and Transport: Quartier Administratif, Chellah, Rabat; tel. (3) 7762811; fax (3) 7765505; e-mail ghellab@mtpnet.gov.ma; internet www.mtpnet.gov.ma.

Ministry of Finance and Privatization: Quartier Administratif, Chellah, Rabat; tel. (3) 7677501; fax (3) 7677527; e-mail daag@daag.finances.gov.ma; internet www.finances.gov.ma.

Ministry of Foreign Affairs and Co-operation: ave Franklin Roosevelt, Rabat; tel. (3) 7761583; fax (3) 7765508; e-mail mail@maec.gov.ma; internet www.maec.gov.ma.

Ministry of Foreign Trade: 63 ave Moulay Youssef, Rabat; e-mail ministere@mce.gov.ma; internet www.mce.gov.ma.

Ministry of Habous (Religious Endowments) and Islamic Affairs: Al-Mechouar Essaid, Rabat; tel. (3) 7766801; fax (3) 7765282; e-mail infos@habous.gov.ma; internet www.habous.gov.ma.

Ministry of Health: 335 blvd Muhammad V, Rabat; tel. (3) 7761121; fax (3) 7768401; e-mail inas@sante.gov.ma; internet www.sante.gov.ma.

Ministry of Housing and Town Planning: Rues al-Jouaze and al-Joumaize, Hay Ryad, Secteur 16, 10000 Rabat; tel. (3) 7577000; fax (3) 7577373; e-mail mhu@mhu.gov.ma; internet www.mhu.gov.ma.

Ministry of Industry, Commerce and Economic Development: Rabat; tel. (3) 7761868; fax (3) 7766265; e-mail webmaster@mcinet.gov.ma; internet www.mcinet.gov.ma.

Ministry of the Interior: Quartier Administratif, Rabat; tel. (3) 7761868; fax (3) 7762056.

Ministry of Justice: Place Mamounia, Rabat; tel. (3) 7732941; fax (3) 7730772; e-mail kourout@justice.gov.ma; internet www.justice.gov.ma.

Ministry of the Modernization of the Public Sector: Quartier Administratif, rue Ahmed Cherkaoui, Agdal, BP 1076, Rabat; tel. (3) 7773106; fax (3) 7778438; e-mail info@mmsp.gov.ma; internet www.mmsp.gov.ma.

Ministry of National Education, Higher Education, Training and Scientific Research: Bab Rouah, Rabat; tel. (3) 7774839; fax (3) 7779001; internet www.men.gov.ma.

Ministry in charge of Relations with Parliament: Nouveau Quartier Administratif, Agdal, Rabat; tel. (3) 7775159; fax (3) 7777719; e-mail mirepa@mcrp.gov.ma; internet www.mcrp.gov.ma.

Ministry of Territorial Administration, Water Resources and the Environment: 36 ave el-Abtal, Agdal, Rabat; tel. (3) 7772634; fax (3) 7772756; e-mail info@minenv.gov.ma; internet www.minenv.gov.ma.

Ministry of Youth and Sports: blvd ibn Sina, Rabat; tel. (3) 7680028; fax (3) 7680145; internet www.mjs.gov.ma.

Legislature

MAJLIS AN-NUAB
(Chamber of Representatives)

President: ABDELWAHAD RADI (USFP).

General Election, 27 September 2002

Party	% of votes	Seats
Union socialiste des forces populaires (USFP)	15.38	50
Istiqlal	14.77	48
Parti de la justice et du développement (PJD)	12.92	42
Rassemblement national des indépendants (RNI)	12.62	41
Mouvement populaire (MP)	8.31	27
Mouvement national populaire (MNP)	5.54	18
Union constitutionnelle	4.92	16
Front des forces démocratiques (FFD)	3.69	12
Parti national démocrate (PND)	3.69	12
Parti du progrès et du socialisme (PPS)	3.38	11
Union démocratique (UD)	3.08	10
Mouvement démocratique social (MDS)	2.15	7
Parti socialiste démocratique (PSD)	1.85	6

MOROCCO

Party—continued	% of votes	Seats
Parti Al Ahd	1.54	5
Alliance des libertés (ADL)	1.23	4
Parti de la gauche socialiste unifiée (PGSU)	0.92	3
Parti de la réforme et du développement (PRD)	0.92	3
Parti marocain libéral (PML)	0.92	3
Parti des forces citoyennes (PFC)	0.62	2
Parti de l'environnement et du développement (PED)	0.62	2
Parti démocratique et de l'indépendance (PDI)	0.62	2
Congrès national ittihadi (CNI)	0.31	1
Total	**100.00**	**325***

* 30 of the 325 seats were reserved for women. Of these 30 seats, five were won by the USFP; Istiqlal, the PJD and the RNI each took four seats; the MP, the MNP, the UC, the PND, the FFD and PPS all secured two seats; and the UD received one seat.

MAJLIS AL-MUSTASHARIN
(Chamber of Advisers)

President: MUSTAPHA OKACHA.

Election, 5 December 1997*

	Seats
Rassemblement national des indépendants (RNI)	42
Mouvement démocratique et social (MDS)	33
Union constitutionnelle (UC)	28
Mouvement populaire (MP)	27
Parti national démocrate (PND)	21
Istiqlal	21
Union socialiste des forces populaires (USFP)	16
Mouvement national populaire (MNP)	15
Parti de l'action (PA)	13
Front des forces démocratiques (FFD)	12
Parti du progrès et du socialisme (PPS)	7
Parti social et démocratique (PSD)	4
Parti démocratique pour l'indépendance (PDI)	4
Trade unions	
Confédération Démocratique du Travail (CDT)	11
Union Marocaine du Travail (UMT)	8
Union Générale des Travailleurs Marocains (UGMT)	3
Others	5
Total	**270**

* Of the Chamber of Advisers' 270 members, 162 were elected by local councils, 81 by chambers of commerce and 27 by trade unions.
Note: On 8 September 2000 elections were held to renew one-third of the seats in the Chamber of Advisers. 54 members were elected by local councils and 27 by chambers of commerce. The seats were allocated accordingly: RNI 14 seats; MNP 12; PND 10; MP 9; UC 8; Istiqlal 7; MDS 6; FFD 5; USFP 3; PPS 2; PA 2; PSD 2; PDI one. Of the nine seats elected by trade unions, the CDT won 4; the UMT 2; the UGTM 2; and the l'Union Nationale des Travailleurs du Maroc (UNMT) won one seat. Further elections were held to renew one-third of the seats in the Chamber of Advisers on 6 October 2003.

Political Organizations

Congrès national ittihadi (CNI): 209 blvd Strasbourg, Résidence C, 2ème étage, Casablanca; tel. and fax (2) 2447664; f. 2001 by dissident members of the USFP; Sec.-Gen. ABDELMAJID BOUZOUBÂA.

Front des forces démocratiques (FFD): 13 blvd Tariq ibn Ziad, Journal Al-Mounaâtaf, Rabat; tel. (3) 7661625; fax (3) 7660621; e-mail www.info.ffd@menara.ma; internet www.ffd.ma; f. 1997 after split from PPS; Sec.-Gen. THAMI EL-KHIARI.

Istiqlal (Independence): 4 ave Ibnou Toumert, Bab el-Had, Rabat; tel. (3) 7730951; fax (3) 7736329; internet www.istiqlal.ma; f. 1944; aims to raise living standards and to confer equal rights on all; emphasizes the Moroccan claim to Western Sahara; Sec.-Gen. ABBAS EL-FASSI.

Mouvement démocratique et social (MDS): 471 ave Muhammad V, Rabat; tel. (3) 7709110; f. 1996 as Mouvement national démocratique et social after split from MNP; adopted current name in Nov. 1996; Leader MAHMOUD ARCHANE.

Mouvement national populaire (MNP): 2 blvd Tarik ibn Zyad, Hassan, Rabat; tel. (3) 7761552; fax (3) 7761479; f. 1991; centre party; Leader MAHJOUBI AHERDANE.

Mouvement populaire (MP): 66 rue Patrice Lumumba, Rabat; tel. (3) 7766431; fax (3) 7767537; e-mail webmaster@harakamp.org.ma; internet www.harakamp.org.ma; f. 1958; liberal; Sec.-Gen. MOHAND LAENSER.

Mouvement populaire pour la démocratie (MPD): Leader M. EL-KHATIB.

Organisation de l'action démocratique et populaire (OADP): Casablanca; tel. (2) 2262433; fax (2) 2278442; e-mail organisation.oadp@caramail.com; f. 1983; Sec.-Gen. MUHAMMAD BEN SAÏD AÏT IDDER.

Parti de l'action (PA): 113 ave Allal ben Abdallah, Rabat; tel. (3) 7206661; f. 1974; advocates democracy and progress; Sec.-Gen. MUHAMMAD EL-IDRISSI.

Parti Al Ahd: 14 rue Idriss al-Akbar, rue Tafraout, Hassan, Rabat; tel. (3) 7204816; fax (3) 7204786; e-mail alhakika@iam.net.ma; f. 2002; Chair. NAJIB EL-OUAZZANI.

Parti de l'avant-garde démocratique socialiste (PADS): BP 2091, 54 ave de la Résistance Océan, Rabat; tel. (3) 7200559; fax (3) 7708491; an offshoot of the USFP; legalized in April 1992; Sec.-Gen. AHMAD BENJELLOUNE.

Parti démocratique et de l'indépendance (PDI): Casablanca; tel. (2) 2223359; f. 1946; Sec.-Gen. ABDELWAHED MAÂCH.

Parti de l'environnement et du développement (PED): 3 rue Azilal, Hassan, Rabat; tel. (3) 7702174; fax (3) 7702174; e-mail alamiahmed@hotmail.com; internet www.geocities.com/ped_maroc; f. 2002; Sec.-Gen. AHMAD AL-ALAMI.

Parti des forces citoyennes (PFC): 353 blvd Muhammad V, 9ème étage, Casablanca; tel. (2) 2400608; fax (2) 2400613; e-mail citoyennes@iam.net.ma; f. 2001; Sec.-Gen. ABDERRAHIM LAHJOUJI.

Parti de la gauche socialiste unifiée (PGSU): 29 ave Lalla Yacout, Apartment No. 1, BP 15797, Casablanca; f. 2001; left-wing coalition comprising the OADP, the MPD, the Activistes de gauche and the Démocrates indépendants; Pres. MUHAMMAD BEN SAÏD AÏT IDDER.

Parti de la justice et du développement (PJD): ave Abdelwahed Elmorakechi, rue Elyafrani, 4 les Orangers, Rabat; tel. (3) 7208862; fax (3) 7208854; e-mail info@pjd.ma; internet www.pjd.ma; f. 1967 as the Mouvement populaire constitutionnel et démocratique (MPCD); breakaway party from MP; formally absorbed members of the Islamic asscn Al Islah wa Attajdid in June 1996 and adopted current name in Oct. 1998; Sec.-Gen. SAÂDEDDINE OTHMANI.

Parti marocain libéral (PML): 114 ave Allal ben Abdallah, 2ème étage, Rabat; tel. (3) 7733670; fax (3) 7733611; e-mail pml@menara.ma; f. 2002; Nat. Co-ordinator MUHAMMAD ZIANE.

Parti national démocrate (PND): 18 rue de Tunis, Hassan, Rabat; tel. (3) 7732127; fax (3) 7720170; internet www.pnd.ma; f. 1981 from split within RNI; Sec.-Gen. ABDELLAH KADIRI.

Parti de la réforme et du développement (PRD): 34 ave Pasteur, Rabat; tel. (3) 7703801; fax (3) 7655468; f. 2001; by fmr members of the RNI; Leader ABD AR-RAHMANE EL-KOUHEN.

Parti de la Renaissance et de la Vertu (Renaissance and Virtue Party): Bouznika; f. 2005; national democratic party based on the principles of Islam; Sec.-Gen. MUHAMMAD KHALIDI.

Parti du progrès et du socialisme (PPS): 29 ave John Kennedy, Youssoufia, Rabat; tel. (3) 7759464; fax (3) 7759476; e-mail sg@pps.maroc.org; f. 1974; successor to the Parti communiste marocain (banned in 1952), and the Parti de la libération et du socialisme (banned in 1969); left-wing; advocates modernization, social progress, nationalization and democracy; 35,000 mems; Sec.-Gen. ISMAÏL ALAOUI.

Parti socialiste démocratique (PSD): 1 rue ibn Moqla, angle les Orangers, Rabat; tel. and fax (3) 7208576; e-mail dsp1@iam.net.ma; f. 1996; breakaway party from OADP; Leader ISSA OUARDIGHI.

Rassemblement national des indépendants (RNI): 6 rue Laos, ave Hassan II, Rabat; tel. (3) 7721420; fax (3) 7733824; f. 1978 from the pro-govt independents' group that then formed the majority in the Chamber of Representatives; Leader AHMAD OUSMAN.

Union constitutionnelle (UC): 158 ave des Forces Armées Royales, Casablanca; tel. (2) 2441144; fax (2) 2441141; e-mail union_constit@menara.ma; f. 1983; 25-member Political Bureau; Leader MUHAMMAD ABIED.

Union démocratique (UD): 75 ave John Kennedy, Rabat; tel. (3) 7636616; fax (3) 7636594; f. 2001; Pres. BOUAZZA IKKEN.

Union nationale des forces populaires (UNFP): 28–30 rue Magellan, BP 747, Casablanca; tel. (2) 2302023; fax (2) 2319301; f. 1959 by Mehdi ben Barka from a group within Istiqlal; left-wing; in 1972 a split occurred between the Casablanca and Rabat sections of the party; Leader (vacant).

Union socialiste des forces populaires (USFP): 17 rue Oued Souss, Agdal, Rabat; tel. (3) 7773905; fax (3) 7773901; e-mail webmaster@usfp.ma; internet www.usfp.ma; f. 1959 as UNFP;

MOROCCO

became USFP in 1974; left-wing progressive party; 100,000 mems; First Sec. MUHAMMAD EL-YAZGHI.

The following group is active in the disputed territory of Western Sahara:

Frente Popular para la Liberaciόn de Saguia el-Hamra y Río de Oro (Frente Polisario) (Polisario Front): BP 10, el-Mouradia, Algiers; tel. (2) 747907; fax (2) 747206; e-mail dgmae@mail.wissal.dz; f. 1973 to gain independence for Western Sahara, first from Spain and then from Morocco and Mauritania; signed peace treaty with Mauritanian Govt in 1979; supported by Algerian Govt; in February 1976 proclaimed the Sahrawi Arab Democratic Republic (SADR); admitted as the 51st member of the OAU in Feb. 1982 and currently recognized by more than 75 countries worldwide; its main organs are a 33-member National Secretariat, a 101-member Sahrawi National Assembly (Parliament) and a 13-member Govt; Sec.-Gen. of the Polisario Front and Pres. of the SADR MUHAMMAD ABD AL-AZIZ; Prime Minister of the SADR BOUCHRAYA HAMMOUDI BAYOUNE.

Diplomatic Representation

EMBASSIES IN MOROCCO

Algeria: 46–48 blvd Tariq ibn Ziad, BP 448, 10001 Rabat; tel. (3) 7661574; fax (3) 7762237; e-mail algerabat@iam.net.ma; Ambassador LARBI BELKHEIR.

Angola: km 5, 53 Ahmed Rifaï, BP 1318, Soussi, Rabat; tel. (3) 7659239; fax (3) 7653707; e-mail amb.angola@iam.net.ma; Ambassador Dr LUIS JOSÉ DE ALMEIDA.

Argentina: 12 rue Mekki Bitaouri, Souissi, 10000 Rabat; tel. (3) 7755120; fax (3) 7755410; e-mail emarr@mrecic.gov.ar; Ambassador ALBERTO DE NUÑEZ.

Austria: 2 rue de Tiddes, BP 135, 10000 Rabat; tel. (3) 7761698; fax (3) 7765425; e-mail rabat-ob@bmaa.gv.at; Ambassador Dr GERHARD DEISS.

Bahrain: rue beni Hassan, km 6.5, route des Zaêrs, Soussi, Rabat; tel. (3) 7633500; fax (3) 7630732; e-mail bahrain@mtds.com; Ambassador KHALID BIN SALMAN AL-KHALIFA.

Bangladesh: 25 ave Tarek ibn Ziad, BP 1468, Rabat; tel. (3) 7766731; fax (3) 7766729; e-mail bdoot@mtds.com; internet www.bangladeshembassy-morocco.org; Ambassador MOHAMMAD AL-HAROON.

Belgium: 6 ave de Muhammad el-Fassi, Tour Hassan, Rabat; tel. (3) 7268060; fax (3) 7767003; e-mail rabat@diplobel.org; internet www.diplomatie.be/rabat; Ambassador PATRICK VERCAUTEREN.

Benin: 30 ave Mehdi ben Barka, BP 5187, Souissi, 10105 Rabat; tel. (3) 7754158; fax (3) 7754156; Ambassador ISSIRADJOU IBRAHIM GOMINA.

Brazil: 10 ave el-Jacaranda, Secteur 2, Hay Riad, 10000 Rabat; tel. (3) 7714613; fax (3) 7714808; e-mail brabat@iam.net.ma; Ambassador CARLOS ALBERTO SIMAS MAGALHÃES.

Bulgaria: 4 ave Ahmed el-Yazidi, BP 1301, 10000 Rabat; tel. (3) 7765477; fax (3) 7763201; e-mail bulemrab@wanadoo.net.ma; Ambassador KATIA PETROVA TODOROVA.

Burkina Faso: 7 rue al-Bouziri, BP 6484, Agdal, 10101 Rabat; tel. (3) 7675512; fax (3) 7675517; e-mail ambfrba@smirt.net.ma; Ambassador Brig.-Gen. IBRAHIM TRAORÉ.

Cameroon: 20 rue du Rif, BP 1790, Souissi, Rabat; tel. (3) 7754194; fax (3) 7750540; e-mail ambacamrabat@ifrance.com; Ambassador MAHAMAT PABA SALÉ.

Canada: 13 bis rue Jaâfar as-Sadik, BP 709, Agdal, Rabat; tel. (3) 7687400; fax (3) 7687430; e-mail rabat@dfait-maeci.gc.ca; internet www.dfait-maeci.gc.ca/morocco; Ambassador CARMEN SYLVAIN.

Central African Republic: Villa No 4, ave Souss, Cité Saâda, Quartier Administratif, BP 770, Agdal, 10000 Rabat; tel. (3) 7631654; fax (3) 7631655; e-mail centrafricaine@iam.net.ma; Ambassador ISMAÏLA NIMAGA.

Chile: 35 ave Ahmed Balafrej, Souissi, Rabat; tel. (3) 7636065; fax (3) 7636067; e-mail echilema@menara.net.ma; Ambassador ALEJANDRO CARVAJAL.

China, People's Republic: 16 ave Ahmed Balafrej, 10000 Rabat; tel. (3) 7754056; fax (3) 7757519; Ambassador CHENG TAO.

Colombia: Résidence place Otman Ibnou Affane, 3e étage, App. no 12, angle ave 16 Novembre et rue Honaine, Agdal, 10000 Rabat; tel. (3) 7670804; fax (3) 7670802; e-mail emcora@smirt.net.ma; Ambassador GUILLERMO SALAH ZULETTA.

Congo, Democratic Republic: 34 ave de la Victoire, BP 553, 10000 Rabat; tel. (3) 7262280; fax (3) 7262280.

Congo, Republic: ave Imam Malik, 7 rue Senhaja, Soussi, Rabat; tel. (3) 7659966; fax (3) 7659959; Ambassador JEAN-MARIE EWENGUE.

Côte d'Ivoire: 21 rue de Tiddas, BP 192, 10001 Rabat; tel. (3) 7763151; fax (3) 7762792; e-mail ambcim@clam.net.ma; Ambassador SIA BI SEI.

Croatia: 73 rue Marnissa, Souissi, Rabat; tel. (3) 7638824; fax (3) 7638827; e-mail croamb@menara.ma; Ambassador DUBRAVCO ZIPOVČIĆ.

Czech Republic: 4m 4.5 route des Zaêrs, Zankat Aït Melloul, villa Merzaâ, Souissi, Rabat; tel. (3) 7755421; fax (3) 7755493; e-mail rabat@embassy.mzv.cz; internet www.mzv.cz/rabat; Ambassador ELEONORA URBANOVA.

Egypt: 31 rue al-Jazair, 10000 Rabat; tel. (3) 7731833; fax (3) 7706821; e-mail embegypt@mtds.com; Ambassador ACHRAF YOUSUF ABDELHALIM ZAÂZAÂ.

Equatorial Guinea: ave President Roosevelt, angle rue d'Agadir 9, Rabat; tel. (3) 7769454; fax (3) 7769454; Ambassador JUAN NDONG NGUEMA MBENGONO.

Finland: 145 rue Soufiane ben Wahb, OLM, Rabat; tel. (3) 7762312; fax (3) 7762352; e-mail admin@ambafinrab.org.ma; Ambassador SAULI ERIK FEODOROW (resident in Lisbon, Portugal).

France: 3 rue Sahnoun, Rabat; tel. (3) 7689700; fax (3) 7689720; e-mail webmestre@ambafrance-ma.org; internet www.ambafrance-ma.org; Chargé d'affaires a.i. BRUNO AUBERT.

Gabon: ave Imam Malik, km 3.5, BP 1239, 10100 Rabat; tel. (3) 7751968; fax (3) 7757550; Ambassador FRANÇOIS BANGA EBOUMI.

Gambia: 11 rue Cadi ben Hammadi Senhaji, Soussi, Rabat; tel. (3) 7638045; fax (3) 7638189; Ambassador MAUDO HARLEY NURU TOURAY.

Germany: 7 Zankat Madnine, BP 235, 10000 Rabat; tel. (3) 7709662; fax (3) 7706851; e-mail amballma@mtds.com; internet www.amballemagne-rabat.ma; Ambassador Dr GOTTFRIED HAAS.

Greece: km 5 route des Zaêrs, Villa Chems, Soussi, 10000 Rabat; tel. (3) 7638964; fax (3) 7638990; e-mail ambagrec@iam.net.ma; Ambassador MICHEL CAMBANIS.

Guinea: 15 rue Hamzah, Agdal, Rabat; tel. (3) 7674148; fax (3) 7672513; Ambassador MAHMADOU SALIOU SYLA.

Holy See: rue Béni M'tir, BP 1303, Souissi, Rabat (Apostolic Nunciature); tel. (3) 7772277; fax (3) 7756213; e-mail nuntius@iam.net.ma; Apostolic Nuncio Most Rev. ANTONIO SOZZO (Titular Archbishop of Concordia).

Hungary: route des Zaêrs, 17 Zankat Aït Melloul, BP 5026, Souissi, Rabat; tel. (3) 7750757; fax (3) 7754123; e-mail huembrba@mtds.com; Ambassador LÁSZLÓ VÁRADI.

India: 13 ave de Michlifen, 10000 Rabat; tel. (3) 7671339; fax (3) 7671269; e-mail india@menara.ma; internet www.indianembassymorocco.ma; Ambassador PRABHU DAYAL.

Indonesia: 63 rue Béni Boufrah, km 5.9 route des Zaêrs, BP 576, 10105 Rabat; tel. (3) 7757860; fax (3) 7757859; e-mail kbrirabat@iam.net.ma; Ambassador SJACHWIEN ADENAN.

Iran: ave Imam Malik, BP 490, 10001 Rabat; tel. (3) 7752167; fax (3) 7659118; e-mail iranembassy@iam.net.ma; Ambassador MOHAMMED MASJED JAME'I.

Iraq: 39 blvd Mehdi ben Barka, 10100 Rabat; tel. (3) 7754466; fax (3) 7759749; e-mail rbtemb@iraqmofamail.net; Ambassador GHAZY HAMAD AWAD.

Italy: 2 rue Idriss al-Azhar, BP 111, 10001 Rabat; tel. (3) 7706592; fax (3) 7706882; e-mail ambasiata@ambitalia.ma; internet www.ambitalia.ma; Ambassador ALBERTO CANDILIO.

Japan: 39 ave Ahmed Balafrej, Souissi, 10100 Rabat; tel. (3) 7631782; fax (3) 7750078; e-mail amb-japon@fusion.net.ma; internet www.ma.emb-japan.go.jp; Ambassador SEIJI HINATA.

Jordan: 65 Villa al-Wafaa, Souissi, 10000 Rabat; tel. (3) 7759270; fax (3) 7758722; Ambassador NABIL ASH-SHARIF.

Korea, Republic: 41 ave Mehdi ben Barka, Souissi, 10100 Rabat; tel. (3) 7756791; fax (3) 7750189; e-mail morocco@mofat.go.kr; internet www.mofat.go.kr/morocco; Ambassador (vacant).

Kuwait: ave Imam Malik, km 4.3, BP 11, 10001 Rabat; tel. (3) 7631111; fax (3) 7753591; Ambassador SALAH MUHAMMAD AL-BIJAN.

Lebanon: 19 ave Abd al-Karim ben Jalloun, 10000 Rabat; tel. (3) 7760728; fax (3) 7766667; Ambassador AHMAD OTHMANE ABDELLAH.

Liberia: Lotissement no 7, Napabia, rue Ouled Frej, Souissi, Rabat; tel. (3) 7638426; Ambassador (vacant).

Libya: 1 rue Chouaïb Doukkali, BP 225, 10000 Rabat; tel. (3) 7769566; fax (3) 7705200; Ambassador NASSER HAMALI EL-LAFI.

Malaysia: 17 ave Bir Kacem, Soussi, Rabat; tel. (3) 7658324; fax (3) 7658363; e-mail mwrabat@menara.ma; internet myperwakilan.mfa.gov.my/af/rabat; Ambassador (vacant).

Mali: 58 cité Olm, Souissi, Rabat; tel. (3) 7759125; fax (3) 7754742; Ambassador MOUSSA COULIBALY.

Mauritania: 6 rue Thami Lamdour, BP 207, Souissi, 10000 Rabat; tel. (3) 7656678; fax (3) 7656680; e-mail ambassadeur@mauritanie.org.ma; Ambassador CHIAKH OULD AÂL.

MOROCCO

Mexico: 6 rue Cadi Mohamed Brebi, BP 1789, Souissi, Rabat; tel. (3) 7631969; fax (3) 7631971; e-mail embamexmar@smirt.net.ma; Ambassador Juan Antonio Mateos Cicero.
Netherlands: 40 rue de Tunis, BP 329, 10001 Rabat; tel. (3) 7219600; fax (3) 7219665; e-mail nlgovrab@mtds.com; internet www.ambassadepaysbasrabat.org; Ambassador Sjoerd Leenstra.
Niger: 14 Bis, rue Jabal al-Ayachi, Agdal, Rabat; tel. (3) 7674615; fax (3) 7674629; Ambassador Ramatou Diori Hamani.
Nigeria: 70 ave Omar ibn al-Khattab, BP 347, Agdal, Rabat; tel. (3) 7671857; fax (3) 7672739; e-mail nigerianrabat@menara.ma; Ambassador Alhaji Abubakar Shehu Wurno.
Norway: 9 rue Khénifra, BP 757, Agdal, Rabat; tel. (3) 7764085; fax (3) 7764088; e-mail emb.rabat@mfa.no; internet www.norvege.ma; Ambassador Arne Aasheim.
Oman: 21 rue Hamza, Agdal, 10000 Rabat; tel. (3) 7673788; fax (3) 7674567; Ambassador Abdullah bin Muhammad bin Abdullah al-Farissi.
Pakistan: 37 ave Ahmed Balafrej, Souissi, Rabat; tel. (3) 7762402; fax (3) 7766742; e-mail pareprabat@iam.net.ma; Ambassador Attiya Mahmood.
Peru: 16 rue d'Ifrane, 10000 Rabat; tel. (3) 7723236; fax (3) 7702803; e-mail lepruab@msn.com; Ambassador Jorge Abarca del Carpio.
Poland: 23 rue Oqbah, Agdal, BP 425, 10000 Rabat; tel. (3) 7771173; fax (3) 7775320; e-mail apologne@iam.net.ma; internet www.ambpologne.ma; Ambassador Joanna Wronecka.
Portugal: 5 rue Thami Lamdouar, Souissi, 10100 Rabat; tel. (3) 7756446; fax (3) 7756445; e-mail embport-rabat@hotmail.com; Ambassador (vacant).
Qatar: 4 ave Tarik ibn Ziad, BP 1220, 10001 Rabat; tel. (3) 7765681; fax (3) 7765774; e-mail rabat@mofa.gov.qa; Ambassador Saqr Mubarak al-Mansouri.
Romania: 10 rue d'Ouezzane, Hassan, Rabat; tel. (3) 7724694; fax (3) 7700196; e-mail amb.roumanie@menara.ma; Ambassador Vasile Popovici.
Russia: km 4 route des Zaêrs, 10100 Rabat; tel. (3) 7753509; fax (3) 7753590; e-mail ambrus@iam.net.ma; Ambassador Alexander Tokovinin.
Saudi Arabia: 322 ave Imam Malik, km 6, route des Zaêrs, Rabat; tel. (3) 657789; fax (3) 7768587; e-mail ambassd@goodinfo.net.ma; Ambassador Dr Muhammad Abd ar-Rahman bin Abd al-Aziz Bachar.
Senegal: 17 rue Cadi ben Hamadi Senhaji, Souissi, 10000 Rabat; tel. (3) 7754171; fax (3) 7754149; e-mail ambassene@iam.net.ma; Ambassador Ibou Idiaye.
Serbia and Montenegro: 23 ave Mehdi ben Barka, Souissi, BP 5014, 10105 Rabat; tel. (3) 7772201; fax (3) 7753258; e-mail sermont@menara.ma; Ambassador Mehmed Becović.
South Africa: 34 rue Saâdiens, Rabat; tel. (3) 7706760; fax (3) 7706756; e-mail sudaf@mtds.com; Ambassador M. Mtutuzeli Mpehle.
Spain: 3 rue Aïn Khalouiya, route des Zaêrs, km 5,300, Souissi, 10000 Rabat; tel. (3) 7633900; fax (3) 7630600; e-mail emb.rabat@mae.es; Ambassador Luis Planas Puchades.
Sudan: 5 ave Ghomara, Souissi, 10000 Rabat; tel. (3) 7752863; fax (3) 7752865; e-mail soudanirab@maghrebnet.net.ma; internet www.ambsoudan.ma; Ambassador (vacant).
Sweden: 159 ave John Kennedy, BP 428, 10000 Rabat; tel. (3) 7633210; fax (3) 7758048; e-mail ambassaden.rabat@foreign.ministry.se; internet www.swedenabroad.com/rabat; Ambassador Klas Gierow.
Switzerland: square de Berkane, BP 169, 1001 Rabat; tel. (3) 7268030; fax (3) 7268040; e-mail vertretung@rab.rep.admin.ch; internet www.eda.admin.ch/rabat; Ambassador Christian Dunant.
Syria: km 5.2, route des Zaêrs, BP 5158, Souissi, Rabat; tel. (3) 7755551; fax (3) 7757522; Chargé d'affaires a.i. Khouzama Mustapha.
Thailand: 11 rue de Tiddes, BP 4436, Rabat; tel. (3) 7763328; fax (3) 7763920; e-mail thaima@menara.ma; Ambassador (vacant).
Tunisia: 6 ave de Fès et 1 rue d'Ifrane, 10000 Rabat; tel. (3) 7730636; fax (3) 7730637; Ambassador Salah Baccari.
Turkey: 7 ave Abd al-Karim ben Jelloun, 10000 Rabat; tel. (3) 7661522; fax (3) 7660476; e-mail amb-tur-rabat@iam.net.ma; Ambassador Akin Algan.
Ukraine: rue Mouaouya ben Houdaig, Villa 212, Cité OLM Soussi II, Rabat; tel. (3) 7657840; fax (3) 7754679; e-mail ukremb@iam.net.ma; internet www.ukremb.ma; Ambassador Borys Hudyma.
United Arab Emirates: 11 ave des Alaouines, 10000 Rabat; tel. (3) 7702085; fax (3) 7724145; e-mail emirabat@iam.net.ma; Ambassador Issaa Hamad Bushahab.
United Kingdom: 17 blvd de la Tour Hassan, BP 45, 10001 Rabat; tel. (3) 7238600; fax (3) 7704531; e-mail consular.rabat@fco.gov.uk; internet www.britain.org.ma; Ambassador Charles Gray.
USA: 2 ave de Muhammad el-Fassi, Rabat; tel. (3) 7762265; fax (3) 7765661; e-mail ircrabat@usembassy.ma; internet www.usembassy.ma; Ambassador Thomas T. Riley.
Venezuela: 58 Lotissement OLM, Villa Yasmine, rue Capitaine Abdeslam el-Moudden el-Alami, Soussi, Rabat; tel. (3) 7650315; fax (3) 7650372; e-mail emvenez@iam.net.ma; Ambassador Rebeca Sanchez Bello.
Yemen: 11 rue Abou-Hanifa, Agdal, 10000 Rabat; tel. (3) 7674306; fax (3) 7674769; e-mail yemenembassy@iam.net.ma; Ambassador Ahmad A. al-Basha.

Judicial System

SUPREME COURT

Al-Majlis al-Aala

Hay Ryad, Ave an-Nakhil, Rabat; tel. (3) 7714936; fax (3) 7715106; e-mail coursupreme@coursupreme.ma; internet www.coursupreme.ma; Responsible for the interpretation of the law and regulates the jurisprudence of the courts and tribunals of the Kingdom. The Supreme Court sits at Rabat and is divided into six Chambers.

First President: Driss Dahak.
Attorney-General: Muhammad Abdelmounim el-Mejboud.

The 21 Courts of Appeal hear appeals from lower courts and also comprise a criminal division.

The 65 Courts of First Instance pass judgment on offences punishable by up to five years' imprisonment. These courts also pass judgment, without possibility of appeal, in personal and civil cases involving up to 3,000 dirhams.

The Communal and District Courts are composed of one judge, who is assisted by a clerk or secretary, and hear only civil and criminal cases.

The seven Administrative Courts pass judgment, subject to appeal before the Supreme Court pending the establishment of administrative appeal courts, on litigation with Government departments.

The nine Commercial Courts pass judgment, without the possibility of appeal, on all commercial litigations involving up to 9,000 dirhams. They also pass judgment on claims involving more than 9,000 dirhams, which can be appealed against in the commercial appeal courts.

The Permanent Royal Armed Forces' Court tries offences committed by the armed forces and military officers.

Religion

ISLAM

About 99% of Moroccans are Muslims (of whom about 90% are of the Sunni sect), and Islam is the state religion.

CHRISTIANITY

There are about 69,000 Christians, mostly Roman Catholics.

The Roman Catholic Church

Morocco (excluding the disputed territory of Western Sahara) comprises two archdioceses, directly responsible to the Holy See. At 31 December 2003 there were an estimated 23,510 adherents in the country, representing less than 0.1% of the population. The Moroccan archbishops participate in the Conférence Episcopale Régionale du Nord de l'Afrique (f. 1985), based in Tunis (Tunisia).

Archbishop of Rabat: Most Rev. Vincent Landel, Archevêché, 1 rue Hadj Muhammad Riffaï, BP 258, 10001 Rabat; tel. (3) 7709239; fax (3) 7706282; e-mail landel@wanadoo.net.ma.
Archbishop of Tangier: Most Rev. José Antonio Peteiro Freire, Archevêché, 55 rue Sidi Bouabid, BP 2116, 9000 Tangier; tel. (3) 9932762; fax (3) 9949117; e-mail igletanger@wanadoo.net.ma.

Western Sahara comprises a single Apostolic Prefecture, with an estimated 110 Catholics (2003).

Prefect Apostolic of Western Sahara: Fr Acacio Valbuena Rodríguez, Misión Católica, BP 31, 70001 el-Aaiún; tel. 893270.

The Anglican Communion

Within the Church of England, Morocco forms part of the diocese of Gibraltar in Europe. There are Anglican churches in Casablanca and Tangier.

MOROCCO

Protestant Church

Evangelical Church: 33 rue d'Azilal, 20000 Casablanca; tel. (2) 2302151; fax (2) 2444768; e-mail eeam@lesblancs.com; f. 1920; established in eight towns; Pres. Pastor JEAN-LUC BLANC; 1,000 mems.

JUDAISM

There is a Jewish community of some 8,000. In March 1999 the Moroccan authorities reopened the synagogue in Fez, established in the 17th century.

Grand Rabbi of Casablanca: CHALOM MESSAS (President of the Rabbinical Court of Casablanca, Palais de Justice, place des Nations Unies).

The Press

DAILIES

Casablanca

Assahra al-Maghribia: 88 blvd Muhammad V, Casablanca; tel. (2) 2268860; fax (2) 2203935; f. 1989; Arabic; Dir ABD AL-HAFID ROUISSI.

Al-Bayane (The Manifesto): 62 blvd de la Gironde, BP 13152, Casablanca; tel. (2) 2307882; fax (2) 2308080; internet www.bayanealyaoume.ma; Arabic and French; organ of the Parti du progrès et du socialisme; Dir ISMAÏL ALAOUI; circ. 5,000.

L'Economiste: 201 blvd de Bordeaux, Casablanca; tel. (2) 2271650; fax (2) 2297285; e-mail info@leconomiste.com; internet www.leconomiste.com; f. 1991; French; Pres. ABDELMOUNAÏM DILAMI; Dir-Gen. KHALID BELYAZID; Editor-in-Chief NADIA SALAH; circ. 32,000.

Al-Ittihad al-Ichtiraki (Socialist Unity): 33 rue Emir Abdelkader, BP 2165, Casablanca; tel. (2) 2407385; fax (2) 2619405; Arabic; f. 1983; organ of the Union socialiste des forces populaires; Dir ABDALLAH BOUHLAL; Editor ABD AR-RAHMAN EL-YOUSSOUFI; circ. 110,000.

Libération: 33 rue Emir Abdelkader, BP 2165, Casablanca; tel. (2) 2619400; fax (2) 2620978; e-mail liberation@mis.net.ma; internet www.liberation.press.ma; f. 1964; French; organ of the Union socialiste des forces populaires; Dir MUHAMMAD AL-YAZGHI.

Maroc Soir: 17 rue Othman ben Affan, BP 20000, Casablanca; tel. (2) 2489199; fax (2) 2262969; internet www.marocsoir.ma; f. 2005; French; Editor-in-Chief MEHDI HARIZI.

Le Matin du Sahara: 88 blvd Muhammad V, Casablanca; tel. (2) 2268860; fax (2) 2262969; e-mail contact@lematin.press.ma; internet www.lematin.ma; f. 1971; French; Dir-Gen. HICHAM SENOUSSI; circ. 100,000.

Rissalat al-Oumma (The Message of the Nation): 152 ave des Forces Armées Royales, BP 20005, Casablanca; tel. (2) 2901925; fax (2) 2901926; Arabic; weekly edition in French; organ of the Union constitutionnelle; Dir MUHAMMAD TAMALDOU.

Rabat

Al-Alam (The Flag): ave Hassan II, rue Casablanca, Lot Vita, BP 141, Rabat; tel. (3) 7292642; fax (3) 7291784; e-mail alalam@alalam.ma; internet www.alalam.ma; f. 1946; organ of the Istiqlal party; Arabic; literary supplement on Saturdays; Dir ABD AL-KARIM GHALLAB; circ. 64,000.

Al-Anba'a (Information): ave Allal el-Fassi, BP 65, Rabat; tel. (3) 7683968; fax (3) 7683544; f. 1963; daily; Arabic; publ. by Ministry of Communication; Dir AHMAD YACOUBI.

Assyassa al-Jadida: 43 rue Abou Fares al-Marini, BP 1385, Rabat; tel. (3) 7208571; fax (3) 7208573; e-mail assassjdid@maghrebnet.net.ma; f. 1997; Arabic; organ of the Parti socialiste démocratique; Dir ABD AL-LATIF AOUAD; Editor TALAÂ ASSOUD ALATLASSI.

Al-Maghrib: 6 rue Laos, BP 469, Rabat; tel. (3) 7722702; fax (3) 7722765; f. 1981; French; organ of the Rassemblement national des indépendants; Dir MUSTAPHA IZNASNI; circ. 15,000.

Al-Mithaq al-Watani (The National Charter): 6 rue Laos, BP 469, Rabat; tel. (3) 7722708; fax (3) 7722765; f. 1977; Arabic; organ of the Rassemblement national des indépendants; Dir MUHAMMAD AUAJJAR; circ. 25,000.

An-Nidal ad-Dimokrati (The Democratic Struggle): 18 rue de Tunis, Hassan, Rabat; tel. (3) 7732127; fax (3) 7720170; e-mail annidal@menara.ma; Arabic; f. 1984; organ of the Parti national démocrate; Dir MUHAMMAD ARSALANE EL-JADIDI.

L'Opinion: Ave Hassan II, Rabat; tel. (3) 7293002; fax (3) 7292639; e-mail lopinion@lopinion.ma; internet www.lopinion.ma; f. 1965; French; organ of the Istiqlal party; Dir MUHAMMAD IDRISSI KAÏTOUNI; Editor JAMAL HAJJAM; circ. 60,000.

SELECTED PERIODICALS

Casablanca

Achamal: Casablanca; weekly; Arabic; Editor-in-Chief KHALID MECHBAL.

Bulletin Mensuel de la Chambre de Commerce et d'Industrie de la Wilaya du Grand Casablanca: 98 blvd Muhammad V, BP 423, Casablanca; tel. (2) 2264327; monthly; French; Pres. LAHCEN EL-WAFI.

CGEM Infos: angle ave des Forces Armées Royales et rue Muhammad Arrachid, 20100 Casablanca; tel. (2) 2252696; fax (2) 2253839; e-mail cgem@iam.net.ma; internet www.cgem.ma; weekly; French; Admin. MOUHCINE AYOUCHE.

Challenge Hebdo: ave des Forces Armées Royales, Tour de Habous, 13ème étage, Casablanca; tel. (2) 2548153; fax (2) 2300990; e-mail redaction@challengehebdo.com; internet www.challengehebdo.com; weekly; French; business magazine; circ. 15,000.

Construire: 744 rue Boukraâ, Résidence Hanane Jassim I, Bourgogne, Casablanca; tel. (2) 2220273; fax (2) 2273627; e-mail nlleconstruire@menara.ma; f. 1940; weekly; French; Dir ABDELKRIM TALAL.

Demain: Casablanca; f. 1997; weekly, French; Dir ALI LAMRABET.

Les Echos Africains: Immeuble SONIR, angle blvd Smiha, rue d'Anjou, BP 13140, Casablanca; tel. (2) 2307271; fax (2) 2319680; f. 1972; monthly; French; news, economics; Dir MUHAMMAD CHOUFFANI EL-FASSI; Editor SOODIA FARIDI; circ. 5,000.

La Gazette du Maroc: ave des Forces Armées Royales, Tour de Habous, 13ème étage, Casablanca; tel. (2) 2548150; fax (2) 2318094; e-mail redaction@lagazettedumaroc.com; internet www.lagazettedumaroc.com; weekly; French; Dir KAMAL LAHLOU; circ. 25,000.

Al-Ittihad al-Watani Lilkouate ach-Chaâbia (National Union of Popular Forces): 28–30 rue Magellan, Casablanca; tel. (2) 2302023; fax (2) 2319301; weekly; Arabic; organ of the Union nationale des forces populaires; Dir (vacant).

Le Journal: 61 ave des Forces Armées Royales, Casablanca; tel. (2) 2546670; fax (2) 2446185; e-mail lejournalhebdo@yahoo.fr; internet www.lejournal-hebdo.com; weekly; French; news, politics, economics; Dir ABOUBAKR JAMAÏ.

Lamalif: 6 bis rue Defly Dieude, Casablanca; tel. (2) 2220032; f. 1966; monthly; French; economic, social and cultural magazine; Dir MUHAMMAD LOGHLAM.

La Mañana: 88 blvd Muhammad V, Casablanca; tel. (2) 2268860; fax (2) 2203935; f. 1990; Spanish; Dir ABD AL-HAFID ROUISSI.

Maroc Fruits: 283 blvd Zerktouni, Casablanca; tel. (2) 2363946; fax (2) 2364041; f. 1958; fortnightly; Arabic and French; organ of the Association des Producteurs d'Agrumes du Maroc; Pres. LYOUSSI HASSAN; circ. 6,000.

Maroc Soir: 34 rue Muhammad Smiha, Casablanca; tel. (2) 2301271; fax (2) 2317535; f. 1971; French; Dir ABD AL-HAFID ROUISSI; circ. 30,000.

Matin Hebdo: 34 rue Muhammad Smiha, Casablanca; tel. (2) 2301271; weekly; Dir AHMAD AL-ALAMI.

Matin Magazine: 88 blvd Muhammad V, Casablanca; tel. (2) 2268860; fax (2) 2262969; f. 1971; weekly; French; Dir ABD AL-HAFID ROUISSI.

An-Nidal (The Struggle): 10 rue Cols Bleus, Sidi Bousmara, Médina Kédima, Casablanca; f. 1973; weekly; Arabic; organ of the Parti national démocrate; Dir IBRAHIMI AHMAD.

La Nouvelle Tribune: 320 blvd Zerktouni, Casablanca; tel. (2) 2200030; fax (2) 2200031; e-mail courrier@lanouvelletribune.com; internet www.lanouvelletribune.com; f. 1996; weekly; French; Dir FAHD YATA; circ. 25,000.

Les Nouvelles du Maroc: 28 ave des Forces Armées Royales, Casablanca; tel. (2) 2203031; fax (2) 2277181; weekly; French; Dir KHADIJA S. IDRISSI.

Al-Ousbouaa al-Maghribia: 158 ave des Forces Armées Royales, Casablanca; f. 1984; organ of the Union constitutionnelle; Editor MUSTAFA ALAOUI.

La Quinzaine du Maroc: 53 rue Dumont d'Urville, Casablanca; tel. (2) 22440033; fax (2) 2440426; e-mail mauro@wanadoopro.ma; f. 1951; monthly; English and French; Dir HUBERT MAURO; circ. 20,000.

Revue Marocaine de Droit: 24 rue Nolly, Casablanca; tel. (2) 2273673; quarterly; French and Arabic; Dirs J. P. RAZON, A. KETTANI.

As-Sahifa: Casablanca; weekly; Arabic; Dir ABOUBAKR JAMAÏ.

Les Temps du Maroc: 88 blvd Muhammad V, Casablanca; tel. (2) 2268860; fax (2) 2262969; e-mail contact@lematin.press.ma; f. 1995; weekly; French; Dir ABD AL-HAFID ROUISSI.

Version Homme: ave des Forces Armées Royales, Tour de Habous, 13ème étage, Casablanca; tel. (2) 2450089; fax (2) 2442213; e-mail redaction@versionhomme.com; internet www.versionhomme.com; monthly; lifestyle magazine for men; Dir RAFIK LAHLOU.

La Vie Economique: 5 blvd ben Yacine, 20300 Casablanca; tel. (2) 2443868; fax (2) 2304542; e-mail vieeco@marocnet.net.ma; internet www.lavieeco.com; f. 1921; weekly; French; Pres. and Dir JEAN LOUIS SERVAN-SCHREIBER.

La Vie Industrielle et Agricole: 142 blvd Muhammad V, Casablanca; tel. (2) 2274407; 2 a month; French; Dir AHMAD ZAGHARI.

La Vie Touristique Africaine: 142 blvd Muhammad V, Casablanca; tel. (2) 2274407; fortnightly; French; tourist information; Dir AHMAD ZAGHARI.

Rabat

Al-Aklam (The Pens): Rabat; monthly; Arabic; Dir ABD AR-RAHMAN BEN AMAR.

Al-Anba'a (Information): ave Allal el-Fassi, Rabat; tel. (3) 7683967; fax (3) 7683970; f. 2000; weekly; Arabic; publ. by Ministry of Communication; Dir (Editorial) MUHAMMAD BELGHAZI.

Assiassa Al-Jadida: 8 rue Sanaâ, BP 1385, Rabat; tel. (3) 7208571; fax (3) 7208573; e-mail aouad@nsimail.com; f. 1996; weekly; Arabic; organ of the Partie socialiste démocratique; Dir ABDELLATIF AOUAD.

Ach-Chorta (The Police Magazine): BP 437, Rabat; tel. (3) 7652087; monthly; Arabic; Dir MUHAMMAD AD-DRIF.

Da'ouat al-Haqq (Call of the Truth): al-Michwar as-Said, Rabat; tel. (3) 7760810; publ. by Ministry of Habous (Religious Endowments) and Islamic Affairs; f. 1957; monthly; Arabic.

Al-Haraka: 66 rue Patrice Lumumba, BP 1317, Rabat; tel. (3) 7768667; fax (3) 7768677; weekly; Arabic; organ of the Mouvement populaire; Dir ALI ALAOUI.

Al-Imane: rue Akenssous, BP 356, Rabat; f. 1963; monthly; Arabic; Dir ABOU BAKER AL-KADIRI.

Al-Irchad (Spiritual Guidance): al-Michwar as-Said, Rabat; tel. (3) 7760810; publ. by Ministry of Habous (Religious Endowments) and Islamic Affairs; f. 1967; monthly; Arabic.

Al-Khansa: 154 ave Souss Mohammadia, Rabat; monthly; Arabic; Dir ABOUZAL AÏCHA.

Al-Maghribi: Rabat; tel. (3) 7768139; weekly; Arabic; organ of the Parti de l'action; Dir ABDALLAH AL-HANANI.

At-Tadamoun: Rabat; monthly; Arabic; Dir ABD AL-MAJID SEMLALI EL-HASANI.

La Verité: Rabat; weekly; French; Chief Editor ALLAL EL-MALEH.

La Voix du Centre: Rabat; weekly; French; Editor-in-Chief MUSTAPHA SHIMI.

Tangier

Actualités Touristiques: 80 rue de la Liberté, Tangier; monthly; French; Dir TAYEB ALAMI.

Le Journal de Tanger: 8 rue Cadi Ayyad, Tangier; tel. (3) 7946051; fax (3) 7945709; e-mail redact@journaldetanger.com; internet www.lejournaldetanger.com; f. 1904; weekly; French, English, Spanish and Arabic; Dir ABD AL-HAQ BAKHAT; circ. 10,000.

NEWS AGENCIES

Maghreb Arabe Presse (MAP): 122 ave Allal ben Abdallah, BP 1049, 10000 Rabat; tel. (3) 7764083; fax (3) 7765005; e-mail mapweb@map.co.ma; internet www.map.ma; f. 1959; Arabic, French, English and Spanish; state-owned; Dir-Gen. MUHAMMAD KHABBACHI.

Foreign Bureaux

Agence France-Presse (AFP): 2 bis rue du Caire, BP 118, Rabat; tel. (3) 7768943; fax (3) 7700357; f. 1920; Dir IGNACE DALLE.

Agencia EFE (Spain): 14 ave du Kairouane, Rabat; tel. (3) 7723218; fax (3) 7732195; Bureau Chief ALBERTO MASEGOSA GARCÍA-CALAMARTE.

Informatsionnoye Telegrafnoye Agentstvo Rossii—Telegrafnoye Agentstvo Suverennykh Stran (ITAR—TASS) (Russia): 32 rue de la Somme, Rabat; tel. (3) 7750315; Dir OLEG CHIROKOV.

Inter Press Service (IPS) (Italy): Rabat; tel. (3) 7756869; fax (3) 7727183; e-mail ipseumed@hotmail.com; internet www.ips.org; Dir BOULOUIZ BOUCHRA.

Reuters (United Kingdom): 509 Immeuble es-Saâda, ave Hassan II, Rabat; tel. (3) 7726518; fax (3) 7722499; Chief Correspondent (North Africa) JOHN BAGGALEY.

Xinhua (New China) News Agency (People's Republic of China): 4 rue Kadi Mekki el-Bitaouri, Souissi, Rabat; tel. (3) 7755320; fax (3) 7754319; Dir ZHUGE CANGLIN.

Publishers

Afrique Orient: 159 bis blvd Yacoub el-Mansour, Casablanca; tel. (2) 2259813; fax (2) 2440080.

Belvisi: 17 rue Abbas Ibnou Farnass, BP 8044, Casablanca; tel. (2) 2250973; fax (2) 2986258; f. 1986.

Dar el-Kitab: place de la Mosquée, Quartier des Habous, BP 4018, Casablanca; tel. (2) 2305419; fax (2) 2304581; f. 1948; philosophy, history, Africana, general and social science; Arabic and French; Dir BOUTALEB ABDOU ABD AL-HAY; Gen. Man. KHADIJA EL KASSIMI.

Editions Le Fennec: 89B blvd d'Anfa, 14ème étage, Casablanca; tel. (2) 2209314; fax (2) 2277702; e-mail info@lefennec.com; internet www.lefennec.com; fiction and essays; Dir LAYLA B. CHAOUNI.

Editions La Porte: 281 blvd Muhammad V, BP 331, Rabat; tel. (3) 7709958; fax (3) 7706476; e-mail la_porte@meganet.net.ma; law, guides, economics, educational books.

Les Editions Maghrébines: Quartier Industrial, blvd E, N 15, Sin Sebaâ, Casablanca; tel. (2) 2351797; fax (2) 2355541; f. 1962; general non-fiction.

Malika Editions: 60 blvd Yacoub el-Mansour, 20100 Casablanca; tel. (2) 2235688; fax (2) 2251651; e-mail edmalika@connectcom.net.ma; internet www.malikaedition.com; art publications.

GOVERNMENT PUBLISHING HOUSE

Imprimerie Officielle: ave Yacoub el-Mansour, Rabat-Chellah; tel. (3) 7765024; fax (3) 7765179.

Broadcasting and Communications

TELECOMMUNICATIONS

Regulatory Authority

Agence Nationale de Réglementation des Télécommunications (ANRT): Centre d'Affaires, blvd ar-Ryad, BP 2939, Hay Ryad, 10100 Rabat; tel. (3) 7718400; fax (3) 7203862; e-mail con@anrt.net.ma; internet www.anrt.net.ma; f. 1998; Dir-Gen. MUHAMMAD BENCHAÂBOUN.

Principal Operators

Itissalat al-Maghrib—Maroc Télécom: ave Annakhil Hay Riad, Rabat; tel. (3) 7719000; fax (3) 7714860; e-mail webmaster@iam.ma; internet www.iam.ma; f. 1998 to take over telephone services from the ONPT; privatized in 2004; Vivendi Universal (France) holds a 51% stake; Chair. ABDESSALEM AHIZOUNE.

Méditel: Twin Centre, angle blvd Zerktouni et Massira al-Khadra, Casablanca; internet www.meditel.ma; f. 1999; subsidiary of Telefónica SA and Portugal Telecom; provides national mobile telecommunications services; Dir-Gen. MIGUEL MENCHEN.

BROADCASTING

Morocco can receive broadcasts from Spanish radio stations, and the main Spanish television channels can also be received in northern Morocco.

Radio

Radio Casablanca: c/o Loukt s.a.r.l, BP 16011, Casa Principal, 20001 Casablanca; e-mail i-rc@maroc.net; internet www.maroc.net/rc.

Radio Méditerranée Internationale: 3–5 rue Emsallah, BP 2055, Tangier; tel. and fax (3) 9936363; e-mail medi1@medi1.com; internet www.medi1.com; Arabic and French; Man. Dir PIERRE CASALTA.

Voice of America Radio Station in Tangier: c/o US Consulate-General, chemin des Amoureux, Tangier.

Television

Radiodiffusion-Télévision Marocaine: 1 rue el-Brihi, BP 1042, 1000 Rabat; tel. (3) 7766885; fax (3) 7766888; internet www.rtm.ma; govt station; transmission commenced 1962; 45 hours weekly; French and Arabic; carries commercial advertising; Dir-Gen. and Dir Television FAIÇAL LARAICHI.

SOREAD 2M: Société d'études et de réalisations audiovisuelles, km 7.3 route de Rabat, Aïn-Sebaâ, Casablanca; tel. (2) 2667373; fax (2) 2667392; internet www.2m.tv; f. 1988; transmission commenced 1989; public television channel, owned by Moroccan Government (72%) and by private national foreign concerns; broadcasting in French and Arabic; Man. Dir MOSTAFA BENALI.

MOROCCO   *Directory*

Finance

(cap. = capital; res = reserves; dep. = deposits; m. = million;
brs = branches; amounts in dirhams unless otherwise indicated)

BANKING

Central Bank

Bank Al-Maghrib: 277 ave Muhammad V, BP 445, Rabat; tel. (3) 7702626; fax (3) 7706677; e-mail dai@bkam.gov.ma; internet www.bkam.ma; f. 1959 as Banque du Maroc; bank of issue; cap. 500m., res 4,869.0m., dep. 37,445.6m. (Dec. 2002); Gov. ABDELLATIF JOUAHRI.

Other Banks

Attijariwafa Bank: 2 blvd Moulay Youssef, BP 11141, 20000 Casablanca; tel. (2) 2298888; fax (2) 2294125; e-mail contact@attijariwafa.com; internet www.attijariwafabank.com; f. 2004; 14.5% owned by Grupo Santander; formed by merger between Banque Commerciale du Maroc SA (BCM) and Wafabank; cap. 1,930.0m., res 9,019.1m., dep. 83,845.0m. (Dec. 2004); Chair. and CEO KHALID OUDGHIRI; Gen. Man. OMAR BOUNJOU.

Banque Centrale Populaire (Crédit Populaire du Maroc): 101 blvd Muhammad Zerktouni, BP 10622, 21100 Casablanca; tel. (2) 2202533; fax (2) 2222699; e-mail bcp@banquepopulairemorocco.ma; internet www.cpm.co.ma; f. 1961; 51% state-owned, 49% privately-owned; merged with Société Marocaine de Dépot et Crédit in 2003; cap. 1,348.7m., res 5,089.1m., dep. 83,388.1m. (Dec. 2003); Pres. and Gen. Man. NOUREDDINE OMARY; 458 brs.

Banque Marocaine du Commerce Extérieur SA (BMCE): 140 ave Hassan II, BP 13425, 20000 Casablanca; tel. (2) 2200496; fax (2) 2200512; e-mail sgg@bmcebank.co.ma; internet www.bmcebank.ma; f. 1959; transferred to majority private ownership in 1995; cap. 1,587.5m., res 3,401.4m., dep. 47,305.1m., total assets 57,848.4m. (Dec. 2003); Chair. and CEO OTHMAN BEN JELLOUN; 201 brs.

Banque Marocaine pour l'Afrique et l'Orient: 1 place Bandoeng, BP 11183, 20000 Casablanca; tel. (2) 2307070; fax (2) 2301673; f. 1975 to take over British Bank of the Middle East (Morocco); total assets 1,785.4m., cap. and res -858.8m. (Dec. 2003); Pres. TARIK SIJILMASSI; 29 brs.

Banque Marocaine pour le Commerce et l'Industrie SA (BMCI): 26 place des Nations Unies, BP 15573, Casablanca; tel. (2) 2224101; fax (2) 2224604; e-mail adiba.lahbabi@africa.bnpparibas.com; internet www.bmcinet.com; f. 1964; transferred to majority private ownership in 1995; cap. 775.2m., res 22,187.8m., dep. 17,261.0m. (Dec. 2003); Pres. MUSTAPHA FARIS; Chair. JOËL SIBRAC; Gen. Man. ETIENNE BAREL; 137 brs.

Banque Nationale pour le Développement Economique (BNDE): 12 place des Alaouites, BP 407, 10000 Rabat; tel. (3) 7706040; fax (3) 7703706; f. 1959; 34.2% state-owned, 65.8% privately-owned; cap. 600.0m., res 475.8m., dep. 5,200.6m. (Dec. 1999); Pres. MUSTAPHA FARIS; 14 brs.

Citibank (Maghreb): BP 13362, Zénith Millenium, Immeuble 1, Lotissement Attaoufik, Sidi Maârouf, Casablanca; tel. (2) 2489600; fax (2) 2974197; f. 1967; total assets 1,211.0m.; cap. and res 194.0m. (Dec. 2003); Pres. NUHAD SABILA; 2 brs.

Crédit Immobilier et Hôtelier: 187 ave Hassan II, Casablanca; tel. (2) 2479000; fax (2) 2479999; e-mail cih@cih.co.ma; internet www.cih.co.ma; f. 1920; transferred to majority private ownership in 1995; total assets 22,798.9m., cap. and res 490.8m. (Dec. 2003); Pres. MUHAMMAD EL-ALJ; 91 brs.

Crédit du Maroc SA: 48–58 blvd Muhammad V, BP 13579, 20000 Casablanca; tel. (2) 2477000; fax (2) 2477127; e-mail cdmdai@atlasnet.net.ma; internet www.creditdumaroc.co.ma; f. 1963; cap. 833.8m., res 662.0m., dep. 17,578.5m. (Dec. 2003); Chair. and CEO FRANCIS SAVOYE; 137 brs.

Société Générale Marocaine de Banques SA: 55 blvd Abd al-Moumen, BP 13090, 21100 Casablanca; tel. (2) 2438888; fax (2) 200948; e-mail contact@sgmaroc.com; internet www.sgmaroc.org; f. 1962; total assets 26,844.6m., cap. and res 2,186.8m. (Dec. 2003); Pres. ABD AL-AZIZ TAZI; 132 brs.

Bank Organizations

Association Professionnelle des Sociétés de Bourse du Maroc: angle rue Muhammad Errachid et ave des Forces Armées Royales, 20000, Casablanca; tel. (2) 2542333; fax (2) 2542336; e-mail apsb@apsb.org.ma; internet www.apsb.org.ma; f. 1995; groups all brokers in the stock exchange of Casablanca, for studies, inquiries of general interest and contacts with official authorities; 12 mems; Pres. YOUSUF BENKIRANE; Vice-Pres. OMAR AMINE; Exec. Dir SANAÁ LAROUI.

Groupement Professionnel des Banques du Maroc: 71 ave des Forces Armées Royales, Casablanca; tel. (2) 2314824; fax (2) 2314903; f. 1967; groups all commercial banks for studies, inquiries of general interest, and contacts with official authorities; 18 mems; Pres. ABD AL-LATIF JOUAHRI.

STOCK EXCHANGE

Bourse de Casablanca: ave de l'Armée Royale, Casablanca; tel. (2) 2452626; fax (2) 2452625; e-mail contact@casablanca-bourse.com; internet www.casablanca-bourse.com; f. 1929; Chair. DRISS BENCHEIKH.

INSURANCE

Alliance Africaine: 63 blvd Moulay Youssef, 20000 Casablanca; tel. (2) 2200690; fax (2) 2200694; f. 1975; cap. 20m.; Pres. ABD AR-RAHIM CHERKAOUI; Dir-Gen. KHALID CHEDDADI.

Assurances Al-Amane: 122 ave Hassan II, 20000 Casablanca; tel. (2) 2267272; fax (2) 2265664; f. 1975; cap. 120m.; Pres. and Dir-Gen. MUHAMMAD BOUGHALEB.

Atlanta Assurances: BP 13685, 20001 Casablanca; tel. (2) 2436868; fax (2) 2203011; e-mail info@atlanta.ma; f. 1947; cap. 100m.; Dir-Gen. SELLAM SEKKAT.

Cie Africaine d'Assurances: 120 ave Hassan II, 20000 Casablanca; tel. (2) 2224185; fax (2) 2260150; f. 1950; Dir-Gen. JAMAL HAROUCHI.

Cie d'Assurances et de Réassurances SANAD: 3 blvd Muhammad V, BP 13438, 20000 Casablanca; tel. (2) 2260591; fax (2) 2293813; e-mail contact@sanad.ma; internet www.sanad.ma; f. 1975; Chair. MUHAMMAD HASSAN BENSALAH; Dir-Gen. ABDELTIF TAHIRI.

CNIA Assurance: 216 blvd Muhammad Zerktouni, 20000 Casablanca; tel. (2) 2474040; fax (2) 2206081; f. 1949; cap. 30m.; Pres. ABDELLATIF AR-RAYES; Dir-Gen. SAÏD AHMIDOUCH.

La Marocaine Vie: 37 blvd Moulay Youssef, Casablanca; tel. (2) 2206320; fax (2) 2261971; f. 1978; cap. 12m.; Pres. HAMZA KETTANI.

Mutuelle Centrale Marocaine d'Assurances: 16 rue Abou Inane, BP 27, Rabat; tel. (3) 7766960; Pres. ABD AS-SALAM CHERIF D'OUEZZANE; Dir-Gen. YACOUBI SOUSSANE.

Mutuelle d'Assurances des Transporteurs Unis (MATU): 215 blvd Muhammad Zerktouni, Casablanca; tel. (2) 2367097; Dir-Gen. M. BENYAMNA MUHAMMAD.

RMA Watanya: 83 ave des Forces Armées Royales, 20000 Casablanca; tel. (2) 2312163; fax (2) 2313137; e-mail info@rmawatanya.com; internet www.rmawatanya.com; formed following merger of Al-Watanya and La Royale Marocaine d'Assurances; CEO SÉBASTIEN CASTRO.

Es-Saâda, Cie d'Assurances et de Réassurances: 123 ave Hassan II, BP 13860, 20000 Casablanca; tel. (2) 2222525; fax (2) 2262655; e-mail es-saada@techno.net.ma; f. 1961; cap. 50m.; Pres. MEHDI OUAZZANI; Man. Dir SAÏD OUAZZANI.

Société Centrale de Réassurance: Tour Atlas, place Zallaqa, BP 13183, Casablanca; tel. (2) 2308585; fax (2) 2308672; e-mail scr@scrmaroc.com; internet www.scrmaroc.com; f. 1960; cap. 30m.; Chair. MUSTAPHA BAKKOURY; Man. Dir AHMAD ZINOUN.

Société Marocaine d'Assurances à l'Exportation: 24 rue Ali Abderrazak, BP 15953, Casablanca; tel. (2) 2982000; fax (2) 2252070; e-mail smaex@smaex.com; internet www.smaex.com; f. 1988; insurance for exporters in the public and private sectors; assistance for export promotion; Pres. and Dir-Gen. MUHAMMAD TAZI; Asst Dir-Gen. ABDELKADER DRIOUACHE.

WAFA Assurance: 1–3 blvd Abd al-Moumen, BP 13420, 20001 Casablanca; tel. (2) 2224575; fax (2) 2209103; e-mail webmaster@wafaassurance.com; internet www.attijariwafabank.com; Pres. SAÂD KETTANI; Dir-Gen. JAOUAD KETTANI.

Zurich Cie Marocaine d'Assurances: City Park Centre, 106 rue Abderrahmane Sahraoui, 20000 Casablanca; tel. (2) 2279015; fax (2) 2276718; e-mail saida.el.azhari@zurich.com; Pres. and Dir-Gen. BERTO FISLER.

INSURANCE ASSOCIATION

Fédération Marocaine des Sociétés d'Assurances et de Réassurances: 154 blvd d'Anfa, Casablanca; tel. (2) 2391850; fax (2) 2391854; f. 1958; 17 mem. cos; Pres. HAMZA KETTANI.

Trade and Industry

GOVERNMENT AGENCIES

Centre Marocain de Promotion des Exportations (CMPE): 23 blvd Bnou Majid el-Bahar, BP 10937, Casablanca; tel. (2) 2302210; fax (2) 2301793; e-mail cmpe@cmpe.org.ma; internet www.cmpe.org.ma; f. 1980; state org. for promotion of exports; Dir-Gen. MOUNIR M. BENSAÏD.

Direction de la Privatisation: 1 angle ave ibn Sina et Oued al-Makhazine, Agdal, Rabat; tel. (3) 7689614; fax (3) 7673299; e-mail minpriv@mtds.com; privatization agency integrated with ministries responsible for the economy, finance, privatization and tourism; Dir николNajib Hajoui.

Office National des Hydrocarbures et des Mines (ONHM): 5 ave Moulay Hassan, BP 99, 10001 Rabat; tel. (3) 7702398; fax (3) 7709411; e-mail sammoud@brpm.org.ma; f. 2003 to succeed Bureau de Recherches et de Participations Minières (BRPM) and Office National de Recherches et d'Exploitations Pétrolières (ONAREP); state agency conducting exploration, valorization and exploitation of hydrocarbons and mineral resources; Dir-Gen. Mella Amina Benkhadra.

Société de Gestion des Terres Agricoles (SOGETA): 35 rue Daïet-Erroumi, BP 731, Agdal, Rabat; tel. (3) 7772778; fax (3) 7772765; internet www.sogeta.ma; f. 1973; oversees use of agricultural land; Man. Dir Bachir Saoud.

DEVELOPMENT ORGANIZATIONS

Agence National pour la Promotion de Petite et Moyenne Entreprise (ANPME): 10 rue Gandhi, BP 211, 10001 Rabat; tel. (3) 7708460; fax (3) 7707695; e-mail anpme@anpme.ma; internet www.anpme.ma; f. 1973 as the Office pour le Développement Industriel; name changed as above in 2002; state agency to develop industry; Dir-Gen. Latifa Echihabi.

Caisse de Dépôt et de Gestion: place Moulay el-Hassan, BP 408, 10001 Rabat; tel. (3) 7765520; fax (3) 7763849; e-mail cdg@cdg.org.ma; internet www.cdg.org.ma; f. 1959; finances small-scale projects; cap. and res 2,058.1m. dirhams (Dec. 1998); Dir-Gen. Mustapha Bakkouri; Sec.-Gen. Mustapha Mechahouri.

Caisse Marocaine des Marchés (Marketing Fund): Résidence el-Manar, blvd Abd al-Moumen, Casablanca; tel. (2) 2259118; fax (2) 2259120; f. 1950; cap. 10m. dirhams; Man. Hassan Kissi.

Caisse Nationale de Crédit Agricole (Agricultural Credit Fund): 2 ave d'Alger, BP 49, 10001 Rabat; tel. (3) 7725920; fax (3) 7732580; f. 1961; cap. 1,573.5m. dirhams, dep. 3,471.9m. dirhams; Dir-Gen. Saïd Ibrahimi.

Société de Développement Agricole (SODEA): ave Hadj Ahmed Cherkaoui, BP 6280, Rabat; tel. (3) 7770825; fax (3) 7774798; internet www.sodea.com; f. 1972; state agricultural devt org.; Man. Dir M. Sabbari Hassani Larbi.

Société Nationale d'Investissement (SNI): 60 rue d'Alger, BP 38, 20000 Casablanca; tel. (2) 2268888; fax (2) 2476126; f. 1966; transferred to majority private ownership in 1994; cap. 10,900m. dirhams; Pres. Hassan Bouhemou; Sec.-Gen. Saâd Bendidi.

CHAMBERS OF COMMERCE

La Fédération des Chambres de Commerce et d'Industrie du Maroc: 6 rue d'Erfoud, Rabat-Agdal; tel. (3) 7767078; fax (3) 7767076; f. 1962; groups the 26 Chambers of Commerce and Industry; Pres. Ahmad M'Rabet; Dir-Gen. Muhammad Larbi el-Harras.

Chambre de Commerce, d'Industrie et de Services de la Wilaya de Rabat-Salé: 1 rue Gandhi, BP 131, Rabat; tel. (3) 7202430; fax (3) 7706768; e-mail ccisrs@ccisrs.org.ma; Pres. Omar Derraji; Dir Mounji Zniber.

Chambre de Commerce et d'Industrie de la Wilaya du Grand Casablanca: 98 blvd Muhammad V, BP 423, Casablanca; tel. (2) 2264327; Pres. Lahcen el-Wafi.

INDUSTRIAL AND TRADE ASSOCIATIONS

Office National Interprofessionnel des Céréales et des Légumineuses: 25 ave Moulay Hassan, BP 154, Rabat; tel. (3) 7701735; fax (3) 7709626; f. 1937; Dir-Gen. Abd al-Hai Bouzoubaâ.

Office National des Pêches: Port de Pêche, Casablanca; tel. (2) 2304700; fax (2) 2442334; e-mail onp@onp.co.ma; internet www.onp.co.ma; f. 1969; state fishing org.; Man. Dir Majid Kaissar el-Ghaib.

EMPLOYERS' ORGANIZATIONS

Association Marocaine des Industries Textiles et de l'Habillement (AMITH): 92 blvd Moulay Rachid, Casablanca; tel. (2) 2942085; fax (2) 2940587; e-mail mtazi@amith.org.ma; internet www.amith.org.ma; f. 1958; mems 700 textile, knitwear and ready-made garment factories; Pres. Karim Tazi; Dir-Gen. Muhammad Tazi.

Association des Producteurs d'Agrumes du Maroc (ASPAM): 283 blvd Zerkitoum, Casablanca; tel. (2) 2363746; fax (2) 2364041; f. 1958; links Moroccan citrus growers; has its own processing plants; Pres Lyoussi Hassan.

Association Professionelle des Agents Maritimes, Consignataires de Navires, et Courtiers d'Affrètement du Maroc: 219 blvd des FAR, 5e étage, 20000 Casablanca; tel. (2) 2541112; fax (2) 2541415; e-mail apram@wanadoopro.ma; internet www.apram.ma; Pres. Abdelaziz Mantranch; 45 mems.

Association Professionnelle des Cimentiers: 239 blvd Moulay Ismaïl, Casablanca; tel. (2) 2401342; fax (2) 2248208; cement manufacturers.

Confédération Générale des Entreprises du Maroc (CGEM): angle ave des Forces Armées Royales et rue Muhammad Arrachid, 20100 Casablanca; tel. (2) 2252696; fax (2) 2253839; e-mail cgem@cgem.ma; internet www.cgem.ma; Pres. Hassan Chami.

Union Marocaine de l'Agriculture (UMA): 12 place des Alaouites, Rabat; Pres. M. Nejjai.

UTILITIES

Electricity and Water

Office National de l'Eau Potable (ONEP): 6 bis rue Patrice Lumumba, Rabat; tel. (3) 7650695; fax (3) 7650640; e-mail onepigi@mtds.com; internet www.onep.org.ma; f. 1972; responsible for drinking-water supply; Dir Ali Fassi-Fihri.

Office National de l'Electricité (ONE): 65 rue Othman ben Affan, BP 13498, 20001 Casablanca; tel. (2) 2668080; fax (2) 2220038; e-mail offelec@one.org.ma; internet www.one.org.ma; f. 1963; state electricity authority; Dir-Gen. Younès Maâmar.

Régie Autonome Intercommunale de Distribution d'Eau et d'Electricité de la Wilaya de Chaouia (RADEEC): industrial and commercial public body providing water and power supplies in the Chaouia region.

Régie Autonome Intercommunale de Distribution d'Eau et d'Electricité de la Wilaya de Tanger (RAID): 5 rue Oqba ibn Naffiy, BP 286, Tangier; tel. (3) 7321414; fax (3) 7322156; water, sewerage and electricity network for Tangier.

Régie d'Eau et d'Electricité (RED): Rabat; in 1998 a 30-year concession to manage Rabat's water and power grids was awarded to a consortium of Electricidade de Portugal (Portugal), Urbaser (Spain) and Alborada (Morocco).

Gas

Afriquia Gaz: rue Ibnou el-Ouennanae Aïn Sebaâ; Casablanca; tel. (2) 2352144; fax (2) 2352239; f. 1992; Morocco's leading gas distributor; transfer to private ownership pending; Dir-Gen. Rachid Idrissi Kaitouni.

TRADE UNIONS

Confédération Démocratique du Travail (CDT): 64 rue al-Mourtada, Quartier Palmier, BP 13576, Casablanca; tel. (2) 2994470; fax (2) 2994473; e-mail cdtmaroc@hotmail.com; internet www.cdt.ma; f. 1978; 400,000 mems; Sec.-Gen. Noubir el-Amaoui.

Union Démocratique de l'Agriculture: f. 1997; Sec.-Gen. Abd ar-Rahman Filali.

Union Générale des Travailleurs Marocains (UGTM): 9 rue du Rif, angle route de Médiouna, Casablanca; tel. (2) 2282144; f. 1960; associated with Istiqlal; supported by unions not affiliated to UMT; 673,000 mems; Sec.-Gen. Abd ar-Razzaq Afilal.

Union Marocaine du Travail (UMT): Bourse du Travail, 232 ave des Forces Armées Royales, Casablanca; tel. (2) 2302292; left-wing and associated with the UNFP; most unions are affiliated; 700,000 mems; Sec. Mahjoub ben Seddiq.

Union Syndicale Agricole (USA): agricultural section of UMT.

Union Marocaine du Travail Autonome: Rabat; breakaway union from UMT.

Transport

Office National des Transports (ONT): rue al-Fadila, Quartier Industriel, BP 596, Rabat-Chellah; tel. (3) 7797842; fax (3) 7797850; f. 1958; Dir-Gen. Muhammad Lahbib el-Gueddari.

RAILWAYS

In 2005 there were 1,907 km of railways, of which 418 km were double track; 1,022 km of lines were electrified and diesel locomotives were used on the rest. In that year the network carried some 18.5m. passengers and 32.7m. metric tons of freight. All services are nationalized. A feasibility study was begun in 1998 into the construction of a 28-km metro system in Casablanca.

Office National des Chemins de Fer (ONCF): 8 bis rue Abderrahmane el-Ghafiki, Rabat-Agdal; tel. (3) 7774747; fax (3) 7774480; e-mail ketary@oncf.ma; internet www.oncf.ma; f. 1963; administers all Morocco's railways; Dir-Gen. Muhammad Rabie Khlie.

MOROCCO

ROADS

In 2002 there were 57,694 km of classified roads, of which 56.4% were paved.

Autoroutes du Maroc (ADM): Hay Riad, Rabat; tel. (3) 7711056; fax (3) 7711059; e-mail naitbrahim.ismail@adm.co.ma; internet www.adm.co.ma; responsible for the construction and upkeep of Morocco's motorway network.

Cie de Transports au Maroc (CTM—SA): km 13.5, Autoroute Casablanca–Rabat, Casablanca; tel. (2) 2438282; fax (2) 2765428; e-mail webmaster@ctm.co.ma; internet www.ctm.co.ma; agencies in Tangier, Rabat, Meknès, Oujda, Marrakesh, Agadir, El Jadida, Safi, Casablanca, Essaouira, Fez and Ouarzazate; privatized in 1993, with 40% of shares reserved for Moroccan citizens; Pres. and Dir-Gen. ABDALLAH LAHLOU.

SHIPPING

According to official figures, Morocco's 21 ports handled 61.5m. tons of goods in 2004. The most important ports, in terms of the volume of goods handled, are Casablanca, Jorf Lasfar, Safi and Mohammadia. Tangier is the principal port for passenger services. Construction work on new ports at Tangier (to handle merchandise traffic) and Agadir commenced in 2000.

Office d'Exploitation des Ports (ODEP): 175 blvd Muhammad Zerktouni, 20100 Casablanca; tel. (2) 2232324; fax (2) 2232325; e-mail administrateur@odep.org.ma; internet www.odep.org.ma; f. 1985; port management and handling of port equipment; Gen. Man. MUSTAPHA BARROUG.

Principal Shipping Companies

Agence Med SRA: 3 rue ibn Rochd, 90000 Tangier; tel. (3) 9935875; fax (3) 9933239; e-mail agencemed@menara.ma; f. 1904; owned by the Bland Group; also at Agadir, Casablanca, Jorf Lasfar, Nador and Safi; Operations Man. MUHAMMAD CHATT.

Cie Chérifienne d'Armement: 5 blvd Abdallah ben Yacine, 21700 Casablanca; tel. (2) 2309455; fax (2) 2301186; f. 1929; regular services to Europe; Man. Dir MAX KADOCH.

Cie Marocaine d'Agences Maritimes (COMARINE): 45 ave de l'Armée Royale, BP 60, 20000 Casablanca; tel. (2) 2311941; fax (2) 2312570; e-mail comarine@marocnet.net.ma.

Cie Marocaine de Navigation (COMANAV): 7 blvd de la Résistance, BP 628, Casablanca 20300; tel. (2) 2303012; fax (2) 2308455; e-mail comanav@comanav.co.ma; f. 1946; regular services to Mediterranean, North-west European, Middle Eastern and West African ports; tramping; Chair. MUHAMMAD BENHAROUGA.

Intercona SA: 7 rue Hariri, 4ème étage, Tangier; tel. (3) 9945907; fax (3) 9945909; e-mail intercona@wanadoo.net.ma; f. 1943; daily services from Algeciras (Spain) to Tangier and Ceuta (Spanish North Africa); Pres. VICENTE JORRO.

Limadet-ferry: 3 rue ibn Rochd, Tangier; tel. (3) 933639; fax (3) 937173; f. 1966; operates between Algeciras (Spain) and Tangier, six daily; Dir-Gen. RACHID BEN MANSOUR.

Société Marocaine de Navigation Atlas: 81 ave Houmane el-Fatouaki, 21000 Casablanca; tel. (2) 2224190; fax (2) 2274401; f. 1976; Chair. HASSAN CHAMI; Man. Dir M. SLAOUI.

Union Maritime Maroc-Scandinave (UNIMAR): 12 rue de Foucauld, BP 746, Casablanca; tel. (2) 2279590; fax (2) 2223883; f. 1974; chemicals; Dir-Gen. ABD AL-WAHAB BEN KIRANE.

Voyages Paquet: 65 ave de l'Armée Royale, Casablanca; tel. (2) 2761941; fax (2) 2442108; f. 1970; Pres. MUHAMMAD ELOUALI ELALAMI; Dir-Gen. NAÏMA BAKALI ELOUALI ELALAMI.

CIVIL AVIATION

The main international airports are at Casablanca (King Muhammad V), Rabat, Tangier, Marrakesh, Agadir Inezgane, Fez, Oujda, Al-Hocima, el-Aaiún, Ouarzazate and Agadir al-Massira. Construction of a new international airport at al-Aroui, located 25 km south of Nador, began in late 1998. In November 1999 the Arab Fund for Economic and Social Development granted a loan worth US $32.7m. to finance a project to extend and modernize King Muhammad V airport. A second runway has recently been completed, and the construction of new terminal buildings was under way in early 2006.

Atlas Blue: Aéroport Casablanca—Ménara, BP 440, Casablanca Medina; fax (2) 44424222; e-mail contact@atlas-blue.com; internet www.atlas-blue.com; f. 2004; wholly owned by Royal Air Maroc (RAM); low-cost airline; domestic flights and services to six European countries; Chair ZOUHAIR MUHAMMAD EL-AOUFIR.

Office Nationale des Aéroports: BP 8101, Casablanca-Oasis; tel. (2) 2539040; fax (2) 2539901; e-mail onda@onda.ma; internet www.onda.ma; f. 1990; Dir-Gen. ABDELHANINE BENALLOU.

Regional Airlines: Aéroport de Muhammad V, BP 12518, Casablanca; tel. (2) 2538020; fax (2) 2538411; f. 1997; privately-owned; domestic flights and services to southern Spain, Portugal and the Canary Islands; Pres. and CEO MUHAMMAD HASSAN BENSALAH.

Royal Air Maroc (RAM): Aéroport de Casablanca-Anfa; tel. (2) 2912000; fax (2) 2912087; e-mail callcenter@royalairmaroc.com; internet www.royalairmaroc.com; f. 1953; 94.4% state-owned; scheduled for partial privatization; domestic flights and services to 35 countries in Western Europe, Scandinavia, the Americas, North and West Africa, the Canary Islands and the Middle East; CEO DRISS BENHIMA.

Tourism

Tourism is Morocco's second main source of convertible currency. The country's attractions for tourists include its sunny climate, ancient sites (notably the cities of Fez, Marrakesh, Meknès and Rabat) and spectacular scenery. There are popular holiday resorts on the Atlantic and Mediterranean coasts. In 2004 foreign tourist arrivals totalled 2.75m., compared with 1.63m. in 1996. Tourist receipts, including passenger transport, totalled US $3,369m. in 2003.

Office National Marocain du Tourisme: 31 angle ave al-Abtal et rue Oued Fès, Agdal, Rabat; tel. (3) 7681531; fax (3) 7777437; e-mail contact@tourisme-marocain.com; internet www.tourisme-marocain.com; f. 1918; Dir-Gen. FATHIA BENNIS.

MOZAMBIQUE

Introductory Survey

Location, Climate, Language, Religion, Flag, Capital

The Republic of Mozambique lies on the east coast of Africa, bordered to the north by Tanzania, to the west by Malawi, Zambia and Zimbabwe, and to the south by South Africa and Swaziland. The country has a coastline of about 2,470 km (1,535 miles) on the shores of the Indian Ocean, and is separated from Madagascar, to the east, by the Mozambique Channel. Except in a few upland areas, the climate varies from tropical to sub-tropical. Rainfall is irregular, but the rainy season is usually from November to March, when average temperatures in Maputo are between 26°C (79°F) and 30°C (86°F). In the cooler dry season, in June and July, the average temperatures are 18°C (64°F) to 20°C (68°F). Portuguese is the official language, while there are 39 indigenous languages, the most widely spoken being Makhuwa, Tsonga, Sema and Lomwe. Many of the inhabitants follow traditional beliefs. There are about 5m. Christians, the majority of whom are Roman Catholics, and 4m. Muslims. The national flag (proportions 2 by 3) has three equal horizontal stripes, of green, black and yellow, separated by narrow white stripes. At the hoist is a red triangle containing a five-pointed yellow star, on which are superimposed an open book, a hoe and a rifle. The capital is Maputo (formerly Lourenço Marques).

Recent History

Mozambique became a Portuguese colony in the 19th century and an overseas province in 1951. Nationalist groups began to form in the 1960s. The Frente de Libertação de Moçambique (Frelimo—Mozambique Liberation Front) was formed in 1962 and launched a military campaign for independence in 1964. After the coup in Portugal (q.v.) in April 1974, negotiations between Frelimo and the new Portuguese Government resulted in a period of rule in Mozambique by a transitional Government, followed by full independence on 25 June 1975. The leader of Frelimo, Samora Machel, became the first President of Mozambique. Between September and December 1977 elections took place to local, district and provincial assemblies and, at national level, to the Assembléia Popular (People's Assembly).

In March 1976 Mozambique closed its border with Rhodesia (now Zimbabwe) and applied economic sanctions against that country. Mozambique was the principal base for Rhodesian nationalist guerrillas, and consequently suffered considerable devastation as a result of offensives launched by Rhodesian government forces against guerrilla camps. The border was reopened in January 1980.

After Zimbabwean independence in April 1980, South Africa adopted Rhodesia's role as supporter of the Mozambican opposition guerrilla group, Resistência Nacional Moçambicana (Renamo), also known as the Movimento Nacional da Resistência de Moçambique. The activities of Renamo subsequently increased, causing persistent disruption to road, rail and petroleum pipeline links from Mozambican ports, which were vital to the economic independence of southern African nations from South Africa. In March 1984 Mozambique and South Africa signed a formal joint non-aggression pact, known as the Nkomati accord, whereby each Government undertook to prevent opposition forces on its territory from launching attacks against the other, and a Joint Security Commission was established. The accord effectively implied that South Africa would withdraw its covert support for Renamo in return for a guarantee by Mozambique that it would prevent any further use of its territory by the then banned African National Congress of South Africa (ANC). However, following an intensification of Renamo activity, in 1985 the Frelimo Government appealed to foreign powers for increased military assistance, and in June it was agreed that Zimbabwe would augment its military presence in Mozambique. A major military offensive against Renamo in July resulted in the capture, in August, of the rebels' national operational command centre and of other major rebel bases in the area. Mozambique subsequently alleged that documents discovered at one of the captured Renamo bases revealed that South Africa had repeatedly violated the Nkomati accord by providing material support for the rebels. The Joint Security Commission ceased to meet in 1985.

General elections were scheduled to take place in 1982, but were postponed several times because of the security situation. Legislative elections eventually began in August 1986, but were delayed, owing to the internal conflict. The post of Prime Minister was created in July and allocated to Mário Machungo. President Machel died in an air crash in South Africa in October. The causes of the incident were unclear, and the Mozambican Ministry of Information declared that it did not exclude the possibility of South African sabotage. (In May 1998 it was announced that South Africa's Truth and Reconciliation Commission—TRC—was to examine evidence relating to the crash. The TRC final report stated that the evidence was inconclusive, but a number of questions merited further investigation. In early 2006 the South African Government announced that it was to reopen the inquiry into Machel's death.) In November 1986 the Central Committee of Frelimo appointed Joaquim Alberto Chissano, hitherto Minister for Foreign Affairs, as President. The elections were then resumed. In contrast to the 1977 elections, the voters were given a choice of candidates; nevertheless, all government and party leaders had been re-elected when the poll was completed in December 1986.

In June 1988, following six months of negotiations, Mozambique, South Africa and Portugal signed an agreement to rehabilitate the Cahora Bassa hydroelectric plant in Mozambique (potentially one of the greatest sources of electricity in southern Africa). In May Mozambican and South African officials had agreed to reactivate the Nkomati accord and to re-establish the Joint Security Commission; subsequently a joint commission for co-operation and development was established.

At Frelimo's fifth congress, held in July 1989, the party's exclusively Marxist-Leninist orientation was renounced, and party membership was opened to Mozambicans from all sectors of society. In January 1990 Chissano announced the drafting of a new constitution.

In mid-1989 Presidents Daniel arap Moi of Kenya and Robert Mugabe of Zimbabwe agreed to mediate between the Mozambique Government and Renamo. In August Renamo rejected the Government's peace proposals, and demanded recognition as a political entity, the introduction of multi-party elections and the withdrawal of Zimbabwean troops from Mozambique as preconditions for peace. However, further talks between the Government and the rebels resulted in an agreement, in December 1990, for a partial cease-fire. Under the terms of the agreement, all Zimbabwean troops present in Mozambique were required to retire to the Beira and Limpopo transport 'corridors' linking Zimbabwe to the Mozambican ports of Beira and Maputo. The cease-fire was confined to these areas.

The agreement followed the introduction, on 30 November 1990, of a new Mozambican Constitution, formally ending Frelimo's single-party rule and committing the State to political pluralism and a free-market economy, and enshrining private property rights and guarantees of press freedom. The official name of the country was changed from the People's Republic of Mozambique to the Republic of Mozambique. Renamo refused to recognize the new Constitution, declaring that it had been drafted without democratic consultation. The President was henceforth to be elected by direct universal suffrage, and the legislature was renamed the Assembléia da República (Assembly of the Republic). A new law concerning the formation, structure and function of political parties came into effect in February 1991. In accordance with the Constitution, Renamo would not be recognized as a legitimate political party until it had renounced violence completely.

In December 1990 negotiations between the Government and Renamo resumed in Rome, Italy, and a Joint Verification Commission, comprising independent representatives from 10 nations, in addition to those of the Mozambican Government and Renamo, was established to monitor the partial cease-fire. Further talks took place in Rome in January 1991, but collapsed following the presentation of a report by the Joint Verification Commission containing accusations that Renamo had violated the cease-fire agreement, and did not resume until May.

In August 1991 a Frelimo party congress undertook further structural changes. The Political Bureau was restyled the Political Commission; Chissano was re-elected as President of the party, while Feliciano Salomão Gundana, Minister of the Presidency, was appointed to the new position of Secretary-General.

In October 1991 Renamo and the Government signed a protocol agreeing fundamental principles and containing a set of mutual guarantees as a basis for a peace accord. Throughout the discussions Renamo continued guerrilla attacks, many of which were launched (despite the Nkomati accord) from South Africa. Under the terms of the protocol, Renamo effectively recognized the legitimacy of the Government and agreed to enter the multi-party political framework. In return, the Government pledged not to legislate on any of the points under negotiation in Rome until a general peace accord had been signed. In November a second protocol was signed by both parties, enabling Renamo to begin functioning as a political party immediately after the signing of a general peace accord.

In March 1992, following discussions conducted in Rome, a third protocol was signed establishing the principles for the country's future electoral system. Under its terms, the elections, to be held under a system of proportional representation, were to be supervised by international observers. An electoral commission was to be established, with one-third of its members to be appointed by Renamo. Discussions, which resumed in June, reached an impasse over constitutional issues. In July Chissano announced that he was prepared to meet the Renamo leader, Afonso Macacho Marceta Dhlakama, for direct talks. On 7 August, following three days of discussions in Rome, Chissano and Dhlakama signed a joint declaration committing the two sides to a total cease-fire by 1 October, as part of a General Peace Agreement (Acordo Geral de Paz—AGP). In September Chissano and Dhlakama met in Gaborone, Botswana, to attempt to resolve the deadlocked military and security issues. Chissano offered to establish an independent commission to monitor and guarantee the impartiality of the Serviço de Informação e Segurança do Estado (SISE—State Information and Security Service). In addition, the figure of 30,000 was agreed upon as the number of troops to comprise the joint national defence force.

The AGP was finally signed on 4 October 1992. Under the terms of the agreement, a general cease-fire was to come into force immediately after ratification of the treaty by the legislature. Both the Renamo troops and the government forces were to withdraw to assembly points within seven days of ratification. The new national defence force, the Forças Armadas de Defesa de Moçambique (FADM), would then be created, drawing on equal numbers from each side, with the remaining troops surrendering their weapons to a UN peace-keeping force within six months. A Cease-fire Commission, incorporating representatives from the Government, Renamo and the UN, was to be established to assume responsibility for supervising the implementation of the truce regulations. Overall political control of the peace process was to be vested in a Comissão de Supervisão e Controle (CSC—Supervision and Control Commission), comprising representatives of the Government, Renamo and the UN. In addition, Chissano was to appoint a National Information Commission (COMINFO—Comissão Nacional de Informação), with responsibilities including supervision of the SISE. Presidential and legislative elections were to take place, under UN supervision, one year after the signing of the AGP, provided that it had been fully implemented and the demobilization process completed. The AGP was duly ratified by the Assembléia da República and came into force on 15 October. On that day UN observers arrived in Maputo to supervise the first phase of the cease-fire. However, shortly afterwards the Government accused Renamo of systematically violating the accord. Dhlakama subsequently claimed that Renamo's actions had been defensive manoeuvres and, in turn, accused government forces of violating the accord by advancing into Renamo territory.

In November 1992, owing to considerable delays in the formation of the various peace commissions envisaged in the AGP, the timetable for the cease-fire operations was redrafted. In December the UN Security Council finally approved a plan for the establishment of the UN Operation in Mozambique (ONUMOZ), providing for the deployment of some 7,500 troops, police and civilian observers to oversee the process of demobilization and formation of the FADM, and to supervise the forthcoming elections. However, there were continued delays in the deployment of ONUMOZ. In March the peace process was effectively halted when Renamo withdrew from the CSC and the Cease-fire Commission, protesting that proper provisions had not been made to accommodate its officials, and in April Dhlakama announced that his forces would begin to report to assembly points only when Renamo received US $15m. to finance its transition into a political party. Meanwhile, the first UN troops became operational on 1 April.

In June 1993 Renamo rejoined the CSC. The commission subsequently agreed to a formal postponement of the election date to October 1994. A meeting in Maputo of international aid donors, also in June 1993, produced promises of additional support for the peace process, bringing the total pledged by donors to US $520m., including support for the repatriation of 1.5m. refugees from neighbouring countries, the resettlement of 4m.–5m. displaced people and the reintegration of some 80,000 former combatants into civilian life. The UN also agreed to establish a trust fund of $10m. to finance Renamo's transformation into a political party, with the disbursement of funds dependent on UN approval.

Renamo announced new preconditions to the advancement of the peace process in July 1993, insisting initially on the recognition of its own administration, to operate parallel to that of the Government, and later on the appointment of its members to five of the country's 11 provincial governorships. Under the terms of an agreement signed in September, Renamo was to appoint three advisers to each of the incumbent provincial governors to make recommendations relating to the reintegration of areas under Renamo control into a single state administration. In October 1993 the CSC approved a new timetable covering all aspects of the peace process, including the elections in October 1994. In November 1993 the UN Security Council renewed the mandate of ONUMOZ for a further six months. In addition, it acceded to the joint request by the Government and Renamo for a UN police corps. In the same month consensus was finally reached on the text of the electoral law, which was promulgated at the end of December. At a meeting of the CSC in mid-November an agreement was signed providing for the confinement of troops, to be concluded by the end of the year.

In February 1994 the UN Security Council announced that, in response to demands made by Renamo, it would be increasing the membership of the UN police corps monitoring the confinement areas from 128 to 1,144. By the end of February only 50% of troops had entered designated assembly points, and none had officially been demobilized. In March, in an effort to expedite the confinement process, the Government announced that it was to commence the unilateral demobilization of its troops. Renamo began the demobilization of its troops shortly afterwards. In April Lt-Gen. Lagos Lidimo, the nominee of the Government, and the former Renamo guerrilla commander, Lt-Gen. Mateus Ngonhamo, were inaugurated as the high command of the FADM. In the same month Chissano issued a decree scheduling the presidential and legislative elections for 27–28 October, and in May the UN Security Council renewed the mandate of ONUMOZ for the final period, ending on 15 November.

The confinement and demobilization processes continued to make slow progress, and the deadlines for the completion of confinement and demobilization were extended. On 16 August 1994, in accordance with the provisions of the AGP, the government Forças Armadas de Moçambique were formally dissolved and their assets transferred to the FADM, which was inaugurated as the country's official armed forces on the same day. In December the Cease-fire Commission issued its final report, according to which ONUMOZ had registered a combined total of 91,691 government and Renamo troops during the confinement process, of whom 11,579 had enlisted in the FADM (compared with the 30,000 envisaged in the AGP).

In August 1994 Renamo formally registered as a political party. In the same month the Partido Liberal e Democrático de Moçambique, the Partido Nacional Democrático and the Partido Nacional de Moçambique formed an electoral coalition, the União Democrática (UD). The presidential and legislative elections took place on 27–29 October. The extension of voting to a third day had become necessary following the withdrawal of Renamo from the elections only hours before the beginning of the poll, claiming that conditions were not in place to ensure free and fair elections. However, following concerted international pressure, Renamo abandoned its boycott after the first day. In the presidential election Chissano secured an outright majority (53.3%) of the votes. His closest rival was Dhlakama, who received 33.7% of the votes. In the legislative elections Frelimo also secured an overall majority, winning 129 of the 250 seats in the Assembléia da República; Renamo obtained 112 seats, and the UD the remaining nine. Dhlakama accepted the results of the elections, although he maintained that there had been irregularities. The UN asserted that the irregularities were insufficient to have affected the overall credibility of the poll, which it declared to have been free and fair—a view endorsed by international observers. Later in November the UN Security Council extended the mandate of ONUMOZ until the end of January 1995.

Chissano was inaugurated as President on 9 December 1994, and the new Government, in which all portfolios were assigned to members of Frelimo, was sworn in on 23 December. Demands by Renamo that it be awarded governorships in the five provinces where it won a majority of the votes in the legislative elections were rejected by Chissano. At the first session of the new legislature, which began on 8 December, a dispute resulted in the withdrawal of the Renamo and UD deputies, although both groups abandoned their boycott by the end of December.

By the end of March 1995 only a small unit of ONUMOZ officials remained in the country. In February 1996 the Government proposed that municipal elections, which the Constitution stipulated must be conducted no later than October 1996, be held in 1997. Delays in the election process had resulted from a dispute between the parliamentary opposition, which demanded simultaneous local elections throughout Mozambique, and the Government, which sought to hold elections only in those areas that had attained municipal status. In October 1996 the Assembléia da República approved a constitutional amendment differentiating between municipalities and administrative posts. In August 1997 the Government postponed the elections until 1998, owing to delays in the disbursement by international donors of funding for the voter registration process. In January 1998 Renamo alleged that the voter registration process had been fraudulent, and threatened to boycott the elections unless a further registration of voters was conducted. In April Renamo was among 16 opposition parties that officially withdrew from the elections. Renamo subsequently campaigned vigorously to dissuade the electorate from participating in the ballot. At the elections, which took place on 30 June, Frelimo secured all the mayoral posts and won control of all the municipal authorities contested. Very few opposition parties contested the election, and Frelimo's main competition came from independent candidates. Moreover, the voter turn-out was only 14.6%, prompting Renamo to demand the annulment of the elections.

Under the Constitution, presidential and legislative elections were to take place by November 1999. However, political disputes and administrative delays threatened to force a postponement of the elections. A principal cause of the delay was Renamo's insistence on the need to reregister the entire electorate. In June Frelimo announced that Chissano would stand as its presidential candidate. In the following month 11 opposition parties, led by Renamo, signed an agreement to contest the forthcoming elections as a coalition, styled Renamo—União Eleitoral (Renamo—UE). The coalition was to present a single list of legislative candidates, with Dhlakama as its presidential candidate.

Presidential and legislative elections took place on 3–5 December 1999. In the presidential contest, Chissano defeated Dhlakama (his sole challenger), taking 52.3% of the valid votes cast. Frelimo secured an outright majority in the legislative elections, winning 133 of the 250 seats in the Assembléia da República; Renamo—UE obtained the remaining seats. Renamo rejected the outcome, claiming that the vote had been fraudulent. However, international monitors declared that the vote had been free and fair. In January 2000 the Supreme Court—exercising the functions of the Constitutional Council, which had yet to be established—rejected the appeal by Renamo against the results of the elections. On 15 January Chissano was sworn in for a further five-year presidential term.

In February 2000 massive flooding in southern and central areas caused widespread devastation to the country's social and economic infrastructure. The flooding was the worst ever on record, seriously affecting an estimated 2m. people. Some 10% of Mozambique's cultivated land was destroyed, and most of its livestock was lost. Much of the country's transport infrastructure was destroyed, as were many villages. The World Bank estimated the cost of losses at between US $270m. and $430m.

Renamo boycotted the election of the new Comissão Nacional de Eleicões (CNE—National Elections Commission), officially inaugurated in July 2000, on the grounds that it did not recognise the legitimacy of the current Government, and that a review of the current electoral law was needed. Frelimo appointed eight representatives to the 15-member CNE. Demonstrations held by Renamo in November, in protest at the results of the December 1999 elections, resulted in the deaths of some 41 people, following clashes between Renamo and Frelimo supporters. (In June 2001 several Renamo members were found guilty of armed rebellion in relation to the riots, while several police-officers were also prosecuted; a further 14 Renamo members and supporters were imprisoned in January 2002 for their part in the violence.) Moreover, later in November 2000 one of the country's most influential journalists, Carlos Cardoso, was killed in Maputo. It was alleged by Dhlakama that Cardoso had been murdered as a result of an article, published in his newspaper *Metical*, in which he had criticized the Government's involvement in the protests earlier in November, however, it was announced in March 2001 that three people, including the former manager of a branch of the Banco Comercial de Moçambique—BCM, had been arrested in connection with Cardoso's murder; shortly before his death Cardoso had apparently uncovered details relating to the theft of some 144,000m. meticais from a branch of the BCM in 1996.

In late December 2000 Dhlakama and Chissano held talks (the first since the disputed election of December 1999) in an attempt to resolve the growing tension between their two parties. The two leaders agreed to hold further talks in 2001, and to establish inquiries into the violence of November 2000. Moreover, Dhlakama stated that he was prepared to accept the results of the 1999 elections, and Chissano pledged to consult Renamo about future state appointments. However, comments by Dhlakama, accusing Frelimo of violence and intimidation towards Renamo, subsequently jeopardized the future of talks between the two parties. In a second meeting between the two leaders in January 2001 it was agreed that a number of working groups (including groups on defence and security, constitutional and parliamentary affairs, and the media) would be established in February. At a further meeting, in March, Chissano referred Dhlakama's demand for the appointment of Renamo state governors to the Assembléia da República, whose Frelimo representatives were strongly opposed to accommodating Renamo demands. In protest, Dhlakama ceased negotiations in April.

Floods in central Mozambique in February and March 2001 resulted in some 100 deaths and left an estimated 230,000 people homeless. In July the Government requested some US $132m. in international aid to assist in the reconstruction of damaged infrastructure, and for the development of measures to prevent a recurrence.

President Chissano announced in May 2001 that he would not stand for re-election on the expiry of his term in 2004. At the long-postponed Renamo congress, held in October 2001, Dhlakama was re-elected party President, obtaining over 95% of votes cast; Joaquim Vaz was elected Secretary-General. The holding of a party congress by Renamo for the first time since the end of the civil war, as well as the establishment of a 10-member Political Committee, were regarded as confirmation of the movement's decision to establish itself as a full political party, and to decentralize the party leadership and structure.

In August 2001 António Siba-Siba Macuacua, the interim Chairman of Banco Austral, was murdered while investigating corruption allegations at the bank. Macuacua had published a list of more than 1,000 people, including some government officials, who had failed to repay loans to the bank. The investigation into Macuacua's murder proceeded slowly, raising concerns over the impunity of those connected with organized crime, and by early 2006 no charges had been brought in the case. In November 2001 the Assembléia da República approved legislation prohibiting the process of 'money laundering'. The new measures imposed restrictions on banking and other local financial activities, in an attempt to render them more accountable.

In June 2002, at the party's eighth congress, Frelimo elected Armando Guebuza as its Secretary-General, and thus also its candidate for the 2004 presidential election. During July Renamo's attempt to establish itself as a legitimate opposition party was threatened after Dhlakama dismissed Vaz as Secretary-General, assuming the position himself, and dissolved the party's Political Committee. In October Renamo announced its intention to contest municipal elections (due in 2003) alone, rather than in coalition, while in November 2002 the party regained some stability with the appointment of Viana Magalhaes as Secretary-General. In December, however, further controversy arose when Renamo demanded the exclusion from the Assembléia da República of five deputies who had resigned or been expelled from the party, including Raul Domingos, formerly a senior member of Renamo, who had been expelled from the party in 2000. Renamo protesters caused an estimated US $11,000 of damage to the Assembléia. The former Renamo deputies retained their right to participate in the Assembléia.

Meanwhile, in November 2002, during the trial of six men for Cardoso's murder in 2000, the President's eldest son, Nyimpine Chissano, was accused by three of the defendants of having ordered or paid for the assassination; Nyimpine Chissano denied any involvement in the murder. It was additionally claimed that one of the accused, Aníbal António dos Santos, who had escaped from custody in suspicious circumstances at the beginning of September, was making secret threats against key figures in the trial. In January 2003 all six accused were found guilty of Cardoso's murder; dos Santos, who had been tried *in absentia*, was arrested in South Africa at the end of January, and extradited to Mozambique to serve a prison term of 28 years and six months. He escaped custody again in May 2004 but was subsequently arrested in Canada and extradited to Mozambique in January 2005. The Supreme Court ruled in December 2004 that he should be retried; dos Santos was sentenced to 30 years' imprisonment in January 2006. Nyimpine Chissano continued to deny any involvement in the murder. In June 2004 seven people, including three who were currently serving prison sentences for Cardoso's murder, were convicted of charges relating to the disappearance of funds from the BCM and were sentenced to terms of imprisonment.

In February 2003, in response to Renamo's decision to run alone in the municipal elections, 10 opposition parties announced the formation of a new coalition, the União Eleitoral, led by Domingos, who had previously announced his intention of standing as an independent in the presidential election. In October Domingos founded his own party, the Partido para a Paz, Democracia e Desenvolvimento (PPDD). From mid-2003 divisions became apparent within Frelimo between supporters of its presidential candidate, Guebuza, and Chissano loyalists. The Conselho Constitucional (Constitutional Council), which was to supervise elections and determine the constitutionality of new legislation, was inaugurated in early November, with Rui Baltazar dos Santos Alves as its first Chairman. Municipal elections were held on 19 November. Despite allegations by Renamo of irregularities, the elections proceeded smoothly, and their conduct was later commended by an observer mission from the European Union (EU, see p. 228), although voter turn-out, at 24.2%, was low. Frelimo won a majority in 29 municipalities, while Renamo won a majority in four, including Beira. The results were verified by the Constitutional Council in January 2004.

In mid-February 2004 Luísa Dias Diogo was appointed as Prime Minister, to replace Mocumbi, who resigned the premiership to take up an executive post in an EU-sponsored initiative specializing in clinical research. Diogo retained the responsibilities of Minister of Planning and Finance, the post she had held under Mocumbi.

In mid-2004 the compilation of voter lists for the forthcoming presidential and legislative elections resulted in the registration of a further 1.2m. voters (although there were concerns that some people had registered twice), bringing the total number of those eligible to vote to some 9.1m. In mid-August fighting, in which a member of the security forces was killed, took place between Renamo supporters and the police in Sofala province. Concern was expressed that further violence would occur prior to the December elections.

By the deadline for submissions in October 2004, eight candidates, five of whom were subsequently approved by the Conselho Constitucional, had registered their intention to contest the presidential election. Three candidates were rejected on the grounds that they had not gathered the requisite 10,000 signatures to support their nominations. The five candidates were Guebuza, Dhlakama, Domingos, Yaqub Sabindy of the Partido Independente de Moçambique, reportedly an Islamist party (although the Constitution prohibited religious affiliations in political organizations), and Carlos Alexandre dos Reis, the leader of the União Nacional Moçambicana. 25 political organizations and coalitions registered to contest the legislative elections, although there were serious misgivings regarding the credibility of a number of the parties. In mid-November the Assembléia da República approved changes to the Constitution, which were to take effect on the day following the declaration of the results of the elections. Notably, the President would no longer be afforded immunity from prosecution and a Council of State was to be created. It was also envisaged that elections to provincial assemblies, which were to mirror in structure those to the Assembléia, would take place in 2008.

The presidential and legislative elections took place as scheduled on 1–2 December 2004, and proceeded without notable incident, although 37 voting stations did not open, reportedly owing to bad weather. For the first time Mozambicans living abroad were able to vote. Although national and international observers stated that the elections had been generally free and fair, they did express concern at the lack of access that they had been granted to the counting process and about the low rate of voter participation, which was recorded at just 36.3%. Renamo, later joined by other opposition parties, announced that it would not recognize the results, due to alleged irregularities produced by the computer system used to tabulate the votes and demanded that the elections be rerun. Official results, which were released on 21 December, revealed that Guebuza had won 63.7% of the votes cast at the presidential election, while Dhlakama took 31.7% and Domingos 2.7%. In the legislative elections, Frelimo won 62.0% of the votes, securing 160 of the available 250 seats, while Renamo took 29.7% and 90 seats (a significant decline compared with the 117 seats it had won in the 1999 elections). No other party achieved the minimum of 5% of total votes cast required to secure parliamentary representation. Protests lodged by Renamo with the CNE and the Constitutional Council were rejected in January 2005, and Renamo announced that it would accept the election results and participate in the new legislature.

In mid-January 2005 the election results were approved by the Constitutional Council. The new Assembléia da República was inaugurated on 31 January, and Eduardo Mulémbue was re-elected to the post of Chairman. Guebuza was sworn in as President on 2 February and in his inauguration speech pledged to promote rural development and to take measures to combat corruption and poverty. The new Government, featuring a number of new appointees, was announced the following day. Diogo retained her position as Prime Minister, however, in a reorganization of ministerial functions, Manuel Chang became Minister of Finance, while Aiuba Cuereneia headed the newly created Ministry of Planning and Development. Alcinda Abreu was appointed Minister of Foreign Affairs and Co-operation, while José Pacheco became Minister of the Interior. In mid-February a further three ministers were appointed to the justice, science and technology and veterans' affairs portfolios. In March Chissano resigned as President of Frelimo and was replaced by Guebuza.

Meanwhile, in February 2005 it was reported that members of Dhlakama's guard, protesting against the non-payment of wages and poor living conditions, had taken five Renamo officials hostage. The following month the Government announced plans to integrate the guards (estimated to number 100–150), who had been maintained by Dhlakama as his personal guard following the end of the civil war in 1992, into the state security forces, however such attempts were consistently stalled by Dhlakama. In September 2005 conflict between Frelimo and Renamo supporters led to the deaths of 12 people in Mocimboa da Praia, in Cabo Delgado province, following a disputed by-election earlier in the year.

In November 2005 the Assembléia da República passed legislation providing for the formation of the Council of State, as envisaged in changes to the Constitution approved in late 2004. Members of the Council, including Dhlakama, were subsequently appointed by Guebuza and the Assembléia da República, and took office in late December 2005.

During 1995 the activities, principally in the border province of Manica, of a group of mainly Zimbabwean dissidents, known as Chimwenje, came under increasing scrutiny. The group, which was alleged to have links with Renamo, was believed to be preparing for military incursions into Zimbabwe, where it sought the overthrow of President Mugabe. In early 1996 the Chissano Government announced its intention to expel the dissidents from Mozambique. In June, following a series of armed attacks on both sides of the Mozambique–Zimbabwe border, which were believed to have been perpetrated by Chimwenje, the Governments of Mozambique and Zimbabwe agreed to combine and intensify efforts to combat the activities of the dissidents. The group was suppressed in late 1996. During late 2002 and early 2003 Mozambique resettled a number of white Zimbabwean farmers whose land had been appropriated by the Mugabe regime.

MOZAMBIQUE

After stepping down as President following the election of December 2004, Chissano increasingly took on an international role. In mid-2005, as the UN Secretary-General's special envoy, he monitored the presidential election in Guinea-Bissau, while in August he was appointed mediator for the African Union (see p. 153) in Zimbabwe.

After independence, Mozambique developed strong international links with the USSR and other countries of the communist bloc, and with neighbouring African states: it is a member of the Southern African Development Community (SADC, see p. 358), founded in 1979, as the Southern African Development Co-ordination Conference, then with the aim of reducing the region's economic dependence on South Africa, principally by developing trade routes through Mozambique. In December 1996 Mozambique, Malawi, Zambia and Zimbabwe (also SADC members) formally agreed to establish the Beira Development Corridor as a trading route avoiding South Africa's ports. In 1993 full diplomatic relations were established with South Africa. In July 1994 Mozambique and South Africa established a new Joint Defence and Security Commission, replacing the Joint Security Commission originally established in 1984. In November 1995 Mozambique was admitted, by special dispensation, as a full member of the Commonwealth (see p. 193). In late 2005 Mozambican troops ended their participation in the United Nations Operation in Burundi (see p. 79), following the successful installation of a government of national unity in that country.

Government

The Constitution of 30 November 1990 (amended in 1996 and 2004) provides for a multi-party political system. Legislative power is vested in the Assembléia da República, with 250 members, who are elected for a five-year term. Members are elected by universal, direct adult suffrage in a secret ballot, according to a system of proportional representation. The President of the Republic, who is Head of State, is directly elected for a five-year term; the President holds executive power and governs with the assistance of an appointed Council of Ministers. A Council of State advises the President, who, however, has no obligation to follow its advice. Provincial governors, appointed by the President, have overall responsibility for the functions of government within each of the 11 provinces. For the purposes of local government, Mozambique is divided into 33 municipalities. The 2004 amendments to the Constitution provided for the creation of provincial assemblies, scheduled to be elected in 2008.

Defence

In August 2005 total active armed forces were estimated at 10,200–11,200 (army 9,000–10,000, navy 200, air force 1,000). At that time Mozambican forces were deployed in three overseas peace-keeping missions. Military service is compulsory and lasts for two years. Expenditure on defence was budgeted at an estimated 2,700,000m. meticais in 2005.

Economic Affairs

In 2004, according to estimates by the World Bank, Mozambique's gross national income (GNI), measured at average 2002–04 prices, was US $4,710m., equivalent to $250 per head (or $1,160 per head on an international purchasing-power parity basis). During 1995–2004, it was estimated, the population increased at an average annual rate of 2.1%, while gross domestic product (GDP) per head increased, in real terms, by an average of 6.1% per year. Overall GDP increased, in real terms, at an average annual rate of 8.3% in 1995–2004; growth in 2004 was 7.8%.

Agriculture (including forestry and fishing) contributed an estimated 21.2% of GDP in 2004. In mid-2003 an estimated 80.6% of the economically active population were employed in the sector. Fishing is the principal export activity: fish, crustaceans and molluscs accounted for 9.2% of total export earnings in 2003. The principal cash crops are fruit and nuts, cotton, sugar cane and copra. After production fell sharply in the 1990s, the Government attempted to increase revenue from the cashew crop by promoting production and improving processing facilities. The main subsistence crop is cassava. During 1995–2004, according to the World Bank, agricultural GDP increased by an average of 6.3% per year. Growth in 2004 was 7.9%.

Industry (including mining, manufacturing, construction and power) employed 5.6% of the economically active population in 1997, and provided an estimated 26.7% of GDP in 2004. During 1995–2004, according to the World Bank, industrial GDP increased at an average annual rate of 17.2%; growth in 2004 was 10.0%.

Mining contributed an estimated 0.9% of GDP in 2004, and employed 0.5% of the economically active population in 1997. Only coal, bauxite, marble, gold and salt are exploited in significant quantities, although gravel and crushed rocks are also mined. In November 2004 the Companhia Vale do Rio Doce (Brazil) was granted a coal mining concession in Moatize; production was expected to begin in 2009. The exploitation of commercially viable levels of graphite began in 1994, but production ceased in 2000. Formal production of bentonite also ceased in 2002, although small amounts were still processed. There are reserves of other minerals, including high-grade iron ore, precious and semi-precious stones, and natural gas. Plans began in 1994 to exploit natural gas reserves at Pande, in the province of Inhambane, which were estimated at 55,000m. cu m. A South African company, SASOL Ltd, was granted a 25-year concession to develop gasfields at Pande and Temane (also in Inhambane province); it was anticipated that the Government would receive revenues of some US $900m. from the project, and the construction of a pipeline to transport the gas to South Africa was completed in early 2004. A gas-processing centre opened in Temane in early 2004. In 2003 the Government announced that it was to invest $20m. in gas prospecting in Sofala province. In 1999 the largest reserve of titanium in the world (estimated at 100m. metric tons) was discovered in the district of Chibuto, in the province of Gaza; production from the Limpopo Corridor Sands Project in Chibuto was expected to begin in 2007 and last for some 35 years, providing up to 1m. tons of titanium per year. In 2003 plans were announced for the exploitation of further titanium reserves in Nampula province; it was hoped that production would commence in 2006, providing up to 2.5% of GDP. According to official figures, mining GDP increased at an average annual rate of 21.4% in 1996–2003; growth in 2004 was estimated at 153.7%.

Manufacturing contributed an estimated 13.5% of GDP in 2004, and employed 3.0% of the economically active population in 1997. A large aluminium smelter, Mozal, was opened in 2000 and expanded in 2003, with the completion of Mozal 2, which was expected to double capacity, to some 506,000 metric tons of aluminium ingots per year. Aluminium production was valued at 19,067,000m. meticais in 2003, equivalent to 16.8% of GDP. In 2004 unwrought aluminium and alloys accounted for 60.8% of total export earnings. During 1995–2004, according to the World Bank, manufacturing GDP increased at an average annual rate of 16.8%; growth in 2004 was 10.0%.

Electrical energy is derived principally from hydroelectric power, which provided some 99.7% of total electricity production in 2002. Mozambique's important Cahora Bassa hydroelectric plant on the Zambezi River supplies electricity to South Africa and Zimbabwe. By 2004 an extended power supply from Cahora Bassa to Zambézia, Manica and Sofala was in operation. From 1999 a consortium involving Mozambican, French and German companies financed a feasibility study for the construction of a hydroelectric power plant at Mepanda Uncua, some 70 km downstream of Cahora Bassa, which would help to support the 900-MW energy requirement of the Mozal smelter. Construction of the plant, which would have a generating capacity of 2,500 MW, was projected to cost some US $1,500m. It was envisaged that power from the plant, which would not be completed before 2007, would also be exported to South Africa. Mozambique currently imports all of its petroleum requirements. Imports of mineral fuels and lubricants comprised 16.5% of the value of total imports in 2003.

The services sector engaged 12.3% of the economically active population in 1997, and contributed an estimated 52.1% of GDP in 2004. By the end of the 1990s tourism was the fastest growing sector of the economy, and in 2002 receipts from tourism totalled US $144m. It was hoped that the formal opening, in April 2002, of the Great Limpopo Transfrontier Park, comprising South Africa's Kruger National Park, Zimbabwe's Gonarezhou National Park and Mozambique's Limpopo National Park, would attract additional tourists. The GDP of the services sector increased by an average of 2.8% per year in 1995–2004, according to the World Bank; services GDP increased by 4.7% in 2004.

In 2004 Mozambique recorded a trade deficit of US $345.8m., and there was a deficit of $607.4m. on the current account of the balance of payments. In 2003 the principal source of imports was South Africa (37.3%); the other major suppliers were Australia and the USA. In the same year Belgium was the principal market for exports (receiving 43.5%); South Africa and Spain were the other significant purchasers. The principal exports in 2003 were unwrought aluminium and alloys, food, live animal and tobacco, and mineral fuels and lubricants. The principal imports in 2003 were machinery and transport equipment, mineral fuels and lubricants, food and live animals, and chemicals. Production from the Mozal aluminium smelter provided around 50% the value of total exports in that year.

In 2005 there was an overall budgetary deficit of 5,487,000m. meticais. Mozambique's total external debt was US $4,930m. at the end of 2003, of which $4,381m. was long-term public debt. In that year the cost of debt-servicing was equivalent to 6.9% of the total value of exports of goods and services. The average annual rate of inflation was 3.7% in 1998–2004; consumer prices increased by an average of 14.0% in 2003, and by 8.9% in 2004. The number of unemployed was 118,000 at the end of 1996.

Mozambique is a member of the Southern African Development Community (SADC, see p. 358). In November 2000 Mozambique was invited by the Common Market for Eastern and Southern Africa (COMESA, see p. 191) to rejoin the organization (Mozambique left COMESA in 1993, when it joined SADC).

In terms of average income, Mozambique is one of the poorest countries in the world. During the 1980s economic development was severely frustrated by the effects of the civil war. Since 1990 there has been considerable progress in liberalizing the economy. Increased production in rural areas, continued structural reform and the partial restoration of the infrastructure contributed to significant GDP growth from 1993, and in 1994–98 Mozambique's economy was one of the fastest growing in the world. In June 1999 the Bretton Woods institutions reduced Mozambique's public debt by almost two-thirds, significantly decreasing the country's annual servicing obligations for the period 1999–2005, and the IMF approved a three-year loan for Mozambique, equivalent to some US $78.5m., under the Enhanced Structural Adjustment Facility (later renamed the Poverty Reduction and Growth Facility—PRGF). Strong economic growth was recorded following the opening of the Mozal smelter in 2000 and in the early 2000s, following severe flooding in southern and central Mozambique, much of Mozambique's foreign debt was deferred and later cancelled. In June 2002 the IMF commended Mozambique's rapid post-flood recovery, extending the PRGF arrangement by three years and in December 2005 it announced that Mozambique's outstanding debt to the Fund, worth an estimated $153m., would be cancelled. In February 2006 the IMF completed a review of Mozambique's PRGF facility, and again praised the Government's economic policies, while encouraging the Government to implement policies to raise domestic revenue and decentralize expenditure. (A new tax authority was to be created in 2007.) In late 2004 the Governments of Mozambique, Zambia, Malawi and Tanzania proposed the formation of the Mtwara Development Corridor, linking the four countries and which, it was envisaged, would promote economic growth and improve transport links in the region. In 2005 foreign investment and aid continued to contribute significantly to infrastructural developments, particularly water distribution projects and railways. In late 2005 Portugal announced it was to reduce its stake in the Cahora Bassa hydroelectric plant to 15%, transferring the rest of its holding to the Mozambican Government, for which Mozambique was to reimburse Portugal $950m. for construction and running costs. Also in late 2005 plans were unveiled to redenominate the currency, the metical, by 1,000 to one. The new units were to be introduced in July 2006. In December the Assembléia da República approved the budget for 2006, which anticipated total expenditure of 52,529,500m. meticais, of which almost 60% would be provided in the form of foreign aid. Meanwhile, the Government maintained its commitment to the country's Action Plan for the Reduction of Absolute Poverty; it was estimated that 50% of the population were living below the poverty line in 2004, compared with 69% in 1997. In September 2005 the World Bank approved a credit worth $120m. for the Government's poverty-reduction programme. In 2005 GDP growth was estimated at 8.9%, while inflation was around 14%, although this was predicted to decrease to 7% in 2006.

Education

Education is officially compulsory for seven years from the age of six. Primary schooling begins at six years of age and lasts for seven years. It is divided into two cycles, of five and two years. Secondary schooling, from 13 years of age, lasts for six years and comprises two cycles, each lasting three years. As a proportion of the school-age population, the total enrolment at primary and secondary schools was equivalent to 49% in 2000/01 (males 56%; females 42%). According to UNESCO estimates, in 2002/03 55% of children in the relevant age-group were enrolled at primary schools (males 58%; females 53%), while secondary enrolment included only 12% of children in the relevant age-group (males 14%; females 10%). There were 7,156 students in public higher education in 1997. Two privately owned higher education institutions, the Catholic University and the Higher Polytechnic Institute, were inaugurated in 1996. In late 2003 it was announced that education would no longer take place solely in Portuguese, but also in some Mozambican dialects. In 2005 an estimated 5,000 new teachers were to be recruited. Education was allocated 20.2% of total current government expenditure in 2006.

Public Holidays

2006: 1 January (New Year's Day), 3 February (Heroes' Day, anniversary of the assassination of Eduardo Mondlane), 7 April (Day of the Mozambican Woman), 1 May (Workers' Day), 25 June (Independence Day), 7 September (Victory Day—anniversary of the end of the Armed Struggle), 25 September (Anniversary of the launching of the Armed Struggle for National Liberation, and Day of the Armed Forces of Mozambique), 25 December (National Family Day).

2007: 1 January (New Year's Day), 3 February (Heroes' Day, anniversary of the assassination of Eduardo Mondlane), 7 April (Day of the Mozambican Woman), 1 May (Workers' Day), 25 June (Independence Day), 7 September (Victory Day—anniversary of the end of the Armed Struggle), 25 September (Anniversary of the launching of the Armed Struggle for National Liberation, and Day of the Armed Forces of Mozambique), 25 December (National Family Day).

Weights and Measures

The metric system is in force.

MOZAMBIQUE

Statistical Survey

Source (unless otherwise stated): Instituto Nacional de Estatística, Comissão Nacional do Plano, Av. Ahmed Sekou Touré 21, CP 493, Maputo; tel. 21491054; fax 21490384; e-mail webmaster@ine.gov.mz; internet www.ine.gov.mz.

Area and Population

AREA, POPULATION AND DENSITY

Area (sq km)	799,380*
Population (census results)	
1 August 1980	11,673,725†
1 August 1997	
Males	7,714,306
Females	8,384,940
Total	16,099,246
Population (official projections)	
2003	18,513,826
2004	18,961,503
2005	19,420,036
Density (per sq km) at mid-2005	24.3

* 308,641 sq miles. The area includes 13,000 sq km (5,019 sq miles) of inland water.
† Excluding an adjustment for underenumeration. This was estimated to have been 3.8%, and the adjusted total was 12,130,000.

PROVINCES
(official projections, 2005)

Province	Area (sq km)	Population	Density (per sq km)
Cabo Delgado	82,625	1,617,165	19.6
Gaza	75,709	1,304,798	17.2
Inhambane	68,615	1,381,023	20.1
Manica	61,661	1,320,232	21.4
City of Maputo	300	1,216,873	4,056.2
Maputo Province	26,058	1,044,946	40.1
Nampula	81,606	3,676,003	45.0
Niassa	129,056	999,332	7.7
Sofala	68,018	1,637,821	24.1
Tete	100,724	1,511,832	15.0
Zambézia	105,008	3,710,011	35.3
Total	799,380	19,420,036	24.3

PRINCIPAL TOWNS
(population at 1997 census)

Maputo (capital)	966,837	Nacala-Porto	158,248
Matola	424,662	Quelimane	150,116
Beira	397,368	Tete	101,984
Nampula	303,346	Xai-Xai	99,442
Chimoio	171,056	Gurue	99,335

Mid-2003 (UN estimate, incl. suburbs): Maputo 1,220,632 (Source: UN, *World Urbanization Prospects: The 2003 Revision*).

BIRTHS AND DEATHS

	2001	2002	2003
Birth rate (per 1,000)	41.7	40.9	40.0
Death rate (per 1,000)	15.9	15.4	14.9

Expectation of life (WHO estimates, years at birth): 45 (males 44; females 46) in 2003 (Source: WHO, *World Health Report*).

ECONOMICALLY ACTIVE POPULATION
(persons aged 12 years and over, 1980 census)

	Males	Females	Total
Agriculture, forestry, hunting and fishing	1,887,779	2,867,052	4,754,831
Mining and quarrying	} 323,730	23,064	346,794
Manufacturing			
Construction	41,611	510	42,121
Commerce	90,654	21,590	112,244
Transport, storage and communications	74,817	2,208	77,025
Other services*	203,629	39,820	243,449
Total employed	2,622,220	2,954,244	5,576,464
Unemployed	75,505	19,321	94,826
Total labour force	2,697,725	2,973,565	5,671,290

* Including electricity, gas and water.

Source: ILO, *Yearbook of Labour Statistics*.

1997 (percentage distribution of economically active population at census of 1 August): Agriculture, forestry and hunting: 91.3% of females, 69.6% of males; Mining: 0.0% of females, 1.0% of males; Manufacturing: 0.8% of females, 5.5% of males; Energy: 0.0% of females, 0.3% of males; Construction: 0.3% of females, 3.9% of males; Transport and communications: 0.1% of females, 2.3% of males; Commerce and finance: 4.3% of females, 9.7% of males; Services: 2.2% of females, 3.4% of males; Unknown: 0.9% of females, 1.4% of males.

Mid-2003 (estimates in '000): Agriculture, etc. 7,953; Total labour force 9,870 (Source: FAO).

Health and Welfare

KEY INDICATORS

Total fertility rate (children per woman, 2003)	5.6
Under-5 mortality rate (per 1,000 live births, 2004)	152
HIV/AIDS (% of persons aged 15–49, 2003)	12.2
Physicians (per 1,000 head, 2000)	0.02
Hospital beds (per 1,000 head, 1990)	0.87
Health expenditure (2002): US $ per head (PPP)	50
Health expenditure (2002): % of GDP	5.8
Health expenditure (2002): public (% of total)	71.0
Access to water (% of persons, 2002)	42
Access to sanitation (% of persons, 2002)	27
Human Development Index (2003): ranking	168
Human Development Index (2003): value	0.379

For sources and definitions, see explanatory note on p. vi.

Agriculture

PRINCIPAL CROPS
('000 metric tons)

	2002	2003	2004
Rice (paddy)	168	200	177
Maize	1,236	1,248	1,437
Millet	50	48	53
Sorghum	314	315	337
Potatoes*	80	80	80
Sweet potatoes*	66	66	66
Cassava (Manioc)	5,925	6,150†	6,150†
Sugar cane*	400	400	400
Pulses*	205	205	205
Cashew nuts*	58	58	58
Groundnuts (in shell)	110	110	127
Coconuts*	265	265	265
Copra *	45	45	45
Sunflower seed*	11	11	11
Cottonseed*	24	24	24

MOZAMBIQUE

—continued	2002	2003	2004
Other oil seeds *	6	6	6
Tomatoes*	9	9	9
Other vegetables*	105	105	105
Bananas*	90	90	90
Oranges*	14	14	14
Grapefruits and pomelos*	13	13	13
Mangoes*	24	24	24
Pineapples*	13	13	13
Papayas*	40	43	40
Other fruits*	105	115	105
Cotton (lint)	25†	25*	25*

* FAO estimate(s).
† Unofficial figure.
Source: FAO.

LIVESTOCK
('000 head, year ending September)

	1998	1999	2000
Asses	22	23	23
Cattle	1,300	1,310	1,320
Pigs	176	178	180
Sheep	123	124	125
Goats	388	390	392
Chickens	26,000	27,000	28,000

2001–04: Figures assumed to be unchanged from 2000 (FAO estimates).
Source: FAO.

LIVESTOCK PRODUCTS
(FAO estimates, '000 metric tons)

	2001	2002	2003
Beef and veal	38	38	38
Goat meat	2	2	2
Pig meat	13	13	13
Poultry meat	37	40	36
Cows' milk	60	60	60
Goats' milk	8	8	8
Hen eggs	14	14	14
Cattle hides	5	5	5

2004: Figures assumed to be unchanged from 2003 (FAO estimates).
Source: FAO.

Forestry

ROUNDWOOD REMOVALS
('000 cubic metres, excl. bark)

	1997	1998	1999
Sawlogs, veneer logs and logs for sleepers	129	128	128
Other industrial wood	1,139	1,166	1,191
Fuel wood	16,724	16,724	16,724
Total	17,992	18,018	18,043

2000–04: Production as in 1999 (FAO estimates).
Source: FAO.

SAWNWOOD PRODUCTION
('000 cubic metres, incl. railway sleepers)

	1997	1998	1999
Total	33	28	28

2000–04: Production as in 1999 (FAO estimates).
Source: FAO.

Fishing

(metric tons, live weight)

	2001	2002	2003
Dagaas	5,284	12,156	10,948
Tuna-like fishes	3,241	2,178	1,728
Penaeus shrimps	9,401	9,472	13,551
Knife shrimp	1,738	1,441	1,413
Total catch (incl. others)	30,074	37,139	89,486*

* FAO estimate.
Note: Figures exclude crocodiles, recorded by number rather than by weight. The number of Nile crocodiles caught was: 477 in 2001; 7,322 in 2002; 5,130 in 2003.
Source: FAO.

Mining

('000 metric tons, unless otherwise indicated)

	2002	2003	2004
Bauxite	9.1	11.8	6.7
Coal	43.5	36.7	16.5
Gold (kilograms)*	17	63	56
Quartz (metric tons)	31.4	31.0	173.5
Gravel and crushed rock ('000 cubic metres)	795.7	800.0†	800.0†
Marble (slab) ('000 square metres)	10.0	10.2	13.4
Salt (marine)†	80	80	80
Natural gas (million cu m)	2.0	1.0	1,295

* Figures exclude artisanal gold production; total gold output is estimated at 360 kg–480 kg per year.
† Estimate(s).
Source: US Geological Survey.

Industry

SELECTED PRODUCTS
('000 metric tons, unless otherwise indicated)

	1999	2000	2001
Flour (cereals other than wheat)	9	18	23
Wheat flour	125	114	140
Raw sugar	46	39	31
Beer ('000 hl)	95	989	982
Soft drinks ('000 hl)	100	626	670
Cigarettes (million)	1,084	1,417	1,359
Footwear (excl. rubber, '000 pairs)	7	7	2
Cement	266	348	421
Electric energy (million kWh)*	6,864	6,974	10,673

* Estimates.

2002 ('000 metric tons): Groundnut oil 18.0 (FAO estimate); Beer of barley 48 (FAO estimate); Raw sugar 35; Cement 285.
Sources: FAO; US Geological Survey; UN, *Industrial Commodity Statistics Yearbook*.
2003 ('000 metric tons): Groundnut oil 15.8 (FAO estimate); Beer of barley 48 (FAO estimate); Cement 362 (Sources: FAO; US Geological Survey)
2004 ('000 metric tons): Groundnut oil 20.0 (FAO estimate); Beer of barley 48 (FAO estimate); Cement 350 (estimate) (Sources: FAO; US Geological Survey).

MOZAMBIQUE

Finance

CURRENCY AND EXCHANGE RATES

Monetary Units
100 centavos = 1 metical (plural: meticais).

Sterling, Dollar and Euro Equivalents (30 December 2005)
£1 sterling = 41,456.45 meticais;
US $1 = 24,076.00 meticais;
€1 = 28,402.46 meticais;
100,000 meticais = £2.41 = $4.15 = €3.52.

Average Exchange Rate (meticais per US $)
2003   23,782.3
2004   22,581.3
2004   23,061.0

Note: Between April 1992 and October 2000 the market exchange rate was the rate at which commercial banks purchased from and sold to the public. Since October 2000 it has been the weighted average of buying and selling rates of all transactions of commercial banks and stock exchanges with the public. A proposed devaluation of the metical, with 1 new currency unit becoming equivalent to 1,000 of the former currency, was expected to be implemented on 1 July 2006.

BUDGET
('000 million meticais)

Revenue*	2003	2004	2005
Taxation	13,695	18,993	16,721
Taxes on income	3,235	4,445	4,469
Domestic taxes on goods and services	7,799	11,522	8,936
Customs duties	2,229	2,398	2,816
Other taxes	432	627	500
Non-tax revenue	1,019	1,476	3,662
Total	14,714	20,469	20,383

Expenditure†	2003	2004	2005
Current expenditure	16,342	21,890	20,365
Compensation of employees	7,734	11,045	10,358
Goods and services	2,991	4,908	4,407
Interest on public debt	1,319	1,244	1,248
Transfer payments	3,075	3,778	3,730
Other	1,223	915	622
Capital expenditure	13,369	17,026	13,101
Unallocated	252	—	170
Total	29,963	38,917	33,636

* Excluding grants received ('000 million meticais): 10,590 in 2003; 9,992 in 2004; 9,937 in 2005.
† Excluding net lending ('000 million meticais): 481 in 2003; 1,826 in 2004; 2,171 in 2005.

Source: Banco de Moçambique.

INTERNATIONAL RESERVES
(US $ million at 31 December)

	2002	2003	2004
IMF special drawing rights	0.07	0.08	0.08
Reserve position in IMF	0.01	0.01	0.01
Foreign exchange	802.42	937.41	1,130.86
Total	802.50	937.50	1,130.96

Source: IMF, *International Financial Statistics*.

MONEY SUPPLY
('000 million meticais at 31 December)

	2002	2003	2004
Currency outside banks	3,485.8	4,258.8	5,224.7
Demand deposits at commercial banks	7,850.1	9,768.8	11,054.9
Total money (incl. others)	11,520.8	14,263.4	16,579.1

Source: IMF, *International Financial Statistics*.

COST OF LIVING
(Consumer Price Index; base: 1998=100)

	2002	2003	2004
Food, beverages and tobacco	151	175	187
Clothing and footwear	126	122	125
Firewood and furniture	190	215	263
Health	119	133	134
Transportation and communications	205	232	234
Education, recreation and culture	145	150	151
Other goods and services	136	154	159
All items	157	179	195

Source: IMF, *Republic of Mozambique: Selected Issues and Statistical Appendix* (August 2005).

NATIONAL ACCOUNTS
('000 million meticais at current prices)

National Income and Product

	2001	2002	2003
Compensation of employees	20,446.5	27,012.5	36,346.7
Net operating surplus	11,059.2	11,282.6	11,239.4
Net mixed income	31,949.0	42,114.9	47,406.5
Domestic primary incomes	63,454.8	80,410.1	94,992.6
Consumption of fixed capital	10,401.4	13,865.7	15,079.6
Gross domestic product (GDP) at factor cost	73,856.1	94,275.8	110,072.2
Taxes on production and imports	4,634.2	5,050.1	6,145.3
Less Subsidies	1,945.5	2,442.4	2,314.9
GDP in market prices	76,544.9	96,883.5	113,902.5

Expenditure on the Gross Domestic Product

	2002	2003	2004*
Government final consumption expenditure	10,847.2	14,236.2	16,737.7
Private final consumption expenditure	60,298.7	77,338.0	87,726.4
Increase in stocks	8,506.1	1,346.2	1,927.5
Gross capital formation	20,397.9	29,903.6	28,240.7
Total domestic expenditure	100,049.9	122,824.0	134,632.3
Exports of goods and services	23,174.8	28,927.6	45,172.7
Less Imports of goods and services	26,341.3	37,849.1	46,294.6
GDP in purchasers' values	96,883.5	113,902.5	133,510.4
GDP at constant 1996 prices	54,892.9	59,238.2	63,677.9

* Preliminary estimates.

Gross Domestic Product by Economic Activity

	2002	2003	2004*
Agriculture, livestock and forestry	20,119.8	23,517.5	26,727.6
Fishing	1,486.6	1,707.0	1,577.0
Mining	281.5	379.9	1,142.3
Manufacturing	11,667.1	14,391.6	17,992.0
Electricity and water	3,646.4	5,053.7	7,030.7
Construction	7,701.6	9,207.4	9,365.1
Wholesale and retail trade	23,234.7	24,702.8	28,342.9
Restaurants and hotels	1,219.0	1,412.9	1,691.4
Transport and communications	10,992.8	14,202.1	18,501.6
Financial services	3,703.5	4,211.0	4,326.7
Real estate and business services	1,724.0	1,879.5	1,993.3

MOZAMBIQUE

Statistical Survey

—continued	2002	2003	2004*
Public administration and defence	3,506.2	3,839.1	4,303.9
Education	2,375.6	2,761.6	3,274.9
Health	956.4	1,088.2	1,278.9
Other Services	4,832.1	5,677.5	5,696.8
Sub-total	97,447.5	114,031.7	133,245.0
Less Financial services indirectly measured	2,375.5	2,223.1	2,346.8
Gross value added in basic prices	95,072.0	111,808.6	128,535.4
Taxes on products / *Less* Subsidies on products	1,811.5	2,093.9	2,612.3
GDP in market prices	96,883.5	113,902.5	133,510.4

* Preliminary estimates.

BALANCE OF PAYMENTS
(US $ million)

	2002	2003	2004
Exports of goods f.o.b.	809.8	1,043.9	1,503.9
Imports of goods f.o.b.	−1,476.5	−1,648.1	−1,849.7
Trade balance	−666.6	−604.2	−345.8
Exports of services	339.4	303.9	255.6
Imports of services	−577.0	−573.9	−531.4
Balance on goods and services	−904.2	−874.1	−621.7
Other income received	52.1	55.9	74.5
Other income paid	−655.3	−221.4	−374.0
Balance on goods, services and income	−1,507.4	−1,039.6	−921.2
Current transfers received	827.0	293.2	370.5
Current transfers paid	−188.7	−70.0	−56.7
Current balance	−869.1	−816.5	−607.4
Capital account (net)	222.0	270.7	578.1
Direct investment (net)	347.6	336.7	244.7
Portfolio investment assets	32.2	5.0	−25.4
Other investment assets	−207.7	−77.1	−88.7
Other investment liabilities	−903.8	108.2	−177.1
Errors and omissions (net)	−60.0	208.2	216.4
Overall balance	−1,438.8	35.3	140.7

Source: IMF, *International Financial Statistics*.

External Trade

PRINCIPAL COMMODITIES
(US $ million)

Imports c.i.f.	2002	2003
Food and live animals	187.4	215.7
Cereals	113.1	126.7
Mineral fuels, lubricants etc.	159.6	288.5
Chemicals and related products	86.6	117.1
Plastic and related products	56.9	21.6
Metals and related products	107.6	87.6
Iron and steel	20.7	22.9
Wood pulp and related products	28.1	50.5
Books, magazines, etc.	12.0	27.6
Textiles and related products	29.2	35.7
Machinery and transport equipment	405.6	476.7
General industrial machinery, equipment and parts	89.4	140.4
Electrical machinery, apparatus, etc.	85.4	144.2
Road vehicles and parts	194.9	157.7
General optical and photographic material, etc.	18.4	26.4
Miscellaneous manufactured articles	24.2	27.4
Commodities and transactions not classified elsewhere	402.2	318.5
Total (incl. others)	1,543.0	1,753.0

Exports f.o.b.	2002	2003
Food, live animals and tobacco	204.1	179.8
Fish, crustaceans, molluscs and other seafood	122.4	95.9
Textiles	25.2	45.4
Cotton	16.0	30.8
Mineral fuels, lubricants, etc.	136.0	136.1
Basic manufactures	367.1	574.2
Aluminium and alloys, unwrought	361.4	568.1
Machinery and transport equipment	32.5	44.8
Total (incl. others)	809.8	1,043.9

PRINCIPAL TRADING PARTNERS
(US $ million)

Imports c.i.f.	2002	2003*
Australia	7.5	211.3
France-Monaco	22.5	35.3
Germany	10.2	36.6
India	53.6	72.9
Italy-San Marino-Vatican	10.3	22.1
Japan	42.4	29.8
Malawi	2.3	19.2
Malaysia	n.a.	18.6
Namibia	14.2	6.3
Netherlands	6.9	9.2
Pakistan	6.8	14.3
Portugal	77.5	62.4
Saudi Arabia	25.0	18.4
South Africa	342.2	654.4
Spain	5.8	27.6
Taiwan	16.9	40.6
United Arab Emirates	14.1	11.3
United Kingdom	12.5	19.9
USA	55.6	104.3
Zimbabwe	13.9	9.8
Total (incl. others)	1,262.9	1,753.0

Exports f.o.b.	2002	2003*
Belgium	282.6	454.5
Italy	1.5	30.4
Malawi	10.4	32.8
Netherlands	1.9	29.6
Portugal	29.8	38.9
South Africa	120.4	169.6
Spain	19.0	70.0
Swaziland	0.5	17.4
United Kingdom	0.7	30.6
USA	10.7	15.7
Zimbabwe	39.2	29.5
Total (incl. others)	682.0	1,043.9

* Provisional figures.

Transport

RAILWAYS
(traffic)

	2001	2002	2003
Freight ton-km (million)	605	802	1,362
Passenger-km (million)	142	138	167

Source: IMF, *Republic of Mozambique: Selected Issues and Statistical Appendix* (August 2005).

ROAD TRAFFIC
(motor vehicles in use at 31 December)

	1999	2000	2001
Passenger cars	78,600	81,600	81,600
Lorries and vans	46,900	76,000	76,000

Source: UN, *Statistical Yearbook*.

SHIPPING

Merchant Fleet
(registered at 31 December)

	2002	2003	2004
Number of vessels	131	128	128
Total displacement ('000 grt)	37.2	36.3	36.1

Source: Lloyd's Register-Fairplay, *World Fleet Statistics*.

Freight Handled
('000 metric tons)

	2001	2002	2003
Goods loaded and unloaded	7,423	8,201	8,421

International Sea-borne Freight Traffic
('000 metric tons)

	2001	2002	2003
Goods loaded	2,962	2,780	2,982
Goods unloaded	3,144	4,062	3,837

CIVIL AVIATION
(traffic on scheduled services)

	2001	2002	2003
Kilometres flown (million)	7.5	6.6	6.5
Passengers carried ('000)	266.5	284.2	285.3
Passenger-km (million)	354.7	402.4	410.8

Tourism

TOURIST ARRIVALS BY COUNTRY OF RESIDENCE

Country	2002	2003
Malawi	224,274	121,267
Portugal	19,089	25,392
South Africa	336,657	335,426
Swaziland	37,581	20,018
United Kingdom	13,638	5,798
USA	6,627	5,035
Zimbabwe	233,496	114,936
Total (incl. others)	942,885	726,099

Tourism receipts (US $ million, excl. passenger transport): 64 in 2001; 63 in 2002; 98 in 2003.

Source: World Tourism Organization.

Communications Media

	2002	2003	2004
Telephones ('000 main lines in use)	83.7	n.a.	n.a.
Mobile cellular telephones ('000 subscribers)	254.8	428.9	708.0
Personal computers ('000 in use)	82	n.a.	138
Internet users ('000)	50	n.a.	112

Television receivers ('000 in use): 230 in 2001.

Radio receivers (1997): 730,000 in use.

Facsimile machines (1996): 7,200 in use.

Daily newspapers (1998): 12 (average circulation 43,099).

Non-daily newspapers (1998): 40 (estimated average circulation 205,800).

Periodicals (1998): 32 (average circulation 83,000).

Sources: International Telecommunication Union; UN, *Statistical Yearbook*; UNESCO Institute for Statistics.

Education

(2003)

	Institutions	Teachers	Students
Pre-primary*†	5,689	28,705	1,745,049
Primary	9,027	51,912	3,177,586
Secondary	154	4,112	160,093
Technical	36	924	20,086
Teacher training‡	18	n.a.	9,314

* Public education only.
† 1997 figures.
‡ 2002 figures.

Source: mainly Ministry of Education.

Adult literacy rate (UNESCO estimates): 46.5% (males 62.3%; females 31.4%) in 2002 (Source: UN Development Programme, *Human Development Report*).

Directory

The Constitution

The Constitution came into force on 30 November 1990, replacing the previous version, introduced at independence on 25 June 1975 and revised in 1978. Its main provisions, as amended in 1996 and 2004, are summarized below. There are 306 articles in the Constitution.

GENERAL PRINCIPLES

The Republic of Mozambique is an independent, sovereign, unitary and democratic state of social justice. Sovereignty resides in the people, who exercise it according to the forms laid down in the Constitution. The fundamental objectives of the Republic include:

- the defence of independence and sovereignty;
- the defence and promotion of human rights and of the equality of citizens before the law; and
- the strengthening of democracy, of freedom and of social and individual stability.

POLITICAL PARTICIPATION

The people exercise power through universal, direct, equal, secret, personal and periodic suffrage to elect their representatives, by referendums and through permanent democratic participation. Political parties are prohibited from advocating or resorting to violence.

FUNDAMENTAL RIGHTS AND DUTIES OF CITIZENS

All citizens enjoy the same rights and are subject to the same duties, irrespective of colour, race, sex, ethnic origin, place of birth, religion, level of education, social position or occupation. In realizing the objectives of the Constitution, all citizens enjoy freedom of opinion, assembly and association. All citizens over 18 years of age are entitled to vote and be elected. Active participation in the defence of the country is the duty of every citizen. Individual freedoms are guaranteed by the State, including freedom of expression, of the press, of assembly, of association and of religion. The State guarantees accused persons the right to a legal defence. No Court or

MOZAMBIQUE

Tribunal has the power to impose a sentence of death upon any person.

STATE ORGANS

Public elective officers are chosen by elections through universal, direct, secret, personal and periodic vote. Legally-recognized political parties may participate in elections.

THE PRESIDENT

The President is the Head of State and of the Government, and Commander-in-Chief of the armed forces. The President is elected by direct, equal, secret and personal universal suffrage on a majority vote, and must be proposed by at least 10,000 voters, of whom at least 200 must reside in each province. The term of office is five years. A candidate may be re-elected on only two consecutive occasions, or again after an interval of five years between terms. The President is advised by a Council of State, however, is not obliged to follow its advice.

THE ASSEMBLY OF THE REPUBLIC

Legislative power is vested in the Assembléia da República (Assembly of the Republic). The Assembléia is elected by universal direct adult suffrage on a secret ballot, and is composed of 250 Deputies. The Assembléia is elected for a maximum term of five years, but may be dissolved by the President before the expiry of its term. The Assembléia holds two ordinary sessions each year. The Assembléia, with a two-thirds majority, may impeach the President.

THE COUNCIL OF MINISTERS

The Council of Ministers is the Government of the Republic. The Prime Minister assists and advises the President in the leadership of the Government and presents the Government's programme, budget and policies to the Assembléia da República, assisted by other ministers.

LOCAL STATE ORGANS

The Republic is administered in provinces, municipalities and administrative posts. The highest state organ in a province is the provincial government, presided over by a governor, who is answerable to the central Government. There shall be assemblies at each administrative level.

THE JUDICIARY

Judicial functions shall be exercised through the Supreme Court and other courts provided for in the law on the judiciary, which also subordinates them to the Assembléia da República. Courts must safeguard the principles of the Constitution and defend the rights and legitimate interests of citizens. Judges are independent, subject only to the law.

The Government

HEAD OF STATE

President of the Republic and Commander-in-Chief of the Armed Forces: ARMANDO EMÍLIO GUEBUZA (took office 2 February 2005).

COUNCIL OF MINISTERS
(April 2006)

Prime Minister: LUÍSA DIAS DIOGO.
Minister of Foreign Affairs and Co-operation: ALCINDA ABREU.
Minister of National Defence: Gen. (retd) TOBIAS JOAQUIM DAI.
Minister of Finance: MANUEL CHANG.
Minister of Justice: ESPERANÇA ALFREDO MACHAVELA.
Minister of the Interior: JOSÉ PACHECO.
Minister of Development and Planning: AIUBA CUERENEIA.
Minister of State Administration: LUCAS CHOMERA.
Minister of Agriculture: TOMÁS MANDLATE.
Minister of Fisheries: CADMIEL FILIANE MUTHEMBA.
Minister of Industry and Trade: ANTÓNIO FERNANDO.
Minister of Energy: SALVADOR NAMBURETE.
Minister of Mineral Resources: ESPERANÇA BIAS.
Minister of Transport and Communications: ANTÓNIO FRANCISCO MUNGUAMBE.
Minister of Education and Culture: AIRES BONIFÁCIO ALI.
Minister of Health: PAULO IVO GARRIDO.
Minister of Environmental Co-ordination: LUCIANO ANDRE DE CASTRO.
Minister of Labour: HELENA TAIPO.
Minister of Public Works and Housing: FELÍCIO ZACARIAS.
Minister of Youth and Sport: DAVID SIMANGO.
Minister of Women's Affairs and Social Welfare Co-ordination: VIRGÍLIA BERNARDA NETO ALEXANDRE SANTOS MATABELE.
Minister of Tourism: FERNANDO SUMBANA.
Minister of Veterans' Affairs: FELICIANO SALOMÃO GUNDANA.
Minister of Science and Technology: VENÂNCIO MASSINGUE.
Minister in the Presidency with responsibility for Parliamentary Affairs: ISABEL MANUEL NKAVANDEKA.
Minister in the Presidency with responsibility for Diplomatic Affairs: FRANCISCO CAETANO MADEIRA.

MINISTRIES

Office of the President: Av. Julius Nyerere 1780, Maputo; tel. 21491121; fax 21492065; e-mail gabimprensa@teldata.mz; internet www.presidencia.gov.mz.
Office of the Prime Minster: Praça da Marinha Popular, Maputo; tel. 21426861; fax 21426881; e-mail gabinfo@teledata.mz; internet www.govmoz.gov.mz.
Ministry of Agriculture: Praça dos Heróis Moçambicanos, CP 1406, Maputo; tel. 21460011; fax 21460055; e-mail cda@map.gov.mz.
Ministry of Development and Planning: Praça da Marinha Popular, CP 272, Maputo; tel. 21306808; fax 21306261.
Ministry of Education and Culture: Av. 24 de Julho 167, CP 34, Maputo; tel. 21490677; fax 21492196; internet www.mec.gov.mz.
Ministry of Energy: Maputo.
Ministry of Environmental Co-ordination: Av. Acordos de Lusaka 2115, CP 2020, Maputo; tel. 21466245; fax 21465849; e-mail jwkacha@virconn.com; internet www.micoa.gov.mz.
Ministry of Finance: Maputo.
Ministry of Fisheries: Rua Consiglieri Pedroso 347, CP 1723, Maputo; tel. 21431266; fax 21425087; e-mail alfredo@mozpesca.org; internet www.mozpesca.org.
Ministry of Foreign Affairs and Co-operation: Av. Julius Nyerere 4, CP 2787, Maputo; tel. 21490222; fax 21494070; e-mail minec@zebra.uem.mz.
Ministry of Health: Avs Eduardo Mondlane e Salvador Allende 1008, CP 264, Maputo; tel. 21427131; fax 21427133.
Ministry of Industry and Trade: Praça 25 de Junho 300, CP 1831, Maputo; tel. 21426093; e-mail infomic@mic.gov.mz; internet www.mic.gov.mz.
Ministry of the Interior: Av. Olof Palme 46/48, CP 290, Maputo; tel. 21420131; fax 21420084.
Ministry of Justice: Av. Julius Nyerere 33, Maputo; tel. 21491613; fax 21494264.
Ministry of Labour: Av. 24 de Julho 2351–2365, CP 258, Maputo; tel. 21427051; fax 21421881.
Ministry of Mineral Resources: Av. Fernão de Magalhães 34, CP 2904, Maputo; tel. 21425682; fax 21427103; e-mail minas@minas.co.mz; internet www.minas.co.mz.
Ministry of National Defence: Av. Mártires de Mueda 280, CP 3216, Maputo; tel. 21492081; fax 21491619.
Ministry of Public Works and Housing: Av. Karl Marx 268, CP 268, Maputo; tel. 21420543; fax 21421369; internet www.dna.gov.mz (water); internet www.dnep.gov.mz (roads and bridges).
Ministry of Science and Technology: Av. Patrice Lumumba 770, Maputo; tel. 21352800; fax 21352860; e-mail secretariado@mct.gov.mz; internet www.mct.gov.mz.
Ministry of State Administration: Rua da Rádio Moçambique 112, CP 4116, Maputo; tel. 21426666; fax 21428565; internet www.sdnp.org.mz.
Ministry of Tourism: Av. 25 de Setembro 1018, CP 4101, Maputo; tel. 21313755; fax 21306212; e-mail tourism@mitur.gov.mz; internet www.moztourism.gov.mz.
Ministry of Transport and Communications: Rua Mártires de Inhaminga 336, Maputo; tel. 21420152; fax 21431028; e-mail webmaster@mtc.gov.mz; internet www.mtc.gov.mz.
Ministry of Veterans' Affairs: Rua General Pereira d'Eça 35, CP 3697, Maputo; tel. 21490601.
Ministry of Women's Affairs and Social Welfare Co-ordination: Rua de Tchamba 86, CP 516, Maputo; tel. 21490921; fax 21492757; e-mail vmatabele@mimucas.org.mz; internet www.mimucas.org.mz.
Ministry of Youth and Sport: Av. 25 de Setembro 529, CP 2080, Maputo; tel. 21312172; fax 21300040; e-mail mjd@tvcabo.co.mz; internet www.mjd.gov.mz.

MOZAMBIQUE   Directory

PROVINCIAL GOVERNORS
(April 2006)

Cabo Delgado Province: LÁZARO MATHE.
Gaza Province: DJALMA LOURENÇO.
Inhambane Province: LÁZARO VICENTE.
Manica Province: RAIMUNDO DIOMBO.
Maputo Province: TELMINA PEREIRA.
Nampula Province: FILIPE CHIMOIO PAÚNDE.
Niassa Province: ARNALDO VICENTE BIMBE.
Sofala Province: ALBERTO CLEMENTINO VAQUINA.
Tete Province: ILDEFONSO MUANANTAPHA.
Zambézia Province: CARVALHO MUÁRIA.
City of Maputo: ROSA MANUEL DA SILVA.

President and Legislature

PRESIDENT

Presidential Election, 1–2 December 2004

	Votes	% of votes
Armando Guebuza (Frelimo)	2,004,226	63.74
Afonso Macacho Marceta Dhlakama (Renamo—União Eleitoral)	998,059	31.74
Raul Domingos (PPDD)	85,815	2.73
Yaqub Sabindy (PIMO)	28,656	0.91
Carlos Alexandre dos Reis (FMBG)	27,412	0.87
Total*	**3,144,168**	**100.00**

* Excluding 96,684 blank votes and 81,315 spoilt votes.

LEGISLATURE

Assembléia da República: CP 1516, Maputo; tel. 21400826; fax 21400711; e-mail cdi@sortmoz.com.
Chairman: EDUARDO MULÉMBUE.

General Election, 1–2 December 2004

	Votes	% of votes	Seats*
Frente de Libertação de Moçambique (Frelimo)	1,889,054	62.03	160
Resistência Nacional Moçambicana—União Eleitoral (Renamo—UE)	905,289	29.73	90
Partido para a Paz, Democracia e Desenvolvimento (PPDD)	60,758	2.00	—
Partido para a Liberdade e Solidariedade (PAZS)	20,686	0.68	—
Partido de Reconciliação Nacional (PARENA)	18,220	0.60	—
Partido Independente de Moçambique (PIMO)	17,960	0.59	—
Partido Social de Moçambique (PASOMO)	15,740	0.52	—
Others	117,722	3.87	—
Total (incl. others)†	**3,045,429**	**100.00**	**250**

* Parties must obtain a minimum of 5% of the vote in order to gain representation in the Assembléia da República.
† Excluding 166,540 blank votes and 109,957 spoilt votes.

Election Commission

Comissão Nacional de Eleições (CNE): Maputo; f. 1997.

Political Organizations

In mid-2004 there were five coalitions and 42 parties registered with the Comissão Nacional de Eleiçoes. The parties listed below secured votes in the December 2004 legislative elections.

Congresso dos Democratas Unidos (CDU): Maputo; f. 2001; Leader ANTÓNIO PALANGE.

Frente de Libertação de Moçambique (Frelimo): Rua Pereira do Lago 10, Bairro de Sommerschield, Maputo; tel. 21490181; fax 21490008; e-mail info@frelimo.org.mz; internet www.frelimo.org.mz; f. 1962 by merger of three nationalist parties; reorg. 1977 as a 'Marxist-Leninist vanguard movement'; in 1989 abandoned its exclusive Marxist-Leninist orientation; Pres. ARMANDO GUEBUZA.

Frente de Mudança e Boa Governa (FMBG): f. 2004; comprises:

Partido de Todos os Nativos Moçambicanos (Partonamo): f. 1996; Pres. MUSSAGY ABDUL REMANE.

União Nacional Moçambicana (Unamo): f. 1987; breakaway faction of Renamo; social democratic; obtained legal status 1992; fmr mem. of União Eleitoral; Pres. CARLOS ALEXANDRE DOS REIS; Sec.-Gen. FLORENCIA JOÃO DA SILVA.

Partido Democrático de Libertação de Moçambique (Padelimo): based in Kenya; Pres. JOAQUIM JOSÉ NHOTA.

Partido Independente de Moçambique (PIMO): f. 1993; Islamist; Leader YAQUB SABINDY; Sec.-Gen. MAGALHÃES BRAMUGY.

Partido Liberal e Democrático de Moçambique (Palmo): f. 1991; obtained legal status 1993; Pres. ANTÓNIO MUEDO.

Partido para a Paz, Democracia e Desenvolvimento (PPDD): Quelimane; f. 2003; liberal; Leader RAUL DOMINGOS.

Partido Popular Democrático (PPD): f. 2004; Leader MARCIANO FIJAMA.

Partido de Reconciliação Nacional (PARENA): Maputo; f. August 2004; Leader ANDRÉ BALATE.

Partido Social, Liberal e Democrático (Sol): breakaway faction of Palmo; Leader CASIMIRO MIGUEL NHAMITHAMBO.

Partido Social de Moçambique (Pasomo): Maputo; Leader FRANCISCO CAMPIRA.

Partido do Trabalho (PT): f. 1993; breakaway faction of PPPM; Pres. MIGUEL MABOTE; Sec.-Gen. LUÍS MUCHANGA.

Partido Verde de Moçambique (PVM): Leader BRUNO SAPEMBA.

Resistência Nacional Moçambicana-União Eleitoral (Renamo-UE): f. 1999; coalition comprising Renamo and the União Eleitoral which, in late 2004, consisted of 10 minor parties.

Constituent members include:

Resistência Nacional Moçambicana (Renamo): Av. Julius Nyerere 2541, Maputo; tel. 21493107; also known as Movimento Nacional da Resistência de Moçambique (MNR); f. 1976; fmr guerrilla group, in conflict with the Govt between 1976 and Oct. 1992; obtained legal status in 1994; Pres. AFONSO MACACHO MARCETA DHLAKAMA; Sec.-Gen. OSSUFO MOMADE.

Aliança Independente de Moçambique (Alimo): Maputo; f. 1998; Sec.-Gen. ERNESTO SERGIO.

Frente de Ação Patriótica (FAP): Maputo; f. 1991; Pres. JOSÉ CARLOS PALAÇO.

Frente Democrática Unida—United Democratic Front (UDF): Maputo; Pres. JANEIRO MARIANO.

Frente Unida de Moçambique (Fumo): Av. Mao Tse Tung 230, 1° andar, Maputo; tel. 21494044; in early 2005 the party was reported to have split, with the faction led by Simeão Cuamba and Pedro Loforte supporting a withdrawal from the UE; Sec.-Gen. JOSÉ SAMO GUDO.

Partido de Convenção Nacional (PCN): Av. 25 Setembro 1123, 3° andar, Maputo; tel. 21426891; obtained legal status in 1992; Chair. LUTERO CHIMBIRIMBIRI SIMANGO; Sec.-Gen. Dr GABRIEL MABUNDA.

Partido Ecologista de Moçambique (PEMO): Maputo.

Partido do Progresso do Povo de Moçambique (PPPM): Av. 25 Setembro, 1123, 4° andar, Maputo; tel. 21426925; f. 1991; obtained legal status 1992; Pres. Dr PADIMBE MAHOSE KAMATI; Sec.-Gen. CHE ABDALA.

Partido Renovador Democrático (PRD): obtained legal status 1994; Pres. MANECA DANIEL.

Partido de Unidade Nacional (PUN): TV Sado 9, Maputo; tel. 21419204; Pres. HIPOLITO COUTO.

União para a Salvação de Moçambique (Usamo): f. 2004; coalition comprising the União para a Mudança (UM), PADRES, PSDM, and the PSM; Chair. JULIO NIMUIRE.

Partido Socialista de Moçambique (PSM): Leader JOÃO NKALAMBA.

Other parties obtaining votes at the December 2004 legislative elections were the **Frente do Amplo Oposição (FAO)** (f. 2004), the **Partido Ecologista—Movimento da Terra** (f. 2002), the **Partido para a Liberdade e Solidariedade (PAZS)** (f. 2004), the **Partido para a Reconciliação Democrática (PAREDE)**, and the **União Democrática (UD)** (f. 1994, coalition). In 2005 a coalition comprising 18 small parties, including the **Partido Popular Democrático (PPD)**, the **Partido Nacional de Moçambique (Panamo)** and the **Partido Progressivo e Liberal de Moçambique (PPLM)**, was formed.

Diplomatic Representation

EMBASSIES AND HIGH COMMISSIONS IN MOZAMBIQUE

Algeria: Rua de Mukumbura 121–125, CP 1709, Maputo; tel. 21492070; fax 21490582; e-mail ab220261@virconn.com; Ambassador FOUAD BOUTTOURA.
Angola: Av. Kenneth Kaunda 783, CP 2954, Maputo; tel. 21491883; fax 21493930; Ambassador JOÃO GARCIA BIRES.
Brazil: Av. Kenneth Kaunda 296, CP 1167, Maputo; tel. 21484800; fax 21484806; e-mail ebrasil@teledata.mz; Ambassador PEDRO LUIZ CARNEIRO DE MENDONÇA.
China, People's Republic: Av. Julius Nyerere 3142, CP 4668, Maputo; tel. 21491560; fax 21491196; e-mail emb.chi@tvcabo.co.mz; Ambassador HONG HONG.
Congo, Democratic Republic: Av. Kenneth Kaunda 127, CP 2407, Maputo; tel. 21497154; fax 21494929; Chargé d'affaires a.i. MULUMBA TSHIDIMBA MARCEL.
Congo, Republic: Av. Kenneth Kaunda 783, CP 4743, Maputo; tel. 21490142; Chargé d'affaires a.i. MONSEGNO BASHA OSHEFWA.
Cuba: Av. Kenneth Kaunda 492, CP 387, Maputo; tel. 21492444; fax 21492700; e-mail embacuba.mozambique@tvcabo.com; Ambassador MARCELINA EVANGELINA SEOANE DOMÍNGUEZ.
Denmark: Av. Julius Nyerere 1162, CP 4588, Maputo; tel. 21480000; fax 21480010; e-mail mpmamb@um.dk; internet www.ambmaputo.um.dk; Ambassador MADS SANDAU-JENSEN.
Egypt: Av. Mao Tse Tung 851, CP 4662, Maputo; tel. 21491118; fax 21491489; e-mail egypt2@tropical.co.mz; Ambassador HAMDY ABD ELWAHAB SALEH.
Finland: Av. Julius Nyerere 1128, CP 1663, Maputo; tel. 21490578; fax 21491661; e-mail sanomat.map@formin.fi; Ambassador MARKKU KAUPPINEN.
France: Av. Julius Nyerere 2361, CP 4781, Maputo; tel. 21484600; fax 21484680; e-mail ambafrancemz@tvcabo.co.mz; internet www.ambafrance-mz.org; Ambassador THIERRY VITEAU.
Germany: Rua Damião de Góis 506, CP 1595, Maputo; tel. 21492714; fax 21492888; e-mail germaemb@tvcabo.co.mz; internet www.maputo.diplo.de; Ambassador KLAUS-CHRISTIAN KRAEMER.
Holy See: Av. Kwame Nkrumah 224, CP 2738, Maputo; tel. 21491144; fax 21492217; e-mail namoz.secret@teledata.mz; Apostolic Nuncio Most Rev. GEORGE PANIKULAM (Titular Archbishop of Caudium).
Iceland: Av. Zimbabwe 1694, Maputo; tel. 21483509; fax 21483511; e-mail mozambique@iceida.is; internet www.iceland.org/mo; Chargé d'affaires a.i. JÓHANN PÁLSSON.
India: Av. Kenneth Kaunda 167, CP 4751, Maputo; tel. 21492437; fax 21492364; e-mail hicomind@tvcabo.co.mz; internet www.hicomind-maputo.org; High Commissioner UPENDRA CHANDRA BARO.
Iran: Av. dos Mártires da Machava 1630, Maputo; tel. 21490700; fax 21492005; Ambassador ABDUL ALI TAUAKALI.
Ireland: Av. Julius Nyerere 3332, Maputo; tel. 21491440; fax 21493023; e-mail ireland@virconn.com; Ambassador FRANK SHERIDAN.
Italy: Av. Kenneth Kaunda 387, CP 976, Maputo; tel. 21492229; fax 21492046; e-mail ambasciata@italia.gov.mz; internet www.ambmaputo.esteri.it; Ambassador GUIDO LARCHER.
Japan: Av. Julius Nyerere 2832, CP 2494, Maputo; tel. 21499819; fax 21498957; Ambassador KAWASI BAAH BOAKGE.
Korea, Democratic People's Republic: Rua da Kaswende 167, Maputo; tel. 21491482; Ambassador PAK KUN GWANG.
Malawi: Av. Kenneth Kaunda 75, CP 4148, Maputo; tel. 21491468; fax 21490224; High Commissioner SAM KANDODO BANDA.
Netherlands: Av. Kwame Nkrumah 324, CP 1163, Maputo; tel. 21484200; fax 21484248; e-mail map@minbuza.nl; internet www.nlembassy.org.mz; Ambassador LIDI REMMELZWAAL.
Nigeria: Av. Kenneth Kaunda 821, CP 4693, Maputo; tel. 21490105; fax 21490991; High Commissioner ALBERT G. PIUS OMOTAIO.
Norway: Av. Julius Nyerere 1162, CP 828, Maputo; tel. 21480100; fax 21480107; e-mail emb.maputo@mfa.no; internet www.norway.org.mz; Ambassador THORBJØRN GAUSTADSÆTHER.
Portugal: Av. Julius Nyerere 720, CP 4696, Maputo; tel. 21490316; fax 21491172; e-mail embaixada@embpormaputo.org.mz; Ambassador JOSÉ JOAQUIM ESTEVES DOS SANTOS DE FREITAS FERRAZ.
Russia: Av. Vladimir I. Lénine 2445, CP 4666, Maputo; tel. 21420091; fax 21417515; e-mail embrus@mail.tropical.net; Ambassador VLADIMIR VASLIEVICH ZEMSKIY.
South Africa: Av. Eduardo Mondlane 41, CP 1120, Maputo; tel. 21493030; fax 21493029; e-mail sahc@tropical.co.mz; High Commissioner T. LUJABE-RANKOE.
Spain: Rua Damião de Góis 347, CP 1331, Maputo; tel. 21492048; fax 21494769; e-mail embespmz@correo.mae.es; Ambassador LUÍS ANTÓNIO CALVO CASTAÑO.
Swaziland: Av. Kwame Nkrumah, CP 4711, Maputo; tel. 21491601; fax 21492117; High Commissioner Prince TSHEKEDI.
Sweden: Av. Julius Nyerere 1128, CP 338, Maputo; tel. 21480300; fax 21480390; e-mail ambassaden.maputo@foreign.ministry.se; internet www.swedenabroad.com/maputo; Ambassador MAJ-INGER KLINGVALL.
Switzerland: Av. Ahmed Sekou Touré 637, CP 135, Maputo; tel. 21315275; fax 21315276; tel. vertretung@map.rep.admin.ch; Ambassador RUDOLF BAERFUSS.
Tanzania: Ujamaa House, Av. dos Mártires da Machava 852, CP 4515, Maputo; tel. 21490110; fax 21494782; e-mail ujamaa@zebra.uem.mz; High Commissioner ISSA MOHAMED ISSA.
Timor-Leste: Maputo; Chargé d'affaires a.i. MARINA ALKATIRI.
United Kingdom: Av. Vladimir I. Lénine 310, CP 55, Maputo; tel. 21356000; fax 21356060; e-mail bhc@virconn.com; internet www.britishhighcommission.gov.uk/mozambique; High Commissioner HOWARD PARKINSON.
USA: Av. Kenneth Kaunda 193, CP 783, Maputo; tel. 21492797; fax 21490114; e-mail maputoirc@state.gov; internet www.usembassy-maputo.gov.mz; Ambassador HELEN R. MEAGHER LA LIME.
Zambia: Av. Kenneth Kaunda 1286, CP 4655, Maputo; tel. 21492452; fax 21491893; e-mail zhcmmap@zebra.uem.mz; High Commissioner SIMON GABRIEL MWILA.
Zimbabwe: Av. Kenneth Kaunda 816, CP 743, Maputo; tel. 21490404; fax 21492237; e-mail maro@isl.co.mz; Ambassador DAVID HAMHOZIRIPI.

Judicial System

The Constitution of November 1990 provides for a Supreme Court and other judicial courts, an Administrative Court, courts-martial, customs courts, maritime courts and labour courts. The Supreme Court consists of professional judges, appointed by the President of the Republic, and judges elected by the Assembléia da República. It acts in sections, as a trial court of primary and appellate jurisdiction, and in plenary session, as a court of final appeal. The Administrative Court controls the legality of administrative acts and supervises public expenditure.

President of the Supreme Court: MÁRIO MANGAZE.
Attorney-General: JOAQUIM MADEIRA.

Religion

There are an estimated 5m. Christians and 4m. Muslims, as well as small Hindu, Jewish and Bahá'í communities. In 2004 over 100 religious groups were officially registered.

CHRISTIANITY

There are many Christian organizations registered in Mozambique.
Conselho Cristão de Moçambique (CCM) (Christian Council of Mozambique): Av. Agostino Neto 1584, CP 108, Maputo; tel. 21322836; fax 21321968; e-mail com-ccmhq@isl.co.mz; internet swan.isl.co.mz/ccm; f. 1948; 22 mems; Pres. Rt Rev. ARÃO MATSOLO; Gen. Sec. Rev. DINIS MATSOLO.

The Roman Catholic Church

Mozambique comprises three archdioceses and nine dioceses. At 31 December 2003 adherents represented some 22.3% of the total population.

Bishops' Conference

Conferência Episcopal de Moçambique (CEM), Secretariado Geral da CEM, Av. Paulo Samuel Kankhomba 188/RC, CP 286, Maputo; tel. 21490766; fax 21492174; f. 1982; Pres. Most Rev. JAIME PEDRO GONÇALVES (Archbishop of Beira).

Archbishop of Beira: Most Rev. JAIME PEDRO GONÇALVES, Cúria Arquiepiscopal, Rua Correia de Brito 613, CP 544, Beira; tel. 23322313; fax 23327639; e-mail arquidbeira@teledata.mz.
Archbishop of Maputo: Most Rev. FRANCISCO CHIMOIO, Paço Arquiepiscopal, Avda Eduardo Mondlane 1448, CP 258, Maputo; tel. 21426240; fax 21421873.
Archbishop of Nampula: Most Rev. TOMÉ MAKHWELIHA, Paço Arquiepiscopal, CP 84, 70100 Nampula; tel. 26213025; fax 26214194; e-mail arquidioce.npl@teledata.mz.

The Anglican Communion

Anglicans in Mozambique are adherents of the Church of the Province of Southern Africa. There are two dioceses in Mozambique. The Metropolitan of the Province is the Archbishop of Cape Town, South Africa.

Bishop of Lebombo: Rt Rev. DINIS SALOMÃO SENGULANE, CP 120, Maputo; tel. 21734364; fax 21401093; e-mail libombo@zebra.uem.mz.

Bishop of Niassa: Rev. MARK VAN KOEVERING, CP 264, Lichinga, Niassa; tel. 27112735; fax 27112336; e-mail anglican-niassa@maf.org.

Other Churches

Baptist Convention of Mozambique: Av. Maguiguane 386, CP 852, Maputo; tel. 2126852; Pres. Rev. BENTO BARTOLOMEU MATUSSE; 78 churches, 25,000 adherents.

The Church of Jesus Christ of the Latter-Day Saints: Maputo; 9 congregations, 1,975 mems.

Free Methodist Church: Pres. Rev. FRANISSE SANDO MUVILE; 214 churches, 21,231 mems.

Igreja Congregational Unida de Moçambique: Rua 4 Bairro 25 de Junho, CP 930, Maputo; tel. 21475820; Pres., Sec. of the Synod A. A. LITSURE.

Igreja Maná: Rua Francisco Orlando Magumbwe 528, Maputo; tel. 21491760; fax 21490896; e-mail adm_mocambique@igrejamana.com; Bishop DOMINGOS COSTA.

Igreja Reformada em Moçambique (IRM) (Reformed Church in Mozambique): CP 3, Vila Ulongue, Anogonia-Tete; f. 1908; Gen. Sec. Dr WALLACE E. CHIKAKUDA; 33,000 mems.

Presbyterian Church of Mozambique: Av. Ahmed Sekou Touré 1822, CP 21, Maputo; tel. 21421790; fax 21428623; e-mail ipmoc@zebra.uem.mz; 100,000 adherents; Pres. of Synodal Council Rev. MÁRIO NYAMUXWE.

Seventh-Day Adventist Church: Av. Maguiguana 300, CP 1468, Maputo; tel. and fax 21427200; e-mail victormiconde@teledata.co.mz; 937 churches, 186,724 mems (2004).

Other denominations active in Mozambique include the Church of Christ, the Church of the Nazarene, the Greek Orthodox Church, the United Methodist Church of Mozambique, the Wesleyan Methodist Church, the Zion Christian Church, and Jehovah's Witnesses.

ISLAM

Comunidade Mahometana: Av. Albert Luthuli 291, Maputo; tel. 21425181; fax 21300880; e-mail toranias@zebra.uem.mz; internet www.paginaislamica.8m.com/pg1.htm; Pres. ABDUL ASSIZ OSMAN LATIF.

Congresso Islamico de Moçambique (Islamic Congress of Mozambique): represents Sunni Muslims; Chair. ASSANE ISMAEL MAQBUL.

Conselho Islamico de Moçambique (Islamic Council of Mozambique): Leader Sheikh AMINUDDIN MOHAMAD.

The Press

DAILIES

Correio da Manha: Av. Filipe Samuel Magaia 528, CP 1756, Maputo; tel. 21305322; fax 21305321; e-mail refi@virconn.com; internet www.correiodamanha.co.mz; f. 1997; published by Sojornal, Lda; also publishes weekly Correio Semanal; Dir REFINALDO CHILENGUE.

Diário de Moçambique: Av. 25 de Setembro 1509, 2° andar, CP 2491, Beira; tel. and fax 23427312; f. 1981; under state management since 1991; Dir EZEQUIEL AMBRÓSIO; Editor FARUCO SADIQUE; circ. 5,000 (2003).

Expresso da Tarde: Av. Patrice Lumumba 511, 1° andar, Maputo; tel. 21314912; e-mail expresso@teledata.mz; subscription only; distribution by fax; Dir SALVADOR RAIMUNDO HONWANA.

Mediafax: Av. Amílcar Cabral 1049, CP 73, Maputo; tel. 21430106; fax 21302402; e-mail mediafax@mediacoop.co.mz; internet www.mediacoop.odline.com; f. 1992 by co-operative of independent journalists Mediacoop; news-sheet by subscription only, distribution by fax and internet; Editor JOÃO CHAMUSSE.

Notícias de Moçambique: Rua Joaquim Lapa 55, CP 327, Maputo; tel. 21420119; fax 21420575; f. 1926; morning; f. 1906; under state management since 1991; Dir BERNARDO MAVANGA; Editor HILÁRIO COSSA; circ. 12,793 (2003).

Further newspapers available solely in email or fax format include Diário de Notícias and Matinal.

WEEKLIES

Campeão: Av. 24 de Julho 3706, CP 2610, Maputo; tel. and fax 21401810; sports newspaper; Dir RENATO CALDÉIRA; Editor ALEXANDRE ZANDAMELA.

Correio Semanal: Av. Filipe Samuel Magaia 528, CP 1756, Maputo; tel. 21305322; fax 21305312; Dir REFINALDO CHILENGUE.

Desafio: Rua Joaquim Lapa 55, Maputo; tel. 21305437; fax 21305431; Dir ALMIRO SANTOS; Editor BOAVIDA FUNJUA; circ. 3,890 (2003).

Domingo: Rua Joaquim Lapa 55, CP 327, Maputo; tel. 21431026; fax 21431027; f. 1981; Sun.; Dir JORGE MATINE; Editor MOISES MABUNDA; circ. 10,421 (2003).

Fim de Semana: Rua da Resistência 1642, 1° andar, Maputo; tel. and fax 21417012; e-mail fimdomes@tvcabo.co.mz; internet www.fimdesemana.co.mz; f. 1997; independent.

Savana: c/o Mediacoop, Av. Amílcar Cabral 1049, CP 73, Maputo; tel. 21301737; fax 21302402; e-mail savana@mediacoop.co.mz; internet www.mediacoop.odline.com; f. 1994; Dir KOK NAM; Editor FERNANDO GONÇALVES; circ. 14,000 (2003).

Tempo: Av. Ahmed Sekou Touré 1078, CP 2917, Maputo; tel. 21426191; f. 1970; magazine; under state management since 1991; Dir ROBERTO UAENE; Editor ARLINDO LANGA; circ. 40,000.

Zambeze: Rua José Sidumo, Maputo; tel. 21302019; Dir SALOMÃO MOYANE; circ. 2,000 (2003).

PERIODICALS

Agora: Afrisurvey, Lda, Rua General Pereira d'Eça 200, 1° andar, CP 1335, Maputo; tel. 21494147; fax 21494204; e-mail agora@agora.co.mz; internet www.agora.co.mz; f. 2000; monthly; economics, politics, society; Pres. MARIA DE LOURDES TORCATO; Dir JOVITO NUNES; Editor-in-Chief ERCÍLIA SANTOS; circ. 5,000.

Agricultura: Instituto Nacional de Investigação Agronómica, CP 3658, Maputo; tel. 2130091; f. 1982; quarterly; publ. by Centro de Documentação de Agricultura, Silvicultura, Pecuária e Pescas.

Aro: Av. 24 de Julho 1420, CP 4187, Maputo; f. 1995; monthly; Dir POLICARTO TAMELE; Editor BRUNO MACAME, Jr.

Arquivo Histórico: CP 2033, Maputo; tel. 21321177; fax 21323428; e-mail jneves@zebra.nem.mz; f. 1934; Editor JOEL DAS NEVES TEMBE.

Boletim da República: Av. Vladimir I. Lénine, CP 275, Maputo; govt and official notices; publ. by Imprensa Nacional da Moçambique.

Maderazinco: Maputo; e-mail maderazinco@yahoo.com; internet www.maderazinco.tropical.co.mz; f. 2002; quarterly; literature.

Moçambique–Novos Tempos: Av. Ahmed Sekou Touré 657, Maputo; tel. 21493564; fax 21493590; f. 1992; Dir J. MASCARENHAS.

Mozambiquefile: c/o AIM, Rua da Radio Moçambique, CP 896, Maputo; tel. 21313225; fax 21313196; e-mail aim@tvcabo.co.mz; internet www.sortmoz.com/aimnews; monthly; Dir GUSTAVO MAVIZ; Editor PAUL FAUVET.

Mozambique Inview: c/o Mediacoop, Av. Amílcar Cabral 1049, CP 73, Maputo; tel. 21430722; fax 21302402; e-mail inview@mediacoop.co.mz; internet www.mediacoop.odline.com; f. 1994; 2 a month; economic bulletin in English; Editor FRANCES CHRISTIE.

Portos e Caminhos de Ferro: CP 276, Maputo; English and Portuguese; ports and railways; quarterly.

Revista Médica de Moçambique: Instituto Nacional de Saúde, Ministério da Saúde e Faculdade de Medicina, Universidade Eduardo Mondlane, CP 264, Maputo; tel. 21420368; fax 21431103; e-mail mdgedge@malarins.uem.mz; f. 1982; 4 a year; medical journal; Editor MARTINHO DGEDGE.

NEWS AGENCIES

Agência de Informação de Moçambique (AIM): Rua da Rádio Moçambique, CP 896, Maputo; tel. 21313225; fax 21313196; e-mail aim@tvcabo.co.mz; internet www.sortmoz.com/aimnews; f. 1975; daily reports in Portuguese and English; Dir GUSTAVO LISSETIANE MAVIE.

Foreign Bureaux

Agence France-Presse (AFP): CP 4650, Maputo; tel. 21422940; fax 21422940; Correspondent RACHEL WATERHOUSE.

Agenzia Nazionale Stampa Associata (ANSA) (Italy): Maputo; tel. 21430723; fax 21421906; Correspondent PAUL FAUVET.

Lusa (Agência de Notícias de Portugal, SA): Av. Ho Chi Minh 111, Maputo; tel. 21427591; fax 21421690; e-mail lsa@lusa.pt; Bureau Chief LUÍS ANDRAD DE SÁ.

Xinhua (New China) News Agency (People's Republic of China): Rua Coimbra 258, Maputo; tel. 21414445.

Reuters (UK) is also represented in Mozambique.

Publishers

There are an estimated 30 printing and publishing companies in Mozambique.

Arquivo Histórico de Moçambique: Av. Filipe Samuel Magaia 715, CP 2033, Maputo; tel. 21421177; fax 21423428; e-mail jneves@zebra.uem.mz; internet www.ahm.uem.mz; Dir JOEL DAS NEVES TEMBE.

Central Impressora: c/o Ministério da Saúde, Avs Eduardo Mondlane e Salvador Allende 1008, CP 264, Maputo; owned by the Ministry of Health.

Centro de Estudos Africanos: Universidade Eduardo Mondlane, CP 1993, Maputo; tel. 21490828; fax 21491896; f. 1976; social and political science, regional history, economics; Dir Col SERGIO VIEIRA.

Editora Minerva Central: Rua Consiglieri Pedroso 84, CP 212, Maputo; tel. 2122092; f. 1908; stationers and printers, educational, technical and medical textbooks; Man. Dir J. F. CARVALHO.

Editorial Ndjira, Lda: Av. Ho Chi Minh 85, Maputo; tel. 21300180; fax 21308745; f. 1996.

Empresa Moderna Lda: Av. 25 de Setembro, CP 473, Maputo; tel. 21424594; f. 1937; fiction, history, textbooks; Man. Dir LOUIS GALLOTI.

Fundo Bibliográfico de Língua Portuguesa: Av. 25 Setembro 1230, 7° andar, Maputo; tel. 21429531; fax 21429530; e-mail palop@zebra.uem.mz; f. 1990; state owned; Pres. LOURENÇO ROSÁRIO.

Imprensa Universitária: Universidade Eduardo Mondlane, Praça 19 de Maio, Maputo; internet www.uem.mz/imprensa_universitaris; university press.

Instituto Nacional do Livro e do Disco: Av. 24 de Julho 1921, CP 4030, Maputo; tel. 21434870; govt publishing and purchasing agency; Dir ARMÉNIO CORREIA.

Moçambique Editora: Rua Armando Tivane 1430, Bairro de Polana, Maputo; tel. 21495017; fax 21499071; e-mail info@me.co.mz; internet www.me.co.mz; f. 1996; educational textbooks, dictionaries.

Plural Editores: Av. 24 de Julho 414, Maputo; tel. 21486828; fax 21486829; e-mail plural@pluraleditores.co.mz; internet www.pluraleditores.co.mz; f. 2003; educational textbooks; part of the Porto Editora Group.

GOVERNMENT PUBLISHING HOUSE

Imprensa Nacional de Moçambique: Rua da Imprensa, CP 275, Maputo; tel. 21423383; internet www.imprensanac.gov.mz; part of Ministry of State Administration; Dir VENÂNCIO T. MANJATE.

Broadcasting and Communications

TELECOMMUNICATIONS

TDM currently has a monopoly on fixed lines; however, plans were announced in 2004 to open this sector to competition by 2007.

Telecomunicações de Moçambique, SARL (TDM): Rua da Sé 2, CP 25, Maputo; tel. 21431921; fax 21431944; e-mail jcarvalho@tdm.mz; internet www.tdm.mz; f. 1993; Chair. JOAQUIM RIBEIRO PEREIRA DE CARVALHO; Man. Dir SALVADOR ADRIANO.

Moçambique Celular (mCel): Edif. Mcel, Esquina Av. 25 de Setembro e Rua Belmiro Obede Muianga, CP 1463, Maputo; tel. 21351111; fax 21351119; e-mail mcel@mcel.co.mz; internet www.mcel.co.mz; f. 1997 as a subsidiary of TDM; separated from TDM in 2003; mobile cellular telephone provider.

Vodacom Moçambique: Time Square Complex, Bloco 3, Av. 25 de Setembro, Maputo; tel. 21084111; internet www.vm.co.mz; f. 2002; owned by Vodacom (South Africa); Chair. HERMENGILDO GAMITO; Man. Dir CLIVE TARR.

Regulatory Authority

Instituto Nacional das Comunicações de Moçambique (INCM): Av. Eduardo Mondlane 123–127, CP 1937, Maputo; tel. 21490131; fax 21494435; e-mail info@incm.gov.mz; internet www.incm.gov.mz.

BROADCASTING

Radio

Rádio Encontro: Av. Francisco Manyanga, CP 366, Nampula; tel. 26215588.

Rádio Feba Moçambique: Av. Julius Nyerere 441, Maputo; tel. 21440002.

Rádio Maria: Rua Igreja 156A, Machava Sede, Matola, Maputo; tel. 21750505; fax 21752124; e-mail ramamo@virconn.com; f. 1995; evangelical radio broadcasts; Dir Fr JOÃO CARLOS H. NUNES.

Rádio Miramar: Rede de Comunicação, Av. Julius Nyerere 1555, Maputo; tel. 21488613; fax 21488613; e-mail jose.guerra@tvcabo.co.mz; owned by Brazilian religious sect, the Universal Church of the Kingdom of God.

Rádio Moçambique: Rua da Rádio 2, CP 2000, Maputo; tel. 21431687; fax 21321816; e-mail sepca_mz@yahoo.com.br; internet www.teledata.mz/radiomocambique; f. 1975; programmes in Portuguese, English and vernacular languages; Chair. MANUEL FERNANDO VETERANO.

Rádio Terra Verde: fmrly Voz da Renamo; owned by former rebel movement Renamo; transmitters in Maputo and Gorongosa, Sofala province.

Rádio Trans Mundial Moçambique: Av. Eduardo Mondlane 2998, Maputo; tel. 21407358; fax 21407357.

Television

The Portuguese station, RTP-Africa also broadcasts in Mozambique.

Rádio Televisão Klint (RTK): Av. Agostinho Neto 946, Maputo; tel. 21422956; fax 21493306; Dir CARLOS KLINT.

Televisão Miramar: owned by Brazilian religious sect, the Igrega Universal do Reino de Deus (Universal Church of the Kingdom of God).

Televisão de Moçambique, EP (TVM): Av. 25 de Setembro 154, CP 2675, Maputo; tel. 21308117; fax 21308122; e-mail tvm@tvm.co.mz; internet www.tvm.co.mz; f. 1981; Chair. and CEO SIMÃO JORDÃO ANGUILAZE.

TV Cabo Moçambique: Av. dos Presidentes 68, CP 1750, Maputo; tel. 21480500; fax 21499015; e-mail tvcabo@tvcabo.co.mz; internet www.tvcabo.co.mz; cable television and internet services in Maputo.

Finance

(cap. = capital; res = reserves; dep. = deposits; m. = million; brs = branches; amounts in meticais, unless otherwise stated)

BANKING

Central Bank

Banco de Moçambique: Av. 25 de Setembro 1679, CP 423, Maputo; tel. 21428150; fax 21429721; e-mail info@bancomoc.uem.mz; internet www.bancomoc.mz; f. 1975; bank of issue; cap. 248,952m., res 415,475m., dep. 13,283,222m. (Dec. 2002); Gov. ADRIANO AFONSO MALEIANE; 4 brs.

National Banks

Banco Austral: Av. 25 de Setembro 1184, CP 757, Maputo; tel. 21351739; fax 21301094; e-mail buscentre@teledata.mz; internet www.bancoaustral.com; f. 1977; fmrly Banco Popular de Desenvolvimento (BPD); renationalized in 2001; 80% owned by Amalgamated Banks of South Africa, 20% owned by União, Sociedade e Participacões, Sarl, which represents employees of the bank; cap. 315,000m., res −550m., dep. 2,047,081m. (Dec. 2003); Chair. CASIMIRO FRANCISCO; Man. Dir JOHAN DEODAT STANDER; 52 brs and agencies.

BCI Fomento (BCI) (Banco Comercial e de Investimentos, Sarl): Edif. John Orr's, Av. 25 de Setembro 1465, CP 4745, Maputo; tel. 21307777; fax 21307762; e-mail bci@bci.co.mz; internet www.bci.co.mz; f. 1996; renamed as above following 2003 merger between Banco Comercial e de Investimentos and Banco de Fomento; 42% owned by Caixa Geral de Depósitos (Portugal); 30% Banco Portugues de Investimento; equity 48.5m., dep. 360.0m. (US $, Dec. 2004); Chair. ABDUL MAGID OSMAN; 34 brs.

Banco de Desenvolvimento e de Comércio de Moçambique, SARL (BDCM): Av. 25 de Setembro 420, 1°, sala 8, Maputo; tel. 21313040; fax 21313047; f. 2000; 42% owned by Montepie Geral (Portugal).

Banco Internacional de Moçambique, SARL (BIM): Av. 25 de Setembro 1800, CP 865, Maputo; tel. 21351500; fax 21354808; internet www.mundobim.co.mz; f. 1995; merged with Banco Comercial de Moçambique in 2001; 66.7% owned by Banco Comercial Português, 23.1% by the state; cap. 741,000m., res 52,887m., dep. 13,652,632m. (Dec. 2003); Chair. Dr MÁRIO FERNANDES DA GRAÇA MACHUNGO; Man. Dir JOÃO FILIPE DE FIGUEIREDO, Júnior; 76 brs.

BIM—Investimento (Banco Internacional de Moçambique—Investimento): Av. Zedequias Manganhela 478, Maputo; tel. 21354896; fax 21354897; e-mail mpinto@bim.co.mz; internet www.bimnet.co.mz; f. 1998; 50% owned by Banco Internacional de Moçambique, 25% by BCP Investimento and 15% by International Finance Corpn; total assets US $2.7m. (Dec. 2003); Chair. Dr MÁRIO FERNANDES DA GRAÇA MACHUNGO; Gen. Dir Dr JOSÉ A. FERREIRA GOMES.

Banco Mercantil e de Investimento, Sarl (BMI): Av. 24 de Julho 3549, Maputo; tel. 21407979; fax 21407900.

MOZAMBIQUE

ICB-Banco Internacional de Comércio, SARL: Av. 25 de Setembro 1915, Maputo; tel. 21311111; fax 21314797; e-mail icbm@teledata.mz; internet www.icbank-mz.com; f. 1998; cap. and res 44,923,748m., total assets 164,773,569m. (Dec. 2003); Chair. JOSEPHINE SIVARETNAM; CEO LEE SANG HUAT.

Novo Banco, SARL: Av. do Trabalho 750, Maputo; tel. and fax 21407705; e-mail novobanco@teledata.mz; f. 2000; cap. and res 51,995m., total assets 108,847m. (Dec. 2003).

Standard Bank, SARL (Moçambique): Praça 25 de Junho 1, CP 2086, Maputo; tel. 21352500; fax 21426967; e-mail camal.daude@standardbank.co.mz; internet www.standardbank.co.mz; f. 1966 as Banco Standard Totta de Mozambique; name changed in 2004; 96.0% owned by Stanbic Africa Holdings, UK; cap. 174,000m., res 173,295m., dep. 6,080,437m. (Dec. 2003); Man. Dir CARLOS RAMALHO; 24 brs.

Foreign Banks

African Banking Corporation (Moçambique), SARL: ABC House, Av. Julius Nyerere 999, Polana, CP 1445, Maputo; tel. 21482100; fax 21487474; e-mail abcmoz@africanbankingcorp.com; internet www.africanbankingcorp.com; f. 1999; 100% owned by African Banking Corpn Holdings Ltd (Botswana); fmrly BNP Nedbank (Moçambique), SARL; changed name as above after acquisition in 2002; cap. 65,000m., res 8,642m., dep. 675,833m. (Dec. 2003); Chair. BENJAMIN ALFREDO; Man. Dir ZANDILE CHIRESHE.

African Banking Corporation Leasing, SARL: Rua da Imprensa 256, 7° andar, CP 4447, Maputo; tel. 21300451; fax 21431290; e-mail ulcmoz@mail.tropical.co.mz; 66% owned by African Banking Corpn Holdings Ltd (Botswana); fmrly ULC (Moçambique); changed name as above in 2002; total assets US $1.8m. (Dec. 1998); Chair. ANTÓNIO BRANCO; Gen. Man. VICTOR VISEU.

União Comercial de Bancos (Moçambique), SARL: Av. Friedrich Engels 400, Maputo; tel. 21481900; fax 21498675; e-mail ucb@tvcabo.co.mz; f. 1999; 81.24% owned by Mauritius Commercial Bank Group; total assets US $37,481m. (Dec. 2003); Chair. PHILIPPE ALAIN FORGET; Gen. Man. ROBERT CANTIN.

DEVELOPMENT FUND

Fundo de Desenvolvimento Agrícola e Rural: CP 1406, Maputo; tel. 21460349; fax 21460157; f. 1987; to provide credit for small farmers and rural co-operatives; promotes agricultural and rural development; Sec. EDUARDO OLIVEIRA.

STOCK EXCHANGE

Bolsa de Valores de Moçambique: Av. 25 de Setembro 1230, Prédio 33, 5° andar, Maputo; tel. 21308826; fax 21310559; e-mail jussub@bvm.com; Chair. Dr JUSSUB NURMAMAD.

INSURANCE

In December 1991 the Assembléia da República approved legislation terminating the state monopoly of insurance and reinsurance activities. In 2005 five insurance companies were operating in Mozambique.

Companhia de Seguros de Moçambique, IMPAR: Rua da Imprensa 625, Prédio 33, Maputo; tel. 21429695; fax 21430640; e-mail impar@zebra.uem.mz; f. 1992; Pres. INOCÊNCIO A. MATAVEL; Gen. Man. MANUEL BALANCHO.

Empresa Moçambicana de Seguros, EE (EMOSE): Av. 25 de Setembro 1383, CP 1165, Maputo; tel. 21422095; fax 21424526; f. 1977 as state insurance monopoly; took over business of 24 fmr cos; privatization pending; cap. 150m.; Gen. Dir VENÂNCIO MONDLANE.

Seguradora Internacional de Moçambique: Maputo; tel. 21430959; fax 21430241; e-mail simseg@zebra.uem.mz; Pres. MÁRIO FERNANDES DA GRAÇA MACHUNGO.

Trade and Industry

GOVERNMENT AGENCIES

Centro de Promoção de Investimentos (CPI) (Investment Promotion Centre): Rua da Imprensa 332, CP 4635, Maputo; tel. 21313295; fax 21313325; e-mail cpi@cpi.co.mz; internet www.mozbusiness.gov.mz; f. 1993; encourages foreign investment and IT ventures with foreign firms; evaluates and negotiates investment proposals.

Instituto do Fomento do Caju (INCAJU): Maputo; national cashew institute; Dir CLEMENTIAL MACHUNGO.

Instituto Nacional de Açúcar (INA): Rua da Gávea 33, CP 1772, Maputo; tel. 21326550; fax 21427436; e-mail gpsca.ina@tvcabo.co.mz; Chair. ARNALDO RIBEIRO.

Instituto Nacional de Petróleo: Maputo; f. 2005; regulates energy sector; Dir ARSÉNIO MABOTE.

Instituto para a Promoção de Exportações (IPEX): Av. 25 de Setembro 1008, 3° andar, CP 4487, Maputo; tel. 21307257; fax 21307256; e-mail ipex@tvcabo.co.mz; internet www.ipex.gov.mz; f. 1990 to promote and co-ordinate national exports abroad; Pres. Dr FELISBERTO FERRÃO.

Unidade Técnica para a Reestruturação de Empresas (UTRE): Rua da Imprensa 256, 7° andar, CP 4350, Maputo; tel. 21426514; fax 21421541; e-mail utre@teledata.mz; implements restructuring of state enterprises; Dir MOMADE JUMAS.

CHAMBERS OF COMMERCE

Câmara de Comércio de Moçambique (CCM): Rua Mateus Sansão Muthemba 452, CP 1836, Maputo; tel. 21491970; fax 21490428; e-mail cacomo@teledata.mz; internet www.teledata.mz/cacomo; f. 1980; Pres. JACINTO VELOSO; Sec.-Gen. MANUEL NOTIÇO.

Mozambique-USA Chamber of Commerce: Rua Matheus Sansão Muthema 452, Maputo; tel. 21492904; fax 21492739; e-mail mail@mail.ccmusa.co.mz; internet www.ccmusa.co.mz; f. 1993; Sec. PETER VAN AS.

South Africa-Mozambique Chamber of Commerce (SAMOZACC): internet www.samozacc.co.za; f. 2005; Chair. (Mozambique) ANTÓNIO MATOS.

TRADE ASSOCIATIONS

Associação dos Indústrias do Caju (AICAJU): Maputo; cashew processing industry asscn; Chair. CARLOS COSTA; 12 mem. cos.

Confederação das Associações Económicas (CTA): Av. 10 de Novembro, CP 2975, Maputo; tel. 21311734; fax 21311732; e-mail info@cta.org.mz; internet www.cta.org.mz; Pres. SALIMO ABDULA; Exec. Dir SÉRGIO CHITARÁ; 46 mem. cos.

STATE INDUSTRIAL ENTERPRISES

Empresa Nacional de Carvão de Moçambique (CARBOMOC): Rua Joaquim Lapa 108, CP 1773, Maputo; tel. 21427625; fax 21424714; f. 1948; mineral extraction and export; transfer to private ownership pending; Dir JAIME RIBEIRO.

Empresa Nacional de Hidrocarbonetos de Moçambique (ENH): Av. Fernão de Magalhães 34, CP 4787, Maputo; tel. 21429456; fax 21421608; controls concessions for petroleum exploration and production; Dir MÁRIO MARQUES.

Empresa Nacional de Petróleos de Moçambique (PETROMOC): Praça dos Trabalhadores 9, CP 417, Maputo; tel. 21427191; fax 21430181; f. 1977 to take over the Sonarep oil refinery and its associated distribution co; state directorate for liquid fuels within Mozambique, incl. petroleum products passing through Mozambique to inland countries; Dir MANUEL PATRÍCIO DA CRUZ VIOLA.

UTILITIES

Electricity

Electricidade de Moçambique (EDM): Av. Agostinho Neto 70, CP 2447, Maputo; tel. 21499385; fax 21495154; e-mail ligacaoexpresso@edm.co.mz; internet www.edm.co.mz; f. 1977; 100% state-owned; production and distribution of electric energy; in 2004 plans were announced to extend EDM grid to entire country by 2020, at an estimated cost of US $700m; Pres. MANUEL JOÃO CUAMBE; Dir PASCOAL BACELA; 2,700 employees.

Companhia de Transmissão de Moçambique, SARL (MOTRACO) (Mozambique Transmission Co): Prédio JAT, 4°, Av. 25 de Setembro 420, Maputo; tel. 21313427; fax 21313447; e-mail asimao@motraco.co.mz; internet www.motraco.co.mz; f. 1998; joint venture between power utilities of Mozambique, South Africa and Swaziland; electricity distribution; Gen. Man. FRANCIS MASAWI.

Water

Direcção Nacional de Águas: Av. 25 de Setembro 942, 9° andar, CP 1611, Maputo; tel. 21420469; fax 21421403; e-mail watco@zebra.uem.mz; internet www.dna.mz; Dir AMÉRICO MUIANGA.

TRADE UNIONS

Freedom to form trade unions, and the right to strike, are guaranteed under the 1990 Constitution.

Confederação de Sindicatos Livres e Independentes de Moçambique (CONSILMO): Sec.-Gen. JEREMIAS TIMANE.

Organização dos Trabalhadores de Moçambique—Central Sindical (OTM—CS) (Mozambique Workers' Organization—Trade Union Headquarters): Rua Manuel António de Sousa 36, Maputo; tel. 21426786; fax 21421671; e-mail otmdis@teledata.mz; internet www.otm.org.mz; f. 1983; Pres. AMOS JUNIOR MATSIUHE; Sec.-Gen. (vacant); 15 affiliated unions with over 94,000 mems including:

MOZAMBIQUE

Sindicato Nacional dos Empregadores Bancários (SNEB): Av. Fernão de Magalhães 785, 1°, CP 1230, Maputo; tel. 21428627; fax 21303274; e-mail snebmoz@tvcabo.co.mz; internet www.snebmoz.co.mz; f. 1992; Sec.-Gen. CARLOS MELO.

Sindicato Nacional da Função Pública (SNAPF): Av. Ho Chi Min 365, Maputo; Sec.-Gen. MANUEL ABUDO MOMAD.

Sindicato Nacional dos Profissionais da Estiva e Ofícios Correlativos (SINPEOC): Av. Paulo Samuel Kakhomba 1568, Maputo; tel. and fax 21309535; Sec.-Gen. BENTO MADALA MAUNGUE.

Sindicato Nacional dos Trabalhadores Agro-Pecuários e Florestais (SINTAF): Av. 25 de Setembro 1676, 1° andar, CP 4202, Maputo; tel. 21306284; f. 1987; Sec.-Gen. EUSÉBIO LUÍS CHIVULELE.

Sindicato Nacional dos Trabalhadores da Aviação Civil, Correios e Comunicações (SINTAC): Rua de Silves 24, Maputo; tel. 21309574; Sec.-Gen. LUCAS LUCAZE.

Sindicato Nacional dos Trabalhadores do Comércio, Seguros e Serviços (SINECOSSE): Av. Ho Chi Minh 365, 1° andar, CP 2142, Maputo; tel. 21428561; Sec.-Gen. AMÓS JÚNIOR MATSINHE.

Sindicato Nacional dos Trabalhadores da Indústria do Açúcar (SINTIA): Av. das FPLM 1912, Maputo; tel. 21461772; fax 21461975; f. 1989; Sec.-Gen. ALEXANDRE CÂNDIDO MUNGUAMBE.

Sindicato Nacional dos Trabalhadores da Indústria Alimentar e Bebidas (SINTIAB): Av. Eduardo Mondlane 1267, CP 394, Maputo; tel. 21324709; fax 21324123; f. 1986; Gen. Sec. SAMUEL FENIAS MATSINHE.

Sindicato Nacional dos Trabalhadores da Indústria de Cajú (SINTIC): Rua do Jardim 574, 4° andar, Maputo; tel. 21477732; Sec.-Gen. BOAVENTURA MONDLANE.

Sindicato Nacional dos Trabalhadores da Indústria Metalúrgica, Metalomecânica e Energia (SINTIME): Av. Samora Machel 30, 6°, Maputo; Sec.-Gen. SIMIÃO NHATUMBO.

Sindicato Nacional dos Trabalhadores da Indústria Química, Borracha, Papel e Gráfica (SINTIQUIGRA): Av. Olof Palme 255, CP 4439, Maputo; tel. 21320288; fax 21321096; Sec.-Gen. JOAQUIM M. FANHEIRO.

Sindicato Nacional dos Trabalhadores da Indústria Têxtil Vestuário, Couro e Calçado (SINTEVEC): Av. do Trabalho 1276, 1° andar, CP 2613, Maputo; tel. 21404669; fax 21409295; Sec.-Gen. MARIO RAIMUNDO SITOE.

Sindicato Nacional dos Trabalhadores da Marinha Mercante e Pesca (SINTMAP): Rua Joaquim Lapa 22, 5° andar, No 6, Maputo; tel. 21305593; Sec.-Gen. DANIEL MANUEL NGOQUE.

Sindicato Nacional dos Trabalhadores dos Portos e Caminhos de Ferro (SINPOCAF): Av. Guerra Popular, esquina 24 de Setembro, CP 2158, Maputo; tel. 21403912; fax 21303839; Sec.-Gen. SAMUEL ALFREDO CHEUANE.

Sindicato Nacional de Jornalistas (SNJ): Rua Gen. Pereira d'Eça 12, 1° andar, Maputo; tel. 214998577; fax 21492031; f. 1978; Sec.-Gen. EDUARDO CONSTANTINO.

Transport

Improvements to the transport infrastructure since the signing of the Acordo Geral de Paz (General Peace Agreement) in 1992 have focused on the development of 'transport corridors', which include both rail and road links and promote industrial development in their environs. The Beira Corridor, with rail and road links and a petroleum pipeline, runs from Manica, on the Zimbabwean border, to the Mozambican port of Beira, while the Limpopo Corridor joins southern Zimbabwe and Maputo. Both corridors form a vital outlet for the land-locked southern African countries, particularly Zimbabwe. The Maputo Corridor links Ressano Garcia in South Africa to the port at Maputo, and the Nacala Corridor runs from Malawi to the port of Nacala. Two further corridors were planned: the Mtwara Development Corridor was to link Mozambique, Malawi, Tanzania and Zambia, while the Zambezi Corridor was to link Zambézia province with Malawi. In February 2000 much of the country's infrastructure in the southern and central provinces was devastated as the result of massive flooding. Railway lines, roads and bridges suffered considerable damage.

RAILWAYS

In 2003 the total length of track was 3,114 km, of which 2,072 km was operational. There are both internal routes and rail links between Mozambican ports and South Africa, Swaziland, Zimbabwe and Malawi. During the hostilities many lines and services were disrupted. Improvement work on most of the principal railway lines began in the early 1980s. In the early 2000s work began on upgrading the railway system and in 2004 the World Bank granted €80m. to finance the reconstruction of the Sena railway line to Moatize. Management of the railway companies has been privatized via non-permanent concessions.

Empresa Portos e Caminhos de Ferro de Moçambique (CFM-EP): Praça dos Trabalhadores, CP 2158, Maputo; tel. 21427173; fax 21427746; e-mail cfmnet@cfmnet.co.mz; internet www.cfmnet.co.mz; fmrly Empresa Nacional dos Portos e Caminhos de Ferro de Moçambique; privatized and restructured in 2002; Chair. RUI FONSECA; comprises four separate systems linking Mozambican ports with the country's hinterland, and with other southern African countries, including South Africa, Swaziland, Zimbabwe and Malawi:

CFM—Sul: Praça dos Trabalhadores, CP 2158, Maputo; tel. 21427173; fax 21427746; lines totalling 1,070 km linking Maputo with South Africa, Swaziland and Zimbabwe, as well as Inhambane–Inharrime and Xai–Xai systems; Exec. Dir CARLOS BAMBA NANGHOU; Dir of Railways FERNANDO MAÚSSE.

CFM—Norte: CP 16, Nampula; tel. 26212927; fax 26214320; lines totalling 872 km, including link between port of Nacala with Malawi; management concession awarded to Nacala Corridor Development Company (a consortium 67% owned by South African, Portuguese and US companies) in January 2000; Dir FILIPE NHUSSI; Dir of Railways MANUEL MANICA.

CFM—Zambézia: CP 73, Quelimane; tel. 24212502; fax 24213123; 145-km line linking Quelimane and Mocuba; Dir ORLANDO J. JAIME.

CFM—Centro (CFM—C): CP 472, Beira; tel. 23325200; fax 23324239; lines totalling 994 km linking Beira with Zimbabwe and Malawi, as well as link to Moatize (undergoing rehabilitation); Exec. Dir JOAQUIM VERÍSSIMO.

Beira Railway Co.: Dondo; f. 2004; 51% owned by Rites & Ircon (India), 49% owned by CFM; rehabilitating and managing Sena and Zimbabwe railway lines.

ROADS

In 1999 there were an estimated 30,400 km of roads in Mozambique, of which 5,685 km were paved. Although the road network was improved in the 1990s, the severe floods in February 2000 meant that much of the construction would have to be repeated. In 2001 the Government announced plans to invest US $1,700m. in upgrading and maintaining the road network at the rate of 28,000 km per year. In 2003 827 km of road were built or upgraded. Major constructions in that year included the 315-km road linking Inchope, in Sofala province, to Caia. In 2006 a contract to construct a bridge over the Zambezi river at Caia was awarded to a Portuguese consortium. The bridge was to be completed by 2009.

Administração Nacional de Estradas (ANE): Av. de Moçambique 1225, CP 1294, Maputo; tel. 21475157; fax 21475290; e-mail pce.ane@teledata.mz; internet www.dnep.gov.mz; f. 1999 to replace the Direcção Nacional de Estradas e Pontes; implements government road policy through the Direcção de Estradas Nacionais (DEN) and the Direcção de Estradas Regionais (DER); Pres. Eng. CARLOS FRAGOSO; Dir-Gen. IBRAIMO REMANE.

SHIPPING

Mozambique has three main sea ports, at Nacala, Beira and Maputo, while inland shipping on Lake Niassa and the river system was underdeveloped. At December 2004 Mozambique's registered merchant fleet consisted of 128 vessels, totalling 36,072 grt.

Empresa Portos e Caminhos de Ferro de Moçambique (CFM-EP): Praça dos Trabalhadores, CP 2158, Maputo; tel. 21427173; fax 21427746; e-mail cfmnet@cfmnet.co.mz; internet www.cfmnet.co.mz; fmrly Empresa Nacional dos Portos e Caminhos de Ferro de Moçambique; privatized and restructured in 2002; Port Dir CFM-Sul BOAVENTURA CHAMBAL; Port Dir CFM-Norte AGOSTINHO LANGA, Jr; Port Dir CFM-Centro CHINGUANE MABOTE.

Agência Nacional de Frete e Navegação (ANFRENA): Rua Consiglieri Pedroso 396, CP 492, Maputo; tel. 21427064; fax 21427822; Dir FERDINAND WILSON.

Empresa Moçambicana de Cargas, SARL (MOCARGO): Rua Consiglieri Pedroso 430, 1°–4° andares, CP 888, Maputo; tel. 21421440; fax 21302067; e-mail mocargo1@teledata.mz; internet www.mocargo.co.mz; f. 1982; shipping, chartering and road transport; Man. Dir MANUEL DE SOUSA AMARAL.

Manica Freight Services, SARL: Praça dos Trabalhadores 51, CP 557, Maputo; tel. 21426024; fax 21424595; e-mail achothia@manica.co.mz; international shipping agents; Man. Dir A. Y. CHOTHIA.

Maputo Port Development Company, SARL (MPDC): Port Director's Building, Porto de Maputo, CP 2841, Maputo; tel. 21313920; fax 21313921; e-mail info@portmaputo.com; internet www.portmaputo.com; f. 2002; private-sector international consortium with concession (awarded 2003) to develop and run port of Maputo until 2018; CEO PETER LOWE.

Mozline, SARL: Av. Karl Marx 478, 2° andar, Maputo; tel. 21303078; fax 21303073; e-mail mozline1@virconn.com; shipping and road freight services.

Navique, SARL: Av. Mártires de Inhaminga 4, CP 145, Maputo; tel. 21312706; fax 21426310; e-mail navique_adm@mail.garp.co.mz; Chair. J. A. CARVALHO; Man. Dir PEDRO VIRTUOSO.

CIVIL AVIATION

In 2005 there were six international airports.

Instituto de Aviação Civil de Moçambique (IACM): Maputo; civil aviation institute; Dir ANÍBAL SAMUEL.

Air Corridor: Nampula; f. 2004; domestic carrier; Commercial Dir CESAR MAHUMANE.

Linhas Aéreas de Moçambique, SARL (LAM): Aeroporto Internacional de Maputo, CP 2060, Maputo; tel. 21465137; fax 21422936; e-mail flamingoclub@lam.co.mz; internet www.lam.co.mz; f. 1980; 80% state-owned; operates domestic services and international services to South Africa, Tanzania, Mayotte, Zimbabwe and Portugal; Chair. and Dir-Gen. JOSÉ RICARDO ZUZARTE VIEGAS.

Sociedade de Transportes Aéreos/Sociedade de Transporte e Trabalho Aéreo, SARL (STA/TTA): CP 665, Maputo; tel. 21742366; fax 21491763; e-mail dido@mail.tropical.co.mz; internet www.sta.co.mz; f. 1991; domestic airline and aircraft charter transport services; acquired Empresa Nacional de Transporte e Trabalho Aéreo in 1997; Chair. ROGÉRIO WALTER CARREIRA; Man. Dir JOSÉ CARVALHEIRA.

Other airlines operating in Mozambique include Serviço Aéreo Regional, South African Airlines, Moçambique Expresso, SA—Airlink International, Transairways (owned by LAM) and TAP Air Portugal.

Tourism

Tourism, formerly a significant source of foreign exchange, ceased completely following independence, and was resumed on a limited scale in 1980. There were 1,000 visitors in 1981 (compared with 292,000 in 1972 and 69,000 in 1974). With the successful conduct of multi-party elections in 1994 and the prospect of continued peace, there was considerable scope for development of this sector. By the late 1990s tourism was the fastest growing sector of the Mozambique economy, and in 2000 it was announced that a comprehensive tourism development plan was to be devised, assisted by funding from the European Union. In 2002 there were 45 hotels in Mozambique, offering some 4,129 hotel beds, which represented an increase of 39% on 2000. The opening of the Great Limpopo Transfrontier Park, linking territories in Mozambique with South Africa and Zimbabwe, was scheduled for 2006 and was expected to attract additional tourists. Foreign tourist arrivals in 2003 were 726,099, while tourism receipts totalled US $98m. in that year.

Fundo Nacional do Turismo: Av. 25 de Setembro 1203, CP 2758, Maputo; tel. 21307320; fax 21307324; e-mail futur@futur.org.mz; f. 1993; hotels and tourism; CEO ZACARIAS SUMBANA.

Sociedade do Desenvolvimento do Turismo do Indico (INTUR): Maputo; f. 2001; promotion of tourism in the northern Nacala Development Corridor.

MYANMAR

Introductory Survey

Location, Climate, Language, Religion, Flag, Capital

The Union of Myanmar (Myanma Naing-ngan—formerly Burma) lies in the north-west region of South-East Asia, between the Tibetan plateau and the Malay peninsula. The country is bordered by Bangladesh and India to the north-west, by the People's Republic of China and Laos to the north-east and by Thailand to the south-east. The climate is tropical, with an average temperature of 27°C (80°F) and monsoon rains from May to October. Average annual rainfall is between 2,500 mm and 5,000 mm in the coastal and mountainous regions of the north and east, but reaches a maximum of only 1,000 mm in the lowlands of the interior. Temperatures in Yangon (Rangoon) are generally between 18°C (65°F) and 36°C (97°F). The official language is Myanmar (Burmese), and there are also a number of tribal languages. About 87% of the population are Buddhists. There are animist, Muslim, Hindu and Christian minorities. The national flag (proportions 5 by 9) is red, with a blue canton, in the upper hoist, bearing two ears of rice within a cog-wheel and a ring of 14 five-pointed stars (one for each state), all in white. The capital is Yangon.

Recent History

Burma (now Myanmar) was annexed to British India during the 19th century, and became a separate British dependency, with a limited measure of self-government, in 1937. Japanese forces invaded and occupied the country in 1942, and Japan granted nominal independence under a Government of anti-British nationalists. The Burmese nationalists later turned against Japan and aided Allied forces to reoccupy the country in 1945. They formed a resistance movement, the Anti-Fascist People's Freedom League (AFPFL), led by Gen. Aung San, which became the main political force after the defeat of Japan. Aung San was assassinated in July 1947 and was succeeded by U Nu. On 4 January 1948 the Union of Burma became independent, outside the Commonwealth, with U Nu as the first Prime Minister.

During the first decade of independence Burma was a parliamentary democracy, and the Government successfully resisted revolts by communists and other insurgent groups. In 1958 the ruling AFPFL split into two wings, the 'Clean' AFPFL and the 'Stable' AFPFL, and U Nu invited the Army Chief of Staff, Gen. Ne Win, to head a caretaker Government. Elections to the Chamber of Deputies in February 1960 gave an overwhelming majority to U Nu, leading the 'Clean' AFPFL (which was renamed the Union Party in March), and he resumed office in April. Despite its popularity, however, the U Nu administration proved ineffective, and in March 1962 Gen. Ne Win intervened again, staging a coup to depose U Nu (who was subsequently detained until 1966). The new Revolutionary Council suspended the Constitution and instituted authoritarian control through the government-sponsored Burma Socialist Programme Party (BSPP). All other political parties were outlawed in March 1964.

During the next decade a more centralized system of government was created, in an attempt to win popular support and to nationalize important sectors of the economy. A new Constitution, aiming to transform Burma into a democratic socialist state, was approved in a national referendum in December 1973. The Constitution of the renamed Socialist Republic of the Union of Burma, which came into force in January 1974, confirmed the BSPP as the sole authorized political party, and provided for the establishment of new organs of state. Elections to a legislative People's Assembly took place in January 1974, and in March the Revolutionary Council was dissolved. U Ne Win (who, together with other senior army officers, had become a civilian in 1972) was elected President by the newly created State Council. Burma's economic problems increased, however, and in 1974 there were riots over food shortages and social injustices. Student demonstrations took place in 1976, as social problems increased. Following an attempted coup by members of the armed forces in July, the BSPP reviewed its economic policies, and in 1977 a new economic programme was adopted in an attempt to quell unrest.

An election in January 1978 gave U Ne Win a mandate to rule for a further four years, and in March he was re-elected Chairman of the State Council. In May 1980 a general amnesty was declared for political dissidents, including exiles (as a result of which U Nu, who had been living abroad since 1969, returned to Burma). Gen. San Yu, formerly the Army Chief of Staff, was elected Chairman of the State Council in November 1981. At the fifth Congress of the BSPP, in August 1985, U Ne Win was re-elected for a further four-year term as Chairman. Elections for a new People's Assembly were held in November.

In August 1987, owing to the country's increasing economic problems, an unprecedented extraordinary meeting, comprising the BSPP Central Committee, the organs of the State Council and other state bodies, was convened. U Ne Win proposed a review of the policies of the past 25 years. In September the announcement of the withdrawal from circulation of high-denomination banknotes, coupled with rice shortages, provoked student riots (the first civil disturbances since 1976). Owing to continued economic deprivation, further student unrest in Rangoon (now Yangon) in March 1988 culminated in major protests, which were violently suppressed by riot police under the direct command of U Sein Lwin, the BSPP Joint General Secretary. Further demonstrations started in June. The Government's response was again extremely brutal, and many demonstrators were killed. In July vain attempts were made to counter the growing unpopularity of the Government, including the removal from office of Maj.-Gen. Min Gaung, the Minister of Home and Religious Affairs, and U Thien Aung, the head of the People's Police Force in Rangoon. (The Prime Minister, also, was subsequently dismissed.) Finally, at an extraordinary meeting of the BSPP Congress in July, U Ne Win resigned as party Chairman and asked the Congress to approve the holding of a national referendum on the issue of a multi-party political system. The Congress rejected the referendum proposal and the resignation of four other senior members of the BSPP, including that of U Sein Lwin, but accepted the resignation of U San Yu, the BSPP Vice-Chairman.

The subsequent election of U Sein Lwin to the chairmanship of the BSPP, and his appointment as Chairman of the State Council and as state President, increased popular discontent and provoked further student-led riots. Martial law was imposed on Rangoon, and thousands of unarmed demonstrators were reportedly massacred by the armed forces throughout the country. In August 1988 U Sein Lwin was forced to resign after only 17 days in office. He was replaced by the more moderate Dr Maung Maung, hitherto the Attorney-General, whose response to the continued rioting was conciliatory. Martial law was revoked; Brig.-Gen. Aung Gyi (formerly a close colleague of U Ne Win, now an outspoken critic of the regime), who had been detained under U Sein Lwin, was released; and permission was given for the formation of the All Burma Students' Union. Demonstrations continued, however, and by September students and Buddhist monks had assumed control of the municipal government of many towns. In that month U Nu requested foreign support for his formation of an 'alternative government'. The emerging opposition leaders, Aung Gyi, Aung San Suu Kyi (daughter of Gen. Aung San) and Gen. (retd) Tin Oo (a former Chief of Staff and Minister of Defence), then formed the National United Front for Democracy, which was subsequently renamed the League for Democracy and later the National League for Democracy (NLD).

At an emergency meeting of the BSPP Congress in September 1988 it was decided that free elections would be held within three months and that members of the armed forces, police and civil service could no longer be affiliated to a political party. Now distanced from the BSPP, the armed forces, led by Gen. (later Senior Gen.) Saw Maung, seized power on 18 September, ostensibly to maintain order until multi-party elections could be arranged. A State Law and Order Restoration Council (SLORC) was formed, all state organs (including the People's Assembly, the State Council and the Council of Ministers) were abolished, demonstrations were banned and a night-time curfew was imposed nation-wide. Despite these measures, opposition movements demonstrated in favour of an interim civilian government, and it was estimated that more than 1,000 demonstrators were killed in the first few days following the coup. The SLORC announced the formation of a nine-member Government, with Saw Maung as Minister of Defence and of Foreign Affairs and subsequently also Prime Minister. Although ostensibly in retirement, it was widely believed that U Ne Win retained a controlling influence over the new leaders. The new Government changed the official name of the country to the Union of Burma (as it had been before 1973). The law maintaining the BSPP as the sole party was abrogated, and new parties were encouraged to register for the forthcoming elections. The BSPP registered as the National Unity Party (NUP), with U Tha Kyaw, the former Minister of Transport, as its Chairman. In December 1988, owing to disagreements with Suu Kyi, Aung Gyi was expelled from the NLD after he had founded the Union National Democracy Party. Tin Oo was elected as the new NLD Chairman. U Nu returned to prominence as the leader of a new party, the League for Democracy and Peace (LDP), and also commanded the support of the new Democracy Party.

From October 1988 to January 1989 Suu Kyi campaigned in townships and rural areas across the nation, and elicited much popular support, despite martial law regulations banning public gatherings of five or more people. In March 1989 there were anti-Government demonstrations in many cities, in protest at the increasing harassment of Suu Kyi and the arrest of many NLD supporters and activists. In July Suu Kyi cancelled a rally to commemorate the anniversary of the assassination of her father, owing to the threat of government violence; two days later, both she and Tin Oo were placed under house arrest, accused of 'endangering the State'.

In May 1989 electoral legislation was ratified, providing for multi-party elections to be held on 27 May 1990, and permitting campaigning only in the three months prior to the election date. In June 1989 the SLORC changed the official name of the country to the Union of Myanmar (Myanma Naing-ngan), on the grounds that the previous title conveyed the impression that the population consisted solely of ethnic Burmans. The transliteration to the Roman alphabet of many other place-names was changed, to correspond more closely with pronunciation.

In December 1989 Tin Oo was sentenced by a military tribunal to three years' imprisonment, with hard labour, for his part in the anti-Government uprising in 1988. In the same month U Nu was disqualified from contesting the forthcoming general election, owing to his refusal to dissolve the 'alternative government' that he had proclaimed in September 1988. In January 1990 U Nu and 13 members of the 'alternative government' were placed under house arrest. Five members subsequently resigned and were released. Later in January, Suu Kyi was barred from contesting the election, owing to her 'entitlement to the privileges of a foreigner' (a reference to her marriage to a British citizen) and her alleged involvement with insurgents.

Martial law was revoked in eight townships in November 1989, and in a further 10 in February 1990. It was reported that during 1989 tens of thousands of residents had been forcibly evicted from densely populated areas in major cities, where anti-Government demonstrations had received much support, and resettled in rural areas. In January and April 1989 a prominent human rights organization, Amnesty International, published information regarding violations of human rights in Myanmar, including the torture and summary execution of dissident students. This was followed by criticism from the UN later in the year.

In May 1990 93 parties presented a total of 2,296 candidates to contest 492 seats at the general election for the new assembly; there were also 87 independent candidates. Despite previous efforts to weaken the influence of known leaders and to eliminate dissidents, the voting was reported to be free and orderly. The NLD received 59.9% of the total votes and won 396 of the 485 seats that were, in the event, contested; the NUP obtained 21.2% of the votes, but won only 10 seats. The NLD demanded the immediate opening of negotiations with the SLORC, and progress towards popular rule. However, the SLORC announced that the election had been intended to provide not a legislature but a Constituent Assembly, which was to draft a constitution establishing a 'strong government', and was to be under the direction of a national convention to be established by the SLORC. The resulting draft constitution would have to be endorsed by referendum, and subsequently approved by the SLORC. In July the SLORC announced Order 1/90, stating that the SLORC would continue as the *de facto* Government until a new constitution was drafted. Elected members of the NLD responded (independently of their leadership) with the 'Gandhi Hall Declaration', urging that an assembly of all elected representatives be convened by September.

In August 1990, at an anti-Government protest held in Mandalay to commemorate the killing of thousands of demonstrators in 1988, troops killed four protesters, including two Buddhist monks. In September the SLORC arrested six members of the NLD, including the acting Chairman, Kyi Maung, and acting Secretary-General, Chit Hlaing, on charges of passing state secrets to unauthorized persons. Kyi Maung was replaced as acting NLD Chairman by U Aung Shwe. Also in September NLD representatives discussed plans to declare a provisional government in Mandalay, without the support of the party's Central Executive Committee. Influential monks agreed to support the declaration, but the plan was abandoned after government troops surrounded monasteries. The SLORC subsequently ordered the dissolution of all Buddhist organizations involved in anti-Government activities (all except nine sects) and empowered military commanders to impose death sentences on rebellious monks. More than 50 senior members of the NLD were arrested, and members of all political parties were required to endorse Order 1/90: in acquiescing, the NLD effectively nullified its demand for an immediate transfer of power.

In December 1990 a group of candidates who had been elected to the Constituent Assembly fled to Manerplaw, on the Thai border, and announced a 'parallel government', the National Coalition Government of the Union of Burma (NCGUB), with the support of the Democratic Alliance of Burma (DAB), a broadly based organization uniting ethnic rebel forces with student dissidents and monks. The self-styled Prime Minister of the NCGUB was Sein Win, the leader of the Party for National Democracy (PND) and a cousin of Suu Kyi. The NLD leadership expelled members who had taken part in the formation of the 'parallel government', despite broad support for the move in the NLD. The SLORC subsequently annulled the registration as a political party of the PND, the LDP and two other parties and the elected status of the eight members of the NCGUB. In April 1991 Gen. (later Senior Gen.) Than Shwe, the Vice-Chairman of the SLORC and the Deputy Chief of Staff of the armed forces, officially announced that the SLORC would not transfer power to the Constituent Assembly, as the political parties involved were 'subversive' and 'unfit to rule'. In response to continued pressure from the SLORC, the NLD effected a complete reorganization of the party's Central Executive Committee, replacing Suu Kyi as General Secretary with the previously unknown U Lwin, and Tin Oo with the former acting Chairman, U Aung Shwe.

In July 1991 the SLORC retroactively amended electoral legislation adopted in May 1989, extending the grounds on which representatives of the Assembly could be disqualified or debarred from contesting future elections to include convictions for breaches of law and order. More than 80 elected representatives had already died, been imprisoned or been forced into exile since the election in May 1990. In September 1991 the SLORC declared its intention to remain in charge of state administration for a further five to 10 years. In that month U Ohn Gyaw was appointed Minister for Foreign Affairs in place of Saw Maung, becoming the first civilian in the Cabinet.

In October 1991 Suu Kyi was awarded the Nobel Peace Prize. Sein Win attended the presentation of the award to Suu Kyi's family in Oslo, Norway, in December, gaining the Norwegian Government's *de facto* recognition of the NCGUB. In Myanma students who staged demonstrations (the first since 1989) to coincide with the ceremony were dispersed by security forces. Universities and colleges, which had reopened in May 1991, were closed, and thousands of teaching staff were dismissed or sent for re-education. It was subsequently announced that Suu Kyi had been expelled from the NLD. In January 1992 Tin Oo's expulsion from the NLD was announced in a broadcast.

Three additional members were appointed to the SLORC in January 1992, and the Cabinet was expanded to include seven new ministers, four of whom were civilians. The changes, together with a reorganization of senior ministers in February, were widely perceived to benefit the Chief of Military Intelligence, Maj.-Gen. (later Lt-Gen.) Khin Nyunt (First Secretary of the SLORC). Khin Nyunt was widely regarded as the most powerful member of the SLORC, owing to U Ne Win's continued patronage. Divisions within the ruling junta between Khin Nyunt and the more senior officers were becoming increasingly evident. In March Than Shwe replaced Saw Maung as Minister of Defence, and in April Saw Maung retired as Chairman of the SLORC and Prime Minister for reasons of ill health. Than Shwe was subsequently appointed to both these posts. The SLORC promptly ordered the release of several political prisoners, including U Nu, and announced that Suu Kyi could receive a visit from her family. Than Shwe indicated that he was prepared to meet Suu Kyi personally to discuss her future. In June the first meeting took place between members of the SLORC and opposition representatives from the remaining 10 legal parties, in preparation for the holding of a national convention to draft a new constitution.

In January 1993 the National Convention finally assembled, but was adjourned several times during the year, owing to the objections of the opposition members to SLORC demands for a leading role in government for the armed forces. The SLORC reacted to what it regarded as opposition intransigence by suspending any conciliatory gestures (which had included the revocation of two martial law decrees and amnesties for a total of 534 political prisoners), and many arrests were reported. Towards the end of the year the Chairman of the National Convention's Convening Committee, U Aung Toe (the Chief Justice), announced (seemingly without grounds) that a consensus existed in favour of the SLORC's demands, which comprised: the inclusion, in both the lower and upper chambers of a proposed parliament, of military personnel (to be appointed by the Commander-in-Chief of the Armed Forces); the election of the President by an electoral college; the independent self-administration of the armed forces; and the right of the Commander-in-Chief to exercise state power in an emergency (effectively granting legitimate status to a future coup).

In September 1993 an alternative mass movement to the NUP (which had lost credibility through its election defeat) was formed to establish a civilian front through which the armed forces could exercise control. The Union Solidarity and Development Association (USDA), the aims of which were indistinguishable from those of the SLORC, was not officially registered as a political party, thus enabling civil servants to join the organization, with the incentive of considerable privileges. In January 1994 large numbers of people were apparently coerced into joining USDA rallies to demonstrate support for the constitutional proposals presented by the SLORC.

In January 1994 the National Convention reconvened, and in April it was adjourned, having adopted guidelines for three significant chapters of the future Constitution. Accordingly, Myanmar was to be renamed the Republic of the Union of Myanmar, comprising seven states (associated with some of the country's minority ethnic groups) and seven divisions in central and southern Myanmar (largely representing the areas populated by the ethnic Bamars—Burmans). The Republic would be headed by an executive President, elected by the legislature for five years; proposals for the disqualification of any candidate with a foreign spouse or children would prevent Suu Kyi from entering any future presidential election. Reconvening in September, the Convention again stressed that the central role of the military (as 'permanent representatives of the people') be enshrined in the new Constitution. It was proposed that legislative power be shared between a bicameral Pyidaungsu Hluttaw (Union Parliament) and divisional and state assemblies, all of which were to include representatives of the military. The Pyidaungsu Hluttaw was to comprise the Pyithu Hluttaw and the Amyotha Hluttaw (House of Nationalities): the former would comprise 330 elected deputies and 110 members of the armed forces, and would be elected for five years. The latter would be constituted with equal numbers of representatives from the proposed seven regions and seven states of the Republic, as well as members of the military, and was to comprise a maximum of 224 deputies. A general election was provisionally scheduled for 2 September 1997 (although it was not actually held). The session was adjourned in April 1995.

Meanwhile, in July 1994 Khin Nyunt announced that the SLORC was prepared to hold talks with Suu Kyi. In February a delegation led by a member of the US Congress had been granted permission to visit Suu Kyi, who had expressed her willingness to negotiate with the SLORC. In August a second US Congressman led a delegation to Yangon, meeting with Khin Nyunt. In September, following mediation by a senior Buddhist monk between Suu Kyi and leading members of the SLORC, Suu Kyi was permitted to leave her home to meet Than Shwe and Khin Nyunt. In October Suu Kyi held a second meeting with senior SLORC members. In November it was reported that Suu Kyi had met other detained members of the NLD, including Tin Oo. In January 1995 the SLORC announced that Suu Kyi would be freed only when the new Constitution had been completed; Suu Kyi simultaneously rejected suggestions that she might reach a compromise with the SLORC on the terms for her release. In February leading members of the SLORC held talks in Yangon with an envoy of the UN Secretary-General. In March the Government released 31 political prisoners, including Tin Oo and Kyi Maung.

In July 1995 Suu Kyi was unexpectedly granted an unconditional release from house arrest. The SLORC, which thus hoped to attract greater foreign investment, was in a powerful position: the armed forces were united; political dissent had been effectively suppressed; and cease-fire accords had been reached with nearly all the ethnic insurgent groups. On her release Suu Kyi made a conciliatory speech, urging negotiations with the SLORC and a spirit of compromise. Suu Kyi swiftly reconciled the early leaders of the NLD with the new leadership, which had compromised with the SLORC. Hundreds of supporters gathered daily to hear Suu Kyi speak outside her house in Yangon without being dispersed by security forces. Suu Kyi was reinstated as General Secretary of the NLD in October, in a reorganization of the party's executive committee; Tin Oo and Kyi Maung were named Vice-Chairmen. Aung Shwe, who had led the 'legal' NLD and represented the party at the National Convention, was retained as party Chairman.

In November 1995 the National Convention reconvened. The NLD was becoming increasingly frustrated by the SLORC's failure to open talks with the NLD and its insistence that the National Convention was the proper forum for discussions. (Suu Kyi was, of course, not a member of the National Convention.) The NLD attended the opening session of the Convention, but later withdrew when the SLORC ignored its requests to expand the Convention to make it truly representative. Denouncing the Convention as illegitimate and undemocratic, the NLD for the first time appealed for international support for its cause. The SLORC, which had already begun to imprison NLD supporters for petty crimes, reacted strongly to the NLD boycott, officially expelling the party from the Convention and threatening to 'annihilate' anyone threatening national interests.

During 1996 and 1997 NLD meetings and publications were prohibited, and arrests of its members were frequent. In May 1996 more than 260 members of the NLD (mostly delegates elected to the Constituent Assembly in 1990) were arrested prior to the opening of the party's first congress. The majority were detained for the duration of the congress, which only 18 NLD members were able to attend. The congress resolved to draft an alternative constitution. In June the SLORC intensified its action against the NLD with an order banning any organization that held illegal gatherings or obstructed the drafting of the new Constitution by the National Convention; members of a proscribed party could be liable to between five and 20 years' imprisonment. In September police erected road-blocks around Suu Kyi's house, and again detained NLD activists, in order to prevent the holding of a further congress. Suu Kyi's telephone line was disconnected, and she was unable to deliver her weekly speech for the first time since her release from house arrest. From October the road-block was resumed each week with the purpose of preventing access to Suu Kyi's speech. The SLORC recommenced talks with NLD officials later that month. However, relations quickly deteriorated following an attack on vehicles in which Suu Kyi and other NLD leaders were travelling.

In October 1996 student action in Yangon, in protest against the detention and brutal treatment of fellow students, prompted further repression and numerous arrests (among those detained was Kyi Maung). This was followed in early December by the largest pro-democracy demonstration since 1988, involving more than 2,000 students. The gathering was dispersed peacefully, although some 600 demonstrators were temporarily detained. Smaller student demonstrations continued sporadically until mid-December, when Suu Kyi was briefly confined to her home (although she denied involvement), and tanks were deployed in Yangon; university establishments were closed indefinitely. At the end of December some 50 members of the Communist Party of Burma (CPB) and of the NLD were arrested in connection with the protests. In January 1997 14 people, including at least five NLD members, were convicted of involvement in the unrest and sentenced to seven years' imprisonment.

In January 1997 Suu Kyi was allowed to deliver her weekly speech for the first time in three months. However, the SLORC imposed new restrictions on media access to Suu Kyi, and barricades remained outside her home. In March there were further arrests of NLD members, together with an increased army presence in several towns. Also in March a series of attacks on Muslim targets by Buddhist monks took place across the country. These attacks were rumoured to have been organized by opponents within the regime of Myanmar's application to join the Association of South East Asian Nations (ASEAN, see p. 172), in an attempt to alienate Muslim-dominated members of the grouping. Schools were closed, but reopened in August, while universities remained closed.

In early April 1997 a bomb attack at the home of the Second Secretary of the SLORC, Tin Oo, resulted in the death of his daughter. The Government attributed the bombing to anti-Government groups based in Japan; however, major opposition groups in exile denied involvement in the attack, which was denounced by the NLD. The attack was rumoured to be related to a power struggle between Khin Nyunt, who was increasingly regarded as a moderate, and the more conservative Commander-in-Chief of the Army and Vice-Chair of the SLORC, Gen. Maung Aye, who commanded the support of Tin Oo. The detention of NLD members increased during 1997, while government propaganda vilifying the opposition grew more frequent and Suu Kyi's freedom of movement and association remained restricted. In December the SLORC announced that Kyi Maung had resigned as Vice-Chairman of the NLD as a result of conflict between himself and Suu Kyi, a claim dismissed as false by the NLD. In July 1997, however, Khin Nyunt invited the NLD Chairman, Aung Shwe, to a meeting, which constituted the first high-level contact between the SLORC and the NLD since the release of Suu Kyi from house arrest in July 1995. A further meeting between the SLORC leadership and the NLD was due to take place in September, but was cancelled by the opposition, who insisted that future discussions required the participation of Suu Kyi in her capacity as Secretary-General of the NLD. The SLORC granted permission for an NLD congress to be held in September.

On 15 November 1997 the ruling junta unexpectedly announced the dissolution of the SLORC and its replacement with the State Peace and Development Council (SPDC). The 19-member SPDC comprised exclusively military personnel; younger regional military commanders were included (largely to prevent them from developing local power bases), whilst the four most senior members of the SLORC retained their positions at the head of the new junta: Than Shwe was appointed Chairman, Maung Aye Vice-Chairman, Khin Nyunt First Secretary and Tin Oo Second Secretary. A number of former members of the SLORC were ostensibly promoted to an 'Advisory Group', which was, however, subsequently abolished; five members of this group, who had also held positions in the Cabinet, were placed under house arrest in December, pending investigations into allegations of corruption. The SPDC immediately implemented a reorganization of the Cabinet. The new 40-member Cabinet included 25 former ministers, but, in contrast to the SLORC (the members of which had virtually all held cabinet portfolios), only one member of the SPDC, Than Shwe, was appointed to serve concurrently as a cabinet minister. Among the more junior members of the Cabinet were an increased number of civilian appointees, largely selected from the USDA. The restructuring of the junta and the Cabinet appeared to benefit Khin Nyunt, as several supporters of Maung Aye were removed from power. In December the SPDC announced a further cabinet reorganization and the appointment of a new Chairman (the Minister of Hotels and Tourism, Maj.-Gen. Saw Lwin) and Vice-Chairmen of the National Convention Convening Commission; however, the Convention, which had adjourned in March 1996, remained in recess.

Harassment and persecution of members of the NLD and other opposition movements continued throughout 1998. In March 40 people were arrested on charges of complicity in a conspiracy allegedly led by the exiled All-Burma Students Democratic Front (ABSDF, an armed movement formed in 1988 by students within the DAB, which had officially renounced its armed struggle in 1997) to assassinate leaders of the military junta and initiate terrorist attacks on government offices and foreign embassies. The ABSDF, which rejected the allegations, was accused of complicity with the NLD. Six of the accused were sentenced to death at the end of April. However, the SPDC unexpectedly authorized an NLD party congress, attended by 400 delegates, at the end of May to celebrate the eighth anniversary of the general election. In June the NLD demanded that the SPDC reconvene the Pyithu Hluttaw, in accordance with the results of the 1990 election, by 21 August. Some 40 elected NLD representatives were detained at the end of June, and others were forced to sign pledges restricting their freedom of movement. In July the SPDC ordered NLD elected representatives to report to their local police station twice a day and confined them to their townships. During July and August Suu Kyi attempted to visit NLD members outside the city, in an effort to exert pressure on the SPDC to comply with the NLD's demands. On four separate occasions the opposition leader was prevented from continuing her journey by road-blocks set up by the ruling junta. On one such occasion in July Suu Kyi was forcibly returned to her home by security forces after a six-day protest in her car, following government refusals to comply with her demands for the release of detained opposition members and the commencement of substantive dialogue with the NLD. In a further incident in August, she was returned to her home by ambulance after spending 13 days in her car, prompting considerable international criticism of the SPDC. During Suu Kyi's protest in August Khin Nyunt held a reportedly cordial meeting with the NLD Chairman, Aung Shwe.

Shortly before the NLD's prescribed deadline for convening the Pyithu Hluttaw, the SPDC published an official rejection of the NLD's demands. The NLD responded by declaring its intention unilaterally to convene a 'People's Parliament', which would include elected representatives of all the ethnic minority groups. On the day that Suu Kyi abandoned her protest at the road-block, student demonstrations took place in Yangon (for the first time since December 1996), in support of the NLD's demands. In September thousands of students staged anti-Government demonstrations, which were dispersed by security forces. Arrests of opposition activists increased dramatically, and by early September 193 elected NLD members of the Pyithu Hluttaw and hundreds of party supporters had been detained. In the same month a 10-member Representative Committee, led by Suu Kyi and Aung Shwe, was established by the NLD to act on behalf of the 'People's Parliament' until a legislature could be convened under the 1990 election law. The Committee (which claimed a mandate based on the authorization of more than one-half of the representatives of the Pyithu Hluttaw elected in 1990, many of whom were in detention) asserted that all laws passed by the military junta over the previous 10 years had no legal authority, and also demanded the immediate and unconditional release of all political prisoners. Four parties representing Shan, Mon, Arakanese and Zomi ethnic groups expressed their support for the 'People's Parliament', together with the ABSDF. In the same month 15 senior military officers were reportedly arrested for allegedly planning to meet with Suu Kyi, and a number of large pro-Government rallies were held in Yangon. The NLD condemned the alleged use of coercion, intimidation and threats by government military intelligence units to secure the involuntary resignations of vast numbers of NLD members and the closure of a number of regional party headquarters. Following the death in custody in October of a member of the NLD, detained by the SPDC since early the previous month, the NLD also formally condemned the junta's treatment of detained opposition party members in a letter to Than Shwe. (In August of the same year an elected representative of the NLD, Saw Win, had died in prison while serving an 11-year term of imprisonment, the third NLD member of the Pyithu Hluttaw to die in custody.) In October UN Assistant Secretary-General Alvaro de Soto met with SPDC leaders and also with Suu Kyi during a visit to Myanmar. He reportedly offered large-scale financial and humanitarian aid to the junta in exchange for the initiation of substantive dialogue with the NLD. During October and November about 300 opposition members were released by the Government; however, a further 500 were believed to remain in detention.

In March 1999, despite requests from several foreign Governments, the ruling junta refused to grant a visa to Suu Kyi's terminally ill husband, Michael Aris. The junta instead encouraged Suu Kyi to visit Aris in the United Kingdom; however, Suu Kyi declined to leave the country for fear that she would not be permitted to return. Following Aris's death later the same month, more than 1,000 supporters of Suu Kyi were permitted to attend a Buddhist ceremony at Suu Kyi's home marking her husband's demise.

In April 1999 the UN adopted a unanimous resolution deploring the escalation in the persecution of the democratic opposition in Myanmar. Nevertheless, the harassment and intimidation of NLD members continued, with the resignations from the party of nearly 300 members reported in July 1999; further resignations were reported in November and in January 2000. In December 1999 it was reported that an elected representative of the People's Assembly, U Maung Maung Myint, had been forced to resign by the ruling SPDC. The lack of political progress by the NLD in 1999 led to the formation of a breakaway faction of the party by a prominent party member, Than Tun, who was subsequently expelled from the NLD.

In August 1999 a series of protests was staged by opposition supporters to mark the anniversary of the massacre of thousands of pro-democracy demonstrators by the military Government in 1988. In October the Supreme Court rejected a claim by the NLD that its activities had been 'continuously disrupted, prevented and destroyed' and that hundreds of its members had been illegally detained. In April 2000 Suu Kyi alleged that more than 40 youth members of the NLD had been arrested by the SPDC for their involvement in party activities. In May the NLD called upon the military Government to end the use of forced labour and to recognize the results of the 1990 election.

Opposition radio sources continued to give details of small-scale protests throughout 2000 and 2001. A rare bomb explosion in May 2001 reportedly killed 12 people and injured eight others in a market in Mandalay. In the same month it was reported that religious riots in Toungoo, Pegu province, had led to the deaths of 24 Buddhist monks. The disturbances spread to other towns, prompting allegations that the SPDC had instigated the riots in an attempt to divert public attention from political and economic problems.

Aung San Suu Kyi also continued her persistent opposition to the SPDC. In August 2000 Suu Kyi and 14 NLD colleagues attempted to visit members of the party in Kunyangon, a town just outside Yangon. The group was stopped by a military road-block, but refused to return home. A nine-day stand-off finally ended with Suu Kyi and the NLD members being forcibly returned to Yangon. Suu Kyi and eight others were kept under house arrest for the next two weeks. In early September the SPDC raided the NLD headquarters, and detained a number of other party leaders in their homes. Undeterred, the NLD announced that it was to draft a new constitution for the country, an act declared illegal in 1996 and punishable by 20 years' imprisonment. Later in the month Suu Kyi attempted to leave Yangon again, this time by train to Mandalay, only to be told that all trains were full. The NLD leader was once again returned home and placed under house arrest, while NLD Vice-Chairman Tin Oo and eight other party workers were taken to a government 'guest house'. Pressure on the NLD increased in October 2000, when a deadline for an eviction order for the party to vacate its premises expired. The landladies responsible for the eviction order had been incarcerated by the SPDC for allowing the NLD to use loudspeakers, but claimed that their decision to evict had not been influenced by external coercion.

Despite the sustained suppression of the opposition party and the prevention of protest, the SPDC's treatment of its political rivals became markedly more liberal from mid-2000. In July the SPDC reportedly allowed 60,000 university students to resume their education. The undergraduate universities, however, were relocated in the suburbs, in order to avoid demonstrations in the city centres that might draw in other civilians. Razali Ismail, a Malaysian diplomat newly appointed as the UN Secretary-General's Special Envoy to Myanmar, was allowed access to Suu Kyi during a four-day visit in October 2000, and in the same month James Mawdsley, a British human rights activist sentenced to 17 years' imprisonment in Myanmar in September 1999, was released (see below).

Conciliation between the SPDC and the NLD was confirmed in early January 2001, when it was announced that the two parties had been holding secret talks since October, the first high-level discussions between the opponents since 1994. Lt-Gen. Khin Nyunt met with Suu Kyi several times, although the details of the talks remained closely guarded. Some analysts feared that the resumption of discussions was merely a cynical ploy by the Government to attract foreign investment and curb economic sanctions, a view supported by the fact there was little initial evidence of progress.

In January 2001, in a further placatory gesture, the SPDC ordered the media to stop the regular acrimonious attacks on Suu Kyi and the NLD. In the same month the government-controlled Yangon division court dismissed a lawsuit brought by Suu Kyi's US-based brother, Aung San Oo, who claimed ownership of half of Suu Kyi's house. Although foreigners cannot buy or transfer property in Myanmar, San Oo had been granted an exemption from the Government in July 2000, and thus requested half the family property according to Myanma inheritance law. In October 2001, however, the court rejected Suu Kyi's application to have her brother's claim dismissed. The hearing was subsequently adjourned on several occasions and in December 2003 was postponed until February 2004. At the end of January 2001 the SPDC released NLD Vice-Chairman Tin Oo and 84 other party supporters, who had been detained since Suu Kyi's attempted train journey in September 2000. A few days later a delegation of the European Union (EU, see p. 228) was permitted to meet with Suu Kyi, as was Dr Paulo Sérgio Pinheiro, UN human rights envoy to Myanmar, in April 2001.

In February 2001 Lt-Gen. Tin Oo, the army chief of staff and, as the Council's Second Secretary, the SPDC's fourth most powerful member, was killed in a helicopter crash. While the accident was officially attributed to bad weather and mechanical failure, there were rumours of an assassination, as Lt-Gen. Tin Oo had survived two previous attempts on his life, in 1996 and 1997.

In mid-2001, as discussions continued, the Government ordered the release of a number of NLD members from prison and permitted the reopening of the NLD headquarters and several branch offices in Yangon. However, in July Suu Kyi failed to attend Martyrs' Day ceremonies held in Yangon to commemorate the assassination of her father in 1947, prompting speculation that talks with the Government were foundering, a rumour denied by the SPDC. In August the release of Aung Shwe, Chairman of the NLD, and of Vice-Chairman Tin Oo, was hailed as an indication of progress. Shortly afterwards Ismail held further discussions with Suu Kyi during a visit to Yangon.

In November 2001 two senior army generals—Lt-Gen. Win Myint (widely regarded as the fourth most powerful individual in the country) and Deputy Prime Minister Tin Hla—were dismissed. While no official explanation was given, the two men were under investigation for corruption. As both had expressed only muted support for the ongoing talks with Suu Kyi, there was also speculation that their replacement would be more conducive to the attainment of a political settlement. Two days later the SPDC announced that five government ministers were to retire. While two Deputy Prime Ministers, Rear Adm. Maung Maung Khin and Lt-Gen. Tin Tun, had been expected to step down, the departure of Win Sein, Minister of Culture, Aung San, Minister of Co-operatives, and Saw Tun, Minister of Immigration and Population, had not been foreseen. No official explanation was given for the changes. However, it was thought that their removal constituted an attempt to improve the Government's corrupt and anti-democratic image. In the same month Razali Ismail visited the country again. Upon his departure, Ismail expressed satisfaction with the progress that had been made.

In January 2002 it was reported that Suu Kyi had met privately with Gen. Than Shwe for the first time since 1994, raising hopes that the two sides might be close to reaching a breakthrough. However, in February 2002 international pressure on the SPDC to release all remaining political prisoners (an estimated 1,500, according to Amnesty International) and begin a more substantive dialogue with the NLD increased, prompted by the release of a critical report by the US Government (see below). The Myanma Government responded by releasing five further detainees and expressing its confidence that a successful conclusion to the negotiation process was imminent.

In March 2002 the son-in-law and three grandsons of U Ne Win were arrested on charges of plotting to overthrow the Government. It was alleged that they had intended to abduct three government leaders and force them to form a figurehead government under U Ne Win's influence. Four senior military officials—the Commander-in-Chief of the Air Force, Maj.-Gen. Myint Swe, the Chief of Police, Maj.-Gen. Soe Win, and two regional commanders—were dismissed and questioned in connection with the attempted coup. Ne Win and his daughter, Sandar Win, were placed under house arrest. Despite suspicions that the coup allegations were linked to internal conflicts within the military, owing to the insubstantial nature of the evidence gathered to support the charges, it was announced in April that those arrested would stand trial for high treason. In September, following their trial, U Ne Win's four relatives were convicted and sentenced to death. They entered appeals against the sentences. In December U Ne Win himself died while under house arrest.

In May 2002 Aung San Suu Kyi was finally released from house arrest. The SPDC stated that her release was unconditional and that it would not attempt to impose any restrictions upon her travel. Shortly afterwards Suu Kyi urged the immediate resumption of dialogue with the junta, which had ceased following her liberation. In June she travelled to Mandalay on her first political trip since she was freed; the journey passed without incident. In August Razali Ismail returned to the country with the intention of promoting further political dialogue between the NLD and the SPDC, but made little progress. Meanwhile, Suu Kyi challenged the SPDC to prove its commitment to the achievement of democracy by ordering the release of all political prisoners. In the following month a delegation from the EU visited Myanmar and met with Suu Kyi, but failed to secure a meeting with any members of the SPDC. In November the junta announced the release of 115 prisoners, the largest number to have been freed since negotiations began. However, the releases were dismissed by both the USA and human rights groups as inadequate.

In early 2003 representatives from Amnesty International were permitted to enter Myanmar for the first time and to hold talks with Aung San Suu Kyi. Following the visit, the human rights organization condemned Myanmar's judicial system. Meanwhile, 12 political activists in the country were arrested on suspicion of planning anti-Government activities. In February it was reported that Suu Kyi wanted economic sanctions to be maintained against the Myanma Government until it began a meaningful dialogue with the opposition. In the same month it was announced that Lt-Gen. Soe Win would assume the previously vacant post of Second Secretary of the SPDC. Meanwhile, the Minister of Health, Maj.-Gen. Ket Sein, and the Minister of Finance and Revenue, U Khin Maung Thein, were permitted to retire. They were replaced, respectively, by Dr Kyaw Myint and Maj.-Gen. Hla Tun. In the following month UN envoy Paulo Sérgio Pinheiro restated a UN demand that the junta release all remaining political prisoners, estimated to number 1,200, and enter into serious dialogue with the opposition. Later that month a bomb exploded in Yangon, killing one person, during celebrations being held to commemorate Armed Forces Day. An unexploded bomb was also discovered near the US embassy on the same day.

In April 2003, during a news conference, Aung San Suu Kyi issued a rare criticism of the SPDC for refusing to enter into any substantive dialogue with the opposition. In May 10 members of the NLD were imprisoned on charges that they had organized public protests and participated in clandestine activities. Later in the same month the political situation in Myanmar deteriorated further when violent confrontations occurred in the town of Ye-u, in the north of the country, between government supporters and opposition members travelling with an entourage carrying Aung San Suu Kyi. While the SPDC insisted that the violence had been provoked by the opposition, it was subsequently reported that the clashes had occurred when Suu Kyi and her supporters were ambushed and attacked by pro-Government forces. It was estimated that around 80 members of the entourage had died as a result. On the following day it was reported that Suu Kyi had been taken into 'protective custody' by the SPDC; meanwhile, the headquarters of the NLD, together with NLD offices across the country, were closed down, 17 other members of the NLD were also detained, and all universities under the control of the Ministry of Education were shut indefinitely. In June UN envoy Razali Ismail proceeded with a planned visit to Myanmar. Ismail was permitted to meet with Suu Kyi and confirmed that she had not sustained any injuries during the recent violence. The junta's detention of Suu Kyi prompted widespread international criticism. At a meeting of ASEAN ministers of foreign affairs held later in that month the organization transgressed its traditional policy of non-interference in the affairs of other member states, calling for Suu Kyi to be freed and for Myanmar to make a peaceful transition to democratic practices. Later in June, following the failure of its appeal to the SPDC for the liberation of Suu Kyi, the country's largest aid donor, Japan, announced that it had suspended all economic aid. In July the Government announced that it had freed 91 of the NLD activists detained after the violence of May and permitted a delegation from the International Committee of the Red Cross (ICRC) to visit Suu Kyi; the delegates subsequently confirmed that she was in good health, contradicting reports from the US Department of State, which claimed that she had gone on a hunger strike.

In July 2003 it was reported that three cabinet Ministers—Minister of Industry (No. 1) U Aung Thaung, Minister of Forestry Aung Phone and Minister of Agriculture and Irrigation Maj.-Gen. Nyunt Tin—had all been dismissed. In late August a major reorganization of the Government was announced, during which the former First Secretary of the SPDC, Gen. Khin Nyunt, replaced Field Marshal Than Shwe as Prime Minister. Than Shwe retained the defence portfolio, however. Lt-Gen. Soe Win became First Secretary and was replaced as Second Secretary by Lt-Gen. Thein Sein. Khin Nyunt subsequently announced that the Government intended to reconvene the National Convention, which had been in recess since 1996, in order to draw up a new constitution and move towards the holding of new elections. However, no schedule was announced for the proposed developments, leading to criticism that the announcement was merely an attempt to encourage the removal of international sanctions against the country and the resumption of aid.

In September 2003 it was announced that Aung San Suu Kyi had returned to her home and was being held under house arrest, having undergone major surgery in hospital. A visit to Myanmar by Razali Ismail in the following month failed to secure her release or to end the political deadlock. Paulo Sérgio Pinheiro returned to the country in late October. In November five members of the NLD's Central Executive Committee, who had been held in connection with the violence in May, were released. In December nine people were sentenced to death, having been convicted of high treason; they were amongst 12 people arrested in July for allegedly plotting to overthrow the ruling junta. (Four of the nine people subsequently had their sentences commuted to two years on appeal, and that of another was reduced to five years, while the remaining four were to face life imprisonment.) In January 2004 the release of a further 26 members of the NLD was announced and, in the following month, Vice-Chairman of the NLD Tin Oo was released into house arrest, having been imprisoned since May 2003. Also in January 2004, following a meeting with government officials, representatives from 25 ethnic groups and alliances rejected the proposed 'road map' to democracy outlined by Prime Minister Gen. Khin Nyunt in August 2003 and reiterated demands for the Government to begin talks with the opposition. However, following a visit to the country in March, Razali Ismail expressed confidence that the SPDC would adhere to the 'road map' and proclaimed his trip to have been a success. In April the SPDC released the NLD's Chairman, Aung Shwe, and its Secretary, U Lwin, who had both been under house arrest since May 2003, and reopened the party's headquarters.

The National Convention was reconvened in mid-May 2004, despite a boycott by some ethnic minority groups and the NLD, which demanded that the SPDC release Suu Kyi and Tin Oo from house arrest and reopen the party's branch offices. (It was reported that Khin Nyunt had favoured freeing Suu Kyi to allow her to participate in the Convention, but that Than Shwe had ordered that she be excluded.) More than 1,000 delegates attended the opening session, which was chaired by Lt-Gen. Thein Sein, the SPDC Second Secretary. It was emphasized that the Convention was to be a continuation of the discussions held between 1993 and 1996, at which a number of constitutional provisions had already been drafted (see above). Strict regulations governing the conduct of the delegates were imposed by the SPDC. Criticism of the proceedings could lead to up to 20 years' imprisonment, distribution of unauthorized information from the talks was banned, and delegates were forbidden from expressing disloyalty to the state or discussing any issues not included in the official agenda. The National Convention was adjourned in July. In August courts in Yangon and Mandalay refused to accept petitions from the NLD for the release of Suu Kyi and Tin Oo, and for the reopening of the party's branch offices. Shortly afterwards the UN Secretary-General, Kofi Annan, released a statement urging the Myanma Government to free Suu Kyi and to hold substantive talks with the NLD and other political parties, noting that the National Convention would otherwise lack credibility. Meanwhile, Razali Ismail had been unable to return to Myanmar since his visit in March, as the authorities had rejected his requests for a visa. In September four members of the NLD were reportedly convicted of threatening national security and sentenced to seven years' imprisonment.

In mid-September 2004 a cabinet reorganization took place. Most notably, the civilian Minister of Foreign Affairs, U Win Aung, and his deputy, Khin Maung Win, were replaced by senior military officers Maj.-Gen. Nyan Win and Col Maung Myint, respectively. The changes appeared to reinforce Than Shwe's authority over the Government, as Win Aung was reported to be an ally of Prime Minister Khin Nyunt, who was perceived to be considerably more committed to reform than the SPDC Chairman. Amid reports of a power struggle within the SPDC, Khin Nyunt was removed from the premiership and from his position as Chief of Military Intelligence in October, and was placed under house arrest, apparently owing to his alleged involvement in corruption related to smuggling by military intelligence staff. Lt-Gen. Soe Win was appointed as Prime Minister, while Lt-Gen. Thein Sein replaced Soe Win as First Secretary of the SPDC. The National Intelligence Bureau was abolished, and associates of Khin Nyunt, including several members of his family and many military intelligence officers, were subsequently arrested. In November it was reported that three senior military intelligence officers had been convicted of corruption charges and sentenced to 22 years' imprisonment, and that 12 senior judicial officials, who were either linked to Khin Nyunt or had resisted the purge of those loyal to the former Prime Minister, had been dismissed. Meanwhile, in early November the SPDC announced that the Minister of Home Affairs, Col Tin Hlaing, the Minister of Science and Technology and of Labour, Tin Win, and four deputy ministers had been permitted to retire. It was reported that Tin Hlaing, an ally of Khin Nyunt, had also been placed under house arrest.

In late November 2004 the SPDC ordered the release of 9,248 prisoners who, it claimed, had been wrongly imprisoned owing to improper conduct by the dissolved National Intelligence Bureau. According to the opposition, however, the mass amnesty included only 43 of an estimated 1,300 political prisoners held by the authorities. Moreover, the NLD announced that Aung San Suu Kyi's detention under house arrest had been extended for at least a further year. In mid-December the SPDC freed a further 5,070 prisoners, 11 of whom were reported to be political prisoners, including the Chairman of the Democracy Party, U Thu Wai. However, a number of NLD members were arrested in the same month for allegedly inciting public unrest. In January 2005 widespread rumours of a gun battle involving Maung Aye, Than Shwe, Soe Win and their aides, which were prompted by the unexplained death of Maung Aye's personal assistant, Lt-Col Bo Win Tun, appeared to be unfounded, although speculation about tension within the leadership continued. In the same month it was reported that four associates of Khin Nyunt who had been arrested in October had died in detention, while the closed trials of some 300 others on corruption charges had commenced in a prison in Yangon. The National Convention resumed in mid-February, again without the participation of the NLD and several ethnic minority groups and amid criticism from the EU, the UN and the USA. A few days earlier Tin Oo's detention under house arrest had been extended for a further year.

Following months of speculation, in July 2005 it was announced at the ASEAN Ministerial Meeting held in the Laotian capital of Vientiane that Myanmar was to relinquish the chair of ASEAN, which it had been due to assume in 2006. Myanmar had recently come under increasing pressure from the international community, and in particular from the other member states of ASEAN (a notable departure from the organization's usual policy of non-interference in the internal affairs of members), to forgo its turn to assume the rotating chair in order to enable the Myanma Government instead to focus its attention on addressing the country's human rights situation. Also in July former Prime Minister Khin Nyunt was convicted on eight charges, including corruption and bribery, and was given a suspended prison sentence of 44 years; his two sons were also convicted and sentenced to prison terms. In the same month the Government authorized the release of dozens of political prisoners; however, in September the UN Special Rapporteur for human rights in Myanmar, Paulo Sérgio Pinheiro, stated in an address to the UN General Assembly that approximately 1,100 dissidents remained in detention in Myanmar. Pinheiro's report was based on information derived from various independent sources, as Pinheiro himself had been repeatedly refused entry to Myanmar since November 2003. In August 2005 UN Special Envoy to Myanmar Ali Alatas had been allowed to visit the country, the first special envoy to be granted entry since Razali Ismail in March 2004.

Meanwhile, in August 2005 the World Food Programme published a report stating that one-third of young children in Myanmar were malnourished; in some border areas afflicted by fighting between rival ethnic rebel groups, the figure was believed to be as high as 60%. The report also noted with concern the high number of Myanma children who received little or no formal education. In September Amnesty International released a report detailing the 'unacceptable' use by the military of tens of thousands of ethnic minority citizens to carry out forced labour; the report also drew attention to the military's use of physical abuse against such labourers.

In November 2005 the Government announced that it had initiated the first phase of a relocation of the country's administrative capital from Yangon to Pyinmana, a sparsely populated mountainous region approximately 400 km (nearly 250 miles) to the north of Yangon. Minister of Information Brig.-Gen. Kyaw Hsan announced that the decision to move to Pyinmana had been made owing to its central location and resultant ease of access to and from other parts of the country. However, various popular theories abounded about alternative motives for the transfer, including a fear of invasion by the USA. In the same month the NLD announced that Aung San Suu Kyi's detention under house arrest had again been extended by an additional 12 months.

In January 2006, after having being refused access to the country for almost two years, Razali Ismail, the UN Secretary-General's Special Envoy to Myanmar, relinquished his post. In a statement announcing his decision to resign, Ismail urged ASEAN to adopt a more forceful role in exerting pressure for democratic reform in Myanmar. Earlier that month the US-based organization Human Rights Watch had dismissed the junta's pledges of democratic reform as 'empty rhetoric'. In late January the junta adjourned a session of the National Convention, with a view to reconvening towards the end of 2006. Critics continued to denounce the proceedings as worthless, given that the delegates in attendance had all been selected by the country's military rulers. In February U Win Aung went on trial in Yangon, charged with corruption and bribery; in April the former Minister of Foreign Affairs was convicted and sentenced to seven years' imprisonment. Meanwhile, in February the detention under house arrest of Tin Oo was again extended by a further year. In May UN envoy Ibrahim Gambari was permitted to enter the country. He held discussions with Than Shwe and also had a brief meeting with Suu Kyi.

After Burma gained independence in 1948, various groups conducted armed insurgency campaigns against government forces. The most effective of the ethnic-based insurgency groups was the Karen (Kayin) National Union (KNU), founded in 1948, which led a protracted campaign for the establishment of an independent state for the Karen ethnic group (restyled Kayin in the transliteration changes of 1989), partly through the activities of its military wing, the Karen (Kayin) National Liberation Army (KNLA). The KNU was a member of the National Democratic Front (NDF), an organization which at one time comprised 11 ethnic minority groups—including Kachin, Karenni (Kayinni), Mon, Shan, Pa-O, Palaung, Wa, Arakanese (Rakhine) and Lahu parties—formed in 1975 (by five groups, originally) with the aim of making Burma a federal union and opposing both the Government and, initially, the CPB. The CPB was one of the most well-organized insurgent movements, in military terms, and gained control of significant areas in northern Burma. By May 1986 the various minority groups in the NDF had agreed to relinquish their individual demands for autonomy, in favour of a unified demand for a federal system of government. At the same time, the CPB withdrew its demand for a 'one-party' government and entered into an alliance with the NDF. At the second NDF Congress in June 1987, Maj.-Gen. Bo Mya, the President of the KNU and Chief of Staff of the KNLA, was replaced as NDF President by Saw Maw Reh, a former Chairman of the Karenni (Kayinni) National Progressive Party (KNPP), and further leadership changes removed all KNU representatives from senior NDF positions. The new NDF leaders advocated the establishment of autonomous, ethnic-based states within a Burmese union.

The insurgent groups were sympathetic to anti-Government movements in the major cities. Continued attacks throughout 1988 engaged the government forces in the border areas, leaving fewer of them to impose order in the towns. In September the Karens announced plans to co-operate with protesting students and Buddhist monks to work towards the achievement of democracy. After the armed forces seized power, insurgents intensified operations, aided by at least 3,000 students whom the Karen rebels agreed to train and arm. In November 22 anti-Government groups, led by members of the NDF, formed the DAB. Bo Mya was elected President.

In April 1989 dissatisfaction with the leadership of the CPB led to a mutiny by Wa tribesmen, who constituted an estimated 80%–90% of the CPB's membership. Rebellious Wa soldiers captured the CPB headquarters, and the party's leaders were forced into exile in the People's Republic of China. The leaders of the mutiny subsequently accepted SLORC proposals for the former forces of the CPB army to become government-controlled militia forces in exchange for supplies of rice, financial support and development aid. The former CPB troops agreed to use their main forces against the 25,000-strong rebel separatist Mong Tai

(Shan State) Army (formerly the Shan United Army), whose leader, Khun Sa, controlled much of the drug trade in the 'Golden Triangle', the world's major opium-producing area, where the borders of Myanmar, Laos and Thailand meet. The SLORC also approached members of the NDF, and was successful in securing agreements with the Shan State Progressive Party in September 1989, the Pa-O National Organization in March 1991 and the Palaung State Liberation Organization in May of that year. In July, at the third NDF Congress, these three movements were expelled, reducing the NDF's membership to eight organizations, and Nai Shwe Kyin was elected as the NDF's new President.

In December 1988, following a visit by the Prime Minister of Thailand, the SLORC granted licences to Thai business interests to exploit raw materials in Burma, in return for much-needed foreign exchange. Although there was no announcement of any official Thai-Burmese agreement, subsequent offensives by government forces against rebel groups achieved unprecedented success, with troops frequently attacking insurgent bases from Thai territory. By December 1989 six KNU bases along the Thai border had been captured, and in January 1990 two more camps, harbouring a large number of student dissidents, were seized. In January 1990 the armed forces launched an offensive against Mon separatists. In February they succeeded in capturing Three Pagodas Pass, a principal 'black market' trade route between Thailand and Myanmar, and the headquarters of the New Mon State Party.

Intense fighting between government and rebel forces continued as the KNLA advanced into the lower central Ayeyarwady (Irrawaddy) Delta in late 1991. This potentially diversionary tactic failed to prevent a concerted attempt by government troops to seize control of the KNU and DAB headquarters, which was also the seat of the NCGUB. However, despite the use of sophisticated weaponry purchased from the People's Republic of China, government troops failed to capture the camp at Manerplaw. In March 1992 the Thai Government fulfilled prior threats of strong retaliation, forcing hundreds of Myanma troops out of entrenched positions taken up in order to attack the KNU headquarters from the rear. In April the SLORC officially suspended its offensive against the KNU, 'in the interests of national unity'. In October, however, government troops resumed hostilities, making several incursions into Thai territory. In December the Thai and Myanma Governments agreed to 'relocate' the Myanma armed forces, and in February 1993 they resolved to demarcate their common border.

In February and March 1993 the Kachin Independence Organization (KIO) attended peace talks with the Government in the Kachin state capital of Myitkyina. The Kachins were in a vulnerable position, since they were no longer able to obtain arms from the practically defunct CPB or through Thailand (as the Mong Tai Army controlled the territory between Kachin encampments and the Thai border). The SLORC was anxious to reach an accommodation with the Kachins, as the NCGUB would be severely weakened by the loss of their support (although a *de facto* national cease-fire had been in effect since October 1992). The KIO appeared to have signed a peace agreement in April but, owing to attempts by the Kachins to persuade other members of the DAB to enter discussions with the SLORC, the cease-fire was not announced until October. The agreement was ratified in Yangon in February 1994. The KIO was suspended from the DAB in October 1993 for negotiating separately with the SLORC, and the DAB reiterated its conditions for discussions with the SLORC in a series of open letters. Its stipulations included: the recognition of the DAB as a single negotiating body (the SLORC insisted on meeting each ethnic group separately); the location of the negotiating process in a neutral country; an immediate end to the forcible mass relocation of villagers; a new body to draft a constitution; and the release of all political detainees, beginning with Suu Kyi. Under Thai pressure, however, the DAB policy of negotiating as a front was unofficially abandoned. In February 2001 there were rumours of a coup within the KIO, as Chairman Lt-Gen. Zau Mai was replaced by his deputy, Maj.-Gen. Tu Jai. The rumours were swiftly denied, the reason for the replacement being given as Zau Nai's ill health.

In May 1994 the Karenni (Kayinni) National People's Liberation Front concluded a cease-fire agreement with the SLORC, reportedly the 11th insurgent group to do so. This was followed in July by the declaration of a cease-fire by the Kayan New Land Party, and in October by the declaration of a cease-fire by the Shan State Nationalities Liberation Organization. In December government forces launched a new offensive against the KNU, recapturing its headquarters at Manerplaw in January 1995 (and forcing many hundreds of KNU fighters across the border into Thailand). The virtual defeat of the KNU forces was attributed to their reportedly severe lack of ammunition and funds and also to the recent defection from the Christian-led KNU of a mainly Buddhist faction, which established itself as the Democratic Karen (Kayin) Buddhist Army (DKBA). The DKBA, which had comprised about 10% of the strength of the KNLA, allegedly supported the government forces in their offensive. In February 1995 the Myanma army captured the KNU's last stronghold, and in the following month Bo Mya resigned as the Commander-in-Chief of the KNLA (although he remained the leader of the KNU). In March the KNU declared a unilateral cease-fire, with the aim of initiating negotiations with the SLORC. Earlier in the month the KNPP reportedly became the 14th ethnic insurgent group to abandon its armed struggle against the SLORC. This agreement collapsed in June, however, as government troops entered areas designated in the accord to be under KNPP control. In August 5,000 troops were dispatched to suppress the KNPP rebellion. Clashes continued throughout the year, and in January 1996 government forces captured a major Kayinni stronghold. The KNPP continued fighting, however, with support from the ABSDF. In February 1996 talks between the KNU and the SLORC in Mawlamyine (Moulmein), calling for tripartite negotiations between the NLD, the NCGUB (which had re-elected Sein Win as its head in Sweden in July 1995) and the SLORC, were inconclusive.

Further talks between the SLORC and the KNU began in November 1996, but had collapsed by December. In January 1997 the DKBA, allegedly supported by government forces, attacked Kayin refugee camps in Thailand. The KNU claimed that requests in late January for further peace negotiations were rejected by the SLORC, which then initiated a new offensive against the KNU. Fighting between the KNU and government forces continued in March, forcing several thousand Kayins across the border into Thailand. As a result of the forcible relocation of tens of thousands of Kayins away from KNU bases in Myanmar during 1997, further refugees fled to Thailand. The Thai armed forces denied collusion with the Myanma troops in the process of forced repatriations of Kayin refugees, who were believed to number more than 100,000 in mid-1997. In March 1998 the DKBA, supported by government troops, launched two further attacks on Kayin refugee camps in Thailand, prompting a retaliatory attack by the KNU on DKBA forces. In April 1999 the KNU issued a statement confirming the deaths of seven members of a group of 13 government officials whom they had abducted in February; the remaining six were said to have been released unharmed.

In January 2000 it was reported that 800–1,000 Kayins had fled across the border into Thailand, following clashes between government forces and the KNU. In the same month Gen. Bo Mya was succeeded as the leader of the KNU by the former Secretary-General of the organization, Saw Ba Thin. Following his appointment as leader, Ba Thin announced that, while the KNU intended to continue its struggle against the ruling SPDC, the movement was prepared to negotiate a political settlement with the military regime. It was subsequently reported by both government and independent sources that an initial but inconclusive round of talks between the KNU and the SPDC was held in February, followed by further discussions in March. However, in late 2000 the Government began to use 'scorched-earth' tactics to deprive the KNU of its support base, displacing up to 30,000 people in eastern Myanmar.

In January 2001 Johnny and Luther Htoo, teenage leaders of the Karen rebel group, God's Army, surrendered with 12 of their followers to the Thai authorities. While much smaller than the KNU or the KNLA, God's Army had gained international notoriety owing to the leadership of the twin boys, thought to be aged 13 or 14. Two of the 12 members who surrendered were believed to have been involved in a raid on a Thai village that had left six civilians dead in December 2000.

In April 2003 the KNU claimed responsibility for a series of explosions that had destroyed sections of a gas pipeline in Karen State over the previous two months, declaring that they had intended to draw the attention of the international community to the human rights abuses being perpetrated by government troops in the area. Several bombings along the border with Thailand in the following month were also attributed to the KNU. In December, however, Vice-Chairman of the KNU Bo Mya led a personal delegation to Yangon to explore the possibility of a potential cease-fire arrangement with the Government. In January 2004, having unified the KNU behind his initiative, Bo Mya and other KNU officials held talks with government representatives in Yangon, which resulted in the conclusion of an informal cease-fire arrangement between the two sides. Bo Mya had previously made any peace agreement conditional both on the release of Aung San Suu Kyi and other NLD detainees and on the Government's adherence to UN resolutions delineating a return to democracy for the country. At further talks, held in Mawlamyine in February, the KNU and the Government discussed the demarcation of KNU territory, the relocation of the armed forces and the resettlement of some 200,000 internally displaced civilians in Karen State. However, despite the informal cease-fire, sporadic fighting continued between government troops and the KNLA. Further negotiations in Yangon in October were curtailed at the Government's request following the dismissal of Prime Minister Khin Nyunt. Bo Mya retired as Vice-Chairman of the KNU in December because of ill health; he was replaced by Gen. Tamalabaw. In January 2005 10 government troops were reportedly killed in clashes with the KNU after attacking one of the group's bases near the border with Thailand. Later that month the KNU demanded a resumption of the peace talks, which remained stalled. In the mean time, government forces were reported to have launched an offensive against a KNPP stronghold in Yamu, again close to the Thai border.

Meanwhile, in December 1993 the SLORC initiated a major offensive against Khun Sa's Mong Tai Army encampments on the Thai border. During that month Khun Sa convened a Shan 'parliament' in his base of Homong, which was attended by hundreds of delegates. This was followed, in May 1994, by Khun Sa's declaration of an independent Shan State, of which he declared himself 'President'. In the same month fighting intensified between government forces and the Mong Tai Army near the Thai border, with heavy losses reported on both sides. However, Khun Sa claimed that his army retained control of two-thirds of the Shan State. In July he was reported to have offered to end opium cultivation and to surrender to the government forces, in exchange for their withdrawal from the Shan State and a guarantee of Shan independence. In March 1995 government forces launched an intensive campaign, lasting several months, against the Mong Tai Army. In August a faction calling itself the Shan State National Army broke away from the Mong Tai Army, accusing Khun Sa of using Shan nationalism as a 'front' for drugs-trafficking. Khun Sa subsequently offered to relinquish areas under his control to an international force that could ensure the safety of the Shan whilst eradicating illicit drugs. Khun Sa's position was considerably weakened in September, as improving relations between Thailand and Myanmar led to a Thai pledge to close the common border, thus obstructing his supply routes, and cease-fires with neighbouring ethnic groups allowed the Government to deploy troops in hitherto inaccessible areas. Certain ethnic groups, notably the Wa, were also actively engaged in fighting the Mong Tai Army to gain control of the opium trade. In November Khun Sa announced his retirement from all political and military positions, citing his betrayal by the breakaway group. In January 1996 government troops entered Homong without resistance, and thousands of his former supporters surrendered. Although no formal agreement with the SLORC was announced, it was widely believed that Khun Sa had previously negotiated a settlement with the authorities since he was not detained and it was officially announced that he would not be extradited to the USA on drugs-trafficking charges. (Khun Sa was, moreover, later accorded the status of an honoured elder.) The Mong Tai Army was subsequently transformed into a militia volunteer unit under the command of the armed forces.

Between November 1996 and February 1997 there were reports of clashes between the Shan United Revolutionary Party (a faction of the Mong Tai Army that had not surrendered in January 1996) and government forces. In September 1997 the alliance between three of the major Shan groups who continued their resistance—including the Shan State National Army (SSNA), remnants of the MTA, and the Shan State Peace-keeping Council (SSPC) and its military wing, the Shan State Army (SSA)—was formalized, and the groups joined together in an enlarged SSA. In November it was reported that Shan separatist groups had launched a further offensive against government troops. In May 1999 it was reported that at least 300,000 Shan had been forced from their villages into resettlement camps by government troops. Clashes between SSA units and government forces were reported in December. In March 2000, following the group's announcement that it wished to seek a peaceful settlement with the ruling junta, the SSA issued a statement outlining cease-fire terms. It was later claimed by the SSA that these terms had been misinterpreted by the Government. In May several senior army officers died in an SSA ambush. In the following month more than 60 Shan and hill tribespeople, who had been forcibly relocated and had then attempted to return to their village, were reportedly killed by the Myanma military in a retaliatory attack. In similar incidents in the region in June, as many as 50 other villagers were believed to have been murdered. In 2001 the Government launched several offensives against SSA border camps, causing hundreds more Shan to flee the area. In September 2001 the leader of the SSA, Col Yodsuek, stated that the group would be willing to enter into peace talks with the SPDC.

In late 1996 Gen. Maung Aye ordered that the forces of the United Wa State Army (UWSA—who reached an accommodation with the SLORC in 1989) should withdraw from its principal base or surrender to the Government by the end of 1997. As the deadline approached, tension between the two sides increased until the UWSA was given permission to remain at the base for a further year. In January 2000 it was reported that the SPDC was to launch an operation to relocate 50,000 people from UWSA-controlled opium-growing areas with the alleged intention of eradicating the production of drugs in the areas by 2005. The relocation programme began to cause ethnic tension early in 2001, as the Shan complained that the Wa tribespeople were occupying land that they had previously owned. It was also claimed that the Wa were still growing opium, in spite of the fact that the scheme had been introduced supposedly to prevent heroin production. In February 2001 the office of the UN High Commissioner for Refugees (UNHCR) investigated reports that 300,000 Shan had fled over the border to Thailand as a result of the Wa influx.

In late 1989 the SLORC began resettling Bamar (Burman) Buddhists in the predominantly Muslim areas of Arakan (renamed Rakhine), displacing the local Rohingya Muslims. In April 1991 Rohingya refugees were forced over the border into Bangladesh, as a result of the brutal operations of the Myanma armed forces, including the destruction of villages, widespread killings and pillaging. The Rohingyas had been similarly persecuted in 1976–78, when more than 200,000 of them had sought refuge in Bangladesh. The Rohingyas had finally been repatriated, only to lose their citizenship following the introduction of new nationality legislation in 1982. In November 1991 the SLORC pledged to repatriate genuine Myanma citizens, but claimed that many of the refugees were illegal Bengali immigrants. In April 1992 the Myanma and Bangladeshi Governments signed an agreement providing for the repatriation of those Rohingya refugees in possession of official documentation. The repatriation programme was delayed, however, owing to the continuing flow of refugees to Bangladesh (reaching an estimated 270,000 by the end of June). The first Rohingya refugees were returned to Myanmar in September, without the supervision of UNHCR. Despite demonstrations by Rohingyas in Bangladesh against forced repatriation, refugees continued to be returned to Myanmar. The SLORC's agreement, in November 1993, to allow UNHCR access to repatriated Rohingyas was expected to accelerate the programme. In April 1994 guerrillas of the Rohingya Solidarity Organization carried out attacks in the Maungdaw area of Rakhine. By May 1995 more than 216,000 refugees had been repatriated. In July 1999, however, about 20,000 Rohingya refugees remained in camps in Bangladesh, despite the expiry of the official deadline for their repatriation in August 1997. In April 2000 the International Federation of Human Rights Leagues (FIDH) issued a report condemning the treatment of Rohingya Muslims by the Myanma Government, including forced labour, punitive taxes and extrajudicial killings. The FIDH claimed that the regime was attempting to force the exodus of Rohingyas from their native Rakhine and criticized UNHCR for its effective complicity with the Myanma regime in designating the more recent refugees as economic migrants. In February 2001 violence between Buddhist and Muslim communities in the state capital, Sittwe, was reported to have resulted in at least 12 deaths, prompting the Government to regulate further the movement of Rohingya and other Muslims in and out of Rakhine. In 2003 UNHCR assisted more than 3,000 refugees to return to Myanmar from Bangladesh, following the removal of technical restrictions on their repatriation. Nevertheless, around 18,500 remained in camps in Bangladesh, many of whom were reportedly unwilling to return to Myanmar.

The People's Republic of China restored diplomatic relations with Burma in 1978. From 1988, as Burma's international isolation deepened, China assumed an increasingly important role. It became Myanmar's principal aid donor, arms supplier and source of consumer goods, and delayed the passage of UN resolutions that were strongly critical of the SLORC's violations of human rights. In May 1997 an agreement was reached to establish a trade route through Myanmar to provide the Chinese province of Yunnan with access to the Indian Ocean. In the same year the Chinese Government signed a 30-year agreement with Myanmar that allowed for more than 200 Chinese fishing boats to operate in Myanma waters; the agreement was widely perceived as an indication of increasing Chinese influence in Myanmar. Furthermore, China announced the construction in Myanmar of two liquefied petroleum gas plants in October 2000 and also of a dry dock in February 2001. In December 2001 the Chinese President, Jiang Zemin, travelled to Myanmar, becoming the first Chinese Head of State to visit the country since 1985. Before his arrival the Government announced that it had ordered the release of more than 200 Chinese prisoners as a gesture of goodwill. Following successful discussions, the two Governments signed a series of bilateral agreements intended to enhance co-operative ties. It was reported that China had offered Myanmar US $100m. in aid and investment, although this was thought to be linked to Chinese demands that the ruling junta increase its efforts to eradicate the drug trade between the two countries. Relations between the two countries were further strengthened in March 2004, during a visit to Yangon by Chinese Vice-Premier Wu Yi, by the signing of 24 agreements on economic and technical co-operation and, in February 2006, by a visit to Beijing by the Prime Minister of Myanmar, Lt-Gen. Soe Win, during which the two heads of states agreed further to promote cordial bilateral relations.

Japan and the member states of ASEAN were anxious to halt Myanmar's excessive dependence on China for aid and trade. Myanmar, in its turn, applied to join ASEAN (which maintained a policy of 'constructive engagement' in relation to Myanmar) in an attempt to end its isolation, accelerate economic growth and gain protection from Western criticism of its internal affairs. In July 1994 Myanmar was invited to attend the annual meeting of ASEAN ministers responsible for foreign affairs, and in July 1995 it signed the organization's founding Treaty of Amity and Co-operation, a precursor to full membership. In July 1996 Myanmar was granted observer status, and in July 1997 the country was admitted as a full member of the organization. In May 1996 Myanmar joined the ASEAN Regional Forum (ARF, see p. 176) and in May 2000 the country hosted a high-level meeting of the economic ministers of the ASEAN member countries; the meeting, which was also attended by ministers from the People's Republic of China, Japan and the Republic of Korea, attracted strong criticism from the NLD. Myanmar enjoyed particularly cordial relations with Indonesia, and the military regime aspired to Indonesia's internationally accepted political system, in which the dominant role of the armed forces was enshrined in the Constitution. ASEAN links were strengthened by official visits from the Prime Minister of Cambodia, Hun Sen, in February 2000, and the Vietnamese Minister of Foreign Affairs, Nguyen Dy Nien, in October of the same year. In January 2001 Dr Mahathir Mohamad, Prime Minister of Malaysia and an integral figure in gaining entry for Myanmar into ASEAN, visited Yangon. Gen. Than Shwe and Gen. Khin Nyunt paid a reciprocal visit in September. Mahathir visited the country again in August 2002.

In the late 1990s bilateral relations between Myanmar and Thailand were rather less cordial than previously, with the Thai Government advocating a more limited 'flexible engagement' with Myanmar, in place of the ASEAN policy of 'constructive engagement' formerly endorsed by the country. Relations between the two countries were placed under some strain in late 1999 when a group of armed Myanma student activists, styled the Vigorous Burmese Student Warriors, seized control of the Myanma embassy in Bangkok in early October, demanding the release of all political prisoners in Myanmar and the opening of a dialogue between the military Goverment and the opposition. All 89 hostages were released by the activists within 24 hours, in exchange for the Thai Government's provision of helicopter transport to the Thai–Myanma border. The Thai Government's release of the perpetrators angered the ruling junta in Myanmar, and Myanmar closed its border with Thailand immediately after the incident. The border was re-opened to commerce in late November, although relations between the two countries remained strained. In January 2000 Thai troops shot dead 10 armed Myanma rebels who had taken control of a hospital in Ratchaburi, holding hundreds of people hostage. The rebels, who were reported by some sources to be linked to the Kayin insurgent group, God's Army, had issued several demands, including that the shelling of their base on the Thai–Myanma border by the Thai military be halted, that co-operation between the Thai and Myanma armies against the Kayins should cease, and that Kayin tribespeople be allowed to seek refuge in Thailand. Whilst the Thai Government denied reports that the perpetrators had been summarily executed after handing over their weapons, the brutal resolution of the incident was praised by the military Government in Myanmar.

There was renewed tension on the Thai–Myanma border in October 2000 when a Thai soldier was killed and two others were injured. It was unclear whether the clash was with Myanma troops or a faction allied to the Government. Tension was further heightened in November as 2,000 Myanma troops were deployed along the border, in preparation for an offensive against the KNU. In January 2001 it was reported that a Thai F-16 fighter aircraft had intruded into Myanma airspace, prompting the Government to announce the building of air defence systems along the border. Another border transgression occurred in February, when five Myanma soldiers were arrested by the Thai Border Patrol Police (BPP). The soldiers claimed that they were searching for food, whereas the BPP believed them to be gathering intelligence on Thai positions. On the previous day an offensive had been launched against the KNU, involving 300 Myanma troops, of whom five were killed. In mid-February there was a major incursion into Thai territory by some 200 Myanma troops, in pursuit of 100 SSA rebels. The troops clashed with Thai soldiers and occupied a hill that was within Thai territory for two days. At least two Thai villagers were killed, and officially 14 Myanma soldiers and two civilians also died. A cease-fire was signed, but this did not prevent Myanmar from ordering all SPDC troops on the border to be placed on full combat-ready status. By the end of February Thailand had detained 40 Myanma nationals for spying, according to Myanma figures, while the SPDC accused Thailand of providing support to the SSA.

In May 2001 Thai-Myanma relations deteriorated further when the Thai Government lodged a formal protest over an incident in which members of the DKBA had allegedly attacked a military unit situated in a Thai border village, causing the deaths of three civilians. A further protest was made several days later when the UWSA captured a hill believed to lie within Thai territory; the hill was later recaptured by Thai troops. In response, the Myanma Government demanded the withdrawal of Thai troops from 35 border outposts and claimed that the Thai army had launched air strikes into its territory, an accusation denied by the Thai authorities. The situation was further exacerbated by the publication of an article in a Myanma newspaper that Thailand claimed was insulting to its monarchy. In June Thai Prime Minister Thaksin Shinawatra arrived in Yangon for discussions, which defused the tensions, although the two sides failed to reach any firm agreement as to how they would overcome the problems affecting their relations. In the following month the Thai Minister of Defence, Chavalit Yongchaiyudh, visited Myanmar and agreed to work with the SPDC to aid the forced repatriation of refugees on the Thai–Myanma border. In September Gen. Khin Nyunt made a three-day trip to Thailand, which was seen by many to constitute a starting point for a new era of improved bilateral relations. In January 2002 a joint Thai-Myanma commission (meeting for the first time since 1999) agreed to establish a task force to assist in the repatriation of illegal workers. In February the Thai Minister of Foreign Affairs, Surakiart Sathirathai, visited Yangon. During his stay both countries agreed to co-operate in controlling the cross-border drugs trade.

In mid-2002 relations with Thailand deteriorated sharply when fighting broke out on the border between government troops, allied with the UWSA, and the SSA. It was alleged that Thai troops had fired shells into the country, in the belief that the fighting had encroached upon Thai territory. In response, the Myanma Government again accused Thailand of lending its support to the SSA. The joint border was closed shortly afterwards as tensions escalated. Border incursions continued as the bilateral relationship worsened. In August Surakiart Sathirathai met with leaders of the SPDC in an attempt to defuse the tensions; the border subsequently reopened in October. Relations continued to improve, owing in large part to the adaptation of a policy of 'soft engagement' by the Thai Government and, in early 2003, the two countries signed an unprecedented agreement pledging that future military exercises would be conducted at a suitable distance from the border.

In December 2003 Thailand hosted an international forum, called the 'Bangkok Process', at which the Myanma Minister for Foreign Affairs, U Win Aung, presented the 'road map' to government representatives from 10 other Asian and European countries. In early 2004, in a reflection of the improved relationship between Myanmar and Thailand, Myanmar announced that it was to award Thailand fishing concessions in its waters for one year. Fishing rights had been terminated in May 2001 following tensions on the joint border. A second 'Friendship Bridge' linking the two countries opened in January 2006. However, a second round of talks in the 'Bangkok Process', scheduled for late April 2004, was postponed indefinitely earlier that month at Myanmar's request. Prime Minister Khin Nyunt visited Thailand in June, and discussed various economic, development and border issues with Prime Minister Thaksin Shinawatra. In December the Thai Prime Minister paid a visit to Myanmar, his first since the ousting of Khin Nyunt, and held talks with the new Prime Minister, Lt-Gen. Soe Win. In January 2005 Thailand increased security along the border with Myanmar, amid renewed concerns that fighting between Myanma troops and KNPP rebels might encroach upon Thai territory. In April Thailand again intensified security along its border with Myanmar in response to renewed fighting between the UWSA and the SSA close to Thai territory. In December the Thai Government announced that it was not prepared to host the delayed second meeting of the 'Bangkok Process' since Myanmar had not kept it sufficiently informed of its progress towards democracy; it was unclear whether any future efforts would be made to revive the initiative.

In October 2002 the Australian Minister of Foreign Affairs, Alexander Downer, arrived in Myanmar; he was the most senior Australian politician to have visited the country for 20 years. During his stay he met with senior members of the SPDC and with Aung San Suu Kyi. However, following his departure Suu Kyi reportedly claimed that she would prefer Australia to lend its support to the international sanctions against the country rather than attempt to engage with its leaders.

Despite the killing of three Indian soldiers in a clash with Myanma troops in October 2000, relations between the two countries subsequently improved. Gen. Maung Aye paid a seven-day visit to India in November 2000, meeting both the country's President and Prime Minister. In mid-February 2001 India's Minister of External Affairs, Jaswant Singh, visited Myanmar, the first Indian cabinet minister to do so since the SLORC's assumption of power in 1988. While there, Singh officially opened the Tamu–Kalewa highway, a road built by India at a cost of US $22m. in order to increase bilateral trade with Myanmar. In January 2003 Minister of Foreign Affairs U Win Aung paid a visit to India, during which he met with the Prime Minister and several cabinet ministers. The two Governments agreed to hold regular consultations and to co-operate in counter-terrorism activities. In October 2004 the Chairman of the SPDC, Than Shwe, paid the first visit to India by a Myanma Head of State in 24 years, agreeing to further bilateral co-operation at meetings with the Indian President and Prime Minister. Following discussions between the two countries' respective Ministers of Home Affairs in October 2005, Myanmar and India agreed to a policy of joint interrogation of persons arrested for militant activities and on charges of smuggling drugs or weapons. In March 2006 President Aavul Pakkiri Jainulabidin Abdul Kalam visited Yangon, the first ever state visit to Myanmar by an Indian President.

Following the release of Suu Kyi from house arrest in July 1995, Japan resumed substantial economic aid to Myanmar, which had been halted in 1988. In November 1999 the Japanese Prime Minister met with Senior Gen. Than Shwe during an ASEAN summit meeting in Manila; the meeting was the first between the leader of a major world power and a senior member of the military Government since the junta's suppression of the democratic opposition in 1988. In April 2001 Japan accelerated its policy of engagement, promising a US $28m. aid programme intended to facilitate the upgrading of a hydroelectric power plant in Kayah (see Economic Affairs). The renewal of aid to the country was widely perceived to be a political gesture intended to reward the SPDC for its efforts to reach a settlement with the NLD. The international community criticized Japan's decision to resume aid as being premature in the light of Myanmar's failure to end forced labour and other human rights abuses in the country. In June 2003, following the junta's reimprisonment of Suu Kyi in May of that year, the Japanese Government suspended all economic aid to Myanmar. However, in early 2004 it was announced that Japan was to resume aid once again, having been satisfied that the release of some political prisoners by the SPDC constituted adequate progress towards democracy in the country.

In July 1996, as repression increased, Suu Kyi for the first time urged the imposition of international economic sanctions against Myanmar. From March 1997 the EU withdrew Myanmar's special trading status, in response to concerns over Myanmar's human rights record; later that year a meeting scheduled to take place in November between the EU and ASEAN was cancelled by the EU, owing to its objection to the representation of Myanmar at the talks. In early 1999 a further meeting between the EU and ASEAN, scheduled to be held in February, was postponed indefinitely as a result of continued disagreement between the two organizations regarding the proposed representation of Myanmar. However, an agreement was subsequently reached by the two sides to allow Myanmar to take a 'passive role' in the Joint Co-operation Committee meeting between the EU and ASEAN scheduled to take place in May. The SPDC became more open to the development of external relations when it allowed an EU delegation to visit Myanmar and hold talks with Suu Kyi in January 2001. Despite this, the EU extended its sanctions against Myanmar for a further six months in April 2001, owing to the human rights situation. However, in October the EU announced that it had decided to ease its sanctions. After Razali Ismail's fourth visit to Myanmar in November 2001, plans for a US $16m. HIV/AIDS prevention programme were mooted. Several countries, particularly Japan and the EU, indicated that they would be willing to support a carefully monitored international aid programme, and it was hoped that the prospect of the resumption of limited aid would encourage the Government to release more political prisoners. In January 2003 the Myanma Deputy Minister of Foreign Affairs, Khin Maung Win, was permitted to attend an EU-ASEAN summit meeting for the first time since Myanmar's suspension from the meetings in 1997. However, in April the EU elected to extend its sanctions against the country and to increase the list of SPDC officials subject to visa sanctions and 'freezing' of their assets. Relations between the EU and ASEAN were strained by pressure from some EU member states to exclude ASEAN's three newest members (Cambodia, Laos and Myanmar) from an Asia-Europe Meeting of heads of government (ASEM) in Viet Nam in October 2004. The EU initially insisted that the SPDC should release Aung San Suu Kyi from house arrest and commit to a number of other reforms before Myanmar be allowed to attend. However, ASEAN responded that if its new members were not allowed to participate, then the EU's 10 new members should also be excluded. The result was that Myanmar was represented at the summit meeting by a lower-level delegation, led by the newly appointed Minister of Foreign Affairs, Maj.-Gen. Nyan Win. Two days after the ASEM summit EU ministers responsible for foreign affairs implemented an earlier threat to broaden sanctions against Myanmar if the country did not make progress towards democratization in time for the meeting. The ministers agreed to widen the list of Myanma officials subject to visa sanctions and to co-ordinate international bans on investment in the country (although France secured an exclusion from such a ban for European countries that had already invested in Myanmar).

In September 1999, meanwhile, a diplomatic dispute began between Myanmar and the United Kingdom after British consular staff were refused permission to visit two Britons in detention in Myanmar for their separate involvement in pro-democracy protest action. The British Government expressed its grave concern over their treatment. One of the two Britons was released in November. The second detainee, James Mawdsley, who had received a prison sentence of 17 years for entering the country illegally and carrying pro-democracy leaflets, was released in October 2000, following international pressure; he confirmed that he had been beaten heavily while in captivity.

In May 1997 the USA imposed trade sanctions in protest at persistent and large-scale repression by the SLORC. The sanctions prohibited further investment in Myanmar, but did not affect existing US interests in the country. In July 1997, at a ministerial meeting that followed the ASEAN conference, the US Secretary of State, Madeleine Albright, denounced Myanmar publicly for its poor human rights record and the country's lack of progress towards democracy. During 1998 the USA criticized the military junta in Myanmar for its treatment of Suu Kyi and also demanded the release of hundreds of political prisoners. In March 1999 Albright publicly criticized the regime for taking insufficient action to combat the production of and trade in narcotics within Myanmar. The USA showed its support for the SPDC-NLD talks with a visit by a senior Department of State official to Suu Kyi in February 2001. However, whilst welcoming the discussions, the US Government renewed its sanctions later in the year. In December pro-democracy activists in Myanmar accused the USA of neglecting their cause after a reappraisal of its foreign policy in the wake of the terrorist attacks on the country in September 2001 (see the chapter on the USA). They claimed that the US Government had moderated its criticism of the ruling military junta on the grounds that it suspected the international terrorist network, al-Qa'ida, had a presence in the country. In February 2002 a report issued by the US Government offered the prospect of an easing of sanctions, but only if the military junta released all remaining political prisoners and made further tangible progress towards democracy. However, following the detention of Aung San Suu Kyi in May 2003, in July the US President approved the Burmese Freedom and Democracy Act, already passed by Congress, banning all imports from Myanmar for three years and extending visa sanctions already imposed on SPDC officials. The USA extended economic sanctions against Myanmar for another year in May 2004 and again in July 2005.

In November 1998 the SPDC strongly denied claims made by the UN that the Myanma Government was responsible for the widespread abuse of human rights within the country. However, a report published in August by the International Labour Organization (ILO, see p. 98), following an investigation into the alleged use of forced labour and the suppression of trade unions in Myanmar, found the use of forced labour to be 'pervasive' throughout the whole country, and accused the military regime of using beatings, torture, rape and murder in the exaction of its forced labour policy, constituting a 'gross denial of human rights'. In June 1999 a resolution condemning Myanmar for its widespread use of forced labour was adopted by the member countries of the ILO, and the country was barred from participating in any ILO activities. (In the same month the ruling junta was accused by the human rights organization Amnesty International of perpetrating widespread abuses against ethnic minority groups.) Following the failure of the military Government to carry out the recommendations made by the ILO Commission of Inquiry in 1998 after the organization's initial investigation, in March 2000 the governing body of the ILO recommended that at its meeting in June the International Labour Conference take action to secure compliance by the ruling junta with the ILO's recommendations. In a statement issued in late March, the SPDC categorically rejected the governing body's decision and recommendations. Despite the Government's assurance in November 2000 that it would accept ILO monitors to verify the cessation of forced labour practices, the UN labour body voted to proceed with sanctions against Myanmar. This was the first time such action, the strongest available to the ILO, had been undertaken in the organization's 81-year history. The ILO subsequently requested its members to review their relations with Myanmar and to adopt sanctions. China, India, Malaysia and Russia voted against the action.

In September 2001 an ILO contingent arrived in Myanmar for a three-week visit intended to ascertain whether the military junta had honoured its promise to bring about the abolition of forced labour. In November the ILO issued a report concluding that, while some progress had been made, the practice was still endemic in many parts of the country. It recommended that a permanent ILO presence be established in Myanmar to monitor continued efforts to end forced labour in the region; discussions as to how this could be implemented headed the agenda during a further visit by the ILO in February 2002. The ILO delegation, however, was not permitted to see the NLD leader, Suu Kyi, during its visit and, upon departure, the head of the delegation expressed disappointment at the lack of co-operation it had received from the Myanma authorities. Despite this, in March the ILO agreed to establish a liaison office in the country and, in October, an ILO mission visited the country to assist further in the development of good labour practices. In early 2004, following a visit by an ILO envoy, the SPDC agreed to allow ILO representatives to work freely towards the elimination of forced labour practices in the country. At the ILO's annual International Labour Conference in June, it was reported that the use of forced labour remained widespread in Myanmar, particularly on local infrastructure projects and by the army, although there had been some improvement since the 1990s, with forced labour no longer routinely used on national infrastructure projects.

In October 1999 the UN Secretary-General's Special Envoy for Myanmar, Alvaro de Soto, arrived in the country to attempt, for the fifth time, to promote a dialogue between the military Government and the NLD; de Soto's efforts were, however, fruitless. In April 2000 de Soto was replaced as Special Envoy for Myanmar by Razali Ismail, a Malaysian diplomat, who subsequently arranged the secret dialogue between Suu Kyi and Lt-Gen. Khin Nyunt in October. In November the UN human rights envoy to Myanmar, Rajsoomer Lallah, resigned from his position, citing lack of financial and administrative assistance. Lallah had previously produced a damning report of Myanmar's human rights situation, but had not been granted a visa throughout his four-year term. His successor, Dr Paulo Sérgio Pinheiro, was able to visit Myanmar in April 2001, within six months of taking office. He returned for a further visit in October, but was criticized by the NLD for his failure to spend enough time consulting with local communities. His visit had to be curtailed for reasons of ill health. In February 2002 Pinheiro visited the country for a third time and held further discussions with senior members of the SPDC and with Suu Kyi and other political prisoners. The Government released 11 political prisoners during his stay and, upon leaving, he declared his visit to have been a success. In October Pinheiro travelled to the country again; during his time there he investigated allegations, made by several human rights groups, that members of the Myanma armed forces routinely raped ethnic women along the border with Thailand. He also met with Suu Kyi. In March 2003 he paid a further visit to the country but curtailed his stay, having discovered a hidden microphone in a room where he was interviewing NLD prisoners. He later urged the SPDC to release all remaining political prisoners and enter into a serious dialogue with the opposition. In the first half of 2004 Pinheiro was twice denied entry to Myanmar, and in June he described the ongoing National Convention as a 'meaningless and undemocratic exercise' owing to the restrictions imposed on free discussion and to the absence of the NLD.

In May 1999 the ICRC, which had withdrawn from Myanmar in 1995 but reopened its office there in October 1998, regained permission from the ruling junta to visit a limited number of prisons in the country. Despite having been initially critical of the ICRC for reaching an agreement with the SPDC, Suu Kyi was reported subsequently to have expressed her support for the Committee's work with political prisoners. The ICRC sent a delegation to the country in July 2003, in order to ascertain that Suu Kyi was in good health following her recent imprisonment by the SPDC.

In July 2001 Minister of Foreign Affairs Win Aung travelled to Russia in order to finalize arrangements for the construction of Myanmar's first nuclear research reactor. In January 2002 the Government officially confirmed that it was to proceed with the construction with Russian assistance.

Government

Following the military coup of September 1988, all state organs, including the People's Assembly, the State Council and the Council of Ministers, were abolished by the State Law and Order Restoration Council (SLORC), and the country was placed under martial law. Legislative elections took place in May 1990, but the SLORC subsequently announced that the opposition-dominated elected body was a Constituent Assembly, which was accorded no legislative power. During September 1992 a night curfew, imposed in 1988, and two martial law decrees, in force for three years, were revoked. A ban remained, however, on gatherings of more than five people. In early 1993 a National Convention, comprising members of the SLORC and representatives of the opposition parties, met to draft a new constitution; discussions continued until March 1996, when the National Convention was adjourned. In November 1997 the ruling military junta announced the dissolution of the SLORC and its replacement by the newly created State Peace and Development Council (SPDC). In August 2003 the SPDC announced its intention to reconvene the National Convention, which had remained in recess since 1996, in order that proceedings for the drafting of a new constitution could begin.

Defence

Myanmar maintains a policy of neutrality and has no external defence treaties. The armed forces are largely engaged in internal security duties. In August 2005 the armed services totalled some 428,000 men, of whom a reported 350,000 were in the army, an estimated 13,000 in the navy and 12,000 in the air force. Paramilitary forces included the People's Police Force of 72,000 men and the People's Militia of 35,000 men. In 2005 the defence budget was an estimated US $6,850m.

Economic Affairs

In 1986, according to estimates by the World Bank, Myanmar's gross national income (GNI), measured at average 1984–86 prices, was US $7,450m., equivalent to $200 per head. In 1995–2004, it was estimated, the population increased at an annual average rate of 1.4%, while gross domestic product (GDP) per head increased, in real terms, by an average of 7.0% per year. Overall GDP increased, in real terms, by an annual average of 9.4% between 1995 and 2004. According to the Asian Development Bank (ADB), real GDP expanded by 13.6% in 2003/04 and by 12.2% in 2004/05.

According to the ADB, agriculture (including forestry and fishing) contributed an estimated 54.6% of GDP in 2002/03. The sector engaged an estimated 69.3% of the employed labour force in mid-2003. Rice is the staple crop, and has traditionally been among Myanmar's principal export commodities. Exports of rice and rice products provided 21.6% of total export earnings in 1994/95; however, the proportion had declined to 4.4% by 2001/02. In 2003 the Government announced plans intended to liberalize the rice trade. However, in January 2004 it banned the export of rice for six months, a ban that resulted in significant overproduction and a consequent decline in domestic rice prices. In 2003/04 rice production increased to 23.3m. metric tons, from 21.5m. tons in the previous year; exports, however, declined to 168,400 tons in 2003/04, from 793,500 tons in the previous year. In 2002/03 pulses and beans accounted for 8.8% of total exports. Other crops include sugar cane, maize, dry beans, groundnuts, sesame seed, tobacco and rubber. The fishing sector is also important. Sales of teak and other hardwood provided 9.4% of total export revenue in 2002/03. (Teak is frequently felled illegally and smuggled across the border into Thailand.) Myanmar is the largest source of illicit opium in South-East Asia, and it has been speculated that the Government is involved in its export. In 2003, according to a survey conducted by the UN Office on Drugs and Crime (formerly the UN Office of Drug Control and Crime Prevention, see p. 44), Myanmar was the world's second biggest producer of opium, behind Afghanistan. However, ongoing government efforts to eradicate illicit poppy cultivation were achieving considerable success. In 2005 the area under opium poppy cultivation stood at an estimated 32,800 ha, a reduction of 80% from the peak of 1996. Raw opium production declined to an estimated 312 metric tons in 2005, a decrease of approximately 82% compared with 1996. The number of households involved in opium cultivation in 2005 was estimated to be 193,000, a decline of 26% compared with the previous year. Farmers who had previously relied on the crop were given 3 kg of rice and a daily monetary allowance by the UN to compensate for their loss of earnings. Between 1990/91 and 2000/01, according to the ADB, the real GDP of the agricultural sector increased by an annual average of 5.8%. Annual agricultural GDP growth reportedly measured 8.7% in 2001/02, declining to 6.0% in 2002/03 before rising to 11.7% in 2003/04.

Industry (including mining, manufacturing, construction and utilities) provided an estimated 13.0% of GDP in 2002/03, according to the ADB. The industrial sector engaged 12.2% of the employed labour force (excluding activities not adequately defined) in 1997/98. Between 1990/91 and 2000/01, according to the ADB, industrial GDP increased by an annual average of 10.7%. The industrial sector's GDP growth was reported to have reached 21.8% in 2001/02 and 35.0% in 2002/03, before declining to 20.7% in 2003/04.

Mining and quarrying contributed an estimated 0.4% of GDP in 2002/03 and engaged 0.7% of the employed labour force in 1997/98. Production of crude petroleum decreased steadily from 1980, and from 1988 Myanmar was obliged to import petroleum. Significant onshore and offshore discoveries of natural gas and petroleum have resulted from exploration and production-sharing agreements with foreign companies, the first of which was signed in 1989. Asian firms, in particular, have continued to invest in the sector. During the latter half of 2004 agreements were signed with Chinese and Singaporean companies, permitting onshore exploration in the Kyaukpyu area and offshore exploration in the Gulf of Mottama. In March 2005, however, the Government announced that, in future, all onshore oil and gas blocks would be exclusively operated by the Myanma Oil and Gas Enterprise under the Ministry of Energy. Other important minerals that are commercially exploited include tin, zinc, copper, tungsten, coal, lead, jade, gemstones, silver and gold; however, some of Myanmar's potentially lucrative mineral resources remain largely unexploited. According to the ADB, the GDP of the mining sector increased by an annual average of 18.3% between 1990/91 and 2000/01. Growth in the GDP of the mining sector measured 36.3% in 1999/2000 and 28.0% in 2000/01.

Manufacturing contributed an estimated 9.2% of GDP in 2002/03 and engaged 9.1% of the employed labour force in 1998. The most important branches are food and beverage processing, the production of industrial raw materials (cement, plywood and fertilizers), petroleum refining and textiles. The sector is adversely affected by shortages of electricity and the high price of machinery and spare parts. From mid-2003 a US ban on imports from Myanmar had a serious impact upon the textile sector; textiles and garments had previously constituted the majority of Myanmar's exports to the USA. The real GDP of the manufacturing sector increased, according to the ADB, at an average rate of 8.4% per year between 1990/91 and 2000/01. Manufacturing GDP rose by 14.5% in 1999/2000 and by 23.0% in 2000/01.

Energy is derived principally from natural gas, which accounted for 57.0% of electricity production in 2002; hydroelectric power contributed 33.7% and petroleum 9.3%. In January 2002 the Government announced that its third Five-Year Plan would give priority to the construction of three hydropower plants, in order to accelerate the development of the country's industrial sector. In March 2005 a 280-MW hydropower plant, financed by a Chinese company at an estimated cost of US $160m., was opened at Paung Laung. The same Chinese company was also involved in the ongoing construction of the 790-MW Yeywa hydropower station in Mandalay, and the Shweli Hydel hydro-electric power project in northern Shan State, which was expected to generate 3,042m. kWh annually. In early 2005 it was announced that India's Bharat Petroleum Corporation Ltd was shortly to begin trial exports of diesel fuel to Myanmar; it was expected that the arrangement would be considerably more cost-effective than importing fuel from Malaysia, Myanmar's existing primary source of diesel. Imports of mineral fuels, lubricants, etc. accounted for 14.1% of total imports in 2002/03.

The services sector contributed 32.3% of GDP in 2002/03 and engaged 25.1% of the employed labour force in 1997/98. Tourism revenue increased substantially over the period 1992–95, and became the country's second largest source of foreign exchange in 1995/96. Tourist arrivals reached 217,212 in 2002, and receipts (including passenger transport) totalled US $116m. In 2003 the number of arrivals declined to 205,610 and receipts decreased to $68m. In late 2004 a second international airline, Air Myanmar, was launched, providing services from Yangon to Sydney via Singapore, and to Fukuoka via Bangkok, Shanghai and Seoul. According to figures from the ADB, the GDP of the services sector increased by an average of 7.3% per year between 1990/91 and 2000/01. GDP growth in the sector was reported to have reached 12.9% in 2001/02, 14.8% in 2002/03 and 14.5% in 2003/04.

In 2004 Myanmar recorded a visible trade surplus of US $928.0m., and there was a surplus of $111.5m. on the current account of the balance of payments. In 2004 the principal sources of imports were the People's Republic of China (which supplied 28.3% of the total) and Singapore (20.6%); other major suppliers were Thailand, the Republic of Korea and Malaysia. The principal market for exports (37.0%) was Thailand; other significant purchasers were India (14.0%), the People's Republic of China (6.2%), Japan and the United Kingdom. Illegal trade is widespread, and was estimated to be equivalent to 50% of official trade in 1995/96. The principal imports in 2002/03 were basic manufactures, machinery and transport equipment and mineral fuels and lubricants. The principal exports in that year were teak and other hardwood, pulses and beans and rice and rice products. It was reported that by 2005 sales of natural gas to neighbouring Thailand accounted for more than 30% of Myanmar's total export revenue.

In the financial year ending 31 March 2001 there was an estimated budgetary surplus of 18,109m. kyats, equivalent to 0.7% of GDP. Myanmar's external debt at the end of 2003 totalled US $7,318.4m., of which $5,857.3m. was long-term public debt; in that year the cost of servicing external debt was equivalent to 4.2% of exports of goods and services. The annual rate of inflation averaged 22.4% in 1997–2004. Consumer prices increased by

57.1% in 2002, by 36.6% in 2003 and by 4.5% in 2004, according to the International Labour Organization (ILO). The number of registered unemployed persons in 1998 was equivalent to 2.4% of the labour force.

Myanmar is a member of the UN Economic and Social Commission for Asia and the Pacific (ESCAP, see p. 33), the Asian Development Bank (ADB, see p. 169) and the Colombo Plan (see p. 385), which promote economic development in the region. In July 1997 Myanmar acceded to the Association of South East Asian Nations (ASEAN, see p. 172). Myanmar was granted a 10-year period from 1 January 1998 to comply with the tariff reductions (to between 0% and 5%) required under the ASEAN Free Trade Area (AFTA), which was formally established on 1 January 2002.

In March 2001 the Government implemented its third Five-Year Plan, which projected average annual GDP growth rates in excess of 8% until 2005/06. The main aims of the plan were: to promote the establishment of agro-based industries; to develop the power and energy sectors; to expand the agriculture, meat and fish sectors in order to meet local demand and provide a surplus for export; to establish forest reserves; to extend the health and education sectors; and to develop the rural areas. From the late 1990s, however, Myanmar was effectively sustained by a 'parallel' economy, mainly comprising unofficial border trade with the People's Republic of China, Thailand and India. The currency continued to depreciate sharply. By September 2002 the kyat had declined to a low point of 1,150 to the US dollar, fluctuating thereafter, and it was reported to stand at 1,330 to the dollar in September 2005. The official exchange rate, meanwhile, remained at above six kyats to the dollar until 2004, when it reached an annual average of 5.7 kyats. By early 2006 the ratio of the parallel rate to the official rate was believed to have reached almost 200:1. Although GDP growth in 2004/05 was reported to have reached 13.6% in 2004/05, significantly less favourable results in several crucial areas of production (including agricultural production, electricity generation and the use of crude petroleum and natural gas) offered a markedly different account of Myanmar's economic performance. The vast disparity between the official and market values of the kyat was largely responsible for the conflicting statistics, which were hindering the formulation of apposite economic policies; however, in early 2006 there was no suggestion that Myanmar would adopt a unified exchange rate in the foreseeable future. Despite warnings that the regular financing of the annual budget deficit through an expansion of credit from the country's central bank was unsustainable in the long term, in the mid-2000s the junta continued to adhere to this policy, which had resulted in sharply rising inflation rates and a severe lack of public funding for health, welfare and education. Myanmar's economic prospects deteriorated further in May 2003 when Japan, previously the most important foreign donor, announced the suspension of economic aid, and the USA and the European Union (EU) both strengthened their sanctions against the country, with the USA effectively banning all imports from Myanmar. Although Japan resumed aid donations to the country in mid-2004, both the USA and the EU decided to renew their bans, in May and September 2004 respectively, and there were widespread consumer boycotts of Myanma products. In July and April 2005, respectively, the USA and the EU again renewed their bans on Myanma imports. China extended an official offer of support during Prime Minister General Khin Nyunt's visit to the country in July 2004. Foreign direct investment, meanwhile, had declined from US $208m. in 2000 to $128m. in 2003. In March 2005 the Myanma Government revealed that it was drafting new legislation to combat the problem of international 'money-laundering', in the hope of improving the country's prospects of attracting assistance from international financial institutions. Following its annual review in February 2006, however, the Paris-based Financial Action Task Force (FATF—established in 1989 on the recommendation of the Group of Seven (G-7) industrialized nations (see p. 389)) decided that Myanmar should remain on the group's list of non-co-operative countries and territories, owing to Myanmar's failure to implement effective measures to combat the practice of 'money-laundering'. In June the ILO reactivated a resolution, first approved in June 2000, against the Myanma Government for alleged violations of human rights; this was expected adversely to affect the future provision of international assistance for Myanmar. In September 2005 the rate of tax levied on utilities was raised, and further tax increases were feared following the announcement in late March 2006 that government workers' salaries were to be increased 10-fold, effective from 30 April; the wage increase was also expected to exacerbate the rate of inflation. Furthermore, an eight-fold increase in fuel prices was reported to have been implemented in October 2005. Much work was required to improve Myanmar's basic infrastructure, although some progress was being made. In February 2005 work began on the Taungbro Bridge, which was to provide a direct land-link between Myanmar and Bangladesh and would ultimately connect both countries to China and Thailand; the project was scheduled for completion in 2011. It was hoped that the opening of the second Myanmar-Thailand 'Friendship Bridge' in January 2006 would facilitate the movement of goods and people between the two countries. Also, the Mekong River Bridge, the first bridge between Myanmar and Laos, was scheduled for completion in late 2006. It was hoped that the improvements in transport and communication achieved by such projects would lead to significantly enhanced economic performance. However, it remained imperative that Western states be persuaded to remove their sanctions and to accept Myanmar back into the international community. Consequently, achieving marked improvements in both the country's political situation and its human rights record continued to be of the utmost importance for the Myanma Government if meaningful long-term economic reform were to be effected.

Education

Education is provided free of charge, where available, and is compulsory at primary level. Primary education begins at five years of age and lasts for five years. Primary enrolment was equivalent to 81.9% of children in the relevant age-group in 2001. Secondary education, beginning at 10 years of age, lasts for a further six years, comprising a first cycle of four years and a second of two years. In 2002 enrolment at secondary schools was equivalent to 40% of males and 38% of females in the relevant age-group. In 1994 total enrolment at tertiary level was equivalent to 5.4% of the relevant age-group (males 4.2%; females 6.7%). Emphasis is placed on vocational and technical training. Current expenditure on education by the central Government in 2000/01 was 31,345m. kyats, representing 14.2% of total expenditure.

Public Holidays

2006: 4 January (Independence Day), 12 February (Union Day), 2 March (Peasants' Day, anniversary of the 1962 coup), 13 March* (Full Moon of Tabaung), 27 March (Armed Forces' Day), 13–16 April* (Maha Thingyan—Water Festival), 17 April* (Myanma New Year), 1 May (Workers' Day), 11 May* (Full Moon of Kason), 10 July* (Full Moon of Waso and beginning of Buddhist Lent), 19 July (Martyrs' Day), 6 October* (Full Moon of Thadingyut and end of Buddhist Lent), 21 October* (Deepavali), 3 November* (Tazaungdaing Festival), 6 December* (National Day), 23 December* (Kayin New Year), 25 December (Christmas Day).

2007: 4 January (Independence Day), 12 February (Union Day), February/March* (Full Moon of Tabaung), 2 March (Peasants' Day, anniversary of the 1962 coup), 27 March (Armed Forces' Day), 13–16 April* (Maha Thingyan—Water Festival), 17 April* (Myanma New Year), April/May* (Full Moon of Kason), 1 May (Workers' Day), 19 July (Martyrs' Day), 21 July* (Full Moon of Waso and beginning of Buddhist Lent), October* (Full Moon of Thadingyut and end of Buddhist Lent), November* (Tazaungdaing Festival), 9 November* (Deepavali), 6 December* (National Day), 23 December* (Kayin New Year), 25 December (Christmas Day).

* A number of holidays depend on lunar sightings.

Weights and Measures

The imperial system is in force.

MYANMAR

Statistical Survey

Source (unless otherwise stated): Ministry of National Planning and Economic Development, Minister's Office, Theinbyu St, Botahtaung Township, Yangon; tel. (1) 272009; fax (1) 243791; e-mail ministry.nped@mptmail.net.mm; internet www.mnped.gov.mm.

Area and Population

AREA, POPULATION AND DENSITY

Area (sq km)	676,552*
Population (census results)	
31 March 1973	28,885,867
31 March 1983†	
Males	17,507,837
Females	17,798,352
Total	35,306,189
Population (UN estimates at mid-year)‡	
2002	48,900,000
2003	49,463,000
2004	50,004,000
Density (per sq km) at mid-2004	73.9

* 261,218 sq miles.
† Figures exclude adjustment for underenumeration. Also excluded are 7,716 Myanma citizens (males 5,704, females 2,012) abroad.
‡ Source: UN, *World Population Prospects: The 2004 Revision*.

PRINCIPAL TOWNS
(population at census of 31 March 1983)

Yangon (Rangoon)	2,513,023	Pathein (Bassein)	144,096
Mandalay	532,949	Taunggyi	108,231
Mawlamyine (Moulmein)	219,961	Sittwe (Akyab)	107,621
Bago (Pegu)	150,528	Manywa	106,843

Source: UN, *Demographic Yearbook*.

Mid-2003 (UN estimate, incl. suburbs): Yangon 3,873,739 (Source: UN, *World Urbanization Prospects: The 2003 Revision*).

BIRTHS AND DEATHS
(UN estimates, annual averages)

	1990–95	1995–2000	2000–05
Birth rate (per 1,000)	29.7	24.0	20.8
Death rate (per 1,000)	11.5	10.3	9.7

Source: UN, *World Population Prospects: The 2004 Revision*.

Expectation of life (WHO estimates, years at birth): 59 (males 56; females 63) in 2003 (Source: WHO, *World Health Report*).

ECONOMICALLY ACTIVE POPULATION*
(official estimates, '000 persons)

	1997	1998
Agriculture, hunting, forestry and fishing	11,381	11,507
Mining and quarrying	132	121
Manufacturing	1,573	1,666
Electricity, gas and water	21	48
Construction	378	400
Trade, restaurants and hotels	1,746	1,781
Transport, storage and communications	470	495
Financing, insurance, real estate and business services	577	597
Community, social and personal services†	1,686	1,744
Total employed	17,964	18,359
Unemployed‡	535	452
Total labour force	18,499	18,811

* Excludes members of the armed forces.
† Includes activities not adequately defined.
‡ Persons aged 18 years and over.

Unemployed ('000 persons aged 18 years and over): 382 in 2000; 398 in 2001; 434 in 2002.

Source: UN, *Statistical Yearbook for Asia and the Pacific*.

Mid-2003 (estimates in '000): Agriculture, etc. 18,671; Total labour force 26,954 (Source: FAO).

Health and Welfare

KEY INDICATORS

Total fertility rate (children per woman, 2003)	2.8
Under-5 mortality rate (per 1,000 live births, 2004)	106
HIV/AIDS (% of persons aged 15–49, 2003)	1.2
Physicians (per 1,000 head, 2000)	0.30
Hospital beds (per 1,000 head, 1990)	0.64
Health expenditure (2002): US $ per head (PPP)	30
Health expenditure (2002): % of GDP	2.2
Health expenditure (2002): public (% of total)	18.5
Access to water (% of persons, 2002)	80
Access to sanitation (% of persons, 2002)	73
Human Development Index (2003): ranking	129
Human Development Index (2003): value	0.578

For sources and definitions, see explanatory note on p. vi.

Agriculture

PRINCIPAL CROPS
('000 metric tons)

	2002	2003	2004
Wheat	107	124	130*
Rice (paddy)	21,805	23,136	22,000*
Maize	603	704	600*
Millet	166	176	150*
Potatoes	351	403	400†
Sweet potatoes†	60	60	45
Cassava	126	130†	130†
Sugar cane	6,170	6,485	6,368
Other sugar crops	306	310†	310†
Dry beans	1,527	1,538	1,550†
Dry peas	33	35†	36†
Chick-peas	212	228	230†
Dry cow peas	104	123	130†
Pigeon peas	466*	485	500†
Areca (Betel) nuts†	55	57	57
Soybeans (Soya beans)	124	125†	130†
Groundnuts (in shell)	757	878	715*
Coconuts	365	350†	350†
Sunflower seed	279	339	350†
Sesame seed	399	501	550†
Cottonseed*	94	112	120
Dry onions	647	738*	738†
Garlic	97	100*	100†
Other vegetables†	2,900	3,000	3,000
Plantains	505	530†	530†
Other fruits†	1,120	1,140	1,140
Tea (made)	23*	25*	25†
Pimento and allspice	69	70†	70†
Jute	47	26	26†
Tobacco (leaves)	49	49†	49†
Cotton (lint)*	47	56	60
Natural rubber	37	40	36*

* Unofficial figure(s).
† FAO estimate(s).

Source: FAO.

3110

MYANMAR

LIVESTOCK
('000 head, year ending September)

	2002	2003	2004
Horses*	120	120	120
Cattle	11,551	11,728	11,939
Buffaloes	2,552	2,600*	2,650*
Pigs	4,499	4,840	5,217
Sheep	432	482†	492†
Goats	1,542	1,722†	1,756†
Chickens	57,128	58,000*	57,000*
Ducks*	6,100	6,300	6,500
Geese*	500	500	500

* FAO estimate(s).
† Unofficial figure.

Source: FAO.

LIVESTOCK PRODUCTS
('000 metric tons)

	2002	2003	2004
Beef and veal*	108.0	111.6	114.0
Buffalo meat*	22.1	22.4	23.0
Goat meat	7.8	8.7*	8.7*
Pig meat*	122.7	132.0	132.0
Poultry meat	256.6	261.0*	256.5*
Cows' milk	525.1	533.0†	542.8†
Buffaloes' milk	116.0	120.0*	124.0*
Goats' milk	8.1	8.5*	8.2*
Butter*	11.6	11.7	11.9
Cheese*	33.0	33.4	34.0
Hen eggs	101.7	114.3†	135.0†
Other poultry eggs	11.0	12.5*	13.5*
Cattle hides (fresh)*	22.0	23.5	24.0

* FAO estimate(s).
† Unofficial figure.

Source: FAO.

Forestry

ROUNDWOOD REMOVALS
('000 cubic metres, excl. bark)

	2002	2003	2004
Sawlogs, veneer logs and logs for sleepers	2,613	2,885	2,816
Other industrial wood	1,326	1,353	1,380
Fuel wood	34,939	37,954	37,560
Total	38,877	42,192	41,756

Source: FAO.

SAWNWOOD PRODUCTION
('000 cubic metres, incl. railway sleepers)

	2002	2003	2004
Total (all broadleaved)	1,012	1,001	1,059

Source: FAO.

Fishing

('000 metric tons, live weight, year ending 31 March)

	2000/01	2001/02	2002/03
Capture*	1,166.9	1,312.6	1,349.2
Freshwater fishes	235.4	304.5	288.9
Marine fishes	900.5	975.1	1,026.3
Aquaculture	121.3*	121.3*	257.1
Roho labeo	85.8	76.2	100.0
Total catch*	1,288.1	1,433.9	1,606.3

* FAO estimate(s).

Source: FAO.

Mining

(metric tons, unless otherwise indicated)

	2001	2002*	2003*
Coal and lignite	41,736	57,000	57,000
Crude petroleum ('000 barrels)	4,696	4,920	5,000
Natural gas (million cu m)†	8,804	8,500	8,500
Copper ore‡	25,900	27,500	27,900
Lead ore*‡	900	900	500
Zinc ore‡	467	500	500
Tin concentrates‡	212	210	210
Chromium ore (gross weight)*	3,000	3,000	3,000
Tungsten concentrates‡	49	30	30
Silver ore (kilograms)‡	1,804	1,500	1,500
Gold ore (kilograms)‡§	200*	200	100
Feldspar*§	10,000	10,000	10,000
Barite (Barytes)	31,015	18,000	20,000
Salt (unrefined, excl. brine)*	35,000	35,000	35,000
Gypsum (crude)	64,609	113,000	100,000
Rubies, sapphires and spinel ('000 metric carats)§	8,630	4,770	4,700
Jade	8,200	10,800	11,000

* Estimated production.
† Marketed production.
‡ Figures refer to the metal content of ores and concentrates (including mixed concentrates).
§ Twelve months beginning 1 April of year stated.

Source: US Geological Survey.

Industry

SELECTED PRODUCTS
('000 metric tons, unless otherwise indicated)

	2000	2001	2002
Raw sugar*	60	103	126
Refined sugar†	60	n.a.	89
Cigarettes (million)†	2,512	2,650	2,657
Cotton yarn†	5.7	5.5	4.1
Plywood ('000 cu m)	55	50	19
Printing and writing paper	18	15	15
Nitrogenous fertilizers‡	71	n.a.	n.a.
Petroleum refinery products ('000 barrels)§‖	5,536	5,286	5,500
Cement§	393,355	377,961	400,000
Tin—unwrought (metric tons)§	212	212	210
Electric energy (million kWh, net)	2,930	3,017	n.a.

Beer (hectolitres): 13,000 in 1994.

Woven cotton fabrics (million sq m): 16 in 1995.

* Data from FAO.
† Production by government-owned enterprises only.
‡ Production in terms of nitrogen during twelve months ending 30 September of stated year.
§ Twelve months beginning 1 April of year stated. Data from US Geological Survey.
‖ Figure includes gasoline, jet fuel, kerosene, diesel, distillate fuel oil and residual fuel oil.

Source (unless otherwise specified): UN, *Statistical Yearbook for Asia and the Pacific*.

MYANMAR

Finance

CURRENCY AND EXCHANGE RATES

Monetary Units
100 pyas = 1 kyat.

Sterling, Dollar and Euro Equivalents (30 December 2005)
£1 sterling = 10.2505 kyats;
US $1 = 5.9530 kyats;
€1 = 7.0228 kyats;
1,000 kyats = £97.56 = $167.98 = €142.39.

Average Exchange Rate (kyats per US $)
2003   6.0764
2004   5.7459
2005   5.7610

Note: Since January 1975 the value of the kyat has been linked to the IMF's special drawing right (SDR). Since May 1977 the official exchange rate has been fixed at a mid-point of SDR 1 = 8.5085 kyats. On 1 June 1996 a new customs valuation exchange rate of US $1 = 100 kyats was introduced. In September 2001 the free market exchange rate was $1 = 450 kyats.

CENTRAL GOVERNMENT BUDGET
(million kyats, year ending 31 March)

Revenue*	1998/99	1999/2000	2000/01
Tax revenue	56,653	60,294	75,727
Taxes on income, profits and capital gains	20,515	21,169	26,140
Domestic taxes on goods and services	30,748	33,750	44,101
General sales, turnover or value-added tax	22,720	24,576	32,961
Taxes on international trade and transactions	5,390	5,375	5,486
Other revenue	59,334	62,390	58,324
Entrepreneurial and property income	43,689	47,269	41,144
Administrative fees, non-industrial and incidental sales	15,645	15,121	17,180
Capital revenue	79	211	257
Total	116,066	122,895	134,308

Expenditure†	1998/99	1999/2000	2000/01
Current expenditure	63,095	81,608	134,068
General public services, incl. public order	15,011	23,562	20,435
Defence	39,627	45,040	63,453
Education	9,572	12,132	31,345
Health	3,233	4,144	7,388
Social security and welfare	1,599	2,436	4,993
Recreational, cultural and religious affairs	2,114	2,013	2,668
Economic affairs and services	41,015	46,641	66,132
Agriculture, forestry, fishing and hunting	17,918	19,479	38,447
Transportation and communication	22,161	26,279	25,917
Other current expenditure	11,588	17,332	24,475
Capital expenditure	60,969	71,889	87,187
Total	124,064	153,497	221,255

* Excluding grants received from abroad (million kyats): 524 in 1998/99; 221 in 1999/2000; 242 in 2000/01.
† Excluding lending minus repayments (million kyats): –528 in 1998/99; 63 in 1999/2000; –127 in 2000/01.

Source: IMF, *Government Finance Statistics Yearbook*.

INTERNATIONAL RESERVES
(US $ million at 31 December)

	2002	2003	2004
Gold (national valuation)	11.0	12.0	12.6
IMF special drawing rights	0.1	0.1	0.1
Foreign exchange	469.9	550.1	672.1
Total	481.0	562.2	684.8

Source: IMF, *International Financial Statistics*.

MONEY SUPPLY
(million kyats at 31 December)

	2002	2003	2004
Currency outside banks	718,633	1,102,940	1,347,600
Demand deposits at deposit money banks	290,520	82,948	139,880
Total money (incl. others)	1,009,470	1,186,100	1,487,650

Source: IMF, *International Financial Statistics*.

COST OF LIVING
(Consumer Price Index; base: 2000 = 100)

	2002	2003	2004
Food (incl. beverages)	201.2	274.3	277.5
Fuel and light	163.3	219.3	258.1
Clothing (incl. footwear)	195.8	272.8	300.5
Rent	175.3	245.4	272.2
All items (incl. others)	190.2	259.8	271.6

Source: ILO.

NATIONAL ACCOUNTS
(million kyats at current prices, year ending 31 March)

National Income and Product

	1996/97	1997/98	1998/99
Domestic factor incomes	773,940	1,087,997	1,534,089
Consumption of fixed capital	18,040	21,557	25,907
Gross domestic product (GDP) at factor cost	791,980	1,109,554	1,559,996
Indirect taxes, *less* subsidies	—	—	—
GDP in purchasers' values	791,980	1,109,554	1,559,996
Net factor income from abroad	–116	–69	–220
Gross national product	791,864	1,109,485	1,559,776
Less Consumption of fixed capital	18,040	21,557	25,907
National income in market prices	773,824	1,087,928	1,533,869

Source: UN, *National Accounts Statistics*.

Expenditure on the Gross Domestic Product

	2000/01	2001/02	2002/03
Final consumption expenditure	2,237,476	3,139,827	4,946,534
Increase in stocks	16,709	–2,509	22,456
Gross fixed capital formation	300,981	413,182	552,965
Total domestic expenditure	2,555,166	3,550,500	5,521,955
Exports of goods and services	12,627	16,350	19,955
Less Imports of goods and services	15,060	18,378	14,910
GDP in purchasers' values	2,552,733	3,548,472	5,527,000
GDP at constant 2000/01 prices	n.a.	2,842,314	3,126,546

Source: Asian Development Bank, *Key Indicators of Developing Asian and Pacific Countries*.

Gross Domestic Product by Economic Activity

	2000/01	2001/02	2002/03
Agriculture, hunting, forestry and fishing	1,461,150	2,025,084	3,019,693
Mining and quarrying	15,032	17,334	24,409
Manufacturing	182,897	277,795	508,737
Electricity, gas and water	3,444	3,202	4,540
Construction	46,044	77,115	182,455
Wholesale and retail trade	613,686	858,083	1,304,516
Transport, storage and communications	153,371	191,810	344,149
Finance	2,641	3,299	4,189
Government services	39,354	44,686	49,775
Other services	35,114	50,064	84,537
GDP in purchasers' values	2,552,733	3,548,472	5,527,000

Source: Asian Development Bank, *Key Indicators of Developing Asian and Pacific Countries*.

MYANMAR

BALANCE OF PAYMENTS
(US $ million)

	2002	2003	2004
Exports of goods f.o.b.	2,421.1	2,709.7	2,926.7
Imports of goods f.o.b.	−2,022.1	−1,911.6	−1,998.7
Trade balance	399.0	798.1	928.0
Exports of services	426.0	249.1	254.7
Imports of services	−309.5	−420.0	−459.6
Balance on goods and services	515.5	627.3	723.0
Other income received	36.6	29.4	40.4
Other income paid	−619.7	−771.0	−785.8
Balance on goods, services and income	−67.6	−114.2	−22.4
Current transfers received	187.6	118.0	160.6
Current transfers paid	−23.4	−23.0	−26.7
Current balance	96.6	−19.3	111.5
Direct investment from abroad	152.1	251.5	213.5
Other investment liabilities	−184.1	−114.3	−88.3
Net errors and omissions	−19.2	−78.9	−142.7
Overall balance	45.4	38.9	94.0

Source: IMF, *International Financial Statistics*.

External Trade

PRINCIPAL COMMODITIES
(distribution by SITC, million kyats, year ending 31 March)

Imports c.i.f.	2000/01	2001/02	2002/03
Food and live animals	586	838	684
Mineral fuels, lubricants, etc.	1,145	3,839	2,105
Animal and vegetable oils, fats and waxes	412	253	272
Chemicals and related products	1,924	1,787	1,760
Basic manufactures	4,401	4,548	4,091
Machinery and transport equipment	3,754	5,110	3,558
Miscellaneous manufactured articles	1,000	726	557
Total (incl. others)	15,073	18,378	14,910

Exports f.o.b.	2000/01	2001/02	2002/03
Food and live animals	3,206	3,774	3,789
Dried beans, peas, etc. (shelled)	1,658	1,898	1,760
Crude materials (inedible) except fuels	1,401	2,750	2,404
Teak and other hardwood	803	1,880	1,871
Mineral fuels, etc.	1,180	4,247	5,919
Basic manufactures	1,240	168	564
Miscellaneous manufactured articles	1,570	104	88
Total (incl. others)	12,736	17,131	19,955

Source: Asian Development Bank, *Key Indicators of Developing Asian and Pacific Countries*.

PRINCIPAL TRADING PARTNERS
(US $ million, year ending 31 December)

Imports	2002	2003	2004
China, People's Republic	797.3	998.5	986.3
Hong Kong	69.9	48.4	48.7
India	63.1	93.9	99.8
Indonesia	59.8	50.2	62.9
Japan	126.9	137.0	115.8
Korea, Republic	157.8	202.4	215.1
Malaysia	263.1	154.3	164.3
Singapore	576.6	716.0	717.1
Thailand	355.9	483.3	665.9
Ukraine	34.4	44.6	47.4
Total (incl. others)	2,951.3	3,219.1	3,487.9

Exports	2002	2003	2004
China, People's Republic	124.5	154.1	198.2
France	79.5	56.7	71.2
Germany	73.1	94.0	113.7
India	195.2	355.2	444.8
Japan	100.3	126.9	163.5
Malaysia	69.8	72.6	97.1
Singapore	97.3	76.2	64.5
Thailand	831.2	827.0	1,177.5
United Kingdom	87.8	92.6	127.3
USA	345.4	268.6	—
Total (incl. others)	2,653.7	2,750.2	3,179.9

Source: Asian Development Bank, *Key Indicators of Developing Asian and Pacific Countries*.

Transport

RAILWAYS
(traffic, million)

	2001/02	2002/03	2003/04
Passenger-miles	2,798	2,926	2,679
Freight ton-miles	720	723	599

ROAD TRAFFIC
(registered motor vehicles at 31 March)

	1994	1995	1996
Passenger cars	119,126	131,953	151,934
Trucks	39,939	36,728	42,828
Buses	19,183	14,624	15,639
Motorcycles	71,929	82,591	85,821
Others	8,377	6,251	6,611
Total	258,554	272,147	302,833

Source: Department of Road Transport Administration.

Passenger cars: 177,900 in 1997; 177,600 in 1998; 171,100 in 1999; 173,900 in 2000; 175,400 in 2001; 177,500 in 2002 (Source: UN, *Statistical Yearbook for Asia and the Pacific*).

Commercial vehicles: 74,800 in 1997; 75,900 in 1998; 83,400 in 1999; 90,400 in 2000; 98,900 in 2001; 112,600 in 2002 (Source: UN, *Statistical Yearbook for Asia and the Pacific*).

INLAND WATERWAYS
(traffic by state-owned vessels)

	2001/02	2002/03	2003/04
Passenger-miles (million)	475	481	481
Freight ton-miles (million)	355	371	427

MYANMAR

SHIPPING

Merchant Fleet
(registered at 31 December)

	2002	2003	2004
Number of vessels	124	122	127
Displacement ('000 grt)	402.2	433.0	444.3

Source: Lloyd's Register-Fairplay, *World Fleet Statistics*.

International Sea-Borne Traffic
('000 metric tons)

	2000	2001	2002
Vessels ('000 grt):			
vessels entered	4,545	5,771	3,367
vessels cleared	2,252	981	797
Goods ('000 metric tons):			
goods loaded	3,257	1,017	810
goods unloaded	5,546	5,958	3,422

Source: UN, *Statistical Yearbook for Asia and the Pacific*.

CIVIL AVIATION
(traffic on scheduled services)

	1998	1999	2000
Kilometres flown (million)	9	9	4.1
Passengers carried ('000)	522	537	n.a.
Passenger-km (million)	345	355	225
Total ton-km (million)	40	40	17

Source: UN, *Statistical Yearbook for Asia and the Pacific*.

Tourism

TOURIST ARRIVALS BY COUNTRY OF NATIONALITY

	2001	2002	2003
Australia	4,442	5,194	4,950
China, People's Republic	16,788	17,732	15,564
France	12,461	14,108	13,125
Germany	11,450	12,952	13,341
India	5,572	5,691	6,291
Italy	6,618	7,908	6,129
Japan	20,118	20,744	18,799
Korea, Republic	7,581	7,890	8,399
Malaysia	11,296	12,532	10,003
Singapore	9,939	11,310	10,373
Taiwan	26,020	22,849	19,645
Thailand	17,123	16,936	22,214
United Kingdom	8,424	8,620	7,848
USA	13,524	14,477	13,256
Total (incl. others)	204,862	217,212	205,610

Tourism receipts (US $ million, incl. passenger transport): 132 in 2001; 116 in 2002; 68 in 2003.

Source: World Tourism Organization.

Communications Media

	2002	2003	2004
Telephones ('000 main lines in use)	341.3	363.0	424.9
Mobile cellular telephones ('000 subscribers)	48.0	66.5	92.0
Personal computers ('000 in use)	250	300	325
Internet users ('000)	25	28	63.7

Book production (1999): 227 titles.

Newspapers (1998): 4 dailies (average circulation 400,000).

Facsimile machines (number in use): 2,540 in 1999.

Radio receivers ('000 in use): 3,157 in 1999.

Television receivers ('000 in use): 344.3 in 2000.

Sources: International Telecommunication Union; UNESCO, *Statistical Yearbook*; UN, *Statistical Yearbook*.

Education

(1994/95, provisional)

	Institutions	Teachers	Students
Primary schools*	35,856	169,748	5,711,202
Middle schools	2,058	53,859	1,390,065
High schools	858	18,045	389,438
Vocational schools	86	1,847	21,343
Teacher training	17	615	4,031
Higher education	45	6,246	247,348
Universities	6	2,901	62,098

* Excluding 1,152 monastic primary schools with an enrolment of 45,360.

2001/02 (provisional): *Primary:* Institutions 36,010, Teachers 143,490, Students ('000) 4,793.5; *General Secondary:* Institutions 2,110, Teachers 53,896, Students ('000) 1,600.9; *Tertiary:* Institutions 958, Teachers 15,947, Students ('000) 587.3 (Source: UN, *Statistical Yearbook for Asia and the Pacific*).

Adult literacy rate (UNESCO estimates): 89.7% (males 93.7%; females 86.2%) in 2003 (Source: UN Development Programme, *Human Development Report*).

Directory

The Constitution

On 18 September 1988 a military junta, the State Law and Order Restoration Council (SLORC), assumed power and abolished all state organs created under the Constitution of 3 January 1974. The country was placed under martial law. The state organs were superseded by the SLORC at all levels with the Division, Township and Village State Law and Order Restoration Councils. The SLORC announced that a new constitution was to be drafted by the 485-member Constituent Assembly that was elected in May 1990. In early 1993 a National Convention, comprising members of the SLORC and representatives of opposition parties, met to draft a new constitution; however, the Convention was adjourned in March 1996 and remained in recess in early 2004. In November 1997 the SLORC was dissolved and replaced by the newly formed State Peace and Development Council (SPDC). In August 2003 the SPDC announced that it planned to reconvene the National Convention in 2004 in order that it could commence the drafting of a new constitution.

The Government

HEAD OF STATE

Chairman of the State Peace and Development Council: Field Marshal THAN SHWE (took office as Head of State 23 April 1992).

MYANMAR

STATE PEACE AND DEVELOPMENT COUNCIL
(April 2006)

Chairman: Field Marshal THAN SHWE.
Vice-Chairman: Dep. Senior Gen. MAUNG AYE.
First Secretary: Lt-Gen. THEIN SEIN.
Second Secretary: (vacant).
Third Secretary: (vacant).
Other members: Rear-Adm. KYI MIN, Lt-Gen. KYAW THAN, Lt-Gen. AUNG HTWE, Lt-Gen. YE MYINT, Lt-Gen. KHIN MAUNG THAN, Maj.-Gen. KYAW WIN, Maj.-Gen. THURA SHWE MANN, Maj.-Gen. MYINT AUNG, Lt-Gen. MAUNG BO, Maj.-Gen. THIHA THURA TIN AUNG MYINT OO, Lt-Gen. TIN AYE.

CABINET
(April 2006)

Prime Minister: Lt-Gen. SOE WIN.
Minister of Defence: Field Marshal THAN SHWE.
Minister of Military Affairs: Maj.-Gen. THIHA THURA TIN AUNG MYINT OO.
Minister of Agriculture and Irrigation: Maj.-Gen. HTAY OO.
Minister of Industry (No. 1): U AUNG THAUNG.
Minister of Industry (No. 2): Maj.-Gen. SAW LWIN.
Minister of Foreign Affairs: Maj.-Gen. NYAN WIN.
Minister of National Planning and Economic Development: U SOE THA.
Minister of Transport: Maj.-Gen. THEIN SHWE.
Minister of Culture: Maj.-Gen. KYI AUNG.
Minister of Co-operatives: Col ZAW MIN.
Minister of Rail Transportation: Maj.-Gen. AUNG MIN.
Minister of Energy: Brig.-Gen. LUN THI.
Minister of Education: CHAN NYEIN.
Minister of Health: Dr KYAW MYINT.
Minister of Commerce: Brig.-Gen. TIN NAING THEIN.
Minister of Communications, Posts and Telegraphs and of Hotels and Tourism: Brig.-Gen. THEIN ZAW.
Minister of Finance and Revenue: Maj.-Gen. HLA TUN.
Minister of Religious Affairs: Brig.-Gen. THURA MYINT MAUNG.
Minister of Construction: Maj.-Gen. SAW TUN.
Minister of Science and Technology and of Labour: U THAUNG.
Minister of Immigration and Population and of Social Welfare, Relief and Resettlement: Maj.-Gen. SEIN HTWA.
Minister of Information: Brig.-Gen. KYAW HSAN.
Minister of Progress of Border Areas, National Races and Development Affairs: Col THEIN NYUNT.
Minister of Electric Power: Maj.-Gen. TIN HTUT.
Minister of Sports: Brig.-Gen. THURA AYE MYINT.
Minister of Forestry: Brig.-Gen. THEIN AUNG.
Minister of Home Affairs: Maj.-Gen. MAUNG OO.
Minister of Mines: Brig.-Gen. OHN MYINT.
Minister of Livestock and Fisheries: Brig.-Gen. MAUNG MAUNG THEIN.
Minister at the Office of the Prime Minister: U KO LAY.

MINISTRIES

Office of the Chairman of the State Peace and Development Council: 15–16 Windermere Park, Yangon; tel. (1) 282445.
Prime Minister's Office: Minister's Office, Theinbyu St, Botahtaung Township, Yangon; tel. (1) 283742.
Ministry of Agriculture and Irrigation: Thiri Mingala Lane, off Kaba Aye Pagoda Rd, Yangon; tel. (1) 665587; fax (1) 664493; e-mail dap.moai@mptmail.net.mm; internet www.myanmar.com/Ministry/agriculture/default_1.html.
Ministry of Commerce: 228–240 Strand Rd, Yangon; tel. (1) 256163; fax (1) 253028; e-mail dotd_dg@commerce.gov.mm@mptmail.net.mm; internet www.commerce.gov.mm.
Ministry of Communications, Posts and Telegraphs: 361 Pyay Rd, nr Hanthawaddy Circus, Sanchaung Township, Yangon; tel. (1) 512775; internet www.mcpt.gov.mm.
Ministry of Construction: 39 Nawaday St, Dagon Township, Yangon; tel. (1) 283938; fax (1) 289531; internet www.construction.gov.mm.
Ministry of Co-operatives: 259–263 Bogyoke Aung San St, Yangon; tel. (1) 277096; fax (1) 287919; internet www.myancoop.gov.mm.
Ministry of Culture: 131 Kaba Aye Pagoda Rd, Bahan Township, Yangon; tel. (1) 274975; fax (1) 283794; internet www.myanmar.com/Ministry/culture.
Ministry of Defence: Ahlanpya Phaya St, Yangon; tel. (1) 281611.
Ministry of Education: Theinbyu St, Botahtaung Township, Yangon; tel. (1) 285588; fax (1) 285480; internet www.myanmar-education.edu.mm.
Ministry of Electric Power: 197–199 Lower Kyimyindaing Rd, Ahlone Township, Yangon; tel. (1) 229366; fax (1) 221006; internet www.energy.gov.mm/MEP_1.htm.
Ministry of Energy: 23 Pyay Rd, Lanmadaw Township, Yangon; tel. (1) 221060; fax (1) 222964; e-mail myanmoe@mptmail.net.mm; internet www.energy.gov.mm.
Ministry of Finance and Revenue: 26A Setmu Rd, Yankin Township, Yangon; tel. (1) 274894; internet www.myanmar.com/Ministry/finance.
Ministry of Foreign Affairs: Pyay Rd, Dagon Township, Yangon; tel. (1) 222844; fax (1) 222950; e-mail mofa.aung@mptmail.net.mm; internet www.mofa.gov.mm.
Ministry of Forestry: Thirimingala Lane, Kaba Aye Pagoda Rd, Yangon; tel. (1) 278647; fax (1) 250198; internet www.energy.gov.mm/MOF_1.htm.
Ministry of Health: Theinbyu St, Botahtaung Township, Yangon; tel. (1) 285245; fax (1) 282834; internet www.myanmar.com/Ministry/health.
Ministry of Home Affairs: cnr of Saya San St and No. 1 Industrial St, Yankin Township, Yangon; tel. (1) 549240; internet www.moha.gov.mm.
Ministry of Hotels and Tourism: 77–91 Sule Pagoda Rd, Kyauktada Township, Yangon; tel. (1) 282705; fax (1) 287871; e-mail dht.mht@myanmar.com.mm; internet www.hotel-tourism.gov.mm.
Ministry of Immigration and Population: cnr of Mahabandoola Rd and Theinbyu St, Botahtaung Township, Yangon; tel. (1) 249090; internet www.myanmar.com/Ministry/imm&popu.
Ministry of Industry (No. 1): 192 Kaba Aye Pagoda Rd, Yangon; tel. (1) 566066; internet www.myanmar.com/Ministry/MOI-1.
Ministry of Industry (No. 2): 56 Kaba Aye Pagoda Rd, Yankin Township, Yangon; tel. (1) 666134; fax (1) 666135; e-mail dmip@mptmail.net.mm; internet www.industry2.gov.mm.
Ministry of Information: 365–367 Bo Sung Kyaw St, Yangon; tel. (1) 245631; fax (1) 289274.
Ministry of Labour: Theinbyu St, Botahtaung Township, Yangon; tel. (1) 278320; fax (1) 256185.
Ministry of Livestock and Fisheries: 460 Konthe Rd, Botahtaung Township, Yangon; tel. (1) 297180; fax (1) 289711; e-mail dolf@mptmail.net.mm; internet www.livestock-fisheries.gov.mm.
Ministry of Military Affairs: Yangon.
Ministry of Mines: 90 Kanbe Rd, Yankin Township, Yangon; tel. (1) 577316; fax (1) 577455; internet www.energy.gov.mm/MOM_1.htm.
Ministry of National Planning and Economic Development: Minister's Office, Theinbyu St, Botahtaung Township, Yangon; tel. (1) 241918; fax (1) 243791; e-mail ministry.nped@mptmail.net.mm; internet www.mnped.gov.mm.
Ministry of Progress of Border Areas, National Races and Development Affairs: Minister's Office, Theinbyu St, Botahtaung Township, Yangon; tel. (1) 280032; fax (1) 285257.
Ministry of Rail Transportation: 88 Theinbyu St, Yangon; tel. (1) 292769.
Ministry of Religious Affairs: Kaba Aye Pagoda Rd, Mayangone Township, Yangon; tel. (1) 665620; fax (1) 665728; internet www.mora.gov.mm.
Ministry of Science and Technology: 6 Kaba Aye Pagoda Rd, Yankin Township, Yangon; tel. (1) 667639; fax (1) 651026.
Ministry of Social Welfare, Relief and Resettlement: Theinbyu St, Botahtaung Township, Yangon; tel. (1) 665697; fax (1) 650002; e-mail social-wel-myan@mptmail.net.mm; internet www.myanmar.gov.mm/ministry/MSWRR/main.htm.
Ministry of Sports: National Indoor Stadium, Thuwunna, Thingangyun Township, Yangon; tel. (1) 577343; fax (1) 571061; e-mail MOCYGN.MYA@mptmail.net.mm; internet http://www.myanmar.com/Ministry/sport/default.htm.
Ministry of Transport: 363–421 Merchant St, Botahtaung Township, Yangon; tel. (1) 296815; fax (1) 296324; internet www.myanmar.com/Ministry/Transport.

In 2005–06 the above ministries were in the process of being relocated, following the SPDC's decision to create a new administrative capital in Pyinmana, a mountainous region 400 km (249 miles) to the north of Yangon.

MYANMAR

Legislature

CONSTITUENT ASSEMBLY

Following the military coup of 18 September 1988, the 489-member Pyithu Hluttaw (People's Assembly), together with all other state organs, was abolished. A general election was held on 27 May 1990. It was subsequently announced, however, that the new body was to serve as a constituent assembly, responsible for the drafting of a new constitution, and that it was to have no legislative power. The next legislative election was provisionally scheduled for September 1997, but did not take place.

General Election, 27 May 1990

Party	% of Votes	Seats
National League for Democracy	59.9	392
Shan Nationalities League for Democracy	1.7	23
Arakan (Rakhine) League for Democracy	1.2	11
National Unity Party	21.2	10
Mon National Democratic Front	1.0	5
National Democratic Party for Human Rights	0.9	4
Chin National League for Democracy	0.4	3
Kachin State National Congress for Democracy	0.1	3
Party for National Democracy	0.5	3
Union Pa-O National Organization	0.3	3
Zomi National Congress		2
Naga Hill Regional Progressive Party		2
Kayah State Nationalities League for Democracy		2
Ta-ang (Palaung) National League for Democracy		2
Democratic Organization for Kayan National Unity		2
Democracy Party		1
Graduates' and Old Students' Democratic Association		1
Patriotic Old Comrades' League	12.8	1
Shan State Kokang Democratic Party		1
Union Danu League for Democracy Party		1
Kamans National League for Democracy		1
Mara People's Party		1
Union Nationals Democracy Party		1
Mro (or) Khami National Solidarity Organization		1
Lahu National Development Party		1
United League of Democratic Parties		1
Karen (Kayin) State National Organization		1
Independents		6
Total	**100.0**	**485**

Political Organizations

A total of 93 parties contested the general election of May 1990. By October 1995 the ruling military junta had deregistered all except nine political parties:

Kokang Democracy and Unity Party: Yangon.

Mro (or) Khami National Solidarity Organization: f. 1988; Leader U SAN THA AUNG.

National League for Democracy (NLD): 97B West Shwegondine Rd, Bahan Township, Yangon; f. 1988; initially known as the National United Front for Democracy, and subsequently as the League for Democracy; present name adopted in Sept. 1988; central exec. cttee of 10 mems; Gen. Sec. Daw AUNG SAN SUU KYI; Chair. U AUNG SHWE; Vice-Chair. U TIN OO, U KYI MAUNG.

National Unity Party (NUP): 93C Windermere Rd, Kamayut, Yangon; tel. (1) 278180; f. 1962 as the Burma Socialist Programme Party; sole legal political party until Sept. 1988, when present name was adopted; 15-mem. Cen. Exec. Cttee and 280-mem. Cen. Cttee; Chair. U THA KYAW; Gen. Secs U TUN YI, U THAN TIN.

Shan Nationalities League for Democracy (SNLD): f. 1988; Chair. KHUN HTUN OO; Sec.-Gen. SAI NYUNT LWIN.

Shan State Kokang Democratic Party: 140 40 St, Kyauktada; f. 1988; Leader U YANKYIN MAW.

Union Karen (Kayin) League: Saw Toe Lane, Yangon.

Union Pa-O National Organization: f. 1988; Leader U SAN HLA.

Wa National Development Party: Byuhar St, Yangon.

The following parties contested the general election of March 1990 but subsequently had their legal status annulled:

Anti-Fascist People's Freedom League: Bo Aung Kyaw St, Bahan Township, Yangon; f. 1988; assumed name of wartime resistance movement which became Myanmar's major political force after independence; Chair. BO KYAW NYUNT; Gen. Sec. CHO CHO KYAW NYEIN.

Democracy Party: f. 1988; comprises supporters of fmr Prime Minister U NU; Chair. U THU WAI; Vice-Chair. U KHUN YE NAUNG.

Democratic Front for National Reconstruction: Yangon; f. 1988; left-wing; Leader Thakin CHIT MAUNG.

Lahu National Development Party: f. 1988; deregistered 1994; Leader U DANIEL AUNG.

League for Democracy and Peace: 10 Wingaba Rd, Bahan Township, Yangon; f. 1988; Gen. Sec. U THEIN SEIN.

Party for National Democracy: Yangon; f. 1988; Chair. Dr SEIN WIN.

Union National Democracy Party (UNDP): 2–4 Shin Saw Pu Rd, Sanchaung Township, Yangon; f. 1988; est. by Brig.-Gen. AUNG GYI (fmr Chair. of the National League for Democracy); Chair. U KYAW MYINT LAY.

United League of Democratic Parties: 875 Compound 21, Ledauntkan St, Sa-Hsa Ward, Thingangyun Township, Yangon; f. 1989.

United Nationalities League for Democracy: Yangon; an alliance of parties representing non-Bamar nationalities; won a combined total of 65 seats at the 1990 election.

Other deregistered parties included the Arakan (Rakhine) League for Democracy, the Mon National Democratic Front, the National Democratic Party for Human Rights, the Chin National League for Democracy, the Kachin State National Congress for Democracy, the Zomi National Congress, the Naga Hill Regional Progressive Party, the Kayah State Nationalities League for Democracy, the Ta-ang (Palaung) National League for Democracy, the Democratic Organization for Kayan National Unity, the Graduates' and Old Students' Democratic Association, the Patriotic Old Comrades' League, the Union Danu League for Democracy, the Kamans National League for Democracy, the Mara People's Party and the Karen (Kayin) State National Organization.

The following groups are, or have been, in armed conflict with the Government:

Burma Democratic Alliance (BDA): f. 2004; opposition alliance comprised of several dissident organizations; Leader Dr NAING AUNG.

Chin National Army: Chin State.

Chin National Front: f. 1988; forces trained by Kachin Independence Army 1989–91; first party congress 1993; conference in March 1996; carried out an active bombing campaign in 1996–97, mainly in the Chin State; Pres. THOMAS TANG NO.

Communist Party of Burma (CPB): f. 1939; reorg. 1946; operated clandestinely after 1948; participated after 1986 in jt military operations with sections of the NDF; in 1989 internal dissent resulted in the rebellion of about 80% of CPB members, mostly Wa hill tribesmen and Kokang Chinese; the CPB's military efficacy was thus completely destroyed; Chair. of Cen. Cttee Thakin BA THEIN TIN (exiled).

Democratic Alliance of Burma (DAB): Manerplaw; f. 1988; formed by members of the NDF to incorporate dissident students, monks and expatriates; Pres. Maj.-Gen. BO MYA; Gen. Sec. U TIN MAUNG WIN; remaining organizations include:

All-Burma Student Democratic Front (ABSDF): Dagwin; f. 1988; in 1990 split into two factions, under U Moe Thi Zun and U Naing Aung; the two factions reunited in 1993; Chair. THAN KHE; Sec.-Gen. MYO WIN.

Karen (Kayin) National Union (KNU): f. 1948; in process of negotiating peace agreement with SPDC in 2004; Chair. SAW BA THIN; Vice-Chair. Gen. TAMALABAW; Sec.-Gen. MAHN SHA; military wing: Karen (Kayin) National Liberation Army (KNLA); c. 6,000 troops; Chief of Staff Gen. MUTU.

Karenni (Kayinni) National Progressive Party: agreement with the SLORC signed in March 1995 but subsequently collapsed; resumed fighting in June 1996; Chair. Gen. AUNG THAN LAY; military wing: Karenni (Kayinni) Revolutionary Army.

God's Army: breakaway faction of the KNU; Leaders JOHNNY HTOO, LUTHER HTOO (surrendered to the Thai authorities in Jan. 2001).

National Democratic Front (NDF): f. 1975; aims to establish a federal union based on national self-determination; largely defunct.

National Socialist Council of Nagaland: Sagaing Division; comprises various factions.

MYANMAR

Shan State Army (SSA): enlarged in Sept. 1997 through formal alliance between the following:

Shan State National Army (SSNA): Shan State; f. 1995; breakaway group from Mong Tai Army (MTA); Shan separatists; 5,000–6,000 troops; Leaders KARN YORD, YEE.

Shan State Peace Council (SSPC): fmrly Shan State Progressive Party; Pres. HSO HTEN; Gen. Sec. KARN YORD; cease-fire agreement signed in Sept. 1989, but broken by SSA elements following establishment of above alliance in Sept. 1997; military wing: original **Shan State Army** (5,000 men); Leaders SAI NONG, KAI HPA, PANG HPA.

Other MTA remnants also participated in the alliance.

Vigorous Burmese Student Warriors (VBSW): f. 1999.

Most of the following groups have signed cease-fire agreements, or reached other means of accommodation, with the ruling military junta (the date given in parentheses indicates the month in which agreement with the junta was concluded):

Democratic Karen (Kayin) Buddhist Organization: Manerplaw; breakaway group from the KNU; military wing: Democratic Karen (Kayin) Buddhist Army.

Kachin Democratic Army: (Jan. 1991); fmrly the 4th Brigade of the Kachin Independence Army; Leader U ZAW MAING.

Kachin Independence Organization (KIO): (Oct. 1993); Chair. U LAMON TU JAI; military wing: Kachin Independence Army.

Karen (Kayin) Solidarity Organization (KSO): f. 1997; fmrly All Karen Solidarity and Regeneration Front; breakaway group from the KNU; 21-mem. exec. cttee; advocates nation-wide cease-fire and the settlement of all national problems through negotiations; Pres. SAW W. P. NI; Sec.-Gen. MAHN AUNG HTAY.

Karenni (Kayinni) National People's Liberation Front: (May 1994); Leader U TUN KYAW.

Kayan National Guard: (Feb. 1992).

Kayan New Land Party: (July 1994); Leader U THAN SOE NAING.

Myanmar National Democracy Alliance: (March 1989).

National Democracy Alliance Army: (June 1989).

New Democratic Army: Kachin; (Dec. 1989).

New Mon State Party: (June 1995); Chair. (vacant); military wing: Mon National Liberation Army.

Palaung State Liberation Organization: (April 1991); military wing: Palaung State Liberation Army; 7,000–8,000 men.

Pa-O National Organization: (Feb. 1991); Chair. AUNG KHAM HTI; military wing: Pa-O National Army.

Shan State Nationalities Liberation Organization: (Oct. 1994); Chair. U THA KALEI.

United Wa State Party: (May 1989); fmrly part of the Communist Party of Burma; military wing: **United Wa State Army** (10,000–15,000 men); Leaders CHAO NGI LAI, PAO YU CHANG.

Since 1991 the National Coalition Government of the Union of Burma, constituted by representatives elected in the general election of 1990, has served as a government-in-exile:

National Coalition Government of the Union of Burma (NCGUB): 77 South Washington Street, Suite 308, Rockville, Maryland 20850, USA; tel. (301) 424-4810; fax (301) 424-4812; e-mail ncgub@ncgub.net; internet www.ncgub.net; Prime Minister Dr SEIN WIN.

Diplomatic Representation

EMBASSIES IN MYANMAR

Australia: 88 Strand Rd, Yangon; tel. (1) 251810; fax (1) 246159; internet www.embassy.gov.au/mn; Ambassador BOB DAVIS.

Bangladesh: 11B Thanlwin Rd, Yangon; tel. (1) 515275; fax (1) 515273; e-mail bdootygn@mptmail.net.mm; Ambassador MOHAMMAD KHAIRUZZAMAN.

Brunei: 51 Golden Valley, Bahan Township, Yangon; tel. (1) 510422; fax (1) 512854; Ambassador Brig.-Gen. Dato' Paduka Haji MOHAMAD YUSOF BIN ABU BAKAR.

Cambodia: 34 Kaba Aye Pagoda Rd, Yangon; tel. (1) 546157; fax (1) 546156; e-mail recyangon@mptmail.net.mm; Ambassador HUL PHANY.

China, People's Republic: 1 Pyidaungsu Yeiktha Rd, Yangon; tel. (1) 221281; fax (1) 227019; e-mail chinaemb_mm@mfa.gov.cn; Ambassador GUAN MU.

Egypt: 81 Pyidaungsu Yeiktha Rd, Yangon; tel. (1) 222886; fax (1) 222865; Ambassador MOHAMED EL MENEISSY.

France: 102 Pyidaungsu Yeiktha Rd, POB 858, Yangon; tel. (1) 212523; fax (1) 212527; e-mail ambafrance-rangoun@diplomatie.gouv.fr; internet www.ambafrance-mm.org; Ambassador JEAN-MICHEL LACOMBE.

Germany: 9 Bogyoke Aung San Museum Rd, POB 12, Yangon; tel. (1) 548951; fax (1) 548899; e-mail post@botschaftrangun.net.mm; Ambassador Dr KLAUS WILD.

India: 545–547 Merchant St, POB 751, Yangon; tel. (1) 243972; fax (1) 254086; e-mail amb.indembygn@mptmail.net.mm; Ambassador BHASKAR KUMAR MITRA.

Indonesia: 100 Pyidaungsu Yeiktha Rd, POB 1401, Yangon; tel. (1) 254465; fax (1) 254468; e-mail kbriygn@indosat.net.id; Ambassador WYOSO PROJOWARSITO.

Israel: 15 Khabaung St, Hlaing Township, Yangon; tel. (1) 515115; fax (1) 515116; e-mail yangon@israel.org; Ambassador RUTH SCHATZ.

Italy: 3 Inya Myaing Rd, POB 866, Golden Valley, Bahan Township, Yangon; tel. (1) 527100; fax (1) 514565; e-mail ambitaly@ambitaly.net.mm; internet www.ambyangon.esteri.it; Ambassador RAFFAELE MINIERO.

Japan: 100 Natmauk Rd, POB 841, Bahan Township, Yangon 11021; tel. (1) 549644; fax (1) 549643; e-mail jembassy@baganmail.net.mm; internet www.mm.emb-japan.go.jp; Ambassador NOBUTAKE ODANO.

Korea, Republic: 97 University Ave, Yangon; tel. (1) 515190; fax (1) 513286; e-mail hankuk@koremby.net.mm; Ambassador LEE JU-HEUM.

Laos: A1 Diplomatic Quarters, Franser Rd, Yangon; tel. (1) 222482; fax (1) 227446; Ambassador CHANTHAVY BODHISANE.

Malaysia: 882 Diplomatic Quarters, Pyidaungsu Yeiktha Rd, Yangon; tel. (1) 220249; fax (1) 221840; e-mail mwyangon@mweb.com.na; Ambassador SHAHARUDDIN BIN MOHAMMAD SOM.

Nepal: 16 Natmauk Yeiktha Rd, POB 84, Tamwe, Yangon; tel. (1) 545880; fax (1) 549803; e-mail rnembygn@datseco.com.mm; Ambassador Lt-Gen. (retd) VICTORY S. J. B. RAHA.

Pakistan: A4 Diplomatic Quarters, Pyay Rd, Dagon Township, Yangon; tel. (1) 222881; fax (1) 221147; e-mail parepygn@myanmar.com.mm; Ambassador MUHAMMAD NAWAZ CHAUDHRY.

Philippines: 50 Saya San Rd, Bahan Township, Yangon; tel. (1) 558149; fax (1) 558154; e-mail phyangon@mptmail.net.mm; Ambassador PHOEBE ABAYA GOMEZ.

Russia: 38 Sagawa Rd, Yangon; tel. (1) 241955; fax (1) 241953; e-mail rusinmyan@mptmail.net.mm; Ambassador OLEG V. KABANOV.

Serbia and Montenegro: 114A Inya Rd, POB 943, Yangon; tel. (1) 515282; fax (1) 504274; e-mail yuamb@yangon.net.mm; Chargé d'affaires a.i. VLADIMIR STAMENOVIĆ.

Singapore: 238 Dhamazedi Rd, Bahan Township, Yangon; tel. (1) 559001; fax (1) 559002; e-mail singemb@seygn.com.mm; internet www.mfa.gov.sg/yangon/; Ambassador T. JASUDASEN.

Sri Lanka: 34 Taw Win Rd, POB 1150, Yangon; tel. (1) 222812; fax (1) 221509; e-mail srilankaemb@mpt.net.mm; Ambassador D. M. M. RANARAJA.

Thailand: 73 Manawhari St, Dagon Township, Yangon; tel. (1) 224647; fax (1) 225929; e-mail thaiygn@mfa.go.th; Ambassador SUPHOT DHIRAKAOSAL.

United Kingdom: 80 Strand Rd, Kyauktada Township, Yangon; tel. (1) 370863; fax (1) 370866; e-mail chancery.Rangoon@fco.gov.uk; Ambassador VICKY BOWMAN.

USA: 581 Merchant St, POB 521, Yangon; tel. (1) 379880; fax (1) 256018; e-mail info.rangoon@state.gov; internet rangoon.usembassy.gov; Chargé d'affaires CARMEN MARIA MARTINEZ.

Viet Nam: 317–319 U Wisara Rd, Sanchaung Township, Yangon; tel. (1) 524285; fax (1) 524658; e-mail vnembmyr@bertech.net.mm; Ambassador PHAM QUANG KHON.

Judicial System

A new judicial structure was established in March 1974. Its highest organ, composed of members of the People's Assembly, was the Council of People's Justices, which functioned as the central Court of Justice. Below this Council were the state, divisional, township, ward and village tract courts formed with members of local People's Councils. These arrangements ceased to operate following the imposition of military rule in September 1988, when a Supreme Court with five members was appointed. A chief justice, an attorney-general and a deputy attorney-general were also appointed. In March 2003 a deputy chief justice, four more justices and two further deputy attorney-generals were appointed.

Office of the Supreme Court

101 Pansodan St, Kyauktada Township, Yangon; tel. (1) 280751.

Chief Justice: U AUNG TOE.

Attorney-General: AYE MAUNG.

Religion

Freedom of religious belief and practice is guaranteed. In 1992 an estimated 87.2% of the population were Buddhists, 5.6% Christians, 3.6% Muslims, 1.0% Hindus and 2.6% animists or adherents of other religions.

BUDDHISM

State Sangha Maha Nayaka Committee: c/o Dept of Promotion and Propagation of the Sasana, Kaba Aye Pagoda Precinct, Mayangone Township, Yangon; tel. (1) 660759.

CHRISTIANITY

Myanmar Naing-ngan Khrityan Athin-dawmyar Kaung-si (Myanmar Council of Churches): Myanmar Ecumenical Sharing Centre, 601 Pyay Rd, University PO, Yangon 11041; tel. (1) 537957; fax (1) 296848; e-mail oikom@yangon.net.mm; f. 1914 as Burma Representative Council of Mission; reconstituted as Burma Council of Churches in 1974; 13 mem. nat. churches, 9 mem. nat. Christian orgs; Pres. Rev. SAW MAR GAY GYI; Gen. Sec. Rt Rev. SMITH N. ZA THAWNG.

The Roman Catholic Church

Myanmar comprises three archdioceses and nine dioceses. At 31 December 2003 an estimated 1.3% of the total population were adherents.

Catholic Bishops' Conference of Myanmar
292 Pyay Rd, POB 1080, Sanchaung PO, Yangon 11111; tel. (1) 525868; fax (1) 527198; e-mail clspcbcm@mptmail.net.mm; f. 1982; Pres. Most Rev. CHARLES MAUNG BO (Archbishop of Yangon).

Archbishop of Mandalay: Most Rev. PAUL ZINGTUNG GRAWNG, Archbishop's House, 81st and 25th St, Mandalay 06011; tel. (2) 33916; e-mail paulgrawng@mandalay.net.mm.

Archbishop of Taunggyi: Most Rev. MATTHIAS U SHWE, Archbishop's Office, Bayint Naung Rd, Taunggyi 06011; tel. (81) 21689; fax (81) 22164; e-mail matthias@myanmar.com.mm.

Archbishop of Yangon: Most Rev. CHARLES MAUNG BO, Archbishop's House, 289 Theinbyu St, Botataung, 11161 Yangon; tel. (1) 246710; fax (1) 379059.

The Anglican Communion

Anglicans are adherents of the Church of the Province of Myanmar, comprising six dioceses. The Province was formed in February 1970, and contained an estimated 45,000 adherents in 1985.

Archbishop of Myanmar and Bishop of Yangon: Most Rev. SAMUEL SAN SI HTAY, Bishopscourt, 140 Pyidaungsu Yeiktha Rd, Dagon PO (11191), Yangon; tel. (1) 285379; fax (1) 251405.

Protestant Churches

Lutheran Bethlehem Church: 181–183 Theinbyu St, Mingala Taung Nyunt PO 11221, POB 773, Yangon; tel. (1) 246585; Pres. Rev. JENSON RAJAN ANDREWS.

Myanmar Baptist Convention: 143 Minye Kyawswa Rd, POB 506, Yangon; tel. (1) 223231; fax (1) 221465; e-mail mbc<mbc@mptmail.net.mm; f. 1865; est. as Burma Baptist Missionary Convention; present name adopted 1954; 650,293 mems (2003); Pres. Rev. Dr HONOR NYO; Gen. Sec. Rev. K. D. TU LOM.

Myanmar Methodist Church: Methodist Headquarters, 22 Signal Pagoda Rd, Yangon; Pres. Bishop ZOTHAN MAWIA.

Presbyterian Church of Myanmar: Synod Office, Falam, Chin State; 22,000 mems; Pres. Rev. SUN KANGLO.

Other denominations active in Myanmar include the Lisu Christian Church and the Salvation Army.

The Press

DAILIES

Botahtaung (The Vanguard): 22–30 Strand Rd, Botahtaung PO, POB 539, Yangon; tel. (1) 274310; Myanmar.

Guardian: 392–396 Merchant St, Botahtaung PO, POB 1522, Yangon; tel. (1) 270150; English.

Kyehmon (The Mirror): 77 52nd St, Dazundaung PO, POB 819, Yangon; tel. (1) 282777; Myanmar.

Myanmar Alin (New Light of Myanmar): 58 Komin Kochin Rd, Bahan PO, POB 21, Yangon; tel. (1) 544309; f. 1963; fmrly Loktha Pyithu Nezin (Working People's Daily); organ of the SPDC; morning; Myanmar; Chief Editor U WIN TIN; circ. 400,000.

New Light of Myanmar: 22–30 Strand Rd, Yangon; tel. (1) 297028; e-mail webmaster@myanmar.com; internet www.myanmar.com/nlm; f. 1963; fmrly Working People's Daily; organ of the SPDC; morning; English; Chief Editor U KYAW MIN; circ. 14,000.

PERIODICALS

A Hla Thit (New Beauty): 46 90th St, Yangon; tel. (1) 287106; international news.

Dana Business Magazine: 72 8th St, Lanmadaw Township, Yangon; tel. and fax (1) 224010; e-mail dana@mptmail.net.mm; economic; Editor-in-Chief WILLIAM CHEN.

Do Kyaung Tha: Myawaddy Press, 184 32nd St, Yangon; tel. (1) 274655; f. 1965; monthly; Myanmar and English; circ. 17,000.

Gita Padetha: Yangon; journal of Myanma Music Council; circ. 10,000.

Guardian Magazine: 392–396 Merchant St, Botahtaung PO, POB 1522, Yangon; tel. (1) 296510; f. 1953; nationalized 1964; monthly; English; literary; circ. 11,600.

Kyee Pwar Yay (Prosperity): 296 Bo Sun Pat St, Yangon; tel. (1) 278100; economic; Editor-in-Chief U MYAT KHINE.

Moethaukpan (Aurora): Myawaddy Press, 184 32nd St, Yangon; tel. (1) 274655; f. 1980; monthly; Myanmar and English; circ. 27,500.

Myanma Dana (Myanmar's Economy): 210A 36th St, Kyauktada PO, Yangon; tel. (1) 284660; economic; Editor-in-Chief U THIHA SAW.

Myanmar Morning Post: Yangon; f. 1998; weekly; Chinese; news; circ. 5,000.

Myanmar Times & Business Review: Level 1, 5 Signal Pagoda Rd, Dagon Township, Yangon; tel. (1) 242711; fax (1) 242669; e-mail myanmartimes@mptmail.net.mm; internet www.mmtimes.com; f. 2000; Editor-in-Chief ROSS DUNKLEY.

Myawaddy Journal: Myawaddy Press, 184 32nd St, Yangon; tel. (1) 274655; f. 1989; fortnightly; news; circ. 8,700.

Myawaddy Magazine: Myawaddy Press, 184 32nd St, Yangon; tel. (1) 274655; f. 1952; monthly; literary magazine; circ. 4,200.

Ngwetaryi Magazine: Myawaddy Press, 184 32nd St, Yangon; tel. (1) 274655; f. 1961; monthly; cultural; circ. 3,400.

Pyinnya Lawka Journal: 529 Merchant St, Yangon; tel. (1) 283611; publ. by Sarpay Beikman Management Board; quarterly; circ. 18,000.

Shwe Thwe: 529 Merchant St, Yangon; tel. (1) 283611; weekly; bilingual children's journal; publ. by Sarpay Beikman Management Board; circ. 100,000.

Taw Win Journal (Royal Journal): 149 37th St, Yangon; news; Editor-in-Chief SOE THEIN.

Teza: Myawaddy Press, 184 32nd St, Yangon; tel. (1) 274655; f. 1965; monthly; English and Myanmar; pictorial publication for children; circ. 29,500.

Thwe Thauk Magazine: Myawaddy Press, 184 32nd St, Yangon; f. 1946; monthly; literary.

Ya Nant Thit (New Fragrance): 186 39th St, Yangon; tel. (1) 276799; international news; Editor-in-Chief U CHIT WIN MG.

NEWS AGENCIES

Myanmar News Agency (MNA): 212 Theinbyu Rd, Botahtaung, Yangon; tel. (1) 270893; f. 1963; govt-controlled; Chief Editors U ZAW MIN THEIN (domestic section), U KYAW MIN (external section).

Foreign Bureaux

Agence France-Presse (AFP) (France): 12L Pyithu Lane, 7th Mile, Yangon; tel. (1) 661069; Correspondent U KHIN MAUNG THWIN.

Agenzia Nazionale Stampa Associata (ANSA) (Italy): POB 270, Yangon; tel. (1) 511663; fax (1) 526400; e-mail mtgroup@myanmar.com.mm; Rep. (vacant).

Associated Press (AP) (USA): 283 U Wisara Rd, Sanchaung PO 11111, Yangon; tel. (1) 527014; Rep. AYE AYE WIN.

Xinhua (New China) News Agency (People's Republic of China): 105 Leeds Rd, Yangon; tel. (1) 221400; Correspondent ZHANG YUHFEI.

Reuters (United Kingdom) and **UPI** (USA) are also represented in Myanmar.

Publishers

Hanthawaddy Press: 157 Bo Aung Gyaw St, Yangon; f. 1889; textbooks, multilingual dictionaries; Man. Editor U ZAW WIN.

Knowledge Publishing House: 130 Bo Gyoke Aung San St, Yegyaw, Yangon; art, education, religion, politics and social sciences.

MYANMAR

Kyipwaye Press: 84th St, Letsaigan, Mandalay; tel. (2) 21003; arts, travel, religion, fiction and children's.

Myawaddy Press: 184 32nd St, Yangon; tel. (1) 276889; journals and magazines; CEO U THEIN SEIN.

Sarpay Beikman Management Board: 529 Merchant St, Yangon; tel. (1) 283611; f. 1947; encyclopaedias, literature, fine arts and general; also magazines and translations; Chair. AUNG HTAY.

Shumawa Press: 146 West Wing, Bogyoke Aung San Market, Yangon; mechanical engineering.

Shwepyidan: 12A Haiaban, Yegwaw Quarter, Yangon; politics, religion, law.

Smart and Mookerdum: 221 Sule Pagoda Rd, Yangon; arts, cookery, popular science.

Thu Dhama Wadi Press: 55–56 Maung Khine St, POB 419, Yangon; f. 1903; religious; Propr U TIN HTOO; Man. U PAN MAUNG.

GOVERNMENT PUBLISHING HOUSE

Printing and Publishing Enterprise: 365–367 Bo Aung Kyaw St, Kyauktada Township, Yangon; tel. (1) 294645; f. 1880 as the Government Printing Office; Man. Dir U AUNG NYEIN.

PUBLISHERS' ASSOCIATION

Myanma Publishers' Union: 146 Bogyoke Market, Yangon.

Broadcasting and Communications

TELECOMMUNICATIONS

Posts and Telecommunications Department: Block 68, Ayeyar Wun Rd, South Dagon Township, Yangon; tel. (1) 591388; fax (1) 591383; e-mail dg.ptd@mptmail.net.mm; internet www.mcpt.gov.mm/ptd/index.htm; regulatory authority responsible for supervising radio communication, telephone, telegraph and post operations; Dir-Gen. U TIN HTWE.

Myanma Posts and Telecommunications (MPT): 839 Bogyoke Aung San Rd, Ahlone Township, Yangon; tel. (1) 297722; fax (1) 251911; internet www.mpt.net.mm; fmrly the Posts and Telecommunications Corpn; Man. Dir Col MAUNG MAUNG TIN.

BROADCASTING

Radio

Myanma TV and Radio Department (MTRD): 426 Pyay Rd, Kamayut 11041, Yangon; POB 1432, Yangon 11181; tel. (1) 531850; fax (1) 530211; internet www.myanmar.com/RADIO_TV.HTM; f. 1946; broadcasts in Bamar, Arakanese (Rakhine), Shan, Karen (Kayin), Kachin, Kayah, Chin, Mon and English; Dir-Gen. U KHIN MAUNG HTAY; Dir of Radio Broadcasting U KO KO HTWAY.

In 1992 the National Coalition Government of the Union of Burma (NCGUB) began broadcasting daily to Myanmar from Norway under the name Democratic Voice of Burma (DVB). In 1995 it was believed that the DVB was being operated by Myanma student activists from the Norway-Burma Council, without any formal control by the NCGUB.

Television

Myanma TV and Radio Department (MTRD): 426 Pyay Rd, Kamayut 11041, Yangon; tel. (1) 531850; fax (1) 530211; internet www.myanmar.com/RADIO_TV.HTM; f. 1946; colour television transmissions began in 1980; Dir-Gen. U KHIN MAUNG HTAY; Dir of Television Broadcasting U MYINT OO.

TV Myawaddy: Hmawbi, Hmawbi Township, Yangon; tel. (1) 620270; f. 1995; military broadcasting station transmitting public information, education and entertainment programmes via satellite.

In 2005 the Democratic Voice of Burma (DVB) began broadcasting Myanmar-language news and educational programmes via satellite from Norway. At the start of operations, the DVB broadcasted two hours of transmissions per week, but planned to expand operations over the latter half of 2005. Despite the existence of strict regulations concerning ownership of satellite receiver equipment in Myanmar, it was believed that a considerable number of Myanma households owned a satellite dish without a licence.

Finance

(cap. = capital; res = reserves; dep. = deposits; m. = million; brs = branches; amounts in kyats)

BANKING

In July 1990 new banking legislation was promulgated, reorganizing the operations of the Central Bank, establishing a state-owned development institution, the Myanma Agricultural and Rural Development Bank, and providing for the formation of private-sector banks and the opening of branches of foreign banks.

Central Bank

Central Bank of Myanmar: 26A Settmu Rd, POB 184, Yankin Township, Yangon; tel. (1) 285300; fax (1) 543621; e-mail cbm.ygn@mptmail.net.mm; f. 1947 as People's Bank of the Union of Burma; name changed as above in 1990; bank of issue; cap. 350m., dep. 13,545m.; Gov. U KYAW KYAW MAUNG; 37 brs.

State Banks

Myanma Economic Bank (MEB): 564 Merchant St, Yangon; tel. (1) 289345; fax (1) 283679; f. 1975; provides domestic banking network throughout the country; Man. Dir U MYAT MAW.

Myanma Foreign Trade Bank: 80–86 Maha Bandoola Garden St, POB 203, Kyauktada Township, Yangon; tel. (1) 284911; fax (1) 289585; e-mail mftb-hoygn@mptmail-net.mm; f. 1976; cap. 110m., res 483.9m., dep. 2,425.9m. (March 1999); handles all foreign exchange and international banking transactions; Chair. U KO KO GYI; Sec. U TIN MAUNG AYE.

Development Banks

Myanma Agricultural Development Bank (MADB): 1–7 cnr of Latha St and Kanna Rd, Yangon; tel. (1) 226734; f. 1953; est. as State Agricultural Bank, reconstituted as Myanma Agricultural and Rural Development Bank 1990 and as above 1996; state-owned; cap. 60.0m., dep. 615.6m. (Sept. 1993); Man. Dir U CHIT SWE.

Myanma Investment and Commercial Bank (MICB): 170/176 Bo Aung Kyaw St, Botahtaung Township, Yangon; tel. (1) 250509; fax (1) 256871; e-mail micb.hoygn@mptmail.net.mm; f. 1989; state-owned; cap. 400m., res 786m., dep. 7,035m. (March 2000); Chair. and Man. Dir U MYA THAN; 1 br.

Private Banks

In 2003 a crisis in Myanmar's private banking sector forced the closure of six of the country's 20 private banks. Following government intervention, three subsequently reopened in early 2004, having been cleared of committing banking irregularities. In 2005, however, the licences of a further two private banks were revoked following a government investigation into allegations of money laundering.

Asian Yangon Bank Ltd: 319–321 Maha Bandoola St, Botahtaung Township, Yangon; tel. (1) 245825; fax (1) 245865; f. 1994 as Asian Yangon International Bank Ltd; name changed as above in 2000; Gen. Man. TUN NYUNT.

Co-operative Bank Ltd: 334–336 Kanna Rd, Yangon; tel. (1) 272641; fax (1) 283063; e-mail cbbank@mptmail.net.mm; f. 1992; Gen. Man. U NYUNT HLAING.

First Private Bank Ltd (FPB): 619–621 Merchant St, Pabedan Township, Yangon; tel. (1) 289929; fax (1) 242320; e-mail fpb.hq@mptmail.net.mm; f. 1992; est. as the first publicly subscribed bank; fmrly the Commercial and Development Bank Ltd; provides loans to private business and small-scale industrial sectors; cap. 1,132.05m. (March 2005); Chair. Dr SEIN MAUNG; 15 brs.

Innwa Bank Ltd: cnr 35th St and Merchant St, Kyauktada Township, Yangon; tel. (1) 254642; f. 1997.

Kanbawza Bank Ltd: 615/1 Pyay Rd, Kamayut Township, Yangon; tel. (1) 538075; fax (1) 538069; e-mail kbz@mptmail.net.mm; f. 1994; Chair. U AUNG KO WIN; 22 brs.

Myanma Citizens Bank Ltd (MCB): 383 Maha Bandoola St, Kyauktada Township, Yangon; tel. (1) 273512; fax (1) 245932; f. 1991; Chair. U HLA TIN.

Myanma Oriental Bank Ltd (MOB): 166–168 Pansodan St, Kyauktada Township, Yangon; tel. (1) 246594; fax (1) 253217; e-mail mobl.ygn@mptmail.net.mm; f. 1993; Chair. U MYAT KYAW; Man. Dir and CEO U WIN MYINT.

Myanma Universal Bank (MUB): 81 Theinbyu Rd, Yangon; tel. (1) 297339; fax (1) 201428; f. 1995.

Myanmar Industrial Development Bank Ltd: 26–42 Pansodan St, Kyauktada Township, Yangon; tel. (1) 249536; fax (1) 249529; f. 1996; cap. US $335m.

Myawaddy Bank Ltd: 24–26 Sule Pagoda Rd, Kyauktada Township, Yangon; tel. (1) 283665; fax (1) 250093; e-mail mwdbankygn@mtpt400.stems.com; f. 1993; Gen. Mans U Tun Kyi, U Mya Min.

Tun Foundation Bank Ltd: 165–167 Bo Aung Gyaw St, Yangon; tel. (1) 270710; e-mail tfbbank@mptmail.net.mm; f. 1997; Chair. U Thein Tun.

Yadanabon Bank Ltd: 58A 26th St, cnr of 84th and 85th Sts, Aung Myay Thar Zan Township, Mandalay; tel. (2) 23577; f. 1992.

Yangon City Bank Ltd: 12–18 Sepin St, Kyauktada Township, Yangon; tel. (1) 289256; fax (1) 289231; f. 1993; auth. cap. 500m.; 100% owned by the Yangon City Development Committee; Chair. Col Myint Aung.

Yoma Bank Ltd: 1 Kungyan St, Mingala Taung Nyunt Township, Yangon; tel. (1) 242138; fax (1) 246548; f. 1993; Chair. Serge Pun.

Foreign Banks

By November 2003 18 foreign banks had opened representative offices in Yangon.

STOCK EXCHANGE

Myanmar Securities Exchange Centre: 1st Floor, 21–25 Sule Pagoda Rd, Yangon; tel. (1) 283984; f. 1996; jt venture between Japan's Daiwa Institute of Research and Myanma Economic Bank; Man. Dir Eiji Suzuki.

INSURANCE

At the end of November 2003 there were three representative offices of foreign insurance companies in Myanmar.

Myanma Insurance: 627–635 Merchant St, Yangon; tel. (1) 256244; fax (1) 250275; e-mail MYANSURE@mptmail.net.com; f. 1976; govt-controlled; Man. Dir Col Thein Lwin.

Trade and Industry

GOVERNMENT AGENCIES

Inspection and Agency Services: 383 Maha Bandoola St, Yangon; tel. (1) 284821; fax (1) 284823; works on behalf of state-owned enterprises to promote business with foreign companies; Man. Dir U Ohn Khin.

Myanmar Investment Commission: Ministry of National Planning and Economic Development, 653–691 Merchant St, Pabedan Township, Yangon; tel. (1) 241918; fax (1) 282101; Chair. U Thaung; Vice-Chair. Maj.-Gen. Tin Htut.

Union of Myanmar Economic Holdings: 72–74 Shwadagon Pagoda Rd, Yangon; tel. (1) 78905; f. 1990; public holding co; auth. cap. 10,000m. kyats; 40% of share capital subscribed by the Ministry of Defence and 60% by members of the armed forces.

CHAMBER OF COMMERCE

Union of Myanmar Federation of Chambers of Commerce and Industry (UMFCCI): 504–506 Merchant St, Kyauktada Township, Yangon; tel. (1) 243151; fax (1) 248177; e-mail umcci@mptmail.net.mm; internet www.umfcci.com.mm; f. 1919 as Burmese Chamber of Commerce; name changed as above in 1999; Pres. U Win Myint; Gen. Sec. U Sein Win Hlaing.

UTILITIES

Electricity

Myanma Electric Power Enterprise (MEPE): 197–199 Lower Kyimyindine Rd, Yangon; tel. (1) 220918; fax (1) 221006; e-mail mepe@mptmail.net.mm; Man. Dir U Yan Naing.

Water

Mandalay City Development Committee (Water and Sanitation Dept): cnr of 26th and 72nd Sts, Mandalay; tel. (2) 36173; internet mandalaycity.net/mcdc/about_mcdc.htm; f. 1992; Head of Water and Sanitation Dept U Tun Kyi.

Water Resources Utilization Department (WRUD): Ministry of Agriculture and Irrigation, Thiri Mingala Lane, off Kaba Aye Pagoda Rd, Yangon; tel. (1) 666359; fax (1) 667456; f. 1995.

Yangon City Development Committee (Water and Sanitation Dept): City Hall, cnr of Maha Bandoola Rd and Sule Pagoda Rd, Kyauktada Township, Yangon; tel. (1) 248112; fax (1) 246016; e-mail priycdc@mptmail.net.mm; internet www.yangoncity.com.mm/ycdc/index.asp; f. 1992; Head of Water and Sanitation Dept U Zaw Win.

CO-OPERATIVES

In 1993/94 there were 22,800 co-operative societies, with a turnover of 23,603m. kyats. This was estimated to have increased to 24,760 societies, with a turnover of 20,927m. kyats, in 1994/95.

Central Co-operative Society (CCS) Council: 334–336 Strand Rd, Yangon; tel. (1) 274550; Chair. U Than Hlang; Sec. U Tin Latt.

Co-operative Department: 259–263 Bogyoke Aung San Rd, Yangon; tel. (1) 277096; Dir-Gen. U Maung Hti.

WORKERS' AND PEASANTS' COUNCILS

Conditions of work are stipulated in the Workers' Rights and Responsibilities Law, enacted in 1964. Regional workers' councils ensure that government directives are complied with, and that targets are met on a regional basis. In January 1985 there were 293 workers' councils in towns, with more than 1.8m. members. They are co-ordinated by a central workers' organization in Yangon, formed in 1968 to replace trade union organizations, which had been abolished in 1964. The Myanma Federation of Trade Unions operates in exile.

Peasants' Asiayone (Organization): Yangon; tel. (1) 82819; f. 1977; peasants' representative org.; Chair. Brig.-Gen. U Than Nyunt; Sec. U San Tun.

Workers' Unity Organization: Central Organizing Committee, 61 Thein Byu St, Yangon; tel. (1) 284043; f. 1968; workers' representative org.; Chair. U Ohn Kyaw; Sec. U Nyunt Thein.

Transport

All railways, domestic air services, passenger and freight road transport services and inland water facilities are owned and operated by state-controlled enterprises.

RAILWAYS

The railway network comprised 3,955 km of track in 1996/97, most of which was single track.

Myanma Railways: 361 Theinbyu Rd, Botataung Township, Yangon; tel. (1) 298585; fax (1) 284220; f. 1877; govt-operated; Man. Dir U Thaung Lwin; Gen. Man. U Saw Clyde.

ROADS

In 1996 the total length of the road network in Myanmar was an estimated 28,200 km, of which an estimated 3,440 km were paved. In 2001/02 the total length of road accessible to motor vehicles was 28,598 km.

Road Transportation Department: 375 Bogyoke Aung San St, Yangon; tel. (1) 284426; fax (1) 289716; f. 1963; controls passenger and freight road transport; in 1993/94 operated 1,960 haulage trucks and 928 passenger buses; Man. Dir U Ohn Myint.

INLAND WATERWAYS

The principal artery of traffic is the River Ayeyarwady (Irrawaddy), which is navigable as far as Bhamo, about 1,450 km inland, while parts of the Thanlwin and Chindwinn rivers are also navigable.

Inland Water Transport: 50 Pansodan St, Yangon; tel. (1) 222399; fax (1) 286500; govt-owned; operates cargo and passenger services throughout Myanmar; 36m. passengers and 3.1m. tons of freight were carried in 1993/94; Man. Dir U Khin Maung.

SHIPPING

Yangon is the chief port. Vessels with a displacement of up to 15,000 tons can be accommodated.

In 2004 the Myanma merchant fleet totalled 127 vessels, with a combined displacement of 444,300 grt.

Myanma Port Authority: 10 Pansodan St, POB 1, Yangon; tel. (1) 280094; fax (1) 295134; f. 1880; general port and harbour duties; Man. Dir U Tin Oo; Gen. Man. U Hlaing Soon.

Myanma Five Star Line: 132–136 Theinbyu Rd, POB 1221, Yangon; tel. (1) 295279; fax (1) 297669; e-mail mfsl.myr@mptmail.net.mm; f. 1959; cargo services to the Far East and Australia; Man. Dir U Khin Maung Kyi; Gen. Man. U Kyaw Zaw; fleet of 26 coastal and ocean-going vessels.

CIVIL AVIATION

Mingaladon Airport, near Yangon, is equipped to international standards. The newly built Mandalay International Airport was inaugurated in September 2000. In 2002 plans for the construction of the country's third international airport, Hanthawaddy International Airport in Bago (Pegu), were finally approved; the airport was scheduled to become operational in 2007.

MYANMAR

Department of Civil Aviation: Mingaladon Airport, Yangon; tel. (1) 665144; fax (1) 665124; e-mail dca.myanmar@mpt.mail.net.mm; Dir-Gen. U WIN MAUNG.

Air Bagan Ltd: 56 Shwe Taung Gyar St, Bahan Township, Yangon; tel. (1) 514861; fax (1) 515102; e-mail info@airbagan.com.mm; internet www.airbagan.com; f. 2004; domestic services to 14 destinations.

Air Mandalay: 146 Dhammazedi Rd, Bahan Township, Yangon; tel. (1) 525488; fax (1) 525937; e-mail info@airmandalay.com; internet www.airmandalay.com; f. 1994; Myanmar's first airline; jt venture between Air Mandalay Holding and Myanma Airways; operates domestic services and regional services to Chiang Mai and Phuket, Thailand, and Siem Reap, Cambodia; Chair. Dr TUN CHIN; Man. Dir ERIC KANG TIAN LYE; 242 employees.

Air Myanmar: Yangon; f. 2004; jt venture between Myanmar Airways, Dawn Light Co, Singapore-based Fast Growth Associates Ltd and Hong Kong-based Cathay Aviation; international services to Sydney, Australia, via Singapore and to Fukuoka, Japan, via Bangkok, Shanghai and Seoul.

Myanmar Airways (MA): 123 Sule Pagoda Rd, Yangon; tel. (1) 80710; fax (1) 255305; e-mail 8mpr@maiair.com.mm; internet www.maiair.com; f. 1993; govt-controlled; internal network operates services to 21 airports; COO PRITHPAL SINGH.

Myanmar Airways International (MAI): 08–02 Sakura Tower, 339 Bogyoke Aung San Rd, Yangon; tel. (1) 255260; fax (1) 255305; e-mail management@maiair.com; internet www.maiair.com; f. 1993; govt-owned; established by Myanmar Airways in jt venture with Highsonic Enterprises of Singapore to provide international services; operates services to Bangkok, Dhaka, Hong Kong, Kuala Lumpur and Singapore; Man. Dir GERARD DE VAZ.

United Myanmar Air: Summit Parkview Hotel, Yangon; internet www.unitedmyanmar.com; f. 2003; jt venture between Myanmar Airways and Sunshine Strategic Investments Holdings of Hong Kong; international services to Bangkok, Hong Kong, Kuala Lumpur and Singapore; CEO EDWARD TAN.

Yangon Airways: MMB Tower, Level 5, 166 Upper Pansodan Rd, Mingalar Taungnyunt Township, Yangon; tel. (1) 383100; fax (1) 383127; e-mail info@yangonair.com; internet www.yangonair.com; f. 1996; domestic services to 13 destinations.

Tourism

Yangon, Mandalay, Taunggyi and Pagan possess outstanding palaces, Buddhist temples and shrines. The number of foreign visitors to Myanmar declined severely following the suppression of the democracy movement in 1988. In the early 1990s, however, the Government actively promoted the revival of the tourism industry, and between 1995 and 1998 alone the number of hotel rooms almost doubled, reaching a total of nearly 14,000. In 2003 there were 205,610 foreign tourist arrivals (compared with only 5,000 in 1989). In 2003 revenue from tourism (including passenger transport) totalled an estimated US $68m.

Myanmar Hotels and Tourism Services: 77–91 Sule Pagoda Rd, Yangon 11141; tel. (1) 282013; fax (1) 254417; e-mail mtt.mht@mptmail.net.mm; govt-controlled; manages all hotels, tourist offices, tourist department stores and duty-free shops; Man. Dir U KYI HTUN.

Myanmar Tourism Promotion Board: Level 3, Business Centre, 223 Signal Pagoda Rd, Yangon; tel. (1) 242828; fax (1) 242800; e-mail mtpb@mptmail.net.mm; internet www.myanmar-tourism.com; Chair. U AUNG MYAT KYAW.

Myanmar Travels and Tours: 77–91 Sule Pagoda Rd, POB 559, Yangon 11141; tel. (1) 382243; fax (1) 254417; e-mail mtt.mht@mptmail.net.mm; internet www.myanmartravelsandtours.com; f. 1964; govt tour operator and travel agent; handles all travel arrangements for groups and individuals; Gen. Man. U HTAY AUNG.

Union of Myanmar Travel Association (UMTA): Bldg 69, No 609B, 6th Floor, Yuzana Condo Tower, cnr Shwegonedaing Rd and Kabaraye Pagoda Rd, Bahan Township, Yangon; tel. (1) 559673; fax (1) 545707; e-mail UMTA@mptmail.net.mm; internet www.umtanet.com; f. 2002; organizes private travel agencies and tour operators; promotes Myanmar as a tourist destination; Chair. U KHIN ZAW.

NAMIBIA

Introductory Survey

Location, Climate, Language, Religion, Flag, Capital

The Republic of Namibia (formerly known as South West Africa) lies in south-western Africa, with South Africa to the south and south-east, Botswana to the east and Angola to the north. The country has a long coastline on the Atlantic Ocean. The narrow Caprivi Strip, between Angola and Botswana in the north-east, extends Namibia to the Zambezi river, giving it a border with Zambia. The climate is generally hot, although coastal areas have relatively mild temperatures. Most of the country is subject to drought and unreliable rainfall. The average annual rainfall varies from about 50 mm (2 ins) on the coast to 550 mm (22 ins) in the north. The arid Namib Desert stretches along the west coast, while the easternmost area is part of the Kalahari Desert. The official language is English; however, most of the African ethnic groups have their own languages. At the 2001 census the most widely-spoken African languages were Oshiwambo (used in 48% of households), Nama/Damara (11%), Rukavango (10%) and Otjiherero (8%). In addition, Afrikaans is spoken (11%) and German is also used. About 90% of the population are Christians. The national flag (proportions 2 by 3) comprises a blue triangle in the upper hoist corner, bearing a yellow sun (a blue-bordered disc, surrounded by 12 triangular rays), separated from a green triangle in the lower fly corner by a white-bordered, broad red stripe. The capital is Windhoek.

Recent History

South West Africa became a German possession in 1884. The territory excluded the port of Walvis Bay and 12 small offshore islands, previously annexed by the United Kingdom and subsequently incorporated into South Africa. During the First World War South African forces occupied South West Africa in 1914, and in 1915 Germany surrendered the territory. In 1920 the League of Nations entrusted South Africa with a mandate to administer South West Africa. In 1925 South Africa granted a Constitution giving limited self-government to European (white) inhabitants only. No trusteeship agreement was concluded with the UN after the Second World War, and in 1946 the UN refused South Africa's request for permission to annex South West Africa. In 1949 the territory's European voters were granted representation in the South African Parliament. In 1950 the International Court of Justice (ICJ) issued a ruling that the area should remain under international mandate and that South Africa should submit it to UN control. South Africa refused to comply with this judgment. In October 1966 South Africa's security and apartheid laws were extended to South West Africa, retrospective to 1950.

Opposition within South West Africa to South African rule led to the establishment of two African nationalist organizations, the South West Africa People's Organisation (SWAPO—founded in 1957 as the Ovamboland People's Congress) and the South West African National Union (SWANU—formed in 1959). During 1966 SWAPO's military wing, the People's Liberation Army of Namibia (PLAN), launched an armed struggle for the liberation of the territory. PLAN operated from bases in Angola and Zambia, and was controlled by the external wing of SWAPO (led by Sam Nujoma—the organization's President from 1959). SWAPO also had a legal wing, which was tolerated in South West Africa.

South Africa was consistently criticized at the UN over its extension of apartheid to the territory. The UN General Assembly voted to terminate South Africa's mandate in October 1966, established a UN Council for South West Africa in May 1967, and changed the name of the territory to Namibia in June 1968. In 1971 the ICJ ruled that South Africa's presence was illegal. In 1973 the UN General Assembly recognized SWAPO as 'the authentic representative of the Namibian people', and appointed a UN Commissioner for Namibia to undertake 'executive and administrative tasks'.

A multiracial constitutional conference on the territory's future, organized by the all-white South West Africa Legislative Assembly, was convened in Windhoek in September 1975, attended by representatives of the territory's 11 main ethnic groups. However, neither the UN nor the Organization of African Unity (OAU, now the African Union, see p. 153) recognized this so-called Turnhalle Conference, owing to its ethnic and non-democratic basis, and the legal wing of SWAPO refused to attend. In 1976 and 1977 proposals for procedures whereby Namibia was to achieve independence and formulate a constitution were made by the Turnhalle Conference, but rejected by SWAPO, the UN and the OAU. In September 1977 South Africa appointed an Administrator-General to govern the territory. In November the Turnhalle Conference was dissolved, and the Democratic Turnhalle Alliance (DTA), a coalition of conservative political groups representing the ethnic groups involved in the Turnhalle Conference, was formed.

In early 1978 talks were held between South Africa, SWAPO and a 'contact group' comprising Canada, France, the Federal Republic of Germany, the United Kingdom and the USA. In September the contact group's proposals for a Namibian settlement, including the holding of UN-supervised elections, a reduction in the numbers of South African troops in Namibia and the release of political prisoners, were conditionally accepted by both South Africa and SWAPO and were incorporated in UN Security Council Resolution 435. However, South Africa continued to implement its own internal solution for Namibia with an election for a Constituent Assembly in December. The election was contested by five parties, but boycotted notably by SWAPO. Of the 50 seats in the Assembly, 41 were won by the DTA. In May 1979 South Africa unilaterally established a legislative National Assembly, without executive powers, from the existing Constituent Assembly. In June, following the detention of about 40 of its activists, the legal wing of SWAPO closed its offices in Windhoek and dissolved its executive council.

All-party negotiations, held under UN auspices in Geneva, Switzerland, in January 1981, failed in their aim of arranging a cease-fire and eventual UN-supervised elections. Later in 1981 the contact group attempted to secure support for a three-phase independence plan. However, South Africa's insistence (supported by the USA) that any withdrawal of South African forces must be linked to the withdrawal of Cuban troops from Angola was rejected by Angola and the UN. Meanwhile, the Ministerial Council, formed in 1980 and chaired by Dirk Mudge (also Chairman of the DTA), assumed much of the Administrator-General's executive power in September 1981. However, the DTA was seriously weakened in early 1982 by the resignation of its President, Peter Kalangula. The Ministerial Council was dissolved in January 1983, when, after several months of disagreement with the South African Government regarding the future role of the DTA in the territory, Mudge resigned as Council Chairman. South Africa disbanded the National Assembly and resumed direct rule of Namibia, with Willem van Niekerk as Administrator-General.

The Multi-Party Conference (MPC) was established in November 1983, grouping, initially, seven internal political parties. Boycotted by SWAPO, it appeared to be promoted by South Africa as a means of settling the independence issue outside the framework of Resolution 435, and of reducing SWAPO's dominance in any future post-independence government for Namibia. None the less, South Africa continued to negotiate on the independence issue with SWAPO and Angola. In February 1984 South Africa and Angola agreed to a cease-fire on the Angola–Namibia border, and set up a joint commission to monitor the withdrawal of all South African troops from Angola. Angola undertook to ensure that neither Cuban nor SWAPO forces would move into the areas vacated by the South African troops. Nujoma pledged support for the agreement, but asserted that SWAPO would not abandon the armed conflict until there was a cease-fire in Namibia itself and until South Africa had agreed to UN-supervised elections. Discussions on the independence issue in mid-1984, involving van Niekerk, SWAPO and the MPC, ended inconclusively, as did negotiations in 1984–86 between the South African Government and the US Assistant Secretary of State for African Affairs.

In April 1985 the South African Government accepted a proposal by the MPC for a 'Transitional Government of National Unity' (TGNU) in Namibia. This was formally established in

Windhoek in June, although the arrangement was condemned in advance by the contact group and was declared 'null and void' by the UN Secretary-General. The TGNU consisted of an executive Cabinet, drawn from a National Assembly of 62 members who were appointed from among the parties constituting the MPC. Its establishment was accompanied by the proclamation of a 'bill of rights', drafted by the MPC, which prohibited racial discrimination. A Constitutional Council was also established to prepare a constitution for an independent Namibia. The South African Government retained responsibility for foreign affairs, defence and internal security, and all legislation was to be subject to approval by the Administrator-General. Louis Pienaar replaced van Niekerk in this post in July.

During 1987, following the liberalization of labour laws and the legalization of trade unions for black workers in 1986, the trade union movement became increasingly active. In mid-1987 the Constitutional Council published a draft document; however, South Africa indicated that it could not accept the lack of a guarantee of minority rights in the proposal. In March 1988 the Namibian Supreme Court declared the 'AG8' law of 1980 (providing for the election of 'second-tier' legislative assemblies and for the administration of education and health facilities on an ethnic, rather than a geographical, basis) to be in conflict with the 1985 'bill of rights'.

Both Angola and Cuba were reported in January 1988 to have accepted, in principle, the US demand for a complete withdrawal of Cuban troops from Angola, but they reiterated that this would be conditional on the cessation of South African support for the insurgent União Nacional para a Independência Total de Angola (UNITA). In July Angola, Cuba and South Africa reached agreement on 14 'essential principles' for a peaceful settlement, and in August it was agreed that the implementation of Resolution 435 would begin on 1 November. Also in August the Governments of South Africa, Cuba and Angola announced a cease-fire, to which SWAPO agreed, and South Africa undertook to withdraw all its forces from Angola. The November deadline was not met, owing to failure to agree on an exact schedule for the evacuation of Cuban troops from Angola. In December Angola, Cuba and South Africa signed a formal treaty designating 1 April 1989 as the implementation date for Resolution 435 and establishing a joint commission to monitor the treaty's implementation. (A further agreement was signed by Angola and Cuba, requiring the evacuation of all Cuban troops from Angola by July 1991.) A Constituent Assembly was to be elected in Namibia on 1 November 1989. South African forces in Namibia were to be confined to their bases, and their numbers reduced to 1,500 by July 1989; all South African troops were to have been withdrawn from Namibia one week after the November election. SWAPO forces were to be confined to bases in Angola in April, before being disarmed and repatriated. A multinational military observer force, the UN Transition Assistance Group (UNTAG), was to monitor the South African withdrawal, and civilian administrators and an international police force were to supervise the election. At the end of February the TGNU was formally disbanded, and on 1 March the National Assembly voted to dissolve itself: until independence the territory was governed by the Administrator-General, in consultation with a Special Representative of the UN Secretary-General, Martti Ahtisaari. Pienaar and Ahtisaari were to be jointly responsible for arranging the November election.

Implementation of Resolution 435 was disrupted by large-scale movements, from April 1989, of SWAPO guerrillas into Namibia from Angola, as a result of which the South African security forces, with the consent of the UN, suspended the cease-fire. About 280 SWAPO troops were reported to have been killed in the subsequent conflict. Following negotiations by the joint monitoring commission, conditions were arranged for an evacuation of the SWAPO forces to Angola, and in May the commission certified the cease-fire to be once more in force. In June most racially-discriminatory legislation was repealed, and an amnesty was granted to Namibian refugees and exiles: by late September nearly 42,000 people, including Nujoma, had returned to Namibia. Meanwhile, South Africa completed its troop reduction ahead of schedule.

Voting proceeded peacefully on 7–11 November 1989, with the participation of more than 95% of the electorate. SWAPO received 57.3% of all votes cast and won 41 of the Constituent Assembly's 72 seats, while the DTA, with 28.6% of the votes, secured 21 seats. (In 1991 the South African Government admitted that it had contributed funds to the electoral campaigns of the DTA and several other political parties opposed to SWAPO.) Following the election, South Africa's remaining troops were evacuated from Namibia, while SWAPO's bases in Angola were decommissioned. The SWAPO Government subsequently reached an agreement with South Africa that no legal action would be taken for atrocities committed by either side. The agreement also precluded the establishment of a truth and reconciliation commission.

In February 1990 the Constituent Assembly adopted a draft Constitution, providing for a multi-party democracy based on universal adult suffrage. Later in the month the Constituent Assembly elected Nujoma as Namibia's first President. On 21 March Namibia finally achieved independence; the Constituent Assembly was redesignated the National Assembly, and Nujoma assumed executive power. A Cabinet, headed by the Constituent Assembly Chairman, Hage Geingob (a long-serving SWAPO activist), was also sworn in.

Following Namibia's independence, the port of Walvis Bay, its surrounding territory of 1,124 sq km and the 12 offshore Penguin Islands remained under South African jurisdiction. In September 1991 the Namibian and South African Governments agreed to administer the disputed territories jointly, pending a final settlement on sovereignty, and in August 1992 the two countries announced the forthcoming establishment of a joint administration authority. In August 1993, however, South Africa's multi-party constitutional negotiating committee instructed the Government to prepare legislation for the transfer of sovereignty over Walvis Bay to Namibia. Accordingly, negotiations between Namibia and South Africa resulted in bilateral agreements regarding the future of South African interests in the Walvis Bay area. Namibia formally took control of Walvis Bay and its islands from 1 March 1994. In August SWAPO won eight seats, and the DTA two, in Walvis Bay's first non-racial local elections.

Namibia's first post-independence presidential and legislative elections in December 1994 resulted in overwhelming victories for Nujoma and SWAPO. Nujoma was elected for a second term as President, securing 76.3% of the votes cast, while SWAPO secured 53 of the elective seats in the National Assembly, with 73.9% of the valid votes cast. The DTA won 15 seats (with 20.8% of the votes), and the United Democratic Front (UDF) two. The remaining two seats were won by the Democratic Coalition of Namibia (an alliance of the National Patriotic Front and the German Union) and the Monitor Action Group (MAG). Although SWAPO now had a two-thirds' majority in the National Assembly, Nujoma gave assurances that no amendments would be made to the Constitution without prior approval by national referendum.

At the SWAPO Congress in May 1997 Nujoma was re-elected unopposed as party President. Among the resolutions endorsed by the Congress was a proposal that Nujoma should seek re-election for a third term as national President. It was agreed that the Constitution, which stipulates that a President may serve no more than two consecutive terms, could be exceptionally amended to allow Nujoma to seek a further mandate, since the incumbent had initially been appointed by the Constituent Assembly, and had only once been elected President on a popular mandate. In August 1998 a senior SWAPO official, Ben Ulenga, resigned as Namibia's High Commissioner to the United Kingdom, in protest at the proposed arrangement to allow Nujoma to seek a renewed mandate. In October the exceptional constitutional amendment was approved by the requisite two-thirds' majority in the National Assembly, having received the support of SWAPO's members; the amendment was similarly endorsed by the National Council in November. In March 1999 it was reported that Ulenga was to establish a new political party, the Congress of Democrats (CoD), with a view to contesting the presidential and legislative elections due later in the year.

In August 1998 the DTA's executive announced the suspension of Mishake Muyongo as party President, and dissociated the party from Muyongo's overt support for the secession of the Caprivi Strip—a narrow area of land extending in the north-east, between Angola and Botswana, as far as the Zambezi river (Namibia's border with Zambia). In November it emerged that Muyongo, leading the so-called Caprivi Liberation Movement (CLM), was among more than 100 people who, apparently armed, had crossed into Botswana in October, and who were now seeking asylum in that country. The Namibian Government stated that it had discovered plans for a secessionist rebellion, led by Muyongo and a chief of the Mafwe tribe, Boniface Mamili, in Caprivi. Representatives of the office of the UN High Commissioner for Refugees (UNHCR) subsequently advised the Botswana authorities that the secessionists' fears of persecution, should they be returned to Namibia, were 'plausible'. In subsequent weeks many more people crossed into Botswana, claiming to be fleeing harassment and persecution by the Namibian security forces: among those who left the country were many San/Bushmen, who were not believed to be associated with the secessionist movement. (In mid-2001 it was reported that many more San/Bushmen were considering leaving Namibia, again alleging harassment by the security forces.) During a visit to Botswana in March 1999 Nujoma reached an agreement with President Festus Mogae of that country, whereby the separatist leaders (whose extradition had hitherto been sought by Namibia in order that they could be tried on terrorist charges) would be accorded refugee status, on condition that they be resettled in a third country. Muyongo and Mamili were subsequently granted asylum in Denmark. The agreement also provided for the return to Namibia, under the auspices of UNHCR and without fear of prosecution or persecution, of the estimated 2,500 refugees who had crossed into Botswana since late 1998.

A period of apparent calm in the Caprivi region ended abruptly in early August 1999 with an armed attack by members of an organization styling itself the Caprivi Liberation Army (CLA), who targeted a military base at Mpacha airport and the police headquarters and offices of the Namibian Broadcasting Corporation in the regional capital, Katima Mulilo. At least eight members of the Namibian security forces and five CLA fighters were killed during the attack and its suppression. Nujoma responded by declaring a state of emergency in the region. While there was support within Namibia for the declaration, the CoD, as well as church leaders and human rights organizations, expressed concern at evidence of the ill-treatment of detainees. Several members of the Government were subsequently reported to have admitted that 'mistakes' were made in the aftermath of the attack; however, the army Chief of Staff maintained that the decisive response of the forces under his command had been justified. Visiting Katima Mulilo in late August, Nujoma announced an end to the state of emergency, although army and police reinforcements were to remain in Caprivi. Initially, 12 alleged rebels were remanded on charges of high treason, murder, public violence and illegal possession of firearms; the prosecution asserted that 17 known leaders of the CLA remained at large. Meanwhile, a further 47 suspects were charged with aiding and abetting the rebels. Repatriations of refugees from Botswana were halted following the attack on Katima Mulilo, although UNHCR expressed the hope that voluntary repatriations would resume as soon as the security situation in Caprivi was adequate to guarantee the safe return of refugees. In early 2000, however, following an escalation of instability in the region of the Namibia–Angola border, a further 400 Namibian nationals were reported to have fled to Botswana. In late 2001 officials from Botswana and Namibia held talks regarding the repatriation of about 500 Namibian refugees. In September of that year, in response to a request from the Namibian Government, the Gaborone Magistrates' Court in Botswana ordered the extradition of a group of suspected Caprivi separatists who were wanted to stand trial for high treason in connection with the attack on Katima Mulilo. The Namibian Government was also seeking to extradite Muyongo from Denmark to answer similar charges; the Danish Government stated that it was awaiting advice from UNHCR before making a decision. In October 2003, after numerous delays, the trial commenced of 121 Namibians charged with offences related to the attack on Katima Mulilo. In February 2004 the trial judge ruled that 13 of the defendants were 'irregularly before the court', as a result of a process of 'disguised extradition' whereby they had been removed from Zambia and Botswana, and ordered their release. The Government indicated that it would seek permission to appeal to the Supreme Court against this ruling. It was reported that the 13 defendants thus acquitted had been immediately rearrested on their release. The trial was ongoing in early 2006.

Meanwhile, presidential and legislative elections, which were held on 30 November and 1 December 1999, resulted in an overwhelming victory for Nujoma and SWAPO, with Ulenga and the CoD apparently winning support at the expense of the DTA. In the presidential election Nujoma was returned for a third (and final) term of office with 76.8% of the votes cast, while Ulenga took 10.5% and Katuutire Kaura (Muyongo's successor as President of the DTA) 9.6%. SWAPO won 55 of the elective seats in the National Assembly, with 76.1% of the votes cast (thus ensuring that it retained the two-thirds' majority required to amend the Constitution); the CoD and the DTA each won seven seats (taking, respectively, 9.9% and 9.5% of the total votes cast).

Geingob was reappointed Prime Minister in a reorganization of the Cabinet announced by Nujoma in March 2000. A further cabinet reshuffle was effected in January 2001. In November Nujoma announced that he would not be standing for a fourth term as President on the expiry of his current mandate in 2004.

In August 2002 Nujoma reorganized his Cabinet; Theo Ben Gurirab was appointed Prime Minister, replacing Geingob, who resigned from the Government, having declined the position of Minister of Regional and Local Government and Housing, which was accepted by Joel Kaapanda. It was reported that Nujoma considered Geingob a threat to his authority. Hidipo Hamutenya became Minister of Foreign Affairs, Information and Broadcasting. In May 2003, in a further reallocation of portfolios, Nangolo Mbumba was replaced as Minister of Finance by Saarah Kuugongelwa-Amadhila, while Mbumba became Minister of Information and Broadcasting. Hamutenya was dismissed without explanation in late May 2004, although many observers regarded the decision as part of a plan by the President to manoeuvre his own choice of successor, the Minister of Lands, Resettlement and Rehabilitation, Hifikepunye Pohamba, into a stronger position. Pohamba was duly selected as the presidential candidate of the SWAPO party later that month. Meanwhile Hamutenya was replaced by the Minister of Labour, Marco Hausiku, and the labour portfolio was awarded to Marlene Mungunda.

At national elections held on 15–16 November 2004 Pohamba was elected President with, according to official results, 76.4% of the votes cast; his nearest rival, Ulenga, secured 7.3%. SWAPO also recorded a decisive victory in the elections to the National Assembly, retaining 55 of the 72 seats with 76.1% of the national vote. The CoD increased its share of the vote but won only five seats, compared with seven in the 1999 elections. The DTA took four seats, the UDF three and the MAG one seat, while two newly reactivated parties, the National Unity Democratic Organization and the Republican Party, won three seats and one seat, respectively. The Electoral Commission of Namibia recorded voter turnout at 85%. (Following claims of electoral irregularities by members of the opposition a recount was held in March 2005: with the exception of the CoD all parties received a smaller number of votes, however, the overall allocation of seats remained the same.) Pohamba was due to take office in March 2005, upon the expiry of Samuel Nujoma's third term as President.

Nujoma duly stood down as President on 21 March 2005, but was expected to remain as leader of SWAPO until 2007. Following his swearing in as President that day, Pohamba unveiled his Cabinet, which included six new appointees. The former Minister of Higher Education, Training and Employment Creation, Nahas Angula, and the former Minister of Health and Social Services, Dr Libertina Amathila, were appointed as Prime Minister and Deputy Prime Minister, respectively. The overall structure of the ministries was reorganized and several were renamed to reflect their changed remits. Responsibility for prisons and correctional services was transferred to the newly created Ministry of Safety and Security under Peter Tshirumbu-Tsheehama, who was also appointed acting Minister of Defence. Albert Kawana was appointed to the newly created post of Minister of Presidential Affairs, while the new Ministry of Education, headed by Nangolo Mbumba, assumed the functions of the former ministries of Higher and Basic Education. The incumbent Attorney-General, Pendukeni Ivula-Ithana, assumed the justice portfolio. Despite the structural changes, the composition of the new Government was interpreted as an indication that it would continue with the policies set down under the previous administration. The National Assembly subsequently unanimously elected the former Prime Minister, Theo-Ben Gurirab, as Speaker.

Meanwhile, in April 2001 the Government announced that it had allocated N $100m. to acquire land for redistribution on a voluntary basis over a five-year period. At that time approximately 4,000 (mainly white-owned) farms occupied 52% of the total land area, while the Government had acquired only some 6% of the land required for resettlement. In October 2002 the Government announced that it was considering the seizure of white-owned farms for redistribution to the landless black population, and criticized white farmers for taking advantage of the voluntary basis for land redistribution by charging excessively high prices for their land. In March 2004 the Government estimated that it would cost more than

US $150m. over a five-year period to redistribute some 9m. ha of land among an estimated 243,000 applicants. (It was reported that land prices had increased three-fold between 1990 and 2005.) By September the Government had bought just over 140 farms at a cost of N $131m.—under the 'willing buyer, willing seller' scheme—and resettled 9,156 people. The expropriation of the first white-owned commercial farm was carried out in November 2005; a further 19 farms were listed for expropriation under compulsory purchase orders. However, an independent report, issued by the Legal Assistance Centre, criticized the Government programme, concluding that the resettlement targets were 'logistically impossible' and 'economically unrealistic'. Most resettlement beneficiaries had no previous experience of farming and the report recommended a shared-ownership programme by which black farm-hands (who did not qualify under the resettlement programme) would remain on farms, developing the necessary skills without harming the farming sector as a whole.

In November 2005 the remains of 13 bodies were discovered at five sites near a former military base at Eenhana in the Ohangwena region. The bodies were believed to be PLAN guerillas killed by South African security forces during fighting in 1989. President Pohamba appealed for those with information about the bodies to come forward. The Minister for Information and Broadcasting, Netumbo Nandi-Ndaitwah, reiterated that under the policy of reconciliation no prosecutions would follow (see above). In early December 2005 the National Assembly approved legislation granting former President Nujoma the title of 'Founding Father'.

In March 1993 UNITA alleged that members of the Namibia Defence Force (NDF) had crossed the border into southern Angola to assist Angolan government forces in offensives against UNITA, and subsequently claimed that some 2,000 Cuban troops had landed at Namibia's southern port of Lüderitz, from where they had been transferred to Angola to assist government forces. The Namibian authorities denied any involvement in the Angolan conflict, however. A 550-km stretch of the Okavango river border was closed from September 1994, following the deaths of three Namibians in an attack attributed by the Namibian authorities to UNITA. In September 1995 the Namibian Government announced the formation of a border control unit to assist police and NDF troops deployed along the Okavango. In November the two countries' defence and security commission agreed new measures aimed at facilitating the work of border patrols. Namibia subsequently announced that the Government was to contribute 200 NDF troops to the UN peace-keeping mission in Angola.

Following the attack on Katima Mulilo by Caprivi separatists in August 1999, the Namibian Government alleged that UNITA was lending military and logistical support to the CLA. (Links were also reported with the separatist Barotse Patriotic Front in Zambia, and the Namibian authorities alleged that the CLA had received training on Zambian territory.) There was considerable speculation that not only was Caprivi an important supply route for UNITA, but also that the Angolan rebel movement was attempting to divert resources of the Namibian armed forces away from the conflict in the DRC (q.v.).

Tensions in the region of the Namibia–Angola border escalated from late 1999, after the two countries began joint patrols targeting UNITA, and the Namibian Government authorized the Angolan armed forces to launch attacks against UNITA from Namibian territory. In February 2000 it was announced that Nujoma and President José Eduardo dos Santos of Angola had agreed to implement measures to restore security in the border region; by June, when a curfew was imposed on the north-eastern border with Angola, more than 50 Namibians had been killed in cross-border raids by the Angolan rebels. Continuing conflict in southern Angola resulted in a large number of refugees entering Namibia (some 6,000 arrived from Angola between November 1999 and August 2000, although increased border security subsequently reduced the flow). In March 2001 President Nujoma ordered a further reinforcement of the Namibian military presence in Caprivi. In October UNITA rebels were reported to have destroyed an electricity substation in the Kavango region, and in November a group of unidentified gunmen killed four people in western Caprivi before escaping to Angola.

In April 2002 the Namibian Government welcomed the signing of a formal cease-fire agreement by the Angolan Government and UNITA, some six weeks after the death of Jonas Savimbi, the UNITA leader. Some stability was restored in the Kavango and Caprivi regions in mid-2002, and in August a number of Angolan refugees were repatriated; the majority of them, estimated at around 20,000, were due to return home in mid-2003, under the auspices of UNHCR. In February 2005 Namibia and Angola reached agreement on a maritime border; negotiations had begun in 1993 but were not formalized until 2003 when a joint commission for delimitation and demarcation was established.

Following independence, Namibia became a member of the UN, the Commonwealth, the OAU and the Southern African Development Co-ordination Conference—now the Southern African Development Community (SADC, see p. 358). Despite expressed concerns at South African dominance of the regional economy, the Nujoma regime has forged close links with post-apartheid South Africa, and in 1994 SWAPO contributed funds to the electoral campaigns of the African National Congress of South Africa and the Pan-Africanist Congress. President Nelson Mandela visited Namibia in August of that year, and in December South Africa announced the cancellation of Namibia's pre-independence bilateral debt; South African property in Namibia was also to be transferred to the Namibian authorities. In February 1997 legislation providing for the cancellation of the debt (now amounting to N $1,200m.) was formally approved by the South African Parliament. Nujoma made his first state visit to South Africa in May 1996. In August 2001 the foreign ministers of Namibia and South Africa held talks regarding their 400 km border; Namibia claimed its southern border extended to the middle of the Orange river, while South Africa claimed that its territory stretched to the northern bank. (When South Africa's borders were reassessed in 1994, following its first democratic elections, the Surveyors-General of both Namibia and South Africa had agreed to place the border in the middle of the river, but the agreement was never signed.) The confusion over the location of the border has led to differences over mineral and fishing rights in the river, as well as grazing rights on its islands.

In February 1995 it was announced that Namibia and Botswana were to refer a dispute regarding the demarcation of their joint border on the Chobe river (specifically, the issue of the sovereignty of the small, uninhabited island of Kasikili-Sedudu) for adjudication by the ICJ. The dispute was formally submitted to the Court in mid-1996. The ICJ ruled in December 1999 that the island formed part of the territory of Botswana; the judgment further ruled that nationals of (and vessels flying the flags of) Botswana and Namibia should enjoy equal treatment in the two channels around the island. In January 1998 the two countries' Joint Commission on Defence and Security held an emergency meeting, following allegations by Namibia that troops from Botswana had taken control of a further island in disputed border territory—Situngu Island in the Caprivi Strip. The Joint Commission agreed to expedite the establishment of a Joint Technical Commission for the demarcation of the border. Relations were complicated by the issue of Caprivi secessionism (see above). Situngu is claimed as Mafwe land; furthermore, Namibia's representative in discussions regarding the island, said to be a member of the secessionist movement, was reported to have fled to Angola. In 2003 Botswana and Namibia accepted the demarcation by a joint commission of their joint border along the Kwando, Linyanti and Chobe rivers.

From August 1998 Namibia, which was participating in regional efforts to resolve the conflict in the DRC, supported a Zimbabwean-led initiative by members of SADC (notably excluding South Africa) for military intervention in support of the regime of President Laurent-Désiré Kabila; as many as 2,000 Namibian troops were subsequently dispatched to the DRC, provoking vociferous criticism by opponents of Nujoma. Namibia's continuing military commitments in the DRC following the failure of the 1999 Lusaka accord (to which Namibia was a signatory), together with the need for additional army resources in north-east Namibia as a result of the Caprivi rebellion and the intensification of operations against UNITA (see above), necessitated the allocation of an additional N $173m. to defence in the supplementary budget for 1999/2000, announced in early 2000.

President Laurent-Désiré Kabila was assassinated in January 2001, and was succeeded by his son, Maj.-Gen. Joseph Kabila. Efforts to resolve the conflict in the DRC were accelerated, and in February proposals for the withdrawal of troops involved in the regional military intervention, including the estimated 2,000 Namibians, were approved by the participating countries, under the aegis of the UN Security Council. In March it was announced that Namibian forces would remain in the DRC until the specified date for withdrawal in May. All but an estimated 150

Namibian troops eventually withdrew from the DRC in September, although other foreign forces were still deployed in large numbers; at least 30 Namibian troops were reported to have been killed in three years of service. All Namibian troops had been withdrawn by the end of 2002.

Germany has been a major aid donor to Namibia since independence, and relations are generally close. In September 1995, none the less, during a visit by the German Chancellor, Helmut Kohl, some 300 members of the Herero ethnic group staged a demonstration outside the German embassy in Windhoek to demand compensation for suffering inflicted on the Herero under German rule. In June 2001 the Herero filed a lawsuit in Washington, DC, USA, against three German companies (Deutsche Bank AG, Woermann Line and Terex Corporation), claiming US $2,000m. in reparation for the alleged exploitation and eventual extermination of some 65,000 Herero in 1904–07; a second lawsuit, for a further US $2,000m., was filed against the German Government in September. The case against Terex Corporation was subsequently withdrawn, after the company claimed that it was under different management at the time of the atrocities. In October 2003 it was reported that the Federal Court in Washington, DC, had ruled that it did not have jurisdiction over the Herero case, and that the Herero were consequently considering filing a lawsuit in New York. In January 2004, at a commemoration of the Herero uprising against German rule in 1904, the Government of Germany expressed its regret for the extermination of Herero, but declared itself unwilling to pay compensation to descendants of the victims. During a visit to Namibia in August 2004 the German Minister of Economic Co-operation and Development, Heidemarie Wieczorek-Zeul, apologized to the Herero Community for the atrocities carried out during 1904–07. During a visit to Germany in early December 2005 President Pohamba rejected an offer of reparations valued at N $160m. Bilateral consultations were scheduled to take place in May 2006 and would include a German proposal to invest N $150m., over a 10-year period, in regions inhabited by descendants of populations that suffered during the colonial occupation. The money would be made available in addition to existing aid commitments, which were reported to amount to some €11m. per year. However, the German Government denied that the additional money was intended as war reparations.

Government

On 21 March 1990 Namibia became independent, and the Constitution took effect. Executive authority is held by the President, who is the Head of State. According to the Constitution, the President shall be directly elected by universal adult suffrage for a term of five years, and permitted to hold office for a maximum of two terms. (In late 1998 legislation was approved whereby the Constitution was to be exceptionally amended to allow the incumbent President to seek a third term of office.) Legislative power is vested in the National Assembly, comprising 72 members directly elected by universal adult suffrage and as many as six non-voting members nominated by the President. The National Assembly has a maximum term of five years. An advisory National Council, comprising two representatives from each of the country's 13 regional councils, elected for a six-year period, operates as the second chamber of parliament. Each region has its own Governor.

Defence

In August 2005 the Namibian Defence Force numbered an estimated 9,000 men; there was also a 200-strong coastguard, operating as part of the Ministry of Fisheries and Marine Resources, and a paramilitary force of 6,000. A naval co-operation agreement was signed with Brazil in 1994, culminating in the establishment of the Namibian Navy in October 2004. Projected budgetary expenditure on defence for 2005 was N $1,100m.

Economic Affairs

In 2004, according to estimates by the World Bank, Namibia's gross national income (GNI), measured at average 2002–04 prices, was US $4,814m., equivalent to US $2,370 per head (or $6,960 per head on an international purchasing-power parity basis). During 1995–2004, it was estimated, the population increased at an average annual rate of 2.4% per year, while gross domestic product (GDP) per head increased, in real terms, by an average of 1.0% per year. Overall GDP increased, in real terms, at an average annual rate of 3.4% in 1995–2004. Real GDP increased by 4.2% in 2004.

Agriculture (including hunting, forestry and fishing) contributed 9.8% of GDP in 2004, according to the Bank of Namibia. About 39.0% of the labour force were employed in the sector in 2003. Government revenue from sales of fishing concessions was projected at N $70m. in the financial year ending 31 March 1999, and exports of fish and fish products provided 24.5% of total export earnings in 2003. The principal agricultural activity is beef production; the production of karakul sheepskins is also important. In addition, sealing and ostrich farming are practised on a commercial basis. The main subsistence crops are root crops, millet and maize, although Namibia remains highly dependent on imports of basic foods, especially in drought years. Plantations of seedless grapes were developed on the banks of the Orange river in the late 1990s, and projected growth in production was expected to increase significantly their contribution to export revenue. In recent years Namibia's traditionally rich fisheries have suffered a reverse. In 2004 the hake sector collapsed; and in February 2006 fishing quotas were further lowered and a five-year moratorium was declared on new fishing rights. Legislation aimed at developing aquaculture was adopted in 2003 and a number of fish farms were established. Agricultural GDP increased at an average annual rate of 2.3% in 1995–2004; it increased by 4.2% in 2004.

Industry (including mining, manufacturing, construction and power) contributed 31.3% of GDP in 2004, and engaged 12.2% of the employed labour force in 2000. During 1995–2004 industrial GDP increased by an average of 2.4% per year. Industrial GDP increased by 4.3% in 2004.

Mining and quarrying contributed 11.3% of GDP in 2004 and engaged 0.9% of the employed labour force in 2000. Namibia has rich deposits of many minerals, and is among the world's leading producers of gem diamonds (some 96% of diamonds mined in Namibia are of gem quality). Diamond-mining contributed 86.2% of the sector's GDP in 2003, and diamonds are the principal mineral export, accounting for 31.9% of export earnings in 2002; in 2000 Namibia produced 5% of world diamond output by value. The following year diamonds with an estimated value of US $500,000m. were reported to be lying on the continental shelf off the Namibian coast. In July 2004 the Israeli company Lev Leviev Diamonds established a diamond-cutting and -polishing factory in Windhoek, the first in Namibia and the largest of its kind in Africa. Copper production, which ceased in 1998, following the liquidation of the Tsumeb Corporation, resumed at the former Tsumeb sites in September 2000. In 2005 the smelter at Tsumeb, operated by Ongopolo, remained the only one in the country; imports of foreign ore accounted for around 40% of its production. The Skorpion zinc mine and refinery near Rosh Pinah, opened in mid-2003 by Anglo American plc, was expected to contribute some 4% of GDP on reaching full production in the second half of 2004. Production of an estimated 150,000 metric tons of zinc per year was anticipated over a period of 15 years. A new uranium mine was expected to begin production at Langer Heinrich in 2007, despite health and environmental concerns; the mine was expected to contribute some N $1,400m. to the economy. In addition, zinc, lead, gold, salt, fluorspar, marble and semi-precious stones are extracted, and there are also considerable deposits of hydrocarbons, lithium, manganese, tungsten, cadmium and vanadium. Namibia is also believed to have substantial reserves of coal, iron ore and platinum. Mining GDP increased at an average annual rate of 2.7% in 1993–2001; the sector's GDP decreased by 1.7% in 2000 and by 6.1% in 2001.

Manufacturing contributed 13.3% of GDP in 2004 and engaged 5.3% of the employed labour force in 2000. The sector has hitherto remained underdeveloped, largely owing to Namibia's economic dependence on South Africa. The principal manufacturing activities are the processing of fish and minerals for export; brewing, meat processing and the production of chemicals are also significant. Manufacturing GDP increased by an average of 3.0% per year in 1995–2004; it increased by 4.3% in 2004.

In 2002 96.8% of Namibia's electricity production was derived from hydroelectric power. There is a hydroelectric station at Ruacana, on the Cunene river at the border with Angola, and a second hydroelectric power station was planned at Divundu on the Okavango river; a project to construct a power station at Epupa remained stalled in 2005, following a disagreement between the Namibian and Angolan Governments over the most appropriate site. Final agreement was expected to be reached on developing the Kudu offshore gasfield in early 2006. An 800-MW 'gas-to-power' plant would supply the domestic market and the surplus would be exported to South Africa under an agreement with that country's Electricity Supply Commission. Construction of the plant was scheduled to begin in 2007, for completion by 2009. Domestic electricity generation increased significantly in 2000, enabling the proportion of electrical energy imported to be reduced to 34.8% in that year. A power transmission line, linking the Namibian and South African electricity grids, was inaugurated in southern Namibia in 1999. Imports of mineral fuels and lubricants accounted for 10.4% of the value of total merchandise imports in 2003. South Africa supplies all of Namibia's petroleum requirements.

The services sector contributed 58.9% of GDP in 2004. Tourism is expanding rapidly, and has been the focus of a major privatization initiative. The acquisition of Walvis Bay in March 1994, and subsequent establishment there of a free-trade zone, was expected to enhance Namibia's status as an entrepôt for regional trade. By March 2004 it was estimated that the free-trade zone had attracted some N $80m. of direct foreign investment. In 2006 the Government remained the largest employer, accounting for some 70,000 jobs. The GDP of the services sector increased at an average annual rate of 3.8% in 1995–2004. Services GDP increased by 4.2% in 2004.

In 2004 Namibia recorded a visible trade deficit of US $282.8m., although there was a surplus of US $572.6m. on the current account of the balance of payments. South Africa remained the dominant source of imports in 2003, providing 80.5% of the total. In that year South Africa was also the principal market for Namibian exports (31.5%), followed by Angola (24.9%), Spain (12.8%) and the United Kingdom (10.4%). The principal exports were food and live animals (notably fish and meat), manufactured goods and diamonds. The principal import groups in that year included machinery and transport equipment, manufactured goods, food and live animals and mineral fuels and lubricants.

In the financial year ending 31 March 2005 Namibia recorded an estimated overall budget deficit of N $872.3m. In 1997 South Africa officially cancelled the external public debt inherited by Namibia at independence. Namibia's external debt was estimated at US $716m. in 2003. The annual rate of inflation averaged 8.6% in 1992–2003; consumer prices increased by 4.2% in 2004 and by 2.2% in 2005. According to the 2001 census some 31% of the labour force were unemployed.

Namibia is a member of the Common Market for Eastern and Southern Africa (see p. 191), of the Southern African Development Community (see p. 358), and of the Southern African Customs Union (with Botswana, Lesotho, South Africa and Swaziland); and is also a signatory to the Cotonou Agreement with the European Union.

Namibia's potential for economic prosperity remains high, given its abundant mineral reserves and well-developed infrastructure, both of which were enhanced in 1994 by the acquisition of sovereignty over Walvis Bay and of important diamond-mining rights. The mining of offshore diamond deposits is of increasing importance: the leading diamond producer in the country, Namdeb (a joint venture between the Government and De Beers), accounts for some 10% of national GDP and 30% of export earnings. However, Namibia's economic progress continues to be largely influenced by its dependence on South Africa. (The Namibian dollar, introduced in 1993, is at par with the rand.) Although the average level of income per head is among the highest in the region, there remain extreme disparities in the distribution of wealth; in 1994 land-reform legislation was enacted in an effort to redress this problem, but implementation has been very slow (see above). The Nujoma Government's first National Development Plan, covering the period 1995–2000, aimed principally to reduce poverty and encourage sustainable economic growth (averaging 5% annually during the plan period) through policies of diversification, in an attempt to prevent potential over-dependence on the mining and fishing sectors. The 1995 Export Processing Zones (EPZ) Act aimed to industrialize the economy, which was dominated by primary-sector industries and by July 2005 companies in the EPZ were reported to have attracted more than N $5,200m. in foreign direct investment and contributed N $11,600m. to the economy. Some 7,000 workers were directly employed within the EPZ, principally in the manufacturing industry, which included automotive parts and rebuilding and reconditioning motor vehicles; zinc and copper refinery; and the production of textiles, garments and leatherwear. In November 2001 Namibia became eligible to export certain products to the USA free from tariffs, under the African Growth and Opportunity Act (AGOA); it was estimated that 90% of products made in Namibia would qualify for duty-free access to the US market until 2008. In December 2002 and 2003 Namibia's eligibility for tariff preferences under AGOA was renewed; however, between 2001 and 2003 the US market accounted for less than 3% of Namibian exports. In relation to AGOA, in February 2006 the US Trade and Development Agency awarded the Namibian Ports Authority a grant worth US $2.4m. for the development and expansion of the port facilities at Walvis Bay and Lüderitz. Economic growth in 2005–2006 was expected to be driven by tourism and the continued expansion of the mining sector (and in particular by exports of diamonds, zinc and uranium). However, despite a number of recent positive economic trends, the high rate of unemployment and that fact that more than 20% of the population was infected with HIV/AIDS, remained causes for serious concern.

Education

Under the Constitution, education is compulsory between the ages of six and 16 years, or until primary education has been completed (whichever is the sooner). Primary education consists of seven grades, and secondary education of five. In 2000/01 total enrolment at primary and secondary schools was equivalent to 94% of the school-age population (males 92%; females 95%). Enrolment at primary schools included 82% of children in the relevant age-group (males 79%; females 84%), while the comparable ratio for secondary enrolment in that year was 38% (males 32%; females 44%). In 2002/03 there were some 455,077 children enrolled in pre-primary and primary education, and 138,099 in secondary education. Higher education is provided by the University of Namibia, the Technicon of Namibia, a vocational college and four teacher-training colleges. In 2002/03 13,536 students were enrolled in tertiary education. Various schemes for informal adult education are also in operation in an effort to combat illiteracy. Under the 2004/05 budget N $2,613.2m. was allocated to education (20.6% of total government expenditure).

Public Holidays

2006: 1 January (New Year's Day), 21 March (Independence Day), 14–17 April (Easter), 1 May (Workers' Day), 4 May (Cassinga Day), 25 May (Ascension Day), 25 May (Africa Day, anniversary of the OAU's foundation), 26 August (Heroes' Day), 7 October (Day of Goodwill), 10 December (Human Rights Day), 25–26 December (Christmas).

2007: 1 January (New Year's Day), 21 March (Independence Day), 6–9 April (Easter), 1 May (Workers' Day), 4 May (Cassinga Day), 17 May (Ascension Day), 25 May (Africa Day, anniversary of the OAU's foundation), 26 August (Heroes' Day), 7 October (Day of Goodwill), 10 December (Human Rights Day), 25–26 December (Christmas).

Weights and Measures

The metric system is in use.

Statistical Survey

Source (unless otherwise indicated): Central Bureau of Statistics, National Planning Commission, Government Office Park, Block D2, Luther St, Windhoek; Private Bag 13356, Windhoek; tel. (61) 2834056; fax (61) 237620; e-mail info@npc.gov.na; internet www.npc.gov.na.

Area and Population

AREA, POPULATION AND DENSITY*

Area (sq km)	824,292†
Population (census results)	
21 October 1991	1,409,920
28 August 2001	
Males	936,718
Females	890,136
Total	1,826,854
Population (UN estimates at mid-year)‡	
2002	1,961,000
2003	1,987,000
2004	2,009,000
Density (per sq km) at mid-2004	2.4

* Including data for Walvis Bay, sovereignty over which was transferred from South Africa to Namibia with effect from March 1994. Walvis Bay has an area of 1,124 sq km (434 sq miles) and had a population of 22,999 in 1991.
† 318,261 sq miles.
‡ Source: UN, *World Population Prospects: The 2004 Revision*.

ETHNIC GROUPS
(population, 1988 estimate)

Ovambo	623,000		Caprivian	47,000
Kavango	117,000		Bushmen	36,000
Damara	94,000		Baster	31,000
Herero	94,000		Tswana	7,000
White	80,000		Others	12,000
Nama	60,000		**Total**	1,252,000
Coloured	51,000			

PRINCIPAL TOWNS
(population at 2001 census)

Windhoek	233,529		Rehoboth	21,300
Rundu	44,413		Otjiwarongo	19,614
Walvis Bay	42,015		Keetmanshoop	15,543
Oshakati	28,255		Gobabis	13,856
Katima Mulilo	22,694		Tsumeb	13,108

Mid-2003 (UN estimate, including suburbs): Windhoek (capital) 236,517 (Source: UN, *World Urbanization Prospects: The 2003 Revision*).

BIRTHS AND DEATHS
(UN estimates, annual averages)

	1990–95	1995–2000	2000–05
Birth rate (per 1,000)	41.5	35.1	29.1
Death rate (per 1,000)	8.7	9.9	14.6

Source: UN, *World Population Prospects: The 2004 Revision*.

Expectation of life (WHO estimates, years at birth): 51 (males 50; females 53) in 2003 (Source: WHO, *World Health Report*).

ECONOMICALLY ACTIVE POPULATION
(persons aged 15 to 69 years, 2000 labour force survey)

	Males	Females	Total
Agriculture, hunting, and forestry	69,782	56,677	126,459
Fishing	4,725	3,075	7,800
Mining and quarrying	3,154	713	3,868
Manufacturing	11,375	11,548	22,922
Electricity, gas and water	3,709	484	4,193
Construction	20,740	1,048	21,788
Wholesale and retail trade, repair of motor vehicles, motorcycles and personal and household goods	17,220	21,683	38,902
Restaurants and hotels	3,006	4,671	7,677
Transport, storage and communications	12,243	2,065	14,308
Financial intermediation	2,489	2,444	4,933
Real estate, renting and business activities	17,880	21,437	39,318
Public administration and defence; compulsory social security	15,372	9,047	24,419
Education	11,742	18,797	30,538
Health and social work	2,993	10,143	13,135
Other community, social and personal services	24,324	21,965	46,289
Private households with employed persons	4,754	17,456	22,210
Extra-territorial organizations and bodies	155	172	327
Not classifiable by economic activity	1,166	1,599	2,765
Total employed	226,828	205,021	431,849
Unemployed	89,350	131,284	220,634
Total labour force	316,178	336,305	652,483

Source: ILO.

Mid-2003 (FAO estimates, '000 persons): Agriculture, etc. 309; Total labour force 793 (Source: FAO).

Health and Welfare

KEY INDICATORS

Total fertility rate (children per woman, 2003)	4.5
Under-5 mortality rate (per 1,000 live births, 2004)	63
HIV/AIDS (% of persons aged 15–49, 2003)	21.30
Physicians (per 1,000 head, 1997)	0.30
Health expenditure (2002): US $ per head (PPP)	331
Health expenditure (2002): % of GDP	6.7
Health expenditure (2002): public (% of total)	70.1
Access to water (% of persons, 2002)	80
Access to sanitation (% of persons, 2002)	30
Human Development Index (2003): ranking	125
Human Development Index (2003): value	0.627

For sources and definitions, see explanatory note on p. vi.

NAMIBIA

Agriculture

PRINCIPAL CROPS
('000 metric tons)

	2002	2003	2004*
Wheat	10.5	8.0†	8.0
Maize	27.8	33.0†	33.0
Millet	56.1	60.0*	60.0
Sorghum	5.6	6.0*	6.0
Roots and tubers*	285	295	295
Pulses*	9	9	9
Cottonseed*	5.7	5.1	5.1
Vegetables*	18	18	18
Grapes*	8.0	8.5	8.5
Other fruit*	14.5	14.5	14.5

* FAO estimate(s).
† Unofficial figure.
Source: FAO.

LIVESTOCK
('000 head, year ending September)

	2002	2003	2004
Horses	47.5	48.0*	48.0*
Mules*	6.6	6.7	6.7
Asses	119.8	120.0*	120.0*
Cattle	2,336	2,509*	2,500*
Pigs*	24	28	28
Sheep	2,877	2,900*	2,900*
Goats	2,082.6	2,100.0*	2,100.0*
Chickens*	2,750	2,800	2,800

* FAO estimate(s).
Source: FAO.

LIVESTOCK PRODUCTS
(FAO estimates, '000 metric tons)

	2002	2003	2004
Beef and veal	60.8	78.4	77.3
Mutton and lamb	12.6	14.0	14.0
Goat meat	4.9	5.0	5.0
Pig meat	0.6	0.6	0.6
Poultry meat	3.6	3.9	3.9
Other meat	6.2	6.9	6.9
Cows' milk	105	109	109
Hen eggs	1.7	1.9	1.9
Wool (greasy)	2.1	2.2	2.2
Cattle hides	6.5	8.4	8.3
Sheepskins	1.4	1.6	1.6
Goatskins	0.8	0.8	0.8

Source: FAO.

Forestry

Separate figures are not yet available. Data for Namibia are included in those for South Africa.

Fishing*

('000 metric tons, live weight)

	2001	2002	2003
Capture	547.5	624.9	636.3
Cape hakes (Stokvisse)	173.3	156.5	192.3
Southern African pilchard	7.9	4.2	22.3
Cape horse mackerel (Maasbanker)	309.4	359.2	366.9
Aquaculture	0.1	0.1	0.1†
Total catch	547.5	624.9	636.3

* Figures include quantities caught by licensed foreign vessels in Namibian waters and processed in Lüderitz and Walvis Bay. The data exclude aquatic mammals (whales, seals, etc.). The number of South African fur seals caught was: 44,223 in 2001; 37,670 in 2002; 35,000 in 2003. The number of Nile crocodiles caught was: 105 in 2000 (FAO estimate).
† FAO estimate.
Source: FAO.

Mining

(metric tons, unless otherwise indicated)

	2001	2002	2003
Copper ore*	12,393	18,012	19,500†
Lead concentrates*	12,088	13,809	18,782
Zinc concentrates*	37,622	42,685	60,500
Silver ore (kilograms)*	20,396	43,632	45,100
Uranium oxide	2,640	2,751	2,401
Gold ore (kilograms)*	2,706	2,644	2,425
Fluorspar (Fluorite)‡	81,551	81,084	79,349
Salt (unrefined)	543,218	630,159	697,914
Diamonds ('000 metric carats)	1,487	1,562	1,481

* Figures refer to the metal content of ores and concentrates.
† Estimated production.
‡ Figures (on a wet-weight basis) refer to acid-grade material.
Source: US Geological Survey.

Industry

SELECTED PRODUCTS
(metric tons)

	2001	2002	2003
Unrefined copper (unwrought)	27,015	26,703	26,036

Cement (estimated production, metric tons): 150,000 in 1999.
Source: US Geological Survey.

Finance

CURRENCY AND EXCHANGE RATES

Monetary Units
100 cents = 1 Namibian dollar (N $).

Sterling, US Dollar and Euro Equivalents (30 December 2005)
£1 sterling = N $10.8910;
US $1 = N $6.3250;
€1 = N $7.4616;
N $1,000 = £91.82 = US $158.10 = €134.02.

Average Exchange Rate (N $ per US $)
2003 7.5648
2004 6.4597
2005 6.3593

Note: The Namibian dollar was introduced in September 1993, replacing (at par) the South African rand. The rand remained legal tender in Namibia.

NAMIBIA

Statistical Survey

CENTRAL GOVERNMENT BUDGET
(N $ million, year ending 31 March)

Revenue*	2002/03	2003/04	2004/05
Taxation	9,329.8	8,762.9	10,660.7
Taxes on income, profits and capital gains	4,442.3	3,618.5	3,827.8
Taxes on property	79.3	75.2	85.0
Domestic taxes on goods and services	2,135.7	1,950.8	2,451.1
Taxes on international trade and transactions	2,596.9	3,035.6	4,206.8
Other taxes	75.6	82.8	90.0
Non-tax revenue	1,121.1	970.5	1,144.3
Entrepreneurial and property income	703.2	488.8	666.6
Fines and forfeitures	19.6	18.9	21.0
Administrative fees and charges	382.3	449.3	420.3
Return on capital from lending and equity	15.9	13.5	36.4
Total	10,450.9	9,733.4	11,805.0

Expenditure†	2002/03	2003/04	2004/05
Current expenditure	9,503.0	10,448.3	10,955.2
Personnel expenditure	4,708.9	5,117.0	5,303.6
Expenditure on goods and other services	1,993.6	2,079.4	1,774.8
Interest payments	907.6	996.0	1,176.0
Subsidies and other current transfers	1,892.8	2,255.9	2,700.8
Capital expenditure	1,246.0	1,397.0	1,802.9
Capital investment	1,158.7	1,293.4	1,594.6
Capital transfers	87.2	103.6	208.3
Total	10,749.0	11,843.4	12,758.1

* Excluding grants received from abroad (N $ million): 111.2 in 2002/03; 34.2 in 2003/04; 80.8 in 2004/05.
† Excluding total lending and equity participation (N $ million): 649.7 in 2002/03; 400.0 in 2003/04; 0.0 in 2004/05.

Source: Bank of Namibia, *Quarterly Bulletin* (December 2004).

INTERNATIONAL RESERVES
(US $ million at 31 December, excl. gold)

	2002	2003	2004
IMF special drawing rights	0.02	0.03	0.03
Reserve position in IMF	0.06	0.08	0.09
Foreign exchange	323.05	325.11	344.94
Total	323.13	325.22	345.06

Source: IMF, *International Financial Statistics*.

MONEY SUPPLY
(N $ million at 31 December)

	2001	2002	2003
Demand deposits at deposit money banks	5,805.2	6,152.4	7,266.8
Total money (incl. others)	6,312.7	6,698.2	7,851.4

Source: IMF, *International Financial Statistics*.

COST OF LIVING
(Consumer Price Index; base: December 2001 = 100)

	2003	2004	2005
Food and non-alcoholic beverages	121.6	122.6	124.4
Alcoholic beverages and tobacco	110.9	121.2	130.1
Housing, fuel and power	114.6	122.4	124.3
Clothing and footwear	108.8	109.3	108.2
All items (incl. others)	115.4	120.2	122.9

NATIONAL ACCOUNTS
(N $ million at current prices)

National Income and Product

	2002	2003	2004
Compensation of employees	12,012	13,064	13,846
Operating surplus	13,793	12,561	13,666
Domestic factor incomes	25,805	25,625	27,512
Consumption of fixed capital	4,073	5,304	5,922
Gross domestic product (GDP) at factor cost	29,878	30,929	33,434
Indirect taxes	3,582	3,051	3,680
Less Subsidies	552	140	213
GDP in purchasers' values	32,908	33,840	36,901
Factor income received from abroad	1,803	2,123	2,374
Less Factor income paid abroad	1,447	391	1,892
Gross national income	33,264	35,572	37,383
Less Consumption of fixed capital	4,073	5,304	5,922
National income in market prices	29,191	30,268	31,461
Other current transfers from abroad	3,202	3,670	4,528
Less Other current transfers paid abroad	308	203	225
National disposable income	32,085	33,735	35,764

Expenditure on the Gross Domestic Product

	2002	2003	2004
Government final consumption expenditure	8,692	8,969	9,049
Private final consumption expenditure	18,289	18,794	19,235
Increase in stocks	−468	220	120
Gross fixed capital formation	6,964	9,867	9,286
Total domestic expenditure	33,476	37,850	37,690
Exports of goods and services	16,320	17,396	17,080
Less Imports of goods and services	16,966	18,616	16,622
Statistical discrepancy	77	−2,790	−1,246
GDP in purchasers' values	32,908	33,840	36,901

Gross Domestic Product by Economic Activity

	2002	2003	2004
Agriculture and forestry	1,687	1,814	1,846
Fishing	1,608	1,757	1,470
Mining and quarrying	4,565	2,975	3,837
Diamond mining	3,427	2,630	3,444
Manufacturing	3,305	3,870	4,519
Manufacture of food products and beverages	1,515	1,650	1,670
Electricity and water	854	1,003	1,166
Construction	725	1,029	1,124
Wholesale and retail trade, repairs, etc.	3,428	3,987	4,147
Hotels and restaurants	576	648	651
Transport, storage and communications	2,083	2,382	2,516
Financial intermediation	1,088	1,246	1,236
Real estate and business services	2,832	3,156	3,405
Government services	6,553	6,863	7,107
Other community, social and personal services	244	281	301
Other services	558	606	637
Sub-total	30,106	31,617	33,962
Less Financial services indirectly measured	359	431	413
GDP at basic prices	29,747	31,185	33,549
Taxes, less subsidies, on products	3,161	2,655	3,353
GDP in purchasers' values	32,908	33,840	36,901

Source: Bank of Namibia, *Quarterly Bulletin* (December 2005).

NAMIBIA

Statistical Survey

BALANCE OF PAYMENTS
(US $ million)

	2002	2003	2004
Exports of goods f.o.b.	1,071.6	1,262.0	1,827.5
Imports of goods f.o.b.	−1,282.5	−1,726.0	−2,110.3
Trade balance	−210.9	−464.0	−282.8
Exports of services	283.2	420.2	482.4
Imports of services	−223.8	−249.4	−385.1
Balance on goods and services	−151.5	−293.2	−185.4
Other income received	172.6	283.9	368.5
Other income paid	−133.9	−54.0	−217.6
Balance on goods, services and income	−112.8	−63.4	−34.6
Current transfers received	270.4	426.2	642.1
Current transfers paid	−29.9	−27.2	−34.9
Current balance	127.7	335.7	572.6
Capital account (net)	40.7	68.3	77.2
Direct investment abroad	4.7	10.8	21.6
Direct investment from abroad	51.2	33.3	88.2
Portfolio investment assets	−144.1	−217.4	−249.9
Portfolio investment liabilities	8.2	3.9	4.5
Other investment assets	−247.2	−452.8	−467.8
Other investment liabilities	−19.7	−41.5	−113.6
Net errors and omissions	−31.8	−69.3	−69.7
Overall balance	−210.3	−329.1	−136.9

Source: IMF, *International Financial Statistics*.

External Trade

PRINCIPAL COMMODITIES
(US $ million)

Imports c.i.f.	2001	2002	2003
Food and live animals	172.1	137.3	161.7
Mineral fuels and lubricants	160.9	159.3	148.5
Petroleum and petroleum products	159.0	149.9	144.0
Chemicals and related products	160.2	110.7	106.0
Basic manufactures	274.1	229.4	270.9
Non-metallic mineral manufactures	52.2	42.2	52.3
Metals and metal products	85.4	75.0	67.7
Machinery and transport equipment	532.0	446.0	459.4
Machinery specialized for particular industries	88.0	57.5	54.6
General industrial machinery, equipment and parts	53.6	63.8	60.4
Telecommunications and sound equipment	38.2	27.0	44.0
Telecommunications equipment, parts and accessories	28.1	17.4	27.9
Electrical machinery, apparatus, etc.	70.2	60.9	69.6
Road vehicles	180.9	132.2	163.3
Passenger motor vehicles (excl. buses)	119.7	83.2	103.1
Other transport equipment	44.4	51.8	14.9
Miscellaneous manufactured articles	185.5	154.1	164.2
Clothing and accessories	46.0	37.1	35.5
Total (incl. others)	1,553.0	1,310.1	1,427.9

Exports f.o.b.	2001	2002	2003
Food and live animals	431.5	388.5	471.4
Fish, shellfish and preparations thereof.	315.9	270.8	318.9
Fresh or frozen fish	293.8	253.6	305.2
Beverages and tobacco	67.2	77.7	139.7
Beverages	65.5	74.3	136.9
Alcoholic beverages	49.0	52.4	68.0
Beer made from malt	43.5	41.0	55.2
Crude materials (inedible) except fuels	132.5	146.7	84.2
Metal ores and scrap	103.5	116.8	49.3
Ores and concentrates of uranium and thorium	102.2	115.8	47.1
Basic manufactures	485.6	472.0	231.4
Non-metallic mineral manufactures	450.3	430.5	151.6
Pearl, precious and semi-precious stones	448.1	425.4	141.3
Diamonds	447.8	424.3	141.0
Machinery and transport equipment	54.6	74.4	112.2
Miscellaneous manufactured articles	176.4	64.2	194.5
Printed matter	154.8	31.0	147.8
Total (incl. others)	1,404.5	1,282.9	1,303.7

Source: UN, *International Trade Statistics Yearbook*.

PRINCIPAL TRADING PARTNERS
(US $ million)

Imports c.i.f.	2001	2002	2003
China, People's Repub.	17.0	11.7	18.3
Germany	30.7	41.2	33.5
South Africa	1,336.0	1,013.4	1,149.0
Spain	13.0	16.3	19.4
United Kingdom	18.2	34.3	17.5
USA	14.0	26.3	14.2
Total (incl. others)	1,553.0	1,310.1	1,427.9

Exports f.o.b.	2001	2002	2003
Angola	82.2	186.7	324.9
Belgium	7.7	7.5	7.1
Canada	0.5	4.1	12.9
Congo, Republic	5.0	9.1	33.8
France	25.2	82.4	23.4
Germany	12.2	14.7	14.5
Italy	24.5	23.3	23.0
Netherlands	19.4	17.3	13.9
South Africa	433.5	326.2	410.7
Spain	184.5	155.8	167.0
United Kingdom	495.6	315.1	135.7
USA	41.7	40.4	35.2
Total (incl. others)	1,404.5	1,282.9	1,303.7

Source: UN, *International Trade Statistics Yearbook*.

Transport

RAILWAYS

	2002/03	2003/04
Freight (million net ton-km)	1,244.6	1,247.4
Passengers carried	125,656	112,033

Source: TransNamib Holdings Ltd, *2004 Annual Report*.

NAMIBIA

ROAD TRAFFIC
(motor vehicles in use at 31 December)

	1994*	1995*	1996
Passenger cars	61,269	62,500	74,875
Buses and coaches	5,098	5,200	10,175
Lorries and vans	60,041	61,300	59,352
Motorcycles and mopeds	1,450	1,480	1,520

Total vehicles in use (excluding road tractors, motorcycles and mopeds): 137,650 in 1997; 137,650 in 1998*; 123,568 in 1999*.

2000: Passenger cars 68,565; Buses and coaches 1,924; Lorries and vans 73,598; Road tractors 2,912; Motorcycles and mopeds 2,849.

* Estimate(s).

Source: International Road Federation, *World Road Statistics*.

SHIPPING

Merchant Fleet
(at 31 December)

	2002	2003	2004
Number of vessels	126	129	157
Displacement (gross registered tons)	69,488	74,524	92,299

Source: Lloyd's Register-Fairplay, *World Fleet Statistics*.

Sea-borne Freight Traffic
(year ending 30 August, unless otherwise indicated)

	1999/2000*	2000/01	2001/02
Port of Lüderitz:			
Goods loaded ('000 freight tons†)	93.6	143.3	171.2
Goods unloaded ('000 freight tons)	39.5	105.1	101.7
Goods transhipped ('000 freight tons)	14.1	10.0	4.6
Containers handled (total TEUs)	2,311	2,320	2,480
Port of Walvis Bay:			
Goods loaded ('000 freight tons)	723.4	720.7	915.8
Goods unloaded ('000 freight tons)	1,460.3	1,452.1	1,443.1
Goods transhipped ('000 freight tons)	40.0	56.6	60.3
Containers handled (total TEUs)	24,859	25,768	31,569

* Year ending 30 September 2000.
† One freight ton = 40 cu ft (1.133 cu m) of cargo capacity.

Source: Namibian Ports Authority.

CIVIL AVIATION
(traffic on scheduled services)

	1999	2000	2001
Kilometres flown (million)	7	8	9
Passengers carried ('000)	201	247	215
Passenger-km (million)	548	740	754
Total ton-km (million)	49	151	151

Source: UN, *Statistical Yearbook*.

Tourism

FOREIGN TOURIST ARRIVALS*

Country of origin	2001	2002	2003
Angola	237,691	278,816	222,752
Botswana	29,699	29,328	22,679
Germany	52,976	61,236	58,036
South Africa	241,809	243,894	222,009
United Kingdom	13,941	19,560	19,291
Zimbabwe	12,970	19,145	17,795
Total (incl. others)	670,497	757,201	695,221

* Excluding same-day visitors: 861,184 in 2001; 947,778 in 2002; 917,000 in 2003.

Tourism receipts (US $ million, excl. passenger transport): 236 in 2001; 218 in 2002; 333 in 2003.

Source: World Tourism Organization.

Communications Media

	2002	2003	2004
Telephones ('000 main lines in use)	121.4	127.4	127.9
Mobile cellular telephones ('000 subscribers)	150.0	223.7	286.1
Personal computers ('000 in use)	133	220	220
Internet users ('000)	50.0	65.0	75.0

Television receivers ('000 in use): 67 in 2000.

Source: International Telecommunication Union.

Radio receivers ('000 in use): 232 in 1997 (Source: UNESCO, *Statistical Yearbook*).

Daily newspapers (1997): 4; average circulation ('000 copies) 10 (Source: UNESCO, *Statistical Yearbook*).

Non-daily newspapers (1997): 5; average circulation ('000 copies) 9 (Source: UNESCO, *Statistical Yearbook*).

Education
(2002/03, unless otherwise indicated)

	Teachers	Students Males	Students Females	Total
Pre-primary	1,314*	22,027	28,267	50,294
Primary	14,330*	202,091	202,692	404,783
Secondary	5,869	65,322	72,777	138,099
Tertiary	931	7,152†	6,384†	13,536†

* Estimate for 2000/01.
† Estimate.

Institutions (1998/99): Primary 1,362.

Source: UNESCO, Institute for Statistics.

Adult literacy rate (UNESCO estimates): 85.0% (males 83.5%; females 86.8%) in 2003 (Source: UN Development Programme, *Human Development Report*).

Directory

The Constitution

The Constitution of the Republic of Namibia took effect at independence on 21 March 1990. Its principal provisions are summarized below:

THE REPUBLIC

The Republic of Namibia is a sovereign, secular, democratic and unitary State and the Constitution is the supreme law.

FUNDAMENTAL HUMAN RIGHTS AND FREEDOMS

The fundamental rights and freedoms of the individual are guaranteed regardless of sex, race, colour, ethnic origin, religion, creed or social or economic status. All citizens shall have the right to form and join political parties. The practice of racial discrimination shall be prohibited.

THE PRESIDENT

Executive power shall be vested in the President and the Cabinet. The President shall be the Head of State and of the Government and the Commander-in-Chief of the Defence Force. The President shall be directly elected by universal and equal adult suffrage, and must receive more than 50% of the votes cast. The term of office shall be five years; one person may not hold the office of President for more than two terms.*

THE CABINET

The Cabinet shall consist of the President, the Prime Minister and such other ministers as the President may appoint from members of the National Assembly. The President may also appoint a Deputy Prime Minister. The functions of the members of the Cabinet shall include directing the activities of ministries and government departments, initiating bills for submission to the National Assembly, formulating, explaining and assessing for the National Assembly the budget of the State and its economic development plans, formulating, explaining and analysing for the National Assembly Namibia's foreign policy and foreign trade policy and advising the President on the state of national defence.

THE NATIONAL ASSEMBLY

Legislative power shall be vested in the National Assembly, which shall be composed of 72 members elected by general, direct and secret ballots and not more than six non-voting members appointed by the President by virtue of their special expertise, status, skill or experience. Every National Assembly shall continue for a maximum period of five years, but it may be dissolved by the President before the expiry of its term.

THE NATIONAL COUNCIL

The National Council shall consist of two members from each region (elected by regional councils from among their members) and shall have a life of six years. The functions of the National Council shall include considering all bills passed by the National Assembly, investigating any subordinate legislation referred to it by the National Assembly for advice, and recommending legislation to the National Assembly on matters of regional concern.

OTHER PROVISIONS

Other provisions relate to the administration of justice (see under Judicial System), regional and local government, the public service commission, the security commission, the police, defence forces and prison service, finance, and the central bank and national planning commission. The repeal of, or amendments to, the Constitution require the approval of two-thirds of the members of the National Assembly and two-thirds of the members of the National Council; if the proposed repeal or amendment secures a majority of two-thirds of the members of the National Assembly, but not a majority of two-thirds of the members of the National Council, the President may make the proposals the subject of a national referendum, in which a two-thirds' majority is needed for approval of the legislation.

* In late 1998 the National Assembly and National Council approved legislation whereby the Constitution was to be exceptionally amended to allow the incumbent President to seek a third term of office.

The Government

HEAD OF STATE

President and Commander-in-Chief of the Defence Force: HIFIKEPUNYE POHAMBA (elected by direct suffrage 15–16 November 2004; took office 21 March 2005).

THE CABINET
(March 2006)

President: HIFIKEPUNYE POHAMBA.
Prime Minister: NAHAS ANGULA.
Deputy Prime Minister: Dr LIBERTINA AMATHILA.
Minister of Presidential Affairs: ALBERT KAWANA.
Minister of Home Affairs and Immigration: ROSALIA NGHIDINWA.
Minister of Safety and Security and Acting Minister of Defence: PETER TSHIRUMBU-TSHEEHAMA.
Minister of Foreign Affairs: MARCO HAUSIKU.
Minister of Information and Broadcasting: NETUMBO NANDI-NDAITWAH.
Minister of Education: NANGOLO MBUMBA.
Minister of Mines and Energy: ERRKI NGHIMTINA.
Minister of Justice and Attorney-General: PENDUKENI IVULA-ITHANA.
Minister of Trade and Industry: IMMANUEL NGATJIZEKO.
Minister of Agriculture, Water and Forestry: Dr NICKEY IYAMBO.
Minister of Finance: SAARAH KUUGONGELWA-AMADHILA.
Minister of Health and Social Services: RICHARD KAMWI.
Minister of Labour and Social Welfare: ALPHEUS NARUSEB.
Minister of Regional and Local Government and Housing: JOHN PANDENI.
Minister of Environment and Tourism: WILLEM KONJORE.
Minister of Works, Transport and Communications: JOEL NATANGWE KAAPANDA.
Minister of Lands, Resettlement and Rehabilitation: JERRY EKANDJO.
Minister of Fisheries and Marine Resources: ABRAHAM IYAMBO.
Minister of Gender Equality and Child Welfare: MARLENE MUNGUNDA.
Minister of Youth, National Service, Sport and Culture: JOHN MUTORWA.
Minister without Portfolio: NGARIKUTUKE TJIRIANGE.

Also attending Cabinet

Dir-Gen. of the Namibia Central Intelligence Agency: Lt-Gen. LUCAS HANGULA.
Dir-Gen. of the National Planning Commission: HELMUT ANGULA.

MINISTRIES

Office of the President: State House, Robert Mugabe Ave, PMB 13339, Windhoek; tel. (61) 2707111; fax (61) 221780; e-mail angolo@op.gov.na; internet www.op.gov.na.
Office of the Prime Minister: Robert Mugabe Ave, PMB 13338, Windhoek; tel. (61) 2879111; fax (61) 230648; internet www.opm.gov.na.
Ministry of Agriculture, Water and Forestry: cnr Robert Mugabe Ave and Peter Muller St, PMB 13184, Windhoek; tel. (61) 2087111; fax (61) 229961.
Ministry of Defence: PMB 13307, Windhoek; tel. (61) 2049111; fax (61) 232518.
Ministry of Education: Troskie House, Uhland St, PMB 13186, Windhoek; tel. (61) 2933111; fax (61) 224277.
Ministry of Environment and Tourism: Swabou Bldg, Post St Mall, PMB 13346, Windhoek; tel. (61) 2842111; fax (61) 221930; e-mail tourism@iwwn.com.na; internet www.tourism.com.na.
Ministry of Finance: Fiscus Bldg, John Meinert St, PMB 13295, Windhoek; tel. (61) 2099111; fax (61) 230179.
Ministry of Fisheries and Marine Resources: Uhland and Goethe Sts, Private Bag X13355, Windhoek; tel. (61) 2059111; fax (61) 233286; e-mail mfmr@mfmr.gov.na; internet www.mfmr.gov.na.
Ministry of Foreign Affairs: Govt Bldgs, Robert Mugabe Ave, PMB 13347, Windhoek; tel. (61) 2829111; fax (61) 223937; e-mail headquarters@mfa.gov.na; internet www.mfa.gov.na.
Ministry of Gender Equality and Child Welfare: Windhoek.
Ministry of Health and Social Services: Old State Hospital, Harvey St, PMB 13198, Windhoek; tel. (61) 2039111; fax (61) 227607.
Ministry of Home Affairs and Immigration: Cohen Bldg, Kasino St, PMB 13200, Windhoek; tel. (61) 2922111; fax (61) 2922185.
Ministry of Information and Broadcasting: Windhoek.
Ministry of Justice: Justitia Bldg, Independence Ave, PMB 13248, Windhoek; tel. (61) 2805111; fax (61) 221615; includes the office of the Attorney-General.
Ministry of Labour and Social Welfare: 32 Mercedes St, Khomasdal, PMB 19005, Windhoek; tel. (61) 2066111; fax (61) 212323.
Ministry of Lands, Resettlement and Rehabilitation: Brendan Simbwaye Bldg, Goethe St, PMB 13343, Windhoek; tel. (61) 2852111; fax (61) 254240.
Ministry of Mines and Energy: 1st Aviation Rd, PMB 13297, Windhoek; tel. (61) 2848111; fax (61) 238643; e-mail info@mme.gov.na; internet www.mme.gov.na.
Ministry of Presidential Affairs: Windhoek.
Ministry of Regional and Local Government and Housing: PMB 13289, Windhoek; tel. (61) 2975111; fax (61) 226049.
Ministry of Safety and Security: Brendan Simbwaye Bldg, Goethe St, PMB 13323; tel. (61) 2846111; fax (61) 233879.
Ministry of Trade and Industry: Govt Bldgs, PMB 13340, Windhoek; tel. (61) 2837111; fax (61) 220148; internet www.mti.gov.na.
Ministry of Works, Transport and Communications: PMB 13341, Windhoek; tel. (61) 2088111; fax (61) 228560.

NAMIBIA

Ministry of Youth, National Service, Sport and Culture: Windhoek.

President and Legislature

PRESIDENT

Presidential Election, 15–16 November 2004

Candidate	Votes	% of votes
Hifikepunye Pohamba (SWAPO)	625,605	76.44
Ben Ulenga (CoD)	59,547	7.28
Katuutire Kaura (DTA)	41,905	5.12
Kuaima Riruako (NUDO)	34,616	4.23
Justus Garoeb (UDF)	31,354	3.83
Henk Mudge (RP)	15,955	1.95
Kosie Pretorius (MAG)	9,738	1.15
Total	**818,360**	**100.00**

NATIONAL ASSEMBLY*

Speaker: THEO-BEN GURIRAB.

General Election, 15–16 November 2004

Party	Votes	% of votes	Seats
South West Africa People's Organisation of Namibia (SWAPO)	620,787	76.11	55
Congress of Democrats (CoD)	59,465	7.29	5
Democratic Turnhalle Alliance of Namibia (DTA)	41,714	5.11	4
National Unity Democratic Organisation (NUDO)	33,874	4.15	3
United Democratic Front (UDF)	29,336	3.60	3
Republican Party	15,965	1.96	1
Monitor Action Group (MAG)	6,920	0.85	1
Namibia Movement for Democratic Change (NMDC)	4,138	0.51	—
South West African National Union (SWANU)	3,438	0.42	—
Total	**815,637**	**100.00**	**72**

* In addition to the 72 directly elected members, the President of the Republic is empowered to nominate as many as six non-voting members.

NATIONAL COUNCIL

Chairman: KANDINDIMA (KANDY) NEHOVA.

The second chamber of parliament is the advisory National Council, comprising two representatives from each of the country's 13 Regional Councils, elected for a period of six years.

Election Commission

Electoral Commission of Namibia (ECN): Daniel Munamava St, POB 13352 Windhoek; tel. (61) 220337; fax (61) 224174; internet www.ecn.gov.na; f. 1992; independent; Chair. VICTOR L. TONCHI; Dir of Elections and CEO PHILEMON H. KANIME.

Political Organizations

Congress of Democrats (CoD): 8 Storch St, POB 40905, Windhoek; tel. (61) 256954; fax (61) 256980; e-mail codemo@mweb.com.na; internet www.cod.org.na; f. 1999 after breaking away from SWAPO; Leader BEN ULENGA; Nat. Chair. TSUDAO GURIRAB; Sec.-Gen. KALA GERTZE.

Democratic Turnhalle Alliance of Namibia (DTA): POB 173, Windhoek 9000; tel. 238530; fax 226494; e-mail m.venaani@parliament.gov.na; f. 1977 as a coalition of 11 ethnically-based political groupings; reorg. as a single party in 1991; Pres. KATUUTIRE KAURA; Chair. JOHAN DE WAAL; Sec.-Gen. ALOIS GENDE.

Monitor Action Group (MAG): POB 80808, Olympia, Windhoek; tel. (61) 252008; fax (61) 229242; e-mail monitor@cyberhost.com.na; f. 1991 by mems of the Action Christian National alliance; Leader and Chair. J. W. F. (KOSIE) PRETORIUS.

Namibia Democratic Movement for Change (NDMC): POB 60043, Katutura; tel. and fax (61) 297795; f. 2004; Pres. FRANS GOAGOSEB; Sec.-Gen. CLAUDIA NAMISES.

National Unity Democratic Organisation (NUDO): POB 60043, Katutura; tel. and fax 297795; f. 1964 by the Herero Chiefs' Council; joined the DTA in 1977; broke away from the DTA in 2003; Pres. Chief KUAIMA RIRUAKO; Sec.-Gen. JOSEPH KAUANDENGE.

Republican Party: 6 Hügel St, POB 20020, Windhoek; tel. (61) 225632; fax (61) 225636; e-mail rp.nam@mweb.com.na; f. 1977 after breaking away from the National Party; joined the DTA later in 1977; dissolved in 1991; reactivated in 2003 after breaking away from the DTA; Pres. HENK MUDGE; Sec.-Gen CAROLA ENGELBRECHT.

SWAPO Party of Namibia (SWAPO): POB 1071, Windhoek; tel. (61) 238364; fax (61) 232368; f. 1957 as the Ovamboland People's Congress; renamed South West Africa People's Organisation in 1960; adopted present name in 1997; Pres. Dr SAMUEL DANIEL NUJOMA; Vice-Pres. HIFIKEPUNYE POHAMBA; Sec.-Gen. NGARIKUTUKE TJIRIANGE.

South West African National Union (SWANU): Windhoek; f. 1959 by mems of the Herero Chiefs' Council; formed alliance with the Workers' Revolutionary Party in 1999; Pres. RIHUPISA KANDANDO.

United Democratic Front (UDF): POB 20037, Windhoek; tel. (61) 230673; fax (61) 237175; f. 1989 as a centrist coalition of eight parties; reorg. as a single party in 1999; Nat. Chair. ERIC BIWA; Pres. JUSTUS GAROEB.

Workers' Revolutionary Party: Windhoek; f. 1989; Trotskyist; Leaders WERNER MAMUGWE, HEWAT BEUKES.

The **Caprivi Liberation Army (CLA)**, f. 1998 as the Caprivi Liberation Movement, seeks secession of the Caprivi Strip; conducts military operations from bases in Zambia and Angola; political wing operates from Denmark as the **Caprivi National Union**, led by MISHAKE MUYONGO and BONIFACE MAMILI.

Diplomatic Representation

EMBASSIES AND HIGH COMMISSIONS IN NAMIBIA

Algeria: 111A Gloudina St, Ludwigsdorf, POB 3079, Windhoek; tel. (61) 221507; fax (61) 236376; e-mail ambalg.wkh@iwwn.com.na; Chargé d'affaires a.i. A. I. BENGUEUEDDA.

Angola: Angola House, 3 Dr Agostinho Neto St, Ausspannplatz, PMB 12020, Windhoek; tel. (61) 227535; fax (61) 221498; Ambassador Dr GARCIA PIRES.

Botswana: 101 Nelson Mandela Ave, POB 20359, Windhoek; tel. (61) 221942; fax (61) 221948; High Commissioner NORMAN MOLEBOGE.

Brazil: 52 Bismarck St, POB 24166, Windhoek; tel. (61) 237368; fax (61) 233389; e-mail orlando@iwwn.com.na; Ambassador ORLANDO GALVÊAS OLIVEIRA.

China, People's Republic: 13 Wecka St, POB 22777, Windhoek; tel. (61) 222089; fax (61) 225544; e-mail chinaemb@iafrica.com.na; Ambassador LIANG YINZHU.

Congo, Republic: 9 Korner St, POB 22970, Windhoek; tel. (61) 257517; fax (61) 240796; Ambassador A. KONDHO.

Cuba: 31 Omuramba Rd, Eros, POB 23866, Windhoek; tel. (61) 227072; fax (61) 231584; e-mail embacuba@iafrica.com.na; Ambassador CIPRIANO CASTRO SAEZ.

Egypt: 10 Berg St, POB 11853, Windhoek; tel. (61) 221501; fax (61) 228856; Ambassador AHMAD HASSAN IBRAHEM DARWISH.

Finland: Sanlam Centre, 5th Floor, Independence Ave, POB 3649, Windhoek; tel. (61) 221355; fax (61) 221349; e-mail sanomat.win@formin.fi; internet www.finland.org.na; Ambassador HEIKKI TUUNANEN.

France: 1 Goethe St, POB 20484, Windhoek; tel. (61) 2276700; fax (61) 276710; e-mail frambwdk@iafrica.na; internet www.ambafrance-na.org; Ambassador PHILIPPE PERRIER DE LA BATHIE.

Germany: Sanlam Centre, 6th Floor, 154 Independence Ave, POB 231, Windhoek; tel. (61) 273100; fax (61) 222981; e-mail germany@iway.na; internet www.windhuk.diplo.de; Ambassador Dr WOLFGANG WILHELM MASSING.

Ghana: 5 Nelson Mandela Ave, POB 24165, Windhoek; tel. (61) 221341; fax (61) 221343; High Commissioner AFUA DAAKU.

India: 97 Nelson Mandela Ave, POB 1209, Windhoek; tel. (61) 226037; fax (61) 237320; e-mail hicomind@mweb.com.na; High Commissioner YOGENDRA KUMAR.

Indonesia: 103 Nelson Mandela Ave, POB 20691, Windhoek; tel. (61) 221914; fax (61) 223811; Ambassador GEDE PUTU ARTISME.

Kenya: Kenya House, 5th Floor, 134 Robert Mugabe Ave, POB 2889, Windhoek; tel. (61) 226836; fax (61) 221409; e-mail kenyanet@mweb.com.na; High Commissioner BINSAI J. CHEPSONGOL.

Libya: 69 Burg St, Luxury Hill, POB 124, Windhoek; tel. (61) 234454; fax (61) 234471; Chargé d'affaires a.i. H. O. ALSHAOSHI.

NAMIBIA

Malawi: 56 Bismarck St, POB 13254, Windhoek; tel. (61) 221391; fax (61) 227056; High Commissioner A. MNTHAMBALA.

Malaysia: 10 Von Eckenbrecker St, POB 312, Windhoek; tel. (61) 259344; fax (61) 259343; e-mail malhicom@iwwn.com.na; High Commissioner HAYATI BT ISMAIL.

Mexico: Southern Life Tower, 3rd Floor, 39 Post St Mall, POB 13220, Windhoek; tel. (61) 229082; fax (61) 229180; e-mail embamexn@iway.na; Charge d'affaires a.i. JOSÉ LUÍS GARCÍA.

Nigeria: 4 Omuramba Rd, Eros Park, POB 23547, Windhoek; tel. (61) 232103; fax (61) 221639; e-mail nignam@web.com.na; High Commissioner OKUN AYODEJI.

Portugal: 24 Robert Mugabe Ave, POB 443, Windhoek; tel. (61) 237928; fax (61) 237929; e-mail emport@mweb.com.na; Ambassador MARIA DO CARMO ALLEGRO DE MAGALHÃES.

Russia: 4 Christian St, POB 3826, Windhoek; tel. (61) 228671; fax (61) 229061; e-mail rusembna@iafrica.com.na; Ambassador VYACHESLAV D. SHUMSKII.

South Africa: RSA House, cnr Jan Jonker and Nelson Mandela Aves, POB 23100, Windhoek; tel. (61) 229765; fax (61) 224140; High Commissioner B. S. S. MABIZELA.

Spain: 58 Bismarck St, POB 21811, Windhoek-West; tel. (61) 223066; fax (61) 223046; e-mail embespna@mail.mae.es; Ambassador MARIA VICTORIA SCOLA PLIEGO.

Sweden: Sanlam Centre, 9th Floor, POB 23087, Windhoek; tel. (61) 2859111; fax (61) 2859222; e-mail ambassaden.windhoek@foreign.ministry.se; Chargé d'affaires a.i. GÖRAN HEDEBRO.

United Kingdom: 116 Robert Mugabe Ave, POB 22202, Windhoek; tel. (61) 274800; fax (61) 228895; e-mail bhc@mweb.com.na; High Commissioner ALASDAIR MACDERMOTT.

USA: 14 Lossen St, Ausspannplatz, PMB 12029, Windhoek 9000; tel. (61) 221601; fax (61) 229792; e-mail healykc2@state.gov; internet www.usembassy.namib.com; Ambassador JOYCE A. BARR.

Ukraine: Windhoek; Ambassador IHOR M. TURYANSKIY.

Venezuela: Southern Life Tower, 3rd Floor, 39 Post St Mall, PMB 13353, Windhoek; tel. (61) 227905; fax (61) 227804; e-mail embaven@com.na; Chargé d'affaires ABRAHAM QUINTERO.

Zambia: 22 Sam Nujoma Dr., cnr Mandume Ndemufayo Rd, POB 22882, Windhoek; tel. (61) 237610; fax (61) 228162; High Commissioner GRIFFITHS NYIRONGO.

Zimbabwe: cnr Independence Ave and Grimm St, POB 23056, Windhoek; tel. (61) 228134; fax (61) 226859; Ambassador STAN CHIGWEDERE.

Judicial System

Judicial power is exercised by the Supreme Court, the High Court and a number of Magistrate and Lower Courts. The Constitution provides for the appointment of an Ombudsman.

Chief Justice: PETER SHIVUTE.

Religion

It is estimated that about 90% of the population are Christians.

CHRISTIANITY

Council of Churches in Namibia: 8 Mont Blanc St, POB 41, Windhoek; tel. (61) 217621; fax (61) 62786; e-mail ccn.windhoek@iafrica.com.na; f. 1978; eight mem. churches; Pres. Bishop HENDRIK FREDERIK; Gen. Sec. NANGULA KATHINDI.

The Anglican Communion

Namibia comprises a single diocese in the Church of the Province of Southern Africa. The Metropolitan of the Province is the Archbishop of Cape Town, South Africa. At mid-2000 there were an estimated 31,000 Anglicans in the country.

Bishop of Namibia: Rt Rev. NATHANIEL NDAXUMA NAKWATUMBAH, POB 57, Windhoek; tel. (61) 238920; fax (61) 225903; e-mail anglican@iafrica.com.na.

Dutch Reformed Church

Dutch Reformed Church in Namibia: 34 Feldstreet, POB 389, Windhoek; tel. (61) 225073; fax (61) 227287; e-mail ngkn@iway.na; internet www.ngkn.com.na; f. 1898; Sec. Rev. CLEM MARAIS; 23,724 mems in 43 congregations.

Evangelical Lutheran

Evangelical Lutheran Church in Namibia (ELCIN): PMB 2018, Ondangwa; tel. (56) 24241; fax (56) 240472; e-mail elcinhq@ednweb.com.na; internet www.elca.org/dgm/country_packet/packets/namibia/elcin.html; Moderator Rev. HERMAN OOSTHUISEN; Presiding Bishop ZEPHANIA KAMEETA.

Evangelical Lutheran Church (Rhenish Mission Church): POB 5069, Windhoek; tel. (61) 224531; fax (61) 226775; f. 1967; Pres. Bishop Dr ZEPHANIA KAMEETA.

German Evangelical-Lutheran Church in Namibia (ELCIN—GELC): POB 233, Windhoek; tel. (61) 224294; fax (61) 221470; e-mail delk@namibnet.com; Pres. Bishop REINHARD KEDING; 5,000 mems.

Methodist

African Methodist Episcopal Church: Windhoek; tel. (61) 62757; Rev. B. G. KARUAERA.

Methodist Church of Southern Africa: POB 143, Windhoek; tel. (61) 228921.

The Roman Catholic Church

Namibia comprises one archdiocese, one diocese and one apostolic vicariate. At 31 December 2003 there were 376,474 adherents of the Roman Catholic Church, representing some 16.8% of the total population.

Bishops' Conference

Namibian Catholic Bishops' Conference, POB 11525, Windhoek 9000; tel. (61) 224798; fax (61) 228126; e-mail ncbc@windhoek.org.na; f. 1996; Pres. (vacant).

Archbishop of Windhoek: LIBORIUS NDUMBUKUTI NASHENDA, POB 272, Windhoek 9000; tel. (61) 227595; fax (61) 229836; e-mail rcarch@iafrica.com.na.

Other Christian Churches

Among other denominations active in Namibia are the Evangelical Reformed Church in Africa, the Presbyterian Church of Southern Africa, Seventh Day Adventists and the United Congregational Church of Southern Africa. At mid-2000 there were an estimated 820,000 Protestants and 192,000 adherents professing other forms of Christianity.

JUDAISM

Windhoek Hebrew Congregation: POB 563, Windhoek; tel. (61) 221990; fax (61) 226444; e-mail steinitz@nweb.com.na.

BAHÁ'Í FAITH

National Spiritual Assembly: POB 20372, Windhoek; tel. (61) 239634; e-mail don@iafrica.com.na; mems resident in 215 localities.

The Press

AgriForum: 114 Robert Mugabe Ave, POB 86641, Windhoek; tel. (61) 256023; fax (61) 256035; e-mail richter@agrinamibia.com.na; quarterly; Afrikaans and English; publ. by the Namibia Agricultural Union; Editor RICHTER ERASMUS; circ. 5,000.

Allgemeine Zeitung: Omurambaweg 11, POB 86695, Eros, Windhoek; tel. (61) 225822; fax (61) 220225; e-mail azinfo@az.com.na; internet www.az.com.na; f. 1916; daily; German; Editor-in-Chief STEFAN FISCHER; circ. 5,300 (Mon.–Thurs.), 6,500 (Fri.).

The Big Issue Namibia: 37 Bahnhof St, POB 97140 Maerua Park, Windhoek; tel. (61) 242216; fax (61) 242232; e-mail bigissue@iway.na; internet www.bigissuenamibia.org; f. 2002; monthly; Editor-in-Chief JO ROGGE.

The Caprivi Vision: Caprivi; tel. and fax (66) 253162; internet www.caprivi-vision.iway.na; e-mail cvnews@iway.na; f. 2002; regional newspaper for Caprivi region; Editor RISCO LUMAMEZI.

Insight Namibia: 42 Best St, Windhoek West; POB 40738 Windhoek; tel. (61) 259106; fax (61) 240385; e-mail editorial@insight.com.na; internet www.insight.com.na; f. 2005; monthly; business and current affairs.

Namib Times: Sam Nujoma Ave, POB 706, Walvis Bay; tel. (64) 205854; fax (64) 204813; 2 a week; Afrikaans, English, German and Portuguese; Editor PAUL VINCENT; circ. 4,300.

Namibia Brief: Independence Ave, POB 2123, Windhoek; tel. and fax (61) 251044; quarterly; English; Editor CATHY BLATT; circ. 7,500.

Namibia Business Journal: POB 9355, Windhoek; tel. (61) 228809; fax (61) 228009; Editor MILTON LOUW; circ. 4,000.

Namibia Economist: 7 Schuster St, POB 49, Windhoek 9000; tel. (61) 221925; fax (61) 220615; e-mail info@economist.com.na; internet www.economist.com.na; f. 1986; weekly; English; business, finance and economics; Editor DANIEL STEINMANN; circ. 8,000.

Namibia Review: Turnhalle Bldg, Bahnhof St, PMB 13344, Windhoek; tel. (61) 222246; fax (61) 224937; e-mail nreview@mib.gov.na; govt-owned; monthly; Editor Elizabeth Kalambo-Mule; circ. 5,000.

Namibia Sport: POB 1246, Windhoek; tel. (61) 224132; fax (61) 224613; e-mail editor@namibiasport.com.na; internet www.namibiasport.com.na; f. 2002; monthly; Editor Helge Schultz; circ. 2,000.

Namibia Today: 21 Johan Albrecht St, POB 24669, Windhoek; tel. (61) 276730; fax (61) 276381; 2 a week; Afrikaans, English, Oshiherero and Oshiwambo; publ. by SWAPO; Editor Kaomo-Vijinda Tjombe; circ. 5,000.

The Namibian: 42 John Meinert St, POB 20783, Windhoek; tel. (61) 279600; fax (61) 279602; e-mail editor@namibian.com.na; internet www.namibian.com.na; daily; English; Editor Gwen Lister; circ. 22,700.

The Namibian Worker: POB 50034, Bachbrecht, Windhoek; tel. (61) 215037; fax (61) 215589; e-mail nunw@mweb.com.na; newsletter publ. by National Union of Namibian Workers; revived in 2003; Afrikaans, English and Oshiwambo; Editor-in-Chief C. Ranga Haikali; circ. 1,000.

New Era: Maerua Mall, Private Mail Bag 13364, Windhoek; tel. (61) 273300; fax (61) 220583; internet www.newera.com.na; e-mail editor@newera.com.na; f. 1991; 2 a week; govt-owned; English; Chair. Vilbard Usiku; CEO Sylvester Black; Editor Rajah Munamava; circ. 10,000.

Plus Weekly: POB 21506, Windhoek; tel. (61) 233635; fax (61) 230478; e-mail info@namibiaplus.com; internet www.namibiaplus.com; publ. by Federsen Publications.

Republikein: 11 Omuramba Rd, POB 3436, Eros, Windhoek; tel. (61) 2972000; fax (61) 223721; e-mail republkn@republikein.com.na; internet www.republikein.com.na; f. 1977; daily; Afrikaans, English and German; publ. by Democratic Media Holdings; organ of the DTA party; Group Gen. Man. Chris Jacobie; Editor Gert Jacobie; circ. 17,500 (Mon.–Wed.), 21,000 (Thur.–Fri.).

Sister Magazine: POB 40092, Windhoek; tel. (61) 230618; fax (61) 236371; e-mail sister@iafrica.com.na; 6 a year; publ. by Sister Namibia human rights org.; Editor Liz Frank.

The Southern Times: Maerua Mall, POB 31413, Windhoek; tel. (61) 273300; fax (61) 220583; e-mail tst@newera.com.na; internet www.southerntimes.com.na; f. 2004; weekly (Sun.); owned by New Era and Zimpapers, Zimbabwe; printed in Zimbabwe; regional; Chair. V. T. Usiku; Editor Moses Magadza.

Windhoek Observer: 49 Stuebel St, POB 2255, Windhoek; tel. (61) 221737; fax (61) 226098; e-mail whkob@africaonline.com.na; f. 1978; weekly; English; Editor Hannes Smith; circ. 14,000.

NEWS AGENCIES

Namibia Press Agency (Nampa): cnr Keller and Eugene Marais Sts, POB 26185, Windhoek 9000; tel. (61) 374000; fax (61) 221713; e-mail admin@nampa.org; internet www.nampa.org; f. 1990; Chair. Maureen Hinda.

Foreign Bureaux

Informatsionnoye Telegrafnoye Agentstvo Rossii—Telegrafnoye Agentstvo Suverennykh Stran (ITAR—TASS) (Russia): POB 24821, Windhoek; tel. and fax (61) 232909; Correspondent Pave Myltsev.

Inter Press Service (IPS) (Italy): POB 20783, Windhoek; tel. (61) 226645; Correspondent Mark Verbaan.

South African Press Association (SAPA): POB 2032, Windhoek; tel. (61) 231565; fax (61) 220783; Representative Carmen Honey.

Xinhua (New China) News Agency (People's Republic of China): POB 22130, Windhoek; tel. (61) 226484; fax (61) 226484; Bureau Chief Teng Wenyi.

Reuters (UK) is also represented in Namibia.

PRESS ASSOCIATION

Press Club Windhoek: POB 2032, Windhoek; tel. (61) 231565; fax (61) 220783; Chair. Carmen Honey.

Publishers

BAUM Publishers: POB 3436, Windhoek; tel. (61) 225411; fax (61) 224843; Publr Nic Kruger.

Clarian Publishers: POB 5861, Windhoek; tel. (61) 251044; fax (61) 237251; Publr Cathy Blatt.

ELOC Printing Press: PMB 2013, Oniipa, Ondangwa; tel. and fax (6756) 40211; f. 1901; Rev. Dr Kleopas Dumeni.

Gamsberg Macmillan Publishers (Pty) Ltd: 19 Faraday St, POB 22830, Windhoek; tel. (61) 232165; fax (61) 233538; e-mail gmp@iafrica.com.na; internet www.macmillan-africa.com; Man. Dir Herman van Wyk.

Longman Namibia: POB 9251, Eros, Windhoek; tel. (61) 231124; fax (61) 224019; Publr Linda Bredenkamp.

National Archives of Namibia: Eugène Marais St, PMB 13250, Windhoek; tel. (61) 2935213; fax (61) 2935217; Man. J. Kutzner.

New Namibia Books (Pty) Ltd: POB 21601, Windhoek; tel. (61) 221134; fax (61) 235279; Publr Jane Katjavivi.

Out of Africa Publishers: POB 21841, Windhoek; tel. (61) 221494; fax (61) 221720; e-mail books@mweb.com.na; Man. Wida Lochner.

PUBLISHERS' ASSOCIATION

Association of Namibian Publishers: POB 21601, Windhoek; tel. (61) 235796; fax (61) 235279; f. 1991; Sec. Peter Reiner.

Broadcasting and Communications

Namibia signed a WTO agreement to liberalize telecommunications in 1999. The mobile cellular telecommunications market was deregulated in 2000. A second mobile cellular telephone licence was expected to be issued in 2006.

TELECOMMUNICATIONS

Telecom Namibia Ltd (Telecom): POB 297, Windhoek; tel. (61) 2019211; fax (61) 248723; internet www.telecom.na; f. 1992; state-owned; Chair. T. Haimbili; Man. Dir Frans Ndoroma.

Mobile Telecommunications Ltd (MTC): POB 23051, Windhoek; tel. (61) 249570; fax (61) 249571; f. 1994; sole mobile cellular telecommunications provider; Man. Dir Bengt Strenge.

BROADCASTING

Radio

In 2004 there were a total of 19 radio stations broadcasting from Windhoek including:

Namibian Broadcasting Corpn (NBC): POB 321, Windhoek; tel. (61) 2913111; fax (61) 216209; e-mail tnandjaa@nbc.com.na; internet www.nbc.com.na; f. 1990; runs nine radio stations, broadcasting daily to 90% of the population in English (24 hours), Afrikaans, German and six indigenous languages (10 hours); Chair. Ponhele Ya France; Dir-Gen. Stanley Simataa (acting).

Channel 7/Kanaal 7: POB 20500, Windhoek; tel. (61) 235815; fax (61) 240190; e-mail channel7@k7.com.na; internet www.k7.com.na; Christian community radio station; English and Afrikaans; Man. Neal van den Bergh.

Katutura Community Radio: POB 22355, Windhoek; tel. (61) 263768; fax (61) 262786; f. 1995 by non-governmental orgs; Dir Frederick Gowaseb.

Kudu FM: 8 Diehl St, Southern Industrial, POB 5369, Windhoek; tel. (61) 247262; fax (61) 247259; e-mail radiokudu@radiokudu.com.na; internet www.radiokudu.com.na; f. 1998; commercial station affiliated to Omulunga Radio; English, Afrikaans and German.

Omulunga Radio: POB 40789, Windhoek; tel. (61) 239706; fax (61) 247259; e-mail omulunga@omulunga.com.na; internet www.omulunga.com.na; f. 2002; Ovambo interest station affiliated to Kudu FM; Oshiwambo and English.

Radio Antenna Namibia (Pty) Ltd (Radio 99): Teinert St, POB 11849, Windhoek; tel. (61) 223634; fax (61) 230964; e-mail radio99@iway.com.na; f. 1994; Man. Dir Mario Aita.

Radio Energy (Radio 100): 17 Bismarck St, Windhoek West; POB 676, Windhoek; tel. (61) 256380; fax (61) 256379; e-mail energyos@mweb.com; internet www.energy100fm.com; commercial radio station; Man. Dir Mario Aita.

Other radio stations included: Kosmos Radio, Radio France International (via relay), Radio 99, and Radio Wave. There were six community radio stations including: Radio Ecclesia (Catholic), Live FM (in Rehoboth), Ohangwenga Community Radio, and UNAM Radio (University of Namibia). A further four community stations were planned in 2005 at Oshakti, Gobabis, Keetmanshoop and Swakopmund.

Television

Namibian Broadcasting Corpn (NBC): POB 321, Windhoek; tel. (61) 2913111; fax (61) 216209; e-mail nbcho@iwwn.com.na; internet www.nbc.com.na; f. 1990; broadcasts television programmes in English to 45% of the population, 18 hours daily; Chair. Uazuva Kaumbi; Dir-Gen. Gerry Munyama.

NAMIBIA

Multi-Choice Namibia: POB 1752, Windhoek; tel. (61) 222222; fax (61) 227605; commercial television channels; Gen. Man. HARRY AUCAMP.

Finance

(cap. = capital; res = reserves; dep. = deposits; m. = million; brs = branches; amounts in Namibian dollars)

BANKING

Central Bank

Bank of Namibia: 71 Robert Mugabe Ave, POB 2882, Windhoek; tel. (61) 2835111; fax (61) 2835228; e-mail general.inquiries@bon.com.na; internet www.bon.com.na; f. 1990; cap. 40.0m., res 1,048.7m., dep. 1,270.5m. (Dec. 2002); Gov. TOM K. ALWEENDO; Dep. Gov. P. HARTMAN.

Commercial Banks

Bank Windhoek Ltd: Bank Windhoek Bldg, 262 Independence Ave, POB 15, Windhoek; tel. (61) 2991122; fax (61) 2991620; e-mail info@bankwindhoek.com.na; internet www.bankwindhoek.com.na; f. 1982; cap. 4.7m., res 283.2m., dep. 2,939.0m. (March 2002); Chair. J. C. 'KOOS' BRANDT; Man. Dir J. J. SWANEPOEL; 22 brs.

First National Bank of Namibia Ltd: 209–211 Independence Ave, POB 195, Windhoek; tel. (61) 2992016; fax (61) 2220979; e-mail info@fnbnamibia.com.na; internet www.fnbnamibia.com.na; f. 1987 as First Nat. Bank of Southern Africa Ltd; present name adopted 1990; total assets 4,731.9m. (June 2003); Chair. H. DIETER VOIGTS; CEO LEONARD J. HAYNES; 28 brs and 12 agencies.

Namibian Banking Corpn: Carl List Haus, Independence Ave, POB 370, Windhoek; tel. (61) 225946; fax (61) 223741; Chair. J. C. WESTRAAT; Man. Dir P. P. NIEHAUS; 3 brs.

Nedbank Namibia: 12–20 Dr Frans Indongo St, POB 1, Windhoek; tel. (61) 2959111; fax (61) 2952120; e-mail martinsh@nedbank.com; internet www.nedbank.com.na; f. 1973; fmrly Commercial Bank of Namibia Ltd; subsidiary of Nedbank Ltd, South Africa; total assets 3,000.0m. (June 2005); Chair. T. J. FRANK; Man. Dir MARTIN KALIE SHIPANGA; 10 brs and 2 agencies.

Standard Bank Namibia Ltd: Standard Bank Centre, cnr Werner List St and Post St Mall, POB 3327, Windhoek; tel. (61) 2942126; fax (61) 2942583; e-mail info@standardbank.com.na; internet www.standardbank.com.na; f. 1915; controlled by Standard Bank Investment Corpn; total assets 7,894.0m. (Dec. 2004); Chair. LEAKE S. HANGALA; Man. Dir THEOFELUS MBERIRUA; 22 brs.

Agricultural Bank

Agricultural Bank of Namibia (AgriBank): 10 Post St Mall, POB 13208, Windhoek; tel. (61) 2074200; fax (61) 2074289; e-mail agribank@iafrica.com.na; f. 1922; total assets 739.1m. (March 2001); Chair. HANS-GUENTHER STIER; CEO IIPUMBU LEONARD NANGOLO.

Development Bank

Development Bank of Namibia (DBN): POB 235, Windhoek; tel. (61) 2908000; fax (61) 2908071; e-mail info@dbn.com.na; internet www.dbn.com.na; f. 2004; Chair. SVEN THIEME; CEO DAVID NUYOMA.

STOCK EXCHANGE

Namibian Stock Exchange (NSX): Shop 8, Kaiserkrone Centre, Post St Mall, POB 2401, Windhoek; tel. (61) 227647; fax (61) 248531; e-mail heikon@nsx.com.na; internet www.nsx.com.na; f. 1992; Chair. Exec. Cttee P. HANGO; Gen. Man. HEIKO NIEDERMEIER.

INSURANCE

Corporate Guarantee and Insurance Co of Namibia Ltd (CGI): Corporate House, Ground Floor, 17 Lüderitz St, POB 416, Windhoek; tel. (61) 259525; fax (61) 255213; e-mail info@corporateguarantee.com; internet www.corporateguarantee.com; f. 1996; wholly-owned subsidiary of Nictus Group Ltd since 2001; Chair. J. L. OLIVER; Man. Dir and Principal Officer F. R. VAN STADEN.

Insurance Co of Namibia (INSCON): POB 2877, Windhoek; tel. (61) 275900; fax (61) 233808; f. 1990; short-term insurance; Chair. CHARLES KAURAISA; Man. Dir FERDINAND OTTO.

Legal Shield: 140–142 Robert Mugabe Ave, POB 11363, Windhoek; tel. (61) 2754200; fax (61) 2754090; e-mail legalshield@tgi.net.na; internet www.legalshield.com.na; f. 2000; legal, funeral and medical insurance; Man. Dir QUINTON VAN ROOYEN.

Metropolitan Namibia: Metropolitan Pl., 1st Floor, cnr Bülow and Stubel Sts, POB 3785, Windhoek; tel. (61) 2973000; fax (61) 248191; e-mail www.metropolitan.com.na; f. 1996; subsidiary of Metropolitan Group, South Africa; acquired Channel Life in 2004; Chair. M. L. SMITH; Man. Dir LEEBA FOUCHÉ.

Mutual and Federal Insurance Co Ltd: Mutual and Federal Centre, 5th–7th Floors, 227 Independence Ave, POB 151, Windhoek; tel. (61) 2077111; fax (61) 2077205; f. 1990; subsidiary of Mutual and Federal, South Africa; acquired CGU Holdings Ltd in 2000 and FGI Namibia Ltd in 2001; Man. Dir G. KATJIMUNE; Gen. Man. J. W. B. LE ROUX.

Namibia National Reinsurance Corpn Ltd (NamibRE): Capital Centre, 5th Floor, Levinson Arcade, POB 716 Windhoek; tel. (61) 256905; fax (61) 256904; e-mail administrator@namibre.com; f. 2001; 100% state-owned; Man. Dir ANNA NAKALE KAWANA.

Old Mutual Life Assurance Co (Namibia) Ltd: Mutual Platz, 5th Floor, Post St Mall, POB 165, Windhoek; tel. (61) 2993999; fax (61) 2993520; e-mail nambusdev@oldmutual.com; internet www.oldmutual.com.na; Chair. G. S. VAN NIEKERK; Chief Exec. BERTIE VAN DER WALT.

Sanlam Namibia: 154 Independence Ave, POB 317, Windhoek; tel. (61) 2947418; fax (61) 2947416; e-mail marketing@sanlam.com.na; internet www.sanlam.com.na; f. 1928; subsidiary of Sanlam Ltd, South Africa; merged with Regent Life Namibia, Capricorn Investments and Nam-Mic Financial Services in Dec. 2004; Chair. ROY ANDERSEN; CEO Dr JOHAN VAN ZYL.

Santam Namibia: 344 Independence Ave, POB 204, Windhoek; tel. (61) 2928000; fax (61) 235225; 60% owned by Santam, South Africa; 33.3% owned by Bank Windhoek Holdings Ltd; acquired Allianz Insurance of Namibia Ltd in 2001; Chief Exec. NAMA SIMON GOABAB.

Swabou Insurance Co Ltd: Swabou Bldg, Post St Mall, POB 79, Windhoek; tel. (61) 2997528; fax (61) 2997551; e-mail gertzee@swabouinsurance.com.na; internet www.swabouinsurance.com.na; f. 1990; acquired by FNB Namibia Holdings Ltd in 2004; short-term insurance; Man. Dir RENIER TALJAARD.

Swabou Life Assurance Co Ltd: 209–211 Independence Ave, POB 79, Windhoek; tel. (61) 2997502; fax (61) 2997550; e-mail tgurirab@fnbnamibia.com.na; internet www.swaboulife.com.na; f. 1990; acquired by FNB Namibia Holdings Ltd in 2004; life assurance; CEO GERHARD MANS.

Trade and Industry

GOVERNMENT AGENCIES

Karakul Board of Namibia—Swakara Fur Producers and Exporters: Private Bag 13300, Windhoek; tel. (61) 2909213; fax (61) 2909300; e-mail agrapels@agra.com.na; internet www.agra.com.na; Chair. H. J. VAN WYK; Man. W. H. VISSER.

Meat Board of Namibia: POB 38, Windhoek; tel. (61) 33180; fax (61) 228310; f. 1935; Chair. JOHN LE ROUX; Gen. Man. PAUL STRYDOM.

Meat Corpn of Namibia (Meatco Namibia): POB 3881, Windhoek; tel. (61) 216810; fax (61) 217045; e-mail hoffice@meatco.com.na; internet www.meatco.com.na; processors of meat and meat products at four abattoirs and one tannery; CEO PHILIP STOFFBERG.

Namibian Agronomic Board: POB 5096, Ausspannplatz, Windhoek; tel. (61) 224741; fax (61) 225371; e-mail christof@nammic.com.na; CEO CHRISTOF BROCK.

National Petroleum Corpn of Namibia (NAMCOR): Petroleum House, 1 Aviation Rd, Private Bag 13196, Windhoek; tel. (61) 2045000; fax (61) 2045000; internet www.namcor.com.na; f. 1965 as Southern Oil Exploration Corpn (South-West Africa) (Pty) Ltd—SWAKOR; present name adopted 1990; state petroleum co; responsible for importing 50% of national oil requirements; Chair. F. KISTING; Man. Dir JOE V. MAZEINGO.

DEVELOPMENT ORGANIZATIONS

Namibia Investment Centre (NIC): Ministry of Trade and Industry, Brendan Simbwaye Sq., Block B, 6th Floor, Goethe St, POB 13340, Windhoek; tel. (61) 2837335; fax (61) 220278; e-mail nic@mti.gov.na; f. 1990; promotes foreign and domestic investment; Exec. Dir BERNADETTE ARTIVOR.

Namibia Non-Governmental Organisation Forum (NANGOF): 18 Axalie Doeseb St, POB 70433 Khomasdal, Windhoek; tel. (61) 239469; fax (61) 239471; e-mail nangof@iafrica.com.na; f. 1991; umbrella body representing 95 community-based orgs; Chair. SANDY TJARONDA.

National Housing Enterprise: 7 Omuramba Rd, Eros, POB 20192, Windhoek; tel. (61) 2927111; fax (61) 222301; e-mail nhe@nhe.com.na; internet www.nhe.com.na; f. 1983; replaced Nat. Building and Investment Corpn; provides low-cost housing; manages Housing Trust Fund; 100% state-owned; total assets N $496.4m. (Dec. 2001); Chair. V. R. RUKORO; CEO K. R. MIKE KAVEKOTORA.

NAMIBIA

CHAMBERS OF COMMERCE

Chamber of Mines of Namibia (CMIN): Channel Life Tower, 4th Floor, Post St Mall, 2895, Windhoek; tel. (61) 237925; fax (61) 222638; e-mail chammin@mweb.com.na; f. 1979; Pres. MARK DAWE; Gen. Man. DON NEWMAN (acting); 59 mems (2005).

Namibia National Chamber of Commerce and Industry (NNCCI): 2 Jenner St, cnr Simpson and Jenner Sts, POB 9355, Windhoek; tel. (61) 228809; fax (61) 228009; e-mail info@ncci.org.na; internet www.ncci.org.na; f. 1990; Chair. Dr ESTHER HOVEKA; CEO TARAH SHAANIKA; c. 2,000 mems (2005).

Windhoek Chamber of Commerce and Industries: SWA Building Society Bldg, 3rd Floor, POB 191, Windhoek; tel. (61) 222000; fax (61) 233690; e-mail whkchamber@lianam.lia.net; f. 1920; Pres. H. SCHMIDT; Gen. Man. T. D. PARKHOUSE; 230 mems.

EMPLOYERS' ORGANIZATIONS

Construction Industries Federation of Namibia: 22 Stein St, POB 1479, Klein Windhoek; tel. (61) 230028; fax (61) 224534; e-mail info@cif.namibia.na; internet www.cif.namibia.na; Pres. RENATE SCMIDT; Sec. RICKI WILSON; 70 mems, 14 trade mems, 1 affiliate mem.

Namibia Agricultural Union (NAU): PMB 13255, Windhoek; tel. (61) 237838; fax (61) 220193; e-mail nau@agrinamibia.com.na; represents commercial farmers; Pres. RAIMAR VON HASE; Exec. Man. SAKKIE COETZEE.

Namibia National Farmers' Union (NNFU): 4 Axalie Doeseb St, Windhoek WestPOB 3117, Windhoek; tel. (61) 271117; fax (61) 271115; e-mail nnfu@mweb.com.na; represents communal farmers; Pres. MANFRED RUKORO.

Namibia Professional Hunting Association (NAPHA): 318 Sam Nujoma Dr., Klein WindhoekPOB 11291, Windhoek; tel. (61) 234455; fax (61) 222567; e-mail napha@natron.net; internet www.natron.net/napha; f. 1974; represents hunting guides and professional hunters; Pres. FRANK HEGER; c. 400 mems.

Retail Motor Industry of Namibia (RMI Namibia): POB 2110, Windhoek; tel. (61) 240280; fax (61) 240276; fmrly Motor Industries Federation of Namibia; present name adopted 2002; affiliated to RMI South Africa; Chair. HAROLD PUPKEWITZ; Pres. NEELS SWIEGERS; 40 mems (2003).

UTILITIES

Namibia Power Corpn (Pty) Ltd (NamPower): NamPower Centre, 15 Luther St, POB 2864, Windhoek; tel. (61) 2054111; fax (61) 232805; e-mail register@nampower.com.na; internet www.nampower.com.na; Chair. ANDRIES LEEVI HUNGAMO; Man. Dir Dr LEAKE S. HANGALA.

Northern Electricity: POB 891, Tsumeb; tel. (67) 222243; fax (67) 222245; private electricity supply co; Man. Dir C. G. N. HUYSEN.

TRADE UNIONS

In 2004 there were 27 unions representing more than 100,000 workers.

Trade Union Federations

National Union of Namibian Workers (NUNW): Mungunda St, Katutura; POB 50034, Windhoek; tel. (61) 215037; fax (61) 215589; f. 1972; affiliated to the SWAPO party; Pres. RISTO KAPENDA; Sec.-Gen. EVILASTUS KAARONDA; c. 70,000 mems.

The NUNW has 10 affiliates which include:

Namibia Farm Workers' Union (NAFWU): POB 21007, Windhoek; tel. (61) 218653; f. 1994; Sec.-Gen. ALFRED ANGULA.

Namibia Financial Institutions Union (NAFINU): POB 61791, Windhoek; tel. (61) 239917; fax (61) 215589; f. 2000; Pres. ALEX KAMAUNDJU.

Namibia Food and Allied Workers' Union (NAFAU): Mungunda St, Katutura; POB 1553, Windhoek; tel. (61) 218213; fax (61) 263714; f. 1986; Pres. DAVID NAMALENGA; Gen. Sec. KIROS SACARIAS; 12,000 mems.

Namibia National Teachers' Union (NANTU): POB 61009, Windhoek; tel. (61) 262247; fax (61) 261926; f. 1989; Pres. NDAPEWA NGHIPANDULWA; Sec.-Gen. MIRIAM HAMUTENYA-KATONYALA; 13,000 mems (2002).

Namibia Public Workers' Union (NAPWU): POB 50035, Windhoek; tel. (61) 262078; f. 1987; Pres. ELIPHAS NDINGARA; Sec.-Gen PETRUS NEVONGA; 11,000 mems.

Namibia Transport and Allied Workers' Union (NATAU): POB 7516, Windhoek; tel. (61) 218514; fax (61) 263767; f. 1988; Pres. DAWID TJOMBE; Gen. Sec. JOHN KWEDHI; 7,500 mems.

Metal and Allied Namibian Workers' Union (MANWU): POB 22771, Windhoek; tel. (61) 263100; f. 1987; Pres. J. NAOBEB; Gen. Sec. MOSES SHIIKWA (acting); 5,500 mems.

Mineworkers' Union of Namibia (MUN): POB 1566, Windhoek; tel. (61) 261723; fax (61) 217684; f. 1986; Pres. ANDRIES EISEB; 12,500 mems.

Trade Union Congress of Namibia (TUCNA): POB 2111, Windhoek; tel. (61) 246143; fax (61) 212828; e-mail tucna@africaonline.com; f. 2002 following the merger of the Namibia People's Social Movement (f. 1992 as the Namibia Christian Social Trade Unions) and the Namibia Federation of Trade Unions (f. 1998); Pres. PAULUS HANGO; c. 45,000 (2005).

TUCNA has 14 affiliates including:

Local Authorities Union of Namibia (LAUN): Frans Indongo St, Windhoek; POB 22060, Windhoek; tel. (61) 234625; fax (61) 230035; Pres. FRANCOIS ADONIS.

Namibia Building Workers' Union (NABWU): 3930 Verbena St, Khomasdal; POB 22679, Windhoek; tel. (61) 212828.

Namibia Seamen and Allied Workers Union (NASAWU): Nataniel Maxuilli St, Walvis Bay; POB 1341, Walvis Bay; tel. (64) 204237; fax (64) 205957; Pres. PAULUS HANGO.

Namibia Wholesale and Retail Workers Union (NWRWU): 19 Verbena St, Khomasdal; POB 22769, Windhoek; tel. (61) 212378; fax (61) 212828; e-mail npsm@iafrica.com.na; Sec.-Gen. JOSHUA MABUKU.

Public Service Union of Namibia (PSUN): 45–51 Kroon Rd, Khomasdal; POB 21662, Windhoek; tel. (61) 213083; fax (61) 213047; e-mail psun@namibnet.com; f. 1991; successor to the Gvmt Service Staff Asscn; Pres. AWEBAHE HOESEB; Sec.-Gen. VICTOR KAZONJATI.

Teachers Union of Namibia (TUN): POB 30800, Windhoek; tel. (61) 229115; fax (61) 246360; Pres. GERT JANSEN.

Transport

RAILWAYS

The main line runs from Nakop, at the border with South Africa, via Keetmanshoop to Windhoek, Kranzberg, Tsumeb, Swakopmund and Walvis Bay. There are three branch lines, from Windhoek to Gobabis, Otavi to Grootfontein and Keetmanshoop to Lüderitz. The total rail network covers 2,382 route-km. There are plans for a railway line connecting Namibia with Zambia as part of a programme to improve transport links among the members of the Common Market for Eastern and Southern Africa; plans to extend the northern railway line by 248 km, from Tsumeb to Ondangwa, were announced in 2001.

TransNamib Holdings Ltd: TransNamib Bldg, cnr Independence Ave and Bahnhof St, PMB 13204, Windhoek; tel. (61) 2981111; fax (61) 227984; e-mail pubrelation@transnamib.com.na; internet www.transnamib.com.na; state-owned; Chair. FOIBE JACOBS; CEO JOHN M. SHAETONHODI.

ROADS

In 2000 the road network comprised 66,467 km of roads, of which 4,470 km were main roads. The percentage of paved road increased from 10.9% in 1991 to 13.6% in 1999. A major road link from Walvis Bay to Jwaneng, northern Botswana, the Trans-Kalahari Highway, was completed in 1998, along with the Trans-Caprivi Highway, linking Namibia with northern Botswana, Zambia and Zimbabwe. The Government is also upgrading and expanding the road network in northern Namibia.

SHIPPING

The ports of Walvis Bay and Lüderitz are linked to the main overseas shipping routes and handle almost one-half of Namibia's external trade. Walvis Bay has a container terminal, built in 1999, and eight berths; it is a hub port for the region, serving land-locked countries such as Botswana, Zambia and Zimbabwe. In 2005 NAMPORT added a N $30m. floating dock to the Walvis Bay facilities with a view to servicing vessels used in the region's expanding petroleum industry. Traditionally a fishing port, a new quay was completed at Lüderitz in 2000, with two berths, in response to growing demand from the offshore diamond industry. At the end of 2004 Namibia's merchant fleet comprised 157 vessels, with a combined displacement of 92,299 gross registered tons.

African Portland Industrial Holdings (APIH): Huvest Bldg, 1st Floor, AE/Gams Centre, Sam Nujoma Dr., POB 40047, Windhoek; tel. (61) 248744; fax (61) 239485; e-mail jacques@apiholdings.com; f. 1984; 80% owned by Grindrod (South Africa); bulk port terminal operator; Man. Dir ATHOL EMERTON; Sec. JACQUES CONRADIE.

Namibian Ports Authority (NAMPORT): 17 Rikumbi Kandanga Rd, POB 361, Walvis Bay; tel. (64) 2082207; fax (64) 2082320; e-mail jerome@namport.com.na; internet www.namport.com.na; f. 1994; Chair. SHAKESPEARE MASIZA; Man. Dir SEBBY KANKONDI.

Pan-Ocean Shipping Services Ltd: POB 2613, Walvis Bay; tel. (64) 203959; fax (64) 204199; e-mail kirovg@iafrica.com.na; f. 1995; Man. Dir JÜRGEN HEYNEMANN; Gen. Man. GEORGE KIROV.

CIVIL AVIATION

There are international airports at Windhoek (Hosea Kutako) and Walvis Bay (Rooikop), as well as a number of other airports throughout Namibia, and numerous landing strips.

Air Namibia: TransNamib Bldg, cnr Independence Ave and Bahnhof St, POB 731, Windhoek; tel. (61) 223019; fax (61) 221910; e-mail aguibeb@airnamibia.com.na; internet www.airnamibia.com.na; f. 1959 as Namib Air; state-owned; part-privatization postponed indefinitely in 2003; domestic flights and services to southern Africa and Western Europe; Chair. JOSEPH SHIPEPE; Man. Dir KOSMOS EGUMBO.

Kalahari Express Airlines (KEA): POB 40179, Windhoek; tel. (61) 245665; fax (61) 245612; e-mail keaadmin@kalahariexpress.com.na; f. 1995; domestic and regional flights; Exec. Dir PEINGONDJABI SHIPOH.

Tourism

Namibia's principal tourist attractions are its game parks and nature reserves, and the development of 'eco-tourism' is being promoted. Tourist arrivals in Namibia in 2003 totalled 695,221. In that year tourism receipts amounted to US $333m.

Namibia Tourism Board: PMB 13346, Capital Bldg, Ground Floor, 272 Independence Ave, Windhoek; tel. (61) 2849111; fax (61) 2842364; e-mail tourism@iwwn.com.na; internet www.iwwn.com.na/namtour; Chair. Dr RUKEE TJINGAETE; CEO GIDEON SHILONGO.

NAURU

Introductory Survey

Location, Climate, Language, Religion, Flag, Capital

The Republic of Nauru is a small island in the central Pacific Ocean, lying about 40 km (25 miles) south of the Equator and about 4,000 km (2,500 miles) north-east of Sydney, Australia. Its nearest neighbour is Banaba (Ocean Island), in Kiribati, about 300 km (186 miles) to the east. The climate is tropical, with a westerly monsoon season from November to February. The average annual rainfall is about 2,060 mm (80 ins), but actual rainfall is extremely variable. Day temperatures vary between 24°C and 34°C (75°–93°F). Of the total population in 1983, 61.7% were Nauruans. Their language is Nauruan, but English is also widely understood. The majority of Nauruans are Christians, mostly adherents of the Nauruan Protestant Church. The national flag (proportions 1 by 2) is royal blue, divided by a narrow horizontal yellow stripe, with a 12-pointed white star at the lower hoist. The island state has no official capital, but the seat of the legislature and most government offices are in Yaren district.

Recent History

Nauru, inhabited by a predominantly Polynesian people, organized in 12 clans, was annexed by Germany in 1888. In 1914, shortly after the outbreak of the First World War, the island was captured by Australian forces. It continued to be administered by Australia under a League of Nations mandate (granted in 1920), which also named the United Kingdom and New Zealand as co-trustees. Between 1942 and 1945 Nauru was occupied by the Japanese, who deported 1,200 islanders to Truk (now Chuuk), Micronesia, where many died in bombing raids or from starvation. In 1947 the island was placed under UN Trusteeship, with Australia as the administering power on behalf of the Governments of Australia, New Zealand and the United Kingdom. The UN Trusteeship Council proposed in 1964 that the indigenous people of Nauru be resettled on Curtis Island, off the Queensland coast. This offer was made in anticipation of the progressive exhaustion of the island's phosphate deposits, and because of the environmental devastation resulting from the mining operations. However, the Nauruans elected to remain on the island. Between 1906 and 1968 41m. metric tons of phosphate were mined. Nauru was accorded a considerable measure of self-government in January 1966, with the establishment of Legislative and Executive Councils, and proceeded to independence on 31 January 1968 (exactly 22 years after the surviving Nauruans returned to the island from exile in Micronesia). In early 1998 Nauru announced its intention to seek UN membership and full Commonwealth membership (Nauru had hitherto been a 'special member' of the Commonwealth, not represented at meetings of Heads of Government). The decision was largely based on the islanders' desire to play a more prominent role in international policies relating to issues that affect them, most notably climate change (see below). Nauru became a full member of the Commonwealth in May 1999, and a member of the UN in September of that year.

The Head Chief of Nauru, Hammer DeRoburt, was elected President in May 1968 and re-elected in 1971 and 1973. Dissatisfaction with his increasingly personal rule led to the election of Bernard Dowiyogo (leader of the recently-established, informal Nauru Party) to the presidency in 1976. Dowiyogo was re-elected President after a general election in late 1977. However, DeRoburt's supporters adopted tactics of obstruction in Parliament, and in December 1977 Dowiyogo resigned, in response to Parliament's refusal to approve budgetary legislation; he was re-elected shortly afterwards, but was again forced to resign in April 1978, following the defeat of a legislative proposal concerning phosphate royalties. Lagumot Harris, another member of the Nauru Party, succeeded him, but resigned three weeks later when Parliament rejected a finance measure, and DeRoburt was again elected President. He was re-elected in December of that year, in December 1980 and in May and December 1983.

In September 1986 DeRoburt resigned, following the defeat of a government budget proposal; he was replaced as President by Kennan Adeang, who was elected in Parliament by nine votes to DeRoburt's eight. However, after holding office for only 14 days, Adeang was defeated in a parliamentary vote of 'no confidence', and DeRoburt subsequently resumed the presidency. Following a general election in December Adeang was again narrowly elected President. However, he was subsequently ousted by another vote of 'no confidence', and DeRoburt was reinstated as President. The atmosphere of political uncertainty generated by the absence of a clear majority in Parliament led DeRoburt to dissolve Parliament in preparation for another general election in January 1987, at which the incumbent was re-elected to the presidency by 11 votes to six. In February Adeang announced the establishment of the Democratic Party of Nauru, essentially a revival of the Nauru Party. Eight members of Parliament subsequently joined the new party, which declared that its aim was to curtail the extension of presidential powers and to promote democracy. In August 1989 a parliamentary motion of 'no confidence' in DeRoburt (proposed by Adeang) was approved by 10 votes to five, and Kenas Aroi, a former Minister for Finance, was subsequently elected President. Aroi resigned in December, owing to ill health, and after a general election in the same month Bernard Dowiyogo was re-elected President, defeating DeRoburt by 10 votes to six. The next presidential election, held shortly after a general election in November 1992, resulted in victory for Dowiyogo, by 10 votes to seven, over Buraro Detudamo.

At a general election held in November 1995, when a total of 67 candidates contested the 18 parliamentary seats, all cabinet members were re-elected. A subsequent presidential election resulted in Lagumot Harris's defeat of the incumbent Dowiyogo by nine votes to eight. The resignation of the Chairman of Air Nauru, following allegations of misconduct, prompted Parliament to vote on a motion of 'no confidence' in the Government in November 1996. The motion was narrowly approved and Harris was replaced by Dowiyogo as President. Later that month, however, Dowiyogo's new Government was itself defeated in a parliamentary vote of 'no confidence', and Kennan Adeang was elected to the presidency. A widespread perception that the new Government lacked experience was thought to be a major factor prompting a further motion of 'no confidence' in December, at which Adeang was similarly removed from office. At a subsequent presidential contest Reuben Kun, a former Minister for Finance, defeated Adeang by 12 votes to five, on the understanding that his administration would organize a general election. An election duly took place on 8 February 1997, at which four new members were elected to Parliament, following an apparent agreement between the supporters of Harris and those of Dowiyogo to end the political manoeuvring that had resulted in several months of instability in Nauru. At the election to the presidency, on 13 February, Kinza Clodumar (nominated by Dowiyogo) defeated Harris by nine votes to eight.

In early 1998 five members of Parliament (including former President Lagumot Harris) were dismissed by Adeang, the Speaker, for refusing to apologize for personal remarks about him that had been published in an opposition newsletter. At the resultant by-elections, held in late February 1998, three of the five members were re-elected. A motion expressing 'no confidence' in the President was approved in June, and Dowiyogo was consequently elected to replace Clodumar. In a further vote of 'no confidence', in late April 1999 Dowiyogo was defeated by 10 votes to seven; his replacement was Rene Harris, previously Chairman of the Nauru Phosphate Corporation. Former President Lagumot Harris died in September 1999.

Following legislative elections held on 8 April 2000, Rene Harris was re-elected President, narrowly defeating Dowiyogo by nine votes to eight. Ludwig Scotty was elected Speaker of Parliament. However, Scotty and his deputy, Ross Cairn, subsequently resigned, stating only that they were unable to continue under the 'current political circumstances'. Harris therefore tendered his resignation and was replaced by Dowiyogo, whereupon Scotty and Cairn were re-elected to their posts in the legislature. Observers attributed the manoeuvring to shifting political allegiances within the legislature.

In early 2001, in another reversal to Dowiyogo's leadership, Anthony Audoa, the Minister for Home Affairs, Culture, Health and Women's Affairs, resigned and requested that Parliament be recalled. He claimed that Dowiyogo had squandered Nauru's wealth during his various tenures as President and that in promoting the island as a tax haven he had allowed Nauru to be used by Russian criminal gangs to 'launder' their illegal funds, prompting speculation that he intended to mount a challenge for the presidency.

In late March 2001 Dowiyogo was ousted from the presidency in a parliamentary vote of 'no confidence' while he was undergoing hospital treatment in Australia. The motion, which was passed by two votes, led to Rene Harris regaining the presidency. In October, however, Harris was flown to Australia for emergency medical treatment for a diabetes-related illness, during which time Remy Namaduk performed the role of acting President. Allegations that Nauru's offshore financial centre was being used extensively by Russian criminal organizations for 'laundering' the proceeds of their illegal activities had led Dowiyogo to order a full review of the industry in March 1999. In early 2000 President Rene Harris announced that Nauru was to suspend its offshore banking services and improve the accountability of existing banks on the island, as part of the Government's efforts to bring Nauru's financial services regulations into conformity with international standards. Dowiyogo similarly reaffirmed his commitment to reform the offshore sector, following his election in April 2000. However, in February 2001 11 members of Nauru's 18-member legislature signed a petition requesting that Dowiyogo attend a special session of Parliament to answer questions relating to the island's alleged role in 'laundering' significant funds from Russian criminal organizations. The allegations originated in claims by Russia's central bank that some US $70,000m. of illegal funds had been processed in offshore banks in Nauru. It was estimated that 400 such banks existed on the island in early 2001. The Government subsequently drew up an Anti-Money Laundering Act in August 2001, but the Paris-based Financial Action Task Force (FATF, see p. 389) found that the new laws contained several deficiencies and imposed sanctions in December. (The FATF had been established in 1989 on the recommendation of the Group of Seven (G-7) industrialized nations.) The Government announced revised anti-money-laundering legislation in the same month, and was considering legal action against the FATF in early 2002. Meanwhile, following Islamist attacks on New York and Washington, DC, on 11 September 2001, Nauru's financial system was subject to international scrutiny, amid suspicion that it might have been used as a conduit for the terrorists' funds.

As a result of continued US pressure, Nauru's Parliament approved a new law in February 2004 to address the problem of 'money-laundering', along with legislation to close down the country's offshore banks. In October 2004 the FATF withdrew counter-measures against the country, and in October 2005, following the implementation of the requisite legislation, Nauru became the last of the Pacific islands to be removed from the FATF list of non-co-operative countries and territories. Nauru's removal from the list coincided with the final preparations for the presentation of the National Sustainable Development Strategy, announced at the international donor meeting held in Nauru at the end of November (see below). In December 2003 following the island's commitment to improve transparency and to exchange information on tax matters with other countries, Nauru had been removed from a list of unco-operative tax havens, issued in April 2002 by the Organisation for Economic Co-operation and Development (OECD, see p. 320).

In January 2003 meanwhile, President Rene Harris was defeated in a motion of 'no confidence' by eight votes to three and was replaced by Bernard Dowiyogo. The vote followed a political crisis resulting from the defeat of the Government's budget proposals at the end of December 2002, as well as reports of increasing dissatisfaction with Harris's alleged economic mismanagement of the country. Nauru's deteriorating financial situation, in addition to the Government's decision to accept more than 1,000 asylum-seekers in return for aid from Australia, were believed to be major factors in the loss of confidence in Harris, which had led to the defection to the opposition of two cabinet ministers, two backbenchers and the Speaker in late 2002. However, Harris applied to the Supreme Court, and on 10 January 2003 an injunction was issued against Dowiyogo accepting the presidency. This decision had been based on the fact that only 11 of the 18 members of Parliament had attended the session when the vote took place, thus rendering it invalid; Harris and his Cabinet had staged a boycott of Parliament when the motion was to be proposed. Despite the injunction, Dowiyogo maintained his position and appointed a new Cabinet. Several days of confusion and political instability ensued. Finally, Harris was reinstated as President, following the intervention of Nauru's Melbourne-based Chief Justice. However, he resigned from the presidency the following day. In the resultant contest Dowiyogo defeated Kinza Clodumar by nine votes to eight to become the new President on 20 January. A lack of support for Dowiyogo within Parliament continued to create problems, however, amid appeals for an early election to resolve the impasse.

Meanwhile, a complete collapse of Nauru's telecommunications system in early January 2003 increased the problems experienced by the island. Nauru, thus, effectively became cut off from the rest of the world with external contact only possible when ships equipped with satellite telephones were calling. A speech by Dowiyogo claiming that Nauru was on the verge of bankruptcy, unable to pay its public servants or to send its sick citizens to Australia for treatment, and appealing to donor countries for emergency assistance, could not be transmitted for almost a month. Telecommunications services were restored in early March following a visit from a technician supplied by Australia's government aid agency, AusAID.

In early March 2003 Dowiyogo travelled to Washington, DC, at the request of the US Government, which had threatened to impose harsh economic sanctions on the island and to repossess Air Nauru's only aircraft, if Nauru did not discontinue its offshore banking services. The administration of George W. Bush was reported to have been angered by the possibility that individuals with links to terrorist organizations might have used the island's financial services to 'launder' their funds; some 400 offshore banks were registered on the island in the early 2000s. Consequently, Dowiyogo agreed to sign executive orders not to renew any banking licences or to issue any further so-called 'investor passports'. Shortly after the meeting, however, Dowiyogo collapsed and, following emergency heart surgery, died on 9 March. Derog Gioura was appointed acting Head of State and on 20 March was elected President by nine parliamentary votes to seven. Legislation providing for the expiry of most offshore banking licences within 30 days (and for the remainder within six months) was passed by Parliament in late March, in accordance with the agreement that Dowiyogo had signed in the USA. At the end of March acting President Derog Gioura himself suffered a heart attack and was flown to Australia for treatment.

A general election took place on 3 May 2003, at which six new members were elected to the legislature. However, the new Speaker resigned one day after his election, and with no further nominations for the position, Parliament was unable to proceed to a presidential election. The impasse was resolved when a Speaker was finally elected in late May and Ludwig Scotty won the subsequent presidential election, defeating Kinza Clodumar with 10 parliamentary votes to seven. Scotty, who named a new six-member Cabinet in June, stated his Government's intention to focus on 'prudent management and financial stability'. However, on 8 August Scotty was ousted from office by a 'no confidence' motion and replaced by Rene Harris, who became the fourth President of 2003. The reasons for Scotty's removal were not clear, although concerns had been expressed about his plans to close the recently opened embassies in Washington, DC, and Beijing, and there had been speculation that he intended to switch Nauru's diplomatic allegiance from the People's Republic of China back to Taiwan (see below).

In August 2003 workers at the Nauru Phosphate Corporation began a strike in support of demands for almost six months of unpaid salaries. Opposition politicians claimed that the dispute was an indication of more widespread dissatisfaction with corruption and mismanagement in the industry and within the Government.

In January 2004 President Rene Harris was flown to Australia amid rumours that he had suffered a physical collapse and was in a poor state of health. Officials declined to respond to queries surrounding the President, merely stating that Derog Gioura would be acting President in his absence. In the following month the Minister for Justice resigned, precipitating a vote of 'no confidence' in the President. The country faced a further political crisis when the motion received an equal number of votes in favour and against. Moreover, when Parliament was unable to agree on the election of a new Speaker, following the resignation of the incumbent in early April, the resulting impasse meant that Parliament could not be formally convened. As the country's financial crisis deepened, President Harris travelled to Australia in mid-April to request assistance in averting imminent bankruptcy for the island. On his return to Nauru Harris faced angry demonstrations by hundreds of government employees protesting at the hardship imposed on them as a result of their salaries having been unpaid for 12 months. Reports indicated that government employees (who constituted the majority of paid employees on the island) were surviving on subsistence diets of fish and coconuts. In the same month receivers were appointed to manage the assets of the Nauru Phosphate Royalties Trust (including Nauru's extensive property portfolio in Australia) which was unable to pay off debts of some $A230m. to US interests. Nauruans working in government-owned buildings in Melbourne and Sydney were served with eviction notices. Meanwhile, with neither the Government nor the opposition willing to nominate a Speaker from among its members (thereby giving the other side a majority in Parliament), the legislature was unable to produce a budget. In May, however, during another of Harris's overseas trips, the opposition elected one of its members as Speaker and immediately approved legislation making it illegal for a government to operate without a budget. In the following month, and before the Supreme Court had ruled on the matter, Kinza Clodumar, the Minister of Finance, crossed the floor, thereby allowing the opposition to approve a motion of 'no confidence' in Harris. Ludwig Scotty was subsequently elected to the presidency. In late July Australian Treasury official Peter Depta arrived in Nauru to take up the post of Financial Secretary, effectively assuming control of the country's finances.

Nauru's precarious political situation deteriorated during September 2004, and by the end of the month President Ludwig Scotty had dissolved Parliament and declared a state of emergency. His action had been prompted by the Speaker Russell Kun's suspension of the Minister of Health, Kieren Keke, on the grounds that he held dual Nauruan and Australian nationality. Keke's suspension had resulted in the loss of the Government's one-seat majority and a consequent stalemate in Parliament, during which budget legislation had been unable to be approved. Scotty assumed sole responsibility over the government of the country until a general election took place on 23 October. At the election all nine members of Scotty's Government retained their seats in the legislature, while seven of the nine opposition members of parliament were not re-elected. The result thus gave President Scotty an ample majority in Parliament. Within days of its election the new Government approved a budget that included a reduction in public-sector salaries and increased import duties. In the following month legislation aimed at discouraging criminals, particularly terrorists, from using the country's financial sector was approved, in addition to the establishment of a procedure for conducting possible future referendums and of reviewing the Constitution.

The sudden death of the Speaker, Vassal Gadoengin, from a heart attack in December 2004 led to the election of Valdon Dowiyogo, a new member of Parliament and son of the former President, to the position in the following month.

In January 2005 a committee of members of Parliament began a review of Nauru's Constitution, motivated partly by a desire to achieve greater political stability in the country.

In September 2001 Nauru agreed to accept 310 of 460 predominantly Afghan asylum-seekers who were on board a Norwegian freighter, the MV Tampa, unable to disembark on Christmas Island as Australia refused to grant them entry into its territory (see the chapter on Christmas Island). The Australian Government agreed to fund the processing of the asylum-seekers and to pay an undisclosed sum to Nauru, which was to house the asylum-seekers for three months while their claims for asylum were assessed. Following the interception of several other boats carrying asylum-seekers in Australian waters later the same month, Nauru received a pledge of $A20m. from the Australian Government for agreeing to host 800 asylum-seekers. In December 2001 Nauru signed an agreement with Australia's Minister for Foreign Affairs to accommodate a total of 1,200 at any one time, in return for a further $A10m. of aid, to be allocated to education, health and infrastructure programmes. Local residents and owners of the land upon which the camps were located expressed concern over the delays in processing the asylum-seekers' claims, which were due to be completed by July 2002. In May Australia offered monetary assistance to Afghan asylum-seekers as an incentive to return to their homeland, and in the following month the President announced that he anticipated that all the asylum-seekers would have left Nauru by the end of the year. However, in December some 700 people remained in the camps, despite the deportation of more than 100 Afghan asylum-seekers to Kabul. In the same month the President signed a new agreement with Australia's Minister for Foreign Affairs to extend the duration of the camps' operations and to accommodate up to 1,500 asylum-seekers.

In mid-2003 the Australian Government was accused of cruelty for detaining some 100 children in the camps on Nauru and for failing to reunite families held in separate camps for extended periods. The Nauruan Government was subject to further criticism when the visa of a Catholic priest and prominent human rights activist was withdrawn hours before he was due to visit refugees detained on the island. It was believed that Nauruan officials had been instructed to cancel the visa by the Australian Government. Concerns about the conditions at the camps and the welfare of the detainees increased during 2003, and in December some of those held began a hunger strike in order to attract attention to their situation. A reported 40 asylum-seekers particpated in the strike, some of whom stitched their lips together. The Nauruan Government's subsequent appeals for medical assistance from Australia to care for the hunger strikers, many of whom required hospital treatment during the following weeks, were refused. The emerging rift between the two countries intensified when Nauru's Minister of Finance, Kinza Clodumar, condemned remarks made by Australia's Minister for Immigration, Amanda Vanstone, who had said that the health of the hunger strikers was of no concern to Australia. Clodumar, who stated that his country's limited medical resources could not cope with a problem of this scale, accused Australia of failing to recognize its obligations in continuing to ignore the plight of the asylum-seekers on Nauru. The strike ended about one month after it had begun, and in mid-January 2004 the Australian Government sent a delegation to inspect medical facilities available to asylum-seekers on the island. The resultant report, however, which found services for those held in detention to be adequate, was widely regarded as flawed, as it had failed to examine any of the detainees and had been compiled solely by Australian government officials. In late June 2004 the first of 146 Afghan refugees, cleared to enter Australia, left the detention centre. In November 2005, after four years of detention on the island, a total of 25 asylum-seekers were transferred to Melbourne. It was reported that only two detainees, who had failed to meet security requirements, remained on Nauru.

In February 1987 representatives of the British, Australian and New Zealand Governments signed documents effecting the official demise of the British Phosphate Commissioners, who from 1919 until 1970 had overseen the mining of Nauru's phosphate deposits. President DeRoburt subsequently expressed concern about the distribution of the Commissioners' accumulated assets, which were estimated to be worth $A55m. His proposal that part of this sum be spent on the rehabilitation of areas of the island that had been mined before independence was rejected by the three Governments involved. DeRoburt subsequently established a commission of inquiry to investigate proposals for rehabilitation. The commission proposed that the three Governments provide one-third ($A72m.) of the estimated rehabilitation costs. In 1989 Australia's refusal to contribute to the rehabilitation of former phosphate-mining areas prompted Nauru to institute proceedings, claiming compensation from Australia for damage to its environment, at the International Court of Justice. However, in 1993, following negotiations between President Dowiyogo and the Australian Prime Minister, Paul Keating, a Compact of Settlement was signed, under which the Australian Government was to pay some $A107m. to Nauru. New Zealand and the United Kingdom subsequently agreed to contribute $A12m. each towards the settlement. An investigation into methods for the rehabilitation of the damaged areas of the island included plans to use landfill to encourage the restoration of vegetation to the mined areas, and the re-establishment of many of the species of flora and fauna that had previously been abundant on the island. In mid-1995 a report commissioned by the Government published details of a rehabilitation programme extending over the next 20–25 years and costing $A230m. The success of the rehabilitation scheme, however, was dependent on the co-operation of landowners, some of whom were expected to continue to allow areas to be mined for residual ore once phosphate reserves had been exhausted. In mid-1997 Parliament approved the Nauru Rehabilitation Corporation (NRC) Act, providing for the establishment of a corporate body to manage the rehabilitation programme. The NRC held its inaugural meeting in May

1999. The rehabilitation programme (which was to be partly financed from the Compact of Settlement with Australia) was expected to transform the mined areas into sites suitable for agriculture, new housing and industrial units. The project, however, was hampered considerably by delays, and in early 2004 the chair of the NRC resigned, reportedly in frustration at problems regarding the implementation of a feasibility study into the mining of residual phosphate. Results published in September 2004 from a series of test sites on the island indicated that the potential for residual phosphate mining might be greater than had been previously thought.

As a result of a strike by pilots of Air Nauru, begun in 1988, the Governments of Australia and New Zealand withdrew certification of the airline, concerned that it was not complying with safety standards. Air Nauru resumed operations in 1989, and diplomatic relations with Australia (which had been suspended in the previous year) were restored. In July 1998 the airline was transferred to the Australian aviation register in order to achieve improved surveillance and safety standards. In February 2001 Nauru's transport links with the rest of the world were severed when Air Nauru suspended all its operations, following a report by the Civil Aviation Safety Authority in Australia. The organization claimed that Air Nauru had failed to maintain an effective management structure, did not have sufficiently qualified staff and that the airport in Nauru did not meet regulatory requirements owing to frequent disruptions to electricity and communications services. The suspension was lifted in the following month. Two new diesel-powered electricity generators were bought later that year in the hope that their installation would resolve some of the problems outlined in the report. However, the Nauruan Government complained that the generators did not function properly, and in November 2005 a US consultancy company was engaged to manage the legal action being brought against the company that had sold the generators.

In December 2005 Air Nauru faced the prospect of closure following a court order for the seizure of the carrier's only aircraft, a Boeing 737-400, on account of the airline's non-payment of loan instalments to the Export-Import Bank of the United States. Discussions with Taiwan began in the hope that Air Nauru, which had consistently operated at a loss, might be revived, and in early January 2006 Nauru's Minister of Civil Aviation announced that Taiwan had agreed to offer support. Meanwhile, Air Pacific (of Fiji), Air Vanuatu and Air Marshall Islands (which had hitherto provided only domestic services) were operating sectors of the routes formerly serviced by Air Nauru.

Nauru was persistently critical of France's use of the South Pacific region for nuclear-weapons testing, and was one of the most vociferous opponents of the French Government's decision in mid-1995 to resume its nuclear-testing programme. Diplomatic relations, suspended between the two countries in 1995, were formally resumed in early 1998.

In early 2001 Nauru voiced strong opposition to the US Government's plans to develop a missile defence system, in which missiles are deployed to shoot down other missiles in flight. Government officials in Nauru expressed fears that testing of the system in the region could result in missile debris landing on the Pacific islands.

The President of Nauru met the Cuban Minister of Foreign Affairs in November 2001 at a UN meeting, where they agreed to establish diplomatic relations between their two countries and discussed a proposed technical and economic co-operation agreement whereby Nauru would be provided with health experts from Cuba.

In 1989 a UN report on the 'greenhouse effect' (the heating of the earth's atmosphere and a resultant rise in sea-level) listed Nauru as one of the countries that might disappear beneath the sea in the 21st century, unless drastic action were taken. The Government of Nauru strongly criticized Australia's refusal, at the December 1997 Conference of the Parties to the Framework Convention on Climate Change (see UN Environment Programme, see p. 58), in Kyoto, Japan, to reduce its emission of pollutant gases known to contribute to the 'greenhouse effect'.

In August 2001 Nauru hosted the Pacific Islands Forum summit meeting, despite a problematic shortage of accommodation, caused by the presence of contingents of officials from Australia, refugee agencies, the UN and Eurest (the company subcontracted to operate Nauru's refugee camp). Fiji had been expected to perform this role, but its participation had been opposed owing to its failure to reinstate democratic rule following the coup of the previous year.

In July 2004 President Ludwig Scotty held emergency discussions with the Presidents of Kiribati and Tuvalu regarding at least US $2m. in outstanding salary payments owed to their nationals employed in Nauru by the Nauru Phosphate Corporation. Nauru's financial crisis (see above) led it to appeal for assistance from the Pacific region and the international community. Consequently, in September 2004 the Pacific Islands Forum offered to help pay the salaries of Nauruan government employees (which had been unpaid for many months, resulting in considerable hardship), while the Cuban Government responded to an appeal for healthcare workers (as discussed in a co-operation agreement in late 2001—see above) by sending 11 doctors to Nauru to alleviate an increasingly serious situation, in which only three doctors were available to sick Nauruans.

In July 2002 a political crisis had emerged after President Rene Harris decided unilaterally to recognize the People's Republic of China, thus ending 22 years of diplomatic relations with Taiwan. Several cabinet ministers opposed the shift in policy, and the controversy increased after Harris immediately accepted US $60m. in aid and US $77m. in debt annulment from the People's Republic of China. Following the switch in allegiance, Taiwan announced that it would take legal action to recover a loan of US $12.5m. which it had arranged to make available to Nauru.

In March 2005 President Ludwig Scotty made an official visit to mainland China where he took part in discussions on bilateral aid and economic and technical co-operation. However, in May the Chinese Government announced that Nauru had severed its diplomatic relations with the People's Republic by switching its allegiance back to Taiwan. In July it was reported that Taiwan was to pay the outstanding salaries of some 1,000 workers from Kiribati and Tuvalu, who had remained stranded on Nauru since the island's financial crisis had resulted in the Government's inability to pay their wages. In March 2006 it was announced that Taiwan was providing US $3m. in overdue salary payments to the former phosphate miners from Kiribati and Tuvalu.

In February 2003 two diplomatic missions were opened, in Washington, DC, and in Beijing, primarily to address US concerns over 'money-laundering' and international terrorism (fears regarding the latter increased when, in the same month, two members of al-Qa'ida were found to be travelling on Nauruan passports). However, in July President Scotty announced plans to close the missions, citing economic constraints and his belief that they were not serving their intended purpose. Representatives in China and the USA expressed surprise at the announcement and queried the President's motives, in particular his commitment to ending the lucrative sale of Nauruan passports.

In February 2004 Nauru announced the establishment of diplomatic relations with Iceland. The two countries cited their common reliance on the sea as a unifying factor between them.

Nauru attracted considerable controversy in June 2005 when, at a meeting of the International Whaling Commission (IWC) in the Republic of Korea, it voted with Japan to remove the moratorium on commercial whaling introduced in 1986. Japan was accused by some observers of encouraging small, developing countries to join the IWC and then of attempting to influence their voting with financial incentives. Nauru, however, denied that it had been subjected to any form of manipulation by the Japanese Government, stating that it had voted to remove the ban on whaling in order to preserve its tuna stocks.

Government

Legislative power is vested in the unicameral Parliament, with 18 members elected by universal adult suffrage for up to three years. Executive authority is vested in a Cabinet, which consists of the President of the Republic, elected by the Parliament, and ministers appointed by him. The Cabinet is collectively responsible to Parliament. Responsibilities for administration are divided between the Nauru Local Government Council and the Government. The Council, an elected body of nine members from the country's 14 districts, elects one of its members to be Head Chief.

Defence

Nauru has no defence forces: under an informal arrangement, Australia is responsible for the country's defence.

Economic Affairs

In 2001, according to UN estimates, Nauru's gross domestic product (GDP), measured at current prices, was US $31m., equivalent to $2,500 per head. In 1995–2001, it was estimated, GDP decreased, in real terms, at an average annual rate of 3.5%.

The population increased by an annual average of 2.0% per year in 1990–2000. According to preliminary estimates from the Asian Development Bank (ADB), GDP declined, in real terms, by 1.0% in 2000 and by 0.8% in 2001, before expanding by 0.9% in 2003 and 2.5% in 2004.

Agricultural activity comprises mainly the small-scale production of tropical fruit, vegetables and livestock, although the production of coffee and copra for export is increasingly significant. In 2004, however, as a result of low rainfall, the agricultural sector remained stagnant. According to FAO, agriculture engaged some 17% of the economically active population in 2003. Coconuts are the principal crop. Bananas, pineapples and the screw-pine (*Pandanus*) are also cultivated as food crops, while the islanders keep pigs and chickens. However, almost all Nauru's requirements (including most of its drinking water) are imported. Increased exploitation of the island's marine resources was envisaged following the approval by Parliament of important fisheries legislation in 1997 and 1998. Funding for a new harbour for medium-sized vessels was secured from the Government of Japan in 1998, and in early 1999 the Marshall Islands Sea Patrol agreed to provide assistance in the surveillance of Nauru's exclusive economic zone. Revenue from fishing licence fees totalled $A8.5m. in 2000. In 2004, however, the island's fishing sector continued to be constrained by lack of equipment.

Until the early 1990s Nauru's economy was based on the mining of phosphate rock, which constituted four-fifths of the island's surface area. Phosphate extraction was conducted largely by indentured labour, notably by I-Kiribati and Tuvaluan workers. Revenue from phosphate sales was invested in a long-term trust fund (the Nauru Phosphate Royalties Trust (NPRT—see below) and the Nauru Local Government Council. Exports of phosphates declined to an average of 0.51m. tons annually in 1990–97 (compared with 1.58m. tons per year in the 1980s), mainly owing to the collapse of the Australian market. As a result of the Asian financial crisis, exports of phosphate declined by almost 18% in 1998 compared with the previous year. Mining production decreased by 7.9% in 2000. Primary deposits of phosphate were expected to be exhausted by 2010 at the latest. In 2004 export earnings failed to cover the cost of production. Feasibility studies were conducted into the mining of secondary and residual deposits, although this activity would be less profitable. An Australian engineering company undertook a detailed survey of the island's potential for secondary phosphate mining in early 2004 (see Recent History). In mid-2005, in an effort to raise primary phosphate output, Astro Pacific of New Zealand was appointed to oversee the Republic of Nauru Phosphate Company (Ronphos), which had recently assumed responsibility for the mining operations of the Nauru Phosphate Corporation. Following Astro Pacific's announcement in late 2005 of its discovery of substantial new deposits of high-grade phosphate, production was expected to increase significantly in 2006. An agreement with an Australian fertilizer company, which undertook to provide mining materials and engineering expertise, was signed in late 2005. In early 2006 it was announced that a Thai company was also to become involved in phosphate-mining operations on Nauru.

Energy is derived principally from imported petroleum. Output of electrical energy totalled 33m. kWh in 2000, the same production level as in the previous year, but declined to 30 kWh in 2001.

The services sector comprises mainly those employed in public service. The sector recorded no growth in 2004, with many salaries remaining in arrears (see Recent History). There is no tourism sector. In 2005 commercial banking services remained effectively unavailable.

The country's trade balance deteriorated significantly in 2001. Although imports decreased by 16.3%, exports declined by 61.5% compared with the previous year, resulting in a trade deficit of US $18.4m. The principal imports are food and live animals (which comprised 83.7% of total imports in 1993/94, while beverages accounted for a further 4.1%), machinery and transport equipment (2.8%) and non-metallic mineral manufactures (4.9%). Phosphates are the most important export, earning $A38.1m. in 1995; exports of crude fertilizers to Australia totalled $A8.5m. in 2001. The principal export markets in 2004 were South Africa (which purchased 37.6% of the total), India (19.6%), and Germany (18.0%). The principal sources of imports were Australia (supplying 59.0%) and Indonesia (16.7%).

Nauru consistently records a budget deficit. In 2004/05, however, a fiscal surplus of $A1.6m. was recorded (see below). A significant deficit was forecast for 2005/06. In 2000 overseas development assistance was estimated at US $4.0m., of which $2.9m. was bilateral aid. Development assistance from Australia was projected at $A4.0m. for 2004/05. Nauru's external debt was estimated at $A280m. in 2000. In that year the cost of debt-servicing was equivalent to an estimated 13% of total revenue from the exports of goods and services, while total public debt was equivalent to 60.8% of GDP. Consumer prices increased by 17.9% in 2000. The annual rate of inflation was estimated to average between 3% and 4% in 2005, resulting from the level of inflation in Australia (Nauru using that country's dollar as its currency) and from increased oil prices. The rate of unemployment among those aged 15–19 years in the late 1990s was estimated by the ADB to be 33% of males and 52% of females.

Nauru is a member of the Pacific Community (see p. 350), of the Pacific Islands Forum (see p. 352) and of the UN Economic and Social Commission for Asia and the Pacific (ESCAP, see p. 33), all of which aim to promote regional development. Nauru is also a member of the Asian Development Bank (ADB, see p. 169).

After gaining independence in 1968, Nauru benefited from sole control of phosphate earnings and, as a result, its income per head was among the highest in the world. This, however, had serious repercussions for the country, which became excessively dependent on expatriate labour, imports of consumer goods and convenience foods, causing health and social problems. Another effect of phosphate mining was to render 80% of the island both uninhabitable and uncultivable, leading to chronic overcrowding. Nauru lost a significant amount of money from the NPRT during the 1990s through theft and fraud. Measures to reform the financial sector, in response to allegations that Nauru's offshore banking services were being abused for the purposes of 'money-laundering', were announced in early 2000. However, serious allegations of 'money-laundering' re-emerged in 2001, when the Financial Action Task Force (FATF—see above) declared Nauru to be one of the worst international offenders. The FATF imposed counter-measures (which remained in place until October 2004), prescribing increased monitoring, surveillance and transparency in financial transactions. Nauru remained on the FATF list until October 2005, when its removal was finally approved. In December 2003, meanwhile, the country was also removed from the OECD's list of unco-operative tax havens. Nevertheless, Nauru's economic outlook remained poor. The country's substantial budgetary deficits had become increasingly unsustainable, having been financed largely from offshore borrowings. The fiscal surplus achieved in 2004/05 was derived mainly from revenue received from a previous investment in the Philippine Phosphate Fertilizer Corporation (from which Nauru was expected to earn $A5m. annually for at least the next five years) and from the receipt of a loan repayment from the Cook Islands. The Government had previously relied upon loans from official bilateral sources, overseas corporations or funds from the NPRT, the assets of which had become seriously depleted. The value of the NPRT was estimated at some $A300m. in 2003, compared with $A1,300m. in 1991, and by mid-2004 Nauru's remaining trust fund assets were in the possession of receivers (see Recent History). In July 2005 a parliamentary select committee began investigating allegations of financial irregularities regarding the NPRT. The committee sought submissions from interested parties, and its remit was extended to incorporate investigations into other irregularities including the sale of assets and questionable loans made by the trust. In September, furthermore, thousands of landowners began legal action, claiming that the NPRT owed them some US $69m. in compensation and royalties for the many years of phosphate-mining operations carried out on their land. An NPRT adviser disputed the figure, on the grounds that in Pacific culture ancestral land was traditionally used for the benefit of all generations, rather than for short-term capital gain. The Bank of Nauru, meanwhile, another previous source of budgetary support and financing of phosphate royalty payments to landowners, was believed to have become practically insolvent. From the early 2000s, furthermore, the repeated suspensions of Air Nauru's operations, owing to financial difficulties, had led to serious disruptions in the provision of food, fuel and other essential supplies to the island. In January 2003 President Dowiyogo broadcast an appeal for emergency aid, claiming that the island was on the verge of bankruptcy. A report published by the ADB in April stated that Nauru's economic situation was very serious and deteriorating. In April 2004 receivers acting on behalf of creditors in the USA seized Nauru's property portfolio, including five buildings in Sydney and Melbourne. The Nauruan

Government had been given until early May to repay a debt of more than US $200m. to a US finance corporation. In February 2004 the Governments of Australia and Nauru signed a memorandum of understanding providing for $A22.5m. in assistance for the period July 2003–June 2005. In July 2004 Australian officials arrived in Nauru to assume management of the country's finances. In late 2004 the Pacific Islands Forum provided a cash grant for the purposes of the payment of outstanding salaries. The Forum also offered support in other areas, including financial auditing and planning. It was reported in mid-2005 that the Forum was working to develop a national strategy with the Government of Nauru and was seeking to co-ordinate a programme of financial aid from Pacific donors by September of that year. In November 2005 Nauru hosted an international donor meeting, attended by representatives of about 20 donor nations and agencies, at which it requested support for its National Sustainable Development Strategy. The aims of this programme included an increase in revenue from phosphate production, better use of fish resources and the encouragement of agricultural activities, with particular emphasis on local food production. Further discussions were held in December to address some of the technical aspects of co-ordinating assistance from the donor community, and it was announced that commitments had been received from aid donors towards the restoration of Nauru's education facilities and governance. In March 2006 it was announced that Taiwan had pledged a total of US $13m. in aid to Nauru, most of which was to finance the purchase of a replacement aircraft for the country's airline (see Recent History).

Education

Education is compulsory for Nauruan children between six and 16 years of age. Primary education begins at the age of six and lasts for seven years. Secondary education, beginning at 13 years of age, lasts for up to four years. In 2003 there were six pre-primary schools, nine primary schools and two secondary schools with a total of 141 teachers. In 2003 there were four vocational level teachers with 38 students. In 2001 Nauruans studying overseas at secondary and tertiary levels numbered 85. There is a university extension centre, linked with the University of the South Pacific in Suva, Fiji. An estimated 1% of the adult population were illiterate in 1993–95. The education sector was particularly badly affected by the country's economic crisis during 2004. With payment of their salaries in arrears, many expatriate teachers left the country. The sector also continued to be constrained by the lack of adequate teaching materials. At an international donor meeting held at the end of 2005 (see Recent History), discussions took place regarding monetary aid, some of which was to be used to improve education standards.

Public Holidays

2006: 1 January (New Year's Day), 31 January (Independence Day), 14–17 April (Easter), 17 May (Constitution Day), 26 October (Angam Day), 25–26 December (Christmas).

2007: 1 January (New Year's Day), 31 January (Independence Day), 6–9 April (Easter), 17 May (Constitution Day), 26 October (Angam Day), 25–26 December (Christmas).

Statistical Survey

Source (unless otherwise stated): General Statistician, Nauru Government Offices, Yaren.

AREA AND POPULATION

Area: 21.3 sq km (8.2 sq miles).

Population: 8,042 (Nauruan 4,964, Other Pacific Islanders 2,134, Asians 682, Caucasians—mainly Australians and New Zealanders—262) at census of 13 May 1983; 9,919 (5,079 males, 4,840 females) at census of 17 April 1992; 10,065 (provisional result) at census of 2002 (figure from Asian Development Bank, *Key Indicators of Developing Asian and Pacific Countries*).

Density (2002 census): 472.5 per sq km.

Principal Towns (population, 1992 census): Aiwo (capital) 600; Anetan 427; Anabar 320; Anibare 165. Source: Thomas Brinkhoff, *City Population* (internet www.citypopulation.de).

Births, Marriages and Deaths (1995): Registered live births 203 (birth rate 18.8 per 1,000); Registered marriages 57 (marriage rate 5.3 per 1,000); Registered deaths 49 (death rate 4.5 per 1,000). *2002:* Registered live births 219; Registered deaths 75.

Expectation of Life (WHO estimates, years at birth): 61 (males 58; females 65) in 2003. Source: WHO, *World Health Report*.

Economically Active Population (census of 30 June 1966): 2,473 (Administration 845, Phosphate mining 1,408, Other activities 220). *Mid-2003* (estimates): Agriculture, etc. 1,000; Total labour force 6,000 (Source: FAO).

HEALTH AND WELFARE
Key Indicators

Total Fertility Rate (children per woman, 2003): 3.8.
Under-5 Mortality Rate (per 1,000 live births, 2004): 30.
Physicians (per 1,000 head, 1995): 1.57.
Health Expenditure (2002): US $ per head (PPP): 1,334.
Health Expenditure (2002): % of GDP: 7.6.
Health Expenditure (2002): public (% of total): 88.8.

For sources and definitions, see explanatory note on p. vi.

AGRICULTURE, ETC.

Principal Crop and Livestock (FAO estimates, 2004): Coconuts 1,600 metric tons; Pigs 2,800 head; Chickens 5,000 head.

Fishing (FAO estimates, metric tons, live weight of capture, 2003): Yellowfin tuna 18; Bigeye tuna 10; Skipjack tuna 4; Rainbow runner 4; Total catch (incl. other marine fishes) 43.

Source: FAO.

MINING

Phosphate Rock ('000 metric tons): 487 in 1998; 600 (estimate) in 1999; 500 (estimate) in 2000. The phosphoric acid content (in '000 metric tons) was: 185 in 1998; 230 (estimate) in 1999; 195 (estimate) in 2000. Source: US Geological Survey.

INDUSTRY

Electric Energy (million kWh): 33 in 1999; 33 in 2000; 30 in 2001. Source: UN, *Industrial Commodity Statistics Yearbook*.

FINANCE

Currency and Exchange Rates: Australian currency: 100 cents = 1 Australian dollar ($A). *Sterling, US Dollar and Euro Equivalents* (30 December 2005): £1 sterling = $A2.3469; US $1 = $A1.3630; €1 = $A1.6079; $A100 = £42.61 = US $73.37 = €62.19. *Average Exchange Rate* (US $ per Australian dollar): 1.5419 in 2003; 1.3598 in 2004; 1.3095 in 2005.

Budget (estimates, $A '000, year ending 30 June 1999): *Revenue:* 38,700; *Expenditure:* 37,200.

EXTERNAL TRADE

Principal Commodities ($A '000, year ending 30 June 1994): *Imports:* Food and live animals 38,420; Beverages 1,890; Non-metallic mineral manufactures 2,268; Non-electrical machinery 758; Transport equipment 534; Total (incl. others) 45,906. *Exports:* Total 45,111.

Principal Trading Partners (US $ million, 2004, year ending 31 December): *Imports:* Australia 13.4; Germany 0.9; Indonesia 3.8; United Kingdom 1.0; USA 0.8; Total (incl. others) 22.7. *Exports:* Germany 3.5; India 3.8; Japan 1.2; Republic of Korea 2.0; South Africa 7.3; Total (incl. others) 19.4. Source: Asian Development Bank, *Key Indicators of Developing Asian and Pacific Countries*.

Trade Totals ($A million, year ending 30 June): *Imports c.i.f.:* 46.6 in 2000; 40.6 in 2001; 46.0 in 2002. *Exports f.o.b.:* 48.3 in 2000; 25.1 in 2001; 16.6 in 2002. Source: Asian Development Bank, *Key Indicators of Developing Asian and Pacific Countries*.

NAURU

TRANSPORT

Road Traffic (1989): 1,448 registered motor vehicles.

Shipping: *Merchant Fleet* (displacement, '000 grt at 31 December): 15 in 1991 (at 30 June); 5 in 1992; 1 in 1993. Source: Lloyd's Register of Shipping. *International Freight Traffic* (estimates, '000 metric tons, 1990): Goods loaded 1,650; Goods unloaded 59. Source: UN, *Monthly Bulletin of Statistics*.

Civil Aviation (traffic on scheduled services, 2001): Kilometres flown (million) 3; Passengers carried ('000) 164; Passenger-km (million) 287; Total ton-km (million) 29. Source: UN, *Statistical Yearbook*.

COMMUNICATIONS MEDIA

Radio Receivers (1997): 7,000 in use*.
Television Receivers (1997): 500 in use*.
Telephones (main lines, 2001): 2,000 in use†.
Mobile Cellular Telephones (2001): 1,500 subscribers†.
Internet Users (2001): 300†.

* Source: UNESCO, *Statistical Yearbook*.
† Source: International Telecommunication Union.

EDUCATION

Pre-primary (2003): 6 schools; 44 teachers; 588 pupils.
Primary (2003): 9 schools; 63 teachers; 1,375 pupils.
Secondary (2003): 2 schools; 34 teachers; 645 pupils.
Vocational (2003): 4 teachers; 38 students.

Source: Department of Education, Yaren, Nauru.

Nauruans studying at secondary and tertiary levels overseas in 2001 numbered 85.

Directory

The Constitution

The Constitution of the Republic of Nauru came into force at independence on 31 January 1968, having been adopted two days previously. It protects fundamental rights and freedoms, and vests executive authority in the Cabinet, which is responsible to a popularly elected Parliament. The President of the Republic is elected by Parliament from among its members. The Cabinet is composed of five or six members, including the President, who presides. There are 18 members of Parliament, including the Cabinet. Voting is compulsory for all Nauruans who are more than 20 years of age, except in certain specified instances.

The highest judicial organ is the Supreme Court and there is provision for the creation of subordinate courts with designated jurisdiction.

There is a Treasury Fund from which monies may be taken by Appropriation Acts.

A Public Service is provided for, with the person designated as the Chief Secretary being the Commissioner of the Public Service.

Special mention is given to the allocation of profits and royalties from the sale of phosphates.

The Government

HEAD OF STATE

President: LUDWIG SCOTTY (re-elected 23 October 2004).

CABINET
(April 2006)

President, Minister of Civil Aviation, Minister of Customs and Immigration and Minister of Public Service: LUDWIG SCOTTY.

Minister of Foreign Affairs, Minister of Finance and Leader of Government Business: DAVID ADEANG.

Minister of Justice: GODFREY THOMA.

Minister of Health, Minister of Culture and Tourism, Minister of Shipping and Minister of Women's Affairs: KIEREN KEKE.

Minister of Island Development and Industry: FREDERICK PITCHER.

Minister of Education and Vocational Training, Minister of Public Works, and Minister of Youth Affairs: BARON WAQU.

MINISTRIES

Office of the President: Yaren, Nauru.
Ministry of Education: Yaren, Nauru; tel. 444-3130; fax 444-3718.
Ministry of Health and Youth Affairs: Yaren, Nauru; tel. 444-3166; fax 444-3136.
Ministry of Finance: Aiwo, Nauru; tel. 444-3140; fax 555-4477.
Ministry of Justice: Yaren, Nauru; tel. 444-3160; fax 444-3108.
Ministry of Works and Community Services: Yaren, Nauru; tel. 444-3177; fax 444-3135.

Legislature

PARLIAMENT

Parliament comprises 18 members. The most recent general election took place on 23 October 2004.

Speaker: VALDON DOWIYOGO.

Political Organizations

Democratic Party of Nauru: c/o Parliament House, Yaren, Nauru; f. 1987; revival of Nauru Party (f. 1975); Leader KENNAN ADEANG.

Naoero Amo (Nauru First): c/o Parliament House, Yaren, Nauru; e-mail visionary@naoeroamo.com; internet www.naoeroamo.com; f. 2001; Co-Leaders DAVID ADEANG, KIEREN KEKE.

Diplomatic Representation

EMBASSY IN NAURU

China (Taiwan): POB 294, Yaren; tel. 444-3239; fax 444-3846.

Judicial System

The Chief Justice presides over the Supreme Court, which exercises original, appellate and advisory jurisdiction. The Resident Magistrate presides over the District Court, and he also acts as Coroner under the Inquests Act 1977. The Supreme Court is a court of record. The Family Court consists of three members, one being the Resident Magistrate as Chairman, and two other members drawn from a panel of Nauruans. The Chief Justice is Chairman of the Public Services Appeals Board and of the Police Appeals Board.

Supreme Court

Yaren; tel. 444-3163; fax 444-3104.
Chief Justice: BARRY CONNELL (non-resident).

DISTRICT COURT

Resident Magistrate: G. N. SAKSENA.

FAMILY COURT

Chairman: G. N. SAKSENA.

Religion

Nauruans are predominantly Christians, adhering either to the Nauruan Protestant Church or to the Roman Catholic Church.

Nauruan Protestant Church: Head Office, Nauru; Moderator (vacant).

Roman Catholic Church: POB 16, Nauru; tel. and fax 444-3708; Nauru forms part of the diocese of Tarawa and Nauru, comprising Kiribati and Nauru. The Bishop resides on Tarawa Atoll, Kiribati.

The Press

Central Star News: Nauru; f. 1991; fortnightly.

Nasero Bulletin: Nauru; tel. 444-3847; fax 444-3153; e-mail bulletin@cenpac.net.nr; fortnightly; English; local and overseas news; Editor SEPE BATSIUA; circ. 500.

The Nauru Chronicle: Nauru; Editor RUBY DEDIYA.

Broadcasting and Communications

TELECOMMUNICATIONS

Nauru Telecommunications Service: Nauru; tel. 444-3324; fax 444-3111; Dir EDWARD W. R. H. DEYOUNG.

BROADCASTING

Radio

Nauru Broadcasting Service: Information and Broadcasting Services, Chief Secretary's Department, POB 77, Nauru; tel. 444-3133; fax 444-3153; e-mail ntvdirector@cenpac.net.nr; f. 1968; state-owned and non-commercial; expected to be corporatized in the late 1990s; broadcasts in the mornings in English and Nauruan; operates Radio Nauru; Station Man. RIN TSITSI; Man. Dir GARY TURNER.

Television

Nauru Television (NTV): Nauru; tel. 444-3133; fax 444-3153; e-mail ntvmanager@cenpac.net.nr; began operations in June 1991; govt-owned; broadcasts 24 hrs per day on 3 channels; most of the programmes are supplied by foreign television companies via satellite or on videotape; a weekly current affairs programme is produced locally; Man. MICHAEL DEKARUBE; Dir of Media GARY TURNER.

Finance

(cap. = capital; res = reserves; dep. = deposits; m. = million; amounts in Australian dollars unless otherwise stated)

BANKING

State Bank

Bank of Nauru: Civic Centre, POB 289, Nauru; tel. 444-3238; fax 444-3203; e-mail bonauru@yahoo.com; f. 1976; state-owned; cap. 12.0m., res 123.0m., dep. 141.0m. (Dec. 1994); Chair. NAGENDRA GOSWAMI.

INSURANCE

Nauru Insurance Corporation: POB 82, Nauru; tel. 444-3346; fax 444-3731; f. 1974; sole licensed insurer and reinsurer in Nauru; Chair. NIMES EKWONA.

Trade and Industry

GOVERNMENT AGENCIES

Nauru Agency Corporation: POB 300, Aiwo, Nauru; tel. 444-3782; fax 444-3730; e-mail nrugrp@cenpac.net.nr; management service to assist entrepreneurs in the incorporation of holding and trading corpns and the procurement of trust and insurance licences; chaired by the President of Nauru; Gen. Man. R. C. MOSES.

Nauru Corporation: Civic Centre, Yaren, Nauru; f. 1925; operated by the Nauru Council; the major retailer in Nauru; Gen. Man. A. EPHRAIM.

Nauru Fisheries and Marine Resources Authority: POB 449, Nauru; tel. 444-3733; fax 444-3812; e-mail nfmra@cenpac.net.nr; f. 1997.

Nauru Phosphate Corporation: Aiwo, Nauru; tel. 444-3839; fax 444-2752; f. 1970; has operated the phosphate industry and several public services of the Republic of Nauru (including provision of electricity and fresh water) on behalf of the Nauruan people; responsibility for phosphate-mining operations assumed by Republic of Nauru Phosphate Company (Ronphos), overseen from 2005 by Astro Pacific Group (New Zealand); Gen. Man. LESI OLSSON; Chair. RIDDELL AKUA.

Nauru Phosphate Royalties Trust (NPRT): Nauru; e-mail nprtnau@cenpac.net.nr; statutory corpn; invests phosphate royalties to achieve govt revenue; extensive international interests, incl. hotels and real estate; Sec. NIRAL FERNANDO.

Nauru Rehabilitation Corporation (NRC): Nauru; f. 1999; manages and devises programmes for the rehabilitation of those parts of the island damaged by the over-mining of phosphate; Chair. ALI AMWANO.

UTILITIES

Nauru Phosphate Corporation: Aiwo, Nauru; tel. 555-6481; fax 555-4111; operates generators for the provision of electricity and supplies the island's water; Chair. ALI AMWANO; Gen. Man. JOSEPH HIRAM.

Transport

RAILWAYS

There are 5.2 km of 0.9-m gauge railway serving the phosphate workings.

ROADS

A sealed road, 16 km long, circles the island, and another serves Buada District. There were 1,448 registered vehicles in 1989.

SHIPPING

As Nauru has no wharves, passenger and cargo handling are operated by barge. In late 1998 finance was secured from the Japanese Government for the construction of a harbour in Anibare district. Work on the project began in 1999.

Nauru Pacific: Government Bldg, Yaren, Nauru; tel. 444-3133; f. 1969; operates cargo charter services to ports in Australia, New Zealand, Asia, the Pacific and the west coast of the USA; Man. Dir (vacant).

CIVIL AVIATION

Air Nauru: Directorate of Civil Aviation, Government of Nauru Offices, POB 40, Yaren, Nauru; tel. 444-3274; fax 444-3705; e-mail write2us@airnauru.com.au; internet www.airnauru.com.au; f. 1970; corporatized in 1996 and moved to Australian aviation register in mid-1997; operates passenger and cargo services to Kiribati, Fiji, New Caledonia, Solomon Islands, Guam, Palau, the Philippines, the Marshall Islands, the Federated States of Micronesia, Hawaii (USA), Australia and New Zealand; Chair. KEN MCDONALD; CEO GEOFFREY BOWMAKER.

NEPAL

Introductory Survey

Location, Climate, Language, Religion, Flag, Capital

The Kingdom of Nepal is a land-locked Asian country in the Himalaya mountain range, with India to the east, south and west, and Tibet (the Xizang Autonomous Region), in the People's Republic of China, to the north. The climate varies sharply with altitude, from arctic on the higher peaks of the Himalaya mountains (where the air temperature is permanently below freezing point) to humid subtropical in the central valley of Kathmandu, which is warm and sunny in summer. Temperatures in Kathmandu, which is 1,337 m (4,386 ft) above sea-level, are generally between 2°C (35°F) and 30°C (86°F), with an annual average of 11°C (52°F). The rainy season is between June and October. Average annual rainfall varies from about 1,000 mm (40 ins) in western Nepal to about 2,500 mm (100 ins) in the east. The official language is Nepali, which was spoken by 48.6% of the population in 2001. Other languages include Maithir (12.3% in 2001) and Bhojpuri (7.5%). Some 80.6% of the population were Hindus in 2001, with 10.7% Buddhists and 4.2% Muslims. The national flag (proportions 4 by 3) is composed of two crimson pennants, each with a blue border. The upper section contains a white crescent moon (horns upwards and surmounted by a disc with eight rays) and the lower section a white sun in splendour. The capital is Kathmandu.

Recent History

Nepal is an hereditary monarchy, but for more than 100 years, until 1951, effective power was held by the Rana family, who created the post of hereditary Prime Minister. A popular revolution, led by the Nepali Congress Party (NCP), ousted the Ranas and restored King Tribhuvan to power. A limited constitutional monarchy was established in 1951. During most of the 1950s government was controlled by the monarchy, first under Tribhuvan and then, after his death in 1955, under his son, Mahendra. In February 1959 King Mahendra promulgated Nepal's first Constitution, providing for a bicameral parliament, including a popularly-elected lower house. Elections held later that month resulted in victory for the NCP, led by Bisweswor Prasad (B. P.) Koirala, who became Prime Minister. However, the King retained a certain degree of power, and persistent differences between the King and the Prime Minister led to a royal coup in December 1960: Nepal's first brief period of democracy was thus brought to an abrupt end. The King dismissed the Council of Ministers and dissolved Parliament. A royal decree of January 1961 banned political parties. King Mahendra accused the Koirala administration of corruption, and in December 1962 he introduced a new Constitution, reasserting absolute royal power and providing for a 'partyless' system of government, based on the Panchayat (village council), with a Prime Minister appointed by the King. This office was filled successively by Dr Tulsi Giri (1962–65), Surya Bahadur Thapa (1965–69) and Kirti Nidhi Bista (1969–70, 1971–73). King Mahendra himself was Prime Minister from April 1970 to April 1971. In January 1972 King Mahendra died and was succeeded by his son, Birendra. Nagendra Prasad Rijal became Prime Minister in July 1973, and held office until December 1975, when Dr Giri was reappointed. The new Government made major changes to the Constitution, which allowed for a widening of the franchise and more frequent elections to the Rashtriya Panchayat (National Assembly), but in no way were the King's powers eroded. In September 1977 Dr Giri resigned and was succeeded by Bista.

B. P. Koirala, the former Prime Minister and an advocate of parliamentary democracy, was acquitted of treason in February 1978. Returning from abroad a year later, he was placed under house arrest in April 1979, but then released, partly to appease students who had been demonstrating for reforms. National unrest grew and, after King Birendra announced in May that there would be a national referendum on whether to restore multi-party democracy, Bista resigned and was succeeded as Prime Minister by Thapa. In the referendum, held in May 1980, 54.8% of the voters supported the Panchayat system with reforms. As a result, the King formed a Constitutional Reforms Commission, and in December he issued a decree under which amendments to the Constitution were made, including the proviso that the appointment of the Prime Minister by the King would henceforth be on the recommendation of the Rashtriya Panchayat. In accordance with the new provisions, direct legislative elections were held in May 1981, the first of their kind since 1959, although still on a non-party basis. Thapa was re-elected by the Rashtriya Panchayat as Prime Minister in June 1981, and the King installed a new Council of Ministers (on the recommendation of the Prime Minister). An extensive ministerial reshuffle took place in October 1982, but this failed to stem increasing official corruption and economic mismanagement. In July 1983, for the first time in the 23-year history of the Panchayat system, the incumbent Prime Minister, Surya Bahadur Thapa, was ousted, and a new Council of Ministers was formed by a former Chairman of the Rashtriya Panchayat, Lokendra Bahadur Chand, who had successfully introduced a motion expressing 'no confidence' in Thapa.

In March 1985 the NCP held a convention in Kathmandu, and in May it embarked upon a campaign of civil disobedience, aimed at restoring a multi-party political system and parliamentary rule under a constitutional monarchy. In June there was a series of bomb explosions, resulting in loss of life. The explosions were apparently co-ordinated by two newly formed anti-monarchist and anti-Government groups, the Janawadi Morcha (Democratic Front) and the Samyukta Mukti Bahini (United Liberation Torch-bearers). These bombings united an otherwise seriously divided legislature against the terrorists, and forced the predominantly moderate opposition to abandon the campaign of civil disobedience and to disclaim any responsibility for the explosions. In August the Rashtriya Panchayat approved a stringent anti-terrorist law, and more than 1,000 people were arrested in connection with the unrest.

In May 1986 a general election was held. About 64% of the electorate voted, in spite of appeals by the NCP and the pro-China faction of the Communist Party of Nepal (CPN) (neither of which presented candidates) for a boycott of the polls. All the candidates in the election were nominally independents, but it was reported that among the 72 new entrants to the Rashtriya Panchayat (40 members retained their seats) there were at least 16 members of the Marxist-Leninist faction of the CPN. In June the King nominated 25 additional members of the new Rashtriya Panchayat, and Marich Man Singh Shrestha (previously Chairman of the Rashtriya Panchayat) was elected unopposed by the Assembly as the new Prime Minister. In late 1986, to counter the growing influence of the communist faction in the Rashtriya Panchayat, several senior figures (including Jog Meher Shrestha, a former government minister, and Chand) established a 'Democratic Panchayat Forum', which expressed full support for the non-party system.

In June 1987, in an apparent attempt to improve the image of the Panchayat system, the Government initiated an anti-corruption campaign, during the course of which several senior officials were arrested for drugs-trafficking and other offences. In early 1988 the Government continued its policy of suppressing opposition. In January the President of the NCP was arrested, and in February more than 100 people, who were planning to demonstrate in support of the NCP mayor of Kathmandu (who had been suspended from office for his anti-Panchayat stance), were also detained.

In September 1989 the Government arrested more than 900 NCP supporters, in a seeming effort to prevent them from celebrating the anniversary of the birth of Nepal's first elected Prime Minister, B. P. Koirala (who died in 1982). During these celebrations the NCP demonstrated in protest against the failings of the country's non-party political system. In November the leaders of the NCP held a meeting in Kathmandu with members of several other left-wing and communist political groups, to discuss the proposed formation of a country-wide peaceful 'movement for the restoration of democracy'. At the meeting they stated that the aims of the movement would be the alleviation of Nepal's severe economic problems (including the trade dispute with India, see below), the restoration of full democracy, the transfer from absolute to constitutional monarchy, the immediate replacement of the Panchayat Government by an interim national government, the removal of the ban on political activities, and the introduction of a multi-party system. In January 1990 a co-ordination committee to conduct the Jana Andolan (People's Movement) was formed by the NCP and the newly formed United Left Front (ULF, which was led by Sahana Pradhan and comprised six factions of the CPN and a labour group), despite the Government's efforts to pre-empt its inauguration by arresting hundreds of activists (including many students) and by banning, or heavily censoring, more newspapers. During the consequent violent confrontations between protesters and police that took place in February, it was officially estimated that 12 people were killed and hundreds more were arrested. Violent demonstrations, strikes and mass arrests continued throughout March. At the end of the month the Minister of Foreign Affairs, Shailendra Kumar Upadhayaya, resigned from his post, following differences with the Prime Minister regarding the Government's management of the crisis. A few days later there was an extensive government reshuffle, including the dismissal of nine ministers who allegedly opposed the Government's acts of repression against the pro-democracy movement. In an effort to end the political unrest, the King dismissed Shrestha's Government on 6 April and nominated a restricted four-member Council of Ministers, under the leadership of the more moderate Chand. King Birendra also offered to establish a body that would examine the possibility of altering the Constitution and to hold discussions with the opposition, and he promised to initiate an official inquiry into the 20 deaths that had occurred during demonstrations since February. Despite these concessions, the situation worsened later the same day. A temporary curfew was imposed on the capital, and many political agitators were arrested. The Government immediately initiated talks with the opposition, and on 8 April the King announced that the 30-year ban on political parties was to be ended, thus enabling the future holding of multi-party elections, and that a commission to study constitutional reform was to be established. At the same time, the Jana Andolan suspended its campaign of demonstrations. Many political activists continued to agitate, however, demanding the removal of the formal structure of the Panchayat system. A week later, the King accepted the resignation of Chand from his post as Prime Minister, dismissed the Council of Ministers and announced the dissolution of the Rashtriya Panchayat. King Birendra then invited the opposition alliance of the NCP and the ULF to form an interim government. On 19 April a new 11-member coalition Council of Ministers (including two ministers nominated by the King and two independents), under the premiership of the President of the NCP, Krishna Prasad (K. P.) Bhattarai, was sworn in. The new Prime Minister announced that a general election would be held, on a multi-party basis, within a year. The principal task of the interim Government was to prepare a new constitution in accordance with the spirit of multi-party democracy and constitutional monarchy. King Birendra stated that he was committed to transforming his role into that of a constitutional monarch, and, following further violent clashes in Kathmandu between anti-royalists and police, he ordered the army and the police to comply with the orders of the interim Government in order to facilitate a smooth transition to democracy.

In mid-May 1990 King Birendra announced a general amnesty for all religious and political prisoners. On 21 May he delegated the legislative powers of the dissolved Rashtriya Panchayat to the new Council of Ministers, so that the Council was empowered to enact, amend and repeal legislation in order to bring about the introduction of a multi-party democracy. At the end of the month the King formed a nine-member Constitutional Recommendation Commission, based on the suggestions of the Prime Minister, which, after consulting the various parties, was to prepare a draft constitution and present it to the King within three months. In July the death sentence was abolished and the laws restricting freedom of the press and freedom of association were repealed. In addition, the King suspended almost one-half of the articles in the Constitution to enable the interim Government to function smoothly. The draft of the new Constitution, which was published at the end of August, recommended the introduction of a constitutional monarchy; a democratic multi-party system and a bicameral legislature, composed of a 205-member House of Representatives (Pratinidhi Sabha) and a 60-member National Assembly (Rashtriya Sabha); the official guarantee of fundamental rights (including freedom of expression); an independent judiciary; and the placing of the army under the control of a three-member National Defence Council, headed by the Prime Minister. The draft Constitution recognized Hinduism as the country's dominant religion. It also, however, guaranteed freedom for religious minorities to practise their beliefs (although restrictions on proselytizing were to remain in force). Under the draft Constitution, the King would be allowed to declare a state of emergency on the advice of the Council of Ministers, but such declarations would have to be approved by the House of Representatives within three months. A crucial clause in the new Constitution required the King 'to obey and protect' the Constitution: under the old regime, the King was considered to be above the Constitution. The draft Constitution was approved by the Council of Ministers on 15 October and sent to the King for his endorsement. King Birendra, however, amended the draft in a final effort to retain sovereign authority and full emergency powers. This retrograde action provoked violent protests. The Council of Ministers rejected most of the proposed amendments in the royal counter-draft, but agreed to the King's proposal to establish a Council of State (Raj Parishad), with a standing committee headed by a royal appointee. The 15-member committee was to be composed of eight royal appointees and seven other members, including the Prime Minister, the Ministers of Defence and Foreign Affairs, the Chief Justice of the Supreme Court and the Chief of Army Staff. Bhattarai stressed, however, that the formation of this committee would not alter the democratic nature of the new Constitution, since it would not function as a parallel body to the Council of Ministers. He also emphasized that the King would only be permitted to act on judicial, executive and legislative matters on the advice of the Council of Ministers. The new Constitution was officially promulgated by the King on 9 November.

The communist movement in Nepal suffered a set-back in December 1990, when four of the seven constituent members of the ULF broke away from the front, citing their lack of representation in the interim coalition Council of Ministers. Sahana Pradhan stated, however, that the three remaining factions would continue to operate as the ULF. In January 1991 two major factions of the CPN (the Marxist and Marxist-Leninist factions) merged to form the CPN (Unified Marxist-Leninist—UML).

The general election was held on 12 May 1991. Of the 44 political parties that had been registered by the Election Commission, however, only 20 actually participated. The NCP decided to contest the election alone and not on the basis of an electoral alignment with any of its former Jana Andolan partners. The communists interpreted the NCP's move as the result of an increased understanding between the palace and the NCP on the basis that both wanted to forestall the rise of communism in the country. Consequently, relations between the NCP and the UML became strained and competitive. The general election was not only peaceful, but was also characterized by a good turn-out (65.2% of the electorate). The NCP won a comfortable majority (110 of the 205 seats in the lower house), but it was soundly defeated by the UML in the eastern hill districts and in some parts of the Terai. In Kathmandu, supposedly an NCP stronghold, the party lost all of the seats but one. By winning 69 seats, the UML established itself as the second largest party in the House of Representatives, followed by the United People's Front (UPF), an amalgam of radical, Maoist groups, with nine seats. Two other communist organizations—the Nepal Workers' and Peasants' Party and a faction of the CPN—received two seats each, thus making a total communist tally in the House of Representatives of 82 seats. The Nepali Sadbhavana Party (NSP), which, despite the constitutional prohibition against regional-based parties, was a plains- or Terai-based party, obtained six seats, all of which were in the Terai. The Rashtriya Prajatantra Party (Chand) and the Rashtriya Prajatantra Party (Thapa), led by the former Prime Ministers of those names, fared badly in the election, winning only four seats—the latter one and the former three. All of the three independent candidates who won seats subsequently joined the NCP. Acting Prime Minister Bhattarai lost his seat in the capital, and was replaced in the premiership by Girija Prasad (G. P.) Koirala, the General Secretary of the NCP and brother of the late B. P. Koirala.

By the end of 1991 unity within the ruling NCP was threatened by growing internal dissent amongst its leadership, particularly between the senior leader, Ganesh Man Singh, and G. P. Koirala. The Government suffered a further set-back in April 1992 when a *bandh* (general strike), organized by the communist and other opposition parties in Kathmandu in protest against price rises, water shortages and alleged government corruption, resulted in the deaths of at least seven demonstrators following violent clashes with the police. Despite the consequent imposition of curfews in the capital and in the neighbouring town of Lalitpur, the opposition staged a number of anti-Government protest marches and demonstrations during the following week. The success of a second general strike, which was held in early May, demonstrated the continuing strength of the radical left. It brought Kathmandu to a standstill and, unlike the earlier general strike, passed off without violent incidents. Despite the strikes and the rising cost of living, the NCP performed well in the local elections held throughout the country in May and June. There were, however, widespread reports of corruption and malpractice.

Under the leadership of G. P. Koirala, the centrist NCP Government shifted to the right. The public image of the monarchy and leading members of the former Panchayat regime were rehabilitated with government support. No charges were brought against senior officials of the former administration for corruption or human rights violations. Replicating the patronage system of the Panchayat regime, the NCP rapidly began to dominate the public administration structure. The ruling party's persistent failure to democratize its internal bodies and the absence of open election to posts in the party leadership met with criticism both within and without the NCP.

In addition to opposition from the leadership of his own party, G. P. Koirala was faced with increasing criticism from the opposition parties themselves, which focused on an agreement drawn up by the Prime Minister in December 1991 granting India access to water from the Tanakpur barrage on the Mahakali River, the terms of which were only subsequently revealed to the Nepalese House of Representatives. Alleging that the agreement constituted a treaty affecting national sovereignty, and therefore requiring a two-thirds' majority in the House of Representatives, the opposition launched a campaign calling for the resignation of Koirala on the grounds of unconstitutional behaviour. An indeterminate Supreme Court ruling in December 1992 on Koirala's action only intensified the protest.

In January–February 1993 the national UML congress abandoned much of the party's Marxist dogma and tacitly acknowledged its commitment to working within a democratic multiparty system. However, the untimely deaths of the party's General Secretary, Madan Bhandari, and Politburo member Jiv Raj Ashrit, following a road accident in mid-May, threw the UML into disarray. The rejection by the UML of the findings of a government inquiry, which concluded that the deaths had been accidental, provoked nation-wide protests in support of demands for an independent inquiry into the so-called 'Dhasdunga Incident'. In late May Madhav Kumar Nepal was appointed as the new General Secretary of the UML.

In the mean time, the rehabilitation of officials of the former Panchayat regime continued. In January 1993 the King appointed senior figures of the old administration, including former Prime Ministers Chand and Shrestha, to the 121-member Council of State (Raj Parishad), in a move designed both to rehabilitate former Panchayat officials and to reassert his leadership role over them. In June the right-wing Rashtriya Prajatantra Party (RPP, formed in February 1992, following a merger of the Chand and Thapa factions) held its first national conference in Kathmandu, an event that would have been inconceivable three years previously, when its leaders were forced into hiding by the democracy movement.

In August 1993 the UML signed an agreement with the NCP, providing for the permanent withdrawal of the UML from anti-Government agitation in return for the ruling party's pledge to establish an independent commission to investigate the 'Dhasdunga Incident'. The UPF and other left-wing groups, however, continued their campaign of nation-wide general strikes and demonstrations. Further serious rifts became apparent within the ruling NCP when the party's President, K. P. Bhattarai, lost a legislative by-election to the UML candidate in Kathmandu in February 1994; his defeat was widely attributed to G. P. Koirala's public opposition to his candidature. In March the Government survived a vote of 'no confidence' (by 113 votes to 81) presented to the House of Representatives by the UML. The opposition itself suffered from internal dissension in mid-1994 when both the UPF and the CPN (Unity Centre) split into competing factions, while the UML continued to be divided between radical and conservative camps. The crisis within the NCP culminated on 10 July when followers of Ganesh Man Singh withdrew their support for Koirala, who thereby lost his parliamentary majority. Consequently the Prime Minister offered his resignation, and on the following day the King dissolved the House of Representatives. Koirala was appointed as interim Prime Minister pending the holding of a general election, which was brought forward from mid-1996 to 15 November 1994. At the general election, which attracted a turn-out of 58%, the UML unexpectedly emerged as the single largest party, winning 88 of the 205 seats in the House of Representatives, while the NCP won 85 seats. At the end of the month the UML formed a minority Government under the premiership of its moderate Chairman, Man Mohan Adhikari. In late December the communist Government won a vote of confidence in the House of Representatives (as required by the Constitution for a new administration to continue in power).

On 11 June 1995 the NCP registered a parliamentary motion of 'no confidence' against the communist Government and, in conjunction with the RPP and the NSP, submitted a memorandum to King Birendra, staking their claim to form an alternative government. On the recommendation of the Prime Minister, who wished to avert the passage of the motion, the King dissolved the legislature on 13 June and announced that fresh elections were to be held on 23 November. Adhikari and his Council of Ministers were to function as a caretaker Government, pending the general election. In an apparent attempt to win popular support in the run-up to the election, Adhikari's interim administration substantially increased budgetary expenditure and implemented a number of welfare programmes. The opposition, angered by the communists' mode of electioneering, challenged the dissolution of the House of Representatives in the Supreme Court. In a controversial ruling, declared on 28 August, the Supreme Court decided that the dissolution of the lower house on the advice of a minority administration (when a majority coalition was ready to assume power) had, indeed, been unconstitutional. The House of Representatives was consequently reconvened and the election abandoned. The UML Government was defeated in a vote of 'no confidence' on 10 September, by 107 votes to 88. On 12 September a coalition Government, composed of members of the NCP, the RPP and the NSP, and headed by the NCP's parliamentary leader, Sher Bahadur Deuba, was formed.

In early March 1996 the Government introduced a number of security measures following a series of violent clashes between a group of Maoist activists and the police in western Nepal, which resulted in the deaths of at least 11 people (by the end of the year more than 100 people had been killed as a result of the insurgency). The left-wing extremists (many of whom were members of the underground Communist Party of Nepal—Maoist and the UPF) had launched a 'people's revolutionary war' in the hills of Nepal in February, demanding the abolition of the constitutional monarchy and the establishment of a republic. In May G. P. Koirala was elected to replace Bhattarai as President of the NCP; for the first time since its foundation, the party elected its leader by ballot. In early December seven RPP members of the Council of Ministers resigned from their posts and the faction of the party led by Chand withdrew from the ruling coalition; the Government, however, which continued to enjoy the support of the RPP faction led by Thapa, narrowly survived a legislative vote of 'no confidence' (presented by the UML) later that month. In early January 1997 five of the former RPP ministers who had resigned from the Government in the previous month reversed their position and pledged their support for Deuba's administration; a few days later four of these politicians were reinstated in the Government as part of a ministerial reshuffle. The Government suffered a set-back at the end of the month when the UML, already the largest party in the House of Representatives, increased its strength from 87 to 90 deputies, following its success in three by-elections. Deuba's administration finally collapsed in early March when it lost a vote of confidence in the House of Representatives. Chand was appointed as the new Prime Minister (for the fourth time) at the head of a coalition Government composed of members of the RPP, the UML, the NSP and the Nepal Workers' and Peasants' Party. The new Government, however, seemed unstable from the outset, since the members of the Thapa faction of the RPP refused to support Prime Minister Chand and the ideological differences between the communists and the former pro-monarchists appeared insuperable. Although Chand held the premiership, the UML, as the largest component of the coalition, was responsible for more ministerial posts than the RPP. In May and June the communists replaced the NCP as the country's dominant force in local government, following resounding successes in local elections. These elections were marred, however, by violent clashes between supporters of the main political parties in which about 30 people were killed. In mid-June more than 10,000 NCP supporters demonstrated in Kathmandu in protest over alleged electoral irregularities on the part of the UML during the recent polls. During 1997 the UML suffered from factional infighting, with a major rift developing between Deputy Prime Minister Bam Dev Gautam and the General Secretary of the party, Madhav Kumar Nepal. This factionalism served to destabilize the coalition Government further. In August a strike organized by an alliance of left-wing groups (known as the National Democratic Front) in protest at the rise in the price of fuel and a proposed anti-terrorist law brought Kathmandu and surrounding towns to a standstill. In the following month an anti-defection bill, the aim of which was to prevent politicians from deserting their own party and thus to bring stability to Nepal's politics, was unanimously approved by the House of Representatives.

On 4 October 1997 the Government lost a parliamentary vote of 'no confidence' tabled by the NCP. A few days later King Birendra appointed Thapa, the President of the RPP, to replace Chand as Prime Minister. A new coalition Government, comprising members of the RPP and the NSP, took office on the following day. In December Prime Minister Thapa expanded the Council of Ministers in a reshuffle that introduced members of the NCP and a number of independents into the coalition. In January 1998 Nepal was once again faced with political upheaval when Thapa recommended to the King that he dissolve the House of Representatives and set a date for mid-term elections. The Prime Minister presented the petition for fresh polls following a decision by the UML and dissident members of the RPP (including Chand) to introduce a parliamentary vote of 'no confidence' against the Government. Uncertain as to how to act in this political impasse, the King referred the matter to the Supreme Court (the first time a Nepalese monarch had ever done so). In early February the Court advised King Birendra to convene a special session of the House of Representatives to discuss a 'no confidence' motion against Thapa's Government. Although the Supreme Court's advice was not binding, the King called the parliamentary session. The 'no confidence' motion, which was presented on 20 February, was, however, narrowly defeated. Meanwhile, in mid-January Chand and nine other rebel deputies were expelled from the RPP; they immediately re-established a breakaway faction known as the RPP (Chand). In March the UML suffered a serious reverse when about one-half of the party's parliamentary deputies formed a breakaway faction entitled the Communist Party of Nepal (Marxist-Leninist) (ML). Bam Dev Gautam was unanimously elected as the new party's leader. The creation of the new party left the UML with 49 deputies, while the ML claimed the support of 40 deputies.

Under an agreement reached in October 1997 when Thapa assumed power, the Prime Minister was to transfer the leadership of the coalition Government to the NCP within an agreed time frame. By early April 1998, however, Thapa appeared reluctant to relinquish his post, and the NCP threatened to withdraw support for the Government unless the Prime Minister resigned immediately. Thapa tendered his resignation, and the President of the NCP, G. P. Koirala, was appointed Prime Minister in mid-April, taking office with only two other ministers. After obtaining a parliamentary vote of confidence, by 144 votes to four, the Prime Minister substantially expanded his Council of Ministers. Koirala stated that amongst the top priorities of the one-party minority Government would be the tackling of the Maoist insurgency (which had escalated in recent months). In August, in a seeming attempt to strengthen his own precarious administration and to encourage the UML's communist rivals, the Prime Minister invited the ML to join in alliance with the NCP and to form a coalition government. A new coalition administration was consequently established on 26 August (with the NCP retaining the most important ministries), giving Prime Minister Koirala an adequate parliamentary majority. Meanwhile, the 'people's war' waged by the Maoist activists in the hills of west Nepal gathered momentum. In May the Government launched a large-scale police operation in an effort to curb the guerrilla violence.

In December 1998 the ML withdrew from the coalition Government, alleging that its ruling partner, the NCP, had failed to implement a number of agreements drawn up between the two parties and other political groups in August. Prime Minister G. P. Koirala tendered his resignation, but was asked to head a new coalition Council of Ministers, which was to hold power in an acting capacity pending the holding of a general election. On the recommendation of the Prime Minister, the King appointed a new coalition administration, comprising members of the NCP, the UML and the NSP, and, for the first time in eight years, a nominee of the King, on 25 December. In mid-January 1999 the acting Government won a convincing vote of confidence in the House of Representatives, and on the following day the King dissolved the legislature in preparation for the forthcoming general election.

In late April 1999 the UML suffered a set-back when its veteran leader and former Prime Minister, Man Mohan Adhikari, died during the electoral campaign. In May the NCP won an outright majority in the general election (held over two rounds), securing 110 of the 205 seats in the lower house; the UML obtained 68 seats and the RPP (Thapa) took 11 seats, while the ML and the RPP (Chand) both failed to win a single seat. Voting was conducted relatively peacefully, according to government sources, despite threats by the Maoist insurgents to disrupt the electoral process. A new Council of Ministers, headed by the veteran NCP leader, K. P. Bhattarai, and composed solely of NCP members, was appointed at the end of the month. In late June the UML won all six seats in elections to the National Assembly, and in August Dr Mohammad Mohasin of the RPP was elected Chairman of the upper house.

In late November 1999, in an effort to resolve the Maoist insurgency, which, according to government sources, now affected (moderately to severely) 31 of Nepal's 75 districts and had led to the deaths of more than 1,000 people, the Prime Minister offered to grant the guerrillas an amnesty and various rehabilitation measures if they surrendered their arms and entered into negotiations with the Government. In response, the insurgents (who were estimated to number 5,000–6,000 and to have the support of about 8,000 sympathizers) stated that they were not prepared to enter into peace talks until arrest warrants issued against their leaders were withdrawn, official investigations were carried out into alleged extrajudicial killings of suspected militants by the police, and imprisoned activists were released. In an attempt to facilitate the peace process, the Government established a six-member high-level negotiation commission under the convenorship of former Prime Minister Sher Bahadur Deuba, which was charged with finding a solution to the Maoist situation that met with the approval of all political parties (including the insurgents themselves).

In mid-December 1999 the ruling NCP, despite a number of by-election victories, was once again beset by internecine strife when about 80 pro-Koirala legislators initiated an attempt to oust (by means of a petition) the Prime Minister from his position as the NCP's parliamentary party leader (which would automatically lead to his removal from the premiership). Koirala had initially been supportive of Bhattarai's premiership, but had since become a vociferous critic of his rival's administration, particularly with regard to the Government's perceived mismanagement of the Maoist crisis. In February 2000 a minor reorganization of the Council of Ministers took place, which included the appointment of Ram Chandra Poudel, a former Speaker of the lower house, as Deputy Prime Minister; the ministerial reshuffle was prompted by the earlier resignation of the Minister of Finance, Mahesh Acharya, following a disagreement with the Prime Minister over the appointment of the new Governor of the Central Bank. A few days after the government reorganization, the Minister of Education, Yog Prasad Upadhyaya, resigned in protest at the appointment of Poudel as Deputy Prime Minister. The political unrest culminated in the registration of a vote of 'no confidence' by 58 dissident NCP legislators against Prime Minister Bhattarai; this move led to the immediate resignation of 11 government ministers. The NCP's parliamentary party was scheduled to vote on the no-confidence motion in late February; however, following the attainment of a secret agreement between the Prime Minister and the NCP President, G. P. Koirala, including Bhattarai's reported assurance that he would stand down voluntarily within a fortnight, the proposal was withdrawn. A second motion of 'no confidence' in Bhattarai was registered by 69 predominantly pro-Koirala legislators in the NCP secretariat in mid-March. Under such pressure, Bhattarai tendered his resignation to the King. It was announced that G. P. Koirala was to be the new Prime Minister (for the fourth time), following his election as parliamentary party leader of the NCP; this election process replaced the party's traditional method of choosing a parliamentary leader through consensus. Koirala and a new Council of Ministers were sworn in by the King on 22 March, and vowed to continue the basic programmes and policies that the previous NCP Government had adopted. In May a Human Rights Commission was formed following accusations by various bodies that both the security forces and the Maoist guerrillas had committed human rights violations, including murder and torture.

In early April 2000 Prime Minister Koirala activated the National Defence Council, which, according to the Constitution, comprised the Prime Minister, the Minister of Defence and the Commander-in-Chief of the Royal Nepal Army, to resolve the Maoist crisis. In comparison to the inadequately-trained and poorly-armed police force, which had suffered numerous casualties, the army was much better equipped to deal with the insurgency, and Koirala expressed his wish to mobilize the armed forces in the ongoing fight against militant activity. The possibility of the deployment of the armed forces met with immediate criticism from various Nepalese human rights groups, which claimed that mobilization of the army would lead to an escalation in corruption.

At the end of August 2000 the Maoist crisis worsened. During two Maoist attacks in Dolpa and Lamjung, 24 police officers were killed and 44 were injured. The Royal Nepal Army was criticized for failing to intervene to protect the police from insurgents. The Minister of Home Affairs, Govinda Raj Joshi, resigned after admitting his failure to 'maintain law and order in the country'. The Prime Minister responded to the confusion over the command and control structure of the army by giving Mahesh Acharya, the Minister of Finance, the additional portfolio of defence. G. P. Koirala had hitherto always retained this portfolio personally, but it had become clear that the Government and army needed an independent defence minister, clarification of the army's ambiguous role and the development of a procedure for mobilizing the army, absent from the 1991 Constitution. It was later decided that the Government would employ a dual approach: using the army, as well as encouraging negotiations, in order to resolve the Maoist crisis. In the mean time, the RPP (Chand) merged with the RPP (Thapa); the Chand-led RPP was formally closed down in late 2000.

At the end of October 2000 the first direct unofficial negotiations began between the Government and the CPN (Maoist); however, they soon ended, and the violence resumed in early November. In the same month the high-level commission charged with finding a solution to the Maoist crisis (see above) produced a report advising the Government and Maoist insurgents to cease violence and participate in negotiations. The report also recommended that the Government improve and modernize its security forces. The UML leader, who had earlier held negotiations with the insurgents, ruled out any alliance with the Maoist group until it abandoned the use of force.

In January 2001 the Minister for Tourism and Civil Aviation, Tarani Datta Chataut, resigned following a controversial agreement to lease an Austrian aircraft to the Royal Nepal Airlines Corporation. In early February leading opposition parties issued a memorandum to the Prime Minister, demanding his resignation over the aircraft deal and also the worsening security situation. Koirala strongly denied his involvement in the leasing of the Austrian aircraft. The King then approved a reorganization of the Council of Ministers, on the recommendation of Prime Minister Koirala. However, shortly after the new cabinet was announced, two ministers withdrew their names, criticizing Koirala for making decisions without consulting other senior leaders. Palten Gurung later reneged on his decision, but Khum Bahadur Khadka refused to join the Council of Ministers. In March the Prime Minister faced increasing opposition from within and outside his party. Further ministerial resignations followed. The opposition continued to disrupt parliamentary proceedings, and, as a result, the King prorogued the National Assembly and House of Representatives in early April. At the end of the month the anti-corruption commission cleared the Prime Minister of involvement in the controversial aircraft agreement, but filed cases against 10 other people, including the former minister, Chataut. At the same time, Koirala was accused of accepting bribes in another aircraft deal. The opposition continued to demand his resignation and organized a nation-wide strike in protest against the Government's alleged misuse of power.

On 1 June 2001 King Birendra, Queen Aishwarya and six other members of the royal family were shot dead; the heir to the throne, Crown Prince Dipendra, was gravely wounded. Another family member, Dhirendra Shah, died later in hospital. Initial reports suggested that Prince Dipendra had shot members of his family before shooting himself, following a dispute between himself and his mother, regarding his intentions to marry Devyani Rani (the daughter of a prominent Nepalese politician), of whom the Queen disapproved. Prince Gyanendra, the deceased King Birendra's brother, however, issued a statement claiming that the deaths were the result of an accidental discharge of an automatic weapon. Immediately after the incident Prince Dipendra was pronounced King, and Prince Gyanendra was appointed regent. On 4 June King Dipendra died and was succeeded by Prince Gyanendra. These events caused unrest in Kathmandu, and a curfew was imposed. In the mean time, rumours about the killings began to spread. Few believed the statement given by Gyanendra. Some suggested that Maoist insurgents were to blame; others claimed India was responsible. Following his accession, King Gyanendra established a commission to investigate the killings. The commission, comprising the Chief Justice, K. P. Upadhyaya and the Speaker of the House of Representatives, T. Ranabhat, duly concluded that Dipendra had been responsible for the shootings and that at the time had been under the influence of drugs and alcohol. King Gyanendra bestowed the title of Queen on his wife, Princess Komal, but did not declare his son the Crown Prince until the end of October, owing to his unpopularity among the public, caused by his profligate behaviour.

In late June 2001 elections to 16 seats in the National Assembly took place. The UML won eight seats, bringing its total to 23 and rendering it the largest bloc in the chamber. In June–July Maoist leaders, taking advantage of the discontent in Nepal, intensified their activities. On 13 July the Deputy Prime Minister, Ram Chandra Poudel, resigned, owing to disagreements with the Prime Minister over policy towards the insurgency. Some few days later a senior Maoist leader declared that he would enter negotiations on the condition that the Prime Minister resigned. On 19 July Prime Minister Koirala resigned, citing his failure to curb the Maoist insurgency and long-standing corruption allegations. A few days later the NCP elected former premier Sher Bahadur Deuba as its new leader; King Gyanendra appointed Deuba as Prime Minister on the same day and a new Council of Ministers was sworn in on 26 July. Prime Minister Deuba retained a number of Koirala's cabinet members in an effort to ensure stability and initially kept many of the major portfolios for himself.

Immediately after his appointment Prime Minister Deuba persuaded the Maoist leaders to reciprocate his offer of a cease-fire and agree to enter dialogue. Prior to the negotiations, both sides took part in a series of confidence-building measures: the Maoist activists released 31 kidnapped police officers, and the Government set free over 30 Maoist leaders and published the names of 273 guerrillas still imprisoned. At the same time Parliament passed legislation to establish an Armed Police Force and to develop the co-ordination of regional development and security. The Government released a further 68 insurgents after the first two rounds of negotiations in August and September 2001. Despite the cease-fire, Maoist insurgents continued to carry out violent acts. During the peace talks tens of thousands of people held demonstrations against the fighting. The third round of negotiations, which took place in November, ended in failure, owing to the Maoists' continued demand for the dissolution of the Constitution, the establishment of an interim government, the election of a constituent assembly and, ultimately, a republic. The Government, in contrast, was prepared to offer a much less radical set of changes. Two days later the CPN (Maoist) leader Pushpa Kamal Dahal announced the end of the cease-fire. The Maoists established a parallel central government, the 'United People's Revolutionary Government', and resumed their violent campaign. The Maoists set up parallel governments in 40 of the country's 75 districts, and established direct rule in 22 districts in western Nepal. The violence escalated; on 26 November the King declared a state of emergency and authorized, for the first time, the deployment of the army to curb the insurgency. The King termed the Maoists as 'terrorists' and promulgated the Terrorist and Disruptive Activities Ordinance 2001, which sanctioned a number of counter-terrorist measures, including the suspension of civil liberties and media restrictions. In mid-December Prime Minister Deuba declared that he would not resume negotiations with the Maoists until they surrendered their arms.

Meanwhile, in early September 2001 the Government implemented a radical land reform programme, which was designed to help poor, landless farmers. The programme was supported by the UML, but opposed by smaller parties. Major landowners who risked losing part of their land opposed the limit to the size of individual landholdings. In mid-August Deuba announced that discrimination against Dalits (or 'untouchables') would henceforth be illegal and pledged to pass legislation ending the caste system. A national commission for Dalit welfare and a National Women's Commission were also to be established.

In January 2002 the Nepal Rastra Bank 'froze' the bank accounts of individuals and organizations associated with Maoist militants. In mid-February Maoist insurgents launched their heaviest-ever offensive against government outposts. More than 150 people, mainly soldiers and police officers, were killed in the fighting. In response to the attacks, the army was instructed to use offensive as well as defensive measures to combat the insurgency. On 21 February the legislature voted to extend the state of emergency for three months. Although the opposition criticized the Government for its handling of the insurgency and for failing to react to warnings that major attacks were imminent, it voted for the extension after the Prime Minister agreed to establish social and economic development programmes in poor rural areas where Maoists were active, and ensured the fair use of the emergency powers.

In the mean time, in mid-February 2002 the UML and its breakaway faction, the ML, merged. The merger of the more moderate communist parties was regarded largely as a move to counter the influence of the Maoist insurgents. Strikes occurred in March, severely affecting businesses and schools. In its first annual report, the Human Rights Commission accused the Maoist insurgents of committing serious human rights abuses. The commission also criticized the Government for violating human rights. In early April the Government reduced the controversial restrictions it imposed on the media and political parties as part of the state of emergency. The violent campaign escalated in mid-April, leading to hundreds of fatalities. In May Deuba tabled a parliamentary motion proposing an extension of the six-month state of emergency (which was due to expire on 25 May), prompting strong opposition from within and outside his party. Members of the governing NCP, led by former premier G. P. Koirala, accused Deuba of not consulting them before recommending an extension and urged the Government to withdraw its parliamentary motion. The rift in the party led King Gyanendra to dissolve unexpectedly the House of Representatives on 22 May, on the recommendation of the Prime Minister. A general election was scheduled to take place on 13 November, and the incumbent Government was instructed to rule the country in the interim. Political leaders strongly condemned this decision. On 23 May Deuba was suspended from his party and three days later was expelled from the NCP for three years. In the mean time, three ministers, including the Minister of Finance, resigned in protest at the calling of early elections. In late May King Gyanendra extended by three months the state of emergency. Meanwhile, in early May the army launched a heavy attack against Maoist insurgents in Rolpa district, resulting in the deaths of, according to government sources, 548 guerrillas, three soldiers and one police officer. A series of counter-attacks and attacks ensued, leading to hundreds of fatalities; by the end of May some reports estimated that more than 4,000 people had been killed since the beginning of the insurgency. On 9 May the Maoist leader made an offer of a one-month cease-fire by e-mail to newspapers in Kathmandu; Deuba promptly rejected the proposal, repeating his request for the insurgents to renounce violence.

In mid-June 2002 the NCP officially split during a 'general convention' held by the Deuba faction. Eventually, in mid-September the Election Commission recognized the faction led by G. P. Koirala as the official NCP. Several days later Deuba's minority breakaway faction registered as a new political party, the Nepali Congress Party—Democratic (NCP—D). Meanwhile, in April the Nepal Sadbhavana Party split into two factions and in July two communist parties, the National People's Front and United People's Front, merged to form the People's Front Nepal.

In the mean time, the state of emergency expired in late August 2002. As a result the Maoists intensified their violent campaign. In mid-September the Government rejected Pushpa Kamal Dahal's offer of a cease-fire, on the grounds that it lacked credibility. In early October Deuba requested King Gyanendra to postpone the general election by one year, citing the deteriorating law and order situation. However, King Gyanendra dismissed the Prime Minister and the interim Council of Ministers for reportedly failing to organize the election. The King assumed executive power and postponed indefinitely parliamentary elections scheduled for November. In October King Gyanendra appointed a nine-member interim Government, headed by the former premier and monarchist Lok Bahadur Chand. The NCP, UML and legal experts condemned the dismissal of Deuba and his Government and the establishment of a new Council of Ministers as unconstitutional. Furthermore, the Maoist argument appeared to be strengthened by the King's act of 'feudal absolutism'. In mid-November the King disregarded demands by political parties to create a new government composed of their members, instead reorganizing and expanding the interim Council of Ministers to include a former UML member, businessmen and independents. At the same time, amid continuing violence and disruption, the Deputy Prime Minister stated that the interim Government was prepared to enter negotiations with the CPN (Maoist) and would consider the latter's demand for an elected constituent assembly. In December the human rights organization Amnesty International issued a damning report on the human rights situation in Nepal since the collapse of peace talks in November 2001. The army and Armed Police Force were severely criticized for the reported 'unprecedented levels' of human rights abuses, including torture, arbitrary detention and deaths in custody. In addition, the report accused Maoist insurgents of torturing and killing captives, taking hostages and recruiting children. The report claimed that nearly one-half of the 4,366 people who had died in the conflict since late 2001 were civilians, killed by both security forces and Maoists.

In January 2003 suspected Maoist militants shot dead the chief of the Armed Police Force, Inspector-General Krishna Mohan Shrestha, in Kathmandu; his wife and bodyguard were also killed. Three days later the CPN (Maoist) and the Government announced an immediate cease-fire and agreed to resume peace negotiations after the Government agreed to declassify Maoist activists as terrorists, to withdraw rewards offered for the arrest of Maoist leaders and to cancel international police warrants issued for the guerrilla leaders. In February a series of informal talks took place; at the end of the month the Maoists presented two conditions for the resumption of formal negotiations: the release of Maoist prisoners and the army to return to the barracks. A 22-point code of conduct was signed by the chief government negotiator and Minister of Physical Planning and Construction, Narayan Singh Pun, and the Maoist leader, Baburam Bhattarai, in mid-March. According to the code, the Government would release prisoners gradually and give Maoists equal access to the state-controlled media; there was no mention of the army moving back to the barracks, however. Both sides also agreed formally to cease hostilities. The following day a Maoist negotiator declared that, while a communist republic continued to be the CPN (Maoist)'s goal, the militant group would comply with the public's decision on the future of the monarchy. In the mean time, Chand continued unsuccessfully to involve political parties in the peace process and therefore to form a broad-based negotiating team. The political parties and the Maoists questioned the interim Government's authority to negotiate with the Maoists.

The interim Government and Maoist representatives commenced formal negotiations at the end of April 2003; it was reported that the CPN (Maoist) demanded the release of Maoist prisoners, participation in an interim government and the creation of a constituent assembly, but did not include the abolition of the monarchy in its agenda. At the second round of peace talks, which took place in May, the Government agreed to release several Maoist detainees and to restrict army troops to within 5 km of their barracks. Both sides also achieved consensus on the composition of a committee to monitor the code of conduct guiding the cease-fire. The third round of negotiations, which eventually took place on 17–19 August, ended in impasse over the Maoists' demand for an elected assembly to draft a new constitution. Although the two sides agreed to meet again in a week's time, on 27 August the leader of the CPN (Maoist), Pushpa Kamal Dahal, ended the seven-month cease-fire and withdrew from the peace process. On the following day the Government reclassified the insurgents as 'terrorists' after violent activity resumed. Thousands of people marched in Kathmandu at the end of August to urge the Government and Maoist militants to resume peace talks.

In the mean time, at the end of May 2003 Prime Minister Chand resigned in response to pressure from leaders of the major political parties. The parties (the NCP, UML, Nepal Workers' and Peasants' Party, Nepali Sadbhavan Party—Anandi Devi, and People's Front Nepal), with the support of students, had held demonstrations against the Chand Government and the King almost relentlessly. On 4 June the King appointed the monarchist and former premier Surya Bahadur Thapa as Prime Minister, rejecting the nomination by the five opposition parties of Madhav Kumar Nepal, the General Secretary of the UML. One week later the King appointed a new interim Council of Ministers, composed entirely of members of the monarchist RPP. Thapa had invited M. K. Nepal and Deuba to join the Government, but the leading politicians refused, maintaining that Thapa's appointment was unconstitutional. Opposition parties held a large demonstration in Kathmandu, demanding Thapa's resignation, the reinstatement of the legislature and the establishment of an all-party government. In late August Nepal's major political parties refused Thapa's appeal for co-operation, instead pledging to launch a new set of nation-wide protests in support for the return of parliamentary democracy. On 1 September, however, the Government banned all demonstrations or public gatherings of five or more people in the Kathmandu valley, owing to fears of infiltration by Maoist guerrillas. None the less, over a week later more than 1,000 pro-democracy protesters, including former premier G. P. Koirala, were arrested for defying the ban and taking part in a demonstration.

The CPN (Maoist) fully resumed its violent campaign in September 2003. In the same month it organized a three-day general strike, which severely affected businesses, transport services and schools throughout most of the country. In mid-September the police filed charges against 21 members of the CPN (Maoist), including Pushpa Kamal Dahal and Baburam Bhattarai, for the murder in January of the Inspector-General of the Armed Police Force and two others (see above). According to a report published at the end of October by the Nepal human rights group the Informal Sector Service Centre (INSEC), more than 1,000 people had died in the violence since the collapse of the cease-fire. Meanwhile, Dahal had issued a statement declaring that the CPN (Maoist) would, henceforth, target US-supported organizations instead of infrastructure targets. In response, the US Administration announced at the end of the month that it had banned the CPN (Maoist), listing the group as a threat to national security (the USA was already providing the Nepalese army with military assistance for its campaign against the Maoist insurgents).

In mid-November 2003 it was reported that a high-ranking Nepalese army officer had died in the violence. At the end of the month the international police agency, Interpol, issued arrest warrants for 11 senior CPN (Maoist) officials, including Dahal and Baburam Bhattarai. In mid-December the Government announced that it would grant an amnesty to anyone who surrendered by mid-February 2004. This message was dismissed by Maoist leaders; however, in a statement issued in January, the CPN (Maoist) spokesman Krishna Bahadur Mahara declared that his organization would accept a constitutional monarchy on condition that the King resigned as Supreme Commander-in-Chief of the army and that he confronted some 250 members of the armed forces who were allegedly 'working against the state'. Mahara also declared that the Maoists were ready for dialogue provided that the King and political parties were prepared for 'change without additional bloodshed'. The Maoist leader Baburam Bhattarai, however, emphasized in an interview two days later that a people's republic remained the chief aim of the CPN (Maoist). In the same month the Maoists announced the formation of autonomous people's governments in 10 districts under their control. At the end of the month the CPN (Maoist) stated that it would give priority to development in these areas, and that representatives of the King and the USA were banned from operating in districts under Maoist influence. At the same time, the Nepalese army announced that 15 soldiers had been convicted of human rights violations and other criminal activities, and sentenced to up to six years' imprisonment; six other soldiers had been dismissed from the army for illegal activity committed during military operations against Maoist guerrillas. It was reported in mid-February that more than 555 Maoist militants had surrendered to security forces since the launch of the amnesty in December 2003; the deadline of the amnesty was extended to 12 April 2004. The violence increased, meanwhile. The Maoists held intermittent nation-wide general strikes, adversely affecting businesses and schools. The number of people killed in the eight-year 'people's war' had risen sharply to more than 9,130 by mid-March, of whom more than 1,500 had died since the collapse of the cease-fire in August 2003. It was also reported that more than 250 people had 'disappeared' since August.

Meanwhile, it was reported in mid-November 2003 that the central committee of the RPP had requested Prime Minister Thapa to resign for failing to form an all-party government following his appointment. Thapa, however, maintained the support of the King and, thus, was able to remain in his position. In January 2004 there were almost daily student-led pro-republic protests in Kathmandu. At the end of the month the five main opposition parties issued a joint statement offering formal support to the student movement. This action provided evidence that the NCP, a committed supporter of the constitutional monarchy, and the UML were reconsidering their views towards the monarchy. In early February, as part of a two-week tour around the troubled mid-western region, King Gyanendra gave a public address in the city of Nepalganj. During the speech, the King appealed for an end to the insurgency and appeared to seek an active role in governing democracy. Opposition parties criticized the King, claiming that he was not committed to multi-party democracy and the constitutional monarchy, and pledged to intensify their protests against 'regression'. Prime Minister Thapa, meanwhile, announced that the interim Government was preparing to hold a general election soon. The opposition, however, maintained that the Thapa Government was illegitimate and should be replaced by an all-party government, which in turn would hold elections and enter a peace process with the Maoist militants. In March the leaders of the five main opposition parties announced that a constitutional monarchy had not been successful and that, henceforth, their movement would be directed at achieving the establishment of a republic; a debate on the relevance of the monarchy would be taken to the village level. Meanwhile, in the same month King Gyanendra reorganized and expanded the Council of Ministers. In early May the Prime Minister tendered his resignation as a result of the continuing political impasse. The resignation prompted the collapse of the entire Government; King Gyanendra authorized Thapa to remain in office in an acting capacity pending the formation of a new administration. Later in the same month the Maoists called a three-day general strike, which disrupted communications throughout the country and brought Kathmandu to a standstill. Violence during the strike resulted in the deaths of at least 45 people.

In June 2004 King Gyanendra appointed Sher Bahadur Deuba as Prime Minister for the third time. Several days later the King appointed two members of the NCP—D to the new Council of Ministers, in which Deuba held most of the portfolios. The Council was expanded in the following month, becoming a 31-member Government, which incorporated ministers from the four-party coalition (comprising the NCP—D, the UML, the RPP and the NSP) that had been formed following the resignation of Prime Minister Thapa.

In August 2004, for the first time since they had begun their campaign in 1996, the Maoists instigated a blockade of Kathmandu, stating that it would be of indefinite duration and would last until the Government released all remaining Maoist prisoners and initiated an investigation into the fates of Maoist activists who had reportedly died while in custody. The blockade was lifted after a week, reportedly in response to pleas from ordinary people, who were suffering significant hardship as the prices of food and other essential items had risen steeply. In response, at the end of the month the Government announced the formation of a peace committee, headed by Prime Minister Deuba, which it was hoped would begin peace talks with the Maoists in an attempt to end the ongoing insurgency. However, the rebels rejected a subsequent offer of peace negotiations. In September a riot in Kathmandu resulted in the deaths of two protesters, who were shot dead by police trying to control the demonstrations. An estimated 3,000 demonstrators had gathered to protest against the murder of 12 Nepalese hostages by Iraqi insurgents during the US-led campaign in Iraq.

In October 2004 the Government agreed to observe a cease-fire that had been proposed by the CPN (Maoist) for the duration of the Hindu religious festival of Dasain. Both sides were reported to have adhered, for the most part, to the halt in military operations during the nine-day festival. In the following month Prime Minister Deuba set the rebels a deadline of 13 January 2005 to commence peace talks with the Government. Deuba stated that, if the Maoists did not agree to begin discussions, he would ensure that legislative elections were held by mid-April 2005, using the mandate that had been granted to him by King Gyanendra. However, the Chairman of the CPN (Maoist), Prachanda, rejected the proposed deadline later in that month. The rejection reportedly led to disagreement within the Government over the feasibility of holding elections amidst the ongoing insurgency. The violence had intensified following the expiry of the cease-fire in late October. The Government was destabilized further in November when the founding President of the RPP, former Prime Minister Thapa, announced that he intended to launch a new political party, effectively creating a split within the RPP.

In February 2005 the political situation in Nepal deteriorated further when King Gyanendra abruptly dismissed Prime Minister Deuba and his Government, declared an indefinite state of emergency in the kingdom and announced that, henceforth, he would rule Nepal directly. All communications links into and out of Nepal were severed temporarily, censorship was imposed on the media and former ministers were placed under house arrest. The King claimed that his actions were a result of the Prime Minister's failure to halt the Maoist insurgency and to hold legislative elections in the country. In an attempt to prevent protests, the King ordered the detention of large numbers of political activists. Maoist rebels subsequently instigated a two-week blockade of national highways in protest at the King's actions. Shortly after he had assumed power, the King appointed a new, 10-member Council of Ministers, under his chairmanship. Former Prime Ministers Dr Tulsi Giri and Kirti Nidhi Bista were appointed to serve as Vice-Chairmen. King Gyanendra's assumption of power met with an unfavourable international response, with Nepal's key allies, India and the United Kingdom, suspending military aid to the country and several countries recalling their ambassadors from Nepal in protest.

In March 2005 Thapa announced the foundation of his new political party, the Rashtriya Jana Shakti Party (RJP—National People's Power Party). In the same month several political leaders who had been detained following the royal coup were released from house arrest, including former Prime Minister Deuba. Meanwhile, protests against the King's actions, orchestrated by an opposition alliance comprising five of the country's main political parties, gathered momentum. At the same time, the Maoist insurgency intensified, with several clashes taking place between rebels and government troops. The state of emergency was lifted at the end of April, although there were few indications that normal political activity would be able to resume. Public meetings and demonstrations continued to be prohibited, and police powers of arrest and detention were extended. Meanwhile, former Prime Minister Deuba was rearrested and charged with corruption offences by the newly established Royal Commission for Corruption Control (RCCC). Deuba refused to acknowledge the legitimacy of the body.

In May 2005 seven political parties, including the NCP, announced a joint agenda for the restoration of democracy in Nepal, calling for King Gyanendra to end his period of direct rule and for the House of Representatives, which had been dissolved in 2002, to be recalled. Later that month the alliance organized a demonstration in Kathmandu in protest against the King. Meanwhile, a rift was reported to have developed in the leadership of the CPN (Maoist) between its Chairman, Prachanda, and Baburam Bhattarai. Bhattarai and his wife were thought to have been suspended from the group's politburo. However, they were reportedly reinstated in July. In June Maoist rebels were responsible for the detonation of a land-mine under a bus in the southern district of Chitwan, which resulted in the deaths of 39 civilians. The Maoists subsequently apologized for the attack, claiming that the bomb had been intended to target security forces, and announced that, henceforth, all attacks on unarmed civilians would be suspended.

In June 2005 Sher Bahadur Deuba and six of his former cabinet colleagues were cleared by the RCCC of charges relating to the misappropriation of money from the Prime Minister's Relief Fund. However, Deuba remained in custody pending a further judgment against him. In the following month Deuba, along with four other defendants, was convicted of charges of embezzlement relating to the issuing of a water contract and sentenced to a two-year prison term. Meanwhile, a reorganization and expansion of the Council of Ministers took place.

In August 2005, as opposition to King Gyanendra's ongoing direct rule intensified, it was announced that the seven-party alliance had decided to begin talks with the CPN (Maoist) and to plan joint protests against the King. It cited positive gestures by the group, such as its suspension of attacks on unarmed civilians, as the reason for co-operation, having consistently maintained that it would be willing to hold discussions with the rebels if they renounced violence. In September the Maoists announced a three-month unilateral cease-fire, an offer welcomed by the international community but one to which the Government responded cautiously. By the middle of that month, according to the INSEC, 12,809 people had been killed since the beginning of the 'people's war' in 1996. In October the Government announced that elections would take place to Nepal's 58 municipal councils in February 2006. The seven-party alliance announced that it intended to boycott the polls, although two of its members, the RPP and the RJP, later announced that they had not yet decided whether to participate. Shortly afterwards King Gyanendra stated that elections to the House of Representatives would take place in April 2007. In November, following talks with the CPN (Maoist), the opposition alliance announced that it had reached a 12-point agreement with the rebels intended to try and restore democracy to Nepal. The agreement included a boycott of the February 2006 municipal elections and the election of a constituent assembly, the latter a traditional Maoist demand.

In December 2005 an extensive reorganization of the Council of Ministers took place, in which eight ministers were dismissed and several ministers from the RPP and RJP were appointed. In the same month the CPN (Maoist) announced that it would extend its cease-fire by one month. However, in January 2006 the Maoists stated that the cease-fire had come to an end, owing to the lack of response from the Government, which had continued to authorize offensive operations against them. The insurgency subsequently intensified. In the following month the municipal elections were held, taking place in only 36 of the 58 municipal councils owing to an insufficient number of candidates and during the course of a four-day general strike, co-ordinated by the Maoists, intended to disrupt the polls. Turn-out reached an estimated 20% of registered voters, according to official figures, although the major opposition parties, which boycotted the polls, claimed that the figure was significantly lower. Later that month the RCCC was outlawed, after the Supreme Court ruled that its orders were not valid. Former Prime Minister Sher Bahadur Deuba was subsequently freed from prison, having been convicted of corruption offences by the body in the previous year. In March the Maoists instigated an indefinite blockade of Kathmandu, in another attempt to force King Gyanendra to end his period of direct rule. Meanwhile, the Government offered an amnesty to any Maoist rebels who surrendered before a mid-June 2006 deadline.

In April 2006 the opposition alliance called a nation-wide general strike. Mass demonstrations followed, in response to which the Government announced the imposition of a 'shoot on sight' curfew. As thousands of protesters defied the curfew and violent clashes ensued, King Gyanendra's position appeared increasingly untenable. Following almost three weeks of popular demonstrations, the King offered to permit the opposition alliance to name a new Prime Minister. However, this offer was rejected and the protests continued to escalate. Several days later, in accordance with opposition demands, the King announced that he would reinstate Parliament, thus quelling the unrest. The Maoists rejected the royal offer and vowed to continue their insurgency, accusing the political parties of betraying the 12-point agreement. They did, however, agree to observe a three-month cease-fire. The opposition alliance subsequently nominated former Prime Minister Girija Prasad Koirala to lead a new Government. The House of Representatives formally convened later in that month and approved legislation enabling the formation of a constituent assembly to redraft the country's Constitution.

In 1978 the old Trade and Transit Treaty between Nepal and India was replaced by two treaties (renewed in the mid-1980s), the one concerning bilateral trade between the two countries, the other allowing Nepal to develop trade with other countries via India. Relations with India deteriorated considerably in March 1989, however, when India decided not to renew the treaties, insisting that a common treaty covering both issues be negotiated. Nepal refused, stressing the importance of keeping the treaties separate, on the grounds that trade issues are negotiable, whereas the right of transit is a recognized basic right of land-locked countries. In response, India closed 13 of the 15 transit points through which most of Nepal's trade is conducted. Severe shortages of food and fuel ensued. It was widely believed that a major issue aggravating the dispute was Nepal's purchase of weapons (including anti-aircraft guns) from the People's Republic of China in 1988, which, according to India, violated the Treaty of Peace and Friendship concluded by India and Nepal in 1950. Diplomatic relations between Nepal and India remained strained throughout 1989, with trade at a virtual standstill. Following several rounds of senior-level talks, a joint communiqué was signed by the two countries in June 1990, restoring trade relations and reopening the transit points, and assuring mutual consultations on matters of security. A few days earlier, as an apparent gesture of goodwill to India, the Nepalese

Government had told the Chinese Government to defer indefinitely the delivery of the final consignment of weapons destined for Nepal. The visit to Kathmandu by the Indian Prime Minister in February 1991 (the first official visit to Nepal by an Indian head of government since 1977) helped to reaffirm the traditionally amicable ties between the two countries. Separate trade and transit treaties (valid for five and seven years respectively) were signed during a visit by Prime Minister Koirala to India in December 1991; these treaties were both subsequently renewed on expiry. A major breakthrough in Indo-Nepalese relations was achieved in February 1996, when the Prime Ministers of the two countries formally signed a treaty in New Delhi regarding the shared utilization of the waters of the Mahakali River basin (for irrigation, general consumption and the production of hydroelectric power). The costs and benefits of the project, which involved the construction of a massive hydroelectric power plant, were to be divided between Nepal and India, although not, some critics claimed, to Nepal's benefit. During a visit to Nepal by the Indian Prime Minister in June 1997, the Mahakali Treaty was formally endorsed and India granted Nepal access to Bangladeshi ports through a new transit facility across Indian territory via the Karkavita-Phulbari road (this facility was extended and improved in 1998). Some tension in Indo-Nepalese relations, nevertheless, remained; this centred on border demarcation disputes and, in particular, on the Indian border police's use of territory that Nepal claims as its own in the far west of the country (namely the strategically-situated Kalapani junction between India, Nepal and China, which covers an area of about 35 sq km). In early August 2000 Prime Minister Koirala paid a visit to India and succeeded in improving Indo-Nepalese relations, which had been strained by the hijacking of an Indian Airlines aircraft from Kathmandu in December 1999. Although Nepal was keen to renegotiate the Treaty of Peace and Friendship concluded by Nepal and India in 1950, India agreed to discuss the treaty only at foreign secretary level; therefore, it was unlikely that a solution would be achieved in the immediate future. In late 2001 India supplied Nepal with two helicopters and arms to assist the neighbouring country in its struggle against the Maoist insurgency. India repeated its offer of financial assistance in early 2002. In March both countries extended for five years the 1996 bilateral trade treaty. The Nepalese and Indian Governments also held talks on the civil disorder problem in Nepal; India promised to provide the necessary support. From early 2003, however, the Indian Government became increasingly concerned about King Gyanendra's perceived disregard for democracy. In February 2005 its concerns were realized when the King dismissed the Government and assumed executive power. India condemned the King's actions and suspended military aid to Nepal. It also intensified security along the shared border, owing to increased fears of infiltration by Maoist insurgents and their possible co-operation with rebels operating in India's fractious north-eastern states. In July India resumed non-lethal military aid to Nepal. In January 2006 the bilateral transit treaty expired; in order to allow time for a review of the agreement, India subsequently extended the term of the treaty by three months.

The People's Republic of China has contributed a considerable amount to the Nepalese economy, and the first meeting of a joint committee on economic co-operation took place in 1984. This committee met for a second time (and thenceforth annually) in Kathmandu in 1986, when China agreed to increase its imports from Nepal in order to minimize trade imbalances. Relations between Nepal and China improved further during the late 1980s and 1990s, as indicated by reciprocal visits made by high-ranking Nepalese and Chinese officials (notably, a state visit to Nepal was conducted by the Chinese President, Jiang Zemin, in 1996). In May 2001 the leaders of Nepal and China signed a six-point co-operation agreement to improve cross-border trade, increase road and aviation links and to promote tourism. In March 2005 the Chinese Minister of Foreign Affairs became the most senior foreign official to visit Nepal since King Gyanendra's declaration of direct rule in the previous month.

In 1985 it was agreed that Nepal's border with Tibet (the Xizang Autonomous Region) should be opened. Following the outbreak of ethnic violence in Tibet in 1989, however, the border between Nepal and Tibet was closed indefinitely. The Nepalese authorities have been consistent in their commitment to the 'One China' policy and in their efforts to repatriate refugees fleeing from Tibet. In 1993 G. P. Koirala paid an informal visit to Tibet—the first visit to the region by a Nepalese Premier since the 1950s. In 1995, however, the Nepalese authorities banned a proposed peace march by Tibetans through Nepalese territory. During a visit to China by the Nepalese Minister of Foreign Affairs in August 2000, an agreement was reached to allow Nepal greater use of a new road in Tibet. Greater technological and economic co-operation was also achieved, therefore noticeably increasing bilateral trade. Nepal provoked strong criticism from the UN and Western governments in late May 2003, after it helped Chinese officials to deport 18 Tibetan refugees from Kathmandu to Tibet. Nepal's usual policy was to transfer Tibetan refugees to officials of the UN High Commissioner for Refugees (UNHCR). It was reported in late June that a further 19 Tibetans had been arrested in the western Nepalese district of Accham.

Ties with Bangladesh are also significant, particularly regarding the utilization of joint water resources. Large-scale migration from Bangladesh has resulted in a notable demographic transformation in Nepal, with the Muslim population increasing from around 4% of the total in the early 1990s to, unofficially, about 10% by the end of the decade. In January 2001 the Nepalese Minister of Foreign Affairs visited Bangladesh, where agreements on greater economic and transport co-operation were reached. In December 1982 Nepal and Pakistan strengthened their trade links by renewing a 1962 agreement, and in 1983 they established a joint economic commission and a regular air link. In March 2005 the joint economic commission met for the first time in 10 years, when a delegation of Pakistani economic officials visited Nepal.

In late 1991 thousands of Bhutanese of Nepalese origin began to arrive at refugee camps in eastern Nepal, following the outbreak of political and ethnic unrest in Bhutan. By early 1996 nearly 100,000 refugees were living in eight camps in the districts of Jhapa and Morang. In the first half of 1993 talks were held between Bhutanese and Nepalese government officials regarding proposals to resolve the issues at stake. The Nepalese Government steadfastly refused to consider any solution that did not include the resettlement in Bhutan of all ethnic Nepalese refugees living in the camps. This proposal was rejected by the Bhutanese Government, which claimed that the majority of the camp population were not actually Bhutanese. The deadlock was apparently broken, however, when a joint statement was signed by the Ministers of Home Affairs of Bhutan and Nepal in July, which committed each side to establishing a 'high-level joint committee' to work towards a settlement (including the categorization of the refugees). In a notable shift in strategy, in January 1996 the Nepalese Government transferred the responsibility of handling the Bhutanese refugee problem from the Ministry of Home Affairs to the Ministry of Foreign Affairs. In April 1997 more than 10,000 Bhutanese refugees gathered at a mass demonstration in the eastern Nepalese town of Damak to call for UN intervention in the crisis. They also demanded that the Nepal Government either resolve the refugee problem or, failing that, 'internationalize' it. Nepal and Bhutan finally achieved a breakthrough at the 10th round of negotiations in December 2000. Both countries agreed that nationality would be verified on the basis of the head of the refugee family for those over 25 years of age. Refugees under 25 years of age would be verified on an individual basis. By the end of January 2001 a Joint Verification Team (JVT) had concluded the inspection of refugee camps; verification of 98,897 people claiming refugee status (including 13,000 minors born in the camp) began at the end of March, commencing with the Khudanabari camp. The Nepalese press criticized the JVT for being too slow: by early July the status of 4,128 individuals had been verified. In late 2001 the verification of individuals in the Khudanabari camp was completed. However, despite two further rounds of negotiations, the process reached a standstill in early 2002, with Bhutan reluctant to accept the individuals already verified, and both Governments undecided over the most suitable way to continue the verification process.

In January 2003 Bhutan hosted the 12th ministerial joint committee (MJC), at which the two Governments finally harmonized their positions on each of the four categories. The 14th MJC in May resolved all the remaining issues in order to finalize the categorization process. Details of the results of the verification process at Khudanabari were published on 18 June: 74 families (293 people) were in Category I (forcefully evicted Bhutanese people); 2,182 families (8,595 people) were in Category II (Bhutanese who had emigrated); 817 families (2,948 people) were in Category III (non-Bhutanese people); and 85 families (347 people) were in Category IV (Bhutanese who had committed criminal acts). Despite the new Nepalese Government from late May criticizing the agreements and several political parties in

Nepal calling for the Nepalese Government to repudiate the deal, arrangements were being made to conduct the repatriation to Bhutan of most of the families in Category I by the end of 2003. The 15th MJC, held in Thimphu, Bhutan, in October, was hailed as very successful by the leader of Nepal's delegation. It was agreed at the meeting that the JVT would return to the Nepalese district of Jhapa in November to review the remaining appeals from people in the Khudunabari camp and then begin verification of the Sanischare camp. The committee also decided that Bhutan would be fully responsible for any Category I persons, while Category II people could apply for either Bhutanese or Nepalese citizenship, in accordance with the respective laws. Any appeals by people in Category III were to be resolved by the end of January 2004. However, on 23 December 2003 the Bhutanese members of the JVT, while explaining the remaining procedures to Sector A residents of the Khudanabari camp, were attacked by several thousand other camp members protesting against the terms and conditions of the agreement. The JVT members were subsequently withdrawn to Thimphu. The attack, described by a Nepalese government spokesman as regrettable, was discussed by the two administrations at the South Asian Association for Regional Co-operation (SAARC, see p. 356) summit meeting in early January. In March 2004 Teknath Rizal, Chairman of the Human Rights Council of Bhutan, began a hunger strike in Nepal, intended to draw international attention to the plight of the refugees. The strike ended in the following month, after Rizal had received assurances from the Nepalese Government that it would attempt to enlist the involvement of UNHCR and India in restarting the stalled repatriation process. In September Rizal led a Nepalese delegation to the headquarters of UNHCR in Geneva, Switzerland, in an attempt to raise the international profile of the refugees. In October US Assistant Secretary of State for Population, Refugees and Migration, Arthur Dewey, visited the area and held discussions on how best to resolve the stalemate. However, in early 2006 it appeared unlikely that there would be any swift resumption of the registration process, owing mainly to the political instability in Nepal.

Nepal pursues a non-aligned foreign policy, and had diplomatic relations with 117 countries in late 2005. Nepal (with six other countries) is a founder member of SAARC, formally established in 1985; the Association's permanent secretariat was established in Kathmandu in 1987. Kathmandu hosted a SAARC summit meeting in January 2002, despite rising tension in the region. Nepal is a signatory to the organization's agreement on the South Asian Free Trade Area (SAFTA), which came into force in January 2006.

Government

Under the provisions of the Constitution promulgated in November 1990, Nepal is a constitutional monarchy. The Constitution provides for a bicameral Parliament, comprising a 205-member House of Representatives (Pratinidhi Sabha) and a 60-member National Assembly (Rashtriya Sabha), as the supreme legislative body. The House of Representatives is elected for a five-year term, and members of the National Assembly hold office for a six-year term. Executive power is vested in the King and the Council of Ministers, which is answerable to the House of Representatives. The King appoints the leader of the party that commands a majority in the House of Representatives as Prime Minister, while other ministers are appointed, from among the members of Parliament, on the recommendation of the Prime Minister.

For the purposes of local administration, Nepal is divided into five development regions, 14 zones, 75 districts, 3,913 village development committees and 58 municipalities.

Defence

In August 2005 Nepal's total armed forces numbered 69,000 men. Paramilitary forces numbered 62,000 men. Military service is voluntary. An Armed Police Force was formed in 2001 to counteract the Maoist insurgency and numbered 15,000 in August 2005. The defence budget for 2004/05 was projected at NRs 10,400m.

Economic Affairs

In 2004, according to estimates by the World Bank, Nepal's gross national income (GNI), measured at average 2002–04 prices, was US $6,538m., equivalent to $260 per head (or $1,470 per head on an international purchasing-power parity basis). During 1995–2004, it was estimated, the population increased at an average annual rate of 2.3%, while gross domestic product (GDP) per head increased, in real terms, by an average of 1.6% per year. Overall GDP increased, in real terms, at an average annual rate of 4.0% in 1995–2004. According to official figures, real GDP increased by 3.4% in 2003/04 and by 2.5% in 2004/05.

Agriculture (including forestry and fishing) contributed an estimated 38.3% of GDP in the fiscal year ending 15 July 2005. The sector engaged an estimated 92.9% of the employed labour force in 2003. The principal crops are rice, maize, millet, wheat, sugar cane, potatoes and vegetables and melons. According to the Asian Development Bank (ADB, see p. 169), during 1995–2004 agricultural GDP increased by an average of 3.4% per year. The agricultural sector grew by 3.9% in 2003/04 and by 2.8% in 2004/05.

Industry (comprising mining, manufacturing, construction and utilities) employed only 9.8% of the labour force in 1999, but provided an estimated 21.2% of GDP in 2004/05. About 60% of Nepal's industrial output comes from traditional cottage industries, and the remainder from modern industries. During 1995–2004 industrial GDP increased at an average annual rate of 4.0%. Industrial production increased by 1.0% in 2003/04 and by 0.7% in 2004/05.

Mining employed only 0.08% of the labour force in 1999, and contributed an estimated 0.5% of GDP in 2004/05. Mining GDP increased at an average annual rate of 4.1% in 1995–2004. Mica is mined east of Kathmandu, and there are also small deposits of lignite, copper, talc, limestone, cobalt and iron ore. Geophysical investigations have indicated that the Siwalik range and the Terai belt are potential prospective areas for petroleum.

Manufacturing contributed an estimated 7.8% of GDP in 2004/05, and employed about 5.8% of the labour force in 1999. Manufacturing GDP increased by an average annual rate of 3.1% in 1995–2004. Manufacturing production increased by 1.7% in 2003/04 and by 2.8% in 2004/05. The principal branches of the sector include textiles, particularly carpets and rugs, food products, wearing apparel and tobacco products. Traditional cottage industries include basket-making and the production of cotton fabrics and edible oils.

Energy is derived principally from traditional sources (particularly fuelwood). Imports of mineral fuel and lubricants (mainly for the transport sector), however, comprised an estimated 16.1% of the cost of total imports in 2003/04. In addition, Nepal's rivers are exploited for hydroelectric power (HEP) production, but in July 2002 it was estimated that only about 1% of the country's huge potential generating capacity (83m. kW) was being utilized. In January 2004 the 144,000-kW Kali Gandaki A HEP plant was officially inaugurated. The project, the country's largest, began generating electricity in 2002. Nepal was hoping to export excess electricity to India. Several other HEP projects were under construction in the early 2000s. In August 2004 Cairn Energy Co of the United Kingdom signed an agreement with the Nepalese Government to explore for oil and gas in a 22,000-sq km area in the Terai plain, near the border with India.

The services sector employed 14.0% of the labour force in 1999. The sector contributed an estimated 40.4% of GDP in 2004/05. The GDP of the services sector increased at an average annual rate of 4.4% in 1995–2004. Sectoral GDP increased by 4.0% in 2003/04 and by 2.1% in 2004/05. By 1996 tourism had emerged as Nepal's major source of foreign exchange; in 1999/2000 revenue from tourism amounted to 12.9% of total foreign-exchange earnings. The ongoing Maoist insurgency has affected visitor levels in the early 2000s. In 2003 tourist arrivals showed some improvement, with 338,132 tourists visiting Nepal in that year. Arrivals increased further in 2004, reaching 385,297. However, in 2005 arrivals declined by 2.5%, to 375,501, owing to the King's assumption of power in February and a concomitant deterioration in the domestic security situation, reflected in a particularly significant decrease in arrivals in the first five months of that year.

In 2004 Nepal recorded a visible trade deficit of US $1,048.9m., and there was a surplus of $51.7m. on the current account of the balance of payments. In 2004/05 India was the principal source of imports (supplying 64.9% of the total) and the principal market for exports (67.7%). Other major trading partners were the People's Republic of China, the USA and Germany. The principal exports in 2003/04 were basic manufactures, manufactured goods and articles and garments. The principal imports were basic manufactures, machinery and transport equipment, and mineral fuels and lubricants.

In 2003/04 there was an estimated overall budget deficit of NRs 16,318m. (equivalent to 3.1% of GDP). Foreign aid plays a vital role in the Nepalese economy. Nepal's total external debt was US $3,253m. at the end of 2003, of which $3,176m. was long-term public debt. In that year the cost of debt-servicing was equivalent to 6.0% of receipts from exports of goods and services. The annual rate of inflation averaged 5.7% in 1995–2004. Inflation increased by 4.0% in 2003/04 and by 3.6% in 2004/05. According to the ADB, in 1999/2000 47% of Nepali workers were underemployed, while urban unemployment, a major problem, particularly among educated youths, stood at 7%.

Nepal is a member of the UN Economic and Social Commission for Asia and the Pacific (ESCAP, see p. 33), the ADB, of the Colombo Plan (see p. 385) and of the South Asian Association for Regional Co-operation (SAARC, see p. 356), all of which seek to encourage regional economic development. Nepal became the 147th member of the World Trade Organization (WTO, see p. 370) in April 2004.

With an inhospitable terrain, comprising isolated valleys and very high mountains, Nepal is among the least developed countries in the world. Successive administrations since 1991 have followed a policy of economic liberalization: many state enterprises have been privatized (although there have been numerous delays in the process), and there have been attempts to reduce the fiscal deficit, to increase revenue mobilization, to restructure and improve the financial sector, and to institute and operate open trade and investment policies. In February 1993, as part of a series of economic reforms introduced in an attempt to develop industry further and to increase exports to countries other than India, the Nepalese rupee was made fully convertible for current-account transactions. In 2001/02, for the first time in 19 years, Nepal's GDP registered a negative growth rate: the economy contracted by 0.6%. Tourism and foreign trade fared particularly poorly, owing to a worsening internal security situation, regional tension and the suicide attacks on the USA. In 2002 the interim Government launched the Tenth Five-Year Plan, which aimed for a 4.3%–6.2% growth rate during 2002–07. One of the objectives of the plan was to reduce the level of poverty to 30% from 42%. In November 2003 the IMF approved a three-year US $72m. Poverty Reduction and Growth Facility for Nepal, in support of the country's poverty reduction strategies. By 2003/04 the level of poverty had declined to 31%, owing in part to an increase in remittances from Nepalese workers overseas. The country's accession to the WTO in April 2004 would, it was hoped, lead to the further integration of Nepal into the global economy. However, the expiry at the beginning of 2005 of the WTO's Multi-fibre Arrangement, which imposed quotas upon textile exports from developing countries, had a significant impact upon the country's garment industry; garment exports declined sharply over the course of the year. The 2005/06 budget, introduced in July 2005, envisaged a significant increase in spending on development, and in particular on the ongoing efforts to alleviate poverty; the projected deficit was equivalent to 2% of GDP. Nepal's short-term economic prospects were negatively affected by the deterioration in the political situation in February 2005, when King Gyanendra dismissed the Government and declared a state of emergency in Nepal. The subsequent withdrawal of a significant amount of international aid, together with a further deterioration in the country's security situation, adversely affected economic performance. Meanwhile, foreign investment in Nepal remained negligible, with significant reforms needed if the country's attractiveness as an investment destination was to increase. In August 2005 Unilever Nepal was forced to close its soap-making factory in the country, having been unable to meet demands from Maoists and trade unions for wage rises for its employees. Furthermore, the ongoing Maoist insurgency continued to impede the progress of many development activities in the country. Overseas remittances were an increasingly important source of foreign exchange, totalling the equivalent of an estimated 12% of GDP in 2004/05, and played an important part in ensuring that the current account of the balance of payments remained in surplus. The IMF forecast GDP growth of between 2.5% and 3.5% in 2005/06, but stressed that future economic performance would depend upon the speed with which the Maoist insurgency was resolved and the ability of the Government to implement critical reforms.

Education

Primary education, beginning at six years of age and lasting for five years, is officially compulsory and is provided free of charge in government schools. Secondary education, beginning at the age of 11, lasts for a further seven years, comprising a first cycle of three years (lower secondary), a second of two years (secondary) and a third of two years (higher secondary). In 2000/01 the total enrolment at primary and secondary schools was equivalent to an estimated 87% of the school-age population. Primary enrolment in that year was equivalent to 118% of children in the relevant age-group (boys 128%, girls 108%), while the comparable ratio for secondary enrolment was 51% (boys 58%, girls 43%). There are four state universities: the Tribhuvan University in Kathmandu, the Mahendra Sanskrit Viswavidyalaya in Beljhundi, Dang, the Purbanchal University and the Pokhara University. In addition, there is one private university in Banepa. Altogether, the universities had more than 120,000 students in 1999/2000. Expenditure on education by the central Government in the 2003/04 budget was NRs 14,317m. (18.6% of total spending). The Eighth Five-Year Plan (1992–97) included proposals to introduce free compulsory secondary education in phases over the next 10 years. By 2000 compulsory education had been implemented in only seven of Nepal's 75 districts.

Public Holidays

The public holidays observed in Nepal vary locally. The dates given below apply to Kathmandu.

2006: 11 January (National Unity Day), 30 January (Martyrs' Day), 2 February (Vasant Panchami—Advent of Spring Day), 19 February (Rashtriya Prajatantra Divas—National Democracy Day), 27 February (Maha Shivaratri—in honour of Lord Shiva), 28 February (Lhosar, Tibetan New Year), 14 March (Phagu Purnima—Holi Festival Day), 29 March (Ghode Jatra—Horse Festival), 6 April (Ram Nawami—Lord Ram's Birthday), 14 April (Navabarsha—New Year's Day), 1 May (Labour Day), 13 May (Lord Gautam Buddha's Birthday), 7 July (King Gyanendra's Birthday), 9 August (Janai Purnima—Sacred Thread Ceremony), 16 August (Janmashtami—Lord Krishna's Birthday, and Children's Day), 26 August (Haratalika Teej, Women's Festival), 17 September (Indra Jatra—Festival of Rain God), 23 September (Ghatasthapana and, over nine days, Dasain), 30 September (Durga Puja), 21 October (Laxmi Puja and, over three days, Diwali—Festival of Lights), 23 October (Bhai Tika—Brother's Day), 9 November (Constitution Day), 29 December (King Birendra's Birthday).

2007: 11 January (National Unity Day), 23 January (Vasant Panchami—Advent of Spring Day), 30 January (Martyrs' Day), 16 February (Maha Shivaratri—in honour of Lord Shiva), 18 February (Lhosar, Tibetan New Year), 19 February (Rashtriya Prajatantra Divas—National Democracy Day), March (Ghode Jatra—Horse Festival), 3 March (Phagu Purnima—Holi Festival Day), 27 March (Ram Nawami—Lord Ram's Birthday), 14 April (Navabarsha—New Year's Day), 1 May (Labour Day), 2 May (Lord Gautam Buddha's Birthday), 7 July (King Gyanendra's Birthday), August (Janai Purnima—Sacred Thread Ceremony), August (Children's Day), September (Haratalika Teej—Women's Festival), 4 September (Janmashtami—Lord Krishna's Birthday), 21 October (Ghatasthapana and, over nine days, Dasain), 28 October (Durga Puja Festival), October/November (Indra Jatra—Festival of Rain God), November (Bhai Tika—Brothers' Day), 9 November (Constitution Day, Laxmi Puja and, over three days, Diwali—Festival of Lights), 29 December (King Birendra's Birthday).

Weights and Measures

The metric system has been officially adopted but traditional local and Indian systems of weights and measures are widely used.

NEPAL

Statistical Survey

Source (unless otherwise stated): National Planning Commission Secretariat, Singha Durbar, POB 1284, Kathmandu; tel. (1) 4225879; fax (1) 4226500; e-mail npcs@wlink.com.np; internet www.npc.gov.np.

Area and Population

AREA, POPULATION AND DENSITY

Area (sq km)	147,181*
Population (census results)	
22 June 1991	18,491,097
22 June 2001†‡	
Males	11,563,921
Females	11,587,502
Total	23,151,423
Population (estimates at mid-year)§	
2002	23,670,000
2003	24,200,000
2004	24,740,000
Density (per sq km) at mid-2004	168.1

* 56,827 sq miles.
† Population is *de jure*.
‡ Includes estimates for certain areas in 12 districts where the census could not be conducted, owing to violence and disruption.
§ Source: Asian Development Bank, *Key Indicators of Developing Asian and Pacific Countries*.

Capital: Kathmandu, population (for urban agglomeration) 1,081,845 at 2001 census.

PRINCIPAL TOWNS
(population at 2001 census)

Kathmandu	671,846	Mahendranagar	80,839
Biratnagar	166,674	Butawal	75,384
Lalitpur	162,991	Janakpur	74,192
Pokhara	156,312	Bhaktapur	72,543
Birgunj	112,484	Hetaunda	68,482
Dharan	95,332	Dhangadhi	67,447
Bharatpur	89,323		

BIRTHS AND DEATHS
(UN estimates, annual averages)

	1990–95	1995–2000	2000–05
Birth rate (per 1,000)	38.1	34.5	30.4
Death rate (per 1,000)	11.9	9.8	8.7

Source: UN, *World Population Prospects: The 2004 Revision*.

2001 (estimates): Birth rate 33.1 per 1,000; Death rate 9.6 per 1,000.

Expectation of life (WHO estimates, years at birth): 61 (males 60; females 61) in 2003 (Source: WHO, *World Health Report*).

ECONOMICALLY ACTIVE POPULATION
(1999 labour force survey, '000 persons aged 15 years and over)

Agriculture, hunting and forestry	7,190
Fishing	13
Mining and quarrying	8
Manufacturing	553
Electricity, gas and water	26
Construction	344
Wholesale and retail trade	408
Hotels and restaurants	114
Transport, storage and communications	135
Financial intermediation	19
Real estate, renting and business activities	32
Public administration and defence	70
Education	164
Health and social work	34
Other community, social and personal services	57
Private households with employed persons	289
Extra-territorial organizations and bodies	8
Total employed	**9,463**

Source: Central Bureau of Statistics, Kathmandu.

Mid-2002 (estimates in '000): Agriculture, etc. 10,897; Total labour force 11,729.

Mid-2003 (estimates in '000): Agriculture, etc. 11,157; Total labour force 12,015.

Source: FAO.

Health and Welfare

KEY INDICATORS

Total fertility rate (children per woman, 2003)	4.2
Under-5 mortality rate (per 1,000 live births, 2004)	76
HIV/AIDS (% of persons aged 15–49, 2003)	0.5
Physicians (per 1,000 head, 2001)	0.05
Hospital beds (per 1,000 head, 1997)	0.17
Health expenditure (2002): US $ per head (PPP)	64
Health expenditure (2002): % of GDP	5.2
Health expenditure (2002): public (% of total)	27.2
Access to water (% of persons, 2002)	84
Access to sanitation (% of persons, 2002)	27
Human Development Index (2003): ranking	136
Human Development Index (2003): value	0.526

For sources and definitions, see explanatory note on p. vi.

Agriculture

PRINCIPAL CROPS
('000 metric tons)

	2002	2003	2004
Wheat	1,258	1,344	1,387
Rice (paddy)	4,133	4,456	4,290
Barley	31	32	31
Maize	1,511	1,569	1,590
Millet	283	283	283
Potatoes	1,473	1,531	1,643
Other roots and tubers*	104	105	110
Sugar cane	2,248	2,343	2,305
Beans, dry*	29	30	30
Pigeon peas*	25	25	26
Lentils	148	150	159
Other pulses	48†	48†	46*
Mustard seed	135	125	133

NEPAL

—continued

	2002	2003	2004
Garlic	16	23	28
Other vegetables and melons	1,736	1,890	1,800*
Oranges	131	139	148
Apples	32	33	34
Other fresh fruit (excl. melons)	473	510	520*
Pimento and allspice*	14	14	14
Other spices	21	22*	22*
Ginger	88	90*	90*
Jute and jute-like fibres	17	17	17
Tobacco (leaves)	4	3	3

* FAO estimate(s).
† Unofficial figure.
Source: FAO.

LIVESTOCK
('000 head, year ending September)

	2002	2003	2004
Cattle	6,979	6,954	6,966
Buffaloes	3,701	3,840	3,953
Pigs	934	932	935
Sheep	840	828	824
Goats	6,607	6,792	6,980
Chickens	21,370	22,261	23,024

Source: FAO.

LIVESTOCK PRODUCTS
('000 metric tons)

	2002	2003	2004
Beef and veal*	46.8	47.6	48.5
Buffalo meat	127.9	130.8	133.6
Mutton and lamb	2.8	2.8	2.8
Goat meat	38.6	39.7	40.5
Pig meat	15.6	15.6	15.4
Poultry meat	14.4	15.0	16.1
Cows' milk	352.1	361.6	368.5
Buffaloes' milk	806.7	834.4	863.3
Goats' milk*	64.0	64.0	65.0
Ghee*	20.1	20.2	20.2
Poultry eggs*	26.1	27.3	27.3

* FAO estimates.
Source: FAO.

Forestry

ROUNDWOOD REMOVALS
(FAO estimates, '000 cubic metres, excl. bark)

	2002	2003	2004
Sawlogs, veneer logs and logs for sleepers	1,260	1,260	1,260
Fuel wood	12,728	12,714	12,702
Total	**13,988**	**13,974**	**13,962**

Source: FAO.

SAWNWOOD PRODUCTION
('000 cubic metres, incl. railway sleepers)

	1999	2000	2001
Coniferous (softwood)*	20	20	20
Broadleaved (hardwood)	610	610	610
Total	**630**	**630**	**630**

* FAO estimates.
2002–04: Production as in 2001 (FAO estimates).
Source: FAO.

Fishing
('000 metric tons, live weight)

	2001	2002	2003
Capture	16.7	17.9	18.9
Aquaculture	16.6	17.1	17.7
Common carp	3.4	3.5	3.6
Bighead carp	2.5	2.6	2.7
Silver carp	5.0	5.2	5.3
Other cyprinids	4.8	5.0	5.1
Total catch	**33.3**	**35.0**	**36.6**

Source: FAO.

Industry

SELECTED PRODUCTS
('000 metric tons unless otherwise indicated, year ending 15 July)

	2002/03	2003/04	2004/05*
Cement	255.2	279.4	277.7
Steel rods	154.6	169.3	166.9
Jute goods	34.9	35.7	36.1
Raw sugar	94.1	96.2	97.8
Tea	9.6	11.4	12.5
Vegetable ghee	75.2	72.1	74.3
Beer and liquor (million litres)	28.0	29.4	30.3
Soft drinks (million litres)	31.6	32.5	33.7
Paper	42.1	42.8	45.3
Cigarettes ('000 million)	6.8	7.3	7.4
Cotton clothing (million metres)	1.4	1.5	1.5
Synthetic clothing (million metres)	28.6	31.2	30.1
Soap	54.6	53.8	55.1

* Provisional figures.

Source: Federation of Nepalese Chambers of Commerce and Industry, Kathmandu.

Finance

CURRENCY AND EXCHANGE RATES

Monetary Units
100 paisa (pice) = 1 Nepalese rupee (NR).

Sterling, Dollar and Euro Equivalents (30 December 2005)
£1 sterling = NRs 127.51;
US $1 = NRs 74.05;
€1 = NRs 87.36;
1,000 Nepalese rupees = £7.84 = $13.50 = €11.45.

Average Exchange Rate (rupees per US $)
2003   76.141
2004   73.674
2005   71.368

NEPAL

BUDGET
(NRs million, year ending 15 July)*

Revenue†	2001/02	2002/03	2003/04
Taxation	39,331	42,587	48,173
Taxes on income and profits	8,920	8,132	9,515
Taxes on property	1,134	1,414	1,698
Domestic taxes on goods and services	16,618	18,804	21,406
Taxes on international trade and transactions	12,659	14,236	15,555
Other revenue	9,226	12,103	12,307
Charges, fees, fines, etc.	1,987	2,368	3,377
Sales of goods and services	1,143	1,274	1,322
Dividends	2,513	2,498	2,661
Interest receipts	1,220	925	1,657
Total	**48,556**	**54,690**	**60,480**

Expenditure	2001/02	2002/03	2003/04
Regular expenditure‡	42,155	45,414	47,657
General administration	7,283	7,283	7,283
Defence	5,860	7,381	8,520
Social services	13,070	13,459	14,038
Education	10,258	10,440	10,921
Health	1,980	2,032	2,121
Economic services	2,948	3,097	3,238
Agriculture-related	508	678	679
Infrastructure	1,121	1,127	1,118
Interest payments	5,770	6,622	6,544
Other purposes	7,224	5,806	6,235
Development expenditure§	29,495	27,493	29,140
Social services	9,410	10,501	11,507
Education	2,755	2,730	3,396
Health	1,877	1,620	1,847
Provision of drinking water	1,904	2,139	2,569
Economic services	20,085	16,992	17,633
Agriculture-related	6,132	4,188	4,352
Infrastructure	9,338	9,446	9,413
Total	**71,650**	**72,907**	**76,797**

* Figures refer to the regular and development budgets of the central Government.
† Excluding grants received (NRs million, estimates): 5,800 in 2001/02; 9,600 in 2002/03; 11,300 in 2003/04.
‡ Excluding amortization payments on domestic and foreign loans.
§ Including net lending and excluding principal repayment from corporations.

Source: IMF, *Nepal: Selected Issues and Statistical Appendix* (February 2006).

2004/05 (NRs million, estimates): *Revenue:* Total 70,320. *Expenditure:* Recurrent 67,608; Capital 31,578; Total 111,690.

Source: Federation of Nepalese Chambers of Commerce and Industry, Kathmandu.

INTERNATIONAL RESERVES
(US $ million at mid-December)

	2002	2003	2004
Gold*	6.5	6.5	6.5
IMF special drawing rights	—	0.8	9.7
Reserve position in IMF	7.8	8.6	—
Foreign exchange	1,009.8	1,213.1	1,452.5
Total	**1,024.1**	**1,229.0**	**1,468.7**

* Valued at US $42.5 per troy ounce.

Source: IMF, *International Financial Statistics*.

MONEY SUPPLY
(NRs million at mid-December)*

	1998	1999	2000
Currency outside banks	32,244	36,929	44,526
Private sector deposits with monetary authorities	2,287	4,346	3,160
Demand deposits at commercial banks	10,979	13,832	15,343
Total money	**45,509**	**55,107**	**63,028**

2001: Currency outside banks 51,699; Private sector deposits 3,570.
2002: Currency outside banks 56,022; Private sector deposits 2,350.
2003: Currency outside banks 58,076; Private sector deposits 2,557.
2004: Currency outside banks 65,767; Private sector deposits 3,315.
* Excluding Indian currency in circulation.

Source: IMF, *International Financial Statistics*.

COST OF LIVING
(National Consumer Price Index; base: 2000 = 100)

	2002	2003	2004
Food (incl. beverages)	104.4	110.1	112.9
Fuel and light	106.3	122.8	130.0
Clothing (excl. footwear)	104.4	106.3	108.4
Rent	110.9	116.4	120.9
All items (incl. others)	**105.9**	**112.0**	**115.2**

Source: ILO.

NATIONAL ACCOUNTS
(NRs million at current prices, year ending 15 July)

Expenditure on the Gross Domestic Product

	2001/02	2002/03	2003/04
Government final consumption expenditure	42,327	46,362	49,568
Private final consumption expenditure	329,199	355,535	383,978
Increase in stocks	20,431	31,612	40,260
Gross fixed capital formation	81,613	86,963	95,091
Total domestic expenditure	**473,570**	**520,472**	**568,897**
Exports of goods and services	77,068	73,085	83,429
Less Imports of goods and services	127,962	137,356	156,990
GDP in purchasers' values	**422,676**	**456,201**	**495,336**
GDP at constant 1994/95 prices	**271,008**	**278,785**	**288,064**

Source: Central Bureau of Statistics, Kathmandu.

Gross Domestic Product by Economic Activity

	2002/03	2003/04*	2004/05†
Agriculture, forestry and fishing	171,104	183,357	193,291
Mining and quarrying	2,188	2,377	2,615
Manufacturing	34,337	36,634	39,494
Electricity, gas and water	10,905	11,340	12,258
Construction	45,068	49,033	52,729
Trade, restaurants and hotels	43,978	49,320	49,478
Transport, storage and communications	38,286	43,664	47,558
Finance and real estate	47,719	51,411	56,088
Community and social services	43,961	46,993	50,590
Sub-total	**437,546**	**474,129**	**504,101**
Less Imputed bank service charges	13,911	15,135	16,367
Indirect taxes, *less* subsidies	33,040	36,595	41,269
GDP in purchasers' values	**456,675**	**495,589**	**529,003**

* Revised estimates.
† Preliminary estimates.

Source: Federation of Nepalese Chambers of Commerce and Industry, Kathmandu.

NEPAL

BALANCE OF PAYMENTS
(US $ million)

	2002	2003	2004
Exports of goods f.o.b.	632.0	703.2	763.6
Imports of goods f.o.b.	−1,425.4	−1,665.9	−1,812.5
Trade balance	−793.4	−962.7	−1,048.9
Exports of services	305.2	372.1	460.9
Imports of services	−236.8	−266.2	−373.1
Balance on goods and services	−724.9	−856.8	−961.2
Other income received	56.9	48.7	63.0
Other income paid	−71.2	−69.0	−78.0
Balance on goods, services and income	−739.2	−877.1	−976.2
Current transfers received	828.1	1,022.5	1,090.6
Current transfers paid	−33.2	−25.4	−62.8
Current balance	55.6	119.9	51.7
Other investment assets	−470.4	−436.7	−350.8
Investment liabilities	71.5	67.8	−157.7
Net errors and omissions	−66.6	309.9	339.9
Overall balance	−313.4	100.6	−101.7

Source: IMF, *International Financial Statistics*.

OFFICIAL DEVELOPMENT ASSISTANCE
(US $ million)

	1998	1999	2000
Bilateral donors	218.8	212.3	234.7
Multilateral donors	189.4	138.8	155.1
Total	408.2	351.1	389.8
Grants	255.1	255.0	251.6
Loans	153.1	96.1	138.2
Per caput assistance (US $)	18.7	15.7	17.0

Source: UN, *Statistical Yearbook for Asia and the Pacific*.

External Trade

PRINCIPAL COMMODITIES
(US $ million, year ending 15 July)

Imports c.i.f.	2001/02	2002/03	2003/04
Food and live animals	82	120	116
Crude materials (inedible) except fuels	87	109	143
Mineral fuels and lubricants	305	256	297
Animal and vegetable oils and fats	102	100	117
Chemicals and pharmaceuticals	161	184	224
Basic manufactures	428	448	495
Machinery and transport equipment	254	266	348
Miscellaneous manufactured articles	74	85	69
Total (incl. others)	1,504	1,556	1,847

Exports f.o.b.	2001/02	2002/03	2003/04
Food and live animals	66	78	85
Animal and vegetable oils and fats	97	55	46
Chemicals and pharmaceuticals	43	42	52
Basic manufactures	226	229	320
Miscellaneous manufactured articles	164	222	209
Total (incl. others)	754	652	749

Exports of carpets (US $ million, year ending 15 July): 80.8 in 2001/02; 68.4 in 2002/03; 76.9 in 2003/04.

Exports of garments (US $ million, year ending 15 July): 101.8 in 2001/02; 152.8 in 2002/03; 129.4 in 2003/04.

Source: IMF, *Nepal: Selected Issues and Statistical Appendix* (February 2006).

PRINCIPAL TRADING PARTNERS
(NRs million, year ending 15 July)

Imports	2002/03	2003/04	2004/05
Australia	720.7	1,271.4	1,521.1
Belgium	1,444.0	1,125.6	824.0
China, People's Republic	9,098.8	9,299.9	12,859.2
France	1,590.2	675.5	668.5
Germany	2,278.3	1,977.9	1,570.9
Hong Kong	2,277.0	1,641.6	1,286.4
India	70,924.2	78,739.5	85,836.2
Indonesia	3,976.7	3,253.8	5,222.7
Japan	1,890.8	1,690.4	2,565.2
Korea, Republic	3,380.3	3,080.6	2,784.6
Malaysia	4,009.6	3,676.4	2,820.9
New Zealand	1,421.7	1,283.7	1,229.7
Saudi Arabia	2,364.0	2,547.9	3,138.5
Singapore	9,039.2	8,698.6	7,746.8
Taiwan	1,267.4	1,175.1	825.7
Thailand	2,989.0	4,320.2	3,117.5
United Kingdom	1,065.3	1,035.5	1,452.2
USA	1,707.7	1,433.3	1,763.6
Total (incl. others)	124,352.1	136,277.1	132,186.8

Exports	2002/03	2003/04	2004/05
China, People's Republic	1,631.0	2,348.2	1,888.5
France	454.0	581.8	617.8
Germany	3,555.3	3,567.0	3,121.7
India	26,430.0	30,777.1	39,448.4
Italy	530.8	589.4	582.8
United Kingdom	1,070.7	1,677.1	1,050.0
USA	12,686.5	9,696.0	7,570.7
Total (incl. others)	49,930.6	53,910.7	58,236.2

Source: Federation of Nepalese Chambers of Commerce and Industry, Kathmandu.

Transport

ROAD TRAFFIC
(vehicles registered)

	2000/01	2001/02	2002/03
Cars, jeeps and vans	5,152	4,374	2,906
Buses and minibuses	1,453	1,343	730
Tractors	3,519	3,189	2,485
Other agro-industrial vehicles	1,271	1,798	1,212
Motorcycles	29,291	38,522	29,404
Total (incl. others)	40,995	49,560	37,610

Source: Department of Transport Management, Kathmandu.

CIVIL AVIATION

Royal Nepal Airlines Corporation
(traffic on scheduled services)

	1999	2000	2001
Kilometres flown (million)	9	10	9
Passengers carried ('000)	583	643	641
Passenger-km (million)	1,023	1,155	1,153
Total ton-km (million)	108	121	119

Source: UN, *Statistical Yearbook*.

Tourism

FOREIGN TOURIST ARRIVALS

Country of residence	2001	2002	2003
Australia	10,711	7,179	7,916
Bangladesh	8,108	5,756	5,215
China, People's Republic	8,564	8,026	5,677
France	20,788	13,135	15,730
Germany	21,809	15,570	14,875
India	63,722	65,743	86,578
Italy	8,503	8,002	8,201
Japan	28,554	22,941	27,267
Korea, Republic	11,380	8,632	13,769
Netherlands	13,049	8,049	8,339
Sri Lanka	9,874	9,756	13,960
Thailand	5,768	5,166	11,392
United Kingdom	31,897	19,679	21,550
USA	31,440	17,076	18,871
Total (incl. others)	361,237	275,468	338,132

Tourism receipts (US $ million, incl. passenger transport): 191 in 2001; 134 in 2002; 232 in 2003.

Source: World Tourism Organization.

Foreign tourist arrivals: 385,297 (90,236 from India) in 2004 (Source: Federation of Nepalese Chambers of Commerce and Industry, Kathmandu).

Communications Media

	2002	2003	2004
Telephones ('000 main lines in use)	327.7	371.8	400.2
Mobile cellular telephones ('000 subscribers)	21.9	50.4	179.1
Personal computers ('000 in use)	85	n.a.	118
Internet users ('000)	80	n.a.	175
Daily newspapers (titles)	n.a.	251	n.a.
Non-daily newspapers (titles)	n.a.	3,490	n.a.

Facsimile machines ('000 in use, year ending 15 July): 8 in 1999.

Radio receivers ('000 in use): 840 in 1997.

Television receivers ('000 in use): 170 in 2000; 193 in 2001.

Sources: UNESCO, *Statistical Yearbook*; International Telecommunication Union.

Education

(2004)

	Institutions*	Teachers	Students
Primary	24,746	101,483	4,030,045
Lower Secondary	7,436	25,962	1,444,997
Secondary	4,547	20,232	543,764

* Including duplication, since many schools offer education at more than one level. The total number of primary, lower secondary and secondary institutions was 26,277.

Pre-primary: 1,471 institutions, 257,121 students in 2003.

Source: Ministry of Education and Sports, Kathmandu.

Adult literacy rate (UNESCO estimates): 48.6% (males 62.7%; females 34.9%) in 2003 (Source: UN Development Programme, *Human Development Report*).

Directory

The Constitution

In May 2006, prior to the convention of a Constituent Assembly, the House of Representatives approved a provisional proclamation significantly curtailing the powers of the King. All existing constitutional provisions that contradicted the proclamation were to be nullified. The most significant declarations of the proclamation were: that Nepal would henceforth be designated a secular state; that all legislative powers in the country would be exercised by the House of Representatives; that all executive authority in Nepal would reside within the Council of Ministers; that the Council of State (Raj Parishad) would be abolished; that the 'Royal Nepal Army' would be renamed the 'Nepali Army'; that the monarch would no longer hold the position of Supreme Commander-in-Chief of the Royal Nepal Army; that the monarch would no longer possess the authority to enact laws concerning the royal succession; that the monarch's acts could henceforth be challenged by both the House of Representatives and the court; and that sessions of the House of Representatives should no longer be convened by the monarch but by the Speaker, on the advice of the Prime Minister. This proclamation effectively overrode the Constitution promulgated by the King on 9 November 1990, the main provisions of which are summarized below:

The preamble to the Constitution envisages the guarantee of the fundamental rights of every citizen and the protection of his liberty, the consolidation of parliamentary government, the constitutional monarchy and the multi-party system, and the provision of an independent judicial system. Sovereignty resides in the Nepalese people. The Constitution is the fundamental law of the land.

Nepal is a multi-ethnic, multi-lingual, democratic, independent, indivisible, sovereign, Hindu and constitutional monarchical kingdom. Nepali is recognized as the national and official language.

FUNDAMENTAL RIGHTS

Part Three of the Constitution provides for the fundamental rights of the citizen: all citizens are equal before the law; no discrimination is to be practised on the basis of religion, race, sex, caste, tribe or ideology; no person can be deprived of his liberty except in accordance with the law; capital punishment remains abolished; freedom of expression, freedom to assemble peaceably and without arms, freedom to form trade unions and associations, and freedom of movement are also guaranteed. Similarly, pre-censorship of publications is prohibited and, thus, the right to press and publications is ensured. In the sphere of criminal justice, the following rights are specified in the Constitution: no person is to be punished unless made punishable by law; no person may be tried more than once for the same offence; no one is compelled to testify against himself; no one is to be given punishment greater than that which the law at the time of the offence has prescribed; cruelty to detainees is prohibited; no person is to be detained without having first been informed about the grounds for such an action; and the detainee must appear before the judicial authorities within 24 hours of his arrest. In addition, provision has also been made to compensate any person who is wrongfully detained. A person's right to property is ensured, and the right to protect and promote one's own language, script and culture, as well as the right to education up to primary level in the child's mother tongue, have been safeguarded. Similarly, the right to practise religion and to manage and protect religious places and trusts has been granted to the country's various religious groups. The right to secrecy and inviolability of the person, residence, property, documents, letters and other information is also guaranteed.

GOVERNMENT AND LEGISLATURE

His Majesty the King is the symbol of Nepalese nationality and of the unity of the people of Nepal. The expenditures and the privileges relating to His Majesty and the royal family are determined by law. His Majesty's income and property are exempt from tax.

NEPAL

The executive powers of the country are vested in His Majesty and the Council of Ministers. The direction, supervision and conduct of the general administration of the Kingdom of Nepal are the responsibility of the Council of Ministers. All official duties undertaken by His Majesty, except those which are within his exclusive domain or which are performed on the recommendation of some other institutions or officials, are discharged only on the advice of, and with the consent of, the Council of Ministers. His Majesty appoints the leader of the party that commands a majority in the House of Representatives as Prime Minister, while other Ministers are appointed, from among the members of Parliament, on the recommendation of the Prime Minister. The Council of Ministers is answerable to the House of Representatives. In the event that no single party holds an outright majority in the House, the member who commands a working majority on the basis of the support of two or more parties shall be asked to form the Government. Should this also not be the case, His Majesty may ask a member of the party with the largest number of deputies to form the Government. In the event of these exceptional circumstances, the leader forming the Government must obtain a vote of confidence in the House within 30 days. If such confidence is lacking, His Majesty is to dissolve the House and to order a fresh election to be held within six months. The Parliament is bicameral, comprising the House of Representatives and the National Assembly. His Majesty, the House of Representatives and the National Assembly together form the Parliament of the country. The House of Representatives has 205 members, and all persons who have attained the age of 18 years are eligible to vote for candidates, on the basis of adult franchise. The National Assembly has 60 members, consisting of 10 nominees of His Majesty, 35 members, including three female members, elected by the House of Representatives, and 15 members elected by the electoral college, which includes the heads of the local committees of various development regions. The tenure of office of the members of the House of Representatives is five years, and that of the members of the National Assembly six years.

THE JUDICIARY

The judicial system has three tiers: the Supreme Court, the Appellate Courts and the District Courts. The Supreme Court is the principal Court and is also a Court of Record. The Supreme Court consists of a Chief Justice and 14 other judges. The appointment of the Chief Justice is made on the recommendation of the Constitutional Council, while other judges of the Supreme Court, the Appellate Courts and the District Courts are nominated on the recommendation of the Judicial Council. All judges are appointed by His Majesty on such recommendations.

OTHER INSTITUTIONS

The Constitution also makes provisions for the establishment of a Council of State (Raj Parishad) and its standing committee, a Public Service Commission, Auditor General, Election Commission, Attorney-General, Abuse of Authority Investigation Commission, etc.

POLITICAL PARTIES

Political parties are required to register with the Election Commission, and, to be officially recognized, at least 5% of the candidates presented by a party must be female and the party should obtain at least 3% of the total votes cast at the election to the House of Representatives. It has been specifically provided that no law that bans, or imposes restrictions on, political parties may be enacted.

EMERGENCY PROVISIONS

If and when there is a grave emergency in the country, caused by threat to the sovereignty, indivisibility or security of the country (owing to war, foreign aggression, armed revolt or extreme economic depression), His Majesty may declare a state of emergency in the country. Such a declaration must obtain the approval of the House of Representatives within three months. During the period of emergency, fundamental rights, with the exception of the right of recourse to *habeas corpus*, may be suspended.

AMENDMENTS

The Constitution may be amended by a two-thirds' majority in each House of Parliament. No changes, however, would be allowed to alter the spirit of the preamble.

DEFENCE

His Majesty is the Supreme Commander-in-Chief of the Royal Nepal Army. The Royal Nepal Army is administered and deployed by His Majesty on the recommendation of the National Defence Council. The Commander-in-Chief is appointed on the recommendation of the Prime Minister. The National Defence Council consists of the Prime Minister, as Chairman, the Minister of Defence and the Commander-in-Chief.

Official matters that involve, *inter alia*, the subjects of defence and strategic alliance, the boundaries of the Kingdom of Nepal, agreements on peace and friendship, and treaties concerning the utilization and distribution of natural resources, have to be approved by a two-thirds' majority of the members of both Houses in a joint session of Parliament.

The Government

HEAD OF STATE

King: HM King GYANENDRA BIR BIKRAM SHAH DEV (succeeded to the throne 4 June 2001).

COUNCIL OF MINISTERS
(May 2006)

Prime Minister and Minister of Defence, of the Royal Palace, of Health, of Population and of Industry, Commerce and Supplies: GIRIJA PRASAD KOIRALA.

Deputy Prime Minister and Minister of Foreign Affairs: K. P. SHARMA OLI.

Minister of Finance: Dr RAM SHARAN MAHAT.

Minister of Law, Justice and Parliamentary Affairs: NARENDRA BIKRAM NEMWANG.

Minister of Agriculture and Co-operatives: MAHANTHA THAKUR.

Minister of Home Affairs: KRISHNA SITAULA.

Minister of Land Reform and Management: PRABHU NARAYAN CHAUDHARI.

Minister of Physical Planning and Works: GOPAL MAN SHRESTHA.

Minister of Local Development: RAJENDRA PANDEY.

Minister of Culture, Tourism and Civil Aviation: PRADIP GYANWALI.

Minister of Education and Sports: MANGAL SIDDHI MANANDHAR.

In addition, there are six State Ministers.

MINISTRIES

Prime Minister's Office: Singha Durbar, Kathmandu; e-mail info@pmo.gov.np; internet www.pmo.gov.np.

Ministry of Agriculture and Co-operatives: Singha Durbar, Kathmandu; tel. (1) 4225108; fax (1) 4225825; e-mail moa@fert.mos.com.np; internet www.moac.gov.np.

Ministry of Culture, Tourism and Civil Aviation: Singha Durbar, Kathmandu; tel. (1) 4225870; fax (1) 4227758; e-mail motca@ntc.net.np; internet www.tourism.gov.np.

Ministry of Defence: Singha Durbar, Kathmandu; tel. (1) 4228089; fax (1) 4228204; e-mail info@rna.mil.np; internet www.rna.mil.np.

Ministry of Education and Sports: Keshar Mahal, Kantipath, Kathmandu; tel. (1) 4411599; fax (1) 4412460; e-mail infomoe@most.gov.np; internet www.moe.gov.np.

Ministry of Finance: Foreign Aid Co-ordination Division, POB 12845, Kathmandu; tel. (1) 4259837; internet www.facd.gov.np.

Ministry of Foreign Affairs: Shital Niwas, Maharajganj, Kathmandu; tel. (1) 4416011; fax (1) 4416016; e-mail mofa@mos.com.np; internet www.mofa.gov.np.

Ministry of Forest and Soil Conservation: Singha Durbar, Kathmandu; tel. (1) 4224892; fax (1) 4223868; internet www.biodiv-nepal.gov.np.

Ministry of General Administration: Harihar Bhavan, Lalitpur; tel. (1) 5525183; fax (1) 5523358; e-mail moga@wlink.com.np; internet www.moga.gov.com.np.

Ministry of Health: Ramshah Path, Kathmandu; tel. (1) 4262587; fax (1) 4262543; e-mail info@moh.gov.np; internet www.moh.gov.np.

Ministry of Home Affairs: Singha Durbar, Kathmandu; tel. (1) 4226996; fax (1) 4227186; e-mail homehmg@wlink.com.np; internet www.moha.gov.np.

Ministry of Industry, Commerce and Supplies: Singha Durbar, Kathmandu; tel. (1) 4251174; fax (1) 4220319; internet www.moics.gov.np.

Ministry of Information and Communications: Singha Durbar, Kathmandu; tel. (1) 4220150; fax (1) 4221729; e-mail moichmg@ntc.net.np; internet www.moic.gov.np.

Ministry of Labour and Transport Management: Tridevi Marg, Kathmandu; tel. (1) 4419252; fax (1) 4419251; internet www.moltm.gov.np.

Ministry of Land Reform and Management: Singha Durbar, Kathmandu; tel. (1) 4221660; fax (1) 4220108.

NEPAL

Ministry of Law, Justice and Parliamentary Affairs: Singha Durbar, Kathmandu; tel. (1) 4222847; fax (1) 4243025; e-mail molaw@wlink.com.np; internet www.moljpa.gov.np.

Ministry of Local Development: Sri Mahal, Pulchowk, Lalitpur; tel. (1) 5521727; fax (1) 5522045; e-mail info@mld.gov.np; internet www.mld.gov.np.

Ministry of Physical Planning and Works: Singha Durbar, Kathmandu; tel. (1) 4228285; fax (1) 4412199.

Ministry of Population and the Environment: Singha Durbar, Kathmandu; tel. (1) 4245367; fax (1) 4242138; e-mail info@mope.gov.np; internet www.mope.gov.np.

Ministry of Science and Technology: Singha Durbar, Kathmandu; tel. (1) 4244608; fax (1) 4225474; e-mail most@most.gov.np; internet www.most.gov.np.

Ministry of Water Resources: Singha Durbar, Kathmandu; tel. (1) 4227347.

Ministry of Women, Children and Social Welfare: Singha Durbar, Kathmandu; tel. (1) 4240408; fax (1) 4241516; e-mail mwcsw@ntc.net.np.

Legislature

PARLIAMENT

Rashtriya Sabha
(National Assembly)

The Rashtriya Sabha has 60 members, consisting of 10 nominees of the King, 35 members (including three women) elected by the Pratinidhi Sabha (House of Representatives), and 15 members elected by the electoral college, which includes the heads of the local committees of various development regions. The tenure of office of the members of the Rashtriya Sabha is six years.

Chairman: RAMPRIT PASHWAN.

Pratinidhi Sabha
(House of Representatives)

The 205-member Pratinidhi Sabha is elected, on the basis of adult franchise, for five years. It was dissolved indefinitely on 22 May 2002, but was finally reconvened by the King, following popular protests, on 28 April 2006.

Speaker: SUBASH NEMWANG.
Deputy Speaker: CHITRA LEKHA YADAV.

General Election, 3 and 17 May 1999

Party	Seats
Nepali Congress Party (NCP)	111
Communist Party of Nepal (Unified Marxist-Leninist—UML)	71
National Democratic Party (NDP)	11
Rashtriya Jana Morcha	5
Nepali Sadbhavana Party	5
Nepal Workers' and Peasants' Party	1
Samyukta Janmorcha Nepal*	1
Total	**205**

* Since disbanded.
Note: Polling was deferred until 8 and 23 June 1999 in four constituencies, owing to the deaths of candidates.

Election Commission

Election Commission of the Kingdom of Nepal: Bahadur Bhawan, Kantipath, Kathmandu; tel. (1) 4228663; fax (1) 4229227; e-mail election@mos.com.np; internet www.election-commission.org.np; independent; appointed by the King on recommendation of a Constitutional Council; Chief Election Commr KESHAV RAJ RAJBHANDARI.

Political Organizations

According to the 1990 Constitution, political parties are required to register with the Election Commission, and, in order to be officially recognized, 5% of the candidates presented by a party must be female and the party should obtain at least 3% of the total votes cast in the election to the House of Representatives. The Constitution also specifies that no law may be adopted that bans, or imposes restrictions on, political parties.

Communist Party of Nepal (Maoist): f. 1990 as Communist Party of Nepal (Unity Centre), renamed as above in 1995; underground political movement; orchestrates 'people's war' in hills of west Nepal (since 1996); advocates abolition of constitutional monarchy and establishment of people's republic; Leader PUSHPA KAMAL DAHAL ('Prachanda').

Communist Party of Nepal (Mashal): Kathmandu; Leader CHITRA BAHADUR.

Communist Party of Nepal (Unified Marxist-Leninist) (UML): Madan Nagar, Balkhu, POB 5471, Kathmandu; tel. (1) 4278081; fax (1) 4278084; e-mail uml@ntc.net.np; internet www.cpnuml.org; f. 1991 when two major factions of the Communist Party of Nepal (CPN; f. 1949; banned 1960; legalized 1990)—the Marxist and Marxist-Leninist factions—merged; the Communist Party of Nepal (Marxist-Leninist—ML) seceded in 1998 and rejoined the UML in 2002; the Communist Party of Nepal (Verma) merged with the UML in 2001; Gen. Sec. MADHAV KUMAR NEPAL.

Communist Party of Nepal (United): Dillibazar, POB 2737, Kathmandu; tel. (1) 4430869; fax (1) 4411642; Leader BISHNU B. MANANDHAR.

Green Nepal Party: Kalikasthan, POB 890, Kathmandu; tel. and fax (1) 4438402; e-mail greennepal@htp.com.np; f. 1997; Pres. PUSP PRASAD LUINTEL.

Janawadi Morcha (Democratic Front): Indrachowk, Itumbahal, Kathmandu; tel. (1) 4211033; Pres. RAM RAJYA PRASAD SINGH.

Nepal Praja Parishad: Battisputali, Kathmandu; tel. (1) 4471616; f. 1936; banned 1961; legalized 1990; Pres. RAM HARI SHRESTHA; Gen. Secs Dr MEENA ACHARYA, MAHESWOR SHARMA.

Nepal Samata Party: Bishalnagar, Kathmandu; f. 2002; aims to promote and safeguard the democratic movement; Pres. Lt-Gen. NARAYAN SINGH PUN.

Nepal Workers' and Peasants' Party: Golmadhi Tole-7, Bhaktapur, Kathmandu; tel. (1) 6610974; fax (1) 6613207; e-mail nwpp@ntc.net.np; Chair. NARAYAN MAN BIJUKCHHEN (Rohit).

Nepali Congress Party (NCP): Bhansar Tole, Teku, Kathmandu; tel. (1) 4227748; fax (1) 4227747; e-mail ncparty@ntc.net.np; internet www.nepalicongress.org.np; f. 1947; banned 1960; legalized 1990; Pres. GIRIJA PRASAD KOIRALA; Gen. Sec. RAM KRISHNA PAUDEL; 135,000 active members, 500,000 ordinary members.

Nepali Congress Party—Democratic (NCP—D): Kathmandu; f. 2002 as a breakaway faction of the NCP; Pres. SHER BAHADUR DEUBA; Gen. Secs BIMALENDRA NIDHI, PRAKASH MAN SINGH.

Nepali Janata Dal: Tripureshwor, Kathmandu; tel. (1) 4212389; f. 1990; advocates the consolidation of the multi-party democratic system and supports the campaign against corruption; Leader KESHAR JUNG RAYAMAJHI.

Nepali National Congress: Lazimpat, Kathmandu; tel. (1) 4411090; Pres. DILLI RAMAN REGMI.

Nepali Sadbhavana Party (NSP) (Nepal Goodwill Party): Shantinagar, New Baneshwor, Kathmandu; tel. (1) 4488068; fax (1) 4470797; f. 1990; promotes the rights of the Madhesiya community, who are of Indian origin and reside in the Terai; demands that the Government recognize Hindi as an official language, that constituencies in the Terai be allocated on the basis of population, and that the Government grant citizenship to those who settled in Nepal before April 1990; in 2003 the party split into two factions, one led by Babri Prasad Mandal, known as the Mandal Group, and the other led by Anandi Devi Singh, known as the Anandi Devi group.

People's Front Nepal (Janamorcha Nepal): Kathmandu; f. 2002 following merger of Rashtriya Jana Morcha (National People's Front) and United People's Front; Pres. AMIK SHERCHAN; Vice-Chair. LILAMANI POKHAREL.

Prajatantrik Nepal Party (Democratic Nepal Party): Lalitpur, Kathmandu; f. 2005; Chair. KESHAR BAHADUR BISTA.

Rashtriya Jana Shakti Party (National People's Power Party): Ramalphokhari, Kathmandu; tel. (1) 4437063; fax (1) 4437064; e-mail rjpnepal@info.com.np; internet www.rjpnepal.org; f. 2005; Leader SURYA BAHADUR THAPA.

Rashtriya Janata Parishad (National People's Council): Dillibazar, Kathmandu; tel. (1) 4415150; f. 1992; royalist; aims to defend democracy, nationalism and sovereignty; Pres. MAITRIKA PRASAD KOIRALA; Vice-Pres. KIRTI NIDHI BISTA.

Rashtriya Prajatantra Party (RPP) (National Democratic Party—NDP): Chabahil; tel. (1) 5532131; fax (1) 4423384; internet www.rppnepal.com; liberal democratic party; Chair. PASHUPATI SHUMSHERE J. B. RANA; Asst Gen. Sec. KHEM RAJ PANDIT.

NEPAL

Diplomatic Representation

EMBASSIES IN NEPAL

Australia: Suraj Niwas, Bansbari, POB 879, Kathmandu; tel. (1) 4371678; fax (1) 4371533; internet www.embassy.gov.au/np; Ambassador GRAEME LADE.
Bangladesh: Maharajgunj Ring Rd, POB 789, Kathmandu; tel. (1) 4372843; fax (1) 4373265; e-mail bdootktm@wlink.com.np; Ambassador HUMAYUN KABIR.
China, People's Republic: Baluwatar, POB 4234, Kathmandu; tel. (1) 4411740; fax (1) 4414045; e-mail culture@chineseembassy.org.np; internet www.chinaembassy.org.np; Ambassador SUN HEPING.
Denmark: 761 Neel Saraswati Marg, Lazimpat, POB 6332, Kathmandu; tel. (1) 4413010; fax (1) 4411409; e-mail ktmamb@um.dk; internet www.ambkathmandu.um.dk; Ambassador FINN THILSTED.
Egypt: Pulchowk, Lalitpur, POB 792, Kathmandu; tel. (1) 5524812; fax (1) 5522975; Ambassador NEVINE SAAD ELDIN ASHMAWAY.
Finland: Lazimpat, POB 2126, Kathmandu; tel. (1) 4416636; fax (1) 4416703; e-mail sanomat.kat@formin.fi; internet www.finland.org.np; Chargé d'affaires a.i. PAULI MUSTONEN.
France: Lazimpat, POB 452, Kathmandu; tel. (1) 4412332; fax (1) 4418288; e-mail ambassade@ambafrance-np.org; internet www.ambafrance-np.org; Ambassador MICHEL JOLIVET.
Germany: Gyaneshwar, POB 226, Kathmandu; tel. (1) 4412786; fax (1) 4416899; e-mail info@kathmandu.diplo.de; internet www.kathmandu.diplo.de; Ambassador FRANZ RING.
India: Lainchaur, POB 292, Kathmandu; tel. (1) 4411940; fax (1) 4413132; e-mail pic@eoiktm.org; internet www.south-asia.com/embassy-India; Ambassador SHIV SHANKAR MUKHERJEE.
Israel: Bishramalaya House, Lazimpat, POB 371, Kathmandu; tel. (1) 4411811; fax (1) 4413920; e-mail info@kathmandu.mfa.gov.il; internet kathmandu.mfa.gov.il; Ambassador DAN STAV.
Japan: Panipokhari, POB 264, Kathmandu; tel. (1) 4426680; fax (1) 4414101; internet www.np.emb-japan.go.jp; Ambassador TSUTOMU HIRAOKA.
Korea, Democratic People's Republic: Jhamsikhel, Lalitpur, Kathmandu; tel. (1) 4521084; Ambassador HWANG YONG HWAN.
Korea, Republic: Ravi Bawanl, Kalimatil, POB 1058, Kathmandu; tel. (1) 4270172; fax (1) 4272041; e-mail konepamb@mos.com.np; Ambassador NAM SANG-JUNG.
Malaysia: Block B, Sanchaya Kosh Bldg, Lalitpur, Kathmandu; tel. (1) 5010004; fax (1) 5010492; e-mail malkatmandu@kln.gov.my; Ambassador MAHINDER SINGH.
Myanmar: Chakupath, Patan Gate, Lalitpur, POB 2437, Kathmandu; tel. (1) 5524788; fax (1) 5523402; e-mail emb@myanmar.wlink.com.np; Ambassador U AUNG KHIN SOE.
Norway: Surya Court, Pulchowk, Lalitpur, POB 20765, Kathmandu; tel. (1) 5545307; fax (1) 5545226; e-mail emb.kathmandu@mfa.no; internet www.norway.org.np; Ambassador TORE TORENG.
Pakistan: Pushpanjali, Maharajgunj, Chakrapath, POB 202, Kathmandu; tel. (1) 4374024; fax (1) 4374012; Ambassador SOHAIL AMIN.
Russia: Baluwatar, POB 123, Kathmandu; tel. (1) 4412155; fax (1) 4416571; e-mail ruspos@info.com.np; internet www.nepal.mid.ru; Ambassador ANDREI LEONIDOVICH TROFIMOV.
Sri Lanka: Chundevi Rd, Maharajgunj, POB 8802, Kathmandu; tel. (1) 4413623; fax (1) 4418128; e-mail embassy@srilanka.info.com.np; Ambassador GRACE A. ASIWARHAM.
Thailand: 167/4 Ward No. 3, Maharajgunj-Bansbari Rd, POB 3333, Kathmandu; tel. (1) 4371410; fax (1) 4371409; e-mail thaiemb@wlink.com.np; internet www.thaiembassy.org/kathmandu; Ambassador (vacant).
United Kingdom: Lainchaur, POB 106, Kathmandu; tel. (1) 4410583; fax (1) 4411789; e-mail britemb@wlink.com.np; internet www.britishembassy.gov.uk/nepal; Ambassador KEITH BLOOMFIELD.
USA: Panipokhari, POB 295, Kathmandu; tel. (1) 4411179; fax (1) 4419963; internet nepal.usembassy.gov; Ambassador JAMES MORIARTY.

Judicial System

According to the 1990 Constitution, the judicial system is composed of three tiers: the Supreme Court (which is also a Court of Record), the Appellate Courts and the District Courts. The Supreme Court consists of a Chief Justice and up to 14 other judges. The Chief Justice, whose tenure of office is seven years, is appointed by the King on the recommendation of the Constitutional Council, while all other judges are appointed on the recommendation of the Judicial Council.

Chief Justice: DILIP KUMAR POUDEL.
Attorney-General: YAGYAMURTI BANJADE.

Religion

At the 2001 census, an estimated 80.6% of the population professed Hinduism (the religion of the royal family), while 10.7% were Buddhists and 4.2% Muslims. The actual number of Muslims in the country was considered to be much higher, owing to immigration from Bangladesh. There were an estimated 101,976 Christians in Nepal in 2001.

BUDDHISM

All Nepal Bhikkhu Association: Vishwa Shanti Vihara (World Peace Temple), 465 Ekadantamarga, Minbhawan, New Baneshwar, POB 8973 NPC-327, Kathmandu; tel. (1) 4482984; fax (1) 4482250; e-mail vishwa@ntc.net.np; Treas. BHIKSHU BODHIJNANA.
Nepal Buddhist Council: Nahtole, Lalitpur 20; tel. (1) 5534277; e-mail nepal_bp@hotmail.com; Contact MAHISWOR RAJ BAJRACHARYA.

CHRISTIANITY

Protestant Church

Presbyterian Church of the Kingdom of Nepal: POB 3237, Kathmandu; tel. and fax (1) 4524450.

The Roman Catholic Church

The Church is represented in Nepal by a single apostolic prefecture. At 31 December 2003 there were an estimated 7,151 adherents in the country.

Apostolic Prefecture: Church of the Assumption, Everest Postal Care P. Ltd, POB 8975 EPC-343, Kathmandu; tel. (1) 5542802; fax (1) 5521710; e-mail anath@wlink.com.np; f. 1983 as Catholic Mission; Prefect Apostolic Fr ANTHONY FRANCIS SHARMA.

The Press

PRINCIPAL DAILIES

The Commoner: Naradevi, POB 203, Kathmandu; tel. (1) 4228236; f. 1956; English; Publr and Chief Editor GOPAL DASS SHRESTHA; circ. 7,000.
Daily News: Bhimsensthan, POB 171, Kathmandu; tel. (1) 4279147; fax (1) 4279544; e-mail manju-sakya@hotmail.com; f. 1983; Nepali and English; Chief Editor MANJU RATNA SAKYA; Publr SUBHA LAXMI SAKYA; circ. 20,000.
Dainik Nirnaya: Bhairawa; tel. (71) 520117; Nepali; Editor P. K. BHATTACHAN.
Gorkhapatra: Dharma Path, POB 23, Kathmandu; tel. (1) 4221478; fax (1) 4222921; f. 1901; Nepali; govt-owned; Editor-in-Chief KRISHNA BHAKTA SHRESTHA; circ. 75,000.
The Himalayan Times: International Media Network Nepal (Pvt) Ltd, APCA House, Baidya Khana Rd, Anam Nagar, POB 11651, Kathmandu; e-mail editorial@thehimalayantimes.com; internet www.thehimalayantimes.com; English; Editor RAM PRADHAN.
Janadoot: Ga 2-549, Kamal Pokhari (in front of the Police Station), Kathmandu; tel. (1) 4412501; f. 1970; Nepali; Editor GOVINDA BIYOGI; circ. 6,500.
Kantipur: Kantipur Complex, Subhidhanagar, POB 8559, Kathmandu; tel. (1) 4480100; fax (1) 4470178; e-mail kanti@kantipur.com.np; internet www.kantipuronline.com; f. 1993; Nepali; Chief Exec. HEM RAJ GYAWALI; Editor NARAYAN WAGLE; circ. 117,000.
Kathmandu Post: Kantipur Complex, Subhidhanagar, POB 8559, Kathmandu; tel. (1) 4480100; fax (1) 4466320; e-mail kpost@kantipur.com.np; internet www.kantipuronline.com; f. 1993; English; Editor PRATEEK PRAHAN; circ. 40,000.
Motherland: POB 1184, Kathmandu; English; Editor MANINDRA RAJ SHRESTHA; circ. 5,000.
Nepal Samacharpatra: Sagarmatha Press, Ramshah Path, Kathmandu; e-mail sadhana@mail.com.np; f. 1945; Nepali; Editor NARENDRA BILAS PANDEY; circ. 1,000.
Nepali Hindi Daily: Maitidevi Phant, Shantinagar 32, POB 49, Kathmandu; tel. (1) 4436374; fax (1) 4435931; e-mail das@ntc.net.np; f. 1954; evening; Hindi; Publr UMA KANT DAS; Chief Editor VIJOY KUMAR DAS; circ. 60,000.
Rajdhani: Kathmandu; internet www.rajdhani.com.np; Editor PURUSHOTTAM DAHAL; circ. 50,000.
Rising Nepal: Dharma Path, POB 1623, Kathmandu; tel. (1) 4227493; fax (1) 4224381; internet www.south-asia.com/news-ktmpost.html; f. 1965; English; Editor-in-Chief GYAN BAHADUR RAI (acting); circ. 20,000.
Samaj: National Printing Press, Dillibazar, Kathmandu; f. 1954; Nepali; Editor MANI RAJ UPADHYAYA; circ. 5,000.

Samaya: Kamal Press, Ramshah Path, Kathmandu; f. 1954; Nepali; Editor MANIK LALL SHRESTHA; circ. 18,000.

Space Time Dainik: Iceberg Bldg, 3rd Floor, Putali Sadak, Kathmandu; tel. (1) 4419133; fax (1) 4419504; e-mail info@spacetimenetwork.com; internet www.spacetimenetwork.com; f. 2000; Nepali; Man. Dir JAMIM SHAH; circ. 60,000.

Swatantra Samachar: Kathmandu; tel. (1) 4419285; f. 1957; Editor MADAN DEV SHARMA; circ. 2,000.

SELECTED PERIODICALS

Agricultural Credit: Agricultural Training and Research Institute, Agricultural Development Bank, Head Office, Ramshah Path, Panchayat Plaza, Kathmandu; tel. (1) 4220756; fax (1) 4225329; 2 a year; publ. by the Agricultural Development Bank; Chair. Dr NARAYAN N. KHATRI; Editor RUDRA PD DAHAL.

Arpan: Bhimsensthan, POB 285, Kathmandu; tel. (1) 4244450; fax (1) 4279544; e-mail manju-sakya@hotmail.com; f. 1964; weekly; Nepali; Publr and Chief Editor MANJU RATNA SAKYA; circ. 18,000.

Awake Weekly Chronicle: Kathmandu; English.

Commerce: Bhimsensthan, POB 171, Kathmandu; tel. (1) 4279636; fax (1) 4279544; e-mail manju-sakya@hotmail.com; f. 1971; monthly; English; Publr and Chief Editor MANJU RATNA SAKYA; Editor SUBHA LAXMI SAKYA; circ. 12,000.

Current: Gautam Marg, Kamalpokhari, Kathmandu; tel. (1) 4419484; fax (1) 4413554; e-mail current@namche.com; internet www.current.com.np; f. 1982; weekly; Nepali; Man. Editor KIRAN GAUTAM; Chief Editor DEVENDRA GAUTAM; circ. 10,000.

Cyber Post: Kathmandu; fortnightly; computers, electronics.

Foreign Affairs Journal: 5/287 Lagon, Kathmandu; f. 1976; 3 a year; articles on Nepalese foreign relations and diary of main news events; Publr and Editor BHOLA BIKRUM RANA; circ. 5,000.

Himal, The South Asian Magazine: POB 7251, Kathmandu; tel. (1) 4543333; fax (1) 4521013; e-mail info@himalmag.com; internet www.himalmag.com; f. 1987; monthly; political, business, social and environmental issues throughout South Asia; Editor-in-Chief KANAK MANI DIXIT; Marketing Man. SUMAN SHAKYA.

The Independent: Shankher Deep Bldg, Khichhapokhari, POB 3543, Kathmandu; tel. (1) 4249256; fax (1) 4226293; e-mail independ@mos.com.np; internet www.nepalnews.com.np/independent.htm; f. 1991; weekly; English; Editor SUBARNA B. CHHETRI.

Janadharana (People's Opinion): Kathmandu; e-mail dharana@nepalimail.com; internet www.nepalnews.com.np/dharana.htm; weekly; left-wing; Managing Editor SUBHASHANKAR KANDEL.

Janmabhumi: Janmabhumi Press, Tahachal, Kathmandu; tel. (1) 4280979; e-mail sirishnp@hotmail.com; internet www.catmando.com; weekly; Nepali; Publr and Editor SHIRISH BALLABH PRADHAN.

Koseli: Kathmandu; weekly; Nepali.

Madhuparka: Dharma Path, POB 23, Kathmandu; tel. (1) 4222278; f. 1986; monthly; Nepali; literary; Editor-in-Chief KRISHNA BHAKTA SHRESTHA; circ. 20,000.

Matribhoomi (Nepali Weekly): Ga 2-549, Kamal Pokhari (in front of the Police Station), Kathmandu; tel. (1) 4412501; weekly; Nepali; Editor GOVINDA BIYOGI.

Mulyankan: Kathmandu; monthly; left-wing; Editor SHYAM SHRESTHA.

Nepal: Kantipur Complex, Subhidhanagar, POB 8559, Kathmandu; tel. (1) 4480100; fax (1) 4470178; e-mail feedback@kantipuronline.com; internet www.kantipuronline.com/Nepal; f. 2000; fortnightly; Nepali; Editor KISHORE NEPAL.

Nepal Chronicle: Maruhiti; weekly; English; Publr and Editor CHANDRA LAL JHA.

Nepal Overseas Trade Statistics: Trade Promotion Centre, Pulchowk, Lalitpur, POB 825, Kathmandu; tel. (1) 5525348; fax (1) 5525464; e-mail tpcnep@mos.com.np; internet www.tpcnepal.org.np; annual; English.

Nepal Trade Bulletin: Trade Promotion Centre, Pulchowk, Lalitpur, POB 825, Kathmandu; tel. (1) 5532642; fax (1) 5525464; e-mail tpcnep@mos.com.np; internet www.tpcnepal.org.np; 3 a year; English; Editor KEWAL BISTA.

Nepali Times: Himalmedia Pvt Ltd, POB 7251, Kathmandu; tel. (1) 5543333; fax (1) 4521013; e-mail editors@nepalitimes.com; internet www.nepalitimes.com; f. 1955; weekly; Nepali; Publr and Editor KUNDA DIXIT; circ. 15,000.

People's Review: Pipalbot, Dillibazar, POB 3052, Kathmandu; tel. (1) 4417352; fax (1) 4438797; e-mail preview@ntc.net.np; internet www.peoplesreview.com.np; weekly; English; Editor-in-Chief PUSHPA RAJ PRADHAN; circ. 15,000.

Rastrabani: Kathmandu; tel. (1) 4410339; weekly; Nepali; Chief Editor HARI LAMSAL.

Sanghu Weekly: Kathmandu; weekly; Editor GOPAL BUDHATHOKI.

Sanibariya: Kathmandu; weekly.

Saptahik Weekly: Kantipur Complex, Subhidhanagar, POB 8559, Kathmandu; tel. (1) 4480100; fax (1) 4470178; internet www.kantipuronline.com/saptahic_html/saptahik; f. 1997; weekly; Nepali; news and entertainment; Editor SUBASH DHAKAL.

Spotlight: POB 7256, Kathmandu; tel. (1) 4410772; e-mail spotlight@mos.com.np; f. 1991; weekly; English; Editor MADHAV KUMAR RIMAL.

Swatantra Manch Weekly: POB 49, Kathmandu; tel. (1) 4436374; fax (1) 4435931; e-mail das@ntc.net.np; f. 1985; independent; weekly; Nepali; Publr and Chief Editor VIJOY KUMAR DAS; circ. 30,000.

The Telegraph: Ghattekulo, Dillibazar, POB 4063, Kathmandu; tel. (1) 4419370; e-mail tgw@ntc.net.np; weekly; English; Chief Editor NARENDRA P. UPADHYAYA.

Vashudha: Makhan, Kathmandu; monthly; English; social, political and economic affairs; Publr and Editor T. L. SHRESTHA.

NEWS AGENCIES

Rastriya Samachar Samiti (RSS): Prithivi Path, POB 220, Kathmandu; tel. (1) 4227912; fax (1) 4227698; e-mail info@rss.com.np; internet www.rss.com.np; f. 1962; state-operated; Gen. Man. KAMAL PRADHAN; Chair. (vacant).

Foreign Bureaux

Agence France-Presse (AFP): Bhote Bahal-South, Hansa Marg, POB 402, Kathmandu; tel. (1) 4253960; fax (1) 4222998; e-mail afpresse@mos.com.np; Chief of Bureau KEDAR MAN SINGH.

Associated Press (AP) (USA): Thapathli Panchayan, POB 513, Kathmandu; tel. (1) 4212767; Correspondent BINAYA GURACHARYA.

Deutsche Presse-Agentur (dpa) (Germany): KH 1-27 Tebahal Tole, POB 680, Kathmandu 44601; tel. (1) 4224557; Correspondent K. C. SHYAM BAHADUR.

Inter Press Service (IPS) (Italy): c/o Nepal Press Institute, POB 4128, Kathmandu; tel. and fax (1) 4228943; Correspondent DHRUBA ADHIKARY.

Kyodo News (Japan): 1773/32 Surya Bikram Gyawali Marg, Battisputali, Kathmandu; tel. (1) 4470106; fax (1) 4480571; e-mail madach@subisu.net.np; f. 1976; Correspondent MADHAV ACHARYA.

Reuters (United Kingdom): POB 3341, Kathmandu; tel. (1) 4372152; fax (1) 4373814.

United Press International (UPI) (USA): POB 802, Kathmandu; tel. (1) 4215684; Correspondent BHOLA BIKRAM RANA.

PRESS ASSOCIATIONS

Federation of Nepalese Journalists (FNJ): Media Village, Sinamangal, Kathmandu; tel. (1) 4490063; fax (1) 4490085; e-mail fnjnepal@mail.com.np; internet www.fnjnepal.org; f. 1956; Pres. BISHNU NISHTHURI; Gen. Sec. MAHENDRA BISTA.

Nepal Journalists' Association (NJA): Maitighar, POB 285, Kathmandu; tel. (1) 4262426; fax (1) 4279544; e-mail info@nja.org.np; internet www.nja.org.np; 5,400 mems; Pres. MANJU RATNA SAKYA; Gen. Sec. NIRMAL KUMAR ARYAL.

Press Council: Sanchargram, Tilganga, POB 3077, Kathmandu; tel. (1) 4469799; fax (1) 4469894; e-mail prescoun_mdf@wlink.com.np; internet www.presscouncil.org; f. 1970; Chair. MATHWAR SINGH BASNET; Admin. Officer BISHNU PRASAD SHARMA.

Publishers

Educational Enterprise (Pvt) Ltd: Mahankalsthan, POB 1124, Kathmandu; tel. (1) 4223749; e-mail ishwarbshrestha@yahoo.com; educational and technical; Dir JYOTSNA SHRESTHA.

International Standards Books and Periodicals (Pvt) Ltd: Bhotahity Bazaar, Chowk Bhitra, POB 3000, Kathmandu 44601; tel. (1) 4262815; fax (1) 4264179; e-mail u2@ccsl.com.np; f. 1991; Chief Man. Dir YOGYNDRA LALL CHHIPA; Chief Exec. and Man. Dir GANESH LALL SINGH CHHIPA.

Lakoul Press: Palpa-Tansen, Kathmandu; educational and physical sciences.

Mahabir Singh Chiniya Main: Makhan Tola, Kathmandu.

Mandass Memorials Publications: Kathmandu; Man. BASANT RAJ TULADHAR.

Pilgrims Book House: Thamel, POB 3872, Kathmandu; tel. (1) 4700942; fax (1) 4700943; e-mail pilgrims@wlink.com.np; internet www.pilgrimsbooks.com; f. 1986; Asian studies, religion and travel; Propr PUSHPA TIWARI.

Pilgrims Publishing Nepal (Pvt) Ltd: Goldhunga, POB 21646, Kathmandu; tel. (1) 4356764; e-mail johnsnepal@wlink.com.np;

NEPAL

internet www.pilgrimsbooks.com; f. 2000; Exec. Dir JOHN SNYDER; Man. Dir BISHOW BHATTA.

Ratna Pustak Bhandar: 71 'Ga' Bank Marg, POB 98, Kathmandu; tel. (1) 4223026; fax (1) 4248421; e-mail rpb@wlink.com.np; f. 1945; textbooks, general, non-fiction and fiction; Propr RATNA PRASAD SHRESTHA.

Royal Nepal Academy: Kamaladi, Kathmandu; tel. (1) 4221241; fax (1) 4221175; f. 1957; languages, literature, social sciences, art and philosophy; Dep. Admin. Chief T. D. BHANDARI.

Sajha Prakashan: Pulchowk, Lalitpur, POB 20259, Kathmandu; tel. (1) 5521118; fax (1) 5544236; e-mail sajhap@wlink.com.np; internet www.sajha.org.np; f. 1964; educational, literary and general; Chair. SHANKAR SHRESTHA; Gen. Man. NAV RAJ KARKI.

Trans Asian Media Pvt Ltd: Thapathali Crossing, POB 5320, Kathmandu; tel. (1) 4242895; fax (1) 4223889; Man. Editor SHYAM GOENKA.

GOVERNMENT PUBLISHING HOUSE

Department of Information: Ministry of Information and Communications, Singha Durbar, Kathmandu; tel. (1) 4220150; fax (1) 4221729.

Broadcasting and Communications

TELECOMMUNICATIONS

Nepal Telecommunications Authority: 768/12 Thir Bam Sadhak, POB 9754, Baluwatar, Kathmandu; tel. (1) 4446001; fax (1) 4446006; e-mail ntra@nta.gov.np; internet www.nta.gov.np; telecommunications regulatory body; Chair. SURESH KUMAR PUDASAINI.

Nepal Telecom (Nepal Doorsanchar Co Ltd): Bhadrakali Plaza, POB 11803, Kathmandu; tel. (1) 4246034; fax (1) 4222424; e-mail rkt@ntc.net.np; internet www.ntc.com.np; f. 1975; monopoly provider; scheduled for transfer to private sector; Man. Dir CHET PRASAD BHATTARAI.

Spice Nepal (Pvt) Ltd (SNPL): Kathmandu; f. 2002; jt venture between Kazakhstan-based Group VISOR (75%), Raj Group (20%) and India-based Spice Cell (5%); operates GSM mobile network; Chair. RAJ BAHADUR SINGH; CEO DAMIR KARASSAYEV.

United Telecom: Ground Floor, Triveni Complex, Putali Sadak, Kathmandu; tel. (1) 2000050; fax (1) 2499999; e-mail info@utlnepal.com; internet www.utlnepal.com.np; f. 2003; jt venture between Indian-owned Mahanagar Telephone Nigam Ltd (26.7%), Videsh Sanchar Nigam Ltd (26.7%), Telecom Consultants India (26.7%), and Nepal Venture (Pvt) Ltd (20%); Chair. Shri G. D. GAIHA.

BROADCASTING

Radio

In July 2005 there were 47 commercial and community radio stations in Nepal. A media ordinance adopted by the King in October of that year banned private radio stations in the country from broadcasting news or information-related programmes.

Radio Nepal: Radio Broadcasting Service, HM Government of Nepal, Singha Durbar, POB 634, Kathmandu; tel. (1) 4241923; fax (1) 4221952; e-mail radio@engg.wlink.com.np; internet www.radionepal.org; f. 1951; broadcasts on short wave, medium wave and FM frequencies in 20 regional languages, incl. Nepali and English, for 18 hours daily (incl. two hours of regional broadcasting in the morning and evening); short-wave station at Khumaltar and medium-wave stations at Bhainsepati, Pokhara, Surkhet, Dipayal, Bardibas and Dharan; FM stations at Kathmandu, Kanchanpur, Rupandehi, Chitwan, Makawanpur, Bara, Jumla, Mustang, Jlam, Simikot and Humla; Exec. Dir TAPANATH SHUKLA.

Himalaya Broadcasting Co (Radio HBC 94 FM): POB 8974, CPC 94, Kathmandu; tel. (1) 4489618; fax (1) 4499788; e-mail info@hbc.com.np; internet www.nbc.com.np; f. 1999.

Hits FM: POB 21912, Baneshwor, Kathmandu; tel. (1) 4780296; fax (1) 4780543; e-mail hitsfm@mos.com.np; internet www.hitsfm.com.np; f. 1996; broadcasts 24 hrs daily; Exec. Dir JEEVAN SHRESTHA.

Image FM (Kath FM): POB 5566, Kathmandu; tel. (1) 4230368; fax (1) 4241260; e-mail kath979@wlink.com.np; internet www.imagechannels.com; f. 1999; Station Man. BHARAT SHAKYA.

Kantipur FM: Kantipur Complex, Subhidhanagar, POB 8559, Kathmandu; tel. (1) 4480100; fax (1) 4470178; e-mail kfm@kanti.mos.com.np; internet www.kantipuronline.com/fm_html/kantipur_fm.htm; f. 1998; broadcasts 24 hrs daily; Man. Dir BINOD RAJ GYAWALI; Station Man. GOPAL JHA.

Radio Lumbini: Aanandabane VDC, Ward No. 3, Manigram, Rupandehi, Lumbini; tel. (71) 61003; fax (71) 61545; e-mail lumbinifm@mos.com.np; internet www.radiolumbini.netfirms.com; f. 2000.

Directory

Radio Sagarmatha: GPOB 6958, Kathmandu; tel. (1) 5528091; fax (1) 5530227; e-mail stationmanager@radiosagarmatha.org; internet www.radiosagarmatha.org; f. 1997; independent; Chair. LAXMAN UPRETI; Station Man. MOHSIN BISTA.

Times FM: GPOB 8975, EPC 906, Jawalakhel, Lalitpur, Kathmandu; tel. and fax (1) 5539171; e-mail timesfm@hotnepal.com; Contact R. K. SHRESTHA.

Television

In 1986 Nepal's first television station began broadcasting within the Kathmandu valley.

Nepalese Television Corporation: Singha Durbar, POB 3826, Kathmandu; tel. (1) 4228447; fax (1) 4228312; internet www.explorenepal.com/ntv; f. 1985; broadcasts 32 hours a week; programmes in Nepali (50%), English (25%) and Hindi/Urdu (25%); regional stations at Pokhara, Biratnagar and Hetuada; Gen. Man. TAPA NATH SHUKLA; Dep. Gen. Man. (Technical) RAVINDRA S. RANA; Dep. Gen. Man. (Productions) DURGA NATH SHARMA.

Avenues TV: Tripureshwor, Kathmandu; tel. (1) 4257876; fax (1) 4227222; e-mail avenues@mos.com.np; f. 2003.

Image Metro: 369 Narayan Gopal Sadak, POB 9581, Lazimpat, Kathmandu; tel. (1) 4433141; fax (1) 4432707; e-mail ichannel@wlink.com.np; internet www.imagechannels.com; f. 2003; privately owned; Chair. R. K. MANANDHAR.

Kantipur Television Network (KTV): Kantipur Complex, Subhidhanagar, POB 8559, Kathmandu; tel. (1) 4480100; fax (1) 4470178; internet www.kantipuronline.com/tv; f. 2003; Chair. HEM RAJ GYAWALI; Man. Dir JEEWA LAMICHHANE.

Space-Time Network: Iceberg Bldg, 3rd Floor, Putali Sadak, Kathmandu; tel. (1) 4419133; fax (1) 4419504; e-mail info@spacetimenetwork.com; internet www.spacetimenetwork.com; f. 1994; satellite transmission service; Man. Dir JAMIM SHAH.

Finance

(auth. = authorized; cap. = capital; p.u. = paid up; m. = million; dep. = deposits; res = reserves; brs = branches; amounts in Nepalese rupees unless otherwise stated)

BANKING

Central Bank

Nepal Rastra Bank: Central Office, Baluwatar, POB 73, Kathmandu; tel. (1) 4419804; fax (1) 4414553; e-mail nrb@mos.com.np; internet www.nrb.org.np; f. 1956; bank of issue; 100% state-owned; cap. 10m., res 23,623.5m., dep. 19,241.2m. (July 2000); Gov. BIJAYA NATH BHATTARAI; 9 brs.

Domestic Commercial Banks

Kumari Bank Ltd: Putalisadak, POB 21128, Kathmandu; tel. (1) 4232112; fax (1) 4231960; e-mail info@kbl.com.np; internet www.kumaribank.com; f. 2001; auth. cap 1,000m. (April 2001); Chair. NOOR PRATAP RANA.

Nepal Bank Ltd: Nepal Bank Bldg, Dharmapath, New Rd, POB 36, Kathmandu; tel. (1) 4222397; fax (1) 4220414; e-mail contact@nepalbank.com.np; internet www.nepalbank.com.np; f. 1937; 41% state-owned, 59% owned by Nepalese public; cap. 378m., res 489.6m., dep. 21,570.5m. (July 1997); CEO J. CRAIG MCALLISTER; 126 brs.

Nepal Industrial and Commercial Bank Ltd (NIC Bank): Kamaladi, Ganeshthan, POB 7367, Kathmandu; tel. (1) 4222336; fax (1) 4241865; e-mail kamaladi@nicbank.com.np; internet www.nicbank.com.np; f. 1998; privately owned; cap. US $6.68m., res US $0.70m., dep. US $42.06m. (March 2004); Chair. JAGDISH PRASAD AGRAWAL; CEO SASHIN JOSHI; 6 brs.

Rastriya Banijya Bank (National Commercial Bank): POB 8368, Singha Durbar Plaza, Kathmandu; tel. (1) 4252595; fax (1) 4252931; e-mail secretary@rbb.com.np; internet www.rbb.com.np; f. 1966; 100% state-owned; cap. 1,172m., res 268m., dep. 33,329m. (July 1999); Chair. BASHDEV RAM JOSHI; CEO BRUCE F. HENDERSON; 212 brs, 4 regional offices.

Joint-venture Banks

Bank of Kathmandu Ltd: Kamal Pokhari, POB 9044, Kathmandu; tel. (1) 4414541; fax (1) 4418990; e-mail info@bok.com.np; f. 1993; 55% owned by Nepalese public, 45% by local promoters; cap. 233.6m., res 41.6m., dep. 5,724.1m. (July 2001); Chair. B. R. SINGH; Man. Dir and CEO RADHESH PANT.

Everest Bank Ltd: POB 13384, EBL House, Lazimpat, Kathmandu; tel. (1) 4481017; fax (1) 4482263; e-mail ebl@mos.com.np; internet www.ebl.com.np; f. 1994; 50% owned by directors, 20% by Punjab National Bank (India), 30% by the Nepalese public; cap.

NEPAL

455.0m., res 117.0m., dep. 6,695.0m. (July 2003); Chair. BAL KRISHNA SHRESTHA; Exec. Dir S. S. DABAS; 14 brs.

Himalayan Bank Ltd: Karmachari Sanchaya Kosh Bldg, Tridevi Marg, Thamel, POB 20590, Kathmandu; tel. (1) 4227749; fax (1) 4222800; e-mail hbl@hbl.com.np; internet www.himalayanbank.com; f. 1993; 20% owned by Habib Bank Ltd (Pakistan); cap. 429.0m., res 511.6m., dep. 21,699.9m. (July 2003); Chair. MANOJ BAHADUR SHRESTHA; CEO ASOKE S. J. B. RANA; 8 brs.

Laxmi Bank Ltd: POB 61, Adarsha Nagar, Birgunj, Parsa; tel. (51) 530394; fax (51) 530393; e-mail info@laxmibankltd.com; internet www.laxmibankltd.com; f. 2001; cap. 330.0m., res –3.2m., dep. 761.8m. (July 2003); Chair. MOHAN GOPAL KHETAN; CEO and Dir SUMAN JOSHI.

Nabil Bank Ltd (Nabil): Nabil House, Kamaladi, POB 3729, Kathmandu; tel. (1) 4429546; fax (1) 4429548; e-mail nabil@nabilbank.com.np; internet www.nabilbankltd.com; f. 1984 as Nepal Arab Bank Ltd, name changed as above Jan. 2002; 50% owned by National Bank of Bangladesh, 30% by the Nepalese public and 20% by Nepalese government financial institutions; cap. 491.7m., res 654.8m., dep. 15,923.7m. (July 2002); Chair. SATYENDRA PYARA SHRESTHA; Vice-Chair. DAYARAM GOPAL AGRAWAL; 17 brs.

Nepal Bangladesh Bank Ltd: Bijulibazar, New Baneshwor, POB 9062, Kathmandu; tel. (1) 4783976; fax (1) 4780316; e-mail nbblho@nbbl.com.np; internet www.nbbl.com.np; f. 1994; 50% owned by International Finance Investment and Commerce Bank Ltd (Bangladesh), 20% by Nepalese promoters and 30% public issue; cap. 359.9m., res 324.0m., dep. 10,580.7m. (July 2003); Man. Dir GANESH PRASAD ADHIKARY; Chair. JEET BAHADUR SHRESTHA; 15 brs.

Nepal Credit and Commerce Bank Ltd: Bagh Bazar, POB 12559, Kathmandu; tel. (1) 4246105; fax (1) 4244610; f. as Nepal Bank of Ceylon, reconstituted as above in Sept. 2002 after Bank of Ceylon (Sri Lanka) sold its shares to NB Group (Nepal); Man. Dir NARENDRA BHATTARAI; 14 brs.

Nepal Investment Bank Ltd: Durbar Marg, POB 3412, Kathmandu; tel. (1) 4228229; fax (1) 4226349; e-mail info@nibl.com.np; internet www.nibl.com.np; f. 1986 as Nepal Indosuez Bank Ltd, name changed as above in June 2002; 50% owned by a consortium of Nepalese investors, 20% by general public, 15% by Rastriya Banijya Bank and 15% by Rastriya Beema Sansthan; cap. 295m., res 343m., dep. 7,923m. (July 2003); Chair. UDAY NEPALI SHRESTHA; Chief Exec. Dir PRITHIVI B. PANDE; 12 brs.

Nepal SBI Bank Ltd: Corporate Office, Hattisar, POB 6049, Kathmandu; tel. (1) 4435516; fax (1) 4435612; e-mail nsblco@nsbl.com.np; f. 1993; 50% owned by State Bank of India, 30% by Nepalese public, 15% by Employees' Provident Fund (Nepal) and 5% by Agricultural Development Bank (Nepal); Chair. B. D. SUMITRA; Man. Dir V. P. DANI.

Nepal Sri Lanka Merchant Bank Ltd: NSLMB Bldg, Kalamadi, POB 12248, Kathmandu; tel. (1) 4440300; fax (1) 4441034; e-mail nslmb@info.com.np; Exec. Dir VED MAN SINGH MALLA.

Standard Chartered Bank Nepal Ltd: Grindlays Bhavan, Naya Baneshwor, POB 3990, Kathmandu; tel. (1) 4246753; fax (1) 4226762; internet www.standardchartered.com/np; f. 1987; 75% owned by Standard Chartered Bank (United Kingdom) and 25% by the Nepalese public; cap. 375m., res 1,563m., dep. 21,240m. (July 2004); Chair. CHRISTOPHER LOW; CEO SUJIT MUNIL; 11 brs.

Banking Organization

Nepal Bankers' Association (NBA): Kathmandu; Pres. RADHESH PANT.

Development Finance Organizations

Agricultural Development Bank: Ramshah Path, Kathmandu; tel. (1) 4262885; fax (1) 4262616; e-mail info@adbn.gov.np; internet www.adbn.gov.np; f. 1968; 93.6% state-owned, 2.1% owned by the Nepal Rastra Bank, and 4.3% by co-operatives and private individuals; specialized agricultural credit institution providing credit for agricultural development to co-operatives, individuals and asscns; receives deposits from individuals, co-operatives and other asscns to generate savings in the agricultural sector; acts as Government's implementing agency for small farmers' group development project, assisted by the Asian Development Bank and financed by the UN Development Programme; operational networks include 14 zonal offices, 37 brs, 92 sub-brs, 52 depots and 160 small farmers' development projects, 3 Zonal Training Centres, 2 Appropriate Technology Units; Chair. SHYAM PRASAD MAINALI; Gen. Man. HARI GOPAL GORKHALI.

Nepal Development Bank: Heritage Plaza, POB 11017, Kamaladi, Kathmandu; tel. (1) 4254639; fax (1) 4245753; e-mail ndb@ccsl.com.np; internet www.ndevbank.com; f. 1998; Chair. and Man. Dir UTTAM PUN.

Nepal Housing Development Finance Co Ltd: POB 5624, Kathmandu; tel. (1) 4490259; fax (1) 4493573; e-mail nhdfc@ntc.net.np; Chief Exec. INDRA PRASHAD KARMACHARYA.

Nepal Industrial Development Corporation (NIDC): NIDC Bldg, Durbar Marg, POB 10, Kathmandu; tel. (1) 4228322; fax (1) 4227428; e-mail nidc@wlink.com.np; internet www.nidc.org.np; f. 1959; state-owned; holds investments of 5,609.9m. in 1,125 industrial enterprises (2000/01); offers financial and technical assistance to private-sector industries; in 2000/01 approved a total of 9.41m. in loans and working capital, and disbursed 8.17m.; Gen. Man. UTTAM NARAYAN SHRESTHA.

STOCK EXCHANGE

Nepal Stock Exchange Ltd (NEPSE): Singha Durbar Plaza, POB 1550, Kathmandu; tel. (1) 4250735; fax (1) 4262538; e-mail nepse@stock.mos.com.np; internet www.nepalstock.com; f. 1976; reorg. 1984; converted in 1993 from Securities Exchange Centre Ltd to Nepal Stock Exchange Ltd; 128 listed cos, 120 scripts; Gen. Man. MUKUNDA NATH DHUNGEL; Man. (Admin. and Market Operations) M. P. SHARMA; Man. (Information, Planning and Development) P. BHATTARAI.

INSURANCE

Alliance Insurance Co Ltd: Durbar Marg, POB 10811, Kathmandu; tel. (1) 4222836; fax (1) 4241411; e-mail sk@aic.wlink.com.np.

Everest Insurance Co Ltd: Hattisar, POB 10675, Kathmandu; tel. (1) 4444717; fax (1) 4444366; e-mail eveinsco@mos.com.np; internet www.everestinsurance.com; Chair. MOHAN GOPAL KHETAN.

Himalayan General Insurance Co Ltd: Durbar Marg, POB 148, Kathmandu; tel. (1) 4231581; fax (1) 4223906; e-mail info@thamel.com; internet www.thamel.com/hgi; f. 1993; CEO MAHENDRA KRISHNA SHRESTHA.

National Insurance Co Ltd: Tripureswor, POB 376, Kathmandu; tel. (1) 4250710; fax (1) 4261289; e-mail natinsur@ccsl.com.np; Man. A. S. KOHLI.

National Life and General Insurance Co Ltd: Lazimpat, POB 4332, Kathmandu; tel. (1) 4412625; fax (1) 4416427; e-mail nlgi@mail.com.np; Chief Exec. S. K. SINGH; Pres. OM SINGH.

Neco Insurance Ltd: Hattisar, POB 12271, Lal Durbar, Kathmandu; tel. (1) 4427354; fax (1) 4418761; e-mail info@necoins.com.np; internet www.necoinsurance.com; f. 1994; Chair. JANARDAN AACHARYA; CEO ANIL SHARMA.

Nepal Insurance Co Ltd: NIC Bldg, Kamaladi, POB 3623, Kathmandu; tel. (1) 4221353; fax (1) 4225446; e-mail nic@wlink.com.np.

The Oriental Insurance Co Ltd: Jyoti Bhavan, POB 165, Kathmandu; tel. (1) 4221448; fax (1) 4223419; e-mail oriental@wlink.com.np; CEO Dr MADHUSUDAN KUMAR.

Premier Insurance Co (Nepal) Ltd: Tripureswor Plaza, Tripureswor, POB 9183, Kathmandu; tel. (1) 4259567; fax (1) 4249708; e-mail premier@picl.com.np; internet www.premier-insurance.com.np; Man. Dir SURESH LAL SHRESTHA.

Rastriya Beema Sansthan (National Insurance Corpn): RBS Bldg, Ramshah Path, POB 527, Kathmandu; tel. (1) 4213882; fax (1) 4262610; e-mail beema@wlink.com.np; f. 1967; Gen. Man. BIR BIKRAM RAXAMAJHI.

Sagarmatha Insurance Co Ltd: Kathmandu Plaza, Block Y, 4th Floor, Kamaladi, POB 12211, Kathmandu; tel. (1) 4240896; fax (1) 4247947; e-mail sagarmatha@insurance.wlink.com.np; Exec. Dir K. B. BASNYAT.

United Insurance Co (Nepal) Ltd: I. J. Plaza, Durbar Marg, POB 9075, Kathmandu; tel. (1) 4246686; fax (1) 4246687; e-mail uic@mail.com.np.

Trade and Industry

GOVERNMENT AGENCY

National Planning Commission (NPC): Singha Durbar, POB 1284, Kathmandu; tel. (1) 4225879; fax (1) 4226500; e-mail npcs@npcnepal.gov.np; internet www.npc.gov.np; Vice-Chair. Dr NARAYAN KHADKA.

DEVELOPMENT ORGANIZATIONS

National Productivity and Economic Development Centre: Balaju, POB 1318, Kathmandu; tel. (1) 4350566; fax (1) 4350530; e-mail npedc@wlink.com.np; internet www.npedc-nepal.org; functions as secretariat of National Productivity Council; provides services for industrial promotion and productivity improvement through planning research, consultancy, training, seminars and information services; Gen. Man. BHARAT GYAWALI.

NEPAL

National Tea and Coffee Development Board (NTCDB): New Baneshwor, POB 9683, Kathmandu; tel. (1) 4495792; fax (1) 4497941; e-mail info@teacoffee.gov.np; internet teacoffee.gov.np; f. 1992 to promote and expand the Nepalese tea industry; Exec. Dir TARANATH SHARMA.

National Trading Ltd: Teku, POB 128, Kathmandu; tel. (1) 4227683; fax (1) 4225151; e-mail natreli@mos.com.np; internet www.nationaltrading.com.np; f. 1962; govt-owned; imports and distributes construction materials and raw materials for industry; also machinery, vehicles and consumer goods; operates bonded warehouse, duty-free shop and related activities; brs in all major towns; Chair. SONAFI YADAV; Gen. Man. (vacant).

Nepal Foreign Trade Association: Bagmati Chamber, 1st Floor, Milan Marg, Teku, POB 541, Kathmandu; tel. (1) 4223784; fax (1) 4247159; e-mail nfta@mos.com.np; f. 1972; Pres. AKHIL KUMAR CHAPATAIN; Vice-Pres. SATISH KUMAR MORE.

Nepal Tea Development Corporation Ltd: Triveni Complex, Putali Sadak, Kathmandu; tel. (1) 4224074; fax (1) 4266133; e-mail ntdc@mos.com.np; internet www.ntdcltd.com; f. 1966; privatized in early 2000s; commercial production of tea.

Trade Promotion Centre (TPC): Pulchowk, Lalitpur, POB 825, Kathmandu; tel. (1) 5525348; fax (1) 5525464; e-mail tpcnep@mos.com.np; internet www.tpcnepal.org.np; f. 1971 to encourage exports; govt-owned; Exec. Dir N. C. LAMICHHANE.

CHAMBERS OF COMMERCE

Federation of Nepalese Chambers of Commerce and Industry (FNCCI): FNCCI Bldg, Pachali Shahid Shukra FNCCI Milan Marg, Teku, POB 269, Kathmandu; tel. (1) 4262061; fax (1) 4261022; e-mail fncci@mos.com.np; internet www.fncci.org; f. 1965; comprises 88 District Municipality Chambers (DCCIs), 59 Commodity Associations, 351 leading industrial and commercial undertakings in both the public and private sector, and 9 Bi-national Chambers; publishes annual statistical profile and biannual directory of members *Nepal and the World*; Pres. RAVI BHAKTA SHRESTHA; Dir-Gen. BADRI PRASAD OJHA.

Birganj Chamber of Commerce and Industries: Birta-4, Birganj; tel. (51) 522290; fax (51) 523653; e-mail bicci@cyberspace.com.np; internet www.bicci.org.np; Pres. OM PRAKASH RUNGTA.

Lalitpur Chamber of Commerce and Industry: Mangal Bazar, Patan Durbar Sq., POB 26, Lalitpur; tel. (1) 5521740; fax (1) 5530331; e-mail lcci@mos.com.np; internet www.lcci.org.np; f. 1967; Pres. UMESH LAL AMATYA; Exec. Sec. PRADHYUMAN LALNARESH KUMAR SHRESTHA.

Nepal Chamber of Commerce: Chamber Bhavan, Kantipath, POB 198, Kathmandu; tel. (1) 4222890; fax (1) 4229998; e-mail chamber@wlink.com.np; internet www.nepalchamber.org; f. 1952; non-profit organization promoting industrial and commercial development; 8,000 regd mems and 16,000 enrolled mems; Pres. RAJESH KAZI SHRESTHA; Sec.-Gen. SURESH KUMAR BASNET.

INDUSTRIAL AND TRADE ASSOCIATIONS

Association of Craft Producers: Ravi Bhavan, POB 3701, Kathmandu; tel. (1) 4275108; fax (1) 4272676; e-mail craftacp@mos.com.np; internet acp.org.np; f. 1984; local non-profit organization providing technical, marketing and management services for craft producers, manufacturer, exporter and retailer of handicraft goods; Programme Co-ordinator REVITA SHRESTHA.

Association of Forest-based Industries and Trade: Thapathali, POB 2798, Kathmandu; tel. (1) 4216020.

Association of Nepalese Rice, Oil and Pulses Industries: POB 20782, Radha Bhawan, Tripureswor, Kathmandu; tel. (1) 2011255; fax (1) 4437990; e-mail kbh@fewanet.com.np; Pres. TOLA RAM DUGAR; Gen. Sec. CHANDRA KRISHNA KARMACHARYA.

Association of Pharmaceutical Producers of Nepal: POB 21721, Anamnagar, Kathmandu; tel. (1) 4231871; fax (1) 5535367; e-mail vaidya@vpharma.wlink.com.np; Pres. PRADEEP MAN VAIDYA; Sec.-Gen. UMESH LAL SHRESTHA.

Cargo Agents Association of Nepal: Thamel, POB 5355, Kathmandu; tel. (1) 4419019; fax (1) 4419858.

Central Carpet Industries Association of Nepal: Bijulibazar, POB 2419, Kathmandu; tel. (1) 4496108; fax (1) 4475291; e-mail ccia@enet.com.np; internet www.nepalcarpet.org; Pres. A. G. SHERPA.

Computer Association of Nepal: 235/39 Dobidhara Marg, Kathmandu; tel. (1) 4432700; fax (1) 4434836; e-mail info@can.org.np; internet www.can.org.np; f. 1992; Pres. BIPLAV MAN SINGH.

Footwear Manufacturers' Association of Nepal: Khichapokhari, POB 648, Kathmandu; tel. (1) 4228131; fax (1) 4416576.

Garment Association of Nepal: Shankhamul Rd, New Baneshwor, POB 21332, Kathmandu; tel. (1) 4780691; fax (1) 4780173; e-mail gan@ntc.net.np; internet www.ganasso.org; Pres. KIRAN P. SAAKHA.

Handicrafts Association of Nepal: POB 784, Upma Marg, Thapathali, Kathmandu; tel. (1) 4244231; fax (1) 4222940; e-mail han@wlink.com.np; internet www.nepalhandicraft.org; f. 1972; Pres. PANCHA RATNA SHAKYA; Sec.-Gen. HEM RATNA SHAKYA.

Himalayan Orthodox Tea Producers' Association of Nepal: Kathmandu; f. 1998; non-profit making organization; represents and promotes the Himalayan tea sector; Chair. SURAJ VAIDYA.

Nepal Association of Tour and Travel Agents: Gairidhara Rd, Goma Ganesh, Naxal, POB 362, Kathmandu; tel. (1) 4419409; fax (1) 4418661; e-mail nata@mail.com.np; internet www.nata.org.np; f. 1966; 270 mems; Pres. DHRUBA NARAYAN SHRESTHA.

Nepal Cottage and Small Industries Association: Teku, Kathmandu; tel. (1) 4212876.

Nepal Forest Industries Association: Gyaneshwor, POB 1804, Kathmandu; tel. (1) 4411865; fax (1) 4413838; e-mail padmasri@ccsl.com.np; Pres. HARI PRASAD GIRI; Sec.-Gen. ROHINI THAPALIYA.

Nepal Leather Industries Association: POB 42, Anamnagar, Kathmandu; tel. (1) 4265248; fax (1) 4240491; e-mail giris@atcnet.com.np; Pres. SANJAY GIRI; Sec.-Gen. PARWEZ AKHTAR.

Nepal Plastic Manufacturers' Association: Kandevsthan, Kupandol, Lalitpur; tel. and fax (1) 5528185; Pres. SHAILENDRA LAL PRADHAN; Sec.-Gen. RAJESWOR LAL JOSHI.

Nepal Tea Planters' Association: Bhadrapur-4, Jhapa; tel. (23) 520183; fax (23) 540499; Pres. CHHATRA B. GIRI; Sec.-Gen. MAHESH KUMAR AGRAWAL.

Nepal Textile Industries Association: Krishna Galli, Lalitpur; tel. (1) 5529290; fax (1) 5520291; Pres. GOPAL P. KSHATRIYA; Sec.-Gen. RAM K. MAHARJAN.

Nepal Trans-Himalayan Trade Association: Jyoti Bhawan, Kantipath, Kathmandu; tel. (1) 4226565; fax (1) 4254048; e-mail syamukapu@unilever.wlink.com.np; Pres. Dr ROOP JYOTI; Sec.-Gen. MAHESH TULADHAR.

UTILITIES

Electricity

Butwal Power Co Ltd: POB 11728, Kumaripati, Kathmandu; tel. (1) 5538404; fax (1) 5527901; e-mail service@bpc.com.np; internet www.bpc.com.np; f. 1966; partially privatized in 2003.

Chilime Hydropower Co Ltd: Kathmandu; 51% owned by Nepal Electricity Authority; Dir DAMBER BAHADUR NEPALI.

Department of Electricity Development: POB 2507, Thapa Gaun, Anamnagar, Kathmandu; tel. (1) 4479507; fax (1) 4480257; e-mail doed@pshdp.wlink.com.np; internet www.doed.gov.np; f. 1993; fmrly Electricity Development Centre; name changed as above 1999; under Ministry of Water Resources; Dir-Gen. JAYA KESHAR MACKAY.

Nepal Electricity Authority: Ratna Park, Kathmandu; tel. (1) 4227725; fax (1) 4227035; e-mail neamd@mos.com.np; internet www.nea.org.np; f. 1985 following merger; govt-owned; Man. Dir Dr J. L. KARMACHARYA.

Water

Nepal Water Supply Corpn: Tripureswor Marg, Kathmandu; tel. (1) 4253656; fax (1) 4223484; f. 1990; govt-owned; Exec. Chair. ARUN KUMAR RANJITKAR.

TRADE UNIONS

Trade unions were banned in Nepal in 1961, but were legalized again in 1990, following the success of the pro-democracy movement and the collapse of the Panchayat system.

Nepal Trade Union Congress (NTUC): POB 5507, Kathmandu; tel. (1) 5527443; fax (1) 5527469; e-mail ntuc@wlink.com.np; internet www.ntuc.org.np; f. 1947; 24 affiliated unions; affiliated to ICFTU; Pres. LAXMAN BASNET; Sec.-Gen. ACHUTA RAJ PANDEY.

Democratic Confederation of Nepalese Trade Unions (DECONT): POB 13440, Kathmandu; tel. (1) 4486987; fax (1) 4488486; e-mail udecont@wlink.com.np; internet www.decont.org; f. 1997; Chair. KHILANATH DAHAL.

General Federation of Nepalese Trade Unions (GEFONT): Man Mohan Labour Bldg, GEFONT Plaza, POB 10652, Kathmandu; tel. (1) 4248072; fax (1) 4248073; e-mail info@gefont.org; internet www.gefont.org; f. 1989; 16 affiliated unions; Chair. MUKUNDA NEUPANE.

Transport

Ministry of Labour and Transport Management: Tridevi Marg, Kathmandu; tel. (1) 4419252; fax (1) 4419251; internet www.moltm.gov.np; Sec. MUKTI PRASAD KAFLE.

Interstate Multi-Modal Transport (Pvt) Ltd: Shiva Sabitri Sadan, 240 Red Cross Marg, Kalimati, Kathmandu; tel. (1) 4271473; fax (1) 4271570; e-mail rauniar@mos.com.np; internet www.rauniar.com; f. 1975; provides freight forwarding, transport contracting, customs clearance, warehousing and shipping services, transport consultancy, terminal operations, logistics solutions; Gen. Man. ANAND S. RAUNIAR.

RAILWAYS

Janakpur Railway: Khajuri, Janakpur; tel. (41) 52082; HQ Jayanagar, India; f. 1937; 53 km open, linking Jayanagar with Janakpur and Bijalpura; narrow gauge; 11 steam engines, 25 coaches and vans, and 20 wagons; Man. J. B. THAPA.

Nepal Government Railway: Birganj; f. 1927; 7 steam engines, 12 coaches and 82 wagons; Man. D. SINGH (acting).

ROADS

In 2005 there were 17,217 km of roads, of which 4,781 km were black-topped and 4,703 km gravel-covered. Around Kathmandu there are short sections of roads suitable for motor vehicles, and there is a 28-km ring road round the valley. A 190-km mountain road, Tribhuwana Rajpath, links the capital with the Indian railhead at Raxaul. The Siddhartha Highway, constructed with Indian assistance, connects the Pokhara valley, in mid-west Nepal, with Sonauli, on the Indian border in Uttar Pradesh. The 114-km Arniko Highway, constructed with Chinese help, connects Kathmandu with Kodari, on the Chinese border. In the early 1990s the final section of the 1,030-km East–West Highway was under construction. A number of north–south roads were also being constructed to connect the district headquarters with the East–West Highway. In November 1999 the World Bank agreed to provide Nepal with a loan of US $54.5m. for the construction and maintenance of roads (particularly in the far west of the country).

A fleet of container trucks operates between Kolkata and Raxaul in India and other points in Nepal for transporting exports to, and imports from, third countries. Trolley buses provide a passenger service over the 13 km between Kathmandu and Bhaktapur.

ROPEWAY

A 42-km ropeway links Hetauda and Kathmandu and can carry 22 metric tons of freight per hour throughout the year. Food grains, construction goods and heavy goods on this route are transported by this ropeway.

CIVIL AVIATION

Tribhuvan International Airport is situated about 6 km from Kathmandu. In 2005 Nepal had 44 airports, of various standards.

Royal Nepal Airlines Corporation (RNAC): RNAC Bldg, Kantipath, POB 401, Kathmandu 711000; tel. (1) 4220757; fax (1) 4225347; e-mail raceo@ntc.net.np; internet www.royalnepal-airlines.com; f. 1958; 100% state-owned (scheduled for transfer to private ownership); scheduled services to 27 domestic airfields and international scheduled flights to 10 destinations in Europe, the Middle East and the Far East; Chair. GOVINDA PRASAD PANDEY; Man. Dir MOHAN PRASAD KHANAL.

The monopoly of the RNAC in domestic air services came to an end in 1992. By 2005 there were about 16 private airlines in Nepal providing domestic cargo and passenger services.

Buddha Air: Jawalakhal, Lalitpur, POB 2167, Kathmandu; tel. (1) 4521015; fax (1) 4537726; e-mail buddhaair@wlink.com.np; internet www.buddhaair.com; f. 1997; domestic passenger services; Man. Dir BIRENDRA BASNET.

Gorkha Airlines: New Baneshwor, POB 9451, Kathmandu; tel. (1) 4487033; fax (1) 4471136; e-mail gorkha@mos.com.np; internet www.yomari.com/gorkha/; f. 1996; scheduled and charter passenger and cargo flights to domestic destinations; Exec. Chair. PRAJJWAAL SHRESTHA.

Lumbini Airways (Pvt) Ltd: Min Bhavan, POB 6215, Kathmandu; tel. (1) 4482725; fax (1) 4483380; e-mail lumbini@resv.wlink.com.np; f. 1996; scheduled passenger and cargo flights to domestic destinations; Man. Dir R. K. SAKYA.

Necon Air Ltd: Kalimatidole, Necon Hamlet, Airport Area, POB 10038, Kathmandu; tel. (1) 4473860; fax (1) 4471679; e-mail info@necon.mos.com.np; internet www.neconair.com; f. 1992; scheduled and charter flights to domestic destinations and to India; Chair. and Man. Dir NARAYAN SINGH PUN.

Tourism

Tourism is being developed through the construction of new tourist centres in the Kathmandu valley, Pokhara valley and Chitwan. Regular air services link Kathmandu with Pokhara and Chitwan. Major tourist attractions include Lumbini, the birthplace of Buddha, the lake city of Pokhara and the Himalaya mountain range, including Mt Everest, the world's highest peak. In 1989, in an effort to increase tourism, the Government abolished travel restrictions in 18 areas of north-western Nepal that had previously been inaccessible to foreigners. Following the restoration of parliamentary democracy in 1990, tourist arrivals in Nepal rose considerably. Further travel restrictions in the remote areas of the kingdom were abolished in 1991, and efforts have been made to attract foreign investment in the Nepalese tourism industry, but the insurgency in the west has hindered development in the early 2000s. Nepal received an estimated 463,646 tourists in 2000. The number of visitor arrivals declined to 361,237 in 2001 and to 275,468 in 2002. In 2003 the number of arrivals rose again, to 338,132, and in 2004 arrivals increased further, to 385,297. However, a deterioration in the domestic security situation in 2005 resulted in a decline in arrivals to 375,501. Tourism receipts declined from US $140m. in 2001 to $107m. in 2002, but increased to $232m. in 2003. Hotel bed capacity increased from 32,214 in 1999 to an estimated 36,163 in 2001. The Government granted access to a further 103 mountains, raising the total number of mountains open to climbers to 263, in an effort to promote tourism.

Nepal Tourism Board: Tourist Service Centre, Bhrikuti Mandap, Kathmandu; tel. (1) 4256909; fax (1) 4256910; e-mail info@ntb.wlink.com.np; internet www.welcomenepal.com; f. 1998.

Association of Tourism: Thamel, Kathmandu; tel. (1) 4424740.

Hotel Association Nepal (HAN): Kamalpokhari, POB 2151, Kathmandu; tel. (1) 4412705; fax (1) 4424914; e-mail info@hotelassociation.org.np; internet www.hotelassociation.org.np; f. 1966; Pres. NARENDRA BAJRACHARYA.

Tourist Guide Association of Nepal: POB 5344, Kamaladi, Kathmandu; tel. (1) 4225102.

Trekking Agents Association of Nepal: Naxal, POB 3612, Kathmandu; tel. (1) 4427473; fax (1) 4419245; e-mail taan@wlink.com.np; internet www.taan.org.np; Pres. DEEPAK MAHAT; Sec.-Gen. HARI PRASAD DHAREL.

THE NETHERLANDS

Introductory Survey

Location, Climate, Language, Religion, Flag, Capital

The Kingdom of the Netherlands is situated in western Europe, bordered to the east by Germany and to the south by Belgium. Its northern and western shores face the North Sea. The climate is temperate: the average temperature in January is 0°C (32°F), and the summer average is 21°C (70°F). The national language is Dutch. There is a Frisian-speaking minority (numbering about 400,000). About one-third of the inhabitants are Roman Catholics and about one-quarter are Protestants, while most of the remainder do not profess any religion. The national flag (proportions 2 by 3) has three equal horizontal stripes, of red, white and blue. The capital is Amsterdam, but the seat of government is The Hague ('s-Gravenhage).

Recent History

The Netherlands was occupied by Germany during the Second World War. Following its liberation in 1945, the country chose to abandon its traditional policy of neutrality, subsequently becoming a member of Western European Union (WEU, see p. 365) and the North Atlantic Treaty Organization (NATO, see p. 314). The Treaty establishing the Benelux Economic Union (see p. 385) between the Netherlands, Belgium and Luxembourg was signed in 1958 and came into force in 1960. The Netherlands was a founder member of the European Community (EC—now European Union—EU, see p. 228). Indonesia, formerly the Netherlands East Indies, was granted independence in 1949, except for West New Guinea, which was transferred to Indonesia in 1963. In 1975 Suriname became independent, leaving the Netherlands Antilles as the only remaining Dutch dependency. Aruba, formerly part of the Netherlands Antilles, was granted separate status within the Kingdom of the Netherlands in 1986. A commission, established jointly by the Governments of the Netherlands and the Netherlands Antilles, recommended in October 2004 that the islands of Curaçao and St Maarten (in the Netherlands Antilles) should be given autonomous status within the Kingdom of the Netherlands (i.e. have *status aparte*, like that of Aruba), while the three other islands of the dependency, Saba, Bonaire and St Eustatius, should be placed under direct rule from The Hague. In a series of non-binding referendums between 2000 and 2005 a majority of voters in St Maarten and Curaçao favoured obtaining *status aparte*, while the electorates of both Bonaire and Saba strongly favoured becoming part of the Kingdom of the Netherlands. St Eustatius was the only island to favour remaining part of the Netherlands Antilles. None the less, in late October 2005 the Dutch Minister of Government Reform and Kingdom Relations, Alexander Pechtold, concluded an outline agreement on constitutional reform with all five islands. Curaçao and St Maarten were to be granted *status aparte*, while Bonaire, Saba and St Eustatius would become *koninkrijkseilanden* (kingdom islands) with direct ties to the Netherlands. At a conference on Kingdom relations in November representatives of the Antillean and Dutch Governments agreed the stages of reform with a view to establishing the new constitutional order by 1 July 2007. A further conference, to define the criteria for the new constitutions and legislative and government institutions, was scheduled to take place in mid-2006.

Queen Juliana, who had reigned since 1948, abdicated in favour of her eldest daughter, Beatrix, in April 1980, following the adoption in February of a constitutional amendment that allowed for the accession of the reigning monarch's eldest child, regardless of gender.

All post-war administrations have been formed by various coalitions between the several 'confessional' Catholic and Protestant and 'progressive' Socialist and Liberal parties. At a general election held in April 1971 the left made substantial gains. In July 1972 the Government was forced to resign after losing its working majority in the Second Chamber of the States-General (see Government, below). Another general election took place in November 1972, at which the 'confessional' parties suffered a major reverse, and in May 1973 a new Government was formed by a left-of-centre coalition under the leadership of Dr Johannes (Joop) den Uyl of the Labour Party (Partij van de Arbeid—PvdA). This administration modified the fiscal structure and guaranteed minimum wage levels for all adult workers.

The coalition collapsed in March 1977, following disagreement over land-reform legislation; a general election followed in May. Attempts to form a left-of-centre coalition between the PvdA, the Christian Democratic Appeal (Christen Democratisch Appèl—CDA)—an alliance of 'confessional' groupings, which united in 1980 to form a single party—and Democraten '66 were unsuccessful, and in December 1977 Andries van Agt (of the CDA) formed a centre-right coalition Government of the CDA and the right-wing People's Party for Freedom and Democracy (Volkspartij voor Vrijheid en Democratie—VVD). The new coalition was supported by only 77 of the 150 members of the Second Chamber and was notably weakened by ministerial disagreements on NATO policy and the extent of reductions in public expenditure. Nevertheless, the Government survived its full term in office. A general election was held in May 1981, and a centre-left coalition was formed in September, led by van Agt and comprising the CDA (the party with the largest representation in the Second Chamber), the PvdA and Democraten '66. The Council of Ministers resigned after only five weeks in office, owing to its failure to agree on economic strategy. In November the three-party coalition accepted a compromise economic programme, but deep divisions within the Government continued to delay effective action on the economy. The coalition collapsed again in May 1982: all six PvdA ministers resigned when their ambitious job-creation plan was cut, after which van Agt led a minority interim Government of the CDA and Democraten '66.

Although at a general election held in September 1982 the PvdA secured the greatest number of seats in the Second Chamber (47), the election produced a significant swing to the right. Talks on the formation of a new administration continued until November, when a centre-right CDA-VVD coalition was established under the leadership of Rudolphus (Ruud) Lubbers, a former Minister of Economic Affairs, who had recently succeeded van Agt as Chairman of the CDA. The CDA-VVD coalition was returned to power at a general election in May 1986, with (as in 1982) the two parties winning 81 of the 150 seats in the Second Chamber. A loss of nine seats by the VVD was offset by a corresponding gain by the CDA, which, with 54 seats, became the party with the largest representation in the Second Chamber. The election did, none the less, produce a shift towards the centrist parties, with the PvdA and Democraten '66 (D66—as the party was restyled) both gaining seats at the expense of smaller radical groups. Following the election, Wim Kok, a former trade unionist, replaced Joop den Uyl as parliamentary leader of the PvdA. A new CDA-VVD coalition was formed in July.

In May 1989 the VVD caused the collapse of the Government by refusing to support Lubbers' proposals for the financing of a 20-year National Environment Policy (NEP), which was to involve a reduction in government spending in sectors such as defence and housing, an increase in taxes on motor fuels, and the abolition of tax concessions for commuters using private transport. A general election was called for September, at which the CDA again secured 54 seats in the Second Chamber, while the PvdA took 49 seats (three fewer than in 1986). The VVD lost five seats to rival parties. An alliance of left-wing organizations, GroenLinks, won six seats. In October 1989 negotiations between the CDA and the PvdA culminated in the formation of a centre-left coalition, again led by Lubbers. The coalition accord envisaged increased welfare provision, to be funded by a reduction in defence expenditure, as well as a programme of job creation and reductions in certain categories of taxation. Wim Kok was appointed Deputy Prime Minister and Minister of Finance. In August 1990 the Government introduced an amended version of the NEP, designated the National Environment Policy Plus (NEPP), which was to be financed by both the Government and the industrial sector. The NEPP was to be implemented at a faster pace than its predecessor, and placed strong emphasis on energy conservation and improvements in waste disposal and recycling. Instead of abolishing the system of tax deductions for car commuters (an unpopular proposal under the NEP), the NEPP advocated limiting the standard tax allowance for motorists and increasing excise duties on fuel. Proposals by the CDA, in mid-1991, to limit government expenditure by reforming the extensive disability benefit programme of the national welfare system were a source of friction with the PvdA. However, the PvdA eventually agreed to a compromise whereby the number of years of entitlement to full disability payments was to be restricted. The Government's decision led to widespread protest actions in September of that year.

In November 1992 the Second Chamber ratified the Treaty on European Union, which had been signed by EC Heads of Government at Maastricht in December 1991; the First Chamber similarly approved the Treaty in December 1992.

The CDA lost its leading position in the Government at the May 1994 general election, winning only 34 seats in the Second Chamber. The PvdA, which had focused its election manifesto on unemployment and reductions in social welfare, became, with 37 seats, the party with the largest representation in the Chamber. Both the VVD and D66 improved upon their performances at the previous general election, securing 31 and 24 seats respectively. The remaining 24 seats were distributed among eight smaller parties and special issue groups, including two organizations representing the interests of the elderly. As the combined seats of the CDA and PvdA amounted to less than an absolute majority, negotiations on a three-party coalition agreement commenced between the PvdA, the VVD and D66. Progress was initially retarded by deeply entrenched disagreement between the VVD and PvdA over the latter's reluctance to sanction severe reductions in social welfare spending. Following several concessions by the PvdA (including the proposed privatization of some social benefits), a PvdA-VVD-D66 coalition, with Wim Kok as Prime Minister, was eventually agreed in August. The CDA (now led by Enneüs Heerma, Lubbers having retired from domestic politics following the May election) was thus excluded from the Council of Ministers for the first time since 1917.

In April 1996 the Government agreed that its liberal policy on the personal consumption of recreational 'soft' drugs should be subject to stricter controls, in response to protests from France and other neighbouring states that drugs-trafficking from the Netherlands would be facilitated by the withdrawal of EU border controls under the Schengen agreement.

The PvdA won increased representation at the general election to the Second Chamber held on 6 May 1998, taking 45 seats. The VVD secured 38 seats, while the CDA's representation was further reduced, to 29 seats. D66 won only 14 seats, having lost votes to GroenLinks and the Socialist Party (Socialistische Partij). None the less, the PvdA, VVD and D66 agreed to renew their coalition (it was considered that D66 would be useful as an intermediary in conflicts of policy between the two leading partners), and a new Government, headed by Wim Kok, was inaugurated in August.

A parliamentary committee was established in October 1998 to investigate the Government's response to the crash, six years earlier, of a cargo aircraft belonging to El Al, the Israeli national carrier, into a densely populated suburb of Amsterdam, in which 43 people had died. The inquiry was ordered after the Israeli Government had confirmed reports published in a Dutch newspaper that the cargo on the flight had included depleted uranium (used as ballast) and chemical components of sarin nerve gas. The inquiry investigated claims that residents and workers who had been in contact with the wreckage had suffered ill health since the disaster, as well as allegations that Dutch ministers had been aware of the nature of the cargo. The committee's report, published in April 1999, found that there was a direct link between the accident and the high incidence of ill health around the site of the crash, and was severely critical of the failure of the Prime Minister to co-ordinate government action with respect to the disaster. El Al was accused of failing to co-operate with accident investigators. The report none the less concluded that there was no evidence of attempts by the Netherlands Government to conceal details of the flight's cargo.

At provincial council elections, held on 3 March 1999, the opposition CDA took the largest share of the votes cast; the VVD outperformed the PvdA, while considerable successes for Groen-Links were largely at the expense of D66. The outcome left the Government with only a slender majority in the First Chamber, which is elected by the Provincial Councils.

In May 1999 the First Chamber rejected the Government's proposal to allow the use of referendums on policy issues, a key demand of D66, after the refusal of a prominent member of the VVD to support the measure. D66 subsequently announced that it could no longer work with the VVD, and withdrew from the ruling coalition, prompting the resignation of the Council of Ministers. However, following a series of talks between the three parties, in early June the Government formally withdrew its resignation. In January 2001 the three coalition parties reached a new agreement on the introduction of the use of referendums. The new proposals were for a judicially non-binding referendum and would not require a change to the Constitution. The temporary referendum law entered into force on 1 January 2002 and expired three years later. Legislation was subsequently adopted to allow a national referendum to be held exceptionally on the proposed EU constitutional treaty in June 2005 (see below).

In mid-1999 it emerged that the province of Zuid-Holland had made loans to listed companies amounting to 1,700m. guilders, more than one-and-a-half times its annual budget. The subsequent government investigation found that the decision by the Provincial Executive of Zuid-Holland to assume banking functions in 1995 had been unauthorized and democratically inadmissible, because it bypassed the Provincial Council, and that many rules and regulations had been transgressed.

In September 2000 the First Chamber approved laws giving same-sex couples the same legal status as heterosexuals, including the right to marriage and adoption (the legislation came into effect in April 2001). Legal recognition of homosexual partnerships had been granted in 1998.

During 1992–93 Parliament debated and approved legislation codifying a procedure for the practice of euthanasia in circumstances where it was repeatedly requested by an incurably ill patient. In April 2001 the First Chamber passed a bill legalizing euthanasia by 46 votes to 28, making the Netherlands the first country in the world to do so. (In November 2000 the Second Chamber had passed the bill by 104 votes to 40.) The practice was to be subject to strict criteria. The key conditions according to which life could lawfully be ended were that the patient was terminally ill and in unbearable pain with no prospect of improvement. Euthanasia became legal in April 2002. In October 2005 the practice was extended to include terminally ill infants in acute suffering, with the express consent of the parents.

In August 2001 Kok announced that he would not seek re-election for a further term in office at the general election, scheduled for May 2002. He also announced that he would step down as Party Leader of the PvdA and subsequently endorsed the appointment of Ad Melkert, the Parliamentary Leader of the party, as his successor. Jaap de Hoop Scheffer, the Parliamentary Leader of the CDA, resigned in September 2001. He was replaced by Pieter (Peter) Balkenende the following month.

In April 2002, following the publication of a report by the Netherlands Institute for War Documentation into the massacre of some 7,000 Bosnian Muslims by Bosnian Serb troops in Srebrenica (Bosnia and Herzegovina) in 1995, which blamed the Dutch Government, the Dutch military and the UN for their respective roles in failing to prevent the atrocity (the report claimed that the 100 lightly armed Dutch peace-keeping troops who had been stationed in the town at the time had been ill-trained and had no clear mandate), the entire Council of Ministers resigned. At the request of Queen Beatrix, the Government agreed to remain in office in a caretaker capacity pending the forthcoming general election, which was scheduled to be held on 15 May 2002. In addition, the Chief of Staff of the army, Gen. Ad van Baal, who had been the second highest ranking officer in the army at the time of the massacre, also resigned.

Further investigations by a parliamentary commission, in November 2002, into the failure of the Dutch authorities to prevent the massacre at Srebrenica in 1995 revealed that the former Government had been aware of the likelihood of atrocities occurring in the UN camp, and that the possibility of such killings had in fact been discussed in a meeting of the Council of Ministers on 11 July 1995, the very day the mass murders had occurred. In January 2003 the parliamentary commission concluded that the Netherlands bore responsibility for the massacre, that the Government had failed adequately to plan the mission and that the Dutch army had suppressed details of its failures. In September 2004 about 50 women who had survived the massacre demonstrated outside Parliament demanding compensation from the Government for the failure of their peace-keepers to protect Srebrenica.

On 6 May 2002 the charismatic and controversial politician Pim Fortuyn was shot dead in Hilversum, in central Netherlands, just days before the general election, in which his newly established party, the populist and anti-immigration Lijst Pim

Fortuyn (LPF), was expected to secure a substantial proportion of votes. Fortuyn had formed the movement following his dismissal in January as leader of the Leefbar Nederland (LN) party for his anti-immigration rhetoric. In November Volkert van der Graaf, an animal-rights activist who had been arrested shortly after Pim Fortuyn's murder, confessed to killing the politician. At his trial, which began in late March 2003, van der Graaf claimed that he believed Fortuyn had presented a threat to vulnerable members of society. He was convicted in April and received a prison sentence of 18 years. Appeals were lodged by van der Graaf and by the prosecution, who demanded life imprisonment; in mid-July, however, the original sentence was upheld.

At the general election of 15 May 2002 the CDA won 43 of the 150 seats in the Second Chamber, with 27.9% of the valid votes cast. The LPF, aided by revulsion at Fortuyn's murder, took 26 seats (with 17.0% of the votes), the VVD won 24 seats (15.4%) and the PvdA obtained 23 seats (15.1%). In the light of their electoral defeats, both the PvdA and the VVD changed their Parliamentary Leaders, to Jeltje van Nieuwenhoven and Gerrit Zalm, respectively.

Balkenende was inaugurated as Prime Minister on 21 July 2002, leading a coalition Government comprising the CDA, the LPF and the VVD. However, the same day, a Suriname-born LPF minister in the Ministry of Emancipation and Family Affairs, Philomena Bijhout, resigned when it was confirmed that she had been linked to a Surinamese militia group involved in political killings in the former Dutch colony in December 1982. The LPF suffered a further setback when allegations were made by a newspaper that their new leader, Mat Herben, had tried unfairly to influence the selection procedure for the LN's electoral candidates when Fortuyn was still leader and Herben a party member. Herben resigned at the end of July and was subsequently replaced by Harry Wijnschenk.

The new Government detailed policies to reform the health insurance and social security system and reduce the number of illegal immigrants to the Netherlands. In early October 2002 the Minister of Immigration and Integration opened a new college for the instruction of Muslim religious leaders, imams, in Dutch values and social conventions. The course was compulsory for new imams, who faced deportation if they practised without passing the exam.

Meanwhile, the LPF was riven by factionalism and personal acrimony. In addition to the expulsion of two party members who objected to Wijnschenk's leadership style, in early October 2002 a feud developed between two ministers. Herman Heinsbroek, the Minister of Economic Affairs, articulated his ambition to assume the deputy premiership, which resulted in a damaging dispute with the incumbent Deputy Prime Minister and Minister of Public Health, Welfare and Sport, Dr Eduard Bomhoff. The party was unable to resolve the deep personal and political rivalry between the two ministers. Despite the subsequent resignations of Heinsbroek and Bomhoff from the Council of Ministers, the LPF's coalition partners refused to co-operate further with the party and the Government resigned on 16 October, after just 87 days in power. Balkenende presided over a minority Government, comprising the CDA and the VVD, pending a general election, which was scheduled for January 2003.

In the general election of 22 January 2003, in which 79.9% of the electorate participated, the CDA won 44 seats in the Second Chamber (securing 28.6% of total votes cast), while the PvdA increased its number of seats from 23 to 42 (27.3%), under its charismatic new leader, Wouter Bos. The LPF, again led by Mat Herben, following the resignation of Wijnschenk in late 2002, secured only eight seats, while the D66 obtained six. Although the popularity of the right-wing LPF had declined sharply, the electoral manifestos of the mainstream parties addressed the issues raised by the movement. Of these, immigration became a prominent subject of debate, the VVD echoing Fortuyn's statement that the Netherlands was already 'full'. In late January 2003 negotiations began regarding the formation of a coalition administration led by Balkenende. Disagreements between the CDA and the PvdA over Dutch support for an impending US-led military campaign to remove the regime of Saddam Hussain in Iraq hampered progress. In mid-March, in his capacity as Prime Minister of the interim administration, Balkenende announced that, while Dutch troops would not assist in the campaign, some units of the armed forces and weapons would be supplied to help defend Turkey, should the conflict escalate. Negotiations resumed in late March and, as the US-led coalition entered Iraq, both parties expressed their support for the military operation. In early April, however, talks collapsed following the failure of the two sides to agree on budgetary expenditure cuts to revive a stagnant economy. The following month the CDA negotiated the formation of a centre-right coalition with the VVD and the D66, thereby gaining a slender majority of six in the 150-seat Second Chamber. The coalition Government, under the renewed premiership of Balkenende, was formally sworn in by Queen Beatrix on 27 May.

In late May 2003 the provincial councils elected a new First Chamber in which the CDA-VVD-D66 coalition also obtained a majority, securing 41 of the 75 seats. The new Council of Ministers largely resembled the caretaker administration formed in October 2002. The CDA held eight portfolios, the VVD six and the D66 held two. Two new Deputy Prime Ministers were appointed: Gerrit Zalm of the VVD, who was also assigned the post of Minister of Finance, and Thomas Carolus (Thom) de Graaf of the D66, who was also named as Minister of Government Reform and Kingdom Relations. One of the stated priorities of the incoming Government was a pledge to tackle the problems of illegal drugs and crime. The new administration proposed the extension of police powers to stop and search people and the introduction of compulsory identity cards for citizens from the age of 14 years.

Meanwhile, in March 2003 Princess Margarita lodged a criminal complaint against former Prime Minister Wim Kok and the Dutch secret service. The princess claimed that the Government had acted illegally in obtaining confidential documents and information relating to her husband (Edwin de Roy van Zuydewijn, a commoner whom she had married in 2001) and herself, which were later released by her aunt, Queen Beatrix, to the public. Balkenende admitted that van Zuydewijn had indeed been subject to background checks, but that these were routine for anyone marrying into the royal family. (In July it was reported that Princess Margarita and Zuydewijn had separated.)

In April 2003 the Dutch important food export industry was adversely affected by an epidemic of avian influenza. By the end of the month more than 18m. chickens had been destroyed in a precautionary cull to prevent the epidemic from spreading to neighbouring countries. During the outbreak the Netherlands, one of the world's largest egg and poultry exporters, was estimated to have suffered losses of around €2m. a day.

Legislation was passed by Parliament in September 2003 providing for the prescription of cannabis for medicinal purposes by the national health service. The drug was to be produced by two authorized growers and rigorously controlled for quality. In the same month the Government announced its intention to reform the Netherlands' generous social security system, which had been rendered increasingly expensive by the combination of a rapidly increasing ageing population and a decline in the workforce. The proposed reforms included the reduction of hospital budgets by 5%, the limitation of free dental care to those aged 18 years or under, and the introduction of charges for non-prescription drugs. The Government planned to increase the involvement of the private sector in health care, thereby transferring certain costs from the State to the individual. Under the proposed reforms, a non-refundable health insurance excess of €250 would be introduced in 2005, and in the following year the public and private health care systems would merge and a standard insurance scheme would be offered by the various private health insurance companies. In an effort to encourage more people to work (the rate of unemployment had risen from only 3% in 2001 to 6.5% in 2004), the Government planned to make the eligibility criteria for disability and unemployment benefits more stringent; in addition, incentives for early retirement were to be abandoned.

In December 2003 Rotterdam City Council adopted a highly controversial policy paper that aimed to restore the city's socio-economic balance by building expensive rather than affordable housing and by restricting the issue of residence permits to those who earned at least 20% more than the minimum wage and who spoke a good level of Dutch. A parliamentary report published the following month highlighted a perceived unwillingness to integrate on the part of some immigrants and judged that the tolerant multiculturalist policies practised over the previous 30 years had generally failed.

The coalition Government that assumed power in May 2003 introduced a number of stringent new policies regarding immigrants and asylum-seekers. In late January 2004 the Government announced that, in order to prevent the destabilization of the employment market, a maximum of 22,000 immigrants from the 10 new EU member states (which were scheduled to join the

EU on 1 May) would be permitted to settle in the Netherlands. In mid-February Parliament approved a bill that would permit the deportation of 26,000 failed asylum-seekers over the following three years. The legislation applied to asylum-seekers who had arrived in the Netherlands before 1 April 2001 and who had exhausted their appeals. It authorized the removal of their welfare benefits, and the provision of a repatriation payment and a free flight to their country of origin. The controversial law, which was condemned by human rights groups and considered too severe by the political left, was welcomed by certain sectors of society (particularly among those with low rates of pay) that felt threatened by the rising level of unemployment. The 'voluntary returns' policy came into effect in June 2003. By early 2005 some 8,636 cases had been processed, of which an estimated 41% were granted residence permits. Of the remainder, the majority had returned to their country of origin of their own volition, while 519 people were compulsorily repatriated. Moreover, emigration from the Netherlands rose by 8.9% in 2004, while the number of immigrants entering the country declined by 10.0% overall and by 33.7% among those from outside Europe.

At elections on 10 June 2004 to the enlarged European Parliament, in which 39.1% of the electorate participated, the CDA and the opposition PvdA each won seven of the 27 Dutch seats, while the VVD obtained four. A new party called Europa Transparant (Transparent Europe), led by Paul van Buitenen, won two seats by campaigning against corruption in the EU. The decline in support for the CDA and the VVD (which had previously held nine and six seats respectively) was interpreted as a protest against the stagnant economy and the deployment of troops to Iraq. None the less, Balkenende subsequently extended the mandate of the troops by eight months to March 2005.

The EU Treaty establishing a Constitution for Europe was signed by the EU Heads of State and of Government in October 2004. It required ratification by all 25 EU member states, either through a referendum or by a vote in the national legislature, before it could come into force. In February 2005 the Council of Ministers confirmed that a non-binding referendum on the EU constitutional treaty would take place on 1 June. As the referendum was consultative, the Parliament would still be competent to ratify the constitution even if it had been rejected in the popular vote. However, the Government pledged to abide by a clear result. At the referendum, which was held, as scheduled, on 1 June, 61.6% of those who voted (63% of the electorate) were opposed to ratifying the treaty. On the following day the Government formally withdrew the proposed legislation. This decisive rejection of the treaty by Dutch voters, and by French voters a few days earlier, prompted several other member states to postpone their own referendums, casting doubt on the future of the constitution.

In September 2004 the Government announced proposals for a stringent austerity budget for 2005, in an attempt to reduce the budget deficit and prepare for the economic effects of an ageing population. The proposed measures included reforms to unemployment and disability benefits, reductions in expenditure in health care and the elimination of tax benefits for those saving for early retirement, resulting in a greater monetary incentive to retire at 65 years age, thus extending the average working life of the population. The proposals gave rise to widespread industrial action in September and October, culminating in a demonstration in Amsterdam in early October attended by some 200,000 protesters. However, as a result of negotiations with representatives of the Government, a compromise was reached in November whereby the trade union leaders accepted the proposed disincentive to early retirement and the restriction of eligibility for disability benefits, and agreed to demand only minimal wage increases over the forthcoming year.

The murder in November 2004 of Theo van Gogh, who had made a controversial film about Islamic culture, raised concerns regarding the threat to the Netherlands' liberalism and tolerance presented by the country's failure to assimilate ethnic minorities. Mohammed Bouyeri, who was convicted of van Gogh' murder and sentenced to life imprisonment in late July 2005, was suspected of membership of a militant Islamist organization, known as the Hofstad group. Other members of this group were arrested in connection with threats to kill prominent politicians who were openly critical of Islam, including the writer of van Gogh's screenplay, Ayaan Hirsi Ali. Following van Gogh's murder, a number of arson attacks and acts of vandalism took place, damaging Islamic schools and mosques and other Muslim community buildings. Retaliatory arson attacks also took place at five churches. An alleged member of the Hofstad group, Samir Azzouz, had been arrested in July 2004. His trial began in February 2005 on charges of planning bomb attacks on Schiphol airport (Amsterdam), the parliament building and a nuclear power station. Azzouz was acquitted of these charges in April on the grounds of a lack of direct evidence, although he was sentenced to three months' imprisonment for the illegal possession of weapons; his acquittal was confirmed on appeal in December. Meanwhile, in October Azzouz was one of seven people arrested on suspicion of attempting to procure heavy firearms and planning terrorist attacks against national politicians and public buildings. In December the trial began of Bouyeri and 13 other alleged members of the Hofstad group on charges of membership of a terrorist organization. In March 2006 nine of the defendants were convicted and sentenced to terms of imprisonment ranging from one year to 15 years. Bouyeri was found guilty of leading the organization. In an attempt to improve security, Parliament adopted legislation in January 2005 requiring all citizens and foreigners to carry official identification.

In March 2005 Thomas de Graaf of the D66 tendered his resignation as Deputy Prime Minister and Minister of Government Reform. His resignation followed the rejection by Parliament of an electoral reform bill that would have introduced direct election of mayors. The governing coalition was further destabilized when the two remaining D66 cabinet members announced that they were also reconsidering their positions. However, following negotiations between representatives of the D66, the CDA and the VVD, an agreement was reached that ensured the continuance of the incumbent Government. Alexander Pechtold, the Chairman of the D66 and the Mayor of Wageningen, was appointed Minister of Government Reform and Kingdom Relations, while the D66 Minister of Economic Affairs, Laurens Jans Brinkhorst, assumed the additional role of Deputy Prime Minister.

In October 2005 the Minister of Immigration and Integration, Rita Verdonk, announced proposals to restrict Muslim attire, which would, most controversially, prohibit the wearing of traditional Islamic dress, such as the burka and other face veils, in certain public places. Despite criticism by Muslim and human rights organizations, a motion in support of such measures was narrowly approved by the Second Chamber in December. In mid-March 2006, however, following an investigation into the implications of human rights law on such a ban, the Government failed to reach an agreement on the issue, and the proposals were to be reconsidered. In the same month further measures to control immigration were introduced, requiring potential immigrants from the majority of non-EU countries to pass an examination in their country of origin on their knowledge of Dutch culture and language.

Government plans to commit troops to a NATO peace-keeping mission to southern Afghanistan prompted fierce opposition in late 2005. (Some 350 soldiers from the Netherlands were already stationed in the provinces of Baghlan and Kabul, in the north and east of Afghanistan, while a further 250 were engaged in counter-terrorism operations.) Opponents of further participation in the International Security Assistance Force referred to events in Srebrenica (see above), and claimed that Afghanistan's southern provinces were not sufficiently stable for peace-keeping exercises. However, following a debate in the Second Chamber, in early February 2006 the Minister of Defence, Henk Kamp, announced that 1,200 military personnel were to join the mission in the province of Uruzgan from August. Dutch troops had been withdrawn from Iraq in March 2005.

Government

The Netherlands is a constitutional and hereditary monarchy. Legislative power is held by the bicameral States-General. The First Chamber has 75 members and is indirectly elected for four years by members of the 12 Provincial Councils. The Second Chamber comprises 150 members and is directly elected by universal adult suffrage for four years (subject to dissolution), on the basis of proportional representation. The Head of State has mainly formal prerogatives, and executive power is exercised by the Council of Ministers, which is led by the Prime Minister and is responsible to the States-General. The monarch appoints the Prime Minister and, on the latter's recommendation, other ministers. Each of the 12 provinces is administered by a directly-elected Provincial Council, a Provincial Executive and a Sovereign Commissioner, who is appointed by Royal Decree.

THE NETHERLANDS

Defence

The Netherlands is a member of the North Atlantic Treaty Organization (NATO, see p. 314). Conscription to the armed forces was ended in August 1996, and a gradual reduction in the number of military personnel is ongoing. The total strength of the armed forces at 1 August 2005 was 53,130: army 23,150, navy 12,130, air force 11,050 and Royal Military Constabulary 6,800. Total reserves stood at 54,400 (army 22,200; navy 5,000; air force 5,000; others 22,200). In August 1995 a joint Dutch-German army corps, numbering 28,000 men, was inaugurated, and in January 1996 the operational units of the Royal Netherlands Navy merged with the Belgian navy under the command of the Admiral of the Benelux. In 2004 defence expenditure totalled €7,780m. By November 2004 the Netherlands was committed to contributing troops to two of 13 European Union (see p. 228) 'battlegroups', one with the participation of Germany and Finland and one with the United Kingdom. The battlegroups were to be ready for rapid deployment to crisis areas by 2007.

Economic Affairs

In 2004, according to estimates by the World Bank, the Netherlands' gross national income (GNI), measured at average 2002–04 prices, was US $515,148m., equivalent to $31,700 per head (or $31,220 per head on an international purchasing-power parity basis). During 1995–2004, it was estimated, the population grew at an average annual rate of 0.6%, while gross domestic product (GDP) per head increased, in real terms, at an average annual rate of 1.7% over the same period. Overall GDP increased, in real terms, at an average annual rate of 2.3% in 1995–2004; GDP declined by 0.9% in 2003, but increased by 1.4% in 2004, according to the World Bank, although the Netherlands Central Bureau of Statistics provisionally recorded a decline of 0.1% in 2003, followed by increases of 1.7% in 2004 and 1.1% in 2005.

Agriculture (including hunting, forestry and fishing) contributed 2.1% of GDP in 2004, according to provisional figures. Although only 3.4% of the employed labour force were engaged in the sector in 2004, according to provisional figures, the Netherlands is a net exporter of agricultural products: in 2005 exports of food and live animals provided 11.6% of total export earnings, according to preliminary figures. The principal crops are potatoes, sugar beet, wheat and onions. The main agricultural activity is horticulture; market gardening is highly developed, and the production of cut flowers and bulbs has traditionally been a significant industry, although its contribution to export earnings has declined in recent years. Livestock farming is also an important activity. During 1995–2002 agricultural GDP increased, in real terms, at an average annual rate of 0.6%; however, the sector's GDP declined by 3.6% in 2001 and by 1.6% in 2002.

Industry (including mining, manufacturing, construction and power) contributed 23.9% of GDP and engaged 20.7% of the employed labour force in 2004, according to provisional figures. Industrial GDP increased, in real terms, at an average annual rate of 1.4% in 1995–2002; it rose by 1.0% in 2001, before declining by 1.5% in 2002.

Mining and quarrying provided 2.7% of GDP and engaged 0.1% of the employed labour force in 2004, according to provisional figures. The principal mineral resource is natural gas. Total extraction in 2003 was an estimated 75,000m. cu m. Reserves of petroleum and salts are also exploited. The GDP of the mining sector declined, in real terms, at an average annual rate of 1.2% in 1995–99; it increased by 19.2% in 2001, but decreased by 10.0% in 2002.

Manufacturing contributed 14.0% of GDP and accounted for 13.3% of the employed labour force in 2004, according to provisional figures. Measured by the value of output, the principal branches of manufacturing in 1999 were food products, beverages and tobacco (accounting for 22.4% of the total), electrical and optical equipment (9.8%) and basic chemicals and man-made fibres (9.8%). Several multinational companies are domiciled in the Netherlands. Manufacturing GDP increased at an average annual rate of 1.4% in 1995–2002; it declined by 0.9% in 2001 and by a further 1.6% in 2002.

In 2002 natural gas provided 59.4% of total electricity production and coal 28.0%. Imports of mineral fuels and lubricants comprised 10.4% of the value of total imports in 2003; by 2005 this figure had increased to 14.7%. In recent years the gradual depletion of the Groningen natural gas field has prompted the exploration of investment possibilities in smaller fields, while successive Governments have sought to promote the utilization of 'renewable' energy resources.

The services sector contributed 74.0% of GDP and engaged 76.0% of the employed labour force in 2004, according to provisional figures. Within the sector, financial services, tourism and transport are of considerable importance. The GDP of the services sector increased, in real terms, at an average annual rate of 3.5% in 1995–2002; it rose by 1.5% in 2001 and by 1.1% in 2002.

In 2004 the Netherlands recorded a visible trade surplus of €26,490m. and there was a surplus of €19,125m. on the current account of the balance of payments. In 2004 the principal source of imports was Germany (contributing 19.6% of the total); other major suppliers were Belgium (11.1%), the USA (8.0%), the United Kingdom (6.5%), the People's Republic of China (6.3%) and France (5.3%). Germany was also the principal market for exports (accounting for 23.8% of the total); other major purchasers in 2004 were Belgium (11.9%), France (9.7%), the United Kingdom (9.3%) and Italy (6.0%). The principal exports in 2005 were machinery and transport equipment (notably office machines and automatic data-processing machines), chemicals and related products, food and live animals and petroleum. The principal imports in that year were also machinery and transport equipment (again notably office machines and automatic data-processing machines), followed by chemicals and related products and petroleum.

In 2004 the Netherlands recorded an overall budgetary deficit of €10,700m., equivalent to 2.2% of GDP. In 2004 government debt, according to IMF figures, was estimated to be equivalent to 55.4% of GDP. In 1995–2005 the annual rate of inflation averaged 2.3%. Consumer prices increased by 1.2% in 2004 and by 1.7% in 2005. The annual average rate of registered unemployment grew from 5.4% in 2003 to 6.5% in 2005.

The Netherlands is a founder member of the European Union (EU, see p. 228), of the Benelux Economic Union (see p. 385), of the Organisation for Economic Co-operation and Development (OECD, see p. 320) and of the European Bank for Reconstruction and Development (EBRD, see p. 224).

In the early 1990s the hitherto buoyant, export-led growth of the Dutch economy was undermined by a series of budget deficits, a high level of unemployment and fluctuations in international prices for natural gas. The administration of Wim Kok (1994–2002), pursuing a policy of economic consensus, sought to reduce public expenditure, to restrain labour costs and to deregulate commercial activity. Between 1995 and 2000 the Netherlands recorded annual rates of economic growth above the EU average. In 1999 the Netherlands recorded its first budgetary surplus (equivalent to about 1% of GDP) for some 25 years. However, the state of the economy deteriorated sharply in 2001–03. The Netherlands was particularly vulnerable to the global economic downturn, as a result of the country's dependence on trade. This was further exacerbated by a decline in competitiveness, owing to a combination of decreasing industrial production and increasing labour costs. Moreover, demographic ageing and rising levels of unemployment increased demands for state-funded pensions, health care and welfare benefits, leading to a decline in government revenue but continuing growth in expenditure. In an attempt to reduce the budget deficit in order to comply with the limit of 3% of GDP imposed by the EU's Stability and Growth Pact, the Government announced plans for a comprehensive reform of the health system, and measures to encourage labour participation by restricting access to unemployment and disability payments, and the planned abolition of early retirement tax benefits. As a result, the Government succeeded in reducing the budget deficit to 2.2% of GDP in 2004, and a deficit of 2.4% was estimated for 2005. Partly owing to a strong recovery in the export sector, the economy experienced a modest recovery in 2004 and 2005, with GDP expanding by 1.7% and 1.1%, respectively, according to the Central Bureau of Statistics. The signs of recovery were supported by the 2006 budget proposals to reduce corporate taxes and taxes on middle-income families, and to increase expenditure on education and the environment. Based on an anticipated increase in private consumption and investment, economic expansion of 2.5% was forecast for 2006, which, if achieved, would be the highest rate of growth since 2000.

Education

There are two types of school in the Netherlands: public schools, which are maintained by municipalities, and attended by about 35% of all school children; and private schools, which are, for the most part, denominational and are attended by almost 65% of the school-going population. Both types of school are fully subsidized by the State. Schools are administered by school boards, respon-

THE NETHERLANDS

sible to the local authorities or to the private organizations that operate them, thus providing teachers with considerable freedom. The Minister of Education, Culture and Science, advised by an education council, is responsible for educational legislation and its enforcement.

Full-time education is compulsory in the Netherlands from five to 16 years of age, and part-time education is compulsory for a further two years. Some 98% of four-year-old children also attend primary schools. Primary education lasts for eight years and is followed by various types of secondary education. In 2002/03 enrolment in primary education included 99.2% of children in the relevant age-group (males 99.8%; females 98.6%), while enrolment in secondary education included 88.9% of children in the relevant age-group (males 88.5%; females 89.3%). Pre-university schools provide various six-year courses that prepare pupils for university education. General secondary education comprises senior and junior secondary schools, providing five- and four-year courses that prepare pupils for higher vocational institutes and senior secondary vocational education respectively. In all types there is latitude in the choice of subjects taken.

In 2004/05 199,350 students were enrolled at the Netherlands' 13 universities, while some 346,210 students were enrolled at the 54 institutes of higher vocational education. In addition, 21,004 students were registered with the Open University at 31 December 2003. Education, culture and science were allocated €25,700m. (equivalent to some 19.1% of total expenditure) by the central Government in the 2004 budget.

Public Holidays

2006: 1 January (New Year's Day), 14 April (Good Friday), 17 April (Easter Monday), 30 April (Queen's Day), 25 May (Ascension Day), 5 June (Whit Monday), 25–26 December (Christmas).

2007: 1 January (New Year's Day), 6 April (Good Friday), 9 April (Easter Monday), 30 April (Queen's Day), 17 May (Ascension Day), 28 May (Whit Monday), 25–26 December (Christmas).

Weights and Measures

The metric system is in force.

Statistical Survey

Source: Netherlands Central Bureau of Statistics, Prinses Beatrixlaan 428, POB 959, 2270 AZ Voorburg; tel. (70) 3373800; fax (70) 3877429; e-mail infoservice@cbs.nl; internet www.cbs.nl.

Area and Population

AREA, POPULATION AND DENSITY

Area (sq km)	
Land	33,873
Inland waters	3,479
Coastal water	4,175
Total	41,528*
Population (census results)†	
1 January 1991‡	15,010,445
1 January 2001‡	
Males	7,909,855
Females	8,077,220
Total	15,987,075
Population (official estimate at 1 January)†	
2004	16,258,032
2005	16,305,526
2006§	16,335,509
Density (per sq km of land) at 1 January 2005	482.3‖

* 16,034 sq miles.
† Population is *de jure*.
‡ Based on a compilation of continuous accounting and sample surveys.
§ Provisional figure.
‖ Land area only.

PROVINCES

	Land area (sq km)*	Population (1 January 2006)†	Density (per sq km)
Groningen	2,340	574,469	245
Friesland	3,356	642,432	191
Drenthe	2,649	484,437	183
Overijssel	3,337	1,113,564	334
Flevoland	1,421	370,672	261
Gelderland	4,983	1,975,856	397
Utrecht	1,363	1,180,175	866
Noord-Holland	2,657	2,607,164	981
Zuid-Holland	2,867	3,458,300	1,206
Zeeland	1,805	380,179	211
Noord-Brabant	4,929	2,416,100	490
Limburg	2,164	1,132,161	523
Total	**33,871**	**16,335,509**	**482**

* Figures refer to area at 1 January 2000.
† Provisional.

PRINCIPAL TOWNS
(population of municipalities at 1 January 2003)*

Amsterdam (capital)†	735,562	Arnhem	141,528
Rotterdam	599,651	Zaanstad	139,464
's-Gravenhage (The Hague)†	463,826	's-Hertogenbosch	132,501
Utrecht	265,151	Amersfoort	131,221
Eindhoven	206,118	Haarlemmermeer	122,902
Tilburg	197,917	Maastricht	121,982
Groningen	177,172	Dordrecht	120,043
Almere	165,106	Leiden	117,689
Breda	164,397	Zoetermeer	112,594
Apeldoorn	156,198	Zwolle	109,955
Nijmegen	155,741	Emmen	108,198
Enschede	152,321	Ede	104,771
Haarlem	147,097		

* Provisional figures.
† Amsterdam is the capital, while The Hague is the seat of government.

BIRTHS, MARRIAGES AND DEATHS

	Live births*		Marriages		Deaths*	
	Number	Rate (per 1,000)	Number	Rate (per 1,000)	Number	Rate (per 1,000)
1997	192,443	12.3	85,059	5.4	135,783	8.7
1998	199,408	12.7	86,956	5.5	137,482	8.8
1999	200,445	12.7	89,428	5.7	140,487	8.9
2000	206,619	13.0	88,074	5.5	140,527	8.8
2001	202,603	12.6	82,091	5.0	140,270	8.7
2002	202,083	12.5	85,808	5.3	142,355	8.8
2003	200,689	12.4	80,427	5.0	141,082	8.7
2004	193,789	11.9	72,231	4.5	136,761	8.4

* Including residents outside the country if listed in a Netherlands population register.

Expectation of life (years at birth): 79 (males 76; females 81) in 2003 (Source: WHO, *World Health Report*).

THE NETHERLANDS

IMMIGRATION AND EMIGRATION

Immigrants from*	2002	2003	2004
Europe	59,500	54,892	54,461
Belgium	2,039	1,952	1,710
France	1,770	1,677	1,621
Germany	4,933	4,719	5,103
Turkey	6,181	6,703	4,580
United Kingdom	4,476	3,779	3,419
Americas	18,023	15,537	12,964
Netherlands Antilles	5,992	4,273	3,043
Suriname	3,413	3,433	2,857
USA	2,181	2,785	2,495
Asia	21,013	18,039	14,849
Afghanistan	2,824	1,838	865
Iraq	1,535	1,311	1,165
Africa	21,410	14,939	10,759
Morocco	5,192	4,894	3,655
Oceania	1,304	1,107	986
Total	**121,250**	**104,514**	**94,019**

Emigrants to†	2002	2003	2004
Europe	50,142	50,585	54,815
Belgium	1,519	1,512	1,255
France	1,552	1,551	950
Germany	4,387	4,142	3,205
Spain	1,230	1,268	914
Turkey	1,601	2,148	1,789
United Kingdom	3,788	3,842	2,310
Americas	7,366	7,972	8,533
Netherlands Antilles	3,772	4,593	3,940
Suriname	1,668	1,805	1,044
USA	2,665	2,686	1,646
Asia	5,033	5,535	6,088
Africa	3,500	4,064	4,907
Oceania	687	729	706
Total	**66,728**	**68,885**	**75,049**

* Including Dutch nationals returning to the Netherlands: 21,442 in 2002; 19,828 in 2003; 21,911 in 2004.
† Excluding estimates for underenumeration.

ECONOMICALLY ACTIVE POPULATION
('000 equivalent full-time jobs)

	2002	2003*	2004*
Agriculture, hunting, forestry and fishing	229.2	224.1	217.7
Mining and quarrying	9.3	9.0	9.1
Manufacturing	924.8	894.9	859.2
Electricity, gas and water supply	31.2	30.5	29.8
Construction	477.9	460.2	436.3
Trade, hotels, restaurants and repair	1,262.8	1,243.9	1,224.1
Transport, storage and communications	426.1	417.9	406.7
Financial, real estate and business activities	1,324.0	1,289.0	1,276.4
Public administration and defence	475.6	485.6	473.3
Education	324.7	331.4	332.5
Health and social work	757.8	796.1	811.0
Other community, social and personal service activities	301.4	305.2	303.4
Private households with employed persons	74.6	74.6	74.6
Total employed	**6,619.5**	**6,562.5**	**6,454.3**

* Provisional figures.

2003 ('000 persons aged 15–64 years, employed for a minimum of 12 hours per week): Total employed 7,001; Unemployed 399; Total labour force 7,401 (males 4,301, females 3,099).

2004 ('000 persons aged 15–64 years, employed for a minimum of 12 hours per week): Total employed 6,919; Unemployed 479; Total labour force 7,398 (males 4,266, females 3,132).

2005 ('000 persons aged 15–64 years, employed for a minimum of 12 hours per week): Total employed 6,918; Unemployed 483; Total labour force 7,401 (males 4,219, females 3,182).

Health and Welfare

KEY INDICATORS

Total fertility rate (children per woman, 2003)	1.7
Under-5 mortality rate (per 1,000 live births, 2004)	6
HIV/AIDS (% of persons aged 15–49, 2003)	0.2
Physicians (per 1,000 head, 2002)	3.1
Hospital beds (per 1,000 head, 2000)	10.8
Health expenditure (2002): US $ per head (PPP)	2,564
Health expenditure (2002): % of GDP	8.8
Health expenditure (2002): public (% of total)	65.6
Access to water (% of persons, 2002)	100
Access to sanitation (% of persons, 2002)	100
Human Development Index (2003): ranking	12
Human Development Index (2003): value	0.943

For sources and definitions, see explanatory note on p. vi.

Agriculture

PRINCIPAL CROPS
('000 metric tons)

	2002	2003	2004
Wheat	1,057	1,228	1,224
Barley	315	372	288
Maize	196	196*	196†
Rye	17	21	17
Triticale (wheat-rye hybrid)	24	32	19
Potatoes	7,363	6,469	7,488
Sugar beet	6,250	6,210	6,292
Cabbages	236	261	260
Lettuce	66	94	90†
Spinach	44	41	40†
Tomatoes	555	595	645
Cauliflower	42	42	42†
Cucumbers and gherkins	433	430	435
Aubergines (Eggplants)	33	39	41
Chillies and green peppers	310	315	318
Green shallots and onions†	6	45	46
Dry onions	883	809	808†
Leeks and other alliaceous vegetables	95	104	101†
Green beans	63*	45†	40†
Green peas	86	84	84†
Carrots	422	432	430†
Mushrooms	270	263	260†
Other vegetables (incl. melons)	215*	199*	237†
Apples	354	359	436
Pears	171	159	208
Strawberries	35	36	35†

* Unofficial figure.
† FAO estimate(s).
Source: FAO.

LIVESTOCK
('000 head, year ending September)

	2002	2003	2004
Horses	121	126	120*
Cattle	3,858	3,759	3,767
Chickens	101,052	79,235	100,000*
Sheep	1,186	1,185	1,236
Goats	255	274	265*
Pigs	11,648	11,169	11,097

* FAO estimate.
Source: FAO.

THE NETHERLANDS

LIVESTOCK PRODUCTS
('000 metric tons)

	2002	2003	2004
Beef and veal	384	364	381
Mutton and lamb	17	15	16
Pig meat	1,377	1,250	1,287
Chicken meat	683*	510*	600†
Turkey meat	61	50†	40†
Cows' milk	10,677	11,075*	10,700*
Cheese	637	654	670†
Butter	119	117	117†
Hen eggs	637	450*	595
Cattle hides (fresh)†	40	48	39

* Unofficial figure.
† FAO estimate(s).
Source: FAO.

Forestry

ROUNDWOOD REMOVALS
('000 cubic metres, excl. bark)

	2002	2003	2004
Sawlogs, veneer logs and logs for sleepers	398	438	393
Pulpwood	189	190	188
Other industrial wood	116	126	155
Fuel wood	136*	290	290*
Total	839*	1,044	1,026*

* FAO estimate.
Source: FAO.

SAWNWOOD PRODUCTION
('000 cubic metres, incl. railway sleepers)

	2002	2003	2004
Coniferous (softwood)	149	164	175
Broadleaved (hardwood)	109	105	98
Total	258	269	273

Source: FAO.

Fishing
('000 metric tons, live weight)

	2001	2002	2003
Capture	518.2	464.0	526.3*
European plaice	33.8	29.1	28.9
Blue whiting	63.6	35.6	57.3
Atlantic herring	66.4	78.6	95.1
European pilchard	11.8	27.6	47.4
Atlantic horse mackerel	84.0	56.6	68.1
Chub mackerel	12.7	23.3	25.2
Atlantic mackerel	33.1	43.5	29.2
Aquaculture	57.1	54.4	67.0
Blue mussel	48.6	45.1	56.2
Total catch	575.2	518.5	593.3*

* FAO estimate.
Note: Figures exclude aquatic plants and aquatic mammals. Aquatic mammals are recorded by number rather than by weight. The number of whales and porpoises caught was: 2 in 2001.
Source: FAO.

Mining

	2001	2002	2003
Crude petroleum ('000 barrels)*	18,000	18,000	18,000
Natural gas (million cu metres)†	74,232	75,000*	75,000*
Salt ('000 metric tons)*	5,000	5,000	5,000

* Estimated production.
† Figures refer to gross volume of production. Marketed output (in million cu m) was: 73,296 in 2001; 74,000 in 2002 (estimate); 74,000 in 2003 (estimate).
Source: US Geological Survey.

Industry

SELECTED PRODUCTS
('000 metric tons, unless otherwise indicated)*

	2000	2001	2002
Sand and quartz	8,333	8,593	8,317
Gravel and crushed stone	7,283	5,847	5,634
Margarine and other prepared fats	403	382	402
Raw sugar	1,153	1,036	1,112
Refined sugar	1,061	953	n.a.
Cocoa powder (metric tons)	200,249	187,979	191,769
Cocoa butter (metric tons)	180,302	206,581	204,048
Prepared animal feeds	14,203	13,118	13,030
Beer ('000 hectolitres)	24,956	24,605	24,774
Mineral waters ('000 hectolitres)	1,521	1,858	1,993
Soft drinks ('000 hectolitres)	17,243	18,039	15,239
Cigars (million)	2,215	2,241	2,379
Veneer sheets ('000 cubic metres)	19	18	11
Mechanical wood pulp	137	130	132
Newsprint	415	399	357
Other printing and writing paper	930	846	890
Wrapping and packaging paper and paperboard	1,854	1,800	1,971
Packing containers of paper or paperboard	1,162	1,155	1,174
Soda ash	350	400	400
Synthetic dyestuffs†	24,916	23,993	19,642
Nitrogenous fertilizers (a)‡	1,109	1,013	n.a.
Phosphate fertilizers (b)‡	53	174	n.a.
Synthetic rubber†	116	97	104
Washing powders and detergents	397	384	356
Jet fuels	7,111	6,655	n.a.
Kerosene	376	413	n.a.
Motor spirit (petrol) and other light oils	14,263	14,423	n.a.
Naphthas	11,303	12,116	n.a.
Gas-diesel (distillate fuel) oil	21,994	22,167	n.a.
White spirit	345	386	n.a.
Residual fuel oils	11,215	10,780	n.a.
Lubricating oils	647	574	n.a.
Petroleum bitumen (asphalt)	740	714	n.a.
Liquefied petroleum gas	3,683	3,974	n.a.
Coke	2,127	2,214	n.a.
Coke-oven gas (terajoules)	18,875	19,268	n.a.
Clay building bricks ('000 cu metres)	1,507	1,394	1,369
Cement§	2,450	3,400	3,400
Pig-iron	4,969	5,305	5,367
Crude steel	5,667	6,037	6,119
Aluminium (unwrought): primary	300	294	300
secondary	119	120	120
Refined lead: secondary§	22	24	22
Zinc (unwrought): primary	217	205	200
Merchant vessels launched ('000 grt)	48	32	33
Bicycles ('000)	1,155	1,042	1,086
Electricity (million kWh)	92,110	93,512	n.a.

* Official figures refer to activity by establishments employing 20 or more persons. For manufactured goods, except for cement, petroleum, coal and basic metal products, such data relate to sales (rather than production) by the relevant establishments.
† Refers to amounts sold.
‡ Output during 12 months ending 30 June of the year stated. Figures are in terms of (a) nitrogen or (b) phosphoric acid.
§ Data from US Geological Survey.

Sources: partly UN, *Industrial Commodity Statistics Yearbook* and *Monthly Bulletin of Statistics*; FAO, *Yearbook of Forest Products*; IRF, *World Road Statistics*.

THE NETHERLANDS

Finance

CURRENCY AND EXCHANGE RATES

Monetary Units
100 cent = 1 euro (€).

Sterling and Dollar Equivalents (30 December 2005)
£1 sterling = 1.4596 euros;
US $1 = 0.8477 euros;
€100 = £68.51 = $117.97.

Average Exchange Rate (euros per US $)
2003   0.8860
2004   0.8054
2005   0.8041

Note: The national currency was formerly the guilder. From the introduction of the euro, with the Netherlands' participation, on 1 January 1999, a fixed exchange rate of €1 = 2.20371 guilders was in operation. Euro notes and coins were introduced on 1 January 2002. The euro and local currency circulated alongside each other until 28 January, after which the euro became the sole legal tender.

BUDGET
(€ million)

Revenue	2002	2003	2004
Taxation	110,900	111,700	106,300
Wage and income taxes	28,300	27,500	26,100
Company tax	19,100	18,100	15,900
Dividend tax	3,700	3,800	3,300
Inheritance tax	1,700	1,600	1,400
Gambling tax	200	200	200
Value-added tax	35,000	36,200	35,500
Motor vehicle taxes	9,300	10,100	9,800
Excise duties	8,000	8,500	9,200
Environmental taxes	3,600	4,000	3,200
Import duties	1,800	1,500	1,500
Consumer tax	200	200	200
Other revenue	18,700	17,600	17,400
Total	129,600	129,300	123,700

Expenditure	2002	2003	2004
Education, culture and science	23,100	24,800	25,700
Social security and employment	19,500	20,600	22,700
General public services	13,300	14,200	13,300
Housing and community amenities	11,900	12,600	11,900
Public health, welfare and sport	8,300	9,500	11,100
Foreign affairs and development cooperation	10,400	9,900	9,400
Transport and public works	8,000	8,700	8,200
Defence	7,000	7,300	7,700
Home affairs	4,500	4,900	5,000
Justice	4,800	4,600	5,000
Finance	3,400	3,700	3,800
Housing, planning regulation and environmental management	3,400	3,500	3,500
Agriculture, nature and food quality	2,100	2,100	1,900
Economic affairs	1,800	1,700	1,600
Other	4,200	4,700	3,600
Total	125,700	132,800	134,400

INTERNATIONAL RESERVES
(US $ million at 31 December)

	2002	2003	2004
Gold (market prices)	9,385	10,430	10,948
IMF special drawing rights	697	778	778
Reserve position in IMF	2,849	3,054	2,667
Foreign exchange	6,017	7,180	6,657
Total	18,948	21,442	21,050

Source: IMF, *International Financial Statistics*.

MONEY SUPPLY
(€ '000 million at 31 December)

	2002	2003	2004
Currency issued*	19.36	21.90	26.45
Demand deposits at banking institutions	152.52	156.07	162.19

* Currency put into circulation by De Nederlandsche Bank: €17,470m. in 2002; €21,040m. in 2003; €23,140m. in 2004.

Source: IMF, *International Financial Statistics*.

COST OF LIVING
(Consumer Price Index; base: 2000 = 100)

	2003	2004	2005
Food	111.7	107.8	106.5
Rent, fuel and light	112.5	116.0	121.4
Clothing (incl. footwear)	101.8	99.9	97.3
Health	107.5	108.2	108.5
Transport	107.6	111.6	116.4
Communications	103.5	102.8	98.8
Recreation and culture	105.6	104.6	104.1
All items (incl. others)	109.9	111.2	113.1

NATIONAL ACCOUNTS

National Income and Product
(€ million at current prices)

	2002	2003*	2004*
Compensation of employees	238,825	246,209	249,943
Net operating surplus/mixed income	106,231	106,340	110,341
Domestic primary incomes	345,056	352,549	360,284
Consumption of fixed capital	69,427	71,329	73,217
Gross domestic product (GDP) at factor cost	414,483	423,878	433,501
Taxes on production and imports	58,890	60,496	63,414
Less Subsidies on production and imports	8,159	8,025	8,273
GDP in market prices	465,214	476,349	488,642
Net primary income from abroad	4,254	827	1,149
Gross national income (GNI)	469,468	477,176	489,791
Less Consumption of fixed capital	69,427	71,329	73,217
Net national income	400,041	405,847	416,574
Net current transfers from abroad	−6,642	−6,127	−6,893
Net national disposable income	393,399	399,720	409,681

* Figures are provisional.

Expenditure on the Gross Domestic Product
(€ million at current prices, quarterly data, seasonally adjusted)

	2002	2003*	2004*
Government final consumption expenditure	110,246	116,018	118,512
Private final consumption expenditure	233,043	236,548	239,156
Increase in stocks	−1,275	−79	839
Gross fixed capital formation	92,862	90,747	94,641
Total domestic expenditure	434,876	443,234	453,148
Exports of goods and services	298,450	301,413	328,111
Less Imports of goods and services	268,112	268,298	292,617
GDP in purchasers' values	465,214	476,349	488,642
GDP at constant 2001 prices	448,073	447,478	455,152

* Figures are provisional.

THE NETHERLANDS

Gross Domestic Product by Economic Activity
(€ million at current prices, quarterly data, seasonally adjusted)

	2002	2003*	2004*
Agriculture, hunting, forestry and fishing	9,633	9,918	9,182
Mining and quarrying	10,018	10,338	11,587
Manufacturing	59,182	59,621	60,897
Electricity, gas and water supply	6,895	7,532	6,907
Construction	23,724	23,880	24,765
Wholesale and retail trade; repair of motor vehicles, motorcycles and personal household goods; hotels and restaurants	65,665	64,821	65,306
Transport, storage and communications	30,523	31,521	32,480
Financial and business activities	110,261	113,313	116,530
General government	47,546	50,029	51,253
Care and other service activities	50,927	54,120	56,277
GDP at basic prices	**414,374**	**425,093**	**435,184**
Taxes, less subsidies, on imports	49,706	51,072	53,849
Value-added tax, *less* imputed bank service charge	1,134	184	–391
GDP in purchasers' values	**465,214**	**476,349**	**488,642**

* Figures are provisional.

BALANCE OF PAYMENTS
(€ million)

	2002	2003	2004
Exports of goods f.o.b.	221,887	224,924	246,726
Imports of goods f.o.b.	–202,356	–202,672	–220,237
Trade balance	**19,531**	**22,250**	**26,490**
Exports of services	59,377	56,314	58,609
Imports of services	–60,483	–56,282	–56,777
Balance on goods and services	**18,425**	**22,284**	**28,321**
Other income received	44,797	46,507	51,021
Other income paid	–42,704	–48,431	–52,993
Balance on goods, services and income	**20,518**	**20,360**	**26,349**
Current transfers received	5,261	5,429	5,742
Current transfers paid	–12,196	–12,411	–12,970
Current balance	**13,585**	**13,373**	**19,125**
Capital account (net)	–581	–1,880	42
Direct investment abroad	–36,022	–33,473	540
Direct investment from abroad	26,604	17,128	–2,319
Portfolio investment assets	–68,898	–49,938	–63,087
Portfolio investment liabilities	53,151	79,872	47,131
Financial derivatives assets	74,903	111,278	133,006
Financial derivatives liabilities	–81,910	–111,614	–134,157
Other investment assets	–29,540	–57,393	–55,500
Other investment liabilities	55,029	30,846	59,105
Net errors and omissions	–6,465	1,068	–4,645
Overall balance	**–147**	**–732**	**–753**

OFFICIAL ASSISTANCE TO DEVELOPING COUNTRIES
(net disbursements, US $ million)

	2001	2002	2003
Total	3,172	3,338	3,981

Source: OECD.

External Trade

PRINCIPAL COMMODITIES
(distribution by SITC, € million)

Imports c.i.f.	2003	2004	2005*
Food and live animals	18,323	18,473	18,963
Crude materials (inedible) except fuels	7,957	9,240	9,789
Mineral fuels, lubricants, etc.	21,560	26,724	36,485
Petroleum, petroleum products, etc.	17,195	21,801	30,272
Crude petroleum	10,813	13,349	18,773
Chemicals and related products	25,017	28,616	32,709
Organic chemicals	6,218	7,471	8,506
Basic manufactures	24,240	26,669	28,361
Machinery and transport equipment	78,161	86,724	88,845
Office machines and automatic data-processing equipment	24,449	27,732	29,186
Telecommunications and sound equipment	8,594	11,694	13,510
Other electrical machinery, apparatus, etc.	15,701	16,254	15,954
Road vehicles (incl. air-cushion vehicles) and parts (excl. tyres, engines, and electrical parts)	13,577	14,583	14,208
Passenger motor vehicles (excl. buses)	6,993	7,422	7,066
Miscellaneous manufactured articles	27,422	27,225	28,780
Total (incl. others)	**206,867**	**228,247**	**248,827**

Exports f.o.b.	2003	2004	2005*
Food and live animals	29,769	31,154	32,618
Vegetables and fruit	8,327	8,303	8,624
Crude materials (inedible) except fuels	12,342	14,187	15,737
Mineral fuels, lubricants, etc.	19,366	22,364	30,786
Petroleum, petroleum products, etc.	12,136	14,517	20,845
Chemicals and related products	38,835	43,492	47,757
Organic chemicals	9,649	11,221	12,421
Plastics in primary form	7,604	8,918	9,764
Basic manufactures	23,518	25,504	27,209
Machinery and transport equipment	76,720	84,215	89,365
Office machines and automatic data-processing equipment	25,716	27,132	29,750
Automatic data-processing machines	16,272	17,677	16,848
Telecommunications and sound equipment	6,924	9,400	11,501
Other electrical machinery, apparatus, etc.	16,661	18,540	17,598
Thermionic tubes, transistors etc.	8,337	9,306	7,843
Road vehicles (incl. air-cushion vehicles) and parts (excl. tyres, engines, and electrical parts)	10,296	10879	10,927
Miscellaneous manufactured articles	25,644	26,848	28,931
Total (incl. others)†	**234,166**	**255,660**	**280,743**

* Preliminary figures.
† Including victuals and stores supplied to foreign ships and aircraft.

THE NETHERLANDS

PRINCIPAL TRADING PARTNERS
(€ million)

Imports c.i.f.	2002	2003	2004*
Belgium	22,593.7	23,533.0	25,361.3
Brazil	2,180.1	2,322.7	2,690.4
China, People's Republic	8,929.5	10,630.5	14,354.2
Denmark	2,115.3	2,088.9	2,505.6
France	11,838.3	11,371.4	12,029.4
Germany	39,932.1	41,084.0	44,841.7
Hong Kong	1,249.6	1,215.9	1,627.1
Ireland	3,690.7	3,973.4	3,631.4
Italy	6,250.8	5,876.0	6,011.3
Japan	6,400.7	6,462.0	6,693.7
Korea, Republic	1,865.4	1,950.6	2,098.9
Malaysia	3,683.0	3,717.9	3,484.3
Norway	3,735.4	3,824.8	4,314.7
Russia	3,784.4	4,618.3	6,038.8
Saudi Arabia	1,568.5	2,013.3	2,947.0
Singapore	3,380.3	2,790.7	3,387.1
Spain	4,389.3	4,447.4	4,920.6
Sweden	4,070.4	4,073.4	4,297.1
Switzerland	2,391.0	2,514.3	2,009.2
Taiwan	3,508.5	4,418.2	5,234.9
United Kingdom	16,476.3	15,028.1	14,779.0
USA	18,248.5	16,242.6	18,199.8
Total (incl. others)	205,574.9	206,866.8	228,407.8

Exports f.o.b.	2002	2003	2004*
Austria	3,343.4	3,562.0	3,939.2
Belgium	27,481.9	27,441.8	30,729.8
Denmark	3,390.1	3,265.1	3,562.0
France	23,399.4	23,459.5	24,974.1
Germany	56,465.5	56,776.6	61,262.1
Italy	14,275.3	14,153.9	15,427.4
Japan	2,363.7	2,186.6	2,214.0
Poland	2,765.3	2,769.5	3,245.1
Spain	8,249.1	8,771.3	10,182.5
Sweden	4,464.4	4,655.5	5,093.9
Switzerland	3,869.0	3,803.7	3,939.2
United Kingdom	25,525.5	25,525.5	23,960.4
USA	11,396.0	11,469.3	12,038.3
Total (incl. others)	232,703.7	234,166.1	257,732.8

* Figures are provisional.

Transport

RAILWAYS
(traffic)

	1996	1997	1998
Passenger-km (million)	14,131	14,485	14,879
Freight ton-km (million)	3,123	3,406	3,778

Passenger-km (million): 13,848 in 2003; 14,097 in 2004 (Source: Nederlandse Spoorwegen NV, *Annual Report 2004*).

ROAD TRAFFIC
('000 motor vehicles)

	2001	2002	2003
Passenger vehicles	6,539	6,711	6,855
Commercial passenger vehicles	753	788	780
Buses and coaches	11	11	11
Vans	756	798	856
Lorries	143	145	144
Motorcycles	438	461	494

SHIPPING

Inland Waterways
(transport fleet at 1 January)

	1997	1998	1999
Number of vessels	5,067	5,003	4,577
Carrying capacity ('000 metric tons)	5,859	5,589	5,212

Inland Waterways
(freight traffic, million metric tons)

	1996	1997	1998
Internal transport: Commercial	61.2	75.7	79.3
Internal transport: Private	28.2	20.9	19.3
International transport	201.1	224.5	219.7

Merchant Fleet
(at 31 December)

	2002	2003	2004
Number of vessels	1,316	1,313	1,276
Displacement ('000 grt)	5,664.3	5,702.6	5,622.9

Source: Lloyd's Register-Fairplay, *World Fleet Statistics*.

Sea-borne Freight Traffic
('000 metric tons)

	1997	1998	1999
Goods loaded	88,667	85,137	92,000
Goods unloaded	312,864	319,684	305,000

CIVIL AVIATION*
(Netherlands scheduled air services—million)

	1999	2000	2001
Kilometres flown	422	445	425
Passengers carried	18,540	19,556	19,261
Passenger-kilometres	70,117	73,030	68,793
Total ton-kilometres	11,204	11,811	11,154

* Figures include data for airlines based in the territories and dependencies of the Netherlands.

Tourism

FOREIGN TOURIST ARRIVALS
('000)*

Country of origin	2001	2002	2003
Belgium	629	705	779
France	455	511	465
Germany	2,657	2,755	2,803
Italy	343	346	339
Spain	259	276	275
United Kingdom	1,939	1,851	1,646
Total (incl. others)	9,500	9,595	9,181

* Arrivals at all accommodation establishments.

Tourism receipts (US $ million, excl. passenger transport): 6,723 in 2001; 7,706 in 2002; 9,162 in 2003 (Source: World Tourism Organization).

THE NETHERLANDS

Communications Media

	2002	2003	2004
Telephone ('000 main lines in use)	10,003	10,004	7,861
Mobile cellular telephones ('000 subscribers)	11,700	12,500	14,821
Personal computers ('000 in use)	6,900	n.a.	11,110
Internet users ('000)	8,590	8,500	10,000

Daily newspapers: 37 in 1998 (circulation 4,680,000).

Non-daily newspapers (regional or local): 58 in 1997 (circulation 564,000).

Book production (1993): 34,067 titles, excluding pamphlets.

Radio receivers ('000 in use): 15,300 in 1997.

Television receivers ('000 in use): 8,600.

Facsimile machines ('000 in use): 600 in 1997.

Sources: UNESCO, *Statistical Yearbook*; UN, *Statistical Yearbook*; International Telecommunication Union.

Education

(2004/05)

	Institutions	Students ('000)
Primary	7,314	1,599.2
Secondary	668	937.9
Higher vocational	54	346.2
University	13	199.4

Directory

The Constitution

The Netherlands' first Constitution was adopted in 1814–15. The present Constitution, the first new one since 1848, came into force on 17 February 1983. Its main provisions are summarized below:

THE KINGDOM OF THE NETHERLANDS

The Kingdom of the Netherlands consists of territories in Europe (the Netherlands) and in the Caribbean (the Netherlands Antilles and Aruba). Under the Charter for the Kingdom of the Netherlands, signed by Queen Juliana in 1954, these territories constitute a single realm, ruled by the House of Orange-Nassau.

THE MONARCHY

The Netherlands is a constitutional monarchy with a parliamentary system of government. The Constitution regulates the royal succession and the regency in great detail. A successor to the Throne may be appointed by Act of Parliament if it appears that there will otherwise be no successor. The Bill for this purpose shall be discussed and decided upon in a joint session of the two Chambers of the States-General (Staten Generaal). The Sovereign is succeeded by his or her eldest child. The age of majority of the Sovereign is 18 years. Until the Sovereign has attained that age, the royal prerogative shall be exercised by a Regent.

ELECTORAL SYSTEM

The Parliament of the Netherlands is the Staten Generaal and is composed of two Chambers, a First and a Second Chamber. The Second Chamber, which is the more important politically, consists of 150 members, and is directly elected for four years on the basis of proportional representation. The First Chamber comprises 75 members and is elected by the (directly elected) members of the Provincial Councils.

Nearly all Dutch nationals who have attained the age of 18 years are entitled to take part in the election for the Second Chamber. Those not entitled to vote are certain groups of non-resident nationals, mentally disordered and legally incompetent persons.

To be eligible for membership of the Staten Generaal, a person must be a Dutch national, must have attained the age of 18 years and must not have been disqualified from voting.

MINISTERIAL RESPONSIBILITY

The Ministers, led by the Prime Minister, are responsible to the Staten Generaal for all acts of government. This means, for example, that the power of the Government (Sovereign and Ministers) to dissolve one or both Chambers of the Staten Generaal is ultimately subject to the judgment of the Staten Generaal. The right to declare war and conclude treaties can, in principle, only be exercised subject to prior parliamentary approval. The Constitution contains provisions concerning the transferral of legislative, executive and judicial power to international institutions and on the legal supremacy of self-executing provisions of treaties.

The Prime Minister and the other Ministers are appointed and dismissed by Royal Decree. Ministries are established by Royal Decree.

A Council of Ministers is formed by a so-called 'formateur' (usually the future Prime Minister), who will have been assured of the support of a majority in the Second Chamber of the Staten Generaal.

A Minister may not be a member of the Staten Generaal. However, Ministers have the right to attend sittings of the Chambers and may take part in the deliberations. They must supply the Chambers, either orally or in writing, with any information requested, provided that this cannot be deemed to conflict with the interests of the State.

A statement of the policy that is to be pursued by the Government is given by the Sovereign every year on the third Tuesday in September before a joint session of the two Chambers of the Staten Generaal.

Acts of Parliament are passed jointly by the Government and the Staten Generaal. Bills, including the draft budget, must be introduced into the Second Chamber. The Second Chamber has the right to amend bills; the First Chamber can only accept or reject a bill. Revision of the Constitution requires two parliamentary readings of the bills that contain the proposed changes. In between the two readings, the Staten Generaal must be dissolved and elections held.

THE COUNCIL OF STATE

The Council of State is the Government's oldest and most important advisory body. It must be consulted on all bills and draft general administrative orders. The Council is also an important court for administrative disputes.

The Sovereign is President of the Council of State, but the day-to-day running of the Council is the responsibility of its Vice-President. Its other members—usually former politicians, scholars, judges and business executives—are appointed for life.

LOCAL GOVERNMENT

The Netherlands is divided into 12 provinces. Provinces may be dissolved and established by Act of Parliament. The provincial administrative organs are the Provincial Council, the Provincial Executive and the Sovereign's Commissioner. The Provincial Council—directly elected, as is the Second Chamber, on the basis of proportional representation—forms the provincial equivalent of the Parliament. Each Provincial Council elects, from among its members, a Provincial Executive.

The Sovereign's Commissioner is appointed and dismissed by Royal Decree. Each Commissioner presides over both the Provincial Council and the Provincial Executive. The provincial administrative organs have the constitutionally guaranteed power to regulate and administer their own internal affairs. They may also be required by, or pursuant to, Act of Parliament to provide regulation and administration. At present there are 636 municipalities in the Netherlands. The municipal administrative organs are the Municipal Council (directly elected by the local inhabitants), the Municipal Executive (chosen by the Council from among its members) and the Burgomaster (appointed and dismissed by Royal Decree). The Burgomaster (Mayor) presides over both the Municipal Council and the Municipal Executive. The Municipal Council has the power to make local regulations.

The Government

HEAD OF STATE

Queen of the Netherlands: HM Queen BEATRIX WILHELMINA ARMGARD (succeeded to the throne 30 April 1980).

COUNCIL OF MINISTERS
(April 2006)

A coalition comprising the Christen-Democratisch Appèl (CDA, Christian Democratic Appeal), the Volkspartij voor Vrijheid en Democratie (VVD, People's Party for Freedom and Democracy) and the Democraten 66 (D66).

Prime Minister, Minister of General Affairs: Dr JAN PIETER (JAN PETER) BALKENENDE (CDA).
Deputy Prime Minister, Minister of Finance: GERRIT ZALM (VVD).
Deputy Prime Minister, Minister of Economic Affairs: LAURENS JANS BRINKHORST (D66).
Minister of Foreign Affairs: Dr BERNARD RUDOLF (BEN) BOT (CDA).
Minister of the Interior and Kingdom Relations: JOHANNES WIJNANDUS (JOHAN) REMKES (VVD).
Minister of Defence: HENRICUS GREGORIUS JOZEPH (HENK) KAMP (VVD).
Minister of Government Reform and Kingdom Relations: ALEXANDER PECHTOLD (D66).
Minister of Immigration and Integration: MARIA CORNELIA FREDERIKA (RITA) VERDONK (VVD).
Minister of Justice: JAN PIET HEIN (PIET HEIN) DONNER (CDA).
Minister of Agriculture, Nature and Food Quality: Dr CORNELIS PIETER (CEES) VEERMAN (CDA).
Minister of Education, Culture and Science: MARIA JOSEPHINA ARNOLDINA VAN DER HOEVEN (CDA).
Minister of Social Affairs and Employment: AART JAN DE GEUS (CDA).
Minister of Public Health, Welfare and Sport: JOHANNES FRANCISCUS (HANS) HOOGERVORST (VVD).
Minister of Housing, Spatial Planning and the Environment: SYBILLA MARIA DEKKER (VVD).
Minister of Development Co-operation: ANNA MARIA AGNES (AGNES) VAN ARDENNE (CDA).
Minister of Transport, Public Works and Water Management: KARLA MARIA HENRIËTTE PEIJS (CDA).
Minister Plenipotentiary for the Netherlands Antilles: PAUL R. J. COMENENCIA.
Minister Plenipotentiary for Aruba: FRANCISCO WALFRIDO (FRIDO) CROES.

There are, in addition, 10 Secretaries of State.

MINISTRIES

Office of the Prime Minister, Ministry of General Affairs: Binnenhof 20, POB 20001, 2500 EA The Hague; tel. (70) 3564100; fax (70) 3564683; internet www.minaz.nl.
Ministry of Agriculture, Nature and Food Quality: Bezuidenhoutseweg 73, POB 20401, 2500 EK The Hague; tel. (70) 3786868; fax (70) 3786100; internet www.minlnv.nl.
Ministry of Defence: Plein 4, POB 20701, 2500 ES The Hague; tel. (70) 3188188; fax (70) 3187888; e-mail defensie.voorlichting@co.dnet.mindef.nl; internet www.mindef.nl.
Ministry of Economic Affairs: Bezuidenhoutseweg 30, POB 20101, 2594 AV The Hague; tel. (70) 3798911; fax (70) 3474081; e-mail ezinfo@postbus51.nl; internet www.ez.nl.
Ministry of Education, Culture and Science: Rijnstraat 50, POB 16375, 2500 BJ The Hague; tel. (70) 4123456; fax (70) 4123450; e-mail info@minocw.nl; internet www.minocw.nl.
Ministry of Finance: Korte Voorhout 7, POB 20201, 2500 EE The Hague; tel. (70) 3427542; fax (70) 3427937; internet www.minfin.nl.
Ministry of Foreign Affairs: Bezuidenhoutseweg 67, POB 20061, 2500 EB The Hague; tel. (70) 3486486; fax (70) 3484848; e-mail minbuza@buza.minbuza.nl; internet www.minbuza.nl.
Ministry of Housing, Spatial Planning and the Environment: Rijnstraat 8, POB 20951, 2500 EZ, The Hague; tel. (70) 3393939; internet www.minvrom.nl.
Ministry of Immigration and Integration: operates under Ministry of Justice (see below).
Ministry of the Interior and Kingdom Relations: Schedelhoekshaven 200, POB 20011, 2500 EA The Hague; tel. (70) 4266426; fax (70) 3639153; e-mail info@minbzk.nl; internet www.minbzk.nl.
Ministry of Justice: Schedelhoekshaven 100, POB 20301, 2500 EH The Hague; tel. (70) 3707911; fax (70) 3707900; e-mail voorlichting@minjus.nl; internet www.justitie.nl.
Ministry of Public Health, Welfare and Sport: Parnassusplein 5, POB 20350, 2500 EJ The Hague; tel. (70) 3407911; fax (70) 3407834; internet www.minvws.nl.
Ministry of Social Affairs and Employment: Anna van Hannoverstraat 4, POB 90801, 2509 LV The Hague; tel. (70) 3334444; fax (70) 3334033; internet www.szw.nl.
Ministry of Transport, Public Works and Water Management: Plesmanweg 1, POB 20901, 2500 EX The Hague; tel. (70) 3516171; fax (70) 3517895; e-mail venwinfo@postbus51.nl; internet www.minvenw.nl.
Office of the Minister Plenipotentiary for Aruba: R. J. Schimmelpennincklaan 1, 2517 JN The Hague; tel. (70) 3566200; fax (70) 3451446; e-mail info@arubahuis.nl; internet www.arubahuis.nl.
Office of the Minister Plenipotentiary for the Netherlands Antilles: Badhuisweg 173–175, POB 90706, 2509 LS The Hague; tel. (70) 3066111; fax (70) 3066110; e-mail info@antillenhuis.nl; internet www.antillenhuis.nl.

Legislature

STATEN GENERAL
(States-General)

President of the First Chamber: YVONNE TIMMERMAN.
President of the Second Chamber: Dr FRANS W. WEISGLAS.

First Chamber
Election, 25 May 2003

	Seats
Christen-Democratisch Appèl	23
Partij van de Arbeid	19
Volkspartij voor Vrijheid en Democratie	15
GroenLinks	5
Socialistische Partij	4
Democraten 66	3
Christen Unie	2
Staatkundig Gereformeerde Partij	2
Lijst Pim Fortuyn	1
Independent	1
Total	**75**

Second Chamber
General Election, 22 January 2003

	Votes	%	Seats
Christen-Democratisch Appèl	2,763,480	28.6	44
Partij van de Arbeid	2,631,363	27.3	42
Volkspartij voor Vrijheid en Democratie	1,728,707	17.9	28*
Socialistische Partij	609,723	6.3	9†
Lijst Pim Fortuyn	549,975	5.7	8‡
GroenLinks	493,802	5.1	8
Democraten 66	393,333	4.1	6
Christen Unie	240,694	2.1	3
Staatkundig Gereformeerde Partij	150,305	1.6	2
Total (incl. others)	9,654,475	100.0	150

* Reduced to 27 seats from 2 September 2004, when Geert Wilders left the party to become an independent.
† Reduced to eight seats from 2 February 2004, when the party expelled Ali Lazrak, who subsequently became an independent.
‡ In August 2004 all eight representatives resigned from their party; they remained as an independent faction in the chamber, continuing to use the name Lijst Pim Fortuyn.

Election Commission

Kiesraad (Dutch Electoral Council): POB 20011, 2500 EA The Hague; tel. (70) 4266266; fax (70) 4267634; e-mail kiesraad@minbzk.nl; internet www.kiesraad.nl; f. 1989; independent; Chair. HENK KUMMELING.

Advisory Councils

Raad van State (Council of State): POB 20019, 2500 EA The Hague; tel. (70) 4264426; fax (70) 3651380; internet www.raadvanstate.nl; up to 28 mems nominated by the Sovereign; advises on legislation, constitutional issues, international treaties and all matters of national importance; Vice-Pres. H. D. TJEENK WILLINK.

Sociaal-Economische Raad (Social and Economic Council): Bezuidenhoutseweg 60, 2594 AW The Hague; POB 90405, 2509 LK The Hague; tel. (70) 3499499; fax (70) 3832535; e-mail ser.info@ser.nl; internet www.ser.nl; f. 1950; tripartite advisory body; to advise Govt on social and economic policy; monitors commodity and industrial boards; 33 mems, of which 11 belong to the Netherlands trade union federations, 11 belong to the employers' organizations, and 11 are independent experts in social and economic affairs appointed by the Crown; Pres. H. H. F. WIJFFELS; Sec.-Gen. N. C. M. VAN NIEKERK.

Political Organizations

Centrumdemocraten (CD) (Centre Democrats): POB 84, 2501 CB The Hague; tel. (70) 3469264; right-wing nationalist party; Chair. JOHANNES JANMAAT; Sec. W. B. SCHUURMAN; 1,500 mems.

Christen-Democratisch Appèl (CDA) (Christian Democratic Appeal): Dr Kuyperstraat 5, POB 30453, 2500 GL The Hague; tel. (70) 3424888; fax (70) 3643417; e-mail bureau@cda.nl; internet www.cda.nl; f. 1980; by merger of three 'confessional' parties; Chair. MARJA VAN BIJSTERVELDT; Parliamentary Leader JAN PIETER (JAN PETER) BALKENENDE; 80,000 mems.

Christen Unie (Christian Union): POB 439, 3800 AK Amersfoort; tel. (33) 4226969; fax (33) 4226968; e-mail bureau@christenunie.nl; internet www.christenunie.nl; f. 2000; by merger of two 'evangelical' parties, the Gereformeerd Politiek Verbond and the Reformatorische Politieke Federatie; interdenominational, based on biblical precepts; mem. of European Christian Political Movment; Chair. P. BLOKHUIS; Parliamentary Leader A. ROUVOET; c. 25,000 mems (2005).

Democraten 66 (D66): Laan van Meerdervoort 50, 2517 AM The Hague; tel. (70) 3566066; fax (70) 3641917; e-mail info@D66.nl; internet www.D66.nl; f. 1966; Chair. ALEXANDER PECHTOLD; Leader BORIS DITTRICH; 12,500 mems.

Europa Transparant (Transparent Europe): POB 37002, 3005 LA Rotterdam; tel. (10) 2085925; fax (10) 2621294; e-mail contact@europatransparant.nl; internet www.europatransparant.nl; f. 2004; aims to eliminate corruption, fraud and waste in the European Union; Pres. PAUL VAN BUITENEN.

Fryske Nasjonale Partij (FNP) (Frisian National Party): FNPhûs, Obrechtstrjitte 32, 8916 EN Ljouwert; tel. (58) 2131422; fax (58) 2131420; e-mail fnphus@globalxs.nl; internet www.fnp.nl; f. 1962; promotes federalism and greater regional autonomy; Leader JOHANNES KRAMER.

GroenLinks (The Green Left): POB 8008, 3503 RA Utrecht; tel. (30) 2399900; fax (30) 2300342; e-mail info@groenlinks.nl; internet www.groenlinks.nl; f. 1990; by merger of the Communistische Partij van Nederland, Evangelische Volkspartij, Pacifistisch Socialistische Partij and Politieke Partij Radikalen; Chair. HERMAN MEŸER; Parliamentary Leader DIANA DE WOLFF; 20,500 mems (Jan. 2004).

De Groenen (Green Party): POB 1251, 3500 BG Utrecht; tel. (40) 2043413; e-mail degroenen@planet.nl; internet www.degroenen.nl; f. 1983; Chair. JACQUES DE COO; Sec. FRANK PLATE.

Leefbaar Nederland (LN) (Liveable Netherlands): POB 18581, 2502 EN The Hague; tel. and fax (47) 5410205; e-mail bestuur@leefbaar.nl; internet www.leefbaar.nl.

Lijst Pim Fortuyn (LPF): Albert Plesmanweg 43 M, 3088 GB Rotterdam; tel. (10) 7507050; fax (10) 7507051; e-mail info@lijst-pimfortuyn.nl; internet www.lijst-pimfortuyn.nl; f. 2002; right-wing, populist, anti-immigration; Leader GERARD VAN AS.

Nieuwe Communistische Partij Nederland (NCPN) (New Communist Party of the Netherlands): Haarlemmerweg 177, 1051 LB Amsterdam; tel. (20) 6825019; fax (20) 6828276; e-mail manifest@wanadoo.nl; internet www.ncpn.nl; f. 1992.

Nieuwe Midden Partij (NMP) (New Centre Party): POB 285, 1250 AG Laren; tel. (30) 2729487; e-mail info@nmp.nl; internet www.sdnl.nl/nmp.htm; f. 1970; campaigns on economic issues; Leader MARTIN DESSING.

Partij van de Arbeid (PvdA) (Labour Party): Herengracht 54, POB 1310, 1000 BH Amsterdam; tel. (20) 5512155; fax (20) 5512250; e-mail pvda@pvda.nl; internet www.pvda.nl; f. 1946; by merger of progressive and liberal organizations; democratic socialist; Chair. RUUD KOOLE; Party Leader WOUTER BOS; 62,000 mems (2005).

Socialistiese Arbeiderspartij (SAP) (Socialist Workers' Party): Sint Jacobsstraat 16, 1012 NC Amsterdam; tel. (20) 6259272; fax (20) 6203774; e-mail redactie@grenzloos.nl; internet www.grenzeloos.org; f. 1974; Trotskyist.

Socialistische Partij (SP) (Socialist Party): Vijverhofstraat 65, 3032 SC Rotterdam; tel. (10) 2435555; fax (10) 2435566; e-mail sp@sp.nl; internet www.sp.nl; f. 1972; Chair. JAN MARIJNISSEN; Gen. Sec. HANS VAN HEIJNINGEN; 44,299 mems (2005).

Staatkundig Gereformeerde Partij (SGP) (Reformed Political Party): Laan van Meerdervoort 165, 2517 AZ The Hague; tel. (70) 3029060; fax (70) 3655959; e-mail partijbureau@sgp.nl; internet www.sgp.nl; f. 1918; Calvinist; female membership banned in 1996; Chair. Rev. A. VAN HETEREN; Parliamentary Leader BAS J. VAN DER VLIES; Sec. P. A. ZEVENBERGEN; 25,900 mems (2005).

Verenigde Senioren Partij (VSP) (Union Party of the Elderly): POB 26, 3100 AA Schiedam; tel. and fax (10) 4262533; e-mail vspnieuwegein@pen.nl; internet www.pen.nl/politiek/vspnieuwegein; Chair. H. J. TROOST.

Volkspartij voor Vrijheid en Democratie (VVD) (People's Party for Freedom and Democracy—Netherlands Liberal Party): POB 30836, 2500 GV The Hague; tel. (70) 3613061; fax (70) 3608276; e-mail alg.sec@vvd.nl; internet www.vvd.nl; f. 1948; advocates free enterprise, individual freedom and responsibility, but its programme also supports social security and recommends the participation of workers in profits and management; Chair. JAN VAN ZAANEN; Parliamentary Leader JOZIAS VAN AARTSEN; 48,000 mems.

Diplomatic Representation

EMBASSIES IN THE NETHERLANDS

Albania: Anna Paulownastraat 109B, 2518 BD The Hague; tel. (70) 4272101; fax (70) 4272083; e-mail embalba@xs4all.nl; Ambassador QIRJAKO QIRKO.

Algeria: Van Stolklaan 1–3, 2585 JS The Hague; tel. (70) 3522954; fax (70) 3540222; Ambassador BENCHAÂ DANI.

Argentina: Javastraat 20, 2585 AN The Hague; tel. (70) 3654836; fax (70) 3924900; e-mail argentina@xs4all.nl; internet www.embassyargentina.nl; Ambassador JOSÉ MARÍA BERRO MADERO.

Australia: Carnegielaan 4, 2517 KH The Hague; tel. (70) 3108200; fax (70) 3107863; internet www.australian-embassy.nl; Ambassador STEPHEN BRADY.

Austria: van Alkemadelaan 342, 2597 AS The Hague; tel. (70) 3245470; fax (70) 3282066; e-mail den-haag-ob@bmaa.gv.at; internet www.aussenministerium.at/denhaag; Ambassador Dr ERWIN KUBESCH.

Bangladesh: Wassenaarseweg 39, 2596 CG The Hague; tel. (70) 3283722; fax (70) 3283524; e-mail amb.vanbangladesh@wanadoo.com; Ambassador ISMAT JAHAN.

Belarus: Anna Paulownastraat 34, 2518 BE The Hague; tel. (70) 3631566; fax (70) 3640555; internet www.witrusland.com; Ambassador VLADIMIR GERASIMOVICH.

Belgium: Alexanderveld 97, 2585 DB The Hague; tel. (70) 3123456; fax (70) 3645579; e-mail thehague@diplobel.org; internet www.diplomatie.be/thehague; Ambassador LUC TEIRLINCK.

Bolivia: Nassaulaan 5, 2514 JS The Hague; tel. (70) 3616707; fax (70) 3620039; e-mail embolned@xs4all.nl; Chargé d'affaires a.i. JUAN LIBERMANN CRUZ.

Bosnia and Herzegovina: Bezuidenhoutseweg 223, 2495 AL The Hague; tel. (70) 3588505; fax (70) 3584367; e-mail ba-emb-nl-hag@wanadoo.nl; internet www.xs4all.nl/~bih; Ambassador ZELJKO JERKIĆ.

Brazil: Mauritskade 19, 2514 HD The Hague; tel. (70) 3023959; fax (70) 3561273; e-mail basemb@dataweb.nl; Ambassador GILBERTO VERGNE SABOIA.

Bulgaria: Duinroosweg 9, 2597 KJ The Hague; tel. (70) 3503051; fax (70) 3584688; e-mail info@embassy-bulgaria.nl; internet www.embassy-bulgaria.nl; Ambassador VALENTIN PORIAZOV.

Cameroon: Amaliastraat 14, 2514 JC The Hague; tel. (70) 3469715; fax (70) 3652979; internet www.cameroon-embassy.nl; Ambassador ISABELLE BASSONG.

Canada: Sophialaan 7, POB 30820, 2500 GV The Hague; tel. (70) 3111600; fax (70) 3111620; internet www.canada.nl; Ambassador SERGE APRIL.

Cape Verde: Burgemeester Patijnlaan 1930, 2585 CB The Hague; tel. (70) 3469623; fax (70) 3467702; e-mail embcuned@worldonline.nl; Ambassador FERNANDO JORGE WAHNON FERREIRA.

Chile: Mauritskade 51, 2514 HG The Hague; tel. (70) 3123640; fax (70) 3616227; e-mail echilenl@echile.nl; internet www.echile.nl; Ambassador JUAN GUILLERMO ESPINOSA.

THE NETHERLANDS

China, People's Republic: Adriaan Goekooplaan 7, 2517 JX The Hague; tel. (70) 3065061; fax (70) 3551651; Ambassador XUE HANQUIN.

Colombia: Groot Hertoginnelaan 14, 2517 EG The Hague; tel. (70) 3614545; fax (70) 3614636; Ambassador GUILLERMO FERNÁNDEZ DE SOTO.

Congo, Democratic Republic: Violenweg 2, 2597 KL The Hague; tel. (70) 3547904; fax (70) 3541373; Ambassador JACQUES MASANGU-A-MWANZA.

Costa Rica: Laan Copes van Cattenburg 46, 2585 GB The Hague; tel. (70) 3540780; fax (70) 3584754; e-mail embajada@embacrica.demon.nl; internet www.ambassade-costarica.nl; Ambassador EDGAR UGALDI ALVAREZ.

Croatia: Amaliastraat 16, 2514 JC The Hague; tel. (70) 3623638; fax (70) 3623195; e-mail croemb.haag@mvp.hr; internet nl.mfa.hr; Ambassador FRANE KRNIĆ.

Cuba: Scheveningseweg 9, 2517 KS The Hague; tel. (70) 3606061; fax (70) 3647586; e-mail embacuba@xs4all.nl; internet www.embacuba.nl; Chargé d'affaires a.i. ENRIQUE PRIETO.

Cyprus: Surinamestraat 15, 2585 GG The Hague; tel. (70) 3466499; fax (70) 3924024; e-mail cyprus@xs4all.nl; Ambassador IOANNA MALLIOTIS.

Czech Republic: Paleisstraat 4, 2514 JA The Hague; tel. (70) 3130031; fax (70) 3563349; e-mail hague@embassy.mzv.cz; internet www.mfa.cz/hague; Ambassador PETR KUBERNÁT.

Denmark: Koninginnegracht 30, 2514 AB The Hague; tel. (70) 3025959; fax (70) 3025950; e-mail haaamb@um.dk; internet www.ambhaag.um.dk; Ambassador KIRSTEN BIERING.

Ecuador: Koninginnegracht 84, 2514 AJ The Hague; tel. (70) 3463753; fax (70) 3658910; e-mail embecua@bart.nl; Ambassador JOSÉ LUÍS GUERRERO MARTÍNEZ.

Egypt: Badhuisweg 92, 2587 CL The Hague; tel. (70) 3542000; fax (70) 3543304; e-mail ambegnl@wanadoo.nl; Ambassador AHMED AMIN FATHALLAH.

Estonia: Parkstraat 15, 2514 JD The Hague; tel. (70) 3029050; fax (70) 3029051; e-mail embassy.haag@mfa.ee; Ambassador PRIIT PALLUM.

Finland: Groot Hertoginnelaan 16, 2517 EG The Hague; tel. (70) 3469754; fax (70) 3107174; Ambassador PEKKA OLAVI SÄILÄ.

France: Smidsplein 1, 2514 BT The Hague; tel. (70) 3125800; fax (70) 3125824; e-mail info@ambafrance-nl.org; internet www.ambafrance-nl.org; Ambassador JEAN-MICHEL GAUSSOT.

Germany: Groot Hertoginnelaan 18–20, 2517 EG The Hague; tel. (70) 3420600; fax (70) 3651957; e-mail ambduits@euronet.nl; internet www.duitse-ambassade.nl; Ambassador Dr EDMUND DUCKWITZ.

Ghana: Laan Copes van Cattenburch 70, 2585 GD The Hague; tel. (70) 3384384; fax (70) 3062800; e-mail info@ghanaembassy.nl; internet www.ghanaembassy.nl; Ambassador Dr GRACE AMPONSAH-ABABIO.

Greece: Amaliastraat 1, 2514 JC The Hague; tel. (70) 3638700; fax (70) 3563040; e-mail grembhag@planet.nl; Ambassador GEORGES J. KAKLIKIS.

Holy See: Carnegielaan 5 (Apostolic Nunciature), 2517 KH The Hague; tel. (70) 3503363; fax (70) 3521461; Apostolic Nuncio Most Rev. FRANÇOIS BACQUÉ (Titular Archbishop of Gradisca).

Hungary: Hogeweg 14, 2585 JD The Hague; tel. (70) 3500404; fax (70) 3521749; e-mail info@hungarianembassy.nl; internet www.hungarianembassy.nl; Ambassador GÁBOR SZENTIVÁNYI.

India: Buitenrustweg 2, 2517 KD The Hague; tel. (70) 3469771; fax (70) 3617072; e-mail ambassador@indianembassy.nl; internet www.indianembassy.nl; Ambassador LEELA PONAPPA.

Indonesia: Tobias Asserlaan 8, 2517 KC The Hague; tel. (70) 3108100; fax (70) 3643331; internet www.indonesia.nl; Ambassador MOHAMMAD JUSUF.

Iran: Duinweg 20–22, 2585 JX The Hague; tel. (70) 3548483; fax (70) 3503224; e-mail info@iranembassy.nl; internet www.iranianembassy.nl; Ambassador HOSSEIN PANAHI AZAR.

Iraq: Johan de Wittlaan 16, 2517 JR The Hague; tel. (70) 3101260; fax (70) 3924958; e-mail info@embassyofiraq.nl; Ambassador SIAMAND BANAA.

Ireland: Dr Kuyperstraat 9, 2514 BA The Hague; tel. (70) 3630993; fax (70) 3617604; e-mail info@irishembassy.nl; internet www.irishembassy.nl; Ambassador RICHARD RYAN.

Israel: Buitenhof 47, 2513 AH The Hague; tel. (70) 3760500; fax (70) 3760555; e-mail ambassade@israel.nl; internet thehague.mfa.gov.il; Ambassador HARRY KNEY-TAL.

Italy: Alexanderstraat 12, 2514 JL The Hague; tel. (70) 3021030; fax (70) 3614932; e-mail embitaly.denhaag@esteri.it; internet www.italy.nl; Ambassador MARIO BRANDO PENSA.

Japan: Tobias Asserlaan 2, 2517 KC The Hague; tel. (70) 3469544; fax (70) 3106341; e-mail japan.cultural@planet.nl; internet www.nl.emb-japan.go.jp; Ambassador KYOJI KOMACHI.

Jordan: Badhuisweg 79, 2587 CD The Hague; tel. (70) 4167200; fax (70) 4167209; e-mail info@jordanembassy.nl; internet www.jordanembassy.nl; Ambassador MAZEN M. ARMOUTI.

Kenya: Nieuwe Parklaan 21, 2597 LA The Hague; tel. (70) 3504215; fax (70) 3553594; e-mail info@kenya-embassy.nl; Ambassador KALIMI MUGAMBI MWORIA.

Korea, Republic: Velengde Tolweg 8, 2517 JV The Hague; tel. (70) 3586076; fax (70) 3504712; Ambassador KEUN SEOP OHM.

Kuwait: Carnegielaan 9, 2517 KH The Hague; tel. (70) 3603813; fax (70) 3924588; internet www.kuwaitembassy.nl; Ambassador MOHAMMAD SAAD OUDAH AL-SALLAL.

Latvia: Balistraat 88, 2585 XX The Hague; tel. (70) 3063934; fax (70) 3062858; e-mail embassy.netherlands@mfa.gov.lv; Ambassador BAIBA BRAŽE.

Lebanon: Frederikstraat 2, 2514 LK The Hague; tel. (70) 3658906; fax (70) 3620779; e-mail amb.lib@wanadoo.nl; Ambassador MUSTAPHA HAMDAN.

Libya: 15 Parkweg, 2585 JH The Hague; tel. (70) 355886; fax (70) 3559075; Sec. of the People's Bureau ZAKIA ABDUSSALAM M. SAHLI.

Luxembourg: Nassaulaan 8, 2514 JS The Hague; tel. (70) 3647589; fax (70) 3462000; e-mail lahaye.amb@mae.etat.lu; Ambassador JEAN GRAFF.

Macedonia, former Yugoslav republic: Laan van Meerdervoort 50c, 2517 AM The Hague; tel. (70) 4274464; fax (70) 4274469; e-mail repmak@wanadoo.nl; Chargé d'affaires a.i. TODOR MIROVSKI.

Malaysia: Rustenburgweg 2, 2517 KE The Hague; tel. (70) 3506506; fax (70) 3506536; e-mail malaysia@euronet.nl; Ambassador NOOR FARIDA BINTI MOHD ARIFFIN.

Mexico: Nassauplein 28, 2585 EC The Hague; tel. (70) 3602900; fax (70) 3560543; e-mail embamex@embamex-nl.com; internet www.embamex-nl.com; Ambassador SANDRA FUENTES-BERAIN.

Morocco: Oranjestraat 9, 2514 JB The Hague; tel. (70) 3469617; fax (70) 3614503; Ambassador ALI EL MHAMDI.

New Zealand: Carnegielaan 10, 2517 KH The Hague; tel. (70) 3469324; fax (70) 3632983; e-mail nzemb@xs4all.nl; Ambassador DAVID PAYTON.

Nicaragua: Laan Copes van Cattenburch 84, 2585 GD The Hague; tel. (70) 3225063; fax (70) 3508331; e-mail embajador@embanic.nl; Ambassador JOSÉ FRANCISCO ARGÜELLO GÓMEZ.

Nigeria: Wagenaarweg 5, 2597 LL The Hague; tel. (70) 3501703; fax (70) 3551110; e-mail nigembassy@nigerianembassy.nl; internet www.nigerianembassy.nl; Ambassador Prof. MARY L. NAR.

Norway: Lange Vijverberg 11, 2513 AC The Hague; tel. (70) 3117611; fax (70) 3659630; e-mail embhague@mfa.no; internet www.noorwegen.nl; Ambassador KÅRE BRYN.

Oman: Nieuwe Parklaan 9, LA The Hague; tel. (70) 3615800; fax (70) 3605364; Ambassador KHADIJA HASSAN SALMAN AL-LAWATI.

Pakistan: Amaliastraat 8, 2514 JC The Hague; tel. (70) 3648948; fax (70) 3106047; e-mail parepnl@planet.nl; internet www.embassyofpakistan.com; Ambassador IFTIKHAR MURSHAD.

Peru: Nassauplein 4, 2585 EA The Hague; tel. (70) 3653500; fax (70) 3651929; e-mail info@embassyofperu.nl; Ambassador JOSÉ ANTONIO ARROSPIDE DEL BUSTO.

Philippines: Laan Copes van Cattenburch 125, 2585 EZ The Hague; tel. (70) 3604820; fax (70) 3560030; e-mail ph@bart.nl; Ambassador ROMEO A. ARGUELLES.

Poland: Alexanderstraat 25, 2514 JM The Hague; tel. (70) 7990100; fax (70) 3602810; e-mail ambhaga@polamb.nl; internet www.polamb.nl; Ambassador JAN MICHAŁOWSKI.

Portugal: Bazarstraat 21, 2518 AG The Hague; tel. (70) 3630217; fax (70) 3615589; e-mail am.portugal@wxs.nl; Ambassador JÚLIO MASCARENHAS.

Romania: Catsheuvel 55, 2517 KA The Hague; tel. (70) 3543796; fax (70) 3541587; e-mail sicrned@tip.nl; internet home.tiscali.nl/romanianembassy; Ambassador IULIAN BUGA.

Russia: Andries Bickerweg 2, 2517 JP The Hague; tel. (70) 3451300; fax (70) 3617960; e-mail ambrucon@ambru.nl; internet www.netherlands.mid.ru; Ambassador KIRLL G. GEVORGIAN.

Saudi Arabia: Alexanderstraat 19, 2514 JM The Hague; tel. (70) 3614391; fax (70) 3561452; e-mail saudiembassy@wanadoo.nl; Ambassador WALEED A. ELKHEREIJI.

Serbia and Montenegro: Groot Hertoginnelaan 30, 2517 EG The Hague; tel. (70) 3632397; fax (70) 3602421; e-mail yuambanl@bart.nl; Ambassador MAJA MITROVIĆ.

Slovakia: Parkweg 1, 2585 JG The Hague; tel. (70) 4167777; fax (70) 4167783; e-mail embassy@haag.mfa.sk; internet www.hague.mfa.sk; Chargé d'affaires a.i MILAN KOLLÁR.

Slovenia: Anna Paulownastraat 11, 2518 BA The Hague; tel. (70) 3108690; fax (70) 36266008; e-mail vhg@mzz-dkp.gov.si; internet www.gov.si/mzz/dkp/vhg/eng; Ambassador Dr TEA PETRIN.

South Africa: Wassenaarseweg 40, 2596 CJ The Hague; tel. (70) 3924501; fax (70) 3460669; e-mail info@zuidafrika.nl; internet www.zuidafrika.nl; Ambassador HLENGIWE BUHLE MKHIZE.

Spain: Lange Voorhout 50, 2514 EG The Hague; tel. (70) 3024999; fax (70) 3617959; e-mail ambassade.spanje@worldonline.nl; internet www.claboral.nl; Ambassador ALFONSO DASTIS QUECEDO.

Sri Lanka: Jacob de Graefflaan 2, 2517 JM The Hague; tel. (70) 3655910; fax (70) 3465596; e-mail nlslmesn@wanadoo.nl; internet www.srilankanembassynl.org; Ambassador LOKUGAMAGE RUPASENA KARUNATILAKA.

Sudan: Laan Copes van Cattenburch 81, 2585 EW The Hague; tel. (70) 3605300; fax (70) 3617975; e-mail sudani@worldonline.nl; Ambassador ABUELGASIM ABDELWAHID SHEIKH IDRIS.

Suriname: Alexander Gogelweg 2, 2517 JH The Hague; tel. (70) 3650844; fax (70) 3617445; Ambassador (vacant).

Sweden: J W Frisolaan 3, 2517, JS The Hague; tel. (70) 4120200; fax (70) 4120211; e-mail ambassaden.haag@foreign.ministry.se; internet www.swedenabroad.com/thehague; Ambassador BJÖRN INGVAR SKALA.

Switzerland: Lange Voorhout 42, 2514 EE The Hague; tel. (70) 3642831; fax (70) 3561238; e-mail vertretung@hay.rep.admin.ch; internet www.eda.admin.ch/denhaag; Ambassador Dr WILHELM SCHMID.

Thailand: Laan Copes van Cattenburch 123, 2585 EZ The Hague; tel. (70) 3450632; fax (70) 3451929; Ambassador THANA DUANGRATANA.

Tunisia: Gentsestraat 98, 2587 HX The Hague; tel. (70) 3512251; fax (70) 3514323; Ambassador HAMIDA MRABET LABIDI.

Turkey: Jan Evertstraat 15, 2514 BS The Hague; tel. (70) 3604912; fax (70) 3617969; e-mail turkishembassy@euronet.nl; Ambassador TACAN ILDEM.

Ukraine: Groot Hertoginnelaan 26, 2517 EG The Hague; fax (70) 3615565; e-mail embukr@wxs.nl; Ambassador DYMTRO MARKOV.

United Kingdom: Lange Voorhout 10, 2514 ED The Hague; tel. (70) 4270427; fax (70) 4270345; internet www.britain.nl; Ambassador LYN PARKER.

USA: Lange Voorhout 102, 2514 EJ The Hague; tel. (70) 3109209; fax (70) 3614688; e-mail julier.moyes@state.gov; internet www.usemb.nl; Ambassador ROLAND ARNALL.

Uruguay: Mauritskade 33, 2514 HD The Hague; tel. (70) 3609815; fax (70) 3562826; e-mail uruholan@wxs.nl; internet www.europanas.com/Uruguay-PBajos.htm; Ambassador Dr CARLOS GIANELLI.

Venezuela: Nassaulaan 2, 2514 JS The Hague; tel. (70) 3651256; fax (70) 3656954; e-mail embvene@xs4all.nl; Ambassador AUGUSTÍN PÉREZ.

Viet Nam: Nassauplein 12, 2585 EB The Hague; tel. (70) 3648917; fax (70) 3648656; Ambassador DINH THI MINH HUYEN.

Yemen: Surinamestraat 9, 2585 GG The Hague; tel. (70) 3653936; fax (70) 3563312; Ambassador ABDULMALIK A. ALERYANI.

Judicial System

Justices and judges must have graduated in law at a Dutch university, and are nominated for life by the Crown. The justices of the Supreme Court are nominated from a list of three compiled by the Second Chamber of the States-General.

SUPREME COURT

De Hoge Raad der Nederlanden

Kazernestraat 52, POB 20303, 2500 EH The Hague; tel. (70) 3611311; fax (70) 3658700; internet www.rechtspraak.nl; f. 1838; For appeals in cassation against decisions of courts of lower jurisdiction. As a court of first instance, the Supreme Court tries offences committed in their official capacity by members of the States-General and Ministers. Dealing with appeals in cassation a court is composed of five or, in more straightforward cases, of three justices (Raadsheren).
President of the Supreme Court: W. J. M. DAVIDS.
Procurator-General: A. S. HARTKAMP.
Secretary of the Court: E. HARTOGS.

COURTS OF APPEAL

Gerechtshoven: Five courts: Amsterdam, Arnhem, 's-Hertogenbosch, Leeuwarden, The Hague. A court is composed of three judges (Raadsheren); appeal is from decisions of the District Courts of Justice. Fiscal Divisions (Belastingkamers) of the Courts of Appeal deal with appeals against decisions relating to the enforcement of the fiscal laws (administrative jurisdiction). The court of Arnhem has a Tenancy Division (Pachtkamer), composed of three judges and two assessors (a tenant and a landlord), and a Penitentiary Division (Penitentiaire Kamer), composed of three judges and two experts. The Tenancy Division hears appeals from decisions of all Canton Tenancy Divisions. The Penitentiary Division hears appeals against refusals of release on license, which is usually granted after two-thirds of a prison sentence longer than one year, unless there are special objections from the Minister of Justice. A Companies Division (Ondernemingskamer) is attached to the court at Amsterdam, consisting of three judges and two experts as assessors

DISTRICT COURTS OF JUSTICE

Arrondissementsrechtbanken: There are 19 courts for important civil and penal cases and for appeals from decisions of the Canton Judges. A court is composed of three judges (Rechter); no jury; summary jurisdiction in civil cases by the President of the Court; simple penal cases, including economic offences, generally by a single judge (Politierechter). Offences committed by juveniles are (with certain exceptions) tried by a specialized judge (Kinderrechter), who is also competent to take certain legal steps when the upbringing of a juvenile is endangered. Economic offences, and in particular environmental offences, are also dealt with by a specialized judge sitting alone.

CANTON COURTS

Kantongerechten: There are 62 courts for civil and penal cases of minor importance. A court consists of a single judge, the Canton Judge (Kantonrechter). Each Canton Court has a Tenancy Division (Pachtkamer), presided over by the Canton Judge who is assisted by two assessors (a landlord and a tenant).

ADMINISTRATIVE COURTS

The administrative courts regulate relations between the authorities and citizens according to the provisions of the General Administrative Law Act. The majority of cases are heard by the Administrative Law Sections of the District Courts, while appeals are heard by the Administrative Law Division of the Council of State (Afdeling Bestuursrechtspraak van de Raad van State), which also acts as the court of sole and last instance in the majority of cases concerning education, the environment and spatial planning. In addition, cases relating to certain areas of administrative law are heard by the following bodies:

Centrale Raad van Beroep (Central Appeals Council): POB 16002, 3500 DA Utrecht; tel. (30) 8502100; fax (30) 8502198; e-mail crvb@rechtspraak.nl; internet www.rechtspraak.nl/Gerechten/CRvBp; hears appeals against decisions of the District Courts in matters concerning the public service and social security.

College van Beroep voor het Bedrijfsleven (Trade and Industry Appeals Tribunal): POB 20021, 2500 EA The Hague; tel. (70) 3813910; fax (70) 3813999; internet www.rechtspraak.nl/Gerechten/CBB; hears in first and last instance appeals against decisions enforcing socio-economic and agricultural legislation made by certain bodies, such as regulatory bodies and Chambers of Commerce, and by certain ministers.

Administration Law Section, Aliens Division, District Court of The Hague: court of sole and last instance in cases involving immigration; brs in Zwolle, Den Bosch, Amsterdam and Haarlem. The introduction of a limited right of further appeal is pending.

Tariefcommissie (Tariff Commission): court of sole and last instance for all customs and excise disputes.

Religion

CHRISTIANITY

Raad van Kerken in Nederland (Council of Churches in the Netherlands): Koningin Wilhelminalaan 5, 3818 HN Amersfoort; tel. (33) 4633844; e-mail rvk@raadvankerken.nl; internet www.raadvankerken.nl; f. 1968; 12 mem. churches; Pres. Prof. Dr A. H. C. VAN EIJK; Gen. Sec. Drs H. J. BAKKER.

The Roman Catholic Church

The Netherlands comprises one archdiocese and six dioceses. At 31 December 2003 there were an estimated 5,044,437 adherents in the country.

Bishops' Conference

Nederlandse Bisschoppenconferentie, Biltstraat 121, POB 13049, 3507 LA Utrecht; tel. (30) 2334244; fax (30) 2332103; e-mail secrbk@rkk.nl; internet www.katholieknederland.nl/rkkerk; f. 1986; Pres. Cardinal Dr ADRIANUS J. SIMONIS (Archbishop of Utrecht).

THE NETHERLANDS

Archbishop of Utrecht: Cardinal Dr ADRIANUS J. SIMONIS, Aartsbisdom, Maliebaan 40, POB 14019, 3508 SB Utrecht; tel. (30) 2338030; fax (30) 2311962; e-mail secretariaat@aartsbisdom.nl; internet www.de-oase.nl.

Protestant Churches

Christelijke Gereformeerde Kerken in Nederland (Christian Reformed Churches in the Netherlands): Vijftien Morgen, POB 334, 3900 AH Veenendaal; tel. (318) 582350; e-mail lkb@cgk.nl; internet www.cgk.nl; f. 1834; Relations Dir Rev. J. G. H. VAN DER VINNE; c. 73,400 mems; 180 churches.

First Church of Christ, Scientist: Andries Bickerweg 1B, 2517 JP The Hague; tel. (70) 3636652; e-mail peter.faas@hccnet.nl; churches at Amsterdam, Haarlem and The Hague.

Deutsche Evangelische Gemeinde (German Evangelical Church): Bleijenburg 3B, 2511 VC, The Hague; tel. (70) 3465727; e-mail deg.haag@tiscali.nl; internet www.evangelischekirche-denhaag.nl; Leaders Pastor E. BENZ-WENZLAFF, Pastor B. WENZLAFF.

Dutch Mennonites: Algemene Doopsgezinde Sociëteit, Singel 454, 1017 AW Amsterdam; tel. (20) 6230914; fax (20) 6278919; e-mail dn@ads.nl; internet www.doopsgezind.nl; f. 1811; Pres. THIJN THIJINK; Sec.-Gen. H. W. STENVERS; 11,000 mems; 121 parishes.

Evangelische Broedergemeente (Hernhutters): Annastr. 5C, 3062 KA Rotterdam; tel. (10) 4049224; internet www.ebg.nl; f. 1746; Pres. Pastor J. W. TL. RAPPARLIÉ; 3,000 mems in Holland; six parishes.

Hersteld Apostolische Zendingkerk (Restored Apostolic Missionary Church): Hogerbeetsstraat 32, 2242 TR Wassenaar; tel. (70) 5113995; fax (70) 5113995; e-mail s.de.jong.hazk@hazknederland.org; internet www.hazknederland.org; f. 1863; Pres. Apostle for the Netherlands H. F. RIJNDERS; Sec. J. L. M. STRAETEMANS; 500 mems; 10 parishes.

Protestante Kerk in Nederland (Protestant Church in the Netherlands): Joseph Haydnlaan 2A, POB 8504, 3503 RM Utrecht; tel. (30) 8801880; fax (30) 8801300; e-mail info@pkn.nl; internet www.pkn.nl; f. 2004; unification of the Nederlandse Hervormde Kerk with the Gereformeerde Kerken in Nederland and the Evangelisch-Lutherse Kerk; 2.5m. mems, 3,000 parishes in 77 districts; Pres. Rev. J. G. HEETDERKS; Sec.-Gen. Rev. Dr B. PLAISIER; 1.9m. mems.

Remonstrantse Broedersschap (Remonstrant Brotherhood): Nieuwe Gracht 27A, 3512 LC Utrecht; tel. (30) 2316970; fax (30) 2311055; e-mail info@remonstranten.org; internet www.remonstranten.org; f. 1619; Pres. Dr W. VAN DER BURG; Gen. Sec. M. A. BOSMAN-HUIZINGA; 10,000 mems; 46 parishes.

Unie van Baptistengemeenten in Nederland (Union of Baptist Churches in The Netherlands): Biltseweg 10, 3735 MC Bosch en Duin; tel. (30) 2255660; fax (30) 2251798; e-mail administratie@baptisten.nl; internet www.baptisten.nl; f. 1881; Pres. J. HOFMAN; 11,500 mems.

Other Christian Churches

Anglikaans Kerkgenootschap (Anglican Church): Ary van der Spuyweg 1, 2585 HA The Hague; tel. (70) 3555359; e-mail churchoffice@stjohn-stphilip.org; internet www.stjohn-stphilip.org; f. 1698; Chaplain Rev. MICHAEL SANDERS.

Katholiek Apostolische Gemeenten (Catholic Apostolic Church): 1E De Riemerstraat 3, 2513 CT The Hague; tel. (70) 3555018; f. 1867; seven parishes in the Netherlands and three in Belgium.

Oud-Katholieke Kerk van Nederland (Old Catholic Church): Kon. Wilhelminalaan 3, 3818 HN Amersfoort; tel. (33) 4620875; fax (33) 4630442; e-mail info@okkn.nl; internet www.okkn.nl; f. 1723 in the Netherlands with Jansenist influence; refuses to accept papal infallibility and other 'new' dogmas of the Roman Catholic Church; full communion with the Anglican Churches since 1931; Leader Archbishop of Utrecht Mgr J. A. O. L. VERCAMMEN (18 parishes); Bishop of Haarlem Mgr Dr J. L. WIRIX-SPEETJENS (11 parishes); Bishop of Deventer (vacant); 10,000 mems; also churches in Europe.

Vrij-Katholieke Kerk (Liberal Catholic Church): Diedenweg 29, 6703 GS Wageningen; tel. (31) 7413679; e-mail frank.den.outer@freeler.nl; internet www.vkk.nl; f. 1916; Regionary Bishop Rt Rev. FRANK R. DEN OUTER; Auxiliary Bishop Rt Rev. PETER BAAIJ; 10 congregations; 2 bishops; 25 priests; 1,000 mems.

JUDAISM

Portugees-Israëlietisch Kerkgenootschap (Portuguese-Israelite Federation): MR Visserplein 3, 1011 RD Amsterdam; tel. (20) 6245351; fax (20) 6254680; e-mail pig-amsterdam@euronet.nl; Pres. J. S. CORONEL.

BAHÁ'Í FAITH

National Spiritual Assembly (Bahá'í Community of the Netherlands): Riouwstraat 27, 2585 GR The Hague; tel. (70) 3554017; fax (70) 3506161; e-mail nsa@bahai.nl; internet www.bahai.nl; f. 1962; mems resident in 186 locations (2005).

The Press

PRINCIPAL DAILIES

Alkmaar

Noordhollands Dagblad: POB 2, 1800 AA Alkmaar; tel. (72) 5196196; fax (72) 5124152; e-mail redactie@nhd.hdc.nl; internet www.nhd.nl; morning; Editors GEERT TEN DAM, JAN-GEERT MAJOOR; circ. 150,000 (2002).

Alphen aan den Rijn

Rijn en Gouwe: POB 1, 2400 AA Alphen a/d Rijn; tel. (172) 487444; fax (172) 487478; internet www.rijnengouwe.nl; f. 1871; morning; circ. 40,000 (2001).

Amersfoort

Amersfoortse Courant: POB 1262, 3800 BG Amersfoortse; tel. (33) 4647911; fax (33) 4647251; e-mail ac.redactie@ad.nl; internet www.amersfoortsecourant.nl; f. 1887; publ. by AD NieuwsMedia; evening; Editor-in-Chief ARJEH KALMANN; circ. 35,000 (2002).

Amsterdam

Het Financieele Dagblad (Financial Daily): 85–87 Weesperstraat, POB 216, 1000 AE Amsterdam; tel. (20) 5928711; fax (20) 5928700; e-mail webred@fd.nl; internet www.fd.nl; f. 1796; morning; Editor A. BAKKER; circ. 52,000.

Het Parool: Czaar Peterstraat 213, POB 433, 1000 AK Amsterdam; tel. (20) 5584444; fax (20) 5584351; e-mail redactie@parool.nl; internet www.parool.nl; f. 1940; evening; Dir F.C.R. CAMPAGNE; Editor ERIK VAN GRUIJTHUIJSEN; circ. 95,120.

De Telegraaf: POB 376, 1000 EB Amsterdam; tel. (20) 5859111; fax (20) 5858017; e-mail redactie@telegraaf.nl; internet www.telegraaf.nl; f. 1893; morning; Editors E. BOS, J. OLDE KALTER; circ. 800,000 (2002).

Trouw (Loyalty): POB 859, 1000 AW Amsterdam; tel. (20) 5629444; fax (20) 6680389; e-mail redactie@trouw.nl; f. 1943; morning; Editor F. VAN EXTER; circ. 130,000.

De Volkskrant (The People's Journal): POB 1002, 1000 BA Amsterdam; tel. (20) 5626222; fax (20) 5622448; e-mail redactie@volkskrant.nl; internet www.volkskrant.nl; f. 1919; morning; Editor PIETER I. BROERTJES; circ. 372,100.

Apeldoorn

Apeldoornse Courant: POB 833, 7301 BB Apeldoorn; tel. (55) 5388388; fax (55) 5388200; e-mail rvbe@wegener.nl; internet www.apeldoornsecourant.nl; f. 1903; evening; Chief Editor GERT SELLES; circ. 150,000.

Deventer Dagblad: Brink 91, 7411 BZ Deventer; tel. (57) 0686468; fax (57) 0686462; e-mail reddeveneterdagblad.nl; internet www.deventerdagblad.nl; f. 1869; Editor L. ENTHOVEN; circ. 34,849.

Reformatorisch Dagblad: POB 670, 7300 AR Apeldoorn; tel. (55) 5390222; fax (55) 5412288; e-mail redactie@refdag.nl; internet www.refdag.nl; f. 1971; evening; Editor-in-Chief W. B. KRANENDONK; Man. Dir B. VISSER; circ. 59,000 (2003).

Assen

Drentse en Asser Courant: POB 36, 9400 AA Assen; tel. (592) 329500; fax (592) 314890; e-mail dgd.redactie@hazewinkel.nl; internet www.drentsecourant.nl; f. 1823; evening; Editor G. VOGELAAR.

Barneveld

Barneveldse Krant: Marconistraat 33, POB 67, 3770 AB Barneveld; tel. (342) 494911; fax (342) 494240; e-mail barneveldsekrant@bdu.nl; internet www.barneveldsekrant.nl; f. 1871; publ. by BDU; evening; Dir ERWIN KLEIN WOLTERINK; Editor J. VAN GINKEL; circ. 11,600.

Nederlands Dagblad: POB 111, 3770 AC Barneveld; tel. (342) 411711; fax (342) 411611; e-mail redactie@nd.nl; internet www.nd.nl; f. 1944; morning; Editor P. A. BERGWERFF; circ. 34,000.

Breda

BN/De Stem (The Voice): POB 3229, 4800 MB Breda; tel. (76) 5312311; fax (76) 5312355; e-mail l.krijneni@uitg-zwn.nl; internet www.bndestem.nl; f. 1998; by merger of Brabants Nieuwsblad and De Stem; owned by Wegener; morning; Man. Dir A. A. M. VERREST; Editor J. VAN UFFELEN; circ. 145,769.

THE NETHERLANDS

Delft

Delftsche Courant: POB 18, 2600 AA Delft; tel. (70) 3190911; internet www.delftschecourant.nl; publ. by AD NieuwsMedia; evening; Dir Jan Bonjer; circ. 11,151 (2001).

Deventer

Gelders-Overijsselse Courant: POB 18, 7400 AA Deventer; tel. (570) 648444; fax (570) 621324; evening.

Dordrecht

De Dordtenaar: POB 54, 3300 AB Dordrecht; tel. (78) 6324711; fax (78) 6324729; e-mail redactie@dordtenaar.nl; f. 1946; morning; Editor H. Kerstiens; circ. 38,000.

Eindhoven

Eindhovens Dagblad: POB 534, 5600 AM Eindhoven; tel. (40) 2336336; fax (40) 2436954; e-mail redactie@eindhovensdagblad.nl; internet www.eindhovensdagblad.nl; owned by Wegener; Editor Joep van der Hart; circ. 130,000 (2002).

Enschede

Dagblad Tubantia: POB 28, 7500 AA Enschede; tel. (53) 4842842; fax (53) 4842230; internet www.tctubantia.nl; f. 1872; evening; Editor G. Driehuis; circ. 152,600 (incl. *De Twentsche Courant Tubantia*, below).

De Twentsche Courant Tubantia: POB 28, 7500 AA Enschede; tel. (53) 4842842; fax (53) 4842230; f. 1844; circ. see *Dagblad Tubantia*, above.

Groningen

Dagblad van het Noorden: POB 60, 9700 MC Groningen; tel. (50) 5844444; fax (50) 5844209; e-mail redactie@dvhn.nl; internet www.dvhn.nl; f. 1888; morning; Editors H. Blanken, P. Sijpersma, E. van Dijk; circ. 180,000.

IJmuider Courant: POB 60, 9700 MC Groningen; tel. (50) 5844444; fax (50) 5844209; e-mail redactie@dvhn.nl; internet www.ijmuidercourant.nl; evening; Editor Pieter Sijpersma.

Haarlem

Haarlems Dagblad: POB 507, 2003 PA Haarlem; tel. (23) 5150150; fax (23) 5310296; e-mail redactie.hd@hdc.nl; internet www.haarlemsdagblad.nl; f. 1656; evening; Editors Geert ten Dam, Jan Geert Majoor; circ. 51,520 (2002).

The Hague

Haagsche Courant: POB 16050, 2500 AA The Hague; tel. (70) 3190922; fax (70) 3906447; e-mail redactie@haagschecourant.nl; internet www.haagschecourant.nl; evening; Editor J. P. ter Horst; circ. 105,000.

Nederlandse Staatscourant: Chr. Plantijnstraat 2, POB 20020, 2500 EA The Hague; tel. (70) 3789422; fax (70) 3855505; e-mail staatscourant@sdu.nl; internet www.staatscourant.nl; f. 1814; morning; circ. 14,600.

Heerlen

Limburgs Dagblad: POB 3100, 6401 DP Heerlen; tel. (45) 739911; fax (45) 5739264; internet www.limburgsdagblad.nl; f. 1918; morning; Editor Hans Goessens; circ. 75,000 (2002).

's-Hertogenbosch

Brabants Dagblad: POB 235, 5201 HB 's-Hertogenbosch; tel. (73) 6157157; fax (73) 6157171; e-mail redactie@brabantsdagblad.nl; internet www.brabantsdagblad.nl; f. 1771; morning; Editor T. van der Meulen; circ. 158,290 (2001).

Eindhovens Dagblad: POB 534, 5600 AM Eindhoven; tel. (40) 2336336; fax (40) 2436954; e-mail redactie@eindhovensdagblad.nl; internet www.eindhovensdagblad.nl; Editor Joep van der Hart; circ. 130,000 (2001).

Hilversum

De Gooi en Eemlander: Seinstraat 14, 1223 DA Hilversum; tel. (35) 6477000; fax (35) 6477108; e-mail redactie.ge@hdc.nl; internet www.gooienemlander.nl; f. 1871; evening; Editors Geert ten Dam, Jan-Geert Majoor; circ. 45,000 (2002).

Hoorn

Dagblad voor West-Friesland: Nieuwe Steen 25, POB 5, 1620 AA Hoorn; tel. (22) 9284901; fax (22) 9284929; e-mail lag.dwf.ec@hdcmedia.nl; publ. by HDC Media.

Enkhuizer Courant: Nieuwe Steen 25, POB 5, 1620 AA Hoorn; tel. (22) 9284901; fax (22) 9284929; e-mail lag.dwf.ec@hdcmedia.nl; publ. by HDC Media.

Leeuwarden

Friesch Dagblad: POB 412, 8901 BE Leeuwarden; tel. (58) 2987654; fax (58) 987540; e-mail fd@frieschdagblad.nl; f. 1903; evening; Editor L. Kooistra; circ. 22,000 (2001).

Leeuwarder Courant: POB 394, 8901 BD Leeuwarden; tel. (58) 2845845; fax (58) 2845409; e-mail redactie@leeuwardercourant.nl; internet www.leeuwardercourant.nl; f. 1752; evening; Editor R. Mulder; circ. 112,000.

Leiden

Leidsch Dagblad: POB 54, 2300 AB Leiden; tel. (71) 5356356; fax (71) 5321429; e-mail stadsredactie@leidschdagblad.nl; internet www.leidschdagblad.nl; f. 1860; publ. by HDC Media; evening; Editors Geert ten Dam, Jan-Geert Majoor; circ. 41,464 (2001).

Maastricht

Dagblad De Limburger: POB 1056, 6201 MK Maastricht; tel. (43) 3502000; fax (43) 3501879; e-mail nieuwsdienst@ld.mgl.nl; internet www.limburger.nl; f. 1845; morning; Editor Fons Veldersen; circ. 180,000.

Nijmegen

De Gelderlander: Voorstadslaan 2, POB 36, 6500 DA Nijmegen; tel. (24) 3650611; fax (24) 3650209; e-mail redactie@gelderlander.nl; internet www.gelderlander.nl; f. 1848; owned by Wegener; morning; Editor L. van de Geijn; circ. 164,300 (2001).

Purmerend

Dagblad Waterland (NNC): POB 14, 1440 AA Purmerend; tel. (299) 314700; fax (299) 314747; e-mail waterland@nhd.nl; internet www.nhd.nl; fmrly Nieuwe Noordhollandse Courant; Contact Winnie de Wit.

Rotterdam

Algemeen Dagblad: Marten Meesweg 35, POB 8983, 3009 TC Rotterdam; tel. (10) 4066206; fax (10) 4066958; e-mail ad@ad.nl; internet www.ad.nl; f. 1946; morning; Editor Jan Bonjer; circ. 380,000 (2001).

NRC Handelsblad BV: Marten Meesweg 35, POB 8987, 3009 TH Rotterdam; tel. (10) 4066111; fax (10) 4066967; e-mail nrc@nrc.nl; internet www.nrc.nl; f. 1970; evening; Editor F. E. Jensma; circ. 262,000 (2003).

Rotterdams Dagblad: POB 2999, 3000 CZ Rotterdam; tel. (10) 4004400; fax (10) 4128449; e-mail rd.redactie@ad.nl; internet www.rotterdamsdagblad.nl; f. 1991; evening; Editor Bart Verkade; circ. 102,222 (2001).

Utrecht

Utrechts Nieuwsblad: POB 500, 3990 DM Houten; tel. (30) 6399911; fax (30) 6399226; e-mail info@wumn.wegener.nl; internet www.utrechtsnieuwsblad.nl; f. 1993; evening; Editor-in-Chief A. Kalmann; circ. 86,840 (2001).

Vlissingen

Provinciale Zeeuwse Courant: POB 31, 4460 AA Goes; tel. (118) 484000; fax (118) 472404; internet www.pzc.nl; f. 1758; morning; Editor A. L. Oosthoek; circ. 61,495 (2001).

Zwolle

Zwolse Courant: POB 29, 8000 AA Zwolle; tel. (38) 4275275; fax (38) 4219453; e-mail zwolsecourant@wugo.wegener.nl; internet www.zwolsecourant.nl; f. 1790; morning; Editor H. Beltman; circ. 37,680.

SELECTED WEEKLIES

Adformatie: POB 75462, 1070 AL Amsterdam; tel. (20) 5733644; fax (20) 6793581; e-mail redactie@adformatie.nl; internet www.adformatie.nl; advertising, marketing and media; Editor-in-Chief Léon Bouwman; circ. 40,000.

Avrobode: s'-Gravelandseweg 52, 1217 ET Hilversum; tel. (35) 6717911; fax (35) 717443; internet www.avrobode.nl; publ. by Algemene Omroepvereniging; radio and TV guide; circ. 791,986.

Boerderij: Hanzestraat 1, POB 4, 7000 BA Doetinchem; tel. (314) 349446; fax (314) 344397; e-mail boerderij@reedbusiness.nl; internet www.boerderij.nl; f. 1915; farming; Editor-in-Chief Marcel Henst; circ. 65,000.

THE NETHERLANDS

Donald Duck: Haaksbergsweg 75, 1101 BR Amsterdam; tel. (20) 4300300; fax (20) 4300315; internet www.donaldduck.nl; f. 1952; children's interest; weekly; Publr SUZAN SCHOUTEN HAAGMANS; Editor JESSICA HAAGMANS; circ. 62,784.

Elsevier: POB 152, 1000 AD Amsterdam; tel. (20) 5159944; fax (20) 5159900; e-mail redactie.elsevier@elsevier.nl; internet www.elsevier.nl; f. 1945; current affairs; Chief Editor ARENDO JOUSTRA; circ. 160,000.

Fancy: POB 1610, 2130 JA Hoofddorp; tel. (23) 5565117; fax (23) 5565116; e-mail fancy@sanoma-uitgevers.nl; internet www.fancy.nl; teenage girls' interest; Editor ANNET NITERINK; circ. 120,000.

HP/De Tijd (The Times): Amsterdam; tel. (20) 5734811; fax (20) 5734406; f. 1845; as daily; changed to weekly in 1974; Christian progressive; current affairs; Dir A. VISSER; circ. 37,580.

Libelle: POB 1742, 2130 JC Hoofddorp; tel. (23) 5564002; fax (23) 5564003; e-mail f.stuy@sanoma-uitgevers.nl; internet www.libelle.nl; f. 1934; women's interest; Editor-in-Chief FRANSKA STUY; circ. 587,754.

Margriet: POB 1640, 2130 JA Hoofddorp; tel. (23) 5564200; e-mail redactie@margriet.nl; internet www.margriet.nl; f. 1939; women's interest; Editor ELSA HINTZPETER; circ. 499,868.

Mikro-Gids: Zeverijnstraat 6, 1216 GK Hilversum; tel. (35) 6726751; fax (35) 6726752; f. 1974; radio and TV guide; Dir H. SCHEENSTRA; circ. 468,280.

NCRV-Gids: POB 25900, 1202 HW Hilversum; tel. (35) 6726801; fax (35) 6726863; internet www.ncrvgids.nl; f. 1966; publ. by Nederlandse Christelijke Radio Vereniging; radio and TV guide; Dir C. ABBENHUIS; circ. 419,363.

Nederlands Tijdschrift voor Geneeskunde (Dutch Journal of Medicine): POB 75971, 1070 AZ Amsterdam; tel. (20) 6620150; fax (20) 6735481; e-mail redactie@ntvg.nl; internet www.ntvg.nl; f. 1856; Editors Prof. Dr J. VAN GIJN, Prof. Dr F. W. A. VERHEUG, Prof. Dr A. J. P. M. OVERBEKE, Dr H. VEEKEN; circ. 30,000.

Nieuwe Revu: POB 23059, 1100 DN Amsterdam; tel. (20) 7518380; fax (20) 7518381; e-mail revu@smm.nl; internet www.nieuwerevu.nl; f. 1968; general interest; Editor-in-Chief MARK KOSTER; circ. 127,802.

Panorama: Ceylonpoort 5–25, 2037 AA Haarlem; tel. (23) 5304304; fax (23) 5361624; internet www.panorama.nl; f. 1913; general interest; Dir R. VAN VUURE; circ. 194,466.

Privé: POB 1980, 1000 BZ Amsterdam; tel. (20) 5853375; fax (20) 5854225; e-mail redactie@prive.nl; internet www.prive.nl; f. 1977; women's interest; Editor EVERT SANTEGOEDS; circ. 490,000.

Story: POB 1760, 2130 JD Hoofddorp; tel. (23) 5564894; fax (23) 5564911; f. 1974; women's interest; Editor PETRA BAKKER-SCHUT; circ. 272,700.

TeleVizier: Zeverijnstraat 6, POB 20002, 1202 AB Hilversum; tel. (35) 6726834; fax (35) 6726712; e-mail redactie.televizier@akn.nl; internet www.televizier.nl; publ. by Algemene Omroepvereniging; radio and TV guide; circ. 258,487.

Tina: Ceylonpoort 5–25, 2037 AA Haarlem; tel. (23) 5304304; fax (23) 5352554; f. 1967; teenage interest; circ. 112,191.

TrosKompas: POB 28600, 1202 LR Hilversum; tel. (35) 6728798; fax (35) 6728631; internet www.troskompas.nl; f. 1966; radio and TV guide; Editor EDGER HAMER.

TV Krant: POB 28600, 1202 LR Hilversum; tel. (35) 6728798; fax (35) 6728631; internet www.troskompas.nl; f. 1990; radio and TV guide; Editor EDGER HAMER.

Vara TV Magazine: POB 175, 1200 AD Hilversum; tel. (35) 6711445; fax (35) 6711429; e-mail tv.magazine@vara.nl; internet omroep.vara.nl; radio and TV guide; circ. 500,000.

Veronica: POB 22000, 1202 CA Hilversum; tel. (35) 6463333; fax (35) 6463300; e-mail bladredactie@veronicapublishing; internet www.veronica.nl; f. 1971; radio and TV guide; Editor PETER CONTANT; circ. 1,250,000.

Viva: POB 1630, 2130 JA Hoofddorp; tel. (23) 5565165; fax (23) 5565200; e-mail redactie@viva.nl; internet www.viva.nl; women's interest; Editor KARIN VAN GILST; circ. 149,461.

VNU: Ceylonpoort 5–25, 2037 AA Haarlem; POB 1, 2000 MA Haarlem; tel. (23) 5463463; fax (23) 5463912; e-mail vnupr@hq.vnu.com; circ. 174,250.

Voetbal International: POB 1050, 1000 BB Amsterdam; tel. (20) 5518711; fax (20) 6229141; internet www.vi.nl; f. 1965; football; Chief Editor C. VAN CUILENBORG; circ. 199,190.

VPRO-Gids: POB 11, 1200 JC Hilversum; tel. (35) 6712665; fax (35) 6712285; e-mail gids@vpro.nl; radio and TV guide; Dir H. VAN DALFSEN; circ. 254,000.

Vrij Nederland: POB 1254, 1000 BG Amsterdam; tel. (20) 5518711; fax (20) 6247476; e-mail redactie.vn@weekbladpers.nl; f. 1940; current affairs; Editor EMILE FALLAUX; circ. 80,000.

SELECTED PERIODICALS

Art, History and Literature

De Architect: POB 34, 2501 AG The Hague; tel. (70) 3045833; fax (70) 3045806; e-mail architect@wkths.nl; internet www.deArchitect.nl; Dir H. TILMAN; circ. 8,000.

Kunstbeeld: POB 318, 2280 AH Rijswijk; tel. (70) 3941007; fax (70) 3938382; monthly; art, especially sculpture; Editor ROBERT ROOS; circ. 15,000 (2002).

Spiegel Historiael: Molukkenstraat 200, E5, 1098 TW Amsterdam; tel. (20) 6652759; fax (20) 6657831; e-mail s.h@inter.nl.net; f. 1966; monthly; history and archaeology; circ. 8,000.

Tableau Fine Arts Magazine: Capellalaan 65, 2132 JL Hoofddorp; tel. (23) 5565377; fax (23) 5565376; e-mail tableau@sanoma-uitgevers.nl; every 2 months; Editor RONALD KRAAYEVELD; circ. 17,000.

Tijdschrift voor Geschiedenis (Historical Review): Instituut voor Geschiedenis RUU, Kromme Nieuwe Gracht 66, 3512 HL Utrecht; tel. (30) 2537868; e-mail tvg@let.uu.nl; f. 1886; quarterly; Chair. M. GREVER.

Economic and Business

Computable: POB 1905, 2003 BA Haarlem; tel. (23) 5463413; fax (23) 5465526; e-mail computable@bp.vnu.com; internet www.computable.nl; Dir E. HVEKSTRA; circ. 96,636.

Elektronica: POB 23, 7400 GA Deventer; tel. (570) 648699; fax (570) 610918; e-mail hdevries@kluwer.nl; internet elektronica.profpages.nl; f. 1953; 11 a year; electronics design; Editor HENK DE VRIES; circ. 7,000.

Intermediair: POB 1900, 2003 BA Haarlem; tel. (23) 5463455; fax (23) 5465530; e-mail redactie@intermediair.nl; internet www.intermediair.nl; f. 1965; weekly; business recruitment; Editor PETER TER HORST; circ. 240,678.

Management Team: VNU Business Publications, POB 1907, 2003 BA Haarlem; tel. (318) 521422; fax (318) 523136; internet www.mt.nl; f. 1980; monthly; management; Editor BEN KUIKEN; circ. 142,000 (2001).

PCM (Personal Computer Magazine): Ceylonpoort 5–25, 2037 AA Haarlem; tel. (23) 5463704; fax (23) 5465524; internet www.pcmweb.nl; f. 1982; monthly; computing; Editor-in-Chief FERDINAND SENNEMA; circ. 94,997.

Trade Channel: Holland Business Press BV, Sophiastraat 1, 2011 VT Haarlem; tel. (23) 5319022; fax (23) 5317974; e-mail pvroom@tradechannel.com; internet www.tradechannel.com; f. 1945; monthly, 2 edns: Trade Channel Consumer Goods and Trade Channel Industrial & Technical Products; promote imports and exports; Editor HENK VAN CAPELLE; circ. 13,286 (consumer edn), 55,000 (technical edn).

Home, Fashion and General

Ariadne at Home: Capellalaan 65, POB 1919, 2130 YM Hoofddorp; tel. (23) 5566770; fax (23) 5361624; internet www.ariadneathome.nl; f. 1946; monthly; home decoration; Editor BRIGITTE SPEEKMAN; circ. 169,198.

Het Beste uit Reader's Digest: POB 23330, 1100 DV Amsterdam; tel. (20) 56789111; fax (20) 6976422; e-mail hetbeste@readersdigest.nl; internet www.readersdigest.nl; f. 1957; monthly; general interest; Man. Dir OALA STEENKS; circ. 304,453.

Cosmopolitan: Capellalaan 65, POB 1730, 2132 JL Hoofddorp; fax (23) 5565259; e-mail h.mulder@sanoma-uitgevers.nl; internet www.cosmopolitan.nl; f. 1982; monthly; women's interest; Editor H. MULDER; circ. 108,406.

Kijk: Ceylonpoort 5–25, 2037 AA Haarlem; tel. (20) 4300455; fax (20) 4300450; sports, science, technology and adventure; circ. 92,993.

Knipmode: Capellalaan 65, POB 1900, 2130 JL Hoofddorp; tel. (23) 5565006; fax (23) 5566771; internet www.knipmode.nl; monthly; DIY fashion; Editor-in-Chief MARGREET HAGDORN; Publr GERT JAAP SCHOPPINK; circ. 124,000.

Nouveau: Ceylonpoort 5–25, 2037 AA Haarlem; tel. (23) 304304; fax (23) 350621; f. 1986; women's interest; Dir K. P. M. VAN DE PAS; circ. 134,669.

Opzij: POB 2748, 1000 CS Amsterdam; tel. (20) 5518525; fax (20) 6227265; e-mail opzij@redactie.weekbladpers.nl; internet www.opzij.nl; f. 1972; monthly; feminist themes; Editor CISCA DRESSELHUYS; circ. 80,000.

Ouders van Nu: POB 740, 2400 AS Alphen Aan Den Ryn; tel. (23) 5565066; fax (23) 5565095; e-mail ouders@jongezinnen.nl; internet www.oudersvannu.nl; f. 1967; monthly; childcare; Editor K. KROONSTUIVER; circ. 156,720.

THE NETHERLANDS

Directory

Playboy: POB 1662, 2130 JB Hoofddorp; tel. (23) 5463369; fax (23) 5463924; e-mail playboy@tijdschriften.vnu.com; internet www.playboy.nl; f. 1983; monthly; Editor Paul Koopal; circ. 85,348.

SEN: Mathenesserlaan 179, 3014 HA Rotterdam; fax (102) 092629; e-mail info@senmagazine.com; internet www.senmagazine.com; f. 2004; monthly; women's interest; Publr Senay Ozdemir; circ. 20,000.

TIP Culinair: POB 1632, 2130 JA Hoofddorp; tel. (23) 5565466; fax (23) 5565488; e-mail tipculinair@sanoma-uitgevers.nl; internet www.tipculinair.nl; f. 1977; monthly; cookery; Gen. Editor Dosia Brewer; circ. 120,000.

VT-Wonen: Ceylonpoort 5-25, 2037 AA Haarlem; tel. (30) 822511; fax (30) 898388; internet www.vtwonen.nl; f. 1964; monthly; home-owning and decorating, circ. 210,374; Editor Makkie Mulder.

Leisure Interests and Sport

Autokampioen: POB 93200, 2509 BA The Hague; tel. (70) 3146688; fax (70) 3146279; e-mail autokampioen@anwb.nl; internet www.autokampioen.nl; f. 1908; publ. by Royal Dutch Touring Club (ANWB); motoring; fortnightly; Chief Editor J. Vroomans; circ. 70,000.

Grasduinen (Browsing): POB 23209, 1100 DT Amsterdam; tel. (20) 7510110; fax (20) 7510111; e-mail grasduinen@smm.nl; internet www.grasduinen.nl; monthly; leisure, healthy living, art; Editor Liees Loogman Kannekens; circ. 51,000.

Kampeer en Caravankampioen: POB 93200, 2509 BA The Hague; tel. (70) 3146691; fax (70) 3146692; e-mail kck@anwb.nl; internet www.kck-online.nl; f. 1941; monthly; camping and caravanning; publ. by Royal Dutch Touring Club (ANWB); Editor-in-Chief F. Voorbergen; circ. 139,601.

Kampioen: POB 93200, 2509 BA The Hague; tel. (70) 3146285; fax (70) 3146983; e-mail kampioen@anwb.nl; internet www.kampioen.nl; f. 1885; monthly; recreation and tourism; publ. by Royal Dutch Touring Club (ANWB); Editor E. Lodewyks; circ. 3,700,000.

101 Woonideeën: POB 1702, 2130 JC Hoofddorp; tel. (23) 5564590; fax (23) 5564505; e-mail 101woonideeen@sanoma-uitgevers.nl; internet www.101woonideeen.nl; f. 1957; monthly; home ideas; Editor M. Wiemeyer; circ. 95,000.

Reizen Magazine: POB 93200, 2509 BA The Hague; tel. (70) 3146670; fax (70) 3147610; e-mail reizen@anwb.nl; internet www.reizen.nl; monthly; tourism, travel; publ. by Royal Dutch Touring Club (ANWB); Editor-in-Chief Harri Theirlynck; circ. 60,000.

Sport International: POB 225, 2800 AE Gouda; tel. (182) 599366; fax (182) 516650; f. 1981; monthly; Editor J. Linse; circ. 47,350.

Waterkampioen: POB 93200, 2509 BA The Hague; tel. (70) 3141470; fax (70) 3147356; e-mail waterkampioen@anwb.nl; internet www.anwbmedia.nl; f. 1927; fortnightly; water sports and yachting; publ. by Royal Dutch Touring Club (ANWB); Editor Ingeborg Berghuijs; circ. 54,000.

Scientific and Medical

Huisarts en Wetenschap: POB 3231, 3502 GE Utrecht; tel. (30) 2881700; fax (30) 2870668; e-mail redactie@nhg-nl.org; monthly; medical; Editor Dr Joost Vaat; circ. 8,500.

Natuur & Techniek: Segment Special Interest Media, POB 75, 6190 AB Beek (L); tel. (46) 4389444; fax (46) 4370161; e-mail natutech@xs4all.nl; internet www.natutech.nl; f. 1932; monthly; Editor R. Dobbelaer; circ. 47,360.

Technische Revue: POB 4, 7000 BA Doetinchem; tel. (314) 349911; fax (314) 361522; internet www.ebi.nl; monthly; review of new products; Chief Editor M. L. Matser; circ. 28,000.

Statistics

Statistisch Jaarboek van het Centraal Bureau voor de Statistiek (Statistical Year Book of the Netherlands): Prinses Beatrixlaan 428, POB 4000, 2270 JM Voorburg; tel. (70) 3373800; fax (70) 3575994; internet www.cbs.nl; f. 1899; also Netherlands Official Statistics (quarterly) and 300 other publs; Dir-Gen. G. van der Veen.

NEWS AGENCY

Algemeen Nederlands Persbureau (ANP) (Netherlands News Agency): POB 1, 2501 AA The Hague; tel. (70) 4141414; fax (70) 4140560; e-mail redactie@anp.nl; f. 1934; official agency of the Netherlands Daily Press Asscn; Man. Dir P. F. E. Tesselaar; Editor-in-Chief R. de Spa.

Foreign Bureaux

Anadolu Agency (Turkey): State de Colombes 56, 1098 VT Amsterdam; tel. (20) 6913714; e-mail amsterdam@anadoluajansi.com.tr.

Deutsche Presse-Agentur (dpa) (Germany): Eisenhowerlaan 150, 2517 KP The Hague; tel. (70) 3584499; fax (70) 3521637; Correspondent Thomas P. Spieker.

Dow Jones Newswires: Stadhouderskade 2, 1054 ES Amsterdam; tel. (20) 5890228; e-mail karel.valkenburg@dowjones.com; internet www.djnewswires.com/eu; Dir Karel Valkenburg.

Informatsionnoye Telegrafnoye Agentstvo Rossii—Telegrafnoye Agentstvo Suverennykh Stran (ITAR—TASS) (Russia): J. van Oldenbarneveltlaan 96, 2582 NZ The Hague; tel. and fax (70) 3553876; e-mail tassol@euronet.nl; internet www.netherlands.mid.ru/itar_e.html; f. 1945; Correspondent N. Teterin.

Reuters (UK): Drentestraat 11, 1083 HK Amsterdam; POB 74734, 1070 BS Amsterdam; tel. (20) 5045000; fax (20) 5045040; e-mail amsterdam.newsroom@news.reuters.com; internet www.reuters.com; Chief Correspondent Emma Thomasson.

Rossiyskoye Informatsionnoye Agentstvo—Novosti (RIA—Novosti) (Russia): Nieuwe Parklaan 15, 2597 LA, The Hague; tel. (70) 3586958; fax (70) 3512108; Dir A. Poskakukhin.

Agence France-Presse (AFP), Agenzia Nazionale Stampa Associata (ANSA) (Italy), Inter Press Service (IPS) (Italy) and UPI (USA) are also represented in the Netherlands.

PRESS ORGANIZATIONS

Buitenlandse Persvereniging in Nederland (Foreign Press Asscn in the Netherlands): Oudezijds Voorburgwal 129, 1012 EP Amsterdam; tel. (20) 4221209; e-mail annettebirschel@euronet.nl; internet www.bpv-fpa.nl; f. 1925; Pres. Annette Birschel; Sec. Maite Rodal; 120 mems.

Centraal Bureau voor Courantenpubliciteit van de Nederlandse Dagbladpers (CEBUCO) (Central Advertising Bureau of the Netherlands Daily Press): Hoogoorddreef 5, POB 12040, 1100 AA Amsterdam; tel. (20) 4309100; fax (20) 4309129; e-mail info@cebuco.nl; internet www.cebuco.nl; f. 1935; Dir Cees Polman.

De Nederlandse Nieuwsbladpers (NNP) (Organization of Local Newsmedia in the Netherlands): Drentsestraat 10, 3821 BP Amersfoort; tel. (33) 4481650; fax (33) 45481650; e-mail nnpnl@nnp.nl; internet www.nnp.nl; f. 1945; asscn of publrs of non-daily local newspapers and other local newsmedia; Pres. T. Roskam; Dir J. P. Bos; 70 mems.

Nederlandse Vereniging van Journalisten (Netherlands Union of Journalists): Joh. Vermeerstraat 22, POB 75997, 1070 AZ Amsterdam; tel. (20) 6766771; fax (20) 6624901; e-mail vereniging@nvj.nl; internet www.villamedia.nl; f. 1884; 9,500 mems.

Vereniging De Nederlandse Dagbladpers (NDP) (Dutch Asscn of Daily Newspaper Publrs): Amsterdam; tel. (20) 6763366; fax (20) 6766777; f. 1908; Chair. W. F. de Pagter; Gen. Sec. J. W. D. Gast; 34 mems.

Publishers

Uitgeverij Altamira BV: Blekersvaartweg 19a, Heemstede; tel. (23) 5286882; e-mail altamira@tip.nl; internet www.altamira-becht.nl; f. 1985; philosophy, psychology, New Age, health and spirituality.

Uitgeverij Ankh-Hermes BV: Smyrnastraat 5, POB 125, 7400 AC Deventer; tel. (57) 0678900; fax (57) 0624632; e-mail info@ankh-hermes.nl; internet www.ankh-hermes.nl; health, eastern and western religions, astrology, alternative medicine, psychology, esoterics; Dir A. Steenbergen; Publrs E. ten Seldam, A. Kluwer.

Ambo Anthos: Herengracht 435–437, 1017 BR Amsterdam; tel. (20) 5245411; fax (20) 4200422; e-mail info@amboanthos.nl; internet www.amboanthos.nl; literature, cultural history, biographies, history, politics; Dir R. Ammerlaan.

APA (Academic Publishers Associated): POB 806, 1000 AV Amsterdam; tel. (20) 6265544; fax (20) 5285298; e-mail info@apa-publishers.com; internet www.apa-publishers.com; f. 1966; subsidiaries: Holland University Press, Fontes Pers, Oriental Press, Philo Press, van Heusden, Hissink & Co; new and reprint edns in the arts, humanities and science; Man. Dir G. van Heusden.

BV Uitgeverij De Arbeiderspers: Herengracht 370–372, POB 2877, 1000 CW Amsterdam; tel. (20) 5247500; fax (20) 6224937; e-mail info@arbeiderspers.nl; internet www.ap-archipel.nl; participant in Weekbladpers holdings group; general, fiction and non-fiction; Dir R. C. Haans.

A. Asher & Co BV: Zeeweg 264, POB 258, 1970 AG Ijmuiden; tel. (25) 5523839; fax (25) 5510352; e-mail info@asherbooks.com; internet www.asherbooks.com; f. 1830; natural history; Dirs M. J. Roos, J. W. Steiner.

Bert Bakker BV: Herengracht 507, POB 1662, 1000 BV Amsterdam; tel. (20) 6241934; fax (20) 6225461; e-mail pbo@pbo.nl; internet www.pbo.nl; f. 1893; Dutch and international literature, sociology, history, politics, science; Dir Mai Spijkers.

THE NETHERLANDS

John Benjamins BV: Klaprozenweg 105, POB 36224, 1020 ME Amsterdam; tel. (20) 6304747; fax (20) 6739773; e-mail customer.services@benjamins.nl; internet www.benjamins.com; f. 1964; linguistics, philology, psychology and art history; antiquarian scholarly periodicals; Man. Dirs J. L. BENJAMINS, C. L. BENJAMINS-SCHALEKAMP, SELINE BENJAMINS.

Uitgeverij De Bezige Bij BV: Van Miereveldstraat 1, POB 75184, 1070 AD Amsterdam; tel. (20) 3059810; fax (20) 3059824; e-mail info@debezigebij.nl; internet www.debezigebij.nl; f. 1945; Publr MICHIEL GAAF.

Erven J. Bijleveld: Janskerkhof 7, 3512 BK Utrecht, POB 1238, 3500 BE Utrecht; tel. (30) 2317008; fax (30) 2368675; e-mail bijleveld.publishers@wxs.nl; internet www.bijleveldbooks.nl; f. 1865; psychology, sociology, philosophy, religion and history; computer books (as Bijleveld Press); Mans J. B. BOMMELJÉ, L. S. BOMMELJÉ.

Boekencentrum Uitgevers: Goudstraat 50, POB 29, 2700 AA Zoetermeer; tel. (79) 3615481; fax (79) 3615489; e-mail info@boekencentrum.nl; internet www.boekencentrum.nl; bibles, books and magazines; Dir N. A. DE WAAL.

Bohn Stafleu Van Hoghum BV: Het Spoor 2, POB 246, 3990 GA Houten; tel. (30) 6385838; fax (30) 6383839; e-mail klantenservice@bsl.nl; internet www.bsl.nl; mem. of Wolters Kluwer NV holdings group; social sciences, humanities, medical, dental and nursing; Dir P. J. A. SNAKKERS.

Boom Uitgeverij BV: Prinsengracht 747–751, 1017 JX Amsterdam; tel. (20) 6226107; fax (20) 6253327; e-mail mail@virgeverijboom.nl; internet www.uitgeverijboom.nl; f. 1842; fmrly Boom Pers BV, Meppel; philosophy, educational and social sciences, environment, history; Man. Dir DRIES VAN INGEN.

Brill Academic Publishers: Plantijnstraat 2, POB 9000, 2300 PA Leiden; tel. (71) 5353500; fax (71) 5317532; e-mail cs@brill.nl; internet www.brill.nl; f. 1683; academic books and periodicals (mainly in English); classics, medieval, renaissance and oriental studies, comparative religion, biology.

A. W. Bruna Uitgevers BV: Kobaltweg 23–25, POB 40203, 3504 AA Utrecht; tel. (30) 2470411; fax (30) 2410018; e-mail helpdesk@awbruna.nl; internet www.awbruna.nl; f. 1868; general fiction and non-fiction; Dir J. A. A. BOEZEMAN.

Uitgeverij Cantecleer BV: Julianalaan 11, POB 309, 3740 AM Baarn; tel. (35) 5486600; fax (35) 5486645; e-mail cancleer@worldonline.nl; f. 1948; mem. of Bosch & Keuning Uitgevers group; Man. Dir H. SCHWURMANS.

Uitgeverij De Fontein BV: Pr. Marielaan 8, POB 1, 3740 AA Baarn; tel. (35) 5486311; fax (35) 5423855; f. 1981; mem. of Bosch & Keuning holding group; commercial fiction, non-fiction and children's books; Dir T. AKUELD.

Uitgeverij Van Gennep BV: Keizersgracht 524, 1017 EK Amsterdam; tel. (20) 6247033; fax (20) 6247035; e-mail vangennep@wxs.nl; history, social theory, political science, biographies, literature.

Uitgeverij J. H. Gottmer/H. J. W. Becht BV: Wilhelminapark 6, POB 317, 2000 AH Haarlem; tel. (23) 5411190; fax (23) 5274404; e-mail info@gottmer.nl; internet www.gottmer.nl; f. 1937; fiction, non-fiction, children's books, religion, spirituality, travel guides; imprints incl. Aramith, Becht, Dominicus and Hollandia; Dir C. G. A. VAN WIJK.

Uitgeverij Hollandia BV: e-mail info@hollandia-boeken.nl; internet www.hollandia-boeken.nl; f. 1899; travel, yachting and nautical books; Dir TONNIS MUNTINGA.

Uitgeverij Holland BV: Spaarne 110, 2011 CM Haarlem; tel. (23) 5323061; fax (23) 5342908; e-mail info@uitgeverijholland.nl; internet www.uitgeverijholland.nl; f. 1922; literature, reference, science, children's books; Publr J. B. VAN ULZEN.

Uitgeversmaatschappij Kok ten Have: Ijsseldijk 31, POB 5019, 8260 GA Kampen; tel. (38) 3392555; fax (38) 3327331; e-mail algemeen@kok.nl; internet www.kok.nl; f. 1894; theology, belles-lettres, science, periodicals; mem. of Veen Bosch & Keuning Uitgevers; nine subsidiaries; Dir B. A. ENDEDIJK.

Ten Have BV: Ijsseldijk 31, POB 5018, 8266 DA Kampen; tel. (38) 3328912; fax (38) 3392500; e-mail info@uitgeverijtenhave.nl; internet www.uitgeverijtenhave.nl; f. 1831; imprint of Uitgeefmaatschappij Kok ten Have; religious; Dir B. ENDEDIJK; Editor P. DE BOER.

Kosmos-Z&K Uitgevers: Maliebaan 74, POB 13288, 3507 LG Utrecht; tel. (30) 2349211; fax (30) 2349247; e-mail info@kosmoszk.nl; internet www.kosmoszk.nl; f. 1992; mem. of Veen Bosch & Keuning Uitgevers; Dir ROBBERT SCHUURMANS.

Lemniscaat BV: Vijverlaan 48, POB 4066, 3006 AB Rotterdam; tel. (10) 2062929; fax (10) 4141560; e-mail info@lemniscaat.nl; internet www.lemniscaat.nl; f. 1963; philosophy, psychology, care of the disabled and mentally handicapped, books for juveniles and young adults, picture books; Dir J. C. BOELE VAN HENSBROEK.

Uitgeverij Leopold BV: Singel 262, POB 3879, 1001 AR Amsterdam; tel. (20) 5511250; fax (20) 4204699; e-mail info@leopold.nl; internet www.leopold.nl; f. 1923; mem. Weekbladpers BV; children's books; Dir MARTINE SCHAAP.

Uitgeverij Luitingh-Sijthoff BV: Leidsegracht 105A, 1017 ND Amsterdam; tel. (20) 5307340; fax (20) 626251; e-mail info@luitingh-sijthoff.nl; Luitingh; f. 1946; Sijthoff; f. 1851; merged in 1989; mem. of Veen Bosch en Keuning Uitgevers publishing group; fiction and popular non-fiction; Man. Dir J. A. B. LEPPINK.

Malmberg BV: Leeghwaterlaan 16, POB 233, 5201 AE Den Bosch; tel. (73) 6288811; fax (73) 6210512; e-mail malmberg@malmberg.nl; internet www.malmberg.nl; f. 1885; educational; Dir J. M. EIJKENS.

J. M. Meulenhoff BV: Nieuwe Spiegelstraat 26, POB 100, 1000 AC Amsterdam; tel. (20) 5533500; fax (20) 6251135; e-mail info@meulenhoff.nl; internet www.meulenhoff.nl; f. 1895; literature, historical, political, social/cultural, art, paperbacks and pocket books; Dir ROB HOGENES.

Nienhuis Montessori International BV: Industriepark 14, POB 16, 7020 AA Zelhem; tel. (314) 627127; fax (314) 627128; e-mail info@nienhuis.nl; internet www.nienhuis.nl; f. 1800; holdings group; publrs and printers specializing in scientific books and periodicals; Dir A. J. NIENHUIS.

Uitgeverij Ploegsma BV: Keizersgracht 616, POB 19857, 1000 GW Amsterdam; tel. (20) 6262907; fax (20) 6242994; subsidiary: Uitgeverij De Brink; Dir M. BRINKMAN.

Em. Querido's Uitgeverij BV: Singel 262, POB 3879, 1001 AR Amsterdam; tel. (20) 5511262; fax (20) 6391968; internet www.querido.nl; f. 1915; subsidiary: Uitgeverij Nijgh & van Ditmar; participant in 'Singel 262' holdings group; general fiction, history, children's books, translations from Latin and Greek texts; Dir ARY T. LANGBROEK.

Reed Elsevier NV: Van de Sande Bakhuyzenstraat 4, 1061 AG Amsterdam; POB 470, 1000 AL Amsterdam; tel. (20) 5159111; fax (20) 6832617; internet www.elsevier.nl; f. 1979; by merger; subholdings include some 60 subsidiaries in the Netherlands and abroad specializing in: reference works, handbooks, weekly magazines, newspapers, trade and technical pubs, (postgraduate) scientific books and journals, audiovisual materials, further education study courses, databases; CEO CRISPIN DAVIS.

> **Excerpta Medica Medical Communications:** Radarweg 29, 1043 NX Amsterdam; tel. (20) 4853975; fax (20) 4853188; e-mail excerptamedica@elsevier.com; internet www.excerptamedica.com; Man. Dir GERARD STOIA.

Uitgeverij La Rivière & Voorhoeve Kampen: Stationsplein 62, POB 133, 3740 AC Baarn; tel. (35) 5418855; fax (35) 5413174; f. 1876; mem. of Kok holdings group; general non-fiction, children's books; Dirs B. A. ENDEDIJK, A. C. VAN DAM; Man. Editors K. VAN DER SCHEER, J. H. TIMMERMAN, N. HARMSEN.

Editions Rodopi BV: Tijnmuiden 7, 1046 AK Amsterdam; tel. (20) 6114821; fax (20) 4472979; e-mail ordeinfo@rodopi.nl; internet www.rodopi.nl; f. 1966; Dir F. A. VAN DER ZEE.

SDU: Prinses Beatrixlaan 116, POB 20025, 2500 EA The Hague; tel. (70) 3789911; fax (70) 3854321; e-mail sdu@sdu.nl; internet www.sdu.nl; Chair. Dr L. JONGSMA.

BV Uitgeverijen 'Singel 262': Singel 262, POB 3879, 1001 AR Amsterdam; tel. (20) 5511262; fax (20) 6203509; holding group; Man. Dir P. F. M. DE JONG.

Springer: van Godewijckstraat 30, POB 989, 3311 GX Dordrecht; tel. (78) 6576050; fax (78) 6576467; internet www.springeronline.com; merged with Kluwer Academic Publrs in 2004; publrs of books and journals in the fields of science, technology and medicine, incl., inter alia, natural sciences, mathematics, engineering, computer science and psychology; CEO DERK HAANK.

A. J. G. Strengholt Boeken, Anno 1928 BV: Hofstede Oud-Bussem, Flevolaan 41, POB 338, 1400 AH Bussum; tel. (35) 6958411; fax (35) 6946173; e-mail tanya.jansen@strengholt.nl; internet www.strengholtsboeken.nl; f. 1928; health, biography, music, current affairs, psychology, parapsychology, sports, cookery; Dir T. M. JANSEN.

Taylor & Francis The Netherlands (T&F NL): Schipholweg 107C, POB 447, 2300 AK Leiden; tel. (71) 5243080; fax (71) 5234571; e-mail pub.nl@tandf.co.uk; internet www.taylorandfrancisgroup.com; f. 1901; as Swets & Zeitlinger Publishers, acquired by Taylor & Francis in 2004; publrs of books and journals in civil engineering and earth sciences; Sr Publr JANJAAP BLOM.

Uitgeverij De Tijdstroom BV: Asschatterweg 44, 3831 JW Leusden; tel. (342) 450867; fax (342) 450365; e-mail info@tijdstroom.nl; internet www.tijdstroom.nl; f. 1921; educational and professional publications on health and welfare, periodicals in these fields; Dir C. H. J. STAVENUITER.

Unieboek BV: Onderdoor 7, POB 97, 3990 DB Houten; tel. (30) 7998300; fax (30) 7998398; e-mail info@unieboek.nl; internet www

.uniebook.nl; f. 1890; holding group incorporating 10 publishing houses; general and juvenile literature, fiction, popular science, history, art, social, economics, religion, textbooks, etc.; Dir W. VAN GILS.

Veen Bosch en Keuning Uitgevers NV: St Jacobsstraat 125, POB 8049, 3503 RA Utrecht; tel. (30) 2349211; fax (30) 2349208; e-mail algemeen@veenboschenkeuning.nl; internet www.veenboschenkeuning.nl; f. 2001; as a result of merger between Veen Uitgevers Groep and Bosch & Keuning; Dirs A. DE GROOT, J. ATEMA.

VNU Business Publications BV: Ceylonpoort 5–25, POB 4020, 2031 EA Haarlem; tel. (23) 5463463; fax (23) 5463931; e-mail info@bp.vnu.com; internet www.vnubp.nl; trade and fashion, careers, IT, personal computer, management, training.

West Friesland BV: Slijksteeg 4, POB 2308, 1620 EH Hoorn; tel. (22) 9248820; fax (22) 9218944; f. 1943; novels, biographies, children's books, paperbacks, young adults; Man. Dir B. E. ENDEDIJK; Editor-in-Chief F. H. JONKERS.

Wolters Kluwer NV: Apollolaan 153, POB 75248; 1070 AE Amsterdam; tel. (20) 6070400; fax (20) 6070490; e-mail info@wolterskluwer.com; internet www.wolterskluwer.com; Chair. HENRY DE RUITER; CEO NANCY MCKINSTRY.

Wolters-Noordhoff BV: Damsport 157, POB 58, 9700 MB Groningen; tel. (50) 5226922; fax (50) 5277599; e-mail info@wolters.nl; f. 1836; educational and scientific books, educational software, geographical and historical atlases and maps; Man. Dir Dr A. M. W. HOLL.

PUBLISHERS' ASSOCIATIONS

Koninklijke Vereniging van het Boekenvak (KVB) (Royal Association for the Book Trade): Frederiksplein 1, POB 15007, 1001 MA Amsterdam; tel. (20) 6240212; fax (20) 6208871; e-mail info@kvb.nl; internet www.kvb.nl; f. 1815; Chair. E. BRINKMAN; Exec. Dir CONNIE VERBERNE; 1,500 mems.

Nederlands Uitgeversverbond (NUV) (Dutch Publrs' Assen): Atlas Kantorenpark, Gebouw Azië, Hoogoorddreef 5, POB 12040, 1100 AA Amsterdam Zuidoost; tel. (20) 4309150; fax (20) 4309179; e-mail info@nuv.nl; internet www.nuv.nl; Chair. Prof. Dr L. M. L. H. A. HERMANS; Sec. Dr A. J. SWARTJES; 140 mems.

Broadcasting and Communications

TELECOMMUNICATIONS
Regulatory Authority

Onafhankelijke Post en Telecommunicatie Autoriteit (OPTA): Babylon Bldg, Tower B, Koningin Julianaplein 30, POB 90420, 2509 LK The Hague; tel. (70) 3153500; fax (70) 3153501; e-mail mail@opta.nl; internet www.opta.nl; f. 1997; supervises compliance with legislation, settles disputes, manages the telephone number database; Chair. JENS C. ARNBAK.

Service Providers

Debitel: POB 6700, 2130 LT Hoofddorp; internet www.debitel.nl.

Dutchtone: POB 95313, 2509 CH The Hague; tel. (70) 8899000; fax (70) 8898000; e-mail info@dutchtone.nl; internet www.orange.nl; 100% owned by Orange SA.

Enertel NV: K. P. van der Mandelelaan 130–144, POB 25226, 3001 HE Rotterdam; tel. (10) 8803800; e-mail info@enertel.nl; internet www.enertel.nl; owned by Greenfield Capital Partners; CEO CEES MEEUWIS.

Koninklijke KPN NV: POB 30000, 2500 GA The Hague; tel. (70) 3434343; fax (70) 3436568; e-mail webmaster@kpn.com; internet www.kpn.com; privatized 1989; operates KPN Mobile; 14.3% state-owned; CEO ADRIANUS SCHEEPBOUWER.

KPN Broadcast: POB 850, 1200 AW Hilversum; tel. (30) 2386238; fax (30) 2386659; e-mail info@kpnbroadcast.com; internet www.kpnbroadcast.com; provides internet services and analogue, digital and satellite broadcasting services.

Xantic: POB 30012, 2500 GA The Hague; tel. (70) 3434543; fax (70) 3434796; e-mail xantic@xantic.net; internet www.xantic.net; provides communications systems; acquisition by Stratos (Canada) scheduled for completion in early 2006.

MCI Nederland BV: Kroonburgh B3, H.J.E. Wenckebachweg 123, 1096 AM Amsterdam; tel. (20) 7112652; e-mail netherlandspressoffice@lists.mci.com; internet global.mci.com/nl/; integrated voice, data and internet telecommunications products.

T-Mobile: Rijswijkseweg 60, POB 16272, 2500 BG The Hague; tel. (61) 4095000; internet www.t-mobile.nl; 100% owned by Deutsche Telekom; mobile telephone operator.

Telfort BV: POB 23079, 1100 DN Amsterdam Zuid-Oost; tel. 0800-1771; internet www.telfort.com; f. 1997; owned by BT wireless, a subsidiary of British Telecom; Gen. Dir TON AAN DE STEGGE.

UPC Nederland NV: POB 80900, 1005 DA Amsterdam; tel. (20) 7755731; fax (20) 7756724; e-mail mediarelations@upc.nl; internet www.upc.nl; subsidiary of UGC Europe; holds cable monopoly in Amsterdam; internet, telephone, television and radio service provider; Vice-Pres. MARK ZELLENRATH.

Vodafone Libertel: POB 1500, 6201 BM Maast; e-mail roaming@libertel.nl; internet www.vodafone.nl; f. 1999; 70% owned by Vodafone/AirTouch; CEO ALEXANDER SCHUIT.

BROADCASTING

Under the Netherlands public broadcasting system the two co-ordinating bodies work with the seven licensed broadcasters to provide a complete range of programmes.

Co-ordinating Bodies

Nederlandse Programma Stichting (NPS) (Dutch National Broadcasting Service): POB 29000, 1202 MA Hilversum; tel. (35) 6779333; fax (35) 6774517; e-mail publiek@nps.nl; internet www.nps.nl; Dir W. J. M. VAN BEUSEKOM.

Publieke Omroep (Netherlands Public Broadcasting): POB 26444, 1202 JJ Hilversum; tel. (35) 6779222; fax (35) 6772649; e-mail voorlichting@omroep.nl; internet www.omroep.nl; f. 1969; co-ordination of Dutch national public broadcasting and news, sports and teletext programmes on five national public radio and three television channels; fmrly Nederlandse Omroep Stichting; Chair. HARM BRUINS SLOT.

Broadcasting Associations

Algemene Omroepvereniging AVRO: 's-Gravelandseweg 80, POB 2, 1200 JA Hilversum; tel. (35) 6717911; fax (35) 6717439; e-mail info@avro.nl; internet www.avro.nl; f. 1923; independent; general broadcaster; 800,000 mems; Pres. M. SANDERS; Vice-Pres. P. SCHNABEL.

Evangelische Omroep (EO): Oude Amersfoortseweg 79, POB 21000, 1202 BA Hilversum; tel. (35) 6474747; fax (35) 6474727; e-mail eo@eo.nl; internet www.eo.nl; f. 1967; Protestant; Chair. A. VAN DER VEER; Man. Dirs A. P. DE BOER, A. G. KNEVEL, H. N. HAGOORT.

Katholieke Radio Omroep (KRO): 's-Gravelandseweg 80, POB 23000, 1202 EA Hilversum; tel. (35) 6713911; fax (35) 6713666; internet www.kro.nl; f. 1925; Catholic; 615,000 mems; Pres. Dr F. C. H. SLANGEN; Sec.-Gen. Dr H. A. M. HOOFT.

Nederlandse Christelijke Radio Vereniging (NCRV): Bergweg 30, POB 25000, 1202 HB Hilversum; tel. (35) 6719911; fax (35) 6719285; e-mail info@ncrv.nl; internet www.ncrv.nl; f. 1924; Protestant; more than 550,000 mems; Chair. LEO BORN; Dir COEN ABBENHUIS.

Omroepvereniging VARA: Sumatralaan 49, POB 175, 1200 AD Hilversum; tel. (35) 6711911; fax (35) 6711333; e-mail vara@vara.nl; internet www.vara.nl; f. 1925; social-democratic and progressive; 515,000 mems; Pres. VERA M. M. KEUR.

Omroepvereniging VPRO: Media Park, Sumatralaan 49, POB 11, 1200 JC Hilversum; tel. (35) 6712911; fax (35) 6712220; e-mail info@vpro.nl; internet www.vpro.nl; f. 1926; progressive; 440,463 mems; Pres. P. VAN LIESHOUT; Gen. Dir P. SCHRURS; Dir of Radio A. J. HEERMA VAN VOSS; Dir of Television D. LUNENBORG.

TROS: Lage Naarderweg 45–47, POB 28450, 1202 LL Hilversum; tel. (35) 6715715; fax (35) 6715236; e-mail publiekservice@tros.nl; internet www.tros.nl; f. 1964; independent; general broadcaster; 573,664 mems; Chair. K. VAN DOODEWAERD.

Radio

There are five privately owned national radio stations that are operated on a public-service basis, as well as 13 regional stations and about 330 local stations.

Television

Television programmes are transmitted on three public channels, each of which is allocated to a different combination of broadcasting associations and other organizations, and on the commercially funded channels RTL4 and RTL5. Nearly all Dutch households are able to receive at least one satellite station.

SBS 6/NET5: Plantage Middenlaan 14, POB 18179, 1001 ZB Amsterdam; e-mail info@sbs6.nl; internet www.sbs6.nl; private broadcaster; Man. JORIS BOUMAN.

United Pan-Europe Communications NV: POB 80900, 1005 DA Amsterdam; tel. (20) 7729729; fax (20) 7729988; e-mail service@upc.nl; internet www.upc.nl; cable broadcaster; Chair. MICHAEL T. FRIES.

Overseas Broadcasting

BVN TV: Witte Kruislaan 55, POB 222, 1200 JG Hilversum; tel. (35) 6724333; fax (35) 6724343; e-mail bvn@rnw.nl; internet www.bvn.nl; f. 1998; by Radio Nederland Wereldomroep, VRT and Nederlandse Omroep Stichting (NOS); daily international transmissions of news and cultural programmes from public-service broadcasters in Flanders and the Netherlands; Dir of Programmes P. LANDMAN.

Radio Nederland Wereldomroep (Radio Netherlands International): Witte Kruislaan 55, POB 222, 1200 JG Hilversum; tel. (35) 6724211; fax (35) 6724352; e-mail marjolein.hulst@rnw.nl; internet www.rnw.nl; f. 1947; public-service broadcaster; daily transmissions in Arabic, Dutch, English, Indonesian, Papiamento, Portuguese and Spanish; programme and transcription services for foreign radio and TV stations; Radio Nederland Training Centre (for students from developing countries); Pres. JAN HOEH.

Finance

(cap. = capital; res = reserves; dep. = deposits; m. = million; brs = branches; all values are given in euros, unless otherwise stated)

BANKING

Central Bank

De Nederlandse Bank NV: Westeinde 1, POB 98, 1000 AB Amsterdam; tel. (20) 5249111; fax (20) 5242500; e-mail info@dnb.nl; internet www.dnb.nl; f. 1815; nationalized 1948; merged with Pensioen- en Verzekeringskamer (Chamber of Insurance and Pensions) in 2004; cap. 500m., res 11,649m., dep. 9,277m. (Dec. 2002); Pres. A. H. E. M. WELLINK; Exec. Dirs H. J. BROUWER, A. SCHILDER, D. E. WITTEVEEN, F. KLOPPER; 4 brs.

Principal Commercial Banks

ABN AMRO Bank NV: Gustav Mahlerlaan 10, POB 283, 1082 PP Amsterdam; tel. (20) 6289393; fax (20) 6287740; e-mail postbox@abnamro.com; internet www.abnamro.com; f. 1991 by merger of Algemene Bank Nederland NV and Amsterdam-Rotterdam Bank NV; cap. 1,732m., res 11,315m., dep. 472,441m. (Dec. 2003); Chair. RIJKMAN W. J. GROENINK; 915 brs nationally.

Bank Nederlandse Gemeenten NV (BNG): Koninginnegracht 2, POB 30305, 2500 GH The Hague; tel. (70) 3750750; fax (70) 3454743; e-mail info@bng.nl; internet www.bng.nl; f. 1914; 50% state-owned; cap. 139m., res 2,194m., dep. 65,473m. (Dec. 2002); Chair. H. O. RUDING; Pres. P. O. VERMEULEN.

Banque Artesia Nederland NV: Herengracht 539–543, POB 274, 1000 AG Amsterdam; tel. (20) 5204911; fax (20) 6247502; e-mail info@artesia.nl; internet www.artesia.nl; f. 1863; fmrly Banque Paribas Nederland; cap. 163.9m. guilders, res 180.5m. guilders, dep. 7,856.0m. guilders (Dec. 2000); Chair. M. LAUWERS; 10 brs.

CenE Bankiers NV: Herculesplein 5, 3584 AA Utrecht; tel. (30) 2560911; fax (30) 2540919; e-mail info@CenEbankiers.nl; internet www.Cenebankiers.nl; f. 1922; present name adopted 1998; owned by ING Bank NV; cap. 5.5m., res 220.6m., dep. 2,882.6m. (Dec. 2002); Gen. Mans P. A. J. VERBAAS, A. A. RÖELL.

Commerzbank AG Kantoor Amsterdam: Strawinskylaan 2501, POB 75444, 1070 AK Amsterdam; tel. (20) 5574911; fax (20) 6272446; e-mail amsterdam@commerzbank.com; internet www.commerzbank.nl; f. 1973; as Europartners Bank (Nederland) NV; name changed to Commerzbank (Nederland) NV in 1984; name changed as above 2006; cap. 40.9m., res 195.6m., dep. 2,503.6m. (Dec. 2002); Gen. Mans DIRK DREISKÄMPER, EUGÈNE VAN DEN BERG.

Dexia Bank Nederland NV: Piet Heinkade 55, POB 808, 1000 AV Amsterdam; tel. (20) 3485000; fax (20) 5571414; e-mail klantenservie@dexiabank.nl; internet www.dexiabank.nl; f. 2001 by merger of Bank Labouchere NV (f. 1990) and Kempen and Co NV; owned by Dexia banking group; dep. 5,398.1m., total assets 7,290.1m. (Dec. 2001); Chair. D. BRUNEEL; 1 br.

Fortis Bank (Nederland) NV: Blaak 555, POB 1045, 3000 BA Rotterdam; tel. (10) 2701010; fax (10) 4148391; e-mail info@fortis.com; internet www.fortisbank.nl; f. 1999 by merger of VSB Bank and Generale Bank Nederland; cap. 566m., res 2,803m., dep. 800m. (Dec. 2003).

Friesland Bank NV: Zuiderstraat 1, POB 397, 8901 BD Leeuwarden; tel. (58) 2994499; fax (58) 2994591; e-mail service@frieslandbank.nl; internet www.frieslandbank.nl; f. 1913; as Coöperatieve Zuivel-Bank; dep. 5,397.8m. euros, total assets 6,242.0m. guilders (Dec. 2001); Chair. Dr W. F. C. CRAMER; Dirs T. BRANBERGEN, A. VLASKAMP; 33 brs.

Indonesische Overzeese Bank NV (Indover Bank): Stadhouderskade 84, POB 526, 1000 AM Amsterdam; tel. (20) 5700700; fax (20) 6626119; e-mail info@indover.com; internet www.indoverbank.com; f. 1965; cap. 48.0m., res 98.9m., dep. 698.7m. (Dec. 2002); Chair. MUKHLIS RASYID; Pres. DJOKO SARWONO; Gen. Man. D. VAN LEEUWEN.

ING Bank NV (ING Barings): POB 1800, De Amsterdamse Poort, 1000 BV Amsterdam; tel. (20) 5415411; fax (20) 5415444; e-mail ing@ing.com; internet www.ingbank.nl; f. 1991; dep. 386,087m., total assets 443,356m. (Dec. 2001); Chair. MICHEL TILMANT; more than 400 brs.

KAS BANK NV: Spuistraat 172, POB 24001, 1000 DB Amsterdam; tel. (20) 5575911; fax (20) 5576100; e-mail info@kasbank.com; internet www.kasbank.com; f. 1806; by merger, name changed as above in Jan. 2002; cap. 15.7m., res 200.8m., dep. 7,715.4m. (Dec. 2003); Man. Dir F. S. VON BALLUSECK; Vice-Chair. T. J. M. VAN HEESE.

F. van Lanschot Bankiers NV: Hooge Steenweg 29, POB 1021, 5200 HC 's-Hertogenbosch; tel. (73) 5483548; fax (73) 5483648; e-mail vanlanschot@vanlanschot.nl; internet www.vanlanschot.nl; f. 1737; dep. 9,217.2m., total assets 10,748,821m. (Dec. 2001); Chair. Prof. Dr B. DE VRIES; Chair. F. G. H. VAN DER DECKERS; 34 brs.

Mizuho Corporate Bank Nederland NV: Apollolaan 171, POB 7075, 1007 JB Amsterdam; tel. (20) 5734343; fax (20) 5734372; e-mail dkbedp@axxel.nl; f. 2000 by merger of Dai Ichi Kangyo Bank Europe NV and Fuji Bank Nederland NV; cap. 111.8m., res 14.7m., dep. 1,164.1m. (Dec. 2002); Man. Dir S. FUKUMOTO.

NIB Capital Bank NV: Carnegieplein 4, POB 380, 2501 BH The Hague; tel. (70) 3425425; fax (70) 3651071; e-mail thehague@nibcapital.com; internet www.nibcapital.com; f. 1945; as Herstelbank; acquisition by JC Flowers & Co LLC (USA) expected to be completed by end of 2005; cap. 1,362m., res 519m., dep. 17,249m. (Dec. 2003); Chair. M. ENDTHOVEN; 1 br.

Postbank NV: Haarlemmerweg 506, POB 21009, 1000 EX Amsterdam; tel. (20) 5846133; fax (20) 5846132; internet www.postbank.nl; f. 1985; retail bank operating through post offices; owned by ING Group NV; Chair. MICHEL TILMANT.

Rabobank Nederland (Coöperatieve Centrale Raiffeisen-Boerenleenbank BA): Croeselaan 18, POB 17100, 3521 CB Utrecht; tel. (30) 2160000; fax (30) 2161973; e-mail rabocomm@rn.rabobank.nl; internet www.rabobank.nl; f. 1898; res 19,418.0m., dep. 319,257.0m., total assets 374,720.0m. (Dec. 2002); Chair. H. HEEMSKERK; 1,727 brs.

SNS Bank NV: Croeselaan 1, 3503 BJ Utrecht; tel. (30) 2915100; fax (30) 2915300; e-mail info@snsbank.nl; internet www.sns.nl; f. 1971; as Bank der Bondsspaarbanken NV, name changed as above in 2002; cap. 340m., res 1,068m., dep. 33,208m. (Dec. 2002); Chair. S. KEULEN; 200 brs.

Staal Bankiers NV: Lange Houtstraat 8, POB 327, 2501 CH The Hague; tel. (70) 3101510; fax (70) 3650819; e-mail info@staalbankiers.nl; internet www.staalbankiers.nl; f. 1916; mem. of Eureko/Achmea Groep; dep. 3,992.5m., total assets 4,571.6m. (Dec. 2001); Chair. PETER A. DE RUIJTER; Man. Dirs H. W. TE BEEST.

Bankers' Association

Nederlandse Vereniging van Banken (Netherlands Bankers' Assen): POB 3543, 1001 AH Amsterdam; tel. (20) 5502888; fax (20) 6239748; e-mail info@nvb.nl; internet www.nvb.nl; f. 1989; Chair. Dr P. W. MOERLAND; Dir H. G. M. BLOCKS.

STOCK EXCHANGES

A supervisory authority, the Netherlands Securities Board, commenced activities in 1989.

Euronext Amsterdam: Beursplein 5, 1012 JW Amsterdam; POB 19163, 1000 GD Amsterdam; tel. (20) 5505555; fax (20) 5504899; e-mail info@euronext.nl; internet www.euronext.com; subsidiary of Euronext NV, formed by merger of Amsterdam, Paris and Brussels exchanges and joined in 2002 by the LIFFE and the Lisbon stock exchange; unitary stock and options exchange; CEO JOOST VAN DER DOES DE WILLEBOIS.

There are also financial futures, grain, citrus fruits and insurance bourses in the Netherlands; a 'spot' market for petroleum operates from Rotterdam.

INSURANCE COMPANIES

AEGON Nederland: AEGONplein 50, POB 202, 2501 CE The Hague; tel. (70) 3443210; fax (70) 3475238; internet www.aegon.nl; f. 1983; by merger; life, accident, health, general and linked activities; Chair. JOHAN VAN DER WERF.

Delta Lloyd Verzekeringsgroep NV: Spaklerweg 4, POB 1000, 1000 BA Amsterdam; tel. (20) 5949111; fax (20) 937968; internet www.deltalloyd.nl; f. 1807; Chair. JACQUES VAN DIJK.

De Eerste Nederlandsche: POB 325, 1170 AH Badhoevedorp; tel. (20) 6143340; fax (20) 6696556; e-mail info@eerste.nl; internet www.eerste.nl; all branches.

THE NETHERLANDS

Fiducia BV: Ruysdaelplein 42, 2282 BJ Rijswijk; tel. (70) 4140404; fax (70) 4140405; e-mail info@fiducia.nl; internet www.fiducia.nl; f. 1990.

Fortis ASR Verzekeringsgroep NV: Weena 70, POB 100, 3000 AC Rotterdam; tel. (10) 4017465; fax (10) 4125490; internet www.asr.nl; f. 2000 by merger of ASR Verzekeringsgroep NV (f. 1720) and AMEV Nederland NV (f. 1883); owned by the Fortis group; Chair. J. C. VAN EK.

Generali Verzekeringsgroep: Diemerhof 42, 1112 XN Diemen; tel. (20) 6604444; fax (20) 3983000; e-mail info@generali.nl; internet www.generali.nl; f. 1870; life and non-life; Gen. Dir FREEK WANSINK.

ING Groep NV: Amstelveenseweg 500, 1081 KL Amsterdam; tel. (70) 5415433; fax (70) 5415412; e-mail mediarelations@ing.com; internet www.ing.com; f. 1963; Chair. C. A. J. HERKSTRÖTER.

Nationale-Nederlanden NV: Weena 505, 3013 AL Rotterdam; tel. (10) 45130303; f. 1863; Chair. LUDO WIJNGAARDEN.

RVS Levensverzekering NV: Weena 505, 3013 AL Rotterdam; tel. (10) 4012911; fax (10) 4012933; e-mail rvs@rvs.nl; internet www.rvs.nl; f. 1838; subsidiary of ING Groep NV; mem. of Internationale-Nederlanden group; life; Chair. H. W. SMID.

Insurance Associations

Verbond van Verzekeraars (Asscn of Insurers): Bordewijklaan 2, POB 93450, 2509 AL The Hague; tel. (70) 3338500; fax (70) 338510; e-mail info@verzekeraars.nl; internet www.verzekeraars.nl; f. 1978; Chair. P. F. M. OVERMARS; Gen. Man. Prof. Dr E. J. FISCHER.

Trade and Industry

GOVERNMENT AGENCIES

Nederlands Centrum voor Handelsbevordering (NCH) (Netherlands Council for Trade Promotion): Bezuidenhoutseweg 181, POB 10, 2501 CA The Hague; tel. (70) 3441544; fax (70) 3853531; internet www.handelsbevordering.nl; Man. Dir G. VAANDRAGER.

Netherlands Foreign Investment Agency: Bezuidenhoutseweg 16A, POB 20101, 2500 EC The Hague; tel. (70) 3798818; fax (70) 3796322; e-mail info@nfia.nl; internet www.nfia.nl; govt agency; facilitates foreign direct investment.

CHAMBERS OF COMMERCE

There are numerous Chambers of Commerce and Industry in the Netherlands. The most important are:

Kamer van Koophandel en Fabrieken voor Amsterdam (Chamber of Commerce and Industry for Amsterdam): De Ruyterkade 5, 1013 AA Amsterdam; POB 2852, 1000 CW Amsterdam; tel. (20) 5314000; fax (20) 5314799; e-mail post@amsterdam.kvk.nl; internet www.amsterdam.kvk.nl; f. 1811; Dir-Gen. Dr JACOB BEVAART.

Kamer van Koophandel Rotterdam (Chamber of Commerce for Rotterdam): Blaak 40, 3011 TA Rotterdam; POB 450, 3000 AL Rotterdam; tel. (10) 4027777; fax (10) 4145754; e-mail post@rotterdam.kvk.nl; internet www.rotterdam.kvk.nl; f. 1803; Pres. F. J. LAVOOIJ.

Kamer van Koophandel voor Haaglanden (The Hague Chamber of Commerce): Koningskade 30, 2596 AA The Hague; POB 29718, 2502 LS The Hague; tel. (70) 3287100; fax (70) 3240684; e-mail info@denhaag.kvk.nl; internet www.denhaag.kvk.nl; Pres. M. J. VAREKAMP; Sec.-Gen. Dr G. ZANDSTEEG.

EMPLOYERS' ORGANIZATIONS

LTO-Nederland (Netherlands Agricultural Organization): Prinsevinkenpark 19, 2585 HK The Hague; POB 29773, 2502 LT The Hague; tel. (70) 3382700; fax (70) 3382810; e-mail info@lto.nl; internet www.lto.nl; f. 1995; Chair. GERARD DOORNBOS; Sec.-Gen. DIRK DUIJZER; 65,000 mems.

Netherlands Elektronica- en Radiogenootschap: POB 39, 2260 AK Leidschendam; tel. (70) 3325112; fax (70) 3326477; internet www.nerg.nl; f. 1921; Chair. Prof. Dr N. H. G. BAKEN; Sec. E. BOTTELIER; 700 mems.

Nederlandsche Maatschappij voor Nijverheid en Handel (NMNH) (Netherlands Society for Industry and Trade): Jan van Nassaustraat 75, 2596 BP Den Haag; tel. (70) 3141940; fax (70) 3247515; e-mail info@nmnh.nl; internet www.nmnh.nl; f. 1777; Dir-Gen. GEERT VAN DER TANG; more than 5,500 mems.

Nederlandse Tuinbouwraad (NTR) (Netherlands Horticultural Council): POB 462, 2800 AL Gouda; tel. (71) 5659596; fax (71) 5659610; e-mail cmoerman@vgb.nl; f. 1908; Chair. Dr HEIN VAN ASPEREN; Sec. J. W. A. GRIEP.

Vereniging VNO-NCW (Confederation of Netherlands Industry and Employers): Bezuidenhoutseweg 12, POB 93002, 2509 AA The Hague; tel. (70) 3490349; fax (70) 3490300; e-mail informatie@vno-ncw.nl; internet www.vno-ncw.nl; f. 1997 as merger of Verbond van Nederlandse Ondernemingen (VNO) and Nederlands Christelijk Werkgeversverbond (NCW); represents almost all sectors of the Dutch economy; Pres. B. E. M. WIENTJES; mems: 180 asscns representing more than 115,000 enterprises.

UTILITIES

Electricity

E.ON Benelux BV: POB 909, 2270 AX Voorburg; tel. (70) 3820028; fax (70) 3383901; e-mail info@eon-benelux.com; internet www.eon-benelux.com; f. 2000; replaced Electriciteitsbedrijf Zuid Holland (EZH—f. 1941); supplies energy to large-volume customers and distributors.

ENECO: POB 96, 2900 AB Capelle a/d Ijssel; tel. (10) 4576979; fax (10) 4577784; internet www.eneco.nl; Chair. R. BLOM; 5,000 employees.

Essent: POB 9501, 9703 LM Groningen; internet www.essent.nl; f. 1999 by merger of Edon Group and Pnem Mega Group; electricity and gas supply; Chair. Dr J. V. H. PENNINGS.

Nuon ENW: POB 40021, 6803 HA Arnhem; e-mail nuon@nuon.com; internet www.nuon.com; f. 1999; energy and water; Chair. W. MEIJER; CEO LUDO M. J. VAN HALDEREN.

Tennet BV: Utrechtseweg 310, POB 718, 6812 AS Arnhem; tel. (26) 3731111; fax (26) 3731112; e-mail servicedesk@tennet.org; internet www.tennet.org; f. 1999; independent; Dutch Transmission System Operator; manages 220/380 kW national grid and supplies electricity to direct suppliers; Dir MEL KROON.

Gas

Full liberalization of the gas market in the Netherlands took effect from the beginning of July 2004 (postponed from January 2003). Although retaining ownership of the main transport network, NV Nederlandse Gasunie passed the legal tasks of the national transmission system operator to a new, state-owned organization, Gas Transport Services BV, founded on 2 July 2004.

ENECO: see above.

Essent: see above.

Gas Transport Services BV: POB 181, 9700 AD Groningen; tel. (50) 3626000; fax (50) 3626100; e-mail info@gastransport.nl; internet www.gastransportservices.nl; f. 2004; independent; transmission system operator; Chair. C. GRIFFIOEN; CEO PIETER E. G. TRIENEKENS.

NV Nederlandse Gasunie: Concourslaan 17, POB 19, 9700 MA Groningen; tel. (50) 5219111; fax (50) 5211999; internet www.nvnederlandsegasunie.nl.

RWE Obragas NV: POB 300, 5700 AH Helmond; tel. (49) 2594888; fax (49) 2594990; internet www.rwe.nl.

Water

Nuon: see above.

VEWIN: POB 1019, 2280 CA Rijswijk; tel. (70) 4144750; fax (70) 4144420; e-mail vewin@vewin.nl; internet www.vewin.nl; Man. Dir J. J. SCHMITZ.

TRADE UNIONS

Central federations and affiliated unions are mainly organized on a religious, political or economic basis. The most important unions are those of the transport, metal, building and textile industries, the civil service and agriculture.

Central Federations

Christelijk Nationaal Vakverbond in Nederland (CNV) (Christian National Federation of Trade Unions): Ravellaan 1, POB 2475, 3500 GL Utrecht; tel. (30) 2913911; fax (30) 2946544; e-mail cnv@cnv.nl; internet www.cnv.nl; f. 1909; Pres. RENÉ PAAS; Gen. Sec. YVON VAN HOUDT; 360,000 mems.

Eleven affiliated unions, of which the principal unions are:

CNV Bedrijvenbond (Industry, Food and Transport): Prins Bernhardweg 69, POB 327, 3990 GC Houten; tel. (30) 6348348; fax (30) 6348200; e-mail info@cnv.net; internet www.cnv.net; Chair. JAAP JONGEJAN.

CNV Dienstenbond (Service Industries, Media and Printing): Polarisave 175, POB 3135, 2130 KC Hoofddorp; tel. (23) 5651052; fax (23) 5650150; e-mail cnvdienstenbond@cnvdibo.nl; internet www.cnvdienstenbond.nl; f. 1894; Pres. D. SWAGERMAN; Sec. R. J. ROTSHUIZEN; 36,000 mems.

CNV Publieke Zaak (Public-Sector Union): Carnegielaan 1, POB 84500, 2508 AM The Hague; tel. (70) 4160600; fax (70) 4160690; e-mail denhaag@cnvpubliekezaak.nl; internet www.cnvpubliekezaak.nl; Pres. P. J. KOESLAG; Sec. K. KRUITHOF; 84,000 mems.

Hout- en Bouwbond CNV (Wood and Building): Oude Haven 1, 3984 KT Odijk; tel. (30) 6597711; fax (30) 6571101; e-mail info@hbbcnv.nl; internet www.hbbcnv.nl; f. 1900; Chair. A. A. VAN WIJNGAARDEN; Gen. Sec. J. T. SLOK; 50,000 mems.

Onderwijsbond CNV (Education): Boerhaavelaan 5, POB 732, 2700 AS Zoetermeer; tel. (79) 3202020; fax (79) 3202195; e-mail algemeen@ocnv.nl; internet www.ocnv.nl; f. 2000; Pres. MARLEEN BARTH.

Federatie Nederlandse Vakbeweging (FNV) (Netherlands Trade Union Confederation): POB 8456, 1005 AL Amsterdam; tel. (20) 5816300; fax (20) 6844541; e-mail persvoorlichting@vc.fnv.nl; internet www.fnv.nl; f. 1975; as confederation of the Netherlands Federation of Trade Unions (f. 1906) and the Netherlands Catholic Trade Union Federation (f. 1909); Pres. L. J. DE WAAL; Vice-Pres. C. E. ROOZEMOND; Gen. Sec. A. REGEER; 1,234,361 mems.

Seventeen affiliated unions, of which the principal are:

ABVAKABO FNV (Government Personnel, Civil Servants, Private Health Workers, Social Workers, Post and Telecom Workers, Public Utility Workers): Boerhaavelaan 1, POB 3010, 2700 KT Zoetermeer; tel. (79) 3536161; fax (79) 3521226; e-mail post@abvakabo.nl; internet www.abvakabo.nl; f. 1982; Pres. E. SNOEY; Gen. Sec. X. DEN UYL; 360,000 mems.

Algemene Onderwijsbond (AOb) (Education): POB 2875, 3500 GW Utrecht; tel. (30) 2989898; fax (30) 29880; e-mail info@aob.nl; internet www.aob.nl; f. 1997 as merger between Algemene Bond van Onderwijspersoneel and NGL—Dordrecht; Pres. J. TICHELAAR; Gen. Sec. MARTIN KNOOP; 75,000 mems.

FNV Bondgenoten (Transport, Metal and Steel, Information Technology, Electrotechnical, Textiles, Financial Services, Retail, Wholesale, Foods, Agriculture): Varrolaan 100, POB 9208, 3506 GE Utrecht; tel. (30) 2738222; fax (30) 2738225; internet www.bondgenoten.fnv.nl; f. 1998; by merger; Pres. H. VAN DER KOLK; Sec. E. C. DEKKERS; 500,000 mems.

FNV Bouw (Building): Houttuinlaan 3, POB 520, 3440 AM Woerden; tel. (348) 575575; fax (348) 414970; e-mail info@fnvbouw.nl; internet www.fnvbouw.nl; f. 1917; Pres. D. VAN HAASTER; Int. Sec. AGNES JONGERIUS; 150,000 mems.

FNV KIEM (Printing and Allied Trades): J. Tooropstraat, POB 9354, 1006 AJ Amsterdam; tel. (20) 3553636; fax (20) 3553737; e-mail algemeen@fnv-kiem.nl; internet www.fnv.nl/kiem; Chair. LUCIA VAN WESTERLAAK; Gen. Sec. HERMAN LEISINK; 48,000 mems.

Nederlandse Politiebond (Police): Boerhaavelaan 1, POB 393, 2700 AJ, Zoetermeer; tel. (79) 3536161; fax (79) 3521226; e-mail info@politiebond.nl; internet www.politiebond.nl; f. 1946; Pres. J. F. W. VAN DUIJN; Gen. Sec. FRANS VAN DER HEIDEN; 22,500 mems.

Consultative Organization

Stichting van de Arbeid (Labour Foundation): Bezuidenhoutseweg 60, 2594 AW The Hague; tel. (70) 3499577; fax (70) 3499796; internet www.stvda.nl; f. 1945; central organ of co-operation and consultation between employers and employees; 16 bd mems; Jt Pres B. E. M. WIENTJES, Dr A. M. JONGERIUS.

Land Reclamation and Development

Without intensive land-protection schemes, nearly the whole of the north and west of the Netherlands (about one-half of the total area of the country) would be inundated by sea-water twice a day. A large part of the country (including a section of the former Zuiderzee, now the Ijsselmeer) has already been drained.

The Delta Plan, which was adopted in 1958 and provided for the construction of eight dams, a major canal, several locks and a system of dykes, aimed to shorten the southern coastline by 700 km and to protect the estuaries of Zeeland and Southern Holland. The final cost of the delta works project, which had originally been projected at 2,500m. guilders, totalled around 14,000m. guilders, as the result of a complex adaptation to ensure the preservation of the delta's ecological balance.

The Ministry of Transport, Public Works and Water Management is responsible for land reclamation and waterways.

Transport

RAILWAYS

About 70% of the Dutch railway network is electrified; the remaining track carries diesel electric and diesel stock. There were 2,808 km of state-operated railways in 1999, providing mainly passenger services. The infrastructure of the Dutch railway network remains wholly under public ownership. Until early 2002 the main railway operator, Nederlandse Spoorwegen (NS), was partially privatized, but, following a sharp deterioration in the quality of service, it was taken back under government control. NS retains a majority of the passenger and freight rolling stock, and station premises, while there is a small number of additional, privately owned network service providers. Construction of a high-speed rail link connecting Amsterdam and Rotterdam to Antwerp and Brussels, Belgium, and to Paris, France, was expected to be completed by 2007.

Nederlandse Spoorwegen NV (NS): Antwoordnummer 4470, POB 2025, 3500 VE Utrecht; tel. (30) 2359111; fax (30) 2332458; internet www.ns.nl; f. 1937; partially privatized until early 2002, when the Government reasserted management control; operates most railway lines in the Netherlands; Mems of Exec. Bd A. W. VEENMAN, A. MEERSTADT, M. NIGGEBRUGGE.

NS Stations: Laan van Puntenburg 100, POB 2025, 3500 HA, Utrecht; tel. (30) 2354000; fax (30) 2311490; internet www.ns.nl; station management co; Dir AAD W. VEENMAN.

NS Vastgoed: POB 2319, 3500 GH, Utrecht; tel. (30) 3004300; fax (30) 3004400; e-mail info@vastgoed.ns.nl; internet www.ns.nl; f. 1995; property management and property development co; Dir PAUL RUTTE.

NoordNed Personenvervoer BV: Stationsplein 4, POB 452, 8901 BG Leeuwarden; tel. (58) 2335646; fax (58) 2335636; e-mail t.degnua@noordned.com; internet www.noordned.com; f. 1999; subsidiary of Arriva Nederland; operates train and bus services in North and South-West Friesland.

Railion Benelux NV: POB 2060, 3500 GB Utrecht; tel. (30) 2354004; fax (30) 2354334; e-mail info@railion.nl; internet www.railion.nl; international goods transport by rail; Man. Dir CAREL ROBBESON.

ROADS

In 1999 there were 2,235 km of motorway, 6,650 km of main roads, 57,500 km of secondary roads and 59,400 km of other roads in the Netherlands. Cycling is a popular means of transport in the Netherlands, and in 1996 there were 19,100 km of cycle paths.

INLAND WATERWAYS

An extensive network of rivers and canals navigable for ships of 50 metric tons and over, totalling 5,046 km, has led to the outstanding development of Dutch inland shipping. About one-third of goods transported inside the Netherlands are carried on the canals and waterways. Dutch inland shipping has access to Germany and France along the Rhine and its branch rivers, and to France and Belgium along the Meuse and Scheldt (including the Rhine-Scheldt link). Ocean traffic reaches Rotterdam via the New Waterway, and the 21-km long North Sea Canal connects Amsterdam to the North Sea. Following severe river flooding in early 1995, the Government announced the inauguration of a five-year programme to improve and strengthen the Netherlands' river dykes defence system.

SHIPPING

The Netherlands is one of the world's leading shipping countries. At the end of 2004 the merchant fleet comprised 1,276 vessels, with a combined displacement of 5.6m. gross registered tons. The Rotterdam complex, incorporating the Europoort for large oil tankers and bulk carriers, is the main European Union port and the busiest in the world, handling some 322m. metric tons of cargo in 2002.

Principal Companies

Amasus Chartering BV: Zijlvest 26, Farmsum, POB 250, 9930 Delfzijl; tel. (596) 610744; fax (596) 616551; e-mail chartering@amasus.nl; internet www.amasus.nl; shipowners, managers and operators.

Hudig Freight Services: Debussystraat 2, POB 1030, 3160 AE Rhoon; tel. (10) 5066550; fax (10) 5012827; e-mail info@hudig.nl; internet www.hudig.com; f. 1795; international freight services; Man. Dir A. D. FONTEIN.

Koninklijke Vopak NV: Westerlaan 10, POB 863, 3000 AW Rotterdam; tel. (10) 4002911; fax (10) 4139829; e-mail info@vopak.com; internet www.vopak.com; f. 1999; Chair. JOHN PAUL BROEDERS.

Seatrade Groningen BV: Laan Corpus den Hoorn 200, POB 858, JS Groningen; tel. (50) 5215300; fax (50) 5215300; e-mail info@seatrade.nl; internet www.seatrade.nl; shipowners, managers and operators; Man. Dir KARL-HEINZ HILBIG.

Spliethoff's Bevrachtingskantoor BV: Radarweg 36, POB 409, 1000 AK Amsterdam; tel. (20) 4488400; fax (20) 4488500; e-mail gogracht@spliethoff.com; internet www.spliethoff.nl; shipowners, managers and operators; Man. ROLF G. W. ERIKSSON.

Stena Line: Stationsweg 10, POB 2, 3150 AA Hoek van Holland; tel. (17) 4389333; fax (17) 4389309; e-mail info.nl@stenaline.nl; internet www.stenaline.com; operates daily (day and night) ferry services for accompanied private cars, commercial freight vehicles and trailers between Hoek van Holland and Harwich (UK); Man. Dir GUNNAR BLOMDAHL.

Van Uden Maritime BV: POB 1123, 3000 BC, Rotterdam; tel. (10) 2973100; fax (10) 4851044; e-mail group@van-uden.nl; internet www.van-uden.nl; f. 1848; agencies in Rotterdam, Antwerp, Amsterdam; liner operators and representatives; international chartering; Man. D. P. F. DUTILH.

Vroon BV: Haven Westzijde 21, POB 28, 4510 AA Breskens; tel. (117) 384910; fax (117) 384218; e-mail office@vroon.nl; internet www.vroon.nl; shipowners, managers and operators; Chair. and Man. Dir P. W. VROON.

Wagenborg Shipping BV: Marktstraat 10, POB 14, 9930 AA Delfzyl; tel. (596) 636911; fax (596) 636250; e-mail info@wagenborg.com; internet www.wagenborg.com; shipowners, managers and operators; Man. Dirs Dr E. VUURSTEEN, Dr G. R. WAGENBORG.

Wijnne & Barends' Cargadoors- en Agentuurkantonen BV: Handelskade Oost 5, POB 123, 9930 AC Delfzyl; tel. (596) 637777; fax (596) 637790; e-mail info@wijnne-barends.nl; internet www.wijnne-barends.nl; f. 1855; became part of Spliethoff Group in 2003; shipowners, managers and operators; cargo services and agents; Man. Dir D. P. MAKKINJE.

Shipping Associations

Federatie van Werknemers in de Zeevaart (Dutch Seafarers' Federation): Heemraadssingel 323, POB 25131, 3001 HC Rotterdam; tel. (10) 4771188; fax (10) 4773846; e-mail fwz.nl@wxs.nl.

Koninklijke Vereniging van Nederlandse Reders (KVNR) (Royal Asscn of Netherlands' Shipowners): Wijnhaven 65B, POB 2442, 3000 CK Rotterdam; tel. (10) 4146001; fax (10) 2330081; e-mail kvnr@kvnr.nl; internet www.kvnr.nl; f. 1905; Chair. A. KORTELAND; Man. Dir G. X. HOLLEER; 300 mems.

Vereniging Nederlandse Scheepsbouw Industrie (Netherlands Shipbuilding Industry Association): Boerhaavelaan 40, POB 138, 2700 AC Zoetermeer; tel. (79) 3531165; fax (79) 3531155; e-mail info@vnsi.nl; internet www.vnsi.nl; promotes Dutch shipbuilding on a national basis; Man. Dir R. J. SCHOUTEN; 95 mems.

CIVIL AVIATION

The main Dutch airport is at Schiphol, near Amsterdam. There are also international airports at Zestienhoven for Rotterdam, Beek for Maastricht and at Eelde for Groningen. Schiphol expanded rapidly during the late 1990s, from 25.3m. passengers in 1995 to 40.7m. in 2002. A fifth runway was opened in early 2003, while it was intended that the scheduled privatization of Schiphol would attract further investment in the airport's infrastructure.

KLM (Koninklijke Luchtvaart Maatschappij NV) (Royal Dutch Airlines): Schiphol Airport, POB 7700, 1117 ZL Schiphol; head office: Amsterdamseweg 55, 1182 GP Amstelveen; tel. (20) 6499123; fax (20) 6488069; internet www.klm.com; f. 1919; world's oldest commercial airline; regular international air services; merged with Air France in 2004 to create Europe's largest airline; in September 2004 KLM together with Northwest Airlines and Continental Airlines of the USA joined the global Sky Team alliance, which included Air France, Alitalia (Italy), Delta Air Lines (USA), and Korean Air; subsidiaries: KLM Cityhopper, KLM UK; Pres. and CEO LEO VAN WIJK; Gen. Sec. H. E. KUIPÉRI.

Martinair Holland NV: POB 7507, 1118 ZG Schiphol Airport; tel. (20) 6011222; fax (20) 6011303; internet www.martinair.nl; f. 1958; 50% owned by Nedlloyd; world-wide passenger and cargo services; Pres. and CEO AMIE VERBERK.

Schreiner Airways: Diamantlaan 1, POB 381, 2130 AJ Hoofddorp; tel. (23) 5555555; fax (23) 5555500; e-mail info-sag@schreiner.aero; internet www.schreiner.nl; f. 1945; scheduled flights and leasing services; CEO HEIN VERLOOP.

transavia.com: POB 7777, 1118 ZM Schiphol Airport; tel. (20) 6046555; fax (20) 6484637; internet www.transvia.com; f. 1966; scheduled and charter services to leisure destinations; wholly owned by KLM; Pres. ONNO P. M. VAN DEN BRINK.

Tourism

The principal tourist attractions in the Netherlands are the cosmopolitan city of Amsterdam, which receives nearly one-half of all tourist visits, the old towns, the canals, the cultivated fields of spring flowers, the outlying islands, the art galleries and modern architecture. Some 9.2m. foreign tourists stayed in hotels and boarding houses in the Netherlands in 2003. Receipts from tourism totalled an estimated US $9,162m. in the same year.

Toerisme Recreatie Nederlands (Netherlands Board of Tourism): Vlietweg 15, POB 458, 2260 MG Leidschendam; tel. (70) 3705705; fax (70) 3201654; e-mail info@holland.com; internet www.holland.com; f. 1968; Man. Dir HANS VAN DRIEM.

Royal Dutch Touring Club ANWB: POB 93200, 2596 EC The Hague; tel. (70) 3147147; fax (70) 3146969; f. 1883; CEO GUIDO H. N. L. VAN WOERKOM; 55 brs in Europe; 4m. mems.

NETHERLANDS DEPENDENCIES

ARUBA

Introductory Survey

Location, Climate, Language, Religion, Flag, Capital

Aruba is one of the group of Benedenwindse Eilands or 'Leeward Islands', which it forms with part of the Netherlands Antilles (q.v.), and lies in the southern Caribbean Sea, 25 km north of Venezuela and 68 km west of the island of Curaçao (Netherlands Antilles). The climate is tropical, with an average annual temperature of 28°C (82°F), but is tempered by north-easterly winds. Rainfall is very low, averaging only about 425.5 mm (16.8 ins) annually. The official language is Dutch, but the dominant language is Papiamento (a mixture of Dutch, Spanish, English, Arawak Indian and several West African dialects). Spanish and English are also spoken. Most of the inhabitants profess Christianity and belong to the Roman Catholic Church, although a wide variety of other denominations are represented. The national flag (proportions 2 by 3) is blue, with two narrow yellow horizontal stripes in the lower section and a white-bordered four-pointed red star in the upper hoist. The capital is Oranjestad.

Recent History

The Caribbean island of Aruba was claimed for Spain in 1499, but was first colonized by the Dutch in 1636 and subsequently formed part of the Dutch possessions in the West Indies. Administered from Curaçao after 1845, in 1954 Aruba became a member of the autonomous federation of the Netherlands Antilles. The establishment in 1929 of a large petroleum refinery on the island, at San Nicolaas, led to the rapid expansion of the economy and a high standard of living for the islanders. However, many Arubans resented the administrative dominance of Curaçao, and what they regarded as the excessive demands made upon Aruban wealth and resources by the other five islands within the Netherlands Antilles. The island's principal political party, the Movimentu Electoral di Pueblo (MEP), campaigned, from its foundation in 1971 onwards, for Aruban independence and separation from the other islands. In a referendum held in Aruba in March 1977 82% of voters supported independence and withdrawal from the Antillean federation. The MEP used its position in the coalition Government of the Netherlands Antilles, formed in 1979, to press for concessions from the other islands towards early independence for Aruba. In 1981 (after the MEP had withdrawn from the Government of the Netherlands Antilles) a provisional agreement regarding Aruba's future was reached between the Dutch and Antillean Governments. Following further discussions, it was agreed in March 1983 that Aruba should receive separate status (*status aparte*), within the Kingdom of the Netherlands, from 1 January 1986, achieving full independence in 1996. The Dutch Government would remain responsible for defence and external relations until independence, while Aruba was to form a co-operative union with the Netherlands Antilles (the Antilles of the Five) in economic and monetary affairs.

At local elections in April 1983 the MEP increased its representation to 13 of the 21 seats in the Staten (parliament), and the leader of the MEP, Gilberto F. (Betico) Croes, remained as leader of the island Government. Austerity measures, introduced in an attempt to alleviate the adverse effects of the closure (announced in October 1984) of the San Nicolaas petroleum refinery, provoked a series of strikes and demonstrations by civil servants in protest at wage reductions and price rises. The MEP consequently lost popular support and, following elections to the Staten in November 1985, was succeeded in government by a coalition of four opposition parties led by the Arubaanse Volkspartij (AVP). Aruba achieved separate status, as planned, on 1 January 1986, and Jan Hendrik Albert (Henny) Eman, leader of the AVP, became its first Prime Minister. Croes died in November 1986; he was succeeded as leader of the MEP by Nelson O. Oduber.

From 1988 Aruba began to enjoy an economic recovery, based on tourism. However, the MEP claimed that the benefits to the whole community were limited, and also criticized Eman's stated reservations about independence in 1996 and his refusal to negotiate with the Netherlands about transitional arrangements. At a general election in January 1989 the MEP came within 28 votes of securing an absolute majority in the Staten. The number of seats held by the MEP increased from eight to 10, and in February Oduber formed a Government in coalition with the Partido Patriótico Arubano (PPA) and the Accion Democratico Nacional (ADN). (Both these parties had been in the previous Government, and retained one seat each at the election.)

The MEP and the AVP each secured nine seats in the Staten at the January 1993 general election, while the three remaining seats were won by the ADN, the PPA and the Organisacion Liberal Arubano (OLA). Despite gaining fewer votes than the AVP, the MEP administration remained in office, renewing the coalition with the ADN and the PPA. In April 1994, however, Oduber announced the Government's resignation, following the withdrawal of the ADN and the PPA from the coalition. In May, following lengthy inter-party negotiations, it was agreed that a fresh general election would be held. Government functions were to be undertaken in the interim by the MEP. The general election was held on 29 July: the AVP secured 10 seats, while the MEP won nine seats and the OLA the remaining two. In late August Eman formed a Government in coalition with the OLA.

In March 1994 the Governments of Aruba, the Netherlands and the Netherlands Antilles convened in The Hague, the Netherlands, and decided to cancel plans for Aruba's transition to full independence, due to take place in 1996. The possibility of a transition to full independence at a later date was not excluded, but was not considered a priority, and would, moreover, require the approval of the Aruban people, by referendum, as well as the support of a two-thirds' majority in the Staten.

In September 1997 the Staten was dissolved after the OLA withdrew from the coalition. A general election was thus held on 12 December; this resulted in a political composition identical to that of the 1993 polls. Following protracted negotiations, the AVP and the OLA renewed their coalition in mid-1998, and a new Council of Ministers, headed by Eman, was appointed.

In June 2001 the governing coalition collapsed, following the withdrawal of the OLA's support for the AVP's plan to privatize the Aruban Tourism Authority. As a result, the legislative elections that had been scheduled to be held in December were brought forward to 28 September. The MEP comfortably defeated the incumbent AVP in the elections, securing 52% of the votes cast and 12 seats in the Staten. The AVP legislative representation was reduced to six seats. The three remaining seats were shared between the PPA (two) and the OLA (one). Oduber was once again appointed Prime Minister and a new single-party Government, with an unprecedented opportunity to pass legislation through the Staten, took office in November.

In early 2004 after several months of discussion, the Aruban and Dutch Governments agreed to appoint Fredis Refunjol, hitherto Minister of Education, as Governor. The Dutch Government objected to the fact that there was only one candidate for the position and argued that the appointment was overtly political. Nevertheless, since Refunjol's candidature had strong cross-party support in the Staten, he was duly sworn in on 7 May. The erstwhile President of the Staten, Francisco Walfrido Croes, assumed the vacant education portfolio. Meanwhile, in January the Staten voted against becoming an Ultra Periphery Area of the European Union (EU, see p. 228). The island thus remained an Overseas Territory of the EU.

At a general election on 23 September 2005 the MEP again won a majority of seats (11, from 43% of the popular vote) in the 21-seat Staten. The victory came in spite of broad public criticism of the Government's unwillingness to defend wage levels from the downward pressure caused by large-scale immigration from South America. Notably, the minimum wage had not been adjusted for five years. The AVP won eight seats, an improvement on its result in the 2001 election, and the PPA and Network each won one legislative seat. The electoral turn-out among those eligible to vote was 85%. Oduber, who continued as Prime Minister, defended his economic policies and pledged to continue to develop the tourism sector and to balance the budget, which is heavily dependent on external creditors, by 2009.

Aruba's relations with the Antilles of the Five improved after 1986. In 1987 Aruba agreed to undertake economic co-operation, and in 1988 the three Dutch 'Leeward Islands' initiated a joint project for the development of tourism. Aruba's relations with the 'metropolitan' Netherlands were dominated at this time by the latter's pressure for more control to be exercised over the large amount of aid that it gave to Aruba, and by the issue of independence, in particular the future arrangements for the island's security: Aruba's strategic position, close to the South American mainland, and the possibility of its being used as a base for drugs-trafficking, were matters of particular concern. In September 1990 Aruba announced that it was to adopt the 1988 UN Convention on measures to combat trade in illegal drugs; a joint Dutch and Aruban team was formed to conduct investigations. In December 1996, however, the USA included Aruba on its list of major drugs-producing or transit countries. New legislation to facilitate the extradition of suspected drugs-traffickers and money-launderers took effect in October 1997. US naval and air force patrols began operating from a base in Aruba in May 1999 in an effort to counter the transport of illicit drugs. In 2001 the Caribbean Financial Action Task Force commended the Government on its efforts in combating money-laundering. In the same year the territory was removed from the list of so-called 'non-co-operative tax havens' drawn up by the Organisation for Economic Co-operation and Development (OECD, based in Paris, France), after the Government pledged to reform the territory's financial sector in order to conform to OECD's guide-lines by 2005. In October the Minister of Justice, Rudy Croes, visited The Hague to discuss the issue of independence with the Dutch Government. Relations between Aruba and the Netherlands deteriorated, however, when the Dutch Government forced Aruba to introduce a more stringent policy on visa conditions. In November 2003 Aruba signed an agreement with the USA to exchange tax information in order to combat illegal financial activities, such as money-laundering, that are associated with international terrorism and drugs-trafficking. The issue of immigration arose again in late 2004: in the first 10 months of the year Aruba deported 864 Colombians, most of whom arrived on the island from Venezuela.

In May 2005 the disappearance of a US teenager, Natalee Holloway, on the island and the attendant negative publicity in her home country led to tension in the relationship between Aruba and the USA and placed severe strain on the island's crucial tourism industry, which is heavily dependent upon US custom. Later in the year the Governor of Alabama, the missing girl's home state, blamed the Aruban Government for the failure to discover her whereabouts and, backed by overwhelming US public support (and, in January 2006, by the Alabama Senate), unsuccessfully requested that the US Government impose sanctions on Aruba.

After acquiring separate status, Aruba fostered relations with some of its Caribbean neighbours and with countries in Latin America. This included the development of ties with Venezuela, which had traditionally laid claim to the Dutch 'Leeward Islands', including Aruba.

Government

Aruba has separate status within the Kingdom of the Netherlands. Legislative power is held by the unicameral Staten (parliament) of 21 members, elected by universal adult suffrage for four years (subject to dissolution). Executive power in all domestic affairs is vested in the Council of Ministers (led by the Prime Minister), responsible to the Staten. The Governor, appointed by the Dutch Crown for a term of six years, represents the monarch of the Netherlands on Aruba and holds responsibility for external affairs and defence. The Governor is assisted by an advisory council.

Defence

The Netherlands is responsible for Aruba's defence and military service is compulsory. The Governor is Commander-in-Chief of the armed forces on the island. A Dutch naval contingent is stationed in Aruba, primarily to combat drugs-trafficking and organized crime. In May 1999 the USA began air force and navy patrols from a base on Aruba as part of efforts to prevent the transport of illegal drugs.

Economic Affairs

In 2000, according to the UN, Aruba's gross national income (GNI), was US $1,756m. During 1995–2004 the population increased at an average annual rate of 2.3% per year, while gross domestic product (GDP) per head increased, in real terms, by an average of 3.1% per year. Overall GDP increased, in real terms, at an average annual rate of 2.4% in 1995–2004. Real GDP increased by an estimated 3.5% in 2004.

Owing to the poor quality of the soil and the prohibitive cost of desalinated water, the only significant agricultural activity is the cultivation of aloes (used in the manufacture of cosmetics and pharmaceuticals); aloe-based products are exported. Some livestock is raised, and there is a small fishing industry (although in the mid-1990s fishing production contributed only some 12.5% of Aruba's annual consumption of fish and fish products). In 2000 the agricultural sector engaged 0.6% of the employed labour force and contributed 0.4% of total GDP.

The industrial sector, and the island's economy, was formerly based on the refining and transhipment of imported petroleum and petroleum products. In the early 1980s this sector accounted for one-quarter of GDP and provided almost all Aruba's exports. The San Nicolaas petroleum refinery ceased operations in 1985; however, in 1990 the plant partially reopened, following renovation; after more construction and revision works, production reached an estimated 202,000 barrels per day (b/d) in 1999, an increase of 26% on the previous year's total. Following a further US $250m. renovation in 2000, production increased to 280,000 b/d. In March 2004 the refinery was purchased by the US-based Valero Energy Corporation, which, in 2005, announced that it was considering a US $6,000m. expansion of the plant in order to increase production to as much as 800,000 b/d by about 2012. There is a large petroleum transhipment terminal on Aruba, and a small petrochemicals industry. An advanced-technology coker plant opened in 1995 to supply liquefied petroleum gas, largely for export to the USA. There are believed to be exploitable reserves of hydrocarbons within Aruban territory, and Aruba also has reserves of salt. The industrial sector comprised 15.6% of GDP in 2000.

Light industry is limited to the production of beverages, building materials, paints and solvents, paper and plastic products, candles, detergents, disinfectants, soaps and aloe-based cosmetics. There is a 'free zone', and the ports of Oranjestad and Barcadera provide bunkering and repair facilities for ships. In 1996 the Ports of Aruba Masterplan was presented, proposing the relocation (over a 20-year period) of all cargo operations to Barcadera, leaving Oranjestad's port to accommodate commercial, recreation and resort activities. The construction sector, which grew steadily in the 1980s, declined in importance following a moratorium on the construction of new hotels in 1992. In 2005–07, however, some US $150m. was scheduled to be invested in the renovation and expansion of existing hotels and resorts, thereby reinvigorating the construction sector. Industry (including mining, manufacturing, construction and power) engaged 16.4% of the employed labour force in 2000.

The service industries are Aruba's principal economic activity, employing 83.0% of the active labour force and contributing 83.9% of the island's GDP in 2000. Financial services are well established in Aruba, particularly the data-processing sector, an important service to US companies in particular. Aruba's principal source of income is tourism; the hotels and restaurants sector alone was estimated to provide 10.5% of Aruba's GDP in 2002. In 2001 there was a slight decrease in the number of visitor arrivals, attributed mainly to the global economic slowdown and to the effects on tourism of the terrorist attacks on the USA in September of that year. The number of stop-over visitors decreased by 4.3%, to 691,420, while the number of cruise-ship passengers contracted by 0.6%, to 487,296. In 2002 the overall number of visitor arrivals increased, by 3.9%, but this merely served to disguise a further 7.1% decrease in the number of stop-over visitors, to 642,627. The number of cruise-ship passengers increased by 19.5%, to 582,195. Strong growth in the first two months of 2003 was undermined by the repercussions of the US-led military campaign in Iraq; as a result, an overall decline in the tourism sector was recorded in that year. The number of stop-over visitors decreased slightly, to 641,906, and the number of cruise-ship passengers fell by 6.8%, to 542,327. In 2004 the sector finally recorded positive growth again when the number of stop-over arrivals increased by 13.4%, to 728,157. The number of cruise-ship passengers also increased significantly in that year (by 6.3%, to 567,320) and receipts from tourism increased by 24.0%, to a total of A. Fl. 1,872.3m. The first nine months of 2005 saw a further 3.4% increase in the number of visitor arrivals, compared with the equivalent period in 2004.

Aruba is obliged to import most of its requirements, particularly machinery and electrical equipment, chemical products and foodstuffs; in 2004 the island recorded a visible trade deficit of A Fl. 485.2m., but there was a surplus on the current account of the balance of payments of A Fl. 17.9m. In the same year the principal source of imports, excluding the petroleum sector and the 'free zone', was the USA (58.8% of the total); other major sources were the Netherlands, Venezuela and the Netherlands Antilles. The principal market for exports in 2004 was also the USA (accounting for 35.6% of the total), followed by the Netherlands Antilles, the Netherlands and Venezuela.

In 2004 the budget deficit was A Fl. 326.5m. At the end of 2004 total government debt was A Fl. 1,700.2m. (equivalent to 44.5% of GDP), of which 49.1% was owed to external creditors, primarily the Government of the Netherlands. The average annual rate of inflation was 6.3% in 1998–2004. Consumer prices increased by 2.6% in 2004. Some 7.6% of the labour force were unemployed in 2004.

As part of the Kingdom of the Netherlands, Aruba is classed as an Overseas Territory in association with the European Union (see p. 228). It forms a co-operative union with the Antilles of the Five in monetary and economic affairs. Aruba also has observer status with the Caribbean Community and Common Market (CARICOM, see p. 183).

The closure of the San Nicolaas petroleum refinery in 1985 and Aruba's separation from the rest of the Netherlands Antilles in 1986 prompted the Aruban administration to institute a policy of retrenchment and austerity, except for investment in tourism development. In 1992, following six consecutive years of rapid economic growth, during which period there was a threefold increase in hotel capacity, a moratorium was imposed on construction in the tourism industry, partly in recognition of the adverse environmental impact on the island and also to preserve the island's reputation as an exclusive holiday destination for the wealthy. Economic growth subsequently slowed to a more sustainable level during the remainder of the decade, with real GDP growth rates at an average of between 3%–4% annually. Aruba also maintained reasonably low levels of inflation

NETHERLANDS DEPENDENCIES

and of unemployment, and was considered to be one of the most prosperous islands in the Caribbean. Concern has, however, been expressed that Aruba's high public-sector wage bill and the generous nature of the island's social welfare system, combined with its ageing population, will threaten the future stability of public finance, already hindered by a narrow taxation base and poor revenue collection. The budgetary deficit has increased markedly in recent years and in May 2005 the IMF re-emphasized the need for the Government to gain control of the worsening ratio of public debt to GDP. Despite damage inflicted by 'Hurricane Ivan' in September 2004, the economy expanded by about 3.5% in that year and was forecast to expand by a further 3.0% in 2005. The positive economic outlook was predicated on the number of US tourists attracted to Aruba continuing to increase and on the related expansion of the construction sector. However, in 2005 the unpredictability of the tourism industry threatened to undermine the rest of the economy when the disappearance in May of a US teenager on the island, coupled with an apparently poorly managed police investigation, generated large amounts of negative publicity in North America. Tourist occupancy rates in September 2005 were 6.2% lower than the comparative figure in 2004.

Education

A Compulsory Education Act was introduced in 1999, to cover the four-to-16 age group. Kindergarten begins at four years of age. Primary education begins at six years of age and lasts for six years. Secondary education, beginning at the age of 12, lasts for up to six years. The main language of instruction is Dutch, but Papiamento (using a different spelling system from that of the Antilles of the Five) is used in kindergarten and primary education and in the lower levels of technical and vocational education. Papiamento is also being introduced onto the curriculum in all schools. In Aruba there are two institutes of higher education: the University of Aruba, comprising the School of Law and the School of Business Administration, which had 208 students in 1999/2000; and the Teachers' College, which had 180 students in 2000/01. There is also a community college. The majority of students, however, continue their studies abroad, generally in the Netherlands. The Government allocated a planned 12.6% of budget expenditure to education in 1999, equivalent to an estimated 3.4% of GDP.

Public Holidays

2006: 1 January (New Year's Day), 25 January (Gilberto F. (Betico) Croes' Birthday), 27 February (Lenten Carnival), 18 March (National Anthem and Flag Day), 14–17 April (Easter), 30 April (Queen's Day), 1 May (Labour Day), 25 May (Ascension Day), 25–26 December (Christmas).

2007: 1 January (New Year's Day), 25 January (Gilberto F. (Betico) Croes' Birthday), 19 February (Lenten Carnival), 18 March (National Anthem and Flag Day), 6–9 April (Easter), 30 April (Queen's Day), 1 May (Labour Day), 17 May (Ascension Day), 25–26 December (Christmas).

Weights and Measures

The metric system is in force.

Statistical Survey

Sources (unless otherwise stated): Department of Economic Affairs, Commerce and Industry (Direktie Economische Zaken, Handel en Industrie), Sun Plaza Bldg, L. G. Smith Blvd 160, Oranjestad; tel. 5821181; fax 5834494; e-mail deaci@setarnet.aw; internet www.arubaeconomicaffairs.aw; Centrale Bank van Aruba, J. E. Irausquin Blvd 8, POB 18, Oranjestad; tel. 5822509; fax 5832251; e-mail cbaua@setarnet.aw; internet www.cbaruba.org.

AREA AND POPULATION

Area: 193 sq km (74.5 sq miles).

Population: 66,687 (males 32,821, females 33,866) at census of 6 October 1991; 97,518 in mid-2004 (official estimate).

Density (mid-2004): 505.3 per sq km.

Principal Towns (population estimates, 2002): Oranjestad (capital) 20,700; Sint Nicolaas 17,400. Source: Stefan Helders, *World Gazetteer* (internet www.world-gazetteer.com). *Mid-2003* (UN estimate, incl. suburbs): Oranjestad 28,817 (Source: UN, *World Urbanization Prospects: The 2003 Revision*).

Births and Deaths (2001): Registered live births 1,266 (birth rate 13.8 per 1,000); Registered deaths 477 (death rate 5.2 per 1,000).

Expectation of Life (years at birth, 2000): Males 70.0; Females 76.0.

Economically Active Population (persons aged 15 years and over, 2000): Agriculture, hunting and forestry 251; Manufacturing electricity, gas and water 2,940; Construction 3,892; Wholesale and retail trade, repairs 7,112; Hotels and restaurants 7,651; Transport, storage and communications 2,905; Financial intermediation 1,485; Real estate, renting and business activities 3,722; Public administration, defence and social security 3,573; Education 1,431; Health and social work 1,986; Other community, social and personal services 2,776; Private households with employed persons 1,870; Other 324; Total employed 41,918; Unemployed 3,118; Total labour force 45,036.

HEALTH AND WELFARE

Under-5 Mortality Rate (per 1,000 live births, 1996): 4.1.

Physicians (per 1,000 head, 1999): 1.28.

Hospital Beds (per 1,000 head, 1995): 37.0.

Health Expenditure (% of GDP, 1998): 2.5.

Access to Water (% of persons, 2002): 100.

Access to Sanitation (% of persons, 1995): 100.

Source: partly Pan American Health Organization.

For definitions, see explanatory note on p. vi.

FISHING

Total catch (FAO estimates, metric tons, live weight, 2003): 150 (Groupers 15, Snappers and jobfishes 45, Wahoo 50, Other marine fishes 40). Source: FAO.

INDUSTRY

Electric Energy (million kWh, 2002): 824.6.

FINANCE

Currency and Exchange Rates: 100 cents = 1 Aruban gulden (guilder) or florin (A Fl.). *Sterling, Dollar and Euro Equivalents* (30 December 2005): £1 sterling = A Fl. 3.082; US $1 = A Fl. 1.790; €1 = A Fl. 2.112; A Fl. 100 = £32.44 = $55.87 = €47.36. Note: The Aruban florin was introduced in January 1986, replacing (at par) the Netherlands Antilles guilder or florin (NA Fl.). Since its introduction, the currency has had a fixed exchange rate of US $1 = A Fl. 1.79.

Budget (A Fl. million, 2004): *Revenue:* Tax revenue 707.1 (Taxes on income and profits 321.9, Taxes on commodities 255.4, Taxes on property 43.0, Taxes on services 60.7, Foreign exchange commission 26.2); Other current revenue 77.8; Total 784.9, excluding grants received (31.1). *Expenditure:* Wages 286.2; Employers' contributions 184.3; Wage subsidies 122.7; Goods and services 191.1; Interest payments 85.2; Development fund spending 32.9; Investments 34.2; Other expenditure 205.8; Total 1,142.5.

International Reserves (US $ million at 31 December 2004): Gold 48.66; Foreign exchange 295.42; Total 344.08. Source: IMF, *International Financial Statistics*.

Money Supply (A Fl. million at 31 December 2004): Currency outside banks 130.83; Demand deposits at commercial banks 826.71; Total money (incl. others) 960.99. Source: IMF, *International Financial Statistics*.

Cost of Living (Consumer Price Index at December; base: September 2000 = 100): 107.7 in 2002; 110.1 in 2003; 113.2 in 2004.

Gross Domestic Product (A. Fl. million at current prices): 3,421 in 2002; 3,599 in 2003; 3,819 in 2004 (preliminary).

Expenditure on the Gross Domestic Product (A. Fl. million at current prices, 2004, preliminary): Final consumption expenditure 3,024; Gross capital formation 1,129; *Total domestic expenditure* 4,153; Exports of goods and services 2,454; *Less* Imports of goods and services 2,788; *GDP in purchasers' values* 3,819.

Gross Domestic Product by Economic Activity (A. Fl. million at current prices, 2000): Agriculture, hunting, forestry and fishing, and mining and quarrying 14; Manufacturing 91; Electricity, gas and water (incl. petroleum refining) 212; Construction 202; Trade 440; Restaurants and hotels 355; Transport, storage and communications 287; Finance, insurance, real estate and business services 877; Government services 390; Other community, social and personal services 365; *Sub-total* 3,234; *Less* Imputed bank service charges 163; Indirect taxes, *less* subsidies 255; *GDP in purchasers' values* 3,326. Source: UN, *National Accounts Statistics*.

Balance of Payments (A Fl. million, 2004): Exports of goods f.o.b. 4,860.2; Imports of goods f.o.b. −5,345.4; *Trade balance* −485.2; Exports of services 2,218.9; Imports of services −1,425.4; *Balance on goods and services* 308.3; Other income received 65.1; Other income paid −168.5; *Balance on goods, services and income* 204.9; Current transfers received 71.8; Current transfers paid −258.8; *Current bal-*

ance 17.9; Capital account (net) 32.9; Direct investment abroad 1.4; Direct investment from abroad 233.8; Portfolio investment assets −32.3; Portfolio investment liabilities 114.0; Other investment (net) −359.1; Net errors and omissions 2.6; *Overall balance* 11.2.

EXTERNAL TRADE

Principal Commodities (A Fl. million, 2004): *Imports c.i.f.:* Live animals and animal products 94.8; Food products 169.4; Chemical products 158.7; Base metals and articles thereof 104.6; Machinery and electrical equipment 234.3; Transport equipment 134.7; Total (incl. others) 1,478.9. *Exports f.o.b.:* Live animals and animal products 2.6; Machinery and electrical equipment 5.4; Transport equipment 3.5; Art objects and collectors' items 7.6; Total (incl. others) 40.5. Note: Figures exclude transactions of the petroleum sector and those of the Free Trade Zone of Aruba.

Principal Trading Partners (A Fl. million, 2004): *Imports c.i.f.:* Japan 36.9; Netherlands 205.1; Netherlands Antilles 44.5; USA 869.8; Venezuela 50.5; Total (incl. others) 1,478.9. *Exports f.o.b.:* Colombia 1.7; Netherlands 6.9; Netherlands Antilles 8.2; USA 14.4; Venezuela 3.7; Total (incl. others) 40.5. Note: Figures exclude transactions of the petroleum sector and those of the Free Trade Zone of Aruba.

TRANSPORT

Road Traffic (motor vehicles in use, December 2002): Passenger cars 42,802; Lorries 804; Buses 391; Taxis 398; Rental cars 3,324; Other cars 549; Motorcycles 960; Total 49,228.

Shipping (2004): *Arrivals:* 1,833 vessels.

Civil Aviation: *Aircraft Landings:* 16,874 in 2002; 15,642 in 2003; 17,866 in 2004. *Passenger Arrivals:* 759,085 in 2002; 761,085 in 2003; 875,021 in 2004.

TOURISM

Tourist Arrivals: 1,224,822 (642,627 stop-over visitors, 582,195 cruise-ship passengers) in 2002; 1,184,233 (641,906 stop-over visitors, 542,327 cruise-ship passengers) in 2003; 1,304,477 (728,157 stop-over visitors, 576,320 cruise-ship passengers) in 2004.

Tourism Receipts: A. Fl. 1,872.3m. in 2004.

COMMUNICATIONS MEDIA

Radio Receivers (1997): 50,000 in use.

Television Receivers (1997): 20,000 in use.

Telephones (2001): 37,132 main lines in use.

Facsimile Machines (1996): 3,600 in use.

Mobile Cellular Telephones (2001): 53,000 subscribers.

Internet Users (2001): 7,912.

Daily Newspapers (1996): 13 titles (estimated circulation 73,000 copies per issue).

Sources: mainly UNESCO, *Statistical Yearbook*; International Telecommunication Union; UN, *Statistical Yearbook*.

EDUCATION

Pre-primary (2000/01): 23 schools; 2,737 pupils; 105 teachers.

Primary (2000/01): 33 schools; 8,849 pupils; 415 teachers.

General Secondary (2000/01): 10 schools; 4,251 pupils; 242 teachers.

Technical-Vocational (2000/01): 2 schools; 3,237 pupils; 263 teachers.

Community College (1999/2000): 1 school; 1,187 pupils; 106 teachers.

University (1999/2000): 1 university; 208 students; 24 tutors.

Teacher Training (2000/01): 1 institution; 180 students; 25 teachers.

Special Education (2000/01): 4 schools; 272 pupils; 56 teachers.

Private, Non-aided (1999/2000): 4 schools; 553 pupils; 58 teachers.

International School (2000/01): 154 pupils; 25 teachers.

Adult Literacy Rate (official estimates, 2000): Males 97.6%; Females 97.1%.

Directory

The Constitution

On 1 January 1986 Aruba acquired separate status (*status aparte*) within the Kingdom of the Netherlands. The form of government is similar to that for the Netherlands Antilles, which is embodied in the Charter of the Kingdom of the Netherlands (operational from 20 December 1954). The Netherlands, the Netherlands Antilles (Antilles of the Five) and Aruba each enjoy full autonomy in domestic and internal affairs, and are united on a basis of equality for the protection of their common interests and the granting of mutual assistance. In economic and monetary affairs there is a co-operative union between Aruba and the Antilles of the Five, known as the 'Union of the Netherlands Antilles and Aruba'.

The Governor, who is appointed by the Dutch Crown for a term of six years, represents the monarch of the Netherlands in Aruba. The Government of Aruba appoints a minister plenipotentiary to represent it in the Government of the Kingdom. Whenever the Netherlands Council of Ministers is dealing with matters coming under the heading of joint affairs of the realm (in practice mainly foreign affairs and defence), the Council assumes the status of Council of Ministers of the Kingdom. In that event, Aruba's Minister Plenipotentiary takes part, with full voting powers, in the deliberations.

A legislative proposal regarding affairs of the realm and applying to Aruba as well as to the metropolitan Netherlands is sent, simultaneously with its submission, to the Staten Generaal (the Netherlands parliament) and to the Staten (parliament) of Aruba. The latter body can report in writing to the Staten Generaal on the draft Kingdom Statute and designate one or more special delegates to attend the debates and furnish information in the meetings of the Chambers of the Staten Generaal. Before the final vote on a draft the Minister Plenipotentiary has the right to express an opinion on it. If he disapproves of the draft, and if in the Second Chamber a three-fifths' majority of the votes cast is not obtained, the discussions on the draft are suspended and further deliberations take place in the Council of Ministers of the Kingdom. When special delegates attend the meetings of the Chambers this right devolves upon the delegates of the parliamentary body designated for this purpose.

The Governor has executive power in external affairs, which he exercises in co-operation with the Council of Ministers. He is assisted by an advisory council which consists of at least five members appointed by him.

Executive power in internal affairs is vested in a nominated Council of Ministers, responsible to the Staten. The Aruban Staten consists of 21 members, who are elected by universal adult suffrage for four years (subject to dissolution), on the basis of proportional representation. Inhabitants have the right to vote if they have Dutch nationality and have reached 18 years of age. Voting is not compulsory.

The Government

HEAD OF STATE

Queen of the Netherlands: HM Queen BEATRIX.

Governor: FREDIS J. REFUNJOL (took office 7 May 2004).

COUNCIL OF MINISTERS
(April 2006)

Prime Minister and Minister of General Affairs and Utilities: NELSON ORLANDO ODUBER.

Deputy Prime Minister and Minister of Education, Social Affairs and Infrastructure: MARISOL J. TROMP.

Minister of Finance and Economic Affairs: NILO J. J. SWAEN.

Minister of Justice: HYACINTHO RUDY CROES.

Minister of Public Health and the Environment: CANDELARIO A. S. D. (BOOSHI) WEVER.

Minister of Sports, Culture and Labour: TAI FOO RAMON LEE.

Minister of Tourism and Transportation: EDISON BRIESEN.

Minister Plenipotentiary and Member of the Council of Ministers of the Realm for Aruba in the Netherlands: FRANCISCO WALFRIDO CROES.

Minister Plenipotentiary of the Realm for Aruba in Washington, DC (USA): HENRY BAARH.

MINISTRIES

Office of the Governor: Plaza Henny Eman 3, Oranjestad.

Office of the Prime Minister: Government Offices, L. G. Smith Blvd 76, Oranjestad; tel. 5880300; fax 5880024.

NETHERLANDS DEPENDENCIES

Ministry of Education, Social Affairs and Infrastructure: L. G. Smith Blvd 76, Oranjestad; tel. 5880700; fax 5880032; e-mail minszi@setarnet.aw; internet www.minszi.aw.

Ministry of Finance and Economic Affairs: L. G. Smith Blvd 76, Oranjestad; tel. 5880269; fax 5880347; e-mail minfin.ecaffairs@setarnet.aw.

Ministry of General Affairs and Utilities: L. G. Smith Blvd 76, Oranjestad; tel. 5839022; fax 5838958.

Ministry of Justice: L. G. Smith Blvd 76, Oranjestad; tel. 5839131; fax 5825388.

Ministry of Public Health and the Environment: L. G. Smith Blvd 76, Oranjestad; tel. 5834966; fax 5835082.

Ministry of Sports, Culture and Labour: L. G. Smith Blvd 76, Oranjestad; tel. 5839695; fax 5835985.

Ministry of Tourism and Transportation: L. G. Smith Blvd 76, Oranjestad; tel. 5839035; fax 5835084.

Office of the Minister Plenipotentiary for Aruba: R. J. Schimmelpennincklaan 1, 2517 JN The Hague, Netherlands; tel. (70) 3566200; fax (70) 3451446; e-mail info@arubahuis.nl; internet www.arubahuis.nl.

Legislature

STATEN

President: MARLON WERLEMAN, Staten, L. G. Smith Blvd 72, Oranjestad.

General Election, 23 September 2005

Party	Seats
Movimentu Electoral di Pueblo	11
Arubaanse Volkspartij	8
Movimentu Patriótico Arubano	1
Network	1
Total	**21**

Political Organizations

Acción Democratico Nacional (ADN) (National Democratic Action): Oranjestad; f. 1985; Leader PEDRO CHARRO KELLY.

Aliansa Democratico Arubano (Aruban Democratic Alliance): Oranjestad; Leader ROBERT FREDERICK WEVER.

Arubaanse Volkspartij (AVP) (Aruba People's Party): Oranjestad; tel. 5833500; fax 5837870; f. 1942; advocates Aruba's separate status; Leader MICHIEL GODFRIED EMAN.

Conscientisacion y Liberacion Arubano (CLA) (Concentration for the Liberation of Aruba): Oranjestad; Leader MARIANO DUVERT BLUME.

Democracia Real (Real Democracy): Oranjestad; satellite party of the AVP.

Movimentu Electoral di Pueblo (MEP) (People's Electoral Movement): Santa Cruz 74D, Oranjestad; tel. 5854495; fax 5850768; e-mail mep@setarnet.aw; internet www.mep.aw; f. 1971; socialist; 1,200 mems; Pres. and Leader NELSON ORLANDO ODUBER.

Movimentu Patriótico Arubano (MPA) (Aruban Patriotic Movement): Oranjestad; Leader MONICA KOCK ARENDS.

Organisacion Liberal Arubano (OLA) (Aruban Liberal Organization): Oranjestad; f. 1991; Leader GLENBERT FRANCOIS CROES.

Partido Patriótico Arubano (PPA) (Patriotic Party of Aruba): Oranjestad; f. 1949; social democratic; opposed to complete independence for Aruba; Leader BENEDICT (BENNY) JOCELYN MONTGOMERY NISBETT.

RED (Network): Oranjestad; Leader FATHER LAMPE.

Judicial System

Legal authority is exercised by the Court of First Instance. Appeals are heard by the Joint High Court of Justice of the Netherlands Antilles and Aruba.

Attorney-General of Aruba: RUUD ROSINGH.

Courts of Justice: J. G. Emanstraat 51, Oranjestad; tel. 5822294; fax 5821241; e-mail griffiekopie@setarnet.aw.

Religion

Roman Catholics form the largest religious community, numbering more than 80% of the population. The Anglicans and the Methodist, Dutch Protestant and other Protestant churches have a total membership of about 6,500. There are approximately 130 Jews.

CHRISTIANITY

The Roman Catholic Church

Aruba forms part of the diocese of Willemstad, comprising the Netherlands Antilles and Aruba. The Bishop resides in Willemstad (Curaçao, Netherlands Antilles).

Roman Catholic Church: J. Yrausquin Plein 3, POB 702, Oranjestad; tel. 5821434; fax 5821409.

The Anglican Communion

Within the Church in the Province of the West Indies, Aruba forms part of the diocese of the North Eastern Caribbean and Aruba. The Bishop is resident in The Valley, Anguilla.

Anglican Church: Holy Cross, Weg Seroe Pretoe 31, Sint Nicolaas; tel. 5845142; fax 5843394; e-mail holycross@setarnet.aw.

Protestant Churches

Baptist Church: Aruba Baptist Mission, SBC, Paradera 98-C; tel. 5883893.

Church of Christ: Pastoor Hendrikstraat 107, Sint Nicolaas; tel. 5848172.

Dutch Protestant Church: Wilhelminastraat 1, Oranjestad; tel. 5821435.

Evangelical Church: C. Huygenstraat 17, POB 272, Oranjestad; tel. 5822058.

Faith Revival Center: Rooi Afo 10, Paradera; tel. 5831010.

Iglesia Evangelica Pentecostal: Asamblea di Dios, Reamurstraat 2, Oranjestad; tel. 5831940.

Jehovah's Witnesses: Guyabastraat 3, Oranjestad; tel. 5828963.

Methodist Church: Longfellowstraat, Oranjestad; tel. 5845243.

New Apostolic Church: Goletstraat SA, Oranjestad; tel. 5833762.

Pentacostal Apostolic Assembly: Bernhardstraat 185; tel. 5848710.

Seventh-day Adventist: Weststraat, Oranjestad; tel. 5845896.

JUDAISM

Beth Israel Synagogue: Adriaan Laclé Blvd, Oranjestad; tel. 5823272; fax 5823534.

BAHÁ'Í FAITH

Spiritual Assembly: Bucutiweg 19, Oranjestad; tel. 5823104.

The Press

DAILIES

Amigoe di Aruba: Patriastraat 13, POB 323, Oranjestad; tel. 5824333; fax 5822368; e-mail amigoearuba@setarnet.aw; internet amigoe.com; f. 1884; Dutch; Man. RICKY BEAUJOHN; circ. 12,000 (in Aruba and Netherlands Antilles).

Aruba Today: Weststraat 22, Oranjestad; tel. 5827800; fax 5827093; e-mail news@arubatoday.com; internet www.arubatoday.com; Editor-in-Chief JULIA C. RENFRO.

Bon Dia Aruba: Weststraat 22, Oranjestad; tel. 5827800; fax 5827044; e-mail noticia@cspnv.com; internet www.bondia.com; Dir JOHN CHEMALY, Jr.

Diario: Engelandstraat 29, POB 577, Oranjestad; tel. 58826747; fax 58828551; e-mail diario@setanet.aw; internet www.diarioaruba.com; f. 1980; Papiamento; morning; Editor/Man. JOSSY M. MANSUR; circ. 15,000.

Extra: Dominicanessenstraat 17, Oranjestad; tel. 58834034; fax 5821639; Papiamento; Dir C. FRANKEN.

The News: Italiestraat 5, POB 300, Oranjestad; tel. 5824725; fax 5826125; e-mail thenewsaruba@setarnet.aw; f. 1951; English; Publr GERARDUS J. SCHOUTEN; Editor BEN BENNET; circ. 6,900.

Nobo: Dominicanessenstraat 17, Oranjestad; tel. 5834034; fax 5827272; Papiamento; Dir ADRIAAN ARENDS.

La Prensa: Bachstraat 6, POB 566 Oranjestad; tel. 5821199; fax 5828634; e-mail laprensa@laprensacur.com; internet www.laprensacur.com; f. 1929; Papiamento; Editor THOMAS C. PIETERSZ.

NEWS AGENCIES

Algemeen Nederlands Persbureau (ANP) (The Netherlands): Caya G. F. (Betico) Croes 110, POB 323, Oranjestad; tel. 5824333; fax 5822368; internet www.anp.nl.

Aruba News Agencies: Bachstraat 6, Oranjestad; tel. 5821243.

Publishers

Aruba Experience Publications NV: Verbindingsweg 2, POB 634, Oranjestad; tel. 5834467; fax 5384520; e-mail info@arubaexperience.com; internet www.arubaexperience.com; f. 1985; Gen. Man. MICHEL J. M. JANSSEN.

Caribbean Publishing Co Ltd (CPC): L. G. Smith Blvd 116, Oranjestad; tel. 5820485; fax 5820484.

De Wit Stores NV: L. G. Smith Blvd 110, POB 386, Oranjestad; tel. 5823500; fax 5821575; e-mail dewitstores@setarnet.aw; f. 1948; Gen. Man. LYANNE BEAUJON.

Gold Book Publishing: L. G. Smith Blvd 116, Oranjestad; tel. 5820485; fax 5820484; e-mail drosario@caribbeanhotels.org; internet www.caribbeanhotels.org; a division of the Caribbean Hotel Asscn, based in the Cayman Islands.

Oranjestad Printing NV: Italiestraat 5, POB 300, Oranjestad; Man. Dir GERARDUS J. SCHOUTEN.

ProGraphics Inc: Italiestraat 5, POB 201, Oranjestad; tel. 5824550; fax 5822526; e-mail vadprinting@setarnet.aw; f. 2001; fmrly VAD Printers Inc.

Publicidad Aruba NV: Emanstraat 110, POB 295, Oranjestad; tel. 5835139.

Publicidad Exito Aruba SA: Domenicanessenstraat 17, POB 142, Oranjestad; tel. 5822020; fax 5824242; f. 1958.

Rozenstand Publishing Co: Cuquisastraat 1, Oranjestad; tel. 5824482.

Van Dorp Aruba NV: Caya G. F. (Betico) Croes 77, POB 596, Oranjestad; tel. 5823076; fax 5823573.

Broadcasting and Communications

TELECOMMUNICATIONS

Digicel Aruba: POB 662, Oranjestad; e-mail customercare@digicelaruba.com; internet www.digicelaruba.com; f. 2003; owned by an Irish consortium; Chair. DENIS O'BRIEN.

Servicio di Telecomunicacion di Aruba NV (SETAR): Seroe Blanco z/n, POB 13, Oranjestad; tel. 5251576; fax 5836970; e-mail setar@setarnet.aw; internet www.setar.aw; f. 1986; Man. Dir PATRICIO NICOLAS.

BROADCASTING

Radio

Canal 90 FM Stereo: Van Leeuwenhoekstraat 26, Oranjestad; tel. 5828952; fax 837340; e-mail info@canal90fm.aw.

Cristal Sound 101.7 FM: J. G. Emanstraat 124A, Oranjestad; tel. 5827726; fax 5820144.

Hit 94 FM: Oranjestad; e-mail hit94fm@hotmail.com; internet www.hit94fm.com; f. 1993; Dir JOHNNY HABIBE.

Magic 96.5 FM: Oranjestad; internet www.magic965.com.

Radio 1270: Bernardstraat 138, POB 28, Sint Nicolaas; tel. 5845602; fax 5827753; commercial station; programmes in Dutch, English, Spanish and Papiamento; Dir F. A. LEAUER; Station Man. J. A. C. ALDERS.

Radio Carina FM: Datustraat 10A, Oranjestad; tel. 5821450; fax 5831955; commercial station; programmes in Dutch, English, Spanish and Papiamento; Dir-Gen. ALBERT R. DIEFFENTHALER.

Radio Caruso Booy FM: G. M. de Bruynewijk 49, Savaneta; tel. 5847752; fax 5843351; e-mail sira@setarnet.aw; internet www.geocities.com/carusobooy; commercial station; broadcasts for 24 hrs a day; programmes in Dutch, English, Spanish and Papiamento; Pres. HUBERT ERQUILLES ANTONIO BOOY; Gen. Man. SIRA BOOY.

Radio Galactica FM: J. G. Emanstraat 120, Oranjestad; tel. 5830999; fax 5838999; e-mail radiogalactica@hotmail.com; internet www.galactica999fm.aw; f. 1990; Dir MODESTO J. ODUBER; Station Man. MAIKEL J. ODUBER.

Radio Kelkboom: Bloemond 14, POB 146, Oranjestad; tel. 5821899; fax 5834825; e-mail radiokelkboom@setarnet.aw; internet www.watapana-aruba.com; f. 1954; commercial radio station; programmes in Dutch, English, Spanish and Papiamento; Owners CARLOS A. KELKBOOM, E. A. M. KELKBOOM; Dir EMILE A. M. KELKBOOM.

Radio Victoria: Washington 23, POB 5291, Oranjestad; tel. 5873444; fax 5873444; e-mail radiovictoria@setarnet.aw; internet www.setarnet.aw/users/radiovictoria; f. 1958; religious and cultural FM radio station owned by the Radio Victoria Foundation; programmes in Dutch, English, Spanish and Papiamento; Pres. N. J. F. ARTS.

Voz di Aruba (Voice of Aruba): Van Leeuwenhoekstraat 26, POB 219, Oranjestad; tel. 5824134; commercial radio station; programmes in Dutch, English, Spanish and Papiamento; also operates Canal 90 on FM; Dir A. M. ARENDS, Jr.

Television

ABC Aruba Broadcasting Co NV (ATV): Royal Plaza Suite 223, POB 5040, Oranjestad; tel. 5838150; fax 5838110; e-mail 15atv@setarnet.aw.

Telearuba NV: Pos Chiquito 1A, POB 392, Oranjestad; tel. 5857302; fax 5851683; e-mail telearuba@hotmail.com; internet www.telearuba.aw; f. 1963; fmrly operated by Netherlands Antilles Television Co; commercial; acquired by SETAR (q.v.) in March 2005; Gen. Man. M. MARCHENA.

Finance

(cap. = capital; res = reserves; dep. = deposits; m. = million; brs = branches; amounts in Aruban florin, unless otherwise stated)

BANKING

Central Bank

Centrale Bank van Aruba: J. E. Irausquin Blvd 8, POB 18, Oranjestad; tel. 5252100; fax 5252101; e-mail cbaua@setarnet.aw; internet www.cbaruba.org; f. 1986; cap. 10.0m., res 130.7m., dep. 329.8m. (Dec. 2003); Pres. A. R. CARAM; Exec. Dirs K. A. H. POLVLIET, J. R. FIGAROA-SEMELEER.

Commercial Banks

Aruba Bank NV: Caya G. F. (Betico) Croes 41, POB 192, Oranjestad; tel. 5821550; fax 5829152; e-mail customersupport@arubabank.com; internet www.arubabank.com; f. 1925; acquired Interbank Aruba NV in Dec. 2003; total assets US $260m. (Dec. 2004); Man. Dir and CEO ILDEFONS D'ANDELO SIMON; 5 brs.

Banco di Caribe NV: Vondellaan 31, POB 493, Oranjestad; tel. 5232000; fax 5832422; e-mail bdcaua@setarnet.aw; internet www.bancodicaribe.com; f. 1987; Gen. Man. EDUARDO A. DE KORT; 1 br.

Caribbean Mercantile Bank NV: Caya G. F. (Betico) Croes 53, POB 28, Oranjestad; tel. 5823118; fax 5824373; e-mail executive_office@cmbnv.com; internet www.cmbnv.com; f. 1963; cap. 4.0m., res 43.0m., dep. 835.3m. (Dec. 2003); Pres. L. CAPRILES II; Man. Dir W. G. CARSON; 6 brs.

RBTT Bank Aruba NV: Italiestraat 36, Sasakiweg, Oranjestad; tel. 5833221; fax 58821756; e-mail firstet@setarnet.aw; internet www.rbtt.co.tt; f. 2001; fmrly First National Bank of Aruba NV (f. 1985 and acquired by Royal Bank of Trinidad and Tobago Ltd in 1998); total assets US $125.3m. (Dec. 2000); Chair. PETER J. JULY; Pres. EDWIN L. TROMP; 6 brs.

Investment Bank

AIB NV: Wilhelminastraat 34–36, POB 1011, Oranjestad; tel. 5827327; fax 5827461; e-mail aib@setarnet.aw; f. 1987 as Aruban Investment Bank; name changed as above in April 2004; Pres. P. C. M. VAN DER VOORT VAN ZIJP.

Mortgage Bank

Fundacion Cas pa Comunidad Arubano (FCCA): Sabana Blanco 66, Oranjestad; tel. 5238800; fax 5836272; e-mail info@fcaa.com; internet www.fcca.com; f. 1979.

'Offshore' Bank

Citibank NA: J. G. Emanstraat 61, Oranjestad; tel. 5822138; fax 5832363.

INSURANCE

There were eight life insurance companies and 14 non-life insurance companies active in Aruba in December 2005.

Association

Insurance Association of Aruba (IAA): L. G. Smith Blvd 160, Oranjestad; tel. 5821111; fax 5826138.

Trade and Industry

DEVELOPMENT ORGANIZATION

Department of Economic Affairs, Commerce and Industry (Directie Economische Zaken, Handel en Industrie): Sun Plaza Bldg, L. G. Smith Blvd 160, Oranjestad; tel. 5821181; fax 5834494; e-mail deaci@setarnet.aw; internet www.arubaeconomicaffairs.aw; Dir MARIA DIJKHOFF-PITA.

NETHERLANDS DEPENDENCIES

CHAMBER OF COMMERCE AND INDUSTRY

Aruba Chamber of Commerce and Industry: J. E. Irausquin Blvd 10, POB 140, Oranjestad; tel. 5821120; fax 5883200; e-mail secretariat@arubachamber.com; internet www.arubachamber.com; f. 1930; Pres. EDWIN V. ROOS; Exec. Dir LORRAINE C. DE SOUZA.

TRADE ASSOCIATION

Aruba Trade and Industry Association (ATIA): ATIA Bldg, Pedro Gallegostraat 6, POB 562, Oranjestad; tel. 5827593; fax 5833068; e-mail atiaruba@setarnet.aw; internet www.atiaruba.org; f. 1945; Pres. SERGE MANSUR.

UTILITIES

Electricity and Water

Utilities Aruba NV: govt-owned holding co.

Electriciteit-Maatschappij Aruba (ELMAR) NV: Wilhelminastraat 110, Oranjestad; tel. 5823700; fax 5828991; e-mail info@elmar.aw; internet www.elmar.aw; independently managed co, residing under Utilities Aruba NV; electricity distribution; Man. Dir A. O. RAFINÉ.

Water en Energiebedrijf Aruba (WEB) NV: Balashi 76, POB 575, Oranjestad; tel. 5254600; fax 5857681; e-mail info@webaruba.com; f. 1991; independently managed co, residing under Utilities Aruba NV; production and distribution of industrial and potable water, and electricity generation; Gen. Dir JOSÉ LACLÉ.

Gas

Aruba Gas Supply Company Ltd (ARUGAS): Barcadera z/n, Oranjestad; tel. 5851198; fax 5852187; e-mail arubagas@setarnet.aw.

BOC Gases Aruba: POB 387, Oranjestad; tel. 5852173; fax 5852823; e-mail bocaruba@mail.setarnet.aw; internet www.boc.com.

TRADE UNIONS

Federashon di Trahadornan di Aruba (FTA) (Aruban Workers' Federation): Bernardstraat 23, Sint Nicolaas; tel. 5845448; fax 5845504; e-mail federacion@hotmail.com; f. 1964; independent; affiliated to World Confederation of Labour; Sec.-Gen. JOSÉ RUDOLF GEERMAN.

There are also several unions for government and semi-government workers and employees.

Transport

There are no railways, but Aruba has a network of all-weather roads.

Arubus NV: Sabana Blanco 67, Oranjestad; tel. 5827089; fax 5828633; internet www.arubus.com; f. 1979; state-owned company providing public transport services; runs a fleet of 37 buses.

SHIPPING

The island's principal seaport is Oranjestad, whose harbour can accommodate ocean-going vessels. There are also ports at Barcadera and Sint Nicolaas, the latter administered by the Valero Aruba Refining Company.

Aruba Ports Authority NV: L. G. Smith Blvd 23, Oranjestad; tel. 5826633; fax 5832896; e-mail info@arubaports.com; internet www.arubaports.com; f. 1981; responsible for the administration of the ports of Oranjestad and Barcadera; Man. Dir JUAN ALFONSO BOEKHOUDT.

Valero Aruba Refining Co NV: Seroe Colorado, POB 2150, Sint Nicolaas; tel. 5894904; fax 5849087; internet www.valero.com; f. 1989; petroleum refinery, responsible for the administration of the port of Sint Nicolaas; acquired by Valero in 2004; Gen. Man. DAVID LAM.

Principal Shipping Companies

Beng Lian Shipping S. de R. L. A. V. V.: Dominicanessenstraat 22, Oranjestad.

Magna Shipping Co: Koningstraat 52, Oranjestad; tel. 5824349.

Rodoca Shipping and Trading SA: Parkietenbos 30, Barcadera Harbour; tel. 5850096; fax 5823371; fmrly Aruba Shipping and Chartering Co NV.

Windward Island Agencies: Heyligerweg, POB 66, Oranjestad.

CIVIL AVIATION

The Queen Beatrix International Airport (Aeropuerto Internacional Reina Beatrix), about 2.5 km from Oranjestad, is served by numerous airlines, linking the island with destinations in the Caribbean, Europe, the USA and Central and South America. After renovation and expansion, the airport was expected to be able to handle 2.6m. passengers per year by 2010. In November 2000 the national carrier, Air Aruba, was declared bankrupt.

Tourism

Aruba's white sandy beaches, particularly along the southern coast, are an attraction for foreign visitors, and tourism is a major industry. The number of hotel rooms totalled 7,226 in 2004. In that year most stop-over visitors came from the USA (73.5%), Venezuela (8.1%) and the Netherlands (5.2%). In 2004 728,157 stop-over visitors and 576,320 cruise-ship passengers visited Aruba. Receipts from tourism totalled A. Fl. 1,872.3m. in 2004.

Aruba Cruise Tourism: POB 5254, Suite 230, Royal Plaza Mall, L. G. Smith Blvd 94, Oranjestad; tel. 5833648; fax 5835088; e-mail int1721@setarnet.aw; internet www.arubabycruise.com; f. 1995 as the Cruise Tourism Authority—Aruba; name changed as above in 2005; non-profit government organization; Exec. Dir KATHLEEN ROJER.

Aruba Hotel and Tourism Association (AHATA): L. G. Smith Blvd 174, POB 542, Oranjestad; tel. 5822607; fax 5824202; e-mail info@ahata.com; internet www.ahata.com; f. 1965; 85 mems; represents some 6,000 guest rooms; CEO JORGE PESQUERA.

Aruba Tourism Authority (ATA): L. G. Smith Blvd 172, Oranjestad; tel. 5823777; fax 5834702; e-mail ata.aruba@aruba.com; internet www.aruba.com; f. 1953; Man. Dir MYRNA JANSEN-FELICIANO.

THE NETHERLANDS ANTILLES

Introductory Survey

Location, Climate, Language, Religion, Flag, Capital

The Netherlands Antilles (Antilles of the Five) consists of two groups of islands in the Caribbean Sea, about 800 km (500 miles) apart. The main group, lying off the coast of Venezuela, consists of Bonaire and Curaçao which (together with Aruba, 68 km to the east of Curaçao) are known as the Benedenwindse Eilands or 'Leeward Islands'; to the north-east lie the small volcanic islands of St (Sint) Eustatius (also known as Statia), Saba and St (Sint) Maarten (the northern half of the last island being a dependency of the French overseas department of Guadeloupe), known as the Bovenwindse Eilands or 'Windward Islands' (although actually in the Leeward group of the Lesser Antilles). The climate is tropical, moderated by the sea, with an average annual temperature of 27.5°C (81°F) and little rainfall. The official languages are Dutch and Papiamento (a mixture of Dutch, Spanish, Portuguese, English, Arawak Indian and several West African dialects), which is the dominant language of the 'Leeward Islands'. English is the official and principal language of the 'Windward Islands'. Spanish is also widely spoken. Almost all of the inhabitants profess Christianity: the people of the 'Leeward Islands' and Saba are predominantly Roman Catholics, while those of St Eustatius and St Maarten are predominantly Protestants. The state flag (proportions 2 by 3) is white, with a red vertical stripe in the centre, crossed by a horizontal blue stripe on which there are five white five-pointed stars (one for each of the main islands) arranged in an oval. The capital is Willemstad, on the island of Curaçao.

Recent History

The 'Leeward Islands', already settled by communities of Arawak Indians, were discovered by the Spanish in 1499 and were seized by the Dutch in the 1630s. Curaçao became prosperous in the late 17th and 18th centuries as an entrepôt for trade in the Caribbean. The Dutch settled the 'Windward Islands', once settled by Carib Indians, in the mid-17th century. After frequent changes in possession, the islands (including Aruba) were finally confirmed as Dutch territory in 1816. The two groups were administered as Curaçao and Dependencies between 1845 and 1948. Slavery was abolished in 1863, and the islands suffered from an economic decline until the establishment of petroleum refineries on Curaçao and Aruba, in 1918 and

1929, respectively. During the Second World War Queen Wilhelmina of the Netherlands promised independence, and in 1954 a Charter gave the federation of six islands full autonomy in domestic affairs, and declared it to be an integral part of the Kingdom of the Netherlands.

Divisions of political allegiance within the territory have been along island, rather than policy, lines, and a series of coalition Governments has frequently paralysed decision-making. In 1969 serious rioting and looting broke out in Willemstad after a demonstration by workers in the petroleum industry. Troops had to be sent from the Netherlands to quell the disturbances and to restore order. In February 1970 the socialist Government of Ciro Kroon resigned over the nomination of a new Governor, and in 1971 the Government of E. Petronia resigned over the rejection by the Staten (parliament) of new financial measures.

Following elections to the Staten in June 1977, a coalition Government was formed, with the leader of the Democratische Partij (DP), Silvio Rozendal, as Prime Minister. After a boycott of the session by the Movimentu Electoral di Pueblo (MEP) of Aruba and the Frente Obrero i Liberashon 30 di mei (FOL), the Staten was eventually convened by a Governor's decree in October. Rozendal resigned in April 1979, and elections were held in July. A coalition administration was formed by the Movimentu Antiyas Nobo (MAN), the MEP and the Unión Patriótico Bonairiano (UPB), with Dominico (Don) Martina, the leader of the MAN, as Prime Minister. The DP joined the coalition Government in December 1980.

In Aruba resentment of the administrative dominance of Curaçao resulted, in 1971, in the establishment of the pro-independence MEP. In 1981 a series of talks regarding Aruba's future began with the Netherlands Government. However, in September the MEP representatives in the Staten withdrew their support for the Government on the question of Aruba's rights to possible discoveries of petroleum off its coast. The Government's majority was restored by the inclusion of the DP—St Maarten (DP—StM) member for the 'Windward Islands' in the coalition, but a DP resignation in January 1982 precipitated a further crisis. A general election in June failed to resolve the situation, and it was not until October that agreement was reached on the formation by Martina of a new coalition, which excluded the MEP.

In March 1983 agreement was finally reached whereby Aruba would be given separate status (*status aparte*) within the Kingdom of the Netherlands from January 1986, with the prospect of full independence in 1996 (for further details, see Aruba, q.v.). Arguments persisted regarding the division of the Antilles' financial reserves, and over rights to explore for petroleum and other minerals. In June 1984 Martina's coalition Government resigned. A five-party coalition was eventually formed in September, with Maria Liberia-Peters of the conservative Partido Nashonal di Pueblo (PNP) as Prime Minister.

At a general election in November 1985 the PNP gained the largest number of seats in the Staten for the Antilles of the Five (six out of 22), but was unable to secure enough support from other parties to form a government. Martina once again became Prime Minister and formed a coalition Government. During 1986–87 the Government was forced to introduce a series of economic austerity measures, following Aruba's separation from the Netherlands Antilles and the decline of both the petroleum-refining industry and 'offshore' financial services. The Government resigned in March 1988, after losing the support of the DP—StM and the FOL. In May Liberia-Peters formed a coalition with all the parties represented in the Staten except for the MAN and the DP—Curaçao (DP—C).

In January 1989 Martina revealed that successive Curaçao administrations had diverted revenues from the 'offshore' financial sector into a fund that had not been declared to The Hague during negotiations for budgetary support. The Netherlands had recently exerted pressure for more control to be exercised over the large amount of aid that it provided for the Netherlands Antilles. By the early 1990s it appeared that, while the 'metropolitan' Government was unwilling to allow the complete disintegration of the federation, it was prepared to consider a less centralized system or the creation of two federations in the separate island groups.

At a general election in March 1990 the PNP increased the number of its seats (all on Curaçao) to seven, again making it the largest single party in the Staten, and, after some weeks of negotiations, Liberia-Peters assumed the leadership of a broadly based coalition. In March 1992 the FOL and its partner at the 1990 election, the Social Independiente, withdrew from the Government. Liberia-Peters formed a new coalition with the DP—StM, the UPB and the DP—C. In September 1993 the DP—StM withdrew, although the Government maintained its majority in the Staten with the support of an independent deputy and subsequently that of the Windward Islands People's Movement (WIPM).

A referendum was conducted on Curaçao in November 1993 regarding its constitutional status; 74% of the electorate voted for a continuance of the island's status as a member of the Antillean federation. The option of *status aparte* within the Kingdom of the Netherlands, favoured by the Government, received only 18% of the votes cast. As a result of this defeat, the WIPM and the UPB withdrew their support, thus leaving the Government without a majority in the Staten. Liberia-Peters resigned, and Alejandro Felippe Paula, a professor at the University of the Netherlands Antilles, subsequently agreed to head an interim Government. A general election took place in February 1994, at which a new, Curaçao-based party, the Partido Antía Restrukturá (PAR), led by Miguel A. Pourier, became the largest single party (with eight seats) in the Staten. Pourier assumed the leadership of a broadly based coalition Government, which was inaugurated in March.

Referendums on status were conducted on St Maarten, St Eustatius, Saba and Bonaire in October 1994. On St Maarten 60% of the electorate voted to remain within the Antillean federation, while the option of *status aparte* received 32% of the vote. On St Eustatius 86% of voters opted for continued membership of the Antillean federation, while the equivalent vote on Saba was 91%. On Bonaire (where voting took place one week later) some 88% of voters favoured continued federation.

A general election was held on 30 January 1998, at which the PAR lost four of its eight seats in the Staten. The PNP retained its three seats, while a new party, the Partido Laboral Krusada Popular (PLKP), also took three seats. The loss of support for the PAR was attributed to the unpopularity of austerity measures imposed by the outgoing Government. Pourier failed in his attempts to form a new coalition, largely owing to opposition to the PAR's economic policies. A new coalition Government, with Susanne F. C. Camelia-Römer of the PNP as Prime Minister, was finally agreed in early May, only to collapse later in the month, when it was revealed that a designated cabinet member was under criminal investigation. A new Government was sworn in on 1 June. The coalition comprised six parties, with the support of 13 of the 22 members of the Staten.

In late 1998 the Government adopted a National Recovery Plan, which aimed both to reduce the government's fiscal deficit and also to generate growth in the economy through the introduction of measures intended to stimulate investment. However, the Government's subsequent attempts to reduce state expenditure proved to be highly controversial, and proposals to reduce the public-sector work-force by some 2,400—principally through cuts in the civil service of the central Government and of the island Government of Curaçao—caused great tension between Camelia-Römer's PNP and its fellow Curaçao-based coalition partners, the PLKP and the FOL, which led, in October 1999, to the collapse of both the central Government and the island Government of Curaçao.

In November 1999 former Prime Minister Pourier formed a new broadly based coalition Government, which had the support of 18 of the 22 members of the Staten. Concerns were, however, expressed that Pourier's Government would face the same problems as the previous administration in its attempt fully to implement the National Recovery Plan, and this was, to some extent, anticipated by Pourier's appointment of Camelia-Römer as Minister for the National Recovery Plan and Economic Affairs.

A referendum on the constitutional future of St Maarten took place on 23 June 2000. Only 4% of participants in St Maarten favoured maintaining the *status quo*. Some 69% favoured obtaining *status aparte* within the Kingdom of the Netherlands, 14% favoured complete independence and 12% preferred a restructuring of the Antilles of the Five. Although the Dutch Government indicated that it would not support a request by St Maarten to receive *status aparte*, it supported the establishment of a commission to explore the possibilities of St Maarten adopting *status aparte*. In February 2003 Johan Remkes, the Dutch Minister of Interior and Kingdom Relations, confirmed the Netherlands would not permit St Maarten to leave the federation. Despite this set-back, St Maarten had signed an agreement with the central Government in August 2002 that would permit the island's executive council to take out loans on its own initiative, without seeking permission from the central bank. Furthermore, in late 2002 the executive council proposed to the central bank that discussions should begin on a separate monetary system for St Maarten.

In December 2000 an agreement was reached with the Dutch Government on the compulsory acculturation of Antillean migrants to the Netherlands. The high level of unemployment, particularly among the younger members of the Antillean community in the Netherlands, and the steady influx of new migrants in recent years had led the Dutch Government to propose that the Netherlands Antilles adopt legislation whereby those under 25 years of age would be granted permission to emigrate to the Netherlands only after attending acculturation classes designed to facilitate their integration into Dutch society. In May 2005 the Netherlands announced plans to introduce legislation to require citizens of the Netherlands Antilles aged between 16 and 24 years to find work or begin studies within three months of arriving in the Netherlands, or face deportation; it was estimated by the Dutch Government that immigrants from the Netherlands Antilles aged under 25 years were four times more likely to turn to crime than the general Dutch population. Prime Minister Ys described the policy as discriminatory and threatened to take the Dutch Government to court.

The elections of 18 January 2002 were won by the FOL, led by Anthony Godett, which had campaigned against the stringent measures imposed by the IMF. The FOL won five seats in the 22-seat Staten, Pourier's party, the PAR, won four legislative seats, the PNP won three seats, the PLKP, the DP—StM and the UPB each won two seats, and the WIPM, the Democratische Partij—Statia (DP—StE), the Democratische Partij—Bonaire (DP—B) and the National Alliance (NA—comprising the National Progressive Party and the St Maarten Patriotic Alliance) each secured one legislative seat. None the less, despite the party's victory, attempts by the FOL to form a coalition Government failed because of allegations of corruption and mismanagement of funds by party leaders. Eventually, in June 2002 a coalition Government that included representatives of the PAR, the PNP, the PLKP, the DP—StM, the UPD and the DP—StE took office, under the leadership of the new PAR leader, Etienne Ys, replacing Pourier's caretaker Government.

Local elections in Curaçao in May 2003 were won by the FOL under the leadership of Anthony Godett, who had been detained by the police in April for alleged corrupt activities. The victory of Godett's party, known for its independent and assertive attitude towards the Netherlands and the IMF, was expected to impact negatively on the implementation of IMF measures and the island's political relationship with the Netherlands, which had improved under the PAR leadership. Later in the same month Prime Minister Ys' cabinet resigned to allow the FOL to form a fresh governing coalition (comprised of the FOL, the PNP, the PLKP, the UPB, the DP—StE and the WIPM), based on new local political alliances. In late July Ben Komproe of the FOL was sworn in as Prime Minister on a temporary basis, as Godett could not be approved for the post while he faced corruption charges. On 11 August Mirna Luisa Godett, the sister of the FOL leader, was elected by the party to the post of Prime Minister, despite not being a member of the Staten. Komproe, meanwhile, was appointed Minister of Justice. Following the conviction in December of Anthony Godett (and 16 other party members, business leaders and officials) for fraud, embezzlement and corruption charges, in January 2004 the governing coalition almost lost control of the legislature when the WIPM and the UPB withdrew their support. The Government managed to retain its majority, however, when the DP—B agreed to join the coalition later in the same month. In February the Staten rejected a motion proposed by the opposition (and directed at Anthony Godett) that legislators found guilty of corruption be prevented from retaining their parliamentary seats.

Meanwhile, as anticipated, relations between the Netherlands Antilles and the Dutch Government worsened following the advent of the FOL-dominated Government. In August 2003 Mirna Luisa Godett announced that a delegation of Dutch MPs would not be officially received when they visited the territory. Furthermore, she vowed not to speak Dutch, only English. The Dutch Minister of Kingdom Relations responded by pledging to speak only Dutch, since neither the Netherlands Antilles nor the Netherlands were 'part of the British Empire'. Godett's administration further alienated the Dutch Government by its support of a proposal to remove a body scanner at Curaçao's international airport, which had been installed in an attempt to combat the increasing drugs trade between Amsterdam and the Caribbean. Relations continued to worsen during the remainder of 2003 and in January 2004 Godett accused Dutch officials of spying on her Government after it emerged that local justice officials had met two visiting Dutch ministers without her knowledge. Tension was further exacerbated by Godett's rejection of a Dutch proposal to ban known drugs-traffickers from Antillean airlines.

The Government lost its parliamentary majority on 5 April 2004 after four parties (the PNP, the PLKP, DP—B and the DP—StE) withdrew from the FOL-led coalition after failing to effect the resignation of the Minister of Justice, Ben Komproe. The coalition partners accused Komproe of allowing the FOL's main political donor, Nelson Monte, who was serving a custodial sentence for corruption, to stay in a luxury hospital rather than be jailed. After the Staten voted in favour of a 'no confidence' motion against the Government, the Prime Minister submitted her resignation on 6 April; Komproe, Richard Salas, the Minister of Transport and Communications, and Maurice Adriaens, the Minister Plenipotentiary and Member of the Council of Ministers of the Realm of the Netherlands Antilles, also resigned. Komproe's position had already been weakened by his failure to reverse the rising crime rate on Curaçao and by his brother's alleged involvement in fraud. In the wake of the resignations, the Governor, Fritz Goedgedrag, assumed the task of forming a new government; a seven-party coalition (consisting of the PAR, the PNP, the PLKP, the UPB, the DP—StM, the DP—StE and the WIPM) led by Etienne Ys was duly appointed in June and charged with the responsibility of repairing the territory's relationship with the Netherlands and reducing the huge national debt. Meanwhile, in July Anthony Godett was sentenced to 15 months in jail on corruption-related charges; the sentence was confirmed by the High Court in The Hague, the Netherlands, in September 2005.

On 8 October 2004 the Jesurun Commission, established by the Dutch and Antillean Governments and headed by Edsel Jesurun—a former Governor of the territory, recommended the dissolution of the Netherlands Antilles; support for the federation had, it was argued, virtually disintegrated on most of the islands. In particular, changes were needed to combat the rise in unemployment, poverty, violent crime and drugs-smuggling in the territory. The Commission proposed that Curaçao and St Maarten should become autonomous states within the Netherlands (i.e., have *status aparte*), while Saba, Bonaire and St Eustatius should be directly administered by the Dutch Government. In September and November, respectively, in official referendums, a majority of voters on both Bonaire (59%) and Saba (86%) strongly favoured becoming part of the Netherlands. Further referendums on the constitutional futures of Curaçao and St Eustatius took place on 8 April 2005: 68% of participants in Curaçao favoured *status aparte*, in line with the recommendations of the Commission, 23% voted for closer ties with the Netherlands and 5% voted for complete independence—there was a 54% voter turn-out. In St Eustatius, from a voter turn-out of 55%, 76% of the electorate favoured remaining part of the Netherlands Antilles, while 20% voted for closer ties with the Netherlands and 1% preferred to seek complete independence for the tiny island. Taking into account the results of the referendum on St Maarten in 2000 (see above), since St Eustatius was the only island of the dependency to favour the *status quo*, the future of the Antillean federation appeared to be limited. On 3 December 2005 an agreement with the Dutch Government that the extant federation be dissolved by 1 July 2007 was duly signed in Curaçao. Under the new structure, Curaçao and St Maarten were, as expected, to become autonomous members of the Kingdom of the Netherlands, while Saba, Bonaire and St Eustatius were to become 'Kingdom Islands', an as yet undefined status that was likely to be equivalent to that of a Dutch province.

In November 2005 Ys announced that the PAR-led Government had lost its slim majority following the withdrawal from the coalition of the UPB. (The UPB was reportedly dissatisfied with the central Government's financial support for Bonaire's San Francisco Hospital and Flamingo Field Airport.) A general election, intended to be the final election to the Netherlands Antilles Staten, was consequently held on 27 January 2006. The PAR, led by Ys, secured the largest number of seats (five) in the 22-seat legislature. In addition, the MAN won three seats, the PNP, the NA, the UPB, the FOL and Forsa Kòrsou each won two seats and the DP—StM, the WIPM, the DP—StE and the DP—B each secured one legislative seat. In total, 27 parties contested the election. Negotiations to form a new coalition government were, as usual, protracted. Eventually, on 26 March, a coalition Government comprising representatives of the PAR, the MAN, the PNP, the NA, the UPB, the DP—StE and the WIPM, and headed by the PAR leader, Emily de Jongh-Elhage, was sworn into office. (The DP—StE and the WIPM had representatives at the rank of State Secretary rather than at full ministerial level.) De Jongh-Elhage pledged to ensure that the best interests of all the constituent parts of the federation would be considered during the transition period, and that education and the eradication of poverty would be her Government's main concerns.

Meanwhile, in December 2004 the Dutch Government pledged to send 60 policemen to the Netherlands Antilles, primarily Curaçao, to combat the increase in crime on the islands. In addition, 25 Dutch customs and military officials were sent to Curaçao and Bonaire airports in January 2005 to improve security against drugs-transhipment between the Netherlands and its dependent territory.

Government

The Governor of the Netherlands Antilles, appointed by the Dutch Crown for a term of six years, represents the monarch of the Netherlands in the territory, and has executive power over external affairs. The Governor is assisted by an advisory council. Executive power in internal affairs is vested in the Council of Ministers. The Council is responsible to the Staten (parliament), which has 22 members elected by universal adult suffrage for four years (subject to dissolution). The administration of each island is conducted by its own Island Council, Executive Council and Lieutenant-Governor.

Defence

Although defence is the responsibility of the Netherlands, compulsory military service is laid down in an Antilles Ordinance. The Governor is the Commander-in-Chief of the armed forces in the islands, and a Dutch contingent is stationed in Willemstad, Curaçao. The Netherlands also operates a Coast Guard Force (to combat organized crime and drugs-smuggling, based at St Maarten and Aruba. In May 1999 the US air force and navy began patrols from a base on Curaçao to combat the transport of illegal drugs.

Economic Affairs

In 1994 the gross national income (GNI) of the Netherlands Antilles, measured at current prices, was an estimated US $1,550m., equivalent to some $8,800 per head. In 1995–2004 the population increased by an average of 0.9% per year, while gross domestic product (GDP) per head increased, in real terms, by an average of 1.7% per year in the same period. Overall GDP increased, in real terms, by an annual average rage of 0.4% during 1990–95. GDP stood at some $3,073m. in 2004 (equivalent to $16,564 per head). Real GDP increased by 1.0% in 2004.

Agriculture, together with forestry, fishing and mining, contributed only 0.8% of GDP in 2003. The sector employed 0.8% of the working population on Curaçao in 2004–05. Some 8% of the total land area is cultivated. The chief products are aloes (Bonaire is a major exporter), sorghum, divi-divi, groundnuts, beans, fresh vegetables and tropical fruit. A bitter variety of orange is used in the production of Curaçao liqueur. There is also some fishing.

Industry (comprising manufacturing, construction, power and water) contributed 13.9% of GDP in 2003 and employed 14.8% of the working population on Curaçao in 2004–05.

The mining and quarrying sector employed only 0.3% of the working population on Curaçao in 2000. Apart from some phosphates on Curaçao (exploited until the mid-1980s), and some limestone and salt on Bonaire, the islands have no other significant mineral reserves. Aggregate is quarried on St Maarten and consumed primarily by the local construction industry.

Manufacturing contributed 5.5% of GDP in 2003, and employed 7.0% of the working population on Curaçao in 2004–05; activities include food-processing, production of Curaçao liqueur, and the manufacture of paint, paper, soap and cigarettes. Bonaire has a textile factory, and Curaçao's 'free zone' is of considerable importance in the economy, but the 'Windward Islands' have very few manufacturing activities. Petroleum-refining (using petroleum imported from Venezuela) is the islands' principal industrial activity, with the Curaçao refinery leased to the Venezuelan state petroleum company. Production capacity at the refinery was 116.8m. barrels per year in 2001, according to the US Geological Survey; however, industrial action in Venezuela led to the closure of the refinery during December 2002–March 2003, impacting heavily upon the islands' economy. Petroleum transhipment is also important, and ship repairs at the Curaçao dry dock make a significant contribution to the economy. In 2002 petroleum imports comprised 68.4% of total merchandise imports.

The services sector contributed 85.3% of GDP in 2003, and engaged 84.4% of the employed labour force on Curaçao in 2004–05. The Netherlands Antilles is a major 'offshore' financial centre. In June 2000 the Netherlands Antilles was urged by the Organisation for Economic Co-operation and Development (OECD) to improve the accountability and transparency of its financial services; in response, the Government announced that it was to review its taxation legislation to comply more closely with OECD's standards. In April 2002 the Netherlands Antilles was removed from the list of those countries deemed to be un-co-operative tax 'havens' after OECD favourably assessed the Government's legislative amendments. In the same month an agreement was signed with the USA, pledging to share information on tax matters, with the aim of combating money-laundering and associated criminal activities. The financial and business services sector contributed 26.8% of GDP in 2003, and employed 16.7% of the Curaçao working population in 2004–05. Operational income from the 'offshore' sector increased significantly from the 1990s. A major industry for all the islands (particularly St Maarten) is tourism, which is the largest employer after the public sector. Significant improvements in the number of stop-over tourists, the number of cruise-ship passengers and the level of tourism revenue were recorded in 2003 and 2004. Figures for the whole of the latter year were the best since 1994. In addition to tourism, Curaçao, in particular, has sought to establish itself as a centre for regional trade, exploiting its excellent harbours. In 1998 a free trade zone was established at the island's airport, which further enhanced Curaçao's entrepôt status.

In 2004 the Netherlands Antilles recorded a visible trade deficit (excluding most transactions in petroleum) of NA Fl. 1,167.9m., much of which was offset by revenue from services; there was a deficit of NA Fl. 92.1m. on the current account of the balance of payments. The petroleum industry dominates the trade figures of the Netherlands Antilles, particularly of the 'Leeward Islands'. In 2002 the principal source of imports (60.4%) was Venezuela (which provides crude petroleum), and the principal market for exports (22.1%) was the USA. The USA is an important trading partner for all the islands of the Netherlands Antilles, as are the Netherlands and other Caribbean countries. Petroleum is the principal commodity for both import and export, and accounted for 68.4% of imports and 94.7% of exports in 2002. The Netherlands Antilles also imports machinery and transport equipment, manufactured goods, and chemicals and related products, while it exports aloes, Curaçao liqueur and some light manufactures.

In 2004 the general Government (including island governments) recorded a budgetary deficit of NA Fl. 341.1m., which was equivalent to 6.2% of GDP. In the same year the central Government recorded a deficit of NA Fl. 206.1m. on its budget. The administrations of the islands tend to operate with deficits. At the end of June 2005 the combined public domestic debts of the central Government and the island Government of Curaçao were NA Fl. 4,685.5m. (83.7% of GDP). Total foreign debt stood at NA Fl. 717.7m. (12.8% of GDP), 96.2% of which was owed to the Netherlands. The average annual rate of inflation was 1.9% in 1998–2004. Consumer prices increased by an average of 2.1% in 2003 and by 1.3% in 2004. The rate of unemployment in the labour force was an estimated 15.1% for the Netherlands Antilles as a whole in June 2005. According to a sample survey of the labour force, 18.2% of the Curaçao work-force were unemployed in 2004–05. Figures from the 2001 census showed that the rate of unemployment in St Maarten stood at 12.2%, with the rate of youth unemployment at 24.1%.

The Netherlands Antilles, as part of the Kingdom of the Netherlands, has the status of an Overseas Territory in association with the European Union (see p. 228). The Netherlands Antilles enjoys observer status in the Caribbean Community and Common Market (CARICOM, see p. 183).

The relative isolation of the individual islands has led to the development of semi-independent economies, and economic conditions vary considerably between them. Notwithstanding, the Netherlands Antilles experienced relatively strong economic growth in the early 1990s, but, owing mainly to a decline in both the financial services and the petroleum-refining sectors, the past decade witnessed a progressive weakening of the economy, leading to a prolonged recession, high unemployment and increasing rates of emigration. Under the terms of the structural adjustment programme (SAP), undertaken from 1996 in consultation with the IMF, which aimed to eliminate the fiscal deficit over a period of four years, the civil service was to be rationalized, public-sector wages were to be 'frozen' and pension arrangements reviewed, while new indirect taxes were to be introduced. Successive administrations, however, recorded only limited success in implementing the terms of the SAP and its successor, the National Recovery Plan, which was adopted in late 1998, in part owing to the great unpopularity of many of the measures to be undertaken. Following stringent measures announced by the Pourier Government in 2001, the Dutch Government released NA Fl. 153m. (to be spent in 2002–06) to encourage sustained economic development and to support the Netherlands Antilles Government in improving the quality of its administration and education systems. The Netherlands approved the release of €125m. in additional funds in 2003, and the Dutch and Netherlands Antilles Governments agreed on a more prominent role for the Central Bank in the monitoring and implementation of the IMF targets. In 2002–05 the long formation periods of four successive Governments and the consequent lack of a central programme, coupled with the effects of the weak US dollar and, in the earlier part of the period, an under-performing international tourism market, damaged confidence, leading to only small increases in real GDP, according to central bank figures. After growth of only 1.0% in 2004 and 0.5% in 2005, an expansion of a further 1.0% was forecast for 2006. Some optimism was engendered by the improving tourism industry: the first quarter of 2005 saw the number of stop-over arrivals increase by a further 1.8% compared with the equivalent period in 2004, itself a record year for the sector. Growth in activity in Curaçao's free trade zone and a consequent increase in arrivals from Venezuela and the Dominican Republic was reportedly an important boost for the tourism and retail sectors. Under the agreement to dissolve the Netherlands Antilles by July 2007 (see Recent History), announced in December 2005, the Dutch Government agreed to help restructure the islands' public debt, which was equivalent to some US $2,800m. at the end of 2005, a large proportion of which was owed to the Netherlands.

Education

Education was made compulsory in 1992. The islands' educational facilities are generally of a high standard. The education system is the same as that of the Netherlands. Dutch is used as the principal language of instruction in schools on the 'Leeward Islands', while English is used in schools on the 'Windward Islands'. Instruction in Papiamento (using a different spelling system from that adopted by Aruba) has been introduced in primary schools. Primary education begins at six years of age and lasts for six years. Secondary education lasts for a further five years. The University of the Netherlands Antilles, sited on Curaçao, had 1,355 students in 2004/05. In April 2002 the Netherlands Government made more than €12.7m. available for improvements to education provision in the Netherlands Antilles. In 1995 local government expenditure on education in the Antilles of the Five was NA Fl. 178.9m. (19.3% of total spending by the island governments).

Public Holidays

2006: 1 January (New Year's Day), 19 January (Bonaire only: Carnival Rest Day), 27 February (Curaçao and Bonaire only: Lenten Carnival), 14–17 April (Easter), 30 April (Queen's Day), 1 May (Labour Day), 8 May (St Maarten, Saba and St Eustatius only: Celebration of World War II Victory), 25 May (Ascension Day), 5 June (St Maarten, Saba and St Eustatius only: Whit Monday), 1 July (Emancipation Day), 2 July (Curaçao Day), 21 July (St Maarten,

NETHERLANDS DEPENDENCIES

Saba and St Eustatius only: Schoelcher Day), 31 July (Carnival), 6 September (Bonaire Day), 21 October (Antillian Day), 1 November (St Maarten, Saba and St Eustatius only: All Saints' Day), 11 November (St Maarten Day), 16 November (St Eustatius Day), 6 December (Saba Day), 15 December (St Maarten, Saba and St Eustatius only: Kingdom Day), 25–26 December (Christmas).

2007: 1 January (New Year's Day), 19 January (Bonaire only: Carnival Rest Day), 19 February (Curaçao and Bonaire only: Lenten Carnival), 6–9 April (Easter), 30 April (Queen's Day), 1 May (Labour Day), 8 May (St Maarten, Saba and St Eustatius only: Celebration of World War II Victory), 17 May (Ascension Day), 28 May (St Maarten, Saba and St Eustatius only: Whit Monday), 1 July (Emancipation Day), 2 July (Curaçao Day), 21 July (St Maarten, Saba and St Eustatius only: Schoelcher Day), 30 July (Carnival), 6 September (Bonaire Day), 21 October (Antillian Day), 1 November (St Maarten, Saba and St Eustatius only: All Saints' Day), 11 November (St Maarten Day), 16 November (St Eustatius Day), 6 December (Saba Day), 15 December (St Maarten, Saba and St Eustatius only: Kingdom Day), 25–26 December (Christmas).

Weights and Measures
The metric system is in force.

Statistical Survey

Sources (unless otherwise stated): Centraal Bureau voor de Statistiek, Fort Amsterdam, Willemstad, Curaçao; tel. (9) 461-1031; fax 461-1696; internet www.central-bureau-of-statistics.an; Bank van de Nederlandse Antillen, Simon Bolivar Plein 1, Willemstad, Curaçao; tel. (9) 434-5500; fax (9) 461-5004; e-mail info@centralbank.an; internet www.centralbank.an.

AREA AND POPULATION

Area (sq km): Curaçao 444; Bonaire 288; St Maarten (Dutch sector) 34; St Eustatius 21; Saba 13; Total 800 (309 sq miles).

Population: 189,474 at census of 27 January 1992 (excluding adjustment for underenumeration, estimated at 3.2%); 175,653 (males 82,521, females 93,132) at census of 29 January 2001; 185,513 at 1 January 2005 (estimate). *By Island* (2001 census): Curaçao 130,627; Bonaire 10,791; St Maarten (Dutch sector) 30,594; St Eustatius 2,292; Saba 1,349.

Density (per sq km, 2001 census): Curaçao 294.2; Bonaire 37.5; St Maarten (Dutch sector) 899.8; St Eustatius 109.1; Saba 103.8; Total 219.6. *1 January 2005:* Total 231.9.

Principal Town: Willemstad (capital), population (UN estimate, incl. suburbs): 134,003 at mid-2003. Source: UN, *World Urbanization Prospects: The 2003 Revision*.

Births, Marriages and Deaths (2004): Registered live births 2,357; Registered marriages 710 (marriage rate 3.9 per 1,000); Registered deaths 1,412 (death rate 7.7 per 1,000).

Expectation of Life (years at birth): 76.7 (males 73.6; females 79.5) in 2004. Source: Pan-American Health Organization.

Economically Active Population (sample survey, Curaçao only, persons aged 15 years and over, average 2004–05): Agriculture, forestry, fishing and mining 404; Manufacturing 3,583; Electricity, gas and water 612; Construction 3,429; Wholesale and retail trade, repairs 9,719; Hotels and restaurants 4,046; Transport, storage and communications 3,296; Financial intermediation 3,673; Real estate, renting and business activities 4,878; Public administration, defence and social security 4,885; Education 2,254; Health and social work 4,362; Other community, social and personal services 3,596; Private households with employed persons 2,482; Extra-territorial organizations and bodies 125; *Total employed* 51,343 (males 25,316, females 26,027); Unemployed 11,392 (males 5,227, females 6,165); *Total labour force* 62,735 (males 30,543, females 32,192).

HEALTH AND WELFARE

Total Fertility Rate (children per woman, 2004): 2.0.
Under-5 Mortality Rate (per 1,000 live births, 2002): 14.2.
Physicians (per 1,000 head, 1999): 1.4.
Hospital Beds (per 1,000 head, 2002): 7.24.
Health Expenditure: % of GDP (1995): 4.5.
Source: Pan American Health Organization.

For definitions, see explanatory note on p. vi.

The Netherlands Antilles

AGRICULTURE, ETC.

Livestock (FAO estimates, '000 head, year ending September 2004): Asses 2.6; Cattle 0.6; Pigs 2.5; Goats 13.5; Sheep 9.0; Poultry 135.

Livestock Products (FAO estimates, metric tons, 2004): Pig meat 188; Poultry meat 300; Cows' milk 410; Hen eggs 510.

Fishing (metric tons, live weight, 2003): Skipjack tuna 12,084; Yellowfin tuna 6,667; Bigeye tuna 3,203; *Total catch* (incl. others) 23,070 (FAO estimate).

Source: FAO.

MINING

Production ('000 metric tons, 2003, estimate): Salt 500. Source: US Geological Survey.

INDUSTRY

Production ('000 metric tons, 2001, unless otherwise indicated): Jet fuel 915; Kerosene 46 (estimate); Residual fuel oils 5,115; Lubricating oils 395 (estimate); Petroleum bitumen (asphalt) 1,025 (estimate); Liquefied petroleum gas 100; Motor spirit (petrol) 1,750; Aviation gasoline 14; Distillate fuel oils (gas-diesel oil) 2,528 (estimate); Sulphur (recovered) 30 (2002); Electric energy (million kWh) 1210 (2004).

Sources: mainly UN, *Industrial Commodity Statistics Yearbook*, and US Geological Survey.

FINANCE

Currency and Exchange Rates: 100 cents = 1 Netherlands Antilles gulden (guilder) or florin (NA Fl.). *Sterling, Dollar and Euro Equivalents* (30 December 2005): £1 sterling = NA Fl. 3.082; US $1 = NA Fl. 1.790; €1 = NA Fl. 2.112; NA Fl. 100 = £32.44 = $55.87 = €47.36. *Exchange Rate:* In December 1971 the central bank's mid-point rate was fixed at US $1 = NA Fl. 1.80. In 1989 this was adjusted to $1 = NA Fl. 1.79. The US dollar also circulates on St Maarten.

Central Government Budget (NA Fl. million, 2004): *Revenue:* Tax revenue 577.2 (Taxes on goods and services 420.7, Taxes on international trade and transactions 127.0, Other taxes 29.5); Non-tax revenue 79.8; Grants (from other levels of government, excluding overseas development aid) 35.3; Total 692.3. *Expenditure:* Wages and salaries 292.9; Other goods and services 107.2; Interest payments 142.0; Subsidies 1.7; Current transfers 324.3; Capital expenditure (incl. transfers and net lending) 30.3; Total 898.4. *Total General Government Budget* (incl. island governments, NA Fl. million, 2004): *Revenue:* Tax revenue 1,205.0; Non-tax revenue 144.3; Total 1,349.2. *Expenditure:* Current expenditure 1,625.6; Capital expenditure 64.7; Total 1,690.3.

International Reserves (US $ million at 31 December 2004): Gold (national valuation) 152; Foreign exchange 415; Total 567. Source: IMF, *International Financial Statistics*.

Money Supply (NA Fl. million at 31 December 2004): Currency outside banks 231.3; Demand deposits at commercial banks 1,096.8; Total (incl. others) 1,406.5. Source: IMF, *International Financial Statistics*.

Cost of Living (Consumer Price Index; base: 2000 = 100): All items 102.2 in 2002; 104.3 in 2003; 105.7 in 2004. Source: IMF, *International Financial Statistics*.

Expenditure on the Gross Domestic Product (million NA Fl. at current prices, 2003): Final consumption expenditure 4,142.7 (Government 1,146.3, Households and non-profit institutions serving households 2,996.4); Gross fixed capital formation 1,266.2; Changes in inventories 3.4; *Total domestic expenditure* 5,412.3; Exports of goods and services 4,451.9; *Less* Imports of goods and services 4,496.6; Statistical discrepancy 5.9; *GDP in market prices* 5,373.6.

Gross Domestic Product (million NA Fl. at current prices, 2003): Agriculture, fishing, mining, etc. 40.1; Manufacturing 268.0; Electricity, gas and water 198.8; Construction 204.9; Wholesale and retail trade 735.3; Hotels and restaurants 212.5; Transport, storage and communications 437.1; Financial intermediation 836.4; Real estate, renting and business activities 462.0; Public administration, defence, etc. 348.9; Education 508.4; Health care and social services 444.0; Other community, social and personal services 137.2; Private households with employed persons 10.6; *Gross value added at basic prices* 4,844.4; Taxes, less subsidies, on products 529.2; *Gross domestic product in market prices* 5,373.6.

Balance of Payments (US $ million, 2004): Exports of goods f.o.b. 799.8; Imports of goods f.o.b. –1,967.6; *Trade balance* –1,167.9; Exports of services 1,855.7; Imports of services –835.0; *Balance on goods and services* –147.3; Other income received 94.7; Other income paid –105.0; *Balance on goods, services and income* –157.6; Current transfers received 319.6; Current transfers paid –254.0; *Current balance* –92.1; Capital transfers (net) 79.3; Direct investment abroad –25.2; Direct investment from abroad –25.5; Portfolio investment assets –93.9; Portfolio investment liabilities –1.7; Other investment assets –84.0; Other investment liabilities 177.5; Net errors and omissions 71.3; *Overall balance* 5.8. Source: IMF, *International Financial Statistics*.

EXTERNAL TRADE

Principal Commodities (US $ million, 2002): *Imports c.i.f.:* Food and live animals 145.5; Petroleum, petroleum products, etc. 1,552.1 (Crude petroleum 1,354.4); Basic manufactures 110.4; Machinery and transport equipment 126.3 (Road vehicles 72.9); Total (incl. others) 2,268.5. *Exports f.o.b.:* Refined petroleum products 1,609.0; Total (incl. others) 1,699.2. Source: UN, *International Trade Statistics Yearbook*.

Principal Trading Partners (US $ million, 2002): *Imports c.i.f.:* Colombia 30.3; Germany 39.0; Iraq 151.1; Japan 36.7; Netherlands 187.4; USA 305.1; Venezuela 1,370.9; Total (incl. others) 2,268.5. *Exports f.o.b.:* Antigua and Barbuda 22.0; Aruba 22.7; Bahamas 129.9; Belize 26.1; Canada 68.6; Colombia 18.2; Cuba 61.5; El Salvador 80.0; Guatemala 66.5; Guyana 69.7; Haiti 34.2; Honduras 74.2; Netherlands 73.7; Nicaragua 36.3; Panama 68.0; Suriname 24.1; United Arab Emirates 40.6; USA 375.0; Venezuela 169.9; Total (incl. others) 1,699.2. Source: UN, *International Trade Statistics Yearbook*.

TRANSPORT

Road Traffic (Curaçao and Bonaire, motor vehicles registered, excl. government-owned vehicles, 2004): Passenger cars 64,729; Lorries 14,873; Buses 462; Taxis 218; Other cars 207; Motorcycles 1,498.

Shipping: *International Freight Traffic* (Curaçao, '000 metric tons, excl. petroleum, 1997): Goods loaded 215.2; Goods unloaded 516.7. *Merchant Fleet* (registered at 31 December 2004): Number of vessels 214; Total displacement 1,661,631 grt (Source: Lloyd's Register-Fairplay, *World Fleet Statistics*).

TOURISM

Tourist Arrivals: *Stop-overs*: 668,425 in 2002; 728,402 in 2003; 779,325 in 2004. *Cruise-ship Passengers* (Bonaire, Curaçao and St Maarten only): 1,416,288 in 2002; 1,495,713 in 2003; 1,621,178 in 2004.

Tourism Receipts (NA Fl. million, incl. passenger transport): 1,683.5 in 2002; 1,761.0 in 2003; 1,906.5 in 2004.

COMMUNICATIONS MEDIA

Radio Receivers (1997): 217,000 in use.

Television Receivers (1999): 71,000 in use.

Telephones (2001, UN estimate): 81,000 main lines in use.

Mobile Cellular Telephones (1998): 16,000 subscribers.

Internet Users (1999, UN estimate): 2,000.

Daily Newspapers (1996): 6 titles (estimated circulation 70,000 copies per issue).

Sources: UNESCO, *Statistical Yearbook*; UN, *Statistical Yearbook*; International Telecommunication Union.

EDUCATION

Pre-primary (2000/01): 6,811 pupils; 316 teachers.
Primary (2000/01): 22,140 pupils; 1,022 teachers.
Secondary (2000/01): 13,392 pupils; 1,167 teachers.
English Language Secondary (2000/01): 377 pupils.
Vocational (2000/01): 1,747 pupils.
Special Education (2000/01): 2,337 pupils; 178 teachers.
Teacher Training (2000/01): 133 students; 22 teachers.
University (2000/01): 795 students; 131 teachers.
Adult Literacy Rate (2001 census): 96.3% (males 96.7%; females 96.1%).

Directory

The Constitution

The form of government for the Netherlands Antilles is embodied in the Charter of the Kingdom of the Netherlands, which came into force on 20 December 1954. The Netherlands, the Netherlands Antilles and, since 1986, Aruba each enjoy full autonomy in domestic and internal affairs and are united on a basis of equality for the protection of their common interests and the granting of mutual assistance.

The monarch of the Netherlands is represented in the Netherlands Antilles by the Governor, who is appointed by the Dutch Crown for a term of six years. The central Government of the Netherlands Antilles appoints a Minister Plenipotentiary to represent the Antilles in the Government of the Kingdom. Whenever the Netherlands Council of Ministers is dealing with matters coming under the heading of joint affairs of the realm (in practice mainly foreign affairs and defence), the Council assumes the status of Council of Ministers of the Kingdom. In that event, the Minister Plenipotentiary appointed by the Government of the Netherlands Antilles takes part, with full voting powers, in the deliberations.

A legislative proposal regarding affairs of the realm and applying to the Netherlands Antilles as well as to the 'metropolitan' Netherlands is sent, simultaneously with its submission, to the Staten Generaal (the Netherlands parliament) and to the Staten (parliament) of the Netherlands Antilles. The latter body can report in writing to the Staten Generaal on the draft Kingdom Statute and designate one or more special delegates to attend the debates and furnish information in the meetings of the Chambers of the Staten Generaal. Before the final vote on a draft the Minister Plenipotentiary has the right to express an opinion on it. If he disapproves of the draft, and if in the Second Chamber a three-fifths' majority of the votes cast is not obtained, the discussions on the draft are suspended and further deliberations take place in the Council of Ministers of the Kingdom. When special delegates attend the meetings of the Chambers this right devolves upon the delegates of the parliamentary body designated for this purpose.

The Governor has executive power in external affairs, which he exercises in co-operation with the Council of Ministers. He is assisted by an advisory council, which consists of at least five members appointed by him.

Executive power in internal affairs is vested in the nominated Council of Ministers, responsible to the Staten. The Netherlands Antilles Staten consists of 22 members, who are elected by universal adult suffrage for four years (subject to dissolution). Each island forms an electoral district. Curaçao elects 14 members, Bonaire three members, St Maarten three members and Saba and St Eustatius one member each. In the islands where more than one member is elected, the election is by proportional representation. Inhabitants have the right to vote if they have Dutch nationality and have reached 18 years of age. Voting is not compulsory. Each island territory also elects its Island Council (Curaçao 21 members, Bonaire 9, St Maarten 7, St Eustatius and Saba 5), and its internal affairs are managed by an executive council, consisting of the Gezaghebber (Lieutenant-Governor), and a number of commissioners. The central Government of the Netherlands Antilles has the right to annul any local island decision which is in conflict with the public interest or the Constitution. Control of the police, communications, monetary affairs, health and education remain under the jurisdiction of the central Government.

On 1 January 1986 Aruba acquired separate status (*status aparte*) within the Kingdom of the Netherlands. However, in economic and monetary affairs there is a co-operative union between Aruba and the Antilles of the Five, known as the 'Union of the Netherlands Antilles and Aruba'.

The Government

HEAD OF STATE

Queen of the Netherlands: HM Queen BEATRIX.
Governor: Dr FRITZ M. DE LOS SANTOS GOEDGEDRAG.

COUNCIL OF MINISTERS
(April 2006)

The Government comprised a seven-party coalition of the Partido Antía Restrukturá (PAR), the Movimentu Antiyas Nobo (MAN), Partido Nashonal di Pueblo (PNP), the National Alliance (NA), the Unión Patriótico Bonairiano (UPB), the Democratic Partij—Statia (DP—StE) and the Windward Islands People's Movement (WIPM).

Prime Minister: EMILY DE JONGH-ELHAGE (PAR).
Minister of Economic Affairs: BURNEY ELHAGE (UPB).

NETHERLANDS DEPENDENCIES

Minister of Constitutional and Internal Affairs: Roland Duncan (NA).

Minister of Finance: Ersilia T. M. de Lannoy (PNP).

Minister of Justice: David Dick (PAR).

Minister of Education, Culture, Youth and Sports: Omayra Leeflang (PAR).

Minister of Transport and Telecommunications: Kenneth Gijsbertha (MAN).

Minister of Public Health and Social Development: Sandra Smith (MAN).

Minister Plenipotentiary and Member of the Council of Ministers of the Realm of the Netherlands Antilles: Paul R. J. Comenencia (PAR).

Attorney-General of the Netherlands Antilles: Dick A. Piar.

GEZAGHEBBERS
(Lieutenant-Governors)

Bonaire: Richard N. Hart, Wilhelminaplein 1, Kralendijk, Bonaire; tel. 717-5330; fax 717-5100; e-mail gezag@bonairelive.com.

Curaçao: Lizanne M. Richards-Dindial, Centraal Bestuurskantoor, Concordiastraat 24, Willemstad, Curaçao; tel. (9) 461-2900; e-mail info@curacao-gov.an; internet www.curacao-gov.an.

Saba: Antoine J. M. Solagnier, The Bottom, Saba; tel. 416-3215; fax 416-3274; e-mail antoine@solagnier.com.

St Eustatius: Irwin E. Temmer, Oranjestad, St Eustatius; tel. 318-2213.

St Maarten: Franklyn E. Richards, Central Administration, Secretariat, Clem Labega Sq., POB 943, Philipsburg, St Maarten; tel. 542-6085; fax 542-4172; e-mail governor@governorsxm.com; internet www.governorsxm.com.

MINISTRIES

Office of the Governor: Fort Amsterdam 2, Willemstad, Curaçao; tel. (9) 461-2000; fax (9) 461-1412; e-mail kabinet@kgna.an; internet www.gouverneur.an.

Ministry of Constitutional Affairs and Internal Affairs: Willemstad, Curaçao.

Ministry for Economic Affairs and Labour: Scharlooweg 106, Willemstad, Curaçao; tel. (9) 465-6236; fax (9) 465-6316; e-mail info.dez@ibm.net.

Ministry of Education, Culture, Youth and Sports: Boerhavestraat 16, Otrobanda, Willemstad, Curaçao; tel. (9) 462-4777; fax (9) 462-4471.

Ministry of Finance: Pietermaai 17, Willemstad, Curaçao; tel. (9) 432-8000; fax (9) 461-3339; e-mail g.d.dirfin@curinfo.an.

Ministry of General Affairs and Foreign Relations: Plasa Horacio Hoyer 9, Willemstad, Curaçao; tel. (9) 461-1866; fax (9) 461-1268.

Ministry of Justice: Willhelminaplein, Willemstad, Curaçao; tel. (9) 463-0299; fax (9) 465-8083.

Ministry of Public Health and Social Development: Santa Rosaweg 122, Willemstad, Curaçao; tel. (9) 736-3530; fax (9) 736-3531; e-mail vornil@cura.net.

Ministry of Transport and Telecommunications: Fort Amsterdam 17, Willemstad, Curaçao; tel. (9) 461-3988.

Office of the Minister Plenipotentiary of the Netherlands Antilles: Antillenhuis, Badhuisweg 173–175, POB 90706, 2509LS The Hague, the Netherlands; tel. (70) 3066111; fax (70) 3066110; e-mail info@antillenhuis.nl; internet www.antillenhuis.nl.

Legislature

STATEN

Speaker: D. A. S. Lucia (PNP).

General Election, 27 January 2006

Party	Seats
Partido Antía Restrukturá	5
Movimentu Antiyas Nobo	3
Frente Obrero i Liberashon 30 di mei	2
Partido Nashonal di Pueblo	2
Forsa Kòrsou	2
National Alliance	2
Unión Patriótico Bonairiano	2
Democratic Party—St Maarten	1
Democratische Partij—Bonaire	1
Democratic Party—Statia	1
Windward Islands People's Movement	1
Partido Laboral Krusado Popular	—
Pueblo Soberano	—
Democratische Partij—Curaçao	—
Total (incl. others)	22

Political Organizations

Democratische Partij—Bonaire (DP—B) (Democratic Party—Bonaire): Kaya America 13A, POB 294, Kralendijk, Bonaire; tel. 717-8903; fax 717-5923; f. 1954; also known as Partido Democratico Boneriano; liberal; Leader Jopie Abraham.

Democratische Partij—Curaçao (DP—C) (Democratic Party—Curaçao): Neptunusweg 28, Willemstad, Curaçao; f. 1944; Leader Raymond Bentoera.

Democratische Partij—Sint Maarten (DP—StM): Tamarind Tree Dr. 4, Union Rd, Cole Bay, St Maarten; tel. 543-1166; fax 542-4296; Leader Sarah Wescott-Williams.

Democratische Partij—Statia (DP—StE): Oranjestad, St Eustatius; Leader Kenneth van Putten.

Forsa Kòrsou: Willemstad, Curaçao.

Frente Obrero i Liberashon 30 di mei (FOL) (Workers' Liberation Front of 30 May): Mayaguanaweg 16, Willemstad, Curaçao; tel. (9) 461-8105; internet www.fol.an; f. 1969; socialist; Leaders Anthony Godett, Rignald Lak, Editha Wright.

Movimentu Antiyas Nobo (MAN) (Movement for a New Antilles): Landhuis Morgenster, Willemstad, Curaçao; tel. (9) 468-4781; internet www.man.an; f. 1971; socialist; Leader Dominico (Don) F. Martina.

National Alliance (NA): Willemstad, Curaçao; Leader William Marlin.

National Progressive Party: Willemstad, Curaçao; contested the 2002 and 2006 elections as the National Alliance with the St Maarten Patriotic Alliance (q.v.).

St Maarten Patriotic Alliance (SPA): Frontstraat 69, Philipsburg, St Maarten; tel. 543-1064; fax 543-1065; contested the 2002 and 2006 elections as the National Alliance with the National Progressive Party (q.v.); Leader Vance James, Jr.

Partido Antía Restrukturá (PAR) (Restructured Antilles Party): Fokkerweg 28, Willemstad, Curaçao; tel. (9) 465-2566; fax (9) 465-2622; f. 1993; social-Christian ideology; Leader Emily de Jongh-Elhage.

Partido Laboral Krusado Popular (PLKP): Schouwburgweg 44, Willemstad, Curaçao; tel. (9) 737-0644; fax (9) 737-0831; internet www.cura.net/krusada; f. 1997; progressive; Leader Errol A. Cova.

Partido Nashonal di Pueblo (PNP) (National People's Party): Winston Churchillweg 133, Willemstad, Curaçao; tel. (9) 869-6777; fax (9) 869-6688; internet www.pnp.an; f. 1948; also known as Nationale Volkspartij; social christian party; Pres. Maria Liberia-Peters; Leader Susanne F. C. Camelia-Römer.

Partido Union den Reino Ulandés (PURU): Binnenweg 11, Willemstad, Curaçao; Leader Freddy I. Antersun.

People's Democratic Party (PDP): Philipsburg, St Maarten; tel. 542-2696; Leader Millicent de Weever.

People's Progressive Party: Philipsburg, St Maarten.

Pueblo Soberano: Willemstad, Curaçao.

Saba United Democratic Party (SUDP): Saba; tel. 416-3311; fax 416-3434; Leader Steve Hassell.

Saint Eustatius Alliance (SEA): Oranjestad, St Eustatius; Leader Ingrid Whitfield.

Social Independiente (SI): Willemstad, Curaçao; f. 1986 by fmr PNP mems in Curaçao; formed electoral alliance with FOL for 1990 election; Leader George Hueck.

Unión Patriótico Bonairiano (UPB) (Patriotic Union of Bonaire): Kaya Sabana 22, Kralendijk, Bonaire; tel. 717-8906; fax 717-5552;

2,134 mems; Christian-democratic; Leader Ramonsito T. Booi; Sec.-Gen. C. V. Winklaar.

Windward Islands People's Movement (WIPM): Windwardside, POB 525, Saba; tel. 416-2244; Chair. and Leader Will Johnston; Sec.-Gen. Dave Levenstone.

Judicial System

Legal authority is exercised by the Court of First Instance (which sits in all the islands) and in appeal by the Joint High Court of Justice of the Netherlands Antilles and Aruba. The members of the Joint High Court of Justice sit singly as judges in the Courts of First Instance. The Chief Justice of the Joint High Court of Justice, its members (a maximum of 30) and the Attorneys-General of the Netherlands Antilles and of Aruba are appointed for life by the Dutch monarch, after consultation with the Governments of the Netherlands Antilles and Aruba.

Joint High Court of Justice

Wilhelminaplein 4, Willemstad, Curaçao; tel. (9) 463-4111; fax (9) 461-8341; e-mail hofcur@cura.net.

Chief Justice of the Joint High Court: Dr Luis Alberto José de Lannoy.

Attorney-General of the Netherlands Antilles: Dick A. Piar.

Secretary-Executive of the Joint High Court: M. E. N. Rojer-de Freitas (acting).

Religion

CHRISTIANITY

Most of the population were Christian, the predominant denomination being Roman Catholicism. According to the 1992 census, Roman Catholics formed the largest single group on four of the five islands: 82% of the population of Bonaire, 81% on Curaçao, 65% on Saba and 41% on St Maarten. On St Eustatius the Methodists formed the largest single denomination (31%). Of the other denominations, the main ones were the Anglicans and the Dutch Reformed Church. There were also small communities of Jews, Muslims and Bahá'ís.

Curaçaose Raad van Kerken (Curaçao Council of Churches): Barenblaan 11, Willemstad, Curaçao; tel. (9) 737-3070; fax (9) 736-2183; f. 1958; six member churches; Chair. Ida Visser; Exec. Sec. Paul van der Waal.

The Roman Catholic Church

The Netherlands Antilles and Aruba together form the diocese of Willemstad, suffragan to the archdiocese of Port of Spain (Trinidad and Tobago). At 31 December 2003 the diocese numbered an estimated 224,809 adherents (about 78% of the total population). The Bishop participates in the Antilles Episcopal Conference, currently based in Trinidad and Tobago.

Bishop of Willemstad: Rt Rev. Luigi Antonio Secco, Bisdom, Breedestraat 31, Otrobanda, Willemstad, Curaçao; tel. (9) 462-5857; fax (9) 462-7437; e-mail bisdomwstad@curinfo.an.

The Anglican Communion

Saba, St Eustatius and St Maarten form part of the diocese of the North Eastern Caribbean and Aruba, within the Church in the Province of the West Indies. The Bishop is resident in The Valley, Anguilla.

Other Churches

Iglesia Protestant Uni (United Protestant Church): Fortkerk, Fort Amsterdam, Willemstad, Curaçao; tel. (9) 461-1139; fax (9) 465-7481; f. 1825; by union of Dutch Reformed and Evangelical Lutheran Churches; Pres. D. J. Lopes; 3 congregations; 11,280 adherents.

Methodist Church: Oranjestad, St Eustatius.

Other denominations active in the islands include the Moravian, Apostolic Faith, Wesleyan Holiness and Norwegian Seamen's Churches, the Baptists, Calvinists, Jehovah's Witnesses, Evangelists, Seventh-day Adventists, the Church of Christ and the New Testament Church of God.

JUDAISM

Reconstructionist Shephardi Congregation Mikvé Israel-Emanuel: Hanchi di Snoa 29, POB 322, Willemstad, Curaçao; tel. (9) 461-1067; fax (9) 465-4141; e-mail information@snoa.com; internet www.snoa.com; f. 1732 on present site; about 350 mems.

Congregation 'Shaarei Tsedek' Ashkenazi Orthodox Jewish Community: Lelieweg 1A, Willemstad, Curaçao; tel. and fax (9) 737-5738; e-mail ariel@cura.net; 100 mems; Rabbi Ariel Yeshurun.

The Press

Algemeen Dagblad: Daphneweg 44, POB 725, Willemstad, Curaçao; tel. (9) 747-2200; fax (9) 747-2257; e-mail adcarib@cura.net; internet www.ad-caribbean.com; daily; Dutch; Editor Noud Köper.

Amigoe: Kaya Fratumam di Skirpiri z/n, POB 577, Willemstad, Curaçao; tel. (9) 767-2000; fax (9) 767-4084; e-mail management@amigoe.com; internet www.amigoe.com; f. 1884; Christian; daily; evening; Dutch; Dir Ingrid de Maaljer-Hollander; Editor-in-Chief Michael Willemse; circ. 12,000.

Bala: Noord Zapateer nst 13, Willemstad, Curaçao; tel. (9) 467-1646; fax (9) 467-1041; daily; Papiamento.

Beurs- en Nieuwsberichten: A. M. Chumaceiro Blvd 5, POB 741, Willemstad, Curaçao; tel. (9) 465-4544; fax (9) 465-3411; f. 1935; daily; evening; Dutch; Editor L. Schenk; circ. 8,000.

Bonaire Holiday: POB 569, Curaçao; tel. (9) 767-1403; fax (9) 767-2003; f. 1971; tourist guide; English; 3 a year; circ. 95,000.

Bonaire Reporter: Kaya Gob. Debrot 200-6, Bonaire; tel. and fax 717-8988; e-mail reporter@bonairereporter.com; internet bonairereporter.com; English; weekly.

The Business Journal: Indjuweg 30A, Willemstad, Curaçao; tel. (9) 461-1367; fax (9) 461-1955; monthly; English.

Colors: Liberty Publications, Curaçao; tel. and fax (9) 869-6066; e-mail colors@curacao-online.net; internet www.curacao-online.net/colors; f. 1998; general interest magazine; 4 a year; Publr Tirzah Z. B. Libert.

De Curaçaosche Courant: Frederikstraat 123, POB 15, Willemstad, Curaçao; tel. (9) 461-2766; fax (9) 462-6535; f. 1812; weekly; Dutch; Editor J. Koridon.

Curaçao Holiday: POB 569, Curaçao; tel. (9) 767-1403; fax (9) 767-2003; f. 1960; tourist guide; English; 3 a year; circ. 300,000.

Daily Herald: Bush Rd 22, POB 828, Philipsburg, St Maarten; tel. 542-5253; fax 542-5913; e-mail editorial@thedailyherald.com; internet www.thedailyherald.com; daily; English.

Extra: W. I. Compagniestraat 41, Willemstad, Curaçao; tel. (9) 462-4595; fax (9) 462-7575; daily; morning; Papiamento; Man. R. Yrausquin; Editor Mike Oehlers; circ. 20,000.

Newsletter of Curaçao Trade and Industry Association: Kaya Junior Salas 1, POB 49, Willemstad, Curaçao; tel. (9) 461-1210; fax (9) 461-5422; f. 1972; monthly; English and Dutch; economic and industrial paper.

Nobo: Scherpenheuvel w/n, POB 323, Willemstad, Curaçao; tel. (9) 467-3500; fax (9) 467-2783; daily; evening; Papiamento; Editor Carlos Daantje; circ. 15,000.

Nos Isla: Refineria Isla (Curazao) SA, Emmastad, Curaçao; 2 a month; Papiamento; circ. 1,200.

La Prensa: W. I. Compagniestraat 41, Willemstad, Curaçao; tel. (9) 462-3850; fax (9) 462-5983; e-mail laprensa@laprensacur.com; internet www.laprensacur.com; f. 1929; daily; evening; Papiamento; Man. R. Yrausquin; Editor Sigfried Rigaud; circ. 10,750.

Saba Herald: The Level, Saba; tel. 416-2244; f. 1968; monthly; news, local history; Editor Will Johnson; circ. 500.

St Maarten Guardian: Vlaun Bldg, Pondfill, POB 1046, Philipsburg, St Maarten; tel. 542-6022; fax 542-6043; e-mail guardian@sintmaarten.net; f. 1989; daily; English; Man. Dir Richard F. Gibson; Man. Editor Joseph Dominique; circ. 4,000.

St Maarten Holiday: POB 569, Curaçao; tel. (9) 767-1403; fax (9) 767-2003; f. 1968; tourism guide; English; 3 a year; circ. 175,000.

Teen Times: c/o The Daily Herald, Bush Rd 22, POB 828, Philipsburg, St Maarten; tel. 542-5597; e-mail info@teentimes.com; internet www.teentimes.com; for teenagers by teenagers; sponsored by The Daily Herald; English; Editor-in-Chief Michael Granger.

Ultimo Noticia: Frederikstraat 123, Willemstad, Curaçao; tel. (9) 462-3444; fax (9) 462-6535; daily; morning; Papiamento; Editor A. A. Jonckheer.

La Unión: Rotaprint NV, Willemstad, Curaçao; weekly; Papiamento.

NEWS AGENCIES

Algemeen Nederlands Persbureau (ANP) (Netherlands): Panoramaweg 5, POB 439, Willemstad, Curaçao; tel. (9) 461-2233; fax (9) 461-7431; Representative Ronnie Rens.

Associated Press (AP) (USA): Roodeweg 64, Willemstad, Curaçao; tel. (9) 462-6586; Representative Orlando Cuales.

Publishers

Curaçao Drukkerij en Uitgevers Maatschappij: Willemstad, Curaçao.

Ediciones Populares: W. I. Compagniestraat 41, Willemstad, Curaçao; f. 1929; Dir RONALD YRAUSQUIN.

Drukkerij Scherpenheuvel NV: Scherpenheuvel, POB 60, Willemstad, Curaçao; tel. (9) 467-1134.

Drukkerij de Stad NV: W. I. Compagniestraat 41, Willemstad, Curaçao; tel. (9) 462-3566; fax (9) 462-2175; e-mail kenrick@destad.an; f. 1929; Dir KENRICK A. YRAUSQUIN.

Holiday Publications: POB 569, Curaçao; tel. (9) 767-1403; fax (9) 767-2003.

Offsetdrukkerij Intergrafia NV: Essoweg 54, Willemstad, Curaçao; tel. (9) 464-3180.

Broadcasting and Communications

TELECOMMUNICATIONS

Curaçao Telecom: Schottegatweg Oost 19, Willemstad, Curaçao; tel. 736-1056; fax 736-1057; internet www.curacaotelecom.com; f. 1999; bought by Digicel (Ireland) in 2005; telephone and internet services; Chair. DENIS O'BRIEN.

East Caribbean Cellular NV (ECC): 13 Richardson St, Philipsburg, St Maarten; tel. 542-2100; fax 542-5675; e-mail info@eastcaribbeancellular.com; internet www.eastcaribbeancellular.com; f. 1989.

Servicio de Telekomunikashon (SETEL): F. D. Rooseveltweg 337, POB 3177, Willemstad, Curaçao; tel. (9) 833-1222; fax (9) 868-2596; e-mail setel@curinfo.an; internet www.curinfo.an; f. 1979; telecommunications equipment and network provider; state-owned, but expected to be privatized; Pres. ANGEL R. KOOK; Man. Dir JULIO CONSTANSIA; 400 employees.

Smitcoms NV: Dr A. C. Wathey Cruise & Cargo Facility, St Maarten; tel. 542-9140; fax 542-9141; e-mail matthews@sintmaarten.net; internet smitcomsltd.com; f. 2000; international telephone network provider; Man. Dir CURTIS K. HAYNES.

St Maarten Telephone Co (TelEm): C. A. Cannegieter St 17, POB 160, Philipsburg, St Maarten; tel. 542-2278; fax 542-3101; e-mail lpeters@telem.an; internet www.sinmaarten.net; f. 1975; local landline and value-added services, also operates TelCell digital cellular service; 15,000 subscribers; Man. Dir CURTIS K. HAYNES.

United Telecom Services (UTS): Schouwburgweg 22, POB 103, Willemstad, Curaçao; tel. (9) 777-0101; fax (9) 777-1238; e-mail info@antele.com; f. 1908; fmrly called Antelecom NV; Chair. DAVID DICK; Man. Dir HENDRIK J. EIKELENBOOM.

BROADCASTING

Radio

Easy 97.9 FM: Arikokweg 19A, Willemstad, Curaçao; tel. (9) 462-3162; fax (9) 462-8712; e-mail radio@easyfm.com; internet www.easyfm.com; Dir KEVIN CARTHY.

Radio Caribe: Ledaweg 35, Brievengat, Willemstad, Curaçao; tel. (9) 736-9555; fax (9) 736-9569; f. 1955; commercial station; programmes in Dutch, English, Spanish and Papiamento; Dir-Gen. C. R. HEILLEGGER.

Radio Curom (Curaçaose Radio-Omroep Vereniging): Roodeweg 64, POB 2169, Willemstad, Curaçao; tel. (9) 462-6586; fax (9) 462-5796; f. 1933; broadcasts in Papiamento; Dir ORLANDO CUALES.

Radiodifusión Boneriana NV: Kaya Gobernador Debrot 2, Kralendijk, Bonaire; tel. 717-8273; fax 717-8220; e-mail vdb@vozdibonaire.com; internet www.vozdibonaire.com; f. 1980; Owner FELICIANO DA SILVA PILOTO.

Alpha FM: broadcasts in Spanish.

Mega FM: broadcasts in Dutch.

Voz di Bonaire (PJB2) (Voice of Bonaire): broadcasts in Papiamento.

Radio Exito: Wolkstraat 15, Willemstad, Curaçao; tel. (9) 462-5577; fax (9) 462-5580.

Radio Hoyer NV: Plasa Horacio Hoyer 21, Willemstad, Curaçao; tel. (9) 461-1678; fax (9) 461-6528; e-mail hoyer@cura.net; internet www.radiohoyer.com; f. 1954; commercial; two stations: Radio Hoyer I (mainly Papiamento, also Spanish) and II (mainly Dutch, also English) in Curaçao; Man. Dir HELEN HOYER.

Radio Korsou FM: Bataljonweg 7, POB 3250, Willemstad, Curaçao; tel. (9) 737-3012; fax (9) 737-2888; e-mail master@korsou.com; internet www.korsou.com; 24 hrs a day; programmes in Papiamento and Dutch; Gen. Man. ALAN H. EVERTSZ.

Laser 101 (101.1 FM): tel. (9) 737-7139; fax (9) 737-5215; e-mail master@laser101.com; internet www.laser101.fm; 24 hours a day; music; English and Papiamento; Gen. Man. ALAN H. EVERTSZ.

Radio Paradise: ITC Bldg, Piscadera Bay, POB 6103, Curaçao; tel. (9) 463-6103; fax (9) 463-6404; Man. Dir J. A. VISSER.

Radio Tropical: Willemstad, Curaçao; Dir DWIGHT RUDOLPHINA.

Ritme FM (PJB4): broadcasts in Dutch.

Trans World Radio (TWR): Kaya Gouverneur N. Debrotweg 64, Kralendijk, Bonaire; tel. 717-8800; fax 717-8808; e-mail 800am@twr.org; internet www.twrbonaire.com; f. 1964; religious, educational and cultural station; programmes to South, Central and North America, Caribbean in six languages; Pres. Dr DAVID TUCKER, Jr; Station Dir RICHARD FULLER.

Voice of St Maarten (PJD2 Radio): Plaza 21, Backstreet, POB 366, Philipsburg, St Maarten; tel. 542-2580; fax 542-4905; also operates PJD3 on FM (24 hrs); commercial; programmes in English; Gen. Man. DON R. HUGHES.

Voice of Saba (PJF1): The Bottom, POB 1, Saba; studio in St Maarten; tel. 546-3213; also operates The Voice of Saba FM; Man. MAX W. NICHOLSON.

There is a relay station for Radio Nederland on Bonaire.

Television

Antilliaanse Televisie Mij NV (Antilles Television Co): Berg Arraret, POB 415, Willemstad, Curaçao; tel. (9) 461-1288; fax (9) 461-4138; f. 1960; operates Tele-Curaçao (fmrly operated Tele-Aruba); commercial; govt-owned; also operates cable service, offering programmes from US satellite television and two Venezuelan channels; Dir JOSÉ M. CIJNTJE; Gen. Man. NORMAN K. RICHARDS.

Leeward Broadcasting Corporation—Television: Philipsburg, St Maarten; tel. (5) 23491; transmissions for approx. 10 hours daily.

Five television channels can be received on Curaçao, in total. Relay stations provide Bonaire with programmes from Curaçao, St Maarten with programmes from Puerto Rico, and Saba and St Eustatius with programmes from St Maarten and neighbouring islands. Curaçao has a publicly owned cable television service, TDS.

Finance

(cap. = capital; res = reserves; dep. = deposits; m. = million; brs = branches; amounts in Netherlands Antilles guilders unless otherwise stated)

BANKING

Central Bank

Bank van de Nederlandse Antillen (Bank of the Netherlands Antilles): Simon Bolivar Plein 1, Willemstad, Curaçao; tel. (9) 434-5500; fax (9) 461-5004; e-mail info@centralbank.an; internet centralbank.an; f. 1828 as Curaçaosche Bank, name changed as above 1962; cap. 30.0m., res 111.4m., dep. 688.6m. (Dec. 2002); Chair. RALPH PALM; Pres. Dr EMSLEY D. TROMP; 2 brs on St Maarten and Bonaire.

Commercial Banks

Banco di Caribe NV: Schottegatweg Oost 205, POB 3785, Willemstad, Curaçao; tel. (9) 432-3000; fax (9) 461-5220; e-mail info@bancodicaribe.com; internet www.bancodicaribe.com; f. 1973; dep. 941.4m., total assets 1,025.3m. (Dec. 2004); Chair. W.J. CURIEL; CEO and Gen. Man. Dir E. DE KORT; Dir K. ABRAHAM; 5 brs.

Banco Mercantil CA (Banco Universal): Abraham de Veerstraat 1, POB 565, Willemstad, Curaçao; tel. (9) 461-8241; fax (9) 461-1824; f. 1988; Gen. Man. FRANK GIRIGORI.

Banco de Venezuela NV: POB 131, c/o Amicorp NV, Bronsweg 8A, Willemstad, Curaçao; tel. (9) 434-3500; fax (9) 434-3533; f. 1993; Man. Dirs H. P. F. VON AESCH, R. YANES, V.E. BORBERG.

Bank of Nova Scotia NV (Canada): Backstreet 64, POB 303, Philipsburg, St Maarten; tel. 542-3317; fax 542-2562; f. 1969; Man. ROBERT G. JUDD.

Barclays Bank plc (United Kingdom): 29 Front St, POB 941, Philipsburg, St Maarten; tel. 542-3511; fax 542-4531; f. 1959; Man. EDWARD ARMOGAN (offices in Saba and St Eustatius).

Chase Manhattan Bank NA (USA): Chase Financial Center, Vlaun Bldg, Cannegieter Rd (Pondfill) and Mullet Bay Hotel, POB 921, Philipsburg, St Maarten; tel. 542-3726; fax 542-3692; f. 1971; Gen. Man. K. BUTLER.

CITCO Banking Corporation NV: Kaya Flamboyan 9, POB 707, Willemstad, Curaçao; tel. (9) 732-2322; fax (9) 732-2330; e-mail cbc@citco.com; f. 1980 as Curaçao Banking Corpn NV; Man. Dir and Gen. Man. R. F. IRAUSQUIN; Man. Dir A. A. HART.

FirstCaribbean International Bank (Curaçao) NV: De Ruyterkade 61, POB 3144, Willemstad, Curaçao; tel. (9) 433-8000; fax (9) 433-8198; e-mail bank.curacao@firstcaribbeanbank.com; internet www.firstcaribbeanbank.an; f. 1964 as ABN AMRO Bank NV; part of FirstCaribbean Group, based in Barbados; Man. Dir W. M. VAN DER BERG; 6 brs.

Fortis Bank (Curaçao) NV: Berg Arrarat 1, POB 3889, Willemstad, Curaçao; tel. (9) 463-9300; fax (9) 461-3769; internet www.fortisbank.com; f. 1952 as Pierson, Heldring and Pierson (Curaçao) NV; became Meespierson (Curaçao) NV in 1993, name changed as above in 2000; international banking/trust company; Man. Dir GREGORY ELIAS.

Giro Curaçao NV: Scharlooweg 35, Willemstad, Curaçao; tel. (9) 433-9999; fax (9) 461-7861; Gen. Dir L. C. BERGMAN; Financial Dir H. L. MARTHA.

ING Bank NV (Internationale Nederlanden Bank NV): Kaya W. F. G. (Jombi) Mensing 14, POB 3895, Willemstad, Curaçao; tel. (9) 732-7000; fax (9) 732-7502; f. 1989 as Nederlandse Middenstandsbank NV; name changed as above 1992; Gen. Man. MARK SCHNEIDERS.

Maduro & Curiel's Bank NV: Plaza Jojo Correa 2–4, POB 305, Willemstad, Curaçao; tel. (9) 466-1100; fax (9) 466-1130; e-mail info@mcb-bank.com; internet www.mcb-bank.com; f. 1916 as NV Maduro's Bank; merged with Curiel's Bank in 1931; affiliated with Bank of Nova Scotia NV, Toronto; cap. 50.2m., res 119.3m., dep. 3,079.7m. (Dec. 2003); Chair. N. D. HENRÍQUEZ; Man. Dirs WILLIAM H. L. FABRO, RON GOMES CASSERES; 25 brs.

Orco Bank NV: Dr Henry Fergusonweg 10, POB 4928, Willemstad, Curaçao; tel. (9) 737-2000; fax (9) 737-6741; e-mail info@orcobank.com; internet www.orcobank.com; f. 1986; cap. 30.7m., res 27.5m., dep. 523.9m. (Dec. 1999); Chair. E. L. GARCIA; Man. Dir I. D. SIMON; 1 br.

Rabobank Curaçao NV: Zeelandia Office Park, Kaya W. F. G. (Jombi), Mensing 14, POB 3876, Willemstad, Curaçao; tel. (9) 465-2011; fax (9) 465-2066; e-mail l.an.curacao.ops@rabobank.com; internet www.rabobank.com; f. 1978; cap. US $53.0m., res US $17.8m., dep. US $4,535.2m. (Dec. 2003); Chair. S. SCHAT; Gen. Man. J. S. KLEP.

RBTT Bank NV: Kaya Flamboyan 1, Willemstad; tel. (9) 763-8000; fax (9) 763-8449; e-mail info@tt.rbtt.com; internet www.rbtt.com; f. 1997 as Antilles Banking Corpn; name changed to RBTT Bank Antilles in 2001; name changed as above in 2002; Pres. RODNEY S. PRASAD; Chair. PETER J. JULY; 4 brs.

SFT Bank NV: Schottegatweg Oost 44, POB 707, Willemstad, Curaçao; tel. (9) 732-2900; fax (9) 732-2902.

Windward Islands Bank Ltd: Clem Labega Sq. 7, POB 220, Philipsburg, St Maarten; tel. 542-2313; fax 542-4761; affiliated to Maduro and Curiel's Bank NV; f. 1960; cap. and res 3.6m., dep. 53.6m. (Dec. 1984); Man. Dirs VICTOR P. HENRÍQUEZ, W. G. H. STRIJBOSCH.

'Offshore' Banks
(without permission to operate locally)

Abu Dhabi International Bank NV: Kaya W. F. G. (Jombi), Mensing 36, POB 3141, Willemstad, Curaçao; tel. (9) 461-1299; fax (9) 461-5392; internet www.adibwash.com; f. 1981; cap. US $20.0m., res $30.4m., dep. $329.3m. (Dec. 2001); Pres. QAMBARAL MULLA; Man. Dir NAGY S. KOLTA.

Banco Caracas NV: Kaya W. F. G. (Jombi) Mensing 36, POB 3141, Willemstad, Curaçao; tel. (9) 461-1299; fax (9) 461-5392; f. 1984; Pres. GEORGE L. REEVES.

Banco Consolidado NV: Handelskrade 12, POB 3141, Willemstad, Curaçao; tel. (9) 461-3423; f. 1978.

Banco Latino NV: De Ruyterkade 61, POB 785, Willemstad, Curaçao; tel. (9) 461-2987; fax (9) 461-6163; f. 1978; cap. US $25.0m., res $12.3m., dep. $450.8m. (Nov. 1992); Chair. Dr GUSTAVO GÓMEZ LÓPEZ; Pres. FOLCO FALCHI.

Banco Provincial Overseas NV: Santa Rosaweg 51–55, POB 5312, Willemstad, Curaçao; tel. (9) 737-6011; fax (9) 737-6346; Man. E. SUARES.

Banque Artesia Curaçao NV: Castorweg 22–24, POB 155, Willemstad, Curaçao; tel. (9) 461-8061; fax (9) 461-5151; f. 1976 as Banque Paribas Curaçao NV; name changed as above 1998.

Caribbean American Bank NV: POB 6087, TM1 10, WTC Bldg, Piscadera Bay, Willemstad, Curaçao; tel. (9) 463-6380; fax (9) 463-6556; Man. Dir Dr MARCO TULIO HENRÍQUEZ.

First Curaçao International Bank NV: Office Park Zeelandia, Kaya W. F. G. (Jombi) Mensing 18, POB 299, Willemstad, Curaçao; tel. (9) 737-2100; fax (9) 737-2018; f. 1973; cap. and res US $55m., dep. $244m. (1988); Pres. and CEO J. CH. DEUSS; Man. M. NEUMAN-ROUIRA.

FirstCaribbean International Wealth Management (Curaçao) NV: De Ruyterkade 61, Curaçao; tel. (9) 433-8361; fax (9) 433-8360; f. 1976 as ABN AMRO Bank Asset Management (Curaçao) NV; acquired by FirstCaribbean Bank in Dec. 2005; Man. Dir E. J. W. HERMENS.

F. Van Lanschot Bankiers (Curaçao) NV: Schottegatweg Oost 32, POB 4799, Willemstad, Curaçao; tel. (9) 737-1011; fax (9) 737-1086; f. 1962; Man. A. VAN GEEST.

Toronto Dominion (Curaçao) NV: c/o SCRIBA NV, Polarisweg 31–33, POB 703, Willemstad, Curaçao; tel. (9) 461-3199; fax (9) 461-1099; f. 1981; Man. E. L. GOULDING.

Union Bancaire Privée (TDB): J. B. Gorsiraweg 14, POB 3889, Willemstad, Curaçao; tel. (9) 463-9300; fax (9) 461-4129.

Other 'offshore' banks in the Netherlands Antilles include American Express Overseas Credit Corporation NV, Banco Aliado NV, Banco del Orinoco NV, Banco Mercantil Venezolano NV, Banco Principal NV, Banco Provincial International NV, Banunion NV, CFM Bank NV, Citco Banking Corporation NV, Compagnie Bancaire des Antilles NV, Deutsche Bank Finance NV, Ebna Bank NV, Exprinter International Bank NV, Integra Bank NV, Lavoro Bank Overseas NV, Lombard-Atlantic Bank NV, Middenbank (Curaçao) NV, Netherlands Caribbean Bank NV, Noro Bank NV, Premier Bank International NV.

Development Banks

Ontwikkelingsbank van de Nederlandse Antillen NV: Schottegatweg Oost 3C, POB 267, Willemstad, Curaçao; tel. (9) 747-3000; fax (9) 747-3320; e-mail obna@curinfo.an; f. 1981.

Stichting Korporashon pa Desaroyo di Korsou (KORPDEKO): Breedestraat 29C, POB 656, Willemstad, Curaçao; tel. (9) 461-6699; fax (9) 461-3013.

Other Banks

Postspaarbank van de Nederlandse Antillen: Waaigatplein 7, Willemstad, Curaçao; tel. (9) 461-1126; fax (9) 461-7561; f. 1905; post office savings bank; Chair. H. J. J. VICTORIA; cap. 21m.; 20 brs.

Spaar- en Beleenbank van Curaçao NV: MCB Salinja Bldg, Schottegatweg Oost 130, Willemstad, Curaçao; tel. (9) 466-1585; fax (9) 466-1590.

There are also several mortgage banks and credit unions.

Banking Associations

Association of International Bankers in the Netherlands Antilles (IBNA): Chumaceiro Blvd 3, POB 220, Curaçao; tel. (9) 461-5367; fax (9) 461-5369; e-mail info@ibna.an; internet www.ibna.an; f. 1980; 32 mems; Pres. HANS F. C. BLANKVOORT.

Bonaire Bankers' Association: POB 288, Kralendijk, Bonaire.

Curaçao Bankers' Association (CBA): A. M. Chumaceiro Blvd 3, Willemstad, Curaçao; tel. (9) 465-2486; fax (9) 465-2476; e-mail florisela.bentoera@an.rbtt.com; f. 1972; Pres. RODNEY PRASAD; Sec. FLORISELA BENTOERA.

Federashon di Kooperativanan di Spar i Kredito Antiyano (Fekoskan): Curaçaostraat 50, Willemstad, Curaçao; tel. (9) 462-3676; fax (9) 462-4995; e-mail fekoskan@attglobal.net.

International Bankers' Association in the Netherlands Antilles: Scharlooweg 55, Willemstad, Curaçao.

The Windward Islands Bankers' Association: Clem Labega Sq., Philipsburg, St Maarten; tel. 542-2313; fax 542-4761.

INSURANCE

Amersfoortse Antillen NV: Kaya W. F. G. Mensing 19, Willemstad, Curaçao; tel. (9) 461-6399; fax (9) 461-6709.

Aseguro di Kooperativa Antiyano (ASKA) NV: Scharlooweg 15, Willemstad, Curaçao; tel. (9) 461-7765; fax (9) 461-5991; accident and health, motor vehicle, property.

Ennia Caribe Schaden NV: J. B. Gorsiraweg 6, POB 581, Willemstad, Curaçao; tel. (9) 434-3800; fax (9) 434-3873; e-mail mail@ennia.com; f. 1948; general; life insurance as Ennia Caribe Leven NV; Pres. DONALD BAKHUIS; Man. Dir ALBARTUS WILLEMSEN.

ING Fatum: Cas Coraweg 2, Willemstad, Curaçao; tel. (9) 777-7777; fax (9) 461-2023; f. 1904; property insurance.

MCB Group Insurance NV: MCB Bldg Scharloo, Scharloo, Willemstad, Curaçao; tel. (9) 466-1370; fax (9) 466-1327.

Netherlands Antilles and Aruba Assurance Company (NA&A) NV: Pietermaai 135, Willemstad, Curaçao; tel. (9) 465-7146; fax (9) 461-6520; accident and health, motor vehicle, property.

Seguros Antilliano NV: S. b. N. Doormanweg/Reigerweg 5, Willemstad, Curaçao; tel. (9) 736-6877; fax (9) 736-5794; general.

A number of foreign companies also have offices in Curaçao, mainly British, Canadian, Dutch and US firms.

Insurance Association

Insurance Association of the Netherlands Antilles (NAVV): c/o Ing Fatum, Cas Coraweg 2, POB 3002, Willemstad, Curaçao; tel. (9) 777-7777; fax (9) 736-9658; Pres. R. C. MARTINA-JOE.

Trade and Industry

DEVELOPMENT ORGANIZATIONS

Curaçao Industrial and International Trade Development Company NV (CURINDE): Emancipatie Blvd 7, Landhuis Koninsplein, Curaçao; tel. (9) 737-6000; fax (9) 737-1336; e-mail info@curinde.com; internet www.curinde.com; f. 1980; state-owned; manages the harbor free zone, the airport free zone and the industrial zone; Man. Dir E. R. SMEULDERS.

Foreign Investment Agency Curaçao (FIAC): Scharlooweg 174, Curaçao; tel. (9) 465-7044; fax (9) 461-5788; e-mail fiac@curinfo.an.

World Trade Center Curaçao: POB 6005, Piscadera Bay, Curaçao; tel. (9) 463-6100; fax (9) 462-4408; e-mail info@wtccuracao.com; internet www.wtccuracao.com; Man. Dir JOSÉ VICENTE SANCHES PIÑA.

CHAMBERS OF COMMERCE

Bonaire Chamber of Commerce and Industry: Princess Mariestraat, POB 52, Kralendijk, Bonaire; tel. 717-5595; fax 717-8995.

Curaçao Chamber of Commerce and Industry: Kaya Junior Salas 1, POB 10, Willemstad, Curaçao; tel. (9) 461-3918; fax (9) 461-5652; e-mail businessinfo@curacao-chamber.an; internet www.curacao-chamber.an; f. 1884; Chair. RUUD THUIS; Exec. Dir JOHN JACOBS.

St Maarten Chamber of Commerce and Industry: C. A. Cannegieterstraat 11, POB 454, Philipsburg, St Maarten; tel. 542-3590; fax 542-3512; e-mail coci@sintmaarten.net; f. 1979; Exec. Dir J. M. ARRINDELL VAN WINDT.

INDUSTRIAL AND TRADE ASSOCIATIONS

Association of Industrialists of the Netherlands Antilles (ASINA): Kaya Junior Salas 1, Willemstad, Curaçao; tel. (9) 461-2353; fax (9) 465-8040; e-mail asina@cura.net; f. 1981; Pres. E. ZIMMERMAN.

Bonaire Trade and Industry Assen (Vereniging Bedrijfsleven Bonaire): POB 371, Kralendijk, Bonaire.

Curaçao Exporters' Association (CEA): c/o Seawings NV, Maduro Plaza z/n CEA, POB 6049, Curaçao; tel. (9) 733-1591; fax (9) 733-1599; e-mail albert.elens@seawings-curacao.com; f. 1903; Dir ALBERT ELENS.

Curaçao International Financial Services Assen (CIFA): Chumaceiro Blvd 3, POB 220, Curaçao; tel. (9) 461-5371; fax (9) 461-5378; e-mail info@cifa.an; internet www.cifa.an; Chair. HERMAN J. BEHR.

Curaçao Trade and Industry Assen (Vereniging Bedrijfsleven Curaçao—VBC): Kaya Junior Salas 1, POB 49, Willemstad, Curaçao; tel. (9) 461-1210; fax (9) 461-5652; e-mail vbc1@cura.net; f. 1944; Pres. B. KOOYMAN; Exec. Dir R. P. J. LIEUW.

UTILITIES

Electricity and Water

Aqualectra Production NV (KAE): Rector Zwijsenstraat 1, POB 2097, Curaçao; tel. (9) 433-2200; fax (9) 462-6685; e-mail mgmt@aqualectra.com; internet www.aqualectra.com; present name adopted in 2001 following the restructuring of Curaçao's energy sector; Dir S. MARTINA.

GEBE NV: Pond Fill, W. J. A. Nisbeth Rd, POB 123, St Maarten; tel. 542-2213; fax 542-4810; f. 1961; Man. Dir J. A. LAMBERT.

Water & Energiebedrijf Bonaire (WEB) NV: Carlos Nicolaas 3, Kralendijk; tel. 717-8244.

TRADE UNIONS

Algemene Bond van Overheidspersoneel (ABVO) (General Union of Civil Servants): POB 3604, Willemstad, Curaçao; tel. (9) 737-6097; fax (9) 737-3145; e-mail abvo_na@cura.net; internet www.abvo-informa.org; f. 1936; Pres. ROLAND H. IGNACIO; Sec. W. E. CALMES; 4,000 mems.

Algemene Federatie van Bonaireaanse Werknemers (AFBW): Kralendijk, Bonaire.

Central General di Trahado di Corsow (CGTC) (General Headquarters for Workers of Curaçao): POB 2078, Willemstad, Curaçao; tel. (9) 737-6097; fax (9) 737-3145; e-mail abvo-na@cura.net; f. 1949; Sec.-Gen. ROLAND H. IGNACIO.

Curaçaosche Federatie van Werknemers (Curaçao Federation of Workers): Schouwburgweg 44, Willemstad, Curaçao; f. 1964; Pres. WILFRED SPENCER; Sec.-Gen. RONCHI ISENIA; 204 affiliated unions; about 2,000 mems.

Federashon Bonaireana di Trabou (FEDEBON): Kaya Krabè 6, Nikiboko, POB 324, Bonaire; tel. and fax 717-8845; Pres. GEROLD BERNABELA.

Petroleum Workers' Federation of Curaçao: Willemstad, Curaçao; tel. (9) 737-0255; fax (9) 737-5250; affiliated to Int. Petroleum and Chemical Workers' Fed; f. 1955; Pres. R. G. GIJSBERTHA; approx. 1,500 mems.

Sentral di Sindikatonan di Korsou (SSK) (Confederation of Curaçao Trade Unions): Schouwburgweg 44, POB 3036, Willemstad; tel. (9) 737-0794; 6,000 mems.

Sindikato di Trahado den Edukashon na Korsou (SITEK) (Curaçao Schoolteachers' Trade Union): Landhuis Stenen Koraal, Willemstad, Curaçao; tel. (9) 468-2902; fax (9) 469-0552; 1,234 mems.

Windward Islands' Federation of Labour (WIFOL): Pond Fill, Long Wall Rd, POB 1097, St Maarten; tel. 542-2797; fax 542-6631; e-mail wifol@sintmaarten.net; Pres. THEOPHILUS THOMPSON.

Transport

RAILWAYS

There are no railways.

ROADS

All the islands have a good system of all-weather roads. There were 590 km of roads in 1992, of which 300 km were paved.

SHIPPING

Curaçao is an important centre for the refining and transhipment of Venezuelan and Middle Eastern petroleum. Willemstad is served by the Schottegat harbour, set in a wide bay with a long channel and deep water. Facilities for handling containerized traffic at Willemstad were inaugurated in 1984. A Mega Cruise Facility, with capacity for the largest cruise ships, has been constructed on the Otrobanda side of St Anna Bay. Ports at Bullen Bay and Caracas Bay also serve Curaçao. St Maarten is one of the Caribbean's leading ports for visits by cruise ships and in January 2001 new pier facilities were opened which could accommodate up to four cruise ships and add more cargo space. Each of the other islands has a good harbour, except for Saba, which has one inlet, equipped with a large pier. In May 2002 the Netherlands provided NA Fl. 9.6m. for the repair of Saba's port, which sustained severe hurricane damage in 1999. Many foreign shipping lines call at ports in the Netherlands Antilles.

Curaçao Ports Authority: Werf de Wilde, POB 3266, Willemstad, Curaçao; tel. (9) 461-4422; fax (9) 461-3907; e-mail cpamanag@cura.net; internet curports.com; Man. Dir RICHARD LÓPEZ-RAMÍREZ.

Curaçao Shipping Association (SVC): c/o Dammers & van der Heide (Antilles) Inc, Kaya Flamboyan 11, Willemstad, Curaçao; tel. (9) 737-0600; fax (9) 737-3875; Pres. K. PONSEN.

St Maarten Ports Authority: J. Yrausquin Blvd, POB 146, Philipsburg, St Maarten; tel. 542-2307; fax 542-5048; e-mail smpa1shh@sintmaarten.net; internet www.portofstmaarten.com; Man. Dir KEITH FRANCA.

Principal Shipping Companies

Caribbean Cargo Services NV: Jan Thiel w/n, POB 442, Willemstad, Curaçao; tel. (9) 467-2588.

Curaçao Dry-dock Co Inc: POB 3012, Curaçao; tel. (9) 733-0000; fax (9) 736-5580; e-mail marketing@cdmnv.com; internet www.cdmnv.com; f. 1958; Man. Dir MARIO RAYMOND EVERTSZ.

Curaçao Ports Authority (CPA) NV: Werf de Wilde z/n, POB 689, Curaçao; tel. (9) 434-5999; fax (9) 461-3907; e-mail cpamanag@cura.net; internet www.curports.com; Man. Dir RICHARD LÓPEZ-RAMÍREZ.

Curaçao Ports Services Inc NV (CPS): Curaçao Container Terminal, POB 170, Curaçao; tel. (9) 461-5079; fax (9) 461-6536; e-mail cps@ibm.net; Man. Dir KAREL JAN O. ASTER.

Dammers & van der Heide, Shipping and Trading (Antilles) Inc: Kaya Flamboyan 11, POB 3018, Willemstad, Curaçao; tel. (9) 737-0600; fax (9) 737-3875; e-mail general@dammers-curacao.com; internet www.dammers-curacao.com; f. 1964; Man. Dir J. J. PONSEN.

Gomez Transport NV: Zeelandia, Willemstad, Curaçao; tel. (9) 461-5260; fax (9) 461-3358; e-mail gomez-shipping@ibm.net; Man. FERNANDO DA COSTA GÓMEZ.

Hal Antillen NV: De Ruyterkade 63, POB 812, Curaçao.

Intermodal Container Services NV: Fokkerweg 30, Willemstad, POB 3747, Curaçao; tel. (9) 461-3330; fax (9) 461-3432; Mans A. R. BEAUJON, N. N. HARMS.

Kroonvlag Curaçao NV: Maduro Plaza, POB 231, Curaçao; tel. (9) 737-6900; fax (9) 737-1266; e-mail hekro@cura.net.

Lagendijk Maritime Services: POB 3481, Curaçao; tel. (9) 465-5766; fax (9) 465-5998; e-mail ims@ibm.net.

S. E. L. Maduro & Sons (Curaçao) Inc: Maduro Plaza, POB 3304, Willemstad, Curaçao; tel. (9) 733-1501; fax (9) 733-1506; e-mail hmeijer@madurosons.com; Man. Dir H. MEIJER; Vice-Pres. R. CORSEN.

St Maarten Port Services: POB 270, Philipsburg, St Maarten; tel. 542-2304.

Anthony Veder & Co NV: Zeelandia, POB 3677, Curaçao; tel. (9) 461-4700; fax (9) 461-2576; e-mail anveder@ibm.net; Man. Dir JOOP VAN VLIET.

CIVIL AVIATION

There are international airports at Curaçao (Dr Albert Plesman, or Hato, 12 km from Willemstad), Bonaire (Flamingo Field) and St Maarten (Princess Juliana, 16 km from Philipsburg); and airfields for inter-island flights at St Eustatius and Saba. In 1998 a free trade zone was inaugurated at the international airport on Curaçao. The second phase of a US $118m. project to expand Princess Juliana Airport commenced in June 2004. Financing was secured for the construction of new passenger terminal building at Dr Albert Plesman Airport in September 2003. The national carrier of the Netherlands Antilles, known as Dutch Caribbean Airlines (DCA) from 2002, was declared bankrupt in late 2004.

Windward Islands Airways International (WIA—Winair) NV: Princess Juliana Airport, POB 2088, Philipsburg, St Maarten; tel. 545-2568; fax 545-4229; e-mail info@fly-winair.com; internet www.fly-winair.com; f. 1961; govt-owned since 1974; scheduled and charter flights throughout north-eastern Caribbean; Man. Dir EDWIN HODGE.

Tourism

Tourism is a major industry on all the islands. The principal attractions for tourists are the white, sandy beaches, marine wildlife and diving facilities. There are marine parks in the waters around Curaçao, Bonaire and Saba. The numerous historic sites are of interest to visitors. The largest number of tourists visit St Maarten, Curaçao and Bonaire. In 2004 stop-over visitors totalled some 779,325 (of whom 61.0% were on St Maarten). In the same year 1,621,178 cruise-ship passengers visited St Maarten, Curaçao and Bonaire (of whom 83.2% were on St Maarten).

Tourism Corporation Bonaire (TCB): Kaya Grandi 2, Kralendijk, Bonaire; tel. 717-8322; fax 717-8408; e-mail info@tourismbonaire.com; internet www.infobonaire.com; Dir RONELLA CROES.

Curaçao Tourism Development Bureau (CTDB): Pietermaai 19, POB 3266, Willemstad, Curaçao; tel. (9) 434-8200; fax (9) 461-2305; e-mail info@ctbd.net; internet www.curacao-tourism.com; f. 1989; Dir JAMES HEPPLE.

Saba Tourist Office: Windwardside, POB 527, Saba; tel. 416-2231; fax 416-2350; e-mail iluvsaba@unspoiledqueen.com; internet www.sabatourism.com; Dir GLENN C. HOLM.

St Eustatius Tourist Office: Fort Oranje Straat z/n, Oranjestad, St Eustatius; tel. and fax 318-2433; e-mail euxtour@goldenrock.net; internet www.statiatourism.com; Dir ALIDA FRANCIS.

St Maarten Tourist Bureau: Vineyard Office Park, W. G. Buncamper Rd 33, Philipsburg, St Maarten; tel. 5422-337; fax 542-2734; e-mail info@st-maarten.com; internet www.st-maarten.com; Dir REGINA LA BEGA.

HOTEL ASSOCIATIONS

Bonaire Hotel and Tourism Association: Kralendijk, Bonaire; e-mail info@bonhata.org; internet www.bonhata.org; Man. Dir JACK CHALK.

Curaçao Hospitality and Tourism Association (CHATA): POB 6115, Kurason Komèrsio, Curaçao; tel. (9) 465-1005; fax (9) 465-1052; e-mail information@chata.org; internet www.chata.org; f. 1967 as Curaçao Hotel Asscn; Pres. ROLF SPRECHER.

St Maarten Hospitality and Trade Association: W. J. A. Nisbeth Rd 33A, POB 486, Philipsburg, St Maarten; tel. 542-0108; fax 542-0107; e-mail info@shta.com; internet www.shta.com; Pres. EMIL LEE.

NEW ZEALAND

Introductory Survey

Location, Climate, Language, Religion, Flag, Capital

The Dominion of New Zealand lies in the South Pacific Ocean, about 1,750 km (1,100 miles) south-east of Australia. It consists of North Island and South Island, separated by the narrow Cook Strait, and several smaller islands, including Stewart Island (or Rakiura) in the south. The climate is temperate and moist, with an average temperature of 12°C (52°F), except in the far north, where higher temperatures are reached. The official language is English, but the indigenous Maori inhabitants (an estimated 14.1% of the total population at the census of March 2001) also use their own language. At the 2001 census, 15.7% of respondents professed adherence to the Anglican Church, 13.0% being Roman Catholics and 11.5% Presbyterians. The national flag (proportions 1 by 2) is dark blue, with a representation of the United Kingdom flag as a canton in the upper hoist. In the fly are four five-pointed red stars, edged in white, in the form of the Southern Cross constellation. The capital is Wellington, on North Island.

Recent History

New Zealand is a former British colony. It became a dominion, under the British Crown, in 1907 and achieved full independence by the Statute of Westminster, adopted by the British Parliament in 1931 and accepted by New Zealand in 1947.

In 1962 Western Samoa (now Samoa, q.v.), formerly administered by New Zealand, achieved independence, and in 1965 the Cook Islands attained full internal self-government, but retained many links, including common citizenship, with New Zealand. In October 1974 Niue, one of New Zealand's island territories, obtained similar status 'in free association with New Zealand'. New Zealand retains two Dependent Territories, Ross Dependency and Tokelau (see the chapter on New Zealand's Dependent Territories).

In December 1972 the first Labour Government for more than 12 years came to power, under the leadership of Norman Kirk, after a succession of New Zealand National Party administrations. The New Zealand Labour Party took office at a time when the economy was thriving, mainly as a result of a sharp increase in international prices for agricultural commodities. However, this prosperity was accompanied by inflation. Higher domestic demand and the international energy crisis of 1973–74 led to a rapid rise in imports, a reduction in exchange reserves and a severe balance-of-payments problem. The Labour Government's foreign policy was more independent than that of its predecessors. It phased out New Zealand's military commitments under the South-East Asia Treaty Organization and established diplomatic relations with the People's Republic of China.

Norman Kirk died in August 1974, and Wallace Rowling, hitherto Minister of Finance, became Prime Minister in September. The economic recession worsened, and in November 1975 a general election resulted in victory for the National Party, which won 55 of the 87 seats in the House of Representatives, while the Labour Party took the remaining 32 seats. The new Government, under Robert (later Sir Robert) Muldoon, who had led the National Party since July 1974, introduced austere economic policies, and in 1976 reduced the annual intake of migrants from 30,000 to 5,000, while conducting a campaign against illegal immigrants.

New Zealand continued to suffer a very low rate of economic growth and increasing unemployment. Popular dissatisfaction with Muldoon's sometimes controversial leadership was reflected at the general election in November 1978. The National Party retained power, with 50 of the 92 seats in the enlarged House of Representatives, but its share of the total vote fell from 47.2% in 1975 to 39.8%. Labour won more votes (40.4% of the total) but fewer seats (41). The Social Credit Party received 17.1% of the total votes, compared with only 7.4% in 1975, but obtained only one seat. In the November 1981 election Muldoon's majority was further reduced. The National Party won 47 of the 92 seats in the House, while Labour, which again received more votes, won 43 seats and Social Credit (despite obtaining 20.6% of votes cast) only two.

In February 1984 Muldoon's Government antagonized New Zealand's trade unions by effecting legislation to ban 'closed shop' agreements with employers, thus giving employees the right to choose whether or not to join a trade union. Further legislation was used in June to compel striking construction workers to return to work. In the same month, faced with dissent within his own party, Muldoon called an early general election for July. The Labour Party obtained 43% of the total votes and secured 56 of the 95 seats in an enlarged House of Representatives, while the National Party, with 36% of the votes, took 37 seats: it was thought that the National Party had lost considerable support to the newly formed New Zealand Party, a right-wing party which won 12.3% of the votes (but no seats) after campaigning for a minimum of government intervention in the economy. David Lange (the leader of the Labour Party since February 1983) became Prime Minister. James McLay, who had been deputy leader of the National Party since March 1984, defeated Muldoon in an election for the leadership of the party in November 1984, but he was replaced as party leader by his deputy, James (Jim) Bolger, in March 1986.

The Labour Government introduced controversial deregulatory measures to improve the country's economic situation. The initial success of these measures, together with widespread popular support for the Government's anti-nuclear policy (see below), contributed to a second victory for the Labour Party in a general election in August 1987. Of the 97 seats in the enlarged House of Representatives, the Labour Party secured 58, and the National Party 39. (The Democratic Party lost both the seats that its predecessor, the Social Credit Party, had won at the 1984 election.) Of the votes cast, the Labour Party received 47.4%, and the National Party 42.8%.

In 1987 Lange's Government initiated a controversial policy of 'privatization' of state-owned enterprises. In November 1988 policy disagreements prompted Lange to dismiss the minister responsible for the privatization programme, Richard Prebble. Lange was accused by cabinet colleagues of acting without consultation, and in December Roger (later Sir Roger) Douglas, the Minister of Finance, declared that he would not serve another term under Lange. Douglas was promptly dismissed from office, and later that month unsuccessfully challenged Lange for the leadership of the Labour Party. In May 1989 the formation of the NewLabour Party (led by a former president of the Labour Party, Jim Anderton) was announced: the party aimed to appeal to disillusioned Labour supporters. In early August Douglas was elected by Labour MPs to a vacant cabinet post, thus prompting Lange to resign. Shortly afterwards, Geoffrey Palmer, hitherto the deputy leader of the Labour Party, was elected the Labour Party's parliamentary leader and Prime Minister.

In January 1990 Palmer undertook a wide-ranging government reshuffle. The return of Richard Prebble to the Cabinet, in his former post as Minister for State-Owned Enterprises, provoked considerable anger within the Labour Party. The Government aroused further hostility by its introduction of a substantial fee for tertiary-level students. The continued sale of state assets, especially that of the telecommunications company, Telecom, was also unpopular. In September 1990, less than eight weeks before the next general election, Palmer resigned as Prime Minister. Public opinion polls had indicated that Labour, under his leadership, had lost support to the National Party, and members of the Cabinet had consequently urged him to resign. Michael Moore, the Minister of External Relations and Trade (who had also contested the August 1989 leadership election), replaced Palmer as Prime Minister and Labour Party leader. Moore promised to act promptly to avert the enormous budget deficit forecast for 1991/92 and, two weeks later, he secured an agreement with the country's trade union leaders regarding restricted pay settlements. In October 1990, none the less, the National Party won 47.8% of the votes at the general election, taking 67 of the 97 seats in the House of Representatives. The Labour Party, with 35.1% of the votes, won 29 seats, while the NewLabour Party retained its sole seat, obtaining 5.2% of the votes. Jim Bolger, as leader of the National Party, thus became

Prime Minister at the head of a Government that promised to continue Labour's strict budgetary and monetary controls. The sale of state assets would also continue.

In November 1990 the new Government's first economic proposals were outlined. They included the repeal of legislation on equal pay for women, and envisaged reductions in public spending, particularly in the field of social welfare. In December the Government announced measures that entailed proposed reductions in unemployment benefit, family benefits, and in medical and sickness payments, and prepared for the introduction of a system whereby users of medical and educational services (hitherto provided free of charge) would be required to pay, according to a means test. These measures were received with anger by social and church groups. Protest marches took place in April 1991, and plans for a 'freeze' in the levels of old-age pensions prompted groups representing the elderly unsuccessfully to petition the British monarch (through the Governor-General) to dismiss the Government. Two National Party members of the House of Representatives resigned from the party in August, in protest against the proposals, and the Minister of Maori Affairs, Winston Peters (who had openly criticized the Government's economic strategy), was dismissed in October. In November Sir Robert Muldoon announced that he would resign from the legislature in early 1992, in protest against the Government's economic policies. Earlier in the month criticism had prompted the Government to withdraw its stringent means-testing measures for the allocation of state pensions, but the overall level of payments remained lower than previously.

In December 1991 a coalition was formed by minor parties as a challenge to the two main parties. The grouping, known as the Alliance, consisted of the NewLabour Party, the New Zealand Democratic Party, the Green Party of Aotearoa—New Zealand and Mana Motuhake. In its first electoral test (the by-election in February 1992 that had been precipitated by Muldoon's resignation) the Alliance campaigned for the provision of education and health care free of charge and the return to the public sector of 'privatized' state assets. The National Party retained the seat in the by-election, but with a greatly reduced majority. The Alliance secured 38% of the votes, only 5% less than the National Party.

In September 1992 a preliminary referendum on proposed electoral reform was held. The electorate voted overwhelmingly in favour of the abolition of the 'first-past-the-post' system and for its replacement by a form of proportional representation; of the four alternatives offered, the mixed member proportional (MMP) system (similar to that used in Germany) received the greatest support. The new rules were to be implemented at the 1996 election, following a second, binding referendum.

In March 1993 the outspoken Winston Peters, who had continued to embarrass the Government, resigned from his parliamentary seat in order to stand for re-election as an independent candidate. The by-election in April resulted in an overwhelming victory for Peters, the major political parties having declined to present candidates. In July Peters established New Zealand First, and announced that the party would contest all 99 seats at the forthcoming general election.

At the election, held on 6 November 1993, the National Party, which had campaigned mainly on the Government's record of economic recovery, was narrowly returned to office, receiving 35.2% of the total votes cast and securing 50 seats in the House of Representatives. The Labour Party, with 34.7% of the votes, won 45 seats, the Alliance two and New Zealand First two. At a concurrent, second referendum on electoral reform, 54% of voters favoured the adoption of the MMP system. A new Government was appointed in late November.

In October 1994 Peter Dunne, a former cabinet minister, resigned from the Labour Party, following differences over the party's policy on taxation, and declared his intention to remain in the House of Representatives as an independent member. He subsequently established a new party, Future New Zealand. The traditional two-party system was further challenged in early 1995, when support for ACT New Zealand, co-founded by Sir Roger Douglas (reformist Minister of Finance in 1984–88), who had recently announced his return to politics, began to increase rapidly. In June 1995, however, the position of the ruling party was strengthened by the formation of United New Zealand by seven members of the House of Representatives (four National, two Labour and the leader of Future New Zealand, Peter Dunne). The new grouping pledged its support for the Government on issues of confidence. In February, for the first time since the early 1930s, a formal coalition Government was established when the National Party formed an official alliance with United New Zealand. In the ensuing government reorganization, Peter Dunne joined the Cabinet as Minister of Revenue and Internal Affairs. As a result of a number of parliamentary defections and realignments, by April 1996 the number of parliamentary seats held by the National Party had been reduced to 41. In March, meanwhile, Sir Michael Hardie Boys replaced Dame Catherine Tizard as Governor-General.

The first general election under the MMP system was held on 12 October 1996. No party achieved an outright majority. The National Party, with 34.1% of the votes, won 44 of the 120 seats in the expanded House of Representatives, the Labour Party (28.3%) secured 37 seats and New Zealand First (13.1%) garnered 17 seats, while the Alliance won 13 seats, ACT New Zealand eight and United New Zealand one. A notable development was the increase in the number of Maori MPs from six to 15, a figure almost equivalent to the proportion of Maori (the country's aboriginal inhabitants) in the population as a whole. Although the election result initially appeared to favour the formation of a centre-left coalition under the leadership of Helen Clark, complex negotiations finally led to the establishment in December of an alliance between the National Party and New Zealand First, led by Winston Peters.

Jim Bolger thus continued as Prime Minister, while Winston Peters was appointed Deputy Prime Minister and Treasurer, the latter newly created post carrying responsibility for the drafting of the country's budget. Although Peters had previously discounted the possibility of a reconciliation and of entering into a coalition with the National Party, he had unexpectedly altered his stance in exchange for concessions on economic policy. The incoming Cabinet incorporated a total of five members of New Zealand First. Don McKinnon of the National Party retained the foreign affairs portfolio, and Bill Birch continued to hold nominal responsibility for finance.

In September 1997 proposals for the introduction of a compulsory retirement savings scheme were overwhelmingly rejected by the electorate in a referendum. The holding of the referendum had been a condition of New Zealand First's participation in the ruling coalition, but the Prime Minister had also actively supported the proposed pension reforms. In the following month thousands of protesters took to the streets to demand the resignation of the Government, the latter's policies on health and education having drawn particular criticism.

In November 1997, following a leadership challenge from Jenny Shipley, a cabinet minister whose portfolios now included transport and women's affairs, the Prime Minister announced his intention to resign. Shipley was thus sworn in as New Zealand's first woman Prime Minister in December, reiterating the National Party's commitment to a continuation of the partnership with New Zealand First. In the ensuing government reorganization, most supporters of Jim Bolger retained their portfolios but were downgraded. Winston Peters continued as Deputy Prime Minister, while other members of New Zealand First also remained in the Cabinet.

In November 1997, meanwhile, following the Alliance's rejection of a Greens' proposal to establish a coalition arrangement, the Green Party of Aotearoa decided that at the next general election it would stand as a separate political party but would remain a member of the Alliance until that time. In January 1998 the Liberal Party announced that it was to be dissolved and would merge with the Alliance.

In May 1998 the outcome of a parliamentary by-election to fill the seat vacated by Jim Bolger confirmed the electorate's growing disillusionment with the coalition Government. Although the seat was retained by the National Party, its majority was decimated. In August, following an acrimonious dispute regarding the sale of the Government's stake in Wellington airport, Winston Peters was dismissed from the post of Deputy Prime Minister and Treasurer and the dissolution of the coalition Government was announced. Rejecting demands for an early general election, Jenny Shipley reallocated many cabinet portfolios. Although Tau Henare (who in late 1998 founded a new party, Mauri Pacific, having been removed as deputy leader of New Zealand First in July), the Minister of Maori Affairs, was the only former New Zealand First minister to retain his post within the Cabinet, three other erstwhile members of the National Party's former coalition partner remained as ministers outside the Cabinet. Despite the defection of Winston Peters to the opposition, the Prime Minister was able to secure the support of eight of the 16 New Zealand First representatives in the legislature, and in September she survived a vote of confidence in the House. In the same month, in an attempt to raise public concern over the social effects of government policy, in particular the plight of low-income families, the Anglican Church initiated an ecumenical 'Hikoi of Hope', in which protesters from both ends of the country marched to Wellington and converged upon the House of Representatives.

In December 1998 the minority Government's position was further weakened by the unexpected resignation of a supporting independent (and former New Zealand First) MP, following the administration's decision to proceed with its acquisition of 28 F-16 fighter aircraft from the USA. (The contract to lease the aircraft, however, was cancelled in March 2000 by the new Labour Government.) The Prime Minister was placed under further pressure in early 1999, when it was alleged that the Minister of Tourism, Murray McCully, had acted inappropriately with regard to the handling of a major contract for the advertising business of the New Zealand Tourism Board. In February, as the Prime Minister became personally implicated in the affair and as opposition MPs accused her of deliberately misleading the legislature over her association with the head of the advertising agency in question, the Government won a motion of 'no confidence' by 61 votes to 59. Claiming that the ruling party had intended to exploit its links with the agency during the next general election campaign, the Labour Party demanded an inquiry into the Government's alleged payments to departing members of the New Zealand Tourism Board and into the Board's expenditure on overseas promotions. In March the $NZ53m. marketing contract with the agency was terminated. McCully relinquished the tourism portfolio in April.

At the general election, conducted on 27 November 1999, the opposition Labour Party won the largest share of votes cast. A recount of votes in one constituency, where the Green Party candidate then unexpectedly took the seat from the incumbent National MP, combined with the incorporation of 'special votes' (which included those cast by New Zealanders overseas), led to a substantial modification of the initial results. Having secured 38.7% of the votes cast, the Labour Party was finally allocated 49 of the 120 seats in the House of Representatives, while the National Party, which had won 30.5% of the votes, received 39 seats. The Alliance was allocated 10 seats and ACT New Zealand nine seats. Under the recently-introduced system of proportional representation, the Green Party's victory in the one constituency automatically entitled the movement to a further six seats in the legislature. New Zealand First's representation declined to five seats; the party's leader, Winston Peters, only narrowly retained his seat. United New Zealand took the one remaining seat. Having previously discounted any co-operation with the Green Party, the Labour Party was thus obliged to seek the support not only of the Alliance but also of the seven Green MPs.

The leader of the Labour Party, Helen Clark (who had served as Deputy Prime Minister in 1989–90), thus became Prime Minister. The minority Government, which incorporated several members of the Alliance, took office in December 1999. Jim Anderton, the leader of the Alliance, was appointed Deputy Prime Minister, Minister for Economic Development and Minister for Industry and Regional Development. The treasury and finance portfolios were assigned to Dr Michael Cullen, while Phil Goff became Minister of Foreign Affairs and Trade and also assumed responsibility for the justice portfolio.

In a non-binding, citizen-initiated referendum held on the same day as the general election, a majority of voters favoured a reduction in the number of members of the House of Representatives from 120 to 99; voters also favoured a reform of the criminal justice system, including the placing of greater emphasis on the needs of victims of crime.

One of the new Government's stated priorities was the 'Closing the Gaps' initiative, which aimed to address the socio-economic disparities between the Maori and non-Maori communities, particularly in health, housing, education, income and the incidence of crime. Among its first actions were the repeal of the Employment Contracts Act, the restoration of the state monopoly in the provision of accident compensation and the cancellation of the contract to lease 28 F-16 fighter aircraft from the USA. The new Government was strongly criticized by opposition politicians and accused of racism, following its decision in mid-2000 to sell a 25% share of a lucrative radiowaves company (which auctions high frequency radio positions to telecommunications companies) to a Maori trust under its 'Closing the Gaps' policy.

In June 2000 the Prime Minister was obliged to dismiss the Minister of Maori Affairs, Dover Samuels, following allegations of sexual misconduct. On 4 April 2001 Dame Silvia Cartwright (New Zealand's first female High Court Judge) took office as Governor-General. Her appointment represented a significant achievement for women in New Zealand public life, and created an unprecedented situation in which the five most important public roles in the country (those of Prime Minister, Leader of the Opposition, Attorney-General, Chief Justice and Governor-General) were all occupied by women.

In October 2001 Jenny Shipley resigned as leader of the National Party and was replaced by Bill English, a former Minister of Health. The incoming leader renamed the party the New National Party. In December Jim Anderton was placed under considerable pressure from left-wing members of the Alliance to withdraw his support for the Government's military involvement in Afghanistan, following the Prime Minister's confirmation that New Zealand Hercules transport aircraft had landed in Afghanistan, to assist in the US-led military campaign there (see the chapter on Afghanistan). In early April 2002, after months of wrangling, the Alliance split. Anderton and six other members of the party agreed to form a breakaway party, later named the Progressive Coalition, but continued to support the ruling coalition. The seven members of the legislature were expelled from the Alliance in late April. At the same time Laila Harré, Minister of Women's Affairs, Youth Affairs and Statistics, succeeded Anderton as leader of the Alliance and confirmed her support for the Government until the next legislative elections. In June the Prime Minister announced that the next general election was to be held earlier than planned, in late July, largely owing to the collapse of the Alliance, and a dispute between the Labour Party and the Greens over the Government's decision not to renew a moratorium banning the commercial release of genetically modified organisms (which expired in October 2003).

In April 2002, following extensive consultations, the Government announced the proposed replacement of the monarch's Privy Council (based in London, United Kingdom) as New Zealand's court of final appeal by an independent Supreme Court, consisting of five judges headed by the Chief Justice. The requisite legislation was passed in October 2003; the new court began functioning in July 2004.

Some 77% of the registered voters participated in the general election, which took place on 27 July 2002. The Labour Party won 41% of the party votes, thereby securing a second term in office. The party failed, however, to secure an overall majority in the House of Representatives, winning 52 of the 120 seats. New Zealand First received 10% of the vote (13 seats); ACT New Zealand 7% (nine seats); the Greens 7% (nine seats) and United Future New Zealand 7% (eight seats). The Progressive Coalition won 1.7% of the party votes and secured two seats, while the Alliance failed to secure any parliamentary representation. The National Party performed badly at the election, winning only 21% of the party votes; its representation declined by 12 seats to 27. Clark, unable to reach an agreement with the Greens on the issue of genetically modified organisms, formed a minority coalition Government with the Progressive Coalition. The Labour Party leader secured the support of United Future New Zealand. In May 2003 the Prime Minister carried out a government reorganization.

In June 2003 Clark announced that the Government intended to draw up new legislation to ensure that the country's coastline and seabed were owned by the Crown, following a ruling by the Court of Appeal that Maori tribes could pursue their own claims to ownership of the Malborough Sands foreshore and seabed in South Island. Maori attacked the Government's 'draconian' and 'colonialist' actions. In late June the House of Representatives approved the Prostitution Reform Bill, which decriminalized prostitution and provided a legal framework for the sex industry. In October the legislature voted overwhelmingly in favour of the Anti-Terrorism Act, which extended the powers of the police force. The act, an extension of the 2002 Terrorism Suppression Act, created new offences including: improperly dealing with nuclear and radioactive materials; causing the infection of animals; contaminating products, such as food and water; and harbouring a terrorist. The Green Party opposed the legislation, claiming that the law would infringe upon civil liberties.

In February 2004 the Minister of Commerce and of Immigration, Lianne Dalziel, was forced to resign after it transpired that she had lied over the disclosure to the media of a document relating to the deportation of a Sri Lankan youth. The Prime Minister ordered an inquiry into the obtaining by Dalziel of a confidential legal document and into officials' involvement in its subsequent circulation. A cabinet reshuffle was subsequently effected. Meanwhile, in the same month the new leader of the opposition National Party, Don Brash, a former governor of the central bank, announced that if he won power he would discontinue all forms of positive discrimination for Maori, considering the 'special privileges' to be unnecessary and divisive. Brash also pledged to abolish the parliamentary seats reserved for Maori and to repeal 'divisive, race-based' legislation. Clark accused Brash of creating disharmony by breaking the national consensus on dealing with Maori affairs; nevertheless, two days later she promised a review of state assistance for Maori, agreeing that policies should be based on need and not on any perceived privilege. In the February government reorganization, Clark also created the post of Co-ordinating Minister for Race Relations after opinion polls showed a decline in support for her administration over its policies towards the Maori. The portfolio was assigned to the Minister of Education, of State Services, and for Sport and Recreation, Trevor Mallard; he was given the immediate responsibility of conducting a full review of government policy.

In April 2004 the Progressive Coalition renamed itself the Progressive Party. In the same month Clark dismissed the Associate Minister of Maori Affairs, Tariana Turia, after Turia stated that she intended to vote against the Government's Seabed and Foreshore Bill, which ensured that coastal areas were owned by the Crown, on the grounds that the new legislation was in contravention of the rights of indigenous Maori. Following her dismissal, in the following month Turia resigned from the Labour Party and the House of Representatives. In May the Prime Minister secured a narrow victory in a vote of 'no confidence' precipitated by Turia's resignation. Meanwhile, a two-week hikoi (protest march) against the planned legislation, which had commenced in mid-April, arrived outside Parliament in Wellington.

In July 2004 Tariana Turia secured victory in a by-election to the seat of Te Tai Hauauru on North Island, necessitated by her resignation from the House of Representatives in the previous month. Turia was the candidate of the newly formed Maori Party. In November the controversial Seabed and Foreshore Bill was finally passed by the House of Representatives, with the Government securing a narrow victory in the vote owing to the support of New Zealand First. In the same month the Minister of Youth Affairs, for Land Information and of Statistics, John Tamihere, resigned following the revelation that a report on his activities had been sent to the Serious Fraud Office for investigation. In the following month a major government reorganization was announced, in which Tamihere's portfolios were reassigned. The appointments came into effect in February 2005, when Attorney-General Margaret Wilson left the Cabinet in order to succeed Jonathan Hunt as Speaker of the House of Representatives. Deputy Prime Minister Michael Cullen became the new Attorney-General, while retaining his existing portfolios. In March the Serious Fraud Office announced that, following its investigation, it did not intend to charge Tamihere with any offence.

In May 2005 Minister of Fisheries David Benson-Pope resigned from his cabinet post, following the commencement of a police inquiry into allegations that he had abused children during his former career as a teacher. He was, however, reinstated to the Cabinet in the following month. In July Prime Minister Helen Clark announced that a general election would take place in September. At the election, which was held on 17 September, Clark's Labour Party secured victory by a narrow margin, winning 41.1% of the vote and 50 seats, compared with 39.1% of the vote and 48 seats for the National Party, which had improved significantly on its performance at the 2002 election. The newly formed Maori Party secured 2.1% of the vote, winning four of the seven seats reserved for Maoris. As the Labour Party had failed to gain an overall majority, it subsequently entered into a coalition with the Progressive Party, which had won only one seat. With the support of New Zealand First and United Future New Zealand, secured on a more informal basis, this brought the total number of seats controlled by the Government in the new legislature to 61.

In October 2005 the new Government was sworn in. Controversial New Zealand First leader Winston Peters was appointed Minister of Foreign Affairs, while Peter Dunne was allocated the revenue portfolio, but with the unusual provision that both would remain outside the Cabinet. The appointment of Peters met with widespread criticism, owing largely to his anti-immigration views. In March 2006 David Parker, who had been appointed to the post of Attorney-General in the new Government, resigned from the position, having admitted that he had made an error while filing an annual return for a company with which he was involved. He retained the cabinet portfolios of energy and transport, however. Deputy Prime Minister Michael Cullen subsequently became Attorney-General for the second time, holding the post concurrently with the finance and tertiary education portfolios. Meanwhile, in the same month Maj.-Gen. Jerry Mateparae, hitherto Chief of the Army, became the first Maori to be appointed Chief of the New Zealand Defence Force; he took up the position in May. In April it was announced that Anand Satyanand, a retired judge of Indo-Fijian descent, was to replace Dame Silvia Cartwright as Governor-General upon the expiry of her term of office in August 2006.

During 1987, meanwhile, there were protests by the Maori concerning their cultural and economic rights and, in particular, their claims to land in accordance with the Treaty of Waitangi, concluded in 1840 by the British Government and Maori leaders, whereby sovereignty had been ceded to the United Kingdom in return for the Maori people's retention of hunting and fishing grounds. In November 1987 a ruling by the Waitangi Tribunal, reconvened in 1975 to consider retrospectively the claims of Maori land rights activists, recommended the restoration of an Auckland harbour headland to the Maori people. By 1994 about 75% of the country was subject to land claims by Maori groups. In December of that year the Government offered the sum of $NZ1,000m., payable over a 10-year period from September 1992, in full and final settlement of outstanding claims for compensation. The condition that all future land claims be renounced, however, was rejected by most Maori groups. In the same month an historic agreement between the Government and the Tainui people of Waikato provided for the return of land confiscated in 1863 and for the deposit over a period of five years of $NZ65m. in a land acquisition trust.

In May 1995 the Prime Minister and the Queen of the Tainui people signed an agreement relating to a full and final settlement, valued at $NZ170m., of land grievances dating back to 1863. Increasing ethnic tension, however, was demonstrated by the destruction in September 1995 of an old school building by Maori protesters involved in a land dispute and by the burning down in October of an historic church, known as the 'Maori Cathedral', at Otaki, in an apparent retaliatory arson attack by white extremists. In November, in a significant ceremony in Wellington, Queen Elizabeth II gave her personal assent to the legislation ending the Tainui grievances when she signed the Waikato Raupatu Claims Settlement Act, which implemented the $NZ170m. agreement, including the return of 15,780 ha of land, and which incorporated an apology from the Crown for the loss of lives and for the confiscation of property. A final settlement payment of $NZ13m. was made to the Tainui tribe in late 2000. In October 1996, as more modest agreements continued to be reached, the Government announced a $NZ170m. provisional settlement with the South Island's Ngai Tahu (one of New Zealand's smallest Maori tribes) regarding the group's long-standing claim for compensation. In early 1997 Maori leaders, pursuing a claim first lodged by tribal advocates in 1991, embarked upon a lawsuit aimed at the official alteration of New Zealand's name to Aotearoa ('Land of the Long White Cloud').

In July 1997 a Maori tribe that had been driven off its land in the 1840s lodged a claim to the site of the Parliament building in Wellington. The Ngati Tama also presented claims to other areas of the capital, while declaring their willingness to negotiate. At a ceremony in Wellington in September 1997, following six years of negotiations, the Government and the Ngai Tahu reached a formal agreement, subject to approval by the tribe's members, regarding the compensation of $NZ170m. The Government's offer also included the right to name mountains and rivers, often in combination with the English equivalents, and incorporated a full apology from the Crown. In November, the tribal beneficiaries having voted overwhelmingly in favour of the arrangements, the historic deed of full and final settlement was signed by the Prime Minister and representatives of the Ngai Tahu. In March 1998 the Ngai Tahu Claims Settlement Bill was duly submitted to the House of Representatives, where it received approval six months later. In July, exercising for the first time its power of compulsory recommendation, the Waitangi Tribunal ordered the Government to return to the Ngati Turangitukua land (now valued at $NZ6.1m.) which had been confiscated from its Maori owners more than 30 years previously to permit the construction of housing for workers engaged on an electric power project in the central North Island. In early 2000 a joint land claim was lodged by five Maori tribes of the central North Island. With the forestry claim alone worth an estimated $NZ588m., the application was potentially the largest ever submitted to the Waitangi Tribunal. In March 2001 the Ngati Ruanui became the first Taranaki tribe to conclude a deed of settlement with the Government, amounting to $NZ41m. In early 2003 the Ngati Awa voted in favour of a treaty settlement with the Government, which included an apology from the Crown, the return of 64 ha of land and $NZ42m. In August 2005 Prime Minister Helen Clark announced that all Maori land claims under the Treaty of Waitangi would have to be filed by 1 September 2008, in order that they could be settled by 2020. The announcement constituted one of the Labour Party's election pledges, in advance of the general election scheduled to take place in the following month.

In response to Maori grievances over fishing rights, the Government introduced, in 1988, a Maori Fisheries Bill, under the provisions of which 2.5% of current fishing quotas were to be restored to the Maori people annually for the following 19 years. However, Maori activists alleged that the proposed legislation was racially discriminatory, since it stipulated that no other Maori fishing claim would be considered by the Waitangi Tribunal until the 19 years had elapsed. The bill was also condemned by some white New Zealanders, as, if implemented as proposed, it would guarantee the Maori people about 50% of the country's entire fishing rights by the year 2008. In August 1992, finding that the Government had failed to honour its obligations under the Treaty of 1840, the Waitangi Tribunal recommended that ownership of most of the fisheries of South Island be transferred to the Ngai Tahu. In November 1992, in the hope of reaching a permanent settlement, the Government advanced the sum of $NZ150m. to a Maori consortium to enable the latter's purchase of a 50% stake in the country's biggest inshore fishing company. In early 1996 the Treaty of Waitangi Fisheries Commission, established to resolve the issue of the allocation among Maori of resources valued at $NZ200m., had yet to deliver its recommendations. In April the Court of Appeal declared that, despite having no coastline, urban Maori constituted an *iwi* (tribe) and were therefore directly entitled to a share of these fishery assets. The case was subsequently referred to the Privy Council in London. Its decision, announced in January 1997, overruled the Court of Appeal's definition of an *iwi*. In mid-1998 the Waitangi Tribunal ruled that urban Maori without blood ties should be accorded similar negotiating rights to those of traditional *iwi*. The historic decision thus acknowledged urban Maori trusts as modern tribes. In August, however, a High Court judge ruled in favour of traditional Maori tribes, effectively declaring that urban Maori groups had no claim to fishery assets. In October 1999, furthermore, the urban Maori claim was rejected by the Court of Appeal. In June 2004 it was reported that Maori tribes had been offered 20% of all new aquaculture or marine farming areas and 20% of aquaculture areas that had been allocated since 1992 in an attempt to resolve the 1992 fisheries settlement. The offer was believed to be, in part, an inducement to Maori to accept the controversial Seabed and Foreshore Bill (see above).

In April 1997 urban Maori were outraged at a proposal by the Treaty of Waitangi Fisheries Commission to allocate up to $NZ300m. of fishery assets on a tribal basis, rather than according to *iwi* size as the populous northern tribes demanded. The Ngai Tahu and other *iwi*, meanwhile, argued that the length of coastline and traditional fishing grounds should determine the allocation of assets. In early 1998, following an incident in late 1997 when a fishing boat reportedly landed several metric tons of snapper without commercial quota rights, it was announced that new regulations were to govern the management of 'customary' fishing by *tangata whenua* (people of the land), whereby Maori are permitted to take an unlimited amount of seafood provided that it is not for pecuniary gain.

From 1984 the Lange Government's pledge to ban from New Zealand's ports all vessels believed to be carrying nuclear weapons or powered by nuclear energy caused considerable strain in the country's relations with Australia and the USA, its partners in the ANZUS military pact (see p. 395). The ban was duly imposed in February 1985. In July 1986 the US Government announced its intention to devise new, bilateral defence arrangements with Australia, and in August the USA's military obligations to New Zealand under the ANZUS Treaty were formally suspended. In February 1987 the US Government announced its decision not to renew a 1982 memorandum of understanding (due to be renegotiated in June of that year), whereby New Zealand was able to purchase military equipment from the USA at favourable prices. The Lange Government subsequently defined a new defence strategy, based on increased self-reliance for the country's military forces. In June 1987 legislation banning nuclear-armed ships was formally enacted by the House of Representatives, despite strong opposition from the National Party. In September 1989 New Zealand agreed the terms for a joint venture with Australia to build as many as 12 naval frigates to patrol the South Pacific. The decision proved to be very contentious because of the high costs and because of allegations that the Government was succumbing to political pressure from Australia to return to the ANZUS alliance and abandon its independent anti-nuclear stance. In March 1990 the opposition National Party announced its support for the anti-nuclear policy, a position that it retained after its election to office in October.

Following the US Government's decision, in September 1991, to remove nuclear weapons from surface naval vessels, Bolger announced that his administration would reconsider the law banning visits from nuclear-armed and nuclear-propelled warships. The review would focus on the nuclear propulsion ban, which was seen as the obstacle to a renegotiated alliance with Australia and the USA. In July 1992 the USA announced that its warships no longer carried tactical nuclear weapons. In December the report commissioned by the Prime Minister was released. The committee of scientists concluded that the dangers of permitting nuclear-powered vessels to enter New Zealand waters were minimal. Despite these findings, no immediate change to the anti-nuclear legislation was envisaged. In February 1994 the Prime Minister welcomed the US decision to resume senior-level contacts with New Zealand, suspended since 1985. As relations continued to improve, in December 1994 the USA announced that nuclear-armed warships would not be dispatched to New Zealand, thus acknowledging the latter's ban. In August 1998, during a visit by the US Secretary of State, the Prime Minister of New Zealand strongly reiterated her country's long-standing ban on visits by nuclear-armed or nuclear-powered vessels. In July 2005 a private member's bill proposing the removal of the ban was rejected by a large majority by the House of Representatives. Following his attendance at the summit meeting of the Asia-Pacific Economic Co-operation (APEC) forum held in Auckland in September 1999, President Bill Clinton announced the end of the 14-year ban on New Zealand's participation in military exercises with the USA, in preparation for the dispatch of a multinational peace-keeping force to East Timor (now Timor-Leste—q.v.), of which New Zealand troops were to form part.

Meanwhile, New Zealand's trading relations with the USA were strained during 1999 by the latter's imposition of tariffs on imports of New Zealand lamb. However, in December 2000 the World Trade Organization (WTO, see p. 370) ruled in favour of New Zealand's case against the tariffs, and upheld the decision when the USA appealed against the ruling. The Prime Minister visited the USA in March 2002 for a series of meetings with the US President, Secretary of State and other senior officials, raising hopes among members of New Zealand's business community that a free-trade agreement between the two nations could be achieved, despite New Zealand's adherence to its anti-nuclear policy.

The Government quickly expressed support for the USA following the suicide attacks of 11 September 2001 and offered to share intelligence in the effort to combat terrorism. In October the administration provided troops from the Special Air Service (SAS) for the US-led military campaign against the al-Qa'ida (Base) organization, held principally responsible for the attacks, and its Taliban hosts in Afghanistan. US policy in the 'war on terror', however, was a source of concern in New Zealand. In 2003, during the build-up to the US-led military campaign to remove the regime of Saddam Hussain in Iraq, the Government stated that it would favour action in Iraq only through the UN, a stance that was popularly supported in New Zealand. Relations with the US Administration were affected as a result. This was unlikely to help New Zealand's attempts to achieve a free-trade agreement between the two nations. In May Prime Minister Clark warned the USA and the United Kingdom that by invading Iraq without the endorsement of a UN resolution, they had set a dangerous precedent, and that they might later regret unleashing the 'law of the jungle', particularly as China was set to become a dominant world power. New Zealand, however, decided to provide humanitarian support for Iraq and sent a team of army engineers and defence force staff to assist in the rehabilitation of the country once the UN authorized reconstruction efforts following the ousting of Saddam Hussain. The Government had already sent forces to Afghanistan to assist in the reconstruction there and in March 2004 agreed to send SAS troops back to the South Asian country to take part in the search for senior al-Qa'ida leaders. In February 2005 the Prime Minister announced that the New Zealand Defence Force would remain in Afghanistan for a further year from September, when the deployment had been originally scheduled to end.

In July 1985 the *Rainbow Warrior*, the flagship of the anti-nuclear environmentalist group, Greenpeace (which was to have led a flotilla to Mururoa Atoll, in French Polynesia, to protest against France's testing of nuclear weapons in the South Pacific), was blown up and sunk in Auckland Harbour. One member of the crew was killed as a result of the explosion. Two agents of the French secret service were tried for manslaughter in November and sentenced to 10 years' imprisonment, initially in Auckland. The French Government made repeated requests for the release or repatriation of the agents, and in July 1986 the two Governments eventually reached an agreement, whereby the agents were to be transferred to detention on Hao Atoll, in French Polynesia, for three years. The French Government made a formal apology for its part in the sabotage operation, and paid the New Zealand Government $NZ7m. in compensation. By May 1988, however, both the agents had been taken back to France, ostensibly for medical reasons. When neither agent was returned to the atoll, Lange referred the matter to the UN: in May 1990 an arbitration panel ruled that France's repatriation of the agents constituted a substantial violation of the 1986 agreement, but it announced that the agents would not be required to return to Hao Atoll. France agreed to pay an initial US $2m. into a joint fund intended to foster close and friendly relations between the two countries. In April 1991 the French Prime Minister, Michel Rocard, visited New Zealand and again apologized for the sinking of the *Rainbow Warrior*, while reiterating that French testing of nuclear weapons in the Pacific was to continue. However, relations between the two countries deteriorated in July, following the French Government's announcement that it had conferred an honour for distinguished service on one of the two agents responsible for the sabotage of the *Rainbow Warrior*. The issue re-emerged in November, when a third French agent, also suspected of involvement in the 1985 incident, was arrested, at New Zealand's instigation, in Switzerland. In December 1991, however, the New Zealand Government decided against seeking the man's extradition, on the grounds that the case was now considered to be closed. In July 2005 an article in a French newspaper confirmed that the sinking of the *Rainbow Warrior* had been authorized by the then French President, François Mitterrand. France announced the suspension of its nuclear testing in the South Pacific in April 1992. In May 1993 the first French warship to visit New Zealand since 1985 entered Auckland Harbour. (Similarly, in June 1995 the first British warship to visit New Zealand for 12 years arrived in Wellington.)

In June 1995 President Chirac's announcement that France was to resume its nuclear-testing programme in the South Pacific aroused international condemnation. New Zealand suspended military relations with France, and the New Zealand ambassador to Paris was recalled. In August, in response to public pressure, the New Zealand Government dispatched a naval research vessel to the test area. The first in the new series of tests was carried out in early September. Later in the month the International Court of Justice ruled that it could not reopen New Zealand's case against France, brought in 1973. France's continuation of its testing programme, in defiance of world opinion, was a major issue at the Commonwealth heads of government meeting held in Auckland in November 1995. New Zealand's relations with the United Kingdom were strained by the British Prime Minister's apparent support for France's position; upon his arrival in Auckland, thousands of anti-nuclear demonstrators took to the streets to express their outrage. In March 1996 (the French tests having been concluded) France, the United Kingdom and the USA finally acceded to the South Pacific Nuclear-Free Zone Treaty (Treaty of Rarotonga—Pacific Islands Forum, see p. 352), thus opening the way to improved relations with New Zealand and other Pacific nations. In October 1997, following a two-day official visit to Paris by the New Zealand Prime Minister, the resumption of normal relations with France was declared.

Although New Zealand's trade with the People's Republic of China is of increasing significance, relations have been strained by the issue of China's nuclear-testing programme. Relations were further strained in September 1996 when the Dalai Lama, the exiled spiritual leader of Tibet, paid a four-day visit to New Zealand, where he was welcomed by the Prime Minister. In September 1997, however, the New Zealand Deputy Prime Minister expressed support for China's bid to join the WTO. In November 1998 New Zealand's decision to accord Taiwanese government officials similar privileges to those granted to representatives of the People's Republic provoked serious concern in China. During a visit to China in July 1999, however, the Prime Minister of New Zealand reaffirmed her country's support for the 'one China' policy. An official visit to China by the Prime Minister in April 2001 was intended to improve New Zealand's trading position with the country, prior to its accession to the WTO. A senior Chinese official, on a diplomatic tour of the Asia-Pacific region, met with New Zealand's Deputy Prime Minister in April 2002, when New Zealand reconfirmed its 'one China' policy.

New Zealand remained committed to its aim of the global elimination of all nuclear weapons, and in November 1996 was a co-sponsor of a UN resolution, overwhelmingly adopted by the General Assembly, to promote the establishment of a nuclear-weapons-free southern hemisphere. In December the Deputy Prime Minister of New Zealand announced that the Government was to finance a lawsuit against the United Kingdom that was being prepared by former servicemen (and veterans' widows) who had long campaigned for compensation for their exposure to the effects of British hydrogen bomb tests conducted in the South Pacific region in the late 1950s. In January 1997 New Zealand lodged a strong protest with the Japanese Government regarding the proposed route of a ship transporting nuclear waste to Japan from France. In March 1998 the New Zealand Prime Minister travelled to Japan, the first official visit by the country's head of government for 22 years. Relations with Japan, however, continued to be strained by a fishing dispute relating to Japan's perceived failure to conserve stocks of southern bluefin tuna, as agreed in a treaty of 1993, of which Australia was also a signatory. (In July 1998, following a protest to Japan's ambassador in Wellington, New Zealand closed its ports to all Japanese tuna-fishing vessels.) In August 1999 an international tribunal ruled in favour of New Zealand and Australia. In early 2000, the Labour Party's commitment to the protection of the environment having been reaffirmed, the new Government of New Zealand became embroiled in a further dispute with Japan, this time relating to the latter's controversial whaling programme. The Prime Minister, Helen Clark, announced her intention to raise the issue with Japan on an official visit to that country in April 2001, and expressed her Government's desire to pursue proposals for a southern seas whale sanctuary through the International Whaling Commission (see p. 378). In December 2000 New Zealand reiterated its opposition to nuclear waste shipments in response to the news that a shipment of high-level waste had left the United Kingdom for Japan, warning that the vessel must not enter New Zealand's exclusive economic zone. In October of that year New Zealand had ratified the Waigani Convention (signed by all South Pacific Forum members in 1995, except Marshall Islands and Tuvalu), which bans the export of hazardous and radioactive waste to the Pacific Islands.

Meanwhile, New Zealand continued to play an active role in Pacific island affairs. In 1997, in the quest for peace in Papua New Guinea, it participated in a peace-keeping force on the secessionist island of Bougainville. New Zealand hosted discussions between the Papua New Guinea Government and representatives of the secessionist movement, and in January 1998 a permanent ceasefire agreement was signed in Christchurch. The agreement was successfully implemented at the end of April. New Zealand strongly condemned the coup in Fiji in May 2000, which led to the overthrow of the Indian-led, elected Government of the country and prompted outbreaks of racially-motivated violence throughout the islands. New Zealand's Minister of Foreign Affairs and Trade, Phil Goff, led a Commonwealth delegation, together with his Australian counterpart, to negotiate with the ethnic militias involved in a coup in Solomon Islands in June 2000. The New Zealand naval frigate, *Te Kaha*, was dispatched to the islands to serve as a venue for peace talks, and the country pledged to contribute to a group of international peace-keepers following the signing of a ceasefire agreement in October. In mid-2003 New Zealand troops joined forces from Australia and several Pacific Islands to provide a peace-keeping force in Solomon Islands.

In September 2001 relations with Australia were strained by the failure of Ansett, the Melbourne-based airline. Ansett's owner, Air New Zealand, had been unable to find a purchaser for the loss-making company, which was therefore placed in receivership. In Melbourne irate Ansett staff blockaded an aircraft upon which the New Zealand Prime Minister was due to travel, and the Australian media demanded a boycott of New Zealand products. Nevertheless, in the same month the New Zealand Government helped Australia to resolve an international crisis, when it agreed to accept up to 150 of the refugees stranded aboard the Norwegian vessel, the *MV Tampa* (see the chapter on Christmas Island). Despite international pressure, neither Australia nor Indonesia (where they had embarked) were willing to accept the asylum-seekers for the duration of the processing of their claims. The Indonesian President, meanwhile, had paid an historic official visit to New Zealand in June 2001.

Following lengthy negotiations, New Zealand established diplomatic relations at ambassadorial level with the Democratic People's Republic of Korea in March 2001.

In July 2004 New Zealand's relations with Israel were strained when two alleged agents from the Israeli secret service, Mossad, were fined and sentenced to six-month prison terms by the Auckland High Court, having been convicted of fraudulently attempting to obtain New Zealand passports. Prime Minister Helen Clark stated that the available evidence strongly suggested that the men were acting as Israeli agents, but that no explanation had been forthcoming from the Israeli Government. New Zealand subsequently suspended senior-level diplomatic contact with Israel, demanding an apology for the incident. In connection with the deterioration in bilateral relations, in July several graves in a Jewish cemetery in Wellington were desecrated, in what was believed to have been the first anti-Semitic attack to take place in the country. In September, having been released from prison early, the Israelis were deported from the country. Relations remained strained into 2005. However, in June of that year the Israeli Government issued a formal apology for the incident, following which cordial diplomatic relations were restored.

As part of her golden jubilee tour of the Commonwealth, Queen Elizabeth II visited New Zealand in February 2002. Having previously stated that New Zealand's eventual transition to a republic was inevitable, the Prime Minister attracted some criticism for her absence from the country on the day of the Queen's arrival. In response to the international condemnation of the conduct of Zimbabwe's presidential election of March 2002, which subsequently led to that country's suspension from the Commonwealth, New Zealand followed the European Union, Canada and the USA in imposing a travel ban on senior members of the Zimbabwe Government in April. New Zealand also announced a ban on sales of armaments to Zimbabwe and that any New Zealand-based assets and investments found to belong to the Zimbabwean President or his associates would be 'frozen'.

Government

Executive power is vested in the British monarch, as Head of State, and is exercisable by an appointed representative, the Governor-General, who must be guided by the advice of the Executive Council (Cabinet), led by the Prime Minister. Legislative power is vested in the unicameral House of Representatives, elected for three years by universal adult suffrage. A system of mixed member proportional representation was introduced at the election of October 1996, when the legislature was expanded to 120 seats: 65 electorate members, including five seats reserved for Maori, and 55 being chosen from party lists (adjusted to 67, six and 53, respectively, at the 1999 election). The Governor-General appoints the Prime Minister and, on the latter's recommendation, other Ministers. The Cabinet is responsible to the House.

Defence

The ANZUS Security Treaty (see p. 395) was signed by New Zealand in 1951. New Zealand also participates in the Five-Power Defence Arrangements with Australia, Malaysia, Singapore and the United Kingdom. The total strength of active forces in August 2005 was 8,660: army 4,430, navy 1,980, air force 2,250. Reserves totalled 10,800. The defence budget for 2004/05 was estimated at $NZ2,010m.

Economic Affairs

In 2004, according to estimates by the World Bank, New Zealand's gross national income (GNI), measured at average 2002–04 prices, was US $82,465m., equivalent to US $20,310 per head (or US $22,130 per head on an international purchasing-power parity basis). During 1995–2004, it was estimated, the population increased at an average annual rate of 1.1%, while gross domestic product (GDP) per head increased, in real terms, by an average of 2.0% per year. Overall GDP increased, in real terms, at an average annual rate of 3.2% in 1995–2004. According to official figures, growth was 4.8% in 2004 and an estimated 2.7% in 2005.

Agriculture (including hunting, fishing and forestry) contributed 6.1% of GDP (in constant prices) in the year ending March 2005. About 7.5% of the employed labour force were engaged in the sector in 2004. The principal crops are barley, wheat and maize. Fruit (particularly kiwi fruit, apples and pears) and vegetables are also cultivated. New Zealand is a major producer of wool, although its significance as a source of export earnings has declined in recent years. In 2005 exports of wool were worth $NZ651m. Meat and dairy products are important, contributing 15.1% and 16.7% of export earnings, respectively, in that year. The forestry industry showed strong expansion in the early 1990s. In 2005 exports of logs and wood totalled $NZ1,914m. (equivalent to 6.2% of total export earnings). The fisheries sector is of increasing significance, exports in 2005 being worth $NZ1,132m. (equivalent to 3.7% of total export earnings). Between 1995/96 and 2004/05 agricultural GDP (including hunting, fishing and forestry) increased by an average of 1.4% per year. Compared with the previous year, agricultural GDP increased by 0.4% in 2003/04, but contracted by 0.8% in 2004/05.

Industry (including mining, manufacturing, construction and utilities) engaged 22.7% of the employed labour force in 2004. The industrial sector provided 23.9% of GDP (at constant prices) in the year ending March 2005. Between 1995/96 and 2004/05 industrial GDP increased at an average annual rate of 2.3%. Compared with the previous year, industrial GDP increased by 2.7% in 2003/04 and by 3.0% in 2004/05.

Mining contributed only 1.0% of GDP in the year ending March 2005, and employed 0.2% of the working population in 2004. New Zealand has substantial coal reserves; petroleum, natural gas, iron, gold and silica are also exploited. A considerable amount of natural gas is used to produce synthetic petrol. In November 2005 Crown Minerals announced that 40 new petroleum blocks in the offshore Great South Basin were to be tendered out to oil exploration companies in 2006. Compared with the previous year, mining GDP contracted by 12.9% in 2003/04, but expanded by 0.2% in 2004/05.

Manufacturing contributed an estimated 15.8% of GDP (at constant prices) in the year ending March 2005. The sector engaged 14.5% of the employed labour force in 2004. The principal branches of manufacturing are food products, printing and publishing, wood and paper products, chemicals, metals and metal products, machinery and transport equipment. Between 1995/96 and 2004/05 manufacturing GDP increased by an average of 1.8% per year. Manufacturing GDP expanded by 1.6% in 2003/04 and by 1.7% in 2004/05.

Energy is derived mainly from domestic supplies of natural gas, petroleum and coal. Hydroelectric power supplied about 60.7% of total energy output in 2002. Imports of petroleum and its products comprised 11.8% of the total value of merchandise imports in 2005.

The services sector provided 70.0% of GDP (in constant prices) in 2004/05. This sector engaged 69.8% of the employed labour force in 2004. In the year ending March 1988 tourism became the single largest source of foreign exchange. Receipts (excluding international air fares) totalled $NZ6,313m. in 2003/04. Visitor arrivals reached 2.38m. in 2005. Between 1995/96 and 2004/05 the GDP of the services sector increased at an average annual rate of 3.8%. Compared with the previous year, it expanded by 4.0% in 2003/04 and by 4.5% in 2004/05.

In 2004 New Zealand recorded a visible trade deficit of US $1,431m., and there was a deficit of US $6,199m. on the current account of the balance of payments. In 2005 the principal sources of imports were Australia (20.6%), Japan (11.0%) and the USA (10.9%), which were also the principal markets for exports in that year (Australia 21.4%, the USA 14.2% and Japan 10.6%). The United Kingdom, other members of the European Union and Asian countries are also important trading partners. The principal exports in 2005 were dairy products, meat, logs, wood and wood articles, mechanical machinery and equipment and fruit. The principal imports were road vehicles and other machinery and transport equipment, petroleum and petroleum products and electrical machinery and equipment.

In the year ending June 2004 an estimated budgetary surplus of $NZ5,300m. was recorded, equivalent to 3.8% of GDP. In March 2004 New Zealand's external debt stood at an estimated $NZ142,100m., of which $NZ18,200m. was official government debt. The average rate of unemployment decreased from 7.5% of the labour force in 1998 to 3.6% in 2005. Annual inflation averaged 1.8% in 1995–2004. Consumer prices increased by 2.3% in 2004 and by 3.1% in 2005.

New Zealand is a member of the Organisation for Economic Co-operation and Development (see p. 320), Asia-Pacific Economic Co-operation (APEC, see p. 164), the Pacific Community (see p. 350), the Pacific Islands Forum (see p. 352) and of the Cairns Group (see p. 435). New Zealand is also a member of the Colombo Plan (see p. 385) and the UN Economic and Social Commission for Asia and the Pacific (ESCAP, see p. 33). In 1982 New Zealand signed an agreement for a 'closer economic relationship' (CER) with Australia; trade barriers between the two countries were eliminated in July 1990.

Upon taking office in late 1999, the minority Labour Government embarked upon a programme of reforms in the health, education and housing sectors. In addition, some $NZ175m. was allocated for projects aimed at the Maori population. These proposals were to be financed by an increase in income tax on those earning more than $NZ60,000 annually. The new Government also planned to curb the programme of transferring state assets to the private sector. Having been sold to private interests in 1989, Air New Zealand was returned to state ownership in late 2001, following heavy financial losses. In October, in an arrangement costing $NZ885m., the Government announced that it was purchasing an 83% stake in the airline, the continued operations of which remained vital to the country's tourism industry. Following strong growth in 2002 and 2003, despite predictions of an economic slowdown in 2004 GDP increased by 4.8%. Expansion was driven by an ongoing improvement in the performance of the tourism industry, and the strength of the construction sector; housebuilding permits continued to increase, despite the negative impact of the decline in net immigration on housing demand. In December 2004 New Zealand's unemployment rate reached a 20-year low of 3.6%, owing to high levels of job creation. Future trade prospects were enhanced by the commencement of negotiations for a free-trade agreement with the People's Republic of China in December 2004. In addition, in April 2005 an agreement for a 'closer economic partnership' (CEP) was concluded with Thailand and in July of that year New Zealand formed a Trans-Pacific Strategic Economic Partnership with Singapore, Chile and Brunei, which resulted in the liberalization of trade with those countries. In an attempt to encourage employees in New Zealand to save more towards their retirement, the budget for 2005/06, announced in May 2005, introduced the 'KiwiSaver' work-based savings scheme, which also included provision for a government subsidy for all first-time home-buyers. Having been returned to power at the general election in September 2005, the minority Labour Government was expected to increase spending on health and education, in line with its election pledges. Economic growth decelerated somewhat in 2005; GDP grew by an estimated 2.7% in that year. GDP growth was expected to slow further, to around 1.7%, in the financial year ending March 2007.

Education

State education is free and, for children between six and 16 years of age, compulsory. Primary education lasts from five to 11 years of age, after which children transfer to secondary schools until a maximum age of 18. As a proportion of children in the relevant age-groups, the enrolment ratios in 1997 were 100% in primary schools and 90% in secondary schools. In July 2004 a total of 450,196 students were enrolled in primary schools and 264,522 in secondary schools. In addition, 39,268 pupils attended composite schools, providing both primary and secondary education. There are eight universities, as well as 20 polytechnics, offering education at the post-secondary level. Changes introduced in 1991 obliged most students to pay part of their fees: parental income is tested to determine the level of allowances. Budgetary expenditure on education by the central Government in the financial year ending 30 June 2004 was estimated at $NZ7,585m., representing 18.2% of total spending.

Public Holidays

2006: 1–2 January (New Year), 6 February (Waitangi Day, anniversary of 1840 treaty), 14–17 April (Easter), 25 April (ANZAC Day, anniversary of 1915 landing at Gallipoli), 5 June (Queen's Official Birthday), 23 October (Labour Day), 25 December (Christmas Day), 26 December (Boxing Day).

2007: 1–2 January (New Year), 6 February (Waitangi Day, anniversary of 1840 treaty), 6–9 April (Easter), 25 April (ANZAC Day, anniversary of 1915 landing at Gallipoli), 4 June (Queen's Official Birthday), 22 October (Labour Day), 25 December (Christmas Day), 26 December (Boxing Day).

In addition to these national holidays, each region celebrates an anniversary day.

Weights and Measures

The metric system is in force.

Statistical Survey

Source (unless otherwise stated): Statistics New Zealand, Aorangi House, 85 Molesworth St, POB 2922, Wellington 1; tel. (4) 495-4600; fax (4) 472-9135; e-mail info@stats.govt.nz; internet www.stats.govt.nz.

Area and Population

AREA, POPULATION AND DENSITY

Area (sq km)	270,534*
Population (census results)†	
5 March 1996	3,618,303
6 March 2001	
Males	1,823,004
Females	1,914,273
Total	3,737,277
Population (official estimates at mid-year)	
2003	4,009,200
2004	4,061,400
2005	4,098,900
Density (per sq km) at mid-2005	15.2

* 104,454 sq miles.
† Figures refer to the population usually resident. The total population (including foreign visitors) was: 3,681,546 in 1996; 3,820,749 in 2001.

ADMINISTRATIVE REGIONS
(census of March 2001)

	Area (sq km)	Population	Density (per sq km)
North Island			
Northland	13,296	140,133	10.5
Auckland	5,048	1,158,891	229.6
Waikato	26,170	357,726	13.7
Bay of Plenty	11,428	239,412	21.0
Gisborne	8,355	43,974	5.3
Hawke's Bay Region	13,764	142,947	10.4
Taranaki	7,227	102,858	14.2
Manawatu-Wanganui	22,687	220,089	9.7
Wellington	8,056	423,765	52.6
Total North Island	116,031	2,829,798	24.4

NEW ZEALAND

—continued

	Area (sq km)	Population	Density (per sq km)
South Island			
Tasman	14,538	41,352	2.8
Nelson	444	41,568	93.6
Marlborough	12,493	39,558	3.2
West Coast	23,351	30,303	1.3
Canterbury	45,845	481,431	10.5
Otago	31,476	181,542	5.8
Southland	25,392	91,005	3.6
Total South Island	153,540	906,753	5.9
Area outside regions	963	726	0.8
Total	270,534	3,737,277	13.8

PRINCIPAL CENTRES OF POPULATION
(population at census of 6 March 2001)

Auckland	1,074,507	Palmerston North	72,681
Wellington (capital)	339,747	Hastings	58,139
Christchurch	334,107	Napier	54,534
Hamilton	166,128	Nelson	53,685
Dunedin	107,088	Rotorua	52,608
Tauranga	95,694		

BIRTHS, MARRIAGES AND DEATHS

	Live births* Number	Rate (per '000)	Marriages† Number	Rate (per '000)	Deaths* Number	Rate (per '000)
1998	57,251	15.1	20,135	5.3	26,206	6.9
1999	57,053	15.0	21,085	5.5	28,117	7.4
2000	56,605	14.7	20,655	5.4	26,660	7.0
2001	55,799	14.5	19,972	5.1	27,825	7.0
2002	54,021	13.7	20,690	5.3	28,065	7.1
2003	56,134	14.0	21,419	5.3‡	28,010	7.0
2004	58,073	14.3	21,006	n.a.	28,419	7.0
2005	57,745	14.1‡	n.a.	n.a.	27,034	6.6‡

* Data for births and deaths are tabulated by year of registration rather than by year of occurrence.
† Based on the resident population concept, replacing the previous *de facto* concept.
‡ Provisional figure.

Expectation of life (WHO estimates, years at birth): 79 (males 77; females 82) in 2003 (Source: WHO, *World Health Report*).

IMMIGRATION AND EMIGRATION

	2003	2004	2005
Long-term immigrants*	92,660	80,480	78,960
Long-term emigrants†	57,750	65,370	71,990

* Figures refer to persons intending to remain in New Zealand for 12 months or more, and New Zealand citizens returning after an absence of 12 months or more.
† Figures refer to New Zealand citizens intending to remain abroad for 12 months or more, and overseas migrants departing after a stay of 12 months or more.

ECONOMICALLY ACTIVE POPULATION
('000 persons aged 15 years and over, excl. armed forces)

	2002	2003	2004
Agriculture, hunting, forestry	161.3	152.8	148.5
Fishing	3.6	3.9	3.1
Mining and quarrying	3.7	3.3	3.9
Manufacturing	290.8	278.7	292.1
Electricity, gas and water	9.8	8.5	9.5
Construction	120.7	138.6	152.3
Wholesale and retail trade; repair of motor vehicles, motorcycles and personal and household goods	316.8	347.7	359.3
Restaurants and hotels	106.9	94.8	94.2
Transport, storage and communications	113.3	111.0	118.5
Financial intermediation	53.7	54.1	60.6

—continued

	2002	2003	2004
Real estate, renting and business activities	190.2	196.8	218.1
Public administration and defence; compulsory social security	84.5	110.6	114.2
Education	146.7	151.3	161.1
Health and social work	172.8	173.4	180.3
Other community, social and personal service activities	92.2	89.9	94.9
Private households with employed persons	6.6	2.5	2.6
Extra-territorial organizations and bodies	1.0	—	—
Activities not adequately defined	2.2	3.2	3.9
Total employed	1,876.8	1,921.0	2,017.1
Unemployed	102.5	93.9	82.0
Total labour force	1,979.2	2,014.9	2,099.1
Males	1,079.7	1,093.1	1,134.3
Females	899.6	921.8	964.7

Source: ILO.

Health and Welfare

KEY INDICATORS

Total fertility rate (children per woman, 2003)	2.0
Under-5 mortality rate (per 1,000 live births, 2004)	6
HIV/AIDS (% of persons aged 15–49, 2003)	0.1
Physicians (per 1,000 head, 2002)	2.1
Hospital beds (per 1,000 head, 1998)	6.2
Health expenditure (2002): US $ per head (PPP)	1,857
Health expenditure (2002): % of GDP	8.5
Health expenditure (2002): public (% of total)	77.9
Human Development Index (2003): ranking	19
Human Development Index (2003): value	0.933

For sources and definitions, see explanatory note on p. vi.

Agriculture

PRINCIPAL CROPS
('000 metric tons)

	2002	2003	2004
Wheat	301	321	271
Barley	441	378	380
Maize	149	158	170
Oats	35	32	35*
Potatoes	500	500	500*
Dry peas	29	31	31*
Cabbages	30	30	30*
Lettuce	30	31	31*
Tomatoes	87	87	88*
Cauliflower	53	54	55*
Pumpkins, squash and gourds*	156	156	156
Green onions and shallots*	210	220	242
Green peas	45	55	55*
Carrots	57	56	56*
Green corn*	100	100	112
Other vegetables (excl. watermelons)*	149	149	173
Grapes	119	76	166
Apples	531	501	464†
Pears	42	40	40*
Kiwi fruit	248	261	320†

* FAO estimate(s).
† Unofficial figure.

Source: FAO.

NEW ZEALAND

LIVESTOCK
('000 head at 30 June)

	2002	2003	2004
Cattle	9,637	9,656	9,617
Sheep	39,572	39,552	39,255
Goats	153	155	153
Pigs	341	377	389
Horses	76	80	83*
Chickens	17,128	18,049	20,000*
Ducks*	180	180	180
Geese*	68	68	70
Turkeys*	70	75	75

* FAO estimate(s).

Source: FAO.

LIVESTOCK PRODUCTS
('000 metric tons)

	2002	2003	2004
Beef and veal*	576.3	660.3	685.6
Mutton and lamb*	521.3	546.4	509.0
Pig meat*	46.7	48.3	51.8
Poultry meat*	128.9	138.1	149.1
Game meat*	25.6	29.0	31.0‡
Cows' milk†	13,865.9	14,354.1	14,780.0§
Butter†	414.6	462.0	473.0
Cheese†	307.0	275.0	285.0§
Hen eggs	45.7	46.1	47.9§
Other poultry eggs	2.4	2.4‡	2.4‡
Honey	4.7	12.3	12.0‡
Wool: greasy	228.3	229.6	217.7
Wool: scoured	195.3	193.0§	183.0§
Cattle hides (fresh)‡	51.0	58.0	59.0
Sheepskins (fresh)‡	98.0	102.0	140.0

* Twelve months ending 30 September of year stated.
† Twelve months ending 31 May of year stated.
‡ FAO estimate(s).
§ Unofficial figure.

Source: FAO.

Forestry

ROUNDWOOD REMOVALS
('000 cubic metres, year ending 31 March, estimates)

	2001/02	2002/03	2003/04
Sawlogs	7,382	8,386	7,750
Pulp logs	3,504	3,288	3,057
Export logs and chips	7,838	8,435	7,591
Other	2,216	2,342	2,490
Total	20,940	22,451	20,888

2004/05 ('000 cubic metres, year ending 31 March): Total roundwood removals 19,213.

Source: Forestry Statistics Section, Ministry of Agriculture and Forestry, Wellington.

SAWNWOOD PRODUCTION
('000 cubic metres, year ending 31 March)

Species	2001/02	2002/03	2003/04
Radiata pine	3,678	4,214	3,980
Other introduced pines	5	9	8
Douglas fir	124	164	178
Rimu and miro	13	5	5
Total (incl. others)	3,864	4,436	4,209

2004/05 ('000 cubic metres, year ending 31 March, provisional figure): Total sawnwood production 4,343.

Source: Forestry Statistics Section, Ministry of Agriculture and Forestry, Wellington.

Fishing
('000 metric tons, live weight)

	2001	2002	2003
Capture*	567.5	576.1	549.1
Southern blue whiting	29.8	42.1	28.1
Blue grenadier (Hoki)	223.7	192.5	181.1
Pink cusk-eel	18.6	20.3	19.5
Oreo dories	24.2	17.6	15.3
Jack and horse mackerels	28.5	32.3	37.7
Snoek (Barracouta)	25.2	23.1	21.7
Wellington flying squid	35.1	50.0	43.7
Aquaculture	76.0	86.6	84.6
New Zealand mussel	64.0	78.0	78.0
Total catch	643.5	662.7	633.8

* Excluding catches made by chartered vessels and landed outside New Zealand.

Note: Figures exclude aquatic mammals (recorded by number rather than by weight) and sponges. The number of whales and dolphins caught was: 19 in 2001; 13 in 2002; 33 in 2003. The catch of sponges (in metric tons) was: 23 in 2001; 0 in 2002; 0 in 2003.

Source: FAO.

Mining
('000 metric tons, unless otherwise indicated)

	2001	2002	2003
Coal (incl. lignite)	3,911	4,459	5,180
Gold (kg)	9,850	9,770	9,300
Crude petroleum ('000 barrels)	12,400	13,000*	8,711
Gross natural gas (million cu m)	5,000*	5,000*	4,926
Liquid petroleum gas ('000 barrels)*	2,000	2,100	193,953†
Iron sands	1,636	1,740	n.a.
Silica sand	36.0	59.4	48.4
Limestone	4,746	5,294	4,876

* Estimate(s).
† Official figure quoted in metric tons.

Sources: Ministry of Economic Development, Wellington; US Geological Survey.

Industry

SELECTED PRODUCTS
(metric tons, unless otherwise indicated)

	2000	2001	2002
Wine ('000 hectolitres)	570	537	586
Beer (sales, '000 hectolitres)	2,980	3,070	3,093
Wool yarn (pure and mixed)	22,200	n.a.	n.a.
Knitted fabrics*	3,600	3,500	n.a.
Chemical wood pulp†	753,885	744,991	723,054
Mechanical wood pulp†	773,680	827,286	800,676
Newsprint†	360,623	380,614	334,058
Other paper and paperboard†	469,189	490,993	512,669
Fibre board (cu m)†	744,879	801,493	821,994
Particle board (cu m)†	188,054	204,524	198,347
Veneer (cu m)†	378,282	401,590	460,619

NEW ZEALAND

Statistical Survey

—continued	2000	2001	2002
Plywood (cu m)†	239,947	243,702	263,332
Jet fuels ('000 metric tons)	838	815	n.a.
Motor spirit—petrol ('000 metric tons)	1,429	1,500	n.a.
Gas-diesel (Distillate fuel) oils ('000 metric tons)	1,983	1,909	n.a.
Residual fuel oils ('000 metric tons)	363	331	n.a.
Cement ('000 metric tons)	950	950	950
Aluminium—unwrought ('000 metric tons)			
Primary	328.4	322.3	335.0
Secondary	21.5‡	21.5‡	n.a.
Electric energy (million kWh)	39,010	39,910	n.a.

* Twelve months ending 30 September of year stated.
† Twelve months ending 31 March of year stated. Source: Ministry of Agriculture and Forestry, Wellington.
‡ Estimate.

2003: Wine ('000 hectolitres) 550; Electrical energy (million kWh) 36,256.

2004 (year ending 31 March): Chemical wood pulp (metric tons) 654,291; Mechanical wood pulp (metric tons) 808,365; Newsprint (metric tons) 368,421; Other paper and paperboard (metric tons) 477,001; Fibre board (cu m) 873,112; Particle board (cu m) 230,378; Veneer (cu m) 628,747; Plywood (cu m) 345,102 (Source: Ministry of Agriculture and Forestry, Wellington).

Sources (unless otherwise stated): UN, *Industrial Commodity Statistics Yearbook* and *Monthly Bulletin of Statistics*; US Geological Survey; New Zealand Wines Online.

Finance

CURRENCY AND EXCHANGE RATES

Monetary Units
100 cents = 1 New Zealand dollar ($NZ).

Sterling, US Dollar and Euro Equivalents (30 December 2005)
£1 sterling = $NZ2.5270;
US $1 = $NZ1.4676;
€1 = $NZ1.7313;
$NZ100 = £39.57 = US $68.14 = €57.76.

Average Exchange Rate (New Zealand dollars per US $)
2003 1.7221
2004 1.5087
2005 1.4203

BUDGET
($NZ million, year ending 30 June)

Revenue	2000/01	2001/02	2002/03
Direct taxation	23,863	24,557	26,778
Indirect taxation	12,875	13,863	13,007
Compulsory fees, fines, penalties and levies	385	520	2,763
Operational revenue	2,369	2,702	14,479
Total	39,492	41,642	57,027

Expenditure	2000/01	2001/02	2002/03
Core government services	1,817	1,602	1,655
Defence	1,267	1,197	1,154
Law and order	1,560	1,755	1,911
Education	6,690	7,124	7,788
Health	7,342	7,713	7,412
Transport and communications	1,026	1,120	5,619
Social security and welfare	13,216	13,487	17,084
Economic and industrial services	1,141	1,157	4,280
Total (incl. others)	38,186	39,699	55,224

Source: New Zealand Treasury, Wellington.

INTERNATIONAL RESERVES
(US $ million at 31 December)

	2002	2003	2004
IMF special drawing rights	22	28	34
Reserve position in IMF	459	644	474
Foreign exchange	3,258	4,206	4,786
Total	3,739	4,878	5,294

Source: IMF, *International Financial Statistics*.

MONEY SUPPLY
($NZ million at 31 December)

	2002	2003	2004
Currency outside banks	2,451	2,597	2,188
Demand deposits at banking institutions	17,487	19,068	19,578
Total money (incl. others)	20,018	21,705	21,789

Source: IMF, *International Financial Statistics*.

COST OF LIVING
(Consumer Price Index; base: 2000 = 100)

	2002	2003	2004
Food (incl. beverages)	109.4	109.4	110.3
Fuel and light	105.6	112.3	122.7
Clothing (incl. footwear)	102.9	102.4	101.8
Rent	91.8	94.7	97.6
All items (incl. others)	105.4	107.2	109.7

Source: ILO.

NATIONAL ACCOUNTS

National Income and Product
($NZ million at current prices, year ending 31 March)

	2002/03	2003/04	2004/05
Compensation of employees	54,904	58,693	62,918
Gross operating surplus	59,555	63,022	66,954
Taxes on production and imports	16,810	17,950	19,170
Less Subsidies	412	440	485
GDP in market prices	130,857	139,225	148,557
Net factor income from abroad	−7,044	−7,406	−9,964
Gross national income	123,813	131,819	138,593
Less Consumption of fixed capital	18,388	19,056	20,074
Net national income	105,425	112,763	118,519
Other current transfers from abroad (net)	113	391	494
Net national disposable income	105,538	113,154	119,013

Expenditure on the Gross Domestic Product
($NZ million at current prices, year ending 31 March)

	2002/03	2003/04	2004/05
Government final consumption expenditure	22,863	24,307	26,483
Private final consumption expenditure	76,708	81,728	87,531
Change in inventories	769	1,159	1,638
Gross fixed capital formation	27,749	31,527	34,923
Total domestic expenditure	128,090	138,721	150,574
Exports of goods and services	42,339	40,455	43,142
Less Imports of goods and services	40,095	40,159	44,732
GDP in market prices	130,334	139,016	148,984
GDP at constant 1995/96 prices	115,702	119,947	124,286

NEW ZEALAND

Gross Domestic Product by Economic Activity
($NZ million in current prices)

	1999/2000	2000/01	2001/02
Agriculture	5,926	7,963	9,349
Hunting and fishing	335	351	350
Forestry and logging	1,109	1,270	1,216
Mining and quarrying	1,200	1,384	1,444
Manufacturing	16,745	18,040	19,118
Electricity, gas and water	2,896	2,835	2,966
Construction	4,847	4,795	5,204
Wholesale and retail trade	13,829	14,220	16,019
Hotels and restaurants	1,887	2,086	2,253
Transport, storage and communications	7,808	7,929	8,433
Financial intermediation (incl. insurance)	5,946	6,270	6,832
Property and business activities	14,906	15,219	16,612
Ownership of dwellings	8,307	8,330	8,411
Public administration and defence	4,712	4,864	5,076
Education	4,463	4,642	4,852
Health and community services	5,443	5,802	6,254
Cultural and recreational services	2,270	2,437	2,572
Personal and other services	1,588	1,669	1,768
Sub-total	104,218	110,106	118,729
Less Financial intermediation services indirectly measured	3,533	3,575	3,939
Gross value added at basic prices	100,685	106,529	114,791
Goods and services tax on production	7,312	7,571	8,098
Import duties	612	633	643
Other taxes on production (net)	−40	—	—
GDP in market prices	108,570	114,733	123,532

BALANCE OF PAYMENTS
(US $ million)

	2002	2003	2004
Exports of goods f.o.b.	14,517	16,835	20,458
Imports of goods f.o.b.	−14,351	−17,291	−21,889
Trade balance	166	−456	−1,431
Exports of services	5,161	6,443	7,847
Imports of services	−4,718	−5,587	−6,902
Balance on goods and services	608	399	−486
Other income received	1,077	1,380	1,527
Other income paid	−4,041	−5,281	−7,320
Balance on goods, services and income	−2,355	−3,502	−6,279
Current transfers received	616	793	828
Current transfers paid	−496	−647	−748
Current balance	−2,235	−3,357	−6,199
Capital account (net)	765	508	302
Direct investment abroad	−185	−299	825
Direct investment from abroad	738	2,438	2,271
Portfolio investment assets	−935	−856	−2,044
Portfolio investment liabilities	2,400	2,184	7,297
Other investment assets	−1,086	317	−919
Other investment liabilities	107	−430	1,428
Net errors and omissions	1,516	277	−2,334
Overall balance	1,086	783	629

Source: IMF, *International Financial Statistics*.

External Trade

PRINCIPAL COMMODITIES
($NZ million)

Imports (c.i.f.)	2003	2004	2005*
Vehicles, parts and accessories	5,067	5,439	5,408
Mechanical machinery and equipment	4,260	4,785	5,055
Petroleum, petroleum products, etc.	2,898	3,552	4,393
Electrical machinery and equipment	2,813	3,251	3,289
Textiles and textile articles	1,580	1,630	1,677
Plastic and plastic articles	1,201	1,322	1,400
Iron and steel and articles	965	1,199	1,294
Optical, medical and measuring equipment	988	1,076	1,104
Total (incl. others)	31,782	34,915	37,261

* Provisional figures.

Exports f.o.b.	2003	2004	2005*
Milk powder, butter and cheese	4,725	4,970	5,158
Meat and edible offal	4,160	4,576	4,656
Logs, wood and wood articles	2,081	2,101	1,914
Mechanical machinery and equipment	1,398	1,603	1,683
Fruit	999	1,390	1,167
Fish, crustaceans and molluscs	1,068	1,130	1,132
Aluminium and aluminium articles	931	1,061	1,085
Electrical machinery and equipment	900	1,026	1,010
Total (incl. others)†	28,397	30,712	30,820

* Provisional figures.
† Including re-exports ($NZ million): 1,091 in 2003; 1,203 in 2004; 1,346 (provisional figure) in 2005.

PRINCIPAL TRADING PARTNERS
($NZ million)

Imports (c.i.f.)*	2003	2004	2005
Australia	7,175	7,812	7,684
Belgium	340	331	314
Canada	567	622	480
China, People's Republic	2,848	3,376	4,034
France	895	1,038	1,005
Germany	1,683	1,817	1,804
Indonesia	377	422	586
Italy	778	836	875
Japan	3,718	3,895	4,082
Korea, Republic	849	993	1,024
Malaysia	725	839	927
Netherlands	n.a.	286	386
Singapore	630	973	1,232
Sweden	336	354	366
Taiwan	693	798	880
Thailand	572	662	952
United Arab Emirates	458	343	513
United Kingdom	1,055	1,172	1,192
USA	3,722	3,917	4,065
Total (incl. others)	31,782	34,915	37,261

* Excluding specie and gold.

Exports*	2003	2004	2005
Australia	6,119	6,400	6,593
Belgium	632	519	515
Canada	548	521	524
China, People's Republic	1,376	1,745	1,565
Fiji	269	341	353
France	373	373	387
Germany	746	727	789
Hong Kong	559	560	525
Indonesia	383	411	465
Italy	444	439	446
Japan	3,123	3,443	3,261
Korea, Republic	993	1,165	1,082

NEW ZEALAND

Exports*—continued	2003	2004	2005
Malaysia	545	523	468
Mexico	411	394	437
Philippines	489	500	504
Saudi Arabia	n.a.	326	379
Singapore	307	362	428
Taiwan	626	704	773
Thailand	333	365	n.a.
United Kingdom	1,363	1,456	1,432
USA	4,119	4,436	4,373
Total (incl. others)	28,397	30,712	30,820

* Including re-exports, but excluding specie and gold.

Transport

RAILWAYS
(traffic, year ending 30 June)

	2000/01	2001/02	2002/03
Freight ('000 metric tons)	14,461	14,330	14,822
Passengers ('000)	12,714	12,521	12,300*

* Excludes passengers on the Tranz Scenic network.

Source: Tranz Rail Ltd, Wellington.

ROAD TRAFFIC
(vehicles licensed at 31 March)

	2000	2001	2002
Passenger cars	1,877,850	1,909,480	1,960,503
Goods service vehicles	368,964	364,928	366,639
Taxis	7,479	7,181	7,366
Buses and service coaches	12,264	12,667	13,339
Trailers and caravans	359,400	368,994	381,914
Motorcycles and mopeds	48,722	47,670	47,423
Tractors	20,526	21,377	22,914

Source: Ministry of Transport, Wellington.

SHIPPING

Merchant Fleet
(registered at 31 December)

	2002	2003	2004
Number of vessels	173	170	173
Displacement (grt)	180,435	205,188	206,415

Source: Lloyd's Register-Fairplay, *World Fleet Statistics*.

Vessels Handled
(international, '000 grt)

	1993	1994	1995
Entered	37,603	39,700	48,827
Cleared	35,128	37,421	42,985

Source: UN, *Statistical Yearbook*.

International Sea-borne Freight Traffic
('000 metric tons, year ending 30 June)

	2001/02	2002/03	2003/04*
Goods loaded	24,671	25,336	22,589
Goods unloaded	15,447	16,155	17,707

* Provisional.

CIVIL AVIATION
(domestic and international traffic on scheduled services)

	1997	1998	1999
Kilometres flown (million)	173	174	172
Passengers carried ('000)	9,435	8,655	8,892
Passenger-km (million)	20,983	19,014	19,322
Total metric ton-km (million)	2,816	2,700	2,746

Source: UN, *Statistical Yearbook*.

Tourism

VISITOR ARRIVALS

Country of residence	2003	2004	2005
Australia	702,162	855,933	874,738
China, People's Republic	65,989	84,368	87,850
Germany	52,534	55,736	57,549
Japan	150,851	165,023	154,925
Korea, Republic	112,658	113,908	112,005
United Kingdom	264,819	283,700	306,815
USA	211,624	218,345	214,507
Total (incl. others)	2,104,420	2,347,672	2,382,950

Tourism receipts ($NZ million, year ending 31 March): 5,544 in 2001/02; 6,192 in 2002/03; 6,313 in 2003/04.

Source: Tourism Research Council, Wellington.

Communications Media

	2002	2003	2004
Telephones ('000 main lines in use)	1,765.0	1,798.0	1,800.5
Mobile cellular telephones ('000 subscribers)	2,449	2,599	3,027
Personal computers ('000 in use)	1,630	n.a.	1,924
Internet users ('000)	1,908	2,110	3,200

Television receivers ('000 in use): 2,130 in 2001.

Radio receivers ('000 in use): 3,750 in 1997.

Facsimile machines ('000 in use, year ending 31 March 1996): 65.

Daily newspapers: 26 (circulation 850,000 copies, 2002).

Non-daily newspapers: 2 (circulation 311,380 copies, 2002).

Book production (1999): 4,800 titles.

Sources: partly International Telecommunication Union; UNESCO, *Statistical Yearbook*; UN, *Statistical Yearbook*.

Education

(July 2004)

	Institutions	Teachers (full-time equivalent)	Students
Early childhood services	4,374	11,485[1,4]	184,513[2]
Primary schools[3]	2,124	26,011[4]	450,196
Composite schools[5]	147	2,403[4]	39,268
Secondary schools[6]	352	19,180[4]	264,522
Special schools	47	945[4]	2,672
Polytechnics	20[7]	4,223[7]	117,514
Colleges of education	4[7]	491[7]	11,107
Universities	8[7]	6,562[7]	138,583
Wananga[8]	3[7]	781[7]	41,644
Private training establishments receiving government grants	522[7]	4,177[7]	59,158

[1] Excludes 1,205 playcentre teaching staff and Te Kohanga Reo personnel (responsible for Maori 'Language Nests').
[2] Includes children on the regular roll of the Correspondence School, kindergartens, playcentres, Te Kohanga Reo, Early Childhood Development Unit funded playgroups, Early Childhood Development Unit funded Pacific Islands language groups, education and care centres (incl. home-based childcare).
[3] Primary schools include Full Primary Years 1–8, Contributing Years 1–6, Intermediate Years 7–8.
[4] Teachers employed in state schools at 1 March 2004.
[5] Composite schools provide both primary and secondary education (includes area schools and the Correspondence School).
[6] Secondary schools include Years 7–15, Years 9–15.
[7] 2003 figure.
[8] Tertiary institutions providing polytechnic and university level programmes specifically for Maori students, with an emphasis on Maori language and culture.

Source: Ministry of Education, Wellington.

Directory

The Constitution

New Zealand has no written constitution. The political system is closely modelled on that of the United Kingdom (with an element of proportional representation introduced to the legislature in 1996). As in the United Kingdom, constitutional practice is an accumulation of convention, precedent and tradition. A brief description of New Zealand's principal organs of government is given below:

HEAD OF STATE

Executive power is vested in the monarch and is exercisable in New Zealand by the monarch's personal representative, the Governor-General.

In the execution of the powers and authorities vested in him or her, the Governor-General must be guided by the advice of the Executive Council.

EXECUTIVE COUNCIL

The Executive Council consists of the Governor-General and all the Ministers. Two members, exclusive of the Governor-General or the presiding member, constitute a quorum. The Governor-General appoints the Prime Minister and, on the latter's recommendation, the other Ministers.

HOUSE OF REPRESENTATIVES

Parliament comprises the Crown and the House of Representatives. At the 1996 general election, a system of mixed member proportional representation was introduced. The House of Representatives comprises 120 members: 67 electorate members (five seats being reserved for Maoris) and 53 members chosen from party lists. They are designated 'Members of Parliament' and are elected for three years, subject to the dissolution of the House before the completion of their term.

Everyone over the age of 18 years may vote in the election of members for the House of Representatives. Since August 1975 any person, regardless of nationality, ordinarily resident in New Zealand for 12 months or more and resident in an electoral district for at least one month is qualified to be registered as a voter. Compulsory registration of all electors except Maoris was introduced at the end of 1924; it was introduced for Maoris in 1956. As from August 1975, any person of the Maori race, which includes any descendant of such a person, may enrol on the Maori roll for the particular Maori electoral district in which that person resides.

By the Electoral Amendment Act 1937, which made provision for a secret ballot in Maori elections, Maori electors were granted the same privileges, in the exercise of their vote, as general electors.

In local government the electoral franchise is the same.

The Government

Head of State: HM Queen ELIZABETH II (acceded to the throne 6 February 1952).

Governor-General and Commander-in-Chief: Dame SILVIA CARTWRIGHT (until 4 August 2006), Judge ANAND SATYANAND (from 4 August 2006).

CABINET
(May 2006)

A coalition of the Labour Party and the Progressive Party.

Prime Minister and Minister for Arts, Culture and Heritage: HELEN CLARK.
Deputy Prime Minister, Attorney-General, Minister of Finance, Minister for Tertiary Education and Leader of the House: Dr MICHAEL CULLEN.
Minister of Agriculture, for Biosecurity, of Fisheries and of Forestry: JIM ANDERTON.
Minister of Education, of Broadcasting, of Research, Science and Technology and for Crown Research Institutes: STEVE MAHAREY.
Minister of Defence, of Trade, of Pacific Island Affairs and for Disarmament and Arms Control: PHIL GOFF.
Minister of State Services, of Police, of Transport and for Food Safety: ANNETTE KING.
Minister for Economic Development, for Industry and Regional Development, for State Owned Enterprises and for Sport and Recreation: TREVOR MALLARD.
Minister of Health: PETE HODGSON.
Minister of Maori Affairs: PAREKURA HOROMIA.
Minister of Justice and of Local Government and in Charge of Treaty of Waitangi Negotiations: MARK BURTON.
Minister of Labour, for Accident Compensation Corporation and for Senior Citizens: RUTH DYSON.
Minister of Conservation and of Housing: CHRIS CARTER.
Minister of Internal Affairs, of Civil Defence, for Courts and of Veterans' Affairs: RICK BARKER.
Minister for Social Development and Employment and for the Environment: DAVID BENSON-POPE.
Minister of Commerce and of Women's Affairs: LIANNE DALZIEL.
Minister of Corrections and of Tourism: DAMIEN O'CONNOR.
Minister of Immigration, of Communications and for Information Technology: DAVID CUNLIFFE.
Minister of Energy and for Land Information: DAVID PARKER.
Minister of Customs and of Youth Development: NANAIA MAHUTA.
Minister for Building Issues and of Statistics: CLAYTON COSGROVE.
Minister of State: JIM SUTTON.

MINISTERS OUTSIDE CABINET
(May 2006)

Minister of Foreign Affairs and for Racing: WINSTON PETERS.
Minister of Revenue: PETER DUNNE.
Minister of Consumer Affairs: JUDITH TIZARD.
Minister for Transport Safety: HARRY DUYNHOVEN.
Minister for the Community and Voluntary Sector: WINNIE LABAN.
Ministers of State: DOVER SAMUELS, MITA RIRINUI, MAHARA OKEROA.

MINISTRIES AND GOVERNMENT DEPARTMENTS

Department of the Prime Minister and Cabinet: Executive Wing, Parliament Bldgs, Wellington; tel. (4) 471-9035; fax (4) 473-2508; internet www.dpmc.govt.nz.
Ministry of Agriculture and Forestry: 25 The Terrace, POB 2526, Wellington; tel. (4) 819-0100; fax (4) 474-4111; e-mail info@maf.govt.nz; internet www.maf.govt.nz.
Department of Building and Housing: 256 Lambton Quay, POB 10-729, Wellington; tel. (4) 494-0260; fax (4) 494-0290; e-mail info@dbh.govt.nz; internet www.dbh.govt.nz.
Ministry of Civil Defence and Emergency Management: Level 9, 22 The Terrace, POB 5010, Wellington; tel. (4) 473-7363; fax (4) 473-7369; e-mail emergency.management@dia.govt.nz; internet www.civildefence.govt.nz.
Department of Conservation: POB 10-420, Wellington; tel. (4) 471-0726; fax (4) 471-1082; e-mail tsmith@doc.govt.nz; internet www.doc.govt.nz.
Ministry for Culture and Heritage: POB 5364, Wellington; tel. (4) 499-4229; fax (4) 499-4490; e-mail info@mch.govt.nz; internet www.mch.govt.nz.
Ministry of Defence: POB 5347, Lambton Quay, Wellington; tel. (4) 496-0999; fax (4) 496-0859; e-mail info@defence.govt.nz; internet www.defence.govt.nz.
Ministry of Economic Development: POB 1473, 33 Bowen St, Wellington; tel. (4) 472-0030; fax (4) 473-4638; e-mail info@med.govt.nz; internet www.med.govt.nz.
Ministry of Education: Level 7, St Paul's Square, 45–47 Pipitea St, Thorndon, Wellington; tel. (4) 463-8000; fax (4) 463-8001; e-mail enquiries.national@minedu.govt.nz; internet www.minedu.govt.nz.
Ministry for the Environment: 23 Kate Sheppard Place, POB 10-362, Wellington; tel. (4) 439-7400; fax (4) 439-7700; e-mail library@mfe.govt.nz; internet www.mfe.govt.nz.
Ministry of Fisheries: ASB Bank House, 101–103 The Terrace, POB 1020, Wellington; tel. (4) 470-2600; fax (4) 470-2601; e-mail info@fish.govt.nz; internet www.fish.govt.nz.
Ministry of Foreign Affairs and Trade: Private Bag 18901, Wellington; tel. (4) 439-8000; fax (4) 472-9596; e-mail enquiries@mfat.govt.nz; internet www.mfat.govt.nz.
Ministry of Health: 133 Molesworth St, POB 5013, Wellington; tel. (4) 496-2000; fax (4) 496-2340; e-mail emailmoh@moh.govt.nz; internet www.moh.govt.nz.
Department of Internal Affairs: 46 Waring Taylor St, POB 805, Wellington; tel. (4) 495-7200; fax (4) 495-7222; e-mail info@dia.govt.nz; internet www.dia.govt.nz.

NEW ZEALAND

Ministry of Justice: POB 180, Wellington; tel. (4) 918-8800; fax (4) 918-8820; e-mail reception@justice.govt.nz; internet www.justice.govt.nz.

Department of Labour: POB 3705, Wellington; tel. (4) 915-4444; fax (4) 915-0891; e-mail info@dol.govt.nz; internet www.dol.govt.nz.

Ministry of Maori Development (Te Puni Kokiri): POB 3943, Wellington 6015; tel. (4) 922-6000; fax (4) 922-6299; e-mail tpkinfo@tpk.govt.nz; internet www.tpk.govt.nz.

Ministry of Pacific Island Affairs: POB 833, Wellington; tel. (4) 473-4493; fax (4) 473-4301; e-mail contact@minpac.govt.nz; internet www.minpac.govt.nz.

Ministry of Research, Science and Technology: POB 5336, Wellington; tel. (4) 917-2900; fax (4) 471-1284; e-mail talk2us@morst.govt.nz; internet www.morst.govt.nz.

Ministry of Social Development: Bowen State Bldg, Bowen St, POB 12136, Wellington; tel. (4) 916-3300; fax (4) 918-0099; e-mail information@msd.govt.nz; internet www.msd.govt.nz.

State Services Commission: POB 329, Wellington; tel. (4) 495-6600; fax (4) 495-6686; e-mail commission@ssc.govt.nz; internet www.ssc.govt.nz.

Statistics New Zealand (Tatauranga Aotearoa): POB 2922, Wellington; tel. (4) 931-4600; fax (4) 931-4610; e-mail info@stats.govt.nz; internet www.stats.govt.nz.

Ministry of Tourism: POB 5640, Wellington; tel. (4) 498-7440; fax (4) 498-7445; e-mail info@tourism.govt.nz; internet www.tourism.govt.nz.

Ministry of Transport: POB 3175, Wellington; tel. (4) 472-1253; fax (4) 473-3697; e-mail reception@transport.govt.nz; internet www.transport.govt.nz.

Treasury: POB 3724, Wellington 6001; tel. (4) 472-2733; fax (4) 473-0982; e-mail information@treasury.govt.nz; internet www.treasury.govt.nz.

Ministry of Women's Affairs: POB 10-049, Wellington; tel. (4) 915-7112; fax (4) 916-1604; e-mail mwa@mwa.govt.nz; internet www.mwa.govt.nz.

Ministry of Youth Development: POB 1556, Wellington; tel. (4) 916-3300; fax (4) 918-0091; e-mail mydinfo@myd.govt.nz; internet www.myd.govt.nz.

Legislature

HOUSE OF REPRESENTATIVES

Speaker: MARGARET WILSON.
General Election, 17 September 2005

Party	Number of votes	% of votes	Party seats	List seats	Total seats
NZ Labour Party	935,319	41.10	31	19	50
NZ National Party	889,813	39.10	31	17	48
New Zealand First	130,115	5.72	—	7	7
Green Party	120,521	5.30	—	6	6
Maori Party	48,263	2.12	4	—	4*
United Future NZ	60,860	2.67	1	2	3
ACT New Zealand	34,469	1.51	1	1	2
Progressive Party	26,441	1.16	1	—	1
Total (incl. others)	2,286,190	100.00	69	52	121

* Includes two guaranteed seats.

Election Commission

Electoral Commission of New Zealand: POB 3050, Wellington; tel. (4) 474-0670; fax (4) 474-0674; e-mail info@elections.govt.nz; internet www.elections.org.nz; independent; Pres. ANTHONY ELLIS; Chief Exec. HELENA CATT.

Political Organizations

In August 2005 19 political parties were registered.

ACT New Zealand: Unit A, 11–13 Clovernook Rd, POB 99-651, Newmarket, Auckland; tel. (9) 523-0470; fax (9) 523-0472; e-mail info@voteact.org.nz; internet www.act.org.nz; f. 1994; supports free enterprise, tax reform and choice in education and health; Pres. GARRY MALLETT; Leader RODNEY HIDE.

Destiny New Zealand: POB 511-55, Pakuranga, Auckland; tel. and fax (9) 574-5085; e-mail office@destinynz.org.nz; internet www.destinynz.org.nz; f. 2003; Leader RICHARD LEWIS; Pres. STEPHEN BROWN.

Direct Democracy Party: POB 8128, Taurange, Bay of Plenty; tel. (7) 286-8789; e-mail secretary@directdemocracy.net.nz; internet www.directdemocracy.co.nz; f. 2005; Leader KELVYN ALP.

Green Party of Aotearoa—New Zealand: POB 11-652, Wellington; tel. (4) 801-5102; fax (4) 801-5104; e-mail greenparty@greens.org.nz; internet www.greens.org.nz; f. 1989; fmrly Values Party, f. 1972; Leader JEANETTE FITZSIMONS.

Mana Motuhake o Aotearoa (New Zealand Self-Government Party): Private Bag 68-905, Newton, Auckland; f. 1979; pro-Maori; promotes bicultural policies; Leader WILLIE JACKSON.

Maori Party: PO Box 20683, Glen Eden, Waitakere City; tel. (9) 813-9204; fax (9) 813-9206; e-mail enquiry@maoriparty.com; internet www.maoriparty.com; f. 2004; Co-Leaders Dr PITA SHARPLES, Hon. TARIANA TURIA, Dr WHATARANGI WINIATA.

The New Zealand Democratic Party Inc: 414 Glenfield Rd, POB 40364, Glenfield, North Shore City; tel. (9) 442-2364; fax (9) 442-2438; e-mail nzdp.inc@xtra.co.nz; internet www.democrats.org.nz; f. 1953 as Social Credit Political League; adopted present name 1985; liberal; Pres. NEVILLE AITCHISON; Leader STEPHNIE DE RUYTER.

New Zealand First: c/o House of Representatives, Wellington; fax (4) 472-8557; e-mail nzfirst@parliament.govt.nz; f. 1993 by fmr National Party mems; Leader WINSTON PETERS; Pres. DAIL JONES.

New Zealand Labour Party: 160–162 Willis St, POB 784, Wellington; tel. (4) 384-7649; fax (4) 384-8060; e-mail nzlpho@labour.org.nz; internet www.labour.org.nz; f. 1916; advocates an organized economy guaranteeing an adequate standard of living to every person able and willing to work; Pres. MIKE WILLIAMS; Parl. Leader HELEN CLARK; Gen. Sec. MIKE SMITH.

New Zealand National Party: Willbank House, 14th Floor, 57 Willis St, POB 1155, Wellington 60015; tel. (4) 472-5211; fax (4) 478-1622; e-mail hq@national.org.nz; internet www.national.org.nz; f. 1936; centre-right; supports private enterprise and competitive business, together with maximum personal freedom; Pres. JUDY KIRK; Parl. Leader DON BRASH.

Progressive Party: POB 33-243, Christchurch; tel. (3) 377-7679; fax (3) 377-7673; e-mail contact@progressive.org.nz; internet www.progressive.org.nz; f. 2002 as the Progressive Coalition to contest the general election; name changed as above April 2004; Leader JIM ANDERTON.

United Future New Zealand (UFNZ): c/o House of Representatives, Wellington; e-mail unitedfuture@parliament.govt.nz; internet www.unitedfuture.org.nz; f. 1995 by four mems of National Party, two mems of Labour Party and leader of Future New Zealand; joined by New Zealand Conservative Party in 1998; Pres. GRAEME REEVES.

Other parties that contested the 2005 election included the Alliance, the Aotearoa Legalise Cannabis Party, the Christian Heritage Party, Libertarianz, the New Zealand Family Rights Protection Party, the 99 MP Party, the One New Zealand Party and the Republic of New Zealand Party.

Diplomatic Representation

EMBASSIES AND HIGH COMMISSIONS IN NEW ZEALAND

Argentina: Sovereign Assurance House, 14th Floor, 142 Lambton Quay, POB 5430, Lambton Quay, Wellington; tel. (4) 472-8330; fax (4) 472-8331; e-mail enzel@arg.org.nz; internet www.arg.org.nz; Ambassador PEDRO R. HERRERA.

Australia: 72–78 Hobson St, Thorndon, POB 4036, Wellington; tel. (4) 473-6411; fax (4) 498-7118; e-mail nzinbox@dfat.gov.au; internet www.australia.org.nz; High Commissioner JOHN DAUTH.

Brazil: Wool House, Level 9, 10 Brandon St, Wellington; tel. (4) 473-3516; fax (4) 473-3517; e-mail brasemb@brazil.org.nz; internet www.brazil.org.nz; Ambassador SÉRGIO BARBOSA SERRA.

Canada: 61 Molesworth St, POB 12049, Wellington 1; tel. (4) 473-9577; fax (4) 471-2082; e-mail wlgtn@international.gc.ca; internet www.dfait-maeci.gc.ca/newzealand; High Commissioner PENNY REEDIE.

Chile: 19 Bolton St, POB 3861, Wellington; tel. (4) 471-6270; fax (4) 472-5324; e-mail embchile@ihug.co.nz; Ambassador JUAN A. SALAZAR SPARKS.

China, People's Republic: 2–6 Glenmore St, POB 17-257, Karori, Wellington; tel. (4) 472-1382; fax (4) 499-0419; e-mail info@chinaembassy.org.nz; internet www.chinaembassy.org.nz; Ambassador ZHANG YUANYUAN.

Fiji: 31 Pipitea St, Thorndon, POB 3940, Wellington; tel. (4) 473-5401; fax (4) 499-1011; e-mail viti@paradise.net.nz; internet www.fiji.org.nz; High Commissioner BAL RAM.

NEW ZEALAND

Directory

France: Sovereign House, 12th Floor, 34–42 Manners St, POB 11-343, Wellington; tel. (4) 384-2555; fax (4) 384-2577; e-mail amba.france@actrix.gen.fr; internet www.ambafrance-nz.org; Ambassador JEAN-MICHEL MARLAUD.

Germany: 90–92 Hobson St, POB 1687, Wellington; tel. (4) 473-6063; fax (4) 473-6069; e-mail german.embassy@iconz.co.nz; internet www.wellington.diplo.de; Ambassador JOERG HANS ZIMMERMANN.

Greece: 5–7 Willeston St, 10th Floor, POB 24-066, Wellington; tel. (4) 473-7775; fax (4) 473-7441; e-mail info@greece.org.nz; Ambassador EVANGELOS DAMIANAKIS.

Holy See: Apostolic Nunciature, 112 Queen's Drive, Lyall Bay, POB 14-044, Wellington 6041; tel. (4) 387-3470; fax (4) 387-8170; e-mail nuntius@ihug.co.nz; Apostolic Nuncio Most Rev. CHARLES D. BALVO (Titular Archbishop of Castello).

India: 180 Molesworth St, POB 4045, Wellington 1; tel. (4) 473-6390; fax (4) 499-0665; e-mail hicomind@xtra.co.nz; internet www.hicomind.org.nz; High Commissioner K. P. ERNEST.

Indonesia: 70 Glen Road, Kelburn, POB 3543, Wellington; tel. (4) 475-8699; fax (4) 475-9374; e-mail kbriwell@ihug.co.nz; internet www.indonesianembassy.org.nz; Chargé d'affaires a.i. MARLINA S. TAHRIR.

Iran: The Terrace, POB 10-249, Wellington; tel. (4) 386-2983; fax (4) 386-3065; e-mail embassy.of.iran@xtra.co.nz; Ambassador KAMBIZ SHAYKH HASANI.

Israel: Equinox House, 13th Floor, 111 The Terrace, POB 2171, Wellington; tel. (4) 472-2368; fax (4) 499-0632; e-mail israel@central.co.nz; internet users.iconz.co.nz/israel; Ambassador NAFTALI TAMIR (resident in Australia).

Italy: 34–38 Grant Rd, Thorndon, POB 463, Wellington 1; tel. (4) 473-5339; fax (4) 472-7255; e-mail ambwell@xtra.co.nz; internet www.italy-embassy.org.nz/em_well.html; Ambassador Dr LIANA MAROLLA.

Japan: Majestic Centre, Levels 18–19, 100 Willis St, POB 6340, Wellington 1; tel. (4) 473-1540; fax (4) 471-2951; e-mail japan.emb@eoj.org.nz; Ambassador MASAKI SAITO.

Korea, Republic: ASB Bank Tower, Level 11, 2 Hunter St, POB 11-143, Wellington; tel. (4) 473-9073; fax (4) 472-3865; e-mail korembec@world-net.co.nz; internet www.koreanembassy.org.nz; Ambassador SHIN JUNG-SEUNG.

Malaysia: 10 Washington Ave, Brooklyn, POB 9422, Wellington; tel. (4) 385-2439; fax (4) 385-6973; e-mail mwwelton@xtra.co.nz; High Commissioner Dato' SOPIAN BIN AHMAD.

Mexico: Perpetual Trust House, Level 8, 111–115 Customhouse Quay, Manners St, POB 11-510, Wellington; tel. (4) 472-0555; fax (4) 496-3559; e-mail mexico@xtra.co.nz; internet www.mexico.org.nz; Ambassador MARÍA ANGÉLICA ARCE MORA.

Netherlands: Investment House, 10th Floor, cnr Featherston and Ballance Sts, POB 840, Wellington; tel. (4) 471-6390; fax (4) 471-2923; e-mail wel@minbuza.nl; internet www.netherlandsembassy.co.nz; Ambassador HENRICA E. C. M. TER BRAACK.

Papua New Guinea: 279 Willis St, POB 197, Wellington; tel. (4) 385-2474; fax (4) 385-2477; e-mail pngnz@globe.net.nz; High Commissioner BERNARD NAROKOBI.

Peru: Cigna House, Level 8, 40 Mercer St, POB 2566, Wellington; tel. (4) 499-8087; fax (4) 499-8057; e-mail embassy.peru@xtra.co.nz; internet www.embassyofperu.org.nz; Ambassador JAVIER LEÓN.

Philippines: 50 Hobson St, Thorndon, POB 12-042, Wellington; tel. (4) 472-9848; fax (4) 472-5170; e-mail embassy@wellington-pe.co.nz; Ambassador Dr BIENEVENIDO V. TEJANO.

Poland: 17 Upland Rd, Kelburn, POB 10211, Wellington; tel. (4) 475-9453; fax (4) 475-9458; e-mail polishembassy@xtra.co.nz; internet poland.org.nz; Ambassador LECH MASTALERZ.

Russia: 57 Messines Rd, Karori, Wellington; tel. (4) 476-6113; fax (4) 476-3843; e-mail embassyofrussia@xtra.co.nz; internet www.rus.co.nz; Ambassador MIKHAIL LYSENKO.

Samoa: 1A Wesley Rd, Kelburn, POB 1430, Wellington; tel. (4) 472-0953; fax (4) 471-2479; e-mail shc@paradise.net.nz; High Commissioner ASI TUIATAGA J. F. BLAKELOCK.

Singapore: 17 Kabul St, Khandallah, POB 13140, Wellington; tel. (4) 470-0850; fax (4) 479-4066; e-mail shcwlg@xtra.co.nz; internet www.mfa.gov.sg/wellington; High Commissioner SEETOH HOY CHENG.

Switzerland: Panama House, 22 Panama St, POB 25004, Wellington; tel. (4) 472-1593; fax (4) 499-6302; e-mail vertretung@wel.rep.admin.ch; Ambassador Dr BEAT NOBS.

Thailand: 2 Cook St, Karori, Wellington; tel. (4) 476-8616; fax (4) 476-3677; e-mail thaiembassynz@xtra.co.nz; internet www.thaiembassynz.org.nz; Ambassador NORACHIT SINHASENI.

Turkey: 15–17 Murphy St, Level 8, POB 12-248, Wellington; tel. (4) 472-1292; fax (4) 472-1277; e-mail turkem@xtra.co.nz; Ambassador UGUR ERGUN.

United Kingdom: 44 Hill St, POB 1812, Wellington; tel. (4) 924-2888; fax (4) 473-4982; e-mail ppa.mailbox@fco.gov.uk; internet www.britain.org.nz; High Commissioner RICHARD FELL.

USA: 29 Fitzherbert Terrace, POB 1190, Wellington; tel. (4) 462-6000; fax (4) 472-3537; internet usembassy.org.nz; Ambassador WILLIAM P. MCCORMICK.

Viet Nam: Level 2, Grand Plimmer Tower, 2–6 Glimer Terrace, Wellington; tel. (4) 473-5912; fax (4) 473-5913; e-mail embassyvn@paradise.net.nz; Ambassador TRAN HAI HAU.

Judicial System

The Judicial System of New Zealand comprises a Supreme Court, a Court of Appeal, a High Court and District Courts, all of which have civil and criminal jurisdiction, and the specialist courts, the Employment Court, the Family Court, the Youth Court and the Maori Land Court. Until the establishment of the Supreme Court on 1 January 2004, final appeal was to the Judicial Committee of the Privy Council in the United Kingdom. After 1 January 2004 the Supreme Court replaced the Privy Council as the final appellate court. The right to appeal to the Supreme Court was granted only if the Court was satisfied that the case involved a matter of general or public importance or commercial significance, or in order to correct or prevent a substantial miscarriage of justice.

The Court of Appeal hears appeals from the High Court and from District Court Jury Trials, although it does have some original jurisdiction. Its decisions are final, except in cases that may be appealed to the Supreme Court. Appeals regarding convictions and sentences handed down by the High Court or District Trial Courts are by leave only.

The High Court has jurisdiction to hear cases involving crimes, admiralty law and civil matters. It hears appeals from lower courts and tribunals, and reviews administrative actions.

District Courts have an extensive criminal and civil law jurisdiction. They hear civil cases up to $NZ200,000, unless the parties agree to litigate a larger sum (up to $NZ62,500 per year for rent and up to $NZ500,000 for real estate). Justices of the Peace can hear minor criminal and traffic matters if less than $NZ5,000. The Family Court, which is a division of the District Courts, has the jurisdiction to deal with dissolution of marriages, adoption, guardianship applications, domestic actions, matrimonial property, child support, care and protection applications regarding children and young persons, and similar matters.

The tribunals are as follows: the Employment Tribunal (administered by the Department of Labour), Disputes Tribunal, Complaints Review Tribunal, Residential Tenancies Tribunal, Waitangi Tribunal, Environment Court, Deportation Review Tribunal and Motor Vehicles Disputes Tribunal. The Disputes Tribunal has the jurisdiction to hear civil matters involving sums up to $NZ7,500. If the parties agree, it can hear cases involving sums up to $NZ12,000.

In criminal cases involving indictable offences (major crimes), the defendant has the right to a jury. In criminal cases involving summary offences (minor crimes), the defendant may elect to have a jury if the sentence corresponding to the charge is three months or greater.

Attorney-General: Dr MICHAEL CULLEN.

Chief Justice: Dame SIAN ELIAS.

THE SUPREME COURT

Judges: Dame SIAN ELIAS, THOMAS MUNRO GAULT, Sir KENNETH KEITH, PETER BLANCHARD, ANDREW PATRICK CHARLES TIPPING.

THE COURT OF APPEAL

President: NOEL CROSSLEY ANDERSON.

Judges: Justice JOHN J. MCGRATH, Justice SUSAN GLAZEBROOK, Justice ROBERT GRANT HAMMOND, Justice WILLIAM YOUNG, Justice CHAMBERS, Justice O'REGAN.

THE HIGH COURT

Permanent Judges: Chief Justice Dame SIAN ELIAS (*ex officio*), Justice JOHN ANTHONY DOOGUE, Justice JAMES BRUCE ROBERTSON, Justice LOWELL GODDARD, Justice J. WARWICK GENDALL, Justice WILD, Justice E. T. DURIE, Justice RONALD YOUNG, Justice SIMON FRANCE, Justice NEAZOR, Justice MACKENZIE, Justice MILLER, Justice MCGECHAN, Justice HUGH WILLIAMS, Justice DAVID BARAGWANATH, Justice PETER M. SALMON, Justice BARRY J. PATERSON, Justice JUDITH M. POTTER, Justice JOHN A. LAURENSON, Justice TONY RANDERSON, Justice NICHOLSON, Justice RODNEY HANSEN, Justice PRIESTLEY, Justice HARRISON, Justice HEATH, Justice FRATER, Justice G. J. VENNING, Justice KEANE, Justice COOPER, Justice JOHN HANSEN, Justice PANCKHURST, Justice CHISHOLM, Justice FOGARTY, Justice DENIS KIERAN CLIFFORD.

NEW ZEALAND

Religion

CHRISTIANITY

Te Runanga Whakawhanaunga i Nga Hahi o Aotearoa (Maori Council of Churches in New Zealand): Private Bag 11903, Ellerslie, Auckland, Aotearoa-New Zealand; tel. (9) 525-4179; fax (9) 525-4346; f. 1982; four mem. churches; Administrator TE RUA GRETHA.

The Anglican Communion

The Anglican Church in Aotearoa, New Zealand and Polynesia comprises Te Pihopatanga o Aotearoa and eight dioceses (one of which is Polynesia). In 1996 the Church had an estimated 631,764 members in New Zealand.

Primate of the Anglican Church in Aotearoa, New Zealand and Polynesia, and Bishop of Auckland: Rt Rev. JOHN CAMPBELL PATERSON, POB 37-242, Parnell, Auckland; tel. (9) 302-7201; fax (9) 377-6962.

General Secretary and Treasurer of the Anglican Church in Aotearoa, New Zealand and Polynesia: ROBIN NAIRN, POB 885, Hastings; tel. (6) 878-7902; fax (6) 878-7905; e-mail gensec@hb.ang.org.nz; internet www.anglican.org.nz.

The Roman Catholic Church

For ecclesiastical purposes, New Zealand comprises one archdiocese and five dioceses. At 31 December 2003 there were an estimated 461,860 adherents.

Bishops' Conference

New Zealand Catholic Bishops' Conference, POB 1937, Wellington; tel. (4) 496-1747; fax (4) 496-1746; e-mail adickinson@nzcbc.org.nz; f. 1974; Pres. Most Rev. DENIS BROWNE (Bishop of Hamilton); Sec. Archbishop JOHN A. DEW (Archbishop of Wellington); Exec. Officer ANNE DICKINSON.

Archbishop of Wellington: Most Rev. JOHN A. DEW, POB 1937, Wellington 6015; tel. (4) 496-1766; fax (4) 496-1330; e-mail j.dew@wn.catholic.org.nz.

Other Christian Churches

Baptist Churches of New Zealand: 8 Puhinui Rd, Manukau City, POB 97543, South Auckland; tel. (9) 278-7494; fax (9) 278-7499; e-mail info@baptist.org.nz; internet www.baptist.org.nz; f. 1882; 22,456 mems; Pres. MARJORY GIBSON; Nat. Leader Rev. BRIAN WINSLADE.

Congregational Union of New Zealand: 10 The Close, 42 Arawa St, New Lynn, Auckland; tel. and fax (9) 827-3708; e-mail cunz@xtra.co.nz; f. 1884; 786 mems, 15 churches; Gen. Sec. BOB FRANKLYN; Chair. BARBARA KENNETT.

Methodist Church of New Zealand: Connexional Office, POB 931, Christchurch; tel. (3) 366-6049; fax (3) 366-9439; e-mail info@methodist.org.nz; internet www.methodist.org.nz; 18,548 mems; Gen. Sec. Rev. JILL VAN DE GEER.

Presbyterian Church of Aotearoa New Zealand: 100 Tory St, POB 9049, Wellington; tel. (04) 801-6000; fax (04) 801-6001; e-mail assemblyoffice@presbyterian.org.nz; internet www.presbyterian.org.nz; 50,000 mems; Moderator Rt Rev. GARRY MARQUAND; Assembly Exec. Sec. Rt Rev. Dr KERRY ENRIGHT.

There are several Maori Churches in New Zealand, with a total membership of over 30,000. These include the Ratana Church of New Zealand, Ringatu Church, Church of Te Kooti Rikirangi, Absolute Maori Established Church, Destiny Church and United Maori Mission. The Antiochian Orthodox Church, the Assemblies of God, the Greek Orthodox Church of New Zealand, the Liberal Catholic Church and the Society of Friends (Quakers) are also active.

BAHÁ'Í FAITH

National Spiritual Assembly of the Bahá'ís of New Zealand: POB 21-551, Henderson, Auckland 1231; tel. (9) 837-4866; fax (9) 837-4898; e-mail natsec@nsa.org.nz; internet www.bahai.org.nz; CEO SUZANNE MAHON.

The Press

NEWSPAPERS AND PERIODICALS

Principal Dailies

In 2001 there were 25 daily newspapers in New Zealand (seven morning, 18 evening).

Bay of Plenty Times: 108 Durham St, Private Bag 12002, Tauranga; tel. (7) 577-7770; fax (7) 578-0047; e-mail news@bopp.co.nz; internet www.mytown.co.nz/bayofplenty; f. 1872; evening; Mon.–Sat.; Gen. Man. ROD HALL; Editor CRAIG NICHOLSON; circ. 23,285.

The Daily News: Currie St, POB 444, New Plymouth; tel. (6) 758-0559; fax (6) 758-6849; e-mail editor@dailynews.co.nz; f. 1857; morning; Gen. Man. KEVIN NIELSEN; Editor (vacant); circ. 27,316.

The Daily Post: 1143 Hinemoa St, POB 1442, Rotorua; tel. (7) 348-6199; fax (7) 346-0153; e-mail daily@dailypost.co.nz; f. 1885; evening; Gen. Man. MIKE FLETCHER; Editor KARYN SCHERER; circ. 12,100.

Dominion Post: Dominion Post House, 40 Boulcott St, POB 3740, Wellington; tel. (4) 474-0222; fax (4) 474-0350; e-mail editor@dompost.co.nz; internet www.stuff.co.nz; f. 2002 following merger of *The Evening Post* and *The Dominion*; morning; Gen. Man. PAUL ELENIO; Editor TIM PANKHURST; circ. 98,229.

Gisborne Herald: 64 Gladstone Rd, POB 1143, Gisborne; tel. (6) 868-6655; fax (6) 867-8048; e-mail editorial@gisborneherald.co.nz; f. 1874; evening; Man. Dir M. C. MUIR; Editor IAIN GILLIES; circ. 9,587.

Hawke's Bay Today: 113 Karamu Rd, POB 180, Hastings; tel. (6) 873-0800; fax (6) 873-0805; e-mail hb_news@hbtoday.co.nz; f. 1999; evening; conservative; Gen. Man. RON D. HALL; Editor LOUIS PIERARD; circ. 33,000.

Manuwatu Standard: POB 3, Palmerston North; tel. (6) 356-9009; fax (6) 350-9545; e-mail editor@msl.co.nz; f. 1880; evening; Gen. Man. PAUL ELENIO; Editor JO MYERS; circ. 20,566.

Marlborough Express: 62–64 Arthur St, POB 242, Blenheim; tel. (3) 577-2950; fax (3) 577-2953; e-mail laurab@marlexpress.co.nz; internet www.marlboroughexpress.co.nz; f. 1866; Gen. Man. ROGER G. ROSE; Editor LAURA BASHAM; circ. 10,431.

The Nelson Mail: 15 Bridge St, POB 244, Nelson; tel. (3) 548-7079; fax (3) 546-2802; e-mail billm@nelsonmail.co.nz; f. 1866; evening; Business Man. MARK HUGHES; Editor BILL MOORE; circ. 18,555.

New Zealand Herald: 46 Albert St, POB 32, Auckland; tel. (9) 379-5050; fax (9) 373-6421; internet www.nzherald.co.nz; f. 1863; morning; Editor TIM MURPHY; circ. 215,000.

The Northern Advocate: 36 Water St, POB 210, Whangarei; tel. (9) 438-2399; fax (9) 430-5669; e-mail daily@northernadvocate.co.nz; internet www.wilsonandhorton.co.nz; f. 1875; evening; Gen. Man. J. E. P. HENTON; Editor A. VERDON; circ. 15,112.

Otago Daily Times: Lower Stuart St, POB 517, Dunedin; tel. (3) 477-4760; fax (3) 474-7422; e-mail odt.editor@alliedpress.co.nz; internet www.odt.co.nz; f. 1861; morning; Man. Dir JULIAN C. S. SMITH; Editor ROBIN CHARTERIS; circ. 44,500.

The Press: Cathedral Sq., Private Bag 4722, Christchurch; tel. (3) 379-0940; fax (3) 364-8492; e-mail editorial@press.co.nz; internet www.press.co.nz; f. 1861; morning; Gen. Man. CHRIS JAGUSCH; Editor PAUL THOMPSON; circ. 92,000.

Southland Times: 67 Esk St, POB 805, Invercargill; tel. (3) 218-1909; fax (3) 214-9905; e-mail editor@stl.co.nz; internet www.southlandtimes.co.nz; f. 1862; morning; Gen. Man. BARRY APPLEBY; Editor FRED TULETT; circ. 29,928.

Taranaki Daily News: 49–65 Currie St, New Plymouth; tel. (6) 759-0800; fax (6) 758-4653; e-mail dailynews@newszone.co.nz; f. 1857; morning; Editor LANCE GIRLING-BUTCHER; circ. 26,754.

Timaru Herald: 52 Bank St, POB 46, Timaru; tel. (3) 684-4129; fax (3) 688-1042; e-mail editor@timaruherald.co.nz; f. 1864; morning; Man. CHRIS MCAUSLIN; Editor DAVE WOOD; circ. 14,141.

Waikato Times: Private Bag 3086, Hamilton; tel. (7) 849-6180; fax (7) 849-9603; e-mail news@waikatotimes.co.nz; f. 1872; evening; independent; Gen. Man. S. MCPHERSON; Editor BRYCE JOHNS; circ. 42,000.

Wanganui Chronicle: 59 Taupo Quay, POB 433, Wanganui; tel. (6) 349-0710; fax (6) 349-0722; e-mail news@wanganuichronicle.co.nz; f. 1856; morning; Gen. Man. R. A. JARDEN; Editor J. MASLIN; circ. 13,000.

Weeklies and Other Newspapers

Best Bets: POB 1327, Auckland; fax (9) 366-4565; Sun. and Thur.; horse-racing, trotting and greyhounds; Editor MIKE BROWN; circ. 10,000.

Christchurch Star: 293 Tuam St, POB 1467, Christchurch; tel. (3) 379-7100; fax (3) 366-0180; e-mail bob_cotton@christchurchstar.co.nz; f. 1868; 2 a week; Chief Reporter BOB COTTON; circ. 118,170.

Herald on Sunday: 58 Albert St, POB 32, Auckland; tel. (9) 373-9323; fax (9) 373-9372; internet www.heraldonsunday.co.nz; f. 2004; Editor SHAYNE CURRIE.

MG Business: 8 Sheffield Cres., Christchurch 8005; tel. (3) 358-3219; fax (3) 358-4490; f. 1876; fmrly Mercantile Gazette; fortnightly; Mon; economics, finance, management, stock market, politics; Editor BILL HORSLEY; circ. 16,300.

The National Business Review: Bank of New Zealand Tower, Level 26, 125 Queen St, POB 1734, Auckland; tel. (9) 307-1629; fax (9) 307-5129; e-mail editor@nbr.co.nz; f. 1970; weekly; Editor NEVIL GIBSON; circ. 14,328.

NEW ZEALAND

New Truth and TV Extra: News Media (Auckland) Ltd, 155 New North Rd, POB 1327, Auckland; tel. (9) 302-1300; fax (9) 307-0761; e-mail editor@truth.co.nz; f. 1905; Friday; local news and features; TV and entertainment; sports; Editor CLIVE NELSON; circ. 22,000.

New Zealand Gazette: Dept of Internal Affairs, POB 805, Wellington; tel. (4) 470-2930; fax (4) 470-2932; e-mail gazette@parliament.govt.nz; internet www.gazette.govt.nz; official government publication; f. 1840; weekly; Man. JANET GOOTJES; circ. 1,000.

North Shore Times: POB 33-235, Takapuna, Auckland; tel. (9) 489-4189; fax (9) 486-1950; e-mail janet.ainsworth@snl.co.nz; 3 a week; Man. JANET AINSWORTH; Editor PETER ELY; circ. 75,000.

Sunday News: POB 1327, Auckland; tel. (9) 302-1300; fax (9) 358-3003; e-mail editor@sunday-news.co.nz; internet www.sundaynews.co.nz; Editor CLIVE NELSON; circ. 113,422.

Sunday Star-Times: POB 1409, Auckland; tel. (9) 302-1300; fax (9) 309-0258; e-mail letters@star-times.co.nz; internet www.sundaystartimes.co.nz; f. 1994 by merger; Editor CATE BRETT; circ. 210,510.

Taieri Herald: POB 105, Mosgiel; tel. (3) 489-7123; fax (3) 489-7668; f. 1962; weekly; Man. Editor LEE HARRIS; circ. 10,700.

Waihi Gazette: Waihi; weekly; Editor FRITHA TAGG; circ. 8,650.

Wairarapa News: POB 87, Masterton; tel. (6) 370-5690; fax (6) 379-6481; f. 1869; Editor ERIC TURNER; circ. 18,200.

Other Periodicals

AA Directions: AA Centre, cnr Albert and Victoria Sts, Auckland; tel. (9) 966-8800; fax (9) 966-8975; e-mail editor@aa.co.nz; internet www.aa.co.nz/Online; quarterly; official magazine of The New Zealand Automobile Association; Editor JOHN CRANNA; circ. 559,005.

Air New Zealand Inflight Magazine: Private Bag 47-920, Ponsonby, Auckland; tel. (9) 379-8822; fax (9) 379-8821; e-mail nzsales@pol.net.nz; monthly; in-flight magazine of Air New Zealand; circ. 61,000.

Architecture New Zealand: AGM Publishing Ltd, Private Bag 99-915, Newmarket, Auckland; tel. (9) 846-4068; fax (9) 846-8742; e-mail johnw@agm.co.nz; f. 1987; every 2 months; Editor JOHN WALSH; circ. 10,000.

Australian Women's Weekly (NZ edition): Private Bag 92-512, Wellesley St, Auckland; tel. (9) 308-2735; fax (9) 302-0667; monthly; Editorial Dir LOUISE WRIGHT; circ. 90,651.

Computer Buyer New Zealand: 246 Queen St, Level 8, Auckland; tel. (9) 377-9902; fax (9) 377-4604; every 2 months; Man. Editor DON HILL; circ. 120,968.

Dairying Today: POB 3855, Auckland; tel. (9) 307-0399; fax (9) 307-0122; e-mail editor@ruralnews.co.nz; internet www.ruralnews.co.nz; monthly; Editor ADAM FRICKER; circ. 25,979.

Fashion Quarterly: ACP Media Centre, Private Bag 92-512, Auckland; tel. (9) 308-2735; fax (9) 302-0667; e-mail fq@acpmedia.co.nz; f. 1982; 5 a year; Editor LEONIE BARLOW; circ. 31,500.

Friday Flash: 155 New North Rd, POB 1327, Auckland; tel. (9) 302-1300; fax (9) 366-4565; e-mail editor@friday-flash.co.nz; weekly; racing; Editor MIKE BROWN; circ. 7,926.

Grapevine: Private Bag 92-124, Auckland; tel. (9) 624-3079; fax (9) 625-8788; monthly; family magazine; Editor JOHN COONEY; circ. 149,658.

Info-Link: AGM Publishing Ltd, Private Bag 99-915, Newmarket, Auckland; tel. (9) 846-4068; fax (9) 846-8742; e-mail pengelly@agm.co.nz; internet www.info-link.co.nz; quarterly; Editors SALLY LINDSAY, REBECCA WOOD; circ. 22,000.

Inwood Magazine: POB 89-027, 7 Tipau St, Torbay; tel. (9) 473-1901; fax (9) 473-1853; e-mail magazines@npl.net.nz; internet www.inwoodmag.com; f. 1993; monthly; forestry; Publr TONY NEILSON; circ. 8,000.

Landfall: University of Otago Press, POB 56, Dunedin; tel. (3) 479-8807; fax (3) 479-8385; e-mail landfall@otago.ac.nz; internet www.otago.ac.nz/press/landfall; f. 1947; 2 a year; literary; circ. 1,200.

Mana Magazine: POB 1101, Rotorua; tel. (7) 349-0260; fax (7) 349-0258; e-mail editor@manaonline.co.nz; internet www.manaonline.co.nz; Maori news magazine; Editor DEREK FOX.

Management: Wellesley St, POB 5544, Auckland; tel. (9) 630-8940; fax (9) 630-1046; e-mail editor@management.co.nz; internet www.profile.co.nz; f. 1954; monthly; business; Editor REG BIRCHFIELD; circ. 12,000.

New Idea New Zealand: 48 Greys Ave, 4th Floor, Auckland; tel. (9) 979-2700; fax (9) 979-2721; weekly; women's interest; Editor (vacant); circ. 59,039.

New Truth: 155 New North Rd, Auckland 1; tel. (9) 302-1300; fax (9) 307-0761; e-mail editor@truth.co.nz; weekly; Editor CLIVE NELSON; circ. 22,000.

New Zealand Dairy Exporter: POB 5544, Wellesley St, Auckland; tel. (9) 630-1624; fax (9) 630-1046; e-mail glenys@dairymag.co.nz; internet www.dairymag.co.nz; f. 1925; monthly; Editor GLENYS CHRISTIAN; circ. 22,739.

New Zealand Gardener: POB 6341, Wellesley St, Auckland; tel. (4) 293-4495; f. 1944; monthly; Editor P. McGEORGE; circ. 77,077.

New Zealand Horse and Pony: POB 12965, Penrose, Auckland; tel. (9) 634-1800; fax (9) 634-2948; e-mail editor@horse-pony.co.nz; internet www.horse-pony.co.nz; f. 1959; monthly; Editor ROWAN DIXON; circ. 11,941.

New Zealand Medical Journal: Department of Surgery, Christchurch Hospital, POB 4345, Christchurch; tel. (3) 364-1277; fax (3) 364-1683; e-mail frank.frizelle@cdhb.govt.nz; internet www.nzma.org.nz; 2 a month; Editor Prof. FRANK A. FRIZELLE; circ. 5,000.

New Zealand Science Review: POB 1874, Wellington; fax (4) 389-5095; e-mail mberridge@malaghan.org.nz; internet www.rsnz.govt.nz/clan/nzmss; f. 1942; 4 a year; reviews, policy and philosophy of science; Editor M. V. BERRIDGE.

New Zealand Woman's Day: Wellesley St, Private Bag 92-512, Auckland; tel. (9) 308-2700; fax (9) 357-0978; e-mail wdaynz@acp.nz.co.nz; weekly; Editor-in-Chief LOUISE WRIGHT; circ. 143,420.

New Zealand Woman's Weekly: NZ Magazines Ltd, POB 90-119, Auckland Mail Centre, Auckland; tel. (9) 360-3820; fax (9) 360-3826; e-mail editor@nzww.co.nz; internet www.on-line.co.nz; f. 1932; Mon.; women's issues and general interest; Editor NICKY PELLEGRINO; circ. 130,706.

Next: Level 4, cnr Fanshawe and Beamont Sts, Westhaven, Private Bag 92-512, Auckland 1036; tel. (9) 308-2773; fax (9) 377-6725; e-mail next@acpmedia.co.nz; f. 1991; monthly; home and lifestyle; Editor SUSANNAH WALKER; circ. 63,000.

North & South: Wellesley St, Private Bag 92-512, Auckland; tel. (9) 308-2700; fax (9) 308-9498; e-mail northsouth@acpmedia.co.nz; f. 1986; monthly; current affairs and lifestyle; Editor ROBYN LANGWELL; circ. 35,959.

NZ Catholic: POB 147-000, Ponsonby, Auckland 1034; tel. (9) 378-4380; fax (9) 360-3065; e-mail catholic@iconz.co.nz; internet www.nzcatholic.org.nz; f. 1996; fortnightly; Roman Catholic; Editor PAT MCCARTHY; circ. 7,000.

NZ Home and Entertaining: ACP Media Centre, cnr Fanshawe and Beaumont Sts, Private Bag 92-512, Auckland; tel. (9) 308-2700; e-mail cmccall@acpmedia.co.nz; f. 1936; bi-monthly, design, architecture, lifestyle; Editor JEREMY HANSEN; circ. 23,000.

NZ House and Garden: 131 New North Rd, Eden Terrace, Auckland; tel. (9) 353-1010; fax (9) 353-1020; internet www.nzhouse-garden.co.nz; monthly; circ. 76,461.

NZ Listener: POB 90-783, Auckland Mail Centre, Level 4, APN Bldg, 46 Albert St, Auckland; tel. (9) 373-9400; fax (9) 373-9406; internet www.listener.co.nz; f. 1939; weekly; current affairs and entertainment; Editor PAMELA STIRLING; Publr and Chief Exec. RICK NEVILLE; circ. 73,404.

Otago Southland Farmer: POB 105, Mosgiel; tel. (3) 489-7123; fax (3) 489-7668; e-mail suzanne.muir@stl.co.nz; fortnightly; Editor MARGARET PHILLIPS; Reg. Man. SUZANNE MUIR; circ. 22,080.

Pacific Wings: NZ Wings Ltd, Harewood, POB 39-099, Christchurch; tel. (3) 359-0256; fax (3) 982-3595; e-mail editor@nzwings.co.nz; internet www.nzwings.co.nz; f. 1932; monthly; Editor CALLUM MACPHERSON; circ. 20,000.

Prodesign: AGM Publishing Ltd, Private Bag 99-915, Newmarket, Auckland; tel. (9) 846-4068; fax (9) 846-8742; e-mail greg@agm.co.nz; f. 1993; every 2 months; publ. of the Designers' Institute of New Zealand; Editor GREG FRAME; circ. 8,000.

PSA Journal: PSA House, 11 Aurora Terrace, POB 3817, Wellington 1; tel. (4) 917-0333; fax (4) 917-2051; e-mail enquiries@psa.org.nz; internet www.pas.org.nz; f. 1913; 4 a year; journal of the NZ Public Service Asscn; circ. 52,000.

Reader's Digest: POB 90-489, Auckland; e-mail editors.au@readersdigest.com; internet www.readersdigest.co.nz; f. 1950; monthly; Editor TONY SPENCER-SMITH; circ. 85,036.

RSA Review: 181 Willis St, POB 27-248, Wellington; tel. (4) 384-7994; fax (4) 385-3325; e-mail rsareview@rnzrsa.org.nz; internet www.rsa.org.nz; quarterly; official magazine of the Royal New Zealand Returned And Services' Asscn; Editor PAUL HARRISON; circ. 95,000.

Rural News: POB 3855, Auckland; tel. (9) 307-0399; fax (9) 307-0122; e-mail rural_news@clear.net.nz; fortnightly; Editor ADAM FRICKER; circ. 88,366.

SHE Magazine: Wellesley St, Private Bag 92-512, Auckland; tel. (9) 308-2735; fax (9) 302-0667; e-mail she@acpmedia.co.nz; Editor LEONIE BARLOW.

Spanz: POB 9049, Wellington; tel. (4) 801-6000; fax (4) 801-6001; e-mail commsmanager@presbyterian.org.nz; internet www

.presbyterian.org.nz; f. 1987; bi-monthly; magazine of Presbyterian Church; circ. 21,500.

Straight Furrow: c/o Rural Press, POB 4233, Auckland; tel. (9) 376-9786; fax (9) 376-9780; e-mail straightfurrow@ruralpress.com; internet www.straightfurrow.co.nz; f. 1933; fortnightly; Editor SUSAN TOPLESS; circ. 85,000.

Time New Zealand: Hopetoun St, Level 8, Newton; fax (9) 366-4706; internet www.timepacific.com; weekly; circ. 35,467.

TV Guide (NZ): POB 1327, Auckland; tel. (9) 302-1300; fax (9) 373-3036; e-mail editor@tv-guide.co.nz; f. 1986; weekly; Editor JULIE ELEY; circ. 207,894.

UNANewZ: UN Asscn of NZ, POB 12324, Wellington; tel. (4) 473-0441; fax (4) 473-2339; e-mail unanz@xtra.co.nz; internet www.converge.org.nz/unanz; f. 1945; quarterly; Editor (vacant).

NEWS AGENCIES

New Zealand Press Association: Newspaper House, 93 Boulcott St, POB 1599, Wellington; tel. (4) 472-7910; fax (4) 473-7480; e-mail news@nzpa.co.nz; internet www.nzpa-online.co.nz; f. 1879; non-political; Chair. JULIAN SMITH.

South Pacific News Service Ltd (Sopacnews): Lambton Quay, POB 5026, Wellington; tel. and fax (3) 472-8329; f. 1948; Man. Editor NEALE MCMILLAN.

Foreign Bureaux

Agence France-Presse (AFP): Manners St, POB 11-420, Wellington; tel. (021) 688438; fax (021) 471085; e-mail afpnz@clear.net.nz; Correspondent MICHAEL FIELD.

Reuters New Zealand Ltd (United Kingdom): POB 11-744, Wellington; tel. (4) 471-4234; e-mail wellington.newsroom@reuters.com; Correspondent GYLES BECKFORD.

United Press International (UPI) (USA): Press Gallery, Parliament Bldgs, Wellington; tel. (4) 471-9552; fax (4) 472-7604; Correspondent BRENDON BURNS.

Xinhua (New China) News Agency (People's Republic of China): 136 Northland Rd, Northland, Wellington; tel. (4) 475-7607; fax (4) 475-7607; e-mail xinhua@ihug.co.nz; Correspondent ZHOU CIPU.

PRESS COUNCIL

New Zealand Press Council: The Terrace, POB 10879, Wellington; tel. (4) 473-5220; fax (4) 471-1785; e-mail presscouncil@asa.co.nz; internet www.presscouncil.org.nz; f. 1972; Chair. BARRY PATERSON; Sec. M. E. MAJOR.

PRESS ASSOCIATIONS

Commonwealth Press Union (New Zealand Section): POB 1066, Wellington; tel. (4) 472-6223; fax (4) 471-0987; Chair. T. PANKHURST; Sec. L. GOULD.

Newspaper Publishers' Association of New Zealand (Inc): Newspaper House, 93 Boulcott St, POB 1066, Wellington 1; tel. (4) 472-6223; fax (4) 471-0987; e-mail npa@npa.co.nz; internet wwww.npa.gov.nz; f. 1898; 31 mems; Pres. J. SANDERS; CEO L. GOULD; Corporate Affairs Man. H. SOUTER.

Publishers

Auckland University Press: Private Bag 92-019, University of Auckland, Auckland; tel. (9) 373-7528; fax (9) 373-7465; e-mail aup@auckland.ac.nz; internet www.auckland.ac.nz/aup; f. 1966; scholarly; Dir ELIZABETH P. CAFFIN.

Christchurch Caxton Press Ltd: 113 Victoria St, POB 25-088, Christchurch 1; tel. (3) 366-8516; fax (3) 365-7840; f. 1935; human and general interest, local and NZ history, tourist pubs; Man. Dir BRUCE BASCAND.

Dunmore Publishing Ltd: POB 250-80, Wellington; tel. (4) 472-2705; fax (4) 471-0604; e-mail books@dunmore.co.nz; internet www.dunmore.co.nz; f. 1975; non-fiction, educational; Publrs MURRAY GATENBY, SHARMIAN FIRTH.

Hachette Livre NZ Ltd: POB 100-749, North Shore Mail Centre, Auckland 1330; tel. (9) 478-1000; fax (9) 478-1010; e-mail admin@hachette.co.nz; f. 1971; fmrly Hodder Moa Beckett Publishers Ltd; Man. Dir KEVIN CHAPMAN.

HarperCollins Publishers (New Zealand) Ltd: 31 View Rd, Glenfield, Auckland; tel. (9) 443-9400; fax (9) 443-9403; f. 1888; general and educational; Man. Dir BARRIE HITCHON.

Learning Media Ltd: POB 3293, Wellington; tel. (4) 472-5522; fax (4) 472-6444; e-mail info@learningmedia.co.nz; internet www.learningmedia.com; f. 1947 as School Publications; became Crown-owned company in 1993; general and educational books, audio cassettes, videos and computer software in English, Spanish, Maori, etc.; International Man. TRISH STEVENSON.

Legislation Direct: POB 12-418, Wellington; tel. (4) 495-2882; fax (4) 495-2880; e-mail idenquiries@legislationdirect.co.nz; internet www.legislationdirect.co.nz; general publishers and leading distributor of government pubs; fmrly Govt Printing Office/GP Publications; Publications Man. WENDY CAYLOR.

LexisNexis NZ Ltd: 205–207 Victoria St, POB 472, Wellington; tel. (4) 385-1479; fax (4) 385-1598; e-mail customer.relations@lexisnexis.co.nz; internet www.lexisnexis.co.nz; legal; Country Man. STEPHEN DUNN.

McGraw-Hill Book Co, New Zealand Ltd: Westfield Tower, 2nd Floor, Westfield Shopping Town, Manukau City, POB 97082, Wiri; tel. (9) 262-2537; fax (9) 262-2540; e-mail cservice_auckland@mcgraw-hill.com; f. 1974; educational; Man. FIRGAL ADAMS.

New Zealand Council for Educational Research: POB 3237, Wellington; tel. (4) 384-7939; fax (4) 384-7933; e-mail sales@nzcer.org.nz; internet www.nzcer.org.nz; f. 1934; scholarly, research monographs, educational, academic, periodicals; Chair. Prof. RUTH MANSELL; Dir ROBYN BAKER.

Pearson Education New Zealand Ltd: Private Bag 102-908, North Shore Mail Centre, Glenfield, Auckland 10; tel. (9) 414-9980; fax (9) 414-9981; e-mail rosemary.stagg@pearsoned.co.nz; f. 1968; fmrly Addison Wesley Longman; educational; Dirs ROSEMARY STAGG, P. FIELD.

Penguin Group (NZ) Ltd: cnr Airborne and Rosedale Rds, Albany, Private Bag 102-902, North Shore Mail Centre, Auckland; tel. (9) 415-4700; fax (9) 415-4701; e-mail geoff.walker@penguin.co.nz; internet www.penguin.co.nz; f. 1973; Publ. Dir GEOFF WALKER; Man. Dir TONY HARKINS.

Wendy Pye Ltd: Private Bag 17-905, Greenlane, Auckland; tel. (9) 525-3575; fax (9) 525-4205; e-mail admin@sunshine.co.nz; children's fiction and educational; Man. Dir WENDY PYE.

Random House New Zealand Ltd: Private Bag 102-950, North Shore Mail Centre, Glenfield, Auckland; tel. (9) 444-7197; fax (9) 444-7524; e-mail admin@randomhouse.co.nz; internet www.randomhouse.co.nz; f. 1977; general; Man. Dir MICHAEL MOYNAHAN.

Reed Publishing (NZ) Ltd: Private Bag 34-901, Birkenhead, Auckland 10; tel. (9) 441-2960; fax (9) 480-4999; e-mail info@reed.co.nz; internet www.reed.co.nz; children's and general non-fiction; Heinemann Education primary, secondary, tertiary and library; Man. Dir ALAN L. SMITH.

University of Otago Press: POB 56, Dunedin; tel. (3) 479-8807; fax (3) 479-8385; e-mail university.press@otago.ac.nz; internet www.otago.ac.nz/press; f. 1958; publishes titles on New Zealand, the Pacific and Asia, with special emphasis on history, literature, the arts and natural and social sciences; also educational titles and journals; Publr WENDY HARREX.

Whitcoulls Ltd: 210 Queen St, 3rd Floor, Private Bag 92-098, Auckland 1; tel. (9) 356-5410; fax (9) 356-5423; NZ, general and educational; Gen. Man. S. PRESTON.

PUBLISHERS' ASSOCIATION

Book Publishers' Association of New Zealand Inc: POB 36-477, Northcote, Auckland 1309; tel. (9) 480-2711; fax (9) 480-1130; e-mail bpanz@copyright.co.nz; internet www.bpanz.org.nz; f. 1977; Pres. ELIZABETH CAFFIN.

Broadcasting and Communications

TELECOMMUNICATIONS

Compass Communications Ltd: POB 2533, Auckland; tel. (9) 965-2200; fax (9) 965-2270; e-mail helpdesk@compass.net.nz; internet www.compass.net.nz; f. 1995; CEO KARIM HUSSONA.

Global One Communications Ltd: Phillips Fox Tower, Level 15, 209 Queen St, Auckland; tel. (9) 357-3700; fax (9) 357-3737.

NewCall Group Ltd: POB 8703, Level 2, NewCall Tower, Symonds St, 44 Khyber Pass, Auckland; tel. (9) 917-6572; fax (9) 917-8338; e-mail info@newcall.co.nz; internet www.newcall.co.nz; Man. Dir G. JAMES BRACKNELL, Jr.

Singtel Optus Ltd: ASB Centre, Level 14, 135 Albert St, Auckland; tel. (9) 356-2660; fax (9) 356-2669.

Telecom Corpn of New Zealand Ltd: Telecom Networks House, 68 Jervois Quay, POB 570, Wellington; tel. (4) 801-9000; fax (4) 385-3469; internet www.telecom.co.nz; Chair. RODERICK DEANE; Chief Exec. THERESA GATTUNG.

TelstraClear: TelstraClear Centre, cnr Northcote and Taharoto Rds, Takapuna, Private Bag 92-143, Auckland; tel. (9) 912-4200; fax (9) 912-4442; e-mail webmaster@telstraclear.co.nz; internet www.telstraclear.co.nz; f. 1990 as Clear Communications Ltd; merged

NEW ZEALAND

Directory

with TelstraSaturn Ltd 2001; business solutions, local and toll services, enhanced internet, etc.; Chair. JOHN B. EDE; CEO ROSEMARY HOWARD; Man. Dir STEVE BURDON.

Vodafone New Zealand Ltd: 21 Pitt St, Private Bag 92-161, Auckland; tel. (9) 357-5100; fax (9) 357-4836; internet www.vodafone.co.nz; fmrly Bell South; cellular network; CEO RUSSELL STANNERS.

Woosh Wireless Ltd: 11–15 Railway St, POB 9635, Newmarket, Auckland; fax (9) 520-3447; internet www.woosh.com; f. 1999 as Walker Wireless Ltd; name changed as above 2003; provides internet and telephony services; Chair. ROD INGLIS; CEO BOB SMITH.

WorldxChange Communications Ltd: 55 Shortland St, POB 3296, Auckland; tel. (9) 308-1300; e-mail info@wxc.co.nz; internet www.wxc.co.nz.

Regulatory Authority

Telecommunications Policy Section, Ministry of Economic Development: 33 Bowen St, POB 1473, Wellington; tel. (4) 472-0030; fax (4) 499-0969; e-mail info@med.govt.nz; internet www.med.govt.nz/pbt/telecom.html.

BROADCASTING

In December 1995 Radio New Zealand Commercial (RNZC) and New Zealand Public Radio Ltd (NZPR) became independent entities, having assumed responsibility for, respectively, the commercial and non-commercial activities of Radio New Zealand. RNZC was sold to the New Zealand Radio Network Consortium in 1996, and NZPR, which remained a Crown-owned company, assumed the name of its now-defunct parent company, to become Radio New Zealand Ltd. In late 1999 there were 190 radio stations broadcasting on a continuous basis, of which 170 were operating on a commercial basis.

Radio

Radio Broadcasters' Association (NZ) Inc: POB 3762, Auckland; tel. (9) 378-0788; fax (9) 378-8180; e-mail rba@xtra.co.nz; represents commercial radio industry; Exec. Dir D. N. G. INNES; Sec. JANINE BLISS; 142 mems.

Radio New Zealand Ltd: RNZ House, 155 The Terrace, POB 123, Wellington; tel. (4) 474-1999; fax (4) 474-1459; e-mail rnz@radionz.co.nz; internet www.radionz.co.nz; f. 1936; Crown-owned entity, operating non-commercial national networks: National Radio and Concert FM; parliamentary broadcasts on AM Network; Radio New Zealand News and Current Affairs; the short-wave service, Radio New Zealand International; and archives; Chair. BRIAN CORBAN; Dep. Chair. ALISON TIMMS.

The Radio Network of New Zealand Ltd: 54 Cook St, Private Bag 92-198, Auckland; tel. (9) 373-0000; e-mail enquiry@radionetwork.co.nz; internet www.radionetwork.co.nz; operates 117 commercial stations, reaching 1.3m. people; Chief Exec. JOHN MCELHINNEY.

Television

Television New Zealand (TVNZ) Ltd: Television Centre, 100 Victoria St West, POB 3819, Auckland; tel. (9) 916-7000; fax (9) 916-7934; internet www.tvnz.co.nz; f. 1960; the television service is responsible for the production of programmes for two TV networks, TV One and 2; networks are commercial all week and transmit in colour; both channels broadcast 24 hours a day, seven days a week, and reach 99.9% of the population; Chair. Sir JOHN ANDERSON.

Maori Television: 9–15 Davis Crescent, POB 113-017, Newmarket, Auckland; tel. (9) 539-7000; fax (9) 539-7199; e-mail info@maoritelevision.com; internet www.maoritelevision.com; f. 2003; broadcasts Maori- and English-language programmes for 7.5 hrs daily; Chair. WAYNE WALDEN.

Private Television

Auckland Independent Television Services Ltd: POB 1629, Auckland.

Bay Satellite TV Ltd: Hastings; tel. (6) 878-9081; fax (6) 878-5994; Man. Dir JOHN LYNAM.

Broadcast Communications Ltd: POB 2495, Auckland; tel. (9) 916-6400; fax (9) 916-6404; internet www.bclnz.co.nz; principal shareholder is Television New Zealand (TVNZ) Ltd; Man. Dir GEOFF LAWSON.

Sky Network Television Limited: 10 Panorama Rd, POB 9059, Newmarket, Auckland; tel. (9) 579-9999; fax (9) 579-0910; internet www.skytv.co.nz; f. 1990; UHF service on six channels, satellite service on 18 channels; Chair. T. MOCKRIDGE; CEO J. FELLET.

TV3 Network Services Ltd: Symonds St, Private Bag 92-624, Auckland; tel. (9) 377-9730; fax (9) 366-5999; internet www.tv3.co.nz; f. 1989; owned by CanWest Global Corpn; Man. Dir RICK FRIESEN.

TV4 Network Ltd: Symonds St, Private Bag 92-624, Auckland; tel. (9) 377-9730; fax (9) 366-5999; e-mail di.winks@tv3.co.nz; internet www.ctv4.co.nz; 'free-to-air' entertainment channel; Man. Dir RICK FRIESEN.

Finance

(cap. = capital; res = reserves; dep. = deposits; m. = million; amounts in New Zealand dollars)

BANKING

Central Bank

Reserve Bank of New Zealand: 2 The Terrace, POB 2498, Wellington; tel. (4) 472-2029; fax (4) 473-8554; e-mail rbnz-info@rbnz.govt.nz; internet www.rbnz.govt.nz; f. 1934; res 416.2m., dep. 8,215.3m. (June 2003); Gov. ALAN BOLLARD; Dep. Gov. ADRIAN ORR.

Registered Banks

As a result of legislation which took effect in April 1987, several foreign banks were incorporated into the domestic banking system.

ANZ National Bank Ltd: Level 10, 2 Hunter St, Wellington; tel. (4) 496-7000; fax (4) 494-4000; internet www.anz.com/nz; f. 1979; subsidiary of Australia and New Zealand Banking Group Ltd of Melbourne, Australia; fmrly ANZ Banking Group (New Zealand) Ltd; name changed as above 2004 following merger with National Bank of New Zealand Ltd; cap. 5,943m., dep. 60,675m. (March 2004); Chair. R. S. DEANE; Chief Exec. GRAHAM HODGES; 143 brs and sub-brs.

ASB Bank Ltd: ASB Bank Centre, cnr Wellesley and Albert Sts, POB 35, Auckland 1; tel. (9) 377-8930; fax (9) 358-3511; e-mail helpdesk@asbbank.co.nz; internet www.asbbank.co.nz; f. 1847 as Auckland Savings Bank, name changed 1988; cap. 523.1m., res 786.8m., dep. 25,620.5m. (June 2003); Chair. G. J. JUDD; Man. Dir G. HUGH BURRETT; 123 brs.

Bank of New Zealand (BNZ): BNZ Centre, 1 Willis St, POB 2392, Wellington; tel. (4) 474-6999; fax (4) 474-6861; internet www.bnz.co.nz; f. 1861; owned by National Australia Bank; cap. 2,063m., dep. 30,762m. (Sept. 2002); Chair. T. K. MCDONALD; Man. Dir P. THODEY; 241 brs and sub-brs.

Citibank NA (USA): 23 Customs Street East, POB 3429, Auckland; tel. (9) 302-3128; fax (9) 308-9928; internet www.citibank.com.au; CEO ANDREW AU; 2 brs.

Deutsche Bank AG: Wellesley St, POB 6900, Auckland; tel. (9) 351-1000; fax (9) 351-1001; internet www.deutsche-bank.co.nz; f. 1986; fmrly Bankers Trust New Zealand; Chief Country Officer BRETT SHEPHERD.

Hongkong and Shanghai Banking Corporation Ltd (Hong Kong): 1 Queen St, Level 9, POB 5947, Auckland; tel. (9) 308-8888; fax (9) 308-8997; e-mail hsbcplb@clear.net.nz; internet www.hsbc.co.nz; CEO NORMAN A. WILSON; 6 brs.

Kiwibank Ltd: Private Bag 39888, Wellington; tel. (4) 462-7900; fax (4) 462-7996; internet www.kiwibank.co.nz; f. 2001; 100% New Zealand-owned; savings bank for small depositors; Chair. JIM BOLGER; Chief Exec. SAM KNOWLES.

Rabobank (New Zealand): POB 38-396, Wellington Mail Centre, Wellington; tel. (4) 462-5650; fax (4) 462-5660; e-mail wellington.enquiry@rabobank.com; internet www.rabobank.co.nz; f. 1996; full subsidiary of Rabobank Nederland; CEO BRUCE DICK.

TSB Bank Ltd: POB 240, New Plymouth; tel. (6) 968-3810; fax (6) 968-3815; internet www.tsbbank.co.nz; f. 1850; dep. 2,300m. (March 2006); Man. Dir K. W. RIMMINGTON; 15 brs.

Westland Bank Ltd: 99 Revell St, POB 103, Hokitika; tel. (3) 755-8680; fax (3) 755-8277; full subsidiary of ASB Bank Ltd; cap. and res 6,176m., dep. 108m. (June 1992); Man. Dir K. J. BEAMS; 9 brs.

WestpacTrust: 318 Lambton Quay, POB 691, Wellington; tel. (4) 498-1000; fax (4) 498-1350; e-mail customer_support@westpac.co.nz; internet www.westpac.co.nz; acquired Trust Bank New Zealand; New Zealand division of Westpac Banking Corpn (Australia); Chief Exec. D. T. GALLAGHER.

Other Banks

Postbank: 58–66 Willis St, Wellington 1; tel. (4) 729-809; f. 1987; owned by Australia and New Zealand Banking Corpn; 550 brs.

Association

New Zealand Bankers' Association: POB 3043, Wellington; tel. (4) 472-8838; fax (4) 473-1698; e-mail nzba@nzba.org.nz; internet www.nzba.org.nz; f. 1891; Chief Exec. ALAN YATES.

STOCK EXCHANGES

Dunedin Stock Exchange: POB 298, Dunedin; tel. (3) 477-5900; Chair. E. S. EDGAR; Sec. R. P. LEWIS.

NEW ZEALAND

New Zealand Exchange Ltd: Level 2, NSX Centre, 11 Cable St, POB 2959, Wellington 1; tel. (4) 472-7599; fax (4) 496-2893; e-mail info@nzx.com; internet www.nzx.com; Chair. SIMON ALLEN; CEO MARK WELDON.

Supervisory Body

New Zealand Securities Commission: POB 1179, Wellington; tel. (4) 472-9830; fax (4) 472-8076; e-mail seccom@sec-com.govt.nz; internet www.sec-com.govt.nz; f. 1979; Chair. JANE DIPLOCK.

INSURANCE

ACE Insurance NZ Ltd: POB 734, Auckland; tel. (9) 377-1459; fax (9) 303-1909; e-mail scott.pickering@ace-ina.com; Man. Dir SCOTT PICKERING.

AMI Insurance Ltd: 29–35 Latimer Sq., POB 2116, Christchurch; tel. (3) 371-9000; fax (3) 371-8314; e-mail amichch@es.co.nz; internet www.ami.co.nz; f. 1926; Chair. KERRY G. L. NOLAN; CEO JOHN B. BALMFORTH.

ANZ Life Assurance Co Ltd: POB 1492, Wellington; tel. (4) 496-7000; fax (4) 470-5100; Man. R. A. DEAN.

AXA New Zealand Ltd: POB 1692, Wellington; tel. (4) 474-4500; fax (4) 472-5069; internet www.axa.co.nz; CEO RALPH STEWART.

BNZ Life Insurance Ltd: POB 1299, Wellington; tel. (4) 382-2577; fax (4) 474-6883; e-mail rodger-murphy@bnz.co.nz; internet www.bnz.co.nz; Gen. Man. R. J. MURPHY.

Farmers' Mutual Group: 68 The Square, POB 1943, Palmerston North 5330; tel. (6) 356-9456; fax (6) 356-4603; e-mail enquiries@fmg.co.nz; internet fmg.co.nz; comprises Farmers' Mutual Insurance Asscn, Farmers' Mutual Insurance Ltd and other cos; fire, accident, motor vehicle, marine, life; Chair. PETER JENSEN.

Gerling NCM EXGO: POB 3933, Wellington 6015; tel. (4) 472-4142; fax (4) 472-6966; e-mail info@gerlingEXGO.co.nz; internet www.gerlingEXGO.co.nz; trade credit insurance services; division of Gerling NZ Ltd since December 2001; Gen. Man. ARTHUR C. DAVIS.

ING Life (NZ) Ltd: 205 Wairau Rd, Glenfield, Auckland 1310; tel. (9) 442-4800; fax (9) 442-4801; e-mail enquiries@inglife.co.nz; internet www.inglife.co.nz; Man. Dir NAOMI BALLANTYNE.

New Zealand Insurance: IAG House, 151 Queen St, Private Bag 92130, Auckland 1030; tel. (9) 309-7000; fax (9) 309-7097; internet www.nzi.co.nz; owned by Insurance Australia Group New Zealand Ltd; Chief Exec. DAVID SMITH.

New Zealand Local Government Insurance Corporation Ltd (Civic Assurance): Local Government Bldg, 114–118 Lambton Quay, POB 5521, Wellington; tel. (4) 978-1250; fax (4) 978-1260; e-mail tim.sole@civicassurance.co.nz; internet www.civicassurance.co.nz; f. 1960; fire, motor, all risks, accident; Chief Exec. TIM SOLE; Gen. Man. GEOFF MERCER.

Promina Group: 48 Shortland St, Auckland; tel. (9) 363-2222; internet www.promina.co.nz; f. 1878; fmrly Royal & SunAlliance; comprises AA Insurance, Vero Insurance New Zealand Ltd and other cos; fire, accident, marine, general; CEO MICHAEL WILKINS.

QBE Insurance (International) Ltd: POB 44, Auckland; tel. (9) 366-9920; fax (9) 366-9935; e-mail gevans@qbe.co.nz; f. 1890; Gen. Man. GRAEME EVANS.

Sovereign Ltd: Sovereign House, 33–45 Hurstmere Rd, Private Bag Sovereign, Auckland; tel. (9) 486-9500; fax (9) 486-9501; e-mail emailus@sovereign.co.nz; internet www.sovereign.co.nz; f. 1989; life insurance and investment.

State Insurance Ltd: Microsoft House, 3–11 Hunter St, POB 5037, Wellington 1; tel. (4) 496-9600; fax (4) 476-9664; internet www.state.co.nz; f. 1905; mem. NRMA Insurance Group; Man. Dir T. C. SOLE.

Tower Insurance Ltd: 22 Fanshawe St, POB 90-347, Auckland; tel. (9) 369-2200; fax (9) 369-2128; internet www.towerlimited.com; f. 1873; fmrly National Insurance Co of New Zealand; CEO P. LINDHOUT.

Associations

Insurance Council of New Zealand: POB 474, Wellington; tel. (4) 472-5230; fax (4) 473-3011; e-mail icnz@icnz.org.nz; internet www.icnz.org.nz; CEO CHRISTOPHER RYAN.

Investment Savings and Insurance Association of New Zealand Inc: POB 1514, Wellington; tel. (4) 473-8730; fax (4) 471-1881; e-mail isi@isi.org.nz; internet www.isi.org.nz; f. 1996 from Life Office Asscn and Investment Funds Asscn; represents cos that act as manager, trustee, issuer, insurer, etc. of managed funds, life insurance and superannuation; Chief Exec. VANCE ARKINSTALL; Exec. Officer DEBORAH KEATING.

Trade and Industry

GOVERNMENT AGENCY

New Zealand Trade and Enterprise: POB 2878, Wellington; tel. (4) 910-4300; fax (4) 910-4309; e-mail info@nzte.govt.nz; internet www.nzte.govt.nz; f. 2003; national government development agency with global network of 48 offices; provides businesses, organizations and investors with access to quality New Zealand goods and services and acts as a gateway to partnerships with New Zealand businesses and to investment opportunities in New Zealand; CEO TIM GIBSON; Chair. PHIL LOUGH.

CHAMBERS OF COMMERCE

Auckland Regional Chamber of Commerce and Industry: POB 47, Auckland; tel. (9) 309-6100; fax (9) 309-0081; e-mail mbarnett@chamber.co.nz; internet www.chamber.co.nz; CEO MICHAEL BARNETT; Pres. DAVID TRUSCOTT.

Canterbury Employers' Chamber of Commerce: 57 Kilmore St, POB 359, Christchurch; tel. (3) 366-5096; fax (3) 379-5454; e-mail info@cecc.org.nz; internet www.cecc.org.nz; Chief Exec. PETER TOWNSEND.

Otago Chamber of Commerce and Industry Inc: Westpac Trust Bldg, Level 7, 106 George St, Dunedin; tel. (3) 477-0341; fax (3) 643-0341; e-mail office@otagochamber.co.nz; internet www.otagochamber.co.nz; f. 1861; CEO J. A. CHRISTIE; Pres. N. SMITH.

Wellington Regional Chamber of Commerce: 109 Featherston St, 9th Floor, POB 1590, Wellington; tel. (4) 914-6500; fax (4) 914-6524; e-mail info@wgtn-chamber.co.nz; internet www.wgtn-chamber.co.nz; f. 1856; Chief Exec. CHARLES FINNY; Pres. SIMON ARNOLD; 1,000 mems.

INDUSTRIAL AND TRADE ASSOCIATIONS

Canterbury Manufacturers' Association: POB 13-152, Armagh, Christchurch; tel. (3) 353-2540; fax (3) 353-2549; e-mail cma@cma.org.nz; internet www.cma.org.nz; f. 1879; CEO JOHN WALLEY; 500 mems.

Employers' and Manufacturers' Association (Central Inc): Federation House, 95–99 Molesworth St, POB 1087, Wellington; tel. (4) 473-7224; fax (4) 473-4501; e-mail ema@emacentral.org.nz; f. 1997 by merger of Wellington Manufacturers' Asscn and Wellington Regional Employers' Asscn; Pres. R. KERR-NEWELL; 2,200 mems.

Employers' and Manufacturers' Association (Northern Inc): 159 Khyber Pass Rd, Grafton, Private Bag 92066, Auckland; tel. (9) 367-0900; fax (9) 367-0902; e-mail ema@ema.co.nz; internet www.ema.co.nz; f. 1886; fmrly Auckland Manufacturers' Asscn; Pres. T. ARNOLD; 5,000 mems.

ENZAFRUIT: POB 279, Hastings; tel. (6) 878-1898; fax (6) 878-1850; e-mail info@enza.co.nz; fmrly New Zealand Apple and Pear Marketing Board; Man. Dir MICHAEL DOSSOR; Chair. B. BIRNIE.

Federated Farmers of New Zealand (Inc): POB 715, Wellington; tel. (4) 473-7269; fax (4) 473-1081; e-mail wellingtonoffice@fedfarm.org.nz; internet www.fedfarm.org.nz; f. 1946; Pres. ALISTAIR POLSON; CEO TONY ST CLAIR; 16,000 mems.

Kiwifruit New Zealand: POB 4246, Mt Maunganui South; tel. (7) 574-7139; fax (7) 574-7149; f. 2000; Chair. Sir BRIAN ELWOOD.

National Beekeepers' Association of New Zealand (Inc): 10 Nikau Lane, RD 1, Otaki 5569; tel. (6) 363-6301; fax (6) 362-6302; e-mail jimedwards@xtra.co.nz; internet www.nba.org.nz; f. 1913; 400 mems; Pres. JANE LORIMER; Sec. PAM EDWARDS.

New Zealand Animal By-Products Exporters' Association: 11 Longhurst Terrace, POB 12-222, Christchurch; tel. (3) 332-2895; fax (3) 332-2825; 25 mems; Sec. J. L. NAYSMITH.

New Zealand Berryfruit Growers' Federation (Inc): POB 10-050, Wellington; tel. (4) 473-5387; fax (4) 473-6999; e-mail berryfed@xtra.co.nz; 530 mems; Pres. JOHN GARELJA; Executive Officer PETER ENSOR.

New Zealand Council of Wool Exporters Inc: POB 2857, Christchurch; tel. (3) 353-1049; fax (3) 374-6925; e-mail cwe@woolexport.net; internet www.woolexport.net; f. 1893; Exec. Man. R. H. F. NICHOLSON; Pres. JOHN HENDERSON.

The New Zealand Forest Owners' Association: POB 1208, Wellington; tel. (4) 473-4769; fax (4) 499-8893; e-mail robmcl@nzfoa.org.nz; internet www.nzfoa.nzforestryco.nz; CEO ROB MCCLAGAN.

New Zealand Fruitgrowers' Federation: Huddart Parker Bldg, POB 2175, Wellington, 6015; tel. (4) 472-6559; fax (4) 472-6409; e-mail hans@fruitgrowers.org.nz; internet www.fruitgrowers.org.nz; f. 1928; 5,000 mems; CEO P. R. SILCOCK.

New Zealand Fruit Wine and Cider Makers Inc: POB 912, New Plymouth, Taranaki; tel. and fax (6) 757-8049; e-mail admin@

NEW ZEALAND

fruitwines.co.nz; internet www.fruitwines.co.nz; f. 1987; 30 mems; Chair. BRIAN SHANKS; Exec. Officer CHRIS GARNHAM.

New Zealand Meat Board: Price Waterhouse Coopers Tower, 113–119 The Terrace, Wellington; tel. (4) 473-9150; fax (4) 474-0800; e-mail help@meatnz.co.nz; internet www.meatnz.co.nz; f. 1922; Chair. JEFF GRANT; Sec. A. DOMETAKIS; 10 mems.

New Zealand Pork Industry Board: POB 4048, Wellington; tel. (4) 385-4229; fax (4) 385-8522; e-mail info@pork.co.nz; internet www.pork.co.nz; f. 1937; Chair. C. TRENGROVE; CEO A. DAVIDSON.

New Zealand Retailers' Association Inc: Willbank House, 8th Floor, 57 Willis St, Wellington; tel. (4) 472-3733; fax (4) 472-1071; e-mail bhellberg@retail.org.nz; internet www.retail.org.nz; direct membership 5,000; Pres. BRUCE GREGORY; CEO JOHN ALBERTSON.

New Zealand Seafood Industry Council: Private Bag 24-901, Wellington; tel. (4) 385-4005; fax (4) 384-2727; e-mail info@seafood.co.nz; internet www.seafood.co.nz; CEO OWEN SYMMANS; Chair. DAVID SHARP.

New Zealand Timber Industry Federation: 2–8 Maginnity St, POB 308, Wellington; tel. (4) 473-5200; fax (4) 473-6536; e-mail enquiries@nztif.co.nz; internet www.nztif.co.uk; 350 mems; Exec. Dir W. S. COFFEY.

New Zealand Vegetable and Potato Growers' Federation (Inc): POB 10232, Wellington 1; tel. (4) 472-3795; fax (4) 471-2861; e-mail information@vegfed.co.nz; internet www.vegfed.co.nz; 4,000 mems; Pres. B. GARGIULO; CEO P. R. SILCOCK.

New Zealand Wool Board: 10 Brandon St, Box 3225, Wellington; tel. (4) 472-6888; fax (4) 473-7872; e-mail info@woolboard.co.nz; internet www.woolboard.co.nz; assists research, development, production and marketing of NZ wool; Chair. B. C. MUNRO; CEO MARK O'GRADY.

NZMP: 25 The Terrace, POB 417, Wellington; tel. (4) 462-8096; fax (4) 471-8600; internet www.nzmp.com; f. 2001 through merger of New Zealand Dairy Board and Fonterra Co-operative.

Registered Master Builders' Federation (Inc): 234 Wakefield St, Level 6, POB 1796, Wellington; tel. (4) 385-8999; fax (4) 385-8995; internet www.masterbuilder.org.nz; Chief Exec. C. PRESTON.

EMPLOYERS' ORGANIZATION

Business New Zealand: Lumley House, Level 6, 3–11 Hunter St, Wellington; tel. (4) 496-6555; fax (4) 496-6550; e-mail admin@businessnz.org.nz; internet www.businessnz.org.nz; f. 2001; Chief Exec. PHIL O'REILLY.

UTILITIES

Energy Efficiency and Conservation Authority (EECA): NGC Bldg, Level 1, 44 The Terrace, Wellington; tel. (4) 470-2200; fax (4) 499-5330; e-mail eecainfo@eeca.govt.nz; internet www.eeca.govt.nz; f. 2000; Chair. MARK FORD; Chief Exec. HEATHER STALEY.

Electricity

Electricity Commission: Level 7, ASB Bank Tower, 2 Hunter St, POB 10-041, Wellington; tel. (4) 460-8860; fax (4) 460-8879; e-mail info@electricitycommission.govt.nz; internet www.electricitycommission.govt.nz; f. 2003; independent; regulatory body supervising electricity sector; Chair. ROY HEMMINGWAY.

Bay of Plenty Electricity Ltd: 52 Commerce St, POB 404, Whakatane 3080; tel. (7) 922-2700; fax (7) 307-0922; e-mail bopelec@bopelec.co.nz; internet www.bopelec.co.nz; f. 1995; generation, purchase and supply of electricity and natural gas; Commercial Man. CHRIS POWER; CEO DAVID BULLEY.

Contact Energy Ltd: Harbour City Tower, Level 1, 29 Brandon St, Wellington; tel. (4) 449-4001; fax (4) 499-4003; e-mail investor.centre@mycontact.co.nz; internet www.contactenergy.co.nz; f. 1996; generation of electricity, wholesale and retail of energy; transferred to the private sector in 1999; Chair. PHIL PRYKE; CEO and Man. Dir STEPHEN BARRETT.

Genesis Energy Ltd: 602 Great South Rd, POB 17-188, Greenlane, Auckland; tel. (9) 580-2094; fax (9) 580-4891; e-mail info@genesisenergy.co.nz; internet www.genesisenergy.co.nz; f. 1999; state-owned; generation and retail of electricity and gas; Chair. BRIAN CORBAN; Chief Exec. MURRAY JACKSON.

The Marketplace Co Ltd (M-CO): Wool House, Level 2, 10 Brandon St, POB 5422, Wellington; tel. (4) 473-5240; fax (4) 473-5247; e-mail info@m-co.co.nz; internet www.m-co.co.nz; administers wholesale electricity market; Chief Exec. CHRIS RUSSELL.

Meridian Energy Ltd: POB 2128, Christchurch; tel. (3) 353-9500; fax (3) 353-9501; internet www.meridianenergy.co.nz; state-owned; generation and retail of electricity; Chair. Dr FRANCIS SMALL; Chief Exec. Dr KEITH TURNER.

Mighty River Power Ltd: Level 19, 1 Queen St, POB 90-399, Auckland; tel. (9) 308-8200; fax (9) 308-8209; e-mail enquiries@mightyriver.co.nz; internet www.mightyriverpower.co.nz; f. 1999; electricity generation and retail; Chair. CAROLE DURBIN; Chief Exec. DOUG HEFFERMAN.

Todd Energy Ltd: POB 3141, Wellington; tel. (4) 471-6555; fax (4) 472-2474; e-mail energy@toddenergy.co.nz; internet www.toddenergy.co.nz; Man. Dir and CEO RICHARD TWEEDIE.

Transpower New Zealand Ltd: Unisys House, 56 The Terrace, POB 1021, Wellington; tel. (4) 495-7000; fax (4) 495-7100; internet www.transpower.co.nz; manages national grid; Chair. Sir COLIN MAIDEN; Chief Exec. RALPH CRAVEN.

TrustPower Ltd: Private Bag 12-023, Tauranga, Auckland; tel. (7) 574-4800; fax (7) 574-4825; e-mail trustpower@trustpower.co.nz; internet www.trustpower.co.nz; f. 1920 as Tauranga Electric Power Board; independent generator; Chair. HAROLD TITTER.

Vector Electricity Ltd: POB 99-882, Newmarket, Auckland; tel. (9) 978-7788; fax (9) 978-7799; internet www.vectorelectricity.co.nz; fmrly Mercury Energy Ltd; operates power networks in Auckland, Manukau and Papakura; CEO MARK FRANKLIN.

Gas

Bay of Plenty Electricity Ltd: see Electricity, above.

E-gas Ltd: Level 13, Forsyth Barr House, cnr Lambton Quay and Johnston St, POB 2577, Wellington; tel. (4) 499-4964; fax (4) 499-4965; e-mail info@e-gas.co.nz; internet www.e-gas.co.nz; supplier of natural gas.

Genesis Energy Ltd: see Electricity, above.

NGC Holdings Ltd: Level 8, NGC Bldg, 44 The Terrace, Private Bag 39-980, Wellington Mail Centre, Wellington; tel. (4) 462-8700; fax (4) 462-8600; e-mail information@ngc.co.nz; internet www.ngc.co.nz; f. 1992; fmrly Natural Gas Corpn Holdings Ltd; name changed as above 2002; purchase, processing and transport of natural gas; wholesale and retail sales; Chair. MICHAEL STIASSNY; Chief Exec. BRYAN CRAWFORD.

Nova Gas Ltd: 11th Floor, Todd Bldg, 95 Customhouse Quay, POB 10-141, Wellington; tel. (4) 472-6263; fax (4) 472-6264; e-mail info@novagas.co.nz; internet www.novagas.co.nz; Group Gas Man. HAMISH TWEEDIE.

Vector Gas Ltd: 101 Carlton Gore Rd, Newmarket, Auckland; tel. (9) 978-7788; fax (9) 978-7799; e-mail info@vectorgas.co.nz; internet www.vectorgas.co.nz; distribution of natural gas in Auckland.

Wanganui Gas Ltd: 179 Hill St, POB 32, Wanganui; tel. (6) 349-0909; fax (6) 345-4931; e-mail enquiries@wanganuigas.co.nz; internet www.wanganuigas.co.nz; f. 1879; supplier of gas on North Island; Chair. CHARLES POYNTER; Chief Exec. TREVOR GOODWIN.

Water

Waste Management NZ Ltd: 86 Lunn Ave, Mt Wellington, Auckland; tel. (9) 527-1300; fax (9) 570-5595; internet www.wastemanagement.co.nz; f. 1985; waste collection, recovery and disposal; liquid waste collection and processing; recycling; Chair. JIM SYME; Man. Dir K. R. ELLIS.

Watercare Services Ltd: Private Bag 92-521, Wellesley St, Auckland 1036; tel. (9) 379-4440; fax (9) 302-8013; e-mail info@water.co.nz; internet www.watercare.co.nz; f. 1993; provides water and waste water services in the Auckland area; Chair. GRAEME HAWKINS; Chief Exec. MARK FORD.

TRADE UNIONS

In December 2000 a total of 134 unions were in operation; 318,519 workers belonged to a union.

New Zealand Council of Trade Unions: Education House, West Block, 178–182 Willis St, POB 6645, Wellington 1; tel. (4) 385-1334; fax (4) 385-6051; internet www.union.org.nz; f. 1937; present name since 1987; affiliated to ICFTU; 34 affiliated unions with 250,000 mems; Pres. ROSS WILSON; Sec. CAROL BEAUMONT.

Principal Affiliated Unions

Association of Staff in Tertiary Education (ASTE)/Te Hau Takitini o Aotearoa: POB 27141, Wellington; tel. (4) 801-5098; fax (4) 385-8826; e-mail enquiry@aste.ac.nz; 3,500 mems; Nat. Sec. SHARN RIGGS.

Association of University Staff (AUS): POB 11-767, Wellington; tel. (4) 915-6690; fax (4) 915-6699; e-mail national.office@aus.ac.nz; internet www.aus.ac.nz; 6,000 mems; Gen. Sec HELEN KELLY.

Central Amalgamated Workers Union (AWUNZ): POB 27-291, 307 Willis St, Wellington; tel. (4) 384-4049; fax (4) 801-7306; e-mail centralawunz@xtra.co.nz; Sec. JACKSON SMITH.

FinSec Finance and Information Workers Union: POB 27-355, Wellington; tel. (4) 385-7723; fax (4) 385-2214; e-mail union@finsec.org.nz; internet www.finsec.org.nz/; Pres. SUE BORASTON; Sec. ANDREW CASIDY.

NEW ZEALAND

Maritime Union of New Zealand: POB 27004, Wellington; tel. (4) 385-0792; fax (4) 384-8766; e-mail trevor.hanson@muno.org.nz; 2,800 mems; Sec. TREVOR HANSON.

Meat and Related Trades Workers Union of Aotearoa: POB 17056, Greenlane, Auckland; tel. (9) 520-0034; fax (9) 523-1286; e-mail meat.union@xtra.co.nz; Sec. GRAHAM COOKE.

New Zealand Dairy Workers Union, Inc: POB 9046, Hamilton; tel. (7) 839-0239; fax (7) 838-0398; e-mail nzdwu@nzdwu.org.nz; internet www.nzdwu.org.nz; f. 1992; 6,400 mems; Sec. JAMES RITCHIE; Pres. JOHN SMITH.

New Zealand Educational Institute (NZEI) (Te Riu Roa): POB 466, Wellington; tel. (4) 384-9689; fax (4) 385-1772; e-mail nzei@nzei.org.nz; internet www.nzei.org.nz; f. 1883; Pres. IRENE COOPER; Sec. LYNNE BRUCE.

New Zealand Engineering, Printing & Manufacturing Union (EPMU): POB 31-546, Lower Hutt; tel. (4) 568-0086; fax (4) 576-1173; e-mail andrew.little@epmu.org.nz; internet www.epmu.org.nz; Sec. ANDREW LITTLE.

New Zealand Meat Workers and Related Trades Union: POB 13-048, Armagh, Christchurch; tel. (3) 366-5105; fax (3) 379-7763; e-mail nzmeatworkersunion@clear.net.nz; 8,439 mems; Pres. J. REID; Gen. Sec. D. W. EASTLAKE.

New Zealand Nurses' Organisation: POB 2128, Wellington; tel. (4) 385-0847; fax (4) 382-9993; e-mail nurses@nzno.org.nz; internet www.nzno.org.nz; 32,000 mems; CEO GEOFF ANNALS.

New Zealand Post Primary Teachers' Association: POB 2119, Wellington; tel. (4) 384-9964; fax (4) 382-8763; e-mail gensec@ppta.org.nz; internet www.ppta.org.nz; Pres. DEBBIE TE WHAITI; Gen. Sec. KEVIN BUNKER.

NZ PSA (New Zealand Public Service Association): PSA House, 11 Aurora Terrace, POB 3817, Wellington 1; tel. (4) 917-0333; fax (4) 917-2051; e-mail enquiries@psa.org.nz; internet www.psa.org.nz; 47,000 mems; Pres. KEITH GUTSELL.

Rail & Maritime Transport Union Inc: POB 1103, Wellington; tel. (4) 499-2066; fax (4) 471-0896; e-mail admin@rmtunion.org.nz; internet rmtunion.org.nz; 3,497 mems; Pres. J. KELLY; Sec. W. BUTSON.

Service and Food Workers' Union: Private Bag 68-914, Newton, Auckland; tel. (9) 375-2680; fax (9) 375-2681; e-mail darien.fenton@sfwu.org.nz; internet www.sfwu.org.nz; 23,000 mems; Pres. DAELE O'CONNOR; Sec. DARIEN FENTON.

Other Unions

Manufacturing & Construction Workers Union: Manners St, POB 11-123, Wellington; tel. (4) 385-8264; fax (4) 384-8007; e-mail M.C.Union@TradesHall.org.nz; Gen. Sec. GRAEME CLARKE.

National Distribution Union (NDU): 120 Church St, Private Bag 92-904, Onehunga, Auckland; tel. (9) 622-8355; fax (9) 622-8353; e-mail ndu@nduunion.org.nz; internet www.nduunion.org.nz; 18,500 mems; Pres. BILL ANDERSEN; Sec. MIKE JACKSON; Vice Pres. DENNIS DAWSON.

New Zealand Building Trades Union: Manners St, POB 11-356, Wellington; tel. (4) 385-1178; fax (4) 385-1177; e-mail nzbtu@tradeshall.org.nz; Pres. P. REIDY; Sec. ASHLEY RUSS.

New Zealand Seafarers' Union: Marion Square, POB 9288, Wellington; tel. (4) 385-9288; fax (4) 384-9288; e-mail admin@seafarers.org.nz; f. 1993; Pres. DAVE MORGAN.

Transport

RAILWAYS

There were 3,898 km of railways in New Zealand in 2003, of which more than 500 km were electrified.

Toll Rail Ltd: Smales Farm, cnr Northcote Rd and Taharoto Drive, Takapuna, Auckland; tel. (4) 498-3000; fax (4) 498-3259; e-mail freight@tollnz.co.nz; internet www.tollrail.co.nz; acquired Tranz Rail Ltd 2003; 3,898 km of railway; Gen. Man. GARY TAYLOR.

ROADS

In June 2003 there were a total of 92,494 km of maintained roads in New Zealand, including 10,791 km of state highways and motorways.

Land Transport New Zealand: NZ Post House, 7–27 Waterloo Quay, POB 2840, Wellington; tel. (4) 931-8700; fax (4) 931-8701; internet www.landtransport.govt.nz; f. 2003; Crown entity charged with contributing to an integrated, safe, responsive and sustainable land transport system; Chair. Dr JAN WRIGHT; Chief Exec. WAYNE DONNELLY.

Transit New Zealand: 20–26 Ballance St, POB 5084, Wellington; tel. (4) 499-6600; fax (4) 496-6666; e-mail deborah.willett@transit.govt.nz; internet www.transit.govt.nz; Crown agency responsible for management and development of the state highway network; Chair. DAVID STUBBS; CEO RICK VAN BARNEVELD.

SHIPPING

There are 13 main seaports, of which the most important are Auckland, Tauranga, Wellington, Lyttleton (the port of Christchurch) and Port Chalmers (Dunedin). In December 2004 the New Zealand merchant fleet comprised 173 vessels, with a total displacement of 206,415 grt.

Principal Companies

P & O Nedlloyd Ltd: Level 4, Panasonic House, 40 Taranaki St, POB 1699, Wellington; tel. (4) 803-5000; fax (4) 803-5055; internet www.ponl.com; world-wide shipping services; Man. Dir TONY GIBSON.

Sofrana Unilines NZ Ltd: 396–404 Queen St, POB 3614, Auckland; tel. (9) 356-1400; fax (9) 356-1407; e-mail info@sofrana.co.nz; internet www.sofrana.co.nz; Chair DIDIER LEROUX; Man. Dir BENOIT MARCENAC.

Other major shipping companies operating services to New Zealand include Blue Star Line (NZ) Ltd and Columbus Line, which link New Zealand with Australia, the Pacific Islands, South-East Asia and the USA.

CIVIL AVIATION

There are international airports at Auckland, Christchurch and Wellington.

Civil Aviation Authority of New Zealand: Aviation House, 10 Hutt Rd, Petone, POB 31441, Lower Hutt; tel. (4) 560-9400; fax (4) 569-2024; e-mail info@caa.govt.nz; internet www.caa.govt.nz; Dir of Civil Aviation JOHN JONES.

Principal Airlines

Air Nelson: Private Bag 32, Nelson 7030; tel. (3) 547-8700; fax (3) 547-8788; e-mail john.hambleton@airnewzealand.co.nz; internet www.airnewzealand.com; f. 1979; owned by Air New Zealand; changed to present name 1986; operates services throughout New Zealand; Gen. Man. JOHN HAMBLETON.

Air New Zealand: Quay Tower, 29 Customs St West, Private Bag 92007, Auckland 1; tel. (9) 366-2400; fax (9) 366-2401; e-mail investor@airnz.co.nz; internet www.airnz.co.nz; f. 1942; privatized in 1989, recapitalized by govt 2001; 80% govt-owned; services to Australia, the Pacific Islands, Asia, Europe and North America, as well as regular daily services to 25 cities and towns in New Zealand; Chair. JOHN PALMER; CEO ROB FYFE.

Freedom Air: Quay Tower, 29 Customs St West, Private Bag 92007, Auckland; tel. (9) 366-2400; fax (9) 366-2401; internet www.freedomair.co.nz; f. 1995; subsidiary of Air New Zealand; operates regional services; Man. Dir STEPHEN JONES.

Pacific Blue Airlines (NZ) Ltd: internet www.flypacificblue.com; f. 2004; wholly-owned subsidiary of Australian Virgin Blue; services to Pacific Islands; CEO TONY MARKS.

Tourism

New Zealand's principal tourist attractions are its high mountains, lakes, forests, volcanoes, hot springs and beaches. In 2005 New Zealand received 2,382,950 visitors. Receipts from tourism totalled $NZ6,313m. in 2003/04.

Tourism New Zealand: POB 95, Wellington; tel. (4) 917-5400; fax (4) 915-3817; e-mail reception@tnz.govt.nz; internet www.newzealand.com; f. 1901; responsible for marketing of New Zealand as a tourism destination; offices in Auckland, Wellington and Christchurch; 13 offices overseas; Chair. WALLY STONE; Chief Exec. GEORGE HICKTON.

NEW ZEALAND'S DEPENDENT TERRITORIES

New Zealand's two Dependent Territories are the Ross Dependency, which is situated in Antarctica, and Tokelau, located in the Pacific Ocean.

ROSS DEPENDENCY

The Ross Dependency comprises the sector of Antarctica between 160°E and 150°W (moving eastward) and the islands lying between those degrees of longitude and south of latitude 60°S. It has been administered by New Zealand since 1923 and has a total area of 750,310 sq km (289,700 sq miles), comprising a land area of 413,540 sq km and an ice shelf of 336,770 sq km. The Territory rises to a height of 3,794 m above sea-level at the peak of the volcano, Mount Erebus.

Scott Base was established in 1957 on Ross Island, and in the following year the Ross Dependency Research Committee was formed to supervise New Zealand activity on the Territory. In 1968 a new scientific station was set up at Lake Vanda, about 130 km (80 miles) west of Scott Base. In 1986 traces of petroleum were discovered in the Territory, more than 600 m below the sea-bed. The Ross Dependency Research Committee was disbanded in 1995. Legislation approved in the mid-1990s consolidated measures aimed at conserving the region's flora and fauna (which includes 18 species of penguin, six species of seal and several rare species of whale) included in the Antarctic Treaty (see p. 545), and reinforced the Convention for the Conservation of Antarctic Marine Living Resources. Since 1997 New Zealand has conducted exploratory fishing for toothfish in the Ross Sea. In April 2006 it was announced that an Estonian summer-only research station was to be built at Edmonson Point South, 350 km north-west of Scott Base, to provide facilities for six people.

TOKELAU

Introductory Survey

Location, Climate, Language, Religion, Flag, Capital

Tokelau consists of three atolls (Atafu, Nukunonu and Fakaofo), which lie about 480 km (300 miles) north of Samoa, in the Pacific Ocean. The annual average temperature is 28°C (82°F), July being the coolest month and May the warmest; rainfall is heavy but inconsistent. The principal language is Tokelauan (a Polynesian language), although English is also widely spoken. The population is almost entirely Christian, with 67% adhering to the Congregational Christian Church of Samoa (a Protestant denomination) and 30% to the Roman Catholic Church. The New Zealand flag (see p. 3216) is used in the Territory. Tokelau has no capital, each atoll having its own administrative centre. However, the seat of government, the Office of the Tokelau Council for Ongoing Government (formerly the Council of Faipule) is recognized as 'the capital' and is rotated on a yearly basis among the three atolls.

Recent History

The Tokelau (formerly Union) Islands became a British protectorate in 1877. At the request of the inhabitants, the United Kingdom annexed the islands in 1916 and included them within the Gilbert and Ellice Islands Colony (now Kiribati and Tuvalu). The British Government transferred administrative control of the islands to New Zealand by legislation enacted in 1925, effective from February 1926. The group was officially designated the Tokelau Islands in 1946, and sovereignty was transferred to New Zealand by legislation of 1948, effective from January 1949. From 1962 until the end of 1971 the High Commissioner for New Zealand in Western Samoa (now Samoa) was also the Administrator of the Tokelau Islands. In November 1974 the administration of the Tokelau Islands was transferred to the Ministry of Foreign Affairs in New Zealand. In 1976 the Tokelau Islands were officially redesignated Tokelau.

New Zealand has undertaken to assist Tokelau towards increased self-government and economic self-sufficiency. The Territory was visited by the UN Special Committee on Decolonization in 1976 and 1981, but on both occasions the mission reported that the people of Tokelau did not wish to change the nature of the existing relationship between Tokelau and New Zealand. This opinion was reiterated by an emissary of the General Fono, the Territory's highest advisory body, in 1987, and by the Official Secretary in 1992. In June 1987, however, in a statement to the UN Special Committee, Tokelau had expressed a desire to achieve a greater degree of political autonomy, while maintaining its relationship with New Zealand. A report by the UN Special Committee in 2002 listed Tokelau as one of 16 dependent territories it was seeking to encourage towards independence. However, a UN decolonization mission which visited the islands in September of that year was told that the majority of Tokelauans wanted to remain part of New Zealand and that the Territory was far too dependent on that country to change its status.

In December 1980 New Zealand and the USA signed a treaty whereby a US claim to Tokelau, dating from 1856, was relinquished. At the same time New Zealand abandoned a claim, on behalf of Tokelau, to Swains Island, which had been administered by the USA since 1925 as part of American Samoa. The treaty was ratified in August 1983, although there was some dissent in Tokelau.

In 1989 Tokelau supported efforts by the South Pacific Forum to impose a regional ban on drift-net fishing (which was believed to have resulted in a serious depletion in tuna stocks). In November New Zealand prohibited drift-net fishing within Tokelau's exclusive economic zone (which extends to 200 nautical miles (370 km) from the islands' coastline). At the Pacific Islands Forum annual meeting in August 2002 New Zealand endorsed Tokelau's membership of the Forum Fisheries Agency.

In 1989 a UN report on the 'greenhouse effect' (the heating of the earth's atmosphere as a result of pollution) listed Tokelau as one of the island groups that would completely disappear beneath the sea in the 21st century, unless drastic action were taken.

A programme of constitutional change, agreed in 1992 and formalized in January 1994, provided for a more defined role for Tokelau's political institutions, as well as for their expansion. A process of relocating the Tokelau Public Service (hitherto based in Apia, Western Samoa, now Samoa) to the Territory began in 1994, and by 1995 all government departments, except Transport and Communications and part of the Administration and Finance Department, had been transferred to Tokelauan soil. The Tokelau Apia Liaison Office (formerly the Office for Tokelau Affairs) was, however, to remain in Western Samoa, owing to that country's more developed communications facilities.

The development of Tokelau's institutions at a national level prompted renewed interest in the islands' prospects for greater internal autonomy. In June 1994 the General Fono adopted a National Strategic Plan, which gave details of Tokelau's progression (over the next five to 10 years) towards increased self-determination and, possibly, free association with New Zealand. The executive and administrative powers of the Administrator were formally transferred, in that year, to the General Fono and, when the Fono was not in session, to the Council of Faipule (cabinet). A draft Constitution was subsequently drawn up. In May 1996 the New Zealand House of Representatives approved the Tokelau Amendment Bill, granting the General Fono the power to enact legislation, to impose taxes and to declare public holidays, effective from 1 August 1996 (although New Zealand was to retain the right to legislate for Tokelau). A visit to the islands by the Prime Minister of Tuvalu in mid-1996, for the signing of a mutual co-operation agreement (covering shipping, trade and fisheries), was widely interpreted as an indication of Tokelau's increased autonomy. A further co-operation agreement was established in March 2003, following a five-day visit to the islands by the Prime Minister of Samoa. Tokelau's traditional leaders agreed a framework for annual meetings with the Samoan Government to discuss issues of concern and mutual benefit in what was regarded as a sign of the growing relationship between the two parties.

Following electoral reforms introduced in the latter half of the 1990s, delegates were, for the first time, elected to the General Fono for a three-year term in January 1999; they had previously been nominated by each Taupulega (Island Council or Council of Elders). As part of the same reform process, the number of delegates to the General Fono was reduced from 27 to 18. At the elections two of the Territory's Faipule (political leaders) were re-elected, while the remaining Faipule and three Pulenuku (village mayor) posts were secured by new candidates. At elections in January 2002 all three incumbent Faipule and one Pulenuku were re-elected to office; two new Pulenuku were elected. In January 2005 again the three Faipule were re-elected, along with one of the Pulenuku; two new Pulenuku were chosen.

Mounting fears among islanders that, despite their wishes, New Zealand was seeking to loosen its ties with Tokelau, led the New Zealand Minister of Foreign Affairs and Trade to state in April 2000 that his country would not impose independence on the Territory and that any change in its political status would only occur with the consent of Tokelauans. In early 2001 the head of the Tokelau Public Service Commission, Aleki Silau, reiterated the islanders' reluctance to renounce New Zealand citizenship, and emphasized that both sides had until 2010 to reach a decision. A mission from the UN Special Committee on Decolonization visited the islands in September 2002 (see above). Under legislation approved in 1999, management of the islands' public service was formally transferred to Tokelau in July 2001. In July 2003 responsibility for the islands' budget was transferred to the General Fono. In October of that year a number of constitutional changes were instituted. The Council of Faipule was renamed the Tokelau Council for Ongoing Government, henceforth to comprise the three Faipule and the three Pulenuku. In the following month New Zealand's Governor-General, Dame Sylvia Cartwright, made an official visit to Tokelau to sign the Principles of Partnership agreement. The document was described by New Zealand's Minister of Foreign Affairs, Phil Goff, as a step closer to decolonization for the islands. Goff reiterated that the final decision on Tokelau's future would be made by its inhabitants, although he also confirmed that he expected the islands to adopt a system of self-government in free association with New Zealand, similar to that existing in Niue and the Cook Islands. In March 2004 it was announced that new powers were to be granted to the three atolls' Taupulega, giving them greater control over local affairs. In May a senior government member reiterated the view that, despite the ambition of New Zealand and the UN for Tokelau to achieve self-determination, the islanders themselves were extremely reluctant to change their status. In June the Administrator's powers were formally transferred from the General Fono to the three Taupulega, as part of the Modern House of Tokelau Project.

In mid-August 2004 New Zealand's Prime Minister Helen Clark made an official visit to Tokelau (the first such visit in more than 20 years). During the visit Clark announced the provision of a grant worth some US $0.3m. towards improvements for boat access to the islands and a review of the islands' communications infrastructure. The Prime Minister also expressed her confidence that the islanders would vote in favour of free association with New Zealand when the issue was finally put to a referendum. In early November leaders from Tokelau travelled to New Zealand for a series of meetings with the latter's Minister of Foreign Affairs, Phil Goff, following which certain elements to be included in a treaty of free association with New Zealand were agreed upon. Contrary to the New Zealand Government's expectations, however, at a referendum on the issue of the future status of Tokelau held between 11 and 15 February 2006 the requisite two-thirds' majority in favour of the proposed change to free association with New Zealand was not received: 349 votes were cast in favour of greater self-government, while 232 voters wanted Tokelau to remain a Dependent Territory. The referendum was observed by several international organizations, including representatives of the UN. The result was regarded as a major set-back for the New Zealand Government.

In February 2005, meanwhile, all three atolls were struck by Cyclone Percy, which caused widespread damage to infrastructure, homes and crops. Nukunonu was subjected to severe flooding as a result of the storm. The New Zealand Government approved some $NZ0.5m. in emergency aid in the form of food supplies and temporary shelter (to be shipped from Samoa) and the restoration of essential services.

New Zealand is responsible for the external relations of Tokelau. Strong links are maintained with Samoa, to the people of which the Tokelauans are closely related. There is considerable co-operation in health and education matters.

Government

The administration of Tokelau is the responsibility of the Minister of Foreign Affairs and Trade of New Zealand, who is empowered to appoint an Administrator to the Territory. In practice, most of the Administrator's powers are delegated to the Official Secretary, who heads the Tokelau Apia Liaison Office, as well as to the General Fono and the Tokelau Council for Ongoing Government (formerly the Council of Faipule). Each atoll has its own Taupulega (Island Council or Council of Elders), which comprises the heads of family groups together with two elected members, the Faipule and the Pulenuku. The Faipule represents the atoll in its dealings with the administering power and the public service, and presides over the Council and the court. The Pulenuku is responsible for the administration of village affairs. The Faipule and the Pulenuku are democratically elected by universal adult suffrage every three years. The three Faipule, who hold ministerial portfolios and along with the three Pulenuku form the six-member Tokelau Council for Ongoing Government, choose one of their number to hold the title Ulu-O-Tokelau (Head of Tokelau) for a term of one year. The Ulu-O-Tokelau chairs sessions of the territorial assembly, the General Fono. The General Fono is a meeting of 18 delegates, who are elected by universal adult suffrage for a three-year term (including the three Faipule and the three Pulenuku) and who represent the entire Territory. There are two or three meetings of the General Fono each year, which may take place on any of the atolls.

Economic Affairs

According to estimates by the UN Development Programme, in 1982 Tokelau's gross national product (GNP) was US $1.2m., equivalent to US $760 per head. Gross domestic product (GDP) was estimated at US $1.5m. in 1993.

Agriculture (including fishing) is, excluding copra production, of a basic subsistence nature. Coconuts (the source of copra) are the only cash crop, for which there is an increasingly limited market. Pulaka, breadfruit, papayas, the screw-pine (*Pandanus*) and bananas are cultivated as food crops. Livestock comprises pigs, ducks and other poultry. Ocean and lagoon fish and shellfish are staple constituents of the islanders' diet. In early 2004 the Pacific Community Secretariat produced a fisheries management plan for Tokelau. The plan, which was to be implemented in mid-2004, focused on community-based activities and included the increased exploitation of the islands' giant-clam resources. In early 2006 a five-year development plan for the fisheries sector was in the process of being drafted for 2006–10. Meanwhile, the sale to foreign fleets of fishing licences permitting them to operate in Tokelau's exclusive economic zone (EEZ) provides an important, albeit fluctuating, source of income (see below).

The industrial sector has been constrained by a lack of resources. Manufacturing comprises mainly the production of handicrafts, notably woven items such as mats. However, the opening on Atafu, in 1990, of a factory processing highly priced yellowfin tuna provided another important source of income. The principal markets for the product were New Zealand and Japan.

Energy is provided by diesel-powered generators, the fuel for which is imported via Samoa. With funding from New Zealand, a major power project was initiated in 2002. The implementation of this scheme, which was ultimately to supply all three atolls with a more reliable source of electricity, was scheduled for completion in 2006. In the longer term, greater emphasis was to be given to renewable forms of energy, particularly solar power.

The services sector is limited, with tourism remaining undeveloped owing to the lack of air services and the difficulty of access. There is just one recognized hotel, on the central atoll of Nukunonu. Fewer than 30 tourists visited the islands in 2001. Since 1982 the General Fono has levied a tax on the salaries of public servants who are unavailable for the community service labour levy. In the mid-1990s, when the public service (the principal employer) engaged approximately 160 people, the tax was equivalent to 6%–12% of public servants' salaries. Public salaries and employment account for the single largest item of government expenditure (about one-third in the early 1990s).

Imports to the value of $NZ1.7m. were purchased in 2002. The principal imports in that year were food and live animals (which cost 55.2% of total imports), mineral fuels (11.6%) and miscellaneous manufactured goods (11.0%).

In 1999/2000 there was a budgetary deficit of $NZ0.9m. Tokelau's budget for 2001/02 was to include at least $NZ4.2m. from New Zealand and an estimated $NZ1.7m. to be obtained from local revenues such as fisheries licensing, duty, taxes, philatelic sales, freight charges and interest earned. Local revenue was estimated to have reached about $NZ2m. in 2005. Receipts from EEZ fees rose from $NZ286,000 in 2004 to an estimated $569,000 in 2005. Fees from shipping, radio excises and customs duties have provided another source of revenue; local receipts from such duties increased from $NZ372,000 in 2004 to an estimated $388,000 in 2005. The sale of postage stamps and souvenir coins (which are legal tender, although New Zealand currency is in general use) also makes a significant contribution to the Territory's income. Receipts from this source increased from $NZ54,000 in 2004 to an estimated $70,000 in 2005. Some revenue is provided by remittances from Tokelauans working abroad, mainly in New Zealand. Since mid-2003 most of New Zealand's bilateral assistance has been transferred directly to the Territory's budget, thereby enabling Tokelau to finance its recurrent expenditure on services such as transport, education and health. Official development assistance from New Zealand increased from a total of $NZ9.0m. in 2004/05 to $9.5m. in 2005/06. In addition to its links to New Zealand, Tokelau maintains a bilateral development assistance plan with Australia, centred upon human resource development. Australia provides scholarships for Tokelauan students to study in Australia or at regional academic institutions. The level of annual development assistance from Australia remained at around $A100,000 in 2004/05.

Tokelau is a member of the Pacific Community (see p. 350), and, as a Dependent Territory of New Zealand, has been represented by that country in the Pacific Islands Forum (see p. 352) and other international organizations. In October 2005 Tokelau was granted observer status at the Pacific Islands Forum.

Tokelau's agricultural development has been constrained by the lack of suitable cultivable soil and by the adverse effects of inclement weather, particularly cyclones. Moreover, the Territory's small size, remote situation, lack of land-based resources and the population's continuing migration to New Zealand severely hinder economic development. The vulnerability of Tokelau's communications was highlighted in January 2005 when a satellite covering that area of the Pacific drifted from its course, resulting in the islands' links with the rest of the world temporarily being completely severed. In September 2002 renewed proposals were announced for the construction of wharves and improved access for shipping to facilitate the export of fish, and of an airport to encourage tourism. It was hoped that Tokelau would derive greater benefits from its fisheries resources as a result of a plan initiated by the Pacific Community Secretariat in 2004 (see above). In 2004 Tokelau signed a three-year agreement relating to New Zealand's budgetary support, along with arrangements for reporting and monitoring, which were to remain in place until 2006/07. The agreement also provided for joint reviews of sectors such as shipping, to be conducted on an annual basis, and for regular financial reviews. In 2001 the sum of $NZ0.68m. derived from the income from fisheries licensing was used to found the Tokelau Trust Fund. The fund was established with assistance from New Zealand and with the aim of enhancing the Territory's long-term self-reliance. By early 2006 the assets of the fund had exceeded $NZ25m. It was hoped that eventually the fund would attract international contributions. Under the Administrative Assistance scheme (part of the the Principles of Partnership agreement—see Recent History), the limited capacity of the Tokelau Public Service is supplemented by the resources of various New Zealand government departments. In February 2005 Cyclone Percy caused serious destruction on the islands, coinciding with 'king tides' that flooded the Territory resulting in widespread damage.

Education

Education is provided free of charge, and is compulsory between the ages of five and 14 years. The provision of an additional year for 15-year-olds is rotated among the Territory's three schools every five years. Government expenditure on education in 1998/99 totalled $NZ0.8m. (equivalent to 18% of total budgetary expenditure). The New Zealand Department of Education provides advisory services and some educational equipment. Scholarships are awarded for secondary and tertiary education and vocational training in Samoa, Fiji, Niue, Tonga and New Zealand. In 2004 a total of 53 Tokelauans over the age of 15 years were studying overseas under the Tokelau Sponsorship Scheme (34 in Samoa, 12 in New Zealand and seven in Fiji). In 2003 there were some 176 Tokelauan pupils enrolled at the Samoa Secondary School. Australia also provides scholarships. There was a total of 358 pupils enrolled in primary and secondary education and 54 teachers on the islands in 2003.

Public Holidays

2006: 1 January (New Year's Day), 6 February (Waitangi Day, anniversary of 1840 treaty), 14–17 April (Easter), 25 April (ANZAC Day, anniversary of 1915 landing at Gallipoli), 5 June (Queen's Official Birthday), 23 October (Labour Day), 25 December (Christmas Day), 26 December (Boxing Day).

2007: 1 January (New Year's Day), 6 February (Waitangi Day, anniversary of 1840 treaty), 6–9 April (Easter), 25 April (ANZAC Day, anniversary of 1915 landing at Gallipoli), 4 June (Queen's Official Birthday), 22 October (Labour Day), 25 December (Christmas Day), 26 December (Boxing Day).

Weights and Measures

The metric system is in force.

Statistical Survey

Source (unless otherwise indicated): Tokelau Apia Liaison Office, POB 805, Apia, Samoa; tel. 20822; fax 21761; e-mail f.aukuso@clear.net.nz.

AREA AND POPULATION

Area: Atafu 3.5 sq km; Nukunonu 4.7 sq km; Fakaofo 4.0 sq km; Total 12.2 sq km (4.7 sq miles).

Population (census of March 1991): Total 1,577 (Atafu 543, Nukunonu 437, Fakaofo 597). *Tokelauans Resident in New Zealand:* 2,802. *Census of 1996* (incl. temporary visitors): Total 1,507 (Atafu 499, Fakaofo 578, Nukunonu 430); Total resident population 1,487. *Mid-2001* (estimate): 1,537.

Density (mid-2001): 126.0 per sq km.

Births and Deaths (1996): Birth rate 33.1 per 1,000; Death rate 8.2 per 1,000. *2003:* Live births 24.

Expectation of Life (official estimates, years at birth, 1996): Males 68; Females 70. Source: Ministry of Foreign Affairs and Trade, Wellington.

Economically Active Population (2001 census, persons aged 15 years and over): Construction 78; Retail trade 12; Hotels and restaurants 4; Transport 7; Communications 20; Village services 182; Public administration 59; Education 53; Medical 23; *Total* 438.

HEALTH AND WELFARE

Access to Water (% of households, 2001): 89.5.

AGRICULTURE, ETC.

Crop Production (FAO estimates, metric tons, 2004): Coconuts 3,000; Copra 45; Roots and tubers 300; Bananas 15; Other tropical fruits 46.

Livestock (FAO estimates, year ending September 2004): Pigs 1,000; Chickens 5,000.

Livestock Products (FAO estimates, metric tons, 2004): Pig meat 20; Chicken meat 5; Hen eggs 8.

Fishing (FAO estimates, metric tons, live weight, 2003): Total catch 200.

Source: FAO.

INDUSTRY

Production (estimate, 1990): Electric energy 300,000 kWh.

FINANCE

Currency and Exchange Rates: New Zealand currency is legal tender. Tokelau souvenir coins have also been issued. New Zealand currency: 100 cents = 1 New Zealand dollar ($NZ); *Sterling, US Dollar and Euro Equivalents* (30 December 2005): £1 sterling = $NZ2.5270; US $1 = $NZ1.4676; €1 = $NZ1.7313; $NZ100 = £39.57 = US $68.14 = €57.76. *Average Exchange Rate* (US $ per $NZ): 1.7229 in 2003; 1.5087 in 2004; 1.4203 in 2005.

Budget ($NZ, year ending 30 June 1998): *Revenue:* Local 734,950; New Zealand subsidy 4,600,000; Total 5,334,950. *Expenditure:* Total 5,208,449.

Overseas Aid (projection, $NZ '000, 2002/03): Official development assistance from New Zealand 8,100 (of which Budget support 4,750, Projects and training 2,650). *2004/05:* Total development assistance from New Zealand $NZ9.0m. Source: Ministry of Foreign Affairs and Trade, Wellington.

EXTERNAL TRADE

Principal Commodities ($NZ, 2002): *Imports:* Food and live animals 923,766; Beverages and tobacco 275; Mineral fuels, etc. 194,779; Animal and vegetable oils, fats and waxes 50,012; Chemicals and related products 45,429; Manufactured goods 183,488; Total (incl. others) 1,673,389.

COMMUNICATIONS MEDIA

Radio Receivers (estimate, 1997): 1,000 in use.

EDUCATION

Schools (1999): 3 (one school for all levels on each atoll).

Teachers (2003): Primary 31; Secondary 23.

Pupils (2003): Primary 182; General secondary 176.

Students Overseas (1999): Secondary 22; Tertiary 20.

Directory

The Constitution

Tokelau is administered under the authority of the Tokelau Islands Act 1948 and subsequent amendments and regulations. The Act declared Tokelau (then known as the Tokelau Islands) to be within the territorial boundaries of New Zealand. The Administrator is the representative of the Crown and is responsible to the Minister of Foreign Affairs and Trade in the New Zealand Government. The office of Administrator is normally held conjointly with that of New Zealand's Secretary of Foreign Affairs and Trade, but provision is made for the offices to be held separately. Most of the powers of the Administrator are delegated to the Tokelau Apia Liaison Office, the General Fono and the Tokelau Council for Ongoing Government (formerly the Council of Faipule). The chief representative of the Administrator (and the Crown) on each atoll is the highest elected official, the Faipule, who exercises executive, political and judicial powers. The three Faipule, who hold ministerial portfolios and along with the three Pulenuku form the six-member Tokelau Council of Faipule, act as the representatives of the Territory in dealings with the administration and at international meetings, and choose one of their number to hold the title Ulu-O-Tokelau (Head of Tokelau) for a term of one year. The Ulu-O-Tokelau chairs sessions of the territorial assembly, the General Fono. The General Fono is a meeting of 18 delegates (including the Faipule and the Pulenuku—Village Mayor—from each atoll), representing the entire Territory. There are two or three meetings each year, which may take place on any of the atolls. The General Fono is the highest advisory body and the administration must consult it about all policy affecting the Territory. The assembly has responsibility for the territorial budget and has the power to enact legislation, to impose taxes and to declare public holidays. There are a number of specialist committees, such as the Budget Committee and the Law Committee.

Tokelau is an association of three autonomous atoll communities. Local government consists of the Faipule, the Pulenuku and the Taupulega (Island Council or Council of Elders). The Faipule, the Pulenuku and delegates to the General Fono are elected every three years on the basis of universal adult suffrage (the age of majority being 21). The Faipule represents the atoll community, liaises with the administration and the Tokelau Public Service, acts as a judicial commissioner and presides over meetings of the Taupulega. The Pulenuku is responsible for the administration of village affairs, including the maintenance of water supplies and the inspection of plantations, and, in some instances, the resolution of land disputes (practically all land is held by customary title, by the head of a family group, and may not be alienated to non-Tokelauans). The Taupulega is the principal organ of local government. The Taupulega also appoints the Failautuhi (Island Clerk), to record its meetings and transactions. The Taupulega in Atafu consists of the Faipule, the Pulenuku and the head of every family group; in Nukunonu it consists of the Faipule, the Pulenuku, the elders of the community and the nominated heads of extended families; in Fakaofo it consists of the Faipule, the Pulenuku and the elders (meetings of all the heads of family groups take place only infrequently).

The Government

(April 2006)

Administrator: NEIL DOUGLAS WALTER (took office March 2003).

FAIPULE

At elections in January 2005, all three incumbent Faipule were re-elected to office.
Faipule of Fakaofo: KOLOUEI O'BRIEN.
Faipule of Nukunonu: PIO TUIA.
Faipule of Atafu: KURESA NASAU.

PULENUKU

At elections in January 2005, two new Pulenuku were elected to office and one was re-elected.
Pulenuku of Fakaofo: KELI NEEMIA.
Pulenuku of Nukunonu: VASA TAVITE.
Pulenuku of Atafu: IOSUA ALENI.

GOVERNMENT OFFICES

Tokelau Apia Liaison Office/Ofiha o Fehokotakiga Tokelau Ma Apia: POB 865, Apia, Samoa; tel. 32325; fax 32328; e-mail f.aukuso@clear.net.nz; responsible for transport, accounting and consular functions; Gen. Man. FALANI AUKUSO.

The Tokelau Public Service has seven departments, divided among the three atolls, with a supervising administrative official located in each village. Two departments are established on each atoll, while the seventh department, the Office of the Tokelau Council for Ongoing Government (formerly the Council of Faipule), rotates on a yearly basis in conjunction with the position of Ulu-O-Tokelau. Management of the Tokelau Public Service was formally transferred to Tokelau in July 2001.

Judicial System

Tokelau's legislative and judicial systems are based on the Tokelau Islands Act 1948 and subsequent amendments and regulations. The Act provided for a variety of British regulations to continue in force and, where no other legislation applies, the law of England and Wales in 1840 (the year in which British sovereignty over New Zealand was established) was to be applicable. New Zealand statute law applies in Tokelau only if specifically extended there. In 1986 legislation formalized the transfer of High Court civil and criminal jurisdiction from Niue to New Zealand. Most cases are judged by the Commissioner established on each atoll, who has limited jurisdiction in civil and criminal matters. Commissioners are appointed by the New Zealand Governor-General, after consultation with the elders of the atoll.

Commissioner of Fakaofo: LUI KELEKOLIO.
Commissioner of Nukunonu: ATONIO EGELIKO.
Commissioner of Atafu: MAKA TOLOA.

Religion

On Atafu almost all inhabitants are members of the Tokelau Congregational Christian Church, on Nukunonu all are Roman Catholic, while both denominations are represented on Fakaofo. In the late 1990s some 70% of the total population adhered to the Congregational Christian Church, and 30% to the Roman Catholic Church.

CHRISTIANITY

Roman Catholic Church

The Church is represented in Tokelau by a Mission, established in 1992. There were an estimated 500 adherents at 31 December 2003.
Superior: Mgr PATRICK EDWARD O'CONNOR, Catholic Mission, Nukunonu, Tokelau (via Apia, Samoa); tel. 4160; fax 4236; e-mail dr.tovite@clear.net.n3.

Broadcasting and Communications

Each atoll has a radio station to broadcast shipping and weather reports. Radio-telephone provided the main communications link with other areas until the late 1990s. A new telecommunications system established at a cost of US $2.76m. (US $1m. of which was provided by New Zealand) and operating through an earth station, linked to a communications satellite, on each atoll, became operational in 1997. A new weekly radio programme, called Vakai, broadcast by Samoa Broadcasting Service to Tokelau's three atolls, began in October 2004.

TELECOMMUNICATIONS

TeleTok: Fenuafala, Fakaofo.

Finance

In 1977 a savings bank was established on each atoll; commercial and other banking facilities are available in Apia, Samoa.

Trade and Industry

A village co-operative store was established on each atoll in 1977. Local industries include copra production, woodwork and plaited craft goods, and the processing of tuna. Electricity is provided by diesel generators based in the village on each atoll.

Transport

There are no roads or motor vehicles. Unscheduled inter-atoll voyages, by sea, are forbidden because the risk of missing landfall is too great. Passengers and cargo are transported by vessels that anchor off shore, as there are no harbour facilities. A scheme to provide wharves (primarily to facilitate the export of fish) was proposed in September 2002. Most shipping links are with Samoa, but a monthly service from Fiji was introduced in 1986. The vessel *Forum Tokelau*, operated by Pacific Forum Line, began a monthly service between Tokelau and Apia, Samoa, in mid-1997. A New Zealand-funded inter-atoll vessel commenced service in 1991, providing the first regular link between the atolls for 40 years. Plans to construct an airstrip on each atoll were postponed in 1987 in favour of the development of shipping links. In late 2002, however, proposals for the construction of an airport were again under consideration.

NEW ZEALAND'S ASSOCIATED STATES

New Zealand's two Associated States are the self-governing Cook Islands and Niue, both of which are situated in the Pacific Ocean.

COOK ISLANDS

Introductory Survey

Location, Climate, Language, Religion, Flag, Capital

The 13 inhabited and two uninhabited islands of the Cook Islands are located in the southern Pacific Ocean and lie between American Samoa, to the west, and French Polynesia, to the east. The islands extend over about 2m. sq km (more than 750,000 sq miles) of ocean, and form two groups: the Northern Cooks, which are all atolls and include Pukapuka, Rakahanga and Manihiki, and the Southern Cooks, including Aitutaki, Mangaia and Rarotonga, which are all volcanic islands. From December to March the climate is warm and humid, with the possibility of severe storms; from April to November the climate is mild and equable. The average annual rainfall on Rarotonga is 2,012 mm (79 ins). The official languages are English and Cook Islands Maori. The principal religion is Christianity, with about 70% of the population adhering to the Cook Islands Congregational Christian Church. The islands' flag (proportions 1 by 2) displays 15 five-pointed white stars (representing the islands of the group) on a royal blue field, with the United Kingdom's Union Flag as a canton in the upper hoist. The capital is Avarua, on Rarotonga.

Recent History

The first Europeans to visit the islands were members of a British expedition, led by Capt. James Cook (after whom the islands are named), in 1773. The Cook Islands were proclaimed a British protectorate in 1888, and a part of New Zealand in 1901.

On 4 August 1965 the Cook Islands became a self-governing Territory in free association with New Zealand. The people are New Zealand citizens. Sir Albert Henry, leader of the Cook Islands Party (CIP), was elected Premier in 1965 and re-elected in 1971, 1974 and March 1978. However, in July 1978, following an inquiry into alleged electoral malpractice, the Chief Justice disallowed votes cast in the elections to the Legislative Assembly (later renamed Parliament) by Cook Islands expatriates who had been flown from New Zealand, with their fares paid from public funds. The amended ballot gave a majority to the Democratic Party (DP), and its leader, Dr (later Sir) Thomas Davis, was sworn in as Premier by the Chief Justice. In August 1979 Sir Albert Henry was convicted of conspiracy to defraud, and was formally stripped of his knighthood.

In May 1981 the Cook Islands' Constitution was amended to increase the membership of Parliament from 22 to 24, and to extend the parliamentary term from four to five years. In March 1983 Sir Thomas Davis lost power to the CIP, under Geoffrey (later Sir Geoffrey) Henry, cousin of the former Premier. However, with one seat already subject to re-election, Henry's majority of three was reduced by the death of one CIP member of Parliament and the transfer of allegiance to the DP by another. Henry resigned in August, and a general election in November returned the DP to power under Davis. In August 1984 Davis announced wide-ranging government changes, with three of the seven posts going to members of the CIP, to form a coalition Government, with Henry as Deputy Prime Minister. In mid-1985, however, Davis dismissed Henry, who had endorsed an unsuccessful motion expressing 'no confidence' in the Government, and Henry's supporters withdrew from the coalition. Henry's successor as Deputy Prime Minister was Dr Terepai Maoate, one of four CIP members who continued to support the Davis Government, in defiance of the CIP central committee.

Davis was forced to resign as Prime Minister in July 1987, after a parliamentary motion expressing 'no confidence' in his administration was approved. He was succeeded by Dr Pupuke Robati, a member of the Cabinet and a leading figure in the DP. Geoffrey Henry again became Prime Minister following a general election victory for the CIP in January 1989. The defection in mid-1990 of a member of Parliament, from the DP to the CIP provided the CIP with 15 seats in Parliament and thus the minimum two-thirds' majority support necessary to amend the Constitution. In August 1991 a constitutional amendment was approved to increase the number of members of Parliament to 25 and, at an election to the newly created seat, a CIP candidate was successful. The amendment also provided for an increase in the number of cabinet members from seven to nine (including the Prime Minister).

At a general election in March 1994 the CIP increased its majority, winning 20 seats in Parliament; the DP secured three seats and the Alliance Party (established in 1992 by Norman George, the former DP parliamentary whip, who had been expelled from the party following a dispute over spending) two. Davis, who failed to win a seat, subsequently resigned as leader of the DP. A referendum held simultaneously revealed that a majority of the electorate favoured retaining the current name (69.8% of voters), national anthem (80.2%) and flag (48.5%) of the Cook Islands. (At subsequent by-elections the CIP lost two seats and the DP and Alliance Party each gained one seat.)

A financial scandal was narrowly averted following reports that during 1994 the Government had issued loan guarantees for foreign companies worth more than $NZ1,200m. (the island's total revenue for 1994/95 was estimated at $NZ50m.). An investigation into the affair by the New Zealand Reserve Bank found that the Government had not been guilty of fraud, but rather had been coerced into the activity by unscrupulous foreign business interests. However, the affair led many investors to remove their funds from the islands, provoking a financial crisis that resulted in Henry's decision in mid-1995 to withdraw the Cook Islands dollar from circulation, and to implement a programme of retrenchment measures. The crisis deepened during 1995 as new allegations emerged, and Henry's Government was severely criticized by New Zealand for failing to co-operate with an official inquiry into accusations of fraud and tax evasion involving several New Zealand companies. Henry maintained that the islands' bank secrecy laws prevented the disclosure of information relating to financial transactions. The situation deteriorated further when it was revealed that the Government had defaulted on a debt of some US $100m. to an Italian bank. In response to pressure from New Zealand, and in an attempt to restore a degree of financial stability to the islands, Henry (whose management of the crisis had been questioned both by his own party and by the opposition) announced a severe restructuring programme in April 1996. The measures included a 50% reduction in the pay of public sector workers, the closure of almost all diplomatic missions overseas, a 60% reduction in the number of government departments and ministries, and the privatization of the majority of government-owned authorities. A marked increase in 1995/96 in the emigration rate and a decline in the number of Cook Islanders returning to the islands following a period of residency overseas was attributed to the austere economic conditions created by the financial crisis.

In August 1997 Parliament approved the Outer Islands Local Government Act, providing for a new budgetary system to allocate funds for projects in the outer islands and for increased powers for local authorities, with the aim of reducing significantly central government administration of the outer islands. As part of the plan, three new government bodies were elected in April 1998.

Henry's administration continued to attract controversy, with the announcement in December 1997 of the closure of the Ministry of Public Works, Survey, Housing, Water Supply and Environment Services for exceeding its budget. The minister responsible, Tihina Tom Marsters, resigned in protest at the closure, which resulted in the loss of more than 100 public servants' jobs, problems with the supply of utilities (particularly water) and the suspension of several development projects.

In November 1997 the northern Cook Islands were devastated by Cyclone Martin, which killed at least eight people and destroyed virtually all crops and infrastructure. The islands' important black pearl industry suffered severe losses as a result of extensive damage on Manihiki Atoll.

At legislative elections in June 1999 the CIP won 11 of the 25 seats in Parliament, the Democratic Alliance Party (DAP, a grouping that included the Democratic Party) 10 seats and the New Alliance Party (NAP, formerly the Alliance Party) four seats. Sir Geoffrey Henry of the CIP was reappointed Prime Minister and formed a new Cabinet, following the establishment of a political coalition with the NAP; the leader of the NAP, Norman George, became Deputy Prime Minister. However, three members of the CIP subsequently left the party to form a coalition with the DAP, in protest at the alliance with the NAP, and at the end of July Henry resigned and was replaced by a 'rebel' CIP member, Dr Joe Williams. Williams was confirmed as the new Prime Minister by 13 votes to 12 in a vote of confidence by the Parliament. Williams' appointment provoked a public protest in

Rarotonga, exacerbated by general discontent at the nomination of a Prime Minister whose parliamentary constituency was outside the Cook Islands. Electors also voted in a referendum on whether the parliamentary term should be reduced from five years to four. The shorter term was favoured by 63% of voters, and thus narrowly failed to receive the support of the two-thirds' majority required to amend the Constitution. The result of the contest for the Pukapuka seat, which had been won by former Prime Minister Inatio Akaruru by just one vote, was challenged by the DAP. The matter was taken to the Court of Appeal, which subsequently declared the result invalid, stripping the Government of its one-seat majority. A by-election was held in late September 1999 to decide the Pukapuka seat, however the result was again said to be invalid and a further by-election was scheduled. The Government became a minority administration in mid-October when the Prime Minister dismissed his deputy, Norman George, along with the Minister of Education, following their defection to the opposition. Despite the appointment of three new ministers, Williams failed to regain a majority in Parliament. In November Williams resigned, shortly before a vote of 'no confidence' was to be tabled against him by Dr Terepai Maoate, the leader of the opposition DAP. Maoate won the vote by 14 votes to 11 and was appointed Prime Minister, forming a new coalition Government with the NAP. He subsequently reappointed Norman George to the post of Deputy Prime Minister.

In February 2001 Maoate removed the transport portfolio from among the responsibilities of Dr Robert Woonton (whose other duties included that of Minister of Foreign Affairs). Maoate underwent medical treatment in March, prompting speculation that he might stand down as Prime Minister later in the year. In July Maoate dismissed Norman George on the grounds that he was working to undermine him; this was the second time that George had lost the position of Deputy Prime Minister. He was replaced by Dr Robert Woonton. Woonton, however, strongly criticized Maoate's leadership in the same month.

In late 2001 the rift between the Prime Minister and his Cabinet widened. Woonton announced his resignation, which Maoate refused to accept. This led to a motion of 'no confidence' in the Prime Minister, which he only narrowly survived. In February 2002 Maoate's leadership was again challenged: 15 of the 25 members of Parliament voted against him in a second motion of 'no confidence'. He was therefore replaced by Robert Woonton. In an extensive ministerial reorganization Sir Geoffrey Henry returned to the Cabinet as Deputy Prime Minister. Woonton declared his priorities to be the encouragement of emigrant workers to return to the islands through income tax incentives and an ambitious redevelopment plan for the capital, Avarua.

The Government's decision not to name a senior civil servant in the Prime Minister's office who had been arrested and charged with fraud in August 2002 led to accusations of secrecy by the opposition. Criticism of the Government's position increased in the following month with the introduction of new media laws (which many observers believed would serve to suppress opposition to government policy), particularly when a government official stated his desire for 'Zimbabwe-style legislation to stop inaccurate reporting'.

In November 2002 Parliament approved a constitutional amendment abolishing the requirement for electoral candidates to reside in the islands for a qualifying period of three months. This action was widely interpreted as a way of retaining the overseas parliamentary seat for the CIP leader, Dr Joe Williams, who lived permanently in New Zealand. In the same month the CIP and the DP formed a coalition government (the fifth such coalition since the previous election) which left Norman George, who had been recently dismissed from his position in the Cabinet, as the sole opposition member of Parliament. The Government's action prompted a demonstration outside the parliament building by some 150 people, organized by a recently formed organization, the Group for Political Change. The protesters claimed that the virtual absence of an opposition constituted an erosion of democracy and appealed to the Prime Minister to commit to an early general election. However, in late January 2003 the CIP was ousted from the coalition. The continued political manoeuvring was widely denounced, particularly among the business community, for creating a climate of instability in the islands. Public dissatisfaction with the situation resulted in the presentation of a petition to Government in March signed by a significant percentage of the population. The petition called for a number of political reforms including a reduction in the number of members of Parliament, the introduction of a shorter parliamentary term and the abolition of the overseas seat. Moreover, businessman Teariki Heather announced the formation of a new political party, the Cook Islands National, in the same month. In September 2003 legislation was approved providing for the abolition of the overseas seat and for a referendum (to be held concurrently with the next general election) on a proposal to shorten the parliamentary term from five years to four.

In early November 2003 the Deputy Prime Minister, Terepai Maoate, and the Minister of Justice, Tangata Vavia, resigned following an unsuccessful attempt by Maoate to propose a motion of 'no confidence' in the Government. The Government was the focus of further criticism in December when about 200 people marched through Avarua to protest at the granting of a residency permit to New Zealander Mark Lyon. The protesters claimed that Lyon, a wealthy businessman with recent convictions for weapons possession and a reputation for behaviour deemed disrespectful to island traditions, was not a suitable candidate for residency in the islands. Moreover, the demonstrators demanded the resignation of the Prime Minister and his chief adviser, Norman George, over the matter, stating that the islands should not be obliged to host undesirable characters, regardless of their ability to finance important business projects.

The reputation of the public service suffered a reversal in November 2003 when the former Chief of Staff in the Office of the Prime Minister, Edward Drollet, was convicted of seven charges of receiving secret commissions and one of forgery and was sentenced to more than two years' imprisonment.

At a general election in September 2004 the DP won 14 of the 24 seats, the CIP secured nine and an independent candidate won the remaining seat. Prime Minister Robert Woonton regained his seat by only four votes, amid accusations that he had secured the support of some voters through bribery. In a referendum held concurrently, 82.3% of participating voters indicated their support for the shortening of the parliamentary term from five years to four. The period immediately after the election was characterized by political manoeuvring and the initiation of several legal cases challenging the outcome in a number of constituencies. In mid-November Woonton announced that his party was to form a coalition government with the CIP. This decision was widely opposed within the DP, whose leadership questioned its legality, and prompted the resignation of the Deputy Prime Minister, Aunty Mau Munokoa. Further controversy was caused by the appointment of the defeated former MP, Norman George, to the position of Speaker. In mid-December, with the DP effectively divided over Woonton's actions, Jim Marurai, of the minority Democratic Tumu Party, was elected Prime Minister and a governing coalition was formed between his party and the CIP. It was understood that Marurai would serve as Prime Minister for the first two years of the parliamentary term and would then be replaced by Sir Geoffrey Henry of the CIP. However, in August 2005 Henry was dismissed and replaced by DP leader Dr Terepai Maoate. In September two further CIP cabinet ministers were dismissed and replaced by DP members. Marurai declared that the coalition had been dissolved, claiming that the action followed threats to his leadership.

The islands suffered considerable damage in February and March 2005 when five cyclones struck in just over four weeks. The resultant damage to housing, infrastructure and crops was estimated at $NZ25m. A rehabilitation programme was implemented, and in October 2005 discussions took place between Jim Marurai and the Prime Minister of New Zealand, Helen Clark, regarding the progress made. The islands' economic situation was also discussed.

In October 2005 Peri Vaevae Pare, the Minister of Health and Internal Affairs, whose other portfolios included social services, was suspended from office pending police investigations into allegations of fraud. In November he was convicted on three charges of intent to defraud and gain pecuniary advantage, each conviction carrying a maximum sentence of five years' imprisonment. In early 2006 the Prime Minister requested the formal resignation of the suspended Minister, who was subsequently replaced. Dr Terepai Maoate continued as Deputy Prime Minister, retaining responsibility for the finance portfolio, while Wilkie Rasmussen remained responsible for foreign affairs.

The rate of emigration, meanwhile, continued to increase. In late 2000 it was announced that some 1,400 residents had left the islands during that year (compared with 641 in the previous year). This resulted in a reduction in the population of the islands to its lowest level in more than 50 years, the majority of the loss being from the outer islands, and prompted the Government to campaign in Australia and New Zealand to encourage former citizens to return to the Cook Islands. Private-sector businesses, many of which had experienced difficulties in recruiting workers in sufficient numbers, were also involved in the campaign. At the census of 2001 the resident population was recorded at only 14,990. In August 2002 the Government announced that it would allocate US $23,350 for the campaign.

In early 2000 the islands of Penrhyn, Pukapuka, Rakahanga and Manihiki expressed their desire to become fully devolved and to take sole control over areas such as administration, public expenditure and justice. In response, the Government pledged gradually to phase out the Ministry of Outer Islands Development, as well as the post of Government Representative in the outer islands. In December of that year an additional US $2m. in funding under the Cotonou agreement was designated for projects on the outer islands.

A reported increase in the number of Russian nationals opening accounts in the Cook Islands led to allegations in early 1999 that the islands' offshore financial centre was being used extensively by criminal organizations for 'laundering' the proceeds of their activities. (The facility had regularly generated some 8% of annual GDP.)

NEW ZEALAND'S ASSOCIATED STATES

The claims were vigorously denied by officials in the sector. However, in June 2000 the naming of the islands by the Paris-based Financial Action Task Force (FATF, see p. 389) as one of a number of countries and territories that had failed to co-operate in regional efforts to combat 'money-laundering', along with the islands' identification by the Organisation for Economic Co-operation and Development (OECD, see p. 320) as a tax 'haven' that lacked financial transparency, led to increased international pressure on the Government to implement stricter controls over its offshore financial centre. Consequently, legislation was approved in August of that year providing for the creation of the Money Laundering Authority and the introduction of new regulations aimed at reducing criminal activity in the sector. In February 2005 the Cook Islands were finally removed from the FATF list of non-co-operative countries and territories.

In August 1985 eight members of the South Pacific Forum (subsequently restyled the Pacific Islands Forum, see p. 352), including the Cook Islands, signed a treaty on Rarotonga, designating a 'nuclear-free' zone in the South Pacific. The treaty imposed a ban on the manufacture, testing, storage and use of nuclear weapons, and the dumping of nuclear waste, in the region.

In January 1986, following the rift between New Zealand and the USA in respect of the ANZUS (see p. 395) security arrangements, Sir Thomas Davis declared the Cook Islands a neutral country, because he considered that New Zealand (which has control over the islands' defence and foreign policy) was no longer in a position to defend the islands. The proclamation of neutrality meant that the Cook Islands would not enter into a military relationship with any foreign power, and, in particular, would prohibit visits by US warships. Visits by US naval vessels were allowed to resume by Henry's Government. In October 1991 the Cook Islands signed a treaty of friendship and co-operation with France, covering economic development, trade and surveillance of the islands' exclusive economic zone (EEZ). The establishment of closer relations with France was widely regarded as an expression of the Cook Islands' Government's dissatisfaction with existing arrangements with New Zealand. However, relations deteriorated considerably when the French Government resumed its programme of nuclear-weapons testing at Mururoa Atoll in September 1995. Henry was fiercely critical of the decision and dispatched a *vaka* (traditional voyaging canoe) with a crew of Cook Islands' traditional warriors to protest near the test site. The tests were concluded in January 1996. Full diplomatic relations with France were established in early 2000. Meanwhile, the islands established diplomatic relations at ambassadorial level with the People's Republic of China in July 1997. In November 1998 Henry made an official visit to China, during which the two countries signed a bilateral trade agreement and each conferred the status of 'most favoured nation' on the other. Henry stated that the move constituted a further attempt by his Government to reduce the islands' dependence on New Zealand. During her visit to the islands in June 2001, Helen Clark, the New Zealand Prime Minister, stated that if the Cook Islands desired complete independence, and membership of international organizations, the process would not be obstructed by New Zealand. Cook Islanders, however, would then be obliged to renounce their New Zealand citizenship.

Government

The Cook Islands is an internally self-governing state in free association with New Zealand, which is responsible for the Cook Islands' external affairs and defence (although the Territory has progressively assumed control over much of its foreign policy). Executive authority is vested in the British monarch, who is Head of State, and is exercised through her official representative; a representative of the New Zealand Government (redesignated High Commissioner in 1994) resides on Rarotonga. Executive government is carried out by the Cabinet, consisting of the Prime Minister and between five and seven other ministers. The Cabinet is collectively responsible to the Parliament, which is formed of 24 members (decreased from 25 in 2004, following the abolition of the seat for a member chosen by non-resident voters) who are elected by universal adult suffrage every four years (reduced from five years by a referendum in 2004). The House of Ariki, which comprises up to 15 members who are hereditary chiefs, can advise the Government, but has no legislative powers. The Koutu Nui is a similar body, comprising sub-chiefs. Each of the main islands, except Rarotonga, has an elected island council, and a government representative who is appointed by the Prime Minister.

Economic Affairs

In 2003, according to the Asian Development Bank (ADB), the Cook Islands' gross domestic product (GDP), measured at current prices, totalled an estimated $NZ238.6m. GDP was estimated to have increased, in real terms, at an average annual rate of 3.0% in 1995–2003. In 2003 GDP per head was estimated at $NZ12,965, compared with $NZ 12,006 the previous year. During 1995–2004, it was estimated, the population increased at an average annual rate of about 0.5%. According to ADB estimates, compared with the previous year overall GDP rose by 4.2% in 2004, with growth being estimated at 3.0% in 2005.

According to estimates by the ADB, agriculture (including forestry and fishing) contributed 15.3% of GDP in 2003. In that year the sector engaged some 28.6% of the economically active population, according to FAO estimates. In 2000 only 35% of Rarotonga households were classified as being agriculturally active, compared with 74% in the southern outer islands. According to ADB figures, the real GDP of the agricultural sector increased by an average of 8.3% per year in 1995–2003. Compared with the previous year, the sector's GDP increased by 28.3% in 2003 and by 15.1% in 2004. In 2002 the sector provided 32.6% of export earnings (compared with 5.3% in the previous year). Papaya is the Cook Islands' most important export crop. Export earnings from the fruit, however, declined to some $NZ122,000 in 2004, equivalent to only 1.1% of total export revenue. Other important cash crops are coconuts and tropical fruits such as mangoes, pineapples and bananas. Cassava, sweet potatoes and vegetables are cultivated as food crops. Pigs and poultry are kept. Aquaculture, in the form of giant clam farming and pearl oyster farming, was developed during the 1980s. The pearl industry expanded considerably during the 1990s. Pearl oyster farming at Manihiki and Penrhyn Island was the islands' most important industry, and pearls were the most important export commodity by 2000, when they contributed 92.1% of total export earnings. The industry was adversely affected, however, by Cyclone Martin which devastated Manihiki Atoll in late 1997 and by a bacterial pearl shell disease in 2000. In response to the infection, the pearl industry agreed to a number of measures designed to protect the environment and reduce overfarming. The value of pearl exports decreased from $NZ14.6m. in 2001 to $NZ6.4m. in 2002, the latter figure nevertheless being equivalent to 58.6% of total export earnings in that year. In 2003, partly owing to low international prices, revenue from pearl exports continued to decline, decreasing to only $NZ2.8m. Earnings from this source rose to almost $NZ3.2m. in 2004, when they accounted for 29.5% of total export receipts. Export earnings were expected to rise to $NZ4.2m. in 2006. The sale of fishing licences to foreign fleets provides an important source of income. However, illegal fishing in the islands' exclusive economic zone (EEZ) increased during the 1990s, and in March 2003 the Government announced harsher penalties in an attempt to deal with this problem. The long-term viability of the fishing sector, furthermore, was threatened by the lack of any regional strategy to address the problem of overfishing of stocks. Revenue from the export of fresh and chilled fish increased from $NZ2.3m. in 2002 to almost $NZ8.3m. in 2003, when for the first time it superseded receipts from pearl exports, but declined to less than $NZ2.9m. (equivalent to 26.9% of total export earnings) in 2004. Some 44 fishing vessels had been in operation during 2003, compared with 19 in 2002.

According to ADB estimates, industry (comprising mining and quarrying, manufacturing, construction and utilities) provided 7.7% of GDP in 2003. The sector engaged 12.1% of employees in 1993. Industrial GDP increased, in real terms, at an average rate of 7.4% per year during 1995–2003. Compared with the previous year, the industrial sector's GDP decreased by 0.3% in 2002 before increasing by 16.2% in 2003 and 14.1% in 2004.

Manufacturing contributed 4.1% of GDP in 1995, and engaged 4.5% of employees in 1993. The manufacturing and mining sectors together accounted for an estimated 3.3% of GDP in 2003. The real GDP of manufacturing and mining increased at an average rate of 5.9% per year during 1995–2003. Compared with the previous year, however, the two sectors' GDP increased by 3.5% in 2001, before decreasing by 2.6% in 2002 and increasing by 1.5% in 2003. The most important industrial activities are fruit-processing, brewing, the manufacture of garments (1.9% of total export earnings in 2004) and handicrafts. Construction contributed an estimated 2.9% of GDP in 2003 and engaged 3.4% of the employed labour force in 1993.

The islands depend on imports for their energy requirements. Mineral fuels accounted for 21.9% of total imports in 2003. In September 1997 the Government signed an agreement with a consortium of Norwegian companies to mine cobalt, nickel, manganese and copper by extracting mineral-rich nodules found in the islands' EEZ between Aitutaki and Penrhyn. It was estimated that the deep-sea mining project, which was expected to begin in 2003/04, could earn the islands up to US $15m. per year and US $600m. in total. Trial operations began in 1999.

Service industries contributed an estimated 77.0% to GDP in 2003 and engaged 80.8% of the employed labour force in 1993. According to figures from the ADB, the GDP of the services sector increased at an average annual rate of almost 1.9% in 1995–2003. Compared with the previous year the GDP of the sector rose by 3.5% in 2003 and by 2.4% in 2004. Tourism expanded considerably from the late 1980s, and generated an estimated $NZ108.5m. in 2004/05. Visitor arrivals rose from 78,328 in 2003 to 83,333 in 2004 and to an estimated 87,449 in 2005. The trade, restaurants and hotels sector contributed 35.7% of GDP in 2003 and engaged 20.9% of the employed labour force in 1993. Offshore banking, introduced to the islands in 1982, expanded rapidly, with more than 2,000 international companies registered by

1987. In 1992 the islands were established as an alternative domicile for companies listed on the Hong Kong Stock Exchange. The financial and business services sector provided 8.3% of GDP in 2003 and engaged 3.6% of the employed labour force in 1993. A significant proportion of the islands' revenue is provided by remittances from migrants (who outnumber the residents of the islands).

The trade deficit rose from US $62m. to $69m. in 2004. In 2003 there was a surplus on the current account of the balance of payments of $12m, equivalent to 8.7% of GDP. The principal exports in 2004 were food and live animals (which accounted for 62.5% of total exports). The principal imports were food and live animals (which cost 23.6%), machinery and transport equipment (21.9% of total imports), and basic manufactures (18.4%). The principal source of imports in 2004 was New Zealand (82.9% of the total). Japan and New Zealand were the principal markets for exports (39.0% and 18.9% respectively). From July 2006 import levies were to be removed, leading to an estimated reduction of 2.2% in overall market prices.

According to ADB estimates, in the financial year ending June 2003 there was an overall budgetary deficit of $NZ1.9m.; this deficit decreased to less than $NZ1.5m. in 2003/04. Development assistance from New Zealand totalled $NZ6.24m. in 2004/05, and in the same year assistance from Australia totalled $A2.8m. In mid-2004 New Zealand and Australia agreed to combine their programmes of aid to the Cook Islands in order to improve their effectiveness. The combined allocation for 2005/06 was $NZ8.87m., comprising aid of $NZ7.65m. from New Zealand and $NZ1.22m. from Australia. The islands were also to receive $NZ1m. per year between 2003 and 2008 (to be spent on education, health and outer islands development) under the Cotonou Agreement with the European Union. New Zealand is the guarantor of the Cook Islands' borrowing from the ADB, and at the end of 2004 the cumulative total of approved loans had reached US $26.67m. An additional $3.43m., including technical assistance to the value of $0.60m., was approved for 2005. It was estimated by the ADB that the islands' external debt at the end of 2001 amounted to some US $53m. The cost of debt-servicing in that year was equivalent to 3.5% of the value of exports of goods and services. By 2004 the total debt stood at an estimated $66m. The annual rate of inflation, according to the ADB, averaged 2.1% in 1995–2004. Consumer prices rose by 3.5% in in the 12 months to December 2005. The ADB estimated the unemployment rate to be 13.1% in 2001.

The Cook Islands is a member of the Pacific Community (see p. 350) and the Pacific Islands Forum (see p. 352) and an associate member of the UN Economic and Social Commission for Asia and the Pacific (ESCAP, see p. 33). In late 1999 the Cook Islands were granted observer status at the Lomé Conventions with the European Union (superseded by the Cotonou Agreement, see p. 277).

From the 1990s development plans sought to expand the economy by stimulating investment in the private sector and developing the islands' infrastructure. The financial regulations of the islands' offshore sector, however, were severely criticized by the Financial Action Task Force (FATF—see Recent History), which until early 2005 continued to include the Cook Islands on a list of countries and territories of which the banking systems were allegedly being used for the purposes of 'money-laundering'. In February 2005 the FATF removed the Cook Islands from this list, subject to a strict monitoring period that was to prevail for at least 12 months. The implementation of new legislation (see above) had led to the foundation in 2003 of the Commission of Offshore Financial Services, as well as new laws relating to banking and financial transactions. As a result, it was hoped that the Cook Islands would be able to resume the expansion of its offshore financial services sector. Offshore financial activity was reported to have made a good recovery in 2005. Large-scale emigration remained a serious and deepening concern for the Cook Islands' economy from the late 1990s, and in 2002 the Government announced that it would allocate US $23,350 to the campaign to encourage islanders resident abroad to return. Another major challenge facing the Government was that of delivering basic services to the outer islands. The principal focus of the joint aid programme being financed by New Zealand and Australia, therefore, was the improvement of the outer islands' infrastructure, such as the upgrading of harbour facilities and the provision of power and water. Under the Development Partnership Agreement signed in September 2005, a total of $NZ7m. was to be allocated over the next three years to development projects in the outer islands. Meanwhile, the success of the tourist industry and the dramatic increase in arrivals to the islands led to expressions of concern that Rarotonga, in particular, was unable to sustain the growth. Reports indicated that waste disposal and energy provision were inadequate in relation to the demands of large numbers of visitors and that pollution of the lagoon was occurring as a result. Fears for the islands' traditional culture were also expressed. In January 2003 the Cook Islands Tourism Corporation appealed for a moratorium on all new tourism projects following an independent report into the environmental and social impact of the industry on the islands. In mid-2004 Air New Zealand introduced less expensive fares to the Cook Islands, and in December the carrier expanded its services. Furthermore, a project to expand the runway at Rarotonga airport, allowing for the arrival of larger aircraft, was expected to be completed by 2005. In February 2006 it was announced that two major construction projects, including a cyclone-proof road to encompass the flood-prone area west of Rarotonga airport, were to be initiated with aid from the People's Republic of China. The removal of import levies, scheduled to take effect in mid-2006, was expected to lead to a reduction in market prices.

Education

Free secular education is compulsory for a period of 10 years between six and 15 years of age. Primary education, from the age of five, lasts for six years. Secondary education, beginning at 11 years of age, comprises two cycles, each of three years. In 2000 there were 28 primary schools and 23 secondary schools. In that year 2,596 pupils were enrolled in primary and 1,750 in secondary schools and there was a total of 144 primary school teachers and 129 teachers at secondary level. Tertiary education is provided at a teacher-training college, a nursing school and through an apprenticeship scheme. Under the New Zealand Training Scheme, the New Zealand Government offers overseas scholarships in New Zealand, Fiji, Papua New Guinea, Australia and Samoa for secondary and tertiary education, career-training and short-term in-service training. There is an extension centre of the University of the South Pacific (based in Fiji) in the Cook Islands. One primary school on Mauke was closed down at the end of 2005 owing to a decline in the number of pupils enrolled. The 40 children enrolled for 2006 were therefore transferred to another school.

Public Holidays

2006: 1 January (New Year's Day), 14–17 April (Easter), 25 April (ANZAC Day, anniversary of 1915 landing at Gallipoli), 8 May (Mothers' Day), 5 June (Queen's Official Birthday), 4 August (Constitution Day), 26 October (Cook Islands Gospel Day), 25 December (Christmas Day), 26 December (Boxing Day).

2007: 1 January (New Year's Day), 6–9 April (Easter), 25 April (ANZAC Day, anniversary of 1915 landing at Gallipoli), 13 May (Mothers' Day), 4 June (Queen's Official Birthday), 4 August (Constitution Day), 26 October (Cook Islands Gospel Day), 25 December (Christmas Day), 26 December (Boxing Day).

Weights and Measures

The metric system is in force.

Statistical Survey

Sources (unless otherwise stated): Statistics Office, POB 125, Rarotonga; tel. 29390; Prime Minister's Department, Government of the Cook Islands, Avarua, Rarotonga; tel. 29300; fax 22856.

AREA AND POPULATION

Area: 237 sq km (91.5 sq miles).

Population: 19,103 (males 9,842, females 9,261) at census of 1 December 1996; 18,027 (males 9,303, females 8,724) at census of December 2001 (provisional). *Resident Population:* 18,034 (males 9,297, females 8,737) at 1996 census; 14,990 (males 7,738, females 7,252) at 2001 census. *Mid-2004:* 20,300 (estimate from Asian Development Bank, *Key Indicators of Developing Asian and Pacific Countries*. *By Island* (resident population, 1996 census): Rarotonga (including the capital, Avarua) 10,337; Aitutaki 2,272; Atiu 942; Mangaia 1,083; Manihiki 656; Mauke 643; Mitiaro 318; Nassau 99; Palmerston (Avarua) 49; Penrhyn (Tongareva) 604; Pukapuka 778; Rakahanga 249; Suwarrow 4. *Cook Island Maoris Resident in New Zealand* (census of 6 March 2001): 52,569.

Density (resident population, mid-2004): 85.7 per sq km.

Principal Town (UN population estimate at mid-2003, incl. suburbs): Avarua (capital) 12,507. Source: UN, *World Urbanization Prospects: The 2003 Revision*.

Births and Deaths (2004): Registered live births: 295 (birth rate 21.9 per 1,000); Registered deaths: 99 (death rate 7.3 per 1,000).

Expectation of Life (WHO estimates, years at birth): 71 (males 68; females 74) in 2003. Source: WHO, *World Health Report*.

Employment (September 1993): Agriculture, hunting, forestry and fishing 457; Mining and quarrying 16; Manufacturing 290; Electricity, gas and water 254; Construction 215; Trade, restaurants and hotels 1,338; Transport, storage and communications 770; Financing, insurance, real estate and business services 231; Community, social and personal services 2,835; *Total employees* 6,406 (males 4,069, females 2,337) (Source: ILO, *Yearbook of Labour Statistics*). *2001* (rounded figures): Agriculture, hunting, forestry and fishing

NEW ZEALAND'S ASSOCIATED STATES

Cook Islands

400; Manufacturing, mining and quarrying 400; Activities not adequately defined 5,100; Total employed 5,100; Unemployed 900; Total labour force 6,800 (Source: Asian Development Bank, *Key Indicators of Developing Asian and Pacific Countries*).

HEALTH AND WELFARE
Key Indicators

Total Fertility Rate (children per woman, 2003): 3.2.

Under-5 Mortality Rate (per 1,000 live births, 2004): 21.

Physicians (per 1,000 head, 1997): 0.90.

Health Expenditure (2002): US $ per head (PPP): 697.

Health Expenditure (2002): % of GDP: 4.6.

Health Expenditure (2002): public (% of total): 93.0.

Access to Water (% of persons, 2002): 95.

Access to Sanitation (% of persons, 2002): 100.

For sources and definitions, see explanatory note on p. vi.

AGRICULTURE, ETC.

Principal Crops (mainly FAO estimates, metric tons, 2004): Cassava 1,250; Sweet potatoes 550; Coconuts 1,800; Vegetables and melons 1,301; Tomatoes 250; Mangoes 250; Papayas 650; Pineapples 15; Bananas 50; Avocados 15.

Livestock (mainly FAO estimates, head, year ending September 2004): Pigs 32,000; Goats 1,000; Poultry 15,000; Horses 300.

Livestock Products (metric tons, 2004): Hen eggs 25; Goatskins 0; Pigmeat 550; Poultry meat 14.

Fishing (FAO estimates, metric tons, live weight, 2003): Total catch 2,605 (Albacore 1,457; Yellowfin tuna 179; Bigeye tuna 200; Groupers 50; Flyingfishes 30; Jacks and crevalles 40; Marlins and sailfishes 97; Swordfish 167; Sharks, rays and skates 20; Octopuses 30; Other marine fishes 300). Figures exclude trochus shells: 8 metric tons (FAO estimate).

Source: FAO.

INDUSTRY

Electric Energy (million kWh): 26 in 2001; 28 in 2002; 29 in 2003.

FINANCE

Currency and Exchange Rates: New Zealand currency is legal tender. In mid-1995 it was announced that the Cook Islands dollar (formerly the local currency, at par with the New Zealand dollar) was to be withdrawn from circulation. New Zealand currency: 100 cents = 1 New Zealand dollar ($NZ); for details of exchange rates, see Tokelau.

Budget ($NZ '000, year ending 30 June 2004): *Revenue:* Total revenue 71,339 (Tax 60,077, Non-tax 6,642, Capital 4,620). Excludes grants (10,040). *Expenditure:* Total expenditure and net lending 82,850 (Current 76,458, Capital 6,392). Source: Asian Development Bank, *Key Indicators of Developing Asian and Pacific Countries*.

Overseas Aid ($NZ '000): Official development assistance from New Zealand 6,200 in 2002/03; 6,240 in 2003/04 and 2004/05. Source: Ministry of Foreign Affairs and Trade, Wellington.

Cost of Living (Consumer Price Index for Rarotonga; base: December 1998 = 100): 121.61 in 2004; 125.87 in 2005.

Gross Domestic Product by Economic Activity ($NZ '000 in current prices, 2003): Agriculture, forestry and fishing 37,357; Mining, quarrying and manufacturing 8,150; Electricity, gas and water 3,418; Construction 7,207; Trade, restaurants and hotels 87,183; Transport and communications 34,630; Financial and business services 20,179; Public administration 27,531; Other services 18,762; *Sub-total* 244,417; *Less* Imputed bank service charge 5,854; *GDP in purchasers' values* 238,564. Source: Asian Development Bank, *Key Indicators of Developing Asian and Pacific Countries*.

Gross Domestic Product at Constant 2000 Prices ($NZ '000): 186,566 in 2001; 193,877 in 2002; 199,974 in 2003. Source: Asian Development Bank, *Key Indicators of Developing Asian and Pacific Countries*.

EXTERNAL TRADE

Principal Commodities (distribution by SITC, $NZ '000, 2004): *Imports c.i.f.:* Food and live animals 26,363; Mineral fuels, lubricants, etc. 9,307; Chemicals 7,353; Basic manufactures 20,511; Machinery and transport equipment 24,371; Miscellaneous manufactured articles 15,899; Total (incl. others) 111,504. *Exports f.o.b.:* Food and live animals 6,736; Basic manufactures 3,271; Miscellaneous manufactured articles 701; Total (incl. others) 10,771.

Principal Trading Partners ($NZ '000, 2004): *Imports:* New Zealand 92,412; Australia 4,757; USA 914; Japan 1,888; Fiji 7,861; Total (incl. others) 111,504. *Exports:* Japan 4,204; New Zealand 2,037; Australia 284; USA 465; Total (incl. others) 10,771.

TRANSPORT

Road Traffic (registered vehicles, April 1983): 6,555. *New Motor Vehicles Registered* (Rarotonga, 2004): Motorcycles 1,151; Cars and jeeps 293; Vans and pick-ups 89; Trucks and buses 41; Others 14; *Total* 1,588.

Shipping: *Merchant Fleet* (registered at 31 December 2004): 52 vessels, displacement 26,108 grt (Source: Lloyd's Register-Fairplay, *World Fleet Statistics*); *International Sea-borne Freight Traffic* (estimates, '000 metric tons): Goods unloaded 32.6 (2001); Goods loaded 9; Goods unloaded 32 (1990) (Source: UN, *Monthly Bulletin of Statistics*).

Civil Aviation (2004): *Aircraft Movements:* 670. *Freight Traffic* (metric tons): Goods loaded 671; Goods unloaded 765.

TOURISM

Foreign Tourist Arrivals: 72,781 in 2002; 78,328 in 2003; 83,333 in 2004.

Tourist Arrivals by Place of Residence (2004): Australia 11,850; Canada 2,419; Europe 20,410; New Zealand 38,755; USA 6,026; Total (incl. others) 83,333.

Tourism Revenue (US $ million, incl. passenger transport): 36 in 2000; 38 in 2001; 46 in 2002. Source: World Tourism Organization.

COMMUNICATIONS MEDIA

Radio Receivers (1997): 14,000 in use*.

Television Receivers (1997): 4,000 in use*.

Telephones (main lines, 2002): 6,000 in use†.

Mobile Cellular Telephones (2002): 1,499 subscribers†.

Facsimile Machines (1990): 230 in use‡.

Internet Users (2002): 3,600.

Daily Newspaper (1996): 1; circulation 2,000*.

Non-daily Newspaper (1996): 1; circulation 1,000*.
* Source: UNESCO, *Statistical Yearbook*.
† Source: International Telecommunication Union.
‡ Source: UN, *Statistical Yearbook*.

EDUCATION

Pre-primary (2000): 26 schools (1998); 31 teachers; 423 pupils.

Primary (2000): 28 schools (1998); 144 teachers; 2,596 pupils.

Secondary* (1998): 23 schools; 129 teachers; 1,750 pupils (2000).

Higher (1980): 41 teachers; 360 pupils†.
* Includes high school education.
† Source: UNESCO, *Statistical Yearbook*.

Directory

The Constitution

On 5 August 1965 a new Constitution was proclaimed, whereby the people of the Cook Islands have complete control over their own affairs in free association with New Zealand, but they can at any time move into full independence by a unilateral act if they so wish.

Executive authority is vested in the British monarch, who is Head of State, and exercised through an official representative. The New Zealand Government also appoints a representative (from 1994 redesignated High Commissioner), resident on Rarotonga.

Executive powers are exercised by a Cabinet consisting of the Prime Minister and between five and seven other ministers including a Deputy Prime Minister. The Cabinet is collectively responsible to Parliament.

Legislation approved in September 2003 resulted in the abolition of the seat for one member elected by voters living overseas and consequently Parliament consists of 24 members elected by universal suffrage and presided over by the Speaker. Moreover, as a result of a referendum held concurrently with the general election of September 2004, the parliamentary term was shortened from five years to four. The House of Ariki comprises up to 15 members who are hereditary chiefs; it can advise the Government, particularly on matters relating to land and indigenous people but has no legislative powers. The Koutu Nui is a similar organization comprised of sub-chiefs, which was established by an amendment in 1972 of the 1966 House of Ariki Act.

Each of the main islands, except Rarotonga (which is divided into three tribal districts or *vaka*), has an elected mayor and a government representative who is appointed by the Prime Minister. In January 2000 it was announced that the post of Government Representative in the outer islands was to be phased out over two years.

The Government

Queen's Representative: Sir FREDERICK GOODWIN.
New Zealand High Commissioner: JOHN BRYAN.

CABINET
(April 2006)

Prime Minister, Minister of Information and Technology, Education, National Human Resources, Office of the Head of State, and Police: JIM MARURAI.
Deputy Prime Minister and Minister of Finance and Economic Development, Financial Intelligence Unit, Public Expenditure and Review Committee, Health, Ombudsman, Development Investment Board, Small Business Enterprise Centre, Attorney-General, Commerce Commission, National Superannuation and Parliamentary Services: Dr TEREPAI MAOATE.
Minister of Foreign Affairs and Immigration, Tourism, Cultural Development and Marine Resources: WILKIE RASMUSSEN.
Minister of Agriculture, Internal Affairs, Youth and Sport, Punanganui Market, Non-Government Organizations and Works: NGAMAU ('AUNTY MAU') MUNOKOA.
Minister of Transport, Justice, Public Service Commission and Cook Islands Investment Corporation: TANGATA VAVIA.
Minister of Environment, Outer Islands Administration, House of Ariki and Kotou Nui: TEINA BISHOP.

GOVERNMENT OFFICES

Office of the Queen's Representative: POB 134, Titikaveka, Rarotonga; tel. 29311.
Office of the Prime Minister: Government of the Cook Islands, Avarua, Rarotonga; tel. 21150; fax 23792; e-mail coso@pmoffice.gov.ck.
Office of the Public Service Commissioner: POB 24, Rarotonga; tel. 29421; fax 21321; e-mail pscom@oyster.net.ck.
Department of Tourism and Transport: POB 61, Rarotonga; tel. 28810; fax 28816; e-mail tourism@cookislands.gov.ck.
New Zealand High Commission: 1st Floor, Philatelic Bureau Bldg, Takuvaine Rd, POB 21, Avarua, Rarotonga; tel. 22201; fax 21241; e-mail nzhraro@oyster.net.ck.

Ministries

Ministry of Agriculture: POB 96, Rarotonga; tel. 28711; fax 21881; e-mail cimoa@oyster.net.ck.
Ministry of Cultural Development: POB 8, Rarotonga; tel. 20725; fax 23725; e-mail culture1@oyster.net.ck; internet www.cinews.co.ck/culture/index.htm.
Ministry of Education: POB 97, Rarotonga; tel. 29357; fax 28357; e-mail dieducat@oyster.net.ck.
Ministry of Energy: POB 72, Rarotonga; tel. 24484; fax 24485.
Ministry of Finance and Economic Management: POB 120, Rarotonga; tel. 22878; fax 23877; e-mail finsec@oyster.net.ck; internet www.mfem.gov.ck.
Ministry of Foreign Affairs and Immigration: POB 105, Rarotonga; tel. 29347; fax 21247; e-mail secfa@foraffairs.gov.ck.
Ministry of Health: POB 109, Rarotonga; tel. 22664; fax 23109; e-mail aremaki@oyster.net.ck.
Ministry of Internal Affairs: POB 98, Rarotonga; tel. 29370; fax 23608; e-mail sec1@intaff.gov.ck.
Ministry of Justice: POB 111, Rarotonga; tel. 29410; fax 29610; e-mail offices@justice.gov.ck.
Ministry of Marine Resources: POB 85, Rarotonga; tel. 28721; fax 29721; e-mail rar@mmr.gov.ck.
Ministry of Outer Islands' Administration: POB 383, Rarotonga; tel. 20321; fax 24321.
Ministry of Works and Physical Planning: POB 102, Rarotonga; tel. 20034; fax 21134; e-mail herman@mow.gov.ck.

Advisory Chambers

House of Ariki: POB 13, Rarotonga; tel. 26500; fax 21260; Pres. TOU TRAUEL ARIKI; Vice-Pres. TAMATOA ARIKI.
Koutu Nui: POB 13, Rarotonga; tel. 29317; fax 21260; e-mail nvaloa@parliament.gov.ck; Pres. TETIKA MATAIAPO DORICE REID.

Legislature

PARLIAMENT

Parliamentary Service
POB 13, Rarotonga; tel. 26500; fax 21260; e-mail nvaloa@parliament.gov.ck.
Speaker: NORMAN GEORGE.
Clerk of Parliament: NGA VALOA.
General Election, 7 September 2004

Party	Seats
Democratic Party (DP)	14
Cook Islands Party (CIP)	9
Independent	1
Total	24

Political Organizations

Cook Islands Labour Party: Rarotonga; f. 1988; anti-nuclear; Leader RENA ARIKI JONASSEN.
Cook Islands National: Rarotonga; f. 2003; Leader TEARIKI HEATHER.
Cook Islands Party (CIP): Rarotonga; f. 1965; Gen. Sec. TIHINA TOM MARSTERS; Leader Dr JOE WILLIAMS.
Democratic Party (DP): POB 73, Rarotonga; tel. 21224; e-mail demo1@oyster.net.ck; f. 1972; Pres. MAKIUTI TONGIA; Leader TEREPAI MAOATE.
Democratic Tumu Party (DTP): POB 492, Rarotonga; tel. 21224; fax 22520; split from Democratic Party in 1985; Leader VINCENT A. K. T. INGRAM.

Judicial System

High Court
Avarua, Rarotonga; e-mail offices@justice.gov.ck.

The judiciary comprises the Privy Council, the Court of Appeal and the High Court.

The High Court exercises jurisdiction in respect of civil, criminal and land titles cases on all the islands, except for Mangaia, Pukapuka and Mitiaro, where disputes over land titles are settled according to custom. The Court of Appeal hears appeals against decisions of the High Court. The Privy Council, sitting in the United Kingdom, is the final appellate tribunal for the country in civil, criminal and land matters.

Attorney-General: Dr TEREPAI MAOATE.
Solicitor-General: JANET GRACE MAKI.
Chief Justice of the High Court: DAVID ARTHUR RHODES WILLIAMS.
Judges of the High Court: GLENDYN CARTER, NORMAN SMITH, COLIN HICHOLSON, HETA HINGSTON.

Religion

CHRISTIANITY

The principal denomination is the Cook Islands (Congregational) Christian Church, to which about 58% of the islands' population belong, according to figures recorded in the census conducted in 1996.

Religious Advisory Council of the Cook Islands: POB 31, Rarotonga; tel. 22851; fax 22852; f. 1968; four mem. churches; Pres. KEVIN GEELAN; Gen. Sec. TUNGANE POKURA.

The Roman Catholic Church

The Cook Islands form the diocese of Rarotonga, suffragan to the archdiocese of Suva (Fiji). At 31 December 2003 the diocese contained an estimated 2,519 adherents. The Bishop participates in the Catholic Bishops' Conference of the Pacific, based in Suva.

Bishop of Rarotonga: Rt Rev. STUART FRANCE O'CONNELL, Catholic Diocese, POB 147, Rarotonga; tel. 20817; fax 29817; e-mail sbish@oyster.net.ck.

The Anglican Communion

The Cook Islands are within the diocese of Polynesia, part of the Church of the Province of New Zealand. The Bishop of Polynesia is resident in Fiji.

Protestant Churches

Cook Islands Christian Church: Takamoa, POB 93, Rarotonga; tel. 26452; 11,193 mems (1986); Pres. Rev. TANGIMETUA TANGATATUTA; Gen. Sec. WILLIE JOHN.

Seventh-day Adventists: POB 31, Rarotonga; tel. 22851; fax 22852; e-mail umakatu@oyster.net.ck; 732 mems (1998); Pres. UMA KATU.

Other churches active in the islands include the Assembly of God, the Church of Latter-day Saints (Mormons), the Apostolic Church, the Jehovah's Witnesses and the Baptist Church.

BAHÁ'Í FAITH

National Spiritual Assembly: POB 1, Rarotonga; tel. 20658; e-mail nsacooks@bahai.org.ck; mems resident in six localities; Sec. JOHNNY FRISBIE.

The Press

Cook Islands Herald: POB 126, Tutakimoa, Rarotonga; e-mail bestread@ciherald.co.ck; internet www.ciherald.co.ck; weekly; Publr GEORGE PITT.

Cook Islands News: POB 15, Avarua, Rarotonga; tel. 22999; fax 25303; e-mail editor@cookislandsnews.com; internet www.cookislandsnews.com; f. 1954; by Govt, transferred to private ownership 1989; daily; mainly English; Man. Dir PHIL EVANS; Editor JOHN WOODS; circ. 2,000.

Cook Islands Star: POB 798, Rarotonga; tel. 29965; e-mail jason@oyster.net.ck; fortnightly; Chief Reporter JASON BROWN.

Cook Islands Sun: POB 753, Snowbird Laundry, Arorangi, Rarotonga; f. 1988; tourist newspaper; twice a year; Editor WARREN ATKINSON.

Broadcasting and Communications

TELECOMMUNICATIONS

Telecom Cook Islands Ltd: POB 106, Rarotonga; tel. 29680; fax 20990; e-mail stu@telecom.co.ck; internet www.telecom.co.ck; CEO STUART DAVIES.

BROADCASTING

Radio

Cook Islands Broadcasting Corpn (CIBC): POB 126, Avarua, Rarotonga; tel. 29460; fax 21907; f. 1989; to operate new television service, and radio service of former Broadcasting and Newspaper Corpn; state-owned; Gen. Man. EMILE KAIRUA.

Radio Cook Islands: tel. 20100; broadcasts in English and Maori 18 hours daily.

KC Radio: POB 521, Avarua, Rarotonga; tel. 23203; f. 1979; as Radio Ikurangi; commercial; operates station ZK1ZD; broadcasts 18 hours daily on FM; Man. Dir and Gen. Man. DAVID SCHMIDT.

Television

Cook Islands Broadcasting Corpn (CIBC): see Radio

Cook Islands TV: POB 126, Rarotonga; tel. 20101; fax 21907; f. 1989; broadcasts nightly, in English and Maori, from 5 p.m. to 10.15 p.m; 10 hours of local programmes per week; remainder provided by Television New Zealand.

In early 1999 the French Société Nationale de Radio-Télévision Française d'Outre-Mer agreed to operate two or three new television channels in the islands.

Finance

Commission of Offshore Financial Services: Rarotonga; tel. 20798; fax 21798; e-mail comm@oyster.net.ck; f. 2003; Commissioner MATHILDA UHRLE; Chair. TREVOR CLARKE.

Financial Supervisory Commission: POB 594, Rarotonga; tel. 20798; fax 21798; e-mail commissionerfsc@oyster.net.ck; f. 1981 as Cook Islands Monetary Board, name changed as above in 2003; supervises banks and insurance companies; regulates trustee companies; registers international companies, trusts, financial institutions, etc.; Commissioner B. WORTH.

Trustee Companies Association (TCA): Rarotonga; controlling body for the 'offshore' financial sector; Sec. LOU COLVEY.

BANKING

Development Bank

Bank of Cook Islands (BCI): POB 113, Avarua, Rarotonga; tel. 29341; fax 29343; e-mail bci@oyster.net.ck; f. July 2001 when Cook Islands Development Bank merged with Cook Islands Saving Bank; finances development projects in all areas of the economy and helps islanders establish small businesses and industries by providing loans and management advisory assistance; Gen. Man. UNAKEA KAUVAI; brs on Rarotonga and Aitutaki.

Commercial Banks

Australia and New Zealand (ANZ) Banking Corpn: 1st Floor, Development Bank Bldg, POB 907, Avarua, Rarotonga; tel. 21750; fax 21760; e-mail lancaster@gatepoly.co.ck; Gen. Man. GAYLE STAPLETON.

The Wall Street Banking Corp Ltd: POB 3012, CITC House, Avarua, Rarotonga; tel. 23445; fax 23446; e-mail info@wallbank.co.ck; internet www.wallstreetbankingcorp.com; f. 1992; 100% owned by Natar Holdings Co Ltd; cap. US $15.0m., dep. US $74.9m. (March 2001); Exec. Dir RIAZ PATEL.

Westpac Banking Corpn (Australia): Main Rd, POB 42, Avarua, Rarotonga; tel. 22014; fax 20802; e-mail bank@westpac.co.ck; Man. TERRY SMITH.

Legislation was adopted in 1981 to facilitate the establishment of 'offshore' banking operations.

INSURANCE

Cook Islands Insurance: POB 44, Rarotonga.

Trade and Industry

GOVERNMENT AGENCIES

Cook Islands Development Investment Board: Private Bag, Avarua, Rarotonga; tel. 24296; fax 24298; e-mail cidib@cidib.gov.ck; internet www.cookislands-invest.com; f. 1996; as replacement for Development Investment Council; promotes, monitors and regulates foreign investment, promotes international trade, advises the private sector and Government and provides training in business skills; CEO MARK SHORT.

Cook Islands Investment Corporation: Rarotonga; tel. 29391; fax 29381; e-mail ciic@oyster.net.ck; f. 1998; manages government assets and shareholding interests; Chair. JOHN SHORT; CEO TEMU OKOTAI.

Cook Islands Public Service Commission: POB 24, Rarotonga; tel. 29421; fax 21321; e-mail pscom@oyster.net.ck; Commissioner JOSEPH CAFFERY.

Cook Islands Trading Corporation: Private Bag 1, Avarua, Rarotonga; tel. 22000; fax 20857; e-mail shop@citc.co.ck.

CHAMBER OF COMMERCE

Chamber of Commerce: POB 242, Rarotonga; tel. 20925; fax 20969; f. 1956; Pres. EWAN SMITH.

INDUSTRIAL AND TRADE ASSOCIATIONS

Pearl Federation of the Cook Islands, Inc: Manihiki; tel. and fax 43363; f. 1995; following the dissolution of the govt-owned Cook Islands Pearl Authority; oversees the activities and interests of pearl-producers in the northern Cook Islands.

Pearl Guild of the Cook Islands: Rarotonga; e-mail trevon@oyster.net.ck; f. 1994; monitors standards of quality within the pearl industry and develops marketing strategies; Pres. TREVON BERGMAN.

UTILITIES

Electricity

Te Aponga Uira O Tumutevarovaro (TAUOT) (Rarotonga Electricity Authority): POB 112, Rarotonga; tel. 20054; fax 21944; Chair. TAMARII TUTANGATA.

Water

Water Supply Department: POB 102, Arorangi, Rarotonga; tel. 20034; fax 21134.

TRADE UNIONS

Airport Workers' Association: Rarotonga Int. Airport, POB 90, Rarotonga; tel. 25890; fax 21890; f. 1985; Pres. NGA JESSIE; Gen. Sec. (vacant).

Cook Islands Industrial Union of Waterside Workers: Avarua, Rarotonga.

Cook Islands Workers' Association (CIWA): POB 403, Avarua, Rarotonga; tel. 24422; fax 24423; largest union in the Cook Islands; Pres. MIRIAMA PIERRE; Gen. Sec. NGAMETUA ARAKUA.

Transport

ROADS

On Rarotonga a 33-km sealed road encircles the island's coastline. A partly sealed inland road, parallel to the coastal road and known as the Ara Metua, is also suitable for vehicles. Roads on the other islands are mainly unsealed.

SHIPPING

The main ports are on Rarotonga (Avatiu), Penrhyn, Mangaia and Aitutaki. The Cook Islands National Line operates a three-weekly cargo service between the Cook Islands, Tonga, Samoa and American Samoa. In August 2002 the Government approved proposals to enlarge Avatiu Harbour. The project received additional funding from the Ports Authority and from New Zealand.

Apex Maritime: POB 378, Rarotonga; tel. 27651; fax 21138.
Cook Islands National Line: POB 264, Rarotonga; tel. 20374; fax 20855; 30% govt-owned; operates three fleet cargo services between the Cook Islands, Niue, Samoa, Norfolk Island, Tonga and New Zealand; Dirs CHRIS VAILE, GEORGE ELLIS.
Cook Islands Shipping Ltd: POB 2001, Arorangi, Rarotonga; tel. 24905; fax 24906.
Ports Authority: POB 84, Rarotonga and Aitutaki; tel. 21921; fax 21191; Chair. DON BEER.
Reef Shipping Company: Rarotonga; operates services between Rarotonga and Aitutaki.
Taio Shipping Ltd: Teremoana Taio, POB 2001, Rarotonga; tel. 24905; fax 24906.
Triad Maritime (1988) Ltd: Rarotonga; fax 20855.

CIVIL AVIATION

An international airport was opened on Rarotonga in 1974. Air New Zealand is among the airlines operating services between Rarotonga and other airports in the region. Air Pacific (Fiji) began a twice-weekly service between Nadi and Rarotonga in June 2000, and in August of that year Air New Zealand began a direct service from Rarotonga to Los Angeles, USA.

Airport Authority: POB 90, Rarotonga; CEO JOE NGAMATA.
Air Rarotonga: POB 79, Rarotonga; tel. 22888; fax 23288; e-mail bookings@airraro.co.ck; f. 1978; privately owned; operates internal passenger and cargo services and charter services to Niue and French Polynesia; Man. Dir EWAN F. SMITH.

Tourism

Tourism is the most important industry in the Cook Islands, and there were 83,333 foreign tourist arrivals in 2004, compared with 25,615 in 1984. Of total visitors in 2004, 46.5% came from New Zealand, 14.2% from Australia and 24.5% from Europe (of whom the largest group came from the United Kingdom). There were 1,874 beds available at hotels and similar establishments in the islands in 1999. Most of the tourist facilities are to be found on Rarotonga and Aitutaki, but the outer islands also offer attractive scenery. Revenue from tourism was estimated at some $NZ93.9m. in 2000/01.

Cook Islands Tourism Corporation: POB 14, Rarotonga; tel. 29435; fax 21435; e-mail tourism@cookislands.gov.ck; internet www.cook-islands.com; CEO CHRIS WONG.

NIUE

Introductory Survey

Location, Climate, Language, Religion, Flag, Capital

Niue is a coral island, located in the Pacific Ocean, about 480 km (300 miles) east of Tonga and 930 km (580 miles) west of the southern Cook Islands. Rainfall occurs predominantly during the hottest months, from December to March, when the average temperature is 27°C (81°F). Average annual rainfall is 7,715mm (298 ins). Niuean, a Polynesian language, and English are spoken. The population is predominantly Christian, with 66% belonging to the Ekalesia Niue, a Protestant church, in 1991. Niue's flag (proportions 1 by 2) is yellow, bearing, in the upper hoist corner, the United Kingdom's Union Flag with a yellow five-pointed star on each arm of the cross of St George and a slightly larger yellow five-pointed star on a blue disc in the centre of the cross. Some 30% of the population resides in Alofi, which is the capital and administrative centre of Niue. Plans to relocate the capital to Fonuakula on the upper plateau of the island were announced following the widespread devastation caused by Cyclone Heta in January 2004.

Recent History

The first Europeans to discover Niue were members of a British expedition, led by Capt. James Cook, in 1774. Missionaries visited the island throughout the 19th century, and in 1900 Niue was declared a British protectorate. In 1901 Niue was formally annexed to New Zealand as part of the Cook Islands, but in 1904 it was granted a separate administration.

In October 1974 Niue attained 'self-government in free association with New Zealand'. Niueans retain New Zealand citizenship, and a sizeable resident Niuean community exists in New Zealand. The 1991 population census revealed an 11.5% decrease since 1986, and many more Niueans live in New Zealand than on Niue. Robert (from 1982, Sir Robert) Rex, who had been the island's political leader since the early 1950s, was Niue's Premier when it became self-governing, and retained the post at three-yearly general elections in 1975–90.

The migration of Niueans to New Zealand has been a cause of concern, and in October 1985 the Government of New Zealand announced its intention to review its constitutional relationship with Niue, with the express aim of preventing further depopulation of the island. In 1987 a six-member committee, comprising four New Zealanders and two Niueans, was formed to examine Niue's economic and social conditions, and to consider the possibility of the island's reversion to the status of a New Zealand-administered territory.

At the 1987 general election all except three of the 20 members of the Niue Assembly were re-elected. The newly founded Niue People's Action Party (NPAP) secured one seat. The NPAP, Niue's only political party, criticized the Government's economic policy, and in particular its apparent inability to account for a substantial amount of the budgetary aid received from New Zealand. A declared aim of the party was to persuade Niueans residing in New Zealand to invest in projects on Niue.

In April 1989 the New Zealand Auditor-General issued a report which was highly critical of the Niuean Government's use of aid money from New Zealand, in particular Rex's preferential treatment of public servants in the allocation of grants. In June Young Vivian, leader of the unofficial NPAP opposition in the Niue Assembly, proposed a motion expressing 'no confidence' in the Government, which was defeated by 13 votes to seven. In November proposed legislation which included the replacement of New Zealand's Governor-General by a Niuean citizen was rejected by the Niue Assembly, owing to the implications for relations with New Zealand.

At the 1990 general election candidates of the NPAP and its sympathizers won 12 of the 20 seats. Earlier disagreements in the NPAP leadership, however, allowed Rex to secure the support of four members previously opposed to his Government. Rex therefore remained Premier.

The announcement in mid-1991 by the New Zealand Government that it was to reduce its aid payments to Niue by about $NZ1m. (a decrease of some 10% on the average annual allocation) caused considerable concern on the island. More than one-quarter of the paid labour force on Niue were employed by the Niue Government, and, following the reduction in aid in July, about 150 (some 25%) lost their jobs. Members of the Government subsequently travelled to New Zealand to appeal against the decision and to request the provision of redundancy payments for the dismissed employees. Their attempts failed, however, with the New Zealand Government reiterating its claim that aid had been inefficiently used in the past.

In December 1992 Sir Robert Rex died, and Young Vivian (who had been serving as acting Premier at the time of Rex's death) was unanimously elected Premier by the Government. Legislative elections took place in February 1993, and in the following month the Niue Assembly elected Frank Lui, a former cabinet minister, as Premier. Lui, who defeated Young Vivian by 11 votes to nine, announced a new Cabinet following the election; among the new Premier's stated objectives were the development of tourism and further plans to encourage Niueans resident in New Zealand to return to the island.

In March 1994 Vivian proposed an unsuccessful motion of 'no confidence' in the Government, and a further attempt by the opposition to introduce a similar motion was invalidated in the High Court in October on a procedural matter. However, during the ensuing debate, the Minister of National Planning and Economic Development, Sani Lakatani, resigned in order to join the opposition as its deputy leader, thus leaving the Government with only 10 official supporters in the Assembly. Subsequent opposition demands for the intervention of the Governor-General of New Zealand in dissolving the legislature, in preparation for a fresh general election, were rejected, and, despite Lui's assurance that an early election would take place in order to end the atmosphere of increasing political uncertainty, polls were not held until February 1996. The Premier and his three cabinet ministers were re-elected to their seats, although support among the electorate for candidates of the Niue People's Party (NPP, as the NPAP had been renamed in 1995) and independents appeared fairly equally divided; in one village the result was decided by the toss of a coin when both candidates received an equal number of votes. Frank Lui was re-elected by the Niue Assembly as Premier, defeating Robert Rex, Jr (son of Niue's first Premier) by 11 votes to nine.

The issue of Niue's declining population continued to cause concern, particularly when provisional census figures, published in late 1997, revealed that the island's population was at its lowest recorded level. The Government expressed disappointment that its policy of encouraging Niueans resident in New Zealand to return to the island had failed and announced its intention to consider introducing more lenient immigration laws in an attempt to increase the population.

At a general election on 19 March 1999 Lui lost his seat and subsequently announced his retirement from politics. The Minister of Finance, Aukuso Pavihi, also failed to be re-elected. On 29 March Sani Lakatani, leader of the NPP, was elected Premier by the new Assembly, defeating O'Love Jacobsen by 14 votes to six. Lakatani's stated priority as Premier was to increase Niue's population to at least 3,000; he claimed that the sharp decline in the number of residents constituted a threat to the island's self-governing status.

It was reported in May 1999 that New Zealand was to phase out aid to Niue by 2003; New Zealand's aid programme to the island had been reduced by $NZ250,000 annually over the previous five years. However, doubts were expressed over the legality of the New Zealand Government's action, and it was suggested that New Zealand was required by law to provide financial assistance under the 1974 act that established Niue as a self-governing state.

In December 1999 a motion of 'no confidence' in Lakatani was proposed by a number of opposition ministers, in protest at the Government's plans to fund a new national airline (Coral Air Niue). The result of the vote was inconclusive, with an equal number of votes cast for and against the motion. The proposed airline did not materialize, and the Government lost $NZ400,000 of its initial investment in the project. The New Zealand Government subsequently criticized officials in Niue for failing to secure a business plan or feasibility study for the proposed airline.

In late 1999 allegations made by a foreign news agency that Niue was being used by criminal organizations for 'laundering' the proceeds of their illegal activities were strongly denied by Lakatani. However, the naming of the island in a report by the Financial Action Task Force (FATF, see p. 389) in June 2000 as one of a number of countries and territories that had failed to co-operate in regional efforts to combat 'money-laundering' led the Government to suspend the issue of any further offshore banking licences until stricter regulations governing the financial sector had been introduced. In early 2001 the USA imposed sanctions on Niue (including a ban on transactions with US banks), claiming that the island had not implemented all the recommendations of the report. Lakatani appealed directly to President George W. Bush to end the embargo, which he said was having a devastating effect on Niue's economy. The Government stressed its commitment to meeting international requirements in its financial sector but claimed that it was having difficulty doing so, given its limited legal resources. Moreover, the Premier expressed strong disapproval that a nation as powerful as the USA should choose to inflict such hardship on a small, economically-vulnerable island, and urged other Pacific islands targeted by the report to unite in protest against such impositions. In June 2001 the Government engaged a US law firm in an effort to persuade two banks, Chase Manhattan and Bank of New York, to remove their bans on the transfer of some $NZ1m. to Niue via the business registry in Panama that the Government used for its offshore tax activity.

Having failed to meet an FATF deadline in August 2001, in February 2002 Niue pledged to repeal its offshore banking legislation. Premier Sani Lakatani was also considering closing down international business registrations based in Niue. The FATF announced in April 2002 that, in view of the island's commitment to improving the transparency of its tax and regulatory systems, the organization was to remove Niue from its list of non-co-operative territories; the decision was duly implemented in October. The bank-licensing legislation was repealed in June.

In December 2001 the Alliance of Independents, a new political party led by Frank Lui, was formed to contest the forthcoming general election. The party's spokesperson, O'Love Jacobsen,

announced that the Alliance would campaign for a direct air link to New Zealand and for increased spending on public health.

At the general election, held on 20 April 2002, all 20 incumbent members were returned to the Niue Assembly. Independent candidate Toke Talagi polled the highest number of votes (445), but overall the NPP was victorious. However, despite having polled the second-highest number of votes (428), Sani Lakatani did not command the general support of his party, and faced a leadership challenge from his deputy, Young Vivian. Following several days of lobbying within the NPP, Vivian was chosen as Premier. Vivian announced that the party had the support of 10 elected members, having formed a coalition with several independents associated with Toke Talagi. Lakatani was appointed Deputy Premier, however, later that year and following a period of ill health, the former Premier indicated that he might withdraw from politics.

In July 2003 Niue's only formal political party, the Niue People's Party, was dissolved as a result of ongoing disagreement among its membership and the failure of several projects (the most prominent of which was the attempted establishment of Coral Air Niue, see above). Opposition member Terry Coe expressed satisfaction with the news, stating that he hoped that party politics would cease henceforth in Niue. Observers also commented that Robert Rex (Niue's widely respected first Premier) had strongly opposed party politics, believing it to cause rifts in families and communities.

In September 2003 the opposition expressed concern that too many government members were travelling overseas on business, and that a significant amount of public money was being used to fund these trips. At the time of the statement seven of the Niue Assembly's 20 members (including two cabinet ministers) were absent on engagements overseas. In the same month it was announced that Niue was to receive US $90,000 from the People's Republic of China in order to build new accommodation for the 300 delegates and visitors who were expected to visit the island for the Pacific Islands Forum summit meeting in 2004. The meeting was relocated, however, following the widespread devastation of the island by a cyclone in early 2004 (see below).

In October 2003 Niue's Premier issued a statement inviting the residents of Tuvalu (whose continued existence on those islands was increasingly threatened by rising sea levels) to migrate to Niue. The Government of Tuvalu subsequently requested that Niue produce a memorandum of understanding giving formal details of this invitation and of the rights that Tuvaluans would enjoy on Niue. Further discussions between officials from the two Governments took place in June 2005.

In early January 2004 Niue was devastated by Cyclone Heta. Damage caused by the storm, which was described as the worst in the island's recent history, included the destruction of many buildings, the loss of most food crops, the death of two people and serious injury of several others and extensive damage to Niue's infrastructure, communications and coral reef. Relief supplies were sent from New Zealand as part of an initial aid programme worth some US $3.5m. It was estimated that US $23m. would be needed for a rebuilding programme to be carried out over a five-year period. The destruction of Alofi was so severe that the Government announced plans to relocate the island's capital to Fonuakula on the upper plateau. However, fears for the continued feasibility of the island were expressed by some observers, who suggested that many Niueans might exercise their right to take up residency in New Zealand, leaving the community on Niue unviable. As work began to repair or rebuild some 300 homes under the Government's New Niue or Niue Foou recovery plan, it was announced that efforts would be made to attract expatriate Niueans back to the island. A fish-processing plant due to open later in the year, as well as a number of new agricultural projects, were expected to provide some employment opportunities. In October New Zealand's Prime Minister Helen Clark made an official visit to Niue to celebrate the 30-year anniversary of the island's attainment of self-governing status. She used the visit to urge expatriate Niueans to return to the island and support efforts to regenerate its infrastructure and economy. Moreover, she announced a programme to introduce the Niuean language into the education curriculum from pre-school level onwards by 2006, as part of Taoga Niue, an initiative aimed at preserving traditional customs and cultural practices on the island. In addition, Clark confirmed that $NZ6m. was to be made available to rebuild the hospital destroyed by Cyclone Heta. Construction of the hospital, located at Kaimiti, began in January 2005.

In March 2000, meanwhile, a Niue-New Zealand joint consultative committee met, for the first time, in Alofi to consider the two sides' future constitutional relationship. Later that year the committee proposed to conduct a survey of islanders' views and to consider all options, from reintegration with New Zealand to full independence. A meeting of the joint committee took place in March 2001 in Wellington at which the issues of New Zealand aid and reciprocal immigration laws were discussed, as well as options for Niue's future constitutional status. In early 2001 Hima Takelesi was appointed Niue's first High Commissioner to New Zealand. New Zealand remained committed to annual assistance of $NZ6.3m. in the years

2001–03. At New Zealand's 2001 census, a total of 20,148 Niueans were recorded as resident in New Zealand. Discussions took place in Wellington in March 2003 between the New Zealand Prime Minister, Helen Clark, and Niue's Premier, Young Vivian. Topics debated included budgetary assistance, a review of the island's development plan and the continued migration of islanders from the territory to New Zealand.

The Government conducted a survey in September 2004 to assess the current population of the island. However, its apparent reluctance to release the information prompted speculation that more people had left Niue than official reports had previously indicated. When its findings were made public in October some observers disputed the figure of 1,550 (which many believed was higher than the reality, in order to attract more favourable levels of economic assistance). A local newspaper conducted a similar survey and estimated a resident population of some 1,300. In July 2005 the Premier announced that efforts to attract Niueans back to the island, notably by promoting the farming and fisheries sectors, were to be increased. The people of Niue were also to be granted better access to health care following an agreement concluded in November 2005 between the Niue Ministry for Health and the Counties Manukau District Health Board of New Zealand. The agreement was expected to facilitate the referral of Niuean patients to New Zealand.

In November 2004 Niue's High Commissioner to New Zealand, Hima Takelesi, announced his intention to return to the island to stand for parliament in the forthcoming elections. His stated motivation was a desire to form a stronger partnership with the 20,000 Niueans resident in New Zealand, in an attempt to ensure that Niue retained its current status and did not become incorporated into New Zealand. At the election, held on 30 April 2005, candidates in two constituencies (one of whom was the Minister of Finance) received equal numbers of votes. The allocation of the seat was eventually determined by the procedure of drawing names out of a hat. Young Vivian was re-elected Premier several days later, defeating O'Love Jacobsen by 17 votes to three. Vivian's stated priorities for the new Legislative Assembly included ongoing efforts to increase Niue's population (see above), the clearing of some 350 derelict homes and continued efforts to increase economic prospects for the island. Moreover, in June Vivian announced his intention to propose political reforms to the Legislative Assembly, including an increase in the parliamentary term from three years to five years and an increase in the number of cabinet ministers from four to six members.

In February 2006 Anton Ojala replaced Kurt Meyer as New Zealand High Commissioner to Niue.

Following almost 10 years of technical and political consultations, Niue and the USA signed a maritime boundary treaty in May 1997, delineating the precise boundary between the territorial waters of Niue and American Samoa.

Government

Niue enjoys self-government in free association with New Zealand. The New Zealand Government, however, remains responsible for the island's defence and external affairs. Executive government is carried out by the Premier and three other ministers. Legislation is the responsibility of the Niue Assembly, which has 20 members (14 village representatives and six elected on a common roll), but New Zealand, if called upon to do so by the Assembly, will also legislate for the island. There is a New Zealand representative in Niue, whose status was upgraded to that of High Commissioner in 1993.

Economic Affairs

Niue's gross domestic product (GDP) was estimated at $NZ17.3m. in 2003, when GDP per head was estimated at $NZ10,048. The population decreased at an average annual rate of 1.8% in 1986–97, and this declining trend subsequently continued.

Agriculture, forestry and fishing contributed 23.3% of GDP in 2003. According to the census of 2001, the sector engaged 9.5% of the employed labour force. A majority of households, however, practise subsistence gardening. The principal crops are coconuts, taro, yams, cassava and sweet potatoes. A taro export scheme was successfully introduced in the early 1990s, and production of the crop increased by more than 500% in 1993. Exports of taro, principally to New Zealand, contributed nearly 93% of total export earnings in 2003, being facilitated by a new regular shipping service. Plans to increase the production of vanilla as an export crop were discussed in 2003, but the promising crop was destroyed by the cyclone of early 2004. The reintroduction of vanilla cultivation, as well as that of organic nonu (or noni, a fruit renowned for its medicinal properties), for export was initiated during 2004 as part of the Government's post-cyclone recovery programme. Honey is also produced for export. Pigs, poultry, goats and beef cattle are raised, mainly for local consumption. An island development plan for 2003 included proposals to develop Niue's fishing industry by employing a fleet of used Korean fishing vessels. A fish-processing factory at Amanau opened in October 2004. It was estimated that the new plant could raise some $NZ9m. annually in revenue. However, a series of problems resulted in the plant remaining unable to begin operations in mid-2005, despite the issuing of five fishing licences to New Zealand vessels and four to Samoan vessels.

Industry (including mining, manufacturing, construction and utilities) contributed only 2.8% of GDP in 2003 but engaged 21.3% of the labour force in 2001. The manufacturing sector has been very limited, accounting for only 1.5% of GDP in 2003. However, in addition to the fish-processing plant (see above), a noni juice factory also opened in October 2004. Exploration for deposits of uranium continued on the island in 2005, but in November it was announced that no commercially viable resources had been identified. The extensive damage caused by Cyclone Heta led to much activity in the construction sector from early 2004, as rebuilding programmes commenced.

The island remains dependent upon imported diesel fuel for its energy requirements. In collaboration with the international environmentalist group Greenpeace, however, in December 2005 Niue confirmed its commitment to the development of wind power, hoping to become one of the first locations in the world to be completely reliant on renewable energy sources.

The services sector contributed 73.9% of GDP in 2003. The sector engaged 64.8% of the labour force in 2001. The Government is the most important employer, engaging 502 members of the paid labour force at mid-2004, when 210 people were employed in the private sector. Tourism has begun to make a significant contribution to the economy, and the sector earned some US $1.0m. in 1998. Polynesian Airlines, the Samoan carrier, signed a five-year agreement in October 2002 to provide a weekly direct air link between Niue and Auckland, New Zealand. This was increased to a twice-weekly service in 2003. Compared with the previous year, tourist arrivals by air increased by 44% to reach 2,758 in 2003. Following the cyclone of January 2004, however, the service was reduced to a weekly flight. Analysts suggested that the island's tourist industry was unlikely to recover within the near future, but in 2004 arrivals reached a total of 2,558. The industry's prospects suffered a further set-back in 2005 when it was announced that Polynesian Airlines was to establish a joint venture with Virgin Blue, the Australian airline and that, as result of proposed route changes, the direct flight between Niue and Auckland was likely to be withdrawn. However, in October 2005 it was announced that Air New Zealand was to begin a weekly service between Auckland and Niue. Meanwhile, the New Zealand Government was providing support to Niue in its attempts to rebuild tourist facilities.

Niue records an annual trade deficit, with imports generally far exceeding exports. The principal exports in 1993 were root crops (which provided 87.1% of total export earnings), coconuts (1.9%), honey and handicrafts. The principal imports were foodstuffs (which constituted 28.0% of the total cost of imports), electrical goods (11.8%), motor vehicles (10.6%) and machinery (5.4%). Niue's most significant exports normally include taro, coconuts, honey and vanilla. New Zealand is the island's main trading partner. The value of New Zealand's export to Niue totalled an estimated $NZ11.63m. in 2004, while that country's imports from Niue were worth less than $NZ0.3m.

Record budgetary expenditure was projected for 2004/05 as part of ongoing efforts to regenerate Niue's economy after Cyclone Heta. In that year New Zealand provided budgetary support of $NZ5.75m., while an additional $1m. was redirected from project assistance. The fiscal balance was further improved by modest reductions, totalling $NZ0.35m., in government expenditure. As a result, the budget was almost balanced in 2004/05, thus reversing the trend of the previous three years during which substantial deficits had been recorded. Total development assistance from New Zealand reached $NZ10.4m. in 2004/05 and $8.25m. in 2005/06. In addition, an aid programme totalling $NZ20m. over five years was announced in late 2004 and a trust fund was established with $NZ10m. from New Zealand and Australia (despite the New Zealand Government's announcement in mid-1999 of its intention to phase out aid to Niue by 2003). By mid-2005 the trust fund's assets stood at $NZ12m. In May 2006 it was announced that, in response to a request from the Premier of Niue, New Zealand had agreed to provide advance funding equivalent to almost US $190,000 in budgetary support. The annual rate of inflation averaged 2.5% in 1995–2003. Compared with the previous year, consumer prices increased by about 3.8% in the last three quarters of 2004. The unemployment rate was estimated at 13.8% in 2001.

Niue is a member of the Pacific Community (see p. 350) and the Pacific Islands Forum (see p. 352), and an associate member of the UN Economic and Social Commission for Asia and the Pacific (ESCAP, see p. 33). In 2000 Niue became a signatory of the Cotonou Agreement (see p. 277) with the European Union (EU).

Niue's economic development has been adversely affected by inclement weather, inadequate transport services and the annual migration of about 10% of the population to New Zealand. Two-thirds of the land surface is uncultivable, and marine resources are variable. Despite measures aimed at encouraging the return to the island of Niueans resident in New Zealand, the population has continued to decline. In late 2003 the Government extended an invitation to the residents of Tuvalu to move to Niue (see above). In 1994 the Niue Assembly approved legislation allowing the island to become an offshore financial centre. The Government predicted that Niue could earn up to $NZ11m. annually in fees from a financial services industry. By mid-1996 the offshore centre was believed to have attracted some US $280,000. However, following the threat of financial sanctions from the Paris-based Financial Action Task Force (FATF, see Recent History), Niue declared its intention to repeal its offshore banking legislation, despite fears that this would result in annual revenue losses of some US $80,000 in bank licence fees and more than US $500,000 in company registration fees. Further attempts to secure additional sources of revenue in Niue included the leasing of the island's telecommunications facilities to foreign companies for use in specialist telephone services. However, this enterprise (which earned the island an estimated $NZ1.5m. per year) caused considerable controversy when it was revealed that Niue's telephone code had been made available to companies offering personal services considered indecent by the majority of islanders. In addition, the island earned some US $0.5m. between 1997 and 2000 from the sale of its internet domain name '.nu', although similar controversy ensued when a report published in July 2004 claimed that the island was hosting some 3m. pages of pornographic material via its .nu domain. (According to the report, Niue's internet suffix was the fourth largest host of pornography in the world.) In mid-2003 Niue became the first location in the world to have a national wireless internet system, allowing internet access from anywhere by means of solar-powered aerials attached to coconut palms. The imposition of harsh economic sanctions by the US Government in 2001, following accusations that the island was still allowing criminal organizations to 'launder' their funds through the territory's offshore financial centre, led Niue's Government to investigate various alternative activities for generating revenue. In June 2002 the Legislative Assembly voted to end the issuing of banking licences, and Niue was removed from the FATF list of non-co-operative countries and territories. In February 2005 Niue announced the virtual closure of its offshore financial centre and the expected cessation of its international business registry in 2006. In November 2001 Premier Sani Lakatani had announced that the Government was negotiating a deal with a US company interested in using Niue as the call-centre of a satellite service. In March 2002 Niue was in the process of concluding a 20-year development programme with the EU. Initial assistance of €2.6m., to be released in 2003, was to be used to finance renewable energy projects. In late 2005 the announcement of the withdrawal of the Australian company that had been investigating the possibility of mining uranium on Niue, following its failure to find exploitable deposits, was a set-back for the island's economic prospects, although serious concerns had been raised with regard to the potential implications of uranium mining for public health and environmental safety. Niue's entire economy was severely affected by Cyclone Heta which struck the island in January 2004 causing extensive damage to housing, crops and infrastructure (see above). The subsequent recovery programme, known as New Niue or Niue Foou, emphasized rebuilding works and included the fish-processing plant at Amanau and the establishment of an industrial park at Fonuakula, at a cost of $NZ0.4m., upon which work began in mid-2005. The Government was also hoping to decrease the working hours of the island's public servants, in an attempt to reduce salary expenses and to encourage more people to participate in both subsistence agriculture and the cultivation of vanilla and nonu for export. During 2005 the New Zealand Government continued to assist Niue's post-cyclone recovery programme. Major priorities were the completion of the new hospital, which was scheduled for December, and investment in the heavy equipment required for other major construction projects, which included the development of wharf and airport facilities. New Zealand was also providing funding in areas such as government housing.

Education

Education is provided free of charge, and is compulsory for 10 years between five and 16 years of age. The school-leaving age was raised from 14 to 16 in 1998. Primary education, from the age of five, lasts for six years, and is followed by six years of secondary education. In 2005 a total of 190 children were enrolled in pre-primary and primary schools. A total of 206 pupils were enrolled in secondary education in the same year. A number of school-leavers take up tertiary education, mainly in the Pacific region and, to a lesser extent, in New Zealand. There is an extension centre of the University of the South Pacific in Niue. An estimated 50 students were engaged in tertiary education in 1991. A private medical school opened in 2000 but subsequently closed. A private university offering online information technology and business management courses opened in late 2003. The budget for 1998 allocated $NZ1,190,386 to education. A long-term programme between Niue and the Dunedin College of Education, funded by New Zealand, concluded at the end of 2005.

Public Holidays

2006: 1 January (New Year's Day), 2 January (Commission Day), 6 February (Waitangi Day, anniversary of 1840 treaty), 14–17 April (Easter), 25 April (ANZAC Day, anniversary of 1915 landing at Gallipoli), 5 June (Queen's Official Birthday), 19–20 October (Constitution Day celebrations), 23 October (Peniamina's Day), 25 December (Christmas Day), 26 December (Boxing Day).

2007: 1 January (New Year's Day), 2 January (Commission Day), 6 February (Waitangi Day, anniversary of 1840 treaty), 6–9 April (Easter), 25 April (ANZAC Day, anniversary of 1915 landing at Gallipoli), 4 June (Queen's Official Birthday), 19–20 October (Constitution Day celebrations), 22 October (Peniamina's Day), 25 December (Christmas Day), 26 December (Boxing Day).

Weights and Measures

The metric system is in force.

Statistical Survey

Source (unless otherwise stated): Economics, Planning, Development and Statistics Unit, POB 40, Alofi; tel. and fax 4219; internet www.gov.nu/statsniue.

AREA AND POPULATION

Area: 261.5 sq km (100.9 sq miles).

Population: 2,088 at census of 17 August 1997; 1,788 (males 897, females 891) at census of 7 September 2001. An estimated 20,145 Niueans lived in New Zealand at the time of the 2001 census. *2004* (official estimate at 7 September): 1,761 (males 866, females 895).

Density (at 7 September 2004): 6.7 per sq km.

Ethnic Groups (2001 census, declared ethnicity): Niueans 1,399; Caucasian 81; Pacific Islander 182; Niuean/Caucasian 28; Niuean/Pacific Islander 42; Asian 4.

Religion (2001 census, declared adherence): Ekalesia Niue 1,093; Church of Jesus Christ of Latter-day Saints 158; Roman Catholic 128; Jehovah's Witnesses 43; Seventh-day Adventist 25; Other 151.

Principal Towns (population, 2001 census): Alofi (capital) 614; Hakupu 227. Source: Thomas Brinkhoff, *City Population* (internet www.citypopulation.de). *Mid-2003* (UN estimate, incl. suburbs): Alofi 689. Source: UN, *World Urbanization Prospects: The 2003 Revision*.

Births, Marriages and Deaths (2001 census): Crude birth rate 18.5 per 1,000; Death rate 7.8 per 1,000. *2002:* Live births 25; Marriages 15; Deaths 13.

Expectation of Life (WHO estimates, years at birth): 71 (males 68; females 74) in 2003. Source: WHO, *World Health Report*.

Immigration and Emigration (2002): Arrivals 3,155; Departures 3,017.

Economically Active Population (2001 census, persons aged 15 years and over): Agriculture, forestry and fishing 60; Mining 17; Manufacturing 19; Electricity, gas and water 27; Construction 72; Trade 48; Restaurants and hotels 29; Transport 64; Finance 35; Real estate, etc. 3; Public administration 96; Education 63; Health, etc. 72; *Total employed* (incl. others) 633; Unemployed 21; *Total labour force* 654. Note: Figures exclude 63 subsistence workers.

HEALTH AND WELFARE

Key Indicators

Total Fertility Rate (children per woman, 2003): 2.9.

Physicians (per 1,000 head, 1996): 1.30.

Health Expenditure (2002): US $ per head (PPP): 149.

Health Expenditure (2002): % of GDP: 9.7.

Health Expenditure (2002): public (% of total): 98.4.

Access to Water (% of persons, 2002): 100.

Access to Sanitation (% of persons, 2002): 100.

For sources and definitions, see explanatory note on p. vi.

AGRICULTURE, ETC.

Principal Crops (FAO estimates, metric tons, 2004): Taro 3,200; Other roots and tubers 3,606; Coconuts 2,500; Bananas 70; Lemons and limes 110. Source: FAO.

Livestock (FAO estimates, 2004): Cattle 112; Pigs 1,900; Chickens 15,000. Source: FAO.

Livestock Products (FAO estimates, year ending September 2004): Pigmeat 55; Poultry meat 18; Hens eggs 12; Honey 6. Source: FAO.

Forestry (cu m, 1985): Roundwood removals 613; Sawnwood production 201.

Fishing (FAO estimates, metric tons, 2003): Total catch 200. Source: FAO.

INDUSTRY

Production (2001, estimate): Electric energy 3 million kWh. Source: UN, *Industrial Commodity Statistics Yearbook*.

FINANCE

Currency and Exchange Rates: 100 cents = 1 New Zealand dollar ($NZ). For details, see Tokelau.

Budget ($NZ '000, year ending 30 June 2003): Recurrent revenue 13,263 (New Zealand budgetary support 3,750, Internal revenue 9,513); Other 3,425; *Total revenue* 16,689; Recurrent 12,458; Capital 486; Corporations 5,437; *Total expenditure* 18,381. *2003/04:* Recurrent revenue 15,929; Total expenditure 17,697 (Recurrent 16,976, Capital 150, Corporations 571) *2004/05* (forecast): Expenditure 24,300.

Overseas Aid ($NZ '000, 2004/05): Official development assistance from New Zealand 10,403. Source: Ministry of Foreign Affairs and Trade, Wellington.

Cost of Living (Consumer Price Index; base: Sept. 2003 = 100): 99.8 in 2003; 103.6 in 2004.

Gross Domestic Product ($NZ '000 in current prices): 16,711 in 2001; 16,245 in 2002; 17,252 in 2003.

GDP by Economic Activity ($NZ '000 in current prices, 2003): Agriculture, forestry and fishing 4,062; Mining and quarrying –12; Manufacturing 268; Electricity, gas and water 201; Construction 36; Trade 2,181; Restaurants and hotels 566; Transport, storage and communications 1,395; Financial and business services; real estate, etc. 1,434; Public administration 6,800; Other community, social and personal services 519; *Sub-total* 17,450; Net services and duties –198; *GDP in purchasers' values* 17,252.

EXTERNAL TRADE

Principal Commodities ($NZ '000, 2002): *Imports c.i.f.:* Total 3,246. *Exports f.o.b.:* Total 135. *2003* (Exports only): Taro 199; Coconuts 16; Total 215.

Principal Trading Partners ($NZ '000, 1993): *Imports c.i.f.:* Australia 101.7; Fiji 140.9; Japan 358.3; New Zealand 5,993.8; Samoa 47.2; USA 197.2; Total (incl. others) 6,962.1. *Exports f.o.b.:* Total 543.2. *2002/03* ($NZ '000): Trade with New Zealand: *Imports c.i.f.:* 3,684; *Exports f.o.b.:* 223. Source: Ministry of Foreign Affairs and Trade, Wellington.

TRANSPORT

Road Traffic (2001 census): Passenger cars 323; Motorcycles 134; Vans 170; Trucks 74; Pick ups 76; Buses 11.

International Shipping: *Ship Arrivals* (1989): Yachts 20; Merchant vessels 22; Total 42. *Freight Traffic* (official estimates, metric tons, 1989): Unloaded 3,410; Loaded 10.

Civil Aviation: *Passengers* (1992): Arrivals 3,500; Departures 3,345; Transit n.a. *Freight Traffic* (metric tons, 1992): Unloaded 41.6; Loaded 15.7.

TOURISM

Foreign Tourist Arrivals (by air): 1,632 in 2002; 2,758 in 2003; 2,558 in 2004.

Tourist Arrivals by Country of Residence (2000): Australia 172; Fiji 58; New Zealand 1,000; Tonga 58; United Kingdom 32; USA 145; Total (incl. others) 2,010.

Tourism Receipts (US $ million): 1 in 1996; 2 in 1997; 1 in 1998.

Source: mainly World Tourism Organization, *Yearbook of Tourism Statistics*.

COMMUNICATIONS MEDIA

Telephones (2002): 1,000 main lines in use.
Mobile Cellular Telephones (2001 census): 225 units in use*.
Radio Receivers (2001 census): 605 in use†.
Television Receivers (2001 census): 451 in use.
Personal Computers (2001 census): 77 in use.
Internet Users (2002): 900.
Non-daily Newspaper (1996, estimate): 1, circulation 2,000†.
* Source: International Telecommunication Union.
† Source: UNESCO, *Statistical Yearbook*.

EDUCATION

Pre-primary and Primary (2005): 1 school; 190 pupils; 24 teachers.
Secondary (2005): 1 school; 206 pupils; 31 teachers.

Source: Department of Education, Niue.

Directory

The Constitution

In October 1974 Niue gained self-government in free association with New Zealand. The latter, however, remains responsible for Niue's defence and external affairs and will continue economic and administrative assistance. Executive authority in Niue is vested in the British monarch as sovereign of New Zealand but exercised through the government of the Premier, assisted by three ministers. Legislative power is vested in the Niue Assembly or Fono Ekepule, which comprises 20 members (14 village representatives and six elected on a common roll), but New Zealand, if requested to do so by the Assembly, will also legislate for the island. There is a New Zealand representative in Niue, the High Commissioner, who is charged with liaising between the Governments of Niue and New Zealand.

The Government

New Zealand High Commissioner: ANTON OJALA.
Secretary to Government: SISILIA TALAGI.

CABINET
(April 2006)

Premier and Minister responsible for the Legislative Assembly, Premier's Department and Cabinet, Civil Aviation, Crown Law Office, Economic Development Planning and Statistics, External Affairs and Niueans Abroad, Niue Public Service Commission, Niue Broadcasting Corporation, Finance, Customs and Revenue, Police and National Security, Administration Department and National Training, Information Technology and Communication, Environment, Niue Tourism and Public Works (Civil and Quarry, Outside Services and Heavy Plant): YOUNG VIVIAN.

Minister of Agriculture, Forestry and Fisheries, Niue Development Bank, Shipping, Investment and Trade, Post and Telecommunications, Business Sector, Immigration and Public Works Department (including Housing, Water Supply and Building): BILL VAKAAFI MOTUFOOU.

Minister of Education, Women's Affairs, Taoga Niue and Culture, Justice, Lands and Survey: VA'AIGA PAOTAMA TUKUI-TONGA.

Minister of Health, Community Affairs, Village Councils, Religious Affairs, Youth and Sports, Meteorological Services, Non-Government Organisations, Niue Power and Energy, Bulk Fuel and Disaster Management: FISA IGILISI PIHIGIA.

GOVERNMENT OFFICES

All ministries are in Alofi.
Office of the New Zealand High Commissioner: POB 78, Tapeu, Alofi; tel. 4022; fax 4173.
Office of the Secretary to Government: POB 40, Alofi; tel. 4200; fax 4232; e-mail secgov.premier@mail.gov.nu.

Legislature

ASSEMBLY

The Niue Assembly or Fono Ekepule has 20 members (14 village representatives and six members elected on a common roll). The most recent general election was held on 30 April 2005.
Speaker: ATAPANA SIAKIMOTU.

Political Organization

Alliance of Independents: Alofi; f. 2001; Leader FRANK LUI; Spokesperson O'LOVE JACOBSEN.

Judicial System

The Chief Justice of the High Court and the Land Court Judge visit Niue quarterly. In addition, lay justices are locally appointed and exercise limited criminal and civil jurisdiction. Appeals against High Court judgments are heard in the Court of Appeal of Niue (created in 1992).

The High Court: exercises civil and criminal jurisdiction.
The Land Court: is concerned with litigation over land and titles.

Land Appellate Court
Hears appeals over decisions of the Land Court.
Chief Justice: NORMAN F. SMITH.

Religion

About 63% of the population belong to the Ekalesia Niue, a Protestant organization, which had 1,093 adherents at the time of the 2001 census. Within the Roman Catholic Church, which has 128 adherents (equivalent to 7.4% of the population) in 2001, Niue forms part of the diocese of Tonga. The Church of Jesus Christ of Latter-day Saints (Mormon—which had 158 adherents in 2001), the Seventh-day Adventists, the Jehovah's Witnesses and the Church of God of Jerusalem are also represented.

Ekalesia Niue: Head Office, POB 25, Alofi; tel. 4195; fax 4352/4010; e-mail ekalesia.niue@niue.nu; f. 1846; by London Missionary Society, became Ekalesia Niue in 1966; Pres. Rev. MATAGI VILITAMA; Gen. Sec. Rev. ARTHUR PIHIGIA.

The Press

Niue Economic review: POB 91, Alofi; tel. 4235; monthly.
Niue Star: POB 151, Alofi; tel. 4207; weekly; Niuean and English; publ. by Jackson's Photography and Video; circ. 600.

Broadcasting and Communications

TELECOMMUNICATIONS
Director of Posts and Telecommunications: Alofi; tel. 4002.
Niue Telecom: Alofi; tel. 4000; internet www.niuenet.com; Man. RICHARD HIPA.

BROADCASTING

Radio
Broadcasting Corporation of Niue: POB 68, Alofi; tel. 4026; fax 4217; operates television service and radio service; govt-owned; Chair. NEAL MORRISSEY; CEO TREVOR TIAKIA; Gen. Man. PATRICK LINO.
Radio Sunshine: broadcasts in English and Niuean between 6 a.m. and 10 p.m. Mon.–Sat.

Television
Broadcasting Corporation of Niue: see Radio
Television Niue: broadcasts in English and Niuean, six days a week from 5 p.m. to 11 p.m.

Finance

DEVELOPMENT BANK
Fale Tupe Atihake Ha Niue (Development Bank of Niue): POB 34, Alofi; tel. 4335; fax 4290; e-mail devbank@niue.nu; f. 1993; began operations July 1994; Gen. Man. ANGELA TUHIPA.

COMMERCIAL BANK
Bank of South Pacific Ltd: Main St, Alofi; tel. 4221; fax 4043; acquired from Westpac Banking Corpn in Sept. 2004; Man. R. J. COX.

Trade and Industry

GOVERNMENT AGENCIES
Business Advisory Service: Alofi; tel. 4228.
Office of Economic Affairs, Planning and Development, Statistics and Trade and Investment: POB 42, Alofi; tel. 4148; e-mail business.epdsu@mail.gov.nu; responsible for planning and financing activities in the agricultural, tourism, industrial sectors, business advisory and trade and investment.

UTILITIES
Niue Power Corporation: POB 198, Alofi; tel. 4119; fax 4385; e-mail gm.npc.@mail.gov.nu.

TRADE UNION
Public Service Association: Alofi.

Transport

ROADS
There are 123 km of all-weather roads and 106 km of access and plantation roads. A total of 788 motor vehicles were registered in 2001. The road network was extensively damaged by Cyclone Heta in January 2004. In mid-2004 it was estimated that some 48 km of sealed roads were clear and in good condition.

SHIPPING
The best anchorage is an open roadstead at Alofi, the largest of Niue's 14 villages. Work to extend a small wharf at Alofi began in mid-1998 with US assistance. The New Zealand Shipping Corporation operates a monthly service between New Zealand, Nauru and Niue. Fuel supplies are delivered by a tanker (the *Pacific Explorer*) from Fiji. In December 2002 the Government signed an agreement with Reef Shipping Ltd to provide a service to New Zealand every three–four weeks.

CIVIL AVIATION
Hanan International Airport has a total sealed runway of 2,350 m, following the completion of a 700-m extension in 1995, with New Zealand assistance. Air links were seriously affected by the cessation of the Air Nauru service in 1989. In 1995 Royal Tongan Airlines began operating a weekly service between Niue and Tonga, with connections to Auckland, New Zealand, which in 1996 became twice-weekly. However, Royal Tongan Airlines discontinued its service to Niue in October 2002. Air Rarotonga (Cook Islands) operates occasional charter flights to Niue. In October 2002 the Niue Government concluded negotiations with Polynesian Airlines of Samoa to introduce direct weekly flights from Niue to Auckland, New Zealand, for a five-year period. The service was increased to a twice-weekly flight in 2003. However, in late 2005 there was uncertainty over the future of this service following the announcement of the establishment of a joint venture between Polynesian Airlines and Virgin Blue, an Australian airline.

Niue Airways Ltd (NAL): Hanan International Airport; f. 1990; registered in New Zealand; Dir RAY YOUNG.

Tourism

Niue has a small but significant tourism industry (specializing in holidays based on activities such as diving, rock-climbing, caving and game fishing), which was enhanced by an increase in the frequency of flights between the island and New Zealand in the early 1990s. The industry earned about US $1m. in 1998. The prospects for the island's tourist industry were severely hampered by the extensive damage caused by Cyclone Heta in January 2004. Experts believed that it would be several years before a recovery could be achieved. However, the island's Matavai resort was operating in mid-2004 and offering 33 rooms for visitors. A total of 2,558 people arrived by air (about 50% of whom were from New Zealand) to visit Niue in 2004.

Niue Tourist Office: POB 42, Alofi; tel. 4224; fax 4225; e-mail niuetourism@mail.gov.nu; internet www.niueisland.com; Dir of Tourism IDA TALAGI HEKESI.

NICARAGUA

Introductory Survey

Location, Climate, Language, Religion, Flag, Capital

The Republic of Nicaragua lies in the Central American isthmus, bounded by the Pacific Ocean to the west and by the Caribbean Sea to the east. Its neighbours are Honduras, to the north, and Costa Rica, to the south. The climate is tropical, with an average annual temperature of 25.5°C (78°F). The rainy season extends from May to October. The national language is Spanish, although English is spoken by some indigenous Indians along the Caribbean coast. Almost all of the inhabitants profess Christianity, and the great majority are Roman Catholics. The national flag (proportions 3 by 5) has three equal horizontal stripes, of blue, white and blue, with the state emblem (a triangle enclosing a dark blue sea from which rise five volcanoes, in green, surmounted by a Phrygian cap from which extend white rays and, at the top, a rainbow, all encircled by the words, in gold capitals, 'República de Nicaragua' and 'América Central') in the centre of the white stripe; the same flag without the state emblem is an alternative version of the civil flag. The capital is Managua.

Recent History

Nicaragua was under Spanish rule from the 16th century until 1821. It then became part of the Central American Federation until 1838. From 1927 US troops were based in Nicaragua at the request of the Government, which was opposed by a guerrilla group, led by Augusto César Sandino. In 1933, following the establishment of the National Guard (commanded by Gen. Anastasio Somoza García), the US troops left Nicaragua. Sandino was assassinated in 1934, but some of his followers ('Sandinistas') continued actively to oppose the new regime. Somoza seized power in a coup in 1935 and took office as President in 1936. Apart from a brief interlude in the late 1940s, Somoza remained as President until September 1956, when he was assassinated. However, the Somoza family continued to dominate Nicaraguan politics until 1979.

In 1962 the left-wing Frente Sandinista de Liberación Nacional (FSLN, the Sandinista National Liberation Front) was formed with the object of overthrowing the Somozas by revolution. Gen. Anastasio Somoza Debayle, son of the former dictator, became President in May 1967, holding office until April 1972. The Congreso Nacional (National Congress) was dissolved, and a triumvirate ruled until Gen. Somoza was re-elected President in September 1974. In January 1978 the murder of Pedro Joaquín Chamorro Cardenal, the leader of the opposition coalition and the editor of *La Prensa* (the country's only independent newspaper), provoked violent demonstrations against the Government.

In June 1979 the FSLN announced the formation of a provisional Junta of National Reconstruction. With the FSLN in command of many towns and preparing for the final onslaught on Managua, President Somoza resigned and left the country on 17 July 1979. (He was assassinated in Paraguay in September 1980.) After the Sandinistas had gained control of the capital, the Junta and its Provisional Governing Council took power on 20 July as the Government of National Reconstruction. The 1974 Constitution was abrogated, and the bicameral Congreso Nacional dissolved. The National Guard was disbanded and replaced by the Ejército Popular Sandinista (EPS—Sandinista People's Army), officially established in August. In August the Junta issued a 'Statute on Rights and Guarantees for the Citizens of Nicaragua', providing for basic personal freedoms and restoring freedom of the press and broadcasting. Civil rights were restored in January 1980.

On taking office, the Junta had issued a Basic Statute, providing for the creation of an appointed Council of State to act as an interim legislature. In March 1981 Commdr Daniel Ortega Saavedra was appointed Co-ordinator of the Junta and of its new consultative body, the Council of Government.

By 1981 discontent at the postponement of elections and the increasing hegemony of the Sandinistas had led to the creation of counter-revolutionary forces ('Contras'), who were mostly members of the former National Guard and operated from camps in Honduras. Meanwhile, relations between the US and Nicaraguan Governments had seriously deteriorated, culminating in the suspension of US economic aid in April. In the same year the US Government donated US $10m. in support of the Contras, while covert operations by the US Central Intelligence Agency (CIA) attempted to destabilize the Sandinista regime. In March 1982 the Sandinista Government declared a state of emergency. However, the intensity of attacks by the Fuerzas Democráticas Nicaragüenses (FDN), anti-Sandinista guerrillas based in Honduras, increased. A Contra group, the Alianza Revolucionaria Democrática (ARDE), was also established in Costa Rica, led by Edén Pastora Gómez, a prominent figure in the revolution who had become disillusioned with the Sandinistas. In December the Sandinistas reaffirmed their support for the initiatives of the 'Contadora group' (Colombia, Mexico, Panama and Venezuela), which was attempting to find peaceful solutions to the disputes involving Central America, and adopted a more conciliatory approach towards the opposition.

In June 1984 talks commenced between the Nicaraguan and US Governments in order to foster the peace negotiations proposed by the Contadora group. However, although the Sandinistas agreed in September to sign a peace agreement, the USA rejected the agreement on the grounds that the forthcoming Nicaraguan elections would not be fairly conducted. In June 1985 the US Congress voted to allocate US $27m. in non-military aid to the Contras. None the less, the Nicaraguan Government reaffirmed its desire to resume negotiations with the USA. Concurrently, however, the civil conflict escalated, and clashes along Nicaragua's borders with Costa Rica and Honduras became increasingly frequent. In July thousands of Miskito Indians, who had allied themselves with the Contras in the early 1980s, began to return to their ancestral homelands in northern Nicaragua, following talks with the Government concerning autonomy for the region.

A presidential election and elections to a constituent assembly were held on 4 November 1984. The assembly was to draw up a constitution within two years of taking office. In August the Government had restored the majority of the civil rights that had been suspended in September 1982, in order to permit parties to campaign without restrictions. In the presidential ballot the FSLN candidate, Daniel Ortega Saavedra, received 67% of the votes cast, and the party won 61 of the 96 seats in the National Constituent Assembly, which replaced the Council of State. Ortega's new Government and the National Constituent Assembly were inaugurated in January 1985.

In August 1986 the US Congress approved assistance for the Contras worth US $100m. In November the US Government disclosed that funds accruing from its clandestine sales of military equipment to Iran had been used to support the Contras.

In January 1987 a new Constitution was promulgated; on the same day, however, civil liberties, guaranteed in the Constitution, were again suspended by the renewal of the five-year-old state of emergency.

In February 1987 the Governments of Costa Rica, El Salvador, Guatemala and Honduras approved a peace plan for Nicaragua, largely based on earlier Contadora proposals, but placing greater emphasis on democratization within Nicaragua, including the ending of the state of emergency. The proposal subsequently underwent some modification, and in August the peace plan was signed by the Presidents of the five nations, in Guatemala. In accordance with the plan's requirements, a four-member National Commission for Reconciliation was created in Nicaragua in August: it was chaired by Cardinal Miguel Obando y Bravo, the Archbishop of Managua, a leading critic of the Government. In January 1988 the Government ended the state of emergency, and consented to participate directly in negotiations with the Contras. In March negotiations between representatives of the Government and the Contras resulted in agreement on a 60-day cease-fire (with effect from 1 April), as a prelude to detailed peace negotiations (this was later unilaterally extended by the Government until November 1989). The Government agreed to the gradual release of political prisoners and to permit the participation of the Contras in domestic political dialogue and, eventually, in elections. In August 1988 the US Senate approved the provision of US $27m. in humanitarian aid for the Contras. As the hope of further military aid diminished, the Contras retreated into Honduras.

In February 1989 the five Central American Presidents met in El Salvador to discuss the reactivation of the regional peace plan. At the meeting it was agreed that, in return for the dismantling of Contra bases in Honduras, there would be moves towards greater democracy in Nicaragua. These included a pledge to hold a general election, open to opposition parties, by February 1990. A number of electoral reforms were introduced: Contra rebels were to be permitted to return to vote, on condition that they relinquished their armed struggle under a proposed demobilization plan. In June 1989 the Unión Nacional Opositora (UNO) was formed by 14 opposition parties of varying political views: the UNO was to present a joint presidential candidate and a single programme in the forthcoming elections.

In August 1989 the five Central American Presidents met in Tela, Honduras, where they signed an agreement providing for the voluntary demobilization, repatriation or relocation of the Contra forces within a 90-day period. To facilitate this process, an International Commission of Support and Verification (CIAV) was established by the UN and the Organization of American States (OAS, see p. 333). Following mediation (conducted by the former US President, Jimmy Carter), the Government concluded an agreement with the leaders of the Miskito Indians of the Caribbean coast. The rebels agreed to renounce their armed struggle and to join the political process. Meanwhile, the UNO designated Violeta Barrios de Chamorro (the owner and director of *La Prensa* since the assassination of her husband, Pedro Chamorro, in 1978), as its presidential candidate in the forthcoming election. Daniel Ortega was nominated as the candidate of the FSLN.

In November 1989 President Ortega declared the ending of the cease-fire with the Contras, on the grounds that the rebels had made insufficient progress in implementing the Tela agreement and disbanding their forces stationed in Honduras. In response to these events, the UN Security Council established the UN Observer Group in Central America (ONUCA) to monitor compliance with the Tela agreement, to prevent cross-border incursions by rebels and to assist in supervising the forthcoming Nicaraguan elections.

The elections proceeded on 25 February 1990, resulting in an unexpected victory for Violeta Chamorro, the UNO candidate, who obtained some 55% of votes in the presidential election, while Ortega received 41%. Foreign observers confirmed the conduct of the polls to have been free and fair. After the elections, the Sandinista Government decreed an immediate cease-fire. The President-elect pledged to 'depoliticize' the military and security forces, and urged the Contra rebels to disband and return to civilian life. However, the UNO had not secured a sufficient majority of seats in the Asamblea Nacional to make amendments to the Constitution. In the interim period before the transfer of power on 25 April 1990, Ortega introduced a number of reforms. A General Amnesty and National Reconciliation Law was adopted: this was designed to pre-empt retaliatory measures against outgoing officials and to quash legal proceedings against those who had committed politically motivated crimes against the State since 1979. In addition, legislation was introduced to protect the rights of public-sector employees.

On 19 April 1990 a cease-fire was agreed by the Contras and the Sandinista armed forces. The Contras agreed to surrender their weapons by 10 June, and to assemble in 'security zones' supervised by UN troops. A transitional agreement between the outgoing Sandinista Government and the newly elected UNO coalition provided for a reduction in the strength of the security forces and their subordination to civilian authority. Upon taking office President Chamorro assumed the post of Minister of National Defence, but allowed the previous minister, Gen. Humberto Ortega Saavedra, temporarily to retain the post of Chief of the EPS: this provoked considerable controversy within the UNO and the Contra leadership. However, in return for a commitment from the Contras to sign the demobilization accords, the Government agreed to the establishment of a special police force, composed of former Contra rebels, in order to guarantee security within the demobilization zones. Demobilization of the Contra rebels was officially concluded on 27 June, signifying the end of 11 years of civil war in Nicaragua.

On assuming office, the UNO Government immediately attempted to reverse much Sandinista policy. The suspension of the civil service law in May 1990 provoked a public-sector strike, which paralysed the country. Chamorro was forced to concede wage increases of 100% and the establishment of a joint commission of trade union and government representatives to revise the civil service law. In July another general strike, involving 100,000 workers, was held in support of demands for wage increases and also in protest at the implementation of legislation allowing the restoration to private ownership of land that had been nationalized and redistributed under the Sandinista regime. Once again the Government made concessions, including a wage increase and the suspension of the programme to privatize land. The agreement was condemned by the Vice-President, Virgilio Godoy Reyes, who accused Chamorro of capitulating too readily to the demands of the FSLN. In October the Government announced the formation of a National Agrarian Commission to study problems of land distribution and illegal land seizures. The commission was to include members of the trade unions and former Contras. In mid-1991, however, the emergence of groups of rearmed Contra rebels (known as Re-contras) became apparent with the reported occupation of several cities in the northern province of Jinotega. The Re-contras' stated aim was to publicize the grievances of thousands of demobilized Contras in the north of the country who had not received land and aid promised them under the terms of the Government's resettlement plan.

In August 1991 a National Security Commission, including a 150-strong special disarmament brigade, was established to disarm civilians. In the same month the FSLN-operated Radio Sandino acknowledged the existence of groups of rearmed Sandinistas (Re-compas), claiming that these had been formed to counter the military operations of the Re-contras. In spite of the efforts of the National Security Commission, reports of hostilities between Re-contras and Re-compas continued. The phased disarmament of the Re-contras and the Re-compas began in January 1992. However, in April groups of the former combatants began joining forces to form the Revueltos, demanding land and credit promised to them prior to demobilization. In May the Government allocated 800 plots of land outside the capital to the Revueltos, as a gesture of its intention to address the groups' grievances. However, rebel activity continued in 1992–94, despite successive government ultimatums requiring the rebels to disarm or face military intervention. On 24 February 1994, following the mediation of Cardinal Obando y Bravo and the OAS, a peace agreement was signed that provided for the demobilization of a prominent Re-contra group, the Frente Norte 3-80, by mid-April, in return for which the rebels were granted an amnesty and the right to be incorporated into the national police force. Nevertheless, violent incidents involving further groups of Re-contras continued in northern and central Nicaragua. In response the Government deployed security forces to combat the rebels' activities, which, it asserted, were criminal and not related to legitimate demands for land.

In June 1991 the FSLN withdrew indefinitely its 39 deputies from the Asamblea Nacional, in protest against the introduction by conservative deputies of a draft bill revoking two laws concerning redistribution of property. The so-called *piñata* laws had been introduced by the FSLN in March 1990, immediately prior to the transfer of power to the Chamorro administration. They guaranteed the property rights of the thousands of people who had benefited from the land expropriation that had been conducted by the Sandinistas. In August 1991 the legislature approved the abrogation of the *piñata* laws, but in the following month President Chamorro vetoed parts of the bill that she deemed to be unconstitutional. In response, right-wing supporters of Vice-President Godoy accused Chamorro of yielding to pressure exerted by the Sandinistas. Disagreement over the property issue had by now led to the alienation by Chamorro of the majority of UNO deputies, and the legislature only narrowly failed to overturn the veto in December. In July, meanwhile, the first congress of the FSLN appointed Daniel Ortega to the newly created post of General Secretary.

In April 1992 Antonio Lacayo Oyanguren (son-in-law of Violeta Chamorro and widely considered to be the principal architect of government policy) announced that the Government was seeking 'fundamental agreements' with the FSLN. This announcement served to fuel the anger of right-wing and liberal members of the UNO who accused both Lacayo and Chamorro of being in league with the Sandinistas. In May the US Congress suspended the release of US $116m. in aid to Nicaragua, on the grounds that the Nicaraguan Government had failed to compensate US citizens for land expropriated under the Sandinista regime. In September Chamorro signed decrees establishing a property ombudsman's office and other provisions to expedite the processing of property claims. In addition, the President signed an agreement specifying that all unjustly confiscated property would be returned (or the rightful owners compensated).

A serious legislative crisis arose in September 1992, when César convened the legislature in the absence of the deputies of the FSLN and the Grupo de Centro (GC—a group of eight dissident UNO deputies who had maintained their allegiance to the Government, thus depriving the UNO of its parliamentary majority), recruiting substitute deputies in order to elect new legislative authorities. Chamorro subsequently announced that no laws approved by the legislature would be promulgated until the assembly recognized a Supreme Court decision ruling César's actions to be unconstitutional and declaring all subsequent rulings by the legislature null and void. In late December Chamorro ordered the army to occupy the assembly building and appointed a provisional administration to manage parliamentary affairs pending the election of new legislative authorities. In January 1993 Chamorro announced a cabinet reorganization. Excluded from the new Government, the UNO declared itself an opposition party, as the Alianza Política Opositora (APO), expelling four member parties for their involvement with the GC. The APO continued to boycott the Asamblea Nacional and to demand the expulsion of Sandinistas from the Government.

In May 1993, in an attempt to resolve the legislative dispute, the Government held separate talks with the APO, the FSLN and representatives of the trade unions and the private sector, with a view to establishing an agenda for multilateral discussions. However, the APO withdrew from the talks, insisting that it would not participate in a national dialogue until its parliamentary majority had been restored and Lacayo and Humberto Ortega had been dismissed. Bilateral discussions between the APO and the Government resumed in September, following the announcement by Chamorro that Humberto Ortega would be replaced as Chief of the EPS in 1994.

In October 1993 unprecedented discussions between the APO and the FSLN resulted in a joint demand for a complete restructuring of the Government's economic policy. In addition, it was agreed that Humberto Ortega should resign as soon as a new law regulating the armed forces was enacted. Constitutional issues were also discussed, with the APO proposing the election of a constituent assembly, while the FSLN favoured the implementation of partial constitutional reform by the incumbent legislature. In late October the APO and the FSLN signed an agreement providing for the implementation of partial constitutional reforms, on condition that a consensus was reached on the substance of the reforms by the end of November (subsequently extended to mid-December). The APO stipulated that it would support the reforms only on condition that its parliamentary majority be restored (through the dismissal of the GC deputies and their replacement by APO members) and that it gain control of the legislative authorities. However, divisions within the APO resulted in the Unión Demócrata Cristiana (UDC), the Movimiento Democrático Nicaragüense (MDN) and the Alianza Popular Conservadora (APC) breaking away from the alliance. The Asamblea Nacional reconvened in January 1994, and a new working alliance, including the FSLN, the GC, the UDC, the MDN and the APC, elected new legislative authorities. The APO subsequently abandoned its boycott of the legislature.

In February 1994 a widening division within the FSLN became apparent when Daniel Ortega founded the Izquierda Democrática Sandinista, an internal faction comprising what were termed 'orthodox revolutionaries' and intended to maintain the party's role as a revolutionary force; the faction declared support for 'all forms of struggle', aims not shared by the party's 'renewalist' faction, led by Sergio Ramírez Mercado. In May, following internal elections, the orthodox faction of the party secured control of the party's national directorate and of the party assembly, the Asamblea Sandinista, which subsequently approved a policy of opposition to the Government.

In November 1994 the Asamblea Nacional approved amendments to some 67 of the Constitution's 202 articles, which adjusted the balance of authority in favour of the legislature. In particular, the Government would be required to seek legislative approval for external loans, debt negotiations and international trade agreements. A further amendment, prohibiting close relatives of a serving President from contesting the presidential election, was widely considered to be intended specifically to prevent Lacayo, Chamorro's son-in-law and Minister of the Presidency, from securing presidential office at the next election, due in 1996. Other reforms included a reduction in the presidential and legislative terms, from six to five years, and the withdrawal of the absolute ban on presidential re-election, although consecutive terms remained prohibited. The set of amendments was deemed illegal by the FSLN leadership but won the support of 32 of the 39 deputies in the FSLN bloc, reflecting the seemingly irreconcilable division within the party. Amendments were also introduced enshrining civilian authority over the depoliticized security forces. The armed forces, which under the Constitution had previously been entitled the Ejército Popular Sandinista, were thenceforth referred to as the Ejército de Nicaragua (Nicaraguan Army).

In January 1995 the disunity within the FSLN finally resulted in members of the renewalist faction forming a separate political party, the Movimiento Renovador Sandinista (MRS). In the following month the constitutional amendments were signed and submitted to Chamorro for approval within 15 days. However, following Chamorro's refusal to promulgate the reforms, on 24 February the Asamblea Nacional released the amendments for publication, thereby enacting them. Chamorro condemned the decision as unconstitutional. In June a resolution to the dispute concerning the constitutional amendments was achieved by the signing of a political accord between the Government and the legislature. Under the terms of the agreement, many of the amendments intended to reduce presidential authority were to be moderated. Legislation defining the interpretation and implementation of the amendments was approved by the Asamblea Nacional in July, and was subsequently promulgated by Chamorro.

In May 1995 a national strike in opposition to government austerity policies received widespread support—in particular from transport workers and agricultural producers protesting, respectively, at rising fuel prices and the scarcity of available credit from state-owned banks. In June some 40 rural workers belonging to the FSLN-affiliated trade union, the Frente Nacional de Trabajadores, occupied the Asamblea Nacional building to support demands for the granting of titles to land allocated under the agrarian reforms of the former FSLN Government. The protest, which lasted three weeks, concluded following a government undertaking to expedite the process of issuing land titles. In November legislation was introduced legalizing the land titles of more than 200,000 families granted land under Sandinista agrarian reform.

Presidential and legislative elections were held on 20 October 1996. Arnoldo Alemán Lacayo of the Partido Liberal Constitucionalista (PLC), the presidential candidate of the Alianza Liberal (an electoral alliance comprising mainly liberal parties) secured 51% of the votes, while Ortega won 38%. However, although international observers declared the ballot to have been generally free and fair, the FSLN and several other parties disputed the result as fraudulent. Many of the provisional results were subsequently revised and, while the Consejo Supremo Electoral (CSE—Supreme Electoral Tribunal) acknowledged the existence of serious anomalies, it maintained that these had been insufficient to affect the overall outcome of the poll. The Alianza Liberal also won the largest number of seats (42) in the Asamblea Nacional, although it failed to gain a majority. The FSLN obtained 35 seats. The day before Alemán took office, in January 1997, the FSLN boycotted the newly inaugurated Asamblea Nacional in protest at the decision of the CSE to conduct an open ballot (rather than a secret vote) to elect the legislative authorities.

In April 1997 the FSLN organized national protests in opposition to the Government's policy concerning the return of property expropriated under the Sandinista regime. Multi-party commissions were established to seek a solution to the property disputes, and to address other issues arising from Alemán's austerity programme, including the rationalization of the civil service. However, the commissions failed to produce agreement. In June a 'national dialogue', involving representatives of more than 50 political parties and civic organizations, was convened by the Government with a view to reaching a consensus on the resolution of issues including poverty, unemployment and property rights. The FSLN, however, declined to participate in the talks. In September the Government and the FSLN reached an agreement in principle on draft legislation concerning the property issue. The bill was subsequently submitted to the 'national dialogue' for consultation. In November the Asamblea Nacional approved the new legislation, the Ley de la Propiedad Reformada, Urbana y Agraria, under the terms of which occupants of small expropriated properties would be granted legal ownership of the land, while those of larger such properties would be required to return them or to compensate fully the original owners over a 15-year period.

In April 1999 attempts by the security services to disperse a student demonstration in the capital led to violent confrontations that resulted in the death of a student. Later that month Alemán again deployed the security services to restore order in the capital after a strike by transport workers to protest against rising fuel prices degenerated into widespread rioting. In early May the Government conceded a 9% reduction in fuel prices in order to end the strike (the strikers had sought a 40% reduction). At the same time, agreement was reached with the student demonstrators on increased university funding. Both the student and the transport workers' protests had been strongly supported by the FSLN, reflecting the progressive political polarization of the Government and the principal opposition party.

In November 1999 the Comptroller-General, Agustín Jarquín, was arrested on charges of committing fraud against the State. Jarquín, a vigorous critic of corruption in the Government, had launched numerous investigations into corrupt practices by members of the Alemán administration, the most notable of which had resulted in the publication of a report, revealing that Alemán had increased his personal wealth by 900% during his terms of office as Mayor of Managua and as President, and that he had failed to declare these assets to the Office of the Comptroller-General, as required by law. Following his detention Jarquín supporters alleged that the accusations made against him were politically motivated. The arrest had serious consequences for the international reputation of the Alemán administration and for the country's economy. Representatives of donor nations and multilateral organizations expressed concern over the case, and both Germany and Sweden suspended funding for various projects as a result of Jarquín's detention. In late December Jarquín was acquitted of the charges against him, and later that month he formally renewed the corruption charges against Alemán.

In June 1999 the Government and the FSLN reached an agreement to begin negotiations on constitutional and electoral reform. This co-operation prompted the formation of an anti-Ortega faction within the FSLN, led by the party's former parliamentary leader, Víctor Hugo Tinoco. In July these dissident Sandinistas, in alliance with former Contras and various minor right-wing and centre-right parties, protested in Managua against the pact. In January 2000 a series of constitutional reforms resulting from the negotiations came into force. The principal amendments included a reduction in the proportion of votes necessary for a President to be elected outright from 45% to 35%, thus increasing the likelihood of an FSLN victory. In return, Alemán was guaranteed a seat in the Asamblea Nacional after leaving office, thus making him virtually immune from prosecution. Other reforms included the restructuring of the judiciary, electoral authorities and the Office of the Comptroller-General—which was to be headed by a five-member board, thereby effectively removing the threat to the Alemán administration of Jarquín.

In January 2001 the Vice-President, Enrique Bolaños Geyer, resigned his position and announced his presidential candidacy, representing the PLC. If elected, Bolaños pledged to investigate legislative corruption and to reduce civil service salaries. Ortega, who was the FSLN nominee, sought to reassure the electorate that he had renounced the more militaristic policies of his past, pledging to demilitarize the border with Costa Rica and to return property belonging to US citizens confiscated by his Government during the 1980s. Nevertheless, Ortega proved to be a controversial choice of candidate for the FSLN. From 1998 his stepdaughter, Zoilamérica Narváez Murillo, had made accusations of sexual abuse against him, and Bolaños, his main opponent, made much of the FSLN's links with the Cuban regime of Fidel Castro Rúz and with the Libyan leader, Col Muammar Al-Qaddafi.

Presidential and legislative elections took place on 4 November 2001, amid tight security. The final results gave Bolaños 56.3% of votes cast, while Ortega secured 42.3% and Alberto Saborío of the Partido Conservador de Nicaragua (PCN), 1.4%. The PLC also won a majority of votes (53.2%) in the elections to the Asamblea Nacional, securing 47 seats; the FSLN won 43 seats and the PCN the remaining two. In the weeks following the election the FSLN made allegations of electoral irregularities. Three FSLN magistrates on the seven-member electoral council objected to the party's allocation of seats in the Asamblea Nacional and resigned their positions in protest. However, the complaint was rejected by the Supreme Constitutional Court.

Bolaños took office on 10 January 2002. Almost immediately he encountered opposition from within his own party, when members of the PLC rejected his preferred candidate for President of Congress, Jaime Cuadra, in favour of former President Alemán. Alemán, who still enjoyed strong support from within the PLC, had already indicated that he intended to stand for re-election in 2007 and to use his position to obstruct legislation proposed by the new President. The new Cabinet, which was appointed in January, included few members of the Alemán faction of the PLC.

In late March 2002 the Attorney-General announced that former President Alemán was to face charges of fraud and embezzlement relating to the state television company, Sistema Nacional de Television Canal 6 (SNTV Canal 6). In the months that followed President Bolaños made several attempts to remove Alemán's congressional immunity. However, internal divisions within the PLC (which had divided into pro-Alemán and pro-Bolaños factions) meant that the President lacked the votes necessary to have the motion approved. As President of the Asamblea Nacional, Alemán obstructed approval of the budget and several reforms to the tax system which the Government needed to introduce in order to negotiate credit from the IMF. At the end of August thousands of protesters marched through Managua to demand an end to the former head of state's immunity.

In September 2002 several of Alemán's relatives and former members of his Government were convicted of 'laundering' some US $100m. from state communications, infrastructure, insurance and petroleum enterprises. Alemán faced the same charges and, on sentencing the guilty parties, the judge urged the Asamblea Nacional to lift the former President's immunity. One week later Alemán suspended a parliamentary session at which the removal of his congressional immunity was to be discussed. The following day FSLN members joined the Bolaños faction of PLC to vote in favour of Alemán's dismissal. Jaime Cuadra was installed as President of the Asamblea and a new legislative commission, comprising supporters of Bolaños, was formed to determine whether Alemán's immunity should be revoked. The former President's financial assets in Panama and those of his family in the USA were 'frozen' while investigations into the charges were made. The USA also suspended Alemán's right to enter its territory; several members of his family and former administration had already fled the country. On 13 December the Asamblea Nacional approved a motion revoking Alemán's congressional immunity by a narrow majority; the former President was immediately put under house arrest.

In late October 2002 Bolaños himself became the subject of allegations of fraud. In response to charges filed with the Supreme Court, that he and his Vice-President, José Rizo Castellón, had used an illegal fund controlled by Alemán to finance his 2001 electoral campaign, Bolaños promised to renounce his presidential immunity at a date named by his prosecutors. In early November Bolaños and Rizo Castellón were formally charged with embezzling US $4.1m. from public funds.

Alemán's arrest further deepened divisions within the PLC. In January 2003 Bolaños' veto of parts of the budget, in order to comply with conditions stipulated by the IMF for Nicaragua to qualify for financial assistance and debt relief, was opposed by both the pro-Alemán faction of the PLC and the FSLN (the Sandinistas had supported the President in his attempts to remove Alemán). In late March the pro-Alemán faction of the PLC officially announced that they were in opposition to the Government, in protest at the Government's alliance with the FSLN. The departure of the deputies left Bolaños with the unconditional support of only nine PLC members in the Asamblea (although six members of the Alemán faction later declared their allegiance to the President).

In June 2003 the pro-Aleman faction of the PLC formed an alliance with the FSLN in order successfully to approve in the legislature the appointment of nine Supreme Court judges with FSLN or pro-Alemán sympathies. The PLC faction believed that the appointments would increase the likelihood that Alemán would be acquitted of the charges against him. Nevertheless, in August a FSLN-appointed Supreme Court judge, Juana Méndez, ruled that the cost of keeping Alemán under house arrest was too great, and the former President was transferred to an specially refurbished prison cell in El Chipote prison in Managua. However, in late November Méndez allowed Alemán to return to house arrest, allegedly following an agreement between the pro-Alemán faction of the PLC and the FSLN. In return for the support of the FSLN in the release of Alemán, the PLC agreed to support FSLN attempts to postpone municipal elections to 2006, and to replace the country's presidential system with a parliamentary one. The supreme court ruling was strongly opposed by many traditionalist members of the FSLN and damaged Ortega's standing within the party. The move provoked a strong reaction from the international community, particularly the USA, which declared Ortega and Alemán to be discredited figures who ought to have no further role in Nicaraguan politics. Concern was also expressed at opposition efforts to impeach President Bolaños on charges of electoral fraud. The USA suspended US $4.9m. in aid for judicial reform, and threatened to obstruct Nicaragua's access to the IMF debt-reduction programme.

On 7 December 2003 former President Alemán was found guilty of charges of money-laundering, fraud, and theft of state funds and sentenced to 20 years' imprisonment. He was also fined US $17m. Owing to ill health, however, he was to serve his prison term under house arrest. He was also stripped of his seat in the Asamblea Nacional and was barred from standing as a presidential candidate during his sentence. The trial was considered to be a test of Nicaragua's judiciary and the outcome was welcomed by the international community. In the same month the alliance between the FSLN and the dissident PLC members collapsed, following the latter's insistence that the release of Alemán was essential if the pact were to continue. One week later the pro-Alemán PLC deputies joined with the pro-Bolaños faction of the party to approve the budget for 2004, essential to gain IMF funding. In January 2004 the two factions of the ruling party attempted a fragile truce in order to select a new directorate of the Asamblea. The new legislative President, Carlos Noguera Pastora, was an Alemán supporter, while the six remaining seats were divided evenly between the two factions of the party. In early December 2004 a court of appeal acquitted Alemán of the charge of appropriating some US $1.5m. from SNTV Canal 6. However, he continued to serve, under house arrest, his sentence for money-laundering.

In late March 2004 the Asamblea began to debate a series of measures proposed by President Bolaños. The proposed reforms included: the introduction of an independently appointed judiciary; adoption of a five-year national budget; and reform of the electoral system. The proposed judicial reform prompted protests in the Asamblea from judges. Bolaños declared he was willing to engage in all-party dialogue on his proposals. Throughout most of 2004 the PLC- and FSLN-dominated Asamblea blocked the reform proposals, although in mid-October the creation of an independent judicial council to appoint judges did receive legislative approval.

Also in late March 2004 President Bolaños, Vice-President Rizo Castellón and 31 other senior members of the PLC were accused of illegal campaign-financing during the previous presidential election. Seven PLC members were arrested, including party president Jorge Castillo Quant. In October the Comptroller-General, Juan Gutiérrez, requested that President Bolaños be removed from power and fined two months' wages for withholding information regarding the financing of his 2001 election campaign. Supporters of the President claimed the request was politically motivated, as the office of the Comptroller-General was controlled by the FSLN and the anti-Bolaños faction of the PLC. At the invitation of Bolaños, a delegation arrived from the OAS to investigate the Comptroller-General's findings. Following a meeting with the OAS representatives, Ortega agreed to withdraw FSLN support for the initiation of impeachment proceedings against the President until after the November municipal elections.

The FSLN won a decisive victory in the local elections of 7 November 2004, securing control of 84 of the 151 municipalities, including Managua. The PLC won power in 57 municipalities and the Alianza por la República (APRE—a pro-Bolaños alliance founded in July 2004) obtained control of six local councils. The following day a two-thirds' majority in the Asamblea Nacional voted in support of constitutional reform legislation limiting presidential powers. The reforms would require the President to seek legislative ratification for key appointments such as ministers, ambassadors, the chief prosecutor and banking superintendent, and would enable the Asamblea to remove officials deemed to be incompetent. However, the most serious proposal was the curtailment of the presidential veto by enabling the legislature to overturn it by a simple majority vote rather than by a two-thirds' majority. On 24 November the PLC and the FSLN approved a law to transfer control of the state energy, water and telecommunications services from the President to one regulatory body, the Superintendencia de Servicios Públicos (Sisep).

On 22 December 2004 President Bolaños appealed to the Supreme Court of Justice, contending that the reforms supported by the FSLN and the PLC would engender irreconcilable tension between the Government and the legislature. Furthermore, Bolaños asserted that the legislation was unconstitutional and that such an attempt to redefine the powers of the executive and legislative branches of government exceeded the remit of the Asamblea Nacional. On 6 January 2005 the Central American Court of Justice (CCJ) ruled that ratification of the controversial constitutional amendments should be suspended. None the less, one week later the Asamblea approved the legislation. On 16 January, two days before the legislation was due to come into effect, the Presidents of El Salvador, Guatemala and Honduras issued a joint statement of support for President Bolaños. Following further negotiations between factions supporting Bolaños, Ortega and Alemán, the President agreed to promulgate the controversial reforms in return for an opposition pledge that it would work towards a consensus with the executive on such matters as the budget and social security reform. Nevertheless, on 29 March the CCJ declared the constitutional reforms to be illegal, ruling that they could only be approved by a specially convened constituent assembly. On the same day the Supreme Court declared the reforms valid.

On 15 December 2004 Eduardo Montiel tendered his resignation as Minister of Finance and Public Credit, stating that disagreements with President Bolaños over economic policies had rendered his position untenable. In early January 2005 Montiel was replaced by Mario Arana Sevilla, hitherto Minister of Development, Industry and Trade. He was succeeded in his former post in the following month by Azucena Castillo de Solano.

On 18 January 2005, in advance of the presidential election that was due in November 2006, the FSLN ruled that its prospective presidential nominees should have been party members for a minimum of 10 years. It was widely believed that the rule was intended to prevent Herty Lewites, the popular former mayor of Managua, from challenging Ortega in party's primary elections (Lewites had represented another party in the 1996 mayoral election). Lewites and a number of his supporters were expelled from the party in the following month, after having been accused of 'abandoning anti-imperialist principles', and in early March the FSLN national congress duly selected Ortega as its presidential candidate. On 13 March Lewites staged a rally in Masaya, south of Managua, attended by some 10,000 people, to protest against the decision and to promote his own candidacy for the presidential ballot.

On 25 April 2005 a 20% increase in bus fares as a result of the increasing cost of fuel imports led to two days of protests in Managua by thousands of students, transport workers and trade-union members. President Bolaños was presented with a petition calling for his resignation, signed by 96 of the country's 152 mayors. However, following negotiations with representatives of the universities and the municipality of Managua, a three-month subsidy was agreed to maintain the former price level, to be funded jointly by the national and municipal governments.

On 25 July 2005 Alemán was released on probation for the remainder of his sentence, allegedly for health reasons. The Court of Appeal overruled the decision three days later, ordering that he return to house arrest. However, the ruling of 25 July was upheld on 30 August by the Supreme Court of Justice, thereby permitting the former President to travel within the province of Managua and to participate in political activities. The Supreme Court of Justice also ratified the constitutional amendment to restrict presidential powers, which had been approved by Asamblea Nacional in January. Ernesto Leal, the Secretary to the Presidency, criticized the ruling, asserting that the executive would adhere to the CCJ ruling that declared the reforms to be illegal.

Accusations against Bolaños' and his associates of illegal campaign-financing during the 2001 elections persisted in 2005. On 5 September seven Central American heads of state gathered in Managua to demonstrate their support for Bolaños. None the less, on 22 September the Asamblea Nacional removed the immunity from prosecution from the Minister of Government, Dr Julio Vega Pasquier, and, in the following week, from the Minister of Education, Culture and Sports, Miguel Angel García Gutiérrez, and the Minister of the Environment and Natural Resources, Arturo Harding Lacayo. Bolaños, however, retained his immunity from prosecution and on 25 October the PLC pledged to withhold support from any motion to remove it.

Dissension over the proposed constitutional reforms impeded the Government's legislative agenda throughout much of 2005. The political impasse meant that the Government failed to gain legislative approval for, inter alia, the proposed Dominican Republic-Central American Free Trade Agreement (DR-CAFTA, comprising Nicaragua, Costa Rica, the Dominican Republic, El Salvador, Guatemala, Honduras and the USA). In early October the US Assistant Secretary of State publicly criticized the PLC-FSLN legislative pact and proposed the implementation of DR-CAFTA without Nicaragua. This intervention, combined with the ongoing efforts to promote dialogue by the OAS, were widely seen as instrumental in resolving the political crisis: on 9 October the FSLN withdrew its opposition to DR-CAFTA and the following day the proposed free trade agreement was approved by the Asamblea Nacional. In addition, Ortega and Bolaños reached an agreement to delay the implementation of the constitutional reforms until the end of Bolaños' mandate in January 2007. Revised reforms were subsequently proposed by the PLC and approved by the legislature on 18 October. Following the deferment of the reforms and the dissolution of the PLC-FSLN pact, US military aid—suspended since April 2005—was renewed.

There were several changes to President Bolaños' Cabinet in 2005 and early 2006. In June 2005 the Minister of National Defence, José Adán Guerra, tendered his resignation. He was succeeded by Avil Ramírez Valdivia, who continued the Government's attempts to introduce legislation providing for the destruction of the country's remaining surplus surface-to-air missiles (see below). Following the resignation of Vice-President José Rizo Castellón in late September, in order to pursue the presidential candidature of the PLC (see below), the vice-presidency was assumed on 10 October by Alfredo Gómez Urcuyo. Then, in early November, Pedro Solórzano submitted his resignation as Minister of Transport and Infrastructure, as did the Minister of Development, Industry and Trade, Azucena Castillo de Solano. Ricardo Vega Jackson was appointed Minister of Transport and Infrastructure, while Castillo de Solano's ministerial duties were subsequently assumed by Alejandro Argüello Choiseul. On 6 January 2006 Leonardo Somarriba González was appointed Secretary to the Presidency, succeeding Ernesto Leal. The following month Cristóbal Sequeira González replaced Harding Lacayo as Minister of the Environment and Natural Resources.

Presidential and legislative elections were scheduled to be held on 5 November 2006. In preparation for these, in mid-August 2005 a centre-left alliance of the MRS and the Alternativa Cristiana (AC), both former FSLN factions, nominated Lewites as its presidential nominee. (The AC withdrew from the alliance, however, in March 2006.) Also in August 2005, former PLC Secretary to the Presidency, Eduardo Montealegre Rivas, presented his candidacy on behalf of the right-wing alliance Alianza Liberal Nicaragüense-Partido Conservador (ALN-PC). Ortega was again the FSLN's presidential candidate in March, while APRE nominated José Antonio Alvarado to be its nominee. In late March 2006 former Vice-President José Rizo Castellón secured the presidential candidature of the PLC. The PLC and the FSLN both performed well in the November 2005 regional elections in the autonomous Atlántico Norte and Atlántico Sur regions, but in early 2006 opinion polls favoured Lewites and Montealegre Rivas to succeed Bolaños as President.

In May 2001 Nicaragua and the USA re-established full military relations, suspended since 1980. In 2003 the Government resisted pressure from the USA to destroy its stockpile of surface-to-air missiles, claiming that a certain number were necessary for defence against terrorism. However, in March 2004 it was reported that the Government had agreed to destroy one-half of the 2,000 weapons. In mid-November President Bolaños announced that about one-half of the remaining surface-to-air missiles (an estimated 1,334) would be destroyed within 18 months. However, in the following month the opposition-controlled Asamblea approved legislation granting it authority to decide on the acquisition and disposal of armaments. The measure formed part of the controversial reforms intended to curtail President Bolaños' powers (see above). Although Bolaños vetoed the legislation, this was overridden in February 2005 by the PLC-FSLN parliamentary bloc. The issue gathered momentum in the previous month following reports in a US newspaper that Nicaraguan missiles were being sold to would-be terrorists. The outgoing Commander-in-Chief of the Armed Forces, Gen. Javier Carrión, rejected the reports; however, on 18 February two men were convicted of selling a surface-to-air missile on the 'black' (parallel, illegal) market. As a result, the Government pledged to destroy 79% of the remaining stockpile of missiles. US military aid to Nicaragua was suspended in April–October, when legislation to reduce the stockpile was finally approved.

In June 1995, prompted by frequent disputes concerning fishing rights in the Gulf of Fonseca, Nicaragua signed an accord with Honduras providing for the visible demarcation of each country's territorial waters. Despite this agreement, in December the Honduran Government issued an official protest to Nicaragua at what it claimed to be the illegal seizure of Honduran fishing vessels by a Nicaraguan naval patrol in Honduran waters. In May 1997 a further incident, in which Nicaraguan and Honduran naval patrols exchanged fire following the seizure by the Nicaraguan navy of Honduran fishing boats, gave renewed impetus to the demarcation issue. However, the demarcation process did not begin until May 1998. In December 1999, following further confrontations, Nicaragua initiated proceedings at the International Court of Justice (ICJ, see p. 19) in The Hague, Netherlands, to determine the maritime delimitation in the Gulf of Fonseca. In that month a dispute arose prompting Nicaragua to sever commercial ties with, and impose import taxes on, Honduras, in direct contravention of Central American free trade undertakings (Nicaragua also imposed similar tariffs on Colombia, thereby violating commitments entered into with the World Trade Organization). Following mediation by the OAS, in January 2000 Nicaragua ended its trade sanctions against Honduras, and in March both countries signed an accord committing them to observe a maritime exclusion zone in the Caribbean and to reduce troop numbers on their common border. In addition, both countries agreed to submit all issues pertaining to maritime space in the Caribbean Sea to the ruling of the ICJ. An agreement was also made to mount co-ordinated naval patrols in the Gulf of Fonseca. However, shortly after conflict again ensued over a small islet in the disputed territory, which Nicaragua claimed had been occupied by the Honduran armed forces. Furthermore, in February 2001 the Minister of Defence, José Adán Guerra, accused Honduras of violating the March 2000 accords by carrying out military exercises in the area and, in the following month, Nicaragua submitted documentation to the ICJ contesting the Treaty. Nicaragua also refused to participate in the joint patrol of the Gulf of Fonseca. In March 2001 delegates from both Governments attended OAS-sponsored discussions in Washington, DC, USA. In June Nicaragua and Honduras concluded a confidence-building agreement, which provided for OAS observers to monitor the actions of army and navy forces on both sides of the common border. However, in August, the Nicaraguan Government claimed that Honduras was planning to launch an attack on its border. In July 2002 the situation further deteriorated when the Nicaraguan Government announced plans to sell oil-drilling rights in the disputed area. The ICJ was yet to rule on the dispute in early 2006.

In 1997 relations with Costa Rica became strained when, following a change in that country's immigration policy, it began deporting Nicaraguans who were residing illegally in the country. Remittances from Nicaraguans in Costa Rica represented a significant contribution to the Nicaraguan economy, averaging US $240m.–$300m. per year. In February 1999 Costa Rica offered one-year renewable residence permits to registering illegal Nicaraguan immigrants. Further antagonism had developed between the two countries in July 1998 when Nicaragua prohibited Costa Rican civil guards from carrying arms while navigating the San Juan river, which forms the border between the two countries. According to a long-standing treaty, the river, which is Nicaraguan territory, was only to be used by Costa Rica for commercial purposes. Following protests by Costa Rica, agreement was reached allowing for that country's civil guard to carry arms on the river while under escort by the Nicaraguan authorities. In August, however, following concerted pressure by opposition parties, the media and the Roman Catholic Church in Nicaragua, which accused the Government of surrendering part of the nation's sovereignty, Nicaragua annulled the accord. In June 2000 both Governments agreed a procedure that would allow armed Costa Rican police-officers to patrol the river. In October 2001 President Alemán further announced that Costa Rican guards could patrol the river, providing they had first obtained permission from his Government, but rejected Costa Rica's submission of the dispute to the ICJ. In September 2002 the two countries appeared to have made some progress towards resolving the dispute when Nicaragua agreed to discontinue the fees charged to Costa Ricans crossing the river in exchange for the abolition of charges levied on visas and tourist permits required by Nicaraguans to enter Costa Rica. Costa Rica also announced that it would relinquish plans to refer the matter to the ICJ. In October bilateral discussions began on the Nicaraguan Government's plans to sell oil-exploration rights in an area of the Caribbean Sea and Pacific Ocean claimed by Costa Rica. Failure to agree on the issue within the stipulated three years prompted Costa Rica, on 28 September 2005, to refer the matter to the ICJ. In response, President Bolaños recalled the Nicaraguan ambassador to Costa Rica, ordered the troops patrolling the border area to prohibit the passage of armed Costa Rican police-officers, and imposed a 35% tariff on Costa Rican imports. Furthermore, in November the Nicaraguan Government declared an interest in reclaiming the province of Guanacaste, annexed by Costa Rica in 1825.

In early November 2001 a dispute with Colombia arose after a Nicaraguan fishing vessel was captured allegedly in Colombian waters. The Colombian authorities charged the crew with violating its sovereignty and misappropriating its natural resources. It was the third time in that year that a Nicaraguan vessel had been apprehended in Colombian waters. In the following month, Nicaragua presented a request to the ICJ that its claim over territorial waters in the Caribbean Sea and around the islands of San Andrés and Providencia be recognized. In July 2003 the Colombian Minister of Foreign Affairs formally objected to the ICJ's involvement in the case. The case was still pending at the ICJ in 2006.

Government

Executive power is vested in the President, who is elected by popular vote for a five-year term. The President is assisted by a Vice-President and an appointed Cabinet. Legislative power is held by the Asamblea Nacional (National Assembly), elected by universal adult suffrage, under a system of proportional representation, for a five-year term.

Defence

In August 2005 the armed forces were estimated to total 14,000 (army 12,000, navy 800, air force 1,200). Compulsory military service was abolished in April 1990. In 1995 the armed forces were renamed the Ejército de Nicaragua, following a constitutional amendment removing their Sandinista affiliation. The defence budget for 2005 totalled US $34.7m.

Economic Affairs

In 2004, according to estimates by the World Bank, Nicaragua's gross national income (GNI), measured at average 2002–04 prices, was US $4,452.1m., equivalent to $790 per head (or $3,300 per head on an international purchasing-power parity basis). During 1995–2004, according to IMF estimates, the population increased at an average annual rate of 2.7%, while gross domestic product (GDP) per head increased, in real terms, by an average of 1.2% per year. According to the IMF, Nicaragua's gross domestic product (GDP) increased, in real terms, by an average of 3.9% per year in 1995–2004; GDP increased by 5.1% in 2004.

Agriculture (including forestry and fishing) contributed an estimated 18.3% of GDP in 2004 and engaged an estimated 43.4% of the employed work-force in 2001. The principal cash crops are coffee (which accounted for 16.8% of export earnings in 2004), groundnuts, sugar cane and beans. Maize, rice and beans are the principal food crops. Production of shellfish became increasingly important in the 1990s, and by 2000 shrimps and lobsters accounted for some 17.4% of export earnings, although this decreased to 10.7% by 2004. Meat and meat products accounted for 14.6% of export earnings in 2004. Agricultural GDP increased at an average annual rate of 3.7% during 1995–2004; the sector's GDP increased by 3.2% in 2003 and by a modest 0.2% in 2004.

Industry (including mining, manufacturing, construction and power) engaged an estimated 15.0% of the employed labour force in 2001 and provided an estimated 29.2% of GDP in 2004. Industrial GDP increased by an average of 3.6% per year during 1995–2004; it increased by 2.4% in 2003 and by 0.5% in 2004.

Mining contributed an estimated 1.1% of GDP in 2004 and engaged an estimated 0.6% of the employed labour force in 2001. Nicaragua has workable deposits of gold, silver, copper, lead, antimony, zinc and iron; its non-metallic minerals include limestone, gypsum, bentonite and marble. In 2004 gold accounted for some 6.0% of export earnings. The GDP of the mining sector increased at an average annual rate of 11.4% in 1990–2001; the sector's GDP decreased by about 20% in 2000, but grew by an estimated 2.5% in 2001.

Manufacturing contributed some 19.2% of GDP in 2004 and engaged an estimated 7.7% of the employed labour force in 2001. The principal branches of manufacturing were food products, beverages and tobacco (about 67% of the total), machinery and metal products and petroleum derivatives and rubber products. The *maquila*, or assembly, sector expanded rapidly in the early 1990s, although growth slowed in the early 2000s. The principal products were clothing, footwear, aluminium frames and jewellery. Manufacturing GDP increased by an average of 3.6% per year in 1995–2004; the sector's GDP grew by 2.4% in 2003 and by a further 0.5% in 2004.

Energy is derived principally from imported petroleum, although two hydroelectric plants in the department of Jinotega account for one-10th of the electrical energy generated in the country. Imports of mineral fuels and lubricants comprised an estimated 10.7% of the total value of imports in 2004. In 2001 Nicaragua produced an estimated 2,613.7m. kWh of electrical energy.

The services sector contributed an estimated 52.6% of GDP in 2003 and engaged an estimated 41.9% of the employed labour force in 2001. The tourism sector expanded throughout the 1990s; in 2003 annual income totalled US $155m., with arrivals put at 525,775, an 11.5% increase on the previous year's figures. The GDP of the services sector increased by an average of 3.9% per year in 1995–2004; the sector grew by 2.1% in 2003, before declining by 0.3% in 2004.

In 2004 Nicaragua recorded a visible trade deficit of about US $1,089.1m., and there was a deficit of $772.2m. on the current account of the balance of payments. In 2004 the principal source of imports (an estimated 22.2%) was the USA; other major suppliers were Nicaragua's partners in the Central American Common Market (CACM—Costa Rica, El Salvador, Guatemala and Honduras, see p. 188), as well as Venezuela and Mexico. The USA was also the principal market for exports (an estimated 34.9%) in 2004; other notable purchasers were the countries of the CACM, Mexico and Canada. The principal exports in 2004 were coffee, meat and gold. The principal imports were non-durable consumer goods, primary materials, intermediate and capital goods for industry and crude petroleum.

In 2004 Nicaragua recorded a budgetary deficit of an estimated 6,930.2m. gold córdobas (equivalent to 9.5% of GDP). At the end of 2003 Nicaragua's total external debt was $6,915m., of which $6,106m. was long-term public debt. The cost of servicing external debt in that year was equivalent to 11.7% of the value of goods and services. In 2000–04 the average annual rate of increase in consumer prices was 6.2%. Consumer prices increased by an annual average of 5.2% in 2003 and by 8.4% in 2004. An estimated 6.5% of the labour force was unemployed in 2004.

Nicaragua is a member of the CACM (see p. 188), which aims eventually to liberalize intra-regional trade, and of the Inter-American Development Bank (IDB, see p. 284). Negotiations towards a free trade agreement, to be known as the Central American Free Trade Agreement, were concluded between El Salvador, Guatemala, Honduras, Nicaragua and the USA in December 2003. The agreement entailed the gradual elimination of tariffs on most industrial and agricultural products over the next 10 and 20 years, respectively. Ratification of the Dominican Republic-Central American Free Trade Agreement (DR-CAFTA, as the agreement was restyled in 2004) was finally approved by the Nicaraguan legislature on 10 October 2005. DR-CAFTA was expected to be inaugurated in 2006.

The implementation of a comprehensive economic reform programme, supported by the IMF, following the end of the civil war in 1990 succeeded in bringing inflation under control, increasing foreign reserves and reducing the fiscal deficit. In December 2000 Nicaragua qualified for debt relief of some US $4,500m. under the World Bank's heavily indebted poor countries (HIPC) initiative. In December 2001 the IDB approved a debt-relief programme of $386m. for Nicaragua, to be implemented annually until 2019. In October 2002 the new Government of Enrique Bolaños Geyer secured an IMF loan of $100m., dependent on certain conditions, including the reduction of the fiscal deficit to 14% of GDP over the next three years, the complete privatization of the state telecommunications concern and a reduction in domestic public debt. The 'Paris Club' of creditor nations also agreed to cancel $405m. of public external debt and to reschedule remaining payments. In early 2003 Nicaragua qualified for a gradual debt reduction under the HIPC initiative of up to 73% of the nation's total external debt. This financial relief remained dependent on the Government meeting targets set by the IMF and the World Bank. In January 2004 the transfer to the private sector of Empresa Nicaragüense de Telecomunicaciones (Enitel) was completed, after the Government sold its remaining 49% stake in the company. In the same month Nicaragua qualified for an estimated $4,500m. in loans, under the enhanced HIPC initiative. In April France, Germany and Spain agreed to forgive $263m. of the country's debts, in keeping with the agreement signed in late 2003 with the 'Paris Club'. However, the continuing legislative impasse (see Recent History) impeded efforts by the Bolaños Government to introduce fiscal reform in 2005, which led to the mid-year suspension of funding under the HIPC initiative, as well as from the USA. In spite of this, in June Nicaragua was among 18 countries to be granted 100% debt relief on multilateral debt incurred prior to 2005 agreed by the Group of Eight (G-8) leading industrialized nations, subject to the approval of the lenders. This cancellation was approved by the IMF in December, under the Multilateral Debt Relief Initiative. The relief totalled some US $201m. (US $132m., excluding the remaining HIPC funding) and was expected to be available from January 2006. In late 2005 the Government finally secured legislative approval on the 2006 budget, and on a series of reforms to the pension system and to tax and banking law. A steep rise in international oil prices put pressure on the country's finances in 2005, contributing to continued high inflation of 9.6%. Economic growth declined slightly in 2005, to an estimated 4.0%; the economy was forecast to expand by 3.5% in 2006.

Education

Primary and secondary education have been provided free of charge since 1979. Primary education, which is officially compulsory, begins at seven years of age and lasts for six years. Secondary education, beginning at the age of 13, lasts for up to five years, comprising a first cycle of three years and a second of two years. In 2002/03 total enrolment at primary schools was equivalent to 85.5% of the relevant age-group (males 85.7%; females 85.3%). Secondary enrolment in that year was equivalent to 39.0% of children in the relevant age-group (males 35.8%; females 42.2%). There are many commercial schools and eight universities. In 2002/03 a total of 100,363 students attended universities and other higher education institutes. In that year public expenditure on education accounted for 15.0% of total government expenditure.

Public Holidays

2006: 1 January (New Year's Day), 13 April (Maundy Thursday), 14 April (Good Friday), 1 May (Labour Day), 19 July (Liberation Day), 1 and 10 August (Managua local holidays), 14 September (Battle of San Jacinto), 15 September (Independence Day), 2 November (Day of the Dead), 8 December (Immaculate Conception), 25 December (Christmas).

2007: 1 January (New Year's Day), 5 April (Maundy Thursday), 6 April (Good Friday), 1 May (Labour Day), 19 July (Liberation Day), 1 and 10 August (Managua local holidays), 14 September (Battle of San Jacinto), 15 September (Independence Day), 2 November (Day of the Dead), 8 December (Immaculate Conception), 25 December (Christmas Day).

A considerable number of local holidays are also observed.

Weights and Measures

The metric system is officially used, although some Spanish and local units are also in general use.

Statistical Survey

Sources (unless otherwise stated): Banco Central de Nicaragua, Carretera Sur, Km 7, Apdos 2252/3, Zona 5, Managua; tel. (2) 65-0500; fax (2) 65-2272; e-mail bcn@cabcn.gob.ni; internet www.bcn.gob.ni; Instituto Nacional de Estadísticas y Censos (INEC), Las Brisas, Frente Hospital Fonseca, Managua; tel. (2) 66-2031; internet www.inec.gob.ni.

Area and Population

AREA, POPULATION AND DENSITY

Area (sq km)	
Land	120,340
Inland water	10,034
Total	130,373*
Population (census results)	
20 April 1971	1,877,952
25 April 1995	
Males	2,147,105
Females	2,209,994
Total	4,357,099
Population (official estimates at mid-year)	
2002	5,341,883
2003	5,482,340
2004	5,626,492
Density (per sq km) at mid-2004	46.8†

* 50,337 sq miles.
† Land area only.

ADMINISTRATIVE DIVISIONS
(official estimates at mid-2004)

	Area (sq km)	Population	Density (per sq km)	Capital
Departments:				
Chinandega	4,822.4	452,190	93.8	Chinandega
León	5,138.0	402,710	78.4	León
Managua	3,465.1	1,413,257	407.9	Managua
Masaya	610.8	324,855	531.9	Masaya
Carazo	1,081.4	182,640	168.9	Jinotepe
Granada	1,039.7	196,275	188.8	Granada
Rivas	2,161.8	172,119	79.6	Rivas
Estelí	2,229.7	220,521	98.9	Estelí
Madriz	1,708.2	137,111	80.3	Somoto
Nueva Segovia	3,491.3	217,444	62.3	Ocotal
Jinotega	9,222.4	305,818	33.2	Jinotega
Matagalpa	6,803.9	497,931	73.2	Matagalpa
Boaco	4,176.7	173,444	41.5	Boaco
Chontales	6,481.3	186,672	28.8	Juigalpa
Río San Juan	7,540.9	97,825	13.0	San Carlos
Autonomous Regions:				
Atlántico Norte (RAAN)	32,819.7	256,440	7.8	Bilwi
Atlántico Sur (RAAS)	27,546.3	389,240	14.1	Bluefields
Total	120,339.5	5,626,492	46.8	—

NICARAGUA

PRINCIPAL TOWNS
(population at 1995 census)

Managua (capital)	864,201	Granada	71,783
León	123,865	Estelí	71,550
Chinandega	97,387	Tipitaga	67,925
Masaya	88,971	Matagalpa	59,397

Mid-2003 (UN estimate, including suburbs): Managua 1,097,611 (Source: UN, *World Urbanization Prospects: The 2003 Revision*).

BIRTHS AND DEATHS
(UN estimates, annual averages)

	1990–95	1995–2000	2000–05
Birth rate (per 1,000)	36.0	32.4	29.1
Death rate (per 1,000)	6.3	5.5	5.0

Source: UN, *World Population Prospects: The 2004 Revision*.

2001: Registered births 103,593 (19.9 per 1,000); Registered deaths 10,071 (1.9 per 1,000).

2002: Registered births 103,643 (19.4 per 1,000); Registered deaths 10,830 (2.0 per 1,000).

Expectation of life (WHO estimates, years at birth): 70 (males 68; females 73) in 2003 (Source: WHO, *World Health Report*).

ECONOMICALLY ACTIVE POPULATION
('000 persons)

	1999	2000	2001
Agriculture, forestry and fishing	655.3	711.8	739.0
Mining and quarrying	11.7	9.4	9.6
Manufacturing	125.3	127.8	131.6
Electricity, gas and water	5.8	5.9	6.1
Construction	88.1	97.3	102.3
Trade, restaurants and hotels	259.2	268.3	279.8
Transport and communications	49.7	51.2	52.9
Financial services	20.1	21.8	22.6
Government services	67.5	65.0	63.5
Other services	261.5	278.8	294.3
Total employed	1,544.2	1,637.3	1,701.7
Unemployed	184.7	178.0	198.7
Total labour force	1,728.9	1,815.3	1,900.4

2002: Total employed 1,976.2; Unemployed 135.6; Total labour force 2,111.8.

2003: Total employed 1,917.0; Unemployed 160.5; Total labour force 2,077.4.

2004: Total employed 1,973.1; Unemployed 138.0; Total labour force 2,111.1.

Health and Welfare

KEY INDICATORS

Total fertility rate (children per woman, 2003)	3.7
Under-5 mortality rate (per 1,000 live births, 2004)	38
HIV/AIDS (% of persons aged 15–49, 2003)	0.2
Physicians (per 1,000 head, 1997)	0.86
Hospital beds (per 1,000 head, 1996)	1.48
Health expenditure (2002): US $ per head (PPP)	206
Health expenditure (2002): % of GDP	7.9
Health expenditure (2002): public (% of total)	49.1
Access to water (% of persons, 2002)	81
Access to sanitation (% of persons, 2002)	66
Human Development Index (2003): ranking	122
Human Development Index (2003): value	0.690

For sources and definitions, see explanatory note on p. vi.

Agriculture

PRINCIPAL CROPS
('000 metric tons)

	2002	2003	2004
Rice (paddy)	283.9	267.6	241.7
Maize	499.5	588.6	521.9
Sorghum	117.8	115.9	114.0
Cassava (Manioc)	107.9	105.8	117.3
Sugar cane	3,119.4	4,100.5	4,090.9
Dry beans	196.9	230.3	223.7
Groundnuts (in shell)	60.4	93.9	99.5
Oil palm fruit*	53.0	53.0	54.0
Bananas	56.4	59.0	61.1
Plantains*	40.0	40.5	41.0
Oranges*	66.0	70.0	75.0
Pineapples*	46.0	48.0	50.0
Coffee (green)	60.2	59.7	70.9

* FAO estimates.
Source: FAO.

LIVESTOCK
('000 head, year ending September)

	2002	2003	2004
Cattle	3,350	3,500	3,400*
Pigs†	430	440	450
Goats†	6.7	6.8	7.0
Horses†	250	260	265
Asses†	8.8	8.9	9.0
Mules†	46.5	47.0	48.0
Poultry†	15,100	16,000	16,500

* Unofficial estimate.
† FAO estimates.
Source: FAO.

LIVESTOCK PRODUCTS
('000 metric tons)

	2002	2003	2004
Beef and veal	60.1	65.6	70.5
Pig meat	6.3	6.5	6.5
Horse meat*	1.9	2.0	2.0
Poultry meat	56.1	61.5	62.3
Cows' milk	611.4	640.7	641.1
Butter	0.6	0.6	0.6
Cheese*	23.2	23.5	24.0
Hen eggs	22.4	22.3	23.2
Cattle hides*	8.7	8.7	8.7

* FAO estimates.
Source: FAO.

Forestry

ROUNDWOOD REMOVALS
('000 cubic metres, excl. bark)

	2002	2003	2004
Sawlogs, veneer logs and logs for sleepers	124	93	93*
Fuel wood*	5,827	5,866	5,906
Total	5,951	5,959	5,999*

* FAO estimate(s).
Source: FAO.

NICARAGUA

SAWNWOOD PRODUCTION
('000 cubic metres, incl. railway sleepers)

	2001	2002	2003*
Coniferous	55	16	16
Broadleaved	10	29	29
Total	65	45	45

* FAO estimates.
2004: Production assumed to be unchanged from 2003 (FAO estimates).
Source: FAO.

Fishing

('000 metric tons, live weight)

	2001	2002	2003
Capture	19.5	16.4	15.3
Snooks	1.4	1.4	1.5
Snappers	1.9	2.2	2.2
Yellowfin tuna	3.5	n.a.	n.a.
Common dolphinfish	1.4	1.4	0.7
Caribbean spiny lobsters	3.9	4.3	3.9
Penaeus shrimp	4.2	4.0	3.7
Aquaculture	5.8	6.1	7.0
Whiteleg shrimp	5.6	6.0	6.9
Total catch	25.3	22.5	22.3

Source: FAO.

Mining

	2001	2002	2003*
Gold ('000 troy ounces)	123.5	126.5	108.3
Silver ('000 troy ounces)	81.4	70.7	65.7
Sand ('000 cubic metres)	401.4	256.0	259.1
Limestone ('000 cubic metres)	231.2	290.0	186.6
Gypsum ('000 metric tons)	34.4	28.2	14.8

* Provisional figures.

Industry

SELECTED PRODUCTS
('000 barrels, unless otherwise indicated)

	2001	2002*	2003†
Raw sugar ('000 metric tons)	354	363	346
Liquid gas	219	194	230
Motor spirit	905	872	855
Kerosene	451	383	359
Diesel	1,578	1,485	1,436
Fuel oil	3,174	2,726	2,668
Bitumen (asphalt)	57	35	71
Cement ('000 metric tons)	595	549	577
Cardboad boxes ('000 sq m)	9,879	8,212	4,673
Electric energy (million kWh)	2,614	n.a.	n.a.
Soap (kgs)	10,000	10,200	n.a.
Rum ('000 litres)	8,595	7,216	8,345

* Preliminary figures.
† Estimates.

Finance

CURRENCY AND EXCHANGE RATES

Monetary Units
100 centavos = 1 córdoba oro (gold córdoba).

Sterling, Dollar and Euro Equivalents (30 December 2005)
£1 sterling = 29.523 gold córdobas;
US $1 = 17.146 gold córdobas;
€1 = 20.227 gold córdobas;
1,000 gold córdobas = £33.87 = $58.32 = €49.44.

Average Exchange Rate (gold córdobas per US dollar)
2003 15.11
2004 15.94
2005 16.73

Note: In February 1988 a new córdoba, equivalent to 1,000 of the former units, was introduced, and a uniform exchange rate of US $1 = 10 new córdobas was established. Subsequently, the exchange rate was frequently adjusted. A new currency, the córdoba oro (gold córdoba), was introduced as a unit of account in May 1990 and began to be circulated in August. The value of the gold córdoba was initially fixed at par with the US dollar, but in March 1991 the exchange rate was revised to $1 = 25,000,000 new córdobas (or 5 gold córdobas). On 30 April 1991 the gold córdoba became the sole legal tender.

BUDGET
(million gold córdobas)

Revenue*	2002	2003	2004†
Taxation	7,738.9	9,422.4	11,252.5
Income tax	1,609.8	2,447.9	3,176.0
Value-added tax	3,355.9	3,812.9	4,575.1
Taxes on petroleum products	1,399.4	1,566.4	1,618.4
Taxes on imports	641.9	628.2	684.4
Other revenue	824.4	728.6	983.1
Total	8,563.3	10,151.0	12,235.6

Expenditure‡	2002	2003	2004†
Compensation of employees	3,443.5	3,834.4	4,178.0
Goods and services	1,332.6	1,246.3	1,468.3
Interest payments	1,286.8	1,918.9	1,478.1
Current transfers	2,504.2	3,050.1	4,240.0
Social security contributions	157.1	223.2	227.4
Other expenditure	360.7	300.5	339.9
Total	9,085.0	10,573.5	11,931.6

* Excluding grants received (million gold córdobas): 1,522.3 in 2002; 2,079.0 in 2003; 2,373.6 in 2004 (preliminary).
† Preliminary figures.
‡ Excluding net acquisition of non-financial assets (million gold córdobas): 2,416.3 in 2002; 3,420.2 in 2003; 4,252.6 in 2004 (preliminary).

INTERNATIONAL RESERVES*
(US $ million at 31 December)

	2003	2004	2005
IMF special drawing rights	0.06	0.50	0.31
Foreign exchange	502.00	667.70	727.50
Total	502.06	668.20	727.81

* Excluding gold reserves (US $ million at 31 December): 4.10 in 1993.
Source: IMF, *International Financial Statistics*.

MONEY SUPPLY
(million gold córdobas at 31 December)

	2002	2003	2004
Currency outside banks	2,085.8	2,506.6	3,103.3
Demand deposits at commercial banks	1,280.5	1,696.0	1,702.3
Total money (incl. others)	3,368.1	4,208.3	4,806.7

Source: IMF, *International Financial Statistics*.

NICARAGUA

COST OF LIVING
(Consumer Price Index; base: 2000 = 100)

	2001	2002	2003
Food (incl. beverages)	108.6	111.8	115.9
Clothing (incl. footwear)	102.4	104.6	106.4
Rent, fuel and light	98.3	102.7	108.7
All items (incl. others)	107.4	111.6	117.4

2004: All items 127.3.

Source: ILO.

NATIONAL ACCOUNTS
(million gold córdobas at current prices)

Expenditure on the Gross Domestic Product

	2002	2003	2004
Government final consumption expenditure	9,973.1	11,157.9	12,764.5
Private final consumption expenditure	47,535.7	51,858.2	59,154.5
Increase in stocks	695.8	1,008.7	1,752.6
Gross fixed capital formation	14,261.8	15,334.2	18,870.4
Total domestic expenditure	72,466.4	79,359.0	92,542.0
Exports of goods and services	12,846.4	15,202.3	19,120.9
Less Imports of goods and services	27,936.4	31,887.5	39,059.6
GDP in purchasers' values	57,376.3	62,673.8	72,603.3
GDP at constant 1994 prices	28,087.5	28,721.2	30,199.9

Gross Domestic Product by Economic Activity

	2002	2003*	2004†
Agriculture, hunting, forestry and fishing	9,809.9	10,435.4	12,388.1
Mining and quarrying	603.3	585.7	736.2
Manufacturing	10,279.2	11,184.3	12,995.5
Electricity, gas and water	1,307.8	1,507.7	1,694.0
Construction	2,977.1	3,358.1	4,342.7
Wholesale and retail trade	8,029.9	8,695.5	9,967.1
Transport and communications	3,085.4	3,459.5	3,967.2
Finance, insurance, real estate and business services	6,973.7	7,689.2	9,044.8
Other private services	4,110.1	4,426.7	4,935.5
Government services	6,163.6	6,812.5	7,737.0
Sub-total	53,340.1	58,154.7	67,808.2
Net taxes on products	6,141.4	7,001.2	8,106.3
Less Imputed bank service charge	2,105.2	2,482.1	3,311.2
GDP in purchasers' values	57,376.3	62,673.8	72,603.3

* Preliminary figures.
† Estimates.

BALANCE OF PAYMENTS
(US $ million)

	2002	2003	2004
Exports of goods f.o.b.	916.8	1,049.6	1,362.9
Imports of goods f.o.b.	−1,834.4	−2,021.3	−2,452.0
Trade balance	−917.6	−971.7	−1,089.1
Exports of services	225.5	257.6	289.7
Imports of services	−337.2	−363.4	−399.3
Balance on goods and services	−1,029.3	−1,077.5	−1,198.7
Other income received	9.2	6.7	9.3
Other income paid	−209.6	−197.4	−201.6
Balance on goods, services and income	−1,229.7	−1,268.2	−1,391.0
Current transfers (net)	462.4	518.9	618.8
Current balance	−767.3	−749.3	−772.2
Capital (net)	248.2	286.0	283.5
Direct investment from abroad	203.9	201.3	250.0
Other investment assets	2.9	−16.0	−10.5
Other investment liabilities	−18.0	−102.2	−178.5
Net errors and omissions	−70.7	−89.3	30.1
Overall balance	−401.0	−469.5	−397.6

Source: IMF, *International Financial Statistics*.

External Trade

PRINCIPAL COMMODITIES
(US $ million)

Imports c.i.f.	2002	2003	2004*
Consumer goods	571.4	631.6	733.7
Non-durable consumer goods	452.0	489.4	569.8
Durable consumer goods	119.4	142.2	163.9
Petroleum, mineral fuels and lubricants	253.7	328.3	425.9
Crude petroleum	149.5	194.4	235.7
Mineral fuels and lubricants	103.8	133.5	190.2
Intermediate goods	508.9	557.6	646.1
Primary materials and intermediate goods for agriculture and fishing	55.8	60.2	67.6
Primary materials and intermediate good for industry	365.1	403.2	452.2
Construction materials	88.0	94.2	126.3
Capital goods	414.8	359.3	404.6
For agriculture and fishing	27.8	19.5	17.5
For industry	237.9	221.1	250.4
For transport	149.1	118.7	136.7
Miscellaneous	4.9	2.6	1.9
Total	1,753.7	1,879.4	2,212.3

* Preliminary figures.

Exports f.o.b.	2002	2003*	2004*
Coffee	73.6	85.5	126.8
Groundnuts	24.2	28.4	39.7
Cattle on hoof	23.3	25.9	35.9
Beans	18.2	20.1	18.8
Bananas	11.0	12.0	10.7
Raw tobacco	4.9	7.2	7.3
Lobster	45.5	36.1	43.4
Shrimp	33.1	33.0	37.2
Gold	35.0	35.0	45.2
Meat and meat products	78.0	83.8	110.4
Refined sugars, etc.	28.6	25.7	36.8
Cheese	13.4	20.5	22.2
Instant coffee	8.9	7.6	9.1
Wood products	17.7	13.4	12.7
Chemical products	15.7	21.9	26.7
Refined petroleum	9.2	7.8	8.0
Porcelain products	9.9	10.2	11.3
Total (incl. others)	561.0	604.5	755.6

* Preliminary figures.

PRINCIPAL TRADING PARTNERS
(US $ million)

Imports c.i.f.	2002	2003	2004*
Canada	19.2	15.7	21.4
Costa Rica	151.3	168.6	189.2
Ecuador	18.3	26.0	38.1
El Salvador	102.7	91.9	103.6
Germany	27.6	42.1	41.7
Guatemala	136.8	137.3	157.4
Honduras	9.7	32.4	51.5
Japan	93.8	81.9	95.5
Mexico	112.2	158.8	163.0
Panama	22.4	18.9	16.6
Spain	32.4	26.8	29.2
Sweden	21.2	32.8	6.5
Taiwan	19.1	17.1	16.0
USA	475.1	462.5	491.9
Venezuela	196.1	183.2	320.1
Total (incl. others)	1,753.7	1,879.4	2,212.3

* Preliminary figures.

NICARAGUA

Exports f.o.b.

	2002	2003*	2004*
Belgium	3.5	3.8	11.7
Canada	19.4	21.3	34.9
Costa Rica	48.4	49.2	50.6
El Salvador	86.7	104.4	109.3
France	9.2	6.0	13.0
Germany	13.0	9.5	14.1
Guatemala	23.2	25.9	32.3
Honduras	38.4	43.5	56.6
Italy	15.3	19.0	17.6
Mexico	21.4	27.9	39.9
Puerto Rico	16.1	15.2	19.4
Russia	13.4	14.5	1.2
Spain	11.2	15.9	23.6
USA	205.2	201.9	263.4
Total (incl. others)	**561.0**	**604.5**	**755.6**

* Preliminary figures.

Transport

RAILWAYS (traffic)

	1990	1991	1992
Passenger-km (million)	3	3	6

Freight ton-km (million): 4 in 1985.

Source: UN, *Statistical Yearbook*.

ROAD TRAFFIC (motor vehicles in use)

	2000	2001	2002
Cars	61,357	70,372	83,168
Buses and coaches	5,460	6,078	6,947
Goods vehicles	87,358	95,986	108,308
Motorcycles and mopeds	23,857	26,654	28,973

SHIPPING

Merchant fleet (registered at 31 December)

	2002	2003	2004
Number of vessels	26	26	27
Total displacement ('000 grt)	3.6	3.6	5.0

Source: Lloyd's Register-Fairplay, *World Fleet Statistics*.

International Sea-Borne Freight Traffic ('000 metric tons)

	1997	1998	1999
Imports	1,272.7	1,964.7	1,180.7
Exports	329.3	204.5	183.6

Total freight traffic ('000 metric tons): 2,215.9 in 2000; 2,363.0 in 2001; 2,093.8 in 2002.

CIVIL AVIATION (traffic on scheduled services)

	1998	1999	2000
Kilometres flown (million)	1.2	0.8	0.8
Passengers carried ('000)	52	59	61
Passenger-km (million)	93	67	72
Freight ton-km (million)	n.a.	0.5	0.5

Source: UN Economic Commission for Latin America and the Caribbean.

Tourism

TOURIST ARRIVALS BY COUNTRY OF ORIGIN

	2001	2002	2003
Canada	11,138	9,800	13,124
Costa Rica	62,055	57,824	76,659
El Salvador	71,886	69,691	73,806
Guatemala	38,311	36,964	40,132
Honduras	118,282	111,947	107,365
Panama	10,720	10,545	11,988
USA	88,375	97,863	117,156
Total (incl. others)	**482,869**	**471,622**	**525,775**

Tourism receipts (US $ million, incl. passenger transport): 138 in 2001; 138 in 2002; 155 in 2003.

Sources: World Tourism Organization.

Communications Media

	2002	2003	2004
Telephones ('000 main lines in use)	171.6	205.0	214.5
Mobile cellular telephones ('000 subscribers)	239.9	466.7	738.6
Personal computers ('000 in use)	150	n.a.	200
Internet users ('000)	90	n.a.	125

Radio receivers ('000 in use): 1,240 in 1997.

Television receivers ('000 in use): 350 in 2000.

Daily newspapers: 4 in 1996 (average circulation 135,000 copies).

Sources: UNESCO, *Statistical Yearbook*; International Telecommunication Union.

Education

(2002, unless otherwise indicated)

	Institutions	Teachers	Males	Females	Total
Pre-primary	5,980	3,672*	88,916	88,618	177,534
Primary	8,251	21,020*	471,656	451,735	923,391
Secondary: general	1,249	5,970*	160,399	203,613	364,012
Tertiary: university level	35	3,630†	n.a.	n.a.	70,925†
Tertiary: other higher	73	210†	8,615	9,898	18,513

* 1996 figure.
† 2001 figure.

Sources: UNESCO, *Statistical Yearbook*; Ministry of Education, Culture and Sports.

Adult literacy rate (UNESCO estimates): 76.7% (males 76.8%; females 76.6%) in 2003 (Source: UN Development Programme, *Human Development Report*).

Directory

The Constitution

Shortly after taking office on 20 July 1979, the Government of National Reconstruction abrogated the 1974 Constitution. On 22 August 1979 the revolutionary junta issued a 'Statute on Rights and Guarantees for the Citizens of Nicaragua', providing for the basic freedoms of the individual, religious freedom and freedom of the press and abolishing the death penalty. The intention of the Statute was formally to re-establish rights which had been violated under the deposed Somoza regime. A fundamental Statute took effect from 20 July 1980 and remained in force until the Council of State drafted a political constitution and proposed an electoral law. A new Constitution was approved by the National Constituent Assembly on 19 November 1986 and promulgated on 9 January 1987. Amendments to the Constitution were approved by the Asamblea Nacional (National Assembly) in July 1995 and January 2000. The following are some of the main points of the Constitution.

Nicaragua is an independent, free, sovereign and indivisible state. All Nicaraguans who have reached 16 years of age are full citizens.

POLITICAL RIGHTS

There shall be absolute equality between men and women. It is the obligation of the State to remove obstacles that impede effective participation of Nicaraguans in the political, economic and social life of the country. Citizens have the right to vote and to be elected at elections and to offer themselves for public office. Citizens may organize or affiliate with political parties, with the objective of participating in, exercising or vying for power. The supremacy of civilian authority is enshrined in the Constitution.

SOCIAL RIGHTS

The Nicaraguan people have the right to work, to education and to culture. They have the right to decent, comfortable and safe housing, and to seek accurate information. This right comprises the freedom to seek, receive and disseminate information and ideas, both spoken and written, in graphic or any other form. The mass media are at the service of national interests. No Nicaraguan citizen may disobey the law or prevent others from exercising their rights and fulfilling their duties by invoking religious beliefs or inclinations.

LABOUR RIGHTS

All have a right to work, and to participate in the management of their enterprises. Equal pay shall be given for equal work. The State shall strive for full and productive employment under conditions that guarantee the fundamental rights of the individual. There shall be an eight-hour working day, weekly rest, vacations, remuneration for national holidays and a bonus payment equivalent to one month's salary, in conformity with the law.

EDUCATION

Education is an obligatory function of the State. Planning, direction and organization of the secular education system is the responsibility of the State. All Nicaraguans have free and equal access to education. Private education centres may function at all levels.

LEGISLATIVE POWER

The Asamblea Nacional exercises Legislative Power through representative popular mandate. The Asamblea Nacional is composed of 90 representatives elected by direct secret vote by means of a system of proportional representation, of which 70 are elected at regional level and 20 at national level. The number of representatives may be increased in accordance with the general census of the population, in conformity with the law. Representatives shall be elected for a period of five years. The functions of the Asamblea Nacional are to draft and approve laws and decrees; to decree amnesties and pardons; to consider, discuss and approve the General Budget of the Republic; to elect judges to the Supreme Court of Justice and the Supreme Electoral Council; to fill permanent vacancies for the Presidency or Vice-Presidency; and to determine the political and administrative division of the country.

EXECUTIVE POWER

The Executive Power is exercised by the President of the Republic (assisted by the Vice-President), who is the Head of State, Head of Government and Commander-in-Chief of the Defence and Security Forces of the Nation. The election of the President (and Vice-President) is by equal, direct and free universal suffrage in secret ballot. Should a single candidate in a presidential election fail to secure the necessary 35% of the vote to win outright in the first round, a second ballot shall be held. Close relatives of a serving President are prohibited from contesting a presidential election. The President shall serve for a period of five years and may not serve for two consecutive terms. All outgoing Presidents are granted a seat in the Asamblea Nacional.

JUDICIAL POWER

The Judiciary consists of the Supreme Court of Justice, Courts of Appeal and other courts of the Republic. The Supreme Court is composed of at least seven judges, elected by the Asamblea Nacional, who shall serve for a term of six years. The functions of the Supreme Court are to organize and direct the administration of justice. There are 12 Supreme Court justices, appointed for a period of seven years.

LOCAL ADMINISTRATION

The country is divided into regions, departments and municipalities for administrative purposes. The municipal governments shall be elected by universal suffrage in secret ballot and will serve a six-year term. The communities of the Atlantic Coast have the right to live and develop in accordance with a social organization which corresponds to their historical and cultural traditions. The State shall implement, by legal means, autonomous governments in the regions inhabited by the communities of the Atlantic Coast, in order that the communities may exercise their rights.

The Government

HEAD OF STATE

President: ENRIQUE BOLAÑOS GEYER (took office 10 January 2002).
Vice-President: ALFREDO GÓMEZ URCUYO.

CABINET
(April 2006)

Minister of Foreign Affairs: NORMAN CALDERA CARDENAL.
Minister of Government: Dr JULIO VEGA PASQUIER.
Minister of National Defence: AVIL RAMÍREZ VALDIVIA.
Minister of Finance and Public Credit: MARIO FLORES.
Minister of Development, Industry and Trade: ALEJANDRO ARGÜELLO CHOISEUL.
Minister of Labour: Dr VIRGILIO JOSÉ GURDIÁN CASTELLÓN.
Minister of the Environment and Natural Resources: CRISTÓBAL ('TITO') SEQUEIRA GONZÁLEZ.
Minister of Transport and Infrastructure: RICARDO VEGA JACKSON.
Minister of Agriculture and Forestry: MARIO SALVO H.
Minister of Health: MARGARITA GURDIÁN LÓPEZ.
Minister of Education, Culture and Sports: MIGUEL ANGEL GARCÍA GUTIÉRREZ.
Minister of the Family: IVANIA DEL SOCORRO TORUÑO PADILLA.
Secretary to the Presidency: LEONARDO SOMARRIBA GONZÁLEZ.

There are, in addition, five Secretaries of State.

MINISTRIES

Ministry of Agriculture and Forestry: Km 8½, Carretera a Masaya, Managua; tel. (2) 76-0235; e-mail prensa@magfor.gob.ni; internet www.magfor.gob.ni.
Ministry of Development, Industry and Trade: Edif. Central, Km 6, Carretera a Masaya, Apdo 8, Managua; tel. (2) 78-8702; fax (2) 70-095; e-mail webmaster@mific.gob.ni; internet www.mific.gob.ni.
Ministry of Education, Culture and Sports: Complejo Cívico Camilo Ortega Saavedra, Managua; tel. (2) 65-1451; e-mail rivash@mecd.gob.ni; internet www.mecd.gob.ni.
Ministry of the Environment and Natural Resources: Km 12½, Carretera Norte, Apdo 5123, Managua; tel. (2) 33-1111; fax (2) 63-1274; e-mail cap@marena.gob.ni; internet www.marena.gob.ni.
Ministry of the Family: Managua; tel. (2) 78-1620; e-mail webmaster@mifamilia.gob.ni; internet www.mifamilia.gob.ni.
Ministry of Finance and Public Credit: Frente a la Asamblea Nacional, Apdo 2170, Managua; tel. (2) 22-6530; fax (2) 22-6430; e-mail webmaster@mhcp.gob.ni; internet www.hacienda.gob.ni.
Ministry of Foreign Affairs: Del Cine González al Sur sobre Avda Bolivar, Managua; tel. (2) 44-8000; fax 28-5102; e-mail despacho.ministro@cancilleria.gob.ni; internet www.cancilleria.gob.ni.
Ministry of Government: Apdo 68, Managua; tel. (2) 28-2284; fax (2) 22-2789; e-mail webmaster@migob.gob.ni; internet www.migob.gob.ni.

NICARAGUA

Ministry of Health: Complejo Cívico Camilo Ortega Saavedra, Managua; tel. (2) 89-7164; e-mail secretaria@minsa.gob.ni; internet www.minsa.gob.ni.

Ministry of Labour: Estadio Nacional, 400 m al norte, Apdo 487, Managua; tel. (2) 28-2028; fax (2) 28-2103.

Ministry of National Defence: Casa de la Presidencia, Managua; tel. (2) 66-3580; fax (2) 28-7911; internet www.midef.gob.ni.

Ministry of Tourism: Hotel Intercontinental 1c, Managua; tel. (2) 22-3333; internet www.intur.gob.ni.

Ministry of Transport and Infrastructure: Frente al Estadio Nacional, Apdo 26, Managua; tel. (2) 28-2061; fax (2) 22-5111; e-mail webmaster@mti.gob.ni; internet www.mti.gob.ni.

President and Legislature

PRESIDENT

Election, 4 November 2001

Candidate	Votes	% of total
Enrique Bolaños Geyer (Partido Liberal Constitucionalista)	1,216,863	56.3
Daniel Ortega Saavedra (Frente Sandinista de Liberación Nacional)	915,417	42.3
Alberto Saborío (Partido Conservador de Nicaragua)	29,933	1.4
Total	**2,162,213**	**100.0**

ASAMBLEA NACIONAL
(National Assembly)

Asamblea Nacional
Avda Bolívar, Contiguo a la Presidencia de la República, Managua; e-mail webmaster@correo.asamblea.gob.ni; internet www.asamblea.gob.ni.

President: EDUARDO GÓMEZ.
First Vice-President: SANTOS RENÉ NÚÑEZ TÉLLEZ.
Second Vice-President: GUILLERMO ANTONIO OSORNO MOLINA.
Third Vice-President: Dr ORLANDO J. TARDENCILLA ESPINOZA.

Election, 4 November 2001

Party	Seats
Partido Liberal Constitucionalista (PLC)	47
Frente Sandinista de Liberación Nacional (FSLN)	42
Partido Conservador de Nicaragua (PCN)	1
Total	**90***

* In addition to the 90 elected members, supplementary seats in the Asamblea Nacional are awarded to the unsuccessful candidates at the presidential election who were not nominated for the legislature but who received, in the presidential poll, a number of votes at least equal to the average required for one of the 70 legislative seats decided at a regional level. On this basis, the FSLN obtained one additional seat in the Asamblea Nacional. A legislative seat is also awarded to the outgoing President. Thus, the PLC also gained an additional seat, bringing the total number of seats in the Asamblea Nacional to 92.

Election Commission

Consejo Supremo Electoral (CSE): Iglesia Las Palmas, 1 c. al sur, Apdo 2241, Managua; tel. (2) 68-7948; e-mail info@cse.gob.ni; internet www.cse.gob.ni; Pres. ROBERTO RIVAS REYES.

Political Organizations

Alianza Liberal Nicaragüense (ALN): Managua; fmrly Movimiento de Salvación Liberal; name changed as above in 2006; formed alliance with Partido Conservador (PC) ahead of 2006 elections; Pres. ELISEO NÚÑEZ HERNÁNDEZ.

Alianza por la República (APRE): Casa 211, Col. Los Robles, Funeraria Monte de los Olivos 1.5 c. al norte, Managua; f. 2004 by supporters of President Enrique Bolaños; Pres. MIGUEL LÓPEZ BALDIZÓN.

Movimiento Democrático Nicaragüense (MDN): Casa L-39, Ciudad Jardín Bnd, 50 m al sur, Managua; tel. (2) 43898; f. 1978; Leader ROBERTO SEQUEIRA GÓMEZ.

Partido Conservador (PC): Colegio Centroamérica, 500 m al sur, Managua; tel. (2) 67-0484; internet www.partidoconservador.org.ni; f. 1992 following merger between Partido Conservador Demócrata (PCD) and Partido Socialconservadurismo; formed alliance with Alianza Liberal Nicaragüense (ALN) ahead of 2006 elections; Pres. MARIO RAPPACCIOLI MCGREGOR.

Partido Social Cristiano (PSC): Ciudad Jardín, Pizza María, 1 c. al lago, Managua; tel. (2) 22-026; f. 1957; 42,000 mems; Pres. ABEL REYES.

Alternativa Cristiana (AC): Managua; fmr faction of Frente Sandinista de Liberación Nacional; Pres. Dr ORLANDO J. TARDENCILLA ESPINOZA.

Camino Cristiano Nicaragüense (CCN): Managua; Pres. GUILLERMO ANTONIO OSORNO MOLINA.

Frente Sandinista de Liberación Nacional (FSLN) (Sandinista National Liberation Front): Costado Oeste Parque El Carmen, Managua; tel. and fax (2) 66-8173; internet www.fsln.org.ni; f. 1960; led by a 15-mem. directorate; embraces Izquierda Democrática Sandinista 'orthodox revolutionary' faction, led by Daniel Ortega Saavedra; 120,000 mems; Gen. Sec. DANIEL ORTEGA SAAVEDRA.

Movimiento Renovador Sandinista (MRS): Tienda Katty 1 c. abajo, Apdo 24; tel. (2) 78-0279; fax (2) 78-0268; f. 1995; fmr faction of Frente Sandinista de Liberación Nacional; Pres. DORA MARÍA TÉLLEZ.

Partido Indígena Multiétnico (PIM): Residencial Los Robles, de Farmacentro 1 c. al este, 80 varas al sur, Managua; Pres. CARLA WHITE HODGSON.

Partido Liberal Constitucionalista (PLC): Semáforos Country Club 100 m al este, Apdo 4569, Managua; tel. (2) 78-8705; fax (2) 78-1800; e-mail plc@ibw.com.ni; internet www.plc.org.ni; f. 1967; Pres. JORGE CASTILLO QUANT; Nat. Sec. Dr NOEL RAMÍREZ SÁNCHEZ.

Partido Liberal Independiente (PLI): Ciudad Jardín, H-4, Calle Principal, Managua; tel. (2) 44-3556; fax (2) 48-0012; f. 1944; Leader VIRGILIO GODOY REYES.

Partido Liberal Nacionalista (PLN): Managua; f. 1913; Pres. CONSTANTINO VELÁSQUEZ ZEPEDA.

Partido Movimiento de Unidad Costeña (PAMUC): Bilwi Puerto Cabeza; Pres. KENNETH SERAPIO HUNTER.

Partido Neo-Liberal (Pali): Cine Dorado, 2 c. al sur, 50 m arriba, Managua; tel. (2) 66-5166; f. 1986; Pres. Dr RICARDO VEGA GARCÍA.

Partido Resistencia Nicaragüense (PRN): Edif. VINSA, frente a Autonica, Carretera Sur, Managua; tel. and fax (2) 70-6508; e-mail salvata@ibw.com.ni; f. 1993; nationalist party; Pres. SALVADOR TALAVERA ALANIZ.

Partido Socialista (PS): Hospital Militar, 100 m al norte, 100 m al oeste, 100 m al sur, Managua; tel. (2) 66-2321; fax (2) 66-2936; f. 1944; social democratic party; Sec.-Gen. Dr GUSTAVO TABLADA ZELAYA.

Partido Unionista Centroamericano (PUCA): Cine Cabrera, 1 c. al este, 20 m al norte, Managua; tel. (2) 27-472; f. 1904; Pres. BLANCA ROJAS ECHAVERRY.

Unión Demócrata Cristiana (UDC): De Iglesia Santa Ana, 2 c. abajo, Barrio Santa Ana, Apdo 3089, Managua; tel. (2) 66-2576; f. 1976 as Partido Popular Social Cristiano; name officially changed as above in Dec. 1993; Pres. AGUSTÍN JARQUÍN.

Yatama (Yapti Tasba Masraka Nanih Aslatakanka): Of. de Odacan, Busto José Martí, 1 c. al este y ½ c. al norte, Managua; tel. (2) 28-1494; Atlantic coast Miskito org.; Leader BROOKLYN RIVERA BRYAN.

Diplomatic Representation

EMBASSIES IN NICARAGUA

Argentina: Semáforos de Villa Fontana, 2 c. abajo, 1 al sur, 1 abajo, 75 varas oeste, Casa 133, Apdo 703, Managua; tel. (2) 83-7066; fax (2) 70-2343; e-mail embargentina@teranet.com.ni; Ambassador HORACIO ALBERTO AMOROSO.

Brazil: Km 7¾, Carretera Sur, Quinta los Pinos, Apdo 264, Managua; tel. (2) 65-0035; fax (2) 65-2206; e-mail ebrasil@ibw.com.ni; Ambassador VICTORIA ALICE CLEAVER.

Chile: Entrada principal los Robles, 1 c. abajo, 1 c. al sur, Apdo 1289, Managua; tel. (2) 78-0619; fax (2) 70-4073; e-mail echileni@cablenet.com.ni; Ambassador CARLOS GONZÁLEZ MÁRQUEZ.

China (Taiwan): Planes de Altamira, 19–20, frente a la cancha de tenis, Apdo 4653, Managua 5; tel. (2) 77-1333; fax (2) 67-4025; e-mail embchina@ibw.com.ni; Ambassador MING-TA HUNG.

NICARAGUA

Colombia: 2da Entrada a las Colinas, 1 c. arriba, ½ c. al lago, Casa 97, Managua; tel. (2) 76-2149; e-mail emanagua@minrelext.gov.co; Ambassador MELBA MARTÍNEZ LÓPEZ.

Costa Rica: Edif. Car, 3°, 4½ km Carretera a Masaya, Managua; tel. (2) 70-3779; fax (2) 70-3780; e-mail info@embajadadecostarica.com; Ambassador RODRIGO CARRERAS JIMÉNEZ.

Cuba: Carretera a Masaya, 3a Entrada a las Colinas, Managua; tel. (2) 76-0742; fax (2) 76-0166; e-mail embacuba@cablenet.com.ni; Chargé d'affaires a.i. MANUEL GUILLOT PÉREZ.

Denmark: De la Plaza España l c. abajo, 2 c. al lago, ½ c. abajo, Apdo 4942, Managua; tel. (2) 68-0250; fax (2) 66-8095; e-mail mgaambu@um.dk; internet www.ambmanagua.um.dk; Ambassador THOMAS NEWHOUSE TRIGG SCHJERBECK.

Dominican Republic: Reparto Las Colinas, Prado Ecuestre 100, con Curva de los Gallos, Apdo 614, Managua; tel. (2) 76-2029; fax (2) 76-0654; e-mail embdom@alfanumeric.com.ni; Ambassador HÉCTOR DARÍO FREITES CAMINERO.

Ecuador: De los Pipitos 1½ c. abajo, Apdo C-33, Managua; tel. (2) 68-1098; fax (2) 66-8081; e-mail ecuador@ibw.com.ni; Ambassador GONZALO ANDRADE RIVERA.

El Salvador: Reparto Las Colinas, Avda del Campo y Pasaje Los Cerros 142, Apdo 149, Managua; tel. (2) 76-0712; fax (2) 76-0711; e-mail embelsa@cablenet.com.ni; Ambassador JOSÉ ROBERTO FRANCISCO IMENDIA MAZA.

Finland: Sucursal Jorge Navarro, Apdo 2219, Managua; tel. (2) 66-3415; fax (2) 66-3416; e-mail sanomat.mgu@formin.fi; Ambassador INGER HIRVELÄ LÓPEZ (non-resident).

France: Iglesia el Carmen 1½ c. abajo, Apdo 1227, Managua; tel. (2) 22-6210; fax (2) 28-1057; e-mail ambafrance-mnga@tmx.com.ni; internet www.ambafrance-ni.org; Ambassador JEAN-PIERRE LAFOSSE.

Germany: Bolonia, de la Rotonda El Güegüense, 1½ c. al lago, contiguo a Optica Nicaragüense, Apdo 29, Managua; tel. (2) 66-3917; fax (2) 66-7667; e-mail alemania@ibw.com.ni; internet www.managua.diplo.de; Ambassador GREGOR KOEBEL.

Guatemala: Km 11½, Carretera a Masaya, Apdo E-1, Managua; tel. (2) 79-9609; fax (2) 79-9610; e-mail embnicaragua@minex.gob.gt; Ambassador JORGE ROLANDO ECHEVERRÍA ROLDÁN.

Holy See: Apostolic Nunciature, Km 10.8, Carretera Sur, Apdo 506, Managua; tel. (2) 65-8657; fax (2) 65-7416; e-mail nuntius@cablenet.com.ni; Apostolic Nuncio Most Rev. JEAN-PAUL AIMÉ GOBEL (Titular Archbishop of Galazia in Campania).

Honduras: Reparto San Juan 312, del Gimnasio Hércules 1 c. al sur y 1½ arriba, Apdo 321, Managua; tel. (2) 78-4133; fax (2) 78-3043; e-mail embhonduras@cablenet.com.ni; Ambassador JORGE ALBERTO MILLA REYES.

Italy: Rotonda El Güegüense, 1 c. al norte, Apdo 2092, ½ c. abajo, Managua 4; tel. (2) 66-2961; fax (2) 66-3987; e-mail embitaliasegr@cablenet.com.ni; internet www.ambitaliamanagua.org; Ambassador Dr ALBERTO BONIVER.

Japan: Plaza España, 1 c. abajo y 1 c. al lago, Bolonia, Apdo 1789, Managua; tel. (2) 66-8668; fax (2) 66-8566; e-mail embjpnic@cablenet.com.ni; internet www.ni.emb-japan.go.jp; Ambassador MITSUHIRO KAGAMI.

Korea, Democratic People's Republic: Managua; Ambassador RI KANG SE.

Libya: Mansión Teodolinda, 1 c. al sur, ½ c. abajo, Managua; tel. (2) 66-8540; fax (2) 66-8542; e-mail ofilibia@ibw.com.ni; Sec. of the People's Bureau MOHAMED KHALIFA MAJDOUB.

Mexico: Contiguo a Optica Matamoros, Km 4½, Carretera a Masaya, Apdo 834, Managua; tel. (2) 78-1859; fax (2) 78-2886; e-mail embamex@cablenet.com.ni; Ambassador COLUMBA CALVO VARGA.

Netherlands: Col. los Robles III etapa, de Plaza el Sol 1 c. al sur 1½ c. al oeste, Apdo 3688, Managua; tel. (2) 70-4505; fax (2) 70-0399; e-mail mng@minbuza.nl; internet www.embholanda.org.ni; Ambassador LAMBERTUS PETRUS MARIA VAN GEEL.

Norway: Plaza España, Apdo 2090, Correo Central, Managua; tel. (2) 66-4199; fax (2) 66-3303; e-mail emb.managua@norad.no; internet www.noruega.org.ni; Ambasssador KRISTEN CHRISTENSEN.

Panama: Casa 93, Reparto Mántica, del Cuartel General de Bomberos 1 c. abajo, Apdo 1, Managua; tel. (2) 66-2224; fax (2) 66-8633; e-mail embdpma@ibw.com.ni; Ambassador MIGUEL LECARO BÁRCENAS.

Peru: Casa 325, Barrio Bolonia, del Hospital Militar 'Alejandró Dávila', 1 c. al lago y 2 c. abajo, Apdo 211, Managua; tel. (2) 66-8677; fax (2) 66-1408; e-mail peru1@ibw.com.ni; Ambassador EDUARDO CARRILLO HERNÁNDEZ.

Russia: Reparto Las Colinas, Calle Vista Alegre 214, Entre Avda Central y Paseo del Club, Apdo 249, Managua; tel. (2) 76-0374; fax (2) 76-0179; e-mail rossia@ibw.com.ni; Ambassador IGOR SERGUEEVICH KONDRAHEV.

Spain: Avda Central 13, Las Colinas, Apdo 284, Managua; tel. (2) 76-0966; fax (2) 76-0937; e-mail embespni@correo.mae.es; internet www.mae.es/Embajadas/Managua; Ambassador JAIME LACADENA HIGUERA.

Sweden: Plaza España, 1 c. abajo, 2 c. al lago y ½ c. al oeste, Apdo 2307, Managua; tel. (2) 55-8400; fax (2) 66-6778; e-mail ambassaden.managua@sida.se; internet www.swedenabroad.se/managua; Ambassador EVA ZETTERBERG.

USA: Km 4½, Carretera Sur, Apdo 327, Managua; tel. (2) 66-6010; fax (2) 66-3861; e-mail consularmanagua@state.gov; internet managua.usembassy.gov; Ambassador PAUL A. TRIVELLI.

Venezuela: Edif. Málaga, 2°, Plaza España, Módulo A-13, Apdo 406, Managua; tel. (2) 72-0267; fax (2) 72-2265; e-mail embaveznica@cablenet.com.ni; Ambassador MIGUEL ANTONIO GÓMEZ NUÑEZ.

Judicial System

The Supreme Court

Km 7½, Carretera Norte, Managua; tel. (2) 33-0083; fax (2) 33-0581; e-mail cdocumentacon@csj.gob.ni; internet www.csj.gob.ni; Deals with both civil and criminal cases, acts as a Court of Cassation, appoints Judges of First Instance, and generally supervises the legal administration of the country.

President: Dr JOSÉ MANUEL MARTÍNEZ SEVILLA.
Vice-President: Dr RAFAEL SOLÍS CERDA.
Attorney-General: ALBERTO NOVOA.

Religion

All religions are tolerated. Almost all of Nicaragua's inhabitants profess Christianity, and the great majority belong to the Roman Catholic Church. The Moravian Church predominates on the Caribbean coast.

CHRISTIANITY

The Roman Catholic Church

Nicaragua comprises one archdiocese, six dioceses and the Apostolic Vicariate of Bluefields. At 31 December 2003 there were an estimated 5,213,778 adherents, representing about 80% of the total population.

Bishops' Conference

Conferencia Episcopal de Nicaragua, Ferretería Lang 1 c. al norte, l c. al este, Zona 3, Las Piedrecitas, Apdo 2407, Managua; tel. (2) 66-6292; fax (2) 66-8069; e-mail cen@tmx.com.ni; f. 1975; statute approved 1987; Pres. LEOPOLDO JOSÉ BRENES SOLÓRZANO (Archbishop of Managua).

Archbishop of Managua: LEOPOLDO JOSÉ BRENES SOLÓRZANO, Arzobispado, Apdo 3058, Managua; tel. (2) 77-1754; fax (2) 76-0130; e-mail mob@adm.unica.edu.ni.

The Anglican Communion

Nicaragua comprises one of the five dioceses of the Iglesia Anglicana de la Región Central de América.

Bishop of Nicaragua: Rt Rev. STURDIE W. DOWNS, Apdo 1207, Managua; tel. (2) 22-5174; fax (2) 22-6701; e-mail episcnic@tmx.com.ni.

Protestant Churches

Baptist Convention of Nicaragua: Apdo 2593, Managua; tel. (2) 25785; fax (2) 24131; e-mail cbn@ibw.com.ni; f. 1917; 135 churches, 20,000 mems (2006); Pres. Rev. GUADALUPE GÓMEZ; Gen. Sec. Rev. ELÍAS GONZÁLEZ ARGÜELLO.

The Nicaraguan Lutheran Church of Faith and Hope: Apdo 151, Managua; tel. (2) 66-4467; fax (2) 66-4609; e-mail luterana@ibw.org.ni; f. 1994; 4,000 mems (2006); Pres. Rev. VICTORIA CORTEZ RODRÍGUEZ.

The Press

NEWSPAPERS AND PERIODICALS

Bolsa de Noticias: Col. Centroamérica 852, Apdo VF-90, Managua; tel. (2) 70-0546; fax (2) 77-4931; e-mail prensa@bolsadenoticias.com.ni; internet www.grupoese.com.ni/BolsadeNoticias; f. 1974; daily; Dir MARÍA ELSA SUÁREZ GARCÍA.

NICARAGUA

Confidencial: De la Iglesia El Carmen 1 c. al lago, ½ c. abajo, Managua; tel. (2) 68-0129; fax (2) 68-4650; e-mail revista@confidencial.com.ni; internet www.confidencial.com.ni; weekly; political analysis; Editor CARLOS F. CHAMORRO.

La Gaceta, Diario Oficial: Semáforos de Plaza Inter, 1 c. arriba, 1½ c. al lago, Managua; tel. (2) 28-3791; e-mail lagaceta@ibw.com.ni; f. 1912; morning; official.

Novedades: Pista P. Joaquín Chamorro, Km 4, Carretera Norte, Apdo 576, Managua; daily, evening.

Nuevo Diario: Pista P. Joaquín Chamorro, Km 4, Carretera Norte, Apdo 4591, Managua; tel. (2) 49-1190; fax (2) 49-0700; e-mail info@elnuevodiario.com.ni; internet www.elnuevodiario.com.ni; f. 1980; morning, daily; independent; Editor XAVIER CHAMORRO CARDENAL; Gen. Man. GABRIELA SALGADO; circ. 45,000.

El Observador Económico: Antiguo Hospital el Retiro, 2 c. al lago, Apdo 2074, Managua; tel. (2) 66-8708; fax (2) 66-8711; e-mail amc@elobservadoreconomico.com; internet www.elobservadoreconomico.com; Dir-Gen. ALEJANDRO MARTÍNEZ CUENCA.

El Popular: Managua; tel. (2) 66-2936; monthly; official publication of the Partido Socialista Nicaragüense.

La Prensa: Km 4½, Carretera Norte, Apdo 192, Managua; tel. (2) 49-8405; fax (2) 49-6926; e-mail info@laprensa.com.ni; internet www.laprensa.com.ni; f. 1926; morning, daily; independent; Pres. JAIME CHAMORRO CARDENAL; Editor EDUARDO ENRÍQUEZ; circ. 30,000.

Prensa Proletaria: Managua; tel. (2) 22-594; fortnightly; official publication of the Movimiento de Acción Popular Marxista-Leninista.

Revista Ambiente: 27 Avda 6901, Managua; tel. and fax (2) 66-8206.

Revista Envío: Edif. Nitlapán, 2°, Universidad Centroamericana, Apdo A-194, Managua; tel. (2) 78-2557; fax (2) 78-1402; e-mail info@envio.org.ni; internet www.envio.org.ni; f. 1981; 11 a year; political analysis; Dir ANDREU OLIVA; Chief Editor MARÍA LÓPEZ VIGIL.

Revista Encuentro: Universidad Centroamericana, Apdo 69, Managua; tel. (2) 78-3923; fax (2) 67-0106; e-mail dirinv@ns.uca.edu.ni; internet www.uca.edu.ni/publicaciones; f. 1968; termly; academic publ. of the Universidad Centroamericana.

Revista 7 Días: Altamira de lo Vicky, 5½ al lago, Managua; e-mail 7dias@ibw.com.ni; internet www.7dias.com.ni.

La Semana Cómica: Centro Comercial Bello Horizonte, Módulos 7 y 9, Apdo SV-3, Managua; tel. (2) 44-909; e-mail bmejia@lasemanacomica.com; internet www.lasemanacomica.com; f. 1980; weekly; Dir RÓGER SÁNCHEZ; circ. 45,000.

Tiempos del Mundo: Apdo 3525, Managua; tel. (2) 70-3418; fax (2) 70-3419; e-mail tiempos@tdm.com.ni; f. 1996; weekly; Gen. Man. TAKUYA ISHII; circ. 5,000.

La Tribuna: Detrás del Banco Mercantil, Plaza España, Apdo 1469, Managua; tel. (2) 66-9282; fax (2) 66-5167; e-mail tribuna@latribuna.com.ni; internet www.latribuna.com.ni; f. 1993; morning, daily; Dir HAROLDO J. MONTEALEGRE; Gen. Man. MARIO GONZÁLEZ.

Vision Sandinista: Costado Este, Parque El Carmen, Managua; tel. and fax (2) 68-1565; internet www.vsandinista.com; f. 1980; weekly; official publ. of the Frente Sandinista de Liberación Nacional; Dir MAYRA REYES SANDOVAL.

Association

Unión de Periodistas de Nicaragua (UPN): Apdo 4006, Managua; Pres. CARLOS SALGADO.

NEWS AGENCIES

Foreign Bureaux

Agencia EFE (Spain): Ciudad Jardín S-22, Apdo 1951, Managua; tel. (2) 24-928; Bureau Chief FILADELFO MARTÍNEZ FLORES.

Deutsche Presse-Agentur (dpa) (Germany): Apdo 2095, Managua; tel. (2) 78-1862; fax (2) 78-1863; Correspondent JOSÉ ESTEBAN QUEZADA.

Informatsionnoye Telegrafnoye Agentstvo Rossii—Telegrafnoye Agentstvo Suverennykh Stran (ITAR—TASS) (Russia): Col. Los Robles, Casa 17, Managua; internet www.itar-tass-com; Correspondent ALEKSANDR TRUSHIN.

Notimex (Mexico): Reparto San Juan, esq. enfrente del Gimnasio Hercules, Managua; tel. (2) 78-4540; fax (2) 67-0413.

Prensa Latina (Cuba): Casa 280, de los Semáforos del Portón de Telcor de Villa Fontana, 25 m al este, 2 c. al lago, Managua; tel. (2) 72-697; e-mail platina@ibw.com.ni; internet www.prensa-latina.com; Correspondent NÉSTOR MARÍN.

United Press International (USA): 165 Col. del Periodista, Managua; tel. and fax (2) 78-1712; Correspondent DAVID GUTIÉRREZ.

Directory

Xinhua (New China) News Agency (People's Republic of China): De Policlínica Nicaragüense, 80 m al sur, Apdo 5899, Managua; tel. (2) 62-155; Bureau Chief LIU RIUCHANG.

Publishers

Academia Nicaragüense de la Lengua: Calle Central, Reparto Las Colinas, Apdo 2711, Managua; f. 1928; languages; Dir PABLO ANTONIO CUADRA; Sec. JULIO YCAZA TIGERINO.

Editora de Arte SA: 53 Reparto Los Robles III, Managua; tel. (2) 78-5854.

Editorial Nueva Nicaragua: Paseo Salvador Allende, Km 3½, Carretera Sur, Apdo 073, Managua; fax (2) 66-6520; f. 1981; Pres. Dr SERGIO RAMÍREZ MERCADO; Dir-Gen. ROBERTO DÍAZ CASTILLO.

Editorial Unión: Avda Central Norte, Managua; travel.

Librería Hispaniamericana (HISPAMER): Costado Este de la UCA, Apdo A-221, Managua; e-mail hispamer@hispamer.com.ni; internet www.hispamer.com.ni; f. 1991.

UCA Publicaciónes: Rectoría de la Universidad Centroamericana, Apdo 69, Managua; tel. (2) 78-3923; e-mail ucapubli@ns.uca.edu.ni; internet www.uca.edu.ni/publicaciones; academic publishing dept of the Universidad Centroamericana.

Universidad Nacional Agraria: Km 12½ Carretera Norte, Apdo 453, Managua; tel. (2) 33-1950; e-mail info@una.edu.ni; internet www.una.edu.ni; sciences.

Broadcasting and Communications

TELECOMMUNICATIONS

Regulatory Bodies

Instituto Nicaragüense de Telecomunicaciones y Correos (Telcor): Edif. Telcor, Avda Bolivar diagonal a Cancillería, Apdo 2264, Managua; tel. (2) 22-7350; fax (2) 22-7554; e-mail webmaster@telcor.gob.ni; internet www.telcor.gob.ni; Dir-Gen. MARTA JULIA LUGO.

Superintendencia de Servicios Públicos (Sisep): Managua; f. Feb. 2005 to oversee the telecommunications, energy and water sectors; operations suspended in June 2005; Supt VÍCTOR MANUEL GUERRERO.

Major Service Providers

ALÓ (PCS de Nicaragua): Managua; e-mail atencion.cliente@alo.com.ni; internet www.alo.com.ni; subsidiary of América Móvil (Mexico); mobile cellular telephone operator; awarded licence in 2002.

Empresa Nicaragüense de Telecomunicaciones (Enitel): Villafontana 2°, Apdo 232, Managua; tel. (2) 77-3057; fax (2) 70-2128; internet www.enitel.com.ni; f. 1925; 99.2% owned by Mexican operator América Móvil; Chair. FREDDY NAZER.

Telefónica Móviles Nicaragua: Km 6½, Carretera a Masaya, Managua; tel. (2) 77-0731; internet www.movistar.com.ni; fmrly BellSouth; owned by Grupo Telefónica Móviles (Spain); mobile cellular telephone provider; Vice-Pres. ANTONIO MELGUIZO ALVARO; Gen. Man. CLAUDIO ANDRÉS HIDALGO SÁEZ.

BROADCASTING

Radio

Radio Cadena de Oro: Altamira 73, Managua; tel. (2) 67-0035; fax (2) 78-1220; f. 1990; Dir ALLAN DAVID TEFEL ALBA.

Radio Católica: Altamira D'Este 621, 3°, Apdo 2183, Managua; tel. (2) 78-0836; fax (2) 78-2544; e-mail catolica@ibw.com.ni; internet www.radiocatolica.org; f. 1961; controlled by Conferencia Episcopal de Nicaragua; Dir Fr ROLANDO ÁLVAREZ; Gen. Man. ALBERTO CARBALLO MADRIGAL.

Radio Corporación, Gadea y Cía: Ciudad Jardín Q-20, Apdo 24242, Managua; tel. (2) 49-1619; fax (2) 44-3824; e-mail rc540@cablenet.com.ni; internet www.radio-corporacion.com; f. 1995; Gen. Man. FABIO GADEA MANTILLA; Asst Man. CARLOS GADEA MANTILLA.

Radio Estrella: Sierritas de Santo Domingo, Frente al Cementerio, Apdo UNICA 104, Managua; tel. (2) 76-0241; fax (2) 76-0062; e-mail radiosm@radioestrelladelmar.com; internet www.radioestrelladelmar.com.

Radio Mundial: 36 Avda Oeste, Reparto Loma Verde, Apdo 3170, Managua; tel. (2) 66-6767; fax (2) 66-4630; commercial; Pres. MANUEL ARANA VALLE; Dir-Gen. ALMA ROSA ARANA HARTIG.

Radio Nicaragua: Villa Fontana, Contiguo a Enitel, Apdo 4665, Managua; tel. (2) 27-2330-1; fax (2) 67-1448; e-mail radio.nicaragua@

netport.com.ni; internet www.radionicaragua.com.ni; f. 1960; government station; Dir-Gen. Ramón Rodríguez Salinas.

Radio Ondas de Luz: Costado Sur del Hospital Bautista, Apdo 607, Managua; tel. and fax (2) 49-7058; f. 1959; religious and cultural station; Pres. Guillermo Osorno Molina; Dir Eduardo Gutiérrez Narváez.

Radio Sandino: Paseo Tiscapa Este, Contiguo al Restaurante Mirador, Apdo 4776, Managua; tel. (2) 28-1330; fax (2) 62-4052; f. 1977; station controlled by the Frente Sandinista de Liberación Nacional; Pres. Bayardo Arce Castaño; Dir Conrado Pineda Aguilar.

Radio Segovia: Ocotal, Nueva Segovia; internet www.radiosegovia.net; f. 1980; commercial.

Radio Tiempo: Reparto Pancasan 217, 7°, Apdo 2735, Managua; tel. (2) 78-2540; f. 1976; Dir Danilo Lacayo Lanzas.

Radio Universidad: Avda Card, 3 c. abajo, Apdo 2883, Managua; tel. (2) 78-4743; fax (2) 77-5057; f. 1984; Dir Luis López Ruiz.

Radio Ya: Pista de la Resistencia, Frente a la Universidad Centroamericana, Managua; tel. (2) 78-5600; fax (2) 78-6000; e-mail webmaster@nuevaya.com.ni; internet www.nuevaya.com.ni; f. 1990; Dir Dennis Schwartz.

There are some 50 other radio stations.

Television

Nicavisión, Canal 12: Bolonia Dual Card, 1 c. abajo, $\frac{1}{2}$ c. al sur, Apdo 2766, Managua; tel. (2) 66-0691; fax (2) 66-1424; e-mail info@tv12-nic.com; internet www.tv12-nic.com; f. 1993; Dir Mariano Valle Peters.

Nueva Imagen, Canal 4: Montoya, 1 c. al sur, 2 c. arriba, Managua; tel. (2) 28-1310; fax (2) 22-4067; Pres. Dionisio Marenco; Gen. Man. Orlando Castilllo.

Sistema Nacional de Televisión Canal 6 (SNTV Canal 6): Km $3\frac{1}{2}$, Carretera Sur, Contiguo a Shell, Las Palmas, Apdo 1505, Managua; tel. (2) 66-4958; fax (2) 66-1520; state-owned; Dir Walter René Pérez.

Televicentro de Nicaragua, SA, Canal 2: Casa del Obrero, $6\frac{1}{2}$ c. al Sur, Apdo 688, Managua; tel. (2) 68-2222; fax (2) 66-3688; e-mail canal2@canal2.com.ni; internet www.canal2.com.ni; f. 1965; Pres. Octavio Sacasa Raskosky; Gen. Man. Alejandro Sacasa Pasos.

Televisora Nicaragüense, SA, Telenica 8: De la Mansión Teodolinda, 1 c. al sur, $\frac{1}{2}$ c. abajo, Bolonia, Apdo 3611, Managua; tel. (2) 66-5021; fax (2) 66-5024; e-mail cbriceno@nicanet.com.ni; f. 1989; Pres. Carlos A. Briceño Lovo.

Televisión Internacional, Canal 23: Casa L-852, Col. Centroamérica, Managua; tel. (2) 68-7466; fax (2) 66-0625; e-mail canal23@ibw.com.ni; f. 1993; Pres. César Riguero.

Ultravisión de Nicaragua, SA: Casa 567, Rotonda los Cocos, Altamira, Managua; tel. (2) 77-3524; Pres. Criseyda Olivas Vega.

Finance

(cap. = capital; res = reserves; dep. = deposits; m. = million; amounts in gold córdobas unless otherwise stated)

BANKING

All Nicaraguan banks were nationalized in July 1979. Foreign banks operating in the country are no longer permitted to secure local deposits. All foreign exchange transactions must be made through the Banco Central or its agencies. Under a decree issued in May 1985, the establishment of private exchange houses was permitted. In 1990 legislation allowing for the establishment of private banks was enacted.

Supervisory Authority

Superintendencia de Bancos y de Otras Instituciones Financieras: Edif. SBOIF, Km 7, Carretera Sur, Apdo 788, Managua; tel. (2) 65-1555; fax (2) 65-0965; e-mail correo@sibiof.gob.ni; internet www.superintendencia.gob.ni; f. 1991; Supt Dr Victor M. Urcuyo Vidaurre.

Central Bank

Banco Central de Nicaragua: Carretera Sur, Km 7, Apdos 2252/3, Zona 5, Managua; tel. (2) 65-0500; fax (2) 65-0561; e-mail bcn@bcn.gob.ni; internet www.bcn.gob.ni; f. 1961; bank of issue and govt fiscal agent; cap. 10.6m., res 21.1m., dep. 15,176.9m. (Dec. 2002); Pres. Dr Mario Arana Sevilla; Gen. Man. José de Jesús Rojas Rodríguez.

Private Banks

Banco de América Central (BAC): Pista Sub-Urbana, Frente a Lotería Popular, Managua; tel. (2) 67-0220; fax (2) 67-0224; e-mail info@bancodeamericacentral.com; internet www.bancodeamericacentral.com; f. 1991; total assets 10,516m. (1999); Pres. Carlos Pellas Chamorro; Gen. Man. Carlos Matus Tapia.

Banco de Crédito Centroamericano (BANCENTRO): Edif. BANCENTRO, Km $4\frac{1}{2}$ Carretera a Masaya, Managua; tel. (2) 78-2777; fax (2) 78-6001; e-mail info@bancentro.com.ni; internet www.bancentro.com.ni; f. 1991; total assets 5,249m. (1999); Pres. Roberto J. Zamora Llanes; Gen. Man. Carlos A. Briceño Ríos.

Banco Uno, SA: Plaza España, Rotonda el Güegüense 20 m al oeste, Managua; tel. (2) 78-7171; fax (2) 77-3154; e-mail info@banexpo.com.ni; internet www.bancouno.com.ni; dep. 2,372m. (Dec. 2002); fmrly Banco de la Exportación (BANEXPO), present name adopted in Nov. 2002; Dir Adolfo Argüello Lacayo.

STOCK EXCHANGE

Bolsa de Valores de Nicaragua: Edif. Oscar Pérez Cassar, Centro BANIC, Km $5\frac{1}{2}$, Carretera Masaya, Apdo 121, Managua; tel. (2) 78-3830; fax (2) 78-3836; e-mail info@bolsanic.com; internet bolsanic.com; f. 1993; Pres. Dr Raúl Lacayo Solórzano; Gen. Man. Carolina Solórzano de Barrios.

INSURANCE

State Company

Instituto Nicaragüense de Seguros y Reaseguros (INISER): Centro Comercial Camino de Oriente, Km 6, Carretera a Masaya, Apdo 1147, Managua; tel. (2) 66-6772; fax (2) 66-5636; e-mail iniser@iniser.com.ni; internet www.iniser.com.ni; f. 1979; to assume the activities of all the pre-revolution national private insurance companies; Exec. Pres. Manuel R. Gurdián Ubago; Vice-Pres. Roberto Ernesto Quintana Cardoze.

Private Companies

Compañía de Seguros del Pacifico, SA: Edif. Telefonica, 3°, Km $6\frac{1}{2}$ Carretera a Masaya, Managua; tel. (2) 68-2454; fax (2) 70-8443; e-mail segurosp@segurospacifico.com.ni; internet www.segurospacifico.com.ni; f. 1997; Gen. Man. Mariangeles Morales Barcenas.

Metropolitana Compañía de Seguros, SA: Reparto Serrano Plaza El Sol, 400 m al norte, Managua; tel. (2) 78-8538; fax (2) 78-2621; e-mail luciaramirez@metroseg.com; Pres. Dr Leonel Argüello Ramírez; Sec. Lucía Ramirez Sanchez.

Seguros América, SA: Centro BAC, Km $5\frac{1}{2}$ Carretera a Masaya, Apdo 6114, Managua; tel. (2) 74-4200; fax (2) 74-4202; e-mail sergioulvert@segamerica.com.ni; f. 1996; Pres. Carlos F. Pellas Chamorro; Man. Sergio Ulvert Sanchez.

Seguros Lafise, SA: Centro Financiero Lafise, Km $5\frac{1}{2}$ Carretera a Masaya, Managua; tel. (2) 70-3505; fax (2) 70-3558; e-mail seguros@seguroslafise.com.ni; internet www.seguroslafise.com.ni; fmrly Seguros Centroamericanos (Segurossa); Pres. Roberto Zamora Llanes; Gen. Man. Claudio Taboada Rodríguez.

Trade and Industry

GOVERNMENT AGENCIES

Empresa Nicaragüense de Alimentos Básicos (ENABAS): Salida a Carretera Norte, Apdo 1041, Managua; f. 1979; controls trading in basic foodstuffs; Dir Mariano Vega Noguera.

Instituto de Desarrollo Rural (IDR) (Institute of Rural Development): B3, Camino de Oriente, Apdo 3593, Managua; tel. (2) 78-4940; e-mail divulgacion@idr.gob.ni; internet www.idr.gob.ni; f. 1995; Exec. Pres. Mario Rosales Pasquier; Dir José Ramón Kontorovsky.

Instituto Nicaragüense de Apoyo a la Pequeña y Mediana Empresa (INPYME): De la Shell Plaza el Sol, 1 c. al sur, 300 m abajo, Apdo 449, Managua; tel. (2) 77-0599; fax (2) 77-0598; internet www.inpyme.gob.ni; supports small and medium-sized enterprises; Exec. Dir Harold Antonio Rocha Solís.

Instituto Nicaragüense de Tecnología Agropecuaria (INTA): Managua; tel. 278-0469; fax 278-1259; e-mail mapache@inta.gob.ni; internet www.inta.gob.ni; f. 1993; Pres. Luis A. Osorio; Dir-Gen. Dr Noel Pallais Checa.

Instituto de la Vivienda Urbana y Rural: Managua; e-mail evigil@invur.gob.ni; internet www.invur.gob.ni; housing devt; Pres. Eduardo Vigil.

DEVELOPMENT ORGANIZATIONS

Asociación de Productores y Exportadores de Nicaragua (APEN): Del Hotel Intercontinental, 2 c. al sur y 2 c. abajo, Bolonia, Managua; tel. (2) 66-5038; fax (2) 66-5039; Gen. Man. Jorge Brenes.

NICARAGUA

Cámara de Industrias de Nicaragua: Rotonda el Güegüense, 300 m al sur, Apdo 1436, Managua; tel. (2) 66-8847; fax (2) 66-1891; e-mail cadin@cadin.org.ni; internet www.cadin.org.ni; Pres. GABRIEL PASOS LACAYO.

Cámara Nacional de la Mediana y Pequeña Industria (CONAPI): Plaza 19 de Julio, Frente a la UCA, Apdo 153, Managua; tel. (2) 78-4892; fax (2) 67-0192; e-mail conapi@nicarao.org.ni; Pres. FLORA VARGAS; Gen. Man. URIEL ARGAÑEL C.

Cámara Nicaragüense de la Construcción (CNC): Bolonia de Aval Card, 2 c. abajo, 50 varas al Sur, Managua; tel. (2) 26-3363; fax (2) 66-3327; e-mail cncsecre@nicarao.org.ni; f. 1961; construction industry; Pres. ALEJANDRO TERÁN.

Instituto Nicaragüense de Fomento Municipal (INIFOM): Edif. Central, Carretera a la Refinería, entrada principal residencial Los Arcos, Apdo 3097, Managua; tel. (2) 66-6050; fax (2) 66-6050; internet www.inifom.gob.ni; Pres. CARLOS MIGUEL DUARTE AREAS.

CHAMBERS OF COMMERCE

Cámara de Comercio de Nicaragua (CACONIC): Rotonda El Güegüense 300 m al sur, 20 m al oeste; tel. (2) 68-3505; fax (2) 68-3600; e-mail comercio@ibw.com.ni; internet www.caconic.org.ni; f. 1892; 530 mems; Pres. JOSÉ ADÁN AGUERRI CHAMORRO; Gen. Man. CARMEN DOLORES CÓRDOVA.

Cámara de Comercio Americana de Nicaragua: Semáforos ENEL Central, 500 m al sur, Apdo 2720, Managua; tel. (2) 67-3099; fax (2) 67-3098; e-mail amcham@ns.tmx.com.ni; f. 1974; Pres. RENÉ GONZÁLEZ.

Cámara Oficial Española de Comercio de Nicaragua: Restaurante la Marseilleisa, ½ c. arriba, Los Robles, Apdo 4103, Managua; tel. (2) 78-9047; fax (2) 78-9088; e-mail gerencia.camacoes@cablenet.com.ni; Pres. JOSÉ ESCALANTE ALVARADO; Sec.-Gen. AUXILIADORA MIRANDA DE GUERRERO.

EMPLOYERS' ORGANIZATIONS

Asociación de Café Especiales de Nicaragua (ACEN): Managua; coffee producers and exporters; Pres. ROBERTO BENDAÑA; Gen. Man. CLAUDIA CASTELLÓN.

Consejo Superior de la Empresa Privada (COSEP): De Telcor Zacarías Guerra, 1 c. abajo, Apdo 5430, Managua; tel. (2) 28-2030; fax (2) 28-2041; e-mail cosep@nic.gbm.net; f. 1972; private businesses; consists of Cámara de Industrias de Nicaragua (CADIN), Unión de Productores Agropecuarios de Nicaragua (UPANIC), Cámara de Comercio, Cámara de la Construcción, Confederación Nacional de Profesionales (CONAPRO), Instituto Nicaragüense de Desarrollo (INDE); mem. of Coordinadora Democrática Nicaragüense; Vice-Pres. ROBERTO TERÁN; Sec. ORESTES ROMERO ROJAS.

Instituto Nicaragüense de Desarrollo (INDE): Camas Lunes 1 c. al oeste, Calle 27 de Mayo, Apdo 2598, Managua; tel. and fax (2) 68-1900; f. 1963; private business org.; 650 mems; Pres. GABRIEL SOLÓRZANO.

Unión Nacional de Agricultores y Ganaderos (UNAG): Managua; Pres. ALVARO FIALLOS.

Unión de Productores Agropecuarios de Nicaragua (UPANIC): Reparto San Juan No 300, detrás del Ginmasio Hércules, Managua; tel. (2) 78-3382; fax (2) 78-3291; e-mail upanic@ibw.com.ni; private agriculturalists' asscn; Pres. OSCAR ALEMÁN; Exec. Sec. ALEJANDRO RASKOSKY.

UTILITIES

Regulatory Bodies

Comisión Nacional de Energía: Managua; Exec. Sec. RAÚL SOLÓRZANO.

Instituto Nicaragüense de Acueductos y Alcantarillados (INAA): De la Mansión Teodolinda, 3 c. al sur, Bolonia, Apdo 1084, Managua; tel. (2) 66-7882; fax (2) 66-7917; e-mail inaa@inaa.gob.ni; internet www.inaa.gob.ni; f. 1979; water regulator; Exec. Pres. ALFREDO GUERRERO.

Instituto Nicaragüense de Energía (INE): Edif. Petronic, 4°, Managua; tel. (2) 28-1142; fax (2) 28-2049; internet www.ine.gob.ni; Pres. OCTAVIO SALINAS MORAZÁN.

Electricity

Unidad de Reestructuración de la Empresa Nicaragüense de Electricidad (URE): Altamira d'Este 141, de la Vicky 1 c. abajo, 1 c. al sur, Managua; tel. (2) 70-9989; fax (2) 78-2284; e-mail ure@ibw.com.ni; internet www.ure.gob.ni; f. 1999 to oversee the privatization of the state-owned distribution and generation companies of ENEL; Exec. Dir SALVADOR QUINTANILLA.

Empresa Nicaragüense de Electricidad (ENEL): Ofs Centrales, Pista Juan Pablo II y Avda Bolívar, Managua; tel. (2) 67-4159; fax (2) 67-2686; e-mail relapub@ibw.com.ni; Pres. FRANK JOHN KELLY; responsible for planning, organization, management, administration, research and development of energy resources; split into a transmission company, 2 distribution businesses and 4 generation companies in 1999.

Empresa Nacional de Transmisión Eléctrica, SA (ENTRESA): Intersección Bolívar y Pista Juan Pablo II, Managua; tel. (2) 77-4159; internet www.entresa.com.ni; operates the electricity transmission network; Gen. Man. HUMBERTO SALVO LABREAU.

GECSA: electricity generation company; 79 MW capacity thermal plant; almost obsolete and therefore difficult to privatize, GECSA was likely to be retained for emergency purposes.

GEOSA: electricity generation company; 112 MW capacity thermal plant; sold to Coastal Power International (USA) in Jan. 2002.

HIDROGESA: electricity generation company; 94 MW capacity hydroelectric plant; privatized in 2002; however, sale annulled in July 2003 owing to alleged irregularities.

ORMAT Momotombo Power Company: Momotombo; internet www.ormat.com; f. 1999 on acquisition of 15-year concession to rehabilitate and operate Momotombo power plant; subsidiary of ORMAT International, Inc; 30 MW capacity geothermal plant.

Unión Fenosa DISSUR y DISNORTE: Managua; electricity distribution company; privatized in 2000; distributes some 1460 GWh (DISSUR 658 GWh, DISNORTE 802 GWh); Dir JOSÉ LEY LAU.

Water

Empresa Nicaragüense de Acueductos y Alcantarillados Sanitarios (ENACAL): 5 Km Carretera Sur 505, Asososca; tel. (2) 66-7863; internet www.enacal.com.ni; Exec. Pres. LUIS DEBAYLE SOLIS.

TRADE UNIONS

Asociación Nacional de Educadores de Nicaragua (ANDEN): Managua; e-mail anden@guegue.com.ni; Sec.-Gen. JOSÉ ANTONIO ZEPEDA; 19 affiliates, 15,000 mems.

Asociación de Trabajadores del Campo (ATC) (Association of Rural Workers): Apdo A-244, Managua; tel. (2) 23-2221; e-mail atcnic@ibw.com.ni; f. 1977; Gen. Sec. EDGARDO GARCÍA; 52,000 mems.

Central Sandinista de Trabajadores (CST): Iglesia del Carmen, 1 c. al oeste, ½ c. al sur, Managua; tel. (2) 65-1096; fax (2) 40-1285; e-mail cts/cor@alfamumeric.com.ni; Sec.-Gen. ROBERTO GONZÁLEZ GAITÁN.

Central de Trabajadores de Nicaragua (CTN) (Nicaragua Workers' Congress): De la Iglesia del Carmen, 1 c. al sur, ½ c. arriba y 75 varas al sur, Managua; tel. (2) 68-3061; fax (2) 652056; e-mail ctn@alfanumeric.com.ni; f. 1962; mem. of Coordinadora Democrática Nicaragüense; Sec.-Gen. CARLOS HUEMBES.

Confederación de Acción y Unidad Sindical (CAUS) (Confederation for Trade Union Action and Unity): Semáforos de Rubenia, 2 c. abajo y 2 c. al lago, Barrio Venezuela, Managua; tel. and fax (2) 44-2587; f. 1973; trade-union wing of Partido Comunista de Nicaragua; Sec.-Gen. EMILIO MÁRQUEZ.

Confederación General de Trabajadores Independientes (CGT(I)) (Independent General Confederation of Labour): Centro Comercial Nejapa, 1 c. arriba y 3 c. al lago, Managua; tel. (2) 22-5195; fax (2) 28-7505; f. 1953; Sec.-Gen. NILO M. SALAZAR; 4,843 mems (est.) from six federations with 40 local unions, and six non-federated local unions.

Confederación de Unificación Sindical (CUS) (Confederation of United Trade Unions): Casa Q3, del Colegio la Tenderi 2½ c. arriba, Ciudad Jardín, Managua; tel. (2) 48-3681; fax (2) 40-1330; e-mail sindicatocus@yahoo.com; f. 1972; affiliated to the Inter-American Regional Organization of Workers, etc.; mem. of Coordinadora Democrática Nicaragüense; Sec.-Gen. JOSÉ ESPINOZA.

Federation Enrique Schmidt (FESC): Managua; e-mail fschmidt@tmx.com.ni; communications and postal workers' union.

Federación de Trabajadores Nicaragüenses (FTN): workers' federation; Leader DOMINGO PÉREZ.

Federación de Trabajadores de la Salud (FETSALUD) (Federation of Health Workers): Optica Nicaragüense, 2 c. arriba ½ c. al sur, Apdo 1402, Managua; tel. and fax (2) 66-3065; e-mail fntsid@ibw.com.ni; Dir DAVE GODSON; 25,000 mems.

Federación de Transportadores Unidos Nicaragüense (FTUN) (United Transport Workers' Federation of Nicaragua): De donde fue el Vocacional, esq. este, 30 m al sur, Apdo 945, Managua; f. 1952; Pres. MANUEL SABALLOS; 2,880 mems (est.) from 21 affiliated associations.

Frente Nacional de los Trabajadores (FNT) (National Workers' Front): Residencial Bolonia, de la Optica Nicaragüense, 2 c. arriba, 30 varas al sur, Managua; tel. and fax (2) 66-3065; e-mail fnt@ibw.com.ni; f. 1979; affiliated to Frente Sandinista de Liberación

NICARAGUA

Nacional; Leader Dr Gustavo Porras Cortés; Sec.-Gen. José A. Bermúdez.

Unión Nacional de Agricultores y Ganaderos (UNAG) (National Union of Agricultural and Livestock Workers): Contiguo Edif. Julia Pasos, Reparto Las Palmas, $3\frac{1}{2}$ km Carretera Sur, Managua; tel. (2) 66-1675; fax (2) 66-2135; e-mail unag@unag.org.ni; internet www.unag.org.ni; f. 1981; Pres. Alvaro Fiallos Oyanguren.

Unión Nacional de Caficultores de Nicaragua (UNCAFENIC) (National Union of Coffee Growers of Nicaragua): Reparto San Juan, Casa 300, Apdo 3447, Managua; tel. (2) 78-2586; fax (2) 78-2587; Pres. Freddy Torres.

Unión Nacional de Empleados (UNE): Managua; e-mail cocentrafemenino@xerox.com.ni; f. 1978; public sector workers' union; Sec.-Gen. Domingo Pérez; 18,000 mems.

Unión de Productores Agropecuarios de Nicaragua (UPANIC) (Union of Agricultural Producers of Nicaragua): Reparto San Juan, Casa 300, Apdo 2351, Managua; tel. (2) 78-3382; fax (2) 78-2587; Pres. Manuel Alvarez.

Transport

RAILWAYS

Ferrocarril de Nicaragua: Plantel Central Casimiro Sotelo, Del Parque San Sebastián, 5 c. al lago, Apdo 5, Managua; tel. (2) 22-2160; fax (2) 22-2542; f. 1881; govt-owned; main line from León via Managua to Granada on Lake Nicaragua (132 km), southern branch line between Masaya and Diriamba (44 km), northern branch line between León and Río Grande (86 km) and Puerto Sandino branch line between Ceiba Mocha and Puerto Sandino (25 km); total length 287 km; reported to have ceased operations in 1994.

ROADS

In 2000 there were an estimated 19,032 km of roads, of which 2,093 km were paved. Of the total, only some 9,000–10,000 km were accessible throughout the entire year. Some 8,000 km of roads were damaged by 'Hurricane Mitch', which struck in late 1998. The Pan-American Highway runs for 384 km in Nicaragua and links Managua with the Honduran and Costa Rican frontiers and the Atlantic and Pacific Highways connecting Managua with the coastal regions.

SHIPPING

Corinto, Puerto Sandino and San Juan del Sur, on the Pacific, and Puerto Cabezas, El Bluff and El Rama, on the Caribbean, are the principal ports. Corinto deals with about 60% of trade. In 2001 the US-based company Delasa was given a 25-year concession to develop and modernize Puerto Cabezas port. It was to invest some US $200m.

Empresa Portuaria Nacional (EPN): Apdo 2727–3570, Managua; tel. (2) 22-3827; fax (2) 66-3488; e-mail epn_puertos@epn.com.ni; internet www.epn.com.ni; Pres. Alejandro Fiallos Navarro.

Administración Portuaria de Bluefields-Bluff: tel. (8) 22-2632; e-mail puertobluff@epn.com.ni.

Administración Portuaria de Corinto: De Telcor, 1 c. al oeste, Corinto; tel. (3) 42-2768; e-mail puertocorinto@epn.com.ni; f. 1956.

Administración Portuaria de San Juan del Sur: tel. (4) 58-2336; e-mail puertosanjuan@epn.com.ni.

Administración Portuaria de Puerto Cabezas: tel. (2) 82-2331.

Administración Portuaria de Sandino: tel. (3) 12-2212; e-mail puertosandino@epn.com.ni.

CIVIL AVIATION

The principal airport is the Augusto Sandino International Airport, in Managua. There are some 185 additional airports in Nicaragua.

Empresa Administradora de Aeropuertos Internacionales (EAAI): POB 5179, 11 Km Carretera Norte, Managua; tel. (2) 33-1624; fax (2) 63-1072; e-mail webm@eaai.com.ni; internet www.eaai.com.ni; autonomous govt entity; operates Managua International Airport and three national airports: Bluefields, Puerto Cabezas and Corn Island; Pres. Danilo Lacayo Rappacioli; Gen. Man. Alfredo Chamorro.

Atlantic Airlines: Estatua José Martí, 150 m este, Managua; tel. (2) 22-3037; fax (2) 28-5614; e-mail reservaciones@atlanticairlines.com.ni; internet www.atlanticairlines.com.ni; scheduled domestic services, charters, cargo transportation and courier services; Gen. Man. Luis Arévalo.

La Costeña: Managua International Airport, Managua; tel. (2) 63-2142; fax (2) 63-1281; e-mail info@flycostena.com.ni; internet www.tacaregional.com/costena/; Gen. Man. Alfredo Caballero.

Tourism

In 2003 tourist arrivals totalled 525,775 and receipts from tourism totalled US $155m.

Instituto Nicaragüense de Turismo (INTUR): Del Hotel Intercontinental Managua, 1 c. al sur, 1 c. al oeste, Managua; tel. (2) 22-6460; fax (2) 22-6610; e-mail promocion@intur.gob.ni; internet www.visit-Nicaragua.com; f. 1998; Pres. María Nelly Rivas Blanco; Vice-Pres. Ruth Sequeira.

Asociación Nicaragüense de Agencias de Viajes y Turismo (ANAVYT): Edif. Policlínica Nicaragüense, Reparto Bolonia, Apdo 1045, Managua; tel. (2) 66-9742; fax (2) 66-4474; e-mail aeromund@cablenet.com.ni; f. 1966; Pres. Ana María Rocha C.

Cámara Nacional de Turismo (CANATUR): Contiguo al Ministerio de Turismo, Apdo 2105, Managua; tel. (2) 66-5071; fax (2) 66-5071; e-mail canatur@munditel.com.ni; f. 1976.

NIGER

Introductory Survey

Location, Climate, Language, Religion, Flag, Capital

The Republic of Niger is a land-locked country in western Africa, with Algeria and Libya to the north, Nigeria and Benin to the south, Mali and Burkina Faso to the west, and Chad to the east. The climate is hot and dry, with an average temperature of 29°C (84°F). The official language is French, but numerous indigenous languages, including Hausa (spoken by about one-half of the population), Tuareg, Djerma and Fulani, are also used (the 1991 sovereign National Conference identified 10 'national' languages). Some 95% of the population are Muslims, the most influential Islamic groups being the Tijaniyya, the Senoussi and the Hamallists. Most of the remainder of the population follow traditional beliefs, and there is a small Christian minority. The national flag (proportions 6 by 7) has three equal horizontal stripes, of orange, white and green, with an orange disc in the centre of the white stripe. The capital is Niamey.

Recent History

Formerly a part of French West Africa, Niger became a self-governing member of the French Community in December 1958 and was granted independence on 3 August 1960. Hamani Diori, leader of the Parti progressiste nigérien (the local section of the Ivorian-dominated Rassemblement démocratique africain) and Prime Minister since December 1958, became Head of State. Following the suppression of Djibo Bakary's left-wing nationalist Union nigérienne démocratique—Sawaba in 1959, Diori was elected President in November 1960, and re-elected in 1965 and 1970. Close links were maintained with France.

The Sahelian drought of 1968–74 was particularly damaging to the Nigerien economy and was a major factor in precipitating a military coup in April 1974. Diori was arrested, and Lt-Col (later Maj.-Gen.) Seyni Kountché, the armed forces Chief of Staff, became President. The new administration, headed by a Conseil militaire suprême (CMS), suspended the Constitution; the legislature was replaced by a consultative Conseil national de développement (CND), and political activity was banned. Kountché obtained the withdrawal of French troops and reduced French influence over the exploitation of Niger's deposits of uranium (which France had initiated in 1968). In August 1975 Djibo Bakary (who had returned to Niger from exile following the coup) was arrested, together with the Vice-Chairman of the CMS and the head of the national groundnut company, on charges of plotting to seize power.

From 1977 the proportion of army officers in the Government was progressively reduced. Senior members of Diori's administration and other political prisoners were released in 1978, and in 1980 Diori and Bakary were released from prison, although Diori was kept under house arrest. In January 1983 a civilian, Oumarou Mamane, was appointed to the newly created post of Prime Minister. In October, while Kountché was overseas, ministers loyal to his regime thwarted a coup attempt by military officers. Two government ministers were among those arrested, although the suspected architects of the plot fled Niger. In November Mamane, who in August had been appointed President of the CND, was replaced as premier by Hamid Algabid.

A draft 'national charter' was approved by a reported 99.6% of voters in a referendum in June 1987. In November Kountché died while undergoing medical treatment in France, and Col (later Brig.) Ali Saïbou, the army Chief of Staff, was inaugurated as Chairman of the CMS and Head of State. Diori was released from house arrest, and an appeal was made to exiled Nigeriens to return to the country. (Diori died in Morocco in 1989.) In December 1987 an amnesty was proclaimed for all political prisoners. In July 1988 Mamane (who had been replaced as President of the CND in September 1987) was reinstated as Prime Minister, and the CND was given the task of drafting a new constitution. In August 1988 Brig. Saïbou formed a new ruling party, the Mouvement national pour la société de développement (MNSD). In October four of those who had been implicated in the 1983 coup attempt were sentenced, in absentia, to death; 16 others received prison sentences.

In May 1989 an MNSD congress elected a Conseil supérieur d'orientation nationale (CSON) to succeed the CMS. The draft Constitution was endorsed by a reported 99.3% of voters in a referendum in September. At elections in December Saïbou (as President of the CSON, the sole candidate) was confirmed as President of the Republic, for a seven-year term, by 99.6% of those who voted, while 99.5% of voters endorsed a single list of CSON-approved deputies to a new, 93-member Assemblée nationale. It was subsequently announced that Niger's two remaining political prisoners were to be released, to commemorate Saïbou's inauguration as President of what was designated the Second Republic. In March 1990 a prominent industrialist, Aliou Mahamidou, was appointed Prime Minister in an extensive government reorganization. In June the CSON announced that the Constitution was to be amended to facilitate a transition to political pluralism. In November Saïbou announced that a multi-party political system would be established. A national conference on political reform was to be convened in mid-1991, and multi-party national elections would take place in 1992.

In March 1991 the armed forces Chief of Staff announced that the armed forces were to distance themselves from the MNSD with immediate effect. In July Saïbou resigned as Chairman of the MNSD, in preparation for the National Conference, which was convened in Niamey later that month and attended by about 1,200 delegates, including representatives of the organs of state, 24 political organizations, the military and civil society. It declared itself sovereign, voting to suspend the Constitution and dissolve the legislature. Saïbou would remain in office as Head of State on an interim basis, but the Conference would supervise the exercise of his (now largely ceremonial) powers. The Government was dissolved in September, and in October the Conference appointed Cheiffou Amadou to head a transitional Council of Ministers, which was intended to hold office until the inauguration of democratically elected institutions, now scheduled for early 1993. Prior to the conclusion of the Conference, in November 1991, its President, André Salifou, was designated Chairman of a 15-member interim legislative body, the Haut conseil de la République (HCR), which was, inter alia, to supervise the drafting of a new constitution.

The new Constitution was approved by 89.8% of those who voted in a referendum held on 26 December 1992. The MNSD won the greatest number of seats (29) at elections to the 83-member Assemblée nationale, held on 14 February 1993 and contested by 12 political parties, but was prevented from resuming power by the rapid formation, following the elections, of the Alliance des forces de changement (AFC) by six parties with a total of 50 seats in the legislature. Principal members of the AFC were the Convention démocratique et sociale—Rahama (CDS), the Parti nigérien pour la démocratie et le socialisme—Tarayya (PNDS), and the Alliance nigérienne pour la démocratie et le progrès social—Zaman Lahiya (ANDP). At the first round of the presidential election, held on 27 February and contested by eight candidates, Col (retd) Mamadou Tandja, Saïbou's successor as leader of the MNSD, won the greatest proportion of votes cast (34.2%). He and his nearest rival, Mahamane Ousmane (the leader of the CDS, with 26.6%), proceeded to a second round on 27 March, at which Ousmane was elected President by 55.4% of voters; his inauguration took place on 16 April. Ousmane appointed Mahamadou Issoufou of the PNDS, as Prime Minister. Despite an attempt by the MNSD to block the appointment, in May, Moumouni Adamou Djermakoye of the ANDP, became President of the Assemblée nationale.

The new regime's efforts to curb public expenditure, combined with the effects of the 50% devaluation of the CFA franc in January 1994, provoked considerable disquiet among workers and students. In September the PNDS withdrew from the AFC, and Issoufou resigned the premiership, in protest at the perceived transfer of certain prime ministerial powers to the President. A new minority Government, led by Souley Abdoulaye of the CDS, failed to withstand a parliamentary motion of 'no confidence' proposed by the MNSD and the PNDS in October. Ousmane therefore dissolved the Assemblée nationale.

At legislative elections held in mid-January 1995 the MNSD won 29 seats and subsequently led a 43-strong majority group in the Assemblée nationale. Although the CDS increased its representation to 24 seats, the AFC secured only 40 seats. Ousmane declined to accept the new majority's nominee to the premiership, Hama Amadou (the Secretary-General of the MNSD), instead appointing another member of that party, Amadou Aboubacar Cissé, a former official of the World Bank. The MNSD and its allies announced that they would not co-operate with his administration, and Cissé was expelled from the party. Meanwhile, Issoufou was elected President of the Assemblée nationale. In February the legislature approved a motion of censure against Cissé, and Ousmane accepted the nomination of Amadou as Prime Minister. This political 'cohabitation' encountered serious difficulties, as the President and Prime Minister disputed their respective competencies, in particular with regard to a proposed programme for the reorganization and privatization of state enterprises, which Ousmane opposed. Following several months of industrial unrest, Ousmane's rejection of the Government's draft budget, in January 1996, resulted in a new impasse in relations.

On 27 January 1996 the elected organs of state were overthrown by the military. The coup leaders, who formed a Conseil de salut national (CSN), chaired by Col (later Brig.-Gen.) Ibrahim Baré Maïnassara, armed forces Chief of Staff since March 1995 and a former aide-de-camp to Kountché, asserted that their seizure of power had been necessitated by Niger's descent into political chaos. The CSN suspended the Constitution and dissolved the Assemblée nationale, while political parties were suspended. A national forum was to be convened to consider the revision of the Constitution and the electoral code, and to determine a timetable for a return to civilian rule. The CSN appointed Boukary Adji, the Deputy Governor of the Banque centrale des états de l'Afrique de l'ouest (and Minister of Finance in 1983–87) as Prime Minister. Adji's transitional Government, named in February 1996, was composed entirely of civilians, including the former HCR President, André Salifou, although military officers were appointed to regional governorships. In that month Ousmane, Amadou and Issoufou signed a joint text, in Maïnassara's presence, which effectively endorsed the legitimacy of the CSN and stated that the assumption of power by the military had been necessitated by the prolonged administrative difficulties that had preceded it.

Two consultative bodies were established to prepare for the restoration of civilian government, the advisory Conseil des sages (which elected Saïbou as its Chairman) and the co-ordinating committee of the national forum. The National Forum for Democratic Renewal, which was convened in April 1996, adopted revisions to the Constitution that aimed to guarantee greater institutional stability, essentially by conferring executive power solely on the President. In April Ousmane, Amadou and Issoufou accompanied Maïnassara to northern Niger to celebrate National Concord Day, on the first anniversary of the signing of the peace agreement with the Tuareg movement (see below).

By May 1996 Maïnassara had confirmed reports of his intention, which he had initially denied, to seek election as President. The revised Constitution was approved by some 92.3% of the votes cast at a referendum on 12 May (about 35% of the electorate participated). The ban on political activity was lifted shortly afterwards. Ousmane, Issoufou, Tandja and Djermakoye swiftly announced their intention to contest the presidential election. There was much criticism among opposition groups of the appointment of a new High Court of Justice, which was to be solely responsible for trying cases of high treason and other offences committed by public figures (including past officials) in the exercise of their state duties. Moreover, tensions between the authorities and the Commission électorale nationale indépendante (CENI) became increasingly evident, as the Government disregarded the latter's recommendation that the presidential election be postponed, in response to various logistical delays.

Voting in the presidential election commenced, as scheduled, on 7 July 1996, but was quickly halted in several areas where preparations were incomplete: polling took place in these areas on 8 July. Shortly before the end of voting the authorities announced the dissolution of the CENI, citing its alleged obstruction of the electoral process. A new commission was appointed to collate the election results. Meanwhile, Maïnassara's four rivals for the presidency were placed under house arrest. According to provisional results, announced by the new commission, Maïnassara won the election, with some 52.2% of the votes cast, Ousmane secured 19.8%, and Tandja 15.7%. The Supreme Court validated the election results on 21 July, and the release from house arrest of the defeated candidates was announced on the following day. Maïnassara was installed as President on 7 August 1996. A new Government, with Adji as Prime Minister, also included Abdoulaye and Cissé. Members of the CDS, the MNSD and the PNDS who had accepted government posts were subsequently expelled from these parties.

In August 1996 the legislative elections, which had been scheduled for September, were postponed until 10 November. The Conseil des sages recommended a further delay, pending the resolution of difficulties, including the threatened boycott by the main opposition parties, now grouped in a Front pour la restauration et la défense de la démocratie (FRDD). At Maïnassara's instigation, the Government undertook inter-party negotiations, mediated by the Conseil des sages. The Government agreed to permit opposition access to the state media and to rescind the ban (in force since the presidential election) on public meetings and demonstrations, and in October announced the further postponement of the legislative elections, to 23 November, and the restoration of the CENI, with the same composition as that which had overseen the 1995 election. The commission's prerogatives were, however, amended, and the FRDD responded that it would not participate in the forthcoming poll unless the CENI was reinstated with its original powers and the presidential election annulled.

The legislative elections proceeded on 23 November 1996, contested by 11 parties and movements. According to official results, the pro-Maïnassara Union nationale des indépendants pour le renouveau démocratique (UNIRD) won 52 of the Assemblée nationale's 83 seats. International observers pronounced themselves satisfied with the organization and conduct of the election. (The Supreme Court later annulled the results in three constituencies won by the UNIRD, on the grounds of fraud.) A new Government was formed, with Cissé as Prime Minister. The FRDD rejected an invitation to participate in the Government, and the deputy leader of the CDS, Sanoussi Jackou, was expelled from the party after accepting a ministerial post.

In January 1997 an unauthorized opposition demonstration in Niamey degenerated into clashes with the security forces. Some 62 people were arrested, among them Ousmane, Tandja and Issoufou, who were to be tried by the recently restored State Security Court. In response to opposition claims that neither the Constitution nor the penal code made provision for the Court (which had been in existence under the Kountché regime), the Government cited constitutional provisions that ensured the continued validity of laws in force at the time of the promulgation of the Constitution, unless specifically repealed. Nine days later, following clashes in Zinder and a further protest in Niamey, the opposition leaders were released, reportedly on Maïnassara's direct order. The FRDD rejected an invitation by the President to participate in a government of national unity, demanding the dissolution of the Assemblée nationale and the holding of free and fair elections.

In November 1997 Maïnassara dismissed the entire Government: a resumption of hostilities in the north had been compounded by poor harvests and by further labour unrest. Maïnassara appointed Ibrahim Hassane Maiyaki, hitherto Minister of Foreign Affairs and Co-operation, as Prime Minister and named a new Council of Ministers in December.

In January 1998 it was announced that members of a commando unit had been arrested and charged with attempting to overthrow Maïnassara and other senior officials. Four of the accused made a televised confession, stating that they had been operating on the direct orders of former Prime Minister Amadou, who was himself arrested. Amadou was released on bail shortly afterwards, charged with forming a militia, criminal conspiracy and illegal possession of weapons. In February soldiers at three military garrisons in the Diffa region, in the south-east, mutinied, taking hostage local military commanders and civilian administrators. The rebels imposed a curfew and demanded the payment of four months' salary arrears. Despite reassurances from the Government, the mutiny spread to the north—to Agadez and Arlit—and to Zinder. All the rebellions had been abandoned by early March, after the Government promised payment of two months' salary arrears and undertook to establish a minimum standard of living for all military personnel.

In February 1998 three parties of the presidential group, including the ANDP, formed the Alliance des forces démocratiques et sociales (AFDS). However, the AFDS subsequently protested against its perceived marginalization in the political process and in the state media, observing that the alliance was increasingly associated with the opposition. Clashes in Tahoua in April between the security forces and FRDD activists, who were demanding Maïnassara's resignation, were followed by violent protests by the FRDD in Maradi and in Zinder. In July the Government and the FRDD and the AFDS signed an agreement that was intended to facilitate opposition participation in the local elections. Revisions to electoral procedures and institutions were outlined, while the equal access of all political groups to the state media and the freedom to demonstrate were to be guaranteed. However, following a dispute over the President of the CENI, in October the CENI postponed voting until February 1999.

Voting in the regional, district and municipal elections took place on 7 February 1999, one day after the Minister of the Interior, Souley Abdoulaye, had presented a document purportedly giving evidence of an opposition plot to obtain full control of the state. Following the discovery of overt irregularities, the CENI emphasized that it favoured by-elections in affected areas. Full results, which were not released by the Supreme Court until 7 April, gave the 11 opposition parties a slim overall majority of seats in those municipal, district and regional assemblies where the elections were deemed valid. Voting was to be rerun at some 4,000 polling stations nation-wide. The FRDD and AFDS denounced Maïnassara as personally responsible for the disruption to voting and demanded the President's resignation.

On 9 April 1999 Maiyaki made a broadcast to the nation, announcing the death of Maïnassara in an 'unfortunate accident' at a military airbase in Niamey. The Prime Minister stated that the defence and security forces would continue to be the guarantors of republican order and national unity, and announced the dissolution of the Assemblée nationale, as well as the temporary suspension of all party political activity. Despite the official explanation for his death, it was generally perceived that members of the presidential guard had assassinated Maïnassara in a *coup d'état*. Although members of the Assemblée nationale initially rejected its dissolution, on 11 April the Constitution was suspended, and its institutions dissolved. The February local elections were annulled. A military Conseil de réconciliation nationale (CRN), under the chairmanship of Maj. Daouda Mallam Wanké (hitherto head of the presidential guard), was to exercise executive and legislative authority during a nine-month transitional period, prior to the restoration of elected civilian institutions. Wanké immediately signed an ordinance on interim political authority, which was to function as a constitutional document during the transitional period. Maiyaki was reappointed as Prime Minister of the transitional Government on 12 April; a new Council of Ministers was named shortly afterwards. Moussa Moumouni Djermakoye, who had been succeeded as armed forces Chief of Staff by Lt-Col Soumara Zanguina, became Minister of National Defence. In July, in a minor reshuffle, the Minister of the Interior and Territorial Administration, Lt-Col Moumouni Boureima, was appointed armed forces Chief of Staff, while Zanguina became an adviser to the Head of State.

The new draft Constitution was submitted to referendum on 18 July 1999, when it was approved by 89.6% of those who voted (about one-third of the registered electorate). The Constitution, promulgated by Wanké on 9 August, envisaged a balance of powers between the President, the Government and the legislature, but, none the less, vested strong powers in the Head of State, who was to be politically liable only in the case of high treason. The Government, under a Prime Minister appointed by the President, was to be responsible to the Assemblée nationale, which would be competent to remove the Prime Minister by vote of censure. A clause in the Constitution guaranteeing all those involved in the military take-overs of 1996 and 1999 immunity from prosecution provoked controversy and was condemned by Amnesty International, in a report in September, as undermining the rule of law. The report was regarded as particularly significant in that it published the testimony of a witness who alleged that Maïnassara had been killed by the presidential guard under Wanké's command. The Wanké regime continued to assert that Maïnassara's death had been accidental, and that a commission of inquiry into the death had been ordered in response to a complaint lodged by the late President's family.

Voting at the presidential election, which was contested by seven candidates, took place on 17 October 1999, and was considered both by the CENI and by independent observers to have been largely transparent and peaceful. Mamadou Tandja, of the MNSD, won 32.3% of the votes cast, followed by Issoufou, of the PNDS, with 22.8%, and Ousmane, of the CDS, with 22.5%. The rate of participation by voters was 43.7%. Tandja and Issoufou proceeded to a second round on 24 November. Having secured the support of Ousmane, Tandja was elected President, with 59.9% of the votes cast. About 39% of the registered electorate voted. The MNSD was similarly successful in the concurrent elections to the Assemblée nationale, winning 38 of the 83 seats; the CDS took 17, the PNDS 16, the pro-Maïnassara Rassemblement pour la démocratie et le progrès—Djamaa (RDP) eight and the ANDP four. Tandja, who had served in the CMS under Kountché and was Minister of the Interior in the early 1990s, was inaugurated as President on 22 December. Hama Amadou was subsequently appointed Prime Minister, and a new Council of Ministers was named in January 2000.

In January 2000 the Assemblée nationale adopted draft amnesty legislation, as provided for in the Constitution. The amnesty was opposed by the RDP, and many activists of the party joined a demonstration in February to denounce the legislation and to demand an international inquiry into the death of Maïnassara. In March 12 opposition parties, led by the PNDS, formed a coalition, the Coordination des forces démocratiques (CFD). Similarly, 17 parties loyal to the President, most notably the MNSD and the CDS, formed the Alliance des forces démocratiques (AFD). In May Col Bourahima Moumouni was appointed armed forces Chief of Staff. None the less, rumours persisted of dissent within the army; in June Amadou warned that, without a restoration of military discipline, the threat of further uprisings could not be ignored. Also in that month 10 soldiers were arrested, following the kidnapping and arrest of Maj. Djibrilla Hima, a spokesman for the former Wanké regime.

In September 2001 President Tandja reshuffled the Council of Ministers, retaining Prime Minister Amadou and 10 of his ministers, although there were some 13 new appointments. In October opposition parties tabled a further censure motion against the Government in the Assemblée nationale, although the motion was withdrawn before voting could proceed, in response to concerns that it would negatively affect the Government's ongoing negotiations with the World Bank and the European Union (EU, see p. 228).

In the early 2000s demands for the introduction of Islamic *Shari'a* law became a source of tension in Niger. In November 2000 violent protests erupted in Niamey and Maradi in response to a fashion show held in the capital. Following the demonstrations, some 270 people, reportedly including prominent religious leaders, were arrested, although 240 of the protesters were released promptly without charge. Islamist leaders, who condemned the show as an incitement to debauchery, had instigated the protests. In early July 2002 two Islamist activists, who had demanded the introduction of the *Shari'a* in a letter to Tandja, were charged with incitement to revolt.

In July 2002 the ANDP withdrew from the opposition CFD alliance and joined the AFD, thereby increasing the Government's parliamentary majority by four seats. Explaining his party's shift in allegiances, the leader of the ANDP, Moumouni Adamou Djermakoye, accused the CFD of intolerance and of failing to ease social tensions.

In late July 2002 a further mutiny broke out at a barracks in Diffa. The mutineers arrested several officers, and the mayor of Diffa and the regional governor, and took control of a radio station to broadcast their demands for improved pay and conditions, including the payment of wage arrears. The Government declared a state of emergency in Diffa and dispatched troops to bring the rebellion, which continued for 10 days, to a halt. Six soldiers, including three officers, were arrested in connection with the rebellion, but other rebel soldiers were reported to have fled the region, while a further uprising, at a barracks to the east of Diffa, was rapidly quashed. In early August, meanwhile, a military uprising broke out in Niamey, although government forces quickly restored order in the capital. By mid-September special security measures in the Diffa region had been relaxed. Amadou claimed that the rebellion in Diffa had been intended to serve as a distraction, while a *coup d'état* was being prepared in Niamey. In mid-September the President and Vice-President of the Constitutional Court resigned, following a ruling by the Court, earlier in the month, that two decrees announced by President Tandja in relation to the suppression of the rebellion were unconstitutional; in particular, the imposition of emergency measures by the Head of State without consulting the Prime Minister, the Assemblée nationale and the Constitutional Court was deemed a breach of constitutional requirements, while a further decree, which restricted media coverage of the uprising, was also determined to be illegal.

Tandja implemented a major government reshuffle in November 2002, as a result of which the position of allies of Prime Minister Amadou was reportedly strengthened. Among the 13 new ministerial appointments was Moumouni Adamou Djermakoye as Minister of State, responsible for African Integration and the NEPAD (New Partnership for Africa's Development, see p. 157) Programmes, while seven ministers left the Government. Although several principal positions remained unchanged, new appointments were made to the Ministries of National Defence and of the Interior and Decentralization. At the end of December the Assemblée nationale approved legislation providing for the creation of a special military tribunal to try those accused of involvement in the rebellion earlier in the year (a total of 268 arrests were reported); elements within the opposition alleged that the legislation violated several articles of the Constitution. However, many soldiers were reportedly released during 2003, owing to a lack of evidence, and the three highest-ranking officers arrested were provisionally freed in February 2004. (Six of the mutineers were awarded custodial sentences at a military tribunal in early 2006.)

In June 2003 the Assemblée nationale approved amendments to the electoral code proposed by President Tandja. Henceforth, ministers seeking elected office would no longer be obliged to resign from their government posts, while the requirement that the CENI be chaired by a judge was to be abolished. Opposition parties boycotted the vote, stating that reforms to electoral law had hitherto been decided by consensus, and the CFD declared its intention to challenge the revised code at the Constitutional Court. Following an attempt by the opposition to introduce a vote of censure against the Government, Amadou closed the legislative session before such a vote could be held. However, by August tensions between the Government and the opposition regarding the CENI had abated, and a Chairman (a judge, Hamidou Salifou Kane) was appointed, with the support of the CFD. In mid-October the Council of Ministers announced proposals to increase the number of deputies in the Assemblée nationale from 83 to 113, in order to reflect the growth in the population recorded between the national censuses of 1988 and 2001. A minor government reshuffle was effected later in October 2003. Also in that month the Council of Ministers approved the abolition of the State Security Court.

In early February 2004 it was announced that municipal elections, initially scheduled to be held on 28 March, had been postponed until 29 May, owing to logistical difficulties experienced by several political parties. In mid-February Rhissa Ag Boula a former Tuareg rebel leader (see below), was dismissed as Minister of Tourism and Crafts, following allegations that he was implicated in the murder of an MNSD activist earlier in the year; he was subsequently arrested and charged with complicity in the murder. Meanwhile, another former Tuareg rebel leader, Mohamed Anako, was appointed as Minister-delegate at the Ministry of the Economy and Finance, responsible for the Taxation of Local Communities and the Informal Sector.

In mid-May 2004 the CDS announced that the party's Chairman, former President Ousmane, would be its candidate in the presidential election due to be held in December. Later that month several trade unions organized a series of strikes in support of demands for improved working and living conditions for public-sector workers following the failure of negotiations with the authorities. The municipal elections, which had been further postponed in May, were held on 24 July. According to provisional results, pro-presidential parties won a total of 2,335 of the 3,747 seats in the country's 265 communes (the MNSD 1,388, the CDS 748 and the ANDP 199), while, of the opposition parties, the PNDS secured 821 seats, coming second overall, and the RDP 217. The non-aligned Rassemblement social-démocratique—Gaskiya (RSD), which had been formed following a split in the CDS, also unexpectedly won 217 seats; the turn-out was 43.6%. In mid-August press freedom groups expressed concern at the detention of Moussa Kaka, the director of an independent radio station, Saraounia, following an interview broadcast by the station with an apparent member of the FLAA (see below), who claimed responsibility for a recent attack on three buses in the north of the country, in which three passengers had died.

In the first round of the presidential election, held on 16 November 2004 and contested by six candidates, Tandja won 40.7% of votes cast, followed by Issoufou, who received 24.6%, and Ousmane, who took 17.4%. Tandja and Issoufou therefore proceeded to a second round of voting, while the four eliminated candidates (representing the CDS, the RSD, the ANDP and the RDP) all urged their supporters to transfer their allegiance to Tandja. In the second round of voting, held on 4 December, Tandja was victorious, receiving 65.5% of votes cast. (Turn-out in the first round was reported to be 48.5% of registered voters, declining slightly, to 45.0%, in the second round.) At elections to the newly enlarged 113-seat Assemblée nationale, held concurrently with the second round of voting in the presidential election, the MNSD won the largest number of seats, obtaining 47, while allied pro-presidential parties secured a further 41 seats—22 were taken by the CDS, seven by the RSD, six by the RDP, five by the ANDP and one seat by the Parti Social Démocrate du Niger—Alheri (PSDN). An opposition coalition formed around the PNDS, which also comprised the Parti nigérien pour l'autogestion (PNA), the Parti progressiste nigérien pour le rassemblement démocratique africain (PPN-RDA), the Union pour la démocratie et la République (UDR) and the Union nigérienne des indépendants (UNI), won a total of 25 seats. Ousmane was subsequently re-elected as President of the Assemblée nationale, 13 seats in which, in accordance with legislation adopted in 2001, were reserved for women. The elections were pronounced 'free, fair and transparent' by international observers, although the PNDS claimed that various electoral irregularities had occurred, including the use of state funds to finance the campaign of the MNSD. Later in December President Tandja announced the formation of a new Government, in which Amadou remained as Prime Minister. The new Government comprised 27 ministers; nine ministers were retained from the previous cabinet. During the course of 2005 several observers noted an increasing degree of political consensus in Niger between the Government and the opposition; in particular, it was reported that Issoufou was involved in regular consultations with the authorities.

The Government was criticized by human rights groups in early March 2005, after the cancellation of a ceremony at which some 7,000 people purported to be slaves were to be 'freed'; the Government denied that slavery (which had been criminalized in May 2003) continued to exist in Niger, although activists estimated that at least 43,000 people remained in slavery across the country. In early May 2005 two anti-slavery campaigners were arrested and charged with fraud for allegedly attempting to elicit funds illegally from foreign donors. Later that month some 2,000 people participated in a march in Niamey to demand their release; they were freed on bail in mid-June.

In mid-March 2005 up to 20,000 people were reported to have participated in demonstrations in Niamey against the recent introduction of a 19% value-added tax on basic commodities. The demonstration, which ended in isolated incidents of violence against property, was organized by an alliance of some 30 groups, including trade unions, human rights organizations and consumer movements known as the Coalition contre la vie chère (CCVC). In the following week, after the Government refused to authorize a second protest march, the CCVC staged a one-day strike, which halted most activity in the capital. The authorities subsequently agreed to hold talks with the CCVC, although they emphasized that the tax would not be withdrawn. However, before the proposed meeting, five leaders of the Coalition were arrested and accused of establishing an unauthorized association and plotting against state security. The radio station Alternative FM, which had broadcast interviews with prominent supporters of the CCVC, and was also closed by police, prompting protests from international press freedom groups. (The director of the station, Moussa Tchangari, was among those arrested.) During a further one-day strike, held a few days later, protesters erected barricades and burned tyres in Maradi and Tahoua, leading to further arrests. A third strike was suspended by the Coalition in early April in the hope that a compromise could be reached with the Government. The five leaders of the CCVC were subsequently released and, following negotiations between the Government and the leadership of the CCVC, agreement was released on numerous concessions; notably flour and milk were to be exempted from the tax, and special arrangements were to be made to limiting the effect of the tax on the cost of water and electricity.

None the less, public discontent with the Government arose again in mid-2005 over severe food shortages, which had largely resulted from a poor harvest in 2004, when low rainfall had been combined with an invasion of locusts. According to the Ministry of Agricultural Development, there was a shortfall of more than 223,000 metric tons of grain, representing the country's largest deficit for more than 20 years. In early June up to 2,000 people marched through Niamey in protest at the Government's failure to respond adequately to the crisis and in support of opposition-backed demands for the distribution of free food. The march was organized by a group of civil society organizations, which accused the authorities of being ill-prepared despite having had sufficient warning of the shortages. Meanwhile, in early May 11 people were killed in Dosso, some 140 km south-east of Niamey, when clashes broke out between nomadic herdsmen and local landowners in a dispute over scarce grazing land. The Government, which had been supplying cereals at subsidized prices in the most stricken areas, appealed for international assistance (the response to a UN appeal for Niger, launched in late 2004, had been extremely limited), but insisted that it did not have the resources to distribute free food and instead announced plans to 'loan' grain to farmers most at risk until they could reimburse the Government after the harvest later in the year. As people reportedly began fleeing to Nigeria, government ministers and officials contributed financially to efforts to alleviate the crisis. In mid-July the UN World Food Programme appealed for further international aid for Niger, noting that its ability to assist those in need had been hampered by a slow response from donors.

Ethnic unrest followed the return to northern Niger, during the late 1980s, of large numbers of Tuareg nomads who had migrated to Libya and Algeria in the early 1980s to escape the Sahelian drought. It was widely believed that the perceived failure of the Saïbou administration to assist in the rehabilitation of returnees was a significant factor contributing to the subsequent Tuareg uprising. In May 1990 some 100 deaths were reported when the military suppressed a Tuareg attack on the prison and gendarmerie at Tchin-Tabaraden. In April 1991 44 Tuaregs were reportedly acquitted of involvement in the attack. In a renewed offensive, which began in October, numerous attacks were directed against official targets in the north, and several members of the armed forces were kidnapped. In January 1992 the transitional authorities intensified security measures in the north and, for the first time, formally acknowledged that there was a rebellion in the country. Rhissa Ag Boula, the leader of the rebel Front de libération de l'Aïr et l'Azaouad (FLAA), subsequently stated that the Tuareg rebels were seeking to achieve the establishment of a federal system of governance. Although the Government and the FLAA concluded a truce agreement in May, violence swiftly resumed. In August the security forces launched a major offensive against rebel Tuareg groups. Military authority was reinforced in October by the appointment of senior members of the security forces to northern administrative posts. In November, none the less, a commission that had been appointed by the transitional Government recommended a far-reaching programme of decentralization, according legal status and financial authority to local communities. In December the Government announced the release from custody of 57 Tuaregs.

In January 1993 five people were killed in a Tuareg attack on a meeting of the MNSD attended by Mamadou Tandja (who was Minister of the Interior at the time of the suppression of the Tchin-Tabaraden raid) in the northern town of Abala. Later in January 81 Tuaregs were released from detention, and a Minister of State for National Reconciliation, whose main responsibility would be to seek a solution to the Tuareg issue, was appointed to the Government. In March, following Algerian mediation, Ag Boula (who was based in Algeria) agreed that the FLAA would observe a truce for the duration of the campaign for the second round of the presidential election. Shortly afterwards Tuareg representatives in Niamey signed a similar (French-brokered) agreement. In April the outgoing transitional Government and the FLAA agreed to extend the truce indefinitely; the remaining Tuareg prisoners were subsequently released from detention, and the rebels released their hostages.

The Ousmane administration identified the resolution of the Tuareg issue as a priority. In mid-1993 a three-month truce agreement between representatives of the Government and the Tuaregs, which provided for the demilitarization of the north, and envisaged negotiations on the Tuaregs' political demands, was signed in Paris, France. However, a new group, the Armée révolutionnaire de libération du nord-Niger (ARLN), emerged to denounce the truce, and supporters of the truce (led by Mano

Dayak, the Tuareg signatory to the agreement) broke away from the FLAA to form the Front de libération de Tamoust (FLT): Ag Boula and the remainder of the FLAA stated that they could not support any agreement that contained no specific commitment to discussion of federalism. In September the FLT and the Government agreed to extend the truce for a further three months. Although the FLAA and the ARLN refused to sign the accord, in October they joined with the FLT in a Coordination de la résistance armée (CRA), with the aim of presenting a cohesive programme in future negotiations.

Despite an escalation of violence during May 1994, as a result of which as many as 40 deaths were recorded, negotiations took place in Paris in June. Tentative agreement was reached on the creation of ethnically based autonomous regions, each of which was to have its own elected assembly and governor to function in parallel with the organs of central government. Despite renewed unrest, in September the CRA presented Nigerien government negotiators with a plan for the restoration of peace. Formal negotiations resumed, with mediation by the Burkinabè President, Blaise Compaoré, as well as representatives of France and Algeria, in Ouagadougou (Burkina Faso) in October. A new peace accord resulted, emphasizing that Niger was 'unitary and indivisible', while proposing the establishment of elected assemblies or councils for territorial communities, which would be responsible for the implementation of economic, social and cultural policies. The Government was to take immediate measures to ensure the rehabilitation and security of areas affected by the conflict. Provisions were also to be made to facilitate the return and resettlement of refugees. A renewable three-month truce was to take immediate effect, to be monitored by French and Burkinabè military units. By the time of the conclusion of the Ouagadougou agreement the number of deaths since the escalation of the Tuareg rebellion in late 1991 was officially put at 150. A commission was established in January 1995 to consider the administrative reorganization of the country.

Ag Boula, who had withdrawn from the CRA, and refused to participate in the decentralization committee, in protest at alleged delays in the implementation of the provisions of the October 1994 agreement, emerged as the leader of the Tuareg delegation (now renamed the Organisation de la résistance armée—ORA) at negotiations in Ouagadougou in March 1995. In April it was announced that a lasting peace agreement had been reached. Demobilized rebels were to be integrated into the Nigerien military and public sector; particular emphasis was to be placed on the economic, social and cultural development of the north, and the Government undertook to support the decentralization process. There was to be a general amnesty for all parties involved in the Tuareg rebellion and its suppression, and a day of national reconciliation was to be instituted in memory of the victims of the conflict. The peace agreement was formally signed by Ag Boula and a representative of the Nigerien Government on 24 April 1995, one day before the cease-fire took effect.

Meanwhile, there was increasing ethnic unrest in the Lake Chad region of south-east Niger, where several thousand (mainly Toubou) Chadian refugees had settled since the overthrow of President Hissène Habré in late 1990. The Front démocratique du renouveau (FDR) emerged in October 1994 to demand increased autonomy for the Toubou population of the south-east. In November, in compliance with a request by the UN, Niger established a committee whose stated aim was to disarm militias and to combat arms-trafficking, which was reportedly well-established in the Agadez and Lake Chad regions. A Comité spécial de la paix (CSP) was inaugurated in May 1995, and a military observer group, comprising representatives of Burkina and France, was deployed in the north in July. The Prime Minister approved an amnesty in that month, and all Tuareg prisoners were reported to have been released shortly afterwards. The peace process was undermined, however, by evidence that Dayak and other Tuareg groups in a revived CRA were making common cause with the FDR in demanding autonomy for their respective regions. In October clashes in the north-east involving rebel Tuaregs and the armed forces were attributed to elements of the CRA. In the same month bilateral and international donors pledged some 18,700m. francs CFA in support of a two-year emergency programme for the development of the north. In December Dayak was one of three leading CRA members to be killed in an air crash. In January 1996 the new leader of the FLT (and acting leader of the CRA), Mohamed Akotai, indicated that his movement favoured inter-Tuareg reconciliation and a dialogue with the Government.

Following the *coup d'état* of January 1996, the CSN expressed its commitment to the peace process. The new administration, the ORA and the CRA all expressed the view that direct contacts between the military and the Tuareg movements would expedite the peace process. Although the FDR also expressed its willingness to co-operate with the new authorities, an armed assault on Dirkou in February by members of that movement, and an army counter-attack, resulted in 12 deaths. In March the Nigerien authorities, the office of the UN High Commissioner for Refugees (UNHCR) and the Governments of Algeria and Burkina signed agreements on refugee repatriation. Shortly afterwards the CRA, including the FDR, affirmed its recognition of the April 1995 agreement, and announced that it would observe a unilateral truce for one month, while negotiations continued. In April 1996 the Government and the CRA signed an agreement formalizing the latter's adherence to the peace process. The following month the ORA and the CRA agreed to establish a joint committee to co-ordinate their activities and to represent their interests in negotiations. In July the CSP and the resistance movements recommended measures aimed at curbing ongoing insecurity in northern areas. In September joint peace-keeping patrols of the Nigerien armed forces and former rebels were inaugurated in the north.

In late September 1996 Ag Boula announced that the ORA no longer considered itself bound by the peace treaty. The authorities asserted that this abandonment of the 1995 accord was linked primarily to the arrest of ORA members in connection with the diversion, some months previously, of a large consignment of cigarettes bound for the north. In an apparent gesture of reconciliation, the detainees were released at the end of October 1996, and the ORA surrendered the consignment to the authorities. In November it was reported that a new group had emerged from among the ORA and the CRA; led by Mohamed Anako, the Union des forces de la résistance armée (UFRA) affirmed its commitment to the peace accord. Following a meeting between Maïnassara and Ag Boula in January 1997, and assurances regarding the implementation of provisions of the 1995 accord, the ORA declared its renewed support; it was announced, moreover, that the FLAA and FLT would establish a joint patrol aimed at combating insecurity and banditry, and other measures intended to facilitate the reintegration of former rebels proceeded.

Insecurity persisted, none the less, particularly in the east. Violent clashes were reported in March 1997, involving several hundred soldiers and Toubou rebels: the FDR protested that the operation, which was attributed by the authorities to the need to eliminate isolated groups of armed bandits, was endangering the peace accord. In July, however, the FDR announced its withdrawal from the peace process, stating that Nigerien and Chadian military units had attacked one of its bases; the FDR reported that 17 members of the armed forces had been killed in clashes with its fighters. The Nigerien authorities, however, denied that any engagement had taken place. The conclusion of the disarmament process was officially celebrated in Tchin-Tabaraden in late October. The armed forces subsequently undertook an offensive against positions held by rebel groups. In November, following two weeks of talks, a peace accord, known as the Algiers addendum protocol, providing for an immediate cease-fire, was signed in Algeria between the Nigerien Government, the UFRA and the Forces armées révolutionnaires du Sahara (FARS), which comprised both Toubou and Arab elements. In March 1998 the ORA and CRA surrendered their weapons stocks at Agadez. Meanwhile, Ag Boula was appointed as Minister-delegate responsible for Tourism in December 1997.

In June 1998 it was reported that the last units of the UFRA had disarmed at a ceremony near Agadez. A peace agreement was signed with the FDR in August. Following the death of President Maïnassara, in April 1999, the military CRN gave assurances that the peace process would be continued. Ag Boula was promoted to the rank of minister in the transitional Government, while Anako was appointed as special adviser to Wanké. Ag Boula retained his ministerial post in the new Government of Hama Amadou, formed in January 2000. In June the final groups of fighters from the UFRA and other movements participating in the peace process were disarmed near Agadez, prior to their intended integration into the national forces. Concerns remained, however, that progress still had to be made in the implementation of moves towards greater administrative decentralization, as well as regarding the delayed fulfilment of quotas for Tuaregs in military formations. In late September more than 1,200 guns, surrendered by the disarmed factions, were ceremoniously burned in Agadez, in the presence of President Mamadou Tandja, leaders of other West African nations and UN representatives. At the ceremony, Anako announced the dissolution of several of the rebel groups and militias. In September 2001 Chahayi Barkaye, the leader of the FARS, the principal rebel group to have refused disarmament, was killed in heavy fighting with Nigerien soldiers near the Libyan border.

In February 2004 Ag Boula was dismissed from his ministerial post and detained on a charge of complicity in the murder of an MNSD activist (in order to maintain Tuareg representation in the Government, Anako was appointed as a Minister-delegate at the Ministry of the Economy and Finance). The Government subsequently denied rumours that elements of FLAA had resumed insurgent activities in the north; however, following a clash with government forces in October, in which five people were reported to have died, Ag Boula's brother, Mohammed Ag Boula, claimed responsibility for the attack during an interview with French radio broadcaster Radio France Internationale, citing the failure of the Government to implement the 1995 peace agreements, and the continuing detention of certain former insurgents, as motivation for the attack. Also in late 2004 four government soldiers were taken hostage in northern Niger; once more, Mohammed Ag Boula declared responsibility for the action, as the leader of a revived FLAA. Following mediation by the Libyan authorities, the hostages were released, after some five months in captivity, in February 2005; Rhissa Ag Boula was released from prison one month later where he had been awaiting trial. The authorities reportedly denied Ag Boula's release was linked to that of the hostages, although Mohamed Ag Boula had previously refused to free the kidnapped soldiers while his brother remained in detention.

In foreign affairs, there was a notable deterioration in relations with the USA in the immediate aftermath of the 1996 presidential election in Niger. The assumption of power by the CRN in April 1999, following the death of Maïnassara, was condemned by the USA, France and Niger's other Western creditors. (The US Department of State was a principal source of reports that a coup had taken place.) Relations with the USA improved following the re-installation of an elected Government; in February 2000 Niger's Minister of Foreign Affairs, Co-operation and African Integration visited Washington, DC and in March the USA announced an end to the sanctions imposed after Maïnassara's death. In August President Tandja met President Bill Clinton and other US representatives in Abuja, Nigeria, where the USA announced increased support for Niger in areas including food security, the promotion of democracy, education and health care.

Countries of the region with which Maïnassara had forged close relations also condemned the military take-over of April 1999: Libya notably denounced the new regime, although relations between the CRN and the Libyan Government had normalized by the end of the year. In December the two countries signed an agreement envisaging the establishment of a joint company to distribute oil and liquefied natural gas; it was also agreed to expedite the establishment of a joint company for petroleum exploration and production. In January 2000 President Tandja undertook an official visit to Libya and met the country's leader, Col Muammar al-Qaddafi. On a visit to Agadez in early July, Qaddafi pledged support for the Tuareg peace process. Later that month Prime Minister Amadou visited Libya and met Qaddafi. In November Libya pledged to grant financial support for several construction and development projects in Niger. Meanwhile, some 1,000 Nigerien citizens were repatriated from Libya in October, following instances of inter-ethnic violence between Libyan Arabs and black Africans in that country.

The EU suspended all assistance to Niger in the aftermath of the military take-over in April 1999 and made its resumption dependent on a full investigation into Maïnassara's death; the CRN subsequently stated that its report had been lodged with organizations including the EU, and EU aid recommenced in June 2000. France also suspended military and civilian co-operation with Niger in April 1999. Following a visit to France by Mamadou Tandja in January 2000, when the newly installed Nigerien President met President Jacques Chirac and Prime Minister Lionel Jospin, the resumption of French co-operation was formalized, with the announcement of exceptional assistance principally to allow payment of outstanding salaries in the public sector. Chirac visited Niger in October 2003, when he praised 'the return of democratic life' to the country.

In May 2000 a long-term dispute between Niger and Benin regarding the ownership of a number of small islands along their common border at the Niger river escalated, reportedly following the sabotage of a Beninois administrative building on the island of Lété, apparently by Nigerien soldiers. A meeting between representatives of the two Governments failed to resolve the dispute, which was subsequently referred to the Organization of African Unity (OAU, now the African Union, see p. 153) for arbitration. Further clashes between rival groups of farmers were reported on Lété in late August. In April 2002 the two Governments officially ratified an agreement (signed in 2001) to refer the issue of ownership of the islands to the International Court of Justice (ICJ) in The Hague, Netherlands, for arbitration. Benin and Niger filed confidential written arguments with the Court, and in November 2003 a five-member chamber formed to consider the case held its first public sitting. Both countries subsequently submitted counter-arguments, and a third written pleading was submitted by both parties in December of that year. The public hearings in the case took place before the Chamber of the ICJ in March 2005. Meanwhile, in late 2004 Nigerien traders and haulage contractors boycotted Cotonou port in Benin in reaction to the shooting of two Nigerien citizens by Beninois gendarmes in the city in September. The boycott was ended in January 2005 following a visit to Niamey by the Beninois Minister of Foreign Affairs and African Integration, Rogatien Biaou, during which he announced that the Beninois Government would compensate the victims' families. In July 2005 the ICJ issued a final ruling to the effect that 16 of the 25 disputed islands, including Lété, belonged to Niger; the Governments of both countries announced their acceptance of the ruling.

In June 2001 Niger and Nigeria announced that joint border patrols of their common frontier would be instigated, in order to combat increasing cross-border crime and smuggling in the region. It was reported that the introduction of *Shari'a* law in several northern Nigerian states, from 2000, had been instrumental in encouraging Nigerian criminal gangs to operate from within Niger. Further concerns regarding regional security were raised in early 2004, when Islamic militants belonging to the Algerian-based Groupe salafiste pour la prédication et le combat (GSPC) reportedly attacked a group of tourists in northern Niger. In March clashes between the militants and Chadian and Nigerien troops reportedly resulted in the deaths of some 43 GSPC fighters in northern Niger. It was reported in that month that the Governments of Algeria, Chad, Mali and Niger were to reinforce security co-operation in the regions of their common borders. In January 2005 President Tandja was elected Chairman of the Economic Community of West African States (see p. 217); paramount among the organization's concerns during the first months of his chairmanship were common agricultural policy and the political crises in Côte d'Ivoire and Togo. In June 2005 Niger, Algeria, Chad, Mali and Nigeria were among nine North and West African countries that participated in US-led military exercises aimed at increasing co-operation in combating cross-border banditry and militancy in the region.

Government

Following the death of President Ibrahim Baré Maïnassara, in April 1999, a military Conseil de réconciliation nationale (CRN) was established, under the chairmanship of Maj. Daouda Mallam Wanké, to exercise executive and legislative authority during a nine-month transitional period prior to the restoration of elected organs of government. A new constitution was approved in a national referendum in July 1999. The Constitution of the Fifth Republic, promulgated on 9 August, envisages a balance of powers between the President, Government and legislative Assemblée nationale. The President, who is elected by universal adult suffrage, is Head of State, and is accorded 'broad ordinary and arbitral powers'. The Government, under a Prime Minister appointed by the President, is responsible to the Assemblée nationale, which is competent to remove the Prime Minister by vote of censure. The Assemblée nationale is similarly elected by direct adult suffrage. The new President and legislature were inaugurated in December 1999.

For the purposes of local administration, Niger comprises seven regions and the municipality of Niamey. A reorganization of Niger's administrative structures, with the aim of devolving increased autonomy to local and regional authorities, was undertaken in the second half of the 1990s.

Defence

In August 2005 Niger's armed forces totalled 5,300 men (army 5,200; air force 100). Paramilitary forces numbered 5,400 men, comprising the gendarmerie (1,400), the republican guard (2,500) and the national police force (1,500). Conscription to the armed forces is selective and lasts for two years. Budgetary expenditure on defence in 2005 was estimated at 16,000m. francs CFA.

Economic Affairs

In 2004, according to estimates by the World Bank, Niger's gross national income (GNI), measured at average 2002–04 prices, was US $2,836m., equivalent to $230 per head (or $830 on an international purchasing-power parity basis). During 1995–2004, it was estimated, the population increased at an average annual rate of 3.3%, while gross domestic product (GDP) per head increased, in real terms, by an average of 0.1% per year. Overall GDP increased, in real terms, at an average annual rate of 3.4% in 1995–2004; growth was 0.9% in 2004.

Agriculture (including hunting, forestry and fishing) contributed 42.0% of GDP in 2003. About 87.1% of the labour force were employed in the sector in that year. The principal cash crops are cow-peas, onions, groundnuts and cotton. The principal subsistence crops are millet, sorghum and rice. Niger is able to achieve self-sufficiency in basic foodstuffs in non-drought years. A record grain surplus of 440,000 metric tons was achieved in 2003/04; however, agricultural production in northern Niger in 2004/05 was severely affected by drought and by the swarms of locusts that invaded the Sahel region from mid-2004, resulting in a grain deficit of 223,487 tons for that agricultural year. The effects of drought and locust invasion were also thought to have caused significant damage to pasture land: livestock-rearing in Niger is especially important among the nomadic population, and live animals intended chiefly for food accounted for 18.0% of total export earnings in 2003, constituting the second most important source of export revenue, after uranium. Major anti-desertification and reafforestation programmes are in progress. According to the World Bank, agricultural GDP increased by an average of 3.6% per year in 1995–2003. Agricultural GDP increased by 6.0% in 2003.

Industry (including mining, manufacturing, construction and power) contributed 12.7% of GDP in 2003. Only 3.6% of the labour force were employed in industrial activities at the time of the 1988 census. According to the World Bank, industrial GDP increased by an average of 3.3% per year in 1995–2003; growth was 4.0% in 2003.

Mining contributed 2.3% of GDP in 2003, but employed only 0.2% of the labour force in 1988. Niger is among the world's foremost producers of uranium (the third largest, after Canada and Australia, in 2002), although the contribution of uranium-mining to the domestic economy has declined, as production costs have exceeded world prices for the mineral. In 2003 exports of uranium accounted for 54.0% of total export earnings. In addition, gypsum, coal, salt and cassiterite are also extracted, and commercial exploitation of gold (previously mined on a small scale) at the Samira Hill mine began in 2004, with total production of 120,000 ounces of gold forecast for 2005. In 2000 the Government awarded two permits for petroleum exploration in eastern Niger to two US companies. According to the IMF, the GDP of the mining sector increased at an average annual rate of 1.1% in 1997–2003; mining GDP increased by an estimated 1.3% in 2003.

Manufacturing contributed 6.5% of GDP in 2003, and employed 2.7% of the labour force in 1988. The processing of agricultural products (groundnuts, cereals, cotton and rice) constitutes the principal activity. Some light industries, including a textiles plant, a brewery and a cement works, supply the internal market. According to the World Bank, manufacturing GDP increased by an average of 4.0% per year in 1995–2003. Manufacturing GDP increased by 5.1% in 2003.

The domestic generation of electricity (almost entirely thermal) provides a little less than one-half of Niger's electrical energy requirements, much of the remainder being imported from Nigeria. Construction of a hydroelectric installation at Kandadji, on the Niger, is planned. Imports of mineral fuels accounted for 16.9% of the value of merchandise imports in 2003.

The services sector contributed 45.3% of GDP in 2003, and employed 15.0% of the labour force in 1988. The GDP of the sector increased by an average of 4.0% per year in 1995–2003, according to the World Bank; growth was 5.2% in 2003.

In 2003 Niger recorded a visible trade deficit of an estimated 72,300m. francs CFA, while there was a deficit of 98,700m. francs CFA on the current account of the balance of payments. France was Niger's principal source of imports in 2001, supplying 14.6%; other major suppliers were Côte d'Ivoire, the People's Republic of

China, the USA and Nigeria. The principal markets for exports in that year were France (36.5%), Nigeria and Japan. The principal exports in 2003 were uranium (most of which is purchased by France), live animals and vegetables (principally cow-peas and onions). The principal imports in that year were food and live animals (22.2% of total imports, of which around one-half was accounted for by cereals and cereal preparations), machinery and transport equipment, refined petroleum products and fixed vegetable oils and fats (notably palm oil).

Niger's overall budget deficit for 2003 was estimated at 51,000m. francs CFA (equivalent to 3.3% of GDP). Niger's total external debt was US $2,116m. at the end of 2003, of which $1,945m. was long-term public debt. Consumer prices increased by an annual average of 1.7% during 1996–2004. Consumer prices increased by 3.9% in 2003 and by 0.2% in 2004. Some 20,926 people were registered as unemployed in 1991.

Niger is a member of numerous regional organizations, including the Economic Community of West African States (see p. 217), the West African organs of the Franc Zone (see p. 282), the Conseil de l'Entente (see p. 385), the Lake Chad Basin Commission (see p. 386), the Liptako–Gourma Integrated Development Authority (see p. 386), the Niger Basin Authority (see p. 387) and the Permanent Inter-State Committee on Drought Control in the Sahel (see p. 387).

Niger is one of the world's poorest countries, and has consistently been among the lowest ranking countries in the United Nations Development Programme's Human Development Report, while literacy levels are also among the lowest in the world. Niger's narrow export base, which is dominated by uranium, meant that the country benefited less than most countries of the region from the 50% devaluation of the CFA franc in 1994. Political instability in the mid-1990s had a negative impact on economic performance, and most major creditors withdrew support after the military take-over that followed the death of President Maïnassara in 1999. Following the restoration of civilian rule, France resumed aid and debt relief to Niger in early 2000, and in December the IMF and the World Bank announced that Niger would receive US $890m. in debt-service relief under the enhanced framework of the initiative for heavily indebted poor countries. Also in December the IMF announced the approval of a three-year loan, worth $76m., for Niger under the Poverty Reduction and Growth Facility (PRGF); in November 2003 the IMF extended this arrangement until the end of June 2004, and in January 2005 an additional PRGF arrangement, worth $10m. over three years, was concluded. In July 2005 Niger was among 18 countries to be granted 100% debt relief on multilateral debt agreed by the Group of Eight leading industrialized nations (G-8), subject to the approval of the lender. Economic performance improved steadily in 2001–03, largely owing to a series of successful harvests and the maintenance of relative political stability; however, the combined effect of drought and locust invasions on the agricultural sector was expected to impact negatively on growth for 2004 and to generate high inflation in food prices in 2005. Indeed, widespread food insecurity in that year, and public protests against the introduction of a 19% value-added tax resulted in several staple goods, including milk and flour, being exempted from the tax, and in an effective lowering of the rate of the tax on water and electricity (see Recent History). None the less, it remained unclear whether these modifications would have a significant impact on the poorer, rural, regions of Niger. Majority shares in the state water and telecommunications companies were transferred to the private sector in 2001, while the divestiture of the state petroleum company and, following major restructuring, of the state electricity company were ongoing priorities in 2006, although progress in privatization and other economic reform programmes had been delayed as a result of the food insecurity experienced in the previous year. Real GDP growth of 4.5% was forecast by the IMF for 2005, with similar levels of growth anticipated in both 2006 and 2007.

Education

Education is available free of charge, and is officially compulsory for eight years between the ages of seven and 15 years. Primary education begins at the age of seven and lasts for six years. Secondary education begins at the age of 13 years, and comprises a four-year cycle followed by a three-year cycle. Primary enrolment in 2000/01 included 30% of children in the appropriate age-group (boys 36%; girls 24%). Secondary enrolment in that year included only 5% of the relevant age-group (boys 6%; girls 4%). The Abdou Moumouni University (formerly the University of Niamey) was inaugurated in 1973, and the Islamic University of Niger, at Say (to the south of the capital), was opened in 1987. In December 2001 the Assemblée nationale approved legislation providing for the introduction of teaching in all local languages, with the aim of improving the literacy rate. Expenditure on education in 2000 was 32,500m. francs CFA, representing 15.5% of total spending.

Public Holidays

2006: 1 January (New Year's Day), 10 January*† (Tabaski, Feast of the Sacrifice), 31 January* (Islamic New Year), 10 April* (Mouloud, Birth of the Prophet), 17 April (Easter Monday), 24 April (National Concord Day), 1 May (Labour Day), 3 August (Independence Day), 23 October* (Aïd al-Fitr, end of Ramadan), 18 December (Republic Day), 31 December*† (Tabaski, Feast of the Sacrifice).

2007: 1 January (New Year's Day), 20 January* (Islamic New Year), 31 March* (Mouloud, Birth of the Prophet), 9 April (Easter Monday), 24 April (National Concord Day), 1 May (Labour Day), 3 August (Independence Day), 13 October* (Aïd al-Fitr, end of Ramadan), 18 December (Republic Day), 20 December* (Tabaski, Feast of the Sacrifice).

* These holidays are dependent on the Islamic lunar calendar and may vary by one or two days from the dates given.

† This festival occurs twice (in the Islamic years AH 1426 and 1427) within the same Gregorian year.

Weights and Measures

The metric system is in force.

NIGER

Statistical Survey

Source (unless otherwise stated): Direction de la Statistique et de l'Informatique, BP 720, Niamey; tel. 72-23-74; fax 73-33-71.

Area and Population

AREA, POPULATION AND DENSITY

Area (sq km)	1,267,000*
Population (census results)	
20 November 1977	5,098,427
20 May 1988	
Males	3,590,070
Females	3,658,030
Total	7,248,100
1 June 2001 (provisional result)	10,790,352
Population (UN estimates at mid-year)†	
2002	12,617,000
2003	13,052,000
2004	13,499,000
Density (per sq km) at mid-2004	10.7

* 489,191 sq miles.
† Source: UN, *World Population Prospects: The 2004 Revision*.

Ethnic Groups (Percentage of total, 1995): Hausa 52.8; Djerma 14.7; Peul 10.4; Kanori 8.7; Songhaï 8.1; Tuareg 3.0; Toubou 0.5; Others 1.8 (Source: La Francophonie).

PROVINCES
(population at 1988 census, rounded figures)

Tillabéri*	1,725,700	Dosso		1,018,900
Zinder	1,411,100	Agadez		208,800
Maradi	1,389,400	Diffa		189,100
Tahoua	1,308,600			

* Includes Niamey, which subsequently became a separate administrative unit.

PRINCIPAL TOWNS
(population at 1988 census)

Niamey (capital)	398,265*	Tahoua		51,607
Zinder	120,892	Agadez		50,164
Maradi	112,965	Arlit		31,993

* Figure refers to Niamey city only. Population of the Niamey agglomeration was 550,000.

Mid-2003 (UN estimate, incl. suburbs): Niamey 889,977 (Source: UN, *World Urbanization Prospects: The 2003 Revision*).

BIRTHS AND DEATHS
(UN estimates, annual averages)

	1990–95	1995–2000	2000–05
Birth rate (per 1,000)	56.4	57.2	55.1
Death rate (per 1,000)	24.8	22.9	21.2

Source: UN, *World Population Prospects: The 2004 Revision*.

Expectation of life (WHO estimates, years at birth): 41 (males 42; females 41) in 2003 (Source: WHO, *World Health Report*).

ECONOMICALLY ACTIVE POPULATION
(persons aged 10 years and over, 1988 census, provisional)

	Males	Females	Total
Agriculture, hunting, forestry and fishing	1,549,600	243,950	1,793,550
Mining and quarrying	4,790	960	5,750
Manufacturing	28,060	35,630	63,690
Electricity, gas and water	2,330	60	2,390
Construction	14,040	390	14,430
Trade, restaurants and hotels	95,670	112,700	208,370
Transport, storage and communications	14,400	470	14,870
Financing, insurance, real estate and business services	1,400	450	1,850
Community, social and personal services	100,620	29,110	129,730
Activities not adequately defined	21,250	50,270	71,520
Total employed	1,832,160	473,990	2,306,150
Unemployed	44,210	16,360	60,570
Total labour force	1,876,370	490,350	2,366,720

Source: UN, *Demographic Yearbook*.

Mid-2003 (estimates in '000): Agriculture, etc. 4,777; Total labour force 5,486 (Source: FAO).

Health and Welfare

KEY INDICATORS

Total fertility rate (children per woman, 2003)	8.0
Under-5 mortality rate (per 1,000 live births, 2004)	259
HIV/AIDS (% of persons aged 15–49, 2003)	1.2
Physicians (per 1,000 head, 2002)	0.03
Hospital beds (per 1,000 head, 1998)	0.12
Health expenditure (2002): US $ per head (PPP)	27
Health expenditure (2002): % of GDP	4.0
Health expenditure (2002): public (% of total)	50.8
Access to water (% of persons, 2002)	46
Access to sanitation (% of persons, 2002)	12
Human Development Index (2003): ranking	177
Human Development Index (2003): value	0.281

For sources and definitions, see explanatory note on p. vi.

Agriculture

PRINCIPAL CROPS
('000 metric tons)

	2000	2001	2002
Wheat	10.9	6.3	3.3*
Rice (paddy)	60.5	76.4	76.5*
Maize	3.9	6.4	7.0*
Millet	1,697.2	2,414.4	2,500.0†
Sorghum	370.7	655.7	700.0†
Potatoes	7.6	4.2	4.2*
Sweet potatoes	46.6	29.4	30.0*
Cassava (Manioc)	164.5	105.5	100.0*
Sugar cane	200.0	211.4	220.0*
Dry cow-peas	268.7	350.0*	400.0*
Other pulses*	20.0	20.1	22.2
Groundnuts (in shell)	113.2	129.3	100.0†
Sesame seed	14.1	21.7	22.0*
Cottonseed*	3.5	3.0	3.0
Cabbages	119.0	120.0*	120.0*
Lettuce	42.0	40.0*	40.0*
Tomatoes	139.9	99.2	100.0*
Chillies and green peppers	17.2	17.0*	17.0*

NIGER

Statistical Survey

—continued	2000	2001	2002
Dry onions	356.2	271.2	270.0*
Garlic	8.2	8.0*	8.0*
Green beans*	22	22	23
Carrots	18.8	18.0*	18.0*
Other vegetables*	47.6	48.7	48.7
Dates*	7.6	7.7	7.7
Other fruit*	42	42	43
Cotton (lint)	6.4	6.9	7.0*
Spices*	5.3	5.3	5.3
Tobacco (leaves)	4.4	0.2	1.0†

* FAO estimate(s).
† Unofficial figure.
Source: FAO.

2003 ('000 metric tons): Sorghum: 720.0 (unofficial figure); Dry cow-peas 549.0 (unofficial figure); Groundnuts (in shell) 209.4 (unofficial figure); Dates 7.8 (FAO estimate); Spices 5.4 (FAO estimate). Note: All other figures assumed to be unchanged from 2002 (FAO estimates).

2004 ('000 metric tons): Sorghum: 580.0 (unofficial figure); Dry cow-peas 549.0 (FAO estimate); Groundnuts (in shell) 209.4 (FAO estimate); Dates 7.8 (FAO estimate); Spices 5.4 (FAO estimate). Note: All other figures assumed to be unchanged from 2002 and 2003 (FAO estimates).

LIVESTOCK
(FAO estimates, '000 head, year ending September)

	2001	2002	2003
Cattle	2,260	2,260	2,260
Sheep	4,500	4,500	4,500
Goats	6,900	6,900	6,900
Pigs	39.0	39.5	39.5
Horses	105	105	106
Asses	580	580	580
Camels	415	415	420
Chickens	24,000	24,500	25,000

2004: Figures assumed to be unchanged from 2003 (FAO estimates).
Source: FAO.

LIVESTOCK PRODUCTS
('000 metric tons)

	2000	2001	2002*
Beef and veal	41.0†	42.1†	35.0
Mutton and lamb	14.7*	15.7*	12.8
Goat meat	24.6*	25.2*	25.2
Camel meat	6.8*	7.5*	7.5
Game meat	15*	15*	15
Chicken meat	27.2*	27.8*	28.4
Other meat	3.3*	3.7*	3.7
Cows' milk	180*	184*	184
Sheep's milk	15.4*	15.6*	15.6
Goats' milk	100*	105*	105
Camels' milk	10.7*	10.8*	10.8
Cheese	14.1*	14.7*	14.7
Butter	5.0*	5.1*	5.1
Hen eggs	10.2*	10.4*	10.5
Cattle hides	6.3*	6.4*	5.2
Sheepskins	1.8*	2.0*	1.6
Goatskins	3.6*	4.2*	4.2

* FAO estimate(s).
† Unofficial figure.

2003 (FAO estimates, '000 metric tons): Mutton and lamb 15.2; Camel meat 7.8; Chicken meat 29.0; Sheepskins 1.9. Note: All other figures assumed to be unchanged from 2002.

2004 (FAO estimates, '000 metric tons): Note: All figures assumed to be unchanged from 2003.

Source: FAO.

Forestry

ROUNDWOOD REMOVALS
(FAO estimates, '000 cubic metres, excl. bark)

	2002	2003	2004
Industrial wood	411	411	411
Fuel wood	8,190	8,391	8,596
Total	8,601	8,802	9,007

Source: FAO.

SAWNWOOD PRODUCTION
(FAO estimates, '000 cubic metres, incl. railway sleepers)

	1991	1992	1993
Total (all broadleaved)	0	1	4

Source: FAO.

1994–2004: Figures assumed to be unchanged from 1993 (FAO estimates).

Fishing
(metric tons, live weight)

	2001	2002	2003
Capture (freshwater fishes)	20,800	23,560	55,860
Aquaculture	21	40	40
Total catch	20,821	23,600	55,900

Source: FAO.

Mining
('000 metric tons, unless otherwise indicated)

	2001	2002	2003
Hard coal	163.3	182.9	183.0*
Tin (metric tons)†	9	11	11*
Uranium (metric tons)†	2,920	3,076	3,143‡
Gold (kg)§	30	28	28*
Salt*	2	2	2
Gypsum	3.2	17.7	17.7*

* Estimated production.
† Data refer to the metal content of ore.
‡ Reported production.
§ Does not include unreported production. Total output of gold was estimated at roughly 1,000 kg per year.

Source: US Geological Survey.

Industry

SELECTED PRODUCTS
('000 metric tons, unless otherwise indicated)

	2001	2002	2003
Raw sugar ('000 metric tons)*	21.1	22.0	22.0
Cement	47.0	54.7	63.7
Soap	7.5	8.7	10.4
Textile fabrics (million metres)	6.7	7.0	5.6
Beer ('000 bottles)	124.4	120.4	116.5
Electric energy (million kWh)	199.2	39.6	45.8

* FAO estimates.

Source: mostly IMF, *Niger: Statistical Annex* (July 2004).

NIGER

Statistical Survey

Finance

CURRENCY AND EXCHANGE RATES

Monetary Units
100 centimes = 1 franc de la Communauté financière africaine (CFA).

Sterling, Dollar and Euro Equivalents (30 December 2005)
£1 sterling = 957.440 francs CFA;
US $1 = 556.037 francs CFA;
€1 = 655.957 francs CFA.
10,000 francs CFA = £10.44 = $17.98 = €15.24.

Average Exchange Rate (francs CFA per US $)
2003 581.20
2004 528.29
2005 527.47

Note: An exchange rate of 1 French franc = 50 francs CFA, established in 1948, remained in force until January 1994, when the CFA franc was devalued by 50%, with the exchange rate adjusted to 1 French franc = 100 francs CFA. This relationship to French currency remained in effect with the introduction of the euro on 1 January 1999. From that date, accordingly, a fixed exchange rate of €1 = 655.957 francs CFA has been in operation.

BUDGET
('000 million francs CFA)

Revenue*	2001	2002	2003
Tax revenue	125.6	144.6	152.1
Taxes on income, profits, payroll and work force	22.6	23.1	28.3
Taxes on goods and services	30.4	30.6	34.1
Taxes on corporate profits	10.4	11.9	17.0
Excise taxes	7.9	7.6	7.5
Taxes on uranium production	3.7	3.3	3.4
Import duties	58.1	65.9	63.4
Taxes on international trade and transactions	64.8	82.9	79.9
Non-tax revenue	4.1	3.8	1.2
Settlement of reciprocal debts	0.0	8.4	0.0
Annexed budgets and special accounts	3.2	4.1	3.4
Total	**133.0**	**160.9**	**156.7**

Expenditure†	2001	2002	2003
Current expenditure	157.5	161.7	156.7
Defence	18.2	14.4	14.3
Security	10.9	8.6	8.5
Education	24.2	31.0	29.6
Health	10.2	10.2	10.3
Social affairs	0.3	0.4	0.4
Agriculture	3.9	3.1	2.9
Mining	0.4	0.4	0.3
Road infrastructure	5.6	3.5	0.6
Transport and communications	0.7	0.1	0.1
Interest payments	25.4	22.6	17.4
Capital expenditure	89.0	116.5	115.5
Total	**246.5**	**278.2**	**272.2**

* Excluding grants received ('000 million francs CFA): 59.3 in 2001; 58.4 in 2002; 64.5 in 2003.
† Excluding net lending ('000 million francs CFA): −0.8 in 2001; −0.2 in 2002; 0.0 in 2003.

Source: IMF, *Niger: Statistical Annex* (July 2004).

INTERNATIONAL RESERVES
(US $ million at 31 December, excl. gold)

	2002	2003	2004
IMF special drawing rights	0.7	2.7	0.9
Reserve position in IMF	11.6	12.7	13.3
Foreign exchange	121.6	244.7	243.7
Total	**133.9**	**260.1**	**258.0**

Source: IMF, *International Financial Statistics*.

MONEY SUPPLY
('000 million francs CFA at 31 December)

	2002	2003	2004
Currency outside banks	39.3	84.9	96.8
Demand deposits at deposit money banks*	54.2	61.6	81.8
Checking deposits at post office	1.7	2.4	3.2
Total money (incl. others)*	**95.6**	**149.5**	**181.9**

* Excluding the deposits of public enterprises of an administrative or social nature.

Source: IMF, *International Financial Statistics*.

COST OF LIVING
(Consumer Price Index for Niamey; base: 1996 = 100)

	2002	2003	2004
Food, beverages and tobacco	113.9	117.9	116.2
Clothing	92.1	106.0	104.2
Housing, water, electricity and gas	114.7	107.4	108.9
All items (incl. others)	**110.0**	**114.3**	**114.5**

Source: Banque centrale des états de l'Afrique de l'ouest.

NATIONAL ACCOUNTS
('000 million francs CFA at current prices)

Expenditure on the Gross Domestic Product

	2001	2002	2003
Final consumption expenditure	1,228.8	1,363.6	1,397.0
Households			
Non-profit institutions serving households	1,069.6	1,189.8	1,223.7
General government	159.2	173.8	173.3
Gross capital formation	155.9	201.4	241.2
Gross fixed capital formation	153.1	198.6	238.4
Changes in inventories			
Acquisitions, less disposals, of valuables	2.8	2.8	2.8
Total domestic expenditure	**1,384.7**	**1,565.0**	**1,638.2**
Exports of goods and services	217.6	235.0	235.7
Less Imports of goods and services	316.5	379.6	385.3
GDP in market prices	**1,285.8**	**1,420.4**	**1,488.6**

Gross Domestic Product by Economic Activity

	2001	2002	2003
Agriculture, hunting, forestry and fishing	494.7	568.0	591.9
Mining and quarrying	31.8	32.2	32.6
Manufacturing (incl. handicrafts)	80.3	85.1	91.3
Electricity and water	15.5	15.7	16.6
Construction and public works	31.0	34.0	37.8
Trade	188.0	195.5	208.2
Transport	79.0	83.3	91.7
Non-market services	172.9	187.8	197.9
Other services	127.9	135.9	140.7
Sub-total	**1,221.1**	**1,337.5**	**1,408.7**
Import taxes and duties	64.7	82.9	79.9
GDP in purchasers' values	**1,285.8**	**1,420.4**	**1,488.6**

Source: Banque centrale des états de l'Afrique de l'ouest.

NIGER

BALANCE OF PAYMENTS
('000 million francs CFA)

	2001	2002	2003
Exports of goods f.o.b.	199.7	194.8	203.3
Imports of goods f.o.b.	−243.1	−258.7	−275.7
Trade balance	−43.3	−63.8	−72.3
Services (net)	−66.3	−70.9	−77.3
Balance on goods and services	−109.6	−134.7	−149.6
Income (net)	−11.0	−16.8	−7.9
Balance on goods, services and income	−120.6	−151.5	−157.5
Private unrequited transfers (net)	10.5	8.6	7.0
Public unrequited transfers (net)	42.2	43.9	51.8
Current balance	−67.9	−99.0	−98.7
Capital account (net)	34.2	53.8	42.6
Direct investment (net)	19.4	2.9	1.5
Portfolio investment (net)	2.7	1.0	1.0
Other investment (net)	−3.5	19.9	21.5
Net errors and omissions	−9.2	−21.6	−7.4
Overall balance	−24.3	−43.0	−39.5

Source: Banque centrale des états de l'Afrique de l'ouest.

External Trade

PRINCIPAL COMMODITIES
(Distribution by SITC, US $ million)

Imports c.i.f.	2001	2002	2003
Food and live animals	105.8	113.7	122.3
Dairy products and birds' eggs	11.2	11.8	13.0
Milk and cream	10.8	11.5	12.6
Milk and cream, preserved, concentrated or sweetened	10.6	11.4	12.4
Cereals and cereal preparations	62.8	71.4	63.4
Rice, semi-milled or wholly milled	39.4	47.5	37.2
Rice, semi-milled or milled (unbroken)	38.2	47.5	36.0
Meal of flour of wheat or of meslin	11.2	12.7	12.8
Flour of wheat or of meslin	11.2	12.7	10.8
Sugar, sugar preparations and honey	14.1	11.3	24.5
Refined sugar, etc.	13.5	10.5	23.6
Beverages and tobacco	15.2	20.6	21.7
Cigarettes	13.3	19.2	19.3
Crude materials (inedible) except fuel	9.8	18.2	30.5
Textile fibres (not wool tops) and their wastes (not in yarn)	2.2	10.6	21.1
Bulk textile waste, old clothing, traded in bulk or in bales	1.9	10.4	20.6
Mineral fuels, lubricants, etc., (incl. electric current)	40.7	59.2	93.3
Petroleum, petroleum products, etc.	32.7	48.6	79.9
Petroleum products, refined	32.5	46.4	75.3
Motor spirit, incl. aviation spirit	14.5	18.9	38.8
Kerosene and other medium oils	14.8	24.6	33.3
Kerosene (incl. kerosene type jet fuel)	12.0	18.7	25.2
Animal and vegetable oils, fats and waxes	22.3	29.4	40.6
Fixed vegetable oils and fats	21.2	27.8	37.6
Palm oil	16.4	23.0	32.2
Chemicals and related products	28.7	35.7	43.0
Medicinal and pharmaceutical products	9.3	12.0	16.5
Basic manufactures	35.8	57.8	67.4

Imports c.i.f.—continued	2001	2002	2003
Textile yarn, fabrics, made-up articles, etc.	7.3	20.6	21.8
Cotton fabrics, woven (not incl. narrow or special fabrics)	3.1	15.0	16.3
Machinery and transport equipment	48.7	76.1	108.1
Telecommunications, sound recording and reproducing equipment	3.6	15.3	22.6
Other telecommunications equipment, parts and accessories, etc.	2.8	14.6	21.5
Electrical line telephonic and telegraphic apparatus	1.1	13.1	18.0
Road vehicles	20.9	25.1	37.5
Passenger motor vehicles (excl. buses)	12.7	13.5	17.5
Miscellaneous manufactured articles	16.2	19.9	24.2
Total (incl. others)	324.5	430.9	551.0

Exports f.o.b.	2001	2002	2003
Food and live animals	58.5	68.2	55.0
Live animals chiefly for food	41.0	35.6	37.1
Animals of the bovine species (incl. buffaloes), live	16.0	13.5	16.5
Sheep and goats, live	22.4	19.0	18.2
Fish, crustaceans and molluscs, and preparations thereof	4.3	6.3	4.0
Vegetables and fruit	12.2	24.7	12.1
Vegetables, fresh or simply preserved; roots and tubers	11.5	23.9	11.7
Other fresh or chilled vegetables	8.4	21.2	9.1
Alliaceous vegetables, fresh or chilled	5.8	18.9	7.7
Beverages and tobacco	0.1	9.8	5.1
Cigarettes	—	9.7	4.8
Crude materials (inedible) except fuels	88.2	98.8	122.3
Textile fibres (not wool tops) and their wastes (not in yarn)	0.3	6.8	7.2
Ores and concentrates of uranium and thorium	86.2	90.2	111.4
Basic manufactures	1.3	12.4	12.4
Fabrics, woven, 85% plus of cotton, bleached, dyed, etc., or otherwise finished	0.5	11.4	11.6
Total (incl. others)	154.0	200.9	206.2

Source: UN, *International Trade Statistics Yearbook*.

PRINCIPAL TRADING PARTNERS
(US $ million)

Imports c.i.f.	2001	2002	2003
Bahrain	2.9	10.7	7.1
Belgium	3.6	5.9	8.0
Benin	6.3	9.8	14.5
Brasil	2.5	8.3	16.9
Burkina Faso	7.7	4.8	11.0
China, People's Republic	20.9	39.2	51.7
Côte d'Ivoire	47.3	64.2	73.6
France	62.2	67.2	80.5
Germany	4.3	5.8	10.0
Ghana	6.4	8.1	8.0
India	1.7	17.5	17.8
Israel	5.1	0.5	0.4
Italy	4.7	7.3	6.4
Japan	15.6	20.5	24.8

NIGER

Imports c.i.f.—continued	2001	2002	2003
Netherlands	5.3	12.2	12.0
Nigeria	33.3	30.5	39.8
Pakistan	20.2	4.5	0.4
South Africa	1.8	2.5	25.1
Spain	2.6	4.6	8.0
Togo	8.7	13.5	15.0
Tunisia	4.0	7.8	9.3
United Kingdom	7.1	11.5	17.3
USA	18.9	36.1	45.3
Total (incl. others)	324.5	430.9	551.0

Exports f.o.b.	2001	2002	2003
Algeria	0.3	0.6	0.5
Belgium	—	—	0.2
Benin	1.7	5.1	2.2
Burkina Faso	0.8	1.0	1.5
Chad	0.6	0.1	0.1
China, People's Republic	—	0.2	0.1
Côte d'Ivoire	2.3	7.0	5.4
France (incl. Monaco)	56.2	65.1	75.3
Germany	0.1	0.1	0.2
Ghana	1.9	9.0	3.8
India	—	—	0.3
Japan	25.4	23.4	30.7
Libya	0.2	0.7	1.3
Mali	0.2	0.2	0.2
Netherlands	—	1.1	3.9
Nigeria	57.1	64.4	56.7
South Africa	—	—	0.7
Spain	5.8	6.1	8.3
Switzerland-Liechtenstein	0.2	0.1	0.1
Togo	0.1	1.1	0.3
United Arab Emirates	—	—	0.7
United Kingdom	—	1.5	2.6
USA	0.5	13.1	9.4
Venezuela	—	0.6	—
Viet Nam	—	—	0.4
Total (incl. others)	154.0	200.9	206.2

Source: UN, *International Trade Statistics Yearbook*.

Transport

ROAD TRAFFIC
(estimates, motor vehicles in use)

	1994	1995	1996
Passenger cars	38,610	37,620	38,220
Lorries and vans	13,160	14,100	15,200

Source: IRF, *World Road Statistics*.

CIVIL AVIATION
(traffic on scheduled services)*

	1999	2000	2001
Kilometres flown (million)	3	3	1
Passengers carried ('000)	84	77	46
Passenger-km (million)	235	216	130
Total ton-km (million)	36	32	19

* Including an apportionment of the traffic of Air Afrique.

Source: UN, *Statistical Yearbook*.

Tourism

FOREIGN TOURIST ARRIVALS BY ORIGIN
(rounded figures)*

	2000	2001	2002
Africa	28,000	37,000	26,000
America	2,700	2,000	2,000
USA	1,500	1,000	1,000
Europe	14,000	11,000	9,000
France	n.a.	7,000	6,000
Total (incl. others)	45,700	52,000	39,000

* Figures refer to arrivals at national borders.

Tourism receipts (US $ million, incl. passenger transport): 28 in 2000; 32 in 2001; 28 in 2002; 34 in 2003.

Source: World Tourism Organization.

Communications Media

	2002	2003	2004
Telephones ('000 main lines in use)	22.4	n.a.	24.1
Mobile cellular telephones ('000 subscribers)	16.6	76.6	148.3
Personal computers ('000 in use)*	7	n.a.	9
Internet users ('000)*	15.0	n.a.	24.0

* Estimates.

1995: Facsimile machines 327 in use.

1996: Daily newspapers 1 (average circulation 2,000 copies); Non-daily newspapers 5 (average circulation 14,000 copies).

1997 ('000 in use): Radio receivers 680; Daily newspapers 1 (average circulation 2,000 copies).

1998 ('000 in use): Daily newspapers 1 (average circulation 2,000 copies).

2000 ('000 in use): Television receivers 395.

Books published (first editions, 1991): titles 5; copies ('000) 11.

Sources: UNESCO, *Statistical Yearbook*; UNESCO Institute for Statistics; UN, *Statistical Yearbook*; International Telecommunication Union.

Education

(2002/03, unless otherwise indicated)

	Institutions*	Teachers	Males	Females	Total
Pre-primary	193	684	8,700	8,564	17,264
Primary	5,975	20,533	513,279	344,313	857,592
Secondary	n.a.	4,063	76,292	48,497	124,789
Tertiary	n.a.	806†	10,416*	3,438*	13,854*

* 2001/02.
† 2000/01.

Source: mainly UNESCO Institute for Statistics.

Adult literacy rate (UNESCO estimates): 14.4% (males 19.6%; females 9.4%) in 2003 (Source: UN Development Programme, *Human Development Report*).

Directory

The Constitution

Following the death of President Ibrahim Baré Maïnassara, on 9 April 1999, a military Conseil de réconciliation nationale (CRN) was formed to exercise executive and legislative authority during a transitional period prior to the restoration of elected organs of government. A new Constitution, of what was to be designated the Fifth Republic, was approved by national referendum on 18 July 1999. The Constitution of the Fifth Republic, promulgated on 9 August, envisages a balance of powers between the President, Government and legislative Assemblée nationale. The President, who is elected by universal adult suffrage, is Head of State, and is

NIGER

accorded 'broad ordinary and arbitral powers'. The Government, under a Prime Minister appointed by the President, is responsible to the Assemblée nationale, which is competent to remove the Prime Minister by vote of censure. The Assemblée nationale is similarly elected by direct adult suffrage. The new President and legislature were inaugurated in December 1999.

Enshrined in the Constitution is a clause granting immunity from prosecution for all those involved in the *coups d'état* of January 1996 and April 1999. Legislation to this effect was adopted by the Assemblée nationale in January 2000.

Among regulatory bodies provided for in the Constitution are the Conseil supérieur de la communication, responsible for the broadcasting and communications sector, and the Conseil supérieur de la défense nationale, which advises the Head of State on defence matters.

The Government

HEAD OF STATE

President: Col (retd) MAMADOU TANDJA (inaugurated 22 December 1999, re-elected 4 December 2004).

COUNCIL OF MINISTERS
(April 2006)

Prime Minister: HAMA AMADOU.
Minister of State, Minister of Water, the Environment and the Fight against Desertification: ABDOU LABO.
Minister of State, Minister of Capital Works: SEYNI OUMAROU.
Minister of Trade, Industry and the Promotion of the Private Sector: HABI MAHAMADOU SALISSOU.
Minister of Public Health and the Fight against Epidemics: ARI IBRAHIM.
Minister of National Defence: HASSAN SOULEY BONTO.
Minister of Justice, Keeper of the Seals: El Hadj MATI MOUSSA.
Minister of Foreign Affairs, Co-operation and African Integration: AÏCHATOU MINDAOUDOU.
Minister of Transport: SOULEYMANE KANE.
Minister of the Economy and Finance: ALI LAMINE ZÈNE.
Minister of Land Management and Community Development: MAHAMANE MOUSSA.
Minister of Youth, Sports and the Games of La Francophonie: MOUSSA ABDOURAHMANE SEYDOU.
Minister of Tourism and Crafts: AMADOU NOUHOU.
Minister of Town Planning, Living Conditions and the Land Register: DIALLO AÏSSA ABDOULAYE.
Minister of Mines and Energy: MOHAMED ABDOULAHI.
Minister of the Interior and Decentralization: MOUKAÏLA MODI.
Minister of Basic Education and Literacy: HAMANI HAROUNA.
Minister of Animal Resources: ABDOULAYE DJINNA.
Minister of Agricultural Development: LABO MOUSSA.
Minister of Secondary and Higher Education, Research and Technology: OUSMANE GALADIMA.
Minister of the Civil Service and Labour: KANDA SIPTEY.
Minister responsible for Relations with Institutions and Government Spokesman: MOHAMED BEN OMAR.
Minister of Population and Social Action: BOUKARI ZILHA MAHAMADOU.
Minister of Culture, the Arts and Communication: OUMAROU HADARI.
Minister of Privatization and the Restructuring of Enterprises: GAZOBI LAOULI RAHAMOU.
Minister of Professional and Technical Training, responsible for Youth Employment: ABDOU DAOUDA.
Minister for the Promotion of Women and the Protection of Children: OUSMANE ZEÏNABOU MOULAYE.

MINISTRIES

Office of the President: BP 550, Niamey; tel. 72-23-80; fax 72-33-96; internet www.delgi.ne/presidence.
Office of the Prime Minister: BP 893, Niamey; tel. 72-26-99; fax 73-58-59.
Ministry of Agricultural Development: BP 12091, Niamey; tel. 73-35-41; fax 73-20-08.
Ministry of Animal Resources: BP 12091, Niamey; tel. 73-79-59; fax 73-31-86.
Ministry of Basic Education and Literacy: BP 557, Niamey; tel. 72-28-33; fax 72-21-05; e-mail scdameb@intnet.ne.
Ministry of Capital Works: BP 403, Niamey; tel. 73-53-57; fax 72-21-71.
Ministry of the Civil Service and Labour: BP 11107, Niamey; tel. 73-22-31; fax 73-61-69; e-mail sani.yakouba@caramail.com.
Ministry of Culture, the Arts and Communication: BP 452, Niamey; tel. 72-28-74; fax 73-36-85.
Ministry of the Economy and Finance: BP 389, Niamey; tel. 72-23-74; fax 73-59-34.
Ministry of Foreign Affairs, Co-operation and African Integration: BP 396, Niamey; tel. 72-29-07; fax 73-52-31.
Ministry of the Interior and Decentralization: BP 622, Niamey; tel. 72-32-62; fax 72-21-76.
Ministry of Justice: BP 466, Niamey; tel. 72-31-31; fax 72-37-77.
Ministry of Land Management and Community Development: BP 403, Niamey; tel. 73-53-57; fax 72-21-71.
Ministry of Mines and Energy: BP 11700, Niamey; tel. 73-45-82; fax 73-28-12.
Ministry of National Defence: BP 626, Niamey; tel. 72-20-76; fax 72-40-78.
Ministry of Population and Social Action: BP 11286, Niamey; tel. 72-23-30; fax 73-61-65.
Ministry of Privatization and the Restructuring of Enterprises: Immeuble CCCP, BP 862, Niamey; tel. 73-27-50; fax 73-59-91; e-mail ccpp@intnet.ne.
Ministry of Professional and Technical Training: BP 628, Niamey; tel. 72-26-20; fax 72-40-40.
Ministry for the Promotion of Women and the Protection of Children: BP 11286, Niamey; tel. 72-23-30; fax 73-61-65.
Ministry of Public Health and the Fight against Epidemics: BP 623, Niamey; tel. 72-28-08; fax 73-35-70.
Ministry of Secondary and Higher Education, Research and Technology: BP 628, Niamey; tel. 72-26-20; fax 72-40-40; e-mail mesnt@intnet.ne.
Ministry of Tourism and Crafts: BP 480, Niamey; tel. 73-65-22; fax 72-23-87.
Ministry of Town Planning, Living Conditions and the Land Register: BP 403, Niamey; tel. 73-53-57; fax 72-21-71.
Ministry of Trade, Industry and the Promotion of the Private Sector: BP 480, Niamey; tel. 73-29-74; fax 73-21-50; e-mail nicom@intnet.ne.
Ministry of Transport: BP 12130, Niamey; tel. 72-28-21; fax 73-36-85.
Ministry of Water, the Environment and the Fight against Desertification: BP 257, Niamey; tel. 73-47-22; fax 72-40-15.
Ministry of Youth, Sports and the Games of La Francophonie: BP 215, Niamey; tel. 72-32-35; fax 72-23-36.

President and Legislature

PRESIDENT

Presidential Election, First Round, 16 November 2004

Candidate	Votes	% of votes
Mamadou Tandja (MNSD)	991,764	40.67
Mahamadou Issoufou (PNDS)	599,792	24.60
Mahamane Ousmane (CDS)	425,052	17.43
Cheiffou Amadou (RSD)	154,732	6.34
Moumouni Adamou Djermakoye (ANDP)	147,957	6.07
Hamid Algabid (RDP)	119,153	4.89
Total	**2,438,450**	**100.00**

Second Round, 4 December 2004

Candidate	Votes	% of votes
Mamadou Tandja (MNSD)	1,509,905	65.53
Mahamadou Issoufou (PNDS)	794,397	34.47
Total	**2,304,302**	**100.00**

LEGISLATURE

Assemblée nationale
pl. de la Concertation, BP 12234, Niamey; tel. 72-27-38; fax 72-43-08; e-mail webmestre@assemblee.ne; internet www.assemblee.ne.

NIGER

President: El Hadj MAHAMANE OUSMANE.
General Election, 4 December 2004

Party	Seats
Mouvement national pour la société de développement—Nassara (MNSD)	47
Parti nigérien pour la démocratie et le socialisme—Tarayya (PNDS)	25*
Convention démocratique et social—Rahama (CDS)	22
Rassemblement social–démocratique—Gaskiya (RSD)	7
Rassemblement pour la démocratie et le progrès—Jama'a (RDP)	6
Alliance nigérienne pour la démocratie et le progrès social—Zaman Lahiya (ANDP)	5
Parti Social Démocrate du Niger—Alheri	1
Total	**113**

* Including eight seats won by parties running in coalition with the PNDS, namely the Parti nigérien pour l'autogestion (PNA), the Parti progressiste nigérien pour le rassemblement démocratique africain (PPN—RDA), the Union pour la démocratie et la République (UDR) and the Union nigérienne des indépendants (UNI).

Election Commission

Commission électorale nationale indépendante (CENI): Niamey; Chair. HAMIDOU SALIFOU KANE.

Political Organizations

In mid-2005 there were some 39 political parties registered in Niger, of which the following were among the most prominent:

Alliance nigérienne pour la démocratie et le progrès social—Zaman Lahiya (ANDP): Quartier Abidjan, Niamey; tel. 74-07-50; fmrly mem. of opposition Coordination des forces démocratiques (CFD); joined pro-Govt Alliance des forces démocratiques (AFD) in 2002; Leader Col (retd) MOUMOUNI ADAMOU DJERMAKOYE.

Alliance pour la démocratie et le progrès—Zuminci (ADP): Niamey; Chair. ISSOUFOU BACHAR.

Convention démocratique et social—Rahama (CDS): place Toumo, Niamey; tel. 74-19-58; f. 1991; supports Govt of Hama Amadou; mem. of Alliance des forces démocratiques (AFD); Pres. MAHAMANE OUSMANE.

Mouvement national pour la société de développement—Nassara (MNSD): rue du Stade, Niamey; tel. 73-39-07; e-mail webmaster@mnsd.ne; internet www.mnsd.ne; f. 1988; sole party 1988–90; Chair. Col (retd) MAMADOU TANDJA; Pres. HAMA AMADOU.

Parti nigérien pour l'autogestion—al Umat (PNA): Quartier Zabarkian, Niamey; tel. 72-33-05; f. 1997; contested legislative elections in Dec. 2004 in coalition with the PNDS; Leader SANOUSSI JACKOU.

Parti nigérien pour la démocratie et le socialisme—Tarayya (PNDS): place Toumo, Niamey; tel. 74-48-78; f. 1990; mem. of Coordination des forces démocratiques (CFD); Sec.-Gen. MAHAMADOU ISSOUFOU.

Parti progressiste nigérien—Rassemblement démocratique africain (PPN—RDA): Quartier Sonni, Niamey; tel. 74-16-70; associated with the late Pres. Diori; mem. of Coordination des forces démocratiques (CFD); contested legislative elections in Dec. 2004 in coalition with the PNDS; Chair. ABDOULAYE DIORI.

Parti social-démocrate nigérien—Alheri (PSDN): Leader KAZELMA OUMAR TAYA.

Rassemblement pour la démocratie et le progrès—Djamaa (RDP): place Toumo, Niamey; tel. 74-23-82; party of late Pres. Maïnassara; Chair. HAMID ALGABID; Sec.-Gen. MAHAMANE SOULEY LABI.

Rassemblement social-démocratique—Gaskiya (RSD): Quartier Poudrière, Niamey; tel. 74-00-90; f. 2004 following split in the CDS; Pres. CHEIFFOU AMADOU.

Rassemblement pour un Sahel vert—Nima (RSV): BP 12515, Niamey; tel. and fax 74-11-25; e-mail agarba_99@yahoo.com; Pres. ADAMOU GARBA.

Union pour la démocratie et le progrès—Amici (UDP): supports Govt of Hama Amadou; mem. of Alliance des forces démocratiques (AFD); Leader ABDOULAYE TONDI.

Union pour la démocratie et le progrès social—Amana (UDPS): represents interests of Tuaregs; mem. of Coordination des forces démocratiques (CFD); Chair. ISSOUF BAKO.

Union pour la démocratie et la République—Tabbat (UDR): Quartier Plateau, Niamey; f. 2002; contested legislative elections in Dec. 2004 in coalition with the PNDS; Pres. AMADOU BOUABACAR CISSÉ.

Union des forces populaires pour la démocratie et le progrès—Sawaba (UFPDP): Niamey.

Union des Nigeriens indépendants (UNI): Quartier Zabarkan, Niamey; tel. 74-23-81; contested legislative elections in Dec. 2004 in coalition with the PNDS; Leader AMADOU DJIBO.

Union des patriotes démocratiques et progressistes—Shamuwa (UPDP): Niamey; tel. 74-12-59; Chair. Prof. ANDRÉ SALIFOU.

Union des socialistes nigériens—Talaka (USN): f. 2001 by mems of the UFPDP; Leader ISSOUFOU ASSOUMANE.

In March 2001 12 opposition parties, led by the PNDS, formed the **Coordination des forces démocratiques (CFD)** (Zabarkan, rue du SNEN, BP 5005, Niamey; tel. 74-05-69), while 17 parties loyal to Prime Minister Hama Amadou, headed by the MNSD, formed the **Alliance des forces démocratiques (AFD)**. In July 2002 the ANDP withdrew from the CFD and joined the AFD.

Diplomatic Representation

EMBASSIES IN NIGER

Algeria: route des Ambassades-Goudel, BP 142, Niamey; tel. 72-35-83; fax 72-35-93; Ambassador HAMID BOUKRIF.

Benin: BP 11544, Niamey; tel. 72-28-60; Ambassador TAÏROU MAMADOU DJAOUGA.

Chad: Niamey; tel. 77-34-64; fax 72-43-61; Ambassador ALI ABDOULAYE SABRE.

China, People's Republic: BP 873, Niamey; tel. 72-32-83; fax 72-32-85; e-mail embchina@intnet.ne; Ambassador (vacant).

Cuba: rue Tillaberi, angle rue de la Cure Salée, face lycée Franco-Arabe, Plateau, BP 13886, Niamey; tel. 72-46-00; fax 72-39-32; e-mail amcbauba@intnet.ne; Ambassador SERAFIN GIL RODRÍGUEZ VALDÉS.

Egypt: Terminus Rond-Point Grand Hôtel, BP 254, Niamey; tel. 73-33-55; fax 73-38-91; Ambassador MOHAMED MAHMOUD MOUSTAFA EL-ASHMAWI.

France: route de Tondibia, quartier Yantala, BP 10660, Niamey; tel. 72-24-32; fax 72-20-66; e-mail webmestre@mail.com; internet www.ambafrance-ne.org; Ambassador FRANÇOIS PONGE.

Germany: 71 ave du Général de Gaulle, BP 629, Niamey; tel. 72-35-10; fax 72-39-85; e-mail amballny@intnet.ne; Ambassador HEIKE THIELE.

Iran: 11 rue de la Présidence, BP 10543, Niamey; tel. 72-21-98; fax 72-28-10; Ambassador MOHAMMAD AMIN NEJAD.

Korea, Democratic People's Republic: Niamey; Ambassador PAK SONG IL.

Libya: route de Goudel, BP 683, Niamey; tel. 72-40-19; fax 72-40-97; e-mail boukhari@intnet.ne; Ambassador BOUKHARI SALEM HODA.

Morocco: ave du Président Lubke, face Clinique Kaba, BP 12403, Niamey; tel. 73-40-84; fax 73-80-27; e-mail ambmang@intnet.ne; Ambassador MOHAMED JABER.

Nigeria: rue Goudel, BP 11130, Niamey; tel. 73-24-10; fax 73-35-00; Ambassador Dr YAKUBU KWARI.

Pakistan: ave des Zarmakoye, Yantala Plateau, BP 10426, Niamey; tel. 75-32-57; fax 75-32-55; e-mail ambny00@intnet.ne; Ambassador SOHAIL ITIEHAD HUSSAIN.

Saudi Arabia: route de Tillabery, BP 339, Niamey; tel. 75-32-15; fax 75-24-42; e-mail neemb@mofa.gov.sa; Chargé d'affaires a.i. FAHAD ALI ALDOSARY.

USA: rue des Ambassades, BP 11201, Niamey; tel. 73-31-69; fax 73-55-60; e-mail usis@intnet.ne; internet niamey.usembassy.gov; Ambassador BERNADETTE MARY ALLEN (designate).

Judicial System

The Supreme Court was dissolved following the death of President Ibrahim Baré Maïnassara in April 1999, but was re-established following the return to constitutional order later in that year. In accordance with the Constitution of the Fifth Republic, promulgated in August 1999, a Constitutional Court was established to replace the former Constitutional Chamber of the Supreme Court.

High Court of Justice: Niamey; internet www.assemblee.ne/organes/hjc.htm; competent to indict the President of the Republic and all other state officials (past and present) in relation to all matters of state, including high treason; comprises seven perm. mems and three rotating mems; Pres. MOUMOUNI ADAMOU DJERMAKOYE.

NIGER

Supreme Court: Niamey; tel. 74-26-36; comprises three chambers; in 2002 the Government announced proposals to replace the Supreme Court with three separate courts: a Court of Cassation, a Council of State and an Audit Court; Pres. MAMADOU MALLAM AOUMI; Vice-Pres. SALIFOU FATIMATA BAZEYE; Pres. of the Administrative Chamber DILLE RABO; Pres. of the Judicial Chamber (vacant); Pres. of the Chamber of Audit and Budgetary Discipline SIKKOSO MORY OUSMANE; Prosecutor-Gen. MAHAMANE BOUKARY.

Constitutional Court: BP 10779, Niamey; tel. 72-30-81; fax 72-35-40; e-mail cconstit@intnet.ne; f. 1999; comprises a President, a Vice-President and five Councillors; Pres. ABBA MOUSSA ISSOUFOU; Vice-Pres. ABDOU HASSAN.

Courts of First Instance: located at Niamey (with sub-divisions at Dosso and Tillabéri), Maradi, Tahoua (sub-divisions at Agadez, Arlit and Birni N'Konni) and Diffa (sub-division at Diffa).

Labour Courts: function at each Court of the First Instance and sub-division thereof.

Religion

It is estimated that some 95% of the population are Muslims, 0.5% are Christians and the remainder follow traditional beliefs.

ISLAM

The most influential Islamic groups in Niger are the Tijaniyya, the Senoussi and the Hamallists.

Association Islamique du Niger: Niamey; Dir CHEIKH OUMAROU ISMAEL.

CHRISTIANITY

Various Protestant missions maintain 13 centres, with a personnel of 90.

The Roman Catholic Church

Niger comprises two dioceses, directly responsible to the Holy See. The Bishops participate in the Bishops' Conference of Burkina Faso and Niger (based in Ouagadougou, Burkina Faso). At 31 December 2003 there were an estimated 16,031 adherents in Niger.

Bishop of Maradi: Rt Rev. AMBROISE OUÉDRAOGO, Evêché, BP 447, Maradi; tel. and fax 41-03-30; fax 41-13-86; e-mail ambroiseoued@yahoo.fr.

Bishop of Niamey: Rt Rev. MICHEL CHRISTIAN CARTATÉGUY, Evêché, BP 10270, Niamey; tel. 73-32-59; fax 73-80-01; e-mail cartateguymi@voila.fr; internet www.multimania.com/cathoniger.

The Press

The published press expanded considerably in Niger after 1993, when the requirement to obtain prior authorization for each edition was lifted, although legislation continued to require that a copy of each publication be deposited at the office of the Procurator of the Republic. For the most part, however, economic difficulties have ensured that few publications have maintained a regular, sustained appearance. The following were among those newspapers and periodicals believed to be appearing regularly in early 2005:

L'Action: Quartier Yantala, Niamey; tel. 96-92-22; e-mail action_ne@yahoo.fr; internet www.tamtaminfo.com/action.pdf; f. 2003; fortnightly; popular newspaper intended for youth audience; Dir of Publication BOUSSADA BEN ALI; circ. 2,000 (2003).

L'Alternative: BP 10948, Niamey; tel. 74-24-39; fax 74-24-82; e-mail alter@intnet.ne; internet www.alternative.ne; f. 1994; weekly; in French and Hausa; Dir MOUSSA TCHANGARI; Editor-in-Chief ABDRAMANE OUSMANE.

Anfani: Immeuble DMK, rue du Damagaram, BP 2096, Niamey; tel. 74-08-80; fax 74-00-52; e-mail anfani@intnet.ne; f. 1992; 2 a month; Editor-in-Chief IBBO DADDY ABDOULAYE; circ. 3,000.

As-Salam: BP 451, Niamey; tel. 74-29-12; e-mail assa_lam@yahoo.fr; monthly; Dir IBBO DADDY ABDOULAYE.

Le Canard Déchaîné: BP 383, Niamey; tel. 92-66-64; satirical; weekly; Dir of Publication ABDOULAYE TIÉMOGO; Editor-in-Chief IBRAHIM MANZO.

Le Canard Libéré: BP 11631, Niamey; tel. 75-43-52; fax 75-39-89; e-mail canardlibere@caramail.com; satirical; weekly; Dir of Publication TRAORÉ DAOUDA AMADOU; Editorial Dir OUMAROU NALAN MOUSSA.

Le Démocrate: 21 rue 067, NB Terminus, BP 11064, Niamey; tel. 73-24-25; e-mail le_democrate@caramail.com; internet www.tamtaminfo.com/democrate.pdf; weekly; independent; f. 1992; Dir of Publication ALBERT CHAÏBOU; Editor-in-Chief OUSSEINI ISSA.

Les Echos du Sahel: Villa 4012, 105 Logements, BP 12750, Niamey; tel. and fax 74-32-17; e-mail ecosahel@intnet.ne; f. 1999; rural issues and development; quarterly; Dir IBBO DADDY ABDOULAYE.

L'Enquêteur: BP 172, Niamey; tel. 90-18-74; e-mail lenqueteur@yahoo.fr; fortnightly; Publr TAHIROU GOURO; Editor IBRAHIM SOULEY.

Haské: BP 297, Niamey; tel. 74-18-44; fax 73-20-06; e-mail webmaster@planetafrique.com; internet www.haske.uni.cc; f. 1990; weekly; also Haské Magazine, quarterly; Dir CHEIKH IBRAHIM DIOP.

La Jeune Académie: BP 11989, Niamey; tel. 73-38-71; e-mail jeune.academie@caramail.com; monthly; Dir ABDOULAYE HASSOUMI GARBA.

Journal Officiel de la République du Niger: BP 116, Niamey; tel. 72-39-30; fax 72-39-43; f. 1960; fortnightly; govt bulletin; Man. Editor BONKOULA AMINATOU MAYAKI; circ. 800.

Libération: BP 10483, Niamey; tel. 97-96-22; f. 1995; weekly; Dir BOUBACAR DIALLO; circ. 1,000 (2003).

Matinfo: BP 11631, Niamey; tel. 75-43-52; fax 75-39-89; e-mail matinfo@caramail.com; daily; independent; Dir DAOUDA AMADOU TRAORÉ.

Nigerama: BP 11158, Niamey; tel. 74-08-09; e-mail anpniger@intnet.ne; quarterly; publ. by the Agence Nigérienne de Presse.

L'Opinion: BP 11116, Niamey; tel. 74-09-84; e-mail lopinion@dounia.ne; Dir ALZOUMA ZAKARI.

Le Regard: ; tel. 73-84-07; e-mail le_regard@usa.net; Dir MAHAMADOU TOURÉ.

Le Républicain: Nouvelle Imprimerie du Niger, place du Petit Marché, BP 12015, Niamey; tel. 73-47-98; fax 73-41-42; e-mail webmasters@republicain-niger.com; internet www.republicain-niger.com; f. 1991; weekly; independent; Dir of Publication MAMANE ABOU; circ. 2,500.

La Roue de l'Histoire: Zabarkan, rue du SNEN, BP 5005, Niamey; tel. 74-05-69; internet www.tamtaminfo.com/roue.pdf; weekly; Propr SANOUSSI JACKOU; Dir ABARAD MOUDOUR ZAKARA.

Le Sahel Quotidien: BP 13182, ONEP, Niamey; tel. 73-34-87; fax 73-30-90; f. 1960; publ. by Office National d'Edition et de Presse; daily; Dir IBRAHIM MAMANE TANTAN; Editor-in-Chief ALASSANE ASOKOFARE; circ. 5,000; also Sahel-Dimanche, Sundays; circ. 3,000.

Sauyi: BP 10948, Niamey; tel. 74-24-39; fax 74-24-82; e-mail sarji@alternative.ne; fortnightly; Hausa; publ. by Groupe Alternative; Hausa; rural interest; Dir SAÏDOU ARJI.

Stadium: BP 10948, Niamey; tel. 74-08-80; e-mail kiabba@yahoo.fr; sports; 2 a month; Dir ABDOU TIKIRÉ.

Le Témoin: BP 10483, Niamey; tel. 96-58-51; e-mail istemoin@yahoo.fr; internet www.tamtaminfo.com/temoin.pdf; 2 a month; Dir of Publication IBRAHIM SOUMANA GAOH; Editors AMADOU TIÉMOGO, MOUSSA DAN TCHOUKOU, I. S. GAOH; circ. 1,000 (2005).

Ténéré Express: BP 13600, Niamey; tel. 73-35-76; fax 73-77-75; e-mail tenerefm@intnet.ne; daily; independent; current affairs; Dir ABDOULAYE MOUSSA MASSALATCHI.

La Tribune du Peuple: Niamey; tel. 73-34-28; e-mail tribune@intnet.ne; f. 1993; weekly; Man. Editor IBRAHIM HAMIDOU.

Le Trophée: BP 2000, Niamey; tel. 74-12-79; e-mail strophee@caramail.com; sports; 2 a month; Dir ISSA HAMIDOU MAYAKI.

NEWS AGENCIES

Agence Nigérienne de Presse (ANP): BP 11158, Niamey; tel. 74-08-09; e-mail anpniger@intnet.ne; f. 1987; state-owned; Dir YAYE HASSANE.

Sahel—Office National d'Edition et de Presse (ONEP): BP 13182, Niamey; tel. 73-34-86; f. 1989; Dir ALI OUSSEÏNI.

Publishers

La Nouvelle Imprimerie du Niger (NIN): place du Petit Marché, BP 61, Niamey; tel. 73-47-98; fax 73-41-42; e-mail nin@intnet.ne; f. 1962 as Imprimerie Nationale du Niger; govt publishing house; brs in Agadez and Maradi; Dir E. WOHLRAB.

Réseau Sahélien de Recherche et de Publication: Niamey; tel. 73-36-90; fax 73-39-43; e-mail resadep@ilimi.uam.ne; press of the Université Abdou Moumouni; Co-ordinator BOUREIMA DIADIE.

Broadcasting and Communications

REGULATORY AUTHORITY

Conseil Supérieur de la Communication (CSC): Plateau, Niamey; tel. 72-23-56; comprises 15 mems; one representative of the President of the Republic, one representative of the President of the

NIGER

Assemblée nationale, one representative of the Prime Minister, one representative apiece of the Ministers of Culture, the Arts and Communication, of the Interior and Decentralization, and of Justice, three representatives of the publicly owned communications sector, four representatives of civil society, and one representative each of private-sector employees and employers in the domain of communication; Pres. MARIAMA KEÏTA.

TELECOMMUNICATIONS

Celtel Niger: Niamey; tel. 73-85-43; fax 73-23-85; e-mail b-sghir@intnet.ne; f. 2001 to operate mobile cellular telecommunications network in Niamey and Maradi; 70% owned by Celtel International (United Kingdom), 30% owned by Caren Assurance; Dir-Gen. COLIN CAMPBELL.

Société Nigérienne des Télécommunications (SONITEL): BP 208, Niamey; tel. 72-20-00; fax 73-58-12; e-mail sonitel@intnet.ne; internet www.intnet.ne; f. 1998; 51% jtly-owned by ZTE Corpn (People's Republic of China) and Laaico (Libya), 46% state-owned; Dir-Gen. MOUSSA BOUBACAR.

Sahel Com: BP 208, Niamey; f. 2002; mobile cellular telecommunications in Niamey.

Telecel Niger: Niamey; f. 2001 to operate mobile cellular telecommunications network, initially in Niamey and western regions, expanding to cover Maradi and Zinder by 2003, and Tahoua and Agadez by 2004; 68% owned by Orascom Telecom (Egypt); Dir HIMA SOULEY.

BROADCASTING

Radio

Independent radio stations have been permitted to operate since 1994, although the majority are concentrated in the capital, Niamey. In 2000 the first of a network of rural stations, RURANET, which were to broadcast mainly programmes concerned with development issues, mostly in national languages, was established. Several local radio stations, funded by the Agence intergouvernementale de la francophonie, were expected to commence operations in the early 2000s.

Anfani FM: blvd Nali-Béro, BP 2096, Wadata, Niamey; tel. 74-08-80; fax 74-00-52; e-mail anfani@intnet.ne; private radio station, broadcasting to Niamey, Zinder, Maradi and Diffa; Dir ISMAËL MOUTARI.

Office de Radiodiffusion-Télévision du Niger (ORTN): BP 309, Niamey; tel. 72-31-63; fax 72-35-48; state broadcasting authority; Dir-Gen. YAYÉ HAROUNA.

La Voix du Sahel: BP 361, Niamey; tel. 72-22-02; fax 72-35-48; e-mail ortny@intnet.ne; f. 1958; govt-controlled radio service; programmes in French, Hausa, Djerma, Kanuri, Fulfuldé, Tamajak, Toubou, Gourmantché, Boudouma and Arabic; Dir IBRO NA-ALLAH AMADOU.

Ténéré FM: BP 13600, Niamey; tel. 73-65-76; fax 73-46-94; e-mail tenerefm@intnet.ne; f. 1998; Dir ABIBOU GARBA; Editor-in-Chief SOULEYMANE ISSA MAÏGA.

Ruranet: Niamey; internet membres.lycos.fr/nigeradio; f. 2000; network of rural radio stations, broadcasting 80% in national languages, with 80% of programmes concerned with development issues; 31 stations operative in April 2002.

La Voix de l'Hémicycle: BP 12234, Niamey; f. 2002 as the radio station of the Assemblée nationale; broadcasts parliamentary debates and analysis for 15 hours daily in French and national languages to Niamey and environs.

Sudan FM: Dosso; auth. 2000; private radio station; Dir HIMA ADAMOU.

Television

Office de Radiodiffusion-Télévision du Niger (ORTN): see Radio

Télé-Sahel: BP 309, Niamey; tel. 72-31-55; fax 72-35-48; govt-controlled television service; broadcasts daily from 13 transmission posts and six retransmission posts, covering most of Niger; Dir-Gen. ABDOU SOULEY.

Télévision Ténéré (TTV): BP 13600, Niamey; tel. 73-65-76; fax 73-77-75; e-mail tenerefm@intnet.ne; f. 2000; independent broadcaster in Niamey; Dir ABIBOU GARBA.

The independent operator, Télé Star, broadcasts several international or foreign channels in Niamey and environs, including TV5, Canal Horizon, CFI, RTL9, CNN and Euro News

Finance

(cap. = capital; res = reserves; dep. = deposits; m. = million; brs = branches; amounts in francs CFA)

BANKING

Central Bank

Banque Centrale des Etats de l'Afrique de l'Ouest (BCEAO): BP 487, Niamey; tel. 72-24-91; fax 73-47-43; HQ in Dakar, Senegal; f. 1962; bank of issue for the mem. states of the Union économique et monétaire ouest-africaine (UEMOA, comprising Benin, Burkina Faso, Côte d'Ivoire, Guinea-Bissau, Mali, Niger, Senegal and Togo); cap. and res 859,313m., total assets 5,671,675m. (Dec. 2002); Gov. CHARLES KONAN BANNY; Dir in Niger ABDOULAYE SOUMANA; brs at Maradi and Zinder.

Commercial Banks

Bank of Africa—Niger (BOA-Niger): Immeuble Sonara II, ave de la Mairie, BP 10973, Niamey; tel. 73-36-20; fax 73-38-18; e-mail boafrni@intnet.ne; internet www.bkofafrica.net/niger.htm; f. 1994 to acquire assets of Nigeria International Bank Niamey; 42.6% owned by African Financial Holding; cap. and res 2,658m., total assets 26,669m. (Dec. 2003); Pres. PAUL DERREUMAUX; Dir-Gen. MAMADOU SÉNÉ; 2 brs.

Banque Commerciale du Niger (BCN): Rond-Point Maourey, BP 11363, Niamey; tel. 73-39-15; fax 73-21-63; f. 1978; 83.15% owned by Libyan Arab Foreign Bank, 16.85% state-owned; cap. and res 1,477m., total assets 14,618m. (Dec. 2003); Administrator IBRAHIM MAJDOUB NAJI (acting).

Banque Internationale pour l'Afrique au Niger (BIA—Niger): ave de la Mairie, BP 10350, Niamey; tel. 73-31-01; fax 73-35-95; e-mail bia@intnet.ne; internet www.bianiger.com; f. 1980; 35% owned by Groupe Belgolaise (Belgium); cap. 2,800.0m., res 1,335.1m., dep. 42,263.9m. (Dec. 2003); Pres. AMADOU HIMA SOULEY; Dir-Gen. DANIEL HASSER; 11 brs.

Banque Islamique du Niger pour le Commerce et l'Investissement (BINCI): Immeuble El Nasr, BP 12754, Niamey; tel. 73-27-30; fax 73-47-35; e-mail binci@intnet.ne; f. 1983; fmrly Banque Masraf Faisal Islami; 33% owned by Dar al-Maal al-Islami (Switzerland), 33% by Islamic Development Bank (Saudi Arabia); cap. 1,810m., total assets 7,453m. (Dec. 2003); Pres. ABDERRAOUF BENESSAÏAH; Dir-Gen. AÏSSANI OMAR.

Ecobank Niger: blvd de la Liberté, angle rue des Bâtisseurs, BP 13804, Niamey; tel. 73-71-81; fax 73-72-04; e-mail ecobankni@ecobank.com; internet www.ecobank.com; f. 1999; 59.4% owned by Ecobank Transnational Inc. (Togo, operating under the auspices of the Economic Community of West African States), 28.6% by Ecobank Benin, 11.9% by Ecobank Togo; cap. and res 2,265.6m., total assets 26,959.2m. (Dec. 2003); Chair. MAHAMADOU OUHOUMOUDOU; Dir-Gen. FELIX BIKPO.

Société Nigérienne de Banque (SONIBANK): ave de la Mairie, BP 891, Niamey; tel. 73-45-69; fax 73-46-93; e-mail sonibank@intnet.ne; f. 1990; 25% owned by Société Tunisienne de Banque; cap. 2,000.0m., res 4,728.5m., dep. 41,725.5m. (Dec. 2004); Pres. ILLA KANÉ; Dir-Gen. MOUSSA HAITOU; 6 brs.

Development Banks

Caisse de Prêts aux Collectivités Territoriales (CPCT): route Torodi, BP 730, Niamey; tel. 72-34-12; fax 72-30-80; f. 1970; 100% state-owned (94% by organs of local govt); cap. and res 744m., total assets 2,541m. (Dec. 2003); Admin. ABDOU DJIBO (acting).

Crédit du Niger (CDN): 11 blvd de la République, BP 213, Niger; tel. 72-27-01; fax 72-23-90; e-mail cdb-nig@intnet.ne; f. 1958; 54% state-owned, 20% owned by Caisse Nationale de Sécurité Sociale; transfer to full private ownership pending; cap. and res 1,058m., total assets 3,602m. (Dec. 2003); Administrator ABDOU DJIBO (acting).

Fonds d'Intervention en Faveur des Petites et Moyennes Entreprises Nigériennes (FIPMEN): Immeuble Sonara II, BP 252, Niamey; tel. 73-20-98; f. 1990; state-owned; cap. and res 124m. (Dec. 1991); Chair. AMADOU SALLA HASSANE; Man. Dir IBRAHIM BEIDARI.

Savings Bank

Office National de la Poste et de l'Epargne: BP 11778, Niamey; tel. 73-24-98; fax 73-35-69; fmrly Caisse Nationale d'Epargne; Chair. Mme PALFI; Man. Dir HASSOUME MATA.

STOCK EXCHANGE

Bourse Régionale des Valeurs Mobilières (BRVM): c/o Chambre de Commerce et d'Industrie du Niger, Place de la Concertation, BP 13299, Niamey; tel. 73-66-92; fax 73-69-47; e-mail imagagi@brvm.org; internet www.brvm.org; f. 1998; national branch of BRVM

NIGER

(regional stock exchange based in Abidjan, Côte d'Ivoire, serving the member states of UEMOA); Man. IDRISSA S. MAGAGI.

INSURANCE

Agence d'Assurance du Sahel: BP 10661, Niamey; tel. 74-05-47.

Agence Nigérienne d'Assurances (ANA): place de la Mairie, BP 423, Niamey; tel. 72-20-71; f. 1959; cap. 1.5m.; owned by L'Union des Assurances de Paris; Dir JEAN LASCAUD.

Caren Assurance: BP 733, Niamey; tel. 73-34-70; fax 73-24-93; e-mail carenas@intnet.ne; insurance and reinsurance; Dir-Gen. IBRAHIM IDI ANGO.

Leyma—Société Nigérienne d'Assurances et de Réassurances (SNAR—Leyma): BP 426, Niamey; tel. 73-57-72; fax 73-40-44; f. 1973; restructured 2002; Pres. AMADOU OUSMANE; Dir-Gen. MAMADOU MALAM AOUAMI.

La Nigérienne d'Assurance et de Réassurance: BP 13300, Niamey; tel. 73-63-36; fax 73-73-37.

Union Générale des Assurances du Niger (UGAN): rue de Kalley, BP 11935, Niamey; tel. 73-54-06; fax 73-41-85; f. 1985; cap. 500m.; Pres. PATHÉ DIONE; Dir-Gen. MAMADOU TALATA; 7 brs.

Trade and Industry

GOVERNMENT AGENCIES

Cellule de Coordination de la Programme de Privatisation: Immeuble Sonibanque, BP 862, Niamey; tel. 73-29-10; fax 73-29-58; responsible for co-ordination of privatization programme; Co-ordinator IDÉ ISSOUFOU.

Office des Eaux du Sous-Sol (OFEDES): BP 734, Niamey; tel. 74-01-19; fax 74-16-68; govt agency for the maintenance and development of wells and boreholes; Pres. DJIBO HAMANI.

Office du Lait du Niger (OLANI): BP 404, Niamey; tel. 73-23-69; fax 73-36-74; f. 1971; development and marketing of milk products; transferred to majority private ownership in 1998; Dir-Gen. M. DIENG.

Office National de l'Energie Solaire (ONERSOL): BP 621, Niamey; tel. 73-45-05; govt agency for research and development, commercial production and exploitation of solar devices; Dir ALBERT WRIGHT.

Office National des Ressources Minières du Niger (ONAREM): Rond-Point Kennedy, BP 12716, Niamey; tel. 73-59-28; fax 73-28-12; f. 1976; govt agency for exploration, exploitation and marketing of all minerals; Pres. MOUDY MOHAMED; Dir-Gen. A. A. ASKIA.

Office des Produits Vivriers du Niger (OPVN): BP 474, Niamey; tel. 73-44-43; fax 74-27-18; govt agency for developing agricultural and food production; Dir-Gen. M. ISSAKA.

Riz du Niger (RINI): BP 476, Niamey; tel. 71-13-29; fax 73-42-04; f. 1967; cap. 825m. francs CFA; 30% state-owned; transfer to 100% private ownership proposed; production and marketing of rice; Pres. YAYA MADOUGOU; Dir-Gen. M. HAROUNA.

DEVELOPMENT ORGANIZATIONS

Agence Française de Développement (AFD): 203 ave du Gountou-Yéna, BP 212, Niamey; tel. 72-33-93; fax 72-26-05; e-mail afdniamey@groupe-afd.org; internet www.afd.fr; Country Dir FRANÇOIS GIOVALUCCHI.

Mission Française de Coopération et d'Action Culturelle: BP 494, Niamey; tel. 72-20-66; administers bilateral aid from France; Dir JEAN BOULOGNE.

SNV (Société Néerlandais de Développement): ave des Zarmakoye, BP 10110, Niamey; tel. 75-36-33; fax 75-35-06; e-mail snvniger@snv.ne; internet www.snv.ne; present in Niger since 1978; projects concerning food security, agriculture, the environment, savings and credit, marketing, water and communications; operations in Tillabéri, Zinder and Tahoua provinces.

CHAMBERS OF COMMERCE

Chambre de Commerce d'Agriculture, d'Industrie et d'Artisanat du Niger: BP 209, Niamey; tel. 73-22-10; fax 73-46-68; e-mail cham209n@intnet.ne; internet www.ccaian.org; BP 201, Agadez; tel. 44-01-61; BP 91, Diffa; tel. 54-03-92; BP 79, Maradi; tel. 41-03-76; BP 172, Tahoua; tel. 61-03-84; BP 83, Zinder; tel. 51-00-78; f. 1954; comprises 80 full mems and 40 dep. mems; Pres. IBRAHIM IDI ANGO; Sec.-Gen. SADOU AISSATA.

INDUSTRIAL AND TRADE ORGANIZATIONS

Centre Nigérien du Commerce Extérieur (CNCE): place de la Concertation, BP 12480, Niamey; tel. 73-22-88; fax 73-46-68; f. 1984; promotes and co-ordinates all aspects of foreign trade; Dir AÏSSA DIALLO.

Société Nationale de Commerce et de Production du Niger (COPRO-Niger): Niamey; tel. 73-28-41; fax 73-57-71; f. 1962; monopoly importer of foodstuffs; cap. 1,000m. francs CFA; 47% state-owned; Man. Dir DJIBRILLA HIMA.

EMPLOYERS' ORGANIZATIONS

Syndicat des Commerçants Importateurs et Exportateurs du Niger (SCIMPEXNI): Chambre de Commerce, d'Agriculture, d'Industrie et d'Artisanat du Niger, Niamey; tel. 73-33-17; Pres. M. SILVA; Sec.-Gen. INOUSSA MAÏGA.

Syndicat National des Petites et Moyennes Entreprises et Industries Nigériennes (SYNAPEMEIN): Chambre de Commerce, d'Agriculture, d'Industrie et d'Artisanat du Niger, Niamey; Pres. SEYBOU SLAEY; Sec.-Gen. ADOLPHE SAGBO.

Syndicat Patronal des Entreprises et Industries du Niger (SPEIN): BP 415, Niamey; tel. 73-24-01; fax 73-47-07; f. 1994; Pres. AMADOU OUSMANE; Sec.-Gen. NOUHOU TARI.

UTILITIES

Electricity

Société Nigérienne d'Electricité (NIGELEC): 46 ave du Gen. de Gaulle, BP 11202, Niamey; tel. 72-26-92; fax 72-32-88; e-mail nigelec@intnet.ne; f. 1968; 95% state-owned; 51% transfer to private ownership proposed; production and distribution of electricity; Dir-Gen. IBRAHIM FOUKORI.

Water

Société d'Exploitation des Eaux du Niger (SEEN): blvd Zarmaganda, BP 12209, Niamey; tel. 72-25-00; fax 73-46-40; fmrly Société Nationale des Eaux; 51% owned by Veolia Environnement (France); production and distribution of drinking water; Pres. ABARY DAN BOUZOUA SOULEYMENE; Dir-Gen. SEYNI SALOU.

TRADE UNION FEDERATIONS

Confédération des Travailleurs du Niger (CTN): Niamey; Sec.-Gen. ISSOUFOU SEYBOU.

Entente des Travailleurs du Niger (ETN): Bourse du Travail, BP 388, Niamey; tel. and fax 73-52-56; f. 2005 by merger of Confédération Nigérienne du Travail, Union Generale des Travailleurs du Niger and Union des Syndicats des Travailleurs du Niger.

Transport

ROADS

Niger is crossed by highways running from east to west and from north to south, giving access to neighbouring countries. A road is under construction to Lomé, Togo, via Burkina Faso, and the 428-km Zinder–Agadez road, scheduled to form part of the Trans-Sahara Highway, has been upgraded. Niger and Algeria appealed jointly in mid-1998 for international aid to fund construction of the Trans-Sahara Highway, development of which was suspended in the mid-1990s because of the conflict in northern Niger. Some 2,100m. francs CFA of the budget for 2001 was allocated to road maintenance.

In 2000 there were an estimated 14,000 km of classified roads, of which 3,621 km were paved.

Société Nationale des Transports Nigériens (SNTN): BP 135, Niamey; tel. 72-24-55; fax 74-47-07; e-mail stratech@intnet.ne; f. 1963; operates passenger and freight road-transport services; 49% state-owned; Chair. MOHAMED ABDOULAHI; Man. Dir BARKE M. MOUSTAPHA.

RAILWAYS

There are as yet no railways in Niger.

Organisation Commune Bénin-Niger des Chemins de Fer et des Transports (OCBN): BP 38, Niamey; tel. 73-27-90; f. 1959; 50% owned by Govt of Niger, 50% by Govt of Benin; manages the Benin-Niger railway project (begun in 1978); also operates more than 500 km within Benin (q.v.); extension to Niger proposed; transfer to private ownership proposed; Dir-Gen. FLAVIEN BALOGOUN.

INLAND WATERWAYS

The River Niger is navigable for 300 km within the country. Access to the sea is available by a river route from Gaya, in south-western Niger, to the coast at Port Harcourt, Nigeria, between September and March. Port facilities at Lomé, Togo, are used as a commercial outlet for land-locked Niger: some 126,000 metric tons of goods imported by Niger pass through Lomé annually. An agreement providing import

NIGER

facilities at the port of Tema was signed with Ghana in November 1986.

Niger-Transit (NITRA): Zone Industrielle, BP 560, Niamey; tel. 73-22-53; fax 73-26-38; f. 1974; 48% owned by SNTN; customs agent, freight-handling, warehousing, etc; manages Nigerien port facilities at Lomé, Togo; Pres. OUMAROU ALI BEÏOLI; Man. Dir SADE FATIMATA.

Société Nigérienne des Transports Fluviaux et Maritimes (SNTFM): Niamey; tel. 73-39-69; river and sea transport; cap. 64.6m. francs CFA; 99% state-owned; Man. Dir BERTRAND DEJEAN.

CIVIL AVIATION

There are international airports at Niamey (Hamani Diori), Agadez (Mano Dayak) and Zinder, and major domestic airports at Diffa, Maradi and Tahoua.

Air Continental: Niamey; f. 2003 to replace Air Niger International (f. 2002); 60% owned by private Nigerian interests, 20% by private Nigerien interests, 5% by Govt of Niger; regional and international services.

Air Inter Afrique: Niamey; tel. 73-85-85; fax 73-69-73; f. 2001; operates services within West Africa; CEO CHEIKH OUSMANE DIALLO.

Air Inter Niger: Agadez; f. 1997 to operate services to Tamanrasset (Algeria).

Niger Air Continental: Niamey; e-mail info@nigeraircontinental.com; f. 2003.

Nigeravia: BP 10454, Niamey; tel. 73-30-64; fax 74-18-42; e-mail nigavia@intnet.ne; internet www.nigeravia.com; f. 1991; operates domestic, regional and international services; Pres. and Dir-Gen JEAN SYLVESTRE.

Société Nigérienne des Transports Aériens (SONITA): Niamey; f. 1991; owned by private Nigerien (81%) and Cypriot (19%) interests; operates domestic and regional services; Man. Dir ABDOULAYE MAIGA GOUDOUBABA.

Tourism

The Aïr and Ténéré Nature Reserve, covering an area of 77,000 sq km, was established in 1988. Tourism was hampered by insecurity in the north and east during the 1990s. However, the number of foreign arrivals at hotels and similar establishments increased from 39,190 in 1997 to 42,433 in 1999, when tourism receipts amounted to US $24m. In 2002 some 39,000 tourists entered Niger, while receipts from tourism totalled $34m. in 2003.

Office National du Tourisme (ONT): ave de Président H. Luebke, BP 612, ave Luebke, Niamey; tel. 73-24-47; fax 73-39-40.

NIGERIA

Introductory Survey

Location, Climate, Language, Religion, Flag, Capital

The Federal Republic of Nigeria is a West African coastal state on the shores of the Gulf of Guinea, with Benin to the west, Niger to the north, Chad to the north-east, and Cameroon to the east and south-east. The climate is tropical in the southern coastal areas, with an average annual temperature of 32°C (90°F) and high humidity. It is drier and semi-tropical in the north. Average annual rainfall is more than 2,500 mm (98 ins) in parts of the south-east, but in certain areas of the north is as low as 600mm (24 ins). In 1963 the most widely spoken languages were Hausa (20.9%), Yoruba (20.3%), Ibo (16.6%) and Fulani (8.6%). English is the country's official language. In 1963 the principal religious groups were Muslims (47.2%) and Christians (34.5%), while 18% of the total population followed animist beliefs. The national flag (proportions 1 by 2) has three equal vertical stripes, of green, white and green. The capital is Abuja, to which the Federal Government was formally transferred in December 1991; however, many non-government institutions remained in the former capital, Lagos.

Recent History

The territory of present-day Nigeria, except for the section of former German-controlled Cameroon (see below), was conquered by the United Kingdom, in several stages, during the second half of the 19th century and the first decade of the 20th century. The British dependencies of Northern and Southern Nigeria were merged into a single territory in 1914, administered largely by traditional native rulers, under the supervision of the colonial authorities. In 1947 the United Kingdom introduced a new Nigerian Constitution, establishing a federal system of government, based on three regions: Northern, Western and Eastern. The federal arrangement was an attempt to reconcile religious and regional tensions, and to accommodate Nigeria's diverse ethnic groups, notably the Ibo (in the east), the Yoruba (in the west) and the Hausa and Fulani (in the north). The Northern Region, which was predominantly Muslim, contained about one-half of Nigeria's total population.

In 1954 the federation became self-governing, and the first federal Prime Minister, Alhaji Abubakar Tafawa Balewa (a Muslim northerner), was appointed in August 1957. A constitutional conference, convened in 1958, agreed that Nigeria should become independent in 1960, and elections to an enlarged federal legislature took place in December 1959. The Northern People's Congress (NPC), which was politically dominant in the north, became the single largest party in the new legislature, although lacking an overall majority. Tafawa Balewa (a prominent member of the NPC) continued to head a coalition government of the NPC and the National Council for Nigeria and the Cameroons (NCNC), which attracted most support in the Eastern Region.

On 1 October 1960, as scheduled, the Federation of Nigeria achieved independence, initially as a constitutional monarchy. In June 1961 the northern part of the UN Trust Territory of British Cameroons was incorporated into Nigeria's Northern Region as the province of Sardauna, and in August 1963 a fourth region, the Mid-Western Region, was created by dividing the existing Western Region. On 1 October a revised Constitution was adopted, and the country was renamed the Federal Republic of Nigeria, although it remained a member of the Commonwealth. Dr Nnamdi Azikiwe of the NCNC took office as Nigeria's first President (then a non-executive post).

The first national election after independence, to the federal House of Representatives, took place in December 1964. Widespread violence was reported during the election campaign, prompting a boycott of the poll by the main opposition grouping, the United Progressive Grand Alliance (UPGA), a coalition of four parties, dominated by the NCNC (previously renamed the National Convention of Nigerian Citizens). The election resulted in a large majority for the Nigerian National Alliance, a seven-party coalition, which was dominated by the NPC.

On 15 January 1966 Tafawa Balewa's civilian Government was overthrown (and the Prime Minister killed) by junior army officers (mainly Ibos from the Eastern Region). Surviving federal ministers transferred power to the Commander-in-Chief of the Army, Maj.-Gen. Johnson Aguiyi-Aronsi (an Ibo), who formed a Supreme Military Council, suspended the Constitution and imposed emergency rule. On 29 July Aguiyi-Aronsi was killed in a further coup, staged by northern troops, and power was transferred to the Chief of Staff of the Army, Lt-Col (later Gen.) Yakubu Gowon, a Christian northerner. Gowon subsequently reintroduced the federal system, which had been suppressed after the January coup.

In early 1967 there was a rapid deterioration in relations between the Federal Government and the military Governor of the Eastern Region, Lt-Col Chukwuemeka Odumegwu Ojukwu, following a dispute between the federal and regional authorities concerning the distribution of petroleum revenues. The increasing tensions in Nigeria's federal structure prompted Gowon to propose the replacement of the four existing regions by 12 states. On 30 May Ojukwu announced the secession of the Eastern Region from the Federation, and proclaimed its independence as the Republic of Biafra. Fighting between the forces of Biafra and the Federal Government began in July; federal forces eventually suppressed the rebellion in December 1969, following Ojukwu's departure into exile, and Biafran forces formally surrendered in January 1970. Meanwhile, the proposed 12-state structure replaced the four federal regions in April 1968.

In October 1974 Gowon postponed the restoration of civilian rule indefinitely. However, increasing opposition to Gowon's regime culminated in his overthrow by other senior officers in a bloodless coup on 29 July 1975. He was replaced as Head of State by Brig. (later Gen.) Murtala Ramat Muhammed, hitherto Federal Commissioner for Communications, who, in October 1975, announced a detailed timetable for a transition to civilian rule. In February 1976, however, Muhammed was assassinated during an unsuccessful coup attempt. Power was immediately assumed by Lt-Gen. (later Gen.) Olusegun Obasanjo, the Chief of Staff of the Armed Forces, who promised to fulfil his predecessor's programme for the restoration of civilian rule.

In March 1976 the number of states was increased from 12 to 19, and it was announced that a new federal capital was to be constructed near Abuja, in central Nigeria. In September 1978 a new Constitution was promulgated, and the state of emergency, in force since 1966, was ended. At the same time the 12-year ban on political activity was revoked. Elections took place in July 1979 to a new bicameral National Assembly (comprising a Senate and a House of Representatives), and for State Assemblies and State Governors. The National Party of Nigeria (NPN), which included many prominent members of the former NPC, received the most widespread support in all the elections. The NPN's presidential candidate, Alhaji Shehu Shagari (who had served as an NPC federal minister prior to 1966 and as a federal commissioner in 1970–75), was elected to the new post of executive President in August 1979. He took office on 1 October, whereupon the military regime transferred power to the newly elected civilian authorities and the new Constitution came into effect.

In August–September 1983 local government, state and federal elections took place. In the presidential election Shagari was returned for a second term of office. The NPN won 13 of the 19 state governorships, and achieved substantial majorities in the Senate and the House of Representatives. On 31 December, however, the civilian Government was deposed in a bloodless military coup, led by Maj.-Gen. Muhammadu Buhari, who had been Federal Commissioner for Petroleum in 1976–78. The Government was replaced by a Supreme Military Council (SMC), headed by Buhari; the National Assembly was dissolved, and all political parties were banned. Hundreds of politicians, including former President Shagari, were arrested on charges of corruption, and legislation that severely restricted the freedom of the press was introduced.

On 27 August 1985 Buhari's administration was deposed in a bloodless coup, led by Maj.-Gen. (later Gen.) Ibrahim Babangida, the Chief of Staff of the Army and a member of the SMC. A new military administration, the Armed Forces Ruling Council (AFRC), was established, with Babangida as President. The decree on press censorship was revoked, and a number of journalists and other political detainees were released. (Shagari and 17 other former government officials were released in July 1986, having been acquitted of corruption charges.) In December 1985 the AFRC suppressed a coup attempt by disaffected army officers; 10 of the alleged conspirators were later executed.

In February 1986 Babangida's announcement that Nigeria had been accepted as a full member of the Organization of the Islamic Conference (OIC, see p. 340) prompted concern in the non-Muslim sector of the population at increasing 'Islamization' in Nigeria. In July 1987 Babangida announced details of a programme to transfer power to a civilian government on 1 October 1992. The ban on party politics was to be revoked in 1989, and a maximum of two associations were to be approved to contest elections. In August 1987 the Government established a National Electoral Commission (NEC); in September the number of states was increased to 21. The local government elections contested by some 15,000 non-party candidates took place in December. In May 1988 a Constituent Assembly, comprising 450 members elected by local government and 117 members nominated by the AFRC, commenced preparation of a draft constitution. The progress of the Constituent Assembly was impeded, however, by controversy over the proposed inclusion of Islamic (*Shari'a*) courts in the new document.

In April 1989 the Constituent Assembly presented a draft Constitution to Babangida. In May Babangida announced the end of the prohibition on political parties, and the new Constitution (which was scheduled to take effect on 1 October 1992) was promulgated. Only 13 of the existing parties managed to fulfil the requirements for registration by the stipulated date in July 1989. In September the NEC submitted six political associations to the AFRC; in October, however, it was decided to dissolve all the newly formed political parties, on the grounds that they were too closely associated with discredited former parties. In their place, the AFRC created two new organizations, the Social Democratic Party (SDP) and the National Republican Convention (NRC), provoking widespread criticism.

On 22 April 1990 a coup attempt, staged by junior army officers, led by Maj. Gideon Orkar (who claimed to be acting on behalf of Nigerians in the centre and south of the country), was suppressed; some 160 members of the armed forces were subsequently arrested. In July, following their conviction by a military tribunal on charges of conspiring to commit treason, 69 prisoners, including Orkar, were executed.

Following the completion of registration for membership of the SDP and the NRC, party executives were elected for each state in July 1990, replacing government-appointed administrators. Later in August Babangida replaced: nine government ministers, and the position of Chief of General Staff, held by Vice-Adm. (later Adm.) Augustus Aikhomu, was replaced by the office of Vice-President (to which Aikhomu was immediately appointed). Babangida subsequently announced plans to reduce substantially the size of the armed forces. In September, in an attempt to restrict military influence within the Government, three ministers were obliged to retire from the armed forces. Local government elections (postponed from the previous year) took place in early December, with only an estimated 20% of registered voters participating.

In October 1990 the Movement for the Survival of the Ogoni People (MOSOP) was formed to co-ordinate opposition to the exploitation of petroleum reserves in territory of the Ogoni ethnic group (Ogoniland), in the south-central Rivers State, by the Shell Petroleum Development Company of Nigeria. Following a demonstration, organized by MOSOP in protest at environmental damage resulting from petroleum production, it was reported that security forces had killed some 80 Ogonis.

In September 1991, in an apparent attempt to relieve ethnic tensions prior to the elections, nine new states were created, increasing the size of the federation to 30 states. On 12 December the Federal Government was formally transferred from Lagos to Abuja, the new federal capital. In the gubernatorial and state assembly elections, which took place on 14 December, the NRC secured a majority in 14 State Assemblies, while the SDP won control of 16 State Assemblies; candidates representing the NRC were elected as State Governors in 16 states. Both the SDP and the NRC disputed the election results in a number of states, on the grounds of malpractice.

In January 1992 Babangida formed a new Council of Ministers, in which several portfolios were restructured. In the same month the Government announced that elections to a bicameral National Assembly, comprising a 593-member House of Representatives and a 91-member Senate, would take place on 7 November, and would be followed by a presidential election on 5 December. The formal installation of a civilian government (and the implementation of the new Constitution) was consequently scheduled for 2 January 1993, rather than, as previously planned, on 1 October 1992.

In May 1992 some 300 people were reported to have been killed in renewed violence between the Hausa ethnic group (which was predominantly Muslim) and the Kataf (predominantly Christian) in Kaduna. Shortly afterwards the Government announced that all organizations with religious or ethnic interests were to be prohibited. Later in May further rioting occurred in Lagos, following the arrest of the Chairman of the Campaign for Democracy (CD—an informal alliance of Nigerian human rights organizations, which had been established in late 1991), Dr Beko Ransome-Kuti, who had accused the Government of deliberately provoking unrest in order to delay the transition to civilian rule. In June several human rights activists, including Ransome-Kuti, were released, pending their trial (which was later deferred) on charges of conspiring to incite the previous month's riots.

At elections to the bicameral National Assembly, which had been brought forward to 4 July 1992, the SDP secured a majority in both chambers, with 52 seats in the Senate and 314 seats in the House of Representatives, while the NRC won 37 seats in the Senate and 275 seats in the House of Representatives. The formal inauguration of the National Assembly, due to take place on 27 July, was, however, postponed until 5 December, the stipulated date for the presidential election, prompting concern at the AFRC's apparent reluctance to relinquish legislative power.

Voting in primary elections for presidential candidates took place in September 1992. In October, however, shortly before a final round of voting was due to take place, Babangida suspended the primary elections, pending the outcome of an investigation by the NEC into alleged incidents of electoral malpractice. Later that month, following a report by the NEC that confirmed malpractice, Babangida announced that the leaders of the NRC and the SDP were to be removed from office.

In November 1992 Babangida postponed the presidential election until 12 June 1993. On 2 January 1993 (hitherto the stipulated date for the completion of the transition to civilian rule) the AFRC was to be replaced by a 14-member ruling National Defence and Security Council (NDSC), and the existing Council of Ministers by a civilian Transitional Council, pending the installation of a civilian government, which was to take place on 27 August. Babangida further announced that the 23 prospective presidential candidates who had contested the discredited primary elections were to be prohibited from political activity during the transitional period: new candidates were to be nominated at a series of party congresses, to be conducted at ward, local government, state and national level.

On 5 December 1992 Babangida inaugurated the National Assembly. On 2 January 1993 the AFRC and the Council of Ministers were duly dissolved, and the Transitional Council and the NDSC (which comprised the President, Vice-President, the heads of the armed forces and senior members of the Transitional Council) were formally installed. The Chairman of the Transitional Council, Chief Ernest Adegunle Shonekan, was officially designated Head of Government (although supreme power was vested in the NDSC and the President), while Aikhomu retained the post of Vice-President. In accordance with the new programme for the transition to civilian rule, party congresses to select presidential candidates were conducted in February–March; the NRC elected Alhaji Bashir Othman Tofa and the SDP Chief Moshood Kastumawo Olawale Abiola to contest the presidential election.

In June 1993 the Association for a Better Nigeria (ABN), a newly formed pro-Babangida pressure group, obtained an interim injunction in the Abuja High Court prohibiting the NEC from conducting the presidential election, pending an appeal by the ABN for the extension of military rule until 1997. The NEC, however, announced that the injunction was invalid, and that the election would take place as scheduled. Owing, in part, to confusion caused by the court action, only about 30% of the registered electorate voted in the presidential election, which took place on 12 June. Initial results indicated that Abiola had secured the majority of votes in 11 of 15 states. Shortly afterwards, however, the ABN obtained a further injunction suspending the promulgation of the election results. The court ruling prompted widespread demands that the results be released, and several applications were lodged in an attempt to reverse the injunction. Later in June the CD released election results (which it claimed to be official) indicating that Abiola had secured the majority of votes in 19 states, and Tofa in 11; Abiola subsequently proclaimed himself President. Amid increasing tension, the Abuja High Court declared the election results to be invalid, on the grounds that the NEC had failed to comply with the ruling that had cancelled the poll.

On 23 June 1993, in what it claimed was an effort to uphold the judicial system, the NDSC annulled the results of the presidential election, suspended the NEC and halted all proceedings pertaining to the election. Babangida subsequently announced that the poll had been marred by widespread irregularities (despite reports by international observers that voting had been conducted fairly), but insisted that he remained committed to the transition to civilian rule on 27 August. The SDP and the NRC were to select two new presidential candidates, under the supervision of a reconstituted NEC; prospective candidates would be required to comply with new electoral regulations, which effectively precluded Abiola and Tofa from contesting a further poll. (Abiola, however, continued to claim, with much popular support, that he had been legitimately elected to the presidency.) The annulment of the election attracted international criticism, particularly from the USA and the United Kingdom, which announced the imposition of military sanctions against Nigeria.

In July 1993 a general strike, organized by the CD in support of demands that Abiola be installed as President, culminated in rioting; some 20 people were subsequently killed when security forces violently suppressed the unrest. Shortly afterwards the NDSC announced that a new presidential election was to take place on 14 August, in order to fulfil the pledge to transfer power to a civilian government on 27 August. The new electoral schedule was generally viewed with scepticism, while the SDP declared its intention to boycott the poll, on the grounds that it had legitimately won the previous election. Legal proceedings initiated by Abiola in the Lagos Supreme Court, in an attempt to uphold his claim to the presidency, were abandoned after Babangida introduced legislation that prohibited any legal challenges to the annulment of the election.

At the end of July 1993 Babangida announced that an Interim National Government (ING) was to be established, on the grounds that there was insufficient time to permit the scheduled transition to civilian rule on 27 August. In August the CD continued its campaign of civil disobedience in protest at the annulment of the election, appealing for a three-day general strike (which was widely observed in the south-west of the country, where Abiola received most popular support). Later in August Babangida resigned, reportedly as a result of pressure from prominent members of the NDSC, notably the Secretary of Defence, Gen. Sani Abacha. On 27 August a 32-member interim Federal Executive Council (FEC), headed by Shonekan, was installed, while the transitional period for the return to civilian rule was extended to 31 March 1994. (Shonekan was later designated Head of State and Commander-in-Chief of the Armed Forces.) Supporters of democracy criticized the inclusion in the ING of several members of the now-dissolved NDSC, including Abacha, who was appointed to the new post of Vice-President.

At the end of August 1993 the CD staged a further three-day strike, while the Nigerian Labour Congress (NLC) and the National Union of Petroleum and Natural Gas Workers (NUPENG) also announced industrial action in support of the installation of a civilian administration, headed by Abiola. The combined strike action resulted in a severe fuel shortage and the suspension of most economic activity. Following the establishment of the ING, Shonekan pledged his commitment to the democratic process and, in an effort to restore order, initiated negotiations with the NLC and effected the release of several journalists and prominent members of the CD, including Ransome-Kuti, who had been arrested in July. In early September the NLC and NUPENG provisionally suspended strike action, after the ING agreed to consider their demands.

In September 1993 a series of military appointments, which included the nomination of Lt-Gen. Oladipo Diya to the office of Chief of Defence Staff, effectively removed supporters of Babangida from significant posts within the armed forces, thereby strengthening Abacha's position. Later in September the NRC and SDP agreed to a new timetable whereby local government elections and a presidential election would take place concurrently in February 1994. The CD subsequently announced the resumption of strike action in support of demands for the installation of Abiola as President, and Ransome-Kuti and other prominent members of the CD were again arrested. In October 1993 the SDP demanded that he be inaugurated as President, and refused to participate in the new elections.

In November 1993 the President of the Senate, a strong supporter of Abiola, was removed from office. Shortly afterwards the Lagos High Court ruled in favour of an application by Abiola, declaring the establishment of the ING to be invalid under the terms of the 1979 Constitution (whereby the President of the Senate was to act as interim Head of State). In the same month the ING dissolved the government councils, prior to local elections, and withdrew state subsidies on petroleum products. The resultant dramatic increase in the price of fuel prompted widespread anti-Government demonstrations, and the NLC announced the resumption of strike action. Meanwhile, the scheduled revision of the electoral register ended in failure, owing to a boycott by supporters of the SDP, and it became apparent that the new schedule for the transition to civilian rule was unviable.

On 17 November 1993, following a meeting with senior military officials, Shonekan resigned as Head of State and immediately transferred power to Abacha (confirming widespread speculation that the latter had effectively assumed control of the Government following Babangida's resignation). On the following day Abacha dissolved all state institutions that had been established under the transitional process, replaced the State Governors with military administrators, prohibited political activity (thereby proscribing the NRC and the SDP), and announced the formation of a Provisional Ruling Council (PRC), which was to comprise senior military officials and principal members of a new FEC. He insisted, however, that he intended to relinquish power to a civilian government, and pledged to convene a conference with a mandate to determine the constitutional future of the country. Restrictions on the media were revoked. On 21 November Abacha introduced legislation that formally restored the 1979 Constitution and provided for the establishment of the new government organs. In an apparent attempt to counter domestic and international criticism, several prominent supporters of Abiola, including Kingibe, and four former members of the ING were appointed to the PRC and FEC, which were installed on 24 November. Abacha subsequently removed 17 senior military officers who were believed to be loyal to Babangida. In the same month the NLC agreed to abandon strike action after the Government acted to limit the increase in the price of petroleum products.

In December 1993 the United Kingdom announced that member nations of the European Union (EU, see p. 228) were to impose further sanctions against Nigeria, including restrictions on the export of armaments. In April 1994 the Government announced a programme for the establishment of a National Constitutional Conference (NCC): some 273 delegates were to be elected in May, while 96 delegates were to be nominated by the Government from a list of eligible citizens submitted by each state. The NCC was to be convened at the end of June, and was to submit recommendations, including proposals for a new draft constitution, to the PRC in October. The ban on political activity was to end in January 1995. In May 1994 a new pro-democracy organization, comprising former politicians, retired military officers and human rights activists, the National Democratic Coalition (NADECO), demanded that Abacha relinquish power by the end of that month and urged a boycott of the NCC. In the same month the leader of MOSOP, Ken Saro-Wiwa, was arrested in connection with the deaths, during political violence, of four Ogoni traditional leaders. Saro-Wiwa was alleged to have incited his supporters to commit the murders, although many critics of the Nigerian authorities believed that the charges had been fabricated by the Government in an effort to suppress the activities of MOSOP.

In June 1994 a number of prominent opposition members, including Ransome-Kuti, were also arrested after the CD urged a campaign of civil disobedience, supported by NADECO. Following a public gathering, at which Abiola declared himself Head of State and President of a parallel government, a warrant was issued for his arrest on charges of treason; the authorities claimed that he intended to organize an uprising to force the military administration to relinquish power. Later in June he was arrested by security forces, prompting protests from pro-democracy organizations and from the Governments of the United Kingdom and the USA. Further demonstrations in support of demands for an immediate suspension of military rule and the installation of Abiola as President ensued. At the initial session of the NCC, which was convened as scheduled,

Abacha pledged to relinquish power at a date that would be determined by the conference.

In July 1994 Abiola was arraigned before a special High Court in Abuja and charged with treason. NUPENG initiated strike action in support of demands for Abiola's release and installation as President, and an improvement in government investment in the petroleum industry. By mid-July several affiliated unions had joined the strike action, resulting in an effective suspension of economic activity in Lagos and other regions in the south-west of the country. At the end of the month it was reported that some 20 people had been killed when security forces violently suppressed anti-Government demonstrations. In September the union leaders announced the suspension of strike action, in view of the ensuing widespread hardship. Later in September Abacha enlarged the PRC from 11 to 25 members, all senior military officials.

Meanwhile, Abiola's trial was repeatedly adjourned, following his legal action, in August 1994, challenging the jurisdiction of the special High Court in Abuja with regard to an offence that had been allegedly committed in Lagos. Despite reports that he was suffering from a medical condition necessitating immediate treatment, Abiola had refused to accept the stipulated conditions for bail, requiring him to refrain from political activity.

In January 1995 the NCC, which had been scheduled to complete the preparations for a draft constitution in October 1994, adjourned until March 1995, prompting increasing concern that its protracted deliberations served to prolong the tenure of the military administration. The trial of Saro-Wiwa and a further 14 Ogoni campaigners, on charges of complicity in the murder of the four Ogoni traditional leaders, commenced in mid-January; the defendants were to challenge the legitimacy of the government-appointed Special Military Tribunal, at Port Harcourt. In February the Federal Court of Appeal dismissed Abiola's legal action challenging the jurisdiction of the High Court in Abuja.

In February 1995 Abacha dissolved the FEC, after a number of ministers announced their intention of engaging in political activity in the forthcoming transitional period. In March some 150 military officials were arrested, and the authorities subsequently confirmed reports of a conspiracy to overthrow the Government. (However, opponents of the Abacha administration claimed that the Government had fabricated a coup attempt, with the aim of suppressing dissent within the armed forces.) The arrest of the former Head of State, Olusegun Obasanjo, and his former deputy, Maj.-Gen. (retd) Shehu Musa Yar'Adua, together with other prominent critics of the Government, prompted international protests. In mid-March Abacha appointed a new, 36-member FEC. In May more than 40 people, including Obasanjo, Yar'Adua and Ransome-Kuti, were arraigned before a Special Military Tribunal in Lagos, in connection with the alleged coup attempt in March.

In late June 1995 the NCC submitted a draft Constitution to Abacha, who rescinded the ban on political activity; a programme for transition to civilian rule was to be announced on 1 October. (A number of political organizations subsequently emerged, in response to the removal of the ban.) At the end of June it was reported that Yar'Adua and a further 13 military officers had been sentenced to death for conspiring to overthrow the Government, while several other defendants, including Obasanjo and Ransome-Kuti, received custodial terms. The Government subsequently confirmed that a total of 43 had been convicted in connection with the coup attempt, prompting protests and appeals for clemency from the international community. On 1 October, however, Abacha officially commuted the death sentences to terms of imprisonment and reduced the custodial sentences (although he did not withdraw the capital charges against Abiola). At the same time he announced the approval of the new Constitution (which was due to be formally endorsed later that year) and the adoption of a three-year programme for transition to civilian rule, whereby a new President was to be inaugurated on 1 October 1998, following elections at local, state and national level. (The duration of the transitional period was received with disapproval by the international community.)

At the end of October 1995 Saro-Wiwa and a further eight Ogoni activists were sentenced to death by the Special Military Tribunal in Port Harcourt, having been convicted of involvement in the murder of the four Ogoni leaders in May 1994; six defendants were acquitted. Although the defendants were not implicated directly in the incident, the nine convictions were based on the premise that the MOSOP activists had effectively incited the killings. An international campaign against the convictions and numerous appeals for clemency ensued. However, on 10 November the nine convicted Ogonis were executed, prompting immediate condemnation by the international community. Nigeria was suspended from the Commonwealth, and threatened with expulsion if the Government failed to restore democracy within a period of two years. Later that month the EU reaffirmed its commitment to existing sanctions that had been imposed in 1993 (notably an embargo on the export of armaments and military equipment to Nigeria), and extended visa restrictions to civilian members of the administration. The Governments of the USA, South Africa and the EU member nations recalled their diplomatic representatives from Nigeria in protest at the executions. The Nigerian Government condemned the imposition of sanctions and, in turn, withdrew its diplomatic representatives from the USA, South Africa and the EU member countries. Additional security forces were dispatched to Ogoniland to deter any protests against the executions, while a further 19 Ogonis were charged with complicity in the May 1994 murders. (However, their trial was subsequently postponed, pending an appeal to the effect that the Special Military Tribunal at Port Harcourt was unconstitutional.)

In December 1995 Abacha approved the establishment of a number of committees, including the National Electoral Commission of Nigeria (NECON), to implement the transitional programme. NECON subsequently divided the country into seven regions (rather than six, as originally envisaged), prior to local government elections in early 1996. Later in December the Commonwealth Ministerial Action Group (CMAG—comprising the ministers with responsibility for foreign affairs of eight member countries), which had been established at the summit meeting in November, met to discuss further measures to be taken if the Nigerian Government failed to restore democracy, and announced that five of the ministers were to visit Nigeria to initiate negotiations with the military administration. (The diplomatic representatives who had been withdrawn following the executions in November subsequently returned to Lagos, in order to facilitate the Commonwealth mission.) In January 1996 the Government refused the Commonwealth delegation permission to visit Nigeria, and demanded that the decision to suspend Nigeria be reviewed. At the end of January the Government announced that the new Constitution would be formally adopted in 1998, upon the completion of the transitional period (rather than in late 1995).

In February 1996 the 19 Ogonis who remained in detention pending their trial appealed to the Commonwealth for assistance in securing their release. In March local government elections were contested, on a non-party basis, as part of the transitional programme; although opposition leaders had urged a boycott, NECON claimed that a high level of voter participation had been recorded. In April a UN mission visited Ogoniland to investigate the trial and execution of the nine Ogoni activists in 1995; it was reported that Ogoni and other opposition representatives were prevented from meeting the delegation. Later that month, following the Government's continued refusal to enter into negotiations with CMAG regarding human rights issues and the restoration of democracy, the Commonwealth proposed to adopt a number of sanctions against Nigeria.

In June 1996 Nigerian officials met CMAG in an attempt to avert the threatened imposition of sanctions against Nigeria; the Nigerian delegation demanded that Nigeria be readmitted to the Commonwealth in exchange for the Government's adoption of the programme for transition to civilian rule by October 1998. The Commonwealth dismissed the programme as unsatisfactory, but remained divided regarding the adoption of consequent measures. It was finally agreed that the Commonwealth would suspend the adoption of sanctions, but that the situation would subsequently be reviewed. Canada, however, announced its opposition to this decision and unilaterally imposed a number of sanctions (similar to those already adopted by the EU). In September 1996 CMAG agreed that the Commonwealth delegation would visit Nigeria, despite conditions imposed by the military authorities, which insisted that it would not be permitted access to opposition activists or political prisoners.

In June 1996 legislation governing the formation of political parties was promulgated. Five of 15 political organizations that applied for registration were granted legal status in September. NADECO condemned the disqualification of the remaining 10 parties, which were subsequently dissolved by decree; it was widely believed that the associations that had been granted registration were largely sympathetic towards the military administration. In October Abacha announced the creation of a further six states, increasing the total size of the federation to 36 states.

International observers declared that the local government elections, which finally took place in March 1997, had been conducted peacefully; it was reported that the United Nigerian Congress Party (UNCP) had secured the highest number of seats in the municipal councils.

In early 1997 escalating tension between the Ijaw and Itsekiri ethnic groups in the town of Warri, in south-western Nigeria, severely disrupted operations in the region of the Niger Delta by the Shell Petroleum Development Company of Nigeria. In March a demonstration by members of the Ijaw ethnic group in Warri precipitated violent clashes. Protesters seized Shell installations and took about 100 employees hostage, in an attempt to force the Government to accede to their demands. A curfew was subsequently imposed in the region in an attempt to restore order. By mid-April it was reported that about 70 people had been killed in the disturbances, while the disruption in petroleum production had resulted in a national fuel shortage, effectively suspending the transportation system in much of the country. Further clashes and attacks on Shell installations in May were reported. Later that month the authorities established a commission of inquiry to investigate the cause of the unrest and submit recommendations for restoring order in the region.

In April 1997 Abacha issued a decree empowering himself to replace the mayors who had been elected in March and to dissolve local municipal councils if he considered that they were acting contrary to national interests. In May some 22 pro-democracy and human rights organizations, including MOSOP and the CD, formed a loose alliance, the United Action for Democracy (UAD), with the aim of campaigning for the restoration of democracy in Nigeria.

At a summit meeting of the Commonwealth Heads of Government, which took place in Edinburgh, United Kingdom, in October 1997, Nigeria's suspension from the organization was extended for an additional year; it was further indicated that the country would be expelled from the Commonwealth, if Abacha reneged on his pledge to restore democratic rule by 1 October 1998. The Government had announced a new electoral timetable: elections to the State Assemblies were to take place in December 1997, followed by elections to the National Assembly on 25 April 1998, and presidential and gubernatorial elections on 1 August of that year (although it was maintained that the new elected organs of government would be installed by 1 October 1998). Elections to the state legislatures, which were contested by the five registered parties, took place accordingly on 6 December 1997; the UNCP won 637 of the 970 contested seats, securing a majority in 29 of the 36 State Assemblies. The other four parties (the Congress for National Consensus, the Democratic Party of Nigeria, the Grassroots Democratic Movement and the National Centre Party of Nigeria) subsequently attributed the electoral success of the UNCP to malpractice on the part of the authorities, and threatened to withdraw from the remainder of the electoral process. In mid-December Abacha nominated a new FEC, in which most of the ministers who had served in the previous administration were replaced. Later that month, following reports of a bomb attack at the presidential wing of the airport at Abuja, the Government announced that an attempted coup had been thwarted. About 100 people, notably several prominent military officials (including Lt-Gen. Diya), were subsequently detained. However, there was widespread speculation that government claims of a coup attempt were a pretext for the removal of a number of army officers who were perceived to be a threat to Abacha. The incident also served to divert attention from the death in detention of Yar'Adua earlier that month. In February 1998, following the report of a special board of investigation, 26 people, including Diya and two ministers who had served in the previous FEC, were charged with conspiring to overthrow the Government.

In March 1998 a number of associations that supported Abacha conducted rallies in favour of his re-election in August. UAD organized counter-demonstrations (which resulted in the arrest of a number of protesters by the security forces), and announced that it was to initiate a campaign of civil disobedience to oppose Abacha's candidacy in the presidential election. In April all five registered parties voted separately to nominate Abacha as the sole presidential candidate; Abacha was therefore to contest the presidential election in August unopposed.

On 8 June 1998 Abacha died unexpectedly from heart failure. The PRC designated the Chief of Defence Staff, Maj.-Gen. Abdulsalami Abubakar, as Abacha's successor, and on 9 June he was inaugurated as Head of State (having been promoted to the rank of General). Abubakar pledged to continue the Abacha Government's scheduled transition to civilian rule. The UAD, however, urged continued protests against the military administration. In mid-June Abubakar ordered the release of about 26 political prisoners, including Obasanjo (ostensibly on grounds of ill health). In July, following discussions with UN officials, the authorities agreed to release Abiola from detention. Shortly after his release, however, Abiola collapsed and subsequently died. Violent rioting ensued, amid widespread speculation that the authorities were responsible for Abiola's death. Although an autopsy confirmed that he had died of heart failure, it was indicated that his period in detention had contributed to his poor health. Later in July Abubakar announced that the transition to civilian rule would be completed on 29 May 1999 (rather than 1 October 1998). The Government annulled the results of the elections that had previously been conducted, and dissolved the five authorized political parties, NECON and other electoral bodies. In August a new, 31-member FEC, which included a number of civilians, was appointed to remain in office pending the formal transition to civilian rule; an Independent National Electoral Commission (INEC) was also established. Later that month the INEC announced that local government elections would take place on 5 December 1998 and state legislative elections on 9 January 1999, followed by elections to a bicameral national legislature on 20 February and a presidential election on 27 February. On 7 September 1998 the Government published the draft Constitution that had been submitted by the NCC in June 1995. Abubakar announced that all charges against Nigerian exiles abroad had been abandoned, and that the 19 Ogoni activists who had been detained in connection with the killing of the four Ogoni leaders in May 1994 had been granted an unconditional release.

Some 25 new political organizations had submitted applications for registration to the INEC by the stipulated deadline, which was extended to early October 1998. The commission provisionally approved nine political associations, notably the People's Democratic Party (PDP), which principally comprised former opponents of the Abacha administration. In the same month CMAG recommended that Commonwealth member states end sanctions against Nigeria, in preparation for the country's readmission to the Commonwealth. At the end of that month, in response to the democratization measures undertaken by the Government, the EU ended a number of sanctions against Nigeria (while maintaining the embargo on the export of armaments).

In November 1998 Obasanjo (who had joined the PDP in October) announced that he intended to seek nomination as the party's presidential candidate. At elections to Nigeria's 768 local municipal councils, which took place, as scheduled, on 5 December, the PDP secured about 60% of the votes cast. The INEC subsequently declared that the PDP, the All Nigeria People's Party (ANPP) and the Alliance for Democracy (AD) were the only political organizations to qualify for final registration, having achieved the requisite minimum of 5% of the votes cast in 24 seats. The state legislative elections, which were consequently contested only by the PDP, APP and AD, took place on 9 January 1999. The PDP, with about 50% of votes cast, secured 20 state governorships, while the ANPP obtained nine and the AP six. Elections in Bayelsa State were postponed, owing to clashes between the security forces and Ijaw activists (whose continued attacks against petroleum installations resulted in the imposition of a state of emergency at the end of December 1998).

In January 1999 several prominent members of former administrations announced that they intended to seek nomination to contest the forthcoming presidential election. In early February the ANPP and AD, which, despite the stated opposition of the INEC, had established an electoral alliance, nominated a joint candidate, Samuel Oluyemisi Falae (a former Minister of Finance in the Babangida administration). Later that month Obasanjo was elected as the presidential candidate of the PDP, defeating a former civilian Vice-President, Alex Ekwueme. At the elections to the bicameral legislature, which took place on 20 February, the PDP secured 215 seats in the 360-member House of Representatives and 66 seats in the 109-member Senate. (Voting in the Niger Delta region was postponed, owing to continued unrest, and a further by-election for the vacant seat to the National Assembly took place in March.)

On 27 February 1999 Obasanjo was elected to the presidency, with 62.8% of votes cast. Voting irregularities were reported, and

Falae submitted a legal challenge to the electoral results at the Court of Appeal on the grounds of malpractice. In March the Government ordered the release of some 95 prisoners, including Diya, who had been detained in connection with the alleged coup attempt in December 1997. In April 1999 the Court of Appeal dismissed Falae's challenge to the declaration of Obasanjo as President-elect, and a further legal appeal at the Supreme Court was also rejected. The Constitution was formally promulgated on 5 May. Obasanjo was formally inaugurated as President on 29 May; on the same day Nigeria was readmitted as a full member of the Commonwealth. Obasanjo announced that measures to combat corruption would be introduced, and that all contracts awarded since the beginning of 1999 would be reviewed, following reports that the outgoing military Government had perpetrated large-scale embezzlement of state funds and assets. On 3 June the inaugural session of the National Assembly took place. Obasanjo nominated a new Cabinet, principally comprising members of the PDP, which was approved by the Senate later that month. He also undertook a reorganization of the armed forces, removing more than 150 military officers who had served under the Abacha Government.

In October 1999 the Governor of the predominantly Muslim Zamfara State, in northern Nigeria, announced the introduction of Islamic *Shari'a* law in the state, in response to endemic crime. Obasanjo subsequently declared that the state imposition of *Shari'a* was in contravention of the federal Constitution. In November government troops were deployed to suppress unrest in the town of Odi, in Bayelsa State, following the killing of 12 members of the security forces by Ijaw activists. Obasanjo denied subsequent reports of retaliatory atrocities perpetrated by government forces against the local civilian population. Measures were subsequently introduced to grant states a higher proportion of revenue generated locally, in an effort to reduce ethnic tension in the Niger Delta. The Government had also demanded that multinational enterprises operating in the Niger Delta adopt long-term measures in response to environmental damage. Later in November about 50 people were killed in clashes between the Yoruba and Hausa in an outskirt of Lagos. Obasanjo (himself a Yoruba) accused a Yoruba nationalist organization, the O'odua People's Congress (OPC), of precipitating the violence.

In December 1999 Kano State, in the north, announced the adoption of *Shari'a* law. However, the Christian Association of Nigeria threatened to initiate a legal challenge to the introduction of *Shari'a* law by Kano and Zamfara States, on the grounds that it contravened the principle of secularity enshrined in the Constitution. In January 2000 the adoption of *Shari'a* was formally ratified by the Governor of Zamfara State. In February a demonstration by Christians in the northern town of Kaduna in protest at the proposed imposition of *Shari'a* in Kaduna State precipitated violent hostilities between Muslims and Christians, in which more than 300 people were killed; government troops eventually suppressed the unrest, and a curfew was imposed in the town. However, more than 50 people were killed in further clashes between Christians and Muslims in the south-eastern towns of Aba and Umuahia, which ensued in reprisal for the violence in the north. By the end of the month thousands of Christians had fled the north of the country, fearing possible retaliatory massacres. At an emergency meeting at the end of February, chaired by Obasanjo, the Governors of the 18 northern states agreed, in the interests of peace, to withdraw the new legislation introducing *Shari'a* law, and to revert to the provisions for *Shari'a* in the existing penal code, in accordance with the federal Constitution. However, the Governors of a number of the states subsequently announced that they would not comply with the federal government order, but would proceed with the implementation of *Shari'a* law. In March religious rioting in Niger State (where the adoption of the *Shari'a* law had been declared) was reported. In May some 150 people were killed in further clashes between Christians and Muslims in Kaduna; government troops were again deployed in the town to restore order. In early June Obasanjo reorganized the Cabinet, following media criticism of a number of ministers. In the same month a government announcement of a reduction in subsidies on domestic fuel precipitated riots by students in the south-west of the country and a general strike, organized by the NLC (which ended a few days later, after the authorities agreed to limit the increase in the price of fuel).

In August 2000, following persistent dissension between the executive and the legislature over the issue of government corruption, the President of the Senate was removed from office and charged with misusing public funds. In the same month *Shari'a* law was formally adopted in the northern states of Katsina, Jigawa and Yobe (to enter into effect later that year). In September the Governor of Borno State also announced the adoption of *Shari'a*. Although the Governors of most of these states had declared that Christians would be exempt from the provisions of *Shari'a*, social segregation of men and women and the application of punishments stipulated under Islamic law had been widely implemented in Zamfara and Kano States. In view of the violence in Kaduna State, the Governor announced that the form of *Shari'a* to be introduced in the state was to be modified to allow Islamic courts to exist in conjunction with special courts upholding secular laws. In early October some 100 people were killed in further severe ethnic clashes in Lagos between the Hausa and members of the Yoruba OPC; security forces, supported by troops, finally restored order in the capital. Later that month Obasanjo banned the OPC and ordered the arrest of more than 200 of the movement's prominent members, including the leader, Frederick Faseun.

At the end of January 2001 Obasanjo replaced 10 members of the Cabinet in an extensive reorganization, following widespread criticism of the Government's failure to resolve economic and social difficulties. In late March the Governors of Nigeria's 17 southern states, meeting in Benin City, urged that the Constitution be amended to provide for greater government decentralization, including the right for states to establish separate security forces. In the same month the US Supreme Court ruled that the relatives of Ken Saro-Wiwa and the other Ogoni activists executed in 1995 were entitled to continue legal proceedings against the multinational petroleum group, Royal Dutch Shell, for the alleged complicity of its Nigerian subsidiary in the human rights violations perpetrated against the Ogoni ethnic group (see above). In April Obasanjo replaced the heads of the three branches of the armed forces, notably the Chief of Army Staff, who had served under Abacha.

In mid-June 2001 religious and ethnic unrest in northern and central Nigeria intensified; some 1,000 people were killed in fighting between Christians and Muslims in Bauchi (which had become the 10th northern state to adopt *Shari'a* law). In early September hostilities between Christians and Muslims also erupted in the central town of Jos, where Christians had objected to the appointment of a Muslim to an influential post heading the state's poverty alleviation programme; it was reported that some 500 people were killed, before armed forces were deployed to restore control. In October it was reported that a further 200 civilians had been killed in Jos and the northern town of Kano, in clashes precipitated by Muslim protests at the US offensive in Afghanistan (following the terrorist attacks against the USA on 11 September). Government troops were reported to have perpetrated a massacre of about 200 Tiv villagers in the eastern state of Benue later that month, in retaliation for the abduction of 19 members of the armed forces, who had been deployed to quell unrest in the region.

In December 2001 the incumbent Minister of Justice, a close associate of Obasanjo, was shot and killed in the south-west town of Ibidjan (where a curfew was subsequently imposed); general speculation regarding the identity of his assailants was focused on rivalries within the Yoruba community.

In early 2002 the death sentence imposed on a woman in northern Sokoto State, who had been convicted in October 2001 under *Shari'a* law on charges of adultery, attracted increasing international attention. Following pressure from the international community, in March the Minister of Justice urged the 12 State Governors who had adopted *Shari'a* law to discontinue its strict enforcement, on the grounds that it contravened the Constitution for reasons of discrimination (applying only to Muslims). A Court of Appeal subsequently overturned the sentence against the convicted woman, ruling that there was insufficient evidence to justify the death penalty. However, the Governors of several northern states insisted that they would continue to implement *Shari'a*.

In April 2002 the Federal Government reached an agreement with Abacha's relatives and business associates, whereby Swiss banks were to return state funds appropriated by the former President, and the Nigerian authorities were to abandon legal proceedings against several members of Abacha's family. Also in April Obasanjo announced that he intended to seek a second term in office, while the former Head of State, Muhammadu Buhari, stated that he planned to contest the forthcoming presidential election on behalf of the ANPP. In June the INEC announced that, of 24 political parties that had applied for official registration, only three had been recognized (increasing the total number of legal associations to six). In July several people were killed during violence in the Niger Delta, following a dispute over selecting a political candidate for forthcoming local government elections (which, however, were subsequently postponed indefinitely owing to lack of preparation). Meanwhile, in June, after a long-standing dispute between Obasanjo and the Senate over control of public finances, the President survived an impeachment attempt by the upper chamber. In August the House of Representatives adopted by an overwhelming majority a resolution demanding that Obasanjo resign from office or face impeachment, on charges of mismanagement and abuse of power. Obasanjo refused to comply with the resolution, and at the end of that month the PDP voted in favour of drafting a list of charges against the President.

In August 2002 the *Shari'a* Court of Appeal in Katsina State upheld a sentence of death by stoning imposed in March against a woman, Amina Lawal, who had been convicted for having extramarital sexual intercourse. The case attracted international outrage, and the Minister of Justice announced that the Federal Government was opposed to the death sentence. (A further appeal against the sentence was submitted at federal level.) In the same month a *Shari'a* court in Jigawa State imposed a death sentence against a man who had been convicted for rape of a minor. In October the Federal Government announced that it would not permit executions under *Shari'a* law, after contestants threatened to boycott a 'Miss World' beauty pageant, due to be staged in Kaduna in December. Following increasing controversy over the pageant, an article in the newspaper *This Day*, referring to the Prophet Mohammed in connection with the contestants, precipitated violent protests by Muslims. Some 200 people were killed in ensuing clashes between Muslims and Christians in Kaduna, and the pageant was finally relocated to London, United Kingdom. The Deputy Governor of Zamfara State issued a *fatwa* against the female journalist responsible for the article (who had fled abroad).

In December 2002 the INEC granted registration to a further 24 political associations, after the Supreme Court upheld an appeal by five opposition parties against their exclusion, and ordered less restrictive regulations for legalization. Later that month the Commission announced that legislative elections were to be conducted on 12 April 2003, followed by a presidential election on 19 April, and elections to regional Houses of Assembly on 3 May. In January Obasanjo was formally elected as the presidential candidate of the PDP. A further 18 political leaders subsequently announced their intention to contest the presidential election. In March the killing of a prominent member of the ANPP in Abuja was declared by the authorities to have been politically motivated. In the same month further clashes between members of the Ijaw and Itsekiri ethnic group near Warri forced the suspension of the operations of a number of international petroleum companies; government troops were dispatched to the region to suppress the violence.

Incidences of violence and malpractice were reported during the federal legislative elections on 12 April 2003. The PDP emerged with an overwhelming majority in both legislative chambers (213 seats in the House of Representatives and 73 in the Senate), while the ANPP was the only other party to secure significant representation (95 seats in the House of Representatives and 28 in the Senate). At the presidential election on 19 April (the first to be organized by civilian authorities for 19 years), Obasanjo was elected for a second term by 61.9% of the valid votes cast, while Buhari received 32.2% of votes. Opposition leaders, notably Buhari, contested the results, claiming that widespread electoral malpractice had been perpetrated, and indicated that violent protests might ensue. International monitors, although generally satisfied with the organization of the elections, declared that irregularities had taken place, particularly in the region of the Niger Delta. At gubernatorial elections, which also took place on 19 April, the PDP gained eight state governorships from the ANPP and AD, losing only one (that of Kano). Later that month Obasanjo criticized a statement by EU monitors, who claimed that they had obtained evidence of electoral malpractice perpetrated in 13 states. Meanwhile, at the end of April four offshore petroleum rigs, operated by a US enterprise, Transocean, in the Niger Delta were seized by protesting Nigerian employees, who took hostage 97 foreign national workers. Military naval forces were dispatched to the region. Following negotiations between officials of NUPENG, the NLC and Transocean, all hostages were airlifted from the rigs.

Obasanjo officially dissolved the Federal Government on 21 May 2003. He was sworn in on 29 May (after a legal challenge against his inauguration by Buhari was rejected by the federal Court of Appeal), and in early June began to nominate ministers to his new administration. On 17 July Obasanjo finally inaugurated the new, 40-member Federal Government, which included the hitherto Vice-President of the World Bank, Dr Ngozi Okonja-Iweala, as the new Minister of Finance and the Economy (an appointment that reflected the authorities' stated intention to eliminate corruption and implement economic reforms).

In September 2003 the *Shari'a* Court of Appeal in Katsina State overturned the sentence of death by stoning imposed on Amina Lawal, on the grounds that procedural irregularities had discredited the previous judgment. The case had attracted international protests on Lawal's behalf. Meanwhile, legislation to repeal the death penalty was under debate at the National Assembly; the proposed abrogation was strongly opposed by the Muslim community, which perceived it as a infringement of *Shari'a* law. In January 2004 a newly established group of Islamist fundamentalist militants, known as the Taliban (styled on the Afghanistan movement of that name), attacked police stations in the capital of Yobe State, Damaturu, reportedly killing a police officer. Government troops dispatched to Yobe State restored order, killing many members of the organization, which was believed to be connected to extremist student supporters of the establishment of an Islamic state. Local government elections, conducted at the end of March, were marred by violent incidents; some 20 people were killed in ethnic clashes in central Plateau State on the day prior to the ballot. Initial results indicated that the PDP had secured about two-thirds of the contested seats, but widespread malpractice was also reported.

In early April 2004 the Government announced that some 20 army officials had been arrested, following the discovery of a conspiracy to seize power, believed to have been instigated by a former head of security in the Abacha administration, Maj. Hama al-Mustapha. (In October three senior military officers, including al-Mustapha, were charged with planning to overthrow the Government with an attack on the presidential helicopter.) Later in April reports emerged of severe clashes between Christian and Muslim tribes in farming villages on the border of Plateau State, reportedly as a result of land ownership disputes; by early May it was estimated that a total of 650 people, mainly Muslims, had been killed in the fighting. Muslims subsequently rioted in Kano in reprisal for the deaths; the Christian Association of Nigeria announced that 600 Christians had been killed and that a further 30,000 had fled from the region. Later in May Obasanjo dispatched security forces to restore order and imposed emergency powers in Plateau State, replacing the Governor with a former military officer and dissolving its legislature. (In November Obasanjo ended the state of emergency imposed in Plateau State, and reinstated the elected Governor, who, however, had been detained in London, on suspicion of financial malpractice.) In early June some 50 people were killed in further religious clashes in Numan, near the border with Cameroon (reportedly over the proposed construction of a mosque).

In June 2004 the NLC organized a national strike, which was widely observed, in protest at a further increase in the price of fuel. In September renewed hostilities between the Ijaw and Ijekiri in the Niger Delta prompted further concern on the part of the authorities, particularly after an Ijaw militia, the Niger Delta People's Volunteer Force, threatened a campaign to disrupt petroleum supplies by attacking installations. Consequently, the Government announced a further substantial increase in the price of fuel in that month, prompting the NLC to organize a general strike in early October. Further planned strike action by the NLC and allied organizations was suspended in mid-November, after the Government agreed to a reduction in the price. Following a peace accord between the Government and the activists, reached in October, fighting in the region declined significantly. However, Ijaw militia had failed to disarm by the scheduled date at the end of December, and a campaign of peaceful protests was threatened, on the grounds that the Government had not complied with the terms of the agreement.

In early January 2005 the Inspector-General of the security forces was removed, after being implicated in charges of malpractice involving government revenue. In late February a three-month national conference, comprising 400 government appointed delegates, was convened to decide on political reform, including possible constitutional amendments, prior to the elections in 2007; however, the conference was boycotted by the opposition and was refused funding by the legislature. At the end of March the Government introduced new legislation permitting the establishment of unions independent of the NLC and prohibiting strikes in essential service sectors, with the aim of restricting the influence of the Congress.

In March 2005 the Minister of Education, Fabian Osuji, was dismissed for offering financial incentives to parliamentary deputies, including the Speaker of the Senate (who was subsequently also removed), with the intention of securing a substantial increase in the education budget for 2005. Osuji denied the charges, and submitted a legal appeal against his dismissal, which had been announced by Obasanjo through the national media. In early April Obasanjo dismissed the minister responsible for housing, who was accused of the clandestine sale of state property to government members. In May the trial of Osuji, together with six former senators (including the dismissed Speaker), on corruption charges commenced in Abuja. In August 2005 Abubakar (who was expected to contest the presidential election in 2007) became the subject of controversy, after it emerged that he was under investigation by Federal Bureau of Investigation agents in the USA for allegedly receiving payments from a member of the US Congress.

In September 2005 tension increased in the Niger Delta region, following the arrest of the leader of a prominent militant movement, the Niger Delta People Volunteer Force; Mujahid Dokubo-Asari had threatened to continue hostilities unless his demands that the Ijaw people of the region be granted self-determination were met. Petroleum installations, which had temporarily closed, resumed operations after Dokubo-Asari urged his supporters to maintain civil order. In early October he was officially charged with treason before the Abuja Federal High Court. Later that month the leader of the Movement for the Actualization of the Sovereign State of Biafra (MASSOB), Chief Ralph Uwazuruike, was arrested and subsequently charged with treason (on the grounds that he had attempted to overthrow the Federal Government). In December Obasanjo placed defence and security personnel in the region on alert, following a petroleum pipeline explosion, in which several people were killed. Protests by members of MASSOB against the arrest of their leader ended in clashes, in which some 20 people were killed. In January 2006 four foreign nationals employed by companies subcontracted by Shell were seized by militants in Bayelsa State; a hitherto unknown Movement for the Emancipation of the Niger Delta (MEND) claimed responsibility for taking the hostages. Following the explosion of a further petroleum pipeline, the Shell Petroleum Development Company was obliged to suspend production from that offshore field (equivalent to one-tenth of the country's total output). MEND demanded that the Shell Petroleum Development Company pay US $1,500m. in compensation for environmental damage, and the release from custody of Dokubo-Asari and the Governor of Bayelsa State (who had been arrested in the United Kingdom and charged with financial malpractice). At the end of January MEND announced the release of the hostages on humanitarian grounds, but maintained that it would continue attacks in the Niger Delta region. Following further clashes in the region in February, members of MEND seized a further nine foreign nationals employed by a subcontracted US enterprise, Willbros. Six of the hostages were released one week later, while the remaining three (two US and one British national) were released in late March. Also in February a High Court in Port Harcourt ruled that the Shell Petroleum Development Company pay US $1,500m. in compensation to the Ijaw population in the Niger Delta for environmental damage, in compliance with a decision by the National Assembly in 2000. In March 2006 the Federal High Court in Abuja rejected an appeal by 11 MASSOB leaders, including Uwazuruike, against treason charges levelled against them (on grounds of attempting to overthrow the Federal Government). Meanwhile, in February more than 150 people were killed in religious rioting, after Muslim protests in the north of the country over cartoons in a Danish newspaper perceived as insulting the Prophet Mohammed and subsequent reprisal attacks by Christians in the south-eastern towns of Onitsha and Enugu.

In early 2006 the Nigerian Constitutional Committee conducted a series of public debates on proposed amendments to the Constitution, which would allow Obasanjo to seek a third term in office. A national census, conducted in late March, was extended for two days, as a result of shortage and the misappropriation of enumeration materials. Attacks on census officials by members of MASSOB, who supported a boycott of the operation, were reported in the south-east, and the exercise was completed amid complaints that civilians in remote parts of the country had not been included. In early April hostility worsened between Obasanjo and Abubakar (who protested at the proposals to end the constitutional restriction on two presidential terms).

Nigeria has taken a leading role in African affairs and is a prominent member of the Economic Community of West African States (ECOWAS, see p. 217) and other regional organizations. The Nigerian Government has contributed a significant number of troops to the ECOWAS Monitoring Group (ECOMOG, see p. 220), which was deployed in Liberia from August 1990 in response to the conflict between government forces and rebels in that country (see the chapter on Liberia). In 1993 Nigerian troops were dispatched to Sierra Leone, in response to a formal request by the Sierra Leonean Government for military assistance to repulse attacks by rebels in that country. Following the completion of the transition to civilian rule in Nigeria in May 1999, a phased withdrawal of Nigerian troops from Sierra Leone commenced. By the end of April 2000 all Nigerian troops belonging to ECOMOG had left Sierra Leone; however, Nigeria continued to contribute troops to the UN Mission in Sierra Leone (UNAMSIL). In September an official visit to Nigeria by the US President, Bill Clinton, the first by a US Head of State since 1978, provided for a number of new trade and development initiatives. After further full-scale conflict in Liberia in mid-2003 (see the chapter on Liberia), the Liberian President, Charles Taylor, finally accepted an offer of asylum from Obasanjo, following pressure from the international community, and took up residence in Calabar, in south-eastern Nigeria, in early August. Some 1,500 Nigerian troops, which were deployed in the country, under an ECOWAS mandate, at the end of August, were instrumental in restoring peace and were incorporated into the replacement contingent, the UN Mission in Liberia (UNMIL, see p. 76), on 1 October. In October the Nigerian Government strongly protested at the US authorities' approval of a reward of some US $2m. for the arrest of Taylor (who had been indicted by the Special Court established in Sierra Leone to try war crime suspects.) In March 2006 Nigeria announced that it had received a formal request from the new Liberian Government (see chapter on Liberia) to extradite Taylor to the Special Court. Obasanjo agreed to return him to the Liberian authorities, but failed to comply with demands by the Chief Prosecutor of the Special Court and the USA to take him into custody. Taylor fled from his residence in Calabar, but was apprehended two days later in Borno State, near the border with Cameroon, and dispatched to Liberia, from where he was immediately extradited by UNMIL peace-keepers to the Special Court.

In 1991 the Nigerian Government claimed that Cameroonian security forces had annexed several Nigerian fishing settlements in Cross River State (in south-eastern Nigeria), following a long-standing border dispute, based on a 1913 agreement between Germany and the United Kingdom that ceded the Bakassi peninsula in the Gulf of Guinea (a region with significant petroleum reserves) to Cameroon. Subsequent negotiations between Nigerian and Cameroonian officials in an effort to resolve the dispute achieved little progress. In December 1993 some 500 Nigerian troops were dispatched to the region, in response to a number of incidents in which Nigerian nationals had been killed by Cameroonian security forces. Later that month the two nations agreed to establish a joint patrol at the disputed area, and to investigate the cause of the incidents. In February 1994, however, the Nigerian Government increased the number of troops deployed in the region. Later in February the Cameroonian Government announced that it was to submit the dispute for adjudication by the UN, the Organization of African Unity (OAU, now the African Union, see p. 153) and the International Court of Justice (ICJ), and requested military assistance from France. Subsequent reports of clashes between Cameroonian and Nigerian forces in the region prompted fears of a full-scale conflict between the two nations.

In February 1996 renewed hostilities between Nigerian and Cameroonian forces in the Bakassi region resulted in several casualties. Later that month, however, Nigeria and Cameroon agreed to refrain from further military action, and delegations from the two countries resumed discussions, with mediation by President Gnassingbe Eyadéma of Togo, in an attempt to resolve the dispute. In March the ICJ ruled that Cameroon had failed to provide sufficient evidence to support its contention that Nigeria had instigated the border dispute, and ordered both nations to cease military operations in this respect, to withdraw troops to former positions, and to co-operate with a UN investigative mission that was to be dispatched to the region. In April, however, clashes continued, with each Government accusing the other of initiating the attacks. Although tension in the region remained high, diplomatic efforts to avoid further conflict increased in May; in that month a Cameroonian delegation visited Nigeria, while Abacha accepted an invitation to attend an OAU summit meeting, which was to be convened in Yaoundé in July. The UN investigative mission visited the Bakassi region in September. In May 1997 the Cameroonian Government denied further allegations by Nigeria that it had initiated hostilities; the UN requested that the Togolese President continue mediation efforts. Further clashes between Nigerian and Cameroonian forces were reported in December 1997 and February 1998. In March the Nigerian Government contested the jurisdiction of the ICJ to rule on the Bakassi issue, on the grounds that the two countries had agreed to settle the dispute through bilateral negotiations. In June, however, the Court pronounced that it had the necessary jurisdiction.

In October 2002 the ICJ finally ruled that the disputed Bakassi region was part of Cameroon, under the terms of the 1913 agreement. Obasanjo criticized the decision, in support of strong opposition expressed by the Nigerian majority inhabitants of the peninsula, although he subsequently pledged to abide by the ruling. In August 2003, following UN mediation, Nigeria and Cameroon finally adopted a framework agreement for the implementation of the ICJ's judgment; all military and administrative personnel were to be withdrawn from the Bakassi region, and a commission, comprising Nigerian, Cameroonian and UN officials, was to resolve outstanding issues for the redemarcation of boundaries between the two countries, in a process that was expected to continue for up to three years. In December the Nigerian Government ceded control of some 33 villages on its north-eastern border to Cameroon, but sovereignty over the disputed territory with petroleum resources remained under discussion by the commission. However, the Nigerian Government announced that the transfer of authority in the peninsula, scheduled for September 2004, had been postponed, citing technical difficulties in the final redemarcation of the joint border. Following a meeting in May 2005 between Obasanjo and the Head of State of Cameroon, conducted in Geneva, Switzerland, under the aegis of the UN Secretary-General, it was announced that the two sides had agreed to draft a new programme for Nigeria's withdrawal from the Bakassi peninsula.

Government

Under the terms of the Constitution of the Federal Republic of Nigeria, which entered into effect on 31 May 1999, executive power is vested in the President, who is the Head of State. The President, who is elected for a term of four years (and is restricted to two mandates), nominates a Vice-President and a Cabinet, subject to confirmation by the Senate. Legislative power is vested in the bicameral National Assembly, comprising a 360-member House of Representatives and a 109-member Senate, which is elected by universal suffrage for a four-year term. Nigeria is a federation of 36 states, comprising 774 local government areas. The executive power of a state is vested in the Governor of that state, who is elected for a four-year term, and the legislative power in the House of Assembly of that state.

Defence

In August 2005 Nigeria's total armed forces numbered 78,500 (army 62,000, navy 7,000 and air force 9,500). There was also a paramilitary force of 82,000. Military service is voluntary. Expenditure on defence by the Federal Government in 2005 was budgeted at ₦111,000m.

Economic Affairs

In 2004, according to estimates by the World Bank, Nigeria's gross national income (GNI), measured at average 2002–04 prices, was US $53,983m., equivalent to $390 per head (or $930 per head on an international purchasing-power parity basis). During 1995–2004, it was estimated, the population increased, in real terms, at an average annual rate of 2.6%, while gross domestic product (GDP) per head rose by 1.0%. Overall GDP increased, in real terms, at an average annual rate of 3.6% in 1995–2004; growth was 10.7% in 2003 and 3.6% in 2004.

Agriculture (including hunting, forestry and fishing) contributed an estimated 26.4% of GDP in 2003. An estimated 30.6% of the labour force were employed in the sector in that year. The principal cash crops are cocoa (which accounted for only 0.7% of total merchandise exports in 1995), rubber and oil palm. Staple food crops include rice, maize, taro, yams, cassava, sorghum and millet. Timber production, the raising of livestock (principally goats, sheep, cattle and poultry), and artisanal fisheries are also important. According to the World Bank, agricultural GDP increased at an average annual rate of 4.1% in 1995–2004. Growth in agricultural GDP was 4.3% in 2004.

Industry (including mining, manufacturing, construction and power) engaged an estimated 6.9% of the employed labour force in 1990, and contributed an estimated 49.5% of GDP in 2003. According to the World Bank, industrial GDP increased at an average annual rate of 2.2% in 1995–2004. It increased by 22.4% in 2003, but declined by 4.0% in 2004.

Mining contributed 44.8% of GDP in 2003, although the sector engaged less than 0.1% of the employed labour force in 1986. The principal mineral is petroleum, of which Nigeria is Africa's leading producer (providing an estimated 88.5% of total export earnings in 2004). In addition, Nigeria possesses substantial deposits of natural gas and coal. In late 1999 the Nigerian Government commenced exports of liquefied natural gas, and by 2004 natural gas accounted for 8.8% of earnings. A 600-km pipeline, which would transport natural gas from the Escravos field, in Delta State, to Benin, Togo and Ghana, was under development and was scheduled to become operational in 2006. Tin and iron ore are also mined, while there are plans to exploit deposits of uranium. The GDP of the mining sector was estimated by the IMF to have declined by an average of 0.1% per year in 1997–2001; mining GDP increased by 0.6% in 2001.

Manufacturing contributed 4.0% of GDP in 2003, and engaged about 4.3% of the employed labour force in 1986. The principal sectors are food-processing, brewing, petroleum-refining, iron and steel, motor vehicles (using imported components), textiles, cigarettes, footwear, pharmaceuticals, pulp and paper, and cement. According to the World Bank, manufacturing GDP increased at an average annual rate of 3.5% in 1995–2003. Manufacturing GDP increased by 6.2% in 2003.

Energy is derived principally from natural gas, which provided some 44.0% of electricity in 2002, and hydroelectric power (46.2%). Mineral fuels comprised an estimated 1.8% of the value of merchandise imports in 2000.

The services sector contributed an estimated 24.2% of GDP in 2003, and engaged 48.5% of the employed labour force in 1986. According to World Bank estimates, the GDP of the services sector increased at an average annual rate of 4.7% in 1995–2004. The GDP of the services sector increased by 9.3% in 2004.

In 2004 Nigeria recorded an estimated trade surplus of US $12,561m., and there was a surplus of $12,264m. on the current account of the balance of payments. In 2003 the principal source of imports (9.3%) was the People's Republic of China; other major suppliers were the United Kingdom, France, the USA, the Netherlands and Germany. The USA was the principal market for exports (40.2%) in that year; other significant purchasers were Spain, Brazil, France, Indonesia and Japan. The main exports in 2004 were petroleum and natural gas. The principal imports in 2000 were machinery and transport equipment (particularly road vehicles), chemicals, manufactured goods, and food and live animals.

Nigeria's overall budget deficit for 2004 was ₦142,700m., equivalent to 1.7% of GDP. The country's external debt totalled US $34,963m. at the end of 2003, of which $31,563m. was long-term public debt. In that year the cost of debt-servicing was equivalent to 8.0% of the value of exports of goods and services. The annual rate of inflation averaged 24.5% in 1992–2004; consumer prices increased by 15.0% in 2004. An estimated 4.5% of the labour force were unemployed at the end of 1997.

Nigeria is a member of the African Development Bank (see p. 151), of the Economic Community of West African States (see p. 217), which aims to promote trade and co-operation in West Africa, and of the Organization of the Petroleum Exporting Countries (see p. 344).

Following high levels of economic growth in the 1970s, Nigeria's economy deteriorated as a result of the subsequent decline in international prices for petroleum. In response to democratization measures initiated by a new military Head of State in mid-1998, the European Union ended a number of sanctions against Nigeria later that year. In January 1999 the Government abolished the dual exchange rate system and ended restrictions on foreign investment. The new civilian Government, which was installed in June, benefited greatly from an increase in the international price of petroleum, and some fiscal recovery ensued. Continuing violent protests in the Niger Delta region

NIGERIA

disrupted petroleum production, however, and, together with severe religious and ethnic violence from 2000 (see Recent History), deterred potential foreign investors. The Government failed to adhere to a one-year IMF-endorsed economic programme, which expired in August 2001, and the IMF suspended formal relations with Nigeria in March 2002, thereby ending the immediate prospect of concessionary debt relief. Despite widespread discontent over his perceived failure to reduce corruption, Obasanjo was returned to the presidency in April 2003. His new Government included several proponents of economic reform, notably the hitherto Vice-President of the World Bank as the new Minister of Finance and the Economy. In early 2004 the administration promulgated its new reform policy, the National Economic Empowerment and Development Strategy (NEEDS). The NEEDS programme, which was to continue for a period of three years, comprised the main objectives of accelerated privatization and deregulation, budgetary restraint, increased productivity, administrative reform, greater state accountability, and improved conditions for private investment. Despite slowed growth in 2004, an IMF review welcomed progress in that year under the NEEDS programme as a transition towards a comprehensive new policy of fiscal prudence. In June 2005 the 'Paris Club' of creditor nations reached agreement, in principle, on a restructuring arrangement to address the country's exceptionally high levels of debt. In October the IMF endorsed the Nigerian Government's economic reform strategy detailed in NEEDS, with the approval of a two-year Policy Support Instrument (PSI) arrangement (as an alternative to a full IMF programme). Later that month the 'Paris Club' formally signed an agreement providing for the cancellation of US $18,000m. of a total $31,000m. owed to foreign Governments; Nigeria was to pay all arrears, receive the partial cancellation of debt and buy the remainder of debt with petroleum revenue generated by the higher international price, thereby securing a considerable reduction in debt-servicing charges. In early 2006 an escalation of unrest in the Niger Delta region, with a series of attacks against petroleum pipelines and seizures of foreign nationals as hostages, threatened national stability. The violence had resulted in the temporary closure of an offshore field and ensuing significant reduction in petroleum exports and in national power generation, exacerbating energy shortages. In February a High Court ruled that the Shell Petroleum Development Company pay $1,500m. in compensation to the Ijaw population in the Niger Delta for environmental damage. Nevertheless, militant groups in the region continued to demand the withdrawal of all foreign enterprises exploiting the country's resources. Also in February an outbreak of a lethal strain (H5NI) of highly contagious avian influenza was confirmed in three northern states, necessitating the imposition of emergency measures including the cull of poultry and payment of compensation to farmers. In early 2006 implementation of reforms under the NEEDS programme (which was due to conclude in 2007) was perceived as limited, although the Government had made progress in budgetary management, privatization of the energy industry and restructuring of the banking sector.

Education

Education is partly the responsibility of the state governments, although the Federal Government has played an increasingly important role since 1970. Primary education begins at six years of age and lasts for six years. Secondary education begins at 12 years of age and lasts for a further six years, comprising two three-year cycles. Education to junior secondary level (from six to 15 years of age) is free and compulsory. In 2002/03 some 67% of children in the relevant age-group (males 74%; females 60%) were enrolled in primary education, while the comparable ratio for secondary enrolment was only 29% (males 32%; females 26%). In 1993 383,488 students were enrolled in 133 higher education institutions. Expenditure on education by the Federal Government in 2001 was ₦59,745m., equivalent to 7.5% of total expenditure in the federal budget.

Public Holidays

2006: 1 January (New Year's Day), 10 January*† (Id al-Kabir, Feast of the Sacrifice), 10 April* (Mouloud, Birth of the Prophet), 14–17 April (Easter), 1 October (National Day), 23 October* (Id al-Fitr, end of Ramadan), 25–26 December (Christmas), 31 January*† (Id al-Kabir, Feast of the Sacrifice).

2007: 1 January (New Year's Day), 31 March* (Mouloud, Birth of the Prophet), 6–9 April (Easter), 1 October (National Day), 13 October* (Id al-Fitr, end of Ramadan), 20 December* (Id al-Kabir, Feast of the Sacrifice), 25–26 December (Christmas).

* These holidays are dependent on the Islamic lunar calendar, and may vary by one or two days from the dates given.

† This festival occurs twice (in the Islamic years AH 1426 and 1427) within the same Gregorian year.

Weights and Measures

The metric system is in force.

Statistical Survey

Source (unless otherwise stated): Federal Office of Statistics, Plot 205, Bacita Close, Garki, Abuja; tel. 803-3153401; e-mail eteamah@yahoo.comt; internet www.bosng.org.

Area and Population

AREA, POPULATION AND DENSITY

Area (sq km)	923,768*
Population (census results, 28–30 November 1991)†	
Males	44,529,608
Females	44,462,612
Total	88,992,220
Population (UN estimates at mid-year)‡	
2002	123,134,000
2003	125,912,000
2004	128,709,000
Density (per sq km) at mid-2004	139.3

* 356,669 sq miles.
† Revised 15 September 2001.
‡ Source: UN, *World Population Prospects: The 2004 Revision.*

STATES
(unrevised census of November 1991)*

	Population	Capital
Abia	2,297,978	Umuahia
Adamawa	2,124,049	Yola
Akwa Ibom	2,359,736	Uyo
Anambra	2,767,903	Awka
Bauchi	4,294,413	Bauchi
Benue	2,780,398	Makurdi
Borno	2,596,589	Maiduguri
Cross River	1,865,604	Calabar
Delta	2,570,181	Asaba
Edo	2,159,848	Benin City
Enugu	3,161,295	Enugu
Imo	2,485,499	Owerri
Jigawa	2,829,929	Dutse
Kaduna	3,969,252	Kaduna
Kano	5,632,040	Kano
Katsina	3,878,344	Katsina
Kebbi	2,062,226	Birnin Kebbi
Kogi	2,099,046	Lokoja
Kwara	1,566,469	Ilorin
Lagos	5,685,781	Ikeja
Niger	2,482,367	Minna
Ogun	2,338,570	Abeokuta

NIGERIA

—continued	Population	Capital
Ondo	3,884,485	Akure
Osun	2,203,016	Oshogbo
Oyo	3,488,789	Ibadan
Plateau	3,283,704	Jos
Rivers	3,983,857	Port Harcourt
Sokoto	4,392,391	Sokoto
Taraba	1,480,590	Jalingo
Yobe	1,411,481	Damaturu
Federal Capital Territory	378,671	Abuja
Total	88,514,501	

* In October 1996 the Government announced the creation of six new states: Bayelsa, Ebonyi, Ekiti, Gombe, Nassarawa and Zamfara (with capitals at Yenogoa, Abakaliki, Ado-Ekiti, Gombe, Lafia and Gusau respectively).

PRINCIPAL TOWNS
(unrevised census of November 1991)

Lagos (federal capital)*	5,195,247	Enugu		407,756
Kano	2,166,554	Oyo		369,894
Ibadan	1,835,300	Warri		363,382
Kaduna	933,642	Abeokuta		352,735
Benin City	762,719	Onitsha		350,280
Port Harcourt	703,421	Sokoto		329,639
Maiduguri	618,278	Okene		312,775
Zaria	612,257	Calabar		310,839
Ilorin	532,089	Katsina		259,315
Jos	510,300	Oshogbo		250,951
Aba	500,183	Akure		239,124
Ogbomosho	433,030	Bauchi		206,537

* Federal capital moved to Abuja (population 107,069) in December 1991.

Mid-2003 (UN estimates, incl. suburbs): Lagos 10,103,459; Kano 2,762,800; Ibadan 2,284,396; Kaduna 1,272,541.

Source: UN, *World Urbanization Prospects: The 2003 Revision.*

BIRTHS AND DEATHS
(UN estimates, annual averages)

	1990–95	1995–2000	2000–05
Birth rate (per 1,000)	46.1	43.9	42.0
Death rate (per 1,000)	18.4	19.0	19.4

Source: UN, *World Population Prospects: The 2004 Revision.*

Expectation of life (WHO estimates, years at birth): 45 (males 45; females 46) in 2003 (Source: WHO, *World Health Report*).

ECONOMICALLY ACTIVE POPULATION
(sample survey, '000 persons aged 14 years and over, September 1986)

	Males	Females	Total
Agriculture, hunting, forestry and fishing	9,800.6	3,458.4	13,259.0
Mining and quarrying	6.8	—	6.8
Manufacturing	806.4	457.3	1,263.7
Electricity, gas and water	127.0	3.4	130.4
Construction	545.6	—	545.6
Trade, restaurants and hotels	2,676.6	4,740.8	7,417.4
Transport, storage and communications	1,094.7	17.2	1,111.9
Financing, insurance, real estate and business services	109.8	10.3	120.1
Community, social and personal services	3,939.5	962.6	4,902.1
Activities not adequately defined	597.1	147.8	744.9
Total employed	19,704.1	9,797.8	29,501.9
Unemployed	809.8	453.8	1,263.6
Total labour force	20,513.9	10,251.6	30,765.5

Note: Figures are based on a total estimated population of 98,936,800, which may be an overestimate.

Source: ILO, *Yearbook of Labour Statistics.*

Mid-2003 (estimates in '000): Agriculture, etc. 15,178; Total labour force 49,560 (Source: FAO).

Health and Welfare

KEY INDICATORS

Total fertility rate (children per woman, 2003)	5.4
Under-5 mortality rate (per 1,000 live births, 2004)	197
HIV/AIDS (% of persons aged 15–49, 2003)	5.4
Physicians (per 1,000 head, 2000)	0.27
Hospital beds (per 1,000 head, 1990)	1.67
Health expenditure (2002): US $ per head (PPP)	43
Health expenditure (2002): % of GDP	4.7
Health expenditure (2002): public (% of total)	25.6
Access to water (% of persons, 2002)	60
Access to sanitation (% of persons, 2002)	38
Human Development Index (2003): ranking	158
Human Development Index (2003): value	0.453

For sources and definitions, see explanatory note on p. vi.

Agriculture

PRINCIPAL CROPS
('000 metric tons)

	2002	2003	2004
Wheat	77	71	71
Rice (paddy)	3,192	3,373	3,542
Maize	4,688	4,779	4,779
Millet	6,100	6,282	6,282
Sorghum	7,704	8,028	8,028
Fonio	83	83	81
Potatoes	629	657	657
Sweet potatoes	2,503	2,516	2,516
Cassava	32,749	32,913	38,179
Taro (Coco yam)	3,929	4,027	4,027
Yams	26,258	26,324	26,587
Sugar cane	747	739	776
Dry cow peas	2,174	2,228	2,317
Other pulses*	50	50	50
Cashew nuts	186	209	213
Kolanuts*	85	85	85
Soybeans	437	449	465
Groundnuts (in shell)	2,699	2,797	2,937
Coconuts	161	166	166
Oil palm fruit*	8,500	8,632	8,700
Karite nuts (Sheanuts)	371	410	414
Sesame seed†	73	74	75
Melonseed	347	341	346
Cottonseed*	250	250	250
Tomatoes*	889	889	889
Green chillies and peppers*	720	720	720
Green onions and shallots*	220	220	220
Dry onions*	600	615	615
Carrots*	235	235	235
Okra*	730	730	730
Green corn (maize)*	576	576	576
Other fresh vegetables (incl. melons)	4,276	4,300*	4,285
Plantains	2,058	2,103	2,103
Citrus fruits*	3,250	3,250	3,250
Mangoes*	730	730	730
Pineapples*	889	889	889
Papayas*	755	755	755
Other fruit (excl. melons)*	1,400	1,400	1,400
Cocoa beans	340	361	366
Pimento and allspice*	48	48	48
Ginger	106	110*	110*
Cotton (lint)*	150	140	140
Tobacco (leaves)*	9	9	9
Natural rubber (dry weight)	112	142	142

* FAO estimate(s).
† Unofficial figures.

Source: FAO.

NIGERIA

Statistical Survey

LIVESTOCK
('000 head, year ending September)

	2002	2003	2004
Horses*	205	205	206
Asses*	1,000	1,000	1,050
Cattle	15,149	15,164	15,200*
Camels*	18	18	18
Pigs	6,112	6,356	6,611
Sheep*	22,000	22,500	23,000
Goats*	27,000	27,000	28,000
Poultry	131,125	137,680	140,000*

* FAO estimate(s).
Source: FAO.

LIVESTOCK PRODUCTS
(FAO estimates, '000 metric tons)

	2002	2003	2004
Beef and veal	279.5	279.5	280.0
Mutton and lamb	96.8	99.0	100.7
Goat meat	142.2	142.2	147.1
Pig meat	192.5	200.2	208.2
Poultry meat	190.0	201.0	211.0
Game meat	120	120	120
Cows' milk	432	432	432
Butter and ghee	9.8	9.8	9.8
Cheese	7.8	7.8	7.8
Poultry eggs	450	460	476
Cattle hides	43.0	43.0	43.1
Sheepskins	17.6	18.0	18.3
Goatskins	22.4	22.4	23.2

Source: FAO.

Forestry

ROUNDWOOD REMOVALS
(FAO estimates, '000 cubic metres, excluding bark)

	2002	2003	2004
Sawlogs, veneer logs and logs for sleepers	7,100	7,100	7,100
Pulpwood	39	39	39
Other industrial wood	2,279	2,279	2,279
Fuel wood	60,064	60,449	60,852
Total	69,482	69,867	70,270

Source: FAO.

SAWNWOOD PRODUCTION
('000 cubic metres, including railway sleepers)

	1995	1996	1997
Broadleaved (hardwood)	2,356	2,178	2,000

1998–2004: Broadleaved (hardwood) production as in 1997.
Source: FAO.

Fishing

('000 metric tons, live weight)

	2001	2002	2003
Capture	452.1	481.1	475.2
Tilapias	18.3	17.2	31.2
Elephant snout fishes	17.5	5.6	15.4
Torpedo-shaped catfishes	21.3	15.0	27.0
Sea catfishes	16.5	21.2	18.3
West African croakers	15.1	11.9	13.5
Sardinellas	73.9	71.5	79.1
Bonga shad	19.0	22.0	21.6
Southern pink shrimp	18.8	13.4	13.2
Other shrimps and prawns	0.9	17.1	15.0
Aquaculture	24.4	30.6	30.7
Total catch	476.5	511.7	505.8

Source: FAO.

Mining
(metric tons unless otherwise indicated)

	2002	2003	2004
Coal, bituminous	43,482	23,089	9,000
Kaolin	200,000	200,000	200,000
Gypsum	300,000	100,000	100,0000
Crude petroleum ('000 barrels)*	773,000	825,000	900,400
Natural gas (million cu m)	50,000	53,000	57,747
Tin concentrates†	790	1,800	1,000

* Estimates.
† Metal content.
Source: US Geological Survey.

Industry

SELECTED PRODUCTS
('000 metric tons, unless otherwise indicated)

	2001	2002	2003
Palm oil*	903	908	915
Raw sugar*†	40	40	40
Wheat flour*†	1,564	1,730	1,598
Beer of barley*†	956	1,171	1,170
Beer of sorghum*†	698	760	794
Plywood ('000 cubic metres)*†	55	55	55
Wood pulp*†	23	23	23
Paper and paperboard*†	19	19	19
Liquefied petroleum gas ('000 barrels)†	1,000	2,300	2,000
Motor spirit—petrol ('000 barrels)†	24,400	22,400	20,000
Kerosene ('000 barrels)†	12,500	11,800	12,000
Gas-diesel (distillate fuel) oil ('000 barrels)†	18,900	18,800	19,000
Residual fuel oils ('000 barrels)†	21,500	17,200	17,000
Cement†	2,400	2,100	2,100
Tin metal—unwrought (metric tons)†	25	25	25
Electric energy (million kWh)‡	18,107	n.a.	n.a.

* Source: FAO.
† Estimates.
‡ Source: UN, *Industrial Commodity Statistics Yearbook*.
Source (unless otherwise indicated): US Geological Survey.

Finance

CURRENCY AND EXCHANGE RATES

Monetary Units
  100 kobo = 1 naira (₦).

Sterling, Dollar and Euro Equivalents (31 October 2005)
  £1 sterling = 230.24 naira;
  US $1 = 129.53 naira;
  €1 = 155.73 naira;
  1,000 naira = £4.34 = $7.72 = €6.42.

Average Exchange Rate (naira per US $)
  2002   120.578
  2003   129.222
  2004   132.888

NIGERIA

FEDERAL BUDGET
(₦ million)*

Revenue†	2000	2001	2002
Distribution from Federation Account	514,969	530,658	545,438
Drawdown of Federation Stabilization Account	—	64	—
Share of value-added tax (VAT)	8,770	13,359	15,747
Independent revenue‡	38,057	44,405	68,134
Education Trust Fund	8,302	16,214	9,570
Customs levies	14,182	24,195	20,000
First-charge deductions from federation revenue	783,953	680,070	496,798
External debt-servicing	175,034	232,192	143,867
National priority projects	42,459	18,124	—
Nigerian National Petroleum Corporation (NNPC) cash calls and priority projects	284,750	429,754	352,932
Other	—	53,737	—
Total	1,368,233	1,362,701	1,155,688

Expenditure§	2000	2001	2002
Recurrent expenditure	633,035	670,140	1,024,389
General administration	59,332	75,080	146,807
National Assembly	4,766	19,804	20,163
Defence	31,046	47,072	86,054
Internal security	26,154	38,855	78,713
Agriculture and water resources	4,806	7,065	12,439
Construction	11,480	7,202	9,276
Transport and communications	2,428	33,935	36,579
Other economic services	11,102	4,809	7,616
Education	39,034	39,885	100,240
Health	11,580	24,524	50,563
Other social and community services	8,189	15,226	38,628
Interest payments due	279,911	326,638	360,956
Other transfers¶	143,206	30,046	76,355
Capital expenditure	239,451	438,697	321,378
General administration	36,560	28,032	36,572
National Assembly	1,889	9	1,472
Defence	6,444	16,400	22,094
Internal security	8,397	4,814	13,440
Agriculture and water resources	8,803	57,879	32,364
Roads and construction	7,006	21,440	35,850
Manufacturing, mining and quarrying	10,514	7,284	39,663
Transport and communications	7,177	19,241	17,083
Housing	—	56,356	44,479
National priority projects	40,377	18,124	—
Other economic services	37,629	79,434	45,894
Education	10,529	19,860	9,215
Health	8,866	20,128	12,608
Other social and community services	8,570	13,348	10,644
Transfers	46,698	76,348	—
Total	872,486	1,108,837	1,345,767

* Figures refer to the operations of the Federal Government, the 'first charges' and the Petroleum Special Trust Fund (PSTF).
† Figures for government revenue refer to federally retained revenue. This includes 48.5% of total distributed revenue of the Federation Account, more than one-half of which consists of proceeds from the operations of the NNPC and foreign petroleum companies. The remainder of Federation Account revenue is allocated to state governments (24%), local governments (20%) and five special funds (7.5%). The Federal Government retains 20% of federally collected VAT.
‡ Including loan repayments and proceeds from the privatization or commercialization of state enterprises.
§ Figures exclude the operations of extrabudgetary accounts. Including supplementary and extrabudgetary outlays, total expenditure (in ₦ million) was: 1,220,744 in 2000; 1,625,255 in 2001; 1,420,406 in 2002.
¶ Including pensions, gratuities, grants, subventions and losses from transactions in foreign exchanges.

Source: IMF, *Nigeria: Selected Issues and Statistical Appendix* (August 2004).

INTERNATIONAL RESERVES
(US $ million at 31 December)

	2002	2003	2004
Total*	7,331	7,128	16,956

* Almost exclusively foreign exchange, and excluding gold reserves (687,000 troy ounces each year).

Source: IMF, *International Financial Statistics*.

MONEY SUPPLY
(₦ million at 31 December)

	2002	2003	2004
Currency outside banks	386,942	412,155	458,587
Demand deposits at commercial banks	503,870	577,664	728,552
Total money (incl. others)	946,253	1,225,559	1,330,658

Source: IMF, *International Financial Statistics*.

COST OF LIVING
(Consumer Price Index for September of each year; base: May 2003 = 100)

	2001	2002	2003
Food (excl. beverages)	94.5	99.9	106.2
Beverages, tobacco and kola	77.7	96.5	105.3
Clothing (incl. footwear)	87.5	97.6	120.1
Rent, fuel and light	71.5	85.9	138.2
Household goods	80.9	96.2	108.4
Medical care and health	81.5	107.1	125.3
Transport	71.9	80.2	108.7
Recreation and education	82.2	96.7	111.0
All items (incl. others)	87.1	95.8	113.4

Source: IMF, *Nigeria: Selected Issues and Statistical Appendix* (August 2004).

NATIONAL ACCOUNTS
(₦ million at current prices)

National Income and Product*

	1992	1993	1994
Compensation of employees	59,100	74,546	81,048
Operating surplus	468,880	604,200	808,817
Domestic factor incomes	527,980	678,746	889,865
Consumption of fixed capital	16,351	17,240	18,629
Gross domestic product (GDP) at factor cost	544,331	695,986	908,494
Indirect taxes	5,762	5,689	6,042
Less Subsidies	284	202	202
GDP in purchasers' values	549,809	701,473	914,334
Factor income received from abroad	2,799	1,338	1,170
Less Factor income paid abroad	67,203	74,900	66,878
Gross national product (GNP)	485,405	627,911	848,626
Less Consumption of fixed capital	16,351	17,240	18,629
National income in market prices	469,053	610,671	829,997
Other current transfers from abroad	15,240	21,386	13,164
Less Other current transfers paid abroad	2,560	3,592	2,211
National disposable income	481,733	628,465	840,950

* Figures are provisional.

Source: UN, *National Accounts Statistics*.

2001 (₦ million): GDP in purchasers' values 5,339,063; Net factor income from abroad −476,732; Gross national product 4,862,331 (Source: IMF, *Nigeria: Selected Issues and Statistical Appendix*—August 2004).

2002 (₦ million): GDP in purchasers' values 5,632,308; Net factor income from abroad −782,179; Gross national product 4,850,129 (Source: IMF, *Nigeria: Selected Issues and Statistical Appendix*—August 2004).

2003 (₦ million, preliminary figures): GDP in purchasers' values 7,545,263; Net factor income from abroad −1,104,976; Gross national product 6,440,287 (Source: IMF, *Nigeria: Selected Issues and Statistical Appendix*—August 2004).

NIGERIA

Statistical Survey

Expenditure on the Gross Domestic Product
(₦'000 million at current prices)

	2002	2003	2004
Government final consumption expenditure	478	450	493
Private final consumption expenditure	4,015	5,493	6,470
Increase in stocks	} 501	} 867	} 1,383
Gross fixed capital formation			
Total domestic expenditure	4,994	6,810	8,346
Exports of goods and services	2,564	3,479	4,358
Less Imports of goods and services	1,954	3,098	4,150
GDP in purchasers' values	5,603	7,191	8,553

Source: IMF, *International Financial Statistics*.

Gross Domestic Product by Economic Activity
(₦ million at current prices)

	2001	2002	2003*
Agriculture, hunting, forestry and fishing	1,584,312	1,700,451	1,940,587
Mining and quarrying	2,229,675	2,095,245	3,297,206
Manufacturing	201,393	250,187	293,083
Electricity, gas and water	2,438	4,234	5,153
Construction	40,755	39,191	44,753
Trade, restaurants and hotels	650,112	781,012	1,050,928
Transport, storage and communications	147,775	182,392	243,015
Finance, insurance, real estate and business services	226,151	286,075	346,696
Government services	40,176	48,974	50,812
Other community, social and personal services	55,385	66,405	87,907
GDP at factor cost	5,178,171	5,454,165	7,360,139
Taxes on products	163,392	180,643	187,625
Less Subsidies	2,500	2,500	2,500
GDP in purchasers' values	5,339,063	5,632,308	7,545,263

* Preliminary figures.

Source: IMF, *Nigeria: Selected Issues and Statistical Appendix* (August 2004).

BALANCE OF PAYMENTS
(US $ million)

	2002	2003	2004
Exports of goods f.o.b.	15,613	22,629	23,657
Imports of goods f.o.b.	−10,876	−10,499	−11,096
Trade balance	4,738	12,130	12,561
Exports of services	2,524	3,473	3,336
Imports of services	−4,922	−5,715	−4,969
Balance on goods and services	2,340	9,889	10,929
Other income received	184	82	157
Other income paid	−2,854	−1,518	−1,074
Balance on goods, services and income	−330	8,453	10,012
Current transfers received	1,422	1,063	2,273
Current transfers paid	−9	−12	−21
Current balance	1,083	9,504	12,264
Direct investment from abroad	1,874	2,006	1,875
Portfolio investment assets	134	147	352
Other investment assets	−5,890	−10,115	−2,288
Other investment liabilities	−4,673	−3,838	−4,426
Net errors and omissions	2,782	1,035	714
Overall balance	−4,689	−1,260	8,491

Source: IMF, *International Financial Statistics*.

External Trade

PRINCIPAL COMMODITIES
(US $ million)

Imports c.i.f.	1998	1999	2000
Food and live animals	1,100.5	1,171.9	1,095.9
Milk and cream	109.1	232.4	130.4
Fish and fish preparations*	218.0	176.8	248.8
Cereals and cereal preparations	512.8	605.9	412.1
Wheat and meslin, unmilled	297.0	434.1	251.3
Rice	186.5	107.4	119.7
Sugar and honey	203.6	116.0	146.7
Chemicals and related products	1,061.2	701.7	1,165.6
Organic chemicals	174.2	109.3	163.2
Manufactured fertilizers	56.3	5.8	203.0
Artificial resins and plastic materials and cellulose esters	267.0	215.0	295.8
Polymerization and copolymerization products	210.0	152.0	244.2
Basic manufactures	1,066.9	891.5	1,103.2
Paper and paperboard	160.6	115.2	211.0
Cement	114.5	268.2	158.8
Iron and steel	359.9	210.8	361.0
Universals, sheets and plates	176.6	104.5	218.5
Machinery and transport equipment	1,968.2	1,240.0	1,944.5
Power-generating machinery and equipment	225.4	146.9	200.8
Machinery specialized for particular industries	360.2	170.9	289.4
General industrial machinery and parts	371.4	228.4	271.0
Electric machinery, apparatus and parts	192.7	107.7	310.5
Road vehicles	445.6	350.0	603.4
Passenger motor vehicles (excl. buses)	156.3	128.0	208.4
Lorries and special purpose motor vehicles	85.9	50.4	177.2
Miscellaneous manufactured articles	278.4	219.2	241.6
Total (incl. others)	5,764.3	4,482.5	5,805.5

* Including crustacea and molluscs.

Exports f.o.b.	1998	1999	2000
Crude petroleum	6,658.7	15,952.4	26,956.1
Total (incl. others)	6,868.9	16,123.5	27,055.2

Source: UN, *International Trade Statistics Yearbook*.

NIGERIA

PRINCIPAL TRADING PARTNERS
(US $ million)*

Imports c.i.f.	1999	2000	2001
Belgium	144.0	314.5	438.2
Benin	3.4	36.0	176.7
Brazil	152.9	178.8	174.6
China, People's Repub.	177.3	252.3	526.8
France (incl. Monaco)	306.4	324.5	371.7
Germany	360.6	593.5	780.8
Greece	191.9	38.5	43.6
Hong Kong	58.3	87.7	96.4
India	198.6	198.7	315.7
Indonesia	36.9	45.3	107.8
Ireland	91.5	34.6	35.4
Italy	149.1	271.9	200.8
Japan	139.2	283.9	360.3
Korea, Repub.	85.1	127.1	216.1
Mauritania	71.4	51.6	54.2
Netherlands	297.8	251.3	391.7
Russia	16.0	195.0	115.7
Singapore	57.4	61.2	103.7
South Africa	85.8†	67.8	231.4
Spain	61.5	75.7	108.3
Sweden	19.1	62.0	52.6
Switzerland-Liechtenstein	45.0	98.8	96.6
Thailand	88.4	114.3	115.6
United Kingdom	491.9	753.9	1,069.8
USA	700.1	659.0	822.8
Total (incl. others)	4,482.5	5,805.5	7,958.2

Exports f.o.b.	1999	2000	2001
Brazil	716.0	668.3	1,051.3
Cameroon	186.8	246.7	125.0
Canada	370.0	616.5	357.3
Chile	134.8	281.2	110.2
China, People's Repub.	186.0	140.6	127.0
Côte d'Ivoire	574.4	843.9	341.5
France (incl. Monaco)	1,438.4	1,660.4	1,142.3
Germany	36.9	112.3	243.6
Ghana	294.1	262.8	271.2
India	2,857.3	3,927.6	2,083.3
Indonesia	87.5	607.6	537.2
Italy	496.7	1,119.5	854.0
Korea, Repub.	347.2	231.1	49.7
Netherlands	123.2	254.1	364.8
Portugal	407.4	688.0	461.4
Senegal	172.7	247.3	174.8
South Africa	347.9†	266.9	197.7
Spain	984.3	2,350.7	1,175.6
USA	5,470.1	11,521.4	7,320.9
Total (incl. others)	16,123.5	27,055.2	17,796.5

* Imports by country of consignment; exports by country of destination.
† Figure refers to the Southern African Customs Union.

Source: UN, *International Trade Statistics Yearbook*.

Transport

RAILWAYS
(traffic)

	1995	1996	1997
Passenger-km (million)	161	170	179
Freight ton-km (million)	108	114	120

Source: UN, *Statistical Yearbook*.

ROAD TRAFFIC
(estimates, motor vehicles in use)

	1995	1996
Passenger cars	820,069	885,080
Buses and coaches	1,284,251	903,449
Lorries and vans	673,425	912,579
Motorcycles and mopeds	481,345	441,651

Source: IRF, *World Road Statistics*.

1997 ('000 vehicles): Passenger cars 52.3; Commercial vehicles 13.5 (Source: *UN Statistical Yearbook*).

SHIPPING

Merchant Fleet
(registered at 31 December)

	2002	2003	2004
Number of vessels	303	311	330
Displacement ('000 grt)	410.6	418.7	429.0

Source: Lloyd's Register-Fairplay, *World Fleet Statistics*.

International Sea-borne Freight Traffic
(estimates, '000 metric tons)

	1991	1992	1993
Goods loaded	82,768	84,797	86,993
Goods unloaded	10,960	11,143	11,346

Source: UN Economic Commission for Africa, *African Statistical Yearbook*.

CIVIL AVIATION
(traffic on scheduled services)

	1999	2000	2001
Kilometres flown (million)	4	2	1
Passengers carried ('000)	162	48	33
Passenger-km (million)	370	63	25
Total ton-km (million)	61	8	3

Source: UN, *Statistical Yearbook*.

Tourism

ARRIVALS BY NATIONALITY
(estimates)*

Country	2001	2002	2003
Benin	230,849	271,248	318,716
Cameroon	62,881	73,885	86,815
Chad	49,947	58,688	68,958
France	36,323	42,680	50,149
Germany	35,430	41,630	48,915
Ghana	121,081	142,270	167,167
Italy	38,509	45,248	53,166
Liberia	63,054	74,088	87,053
Niger	364,375	428,141	503,066
Sudan	37,013	43,490	51,101
Total (incl. others)	1,754,948	2,061,726	2,422,530

* Figures refer to arrival at frontiers of visitors from abroad, including same-day visitors (excursionists).

Tourism receipts (US $ million, incl. passenger transport): 232 in 2001; 263 in 2002.

Source: World Tourism Organization.

Communications Media

	2002	2003	2004
Telephones ('000 main lines in use)	702.0	853.1	1,027.5
Mobile cellular telephones ('000 in use)	1,607.9	3,149.5	9,147.2
Personal computers ('000 in use)	853	860	867
Internet users ('000)	420	750	1,770

Radio receivers ('000 in use): 23,500 in 1997.

Television receivers ('000 in use): 12,000 in 2001.

Book production (titles, including pamphlets): 1,314 in 1995.

Daily newspapers: 25 (estimated average circulation 2,760,000 copies) in 1998.

Sources: International Telecommunication Union; UNESCO Institute for Statistics.

Education

(1994)

	Institutions	Teachers	Males	Females	Total
Primary	38,649	435,210	9,056,367	7,134,580	16,190,947
Secondary	6,162*	152,596	2,419,782	2,031,547	4,451,329
Teacher training†	135	4,531	n.a.	n.a.	108,751
Technical and vocational†	240	5,115	n.a.	n.a.	89,536
Higher education	133*	19,601‡	n.a.	n.a.	383,488*

* 1993 figure.
† 1987 figures.
‡ 1989 figure.

Sources: Federal Ministry of Education, Lagos; UNESCO, *Statistical Yearbook*.

Adult literacy rate (UNESCO estimates): 66.8% (males 74.4%; females 59.4%) in 2002 (Source: UN Development Programme, *Human Development Report*).

Directory

The Constitution

The Constitution of the Federal Republic of Nigeria was promulgated on 5 May 1999, and entered into force on 31 May. The main provisions are summarized below:

PROVISIONS

Nigeria is one indivisible sovereign state, to be known as the Federal Republic of Nigeria. Nigeria is a Federation, comprising 36 States and a Federal Capital Territory. The Constitution includes provisions for the creation of new States and for boundary adjustments of existing States. The Government of the Federation or of a State is prohibited from adopting any religion as a state religion.

LEGISLATURE

The legislative powers of the Federation are vested in the National Assembly, comprising a Senate and a House of Representatives. The 109-member Senate consists of three Senators from each State and one from the Federal Capital Territory, who are elected for a term of four years. The House of Representatives comprises 360 members, representing constituencies of nearly equal population as far as possible, who are elected for a four-year term. The Senate and House of Representatives each have a Speaker and Deputy Speaker, who are elected by the members of the House from among themselves. Legislation may originate in either the Senate or the House of Representatives and, having been approved by the House in which it originated by a two-thirds majority, will be submitted to the other House for approval, and subsequently presented to the President for assent. Should the President withhold his assent, and the bill be returned to the National Assembly and again approved by each House by a two-thirds majority, the bill will become law. The legislative powers of a State of the Federation will be vested in the House of Assembly of the State. The House of Assembly of a State will consist of three or four times the number of seats that the State holds in the House of Representatives (comprising not less than 24 and not more than 40 members).

EXECUTIVE

The executive powers of the Federation are vested in the President, who is the Head of State, the Chief Executive of the Federation and the Commander-in-Chief of the Armed Forces of the Federation. The President is elected for a term of four years and must receive not less than one-quarter of the votes cast at the election in at least two-thirds of the States in the Federation and the Federal Capital Territory. The President nominates a candidate as his associate from the same political party to occupy the office of Vice-President. The Ministers of the Government of the Federation are nominated by the President, subject to confirmation by the Senate. Federal executive bodies include the Council of State, which advises the President in the exercise of his powers. The executive powers of a State are vested in the Governor of that State, who is elected for a four-year term and must receive not less than one-quarter of votes cast in at least two-thirds of all local government areas in the State.

JUDICIARY

The judicial powers of the Federation are vested in the courts established for the Federation, and the judicial powers of a State in the courts established for the State. The Federation has a Supreme Court, a Court of Appeal and a Federal High Court. Each State has a High Court, a *Shari'a* Court of Appeal and a Customary Court of Appeal. Chief Judges are nominated on the recommendation of a National Judicial Council.

LOCAL GOVERNMENT

The States are divided into 768 local government areas. The system of local government by democratically-elected local government councils is guaranteed, and the Government of each State will ensure their existence. Each local government council within the State will participate in the economic planning and development of the area over which it exercises authority.

Federal Government

HEAD OF STATE

President and Commander-in-Chief of the Armed Forces: Gen. (retd) OLUSEGUN OBASANJO (inaugurated 29 May 1999; re-elected 19 April 2003).

Vice-President: Alhaji ATIKU ABUBAKAR.

CABINET
(April 2006)

Minister of Finance and the Economy: Dr NGOZI OKONJO-IWEALA.
Minister of Foreign Affairs: AMB OLU ADENIJI.
Minister of Health: Prof. EYITAYO LAMBO.
Minister of Housing: SEGUN MIMIKO.
Minister of Industry: FIDELIS TAPGUN.
Minister of Information: FRANK NWEKE.
Minister of Internal Affairs: MAGAJI MUHAMMED.
Minister of Justice and Attorney-General: BAYO OJO.
Minister of Labour and Productivity: HASSAN LAWAL.
Minister of Police Affairs: BRODERICK BOZIMO.
Minister of Power and Steel: LIYEL IMOKEN.
Minister of Agriculture and Rural Development: ADAMU BELLO.
Minister of Commerce: IDRIS WAZIRI.
Minister of Communications: CORNELIUS ADEBAYO.

NIGERIA

Minister of Defence: Rabiu Musa Kwankwaso.
Minister of Education: Chinwe Nora Obaji.
Minister of the Environment: Dr Iyorchia Ayu.
Minister of the Federal Capital Territory: Mallam Nasir El-Rufai.
Minister of Aviation: Babalola Borishade.
Minister of Culture and Tourism: Chief Franklin Ogbuewu.
Minister of Regional Integration and Co-operation: Lawan Gana Buba.
Minister of Government Affairs: Musa Mohammed.
Minister of Science and Technology: Dr Turner Isoun.
Minister of Solid Minerals: Obiageli Odion Ezekwesili.
Minister of Transport: Abiye Sekibo.
Minister of Water Resources: Mallam Mukhtar Shagari.
Minister of Sports: Saidu Samaila.
Minister of Women's Affairs and Youth: Maryam Ciroma.
Minister of Works: Dr Obafemi Afolarin Anibaba.
There are, in addition, 18 Ministers of State.

MINISTRIES

All ministries are located in Abuja.

Office of the Head of State: New Federal Secretariat Complex, Shehu Shagari Way, Central Area District, Abuja; tel. (9) 5233536.
Ministry of Agriculture and Rural Development: Area 1, Secretariat Complex, Garki, Abuja; tel. (9) 3141185.
Ministry of Aviation: New Federal Secretariat Complex, Shehu Shagari Way, Central Area District, Abuja; tel. (9) 5232132.
Ministry of Commerce: Area 1, Secretariat Complex, Garki, Abuja; tel. (9) 2341884.
Ministry of Communications: New Federal Secretariat Complex, Shehu Shagari Way, Central Area District, Abuja; tel. (9) 5237183.
Ministry of Culture and Tourism: Area 1, Secretariat Complex, Garki, Abuja; tel. (9) 2342727; e-mail ntdc@metrong.com.
Ministry of Defence: Ship House, Central Area, Abuja; tel. (9) 2340534.
Ministry of Education: New Federal Secretariat Complex, Shehu Shagari Way, Central Area District, Abuja; tel. (9) 5232800; fax (9) 619904.
Ministry of the Federal Capital Territory: FCT Secretariat Complex, Area 11, Abuja; tel. (9) 5234014.
Ministry of Finance and the Economy: Olusegun Obasanjo Way, Garki, Abuja; tel. (9) 2344686.
Ministry of Foreign Affairs: Maputo St, Zone 3, Wuse District, Abuja; tel. (9) 5230576.
Ministry of Health: New Federal Secretariat Complex, Shehu Shagari Way, Central Area District, Abuja; tel. (9) 5230576.
Ministry of Industry: Area 1, Secretariat Complex, Garki, Abuja; tel. (9) 5230576.
Ministry of Information: Radio House, Herbert Macaulay Way, Area 11, Garki, Abuja; tel. (9) 5230576.
Ministry of Internal Affairs: Area 1, Secretariat Complex, Garki, Abuja; tel. (9) 2346884.
Ministry of Justice: New Federal Secretariat Complex, Shehu Shagari Way, Central Area District, Abuja; tel. (9) 5235208.
Ministry of Labour and Productivity: New Federal Secretariat Complex, Shehu Shagari Way, Central Area District, Abuja; tel. (9) 5235980.
Ministry of Police Affairs: New Federal Secretariat Complex, Shehu Shagari Way, Central Area District, Abuja; tel. (9) 5230549.
Ministry of Power and Steel: New Federal Secretariat Complex, Shehu Shagari Way, Central Area District, Abuja; tel. (9) 5237064.
Ministry of Science and Technology: New Federal Secretariat Complex, Shehu Shagari Way, Central Area District, Abuja; tel. (9) 5233397.
Ministry of Solid Minerals: New Federal Secretariat Complex, Shehu Shagari Way, Central Area District, Abuja; tel. (9) 5235830.
Ministry of Sports: New Federal Secretariat Complex, Shehu Shagari Way, Abuja; tel. (9) 5235905.
Ministry of Transport: National Maritime Agency Bldg, Central Area, Abuja; tel. (9) 5237053; e-mail permsec@fedtransport-gov.org.
Ministry of Water Resources: Area 1, Secretariat Complex, Garki, Abuja; tel. (9) 2342376.
Ministry of Women's Affairs and Youth: New Federal Secretariat Complex, Shehu Shagari Way; tel. (9) 5237051.
Ministry of Works: Mabushi District, Garki, Abuja; tel. (9) 5211622; fax (9) 2340174.

President and Legislature

PRESIDENT

Election, 19 April 2003

Candidate	Votes	% of votes
Olusegun Obasanjo (People's Democratic Party)	24,456,140	61.94
Muhammadu Buhari (All Nigeria People's Party)	12,710,022	32.19
Ojukwu Chukwuemeka Odumegwu (All Progressive Grand Alliance)	1,297,445	3.29
Others	101,688	2.58
Total*	39,480,489	100.00

* Excluding 2,538,246 invalid votes.

NATIONAL ASSEMBLY

House of Representatives

Speaker of the House of Representatives: Alhaji Bello Aminu Masari.

Election, 12 April 2003

Party	Votes	% of votes	Seats
People's Democratic Party	15,927,807	54.49	223
All Nigeria People's Party	8,021,531	27.44	96
Alliance for Democracy	2,711,972	9.28	34
United Nigeria People's Party	803,432	2.75	2
All Progressive Grand Alliance	397,147	1.36	2
National Democratic Party	561,161	1.92	1
People's Redemption Party	185,764	0.76	1
People's Salvation Party	96,550	0.33	1
Others	527,706	1.67	—
Total	29,233,070	100.00	360

Senate

Speaker of the Senate: Kenechukwu Nnamani.

Election, 12 April 2003

Party	Votes	% of votes	Seats
People's Democratic Party	15,585,538	53.69	76
All Nigeria People's Party	8,091,783	27.87	27
Alliance for Democracy	2,828,082	9.74	6
Others	2,524,704	8.70	—
Total	29,030,107	100.00	109

Election Commission

Independent National Electoral Commission (INEC): Zambezi Cres., Maitama District, PMB 0184, Garki, Abuja; tel. (9) 4134368; e-mail info@inecnigeria.org; internet www.inecnigeria.org; f. 1998; Chair. Sir Abel Guobadia.

Political Organizations

Following the death of the military Head of State in June 1998, the existing authorized political parties were dissolved. The Government established a new Independent National Electoral Commission, which offically approved three political parties to contest elections in February 1999. Prior to legislative and presidential elections in April 2003, three political associations were granted registration in June 2002, as were a further 24 in December.

Abia Democratic Alliance (ADA): Umuahia; f. 2001; allied to the People's Democratic Party.

Alliance for Democracy (AD): Abeokuta St, Area 8, Garki, Abuja; e-mail info@alliancefordemocracy.org; internet www.afrikontakt.com/alliance; f. 1998; contested 1999 elections in alliance with the APP; breakaway faction (Leader Maman Yusuf) f. 2000; Chair. Chief Bisi Akande (acting).

All Nigeria People's Party (ANPP): internet www.appnigeria.org; f. 1998; contested 1999 elections in alliance with the AD; Leader Alhaji Yusuf Garbah Ali.

All Progressive Grand Alliance (APGA): Abuja; regd June 2002; Leader CHEKWAS OKORIE.

Fourth Dimension: f. 2001 by fmr politicians and military officers; Chair. Adm. (retd) AUGUSTUS AIKHOMU.

IBB Vision 2003: f. 2002; supports former Pres. Ibrahim Babangida; Chair. HAMEED MAKAMA.

Ijaw Youth Congress (IYC): f. 1999; Pres. FELIX TUODOLO.

Movement for the Actualization of the Sovereign State of Biafra (MASSOB): f. 1999; Leader Chief RALPH UWAZURIKE.

Movement for the Emancipation of the Niger Delta (MEND): f. 2005; main Ijaw militant group operating in the Niger Delta; Leader Maj.-Gen. GODSWILL TAMUNO.

Movement for the Survival of the Ogoni People (MOSOP): f. 1990 to organize opposition to petroleum production in Ogoni territory; Leader LEDUM MITEE.

National Conscience Party (NCP): 18 Phase 1 Low Cost Housing Estate, Lake City Ave, Gwagwalada, Abuja; tel. (9) 4963508; e-mail info@nigeriancp.net; internet www.nigeriancp.net; Leader GANI FAWEHINMI.

National Democratic Party (NDP): POB 8196, Abuja; tel. (9) 6703366; e-mail info@ndpnigeria.com; internet www.ndpnigeria.com; regd June 2002; Chair. ALIYU HABU FARI.

National Frontier: f. 2001 by fmr Governors and military officers; Chair. Chief EDWIN UME EZEOKE.

National Solidarity Party: f. 2001 by fmr military officers; Chair. SALEH JAMBO.

Niger Delta People's Volunteer Force (NDPVF): prominent Ijaw militant group operating in the Niger Delta; Leader Alhaji MUJAHID DOKUBO-ASARI.

O'odua People's Congress (OPC): f. 1994; banned Oct. 2000; Yoruba nationalist organization; divided into two factions, led by FREDERICK FASEUN and GANIYU ADAMS.

People's Democratic Party (PDP): f. 1998 by fmr opponents of the Govt of Gen. Sani Abacha; supports greater federalism; party of Pres. Gen. (retd) Olusegun Obasanjo; Chair. AHMADU ALI.

People's Redemption Party (PRP): Abuja; regd Dec. 2002; Leader BALARABE MUSA.

People's Salvation Party (PSP): regd Dec. 2002; Chair. Alhaji WADA NAS.

Progressive Liberation Party (PLP): f. 2001; Leader EZEKIEL IZUOGU.

Reform Party of Nigeria (RPN): tel. (1) 6463826342; fax (1) 7753059912; e-mail reformnigeria@reformnigeria.com; internet www.reformnigeria.com.

United Nigeria Development Forum: f. 2001 by fmr military officers of Pres. Sani Abacha; Chair. Brig.-Gen. (retd) LAWAL JA'AFAR ISA.

United Nigeria People's Party (UNPP): Abuja; regd June 2002; Leader SALEH JAMBO.

United Progressive Grand Alliance (UPGA): Enugu; f. 2001; Chair. CHEKWAS OKORIE.

Diplomatic Representation

EMBASSIES AND HIGH COMMISSIONS IN NIGERIA

Algeria: Plot 203, Etim Inyang Cres., POB 55238, Falomo, Lagos; tel. (1) 612092; fax (1) 2624017; Ambassador EL-MIHOUB MIHOUBI.

Angola: 5 Kasumu Ekomode St, Victoria Island, POB 50437, Falomo Ikoyi, Lagos; tel. (1) 2611135; Ambassador B. A. SOZINHO.

Argentina: 93 Awolowo Rd, SW Ikoyi, POB 51940, Lagos; tel. (1) 2690093; fax (1) 2690117; Chargé d'affaires a.i. GUSTAVO FAZZARI.

Australia: 2 Ozumba Mbadiwe Ave, Victoria Island, POB 2427, Lagos; tel. (1) 2613124; fax (1) 2618703; e-mail ahelagos@hyperia.com; High Commissioner ROBERT WHITTY.

Austria: Fabac Centre, 3B Ligali Ayorinde Ave, POB 1914, Lagos; tel. (1) 2616081; fax (1) 2617639; Ambassador Dr WILFRIED ALMOSLECHNER.

Belgium: 67 Mississippi St, Maitama, Abuja; tel. (9) 4137930; fax (9) 4133797; e-mail abuja@diplobel.org; Ambassador DIRK VAN EECKHOUT.

Benin: 4 Abudu Smith St, Victoria Island, POB 5705, Lagos; tel. (1) 2614411; fax (1) 2612385; Ambassador PATRICE HOUNGAVOU.

Brazil: 257 Kofo Abayomi St, Victoria Island, POB 1931, Lagos; tel. (1) 2610135; fax (1) 2613394; e-mail nigbrem@intracom.net.ng; Ambassador ALBERTO FERREIRA GUIMARAES.

Bulgaria: 3 Walter Carrington Cres., Victoria Island, PMB 4441, Lagos; tel. (1) 2611931; fax (1) 2619879; Ambassador (vacant).

Burkina Faso: 15 Norman Williams St, Ikoyi, Lagos; tel. (1) 617985; e-mail ebfn@nova.net.ng; Ambassador DRAMANE YAMÉOGO.

Cameroon: 5 Elsie Femi Pearse St, Victoria Island, PMB 2476, Lagos; tel. (1) 2612226; fax (1) 7747510; High Commissioner ANDRÉ E. KENDECK MANDENG.

Canada: 4 Idowu Taylor St, Victoria Island, POB 54506, Ikoyi Station, Lagos; tel. (1) 2692195; fax (1) 2692919; High Commissioner IAN FERGUSON.

Chad: 2 Goriola St, Victoria Island, PMB 70662, Lagos; tel. (1) 2622590; fax (1) 2618314; Ambassador Dr ISSA HASSAN KHAYAR.

China, People's Republic: Plot 302–303, Central Area, Abuja; tel. (9) 2347081; Ambassador LIANG YINZHU.

Côte d'Ivoire: 3 Abudu Smith St, Victoria Island, POB 7786, Lagos; tel. (1) 610936; fax (1) 2613822; e-mail cotedivoire@micro.com.ng; Ambassador EMILE M'LINGUI KEFFA.

Cuba: Plot 935, Idejo St, Victoria Island, POB 328, Victoria Island, Lagos; tel. (1) 2614836; fax (1) 2617036; Ambassador GIRALDO MAZOLA.

Czech Republic: Plot 1223, Gnassingbé Eyadéma St, Asokoro District, POB 4628, Abuja; tel. (9) 3141245; fax (9) 3141248; e-mail abuja@embassy.mzv.cz; Ambassador JURAJ CHMIEL.

Denmark: 4 Walter Carrington Cres., Victoria Island, POB 2390, Lagos; tel. (1) 2611503; fax (1) 2610841; Ambassador LARS BLINKENBERG.

Egypt: 182B Kofo Abayomi St, POB 538, Lagos; tel. (1) 2612922; fax (1) 261767; Ambassador FUAD YUSUF.

Equatorial Guinea: 7 Bank Rd, Ikoyi, POB 4162, Lagos; tel. (1) 2683717; Ambassador A. S. DOUGAN MALABO.

Ethiopia: Plot 97, Ahmadu Bello Rd, Victoria Island, PMB 2488, Lagos; tel. (1) 2613198; fax (1) 2615055; Ambassador J. K. SHINKAIYE.

Finland: Plot 13, 13 Walter Carrrington Cres., Victoria Island, POB 4433, Lagos; tel. (1) 2610916; fax (1) 2613158; Ambassador HEIKKI LATVANEN.

France: 32 Odi St, off Aso Dr., Maitama, Abuja; tel. (9) 5235506; fax (9) 5235482; e-mail ambafrance.abj@micro.com.ng; internet www.ambafrance-ng.org/emb; Ambassador YVES GAUDEUL.

Gabon: 8 Norman Williams St, SW Ikoyi, POB 5989, Lagos; tel. (1) 2684673; fax (1) 2690692; Ambassador E. AGUEMINYA.

Gambia: 162 Awolowo Rd, SW Ikoyi, POB 873, Lagos; tel. (1) 682192; High Commissioner OMAR SECKA.

Germany: Plot 3323, Amazon St, Abuja; tel. (9) 4130962; fax (9) 4130949; e-mail info@abuja.diplo.de; Ambassador Dr DIETMAR KREUSEL.

Ghana: 21–25 King George V Rd, POB 889, Lagos; tel. (1) 2630015; fax (1) 2630338; High Commissioner Lt-Gen. JOSHUA HAMIDU.

Greece: Plot 1397, 9B Tiamiyu Savage St, Victoria Island, POB 1199, Lagos; tel. (1) 2614852; fax (1) 2611412; Ambassador HARIS KARABARBOUNIS.

Guinea: 8 Abudu Smith St, Victoria Island, POB 2826, Lagos; tel. (1) 2616961; Ambassador KOMO BEAVOGUI.

Holy See: Pope John Paul II Cres., Maitama, PMB 541, Garki, Abuja; tel. (9) 4138381; fax (9) 4136653; e-mail nuntiusabj@hotmail.com; Apostolic Nuncio Most Rev. RENZO FRATINI (Titular Archbishop of Botriana).

Hungary: Plot 1685, Jose Marti Cres., Asokoro, Abuja; tel. (1) 3141180; fax (1) 3141177; e-mail huemblgs@nova.net.ng; Ambassador GYÖRGY SZABÓ.

India: 8A Walter Carrington Cres., POB 2322, Lagos; tel. (1) 2681297; fax (1) 2693803; High Commissioner SATINDER KUMBER UPPAL.

Indonesia: 5 Anifowoshe St, Victoria Island, POB 3473, Marina, Lagos; tel. (1) 2614601; fax (1) 2613301; e-mail indlgs@infoweb.abs.net; Ambassador SUSANTO ISMODIRDJO.

Iran: 2 Udi St, Maitama, Abuja; tel. (1) 5238048; fax (1) 5237785; e-mail irembassy_abuja@yahoo.com; Ambassador JAWAD TORKABADI.

Ireland: Plot 415, Negro Cres., Maitama District, Abuja; tel. (9) 4131751; fax (9) 4131805; Ambassador JOE LYNCH.

Israel: Plot 636, Cowrie House, Adeyemo Alakaja St, Victoria Island, Lagos; tel. (1) 2622055; fax (1) 2622040; Ambassador GADI GOLAN.

Italy: 12 Walter Carrington Cres., Victoria Island, POB 2161, Lagos; tel. (1) 2621046; fax (1) 2619881; e-mail ambitnig@alpha.linkserve.com; Ambassador GIOVANNI GERMANO.

Jamaica: Plot 77, Samuel Adedoyin Ave, Victoria Island, POB 75368, Lagos; tel. (1) 2611085; fax (1) 2610047; High Commissioner ROBERT MILLER (acting).

Japan: 24–25 Apese St, Victoria Island, PMB 2111, Lagos; tel. (1) 2614929; fax (1) 2614035; Ambassador TAKAHISA SASAKI.

Kenya: 52 Oyinkan Abayomi Dr., Ikoyi, POB 6464, Lagos; tel. (1) 2682768; High Commissioner DANIEL MEPUKORI KOIKAI.

NIGERIA

Korea, Democratic People's Republic: 31 Akin Adesola St, Victoria Island, Lagos; tel. (1) 2610108; Ambassador KIM PYONG GI.

Korea, Republic: Plot 934, Idejo St, Victoria Island, POB 4668, Lagos; tel. (1) 2615353; Ambassador CHAI KI-OH.

Lebanon: Plot 18, Walter Carrington Cres., Victoria Island, POB 651, Lagos; tel. (1) 2614511; Ambassador M. SALAME.

Liberia: 3 Idejo St, Plot 162, off Adeola Odeku St, Victoria Island, POB 70841, Lagos; tel. (1) 2618899; Ambassador Prof. JAMES TAPEH.

Libya: 46 Raymond Njoku Rd, SW Ikoyi, Lagos; tel. (1) 2680880; Chargé d'affaires a.i. IBRAHIM AL-BASHAR.

Malaysia: 205 Abiola Segun-Ajayi St, Victoria Island, POB 3729, Lagos; tel. (1) 3200687; fax (1) 3200787; e-mail mwlagos@hyperia.com; High Commissioner MOHAMMED ZAIN ABUBAKAR.

Morocco: Plot 1318, 27 Karimu Katun St, Victoria Island, Lagos; tel. (1) 2611682; Ambassador SAAD EDDINE TAIEB.

Namibia: Tiamiyu Savage St, Victoria Island, PMB 1395, Lagos; tel. (1) 2618606; e-mail namibiahc@alfa.linkserve.com.

Netherlands: 24 Ozumba Mbadiwe Ave, Victoria Island, POB 2426, Lagos; tel. (1) 2613005; fax (1) 617605; Ambassador B. R. KÖRNER.

Niger: 15 Adeola Odeku St, Victoria Island, PMB 2736, Lagos; tel. (1) 2612300; Ambassador Alhaji MAHAMANG DADO MANSOUR.

Norway: 3 Anifowoshe St, Victoria Island, PMB 2431, Lagos; tel. (1) 2618467; fax (1) 2618469; e-mail emb.lagos@mfa.no; Ambassador DAG NISSEN.

Pakistan: 4 Molade Okoya-Thomas St, Victoria Island, POB 2450, Lagos; tel. (1) 613909; fax (1) 614822; High Commissioner ZAFAR A. HILALY.

Philippines: Plot 152, No 302, off Third Ave, Victoria Island, Lagos; tel. (1) 2614048; Ambassador MUKHTAR M. MUALLAM.

Poland: 16 Ona Cres., Maitama, Abuja; tel. (9) 4138280; fax (9) 4138281; e-mail poembabu@linkserve.com.ng; internet www.msz.gov.pl/amb/abuja; Ambassador GRZEGORZ WALINSKI.

Portugal: Plot 1677, Olukunle Bakare Close, Victoria Island, Lagos; tel. (1) 2619037; fax (1) 2616071; Ambassador FILIPE ORLANDO DE ALBUQUERQUE.

Romania: Plot 498, Nelson Mandela St, Zone A4, Asokoro, POB 10376, Abuja; tel. (9) 3142304; fax (9) 3142306; e-mail romnig@nigtel.com; Ambassador GHEORGHE DUMITRU.

Russia: 5 Walter Carrington Cres., Victoria Island, POB 2723, Lagos; tel. (1) 2613359; fax (1) 4619994; e-mail musemlagos@vgccl.net; Ambassador GENNADY V. ILYITEHEV.

Saudi Arabia: Plot 347H, off Adetokunbo Ademola Cres., Wuse 2, Abuja; tel. (9) 4131880; fax (9) 4134906; Ambassador ANWAR A. ABD-RABBUH.

Senegal: 14 Kofo Abayomi Rd, Victoria Island, PMB 2197, Lagos; tel. (1) 2611722; Ambassador ALIOUNE DIAGNE.

Serbia and Montenegro: 7 Maitama Sule St, SW Ikoyi, PMB 978, Lagos; tel. (1) 2680238; Chargé d'affaires a.i. DORBEJOG KAHANSKI.

Sierra Leone: 31 Waziri Ibrahim St, Victoria Island, POB 2821, Lagos; tel. (1) 2614666; High Commissioner JOSEPH BLELL.

Slovakia: POB 1290, Lagos; tel. (1) 2621585; fax (1) 2612103; e-mail obeo.sk@micro.com.ng; Ambassador VASIL HUDÁK.

Somalia: Plot 1270, off Adeola Odeka St, POB 6355, Lagos; tel. (1) 2611283; Ambassador M. S. HASSAN.

South Africa: 4 Maduike St, Ikoyi, Lagos; tel. (1) 2693842; fax (1) 2690448; High Commissioner S. G. NENE.

Spain: 21C Kofo Abayomi Rd, Victoria Island, POB 2738, Lagos; tel. (1) 2615215; fax (1) 2618225; e-mail embespng@mail.mae.es; Ambassador ALFONSO MANUEL PORTABALES VÁZQUEZ.

Sudan: 2B Kofo Abayomi St, Victoria Island, POB 2428, Lagos; tel. (1) 2615889; Ambassador AHMED ALTIGANI SALEH.

Sweden: PMB 569, Garki, Abuja; tel. (9) 3143399; fax (9) 3143398; e-mail ambassaden-abuja@foreign.ministry.se; Ambassador BIRGITTA HOLST ALANI.

Switzerland: Plot 1098, Kwami Nkrumah Cres., Asokoro District, Abuja; tel. (9) 3142307; fax (9) 3148364; Ambassador Dr RUDOLF KNOBLAUCH.

Syria: 25 Kofo Abayomi St, Victoria Island, Lagos; tel. (1) 2615860; Chargé d'affaires a.i. MUSTAFA HAJ-ALI.

Tanzania: 8 Agoro Odiyan St, Victoria Island, POB 6417, Lagos; tel. (1) 613594; fax (1) 618908; High Commissioner CISCO MTIRO (acting).

Thailand: 1 Ruxton Rd, Old Ikoyi, POB 3095, Lagos; tel. (1) 2681337; Ambassador N. SATHAPORN.

Togo: 96 Awolowo Rd, SW Ikoyi, POB 1435, Lagos; tel. (1) 2617449; Ambassador FOLI-AGBENOZAN TETTEKPOE.

Trinidad and Tobago: 3A Tiamiyu Savage St, Victoria Island, POB 6392, Marina, Lagos; tel. (1) 2612087; fax (1) 612732; High Commissioner Dr HAROLD ROBERTSON.

Turkey: 3 Okunola Martins Close, Ikoyi, POB 56252, Lagos; tel. (1) 2691140; fax (1) 2693040; e-mail turkemb@infoweb.abs.net; Ambassador ÖMER SAHINKAYA.

United Kingdom: Shehu Shangari Way, Maitama, Abuja; tel. (9) 4132010; fax (9) 4133552; e-mail consular@abuja.mail.fco.gov.uk; High Commissioner RICHARD GOZNEY.

USA: 7 Mambilla St, off Aso Dr., Maitama District, Abuja; tel. (9) 5230916; fax (9) 5230353; e-mail usabuja@pd.state.gov; internet www.abuja.usembassy.gov; Ambassador JOHN CAMPBELL.

Venezuela: 35B Adetokunbo Ademola St, Victoria Island, POB 3727, Lagos; tel. (1) 2611590; fax (1) 2617350; e-mail embavenez.nig@net.ng; Ambassador ALFREDO ENRIQUE VARGAS.

Zambia: 11 Keffi St, SW Ikoyi, PMB 6119, Lagos; High Commissioner B. N. NKUNIKA (acting).

Zimbabwe: 10A Tiamiyu Savage St, POB 50247, Victoria Island, Lagos; tel. (1) 2619328; Ambassador GIFT PUNUNGUE (acting).

Judicial System

Supreme Court

Three Arms Complex, Central District, PMB 308, Abuja; tel. (9) 2346594; consists of a Chief Justice and up to 15 Justices, appointed by the President, on the recommendation of the National Judicial Council (subject to the approval of the Senate); has original jurisdiction in any dispute between the Federation and a State, or between States, and hears appeals from the Federal Court of Appeal.

Chief Justice: MUHAMMADU LAWAL UWAIS.

Court of Appeal: consists of a President and at least 35 Justices, of whom three must be experts in Islamic (*Shari'a*) law and three experts in Customary law.

Federal High Court: consists of a Chief Judge and a number of other judges.

Each State has a **High Court**, consisting of a Chief Judge and a number of judges, appointed by the Governor of the State on the recommendation of the National Judicial Council (subject to the approval of the House of Assembly of the State). If required, a state may have a **Shari'a Court of Appeal** (dealing with Islamic civil law) and a **Customary Court of Appeal**. **Special Military Tribunals** have been established to try offenders accused of crimes such as corruption, drugs-trafficking and armed robbery; appeals against rulings of the Special Military Tribunals are referred to a **Special Appeals Tribunal**, which comprises retired judges.

Religion

ISLAM

According to the 1963 census, there were more than 26m. Muslims (47.2% of the total population) in Nigeria.

Spiritual Head: Alhaji MOHAMED MACCIDO (the Sultan of Sokoto).

CHRISTIANITY

The 1963 census enumerated more than 19m. Christians (34.5% of the total population).

Christian Council of Nigeria: 139 Ogunlana Dr., Surulere, POB 2838, Lagos; tel. (1) 7923495; f. 1929; 15 full mems and six assoc. mems; Pres. Rt Rev. ROGERS O. UWADI; Gen. Sec. Rev. IKECNUKWU OKORIE.

The Anglican Communion

Anglicans are adherents of the Church of the Province of Nigeria, comprising 61 dioceses. Nigeria, formerly part of the Province of West Africa, became a separate Province in 1979; in 1997 it was divided into three separate provinces. The Church had an estimated 10m. members in 1990.

Archbishop of Province I and Bishop of Lagos: Most Rev. EPHRAIM A. ADEMOW, Archbishop's Palace, 29 Marina, POB 13, Lagos; tel. (1) 2635681; fax (1) 2631264.

Archbishop of Province II and Bishop of Awka: Most Rev. MAXWELL ANIKWENWA, Bishopscourt, Ifite Rd, POB 130, Awka.

Archbishop of Province III and Bishop of Abuja: Most Rev. PETER JASPER AKINOLA, Archbishop's Palace, POB 212, ADCP, Abuja; fax (9) 5230986; e-mail abuja@anglican.skannet.com.ng.

General Secretary: Ven. SAMUEL B. AKINOLA, 29 Marina, POB 78, Lagos; tel. (1) 2635681; fax (1) 2631264.

The Roman Catholic Church

Nigeria comprises nine archdioceses, 36 dioceses, two Apostolic Vicariates and one Apostolic Prefecture. At 31 December 2003 the

NIGERIA — Directory

total number of adherents represented an estimated 14% of the population.

Catholic Bishops' Conference of Nigeria
6 Force Rd, POB 951, Lagos; tel. (1) 2635849; fax (1) 2636680; e-mail cathsecl@infoweb.abs.net; f. 1976; Pres. Most Rev. JOHN O. ONAIYEKAN (Archbishop of Abuja); Sec.-Gen. of Secretariat Rev. Fr MATTHEW HASSAN KUKAH.

Archbishop of Abuja: Most Rev. JOHN O. ONAIYEKAN, Archdiocesan Secretariat, POB 286, Garki, Abuja; tel. (9) 2340661; fax (9) 2340662; e-mail archbuja@infoweb.abs.net.

Archbishop of Benin City: Most Rev. PATRICK E. EKPU, Archdiocesan Secretariat, POB 35, Benin City, Edo; tel. (52) 253787; fax (52) 255763; e-mail cadobc@infoweb.abs.net.

Archbishop of Calabar: Most Rev. JOSEPH EDRA UKPO, Archdiocesan Secretariat, PMB 1044, Calabar, Cross River; tel. (87) 231666; fax (87) 239177.

Archbishop of Ibadan: Most Rev. FELIX ALABA JOB, Archdiocesan Secretariat, 8 Latosa Rd, PMB 5057, Ibadan, Oyo; tel. (22) 2413544; fax (22) 2414855; e-mail archdiocese.ibadan@skannet.com.ng.

Archbishop of Jos: Most Rev. IGNATIUS AYAU KAIGAMA, Archdiocesan Secretariat, 20 Joseph Gomwalk Rd, POB 494, Jos, Plateau; tel. (73) 451548; fax (73) 451547; e-mail josarch@hisen.org.

Archbishop of Kaduna: Most Rev. PETER YARIYOK JATAU, Archbishop's House, Tafawa Balewa Way, POB 248, Kaduna; tel. (62) 246076; fax (62) 240026; e-mail catholickad@email.com.

Archbishop of Lagos: Cardinal ANTHONY OLUBUNMI OKOGIE, Archdiocesan Secretariat, 19 Catholic Mission St, POB 8, Lagos; tel. (1) 2635729; fax (1) 2633841; e-mail arclagos@infoweb.abs.net.

Archbishop of Onitsha: Most Rev. VALERIAN OKEKE, Archdiocesan Secretariat, POB 411, Onitsha, Anambra; tel. (46) 413298; fax (46) 413913; e-mail secretariat@onitsha-archdiocese-org.

Archbishop of Owerri: Most Rev. ANTHONY J. V. OBINNA, Archdiocesan Secretariat, POB 85, Owerri, Imo; tel. (83) 230115; fax (83) 233255; e-mail owcathsec@hotmail.com.

Other Christian Churches

Brethren Church of Nigeria: c/o Kulp Bible School, POB 1, Mubi, Adamawa; f. 1923; 100,000 mems; Gen. Sec. Rev. ABRAHAM WUTA TIZHE.

Church of the Lord (Aladura): Anthony Village, Ikorodu Rd, POB 308, Ikeja, Lagos; tel. (1) 4964749; f. 1930; 1.1m. mems; Primate Dr E. O. A. ADEJOBI.

Lutheran Church of Christ in Nigeria: POB 21, Numan, Adamawa; 575,000 mems; Pres. Rt Rev. Dr DAVID L. WINDIBIZIRI.

Lutheran Church of Nigeria: Obot Idim Ibesikpo, Uyo, Akwa Ibom; tel. and fax (85) 201848; f. 1936; 370,000 mems; Pres. Rev. S. J. UDOFIA.

Methodist Church Nigeria: Wesley House, 21–22 Marina, POB 2011, Lagos; tel. (1) 2631853; 483,500 mems; Patriarch Rev. SUNDAY COFFIE MBANG.

Nigerian Baptist Convention: Baptist Bldg, PMB 5113, Ibadan; tel. (2) 2412267; fax (2) 2413561; e-mail baptconv@skannet.com; 2.5m. mems; Pres. Rev. EMMANUEL O. BOLARINWA; Gen. Sec. Dr ADEMOLA ISHOLA.

Presbyterian Church of Nigeria: 26–29 Ehere Rd, Ogbor Hill, POB 2635, Aba, Imo; tel. (82) 222551; f. 1846; 130,000 mems; Moderator Rt Rev. Dr A. A. OTU; Synod Clerk Rev. UBON B. USUNG.

The Redeemed Church of Christ, the Church of the Foursquare Gospel, the Qua Iboe Church and the Salvation Army are prominent among numerous other Christian churches active in Nigeria.

AFRICAN RELIGIONS

The beliefs, rites and practices of the people of Nigeria are very diverse, varying between ethnic groups and between families in the same group. In 1963 about 10m. persons (18% of the total population) were followers of traditional beliefs.

The Press

DAILIES

Abuja Times: Daily Times of Nigeria Ltd, 2 Hasper Cres., Wuse Zone 7, PMB 115 Gaski, Abuja; tel. (1) 4900850; f. 1992; Editor CLEMENT ILOBA.

Daily Champion: Isolo Industrial Estate, Oshodi-Apapa, Lagos; fax (1) 4526011; e-mail letters@champion-newspapers.com; internet www.champion-newspapers.com; Editor AUGSTEN ADAMU.

Daily Express: Commercial Amalgamated Printers, 30 Glover St, Lagos; f. 1938; Editor Alhaji AHMED ALAO (acting); circ. 20,000.

Daily Sketch: Sketch Publishing Ltd, Oba Adebimpe Rd, PMB 5067, Ibadan; tel. (2) 414851; f. 1964; govt-owned; Chair. RONKE OKUSANYA; Editor ADEMOLA IDOWU; circ. 64,000.

Daily Star: 9 Works Rd, PMB 1139, Enugu; tel. (42) 253561; Editor JOSEF BEL-MOLOKWU.

Daily Times: Daily Times of Nigeria Ltd, New Isheri Rd, Agidingbi, PMB 21340, Ikeja, Lagos; tel. (1) 4900850; f. 1925; 60% govt-owned; Editor OGBUAGU ANIKWE; circ. 400,000.

The Democrat: 9 Ahmed Talib Ave, POB 4457, Kaduna South; tel. (62) 231907; f. 1983; Editor ABDULHAMID BABATUNDE; circ. 100,000.

Evening Times: Daily Times of Nigeria Ltd, New Isheri Rd, Agidingbi, PMB 21340, Ikeja, Lagos; tel. (1) 4900850; Man. Dir Dr ONUKA ADINOYI-OJO; Editor CLEMENT ILOBA; circ. 20,000.

The Guardian: Rutam House, Isolo Expressway, Isolo, PMB 1217, Oshodi, Lagos; tel. (1) 524111; internet www.ngrguardiannews.com; f. 1983; independent; Publr ALEX IBRU; Editor EMEKA IZEZE; circ. 80,000.

National Concord: Concord House, 42 Concord Way, POB 4483, Ikeja, Lagos; f. 1980; Editor NSIKAK ESSIEN; circ. 200,000.

New Nigerian: Ahmadu Bello Way, POB 254, Kaduna; tel. (62) 201420; f. 1965; govt-owned; Chair. Prof. TEKENA TAMUNO; Editor (vacant); circ. 80,000.

Nigerian Chronicle: Cross River State Newspaper Corpn, 17–19 Barracks Rd, POB 1074, Calabar; tel. (87) 224976; fax (87) 224979; f. 1970; Editor UNIMKE NAWA; circ. 50,000.

Nigerian Herald: Kwara State Printing and Publishing Corpn, Offa Rd, PMB 1369, Ilorin; tel. and fax (31) 220506; f. 1973; sponsored by Kwara State Govt; Editor RAZAK EL-ALAWA; circ. 25,000.

Nigerian Observer: The Bendel Newspaper Corpn, 18 Airport Rd, POB 1143, Benin City; tel. (52) 240050; f. 1968; Editor TONY IKEAKANAM; circ. 150,000.

Nigerian Standard: 5 Joseph Gomwalk Rd, POB 2112, Jos; f. 1972; govt-owned; Editor SALE ILIYA; circ. 100,000.

Nigerian Statesman: Imo Newspapers Ltd, Owerri-Egbu Rd, POB 1095, Owerri; tel. (83) 230099; f. 1978; sponsored by Imo State Govt; Editor EDUBE WADIBIA.

Nigerian Tide: Rivers State Newspaper Corpn, 4 Ikwerre Rd, POB 5072, Port Harcourt; f. 1971; Editor AUGUSTINE NJOAGWUANI; circ. 30,000.

Nigerian Tribune: African Newspapers of Nigeria Ltd, Imalefalafi St, Oke-Ado, POB 78, Ibadan; tel. (2) 2313410; fax (2) 2317573; e-mail correspondence@nigerian-tribune.com; internet www.nigerian-tribune.com; f. 1949; Editor FOLU OLAMITI; circ. 109,000.

Post Express: 7 Warehouse Rd, PMB 1186, Apapa, Lagos; tel. (1) 5453351; fax (1) 5453436; e-mail postexpress@nova.net.ng; internet www.postexpresswired.com; Publr Chief S. ODUWU; Man. Dir Dr STANLEY MACEBUH.

The Punch: Skyway Press, Kudeti St, PMB 21204, Onipetsi, Ikeja; tel. (1) 4963580; f. 1976; Editor GBMEIGA OGUNLEYE; circ. 150,000.

This Day: 35 Creek Rd, Apapa, Lagos; tel. (1) 5871432; fax (1) 5871436; e-mail thisday@nova.net.ng; internet www.thisdayonline.com.

Vanguard: Kirikiri Canal, PMB 1007, Apapa; e-mail vanguard@linkserve.com.ng; internet www.vanguardngr.com; f. 1984; Editor FRANK AIGBOGUN.

SUNDAY NEWSPAPERS

Sunday Chronicle: Cross River State Newspaper Corpn, PMB 1074, Calabar; f. 1977; Editor-in-Chief ETIM ANIM; circ. 163,000.

Sunday Concord: Concord House, 42 Concord Way, POB 4483, Ikeja, Lagos; f. 1980; Editor DELE ALAKE.

Sunday Herald: Kwara State Printing and Publishing Corpn, PMB 1369, Ilorin; tel. (31) 220976; f. 1981; Editor CHARLES OSAGIE (acting).

Sunday New Nigerian: Ahmadu Bello Way, POB 254, Kaduna; tel. (62) 245220; fax (62) 213778; e-mail auduson@newnigerian.com; internet www.newnigerian.com; f. 1981; weekly; Editor IBRAHIM AUDUSON; circ. 120,000.

Sunday Observer: PMB 1334, Bendel Newspapers Corpn, 18 Airport Rd, Benin City; f. 1968; Editor T. O. BORHA; circ. 60,000.

Sunday Punch: Kudeti St, PMB 21204, Ikeja; tel. (1) 4964691; fax (1) 4960715; f. 1973; Editor DAYO WRIGHT; circ. 150,000.

Sunday Sketch: Sketch Publishing Co Ltd, PMB 5067, Ibadan; tel. (2) 414851; f. 1964; govt-owned; Editor OBAFEMI OREDEIN; circ. 125,000.

Sunday Standard: Plateau Publishing Co Ltd, Owerri-Egbu Rd, PMB 1095, Owerri; tel. (83) 230099; f. 1978; sponsored by Imo State Govt; Editor EDUBE WADIBIA.

Sunday Sun: PMB 1025, Okoro House, Factory Lane, off Upper Mission Rd, New Benin.

NIGERIA

Sunday Tide: 4 Ikwerre Rd, POB 5072, Port Harcourt; f. 1971; Editor Augustine Njoagwuani.

Sunday Times: Daily Times of Nigeria Ltd, New Isheri Rd, Agidingbi, PMB 21340, Ikeja, Lagos; tel. (1) 4900850; f. 1953; 60% govt-owned; Editor Dupe Ajayi; circ. 100,000.

Sunday Tribune: Imalefalafi St, POB 78, Oke-Ado, Ibadan; tel. (2) 2310886; Editor Wale Ojo.

Sunday Vanguard: Kirikiri Canal, PMB 1007, Apapa; Editor Dupe Ajayi.

WEEKLIES

Albishir: Triumph Publishing Co Ltd, Gidan Sa'adu Zungur, PMB 3155, Kano; tel. (64) 260273; f. 1981; Hausa; Editor Aliyu Umar (acting); circ. 15,000.

Business Times: Daily Times of Nigeria Ltd, New Isheri Rd, Agidingbi, PMB 21340, Ikeja, Lagos; tel. (1) 4900850; f. 1925; 60% govt-owned; Editor Godfrey Bamawo; circ. 22,000.

Gboungboun: Sketch Publishing Co Ltd, New Court Rd, PMB 5067, Ibadan; tel. (2) 414851; govt-owned; Yoruba; Editor A. O. Adebanjo; circ. 80,000.

The Independent: Bodija Rd, PMB 5109, Ibadan; f. 1960; English; Roman Catholic; Editor Rev. F. B. Cronin-Coltsman; circ. 13,000.

Irohin Imole: 15 Bamgbose St, POB 1495, Lagos; f. 1957; Yoruba; Editor Tunji Adeosun.

Irohin Yoruba: 212 Broad St, PMB 2416, Lagos; tel. (1) 410886; f. 1945; Yoruba; Editor S. A. Ajibade; circ. 85,000.

Lagos Life: Guardian Newspapers Ltd, Rutam House, Isolo Expressway, Isolo, PMB 1217, Oshodi, Lagos; f. 1985; Editor Bisi Ogunbadejo; circ. 100,000.

Lagos Weekend: Daily Times of Nigeria Ltd, New Isheri Rd, Agidingbi, PMB 21340, Ikeja, Lagos; tel. (1) 4900850; f. 1965; 60% govt-owned; news and pictures; Editor Sam Ogwa; circ. 85,000.

The News: Lagos; independent; Editor-in-Chief Jenkins Alumona.

Newswatch: 3 Billingsway Rd, Oregun, Lagos; tel. (1) 4935654; fax (1) 4960950; e-mail newswatchngr@aol.com; f. 1985; English; CEO Ray Ekpu; Editor-in-Chief Dan Agbese.

Nigerian Radio/TV Times: Nigerian Broadcasting Corpn, POB 12504, Ikoyi.

Sporting Records: Daily Times of Nigeria Ltd, New Isheri Rd, Agidingbi, PMB 21340, Ikeja, Lagos; tel. (1) 4900850; f. 1961; 60% govt-owned; Editor Cyril Kappo; circ. 10,000.

Tempo: 26 Ijaiye Rd, PMB 21531, Ogba, Ikeja, Lagos; tel. (1) 920975; fax (1) 4924998; e-mail ijc@linkserve.com.ng; news magazine.

Times International: Daily Times of Nigeria Ltd, 3–7 Kakawa St, POB 139, Lagos; f. 1974; Editor Dr Hezy Idowu; circ. 50,000.

Truth (The Muslim Weekly): 45 Idumagbo Ave, POB 418, Lagos; tel. (1) 2668455; f. 1951; Editor S. O. Lawal.

ENGLISH-LANGUAGE PERIODICALS

Afriscope: 29 Salami Saibu St, PMB 1119, Yaba; monthly; African current affairs.

The Ambassador: PMB 2011, 1 peru-Remo, Ogun; tel. (39) 620115; quarterly; Roman Catholic; circ. 20,000.

Benin Review: Ethiope Publishing Corpn, PMB 1332, Benin City; f. 1974; African art and culture; 2 a year; circ. 50,000.

Headlines: Daily Times of Nigeria Ltd, New Isheri Rd, Agindingbi, PMB 21340, Ikeja, Lagos; f. 1973; monthly; Editor Adams Aliu; circ. 500,000.

Home Studies: Daily Times Publications, 3–7 Kakawa St, Lagos; f. 1964; 2 a month; Editor Dr Elizabeth E. Ikem; circ. 40,000.

Insight: 3 Kakawa St, POB 139, Lagos; quarterly; contemporary issues; Editor Sam Amuka; circ. 5,000.

Journal of the Nigerian Medical Association: 3–7 Kakawa St, POB 139, Apapa; quarterly; Editor Prof. A. O. Adesola.

Lagos Education Review: Faculty of Education, University of Lagos Akoka, Lagos; tel. (1) 5820396; fax (1) 4932669; f. 1978; 2 a year; African education; Editor Prof. Duro Ajeyalemi.

The Leader: 19A Assumpta Press Ave, Industrial Layout, PMB 1017, Owerri, Imo; tel. (83) 230932; fortnightly; Roman Catholic; Editor Rev. Kevin C. Akagha.

Management in Nigeria: Plot 22, Idowu Taylor St, Victoria Island, POB 2557, Lagos; tel. (1) 2615105; fax (1) 614116; e-mail nim@rcl.nig.com; quarterly; journal of Nigerian Inst. of Management; Editor Rev. Deji Olokesusi; circ. 25,000.

Marketing in Nigeria: Alpha Publications, Surulere, POB 1163, Lagos; f. 1977; monthly; Editor B. O. K. Nwelih; circ. 30,000.

Modern Woman: 47–49 Salami Saibu St, Marina, POB 2583, Lagos; f. 1964; monthly; Man. Editor Toun Onabanjo.

The New Nation: 52 Iwaya Rd, Onike, Yaba, Surulere, POB 896, Lagos; tel. (1) 5863629; monthly; news magazine.

Nigeria Magazine: Federal Dept of Culture, PMB 12524, Lagos; tel. (1) 5802060; f. 1927; quarterly; travel, cultural, historical and general; Editor B. D. Lemchi; circ. 5,000.

Nigerian Businessman's Magazine: 39 Mabo St, Surulere, Lagos; monthly; Nigerian and overseas commerce.

Nigerian Journal of Economic and Social Studies: Nigerian Economic Society, c/o Dept of Economics, University of Ibadan; tel. (2) 8101701; fax (2) 8100079; e-mail banayochukwu@yahoo.co.uk; internet www.nes.org.ng; f. 1959; 3 a year; Editor Prof. Ben Aigbokhan.

Nigerian Journal of Science: University of Ibadan, POB 4039, Ibadan; publ. of the Science Asscn of Nigeria; f. 1966; 2 a year; Editor Prof. L. B. Kolawole; circ. 1,000.

Nigerian Worker: United Labour Congress, 97 Herbert Macaulay St, Lagos; Editor Lawrence Borha.

The President: New Breed Organization Ltd, Plot 14 Western Ave, 1 Rafiu Shitty St, Alaka Estate, Surulere, POB 385, Lagos; tel. (1) 5802690; fax (1) 5831175; fortnightly; management; Chief Editor Chris Okolie.

Quality: Ultimate Publications Ltd, Oregun Rd, Lagos; f. 1987; monthly; Editor Bala Dan Musa.

Radio-Vision Times: Western Nigerian Radio-Vision Service, Television House, POB 1460, Ibadan; monthly; Editor Alton A. Adedeji.

Savanna: Ahmadu Bello University Press Ltd, PMB 1094, Zaria; tel. (69) 550054; e-mail abupl@wwlkad.com; f. 1972; 2 a year; Editor Prof. J. A. Ariyo; circ. 1,000.

Spear: Daily Times of Nigeria Ltd, New Isheri Rd, Agidingbi, PMB 21340, Ikeja, Lagos; tel. (1) 4900850; f. 1962; monthly; family magazine; Editor Coker Onita; circ. 10,000.

Technical and Commercial Message: Surulere, POB 1163, Lagos; f. 1980; 6 a year; Editor B. O. K. Nwelih; circ. 12,500.

Today's Challenge: PMB 2010, Jos; tel. (73) 52230; f. 1951; 6 a year; religious and educational; Editor Jacob Shaiby Tsado; circ. 15,000.

Woman's World: Daily Times of Nigeria Ltd, New Isheri Rd, Agidingbi, PMB 21340, Ikeja, Lagos; monthly; Editor Toyin Johnson; circ. 12,000.

VERNACULAR PERIODICALS

Abokiyar Hira: Albah International Publishers, POB 6177, Bompai, Kano; f. 1987; monthly; Hausa; cultural; Editor Bashari F. Foukbah; circ. 35,000.

Gaskiya ta fi Kwabo: Ahmadu Bello Way, POB 254, Kaduna; tel. (62) 201420; f. 1939; 3 a week; Hausa; Editor Abdul-Hassan Ibrahim.

NEWS AGENCIES

Independent Media Centre (IMC): POB 894, Benin City; e-mail nigeriaimc@yahoo.com; internet www.nigeria.indymedia.org.

News Agency of Nigeria (NAN): Independence Avenue, Central Business Area, PMB 7006, Garki, Abuja; tel. (9) 2349732; fax (9) 2349735; e-mail nanabujaq@rd.nig.com; internet www.newsagencyofnigeria.org; f. 1978; Man. Dir Akin Osuntokun; Editor-in-Chief Shehu Abui.

Foreign Bureaux

Agence France-Presse (AFP): 11 Awolowo Rd, SW Ikoyi, PMB 2448, Lagos; tel. (1) 2691336; fax (1) 2670925; e-mail afplagos@afp.com; Bureau Chief David Clarke.

Informatsionnoye Telegrafnoye Agentstvo Rossii—Telegrafnoye Agentstvo Suverennykh Stran (ITAR—TASS) (Russia): 401 St, POB 6465, Victoria Island, Lagos; tel. (1) 617119; Correspondent Boris V. Pilnikov.

Inter Press Service (IPS) (Italy): c/o News Agency of Nigeria, PMB 12756, Lagos; tel. (1) 5801290; Correspondent Remi Oyo.

Pan-African News Agency (PANA): c/o News Agency of Nigeria, National Arts Theatre, POB 8715, Marina, Lagos; tel. (1) 5801290; f. 1979.

Xinhua (New China) News Agency (People's Republic of China): 161A Adeola Odeku St, Victoria Island, POB 70278, Lagos; tel. (1) 2612464; Bureau Chief Zhai Jingsheng.

Publishers

Africana First Publishers Ltd: Book House Trust, 1 Africana-First Dr., PMB 1639, Onitsha; tel. (46) 485031; f. 1973; study guides, general science, textbooks; Chair. Ralph O. Ekpeh; Man. Dir J. C. Odike.

Ahmadu Bello University Press: PMB 1094, Zaria; tel. (69) 550054; e-mail abupl@wwlkad.com; f. 1972; history, Africana, social sciences, education, literature and arts; Man. Dir SA'IDU HASSAN ADAMU.

Albah International Publishers: 100 Kurawa, Bompai-Kano, POB 6177, Kano City; f. 1978; Africana, Islamic, educational and general, in Hausa; Chair. BASHARI F. ROUKBAH.

Alliance West African Publishers: Orindingbin Estate, New Aketan Layout, PMB 1039, Oyo; tel. (85) 230798; f. 1971; educational and general; Man. Dir Chief M. O. OGUNMOLA.

Aromolaran Publishing Co Ltd: POB 1800, Ibadan; tel. (2) 715980; f. 1968; educational and general; Man. Dir Dr ADEKUNLE AROMOLARAN.

Cross Continent Press Ltd: 25 Egbeyemi Rd, Ilupeju, POB 282, Yaba, Lagos; tel. and fax (1) 7746348; e-mail crosscontinent@yahoo.com; f. 1974; general, educational and academic; Man. Dir Dr T. C. NWOSU.

Daar Communications Ltd: Communication Village, AIT Rd, Off Lagos–Abeokuta Expressway, Ilapo Village, Alagbado, Lagos; tel. (1) 2644814; fax (1) 2644817; broadcasting and information services; Man. Dir. KENNY OGUNGBE.

Daystar Press: Daystar House, POB 1261, Ibadan; tel. (2) 8102670; f. 1962; religious and educational; Man. PHILLIP ADELAKUN LADOKUN.

ECWA Productions Ltd: PMB 2010, Jos; tel. (73) 52230; f. 1973; religious and educational; Gen. Man. Rev. J. K. BOLARIN.

Ethiope Publishing Corpn: Ring Rd, PMB 1332, Benin City; tel. (52) 243036; f. 1970; general fiction and non-fiction, textbooks, reference, science, arts and history; Man. Dir SUNDAY N. OLAYE.

Evans Brothers (Nigeria Publishers) Ltd: Jericho Rd, PMB 5164, Ibadan; tel. (2) 2414394; fax (2) 2410757; f. 1966; general and educational; Chair. Dr ADEKUNLE OJORA; Man. Dir GBENRO ADEGBOLE.

Fourth Dimension Publishing Co Ltd: 16 Fifth Ave, City Layout, PMB 01164, Enugu; tel. (42) 459969; fax (42) 456904; e-mail nwankwov@infoweb.abs.net; internet www.fdpbooks.com; f. 1977; periodicals, fiction, verse, educational and children's; Chair. ARTHUR NWANKWO; Man. Dir V. U. NWANKWO.

Gbabeks Publishers Ltd: POB 37252, Ibadan; tel. (62) 2315705; e-mail gbabeks@hotmail.com; f. 1982; educational and technical; Man. Dir TAYO OGUNBEKUN.

Heinemann Educational Books (Nigeria) Ltd: 1 Ighodaro Rd, Jericho, PMB 5205, Ibadan; tel. (2) 2412268; fax (2) 2411089; e-mail info@heinemannbooks.com; internet www.heinemannbooks.com; f. 1962; educational, law, medical and general; Chair. AIGBOJE HIGO; Man. Dir AYO OJENIYI.

Heritage Books: The Poet's Cottage, Artistes Village, Ilogbo-Eremi, Badagry Expressway, POB 610, Apapa, Lagos; tel. (1) 5871333; e-mail theendofknowledge@yahoo; internet www.theendofknowledge.com; f. 1971; general; Chair. NAIWU OSAHON.

Ibadan University Press: Publishing House, University of Ibadan, PMB 16, IU Post Office, Ibadan; tel. (2) 400550; f. 1951; scholarly, science, law, general and educational; Dir F. A. ADESANOYE.

Ilesanmi Press Ltd: Akure Rd, POB 204, Ilesha; tel. 2062; f. 1955; general and educational; Man. Dir G. E. ILESANMI.

John West Publications Ltd: Plot 2, Block A, Acme Rd, Ogba Industrial Estate, PMB 21001, Ikeja, Lagos; tel. (1) 4925459; f. 1964; general; Man. Dir Alhaji L. K. JAKAUDE.

Kolasanya Publishing Enterprise: 2 Epe Rd, Oke-Owa, PMB 2099, Ijebu-Ode; general and educational; Man. Dir Chief K. OSUNSANYA.

Literamed Publications Ltd (Lantern Books): Plot 45, Alausa Bus-stop, Oregun Industrial Estate, Ikeja, PMB 21068, Lagos; tel. (1) 3450751; fax (1) 4935258; e-mail information@lantern-books.com; internet www.lantern-books.com; f. 1969; children's, medical and scientific; Chair. O. M. LAWAL-SOLARIN.

Longman Nigeria Ltd: 52 Oba Akran Ave, PMB 21036, Ikeja, Lagos; tel. (1) 4978925; fax (1) 4964370; e-mail longman@linkserve.com; f. 1961; general and educational; Man. Dir J. A. OLOWONIYI.

Macmillan Nigeria Publishers Ltd: Ilupeju Industrial Estate, 4 Industrial Ave, POB 264, Yaba, Lagos; tel. (1) 4962185; e-mail macmillan@hotmail.com; internet www.macmillan.nigeria.com; f. 1965; educational and general; Exec. Chair. J. O. EMANUEL; Man. Dir Dr A. I. ADELEKAN.

Minaj Systems Ltd: Ivie House, 4–6 Ajose Adeogun St, POB 70811, Victoria Island, Lagos; tel. (1) 2621168; fax (1) 2621167; e-mail minaj@minaj.com; broadcasting, printing and publishing; Chair. Chief MIKE NNANYE I. AJEGBO.

Nelson Publishers Ltd: 8 Ilupeju By-Pass, Ikeja, PMB 21303, Lagos; tel. (1) 4961452; general and educational; Chair. Prof. C. O. TAIWO; Man. Dir R. O. OGUNBO.

Northern Nigerian Publishing Co Ltd: Gaskiya Bldg, POB 412, Zaria; tel. (69) 332087; f. 1966; general, educational and vernacular texts; Gen. Man. JA'AFAR D. MOHAMMED.

NPS Educational Publishers Ltd: Trusthouse, Ring Rd, off Akinyemi Way, POB 62, Ibadan; tel. (2) 316006; f. 1969; academic, scholarly and educational; CEO T. D. OTESANYA.

Nwamife Publishers: 10 Ibiam St, Uwani, POB 430, Enugu; tel. (42) 338254; f. 1971; general and educational; Chair. FELIX C. ADI.

Obafemi Awolowo University Press Ltd: Obafemi Awolowo University, Ile-Ife; tel. (36) 230284; f. 1968; educational, scholarly and periodicals; Man. Dir AKIN FATOKUN.

Obobo Books: The Poet's Cottage, Artistes Village, Ilogbo-Eremi, Badagry Expressway, POB 610, Apapa, Lagos; tel. and fax (1) 5871333; e-mail theendofknowledge@yahoo.com; internet www.theendofknowledge.com; f. 1981; children's books; Editorial Dir BAKIN KUNAMA.

Ogunsanya Press Publishers and Bookstores Ltd: SW9/1133 Orita Challenge, Idiroko, POB 95, Ibadan; tel. (2) 310924; f. 1970; educational; Man. Dir Chief LUCAS JUSTUS POPO-OLA OGUNSANYA.

Onibonoje Press and Book Industries (Nigeria) Ltd: Felele Layout, Challenge, POB 3109, Ibadan; tel. (2) 313956; f. 1958; educational and general; Chair. G. ONIBONOJE; Man. Dir J. O. ONIBONOJE.

Pilgrim Books Ltd: New Oluyole Industrial Estate, Ibadan/Lagos Expressway, PMB 5617, Ibadan; tel. (2) 317218; educational and general; Man. Dir JOHN E. LEIGH.

Spectrum Books Ltd: Sunshine House, 1 Emmanuel Alayande St, Oluyole Estate, PMB 5612, Ibadan; tel. (2) 2310145; fax (2) 2318502; e-mail admin1@spectrumbooksonline.com; internet www.spectrumbooksonline.com; f. 1978; educational and fiction; Man. Dir JOOP BERKHOUT.

University of Lagos Press: University of Lagos, POB 132, Akoka, Yaba, Lagos; tel. (1) 825048; e-mail library@rcl.nig.com; university textbooks, monographs, lectures and journals; Man. Dir S. BODUNDE BANKOLE.

University Press Ltd: Three Crowns Bldg, Eleyele Rd, Jericho, PMB 5095, Ibadan; tel. (2) 2411356; fax (2) 2412056; e-mail unipress@skannet.com.ng; f. 1978; associated with Oxford University Press; educational; Man. Dir WAHEED O. OLAJIDE.

University Publishing Co: 11 Central School Rd, POB 386, Onitsha; tel. (46) 210013; f. 1959; primary, secondary and university textbooks; Chair. E. O. UGWUEGBULEM.

Vanguard Media Ltd: Vanguard Ave, off Mile 2/Apapa Expressway, Kirikiri Canal; tel. (1) 5871200; fax (1) 5872662; e-mail vanguard@linkserve.com.ng; Publr SAM AMUKA.

Vista Books Ltd: 59 Awolowo Rd, S. W. Ikoyi, POB 282, Yaba, Lagos; tel. (1) 7746348; e-mail vista-books@yahoo.com; f. 1991; general fiction and non-fiction, arts, children's and educational; Man. Dir Dr T. C. NWOSU.

West African Book Publishers Ltd: Ilupeju Industrial Estate, 28–32 Industrial Ave, POB 3445, Lagos; tel. (1) 4702757; fax (1) 5556854; e-mail w_bookafricapubl@hotmail.com; internet www.wabp.com; f. 1967; textbooks, children's, periodicals and general; Chair. B. A. IDRIS-ANIMASHAUN; Man. Dir FOLASHADE B. OMO-EBOH.

PUBLISHERS' ASSOCIATION

Nigerian Publishers Association: Book House, NPA Permanent Secretariat, Jericho G.R.A., POB 2541, Ibadan; tel. (2) 2413396; f. 1965; Pres. S. B. BANKOLE.

Broadcasting and Communications

TELECOMMUNICATIONS

Nigerian Communications Commission (NCC): Plot 19, Aguata Close, Garki 2, Abuja; tel. (9) 2340330; fax (9) 2344589; e-mail ncc@ncc.gov.ng; internet www.ncc.gov.ng; f. 1932 as an independent regulatory body for the supply of telecommunications services and facilities; Chair. Alhaji AHMED JODI; CEO ERNEST C. A. NDUKWE.

Intercellular Nigeria Ltd: UBA House, 57, Marina, PMB 80078, Victoria Island, Lagos; tel. (1) 4703010; fax (1) 2643014; e-mail hq@intercellular-ng.com; f. 1993; internet and international telephone services; Pres. BASHIR EL-RUFAI.

Motophone Ltd: C. & C. Towers, Plot 1684, Sanusi Fafumwa St, Victoria Island, Lagos; tel. (1) 2624168; fax (1) 2620079; e-mail motophone@hyperia.com; f. 1990; Man. Dir ERIC CHAMCHOUM.

Multi-Links Telecommunication Ltd: 231 Adeola Odeku St, Victoria Island, POB 3453, Marina, Lagos; tel. (1) 7740000; fax (1) 2622452; e-mail ccu@multilink.com; f. 1994; Man. Dir C. K. RAMANI.

NIGERIA   *Directory*

Nigerian Mobile Telecommunications Ltd (M-TEL): 3 M-Tel St, off Mal Aminu Kano Cres., Wuse 2, Abuja; tel. (9) 5237801; fax (9) 409066; f. 1996; Man. Dir Eng. ISMAILA MOHAMMED.

Nigerian Telecommunications (NITEL): 2 Bissau St, off Herbert Macaulay Way, Wuse Zone 6, Abuja; tel. (9) 5233021; Chair. Dr MARTINS IGBOKWE.

Telnet (Nigeria) Ltd: Plot 242, Kofo Abayomi St, Victoria Island, POB 53656, Falomi Ikoyi, Lagos; tel. (1) 2611729; fax (1) 2619945; e-mail info@iteco.com; internet www.telnetng.com; f. 1985; telecommunications engineering and consultancy services; Man. Dir Dr NADU DENLOYE.

BROADCASTING
Regulatory Authority

National Broadcasting Commission: Plot 807, Ibrahim Taiwo Rd, Asokoro District, POB 5747, Garki, Abuja; tel. (9) 3147525; fax (9) 3147522; e-mail info@nbc-ng.org; internet www.nbc-ng.org; Chair. OBONG O. R. AKPAN.

Radio

Federal Radio Corpn of Nigeria (FRCN): Area 11, Garki, PMB 55, Abuja; tel. (9) 2345915; fax (9) 2345914; f. 1976; controlled by the Fed. Govt and divided into five zones: Lagos (English); Enugu (English, Igbo, Izon, Efik and Tiv); Ibadan (English, Yoruba, Edo, Urhobo and Igala); Kaduna (English, Hausa, Kanuri, Fulfulde and Nupe); Abuja (English, Hausa, Igbo and Yoruba); Chair. Y. ALABI.

Imo Broadcasting Corpn: 14 Savage Cres., Enugu, Imo; tel. (42) 250327; operates one radio station in Imo State.

Voice of Nigeria (VON): Radio House, Herbert Macaulay Way, Area 10, Garki, Abuja; tel. (9) 2344017; fax (9) 2346970; e-mail dgovon@nigol.net.ng; internet www.voiceofnigeria.org; f. 1990; controlled by the Fed. Govt; external services in English, French, Arabic, Ki-Swahili, Hausa and Fulfulde; Dir-Gen. TAIWO ALIMI.

Menage Holding's Broadcasting System Ltd: Umuahia, Imo; commenced broadcasting Jan. 1996; commercial.

Ray Power 100 Drive: Abeokuta Express Way, Ilapo, Alagbado, Lagos; tel. (1) 2644814; fax (1) 2644817; commenced broadcasting Sept. 1994; commercial; Chair. Chief RAYMOND DOKPESI.

Television

Nigerian Television Authority (NTA): Television House, Ahmadu Bello Way, Victoria Island, PMB 12036, Lagos; tel. (1) 2615949; f. 1976; controlled by the Fed. Govt; comprises 32 stations (due to be increased to 67), which broadcast local programmes; Chair. YAKUBULL HUSSAINI; Dir-Gen. Alhaji MOHAMMED IBRAHIM.

NTA Aba/Owerri: Channel 6, PMB 7126, Aba, Abia; tel. (83) 220922; Gen. Man. GODWIN DURU.

NTA Abeokuta: Channel 12, PMB 2190, Abeokuta, Ogun; tel. (39) 242971; f. 1979; broadcasts in English and local languages; Gen-Man. VICTOR FOLIVI.

NTA Abuja: PMB 55, Garki, Abuja; tel. (9) 2345915.

NTA Akure: PMB 794, Akure; tel. (34) 230351; fax (34) 243216; e-mail ntaakure2006@yahoo.com; Gen. Man. H. T. OLOWOFELA.

NTA Bauchi: PMB 0146, Bauchi; tel. (77) 42748; f. 1976; Man. MUHAMMAD AL-AMIN.

NTA Benin City: West Circular Rd, PMB 1117, Benin City; Gen. Man. J. O. N. EZEKOKA.

NTA Calabar: 105 Marion Rd, Calabar; Man. E. ETUK.

NTA Enugu: Independence Layout, PMB 01530, Enugu, Anambra; tel. (42) 335120; f. 1960; Gen. Man. G. C. MEFO.

NTA Ibadan: POB 1460, Ibadan, Oyo; tel. (2) 713238; Gen. Man. JIBOLA DEDENUOLA.

NTA Ikeja: Tejuosho Ave, Surulere.

NTA Ilorin: PMB 1478, Ilorin; tel. and fax (31) 224196; Gen. Man. VICKY OLUMUDI.

NTA Jos: PMB 2134, Jos; Gen. Man. M. J. BEWELL.

NTA Kaduna: POB 1347, Kaduna; tel. (62) 216375; f. 1977; Gen. Man. Alhaji BELLO ABUBAKAR.

NTA Kano: PMB 3343, Kano; tel. (64) 640072; Gen. Man. B. B. MUHAMMAD.

NTA Lagos: Ahmadu Bello Way, Victoria Island, PMB 12005, 12036, Ikaji, Lagos; tel. (1) 2622082; fax (1) 2626239; Dir-Gen. BEN MURRAY-BRUCE.

NTA Maiduguri: PMB 1487, Maiduguri; Gen. Man. M. M. MAILAFIYA.

NTA Makurdi: PMB 2044, Makurdi.

NTA Minna: TV House, PMB 79, Minna; tel. (66) 222941; fax (66) 222552; Gen. Man. VICKY OLUMUBI.

NTA Port Harcourt: PMB 5797, Port Harcourt; Gen. Man. JON EZEKOKA.

NTA Sokoto: PMB 2351, Sokoto; tel. (60) 232670; f. 1975; Gen. Man. M. B. TUNAU.

NTA Yola: PMB 2197, Yola; Gen. Man. M. M. SAIDU.

Finance

(cap. = capital; res = reserves; dep. = deposits; m. = million; brs = branches; amounts in naira unless otherwise stated)

BANKING

At the end of 2003 the Nigerian banking system included a total of 89 deposit banks (with 3,300 branches); of these, 11 were estimated by the Central Bank to be insolvent and 24 marginally solvent.

Central Bank

Central Bank of Nigeria: Samuel Ladoke Akintola Way, PMB 0187, Garki, Abuja; tel. (1) 2660100; e-mail info@cenbank.org; internet www.cenbank.org; f. 1958; bank of issue; cap. and res 6,908.8m., dep. 168,187m. (1995); total foreign assets 972,630m. (2003); Gov. Prof. CHARLES C. SOLUDO; 18 brs.

Commercial Banks

Afribank Nigeria Ltd: 51–55 Broad St, PMB 12021, Lagos; tel. (1) 2641566; fax (1) 2664890; e-mail info@afribank.com; internet www.afribank.net; f. 1969 as International Bank for West Africa Ltd; cap. and res 7,748.7m., total assets 86,669.4m. (March 2004); Chair. Alhaji KOLA BELGORE; Man. Dir Chief Alhaji KASHIM M. NJIDDA; 137 brs.

Allstates Trust Bank PLC: Allstates Centre, Plot 1675, Oyin Jolayemi St, POB 73018, Victoria Island, Lagos; tel. (1) 4618445; fax (1) 2612206; e-mail enquiry@allstatesbankng.com; internet www.allstatesbankng.com; cap. 2,476.8m. (Sept. 2001); Man. Dir DUATE PATMORE IYABI.

Bank of the North Ltd: Ahmadu Bello House, 2 Zaria Rd, POB 211, Kano; tel. (64) 660290; fax (64) 661361; e-mail bon@bankofthenorth.com; internet www.bankofthenorth.com; f. 1960; cap. 1,200.0m., res 2,500.4m., dep. 46,572.9m. (Dec. 2002); Chair. ABUBAKAR SADAUKI.

Chartered Bank PLC: 1 Chartered Close, off Idejo St, Victoria Island, Lagos; tel. (1) 2620380; fax (1) 2615094; e-mail info@charteredbank.com; internet www.charteredbank.com; f. 1988; cap. 1,131.7m., res 3,109.4m., dep. 30,419.8m. (March 2003); Chair. Lt-Gen. (retd) MOHAMMED INUA WUSHISHI.

Citizens' International Bank Ltd: 243 Ahmadu Bello Way, Victoria Island, Lagos; tel. (1) 2601030; fax (1) 2615138; e-mail info@citizensbankng.com; internet www.citizensbankng.com; f. 1990; cap. 619.8m., res 1,809.6m., dep. 31,496.3m. (March 2002); Chair. Chief JOYCE D. U. IFEGWU.

City Express Bank Ltd: Adetokunbo Ademola St, Victoria Island, PMB 12637, Marina, Lagos; tel. (1) 2622454; fax (1) 2619024; e-mail ceb@cityexpressbank.com; internet www.cityexpressbank.com; cap. 1,280.7m., 1,088.6m., dep. 10,295.3m. (March 2003); Chair. SAMUEL ADEDOYIN; Pres. and CEO ELIZABETH OLUSOLA ADEOTI.

Ecobank Nigeria Ltd: 2 Ajose Adeogun St, Victoria Island, POB 72688, Lagos; tel. (1) 2626638; fax (1) 2616568; e-mail ecobank@linkserve.com.ng; internet www.ecobank.com; cap. 1,522.9m., res 1,996.0m., dep. 19,979.0m. (Dec. 2003); Chair. OMO-OBA ODIMAYO; Man. Dir FUNKE OSIBODU; 26 brs.

EIB International Bank PLC: Plot 5, Ikeja Commercial Scheme, off Obafemi, Awolowo, Alausa, Ikeja, PMB 12864, Lagos; tel. (1) 4932567; fax (1) 4932565; e-mail ekobank@ekobank.com; internet www.ekobank.com; f. 1986 as Eko International Bank; name changed as above Oct. 2002; cap. 573.0m., res 296.5m., dep. 5,554.1m. (Dec. 2001); Chair. ABUBAKAR A. OLASWERE; 10brs.

Equity Bank of Nigeria Ltd: Kingsway House, 107–113 Broad St, Lagos; tel. (1) 2665142; fax (1) 2660235; e-mail itequity@equity-bank.com.ng; internet www.equity-bank.com.ng; f. 1988 as Meridien Equity of Nigeria Ltd; name changed 1995; cap. and res 1,928.4m., total assets 15,041.7m. (Dec. 2002); Chair. Alhaji ISYAKU UMAR; Man. Dir and CEO AKIN AJAYI.

First Bank of Nigeria PLC: Samuel Asabia House, 35 Marina, POB 5216, Lagos; tel. (1) 2665900; fax (1) 2665934; e-mail fbn@firstbanknigeria.com; internet www.firstbanknigeria.com; f. 1894 as Bank of British West Africa; cap. 1,751.0m., res 36,870.0m., dep. 207,181.0m. (March 2004); Chair. UMAR ABDUL MUTALLAB; CEO and Man. Dir JACOBS M. AJEKIGBE; 302 brs.

FSB International Bank PLC: 23 Awolowo Rd, Ikoyi, PMB 12512, Lagos; tel. (1) 2690739; fax (1) 2690397; e-mail customerservice@fsbint.com; internet www.fsbint.com; f. 1974 as Federal Savings Bank; name changed 1989; cap. 1,016.9m., res 1,593.4m., dep.

21,153.6m. (March 2002); Chair. Alhaji A. O. G. Otiti; Man. Dir Mohammed Hayatu-Deen.

Habib Nigeria Bank Ltd: 7–9 Bank Rd, PMB 2180, Kaduna; tel. (62) 235140; fax (62) 234584; e-mail info@habibbank.com.ng; internet www.habibbank.com.ng; f. 1983; cap. and res 3,735.9m., total assets 36,022.3m. (Dec. 2003); Chair. L. K. Abiola; Man. Dir Abdulfatai Kekere-Ekun; 65 brs.

Intercontinental Bank Ltd: Danmole St, Plot 999c, Adela Odeku, Victoria Island, Lagos; tel. (1) 2622940; fax (1) 2622981; e-mail info@intercontinentalbankplc.com; internet www.intercontinentalbankplc.com; cap. and res 10,181.4m., total assets 96,857.9m. (Dec. 2003); Chair. Raymond C. Obieri; 42 brs.

Investment Banking & Trust Co Ltd (IBTC): I.B.T.C. Place, Walter Carrington Cres., POB 71707, Victoria Island, Lagos; tel. (1) 2626520; fax (1) 2626541; e-mail ibtc@ibtclagos.com; internet www.ibtclagos.com; f. 1989; cap. 1,000.0m., res 3,886.0m., dep. 8,181.5m. (March 2003); Chair. David Dankaro; Man. Dir Atedo A. Peterside.

Lion Bank of Nigeria: 34 Ahmadu Bello Way, PMB 2126, Jos, Plateau; tel. (73) 452223; fax (73) 454602; e-mail itd@lionbankng.com; f. 1987; cap. 1,500.0m., res 2,112.9m., dep. 7,889.4m. (March 2003); Chair. Alhaji Rayyanu Dalhatu.

Magnum Trust Bank: 67 Marina, PMB 12933, Lagos; tel. (1) 2640060; fax (1) 2640069; e-mail magnum@magnum-bank.com; internet www.magnum.addr.com; f. 1991; cap. 600.0m., res 488.0m., dep. 10,763.4m. (Feb. 2002); Chair. Vincent A. Maduka; Man. Dir Wahab Babatunde Dabiri.

NAL Bank PLC: NAL Towers, 20 Marina, PMB 12735, Lagos; tel. (1) 2600420; fax (1) 2633294; e-mail infonal@nalbankplc.com; internet www.nalbankplc.com; f. 1960; cap. 831.78m., res 2,521.1m., dep. 16,915.8m. (June 2003); Chair. Mouftah Baba-Ahmed; Man. Dir Ben Akabueze; 12 brs.

NBM Bank Ltd: 228a Awolowo Rd, POB 52463, Ikoyi, Lagos; tel. (1) 2690380; fax (1) 2693256; e-mail nbm@nbmbank.com; internet www.nbmbank.com; cap. 1,000.0m., res 468.4m., dep. 4,497.6m. (Dec. 2001); Chair. Prince A. Lamuye (acting).

Nigeria International Bank Ltd: Commerce House, 11 Idowu Taylor St, Victoria Island, POB 6391, Lagos; tel. (1) 2622000; fax (1) 2618916; internet www.citibanknigeria.com; f. 1984; cap. 1,000.0m., res 6,791.2m., dep. 37,821.8m. (Dec. 2002); Chair. Chief Charles S. Sankey; 13 brs.

Omegabank (Nigeria) plc: 1 Engineering Cl., PMB 80134, off Idowu Taylor, Victoria Island, Lagos; tel. (1) 2622580; fax (1) 2620761; e-mail omegabank@omegabankplc.com; internet www.omegabankplc.com; f. 1982 as Owena Bank plc; name changed 2001; 30% owned by Ondo State Govt; cap. 2,896.4m., res 208.0m., dep. 11,676.8m. (Dec. 2001); Chair. Chief Anthony Adeniyi; CEO Rev. Dr Segun Agbetuyi.

Société Générale Bank (Nigeria) Ltd: Sarah House, 13 Martins St, PMB 12471, Lagos; tel. (1) 2660315; fax (1) 2663731; e-mail infosgbn@sgbn.com.ng; internet www.sgbn.com.ng; cap. 556.5m., res 597.6m., dep. 14,470.9m. (June 2001); Chair. Dr Sola Saraki.

Trade Bank PLC: 2 Ilofa Rd, PMB 1496, Ilorin; tel. (31) 220062; fax (31) 223532; e-mail tradebnk@info.web.abs.net; internet www.tradebankplc.com; f. 1985; cap. 1,000.0m., res 572.4m., dep. 9,138.9m. (March 2002); Chair. Alhaji Aliyu Alarape Salman; Man. Dir Samuel Ereola Kolawole.

Tropical Commercial Bank PLC: Gidan Muhammad Dankabo, 72b Murtala Mohammed Way, PMB 4636, Kano; tel. (64) 640050; fax (64) 644506; e-mail tcbplc@samdav.com; f. 1974 as Kano Co-operative Bank Ltd; name changed 1988; 883.8m., res 272.5m., dep. 4,490.3m. (Dec. 2002); Chair. Ahmad Muhammad.

Union Bank of Nigeria Ltd: 36 Marina, PMB 2027, Lagos; tel. (1) 2665439; fax (1) 2669873; e-mail askubn@ng.com; internet www.unionbankng.com; f. 1969; as Barclays Bank of Nigeria Ltd; cap. 1,258m., res 29,044m., dep. 204,347m. (March 2002); Chair. Prof. Kalu Ukeh Kalu; CEO G. A. T. Oboh; 235 brs.

United Bank for Africa (Nigeria) Ltd: UBA House, 57 Marina, POB 2406, Lagos; tel. (1) 2644651; fax (1) 2642243; e-mail info@ubaplc.com; internet www.ubaplc.com; f. 1961; cap. and res 14,901m., total assets 203,871m. (March 2003); Chair. Kayode Sofola; Man. Dir Mallam Aliyu Dikko; 213 brs.

Wema Bank Ltd: Wema Towers, PMB 12862, 27 Nnamdi Akkzikwe St, Lagos; tel. (1) 2668105; fax (1) 2669508; e-mail info@wemabank.com; internet www.wemabank.com; f. 1945; cap. and res 1,555.5m., total assets 71,423.8m. (March 2004); Chair. Olapade Mohammed; Man. Dir and CEO Alhaji Alade M. Adeleke; 75 brs.

Merchant Banks

FBN (Merchant Bankers) Ltd: 9/11 Macarthy St, Onikan, POB 12715, Lagos; tel. (1) 2600880; fax (1) 2633600; e-mail bisioni@fbnmb.com; internet www.fbnmb.com; cap. 1,000m. (2003); Chair. Jacobs Moyo Ajekigbe.

Fidelity Bank Ltd: Savannah House, 62-66 Broad St, Lagos; tel. (1) 2610408; fax (1) 2610414; e-mail info@fidelitybankplc.com; internet www.fidelitybankplc.com; f. 1988; cap. and res 1,189.2m., res 1,326.2m., dep. 16,888.1m. (June 2003); Chair. Chief Emmanuel A. Okechukwu; CEO Kenneth O. Aigbinode.

First City Monument Bank Ltd: Primrose Tower, 17a Tinubu St, POB 9117, Lagos; tel. (1) 2665944; fax (1) 2665126; e-mail caf@fcmb-ltd.com; internet www.fcmb-ltd.com; www.fcmb-ltd.com; f. 1983; cap. 1,000.0m., res 1,231.4m., dep. 8,564.4m. (April 2002); Chair. and CEO Otunba M. O. Balogun.

First Interstate Merchant Bank (Nigeria) Ltd: Kingsway Bldg Complex, 2/4 Davies St, off Marina, Victoria Island, POB 72295, Lagos; tel. (1) 2600500; fax (1) 2668273; e-mail merchant@fimb.metrong.com; cap. 507.6m., res 110.4m., dep. 2,055.3m. (March 2000); Chair. Prof. A. L. Mabogunje.

IMB International Bank PLC: IMB Plaza, 1 Akin Adesola St, Victoria Island, PMB 12028, Lagos; tel. (1) 2612204; fax (1) 2616792; internet www.imbplc.com; f. 1974; name changed from International Merchant Bank (Nigeria) Ltd 2001; cap. and res 1,632.7m., total assets 8,786.7m. (June 2001); Chair. Mohammed Shuwa; Man. Dir Edwin Chinye; 10 brs.

MBC International Bank Ltd: 16 Keffi St, S W Ikoyi, POB 53289, Lagos; tel. (1) 2690261; fax (1) 2690767; e-mail mbc@mbc-nig.com; internet www.mbc-nig.com; f. 1982 as Merchant Banking Corpn; name changed 2000; cap. and res 1,714.2m., total assets 15,481.6m. (March 2003); Chair. Dr M. A. Majekodunmi; Man. Dir Raymond A. Bariou.

Nigerian American Bank Ltd: Boston House, 10–12 Macarthy St, PMB 12759, Lagos; tel. (1) 2600360; fax (1) 2631712; e-mail nambl@micro.com.ng; f. 1979; affiliate of First National Bank of Boston (USA); cap. 1,000.0m., res 638.7m., dep. 2,244.5m. (Dec. 2002); Chair. Alhaji Ibrahim Damcida; Man. Dir Osaro Isokpan; 7 brs.

Stanbic Bank Nigeria Ltd: 188 Awolowo Rd, Ikoyi, POB 54746, Lagos; tel. (1) 2690402; fax (1) 2692469; e-mail info@stanbic.com.ng; internet www.stanbic.com.ng; f. 1983 as Grindlays Merchant Bank of Nigeria; cap. 500.0m., res 287.4m., dep. 3,344.2m. (Dec. 2001); Chair. Dr Matthew Tawo Mbu; Man. Dir M. A. Weeks.

Development Banks

Bank of Industry (BOI) Ltd: BOI House, 63/71 Broad St, Lagos; tel. (1) 2663470; fax (1) 2667074; e-mail info@boi-ng.com; internet www.boi-ng.com; f. 1964 as the Nigerian Industrial Development Bank Ltd to provide medium and long-term finance to industry, manufacturing, non-petroleum mining and tourism; name changed as above Oct. 2001; cap. 400m. (Dec. 2001); Man. Dir Dr Lawrence Oss-Afiana; 6 brs.

Guaranty Trust Bank Ltd: The Plural House, Plot 1669, Oyin Jolayemi St, PMB 75455, Victoria Island, Lagos; tel. (1) 2622650; fax (1) 2622706; e-mail corpaff@gtbplc.com; internet www.gtbplc.com; f. 1990; cap. 1,250.0m., res 8,411.4m., dep. 51,067.8m. (Feb. 2003); Chair. Prof. Mosobalaje O. Oyawoye.

Nigerian Agricultural, Co-operative and Rural Development Bank Ltd (NACB): Yakubu Gowoh, PMB 2155, Kaduna; tel. (62) 243590; fax (62) 245012; e-mail nacb@infoweb.abs.net; f. 1973; for funds to farmers and co-operatives to improve production techniques; name changed as above Oct. 2000, following merger with People's Bank of Nigeria; cap. 1,000m. (2002); Chair. Alhaji Isa Tata Yusuf; Man. Dir Alhaji Umar Babale Girei; 200 brs.

Bankers' Association

Chartered Institute of Bankers of Nigeria: 19 Adeola Hopewell St, POB 72273, Victoria Island, Lagos; tel. (1) 2615642; fax (1) 2611306; Chair. Johnson O. Ekundayo; CEO A. A. Adenubi.

STOCK EXCHANGE

Securities and Exchange Commission (SEC): Mandilas House, 96–102 Broad St, PMB 12638, Lagos; f. 1979 as govt agency to regulate and develop capital market and to supervise stock exchange operations; Dir-Gen. Musa Al-Faki.

Nigerian Stock Exchange: Stock Exchange House, 2–4 Customs St, POB 2457, Lagos; tel. (1) 2660287; fax (1) 2668724; e-mail nse@nigerianstockexchange.com; internet www.nigerianstockexchange.com; f. 1960; Pres. Dr Raymond C. Obieri; Dir-Gen. Dr Ndi Okereke-Onyiuke; 6 brs.

INSURANCE

In early 2005 more than 450 registered insurance companies were operating in Nigeria. Since 1978 they have been required to reinsure 20% of the sum insured with the Nigeria Reinsurance Corpn.

NIGERIA

Insurance Companies

African Alliance Insurance Co Ltd: 112 Broad St, POB 2276, Lagos; tel. (1) 2664398; fax (1) 2660943; e-mail alliance@infoweb.abs.net; f. 1960; life assurance and pensions; Man. Dir OPE OREDUGBA; 30 brs.

Aiico International Insurance (AIICO): AIICO Plaza, Plot PC 12, Afribank St, Victoria Island, POB 2577, Lagos; tel. (1) 2610651; fax (1) 2617433; e-mail info@aiicoplc.com; internet www.aiicoplc.com; CEO M. E. HANSEN.

Ark Insurance Group: Glass House, 11A Karimu Kotun St, Victoria Island, POB 3771, Marina, Lagos; tel. (1) 2615826; fax (1) 2615850; e-mail ark@nova.net.ng; internet www.nigeriaweb.com/ark; Chair. F. O. AWOGBORO.

Continental Reinsurance Co Ltd: Reinsurance House, 11th Floor, 46 Marina, POB 2401, Lagos; tel. (1) 2665350; fax (1) 2665370; e-mail crcl@cyberspace.net.ng; CEO ADEYEMO ADEJUMO.

Cornerstone Insurance Co Plc: POB 75370, Victoria Island, Lagos; tel. (1) 2631832; fax (1) 2633079; e-mail marketing@cornerstone.com.ng; internet www.cornerstone.com; f. 1991; Chair. CLEMENT O. BAIYE.

Equity Indemnity Insurance Co Ltd: POB 1514, Lagos; tel. (1) 2637802; fax (1) 2637479; e-mail equity@infoweb.abs.net; f. 1991; Chair. Prof. O. A. SERIKI.

Great Nigeria Insurance Co Ltd: 8 Omo-Osaghie St, off Obafemi Awolono Rd, Ikoyi S/W, Ikoyi, Lagos; tel. (1) 2695805; fax (1) 2693483; e-mail info@greatinsure-ng.com; internet www.greatinsure-ng.com; f. 1960; all classes; Man. Dir M. A. SIYANBOLA.

Guinea Insurance Co Ltd: Guinea Insurance House, 21 Nnandi Azikiwe St, POB 1136, Lagos; tel. (1) 2665201; f. 1958; all classes; CEO AYO BAMMEKE.

Industrial and General Insurance Co Ltd: Plot 741, Adeola Hopewell St, POB 52592, Falomo, Lagos; tel. (1) 2625437; fax (1) 2621146; e-mail info@igi-insurers.com; internet www.igi-insurers.com; Chair. Y. GOWON.

Kapital Insurance Co Ltd: 116 Hadejia Rd, POB 2044, Kano; tel. (64) 645666; fax (64) 636962; CEO MOHAMMED GAMBO UMAR.

Law Union and Rock Insurance Co of Nigeria Ltd: 88–92 Broad St, POB 944, Lagos; tel. (1) 2663526; fax (1) 2664659; fire, accident and marine; 6 brs; CEO S. O. AKINYEMI.

Leadway Assurance Co Ltd: NN 28–29 Constitution Rd, POB 458, Kaduna; tel. (62) 200660; fax (62) 236838; f. 1970; all classes; Man. Dir OYEKANMI ABIODUN HASSAN-ODUKALE.

Lion of Africa Insurance Co Ltd: St Peter's House, 3 Ajele St, POB 2055, Lagos; tel. (1) 2600950; fax (1) 2636111; f. 1952; all classes; Man. Dir G. A. ALEGIEUNO.

National Insurance Corpn of Nigeria (NICON): 5 Customs St, POB 1100, Lagos; tel. (1) 2640230; fax (1) 2666556; f. 1969; all classes; cap. 200m.; Chair. JOHN IRIATA ABUHME; 28 brs.

N.E.M. Insurance Co (Nigeria) Ltd: 22A Borno Way, Ebute, POB 654, Lagos; tel. (1) 5861920; all classes; Chair. Alhaji Dr ALIYU MOHAMMED; Man. Dir J. E. UMUKORO.

Niger Insurance Co Ltd: 47 Marina, POB 2718, Lagos; tel. (1) 2664452; fax (1) 2662196; all classes; Chair. P. M. G. SOARES; 6 brs.

Nigeria Reinsurance Corpn: 46 Marina, PMB 12766, Lagos; tel. (1) 2667049; fax (1) 2668041; e-mail info@nigeriare.com; internet www.nigre.com; all classes of reinsurance; Man. Dir T. T. MIRILLA.

Nigerian General Insurance Co Ltd: 1 Nnamdi Azikiwe St, Tirubu Square, POB 2210, Lagos; tel. (1) 2662552; e-mail odua@odua.com; f. 1951; all classes; Chair. O. O. OKEYODE; Man. Dir J. A. OLANIHUN; 15 brs.

Phoenix of Nigeria Assurance Co Ltd: Mandilas House, 96–102 Broad St, POB 12798, Lagos; tel. (1) 2661160; fax (1) 2662883; e-mail phoenixassce@alpha.linkserve.com; f. 1964; all classes; cap. 10m.; Chair. A. A. OJORA; Man. Dir A. A. AKINTUNDE; 5 brs.

Prestige Assurance Co (Nigeria) Ltd: 19 Ligali Ayorinde St, Victoria Island, POB 650, Lagos; tel. (1) 3204681; fax (1) 3204684; e-mail prestigeassurance@yahoo.co.uk; f. 1952; all classes except life; Chair. Chief C. S. SANKEY; Man. Dir N. S. R. CHANDRAPRASAD.

Royal Exchange Assurance (Nigeria) Group: New Africa House, 31 Marina, POB 112, Lagos; tel. (1) 2663120; fax (1) 2664431; all classes; Chair. Alhaji MUHTAR BELLO YOLA; Man. Dir JONAH U. IKHIDERO; 6 brs.

Sun Insurance Office (Nigeria) Ltd: Unity House, 37 Marina, POB 2694, Lagos; tel. (1) 2661318; all classes except life; Man. Dir A. T. ADENIJI; 6 brs.

United Nigeria Insurance Co Ltd (UNIC): 53 Marina, POB 588, Lagos; tel. (1) 2663201; fax (1) 2664282; f. 1965; all classes except life; CEO E. O. A. ADETUNJI; 17 brs.

Unity Life and Fire Insurance Co Ltd: 25 Nnamdi Azikiwe St, POB 3681, Lagos; tel. (1) 2662517; fax (1) 2662599; all classes; Man. Dir R. A. ODINIGWE.

West African Provincial Insurance Co: WAPIC House, 119 Awolowo Rd, POB 55508, Falomo-Ikoyi, Lagos; tel. (1) 2672770; fax (1) 2693838; e-mail wapic@alpha.linkserve.com; Man. Dir D. O. AMUSAN.

Insurance Association

Nigerian Insurance Association: Nicon House, 1st Floor, 5 Customs St, POB 9551, Lagos; tel. (1) 2640825; f. 1971; Chair. J. U. IKHIDERO.

Trade and Industry

GOVERNMENT AGENCIES

Bureau of Public Enterprises: Secretariat of the National Council on Privatization, 1 Osun Cres., off Ibib Way, Maitama District, PMB 442, Garki, Abuja; tel. (9) 4134636; tel. (9) 4134640; fax (9) 4134657; e-mail bpe@bpeng.org; internet www.bpeng.org; Dir-Gen. Mallam NASIR AHMAD EL-RUFAI.

Corporate Affairs Commission: Area 11, Garki, Abuja; tel. (9) 2342917; fax (9) 2342669; e-mail info@cac.gov.ng; internet www.cac.gov.ng; Sec. HENRIEITA O. M. TALABI.

National Council on Privatisation: Bureau of Public Enterprises, NDIC Bldg, Constitution Ave, Central Business District, PMB 442, Garki, Abuja; tel. (9) 5237405; fax (9) 5237396; e-mail bpegen@micro.com.ng; internet www.bpe.gov.ng.

Nigeria Export Processing Zones Authority: Radio House, Fourth Floor, Herbert Macaulay Way, PMB 037, Garki, Abuja; tel. (9) 2343059; fax (9) 2343061; e-mail info@nepza.com; internet www.nepza.com; Gen. Man. SINA A. AGBOLUAJE.

DEVELOPMENT ORGANIZATIONS

Benin–Owena River Basin Development Authority: 24 Benin-Sapele Rd, PMB 1381, Obayantor, Benin City; tel. (52) 254415; f. 1976 to conduct irrigation; Gen. Man. Dr G. E. OTEZE.

Chad Basin Development Authority: Dikwa Rd, PMB 1130, Maiduguri; tel. (76) 232015; f. 1973; irrigation and agriculture-allied industries; Chair. MOHAMMED ABALI; Gen. Man. Alhaji BUNU S. MUSA.

Cross River Basin Development Authority: 32 Target Rd, PMB 1249, Calabar; tel. (87) 223163; f. 1977; Gen. Man. SIXTUS ABETIANBE.

Federal Institute of Industrial Research, Oshodi (FIIRO): Murtala Muhammed Airport, Bilnd Centre St, Oshodi, Ikeja, PMB 21023, Lagos; tel. (1) 900121; fax (1) 4525880; f. 1956; plans and directs industrial research and provides tech. assistance and information to industry; specializes in foods, minerals, textiles, natural products and industrial intermediates; Dir. Prof. S. A. ODUNFA.

Industrial Training Fund: Miango Rd, PMB 2199, Jos, Plateau; tel. and fax (73) 461887; e-mail dp@itf-nigeria.com; internet www.itf-nigeria.com; f. 1971 to promote and encourage skilled workers in trade and industry; Dir-Gen. Prof. OLU E. AKEREJOLA.

Kaduna Industrial and Finance Co Ltd: Investment House, 27 Ali Akilu Rd, PMB 2230, Kaduna; tel. (62) 240751; fax (62) 240754; e-mail kifc@skannet.com; f. 1989; provides development finance; Chair. (vacant); Man. Dir Alhaji DAHIRU MOHAMMED.

Kwara State Investment Corpn: 109–112 Fate Rd, PMB 1344, Ilorin, Kwara; tel. (31) 220510.

Lagos State Development and Property Corpn: 1 Town Planning Way, Ilupeju, Lagos; tel. (1) 4972243; e-mail isdpc@isdpc.com; internet www.isdpc.com; f. 1972; planning and development of Lagos; Gen. Man. O. R. ASHAFA.

New Nigerian Development Co Ltd: 18/19 Ahmadu Bello Way, Ahmed Talib House, PMB 2120, Kaduna; tel. (62) 249355; fax (62) 245482; e-mail nndc@skannet.com.ng; f. 1949; owned by the Govts of 19 northern States; investment finance; 8 subsidiaries, 83 assoc. cos; Chair. Lt-Gen. (retd) GARBA DUBA.

Niger Delta Development Commission: 6 Olumeni St, Port Harcourt; internet www.nddconline.org; f. 1976; Man. Dir GODWIN OMENE.

Nigerian Enterprises Promotion Board: 15–19 Keffi St, S.W. Ikoyi, Lagos; tel. (1) 2680929; f. 1972 to promote indigenization; Chair. MINSO GADZAMA.

Northern Nigeria Investments Ltd: 4 Waff Rd, POB 138, Kaduna; tel. (62) 239654; fax (62) 230770; f. 1959 to identify and invest in industrial and agricultural projects in 16 northern States; cap. p.u. 20m.; Chair. Alhaji ABUBAKAR G. ADAMU; Man. Dir GIMBA H. IBRAHIM.

Odu'a Investment Co Ltd: Cocoa House, PMB 5435, Ibadan; tel. (2) 417710; fax (2) 413000; f. 1976; jtly owned by Ogun, Ondo and Oyo States; Man. Dir Alhaji R. S. ARUNA.

Plateau State Water Resources Development Board: Jos; incorporates the fmr Plateau River Basin Devt Authority and Plateau State Water Resources Devt Board.

Projects Development Institute: Emene Industrial Layout, Proda Rd, POB 01609, Enugu; tel. (42) 451593; fax (42) 457691; e-mail proda@rmrdc.nig.com; f. 1977; promotes the establishment of new industries and develops industrial projects utilizing local raw materials; Dir BASIL K. C. UGWA.

Raw Materials Research Development Council: Plot 427, Aguiyi, Ironsi St, Maitama, Abuja; tel. (9) 5237417.

Rubber Research Institute of Nigeria: PMB 1049, Benin City; tel. (52) 254792; f. 1961; conducts research into the production of rubber and other latex products; Dir Dr M. M. NADOMA.

Trans Investments Co Ltd: Bale Oyewole Rd, PMB 5085, Ibadan; tel. (2) 416000; f. 1986; initiates and finances industrial and agricultural schemes; Gen. Man. M. A. ADESIYUN.

CHAMBERS OF COMMERCE

Nigerian Association of Chambers of Commerce, Industry, Mines and Agriculture: 15A Ikorodu Rd, Maryland, PMB 12816, Lagos; tel. (1) 4964727; fax (1) 4964737; e-mail naccima@supernet300.com; Pres. CLEMENT OBINEZE MADUAKO; Dir-Gen. L. O. ADEKUNLE.

Aba Chamber of Commerce and Industry: UBA Bldg, Ikot Expene Rd/Georges St, POB 1596, Aba; tel. (82) 352084; fax (82) 352067; f. 1971; Pres. IDE J. C. UDEAGBALA.

Abeokuta Chamber of Commerce and Industry: 29 Kuto Rd, Ishabo, POB 937, Abeokuta; tel. (39) 241230; Pres. Chief S. O. AKINREMI.

Abuja Chamber of Commerce, Industry, Mines & Agriculture: International Trade Fair Complex, KM8, Airport Road, PMB 86, Garki, Abuja; tel. (9) 5239995; tel. (9) 6707428; fax (9) 2348808; e-mail abuccima@hotmail.com; Pres. Sir PETER OKOLO.

Adamawa Chamber of Commerce and Industry: c/o Palace Hotel, POB 8, Jimeta, Yola; tel. (75) 255136; Pres. Alhaji ISA HAMMANYERO.

Akure Chamber of Commerce and Industry: 57 Oyemekun Rd, POB 866, Akure; tel. (34) 242540; f. 1984; Pres. ADEDEJI OMISAMI.

Awka Chamber of Commerce and Industry: 220 Enugu Rd, POB 780, Awka; tel. (45) 550105; Pres. Lt-Col (retd) D. ORUGBU.

Bauchi Chamber of Commerce and Industry: 96 Maiduguri Rd, POB 911, Bauchi; tel. (77) 42620; f. 1976; Pres. Alhaji MAGAJI MU'AZU.

Benin Chamber of Commerce, Industry, Mines and Agriculture: 10 Murtala Muhammed Way, POB 2087, Benin City; tel. (52) 255761; Pres. C. O. EWEKA.

Benue Chamber of Commerce, Industry, Mines and Agriculture: 71 Ankpa Qr Rd, PMB 102344, Makurdi; tel. (44) 32573; Chair. Col (retd) R. V. I. ASAM.

Borno Chamber of Commerce and Industry: Grand Stand, Ramat Sq., off Central Bank, PMB 1636, Maiduguri; tel. (76) 232832; e-mail bsumar@hotmail.com; f. 1973; Pres. Alhaji MUHAMMADU RIJYA; Sec.-Gen. BABA SHEHU BUKAR.

Calabar Chamber of Commerce and Industry: Desan House Bldg, 38 Ndidem Iso Rd, POB 76, Calabar, Cross River; tel. (87) 221558; 92 mems; Pres. Chief TAM OFORIOKUMA.

Enugu Chamber of Commerce, Industry and Mines: International Trade Fair Complex, Abakaliki Rd, POB 734, Enugu; tel. (42) 250575; fax (42) 252186; e-mail eccima@infoweb.abs.net; internet www.enuguchamber.com; f. 1963; Dir S. C. NWAEKEKE.

Franco-Nigerian Chamber of Commerce: Big Leaf House, 7 Oyin Jolayemi St, POB 70001, Victoria Island, Lagos; tel. (1) 2621423; fax (1) 2621422; e-mail fncci@ccife.org; internet www.ccife.org/nigeria; f. 1985; Chair. S. JEGEDE; Pres. AKIN AKINBOLA.

Gongola Chamber of Commerce and Industry: Palace Hotel, POB 8, Jimeta-Yola; tel. (75) 255136; Pres. Alhaji ALIYU IBRAHIM.

Ibadan Chamber of Commerce and Industry: Commerce House, Ring Rd, Challenge, PMB 5168, Ibadan; tel. (2) 317223; Pres. JIDE ABIMBOLA.

Ijebu Chamber of Commerce and Industry: 51 Ibadan Rd, POB 604, Ijebu Ode; tel. (37) 432880; Pres. DOYIN DEGUN.

Ikot Ekpene Chamber of Commerce and Industry: 47 Aba Rd, POB 50, Ikot Ekpene; tel. (85) 400153; Pres. G. U. EKANEM.

Kaduna Chamber of Commerce, Industry and Agriculture: 24 Waff Rd, POB 728, Kaduna; tel. (62) 211216; fax (62) 214149; Pres. Alhaji MOHAMMED SANI AMINU.

Kano Chamber of Commerce, Industry, Mines and Agriculture: Zoo Rd, POB 10, Kano City, Kano; tel. (64) 666936; fax (64) 667138; Pres. MALLAM U. J. KIRU.

Katsina Chamber of Commerce and Industry: 1 Nagogo Rd, POB 92, Katsina; tel. (65) 31014; Pres. ABBA ALI.

Kwara Chamber of Commerce, Industry, Mines and Agriculture: Kwara Hotel Premises, Ahmadu Bello Ave, POB 1634, Ilorin; tel. (31) 223069; fax (31) 224131; e-mail kwaccima@yahoo.com; internet www.kwaccima.com; Pres. Alhaji JANI IBRAHIM; Dir-Gen. ABDULSALAAM A. JIMOH.

Lagos Chamber of Commerce and Industry: Commerce House, 1 Idowu Taylor St, Victoria Island, POB 109, Lagos; tel. (1) 2705386; fax (1) 2701009; e-mail inform@micro.com.ng; f. 1888; 1,267 mems; Pres. Chief OLUSOLA FALEYE.

Niger Chamber of Commerce and Industry: Trade Fair Site, POB 370, Minna; tel. (66) 223153; Pres. Alhaji U. S. NDANUSA.

Nnewi Chamber of Commerce and Industry: 31A Nnobi Rd, POB 1471, Nnewi; tel. (46) 462258; f. 1987; Pres. AJULU UZODIKE.

Osogbo Chamber of Commerce and Industry: Obafemi Awolowo Way, Ajegunle, POB 870, Osogbo, Osun; tel. (35) 231098; Pres. Prince VICTOR ADEMLE.

Owerri Chamber of Commerce and Industry: OCCIMA Secretariat, 123 Okigwe Rd, POB 1439, Owerri; tel. (83) 234849; Pres. Chief OKEY IKORO.

Oyo Chamber of Commerce and Industry: POB 67, Oyo; Pres. Chief C. A. OGUNNIYI.

Plateau State Chambers of Commerce, Industry, Mines and Agriculture: Shama House, 32 Rwang Pam St, POB 2092, Jos; tel. (73) 53918; f. 1976; Pres. Chief M. E. JACDOMI.

Port Harcourt Chamber of Commerce, Industry, Mines and Agriculture: Alesa Eleme, POB 585, Port Harcourt; tel. (84) 239536; f. 1952; Pres. Chief S. I. ALETE.

Remo Chamber of Commerce and Industry: 7 Sho Manager Way, POB 1172, Shagamu; tel. (37) 640962; Pres. Chief S. O. ADEKOYA.

Sapele Chamber of Commerce and Industry: 144 New Ogorode Rd, POB 154, Sapele; tel. (54) 42323; Pres. P. O. FUFUYIN.

Sokoto Chamber of Commerce and Industry: 12 Racecourse Rd, POB 2234, Sokoto; tel. (60) 231805; Pres. Alhaji ALIYU WAZIRI BODINGA.

Umahia Chamber of Commerce: 44 Azikiwe Rd, Umahia; tel. (88) 223373; fax (88) 222299; Pres. GEORGE AKOMAS.

Uyo Chamber of Commerce and Industry: 141 Abak Rd, POB 2960, Uyo, Akwa Ibom; Pres. Chief DANIEL ITA-EKPOTT.

Warri Chamber of Commerce and Industry: Block 1, Edewor Shopping Centre, Warri/Sapele Rd, POB 302, Warri; tel. (53) 233731; Pres. MOSES F. OROGUN.

INDUSTRIAL AND TRADE ASSOCIATIONS

Nigerian Export Promotion Council: Zone 2, Block 312, Wuse, PMB 133, Abuja; tel. (9) 5230930; fax (9) 5230931; f. 1976; Chair. Alhaji ISIAKA ADELEKE.

Nigerian Investment Promotion Commission (NIPC): Plot 1181, Agyuiyi-Ironsi St, Maitama District, Abuja; tel. (9) 4138026; fax (9) 4138021; e-mail nipc@nipc-nigeria.org; internet www.nipc-nigeria.org; Chair. FELIX O. A. OHIWEREI; Exec. Sec. Alhaji MUSTAFA BELLO.

EMPLOYERS' ORGANIZATIONS

Association of Advertising Practitioners of Nigeria: 3 William St, off Sylvia Cres., POB 50648, Anthony Village, Lagos; tel. (1) 4970842.

Chartered Institute of Bankers: Plot PC 19, Adeola Hopewell St, POB 72273, Victoria Island, Lagos.

Institute of Chartered Accountants of Nigeria: Plot 16, Professional Layout Centre, Idowu Taylor St, Victoria Island, POB 1580, Lagos; tel. (1) 2622394; fax (1) 2610304; e-mail info.ican@ican.org.ng; f. 1965; CEO and Registrar O. OLUBUNMI SOWANDE (acting).

Nigeria Employers' Consultative Association: Commercial House, 1–11 Commercial Ave, POB 2231, Yaba, Lagos; tel. (1) 800360; fax (1) 860309; f. 1957; Pres. Chief R. F. GIWA.

Nigerian Institute of Architects: 2 Idowu Taylor St, Victoria Island, POB 178, Lagos; tel. (1) 2617940; fax (1) 2617947; f. 1960; Pres. Chief O. C. MAJOROH.

Nigerian Institute of Building: 45 Opebi Rd, Ikeja, POB 3191, Marina, Lagos; tel. (1) 4930411; f. 1970; Pres. Dr SANI HABU GUMEL.

Nigerian Institution of Estate Surveyors and Valuers: Flat 2B, Dolphin Scheme, Ikoyi, POB 2325, Lagos; tel. (1) 2673131; fax (1) 2694314; e-mail niesv@nova.net.ng; Pres. NWEKE UMEZURUIKE.

NIGERIA

Nigerian Society of Engineers: National Engineering Centre, 1 Engineering Close, POB 72667, Victoria Island, Lagos; tel. and fax (1) 2617315; Pres. Dr O. AJAYI.

UTILITIES
Electricity

Power Holding Company of Nigeria (PHCN): Plot 1071, Area 3, Garki, Abuja; tel. (1) 5231938; f. 1972 as National Electric Power Authority, by merger of the Electricity Corpn of Nigeria and the Niger Dams Authority; renamed as above April 2005; assets were to be diverted to six generating companies and 11 distribution companies, prior to privatization; Man. Dir JOSEPH MAKOJU.

Gas

Nigeria Liquefied Natural Gas Co Ltd (NLNG): C. and C. Towers, Plot 1684, Sanusi Fafunwa St, Victoria Island, PMB 12774, Marina, Lagos; tel. (1) 2624190; fax (1) 2616976; internet www.nigerialng.com; Man. Dir. Dr CHRIS HAYNES.

TRADE UNIONS
Federation

Nigerian Labour Congress (NLC): 29 Olajuwon St, off Ojuelegba Rd, Yaba, POB 620, Lagos; tel. (1) 5835582; f. 1978; comprised 29 affiliated industrial unions in 1999; Pres. ADAMS OSHIOMOLE.

Principal Unions

Amalgamated Union of Public Corpns, Civil Service, and Technical and Recreational Services Employees: 9 Aje St, PMB 1064, Yaba, Lagos; tel. (1) 5863722; Sec.-Gen. SYLVESTER EJIOFOR.

National Union of Journalists: Lagos; Pres. LANRE OGUNDIPE; Sec. MOHAMMED KHALID.

National Union of Petroleum Workers and Natural Gas (NUPENG): Lagos; Sec.-Gen. FRANK KOKORI.

Nigerian Union of Civil Engineering, Construction, Furniture and Woodworkers: 51 Kano St, Ebute Metta, PMB 1064, Lagos; tel. (1) 5800263.

Nigerian Union of Mine Workers: 95 Enugu St, POB 763, Jos; tel. (73) 52401.

Petroleum and Gas Senior Staff Association of Nigeria (PENGASSAN): Lagos; Sec.-Gen. KENNETH NAREBOR.

Transport

RAILWAYS

There are about 3,505 km of mainly narrow-gauge railways. The two principal lines connect Lagos with Nguru and Port Harcourt with Maiduguri.

Nigerian Railway Corpn: Plot 739, Zone A6, Panama St, off IBB Way, Maitama, Abuja; tel. (9) 5231912; f. 1955; restructured in 1993 into three separate units: Nigerian Railway Track Authority; Nigerian Railways; and Nigerian Railway Engineering Ltd; Chair. Alhaji WAZIRI MOHAMMED.

ROADS

In 1999 the Nigerian road network totalled 194,394 km, including 1,194 km of motorways, 26,500 km of main roads and 32,300 km of secondary roads; some 60,068 km were paved.

Nigerian Road Federation: Ministry of Transport, National Maritime Agency Bldg, Central Area, Abuja; tel. (9) 5237053.

INLAND WATERWAYS

Inland Waterways Department: Ministry of Transport, National Maritime Agency Bldg, Central Area, Abuja; tel. (9) 5237053; responsible for all navigable waterways; Chair. Alhaji SULE ONABIYI.

SHIPPING

The principal ports are the Delta Port complex (including Warri, Koko, Burutu and Sapele ports), Port Harcourt and Calabar; other significant ports are situated at Apapa and Tin Can Island, near Lagos. The main petroleum ports are Bonny and Burutu.

National Maritime Authority: Michael Okpara St, Plot 1970, Wuse, Zone 5, Abuja; tel. (9) 5237016; fax (9) 5237015; f. 1987; Dir-Gen. Alhaji BUBA GALADIMA.

Nigerian Ports Authority: Olusegun Obasanjo Way, Plot 126, Central Business District, Garki, Abuja; tel. (9) 2347920; fax (9) 2347930; e-mail telnpo@infoweb.abs.net; internet www.nigeria-ports.com; f. 1955; CEO Chief ADEBAYO SARUMI.

Nigerian Green Lines Ltd: Unity House, 15th Floor, 37 Marina, POB 2288, Lagos; tel. (1) 2663303; 2 vessels totalling 30,751 grt; Chair. Alhaji W. L. FOLAWIYO.

Nigeria Unity Line: Maritime Complex, 34 Creek Rd, PMB 1175, Apapa, Lagos; tel. (1) 5804808; fax (1) 5804807; e-mail nul@hyperia.com; f. 1995 following the dissolution of the Nigerian National Shipping Line; govt-owned; Chair. Chief A. R. DIKIBO.

Association

Nigerian Shippers Council: 4 Park Lane, Apapa, Lagos; tel. (1) 5452307; e-mail info@shipperscouncil.com; internet www.shipperscouncil.com; Chair. G. C. OBIOZOR.

CIVIL AVIATION

The principal international airports are at Lagos (Murtala Mohammed Airport), Kano, Port Harcourt and Abuja. There are also 14 airports for domestic flights. In early 1997 a two-year programme to develop the airports at Lagos, Abuja, Port Harcourt and Kano was announced. Some 27 airlines operate in Nigeria.

Federal Airport Authority of Nigeria: Murtala Mohammed Airport, PMB 21607, Ikeja, Lagos; tel. (1) 4900800; Chair. SARGEANT AWUSE.

Principal Airlines

Virgin Nigeria: 3rd Floor Ark Towers Plot 17, Ligali Ayorinde St Victoria Island Extension, Ikeja, Lagos; tel. (1) 1) 4600505; e-mail commercial@virginnigeria.com; internet www.virginnigeria.com; f. Sept. 2004; private flag carrier; 51% owned by Nigerian institutional investors and 49% by Virgin Atlantic; scheduled domestic regional and international services; CEO CONRAD CLIFFORD.

Tourism

Potential attractions for tourists include fine coastal scenery, dense forests, and the rich diversity of Nigeria's arts. A total of 2,422,530 tourists visited Nigeria in 2003. Receipts from tourism amounted to US $263m. in 2002.

Nigerian Tourism Development Corpn: Old Federal Secretariat, Area 1, Garki, PMB 167, Abuja; tel. (9) 2342764; fax (9) 2342775; e-mail ntdc@metrong.com; internet www.nigeria.tourism.com; Chair. Prince ADESUYI HAASTRUP; CEO OMOTAYO OMOTOSHO.

NORWAY

Introductory Survey

Location, Climate, Language, Religion, Flag, Capital

The Kingdom of Norway forms the western part of Scandinavia, in northern Europe. It is bordered to the east by Sweden and, within the Arctic Circle, by Finland and Russia. A long, indented coast faces the Atlantic Ocean. Norway exercises sovereignty over the Svalbard archipelago, Jan Mayen island and the uninhabited dependencies of Bouvetøya and Peter I Øy. Dronning Maud Land, in Antarctica, is also a Norwegian dependency. Norway's climate is temperate on the west coast but colder inland. Average temperatures range from −2°C (28°F) to 8°C (46°F). There are two forms of the Norwegian language, which are officially recognized as equal. About 80% of children in schools use the older form, Bokmål, as their principal language, whereas only 20% use the newer form, Nynorsk (Neo-Norwegian). Lappish is also spoken by the Sámi population, in northern Norway. Almost all of the inhabitants profess Christianity: the Evangelical Lutheran Church is the established religion, with about 86% of the population professing adherence in 2003. The civil flag (proportions 8 by 11) has a dark blue cross, bordered with white, on a red background, the upright of the cross being to the left of centre; the state flag (16 by 27) displays the same cross, but forms a triple swallow-tail at the fly. The capital is Oslo.

Recent History

Norway, formerly linked to the Swedish crown, declared its independence in 1905. The union with Sweden was peacefully dissolved and the Norwegians elected their own monarch, Prince Karl of Denmark, who took the title of King Håkon VII. He reigned until his death in 1957, and was succeeded by his son, Olav V. Olav's son, Crown Prince Harald (who had acted as regent since his father suffered a stroke in May 1990), became King Harald V upon Olav's death in January 1991.

During the Second World War Norway was occupied by German forces between 1940 and 1945. Norway abandoned its traditional policy of neutrality after the war, joining the North Atlantic Treaty Organization (NATO, see p. 314) in 1949. Norway was also a founder member of the Nordic Council (see p. 397) in 1952 and of the European Free Trade Association (EFTA, see p. 386) in 1960.

Det norske Arbeiderparti (DnA—Norwegian Labour Party) governed from 1935 to 1965, except for the period of German occupation, when a pro-Nazi 'puppet' regime was administered by Vidkun Quisling, and an interlude of one month in 1963. Norway applied for membership of the European Community (EC, now European Union—EU, see p. 228) in 1962, and again in 1967. A general election to the Storting (parliament) in September 1965 resulted in a defeat for the Labour Government of Einar Gerhardsen, who had been Prime Minister almost continuously since 1955. His administration was replaced in October 1965 by a non-socialist coalition under Per Borten, leader of the Senterpartiet (Sp—Centre Party). In March 1971, however, Borten resigned, following revelations that he had deliberately disclosed confidential details of Norway's negotiations with the EC. He was succeeded by a minority DnA Government, led by Trygve Bratteli. The terms of Norway's entry into the EC were agreed in December 1971, and a preliminary Treaty of Accession was signed in January 1972. In September, however, a consultative referendum on the agreed terms produced a 53.3% majority against entering the EC. The application was withdrawn, and Bratteli resigned in October. A coalition of Venstre (Liberals), the Sp and the Kristelig Folkeparti (KrF—Christian Democrats' Party) formed a new minority Government, with Lars Korvald of the KrF as Prime Minister.

Following the general election of September 1973, Bratteli formed another minority DnA Government, dependent on the support of a socialist alliance known from 1975 as the Socialistisk Venstreparti (SV—Socialist Left Party). In January 1976 Bratteli was succeeded as Prime Minister by Odvar Nordli. Nordli resigned in February 1981, for reasons of ill health, and was succeeded by Gro Harlem Brundtland, Norway's first female Prime Minister. At the general election in September the DnA lost support to centre-right groups. In October a minority administration, led by Kåre Willoch, became Norway's first Høyre (Conservative) Government since 1928. In June 1983 a coalition of Høyre with the Sp and the KrF was formed, with 79 of the 165 parliamentary seats. Willoch's Government was returned to power, although lacking an overall majority in the Storting, following the general election in September 1985. In May 1986, however, Willoch resigned when the Storting narrowly rejected a proposal to increase taxation on petrol. The Norwegian Constitution did not permit a general election before the expiry of the Storting's term (due in 1989). Brundtland accepted an invitation by the King to form a minority DnA administration. The new Government devalued the krone by 12%, and a revised budget was approved by the Storting in June 1986.

At the general election in September 1989 both the DnA and Høyre lost support to more radical parties. The SV gained nine seats, to achieve a total of 17 seats in the 165-seat Storting. The Fremskrittspartiet (FrP—Progress Party) increased its representation from two to 22 seats, despite attracting allegations of racism during the election campaign. Brundtland's Government resigned in October, following an agreement made by Høyre, the Sp and the KrF to form a coalition. The new Government, led by Jan Syse (Høyre leader since January 1988), controlled only 62 seats in the Storting and was dependent upon the support of the FrP. Also in September 1989 the Sámi (Lapps) of northern Norway elected 39 representatives for a new Sameting (Consultative Assembly), to be based in Karasjok. This followed an amendment to the Constitution the previous year, which recognized the Sámi as an indigenous people and an ethnic minority. There was considerable support among the Sámi for a degree of autonomy, in order to protect their traditional way of life. The Sámi had officially ceased to exist by 1900, with their culture and language being declared illegal, but by 2000 they had formed a joint council comprising Sámi populations in Norway, Sweden, Finland and Russia, and received a parliament building, opened in November by King Harald V. The issue of land rights, however, remained unresolved. This was aggravated by the discovery, in November 2001, of substantial platinum deposits in Finnmark, an area to which the Sámi laid claim.

While Høyre had supported EC membership since 1988, the Sp remained strongly opposed to it. In October 1990 the Government announced that the Norwegian krone was to be linked to the European Currency Unit (ECU). Later in that month the coalition collapsed, following disagreement between Høyre and the Sp regarding Norwegian demands in the negotiations between EFTA and the EC on the creation of a joint European Economic Area (EEA). In November the DnA formed another minority Government, led by Brundtland.

In October 1991 agreement was finally reached on the terms of the EEA treaty, including arrangements whereby EC countries were to be allowed to take extra quotas of fish from Norwegian waters, while Norwegian fish products were to have increased access to EC markets. Many Norwegians remained opposed to membership of the EC, fearing, in particular, that government subsidies that had allowed the survival of remote rural and coastal communities would no longer be permitted. The EEA treaty was ratified by the Storting in October 1992. (The treaty entered into effect on 1 January 1994, following ratification by all of the countries concerned.) A proposal by Brundtland to apply for EC membership was endorsed by the Storting in November 1992, and an application was duly submitted.

In November 1992 Brundtland resigned from the leadership of the DnA, and was replaced by the party's Secretary-General, Thorbjørn Jagland. At the September 1993 general election the DnA slightly increased its representation in the Storting, from 63 to 67 seats. The Sp (which opposed EC membership) increased its total from 11 to 32 seats, thereby becoming the second largest party in the Storting, while Høyre won only 28 seats, compared with 37 at the previous election.

Negotiations on Norway's entry to the EU, as the EC had been restyled, were concluded in March 1994. However, at a national referendum held on 27–28 November (shortly after Sweden and Finland had voted to join the Union), 52.4% of voters rejected EU membership. The success of the campaign opposing Norway's entry to the EU was attributed to several factors: in particular, farmers feared the impact of an influx of cheaper agricultural goods from the EU, and fisheries workers feared that fish stocks would be severely depleted if EU boats were granted increased access to Norwegian waters. There was also widespread concern that national sovereignty would be compromised by the transfer to the EU of certain executive responsibilities.

At local elections held in September 1995, the DnA received 31% of the votes cast (compared with 37% at the 1993 general election), Høyre obtained 20% and the Sp 12%. The right-wing FrP, which had campaigned for more stringent policies on law and order, doubled its share of the vote to 12%, from 6% at the general election.

In October 1996 Brundtland resigned as Prime Minister. Thorbjørn Jagland, the Chairman of the DnA, succeeded her. Jagland emphasized that he would continue the previous Government's cautious fiscal policy. By the end of the year, however, the Government's credibility had been seriously undermined, after Terje Röd-Larsen, the newly appointed Minister of National Planning, and Grete Faremo, the Minister of Petroleum and Energy, were forced to resign, following, respectively, allegations of financial irregularities and abuse of power.

A general election was conducted on 16 September 1997, at which the DnA attracted the largest level of support, winning 35.0% of the votes cast (65 seats), ahead of the FrP with 15.3% (25 seats), Høyre 14.3% (23 seats) and the KrF 13.7% (25 seats). In October Jagland resigned, honouring a pre-election pledge to stand down should the DnA fail to secure at least the 36.9% of popular support that it attracted at the 1993 poll. Kjell Magne Bondevik, the parliamentary leader of the KrF, had organized an alliance of the KrF, the Sp and Venstre (with representation totalling 42 seats), and was invited to form a coalition government on that basis. The new Council of State was dominated by the KrF. There was some uncertainty regarding the durability of the Government after the Prime Minister took more than three weeks' leave from his post from the end of August 1998, announcing that he was suffering from depression caused by overwork. Bondevik was reported to have been under intense pressure as a result of the recent instability of the economy, largely attributable to the sharp decline in international prices for petroleum; this had notably necessitated the postponement of the introduction of a scheme, promoted by the Prime Minister, to give financial support to parents choosing to look after their children at home. In November, furthermore, the Government was obliged to abandon proposed tax increases in order to secure the support of the FrP (and thus parliamentary approval) for the 1999 budget. Electoral support for the DnA declined further in the local elections held in September, when it received 28.2% of the votes cast; support also declined for the three parties in the coalition Government, while the most significant gains were made by the right-wing FrP, which campaigned on an anti-immigration platform and received the third largest share of the vote.

On 9 March 2000 Bondevik resigned following his defeat in a confidence motion in the Storting by 81 votes to 71. The vote was called to resolve a dispute between the majority in the Storting and the minority Government on whether to postpone the construction of gas-fired power plants pending the introduction of new technology to render them pollution-free. Bondevik favoured postponement as he opposed amending the country's strict anti-pollution laws to allow increased carbon dioxide emissions. Bondevik recommended that Jens Stoltenberg, who had replaced Jagland as leader of the DnA in February, be approached to form a single-party minority government. Stoltenberg took office as Prime Minister on 17 March. The new Council of State, which was drawn exclusively from the DnA, included Jagland as Minister of Foreign Affairs. The new Government pledged to reform the public sector, resume the country's privatization programme, forge stronger links with Europe and continue Norway's role as a mediator in international peace negotiations.

The Deputy Chairman of the FrP, Terje Soeviknes, resigned from his party position in February 2001, following allegations, which he denied, that he had raped a 16-year-old girl at a youth conference the previous year. Soeviknes had been viewed as the next leader of the increasingly influential FrP, and the party suffered a decline in popularity following his resignation. In January the first officially recognized racially motivated murder in Norway took place. Six youths with neo-Nazi sympathies were arrested on suspicion of involvement in the murder of a 15-year-old anti-racist campaigner, whose father was Ghanaian. The Government condemned the murder but counselled caution regarding demands for the banning of neo-Nazi groups. Two of the suspects were convicted of the crime in January 2002, and a third was convicted as an accessory to the crime.

In March 1999 the Storting approved compensation valued at US $57.5m. for the country's Holocaust victims and their descendants. The programme was to include compensation for plundered property, as well as funding for contemporary Jewish community projects. In October 2001 a lawsuit was brought against the Norwegian Government by surviving victims of the Nazi *Lebensborn* (Source of Life) project. The survivors, children of German soldiers and Norwegian women, were conceived during the Nazi occupation of Norway in the Second World War as part of a scheme to create a 'master race'. They alleged that, following the liberation of Norway, they and their mothers were subjected to systematic abuse and discrimination, and that the Government not only allowed this abuse to occur, but also attempted to conceal it. The lawsuit was rejected on the grounds that the alleged offences occurred too long ago to be brought to court. However, in late 2002 the Storting's Justice Committee recommended that the Government 'make amends'.

At a general election conducted on 10 September 2001, the DnA received only 24.3% of the valid votes cast (its poorest electoral performance since 1909), attaining 43 of the 165 parliamentary seats. Høyre secured 21.2% of the votes cast (38 seats), the FrP 14.7% (26 seats), the SV 12.5% (23 seats) and the KrF 12.4% (22 seats). The DnA formed a minority Government, but was unable to attract enough political support to hold a majority in the Storting. Stoltenberg consequently resigned on 17 October, and the DnA was replaced in government by a minority centre-right coalition comprising Høyre, the KrF and Venstre, with Bondevik as Prime Minister. The coalition gained a majority in the Storting with the informal support of the FrP, which was expected to exert a strong influence on government policy.

In February 2003 the Government announced its decision to expel Mullah Krekar, the leader of the Kurdish guerrilla organization Ansar al-Islam, who was suspected by both the USA and the UN of having links to terrorism, and possibly to the Islamist al-Qa'ida (Base) network. However, Krekar, who had stated that he would not leave Norway voluntarily, was not taken into custody or otherwise compelled to leave the country. The following month the Government announced that the case, which was without precedent in Norway, merited further investigation, and that the launch of the US-led military action in Iraq that month posed difficulties for his repatriation, effectively granting Krekar the right to remain in the country for a further two months. A request from Jordan for him to be extradited for drugs offences was also to be investigated. Krekar was eventually detained following an appearance on Dutch television during which he stated that Ansar al-Islam had suicide bombers ready to attack US citizens, but did not remain in custody for long. Krekar was arrested again in December and charged with plotting the murder of his political rivals in Iraq in 2000–01, and was imprisoned in early January 2004 while prosecutors investigated the charges against him. Despite the prosecutors' efforts to keep Krekar in custody, he was eventually freed by the Lagmannsrett (Court of Appeal) in February 2004. The charges against Krekar were withdrawn in June owing to insufficient evidence. In 2005 Krekar's expulsion was further delayed pending a guarantee from the Iraqi authorities that he would not face the death penalty. (Norwegian law forbids extradition to countries with the death penalty.)

In December 2003 the Storting adopted legislation introducing a minimum quota of 40% for female board members for all publicly owned enterprises and public limited-liability companies in the private sector. The rules applying to publicly owned companies took effect in January 2004, but private companies were given until July 2005 to achieve the desired gender representation voluntarily before the legislation would be enforced. In December 2005 the Government concluded that the gender representation requirements would not be reached on a voluntary basis and approved the entry into force of the legislation as regards public limited-liability companies in the private sector from January 2006. Companies were given until the end of 2007 to meet the requirements set by the legislation. Informal gender quotas have operated in Norway since 1981, since when some 40% of government posts have been held by women.

In 2004 Norway introduced transitional rules aimed at limiting (for an initial period of two years) the entry of migrant workers from the eight central and eastern European countries that joined the EU on 1 May. While Norway was not itself a member of the EU, it nevertheless had commitments arising from its membership of the EEA and the EU's Schengen Agreement. The Government had originally planned to allow unrestricted access to Norway's labour markets, but felt compelled to change its position following the introduction of similar prohibitory legislation by neighbouring countries.

Local elections were held on 15 September 2003, at which the participation rate was the lowest since the Second World War. The DnA remained the party with the largest share of the vote, while the KrF performed particularly poorly, receiving just one-half as much support as it had done at the general election in 2001. The biggest gains were made by the SV and the FrP, which achieved its best result in 30 years. In January 2004 Valgerd Svarstad Haugland resigned as Chairperson of the KrF; however, she retained her post as the Minister of Culture and Church Affairs. The Minister of Health, Dagfinn Høybråten, was unanimously elected to replace her as leader of the KrF. In February Jan Petersen announced his decision to step down as Chairman of Høyre, while retaining his post as Minister of Foreign Affairs. Erna Solberg was elected as the new leader of Høyre in May.

On 1 June 2004 legislation, originally approved by the Storting in April 2003, came into force, outlawing smoking in restaurants, cafés, bars and nightclubs in order to protect employees and patrons from the effects of passive smoking. Norway was the second country in the world to adopt such legislation, after Ireland.

A general election was held on 12 September 2005, at which the DnA received 32.7% of the votes cast and won 61 of the 169 seats in the enlarged Storting, thus retaining its position as the largest parliamentary party. The DnA contested the election at the head of a centre-left alliance also comprising the SV (which secured 15 seats, with 8.8% of the votes cast) and the Sp (11 seats, with 6.5%). The FrP won 22.1% of the votes cast (38 seats), a significant increase compared with the 2001 poll, while Høyre secured 14.1% (23 seats), the KrF 6.8% (11 seats) and Venstre 5.9% (10 seats). Some 77.1% of the electorate participated in the election. The DnA, the SV and the Sp subsequently formed the first majority Government since 1985, led by Stoltenberg of the DnA, which was sworn into office in mid-October. The new coalition Government's programme included proposals to increase welfare spending, raise taxes and eradicate social inequality.

In January 2006 the Government announced that the Statens Pensjonsfond (State Pension Fund) would henceforth no longer invest in companies whose activities 'violate fundamental humanitarian principles', including those involved in the production of nuclear weapons. Also in January, a tax was introduced on milk and juice cartons in an attempt to persuade producers and consumers to recycle more of their refuse. The tax was to be removed once recycling levels reached 95%.

During 1993 the Norwegian Government was instrumental in conducting secret negotiations between the Israeli Government and the Palestine Liberation Organization (PLO), which led to agreement on Palestinian self-rule in certain areas occupied by Israel. Norway won international acclaim for its role in furthering peace in the Middle East through these negotiations, and continued to be involved in the advancement of the peace process in the late 1990s and first half of the 2000s.

In February 2000 Norway extended its role as an international mediator, agreeing to broker negotiations between the Sri Lankan Government and Tamil separatists in an attempt to end the 17-year conflict; the negotiations were still continuing, under Norway's auspices, in early 2006. In April 2001 Norway agreed to host peace negotiations between the Philippine Government and the Philippine dissident communist alliance, the National Democratic Front; similarly, Norway's role as mediator was continuing in these negotiations in early 2006.

Norway declared an exclusive economic zone extending to 200 nautical miles (370 km) from its coastline in 1977, and also unilaterally established a fisheries protection zone around its territory of Svalbard. The declaration of an economic zone around Jan Mayen island in 1980 led to agreements with Iceland, in 1980 and 1981, over conflicting claims to fishing and mineral rights. A similar dispute with Denmark, acting for Greenland, was not resolved, and in 1988 Denmark requested arbitration by the International Court of Justice, in The Hague, Netherlands, which gave its judgment on the delimitation of the disputed zones in June 1993 (see under Jan Mayen). During 1994 incidents were reported between vessels of the Norwegian coastguard and Icelandic fishing boats, within the economic zone surrounding the Norwegian island of Spitsbergen (see under Svalbard). In October 2005 Norway detained two Russian vessels that were illegally transferring fish within the same zone.

Following a moratorium on commercial whaling, adopted by the International Whaling Commission (IWC, see p. 378) with effect from 1985, Norway continued to hunt small numbers of whales ostensibly for purposes of scientific research, and in 1992 the Norwegian Government declared that it would allow the resumption of commercial hunting of minke whales in 1993, claiming that (according to the findings of the IWC's scientific commission) this species was plentiful enough to allow whaling on a sustainable basis: the Government argued that many Norwegian coastal communities depended on whaling for their existence. A moratorium on the hunting of seal pups, imposed in 1989, was ended by the Norwegian Government in 1995, although it was emphasized that the killing of seals would be strictly for scientific purposes. Opponents of sealing, however, expressed concern that Norway might seek to resume commercial hunting. Norway continued to campaign against the moratorium on commercial whaling, and made some progress in its attempts to exempt the minke whale from the ban on exports of whale products imposed under the Convention on International Trade in Endangered Species (CITES). In July 1999 journalists revealed that 500 metric tons of blubber had been stockpiled by the Norwegians in anticipation of a resumption of legal trading. In January 2001 the Government announced that it would resume exports of whale meat and products without waiting for the next CITES conference, scheduled for 2004. The announcement attracted criticism from environmental groups; however, many observers (including a number within the IWC) admitted that a return to controlled commercial whaling was becoming inevitable. In March 2002 Norway declared that it was to resume exports of whale meat to Japan. In December 2005 the Norwegian Government announced an increase in its quota for minke whales from 797 in 2005 to 1,052 in 2006, the highest quota since 1993.

Relations between Norway and Sweden were strained in 1999 by disputes arising from negotiations regarding the proposed merger of Telenor and Telia, respectively the Norwegian and Swedish state-owned telecommunications companies, which collapsed acrimoniously in December amidst Swedish accusations of Norwegian nationalism. (Four foreign takeover attempts of major Norwegian petroleum companies and banks failed in 1999.)

In January 2002, following the US-led military campaign against the Taliban and al-Qa'ida militants in Afghanistan in 2001, Norway contributed 180 troops to the International Security Assistance Force (ISAF), deployed in Kabul and at Bagram airbase to help maintain security in the area. In January 2004, at the request of the Loya Jirga (the Afghan Grand Assembly) the Norwegian troops extended their mission in Afghanistan until August 2004. Norway also contributed special forces troops from its Naval Ranger Command and the Norwegian Army's Ranger Command to the US-led operation 'Enduring Freedom', the main aim of which was to combat al-Qa'ida's terrorist network in Afghanistan. In August 2004 the mandate of Norway's ISAF troops in Afghanistan was extended indefinitely. In January 2006 Norway withdraw from 'Enduring Freedom' and instead increased its commitment to the ISAF.

In July 2003 Norway sent 150 soldiers from the Telemark Engineer Squadron to Iraq to help British troops south of Basra repair roads and bridges and to clear land mines, following the success of the US-led military action in removing the regime of Saddam Hussain earlier in the year. Norway had not supported the war, and insisted that its troops were in Iraq as part of a humanitarian 'stabilizing force' mandated by the UN Security Council Resolution 1483, and that they would remain separate from peace-keeping forces dispatched by the USA, the United Kingdom, Denmark and Poland. In December 2003 the Storting voted to extend the troops' presence in Iraq by at least six months. Norway withdrew its troops from Iraq in mid-2004. However, a small number of staff officers, who were attached to a Polish brigade, remained. In December 2005 the last of Norway's troops in Iraq were withdrawn.

From 1999 Norway contributed 520 troops to the KFOR peace-keeping mission in Kosovo, consisting of a mechanized infantry battalion and a smaller rapid reaction force that was specially trained in riot control. In 2004 Norway increased its contribution to KFOR, sending four helicopters and support personnel. In 2005 Norway also had troops in peace-keeping missions in Bosnia and Herzegovina, the Middle East, Ethiopia, Eritrea and Sudan.

Government

Norway is a constitutional monarchy. Legislative power is held by the Storting (parliament), with 165 members elected for four years by universal adult suffrage, on the basis of proportional representation. For the consideration of legislative proposals, the Storting divides itself into two chambers by choosing one-quarter of its members to form the Lagting (upper house), the remainder forming the Odelsting (lower house). Executive power is nominally held by the monarch, but is, in effect, exercised by the Statsråd (Council of State), led by the Prime Minister. The Council is appointed by the monarch in accordance with the will of the Storting, to which the Council is responsible. Norway comprises 19 counties (fylker) and 435 municipalities.

Defence

Norway is a member of the North Atlantic Treaty Organization (NATO, see p. 314), and became an associate member of Western European Union (WEU, see p. 365) in 1992. Every male is liable for 12 months' national service at the age of 19. Periodical refresher programmes are also compulsory until the age of 44. The total strength of the armed forces in August 2005 was 25,800 (including 15,200 conscripts): army 14,700 (8,700 conscripts), navy 6,100 (3,300 conscripts), and air force 5,000 (3,200 conscripts). There is also a mobilization reserve of about 219,000 (army 83,000, navy 22,000, air force 25,000 and Home Guard c. 73,000), a coastguard of 270 and a coastal defence force of 160. In addition, there is naval Home Guard with a mobilization reserve of 4,900 and an air force Home Guard with a mobilization reserve of 2,500. The defence budget for 2005 was projected at 30,300m. kroner.

In December 2004 the Storting gave qualified approval for Norway's participation, with Finland and Sweden, in a joint Nordic battle group as part of a proposed European Union (EU) rapid reaction force. With Norway's participation the group's total strength was to be 1,500. The group, one of six or seven such battle groups envisaged by the EU, was to be ready for international deployment from 2008.

Economic Affairs

In 2004, according to estimates by the World Bank, Norway's gross national income (GNI), measured at average 2002–04 prices, was US $238,398m., equivalent to $52,030 per head (or $38,550 per head on an international purchasing-power parity basis). During 1995–2004, it was estimated, the population increased by an average of 0.6% per year, while gross domestic product (GDP) per head increased, in real terms, by an average of 2.3% per year. Norway's overall GDP increased, in real terms, at an average annual rate of 2.8% in 1995–2004. Real GDP increased by 0.4% in 2003 and by 2.9% in 2004.

The contribution of agriculture (including hunting, forestry and fishing) to GDP in 2005 was estimated at 1.6%. In 2004 the agricultural sector engaged 3.5% of the employed labour force. Around 3.4% of the land surface is cultivated, and the most important branch of the sector is livestock-rearing. Fish-farming has been intensively developed by the Government since the early 1970s. The fishing industry provided an estimated 4.9% of total export revenue in 2004. A temporary emergency ban on cod fishing in parts of the North Sea, agreed between the European Union (EU, see p. 228) and Norway, was announced in January 2001 in an attempt to prevent the collapse of fish stocks through over-fishing. In February 2004 the Government appealed against proposals by the United Kingdom to block salmon imports to the EU from non-EU countries. In 2003 Norway produced some 507,400 metric tons of farmed salmon. Agricultural GDP decreased at an average annual rate of 1.0% during 1995–2003. Agricultural GDP increased by 1.2% in 2002, but declined by 2.9% in 2003.

Industry (including mining, manufacturing, construction, power and public utilities) contributed an estimated 42.3% of GDP in 2005, and engaged 20.9% of the employed labour force in 2004. During 1995–2003 industrial GDP increased, in real terms, at an average annual rate of 1.2%. Industrial GDP rose by 0.5% in 2002, but decreased by 2.0% in 2003.

Mining (including gas and petroleum extraction) provided an estimated 26.1% of GDP in 2005, and engaged 1.5% of the employed labour force in 2004. Extraction of petroleum and natural gas dominates the sector, accounting for 25.9% of GDP in 2005 and 1.3% of employment in 2004. Norway possesses substantial reserves of petroleum and natural gas (exports of petroleum and petroleum products accounted for 48.2% of total export earnings in 2004). Most of the reserves are located off shore. During 1995–2005 the production of crude petroleum from fields on the Norwegian continental shelf decreased at an average annual rate of 0.6%, while output of natural gas grew at an average rate of 11.8% per year, according to the Norwegian Petroleum Directorate. Norway's other mineral reserves include iron ore, iron pyrites, copper, lead and zinc. Substantial deposits of platinum were discovered in the northern county of Finnmark in November 2001—the area was also believed to contain deposits of gold and diamonds. In October 2003 Norway signed a deal to export natural gas from the Ormen Lange gas field to the United Kingdom; it was envisaged that 20,000m. cu m of natural gas per year would be exported from the field. To that end a large terminal was to be constructed in Aukra, on the island of Gossa, from which the gas was to be pumped via a 1,200-km pipeline to the United Kingdom. The construction of the terminal was expected to cost 66,000m. kroner and was to be completed by 2007. In December 2003 the Government announced that it was to open the hitherto unexplored Barents Sea for petroleum and gas extraction; three exploratory wells were drilled in 2004–05. In October 2005 Norsk Hydro ASA announced that it had made six petroleum discoveries along Norway's continental shelf, three of which seemed particularly promising. In March 2006 the Government announced that it was to allow further prospecting in the Barents Sea, but that drilling was to be prohibited until 2010 in a 50-km coastal zone (including the Lofoten Islands) in order to protect the environment and fish stocks.

Manufacturing contributed an estimated 9.5% of GDP in 2005, and employed 11.7% of the working population in 2004. In 1998 the most important branches of manufacturing, measured by gross value of output, were food products (accounting for 20.3% of the total), transport equipment (13.5%), metals and metal products (13.2%), chemicals and chemical products (7.6%), and publishing and printing (7.2%). During 1995–2001 manufacturing GDP increased, in real terms, by an average of 0.8% per year. Manufacturing GDP decreased by 0.7% in 2000 and by 0.4% in 2001.

In 2004, according to provisional figures, some 98.8% of Norway's installed capacity of electric energy was produced by hydroelectric power schemes; domestic energy demands are easily supplied, and Norway has exported hydroelectricity since 1993. Norway's extensive reserves of petroleum and natural gas are mainly exploited for sale to foreign markets, since the domestic market is limited.

The services sector contributed an estimated 56.1% of GDP in 2005, and engaged 75.6% of the employed labour force in 2004. The GDP of the services sector increased, in real terms, by an average of 4.0% per year during 1995–2003; it grew by 1.7% in 2002 and by 2.0% in 2003.

Although shipbuilding has declined since the early 1970s, Norway remains a leading shipping nation. The establishment of the Norwegian International Ship Register in 1987 allowed an expansion of the merchant fleet by more than 300%, in terms of gross tonnage. At 31 December 2004 the combined displacement of the merchant fleet totalled 18.9m. grt, of which the Norwegian International Ship Register accounted for 15.4m. grt.

In 2004, according to IMF figures, Norway recorded a visible trade surplus of US $33,576m., and there was a surplus of $34,445m. on the current account of the balance of payments. In 2004 the EU provided 70.6% of imports and took 79.0% of exports; fellow members of the European Free Trade Association (EFTA, see p. 386) accounted for 1.2% of Norway's imports and 0.7% of exports in the same year. The principal source of imports in 2004 was Sweden (providing 15.7% of the total), followed by Germany (13.5%), Denmark (7.3%) and the United Kingdom (6.5%); the principal market for exports was the United Kingdom (taking 22.6%), followed by Germany (13.2%), the Netherlands (10.2%), France (9.1%) and the USA (7.7%). In 2004 the principal exports were crude petroleum (accounting for 44.7% of total exports), natural gas (13.4%), basic manufactures (12.0%, notably aluminium), machinery and transport equipment (8.8%), and chemicals and related products (5.4%); the principal imports were machinery and transport equipment (38.8%), basic manufactures (17.1%), miscellaneous manufactured articles (15.7%), and chemicals and related products (9.6%).

In 2004 Norway recorded an overall surplus of 200,249m. kroner in the general budget (equivalent to some 11.7% of GDP in purchasers' values). At the end of 2005 Norway's gross external debt was estimated at 1,891,333m. kroner; general government debt amounted to 514,583m. kroner. During 1995–2005 the average annual rate of inflation was 2.0%; consumer prices increased by 0.5% in 2004 and by 1.6% in 2005. The average rate of unemployment was 4.5% in 2004.

In addition to its membership of EFTA, Norway is a member of the European Economic Area (EEA), the Nordic Council (see p. 397) and the Nordic Council of Ministers (see p. 397). Although

NORWAY

Norway is not a member of the EU, it joined the EU's Schengen Agreement (see p. 257) in May 1999 (Denmark, Finland and Sweden—all EU members—had already joined in 1996) by virtue of its membership in the Nordic passport union (Iceland also joined the Schengen Agreement in May 1999).

The Norwegian economy, which is highly dependent on its hydrocarbons sector (Norway is the world's second largest petroleum exporter), experienced a sustained expansion during the 1990s, leading to virtually full employment, as well as rises in real incomes. Norway maintained a stable exchange rate during this period and a prudent fiscal position, and reinvested a substantial proportion of petroleum revenues abroad through the State Petroleum Fund, partly in preparation for future increased demands on pensions and also to offer limited protection to the economy against fluctuations in the petroleum sector. In the first years of the 21st century a strong policy framework underpinned enviable prosperity and a high degree of social equity in Norway. The fiscal guidelines adopted in 2001 formed the basis of a reasonable compromise between the current and future use of petroleum revenues. Norway's traditionally high social cohesiveness and solidarity ensured that the use of the petroleum wealth benefited people at all levels of society, and would continue to benefit future generations well after the petroleum itself was depleted. After a period of weak growth in 2001–03, reflecting economic weakness in Norway's trading partners, Norway's economy recovered in 2004–05, driven by increased investment within the petroleum industry. Moreover, low interest rates and high real income growth stimulated domestic demand, and growth in private consumption and housing investment was strong. This upturn gradually became more broadly based, with exports and business investment also increasing. GDP growth in 2005 was estimated at 2.5%, although mainland Norway experienced stronger growth, of 3.7%, which was attributed to increased activity in the services sector and significant increases in investments in housing, manufacturing and petroleum and natural gas extraction, particularly in the last quarter of the year. The new centre-left Government that took office in October 2005 planned to raise taxes and increase spending in areas such as education, health care and social welfare, while the central bank intended to raise interest rates gradually. Unemployment was forecast to continue its steady decline.

Education

Compulsory education begins at six years of age and lasts for 10 years. Elementary education is divided into a four-year lower stage (barnetrinnet), for children aged six to 10 years, a three-year intermediate stage (mellomtrinnet), for children aged 10 to 13 years, and a three-year upper stage (ungdomstrinnet), from the age of 13. A pupil may then transfer to an upper-secondary school for a course lasting three years.. Primary enrolment in 2002/03 included 100% of children in the relevant age-group, while the comparable ratio for secondary enrolment was 96% (males 96%; females 97%). From the second half of 2002 adults who had not completed compulsory education, or who wished to refresh their competence, were given a statutory right to lower-secondary education. This also applied to special education. With effect from the 2000/01 academic year, everyone had the right to upper-secondary education. Upon completion of a three-year course in general and technical areas of study at an upper-secondary school, a pupil may seek admission to one of Norway's four universities or other colleges. From 2000 persons from the age of 25 had the right to be assessed for admittance to higher education based on non-formal learning. A broader system of higher professional education has been organized on a regional basis, including colleges of education and technology. At 1 October 2003 130,148 students were enrolled at colleges of higher education, with a further 79,611 enrolled at universities and their equivalent. Expenditure on education by all levels of government in 2004 was 102,479m. kroner (equivalent to 13.9% of total government expenditure).

Public Holidays

2006: 1 January (New Year's Day), 13 April (Maundy Thursday), 14 April (Good Friday), 17 April (Easter Monday), 1 May (Labour Day), 5 May (Ascension Day), 17 May (Constitution Day), 5 June (Whit Monday), 24 December (Christmas Eve)*, 25–26 December (Christmas), 31 December (New Year's Eve)*.

2007: 1 January (New Year's Day), 5 April (Maundy Thursday), 6 April (Good Friday), 9 April (Easter Monday), 1 May (Labour Day), 17 May (Ascension Day and Constitution Day), 28 May (Whit Monday), 24 December (Christmas Eve)*, 25–26 December (Christmas), 31 December (New Year's Eve)*.

* Half day from 12 noon.

Weights and Measures

The metric system is in force.

Statistical Survey

Sources (unless otherwise stated): Statistics Norway, Kongensgt. 6, Oslo; tel. 21-09-00-00; fax 21-09-49-73; e-mail biblioteket@ssb.no; internet www.ssb.no; Nordic Statistical Secretariat (Copenhagen), *Yearbook of Nordic Statistics*.

Area and Population

AREA, POPULATION AND DENSITY

Area (sq km)	
Land	304,280
Inland water	19,522
Total	323,802*
Population (census results)	
3 November 1990	4,247,546
3 November 2001	
Males	2,240,281
Females	2,280,666
Total	4,520,947
Population (official estimates at 1 January)	
2004	4,577,457
2005	4,606,363
2006	4,640,219
Density (per sq km) at 1 January 2006†	15.2

* 125,020 sq miles.
† Excluding inland water.

COUNTIES
(1 January 2005)

	Land area (sq km)*	Population	Density (per sq km)
Østfold	3,887	258,542	66.5
Akershus	4,579	494,218	107.9
Oslo	426	529,846	1,243.8
Hedmark	26,082	188,376	7.2
Oppland	23,787	183,174	7.7
Buskerud	13,797	243,491	17.6
Vestfold	2,147	220,736	102.8
Telemark	13,854	166,289	12.0
Aust-Agder	8,312	103,596	12.5
Vest-Agder	6,677	161,276	24.2
Rogaland	8,590	393,104	45.8
Hordaland	14,551	448,343	31.0
Sogn og Fjordane	17,680	107,032	6.1
Møre og Romsdal	14,590	244,689	16.8
Sør-Trøndelag	17,830	272,567	15.4
Nord-Trøndelag	20,777	128,444	6.2
Nordland	36,074	236,825	6.6
Troms	24,884	152,741	6.1
Finnmark	45,757	73,074	1.6
Total	**304,280**	**4,606,363**	**15.1**

* Excluding inland waters, totalling 19,522 sq km.

NORWAY

PRINCIPAL TOWNS
(population of urban settlements at 1 January 2004)

Oslo (capital)	794,356	Tønsberg	44,343
Bergen	211,326	Ålesund	43,655
Stavanger/Sandnes*	169,455	Haugesund	39,987
Trondheim	144,434	Sandefjord	39,069
Fredrikstad/Sarpsborg*	95,994	Moss	34,323
Drammen	89,500	Bodø	33,134
Porsgrunn/Skien*	84,657	Arendal	30,860
Kristiansand	63,020	Hamar	28,296
Tromsø	51,352	Larvik	22,845

* From 1 January 1999 continuous urban settlements are merged to one settlement.

BIRTHS, MARRIAGES AND DEATHS

	Registered live births		Registered marriages*		Registered deaths†	
	Number	Rate (per 1,000)	Number	Rate (per 1,000)	Number	Rate (per 1,000)
1997	59,801	13.6	22,933	5.2	44,595	10.1
1998	58,352	13.2	22,349	5.0	44,112	10.0
1999	59,298	13.3	23,455	5.3	45,170	10.1
2000	59,234	13.2	25,356	5.6	44,002	9.8
2001	56,696	12.6	22,967	5.1	43,981	9.7
2002	55,434	12.3	24,069	5.3	44,465	9.8
2003	56,458	12.4	22,361	4.9	42,478	9.3
2004	56,951	12.4	22,354	4.9	41,200	8.9

* Where bridegroom is resident in Norway.
† Including deaths of residents temporarily abroad.

Expectation of life (WHO estimates, years at birth): 79 (males 77; females 82) in 2003 (Source: WHO, *World Health Report*).

IMMIGRATION AND EMIGRATION

	2002	2003	2004
Immigrants	40,122	35,957	36,482
Emigrants	22,948	24,672	23,271

ECONOMICALLY ACTIVE POPULATION
('000 persons aged 16 to 74 years)*

	2002	2003	2004
Agriculture, hunting and forestry	69	67	63
Fishing	17	16	16
Oil and gas extraction	31	29	30
Mining and quarrying	4	3	3
Manufacturing	289	278	266
Electricity, gas and water	14	17	16
Construction	157	159	160
Trade, restaurants and hotels	401	407	415
Transport and communications	161	149	149
Financing, insurance, real estate and business services	272	272	271
Public administration and defence	145	149	144
Education	188	186	195
Health and social work	440	440	449
Other services	95	94	98
Activities not specified	3	2	1
Total employed	2,286	2,269	2,276
Unemployed	92	107	106
Total labour force	2,378	2,375	2,382
Males	1,262	1,259	1,263
Females	1,116	1,116	1,119

* Figures are annual averages, based on quarterly sample surveys.

Health and Welfare

KEY INDICATORS

Total fertility rate (children per woman, 2003)	1.8
Under-5 mortality rate (per 1,000 live births, 2004)	4
HIV/AIDS (% of persons aged 15–49, 2003)	0.1
Physicians (per 1,000 head, 2001)	3.56
Hospital beds (per 1,000 head, 2000)	14.60
Health expenditure (2002): US $ per head (PPP)	3,409
Health expenditure (2002): % of GDP	9.6
Health expenditure (2002): public (% of total)	83.5
Access to water (% of persons, 2002)	100
Human Development Index (2003): ranking	1
Human Development Index (2003): value	0.963

For sources and definitions, see explanatory note on p. vi.

Agriculture

PRINCIPAL CROPS
('000 metric tons)*

	2002	2003	2004
Wheat	261.5	349.2	409.5
Barley	592.4	585.0	619.3
Rye	9.1	18.1	37.4
Oats	278.5	333.4	359.2
Potatoes	360.8	339.7	349.8
Rapeseed	17.8	11.3	11.0
Cabbages	17.3	16.9	16.1
Tomatoes	9.4	9.1	9.1
Cucumbers and gherkins	12.4	13.0†	13.0†
Green onions and shallots	19.5	17.0†	17.0†
Carrots	35.9	35.3	29.1
Other fresh vegetables	44.7	53.0†	53.6†
Apples	13.7	10.1	11.6

* Figures refer to holdings with at least 0.5 ha of agricultural area in use.
† FAO estimate.
Source: FAO.

LIVESTOCK
('000 head)*

	2002	2003	2004
Horses	29.5	28.2	28.0†
Cattle	950.5	938.6	930.5
Sheep	2,423.9	2,421.7	2,416.3
Goats	64.8	64.9	64.7
Pigs	453.0	497.0	505.4
Chickens	3,329	3,472	3,535

* Figures refer to holdings with at least 0.5 ha of agricultural area in use.
† FAO estimate.
Source: FAO.

NORWAY

LIVESTOCK PRODUCTS
('000 metric tons)

	2002	2003	2004
Beef and veal	85.1	84.8	86.1
Mutton and lamb	25.1	24.5	26.2
Pig meat	104.0	106.0	113.5
Poultry meat	46.0	49.4	54.7
Cows' milk	1,659.9*	1,729.0*	1,700.0†
Goats' milk	21.6	21.5	21.7
Butter	15.2	14.3	12.9*
Cheese	83.2	83.2	83.3
Hen eggs	48.2	50.6	52.8
Honey	1.9	1.5	1.3
Wool: greasy	5.2	5.1	5.2
Wool: scoured	3.4	3.2	3.6†
Cattle hides (fresh)†	8.6	8.3	8.3
Sheepskins (fresh)†	7.2	7.3	7.6

* Unofficial figure.
† FAO estimate(s).
Source: FAO.

Forestry

ROUNDWOOD REMOVALS
('000 cubic metres, excl. bark)

	2002	2003	2004
Sawlogs, veneer logs and logs for sleepers	4,141.7	3,937.9	4,160.0
Pulpwood	3,294.8	3,025.2	3,360.0
Other industrial wood	26.4	26.1	31.0
Fuel wood	1,188.7	1,309.0	1,229.0
Total	8,651.6	8,298.2	8,780.0

Source: FAO.

SAWNWOOD PRODUCTION
('000 cubic metres, incl. railway sleepers)

	2002	2003	2004
Coniferous (softwood)	2,200	2,160	2,203
Broadleaved (hardwood)	25	26	27
Total	2,225	2,186	2,230

Source: FAO.

Fishing

('000 metric tons, live weight)

	2001	2002	2003
Capture	2,687.0	2,740.4	2,550.2
Atlantic cod	209.0	228.1	217.5
Saithe (Pollock)	169.6	203.1	212.2
Blue whiting (Poutassou)	573.7	557.7	851.4
Sandeels (Sandlances)	187.5	176.0	29.6
Capelin	482.8	522.3	249.1
Atlantic herring	581.2	573.8	563.0
Atlantic mackerel	180.8	184.4	163.4
Aquaculture	510.7	551.3	582.0
Atlantic salmon	436.1	462.5	507.4
Total catch	3,197.7	3,291.7	3,132.2

Note: Figures exclude aquatic plants ('000 metric tons, wet weight, capture): 175.9 in 2001; 182.6 in 2002; 153.2 in 2003. Also excluded are aquatic mammals, recorded by number rather than by weight. The number of minke whales caught was: 552 in 2001; 634 in 2002; 647 in 2003. The number of harp seals caught was: 8,192 in 2001; 3,580 in 2002; 7,575 in 2003. The number of hooded seals caught was: 3,820 in 2001; 7,116 in 2002; 5,295 in 2003.

Source: FAO.

Mining

('000 metric tons, unless otherwise indicated, estimates)

	2002	2003	2004
Coal (all grades)	310	300	300
Crude petroleum (million barrels)	1,093	1,041	1,024
Iron ore*	350†	340	408
Natural gas (million cu m)‡	65,501	73,124	78,465

* Metal content of ore.
† Estimate.
‡ Marketed natural gas reported as total methane sales.
Source: US Geological Survey.

Industry

SELECTED PRODUCTS
('000 metric tons, unless otherwise indicated)

	2000	2001	2002
Margarine	52	49	50
Mechanical wood pulp (dry weight)	1,717	1,668	1,616
Chemical wood pulp (dry weight)	622	670	645
Particle board ('000 cu m)	433	428	368
Paper and paperboard	2,300	2,220	2,114
Woven woollen fabrics (metric tons)	575*	649*	n.a.
Motor spirit (petrol, '000 barrels)*	26,000	26,000	26,000
Kerosene ('000 barrels)*	9,000	9,000	9,000
Naphthas ('000 barrels)*	26,000	27,000	27,000
Gas-diesel (distillate fuel) oil ('000 barrels)*	46,000	46,000	46,000
Residual fuel oil ('000 barrels)*	12,000	12,000	12,000
Cement	1,851	1,870*	1,850*
Ferro-silicon (75% basis)*	460	450	390
Other ferro-alloys*	730	670	650
Crude steel	620	635	694
Nickel (refined): primary	58.7	68.2	68.5
Copper (refined): primary and secondary	27.0*	26.7	30.5
Aluminium (refined): primary	1,025.7	1,067.6	1,095.5
Aluminium (refined): secondary	254.6	223.9	271.0
Zinc (refined): primary	125.8	129.3	137.3
Electricity (million kWh)†	143,040	128,646	n.a.

* Estimated or unofficial figure(s).
† Including production in Svalbard and Jan Mayen.
Sources: UN, *Industrial Commodity Statistics Yearbook*; US Geological Survey.

Finance

CURRENCY AND EXCHANGE RATES

Monetary Units
100 øre = 1 Norwegian krone (plural: kroner).

Sterling, Dollar and Euro Equivalents (30 December)
£1 sterling = 11.6573 kroner;
US $1 = 6.7700 kroner;
€1 = 7.9866 kroner;
1,000 Norwegian kroner = £85.78 = $147.71 = €125.21.

Average Exchange Rate (kroner per US $)
2003 7.0802
2004 6.7408
2005 6.4425

NORWAY

Statistical Survey

GENERAL BUDGET
(million kroner)*

Revenue	2002	2003	2004
Taxation†	663,811	677,661	761,956
Taxes on income, profits and wealth†	302,182	309,317	370,851
Social security contributions	151,098	155,507	163,676
Value-added tax and investment levy	135,284	135,755	227,429
Property income	82,278	83,730	87,159
Interest and dividends	80,691	81,705	84,790
Other current transfers	64,366	72,831	85,374
Fines and penalties, etc.	833	1,144	1,364
From public enterprises	58,752	63,468	77,888
Operating surplus	4,478	4,265	3,291
Capital transfers†	1,243	1,532	1,660
Total	816,176	840,019	939,441

Expenditure‡	2002	2003	2004
General public services	73,717	75,336	70,709
Defence	30,121	29,909	29,777
Public order and safety	15,487	15,829	15,983
Economic affairs	63,213	61,976	60,709
Environmental protection	4,194	4,456	5,185
Housing and community amenities	2,485	6,406	6,424
Health	112,872	121,721	125,952
Recreation, culture and religion	16,639	17,621	18,598
Education	90,554	101,000	102,479
Social protection	262,826	283,980	300,182
Unallocated	3,179	3,036	3,194
Total	675,287	721,270	739,192
Current	656,832	699,094	718,649
Capital	18,456	22,176	20,544

* Figures represent a consolidation of the operations of the central Government and local administrations (counties and municipalities), including social security funds and extrabudgetary accounts.
† Inheritance and gift taxes are excluded from tax revenue and are treated as capital transfers.
‡ Excluding lending minus repayments.

INTERNATIONAL RESERVES
(US $ million at 31 December)

	2003	2004	2005
Gold (national valuation)	490.6	—	—
IMF special drawing rights	335.0	360.8	307.1
Reserve position in IMF	994.9	868.5	301.5
Foreign exchange	35,890.2	43,078.2	46,377.4
Total	37,710.7	44,307.5	46,986.0

Source: IMF, *International Financial Statistics*.

MONEY SUPPLY
(million kroner at 31 December)

	2001	2002	2003
Currency outside banks	42,100	40,410	41,690
Demand deposits at commercial and savings banks	616,023	671,850	706,250
Total money (incl. others)	658,123	712,260	747,940

Demand deposits at commercial and savings banks (million kroner at 31 December): 700,070 in 2004; 791,390 in 2005.

Source: IMF, *International Financial Statistics*.

COST OF LIVING
(Consumer Price Index; base: 1998 = 100)

	2003	2004	2005
Food	104.8	106.7	108.4
Alcoholic beverages and tobacco	114.6	123.6	126.7
Housing and maintenance	129.7	130.0	132.2
Fuel and power	174.3	161.5	158.8
Clothing and footwear	79.6	74.1	70.7
Furnishings and household equipment	102.2	100.4	100.0
Health	120.8	126.3	129.8
Transport	113.9	115.8	120.8
Communications	86.2	82.8	82.2
Recreation and culture	105.6	105.7	106.5
Education	135.0	141.5	143.4
Restaurants and hotels	119.6	122.3	124.3
Other goods and services	118.9	119.9	118.9
All items (incl. others)	112.8	113.3	115.1

NATIONAL ACCOUNTS
(million kroner at current prices)

National Income and Product

	2003	2004*	2005*
Compensation of employees	729,502	764,667	800,574
Operating surplus	447,832	527,214	651,373
Domestic factor incomes	1,177,334	1,291,881	1,451,947
Consumption of fixed capital	224,306	235,035	246,996
Gross domestic product (GDP) at factor cost	1,401,640	1,526,916	1,698,943
Indirect taxes	212,838	227,430	244,779
Less Subsidies	37,732	37,414	37,661
GDP in purchasers' values	1,576,746	1,716,932	1,906,061
Factor income received from abroad	89,202	94,422	114,686
Less Factor income paid abroad	75,610	86,958	107,306
Gross national product (GNP)	1,590,338	1,724,396	1,913,441
Less Consumption of fixed capital	224,306	235,035	246,996
National income in market prices	1,366,032	1,489,361	1,666,445
Other current transfers received from abroad	13,972	16,510	17,148
Less Other current transfers paid abroad	34,917	33,796	36,854
National disposable income	1,345,087	1,472,075	1,646,740

* Figures are provisional.

Expenditure on the Gross Domestic Product

	2003	2004*	2005*
Government final consumption expenditure	354,220	370,787	387,889
Private final consumption expenditure	720,025	760,921	799,236
Increase in stocks	14,277	32,552	30,848
Gross fixed capital formation	276,609	309,841	356,065
Total domestic expenditure	1,365,131	1,474,101	1,574,037
Exports of goods and services	637,373	732,444	862,220
Less Imports of goods and services	425,758	489,612	530,195
GDP in purchasers' values	1,576,745	1,716,933	1,906,062

* Figures are provisional.

NORWAY

Statistical Survey

Gross Domestic Product by Economic Activity

	2003	2004*	2005*
Agriculture, hunting and forestry	15,496	15,930	16,365
Fishing and fish farming	6,538	8,091	11,047
Petroleum and gas extraction	276,298	338,100	447,167
Other mining and quarrying	3,045	3,648	3,540
Manufacturing	153,656	162,273	164,515
Electricity, gas and water	38,215	36,106	40,022
Construction	62,432	68,226	75,714
Wholesale and retail trade; repair of motor vehicles	126,329	134,897	144,087
Hotels and restaurants	20,188	20,534	21,166
Transport, storage and communications†	124,928	128,909	131,478
Financing, insurance, real estate and business services	195,755	208,728	225,586
Private services in households	81,630	85,414	89,844
Public administration and defence	71,385	74,555	77,368
Education	70,018	72,841	76,574
Health and social work	131,856	140,456	149,114
Other social and personal services	49,498	51,984	54,816
Sub-total	1,427,267	1,550,692	1,728,404
Value-added tax and investment levy	135,755	145,645	157,668
Other taxes on products (net)	53,912	59,328	63,516
Less Financial intermediation services indirectly measured	40,189	41,690	42,806
Statistical discrepancy	—	2,958	−719
GDP in purchasers' values	1,576,745	1,716,933	1,906,062

* Figures are provisional.
† Including transportation of petroleum and gas by pipeline.

BALANCE OF PAYMENTS
(US $ million)

	2002	2003	2004
Exports of goods f.o.b.	59,616	69,073	82,993
Imports of goods f.o.b.	−35,277	−40,803	−49,418
Trade balance	24,340	28,269	33,576
Exports of services	18,689	21,666	26,111
Imports of services	−16,910	−19,938	−24,139
Balance on goods and services	26,119	29,998	35,547
Other income received	9,322	10,548	12,352
Other income paid	−8,690	−9,260	−10,809
Balance on goods, services and income	26,752	31,286	37,090
Current transfers received	1,810	2,008	2,408
Current transfers paid	−4,089	−4,968	−5,054
Current balance	24,473	28,326	34,445
Capital account (net)	−191	678	−154
Direct investment abroad	−3,850	−2,310	−1,948
Direct investment from abroad	502	2,055	502
Portfolio investment assets	−22,987	−19,287	−38,134
Portfolio investment liabilities	4,675	13,123	9,435
Financial derivatives assets	−4,270	35	−636
Financial derivatives liabilities	−556	−161	501
Other investment assets	−12,474	−25,185	−17,027
Other investment liabilities	29,723	12,358	26,562
Net errors and omissions	−9,320	−9,286	−8,318
Overall balance	5,723	346	5,227

Source: IMF, *International Financial Statistics*.

OFFICIAL ASSISTANCE TO DEVELOPING COUNTRIES
(million kroner)

	2001	2002	2003
Bilateral assistance	7,901	8,493	9,646
Technical assistance	1,140	1,551	1,878
Investments	532	412	378
Sector-related project and programme aid	3,510	3,496	3,310
Non-sector related project and programme aid	2,357	3,132	3,983
Associated financing	9	69	—
Loan assistance	—	—	—
Norfund	61	57	96
Multilateral assistance	3,374	4,400	4,107
Contributions to multilateral organizations	273	—	—
Humanitarian relief work	273	—	—
Administration	595	652	704
Total official development assistance	11,870	13,545	14,457

2004 (million kroner): Bilateral assistance 6,939; Multi-bi assistance 2,622; Multilateral assistance 4,463; Administration 793; Total official development assistance 14,817.

External Trade

(Note: Figures include all ships bought and sold but exclude trade in military supplies under defence agreements.)

PRINCIPAL COMMODITIES
(distribution by SITC, million kroner)

Imports c.i.f.*	2002	2003	2004
Food and live animals	16,003	16,093	17,611
Crude materials (inedible) except fuels	17,967	19,473	23,634
Metalliferous ores and metal scrap	10,047	11,241	14,834
Mineral fuels, lubricants, etc. (incl. electric current)	10,096	13,146	14,723
Petroleum, petroleum products, etc.	7,481	7,805	9,186
Chemicals and related products	27,122	28,624	31,377
Basic manufactures	43,213	45,036	55,815
Metal manufactures	9,728	10,783	13,499
Machinery and transport equipment	111,860	109,281	126,508
Machinery specialized for particular industries	9,589	9,895	11,826
General industrial machinery, equipment and parts	14,156	14,700	15,306
Office machines and automatic data-processing equipment	13,504	13,169	15,458
Automatic data-processing machines and units	7,753	7,806	9,544
Telecommunications and sound equipment	10,296	10,909	13,846
Telecommunications equipment and parts	6,972	7,304	9,486
Other electrical machinery, apparatus, etc.	14,726	14,948	17,279
Road vehicles and parts†	25,424	27,326	34,366
Passenger motor cars (excl. buses)	14,178	14,575	19,258
Other transport equipment†	17,387	12,102	11,362
Ships exceeding 100 grt	2,818	5,873	5,221
Miscellaneous manufactured articles	45,526	46,963	51,308
Clothing and accessories (excl. footwear)	10,787	10,962	11,452
Total (incl. others)	276,433	283,269	325,994

* Equipment imported directly to the Norwegian sector of the continental shelf is excluded.
† Excluding tyres, engines and electrical parts.

NORWAY

Exports f.o.b.	2002	2003	2004
Food and live animals	30,260	27,819	30,010
Fish and fish preparations*	27,387	25,117	27,281
Mineral fuels, lubricants, etc.			
(incl. electric current)	287,461	296,322	353,025
Petroleum, petroleum products, etc.	217,882	222,927	266,830
Crude petroleum	204,972	206,280	247,421
Gas (natural and manufactured)	66,256	70,875	83,905
Natural gas	59,409	62,237	74,016
Chemicals and related products	25,563	26,726	30,104
Basic manufactures	50,079	53,541	66,187
Non-ferrous metals	26,226	29,408	35,280
Aluminium	18,698	20,660	23,770
Machinery and transport equipment	55,747	54,893	48,900
Transport equipment†	21,939	22,393	n.a.
Miscellaneous manufactured articles	14,226	14,205	14,896
Total (incl. others)	472,953	482,933	553,263

* Including crustaceans and molluscs.
† Excluding tyres, engines and electrical parts.

PRINCIPAL TRADING PARTNERS
(million kroner)

Imports c.i.f.	2002	2003	2004
Belgium	5,614.9	5,792.4	7,796.8
Canada	5,701.8	5,730.6	7,622.5
China, People's Repub.	14,679.5	12,397.4	16,180.6
Denmark	21,785.0	22,247.9	23,915.5
Finland	9,116.8	9,150.1	12,991.4
France	12,888.0	12,289.9	13,659.9
Germany	36,095.7	37,491.6	44,105.5
Ireland	3,974.1	3,973.2	4,669.0
Italy	10,652.9	11,213.2	11,483.8
Japan	8,465.7	10,195.9	11,039.5
Korea, Republic	1,700.4	3,199.1	3,023.4
Netherlands	12,857.9	12,681.6	14,296.0
Poland	3,470.3	3,785.3	5,146.0
Russia	5,808.0	5,856.2	7,717.6
Spain	4,335.6	4,481.4	5,621.9
Sweden	42,443.4	45,481.4	51,100.8
Switzerland	3,437.6	3,225.4	3,314.6
Taiwan	2,761.8	2,774.0	3,317.5
United Kingdom	20,127.4	20,287.6	21,291.3
USA	16,906.2	14,547.4	15,815.3
Total (incl. others)	276,432.5	283,269.1	325,994.2

Exports f.o.b.	2002	2003	2004
Belgium	14,241.8	13,019.4	13,978.8
Canada	17,266.4	17,649.6	21,123.5
China, People's Repub.	7,388.0	6,091.4	6,132.1
Denmark	18,997.2	18,496.0	20,382.6
Finland	9,027.4	8,299.7	8,289.3
France	39,971.8	39,541.1	48,522.2
Germany	59,982.5	62,872.0	72,784.5
Ireland	5,841.4	3,801.0	7,355.7
Italy	17,733.4	17,020.1	16,035.8
Japan	8,726.2	6,869.5	6,860.7
Korea, Republic	4,758.0	3,521.3	4,877.4
Netherlands	45,221.2	46,383.6	56,192.2
Spain	7,552.0	11,523.9	15,356.3
Sweden	35,326.6	35,684.8	37,259.2
United Kingdom	91,334.6	102,602.2	125,081.3
USA	41,179.2	41,659.1	42,326.0
Total (incl. others)	472,953.3	482,933.0	533,262.7

Transport

STATE RAILWAYS
(traffic)

	1999	2000	2001
Passengers carried ('000)	50,019	50,773	49,396
Goods carried ('000 metric tons)	8,229	7,959	8,190
Passenger-kilometres (million)	2,668	2,635	2,536
Freight ton-kilometres (million)	2,456	2,399	2,451

2002: Passenger-kilometres (million) 2,477; Net ton-kilometres (million) 3,019 (Source: UN, *Statistical Yearbook*).

ROAD TRAFFIC
(motor vehicles registered at 31 December)

	2002	2003	2004
Passenger cars (incl. station wagons and ambulances)	1,899,767	1,933,660	1,977,922
Buses	34,110	32,374	30,592
Vans	258,133	268,326	284,029
Combined vehicles	95,453	90,600	85,149
Goods vehicles, etc.	77,442	79,356	80,623
Tractors and special-purpose vehicles	234,991	238,726	237,812
Motorcycles	94,645	98,800	103,716
Snow scooters	52,174	53,599	54,362
Mopeds	130,528	140,796	144,855

SHIPPING

Merchant Fleet
(registered at 31 December)

	2002	2003	2004
Number of vessels	2,299	2,253	2,173
Total displacement ('000 grt)	22,194.5	20,509.3	18,936.2

Note: Figures include vessels on the Norwegian International Ship Register.
Source: Lloyd's Register-Fairplay, *World Fleet Statistics*.

International Sea-borne Freight Traffic*
('000 metric tons)

	1998	1999	2000
Goods loaded	154,116	151,116	160,080
Goods unloaded	27,264	25,788	23,400

* Figures exclude transit traffic (other than Swedish iron ore), packing and re-export.

Source: UN, *Monthly Bulletin of Statistics*.

CIVIL AVIATION
(traffic on scheduled services)*

	1999	2000	2001
Kilometres flown (million)	151	149	149
Passengers carried ('000)	15,020	15,182	14,556
Passenger-kilometres (million)	9,874	10,367	10,461
Total ton-kilometres (million)	1,154	1,218	1,224

* Including an apportionment (2/7) of the international services of Scandinavian Airlines System (SAS), operated jointly with Denmark and Sweden.

Source: UN, *Statistical Yearbook*.

Tourism

VISITOR ARRIVALS BY COUNTRY OF ORIGIN*

	2001	2002	2003
Denmark	776,811	736,430	617,141
Finland	69,286	69,899	60,315
France	230,055	229,600	220,013
Germany	814,352	767,787	773,724
Italy	122,126	130,396	142,275
Japan	167,483	147,048	112,559
Netherlands	270,452	280,081	283,355
Spain	171,612	175,803	180,476
Sweden	585,433	549,930	475,234
United Kingdom	516,625	544,693	516,355
USA	381,837	356,227	298,081
Total (incl. others)	4,815,439	4,705,537	4,374,657

* Non-resident staying in all types of accommodation establishments.

Tourism receipts (US $ million, incl. passenger transport): 2,380 in 2001; 2,663 in 2002; 3,082 in 2003.

Source: World Tourism Organization.

Communications Media

	2002	2003	2004
Telephones ('000 main lines in use)	3,343	3,268	2,228*
Mobile cellular telephones ('000 subscribers)	3,840.4	4,163.4	n.a.
Personal computers ('000 in use)	2,405	n.a.	2,630
Internet users ('000)	1,399	1,583	1,792

* Estimate.
Source: International Telecommunication Union.

Television receivers (2000): 3,000,000 in use.
Radio receivers (1997): 4,030,000 in use*.
Books published (1999): 4,985 titles†.
Daily newspapers (2002): 61; net circulation ('000 copies) 2,201‡.

* Source: UNESCO, *Statistical Yearbook*.
† Source: UN, *Statistical Yearbook*.
‡ Issued at least six times a week.

Education

(incl. Svalbard, 1 October 2003)

	Institutions	Teachers*	Students
Pre-primary	5,924	58,422†	205,172
Primary and lower secondary	3,209	65,376	617,577
Upper secondary	462	26,618	218,089
Colleges of higher education	59	6,313	130,148
Universities and their equivalent	11	9,553	79,611

* Full-time.
† Of the total, 19,422 were trained as pre-school teachers.

Directory

The Constitution

The Constitution was promulgated on 17 May 1814.

According to the Constitution, Norway is a 'free, independent, indivisible, inalienable Kingdom'; its form of government a 'limited and hereditary monarchy'. (In May 1990 the law of succession, which stipulated that a male heir should have precedence in succeeding to the throne, was amended to permit men and women an equal right to the throne. The previous law would still apply to those born before 1990.) The Evangelical Lutheran Church is the established religion of the State.

Executive power is vested in the King, legislative power in the Storting (parliament), and judicial power in the Judicature.

EXECUTIVE POWER

The King exercises his power through the Statsråd (Council of State). The Statsråd is composed of a Prime Minister and not fewer than seven other Councillors of State, all at least 30 years of age. The business to be dealt with in the Statsråd is prepared by the various executive Ministries, each with a Councillor of State at its head. These executive departments conduct the administrative work of the country.

The Government submits the budget estimates and introduces bills in the Storting.

Formally, the King appoints the Government, but since the introduction of the parliamentary system in 1884 it is the practice for him to act in accordance with the will of the Storting.

LEGISLATIVE POWER

The Storting is elected quadrennially by universal suffrage. All Norwegian citizens aged 18 years and over are eligible to vote and every qualified voter who has resided in Norway for at least 10 years is eligible to stand for election. In 2005 the Storting was expanded from 165 seats to 169, 150 of which are elected directly, with the remaining 19 (one for each constituency) being allocated by proportional representation among parties receiving a minimum of 4% of the votes cast. The members of the Storting elect one-quarter of their own body to constitute the Lagting (upper house); the other three-quarters compose the Odelsting (lower house). All bills must first be introduced in the Odelsting, either by the Government through a Councillor of State or by a member of the Odelsting. Should the bill be passed by the Odelsting, it is sent to the Lagting, which may adopt it or return it with amendments. If a bill be passed twice by the Odelsting and rejected on both occasions by the Lagting, it is submitted to the entire Storting and decided by a two-thirds' majority. When a bill has thus been passed, it must receive royal assent in the Statsråd.

Bills for the revision of the Constitution must be introduced in the first, second or third session after a new election. However, only the Storting, after the next election, has the power to decide whether the proposed alteration should be adopted. Bills relating to the Constitution are dealt with only by the united Storting. For the adoption of a bill of this nature, a two-thirds' majority is required, and the measure becomes law without royal assent.

The Storting votes all state expenditure and determines state revenue, taxes, customs tariffs and other duties; the Odelsting exercises control over government administration, government appointments and so forth.

The Storting prepares its business through its committees and settles such business, with the exception of bills, in plenum. The Councillors of State may attend the Storting, having the right of speech but not of voting.

The Storting determines the duration of each session. It is opened and prorogued by the King each year. The Storting cannot be dissolved either by the King or by its own resolution until the expiry of the quadrennial period for which it has been elected.

Note: In September 1989 the Sámi (Lapps) of northern Norway elected 39 representatives to a new Sameting (Consultative Assembly). The Sameting is elected quadrennially and is based in the town of Karasjok, in Finnmark.

The Government

HEAD OF STATE

Sovereign: King HARALD V (succeeded to the throne 17 January 1991; sworn in 21 January 1991).

NORWAY

COUNCIL OF STATE
(Statsråd)
(April 2006)

A majority Government, comprising Det norske Arbeiderparti (DnA), the Sosialistisk Venstreparti (SV) and the Senterpartiet (Sp).

Prime Minister: JENS STOLTENBERG (DnA).
Minister of Finance: KRISTIN HALVORSEN (SV).
Minister of Local Government and Regional Development: ÅSLAUG MARIE HAGA (Sp).
Minister of Foreign Affairs: JONAS GAHR STØRE (DnA).
Minister of Defence: ANNE-GRETE STRØM-ERICHSEN (DnA).
Minister of the Environment: HELEN ODDVEIG BJØRNØY (SV).
Minister of Petroleum and Energy: ODD ROGER ENOKSEN (Sp).
Minister of Development Co-operation: ERIK SOLHEIM (SV).
Minister of Trade and Industry: ODD ERIKSEN (DnA).
Minister of Transport and Communications: LIV SIGNE NAVARSETE (Sp).
Minister of Education and Research: ØYSTEIN KÅRE DJUPEDAL (SV).
Minister of Labour and Social Inclusion: BJARNE HÅKON HANSSEN (DnA).
Minister of Justice: KNUT STORBERGET (DnA).
Minister of Children and Equality: KARITA BEKKEMELLEM (DnA).
Minister of Culture and Church Affairs: TROND GISKE (DnA).
Minister of Health and Care Services: SYLVIA KRISTIN BRUSTAD (DnA).
Minister of Government Administration and Reform: HEIDI GRANDE RØYS (SV).
Minister of Agriculture and Food: TERJE RILS-JOHANSEN (Sp).
Minister of Fisheries and Coastal Affairs: HELGA PEDERSEN (DnA).

MINISTRIES

Office of the Prime Minister: Akersgt. 42, POB 8001 Dep., 0030 Oslo; tel. 22-24-90-90; fax 22-24-95-00; e-mail postmottak@smk.dep.no; internet odin.dep.no/smk.

Ministry of Agriculture and Food: Akersgt. 59 (R5), POB 8007 Dep., 0030 Oslo; tel. 22-24-90-90; fax 22-24-95-55; e-mail postmottak@lmd.dep.no; internet odin.dep.no/lmd.

Ministry of Children and Equality: Akersgt. 59, POB 8036 Dep., 0030 Oslo; tel. 22-24-90-90; fax 22-24-95-15; e-mail postmottak@bld.dep.no; internet odin.dep.no/bld.

Ministry of Culture and Church Affairs: Akersgt. 59, POB 8030 Dep., 0030 Oslo; tel. 22-24-90-90; fax 22-24-95-50; e-mail postmottak@kkd.dip.no; internet odin.dep.no/kkd.

Ministry of Defence: Myntgt. 1, POB 8126 Dep., 0032 Oslo; tel. 23-09-80-00; fax 23-09-60-51; e-mail postmottak@fd.dep.no; internet www.mod.no.

Ministry of Education and Research: Akersgt. 44, POB 8119 Dep., 0032 Oslo; tel. 22-24-90-90; fax 22-24-95-40; e-mail postmottak@ufd.dep.no; internet odin.dep.no/ufd.

Ministry of the Environment: Myntgt. 2, POB 8013 Dep., 0030 Oslo; tel. 22-24-90-90; fax 22-24-95-60; e-mail postmottak@md.dep.no; internet odin.dep.no/md.

Ministry of Finance: Akersgt. 40, POB 8008 Dep., 0030 Oslo; tel. 22-24-90-90; fax 22-24-95-10; e-mail postmottak@finans.dep.no; internet odin.dep.no/fin.

Ministry of Fisheries and Coastal Affairs: Grubbegt. 1, POB 8118 Dep., 0032 Oslo; tel. 22-24-90-90; fax 22-24-95-85; e-mail postmottak@fkd.dep.no; internet odin.dep.no/fkd.

Ministry of Foreign Affairs: 7 juni pl. 1, POB 8114 Dep., 0032 Oslo; tel. 22-24-36-00; fax 22-24-95-80; e-mail post@mfa.no; internet odin.dep.no/ud; also incl. Ministry of International Development.

Ministry of Government Administration and Reform: Akersgt. 59, POB 8004 Dep., 0030 Oslo; tel. 22-24-46-60; fax 22-24-95-16; e-mail postmottak@mod.dep.no; internet odin.dep.no/mod.

Ministry of Health and Care Services: Einar Gerhardsens pl. 3, POB 8011 Dep., 0030 Oslo; tel. 22-24-90-90; fax 22-24-95-75; e-mail postmottak@hod.dep.no; internet odin.dep.no/hod.

Ministry of Justice and the Police: Akersgt. 42, POB 8005 Dep., 0030 Oslo; tel. 22-24-90-90; fax 22-24-95-30; e-mail postmottak@jd.dep.no; internet odin.dep.no/jd.

Ministry of Labour and Social Inclusion: Einar Gerhardsens pl. 3, POB 8019 Dep., 0030 Oslo; tel. 22-24-90-90; fax 22-24-95-65; e-mail postmottak@asd.dep.no; internet odin.dep.no/asd.

Ministry of Local Government and Regional Development: Akersgt. 59, POB 8112 Dep., 0032 Oslo; tel. 22-24-90-90; fax 22-24-95-45; e-mail postmottak@krd.dep.no; internet odin.dep.no/krd.

Ministry of Petroleum and Energy: Einar Gerhardsens pl. 1, POB 8148 Dep., 0033 Oslo; tel. 22-24-90-90; fax 22-24-95-65; e-mail postmottak@oed.dep.no; internet odin.dep.no/oed.

Ministry of Trade and Industry: Einar Gerhardsens pl. 1, POB 8014 Dep., 0030 Oslo; tel. 22-24-90-90; fax 22-24-95-65; e-mail postmottak@nhd.dep.no; internet odin.dep.no/nhd.

Ministry of Transport and Communications: Akersgt. 59, POB 8010 Dep., 0030 Oslo; tel. 22-24-90-90; fax 22-24-95-70; e-mail postmottak@sd.dep.no; internet odin.dep.no/sd.

Legislature

STORTING

Stortinget

Karl Johansgt. 22, 0026 Oslo; tel. 23-31-30-50; fax 23-31-38-50; e-mail stortinget.postmottak@stortinget.no; internet www.stortinget.no.

President: THORBJØRN JAGLAND (DnA).
Vice-President: CARL I. HAGEN (FrP).

The Storting has 169 members, one-quarter of whom sit as the upper house, the Lagting, and the rest as the lower house, the Odelsting.

President of the Lagting: INGE LØNNING, (H).
Vice-President: JON LILLETUN (KrF).
President of the Odelsting: BERIT BRØRBY (DnA).
Vice-President: OLAV GUNNAR BALLO (SV).

General Election, 12 September 2005

Party	Votes	% of votes	Seats
Det norske Arbeiderparti (DnA)	862,671	32.69	61
Fremskrittspartiet (FrP)	582,014	22.05	38
Høyre (H)	372,046	14.10	23
Sosialistisk Venstreparti (SV)	233,049	8.83	15
Kristelig Folkeparti (KrF)	179,109	6.79	11
Senterpartiet (Sp)	171,036	6.48	11
Venstre (V)	156,101	5.92	10
Rød Valgallianse (RV)	32,364	1.23	—
Kystpartiet (KP)	21,947	0.83	—
Pensjonistpartiet (Pp)	13,568	0.51	—
Others	15,039	0.57	—
Total	2,638,944	100.00	169

Political Organizations

Arbeidernes Kommunistparti (Workers' Communist Party): Ostarhausgt. 27, 0183 Oslo; tel. 22-98-90-60; fax 22-98-90-55; e-mail akp@akp.no; internet www.akp.no; f. 1973; mem. of Red Electoral Alliance (see below); Leader JORUN GULBRANDSEN.

Fremskrittspartiet (FrP) (Progress Party): Karl Johansgt. 25, 0159 Oslo; tel. 23-13-54-00; fax 23-13-54-01; internet www.frp.no; f. 1973; formerly Anders Lange's Party; anti-tax; favours privatization, the diminution of the welfare state and less immigration; Chair. SIV JENSEN; Sec.-Gen. GEIR MO.

FRIdemokratene (Free Democrats): POB 310 Sentrum, 0103 Oslo; tel. 22-84-45-46; e-mail fridem@online.no; internet www.fridemokratene.no.

Høyre (H) (Conservative): Stortingsgt. 20, POB 1536 Vika, 0117 Oslo; tel. 22-82-90-00; fax 22-82-90-80; e-mail hoyre@hoyre.no; internet www.hoyre.no; f. 1884; aims to promote economic growth and sound state finances, achieve a property-owning democracy, and to uphold democratic government, social security, private property, private initiative and personal liberty; 63,000 mems; Chair. ERNA SOLBERG; Dep. Chair. PER-KRISTIAN FOSS; Leader ODDVARD NILSEN; Sec.-Gen. TROND R. HOLE.

Internasjonale Sosialister (International Socialists): POB 9226 Grønland, 0134 Oslo; tel. 22-20-17-89; fax 22-20-35-70; e-mail intsos@intsos.no; internet www.intsos.no; f. 1985.

Kristelig Folkeparti (KrF) (Christian Democratic Party): Øvre Slottsgt. 18–20, POB 478 Sentrum, 0105 Oslo; tel. 23-10-28-00; fax 23-10-28-10; e-mail krf@krf.no; internet www.krf.no; f. 1933; aims to promote a democratic policy based on Christian outlook; Chair. DAGFINN HØYBRÅTEN; Sec. INGER HELENE VENAAS.

Kystpartiet (Coastal Party): Stortingsgt., POB 207, 0026 Oslo; tel. 23-31-31-63; fax 23-31-38-23; internet www.kystpartiet.no; Leader STEINAR BASTESEN.

Miljøpartiet de Grønne (Green Environmental Party): POB 2169, 7001 Trondheim; tel. 73-53-09-11; fax 73-53-05-15; e-mail gronne@gronne.no; internet www.gronne.no; f. 1988; Chief Officer TORE BERGUM.

Naturlovpartiet (Natural Law Party): 2610 Mesnali; tel. 62-36-31-30; fax 62-36-30-45; e-mail info@nlp.no; internet www.nlp.no; f. 1992; Leader ODD SVERRE LOSET.

Norges Kommunistiske Parti (Communist Party of Norway): POB 9288 Groenland, 0134 Oslo; Helgesensgt. 21, Oslo; tel. 22-71-57-58; fax 22-71-79-09; e-mail nkp@nkp.no; internet www.nkp.no; f. 1923; Chair. ZAFER GOEZET.

Det norske Arbeiderparti (DnA) (Norwegian Labour Party): Youngstorget 2A, POB 8743, 0028 Oslo; tel. 24-14-40-00; fax 24-14-40-01; e-mail dna@dna.no; internet www.dna.no; f. 1887; social democratic; 66,813 mems; Leader JENS STOLTENBERG; Gen. Sec. MARTIN KOLBERG.

Pensjonistpartiet (Pensioners' Party): Nordsetavern 410, 2618 Lillehammer; tel. 61-25-17-70; fax 61-25-06-67; e-mail mona@pensjonistpartiet.no; internet www.pensjonistpartiet.no; Leader GUNNAR BEKKEN.

Rød Valgallianse (Red Electoral Alliance): Osterhausgt. 27, 0183 Oslo; tel. 22-98-90-50; fax 22-98-90-55; e-mail rv@rv.no; internet www.rv.no; f. 1973; left-wing group; Leader TORSTEIN DAHLE.

Senterpartiet (Sp) (Centre Party): Kristian Augustsgt. 7B, 0130 Oslo; tel. 22-98-96-00; fax 22-98-96-10; e-mail epost@senterpartiet.no; internet www.senterpartiet.no; f. 1920 as the Bondepartiet (Agrarian Party), name changed 1959; advocates a decentralized society which will secure employment and diversified settlements in all parts of the country; opposes Norwegian membership of the EU; encourages the development of an ecologically balanced society; Leader ASLAUG MARIA HAGA; Sec.-Gen. DAGFINN SUNDSBØ.

Sosialistisk Venstreparti (SV) (Socialist Left Party): Akersgt. 35, 0158 Oslo; tel. 21-93-33-00; fax 21-93-33-01; e-mail post@sv.no; internet www.sv.no; f. 1975 as a fusion of the Socialist People's Party, the Democratic Socialists and other socialist forces united previously in the Socialist Electoral League; advocates non-alignment and socialism independent of international centres, based on workers' control, decentralized powers, gender equality and ecological principles; Chair. KRISTIN HALVORSEN.

Venstre (V) (Liberal): Møllergt. 16, 0179 Oslo; tel. 22-40-43-50; fax 22-40-43-51; e-mail venstre@venstre.no; internet www.venstre.no; f. 1884; in 1988 reunited with Det Liberale Folkepartiet (Liberal Democratic Party, f. 1972); advocates the promotion of national and democratic progress on the basis of the present system by gradual economic, social and cultural reforms; Leader LARS SPONHEIM; Sec.-Gen. TERJE BREIVIK.

Diplomatic Representation

EMBASSIES IN NORWAY

Afghanistan: 17 Kronprinsens Gt., 0251 Oslo; tel. 22-83-84-10; fax 22-83-84-11; e-mail info@afghanemb.com; Ambassador YAHYA MAROOFI.

Argentina: Drammensvn 39, 0244 Oslo; tel. 22-55-24-48; fax 22-44-16-41; e-mail enoru@online.no; Ambassador ORLANDO R. REBAGLIATI.

Austria: Thomas Heftyesgt. 19–21, 0244 Oslo; tel. 22-55-23-48; fax 22-55-43-61; e-mail oslo-ob@bmaa.gv.at; Ambassador Dr ANTON KOZUSNIK.

Belgium: Drammensvn 103D, 0244 Oslo; tel. 23-13-32-20; fax 22-44-38-08; e-mail oslo@diplobel.org; internet www.diplomatie.be/oslo; Ambassador FRANK RECKER.

Brazil: Sigurd Syrsgt. 4, 0244 Oslo; tel. 22-54-07-30; fax 22-44-39-64; e-mail brasil@brasil.no; internet www.brasil.no; Ambassador CESAR DE FARIA D. MOREIRA.

Bulgaria: Tidemandsgt. 11, 0244 Oslo; tel. 22-55-40-40; fax 22-55-40-24; e-mail bulgemb@online.no; internet www.bulgaria2net.com; Ambassador GANCHO GANEV.

Canada: Wergelandsvn 7, 0244 Oslo; tel. 22-99-53-00; fax 22-99-53-01; e-mail oslo@international.gc.ca; internet www.canada.no; Ambassador JILLIAN STIRK.

Chile: Meltzersgt. 5, 0244 Oslo; tel. 22-44-89-55; fax 22-44-24-21; e-mail embassy@chile.no; internet www.chile.no; Ambassador MANUEL ATRIA.

China, People's Republic: Tuengen allé 2B, Vinderen, 0244 Oslo; tel. 22-49-38-57; fax 22-92-19-78; Ambassador CHEN NAIQING.

Costa Rica: Skippergt. 33, 8th Floor, 0154 Oslo; tel. 22-42-58-23; fax 22-33-04-08; e-mail embassy@costarica.no; internet www.costarica.no; Ambassador XINNIA LUISA GUEVARA-CONTRERAS.

Croatia: Drammensvn 82, 0271 Oslo; tel. 22-44-22-33; fax 22-44-39-00; e-mail embassy@online.no; Ambassador JAGODA VUKUŠIĆ.

Czech Republic: Fritznersgt. 14, 0244 Oslo; tel. 22-12-10-31; fax 22-55-33-95; e-mail oslo@embassy.mzv.cz; internet www.mzv.cz/oslo; Ambassador Dr JAROSLAV HORÁK.

Denmark: Olav Kyrresgt. 7, 0244 Oslo; tel. 22-54-08-00; fax 22-55-46-34; e-mail oslamb@um.dk; internet www.amboslo.um.dk; Ambassador STEN LILHOLT.

Egypt: Drammensvn 90A, 0244 Oslo; tel. 23-08-42-00; fax 22-56-22-68; Ambassador NERMIN ALY MONIR MURAD.

Estonia: Parkvn 51A, 0244 Oslo; tel. 22-54-00-70; fax 22-54-00-71; e-mail embassy.oslo@mfa.ee; internet www.estemb.no; Ambassador JUHAN HARAVEE.

Finland: Thomas Heftyesgt. 1, 0244 Oslo; tel. 22-12-49-00; fax 22-12-49-49; e-mail sanomat.osl@formin.fi; internet www.finland.no; Ambassador PEKKA HUHTANIEMI.

France: Drammensvn 69, 0244 Oslo; tel. 23-28-46-00; fax 23-28-46-70; Ambassador HUBERT DE LA FORTELLE.

Germany: Oscarsgt. 45, 0244 Oslo; tel. 23-27-54-00; fax 22-44-76-72; e-mail info@oslo.diplo.de; internet www.oslo.diplo.de; Ambassador ROLAND MAUCH.

Greece: Nobelsgt. 45, 0244 Oslo; tel. 22-44-27-28; fax 22-56-00-72; e-mail gremb@online.no; Ambassador YANNIS BOUCAOURIS.

Guatemala: Oscarsgt. 59, 0258 Oslo; tel. 22-55-60-04; fax 22-55-60-47; e-mail guatemala@embajada.no; Ambassador LUIS RAUL ESTEVEZ.

Hungary: Sophus Liesgt. 3, 0244 Oslo; tel. 22-55-24-18; fax 22-44-76-93; e-mail huembosl@online.no; Ambassador GYÖRGY KRAUSZ.

Iceland: Stortingsgt. 30, 0244 Oslo; tel. 23-23-75-30; fax 22-83-07-04; e-mail icemb.oslo@mfa.is; internet www.iceland.org/no; Ambassador STEFÁN SKJALDARSON.

India: Niels Juelsgt. 30, 0244 Oslo; tel. 22-55-22-29; fax 22-44-07-20; e-mail india@online.no; Ambassador GOPALKRISHNA GANDHI.

Indonesia: Gange-Rolvsgt. 5, 0244 Oslo; tel. 22-44-11-21; fax 22-55-34-44; e-mail kbrioslo@online.no; Ambassador AMIRUDDIN NOOR.

Iran: Drammensvn 88E, 0244 Oslo; tel. 22-55-24-08; fax 22-55-49-19; Chargé d'affaires a.i. JAVAD KAJOUYAN FINI.

Ireland: Haakon VIIs gt. 1, 0244 Oslo; tel. 22-01-72-00; fax 22-01-72-01; e-mail hibernia@online.no; Ambassador THELMA MARIA DORAN.

Israel: POB 534 Skøyen, 0214 Oslo; tel. 21-01-95-00; fax 21-01-95-30; e-mail israel@oslo.mfa.gov.il; Ambassador MIRYAM SHOMRAT.

Italy: Inkognitogt. 7, 0244 Oslo; tel. 22-55-22-33; fax 22-44-34-36; e-mail ambitalia.oslo@online.no; internet www.ambitalia.no; Ambassador UBERTO PESTALOZZA.

Japan: Parkvn 33B, 0244 Oslo; tel. 22-55-10-11; fax 22-44-25-05; internet www.japan-embassy.no; Ambassador MASAO KAWAI.

Korea, Republic: Inkognitogt. 3, 0244, Oslo; tel. 22-55-20-18; fax 22-56-14-11; Ambassador PARK KYUNG-TAI.

Latvia: POB 3163 Elisenberg, 0208 Oslo; tel. 22-54-22-80; fax 22-54-64-26; e-mail embassy.norway@mfa.gov.lv; Ambassador MARIS KLISANS.

Lithuania: Drammensvn 40, 0244 Oslo; tel. 22-12-92-00; fax 22-12-92-01; e-mail litauens@online.no; internet no.urm.lt; Chargé d'affaires a.i. REGIMANTAS JABLONSKAS.

Morocco: Holtegt. 28, 0355 Oslo; tel. 23-19-71-50; fax 23-19-71-51; Ambassador BOUCHAAB YAHDIH.

Netherlands: Oscarsgt. 29, 0244 Oslo; tel. 23-33-36-00; fax 23-33-36-01; e-mail nlgovosl@online.no; internet www.netherlands-embassy.no; Ambassador D. A. V. E. ADER.

Pakistan: Eckersbergsgt. 20, 0244 Oslo; tel. 23-16-60-80; fax 22-55-50-97; e-mail info@pakistanembassy.no; internet www.pakistanembassy.no; Ambassador SHAHBAZ SHAHBAZ.

Poland: Olav Kyrres pl. 1, 0244 Oslo; tel. 22-55-55-36; fax 22-44-48-39; e-mail ambpol@online.no; Ambassador ANDRZEJ JAROSZYŃSKI.

Portugal: Josefinesgt. 37, 0244 Oslo; tel. 23-33-28-50; fax 22-56-43-55; internet www.dgaccp.pt/oslo; Ambassador MANUEL BARREIROS.

Romania: Oscarsgt. 51, 0244 Oslo; tel. 22-44-15-12; fax 22-4316-74; Chargé d'affaires a.i. ANAMARIA ALMASAN.

Russia: Drammensvn 74, 0244 Oslo; tel. 22-55-32-78; fax 22-55-00-70; e-mail rembassy@online.no; internet www.norway.mid.ru; Ambassador ALEXANDER N. PANOV.

Serbia and Montenegro: Drammensvn 105, 0244 Oslo; tel. 22-44-81-05; fax 22-55-29-92; e-mail yu.amb.oslo@online.no; internet www.sr-cg-embno.com; Ambassador VIDA OGNJENOVIĆ.

Slovakia: Thomas Heftyesgt. 24, 0244 Oslo; tel. 22-04-94-70; fax 22-04-94-74; e-mail slovakr@online.no; internet www.oslo.mfa.sk; Ambassador DUŠAN ROZBORA.

South Africa: Drammensvn 88C, POB 2822 Solli, 0204 Oslo; tel. 23-27-32-20; fax 22-44-39-75; e-mail sa-emb@online.no; Ambassador ISMAIL COOVADIA.

Spain: Oscarsgt. 35, 0244 Oslo; tel. 22-92-66-80; fax 22-92-66-90; e-mail embspain@online.no; Ambassador FERNANDO ALVARGONZÁLEZ.

Sudan: Holtegt. 28, 0355 Oslo; tel. 22-60-33-55; fax 22-69-83-44; Ambassador MOHAMED ALI ELTOM.

Sweden: Nobels gt. 16, 0244 Oslo; tel. 24-11-42-00; fax 22-55-15-96; e-mail ambassaden.oslo@foreign.ministry.se; internet www.sverigesambassad.no; Ambassador MATS RINGBORG.

Switzerland: Bygdøy allé 78, 0244 Oslo; tel. 22-43-05-90; fax 22-44-63-50; e-mail vertretung@osl.rep.admin.ch; Ambassador GIAN FEDERICO PEDOTTI.

Thailand: Eilert Sundtsgt. 4, 0244 Oslo; tel. 22-12-86-60; fax 22-04-99-69; e-mail thaioslo@online.no; Ambassador DOMEDEJ BUNNAG.

Tunisia: Haakon VIIs gt. 5B, 0161 Oslo; tel. 22-83-19-17; fax 22-83-24-12; e-mail ambassade.tunisie.oslo@online.no; Ambassador HOUDA KANOUN.

Turkey: Halvdan Svartesgt. 5, 0244 Oslo; tel. 22-44-99-20; fax 22-55-62-63; e-mail postmaster@oslo-turkish-embassy.com; Ambassador BERHAN EKINCI.

United Kingdom: Thomas Heftyesgt. 8, 0264 Oslo; tel. 23-13-27-00; fax 23-13-27-41; e-mail britemb@online.no; internet www.britain.no; Ambassador DAVID POWELL.

USA: Drammensvn 18, 0244 Oslo; tel. 22-44-85-50; fax 22-43-07-77; e-mail oslo@usa.no; internet www.usa.no; Ambassador BENSON K. WHITNEY.

Venezuela: Drammensvn 82, POB 2820 Solli, 0204 Oslo; tel. 22-43-06-60; fax 22-43-14-70; e-mail consulado@venezuela.no; Ambassador LOURDES MOLINOS.

Judicial System

The judicial system in Norway is organized on three levels. The courts of first instance are the District (Herredsrett) and City (Byrett) Courts. The country is divided into 93 judicial areas, most of which are served by one professional judge and one or two deputies (in the major cities the number of judges ranges from three to 52). The Court of Appeal (Lagmannsrett) consists of six jurisdictions, each with between 10 and 52 judges, and two divisions (Appeals and Criminal Divisions). The Supreme Court (Høyesterett) sits in Oslo and decides cases in the last instance. The Court, which is served by 19 judges appointed by the Crown and presided over by a Chief Justice, is competent to try all factual and legal aspects of cases in civil and criminal cause. In criminal cases, however, the competence of the Court is limited to questions concerning the application of the law, the nature of the penalty, and procedural errors of the lower courts. Appeals to the Supreme Court may not be based on errors in the assessment of evidence in connection with the question of guilt.

SUPREME COURT

Høyesterett
(Supreme Court)

Høyesteretts pl., POB 8016 Dep., 0030 Oslo; tel. 22-03-59-00; fax 22-33-23-55; e-mail post@hoyesterett.no; internet www.hoyesterett.no; f. 1815; pronounces judgment in the final instance; hears both civil and criminal cases, and has jurisdiction in all areas of law; composed of 18 ordinary justices of the Supreme Court and one Chief Justice; individual cases are heard by five justices—in some instances cases are heard by all of the justices sitting in plenary session; works in two parallel and equal divisions; Supreme Court justices also sit on the Appeals Selection Committee of the Supreme Court, which is classed as a separate court; cases brought before the Appeals Selection Committee are heard by three justices; any matter brought before the Supreme Court must initially be considered by the Appeals Selection Committee; justices sit in both divisions of the Supreme Court and on the Appeals Selection Committee in accordance with a rota system.

Chief Justice of the Supreme Court: TORE SCHEI.

Justices of the Supreme Court: GUNNAR AASLAND, LIV GJØLSTAD, KETIL LUND, KARENANNE GUSSGARD, STEINAR TJOMSLAND, KIRSTI COWARD, EILERT STANG LUND, LARS OFTEDAL BROCH, HANS FLOCK, MAGNUS MATNINGSDAL, GEORGE FR. RIEBER-MOHN, KARIN M. BRUZELIUS, JENS EDVIN A. SKOGHØY, KARL ARNE UTGÅRD, INGER-ELSE STABEL, OLE BJØRN STØLE, SVERRE MITSEM, TORIL MARIE ØIE.

COURTS OF APPEAL

Agder Lagmannsrett (Court of Appeal in Skien): Statens hus, Gjerpensgt. 16, 3708 Skien; tel. 35-54-05-00; fax 35-52-10-09; e-mail agder.lagmannsrett@domstol.no; internet www.domstol.no; Presiding Judge ARNE CHRISTIANSEN.

Borgarting Lagmannsrett (Court of Appeal in Oslo): POB 8017 Dep., 0030 Oslo; Oslo Tinghus, C. J. Hambros pl. 4, Oslo; tel. 22-03-52-00; e-mail borgadm@domstol.no; internet www.domstol.no/borgarting; Presiding Judge NILS ERIK LIE.

Eidsivating Lagmannsrett (Court of Appeal in Hamar): Hamar tinghus, Østregt. 41, 2326 Hamar; tel. 62-55-06-00; fax 62-55-06-20; e-mail elag@domstol.no; internet www.domstol.no/elag; Presiding Judge ODD JARL PEDERS.

Frostating Lagmannsrett (Court of Appeal in Trondheim): Trondheim tinghus, Munkegt. 20, 7004 Trondheim; tel. 73-54-24-60; fax 73-54-24-84; e-mail frostating.lagmannsrett@domstol.no; internet www.frostating.no; Presiding Judge KJELL BUER.

Gulating Lagmannsrett (Court of Appeal in Bergen): Bergen tinghus, Tårnpl. 2, POB 7414, 5020 Bergen; tel. 55-23-71-20; fax 55-23-07-24; e-mail gulating@domstol.no; internet www.domstol.no/gulating; Presiding Judge RUNE FJELD.

Hålogaland Lagmannsrett (Court of Appeal in Tromsø): Fr. Nansens pl. 17, POB 2511, 9271 Tromsø; tel. 77-66-00-35; fax 77-66-00-60; e-mail halogaland.lagmannsrett@domstol.no; internet www.domstol.no; Presiding Judge ARILD O. EIDESEN.

CIVIL COURTS

In each municipality there is a Conciliation Board (Forliksråd) consisting of three lay members elected by the municipal council for four years. With a few exceptions, no case may be taken to a court of justice without a prior attempt at mediation by a Conciliation Court. In addition to mediation, the Conciliation Court has a judicial capacity and is intended to settle minor cases in a simple manner without great expense to the parties involved.

The ordinary lower courts are the District and City Courts, which decide all cases not adjudicated upon by the Conciliation Court, and they also act as courts of appeal from judgments given in the Conciliation Court. During the main hearing, the court is generally convened with only one professional judge, but each of the parties may request that the court be convened with two lay judges, in addition to the professional judge. When the court finds it advisable, it may also summon lay judges on its own initiative.

Judgments delivered in the District and City Courts may be taken, on appeal, to the Court of Appeal or to the Supreme Court. In the Court of Appeal cases are judged by three professional judges, but, if requested by one of the parties, lay judges may be summoned.

CRIMINAL COURTS

The criminal courts are: the Court of Examination and Summary Jurisdiction (Forhørsretten), the District and City Courts, the Court of Appeal and the Supreme Court. In the Court of examination and summary jurisdiction the professional judge presides alone, but in the District and City Courts two lay judges also sit. Following the implementation of a major reform in 1995, all criminal cases now begin in a District or City Court. The gravest offences were previously tried directly before a jury in the Court of Appeal and the possibilities for appeal were thus limited. Now, however, the issue of guilt can be appealed to the Court of Appeal in all cases. (Such cases are tried either by three professional judges, and four lay judges with equal votes—meddomsrett, or by three professional judges and a jury of 10 members. For a guilty verdict to be upheld in the latter case, at least seven members of the jury must support the original decision of the lower court. In other cases appeal is directly to the Supreme Court.) The maximum penalty permissible under Norwegian law is 21 years of imprisonment.

OMBUDSMAN

The office of Parliamentary Ombudsman was established in 1962. An Ombudsman is elected by the Storting after every general election for a four-year term (with the possibility of re-election). The Ombudsman is accessible to all citizens, and attempts to ensure against the public administration committing any injustice to the individual citizen. The Ombudsman does not cover private legal affairs, and does not have the right to reverse an official decision, but his pronouncements are normally complied with.

Sivilombudsmannen—Stortingets ombudsmann for forvaltningen (Parliamentary Ombudsman for Public Administration): POB 3 Sentrum, 0101 Oslo; Akersgt. 8, 0158, Oslo; tel. 22-82-85-00; fax 22-82-85-11; e-mail post@sivilombudsmannen.no; internet www.sivilombudsmannen.no; ARNE FLIFLET.

Religion

CHRISTIANITY

Citizens are considered to be members of the National Church unless they explicitly associate themselves with another denomination; 86% of the population (approximately 3.9m. persons) nominally belong to the Church. However, actual church attendance is considered to be rather low. Other Protestant Christian denominations account for some 3.4% of the population. There are a very small number of Orthodox Christians in Norway.

The National Church

Church of Norway

The Church Synod, POB 799 Sentrum, 0106 Oslo; tel. 23-08-12-00; fax 23-08-12-01; e-mail post.kirkeradet@kirken.no; internet www.kirken.no; The Evangelical Lutheran Church, constituted as the State Church; there are 11 dioceses, 103 archdeaconries, 620 clerical districts and 1,298 parishes. The highest representative body of the Church is the Synod, summoned for the first time in 1984. In 2003 approximately 86% of the population belonged to the State Church.

Bishop of Oslo: GUNNAR STÅLSETT.

Bishop of Borg: OLE CHRISTIAN KVARME.

Bishop of Hamar: ROSEMARIE KÖHN.

Bishop of Tunsberg: LAILA RIKSAASEN DAHL.

Bishop of Agder: OLAV SKJEVESLAND.

Bishop of Stavanger: ERNST ODDVAR BAASLAND.

Bishop of Bjørgvin: OLE D. HAGESÆTHER.

Bishop of Møre: ODD BONDEVIK.

Bishop of Nidaros: FINN WAGLE.

Bishop of Sør-Hålogaland: ØYSTEIN I. LARSEN.

Bishop of Nord-Hålogaland: PER OSKAR KJØLAAS.

The Roman Catholic Church

For ecclesiastical purposes, Norway comprises the diocese of Oslo and the territorial prelatures of Tromsø and Trondheim. The diocese and the prelatures are directly responsible to the Holy See. At 31 December 2003 there were an estimated 56,308 adherents in Norway, equivalent to about 1.2% of the population. The Bishop of Oslo participates in the Scandinavian Episcopal Conference (based in Västra Frölunda, Sweden).

Bishop of Oslo: Rt Rev. GERHARD SCHWENZER, Oslo Katolske Bispedømme, Akersvn 5, 0177 Oslo; tel. 23-21-95-00; fax 23-21-95-01; e-mail okb@katolsk.no; internet www.katolsk.no.

Other Churches

Church of England: St. Edmund's Anglican Church, Møllergt. 30, Oslo; tel. 22-69-22-14; fax 22-69-21-63; e-mail trepar@online.no; internet www.osloanglicans.net; 1,600 mems (2001); also in Stavanger, Bergen and Trondheim; Rev. Dr TREVOR PARK (Diocese of Gibraltar in Europe).

Evangelical Lutheran Free Church of Norway: POB 23, Bekkelagshøgda, 1109 Oslo; tel. 22-74-86-00; fax 22-74-86-01; e-mail post@frikirken.no; internet www.frikirken.no; f. 1877; c. 22,000 mems (2004); Chair. of Synod ARNFINN LØYNING.

Norwegian Baptist Union: Michelsesvei 62C, 1368 Stabekk; tel. 67-10-35-60; fax 67-10-35-69; f. 1860; 10,254 mems (2004); Gen. Sec. MAGNAR MAELAND.

Pinse Bevegelsen i Norge (Pentecostal Movement): POB 6717, St Olavs Pl., 0130 Oslo; tel. 22-11-43-00; fax 22-11-43-43; e-mail jeppestol@pinsebevegelsen.no; internet www.pinsebevegelsen.no; 44,977 mems (1998).

United Methodist Church: POB 2744 St Hanshaugen, 0131 Oslo; tel. 23-33-27-00; fax 23-33-27-01; e-mail post@metodistkirken.no; internet www.metodistkirken.no; f. 1856; 12,945 mems (2004); Council Dir GUNNAR BRADLEY.

In 1998 there were 15,113 Jehovah's Witnesses in Norway and 6,188 Seventh-day Adventists. There were 7,934 members of the Missionary Alliance.

OTHER RELIGIONS

In 2004 there were 75,761 Muslims in Norway. Buddhists (of whom there were 6,920 in 1998), Jews (1,048 in 1996), Sikhs and Hindus are present in very small numbers, together comprising considerably less than 1% of the population. The Norwegian Humanist Association—the only national organization for those who do not formally practise any religion, including atheists—had 69,652 registered adult members and claimed 10,000 children as associate members in 2004. (Full membership is restricted to adults.) The Government estimated that an additional 6% of the population (approximately 273,000 persons) did not formally practise religion. A substantial proportion (42%) of the country's religious minorities are concentrated in the Oslo metropolitan area, including 76% of the country's Muslims and the country's entire Buddhist community.

The Press

The principle of press freedom is safeguarded in the Norwegian Constitution. There is no law specifically dealing with the Press. Editors bear wide responsibility in law for the content of their papers, especially regarding such matters as libel. Although a journalist is legally entitled to conceal his source he may be required to disclose this information under penalty of imprisonment, but such instances are rare. A three-member Council of Conduct gives judgments in cases of complaint against a paper or of disputes between papers. It has no powers of enforcement but its judgments are highly respected. The Press Association has a Code of Ethics aimed at maintaining the standards and reputation of the profession.

The Eastern region dominates press activity. Oslo dailies are especially influential throughout this area, and four of these—*Aftenposten*, *Verdens Gang*, *Dagbladet* and *Dagavisen*—have a national readership. Nevertheless, in Norway's other chief cities the large local dailies easily lead in their own districts. In 2002 Norway had 61 daily newspapers, with a combined circulation averaging 2,201,000 copies per issue. A few very large papers are responsible for the bulk of this circulation. In 1996 the most popular newspapers were *Verdens Gang* (Oslo), *Aftenposten* (Oslo), *Dagbladet* (Oslo), *Bergens Tidende* (Bergen) and *Adresseavisen* (Trondheim), with a combined circulation of almost 1m. At the beginning of 1994 the principal media holding company was Schibsted A/S, which owned *Aftenposten* and *Verdens Gang* and had substantial holdings in *Adresseavisen* (33.4%), *Stavanger Aftenblad* (30.5%) and several other newspapers. Orkla Media A/S had holdings of 90% or more in eight regional newspapers (and a 50% share in the major magazine publisher Hjemmet Mortensen—see below). The trade-union-owned Norsk Arbeiderpresse is the principal owner of the left-wing press.

PRINCIPAL NEWSPAPERS

Ålesund

Sunnmørsposten: POB 123, 6001 Ålesund; tel. 70-12-00-00; fax 70-12-46-42; e-mail redaksjon@smp.no; internet www.smp.no; f. 1882; Liberal; Editor HARALD H. RISE; circ. 36,608.

Arendal

Agderposten: POB 8, 4801 Arendal; tel. 37-00-37-00; fax 37-00-38-38; e-mail agderposten@agderposten.no; internet www.agderposten.no; f. 1874; independent; Editor STEIN GAUSLAA; circ. 25,660.

Bergen

Bergens Tidende: Krinkelkroken 1, POB 7240, 5020 Bergen; tel. 55-21-45-00; fax 55-21-48-48; e-mail annonse@bergens-tidende.no; internet www.bergens-tidende.no; f. 1868; Editor HANS ERIK MATRE; circ. 95,455.

Bergensavisen: Chr. Michelsensgt. 4, POB 824 Sentrum, 5807 Bergen; tel. 55-23-50-00; fax 55-23-17-36; e-mail olav.bergo@ba.no; internet www.ba.no; f. 1927; Labour; Editor OLAV TERJE BERGO; circ. 32,000.

Dagen: POB 76/77, 5002 Bergen; tel. 55-31-17-55; fax 55-31-71-06; f. 1919; religious daily; Editor FINN JARLE SÆLE; circ. 12,351.

Billingstad

Asker og Baerums Budstikke: POB 133, 1376 Billingstad; tel. 66-77-00-00; fax 66-77-00-60; e-mail redaksjonen@budstikka.no; internet www.budstikka.no; f. 1898; 6 a week; Conservative; Editor ANDREAS GJØLME; circ. 31,940.

Bodø

Nordlands Framtid: Storgt. 9, 8002 Bodø; tel. 75-50-50-00; fax 75-50-50-10; e-mail redaksjonen@nordlands-framtid.no; internet www.nordlands-framtid.no; f. 1910; Labour; Editor THOR WOJE; circ. 20,257.

Drammen

Drammens Tidende: POB 7033, 3007 Drammen; tel. 32-20-40-00; fax 32-20-42-10; e-mail redaksjonen@dt.no; internet www.dt.no; f. 1832 and 1883; Conservative daily; Dir FINN GRUNDT; Editor HANS ARNE ODDE; circ. 45,000.

Fredrikstad

Fredrikstad Blad: POB 143, 1601 Fredrikstad; tel. 69-38-80-00; fax 69-31-31-81; e-mail tips@f-b.no; internet www.f-b.no; f. 1889; Conservative; Editor ERLING OMVIK; circ. 25,510.

Gjøvik

Oppland Arbeiderblad: POB 24, 2801 Gjøvik; tel. 61-18-93-00; fax 61-17-98-56; internet www.oa-net.no; f. 1924; daily; Labour; Editor-in-Chief JENS O. JENSEN; circ. 28,500.

Hamar

Hamar Arbeiderblad: Torggt. 51, POB 333, 2301 Hamar; tel. 62-51-96-99; fax 62-51-96-18; e-mail post@ha-nett.no; internet www.ha-nett.no; f. 1925; daily; Labour; Editor ROLV AMDAL; circ. 29,000.

Harstad

Harstad Tidende: Storgt. 11, POB 85, 9481 Harstad; tel. 77-01-80-00; fax 77-01-80-05; e-mail redaksjonen@ht.no; internet www.ht.no; f. 1887; Conservative; Editor ODD R. OLSEN; circ. 15,556.

Haugesund

Haugesunds Avis: POB 2024, 5501 Haugesund; tel. 52-72-00-00; fax 52-72-04-44; e-mail redaksjonen@haugesunds-avis.no; internet www.haugesunds-avis.no; f. 1895; independent; Editor-in-Chief TONY NUNDAL; circ. 34,811.

Hønefoss

Ringerikes Blad: POB 68, 3502 Hønefoss; tel. 32-17-95-00; fax 32-17-95-01; e-mail redaksjonen@ringblad.no; internet www.ringblad.no; f. 1845; independent; Editor TORE ROLAND; circ. 13,152.

Kongsvinger

Glåmdalen: Gågt. 20, 2226 Kongsvinger; tel. 62-88-25-00; fax 62-88-25-01; e-mail redaksjon@glomdalen.no; internet www.glomladen.no; f. 1926; daily; Labour; Editor BJORN SAUGE; circ. 22,557.

Kristiansand

Fædrelandsvennen: POB 369, 4664 Kristiansand; tel. 38-11-30-00; fax 38-11-30-01; e-mail fep@fedrelandsvennen.no; internet www.fedrelandsvennen.no; f. 1875; daily; Liberal independent; Editor FINN HOLMER-HOVEN; circ. 44,141.

Lillehammer

Gudbrandsdølen Lillehammer Tilskuer: POB 954, 2601 Lillehammer; tel. 61-28-98-33; fax 61-26-09-60; f. 1841 and 1894; independent; Editor-in-Chief ASBJØRN RINGEN; circ. 30,018.

Lillestrøm

Akershus/Romerikes Blad: POB 235, 2001 Lillestrøm; tel. 63-80-50-50; fax 63-80-50-60; e-mail redaksjonen@rb.no; internet www.rb.no; f. 1913; Labour; Editor-in-Chief TERJE GRANERUD; circ. 42,123.

Molde

Romsdals Budstikke: POB 55, 6401 Molde; tel. 72-15-00-00; fax 71-25-00-11; f. 1843; Conservative independent; Editor ARNT SOMMERLUND; circ. 18,773.

Moss

Moss Avis: POB 248/250, 1501 Moss; tel. 69-20-50-00; fax 69-20-50-03; e-mail jan.tollefsen@moss-avis.no; internet www.moss-avis.no; f. 1876; Liberal/Conservative independent; Editor JAN TOLLEFSEN; circ. 14,561.

Oslo

Aftenposten: Akersgt. 51, POB 1178 Sentrum, 0107 Oslo; tel. 22-86-30-00; fax 22-42-63-25; e-mail aftenposten@aftenposten.no; internet www.aftenposten.no; f. 1860; Conservative independent; Editor-in-Chief EINAR HANSEID; circ. morning 262,362, evening 167,671, Sunday 229,858 (2001).

Akers Avis/Groruddalen Budstikke: POB 100 Grorud, 0905 Oslo; tel. 22-25-01-89; fax 22-16-01-05; f. 1928; 2 a week; non-political; Editor HJALMAR KIELLAND; circ. 12,536.

Dagavisen: POB 1183 Sentrum, 0107 Oslo; tel. 22-72-60-00; fax 22-64-92-82; f. 1884; Labour; Editor-in-Chief ARVID JACOBSEN; circ. 51,786.

Dagbladet: POB 1184 Sentrum, 0107 Oslo; tel. 22-31-06-00; fax 22-31-05-10; e-mail annb@dagbladet.no; internet www.dagbladet.no; f. 1869; daily; Editor-in-Chief THOR GJERMUND ERIKSEN; circ. 183,092.

Dagens Næringsliv: POB 1182 Sentrum, 0107 Oslo; tel. 22-00-10-00; fax 22-00-10-70; e-mail annonser@dn.nhst.no; Editor AMUND DJUVE; circ. 68,663.

Nationen: POB 9390 Grønland, 0135 Oslo; tel. 21-31-00-00; fax 21-31-00-90; e-mail nationen@nationen.no; internet www.nationen.no; f. 1918; daily; Centre; Editor-in-Chief LARS OLAV HAUG; circ. 18,500.

Verdens Gang: Akersgt. 55, POB 1185 Sentrum, 0107 Oslo; tel. 22-00-00-00; fax 22-42-68-70; e-mail redaksjonen@vg.no; internet www.vg.no; f. 1945; independent; Editor-in-Chief BERNT OLUFSEN; circ. 380,190.

Vårt Land: POB 1180 Sentrum, 0107 Oslo; tel. 22-31-03-10; fax 22-31-03-05; e-mail annonse@vl.no; internet www.vl.no; f. 1945; independent, religious daily; Editor HELGE SIMONNES; circ. 28,000.

Sandefjord

Sandefjords Blad: POB 2042, Hasle, 3202 Sandefjord; tel. 33-42-00-00; fax 33-46-29-91; e-mail redaksjonen@sandefjords-blad.no; internet www.sandefjords-blad.no; f. 1861; Conservative; Editor LEIF MAGNE FLEMMEN; circ. 15,000.

Sarpsborg

Sarpsborg Arbeiderblad: POB 87, 1701 Sarpsborg; tel. 69-11-11-11; fax 69-11-11-00; e-mail sa@ostfoldpressen.no; internet www.sarpsborg-arbeiderblad.of.no; f. 1929; independent; Editor TOM HELGESEN; circ. 19,000.

Skien

Telemarksavisa AS: POB 2833, Kjørbekk, 3702 Skien; tel. 35-58-55-00; fax 35-52-82-09; e-mail ove.mellingen@telemarksavisa.no; internet www.telemarksavisa.no; f. 1921; independent; Editor OVE MELLINGEN; circ. 22,000.

Varden: POB 2873 Kjørbekk, 3702 Skien; tel. 35-54-30-00; fax 35-52-83-23; e-mail info@varden.no; internet www.varden.no; f. 1874; Conservative; Editor MAJ-LIS STORDAL; circ. 32,986.

Stavanger

Stavanger Aftenblad: POB 229, 4001 Stavanger; tel. 05150; fax 51-89-30-05; internet www.aftenbladet.no; independent; f. 1893; Editor-in-Chief TOM HETLAND; circ. 69,000.

Steinkjer

Trønder-Avisa: Hamnegt., 7738 Steinkjer; tel. 74-12-12-00; fax 74-12-13-13; e-mail redaksjonen@t-a.no; internet www.t-a.no; Centre/Liberal; Editor OLE ERIK ALMLID; circ. 25,000.

Tønsberg

Tønsbergs Blad: POB 2003, Postterminalen, 3103 Tønsberg; tel. 33-37-00-00; fax 33-37-30-10; e-mail redaksjonen@tb.no; internet www.tb.no; f. 1870; Conservative; Editor-in-Chief MARIT HAUKOM; circ. 33,400.

Tromsø

Nordlys: Rådhusgt. 3, POB 2515, 9272 Tromsø; tel. 77-62-35-00; fax 77-62-35-01; e-mail nyheter@nordlys.no; internet www.nordlys.no; f. 1902; Labour; Editor JONNY HANSEN; circ. 30,924.

Trondheim

Adresseavisen: 7003 Trondheim; tel. 07200; fax 72-50-15-16; e-mail redaksjon@adresseavisen.no; internet www.adressa.no; f. 1767; Editor GUNNAR FLIKKE; circ. 85,839.

POPULAR PERIODICALS

Allers: Stenersgt. 2, 0107 Oslo; tel. 21-30-10-00; fax 21-30-12-04; e-mail allersredaktion@afj.no; family weekly; Editor-in-Chief ORY BJØRHOVDE; circ. 123,578.

Bedre Helse: 0441 Oslo; tel. 22-58-53-37; fax 22-58-58-79; e-mail ann.brendshoi@hm-media.no; health; circ. 33,219 (2000).

Byavisa: Munkegt. 66E, 7011 Trondheim; tel. 73-99-05-50; fax 73-99-05-60; e-mail redaksjon@byavisa.no; internet www.byavisa.no; f. 1996; weekly; circ. 82,000.

Bonytt: 0441 Oslo; tel. 22-58-58-29; fax 22-58-58-09; e-mail bonytt@hm-media.no; internet www.bonytt.com; home and furnishing; 14 a year; Editor ANNA KOLBERG; circ. 68,000 (2003).

Familien: 0441 Oslo; tel. 22-58-57-00; fax 22-58-07-64; family fortnightly; Editor-in-Chief IVAR MOE; circ. 151,303 (2002).

Foreldre & Barn: 0441 Oslo; tel. 22-96-15-00; fax 22-96-13-52; internet www.foreldre.com; 11 a year; for parents of young children; Editor EDDA ESPELAND; circ. 59,210 (2000).

Foreldremagasinet: Gullhaugvn 1, 0483 Oslo; POB 5001 Majorstuen, 0301 Oslo; tel. 22-58-55-39; e-mail vibeke.ostelie@hm-media.no; for parents; circ. 20,470 (2000).

Henne: POB 1169 Sentrum, 0107 Oslo; tel. 21-30-10-00; e-mail tips@henne.no; www.henne.no; women's; Editor-in-Chief ELLEN ARNSTAD; circ. 45,586.

Hjemmepc: Sandakervn 114B, 0483 Oslo; POB 5001 Majorstuen, 0301 Oslo; tel. 22-58-55-14; e-mail hallvard.lunde@hm-media.no; internet www.hjemmepc.no; home computers; circ. 28,963 (2003).

Hjemmet: 0441 Oslo; tel. 22-58-50-00; fax 22-58-05-70; e-mail hjemmet@hm-media.no; internet www.hm-media.no; family weekly; Editor-in-Chief LISE HANSEN; circ. 228,313 (2004).

Hytteliv: 0441 Oslo; tel. 22-58-50-00; fax 22-58-58-59; e-mail turid.roste@hm-media.no; f. 1972; 9 a year; for second-home owners; Editor TURID RØSTE; circ. 55,000 (2000).

I form: Trim.no AS, 6789 Loen; tel. 22-37-30-50; fax 91-38-59-26; e-mail redaksjonen@trim.no; internet www.iform.no; monthly; health and fitness; Editor-in-Chief JENS HENNEBERG; circ. 46,551.

Jærbladet: POB 23, 4341 Bryne; tel. 51-77-99-00; fax 51-48-37-40; 3 days a week; independent; Editor IVAR RUSDAL; circ. 12,477.

KK (Kvinner og Klær): POB 1169 Sentrum, 0107 Oslo; Stenersgt. 2, Oslo; tel. 21-30-10-00; fax 22-63-61-02; e-mail leserservice@kk.no; internet www.kk.no; women's weekly; Editor-in-Chief JUNE TRØNNES HANSSEN; circ. 88,158.

Mann: 0441 Oslo; tel. 22-58-50-00; fax 22-58-05-69; e-mail post@mann.no; internet www.mann.no; men's magazine; Editor-in-Chief ROGER GROENDALEN; circ. 20,000.

Mat & Drikke: Lindbäckveien 28A, 1163 Oslo; tel. 22-29-89-75; fax 22-29-64-85; internet www.matogdrikke.no; 7 a year; food and wine; Editor-in-Chief ARNFINN HANSSEN; circ. 23,032.

Norsk Ukeblad: Gullhaugvn 1, 0483 Oslo; tel. 22-58-53-00; fax 22-58-05-69; family weekly; Editor-in-Chief ULF-ARVID MEJLÆNDER; circ. 178,119 (2000).

Det Nye: 0441 Oslo; tel. 22-58-50-00; fax 22-58-58-09; e-mail detnye@hm-media.no; internet www.detnye.com; for young women; 14 a year; Editor-in-Chief KRISTIN MA BERG; circ. 72,000.

Programbladet: POB 1180 Sentrum, 0107 Oslo; tel. 22-31-03-10; fax 22-31-04-55; f. 1946; radio and television weekly; Editor ØYVIND RISVIK; circ. 65,000.

Se og Hør: POB 1164 Sentrum, 0128 Oslo; tel. 22-41-51-80; fax 22-41-51-70; f. 1978; news weekly (radio and TV); Editors-in-Chief KNUT HÅVIK, ODD J. NELVIK; circ. 366,887.

Shape-Up: Sørkedalsvn 10A, 0301 Oslo; tel. 22-96-15-00; fax 22-96-13-52; 11 a year; health and beauty; Editor EVA SUNDENE LYNGAAS; circ. 30,986 (2000).

TOPP: POB 1164 Sentrum, 0107 Oslo; tel. 22-41-51-80; fax 22-41-51-70; monthly; for young people aged between 10 and 17 years; Editors ODD J. NELVIK, KNUT HÅVIK; circ. 48,011.

Vi Menn: 0441 Oslo; tel. 22-58-50-00; fax 22-58-05-71; e-mail vimenn@hm-media.no; internet www.vimenn.com; men's weekly; Editor-in-Chief SVEIN E. HILDONEN; circ. 106,596 (2002).

SPECIALIST PERIODICALS

Alt om Fiske: Gullhaugvn 1, 0483 Olso; POB 5001 Majorstuen, 0301 Oslo; tel. 22-58-55-13; fax 22-58-06-66; e-mail aud.haugvik@hm-media.no; angling; circ. 22,906 (2005).

Barnemagasinet BAM: 0441 Oslo; Gullhaugvn 1, 0483 Oslo; tel. 23-00-81-80; fax 23-00-81-89; e-mail postmaster@bam.no; internet www.bam.no; for expectant and new parents; three additional titles, *BAM Gravid*, *BAM Nyfødt* and *BAM Spedbarn*; circ. 80,000 (2000).

Batmagasinet: POB 1169 Sentrum, 0107 Oslo; tel. 21-30-10-00; fax 21-30-12-59; e-mail hans.due@afj.no; internet www.batmagasinet.no; f. 1985; Aller Familie-journal AS; 12 a year; boating, powerboats; Editor HANS DUE; circ. 28,555.

Bil: POB 9247 Vaterland, 0134 Oslo; tel. 23-03-66-00; fax 23-03-66-40; e-mail bil@bilforlaget.no; internet www.bilnorge.no; 10 a year; motoring; Editor KJELL-MAGNE AALBERGSJØ; circ. 51,388.

Bondebladet: POB 9367 Grønland, 0135 Oslo; tel. 21-31-44-00; fax 21-31-44-01; e-mail post@bondebladet.no; internet www.bondebladet.no; f. 1974; weekly; farming; Editor BENDIK BENDIKSEN; circ. 85,593.

Familiens Grønne Gleder: 0441 Oslo; Gullhaugvn 1, 0483 Oslo; tel. 22-58-55-13; fax 22-58-05-06; e-mail aud.haugvik@hm-media.no; gardening; circ. 55,000 (2004).

Fjell og Vidde: Den Norske Turistforening, POB 7 Sentrum, 0101 Oslo; tel. 22-82-28-00; fax 22-82-28-01; e-mail redaksjonen@turistforeningen.no; internet www.turistforeningen.no; f. 1967; 6 a year; organ of The Norwegian Mountain Touring Asscn; Editor HELLE ANDRESEN; circ. 128,000.

Fotball: Sørkedalsvn 10A, 0301 Oslo; tel. 22-96-15-00; fax 22-96-13-52; 8 a year; for football players and spectators; Editor ØYVIND STEEN JENSEN; circ. 98,655.

Gravid: Gullhaugvn 1, 0483 Oslo; POB 5001 Majorstuen, 0301 Oslo; tel. 22-58-55-15; e-mail erika-o.asker@hm-media.no; for pregnant women; circ. 15,301 (2000).

Hagen for alle: Nalum., 3294 Stavern; tel. 33-19-56-05; e-mail red-hfa@online.no; internet www.hagen-foralle.no; monthly; gardening; Editor HELENE B. ØKSENHOLT; circ. 30,000.

Hundesport: POB 0163 Bryn, 0611 Oslo; tel. 21-60-09-00; fax 21-60-09-01; e-mail hundesport@nkk.no; internet www.nkk.no; monthly; for dog-owners; circ. 50,000.

Ingeniørnytt: POB 164, 1332 Østerås; Nils Lassons vei 5, 1359 Eiksmarka; tel. 67-16-34-99; fax 67-16-34-55; e-mail ingnytt@online.no; internet www.ingeniornytt.no; every 2 weeks; engineering, architecture; circ. 65,000.

Jakt & Fiske: POB 94, 1378 Nesbru; tel. 66-79-22-00; fax 66-90-15-87; e-mail viggokristiansen@njff.no; monthly; hunting and angling; Editor VIGGO KRISTIANSEN; circ. 76,710.

Jakt, Hund & Våpen: Gullhaugvn 1, 0483 Oslo; POB 5001 Majorstuen, 0301 Oslo; tel. 22-58-55-34; e-mail inger.storodegard@hm-media.no; hunting; circ. 25,908 (2000).

Kampanje: Sandakerv. 114B, 0483 Oslo; tel. 22-58-50-00; fax 22-15-40-86; e-mail redaksjon@kampanje.no; internet www.kampanje.com; marketing and media; Editor-in-Chief GLENN Ø. STØLDAL; circ. 11,340 (2000).

Kapital: POB 444 Vinderen 0319 Oslo; tel. 23-29-65-50; fax 23-29-65-94; e-mail wenchew@kapital.no; internet www.hegnar.no; fortnightly; business, management; circ. 40,000.

Kommuniké: POB 9202, 0134 Oslo; tel. 21-03-36-00; fax 21-03-36-50; f. 1936; 9 a year; organ of Norwegian Confederation of Municipal Employees; Editor AUDUN HOPLAND; circ. 54,000.

Kontor & Finans: POB 14 Røa, 0701 Oslo; tel. 22-52-44-60; fax 22-52-24-80; e-mail ergjerts@sn.no; f. 1977; quarterly; business; Editor THOR O. SANDBERG; circ. 100,000.

LINUXmagasinet: POB 7183 Majorstuen, 0307 Oslo; tel. 23-36-82-00; fax 23-36-82-01; e-mail tosterud@linmag.no; internet www.linmag.no; Linux operating system, open source software; 5 a year; Editor-in-Chief SVEIN ERIK TOSTERUD; circ. 8,000.

Motor: POB 494 Sentrum, 0105 Oslo; tel. 22-34-15-55; fax 22-34-14-90; e-mail redaksjonen@motor.no; internet www.motor.no; monthly; motoring, travel and leisure; Editor SVEIN OLA HOPE; circ. 400,000.

NETTUERK: Lilleiorget 1, 0184 Oslo; tel. 23-06-33-74; fax 23-06-33-66; e-mail harald@lo-media.no; monthly; electricity and electronics; Editor HAROLD OLAU MOEN; circ. 43,500.

Norsk Hagetidend: POB 53 Manglerud, 0612 Oslo; tel. 23-03-16-00; fax 23-03-16-01; e-mail postkasse@hageselskapet.no; internet www.hageselskapet.no; f. 1885; monthly; gardening; Editor BERGLJOT GUNDERSEN; circ. 41,878.

Norsk Landbruk: POB 9303 Grønland, 0135 Oslo; tel. 21-31-44-00; fax 21-31-44-92; e-mail norsk.landbruk@tunmedia.no; internet www.norsklandbruk.no; f. 1882; 2 a year; agriculture, horticulture and forestry; Editor-in-Chief MARIANNE RØHME; circ. 16,172.

Okonomisk Rapport: POB 290 Skøyen, 0213 Oslo; tel. 22-40-41-00; fax 22-40-41-01; e-mail rapport@orapp.no; internet www.orapp.no; business; circ. 24,946 (2000).

PCPro: Sandakervn 114B, 0441 Oslo; POB 5001 Majorstuen, 0301 Oslo; tel. 22-58-59-34; e-mail pcpro@hm-media.no; internet www.pcpro.no; f. 2000; 8 a year; computing; circ. 25,000; Editor-in-Chief KJETIL ENSTAD.

Seilmagasinet: POB 253, 1379 Nesbru; tel. 66-77-40-60; fax 66-77-40-61; e-mail morten.jensen@seilmagasinet.no; internet www.seilmagasinet.no; f. 1975; 10 a year; sailing; Editor MORTEN JENSEN; circ. 14,000.

SKOGeieren: POB 1438 Vika, 0115 Oslo; tel. 22-01-05-50; fax 22-83-40-47; e-mail anders.hals@skog.no; f. 1914; 12 a year; forestry; Editor ANDERS HALS; circ. 46,100.

Snø og Ski: Kongevn 5, 0787 Oslo; tel. 22-92-32-00; fax 22-92-32-50; quarterly; winter and summer sports; Editor KRISTIN MOE KROHN; circ. 42,000.

Teknisk Ukeblad (Technology Review Weekly): POB 5844 Majorstuen, 0308 Oslo; tel. 23-19-93-00; fax 23-19-93-01; e-mail redaksjonen@tu.no; internet www.tu.no; f. 1854; technology, industry, management, marketing and economics journal; Editor-in-Chief TOMMY RUDIHAGEN; circ. 93,542.

Tidsskriftet Sykepleien: POB 456 Sentrum, 0104 Oslo; tel. 22-04-33-04; fax 22-04-33-756; internet www.sykepleien.no; f. 1912; 21 a year; health personnel, nursing; Editor-in-Chief BARTH THOLENS; circ. 69,000.

Tips: Gullhaugvn 1, 0483 Oslo; POB 5001 Majorstuen, 0301 Oslo; tel. 22-58-50-00; fax 22-58-59-19; e-mail firmapost@tips.as; internet www.tips.as; football and betting; circ. 20,000 weekdays, 18,000 weekend (2000).

Utdanning: POB 9191 Grønland, 0167 Oslo; tel. 24-14-00-00; fax 24-14-22-85; e-mail redaksjonen@utdanning.ws; internet www.utdanning.ws; f. 1934; fmrly *Norsk Skoleblad*; weekly; teaching; Editor KNUT HOVLAND; circ. 129,423.

Utsyn: Sinsenvn 25, 0572 Oslo; tel. 22-00-72-00; fax 22-00-72-02; e-mail utsyn@nlm.no; internet www.utsyn.no; 25 a year; organ of Norsk Luthersk Misjonssamband (Norwegian Lutheran Mission); circ. 17,000.

Vi Menn Båt: 0441 Oslo; Gullhaugvn 1, 0483 Oslo; tel. 22-58-50-00; fax 22-58-05-66; e-mail inger.storodegard@hm-media.no; internet

NORWAY

www.vimenn.no; f. 1992; 6 a year; boats; Editor MORTEN MUNCH ERICHSEN; circ. 77,000 (2004).

Vi Menn Bil: 0441 Oslo; Gullhaugvn 1, 0483 Oslo; tel. 22-58-50-00; fax 22-58-05-66; e-mail olaug.gaarder@hm-media.no; internet www.vimenn.no; f. 1996; 10 a year; cars; Editor MORTEN MUNCH ERICHSEN; circ. 105,000 (2004).

Vi Menn Fotball: Gullhaugvn 1, 0483 Oslo; POB 5001 Majorstuen, 0301 Oslo; tel. 22-58-55-15; e-mail erika-o.asker@hm-media.no; football; circ. 30,000 (2000).

Villmarksliv: 0441 Oslo; tel. 22-58-50-00; fax 22-58-52-39; e-mail dag.kjelsaas@hm-media.no; internet www.villmarksinfo.no; f. 1972; monthly; angling, hunting, photography; Editor-in-Chief DAG KJELSAAS; circ. 63,645 (2000).

NEWS AGENCIES

Bulls Pressetjeneste A/S: Ebbellsgt. 3, 0158 Oslo; tel. 22-98-26-60; fax 22-20-49-78; e-mail info@bulls.no; internet www.bulls.no; Man. PAUL E. VATNE.

A/S Norsk Telegrambyrå (NTB) (Norwegian News Agency): Holbergs gt. 1, POB 6817 St Olavs pl., 0130 Oslo; tel. 22-03-44-00; fax 22-20-12-29; e-mail ntb@ntb.no; f. 1867; Editor-in-Chief THOR VIKSVEEN.

Foreign Bureaux

Agence France-Presse (AFP): c/o NTB, Holbergsgt. 1, POB 6817 St Olavs pl., 0130 Oslo; tel. 22-03-44-00; fax 22-20-12-29; Correspondent OLE LUDVIG NYMOEN.

Associated Press (AP) (USA): Holbergsgt. 1, 0166 Oslo; tel. 22-20-10-30; fax 22-20-52-80; Bureau Chief DOUG MELLGREN.

Deutsche Presse-Agentur (dpa) (Germany): Holbergsgt. 1, 0166 Oslo; tel. 22-03-44-00; fax 22-20-12-29; Editor BJØRN VESETH.

Informatsionnoye Telegrafnoye Agentstvo Rossii—Telegrafnoye Agentstvo Suverennykh Stran (ITAR—TASS) (Russia): Fougstadsgt. 9, 0173 Oslo; tel. 22-60-61-91; fax 22-60-63-22; Correspondent IGOR B. PSHENICHNIKOV.

Inter Press Service (IPS) (Italy): Holbergsgt. 1, 0166 Oslo; tel. 22-11-50-80; fax 22-11-50-95; e-mail mail@ipsnor.no; Dir KRISTIN HAVGAR.

Reuters Norge A/S: Stortorvet 10, 0155 Oslo; tel. 22-93-69-00; fax 22-42-50-32; internet www.reuters.no; Country Rep. HENRIK KLAWITTER.

Rossiiskoye Informatsionnoye Agentstvo—Novosti (RIA—Novosti) (Russia): Oslo; tel. 22-55-55-41; fax 22-55-65-20; Editor ALEKSANDR KRASNOV.

United Press International (UPI) (USA): Holbergsgt. 1, 0166 Oslo; tel. 22-03-44-00; fax 22-20-12-29.

PRESS ASSOCIATIONS

Den Norske Fagpresses Forening (Specialized Press Asscn): Akersgt. 41, 0158 Oslo; tel. 24-14-61-00; fax 24-14-61-10.

Mediebedriftenes Landsforening (Norwegian Media Businesses' Asscn): Tollbugt. 27, 0157 Oslo; tel. 22-86-12-00; fax 22-42-26-11; e-mail post@mediebedriftene.no; internet www.mediebedriftene.no; Man. Dir ARVID SAND.

Norsk Journalistlag (Norwegian Union of Journalists): Torggt. 5, 5th Floor, POB 8793 Youngstorget, 0028 Oslo; tel. 22-05-39-50; fax 22-41-33-70; e-mail nj@nj.no; internet www.nj.no; f. 1946; Sec.-Gen. JAHN-ARNE OLSEN; 8,770 mems (2004).

Norsk Presseforbund (Norwegian Press Asscn): Rådhusgt. 17, POB 46 Sentrum, 0101 Oslo; tel. 22-40-50-40; fax 22-40-50-55; e-mail np@presse.no; internet www.presse.no; f. 1910; asscn of newspapermen, editors and journalists; Pres. MARIT HAUKOM; Sec.-Gen. PER EDGAR KOKKVOLD.

Publishers

Andresen & Butenschøn A/S: POB 1153 Sentrum, 0107 Oslo; tel. 23-13-92-40; fax 22-33-58-05; e-mail abforlag@online.no.

Antropos Forlag: Josefinesgt. 12, 0351 Oslo; tel. 22-46-03-74; e-mail forlag@antropos.no; internet www.antropos.no.

Ariel Lydbokforlag A/S: Solfallsv. 67, 1430 Ås; POB 1546 Vika, 0117 Oslo; tel. and fax 64-94-35-10; f. 1988; audiocassettes; Editors-in-Chief INGER SCHJOLDAGER, MARGARETE WIESE.

H. Aschehoug & Co (W. Nygaard): Sehestedsgt. 3, POB 363 Sentrum, 0102 Oslo; tel. 22-40-04-00; fax 22-20-63-95; e-mail epost@aschehoug.no; internet www.aschehoug.no; f. 1872; general non-fiction, fiction, reference, children's, educational, textbooks; Man. Dir WILLIAM NYGÅRD; Asst Man. Dir ERIK HOLST.

Bladkompaniet A/S: Staælfjœra 5, POB 148 Kalbakken, 0902 Oslo; tel. 22-90-24-00; fax 22-90-24-01; e-mail bladkompaniet@bladkompaniet.no; internet www.bladkompaniet.no; f. 1915; general fiction, non-fiction, paperbacks, comics, magazines; Publr CLAUS HUITFELDT; Editorial Dir FINN ARNESEN.

Boksenteret Erik Pettersen & Co A/S: Krusesgt. 11, POB 3125 Elisenberg, 0207 Oslo; tel. 22-54-07-00; fax 22-54-07-07; e-mail bs@boksenteret.no; internet www.boksenteret.no; f. 1999; illustrated, non-fiction, craft, DIY; Man. Dir ERIK PETTERSEN.

Bokvennen Forlag: Trudvangvn 41, 0363 Oslo; tel. 22-60-80-28; fax 22-93-02-88; f. 1989; fiction, essays, biographies; Mans MORTEN CLAUSSEN, JAN M. CLAUSSEN.

F. Bruns Bokhandel og Forlag A/S: Kongensgt. 10–14, 7005 Trondheim; tel. 73-51-00-22; fax 73-50-93-20; f. 1873; local history, technology; Publr FRIDTHJOV BRUN.

Cappelen Akademisk Forlag A/S: POB 350 Sentrum, 0101 Oslo; tel. 22-98-58-00; fax 22-95-58-41; e-mail cafinfo@cappelen.no; internet www.cappelen.no; f. 1946; textbooks for universities and colleges, social sciences, law, economics, medicine, health and nursing, educational science, psychology; Publr ESTER MOEN.

J. W. Cappelens Forlag A/S: Mariboesgt. 13, POB 350 Sentrum, 0101 Oslo; tel. 22-36-50-00; fax 22-36-50-40; e-mail web@cappelen.no; internet www.cappelen.no; f. 1829; general, educational, popular science, fiction, maps, children's, encyclopaedias; Man. Dir SINDRE GULDVOG.

N. W. Damm og Søn A/S: Fridtjof Nansensvei 14, 0055 Oslo; tel. 24-05-70-00; fax 24-05-12-99; e-mail post@damm.no; internet www.damm.no; f. 1843; children's, reference, handbooks; Man. Dir TOM HARALD JENSSEN.

Eide Forlag A/S: Sandbrugt. 11, POB 4081 Dreggen, 5835 Bergen; tel. 55-32-90-40; fax 55-31-90-18; f. 1945; general, children's, textbooks, fiction, non-fiction; Publr TRINE KOLDERUP FLATEN; Man. Dir ROALD FLATEN.

Forlaget Fag og Kultur A/S: POB 6633 Etterstad, Biskop Jens Nilssønsgt. 5, 0607 Oslo; tel. 23-30-24-00; fax 23-30-24-04; e-mail firmapost@fagogkultur.no; internet www.fagogkultur.no; f. 1987; reference; Man. Dir MARI ETTRE OLSEN.

Fagbokforlaget: Huitfeldtsgt. 15, POB 2336 Solli, 0201 Oslo; tel. 22-55-69-06; fax 22-55-41-83; e-mail fagbokforlaget@fagbokforlaget.no; f. 1992; general and scientific; Publrs ARNO VIGMOSTAD, ARNSTEIN BJØRKE.

Falken Forlag: Osterhaugsgt. 8, 0183 Oslo; tel. 22-20-86-40; f. 1946; fiction, non-fiction; Publr KIRSTI KRISTIANSEN.

Fonna Forlag: POB 6912 St Olavs pl., 0130 Oslo; tel. 22-20-13-03; fax 22-20-12-01; e-mail fonna@fonna.no; internet www.fonna.no; f. 1940; limited co; general, fiction; Man. Dir ROALD WAKTSKJOLD.

Fono Forlag AS: Billingstadsletta 30, POB 169, 1376 Billingstad; tel. 66-84-64-90; fax 66-84-75-07; e-mail mail@fonoforlag.no; internet www.fonoforlag.no; f. 1991; audio books; Gen. Man. HALVOR HANEBORG.

Frifant Forlag A/S: Leinvn 10, 1453 Bjørnemyr; tel. 66-91-29-40; fax 66-91-29-41; e-mail frifor@online.no; internet www.frifant.no; f. 1997.

Genesis Forlag: Kongensgt. 22, 0153 Oslo; POB 1180 Sentrum, 0107 Oslo; tel. 22-31-03-10; fax 22-31-02-05; e-mail genesis@genesis.no; internet www.genesis.no; f. 1996; Dir MAGNE LERØ.

John Grieg Forlag A/S: Valkendosfjst. 1A, 5012 Bergen; tel. 55-21-31-80; fax 55-12-00-05; internet www.griegforlag.no; f. 1721; children's books, art, education, aquaculture; Publr SVEIN SKOTHEIM.

Gyldendal Akademisk: Kristian IVs gt. 13, POB 6730 St Olavs pl., 0130 Oslo; tel. 22-03-43-00; fax 22-03-43-05; e-mail akademisk@gyldendal.no; internet www.gyldendal.no/akademisk; f. 1992; university textbooks; Man. Dir FREDRIK NISSEN.

Gyldendal Norsk Forlag A/S: Sehestedsgt. 4, POB 6860 St Olavs pl., 0130 Oslo; tel. 22-03-41-00; fax 22-03-41-05; internet www.gyldendal.no; f. 1925; general, non-fiction, fiction, biography, religion, cookery, school and university textbooks, children's, manuals; Man. Dir BJØRGUN HYSING.

Hjemmet Mortensen A/S: 0441 Oslo; tel. 22-58-50-00; fax 22-58-50-68; f. 1941; fiction, non-fiction, children's; Man. Dir KNUT ENGER.

Imprintforlaget A/S: POB 2336 Solli, 0201 Oslo; tel. 23-13-69-30.

InfoMediaHuset A/S: POB 382 Sentrum, 0102 Oslo; tel. 22-63-64-00; fax 22-63-65-94; e-mail aina@elanders.no; internet www.elanderspublishing.no; f. 1844 as Elanders Forlag; present name adopted 2003; legislation, catalogues; Publr AINA THORSTENSEN.

Kolibri Forlag A/S: Kristian IV'sgt. 15, 0164 Oslo; tel. 22-11-01-53; fax 22-11-01-54; f. 1982; fantasy, non-fiction, cookery, children's, humour, leisure; Publr ELSE LILL BJØNNES.

Kolon Forlag: Sehestedsgt. 4, POB 6860 St Olavs pl., 0130 Oslo; tel. 22-03-42-02; fax 22-03-41-05; e-mail kolon@gyldendal.no; internet www.kolonforlag.no; f. 1995; modern Norwegian poetry and fiction; Publr TORLEIV GRUE.

Kunnskapsforlaget: Gullhaug Torg 1, POB 4432 Nydalen, 0403 Oslo; tel. 22-02-22-00; fax 22-02-22-99; e-mail resepsjonen@kunnskapsforlaget.no; internet www.kunnskapsforlaget.no; f. 1975; reference books, encyclopedias, dictionaries, atlases, electronic reference titles, knowledge games; Man. Dir KRISTIN W. WIELAND; Editorial Dir ØYSTEIN EEK; Editor-in-Chief PETTER HENRIKSEN.

Landbruksforlaget: Schweigaardsgt. 34A POB 9303 Grønland, 0135 Oslo; tel. 21-31-44-00; fax 21-31-44-92; e-mail post@landbruksforlaget.no; internet www.landbruksforlaget.no; f. 1949; outdoor, handicrafts, culture, horses, dogs, children; Editorial Man. HEIDI JANNICKE ANDERSEN.

Libretto Forlag: Eilert Sundtsgt. 32, 0259 Oslo; tel. 22-44-30-11; fax 22-44-30-12; f. 1990; children's, giftbooks and handbooks; Publr TOM THORSTEINSEN.

Lunde Forlag A/S: Sinsenv. 25, 0572 Oslo; tel. 22-00-73-50; fax 22-00-73-73; e-mail lunde@nlm.no; internet www.lunde-forlag.no; f. 1905; religious, general, fiction, children's; Publishing Dir ASBJØRN KVALBEIN.

Luther Forlag: Grensen 15, POB 6640 St Olavs pl., 0129 Oslo; tel. 22-00-87-80; fax 22-00-87-81; e-mail postkasse@lutherforlag.no; internet www.lutherforlag.no; religious, fiction, general; Dir ASLE DINGSTAD.

Lydbokforlaget A/S: Søreggen 2, POB 135, 7223 Melhus; tel. 72-85-60-70; fax 72-85-60-90; e-mail herborg.hongset@lybokforlaget.no; internet www.lybokforlaget.no; f. 1987; owned by H. Aschehoug & Co (33%), Gyldendal Norsk Forlag (33%) and Stiftergruppen (34%).

Messel Forlag: St Olavsgt. 21A, 0165 Oslo; tel. 22-20-29-15; e-mail messelfo@online.no.

NKI Forlaget: Hans Burumsvn 30, POB 111, 1319 Bekkestua; tel. 67-58-88-00; fax 67-58-19-02; f. 1972; textbooks for secondary and technical schools and colleges; Publr JAN B. THOMSEN.

Norsk Bokreidingslag L/L: POB 684, 5807 Bergen; tel. 55-30-18-99; fax 55-32-03-56; e-mail post@bodonihus.no; internet www.bokreidingslaget.no; f. 1939; fiction, folklore, linguistics, cultural history; Man. FROYDIS LEHMANN.

Det Norske Samlaget: Jens Bjelkesgt. 12, POB 4672 Sofienberg, 0506 Oslo; tel. 22-70-78-00; fax 22-68-75-02; e-mail det.norske@samlaget.no; internet www.samlaget.no; f. 1868; general literature, fiction, poetry, children's, textbooks; Man. Dir NINA REFSETH.

Forlaget Oktober A/S: Kr. Augustsgt. 11, POB 6848 St Olavs pl., 0130 Oslo; tel. 23-35-46-20; fax 23-35-46-21; e-mail oktober@aschehoug.no; internet www.aschehoug.no/oktober; f. 1970; fiction, politics, social and cultural books; Publr GEIR BERDAHL.

Orion Forlag: Søkedalsvn 10C, 0369 Oslo; tel. 23-19-60-90; internet www.boknett.no/orion.

Pantagruel Forlag A/S: POB 2370 Solli, 0201 Oslo; tel. 23-27-28-10; e-mail alle@pantagruel.no.

Pax Forlag A/S: Huitfeldtgt. 15, POB 2336 Solli, 0201 Oslo; tel. 23-13-69-00; fax 22-55-41-83; f. 1964; fiction, non-fiction, feminism, social sciences; Man. Dir BJØRN SMITH-SIMONSEN.

Sambåndet Forlag AS: Vetrlidsalm. 1, 5014 Bergen; tel. 55-31-79-63; fax 55-31-09-44; e-mail vestlandskes.bokhandel@vestbok.no; f. 1945; religion, children's, poetry; Dir TARALD UELAND.

Chr. Schibsteds Forlag A/S: POB 6973 St Olavs pl., 0130 Oslo; tel. 24-14-69-00; fax 24-14-69-01; e-mail schibsted.forlag@schibsted.no; internet www.schibsted-forlag.no; f. 1839; reference, biographies, handbooks, hobbies, crafts, children's books, food and drink, sports, foreign language, guides, maps; Man. Dir THOMAS ØYBÖ.

Skolebokforlaget A/S: Stortingsgt. 30, 0161, Oslo; tel. 22-83-77-05; fax 22-83-38-32; f. 1979; educational; Man. Dir HANS B. BUTENSCHØN; Editor SVERRE MØRKHAGEN.

Snøfugl Forlag: POB 95, 7221 Melhus; tel. 72-87-24-11; fax 72-87-10-13; f. 1972; fiction, general; Man. ASMUND SNØFUGL.

Solum Forlag A/S: Hoffsvn 18, POB 140 Skøyen, 0212 Oslo; tel. 22-50-04-00; fax 22-50-14-53; e-mail info@solumforlag.no; internet www.solumforlag.no; f. 1973; fiction, human sciences, general; Man. Dir KNUT ENDRE SOLUM.

Spartacus Forlag A/S: POB 2587 Solli, 0203 Oslo; tel. 22-44-56-70; fax 22-44-46-50; e-mail post@spartacus.no; internet www.spartacus.no; f. 1989.

Spektrum Forlag ANS: POB 363 Sentrum, 0102 Oslo; tel. 23-13-39-03; e-mail cyrus.brantenberg@spektrum-forlag.no.

Stabenfeldt A/S: Aker Base Dusavik, Bygg 19, 4029 Stavanger; tel. 51-84-54-00; fax 51-84-54-90; f. 1920; general fiction, adventure, reference; Man. Dir TOR TJELDFLÅT.

Tell Forlag A/S: Nilsemarka 5C, 1390 Vollen; tel. 66-78-09-18; fax 66-90-05-72; e-mail tell@tell.no; internet www.tell.no; f. 1987; textbooks and educational books; Man. TELL-CHR. WAGLE.

Tiden Norsk Forlag A/S: Kristian Augustsgt. 12, POB 6704 St. Olavs plass, 0130 Oslo; tel. 23-32-76-20; fax 23-32-76-97; e-mail tiden@tiden.no; internet www.tiden.no; f. 1933; literary fiction, crime, thrillers, fantasy, non-fiction; Pub. Dir RICHARD AARØ.

Universitetsforlaget AS: Sehestedsgt. 3, POB 508 Sentrum, 0105 Oslo; tel. 24-14-75-00; fax 24-14-75-01; e-mail post@universitetsforlaget.no; internet www.universitetsforlaget.no; f. 1950; publishers to the Universities of Oslo, Bergen, Trondheim and Tromsø and various learned societies; school books, university textbooks, specialized journals; Man. Dir ARNE MAGNUS.

Verbum Forlag: Underhaugsvn 15, POB 7062 Majorstuen, 0306 Oslo; tel. 22-93-27-00; fax 22-93-27-27; e-mail verbum.forlag@bibelselskapet.no; internet www.verbumforlag.no; f. 1820; Christian literature; Man. TURID BARTH PETTERSEN.

Vett & Viten A/S: Nye Vakås Vn. 56, POB 203, 1379 Nesbru; tel. 66-84-90-40; fax 66-84-55-90; e-mail vv@vettviten.no; internet www.vettviten.no; f. 1987; medical, technical and engineering textbooks; Publr JAN LIEN.

Wigestrand Forlag A/S: POB 621, 4001 Stavanger; tel. 51-89-49-69; e-mail forlag@wigestrand.no.

PUBLISHERS' ASSOCIATION

Den norske Forleggerforening (Norwegian Publishers' Asscn): Øvre Vollgt. 15, 0158 Oslo; tel. 22-00-75-80; fax 22-33-38-30; e-mail dnf@forleggerforeningen.no; internet www.forleggerforeningen.no; f. 1895; Chair. GEIR BERDAHL; Man. Dir PER CHRISTIAN OPSAHL; 52 mem. firms.

Broadcasting and Communications

TELECOMMUNICATIONS

Post- og Teletilsynet (Norwegian Post and Telecommunications Authority): Revierstredt 2, POB 447 Sentrum, 0104 Oslo; tel. 22-82-46-00; fax 22-82-48-90; e-mail firmapost@npt.no; internet www.npt.no; f. 1987; issues and supervises regulations, concessions and licences; expanded to incorporate postal matters in 1997; Dir-Gen. WILLY JENSEN.

Norkring AS: Telenor Broadcast, 1331 Fornebu; tel. 67-89-20-00; fax 67-89-36-14; internet www.norkring.no; Dir TRULS LANGEGGEN.

Telenor AS: Snarøyvn 30, 1331 Fornebu; tel. 67-89-00-00; internet www.telenor.com; state-owned; Pres. and CEO TORMOD HERMANSEN.

BROADCASTING

Radio

Norsk Rikskringkasting (NRK) (Norwegian Broadcasting Corpn): Bj. Bjørnsons pl. 1, 0340 Oslo; tel. 23-04-70-00; fax 23-04-78-80; e-mail info@nrk.no; internet www.nrk.no; autonomous public corpn; operates three national services (including a youth programme), 18 regional services (including one in the language of the Sámi—Lappish) and an international service, Radio Norway International; Chair. of Govs ANNE CARINE TANUM; Dir-Gen. JOHN G. BERNANDER; CEO (Broadcasting) HANS-TORE BJERKAAS.

P4—Radio Hele Norge ASA: Serviceboks, 2626 Lillehammer; tel. 61-24-84-44; fax 61-24-84-45; e-mail p4@p4.no; internet www.p4.no; f. 1993; private commercial station.

Television

Norsk Rikskringkasting (NRK) (Norwegian Broadcasting Corpn): (see Radio, above); Dir of Television HANS-TORE BJERKAAS.

TV-2: POB 2 Sentrum, 0101 Oslo; tel. 02255; fax 21-00-60-03; f. 1992; private commercial station; Man. Dir KARE VALEBROKK; Dir of Programmes NILS K. ANDRESEN.

TV Norge: Oslo; private satellite television service.

Finance

In 2005 there were 15 commercial banks (comprising the major banks, some large regional banks and a number of smaller regional and local banks). In 2005 the commercial banks had total assets of 1,335,425m. kroner. In 2004 there were 126 savings banks, with total assets of 1,231,000m. kroner. There were also 10 publicly financed government banks.

Kredittilsynet (Financial Supervisory Authority of Norway): Østensjøvn 43, POB 100 Bryn, 0611 Oslo; tel. 22-93-98-00; fax 22-63-02-26; e-mail post@kredittilsynet.no; internet www.kredittilsynet.no; finance inspectorate; Dir-Gen. BJØRN SKOGSTAD AAMO.

NORWAY

BANKING

(cap. = capital; res = reserves; dep. = deposits; m. = millions; brs = branches; amounts in kroner)

Central Bank

Norges Bank: Bankplassen 2, POB 1179 Sentrum, 0107 Oslo; tel. 22-31-60-00; fax 22-41-31-05; e-mail central.bank@norges-bank.no; internet www.norges-bank.no; f. 1816; holds the exclusive right of note issue; cap. and res 46,213m., dep. 1,039,777m. (Dec. 2003); Chair. of Supervisory Bd MARY KVIDAL; Gov. SVEIN GJEDREM; 12 brs.

Principal Commercial Banks

Bank 1 Oslo A/S: POB 778 Sentrum, Henrik Ibsens gt. 12, 0106 Oslo; tel. (915) 07040; fax 21-02-81-50; e-mail bank1@sparebank1.no; internet www.sparebank1.no; f. 1898; name changed as above 2000; cap. 291m., res 18m., dep. 10,500m. (Dec. 2003); CEO TORBJØRN VIK; Chair. GUNN WÆRSTED; 7 brs.

DnB NOR Bank ASA (Gjensidige NOR Sparebank ASA): Aker Brygge, Stranden 21, 0021 Oslo; tel. 81-50-05-60; fax 22-31-84-84; internet www.ubn.no; f. 1985 as Sparebanken ABC, by merger of Sparebanken Oslo and Union Bank of Norway; merged with four regional savings banks in 1990; Sparebanken Telemark incorporated in 1997; merged with Gjensidige Bank AS in 1999; merged with Den Norske Bank ASA (f. 1990) and adopted present name in 2004; cap. 16,964m., res 16,608m., dep. 578,062m. (Dec. 2003); Chair. OLAV HYTTA; Pres. and CEO SVEIN AASER; 130 brs.

Fokus Bank ASA: Vestre Rosten 77, 7466 Trondheim; tel. 72-88-20-11; fax 72-88-20-61; e-mail fokus@fokus.no; internet www.fokus.no; f. 1987; Den Danske Bank of Denmark took over Fokus Bank in 1999; cap. 1,863m., dep. 47,298m. (Dec. 2003); Chair. SØREN MØLLER NIELSEN; Man. Dir and CEO THOMAS BORGEN; 60 brs.

Nordea Bank Norge ASA: Middelthunsgt. 17, 0368 Oslo; POB 1166 Sentrum, 0107 Oslo; tel. 22-48-50-00; fax 22-48-47-49; internet www.nordea.com; fmrly Christiana Bank og Kreditkasse ASA, current name adopted 2001; part of Nordea Group (Finland); cap. 1,160m., res 9,527m., dep. 188,689m. (Dec. 2003).

Nordlandsbanken ASA: Molov. 16, 8002 Bodø; tel. 91-50-89-00; fax 75-55-85-10; e-mail post@nordlandsbanken.no; internet www.nordlandsbanken.no; f. 1893; cap. 625m., res 816m., dep. 12,686m. (Dec. 2003); Chair. LEIF TEKSUM; Man. Dir and CEO MORTEN STØVER; 17 brs.

Principal Savings Banks

Sparebanken Hedmark: Torggt. 12–14, POB 203, 2302 Hamar; tel. 62-51-20-00; fax 62-53-29-75; e-mail konsern@sparebanken-hedmark.no; internet www.sparebanken-hedmark.no; f. 1845; cap. 2,666m., dep. 20,248m. (Dec. 2003); Chair. SYVER AALSTAD; Man. Dir HARRY KONTERUD; 12 brs.

Sparebanken Midt-Norge: Sondregt. 4, 7005 Trondheim; tel. 73-58-51-11; fax 73-58-64-50; e-mail smn@smn.no; internet www.smn.no; f. 1823; cap. 607m., res 1,589m., dep. 32,392m. (Dec. 2003); Chair. STEIN ATLE ANDERSEN; Man. Dir FINN HAUGAN; 75 brs.

Sparebanken Møre: Keiser Wilhelmsgt. 29–33, 6002 Ålesund; tel. 70-11-30-00; fax 70-12-99-12; e-mail sparebanken.more@sbm.no; internet www.sbm.no; f. 1985; cap. 631m., res 1,258m., dep. 15,312m. (Dec. 2004); Man. Dir OLAV-ARNE FISKERSTRAND; 55 brs.

Sparebanken Nord-Norge: POB 6800, Storgt. 65, 9298 Tromsø; tel. 91-50-22-44; fax 77-62-20-22; e-mail snow@snn.no; internet www.snn.no; f. 1989; cap. 49,000m., res 729m., dep. 25,000m. (Dec. 2005); CEO HANS OLAV KARDE; Deputy CEO ODDMUND ÅSEN; 90 brs.

Sparebanken Pluss: POB 200, Rådhusgt. 7–9, 4662 Kristiansand; tel. 38-17-35-00; fax 38-02-04-70; e-mail firmapost@sparebankenpluss.no; internet www.sparebankenpluss.no; f. 1824; merged with four savings banks in 1987; total assets 12,811m. (Dec. 2003); Chair. JENS FREUCHEN; Man. Dir STEIN HANNEVIK.

Sparebanken Rogaland: Bjergsted Terrasse 1, 4001 Stavanger; tel. 51-50-90-00; fax 51-53-18-64; e-mail sparebank1@sr-bank.no; internet www.sr-bank.no; f. 1839 (as Egersund Sparebank); merged with 22 savings banks in 1976; cap. 705m., res 2,260m. dep. 53,242m. (Dec. 2004); Pres. TERJE VAREBERG; 57 brs.

Sparebanken Sør: POB 602, 4809 Arendal; Vestervn. 1, 4800 Arendal; tel. 37-02-50-00; fax 37-02-41-50; e-mail international@sor.no; internet www.sor.no; f. 1825; cap. and res 1,445m., dep.15,887m. (Dec. 2003); Chair. JOSTEIN DALANE; Man. Dir HANS A. IVERSEN; 35 brs.

Sparebanken Vest: Kaigt. 4, 5016 Bergen; tel. 55-21-00-00; fax 55-21-74-10; e-mail sparebank1.vest@spv.sparebank1.no; internet www.spv.no; f. 1823; as Bergens Sparebank; merger 1982/83 of 25 savings banks; cap. 250m., res 2,179m., dep. 36,477m. (Dec. 2003). Man. Dir KNUT RAVNÅ; 59 brs.

Bankers' Associations

Finansnaeringens Hovedorganisasjon (Norwegian Financial Services Asscn): Hansteensgt. 2, POB 2473 Solli, 0202 Oslo; tel. 23-28-42-00; fax 23-28-42-01; e-mail fnh@fnh.no; internet www.fnh.no; f. 2000 by merger of Den norske Bankforening (Nowegian Bankers' Asscn) and Norges Forsikringsforbond (Norwegian Insurance Asscn); Chair. SVEIN AASER; Man. Dir ARNE SKAUGE; 28 brs.

Sparebankforeningen i Norge (Savings Banks Asscn): Universitetsgt. 8, POB 6772, 0130 Oslo; tel. 22-11-00-75; fax 22-36-25-33; f. 1914; Pres. KJELL REMVIK (Sparebanken Møre); Man. Dir EINAR FORSBAK; 133 mems.

STOCK EXCHANGE

Oslo Børs: Tollbugt. 2, POB 460 Sentrum, 0105 Oslo; tel. 22-34-17-00; fax 22-41-65-90; e-mail info@oslobors.no; internet www.oslobors.no; f. 1819; part of an alliance (Nordic Exchanges, Norex) with the Copenhagen, Reykjavík and Stockholm Stock Exchanges, launched June 1999; Pres. SVEN ARILD ANDERSEN.

INSURANCE

Assuranceforeningen Skuld: POB 1376 Vika, 0114 Oslo; tel. 22-00-22-00; fax 22-42-42-22; e-mail osl@skuld.com; internet www.skuld.com; f. 1897; mutual, shipowners' protection and indemnity; Chair. ERIK GLØERSEN; Pres. and CEO DOUGLAS JACOBSOHN.

Gjensidige NOR Forsikring: Drammensvn 228, POB 276, 1326 Lysaker; tel. 22-96-80-00; fax 22-96-92-00; e-mail epost@gjensidigenor.no; internet www.gjensidigenor.no; f. 1847; merged with Forenede Norge Forsikring and Forenede Skadeforsikring in 1993; Pres. HELGE KVAMME; CEO LARS AUSTIN.

Norske Liv AS: Drammensvn 21, 0201 Oslo; tel. 22-44-39-50; fax 22-55-79-72; f. 1844; life insurance; CEO K. NORDBY.

Uni Storebrand: Håkon VIIs gt. 10, POB 1380 Vika, 0114 Oslo; tel. 22-31-10-20; f. 1991 by merger of Storebrand (f. 1947) and Uni Forsikring (f. 1984); group includes life, non-life and international reinsurance operations; taken over by govt administrators in 1992 and new holding co (Uni Storebrand New) formed, following suspension of payments to creditors; Chair. ERIK KEISERUD; CEO PER TERJE VOLD.

Vesta Group PLC: Folke Bernadottesvei 50, 5020 Bergen; tel. 55-17-10-00; fax 55-17-18-99; f. 1884; owned by Skandia (Sweden); includes Skadeforsikringsselskapet Vesta A/S (general insurance), Vesta Liv A/S (life insurance), Vesta Finans A/S (financial services); Chair. JAN EINAR GREVE; Man. Dir JOHAN FR. ODFJELL.

Vital Insurance: Folke Bernadottesvei 40, 5020 Bergen; tel. 55-17-80-90; fax 55-17-86-99; internet www.vital.no; f. 1990 by a merger between NKP Forsikring and Hygea; life and pension insurance; Chair. SVEIN AASEN; Pres. BJØRN ØSTBØ.

Insurance Association

Finansnaeringens Hovedorganisasjon (Norwegian Financial Services Asscn): (see Bankers' Associations above).

Trade and Industry

GOVERNMENT AGENCY

Innovasjon Norge (Innovation Norway): Akersgt 13, POB 448 Sentrum, 0104 Oslo; tel. 22-00-25-00; fax 22-00-25-01; e-mail post@invanor.no; internet www.invanor.no; f. 2004 to replace Norges Turistråd (Norwegian Tourist Board), Norges Eksportråd (Norwegian Trade Council), Statens nærings- og distriktsutviklingsfond (SND-Regional Development Fund) and Statens Veiledningskontor for Oppfinnere (SVO-Government Consultative Office for Inventors); state-owned; operates in all Norwegian counties and more than 30 countries world-wide; Pres. STEINAR OLSEN.

CHAMBERS OF COMMERCE

Bergen Chamber of Commerce and Industry: Olav Kyrresgt. 11, 5807 Bergen; tel. 55-55-39-00; fax 55-55-39-01; e-mail firmapost@bergen-chamber.no; internet www.bergen-chamber.no; f. 1915; Pres. EGIL HERMAN SJURSEN; Man. Dir HELGE S. DYRNES.

Oslo Chamber of Commerce: Drammensvn 30, POB 2874 Solli, 0230 Oslo; tel. 22-12-94-00; fax 22-12-94-01; e-mail mail@chamber.no; internet www.chamber.no; Man. Dir LARS-KÅRE LEGERNES.

INDUSTRIAL AND TRADE ASSOCIATION

Norges Skogeierforbund (Norwegian Forest Owners): Roald Amundsengt. 6, POB 1438 Vika, 0115 Oslo; tel. 23-00-07-50; fax 22-42-16-90; e-mail nsf@skog.no; internet www.skog.no; f. 1913; aims to promote the economic and technical interests of the forest owners, a general forest policy in the interests of private ownership and co-operation between the affiliated associations; Man. Dir IVAR KORSBAKKEN; 44,000 mems.

EMPLOYERS' ASSOCIATIONS

Næringslivets Hovedorganisasjon (Confederation of Norwegian Business and Industry): Middelthunsgt. 27, POB 5250 Majorstua, 0303 Oslo; tel. 23-08-80-00; fax 23-08-80-01; e-mail firmapost@nho.no; internet www.nho.no; f. 1989; rep. org. for industry, crafts and service industries; Pres. JENS ULLTVEIT-MOE; Dir-Gen. FINN BERGSEN, Jr; c. 16,500 mems who must also belong to the 23 affiliated national asscns; chief among which are the following:

Entreprenørforeningen—Bygg og Anlegg (General Contractors): POB 5485 Majorstua, 0305 Oslo; tel. 23-08-75-35; fax 23-08-75-30; Admin. Dir ØIVIND SERERGREN; 220 mems.

Fiskerinæringens Landsforening (Fishing Industry): POB 5471 Majorstua, 0305 Oslo; tel. 23-08-87-30; fax 23-08-87-31; Man. Dir TERJE E. MARTINUSSEN.

Flyselskapenes Landsforening (Airlines): POB 5474 Majorstua, 0305 Oslo; tel. 23-08-85-72; fax 22-56-57-90; e-mail tor.sodeland@nho.no; Dir TOR SODELAND.

TBL Møbel- og Innredning (Asscn of Norwegian Furnishing Industries): POB 7072 Majorstuen, 0306 Oslo; tel. 22-59-00-00; fax 22-59-00-01; e-mail tbl@tbl.no; internet www.tbl.no; Exec. Man. EGIL SUNDET.

Næringsmiddelbedriftenes Landsforening (Food and Drink Industry): POB 5472 Majorstua, 0305 Oslo; tel. 23-08-87-00; fax 23-08-87-20; e-mail knut.maroni@nbl.no; internet www.nbl.no; Admin. Dir KNUT MARONI.

NHO Reiseliv (Norwegian Hospitality Asscn): POB 5465 Majorstua, Essendropsgt. 6, 0305 Oslo; tel. 23-08-86-20; fax 23-08-86-21; e-mail firmapost@nhoreiseliv.no; internet www.nhoreiseliv.no; f. 1997 as Reiselivsbedriftenes Landsforening; current name adopted 2005; Admin. Dir KNUT ALMQUIST.

Norges Bilbransjeforbund (Norwegian Motor Car Dealers and Services): Drammensvn 97, POB 2804 Solli, 0204 Oslo; tel. 22-54-21-00; fax 22-44-10-56; e-mail firmapost@nbf.no; internet www.nbf.no; f. 1962; Admin. Dir SYVER LEIVESTAD.

Norges Elektroentreprenørforbund (Norwegian Electrical Contractors' Asscn): Essendropsgt. 3, POB 5467 Majorstua, 0305 Oslo; tel. 23-08-77-00; fax 23-08-77-01; e-mail iso@nelfo.no; internet www.nelfo.no; Admin. Dir JORTEIN SKREE.

Norsk Bryggeri- og Mineralvannindustris Forening (Norwegian Breweries and Soft Drink Producers): POB 7087 Majorstua, 0306 Oslo; tel. 23-08-86-90; fax 22-60-30-04; e-mail firmapost@nbmf.no; internet www.nbmf.no; Man. Dir PER UNDRUM; 21 mems.

Norsk Industri (Fed. of Norwegian Industries): POB 7072 Majorstuen, 0306 Oslo; Oscars gt. 20, 0352 Oslo; tel. 22-59-00-00; fax 22-59-00-01; e-mail post@norskindustri.no; internet www.norskindustri.no; f. 2005 by merger of Teknologibedriftenes Landsforening (Fed. of Norwegian Manufacturing Industries) and Prosessindustriens Landsforening (Fed. of Norwegian Process Industries); Chair. RASMUS SUNDE; Man. Dir STEIN LIER-HANSEN; c. 2,000 mem. cos and c. 110,000 mems.

Oljeserviceselskapenes Landsforening (Oil Industry): Lervigsxn 32, POB 547, 40003 Stavanger; tel. 51-84-65-00; fax 51-84-65-01; e-mail firmapost@olf.no; internet www.olf.no; Admin. Dir FINN ROAR AMODT.

Servicebedriftenes Landsforening (Service Industry): Essendropsgt. 6, 0368 Oslo; tel. 23-08-86-50; fax 23-08-86-59; e-mail petter.furulund@service.no; internet www.sbl.no; Admin. Dir PETTER FURULUND.

Skogbrukets Landsforening (Forestry): Roald Amundsensegt. 6, 0161 Oslo; POB 1630 Vika, 0119 Oslo; tel. 23-00-07-90; fax 22-42-16-90; e-mail firmapost@skogbruk.no; internet www.skogbruk.no; f. 1928; Man. Dir KNUT BERG.

Tekoindustriens Bransjeforening (Textile, Clothing, Shoe, Leather and Sporting Goods Industries): Oscarsgt. 20, POB 7072 Majorstuen, 0306 Oslo; tel. 22-59-00-00; fax 22-59-00-06; f. 1989 by merger of several asscns; Chair. TERJE GORM HANSEN; Man. Dir KARI RØMCKE; 110 mems.

Transportbedriftenes Landsforening (Norwegian Transport Companies): POB 5477 Majorstua, 0305 Oslo; tel. 23-08-86-00; fax 23-08-86-01; Admin. Dir CHRISTIAN AUBERT.

Treforedlingsindustriens Bransjeforening (TFB) (Pulp and Paper): Oscarsgt. 20, POB 7772 Majorstuen, 0306 Oslo; tel. 22-59-00-51; fax 23-08-78-99; e-mail mb@norskindustri.no; internet www.pulp-and-paper.no; Chair. PER A. SOERLIE; 23 mems.

Visuell Kommunikasjon Norge (Norwegian Federation of Visual Communications Enterprises): Tollbugt. 27, 0157 Oslo; tel. 22-47-88-70; fax 22-47-88-70; e-mail viskom@viskom.net; internet www.viskom.net; f. 1906; Man. Dir PÅL STEPHENSEN; 280 mems.

Handels- og Servicenæringens Hovedorganisasjon (Federation of Commercial and Service Enterprises): Drammensvn 30, POB 2900 Solli, 0230 Oslo; tel. 22-54-17-00; fax 22-56-17-00; e-mail info@hsh-org.no; internet www.hsh-org.no; f. 1990 by merger; 10,400 mem. cos; Pres. CARL OTTO LØVENSKIOLD.

UTILITIES

Electricity

Bergenshalvøens Kommunale Kraftselskap A/S: POB 7050, 5020 Bergen; tel. 55-12-70-00; fax 55-12-70-01; e-mail firmapost@bkk.no; internet www.bkk.no; f. 1920.

Hafslund ASA: 0247 Oslo; Drammensvn 144, 0277 Oslo; tel. 22-43-50-00; internet www.hafslund.no; f. 1898; electrical generation (nine hydroelectric plants), sales, distribution, safety, installation, security and network infrastructure; Pres. and CEO RUNE BJERKE; Chair. CHRISTIAN BRINCH.

Haugesund Energi AS: Haugesund; tel. 52-70-80-00; fax 52-70-80-05; e-mail firmapost@haugesund-energi.no; f. 1908; joint stock co; 15,000 customers.

Nedre Eiker Energi: Evjegata 13, POB 153, 3051 Mjøndalen; tel. 32-23-28-70; fax 32-87-72-10.

Nordmøre Energiverk AS: Industrivn 1, POB 2125, 6501 Kristiansund; tel. 71-56-55-00; fax 71-58-15-21; e-mail neas@neas.mr.no.

Nord-Salten Kraftlag AL: POB 70, 8276 Ulvsvåg; tel. 75-77-10-00; fax 75-77-10-01; e-mail nskal@narvikknet.no; f. 1946.

Nord-Trøndelag Elektrisitetsverk: Steinkjer; e-mail nte@nte.nt.no; 70,343 customers.

Oslo Energi AS: Oslo; tel. 22-92-50-00; fax 22-43-50-85; 290,898 customers.

Statkraft SF: POB 200 Lilleaker, 0216 Oslo; tel. 24-06-70-00; fax 24-06-70-01; e-mail info@statkraft.no; internet www.statkraft.no; Pres. and CEO BÅRD MIKKELSEN.

Statnett SF: Husebybakken 28B, POB 5192 Majorstua, 0302 Oslo; tel. 22-52-70-00; fax 22-52-70-01; national power grid co; supervises and co-ordinates the operation of the entire Norwegian power system, also operates own transmission lines and submarine cables, as well as sub-stations and switching stations; state-owned co under the jurisdiction of the Ministry of Petroleum and Energy; Pres. and CEO ODD HÅKON HOELSÆTER.

Statnett Entreprenør AS: ; fax 22-52-71-80; subsidiary specializing in overseas sales.

Other major production and distribution companies include Akershus Energiverk, Aktieselskapet Tysselfaldene, Aust-Agder kraftverk, Bærum Energi AS, Bergen Lysverker, Elkem AS, Fredrikstad Energiverk AS, Hamar-regionen Energiverk, Hedmark Energi AS, Helgelund Kraftlag A/L, Hydro Energi, Kraftlaget Opplandskraft, Kristiansand Energiverk, Lyse Kraft, Østfold Energiverk, I/S Øvre Otta, Sira-Kvina Kraftselskap, Skiensfjorden komm. kraftselskap, Stavanger Energi, Svelvik Everk, Trønder Energi, Trondheim Energiverk, Troms Kraftforsyning and Vest-Agder Energiverk.

TRADE UNIONS

Landsorganisasjonen i Norge (LO) (Norwegian Confederation of Trade Unions): Folkets Hus, Youngsgt. 11, 0181 Oslo; tel. 23-06-10-50; fax 23-06-17-43; e-mail lo@lo.no; internet www.lo.no; f. 1899; Pres. GERD-LIV VALLA; Int. Sec. INGUNN YSSEN; 800,000 mems in 25 affiliated unions (2001).

The member unions are:

Arbeiderbevegelsen Presseforbund (Labour Press Union): POB 8732, Youngstorget, 0028 Oslo; tel. 91-66-39-99; fax 22-41-33-70; f. 1909; Pres. EVA GRØNSETH; 900 mems.

EL & IT Forbundet (Electricians and Information Technology Workers): Youngsgt. 11, 0181 Oslo; tel. 23-06-34-00; fax 23-06-34-01; e-mail firmapost@elogit.no; internet www.elogit.no; f. 1999 by merger of Tele- og Dataforbundet (TD) and Norsk Elektriker- og Kraftstasjonsforbundet (NEKF); Pres. HANS OLAV FELIX; 37,000 mems.

Fellesforbundet (The Norwegian United Federation of Trade Unions): Lilletorget 1, 0184 Oslo; tel. 23-06-31-00; fax 23-06-31-01; e-mail fellesforbundet@fellesforbundet.no; internet www.fellesforbundet.no; f. 1988; Pres. KJELL BJØRNDALEN; 130,000 mems.

Fellesorganisasjonen for barnevernpedagoger, sosionomer og vernepleiere (Social Educators and Social Workers): POB 4693 Sofienberg, 0506 Oslo; tel. 23-06-11-70; fax 23-06-11-14; e-mail kontor@fobsv.no; internet www.fobsv.no; f. 1992; Pres. RANDI REESE; Gen. Sec. HANS CHRISTIAN LILLEHAGEN; 18,500 mems.

Forbundet for Ledelse og Teknikk (Engineers and Managers): POB 8906 Youngsgt. 11, 0028 Oslo; tel. 22-03-10-29; fax 22-03-10-17; f. 1951; Pres. MAGNUS MIDTBØ; 16,376 mems.

NORWAY

Directory

Handel og Kontor i Norge (Commercial and Office Employees): Youngsgt. 11, 0181 Oslo; tel. 22-03-11-80; fax 22-03-12-06; f. 1908; Pres. STURE ARNTZEN; 56,209 mems.

Hotel- og Restaurant Arbeiderforbundet (Hotel and Restaurant Workers): Storgt. 32, 0184 Oslo; tel. 23-06-21-00; fax 23-06-21-01; e-mail hraf@hraf.no; internet www.hraf.no; f. 1931; Pres. ELI LJONGGREN; 14,827 mems.

Musikernes Fellesorganisasjon (Norwegian Musicians' Union): POB 8806 Youngstorget, 0028 Oslo; tel. 23-06-21-50; fax 23-06-21-51; e-mail mfo@musikerorg.no; internet www.musikerorg.no; f. 2001; Pres. ARNFINN BJERKESTRAND; 6,500 mems.

Norges Offiserforbund (Norwegian Military Officers): Møllergt. 10, 0179 Oslo; tel. 22-03-15-72; fax 22-03-15-77; f. 1978; Pres. PETER ANDRE MOE; 4,527 mems.

Norsk Arbeidsmandsforbund (Norwegian General Workers): POB 8704 Youngstorget, 0028 Oslo; tel. 23-06-10-50; fax 23-06-10-92; e-mail norsk@arb-mand.no; internet www.arbeidsmandsforbundet.no; f. 1895; Pres. ERNA C. DYNGE; 31,000 mems.

Norsk Fengselstjenestemannsforbund (Norwegian Prison Officers): Møllergt. 10, 0179 Oslo; tel. 22-03-15-88; fax 22-42-46-48; f. 1918; Pres. ROAR ØVREBØ; 2,438 mems.

Norsk Grafisk Forbund (Norwegian Graphic Workers): Lilletorget 1, 0184 Oslo; tel. 23-06-13-00; fax 23-06-13-25; e-mail ngf@ngf.no; internet www.ngf.no; f. 1882; Pres. ROGER ANDERSEN; 12,971 mems.

Norsk Jernbaneforbund (Norwegian Railway Workers): Møllergt. 10, 0179 Oslo; tel. 23-06-10-50; fax 23-06-13-85; f. 1892; Pres. OVE DALSHEIM; 19,920 mems.

Norsk Kjemisk Industriarbeiderforbund (Norwegian Chemical Workers): Youngsgt. 11, 0181 Oslo; tel. 22-03-13-40; fax 22-03-13-60; f. 1923; Pres. OLAV STØYLEN; 31,999 mems.

Norsk Kommuneforbund (Norwegian Municipal Employees): Kr. Augustsgt. 23, 0164 Oslo; tel. 22-36-47-10; fax 22-36-40-25; f. 1920; Pres. JAN DAVIDSEN; 226,722 mems.

Norsk Lokomotivmannsforbund (National Union of Norwegian Locomotive Workers): Svingen 2, 0196 Oslo; tel. 23-30-21-10; fax 23-30-21-11; e-mail nlf@lokmann.no; internet www.lokmann.no; f. 1893; Pres. ØYSTEIN ASLAKSEN; 1,197 mems.

Norsk Næring- og Nytelsesmiddelforbund (Norwegian Food and Allied Workers): Arbeidersamfunnets pl. 1, 0181 Oslo; tel. 22-20-66-75; fax 22-36-47-84; e-mail firmapost.nnn@loit.no; internet www.nnn.no; f. 1923; Pres. TORBJØRN DAHL; 34,813 mems.

Norsk Olje- og Petrokjemisk Fagforbund (Norwegian Oil and Petrochemical Workers): Kongensgt. 52, 4012 Stavanger; tel. 51-56-79-80; fax 51-56-79-88; f. 1977; Pres. LARS A. MYHRE; 10,654 mems.

Norsk Post- og Kommunikasjonsforbund (Norwegian Union of Postal and Communications Workers): Møllergt. 10, 0179 Oslo; tel. 23-06-22-90; fax 22-42-74-86; e-mail postkom@loit.no; f. 2000; Pres. ODD-CHRISTIAN ØVERLAND; 28,911 mems.

Norsk Sjømannsforbund (Norwegian Seamen): Grev. Wedels pl. 7, 0151 Oslo; tel. 22-82-58-00; fax 22-33-66-18; f. 1910; Pres. ERIK BRATVOLD; 12,500 mems.

Norsk Tjenestemannslag (Norwegian Civil Service Union): Møllergt. 10, 0179 Oslo; tel. 23-06-15-99; fax 23-06-15-55; internet www.ntl.no; f. 1947; Pres. TURID LILLEHEIE; 47,400 mems.

Norsk Transportarbeiderforbund (Norwegian Transport Workers): Youngsgt. 11, 0181 Oslo; tel. 22-20-40-55; fax 22-11-35-72; f. 1896; Pres. WALTER KOLSTAD; 16,018 mems.

Norsk Treindustriarbeiderforbund (Norwegian Wood Workers): Youngsgt. 11, 0181 Oslo; tel. 23-06-13-90; fax 23-06-13-95; e-mail ntafpost@ntaf.no; internet www.ntaf.no; f. 1904; Pres. ANTON SOLHEIM; 5,241 mems.

Skolenes Landsforbund (School Employees): Møllergt. 20, 0179 Oslo; tel. 22-03-13-62; fax 22-03-13-83; f. 1982; Pres. GRO STANDNES; 3,466 mems.

Statstjenestemannskartellet (Government Employees): Møllergt. 10, 0179 Oslo; tel. 22-03-15-78; fax 22-42-00-75; f. 1939; Pres. TERJE MOE GUSTAVSEN; 105,867 mems.

Yrkesorganisasjonenes Sentralforbund (YS): Brugt. 19, 0134 Grønland; tel. 21-01-36-00; fax 21-01-37-20; f. 1977; Pres. RANDI BJØRGEN; 242,000 mems in 19 affiliated unions.

Transport

RAILWAYS

At 31 December 2003 there were 4,077 km of state railways (standard gauge), of which 2,518 km were electrified.

Norges Statsbaner AS (NSB) (Norwegian State Railways): Prinsensgt. 7–9, 0048 Oslo; tel. 23-15-00-00; fax 23-15-33-00; internet www.nsb.no; f. 1854; as private line; govt-owned; CEO E. ENGER.

ROADS

In 2004 there were 91,919 km of public roads in Norway, of which 664 km were motorways and 26,466 km were national main roads. In 2005 a new bridge linking Norway and Sweden was opened in Svinesund.

Vegdirektoratet: Grensevn 92, POB 8142 Dep., 0033 Oslo; tel. 22-07-35-00; fax 22-07-37-68; e-mail firmapost@vegvesen.no; internet www.vegvesen.no; f. 1864; Dir OLAV SØFTELAND.

SHIPPING

At 31 December 2004 the Norwegian merchant fleet numbered 2,173 vessels, with a combined displacement of 18.9m. grt. The total includes vessels on the Norwegian International Ship Register (established in 1987), which numbered 656 vessels at 31 December 2004, with a combined displacement of 15.4m. grt. The Norwegian-controlled fleet represents some 10% of the world's total fleet, making Norway one of the four largest shipping nations in the world. It has been estimated that Norwegian companies control some 23% of the world's cruise vessels, 19% of the world's gas carriers, 19% of the world's chemical tankers and 10.5% of all crude petroleum tankers.

Port Authorities

Ålesund: Ålesund Havn KF, Skansekaia, 6002 Ålesund; tel. 70-16-34-00; fax 70-16-34-01; e-mail post@alesund.havn.no; internet www.alesund.havn.no.

Bergen: Bergen & Omland Havnevesen, Slottsgt. 1, 5003 Bergen; tel. 55-56-89-50; fax 55-56-89-86; e-mail bergen.havn@bergen-kommune.telemax.no; internet www.bergenhavn.no; Harbour Master GUNVALD ISAKSEN.

Bodø: Bodø Havnevesen, POB 138, 8001 Bodø; tel. 75-58-15-80; fax 75-58-59-90; e-mail firmapost@bodo-havnevesen.no; Harbour Master TERJE DOKSRØD.

Borg Harbour: Borg Havnevesen, Oravn 27, POB 1205 Gamle, 1631 Fredrikstad; tel. 69-35-89-00; fax 69-35-89-20; e-mail borghavnevesen@borghavn.of.no; Port Capt. SVEN-JAN JOHANSEN.

Flekkefjord: Flekkefjord Havnevesen, Eschebrygga, 4400 Flekkefjord; tel. 38-32-89-90; fax 38-32-89-91; e-mail helge.nilsen@flekkefjord.kommune.no; internet flekkefjord.kommune.no; Harbour Master HELGE NILSEN.

Flora Hamn og Næring KF: POB 17, 6901 Florø; tel. 57-74-14-28; fax 57-74-09-16.

Grenland: Grenland Havnevesen, POB 20, 3991 Brevik; tel. 35-93-10-00; fax 35-93-10-11; e-mail grenland-havnevesen@grenland-havn.no; internet port.of.grenland.com; Port Capt. TORJUS JOHNSEN.

Halden: Halden Havnevesen, Langbrygga 3, 1750 Halden; tel. 69-18-32-00; fax 69-18-06-80; Harbour Master ØYVIND JOHANNESSEN.

Hammerfest: Hammerfest Havnevesen, POB 123, 9615 Hammerfest; tel. 78-40-74-00; fax 78-40-74-01; e-mail post@hammerfest.havn.no; f. 1828; Harbour Master ROLL STIANSEN.

Haugesund: Karmsund Interkommunale Havnevesen, Garpaskjaerskaien, 5500 Haugesund; tel. 52-70-37-50; fax 52-70-37-69.

Horten: Borre Havnevesen, POB 167, 3192 Horten; tel. 33-03-17-17; fax 33-04-47-27; Harbour Master KJELL FJELLIN.

Kirkenes: Municipality of Sør-Varanger, Rådhusplassen, POB 406, 9915 Kirkenes; tel. 78-97-74-99; fax 78-97-75-87; e-mail post@kirkenes-havn.no.

Kopervik: Karmsund Havnevesen, POB 70, 4291 Kopervik; tel. 52-84-54-70; fax 52-84-54-71; e-mail postmattak@karmsund-havn.no; internet www.karmsund-havn.no; Harbour Master O. E. MAELAND.

Kragerø: Board of Harbour Commissioners, POB 158, 3791 Kragerø; tel. 35-98-17-50; fax 35-99-13-34; e-mail post@kragero-havnevesen.no; Harbour Master Capt. BORGAR F. THORSEN.

Kristiansand S.: Kristiansand Havn KF, Gravane 4, 4661 Kristiansand S.; tel. 38-00-60-00; fax 38-02-70-99; e-mail post@kristiansand-havn.no; internet www.kristiansand-havn.no; Port Dir STEIN E. HAARTVEIT.

Kristiansund N.: Kristiansund Havnevesen, Kaibakken 1, 6509 Kristiansund N.; tel. 40-00-65-04; fax 71-67-14-83; e-mail info@knhavn.noo; Harbour Master JAN OLAV BJERKESTRAND.

Larvik: Larvik Havn KF, POB 246 Sentrum, Havnegt. 5, 3251 Larvik; tel. 33-16-57-50; fax 33-16-57-59; e-mail post@larvik.havn.no; internet www.larvik.havn.no; Port Dir JAN FREDRIK JONAS.

Malm: Fosdalens Bergverks Aktie, 7720 Malm; tel. 74-15-71-00; fax 74-15-78-76; Agent OLAV VAARDAL.

Mandal Port of Agder: Mandal Havnevesen KF, POB 57, 4501 Mandal; tel. 38-27-34-77; fax 38-26-34-76; e-mail havnefogden@

NORWAY

Directory

mandal.kommune.no; internet www.portofagder.no; Harbour Master JONNY O. HANSEN.

Mongstad: Statoil Mongstad, 5954 Mongstad; tel. 56-34-40-00; fax 56-34-47-29; e-mail jja@statoil.com; Port Capt. JON M. JAKOBSEN.

Mosjøen: Mosjøen Havnevesen, 8650 Mosjøen; tel. 75-17-52-65; fax 75-17-03-65; e-mail mosjohavn@enitel.no; Port Man. GUNNAR JOHANSEN.

Moss: Moss Havnevesen, Moss Maritime Centre, Moss; tel. 69-25-11-06; Harbour Master FINN SYVERTSEN.

Narvik: Narvik Havn KF, POB 627, 8508 Narvik; tel. 76-95-03-70; fax 76-95-03-84; e-mail narvikhavn@narvik.kommune.no; internet www.portofnarvik.com; Port Man. RUNE ARNOY.

Odda: Odda Havnevesen, 5750 Odda; tel. 53-64-84-00; fax 53-64-12-92; Harbour Master OLAV BJØERKE.

Orkanger: Orkanger Havnevesen, 7300 Orkanger; tel. 72-48-00-09; fax 72-48-10-03; e-mail tom.hamborg@orkdal.kommune.no; Port Man. TOM HAMBORG.

Oslo: Oslo Havnevesen, POB 230 Sentrum, 0103 Oslo 1; tel. 23-49-26-00; fax 23-79-26-01; e-mail postmottak@havnevesenet.oslo.kommune.no; internet www.ohv.oslo.no; Port Capt. HARRY GRYTBAKK.

Risør: Risør Havnekontor, 4950 Risør; tel. 37-14-96-00; fax 37-14-96-01; Agent KJELL SKARHEIM.

Sandefjord: Sandefjord Havnevesen, Tollbugt. 5, 3200 Sandefjord; tel. 33-45-60-38; fax 33-46-26-13; Harbour Master LEIF ALLUM.

Sauda: Sauda Havnekontor, 4200 Sauda; tel. 52-78-25-85; fax 52-78-15-88; Harbour Master OEYSTEIN TVEIT.

Stavanger: Stavanger Interkommunale Havn IKS, Nedre Strandgt. 51, 4005 Stavanger; tel. 51-50-12-00; fax 51-50-12-22; e-mail info@stavanger.havn.no; internet www.stavanger.havn.no; Port Dir BJØRN HELGOY.

Tønsberg: Tønsberg Havnevesen, Nedre Langgate 36, 3126 Tønsberg; tel. 33-35-45-00; fax 33-33-26-75; e-mail tonsberg.havn@tonsberg.kommune.no; Harbour Master PER SVENNAR.

Tromsø Havn KF: Tromsø Havnevesen, POB 392, 9254 Tromsø; tel. 77-66-18-50; fax 77-66-18-51; e-mail adm@tromso.havn.no; internet www.tromso.havn.no; f. 1827; Port Capt. ASBJØRN NIKOLAI MORTENSEN.

Trondheim: Trondheim Havn, Pirsenteret, 7462 Trondheim; tel. 73-99-17-00; fax 73-99-17-17; Port Capt. SIGURD KLEIVEN.

Vardø: Vardø Havn KF, POB 50, 9951 Vardø; tel. 78-98-72-76; fax 78-98-78-28; Harbour Master INGOLF ERIKSEN.

Shipping Organizations

Nordisk Skibsrederforening (Northern Shipowners' Defence Club): Kristinelundvn 22, POB 3033 Elisenberg, 0207 Oslo; tel. 22-13-56-00; fax 22-43-00-35; e-mail post@nordisk.no; internet www.nordisk.no; f. 1889; Pres. MORTEN WERRING; Man. Dir GEORG SCHEEL.

Norges Rederiforbund (Norwegian Shipowners' Asscn): POB 1452 Vika, 0116 Oslo; tel. 22-40-15-00; fax 22-40-15-15; e-mail post@rederi.no; internet www.rederi.no; f. 1909; 10 regional asscns; Dir-Gen. MARIANNE LIE.

Norsk Skipsmeglerforbund (Norwegian Shipbrokers' Asscn): Fr. Nansens pl. 9, 0160 Oslo; tel. 22-20-14-85; fax 22-42-74-13; e-mail mail@shipbroker.no; internet www.shipbroker.no; f. 1919; Pres. AXEL STOVE LORENTLEN; Gen. Man. GRETE C. NOER; 150 mems.

Det Norske Veritas (DNV): Veritasvn 1, POB 300, 1322 Høvik; tel. 67-57-99-00; f. 1864; classification and certification of ships, other floating structures and fixed offshore structures, petrochemical installations, marine research and development; stations in over 100 countries throughout the world; acts on behalf of 130 national maritime authorities; CEO MIKLOS KONKOLY-THEGE.

Rederienes Landsforening (Federation of Norwegian Coastal Shipping): Essendropsgt. 6, POB 5201 Majorstua, 0302 Oslo; tel. 23-08-85-60; fax 23-08-85-61; e-mail rlf@rlf.no; internet www.rlf.no; Admin. Dir HARALD THOMASSEN.

Principal Companies

Actinor Shipping ASA: Rådhusgt. 27, 0158 Oslo; tel. 22-42-78-30; fax 22-42-72-04; Pres. KRISTIAN EIDESVIK.

Bergesen d.y. ASA: Drammensvn 106, POB 2800 Solli, 0204 Oslo; tel. 22-12-05-05; fax 22-12-05-00; e-mail bergesen@bergesen.no; internet www.bergesen.no; f. 1935; merged with Havtor Management A/S in 1995; Chair. MORTEN SIG. BERGESEN; Man. Dir SVEIN ERIK AMUNDSEN.

Bergshav Management AS: POB 8, 4891 Grimstad; tel. 37-25-63-00; fax 37-25-63-01; e-mail mgmt@bergshav.com; internet www.bergshav.com; Chair. ATLE BERGSHAVEN.

Bona Shipping AS: Rådhusgt. 27, POB 470 Sentrum, 0105 Oslo; tel. 22-31-00-00; fax 22-31-00-01; internet www.bona.no; Pres. RAGNAR BELCK-OLSEN.

Grieg Shipping A/S: POB 781, 5002 Bergen; tel. 55-57-69-50; fax 55-57-69-10; Man. Dir JACOB IRGENS.

Leif Høegh & Co ASA: Wergelandsvn 7, POB 2596 Solli, 0203 Oslo; tel. 22-86-97-00; fax 22-20-14-08; e-mail ihc@hoegh.no; internet www.hoegh.no; f. 1927; vessels for the transport of liquefied gas, ores and other bulk materials, car and ro-ro ships and reefers; world-wide services; Chair. WESTYE HØEGH; Pres. THOR J. GUTTORMSEN.

Jahre-Wallem AS: Strandpromenaden 9, POB 271, 3201 Sandefjord; tel. 33-48-44-44; fax 33-48-44-43; e-mail jawa@jawa.no; Dir HENRIK LIAN.

Jebsens Management A/S: POB 4145 Dreggen, 5015 Bergen; tel. 55-31-03-20; fax 55-31-72-70; f. 1929; services in Scandinavia, and to Europe, Far East, Australia, the Americas; Owner ATLE JEBSEN.

Torvald Klaveness & Co AS: Harbitzalleen 2A, POB 183 Skøyen, 0212 Oslo; tel. 22-52-60-00; fax 22-50-67-31; Chair. T. E. KLAVENESS; Man. Dir NILS HOY-PETERSEN.

Knutsen OAS Shipping A/S: Smedasundet 40, POB 2017, 5501 Haugesund; tel. 52-70-40-00; fax 52-70-40-40; Man. JENS ULLTVEIT MOE.

A/S J. Ludwig Mowinckels Rederi: Bradbenken 1, POB 4070 Dreggen, 5835 Bergen; tel. 55-21-63-00; fax 55-21-63-05; e-mail mailbox@jlmr.no; f. 1898; tankers and cargo services; Man. Dir BØRGE ROSENBERG.

Norbrooker Shipping & Trading A/S: POB 34, 4401 Flekkefjord; Strandgt. 36, 4400 Flekkefjord; tel. 38-32-61-00; fax 38-38-17-01; e-mail norbroke@online.no.

Odfjell ASA: Conrad Mohrsveg 29, 5073 Bergen; POB 6101 Postterminalen, 5892 Bergen; tel. 55-27-00-00; fax 55-28-47-41; e-mail mail@odfjell.com; internet www.odfjell.com; f. 1916; transportation and storage of liquid chemicals; Chair. B. D. ODFJELL, Jr.

Rasmussen Maritime Services A/S: POB 37, 4661 Kristiansand; tel. 38-12-22-00; fax 38-07-03-58; e-mail rms@rasmussen.no; Man. Dir OIVIND STAERK.

Red Band A/S: Prinsens gt. 2B, POB 374 Sentrum, 0101 Oslo; tel. 22-34-11-00; fax 22-42-13-14; e-mail redband@redband.no; Chair. NICOLAS BRUM-LIE.

Det Stavangerske Dampskibsselskab: POB 40, 4001 Stavanger; tel. 51-84-56-11; fax 51-84-56-03; Chair. HENRIK AGER-HANSSEN.

Uglands Rederi A/S: POB 128, 4891 Grimstad; tel. 37-29-26-00; fax 37-04-47-22; e-mail jjuc@jjuc.no; internet www.jjuc.no; f. 1930; part of J. J. Ugland Cos (f. 1996; group of cos with shipping interests; tankers, bulk carriers, crane vessel, barges).

Anders Wilhelmsen & Co AS: Beddingen 8, Aker Brygge, POB 1583 Vika, 0118 Oslo; tel. 22-01-42-00; fax 22-01-43-72; e-mail thagen@awilco.no; Chair. ARNE WILHELMSEN; Man. Dir ENDRE ORDING SUND.

Wilh. Wilhelmsen ASA: Strandvn 20, POB 33, 1324 Lysaker; tel. 67-58-40-00; fax 67-58-40-80; internet www.wilh-wilhelmen.com; f. 1861; regular fast freight services world-wide; Chair. WILHELM WILHELMSEN; Man. Dir INGAR SKAUG.

CIVIL AVIATION

In 1999 there were 53 scheduled airports in Norway, the principal international airport being Gardermøn Airport, 47 km north of Oslo. The airport at Gardermøn opened in October 1998, replacing the previous principal international airport, Fornebu Airport, which ceased operations in the same month.

Civil Aviation Authority

Luftfartstilsynet: POB 243, 8001 Bodø; tel. 75-58-50-00; fax 75-58-50-05; e-mail postmottak@caa.no; internet www.caa.no; f. 2000; independent administrative body under the Ministry of Transport and Communications; Dir-Gen. OTTO LAGARHUS.

Principal Airlines

SAS Norge ASA (Norwegian Airlines Ltd): 0800 Oslo; tel. 64-81-60-50; fax 67-58-08-20; f. 1946; partner in Scandinavian Airlines System (SAS) and SAS Commuter, with Denmark and Sweden (q.v.); Chair. HARALD NORVIK; Gen. Man. JOERGEN LINDEGAARD.

Braathens SAFE (Braathens South-American & Far East Airtransport) ASA: Oksenøyvn 3, POB 55 Lufthavn-Fornebu, 1330 Oslo Airport; tel. 67-59-70-00; fax 67-59-13-09; internet www.braathens.no; f. 1946; scheduled airline and charter company; domestic routes: all main cities in Norway and Longyearbyen, Svalbard; international routes within Europe; Pres. ERIK G. BRAATHEN; Chair. LARS A. CHRISTENSEN.

Norwegian Air Shuttle: Oksenøyvn 10, POB 115 Oslo Lufthavn, 1331 Oslo; tel. 67-58-37-77; fax 67-58-32-77; f. 1966; present name since 1993; charter and contract flights; Man. Dir STIG WILLASSEN.

Scandinavian Airlines System (SAS): Head Office: Snaröyvn 57, 0080 Oslo; tel. 64-81-60-50; internet www.sas.no; f. 1946; the national carrier of Denmark, Norway and Sweden; consortium owned two-sevenths by SAS Danmark A/S, two-sevenths by SAS Norge ASA and three-sevenths by SAS Sverige AB; parent org. is a limited co-owned 50% by Government and 50% by private shareholders; SAS group includes the consortium and the subsidiaries in which the consortium has a majority or otherwise controlling interest; the Board consists of two members from each of the parent cos and the chairmanship rotates among the three national chairmen on an annual basis; strategic alliance with Lufthansa (Germany) formed in 1995; Chair. BO BERGGREN; Pres. and CEO JAN STENBERG.

Widerøe's Flyveselskap ASA: Eyvind Lyches vei 10, POB 312, 1301 Sandvika; tel. 67-11-60-00; fax 67-11-61-95; internet www.wideroe.no; f. 1934; scheduled domestic service; Pres. PER ARNE WATLE.

Widerøe Norsk Air: POB 2047, 3202 Sandefjord; tel. 33-46-98-80; fax 33-47-03-25; f. 1961; acquired by Widerøe in 1989; regional services in Scandinavia; Technical Dir JAN RUNE NORDGARD.

Tourism

Norway is a popular resort for tourists who prefer holidays in rugged, peaceful surroundings. It is also a centre for winter sports. In 2003 receipts from tourism amounted to US $3,082m., compared with $2,663m. in the previous year. In that year visitor arrivals totalled 4.4m.

Innovasjon Norge (Innovation Norway): Akersgt 13, POB 448 Sentrum, 0104 Oslo; tel. 22-00-25-00; fax 22-00-25-01; e-mail post@invanor.no; internet www.visitnorway.com; f. 2004 to replace Norges Turistråd (Norwegian Tourist Board), Norges Eksportråd (Norwegian Trade Council), Statens nærings- og distriktsutviklingsfond (SND-Regional Development Fund) and Statens Veiledningskontor for Oppfinnere (SVO-Government Consultative Office for Inventors); state-owned; operates in all Norwegian counties and more than 30 countries world-wide; Pres. STEINAR OLSEN.

NORWEGIAN EXTERNAL TERRITORIES
SVALBARD

Introductory Survey

Location and Climate

The Svalbard archipelago is the northernmost part of the Kingdom of Norway. It lies in the Arctic Sea, 657 km north of mainland Norway, between latitudes 74°N and 81°N and longitudes 10°E and 35°E, comprising a total area of 61,022 sq km (23,561 sq miles). The group consists of nine principal islands, Spitsbergen (formerly Vestspitsbergen), the main island, Kvitøya, Edgeøya, Barentsøya, Nordaustlandet, Prins Karls Forland, Kong Karls Land, Hopen and Bjørnøya (Bear Island), some 204 km to the south of the main island, together with numerous small islands. Mild Atlantic winds lessen the severity of the Arctic climate, but almost 60% of the land area is covered with glaciers. Average temperatures range from −16°C (3°F) to 6°C (43°F), and precipitation in the lowlands averages some 200 mm per year.

History and Government

The existence of Svalbard has probably been known since Viking exploration in the 12th century. There were conflicting claims to sovereignty by Britain, the Netherlands and Denmark-Norway in the 17th century, when the area was an important centre for whale hunting, but interest subsequently lapsed until the early years of the 20th century, when coal deposits were discovered. On 9 February 1920 14 nations signed a treaty recognizing Norwegian sovereignty over Svalbard. International rights of access and economic exploitation were agreed, but the use of the islands for bellicose purposes and the construction of fortifications were expressly forbidden.

Svalbard has been part of the Kingdom of Norway since it was formally incorporated in 1925. The territory is administered by a Sysselmann (Governor), resident at Longyearbyen, on Spitsbergen, which is the administrative centre of the archipelago. The Sysselmann is responsible to the Polar Department of the Ministry of Justice and the Police. The Norwegian Polar Institute acts in an advisory capacity to the administration. Svalbard lies within the same judicial jurisdiction as the city of Tromsø.

In accordance with the Svalbard Treaty of 1920, the Norwegian Government prescribed a mining code in 1925, regulating all mineral prospecting and exploitation in the islands and their territorial waters extending to 4 nautical miles (7.4 km). The Mining Code is administered by a Commissioner of Mines.

In 1941 the population was evacuated by Allied forces for the duration of the war, and three years later the USSR, to which Svalbard was of considerable strategic interest, unsuccessfully sought Norway's agreement to a revision of the 1920 treaty whereby part of the archipelago would become a Soviet-Norwegian condominium. Russia currently maintains a helicopter station and a mobile radar station adjoining its coal-mining settlement at Barentsburg on Spitsbergen. Russia (and, before it, the USSR) has refused to recognize Norway's unilateral declaration of a fisheries protection zone around Svalbard from 1977.

In June 1994 vessels of the Norwegian coastguard severed the nets of Icelandic fishing boats that were alleged to be fishing within the fisheries protection zone. The Icelandic Government subsequently withdrew its boats from the zone; in August, however, Norway claimed that an Icelandic boat had opened fire on a Norwegian coastguard vessel.

Particularly since a Royal Decree of 1971, the Norwegian administration has endeavoured to protect the flora, fauna and environment of Svalbard. The protected areas, which total 39,815 sq km of land, or 65% of the land area, and 76,293 km of sea, include seven national parks, the most recently created (September 2005) being at Indre Wijdefjorden in northern Spitsbergen.

Apart from a small permanent research station established by Poland, only Norway and Russia maintain permanent settlements on Svalbard. In order to continue Norwegian occupation of Svalbard, thus ensuring its future as a Norwegian territory and protecting it from potential, rival claims for sovereignty, notably from Russia, in 2000 the Svalbard administration proposed the opening of a new coal mine on Spitsbergen to exploit newly discovered reserves. Svalbard has also been promoted as a centre for scientific research; at the end of 2000 there were more than 20 scientific stations from foreign countries on the islands. In January 2004 representatives of the Norwegian Ministry of Foreign Affairs met with Russia's Deputy Minister of Foreign Affairs to discuss possible bilateral co-operation in Svalbard, in the areas of energy, fisheries and environmental protection.

In November 2001 Norwegians resident on Spitsbergen conducted, for the first time, an election for a local council. The new Longyearbyen Council (Longyearbyen Lokalstyre) replaced the incumbent Svalbard Council, which had been partly appointed by the state-owned mining company, Store Norske Spitsbergen Kulkompani. The new 15-seat Council was to exercise only limited power in issues relating to health, education and the Church, which would all continue to be controlled by the State. The rate of participation in the local election was only 51.5% of the electorate; a multi-party grouping received 47.8% of the total votes cast, obtaining eight seats on the Council, while Det norske Arbeiderparti (DnA—Norwegian Labour Party) won 37.9% and secured six seats; Høyre took the remaining seat, with 10.1% of the votes cast. The Kristelig Folkeparti (KrF—Christian Democrats' Party) won 4.2% of the votes cast, but did not gain representation on the Council.

Elections to the Longyearbyen Council were held in 2003. The DnA secured 44.6% of the votes cast and six seats on the Council, while the multi-party grouping won five seats, with 31.0% of the votes cast. The Fremskrittspartiet (FrP—Progress Party) and Høyre each won two seats, respectively receiving 12.3% and 12.1% of the votes cast. The Council's mandate was increased from two to four years.

Social and Economic Affairs

The total population in January 2005 was 2,400, of whom 1,645 were resident in Norwegian settlements, 747 in Russian settlements and eight in Polish settlements. There are limited recreational, transport, financial and educational facilities on Svalbard. There is a hospital in Longyearbyen.

During 1994 a total of 212 expeditions visited Svalbard, of which the majority (169) were tourist expeditions. In 2004 31,004 guests booked in at hotels in Svalbard.

Coal is the islands' main product. In 2004 2,991,166 metric tons were shipped from mines on Svalbard (2,859,089 tons from Norwegian mines). The Norwegian state-owned coal company, Store Norske Spitsbergen Kulkompani (SNSK), directly employed 230 people in 2004. The company was incurring financial losses each year, and the principal motive for continuing to exploit the coal deposits appeared to be political rather than economic. Until 1989 SNSK operated many local services and provided most of the infrastructure, but in that year these functions were assumed by the state company Svalbard Samfunnsdrift, which employed 140 people in 1998. By 1998 the number of people employed in the Norwegian mines had declined to 201 (from 358 in 1991), but the number increased again to 265 in 2004. At the end of 2000 only one Norwegian coal-mining camp, Gruve 7, was operational (compared with seven at the islands' peak), and this was largely to supply the one coal-burning power station, which provides electricity for the capital, Longyearbyen. In early 2004 Longyearbyen Energiverk (the company that operates the power station) was considering alternative sources of energy with which to replace the station. Russia still had two camps on Svalbard at the beginning of 2004, although the one at Pyramiden had only been mined for scrap since 1998 (and even this limited activity was drawing to a close), while the other, at Barentsburg, was still shipping coal to Russia. A new Norwegian mine, at Svea, about 60 km (38 miles) from Longyearbyen, was opened in 2001 to exploit significant newly discovered reserves of coal. The coal was of high calorific value (1,200 kilocalories per kilo more than usual) and therefore burnt more cleanly than normal coal. Svea is extremely well-placed for exporting coal to Europe, being located only 10 km from the port; the mine is linked to the port by road, and in 2004 SNSK constructed a conveyor belt to transport the coal directly to the ships.

Deep drillings for petroleum have been carried out by Norwegian and other companies, but no commercial results have been reported. Svalbard's other mineral resources include reserves of phosphate, asbestos, iron ore, anhydrite, limestone and various sulphides.

Tourism has been encouraged on Svalbard; cruise ships make stops at the islands and there is also a small industry in skiing and trekking across the wilderness. The services sector has grown substantially in recent years, particularly in the areas of education and research. Many jobs are connected to Norwegian government organizations, such as Statsbygg, the state-owned building agency, and Longyearbyen Elementary and High School.

For 2005 the Svalbard budget was 195.2m. kroner, of which 135.9m. kroner was a direct subsidy from the Norwegian state budget. Svalbard raises some revenue from the sale of fishing licences.

Statistical Survey

Source: Statistics Norway, Kongensgt. 6, Oslo; tel. 21-09-00-00; fax 21-09-49-73; e-mail biblioteket@ssb.no; internet www.ssb.no.

AREA AND POPULATION

Area: 61,022 sq km (23,561 sq miles).
Population (1 January 2005): 2,400 (Norwegian 1,645, Russian 747, Polish 8).
Density (1 January 2005): 0.04 per sq km.
Economically Active Population (2003): Mining and quarrying 233; Manufacturing 8; Construction 194; Wholesale and retail trade 107; Hotels and restaurants 100; Transport and storage 177; Supporting and auxiliary transport activities 120; Public administration 147; Education, health and social work 133; Other community, social and personal service activities 15; *Total* 1,234.

MINING

Coal Shipments ('000 metric tons): 2,363.2 (Norwegian mines 2,131.7) in 2002; 3,173.5 (Norwegian mines 2,809.2) in 2003; 2,991.2 (Norwegian mines 2,859.1) in 2004.

FINANCE

(Norwegian currency is used; 100 øre = 1 Norwegian krone)
Budget (million kroner, 2005): : Estimated revenue 195.2 (incl. direct grant of 135.9 from central Govt); Budgeted expenditure 195.2.

TRANSPORT AND TOURISM

Road Traffic (vehicles registered at 31 December 2004): Passenger cars 930; Buses 41; Goods vehicles 394; Mopeds and motorcycles 130; Snow scooters 1,468.
Civil Aviation (2004, metric tons unless otherwise specified): Passengers (number) 86,232; Goods received 641; Goods sent 42; Mail received 412; Mail sent 54.
Guests Arriving at Hotels: 28,654 in 2002; 27,879 in 2003; 31,004 in 2004.

EDUCATION

(2004)

Pre-primary: Schools 3; Teachers 33; Pupils 103.
Primary and Lower Secondary: Schools 1; Pupils 144.
Upper Secondary: Schools 1; Pupils 55.

Directory

The Government

(April 2006)

ADMINISTRATION

Governor (Sysselmann): SVEN OLE FAGERNÆS.
Commissioner of Mines: PER ZAKKEN BREKKE.

OFFICES

Office of the Governor: Kontoret til Sysselmannen på Svalbard, POB 633, 9171 Longyearbyen, Svalbard; tel. 79-02-43-00; fax 79-02-11-66; e-mail firmapost@sysselmannen.svalbard.no; internet www.sysselmannen.svalbard.no.

Ministry of Justice and the Police (Polar Affairs Department): Akersgt. 42, POB 8005 Dep., 0030 Oslo; tel. 22-24-56-01; fax 22-24-95-39; e-mail postmottak@jd.dep.no; responsible for the administration of Svalbard and Jan Mayen, and for the Norwegian 'Antarctic' dependencies.

Norsk Polarinstitutt Svalbard (Norwegian Polar Institute Svalbard): Næringsbygget, POB 505, 9171 Longyearbyen, Svalbard; tel. 79-02-26-00; fax 79-02-26-04; e-mail postmottak@npolar.no; internet www.npolar.no; f. 1928 as Norges Svalbard- og Ishavs-undersøkelser; adopted present name and expanded functions in 1948; branch of Norwegian Polar Institute, Oslo; mapping and research institute; responsible for advising Govt on matters concerning Svalbard, Jan Mayen and the 'Antarctic' dependencies; monitors and investigates environment of the territories; organizes regular Antarctic research expeditions; establishes and maintains aids to navigation in Svalbard waters; Dir ARNHILD RAMSENG.

Norsk Polarinstitutts Forskningsstasjon (Norwegian Polar Institute Research Station): Sverdrupstasjonen, 9173 Ny-Ålesund, Svalbard; tel. 79-02-74-00; fax 79-02-70-02; permanent research base in Svalbard.

Longyearbyen Lokalstyre (Longyearbyen Council): POB 350, 9171 Longyearbyen; tel. 79-02-21-50; fax 79-02-21-51; e-mail postmottak@lokalstyre.no; internet www.lokalstyre.no; f. 2002; first locally elected body in Svalbard; replaced Svalbard Council; Leader SIGMUND SPJELKAVIK.

Svalbard, as an integral part of the Kingdom of Norway, has provision for its Norwegian inhabitants to participate in the national elections. For judicial matters Svalbard lies in the jurisdiction of Tromsø. The state Evangelical Lutheran Church provides religious services.

Press

There is only one newspaper published in the Svalbard archipelago.
Svalbardposten: POB 503, 9171 Longyearbyen; tel. 79-02-47-00; fax 79-02-47-01; e-mail post@svalbardposten.no; internet www.svalbardposten.no; f. 1948; weekly; Editor-in-Chief TORBJORN PEDERSEN; circ. 3,300.

Finance

Norwegian currency is used. Most banking facilities are available.
Sparebanken Nord-Norge: POB 518, 9171 Longyearbyen, Svalbard; tel. 79-02-29-10; fax 79-02-29-11; e-mail kundeservice@snn.sparebank1.no; internet www.snn.no; savings bank.

Trade and Industry

Store Norske Spitsbergen Kulkompani A/S: 9171 Longyearbyen, Svalbard; tel. 79-02-52-00; fax 79-02-18-41; internet www.snsk.no; state-owned; operates coal-mines; 230 employees (2003); Admin. Dir ATLE FORNES.

Store Norske Spitsbergen Grubekompani A/S (SNSG): f. 2002; manages all assets, rights, contractual obligations and liabilities in connection with the Svea Nord mine, responsible for coal production and sales in Longyearbyen and Svea, and for exploration at both its own SNSK's claims.

Store Norske Boliger A/S: f. 2002; manages the group's accommodation in Longyearbyen and some of the accommodation in Svea.

Svalbard Næringsutvikling A/S: 9170 Longyearbyen, Svalbard; tel. 79-02-21-00; fax 79-02-10-19; state-owned; encourages development of industry and trade; Admin. Dir ENDRE HOFLANDSDAL.

Svalbard Samfunnsdrift A/S: POB 475, 9171 Longyearbyen, Svalbard; tel. 79-02-23-00; fax 79-02-23-01; e-mail firmapost@ssd.no; internet www.ssd.no; state-owned; operates most local services, undertakes infrastructure development; 140 employees (1998); Admin. Dir ENDRE HOFLANDSDAL.

Transport

Shipping links operate from June to August, with weekly sailings from Honningsvåg to Longyearbyen and Ny-Ålesund and back via Tromsø. In 1975 an airport was opened near Longyearbyen. SAS and Braathens SAFE operate services to Tromsø up to five times per week. There are air strips at Ny-Ålesund and Svea, and a Russian helicopter facility at Barentsburg. Apart from helicopters, and a fixed-wing service between Longyearbyen and Ny-Ålesund, internal traffic is little developed.

AIRPORT

Svalbard Lufthavn: POB 550, 9171 Longyearbyen, Svalbard; tel. 79-02-38-00; fax 79-02-38-01; e-mail ole.m.rambech@avinor.no; internet www.avinor.no; f. 1975; owned by Avinor; Man. OLE M. RAMBECH.

JAN MAYEN

The lofty volcanic island of Jan Mayen is located in the Arctic Ocean, some 910 km west-north-west of Bodø on the Norwegian mainland, 610 km north-north-east of Iceland and 480 km east of Greenland (Denmark). The island is 53 km in length and has a total area of 377 sq km (145 sq miles). The highest point is the summit of Mt Beerenberg (2,277 m above sea-level). The climate is severe, cold and usually misty.

The sea north and west of Jan Mayen (which was frequented by various whalers and hunters for a brief period in the 17th century) has been an important area for sealing by Norwegians since the mid-19th century. Partly to assist their navigation, the Norwegian Meteorological Institute instigated activities on the island in the early 20th century. In 1922 Jan Mayen was declared annexed by the Institute, and on 8 May 1929 Norwegian sovereignty was proclaimed by Royal Decree. The island was made an integral part of the Kingdom of Norway by the Jan Mayen Act of 1930. Jan Mayen is not included in the Svalbard Treaty.

The island has no known exploitable mineral resources and is largely barren. Fishing in the surrounding waters is intermittently productive, and it was once considered that a base for fishing fleets could be established. This is now believed to be unlikely, particularly because of the high cost of building a harbour. In September 1970 there was a violent volcanic eruption on the island, the first since the early 19th century. In the course of the first few days of the eruption a huge glacier melted and millions of cubic metres of ice disappeared as steam. Lava poured into the sea and formed about 3.5 sq km of new land. The island's main use remains as a meteorological, navigational and radio station.

During the Second World War Jan Mayen remained the only part of Norway under Norwegian rule, following the German invasion of the mainland. Despite some conflict, the Norwegian Government and its allies maintained the strategic meteorological station and established a radio-locating station on the island during the war.

In 1946 a new base was established at Nordlaguna, both as a meteorological and a coastal radio station. As a result of a North Atlantic defence co-operation exercise in 1959–60, a long-range navigation (LORAN) network was established, with one base on Jan Mayen. At the same time, it was decided to build an airstrip near the new LORAN C base, and in 1962 the personnel of the weather and coastal radio services also moved to the same area.

After negotiations with Iceland in 1980, the Norwegian Government declared an economic zone extending for 200 nautical miles (370 km) around the coast of Jan Mayen. In 1981 a further agreement was made with Iceland, regarding mineral and fishing rights. A dispute with Denmark, acting on behalf of Greenland, concerning the delimitation of maritime economic zones between Greenland and Jan Mayen was referred by Denmark to the International Court of Justice (based in The Hague, Netherlands) in 1988. The Court delivered its judgment in June 1993, deciding that 57% of the disputed area belonged to Norway. A subsequent accord on maritime delimitation, agreed between the Governments of Norway, Greenland and Iceland in November 1997, established the boundaries of a 1,934-sq km area of Arctic sea that had been excluded from the terms of the 1993 settlement.

The commanding officer in charge of the LORAN C base is the chief administrative official of the island. The officer is responsible for the 15–25 inhabitants (who usually remain on the island for only one year at a time), and is accountable to the Chief of Police in Bodø, and the Ministry of Justice and the Police (as in Svalbard). The LORAN C commander may grant permission for visits of not more than 24 hours. For longer visits, the Bodø Chief of Police or the Ministry must approve the application. Visits are normally allowed only for scientific purposes and only if private provision has been made for transport. There is no public transport or accommodation on Jan Mayen.

Officer-in-charge: MILDRID RINGSET, LORAN C Base, Jan Mayen; tel. 51-40-22-50; fax 51-40-20-66; e-mail janmayen@ftd.mil.no; internet www.jan-mayen.no.

Chief of Police (Bodø): Kongensgt. 81, POB 1023, 8006 Bodøe-mail politiet@bodo.politiet.no.

For the Ministry of Justice and the Police and the Norsk Polarinstitutt (Norwegian Polar Institute), see under Svalbard.

NORWEGIAN DEPENDENCIES

Norway's so-called 'Antarctic' dependencies are all uninhabited and were acquired as a result of Norwegian whaling interests in the region since the 1890s. The three territories are dependencies of the Kingdom of Norway, and are administered by the Polar Department of the Ministry of Justice and the Police, with the advice of the Norsk Polarinstitutt (Norwegian Polar Institute: for details, see under Svalbard) and the assistance of the Ministry of the Environment.

Bouvetøya

Bouvetøya (Bouvet Island) is a volcanic island in the South Atlantic Ocean, some 2,400 km south-west of the Cape of Good Hope (South Africa) and 1,600 km north of Antarctica. The island lies north of the Antarctic Circle (it is not, therefore, encompassed by the terms of the Antarctic Treaty). Bouvetøya has an area of 49 sq km, but about 93% of the surface is covered by ice. The climate is maritime antarctic, with a mean annual temperature of −1°C and a persistent heavy fog.

Regular landings on the island occurred only as part of Norwegian Antarctic expeditions in the 1920s and 1930s. Bouvetøya was claimed for Norway in 1927, placed under its sovereignty in 1928, and declared a Norwegian dependency in 1930. A Royal Decree of 1971 declared the entire island to be a nature reserve. An automatic weather station was established in 1977, and the island is regularly visited by Norwegian scientific expeditions.

Dronning Maud Land

Dronning Maud Land (Queen Maud Land) is that sector of the Antarctic continent lying between the longitudes of 20°W (adjoining the British Antarctic Territory to the west) and 45°E (neighbouring the Australian Antarctic Territory). The territory is, in area, several times the size of Norway, and 98% of its surface is covered by ice. The climate is severe, the usual temperature always being below 0°C and, in the winter months of mid-year, falling to −60°C on the coast and −88°C inland. The territory's coast is divided into five named sectors (the exact delimitations of which, and of the territory as a whole, have varied at different periods): Kronprinsesse Märtha Kyst (Crown Princess Märtha Coast), Prinsesse Astrid Kyst, Prinsesse Ragnhild Kyst, Prins Harald Kyst and Kronprins Olav Kyst.

The first Norwegian territorial claims in Antarctica were made in 1929, following many years of Norwegian involvement in the exploration and survey of the continent. Further claims were made in 1931 and 1936–37. These claims were formalized by the Norwegian authorities, and the land placed under their sovereignty, only in 1939. The extent of Dronning Maud Land then received its current limits, between the British and Australian claims. Norway now follows a policy which upholds its claim to sovereignty but supports the pattern of international co-operation, particularly that established under the terms of the Antarctic Treaty (see p. 545) (signed in 1959), to which the Kingdom of Norway is an original signatory. There are six wintering stations, staffed by personnel of various nationalities, in Dronning Maud Land.

Peter I Øy

Peter I Øy (Peter I Island) is located in the Bellingshausen Sea, some 450 km north of Antarctica and more than 1,800 km south-west of Chile, the nearest inhabited territory. It covers an area of some 156 sq km, 95% of which is covered by ice. The island lies within the Antarctic Circle and the area covered by the terms of the Antarctic Treaty. The first recorded landing on the island was not made until 1929, by a Norwegian expedition, which then claimed the island. A Royal Proclamation placed Peter I Øy under Norwegian sovereignty in 1931, and the island was declared a dependency in 1933. Few landings have been made since, but in 1987 the Norsk Polarinstitutt (Norwegian Polar Institute) conducted a relatively long survey and established an automatic weather station on the island.

OMAN

Introductory Survey

Location, Climate, Language, Religion, Flag, Capital

The Sultanate of Oman occupies the extreme east and south-east of the Arabian peninsula. It is bordered to the west by the United Arab Emirates (UAE), Saudi Arabia and Yemen. A detached portion of Oman, separated from the rest of the country by UAE territory, lies at the tip of the Musandam peninsula, on the southern shore of the Strait of Hormuz. Oman has a coastline of more than 1,600 km (1,000 miles) on the Indian Ocean, and is separated from Iran by the Gulf of Oman. In Muscat average annual rainfall is 100 mm and the average temperature varies between 21°C (70°F) and 35°C (95°F). Rainfall is heavier on the hills of the interior, and the south-western province of Dhofar is the only part of Arabia to benefit from the summer monsoon. The official language is Arabic. Islam is the official religion. The majority of the population are Ibadi Muslims, while about one-quarter are Hindus. The national flag (proportions 1 by 2) has three equal horizontal stripes, of white, red and green, with a vertical red stripe at the hoist. In the upper hoist is a representation, in white, of the state emblem, two crossed swords and a dagger (*khanjar*), surmounted by a belt. The capital is Muscat.

Recent History

Officially known as Muscat and Oman until 1970, the Sultanate has had a special relationship with the United Kingdom since the 19th century. Full independence was confirmed by a treaty of friendship with the United Kingdom on 20 December 1951, although the armed forces and police retain some British officers on loan service. Sultan Said bin Taimur succeeded his father in 1932 and maintained a strictly conservative and isolationist rule until July 1970, when he was overthrown by his son in a bloodless palace coup. The new Sultan, Qaboos bin Said as-Said, then began a liberalization of the regime, and spending on development was increased.

A Consultative Assembly (comprising representatives of the Government, the private sector and the regions, appointed by the Sultan) was created in 1981, in order to advise Sultan Qaboos on economic and social development. In November 1990 it was announced that the Assembly was to be replaced by a Consultative Council (Majlis ash-Shoura), comprising regional representatives, which was intended to extend participation by Omani citizens in national affairs. A selection process was duly announced whereby representatives of each of the country's 59 districts (*wilayat*) would nominate three candidates; the nominations would then be submitted to the Deputy Prime Minister for Legal Affairs, who, with the Sultan's approval, would choose one representative for each district to join the new Majlis. No government official or civil servant would be eligible for election to the new body. The President of the Consultative Council would be appointed by royal decree; other executive officers and committee members would be designated by, and from among, the 59 local delegates. Although the role of the Majlis was strictly advisory, government ministers were to be obliged to submit reports to the assembly and to answer any questions addressed to them. The Majlis was formally established by royal decree in November 1991 and was convened in January 1992, when its members were sworn in for a three-year term. In 1994 membership of the Majlis was increased from 59 to 80, to include an additional member for any district with 30,000 or more inhabitants. Women were for the first time nominated as candidates in six regions in and around the capital; two women were subsequently appointed to the enlarged Majlis.

In mid-1994 the Government was reported to be employing stringent measures to curb an apparent rise in Islamist militancy in Oman. In August the security forces arrested more than 200 members of an allegedly foreign-sponsored Islamist organization, including two junior ministers, university lecturers, students and soldiers. Most were later released, but in November several of those against whom charges had been brought were sentenced to death, having been found guilty of conspiracy to foment sedition; the Sultan subsequently commuted the death sentences to terms of imprisonment. In November 1995 139 prisoners were released, under a general amnesty granted by Sultan Qaboos.

In November 1996 Sultan Qaboos issued a decree promulgating a Basic Statute of the State, a constitutional document defining for the first time the organs and guiding principles of the State. The Statute provided for a Council of Oman, to be composed of the Majlis ash-Shoura and a new Council of State (Majlis ad-Dawlah). The latter was to be appointed from among prominent Omanis, and would liaise between the Government and the people of Oman. It was subsequently reported that 23 senior government ministers had resigned as directors of public joint-stock companies, in accordance with a stipulation in the Basic Statute that ministers should not abuse their official position for personal gain. In December a Defence Council was established by royal decree, comprising the Minister of the Royal Court, the heads of the armed and police forces, and the chief of internal security. The Basic Statute defined a process of succession to the Sultan, requiring that the ruling family determine a successor within three days of the throne's falling vacant, failing which the Defence Council would confirm the appointment of a successor predetermined by the Sultan.

Voting was organized in October 1997 to select candidates for appointment to the Majlis ash-Shoura. Women from all regions were permitted to seek nomination. Of a total of 736 candidates, 164 were chosen, from whom the Sultan selected the 82 members of the new Majlis in November. The two female members of the outgoing Majlis were returned to office. In December Sultan Qaboos issued a decree appointing the 41 members of the Majlis ad-Dawlah, which was reportedly dominated by former politicians, business leaders and academics. A further decree established the Council of Oman, which was formally inaugurated by the Sultan on 27 December.

Elections to the Majlis ash-Shoura were held on 14 September 2000. For the first time members were directly elected rather than appointed by the Sultan. However, voting rights were restricted to prominent business leaders, intellectuals, professionals and tribal chiefs. Of a total of 541 candidates (21 of whom were women), 83 (including two women) were elected to the Majlis. The number of eligible voters had tripled, to some 150,000, since the previous election; according to official figures, an estimated 90% of the electorate participated in the poll. Publication of final election results was postponed until 20 September, following allegations that there had been incidences of vote-buying; however, the Ministry of the Interior found no evidence of electoral malpractice. A new Majlis ad-Dawlah was appointed in October, and the Council of Oman convened for its second term on 4 November. Government changes were effected in May, June and November 2001, and in February 2002.

From late 2000 the Government undertook measures aimed at reducing the number of expatriates in Oman's labour force, a process termed 'Omanization'. In April 2001 more than 100 suspected illegal immigrants were detained by the Omani authorities, who announced that all foreign nationals employed illegally in the country who had not supplied the correct documentation within a period of two months would be liable to deportation. About 130 alleged illegal immigrants were reportedly arrested in September.

The Government announced in February 2003 that the next elections to the Majlis ash-Shoura were to be held in October; voting rights would be granted to all Omani citizens over 21 years of age—a total of some 820,000 people. In March Sultan Qaboos issued a decree establishing a Public Authority for Craft Industries. The President of the Authority, Sheikha Aisha bint Khalfan bin Jumiel as-Siyabiah, was given the rank of Minister, and thus became the first female to be appointed to that level of government. Few changes to the composition of the Majlis ash-Shoura resulted from the elections, held as expected on 4 October. A total of 506 candidates, 15 of them women, stood for election to the 83-seat Consultative Council. While the electoral process was described by observers as fair and open, the turn-out was a disappointing 32% of the electorate. Critics of the elections claimed that tribal loyalties had guided the decision-making of most voters, resulting in a predictable set of results—a situation that was exacerbated by the lack of legislative power wielded by council members. Only two female candidates secured election to the Majlis, both of whom were already serving members. A royal decree passed in October extended the term of office for members of both the Majlis ash-Shoura and the Majlis ad-Dawlah from three to four years. In November a new Council of State was appointed, with an expanded membership of 57 (including eight women).

In February 2004 Sultan Qaboos announced a limited reorganization of the Council of Ministers: Sheikh Muhammad bin Abdullah bin Isa al-Harthi replaced Malek bin Sulayman al-Ma'amari as Minister of Transport and Telecommunications and the erstwhile Chief of Police, Sheikh Hilal bin Khalid bin Nasser al-Ma'wali, took over responsibility for the civil service portfolio. Meanwhile, al-Ma'amari was promoted to the rank of Lt-Gen. and appointed Chief of Police and Customs with the rank of Minister. A further decree signed in March appointed Dr Rawya bint Saud bin Ahmad al-Busaidiyah as Minister of Higher Education (the first female member of the Council of Ministers) and Sheikh Yahya bin Mahfoudh al-Mantheri as President of the Council of State. In May the Minister of Regional Municipalities and the Environment, Dr Khamis bin Mubarak bin Isa al-Alawi, was named as the new Minister of Housing, Electricity and Water; his former portfolio was assumed by Abdullah bin Salem bin Amer ar-Rawas. In June the Sultan created by royal decree a Ministry of Tourism; another woman, Rajha bint Abd al-Amir bin Ali, was appointed as the new minister. A third woman was appointed to the Council of Ministers when Dr Sharifah bint Khalfan bin Nasser al-Yahiyaia was in October given the role of Minister of Social Development. As part of the same limited reorganization, Qaboos also created a new Ministry of Sports; Ali bin Massoud bin Ali as-Sinaidi was appointed as its head.

In October 2005 31 Omanis were sentenced to gaol terms on charges including bribery and forgery, thus apparently signalling that the Government was keen to combat administrative corruption. Several high-ranking government officials were reportedly among those convicted. Meanwhile, as permitted by the approval of a press and broadcasting law in 2004, the country's first private television and radio stations were expected to receive licences in 2006. Although Omanis can, against the wishes of the state, receive private broadcasts from foreign broadcasters, this represented a significant concession to reformist elements in society. Nevertheless, since two writers had been imprisoned for criticizing the Government in 2005 (one of whom did not receive a trial), the path to liberalization could not be regarded as smooth. There were, in addition, signs in 2005 that militant Islamism was flourishing in the country, and numerous Omanis were arrested in relation to several failed plots against the regime and against expatriate workers.

An agreement on the demarcation of Oman's border with Yemen, which had been the subject of a lengthy dispute with the former People's Democratic Republic of Yemen, was signed in October 1992 and ratified in December; demarcation was completed in June 1995. In July 1996 Oman withdrew an estimated 15,000 troops from the last of the disputed territories on the Yemeni border, in accordance with the 1992 agreement, and in May 1997 the border demarcation maps were signed in Muscat. Several bilateral economic co-operation accords were announced in September 1998, as were plans for the establishment of a free-trade zone. Oman and Yemen agreed in October 2001 to extend co-operation between their hydrocarbon industries. In April 2005 talks were held in Muscat over the enhancement of joint security arrangements.

In response to the invasion of Kuwait by Iraq in August 1990, Oman, together with the other members of the Co-operation Council for the Arab States of the Gulf (Gulf Co-operation Council—GCC, see p. 205), gave its support to the deployment of a US-led defensive force in Saudi Arabia. The Omani Government expressed the view that the imposition of international economic sanctions would compel Iraq to withdraw from Kuwait. In November there was evidence that Oman was attempting to mediate in the crisis, when the Iraqi Minister of Foreign Affairs, Tareq Aziz, visited Oman. By the mid-1990s Oman's stance regarding the continuation of economic sanctions against Iraq appeared ambivalent: Oman and Qatar were, notably, absent from talks held in March 1995 between the US Secretary of State, Warren Christopher, and other GCC members to discuss the issue. In November 1997 and again in early 1998 Oman stated its opposition to possible military action to force Iraq to submit to inspections of its weapons capabilities by the UN Special Commission (UNSCOM, see the Recent History of Iraq), maintaining that the UN should remove the economic sanctions against Iraq once UNSCOM had been permitted to complete its task.

Although Oman was swift to condemn the September 2001 terrorist attacks in New York and Washington, DC, the Omani Government expressed concern that the US-led military campaign in Afghanistan against the al-Qa'ida (Base) network of Osama bin Laden (held by the USA to be principally responsible for the attacks) and the Taliban regime should not be extended to target any Arab state, notably Iraq. Street demonstrations were held in October by Omani students protesting against the war in Afghanistan. During an official visit to Oman by the US Secretary of Defense, Donald Rumsfeld, in that month, it was reported that the USA was to supply Oman with 12 F-16 fighter aircraft and other advanced weaponry, at a cost of some US $1,120m. From 2002 Oman opposed attempts led by the USA, as part of its 'war on terror', to garner international support for a military offensive against the Iraqi regime of Saddam Hussain, and advocated a diplomatic solution to the escalating crisis. In March 2003, as the US-led force began assaults on targets in Iraq, Sultan Qaboos appealed for a swift curtailment of the conflict, which he described as 'unjustified' and 'illegitimate'. During March and April there were frequent anti-war protests in various locations in Oman.

In April 1994 the Israeli Deputy Minister of Foreign Affairs, Yossi Beilin, participated in talks in Oman. This constituted the first official visit by an Israeli government member to an Arab Gulf state since Israel's declaration of independence in 1948. In September 1994, moreover, Oman and the other GCC member states announced the partial ending of their economic boycott of Israel. In December the Israeli Prime Minister, Itzhak Rabin, made an official visit to Oman to discuss the Middle East peace process, and in February 1995 it was announced that low-level diplomatic relations were to be established between Oman and Israel. An Omani trade office was opened in Tel-Aviv in August 1996, despite concerns that bilateral relations would be undermined by the uncompromising stance adopted by the new Israeli Government of Binyamin Netanyahu. In March 1997 ministers responsible for foreign affairs of the countries of the League of Arab States (the Arab League, see p. 306) recommended, in condemnation of Israeli settlement policy, the suspension of involvement in multilateral negotiations with Israel, a reassertion of the primary economic boycott and the ending, by means of closing representative offices in Tel-Aviv, of efforts to normalize bilateral relations. In April Oman prohibited Israeli participation at a Muscat trade fair. Oman attended the Middle East and North Africa economic conference in Doha, Qatar, in November, despite a boycott by most Arab League and GCC members in response to the perceived failure of Israel (which was represented at the conference) to comply with its obligations under the Middle East peace process. In October 2000, in view of the deepening crisis in Israeli–Palestinian relations, Oman closed both its trade office in Tel-Aviv and the Israeli trade office in Muscat. Oman hosted the annual summit meeting of GCC heads of state in December 2001, at the close of which a statement was issued blaming Israel for the collapse of the peace process and expressing support for the Palestinian leadership. Two demonstrations took place in Muscat in April 2002 to demand an end to Israeli military incursions into Palestinian territory.

In July 2004 Oman signed a Trade and Investment Framework Agreement with the USA—regarded as a preliminary step on the path towards a bilateral free-trade agreement (FTA). Negotiations between Oman and the USA concerning the FTA duly took place in March–October 2005 and the deal was signed following their conclusion. The FTA was to be implemented following approval of the legislation by the Majlis ash-Shoura and the US Congress, which was expected in 2006. The developing US-Omani relations were likely to displease the Saudi Government, which had previously argued that the GCC should negotiate a trade deal as a single body and in 2004 claimed that a similar US agreement with Bahrain contravened the GCC's external tariff agreement.

Government

The Basic Statute of the State, which was promulgated by Royal Decree on 6 November 1996, defines Oman's organs of government. The Sultan, who is Head of State, is empowered to promulgate and ratify legislation. He is assisted in formulating and implementing the general policy of the State by a Council of Ministers. Members of the Council of Ministers are appointed by the Sultan, who presides, or may appoint a Prime Minister to preside, over the Council. There is no legislature. However, a Majlis ash-Shoura (Consultative Council) is now elected for four years at national polls. Voters were previously nominated within the country's *wilayat*, or districts, with the franchise effectively limited to prominent business leaders, intellectuals, professionals and tribal chiefs; with effect from elections held in October 2003, however, voting rights were granted to all Omani citizens over 21 years of age. The Majlis is composed of one representative from each *wilaya* with fewer than 30,000 inhabitants, and two from each *wilaya* with 30,000 or more inhabitants. Since the elections of September 2000, the Majlis ash-Shoura has comprised 83 members. A 57-member Majlis ad-Dawlah (Council of State) is appointed by the Sultan from among prominent Omanis; members also serve a four-year term of office. The two Councils together comprise the Council of Oman.

Oman comprises three governorates, subdivided into 59 *wilayat*; each *wilaya* has its own governor (*wali*).

Defence

In August 2005 the Omani armed forces numbered 41,700 (including about 2,000 expatriate personnel): army 25,000; navy 4,200; air force 4,100; royal household 6,400. Paramilitary forces numbered 4,400: tribal home guard (*firqat*) 4,000; police coastguard 400. Military service is voluntary. Government expenditure on defence was budgeted at RO 1,140m. in 2005.

Economic Affairs

In 2003, according to estimates by the World Bank, Oman's gross national income (GNI), measured at average 2001–03 prices, was US $20,509m., equivalent to $7,890 per head (or $13,250 per head on an international purchasing-power parity basis). During 1995–2004, it was estimated, the population increased at an average annual rate of 2.5%, while real gross domestic product (GDP) per head increased, in real terms, by an average of 1.0% per year during 1995–2003. Overall GDP increased, in real terms, at an average annual rate of 3.5% in 1995–2003; growth was 2.0% in 2003 and an estimated 5.6% in 2004.

Agriculture (including fishing) engaged 8.0% of the employed population at the 2003 census, and contributed an estimated 1.8% of GDP in 2004. The major crops are dates, tomatoes, bananas, watermelons and onions. The production of frankincense, formerly an important export commodity, has been revived. Livestock and fishing are also important. The real GDP of the agricultural sector increased by an average of 4.0% annually in 1990–2000. Real agricultural GDP decreased by 2.3% in 2003, but increased by some 5.1% in 2004.

Industry (including mining and quarrying, manufacturing, construction and power) employed 27.9% of the working population in 2003, and provided an estimated 54.3% of GDP in 2004. Real industrial GDP increased by an average of 4.1% annually in 1990–2000. The sector's real GDP decreased by 3.5% in 2003, but increased by 2.7% in 2004.

According to provisional figures, the mining sector contributed 41.6% of GDP in 2004, and engaged 2.8% of the employed labour force in 2003. The main mineral reserves are petroleum and natural gas, which together provided an estimated 41.5% of GDP in 2004. There were proven petroleum reserves of 5,600m. barrels at the end of 2004. Production in 2004 averaged an estimated 785,000 barrels per day (b/d). Petroleum reserves were estimated to be sufficient to sustain production at that level until 2025. Exports of Omani crude petroleum provided 67.9% of total export earnings in 2004. Natural gas is also an important mineral resource; there were proven reserves of some 1,000,000m. cu m at the end of 2004, sustainable for about 57 years at 2004 production levels (output in 2004 totalled 17,600m. cu m—an increase of some 7% compared with the previous year). Budgetary revenue from petroleum and natural gas contributed some 68.9% of the total in 2004. Chromite, gold, silver, salt, marble, gypsum and limestone are also mined, and the exploitation of coal deposits is planned. The GDP of the mining sector increased at an average annual rate of 3.5% in 1990–2000; mining GDP contracted by 8.1% in 2003 and by some 1.8% in 2004.

Manufacturing contributed an estimated 8.4% of GDP in 2004, and engaged 8.2% of the employed labour force in the same year. The most important branches of the sector are petroleum-refining, construction materials, cement production and copper-smelting. Assembly industries, light engineering and food-processing are being encouraged at industrial estates in Muscat, Sohar and Salalah. Completion in 2000 of a US $9,000m. liquefied natural gas (LNG) plant at Sur reduced domestic demand for petroleum and also produced a surplus for export. The GDP of the manufacturing sector increased, in real terms, at an average rate of 7.9% annually in 1990–2000. The sector's real GDP increased by 6.6% in 2003 and by 5.1% in 2004.

Energy is derived almost exclusively from domestic supplies of natural gas (which accounted for 82.0% of electricity produced in 2002) and petroleum. Imports of fuel products comprised just 2.5% of total imports in 2004.

Services provided an estimated 44.0% of GDP in 2004, and engaged 64.0% of the employed population at the 2003 census. With the Government seeking to diversify Oman's petroleum-dependent economy, the construction of several large-scale tourist projects have been initiated in recent years. Pre-eminent among these was Al-Madina az-Zarqa (Blue City) resort, the plans for which were announced in June 2005, and which was expected to cost US $15,000m. and to take some 15 years to complete. The GDP of the services sector increased, in real terms, at an average rate of 5.3% per year during 1990–2000. Real services GDP increased by 6.2% in 2003 and by 7.5% in 2004.

In 2004 Oman recorded a visible trade surplus of RO 2,104m., and there was a surplus of RO 170m. on the current account of the balance of payments. In 2004 the principal sources of imports were the UAE and Japan (which supplied, respectively, 32.4% and 14.0% of Oman's imports). Italy, the United Kingdom, Germany and the USA are also important suppliers. The most important market for non-petroleum exports in 2004 was the UAE (taking 37.2%). Iran and Saudi Arabia were also important markets for non-petroleum exports. Petroleum and natural gas is, by far, the principal export category, comprising 81.4% of the total in 2004. Excluding re-exports (which contributed 10.5% of total export earnings in that year), live animals and animal products made the most notable contribution to export revenue of all non-oil exports of Omani origin. The principal imports in 2004 were machinery and transport equipment, basic manufactures, food and live animals, and chemicals.

Oman recorded an estimated overall budgetary surplus of RO 230.3m. in 2004 (equivalent to 2.4% of GDP in that year). At the end of 2003 Oman's total external debt was US $3,886m., of which $2,642m. was long-term public debt. The cost of debt-servicing in that year was equivalent to 10.3% of the total value of exports of goods and services. Annual inflation declined by an average of 0.4% in 1998–2004; however, consumer prices increased by an annual average of 0.4% in 2004. Although Oman has traditionally relied on a high level of immigrant labour (non-Omanis accounted for 57.6% of the employed labour force in 2003), employment opportunities for young Omanis declined in the early 1990s and, according to census results, unemployment among Omanis stood at 11.9% in 1993; the figure was estimated at 12%–15% in 2006, although unemployment in rural areas was assumed to be far greater.

Oman is a member of the Arab Fund for Economic and Social Development (see p. 161), the Islamic Development Bank (see p. 303) and the Arab Monetary Fund (see p. 163). It was a founder member of the Co-operation Council for the Arab States of the Gulf (the Gulf Co-operation Council—GCC, see p. 205), and of the Indian Ocean Rim Association for Regional Co-operation (see p. 386). Oman is not a member of the Organization of the Petroleum Exporting Countries (OPEC, see p. 344) nor of the Organization of Arab Petroleum Exporting Countries (OAPEC, see p. 338), but it generally respects OPEC's policies regarding levels of petroleum production and pricing. Oman was admitted to the World Trade Organization (see p. 370) in November 2000. In preparation for admittance to the WTO, the Government abolished import fees, raised the limit on foreign ownership of local industries from 49% to 70% (effective from 1 January 2001) and authorized 100% foreign ownership in banking, insurance and brokerage firms (from 1 January 2003). The GCC's six members established a unified regional customs tariff in January 2003, and the organization has undertaken to establish a single market and currency no later than January 2010. The economic convergence criteria for the monetary union were agreed at a GCC summit in Abu Dhabi, the UAE, in December 2005.

Oman's limited petroleum reserves and fluctuations in the price of petroleum have necessitated a series of five-year development plans to diversify the country's economic base, in particular through the expansion of the private sector. Under the seventh Development Plan (2006–10), emphasis was to be placed on the development of the non-petroleum sector (with gas-based industry and tourism being notable targets), and the expansion of the privatization programme (begun in mid-1994). Under the Plan, the Government aimed to achieve annual GDP growth of at least 3% and to maintain low annual rates of inflation. The previous Plan (2001–05) had sought, in particular, to create more jobs for Omani nationals, to increase state funding for their education and training, and to limit the employment of expatriates in certain fields. Omanis were now reported to constitute at least 90% of employees in banking and finance; however, the IMF in December 2005 warned the Government to apply the so-called 'Omanization' policy with flexibility, and to ensure that education and training investment kept pace with the increase in job opportunities for nationals. In July 2004 a royal decree finally mandated the comprehensive privatization of the power sector; in 2006 divestments of the postal service and in the transport sector were either in the planning stages or, in the case of Oman's two major airports, temporarily abandoned after the failure to agree terms with an airport management company. The public offering of shares in Oman Telecommunications Company (Omantel) in July 2005 was hugely oversubscribed by domestic purchasers, although the sale proved less attractive to foreigners when it was opened up in October. Plans for the establishment of a free-trade zone at Salalah, which was expected to create new employment opportunities for Omani nationals and also to encourage foreign investment, were again in progress in 2006; a major investor had departed from the venture in late 2002, alluding to the political instability in the region as a reason for its withdrawal. The development of the non-petroleum sector was also in progress: notably, the contribution of natural gas to total budgetary revenue increased by 47% in 2005. In addition, the relatively new tourism industry was experiencing a construction-led transformation in 2004–06; the largest projects to date were The Wave and Al-Madina az-Zarqa (Blue City) resorts, which were launched in February 2004 and June 2005, respectively. To co-ordinate the nascent industry, the Government established a Ministry of Tourism in June 2004 and Oman joined the World Tourism Organization (see p. 148) in July. In January 2006 the Government announced an expansionist budget, with a projected deficit of RO 650m.; expenditure was planned to increase by some 21.7%. However, since petroleum prices remained considerably stronger than the Government's cautious estimates, the actual figures, as in 2005, would almost certainly represent a significant surplus. An economic growth rate of 5.6% was estimated in 2004, while increases of 4.1% and 4.3% were forecast for 2005 and 2006, respectively. It was also expected that the implementation of a free-trade agreement with the USA (yet to be approved by the US Congress in early 2006) would provide a further boost to economic growth, in particular to the growing services sector.

Education

In 1970 there were only three schools, with a total of 909 pupils. By 2004/05 there were 1,038 schools at the primary, preparatory and secondary levels, as well as 143 private kindergartens and schools regulated by the Ministry of Education; in total, 572,864 students were in state education (at the primary–secondary level) and 25,472 in private education in that year. According to the Basic Statute, the State endeavours to make education available to all; it provides public education and encourages the establishment of private educational institutions. However, education is still not compulsory. Primary education begins at six years of age and lasts for six years. The next level of education, divided into two equal stages, lasts for a further six years. In 1998/99 a new system, comprising 10 years of basic education and two extra years of secondary education, dependent on attainment, was introduced in 17 schools; it was to be implemented gradually throughout the country. Primary enrolment in 2002/03 included 72% of children in the relevant age-group (boys 72%; girls 72%), while preparatory and secondary enrolment included 69% of children in the relevant age-group (boys 69%; girls 70%). In 2004/05 there were six teacher-training colleges and four vocational institutes, together with institutes of health sciences, tourism, law and banking, and five technical colleges. There were seven Islamic colleges in 1995/96. Oman's first national university, named after Sultan Qaboos, was opened in late 1986, and had 12,855 students in 2004. There are four private universities and several private technical colleges. In the 2006 budget, RO 525m. (12.4%) of current and investment expenditure was allocated to education by the central Government.

Public Holidays

2006: 10 January*† (Id al-Adha, Feast of the Sacrifice), 31 January* (Muharram, Islamic New Year), 10 April* (Mouloud, Birth of the Prophet), 21 August* (Leilat al-Meiraj, Ascension of the Prophet), 24 September* (Ramadan begins), 23 October* (Id al-Fitr, end of Ramadan), 18 November (National Day), 19 November (Birthday of Sultan Qaboos), 31 December*† (Id al-Adha, Feast of the Sacrifice).

2007: 20 January* (Muharram, Islamic New Year), 31 March* (Mouloud, Birth of the Prophet), 10 August* (Leilat al-Meiraj, Ascension of the Prophet), 13 September* (Ramadan begins), 13 October* (Id al-Fitr, end of Ramadan), 18 November (National Day), 19 November (Birthday of Sultan Qaboos), 20 December* (Id al-Adha, Feast of the Sacrifice).

* These holidays are dependent on the Islamic lunar calendar and may vary by one or two days from the dates given.

† This festival occurs twice (in the Islamic years AH 1426 and 1427) within the same Gregorian year.

Weights and Measures

The imperial, metric and local systems are all used, although the metric system was officially adopted in 1974.

Statistical Survey

Sources (unless otherwise stated): Information and Publication Centre, Ministry of National Economy, POB 506, Muscat 113; tel. 24604285; fax 24698467; e-mail mone@omantel.net.om; internet www.moneoman.gov.om; Central Bank of Oman, POB 1161, 44 Mutrah Commercial Centre, Ruwi 112; tel. 24702222; fax 24702253; e-mail cboresb@omantel.net.om; internet www.cbo-oman.org.

Area and Population

AREA, POPULATION AND DENSITY

Area (sq km)	309,500*
Population (census results)	
1 December 1993	2,018,074†
1 December 2003	
Males	1,313,239
Females	1,027,576
Total	2,340,815‡
Population (official estimate at mid-year)	
2004	2,416,000
Density (per sq km) at mid-2004	7.8

* 119,500 sq miles.
† Comprising 1,483,226 Omani nationals and 534,848 non-Omanis.
‡ Comprising 1,781,558 Omani nationals and 559,257 non-Omanis.

GOVERNORATES

(2003 census)

	Area (sq km)	Population	Density (per sq km)
Muscat	3,900	632,073	162.1
Al-Batinah	12,500	653,505	52.3
Musandam	1,800	28,378	15.8
Adh-Dhahira	44,000	207,015	4.7
Ad-Dakhliya	31,900	267,140	8.4
Ash-Sharqiya	36,400	313,761	8.6
Al-Wosta	79,700	22,983	0.3
Dhofar	99,300	215,960	2.2
Total	309,500	2,340,815	7.6

OMAN

PRINCIPAL TOWNS
(population at 1993 census)

Salalah	131,802	Nizwa	58,582
Ibri	93,475	Sur	53,504
Suhar	90,814	Al-Buraymi	48,287
Ar-Rustaq	61,984	Muscat (capital)	40,856

Source: Thomas Brinkhoff, *City Population* (internet www.citypopulation.de).

Mid-2003: (UN estimate, incl. suburbs) Muscat 638,115 (Source: UN, *World Urbanization Prospects: The 2003 Revision*).

BIRTHS AND DEATHS
(official estimates, Omani nationals only)

	2002	2003	2004
Birth rate (per 1,000)	25.7	24.4	24.0
Death rate (per 1,000)	3.5	2.7	2.6

Expectation of life (years at birth): 74.27 (males 73.15; females 75.41) in 2004.

EMPLOYMENT
(persons aged 15 years and over, 2003 census)

	Omanis	Non-Omanis	Total
Agriculture and fishing	14,210	43,904	58,114
Mining and quarrying	11,998	8,117	20,115
Manufacturing	13,831	45,661	59,492
Electricity, gas and water	1,826	2,219	4,045
Construction	10,128	108,129	118,257
Trade, hotels and restaurants	24,999	84,158	109,157
Transport, storage and communications	17,202	10,472	27,674
Finance, insurance and real estate	12,657	12,543	25,200
Public administration and defence	144,699	18,043	162,742
Other community, social and personal services	54,923	83,299	138,222
Activities not adequately defined	5,973	7,633	13,606
Total employed	**312,446**	**424,178**	**736,624**
Males	258,655	364,337	622,992
Females	53,791	59,841	113,632

Health and Welfare

KEY INDICATORS

Total fertility rate (children per woman, 2003)	4.9
Under-5 mortality rate (per 1,000 live births, 2004)	13
HIV/AIDS (% of persons aged 15–49, 2003)	0.1
Physicians (per 1,000 head, 2002)	1.26
Hospital beds (per 1,000 head, 2002)	2.0
Health expenditure (2002): US $ per head (PPP)	379
Health expenditure (2002): % of GDP	3.4
Health expenditure (2002): public (% of total)	81.6
Access to water (% of persons, 2002)	79
Access to sanitation (% of persons, 2002)	89
Human Development Index (2003): ranking	71
Human Development Index (2003): value	0.781

For sources and definitions, see explanatory note on p. vi.

Agriculture

PRINCIPAL CROPS
('000 metric tons)

	2002	2003	2004*
Sorghum*	3.0	3.0	3.0
Potatoes	15.5	15.5	15.5
Tomatoes	43.1	41.9	43.0
Dry onions	15.6	17.6	18.0
Other vegetables*	98.0	98.0	98.5
Watermelons	27.0	26.6	27.0
Bananas	32.9	28.8	33.0
Lemons and limes	8.4	6.8	7.5
Mangoes	10.9	10.9	11.0
Dates	238.6	219.8	238.0
Papayas	2.5	2.5	2.5

* FAO estimates.
Source: FAO.

LIVESTOCK
('000 head, year ending September)

	2002	2003	2004*
Asses*	29	29	29
Cattle	320	326	330
Camels	118	120	122
Sheep	361	368	370
Goats	1,018	1,039	1,050
Poultry*	3,700	3,900	4,000

* FAO estimates.
Source: FAO.

LIVESTOCK PRODUCTS
('000 metric tons)

	2002	2003	2004*
Beef and veal*	4.1	4.1	4.2
Camel meat*	6.4	6.5	6.6
Mutton and lamb*	13.1	13.1	13.1
Goat meat*	8.0	10.0	13.8
Poultry meat*	5.6	5.8	5.8
Cows' milk*	18.1	18.5	18.9
Sheep's milk*	3.7	3.7	3.7
Goats' milk*	81.4	81.4	81.4
Hen eggs	8.6	8.2	8.6

* FAO estimates.
Source: FAO.

Fishing

('000 metric tons, live weight)

	2001	2002	2003
Capture	129.9	142.7	138.5
Groupers	3.8	3.3	4.2
Emperors (Scavengers)	6.5	7.2	8.0
Porgies and seabreams	4.0	8.8	5.9
Hairtails and cutlassfishes	2.6	6.6	8.8
Demersal percomorphs	2.4	11.3	5.9
Indian oil sardine	59.0	37.9	32.0
Longtail tuna	6.0	6.9	8.0
Yellowfin tuna	7.9	7.1	10.2
Carangids	1.3	7.8	2.6
Pelagic percomorphs	3.4	5.5	5.0
Sharks, rays, skates, etc.	3.6	3.8	5.9
Cuttlefish and bobtail squids	3.9	8.1	11.4
Aquaculture	—	—	0.4
Total catch	**129.9**	**142.7**	**138.8**

Source: FAO.

OMAN

Mining

('000 metric tons, unless otherwise indicated)

	2002	2003*	2004*
Crude petroleum (million barrels)	328.0	300.0	285.4
Natural gas (dry, million cu m)*	14,800	17,000	17,000
Chromite	27.4	13.0	18.6
Silver (kg)	38	—	—
Gold (kg)*	188	4	—
Marble	135.9	140.0	140.0
Salt	14.4	15.0	15.0
Gypsum	55.7	50.0	60.0

* Estimates.

Source: US Geological Survey.

Industry

SELECTED PRODUCTS
('000 barrels, unless otherwise indicated)

	2002	2003	2004
Jet fuel and kerosene	2,008	2,000*	1,407*
Motor spirit (petrol)	5,428	5,400*	5,215*
Gas-diesel (distillate fuel) oils	6,658	6,700*	6,442*
Residual fuel oils	14,942	15,000*	14,247*
Electric energy (million kWh)	10,331	10,714	11,499

* Estimate.

Source: mainly US Geological Survey.

Finance

CURRENCY AND EXCHANGE RATES

Monetary Units
1,000 baiza = 1 rial Omani (RO).

Sterling, Dollar and Euro Equivalents (30 December 2005)
£1 sterling = 662.1 baiza;
US $1 = 384.5 baiza;
€1 = 453.6 baiza;
100 rials Omani = £151.04 = $260.08 = €220.46.

Exchange Rate: Since January 1986 the official exchange rate has been fixed at US $1 = 384.5 baiza (1 rial Omani = $2.6008).

BUDGET
(RO million)

Revenue	2002	2003	2004
Petroleum revenue (net)	2,200.5	2,316.4	2,676.1
Natural gas revenue	76.6	87.0	106.0
LNG and oil condensates	—	—	373.7
Other current revenue	675.2	875.4	850.0
Taxes and fees	154.4	170.4	191.4
Income tax on enterprises	54.7	61.5	65.3
Customs duties	60.2	65.0	71.0
Non-tax revenue	520.8	704.9	658.6
Electricity	116.6	118.6	116.1
Surplus from public authorities	—	16.6	15.0
Income from government investments	232.9	370.4	319.8
Capital revenue	15.9	10.2	16.6
Capital repayments	41.3	16.3	17.8
Total	**3,009.5**	**3,305.3**	**4,040.2**

Expenditure	2002	2003	2004
Current expenditure	2,273.9	2,373.1	2,661.2
Defence and national security	957.9	1,009.6	1,143.6
Civil ministries	1,148.9	1,184.3	1,304.4
General public services	171.8	167.5	199.2
Education	354.9	382.2	418.1
Health	149.9	152.5	160.2
Social security and welfare	93.1	98.4	91.7
Housing	102.2	117.3	124.7
Cultural and religious affairs	41.2	38.9	43.5
Fuel and energy	151.8	143.3	180.9
Investment expenditure	586.7	700.0	1,034.8
Share of PDO expenditure†	201.3	242.0	257.4
Participation and subsidies	78.9	115.8	113.9
Total	**2,939.5**	**3,188.9**	**3,809.9**

* Preliminary figures.
† Referring to the Government's share of current and capital expenditure by Petroleum Development Oman.

INTERNATIONAL RESERVES
(US $ million at 31 December)

	2002	2003	2004
Gold (national valuation)	0.2	0.3	0.3
IMF special drawing rights	8.9	11.6	13.9
Reserve position in IMF	99.8	115.3	98.9
Foreign exchange	3,064.8	3,466.6	3,484.5
Total	**3,173.7**	**3,593.8**	**3,597.6**

Source: IMF, *International Financial Statistics*.

MONEY SUPPLY
(RO million at 31 December)

	2002	2003	2004
Currency outside banks	289.6	303.8	329.0
Demand deposits at commercial banks	482.0	504.2	582.7
Total money	**771.7**	**808.0**	**911.7**

Source: IMF, *International Financial Statistics*.

COST OF LIVING
(Consumer Price Index for Muscat; base: 2000 = 100)

	2002	2003	2004
Food, beverages and tobacco	n.a.	99.7	100.1
Textiles, clothing and footwear	n.a.	96.6	98.3
Rent, electricity, water and fuel	n.a.	97.7	96.9
All items (incl. others)	98.8	98.7	99.1

NATIONAL ACCOUNTS
(RO million in current prices)

Expenditure on the Gross Domestic Product

	2002	2003	2004*
Government final consumption expenditure	1,800	1,853	2,032
Private final consumption expenditure	3,430	3,656	4,341
Gross fixed capital formation	977	1,307	1,785
Total domestic expenditure	**6,207**	**6,816**	**8,158**
Exports of goods and services	4,494	4,735	5,450
Less Imports of goods and services	2,887	3,175	4,080
GDP in purchasers' values	**7,815**	**8,376**	**9,527**
GDP at constant 1988 prices	**6,230**	**6,355**	**6,713**

OMAN

Gross Domestic Product by Economic Activity

	2002	2003	2004*
Agriculture and livestock	105.3	108.6	112.0
Fishing	53.1	56.7	57.6
Mining and quarrying	3,285.5	3,437.8	4,032.5
Crude petroleum	3,101.3	3,211.7	3,768.3
Natural gas	167.8	212.4	247.9
Non-petroleum	16.4	13.7	16.3
Manufacturing	630.7	719.9	810.8
Electricity and water	79.0	107.6	136.5
Construction	170.6	193.6	279.9
Wholesale and retail trade	914.0	994.9	1,152.0
Hotels and restaurants	59.1	61.3	69.9
Transport, storage and communications	535.3	578.9	654.3
Financial intermediation	322.4	336.9	340.8
Real estate and business activities	435.8	446.7	466.3
Public administration and defence	772.1	817.5	848.2
Education	360.8	404.7	444.3
Health	134.6	144.4	152.0
Other community, social and personal services	106.9	110.7	113.6
Private households with employed persons	16.5	16.5	16.5
Sub-total	7,981.7	8,536.7	9,687.2
Less Financial intermediation services indirectly measured	226.8	225.8	231.1
Gross value added in basic prices	7,754.9	8,310.9	9,456.1
Taxes on imports	60.2	65.0	71.0
GDP in purchasers' values	7,815.1	8,375.9	9,527.1

* Provisional figures.
† Preliminary figures.

BALANCE OF PAYMENTS
(RO million)

	2002	2003	2004
Exports of goods f.o.b.	4,296	4,487	5,131
Imports of goods f.o.b.	−2,167	−2,340	−3,027
Trade balance	2,129	2,147	2,104
Exports of services	198	248	319
Imports of services	−720	−835	−1,053
Balance on goods and services	1,607	1,560	1,370
Other income received	96	95	100
Other income paid	−562	−673	−598
Balance on goods, services and income	1,141	982	872
Current transfers paid	−616	−643	−702
Current balance	525	339	170
Capital account (net)	2	4	8
Direct investment from abroad	10	203	−7
Portfolio investment liabilities	−7	21	106
Other investment assets	0	−59	−258
Other investment liabilities	−248	−273	538
Net errors and omissions	9	22	−359
Overall balance	121	257	198

External Trade

PRINCIPAL COMMODITIES
(RO million)

Imports c.i.f. (distribution by SITC)*	2002	2003	2004
Food and live animals	266.7	288.0	369.1
Dairy products and eggs	61.0	63.2	94.6
Beverages and tobacco	185.2	117.8	43.5
Tobacco and tobacco manufactures	158.4	104.5	27.3
Crude materials (inedible) except fuels	60.3	112.4	104.5
Metalliferous ores and metal scrap	30.8	83.9	68.6
Minerals, fuels, lubricants, etc.	51.1	83.2	83.8
Petroleum and related products	50.6	82.1	83.2
Chemicals and related products	169.6	189.7	246.2
Basic manufactures	352.4	390.4	587.3
Iron and steel	95.8	118.2	217.1
Machinery and transport equipment	966.0	1,087.0	1,564.6
Power generating machinery and equipment	103.5	56.3	122.8
Machinery specialized for particular industries	132.2	169.3	254.5
General industrial machinery, equipment and parts	87.4	106.3	209.0
Telecommunication and sound recording equipment	77.9	58.8	103.6
Road vehicles	391.4	491.5	671.2
Passenger motor cars	233.3	305.8	445.7
Motor vehicles for transport of goods	57.5	82.1	101.6
Miscellaneous manufactured articles	135.4	157.7	183.2
Commodities not elsewhere classified by SITC	109.5	80.6	104.5
Total (incl. others)	2,309.1	2,527.0	3,312.6

Exports f.o.b.	2002	2003	2004
Petroleum and natural gas	3,307.3	3,581.8	4,186.4
Crude petroleum	2,858.3	2,984.5	3,490.9
Refined petroleum	38.3	61.4	61.5
Natural gas	410.7	535.9	634.0
Non-oil and -gas exports	988.3	904.9	958.5
Live animals and animal products	54.0	61.6	91.9
Base metals and articles thereof	32.8	40.0	72.6
Total†	4,295.6	4,486.7	5,144.9

* Excluding unrecorded imports (RO million): 111.7 in 2002; 88.0 in 2003; 96.2 in 2004.
† Including re-exports (RO million): 726.7 in 2002; 600.8 in 2003; 538.2 in 2004.

OMAN

PRINCIPAL TRADING PARTNERS
(RO million)

Imports c.i.f.	2002	2003	2004
Australia	41.7	59.5	72.5
Bahrain	33.3	51.0	31.8
Belgium	39.0	24.4	37.5
China, People's Republic	37.1	61.2	57.5
France	54.9	60.7	131.4
Germany	101.5	111.9	163.2
India	104.3	110.6	121.3
Italy	70.7	61.3	195.2
Japan	372.5	431.8	464.0
Korea, Republic	44.8	82.8	74.9
Malaysia	27.7	32.7	32.1
Netherlands	37.8	39.9	82.0
Saudi Arabia	84.8	86.3	46.5
Singapore	23.1	29.1	37.6
Ukraine	19.1	64.3	12.6
United Arab Emirates	633.0	545.2	1,072.3
United Kingdom	140.1	142.8	164.0
USA	151.3	157.5	163.1
Total (incl. others)	2,309.1	2,527.0	3,312.7

Exports f.o.b.*	2002	2003	2004
Belgium	6.1	8.8	14.6
China, People's Republic	1.9	5.6	15.2
Germany	4.6	5.8	10.2
Hong Kong	11.4	22.6	21.5
India	8.5	8.7	14.0
Iran	199.9	165.2	87.8
Iraq	26.9	9.1	20.1
Jordan	9.4	22.6	27.2
Kenya	12.6	1.0	0.9
Kuwait	10.1	17.0	15.8
Libya	7.2	14.8	10.8
Pakistan	5.2	4.6	11.1
Qatar	13.2	11.5	17.0
Saudi Arabia	69.6	76.0	85.8
Singapore	10.9	17.8	15.0
Syria	3.1	4.8	12.6
Tanzania	27.4	4.6	4.6
United Arab Emirates	387.6	295.7	357.0
United Kingdom	25.1	30.1	26.2
USA	33.0	32.1	34.1
Yemen	19.3	23.8	27.6
Zambia	12.2	0.4	0.1
Total (incl. others)	988.3	904.9	958.5

* Excluding petroleum exports.

Transport

ROAD TRAFFIC
(registered vehicles at 31 December)

	2001	2002	2003
Private cars	309,217	335,771	284,902
Taxis	20,901	23,639	23,761
Commercial	132,920	140,270	109,118
Government	27,788	29,175	14,861
Motorcycles	5,195	5,436	3,977
Diplomatic	1,274	1,386	561
Other	23,631	24,625	7,320
Total	520,926	560,302	444,500

SHIPPING
Merchant Fleet
(registered at 31 December)

	2002	2003	2004
Number of vessels	26	23	26
Total displacement ('000 grt)	19.2	16.0	17.1

Source: Lloyd's Register-Fairplay, *World Fleet Statistics*.

Statistical Survey

International Sea-borne Freight Traffic
('000 metric tons, unless otherwise specified)

	2002	2003	2004
Port Sultan Qaboos:			
Goods loaded onto vessels ('000 US shipping tons)	935	4,627	1,181
Goods unloaded from vessels ('000 US shipping tons)	4,481	1,073	5,415
Goods loaded onto launches	722	—	154
Goods unloaded from launches	26,688	39,399	63,535
Port Salalah:			
Goods loaded	728	762	1,070
Goods unloaded	950	580	464
Mina Al-Fahal Coastal Area			
Petroleum loaded	42,806	39,079	36,889
Petroleum products unloaded	292	211	328

CIVIL AVIATION
(aircraft movements, passengers and cargo handled at Seeb International Airport)

	2002	2003	2004
International flights:			
flights (number)	31,472	34,707	35,803
passengers ('000)	2,154	2,602	3,187
goods handled (metric tons)	45,573	47,020	65,917
Domestic flights:			
flights (number)	8,083	7,623	7,819
passengers ('000)	293	284	274
goods handled (metric tons)	1,361	1,610	1,234

Tourism

FOREIGN TOURIST ARRIVALS*

Country of nationality	2001	2002	2003
Bahrain	18,538	17,609	29,881
Egypt	12,759	16,990	16,886
France	11,522	15,770	14,803
Germany	46,128	33,300	31,133
India	61,891	57,212	83,065
Kuwait	11,378	10,052	11,218
Netherlands	10,095	10,053	9,052
Pakistan	10,076	7,452	12,017
Saudi Arabia	18,543	21,555	22,163
Switzerland	9,614	12,294	9,735
Tanzania	11,499	4,789	6,202
United Arab Emirates	65,122	71,697	87,407
United Kingdom	85,029	76,861	60,532
USA	27,025	25,647	24,620
Total (incl. others)	562,119	602,109	629,986

* Figures refer to international arrivals at hotels and similar establishments.

Tourism receipts (US $ million, incl. passenger transport): 285 in 2001; 349 in 2002; 372 in 2003.

Source: World Tourism Organization.

Communications Media

	2002	2003	2004
Telephones ('000 main lines in use)	233.9	229.7	240.3
Mobile cellular telephones ('000 subscribers)	464.9	593.5	805.0
Personal computers ('000 in use)	95	n.a.	118
Internet users ('000)	180	n.a.	245.0
Daily newspapers (number)	5	5	6
Non-daily newspapers and other periodicals (number)	23	23	n.a.

Television receivers (number in use): 1,430,000 in 2000.

Radio receivers (number in use): 1,400,000 in 1997.

Facsimile machines (number in use): 6,356 in 1997.

Book production (number of titles): 7 in 1996; 136 in 1998; 12 in 1999.

Sources: mainly UNESCO, *Statistical Yearbook*, and International Telecommunication Union.

Education

(state schools, 2004/05)

	Institutions	Teachers	Males	Females	Total
Pre-primary*	5	347	3,792	3,197	6,989
Basic†		16,881	89,302	85,618	174,920
General†:	1,038‡				
Grades 1–6		5,274	65,206	62,878	128,084
Grades 7–9		5,670	75,040	65,349	140,389
Grades 10–12		6,729	65,916	63,555	129,471
Special schools	3	138	387	252	639
Higher§	34	1,608	12,282	11,004	23,286
University	1	955	6,416	6,439	12,855

* Figures refer to 1997/98 (Source: UNESCO, *Statistical Yearbook*).
† The Basic education system began to replace the General education system from 1998/99.
‡ 2001/02.
§ Comprising six teacher-training colleges, the College of *Shari'a* and Law, five technical colleges, the Academy of Tourism and Catering, the College of Banking and Financial Studies, 16 institutes of health and four vocational-training centres.

Adult literacy rate (UNESCO estimates): 74.4% (males 82.0%; females 65.4%) in 2003 (Source: UN Development Programme, *Human Development Report*).

Directory

The Constitution

The Basic Statute of the State was promulgated by royal decree on 6 November 1996, as Oman's first document defining the organs and guiding principles of the State.

Chapter 1 defines the State and the system of government. Oman is defined as an Arab, Islamic and independent state with full sovereignty. Islamic law (*Shari'a*) is the basis for legislation. The official language is Arabic. The system of government is defined as Sultani (Royal), hereditary in the male descendants of Sayyid Turki bin Said bin Sultan. Article 6 determines the procedure whereby the Sultan is designated.

Chapter 2 defines the political, economic, social, cultural and security principles of the State. Article 11 (economic principles) includes the stipulation that 'All natural resources and revenues therefrom shall be the property of the State which will preserve and utilize them in the best manner taking into consideration the requirements of the State's security and the interests of the national economy'. The constructive and fruitful co-operation between public and private activity is stated to be the essence of the national economy. Public property is inviolable, and private ownership is safeguarded. Article 14 (security principles) provides for a Defence Council to preserve the safety and defence of the Sultanate.

Chapter 3 defines public rights and duties. Individual and collective freedoms are guaranteed within the limits of the law.

Chapter 4 concerns the Head of State, the Council of Ministers, Specialized Councils and financial affairs of the State. Article 41 defines the Sultan as Head of State and Supreme Commander of the Armed Forces. The article states that 'His person is inviolable. Respect for him is a duty and his command must be obeyed. He is the symbol of national unity and the guardian of its preservation and protection'. The Sultan presides over the Council of Ministers, or may appoint a person (Prime Minister) to preside on his behalf. Deputy Prime Ministers and other Ministers are appointed by the Sultan. The Council of Ministers and Specialized Councils assist the Sultan in implementing the general policy of the State.

Chapter 5 comprises a single Article (58). This states that the Council of Oman shall consist of the Majlis ash-Shoura (Consultative Council) and the Majlis ad-Dawlah (Council of State). The jurisdiction, terms, sessions, rules of procedure, membership and regulation of each shall be determined by the law.

Chapter 6 concerns the judiciary. Articles 59 and 60 state that the supremacy of the law shall be the basis of governance, and enshrine the dignity, integrity, impartiality and independence of the judiciary. Article 66 provides for a Supreme Council of the judiciary.

Chapter 7 defines the general provisions pertaining to the application of the Basic Statute.

The Government

HEAD OF STATE

Sultan: QABOOS BIN SAID AS-SAID (assumed power on 23 July 1970, after deposing his father).

COUNCIL OF MINISTERS
(April 2006)

Prime Minister and Minister of Foreign Affairs, Defence and Finance: Sultan QABOOS BIN SAID AS-SAID.

Deputy Prime Minister for the Council of Ministers: Sayyid FAHAD BIN MAHMOUD AS-SAID.

Personal Representative of the Sultan: Sayyid THUWAINI BIN SHIHAB AS-SAID.

Minister of National Economy, Supervisor of the Finance Ministry and Deputy Chairman of the Financial Affairs and Energy Resources Council: AHMAD BIN ABD AN-NABI MACKI.

Minister Responsible for Defence Affairs: Sayyid BADR BIN SAUD BIN HAREB.

Minister of Legal Affairs: MUHAMMAD BIN ALI BIN NASIR AL-ALAWI.

Minister of Oil and Gas: Dr MUHAMMAD BIN HAMAD BIN SAIF AR-RUMHI.

Minister of Justice: Sheikh MUHAMMAD BIN ABDULLAH BIN ZAHIR AL-HINAI.

Minister of Awqaf (Religious Endowments) and Religious Affairs: Sheikh ABDULLAH BIN MUHAMMAD BIN ABDULLAH AS-SALIMI.

Minister Responsible for Foreign Affairs: YOUSUF BIN AL-ALAWI BIN ABDULLAH.

Minister of Information: HAMAD BIN MUHAMMAD BIN MUHSIN AR-RASHIDI.

Minister of Housing, Electricity and Water: Dr KHAMIS BIN MUBARAK BIN ISA AL-ALAWI.

Minister of Education: YAHYA BIN SAUD BIN MANSOOR AS-SULAIMI.

Minister of Higher Education: Dr RAWYA BINT SAUD BIN AHMAD AL-BUSAIDIYAH.

Minister of Tourism: RAJHA BINT ABD AL-AMIR BIN ALI.

Minister of Social Development: Dr SHARIFAH BINT KHALFAN BIN NASSER AL-YAHIYAIA.

Minister of Manpower: JUMA BIN ALI BIN JUMA.

Ministry of Sports: ALI BIN MASSOUD BIN ALI AS-SINAIDI.

Minister of Transport and Telecommunications: Sheikh MUHAMMAD BIN ABDULLAH BIN ISA AL-HARTHI.

OMAN

Minister of National Heritage and Culture: Sayyid HAITHAM BIN TARIQ BIN AS-SAID.
Minister of the Interior: Sayyid SAUD BIN IBRAHIM BIN SAUD AL-BUSAIDI.
Minister of Commerce and Industry: MAQBOOL BIN ALI BIN SULTAN.
Minister of Agriculture and Fisheries: Sheikh SALIM BIN HILAL AL-KHALILI.
Minister of Health: Dr ALI BIN MUHAMMAD BIN MOUSA AR-RAISI.
Minister of Regional Municipalities, the Environment and Water Resources: ABDULLAH BIN SALEM BIN AMER AR-RAWAS.
Minister of the Civil Service: Sheikh HILAL BIN KHALID BIN NASSER AL-MA'WALI.
Governor of Muscat and Minister of State: Sayyid AL-MUTASIM BIN HAMOUD AL-BUSAIDI.
Governor of Dhofar and Minister of State: Sheikh MUHAMMAD BIN ALI AL-QATABI.
Minister of the Diwan of the Royal Court: Sayyid ALI BIN HAMOUD BIN ALI AL-BUSAIDI.
Minister of the Palace Office and Head of the Office of the Supreme Commander of the Armed Forces: Maj.-Gen. ALI BIN MAJID AL-MA'AMARI.
Sultan's Adviser on the Environment: Sayyid SHABIB BIN TAYMUR AS-SAID.
Sultan's Adviser on National Heritage Affairs: Sayyid FAISAL BIN ALI BIN FAISAL AS-SAID.

MINISTRIES

Diwan of the Royal Court: POB 632, Muscat 113; tel. 24738711; fax 24739427; internet www.diwan.gov.om.
Ministry of Agriculture and Fisheries: POB 467, Ruwi 113; tel. 24694182; fax 24695909; internet www.maf.gov.om.
Ministry of Awqaf (Religious Endowments) and Religious Affairs: POB 354, Ruwi 112; tel. 24697699; e-mail info@mara.gov.om; internet www.mara.gov.om.
Ministry of the Civil Service: POB 3994, Ruwi 112; tel. 24696000; fax 24601365; internet www.omanmocs.gov.om.
Ministry of Commerce and Industry: POB 550, Muscat 113; tel. 24774290; fax 24817238; e-mail minister@mocioman.gov.om; internet www.mocioman.gov.om.
Ministry of Defence: POB 113, Muscat 113; tel. 24704096; fax 24618205.
Ministry of Education: POB 3, Muscat 113; tel. 24775334; fax 24704465; e-mail info@edu.gov.om; internet www.edu.gov.om.
Ministry of Finance: POB 506, Muscat 113; tel. 24738201; fax 24737028; e-mail info@mof.gov.om; internet www.mof.gov.om.
Ministry of Foreign Affairs: POB 252, Muscat 113; tel. 24699500; fax 24699589.
Ministry of Health: POB 393, Muscat 113; tel. 24602177; fax 24601430; e-mail moh@moh.gov.om; internet www.moh.gov.om.
Ministry of Higher Education: POB 82, Ruwi 112; tel. 24693148; internet www.mohe.gov.om.
Ministry of Housing, Electricity and Water: POB 1491, Ruwi 112; tel. 24603906; fax 24699180; internet www.mhew.gov.om.
Ministry of Information: POB 600, Muscat 113; tel. 24603222; fax 24692345; e-mail informus@omantel.net.om; internet www.omanet.om.
Ministry of the Interior: POB 127, Ruwi 112; tel. 24602244; fax 24696660.
Ministry of Justice: POB 354, Ruwi 112; tel. 24697699; internet www.moj.gov.om.
Ministry of Legal Affairs: POB 578, Ruwi 112; tel. 24605802.
Ministry of Manpower: POB 895, Muscat 113; tel. 24713983; fax 24713721.
Ministry of National Economy: POB 881, Muscat 113; tel. 24698821; fax 24698908; e-mail mone@omantel.net.om; internet www.moneoman.gov.om.
Ministry of National Heritage and Culture: POB 668, Muscat 113; tel. 24602555; fax 24602735; internet www.mnhc.gov.om.
Ministry of Oil and Gas: POB 551, Muscat 113; tel. 24603333; fax 24696972.
Ministry of the Palace Office: POB 2227, Ruwi 112; tel. 24600841.
Ministry of Regional Municipalities, the Environment and Water Resources: POB 323, Muscat 113; tel. 24696444; fax 24602320; e-mail aid@mrmewr.gov.om; internet www.mrmewr.gov.om.
Ministry of Sports: Muscat; e-mail minister@mosa.gov.om; internet www.sportsoman.com.
Ministry of Tourism: Madinat Al-Sultan Qaboos, POB 200, Muscat 115; tel. 24588877; fax 24588844; e-mail info@omantourism.gov.om; internet www.omantourism.gov.om.
Ministry of Transport and Telecommunications: POB 338, Ruwi 112; tel. 24697870; fax 24696817; e-mail pttdiwan@omantel.net.om; internet www.comm.gov.om.

COUNCIL OF OMAN

Majlis ash-Shoura
(Consultative Council)

President: Sheikh ABDULLAH BIN ALI AL-QATABI.

The Majlis ash-Shoura was established by royal decree in November 1991. Initially, members of the Majlis were appointed by the Sultan from among nominees selected at national polls, but from the September 2000 elections, members were directly elected. Two representatives are appointed from four candidates in each *wilaya* (province) of more than 30,000 inhabitants, and one from two candidates in each *wilaya* of fewer than 30,000 inhabitants. Members of the Majlis are appointed for a single four-year term of office. The Majlis elected in October 2003 comprised 83 members. The Majlis is an advisory body, the duties of which include the review of all social and economic draft laws prior to their enactment; public-service ministries are required to submit reports and answer questions regarding their performance, plans and achievements. The President of the Majlis ash-Shoura is appointed by royal decree.

Majlis ad-Dawlah
(Council of State)

President: Sheikh YAHYA BIN MAHFOUDH AL-MANTHERI.

The Majlis ad-Dawlah was established in December 1997, in accordance with the terms of the Basic Statute of the State. It is also an advisory body, comprising 57 members appointed by the Sultan for a four-year term. Its function is to serve as a liaison between the government and the people of Oman. A new Majlis was appointed in November 2003.

Political Organizations

There are no political organizations in Oman.

Diplomatic Representation

EMBASSIES IN OMAN

Algeria: POB 216, Muscat 115; tel. 24601698; fax 24694419; e-mail algeria@omantel.net.om; Ambassador TAYEB SAÂDI.
Austria: Moosa Complex Bldg, No. 477, 2nd Floor, Way No. 3109, POB 2070, Ruwi 112; tel. 24793135; fax 24793669; e-mail maskat-ob@bmaa.gv.at; Ambassador Dr ANDREAS KARABACZEK.
Bahrain: POB 66, Madinat Qaboos, Al-Khuwair; tel. 24605912; fax 24605072; Chargé d'affaires AHMAD MUHAMMAD MAHMOUD.
Bangladesh: POB 3959, Ruwi 112; tel. 24707462; fax 24708495; e-mail bangla@omantel.net.om; Ambassador GOLAM AKBAR KHONDAKAR.
Brunei: POB 91, Ruwi 112; tel. 24603533; fax 24693014; e-mail kbopuni@omantel.net.om; Ambassador Dato SERI SETIA HAJI ADAM AHMAD.
China, People's Republic: Al-Ansherah St, Way No. 1507, House No. 465, Madinat Alalam, POB 315, Muscat 112; tel. 24696698; fax 24602322; e-mail chinaemb_om@mfa.gov.cn; Ambassador DENG SHAOQIN.
Egypt: Jamiat ad-Dowal al-Arabiya St, Diplomatic City, Al-Khuwair, POB 2252, Ruwi 112; tel. 24600411; fax 24603626; e-mail egyembmuscat@hotmail.com; Ambassador HANI RIAD ALI.
France: Diplomatic City, Al-Khuwair, POB 208, Madinat Qaboos 115; tel. 24681800; fax 24681843; e-mail diplofr1@omantel.net.om; internet www.ambafrance-om.org; Ambassador MARC BARETY.
Germany: POB 128, Ruwi 112; tel. 24832482; fax 24835690; e-mail info@maskat.diplo.de; Ambassador HARTMUT BLANKENSTEIN.
India: POB 1727, Ruwi 112; tel. 24813838; fax 24811607; e-mail hom@indemb-oman.org; internet www.indemb-oman.org; Ambassador ASHOK KUMAR ATTRI.
Iran: Diplomatic Area, Jamiat ad-Dowal al-Arabiya St, POB 3155, Ruwi 112; tel. 24696944; fax 24696888; e-mail iranembassy@hotmail.com; internet www.iranembassy.gov.om; Ambassador MUHAMMAD JAVAD ASAYESH.
Iraq: POB 262, Way 1737, House No. 2803, Ruwi 112; tel. 604178; fax 602026; e-mail musemb@iraqmofamail.net; Ambassador ABD AR-RASOOL KADHIM ALWASH.

OMAN

Italy: Shati al-Qurum, Way No. 3034, House No. 2697, POB 3727, Ruwi 112; tel. 24693727; fax 24695161; e-mail ambasciata.mascate@esteri.it; internet www.ambmascate.esteri.it; Ambassador GRAZIELLA SIMBOLOTTI.

Japan: Shati al-Qurum, Villa No. 760, Way No. 3011, Jamiat ad-Dowal al-Arabiya St, POB 3511, Ruwi 112; tel. 24601028; fax 24698720; internet www.oman.emb-japan.go.jp; Ambassador KEJI MORI.

Jordan: Diplomatic City, Arab League St, POB 70, Al-Adhaiba 130; tel. 24692760; fax 24692762; e-mail embhkjom@omantel.net.om; Ambassador NABIL ALI BARTO.

Korea, Republic: POB 377, Madinat Qaboos 115; tel. 24691490; fax 24691495; e-mail emboman@mofat.go.kr; Ambassador KIM EUI-SHICK.

Kuwait: Al-Khuwair Diplomatic Area, Arab League St, Block No. 13, Bldg No. 58, POB 1798, Ruwi 112; tel. 24699626; fax 24604732; Ambassador Sheikh FAISAL AL-HOMOUD AL-MALEK AS-SABAH.

Malaysia: Shati al-Qurum, Villa No. 1611, Way No. 3019, POB 3939, Ruwi 112; tel. 24698329; fax 24605031; e-mail mwmuscat@omantel.net.om; Ambassador SAIPUL ANUAR BIN ABD MUIN.

Morocco: Shati al-Qurum, Villa No. 1758, Way No. 3021, POB 3125, Ruwi 112; tel. 24696152; fax 24601114; e-mail sifamamu@omantel.net.om; Ambassador NOUREDDINE BENOMAR.

Netherlands: Shati al-Qurum, Way No. 3017, Villa No. 1366, POB 3302, Ruwi 112; tel. 24603706; fax 24603778; e-mail mus@minbuza.nl; internet www.nlembassyoman.org; Ambassador ANNELIES BOOGAERDT.

Pakistan: POB 1302, Ruwi 112; tel. 24603439; fax 24697462; e-mail parepmct@omantel.net.om; Ambassador (vacant).

Philippines: POB 420, Madinat Qaboos 115; tel. 24605140; fax 24605176; e-mail muscatpe@omantel.net.om; Ambassador AKMAD D. OMAR.

Qatar: Diplomatic City, Jamiat ad-Dowal al-Arabiya Street, Al-Khuwair, POB 802, Muscat 113; tel. 24691152; fax 24691156; Ambassador ABDULLAH SAAD AL-MANAA.

Russia: Shati al-Qurum, Way No. 3032, Surfait Compound, POB 80, Ruwi 112; tel. 24602894; fax 24604189; Ambassador ALEKSANDR K. PATSEV.

Saudi Arabia: Diplomatic City, Jamiat ad-Dowal al-Arabiya Street, POB 1411, Ruwi 112; tel. 24601744; fax 24603540; e-mail omemb@mofa.gov.sa; internet www.mofa.gov.sa/detail.asp?InService ID=262&intemplatekey=MainPage; Ambassador AHMAD ALI AL-KAHTANI.

Somalia: Mumtaz Street, Villa Hassan Jumaa Baker, POB 1767, Ruwi 112; tel. 24564412; fax 24564965; Ambassador MUHAMMAD SUBAN NUR.

South Africa: Al-Harthy Complex, POB 231, Muscat 118; tel. 24694791; fax 24694792; e-mail southae@omantel.net.om; internet www.saembassymuscat.gov.om; Ambassador YACOOB ABBA OMAR.

Sri Lanka: POB 95, Madinat Qaboos 115; tel. 24697841; fax 24697336; e-mail lankaemb@omantel.net.om; Ambassador (vacant).

Sudan: Diplomatic City, Al-Khuwair, POB 3971, Ruwi 112; tel. 24697875; fax 24699065; Ambassador ABD AL-AZIZ MARHOUM AHMAD.

Syria: Madinat Qaboos, Al-Ensharah Street, Villa No. 201, POB 85, Muscat 115; tel. 24697904; fax 24603895; internet www.syrianembassy.gov.om; Chargé d'affaires ANWAR WEBBI.

Thailand: Shati al-Qurum, Villa No. 1339, Way No. 3017, POB 60, Ruwi 115; tel. 24602683; fax 24605714; e-mail thaimct@omantel.net.om; Ambassador THINAKORN KANASUTA.

Tunisia: Al-Ensharah Street, Way No. 1507, POB 220, Muscat 115; tel. 24603486; fax 24697778; Ambassador HATEM ESSAIEM.

Turkey: Bldg No. 3270, Street No. 3042, Shati al-Qurum, POB 47, Mutrah 115; tel. 24697050; fax 24697053; e-mail turemmus@omantel.net.om; internet www.turkishembassyoman.org; Ambassador ENGIN TÜRKER.

United Arab Emirates: Diplomatic City, Al-Khuwair, POB 551, Muscat 111; tel. 24600302; fax 24604182; Ambassador HAMAD HELAL THABIT AL-KUWAITI.

United Kingdom: POB 185, Mina al-Fahal 116; tel. 24609000; fax 24609010; e-mail enquiries.muscat@fco.gov.uk; internet www.britishembassy.gov.uk/oman; Ambassador Dr NOEL GUCKIAN.

USA: Diplomatic City, POB 202, Muscat 115; tel. 24698989; fax 24693885; e-mail aemctric@omantel.net.om; internet oman.usembassy.gov; Ambassador GARY A. GRAPPO.

Yemen: Shati al-Qurum, Area 258, Way No. 2840, Bldg No. 2981, POB 105, Madinat Qaboos 115; tel. 24600815; fax 24605008; Ambassador AHMAD DAIFALLAH AL-AZEIB.

Judicial System

Oman's Basic Statute guarantees the independence of the judiciary. The foundation for the legal system is *Shari'a* (Islamic law), which is the basis for family law, dealing with matters such as inheritance and divorce. Separate courts have been established to deal with commercial disputes and other matters to which *Shari'a* does not apply.

Courts of the First Instance are competent to try cases of criminal misdemeanour; serious crimes are tried by the Criminal Courts; the Court of Appeal is in Muscat. There are district courts throughout the country. Special courts deal with military crimes committed by members of the armed and security forces.

The Basic Statute provides for a Supreme Council to supervise the proper functioning of the courts.

An Administrative Court, to review the decisions of government bodies, was instituted in April 2001.

The office of Public Prosecutor was established in 1999 and the first such appointment was made in June 2001.

Religion

ISLAM

The majority of the population (estimated at 53.5% in 1994) are Muslims, of whom approximately three-quarters are of the Ibadi sect and about one-quarter are Sunni Muslims.

HINDUISM

According to 1994 estimates, 28.0% of the population are Hindus.

CHRISTIANITY

It was estimated that in 1994 14.7% of the population were Christians.

Protestantism

The Protestant Church in Oman: POB 1982, Ruwi 112; tel. 24702372; fax 24789943; e-mail pcomct@omantel.net.om; internet www.churchinoman.net; joint chaplaincy of the Anglican Church and the Reformed Church of America; four inter-denominational churches in Oman, at Ruwi and Ghala in Muscat, at Sohar and at Salalah; Senior Pastor Rev. MIKE CLARKSON.

The Roman Catholic Church

A small number of adherents, mainly expatriates, form part of the Apostolic Vicariate of Arabia. The Vicar Apostolic is resident in the United Arab Emirates.

The Press

Article 31 of Oman's Basic Statute guarantees the freedom of the press, printing and publishing, according to the terms and conditions specified by the law. Published matter 'leading to discord, harming the State's security or abusing human dignity or rights' is prohibited.

NEWSPAPERS

Oman Daily Newspaper: POB 3303, Ruwi 112; tel. 24701555; e-mail editor@omandaily.com; internet www.omandaily.com; daily; Arabic; Editor-in-Chief HABIB MUHAMMAD NASIB; circ. 15,560.

Ash-Shabiba: POB 3303, Ruwi 112; tel. 24795373; fax 24796711; e-mail shabiba1@omantel.net.om; internet www.shabiba.com; daily; Arabic; culture, leisure and sports.

Al-Watan (The Nation): POB 463, Muscat 113; tel. 24491919; fax 24491280; e-mail alwatan@omantel.net.om; internet www.alwatan.com; f. 1971; daily; Arabic; Editor-in-Chief MUHAMMAD BIN SULAYMAN AT-TAI; circ. 40,000.

English Language

Khaleej Times: POB 3305, Ruwi 112; tel. 24700895; fax 24706512; Reg. Man. SANKAR NARAYAN.

Oman Daily Observer: POB 3303, Ruwi 112; tel. 24703055; fax 24790524; e-mail editor@omanobserver.com; internet www.omanobserver.com; f. 1981; daily; publ. by Oman Establishment for Press, News, Publication and Advertising; Chair. ABDULLAH BIN NASSER AR-RAHBI; Editor SAID BIN KHALFAN AL-HARTHI; circ. 22,000.

Times of Oman: POB 770, Ruwi 112; tel. 24811953; fax 24813153; e-mail times@omantel.net.om; internet www.timesofoman.com; f. 1975; daily; Founder, Propr and Editor-in-Chief MUHAMMAD AZ-ZEDJALI; Man. Dir ANIS BIN ESSA AZ-ZEDJALI; circ. 34,000.

The Week: POB 2616, Ruwi 112, Muscat; tel. 24799388; fax 24793316; internet www.freetheweek.com; weekly; free; published by Apex Press and Publishing; circ. 51,000 (copies distributed).

PERIODICALS

Al-Adwaa' (Lights): POB 580, Muscat 113; tel. 24704353; fax 24798187; weekly; Arabic; economic, political and social; Editor-in-Chief HABIB MUHAMMAD NASIB; circ. 15,600.

Al-'Akidah (The Faith): POB 1001, Ruwi 112; tel. 24701000; fax 24709917; weekly illustrated magazine; Arabic; political; Editor SAID AS-SAMHAN AL-KATHIRI; circ. 10,000.

Business Today: Apex Press and Publishing, POB 2616, Ruwi 112; tel. 24799388; fax 24793316; e-mail editorial@apexstuff.com; internet www.apexstuff.com; monthly; Man. Editor MOHANA PRABHAKAR.

The Commercial: POB 2002, Ruwi 112; tel. 24704022; fax 24795885; e-mail omanad@omantel.net.om; f. 1978; monthly; Arabic and English; business news; Man. AYOOB CHANKALAN; Chief Editor HAMAD BIN AMIR AL-KASBI; circ. 7,000.

Al-Ghorfa (Oman Commerce): POB 1400, Ruwi 112; tel. 24703082; fax 24708497; e-mail alghorfa@chamberoman.com; internet www.chamberoman.com; f. 1978; bi-monthly; English and Arabic; business; publ. by Oman Chamber of Commerce and Industry; Editor HAMOOD HAMAD AL-MAHROUQ; circ. 10,500.

Jund Oman (Soldiers of Oman): POB 113, Muscat 113; tel. 24613615; fax 24613369; f. 1974; monthly; Arabic; illustrated magazine of the Ministry of Defence; Supervisor Chief of Staff of the Sultan's Armed Forces.

Al-Markazi (The Central): POB 1161, Ruwi 112; tel. 24702222; fax 24707913; f. 1975; bi-monthly economic magazine; English and Arabic; publ. by Central Bank of Oman.

Al-Mawared at-Tabeey'iyah (Natural Resources): POB 551, Muscat; publ. by Ministries of Agriculture and Fisheries and of Oil and Gas; monthly; English and Arabic; Editor KHALID AZ-ZUBAIDI.

Al-Mazari' (Farms): POB 467, Muscat; weekly journal of the Ministry of Agriculture and Fisheries; Editor KHALID AZ-ZUBAIDI.

An-Nahda (The Renaissance): POB 979, Muscat 113; tel. 24563104; fax 24563106; weekly illustrated magazine; Arabic; political and social; Editor TALEB SAID AL-MEAWALY; circ. 10,000.

Oman Today: Apex Press and Publishing, POB 2616, Ruwi 112; tel. 24799388; fax 24793316; e-mail editorial@apexstuff.com; internet www.apexstuff.com; f. 1981; monthly; English; leisure and sports; Man. Editor MOHANA PRABHAKAR; circ. 20,000.

Al-Omaniya (Omani Woman): POB 3303, Ruwi 112; tel. 24792700; fax 24707765; monthly; Arabic; circ. 10,500.

Risalat al-Masjed (The Mosque Message): POB 6066, Muscat; tel. 24561178; fax 24560607; issued by Diwan of Royal Court Affairs Protocol Dept (Schools and Mosques Section); Editor JOUMA BIN MUHAMMAD BIN SALEM AL-WAHAIBI.

Ash-Shurta (The Police): Directorate of Public Relations, Royal Oman Police, POB 2, Muscat 113; tel. 24569216; fax 24562341; quarterly magazine of Royal Oman Police; Editor Dir of Public Relations.

Al-Usra (The Family): POB 440, Mutrah 114; tel. 24794922; fax 24795348; e-mail admeds@omantel.net.om; f. 1974; fortnightly; Arabic; socio-economic illustrated magazine; Chief Editor SADEK ABDOWANI; circ. 15,000.

NEWS AGENCY

Oman News Agency: Ministry of Information, POB 3659, Ruwi 112; tel. 24696970; e-mail info@omannews.com; internet www.omannews.com; f. 1986; Dir-Gen. MUHAMMAD BIN SALIM AL-MARHOON.

Publishers

Apex Press and Publishing: POB 2616, Ruwi 112; tel. 24799388; fax 24793316; internet www.apexstuff.com; f. 1980; art, history, trade directories, maps, leisure and business magazines, and guidebooks; Pres. SALEH M. TALIB AZ-ZAKWANI; Man. Editor MOHANA PRABHAKAR.

Arabian Distribution and Publishing Enterprise: Mutrah; tel. 24707079.

Dar al-Usra: POB 440, Mutrah 114; tel. 24794922; fax 24795348; e-mail alusra@omantel.net.om.

Muscat Press and Publishing House SAOC: POB 3112, Ruwi 112; tel. 24795373; fax 24796711.

National Publishing and Advertising LLC: POB 3112, Ruwi 112; tel. 24793098; fax 24708445; e-mail npanet@usa.net; f. 1987; Man. ASHOK SUVARNA.

Oman Establishment for Press, News, Publication and Advertising (OEPNPA): Information City, Al-Qurum, Muscat; f. 1996 as Oman Newspaper House; Chair. ABDULLAH BIN NASSER AR-RAHBI.

Oman Establishment for Printing and Publishing: POB 463, Muscat 113; tel. 24591919; fax 24591280; Editor-in-Chief SAID BIN KHALFAN AL-HARTHY.

Oman Publishing House: POB 580, Muscat; tel. 24704353.

Ash-Shahmi Publishers and Advertisers: POB 6112, Ruwi; tel. 24703416.

Broadcasting and Communications

TELECOMMUNICATIONS

Regulatory Authority

Telecommunications Regulatory Authority: POB 579, Ruwi 112; tel. 24574300; fax 24565464; e-mail traoman@tra.gov.om; internet www.tra.gov.om; f. 2002 to oversee the privatization of Omantel (see below) and to set tariffs and regulate the sale of operating licences; Chair. Sheikh MUHAMMAD BIN ABDULLAH BIN ISA AL-HARTHI.

State-owned Company

Oman Telecommunications Company SAOC (Omantel): POB 789, Ruwi 112; tel. 24631417; fax 24697066; e-mail info@omantel.net.om; internet www.omantel.net.om; f. 1999 as successor to the General Telecommunications Organization, to facilitate transfer to private ownership; Chair. Sheikh MUHAMMAD BIN ABDULLAH BIN ISA AL-HARTHI; Exec. Pres. Eng. MUHAMMAD BIN ALI AL-WAHAIBI.

BROADCASTING

Radio

Radio Sultanate of Oman: Ministry of Information, POB 600, Muscat 113; tel. 24602058; fax 24601393; e-mail omanfm@omanet.com; internet www.oman-radio.gov.om; f. 1970; transmits in Arabic 20 hours daily, English on FM (Oman FM) 15 hours daily; Dir-Gen. NASSER SULAYMAN AS-SAIBANI.

Radio Salalah: f. 1970; transmits daily programmes in Arabic and the Dhofari languages; Dir MUHAMMAD BIN AHMAD AR-ROWAS.

The British Broadcasting Corpn (BBC) has built a powerful medium-wave relay station on Masirah island. It is used to expand and improve the reception of the BBC's Arabic, Farsi, Hindi, Pashtu and Urdu services.

Television

Sultanate of Oman Television: Ministry of Information, POB 600, Muscat 113; tel. 24603222; fax 24605032; internet www.oman-tv.gov.om; began broadcasting in 1974; programmes broadcast via Arabsat and Nilesat satellite networks.

Finance

(cap. = capital; res = reserves; dep. = deposits; m. = million; brs = branches; amounts in rials Omani unless otherwise stated)

BANKING

At the end of December 2005 there were 13 commercial banks (five local and eight foreign) and three specialized banks, with a total network of 355 domestic branch offices operating throughout Oman. Legislation introduced in January 2001 increased the minimum capital requirement for Omani commercial banks from RO 10m. to RO 20m., and set a minimum capital requirement of RO 3m. for foreign banks established in Oman.

Central Bank

Central Bank of Oman: POB 1161, 44 Mutrah Commercial Centre, Ruwi 112; tel. 24702222; fax 24702253; e-mail almarkazi@omantel.net.om; internet www.cbo-oman.org; f. 1974; cap. 300.0m., res 405.1m., dep. 330.1m. (Dec. 2003); 100% state-owned; Exec. Pres. HAMOUD SANGOUR AZ-ZADJALI; 2 brs.

Commercial Banks

Bank Dhofar SAOG: POB 1507, Ruwi 112; tel. 24790466; fax 24797246; e-mail info@bankdhofar.com; internet www.bankdhofar.com; f. 1990 as Bank Dhofar al-Omani al-Fransi SAOG; renamed as above in Jan. 2004 after merger with Majan International Bank SAOC; cap. 42.0m., res 18.5m., dep. 385.0m. (Dec. 2003); Chair. Eng. ABD AL-HAFIDH SALIM RAJAB AL-AUJAILI; CEO AHMAD BIN ALI ASH-SHANFARI; 45 brs.

BankMuscat SAOG: POB 134, Ruwi 112; tel. 24703044; fax 24707806; e-mail banking@bkmuscat.com; internet www.bankmuscat.com; f. 1993 by merger as Bank Muscat Al-Ahli Al-Omani; renamed Bank Muscat International in 1998, and as above in

1999; merged with Commercial Bank of Oman Ltd SAOG in 2000 and with Industrial Bank of Oman in 2002; 89.6% owned by Omani shareholders; cap. 51.5m., res 109.4m., dep. 1,288.8m. (Dec. 2003); Chair. Abd al-Malek bin Abdullah al-Khalili; CEO Abd ar-Razak Ali Issa; 95 brs.

National Bank of Oman SAOG (NBO): POB 751, Ruwi 112; tel. 24708894; fax 24707781; e-mail info@nbo.co.om; internet www.nbo.co.om; f. 1973; 100% Omani-owned; cap. 45.8m., res 49.9m., dep. 810.0m. (Dec. 2002); Chair. Sheikh Suhail Bahwan; CEO Andrew Duff; 49 brs.

Oman Arab Bank SAOC: POB 2010, Ruwi 112; tel. 24706265; fax 24797736; e-mail oabrbobs@omantel.net.om; internet www.omanab.com; f. 1984; purchased Omani European Bank SAOG in 1994; 51% Omani-owned, 49% by Arab Bank PLC (Jordan); cap. 22m., res 19m., dep. 280m. (Dec. 2002); Chair. Rashad Muhammad az-Zubair; CEO Abd al-Qader Askalan; 31 brs.

Oman International Bank SAOG: POB 1727, Muscat 111; tel. 24682500; fax 24682800; e-mail oibintl@omantel.net.om; internet www.oiboman.com; f. 1984; 100% Omani-owned; cap. 62.9m., res 21.6m., dep. 472.7m. (Dec. 2003); Chair. Reem Omar Zawawi; CEO John Carlough; 82 brs.

Foreign Banks

Bank of Baroda (India): Corniche Rd, POB 231, Mutrah 114; tel. 24714559; fax 24714560; e-mail ce.oman@bankofbaroda.com; internet www.bankofbaroda.com; f. 1976; Gen. Man. N. Ramani; 3 brs.

Bank Melli Iran: POB 2643, Ruwi 112; tel. 24815160; fax 24815183; e-mail bmimct@omantel.net.om; f. 1974; Gen. Man. Karim Deravi.

Bank Saderat Iran: POB 1269, Ruwi 112; tel. 24833923; fax 24836478; e-mail bsimct@omantel.net.om; total assets 6.3m. (2000); f. 1976; Gen. Man. Hamid Iranzaid; 1 br.

Habib Bank Ltd (Pakistan): POB 1326, Ruwi 112; tel. 24817139; fax 24815809; e-mail hbloman1@omantel.net.om; f. 1972; Exec. Vice-Pres. and Country Man. Khalid Sher Khan; 9 brs.

HSBC Bank Middle East (United Kingdom): Mutrah Business District, POB 240, Ruwi 112; tel. 24799920; fax 24704241; f. 1948; CEO Robert Bray; 5 brs.

National Bank of Abu Dhabi: As-Safra Bldg, POB 393, Ruwi 112; tel. 24761000; fax 24761060; e-mail saeed.almubarak@nbad.com; internet www.nbad.com; f. 1976; Man. Saeed Salem al-Mubarak; 1 br.

Standard Chartered Bank (UK): Bait al-Falaj St, POB 2353, Ruwi 112; tel. 24703999; fax 24796864; e-mail kukoor.murtadha-m@om.standardchartered.com; internet www.standardchartered.com/om; f. 1968; Man. Murtadha Muhammad Ali Kukoor; 1 br.

State Bank of India: Muscat; f. 2004; 1 br.

Development Banks

Alliance Housing Bank: POB 545, Mina al-Fahal 116; tel. 24568845; fax 24568003; e-mail info@alliance-housing.com; internet www.alliance-housing.com; f. 1997; privately owned; cap. 21.0m., total assets 124.9m. (Dec. 2004); Chair. Ahmad bin Suwaidan al-Balushi; Gen. Man. Laurie Cowell; 7 brs.

Oman Development Bank SAOG: POB 3077, Ruwi 112; tel. 24812507; fax 24813100; e-mail odebe@omantel.net.om; f. 1977; absorbed Oman Bank for Agriculture and Fisheries in 1997; short-, medium- and long-term finance for development projects in industry, agriculture and fishing; state-owned; cap. 20.0m. (Dec. 2004), res 0.4m., dep. 13.5m. (Dec. 2002); Chair. Sheikh Abdulmalik Abdullah al-Hinai; Gen. Man. Samir bin Béchir Said; 10 brs.

Oman Housing Bank SAOC: POB 2555, Ruwi 112; tel. 24704444; fax 24704071; f. 1977; long-term finance for housing development; 100% state-owned; cap. 30.0m., total assets 166.4m. (Dec. 2004); Chair. Darwish Ismail Ali al-Bulushi; Gen. Man. Adnan Haidar Darwish az-Za'abi; 9 brs.

STOCK EXCHANGE

Muscat Securities Market (MSM): POB 3265, Muscat 112; tel. 24812607; fax 24816353; e-mail info@msm.gov.om; internet www.msm.gov.om; 35 cos listed at the end of Dec. 2003; f. 1989; Chair. Abdullah bin Salem as-Salmi; Dir-Gen. Ahmad Saleh al-Marhoon.

Supervisory Body

Capital Markets Authority (CMA): POB 3359, Ruwi 112; tel. 24812722; fax 24816266; e-mail info@cma-oman.gov.om; internet www.omancma.org; f. 2000 to regulate stock exchange; Exec. Pres. Yahya bin Said Abdullah al-Jabri.

INSURANCE

In 2004 there were 15 licensed insurance companies operating in Oman. Of these, seven were local firms and the remainder were branches of non-resident companies.

Al-Ahlia Holding Co SAOG: POB 1463, Ruwi 112; tel. 24709331; fax 24797151; e-mail aais@alahliaoman.com; f. 1985; cap. 2.5m.; Chair. Adel Abdullah ar-Raisi; Gen. Man. P. R. Ramakrishnan.

Dhofar Insurance Co SAOG: POB 1002, Ruwi 112; tel. 24793640; fax 24793641; e-mail dhofar@dhofarinsurance.com; internet www.dhofarinsurance.com; f. 1989; cap. 9.4m. (Feb. 2005); Dir and CEO Taher bin Taleb Kamal al-Heraki.

Al-Ittihad al-Wattani: POB 2279, Ruwi 112; tel. 24700715; fax 24705595; f. 1977; Lebanese co; Area Man. George A. Chidiac.

Muscat Insurance Co SAOG: POB 72, Ruwi 112; tel. 24695897; fax 24695847; e-mail mic@omzest.com; Gen. Man. Malcolm A. Jack.

National Life Insurance Co SAOC: POB 798, Wadi Kabir 117; tel. 24793666; fax 24795222; e-mail natlife@nlicgulf.com; internet www.nlicgulf.com; f. 1983; Gen. Man. S. Venkatachalam.

Oman National Insurance Co SAOC (ONIC): POB 2254, Ruwi 112; tel. 24795020; fax 24702569; f. 1978; cap. 2m.; Chair. Mushtaq bin Abdullah Jaffer as-Saleh; Gen. Man. Michael J. Wright.

Oman United Insurance Co SAOG: POB 1522, Ruwi 112; tel. 24703990; fax 24796327; e-mail ouinsco@omantel.net.om; internet www.ouholding.com; f. 1985; cap. 2m.; Chair. Said Salim bin Nassir al-Busaidi; Gen. Man. Khalid Mansour Hamed.

Trade and Industry

GOVERNMENT AGENCY

Omani Centre for Investment Promotion and Export Development (OCIPED): POB 25, Al-Wadi Kabir 117, Muscat; tel. 24812344; fax 24810890; e-mail info@ociped.com; internet www.ociped.com; f. 1996; promotes investment to Oman and the development of non-oil Omani exports; Chair. Maqbool bin Ali bin Sultan; Exec. Pres. Salem bin Nasser al-Ismaily.

CHAMBER OF COMMERCE

Oman Chamber of Commerce and Industry: POB 1400, Ruwi 112; tel. 24707684; fax 24708497; e-mail pubrel@chamberoman.com; internet www.chamberoman.com; f. 1973; Pres. Eng. Salem Said al-Ghatami; 112,211 mems (2004).

STATE HYDROCARBONS COMPANIES

National Gas Co SAOG: POB 95, Rusayl 124; tel. 24446073; fax 24446307; e-mail natgas@omantel.net.om; f. 1979; bottling of liquefied petroleum gas; Chair. Sheikh Khalid Ahmad Sultan al-Hosni; Gen. Man. Pradyot Kumar Bagchi; 158 employees.

Oman Gas Co SOAC (OGC): POB 799, al–Khuwair 133; tel. 24681600; fax 24681678; e-mail info@oman-gas.com.om; f. 1999; government-owned (80% Ministry of Oil and Gas; 20% Oman Oil Co); operates gas network and builds pipelines to supply power plants and other industries in Oman; Chair. Khalifa Mubarak al-Hinai; CEO Yousuf Muhammad al-Ojaili.

Oman LNG LLC: POB 560, Mina al-Fahal 116; tel. 24609900; fax 24609999; e-mail info@omanlng.co.om; internet www.omanlng.com; f. 1992; 51% state-owned; manages 6.6m. metric-tons-per-year liquefied natural gas plant at Qalhat; manufacturing, shipping and marketing; Chair. Nasser bin Khamis al-Jashmi; CEO and Gen. Man. Dr Agnus Cassens; 225 employees.

Oman Oil Co SAOC (OOC): POB 261, al-Harthy Complex, Ruwi 118; tel. 24567392; fax 24567386; e-mail oman-oil@oman-oil.com; internet www.oman-oil.com; f. late 1980s to invest in foreign commercial enterprises and oil trading operations; 100% state-owned; Chair. Maqbool bin Ali bin Sultan; CEO Ahmad al-Wahaibi.

Oman Refinery Co LLC: POB 3568, Ruwi 112; tel. 24561200; fax 24561384; e-mail orc@refinery.co.om; production of light petroleum products; Man. Dir Kazutoshi Shimmuro; 300 employees.

Petroleum Development Oman LLC (PDO): POB 81, Muscat 113; tel. 24678111; fax 24677106; e-mail external-affairs@pdo.co.om; internet www.pdo.co.om; incorporated in Sultanate of Oman since 1980 by royal decree as limited liability co; 60% owned by Oman Govt, 34% by Royal Dutch Shell; production (2003) averaged 702,000 b/d from some 100 fields, linked by a pipeline system to terminal at Mina al-Fahal, near Muscat; Man. Dir John Malcolm; 4,500 employees.

UTILITIES

As part of its privatization programme, the Omani Government is divesting the utilities on a project-by-project basis. Private investors have already been found for several municipal waste water projects, desalination plants and regional electricity providers. Listed below are the state agencies currently responsible for each utility.

Ministry of Housing, Electricity and Water: (see The Government); plans and supervises the development of the utilities in Oman.

Electricity

Oman National Electric Co SAOG (ONEC): POB 1393, Ruwi 112; tel. 24796353; fax 24704420; e-mail onecctr@omantel.net.om; internet www.onec.org; f. 1978; Chair. MAHMOUD ABDULLAH AL-KHONJI; Gen. Man. Dr IRFAN A. RIZVI.

Water

Ministry of Regional Municipalities, the Environment and Water Resources: (see The Government); assesses, manages, develops and conserves water resources.

Transport

ROADS

A network of adequate graded roads links all the main centres of population and only a few mountain villages are inaccessible by off-road vehicles. In 2004 there were 40,116 km of roads, of which 863 km were dual carriageways and a further 13,821 km were asphalted roads. Several large-scale road-building projects were under way in 2006, including the construction of a ring-road around Muscat, at a cost of US $154m.

Directorate-General of Roads: POB 7027, Mutrah; tel. 24701577; Dir-Gen. of Roads Sheikh MUHAMMAD BIN HILAL AL-KHALILI.

Oman National Transport Co SAOG (ONTC): POB 620, Muscat 113; tel. 24590046; fax 24590152; e-mail info@ontcoman.com; internet www.ontcoman.com; f. 1972; re-established in 1984; operates local, regional and long-distance bus services from Muscat; Chair. MAJID SAID SALIM AR-RUWAHI; Man. Dir SULAYMAN BIN MUHANA AL-ADAWI.

SHIPPING

Port Sultan Qaboos (Mina Sultan Qaboos), at the entrance to the Persian (Arabian) Gulf, was built in 1974 to provide nine deep-water berths varying in length from 250 ft to 750 ft (76 m to 228 m), with draughts of up to 43 ft (13 m), and three berths for shallow-draught vessels drawing 12 ft to 16 ft (3.7 m to 4.9 m) of water. A total of 12 new berths have been opened and two of the existing berths have been upgraded to a container terminal capable of handling 60 containers per hour. The port also has a 3,000-metric-ton-capacity cold store which belongs to the Oman Fisheries Co. In the 1990s Port Sultan Qaboos underwent a further upgrade and expansion. In 2004 1,864 ships visited the port and 2.2m. tons of cargo were handled.

The oil terminal at Mina al-Fahal can also accommodate the largest super-tankers on offshore loading buoys. Similar facilities for the import of refined petroleum products exist at Mina al-Fahal. Mina Raysut, near Salalah (now known as Salalah port), has been developed into an all-weather port, and, in addition to container facilities, has four deep-water berths and two shallow berths. The port is currently undergoing transformation into a free-trade zone. During 2004 601 ships called at Salalah. In 2002 the port handled a reported 2m. 20-ft equivalent units (TEU). The construction of two further deep-water berths was planned, which would increase the port's capacity to some 3m. TEUs per year. Loading facilities for smaller craft exist at Sohar and Khasab (both of which are being expanded), Khaboura, Sur, Marbet, Ras al-Had, Al-Biaa, Masirah and Salalah. The construction of a new port at Duqm, on the Gulf of Masirah, was in the planning stages in early 2006. The project, which was to include two docks capable of accommodating large tankers, was forecast to cost US $500m.

Directorate-General of Ports and Maritime Affairs: POB 684, Ruwi 113; tel. 24700986; fax 24702044; e-mail dgpma@omantel.net.om; Dir-Gen. Eng. JAMAL T. AZIZ.

Port Services Corpn SAOG (PSC): POB 133, Muscat 113; tel. 24714000; fax 24714007; e-mail mktg@pscoman.com; internet www.pscoman.com; f. 1976; cap. RO 7.2m. (2002); jointly owned by the Govt of Oman and private shareholders; Exec. Pres. SAUD BIN AHMAD AN-NAHARI.

Salalah Port Services Co SAOG (SPS): POB 105, Muscat 118; tel. 24600586; fax 24600736; e-mail admin@salalahport.com; internet www.salalahport.com; port authority for Salalah port; CEO and Gen. Man. TIEMEN MEESTER.

CIVIL AVIATION

Domestic and international flights operate from Seeb International Airport. In 2004 3.2m. passengers passed through the airport; it is planned to increase annual passenger capacity to 12.5m. over a 25-year period. Seeb International Airport and Oman's second international airport, at Salalah (completed in 1978), were both effectively privatized in October 2001. Responsibility for the management and refurbishment of the airports passed to Oman Airports Management Company (OAMC); however, following the failure of the Government successfully to agree financial terms for the privatization and ongoing development of the airports with OAMC, the 25-year contract was cancelled in October 2004 and Seeb and Salalah airports were transferred back to state control. There are also airports at Sur, Masirah, Khasab and Diba; most other sizeable towns have airstrips.

Directorate-General of Civil Aviation and Meteorology: POB 1, CPO Seeb Airport, Muscat 111; tel. 24519356; fax 24519880; e-mail dgen@dgcam.gov.om; internet www.dgcam.gov.om; Dir-Gen. Eng. AHMAD BIN SAID BIN SALIM AR-RAWAHY.

Gulf Air: POB 1444, Ruwi 112; tel. 24703222; fax 24793381; e-mail gfmctsls@omantel.net.om; internet www.gulfairco.com; f. 1950 as Gulf Aviation Co; name changed 1974; jointly owned by the Govts of Bahrain, Oman and Abu Dhabi (UAE), although Abu Dhabi announced in Sept. 2005 that it was to withdraw from the business; international services to destinations in Europe, the USA, Africa, the Middle East, the Far East and Australasia; Chair. ABD AL-AZIZ JASIM KANOO; Pres. and CEO JAMES HOGAN; Area Man. ALI ABD AL-KHALIQ.

Oman Aviation Services Co SAOG: POB 58, Seeb International Airport 111; tel. 24519953; fax 24521075; internet www.oman-aviation.com; f. 1981; cap. RO 11m.; 35% of shares owned by Govt, 65% by Omani nationals; air-charter, maintenance, handling and catering; operators of Oman's domestic airline (Oman Air); international services to Bangladesh, India, Kenya, Kuwait, Lebanon, Pakistan, Qatar, Saudi Arabia, Sri Lanka, Tanzania and the UAE; Chair. SAEED BIN HAMDOON BIN SAIF AL-HARTHY; CEO ABD AR-RAHMAN AL-BUSAIDY.

Tourism

Tourism, introduced in 1985, is strictly controlled. Oman's attractions, apart from the capital itself, include Nizwa, ancient capital of the interior, Dhofar and the forts of Nakhl, Rustaq and Al-Hazm. The country also possesses an attractive and clean environment, including around 1,700 km of sandy beaches. The Government promotes, in a limited capacity, high-quality adventure, cultural and marine tourism. In 2003 there were 629,986 visitor arrivals in Oman and tourism receipts totalled US $372m.

Directorate-General of Tourism: Madinat Al-Sultan Qaboos, POB 200, Muscat 115; tel. 24588877; fax 24588844; e-mail info@omantourism.gov.om; internet www.omantourism.gov.om; Dir-Gen. MUHAMMAD ALI SAID.

PAKISTAN

Introductory Survey

Location, Climate, Language, Religion, Flag, Capital

The Islamic Republic of Pakistan lies in southern Asia, bordered by India to the east and by Afghanistan and Iran to the west. It has a short frontier with the People's Republic of China in the far north-east. The climate is dry and generally hot, with an average annual temperature of 27°C (80°F), except in the mountains, which have very cold winters. Temperatures in Karachi are generally between 13°C (55°F) and 34°C (93°F), with negligible rainfall. The principal languages are Punjabi (the language usually spoken in 44.2% of households in 1998), Pushto (Pashtu) (15.4%), Sindhi (14.1%) and Saraiki (10.5%). Urdu (7.6%) is the national language, and English is extensively used. The state religion is Islam, embracing about 97% of the population, the remainder being mainly Hindus or Christians. The national flag (proportions 2 by 3) has a vertical white stripe at the hoist, while the remainder is dark green, with a white crescent moon and a five-pointed star in the centre. The capital is Islamabad.

Recent History

Pakistan was created in August 1947 by the partition of the United Kingdom's former Indian Empire into the independent states of India and Pakistan, in response to demands by elements of the Muslim population in the subcontinent for the establishment of a specifically Islamic state. Pakistan originally comprised two distinct regions: East Pakistan and West Pakistan, separated by some 1,600 km (1,000 miles) of Indian territory, and united only by a common religion. Although the majority of the population lived in the smaller part, East Pakistan, political and military power was concentrated in the west, where the Muslim League was the dominant political movement. The leader of the Muslim League, Muhammad Ali Jinnah, popularly known as Quaid-i-Azam ('Great Leader'), became the first Governor-General of Pakistan but died in 1948. The country, formerly a dominion with the British monarch as Head of State, became a republic on 23 March 1956, when Pakistan's first Constitution was promulgated. At the same time Maj.-Gen. Iskander Mirza became Pakistan's first President.

Pakistan came under military rule in early October 1958, when President Mirza abrogated the Constitution, declared martial law, dismissed the national and provincial governments and dissolved all political parties. In late October, however, Gen. (later Field Marshal) Muhammad Ayub Khan, the Martial Law Administrator appointed by Mirza, removed Mirza from office and became President himself. Ayub Khan's autocratic but modernizing regime lasted until March 1969, when he was forced to resign following widespread unrest. Gen. Agha Muhammad Yahya Khan, the Commander-in-Chief of the Army, replaced him, and martial law was reimposed.

In December 1970 the country's first general election was held for a national assembly. Sheikh Mujibur Rahman's Awami League, which advocated autonomy for East Pakistan, won almost all the seats in the east (thus gaining an absolute majority in the National Assembly), while the Pakistan People's Party (PPP), led by Zulfikar Ali Bhutto, won a majority of seats in the west. Following the failure of negotiations to achieve a coalition government of the two parties, on 23 March 1971 East Pakistan declared its independence as the People's Republic of Bangladesh. Civil war immediately broke out, as Pakistani troops clashed with Bengali irregular forces. In December the Indian army intervened in the conflict to support the Bengalis, and the Pakistani army was forced to withdraw, thus permitting Bangladesh to establish firmly its independence. In the truncated Pakistan that remained in the west, Yahya Khan resigned, military rule was ended, and Bhutto became the new President.

A new Constitution, which came into effect in August 1973, provided for a parliamentary system of government. Bhutto became executive Prime Minister, while Fazal Elahi Chaudry, hitherto Speaker of the National Assembly, became constitutional President. The PPP won an overwhelming majority of seats in elections to the National Assembly in March 1977. However, the opposition Pakistan National Alliance (PNA) accused the PPP of widespread electoral malpractice and launched a nation-wide campaign of civil disobedience. An estimated 1,000 people died in subsequent clashes between troops and demonstrators, and some 40,000 people were arrested. In July the armed forces intervened in the crisis: Bhutto was deposed in a bloodless military coup and a martial law regime was instituted, with Gen. Mohammad Zia ul-Haq, the Army Chief of Staff, as Chief Martial Law Administrator. President Chaudry remained in office as Head of State. Bhutto was subsequently charged with instigating the murder of a PPP dissident and a member of the dissident's family in 1974. He was sentenced to death in March 1978 and executed in April 1979.

In September 1978 President Chaudry resigned and Gen. Zia became President. General elections were postponed several times by the military administration, and in October 1979 Gen. Zia announced an indefinite postponement of the polls. Opposition to the military regime was severely suppressed, particularly after new martial law orders were adopted in May 1980. In March 1981 nine political parties formed an opposition alliance, the Movement for the Restoration of Democracy (MRD), which advocated an end to military rule and a return to a parliamentary system of government. Several opposition politicians were subsequently interned or placed under house arrest. In August 1983 the MRD, led by the PPP, launched a civil disobedience campaign to press for the restoration of parliamentary democracy on the basis of the 1973 Constitution. The campaign enjoyed considerable support in Sindh province, where anti-Government protests resulted in numerous deaths. However, there was limited popular support elsewhere in the country, and the campaign ended in December 1983. Many political leaders and activists, including Benazir Bhutto (daughter of the former President and herself a leading PPP activist), were subsequently imprisoned or went into exile.

Gen. Zia's regime zealously pursued a policy of 'Islamization' of the country's institutions, including the enforcement of Islamic penal codes, and the introduction of Islamic economic principles, such as interest-free banking. In December 1984 a referendum was held, which sought affirmation of the Islamization process and, indirectly, endorsement of a further five-year term for Gen. Zia. The referendum was boycotted by the MRD, but, according to official figures, 98% of those participating supported the proposal. There were, however, widespread allegations of electoral malpractice.

In February 1985 a general election was held for a national assembly, followed shortly afterwards by elections to four provincial assemblies. The elections were held on a non-party basis, but widespread dissatisfaction with the regime was indicated by the defeat of several of Zia's cabinet ministers and close supporters. The largest two groupings in the new National Assembly were formed by a faction of the Pakistan Muslim League (PML, the successor to the Muslim League), known as the Pagara Group, and former members of the PPP. In late March Gen. Zia appointed Muhammad Khan Junejo, a member of the PML (Pagara Group), as Prime Minister, and an almost entirely civilian Cabinet was formed.

In October 1985 the National Assembly approved changes to the Constitution (the 'Eighth Amendment'), proposed by Gen. Zia, which introduced a powerful executive presidency and indemnified all actions of the military regime during the previous eight years. On 30 December Gen. Zia announced the repeal of martial law and the restoration of the Constitution (as amended in October). The military courts were dissolved, and military personnel were removed from civilian posts, with the exception of Gen. Zia, who remained as President and head of the armed forces. Junejo retained the post of Prime Minister in a new Cabinet. However, the MRD continued to demand the restoration of the unamended 1973 Constitution. In April 1986 its cause was strengthened by the return from exile of Benazir Bhutto, who travelled throughout the country holding political rallies which attracted thousands of supporters. She demanded the resignation of President Zia and the holding of a free general election, open to all political parties. In May Benazir Bhutto and her mother, Nusrat Bhutto, were elected as Co-Chairwomen of the PPP. In August the Government adopted a less tolerant approach towards the MRD by banning all rallies scheduled for

Independence Day and by detaining hundreds of opposition members, including Benazir Bhutto. The arrests provoked violent anti-Government demonstrations in a number of cities.

In late 1986 violent clashes occurred in Karachi, Quetta and Hyderabad as a result of disputes between rival ethnic groups (primarily between the Pathans, originally from the North-West Frontier Province—NWFP—and Afghanistan, and the Urdu-speaking Mohajirs, who migrated from India when the subcontinent was partitioned in 1947). The violence was most severe in Karachi, where some 170 people were killed in December. The rise of ethnic communalism in Pakistan was reflected in the results of local elections held throughout the country in November 1987. The party of the Mohajirs, the Mohajir Qaumi Movement (MQM), won the majority of seats in Karachi and was also successful in other urban areas of Sindh province. Nationwide, the government-supported PML received the majority of votes, while the PPP won less than 20% of total seats.

In May 1988, in accordance with the authority vested in him through the Eighth Amendment, President Zia dismissed the Prime Minister and his Cabinet, and dissolved the National Assembly and the four provincial assemblies. Zia became head of an interim administration, which was to govern until a general election was held. In July Zia announced that the elections to the National Assembly and the provincial assemblies would be held in November. On 17 August 1988, however, President Zia was killed in an air crash in eastern Pakistan. Subsequent speculation that the cause of the crash was sabotage was not officially confirmed. The Chairman of the Senate, Ghulam Ishaq Khan, was appointed acting President, and an emergency National Council (composed of senior military officers, the four provincial governors and four federal ministers) was appointed to take charge of government.

Despite the imposition of a state of emergency after the death of Zia, the general election took place, as scheduled, in November 1988. In the elections to the National Assembly the PPP won 93 of the 207 directly-elective seats, and was the only party to secure seats in each of Pakistan's four provinces. The Islamic Democratic Alliance (IDA), a grouping of nine Islamic and right-wing parties (including the PML), gained 54 seats, with the remaining seats going to independents and candidates representing seven smaller parties. The PPP did not achieve such a high level of support, however, in the elections to the provincial assemblies, held three days later. The PPP was able to form coalition governments in Sindh and the NWFP, but the IDA took power in Punjab, the most populous province. At the federal level, a coalition Government was formed by the PPP and the MQM, which together had a working majority in the National Assembly (the MQM had 14 seats). Benazir Bhutto, the leader of the PPP, was appointed Prime Minister on 1 December, thus becoming the first female leader of a Muslim country. The state of emergency was repealed on the same day. A new Cabinet was formed, and later in December an electoral college (comprising the Senate, the National Assembly and the four provincial assemblies) elected Ghulam Ishaq Khan as President.

Benazir Bhutto's attempts, in early 1989, to repeal the Eighth Amendment to the Constitution, which severely constrained her powers as Prime Minister, were unsuccessful. Moreover, the fragile coalitions that the PPP had formed in the provincial assemblies soon came under pressure. In April the coalition Government formed by the PPP and the Awami National Party (ANP) in the NWFP collapsed. In May the coalition with the MQM in Sindh province also failed, following renewed ethnic conflict in the region. In the same month the opposition was strengthened by the formation of an informal parliamentary grouping, the Combined Opposition Party (COP), comprising the IDA, the ANP, Jamiat-e-Ulema-e-Islam (JUI) and the Pakistan Awami Ittehad. In October the Government suffered a serious reversal when the MQM withdrew its parliamentary support for the PPP and transferred it to the opposition, claiming that the PPP had failed to honour any of the promises made in the original co-operation agreement between the two parties. In November a parliamentary motion of 'no confidence', proposed by the COP against the Government, was narrowly defeated. In January 1990 the COP organized a campaign to undermine the Government, accusing it of corruption, political bribery and mismanagement. Rallies and demonstrations in Sindh province culminated in violence between supporters of the PPP and the MQM; in May about 100 people were killed during violent clashes between police and demonstrators in the region. Calm was temporarily restored by the deployment of army units.

By mid-1990 the initial popularity of the PPP Government appeared to have declined considerably: the maintenance of law and order had worsened; no significant new legislation had been introduced; the economic situation was deteriorating; and there were widespread allegations of corruption against high-ranking officials. On 6 August the President, in accordance with his constitutional powers, dissolved the National Assembly, dismissed the Prime Minister and her Cabinet and declared a state of emergency. He also announced that a general election would take place in late October. The President alleged that the ousted Government had violated the Constitution, accusing it of corruption, nepotism and incompetence. Ghulam Mustafa Jatoi, the leader of the COP in the National Assembly, was appointed acting Prime Minister in an interim Government. The four provincial assemblies were also dissolved, and 'caretaker' Chief Ministers appointed. Benazir Bhutto claimed that the dissolution of her administration was illegal and strongly denied the various charges made against her Government. At the end of August several of Benazir Bhutto's former ministers were arrested, and in the following month she herself was indicted on more than 10 charges of corruption and abuse of power. In early October Benazir Bhutto's husband, Asif Ali Zardari, was arrested on charges of extortion, kidnapping and financial irregularities (he was later acquitted on all counts).

At the general election, which took place, as scheduled, on 24 October 1990, the IDA doubled its representation in the National Assembly, leaving it only four seats short of an absolute majority, while the People's Democratic Alliance (PDA, an electoral alliance comprising the PPP and three smaller parties) suffered a heavy defeat. Support for the PPP also declined in the provincial elections, where it unexpectedly lost control of its traditional stronghold in Sindh and fared badly elsewhere. Regional and ethnic parties continued to expand their influence, notably the MQM in urban areas of Sindh, and the ANP in the NWFP. On 6 November Mohammad Nawaz Sharif, the leader of the IDA and the former Chief Minister of Punjab, was elected as the new Prime Minister. He officially ended the three-month-long state of emergency, and appointed a new Cabinet, which included several ministers who had served under President Zia. Nawaz Sharif promised that one of the Government's major priorities was to establish lasting peace in Sindh, where ethnic conflict and general lawlessness continued to prevail. It was alleged, however, that the Government's subsequent campaign of suppression in the province, in response to numerous local murders and kidnappings, was aimed primarily at supporters of the PPP, hundreds of whom were arrested. In January 1991 the IDA won 19 of the 25 by-elections for seats in the National Assembly and the provincial assemblies, and in March won a decisive majority in elections to 42 seats in the Senate.

In May 1991 the National Assembly adopted legislation imposing the incorporation of *Shari'a*, the Islamic legal code, in Pakistan's legal system. The Assembly also adopted legislation providing for the Islamization of the educational, economic and judicial systems. Benazir Bhutto criticized the legislation as being extreme and fundamentalist, while the right-wing JUI claimed that the new law's provisions were not stringent enough.

The fundamentalist Jamaat-e-Islami Pakistan (JIP) left the IDA in May 1992, in protest at the Government's decision to support the new moderate *mujahidin* Government in Kabul, Afghanistan. The JIP accused the Government of abandoning the extremist Afghan guerrilla leader, Gulbuddin Hekmatyar, and also of failing to effect the full Islamization of Pakistan.

In response to continuing violence in Sindh, the Government launched 'Operation Clean-up' in May 1992, whereby the army was to apprehend criminals and terrorists, and seize unauthorized weapons. A violent clash between two factions of the MQM (the majority Altaf faction and the small breakaway Haqiqi faction) in Karachi in June provided the armed forces with the opportunity to suppress the extremist elements within the MQM. More than 500 people were arrested; caches of arms were located and seized; and 'torture cells', allegedly operated by the MQM, were discovered. The leader of the MQM (A), Altaf Hussain, accused the Government of attempting to crush the MQM through the military operation. In protest, 12 of the 15 MQM members in the National Assembly and 24 of the 27 members in the Sindh assembly resigned their seats. The Government, however, repeatedly gave assurances that the operations were against criminals, and not specifically against the MQM.

In mid-November 1992 the PDA intensified its campaign of political agitation and was now supported by the majority of the components of the newly formed opposition National Democratic Alliance (NDA), including the National People's Party (NPP—which had been expelled from the IDA in March). The large-scale demonstrations and marches organized by Benazir Bhutto were, however, ruthlessly suppressed by the Government. By mid-December tensions between the Government and opposition had eased considerably, and in January 1993, in an apparently conciliatory move on the part of Nawaz Sharif's administration, Benazir Bhutto was elected Chairperson of the National Assembly's Standing Committee on Foreign Affairs. Shortly after Benazir Bhutto had accepted the nomination, her husband was released on bail.

In March 1993 a growing rift between the Prime Minister and the President became evident when the Government initiated discussions regarding proposed modifications to the provisions of the Eighth Constitutional Amendment, which afforded the President the power to dismiss the Government and dissolve assemblies, and to appoint judicial and military chiefs. In late March three cabinet ministers resigned in protest at Nawaz Sharif's nomination as President of the PML (Junejo Group), to succeed Muhammad Khan Junejo (who had died earlier that month), and voiced their support for Ghulam Ishaq Khan in his political struggle with the Prime Minister. In a seemingly final attempt at reconciliation, the Cabinet unanimously decided, in early April, to nominate Ghulam Ishaq Khan as the PML's candidate for the forthcoming presidential election. By mid-April, however, a total of eight ministers had resigned from the Cabinet in protest at Nawaz Sharif's continued tenure of the premiership. On 18 April the President dissolved the National Assembly and dismissed the Prime Minister and his Cabinet, accusing Nawaz Sharif of 'maladministration, nepotism and corruption'. The provincial assemblies and governments, however, remained in power, despite demands by the PDA and the NDA for their dissolution. A member of the dissolved National Assembly, Mir Balakh Sher Mazari, was sworn in as acting Prime Minister. It was announced that elections to the National Assembly would be held on 14 July. In late April a broadly-based interim Cabinet, including Benazir Bhutto's husband, was sworn in. In early May the PML (Junejo Group) split into two factions: one led by Nawaz Sharif, the other by Hamid Nasir Chattha (with the support of the President).

On 26 May 1993, in an historic and unexpected judgment, the Supreme Court ordered that the National Assembly, the Prime Minister and the Cabinet (dismissed in April) should be restored to power immediately, stating that President Khan's order had been unconstitutional. The President agreed to honour the Court's ruling, and the National Assembly and Nawaz Sharif's Government were reinstated with immediate effect. On the following day Nawaz Sharif's return to power was consolidated when he won a vote of confidence in the National Assembly. A few days later, however, there was renewed political turmoil following the dissolution, through the machinations of supporters of the President, of the provincial assemblies in Punjab and the NWFP. Lacking effective authority in each of the four provinces, Nawaz Sharif resorted to the imposition of federal government's rule on Punjab through a resolution passed by the National Assembly in late June. However, the Punjab provincial government refused to obey the federal Government's orders, claiming that they subverted provincial autonomy, prompting the Government to threaten the imposition of a military administration. Meanwhile, an All Parties Conference (APC), including, amongst others, Benazir Bhutto and the Chief Ministers of Punjab and the NWFP, convened in Lahore to pass a resolution, urging the President to dissolve the legislature, dismiss Nawaz Sharif's Government and hold fresh elections. In early July the Chief of Army Staff, following an emergency meeting of senior army officers, acted as an intermediary in talks between the President and Prime Minister in an attempt to resolve the political crisis. Benazir Bhutto, supported by her APC collaborators, announced a 'long march' on 16 July, with the intention of laying siege to the federal capital and forcing Nawaz Sharif to resign. Fearing the outbreak of serious violence, the army persuaded Benazir Bhutto to postpone the march, reportedly assuring her that both the President and the Prime Minister would resign and that a general election would be held under a neutral administration. On 18 July, in accordance with an agreement reached under the auspices of the army, both Khan and Nawaz Sharif resigned from their posts, the Federal Legislature and the provincial assemblies were dissolved, the holding of a general election in October was announced, and neutral administrations were established, at both federal and provincial level. As specified in the Constitution, Khan was succeeded by the Chairman of the Senate, Wasim Sajjad Jan, who was to hold the presidency for the remaining tenure of the deposed President. A small, apolitical Cabinet was sworn in, headed by Moeenuddin Ahmad Qureshi, a former Executive Vice-President of the World Bank, as interim Prime Minister.

The general election, held in early October 1993 under military supervision, was widely considered to have been fair, although the turn-out, which some officials estimated to be less than 50%, was disappointing. The polling was closely contested between the PML faction led by Nawaz Sharif—PML (Nawaz—N)—and the PPP (the MQM boycotted the elections to the National Assembly, claiming systematic intimidation by the army, but took part in the provincial assembly elections a few days later). However, neither of the two leading parties won an outright majority in the federal elections, and in the provincial elections an outright majority was only achieved by the PPP in Sindh. Following intensive negotiations with smaller parties and independents in the National Assembly, on 19 October Benazir Bhutto was elected to head a coalition Government. On the following day a PPP-led coalition assumed control of the provincial administration in Punjab (traditionally a PML stronghold). The provincial governments in the NWFP and in Balochistan were, however, headed by alliances led by the PML (N).

In November 1993 the PPP's candidate, the newly appointed Minister of Foreign Affairs, Sardar Farooq Ahmad Khan Leghari, was elected President, having secured 274 votes (62% of the total) in the electoral college. The incumbent acting President, Wasim Sajjad Jan, who stood as the candidate of the PML (N), obtained 168 votes (38%). On assuming office, Leghari stated that he intended to end his political ties with the PPP and that he hoped for the early repeal or modification of the controversial Eighth Constitutional Amendment.

In February 1994 the President dismissed the Chief Minister and government of the NWFP, suspended the provincial legislature and imposed governor's rule, following the thwarted introduction of a vote of 'no confidence' against the PML (N)-led coalition by the PPP. The PPP consolidated its hold on federal power in March by winning the majority of the contested seats in elections to the Senate. In April a PPP member was elected as Chief Minister of the newly revived provincial government in the NWFP; the opposition alliance boycotted the proceedings.

September 1994 witnessed an upsurge in political unrest when Nawaz Sharif organized a nation-wide general strike; in response, the Government arrested hundreds of PML supporters. In November the Government was confronted with a series of uprisings staged by heavily-armed tribesmen in the mountainous regions of Malakand and Swat demanding the enforcement of *Shari'a*. The fundamentalist revolt was suppressed by paramilitary forces (but only after the deaths of several hundred people), and the *Shari'a* measures were implemented in the tribal areas. By the end of the year, however, the police and paramilitary forces appeared to be losing control of Karachi, which was riven by rapidly escalating ethnic and criminal violence; nearly 170 people were killed in the city in December alone, following the lengthy 'Operation Clean-up' and the withdrawal of the army in the previous month. Much of the violence stemmed from the bloody rivalry between the opposing factions of the MQM, whilst other killings were linked to drugs mafias and to sectarian disputes between Sunni and Shi'a Muslims.

In early 1995, despite the arrest of large numbers of suspected Islamist militants, there was an upsurge in religious violence between Sunni and Shi'a Muslims in Karachi. In March the murder of two US consular officials by unidentified gunmen in the troubled Sindh capital provoked international condemnation. There was no respite from the violence in the following months, and by June the security forces had lost control of large areas of Karachi to MQM activists. Negotiations between representatives of the MQM (A) and government officials in mid-1995 proved fruitless and, although there was a temporary abatement in urban violence in the latter half of the year, the city's problems were far from resolved. It was estimated that during 1995 almost 2,000 people (including about 250 members of the security forces) were killed as a result of the political and ethnic violence in Karachi. In September of that year the growing political instability in Pakistan was underlined by the arrest of nearly 40 army officers on suspicion of plotting to overthrow the Government and to establish an Islamist fundamentalist state. In November 18 people were killed when a car bomb exploded at the Egyptian embassy in Islamabad; within hours of the attack three militant Islamist groups in Egypt had claimed responsibility for the bombing. During the previous year the Pakistani Government had been co-operating with Egypt in attempts to apprehend and extradite members of illegal Islamist militant organizations operating in the NWFP or across the border in Afghanistan. (In 1993–95 the Pakistan authorities, concerned at the country's growing reputation as a refuge for Islamist extremists, expelled more than 2,000 Arabs, the majority of whom were reported to have been involved in the civil war in Afghanistan.) Acts of violence and terrorism in Pakistan continued throughout late 1995 and early 1996.

A new political force emerged in Pakistan in early 1996, when the popular former international cricketer Imran Khan (of late a prominent benefactor of charitable causes) established a political reform movement known as the Tehrik-e-Insaf (Movement for Justice), to oppose Benazir Bhutto's administration.

In March 1996 the Supreme Court in Karachi ruled that the Government no longer had the exclusive mandate to appoint judges to the higher courts; these appointments would, in future, be required to have the consent of the Chief Justices of the High Courts and the Chief Justice of Pakistan. This ruling aroused considerable controversy since it deprived the executive of substantial authority within the national judicial system.

The Government's popularity was undermined by the necessary introduction of an austere budget, including the introduction of new taxes, in mid-June 1996, in an attempt to reduce the budget deficit. The volatile political situation was intensified by a bomb explosion at Lahore airport in late July, a series of debilitating public-sector strikes and by a resurgence of violence in Karachi. In addition, the appointment of the Prime Minister's unpopular husband, Asif Ali Zardari, as Minister of Investment as part of a cabinet expansion in July aroused much controversy and criticism. At the end of that month the Government's position appeared even less secure when about 16 opposition parties, including the PML (N), the MQM and the JIP, established an informal alliance with a one-point agenda: to oust Prime Minister Bhutto and her Government. Pakistan was thrown into further political turmoil in mid-September following the fatal shooting of Benazir Bhutto's estranged brother, Mir Murtaza Bhutto, in a gun battle with police in Karachi. A number of opposition politicians accused the Prime Minister and her husband of complicity in the killing, while Benazir Bhutto implied in a number of public statements that she believed that the President and the army were to blame. In 1995 Mir Murtaza Bhutto had established a rival faction of the PPP, known as the PPP (Shaheed Bhutto Group), charging his sister's Government with corruption and misrule; the breakaway faction, however, attracted no substantial support and posed little threat to the Prime Minister. Meanwhile, growing discord between Benazir Bhutto and President Leghari became more apparent.

Amidst mounting public discontent, President Leghari dismissed Prime Minister Benazir Bhutto and her Government and dissolved the National Assembly on 5 November 1996 (the state assemblies were dissolved over the following week), citing the deteriorating law and order situation, severe economic problems, widespread corruption, disregard for judicial authority and the violation of various constitutional provisions as justification for his action. A former Speaker of the National Assembly, Malik Meraj Khaled, who claimed no affiliation to any political party, was named as acting Prime Minister and an interim Cabinet was appointed. Following the dismissal of her Government, it was reported that several leading members of Benazir Bhutto's PPP, including her husband, had been arrested. In mid-November the President promulgated a decree providing for a five-year disqualification from public office of politicians (with the exception of the President and members of the judiciary and armed forces) involved in corruption and abuses of power. At the end of December the JIP announced its intention to boycott the forthcoming general election, accusing the 'caretaker' Government of failing in its much-vaunted anti-corruption drive. Sectarian violence between Sunni and Shi'a Muslims escalated in January 1997, culminating in a bomb blast outside a district court in Lahore, which killed the leader of the Sunni extremist group Sipah-e-Sahaba Pakistan, and 25 others. Meanwhile, in early January the President instituted an official advisory role for the military, with the formation of a 10-member Council of Defence and National Security (CDNS), which was to advise the Government on a broad range of issues from national security to the economy. The President chaired the new body, which comprised the Prime Minister, four senior cabinet ministers, the Chairman of the Joint Chiefs of Staff and the three armed services chiefs, and could refer any matter to it without previously consulting the Prime Minister. In response to this unexpected development, many political parties, including the PPP, but with the notable exception of the PML (N), accused the President of an unconstitutional usurpation of authority. The Government insisted, however, that the role of the CDNS would be purely advisory.

The general election, which was held on 3 February 1997, was marred by an extremely low turn-out (an estimated 30%–40%). The PML (N) won a decisive victory, obtaining 134 of the 204 directly-elective seats in the National Assembly (voting in three seats was deferred until a later date), while the PPP was routed, both at federal and state level, winning only 18 seats. The MQM emerged as the country's third political force (obtaining 12 seats), while Imran Khan's Tehrik-e-Insaf failed to win a single seat. Nawaz Sharif was sworn in as Prime Minister on 17 February and a small Cabinet was appointed the following week. In March the PML (N) and its allies secured a two-thirds' majority in the 87-seat Senate following elections for about one-half of the seats.

Nawaz Sharif's political authority was strengthened considerably in April 1997, when both the National Assembly and the Senate voted unanimously to repeal the major components of the 1985 Eighth Constitutional Amendment, thereby divesting the President of the power to appoint and dismiss the Prime Minister and Cabinet, to dissolve the legislature, to order a national referendum on any national issue, and to appoint provincial Governors, the Chairman of the Joint Chiefs of Staff and the three armed forces chiefs (these functions and appointments were, in future, to be carried out subject to mandatory advice from the Prime Minister). The President thus became a largely ceremonial figure whose main executive role was the appointment of judges. President Leghari was reported to have 'willingly agreed' to the constitutional changes.

In July 1997 Asif Ali Zardari was formally charged with ordering the killing of Mir Murtaza Bhutto; 21 other former officials were simultaneously charged with murder and conspiracy in the death. In September the Swiss police ordered four banks in Geneva to 'freeze' the accounts of Benazir Bhutto and her family after Pakistan's Accountability Commission alleged that up to US $80m. had been illegally transferred to them. In January 1998 the British authorities, at the request of the Pakistani Government, ordered the seizure of documents relating to assets and bank accounts of Benazir Bhutto in the United Kingdom. In March the Sindh High Court issued an arrest warrant for the leader of the PPP on a charge of misuse of power during her final term in office as Prime Minister. In April the High Court in Lahore ordered that all assets belonging to Benazir Bhutto, her husband and her mother be 'frozen' as the government investigation into allegations of corruption continued.

Meanwhile, in the latter half of 1997 a serious rift developed between Nawaz Sharif and the Chief Justice of the Supreme Court, Sajjad Ali Shah, over the appointment of new judges to the Court. In early November, however, a compromise was reached between the Supreme Court and the Government, allowing the former to appoint five new judges while confirming the right of the legislature to determine the total number of judges. Yet, despite this outcome, the crisis was not over and later that month the Supreme Court charged Nawaz Sharif and five other officials with contempt for slandering the Court and defying its orders in the previous month. The Prime Minister, who, if found guilty, was liable to be disqualified from office, denied the charges. The Chief Justice was forced to adjourn Nawaz Sharif's trial in late November, however, when thousands of the Prime Minister's supporters stormed the Supreme Court in Islamabad. The constitutional crisis came to a dramatic end on 2 December when the Chief Justice was suspended from office by rebel members of the Supreme Court; on the same day President Leghari also stood down from office. The Chairman of the Senate, Wasim Sajjad Jan, assumed the position of acting President. It was widely speculated that the army, in tacitly supporting the Prime Minister, had exerted considerable influence in resolving the constitutional impasse. Nawaz Sharif strengthened his hold on power on 31 December when his nominee and fellow Punjabi, Mohammad Rafiq Tarar (a personal acquaintance of the Prime Minister and a former Supreme Court judge), won the presidential election by a record margin (winning more than 80% of the total votes cast by the electoral college).

In January 1998 sectarian violence erupted again in Lahore when at least 24 Shi'a Muslims were massacred by a clandestine

Sunni group. In response, the Government approved measures to control illicit weapons in an attempt to curb terrorism. (A controversial anti-terrorist law had been passed in August 1997, giving the security forces extensive powers of arrest and enabling the Government to ban any group or association without parliamentary approval.) In late February, however, two Iranian engineers were murdered by unidentified terrorists in Karachi, and in the following month more than 20 people were killed in two bomb explosions on passenger trains in Lahore.

Despite the temporary public euphoria and heightened popularity of the Prime Minister arising from the conduct of the controversial nuclear tests in May 1998 (see below), the repercussions (particularly the international sanctions) left Pakistan in dire financial straits. In late August the Prime Minister introduced the Fifteenth Constitutional Amendment Bill to the National Assembly, seeking to replace Pakistan's legal code with *Shari'a*. Nawaz Sharif attempted to allay fears of a move towards Islamist extremism by promising to uphold women's rights and to safeguard minorities. The Bill was passed in the National Assembly in October; it was denounced by human rights activists as 'regressive'.

The Government suffered a severe reverse in late October 1998 when the Muttahida Qaumi Movement—MQM (A)—(formerly known as the Mohajir Qaumi Movement) withdrew its support for the PML (N)-led provincial administration in Sindh. On 30 October the provincial legislature was suspended and the troubled province was placed under governor's rule in an effort to curb the violence. In November the Prime Minister announced the establishment of anti-terrorist military courts in Karachi (which were designed to dispense rapid and punitive justice), and the suspension of civil rights in Sindh.

In April 1999 the Lahore High Court found Benazir Bhutto (now in self-imposed exile abroad) and her husband guilty of corruption; they were each sentenced to five years' imprisonment, their property was confiscated and they were jointly fined US $8.6m. The verdict automatically removed the former Prime Minister and Asif Ali Zardari (who was already in prison serving a separate sentence) from their seats in the National Assembly and Senate, respectively.

Meanwhile, in early January 1999 the Prime Minister escaped an apparent assassination attempt when a bomb exploded near his country residence in Punjab, killing four people. The following day there was an upsurge in sectarian violence in the province when unidentified gunmen murdered 17 worshippers in a Shi'a mosque near Multan. Sindh became the focus of political attention later in the month when the Supreme Court declared unlawful the central Government's decision (made in November 1998) to remove the powers of the speaker and deputy speaker of the suspended Sindh assembly. In mid-February 1999 the Supreme Court ruled that military trials could not be used for cases against civilians, thus sparing 14 people from death sentences imposed in the military tribunals in Sindh and effectively barring the establishment of military courts throughout the country (as the Government had proposed). The Supreme Court ordered the transfer of the cases to civilian anti-terrorist courts.

A dangerous escalation in the Kashmir crisis between Pakistan and India in mid-1999 (see below) and the former's effective defeat in the face of almost universal condemnation and diplomatic isolation appeared to represent a major turning point in the fortunes of the PML Government. Although Nawaz Sharif attempted to ensure that any blame attached to the episode would be diverted to the army, many of his opponents in Pakistan declared that his seeming haste to concede defeat and to agree to a Pakistani withdrawal in the face of US pressure constituted a national 'betrayal'. In mid-September Nawaz Sharif's position looked increasingly precarious following the formation of a Grand Democratic Alliance by 19 conservative and centrist opposition parties, including the PPP, the MQM (A) and the ANP, which demanded the Prime Minister's immediate resignation. The various Islamist parties, including the JIP, also stepped up their anti-Government protests and rallies throughout the country. The opposition was weakened to some extent, however, by the fact that Benazir Bhutto was unwilling to return to Pakistan for fear of being arrested.

Events took a dramatic turn on 12 October 1999, when, shortly after Nawaz Sharif's announcement of a decision to dismiss the Chief of Army Staff and Chairman of the Joint Chiefs of Staff Committee, Gen. Pervez Musharraf, the army chief flew back from an official tour in Sri Lanka and promptly organized a bloodless military coup in Islamabad. Nawaz Sharif and his Government were overthrown, and the deposed Prime Minister was placed under house arrest. On 15 October Gen. Musharraf assumed the position of Chief Executive, declared a nation-wide state of emergency and suspended the Constitution, the National Assembly, the Senate, the four provincial legislatures and all political officials, with the exception of the President and judiciary. He also ensured, by means of a Provisional Constitution Order, that his actions could not be challenged by any court of law, thus imposing virtual martial law. On 18 October the Commonwealth Ministerial Action Group (CMAG) condemned the coup and demanded a time-frame for the restoration of democracy; Pakistan was suspended from participation in meetings of the Commonwealth with immediate effect. Meanwhile, on 22 October Gen. Musharraf appointed four new provincial governors, and on 26 October he installed a three-member Cabinet (which was later expanded) and named the members of a National Security Council (NSC), which was expected to be the supreme executive body of the country.

Following his seizure of power, Gen. Musharraf attempted to win over international opinion by portraying himself as a moderate, liberal leader. He was aided, in this respect, by the fact that the majority of the Pakistani people appeared to support the army's coup (it was a widely-held opinion that the military had no provincial bias and represented all levels of society—rather than purely the landed élite). Although expressing regret at Pakistan's effective suspension from the Commonwealth, the military regime was more concerned with the reaction of the USA and international financial organizations to the coup. The US Government's initial relations with the new administration in Pakistan appeared cautious but conciliatory. Gen. Musharraf promised an eventual return to civilian rule and announced wide-ranging measures to tackle corruption, loan defaulters, tax evasion, regional instability and religious extremism. The new regime's major priority was the revival of the almost bankrupt economy.

In November 1999 Nawaz Sharif and six other senior officials (including Mohammad Shahbaz Sharif, the brother of the ousted Prime Minister and the former Chief Minister of Punjab) were arrested on charges of criminal conspiracy, hijacking (a charge that carries the maximum penalty of the death sentence), kidnapping and attempted murder in relation to the alleged refusal of landing rights to the commercial aircraft carrying Gen. Musharraf from Sri Lanka to Karachi on 12 October; the aircraft ran precariously low on fuel before troops loyal to the army chief seized control of the airport and permission to land was finally granted (although the aircraft was rerouted to Nawabshah). The military authorities also charged Nawaz Sharif and his brother in November with corruption and non-repayment of bank loans. Later that month a new law was enacted barring politicians from holding public office for 21 years if found guilty of corruption or of defaulting on loans. The bill also allowed for the establishment of special courts to conduct trials within 30 days and gave the newly formed National Accountability Bureau far-reaching powers of investigation.

In early April 2000 Nawaz Sharif was sentenced to life imprisonment on charges of terrorism and hijacking, despite the prosecution having demanded the maximum penalty of the death sentence; in addition to the life sentence, all of the former Prime Minister's property in Pakistan was to be confiscated by the State. The six other defendants were acquitted. In May Nawaz Sharif's trial on charges of corruption opened; two months later the deposed Prime Minister was convicted and sentenced to 14 years' imprisonment, and barred from holding public office for 21 years. In August the Chief Executive issued a decree disqualifying those convicted of criminal offences and of terrorist acts from holding public office. The decision was viewed by many as a ban on convicted political leaders, notably former Prime Ministers Benazir Bhutto and Nawaz Sharif. In October the Karachi High Court upheld Nawaz Sharif's conviction and sentence for hijacking, but sustained the deposed Prime Minister's appeal against a conviction for terrorism.

Meanwhile, in late January 2000 Gen. Musharraf was accused of undemocratic conduct and of attempting to erode the independence of the judiciary when he dismissed the country's Chief Justice, Saiduzzaman Siddiqui, together with five other judges of the Supreme Court, following their refusal to swear allegiance to the military regime under a new oath. In May Gen. Musharraf's regime was strengthened by a unanimous decision by the pro-military Supreme Court to validate the October 1999 coup as having been necessary to spare the country from chaos and bankruptcy. At the same time, the Court announced that the

Chief Executive should name a date not later than 90 days before the expiry of the three-year period from 12 October 1999 for the holding of elections to the National Assembly, the provincial assemblies and the Senate. Gen. Musharraf stated that he would comply with the Supreme Court ruling regarding the restoration of democracy.

In July 2000 Gen. Musharraf issued a decree to revive the Islamic provisions of the suspended Constitution and to incorporate them in the Provisional Constitution Order, thereby supporting a ban on the passing of any law that conflicts with Islamic principles. In mid-August the NSC was reconstituted and redefined as the supreme executive body, comprising the three chiefs of staff and the Ministers of Foreign Affairs, of Interior, of Finance and of Commerce.

In late 2000 former leaders Nawaz Sharif and Benazir Bhutto, with 16 other smaller political parties, agreed to form the Alliance for the Restoration of Democracy (ARD), in an effort to end military rule and accelerate a return to democracy. The new alliance superseded the PPP-led Grand Democratic Alliance. On 10 December Nawaz Sharif was unexpectedly released from prison and sent into exile in Saudi Arabia, with his wife and 17 other members of his family. The Government announced that the deposed Prime Minister had been granted a 'presidential pardon' and was allowed to leave the country to seek medical treatment. In return, Nawaz Sharif relinquished his personal and business assets worth approximately Rs 500m., promised not to return to Pakistan for 10 years, and agreed not to take part in Pakistani politics for 21 years. The deal, reportedly negotiated by a member of the Saudi Arabian royal family, weakened Nawaz Sharif's prospects as a serious opponent to the Chief Executive, and adversely affected the credibility of Gen. Musharraf's campaign against political corruption.

In early April 2001 the Supreme Court ordered that Benazir Bhutto's conviction for corruption be set aside and a retrial held. Later that month the court concluded that the verdict had been politically motivated. Meanwhile, Bhutto and her husband faced further charges of corruption. In May a warrant was issued for Bhutto's arrest on her return to Pakistan. However, owing to her continued exile in Dubai (United Arab Emirates), in June she was sentenced, *in absentia,* to three years' imprisonment for failing to appear in court to answer these latest corruption allegations; this criminal conviction effectively disqualified Bhutto from holding further public office in Pakistan.

In late December 2000 the first phase of local elections was held. According to the Government, the turn-out reached 43.5%. The opposition PPP, however, claimed that less than 20% of the electorate had participated, attributing the low turn-out to the ban on political parties. Of a total of 20,076 seats, 33% were reserved for female candidates, but few women were able or willing to participate. The next three phases of local elections took place in March, May and July 2001. Although the elections were conducted on a non-party basis, it was believed that the majority of candidates were sponsored by either the PML (N) or the PPP. Elections to the 40-member legislative assembly for Azad Kashmir also took place in early July. Meanwhile, Musharraf insisted that a ban on party political activity in public would be maintained until after the forthcoming parliamentary elections, and opposition attempts at organizing pro-democracy rallies in March and May were suppressed by the authorities, who detained thousands of ARD supporters prior to the planned demonstrations.

On 20 June 2001 Gen. Musharraf unexpectedly assumed the presidency, having dismissed Mohammad Rafiq Tarar (who had reportedly refused to resign from the post). Musharraf immediately issued a formal dissolution of both houses of the Federal Legislature (which had been suspended since October 1999) in preparation for the elections. In an Independence Day address to the nation in August, Musharraf confirmed that elections to the four provincial legislatures and to the bicameral federal parliament would be conducted between 1 and 11 October 2002, thereby providing for the full restoration of democratic institutions by 12 October (the deadline established by the Supreme Court). Musharraf also announced that certain 'checks and balances' would be contained in constitutional amendments to be promulgated before June 2002; these were expected to include enhanced presidential powers and an advisory executive role for the military.

In response to a continuing escalation in sectarian and ethnically motivated violence, in June 2001 the Government approved new legislation to tackle terrorist activity. Earlier in the month Musharraf had complained that Pakistan's growing reputation as a centre for militant religious intolerance and fundamentalism was having a detrimental effect on the country's international standing and on its economic prospects. In his Independence Day address to the nation in August, Musharraf appealed for greater tolerance and understanding and announced an immediate ban on the activities of two militant Islamist groups: the Sunni Lashkar-e-Jhangvi and the Shi'a Sipah-e-Mohammad.

As one of only three states to have recognized the legitimacy of the Taliban administration in Afghanistan, and as the most significant trading partner and political associate of the regime, Pakistan's support was crucial to the efforts of the US-led antiterrorism coalition in the aftermath of the 11 September 2001 terrorist attacks on the US mainland, and Musharraf was left in little doubt that his refusal to co-operate with the campaign to apprehend those members of the al-Qa'ida (Base) organization held responsible for the attacks would result in Pakistan's increased economic and political isolation. Therefore, Musharraf's political opponents in the PML and PPP appeared to accept his declaration of co-operation with US requests for shared intelligence and use of air space with resignation. (In early November, however, the PML announced that it was transferring its support to those groups opposed to co-operation with the US-led coalition—a move that prompted accusations from other moderate opponents that the party leadership was attempting to make political gains from the crisis.) However, large-scale popular opposition to the decision was inevitable, particularly in the NWFP bordering Afghanistan, which was home to large numbers of Pakhtoon (Pashtun) Pakistanis who were fiercely opposed to any assault on the Pashtun-dominated Taliban. Despite Musharraf's insistence that the US-led activities in the region did not represent an attack on Islam, protests against the action spread throughout the country, and on 21 September a grouping of more than 30 Pakistani militant Islamist organizations known as the Afghan Defence Council (ADC) organized an opposition campaign of demonstrations and industrial action nation-wide. There was further opposition to Pakistan's support for the intervention in Afghanistan from within the armed forces and the Inter-Services Intelligence (ISI) agency, both having enjoyed particularly close links with the Taliban. In early October, having extended indefinitely his term of office as Chief of Army Staff, Musharraf implemented a radical reorganization of the military high command and the intelligence service, replacing a number of senior personnel with known sympathies for the country's militant Islamist cause, including Lt-Gen. Mahmood Ahmed, head of the ISI. However, popular protests against co-operation with the US-led coalition continued. None the less, Musharraf's resolve remained firm (strengthened, in part, by the promise of financial recognition of his political support from the USA and the European Union—EU), and despite the uncompromising response of the security forces to sporadic rioting, an attempt to capture the Jacobad air base in Sindh province (which was providing logistical support to US forces) by some 5,000 demonstrators and an opposition rally attended by around 20,000 protesters in Karachi, there were surprisingly few casualties. In early November the leaders of the JUI and the JIP were detained following allegations that they were continuing to promote anti-Government activities and demonstrations. Earlier in the month a Qatar-based Arab satellite television channel, Al-Jazeera, had broadcast details of a new communication from Osama bin Laden, the Saudi-born leader of the al-Qa'ida organization, in which he issued a renewed call to *jihad* against non-Muslims and urged Pakistanis to rise up and overthrow Musharraf's administration for its part in the US-led campaign. Bin Laden's exhortations were particularly resonant in the border regions of the NWFP and Balochistan, where reports were emerging of large numbers of armed local tribesmen crossing the border as willing recruits for the Taliban. By mid-November there were believed to be significant numbers of Pakistanis fighting in Afghanistan (and reports that supply lines were being maintained into north-western Pakistan), rekindling long-standing animosity with the forces of the United National Islamic Front for the Salvation of Afghanistan (commonly known as the United Front or Northern Alliance), whose impressive territorial gains in Afghanistan (with the support of the US-led coalition) in early November alarmed Musharraf sufficiently for him to request a suspension of all bombing in Afghanistan during the Muslim holy month of Ramadan and to seek assurances that the United Front would not be allowed to occupy Kabul (the Afghan capital) unilaterally, during an official visit to Europe and the USA in the second week of November. However, Musharraf's concerns were overtaken by events, and by mid-November the United Front had taken Kabul, leaving Musharraf to concentrate his efforts in attempting to convince the international community of the need for plural (including Pashtun, perhaps even moderate Taliban) representation in any interim administration in Afghanistan. As the rout of Taliban forces in Afghanistan continued in December and the USA intensified its bombardment of suspected al-Qa'ida positions in the Tora Bora region of southern Afghanistan, Pakistan reinforced security personnel along its northwestern border (believed to number some 125,000 by the end of 2001) in order to intercept fleeing combatants. Many ethnic Pashtuns (both Pakistani and Afghan) were believed to have evaded capture on the border and escaped into north-western Pakistan. Violent exchanges between Pakistani security forces and intercepted (mostly Arab) al-Qa'ida fighters in the border regions resulted in a number of casualties on both sides.

Meanwhile, relations with India had become openly hostile as a result of the deteriorating security situation in Kashmir and the increasingly violent activities of Pakistan's militant Islamist groups in India (see below). Following intense international pressure (particularly from the USA) to address the continuing security risk presented by these groups, in December 2001 the security forces began to detain some of their most prominent members, and financial assets were 'frozen' and offices closed down. Moreover, in January 2002 Musharraf announced an indefinite ban on the activities of five predominantly separatist groups (Tehrik-e-Nifaz-e-Shariat-e-Mohammadi, Sipah-e-Sahaba Pakistan, Jaish-e-Mohammed, Tehrik-e-Jafria and Lashkar-e-Taiba) and plans to reform the country's system of *madrassa* religious schools, many of which were accused of promoting extremism and theocracy. Musharraf's counter-terrorism initiative and new moderate vision drew plaudits from the international community, but the murder of US journalist Daniel Pearl (see below) and several subsequent sectarian attacks, mainly on Shi'a Muslims, appeared to undermine the success of Musharraf's rhetoric. Nevertheless, in mid-June it was announced that the Government had approved an ordinance for the registration of *madrassas*, according to which only *madrassas* that were registered by the Madrassa Education Board within the next six months would be allowed to operate.

During early 2002 Musharraf reiterated his commitment to returning the country to democracy, beginning with the parliamentary elections scheduled for October. In early April the Government approved a plan to hold a national referendum seeking endorsement for Musharraf's term of office as President to be extended by five years and approval of the Government's political and economic programme. Opposition parties and the independent Human Rights Commission of Pakistan condemned the decision as unconstitutional and illegal and resolved to boycott the vote; however, on 27 April the Supreme Court ruled that the referendum was legitimate, allowing the poll to take place three days later. According to official figures, 98% of those participating supported the proposal. There were, however, widespread allegations of gross irregularities and fraud. The Government claimed that the turn-out was 70%, but opposition parties and independent monitors estimated that it was about 5%. In late June Musharraf dismissed the head of the political wing of the ISI and chief organizer of the presidential referendum, Maj.-Gen. Ehtesam Zamir, after being forced to admit that his referendum victory had been fraudulent. In an attempt to reduce the political influence wielded by feudal landowning families, on 24 June the President issued a Chief Executive's Order stipulating that all candidates for future elections to federal and provincial legislatures should hold a university degree. Several days later Musharraf publicly announced a set of radical proposals for constitutional reform. The reforms were strongly criticized by political parties, constitutional experts and human rights groups for attempting to remodel Pakistan's prime-ministerial system into a presidential one and to undermine the authority of any elected government. Among the changes, Musharraf proposed to reduce the parliamentary term from five years to four; to lower the voting age from 21 to 18; to restrict the number of terms premiers or provincial chief ministers could hold in office to two; and to disqualify those members of the legislature who had criminal convictions, had defaulted on loans or had absconded. The last two amendments were widely considered to be aimed at preventing former Prime Ministers Benazir Bhutto and Nawaz Sharif from returning to office. Furthermore, in early July Musharraf issued a decree barring former premiers and chief ministers from seeking a third term in office. Several days later Musharraf announced that elections to the federal and provincial legislatures would be held on 10 October.

Instead of presenting the constitutional amendments before the next legislature, on 21 August 2002 President Musharraf unilaterally enacted the Legal Framework Order, which introduced 29 amendments to the Constitution and validated all the military decrees approved since the coup in 1999. The amendments would take effect from 12 October. As a result, the President's powers were enlarged and the military was ensured influence in decision-making beyond the parliamentary elections in October. The above proposals were endorsed. One of the most significant amendments, the establishment of a National Security Council (NSC), which would include Musharraf in his capacity as President and Chief of Army Staff, as well as the three other armed forces chiefs, the Prime Minister, the provincial chief ministers, the leader of the parliamentary opposition and Speakers of both houses of the Federal Legislature, was also authorized. The NSC would provide consultation to the elected government on strategic issues. The President was also restored the right to dissolve the National Assembly, and to dismiss the Prime Minister and Cabinet; furthermore, he was given the authority to override parliamentary majorities and provincial assemblies in order to appoint a Prime Minister and provincial governors himself if necessary. The amendments allowed the President to appoint Supreme Court judges and to extend his term in office. The changes were heavily criticized by the PML (N) and PPP. Musharraf, however, insisted that a formal role for the military in governing the country was necessary to ensure a stable transition to democracy and to forestall a potential military coup. According to the Legal Framework Order, the size of the National Assembly would be increased to 342 members, with 60 seats reserved for women and 10 seats reserved for non-Muslims. The Senate would consist of 100 members. The PML (N) and PPPP (see below) were permitted to take part in the elections.

Meanwhile, in late July 2002 Benazir Bhutto was re-elected as leader of the PPP. However, the decree barring parties from contesting an election if any of its office-holders have a criminal conviction prompted the PPP in early August to create the Pakistan People's Party Parliamentarians (PPPP) under new leadership to contest the forthcoming general elections. At the same time Shahbaz Sharif was elected leader of the pro-Nawaz PML. Bhutto's plans to return to the political arena were thwarted in late August when election officials in Sindh province rejected her candidacy in the National Assembly elections, owing to her criminal conviction. In response, Nawaz Sharif withdrew his nomination papers (although they had been accepted by the Election Commission), reportedly in solidarity with Bhutto. In mid-September Shahbaz Sharif was disqualified from entering the general election, for defaulting on a bank loan. Meanwhile, a pro-Musharraf faction of the PML, the Quaid-e-Azam group, was reportedly receiving covert support from the Government.

On 9 October 2002 Musharraf declared that he was resigning the title of Chief Executive. The following day elections for the National Assembly and provincial assemblies took place. In elections to the National Assembly the PML (Quaid-e-Azam—Q) won 77 of the 272 directly-elective seats (25.7% of the vote). The PPPP won 25.8% of the vote, but only 63 seats. A surprising outcome was the success of the Muttahida Majlis-e-Amal (MMA), an alliance of six Islamist parties, in securing 45 seats (11.3% of the vote). The PML (N) won only 14 seats (9.4% of the vote). According to the Election Commission, the turn-out at the election was 41.8%; voting to five seats was deferred to a later date. The PML (Q)'s strong performance was to be expected, since Musharraf had publicly voiced his support for the party during the election campaign. Opposition parties, independent analysts and the Human Rights Commission of Pakistan claimed that the army had provided financial and other support to the PML (Q), while hampering other parties' campaign efforts. Meanwhile, Benazir Bhutto claimed that the election had been rigged. EU election monitors reported that the poll was 'seriously flawed'. The emergence of the MMA as a third political force suggested that a significant proportion of the population objected to Musharraf's support for the US-led military action against the Taliban and al-Qa'ida in Afghanistan, and the ongoing campaign against al-Qa'ida in Pakistan. PPPP and PML (N) leaders considered the religious alliance's success to be a result of the military Government's attempts to prevent their parties from achieving power. However, many observers held the opinion that the army and ISI sponsored the MMA in an attempt to convince the West that continued military rule was necessary to contain the religious parties; to gain further concessions from the USA; and to ensure support from the new government for hostile policies towards India, particularly over the Kashmir issue. On 31 October the 60 seats reserved for women and 10 for non-Muslims were allocated by the Election Commission. The three leading parties entered intensive and protracted negotiations on forming a governing coalition: the PML (Q) and PPPP each attempted to gain the support of the MMA. However, the parties failed to reach common ground; neither the PML (Q) or PPPP was able to persuade the MMA to withdraw its candidate for prime minister. By mid-November the parties had failed to reach a compromise; nevertheless, the National Assembly convened and elected a Speaker and Deputy Speaker. Shortly beforehand, the President revived the 1973 Constitution, which had been in abeyance since he assumed power in 1999—it was believed that the Constitution incorporated the controversial Legal Framework Order—and took an oath to begin his new five-year term as President. On 21 November the PML (Q) candidate Zafarullah Khan Jamali was elected Prime Minister by the National Assembly. Jamali's victory ensured a PML (Q)-led, pro-army Government with a slim majority, which was sworn in two days later. Meanwhile, Musharraf agreed to transfer power to the elected Government, but emphasized that he would continue to carry out his 'important role'.

The MMA won a majority in the provincial elections in the NWFP in October 2002 and formed a provincial government in late November, with Muhammad Akram Durrani elected Chief Minister. The MMA and PML (Q) announced a coalition government in the province of Balochistan in late November, led by a PML (Q) Chief Minister. The PML (Q) assumed power in Punjab at the same time. The PPPP emerged as the single largest party in the Sindh assembly but failed to form a coalition government despite support from the MMA. Eventually, in mid-December the PML (Q), MMA and several smaller parties agreed to a power-sharing arrangement with Ali Mohammad Maher, a PML (Q) representative, as Chief Minister. The delay in forming new federal and provincial governments meant that the Senate elections were finally held on 25–27 February 2003. Some 88 of the 100 seats in the Senate were elected by the four provincial assemblies. The remaining 12 seats were chosen by the National Assembly from a list of candidates provided by the Federally Administered Tribal Areas and the federal capital. The PML (Q) secured 34 seats, making it the largest single party in the Senate. The Senate convened on 12 March. The PML (Q) candidate Mian Mohammad Soomro was elected unopposed as Chairman of the Senate after the eight opposition parties boycotted the vote in protest at the President's Legal Framework Order and the alleged military interference in the Senate elections.

At the end of April 2003 the National Assembly suspended its session, following a month of disruption caused by opposition parties. The MMA, PPPP and other opposition parties had refused to allow Musharraf to address the legislature (a constitutional requirement before it could begin to legislate) and repeatedly demanded that the President submit the Legal Framework Order to approval by the National Assembly; however, the President, mindful of the fact that the amendments would not secure the two-thirds' majority required for constitutional change, refused to accede to this demand. A joint committee formed by the Government and opposition to discuss the Order failed to reach an agreement and the consultations collapsed. In late May it was reported that the five political parties of the coalition Government had suggested a compromise plan in an attempt to resolve the impasse in the National Assembly. Significantly, however, the Government's plan did not include Musharraf's resignation as Chief of Army Staff and the compromise was not accepted. In June the opposition presented a motion of 'no confidence' in the Speaker of the National Assembly, Chaudhry Amin Hussain, following his ruling that Musharraf's constitutional amendments were valid and that the legislature should function according to them. The opposition argued that Hussain had contravened the 1973 Constitution (which it regarded as the only legitimate Constitution) by ruling in favour of the Legal Framework Order, and, as a result, the Speaker no longer had the right to the confidence of the Assembly. However, when the Deputy Speaker ruled that the vote would be by secret ballot, the opposition refused to vote and the motion collapsed. In July the opposition withdrew a motion of 'no confidence' in the Deputy Speaker after Jamali offered to resume negotiations with the opposition regarding the constitutional amendments. The opposition's campaign of boycott and agitation of parliamentary proceedings continued, however. Tensions between the MMA and Musharraf increased after an election tribunal barred an MMA legislator from office on educational grounds. Members of the Islamist coalition without a degree were eventually allowed by Musharraf to stand as candidates. The tribunal, however, ruled against the exemption, prompting protests by the MMA. The National Assembly reconvened on 20 August 2003, after being forced to suspend its session for more than two months.

Meanwhile, in early June 2003 the legislative assembly in the NWFP unanimously voted in favour of legislation to implement Shari'a throughout the province (the NWFP Government had already issued a directive requiring civil servants to pray twice a day and introduced legislation forbidding male doctors to examine women). In response to the bill, which gave Islamic law precedence over secular provincial law, Musharraf dismissed two senior NWFP officials—the chief secretary and police chief—for failing to secure law and order in the provincial capital of Peshawar against attacks by militant Islamists. During a visit to the NWFP later that month Musharraf warned against the adoption of Taliban-style Islam, promoting instead the practice of 'tolerant, progressive and civilized' Islam. In July, however, a journalist was sentenced to life imprisonment for blasphemy in Peshawar.

In September 2003 the Cabinet unanimously endorsed a modified version of the Legal Framework Order. Although the PML (N) and PPPP appeared to be ready to compromise on their opposition to the measures, the MMA remained dissatisfied and negotiations between the Government and opposition continued. Finally, in December Musharraf announced seven concessions to the Legal Framework Order, including his commitment to resign as Chief of Army Staff by December 2004. On 29 December 2003 the National Assembly passed the Constitution (Seventeenth Amendment) Bill, which comprised the seven modifications. The opposition ARD (an alliance including the PML (N) and PPPP) had boycotted the parliamentary proceedings, dismissing the concessions as 'cosmetic'; none the less, the amendments received the necessary two-thirds' majority in the National Assembly vote. According to the Bill, which became law on 31 December following the Senate's approval, the existing NSC, which had been inactive since its creation one year previously, disbanded. A new National Security Council (NSC) was to be established by an act of parliament, rather than be incorporated into the Constitution by the Legal Framework Order. Furthermore, while the President would have the right to dismiss the National Assembly, he would have to refer the matter to the Supreme Court within 15 days. Despite the concessions, Musharraf retained most of the special powers that he had awarded himself in 2002. In early January 2004 the federal and provincial legislatures passed votes of confidence in Musharraf, allowing him to complete his five-year term as President (due to expire in 2007). In April the National Assembly passed an item of legislation on the establishment of the NSC amid strong protest by opposition members. The council was to comprise the President, the Prime Minister, the Chairman of the Senate, the Speaker of the National Assembly, the leader of the parliamentary opposition, the provincial chief ministers and the three other chiefs of armed forces. The new Chief of Army Staff (to be appointed in late 2004 after Musharraf's resignation from the position) would also be a member. The NSC law, approved by the Senate several days later, gave the armed forces a formal, albeit supervisory, role in civilian politics for the first time in Pakistan's history.

In the mean time, in late September 2003 the leader of the ARD, Nawabzada Nasrullah Khan, died; he was replaced by Makhdoom Javed Hashmi, the acting President of the PML (N), in early October. In late October, however, Hashmi was arrested on charges of inciting mutiny after circulating a letter at a press conference criticizing the military's involvement in politics that he claimed was written by junior army officers. The authorities claimed the letter, which was also critical of President Musharraf and his alliance with the USA, was a forgery. Hashmi was convicted of inciting mutiny in the army, forgery and defamation in mid-April 2004 and sentenced to 23 years' imprisonment (he received seven different prison sentences—with a maximum of seven years on one count—which were to run concurrently, and was therefore expected to serve a term of no more than seven years). The PML (N) condemned the verdict, claiming that it proved that the judiciary was under the control of Musharraf. Meanwhile, in December 2003 the President of the MMA and leader of Jamiat-e-Ulema-e-Pakistan, Maulana Shah Ahmed

Noorani Siddiqui, died. Amir Qazi Hussain Ahmad was appointed President of the MMA in an acting capacity. In the same month, in a landmark judgment, the Supreme Court ruled that all adult Muslim women were able to marry anyone of their own free will, with or without the consent of their father or guardian (*Wali*). The ruling supported a similar judgment declared by the Federal Shari'a Court in 1981 and overturned 1997 rulings by the Lahore High Court that a marriage without the consent of the *Wali* was invalid.

In mid-August 2003 Asif Ali Zardari was acquitted of all charges relating to the 1998 murder of Sajjad Hussain, the former Chairman of Pakistan Steel Mills. Earlier that month, however, Zardari and Benazir Bhutto were convicted by a Swiss investigative judge in Geneva of money-laundering and receiving bribes from two Swiss companies in 1995. Bhutto and her husband each received a suspended six-month prison sentence and a fine of US $50,000. They were also ordered to repay the Pakistani Government $11.9m. (The Lahore High Court had convicted Bhutto and Zardari in the same case in 1999 but the Supreme Court overturned the verdict two years later, concluding that it had been politically motivated, and ordered a retrial by a state accountability court.) In early November 2003, however, a court in Geneva quashed the prison sentences and fines following an appeal by Benazir Bhutto and her husband. At the same time, opposition parties in Pakistan held widespread protests on the seventh anniversary of Zardari's arrest to demand his release from prison. Zardari, now largely considered a political prisoner, was implicated in 14 pending criminal cases, but had been convicted on only one corruption charge (in September 2002). Meanwhile, Bhutto faced further corruption cases in Pakistan, Switzerland, the United Kingdom and the USA. In June 2004 Bhutto was indicted by a Geneva court on a new, more serious charge of 'money-laundering by profession', relating to alleged commissions and bribes that she had received from Swiss companies in the 1990s. In September the Lahore High Court overturned Zardari's corruption conviction following an appeal. However, Zardari remained in custody owing to another pending case against him. In November the Supreme Court ordered that Zardari be released on bail, following eight years of imprisonment. His freedom initially appeared to be short-lived, as in the following month he was rearrested upon arrival in Islamabad; a judge in Karachi had cancelled bail as Zardari had allegedly failed to attend a hearing into a 1996 murder case in which he was accused of involvement. However, later in that month the decision was overturned and Zardari's bail was restored. In June 2005 Zardari suffered a major heart attack and was admitted to a hospital in Dubai. In September an arrest warrant was issued for him, after he failed to attend a court hearing in Rawalpindi related to ongoing corruption allegations against him. In the same month Bhutto testified at a Geneva court in relation to the money-laundering charges against her and her husband. In November the former Prime Minister was acquitted by a court in Karachi of corruption charges against her. Later in that month Bhutto claimed that President Musharraf had offered to abandon all remaining charges against her, on the condition that she declined to take place in elections scheduled for 2007; she claimed that she was unable to accept the condition.

Attacks by suspected militant Islamists on Western targets, meanwhile, continued to take place in 2003. Although Musharraf decided not to support the USA in its attempt to gain UN endorsement of the planned military campaign to remove the regime of Saddam Hussain in Iraq in March, the President was condemned by some sectors of the Pakistani community for not opposing the war in stronger terms. In November Musharraf proscribed six militant Islamist groups under the 1997 Anti-Terrorist Act. Three of the organizations—Islami Tehrik-e-Pakistan (formerly Tehrik-e-Jafria-e-Pakistan), Millat-e-Islamia Pakistan (formerly Sipah-e-Sahaba) and Khudam ul-Islam (formerly Jaish-e-Mohammed)—had disregarded an earlier ban by changing their names, thus bringing into question the President's commitment to curb militant activity. The activities of Jamiat ul-Furqan, Jamiat ul-Ansar (formerly Harakat ul-Mujahideen) and Hizb-ut-Tahrir were also proscribed. Jamaat-ud-Dawa (considered by some to be the new identity for the banned Lashkar-e-Taiba movement) was placed under surveillance. Some commentators doubted the effectiveness of Musharraf's approach to militant Islamism, claiming that the groups would continue to receive covert support from the army and judiciary. Indeed, in December the President narrowly escaped two assassination attempts by suspected Islamist militants near his residence in Rawalpindi. No one was hurt in the first suicide bomb attack, but the second killed at least 17 people and injured about 50 others. One of the suicide bombers was identified as a member of the banned Khudam ul-Islam. Islamist militants had reportedly become very angry at the Government's agreement to enter negotiations with India (see below), and at Musharraf's decision to allow the UN International Atomic Energy Agency (IAEA, see p. 98) to investigate the sale of Pakistani nuclear technology to Iran, the Democratic People's Republic of Korea (North Korea) and Libya (see below). It was suggested that al-Qa'ida, which in September had issued a death threat to Musharraf, blaming him for the arrest of hundreds of its members, was responsible for organizing the attacks. There was also speculation that the extremists had infiltrated Musharraf's security apparatus in order to gain secret information on his travel plans. In a speech to a convention of Muslim scholars and clerics in mid-February 2004, Musharraf warned religious and political organizations against promoting extremism. At the same time, he asked his audience to play an active role in fostering unity and sectarian harmony and combating Islamist militancy.

From mid-2003 the frequency and scale of sectarian attacks increased. In June gunmen shot dead 11 Shi'a Muslims and wounded nine others in Quetta; 18 members of Sipah-e-Sahaba were arrested on suspicion of involvement in the attacks. In the following month a suicide bomb attack took place in a Shi'a mosque also in Quetta, killing at least 50 Shi'a worshippers and injuring more than 60; the Sunni militant organization Lashkar-e-Jhangvi claimed responsibility for the attack. In early October seven Shi'a Muslims were killed in a gun attack in Karachi by Sunni militants. The Government held a group called 313, a newly formed alliance of Lashkar-e-Jhangvi, Harakat ul-Mujahideen and Harakat ul-Jihad al-Islami, responsible for the attack, claiming that their motives were sectarian and anti-Government. On 6 October the legislator and leader of Sipah-e-Sahaba, Maulana Azam Tariq, was assassinated in Islamabad; a previously unknown Shi'a group, Fedayim Imam Mahdi, claimed responsibility for the attack. The shooting provoked riots in Islamabad and the city of Jhang: Sunni militants, vowing revenge, burnt down a Shi'a shrine and cinema in the capital and a Shi'a mosque in Tariq's home city, Jhang. The leader of the Shi'a extremist Islami Tehrik-e-Pakistan, Allama Sajid Ali Naqvi, was arrested in mid-November, in connection with Tariq's murder. Sectarian strife continued to afflict Quetta: in March 2004 more than 40 Shi'a Muslims were killed and over 150 injured after Sunni extremists attacked a Shi'a procession during a religious ceremony to commemorate the holy day of Ashoura.

In December 2003 the Minister of Information and Media Development, Sheikh Rashid Ahmad, admitted that the authorities were investigating allegations that Pakistan had transferred nuclear technology to other countries, and that Dr Abdul Qadeer Khan, the founder of Pakistan's nuclear weapons programme, and two other nuclear scientists were being questioned. The Government was under tremendous pressure from the USA and IAEA, which had recently concluded that Iran had been supplied with designs for nuclear equipment that originated from Pakistan, to investigate the accusations. The authorities, however, were quick to deny any official involvement, suggesting that 'rogue' individuals motivated by personal greed were to blame. Khan was reportedly placed under house arrest and in late January 2004 was removed from his post as scientific adviser to the Prime Minister. On 4 February, in a dramatic development, Khan confessed on television that during the past 15 years he had provided Iran, North Korea and Libya with designs and technology to develop nuclear weapons (he had already signed a detailed confession). He apologized, asked for forgiveness, and took full responsibility for his actions; he also denied any government involvement and absolved the military and his fellow scientists. Dr Khan's plea for clemency was granted two days later by Musharraf. The President announced that he and the Cabinet had taken into account the nuclear scientist's services to the country before coming to their decision and that Khan would remain under strict surveillance. Musharraf also refused to allow independent investigators to continue their inspection, encouraging speculation that the authorities were trying to protect the Pakistani military. It was widely acknowledged that prosecuting Dr Khan would have led to unrest throughout the country (he had been long revered as the 'father' of Pakistan's nuclear bomb and had the status of a national hero) and political problems (there were fears that if put on trial the scientist would provide evidence that incriminated Pakistani leaders and generals). Musharraf countered allegations that he might have been involved in the sale of weapons, claiming that he tried to curb the proliferation after becoming suspicious three years ago by forcing Khan's retirement from his post as head of the Khan Research Laboratories, and that he delayed holding an investigation into the matter owing to the scientist's popularity and privileged position. He also stated that he was only able to take action once the USA had provided him with enough information in October 2003. Musharraf attempted to evade allegations that Khan was ideologically motivated by attributing the scientist's activities to personal gain. Military analysts, however, continued to doubt that Khan was solely responsible, declaring that it was unlikely that the transfer of nuclear materials could have been conducted without the knowledge and involvement of at least parts of the military. Meanwhile, two former chiefs of army staff, retired Gen. Mirza Aslam Beg and retired Gen. Jehangir Karamat, were questioned and exonerated of any wrongdoing. Musharraf stated that Pakistan would continue to co-operate with the IAEA but would not allow IAEA inspectors to monitor its nuclear programmes. In November 2004 the Supreme Court rejected a petition that Khan be released from house arrest on the grounds of ill health. In February 2005 the Government denied a report in the US magazine Time that Khan had also sold nuclear technology to Saudi Arabia and Egypt.

In the first half of 2004 violence between Sunni and Shi'a Muslims in Karachi escalated. In early May the Shi'a Hyderi mosque was attacked by a suicide bomber, resulting in the deaths of 16 people. Later in that month a senior Sunni cleric and known Taliban supporter, Mufti Nizamuddin Shamzai, was assassinated. In an apparent revenge attack, another Shi'a mosque in the centre of the city was bombed, killing 16 people and prompting an outbreak of rioting in the city. In June the Chief Minister of Sindh, Sardar Ali Mohammed Maher, was forced to resign as a result of Karachi's deteriorating law and order situation; he was replaced by Dr Arbab Ghulam Rahim. In the same month at least 10 people were killed following an attack on the motorcade of the commander of the Karachi army corps, Lt-Gen. Ahsan Saleem Hayat. Shortly afterwards it was announced that 10 suspected members of al-Qa'ida had been apprehended in the city; they allegedly confessed to having participated in Lt-Gen. Hayat's attempted assassination. The men were charged with terrorist offences in September. Meanwhile, in August several more explosions occurred in Karachi.

In the mean time, in June 2004 Prime Minister Jamali tendered his resignation, having been placed under considerable pressure to do so by President Musharraf. Musharraf was reportedly frustrated at the weakness of Jamali's Government and, in particular, its apparent inability to curb sectarian violence in Pakistan. It was also thought that Jamali's suggestion that Musharraf should honour his pledge to step down as army chief at the end of 2004 had been a significant factor. Later in the same month Musharraf's nominee, Chaudhry Shujaat Hussain, President of the newly formed PML (which had been created following the merger of several factions of the PML and the Sindh Democratic Alliance in the previous month), was elected to serve as interim Prime Minister. It was reported that Minister of Finance Shaukat Aziz was Musharraf's choice to serve in the post permanently, but, as Aziz was a Senator, he would first need to be elected to the House of Representatives. In July Hussain announced five new appointments to his Cabinet, including that of Babar Khan Gauri as Minister of Communications. In the same month Shaukat Aziz survived an assassination attempt by an alleged suicide bomber in the town of Attock in Punjab, one of the two constituencies that he was contesting in forthcoming by-elections (the other being that of Tharparkar in Sindh). In late August, following victories in both constituencies, Aziz was elected as Prime Minister and leader of the house by the National Assembly and, on the following day, was formally sworn in to his new office. In the following month a new Cabinet was appointed, which included the 20 members of Chaudhry Shujaat Hussain's interim Government and incorporated an additional 13 members. Aziz retained the finance portfolio, while Aftab Ahmad Khan Sherpao became Minister of the Interior. Rao Sikander Iqbal continued as Minister of Defence.

In October 2004 the National Assembly approved legislation enabling Musharraf to retain his dual role as President and Chief of Army Staff, contrary to his December 2003 pledge that he would resign from his military position by the end of 2004. The opposition protested that the bill was unconstitutional and condemned it strongly, although the Speaker curtailed debate on the issue. The Government claimed that the ongoing terrorist threat necessitated Musharraf's retention of both roles, a claim supported by the state assemblies of Punjab and Sindh, both of which passed motions requesting that Musharraf stay on as army chief. In November, having been approved by the Senate, the bill was signed into law by its Chairman, Mian Mohammad Soomro, who was acting President while Musharraf was out of the country. In December Musharraf formally confirmed that he intended to retain his military position until the end of his presidential term, in 2007. In March 2005 the MMA orchestrated protest marches in Karachi, Quetta, Peshawar and Lahore to protest against Musharraf's actions; its supporters also observed a series of nation-wide strikes, culminating in a general strike in early April. However, this received only limited support. Later that month the Supreme Court dismissed all petitions challenging Musharraf's dual role as unconstitutional. In May it was announced that Musharraf would definitely seek re-election as President following the expiry of his term of office in 2007; the opposition denounced his decision.

Meanwhile, in late 2004 and early 2005 outbreaks of sectarian violence intensified in frequency. In October in Multan two bombs exploded at a Sunni Muslim rally, held to commemorate the first anniversary of the assassination of Maulana Azam Tariq, killing at least 40 people. Minister of the Interior Sherpao announced subsequently that he would order provincial governments to ban all religious gatherings apart from prayers at mosques. There was speculation that the bombing was revenge for a suicide attack on a Shi'a mosque in Sialkot in Punjab earlier in that month, in which an estimated 30 people lost their lives. Meanwhile, in Karachi another prominent Sunni religious leader, Mufti Muhammad Jamil, was assassinated and, on the following day, a suicide bomber attacked a Shi'a mosque in Lahore. In December at least 11 people died when a bomb exploded next to an army vehicle at a market in Quetta; the separatist Balochistan National Army claimed responsibility for the attack, but denied that it had intended to kill civilians, declaring that members of the armed forces were its target. In March 2005 a bomb explosion at a Sufi Muslim shrine, sacred to both Sunni and Shi'a Muslims, in the town of Fatehpur resulted in the deaths of at least 50 pilgrims. Four suspects, believed to be members of the banned Sunni Sipah-e-Sahaba group, were subsequently arrested in connection with the attack. In May a suicide bombing at a Sufi shrine in Islamabad killed at least 20 people. Later in the same month an attack on a Shi'a mosque in Karachi resulted in five deaths.

In January 2005 claims that military personnel had raped and assaulted a female doctor employed by Pakistan Petroleum Ltd in Balochistan precipitated an outbreak of violence in the province, which had become increasingly lawless throughout late 2004. Bugti tribesmen clashed with security forces at the Sui gas processing plant, causing severe damage to the plant and to three gas pipelines and affecting gas supplies throughout the whole of the country (the Sui gas field accounted for some 45% of total gas production in Pakistan). In response to an appeal by the provincial government, the federal Government sent army and paramilitary troops to protect the gas field, resulting in a temporary cessation of the unrest in Sui. However, later in the month three bombs exploded in the provincial capital, Quetta. The violence in the province was seen to some extent to be indicative of local resentment at the federal Government's exploitation of its mineral wealth. It was feared that further clashes between the army and local rebels would encourage Balochi nationalist sentiment. In February a spate of bomb attacks took place in various different areas of Balochistan as the violence continued. Responsibility for several of the attacks was claimed by the Balochistan Liberation Army (BLA), an insurgent group operating in the province. In March more than 60 civilians died during clashes between security forces and tribesmen in the area as the conflict intensified. Following an attack on a military convoy, a stand-off ensued between the two sides, with tribal leader and President of the Jamhuri Watan Party, Nawab Akbar Bugti, refusing to compromise in the tribesmen's struggle to secure political autonomy and a greater share of revenue from Balochistan's gas reserves. Following talks between Bugti and a government delegation that included former Prime Minister Chaudhry Shujaat Hussain, an agreement was reached to defuse the crisis. The process of implementing the agreement, which included the withdrawal of troops by both sides, began in April. Meanwhile, later in March a bomb exploded at a Muslim shrine in the town of Usa Mohammad, killing 35 people. Sporadic unrest continued throughout 2005, intensifying again during a visit by President Musharraf to the province in December of that year. Shortly before Musharraf was scheduled to visit a paramilitary camp in the area, eight rockets were reportedly fired at the camp, an attack for which the BLA later claimed responsibility. The violence continued into 2006.

In June 2005 the trial of nine suspects began in Punjab, in connection with one of the attempted assassination attempts on President Musharraf in December 2003. In August five of the men, including one soldier, were sentenced to death, having been found guilty of involvement in the plot. Three other men were sentenced to lengthy prison terms. In October four junior members of the air force were convicted of involvement in another attempted assassination in the same month and sentenced to death, while a further two people were sentenced to life imprisonment.

In the mean time, the issue of religious extremism continued to resonate in Pakistani society. In July 2005, following the discovery that at least two of the four British Muslim suicide bombers who had attacked the transport network in London, United Kingdom, in that month had previously visited Pakistan and had allegedly received instruction at one of the country's many *madrassas*, President Musharraf announced the implementation of a more stringent policy to prevent the spread of Islamic extremism. Hundreds of suspected Islamist militants were arrested and several *madrassas* suspected of being involved in extremism were raided. Musharraf stressed that he did not believe that the British bombers had been radicalized in Pakistan, however. In August the National Assembly gave its assent to legislation requiring all *madrassas* to register with the Government and to submit annual reports. They were also barred from encouraging militancy and propagating religious hatred. Furthermore, all foreign students studying at *madrassas* in Pakistan were to be expelled. Meanwhile, President Musharraf filed a petition with the Supreme Court objecting to certain sections of legislation passed in the previous month by the provincial assembly of the NWFP. The new laws made provision for 'morality police' in the province, who would enforce prayer attendance, discourage singing and dancing and practise strict media censorship. The legislation had been proposed by the conservative religious alliance the MMA, which dominated the province's assembly. The Supreme Court subsequently ruled that sections of the law relating to the powers of an Islamic *Mohtasib* (moral guardian), which had been established by the bill, were unconstitutional. The increasing dominance of the MMA and its implementation of guidelines to govern social behaviour, in line with Islamic values, provided an indication of the increasing 'Talibanization' of some sections of Pakistani society.

During August to October 2005 local government elections took place, over several stages. Although political parties were theoretically prohibited from participating in the elections, the political allegiances of most candidates were widely known. The polls were marred by violence and intimidation in many areas; in particular, the exercise of the franchise by women and the candidature of some for office attracted controversy, with repolling ordered in several areas as a result of complaints that women had been prevented from voting. Overall, the results indicated a decline in support for religious parties, with more moderate parties reported to have won a majority of seats in local union councils in Punjab and Sindh. Meanwhile, in the NWFP and Balochistan support for the MMA had apparently decreased significantly. However, the results of the polls were called into question by widespread allegations of malpractice and corruption.

Meanwhile, in October 2005 a huge earthquake, the epicentre of which was in the town of Balakot, in the NWFP, devastated Azad Kashmir and much of the NWFP, resulting in the deaths of over 81,000 people and leaving millions more homeless. The response of the Government and armed forces to the tragedy attracted criticism for its tardiness and lack of co-ordination, although the logistical challenge of delivering relief to many of the remote areas affected was considerable. Furthermore, the aid committed by international donors in the aftermath of the disaster was reportedly criticized as inadequate by President Musharraf. At a meeting of donors held in November in Islamabad, a total of US $5,800m. was pledged by the international community for the relief and reconstruction effort, exceeding the Government's target. Most of the aid donated was intended for the long-term effort, however, and funds for immediate humanitarian relief remained slow to arrive, prompting fears that the arrival of winter in the affected region would cause a second 'wave' of deaths.

In February 2006 widespread protests occurred in towns and cities across Pakistan, as demonstrators gathered to condemn the publication of cartoons of the Prophet Mohammed in a Danish newspaper in September 2005. Although the demonstrations began peacefully and on a relatively small scale, they became increasingly violent in some areas, resulting in several deaths. The MMA exploited the protests to increase public opposition to President Musharraf, whose Government had condemned the cartoons but who was widely perceived to be allied with the West. The protests culminated in the withdrawal of the Danish ambassador from the country. Meanwhile, on 6 March elections took place for half the seats in the Senate.

In foreign relations Pakistan has traditionally pursued a policy of maintaining close links with Islamic states in the Middle East and Africa and with the People's Republic of China, while continuing to seek aid and assistance from the USA. Pakistan's controversial nuclear programme prompted the USA to terminate development aid in April 1979, but, as a result of the Soviet invasion of Afghanistan in December of that year, military and economic assistance was renewed in 1981. However, increased concern about Pakistan's ability to develop nuclear weapons and Pakistan's refusal to sign the Treaty on the Non-Proliferation of Nuclear Weapons led to the suspension of military and economic aid by the US Government again in 1990 (under the Pressler Amendment). In February 1992 the Pakistani Government admitted for the first time that Pakistan had nuclear-weapons capability, but added that it had 'frozen' its nuclear programme at the level of October 1989, when its capabilities were insufficient to produce a nuclear device. In September 1995 the US Senate voted in favour of the Brown Amendment, which allowed a limited resumption of defence supplies to Pakistan. The Brown Amendment (which was ratified by the US President, Bill Clinton, in January 1996) also deleted the Pressler Amendment requirements for economic sanctions, thus paving the way for the resumption of US economic aid to Pakistan. In August 1996 the first consignment of US military equipment released by the US Government after a six-year delay arrived in Pakistan. In December 1998 Prime Minister Nawaz Sharif held talks with President Clinton in the US capital in an attempt to gain support for Pakistan's ailing economy and to persuade the US leader further to ease sanctions imposed on Pakistan following nuclear tests carried out by the latter in May (see below). During 1998–99 the USA lifted some of the sanctions imposed on Pakistan and India, whilst reiterating requests that the two countries sign the Comprehensive Test Ban Treaty (CTBT) and exercise restraint in their respective missile development programmes to ensure peace in South Asia. During 2000 US foreign policy appeared to favour closer co-operation with India at the expense of improved relations with Pakistan. However, Pakistan's strategic importance to US efforts to dismantle the Taliban regime in Afghanistan and thus apprehend members of the al-Qa'ida terrorist organization held responsible for the devastating attacks on New York and Washington, DC, USA, in September 2001 resulted in attempts by the USA to promote Pakistan's political rehabilitation in the Western international community. Although in September the US Government withdrew sanctions imposed on Pakistan in May 1998, and Gen. Musharraf was warmly received on official visits to the USA in November 2001 and February 2002, a 1990 suspension order on the delivery to Pakistan of 28 US F-16 fighter aircraft was not lifted, to the evident disappointment of the Pakistani President.

Despite the international acclaim that greeted Musharraf's public declaration of his commitment to the eradication of militant religious extremism in January 2002, US concerns about the proliferation of armed fundamentalist groups in Pakistan's border regions, and the possibility of their assisting scattered al-Qa'ida units to regroup in these areas, persisted. A US journalist, Daniel Pearl, was abducted in Karachi in January by a previously unknown group called the National Movement for the Restoration of Pakistani Sovereignty, which made a number of demands for his safe return, including the release of all Pakistani nationals captured by US forces in Afghanistan and transported (together with other suspected al-Qa'ida members) to a detention centre at the US military base in Guantánamo Bay in Cuba. Despite the prompt arrest by the Pakistani authorities of a British-born militant Islamist, Ahmed Omar Saeed Sheikh, who was believed to have organized the kidnapping, it soon emerged that Pearl had been murdered by his abductors. Confounding speculation that suspects in the case would be extradited for trial in the USA, in March Saeed Sheikh and three alleged accomplices appeared in a specially instituted anti-terrorism court in Karachi on charges of kidnapping, murder and terrorism. The men were convicted of the charges in mid-July; Saeed Sheikh was sentenced to death and his co-defendants were each sentenced to life imprisonment. Following an anti-US grenade attack on the Protestant International Church in Islamabad in March, in which five people (including the wife and daughter of a US diplomat) were killed, Musharraf dismissed five senior police officers for what he considered a serious lapse in security. It was widely believed that intelligence proceeding from Pakistani investigations to discover the identities of the assailants was a crucial factor in the arrest of Abu Zubaydah, one of al-Qa'ida's most senior commanders, by officers of the US Federal Bureau of Investigation (FBI) in Faisalabad at the end of March. However, it was reported that several prominent Islamic clerics and at least 1,300 of their supporters detained in late 2001 were released in early April 2002. In early May a suicide bomber killed 14 people, mostly French engineers, in Karachi. (Three men were convicted on charges of conspiracy relating to the suicide bombing and sentenced to death in June 2003; two of the men were reportedly members of the banned Islamist Harakat ul-Jihad-al-Islami and Harakat ul-Mujahideen.) Another attack occurred in mid-June 2002 outside the US consulate in Karachi, killing 12 people. One month later two Pakistani members of the al-Alami faction of Harakat ul-Mujahideen claimed responsibility for the attack on the US consulate as well as other attacks on Western targets. (In April 2003 four men were convicted of organizing the attack on the consulate; two were sentenced to death. The two were also convicted in October of attempting to assassinate Musharraf in April 2002, along with one other member of Harakat ul-Jihad-al-Islami, and sentenced to 10 years' imprisonment.) In September 2002 Pakistani security forces arrested 12 alleged members of al-Qa'ida in Karachi, including the Yemeni-born Ramzi Binalshibh, a principal suspect in the attacks on the USA on 11 September 2001. The USA took custody of Binalshibh and four other al-Qa'ida suspects. In December Pakistani authorities arrested Dr Ahmed Javed Khawaja, a US citizen, and his brother, for allegedly sheltering and medically treating al-Qa'ida members and their families. The two suspects were charged a month later, prompting criticisms from human rights activists.

In an apparent breakthrough in the campaign against religious extremism, the alleged operations chief of the al-Qa'ida network, Khalid Sheikh Mohammed, suspected of planning the attacks on the USA in September 2001, was arrested in Rawalpindi in March 2003. It was hoped that the suspect, who was promptly taken into US custody, would provide information on the identity and whereabouts of al-Qa'ida cells in Pakistan and elsewhere in the world. Two other suspected Islamist militants were also arrested. The ISI's involvement in the arrest of the alleged militants suggested that the intelligence agency was genuinely attempting to curb militant activity. Furthermore, in early March the ISI declared that since 11 September 2001 Pakistan had arrested 442 suspected foreign militants, of which 346 had been turned over to US custody. However, the discovery of Mohammed in a house owned by an army officer's brother raised questions about links between al-Qa'ida and the Pakistani military. Furthermore, the proprietor's prominent role in the Jamaat-e-Islami generated speculation about the political party's connections with al-Qa'ida. The arrests temporarily eased US pressures to support a UN Security Council resolution authorizing the removal of the regime of Saddam Hussain in Iraq. Later that month Pakistan, influenced by widespread large-scale protest marches against military action in Iraq, decided not to support the USA. In the same month the USA removed all remaining sanctions imposed on Pakistan after the 1999 military coup. In late April 2003 security forces arrested 10 allegedly senior members of the terrorist network and seized a large quantity of weapons in Peshawar. In early April the USA agreed to waive a total of US $1,000m. in debt, in recognition of Pakistan's efforts in the 'war on terror'. During Musharraf's visit to the USA in June, the Pakistani President hoped to secure further pledges of co-operation, economic aid and possibly military sales in return for his support. Indeed, the US President, George W. Bush, offered an aid package of $3,000m. in financial and military assistance over the next five years. The Bush Administration, however, declined to cancel a further $1,800m. debt, owing to reservations over whether enough was being done to curb militant activity and to prevent the infiltration of separatist militants into Indian-controlled Kashmir. There were also concerns about Islamist fundamentalism in Pakistani politics, the country's incomplete return to democratic rule and Pakistan's nuclear weapons programme (the USA had already placed a symbolic two-year ban on trade with Khan Research Laboratories following allegations that the latter had assisted North Korea in supplying nuclear designs).

In early October 2003 Pakistani forces arrested 18 suspected militants in South Waziristan, one of the Federally Administered Tribal Areas. The offensive followed reports of increased militant activity in the region, particularly in conservative Pashtun areas where Taliban members were known to have support. At least eight Taliban and al-Qa'ida suspects were killed during the operation; it was later reported that the majority of the dead were of foreign origin. Later that month the armed forces arrested a further 40 people, including tribal elders who were accused of sheltering al-Qa'ida suspects. However, despite the apparent attempts to combat Taliban activity in the tribal areas, there were claims that Pakistani troops continued to allow Taliban movement across the Afghan–Pakistani border and that senior Taliban members were openly living in Quetta, a city close to Waziristan. In January 2004 Musharraf, during a speech to the Pakistani legislature, attempted to reassure the USA and the rest of the world that Pakistan was committed to defeating militant Islamism. While an army operation in South Waziristan earlier that month largely failed, by the end of January seven al-Qa'ida suspects and the Taliban former governor of Baghis province, Afghanistan, had been arrested. The search for suspected militants remained focused on South Waziristan, where the USA believed bin Laden and other al-Qa'ida leaders were receiving shelter. Several thousands of Pakistani troops were deployed to force al-Qa'ida fugitives across the border into Afghanistan, where US soldiers were active (US troops were not allowed to operate from Pakistani soil). In late February, following the expiry of a deadline for tribal leaders to hand over Islamist fugitives, the army launched another attack, this time arresting 58 suspects. Pakistan's recent efforts were largely in response to the USA's restraint over the nuclear proliferation scandal (see above). However, the reluctance by Pakistani troops to attack Afghanistan's former rulers threatened to affect Musharraf's relations with the US Government. Nevertheless, the USA remained anxious not to destabilize the Pakistani President, who was facing growing domestic opposition owing to his support for the 'war on terror'.

Meanwhile, fighting between Pakistani troops and militants in March 2004 resulted in the deaths of more than 100 people, including the al-Qa'ida intelligence chief, Abdullah. Many other militants were believed to have evaded capture and escaped. The army subsequently offered a temporary amnesty to both the militants and those tribesmen sheltering them. However, by the 30 April deadline only five tribesmen had surrendered. Meanwhile, during a visit to Pakistan in March, the US Secretary of State announced that, in recognition of the close military relations between the two countries, the USA had decided to designate Pakistan a 'major non-North Atlantic Treaty Organization (NATO) ally'. Shortly afterwards President Bush announced that all remaining US sanctions against Pakistan would be lifted. However, concerns continued to be expressed by the USA that more progress was not being made in the campaign against al-Qa'ida. Renewed fighting in June, after a period of calm in Waziristan, resulted in the deaths of 72 people, including the popular Waziri tribal leader and former Taliban commander Nek Mohammed. In the following month it was announced that several suspected al-Qa'ida members, including the Tanzanian Ahmed Khalfan Ghailani, wanted in connection with the 1998 bombing of US embassies in Kenya and Tanzania, had been arrested in the town of Gujrat in Punjab. Ghailani was later placed in the custody of the USA. In August the Government announced that it had thwarted a plan to carry out several attacks in Islamabad, and had subsequently arrested at least 12 al-Qa'ida suspects. Meanwhile, the authorities in the United Arab Emirates had arrested Qari Saifullah Akhtar, believed to be one of bin Laden's chief advisers and the leader of Harakat ul-Jihad-al-Islami, and extradited him to Pakistan. Akhtar was believed to have been involved in the December 2003 plot to assassinate President Musharraf.

In the mean time military operations continued in Waziristan, although it was believed that the death of Nek Mohammed had strengthened local resistance to the army campaign. The fighting escalated in September 2004 and military officials claimed that, as a result of intensified military pressure, al-Qa'ida fighters were being driven out of the area, possibly leaving for Iraq. In the same month it was announced that police had killed a prominent al-Qa'ida figure, Amjad Hussain Farooq, during a gun battle in Nawabshah, north of Karachi. Farooq was believed to have planned the failed assassination attempts on Musharraf in December 2003 and to have been involved in both the murder of Daniel Pearl and in several bombings in Karachi in 2002. In February 2005, following further military activity in Waziristan, the army announced that it had concluded a peace agreement with five tribal leaders under which, in exchange for an amnesty, the leaders had promised that they would not fight the Pakistani army or support Taliban and al-Qa'ida fighters in the area. In the same month, in a move indicative of the improved relations between the two countries, the USA revived the deal that it had suspended in 1990 to supply Pakistan with F-16 fighter aircraft. The agreement constituted part of a US $3,000m., five-year assistance programme. Following the devastating earthquake of October, however, the purchase of the aircraft was postponed, in order that the funds could be allocated instead to the reconstruction effort. Meanwhile, in May it was announced that Abu Faraj al-Libbi, reported to be the operational head of al-Qa'ida in Pakistan, had been captured in the city of Mardan in the NWFP. A further 20 suspected al-Qa'ida operatives were arrested in the following weeks. Al-Libbi was subsequently transferred into US custody for interrogation. In December five militants were reported to have been killed following a missile strike on a house in the town of Mir Ali in North Waziristan.

In January 2006 several civilians were killed in a US air-strike on a house in a village near the border with Afghanistan that intelligence sources claimed was being visited by Ayman al-Zawahiri, a leading al-Qa'ida figure. Al-Zawahiri was, however, not present at the house. In March US President Bush visited Pakistan, although his one-night stay was overshadowed somewhat by a visit that he had made to India several days previously, in which a landmark nuclear co-operation agreement had been announced. Shortly before his arrival in Pakistan, a suicide bomb attack on the US consulate in Karachi resulted in the deaths of three people, including a US diplomat.

Relations with Afghanistan were strained during the 1980s and early 1990s, as rebel Afghan tribesmen (the *mujahidin*) used areas inside Pakistan (notably the city of Peshawar) as bases for their activities. In early 1988 there were an estimated 3.2m. Afghan refugees in Pakistan, most of them in the NWFP. The presence of the refugees prompted cross-border attacks against *mujahidin* bases by Soviet and Afghan government troops. In 1988 Pakistan signed the Geneva Accords on the withdrawal of Soviet troops from Afghanistan, which included agreements on the voluntary repatriation of Afghan refugees from Pakistan. Following the withdrawal of Soviet troops from Afghanistan in 1989, Pakistan maintained its support for the guerrillas' cause, while denying accusations by the Afghan Government that it was taking an active military part in the conflict, or that it was acting as a conduit for arms supplies to the *mujahidin*. The Pakistani Government welcomed the overthrow of the Afghan regime by the guerrillas in April 1992 and supported the interim coalition Government that was formed to administer Afghanistan until the holding of free elections. Relations between Pakistan and Afghanistan deteriorated, however, in 1994. The turbulence and increasing anti-Pakistan feeling in Afghanistan threatened not only to result in an extension of the violence into the Pakhtoon (Pashtun) areas of the NWFP, but also obstructed the trade route from the Central Asian republics of the former USSR to the Arabian Sea at Karachi. The situation worsened in September 1995 when the Pakistani embassy in Kabul was ransacked and burned down by a mob of about 5,000 Afghans protesting at Pakistan's alleged active support for the Islamist Taliban militia. In the following month the Afghan ambassador to Pakistan was expelled from the country. Following the capture of Kabul by Taliban troops in late September 1996 and their assumption of power, the Pakistani Government issued a statement in which it recognized the Taliban militia as the new Afghan Government.

In December 1999 there were signs of distinct changes in Pakistan's policy towards Afghanistan. Following the imposition of UN-mandated sanctions on Afghanistan the previous month for refusing to hand over the terrorist suspect bin Laden, Pakistan appeared to be exerting pressure on the Taliban to accede to Western demands by closing down a number of Afghan banking operations in Pakistan. The Pakistani Government continued to offer financial and diplomatic support to the Taliban, though Gen. Musharraf repeatedly and strongly denied giving military assistance. Allegations regarding the involvement of Pakistan's special forces in the Taliban campaign grew, however, following the latter's successful offensive in August–September 2000. The Pakistani Government agreed to implement the UN sanctions imposed on Afghanistan in January 2001, but announced that it would attempt to mitigate the effect of the restrictions, warning of a steep increase in refugee numbers and a worsening of the civil war. The failure of (somewhat unconvincing) attempts by senior Pakistani military officers to persuade the Taliban administration to comply with US demands that bin Laden and members of his al-Qa'ida terrorist organization thought to be resident in Afghanistan should be handed over to the US authorities to answer charges of responsibility for the September 2001 terrorist attacks on the US mainland ultimately resulted in a US-led military campaign to remove the Taliban from power. Despite considerable opposition from ethnic Pashtuns (who comprised the majority of the Taliban administration) in north-western Pakistan and from elements of the armed forces who had spent years consolidating relations with the Taliban regime, Musharraf was forced to co-operate with the US-led coalition to avoid potentially devastating economic and political isolation. Long-standing enmity between the Pakistani Government and the tribes of the United Front arising from Pakistani sponsorship of the Taliban regime was exacerbated by the participation of Pakistani nationals in the armed resistance to the United Front's renewed military campaign (supported by the international coalition) to recapture Afghanistan (see above). As the United Front continued to make impressive territorial gains in Afghanistan, culminating in the capture of the capital, Kabul, in mid-November, the Pakistani Government announced the closure of all Taliban consular offices in Pakistan, including the embassy in Islamabad. It was hoped that the broad-based ethnicity of the Afghan Interim Administration (which included Pashtun representatives) installed in December would help to foster improved relations between the Pakistani authorities and the tribes of the United Front.

Publicly, Musharraf supported Karzai and the new Afghan Transitional Administration. However, Afghan officials were convinced that the Pakistani ISI was giving sanctuary to senior Taliban members and other anti-Afghan Government military commanders, such as Gulbuddin Hekmatyar. In mid-February 2003 the Pakistani and Afghan military intelligence services held talks in Rome, Italy, in an attempt to resolve deep-rooted differences. Some two months later, during an official visit to Pakistan, President Karzai urged the Pakistani Government to assist in curbing the cross-border attacks by militant Islamists. Relations were strained when Pakistan delivered a formal protest to Afghanistan in June over the dumping of the bodies of some 21 Taliban fighters on its territory; the Afghan authorities were forced to take back the bodies after Pakistani border guards discovered that the dead were, in fact, not Pakistani, but Afghan citizens. One month later, in a seemingly well-planned operation, the Pakistani embassy in Afghanistan was stormed and raided by hundreds of Afghans in protest against alleged incursions by Pakistani border troops into Afghan territory. The crowds were dispersed by Afghan police; Karzai apologized for the incident to the Pakistani President and promised to pay compensation. The embassy was reopened almost two weeks later. In January 2004 the Pakistani Prime Minister paid his first ever official visit to Afghanistan; the two countries agreed to work together to combat cross-border infiltration. In August Karzai visited Islamabad, where he held talks with Musharraf, who insisted that Taliban and al-Qa'ida militants operating in the NWFP and Balochistan would not be permitted to use the areas as bases from which to disrupt the Afghan presidential election, scheduled to take place in October. In March 2005, during a visit by Karzai, who had secured victory in the presidential election, the improvement in bilateral relations was illustrated when the two countries agreed to establish bus services linking Peshawar with the Afghan city of Jalalabad and Quetta with the Afghan city of Qandahar. However, in mid-2005 relations became strained again, when Afghan police apprehended three Pakistani men thought to have been plotting to kill the outgoing US ambassador to Afghanistan. The Afghan Government accused Pakistan of failing to prevent Taliban insurgents hiding in the border regions from perpetrating an increasing number of attacks in its southern and eastern provinces. In response, Musharraf assured Karzai of his continued co-operation in the battle against terrorism. However, questions continued as to the extent of Pakistan's commitment to preventing the resurgence of the Taliban.

In July 2005 Prime Minister Shaukat Aziz visited Kabul and held talks with President Karzai concerning border security issues. In September, following a meeting with US Secretary of State Condoleezza Rice in New York, USA, Musharraf announced a proposal to construct a fence along Pakistan's border with Afghanistan. The fence would serve to prevent insurgents based in Pakistan from launching cross-border raids, while also reducing drugs-smuggling from Afghanistan. The proposal met with criticism from Pakistani opposition parties, and Musharraf admitted that there were no practical plans for the construction of the fence. Meanwhile, additional Pakistani troops were deployed along the border, in order to prevent disruption of the legislative elections in Afghanistan that were to take place in that month. Bilateral relations deteriorated further in early 2006, when Afghan President Karzai gave President Musharraf a list of militants believed to be hiding in Pakistan; Musharraf responded by claiming that the Afghan Government's intelligence on the militants was out of date and accused Karzai of being unaware of security issues in his own country.

Drought conditions in the region contributed to a new influx of Afghan refugees in early 2001 (there were thought to be more than 2m. in Pakistan in March), placing renewed strain on limited resources and threatening to exacerbate the country's deteriorating economy and security situation. Military operations by the US-led anti-terrorism coalition in Afghanistan in October 2001 resulted in a new exodus of refugees. Although Pakistan had officially closed its border with Afghanistan in late September, it was estimated that as many as 80,000 refugees had crossed into Pakistan illegally before the Government agreed, at the end of October, to plans to reopen the border to allow the inflow of as many as 300,000 of the most vulnerable refugees, as part of an agreement with the office of the UN High Commissioner for Refugees (UNHCR) that was to include the establishment of 15 new camps. (In February 2002 it was announced that thousands of refugees had been moved from the notorious Jalozai camp in northern Pakistan—which was subsequently closed—to a new UNHCR-supervised camp near Peshawar.) According to UNHCR, by April 2002 (following the decisive defeat of Taliban forces in most of Afghanistan) repatriation offices in Pakistan were processing the return of as many as 50,000 Afghan refugees each week. At the end of 2002 UNHCR announced that more than 1.5m. Afghan refugees in Pakistan had returned to their homeland, surpassing all expectations; a further 400,000 returned in 2003 and approximately 384,000 in 2004. In early 2005 the Pakistani Government and UNHCR launched a census intended to determine how many Afghan refugees remained in Pakistan, in order to aid the development of policies to assist them. Over the course of that year an estimated 450,000 refugees were repatriated. UNHCR estimated that 400,000 voluntary repatriations to Afghanistan from Pakistan would take place during 2006.

Relations with India have dominated Pakistan's foreign policy since the creation of the two states in 1947. Relations deteriorated during the late 1970s and early 1980s, owing to Pakistan's programme to develop nuclear weapons, and as a result of major US weapons deliveries to Pakistan. The other major contentious issue between the two states was the disputed region of Kashmir, where, since 1949, a cease-fire line, known as the Line of Control (LoC), has separated Indian-controlled Kashmir (the state of Jammu and Kashmir) and Pakistani Kashmir, which comprises Azad (Free) Kashmir and the Northern Areas. While Pakistan demanded that the sovereignty of the region be decided in accordance with earlier UN resolutions (which advocated a plebiscite in both parts of the region), India argued that a solution should be reached through bilateral negotiations.

Relations between Pakistan and India reached a crisis in late 1989, when the outlawed Jammu and Kashmir Liberation Front (JKLF) and several other Muslim groups in Indian-controlled Kashmir intensified their campaigns of terrorism, strikes and civil unrest, in support of demands for an independent Kashmir or unification with Pakistan. In response, the Indian Government dispatched troops to Jammu and Kashmir. By early February 1990 it was officially estimated that about 80 people (mostly civilians) had been killed in resulting clashes between troops and protesters. The opposition parties in Pakistan organized nation-wide strikes, to express their sympathy for the Muslims in Jammu and Kashmir, and urged the Government to adopt more active measures regarding the crisis.

In December 1990 discussions were held between the Ministers of External Affairs of Pakistan and India, at which an agreement not to attack each other's nuclear facilities was finalized, but no solution was found to the Kashmiri problem. Further high-level talks held between the two countries during the first half of the 1990s made no progress in resolving the crisis, and skirmishes between Pakistani and Indian troops along the border in Kashmir continued. In December 1994 Pakistan was successful in securing the passage of a resolution condemning reported human rights abuses by Indian security forces in Kashmir at the summit meeting of the Organization of the Islamic Conference held in Casablanca, Morocco. (In the same month Pakistan's decision to close down its consulate in Mumbai (Bombay), amid claims of Indian support for acts of terrorism in Karachi, provided a further indication of the growing rift between the two countries.) In February 1995 (and again in February 1996) Benazir Bhutto's Government organized a nation-wide general strike to express solidarity with the independence movement in Jammu and Kashmir and to protest against alleged atrocities carried out by the Indian forces. In January 1996 relations between the two countries deteriorated when the Pakistani Government accused the Indian forces of having launched a rocket attack on a mosque in Azad Kashmir, which killed 20 people. The Indian authorities claimed that the deaths had been caused by Pakistani rockets that had been misfired. Tensions between Pakistan and India were also exacerbated in early 1996 by allegations that each side was on the verge of conducting nuclear tests. Later that year, India's decision to hold state assembly elections in Jammu and Kashmir (described as 'farcical' by Benazir Bhutto) and its refusal to sign the CTBT did nothing to encourage an improvement in relations between Islamabad and New Delhi. In March 1997, however, talks (which had been suspended since 1994) were resumed, both at official and at ministerial level. Of most significance were the negotiations between India and Pakistan's foreign secretaries, which took place in Islamabad in June. These talks resulted in an agreement to establish a series of distinct working parties to consider groups of issues. One such group of issues specifically related to Jammu and Kashmir. Little progress was made, however, in improving bilateral relations during a further round of high-level talks held in New Delhi in September and tension increased at the end of the month.

In April 1998 Pakistan provoked stern condemnation from the recently elected right-wing Government in India following its successful test-firing of a new intermediate-range missile (capable of reaching deep into Indian territory). The arms race escalated dramatically and to potentially dangerous proportions in the following month when India conducted five underground nuclear test explosions. The test programme was condemned world-wide, and the USA imposed economic sanctions against India. The US President, Bill Clinton, and the UN Security Council urged Pakistan to show restraint in not carrying out its own retaliatory test explosions. However, at the end of May Pakistan carried out six underground atomic test explosions. In early June the Pakistani Government ordered a 50% reduction in public expenditure in an attempt to mitigate the effects of the resultant economic sanctions imposed by various foreign countries, including the USA. Immediately after the nuclear tests, India and Pakistan announced self-imposed moratoriums on further testing and engaged themselves in intense diplomatic activity. In September, however, the Pakistani Minister of Foreign Affairs categorically stated that Pakistan would not sign the CTBT until all of the sanctions were lifted and other legitimate concerns addressed.

Indo-Pakistani talks at foreign secretary level regarding Kashmir and other issues were resumed in Islamabad in October 1998. In February 1999 relations appeared to improve considerably when the Indian Prime Minister, Atal Bihari Vajpayee, made an historic journey (inaugurating the first passenger bus service between India and Pakistan) over the border to Lahore. Following his welcome by the Pakistani Prime Minister, the two leaders held a summit meeting (the first to be conducted in Pakistan for 10 years), at the end of which they signed the Lahore Declaration, which, with its pledges regarding peace and nuclear security, seemed designed to allay world-wide fears of a nuclear 'flashpoint' in South Asia. The contentious subject of Jammu and Kashmir was, however, largely avoided. Concern over the escalating arms race in South Asia was again deepened in April, following a series of ballistic missile tests carried out first by India and then by Pakistan (both countries, however, appeared to have adhered to the procedures incorporated in the Lahore

Declaration, by informing each other of their test plans well in advance).

In May 1999 the Kashmir conflict intensified to reach what was termed a 'near-war situation' following the reported infiltration of 600–900 well-armed Islamist militants, reinforced by regular Pakistani troops, across the LoC into the area around Kargil in the Indian-held sector of Kashmir. It was widely believed that the incursion of the guerrillas had been planned months in advance by the Pakistani army and intelligence agents; the Pakistani Government, however, claimed that it had no direct involvement whatsoever with the Islamist insurgents. In response, the Indian troops launched a series of airstrikes against the militants at the end of the month, a move that represented a serious provocation to Pakistan since it constituted the first peacetime use of air power in Kashmir. Within days tensions were heightened when a militant Kashmiri group claimed responsibility for shooting down an Indian helicopter gunship and Pakistani troops destroyed two Indian fighter aircraft, which had reportedly strayed into Pakistani airspace. Artillery exchanges increased along the LoC (with both sides suffering heavy casualties) and reports of the massing of troops and evacuation of villages along the international border aroused considerable concern. In early July, however, Indian military dominance combined with US diplomatic pressure prompted Nawaz Sharif's precipitate visit to Washington, DC, in the USA for talks with President Clinton. The resultant Washington Declaration prepared the ground for an end to the Kargil crisis through the Pakistan leader's agreement to the withdrawal of all 'intruders' from Indian-controlled Kashmir. In August there was renewed tension between Pakistan and India when India shot down a Pakistani naval reconnaissance aircraft near Pakistan's border with Gujarat, killing all 16 personnel on board; Pakistan retaliated the following day by opening fire on Indian military aircraft in the same area.

In October–November 1999 there was a notable increase in terrorist incidents in Kashmir, and Indian and Pakistani forces were reported to have resumed skirmishes across the LoC. Relations between the two countries worsened in early November after the success of Vajpayee in promoting an official condemnation of the new Pakistani military regime by the Commonwealth heads of government, following the military coup in Pakistan in mid-October. In December the Indian Government stated that it would not resume dialogue with Pakistan until the latter halted 'cross-border terrorism'.

In late December 1999 the Kashmir conflict came to international attention when five Islamist fundamentalists hijacked an Indian Airlines aircraft and held its passengers captive at Qandahar airport in southern Afghanistan for one week. Among the hijackers' demands was the release of 36 Muslim militants being held in Indian prisons who supported the Kashmiri separatist movement. Under increasing domestic pressure to prioritize the safety of the hostages, the Indian Government agreed to release three of the prisoners in exchange for the safe return of the captive passengers and crew. Despite Indian accusations of complicity, the Pakistani Government denied any links with the hijackers. In late March 2000 the US President's recent visit to the region appeared to have failed to bring Pakistan and India any closer together when Gen. Musharraf's offer of peace talks regarding Kashmir was firmly rejected by the Indian Government (which still seemed deeply suspicious of the Pakistani Chief Executive). India continued to demand that Pakistan cease 'cross-border terrorism' as a precondition for negotiations, and Pakistan repeatedly denied arming and funding militants. On 24 July the Kashmiri militant group, the Hizbul Mujahideen, declared a three-month cease-fire on condition that India curbed human rights violations and military operations against militants. Other militant groups denounced the cease-fire. The Pakistani army continued a policy of not firing first, at the same time emphasizing that the cease-fire was not unilateral. The Government supported the cessation of hostilities, but was allegedly under pressure from separatist groups not to become involved in peace negotiations. The Hizbul Mujahideen later demanded tripartite discussions, which included Pakistan, but India refused to involve its neighbouring state, renouncing it as 'terrorist'. The cease-fire ended in the second week of August.

In mid-August 2000 Pakistan renewed its offer to resume negotiations, despite claims of increased violence by the Indian army towards separatists. Relations, however, remained unchanged and violence in the region intensified. In November the Indian Government declared the suspension of combat operations against Kashmiri militants during the Muslim holy month of Ramadan. The unilateral cease-fire began at the end of November (and was subsequently extended, at intervals, until the end of May); Indian security forces were authorized to retaliate if fired upon. The majority of national parties and foreign governments supported the cessation of hostilities, although the Pakistani authorities described the cease-fire as 'meaningless' without simultaneous constructive dialogue. The All-Party Hurriyat Conference welcomed the development and offered to enter negotiations with Pakistani authorities in order to prepare for tripartite discussions. The Hizbul Mujahideen and other militant groups, however, rejected the offer and continued their campaign of violence, extending their activities as far as the Red Fort in Old Delhi, where three people were shot dead in December. In the same month Pakistan extended an invitation to the All-Party Hurriyat Conference to participate in joint preparations for the establishment of tripartite negotiations. At the end of December India agreed to issue passports to a delegation of All-Party Hurriyat Conference leaders to allow them to visit Pakistan; however, processing of the applications was subsequently stalled. In mid-January 2001 the Indian High Commissioner to Pakistan visited Gen. Musharraf. This meeting signified the first high-level contact since the military coup in Pakistan in 1999. The two officials urged an early resumption of negotiations on the Kashmir question.

Relations with India appeared to improve following the earthquake in Gujarat in January 2001, when Pakistan offered humanitarian relief to India and the leaders of the two countries thus established contact. In May Prime Minister Vajpayee issued an unexpected invitation to Gen. Musharraf to attend bilateral negotiations in Agra in July. However, hopes for a significant breakthrough on the issue of Kashmir were frustrated by the failure of the two leaders to agree to a joint declaration at the conclusion of the dialogue; the divergent views of the two sides on the priority issue in the dispute (cross-border terrorism according to India, and Kashmiri self-determination in the opinion of Pakistan) appeared to be more firmly entrenched than ever. Tension with India was heightened considerably following a guerrilla-style attack on the state assembly building in Srinagar on 1 October. An estimated 38 people (including two of the four assailants) were killed and around 70 were wounded in the attack and in the subsequent confrontation with security forces. The Indian Government attributed responsibility for the attack to the Pakistan-based Jaish-e-Mohammed and Lashkar-e-Taiba groups. Tensions were exacerbated later in the month when Gen. Musharraf rejected official Indian requests to ban the activities of the organization in Pakistan, although he did publicly condemn the attack.

On 13 December 2001 five armed assailants gained access to the grounds of the Indian union Parliament in New Delhi and attempted to launch an apparent suicide attack on the parliament building. Although no parliamentary deputies were hurt in the attack, nine people were killed and some 25 were injured in the botched assault; the five assailants were also killed in the attack. The Indian authorities again attributed responsibility for the attack to the Jaish-e-Mohammed and Lashkar-e-Taiba groups, and suggested that the five assailants appeared to be of Pakistani origin. Pakistan, which had been among the many countries to express immediate condemnation of the attack (which was popularly described as an assault on democracy), now demanded to see concrete proof to support the allegations made by the Indian Government, while the US Government urged the Indian authorities to exercise restraint in their response. Tensions between India and Pakistan continued to mount when Mohammed Afzal, a member of Jaish-e-Mohammed arrested in Kashmir on suspicion of complicity in the incident, admitted his involvement and alleged publicly that Pakistani security and intelligence agencies had provided support to those directly responsible for the attack. India recalled its High Commissioner from Islamabad and announced that overground transport services between the two countries would be suspended from 1 January 2002. As positions were reinforced with troops and weapons (including missiles) on both sides of the LoC, there was considerable international concern that such brinkmanship might propel the two countries (each with nuclear capabilities) into renewed armed conflict. Mindful of the potential detriment to security at Pakistan's border with Afghanistan that could result from escalated conflict in Kashmir, the USA applied increased pressure on the beleaguered Pakistani Government (already facing vociferous domestic opposition to its accommodation of US activities in Afghanistan) to adopt a more conciliatory attitude towards India's security concerns, and in late December the Pakistani authorities followed the US Government's lead in 'freezing' the assets of the two groups held responsible for the attack by India. The leaders of the two groups were later detained by the Pakistani authorities (who arrested some 80 suspected militants in the last week of December), but, despite an evident satisfaction at this development, the Indian Government continued to dismiss much of the Pakistani response as superficial and demanded that the two leaders be extradited (together with 20 other named Pakistan-based militants) to stand trial in India.

It had been hoped that tensions between the two countries might be defused by renewed dialogue between Vajpayee and Musharraf at a summit meeting of the South Asian Association for Regional Co-operation (SAARC) convened in Nepal in the first week of January 2002, but contacts between the two men were minimal, and troops on both sides of the LoC continued to exchange gunfire in the days following the conference. However, on 12 January Musharraf yielded to relentless international pressure by publicly condemning the activities of militant extremists based in Pakistan and announcing the introduction of a broad range of measures to combat terrorist activity and religious zealotry, including the proscription of five extremist organizations (among them Jaish-e-Mohammed and Lashkar-e-Taiba). It was hoped that reports published in late January, which indicated that the number of terrorist incidents in Jammu and Kashmir had halved since the introduction of the counter-insurgency measures, would help foster a more substantial improvement in future relations between the two countries. However, in March 2002 India and (subsequently) Pakistan expelled a number of each other's diplomats for alleged improprieties, and in a somewhat belligerent interview published in April, Musharraf stated that he was prepared to use nuclear weapons in the event of war. In mid-May suspected Islamist militants attacked an Indian army camp in Jammu and Kashmir, killing more than 30 people. India expelled Pakistan's High Commissioner. Indo-Pakistani relations deteriorated further following the assassination of Abdul Ghani Lone, the leader of the moderate All-Party Hurriyat Conference on 21 May, by suspected Islamist militants. India accused the Pakistani Government of supporting the Islamist extremists. Despite US attempts to calm tensions, artillery fire was exchanged along the LoC. More than 1m. soldiers were mobilized on both sides of the border as the two countries appeared to be on the brink of war. Pakistan would not rule out first use of nuclear weapons, and India declared that it would be prepared to go to war after the monsoon season ended (in September) if its neighbour refused to halt 'cross-border terrorism'. Musharraf, however, denied that Pakistan was aiding incursions into Jammu and Kashmir, and ordered several 'routine' tests of its ballistic-missile arsenal at the end of May. An attempt to broker peace at a security summit held in Kazakhstan in early June failed after the Indian Prime Minister refused to meet Musharraf. Following intense diplomatic efforts by British and US officials, the threat of war appeared to diminish. On 10 June India lifted its ban on Pakistani commercial aircraft flying over its territory and prepared to appoint a new High Commissioner to Pakistan, in response to Pakistani pledges to halt cross-border infiltration. India's campaign against 'cross-border terrorism' gained impetus as a result of the US Secretary of Defense Donald Rumsfeld's declaration in mid-June that there were strong indications that al-Qa'ida was operating near the LoC. In late June Rumsfeld announced that Pakistan had significantly reduced cross-border infiltration. However, an attack on Hindus by suspected Islamist militants in Jammu and Kashmir in mid-July disrupted attempts to restore diplomatic relations between India and Pakistan, and the Indian Government decided to delay the appointment of a new High Commissioner to Pakistan. Both countries conducted 'routine' ballistic-missile tests in early October. In mid-October the Indian Minister of Defence stated that India would withdraw a large number of troops from the international border with Pakistan; the number of troops along the LoC would remain unchanged, however. Pakistan reciprocated the announcement shortly afterwards. India's gradual removal of troops began in late October; Pakistan responded by withdrawing a portion of its troops in November. President Musharraf dismissed elections in Jammu and Kashmir in September–October as a 'sham' and 'farcical'.

Relations with India deteriorated in early 2003. Tensions were exacerbated by India's latest set of 'routine' ballistic-missile tests, the violence in Kashmir and India's new military agreement with Russia. In late January India ordered four officials at Pakistan's High Commission in New Delhi to leave the country within 48 hours for 'indulging in activities incompatible with their official status', a euphemism for spying. Pakistan reacted by expelling four officials at the Indian High Commission in Islamabad. In early February India expelled Pakistan's acting High Commissioner, accusing him of funding Kashmiri separatist groups. Four other Pakistani officials were charged with spying and expelled. Pakistan retaliated by giving India's acting High Commissioner and four colleagues 48 hours to leave for allegedly spying. Tensions between India and Pakistan increased after Pakistan responded to India's decision to conduct 'routine' missile tests without advance warning by carrying out a set of its own tests. Nevertheless, in mid-April, during a visit to Jammu and Kashmir, Vajpayee offered to enter dialogue with Pakistan; the Pakistani Prime Minister, Zafarullah Khan Jamali, welcomed the decision and formally invited Vajpayee 10 days later to visit Pakistan. Commentators initially attributed Vajpayee's change in tone to diplomatic pressure from the United Kingdom and USA to begin peace negotiations with Pakistan. However, it soon transpired that the USA had not been notified in advance of the Indian Prime Minister's initiative; indeed, Vajpayee had hardly consulted his Cabinet. In early May the two neighbours agreed to restore diplomatic relations and civil aviation links. Two months later the bus service between Lahore and New Delhi was restored. India, however, continued to insist on a complete cessation of cross-border infiltration as a precondition for peace talks.

In mid-August 2003 President Musharraf proposed a cease-fire along the LoC, but wanted India to reciprocate by reducing its armed personnel in the Srinagar valley and by ending the alleged atrocities committed by the Indian armed forces. India refused Musharraf's offer and continued to hold Pakistan-based militants responsible for the recent rise in attacks in Jammu and Kashmir. Two months later, however, the Indian Minister of External Affairs, Yashwant Sinha, announced 12 confidence-building measures to improve and normalize relations with Pakistan, including offers to enter another round of talks to restore civil aviation links, to introduce more transport links (including a bus service between the capitals of the disputed region across the LoC), to resume full sporting contacts, and to enter dialogue with separatist politicians in Kashmir. Sinha emphasized, however, that no direct talks on Kashmir between India and Pakistan would take place until the latter ceased cross-border infiltration by militant Islamists. Pakistan issued a cautious welcome to most of the proposals, while declaring that bus travellers in Kashmir would need UN travel documents, but was disappointed that there was no offer of a meeting. On 23 November Pakistani Prime Minister Jamali announced a unilateral cease-fire along the LoC, to begin at midnight two days later (on the Muslim festival of Id). Jamali also responded to Vajpayee's offer to discuss transport links by proposing an additional bus service between Lahore and the Indian city of Amritsar. India reciprocated the gesture (but reserved the right to fire at so-called 'infiltrators') and offered to extend the cease-fire across the Actual Ground Position Line in Siachen as well as across the international border. Pakistan agreed to the proposal and at midnight on 25–26 November a cease-fire came into effect. In mid-December the chances of a peace agreement between India and Pakistan improved after Musharraf declared that Pakistan was prepared to cede a long-standing demand for a UN-sponsored plebiscite for the Kashmiri people; India welcomed the initiative. At the same time, Indian and Pakistani officials signed a three-year agreement on the restoration from mid-January 2004 of a passenger and freight train service between New Delhi and Lahore. Direct aviation links were resumed on 1 January 2004. In late December 2003 it was reported that, since the implementation of the cease-fire, separatist-related violence in Jammu and Kashmir had declined. Meanwhile, in November the President banned six Islamist militant groups (three of which had been banned in 2002 but had re-emerged under different names—see above), closed down their offices and 'froze' their bank accounts.

At the ground-breaking SAARC summit meeting in Islamabad in early January 2004, Musharraf assured Vajpayee that he would not permit any territory under Pakistan's control to be used to support terrorism; in return Vajpayee agreed to begin negotiations on all bilateral issues, including Kashmir, in February. Meanwhile, however, Islamist militants who were unhappy with what they perceived as a betrayal by Musharraf continued their violent campaign. Indian and Pakistani senior officials opened discussions in Islamabad in mid-February; a timetable for future dialogue was established. In June several rounds of discussions took place between Indian and Pakistani officials in New Delhi. In a joint statement issued at the end of the month, both sides stressed their renewed commitment to reaching a negotiated final settlement on the Kashmir issue and agreed to restore their diplomatic missions to full strength and, in principle, to reopen their respective consulates in Mumbai and Karachi. An agreement was also reached that each country would, in future, notify the other of any forthcoming missile tests. In September Pakistan and India held their first, official, ministerial-level talks in over three years in New Delhi. As a result, the two sides agreed to implement a series of confidence-building measures, including the restoration of bilateral transport links. In October Musharraf stated, in a speech to the Pakistani press, that a new and radical approach to the Kashmir issue was necessary. In an unprecedented statement, he suggested that Pakistan might be prepared to drop its demands for a UN-sponsored plebiscite on the future of the divided territory if a range of options pertaining to a possible change in Kashmir's status, including independence, joint control, or the placing of Kashmir under UN administration, were considered. India's response to Musharraf's remarks was muted, and it refused to enter into a dialogue with Musharraf over his comments.

In November 2004 Pakistan welcomed a move by India to reduce the number of Indian troops deployed in Jammu and Kashmir. Later in that month Indian Prime Minister Manmohan Singh met with his Pakistani counterpart, Shaukat Aziz, in New Delhi. In the following month further high-level talks on the Kashmir issue were held in Islamabad, but with no tangible progress. In early 2005 tensions resurfaced when each side accused the other of violating the ongoing cease-fire along the LoC. However, in February, following talks between the Indian and Pakistani ministers responsible for foreign affairs, the two countries agreed to open a bus service across the LoC, linking Srinagar with Muzaffarabad. Despite militant threats of disruption, and several attacks on the proposed route, the service opened in early April 2005. Plans were also announced to reopen the consulates in Mumbai and Karachi. In March, in a gesture of goodwill, Musharraf ordered the early release of 700 Indian prisoners, most of them fishermen, who had been imprisoned in Pakistan. Meanwhile, in the same month India made clear its disapproval of the US decision to supply Pakistan with F-16 fighter aircraft, stating its concerns that the deal would exacerbate security tensions in the region. In mid-April Musharraf travelled to India for the first time since 2001 and met with Manmohan Singh in Delhi for further peace talks; the two leaders subsequently issued a statement referring to the peace process as 'irreversible' and agreeing to improve trade and transport links over the LoC.

In October 2005 the devastating consequences of the massive earthquake centred in Azad Kashmir had significant implications for the ongoing peace process. In the aftermath of the disaster, Pakistan accepted an Indian offer of aid. Following a series of negotiations, the two countries subsequently agreed to open a number of crossing points on the LoC, in order to permit the reunification of divided families. The crossing points were finally opened in November. However, continued fears on the part of both countries that the other would take advantage of the situation to conduct military surveillance hampered prospects for more extensive co-operation. Despite speculation that many militants operating in the area had been killed by the earthquake, sporadic separatist violence continued. In an indication of the extent to which bilateral relations had improved, while a bomb attack on New Delhi, India, in late October was believed to have been perpetrated by Pakistani militants, Indian Prime Minister Manmohan Singh refrained from blaming Pakistan directly for the attacks. He stressed instead that he expected Pakistan to take responsibility for the prevention of terrorism directed against India. However, in January 2006 a suggestion by Musharraf in a televised interview that India demilitarize three cities in the Kashmir valley in order to advance the peace process was rejected by the Indian Government. In February a second rail link was opened between the two countries, linking the town of Khokrapar in Sindh with the Indian town of Munabao in Rajasthan.

In March 2006 the peace process advanced further when Manmohan Singh proposed, during the launch of a new bus service linking the two countries, that they sign a treaty of friendship, peace and security, a suggestion welcomed by the Pakistani Government. However, the proposal was criticized for separating the resolution of the Kashmir dispute from other issues affecting the bilateral relationship. It was subsequently agreed that trade links would be further developed, as part of efforts to restore normal relations through the improvement of economic and commercial ties.

Relations with Bangladesh deteriorated in September 2000 when, at the UN Millennium Summit meeting in the USA, the Bangladeshi Prime Minister condemned the Pakistani military leadership, ostensibly as part of a general request for the UN to take action against undemocratic changes of government. Gen. Musharraf subsequently cancelled forthcoming meetings with the Prime Minister of Bangladesh. Later, the Bangladeshi leader demanded that Pakistan apologize for the atrocities committed by its army during the Bangladesh war of liberation and that those involved be brought to justice. In late November Pakistan withdrew its Deputy High Commissioner to Bangladesh, following his insistence that the ruling Bangladesh Awami League, rather than the Pakistani army, was responsible for the bloodshed. The Bangladesh Government declared the diplomat *persona non grata* in mid-December and demanded his immediate departure. During his visit to Bangladesh in late July 2002, President Musharraf apologized unreservedly for the atrocities committed by Pakistani troops during Bangladesh's war of liberation.

Pakistan withdrew from the Commonwealth in January 1972, in protest at the United Kingdom's role in the East Pakistan crisis. Pakistan recognized Bangladesh in February 1974, but attempts to rejoin the Commonwealth in the late 1970s and early 1980s were thwarted by India. In January 1989, however, India announced that it would no longer oppose Pakistan's application to rejoin the organization, and in July, during an official visit to the United Kingdom by Benazir Bhutto, Pakistan was formally invited to rejoin the Commonwealth, which it did on 1 October 1989. In October 1999, however, Pakistan was suspended from participation in meetings of the Commonwealth. In September 2003 the CMAG agreed to maintain Pakistan's suspension from participation in meetings, as it was not convinced that democracy had been completely restored in the country. However, in May 2004 the CMAG agreed to restore fully Pakistan's Commonwealth membership, stating that it had decided that the country had consolidated the progress made towards democracy following the October 2002 general election, owing to President Musharraf's statement that he would step down as Chief of Army Staff by the end of 2004 and the subsequent legislative vote of confidence in his leadership. However, Commonwealth Secretary-General Don McKinnon stated that the Commonwealth would continue to monitor Pakistan and, in particular, progress towards the fulfilment of Musharraf's pledge to become a civilian president. Despite this statement, following the passage of legislation later in that year enabling Musharraf to retain his military role, McKinnon commented that it might be acceptable for Musharraf to keep his dual role as he would do so with parliamentary approval. In February 2005 the CMAG criticized Musharraf for reneging on his pledge and insisted that he must relinquish his military role by 2007.

In early 1992 the Economic Co-operation Organization (ECO, see p. 223), comprising Pakistan, Iran and Turkey, was reactivated, and by the end of the year had been expanded to include Afghanistan, Azerbaijan and the five Central Asian, mainly Muslim, republics of the former USSR; the 'Turkish Republic of Northern Cyprus' joined ECO in 1993. Trade delegations from Turkey and the new republics visited Pakistan, and an agreement for the restoration and construction of highways in Afghanistan, to link Pakistan with these republics, was signed. In 1995 Pakistan, the People's Republic of China, Kazakhstan and Kyrgyzstan signed a transit trade agreement, restoring Pakistan's overland trade route with Central Asia, through China. During a commemorative visit to Pakistan by the Chinese Premier, organized in May 2001 to celebrate 50 years of bilateral relations, the two countries concluded a number of agreements on technical and economic co-operation. Bilateral relations were consolidated and further co-operation agreements were signed during an official visit to China made by Gen. Musharraf in December. Meanwhile, in March Pakistan's Chasma Nuclear Power Plant in Punjab province, which had been built in the 1990s with substantial assistance from the Chinese National Nuclear Corporation, was opened. In early January 2002 it was reported that China had supplied several dozen fighter aircraft and air defence missiles to Pakistan. The two countries were also co-operating to develop a new fighter aircraft. Musharraf visited

China again in August 2002 and reaffirmed the close relations between the two countries. In November President Musharraf made another visit during which various Sino-Pakistani agreements were concluded, including a US $500m. loan to Pakistan, a trade agreement and an extradition treaty. In May 2004 the two countries signed an agreement to construct a second nuclear power plant at Chasma. Further accords on the construction of the plant were signed during a visit to Pakistan by Chinese Premier Wen Jiabao in April 2005. In February 2003, meanwhile, President Musharraf visited Moscow, the first official visit by a Pakistani head of state to the Russian capital in 33 years. Musharraf, reportedly wishing to improve trade relations between the two countries, in return invited the Russian President to visit Pakistan.

Government

The President is a constitutional Head of State, who is normally elected for five years by an electoral college, comprising the Federal Legislature and the four provincial assemblies. The former consists of a lower and upper house.

Pakistan comprises four provinces (each with an appointed Governor and provincial government), the federal capital of Islamabad and the Federally Administered Tribal Areas.

According to the 2002 Legal Framework Order and the 2003 Seventeenth Constitutional Amendment Act, the number of seats in the lower house of the Federal Legislature, called the National Assembly, was increased from 217 to 342, with 272 members directly elected (on the basis of adult suffrage) and 60 seats reserved for women and 10 for non-Muslims. The term of the National Assembly was reduced to four years. The size of the upper house, called the Senate, was increased to 100 seats (from 87). The provincial assemblies directly elected 88 members (of which 16 had to be women and a further 16 technocrats), and the remaining 12 members were chosen by the National Assembly from a list of candidates provided by the Federally Administered Tribal Areas and federal capital. The term of the Senate is six years, with one-half the membership being renewed every three years. The Prime Minister is elected by the National Assembly and he/she and the other ministers in the Cabinet are responsible to it. The powers of the President were greatly enhanced by the constitutional amendments (see The Constitution).

The establishment of a National Security Council was endorsed in 2004, ensuring the military a formal role in government.

Defence

In August 2005 the armed forces totalled 619,000 men (including 513,000 reserves): 550,000 in the army (to be reduced to 50,000 by the end of 2004), 24,000 in the navy and 45,000 in the air force. Active paramilitary forces numbered up to 302,000 (including a National Guard of 185,000 men). The projected defence budget for 2005 was Rs 222,000m. at the federal level. Military service is voluntary.

Economic Affairs

In 2004, according to estimates by the World Bank, Pakistan's gross national income (GNI), measured at average 2002–04 prices, was US $90,663m., equivalent to $600 per head (or $2,160 per head on an international purchasing-power parity basis). During 1995–2004, it was estimated, the population increased at an average annual rate of 2.4%, while gross domestic product (GDP) per head increased, in real terms, by an average of 1.2% per year. Overall GDP increased, in real terms, at an average annual rate of 3.6% in 1995–2004. According to official figures, growth reached 6.4% in 2003/04 and 8.4% in 2004/05.

Agriculture (including forestry and fishing) contributed an estimated 21.6% of GDP in the year ending 30 June 2005. An estimated 43.0% of the employed labour force were engaged in the sector at 30 June 2005. The principal cash crops are cotton (which accounted for around 21.3% of export earnings in 2004/05) and rice; wheat, maize and sugar cane are also major crops. Fishing and leather production provide significant export revenues. In 2004/05 the cotton and wheat harvests reached record levels. During 1995–2004 agricultural GDP increased at an average annual rate of 3.1%; it rose by 2.2% in 2003/04 and by an estimated 7.5% in 2004/05.

Industry (including mining, manufacturing, power and construction) engaged an estimated 20.3% of the employed labour force in June 2005, and provided an estimated 25.1% of GDP in 2004/05. During 1995–2004 industrial GDP increased by an average of 4.4% per year. According to official sources, industrial GDP grew by 12.0% in 2003/04 and by an estimated 10.2% in 2004/05.

Mining and quarrying contributed an estimated 2.0% of GDP in 2004/05, and, according to the Asian Development Bank (ADB, see p. 169), employed 0.1% of the labour force in 2002/03. Petroleum and petroleum products are the major mineral exports. Limestone, rock salt, gypsum, silica sand, natural gas and coal are also mined. In addition, Pakistan has reserves of graphite, copper and manganese. The GDP of the mining sector increased at an average annual rate of 5.2% during 1999/2000–2003/04; mining GDP increased by 3.8% in 2003/04 and by an estimated 5.0% in 2004/05.

Manufacturing contributed an estimated 18.2% of GDP in 2004/05, and, according to the ADB, engaged about 14.4% of the employed labour force in 2003/04. The most important sectors include the manufacture of textiles, food products, automobiles and electrical goods and also petroleum refineries. During 1995–2004 manufacturing GDP increased at an average annual rate of 5.6%; manufacturing GDP increased by 14.1% in 2003/04 and by an estimated 12.5% in 2004/05, according to official figures.

Energy is derived principally from natural gas (providing 35.7% of the total electrical energy supply in 2002), petroleum (32.3%) and hydroelectric power (29.5%). Imports of petroleum and petroleum products comprised about 18.5% of the cost of total imports in 2004/05.

Services engaged 35.6% of the employed labour force in 2000, and provided an estimated 53.3% of GDP in 2004/05. The combined GDP of the service sectors increased at an average rate of 4.3% per year in 1995–2004. The GDP of services expanded by 6.0% in 2003/04 and by an estimated 7.9% in 2004/05, according to official figures.

In 2004 Pakistan recorded a visible trade deficit of US $3,382m., and there was a deficit of $808m. on the current account of the balance of payments. Remittances from Pakistanis working abroad declined substantially during the 1990s, and by 2000/01 had levelled off to about $1,087m. However, the flow of remittances increased significantly to $2,389.1m. in 2001/02 and to $4,236.9m. in 2002/03, before declining to $3,871.6m. in 2003/04. In 2004/05 remittances increased again, to $4,168.8m. The principal source of imports (12.0%) in 2004/05 was Saudi Arabia, and the principal market for exports was the USA (23.9%). Other major trading partners were the United Arab Emirates, the People's Republic of China, Germany, Japan, Kuwait, and the United Kingdom. The principal exports in 2004/05 were textiles and textile articles (particularly cotton), and vegetable products. The principal imports were machinery and mechanical equipment and electrical appliances, mineral products and chemicals and related products.

For the financial year ending 30 June 2005 there was a projected budgetary deficit of Rs 125,700m. (equivalent to approximately 1.9% of GDP). Pakistan's total external debt was US $36,345m. at the end of 2003, of which $31,373m. was long-term public debt. The cost of debt-servicing in that year was equivalent to 16.0% of earnings from exports of goods and services. During 1995–2004 the average annual rate of inflation was 6.0%; according to official figures, consumer prices rose by 4.5% in 2003/04 and by 9.3% in 2004/05. About 7.7% of the labour force were estimated to be unemployed in June 2005.

Pakistan is a member of the South Asian Association for Regional Co-operation (SAARC, see p. 356), of the Asian Development Bank (ADB), of the UN Economic and Social Commission for Asia and the Pacific (ESCAP, see p. 33) and of the Colombo Plan (see p. 385). Pakistan is also a founder member of the Islamic Financial Services Board.

During the 1990s economic growth was constrained by poor investment in manufacturing and inadequate agricultural production, while widespread corruption and inefficient revenue management (particularly in the collection and administration of taxes) undermined attempts to address worsening levels of poverty and deteriorating infrastructure and social services. However, the Musharraf administration that took office in 1999 demonstrated renewed commitment to radical economic reform. In December of that year the IMF agreed to extend a US $1,320m. Poverty Reduction and Growth Facility (PRGF) to Pakistan, in support of a three-year social and economic reform programme, which was implemented during October 2001–September 2004. Despite the economic repercussions of the terrorist attacks on the USA in September 2001, the prolonged drought, and regional and domestic security problems, Pakistan made substantial progress in implementing the programme's crucial objectives, which were: increased potential for economic growth; improved social provisions; and reduced vulnerability to external factors. The economy experienced steady growth, while foreign-exchange reserves increased sharply, owing to an improved trade balance, increased remittances from Pakistanis working abroad and a current-account surplus. Encouraged by the IMF's extension of the PRGF, in December 2001 the 'Paris Club' of creditor governments agreed to reschedule Pakistan's entire bilateral debt stock of $12,500m. In 2003 Pakistan's privatization programme was accelerated. In 2003/04 the Government pledged to use 90% of the proceeds from privatization to pay off some of its foreign debt; the remaining 10% would help to alleviate poverty. There were fears, however, that the political strife, domestic and regional security concerns, bureaucratic obstacles, corruption and inadequate infrastructure would continue to deter potential investors. Nevertheless, in the first half of 2004 the Government was so confident that Pakistan's external accounts would remain strong that it decided not to seek to renew a three-year funding programme from the IMF upon its expiry at the end of the year. In 2005 the Government's privatization programme accelerated significantly, the most significant divestment being the sale of a controlling 26% stake in Pakistan Telecommunications (Pvt) Ltd (PTCL) in June to Dubai-based Emirates Telecommunications. Despite expectations of a slight economic deceleration, in 2004/05 GDP expanded by 8.4%, its fastest rate of expansion for 20 years. Growth was driven by the manufacturing, financial and agricultural sectors. Despite a marked increase in textile exports in the first half of 2005, as the sector benefited from the abolition of global textile quotas in January, the trade deficit widened dramatically over the course of the year as a result of a rapid increase in imports caused by rising global petroleum prices and strong domestic demand. These factors also contributed to a significant increase in the rate of inflation. Largely owing to the widening of the trade deficit, in 2004/05 Pakistan's current-account balance also moved into deficit, having recorded a surplus in the previous three years. The cost of the relief and reconstruction effort necessary in the aftermath of the devastating earthquake that affected the north of the country in October 2005 was expected to have a slight impact upon the size of the budget deficit in 2005/06. However, owing to the remote and largely underdeveloped nature of the areas affected by the disaster, its economic impact was otherwise expected to be limited. The Government targeted GDP growth of 7% in 2005/06, with the State Bank of Pakistan forecasting growth of between 6.0% and 6.6%.

Education

Universal free primary education is a constitutional right, but education is not compulsory. Primary education begins at five years of age and lasts for five years. Secondary education, beginning at the age of 10, is divided into two stages, of three and four years respectively. In 2000/01 enrolment at primary schools was equivalent to 66.2% of children in the relevant age-group (82.9% of boys; 48.4% of girls), while enrolment at secondary level was equivalent to 26.4% of pupils of the relevant age (31.3% of boys; 21.3% of girls). In 2003/04 it was estimated that there were 19,794,000 children enrolled at pre-primary and primary schools (including mosque schools), and 6,119,000 at middle and secondary schools. All institutions, except missions and an increasing number of private schools, are nationalized. From 1976 agrotechnical subjects were introduced into the school curriculum, and 25 trade schools were established in that year. There are 51 universities and degree-awarding institutions. Development expenditure on science and technology and education and training in 2001/02 was projected at Rs 4,343.3m. (only 3.3% of the Government's total development spending).

Public Holidays

2006: 10 January* (Id al-Adha, Feast of the Sacrifice), 31 January* (Muharram, Islamic New Year), 9 February* (Ashoura), 23 March (Pakistan Day, proclamation of republic in 1956), 11 April* (Eid-i-Milad-un-Nabi, Birth of the Prophet), 1 May (Labour Day), 14 August (Independence Day), 6 September (Defence of Pakistan Day), 11 September (Anniversary of Death of Quaid-i-Azam), 24 September* (Ramadan begins), 24 October* (Id al-Fitr, end of Ramadan), 9 November (Allama Iqbal Day), 25 December (Birthday of Quaid-i-Azam), 31 December* (Id al-Adha, Feast of the Sacrifice).

2007: 20 January* (Muharram, Islamic New Year), 29 January* (Ashoura), 20 March* (Eid-i-Milad-un-Nabi, Birth of the Prophet), 23 March (Pakistan Day, proclamation of republic in 1956), 1 May (Labour Day), 14 August (Independence Day), 6 September (Defence of Pakistan Day), 11 September (Anniversary of Death of Quaid-i-Azam), 13 September* (Ramadan begins), 13 October* (Id al-Fitr, end of Ramadan), 9 November (Allama Iqbal Day), 20 December* (Id al-Adha, Feast of the Sacrifice), 25 December (Birthday of Quaid-i-Azam).

* These holidays are dependent on the Islamic lunar calendar and may vary by one or two days from the dates given.

Weights and Measures

The metric system has been officially introduced. Also in use are imperial and local weights, including:

1 maund = 82.28 lb (37.32 kg).
1 seer = 2.057 lb (933 grams).
1 tola = 180 grains (11.66 grams).

PAKISTAN

Statistical Survey

Sources (unless otherwise stated): Federal Bureau of Statistics, 5-SLIC Building, F-6/4, Blue Area, Islamabad; fax (51) 9203233; e-mail statpak@isb.paknet.com.pk; internet www.statpak.gov.pk/depts/index.html; State Bank of Pakistan, Karachi; internet www.sbp.org.pk.

Area and Population

AREA, POPULATION AND DENSITY*

Area (sq km)	796,095†
Population (census results)	
1 March 1981	84,253,644
2 March 1998	
Males	68,873,686
Females	63,478,593
Total	132,352,279
Population (official estimates at 1 January)	
2003	146,750,000
2004	149,650,000
2005	152,530,000
Density (per sq km) at 1 January 2005	191.6

* Excluding data for the disputed territory of Jammu and Kashmir. The Pakistani-held parts of this region are known as Azad ('Free') Kashmir, with an area of 11,639 sq km (4,494 sq miles) and a population of 1,980,000 in 1981, and Northern Areas (including Gilgit and Baltistan), with an area of 72,520 sq km (28,000 sq miles) and a population of 562,000 in 1981. Also excluded are Junagardh and Manavadar. The population figures exclude refugees from Afghanistan (estimated to number 1.1m. in early 2004).
† 307,374 sq miles.

ADMINISTRATIVE DIVISIONS
(population at 1998 census)

	Area (sq km)	Population	Density (per sq km)
Provinces:			
Balochistan	347,188	6,565,885	18.9
North-West Frontier Province	74,522	17,743,645	238.1
Punjab	205,345	73,621,290	358.5
Sindh	140,913	30,439,893	216.0
Federally Administered Tribal Areas	27,221	3,176,331	116.7
Federal Capital Territory:			
Islamabad	906	805,235	888.8
Total	796,095	132,352,279	166.3

PRINCIPAL TOWNS
(population at 1998 census)

Karachi	9,339,023	Bahawalpur	408,395
Lahore	5,143,495	Sukkur	335,551
Faisalabad		Jhang Maghiana	
(Lyallpur)	2,008,861	(Jhang Sadar)	293,366
Rawalpindi	1,409,768	Shekhupura	280,263
Multan	1,197,384	Larkana	270,283
Hyderabad	1,166,894	Gujrat	251,792
Gujranwala	1,132,509	Mardan	245,926
Peshawar	982,816	Kasur	245,321
Quetta	565,137	Rahimyar Khan	233,537
Islamabad (capital)	529,180	Sahiwal	208,778
Sargodha	458,440	Okara	201,815
Sialkot	421,502		

BIRTHS AND DEATHS
(UN estimates, annual averages)

	1990–95	1995–2000	2000–05
Birth rate (per 1,000)	38.3	33.9	31.1
Death rate (per 1,000)	9.8	9.2	8.3

Source: UN, *World Population Prospects: The 2004 Revision*.

Expectation of life (WHO estimates, years at birth): 62 (males 62; females 62) in 2003 (Source: WHO, *World Health Report*).

ECONOMICALLY ACTIVE POPULATION
(ISIC major divisions, '000 persons aged 10 years and over, excl. armed forces, at 30 June)

	2003	2004	2005
Agriculture	17,030	18,180	18,600
Mining and manufacturing	5,630	5,830	5,960
Construction	2,450	2,460	2,520
Electricity and gas distribution	330	280	290
Transport	2,390	2,420	2,480
Trade	6,010	6,250	6,390
Total employed (incl. others)	40,470	42,240	43,220
Unemployed	3,650	3,520	3,600
Total labour force	44,120	45,760	46,820

Source: Ministry of Finance, *Economic Survey, 2004/05*.

Health and Welfare

KEY INDICATORS

Total fertility rate (children per woman, 2003)	5.0
Under-5 mortality rate (per 1,000 live births, 2004)	101
HIV/AIDS (% of persons aged 15–49, 2003)	0.1
Physicians (per 1,000 head, 2001)	0.66
Hospital beds (per 1,000 head, 1993)	0.65
Health expenditure (2002): US $ per head (PPP)	62
Health expenditure (2002): % of GDP	3.2
Health expenditure (2002): public (% of total)	34.9
Access to water (% of persons, 2002)	90
Access to sanitation (% of persons, 2002)	54
Human Development Index (2003): ranking	135
Human Development Index (2003): value	0.527

For sources and definitions, see explanatory note on p. vi.

Agriculture

PRINCIPAL CROPS
('000 metric tons)

	2002	2003	2004
Wheat	18,227	19,183	19,500
Rice (paddy)	6,718	7,272	7,537
Barley	100	100	98
Maize	1,737	1,897	2,797
Millet	189	274	193
Sorghum	203	238	186
Potatoes	1,722	1,946	1,938
Other roots and tubers	439	421	435
Sugar cane	48,042	52,056	53,419
Sugar beet	317	216	250
Dry beans	168	165	148
Chick-peas	362	675	611
Other pulses*	233	233	239
Groundnuts (in shell)	90	115	77
Sunflower seed	184	278	404
Rapeseed	244	353	401
Cottonseed	3,474	3,418	4,853
Tomatoes	294	306	413
Cauliflower	201	200	205
Pumpkins, squash and gourds	245	242	245
Dry onions	1,385	1,427	1,449
Carrots	195	215	232
Okra	103	100	107
Other vegetables	1,458	1,454	1,451
Watermelons†	396	376	386
Cantaloupes and other melons†	265	252	258
Bananas	143	175	148
Oranges†	1,190	1,232	1,169

PAKISTAN

—continued	2002	2003	2004
Tangerines, mandarins, clementines and satsumas†	443	458	434
Lemons and limes†	68	70	67
Apples	315	334	352
Apricots	130	211	215
Peaches and nectarines	76	76	70
Plums	66	64	61
Mangoes	1,037	1,035	1,056
Dates	625	427	622
Other fruits*	968	914	927
Pimento and allspice	99	96	90
Other spices*	42	44	43
Cotton (lint)	1,737	1,709	2,427
Tobacco (leaves)	95	88	86

*FAO estimates.
† Unofficial figures.
Source: FAO.

LIVESTOCK
('000 head, year ending September)

	2002	2003	2004
Cattle	22,858	23,303	23,800
Buffaloes	24,030	24,800	25,500
Sheep	24,398	24,566	24,700
Goats	50,917	52,763	54,700
Horses	318	317	300
Asses	3,966	4,640	4,100
Mules	202	218	200
Camels	758	751	800*
Chickens*	153,000	155,000	160,000
Ducks*	3,500	3,500	3,500

*FAO estimate(s).
Source: FAO.

LIVESTOCK PRODUCTS
('000 metric tons)

	2002	2003	2004
Beef and veal	431	441	451
Buffalo meat	494	508	524
Mutton and lamb	159	161	162
Goat meat	333	345	357
Poultry meat	359.7	376.7	406.7
Other meat*	15.9	15.9	15.9
Cows' milk	8,350	8,620	8,840
Buffaloes' milk	18,022	18,617	19,240
Sheep's milk	31	31	32
Goats' milk	629	652	658
Ghee*	525.3	542.7	560.8
Hen eggs†	360.9	369.4	381.0
Other poultry eggs*	7.2	7.2	7.2
Wool: greasy	39.4	39.7	40.0
Wool: scoured†	23.7	23.9	24.0
Cattle hides*	85.1	87.4	93.6
Buffalo hides*	73.5	77.0	78.8
Sheepskins*	40.7	41.2	41.2
Goatskins*	107.9	111.4	120.0

*FAO estimates.
† Unofficial figures.
Source: FAO.

Forestry

ROUNDWOOD REMOVALS
(FAO estimates, '000 cubic metres, excl. bark)

	2002	2003	2004
Sawlogs, veneer logs and logs for sleepers	1,892	1,892	1,892
Other industrial wood	787	787	787
Fuel wood	25,013	25,304	25,599
Total	**27,692**	**27,983**	**28,278**

Source: FAO.

SAWNWOOD PRODUCTION
('000 cubic metres, incl. railway sleepers)

	1999	2000	2001
Coniferous (softwood)	410	415	435
Broadleaved (hardwood)	665	672	745
Total	**1,075**	**1,087**	**1,180**

2002–04: Production assumed to be unchanged from 2001 (FAO estimates).
Source: FAO.

Fishing

('000 metric tons, live weight)

	2001	2002	2003
Capture	600.8	599.1	564.7
Freshwater fishes	180.1	181.0	165.7
Sea catfishes	38.2	38.5	30.4
Croakers and drums	21.7	22.9	19.7
Largehead hairtail	27.4	28.4	25.7
Indian oil sardine	31.2	31.6	32.9
Other clupeoids	26.9	27.2	25.8
Carangids	33.1	34.0	50.7
Requiem sharks	26.5	27.0	18.7
Skates, rays and mantas	20.8	20.9	13.7
Aquaculture	16.4	12.4	12.1
Total catch	**617.2**	**611.5**	**576.8**

Source: FAO.

Mining

('000 metric tons, unless otherwise indicated, year ending 30 June)

	2001/02	2002/03	2003/04
Barytes (metric tons)	20,629	n.a.	n.a.
Chromite (metric tons)	34,185	22,604	29,230
Limestone	10,820	11,880	13,150
Gypsum	402	420	467
Fireclay (metric tons)	171,056	n.a.	n.a.
Silica sand	162	185	259
Rock salt	1,423	1,412	1,639
Coal and lignite	3,512	3,609	3,325
Crude petroleum ('000 barrels)	23,195	23,457	22,624
Natural gas (million cu ft)	923,758	992,653	1,202,748

Industry

SELECTED PRODUCTS
('000 metric tons, unless otherwise indicated, year ending 30 June)

	2002/03	2003/04	2004/05
Cotton cloth (million sq m)	582.2	683.4	899.0
Cotton yarn	1,915.2	1,929.1	2,111.1
Jute goods	94	102*	n.a.
Refined sugar	3,685.9	4,020.8	n.a.
Vegetable ghee	771.5	888.0	916.8
Cement	10,845	12,862	15,038
Urea	4,401.9	4,431.6	4,606.4
Superphosphate	147.2	167.7	163.1
Sulphuric acid	56.0	64.7	92.4
Soda ash	280.5	286.5	297.7
Caustic soda	164.4	187.5	206.7
Chlorine gas	15.9	17.2	19.1
Cigarettes ('000 million)	49.4	55.4	61.1
Beverages (million bottles)	2,289	2,691*	n.a.
Ammonium nitrate	335.3	350.4	329.9
Nitrophosphate	304.9	363.5	338.9
Pig-iron	1,140.2	1,180.0	1,137.2
Paper and paperboard	376.2	404.7	419.8
Tractors ('000)	26.5	36.1	43.7
Bicycles ('000)	629.7	664.1	587.9
Motor tyres and tubes ('000)	1,698	1,889	2,060
Bicycle tyres and tubes ('000)	14,272	12,898	14,511
Electric energy (million kWh)	75,682	78,290	n.a.

* Provisional figure.

Finance

CURRENCY AND EXCHANGE RATES

Monetary Units
100 paisa = 1 Pakistani rupee.

Sterling, Dollar and Euro Equivalents (30 December 2005)
£1 sterling = 103.02 rupees;
US $1 = 59.83 rupees;
€1 = 70.58 rupees;
1,000 Pakistani rupees = £9.71 = $16.71 = €14.17.

Average Exchange Rate (Pakistani rupees per US $)
2003   57.752
2004   58.258
2005   59.515

CENTRAL GOVERNMENT BUDGET
(million rupees, year ending 30 June)

Revenue	2003/04*	2004/05*	2005/06†
Tax revenue	510,000	590,000	690,000
Income and corporate taxes‡	154,638	175,400	205,900
Other direct taxes	6,862	7,300	9,500
Excise duty	43,500	54,400	59,400
Sales tax‡	218,400	239,000	294,000
Taxes on international trade	86,600	113,900	121,200
Non-tax revenue	180,875	249,017	194,762
Surcharges‡	70,108	36,289	42,638
Total	760,983	875,306	927,400

Expenditure	2003/04*	2004/05*	2005/06†
Current expenditure	714,019	784,680	826,503
General public service	448,430	468,974	503,114
Debt-servicing	317,723	274,717	301,354
Defence‡	180,537	216,258	223,501
Economic affairs	54,758	62,172	56,449
Development expenditure	59,146	82,091	134,593
Capital expenditure	125,348	119,672	132,550
Adjustment	—	14,563	—
Total	898,513	1,001,006	1,093,645

* Revised estimates.
† Budget estimates.
‡ Exclusively federal.

PLANNED DEVELOPMENT EXPENDITURE
(million rupees, year ending 30 June)

	1999/2000*	2000/01†	2001/02†
Sectoral programme:			
Agriculture (incl. subsidy for fertilizers)	329.1	329.2	665.2
Water	11,298.9	10,077.9	} 8,957.7
Power	2,963.0	2,682.5	
Industry	260.1	692.3	364.0
Fuels	1,170.0	2,238.7	—
Minerals	38.0	8.1	—
Transport and communication	3,188.2	4,057.1	754.3
Physical planning and housing	13,274.7	1,748.5	221.4
Science and technology and education and training	7,129.2	4,064.6	4,343.3
Social welfare, culture, tourism, sport and manpower and employment	457.8	263.6	381.5
Health	2,566.4	2,841.4	2,547.5
Population planning	2,200.0	2,200.0	1,800.0
Rural development	117.2	2,419.8	—
Mass media	126.0	126.9	207.3
Special programmes	3,500.0	—	20,170.0
Corporation	—	—	26,678.3
Provincial Development Programme	—	—	30,000.0
Provincial Social Action Programme Tied Allocation	—	—	11,000.0
Total planned development expenditure (incl. others)	116,296.6	120,432.5	130,000.0

* Revised estimates.
† Provisional figures.

Source: Ministry of Finance.

INTERNATIONAL RESERVES
(US $ million, last Thursday of the year)

	2002	2003	2004
Gold*	684	733	817
IMF special drawing rights	2	248	245
Foreign exchange	8,076	10,693	9,554
Total	8,762	11,674	10,616

* Revalued annually, in June, on the basis of London market prices.

Source: IMF, *International Financial Statistics*.

MONEY SUPPLY
(million rupees, last Thursday of the year)

	2002	2003	2004
Currency outside banks	487,745	567,519	655,287
Demand deposits at scheduled banks	628,531	816,587	1,026,569
Total money*	1,118,403	1,387,601	1,687,355

* Including also private-sector deposits at the State Bank.

Source: IMF, *International Financial Statistics*.

PAKISTAN

COST OF LIVING
(Consumer Price Index; base: 2000/01 = 100; year ending 30 June)

	2002/03	2003/04	2004/05
Food, beverages and tobacco	105.4	111.7	125.7
Clothing and footwear	106.8	109.7	113.0
Rent	103.5	102.2	120.4
Fuel and lighting	117.8	121.3	125.8
All items (incl. others)	106.8	111.6	122.0

NATIONAL ACCOUNTS
(million rupees at current prices, year ending 30 June)

Expenditure on the Gross Domestic Product

	2002/03	2003/04	2004/05*
Government final consumption expenditure	428,689	462,462	512,926
Private final consumption expenditure	3,548,157	4,052,901	5,235,382
Increase in stocks	80,629	94,294	103,299
Gross fixed capital formation	736,433	864,701	999,306
Total domestic expenditure	4,793,908	5,474,358	6,850,913
Exports of goods and services	815,158	883,704	1,001,011
Less Imports of goods and services	786,224	825,399	1,304,334
Gross domestic product (GDP) in market prices	4,822,842	5,532,663	6,547,590
GDP at constant 1999/2000 prices	4,185,824	4,453,085	4,799,723

* Provisional figures.

Gross Domestic Product by Economic Activity

	2002/03	2003/04	2004/05*
Agriculture and livestock	1,013,543	1,101,555	1,269,800
Forestry and fishing	45,773	47,574	52,841
Mining and quarrying	84,238	107,990	121,836
Manufacturing	725,434	902,870	1,118,391
Electricity and gas distribution	120,556	150,707	156,301
Construction	100,880	120,487	143,916
Wholesale and retail trade	785,776	922,667	1,107,296
Transport, storage and communications	609,929	699,782	902,247
Banking and insurance	144,989	158,476	210,683
Ownership of dwellings	135,139	146,293	165,456
Public administration and defence	285,854	312,105	337,560
Community, social and personal services	429,301	472,104	543,349
GDP at factor cost	4,481,412	5,142,610	6,129,676
Indirect taxes	403,221	455,549	501,470
Less Subsidies	61,791	65,496	83,556
GDP in market prices	4,822,842	5,532,663	6,547,590

* Provisional figures.

BALANCE OF PAYMENTS
(US $ million)

	2002	2003	2004
Exports of goods f.o.b.	9,832	11,869	13,352
Imports of goods f.o.b.	−10,428	−11,978	−16,735
Trade balance	−596	−109	−3,382
Exports of services	2,429	2,968	2,726
Imports of services	−2,241	−3,294	−5,322
Balance on goods and services	−408	−435	−5,978
Other income received	128	178	220
Other income paid	−2,414	−2,404	−2,582
Balance on goods, services and income	−2,694	−2,659	−8,340
Current transfers received	6,593	6,300	7,672
Current transfers paid	−45	−68	−140

—continued	2002	2003	2004
Current balance	3,854	3,573	−808
Capital account (net)	40	1,138	597
Direct investment abroad	−28	−19	−56
Direct investment from abroad	823	534	1,119
Portfolio investment assets	—	−2	9
Portfolio investment liabilities	−567	−119	393
Other investment assets	−64	−542	−1,338
Other investment liabilities	−948	−1,603	−1,855
Net errors and omissions	974	−52	585
Overall balance	4,084	2,908	−1,355

Source: IMF, *International Financial Statistics*.

OFFICIAL DEVELOPMENT ASSISTANCE
(US $ million)

	1998	1999	2000
Bilateral donors	531.0	435.9	476.0
Multilateral donors	522.0	297.2	226.8
Total	1,053.0	733.1	702.8
Grants	294.1	296.9	206.5
Loans	758.9	436.2	496.3
Per caput assistance (US $)	7.9	5.4	5.0

Source: UN, *Statistical Yearbook for Asia and the Pacific*.

External Trade

Note: Data exclude trade in military goods.

PRINCIPAL COMMODITIES
(US $ million, year ending 30 June)

Imports c.i.f. (excl. re-imports)	1999/2000	2000/01	2001/02
Food and live animals	804.4	901.3	525.2
Crude materials (inedible) except fuels	719.0	635.9	847.8
Mineral fuels, lubricants, etc.	2,873.1	3,395.3	2,869.0
Petroleum, petroleum products, etc.	2,804.4	3,347.3	2,809.5
Animal and vegetable oils, fats and waxes	503.2	432.3	474.1
Fixed vegetable fats and oils	436.1	377.3	411.1
Chemicals and related products	1,997.2	1,903.9	1,871.0
Organic chemicals	593.9	652.8	600.5
Basic manufactures	855.7	883.5	993.1
Iron and steel	304.5	279.0	336.7
Machinery and transport equipment	1,997.7	2,073.4	2,201.9
Machinery specialized for particular industries	595.3	689.6	707.7
Road vehicles and parts (excl. tyres, engines and electrical parts)	345.5	320.6	329.2
Total (incl. others)	10,309.4	10,728.9	10,339.6

PAKISTAN

Statistical Survey

Exports f.o.b. (excl. re-exports)	1999/2000	2000/01	2001/02
Food and live animals	919.8	913.5	947.3
Rice	539.7	527.9	447.8
Crude materials (inedible) except fuels	210.9	283.7	152.1
Basic manufactures	4,628.5	4,852.4	4,832.4
Leather, leather manufactures and dressed furskins	183.8	247.5	250.5
Textile yarn, fabrics, etc.	4,383.7	4,532.2	4,502.7
Miscellaneous manufactured articles	2,550.7	2,720.5	2,770.3
Clothing and accessories (excl. footwear)	1,988.4	2,150.1	2,097.9
Total (incl. others)	8,568.6	9,201.6	9,134.6

2002/03: *Imports (excl. re-imports):* Vegetable products 665.5; Animal or vegetable fats and oil products 667.8; Mineral products 3,230.2 (Mineral fuels and oils and products thereof 3,150.7); Products of the chemical or allied industries 1,801.3 (Organic chemicals 823.1); Plastics, rubber and articles thereof 599.9 (Plastics and articles thereof 448.3); Textiles and textile articles 611.0; Total (incl. others) 12,220.3. *Exports (excl. re-exports):* Vegetable products 954.8 (Cereals 689.2); Raw hides and skins, leather and furskins, etc. 693.1 (Articles of leather, etc. 458.2); Textiles and textile articles 7,794.5 (Cotton 2,351.3; Man-made filaments 602.5; Articles of apparel and clothing accessories, knitted or crocheted 1,152.7; Articles of apparel and clothing accessories, not knitted or crocheted 1,086.6; Miscellaneous made up articles and rags 2,201.8); Total (incl. others) 11,160.3.

2003/04: *Imports (excl. re-imports):* Vegetable products 692.2; Animal or vegetable fats and oil products 768.3; Mineral products 3,426.8 (Mineral fuels and oils and products thereof 3,328.2); Products of the chemical or allied industries 2,300.9 (Organic chemicals 1,065.8); Plastics, rubber and articles thereof 767.6 (Plastics and articles thereof 583.1); Textiles and textile articles 1,010.5; Base metals and articles thereof 945.9; Machinery and mechanical appliances, electrical equipment and parts thereof 2,674.8 (Nuclear reactors, boilers, machinery and mechanical appliances 1,814.8); Vehicles, aircrafts, vessels and associated transport equipment 1,538.2; Total (incl. others) 15,591.8. *Exports (excl. re-exports):* Vegetable products 912.7 (Cereals 640.8); Raw hides and skins, leather and furskins, etc. 732.3 (Articles of leather, etc. 479.7); Textiles and textile articles 8,643.2 (Cotton 2,919.4; Man-made filaments 454.8; Articles of apparel and clothing accessories, knitted or crocheted 1,461.6; Articles of apparel and clothing accessories, not knitted or crocheted 990.4; Miscellaneous made up articles and rags 2,351.5); Total (incl. others) 12,313.3.

Note: Beginning in 2002/03, data are compiled in accordance with a new system of classification, and data for individual commodity groupings may not be comparable with previous years as a result.

PRINCIPAL TRADING PARTNERS
(million rupees, year ending 30 June)

Imports c.i.f. (excl. re-imports)	2002/03	2003/04	2004/05
Australia	11,167.5	17,699.9	33,268.6
Belgium	17,272.2	15,078.7	10,492.9
Canada	7,080.6	11,824.0	11,671.8
China, People's Repub.	49,046.6	66,423.1	109,381.0
France	9,475.5	9,245.2	14,239.0
Germany	32,883.5	18,002.2	50,286.4
Hong Kong	9,184.4	8,416.2	5,619.2
India	9,737.4	22,003.8	32,487.5
Indonesia	15,083.3	20,592.9	34,129.8
Iran	17,691.9	16,349.1	14,374.6
Italy	15,070.2	35,227.3	21,597.3
Japan	47,012.0	53,913.0	86,045.6
Korea, Republic	19,704.7	21,909.5	32,932.8
Kuwait	47,107.6	57,061.9	55,810.4
Malaysia	33,144.6	34,697.0	40,266.0
Netherlands	11,334.0	12,686.0	8,717.7
Saudi Arabia	76,192.5	102,437.0	147,166.5
Singapore	24,935.9	28,291.6	22,172.1
Switzerland	11,072.1	19,013.1	24,155.5
Thailand	13,329.2	15,498.6	24,571.1
Turkey	7,356.5	4,481.5	6,108.5
United Arab Emirates	88,250.3	98,391.8	101,053.7
United Kingdom	20,821.2	25,228.4	31,601.7
USA	42,985.2	76,513.2	92,812.5
Total (incl. others)	714,371.9	897,824.6	1,223,080.0

Exports f.o.b. (excl. re-exports)	2002/03	2003/04	2004/05
Afghanistan	18,380.1	28,393.5	44,320.9
Australia	7,033.9	7,494.1	6,600.3
Bangladesh	6,675.9	11,225.8	12,226.3
Belgium	14,018.5	15,108.7	18,566.8
Canada	12,047.1	10,459.5	11,494.1
China, People's Republic	14,306.5	16,588.3	20,975.6
France	17,028.1	19,502.0	21,794.1
Germany	33,866.7	34,927.4	40,798.7
Hong Kong	30,216.4	33,511.1	33,120.6
Italy	19,919.9	26,147.0	34,835.7
Japan	8,311.7	7,758.9	9,742.7
Korea, Republic	12,831.9	11,625.2	10,965.6
Netherlands	16,768.2	19,296.0	20,053.8
Saudi Arabia	27,844.8	20,071.5	20,782.5
Spain	13,365.9	17,355.6	20,196.3
Turkey	8,538.0	12,598.2	15,321.8
United Arab Emirates	60,647.1	54,308.8	65,054.0
United Kingdom	46,074.5	54,173.6	52,992.9
USA	153,061.3	169,512.0	204,214.4
Total (incl. others)	652,293.8	709,036.1	854,087.8

Transport

RAILWAYS
(year ending 30 June)

	2001/02	2002/03	2003/04
Passenger journeys ('000)	69,000	72,400	75,700
Passenger-km (million)	20,783	22,306	23,045
Freight ('000 metric tons)	5,900	6,180	6,140
Net freight ton-km (million)	4,573	4,820	4,796

Source: Ministry of Finance, *Economic Survey, 2004/05*.

ROAD TRAFFIC
('000 vehicles in use, year ending 30 June)

	2001/02	2002/03	2003/04
Motorcycles and scooters	2,481.1	2,656.2	2,882.5
Passenger cars	1,040.0	1,109.6	1,193.1
Jeeps	43.4	44.4	47.8
Station wagons	122.7	126.4	132.4
Road tractors	630.5	663.2	722.7
Buses	96.6	98.3	100.4
Taxicabs	96.4	104.1	112.6
Rickshaws	80.8	80.9	81.0
Delivery vans and pick-ups	195.2	200.9	205.7
Trucks and tankers	153.7	155.2	157.7

Source: Ministry of Finance, *Economic Survey, 2004/05*.

SHIPPING

Merchant Fleet
(displacement at 31 December)

	2002	2003	2004
Number of vessels	49	50	49
Total displacement ('000 grt)	247.4	321.7	300.7

Source: Lloyd's Register-Fairplay, *World Fleet Statistics*.

International Sea-borne Shipping
(port of Karachi, year ending 30 June)

	2001/02	2002/03	2003/04
Goods ('000 long tons):			
loaded	6,362	6,273	6,081
unloaded	20,330	19,609	21,732

Source: Ministry of Finance, *Economic Survey, 2004/05*.

PAKISTAN

CIVIL AVIATION
(PIA only, domestic and international flights, '000, year ending 30 June)

	2001/02	2002/03	2003/04
Kilometres flown	62,974	63,863	67,164
Passengers carried	4,290	4,391	4,700
Passenger-km ('000)	10,843	11,276	12,808

Source: Ministry of Finance, *Economic Survey, 2004/05*.

Tourism

FOREIGN TOURIST ARRIVALS

Country of nationality	2001	2002	2003
Afghanistan	46,994	98,498	119,368
Canada	11,813	18,150	12,486
China, People's Republic	5,704	8,896	10,055
Germany	9,047	12,243	13,216
India	58,378	2,618	3,380
Japan	7,580	9,975	9,094
United Kingdom	144,408	151,341	128,428
USA	69,067	69,030	65,845
Total (incl. others)	499,719	498,059	479,052

Receipts from tourism (US $ million, incl. passenger transport): 533 in 2001; 562 in 2002; 618 in 2003.

Source: World Tourism Organization.

Communications Media

	2001	2002	2003
Television receivers (number in use)*	3,432,369	3,603,986	3,721,390
Telephones ('000 main lines in use)	3,252.0	3,655.5	3,982.8
Mobile cellular telephones ('000 subscribers)	812.0	1,238.6	2,624.8
Personal computers ('000 in use)	600	n.a.	n.a.
Internet users ('000)	500	1,500	n.a.
Daily newspapers:			
number	168	169	204
average circulation	5,726,494	6,009,135	6,245,775
Other newspapers and periodicals:			
number	595	551	741
average circulation	1,862,642	1,967,042	2,004,860

Radio receivers ('000 in use): 13,500 in 1997.

Facsimile machines ('000 in use): 268 in 1998.

2004: Mobile cellular telephones ('000 in use) 5,020.0; Internet users ('000) 2,000; Telephones ('000 main lines in use) 4,880.0.

* Estimates as at 30 June; includes Azad Kashmir and Northern Areas.

Sources: partly UNESCO, *Statistical Yearbook*; International Telecommunication Union.

Education

(2003/04)

	Institutions	Teachers	Students
Primary*	154,970	432,222	19,794,000†
Middle	28,728	239,351	4,319,000†
Secondary	16,100†	276,900†	1,800,000†
of which secondary vocational institutes	636	8,535	23,000†
Teacher training (pre-degree level)‡	103	1,686	9,587
Higher:			
arts and science colleges	964	27,911	802,000†
professional§	382	9,841	163,852
universities/degree-awarding institutes	51	11,404	218,275

* Including mosque schools.
† Rounded figure.
‡ 2001/02 figure.
§ 2002/03 figure.

Adult literacy rate (UNESCO estimates): 48.7% (males 61.7%; females 35.2%) in 2003 (Source: UN Development Programme, *Human Development Report*).

Directory

The Constitution

The Constitution was promulgated on 10 April 1973, and amended on a number of subsequent occasions (see Amendments, below). Several provisions were suspended following the imposition of martial law in 1977. The (amended) Constitution was restored on 30 December 1985. The Constitution was placed in abeyance on 15 October 1999 following the overthrow of the Government in a military coup. The Constitution, incorporating a Legal Framework Order, was revived on 15 November 2002.

GENERAL PROVISIONS

The Preamble upholds the principles of democracy, freedom, equality, tolerance and social justice as enunciated by Islam. The rights of religious and other minorities are guaranteed.

The Islamic Republic of Pakistan consists of four provinces—Balochistan, North-West Frontier Province, Punjab and Sindh—and the tribal areas under federal administration. The provinces are autonomous units.

Fundamental rights are guaranteed and include equality of status (women have equal rights with men), freedom of thought, speech, worship and the press and freedom of assembly and association. No law providing for preventive detention shall be made except to deal with persons acting against the integrity, security or defence of Pakistan. No such law shall authorize the detention of a person for more than one month.

PRESIDENT

The President is Head of State and acts on the advice of the Prime Minister. He is elected by an electoral college, comprising the two chambers of the Federal Legislature and the four Provincial Assemblies, to serve for a term of five years. He must be a Muslim. The President may be impeached for violating the Constitution or gross misconduct.

FEDERAL LEGISLATURE

The Federal Legislature consists of the President, a lower and an upper house. The lower house, called the National Assembly, has 207 members elected directly for a term of five years, on the basis of universal suffrage (for adults over the age of 21 years), plus 10 members representing minorities. The upper house, called the Senate, has 87 members who serve for six years, with one-half retiring every three years. Each Provincial Assembly is to elect 19 Senators. The tribal areas are to return eight members and the remaining three are to be elected from the Federal Capital Territory by members of the Provincial Assemblies.

There shall be two sessions of the National Assembly and Senate each year, with not more than 120 days between the last sitting of a session and the first sitting of the next session.

The role of the Senate in an overwhelming majority of the subjects shall be merely advisory. Disagreeing with any legislation of the National Assembly, it shall have the right to send it back only once for reconsideration. In case of disagreement in other subjects, the Senate and National Assembly shall sit in a joint session to decide the matter by a simple majority.

GOVERNMENT

The Constitution provides that bills may originate in either house, except money bills. The latter must originate in the National Assembly and cannot go to the Senate. A bill must be passed by both houses and then approved by the President, who may return the bill and suggest amendments. In this case, after the bill has been reconsidered and passed, with or without amendment, the President must give his assent to it.

PROVINCIAL GOVERNMENT

In the matter of relations between Federation and Provinces, the Federal Legislature shall have the power to make laws, including laws bearing on extra-territorial affairs, for the whole or any part of Pakistan, while a Provincial Assembly shall be empowered to make laws for that Province or any part of it. Matters in the Federal Legislative List shall be subject to the exclusive authority of the Federal Legislature, while the Federal Legislature and a Provincial Assembly shall have power to legislate with regard to matters referred to in the Concurrent Legislative List. Any matter not referred to in either list may be subject to laws made by a Provincial Assembly alone, and not by the Federal Legislature, although the latter shall have exclusive power to legislate with regard to matters not referred to in either list for those areas in the Federation not included in any Province.

Four provisions seek to ensure the stability of the parliamentary system. First, the Prime Minister shall be elected by the National Assembly and he and the other Ministers shall be responsible to it. Secondly, any resolution calling for the removal of a Prime Minister shall have to name his successor in the same resolution, which shall be adopted by not less than two-thirds of the total number of members of the lower house. The requirement of a two-thirds' majority is to remain in force for 15 years or three electoral terms, whichever is more. Thirdly, the Prime Minister shall have the right to seek dissolution of the legislature at any time even during the pendency of a no-confidence motion. Fourthly, if a no-confidence motion is defeated, such a motion shall not come up before the house for the next six months.

All these provisions for stability shall apply *mutatis mutandis* to the Provincial Assemblies also.

A National Economic Council, to include the Prime Minister and a representative from each province, shall advise the Provincial and Federal Governments.

There shall be a Governor for each Province, appointed by the President, and a Council of Ministers to aid and advise him, with a Chief Minister appointed by the Governor. Each Province has a provincial legislature consisting of the Governor and Provincial Assembly.

The executive authorities of every Province shall be required to ensure that their actions are in compliance with the Federal laws which apply in that Province. The Federation shall be required to consider the interests of each Province in the exercise of its authority in that Province. The Federation shall further be required to afford every Province protection from external aggression and internal disturbance, and to ensure that every Province is governed in accordance with the provisions of the Constitution.

To further safeguard the rights of the smaller provinces, a Council of Common Interests has been created. Comprising the Chief Ministers of the four provinces and four Central Ministers to decide upon specified matters of common interest, the Council is responsible to the Federal Legislature. The constitutional formula gives the net proceeds of excise duty and royalty on gas to the province concerned. The profits on hydroelectric power generated in each province shall go to that province.

OTHER PROVISIONS

Other provisions include the procedure for elections, the setting up of an Advisory Council of Islamic Ideology and an Islamic Research Institute, and the administration of tribal areas.

AMENDMENTS

Amendments to the Constitution shall require a two-thirds' majority in the National Assembly and the Senate.

In 1975 the Constitution (Third Amendment) Bill abolished the provision that a State of Emergency may not be extended beyond six months without the approval of the National Assembly and empowered the Government to detain a person for three months instead of one month.

In July 1977, following the imposition of martial law, several provisions, including all fundamental rights provided for in the Constitution, were suspended.

An amendment of September 1978 provided for separate electoral registers to be drawn up for Muslims and non-Muslims.

In October 1979 a martial law order inserted a clause in the Constitution establishing the supremacy of military courts in trying all offences, criminal and otherwise.

On 26 May 1980, the President issued a Constitution Amendment Order, which amended Article 199, debarring High Courts from making any order relating to the validity of effect of any judgment or sentence passed by a military court or tribunal granting an injunction; from making an order or entering any proceedings in respect of matters under the jurisdiction or cognizance of a military court or tribunal, and from initiating proceedings against the Chief Martial Law Administrator or a Martial Law Administrator.

By another amendment of the Constitution, the Federal Shari'a Court was to replace the Shari'a Benches of the High Courts. The Shari'a Court, on the petition of a citizen or the Government, may decide whether any law or provision of law is contrary to the injunction of Islam as laid down in the Holy Koran and the Sunnah of the Holy Prophet.

In March 1981 the Government promulgated Provisional Constitution Order 1981, whereby provision is made for the appointment of one or more Vice-Presidents, to be appointed by the Chief Martial Law Administrator, and a Federal Advisory Council (*Majlis-i-Shura*) consisting of persons nominated by the President. All political parties not registered with the Election Commission on 13 September 1979 were to be dissolved and their properties made forfeit to the Federal Council. Any party working against the ideology, sovereignty or security of Pakistan may be dissolved by the President.

The proclamation of July 1977, imposing martial law, and subsequent orders amending the Constitution and further martial law regulations shall not be questioned by any court on any grounds.

All Chief Justices and Judges shall take a new oath of office. New High Court benches for the interior of the provinces shall be set up and retired judges are debarred from holding office in Pakistan for two years. The powers of the High Courts shall be limited for suspending the operation of an order for the detention of any person under any law providing for preventative detention, or release of any person on bail, arrested under the same law.

The Advisory Council of Islamic Ideology, which was asked by the Government to suggest procedures for the election and further Islamization of the Constitution, recommended non-party elections, separate electorates, Islamic qualifications for candidates and a federal structure with greater devolution of power by changing the present divisions into provinces.

Under the Wafaqi Mohtasib Order 1982, the President appointed a Wafaqi Mohtasib (Federal Ombudsman) to redress injustice committed by any government agency.

In March 1985 the President, Gen. Zia ul-Haq, promulgated the Revival of the 1973 Constitution Order, which increased the power of the President by amendments such as those establishing a National Security Council, powers to dismiss the Prime Minister, the Cabinet and provincial Chief Ministers, to appoint judicial and military chiefs, and to call elections, and indemnity clauses to ensure the power of the President. The Constitution was then revived with the exception of 28 key provisions relating to treason, subversion, fundamental rights and jurisdiction of the Supreme Court. In October 1985 the Constitution (Eighth Amendment) Bill became law, incorporating most of the provisions of the Revival of the 1973 Constitution Order and indemnifying all actions of the military regime. In December the enactment of the Political Parties (Amendment) Bill allowed political parties to function under stringent conditions (these conditions were eased in 1988). In December Gen. Zia lifted martial law and restored the remainder of the Constitution.

In March 1987 the Constitution (Tenth Amendment) Bill reduced the minimum number of working days of the National Assembly from 160 days to 130 days.

In April 1997 the Constitution (Thirteenth Amendment) Bill repealed the main components of the Eighth Constitutional Amendment, thus divesting the President of the power to appoint and dismiss the Prime Minister and Cabinet, to dissolve the legislature, to order a national referendum, and to appoint provincial Governors, the Chairman of the Joint Chiefs of Staff and the three armed forces chiefs (these functions and appointments were, in future, to be carried out subject to a mandatory advice from the Prime Minister).

PAKISTAN

In October 1998 the Constitution (Fifteenth Amendment) Bill replaced the country's existing legal code with full *Shari'a*; the bill remained to be ratified by the Senate.

Following the overthrow of the Government in a military coup on 12 October 1999, the Constitution was placed in abeyance on 15 October. On the same day a Provisional Constitution Order was promulgated, according to which executive power was transferred to a National Security Council, under the leadership of a Chief Executive. A federal Cabinet, which was to aid and advise the Chief Executive in the exercise of his functions, was to be appointed by the President on the advice of the Chief Executive. The President was to act on, and in accordance with, the advice of the Chief Executive. The National Assembly, Senate and the Provincial Assemblies were suspended and the Chairman and Deputy Chairman of the Senate ceased to hold office.

In July 2000 the Chief Executive issued a decree to revive the Islamic principles of the suspended Constitution and to incorporate them in the Provisional Constitution Order.

On 20 June 2001 the Proclamation of Emergency (Amendment) Order 2001 was promulgated, according to which the Chief Executive assumed the office of President of Pakistan. The National Assembly, Senate and Provincial Assemblies were dissolved with immediate effect. The Speaker and Deputy Speaker of the National Assembly and Provincial Assemblies ceased to hold office with immediate effect. The President later announced that elections to federal and provincial legislatures would be held on 10 October 2002 (see Recent History).

On 21 August 2002 the Legal Framework Order 2002 was promulgated, which sanctioned the President's 29 amendments to the Constitution, including the restoration of Article 58 (2-B), which authorized the President to dissolve the National Assembly (the article was also amended to allow the President to appoint provincial governors in consultation with the Prime Minister), the restoration of Article 243, which gave the President power to appoint the Chairman of the Joint Chiefs of Staff Committee and the three armed forces chiefs and the power to establish the National Security Council to provide consultation to the elected government on strategic matters. Other amendments included the extension of the President's term in office and role as Chief of Army Staff for five years from the date of the election (10 October 2002). The terms of the National Assembly and Senate were to be decreased to four and five years, respectively, and the number of seats in each house to be increased to 342 and 100, respectively. Part III of the Legal Framework Order sanctioned an amendment to Article 71: a Mediation Committee would be established in instances where the Senate disagrees with legislation of the National Assembly, or vice versa. The Mediation Committee would formulate an agreed item of legislation and place it separately before each house for consideration. According to the amendments, the Prime Minister would continue to have the right to seek dissolution of the legislature at any time, but not during the pendency of a no-confidence motion. Ten Orders endorsed by Musharraf since the establishment of military rule were placed in 'Schedule Six', and therefore could not be altered, repealed or amended without the approval of the President. Constitutional protection was thereby awarded to the offices of the National Accountability Bureau and the Governor of the State Bank of Pakistan. Other provisions granted constitutional protection included the lowering of the voting age from 21 to 18, the Political Parties' Order, the Local Government Ordinances and the autonomy of the Election Commission. The 1973 Constitution, incorporating the Legal Framework Order, was revived on 15 November 2002.

In late December 2003 the legislature passed the Constitution (Seventeenth Amendment) Bill, comprising several amendments to the 2002 Legal Framework Order (in passing this Bill the legislature also endorsed for the first time the validity of the Legal Framework Order). The Bill allowed the President to remain as Chief of Army Staff until 31 December 2004, when he would have to relinquish his military role. The President also retained the right to dissolve the legislature (on the recommendation of the Prime Minister); the matter would then have to be referred to the Supreme Court within 15 days. The Bill endorsed the lowering of the minimum national voting age to 18, and accepted the revised composition of the Senate, National Assembly and provincial assemblies, and clauses relating to political parties.

In April 2004 the legislature approved the National Security Council Bill. This enabled the formation, under the protection of the Constitution, of the National Security Council, a 13-member council chaired by the President and composed of nine civilian politicians and four members of the military. The Council was to serve as a forum for consultation with the Government on matters of national security. Critics protested that the Bill institutionalized the role of the military in national government.

Directory

The Government

HEAD OF STATE

President: Gen. PERVEZ MUSHARRAF (sworn in 20 June 2001).

CABINET
(May 2006)

Prime Minister and Minister of Finance and Revenue, Economic Affairs and Statistics: SHAUKAT AZIZ.
Minister of Defence: RAO SIKANDER IQBAL.
Minister of Commerce: HUMAYUN AKHTAR KHAN.
Minister of Culture: Dr GHAZI GULAB JAMAL.
Minister of Defence Production: Maj. (retd) HABIBULLAH WARRAICH.
Minister of Education: Lt-Gen. (retd) JAVED ASHRAF KAZI.
Minister of the Environment: MAKHDOOM SYED FAISAL SALEH HAYAT.
Minister of Food, Agriculture, Co-operatives and Livestock: SAIKANDAR HAYAT KHAN BOSAN.
Minister of Foreign Affairs: Mian KHURSHID MEHMOUD KASURI.
Minister of Health: MOHAMMAD NASIR KHAN.
Minister of Industries and Production: JEHANGIR KHAN TAREEN.
Minister of Information and Broadcasting: MUHAMMAD ALI DURRANI.
Minister of Housing and Works: SYED SAFWANULLAH.
Minister of Information Technology and Telecommunications: AWAIS AHMAD KHAN LEGHARI.
Minister of the Interior: AFTAB AHMAD KHAN SHERPAO.
Minister of Inter-provincial Co-ordination: SALIM SAIFULLAH.
Minister of Labour, Manpower and Overseas Pakistanis: GHULAM SARWAR KHAN.
Minister of Narcotics Control: GHAUS BAKHISH KHAN MAHR.
Minister of Petroleum and Natural Resources: AMANULLAH KHAN JADOON.
Minister of Political Affairs: Eng. AMIR MUQAM.
Minister of Ports and Shipping: BABAR KHAN GAURI.
Minister of Scientific and Technological Research: CHAUDHRY NOURAIZ SHAKOOR KHAN.
Minister of Social Welfare and Special Education: ZUBAIDA JALAL.
Minister of States and Frontier Regions (SAFRON): Sardar YAR MOHAMMAD RIND.
Minister of Railways: Sheikh RASHID AHMAD.
Minister of Privatisation and Investment: ZAHID HAMID.
Minister of Tourism: NILOFAR BAKHTYAR.
Minister of Communications: MUHAMMAD SHAMIM SIDDIQUI.
Minister of Religious Affairs, Zakat and Ushr: MOHAMMAD IJAZUL HAQUE.
Minister of Kashmir Affairs and Northern Areas: Maj. (retd) TAHIR IQBAL.
Minister of Law, Justice and Human Rights: MUHAMMAD WASI ZAFAR.
Minister of Local Government and Rural Development: Justice (retd) ABDUL RAZZAQ THAHIM.
Minister of the Textiles Industry: MUSHTAQ ALI CHEEMA.
Minister of Population Welfare: CHAUDHRY SHAHBAZ HUSSAIN.
Minister of Parliamentary Affairs: Dr SHER AFGAN KHAN NIAZI.
Minister of Sports: SHAMIM HAIDAR.
Minister of Water and Power: LIAQUAT ALI JATOI.
Minister of Women and Youth Affairs: SUMAIRA MALIK.
Minister of State for Commerce: HAMID YAR HIRAJ.
Minister of State for Communications: SHAHID JAMIL QURESHI.
Minister of State for Economic Affairs: HINA RABBANI KHAR.
Minister of State for Education: ANISA ZEB THAIRKHELI.
Minister of State for the Environment: MALIK AMIN ASLAM KHAN.
Minister of State for Food and Agriculture: MUHAMMAD ALI MALKANI.
Minister of State for Defence: KHALIL KHAN LUND.
Minister of State for Finance: OMAR AYUB KHAN.
Minister of State for Foreign Affairs: MAKHDOOM KHUSRO BAKHTIAR.
Minister of State for Health: Begum SHAHNAZ SHAIKH.

Minister of State for Housing and Works: Sardar MUHAMMAD ASIF NAKAI.
Minister of State for Industries, Production and Special Initiatives: ALI NAWAZ KHAN MAHAR.
Minister of State for Information and Broadcasting: TARIQ AZIM.
Minister of State for Information Technology and Telecommunications: ISHAQ KHAN KHAKWANI.
Minister of State for the Interior: CHAUDHRY ZAFAR IQBAL WARRIACH.
Minister of State for Law, Justice and Human Rights: CHAUDHRY SHAHID AKRAM BHINDER.
Minister of State for Minorities: MUSHTAQ VICTOR.
Minister of State for Overseas Pakistanis: RAZA HAYAT HIRAJ.
Minister of State for Parliamentary Affairs: KAMIL ALI AGHA.
Minister of State for Petroleum and Natural Resources: MIR MUHAMMAD NASEER KHAN MENGAL.
Minister of State for Privatisation and Investment: UMAR AHMAD GHUMAN.
Minister of State for Railways: ALI ASJAD MALHI.
Minister of State for Religious Affairs, Zakat and Ushr: Dr AAMER LIAQUAT HUSSAIN.
Minister of State for Tourism: SUMAIRA MALIK.
Minister of State for Youth Affairs: GHULAM BIBI BHARWANA.
Adviser to the Prime Minister for Foreign Affairs, Law, Justice and Human Rights: SYED SHARIFFUDIN PIRZADA.
Adviser to the Prime Minister for Finance: Dr SALMAN SHAH.
Adviser to the Prime Minister for Irrigation Affairs of the Indus River System Authority (IRSA): FATEH ALI USMAN.

MINISTRIES

Office of the President: Aiwan-e-Sadr, Islamabad; tel. (51) 9206060; fax (51) 9208046.
Office of the Prime Minister's Secretariat: Constitution Ave, F-6/5, Cabinet Division, Cabinet Block, Islamabad; tel. (51) 9206111; internet www.pak.gov.pk.
Ministry of Commerce: Block A, Pakistan Secretariat, Islamabad; tel. (51) 9201816; fax (51) 9205241; e-mail mincom@commerce.gov.pk; internet www.commerce.gov.pk.
Ministry of Culture, Minorities, Sports and Youth Affairs: Block D, Pakistan Secretariat, Islamabad; tel. (51) 9202347; fax (51) 9224697; internet www.heritage.gov.pk.
Ministry of Defence: Pakistan Secretariat, No. II, Rawalpindi 46000; tel. (51) 9271107; fax (51) 9271113.
Ministry of Education: Block D, Pakistan Secretariat, Islamabad; tel. (51) 9212020; fax (51) 9202851; e-mail pak@yahoo.com.
Ministry of Environment, Local Government and Rural Development: Block 4, Old Naval Headquarters, Civic Centre, G-6, Islamabad; tel. (51) 9224291; fax (51) 9202211; e-mail envir@isb.compol.com; internet www.environment.gov.pk.
Ministry of Finance and Revenue: Block Q, Pakistan Secretariat, Islamabad; tel. (51) 9210291; fax (51) 9218062; e-mail finance@isb.paknet.com.pk; internet www.finance.gov.pk.
Ministry of Food, Agriculture, Co-operatives and Livestock: Block B, Pakistan Secretariat, Islamabad; tel. (51) 9210088; fax (51) 9221246.
Ministry of Foreign Affairs: Constitution Ave, Islamabad; tel. (51) 9210335; fax (51) 9224205; e-mail pakfo@yahoo.com; internet www.forisb.org.
Ministry of Health: Block C, Pakistan Secretariat, Islamabad; tel. (51) 9213933; fax (51) 9208139.
Ministry of Housing and Works: Block B, Pakistan Secretariat, Islamabad; tel. (51) 9214121; fax (51) 9202925; internet www.pha.gov.pk.
Ministry of Industries, Production and Special Initiatives: Block A, Pakistan Secretariat, Islamabad; tel. (51) 9212164; fax (51) 9205130; e-mail mind@isb.paknet.com.pk; internet www.moip.gov.pk.
Ministry of Information and Broadcasting: Cabinet Block, Pakistan Secretariat, Islamabad; tel. (51) 9212009; fax (51) 9201350; internet www.infopak.gov.pk.
Ministry of Information Technology and Telecommunications: 4th Floor, Evacuee Trust Complex, Aga Khan Rd, F-5/1, Islamabad; tel. (51) 9201990; fax (51) 9205233; internet www.moitt.gov.pk.
Ministry of the Interior: Block R, Pakistan Secretariat, Islamabad; tel. (51) 9204128; fax (51) 9202642; e-mail info@interior.gov.pk; internet www.interior.gov.pk.
Ministry of Kashmir Affairs, Northern Areas and States and Frontier Regions (SAFRON): Block R, Pakistan Secretariat, Islamabad; tel. (51) 9211405; fax (51) 9202494; e-mail safron@isb.perd.net.pk.
Ministry of Labour, Manpower and Overseas Pakistanis: Block B, Pakistan Secretariat, Islamabad; tel. (51) 9210077; fax (51) 9203462; internet www.labour.gov.pk.
Ministry of Law, Justice and Human Rights: Block S&R, Pakistan Secretariat, Islamabad; tel. and fax (51) 9202658; e-mail molaw1@comsats.net.pk.
Ministry of Petroleum and Natural Resources: 3rd Floor, Block A, Pakistan Secretariat, Islamabad; tel. (51) 9209343; fax (51) 9201770; e-mail info@mpnr.gov.pk; internet www.mpnr.gov.pk.
Ministry of Planning and Development: Block P, Pakistan Secretariat, Islamabad; tel. (51) 9204926; fax (51) 9202704.
Ministry of Population Welfare: Jamil Mohsin Mansion, Civic Centre, Islamabad 44000; tel. (51) 9207383; fax (51) 9201453; e-mail minpop@isb.comsats.net.pk; internet www.mopw.gov.pk.
Ministry of Privatisation and Investment: 5-A, Constitution Ave, EAC Bldg, Islamabad 44000; tel. (51) 9211285; fax (51) 9203076; e-mail info@privatisation.gov.pk; internet www.privatisation.gov.pk.
Ministry of Railways: Block D, Pakistan Secretariat, Islamabad; tel. (51) 9213170; fax (51) 9203867; e-mail railway@isb.paknet.com.pk.
Ministry of Religious Affairs, Zakat and Ushr: G-6, Civic Centre, Islamabad; tel. (51) 9214856; fax (51) 9205833; internet www.mra.gov.pk.
Ministry of Scientific and Technological Research: 4th Floor, Evacuee Trust Complex, Aga Khan Rd, F-5/1, Islamabad; tel. (51) 9208026; fax (51) 9205376; e-mail minister@most.gov.pk; internet www.most.gov.pk.
Ministry of the Textiles Industry: 2nd Floor, FBC Bldg, Islamabad; tel. (51) 9212799; fax (51) 9214015.
Ministry of Tourism: Green Trust Tower Bldg, Jinnah Ave, Blue Area, Islamabad 44000; tel. (51) 9213642; fax (51) 9201696; e-mail secretary@tourism.gov.pk; internet www.tourism.gov.pk.
Ministry of Water and Power: Block A, 15th Floor, Shaheed-e-Millat, Pakistan Secretariat, Islamabad; tel. (51) 9212442; fax (51) 9203187.
Ministry of Women Development, Social Welfare and Special Education: State Life Bldg, No 5, Blue Area, China Chowk, F-6/4, Islamabad; tel. (51) 9201083; fax (51) 9203132; e-mail grapnational@yahoo.com; internet www.mowd.gov.pk.

Federal Legislature

SENATE

The Legal Framework Order, promulgated by the President in August 2002, increased the number of seats in the Senate from 87 to 100. Eighty-eight of the members are elected by the four provincial legislatures; eight are chosen by representatives of the Federally Administered Tribal Areas; and four by the federal capital. Its term of office is six years, but half the membership is renewed after three years. The most recent election was held on 6 March 2006.

Chairman: Mian MOHAMMAD SOOMRO.
Deputy Chairman: JAN MOHAMMAD JAMALI.

Distribution of Seats, March 2006

	Seats
Pakistan Muslim League (Quaid-e-Azam Group)	38
Muttahida Majlis-e-Amal*	17
Pakistan People's Party Parliamentarians	9
Muttahida Qaumi Movement	6
Pakistan Muslim League (Nawaz Group)	4
Pakistan People's Party (Sherpao Group)	3
Pakhtoonkhwa Milli Awami Party	3
Awami National Party	2
Balochistan National Party (Awami)	1
Balochistan National Party (Maingal)	1
Jamhuri Watan Party	1
Jamiat-e-Ulema-e-Islam (F)	1
National Alliance†	1
Pakistan Muslim League (Functional Pir Pagara Group)	1
Independents	12
Total	**100**

PAKISTAN

* Coalition comprising Jamaat-e-Islami Pakistan, Jamiat-e-Ulema-e-Pakistan, Jamiat-e-Ulema-e-Islam (S), Jamiat-e-Ulema-e-Islam (F), Islami Tehreek Pakistan and Jamiat Ahl-e-Hadith.

† Coalition comprising the National People's Party, the Millat Party, the Sindh National Front, the Sindh Democratic Alliance and the National Awami Party.

NATIONAL ASSEMBLY

In accordance with the Legal Framework Order, promulgated by the President in August 2002, the number of seats in the National Assembly increased from 217 to 342, with 60 seats reserved for women and 10 for non-Muslims. Its term of office was reduced by one year to four.

Speaker: CHAUDHRY AMIR HUSSAIN.
Deputy Speaker: Sardar MOHAMMAD YAQOOB.

General Election, 10 October 2002

	Seats
Pakistan Muslim League (Quaid-e-Azam Group)	118
Pakistan People's Party Parliamentarians	81
Muttahida Majlis-e-Amal	60
Pakistan Muslim League (Nawaz Group)	19
Muttahida Qaumi Movement	17
National Alliance	16
Pakistan Muslim League (Functional Pir Pagara Group)	5
Pakistan Muslim League (Junejo Group)	3
Pakistan People's Party (Sherpao Group)	2
Balochistan National Party	1
Pakistan Tehrik-e-Insaf	1
Pakistan Muslim League (Ziaul Haq)	1
Jamhuri Watan Party	1
Muhajir Qaumi Movement	1
Pakistan Awami Tehreek	1
Independents	14
Vacant	1
Total	**342**

Provincial Governments
(May 2006)

Pakistan comprises the four provinces of Sindh, Balochistan, Punjab and the North-West Frontier Province, plus the federal capital and Federally Administered Tribal Areas.

BALOCHISTAN
(Capital—Quetta)

Governor: Sardar AWAIS GHANI.
Chief Minister: JAM MOHAMMAD YOUSUF.
Legislative Assembly: 51 seats (Pakistan Muslim League—Quaid-e-Azam Group 16; Muttahida Majlis-e-Amal 14, National Alliance 5, Balochistan National Movement 3, Jamhuri Watan Party 3, independents and others 8, vacant 2).

NORTH-WEST FRONTIER PROVINCE
(Capital—Peshawar)

Governor: Lt-Gen. (retd) ALI MOHAMMAD JAN ORAKZAI.
Chief Minister: MOHAMMAD AKRAM KHAN DURRANI.
Legislative Assembly: 99 seats (Muttahida Majlis-e-Amal 52, Pakistan People's Party—Sherpao 10, Pakistan People's Party Parliamentarians 8, Awami National Party 8, Pakistan Muslim League—Quaid-e-Azam Group 8, Pakistan Muslim League—Nawaz 4, independents and others 9).

PUNJAB
(Capital—Lahore)

Governor: Lt-Gen. (retd) KHALID MAQBOOL.
Chief Minister: CHAUDHRY PERVEZ ELAHI.
Legislative Assembly: 297 seats (Pakistan Muslim League—Quaid-e-Azam Group 168, Pakistan People's Party Parliamentarians 63, Pakistan Muslim League—Nawaz 38, National Alliance 12, Muttahida Majlis-e-Amal 9, independents and others 7).

SINDH
(Capital—Karachi)

Governor: ISHRATUL EBAD.
Chief Minister: Dr ARBAB GHULAM RAHIM.
Legislative Assembly: 130 seats (Pakistan People's Party Parliamentarians 51, Muttahida Qaumi Movement 31, Pakistan Muslim League—Quaid-e-Azam Group 14, National Alliance 12, Pakistan Muslim League—Functional Pir Pagara Group 9, Muttahida Majlis-e-Amal 8, independents and others 3, vacant 2).

Election Commission

Election Commission of Pakistan: Secretariat, Election House, Constitution Ave, G-5/2, Islamabad; e-mail info@ecp.gov.pk; internet www.ecp.gov.pk; independent; Chief Election Commr Justice (retd) Qazi MUHAMMAD FAROOQ.

Political Organizations

Some 73 parties, issued with election symbols by the Election Commission, contested the general election on 10 October 2002. Three alliances contested the elections: the Alliance for the Restoration of Democracy (Chair. MAKHDOOM AMIN FAHIM; includes the Pakistan Muslim League (Nawaz) and the Pakistan People's Party Parliamentarians); the National Alliance (Chair. GHULAM MUSTAFA JATOI; includes the National People's Party, the Millat Party, the Sindh National Front, the Sindh Democratic Alliance and the National Awami Party); and the Muttahida Majlis-e-Amal (Pres. Amir Qazi HUSSAIN AHMAD; comprises Jamaat-e-Islami Pakistan, Jamiat-e-Ulema-e-Pakistan, Jamiat-e-Ulema-e-Islam (S), Jamiat-e-Ulema-e-Islam (F), Islami Tehreek Pakistan and Jamiat Ahl-e-Hadith).

All Pakistan Jammu and Kashmir Conference: f. 1948; advocates the holding of a free plebiscite in the whole of Kashmir; Pres. Sardar SIKANDAR HAYAT KHAN.

Awami National Party (ANP) (People's National Party): Wali Bagh, Charsadda; tel. (21) 534513; f. 1986 by the merger of the National Democratic Party, the Awami Tehrik (People's Movement) and the Mazdoor Kissan (Labourers' and Peasants' Party); federalist and socialist; Leader KHAN ABDUL WALI KHAN; Pres. ASFANDAR WALI KHAN.

Awami Qiyadat Party (People's Leadership Party): 88 Race Course Rd, St 3, Rawalpindi Cantt; f. 1995; Chair. Gen. (retd) MIRZA ASLAM BAIG.

Balochistan National Party (BNP)—Awami: Quetta; Leader TAHIR BIZENJO.

Balochistan National Party (BNP)—Maingal: Quetta; e-mail bnpwebadmin@balochistan.net; Leader Sardar MOHAMMAD AKHTAR MAINGAL.

Jamaat-e-Islami Pakistan (JIP): Mansoorah, Multan Rd, Lahore 54570; tel. (42) 5419504; fax (42) 5419505; e-mail uroobah@pol.com.pk; internet www.jamaat.org; f. 1941; seeks the establishment of Islamic order through adherence to teaching of Maulana MAUDUDI, founder of the party; revivalist; right-wing; Chair. Amir QAZI HUSSAIN AHMAD; Sec.-Gen. SYED MUNAWAR HASAN; c. 5m. mems (2005).

Jamhuri Watan Party (Bugti) Balochistan: Bugti House, Dera Bugti; Pres. Nawab AKBAR BUGTI.

Jamiat-e-Ulema-e-Islam (JUI): Jamia al-Maarf, al-Sharia, Dera Ismail Khan; f. 1950; advocates adoption of a constitution in accordance with (Sunni) Islamic teachings; Leader Maulana FAZLUR REHMAN.

Jamiat-e-Ulema-e-Pakistan (JUP): Burns Rd, Karachi; f. 1948; advocates progressive (Sunni) Islamic principles and enforcement of Islamic laws in Pakistan; Pres. SHAH FARID UL-HAQ (acting); Gen. Sec. Gen. (retd) K. M. AZHAR KHAN.

Millat Party: 21-E/3, Gulberg III, Lahore; tel. (42) 5757805; fax (42) 5756718; e-mail millat@lhr.comsats.net.pk; advocates 'true federalism'; Chair. FAROOQ AHMAD KHAN LEGHARI.

Millat-e-Islamia Pakistan: Karachi; f. as a breakaway faction of Jamiat-e-Ulema-e-Islam; fmrly known as Sipah-e-Sahaba Pakistan—SSP; Sunni extremist; name changed to above after activities proscribed in January 2002; activities banned again in November 2003; Leader Maulana AHMED LUDHIANVI; Sec.-Gen. HAFIZ AHMED BUKHSH.

Muttahida Qaumi Movement (MQM): 494/8 Azizabad, Karachi; tel. (21) 6313690; fax (21) 6329955; e-mail mqm@mqm.org; internet www.mqm.org; f. 1978 as All Pakistan Mohajir Students Organisation; name changed to Mohajir Qaumi Movement in 1984 and to Muttahida Qaumi Movement in 1997; represents the interests of Muslim, Urdu-speaking immigrants (from India) in Pakistan; seeks the designation of Mohajir as fifth nationality (after Sindhi, Punjabi, Pathan and Balochi); aims to abolish the prevailing feudal political system and to establish democracy; Pres. AFTAB SHEIKH.

National Awami Party: Pir Bakhsh Bldg, Shubah Chowk, Peshawar; Pres. AJMAL KHATAK; Gen. Sec. ARBAB AYUB JAN.

National Democratic Front: Islamabad; fmrly Pakistan National Forum; name changed as above Sept. 2004; Pres. Air Marshal (retd) MOHAMMAD ASGHAR KHAN; Sec.-Gen. Dr GHULAM HUSSAIN.

National Party: Faiz Arbab Saryab Rd, Quetta; f. 2003 following merger of Balochistan National Movement and Balochistan National Democratic Party; Chair. Dr ABDUL HAYAI BALOCH.

National People's Party (NPP): 18 Kh-e-Shamsheer, Defence Housing Authority, Phase V, Karachi; tel. (21) 5854522; fax (21) 5873753; f. 1986; centre left-wing party advocating a just, democratic welfare state for Pakistan; breakaway faction from PPP; Chair. GHULAM MUSTAFA JATOI; Parl. Leader Dr IBRAHIM KHAN.

Pakhtoonkhwa Milli Awami Party (Quetta): Leader SAMAND ACHAKZAI.

Pakistan Awami Tehreek (PAT): 365-M Model Town, Lahore; tel. (42) 5169111; fax (42) 5169114; e-mail info@pat.com.pk; internet www.pat.com.pk; Chair. Dr MUHAMMAD TAHRIR-UL-QADRI.

Pakistan Democratic Party (PDP): f. 1969; advocates democratic and Islamic values; Pres. NAWABZADA MANSOOR AHMED KHAN.

Pakistan Muslim League (PML): Islamabad; f. 2004 following merger of PML Quaid-e-Azam Group, PML (Junejo), PML (Functional), PML (Zia-ul-Haq Shaheed), PML (Jinnah) and the Sindh Democratic Alliance; PML (Functional) subsequently split from party; Pres. CHAUDHRY SHUJAAT HUSSAIN; Sec.-Gen. MUSHAHID HUSSAIN SYED.

Pakistan Muslim League—Functional (PML—F): Islamabad; merged with PML Quaid-e-Azam Group, PML (Junejo), PML (Zia-ul-Haq Shaheed), PML (Jinnah) and the Sindh Democratic Alliance in 2004 but subsequently split from party; Leader PIR PAGARA.

Pakistan Muslim League—Nawaz (PML—N): Camp Office Pakistan Muslim League (Nawaz), 239, St 51, F-10/4, Islamabad; tel. (51) 2213928; e-mail info@pmlnpk.org; internet www.pmlnpk.org; f. 1993 as faction of Pakistan Muslim League (Junejo); Pres. SHAHBAZ SHARIF; Chair RAJA ZAFARUL HAQ.

Pakistan People's Party (PPP): 8, St 63, F-8/4, Islamabad; tel. (51) 2255264; e-mail ppp@ppp.org.pk; internet www.ppp.org.pk; f. 2004 following merger of Pakistan People's Party (Sherpao Group) and Pakistan People's Party Parliamentarians (Patriots); advocates Islamic socialism, democracy and a non-aligned foreign policy; Pres. AFTAB AHMAD KHAN SHERPAO.

Pakistan People's Party (Shaheed Bhutto Group): 71 Clifton, Karachi; f. 1995 as a breakaway faction of the PPP; Chair. GHINWA BHUTTO; Sec.-Gen. Dr MUBASHIR HASAN.

Punjabi Pakhtoon Ittehad (PPI): f. 1987 to represent the interests of Punjabis and Pakhtoons in Karachi; Pres. MALIK MIR HAZAR KHAN.

Sindh National Front: Pres. MUMTAZ BHUTTO.

Sindh Taraqi Passand Party (STPP): Leader Dr QADIR MAGSI.

Tehrik-e-Insaf (Movement for Justice): Lahore; internet www.insaf.org.pk; f. 1996; Leader IMRAN KHAN; Sec.-Gen. MIRAJ MOHAMMAD KHAN.

Tehrik-e-Pakistan (TJP): f. 1987 as Tehrik-e-Jafria-e-Pakistan; Shi'a extremist; renamed as above after activities proscribed in January 2002; activities banned again in November 2003; Leader Allama SAJID ALI NAQVI.

Diplomatic Representation

EMBASSIES AND HIGH COMMISSIONS IN PAKISTAN

Afghanistan: 8, St 90, G-6/3, Islamabad 44000; tel. (51) 2824505; fax (51) 2824504; e-mail afghanem@yahoo.com; Ambassador NANGUYALAI TARZI.

Algeria: 107, St 9, E-7, POB 1038, Islamabad; tel. (51) 2206632; fax (51) 2820912; Ambassador NADIR LARBAOUI.

Argentina: 20, Hill Rd, Shalimar 6/3, POB 1015, Islamabad; tel. (51) 2821242; fax (51) 2825564; e-mail epaki@worldtelmeca.com; Ambassador RODOLFO J. MARTIN SARAVIA.

Australia: Diplomatic Enclave 1, Constitution Ave and Isphani Rd, Sector G-5/4, POB 1046, Islamabad; tel. (51) 2824345; fax (51) 2820112; e-mail ahcisb@isb.compol.com; internet www.embassy.gov.au/pk.html; High Commissioner ZORICA McCARTHY.

Austria: 13, St 1, F-6/3, POB 1018, Islamabad 44000; tel. (51) 2279237; fax (51) 2828366; e-mail Islamabad-ob@bmaa.gv.at; Ambassador Dr GUENTHER GALLOWITSCH.

Azerbaijan: House 14, St 87, G-6/3, Atatürk Ave, Islamabad; tel. (51) 2829345; fax (51) 2820898; e-mail azeremb@isb.paknet.com.pk; internet www.azembassy.com.pk; Ambassador Dr EYNULLA YADALLA OGLU MADATLI.

Bangladesh: 1, St 5, F-6/3, Islamabad; tel. (51) 2279267; fax (51) 2279266; e-mail bdhcisb@sat.net.pk; High Commissioner F. A. SHAMIM AHMED.

Belgium: 14, St 17, F-7/2, Islamabad; tel. (51) 2652635; fax (51) 2652631; e-mail islamabad@diplobel.org; internet www.diplomatie.be/islamabad; Ambassador PATRICK RENAULT.

Bosnia and Herzegovina: House No. 1, Kaghan Rd, F-8/3, Islamabad; tel. (51) 2261041; fax (51) 2261004; e-mail ambassador@bosnianembassypakistan.org; internet www.bosnianembassypakistan.org; Ambassador DAMIR DZONKO.

Brazil: 50, Atatürk Ave, G-6/3, POB 1053, Islamabad; tel. (51) 2279690; fax (51) 2823034; e-mail brasembp@isb.compol.com; Ambassador FAUSTO MARTHA GODOY.

Brunei: 16, St 21, F-6/2, Islamabad; tel. (51) 2823038; fax (51) 2823138; High Commissioner Pehin Dato' Haji Panglima Col (retd) Haji ABDUL JALIL BIN Haji AHMAD.

Bulgaria: Plot No. 6-11, Diplomatic Enclave, Ramna 5, POB 1483, Islamabad; tel. (51) 2279196; fax (51) 2279195; e-mail bul@isb.compol.com; Chargé d'affaires a.i. PLAMEN CHRISTOV PETKOV.

Canada: Diplomatic Enclave, Sector G-5, POB 1042, Islamabad; tel. (51) 2279100; fax (51) 2279110; e-mail isbad@dfait-maeci.gc.ca; internet www.dfait-maeci.gc.ca/islamabad; High Commissioner DAVID COLLINS.

Chile: Islamabad; Ambassador PEDRO BARROS.

China, People's Republic: Ramna 5, Diplomatic Enclave, Islamabad; tel. (51) 2824722; fax (51) 2279602; Ambassador ZHANG CHUNXIANG.

Czech Republic: 49, St 27, Shalimar F-6/2, POB 1335, Islamabad; tel. (51) 2274304; fax (51) 2825327; e-mail islamabad@embassy.mzv.cz; internet www.mzv.cz/islamabad; Ambassador ALEXANDR LANGER.

Denmark: 9, St 90, Ramna 5, POB 1118, Islamabad; tel. (51) 2824722; fax (51) 2823483; e-mail isbamb@um.dk; Ambassador BENT WIGOTSKI.

Egypt: 38–51, UN Blvd, Diplomatic Enclave, Ramna 5/4, POB 2088, Islamabad; tel. (51) 2209072; fax (51) 2279552; Ambassador HUSSEIN KAMEL HARIDY.

Finland: 11, St 88, G-6/3, Islamabad; tel. (51) 2828426; fax (51) 2828427; e-mail finnemb@isd.wol.net.pk; Ambassador TARJA LAITIAINEN.

France: Constitution Ave, G-5, Diplomatic Enclave 1, POB 1068, Islamabad; tel. (51) 2278730; fax (51) 2822583; e-mail ambafra@isb.comsats.net.pk; internet consulfrance-islamabad.org.pk; Ambassador RÉGIS DE BELENET.

Germany: Ramna 5, Diplomatic Enclave, POB 1027, Islamabad 44000; tel. (51) 2007200; fax (51) 2279436; e-mail pregerem@isb.paknet.com.pk; internet www.islamabad.diplo.de; Ambassador Dr GUNTER MULACK.

Greece: 22, Margalla Rd, F-6/3, Islamabad; tel. (51) 2822558; fax (51) 2825161; e-mail greece@isb.paknet.com.pk; internet www.greekembassy.netfirms.com; Ambassador ATHANASSIOS VALASSIDIS.

Holy See: Apostolic Nunciature, St 5, Diplomatic Enclave 1, G-5, POB 1106, Islamabad 44000; tel. (51) 2278218; fax (51) 2820847; e-mail vatipak@isb.comsats.net.pk; Apostolic Nuncio Most Rev. ALESSANDRO D'ERRICO (Titular Archbishop of Carini).

Hungary: 12, Margalla Rd, F-6/3, POB 1103, Islamabad; tel. (51) 2823352; fax (51) 2825256; e-mail hungemb@comsats.net.pk; Ambassador JÓZSEF KOVÁCS.

India: G-5, Diplomatic Enclave, Islamabad; tel. (51) 2828375; fax (51) 2823102; e-mail hicomind@isb.compol.com; High Commissioner SHIV SHANKAR MENON.

Indonesia: Diplomatic Enclave 1, St 5, G-5/4, POB 1019, Islamabad; tel. (51) 2206656; fax (51) 2829145; e-mail unitkom@kbri-islamabad.go.id; internet www.indonesia-embassy.org.pk; Ambassador ANWAR SAN TOSO.

Iran: Plot No. 222, 238, St 2, F-5/1, Islamabad; tel. (51) 2276270; fax (51) 2824839; Ambassador MUHAMMAD EHRAHIM TAHERIAN.

Iraq: 57, St 48, F-8/4, Islamabad; tel. (51) 2214570; fax (51) 2214572; e-mail iraqiya@sat.net.pk; Ambassador KAIS SUBHI AL-YACOUBI.

Italy: 54, Margalla Rd, F-6/3, POB 1008, Islamabad; tel. (51) 2829106; fax (51) 2829026; e-mail segreter@embassy.italy.org.pk; internet www.embassy.italy.org.pk; Ambassador ROBERTO MAZZOTTA.

Japan: Plot No. 53-70, Ramna 5/4, Diplomatic Enclave 1, Islamabad 44000; tel. (51) 2279320; fax (51) 2279340; e-mail japanemb@comsats.net.pk; internet www.pk.emb-japan.go.jp; Ambassador NOBUAKI TANAKA.

Jordan: 99, Main Double Rd, F-10/1, Islamabad; tel. (51) 2297383; fax (51) 2211630; e-mail jordanem@isb.paknet.com.pk; Ambassador MUSA AL-ADWAN.

PAKISTAN

Kazakhstan: 10, St 9, F-8/2, Islamabad; tel. (51) 2262926; fax (51) 2262806; e-mail embkaz@comsats.net.pk; Ambassador BEYBIT ISABAYEV.
Kenya: 8A, Embassy Rd, F-6/4, POB 2097, Islamabad; tel. (51) 2876024; fax (51) 2876027; e-mail kenreppk@apollo.net.pk; High Commissioner MISHI MASIKA MWATSAHU.
Korea, Democratic People's Republic: Diplomatic Enclave, Q. A. U. Rd, Islamabad; tel. and fax (51) 2252754; Ambassador KIM WON GYU.
Korea, Republic: Block 13, St 29, G-5/4, Diplomatic Enclave 2, POB 1087, Islamabad; tel. (51) 2252756; fax (51) 2279391; e-mail emb-pk@mofat.go.kr; Ambassador KIM JOO-SEOK.
Kuwait: Plot Nos 1, 2 and 24, University Rd, G-5, Diplomatic Enclave, POB 1030, Islamabad; tel. (51) 2279380; fax (51) 2279411; Ambassador FAISAL ABDULAZIZ AL-MULAIFI.
Lebanon: 6, St 27, F-6/2, Islamabad; tel. (51) 2278338; fax (51) 2826410; e-mail lebemb@comsats.net.pk; Ambassador WAFIC MUHAMMAD REHAIME.
Libya: 216, Margalla Rd, F-10/3, Islamabad; tel. (51) 2214397; fax (51) 2290093; Ambassador MOHAMMAD SAID MOHAMMAD AL-LAWATI.
Malaysia: 34, St 56, F-7/4, Islamabad; tel. (51) 2279570; fax (51) 2824761; e-mail mwislamb@isb.comsats.net.pk; High Commissioner Gen. Tan Sri MOHAMMAD HASHIM BIN HUSSEIN.
Mauritius: 13, St 26, F-6/2, POB 1084, Islamabad; tel. (51) 2824657; fax (51) 2824656; e-mail mauripak@isb.comsats.net.pk; High Commissioner RHAFIC JANHANGEER.
Morocco: 6, Gomal Rd, E-7, POB 1179, Islamabad; tel. (51) 2829656; fax (51) 2822745; e-mail sifamapak@morocco-embassy.com.pk; internet www.morocco-embassy.com.pk; Ambassador MOHAMED REDA EL FASSI.
Myanmar: 43, St 26, F-6/2, Islamabad; tel. (51) 2822460; fax (51) 2828819; Ambassador U MAUNG NYO.
Nepal: 2, St 8, F-8/3, Islamabad; tel. (51) 2854696; fax (51) 2854722; e-mail nepem@isb.comsats.net.pk; Ambassador (vacant).
Netherlands: PIA Bldg, 2nd Floor, Blue Area, POB 1065, Islamabad; tel. (51) 2279510; fax (51) 2279512; Ambassador Prof. P. M. KURPERFHOEK.
Nigeria: Diplomatic Enclave 1, Isphahani Rd, G-5/4, Islamabad; tel. (51) 2823542; fax (51) 2824104; e-mail nigeria@isb.comsats.net.pk; High Commissioner UMAR EL-GASH MAINA.
Norway: 25, St 19, Shalimar, F-6/2, Islamabad; tel. (51) 2279720; fax (51) 2279726; e-mail emb.islamabad@mfa.no; internet www.norway.org.pk; Ambassador JANIS BJØRN KANAVIN.
Oman: 53, St 48, F-8/4, POB 1194, Islamabad; tel. (51) 2254955; fax (51) 2255074; Ambassador SALIM BIN MOHAMMAD BIN SALIM AL-WAHAIBI.
Philippines: 8, St 60, F-7/4, POB 1052, Islamabad; tel. (51) 2824933; fax (51) 2277389; e-mail isdpe@isb.comsats.net.pk; Ambassador JAIME J. YAMBAO.
Poland: St 24, G-5/4, Diplomatic Enclave 2, POB 1032, Islamabad; tel. (51) 2279491; fax (51) 2279498; e-mail polemb@isb.comsats.net.pk; Ambassador BOGDAN MARCZEWSKI.
Portugal: 40A, Main Margalla Rd, F-7/2, POB 1067, Islamabad 44000; tel. (51) 2279531; fax (51) 2279532; e-mail portugal@isb.paknet.com.pk; Ambassador Dr ANTONIO JOSE DA CAMARA RAMALHO ORUGA.
Qatar: 20, University Rd, Diplomatic Enclave, G-5/4, Islamabad; tel. (51) 2270833; fax (51) 2270207; e-mail qaembpk@yahoo.com; Ambassador HAMAD ALI AL-HINZAB.
Romania: 13, St 88, G-6/3, Islamabad; tel. (51) 2826514; fax (51) 2826515; e-mail romania@isb.comsats.net.pk; Chargé d'affaires a.i. STEFAN MODREA.
Russia: Khayaban-e-Suhrawardy, Diplomatic Enclave, Ramna 4, Islamabad; tel. (51) 2278670; fax (51) 2826552; e-mail russia2@comsats.net.pk; Ambassador SERGEY N. PESKOV.
Saudi Arabia: 14, Hill Rd, F-6/3, Islamabad; tel. (51) 2820156; fax (51) 2278816; Ambassador ALI S. AWADH ASSERI.
Somalia: 21, St 56, F-6/4, Islamabad; tel. (51) 2279789; fax (51) 2826117; Ambassador ABDISALAAM Haji AHMAD LIBAN.
South Africa: House No. 48, Margalla Rd, Khayban-e-Iqbal, Sector F-8/2, Islamabad; tel. (51) 262354; fax (51) 250114; e-mail xhosa@isb.comsats.net.pk; High Commissioner DANIEL JABULANI MAVIMBELA.
Spain: St 6, G-5, Diplomatic Enclave 1, POB 1144, Islamabad; tel. (51) 2279480; fax (51) 2279489; Ambassador JOSE MARIA ROBLES FRAGA.
Sri Lanka: 315C, Khayaban-e-Iqbal, 7/2, Islamabad; tel. (51) 2828723; fax (51) 2828751; e-mail srilanka@isb.comsats.net.pk; High Commissioner Gen. C. S. WEERASOORIYA.
Sudan: 19, St 30, F-8/1, Islamabad; tel. (51) 2263926; fax (51) 2263975; e-mail sudanipk@isb.compol.com; internet www.sudanembassy.co.pk; Ambassador DAFAA ALLAH EL-HAJ ALI.
Sweden: 4, St 5, F-6/3, Islamabad; tel. (51) 2828712; fax (51) 2825284; e-mail ambassaden.islamabad@foreign.ministry.se; Ambassador ANN WILKENS.
Switzerland: St 6, G-5/4, Diplomatic Enclave, POB 1073, Islamabad; tel. (51) 2279291; fax (51) 2279286; e-mail vertretung@isl.rep.admin.ch; Ambassador DENIS FELDMEYER.
Syria: F-81, Islamabad; tel. (51) 2279470; fax (51) 2279472; Ambassador RIAD ISMAT.
Thailand: 10, St 33, Shalimar 8/1, Islamabad; tel. (51) 2280909; fax (51) 2256730; e-mail thailand@isb.comsats.net.pk; Ambassador PISANU CHANVITAN.
Tunisia: 221, St 21, E-7, Islamabad; tel. (51) 2827869; fax (51) 2827871; Ambassador ZOUHEIR DHAOUADI.
Turkey: 58, Atatürk Ave, G-6/3, Islamabad; tel. (51) 2278748; fax (51) 2278752; e-mail turkemb@isb.comsats.net.pk; Ambassador KEMAL GUR.
Turkmenistan: House 22A, Nazim-Ud-Din Rd, Sector F-7/1, Islamabad; tel. (51) 2274913; fax (51) 2278799; e-mail turkmen@comsats.net.pk; Ambassador SAPOR BERDINIYAZOV.
Ukraine: 20, St 18, F-6/2, Islamabad; tel. (51) 2274732; fax (51) 2274913; e-mail ukremb@isb.compol.com; internet www.ukremb.org.pk; Ambassador IGOR POLIKHA.
United Arab Emirates: Plot No. 1-22, Diplomatic Enclave, Quaid-e-Azam University Rd, Islamabad; tel. (51) 2279052; fax (51) 2279063; internet www.uae-embassy.org.pk; Ambassador ALI MOHAMMED ASH-SHAMSI.
United Kingdom: Diplomatic Enclave, Ramna 5, POB 1122, Islamabad; tel. (51) 2012000; fax (51) 2823439; e-mail bhcmedia@isb.comsats.net.pk; internet www.britainonline.org.pk; High Commissioner MARK LYALL GRANT.
USA: Diplomatic Enclave, Ramna 5, POB 1048, Islamabad; tel. (51) 826161; fax (51) 821193; e-mail isl@state.gov; Ambassador RYAN CROCKER.
Uzbekistan: St 21, E-7, Kagan Rd, Islamabad; tel. (51) 2821146; fax (51) 2261739; e-mail uzbekemb@isb.comsats.net.pk; Ambassador OYBEK ORIFBEKOVICH.
Yemen: 220, St 21, E-7, POB 1523, Islamabad 44000; tel. (51) 2653612; fax (51) 2653615; e-mail yemen22@isb.apollo.net.pk; Ambassador ABDUL ELAH MOHAMED HAJAR.

Judicial System

A constitutional amendment bill was passed in the National Assembly in October 1998 replacing the country's existing legal code with full Islamic *Shari'a*. The bill remained to be approved, however, by the Senate.

SUPREME COURT
Chief Justice: IFTIKHAR MOHAMMAD CHAUDHRY.
Attorney-General: MAKHDOOM ALI KHAN.

Federal Shari'a Court
Chief Justice: EJAZ YOUSUF.
Federal Ombudsman: Justice IMTIAZ AHMED SAHIBZADA.

Religion

ISLAM
Islam is the state religion. The majority of the population are Sunni Muslims, while estimates of the Shi'a sect vary between 5% and 20% of the population. Only about 0.001% are of the Ahmadi sect.

CHRISTIANITY
About 3% of the population are Christians.

National Council of Churches in Pakistan: 32-B, Shahrah-e-Fatima Jinnah, POB 357, Lahore 54000; tel. (42) 7592167; fax (42) 7569782; e-mail nccp@lhr.comsats.net.pk; f. 1949; four mem. bodies, nine associate mems; Gen. Sec. VICTOR AZARIAH.

The Roman Catholic Church
For ecclesiastical purposes, Pakistan comprises two archdioceses, four dioceses and one apostolic prefecture. At 31 December 2003 there were an estimated 1,193,293 adherents in the country.

Bishops' Conference

Pakistan Catholic Bishops' Conference, Sacred Heart Cathedral, 1 Mian Mohammad Shafi Rd, POB 909, Lahore 54000; tel. (42) 6366137; fax (42) 6368336; e-mail abishop@lhr.comsats.net.pk; f. 1976; Pres. Most Rev. LAWRENCE J. SALDANHA (Archbishop of Lahore); Sec.-Gen. Rt Rev. ANTHONY LOBO (Bishop of Islamabad-Rawalpindi).

Archbishop of Karachi: Most Rev. EVARIST PINTO, St Patrick's Cathedral, Shahrah-e-Iraq, Karachi 74400; tel. (21) 7781533; fax (21) 7781532.

Archbishop of Lahore: Most Rev. LAWRENCE J. SALDANHA, Sacred Heart Cathedral, 1 Mian Mohammad Shafi Rd, POB 909, Lahore 54000; tel. (42) 6366137; fax (42) 6368336; e-mail abishop@lhr.comsats.net.pk; internet www.rcarchdioceselahore.org.pk.

Protestant Churches

Church of Pakistan: Moderator Rt Rev. SAMUEL AZARIAH (Bishop of Raiwind), 17 Warris Rd, POB 2319, Lahore 3; fax (42) 7577255; f. 1970 by union of the fmr Anglican Church in Pakistan, the United Methodist Church in Pakistan, the United Church in Pakistan (Scots Presbyterians) and the Pakistani Lutheran Church; eight dioceses; c. 700,000 mems (1993); Gen. Sec. (vacant).

Presbyterian Church of Pakistan: 6 Empress Rd, Lahore 54000; tel. (431) 259511; e-mail ajames@brain.net.pk; f. 1961; c. 340,000 mems (1989); Moderator Rev. Dr ARTHUR JAMES; Sec. Rev. Dr MAGSOOD KAMIL.

Other denominations active in the country include the Associated Reformed Presbyterian Church and the Pakistan Salvation Army.

HINDUISM

Hindus comprise about 1.8% of the population.

BAHÁ'Í FAITH

National Spiritual Assembly: 56, Sector H-8/4, Islamabad; tel. (51) 4444699; fax (51) 4444691; e-mail nsapakistan@cyber.net.pk; internet www.bahai.org; f. 1956; Gen. Sec. Prof. MEHRDAD YOSUF.

The Press

The Urdu press comprises almost 800 newspapers, with *Daily Jang, Daily Khabrain, Nawa-i-Waqt* and *Jasarat* among the most influential. The daily newspaper with the largest circulation is *Daily Jang*. Although the English-language press reaches only a small percentage of the population, it is influential in political, academic and professional circles. The three main press groups in Pakistan are Jang Publications (the *Daily Jang, The News,* the *Daily News* and the weekly *Akhbar-e-Jehan*), the Dawn or Herald Group (the *Dawn*, the *Star* and the monthly *Herald* and *Spider*) and the Nawa-i-Waqt Group (the *Nawa-i-Waqt, The Nation* and the weekly *Family*). The establishment of an independent press council was under consideration in 2006.

PRINCIPAL DAILIES

Islamabad

Al-Akhbar: Al-Akhbar House, Markaz, G-8, Islamabad; tel. (51) 852023; fax (51) 256522; Urdu; also publ. in Muzaffarabad; Editor GHULAM AKBAR.

Daily Khabrain: Sitara Market, Markaz, G-7/2, Islamabad; tel. (51) 2204751; fax (51) 2204756.

The Nation: Nawa-i-Waqt House, Zero Point, Islamabad; tel. (51) 277631; fax (51) 278353; e-mail editor@nation.com.pk; internet www.nation.com.pk; English; Editor ARIF NIZAMI; circ. 15,000.

Pakistan Observer: Al-Akhbar House, Markaz, G-8, Islamabad 44870; tel. (51) 2852027; fax (51) 2262258; e-mail observer@comsats.net.pk; internet www.pakobserver.net; f. 1988; English; independent; Editor-in-Chief ZAHID MALIK.

Karachi

Aghaz: 11 Japan Mansion, Preedy St, Sadar, Karachi 74400; tel. (21) 7721688; fax (21) 7722125; e-mail ex101@hotmail.com; internet www.aghaz.com; f. 1962; evening; Urdu; Chief Editor MOHAMMAD ANWAR FAROOQI; circ. 65,000.

Amn: Akhbar Manzil, Elender Rd, off I. I. Chundrigar Rd, Karachi 74200; tel. (21) 2634451; fax (21) 2634454; e-mail amn@aol.net.pk; Urdu; Editor AJMAL DEHLVI.

Business Recorder: Recorder House, 53 Business Recorder Rd, Karachi 74550; tel. (21) 2250071; fax (21) 2222866; e-mail ed.khi@br-mail.com; internet www.brecorder.com; f. 1965; English; Editor WAMIQ A. ZUBERI; Editor-in-Chief M. A. ZUBERI.

Daily Awam: HQ Printing House, I. I. Chundrigar Rd, POB 52, Karachi; tel. (21) 2637111; fax (21) 2636066; f. 1994; evening; Urdu; Editor-in-Chief Mir SHAKIL-UR-RAHMAN.

Daily Beopar: 118 Bombay Hotel, I. I. Chundrigar Rd, Karachi; tel. (21) 214055; Urdu; Man. Editor TARIQ SAEED.

Daily Express: 5 Expressway, off Korangi Rd, Karachi; tel. (21) 5800058; fax (21) 5800051; Urdu; Editor TAHIR NAZIM.

Daily Intekhab: Liaison Office, 3rd Floor, Mashhoor Mahal Bldg, Kucha Haji Usman, off I. I. Chundrigar Rd, Karachi; tel. (21) 2634518; fax (21) 2631092; e-mail intekhab@comsats.net.pk; internet www.dailyintekhab.com; Urdu; also publ. from Hub (Balochistan) and Quetta; Man. Editor NARGIS BALOCH; Publr and Exec. Editor ANWAR SAJIDI.

Daily Jang: HQ Printing House, I. I. Chundrigar Rd, POB 52, Karachi; tel. (21) 2637111; fax (21) 2634395; e-mail jang@jang-group.com.pk; internet www.jang.com.pk; f. 1940; morning; Urdu; also publ. in Quetta, Rawalpindi, Lahore and London; Editor-in-Chief Mir SHAKIL-UR-RAHMAN; combined circ. 750,000.

Daily Khabar: A-8 Sheraton Centre, F. B. Area, Karachi; tel. (21) 210059; Urdu; Exec. Editor FAROOQ PARACHA; Editor and Publr SAEED ALI HAMEED.

Daily Mohasaba: Imperial Hotel, M. T. Khan Rd, Karachi; tel. (21) 519448; Urdu; Editor TALIB TURABI.

Daily News: Al-Rahman Bldg, I. I. Chundrigar Rd, Karachi; tel. (21) 2637111; fax (21) 2634395; f. 1962; evening; English; Editor S. M. FAZIL; circ. 50,000.

Daily Public: Falak Printing Press, 191 Altaf Hussain Rd, New Chhali, Karachi; tel. (21) 5687522; Man. Editor INQUILAB MATRI; Editor ANWAR SANROY.

Daily Sindh Sujag: 15/4, Namco Centre, Campbell St, New Challi, Karachi; tel. (21) 2625282; fax (21) 2623918; Sindhi; political; Editor NASIR DAD BALOCH.

Daily Special: Ahbab Printers, Beauty House, nr Regal Chowk, Abdullah Haroon Rd, Sadar, Karachi; tel. (21) 7771655; fax (21) 7722776; Urdu; Editor MOHAMMAD AT-TAYYAB.

Daily Times: 53 Timber Pond, Keamari, Karachi; tel. (21) 2854838; fax (21) 2854830; e-mail sarfaraz@dailytimes.com.pk; internet www.dailytimes.com.pk; Editor SARFARAZ AHMED.

Dawn: Haroon House, Dr Ziauddin Ahmed Rd, POB 3740, Karachi 74200; tel. (21) 5670001; fax (21) 5682187; e-mail editor@dawn.com; internet www.dawn.com; f. 1947; English; also published from Islamabad and Lahore; Chief Exec. HAMEED HAROON; Editor TAHIR MIRZA; circ. 110,000 (weekdays), 125,000 (Sundays).

Deyanet: Karachi; tel. (21) 2631556; fax (21) 2631888; Urdu; also publ. in Sukkur and Islamabad; Editor NAJMUDDIN SHAIKH.

The Finance: 903–905 Uni Towers, I. I. Chundrigar Rd, Karachi; tel. (21) 2411665; fax (21) 2422560; e-mail tfinance@super.net.pk; English; Chief Editor S. H. SHAH.

Financial Post: Bldg No. 106/C, 11 Commercial St, Phase II, Extension, Defence Housing Authority, Karachi; tel. (21) 5381626; fax (21) 5802760; e-mail fpost@dancom3.com.pk; internet www.dailyfpost.com; f. 1994; English; Chief Editor and CEO QUDSIA K. KHAN; Publr WAJID JAWAD.

Hilal-e-Pakistan: Court View Bldg, 2nd Floor, M. A. Jinnah Rd, POB 3737, Karachi 74200; tel. (21) 2624997; fax (21) 2624996; Sindhi; Editor MOHAMMAD IQBAL DAL.

Jago: Karachi; tel. (21) 2635544; fax (21) 2628137; f. 1990; Sindhi; political; Editor AGHA SALEEM.

Jasarat: Eveready Chambers, Muhammad Bin Qasim Rd, Karachi 74200; tel. (21) 2630391; fax (21) 2632102; e-mail jasarat@cyber.net.pk; f. 1970; Urdu; Editor (vacant); circ. 50,000.

The Leader: Block 5, 609, Clifton Centre, Clifton, Karachi 75600; tel. (21) 5863801; fax (21) 5872206; e-mail info@theleader.com.pk; f. 1958; English; independent; Man. Editor MUNIR M. LADHA; circ. 7,000.

Mazdur: Spencer Bldg, I. I. Chundrigar Rd, Karachi 2; f. 1984; Urdu; Editor MOHAMMAD ANWAR BIN ABBAS.

Millat: 191 Altaf Hussain Rd, Karachi 2; tel. (21) 2411514; internet www.millat.com; f. 1946; Gujarati; independent; Editor INQUILAB MATRI; circ. 22,550.

Mohasib: Karachi; fax (21) 2632763; Urdu; also publ. from Abbotabad; Chief Editor ZAFAR MAJAZI; Editor NAEEM AHMAD.

The Nation: Block-I, Hockey Stadium, off Khayaban-e-Shamsher, Phase V, Defence Housing Authority, Karachi; tel. (21) 5846622; fax (21) 5848892; e-mail editor@nation.com.pk; internet www.nation.com.pk; English; Editor ARIF NIZAMI.

The News International: Al-Rahman Bldg, I. I. Chundrigar Rd, POB 52, Karachi; tel. (21) 2630611; fax (21) 2636976; f. 1990; English; also publ. from Lahore and Rawalpindi/Islamabad; Editor-in-Chief Mir SHAKIL-UR-RAHMAN; Sr Editor HUSUNIA AHMAD.

PAKISTAN

Qaum (Nation): Karachi; Urdu; Editor and Publr Mushtaque Sohail; Man. Editor Mamnoonur Rehman.

Qaumi Akhbar: 14 Ramzan Mansion, Dr Bilmoria St, off I. I. Chundrigar Rd, Karachi; tel. (21) 2633381; fax (21) 2635774; f. 1988; Urdu; Editor Ilyas Shakir.

Roznama Special: Falak Printing Press, 191 Altaf Hussain Rd, Karachi; tel. (21) 5687522; fax (21) 5687579; Publr and Man. Editor Inquilab Matri; Editor Anwar Sen Roy.

Savera: 108 Adam Arcade, Shaheed-e-Millat Rd, Karachi; tel. (21) 419616; Urdu; Editor Rukhsana Saham Mirza.

Sindh Tribune: No. 246-D/6, PECHS, Karachi; tel. (21) 4535227; fax (21) 4332680; English; political; Editor Yousuf Shaheen.

Star: Haroon House, Dr Ziauddin Ahmed Rd, Karachi 74200; e-mail star@dawn.com; evening; English; Editor Kamal Majidulla.

The Times of Karachi: Al-Falah Chambers, 9th Floor, Abdullah Haroon Rd, Karachi; tel. (21) 7727740; e-mail iqbalmir@yahoo.com; evening; English; independent; city news; Editor Mir Iqbal Aziz.

Lahore

Daily Pakistan: 41 Jail Rd, Lahore; tel. (42) 7576301; fax (42) 7586251; internet www.daily-pakistan.com; f. 1990; Urdu; Chief Editor Mujibur Rahman Shami.

Daily Times: Media Times (Pvt) Ltd, 41-N, Industrial Area, Gulberg II, Lahore; tel. (42) 5878614; fax (42) 5878620; e-mail editor@dailytimes.com.pk; Editor Najam Sethi.

Daily Wifaq: 6A Warris Rd, Lahore; tel. (42) 6367467; e-mail dailywiqaf@hotmail.com; Urdu; also publ. in Rawalpindi, Sargodha and Rahimyar Khan; Editor Mazhar Waqar; circ. 20,000.

Mahgribi Pakistan: Lahore; tel. (42) 53490; Urdu; also publ. in Bahawalpur and Sukkur; Editor M. Shafaat.

The Nation: NIPCO House, 4 Sharah-e-Fatima Jinnah, POB 1815, Lahore 54000; tel. (42) 6367580; fax (42) 6367005; e-mail editor@nation.com; internet www.nation.com.pk; f. 1986; English; Chair. Majeed Nizami; Editor Arif Nizami; circ. 52,000.

Nawa-i-Waqt (Voice of the Time): 4 Sharah-e-Fatima Jinnah, Lahore 54000; tel. (42) 6302050; fax (42) 6367583; internet www.nawaiwaqt.com.pk; f. 1940; English, Urdu; also publ. edns in Karachi, Islamabad and Multan; Editor Majid Nizami; combined circ. 560,000.

The Sun International: 15-L, Gulberg III, Ferozepur Rd, Lahore; tel. (42) 5883540; fax (42) 5839951; Editor Mahmood Sadiq.

Tijarat: 14 Abbot Rd, opp. Nishat Cinema, Lahore; Urdu; Editor Jamil Athar.

Rawalpindi

Daily Jang: Murree Rd, Rawalpindi; internet www.jang.com.pk; f. 1940; also publ. in Quetta, Karachi, Lahore and London; Urdu; independent; Editor Mir Javed Rehman; circ. (Rawalpindi) 65,000.

Daily Wifaq: 7A C/A, Satellite Town, Rawalpindi; e-mail dailywifaq@hotmail.com; f. 1959; also publ. in Lahore, Sargodha and Rahimyar Khan; Urdu; Editor Mustafa Sadiq.

The News: Al-Rehman Bldg, Murree Rd, Rawalpindi; tel. (51) 5556223; e-mail thenews@isb.comsats.net.pk; internet www.jang-group.com; f. 1991; also publ. in Lahore and Karachi; English; independent; Chief Editor Mir Shakil-ur-Rahman.

Other Towns

Aftab: Hyderabad; Sindhi; also publ. in Multan; Editor Sheikh Ali Mohammad.

Al Falah: Al Falah Bldg, Saddar Rd, Peshawar; f. 1939; Urdu and Pashtu; Editor S. Abdullah Shah.

Al-Jamiat-e-Sarhad: Kocha Gilania Chakagali, Karimpura Bazar, Peshawar; tel. (91) 2567757; e-mail sagha@brain.net.pk; f. 1941; Urdu and Pashtu; Propr and Chief Editor S. M. Hassan Gilani.

Balochistan Times: Jinnah Rd, Quetta; Editor Syed Fasih Iqbal.

Basharat: Peshawar; Urdu; general; also publ. in Islamabad; Chief Editor Anwar-ul-Haq; Editor Khalid Ather.

Daily Awaz: Peshawar; political; Man. Editor Ali Raza Malik.

Daily Business Report: Railway Rd, Faisalabad; tel. (41) 642131; fax (41) 621207; f. 1948; Editor Abdul Rashid Ghazi; circ. 26,000.

Daily Hewad: 32 Stadium Rd, Peshawar; tel. (521) 270501; Pashtu; Editor-in-Chief Rehman Shah Afridi.

Daily Ibrat Hyderabad: Ibrat Building, Gadi Khata, Hyderabad; tel. (221) 28571; fax (221) 784300; e-mail ibrat@hyd.compol.com; internet www.ibratgroup.com; Sindhi; Man. Editor Qazi Asad Abid.

Daily Khadim-e-Waten: B-2, Civil Lines, Hyderabad; Editor Mushtaq Ahmad.

Daily Rehber: 17-B East Trust Colony, Bahawalpur; tel. (621) 884664; fax (621) 874032; e-mail rehberbwp@yahoo.co.uk; f. 1951; Urdu; Chief Editor Akhter Hussain Anjum; circ. 250,000.

Daily Sarwan: 11-EGOR Colony, Hyderabad; tel. (221) 781382; Sindhi; Chief Editor Ghulam Hussain.

Daily Shabaz: Peshawar; tel. (521) 220188; fax (521) 216483; Urdu; organ of the Awami National Party; Chief Editor Begum Naseem Wali Khan.

Frontier Post: 32 Stadium Rd, Peshawar; tel. (521) 79174; fax (521) 76575; e-mail editor@frontierpost.com.pk; internet www.frontierpost.com.pk; f. 1985; English; left-wing; also publ. in Lahore; closed down temporarily in January 2001, reopened in June; Editor-in-Chief Rehmat Shah Afridi; Editor Muzaffar Shah Afridi.

Jihad: 15A Islamia Club Bldg, Khyber Bazar, Peshawar; tel. (521) 210522; e-mail jehad@pes.comsats.net.pk; also publ. in Karachi, Rawalpindi, Islamabad and Lahore; Editor Sharif Farooq.

Kaleem: Shahi Bazar Thalla, POB 88, Sukkur; tel. (71) 22086; fax (71) 22087; e-mail kaleem1@hyd.paknet.com.pk; Urdu; Editor Shahid Mehr Shamsi.

Kavish: Sindh Printing and Publishing House, Civil Lines, POB 43, Hyderabad; Chief Editor Muhammad Ayub Qazi; Publr/Editor Aslam A. Qazi.

Mashriq: Quetta; Chief Editor Aziz Mazhar.

Nawai Asma'n: Mubarak Ali Shah Rd, Hyderabad; tel. and fax (221) 21925; Urdu, Sindhi and Pashtu; Chief Editor Dost Muhammad.

The News: Qaumi Printing Press, Peshawar; English; Editor Khurshid Ahmad.

Punjab News: Iftikhar Heights, Aminpur Bazar, POB 419, Faisalabad; tel. (41) 633102; fax (41) 615731; e-mail imranlateef1@hotmail.com; internet www.punjabnews.com.pk; f. 1968; Chief Editor and Publr Sheikh Sultan Mahmood; circ. 10,000.

Sarhad: New Gate, Peshawar.

Sindh Guardian: Tulsi Das Rd, POB 300, Hyderabad; tel. and fax (221) 21926; English; Chief Editor Dost Muhammad.

Sindh News: Garikhata, Hyderabad; tel. (221) 20793; fax (221) 781867; Editor Kazi Saeed Akber.

Sindh Observer: POB 43, Garikhata, Hyderabad; tel. (221) 27302; English; Editor Aslam Akber Kazi.

Sindhu: Popular Printers, Ibrat Bldg, Garhhi Khata, Hyderabad; tel. (221) 783571; fax (221) 783570; Sindhi; political.

Watan: 10 Nazar Bagh Flat, Peshawar.

Zamana: Jinnah Rd, Quetta; tel. (81) 71217; Urdu; Editor Syed Fasih Iqbal; circ. 5,000.

SELECTED WEEKLIES

Akhbar-e-Jehan: Printing House, off I. I. Chundrigar Rd, Karachi; tel. (21) 2634368; fax (21) 2635693; e-mail editor-in-chief@akhbar-e-jehan.com; internet www.akhbar-e-jehan.com; f. 1967; Urdu; independent; illustrated family magazine; Editor-in-Chief Mir Javed Rahman; circ. 285,000.

Amal: Shah Qabool Colony, POB 185, Peshawar; tel. (91) 5704673; e-mail maab_kaifi@hotmail.com; f. 1958; Urdu, Pashtu and English; Chief Editor F. M. Zafar Kaifi; Publr Munazima Maab Kaifi.

Badban: Nai Zindagi Publications, Rana Chambers, Old Anarkali, Lahore; Editor Mujibur Rehman Shami.

Chatan: Chatan Bldg, 88 McLeod Rd, Lahore; tel. (42) 6311336; fax (42) 6374690; f. 1948; Urdu; Editor Masud Shorish.

Family Magazine: 4 Shara-i-Fatima Jinnah, Lahore 54000; tel. (42) 6367551; fax (42) 6367583; circ. 100,000.

The Friday Times: 72-F. C. C. Gulberg IV, Lahore; tel. (42) 5673510; fax (42) 5751025; e-mail tft@lhr.comsats.net.pk; internet www.thefridaytimes.com; independent; Editor/Owner Najam Sethi.

Hilal: Hilal Rd, Rawalpindi 46000; tel. (51) 56134605; fax (51) 565017; f. 1951; Friday; Urdu; illustrated armed forces; Editor Mumtaz Iqbal Malik; circ. 90,000.

Insaf: P/929, Banni, Rawalpindi 46000; tel. and fax (51) 5550903; fax (51) 4411038; e-mail insafrwp@isb.paknet.com.pk; f. 1955; Editor Mir Waqar Aziz.

Lahore: Galaxy Law Chambers, 1st Floor, Room 1, Turner Rd, Lahore 5; f. 1952; Editor Saqib Zeervi; circ. 8,500.

Mahwar: D23, Block H, North Nazimabad, Karachi; Editor Shahida Nafis Siddiqi.

Memaar-i-Nao: 39 KMC Bldg, Leamarket, Karachi; Urdu; labour magazine; Editor M. M. Mubasir.

The Muslim World: 49-B, Block 8, Gulshan-e-Iqbal, Karachi 75300; POB 5030, Karachi 74000; tel. (21) 4960738; fax (21) 466878; English; current affairs.

Nairang Khayal: 8 Mohammadi Market, Rawalpindi; f. 1924; Urdu; Chief Editor Sultan Rashk.

PAKISTAN

Nida-i-Millat: 4 Sharah-e-Fatima Jinnah, Lahore 54000.

Noor Jehan Weekly: 32A National Auto Plaza, POB 8833, Karachi 74400; tel. and fax (21) 7723946; f. 1948; Urdu; film journal; Editor KHALID CHAWLA.

Pakistan and Gulf Economist: 1st Floor, 20-C, Sunset Lane 9, Phase 2 Extension, D. H. A., Karachi 75500; tel. (21) 5883967; fax (21) 5883295; e-mail information@pakistaneconomist.com; internet www.pakistaneconomist.com; f. 1960; English; Editor ALI HAIDER GOKAL; circ. 30,000.

Pak Kashmir: Pak Kashmir Office, Soikarno Chowk, Liaquat Rd, Rawalpindi; tel. (51) 74845; f. 1951; Urdu; Editor MUHAMMED FAYYAZ ABBAZI.

Parsi Sansar and Loke Sevak: 8 Mehrabad, 5 McNeil Rd, Karachi 75530; tel. and fax (21) 5656217; e-mail organ@cyber.net.pk; f. 1909; English and Gujarati; Editor MEHERJI P. DASTUR.

Parwaz: Madina Office, Bahawalpur; Urdu; Editor MUSTAQ AHMED.

Qallandar: Peshawar; f. 1950; Urdu; Editor M. A. K. SHERWANI.

Quetta Times: Albert Press, Jinnah Rd, Quetta; f. 1924; English; Editor S. RUSTOMJI; circ. 4,000.

Shahab-e-Saqib: Shahab Saqib Rd, Maulana St, Peshawar; f. 1950; Urdu; Editor S. M. RIZVI.

Takbeer: A-1, 3rd Floor, 'Namco Centre', Campbell St, Karachi 74200; tel. (21) 2626613; fax (21) 2627742; e-mail irfanfaruqi@usa.com; f. 1984; Urdu; Sr. Exec. IRFAN KALIM FAROOQ; circ. 70,000.

Tarjaman-i-Sarhad: Peshawar; Urdu and Pashtu; Editor MOHAMMAD SHAFI SABIR.

Times of Kashmir: P/929, Banni, Rawalpindi 46000; tel. (51) 5550903; fax (51) 4411348; e-mail insafrwp@isb.paknet.com.pk; f. 1982; English; Editor Mir IQBAL AZIZ.

Ufaq: 44H, Block No. 2, PECHS, Karachi; tel. (21) 437992; f. 1978; Editor WAHAJUDDIN CHISHTI; circ. 2,000.

SELECTED PERIODICALS

Aadab Arz: 190 N. Ghazali Rd, Saman Abad, Lahore 54500; tel. (42) 7582449; monthly; Editor KHALID BIN HAMID.

Aalami Digest: B-1, Momin Sq., Rashid Minhas Rd, Gulshan-e-Iqbal, Karachi; monthly; Urdu; Editor ZAHEDA HINA.

Akhbar-e-Watan: 68-C, 13th Commercial St, Phase-II, Extension Defence, Karachi; tel. (21) 5886071; fax (21) 5890179; e-mail akhbarewatan@hotmail.com; f. 1977; monthly; Urdu; cricket; Man. Editor MUNIR HUSSAIN; circ. 63,000.

Albalagh Darul Uloom: Korangi Rd, Karachi; monthly; Editor MOHAMMED TAQI USMANI.

Al-Ma'arif: Institute of Islamic Culture, Club Rd, Lahore 54000; tel. (42) 6363127; f. 1950; quarterly; Urdu; Dir and Editor-in-Chief Dr RASHID AHMAD JALLANDHRI.

Anchal: 24 Saeed Mansion, I. I. Chundrigar Rd, Karachi; monthly.

Architecture and Interiors: B-34, Block 15, Gulshan-e-Iqbal, Karachi; tel. (21) 4977652; fax (21) 4967656; e-mail aplusi@cyberaccess.com.pk; internet www.archpresspk.com; f. 2001; quarterly; English; Editor MUTJUBA HUSSAIN; Man. Editor MURTUZA SHIKOH.

Archi Times: Ghafoor Chambers, 7th Floor, Abdullah Haroon Rd, Karachi; tel. (21) 7772397; fax (21) 7772417; e-mail archtime@cyberaccess.com.pk; f. 1986; monthly; English; architecture; Editor MUJTABA HUSSAIN.

Asia Travel News: 101 Muhammadi House, I. I. Chundrigar Rd, Karachi 74000; tel. (21) 2424837; fax (21) 2420797; fortnightly; travel trade, tourism and hospitality industry; Editor JAVED MUSHTAQ.

Auto Times: 5 S. J. Kayani Shaheed Rd, off Garden Rd, Karachi; tel. (21) 713595; fortnightly; English; Editor MUHAMMAD SHAHZAD.

Bachoon Ka Risala: 108–110 Adam Arcade, Shaheed-e-Millat Rd, Karachi; tel. (21) 419616; monthly; Urdu; Editor RUKHSANA SEHAM MIRZA.

Bagh: 777/18 Federal B Area, POB 485, Karachi; tel. (21) 449662; monthly; Urdu; Editor RAHIL IQBAL.

Bayyenat: Jamia Uloom-e-Islamia, Binnori Town, Karachi 74800; tel. (21) 4927233; f. 1962; monthly; Urdu; religious and social issues.

Beauty: Plot No. 4-C, 14th Commercial St, Defence Housing Authority, Phase II Extension, Karachi; tel. (21) 5805391; fax (21) 5896269; e-mail rmansuri@fascom.com; f. 2000; bi-monthly; English; Chief Editor RIAZ AHMED MANSURI.

Beemakar (Insurer): 85 Press Chambers, I. I. Chundrigar Rd, Karachi; monthly; Urdu; Man. Editor SHAMSHAD AHMAD; Editor A. M. HASHMI.

Chand: 190 N. Ghazali Rd, Saman Abad, Lahore 54500; tel. (42) 7582449; monthly; Editor MASOOD HAMID.

The Cricketer: Plot No. 4-C, 14th Commercial St, Defence Housing Authority, Phase II Extension, Karachi; tel. (21) 5805391; fax (21) 5896269; e-mail rmansuri@fascom.com; f. 1972; monthly; English/Urdu; Chief Editor RIAZ AHMED MANSURI.

Dastarkhuan: Plot No. 4-C, 14th Commercial St, Defence Housing Authority, Phase II Extension, Karachi; tel. (21) 5805391; fax (21) 5896269; e-mail rmansuri@fascom.com; f. 1998; bi-monthly; Urdu; Chief Editor RIAZ AHMED MANSURI.

Defence Journal: 16B, 7th Central St, Defence Housing Authority, POB 12234, Karachi 75500; tel. (21) 5894074; fax (21) 571710; f. 1975; monthly; English; Editor-in-Chief IKRAM SEHGAL; circ. 10,000.

Dentist: 70/7, Nazimabad No. 3, Karachi 18; f. 1984; monthly; English and Urdu; Editor NAEEMULLAH HUSAIN.

Dosheeza: 108–110 Adam Arcade, Shaheed-e-Millat Rd, Karachi; tel. (21) 4930470; fax (21) 4934369; monthly; Urdu; Editor RUKHSANA SEHAM MIRZA.

Duniya-e-Tibb: Eveready Chambers, 2nd Floor, Mohd Bin Qasim Rd, off I. I. Chundrigar Rd, POB 1385, Karachi 1; tel. (21) 2630985; fax (21) 2637624; e-mail mcm@digicom.net.pk; f. 1986; monthly; Urdu; modern and Asian medicine; Editor QUTUBUDDIN; circ. 12,000.

Economic Review: Al-Masiha, 3rd Floor, 47 Abdullah Haroon Rd, POB 7843, Karachi 74400; tel. (21) 7728963; fax (21) 7728957; f. 1969; monthly; economic, industrial and investment research; Editor AHMAD MUHAMMAD KHAN.

Engineering Horizons: 3/II Shadman Plaza, Shadman Market, Lahore 54000; tel. (42) 7581743; fax (42) 7587422; e-mail mahmood@imtiaz-faiz.com; f. 1988; monthly; English.

Engineering Review: 305 Spotlit Chambers, Dr Billimoria St, off I. I. Chundrigar Rd, POB 807, Karachi 74200; tel. (21) 2632567; fax (21) 2639378; e-mail engineeringreview@yahoo.com; internet www.engineeringreview.com.pk; f. 1975; fortnightly; English; circ. 5,000.

Film Asia: 68-C, 13th Commercial St, Phase-II, Extension Defence, Karachi; tel. (21) 5886071; fax (21) 5890179; e-mail akhbarewatan@hotmail.com; f. 1973; monthly; film, television, fashion, art and culture; Man. Editor MUNIR HUSSAIN; circ. 38,000.

Good Food: Plot No. 4-C, 14th Commercial St, Defence Housing Authority, Phase II Extension, Karachi; tel. (21) 5805391; fax (21) 5896269; e-mail rmansuri@fascom.com; f. 1997; bi-monthly; English; Chief Editor RIAZ AHMED MANSURI.

Hamdard-i-Sehat: Institute of Health and Tibbi Research, Hamdard Foundation Pakistan, Nazimabad, Karachi 74600; tel. (21) 6616001; fax (21) 6611755; e-mail hamdardfoundation@hamdard.com.pk; f. 1933; monthly; Urdu; Editor-in-Chief SADIA RASHID; circ. 13,000.

Hamdard Islamicus: Hamdard Foundation Pakistan, Nazimabad, Karachi 74600; tel. (21) 6616001; fax (21) 6611755; e-mail hamdardfoundation@hamdard.com.pk; f. 1978; quarterly; English; Editor-in-Chief SADIA RASHID; circ. 750.

Hamdard Medicus: Hamdard Foundation Pakistan, Nazimabad, Karachi 74600; tel. (21) 6616001; fax (21) 6611755; e-mail hamdardfoundation@hamdard.com.pk; f. 1957; quarterly; English; Editor-in-Chief SADIA RASHID; circ. 1,000.

Hamdard Naunehal: Hamdard Foundation Pakistan, Nazimabad, Karachi 74600; tel. (21) 6616001; fax (21) 6611755; e-mail hamdardfoundation@hamdard.com.pk; f. 1952; monthly; Urdu; Editor MASOOD AHMAD BARAKATI; circ. 34,000.

The Herald: Haroon House, Dr Ziauddin Ahmed Rd, Karachi 74200; tel. (21) 5670001; fax (21) 5687221; e-mail saquib.herald@dawn.com; f. 1970; monthly; English; Editor SAQUIB HANIF; circ. 38,000.

Hikayat: 26 Patiala Ground, Link McLeod Rd, Lahore; monthly; Editor SHAHID JAMIL; circ. 25,000.

Honhar-e-Pakistan: 56 Aurangzeb Market, Karachi; monthly; Editor MAZHAR YUSAFZAI.

Hoor: Hoor St, Lahore; monthly; Editor KHULA RABIA.

Islami Jumhuria: Laj Rd, Old Anarkali, Lahore; monthly; Editor NAZIR TARIQ.

Islamic Studies: Islamic Research Institute, Faisal Masjid Campus, POB 1035, Islamabad 44000; tel. (51) 850751; fax (51) 250821; e-mail amzia555@apollo.net.pk; f. 1962; quarterly; English, Urdu (Fikro-Nazar) and Arabic (Al Dirasat al-Islamiyyah) edns; Islamic literature, religion, history, geography, language and the arts; Editor Dr ZAFAR ISHAQ ANSARI (acting); circ. 3,000.

Jamal: Institute of Islamic Culture, 2 Club Rd, Lahore 54000; tel. (42) 6363127; f. 1950; annual; English; Dir and Editor-in-Chief Dr JULUNDHRI RASHEED.

Journal of the Pakistan Historical Society: c/o Hamdard Foundation, Nazimabad, Karachi 74600; tel. (21) 6616001; fax (21) 6611755; e-mail hamdard@khi.paknet.com.pk; f. 1953; quarterly; English; Editor Dr ANSAR ZAHID KHAN; circ. 700.

Khel-Ke-Duniya: 6/13 Alyusaf Chamber, POB 340, Karachi; tel. (21) 216888.

Khwateen Digest: Urdu Bazar, M. A. Jinnah Rd, Karachi; monthly; Urdu; Editor MAHMUD RIAZ.

PAKISTAN

Kiran: 37 Urdu Bazar, M. A. Jinnah Rd, Karachi; tel. (21) 216606; Editor Mahmud Babar Faisal.

Leather News: Iftikhar Chambers, opp. UNI Plaza, Altaf Hussain Rd, POB 4323, Karachi 74000; fax (21) 2631545; f. 1989; Editor Abdul Rafay Siddiqi.

Medical Variety: 108–110 Adam Arcade, Shaheed-e-Millat Rd, Karachi; tel. (21) 419616; monthly; English; Editor Rukhsana Seham Mirza.

Muslim World Business: 20 Sasi Arcade, 4th Floor, Main Clifton Rd, POB 10417, Karachi 6; tel. (21) 534870; f. 1989; monthly; English; political and business; Editor-in-Chief Muzaffar Hassan.

Naey-Ufaq: 24 Saeed Mansion, I. I. Chundrigar Rd, Karachi; fortnightly.

NGM Communication: Gulberg Colony, POB 3033, Lahore 54660; tel. (42) 5713849; e-mail anjeeam@yahoo.com; internet www.geocities.com/anjeeam; English; lists newly-released Pakistani publications on the internet; updated weekly; Editor Gufraan Nizami.

Pakistan Journal of Applied Economics: Applied Economics Research Centre, University of Karachi, POB 8403, Karachi 75270; tel. (21) 9243168; fax (21) 4829730; e-mail pjae@cyber.net.pk; twice a year; Editor Prof. Dr Shahida Wizarat.

Pakistan Journal of Scientific and Industrial Research: Pakistan Council of Scientific and Industrial Research, Scientific Information Centre, PCSIR Laboratories Campus, off University Rd, Karachi 75280; tel. (21) 4651741; fax (21) 4651738; e-mail pcsirsys@super.net.pk; f. 1958; bi-monthly; English; Exec. Editor Dr Kaniz Fizza Azhar; circ. 1,000.

Pakistan Management Review: Pakistan Institute of Management, Management House, Shahrah Iran, Clifton, Karachi 75600; tel. (21) 9251711; e-mail pimkhi@pim.com.pk; internet www.pim.com.pk; f. 1960; quarterly; English; Editor Iqbal A. Qazi.

Pasban: Faiz Modh Rd, Quetta; fortnightly; Urdu; Editor Molvi Mohd Abdullah.

Phool: 4 Sharah-e-Fatima Jinnah, Lahore 54000; tel. (42) 6367551; e-mail editor@phool.com.pk; internet www.phool.com.pk; f. 1989; monthly; children's; Chief Editor Majid Nizami; Editor M. Shoaib Mirza; circ. 45,000.

Progress: 4th Floor, PIDC House, Dr Ziauddin Ahmed Rd, Karachi 75530; tel. (21) 111-568-568; fax (21) 5680005; e-mail n_nusrat@ppl.com.pk; f. 1956; monthly; publ. by Pakistan Petroleum Ltd; Editor and Publr Nusrat Nasarullah; Chief Exec./Man. Dir S. Munsif Raza.

Qaumi Digest: 50 Lower Mall, Lahore; tel. (42) 7225143; fax (42) 7233261; monthly; Editor Mujibur Rehman Shami.

Sabrang Digest: 47–48 Press Chambers, I. I. Chundrigar Rd, Karachi 1; tel. (21) 211961; f. 1970; monthly; Urdu; Editor Shakeel Adil Zadah; circ. 150,000.

Sach-Chee Kahaniyan: 108–110 Adam Arcade, Shaheed-e-Millat Rd, Karachi; tel. (21) 4930470; fax (21) 4934369; monthly; Urdu; Editor Rukhsana Seham Mirza.

Sayyarah: Aiwan-e-Adab, Urdu Bazar, Lahore 54000; tel. (42) 7321842; f. 1962; monthly; Urdu; literary; Man. Editor Hafeez-ur-Rahman Ahsan.

Sayyarah Digest: 244, Main Market Riwaz Garden, Lahore 54000; tel. (42) 7245412; fax (42) 7325080; e-mail sayyaradigest@brain.com.pk; f. 1963; monthly; Urdu; Chief Editor Amjad Rauf Khan; Editor Kamran Amjad Khan; circ. 40,000.

Science Magazine: Science Book Foundation, Haji Bldg, Hassan Ali Efendi Rd, Karachi; tel. (21) 2625647; monthly; Urdu; Editor Qasim Mahmood.

Seep: Alam Market, Block No. 16, Federal B Area, Karachi; quarterly; Editor Nasim Durrani.

Show Business: 108–110 Adam Arcade, Shaheed-e-Millat Rd, POB 12540, Karachi; tel. (21) 419616; monthly; Urdu; Editor Rukhsana Seham Mirza.

Sindh Quarterly: 36D Karachi Administrative Co-operative Housing Society, off Shaheed-e-Millat Rd, Karachi 75350; tel. (21) 4531988; f. 1973; Editor Sayid Ghulam Mustafa Shah.

Smash: Plot No. 4-C, 14th Commercial St, Defence Housing Authority, Phase II Extension, Karachi; tel. (21) 5805391; fax (21) 5896269; e-mail mansuri@fascom.com; f. 2000; monthly; English; Chief Editor Riaz Ahmed Mansuri.

Spider: Haroon House, Dr Ziauddin Ahmed Rd, Karachi 74200; tel. (21) 111-444-777; fax (21) 5681544; e-mail spider@spider.tm; internet www.spider.tm; f. 1998; internet monthly; Editor Ali Ahsan Halai; CEO Hameed Haroon.

Sports International: Arshi Market, Firdaus Colony, Nazimabad, Karachi 74600; tel. (21) 6602171; fax (21) 6683768; e-mail ibp-khi@cyber.net.pk; f. 1972; fortnightly; Urdu and English; Chief Editor Kanwar Abdul Majeed; Editor Raheel Majeed.

Taj: Jamia Tajia, St 13, Sector 14/B, Buffer Zone, Karachi 75850; monthly; Editor Baba M. Atif Shah Anwari Zaheeni Taji.

Talimo Tarbiat: Ferozsons (Pvt) Ltd, 60 Shahrah-e-Quaid-e-Azam, Lahore 54000; tel. (42) 6301196; fax (42) 6369204; f. 1941; children's monthly; Urdu; Chief Editor A. Salam; circ. 50,000.

Textile Times: Arshi Market, Firdaus Colony, Nazimabad, Karachi 74600; tel. (21) 6683768; e-mail ibp-khi@cyber.net.pk; f. 1993; monthly; English; Chief Editor Kanwar Abdul Majeed; Exec. Editor Raheel Majeed Khan.

Trade Chronicle: Iftikhar Chambers, Altaf Hussain Rd, POB 5257, Karachi 74000; tel. (21) 2631587; fax (21) 2635007; e-mail arsidiqi@fascom.com; f. 1953; monthly; English; trade, politics, finance and economics; Editor Abdul Rab Siddiqi; circ. 6,000.

Trade Link International: Zahoor Mansion, Tariq Rd, Karachi; monthly; English; Man. Editor M. Imran Baig; Editor Ikramullah Qureishi.

TV Times: Plot No. 4-C, 14th Commercial St, Defence Housing Authority, Phase II Extension, Karachi; tel. (21) 5805391; fax (21) 5896269; e-mail rmansuri@fascom.com; f. 1987; monthly; English; Chief Editor Riaz Ahmed Mansuri.

UNESCO Payami: 30 UNESCO House, Sector H-8/1, Islamabad; tel. (51) 434196; fax (51) 431815; monthly; Urdu; publ. by Pakistan National Commission for UNESCO; Editor Dr Munir A. Abro.

The Universal Message: D-35, Block 5, Federal 'B' Area, Karachi 75950; tel. (21) 6349840; fax (21) 6361040; f. 1979; journal of the Islamic Research Acad; monthly; English; literature, politics, economics, religion; Editor Asadullah Khan.

Urdu Digest: 21-Acre Scheme, Samanabad, Lahore 54500; tel. (42) 7589957; fax (42) 7563646; e-mail urdudigest42@hotmail.com; monthly; Urdu; Editor Altaf Hasan Qureshee.

Voice of Islam: Jamiatul Falah Bldg, Akbar Rd, Saddar, POB 7141, Karachi 74400; tel. (21) 7721394; f. 1952; monthly; Islamic Cultural Centre magazine; English; Editor Prof. Abdul Qadeer Saleem; Man. Editor Prof. Waqar Zubairi.

Wings: 101 Muhammadi House, I. I. Chundrigar Rd, Karachi 74000; tel. (21) 2412591; fax (21) 2420797; monthly; aviation and defence; English; Editor and Publr Javed Mushtaq.

Women's Own: Plot No. 4-C, 14th Commercial St, Defence Housing Authority, Phase II Extension, Karachi; tel. (21) 5805391; fax (21) 5896269; e-mail rmansuri@fascom.com; f. 1987; monthly; English; Chief Editor Riaz Ahmed Mansuri.

Yaqeen International: Darut Tasnif (Pvt) Ltd, Main Hub River Rd, Mujahidabad, Karachi 75760; tel. (21) 2814432; fax (21) 2811304; e-mail daruttasnif@yaqeendtl.com; internet www.yaqeendtl.com; f. 1952; English and Arabic; Islamic organ; Editor Dr Hafiz Muhammad Adil.

Yaran-e-Watan: Overseas Pakistanis Foundation, Shahrah-e-Jamhuriate, G-5/2, POB 1470, Islamabad 44000; tel. (51) 9210175; fax (51) 9224518; e-mail opf@comsats.net.pk; f. 1982; monthly; Urdu; publ. by the Overseas Pakistanis Foundation; Editor Haroon Rashid.

Youth World International: 104/C Central C/A, Tariq Rd, Karachi; tel. (21) 442211; f. 1987; monthly; English; Editor Syed Adil Ebrahim.

NEWS AGENCIES

Associated Press of Pakistan (APP): 18 Mauve Area, Zero Point, G-7/1, POB 1258, Islamabad; tel. (51) 2203073; fax (51) 2203074; e-mail appnews@isb.comsats.net.pk; f. 1948; Man. Dir Fazalur Rahman Malik.

National News Agency (NNA): 491-C, Margalla Town, Islamabad 45510; tel. (51) 2840896; fax (51) 2841746; e-mail nnaisb@yahoo.com; f. 1990; Chief Editor Suhail Ilyas.

News Network International: 2nd Floor, Redco Plaza, Islamabad 44000; tel. (51) 2874344; fax (51) 2826289; e-mail nni2005@isb.paknet.com.pk; internet www.nni-news.com; f. 1992; Pakistan's oldest and largest independent international news agency; news in Arabic, Urdu and English; provides services to 435 newspapers and radio and television channels in South Asia, Europe, the Middle East, the Far East and the USA; Editor-in-Chief Qaisar Javed; Editor Muhammad Tahir Khan.

Pakistan—International Press Agency (PPA): 6, St 39, G-6/2, Islamabad 44000; tel. (51) 2279830; fax (51) 2272405; e-mail ppa@ppanews.com.pk; internet www.ppanews.com.pk; Chief Editor Khalid Athar.

Pakistan Press International (PPI): Press Centre, Shahrah Kamal Atatürk, POB 541, Karachi; tel. (21) 2633215; fax (21) 2217069; e-mail ppi@ppinewsagency.com; f. 1956; Chair. Owais Aslam Ali.

United Press of Pakistan (Pvt) Ltd (UPP): 1 Victoria Chambers, Haji Abdullah Haroon Rd, Karachi 74400; tel. (21) 5683235; fax (21)

5682694; e-mail pnrupp2000@yahoo.com; f. 1949; Man. Editor MAHMUDUL AZIZ; 5 brs.

Foreign Bureaux

Agence France-Presse (AFP): 90, Atatürk Ave, G-6/3, Islamabad; tel. (51) 111-237-475; fax (51) 2822203; e-mail islamabad@afp.com; Bureau Chief JEAN-HERVÉ DEILLER.

Agenzia Nazionale Stampa Associata (ANSA) (Italy): Islamabad; Bureau Chief ABSAR HUSAIN RIZVI.

Associated Press (AP) (USA): 6A, St 25, F-8/2, Islamabad; tel. (51) 2260957; fax (51) 2256176; Bureau Chief PAUL B. HAVEN.

Deutsche Presse-Agentur (dpa) (Germany): Islamabad; tel. (51) 821925; Correspondent ANWAR MANSURI.

Inter Press Service (IPS) (Italy): House 10, St 13, F-8/3, Islamabad; tel. (51) 853356; fax (42) 856430; Correspondent MUSHAHID HUSSAIN.

Reuters (United Kingdom): 2nd Floor, Pak Saudi Tower, POB 1069, Islamabad; tel. (51) 2800155; e-mail simon.denyer@reuters.com; Bureau Chief SIMON DENYER.

United Press International (UPI) (USA): Islamabad; tel. (51) 2254470; Bureau Chief ANWAR IQBAL.

Xinhua (New China) News Agency (People's Republic of China): 12A, St 31, F-8/3, Islamabad; tel. (51) 2281490; Chief Correspondent DU ZHENFENG.

PRESS ASSOCIATIONS

All Pakistan Newspaper Employees Confederation: Karachi Press Club, M. R. Kayani Rd, Karachi; f. 1976; confed. of all press industry trade unions; Pres. ABDUL HAMEED CHAPRA; Sec.-Gen. PERVAIZ SHAUKAT.

All Pakistan Newspapers Society: 32 Farid Chambers, Abdullah Haroon Rd, Karachi 3; tel. (21) 5671256; fax (21) 5671310; e-mail theapns@gmail.com; internet www.apns.com.pk; f. 1949; Pres. Mir SHAKIL-UR-REHMAN; Sec.-Gen. KAZI ASAD ABID.

Council of Pakistan Newspaper Editors: c/o United Press of Pakistan, 1 Victoria Chambers, Haji Abdullah Haroon Rd, Karachi 74400; tel. (21) 5682694; fax (21) 5682694; Pres. ARIF NIZAMI; Gen. Sec. QAZI ASLAM.

Publishers

Al-Hamra Publishing: Saudi Pak Tower, Jinnah Ave, Islamabad; tel. (51) 2823862; e-mail contact@alhamra.com.

Anjuman Taraqq-e-Urdu Pakistan: D-159, Block 7, Gulshan-e-Iqbal, Karachi 75300; tel. (21) 461406; f. 1903; literature, religion, textbooks, Urdu dictionaries, literary and critical texts; Pres. AFTAB AHMED KHAN; Hon. Sec. JAMIL UDDIN AALI.

Camran Publishers: Jalaluddin Hospital Bldg, Circular Rd, Lahore; f. 1964; general, technical, textbooks; Propr ABDUL HAMID.

Chronicle Publications: Iftikhar Chambers, Altaf Hussain Rd, POB 5257, Karachi 74000; tel. (21) 2631587; fax (21) 2635007; e-mail arsidiqi@fascom.com; f. 1953; reference, directories, religious books; Dir ABDUL RAUF SIDDIQI.

Dasnavi Book House: Book St, G-6, Mazang Rd, Lahore; tel. (42) 2231518; e-mail bookhome@hotmail.com.

Economic and Industrial Publications: Al-Masiha, 3rd Floor, 47 Abdullah Haroon Rd, POB 7843, Karachi 74400; tel. (21) 7728963; fax (21) 7728434; f. 1965; industrial, economic and investment research.

Elite Publishers Ltd: D-118, SITE, Karachi 75700; tel. (21) 2573435; fax (21) 2564720; e-mail elite@elite.com.pk; internet www.elite.com.pk; f. 1951; Chair. AHMED MIRZA JAMIL; Chief Exec. KHALID JAMIL.

Ferozsons (Pvt) Ltd: 60 Shahrah-e-Quaid-e-Azam, Lahore; tel. (42) 111-626-262; fax (42) 6369204; e-mail support@ferozsons.com.pk; internet www.ferozsons.com.pk; f. 1894; general books, school books, periodicals, maps, atlases, stationery products; Man. Dir A. SALAM; Dir ZAHEER SALAM.

Frontier Publishing Co: 22 Urdu Bazar, Lahore; tel. (42) 7355262; fax (42) 7247323; e-mail masim@brain.net.pk; internet www.brain.net.pk/~masim; academic and general; Execs MUHAMMAD ARIF, MUHAMMAD AMIR, MUHAMMAD ASIM.

Sh. Ghulam Ali and Sons (Pvt) Ltd: 199 Circular Rd, Lahore 54000; tel. (42) 7352908; fax (42) 6315478; e-mail niazasad@hotmail.com; internet www.ghulamali.com.pk; f. 1887; general, religion, technical, textbooks; Dirs NIAZ AHMAD, ASAD NIAZ.

Harf Academy: G/307, Amena Plaza, Peshawar Rd, Rawalpindi.

Idara Taraqqi-i-Urdu: S-1/363 Saudabad, Karachi 27; f. 1949; general literature, technical and professional books and magazines; Propr IKRAM AHMED.

Ilmi Kitab Khana: Kabeer St, Urdu Bazar, Lahore; tel. (42) 62833; f. 1948; technical, professional, historical and law; Propr Haji SARDAR MOHAMMAD.

Inayat Sons: YMCA Bldg, 16 The Mall, Lahore 54000; tel. (42) 8401335; fax (42) 7231896; e-mail general@inayatsons.com; internet www.inayatsons.com; f. 1971; Proprietor S. PERVEZ.

Indus Publications: 25 Fared Chambers, Abdullah Haroon Rd, Karachi; tel. (21) 5660242; e-mail muzaffar_indus@hotmail.com.

Islamic Book Centre: 25B Masson Rd, POB 1625, Lahore 54000; tel. (42) 6361803; fax (42) 6360955; e-mail lsaeed@paknetl.ptc.pk; religion in Arabic, Urdu and English; Islamic history, textbooks, dictionaries and reprints; Propr and Man. Dir SUMBLEYNA SAJID SAEED.

Islamic Publications (Pvt) Ltd: 3 Court St, Lower Mall, Lahore 54000; tel. (42) 7248676; fax (42) 7214974; e-mail islamicpak@hotmail.com; internet www.islamicpak.com.pk; f. 1959; Islamic literature in Urdu and English; Man. Dir Prof. MUHAMMAD AMIN JAVED; Gen. Man. AMANAT ALI.

Jamiatul Falah Publications: Jamiatul Falah Bldg, Akbar Rd, Saddar, POB 7141, Karachi 74400; tel. (21) 7721394; f. 1952; Islamic history and culture; Pres. MUZAFFAR AHMED HASHMI; Sec. Prof. SHAHZADUL HASAN CHISHTI.

Kazi Publications: 121 Zulqarnain Chambers, Ganpat Rd, POB 1845, Lahore; tel. (42) 7311359; fax (42) 7117606; e-mail kazip@brain.net.pk; internet www.brain.net.pk/~kazip/; f. 1978; Islamic literature, religion, law, biographies; Propr/Man. MUHAMMAD IKRAM SIDDIQI; Chief Editor MUHAMMAD IQBAL SIDDIQI.

Lark Publishers: Urdu Bazar, Karachi 1; f. 1955; general literature, magazines; Propr MAHMOOD RIAZ.

Liberty Books (Pvt) Ltd: 3 Rafiq Plaza, M. R. Kayani Rd, Saddar, Karachi; tel. (21) 5683026; fax (21) 5684319; e-mail libooks@cyber.net.pk; internet www.libertybooks.com; f. 1980.

Lion Art Press (Pvt) Ltd: 112 Shahrah-e-Quaid-e-Azam, Lahore 54000; tel. (42) 6304444; fax (42) 6367728; e-mail lionart786@hotmail.com; f. 1919; general publs in English and Urdu; Chief Exec. KHALID A. SHEIKH; Dir ASMA KHALID.

Maktaba Darut Tasnif: Main Hub River Rd, Mujahidabad, Karachi 75760; tel. (21) 2814432; fax (21) 2811307; e-mail daruttasnif@yaqeendtl.com; internet www.yaqeendtl.com; f. 1951; Koran, Majeed and Islamic literature; Dir ABDUL BAQI FAROOQI.

Malik Sirajuddin & Sons: 48/C, Lower Mall, POB 2250, Lahore 54000; tel. (42) 7657527; fax (42) 7657490; e-mail sirajco@brain.net.pk; f. 1905; general, religion, law, textbooks; Man. MALIK ABDUL ROUF.

Malik Sons: Karkhana Bazar, Faisalabad.

Medina Publishing Co: M. A. Jinnah Rd, Karachi 1; f. 1960; general literature, textbooks; Propr HAKIM MOHAMMAD TAQI.

Mehtab Co: Ghazni St, Urdu Bazar, Lahore; tel. (42) 7120071; fax (42) 7353489; e-mail shashraf@brain.net.pk; f. 1978; Islamic literature; Propr SHAHZAD RIAZ SHEIKH.

Mohammad Hussain and Sons: 17 Urdu Bazar, Lahore 2; tel. (42) 7244114; f. 1941; religion, textbooks; Partners MOHAMMAD HUSSAIN, AZHAR ALI SHEIKH, PERVEZ ALI SHEIKH.

Sh. Muhammad Ashraf: 7 Aibak Rd, New Anarkali, Lahore 7; tel. (42) 7353171; fax (42) 7353489; e-mail shashraf@brain.net.pk; f. 1923; books in English on all aspects of Islam; Man. Dir SHAHZAD RIAZ SHEIKH.

National Book Service: 22 Urdu Bazar, Lahore; tel. (42) 7247310; fax (42) 7247323; e-mail masim@brain.net.pk; internet www.brain.net.pk/~masim; academic and primary school books; Execs MUHAMMAD ARIF, MUHAMMAD AMIR, MUHAMMAD ASIM.

Oxford University Press: Plot No. 38, Sector 15, Korangi Industrial Area, Karachi; tel. (21) 111-693-673; fax (21) 5055071; e-mail oup.pk@oup.com; internet www.oup.com.pk; academic, educational and general; Man. Dir AMEENA SAIYID.

Pakistan Law House: Pakistan Chowk, POB 90, Karachi 1; tel. (21) 2212455; fax (21) 2627549; e-mail plh_law_house@hotmail.com; f. 1950; importers and exporters of legal books and reference books; Man. K. NOORANI.

Pakistan Publishing House: Victoria Chambers 2, A. Haroon Rd, Karachi 75400; tel. (21) 5681457; fax (21) 5682036; e-mail danyalbooks@hotmail.com; f. 1959; Propr H. NOORANI; Gen. Man. AAMIR HUSSEIN.

Paramount Books: 152/0, Block 2, PECHS, Karachi 75400; tel. (21) 4310030; e-mail paramount@cyber.net.pk.

Pioneer Book House: 1 Avan Lodge, Bunder Rd, POB 37, Karachi; periodicals, gazettes, maps and reference works in English, Urdu and other regional languages.

Premier Bookhouse: Shahin Market, Room 2, Anarkali, POB 1888, Lahore; tel. (42) 7321174; Islamic and law.

Publishers International: Bandukwala Bldg, 4 I. I. Chundrigar Rd, Karachi; f. 1948; reference; Man. Dir KAMALUDDIN AHMAD.

Publishers United (Pvt) Ltd: 176 Anarkali, POB 1689, Lahore 54000; tel. (42) 7352238; fax (42) 6316015; e-mail smalipub2@hotmail.com; f. 1950; Islamic studies, history, art, archaeology, literature, Oriental studies, geneology, scientific, medical, humanities and social sciences; Man. Dir AHMAD ALI SHEIKH.

Punjab Religious Books Society: Anarkali, Lahore 2; tel. (42) 54416; educational, religious, law and general; Gen. Man. A. R. IRSHAD; Sec. NAEEM SHAKIR.

Reprints Ltd: 16 Bahadur Shah Market, M. A. Jinnah Rd, Karachi; f. 1983; Pakistani edns of foreign works; Chair. A. D. KHALID; Man. Dir AZIZ KHALID.

Royal Book Co: BG-5, Rex Centre, Basement, Fatima Jinnah Rd, Karachi 75530; tel. (21) 5653418; e-mail royalbook@hotmail.com.

Sang-e-Meel Publications: 25 Lower Mall, Lahore 54000; tel. (42) 7220100; fax (42) 7245101; e-mail smp@sang-e-meel.com; internet www.sang-e-meel.com; f. 1962; Senior Man. ALI KAMRAN.

Sindhi Adabi Board (Sindhi Literary and Publishing Organization): Hyderabad; tel. (221) 771276; e-mail sindhiab@yahoo.com; f. 1951; history, literature, culture of Sindh; in Sindhi, Urdu, English, Persian and Arabic; translations into Sindhi, especially of literature and history; chaired by Minister of Education and Literacy, Sindh; Sec. INAM SHEIKH.

Taj Co Ltd: Manghopir Rd, POB 530, Karachi; tel. (21) 294221; f. 1929; religious books; Man. Dir A. H. KHOKHAR.

The Times Press (Pvt) Ltd: C-18, Al-Hilal Society, off University Rd, Karachi 74800; tel. (21) 4932931; fax (21) 4935602; e-mail timekhi@cyber.net.pk; internet www.timespress.8m.com; f. 1948; printers, publishers and stationery manufacturers, including security printing (postal stationery and stamps); registered publishers of Koran, school textbooks, etc.; Dir S. M. MINHAJUDDIN.

Tooba Publishers: 85 Sikandar Block, Allama Iqbal Town, Lahore; tel. (42) 5410185; e-mail haroonkallem@hotmail.com; f. 1983; poetry; Man. HAROON KALEEM USMANI.

Urdu Academy Sind: 16 Bahadur Shah Market, M. A. Jinnah Rd, Karachi 2; tel. (21) 2634185; f. 1947; brs in Hyderabad and Lahore; reference, general and textbooks; Editor and Man. Dir A. D. KHALID.

Vanguard Books (Pvt) Ltd: 72-FCC, Gulberg IV, Lahore; tel. (42) 5763510; fax (42) 5751025; e-mail vbl@brain.net.pk; Chief Exec. NAJAM SETHI.

West-Pak Publishing Co (Pvt) Ltd: 56N, Gulberg II, Lahore; tel. (42) 7230555; fax (42) 7120077; f. 1932; textbooks and religious books; Chief Exec. SYED AHSAN MAHMUD.

GOVERNMENT PUBLISHING HOUSE

Government Publications: Office of the Deputy Controller, Stationery and Forms, nr Old Sabzi Mandi, University Rd, Karachi 74800; tel. (21) 9231989; Dep. Controller MUHAMMAD AMIN BUTT.

PUBLISHERS' ASSOCIATION

Pakistan Publishers' and Booksellers' Association: YMCA Bldg, Shahrah-e-Quaid-e-Azam, Lahore; Chair. SYED AHSAN MAHMUD; Sec. ZUBAIR SAEED.

Broadcasting and Communications

TELECOMMUNICATIONS

Since 2000 the mobile cellular telephone industry has made significant progress in Pakistan. In January 2004 the Government approved legislation providing for enhanced competition in the industry. In 2005 there were 12.49m. mobile cellular telephone subscribers nation-wide.

Pakistan Telecommunication Authority (PTA): F-5/1, Islamabad 44000; tel. (51) 2878143; fax (51) 2878155; e-mail ddpr_pta@yahoo.com; internet www.pta.gov.pk; f. 1997; regulatory authority; Chair. Maj.-Gen. SHAHZADA ALAM MALIK; Dir-Gen. CH. MOHAMMAD DIN.

Burraq Telecom (Pvt) Ltd: House 189, St 69, Sector F-10/3, Islamabad; tel. (51) 111-287-727; fax (51) 2112380; e-mail info@burraqtel.com.pk; internet www.burraqtel.com.pk; f. 2004; jt venture between three telecommunications cos.

Carrier Telephone Industries (Pvt) Ltd: 1-9/2 Industrial Area, POB 1098, Islamabad 44000; tel. (51) 4434978; fax (51) 4449581; e-mail snmctipv@comsats.net.pk; internet www.ctipak.com.pk; f. 1969; Man. Dir MALIK MOHAMMAD AMIN.

Callmate Telips Telecom Ltd: 99-CF, 1/5 Clifton, Karachi; tel. (21) 5867696; fax (21) 5833006; e-mail info@cttelecom.net; internet www.cttelecom.net; f. 2003; telecommunications services.

Instaphone: Pakcom Ltd, World Trade Centre, 10 Khayaban-e-Roomi, Clifton, Karachi; tel. (21) 5871171; fax (21) 5869051; internet www.instaexcite.com; private mobile telephone co.

Mobilink: Orascom Telecom, Kuslum Plaza, 1st Floor, Blue Area, Islamabad; tel. (21) 5670261; fax (21) 5670268; private mobile telephone co.

Pakistan Telecommunications (Pvt) Ltd (PTCL): G-8/4, Islamabad 44000; tel. (51) 4844463; fax (51) 4843991; e-mail gmpr@ptcl.com.pk; internet www.ptcl.com.pk; f. 1990; 74% state-owned; 26% owned by United Arab Emirates co Etisalat; Chair. JUNAID I. KHAN.

Paktel Ltd: 68E, Jinnah Ave, Blue Area, Islamabad 44000; tel. (51) 2271105; fax (51) 2874453; internet www.paktel.com; private mobile telephone co.

TeleCard Ltd: 7th Floor, World Trade Centre, 10 Khayaban-e-Roomi, Block 5, Clifton, Karachi 75600; tel. (21) 111-222-124; e-mail info@gocdma.com.pk; internet www.gocdma.com.pk; Chief Exec. FAISAL HUSSAIN.

Telenor: 13-K, Moaiz Centre, F-7 Markaz, Islamabad; tel. (51) 111-345-700; fax (51) 2651923; internet www.telenor.com.pk; f. 2004; private mobile telephone co; Pres. and CEO TORE JOHNSEN.

Ufone: 13-B, F-7 Markaz, Jinnah Supper Market, Islamabad; internet www.ufone.com; f. 2001; subsidiary of Pakistan Telecommunications (Pvt) Ltd; private mobile telephone co; Chief Exec. BABAR KHAN.

Warid Telecommunications (Pvt) Ltd: 9th Floor, EFU Bldg, Jail Rd, Lahore; e-mail hr@waridtel.com; internet www.waridtel.com; owned by Abu Dhabi Group; CEO HAMID FAROOQ.

Other telecommunications companies operating in Pakistan include Telephone Industries of Pakistan and Alcatel Pakistan Ltd.

RADIO

Pakistan Broadcasting Corporation: National Broadcasting House, Constitution Ave, Islamabad 4400; tel. (51) 9214278; fax (51) 9223827; e-mail cfmpbchq@isb.comsats.net.pk; internet www.radio.gov.pk; f. 1947 as Radio Pakistan; national broadcasting network of 33 stations; home service 24 hrs daily in 17 languages and dialects; external services 11 hrs daily in 15 languages; world service 11.49 hrs daily in two languages; 80 news bulletins daily; Dir-Gen. TARIQ IMMAM.

Azad Kashmir Radio: Muzaffarabad; state-owned; Station Dir MASUD KASHFI; Dep. Controller (Eng.) SYED AHMED.

Capital FM: Islamabad; f. 1995; privately-owned; broadcasts music and audience participation shows 24 hrs daily.

FM-89: Karachi; e-mail info@cityFM89.com; broadcasts in Karachi, Lahore, Islamabad and Faisalabad.

FM-100: Karachi; tel. (21) 2630611; fax (21) 2629311; music station; broadcasts in Karachi, Lahore and Islamabad.

TELEVISION

Geo TV: I. I. Chundrigar Rd, Jang Building, Karachi; tel. (21) 2628614; fax (21) 2636937; e-mail distribution@geo.tv; f. 2003; Pakistan's first private broadcasting network; broadcasts in Urdu; Pres. IMRAN ASLAM.

Indus TV Network: 2nd Floor, Shafi Court, Civil Lines, Mereweather Rd, Karachi; tel. (21) 5693801; fax (21) 5693813; e-mail webmaster@industvnetwork.com; internet www.industvnetwork.com; f. 2000; Pakistan's first independent satellite channel.

I-Plus TV: 2nd Floor, Shafi Court, Mereweather Rd, Karachi; tel. (21) 5652283; fax (21) 5652285; e-mail im@industvnetwork.com.

Pakistan Television Corpn Ltd: Federal TV Complex, Constitution Ave, POB 1221, Islamabad; tel. (51) 9208651; fax (51) 9202202; e-mail md@ptv.com.pk; internet www.ptv.com.pk; f. 1964; transmits 24 hrs daily; four channels; Chair. SHAHID RAFI; Man. Dir ARSHAD KHAN.

Shalimar Television Network (Shalimar Recording and Broadcasting Co Ltd): 36, Sector H-9, POB 1246, Islamabad; tel. (51) 9257396; fax (51) 4434830; e-mail contact@srbc.com.pk; internet www.srbc.com.pk; f. 1989 as People's Television Network; 92.81% state-owned, 7.19% privately-owned; 20 terrestrial stations throughout Pakistan; Chief Exec. ANWAR JAHANGIR; Gen. Man. (Programme Co-ordination) RIFAT KAZMI.

Tele Biz: Techno City, Altaf Hussain Rd, Karachi 74000; tel. (51) 2273886; fax (51) 2278795; e-mail telebiz@cyber.net.pk; Bureau Chief ZAFAR SIDDIQI.

WAQT Television: 4 Sharah Fatimah Jinnah, Lahore; tel. (42) 6278981; fax (42) 6278980.

Finance

(cap. = capital; auth. = authorized; p.u. = paid up; res = reserves; dep. = deposits; m. = million; brs = branches; amounts in rupees unless otherwise stated)

BANKING

In January 1974 all domestic banks were nationalized. In December 1990 the Government announced that it intended to transfer the five state-owned commercial banks to private ownership. By late 1991 the majority of shares in the Muslim Commercial Bank Ltd and the Allied Bank of Pakistan Ltd had been transferred to private ownership. In 1991 the Government granted 10 new private commercial bank licences, the first since banks were nationalized in 1974. In June 2002 the Supreme Court reversed its 1999 ruling that ordered the Government to abolish charging interest. Interest charges, known as 'riba', are forbidden under Islamic law. The ruling would have required all financial institutions to adopt the Islamic style of banking. In late 2002 the State Bank of Pakistan gave banks three options for the launching of Islamic banking: to establish an independent Islamic bank; to open subsidiaries of existing commercial banks; and to establish new branches to carry out Islamic banking operations.

Central Bank

State Bank of Pakistan: Central Directorate, I. I. Chundrigar Rd, POB 4456, Karachi 2; tel. (21) 9212400; fax (21) 9212433; e-mail info@sbp.org.pk; internet www.sbp.org.pk; f. 1948; bank of issue; controls and regulates currency and foreign exchange; cap. 100m., res 63,859m., dep. 308,044m. (June 2003); Gov. SHAMSHAD AKHTER; Dep. Gov. TAWFIQ A. HUSAIN; 17 brs.

Commercial Banks

Allied Bank Ltd: Allied Bank Bldg, Khayaban-e-Iqbal, Main Clifton Rd, Bath Island, Central Office, Karachi 75600; tel. (21) 111-110-110; fax (21) 5217073; e-mail int_div@abl.com.pk; f. 1942 as Australasia Bank Ltd; name changed as above 2005; cap. 10,321m., res 575m., dep. 126,392m. (Dec. 2004); 49% state-owned; Pres., Chair. and Chief Exec. KHALID A. SHERWANI; Exec. Vice-Pres. RASHID MAQSOOD HAMIDI; 734 brs in Pakistan.

Askari Commercial Bank Ltd: AWT Plaza, The Mall, POB 1084, Rawalpindi; tel. (51) 9272150; fax (51) 9272455; e-mail askari@comsats.net.pk; internet www.askaribank.com.pk/; f. 1992; cap. 1,141.7m., res 2,759.6m., dep. 61,656.6m. (Dec. 2003); Chair. Lt-Gen. FAIZ JILANI; Pres. and Chief Exec. KALIM UR-RAHMAN; 57 brs.

Bank Al Habib Ltd: Mackinnons Bldg, I. I. Chundrigar Rd, Karachi; tel. (21) 2412421; fax (21) 2419752; e-mail alhabib@cyber.net.pk; internet www.bankalhabib.com; f. 1991; cap. 1,353m., res 1,398m., dep. 60,341m. (June 2004); Chief Exec. and Man. Dir ABBAS D. HABIB; 65 brs.

Bank Alfalah Ltd: BA Bldg, I. I. Chundrigar Rd, POB 6773, Karachi; tel. (21) 2414030; fax (21) 2417006; e-mail karachi@bankalfalah.com; internet www.bankalfalah.com; f. 1992 as Habib Credit and Exchange Ltd; name changed as above 1998; cap. 2,500.0m., res 1,008.8m., dep. 132,438.7m. (Dec. 2004); 70% owned by Abu Dhabi Consortium, 30% by Habib Bank; Pres. and Chief Exec. MUHAMMAD SALEEM AKHTAR; 13 brs.

The Bank of Khyber: 24 The Mall, Peshawar; tel. (521) 111-959-595; fax (521) 278146; e-mail bokgiant@pes.comsats.net.pk; internet www.bok.com.pk; cap. 1,231.0m., res 614.3m., dep. 19,454.6m. (March 2005); 100% state-owned; the main branch in Peshawar began Islamic banking operations in June 2003; Exec. Dir Qazi MUNIRUL HAQUE; Man. Dir MUNIR AHMED; 29 brs.

The Bank of Punjab: 7 Egerton Rd, POB 2254, Lahore 54000; tel. (42) 9200421; fax (42) 9200297; e-mail info@punjabbank.com; internet www.punjabbank.com; f. 1989; cap. 1,050m., res 1,362m., dep. 41,369m. (March 2004); 51.6% owned by provincial govt; Chair. HAMESH KHAN; Man. Dir and CEO C. R. SHARMA; 241 brs.

Crescent Commercial Bank Ltd: 5th Floor, Sidco Avenue Centre, Maulana Deen Mohammad Wafai Rd, Karachi 74000; tel. (21) 111-999-333; internet www.cresbank.com; f. 2002; Pres. and CEO SHEHZAD NAQVI; Chair. SHAMIM AHMAD KHAN; 18 brs.

Faysal Bank Ltd: 11/13 Trade Centre, I. I. Chundrigar Rd, POB 472, Karachi; tel. (21) 2638011; fax (21) 2637975; e-mail fbl@faysalbank.com.pk; internet www.faysalbank.com.pk; f. 1995; merged with Al-Faysal Investment Bank Ltd 2002; cap. 2,912.6m., res 2,259.1m., dep. 71,039.4m. (March 2005); Pres. and CEO FAROOQ BENGALI; 39 brs.

Habib Bank Ltd: 15 Habib Bank Plaza, I. I. Chundrigar Rd, Karachi 75650; tel. (21) 2418000; fax (21) 2411027; e-mail iuansari@hblpk.com; f. 1941; cap. 6,900m., res 2,644m., dep. 404,629m. (Dec. 2004); transferred to private sector Feb. 2004; Pres. R. ZAKIR MAHMOOD; 1,424 brs in Pakistan.

KASB Bank Ltd: Business and Finance Centre, I. I. Chundrigar Rd, Karachi 74000; tel. (21) 2446772; fax (21) 2446828; e-mail international@kasb.com; internet www.kasbbank.com. f. 1995 as Platinum Commercial Bank Ltd; name changed as above 2003; cap. 2,292.7m., res 84.3m., dep. 15,409.7m. (March 2006); Pres. and CEO MUNEER KAMAL; 16 brs.

Khushhali Bank: 94 West, 4th Floor, Jinnah Ave, Blue Area, POB 3111, Islamabad; fax (51) 9206080; cap. 1,705.0m., res 15,023.4m. (Dec. 2004); Chair. and Man. Dir GHALIB NISHTAR.

MCB Bank Ltd: MCB Tower, I. I. Chundrigar Rd, POB 4976, Karachi 74000; tel. (21) 2414091; fax (21) 2438441; e-mail mcbfid@mcb.com.pk; internet www.mcb.com.pk; f. 1947; cap. 3,709.0m., res 5,612.5m., dep. 248,032.2m. (March 2005); Chair. Mian MUHAMMAD MANSHA; Pres. and CEO MUHAMMAD AFTAB MANZOOR; 1,057 brs in Pakistan, 4 brs abroad.

Meezan Bank Ltd: 3rd Floor, PNSC Bldg, Moulvi Tamizuddin Khan Rd, Karachi 74000; tel. (21) 5610582; fax (21) 5610375; e-mail info@meezanbank.com; internet www.meezanbank.com; f. 1997 as Al-Meezan Investment Bank; became commercial bank 2002 and name changed as above; cap. 1,346.0m., res 256.6m., dep. 16,631.9m. (Dec. 2004); Pres. and CEO IRFAN SIDDIQUI; Gen. Man. NAJMUL HASAN; 12 brs.

Metropolitan Bank Ltd: Spencer's Bldg, I. I. Chundrigar Rd, POB 1289, Karachi; tel. (21) 2636740; fax (21) 2630404; e-mail info@metrobank.com.pk; internet www.metrobank.com.pk; f. 1992; cap. 1,560.0m., res 1,962.0m., dep. 66,287.6m. (March 2005); Pres. and Chief Exec. KASSIM PAREKH; Sr Exec. Vice-Pres. MOHAMADALI R. HABIB; 40 brs.

Mybank Ltd: 10th Floor, Business & Finance Centre, I. I. Chundrigar Rd, Karachi; tel. (21) 111-443-111; fax (21) 2444197; e-mail cok@mybankltd.com; internet www.mybankltd.com; f. 1991; fmrly Bolan Bank Ltd; cap. 1,523.8m., res 101.2m., dep. 11,397.4m. (Dec. 2004); Pres. and CEO MUHAMMAD AZIMUDDIN; Chair. IQBAL ALIMOHAMED; 50 brs.

National Bank of Pakistan (NBP): NBP Bldg, I. I. Chundrigar Rd, POB 4937, Karachi 2; tel. (21) 9212208; fax (21) 9212774; e-mail info@nbp.com.pk; internet www.nbp.com.pk; f. 1949; cap. 4,924.1m., res 11,119.6m., dep. 476,656.5m. (Dec. 2004); 100% state-owned; Pres. ALI RAZA; 1,491 brs in Pakistan and 22 brs abroad.

NIB Bank Ltd: Muhammadi House, I. I. Chundrigar Rd, Karachi; tel. (21) 111-333-111; fax (21) 2417503; e-mail info@nibpk.com; internet www.nibpk.com; f. 2003; Pres. and CEO KHAWAJA IQBAL HASSAN; 27 brs.

Pak-Saudi Bank Ltd: Saudi Pak Tower, 61A Jinnah Ave, Islamabad; tel. (51) 111-222-003; fax (51) 111-222-004; e-mail saudipak@saudipak.com; internet www.saudipak.com; f. 1994 as Prudential Commercial Bank, acquired by Saudi Pak Industrial and Agricultural Investment Co (Pvt) Ltd in 2001; cap. 2,250.0m., res 201.8m., dep. 39,733.7m. (Dec. 2004); Chair./CEO MUHAMMAD RASHID ZAHIR; Vice-Chair. JAWED ANWAR; 30 brs.

PICIC Commercial Bank Ltd: I. I. Chundrigar Rd, POB 572, Karachi 74200; tel. (21) 2637161; fax (21) 2636909; e-mail info@picicbank.com.pk; internet www.picicbank.com.pk; f. 1994 as Schön Bank Ltd; name changed to Gulf Commercial Bank Ltd in 1998; 60% shares and full management of bank acquired by PICIC in February 2001, name changed to above in June 2001; cap. 1,823.3m., res 1,189.9m., dep. 47,299.1m. (Dec. 2004); Chair. MOHAMMAD ALI KHOJA; Pres. and CEO MOHAMMAD BILAL SHEIKH; 20 brs.

Prime Commercial Bank Ltd: 77-Y, Phase III, Defence Housing Authority, Lahore 54792; tel. (42) 5728282; fax (42) 5728181; e-mail primebank@primebank.com.pk; internet www.primebank.com.pk; f. 1991; cap. 2,321.5m., res 1,116.5m., dep. 38,876.1m. (Dec. 2005); Pres. SAEED I. CHAUDHRY; Chair. ABDUL ELAH A. MUKRED; 62 brs.

Soneri Bank Ltd: 87 Shahrah-e-Quaid-e-Azam, POB 49, Lahore; tel. (42) 6368142; fax (42) 6368138; e-mail main.lahore@soneribank.com; f. 1991; cap. 1,271.9m., res 1,592.1m., dep. 45,341.1m. (Dec. 2004); Chair. BADRUDDIN J. FEERASTA; Pres. and CEO SAFAR ALI K. LAKHANI; 44 brs.

Union Bank Ltd: New Jubilee Insurance House, I. I. Chundrigar Rd, Karachi 74200; tel. (21) 2416428; fax (21) 2400842; e-mail ubrokhi@digicom.net.pk; internet www.unionbankpk.com; f. 1991; cap. 2,262.2m., res 709.5m., dep. 74,720.1m. (March 2005); Chair. SHAUKAT TARIN; Man. Dir MUNEER KAMAL; 27 brs.

United Bank Ltd: State Life Bldg, No. 1, I. I. Chundrigar Rd, POB 4306, Karachi 74000; tel. (21) 2417021; fax (21) 2413492; e-mail helpline@ubl.com.pk; internet www.ubl.com.pk; f. 1959; cap. 5,180.0m., res 6,035.2m., dep. 256,716.9m. (March 2005); privatized in 2002; Pres. and CEO ATIF BOKHARI; 1,349 brs in Pakistan and 19 brs abroad.

Principal Foreign Banks

ABN AMRO Bank NV (Netherlands): ABN AMRO Bldg, Abdullah Haroon Rd, POB 4096, Karachi; tel. (21) 5683097; fax (21) 5683432; f. 1948; Country Man. NAVEED A. KHAN; 3 brs.

AlBaraka Islamic Bank (Bahrain): PICIC House, 14 Shahrah-e-Aiwan-e-Tajarat, POB 1686, Lahore 54000; tel. (42) 111-742-742; fax (42) 6309965; e-mail albaraka@albaraka.com.pk; internet www.albaraka.com.pk; Regional Gen. Man. and Country Head SHAFQAAT AHMED; 5 brs.

American Express Bank Ltd (USA): Shaheen Commercial Complex, Dr Ziauddin Ahmed Rd, POB 4847, Karachi; tel. (21) 2634153; fax (21) 2631803; f. 1950; Sen. Dir and Country Man. NADEEM KARAMAT; 4 brs.

Bank of Tokyo-Mitsubishi UFJ Ltd (Japan): Shaheen Complex, 1st Floor, M. R. Kayani Rd, POB 4232, Karachi; tel. (21) 2630171; fax (21) 2631368; e-mail btmkarwr@cyber.net.pk; f. 1953; Gen. Man. K. ENDO; 1 br.

Chase Manhattan Bank, NA (USA): 13th Floor, Commercial Tower, Sidco Ave Centre, 264 R. A. Lines, Karachi; tel. (21) 5683568; fax (21) 5681467; f. 1982; Vice-Pres. RUDOLF VON WATZDORF; 2 brs.

Citibank, NA (USA): No. 1 State Life Bldg, I. I. Chundrigar Rd, Karachi; tel. (21) 2638222; fax (21) 2638211; internet www.citibank.com/pakistan; f. 1961; Gen. Man. ZUBYR SOOMRO; 3 brs.

Deutsche Bank AG (Germany): Avari Towers, Fatimah Jinnah Rd, Karachi; tel. (21) 2416824; fax (21) 2411130; f. 1962; Gen. Man. (Pakistan) ARIF M. ALI; 2 brs.

Doha Bank Ltd (Qatar): 36/6-2 Lalazar Dr., off M. T. Khan Rd, Karachi; tel. (21) 5611313; fax (21) 5610764; Gen. Man. (Pakistan) MASOOD H. KHAN.

Emirates Bank International PJSC (United Arab Emirates): Emirates Bank Bldg, I. I. Chundrigar Rd, POB 831, Karachi; tel. (21) 2416648; fax (21) 2416599; e-mail timgibbs@emiratesbank.com; internet www.emiratesbank.com.pk; f. 1978; Gen. Man. (Pakistan) TIMOTHY P. GIBBS; 10 brs.

Habib Bank AG Zurich (Switzerland): Hirani Centre, I. I. Chundrigar Rd, POB 1424, Karachi; tel. (21) 2630526; fax (21) 2631418; Chief Exec. (Pakistan) MOHAMMAD ZAHIR ESMAIL.

The Hongkong and Shanghai Banking Corpn Ltd (Hong Kong): Shaheen Commercial Complex, M. R. Kayani Rd, POB 121, Karachi; tel. (21) 2632143; fax (21) 2631526; f. 1982; CEO TAHIR SADIQ; Chief Operating Officer RIAZ UL ISLAM; 2 brs.

Mashreq Bank PSC (United Arab Emirates): Ground and 1st Floors, Bahria Complex, 24 M. T. Khan Rd, POB 930, Karachi 74000; tel. (21) 5611271; fax (21) 5610661; f. 1978; Country Man. AZMAT ASHRAF; 3 brs.

Rupali Bank Ltd (Bangladesh): Unitowers, I. I. Chundrigar Rd, POB 6440, Karachi 74000; tel. (21) 2410424; fax (21) 2414322; f. 1976; Country Man. MD SELIM KHAN; 1 br.

Saudi Bahrain Investment Co: Karachi; Man. Dir RASHID ZAHID.

Standard Chartered Bank (United Kingdom): I. I. Chundrigar Rd, POB 4896, Karachi 74000; tel. (21) 2419075; fax (21) 2418788; Chief Exec. (Pakistan) BADAR KAZMI; 6 brs.

Trust Bank Ltd (Kenya): Al-Falah Court, I. I. Chundrigar Rd, Karachi; tel. (21) 2633519; fax (21) 2636534; CEO HUMAYUN ZIA.

Leasing Banks (Modarabas)

The number of leasing banks (modarabas), which conform to the strictures placed upon the banking system by *Shari'a* (the Islamic legal code), rose from four in 1988 to about 45 in 2002. The following are among the most important modarabas in Pakistan.

Asian Leasing Corporation Ltd: 85-B Jail Rd, Gulberg, POB 3176, Lahore; tel. (42) 484417; fax (42) 484418.

Atlas Lease Ltd: Ground Floor, Federation House, Shahrah-e-Firdousi, Main Clifton, Karachi 75600; tel. (21) 5866817; fax (21) 5870543; e-mail all@atlasgrouppk.com; Chair. YUSUF H. SHIRAZI.

B.R.R. International Modaraba: 3rd Floor, Dean Arcade, Block 8, Kehkeshan, Clifton, Karachi 75600; tel. (21) 5835026; fax (21) 5870324; e-mail brr@cyber.net.pk.

Dadabhoy Leasing Co Ltd: 5th Floor, Maqbool Commercial Complex, JCHS Block, Main Shahrah-e-Faisal, Karachi; tel. (21) 4548171; fax (21) 4547301; Man. (Finance) MOHAMMAD AYUB.

English Leasing Ltd: M. K. Arcade, Ground Floor, 32 Davis Rd, Lahore; (42) 6303855; fax (41) 6304251; e-mail englease@hotmail.com. Chair. JAVAID MAHMOOD; CEO MANZOOR ELAHI.

First Habib Bank Modaraba: 18 Habib Bank Plaza, I. I. Chundrigar Rd, Karachi 75650; tel. (21) 2412294; fax (21) 2411860; f. 1991; wholly-owned subsidiary of Habib Bank Ltd; auth. cap. 500.0m., cap. p.u. 397.1m. (1996); CEO MUHAMMAD NAWAZ CHEEMA; Co Sec. NAJEEB MAHMUD.

Orix Leasing Pakistan Ltd: Overseas Investors Chamber of Commerce Bldg, Talpur Rd, Karachi 74000; tel. (21) 2425896; fax (21) 2425897; e-mail olp@orixpakistan.com; internet www.orixpakistan.com; f. 1986; cap. US $10m. (June 2004); Chief Exec. HUMAYUN MURAD.

Pakistan Industrial and Commercial Leasing Ltd: 504 Park Ave, 24-A, Block 6, PECHS, Shahrah-e-Faisal, Karachi 75210; tel. (21) 4551045; fax (21) 4520655; e-mail picl@super.net.pk; f. 1987; Chief Exec. MINHAJ-UL-HAQ SIDDIQI.

Standard Chartered Modaraba: Standard Services of Pakistan (Pvt) Ltd, Standard Bank Bldg, I. I. Chundrigar Rd, POB 5556, Karachi 74000; tel. (21) 223917; fax (21) 2417197; fmrly First Grindlays Modaraba; Man. Dir SHARIQ SALEEM.

Co-operative Banks

In 1976 all existing co-operative banks were dissolved and given the option of becoming a branch of the appropriate Provincial Co-operative Bank, or of reverting to the status of a credit society.

Federal Bank for Co-operatives: State Bank Bldg, G-5, POB 1218, Islamabad; tel. (51) 9205667; fax (51) 9205681; f. 1976; owned jtly by the fed. Govt, the prov. govts and the State Bank of Pakistan; provides credit facilities to each of six prov. co-operative banks and regulates their operations; they in turn provide credit facilities through co-operative socs; supervises policy of prov. co-operative banks and of multi-unit co-operative socs; assists fed. and prov. govts in formulating schemes for development and revitalization of co-operative movement; carries out research on rural credit, etc; share cap. p.u. 200m., res 398m. (1998); Man. Dir M. AFZAL HUSSAIN; 4 regional offices.

Investment Banks

Asset Investment Bank Ltd: Rm 1-B, 1st Floor, Ali Plaza, Khayaban-e-Quaid-e-Azam, Blue Area, Islamabad; tel. (51) 2270625; fax (51) 2272506; Chief Exec. SYED NAVEED ZAIDI.

Atlas Investment Bank Ltd: 3rd Floor, Federation House, Shaheen-e-Firdoosi, Main Clifton, Karachi; tel. (21) 5866817; fax (21) 5870543; e-mail info@atlasbank.com.pk; internet www.atlasbank.com.pk; 15% owned by Bank of Tokyo-Mitsubishi UFJ Ltd; Man. Dir NAEEM KHAN; Pres. and CEO FRAHIM ALI KHAN.

Crescent Standard Investment Bank Ltd: 4th Floor, Crescent Standard Tower, 10-B, Block E-2, Gulberg III, Lahore; tel. (42) 5763306; fax (42) 5870359; e-mail csibl@csibl.com; internet www.csibl.com; f. 1990 as Al-Towfeek Investment Bank Ltd; became First Standard Investment Bank Ltd 2002; name changed as above 2004; cap. 737.7m., res 212.1m., dep. 2,219.4m. (Dec. 2003); Chair. MANZUR UL HAQ; Chief Exec. MAHMOOD AHMED.

Jahangir Siddiqui Investment Bank Ltd: Rm 1031–1303, 13th Floor, Chapel Plaza, Hasrat Mohani Rd, Karachi 74000; tel. (21) 2429445; fax (21) 2429448; e-mail info@js.com; internet www.js.com; f. 1992 as Citicorp Investment Bank (Pak) Ltd; name changed as above 1999; cap. 227.5m., res 313.5m., 364.2m. (Dec. 2003); Chair. MAZHARUL HAQUE SIDDIQUI; CEO SARFARAZ AHMED KHANANI.

Orix Investment Bank Pakistan Ltd: 2nd Floor, Islamic Chamber of Commerce Bldg, Block 9, Clifton, Karachi 75600; tel. (21) 5861266; fax (21) 5868862; e-mail ihalvi@orixbank.com; internet www.orixbank.com; f. 1995; Gen. Man. INTISAR H. ALVI.

Development Finance Organizations

First Women Bank Ltd: S.T.S.M. Foundation Bldg, CL-10/20/2 Beaumont Rd, Civil Lines, Karachi 75530; tel. (21) 111-676-767; fax (21) 5657755; e-mail president@cyber.net.pk; internet www.fwbl.com.pk; f. 1989; cap. and res 590m., dep. 8,690m. (Dec. 2004); Pres. ZARINE AZIZ; 38 brs.

House Building Finance Corpn: Finance and Trade Centre, 3rd Floor, Shahrah-e-Faisal, Karachi 74000; tel. (21) 9202314; fax (21) 9202360; e-mail info@hbfc.com.pk; internet www.hbfc.com.pk; provides loans for the construction and purchase of housing units; Man. Dir ZAIGHAM MEHMOOD RIZVI.

Industrial Development Bank of Pakistan: State Life Bldg No. 2, Wallace Rd, off I. I. Chundrigar Rd, POB 5082, Karachi 74000; tel. (21) 2419160; fax (21) 2411990; e-mail idbp@idbp.com.pk; internet www.idbp.com.pk; f. 1961; provides credit facilities for small and medium-sized industrial enterprises in the private sector; cap. 157.0m., res 342.3m., dep. 20,119.9m. (June 1997); 100% state-owned; Chair. and Man. Dir JAVED SADIQ; 19 brs.

Investment Corpn of Pakistan: NBP Bldg, 5th Floor, I. I. Chundrigar Rd, POB 5410, Karachi 74000; tel. (21) 9212360; fax (21) 9212388; e-mail icp@paknet3.ptc.pk; f. 1966 by the Govt to encourage and broaden the base of investments and to develop the capital market; total assets 4,633.1m., cap. 200.0m., res 413.5m. (June 1997); Man. Dir ISTIQBAL MEHDI; 10 brs.

Khushhali Bank: POB 3111, Islamabad; f. 2000 by the Govt under the Asian Development Bank's micro-finance sector development programme; provides micro-loans to the poor and finances reforms in the micro-finance sector; cap. 1,705m. (Aug. 2000); Pres. GHALIB NISHTAR.

National Investment (Unit Trust) Ltd: NBP Bldg, 6th Floor, I. I. Chundrigar Rd, POB 5671, Karachi; tel. (21) 2419061; fax (21) 2430623; e-mail info@nit.com.pk; internet www.nit.com.pk; f. 1962; an open-ended Mutual Fund, mobilizes domestic savings to meet the requirements of growing economic development and enables investors to share in the industrial and economic prosperity of the country; 67,000 Unit holders (1999/2000); Man. Dir ISTIQBAL MEHDI.

Pakistan Industrial Credit and Investment Corpn Ltd (PICIC): State Life Bldg No. 1, I. I. Chundrigar Rd, POB 5080, Karachi 74000; tel. (21) 2414220; fax (21) 2419100; e-mail contact@picic.com; internet www.picic.com; f. 1957 as an industrial development bank to provide financial assistance in both local and foreign currencies, for the establishment of new industries in the private sector and balancing modernization, replacement and expansion of existing industries; merchant banking and foreign exchange activities; total assets 33,949m., cap. 2,736m., res 4,188m. (June 2005); held 97.9% and 2.1% by local and foreign investors respectively; Man. Dir MOHAMMAD ALI KHOJA; Chair. ALTAF M. SALEEM; 19 brs.

Pakistan Kuwait Investment Co (Pvt) Ltd: Tower 'C', 4th Floor, Finance and Trade Centre, Shahrah-e-Faisal, POB 901, Karachi 74200; tel. (21) 5660750; fax (21) 5683669; jt venture between the Govt and Kuwait to promote investment in industrial and agro-based enterprises; Man. Dir ISTIQBAL MEHDI.

Pak-Libya Holding Co (Pvt) Ltd: Finance and Trade Centre, 5th Floor, Tower 'C', Shahrah-e-Faisal, POB 10425, Karachi 74400; tel. (21) 111-111-115; fax (21) 5682389; e-mail paklibya@paklibya.com.pk; jt venture between the Govts of Pakistan and Libya to promote industrial investment in Pakistan; Man. Dir KHALID SHARWANI.

Regional Development Finance Corpn: Ghausia Plaza, 20 Blue Area, POB 1893, Islamabad; tel. (51) 2825131; fax (51) 2201179; promotes industrial investment in the less developed areas of Pakistan; CEO MIRZA GHAGANFAR BAIG; 13 brs.

Saudi Pak Industrial and Agricultural Investment Co (Pvt) Ltd: Saudi Pak Tower, 61-A Jinnah Ave, Islamabad; tel. (51) 2273514; fax (51) 2273508; e-mail saudipak@saudipak.com; internet www.saudipak.com; f. 1981 jtly by Saudi Arabia and Pakistan to finance industrial and agro-based projects and undertake investment-related activities in Pakistan; cap. 2,000m., res 732m., dep. 5,900m. (March 2001); CEO MUHAMMAD RASHID ZAHIR; Exec. Vice-Pres. ABDUL JALEEL SHAIKH; 1 br.

Small Business Finance Corpn: NBP Bldg, Ground Floor, Civic Centre, Islamabad 44000; tel. (51) 9214296; fax (51) 2826007; provides loans for small businesses; Man. Dir KAISER HANEEF NASEEM.

Youth Investment and Promotion Society: PIA Bldg, 3rd Floor, Blue Area, Islamabad; tel. (51) 815581; Man. Dir ASHRAF M. KHAN.

Zarai Taraqiati Bank Ltd (ZTBL): 1 Faisal Ave, POB 1400, Islamabad; tel. (51) 9220014; fax (51) 812907; e-mail info@ztbl.com.pk; internet www.ztbl.com.pk; f. 1961; provides credit facilities to agriculturists (particularly small-scale farmers) and cottage industrialists in the rural areas and for allied projects; auth. cap. 4,000m., res 1,739m. (June 1999); 100% state-owned; Pres. R. A. CHUGHTAI; 49 regional offices and 349 brs.

Banking Associations

Investment Banks Association of Pakistan: 7th Floor, Shaheen Commercial Complex, Dr Ziauddin Ahmed Rd, POB 1345, Karachi; tel. (21) 2631396; fax (21) 2630678.

Modaraba Association of Pakistan: Chair. WAQAR AJMAL CHAUDHRY.

Pakistan Banks' Association: National Bank of Pakistan, Head Office Bldg, 2nd Floor, I. I. Chundrigar Rd, POB 4937, Karachi 2; tel. and fax (21) 2416686; e-mail pba@cyber.net.pk; Chair. M. YOUNAS KHAN; Sec. A. GHAFFAR K. HAFIZ.

Banking Organizations

Pakistan Banking Council: Habib Bank Plaza, I. I. Chundrigar Rd, Karachi; tel. (21) 227121; fax (21) 222232; f. 1973; acts as a co-ordinating body between the nationalized banks and the Ministry of Finance and Revenue; Chair. MUHAMMAD ZAKI; Sec. Mir WASIF ALI.

Pakistan Development Banking Institute: 4th Floor, Sidco Ave Centre, Stratchen Rd, Karachi; tel. (21) 5688049; fax (21) 5688460.

STOCK EXCHANGES

Securities and Exchange Commission of Pakistan: NIC Bldg, 63 Jinnah Ave, Blue Area, Islamabad; tel. (51) 9207091; fax (51) 9204915; e-mail hilal-bult@secpgov.pk; internet www.secp.gov.pk; oversees and co-ordinates operations of exchanges and registration of companies; registration offices in Faisalabad (356-A, 1st Floor, Al-Jamil Plaza, People's Colony, Small D Ground, Faisalabad; tel. (41) 713841), Karachi (No. 2, 4th Floor, State Life Building, North Wing, Karachi; tel. (21) 2415855), Lahore (3rd and 4th Floors, Associated House, 7 Egerton Rd, Lahore; tel. (42) 9202044), Multan (61 Abdali Rd, Multan; tel. (61) 542609), Peshawar (Hussain Commercial Bldg, 3 Arbab Rd, Peshawar), Quetta (382/3, IDBP House, Shahrah-e-Hall, Quetta; tel. (81) 844138) and Sukkur (B-30, Sindhi Muslim Housing Society, Airport Rd, Sukkur; tel. (71) 30517); Chair. RAZI-UR-RAHMAN KHAN.

Islamabad Stock Exchange: 4th Floor, Stock Exchange Bldg, 101E Faz-ul-haq Rd, Blue Area, Islamabad; tel. (51) 2275045; fax (51) 2275044; e-mail ise@ise.com.pk; internet www.ise.com.pk; f. 1991; 103 mems; Chair. OMAR IQBAL PASHA; Sec. YOUSUF H. MAKHDOOMI.

Karachi Stock Exchange (Guarantee) Ltd: Stock Exchange Bldg, Stock Exchange Rd, Karachi 74000; tel. (21) 2410825; fax (21) 2410824; e-mail gm@kse.com.pk; internet www.kse.com.pk; f. 1947; 200 mems, 701 listed cos; Chair. YASIN LAKHANI; Man. Dir A. M. LODHI.

Lahore Stock Exchange (Guarantee) Ltd: Lahore Stock Exchange Bldg, 19 Khayaban-e-Aiwan-e-Iqbal, Lahore 54000; tel. (42) 6300070; fax (42) 6368484; e-mail lstock@paknet4.ptc.pk; internet www.lahorestock.com; f. 1970; 576 listed cos, 151 mems; Pres. Group Capt. (retd) NASEEM A. KHAN; Man. Dir SAMEER AHMED.

National Commodity Exchange Ltd: 9th Floor, PIC Towers, 32-A Lalazar Drive, M. T. Khan Rd, Karachi; tel. (21) 111-623-623; fax (21) 5611263; e-mail info@ncel.com.pk; internet www.ncel.com.pk; f. 2002; online commodity futures exchange; regulated by Securities and Exchange Commission of Pakistan; Man. Dir ASSIM JANG.

INSURANCE

In 1995 legislation came into effect allowing foreign insurance companies to operate in Pakistan.

Insurance Division: Securities and Exchange Commission, 4th Floor, NIC Bldg, Jinnah Ave, Islamabad; tel. (51) 9208887; fax (51) 9208955; internet www.secp.gov.pk; under the Ministry of Finance and Revenue; Commissioner of Insurance SHARIF EJAZ GHAURI; Exec. Dir SHAFAAT AHMED.

Life Insurance

American Life Insurance Co (Pakistan) Ltd: Laksan Sq., 11th Floor, Bldg 1, Sarwar Shaheed Rd, Karachi 74400; tel. (21) 111-111-711; fax (21) 5688042; e-mail alico@cyber.net.pk.

Metropolitan Life Assurance Co of Pakistan Ltd: 310–313 Qamar House, M. A. Jinnah Rd, Karachi 74000; tel. (21) 2311662; fax (21) 2311667; e-mail myunus@cyber.net.pk; Chief Exec. MAHEEN YUNUS.

Postal Life Insurance Organization: 2nd and 3rd Floors, Karachi GPO Bldg, I. I. Chundrigar Rd, Karachi; tel. (21) 9211102; e-mail gmplikar@paknet.pk.com; f. 1884; life and group insurance; Gen. Man. SHAHAR YARUDDIN.

State Life Insurance Corpn of Pakistan: State Life Bldg No. 9, Dr Ziauddin Ahmed Rd, POB 5725, Karachi 75530; tel. (21) 111-111-888; fax (21) 9202868; e-mail dhasp@statelife.com.pk; internet www.statelife.com.pk; f. 1972; life and group insurance and pension schemes; Chair. SAMEE UL-HASAN.

General Insurance

ACE Insurance Ltd: 6th Floor, NIC Bldg, Abbasi Shaheed Rd, off Shahrah-e-Faisal, Karachi; tel. (21) 5681320; fax (21) 5683935; e-mail zehra.naqvi@ace-ina.com; internet www.ace-ina.com; f. 1853; Chief Exec. ZEHRA NAQVI.

Adamjee Insurance Co Ltd: Adamjee House, 6th Floor, I. I. Chundrigar Rd, POB 4850, Karachi 74000; tel. (21) 2410145; fax (21) 2412627; e-mail info@adamjeeinsurance.com; internet www.adamjeeinsurance.com; f. 1960; Man. Dir and CEO SYED JAWAD GILLANI.

Agro General Insurance Co Ltd: 612, EFU House, M. A. Jinnah Rd, POB 5920, Karachi 74000; tel. (21) 2313182; fax (21) 2313182; f. 1987; Man. Dir M. I. ANSARI.

AIG Pakistan New Hampshire Insurance Co: 2nd Floor, Finlay House, I. I. Chundrigar Rd, Karachi 74000; tel. (21) 111-111-244; fax (21) 2419413; e-mail info-pakistan@aig.com; internet www.aigpakistan.com; f. 1869; Country Man. IQBAL SIDDIQI.

Alpha Insurance Co Ltd: State Life Bldg No. 1B–1C, 2nd Floor, off I. I. Chundrigar Rd, POB 4359, Karachi 74000; tel. (21) 2412609; fax (21) 2419968; f. 1952; Chair. IQBAL M. QURESHI; Man. Dir V. C. GONSALVES; 9 brs.

Amicus Insurance Co Ltd: F-50, Block 7, Feroze Nana Rd, Bath Island, POB 3971, Karachi; tel. (21) 5831082; fax (21) 5870222; f. 1991; Chair. M. IRSHAD UDDIN.

PAKISTAN

Asia Insurance Co Ltd: 19C and 19D, Block L, Gulberg III, Ferozepur Rd, Lahore; tel. (42) 5858532; fax (42) 5865579; e-mail asiains@nexlinx.net.pk; f. 1979; Chief Exec. ZAFAR IQBAL SHEIKH.

Askari General Insurance Co Ltd: 4th Floor, AWT Plaza, The Mall, POB 843, Rawalpindi; tel. (51) 9272425; fax (51) 9272424; e-mail agicoho@agico.com.pk; internet www.agico.com.pk; f. 1995; Pres. and Chief Exec. M. JAMALUDDIN.

Business and Industrial Insurance Co Ltd: 65 East Pak Pavilions, 1st Floor, Fazal-e-Haq Rd, Blue Area, Islamabad; tel. (51) 2278757; fax (51) 2271914; e-mail biic.ltd@yahoo.com; f. 1995; Chair. and Chief Exec. Mian MUMTAZ ABDULLAH.

Capital Insurance Co Ltd: Muradia Rd, Near Lone House, Model Town, Sialkot; tel. (432) 563771; fax (432) 552958; e-mail cicl@skt.comsats.net.pk; f. 1998; Gen. Man. SHAKIL RAZA SYED; Sec. M. I. BUTT.

Central Insurance Co Ltd: Dawood Centre, 5th Floor, M. T. Khan Rd, POB 3988, Karachi 75530; tel. (21) 5684019; fax (21) 5680218; e-mail cicl@khi.wol.net.pk; internet www.coninsure.com; f. 1960; Chief Exec. ABDUR RAHIM.

Century Insurance Co Ltd: 11th Floor, Lakson Square Bldg No. 3, Sarwar Sheheed Rd, POB 4895, Karachi 74200; tel. (21) 5657445; fax (21) 5671665; e-mail cic@cyber.net.pk; f. 1988; Chair. and Chief Exec. IQBALALI LAKHANI; Dir Mir NADIR ALI.

CGU Inter Insurance PLC: 74/1-A, Lalazar, M. T. Khan Rd, POB 4895, Karachi 74000; tel. (21) 5611802; fax (21) 5611456; f. 1861; general and life insurance; Gen. Man. ABDUR RAHIM; 3 brs.

Commerce Insurance Co Ltd: 11 Shahrah-e-Quaid-e-Azam, POB 1132, Lahore 54000; tel. (42) 7325330; fax (42) 7230828; f. 1992; Chief Exec. SYED MOIN-UD-DIN.

Co-operative Insurance Society of Pakistan Ltd: Co-operative Insurance Bldg, Shahrah-e-Quaid-e-Azam, POB 147, Lahore; tel. (42) 7352306; fax (42) 7352794; f. 1949; Chief Exec. and Gen. Man. FAROOQ HAIDER JUNG.

Credit Insurance Co Ltd: Asmat Chambers, 68 Mazang Rd, Lahore; tel. (42) 6316774; fax (42) 6368868; f. 1995; Chief Exec. MUHAMMAD IKHLAQ BUTT.

Crescent Star Insurance Co Ltd: Nadir House, I. I. Chundrigar Rd, POB 4616, Karachi 74000; tel. (21) 2415521; fax (21) 2415474; e-mail crescent_star_ins@hotmail.com; f. 1957; Man. Dir MUNIR I. MILLWALA.

Dadabhoy Insurance Co Ltd: Maqbool Commercial Complex, JCHS Block, Main Shahrah-e-Faisal, Karachi; tel. (21) 4545704; fax (21) 4548625; f. 1983; Chief Exec. USMAN DADABHOY.

Delta Insurance Co Ltd: 101 Baghpatee Bldg, Altaf Hussain Rd, New Challi, Karachi; tel. (21) 2632297; fax (21) 2422942; f. 1991; Man. Dir SYED ASIF ALI.

East West Insurance Co Ltd: 410, EFU House, M. A. Jinnah Rd, POB 6693, Karachi 74000; tel. (21) 2313304; fax (21) 2310821; e-mail ewire@cyber.net.pk; f. 1983; Chair. and Chief Exec. NAVED YUNUS.

EFU General Insurance Ltd: EFU House, M. A. Jinnah Rd, Karachi 74000; tel. (21) 2313471; fax (21) 2310450; e-mail info@efuinsurance.com; internet www.efuinsurance.com; f. 1932; Man. Dir and Chief Exec. SAIFUDDIN N. ZOOMKAWALA.

Excel Insurance Co Ltd: 38/C-1, Block 6, PECH Society, Shahrah-e-Faisal, Karachi 75400; tel. (21) 4548077; fax (21) 4548076; e-mail eicl@cyber.net.pk; f. 1991; Man. Dir GHULAM H. ALI MOHAMMAD.

Gulf Insurance Co Ltd: Gulf House, 1-A Link McLeod Rd, Patiala Grounds, Lahore; tel. (42) 7312028; fax (42) 7234987; f. 1988; Chief Exec. S. ARIF SALAM.

Habib Insurance Co Ltd: Insurance House, 6 Habib Sq., M. A. Jinnah Rd, POB 5217, Karachi 74000; tel. (21) 2424038; fax (21) 2421600; e-mail hic@cyber.net.pk; f. 1942; Chair. HAMID D. HABIB; Man. Dir and Chief Exec. ALI RAZA D. HABIB.

International General Insurance Co of Pakistan Ltd: Finlay House, 1st Floor, I. I. Chundrigar Rd, POB 4576, Karachi 74000; tel. (21) 2424976; fax (21) 2416710; e-mail igikhi@cubexs.net.pk; internet www.igi.com.pk; f. 1953; Gen. Man. AHMED SALAHUDDIN.

Ittefaq General Insurance Co Ltd: H-16 Murree Rd, Rawalpindi; tel. (51) 5771333; f. 1982; Chief Exec. and Man. Dir Dr SYED ISHTIAQ HUSSAIN SHAH.

Jupiter Insurance Co Ltd: 4th Floor, Finlay House, I. I. Chundrigar Rd, POB 4655, Karachi 74000; tel. (21) 2426070; fax (21) 2427660; e-mail jicl20@cyber.net.pk; f. 1994; Chief Exec. MAHMUD HASAN.

Muslim Insurance Co Ltd: 3 Bank Sq., Shahrah-e-Quaid-e-Azam, POB 1219, Lahore; tel. (42) 7320542; fax (42) 7234742; e-mail fariq.rohilla@mickhi.atlasgrouppk.com; f. 1935; Chief Exec. S. C. SUBJALLY.

National General Insurance Co Ltd: 401-B, Satellite Town, nr Commercial Market, Rawalpindi; tel. (51) 4427818; fax (51) 4427361; f. 1969; Gen. Man. F. A. JAFFERY.

National Insurance Corpn: NIC Bldg, Abbasi Shaheed Rd, Karachi 74400; tel. (21) 9202741; fax (21) 9202779; e-mail info@nicl.com.pk; internet www.niclpk.com; govt-owned; sole govt insurance co; Man. Dir M. A. LODHI.

New Jubilee Insurance Co Ltd: 2nd Floor, Jubilee Insurance House, I. I. Chundrigar Rd, POB 4795, Karachi 74000; tel. (21) 2416022; fax (21) 2416728; e-mail nji@cyber.net.pk; internet www.nji.com.pk; f. 1953; Pres., Chief Exec. and Man. Dir MASOOD NOORANI.

North Star Insurance Co Ltd: 37–38 Basement, Sadiq Plaza, 69 The Mall, Lahore 54000; tel. (42) 6314308; fax (42) 6375366; e-mail northstarins@hotmail.com; f. 1995; Chief Exec./Man. Dir M. RAFIQ CHAUDHRY.

Orient Insurance Co Ltd: 2nd Floor, Dean Arcade, Block No. 8, Kahkeshan, Clifton, Karachi; tel. (21) 5865327; fax (21) 5865724; f. 1987; Man. Dir FAZAL REHMAN.

Pak Equity Insurance Co Ltd: M. K. Arcade, 32 Davis Rd, Lahore; tel. (42) 6361536; fax (42) 6365959; f. 1984; Chief Exec. CH. ATHAR ZAHOOR.

Pakistan General Insurance Co Ltd: 3 Bank Sq., Shahrah-e-Quaid-e-Azam, POB 1364, Lahore; tel. (42) 7323569; fax (42) 7230634; f. 1948; Chair. CH. AZFAR MANZOOR; Chief Exec. CH. ATHAR ZAHOOR.

Pakistan Guarantee Insurance Co Ltd: Al-Falah Court, 3rd and 5th Floors, I. I. Chundrigar Rd, POB 5436, Karachi 74000; tel. (21) 2636111; fax (21) 2638740; f. 1965; Chief Exec. SHAKIL RAZA SYED.

Premier Insurance Co of Pakistan Ltd: 2-A State Life Bldg, 5th Floor, Wallace Rd, off I. I. Chundrigar Rd, POB 4140, Karachi 74000; tel. (21) 2416331; fax (21) 2416572; f. 1952; Chair. ZAHID BASHIR; CEO FAKHIR A. RAHMAN.

Prime Insurance Co Ltd: 505–507, Japan Plaza, M. A. Jinnah Rd, POB 1390, Karachi; tel. (21) 7770801; fax (21) 7725427; f. 1989; Chief Exec. ABDUL MAJEED.

Progressive Insurance Co Ltd: 2nd Floor, Sasi Arcade, Block 7, Main Clifton Rd, Clifton, Karachi; tel. (21) 5823560; fax (21) 5823561; f. 1989; Man. Dir and CEO ABDUL MAJEED.

Raja Insurance Co Ltd: Panorama Centre, 5th Floor, 256 Fatimah Jinnah Rd, POB 10422, Karachi 4; tel. (21) 5670619; fax (21) 5681501; f. 1981; Chair. RAJA ABDUL RAHMAN; Man. Dir Sheikh HUMAYUN SAYEED.

Reliance Insurance Co Ltd: Reliance Insurance House, 181-A, Sindhi Muslim Co-operative Housing Society, POB 13356, Karachi 74400; tel. (21) 4539415; fax (21) 4539412; e-mail reli-ins@cyber.net.pk; Chief Exec. and Man. Dir ABDUL RAZAK AHMED.

Royal & SunAlliance Insurance: 8th Floor, Shaheen Complex, POB 4930, M. R. Kayani Rd, Karachi 74000; tel. (21) 2635141; fax (21) 2631369; e-mail rsa@cyber.net.pk; internet www.royalsunalliance.com; f. 1989; Chief Exec. and Man. Dir Dr MUMTAZ A. HASHMI.

Royal Exchange Assurance: P&O Plaza, I. I. Chundrigar Rd, POB 315, Karachi 74000; tel. (21) 2635141; fax (21) 2631369; Man. (Pakistan) Dr MUMTAZ A. HASHMI.

Seafield Insurance Co Ltd: 86-Q, Block 2, Allama Iqbal Rd, PECHS, Karachi; tel. (21) 4527592; fax (21) 4527593; e-mail sifcpk89@hotmail.com; f. 1989; Man. Dir ADNAN HAFEEZ.

Security General Insurance Co Ltd: Nishat House, 53A Lawrence Rd, Lahore; tel. (42) 6279192; fax (42) 6303466; e-mail sgicl@hotmail.com; f. 1996; Man. Dir SYED JAWAD GILLANI.

Shaheen Insurance Co Ltd: 10th Floor, Shaheen Complex, M. R. Kayani Rd, Karachi 74200; tel. (21) 2626870; fax (21) 2626674; e-mail sihifc@cyber.net.pk; internet www.shaheeninsurance.com.pk; f. 1996; Chief Exec. NASREEN RASHID.

Silver Star Insurance Co Ltd: Silver Star House, 2nd Floor, 5 Bank Sq., POB 2533, Lahore 54000; tel. (42) 7324488; fax (42) 7229966; e-mail info@silverstarinsurance.com; internet www.silverstarinsurance.com; f. 1984; Man. Dir and Chief Exec. ZAHIR MUHAMMAD SADIQ; Chair. CHAUDHRY MUHAMMAD SADIQ.

Union Insurance Co of Pakistan Ltd: Adamjee House, 9th Floor, I. I. Chundrigar Rd, Karachi; tel. (21) 2416171; fax (21) 2420174; e-mail unionins@cyber.net.pk; Pres. NISHAT RAFFIQ.

United Insurance Co of Pakistan Ltd: Nizam Chambers, 5th Floor, Shahrah-e-Fatima Jinnah, POB 532, Lahore; tel. (42) 6361471; fax (42) 6375036; f. 1959; Man. Dir and CEO M. A. SHAHID.

Universal Insurance Co Ltd: Universal Insurance House, 63 Shahrah-e-Quaid-e-Azam, POB 539, Lahore; tel. (42) 7353458; fax (42) 7230326; e-mail uic@nexlinx.net.pk; f. 1958; Chief Exec. Begum ZEB GAUHAR AYUB; Man. Dir SARDAR KHAN.

Insurance Associations

Insurance Association of Pakistan: Jamshed Katrak Chamber, G. Allana Rd, POB 4932, Karachi 74000; tel. (21) 2311784; fax (21)

2310798; e-mail iapho@cyber.net.pk; internet www.iap.net.pk; f. 1948; mems comprise 30 cos (Pakistani and foreign) transacting general insurance business; issues tariffs and establishes rules for insurance in the country; regional office in Lahore; Chair. SAIFUDDIN N. ZOOMKAWALA; Sec. N. A. USMANI.

Pakistan Insurance Institute: Shafi Court, 2nd Floor, Mereweather Rd, Karachi 4; f. 1951 to encourage insurance education; Chair. MOHAMMAD CHOUDHRY.

Trade and Industry

GOVERNMENT AGENCIES

Agricultural Marketing and Storage Ltd: Islamabad; tel. (51) 827407; fax (51) 824607.

Alternative Energy Development Board (AEDB): 344-B, Prime Minister's Secretariat, Islamabad; tel. (51) 9223427; fax (51) 9205790; e-mail isesps_pk@yahoo.com; internet www.aedb.org; f. 2003; mandate incl. development of national plans and policies, undertaking promotion and dissemination of activities in field of renewable energy technologies, facilitation of power generation projects using alternative or renewable energy resources; Chair. Air Marshal (retd) SHAHID HAMID.

Board of Investment (BOI): Government of Pakistan, Atatürk Ave, Sector G-5/1, Islamabad; tel. (51) 9206161; fax (51) 9215554; e-mail boipr@isb.comsats.net.pk; internet www.pakboi.gov.pk; Chair. WASIM HAQUEE; Sec. SHUJA SHAH.

Commission for the Islamization of the Economy: Government of Pakistan, Finance Division, House No. 7, St 48, F-8/4, Islamabad 44000; tel. (51) 252834; fax (51) 252835; f. 1991; Chair. MOHAMMAD YAQOOB; Mem./Sec. ZULFIQAR KHAN.

Corporate and Industrial Restructuring Corpn: 13-C-II, M. M. Alam Rd, Gulberg III, Lahore; tel. (42) 5871532; fax (42) 5761650; e-mail info@circ-gov.com; internet www.circ-gov.com.

Earthquake Reconstruction and Rehabilitation Authority (ERRA): Prime Minister's Secretariat (Public), Constitution Ave, Islamabad; tel. (51) 9201254; fax (51) 9209525; f. 2005; Chair. ALTAF SALEEM.

Engineering Development Board: 5-A, Constitution Ave, SEDC Bldg, Islamabad; tel. (51) 9205595; fax (51) 9203584; internet www.engineeringindustry.info; CEO IMTIAZ A. RASTGAR.

Environmental Protection Agency: Govt of Sindh, EPA Complex, ST-2/1, Sector 23, Korangi Industrial Area, Karachi; tel. (21) 5065950; fax (21) 5065940.

Export Processing Zones Authority (EPZA): Landhi Industrial Area Extension, Mehran Highway, Landhi, Karachi 75150; tel. (21) 5082001; fax (21) 5082002; e-mail info@epza.gov.pk; internet www.epza.gov.pk; Chair. RUKHSANA SALEE.

Export Promotion Bureau: 5th Floor, Block A, Finance and Trade Centre, Shahrah-e-Faisal, POB 1293, Karachi; tel. (21) 9201501; fax (21) 9202713; e-mail epb@epb.gov.pk; internet www.epb.gov.pk; Chair. TARIQ IKRAM; Vice-Chair. ZAFAR MAHMOOD.

Family Planning Association of Pakistan: 3-A Temple Rd, Lahore; tel. (42) 111-223-366; fax (42) 6368692; e-mail info@fpapak.org; f. 1953; executes diversified community uplift programmes and activities; CEO MUHAMMAD ASHRAF CHATHA.

Geological Survey of Pakistan: Sariab Rd, POB 15, Quetta; tel. (81) 9211032; fax (81) 9211018; e-mail geophy@gsp.qta.khi.sdnpk.undp.org; Dir-Gen. S. HASAN GAUHAR; Asst Dir MOHSIN ANWAR KAZIM.

Gwadar Port Authority: 2nd Floor, PNSC Bldg, M. T. Khan Rd, Karachi; tel. (21) 9204061; fax (21) 9204196; e-mail gwadarport@hotmail.com.

Higher Education Commission: H-9, Islamabad; tel. (51) 9040305; fax (51) 9290128; e-mail info@hec.gov.pk; internet www.hec.gov.pk; Dir AHMED MALIK.

Information Technology Commission: IT and Telecom Division, Govt of Pakistan, 14, St 61, F-7/4, Islamabad; tel. (51) 9205889; fax (51) 9205992; e-mail secyitc@isb.comsats.net.pk; internet www.itcommission.gov.pk.

Karachi Export Processing Zone (KEPZ): Landhi Industrial Area Extension, Mehran Highway, POB 17011, Karachi 75150; tel. (21) 5082011; fax (21) 5082005; e-mail epza@super.net.pk.

National Accountability Bureau: Government of Pakistan, Islamabad; e-mail info@nab.gov.pk; internet www.nab.gov.pk.

National Aliens Registration Authority (NARA): C-82, Block 2, Clifton, Karachi; tel. (21) 9251083; f. 2001; registers all foreign nationals who wish to work in Pakistan.

National Commission for Human Development: Prime Minister's Secretariat, Level 2, Block D, Islamabad; tel. (51) 9216200; fax (51) 9216164; e-mail info@nchd.org.pk; internet www.nchd.org.pk; f. 2002.

National Database and Registration Authority (NADRA): Ministry of Interior, Awami Markaz, 5-A, Constitution Ave, F-5/1, Islamabad; tel. (51) 9204624; internet www.nadrapk.com.

National Economic Board: f. 1979 by the Govt as an advisory body to review and evaluate the state of the economy and to make proposals, especially to further the adoption of the socio-economic principles of Islam.

National Economic Council: supreme economic body; the governors and chief ministers of the four provinces and fed. ministers in charge of economic ministries are its mems; sr fed. and provincial officials in the economic field are also associated.

National Electric Power Regulatory Authority (NEPRA): OPF Bldg, 2nd Floor, Shahrah-e-Jamhuriat, G-5/2, Islamabad 44000; tel. (51) 9207200; fax (51) 9210215; e-mail info@nepra.org.pk; internet www.nepra.org.pk; Chair. Lt-Gen. (retd) SAEED UZ ZAFAR.

National Energy Conservation Centre (ENERCON): ENERCON Bldg, G-5/2, Islamabad; tel. (51) 9206001; fax (51) 9206004; Man. Dir ARIF ALAUDDIN.

National Highway Authority: 520, Margalla Rd, F-10/2, Islamabad; tel. (51) 9266671; fax (51) 9266153; e-mail nhal2@comsats.net.pk.

National Housing Authority: Prime Minister's Office, Islamabad; tel. (51) 92008539; fax (51) 92008324.

National Tariff Commission: State Life Bldg, No. 5, Jinnah Ave, Islamabad 44000; tel. (51) 9202031; fax (51) 9221205; e-mail ntc@ntc.gov.pk; internet www.ntc.gov.pk; Chair. Dr FAIZULLAH KHILJI.

National Technical Resources Pool: 414-C, National Reconstruction Bureau, Chief Executive's Secretariat II, Islamabad; tel. (51) 9207912.

Oil and Gas Regulatory Authority: Tariq Chambers, Civic Centre, G-6, Islamabad; tel. (51) 9221715; fax (51) 9221714; internet www.ogra.org.pk; regulates oil and gas sector.

Pakistan Electronic Media Regulatory Authority: Islamabad; tel. (51) 9202174; fax (51) 9219634; f. 2002; Chair. IFTIKHAR RASHID; Dir-Gen. Haji AHMAD MALIK.

Pakistan Intellectual Property Rights Organization (PIPRO): 23, St 87, G-6/3, Atatürk Ave, Embassy Rd, Islamabad; tel. (51) 9208581; fax (51) 9208157; f. 2004; oversees issues of copyright, trade marks and patent protection; Dir-Gen. YASIN TAHIR.

Pakistan National Accreditation Council (PNAC): Ministry of Scientific and Technological Research, 4th Floor, Evacuee Trust Complex, Aga Khan Rd, F-5/1, Islamabad; tel. (51) 9222310; fax (51) 9222312; e-mail ismailgulkhatak@yahoo.com; f. 1998; Dir-Gen. ABDUL RASHID KHAN.

Pakistan Revenue Service: national tax authority.

Pakistan Software Export Board (Guarantee) Ltd: 2nd Floor, Evacuee Trust Complex, F-5/1, Aga Khan Rd, Islamabad; tel. (51) 9204074; fax (51) 9204075; e-mail info@pseb.org.pk; internet www.pseb.org.pk; Man. Dir Dr AMIR MATEEN.

Pakistan Standards and Quality Control Authority (PSQCA): Pakistan Secretariat, Block 77, Karachi 74400; tel. and fax (21) 9206263; e-mail psqcadg@super.net.pk; internet www.psqca.com.pk; f. 1996; regulates standards in industry; Dir-Gen. ABDUL GHAFFAR SOOMRO.

Pakistan Telecommunication Authority: F-5/1, Islamabad 44000; tel. (51) 2878143; fax (51) 2878155; e-mail ddpr_pta@yahoo.com; internet www.pta.gov.pk; f. 1997 to regulate telecommunications services; to arrange deregulation of telecommunications; Chair. SHAHZADA ALAM MALIK; Dir-Gen. CH. MOHAMMAD DIN.

Pakistan Tobacco Board: Zonal Office, 152-P Block, Gulberg III, Ferozepur Rd, Lahore; tel. (42) 9230435; Dir EJAZ AHMED HASHMI.

Privatisation Commission: Experts Advisory Cell Bldg, 5A Constitution Ave, Islamabad 44000; tel. (51) 9216514; fax (51) 9203076; e-mail info@privatisation.gov.pk; internet www.privatisation.gov.pk; supervised by Ministry of Privatisation and Investment.

Sindh Katchi Abadi Authority: Karachi; tel. (21) 9211275; fax (21) 9211272; e-mail skaa@khi.compol.com; internet www.skaa.cutecity.com; govt agency established to regulate and improve slums in Pakistan's southern province; Dir-Gen. TASNEEM AHMAD SIDDIQUI.

Sindh Privatisation Commission: Sindh Secretariat, 4-A, Block 15, Court Rd, Karachi; tel. (21) 9202077; fax (21) 9202071; e-mail spcsecretary@yahoo.com; internet www.spc.gov.pk.

Sustainable Development Policy Institute: St 3, UN Blvd, Diplomatic Enclave 1, Islamabad; tel. (51) 2278134; fax (51) 2278135; e-mail msf@sdpi.org; Co-ordinator MOHAMMAD SHAH FARRUKH.

Trading Corporation of Pakistan: Finance and Trade Centre, Main Shahrah-e-Faisal, Karachi 74400; tel. (21) 9202724; fax (21) 9202722; e-mail tepkhi@pk.netsolir.com; f. 1967.

PAKISTAN

Utility Stores Corporation of Pakistan: Plot No. 2039, G-7/F-7, POB 1339, Jinnah Ave, Blue Area, Islamabad; tel. (51) 9210986; fax (51) 9210982; e-mail usc_ho@yahoo.com; internet www.usc.com.pk; f. 1971; Man. Dir Brig. HAFEEZ AHMED.

DEVELOPMENT ORGANIZATIONS

Balochistan Development Authority: Civil Secretariat, Block 7, Quetta; tel. (81) 9202491; created for economic development of Balochistan; exploration and exploitation of mineral resources; development of infrastructure, water resources, etc.

Capital Development Authority: Islamabad; tel. (51) 9201016; fax (51) 9219413; internet www.cda.gov.pk; Chair. KAMRAN LASHARI.

Council for Works and Housing Research (CWHR): F-40, SITE Hub River Rd, Karachi 75730; tel. (21) 2577237; fax (21) 2577235; e-mail whr@comsats.net.pk; internet www.cwhr.gov.pk; f. 1964.

Lahore Development Authority (LDA): LDA Plaza, Egerton Rd, Lahore.

Pakistan Industrial Technical Assistance Centre (PITAC): Maulana Jalaluddin Roomi Rd (old Ferozepur Rd), Lahore 54600; tel. (42) 9230699; fax (42) 9230589; e-mail info@pitac.gov.pk; internet www.pitac.gov.pk; f. 1962 by the Govt to provide prototype tooling facilities and spare parts to manufacturing industries and advanced training to industrial personnel in the fields of metal trades and tool engineering design and related fields; under Ministry of Industries, Production and Special Initiatives; provides human resource development programmes; Chair. ALMAS HYDER; Gen. Man. JAVAID IQBAL SHAIKH.

Pakistan Poverty Alleviation Fund: 6A, Park Rd, F-8/2, Islamabad; tel. (51) 2253178; fax (51) 2251726; e-mail kamran@ppaf.org.pk; internet www.ppaf.org.pk; f. 1997 by the Government; funded by the World Bank; works with non-governmental organizations and private-sector institutions to alleviate poverty; Chief Exec. KAMAL HAYAT.

Peshawar Development Authority (PDA): PDA House, Phase V, Hayatabad, Peshawar; tel. (521) 9217035; fax (521) 9217030.

Quetta Development Authority: Sarai Rd, Quetta; tel. (81) 9211069.

Sarhad Development Authority (SDA): PIA Bldg, Arbab Rd, POB 172, Peshawar; tel. (521) 73076; f. 1972; promotes industrial (particularly mining) and commercial development in the North-West Frontier Province; Chair. KHALID AZIZ.

Small and Medium Enterprises Development Authority (SMEDA): 6th Floor, LDA Plaza, Egerton Rd, Lahore; tel. (42) 6373404; fax (42) 6304926; internet www.smeda.org.pk; f. 1998; 3 brs; CEO SHAHAB KHAWAJA.

CHAMBERS OF COMMERCE

The Federation of Pakistan Chambers of Commerce and Industry: Federation House, Main Clifton, POB 13875, Karachi 75600; tel. (21) 5873691; fax (21) 5874332; e-mail fpcci@cyber.net.pk; internet www.fpcci.com; f. 1950; 163 mem. bodies; Pres. CHAUDHRY MOHAMMAD SAEED; Sec.-Gen. Dr KHALID AMIN.

Islamic Chamber of Commerce and Industry: St 2/A, Block 9, KDA Scheme No. 5, Clifton, Karachi 75600; tel. (21) 5874756; fax (21) 5870765; e-mail icci@icci-oic.org; internet www.icci-oic.org; f. 1979; Pres. Sheikh SALEH BIN ABDUL; Sec.-Gen. AQEEL AHMAD AL-JASSEM.

Overseas Investors' Chamber of Commerce and Industry: Chamber of Commerce Bldg, Talpur Rd, POB 4833, Karachi; tel. (21) 2410814; fax (21) 2427315; e-mail info@oicci.org; internet www.oicci.org.pk; f. 1860 as the Karachi Chamber of Commerce, name changed to above in 1968; 184 mem. bodies; Pres. FAROOQ RAHMATULLAH; Sec.-Gen. ZAHID ZAHEER.

Principal Affiliated Chambers

Azad Jammu and Kashmir Chamber of Commerce and Industry: 9, Sector G/1, Haul Rd, POB 12, Mirpur 10250; tel. (58610) 34760; fax (58610) 34761; e-mail ajkcci@isb.paknet.com.pk; internet www.ajkcci.com; f. 1980; Pres. RAJA MUHAMMAD JAMIL.

Bahawalpur Chamber of Commerce and Industry: 28 C/A, Abbasi Rd, off Shahrah-e-Azia Bhatti Shaheed, Model Town A, Bahawalpur; tel. and fax (621) 883192; fax (621) 889283; e-mail chamber@pakview.com; Pres. Khawaja MOHAMMAD ILYAS.

Balochistan Chamber of Commerce and Industry: Zarghoon Rd, POB 117, Quetta 87300; tel. (81) 2835717; fax (81) 2821948; e-mail qcci@hotmail.com; f. 1984; Pres. Sheikh ABDUL AZIZ; Sec. MUHAMMAD AHMAD.

Chaman Chamber of Commerce and Industry: Commerce House, Chaman; tel. (826) 613308.

Dadu Chamber of Commerce and Industry: 816, 8th Floor, Progressive Plaza, Beaumont Rd, Karachi; tel. (21) 5219026; fax (21) 5650006; e-mail daduchamber@hotmail.com.

Dera Ghazi Khan Chamber of Commerce and Industry: Block 34, Khakwani House, Dera Ghazi Khan, Punjab; tel. (641) 62338; fax (641) 64938; Pres. Khawaja MOHAMMAD YUNUS; Sec. MOHAMMAD MUJAHID.

Dera Ismail Khan Chamber of Commerce and Industry: Circular Rd, POB 5, D. I. Khan; tel. (961) 811334; fax (961) 811334; e-mail sjbdn@epistemics.net.

Faisalabad Chamber of Commerce and Industry: 2nd Floor, National Bank Bldg, Jail Rd, Faisalabad; tel. (41) 616045; fax (41) 615085; e-mail fcci@fsd.paknet.com.pk; Pres. Mian AFTAB AHMAD; Sec. SYED RIAZ HUSSAIN RIZVI.

Gawadar Chamber of Commerce and Industry: Fish Harbour Rd, Gawadar; tel. (864) 211470; Pres. ASGHAR AZIZ SANJARANI.

Gujranwala Chamber of Commerce and Industry: Aiwan-e-Tijarat Rd, Gujranwala; tel. (55) 3256701; fax (55) 3254440; e-mail gcci@gjr.paknet.com.pk; internet www.gcci.org.pk; f. 1978; Pres. ASAD ELAHI; Sec. SYED MUJAHID MUMTAZ.

Gujrat Chamber of Commerce and Industry: 26-A, G. T. Rd, S.I.E. POB 169, Gujrat; tel. (4331) 523012; fax (4331) 523011; Pres. CH. IFTIKHAR AHMED.

Haripur Chamber of Commerce and Industry: 32 Habib Plaza, G. T. Rd, Haripur; tel. (995) 3107; fax (995) 4275; Pres. MALIK MOHAMMAD FAREED.

Hyderabad Chamber of Commerce and Industry: Aiwan-e-Tijarat Rd, Saddar, POB 99, Hyderabad 71000; tel. (22) 2784972; fax (22) 2784977; e-mail hcci@muchomail.com; internet www.hyderabadchamber.com; f. 1961; Pres. MEHMOOD AHMAD; Sec. BASHIR ALI NOORANI.

Islamabad Chamber of Commerce and Industry: Aiwan-e-Sana't-o-Tijarat Rd, Mauve Area, Sector G-8/1, Islamabad; tel. (51) 2250526; fax (51) 2252950; e-mail icci@brain.net.pk; internet www.icci.com.pk; f. 1984; Pres. ZUBAIR AHMED MALIK; Sec. MAJID SHABBIR.

Jhelum Chamber of Commerce and Industry: Rani Nagar, G. T. Rd, Jhelum; tel. (541) 646532; fax (541) 646533; Pres. RAJA TARIQ REHMAN; Sec. Capt. (retd) MUHAMMAD ZAMAN.

Karachi Chamber of Commerce and Industry: Aiwan-e-Tijarat Rd, off Shahrah-e-Liaquat, POB 4158, Karachi 74000; tel. (21) 5873691; fax (21) 5874332; e-mail info@karachichamber.com; internet www.karachichamber.com; f. 1960; 11,705 mems; Pres. HAROON FARUQI; Sec. M. NAZIR ALI.

Khairpur Chamber of Commerce and Industry: Shop 8, Sachal Shopping Centre, Khairpur; tel. (792) 51505.

Lahore Chamber of Commerce and Industry: 11 Shahrah-e-Aiwan-e-Tijarat, POB 597, Lahore; tel. (42) 6305538; fax (42) 6368854; e-mail sect@lcci.org.pk; internet www.lcci.org.pk; f. 1923; 8,000 mems; Pres. YAWAR KHAN; Sec. M. LATIF CHAUDHRY.

Larkana Chamber of Commerce and Industry: 21–23 Kenedy Market, POB 78, Larkana, Sindh; tel. (741) 457136; fax (741) 440709; e-mail president@larkanachamber.com; internet www.larkanachamber.com; Pres. MOHAMMAD ASLAM SHEIKH.

Mirpurkhas Chamber of Commerce and Industry: Khan Chamber, New Town, POB 162, Mirpurkhas, Sindh; tel. (233) 872175; fax (233) 872195; Pres. ABDUL KHALIQUE KHAN; Sec. MOHAMMAD BASIT-ULLAH BAIG.

Multan Chamber of Commerce and Industry: Shahrah-e-Aiwan-e-Tijarat-o-Sanat, Multan; tel. (61) 4517087; fax (61) 4570463; e-mail mccimultan@hotmail.com; Pres. Mian MUGHIS A. SHEIKH; Sec. G. A. BHATTI.

Quetta Chamber of Commerce and Industry: Zarghoon Rd, POB 117, Quetta 87300; tel. (81) 2821943; fax (81) 2821948; e-mail qcci@hotmail.com; Pres. Sheikh ABDUL AZIZ; Sec. MUHAMMAD AHMAD.

Rawalpindi Chamber of Commerce and Industry: 39 Mayo Rd, Civil Lines, Rawalpindi; tel. (51) 5110514; fax (51) 5111055; e-mail rcci@isd.wol.net.pk; f. 1952; Pres. HUSSAIN AHMED OZGAN; Sec. MUHAMMAD IFTIKHAR-UD-DIN.

SAARC Chamber of Commerce and Industry: House No. 5, St No. 59, F-8/4, Islamabad; tel. (51) 2281396; fax (51) 2281390; e-mail saarc@comsats.net.pk; internet www.saarc.sec.org; f. 1993; Pres. MACKY HASHMI.

Sargodha Chamber of Commerce and Industry: 80/2-A, Satellite Town, Sargodha 40100; tel. (48) 9230662; fax (48) 9230663; e-mail sgdacci@hotmail.com; f. 1986; Pres. ABID RAFIQUE KHAWAJA; Sec.-Gen. KASHIF MUKHTAR SHEIKH.

Sarhad Chamber of Commerce and Industry: Sarhad Chamber House, Chacha Younis Park, G. T. Rd, Peshawar; tel. (91) 9213314; fax (91) 9213316; e-mail sccip@brain.net.pk; internet www.scci.pk; f. 1958; 2,509 mems; Pres. MALIK NIAZ AHMED; Sec. MUHAMMAD AYUB.

Sialkot Chamber of Commerce and Industry: Shahrah-e-Aiwan-e-Sanat-o-Tijarat, POB 1870, Sialkot 51310; tel. (52) 4261881; fax (52) 4268835; e-mail research@scci.com.pk; internet www.scci.com.pk; f. 1982; 6,500 mems; Pres. Dr NOUMAN IDRIS BUTT; Sec. NAWAZ AHMED TOOR.

Sukkur Chamber of Commerce and Industry: Sukkur Chamber House, 1st Floor, opp. Mehran View Plaza, Bunder Rd, Sukkur; tel. (71) 23938; fax (71) 23059; Pres. SHAKEEL AHMED MUKHTAR; Sec. MIRZA IQBAL BEG.

Thatta Chamber of Commerce and Industry: PO Shaffiabad, Gharo, Thatta; tel. (14) 7726243; fax (14) 7725122; e-mail malodhi@lodhico.khi2.erum.com.pk.

INDUSTRIAL AND TRADE ASSOCIATIONS

Air Cargo Agents' Association of Pakistan: Suite 305, 3rd Floor, Fortune Centre, 45-A, Block 6, PECHS, Shahrah-e-Faisal, Karachi 75400; tel. (21) 4383501; e-mail acaap@cyberaccess.com.pk; Sec. S. MOHAMMAD ABBAS.

All Pakistan Cement Manufacturers' Association: 5th Floor, Maqbool Commercial Comp., J.C.H.S., Shahrah-e-Faisal, Karachi; tel. (21) 5758360.

All Pakistan Cloth Exporters' Association: 30/7, Civil Lines, Faisalabad; tel. (41) 644750; fax (41) 617985; e-mail apcea@fsd.paknet.com.pk; Chair. AHMAD KAMAL; Sec. AFTAB AHMAD.

All Pakistan Cloth Merchants' Association: 4th Floor, Hasan Ali Centre, Hussaini Cloth Market, nr Mereweather Tower, M. A. Jinnah Rd, Karachi; tel. (21) 2444274; fax (21) 2401423; e-mail pcma@cyber.net.pk; Chair. JAWED CHINOY; Sec.-Gen. RAFIQ KHAN.

All Pakistan Cotton Powerlooms' Association: P-79/3, Montgomery Bazaar, Faisalabad; tel. (411) 612929; fax (411) 28171; Chair. CHAUDRY JAVAID SADIQ.

All Pakistan Furniture Exporters' Association: Karachi; tel. (21) 5861963; Chair. TURHAN BAIG MOHAMMAD.

All Pakistan Textile Mills' Association (APTMA): APTMA House, 44A Lalazar, off Moulvi Tamizuddin Khan Rd, POB 5446, Karachi 74000; tel. (21) 111-700-000; fax (21) 5611305; e-mail aptma@cyber.net.pk; internet www.aptma.org.pk; f. 1959; CEO MUHAMMAD AZAM (acting); Chair. AHMAD KULI KHAN.

Cigarette Manufacturers' Association of Pakistan: Mezzanine 1, Avanti Park View, 141-A, Block 2, PECHS, Allama Iqbal Rd, Karachi 75400; tel. and fax (21) 4526825; e-mail cmaofpak@cyber.net.pk; Sec. TARIQ FAROOQ.

Cotton Board: Dr Abbasi Clinic Bldg, 76 Strachan Rd, Karachi 74200; tel. (21) 215669; fax (21) 5680422; f. 1950; Dep. Sec. Dr MUHAMMAD USMAN.

Federal 'B' Area Industrial Association: F. B. Area, Karachi; Chair. (vacant).

Karachi Cotton Association: The Cotton Exchange, I. I. Chundrigar Rd, Karachi; tel. (21) 2410336; fax (21) 2413035; e-mail kcapak@cyber.net.pk; internet www.kcapak.org; Chair. A. SHAKOOR DADA; Sec. S. A. JAWED.

Korangi Association of Trade and Industry: ST-4/2, 1st Floor, Aiwan-e-Sanat, Sector 23, Korangi Industrial Area, Karachi 74900; tel. (21) 5061211; fax (21) 5061215; e-mail kati@cyber.net.pk; Chair. GULZAR FIROZ; Sec. NIHAL AKHTAR.

Management Association of Pakistan: 36-A/4, Lalazar, opp. Beach Luxury Hotel, Karachi 74000; tel. (21) 5610903; fax (21) 5611683; e-mail info@mappk.org; Pres. SOHAIL WAJAHAT H. SIDDIQUI; Exec. Dir FAROOQ HASSAN.

Pakistan Advertising Association: Rm 318, 3rd Floor, Hotel Metropole, Club Rd, Karachi; tel. (21) 5671567; fax (21) 5671571; e-mail paa@cyberaccess.com.pk.

Pakistan Agricultural Machinery and Implements Manufacturers' Association: Samundari Rd, Faisalabad; tel. (41) 714517; fax (41) 722721; e-mail iqra@fsd.comsats.net.pk.

Pakistan Arms and Ammunition Merchants' and Manufacturers' Association: Metropole Cinema Bldg, Rm 7, Abbot Rd, Lahore; tel. (42) 7239973; fax (42) 7230170; e-mail ssalimali@hotmail.com.

Pakistan Art Silk Fabrics and Garments Exporters' Association: 60, The Mall, Lahore; tel. (42) 6360919; fax (42) 6361291; e-mail pasfgea@hotmail.com; internet www.pasfgea.org; Chair. JAMIL MEHBOOB MAGOON; Sec.-Gen. IFTIKHAR AHMED KHAN.

Pakistan Association of Automotive Parts and Accessories Manufacturers: 894 Circular Rd, nr Nigar Cinema, Lahore; tel. (42) 7312452; fax (42) 7237613; e-mail secypaapam@hotmail.com.

Pakistan Association of Builders and Developers: Abad House, St 1/D, Block 16, Gulistan-e-Jauhar, Karachi; tel. (21) 8113645; fax (21) 8113648; e-mail abadhouse@yahoo.com.

Pakistan Automotive Manufacturers' Association: 11 Ilaco House, Abdullah Haroon Rd, Karachi; tel. (21) 5662493; fax (21) 5687247; e-mail pamauto@cyber.net.pk.

Pakistan Bedwear Exporters' Association: 245-1-V, Block 6, PECHS, Karachi; tel. (21) 4541149; fax (21) 2851429; e-mail dlnash@dlnash.com; Chair. SHABIR AHMED; Sec. S. IFTIKHAR HUSSAIN.

Pakistan Beverage Manufacturers' Association: C, 1st Floor, Kiran Centre, M-28, Model Town Extension, Lahore; tel. (42) 5167306; fax (42) 5167316.

Pakistan Canvas and Tents Manufacturers' and Exporters' Association: 15/63, Shadman Commercial Market, Afridi Mansion, Lahore 3; tel. (42) 7578836; fax (42) 7577572; e-mail pctmea@wol.net.pk; Chair. ABDUL RAZAK CHHAPRA; Sec. IJAZ HUSSAIN.

Pakistan Carpet Manufacturers' and Exporters' Association: 401-A, 4th Floor, Panorama Center, Fatima Jinnah Rd, Saddar, Karachi 75530; tel. (21) 5212189; fax (21) 5679649; e-mail pcmeaho@gerrys.net; internet www.pakistanrug.com.pk; Chair. ABDUL GHAFOOR SAJID; Sec. A. S. HASHMI.

Pakistan Chemicals and Dyes Merchants' Association: Chemical and Dye House, Jodia Bazar, Rambharti St, Karachi 74000; tel. (21) 2432752; fax (21) 2430117; Chair. MOHAMMAD SABIR CHIPPA.

Pakistan Commercial Exporters of Towels Association: PCETA House, 7-H, Block 6, PECHS, Karachi; tel. (21) 4535757; fax (21) 4522372; e-mail pceta@cyber.net.pk; internet www.towelword.com; Chair. JAMIL MAHBOOB MAGOON.

Pakistan Cotton Fashion Apparel Manufacturers' and Exporters' Association: Rm 5, Amber Court, 2nd Floor, Shahrah-e-Faisal, Shaheed-e-Millat Rd, Karachi 75350; tel. (21) 4533936; fax (21) 4546711; e-mail pcfa@cyber.net.pk; f. 1982; 650 mems; Chair. Dr SHAHZAD ARSHAD.

Pakistan Cotton Ginners' Association: 1119–1120, 11th Floor, Uni-Plaza, I. I. Chundrigar Rd, Karachi; tel. (21) 2411406; fax (21) 2423181; e-mail pcga@pgca.org; Pres. MOHAMMAD SAEED; Sec. AIJAZUDDIN GHAURI.

Pakistan Dairy Association: 11/19-B, Link Shami Rd, Lahore; tel. (42) 6680041; fax (42) 6682042; e-mail pakdairy@yahoo.com.

Pakistan Electronic Manufacturers' Association: 1st Floor, Rizvi Chambers, Akbar Rd, Karachi; tel. (21) 7766912; fax (21) 5874546.

Pakistan Engineering Council: Atatürk Ave (East), Sector G-5/2, Islamabad; tel. (51) 2276625; fax (51) 2276224; e-mail info@pec.org.pk; internet www.pec.org.pk; f. 1976.

Pakistan Film Producers' Association: Regal Cinema Bldg, Shahrah-e-Quaid-e-Azam, Lahore; tel. (42) 7322904; fax (42) 7241264; Chair. Mian AMJAD FARZEND; Sec. SAMI DEHLVI.

Pakistan Flour Mills' Association: Taj Complex, Block C-3, 1st Floor, Line Development Area, M. A. Jinnah Rd, Karachi; tel. (21) 5010556; fax (21) 7780137.

Pakistan Footwear Manufacturers' Association: 6-F, Rehman Business Centre, 32-B-III, Gulberg III, Lahore 54660; tel. (42) 5750051; fax (42) 5750052; e-mail pfma@pakfootwear.org; internet www.pakfootwear.org; Chair. WASIM ZAKARIA; Sec. Col (retd) ARSHAD AYYAZ.

Pakistan Gloves Manufacturers' and Exporters' Association: 349 Khadim Ali Rd, G. H. Jones Bldg, Tajpura, POB 1330, Sialkot; tel. (432) 551847; fax (432) 550182; e-mail pgmea@brain.net.pk; Chair. MALIK NASEER AHMED; Sec. GULZAR AHMED SHAD.

Pakistan Hardware Merchants' Association: Mandviwala Bldg, Serai Rd, Karachi 74000; tel. (21) 2420610; fax (21) 2432878; e-mail phmasbcircle@hotmail.com; f. 1961; more than 1,500 mems; Chair. BASIT ALAVI; Sec. SYED ZAFRUN NABI.

Pakistan Hosiery Manufacturers' Association: Karachi; tel. (21) 4522769; fax (21) 4543774; Chair. IMRAN ALI; Sec. YUNUS BIN AIYOOB.

Pakistan Iron and Steel Merchants' Association: Corner House, 2nd Floor, Preedy St, Saddar, Karachi; tel. (21) 5660270; fax (21) 5682724; Pres. MALIK AHMAD HUSSAIN; Gen. Sec. S. S. REHMAN.

Pakistan Jute Mills' Association: 8 Sasi Town Houses, Abdullah Haroon Rd, Civil Lines, Karachi 75530; tel. (21) 5676986; fax (21) 5676463; e-mail pjma@cyber.net.pk; Chair. HUMAYUN MAZHAR; Sec. S. A. H. RIZVI.

Pakistan Knitwear and Sweaters Exporters' Association: Rms Nos 1014–1016, 10th Floor, Park Ave, Block 6, PECHS, Shahrah-e-Faisal, Karachi 95350; tel. (21) 4522604; fax (21) 4525747; Chair. NASIR HUSSAIN.

Pakistan Leather Garments Manufacturers' and Exporters' Association: 92-C, Khayaban-e-Ittehad, DHA Phase II (Extension), Karachi; tel. (21) 5387356; fax (21) 5388799; e-mail info@plgmea.org; internet www.plgmea.org; f. 2002; Chair. AHMAD ZULFIQAR HAYAT.

Pakistan Paint Manufacturers' Association: St 6/A, Block 14, Federal 'B' Area, Karachi 38; tel. (21) 6321103; fax (21) 2560468; f. 1953; Chair. WASSIM A. KHAN; Sec. SYED AZHAR ALI.

Pakistan Petroleum Exploration and Production Companies' Association: 1 St 49, Sector F-6/4, Islamabad; tel. (51) 2823928; fax (51) 2276084; e-mail ppepca@isb.comsats.net.pk; internet www.ppepca.org; f. 1995; Chair. Philip Byrne.

Pakistan Pharmaceutical Manufacturers' Association: 130–131, Hotel Metropole, Karachi; tel. (21) 5211773; fax (21) 5675608.

Pakistan Plastic Manufacturers' Association: 410 Mashrique Shopping Centre, St 6/A, Block No. 14, Gulshan-e-Iqbal, Karachi; tel. (21) 4942336; fax (21) 4944222; e-mail pakppma@pk.netsolir.com; Sec. Fayyaz A. Chaudhry; Pres. Zakaria Usman.

Pakistan Polypropylene Woven Sacks Manufacturers' Association: Karachi; Chair. Shoukat Ahmed.

Pakistan Poultry Association: 219 Mashriq Centre, Block 14, Sir Shah Muhammad Suleman Rd, Gulshan-e-Iqbal, Karachi; tel. (21) 4940362; fax (21) 4940364; e-mail ppasee@cyber.net.pk.

Pakistan Pulp, Paper and Board Mills' Association: 402 Burhani Chambers, Abdullah Haroon Rd, Karachi 74400; tel. (21) 7726150; Chair. Kamran Khan.

Pakistan Readymade Garments Manufacturers' and Exporters' Association: Shaheen View Bldg, Mezzanine Floor, Plot No. 18A, Block 6, PECHS, Shahrah-e-Faisal, Karachi; tel. (21) 4547912; fax (21) 4539669; e-mail info@prgmea.org; Chair. Tahir Aziz.

Pakistan Seafood Industries' Association: A-2, Fish Harbour, West Wharf, Karachi; tel. (21) 2311117; fax (21) 2310939; e-mail psiapk@hotmail.com.

Pakistan Ship Breakers' Association: 608, S. S. Chamber, Siemens Chowrangi, S.I.T.E., Karachi; tel. (21) 293958; fax (21) 256533.

Pakistan Silk and Rayon Mills' Association: Rms Nos 44–48, Textile Plaza, 5th Floor, M. A. Jinnah Rd, Karachi 2; tel. (21) 2410288; fax (21) 2415261; e-mail ctech@edu.pk; f. 1974; Chair. M. Ashraf Sheikh; Sec. M. H. K. Burney.

Pakistan Small Units Powerlooms' Association: 2nd Floor, Waqas Plaza, Aminpura Bazar, POB 8647, Faisalabad; tel. (411) 627992; fax (411) 633567.

Pakistan Soap Manufacturers' Association: 148 Sunny Plaza, Hasrat Mohani Rd, Karachi 74200; tel. (21) 2634648; fax (21) 2563828; e-mail pakistansma@yahoo.com; Chair. Yaqoob Karim.

Pakistan Software Houses Association (PASHA): D-30, Block 9, Clifton, Karachi 75600; tel. (521) 5866595; fax (21) 5869991; e-mail karachi@pasha.org.pk; internet www.pasha.org.pk; f. 1992; Pres. Zain I. Syed.

Pakistan Sports Goods Manufacturers' and Exporters' Association: Paris Rd, Sialkot 51310; tel. (432) 267962; fax (432) 261774; e-mail psga@brain.net.pk; Chair. Sheikh Ahmed Hussain.

Pakistan Steel Melters' Association: 30-S, Gulberg Centre, 84-D/1, Main Boulevard, Gulberg-III, Lahore; tel. (42) 5759284; fax (42) 5712028; e-mail steelmelters@angelfire.com; Chair. Mian Muhammad Saeed.

Pakistan Steel Re-rolling Mills' Association: Rashid Chambers, 6-Link McLeod Rd, Lahore 54000; tel. (42) 7227136; fax (42) 7231154; e-mail steel_re_rollers@hotmail.com; Chair. Mian Manzoor Ahmad; Sec. Lt-Col (retd) S. H. A. Bukhari.

Pakistan Sugar Mills' Association: Mezzanine Floor, 24D Rashid Plaza, Jinnah Ave, Islamabad; tel. (51) 270525; fax (51) 274153; Chair. Chaudhry Zaka Ashraf; Sec.-Gen. K. Ali Qazilbash.

Pakistan Tanners' Association: Plot No. 46-C, 21st Commercial St, Phase II Extension, Defence Housing Authority, Karachi 75500; tel. (21) 5880180; fax (21) 5880093; e-mail pta@fascom.com; Chair. Khwaja Mohammad Yousuf.

Pakistan Tea Association: Suite 307, Business Plaza, Mumtaz Hassan Rd, off I. I. Chundrigar Rd, Karachi; tel. (21) 2422161; fax (21) 2422209; e-mail pta@cyber.net.pk; Chair. Hanif Janoo.

Pakistan Vanaspati Manufacturers' Association: No. 5-B, College Rd, F-7/3, Islamabad; tel. (51) 2274358; fax (51) 2272529; Chair. Sheikh Abdul Razzaque.

Pakistan Wool and Hair Merchants' Association: 27 Idris Chambers, Talpur Rd, Karachi; Pres. Mian Mohammad Siddiq Khan; Sec. Khalid Lateef.

Pakistan Woollen Mills' Association: 25A, Davis Rd, Lahore 54000; tel. (42) 6307691; fax (42) 6306881; e-mail pwma@brain.net.pk; internet www.lcci.org.pk; Chair. Mian Muzaffar Ali; Sec. Muhammad Raheel Chohan.

Pakistan Yarn Merchants' Association: Rms Nos 802–803, Business Centre, 8th Floor, Dunolly Rd, Karachi 74000; tel. (21) 2410320; fax (21) 2424896; e-mail pyma@cubexs.net.pk; Pres. Khurshid A. Sheikh; Sec. Manzoorul Hasan Hashmi.

Rice Exports Association of Pakistan: 4th Floor, Sadiq Plaza, The Mall, Lahore; tel. and fax (42) 6280196; e-mail reaplhr@brain.net.pk; Chair. Haji Abdul Majid.

Towel Manufacturers' Association of Pakistan: 77-A, Block A, Sindhi Muslim Co-operative Housing Society, Karachi 74400; tel. (21) 111-360-360; fax (21) 4551628; e-mail tma@towelassociation.com; internet www.towelassociation.com; Chair. Pervez Ahmed.

EMPLOYERS' ORGANIZATION

Employers' Federation of Pakistan: 2nd Floor, State Life Bldg No. 2, Wallace Rd, off I. I. Chundrigar Rd, POB 4338, Karachi 74000; tel. (21) 2411049; fax (21) 2439347; e-mail efpak@cyber.net.pk; internet www.efpak.com; f. 1950; Pres. Ashraf Wali Mohammad Tabani; Sec.-Gen. Prof. M. Matin Khan.

UTILITIES

Water and Power Development Authority (WAPDA): WAPDA House, Shahrah-e-Quaid-e-Azam, Lahore; tel. (42) 6366911; f. 1958 for development of irrigation, water supply and drainage, building of replacement works under the World Bank-sponsored Indo-Pakistan Indus Basin Treaty; flood-control and watershed management; reclamation of waterlogged and saline lands; inland navigation; generation, transmission and distribution of hydroelectric and thermal power; partial transfer to private ownership carried out in 1996; Chair. Tariq Hamid.

Electricity

National Electric Power Regulatory Authority (NEPRA): OPF Bldg, 2nd Floor, Shahrah-e-Jamhuriat, G-5/2, Islamabad 44000; tel. (51) 9207200; fax (51) 9210215; e-mail info@nepra.org.pk; internet www.nepra.org.pk; f. 1997; fixes the power tariff; Chair. Lt-Gen. (retd) Saeed uz Zafar.

Hub Power Co Ltd (Hubco): Islamic Chamber Bldg, Block No. 9, Clifton, POB 13841, Karachi 75600; tel. (21) 5874677; fax (21) 5870397; e-mail info@hubpower.com; internet www.hubpower.com; f. 1991; supplies electricity; Chair. Mohammad Ali Raza; Chief Exec. Vince Harris.

Karachi Electric Supply Corpn Ltd (KESC): Aimai House, Abdullah Haroon Rd, POB 7197, Karachi; tel. (21) 5685492; fax (21) 5682408; f. 1913; Chair. and Man. Dir Brig. Tariq Soddazai.

Kot Addu Power Co (KAPCO): G.T.P., Kot Addu, District Muzaffargarh; tel. (697) 41336.

National Power Construction Corpn (Pvt) Ltd: 9 Shadman II, Lahore 54000; tel. (42) 7566019; fax (42) 7566022; e-mail npcc@wol.net.pk; internet www.npcc.com.pk; f. 1974; execution of power projects on turnkey basis, e.g. extra high voltage transmission lines, distribution networks, substations, power generation plants, industrial electrification, external lighting of housing complexes, etc.; Man. Dir Muhammad Ajaz Malik; Gen. Man. Tauqir Ahmed Sharifi; project office in Jeddah (Saudi Arabia).

National Power International: D-15, Block 2, Khayaban-e-Ghalib, Clifton, Karachi 75600; tel. (21) 5860328; fax (21) 5860343; e-mail npower@www.fascom.com.

Pakistan Atomic Energy Commission (PAEC): POB 1114, Islamabad; tel. (51) 9209032; fax (51) 9204908; responsible for harnessing nuclear energy for development of nuclear technology as part of the nuclear power programme; operates Karachi Atomic Nuclear Power Plant—KANUPP (POB 3183, nr Paradise Point, Hawksbay Rd, Karachi 75400; tel. (21) 9202222; fax (21) 7737488; e-mail knpc@khi.comsats.net.pk) and Chasma Nuclear Power Plant (CHASNUPP) at Chasma District, Mianwali; building another nuclear power station at Kundian; establishing research centres, incl. Pakistan Institute of Nuclear Science and Technology (PINSTECH); promoting peaceful use of atomic energy in agriculture, medicine, industry and hydrology; searching for indigenous nuclear mineral deposits; training project personnel; Chair. Pervez Butt; Gen. Man. (KANUPP) Qamrul Hoda.

Pakistan Electric Power Co: Lahore; f. 1998; Chair. Javed Burki.

Private Power and Infrastructure Board (PPIB): 50 Nazimuddin Rd, F-7/4, Islamabad; tel. (51) 9205421; fax (51) 9217735; e-mail ppib@ppib.gov.pk; internet www.ppib.gov.pk; f. 1994; facilitates participation of private sector in national power generation; Man. Dir Khalid Rahman.

Quetta Electric Supply Co Ltd: Zarghoon Rd, Quetta Cantt, Balochistan; tel. (81) 9202211; fax (81) 836554; e-mail qesco@qta.infolink.net.pk; f. 1998; CEO Brig. Agha Gul.

Gas

Mari Gas Co Ltd (MGCL): 21 Mauve Area, 3rd Rd, Sector G-10/4, Islamabad; tel. (51) 111410; fax (51) 2297686; e-mail info@marigas.com.pk; internet www.marigas.com.pk; 20% govt-owned; Man. Dir Lt-Gen. (retd) Imtiaz Shaheen.

Oil and Gas Development Corpn Ltd (OGDCL): C-6, Masood Mansion, F-8, Markaz, Islamabad; tel. (51) 9260405; fax (51) 9260467; f. 1961; plans, promotes, organizes and implements programmes for the exploration and development of petroleum and gas

PAKISTAN

resources, and the production, refining and sale of petroleum and gas; transfer to private ownership pending; Man. Dir RAZIUDDIN.

Pakistan Petroleum Ltd (PPL): PIDC House, 4th Floor, Dr Ziauddin Ahmed Rd, Karachi 75530; tel. (21) 111-568-568; fax (21) 5680005; e-mail info@ppl.com.pk; 78.4% govt-owned, 15.5% owned by private Pakistani shareholders and 6.1% owned by International Finance Corpn; Pakistan's largest producer of natural gas; cap. and res Rs 18,393m., sales Rs 10,732m. (July–Dec. 2004); Chief Exec./ Man. Dir S. MUNSIF RAZA.

Sui Northern Gas Pipelines Ltd: Gas House, 21 Kashmir Rd, Lahore; tel. (42) 9201277; fax (42) 9201302; e-mail info@suinorthern.com.pk; internet www.suinorthern.com.pk; f. 1964; 36% state-owned; transmission and distribution of natural gas in northern Pakistan; sales 534,762m. (June 2005); Chair. ALTAF M. SALEEM; Man. Dir ABDUL RASHID LONE.

Sui Southern Gas Co Ltd: 4B Sir Shah Suleman Rd, Block 14, Gulshan-e-Iqbal, Karachi 75000; tel. (21) 9231602; fax (21) 9231604; e-mail info@ssgc.com.pk; f. 1988; 70% state-owned; Chief Exec. MUNAWAR BASEER AHMAD.

Water

Faisalabad Development Authority (Water and Sanitation Agency): POB 229, Faisalabad; tel. (411) 767606; fax (411) 782113; e-mail fwasa@fsd.paknet.com.pk; f. 1978; Man. Dir Lt-Col (retd) SYED GHIAS-UD-DIN.

Karachi Water and Sewerage Board: 9th Mile, Karsaz, Shahrah-e-Faisal, Karachi; tel. (21) 9231882; fax (21) 9231814; e-mail mdkwsb@yahoo.co.uk; f. 1983; Man. Dir Brig. IFTIKHAR HAIDER.

Lahore Development Authority (Water and Sanitation Agency): 4-A Gulberg V, Lahore; tel. (42) 5756739; fax (42) 5752960; f. 1967; Man. Dir IMRAN RAZA ZAIDI.

TRADE UNIONS

National Trade Union Federation Pakistan: Bharocha Bldg, 2-B/6, Commercial Area, Nazimabad No. 2, Karachi 74600; tel. (21) 628339; fax (21) 6622529; e-mail ntuf@super.net.pk; f. 1999; 50 affiliated unions; covers following fields: steel, agriculture, textiles, garments, leather, automobiles, pharmaceuticals, chemicals, transport, printing, food, shipbuilding, engineering and power; Pres. MUHAMMAD RAFIQUE; Gen. Sec. SALEEM RAZA.

Pakistan National Federation of Trade Unions (PNFTU): 406, Qamar House, M. A. Jinnah Rd, Karachi 75890; tel. (21) 6693372; fax (21) 2313077; e-mail pnftu@cyber.net.pk; f. 1962; 177 affiliated feds; 218,468 mems; Pres. MUHAMMAD SHARIF; Sec.-Gen. ABDUL GHAFOOR BALOCH.

The principal affiliated federations are:

All Pakistan Federation of Labour (Durrani Group): Durrani Labour Hall, Khyber Bazar, Peshawar; tel. (91) 216411; fax (91) 274038; f. 1951; 300 affiliated unions, with 445,000 mems; affiliated to the World Federation of Trade Unions (WFTU); Pres. AURANGZEB DURRANI; Sec.-Gen. M. ZAFER IQBAL SAIF.

All Pakistan Federation of Labour (Khalilur Rahman Group): 404–406, International Autoparts Market, Marston Rd, Karachi.

All Pakistan Federation of Trade Unions (APFTU): Bakhtiar Labour Hall, 28 Nisbet Rd, Lahore; tel. (42) 7229419; fax (42) 7239529; e-mail apftu@brain.net.pk; 520,100 mems; Pres. Haji MUHAMMAD AMIN RATHORE; Gen. Sec. KHURSHID AHMED.

Muttahida Labour Federation: 24, Circular Bldg, Risala Rd, Hyderabad; c. 120,000 mems; Pres. KHAMASH GUL KHATTAK; Sec.-Gen. NABI AHMED.

National Labour Federation (NLF): 28, Circular Rd, Hyderabad; Pres. RANA MAHMOOD ALI KHAN.

Pakistan Central Federation of Trade Unions: 220 Al-Noor Chambers, M. A. Jinnah Rd, Karachi; tel. (21) 728891.

Pakistan Railway Employees' Union (PREM): City Railway Station, Karachi; tel. (21) 2415721; Divisional Sec. BASHIRUDDIN SIDDIQUI.

Pakistan Trade Union Federation: Khamosh Colony, Karachi; Pres. KANIZ FATIMA; Gen. Sec. SALEEM RAZA.

Pakistan Transport Workers' Federation: 110 McLeod Rd, Lahore; 17 unions; 92,512 mems; Pres. MEHBOOB-UL-HAQ; Gen. Sec. CH. UMAR DIN.

Other affiliated federations include: Pakistan Bank Employees' Federation, Pakistan Insurance Employees' Federation, Automobile, Engineering and Metal Workers' Federation, Pakistan Teachers Organizations' Council, Sarhad WAPDA Employees' Federation, and Balochistan Ittehad Trade Union Federation.

Transport

RAILWAYS

Pakistan Railways: Empress Rd, Lahore; tel. (42) 9201771; fax (42) 9201760; e-mail gmopr@pakrail.com; internet www.pakrail.com; state-owned; 11,515 km of track and 7,791 route km; seven divisions (Karachi, Lahore, Multan, Quetta, Rawalpindi, Peshawar and Sukkur); Chair. KHURSHEED AHMED KHAN; Gen. Man. SALEEMUR RAHMAN KHAN.

ROADS

The total length of roads was 254,410 km (motorways 339 km, main 6,587 km, secondary 211,846 km, other roads 35,638 km) in 1999. By June 2004 the total length of roads had increased to an estimated 255,856 km, including 8,885 km of highways and motorways.

Government assistance comes from the Road Fund, financed from a share of the excise and customs duty on sales of petrol and from development loans.

National Highways Authority: 27 Mauve Area, G-9/1, Islamabad; tel. (51) 9260717; fax (51) 9260404; e-mail info@nha.gov.pk; internet www.nha.gov.pk; f. 1991; jt venture between Govt and private sector; Chair. Maj.-Gen. (retd) FURRUKH JAVED; Dir-Gen. Maj.-Gen. (retd) HIDAYATULLAH KHAN NIAZI.

Punjab Road Transport Board: Transport House, 11A Egerton Rd, Lahore.

SHIPPING

In 1974 maritime shipping companies were placed under government control. The chief port is Karachi. A second port, Port Qasim, started partial operation in 1980. A third port, Port Gwadar, has been developed as a deep-water seaport; construction was completed in March 2005. Another port, Port Pasni, which is situated on the Balochistan coast, was completed in 1988. In 1991 the Government amended the 1974 Pakistan Maritime Shipping Act to allow private companies to operate.

Mercantile Marine Dept: Government of Pakistan, 70/4, Timber Pond, N. M. Reclamation, Keamari, Karachi; tel. (21) 2852703; fax (21) 2851307; f. 1930; ensures safety of life and property at sea and prevention of marine pollution through implementation of national legislation and international conventions; Chief Officer TARIQ SARDAR.

Ports and Shipping: Government of Pakistan, Plot No. 12, Misc. Area, Mai Kolachi Bypass, Karachi; tel. (21) 9206406; Dir-Gen. Capt. ANWAR SHAH.

Al-Hamd International Container Terminal (Pvt) Ltd: Plot No. 28, O & L Trans Lyari Quarters, Hawkesbay Rd, New Truck Stand, Karachi; tel. (21) 2352651; fax (21) 2351556; e-mail claes.frisk@aictpk.com; internet www.aicpakistan.com.

Engro Vopak Terminal Ltd: 1st Floor, Bahria Complex, 1 M. T. Khan Rd, POB 5736, Karachi 74000; tel. (21) 5610965; fax (21) 5611394; internet www.engro.com.

Karachi International Container Terminal (KICT): Administration Bldg, Berths 28–30, Dockyard Rd, West Wharf, Karachi 74000; tel. (21) 2316401; fax (21) 2313816; internet www.kictl.com; f. 1996; Chief Exec. ROGER L. HAWKE.

Karachi Port Trust (KPT): Eduljee Dinshaw Rd, Karachi 74000; tel. (21) 9214358; fax (21) 9214329; e-mail gmpd@kpt.gov.pk; internet www.kpt.gov.pk; Chair. Rear-Adm. AHMED HAYAT; Sec. FAROZUDDIN.

Karachi Shipyard and Engineering Works Ltd: West Wharf, Dockyard Rd, Karachi; tel. (21) 9214045; fax (21) 9214020; e-mail ksew@cyber.net.pk; internet www.karachishipyard.com.pk; f. 1953; building and repairing ships; general engineering; Man. Dir IFTIKHAR AHMED; Gen. Man. (Business Devt) Cdre N. M. SABIR.

Korangi Fisheries Harbour Authority: Ghashma Goth, Landhi, POB 15804, Karachi 75160; tel. (21) 5013315; fax (21) 5015096; e-mail kfha@sat.net.pk.

National Tanker Co (Pvt) Ltd (Pak): 15th Floor, PNSC Bldg, M. T. Khan Rd, Karachi 74000; tel. (21) 5611843; fax (21) 5610780; f. 1981 by the Pakistan National Shipping Corpn and the State Petroleum Refining and Petrochemical Corpn Ltd; aims to make Pakistan self-reliant in the transport of crude petroleum and petroleum products; Chief Exec. Vice-Adm. A. U. KHAN; Dep. Chief Exec. TURAB ALI KHAN.

Pakistan International Container Terminal Ltd: 2nd Floor, Business Plaza, Mumtaz Hussain Rd, Karachi 74000; tel. (21) 2400404; fax (21) 2400281; e-mail info@pict.com.pk; internet www.pict.com.pk; Chair. Capt. HALEEM A. SIDDIQI.

Pakistan National Shipping Corpn: PNSC Bldg, M. T. Khan Rd, POB 5350, Karachi 74000; tel. (21) 9203980; fax (21) 9203974; e-mail pnsckar@paknet3.ptc.pk; f. 1979 by merger; state-owned; Chair. Vice-Adm. S. T. H. NAQVI; Sec. ARIF SAEED.

Port Qasim Authority (PQA): Bin Qasim, Karachi 75020; tel. (21) 730101; fax (21) 730108; f. 1973; Chair. Vice-Adm. M. ASAD QURESHI; Sec. SYED MUMTAZ HUSSAIN SHAH.

Qasim International Container Terminal: Berths 5–7, Marginal Wharfs, POB 6425, Port Mohammad Bin Qasim, Karachi 75020; tel. (21) 4739100; fax (21) 4730055; e-mail info@qict.net; internet www.qict.net; f. 1994; CEO CHANGEZ NIAZI; Gen. Man. DARAYUS DIVECHA.

Terminals Association of Pakistan: Molasses Exports Wing, Keamari, Karachi; tel. (21) 2410427; fax (21) 2416791; Chair. RASHID JAN MUHAMMAD.

Associations

All Pakistan Shipping Association: 01-E, 1st Floor, Sattar Chambers, West Wharf Rd, Karachi; tel. (21) 2200742; fax (21) 2200743; e-mail mfqshaheen@cyber.net.pk; Chair. MUHAMMAD F. QAISER.

Pakistan Ship Agents' Association: GSA House, 19 Timber Pound, Keamari, Karachi 75620; tel. (21) 2850837; fax (21) 2851528; e-mail psaa@cyber.net.pk; internet www.shipezee.com/psaa; Chair. CYRUS R. COWASJEE.

Terminal Association of Pakistan: 8th Floor, Adamjee House, I. I. Chundrigar Rd, Karachi 74000; tel. (21) 2417131; fax (21) 2416477; e-mail terasspak@cyber.net.pk; Chair. MOHAMMED KASIM HASHAM; Sec. AKHTAR SULTAN.

CIVIL AVIATION

Karachi, Lahore, Rawalpindi, Peshawar and Quetta have international airports. In 2006 plans were under way for the construction of a new international airport at Islamabad, which would cost an estimated US $300m. and would handle 6.5m. passengers annually upon completion.

In 1992 the Government ended the air monopoly held by the Pakistan International Airlines Corpn, and opened all domestic air routes to any Pakistan-based company.

Civil Aviation Authority: Jinnah Terminal, Karachi Airport, Karachi; tel. (21) 9248778; fax (21) 9248770; internet www.caapakistan.com; controls all the civil airports; Dir-Gen. Air Marshal (retd) PERVEZ AKHTAR NAWAZ.

Aero Asia International: 47-E/1, Block 6, PECHS, Karachi 75400; tel. (21) 4544951; fax (21) 4544940; e-mail aeroasia@cyber.net.pk; internet www.aeroasia.com; f. 1993; operates scheduled passenger and cargo services to domestic destinations and to the neighbouring Gulf states; Chair. MOHAMMED YAQUB TABANI; Man. Dir KHURSHID ANWAR.

Air Blue Ltd: Ground Floor, Saudi Pak Bldg, Jinnah Ave, Islamabad; tel. (51) 111-247-258; internet www.airblue.com; f. 2004; Chair. and Man. Dir KHAQAN ABBASI.

Pakistan International Airlines Corpn (PIA): PIA Bldg, Quaid-e-Azam International Airport, Karachi 75200; tel. (21) 4572011; fax (21) 4570419; e-mail info@piac.com.pk; internet www.piac.com.pk; f. 1954; merged with Orient Airways in 1955; 57.7% govt-owned; operates domestic services to 35 destinations and international services to 40 destinations in 31 countries; Chair. and Chief Exec. TARIQ KIRMANI.

Shaheen Air International: 157B Clifton Rd, Clifton, Karachi 75600; tel. (21) 9251921; fax (21) 9251935; e-mail sair@cyber.net.pk; internet www.shaheenair.aero; f. 1993; operates scheduled domestic services and international services to the Gulf region; Man. Dir ATAUR REHMAN.

Tourism

The Himalayan hill stations of Pakistan provide magnificent scenery, a fine climate and excellent opportunities for field sports, mountaineering, trekking and winter sports. The archaeological remains and historical buildings are also impressive.

In 2003 Pakistan received 479,052 foreign visitors and receipts from tourism amounted to around US $618m.

Pakistan Tourism Development Corpn: Aga Khan Rd, Markaz F-6 (Super Market), Islamabad 44000; tel. (51) 9212760; fax (51) 9204027; e-mail tourism@isb.comsats.net.pk; internet www.tourism.gov.pk; f. 1970; Chair. HASHIM KHAN; Man. Dir MUHAMMAD HABIB KHAN.

RELATED TERRITORIES

The status of Jammu and Kashmir has remained unresolved since the 1949 cease-fire agreement, whereby the area was divided into sectors administered by India and Pakistan separately. Pakistan administers Azad (Free) Kashmir and the Northern Areas as *de facto* dependencies, being responsible for foreign affairs, defence, coinage, currency and the implementation of UN resolutions concerning Kashmir.

AZAD KASHMIR

Area: 11,639 sq km (4,494 sq miles).

Population: 1,980,000 (1981 census).

Administration: Government is based on the Azad Jammu and Kashmir Interim Constitution Act of 1974. There are seven administrative districts: Bagh, Bhimber, Kotli, Mirpur, Muzaffarabad, Poonch and Sudhnuti.

Legislative Assembly: consists of 48 members: 40 directly elected and eight indirectly elected, including five women.

Azad Jammu and Kashmir Council: consists of the President of Pakistan as Chairman, the President of Azad Kashmir as Vice-Chairman, five members nominated by the President of Pakistan, six members by the Legislative Assembly, and, *ex officio*, the Pakistan Minister of Kashmir Affairs and Northern Areas..

President of Azad Kashmir: Maj.-Gen. (retd) MOHAMMAD ANWAR KHAN.

Prime Minister: Sardar SIKANDAR HAYAT.

NORTHERN AREAS

Area: 72,520 sq km (28,000 sq miles).

Population: 562,000 (1981 census).

Administration: There are five administrative districts: Gilgit, Skardu, Diamir, Ghizer and Ghanche. The Northern Areas Council consists of 26 members (24 members are elected in a party-based election and two seats are reserved for women), headed by the federal Minister of Kashmir Affairs and Northern Areas.

PALAU

Introductory Survey

Location, Climate, Language, Religion, Flag, Capital

The Republic of Palau (also known as Belau) consists of more than 200 islands, in a chain about 650 km (400 miles) long, lying about 7,150 km (4,450 miles) south-west of Hawaii and about 1,160 km (720 miles) south of Guam. With the Federated States of Micronesia (q.v.), Palau forms the archipelago of the Caroline Islands. Palau is subject to heavy rainfall, and seasonal variations in precipitation and temperature are generally small. Palauan and English are the official languages. The principal religion is Christianity, much of the population being Roman Catholic. The flag (proportions 3 by 5) features a large golden disc (representing the moon), placed off-centre, towards the hoist, on a light blue background. The provisional capital is Koror, on Koror Island: the Constitution provides for the capital to be established on the less developed island of Babeldaob, in Melekeok state.

Recent History

The Republic of Palau's independence, under the Compact of Free Association, in October 1994 marked the end of the Trust Territory of the Pacific Islands, of which Palau was the final component (for history up to 1965, see the chapter on the Marshall Islands). From 1965 there were increasing demands for local autonomy within the Trust Territory. In that year the Congress of Micronesia was formed, and in 1967 a commission was established to examine the future political status of the islands. In 1970 the commission declared Micronesians' rights to sovereignty over their own lands, self-determination, the right to their own constitution and to revoke any form of free association with the USA. In May 1977, after eight years of negotiations, US President Jimmy Carter announced that his Administration intended to adopt measures to terminate the trusteeship agreement by 1981. In the Palau District a referendum in July 1979 approved a proposed local Constitution, which came into effect on 1 January 1981, when the district became the Republic of Palau.

The USA signed the Compact of Free Association with the Republic of Palau in August 1982, and with the Marshall Islands and the Federated States of Micronesia in October. The trusteeship of the islands was due to end after the principle and terms of the Compacts had been approved by the respective peoples and legislatures of the new countries, by the US Congress and by the UN Security Council. Under the Compacts, the four countries (including the Northern Mariana Islands) would be independent of each other and would manage both their internal and foreign affairs separately, while the USA would be responsible for defence and security. In addition, the USA was to allocate some US $3,000m. in aid to the islands.

More than 60% of Palauans voted in February 1983 to support their Compact, but fewer than the required 75% approved changing the Constitution to allow the transit and storage of nuclear materials. A revised Compact, which contained no reference to nuclear issues, was approved by 66% of votes cast in a referendum in September 1984. However, the US Government had hoped for a favourable majority of 75% of the votes cast, which would have allowed the terms of the Compact to override the provisions of the Palau Constitution in the event of a conflict between the two.

In June 1985 President Haruo Remeliik of Palau was assassinated. Relatives of a rival candidate in the 1984 presidential election, Roman Tmetuchl, were convicted of the murder, but remained at liberty pending an appeal; this was upheld, on the grounds of unreliable evidence, by Palau's Supreme Court in August 1987. Lazarus Salii was elected President in September 1985.

In January 1986 representatives of the Palau and US administrations reached a preliminary agreement on a new Compact, whereby the USA consented to provide US $421m. in economic assistance to the islands. However, the proportion of votes in favour of the new Compact at a referendum in the following month was still less than that required for the constitutional ban on nuclear material to be waived. Both Salii and US President Ronald Reagan supported the terms of the Compact, arguing that a simple majority would suffice for its approval, as the USA had guaranteed that it would observe the constitutional ban on nuclear material.

In May 1986 the UN Trusteeship Council endorsed the US Administration's request for the termination of the existing trusteeship agreement with the islands. However, a writ was subsequently submitted to the Palau High Court, in which it was claimed that approval of the Compact with the USA was unconstitutional because it had failed to obtain the requisite 75% of votes. The High Court ruled in favour of the writ, but the Palau Government appealed against the ruling and in October the Compact was approved by the US Congress. At a new plebiscite in December, however, only 66% of Palauans voted in favour of the Compact. Ratification of the Compact thus remained impossible.

A fifth plebiscite on Palau's proposed Compact with the USA, in June 1987, again failed to secure the 75% endorsement required by the Constitution. Under alleged physical intimidation by pro-nuclear supporters of the Compact, the House of Delegates (the lower house of the Palau National Congress) agreed to a further referendum in August. In this referendum an amendment to the Constitution was approved, ensuring that a simple majority would henceforth be sufficient to approve the Compact. This was duly achieved in a further referendum in the same month. When a writ was entered with the Supreme Court challenging the legality of the decision to allow approval of the Compact by a simple majority, a campaign of arson and bombing followed, and one person was murdered.

In February 1988 a team from the US General Accounting Office travelled to Palau to investigate allegations of corruption and intimidation on the part of the Palau Government. Approval of the Compact by the US Congress was to be delayed until the investigators had published their findings. However, in April a ruling by Palau's Supreme Court invalidated the procedure by which the Compact had finally been approved by a simple majority in the previous August. Three government employees, including Salii's personal assistant, were imprisoned in April, after being found guilty of firing on the home of Santos Olikong, Speaker of Palau's House of Delegates. The attack was widely considered to have been prompted by Olikong's public opposition to the Compact.

In August 1988 Salii, the principal subject of the bribery allegations, apparently committed suicide. At an election in November Ngiratkel Etpison was elected President, with just over 26% of the total votes. Although Etpison advocated the proposed Compact and was supported by the pro-Compact Ta Belau Party, his closest challenger, Tmetuchl, opposed it and was supported by the anti-nuclear Coalition for Open, Honest and Just Government, which had demanded that a special prosecutor from the USA be dispatched to Palau to investigate alleged corruption and violent attacks against opponents of the Compact.

Only 60% of voters approved the proposed Compact at a seventh referendum in February 1990. In July the US Department of the Interior declared its intention to impose stricter controls on the administration of Palau, particularly in financial matters. In the following year the leader of Palau's Council of Chiefs (a presidential advisory body), Yutaka Gibbons, initiated proceedings to sue the US Government: his claim centred on demands for compensation for the extensive damage caused to Palau's infrastructure by US forces during the Second World War and the subsequent retardation of the economy, allegedly as a result of the US administration of the islands.

During 1991 the US authorities reopened investigations into the assassination of Remeliik in 1985. In March 1992 Palau's Minister of State, John Ngiraked, his wife, Emerita Kerradel, and Sulial Heinrick (already serving a prison sentence for another killing) were charged with Remeliik's murder. In March 1993 Ngiraked and Kerradel were found guilty of aiding and abetting the assassination of the President, while Heinrick was acquitted.

Legislative and presidential elections were held in November 1992. (The electoral system had been modified earlier in the year to include primary elections for the selection of two presidential candidates.) At the presidential election the incumbent Vice-President, Kuniwo Nakamura, narrowly defeated Johnson Toribiong to become President. A concurrent referendum endorsed a proposal that, in future polls, a simple majority be sufficient to approve the adoption of the Compact of Free Association. Some 62% of voters were in favour of the proposal, which was approved in 14 of Palau's 16 states. A further referendum on the proposed Compact took place in November 1993. Some 68.3% of participating voters approved the proposed Compact, giving the Government a mandate to proceed with its adoption. Nevertheless, opposition to the changes remained fierce, and in January 1994 two legal challenges were mounted that questioned the validity of the amendments and stated that the Compact's approval had been procured by coercion. The challenges failed, however, and on 1 October Palau achieved independence under the Compact of Free Association. At independence celebrations, Nakamura appealed to opponents of the Compact to support Palau's new status. He announced that his Government's principal concern was the regeneration of the country's economy, which he aimed to initiate with an economic programme financed by funds from the Compact. Palau was admitted to the UN in December 1994, and became a member of the IMF in December 1997.

A preliminary round of voting in the presidential election took place in September 1996; Nakamura secured 52.4% of total votes, Toribiong received 33.5%, and Yutaka Gibbons 14.2%. Nakamura and Toribiong were, therefore, expected to proceed to a second election due to take place in November. However, in late September a serious crisis struck Palau when the bridge linking the islands of Koror and Babeldaob collapsed, killing two people and injuring several others. The collapse of the bridge left the capital isolated from the international airport on Babeldaob, with disastrous economic repercussions for Palau, which was reliant on the route for all domestic and international communications. It was subsequently revealed that major repairs had recently been carried out on the bridge, at a cost of US $3.2m., and several reports implied that inappropriate changes made to its structure during the work were responsible for the disaster. Toribiong was harshly critical of Nakamura, who had commissioned the repair work, and demanded his resignation along with those of the public works officials involved. However, following the revelation that Toribiong's running-mate in the election for the vice-presidency was one of the officials involved in the work, Toribiong withdrew his candidacy from the second round of the presidential election. Yutaka Gibbons thus re-entered the contest by default; none the less, at the second round of the presidential poll, held concurrently with legislative elections on 5 November 1996, Nakamura was re-elected with 62.0% of total votes. Meanwhile, the Japanese Government offered to finance the construction of a new bridge linking Koror to Babeldaob; the work was completed in January 2002.

In October 1998 the Senate approved legislation providing for the establishment of an offshore financial centre in Palau. The measure was strongly opposed by Nakamura, who believed that it might attract criminal organizations seeking to 'launder' the proceeds of their illegal activities. In December 1999, following discussions with US government officials, President Nakamura signed an executive order establishing a National Banking Review Commission, with the aim of maintaining a legally responsible banking environment in Palau: both the Bank of New York (of the USA) and Deutsche Bank (of Germany) had alleged that Palau's offshore banks were facilitating money-laundering. The new body was given wide-ranging powers to examine banking operations in the country and to evaluate current banking regulations.

At the presidential election held on 7 November 2000, Thomas E. Remengesau, Jr, hitherto the Vice-President of Palau, was elected with 52% of the votes cast, defeating Senator Peter Sugiyama. Sandra Pierantozzi was elected as Vice-President. Remengesau was officially inaugurated on 19 January 2001. In July 2001 Remengesau introduced a formal resolution proposing the reduction of the legislature to a single chamber, to replace the existing House of Delegates and the Senate, claiming that a unicameral legislature would reduce bureaucracy. However, owing to a lack of legislative progress on the necessary constitutional changes, in early 2004 Remengesau endorsed a congressional resolution to conduct a popular referendum. The poll, which would first require the signatures of 25% of the electorate, was scheduled to take place in November. The proposals included the creation of a unicameral legislature and restrictions on legislators' terms of office; furthermore, it was proposed that Palauans resident in the USA be offered the opportunity of dual citizenship.

Despite President Remengesau's inauguration pledges to improve transparency in public office, there were several instances of fraudulent use of official funds in the early 2000s. In December 2002 the Speaker of the House of Delegates, Mario Gulibert, was arrested on charges relating to the alleged misuse of travel expenses (he was dismissed on unrelated charges in March 2004). In February 2003 the former Governor of Ngardmau state, Albert Ngirmekur, was fined and sentenced to six months' imprisonment following his impeachment for theft. In late 2003 President Remengesau was obliged to veto an attempt by legislators to eliminate the Office of the Special Prosecutor, which had conducted a number of investigations into alleged misuse of public funds. In February 2004, however, members of the National Congress under investigation for alleged misuse of expenses agreed to pay some US $250,000 on condition that the cases against them be withdrawn. In November the Senate overturned President Remengesau's veto of a bill to ease bank-licensing restrictions, although this decision was reversed in December, following the threat of international financial sanctions.

At the presidential election of 2 November 2004, President Remengesau was re-elected with 6,494 of the votes cast; his opponent, Polycarp Basilius, received 3,268 votes. Elias Camsek Chin was elected Vice-President. Following his re-election, Remengesau announced that the priorities of his new administration would include increasing government revenues, promoting economic diversification and tourism, and maintaining programmes of infrastructural development. Concurrent to the presidential election, voters also approved various amendments to the Constitution: to restrict members of the National Congress to three terms of four years, to permit dual US-Palauan citizenship, to provide for the joint election of the country's President and Vice-President as a team and to adjust congressional members' salaries. A proposal to create a unicameral legislature, however, was rejected. A plan to hold a constitutional convention was approved by 5,085 votes (some 53% of the votes cast), with 3,742 votes (some 39%) against the motion. In April 2005 16 state delegates and nine delegates-at-large were elected to the Constitutional Convention, which in mid-June ended its deliberations, following consultations with the general public and special-interest groups. The Convention concluded with 251 proposals, of which 22 were to be submitted for the electorate's consideration at a referendum to be held concurrently with the general elections scheduled for 2008.

In mid-1999 a delegation from Solomon Islands visited Palau to discuss the possibility of allowing Solomon Islanders to work in Palau, in an attempt to resolve the latter's severe labour shortage. In August 2001, however, the Government imposed a ban on the hiring of Indian and Sri Lankan workers, citing rising tensions and disputes with local employers which the Government claimed were largely due to religious differences. The ban was to remain in place until legislation to create official recruitment agencies in Palau had been approved. In July 2002 the Senate approved a bill that would amend the islands' immigration law in order to give greater authority over immigration affairs to the President of Palau. (Non-Palauan nationals were estimated to represent about 73% of the islands' population in 2003.) In March 2003 the Government introduced a measure to extend employment permits for foreign workers, which allowed a new maximum extension of two years. In April some 200 Chinese migrant employees of a failed clothing business were stranded on Palau and placed under house arrest. However, the migrants were subsequently repatriated, following diplomatic intervention from the People's Republic of China.

Diplomatic relations were established, at ambassadorial level, with Taiwan in late 1999; the first Taiwanese ambassador to Palau was formally appointed in April 2000. Reports in December 2000 that the Palau Government was considering establishing diplomatic relations with the People's Republic of China were denied, and President-elect Remengesau reaffirmed Palau's diplomatic ties with Taiwan. In early 2000, meanwhile, Palau and Taiwan signed an agreement pledging to develop bilateral projects in a number of areas, including agriculture, fisheries and tourism. In late January 2005 President Chen Shui-bian of Taiwan visited Palau to discuss economic co-operation and to strengthen bilateral political relations.

In October 2001 the Government sought to establish diplomatic relations with Malaysia and Indonesia in an attempt to facilitate the resolution of disputes about overlapping territorial boundaries, amid concern over increasing instances of illegal fishing in Palauan waters. (Palau introduced more stringent regulations concerning illegal fishing in 2002 and 2003.)

Palau maintains strong diplomatic links with Japan, which has been a leading source of tourist revenue since the 1980s. The Japanese Government provided US $25m. for the reconstruction of the Koror bridge (see above) and contributed to the construction of a new terminal building at Palau International Airport, which opened in May 2003. Construction of an innovative thermal energy generator and desalination plant was scheduled to begin in mid-2003. The project was to be partly funded by the Government of Japan, with technical assistance provided by a Japanese university. In June 2002 President Remengesau undertook his first state visit to the Republic of Korea, his itinerary incorporating visits to a number of infrastructural development projects.

Government

In October 1994 Palau, the last remaining component of the Trust Territory of the Pacific Islands (a United Nations Trusteeship administered by the USA), achieved independence under the Compact of Free Association. Administrative authority was transferred to the Government of Palau (with the USA retaining responsibility for the islands' defence—see below).

A locally drafted Constitution of the Republic of Palau entered into effect on 1 January 1981. Under the Constitution, executive authority is vested in the President, elected by direct suffrage for a four-year term. Legislative power is exercised by the Olbiil era Kelulau ('House of Whispered Decisions', or Palau National Congress), composed of the elected House of Delegates (comprising one Delegate from each of the 16 states of Palau) and the Senate (currently comprising 14 Senators).

Local governmental units are the municipalities and villages. Elected Magistrates and Councils govern the municipalities. Village government is largely traditional.

Defence

The USA is responsible for the defence of Palau, according to the Compact of Free Association implemented in October 1994, and has exclusive military access to its waters, as well as the right to operate two military bases on the islands.

Economic Affairs

In 2004, according to estimates by the World Bank, Palau's gross national income (GNI), measured at average 2002–04 prices, totalled US $137.3m., equivalent to $6,870 per head. During 1995–2004, it was estimated, the population increased at an average annual rate of 1.7%, while gross domestic product (GDP) per head increased, in real terms, by an average of 0.3%. In 1995–2004 overall GDP increased, in real terms, at an average annual rate of 2.0%; growth in 2004 was 2.0%. The Asian Development Bank (ADB) estimated that GDP expanded by 4.9% in 2004 and by 5.5% in 2005.

Agriculture (including fishing) is mainly on a subsistence level, the principal crops being coconuts, root crops and bananas. Pigs and chickens are kept for domestic consumption. Eggs are produced commercially, and the introduction of cattle-ranching on Babeldaob was under consideration in the early 2000s. The agricultural sector, together with mining, engaged 2.0% of the employed labour force in 2003. Agriculture and fisheries (without mining) provided an estimated 4.0% of GDP in 2004. Fishing licences are sold to foreign fleets, including those of Taiwan, the USA, Japan and the Philippines. Palau is a signatory of the Multilateral Fisheries Treaty, concluded by the USA and member states of the South Pacific Forum (now Pacific Islands Forum) in 1987. The islands, however, are believed to lose significant amounts of potential revenue through illegal fishing activity. Revenue from the sale of fishing licences totalled US $39,000 in 1999/2000 and an estimated $76,000 in 2000/01, a considerable decline from the total of $230,000 recorded in 1994/95. Fish have traditionally been a leading export, accounting for some $13m. of exports in 1995, but earnings declined to an estimated $7m. in 2001, reportedly owing to adverse weather conditions. According to the ADB, the agricultural sector's GDP contracted by 2.5% in 2002 and by 1.1% in 2003.

The industrial sector (including mining and quarrying, manufacturing, construction and utilities) provided an estimated 12.7% of GDP in 2004. The only manufacturing activity of any significance is a factory producing garments, which in 1997 employed some 300 (mostly non-resident) workers. In 2004 manufacturing accounted for only 1.4% of GDP. Construction is the most important industrial activity, contributing an estimated 7.8% of GDP in that year and engaging 20.2% of the employed labour force in 2003. Electrical energy is produced by two power plants at Aimeliik and Malakal. According to the ADB, the industrial sector's GDP declined by 5.0% in 2002 but increased by 0.5% in 2003.

Service industries dominate Palau's economy, providing an estimated 83.3% of GDP in 2004, and (with utilities) engaging 73.8% of the employed labour force in 2003. The Government is a significant employer within the sector, public administration engaging some 33.0% of the total employed labour force in 2003. Tourism is an important source of foreign exchange. The trade, hotels and restaurants sector engaged 19.9% of the employed labour force in 2003. In 2003 a total of 65,772 visitors (of whom 41% were from Taiwan and 33% from Japan) arrived in the islands. Visitor arrivals were reported to have increased to 95,000 in 2004, remaining strong in 2005. Expenditure by tourists totalled an estimated US $59m. in 2002. Receipts from visitors to the islands rose from an estimated 40% of GDP in 2003/04 to 80% of GDP in the following year. The GDP of the services sector contracted by 4.8% in 2002 and by 1.1% in 2003, according to the ADB.

In the year ending September 2003 the visible trade deficit was estimated at US $81.8m., rising to $97m. in 2003/04, and falling to a provisional $91.8m. in 2004/05. The deficit on the current account of the balance of payments, including grants, totalled a provisional $15.1m. in 2004/05, equivalent to 10.6% of GDP. Import costs were a provisional US $105.2m. in that year, while revenue from exports totalled a provisional $13.4m. The principal sources of imports in 2002 were the USA (which supplied 42.1% of the total), Guam (12.1%) and Japan (9.8%). The principal imports in 2000/01 were machinery and transport equipment, manufactured goods and food and live animals.

The islands record a persistent budget deficit, projected at US $9.6m. in the year ending 30 September 2004. Financial assistance from the USA contributes a large part of the islands' external revenue. Furthermore, upon implementation of the Compact of Free Association with the USA in 1994, Palau became eligible for an initial grant of US $142m. and for annual aid of $23m. over a period of 14 years. The 2003/04 budget projected total grants of $38.1m., with Compact funds reaching $14.1m. In February 2006 the USA submitted a budget for 2006/07 providing $10.7m. for Palau in direct Compact funding. Palau's external debt was estimated by the ADB to have increased from $18m. in 2003 to $37m. in 2004, while the cost of debt servicing decreased from the equivalent of 66.1% of the value of exports of goods and services in 2003 to just 1.4% in 2004. The annual rate of inflation was thought to average between 1% and 3% in the mid-1990s. The inflation rate was estimated by the ADB at 5.0% in 2004, compared with a rate of 0.9% in the previous year, rising to an estimated 3.0% in 2005. In 2000 2.3% of the total labour force were unemployed.

Palau is a member of the Pacific Community (see p. 350) and of the Pacific Islands Forum (see p. 352); it is also an associate member of the UN Economic and Social Commission for Asia and the Pacific (ESCAP, see p. 33). In early 1996 Palau joined representatives of the other countries and territories of Micronesia at a meeting in Hawaii, at which a new regional organization, the Council of Micronesian Government Executives, was established. The new body aimed to facilitate discussion of economic developments in the region. Palau was admitted to the IMF in late 1997. In December 2002 Palau requested to join the World Trade Organization (WTO, see p. 370), and in December 2003 the country became a member of the Asian Development Bank (ADB, see p. 169).

The economy of Palau has benefited greatly from the substantial aid payments from the US Government that followed the implementation of the Compact of Free Association in 1994 and from the dramatic expansion of tourism in the country. Tourism is expected to remain essential to Palau's economic growth upon the cessation of compact grants, scheduled for 2008/09. In November 2003, however, President Remengesau's decision to veto a bill that would have legalized casino gambling, owing to his fears over the possible social consequences, was thought to have reduced the country's potential attractiveness to visitors of above-average wealth. In 2002 an IMF report claimed that the country's investment laws, specifically the Foreign Investments Act (FIA), which prohibits foreign ownership of land or businesses, contributed to a lack of transparency in financial dealings, particularly in the development of tourism projects. In March 2006 President Remengesau expressed his desire to amend radically the FIA to allow greater foreign investment in tourism projects, provided that it was in partnership with Palauans. A new road along the coastline of Babeldaob, financed under the Compact of Free Association, was none the less widely expected to increase long-term tourism revenues upon its completion in mid-2006. (A new official capital on the island, partly funded by a US $23 loan from Taiwan, was reported to be approaching completion in early 2006.) In December 2001 the Government announced plans to develop a new regional airline, Palau Micronesia Air, to serve Palau and neighbouring countries; this began operations in August 2004 (although flights were temporarily suspended in December 2004 to allow restructuring of the company). Meanwhile, following allegations that Palau's offshore banking system was being used for the purposes of money-laundering (see Recent History), various new banking laws were approved, in an effort to restore the confidence of the international financial community. Although a number of concerns were raised by the Financial Action Task Force on Money Laundering (FATF, see p. 389), Palau was not included on the FATF's list of non-co-operative countries and territories. In June 2002 the legislature approved new measures to regulate the financial sector, which included the creation of a Financial Institutions Commission (FIC). An IMF consultation in March 2006 stressed the need for the FIC to be allocated greater funds and powers, and for the Financial Institutions Act to be amended in order to increase financial scrutiny. Government expenditure was reported to have increased from the equivalent of 57.5% of GDP in 2002/03 to 66.3% of GDP in 2003/04. In May 2005 President Remengesau gave final approval to a government budget envisaging expenditure of US $53.5m. for 2004/05. (In June Remengesau asked Congress to approve a supplement of $1.1m. to the budget.) In July Remengesau submitted a budget proposal for 2005/06, with projected expenditure totalling $55.4m., of which some $52m. was intended for government operations, with the remainder to be allocated to the Hospital Trust Fund and debt servicing. An increase in tax revenue was expected, primarily as a consequence of new hotels opening in Palau. Owing to the decline in Compact funds, in early 2006 the economic priorities of the Remengesau administration included economic diversification, the reduction of public-sector administrative costs and greater involvement of the private sector in the provision of services. The ADB envisaged a GDP growth rate of 5.7% in 2006, with a similar increase projected for 2007.

Education

Education is compulsory for children between the ages of six and 14 years. In 2001/02 an estimated 1,939 pupils attended elementary school. There were 22 public elementary schools in 2004. After eight years of compulsory elementary education, a pupil may enrol in the government-operated high school or one of the five private (church-affiliated) high schools. In 2001/02 an estimated total of 1,898 pupils attended secondary school. The Micronesian Occupational College, based in Palau, provides two-year training programmes. Government spending on education in 1999/2000 totalled US $9.1m., equivalent to 10.7% of total budgetary expenditure.

Public Holidays

2006: 1 January (New Year's Day), 15 March (Youth Day), 5 May (Senior Citizens' Day), 1 June (Presidents' Day), 9 July (Constitution Day), 4 September (Labor Day), 1 October (Independence Day), 24 October (United Nations Day), 23 November (Thanksgiving), 25 December (Christmas).
2007: 1 January (New Year's Day), 15 March (Youth Day), 5 May (Senior Citizens' Day), 1 June (Presidents' Day), 9 July (Constitution Day), 5 September (Labor Day), 1 October (Independence Day), 24 October (United Nations Day), 22 November (Thanksgiving), 25 December (Christmas).

Weights and Measures

With certain exceptions, the imperial system is in force. One US cwt equals 100 lb; one long ton equals 2,240 lb; one short ton equals 2,000 lb. A policy of gradual voluntary conversion to the metric system is being undertaken.

Statistical Survey

AREA AND POPULATION

Area: 508 sq km (196 sq miles); Babeldaob (Babeldaop, Babelthuap) island 409 sq km (158 sq miles).

Population: 17,225 (males 9,213, females 8,012) at census of 9 November 1995; 19,129 at census of 15 April 2000. *Mid-2004:* 20,600 (estimate from Asian Development Bank, *Key Indicators of Developing Asian and Pacific Countries*).

Density (mid-2004): 40.6 per sq km.

Births and Deaths (1999): Live births 250 (birth rate 13.2 per 1,000); Deaths 131 (death rate 6.9 per 1,000). Source: UN, *Population and Vital Statistics Report*.

Expectation of Life (WHO estimates, years at birth): 68 (males 66; females 70) in 2003. Source: WHO, *World Health Report*.

Economically Active Population (2003): Agriculture, fishing and mining 261; Construction 2,678; Manufacturing 6; Transport, communications and utilities 526; Trade, hotels and restaurants 2,639; Finance, insurance and real estate 169; Public administration 4,374; Other services 2,595; *Total employed* 13,248. Source: IMF, *Republic of Palau: Selected Issues and Statistical Appendix* (April 2004).

HEALTH AND WELFARE
Key Indicators

Total Fertility Rate (children per woman, 2003): 2.4.
Under-5 Mortality Rate (per 1,000 live births, 2004): 27.
Physicians (per 1,000 head, 1998): 1.10.
Health Expenditure (2002): US $ per head (PPP): 730.
Health Expenditure (2002): % of GDP: 9.1.
Health Expenditure (2002): public (% of total): 91.0.
Access to Water (% of persons, 2002): 84.
Access to Sanitation (% of persons, 2002): 83.

For sources and definitions, see explanatory note on p. vi

AGRICULTURE, ETC.

Fishing (FAO estimates, metric tons, live weight, 2003): Total catch 1,051 (Marine fishes 877). Source: FAO.

INDUSTRY

Production (2000): Electric energy 210 million kWh. Source: UN, *Statistical Yearbook for Asia and the Pacific*.

FINANCE

Currency and Exchange Rates: United States currency is used: 100 cents = 1 United States dollar (US $). *Sterling and Euro Equivalents* (30 Dec. 2005): £1 sterling = US $1.7219; €1 = US $1.1797; US $100 = £58.08 = €84.77.

Budget (official forecasts, US $'000, year ending Sept. 2004): *Revenue:* Domestic revenue 36,400 (Tax 29,600, Other current revenues 5,300, Local trust fund 1,500); Grants 38,100 (Compact funds 14,100); Total 74,600. *Expenditure:* Current expenditure 62,500 (Wages and salaries 30,600, Purchase of goods and services 26,700, Subsidies and other transfers 4,100, Interest payments and investment fees 1,100); Capital expenditure 21,700; Total 84,200. Source: IMF, *Republic of Palau: Selected Issues and Statistical Appendix* (April 2004).

Cost of Living (Consumer Price Index; base: June 2000 = 100): 100.5 in 2002; 100.1 in 2003; 104.8 in 2004. Source: Asian Development Bank, *Key Indicators of Developing Asian and Pacific Countries*.

Gross Domestic Product by Economic Activity (US $ '000 at current prices, 2004): Agriculture 4,670; Mining 236; Manufacturing 1,690; Electricity, gas and water 3,741; Construction 9,181; Trade 23,860; Transport and communications 10,855; Finance 4,511; Real estate, hotels and restaurants, and business and other services 26,881; Public administration 31,478; *Sub-total* 117,103; Import duties 3,842; *Less* Imputed bank service charges 1,250; *GDP in purchasers' values* 119,695. Source: Asian Development Bank, *Key Indicators of Developing Asian and Pacific Countries*.

Gross Domestic Product at Constant 2000 Prices (US $ '000): 118,524 in 2001; 115,424 in 2002; 115,294 in 2003. Source: Asian Development Bank, *Key Indicators of Developing Asian and Pacific Countries*.

Balance of Payments (estimates, US $ million, year ending Sept. 2003): Exports of goods f.o.b. 11.9; Imports of goods f.o.b. −93.7; *Trade balance* −81.8; Exports of services 57.9; Imports of services −8.7; *Balance on goods and services* −32.6; Other income (net) 3.9; *Balance on goods, services and income* −28.7; Private current transfers (net) −1.3; Official current transfers (net) 24.7; *Current balance* −5.3; Capital grants received 22.8; Loan repayments −0.6; Private direct investment 1.0; Net errors and omissions −21.3; *Overall balance* −3.4. Source: IMF, *Republic of Palau: Selected Issues and Statistical Appendix* (April 2004).

EXTERNAL TRADE

Principal Commodities (US $ '000): *Imports f.o.b.* (2002): Food and live animals 14,381; Beverages and tobacco 7,004; Mineral fuels, lubricants, etc. 12,430; Chemicals 4,860; Basic manufactures 23,647; Machinery and transport equipment 21,902; Miscellaneous manufactured articles 9,921; Total (incl. others) 95,874. *Exports* (2001/02): 11,900 (including trochus, tuna, copra and handicrafts). Source: mainly IMF, *Republic of Palau: Selected Issues and Statistical Appendix*, April 2004.

Principal Trading Partners (US $ '000): *Imports* (2002): Australia 760; China, People's Republic 190; Guam 11,558; Hong Kong 3,457; Japan 9,364; Korea, Republic 8,523; Philippines 4,083; Singapore 7,439; Taiwan 5,439; USA 40,356; Total (incl. others) 95,874. *Exports* (2001/02): Total 11,900. Source: IMF, *Republic of Palau: Selected Issues and Statistical Appendix* (April 2004).

TRANSPORT

International Shipping (1995): *Ship Arrivals:* 280. *Freight Traffic* (metric tons): Goods unloaded 64,034.

TOURISM

Tourist Arrivals: 55,586 in 2000/01; 54,797 in 2001/02; 65,772 in 2002/03.

Tourist Arrivals by Country of Residence (2002/03): Japan 21,620; Philippines 3,409; Taiwan 26,813; USA 9,449.

Tourism Receipts (US $ million, incl. passenger transport): 53 in 2000; 59 in 2001; 59 in 2002.

Sources: IMF, *Republic of Palau: Selected Issues and Statistical Appendix* (April 2004); World Tourism Organization.

COMMUNICATIONS MEDIA

Radio Receivers (1997): 12,000 in use.

Television Receivers (1997): 11,000 in use.

EDUCATION

Primary (2001/02, unless otherwise stated): 22 government schools (1990); 127 teachers (1998/99 estimate); 1,939 pupils (estimate).

Secondary (2001/02, unless otherwise stated): 1 government school (1990); 5 private (church-affiliated) schools (1990); 140 teachers (1999/2000 estimate); 1,898 pupils (estimate).

Tertiary (2001/02 estimates): 46 teachers; 484 students.

2004: 23 government schools (22 elementary; 1 secondary).

Directory

The Constitution

In October 1994 Palau, the last remaining component of the Trust Territory of the Pacific Islands (a United Nations Trusteeship administered by the USA), achieved independence under the Compact of Free Association. Full responsibility for defence lies with the USA, which undertakes to provide regular economic assistance.

From 1986 the three polities of the Commonwealth of the Northern Mariana Islands, the Republic of the Marshall Islands and the Federated States of Micronesia ceased, *de facto*, to be part of the Trust Territory. In December 1990 the United Nations Security Council agreed formally to terminate the Trusteeship Agreement for all the territories except Palau. The agreement with Palau was finally terminated in October 1994.

The islands became known as the Republic of Palau when the locally-drafted Constitution came into effect on 1 January 1981. The Constitution provides for a democratic form of government, with executive authority vested in the directly-elected President and Vice-President. Presidential elections are held every four years. Legislative power is exercised by the Olbiil era Kelulau, the Palau National Congress, which is an elected body consisting of the Senate and the House of Delegates. The Senators represent geographical districts, determined by an independent reapportionment commission every eight years, according to population. There are currently 14 Senators (four from the northern part of Palau, nine from Koror and one from the southern islands). There are 16 Delegates, one elected to represent each of the 16 states of the Republic. The states are: Kayangel, Ngerchelong, Ngaraard, Ngardmau, Ngaremlengui, Ngiwal, Melekeok, Ngchesar, Ngatpang, Aimeliik, Airai, Koror, Peleliu, Angaur, Sonsorol and Tobi. Each state elects its own Governor and legislature.

The Government

HEAD OF STATE

President: THOMAS E. REMENGESAU, Jr (took office 19 January 2001, re-elected 2 November 2004).

Vice-President: ELIAS CAMSEK CHIN.

THE CABINET
(April 2006)

Minister of Health: Dr VICTOR YANO.

Minister of Commerce and Trade: OTOICHI BESEBES.

Minister of Resources and Development: FRITZ KOSHIBA.

Minister of Education: MARIO KATOSANG.

Minister of Justice: ELIAS CAMSEK CHIN.

Minister of Community and Cultural Affairs: ALEXANDER R. MEREP.

Minister of State: TEMMY L. SHMULL.

Minister of Administration and Finance: ELBUCHEL SADANG.

COUNCIL CHIEFS

The Constitution provides for an advisory body for the President, comprising the 16 highest traditional chiefs from the 16 states. The chiefs advise on all traditional laws and customs, and on any other public matter in which their participation is required.

Chairman: Ibedul YUTAKA GIBBONS (Koror).

GOVERNMENT OFFICES AND MINISTRIES

Office of the President: POB 6051, Koror, PW 96940; tel. 488-2541; fax 488-1662; e-mail roppresoffice@palaunet.com.

Department of the Interior, Office of Insular Affairs (OIA): OIA Field Office, POB 6031, Koror, PW 96946; tel. 488-2601; fax 488-2649; internet www.doi.gov/oia/Islandpages/palaupage.htm; Field Rep. J. VICTOR HOBSON, Jr; Co-ordinator HAURO WILLTER.

Ministry of Commerce and Trade: POB 1471, Koror, PW 96940; tel. 488-4343; fax 488-3207.

Ministry of Community and Cultural Affairs: POB 100 Koror, PW 96940; tel. 488-2489; fax 488-2647; internet www.palaugov.net/mincommunity.

Ministry of Education: POB 189, Koror, PW 96940; tel. 488-1464; fax 488-1465; e-mail moe@palaumoe.net; internet www.palaumoe.net.

Ministry of Health: POB 6027, Koror, PW 96940; tel. 488-2552; fax 488-1211; e-mail moh@palau-health.net.

Ministry of Justice: POB 3022, Koror, PW 96940; tel. 488-2487; fax 488-4567; internet www.palaugov.net/minjustice.

Ministry of Resources and Development: POB 100, Koror, PW 96940; tel. 488-2701; fax 488-3380; e-mail mrd@palaunet.com.

All national government offices are based in Koror. Each state has its own administrative headquarters.

PALAU
Directory

President and Legislature

PRESIDENT

At the presidential election held on 2 November 2004, Thomas E. Remengesau, Jr, who won 67% of the votes cast, decisively defeated his opponent, Polycarp Basilius.

OLBIL ERA KELULAU
(Palau National Congress)

President of the Senate: JOHNNY REKLAI.
Vice-President of the Senate: MLIB TMETUCHL.
Speaker of the House of Delegates: AUGUSTINE MESEBELUU.
Vice-Speaker of the House of Delegates: WILLIAM NGIRAIKELAU.

Election Commission

Palau Election Commission: POB 826, Koror, PW 96940; tel. 488-1554; fax 488-3327; Chair. SANTOS BORJA.

Political Organizations

(There are currently no active political parties in Palau)

Palau Nationalist Party: c/o Olbiil era Kelulau, Koror, PW 96940; inactive; Leader JOHNSON TORIBIONG.
Ta Belau Party: c/o Olbiil era Kelulau, Koror, PW 96940; inactive; Leader KUNIWO NAKAMURA.

Diplomatic Representation

EMBASSIES IN PALAU

China (Taiwan): WCTC Bldg, Of. 3F, POB 9087, Koror, PW 96940; tel. 488-8150; fax 488-8151; e-mail embrocb@palaunet.com; Ambassador CLARK K. H. CHEN.
Japan: POB 6050, Palau Pacific Resort, Arakebesang, Koror, PW 96940; tel. 488-6455; fax 488-6458; Ambassador KENRO IINO (resident in Fiji).
Philippines: 2nd Flr, M. Ueki Bldg, Iyebukel Hamlet, POB 1497, Koror, PW 96940; tel. 488-5077; fax 488-6310; e-mail philkor@palaunet.com; Ambassador RAMONCITO MARIÑO.
USA: POB 6028, Koror, PW 96940; tel. 488-2920; fax 488-2911; e-mail usembassykoror@palaunet.com; Chargé d'affaires DEBORAH L. KINGSLAND.

Judicial System

The judicial system of the Republic of Palau consists of the Supreme Court (including Trial and Appellate Divisions), presided over by the Chief Justice, the National Court (inactive), the Court of Common Pleas and the Land Court.

Supreme Court of the Republic of Palau: POB 248, Koror, PW 96940; tel. 488-2482; fax 488-1597; e-mail cjngiraklsong@palaunet.com; Chief Justice ARTHUR NGIRAKLSONG.

Religion

The population is predominantly Christian, mainly Roman Catholic. The Assembly of God, Baptists, Seventh-day Adventists, the Church of Jesus Christ of Latter-day Saints (Mormons), and the Bahá'í and Modignai (or Modeknai) faiths are also represented.

CHRISTIANITY

The Roman Catholic Church

Palau forms part of the diocese of the Caroline Islands, suffragan to the archdiocese of Agaña (Guam). The Bishop, who is resident in Chuuk, Eastern Caroline Islands (see the Federated States of Micronesia), participates in the Catholic Bishops' Conference of the Pacific, based in Suva, Fiji.

MODIGNAI FAITH

Modignai Church: Koror, PW 96940; an indigenous, non-Christian religion; also operates a high school.

The Press

Palau Gazette: POB 100, Koror, PW 96940; tel. 488-3257; fax 488-1662; e-mail roppresoffice@palaunet.com; newsletter publ. by Govt; monthly; Publr ROMAN YANO.
Palau Horizon: POB 487, Meketii, Koror, PW 96940; tel. 488-4588; fax 488-4565; e-mail hprinting@palaunet.com; twice weekly; f. 1998; Publr ABED E. YOUNIS; circ. 1,500.
Rock Islander: POB 1217, Koror, PW 96940; tel. 488-1461; fax 488-1614; e-mail jerome@palaunet.com; quarterly; articles about Palau; Publr JACKSON HENRY.
Roureur Belau: POB 477, Koror, PW 96940; tel. 488-6365; fax 488-4810; e-mail myu@palaunet.com; weekly; Publr CLIFFORD 'SPADE' EBAS.
Tia Belau (This is Palau): POB 477, Koror, PW 96940; tel. 488-6365; fax 488-4810; e-mail myu@palaunet.com; internet www.tiabelau.com; f. 1992; fortnightly; English and Palauan; Editor RAOUL G. BRIONES; Publr MOSES ULUDONG; circ 1,500.

Broadcasting and Communications

BROADCASTING

Radio

KRFM: Sure Save Store, Koror, PW 96940; tel. 488-1359; e-mail rudimch@palaunet.com.
Palau National Communications Corpn (PNCC): POB 99, Koror, PW 96940; tel. 587-9000; fax 587-1888; e-mail pncc@palaunet.com; internet www.palaunet.com; f. 1982; mem. of the Pacific Islands Broadcasting Asscn; operates station WSZB; broadcasts American, Japanese and Micronesian music; 18 hrs daily; Gen. Man. ED CARTER.
T8AA (Eco Paradise): POB 279, Koror, PW 96940; tel. 488-2417; fax 488-1932; broadcasts news, entertainment and music; govt-owned.
WWFM: POB 1327, Koror, PW 96940; tel. 488-4848; fax 488-4420; e-mail wwfm@palaunet.com; internet www.brouhaha.net/palau/wwfm.html; Man. ALFONSO DIAZ.
WSZB Broadcasting Station: POB 279, Koror, PW 96940; tel. 488-2417; fax 488-1932; Station Man. ALBERT SALUSTIANO.
KHBN: POB 66, Koror, PW 96940; tel. 488-2162; fax 488-2163; e-mail hamadmin@palaunet.com; f. 1992; broadcasts religious material; CEO JACKIE MITCHUM YOCKEY.

Television

STV-TV Koror: POB 2000, Koror, PW 96940; tel. 488-1357; fax 488-1207; broadcasts 12 hrs daily; Man. DAVID NOLAN; Technical Man. RAY OMELEN.
Island Cable Television, Inc: POB 39, Koror, PW 96940; tel. 488-1490; fax 587-1888; e-mail nor_ictv@palaunet.com; internet www.palaunet.com/html/ictv.html; owned by the Palau National Communications Corpn.

Finance

(cap. = capital; res = reserves; amounts in US dollars)

BANKING

Bank of Guam: POB 338, Koror, PW 96940; tel. 488-2696; fax 488-1384; internet www.bankofguam.com; Man. KATHRINE C. LUJAN.
Bank of Hawaii (USA): POB 340, Koror, PW 96940; tel. 488-2428; fax 488-2427; internet www.boh.com.
Bank Pacific: POB 1000, Koror, PW 96940; tel. 488-5635; fax 488-4752; Man. JOSEPH KOSHIBA.
National Development Bank of Palau: POB 816, Koror, PW 96940-0816; tel. 488-2578; fax 488-2579; e-mail ndbp@palaunet.com; internet www.ndbp.com; f. 1982; cap. and res 11.5m. (Sept. 2002); 100% govt-owned; Pres. KALEB ADUI, Jr; Chair. NORIWO UBEDEI.
Pacific Savings Bank: POB 399, Koror, PW 96940; tel. 488-1859; fax 488-1858; e-mail bank@palaunet.com; Pres. TIM TAUNTON; Vice-Pres. and COO JOHN DENIRO.

In 1990 there were also 22 registered credit unions, with 1,025 members, but they were severely affected by the financial crisis in Palau.

INSURANCE

Century Insurance Co: POB 318, Koror, PW 96940; tel. 488-8580; fax 488-8632; e-mail knakamura@palaunet.com; internet www.tanholdings.com/cic.asp.

PALAU

Moylan's Insurance Underwriters Palau: POB 156, Koror, PW 96940; tel. 488-2761; fax 488-2744; e-mail palau@moylansinsurance.com; internet www.moylansinsurance.com; Branch Man. KENJI DENGOKL.

NECO Insurance Underwriters Ltd: POB 129, Koror, PW 96940; tel. 488-2325; fax 488-2880; e-mail necogroup@palaunet.com.

Poltalia National Insurance: POB 12, Koror, PW 96940; tel. 488-2254; fax 488-2834; e-mail psata@palaunet.com; f. 1974; Pres. and CEO EPHRAM POLYCARP.

Trade and Industry

CHAMBER OF COMMERCE

Palau Chamber of Commerce: POB 1742, Koror, PW 96940; tel. 488-3400; fax 488-3401; e-mail pcoc@palaunet.com; f. 1984; Pres. SURANGEL WHIPPS, Jr.

CO-OPERATIVES

These include the Palau Fishermen's Co-operative, Palau Boatbuilders' Asscn and the Palau Handicraft and Woodworkers' Guild. In 1990, of the 13 registered co-operatives, eight were fishermen's co-operatives, three consumers' co-operatives (only two in normal operation) and two farmers' co-operatives (one in normal operation).

DEVELOPMENT ORGANIZATION

Palau Conservation Society: POB 1811, Koror, PW 96940; tel. 488-3993; fax 488-3990; e-mail pcs@palaunet.com; internet www.palau-pcs.org; f. 1994; sustainable devt, environmental protection; Exec. Dir TIARE TURANG HOLM.

Transport

ROADS

Macadam and concrete roads are found in the more important islands. Other islands have stone and coral-surfaced roads and tracks. The Government is responsible for 36 km (22 miles) of paved roads and 25 km (15 miles) of coral- and gravel-surfaced roads. Most paved roads are located on Koror and are in a poor state of repair. A major project to construct a new 85-km (53-mile) road around Babeldaob began in 1999 and was scheduled for completion in 2005, subsequently postponed to mid-2006. The project was funded with US $150m. from the Compact of Free Association.

SHIPPING

Most shipping in Palau is government-organized. However, the Micronesia Transport Line operates a service from Sydney (Australia) to Palau. A twice-weekly inter-island service operates between Koror and Peleliu. There is one commercial port at Malakal Harbor, which is operated by the privately owned Belau Transfer and Terminal Company.

CIVIL AVIATION

There is an international airport on Babeldaob. A new terminal building, construction of which was funded by a grant of US 16m. from Japan, opened in May 2003. Domestic airfields (former Japanese military airstrips) are located on Angaur and Peleliu. Continental Micronesia (Northern Mariana Islands and Guam) provides daily flights to Koror from Guam, and twice-weekly flights from Manila (Philippines). Cebu Pacific operates direct flights from Davao (Philippines) to Koror. A civil aviation agreement with Taiwan was signed in 1997, and direct charter flights between Taiwan and Palau began in the following year, operated by the Far Eastern Air Transport Corpn. Palau Trans Pacific also operates from Taiwan. In August 2004 Palau's first locally owned airline, Palau Micronesia Air, made its inaugural flight to Manila. Its routes were to include the Federated States of Micronesia, the Philippines and Australia. However, operations were temporarily suspended in December 2004 in order to permit the restructuring of the company.

Palau Micronesia Air: POB 9048, Ernguul Rd, Topside, Koror, PW 96940; tel. 488-1111; fax 488-8830; e-mail info@palau-air.com; internet www.palau-air.com; serving Chuuk, Yap, Saipan, Manila (Philippines) and Darwin (Australia); operations temporarily suspended in Dec. 2004; Pres. and CEO ALAN SEID.

Rock Island Airlines: managed by Aloha Airlines (Hawaii).

Tourism

Tourism is becoming increasingly important in Palau. The islands are particularly rich in their marine environment, and the Government has taken steps to conserve and protect these natural resources. The myriad Rock Islands, now known as the Floating Garden Islands, are a noted reserve in the lagoon to the west of the main group of islands. There were 1,049 hotel rooms in 2002. In 2003 there were 63,337 visitor arrivals, of whom 46% were from Taiwan and 36% from Japan. Tourist expenditure rose from US $53m. in 1999/2000 to an estimated $59m. in 2002.

Belau Tourism Association: POB 9032, Koror, PW 96940; tel. 488-4377; fax 488-1725; e-mail bta@palaunet.com.

Palau Visitors' Authority: POB 256, Koror, PW 96940; tel. 488-2793; fax 488-1453; e-mail info@visit-palau.com; internet www.visit-palau.com; Man. Dir MARY ANN DELEMEL.

PALESTINIAN AUTONOMOUS AREAS

Introductory Survey

Location, Climate, Language, Religion, Flag, Capital

The Palestinian Autonomous Areas are located in the West Bank and the Gaza Strip. (For a more detailed description of the location of the Palestinian territories, see Government, below.) The West Bank lies in western Asia, to the west of the Jordan river and the Dead Sea, with the State of Israel to the north, west and south. The Gaza Strip lies on the easternmost coast of the Mediterranean, with Israel to the north and east and Egypt to the south. The Interim Agreement of September 1995 (see below) provides for the creation of a corridor, or safe passage, linking the Gaza Strip with the West Bank. A 'southern' safe passage between Hebron and Gaza was opened in October 1999 (although it has been closed since October 2000). Including East Jerusalem, the West Bank covers an area of 5,655 sq km. Precipitation ranges between 600 mm and 800 mm on the Mount Hebron massif and 200 mm in the Jordan valley. Apart from the urban centres of Beit Lahm (Bethlehem) and Al-Khalil (Hebron) to the south, the majority of the Palestinian population is concentrated in the northern localities around Ram Allah (Ramallah), Nabulus (Nablus), Janin (Jenin) and Tulkarm. The Gaza Strip covers an area of 365 sq km. Annual average rainfall is 300 mm. The language of Palestinians in the West Bank and Gaza is Arabic. The majority of the Palestinian population are Muslims, with a Christian minority representing about 2% of the Palestinian population of the territories. This minority, in turn, represents about 45% of all Palestinian Christians. The national flag (proportion 1 by 2) comprises three equal horizontal stripes of black, white and green, with a red triangle with its base corresponding to the hoist. Gaza City is the main population centre and the centre of administration for the Palestinian (National) Authority (PA), appointed in May 1994. Ramallah is the PA's administrative centre in the West Bank. In November 1988 the Palestine National Council (PNC) proclaimed Jerusalem as the capital of the newly declared independent State of Palestine. Israel (q.v.) declares Jerusalem as its capital. In 1967 East Jerusalem was formally annexed by the Israeli authorities, although the annexation has never been recognized by the UN. The permanent status of Jerusalem remains subject to negotiation on so-called 'final status' issues under the Oslo accords (detailed in the Recent History, below).

Recent History

Until the end of the 1948 Arab–Israeli War, the West Bank formed part of the British Mandate of Palestine, before becoming part of the Hashemite Kingdom of Jordan under the Armistice Agreement of 1949. It remained under Jordanian sovereignty, despite Israeli occupation in 1967, until King Hussein of Jordan formally relinquished legal and administrative control on 31 July 1988. Under Israeli military occupation the West Bank was administered by a military government, which divided the territory into seven sub-districts. The Civil Administration, as it was later termed, did not extend its jurisdiction to the many Israeli settlements that were established under the Israeli occupation; settlements remained subject to the Israeli legal and administrative system. By October 2000 approximately 17.2% of the West Bank was under exclusive Palestinian jurisdiction and security control, although Israel retained authority over access to and from the zone; about 23.8% was under Israeli military control, with responsibility for civil administration and public order transferred to the PA; the remaining 59% was under Israeli occupation.

An administrative province under the British Mandate of Palestine, Gaza was transferred to Egypt after the 1949 armistice and remained under Egyptian administration until June 1967, when it was invaded by Israel. Following Israeli occupation the Gaza Strip, like the West Bank, became an 'administered territory'. Until the provisions of the Declaration of Principles on Palestinian Self-Rule (see below) began to take effect, the management of day-to-day affairs was the responsibility of the area's Israeli military commander. Neither Israeli laws nor governmental and public bodies—including the Supreme Court—could review or alter the orders of the military command to any great extent. In 2001 an estimated 42% of the Gaza Strip was under Israeli control, including Jewish settlements, military bases, bypass roads and a 'buffer zone' along the border with Israel. However, Israel withdrew its settlers and military personnel from Gaza in August–September 2005 (see below).

In accordance with the Declaration of Principles on Palestinian Self-Rule of 13 September 1993, and the Cairo Agreement on the Gaza Strip and Jericho of 4 May 1994, the Palestine Liberation Organization (PLO) assumed control of the Jericho area of the West Bank, and of the Gaza Strip, on 17 May 1994. In November and December 1995, under the terms of the Israeli-Palestinian Interim Agreement on the West Bank and the Gaza Strip concluded on 28 September 1995, Israeli armed forces withdrew from the West Bank towns of Nablus, Ramallah, Jenin, Tulkarm, Qalqilya and Bethlehem. (These three agreements and associated accords are referred to collectively as the 'Oslo accords', owing to the role played by Norwegian diplomacy in their negotiation.) In late December the PLO assumed responsibility in some 17 areas of civil administration in the town of Hebron, with a view to eventually assuming full responsibility for civil affairs in the 400 surrounding villages. However, despite a partial withdrawal from Hebron in January 1997, Israeli armed forces were to retain freedom of movement to act against potential hostilities there and also to provide security for some 400 Jewish settlers. Responsibility for security in the rest of Hebron (excluding access roads) passed to the Palestinian police force. Following the first phase of the redeployment and the holding, on its completion, of elections to a Palestinian Legislative Council and for a Palestinian executive president, Israel was to have completed a second redeployment from rural areas by July 1997. The Israeli occupation was to be maintained in military installations, Jewish settlements, East Jerusalem and the settlements around Jerusalem until the conclusion of 'final status' negotiations between Israel and the Palestinians, scheduled for May 1999.

Diplomatic developments within the context of the Oslo peace process led to a new timetable for Israeli redeployment which envisaged two phases, subsequent to the Hebron withdrawal, to be completed by October 1997 and August 1998. Discussions on 'final status' issues—borders, Jerusalem, Jewish settlements and Palestinian refugees—were to commence within two months of the signing of the agreement on Hebron. As guarantor of the Oslo accords, the USA undertook to obtain the release from Israeli custody of Palestinian prisoners, and to ensure that Israel continued to engage in negotiations for the establishment of a Palestinian airport in the Gaza Strip and for safe passage for Palestinians between the West Bank and Gaza. The USA also endeavoured to ensure that the Palestinians would continue to combat terrorism, complete the revision of the Palestinian National Charter (or PLO Covenant), adopted in 1964 and amended in 1968, and consider Israeli requests to extradite Palestinians suspected of involvement in attacks in Israel.

In February 1997 the Israeli Government of Binyamin Netanyahu announced the construction of a new Jewish settlement at Jabal Abu Ghunaim (Har Homa, in Hebrew), near Beit Sahur, which would prejudice 'final status' negotiations concerning Jerusalem because it would effectively separate East Jerusalem from the West Bank. In response, the PA withdrew from 'final status' talks scheduled to commence in March. The start of construction work at Jabal Abu Ghunaim provoked rioting among Palestinians and a resumption of attacks by the military wing of the Islamic Resistance Movement (Hamas) on Israeli civilian targets. Israel responded by ordering a general closure of the West Bank and Gaza. Both the Jabal Abu Ghunaim construction and Israel's unilateral decision to redeploy its armed forces from only 9% of West Bank territory (announced in March) were regarded by many observers as a vitiation of both the Oslo and the subsequent post-Hebron agreements. Moreover, the Israeli daily *Ha'aretz* later reported that Israeli plans, evolved within the framework of the Oslo accords, to relinquish 90% of the West Bank had been revised to a 40% redeployment.

In June 1997 the US House of Representatives voted in favour of recognizing Jerusalem as the undivided capital of Israel and of transferring the US embassy to the city from Tel-Aviv. The vote (which was opposed by US President Bill Clinton) coincided with violent clashes between Palestinian civilians and Israeli troops in Gaza and Hebron. At the end of July, on the eve of a scheduled visit by Dennis Ross, the US Special Co-ordinator to the Middle East, to reactivate negotiations between Israel and the PA, Hamas carried out a suicide bomb attack at a Jewish market in Jerusalem, in which 14 civilians were killed. Ross cancelled his visit and the Israeli Government immediately halted payment of tax revenues to the PA and closed the Gaza Strip and the West Bank. In the aftermath of the bombing the PA undertook a campaign to detain members of Hamas and another militant organization, Islamic Jihad. It was announced at the end of September that, as a result of US diplomacy, Israeli and Palestinian officials had agreed to resume negotiations focusing on the outstanding issues of the Oslo accords in early October.

Meanwhile, the attempted assassination in Amman, Jordan, in late September 1997, of Khalid Meshaal, the head of the Hamas political bureau there, provoked warnings of retaliation against Israel, even before official confirmation that agents of the Israeli security service, Mossad, had been responsible for the attack. In order to secure the release of its agents by the Jordanian authorities, Israel was obliged, at the beginning of October, to free a number of Arab political prisoners, most notably Sheikh Ahmad Yassin, the founder and spiritual leader of Hamas, who had been sentenced to life imprisonment in Israel in 1989 for complicity in attacks on Israeli soldiers. The release of Sheikh Yassin into Jordanian custody was swiftly followed by his return, on 6 October 1997, to Gaza.

It was reported in December 1997 that, under further US pressure, the Israeli Cabinet had agreed in principle to withdraw troops from an unspecified area of the West Bank. However, the Israeli Government subsequently reiterated that it would not conduct such a redeployment until the Palestinian leadership had fulfilled a series of conditions: these included the adoption of effective measures to counter terrorism, a reduction in the strength of its security forces from 40,000 to 24,000, and a revision of the Palestinian National Charter to recognize explicitly Israel's right to exist. Moreover, prior to a summit meeting in January 1998 between Clinton and Netanyahu in Washington, DC, the Israeli Cabinet issued a communiqué detailing 'vital and national interests' in the West Bank (amounting to some 60% of the entire territory) that it was not prepared to relinquish; the document asserted that Israel would, among other areas, retain control of the territory surrounding Jerusalem. In late January, however, direct contacts between Palestinian representatives and the Israeli Prime Minister collapsed.

In late March 1998 it emerged that the USA planned to present new proposals regarding the withdrawal of Israeli armed forces from the West Bank at separate meetings in Europe between US Secretary of State Madeleine Albright and the PA President, Yasser Arafat, and Israeli Prime Minister Netanyahu. However, it was evident that, even if agreement could be reached on the extent of territory involved, the issue of whether a subsequent withdrawal should take place prior to the commencement of 'final status' talks remained far more contentious. The Israeli Cabinet rejected the new US initiative. In April it emerged that, during a visit to Gaza City on behalf of the European Union (EU), the British Prime Minister, Tony Blair, had persuaded Arafat to attend a conference in London, based on the most recent US initiative. Accordingly, in early May Blair hosted a summit meeting attended by Netanyahu, Arafat and Albright. At its conclusion the US Secretary of State invited Netanyahu and Arafat to attend a summit meeting with Bill Clinton in Washington, DC, to discuss the apparent US proposal that Israeli and Palestinian officials could proceed to 'final status' negotiations as soon as the scope of the next Israeli withdrawal from the West Bank had been agreed. In June details of the latest US initiative were unofficially disclosed in the Israeli press: Israel would be required to agree to 'no significant expansion' of Jewish settlements and to relinquish slightly more than 13% of West Bank territory over a period of 12 weeks, in exchange for increased Palestinian co-operation on security issues. The adoption by the Israeli Cabinet later that month of a plan to extend the boundaries of Jerusalem and construct homes there for a further 1m. people prompted accusations by the PA that it amounted to a *de facto* annexation of territories that were officially subject to 'final status' discussions.

On 7 July 1998 the UN General Assembly overwhelmingly approved a resolution to upgrade the status of the PLO at the UN. The new provision, which the USA and Israel had opposed, allowed the PLO to participate in debates, to co-sponsor resolutions, and to raise points of order during discussions of Middle East affairs.

On 19–22 July 1998 Israeli and Palestinian delegations held direct negotiations for the first time since March 1997, in order to discuss the US peace initiative disclosed in June. In late September 1998 Netanyahu and Arafat met in Washington, DC, and agreed to participate in a peace conference in the USA in the following month. The summit meeting, also attended by President Clinton, commenced at the Wye Plantation, Maryland, USA, on 15 October 1998, and culminated in the signing, on 23 October, of the Wye River Memorandum, which was intended to facilitate the implementation of the Oslo accords. Under the terms of the Wye Memorandum, to be implemented within three months of its signing, Israel was to transfer a further 13.1% of West Bank territory from exclusive Israeli control to joint Israeli-Palestinian control. An additional 14% of the West Bank was to be transferred from joint Israeli-Palestinian control to exclusive Palestinian control. The Wye Memorandum also stipulated that: negotiations with regard to a third Israeli redeployment (under the terms of the Oslo accords) should proceed concurrently with 'final status' discussions; the PA should reinforce anti-terrorism measures and arrest 30 suspected terrorists; the strength of the Palestinian police force should be reduced by 25%; Israel should carry out the phased release of 750 Palestinian prisoners (including political detainees); the Palestine National Council (PNC) should annul those clauses of the PLO Covenant deemed to be anti-Israeli; Gaza International Airport was to become operational with an Israeli security presence; and an access corridor between the West Bank and the Gaza Strip should be opened. The Memorandum was endorsed by both the Israeli Cabinet and the Knesset (parliament) by mid-November. On 20 November Israel redeployed its armed forces from about 500 sq km of the West Bank (with the PA assuming responsibilty for all civil affairs and for security affairs in some 400 sq km); released some 250 Palestinian prisoners (although a majority were non-political detainees); and signed a protocol for the opening of Gaza International Airport. Israel retained the right to decide which airlines could use the airport, which was officially inaugurated by Arafat on 24 November.

However, implementation of the Wye Memorandum did not proceed smoothly. In the weeks prior to a visit by Bill Clinton to Israel and the Gaza Strip, planned for December 1998, violent clashes erupted in the West Bank between Palestinians and Israeli security forces. One cause of the unrest was a decision by the Israeli Cabinet to suspend further releases of Palestinian prisoners under the terms of the Wye Memorandum, and its insistence that no Palestinians convicted of killing Israelis, nor members of Hamas or Islamic Jihad, would be released. On 14 December, meanwhile, in the presence of President Clinton, the PNC voted to annul articles of the Palestinian National Charter that were deemed to be anti-Israeli. However, at a summit meeting the following day between Clinton, Netanyahu and Arafat at the Erez check-point between Israel and the Gaza Strip, the Israeli Prime Minister reiterated Israel's stance regarding the release of Palestinian prisoners and further demanded that the Palestinians should honour their commitments by ceasing incitement to violence and formally relinquishing plans for a unilateral declaration of Palestinian statehood on 4 May 1999 (the original deadline as established by the Oslo accords). Netanyahu announced that Israel would not proceed with the second scheduled redeployment of its armed forces (under the Wye Memorandum) on 18 December 1998, and on 20 December the Israeli Cabinet voted to suspend implementation of the agreement.

Palestinians reacted to the death of King Hussein of Jordan in February 1999 with public grief—about 65% of the Kingdom's inhabitants are believed to be of Palestinian origin—especially in the West Bank, which King Hussein ruled for 15 years until June 1967. For Arafat, the death of Hussein was a major political reverse since the King had frequently supported him when the peace process with Israel appeared to be on the verge of collapse. Arafat subsequently surprised many Jordanians by proposing the establishment of a Palestinian-Jordanian confederation. The proposal (which had been put forward as part of a peace initiative in 1985, but was rejected by King Hussein) was not welcomed in Jordan, where it was considered to be premature while the West Bank was still largely under Israeli occupation.

President Arafat came under intense international pressure to postpone a unilateral declaration of Palestinian statehood, at least until after the Israeli elections scheduled for May 1999. In late April PLO chief negotiators Mahmud Abbas (also known as

Abu Mazen) and Saeb Erakat (the Minister of Local Government) visited Washington, DC, in order to secure certain assurances from the USA in return for an extension of the 4 May deadline. Following a meeting of the Palestinian Central Council (PCC), together with Hamas representatives, in Gaza, it was announced that a declaration on Palestinian statehood would be postponed until after the Israeli elections. The decision was applauded internationally, but provoked violent demonstrations among many Palestinians.

Meeting at Sharm esh-Sheikh, Egypt, on 4 September 1999, during a visit to the region by US Secretary of State Albright, Arafat and the new Israeli Prime Minister, Ehud Barak (who had been elected to the premiership in May), signed the Sharm esh-Sheikh Memorandum (or Wye Two accords), outlining a revised timetable for implementation of the outstanding provisions of the original Wye agreement. Under the terms of the Memorandum, on 9 September Israel released some 200 Palestinian 'security' prisoners, and the following day Israel transferred a further 7% of the West Bank to PA control. A ceremonial opening of 'final status' negotiations between Israel and the PA was held at the Erez check-point on 13 September; shortly afterwards details emerged of a secret meeting between Barak and Arafat to discuss an agenda for such talks. However, in early October the Palestinians' chief negotiator and Minister of Culture and Information, Yasser Abd ar-Rabbuh, warned that the PA would boycott 'final status' talks unless Israel ended its settlement expansion programme. In mid-October Barak, also under pressure from left-wing groups in Israel, responded by dismantling 12 'settlement outposts' in the West Bank which he deemed to be illegal. Meanwhile, Israel released a further 151 Palestinian prisoners under the terms of Wye Two. The first 'safe passage' between the West Bank and Gaza was inaugurated on 25 October. Israel asserted that it would maintain almost complete control over the so-called 'southern route', which linked Hebron to the Erez check-point.

'Final status' negotiations between Israel and the PA commenced in Ramallah on 8 November 1999, following a summit meeting held earlier in the month in Oslo, Norway, between Arafat, Barak and Clinton. A further redeployment of Israeli armed forces from 5% of the West Bank, scheduled for 15 November, was postponed owing to disagreement over the areas to be transferred. In early December Palestinian negotiators walked out of the talks, following reports that settlement activity had intensified under Barak. Apparently in response to US pressure, the Israeli Prime Minister subsequently announced a halt to settlement construction until the close of negotiations regarding a framework agreement on 'final status'. In late December Arafat conducted talks in Ramallah with Barak, who became the first Israeli premier to hold peace discussions on Palestinian territory. At the end of the month Israel released some 26 Palestinian 'security' prisoners as a gesture of 'goodwill'. On 6–7 January 2000 Israeli armed forces withdrew from a further 5% of the West Bank; however, Israel announced in mid-January that a third redeployment from 6.1% of the territory (scheduled to take place on 20 January) would be postponed until Barak had returned from revived peace talks with Syria in the USA. During a meeting with Arafat on his return from the USA (where talks on the Israeli-Syrian track had collapsed), Barak was reported to have proposed that the deadline for reaching a framework agreement be postponed for two months. The approval by the Israeli Cabinet of a withdrawal of its troops from a sparsely populated area of the West Bank led the PA to break off negotiations in early February. On 19–20 March Israel released 15 Palestinian 'security' prisoners, and the resumption of 'final status' talks was announced on 21 March. On the same day Israeli armed forces withdrew from a further 6.1% of the West Bank.

In mid-April 2000, following talks between Barak and Clinton in Washington, DC, Israel was said to have agreed to Palestinian demands for greater US involvement in future discussions. Moreover, the Israeli premier reportedly indicated that a Palestinian entity could be established in what was now PA-controlled territory—covering 60%–70% of the West Bank—although he refused to speak of a Palestinian 'state'. Later in April Arafat met with Clinton in Washington, where he sought US intervention in halting Israel's settlement expansion programme. The third round of 'final status' talks between Israel and the PA opened at the Israeli port of Eilat on 30 April, at which Palestinian negotiators denounced a recent decision by the Israeli Government to construct 174 new Jewish homes in the West Bank. At crisis talks between Arafat and Barak in Ramallah in early May, mediated by Dennis Ross, Barak reportedly proposed the transfer to full PA control of three Palestinian villages close to Jerusalem, on condition that the third West Bank redeployment (scheduled to be implemented in June) be postponed. After PA negotiators admitted that the 13 May deadline for reaching a framework agreement would not be met, 'final status' talks were suspended.

At the beginning of May 2000 Palestinians in the West Bank and Gaza initiated mass protests in support of up to 1,000 Palestinian prisoners who had commenced a hunger strike while in Israeli detention. The demonstrations erupted into violence on 15 May (the anniversary of the declaration of the State of Israel in 1948), which was declared to be a 'day of rage'. Three days of violent gun battles ensued between Palestinian police and civilians and Israeli troops, in which seven Palestinians were killed and several hundred injured. Growing anger among Palestinians over the apparent unaccountability of the PA leadership appeared to have contributed to the civil unrest. The hunger strike was called off at the end of the month and the PA detained several Palestinians suspected of involvement in the recent violence. Meanwhile, on 21 May Israel suspended 'secret' talks being conducted between Israeli and Palestinian representatives in Stockholm, Sweden, after an Israeli child was seriously wounded in continuing violence in the West Bank. The Israeli Government also reversed its decision to transfer the three Arab villages to PA control, demanding that Arafat take action to curb Palestinian unrest.

Following a tour of Israel and the Palestinian areas by US Secretary of State Madeleine Albright in early June 2000, President Clinton received Arafat for discussions in Washington, DC, in an attempt to reinvigorate the Israeli-Palestinian track of the Middle East peace process. Four days later Israel released three Palestinian prisoners as a 'goodwill' gesture. On 21 June, two days prior to the scheduled date, the PA reportedly agreed to a postponement of the third redeployment of Israeli forces from the West Bank. The PCC convened on 2 July, and after two days of discussions stated that the PLO would declare a State of Palestine on or before 13 September. On 11 July Bill Clinton inaugurated a peace summit between Arafat and Barak at the US presidential retreat at Camp David, Maryland, with the aim of achieving a framework agreement on 'final status'. However, the talks ended without agreement on 25 July. Despite reported progress regarding the borders of a future Palestinian entity and the question of Palestinian refugees, disagreements over the future status of Jerusalem had been the principal obstacle to an accord. Israel was said to have offered the Palestinians municipal authority over certain parts of East Jerusalem, as well as access to the Islamic holy sites. PA officials, however, demanded full sovereignty over the holy sites (in particular the al-Aqsa Mosque and the Dome of the Rock), with East Jerusalem as the capital of a Palestinian state. Nevertheless, Israel and the PA pledged to continue peace negotiations and to avoid 'unilateral actions'—interpreted as Arafat's threat unilaterally to declare an independent Palestinian state. During a tour principally of Europe, the Middle East and Asia, intense pressure was exerted on Arafat not to announce the establishment of a Palestinian state on 13 September. In early September Bill Clinton held separate talks with Arafat and Barak on the sidelines of the UN Millennium Summit in New York, USA. The PCC convened in Gaza on 9–10 September and agreed to postpone the declaration of statehood for an indefinite period (although 15 November was reportedly designated as the new target date). Later in September negotiations between Israeli and PA officials resumed in the USA, and on 20 September an agreement was signed allowing for construction of the Gaza seaport to begin (the work failed to progress owing to the worsening security situation). On 26 September Barak and Arafat met at the Israeli premier's home for their first direct talks since the Camp David summit.

From late September 2000 the West Bank and Gaza Strip became engulfed in what became known as the al-Aqsa *intifada* (uprising—the first *intifada* began at the end of 1987 and continued for some five years), as Palestinians demonstrated their frustration at the lack of progress in the Oslo peace process and at their failure to achieve statehood. The outbreak of violence was triggered by the visit of Ariel Sharon, leader of Israel's right-wing Likud party, to Temple Mount/Haram ash-Sharif in Jerusalem—the site of the al-Aqsa Mosque and the Dome of the Rock—on 28 September. Sharon's visit to the Islamic holy sites provoked violent protests and stone-throwing by Palestinians, to which Israeli security forces responded forcefully. The clashes spread rapidly to other Palestinian towns: by the end of October at least 140 people had died—all but eight of them Palestinians—and thousands had been wounded. In early October Arafat and Barak travelled to Paris, France, for negotiations led by the US Secretary of State, but no agreement was reached on the composition of an international commission of inquiry into the causes of the violence. The Israeli authorities subsequently sealed off the borders of the West Bank and Gaza, and on 7 October the UN Security Council issued a resolution condemning the 'provocation carried out' at Temple Mount/Haram ash-Sharif and the 'excessive use of force' employed by the Israeli security forces against Palestinians. Meanwhile, Israel accused Arafat of failing to intervene to halt the violence, as members of Arafat's own Fatah movement joined Hamas and other militant groups in the quickly escalating *intifada*. In an attempt to prevent the crisis from developing into a major regional conflict, a US-sponsored summit meeting between Barak and Arafat was convened on 16–17 October at Sharm esh-Sheikh. At the close of the meeting US President Clinton announced that the Israeli and Palestinian leaders had agreed the terms of a 'truce' to halt the spiralling violence. The two sides had also reportedly agreed on the formation of a US-appointed committee to investigate the clashes. Barak, however, demanded that Arafat rearrest some 60 militant Islamists whom the PA had freed in early October. The League of Arab States (the Arab League, see p. 306) held an emergency summit meeting in the Egyptian capital on 21–22 October, and issued a strong condemnation of Israel's actions towards the Palestinians. Barak responded by announcing that Israel was calling a 'time-out' in the peace process.

At the end of October 2000 Islamic Jihad claimed responsibility for a suicide bombing on an Israeli army post in Gaza, signalling a new campaign against Israeli forces by militant Palestinian organizations opposed to the Oslo process. Israel responded by launching air-strikes on Fatah military bases, and declared a new strategy of targeting leading officials of militant Islamist groups suspected of terrorist activities. On 1 November Arafat held a crisis meeting in Gaza with the Israeli Minister for Regional Co-operation, Shimon Peres; the two sides were reported to have agreed a 'cease-fire', based on the truce brokered in Egypt in October. The following day, however, a car bomb exploded in Jerusalem, for which Islamic Jihad claimed responsibility. In early November President Clinton appointed the five-member international commission of inquiry, to be chaired by former US Senator George Mitchell. Meeting with Clinton in the USA shortly afterwards, Arafat demanded that the USA support Palestinian requests for the establishment of a UN peace-keeping force in the self-rule areas (Barak was opposed to such a force). Israel reinforced its closure of the West Bank and Gaza in mid-November, imposing an economic blockade on the territories, and launched air-strikes against PA offices in Gaza later that month, in reprisal for the deaths of two people in the bombing of a school bus for Jewish settlers. At the end of November the Palestinians rejected a partial peace plan, announced by Barak, whereby Israel would withdraw its armed forces from additional West Bank territory provided that the PA agreed to postpone any discussion of the remaining 'final status' issues. In late 2000 Palestinian militants concentrated their attacks against Jewish settlers, while in early December Israel eased some of the sanctions imposed on the Palestinian enclaves at the outbreak of the crisis. In mid-December the US-led commission of inquiry began conducting investigations into the violence.

A further round of peace talks opened in mid-December 2000, at which Clinton was reported to have proposed a peace deal that included plans for a future Palestinian state covering the Gaza Strip and some 95% of the West Bank, as well as granting the Palestinians sovereignty over the Islamic holy sites in the Old City of Jerusalem. However, the US plan also required that Palestinians renounce the right of return for 3.7m. refugees, which the PA deemed unacceptable. The negotiations broke down in late December after two Israelis died in bombings by Palestinian militants in Tel-Aviv and the Gaza Strip. In early January 2001 Arafat visited Washington, DC, to seek official clarification of Clinton's proposals; meanwhile, following a car bomb explosion in northern Israel, the Israeli authorities again tightened their blockade of the West Bank and Gaza. Israel subsequently confirmed its policy of assassinating local Palestinian officials who were regarded as endangering Israeli society, which it referred to as 'targeted killings'.

The election of Ariel Sharon to the Israeli premiership in early February 2001 provoked violent demonstrations by Palestinians, who held Sharon responsible—as Israel's Minister of Defence at that time—for the Phalangist massacre of Palestinian refugees in Lebanese camps in 1982 (see the chapters on Israel and Lebanon). Immediately after Sharon's election Palestinian militants carried out a car bombing in Jerusalem. A few days later another senior Fatah official was killed by Israeli security forces. In mid-February a Palestinian bus driver launched an attack on Israeli soldiers and civilians in Tel-Aviv, killing nine people. Israel responded by again sealing off the Palestinian territories.

At the beginning of June 2001 21 Israelis were killed in a suicide bomb attack, apparently perpetrated by Hamas, at a Tel-Aviv nightclub. The PA agreed the following day to implement the recommendations listed in the final report of the international commission of inquiry under George Mitchell (the Sharm esh-Sheikh Fact-Finding Committee, or 'Mitchell Committee'), published in late May. The Mitchell Report recommended a 'freeze' on Israeli settlement expansion; a clear statement by the PA demanding an end to Palestinian violence; an 'immediate and unconditional' end to the conflict and the disengagement of forces by both sides; and the resumption of security co-operation. Moreover, in mid-June the PA also agreed to an extended cease-fire brokered by the US Central Intelligence Agency (CIA) Director, George Tenet. Although it appeared initially that Palestinian militant groups would maintain the truce, in early July both Hamas and Islamic Jihad formally announced that the cease-fire was ended. In late July Palestinian security forces in Gaza arrested a number of militants, including members of Fatah's military wing, the *tanzim*.

In August 2001 the PA rejected a demand by Israel for the arrest of seven alleged 'terrorists', who headed a 'most wanted' list of about 100 Palestinians suspected of involvement in attacks against Israeli targets. Soon afterwards Israel ordered its armed forces to occupy several PA offices including Orient House, the PA's *de facto* headquarters in East Jerusalem, following a Hamas suicide bombing which killed at least 15 Israelis at a restaurant in central Jerusalem. Israeli troops entered the West Bank town of Jenin in mid-August—the first Israeli reoccupation of territory transferred to full PA control under the terms of the Oslo accords. Palestinian officials called the action a 'declaration of war'. Later in the month Abu Ali Moustafa, the leader of the Popular Front for the Liberation of Palestine (PFLP), was assassinated by Israeli forces in the West Bank.

The unprecedented scale of the suicide attacks launched against New York and Washington, DC, on 11 September 2001—for which the USA held the al-Qa'ida (Base) network led by the Saudi-born militant Islamist Osama bin Laden principally responsible—precipitated efforts by the US Administration to encourage Israel and the PA to end the violence in the Palestinian territories, as President George W. Bush (who had been elected to the presidency in November 2000) sought to garner support for an international 'war on terror'. In mid-September 2001 Yasser Arafat, who had condemned the attacks in the strongest terms, declared that he had ordered militant Palestinian groups to halt their actions against Israelis, while Israel agreed to withdraw from PA-controlled areas of the West Bank. However, Sharon stated that his Government required 48 hours without violence prior to any resumption of peace talks. Arafat and Peres finally met in the Gaza Strip in late September, in an attempt to consolidate the cease-fire arrangements outlined in the Mitchell Report. However, on the first anniversary of the al-Aqsa *intifada* five Palestinians were shot dead by Israeli forces in Gaza, and retaliatory attacks between the two sides resumed.

In early October 2001 President Bush disclosed for the first time that the USA would accept the creation of a Palestinian state, on condition that Israel's existence was not threatened. The assassination in Jerusalem of Israel's ultra-nationalist Minister of Tourism, Rechavam Ze'evi, by three members of the PFLP—apparently in revenge for the murder of the PFLP leader in August—led Israel, in late October, to order its armed forces into six major West Bank towns (rejecting US demands for a swift withdrawal). Shortly after Ze'evi's death Arafat banned all military factions of Palestinian political groups, and his security forces arrested several PFLP militants; however, the PA refused Israeli demands for their extradition. At least five Palestinians reportedly died in Beit Rima, near Ramallah, in a raid by Israeli forces searching for Ze'evi's assassins. Towards the end of October Israel stated that it would carry out a phased withdrawal from the six West Bank towns; however, its 'anti-terrorist' operation continued in Jenin and Tulkarm, and Israeli tanks continued to surround Ramallah.

At the beginning of December 2001 Hamas claimed responsibility for a series of attacks in Jerusalem and Haifa over a 24-hour period, in which at least 25 Israelis were killed. In the week following the attacks Palestinian security forces claimed to have arrested more than 150 (mainly Hamas and Islamic Jihad) militants, mostly in Jenin, and also reportedly placed the spiritual leader of Hamas, Sheikh Ahmad Yassin, under house arrest. Arafat was personally affected by renewed Israeli military operations: an Israeli missile strike on Arafat's official residence in Gaza destroyed two of his helicopters, while in Ramallah Israeli tanks advanced to the edge of the presidential compound, where Arafat was then residing. The Israeli Prime Minister increasingly began to draw parallels between Israel's efforts to suppress the *intifada* and the USA's 'war on terror', describing the PA as a 'terror-supporting entity'. Israel demanded that Arafat arrest 33 militants held to be responsible for recent suicide attacks. In mid-December Israel responded to an assault on a settlers' bus in the West Bank (in which some 10 Israelis died) by declaring the PA leader to be 'irrelevant', owing to his failure to prevent such attacks, and announced that it was severing all contacts with Arafat. The Israeli military launched air-raids across the West Bank and Gaza, reoccupied large areas of Ramallah, and reinforced its military blockade of Arafat's headquarters; several Palestinian police-officers and civilians were killed during the Israeli operations. Meanwhile, the USA again vetoed a proposed UN resolution calling for international observers to be deployed in the Palestinian areas. In a televised speech Arafat issued a strong condemnation of groups that carried out gun attacks and suicide bombings against Israelis, although Sharon insisted that Arafat would not be permitted to leave Ramallah until the PA arrested the perpetrators of Ze'evi's murder.

In January 2002 Arafat ordered an investigation into Israeli and US claims that the PA was complicit in a massive shipment of largely Iranian-produced weaponry—including *Katyusha* rockets, mortar shells and anti-tank missiles—which Israeli forces had intercepted in the Red Sea; the freighter, the *Karine A*, was apparently en route for the Gaza Strip to be used in attacks against Israeli targets. (In February Arafat finally accepted responsibility on behalf of his administration for the shipment.) Following a gun attack by members of another militant group, the Al-Aqsa Martyrs Brigades, that killed six guests at a bar mitzvah ceremony in Hadera, northern Israel, Sharon ordered tanks and armoured vehicles to tighten their blockade of Arafat's Ramallah headquarters (the President had effectively been under house arrest since early December 2001), and also reoccupied Tulkarm in order to arrest known Palestinian 'terrorists'. Although the troops withdrew a day later, it was reported to be the largest military incursion since the start of the al-Aqsa *intifada*. Meanwhile, EU officials increasingly distanced themselves from the US position towards the conflict, reaffirming their support for Arafat as a crucial partner in the peace process. The EU also issued a formal complaint to Israel, listing EU-funded projects in the West Bank and Gaza that had undergone physical damage during recent military operations.

In early February 2002 Israel carried out the 'targeted killing' of at least four members of the radical Democratic Front for the Liberation of Palestine (DFLP) in the Gaza Strip. The violence came at a time of renewed efforts to restart peace negotiations. Ariel Sharon met leading PA representatives, while Shimon Peres held a series of discussions with the PLC Speaker, Ahmad Quray (also known as Abu Ala). However, Israeli officials were angered when a large number of Palestinian militants were freed during Israeli air-strikes on the PA's security headquarters in Nablus. Requests for calm by the UN and attempts by the EU to launch a new peace initiative in the second week of February—reportedly based on the convening of new elections to the PLC—failed to prevent an escalation of violence in the territories, particularly in Gaza. As Hamas appeared to be intensifying its attacks on Israelis by firing a new type of missile, the *Qassam-2*, against Jewish settlers, four Palestinian security officers died during incursions by the Israeli army into three Gazan towns. Israel also accelerated its military offensive in Hebron and Ramallah. In late February up to 30 Palestinians were reportedly killed in Israeli military operations across the West Bank and Gaza in retaliation for the shooting of six Israelis at an army check-point near Ramallah. The Israeli Cabinet subsequently agreed to withdraw its tanks from Arafat's compound in Ramallah but refused to allow the Palestinian leader freedom of movement beyond the town: Sharon stated that the travel ban would remain in place despite the arrest by Palestinian security forces of three militants believed to have been responsible for Ze'evi's murder. The Israeli position led PA security officials to suspend bilateral talks, which had recently been resumed. Gun battles raged across the West Bank at the end of February, despite efforts by Crown Prince Abdullah of Saudi Arabia to promote his proposals for peace in the Middle East prior to a summit meeting of the Arab League Council, due to be held in Beirut, Lebanon, in March. Abdullah's proposals centred on Arab recognition of the State of Israel and the normalization of diplomatic relations, in exchange for agreement by Israel to withdraw from all Arab land occupied since 1967 and on the establishment of a Palestinian state with East Jerusalem as its capital. Arafat announced that he would not attend the Beirut conference owing to threats by Sharon to prevent his return to the West Bank and Gaza should he travel abroad. Meanwhile, the number of fatalities continued to grow: in response to a suicide bombing by a Palestinian woman at an Israeli army check-point, Israel for the first time sent ground troops into two refugee camps in the West Bank which it claimed were centres of Islamist militancy: the Balata camp near Nablus and the camp at Jenin. Fierce fighting ensued, and the PA announced subsequently that it was suspending all contacts with the Israeli Government. The USA, meanwhile, urged Israel to show restraint, while UN and EU officials demanded an immediate Israeli withdrawal from the camps.

PA officials categorically rejected an offer made by Ariel Sharon in early March 2002 that Yasser Arafat should agree to go into voluntary exile. At the same time Israel refused to allow senior UN and EU diplomats to visit Arafat. A number of Palestinians were killed as Israeli forces entered Ramallah, Bethlehem and Tulkarm in an attempt to find those responsible for two attacks apparently perpetrated by the Al-Aqsa Martyrs Brigades, in which 20 Israelis had died. Shortly afterwards Palestinian militants carried out another bus bombing and an assault on a restaurant in Tel-Aviv, leading Israel to launch missiles against targets across the West Bank and Gaza; Arafat's presidential compound in Ramallah and the police headquarters in Gaza were both hit. Three militants—believed to be from the Al-Aqsa Martyrs Brigades, including an aide to the Fatah leader in the West Bank, Marwan Barghouthi (whom Israel claimed was the commander of the Brigades)—died in a helicopter raid in Ramallah. The US Secretary of State, Gen. Colin Powell, publicly criticized Sharon's declared aim of forcing the PA to return to peace talks by defeating them militarily. On 8 March five Jewish settler students were killed by Hamas gunmen in Gaza; an estimated 40 Palestinians died during the fierce fighting that ensued. Meanwhile, Sharon declared that Arafat had met the conditions required for his release after a fifth suspect in Ze'evi's murder was arrested by Palestinian security forces in the first week of March. However, after a suicide bombing in Jerusalem, killing 11 Israelis, and a shooting in Netanya in which two died, Israel's 'inner' Security Cabinet voted to intensify its military offensive. Tanks entered Qalqilya and the Jabalia refugee camp in Gaza (where 18 Palestinians, including four Hamas members, were reported to have been killed), while Arafat's headquarters in Gaza were destroyed by Israeli helicopters and gunboats.

On 11 March 2002 Israel announced that it was lifting its travel ban on Arafat, although the Palestinian leader would still not be permitted to travel abroad. The following day some 20,000 Israeli troops began a massive ground offensive in the Palestinian territories as part of a campaign to dismantle the 'infrastructure of terror'; hundreds of Palestinian men were detained for questioning, and several civilians died during the incursions. This was reported to be the largest Israeli operation against Palestinian militants since the 1982 invasion of Lebanon. Israeli forces again took control of most of Ramallah, with tanks coming to within a short distance of Arafat's presidential compound. On 12 March 2002 the UN Security Council adopted Resolution 1397, affirming its 'vision' of both Israeli and Palestinian states 'within secure and recognized borders'; the US-drafted resolution also demanded an immediate end to 'all acts of violence' by both sides, and called upon Israel and the Palestinians to co-operate in implementation of the Mitchell Report and George Tenet's recommendations. US special envoy to the Middle East Anthony Zinni returned to the region on the following day, and was later accompanied by US Vice-President Dick Cheney. Under pressure to withdraw as a 'goodwill' gesture to Zinni, the Israeli army later withdrew from Ramallah, Tulkarm and Qalqilya, although they continued to surround the towns. Following discussions between Zinni and Arafat, and US-brokered talks between Israeli and PA security officials in Jerusalem, Israel also agreed to redeploy its troops from Bethlehem and Beit Jala. The PA was angered by Cheney's refusal to meet the Palestinian leader until certain cease-fire conditions had been met. After the security talks ended without agreement on 21 March, the Israeli Government again ordered troops into much of the West Bank and detained several alleged militants. A further suicide attack by the Al-Aqsa Martyrs Brigades, which killed three Israelis in central Jerusalem, prompted the USA to add the group to its list of proscribed terrorist organizations.

The Arab League summit proceeded in Beirut on 27–28 March 2002, in the notable absence of both President Hosni Mubarak of Egypt and King Abdullah of Jordan (the two leaders had apparently boycotted the meeting as a gesture of support for the PA President). Palestinian officials were angered when the Lebanese hosts refused to permit Arafat to address the session via a live satellite link from Ramallah: the Lebanese authorities had stated that they feared an Israeli disruption of such a broadcast. At the close of the conference the participating Arab states unanimously endorsed the Saudi peace initiative, which also included a clause calling for a 'just solution' to the question of Palestinian refugees. Israel rejected the plan, however, stating that its terms would lead to the destruction of the Jewish state.

The Israeli–Palestinian crisis deepened at the end of March 2002, following an attack by a Hamas suicide bomber at a hotel in the Israeli town of Netanya, where Jews were celebrating the festival of Passover; 29 people died as a result of the attack and some 140 were injured. Although Arafat personally condemned the bombing, and reportedly ordered the immediate arrest of four prominent West Bank militants, Sharon blamed the PA for its failure to prevent such attacks. In response to what was swiftly called the 'Passover massacre', Israel mobilized about 20,000 army reservists and convened an emergency cabinet meeting, at which 'extensive operational activity against Palestinian terrorism' was agreed. With Arafat effectively isolated at his compound in Ramallah, on 29 March Israeli armed forces began a huge campaign of incursions into West Bank towns—code-named 'Operation Defensive Shield'—with the declared aim of dismantling the Palestinian 'terrorist infrastructure' in order to prevent future suicide bombings against Israeli citizens. During the offensive Israeli forces entered and conducted house-to-house searches for militants in Ramallah, Bethlehem, Beit Jala, Qalqilya, Tulkarm, Jenin and Nablus. On 30 March the UN Security Council met in emergency session and demanded, in Resolution 1402, an immediate Israeli withdrawal from all towns that had been transferred to the PA under the Oslo accords. At the end of the month a Hamas suicide bomber from Jenin killed 15 Israelis at a café in Haifa. Sharon declared that Israel was 'at war', and his 'inner' Security Cabinet gave the army permission to broaden its offensive in the West Bank. Israeli armed forces reoccupied Ramallah and declared it to be a 'closed military area'; many Palestinians were reported to have been killed as a result of the invasion. The US Administration expressed 'grave concern' about the situation in the Palestinian areas, and President Bush urged Arafat to take action to prevent further attacks against Israelis by Palestinian militants.

In early April 2002 Yasser Arafat again dismissed a suggestion by Sharon that the Palestinian leader should go into exile. On 2 April fighting between Israelis and Palestinians in Bethlehem escalated into a siege at the Church of the Nativity—believed to mark the site of Christ's birth. As many as 200 people—Palestinian civilians and priests as well as some 30 armed militants wanted by Israel—sought shelter from Israeli troops inside the church. On 3 April Israeli tanks entered Jenin and its refugee camp. By the following day Israel had effectively reoccupied all but two major towns (Jericho and Hebron) in the West Bank and detained more than 1,000 Palestinians; Bethlehem, like Ramallah, was declared a 'closed military area'. Israel prevented an EU delegation from holding discussions with Arafat, and George W. Bush demanded that Israel withdraw its forces immediately from Palestinian towns and implement the Tenet and Mitchell recommendations for a cease-fire. On 4 April Israeli troops reportedly withdrew from Nablus but entered Hebron. Israel also intensified its offensive in the Jenin refugee camp, the alleged base of several of the suicide bombers. According to PA reports, more than 80 Palestinians died during the first week of Israeli military operations in Jenin. The UN Security Council unanimously adopted a resolution (No. 1403) that demanded the implementation of Resolution 1402 (i.e. an Israeli withdrawal from Palestinian territories) 'without delay'. On 9 April 13 Israeli army reservists were killed in ambushes in the Jenin camp, and the following day, in response to the deaths of at least eight people in a Hamas suicide bombing of a bus near Haifa, Israel ruled out the prospect of further withdrawals from the West Bank while its 'anti-terror' operation remained incomplete. US Secretary of State Powell arrived in Israel on 11 April; he held talks with the besieged Palestinian leader in Ramallah three days later, but stated subsequently that a suggested conference on the Middle East crisis would not necessarily require the personal presence of Arafat. The Secretary of State's mission ended on 17 April without having achieved a cease-fire.

During mid-April 2002 Palestinians made increasingly vocal allegations of an Israeli 'massacre' at the Jenin refugee camp—where many buildings had been destroyed by tanks and bulldozers—and claimed that Israeli armed forces were guilty of war crimes. Palestinian sources suggested that at least 100 Palestinians had died during the Israeli invasion; 23 Israelis were believed to have died. (In early May the US-based Human Rights Watch issued a report stating that Israeli forces had been guilty of 'excessive force' and of war crimes in Jenin, but that there had been no massacre, findings echoed by a UN report released in early August.) Meanwhile, although Israel's forces began to withdraw from some Palestinian-administered towns, a number of Palestinians were killed as Israeli tanks entered the Gazan town of Rafah. Also in mid-April Marwan Barghouthi, the Fatah leader in the West Bank, was arrested by Israeli forces in Ramallah; his trial, on charges of leading Palestinian 'terrorist' groups in the West Bank and of orchestrating a number of suicide bombings against Israeli citizens, began in mid-August. (Barghouthi claimed that the Israeli judiciary had no jurisdiction over him, as an elected member of the PLC.) Meanwhile, Sharon announced on 21 April 2002 that the first stage of Operation Defensive Shield had been completed; however, Israeli forces were to remain in Ramallah and Bethlehem. Some reports stated that more than 4,000 Palestinians were detained during the offensive, although many were subsequently released. According to the Palestine Red Crescent Society, by the end of April at least 1,500 Palestinians had been killed, and more than 19,000 injured, since the start of the al-Aqsa *intifada* in September 2000. According to Israeli sources, more than 470 Israelis had been killed, and many more wounded, as a result of the violence.

Yasser Arafat was freed by the Israeli authorities on 1 May 2002. His release came after the USA secured an arrangement whereby Israel agreed to end its siege of Ramallah, including Arafat's headquarters, on condition that the PA leader handed over six prisoners sheltering in the presidential compound who were wanted by Israel in connection with 'terrorist' activities. In late April four of the prisoners were convicted of direct involvement in the assassination of Rechavam Ze'evi by an *ad hoc* Palestinian court inside the compound and variously sentenced to between one and 18 years' imprisonment. The other two detainees were the PFLP leader, Ahmad Saadat, and a militant implicated in the *Karine A* affair. In early May the six prisoners were moved from Ramallah to a gaol in Jericho, where they were to remain in 'international custody' under US and British guard. Despite Arafat's release, US President Bush declared that he was not yet willing to meet the Palestinian leader. Following protracted negotiations, the siege at the Church of the Nativity in Bethlehem finally came to an end, after more than five weeks, on 10 May, when 13 remaining militants were transferred under international guard to Cyprus pending their dispersal to permanent exile elsewhere in Europe. The agreement ending the siege envisaged that 26 other militants who were removed to the Gaza Strip should be tried by a Palestinian court there. It was reported in mid-June that Israel had begun construction of an electrified (later, partially concrete) 'security fence', which would eventually extend the length of its border with the West Bank, in an attempt to prevent further suicide bombings. There was also a marked increase in violence at this time: in response to a series of fatal suicide attacks against Israeli citizens by Palestinian militants in late June, Israel again ordered its armed forces into several towns in the West Bank and Gaza.

The Israeli Cabinet responded to the latest suicide bombing in Tel-Aviv in late September 2002 by announcing that it would seek to 'isolate' Yasser Arafat. Sharon declared that Arafat had failed to arrest militant Islamists known to advocate violence against Israeli citizens, and Israeli forces began the systematic destruction of Arafat's compound in Ramallah while the Palestinian leader reportedly remained inside one of the office buildings. At the same time Israeli armed forces launched a series of incursions into the Gaza Strip, which increasingly became the focus of Israeli military operations in late 2002 and early 2003. Meanwhile, at the end of September 2002 the Israeli siege of Arafat's headquarters was brought to an end, after the UN Security Council had issued a resolution (No. 1435), demanding the immediate cessation of Israeli military actions in and around Ramallah. However, the Israeli–Palestinian violence continued in subsequent months and the number of people killed since the start of the al-Aqsa *intifada* increased dramatically.

The stalled peace process was temporarily revived by the publication of the 'roadmap' peace plan (sponsored by the Quartet group, comprising the USA, Russia, the UN and the EU) on 30 April 2003. The release of the roadmap, which had originally been agreed in December 2002, was conditional on the announcement of a new Palestinian Cabinet under Prime Minister Mahmud Abbas (see below). However, it also affirmed George W. Bush's pledge to focus attention on Israeli-Palestinian affairs following the successful US-led coalition's campaign during March–April 2003 to overthrow the regime of Saddam Hussain in Iraq. The roadmap envisaged an end to Israeli–Palestinian conflict and the establishment of a sovereign Palestinian state by 2005–06 (for further details, see the chapter on Israel). Broadly speaking, Palestinian responsibilities under the terms of the roadmap were restricted to a commitment to ending militant actions against Israeli targets and the establishment of a civilian and government infrastructure; otherwise, crucial issues concerning the Palestinian population, such as the borders of a future state, the status of refugees and Jerusalem, were to be decided during Israel's negotiations with Lebanon, Syria and other Arab states. Initially, Sharon objected to the issue of the right to return of Palestinian refugees and refused to consider the dismantling of Jewish settlements, but on 25 May 2003 the Israeli Cabinet accepted the terms of the roadmap. At the end of the month Sharon made the unprecedented acknowledgement that Israel was indeed in occupation of the Palestinian areas. In early June Sharon, Abbas and President Bush met in Aqaba, Jordan, to discuss the implementation of the roadmap, particularly the contentious issue of Jewish settlements.

Israeli troops had begun dismantling settlements in the West Bank in early June 2003, but this positive development in the peace process was overshadowed by a resumption of violence: on 10 June Israel attempted to kill the prominent Hamas leader, Abd al-Aziz ar-Rantisi, leading to a retaliatory suicide attack against a bus in Jerusalem, in which 16 people died. Subsequently, Israeli helicopter gunships attacked targets in Gaza. Twenty-six people were killed in the renewed fighting, and the USA condemned the attempted Israeli assassination of ar-Rantisi. Nevertheless, Israel continued to dismantle some Jewish settlements, to withdraw troops from certain areas of the West Bank and Gaza, and to release Palestinian prisoners. This latter development was not a condition of the roadmap, but was viewed as a 'goodwill' gesture to Mahmud Abbas, who was now apparently engaged in a power struggle with Yasser Arafat (see below). Some 400 prisoners were released in mid-August, but they did not include those members of Hamas and Islamic Jihad who had been involved in planning or executing attacks against Israeli targets. Along with Fatah, these two militant groups had declared a three-month cease-fire at the end of June. Following the cease-fire declaration, Israeli troops withdrew from key parts of northern and central Gaza and removed roadblocks from the arterial north–south highway. At the beginning of July Bethlehem was handed over to Palestinian control. The successful implementation of the roadmap was threatened, however, by Israel's ongoing construction of a 'security fence' in the West Bank.

Construction of Israel's 'security fence' in the West Bank had begun in mid-2002. Ostensibly intended to act as a barrier against Palestinian militants who infiltrated Israel to carry out attacks, by mid-2003 Israel was being accused of seeking to annex Palestinian territory. However, construction of the barrier continued despite international criticism, and Israel also maintained its policy of targeting and killing Palestinian militant leaders. A senior commander of Islamic Jihad in Hebron was killed by Israeli forces on 14 August; on 19 August a suicide bomber killed 20 Israelis on a bus in Jerusalem, an attack for which both Hamas and Islamic Jihad claimed responsibility; and Israel raided militant targets in both the West Bank and Gaza Strip. The resumption of hostilities between Israel and the Palestinian militant groups effectively marked the end of the cease-fire declared in June. A prominent member of Hamas, Ismael Abu Shanab, was killed in an Israeli missile attack on 21 August; the following day, Israel reimposed roadblocks on the main north–south highway in the Gaza Strip, a reversal of one of the first initiatives under the terms of the roadmap.

In mid-September 2003 it was reported that the Israeli Cabinet had agreed in principle to the removal of Yasser Arafat as 'a total obstacle to peace'. It was not made clear whether Israel sought to eliminate Arafat or to send him into exile, and although the US Administration declared that it was opposed to either outcome, the USA vetoed a UN Security Council resolution on 16 September condemning Israel's new policy, on the grounds that the resolution did not condemn the actions of Palestinian militant groups. At the end of October Sharon denied that Israel had any intention of 'removing' Yasser Arafat from power. Earlier in the month, the Israeli Cabinet approved the next phase of the 'security fence', and although the new sections were not contiguous to those already built, they would completely enclose Jewish settlements in the West Bank.

Israeli troops raided the West Bank town of Ramallah at the beginning of December 2003, arresting some 30 suspected Palestinian militants. Concurrently, senior Palestinian and Israeli political figures launched a new peace plan in Geneva, Switzerland. Yasser Abd ar-Rabbuh, the former Palestinian Minister of Information, and Yossi Beilin, Israel's former Minister of Justice, were the most prominent supporters of the so-called 'Geneva Accords', which did not have the official approval of either the Israeli or Palestinian administrations. The Geneva Accords outlined a two-state solution to the Israeli–Palestinian issue, including proposals that: Palestinians would receive compensation for giving up the right of return; most settlements in the West Bank and Gaza (except those neighbouring Jerusalem) would be dismantled; and Jerusalem (to become the capital of two states) would be divided administratively rather than physically.

On 19 December 2003 Israel declared that, unless the PA started disarming and disbanding Palestinian militant groups, it was prepared to initiate a 'disengagement plan', consisting of the accelerated construction of the 'security fence' in the West Bank and the physical separation of Israel from the Palestinian territories. In early February 2004 Ariel Sharon announced in an interview published in *Ha'aretz* that a plan had been drawn up for the evacuation of all Jewish settlements in the Gaza Strip. The evacuation would reportedly affect 7,500 settlers in 17 settlements (although details of the plan were subsequently amended—see below). This news was welcomed by the recently appointed Palestinian Prime Minister, Ahmad Quray. On 14 March 10 Israelis were killed in a double suicide bombing at the southern Israeli port of Ashdod, an attack for which both Hamas and the Al-Aqsa Martyrs Brigades claimed responsibility. In retaliation for the attack Ariel Sharon and his inner 'Security Cabinet' ordered Israel's most high profile 'targeted killing'. On 22 March Israeli helicopter gunships in the Gaza Strip attacked the founder and spiritual leader of Hamas, Sheikh Ahmad Yassin, and his entourage as they left a mosque, killing the cleric and several others. Yassin's assassination prompted international condemnation, especially from Iran and from Arab countries, where mass protests took place. However, a UN Security Council resolution condemning the killing was vetoed by the USA, which criticized the absence of any reference to Hamas as a 'terrorist organization'. Immediately after Yassin's assassination, Abd al-Aziz ar-Rantisi was appointed to the leadership of Hamas in Gaza; however, ar-Rantisi himself was killed in a targeted air-strike by Israeli forces in Gaza City on 17 April. EU leaders condemned both of the 'targeted killings' as illegal and unjustified. Hamas did not disclose the identity of ar-Rantisi's successor and reportedly adopted a policy of 'collective leadership' in order to prevent future leaders of the organization from being victims of Israel's strategy of 'targeted killings'. Khalid Meshaal apparently remained the head of the group's political bureau, based in Damascus, Syria. Meanwhile, details of Sharon's 'disengagement plan' were published in Israeli newspapers: the plan combined a complete Israeli withdrawal from the Gaza Strip, and evacuation of all Jewish settlements there, with the consolidation of six settlement blocs in the West Bank. In mid-May the US Secretary of State, Gen. Colin Powell, urged Quray to consider an Israeli withdrawal from the Gaza Strip as a sign of progress towards Palestinian self-sufficiency, while expressing US opposition to the demolition of Palestinian houses there. In late October the Israeli Knesset voted in favour of Sharon's proposal to dismantle all 21 settlements in Gaza, and four in the northern West Bank, entailing the eviction of about 9,000 Jewish settlers. The removal of settlements in Gaza was scheduled to commence in July 2005, but was later postponed until August (see below).

Meanwhile, in mid-May 2004 the Israeli army launched a major offensive in the Gazan town of Rafah in an effort to dismantle tunnels employed by Palestinian militants to smuggle weapons for use in attacks against Israelis. Some 20 people reportedly died when an Israeli helicopter gunship launched two missiles at a peaceful protest against the Israeli assault. Israel claimed that its operation was prompted by the killing by Palestinian militants of 13 of its troops. Some 43 Palestinians, mainly civilians, were killed in the raid, and hundreds of homes were destroyed.

In late May 2004 imprisoned Fatah leader Marwan Barghouthi was convicted by a Tel-Aviv court on five counts of murder and of leading a 'terrorist organization' which had launched Palestinian militant assaults on Israeli forces and settlers, although lack of evidence forced the court to acquit Barghouthi on 33 counts of resistance attacks. The court's verdict provoked strong criticism from the PA, which called the conviction 'illegal, immoral and unjust'. In early June Barghouthi was sentenced to five terms of life imprisonment and two additional 20-year terms.

Following a ruling by the Israeli Supreme Court, in late June 2004 Israel altered the route of part of the 'security fence', including a 30-km section in a Palestinian village, Beit Sourik. In early July the International Court of Justice (ICJ) in the Hague, Netherlands, issued a non-binding ruling that the barrier breached international law and effectively constituted the annexation of Palestinian land. The ICJ urged Israel to remove sections of the fence and to pay compensation to affected Palestinians. Sharon rejected the court's recommendations, while the Palestinian leadership hoped that the decision would mobilize public opinion. In late July the UN General Assembly voted to demand that Israel comply with the ICJ ruling and take down the barrier (the USA voted against the resolution). Meanwhile, Israel continued to build settlements in the West Bank: in mid-August Sharon approved the construction of 1,000 new Jewish homes there.

Palestinian attacks on Israeli targets and violent conflict between Israeli soldiers and Palestinian militants continued in August 2004. Quray condemned such actions as detrimental to the peace process, while Sharon vowed to continue his campaign against 'terrorism'. In early September, following a Hamas double suicide bombing in Beersheba, Israel, in late August which killed 16 people, Israeli tanks and aircraft attacked a Hamas training camp in the centre of the Gaza Strip. In mid-October the UN reported that 135 Palestinians had been killed and an estimated 95 homes destroyed following a 16-day Israeli military assault in northern and southern Gaza, prompted by a Hamas rocket that killed two children in Sderot, close to the border with Gaza.

Following the death of Yasser Arafat in early November 2004 (see below), Sharon expressed hope that the new Palestinian leadership would understand the need to end 'terrorist' attacks before relations between the two sides could be improved and outstanding issues resolved, and international leaders similarly looked forward to positive change, with US President Bush, urged by British Prime Minister Tony Blair, promising to redouble US efforts to assist in the creation of a Palestinian state, which he considered to be possible within four years.

In early December 2004 Israel and Egypt agreed that 750 Egyptian troops would be deployed along the country's border with Gaza in advance of Israel's planned withdrawal; however, Jewish settlers in Gaza vowed to resist eviction. In mid-December Mahmud Abbas issued a call (rejected by Hamas) for an end to the continuing use of violence in resistance to Israeli occupation, while in early January 2005, during the week of the Palestinian presidential election (see below), having earlier criticized Israeli offensives in Gaza as a ploy to disrupt the poll, he demanded that Israel release all Palestinian prisoners before they reached a political agreement. Abbas later strengthened his criticism of Israel, calling it 'the Zionist enemy' when Israeli armed forces responded to Palestinian mortar attacks by firing two shells into a field in Beit Lahiya, killing seven Palestinians. However, Abbas continued to express hopes of implementing the 'roadmap' peace plan and of achieving peace with Israel in the event of his election to the Palestinian presidency. Israel announced that it would withdraw troops from Palestinian areas prior to the election, and that its military would remain outside towns in the West Bank and Gaza Strip for 72 hours. Towards the end of December Israel released 159 Palestinian prisoners as a gesture of 'goodwill' prior to the Palestinian election.

Meanwhile, after it became clear in early January 2005 that Abbas's victory in the polls was a virtual certainty (see below), he announced that his initial aims were to meet Sharon, who had expressed a willingness to hold security talks with him but not full peace negotiations, and to persuade militant groups to cease attacks on Israeli targets. However, Hamas asserted that it had the right to resist Israeli occupation, and, despite repeated calls from Abbas for a cease-fire, Palestinian militant assaults continued, as did offences by Israeli forces (although attacks from both sides were of lesser intensity). Nevertheless, in mid-January the deaths of six Israelis in a Palestinian militant attack at the Karni crossing prompted Sharon to sever ties with the Palestinian leadership and to order the Israeli army to raid several areas of Gaza. Following a demand by the leadership of the PLO that Palestinians should cease all military action against Israel, Sharon called off the offensive in Gaza and announced that Israel would co-operate on security issues, although he instructed his troops to prepare for a full-scale assault on an area in the northern Gaza Strip from where rockets were being fired on Israeli targets, and in late January Palestinian security forces were deployed in the area to prevent such attacks; a marked decrease in violence was reported following the deployment. Meanwhile, in mid-January a first round of talks between Hamas, Islamic Jihad and other militant groups chaired by newly elected PA President Abbas, who was trying to persuade the organizations to declare a cease-fire, was described as 'positive' by Hamas; however, shortly after Abbas arrived in the Gaza Strip for the discussions a suicide bomb attack killed an Israeli and injured several others, and Hamas continued to insist on its right to retaliate against Israeli attacks and demanded that Israel released more than 7,000 Palestinian prisoners and end its policy of targeting militants before it would enter into negotiations.

Security talks between Palestinian and Israeli officials began in late January 2005, and, despite attacks on Palestinian police vehicles by Jewish settlers, the prospect of a meeting between Sharon and the Palestinian leadership was discussed and an agreement reached on the deployment of Palestinian security forces in the southern Gaza Strip within 24 hours to reduce attacks on Israeli targets. (By this time 2,500 Palestinian security forces were patrolling northern Gaza, on the orders of the new Palestinian President.) Hamas and Islamic Jihad dismissed an announcement by Israelis that 'targeted killings' of militants in areas where Palestinian security forces were successfully operating would stop, and Hamas demanded that Israel cease all military action. Israeli attacks continued, however, and Palestinian militants responded by firing mortar rounds against Jewish settlements. Later in the month the former Palestinian Minister of Security, Muhammad Dahlan, and the Israeli Minister of Defence, Lt-Gen. Shaul Mofaz, agreed to the withdrawal of Israeli troops and the deployment of PA security forces in the five West Bank towns of Ramallah, Qalqilya, Tulkarm, Jericho and Bethlehem.

Abbas and Sharon finally met in early February 2005 at a summit meeting held in Sharm esh-Sheikh, with Egypt's President Mubarak and King Abdullah of Jordan also in attendance. At the summit Abbas announced a Palestinian cease-fire and Sharon declared that Israeli military operations would end if Palestinian militant attacks stopped, emphasizing that Israel would not compromise in its fight against 'terrorism'; Sharon also agreed to release 500 Palestinian prisoners as a gesture of 'goodwill'. (The prisoner releases began later that month.) However, although some Palestinian militant groups signed up to the cease-fire, Hamas responded by asserting that it would not be bound by it, criticizing the fact that it had been negotiated unilaterally, and demanded that Israel cease all acts of aggression against Palestinians and release all Palestinian prisoners before agreeing to a formal cease-fire, although they apparently agreed to an informal 'truce'. Soon after the Sharm esh-Sheikh meeting, Israel permitted 56 deported Palestinians to return to the West Bank, and also transferred the bodies of 15 Palestinian bombers to the PA.

Meanwhile, several weeks of relatively little violence were interrupted in late February 2005 by a suicide bomb attack outside a nightclub in Tel-Aviv which killed four Israelis and injured about 50 people, halting Israeli plans to withdraw from the five West Bank towns. The Israeli army launched a raid into a West Bank village and arrested Palestinians suspected of involvement in the attack, but Israeli officials announced that their response would be limited to those who had actually masterminded the bombing (believed to be members of Islamic Jihad), while urging Abbas to intensify his crack-down on Palestinian militant organizations.

In early March 2005, at an international conference in support of the PA hosted by British Prime Minister Tony Blair in London, Abbas expressed his commitment to reforms and to a crack-down on militants, advocating renewed efforts to realize the objectives of the 'roadmap'. Shortly afterwards it was reported that Palestinian militant groups had declared their readiness to cease attacks against Israelis, although this was denied by Hamas, and Israel viewed the declaration with scepticism. Despite initial disagreement regarding the removal of an Israeli army checkpoint at the entrance to the town, in mid-March Israel officially surrendered Jericho to Palestinian security control. Israel also announced plans to remove all 24 of the outposts constructed since Sharon was elected to the premiership in February 2001, after a ministerial report condemned the illegal use of budget funds to develop the outposts. Although the move fulfilled a condition of the 'roadmap', it was criticized for the fact that not all of the 105 outposts, which were deemed by many to be illegal, would be dismantled. In late March 2005 Israeli forces withdrew from the West Bank town of Tulkarm.

Meanwhile, Israel continued to discuss the re-routing of the 'security fence'. In late February 2005 Israel announced plans to alter the route of the barrier so that it would cut out 7% of the territory of the West Bank instead of the 16% outlined in the original route. In mid-March the Israeli Government announced that the barrier (to be completed by the end of 2005) would divide the town of Bethlehem and also separate East Jerusalem and the settlement of Ma'aleh Edomin from the rest of the West Bank; the decision provoked protests by Palestinians, who demanded that the ICJ's recommendations be implemented and expressed concern at the unilateralism of the move and the negative impact that this could have on future peace talks with Israel.

In March and April 2005 there were almost daily reports of confrontations between Palestinian gunmen and security forces in the West Bank and Gaza Strip. In early April the Israeli army killed three young Palestinians in the Rafah refugee camp in Gaza. Although Israel claimed that the three had been attempting to smuggle weapons into Egypt, the sole survivor reportedly asserted that he and his friends had merely been playing football near an Israeli security zone. President Abbas condemned the killings as a breach of the truce, which Hamas and Islamic Jihad were considering revoking.

In late May 2005 Abbas travelled to Washington, DC, for his first meeting with President Bush since becoming President of the PA. Bush reportedly offered US $50m. in direct aid to the PA to develop the Gaza Strip after the Israeli withdrawal. The US President also urged Israel to dismantle illegal settlement outposts in the West Bank, to end the expansion of settlements and to ensure that Israel's 'security fence' did not become a 'political border'. Abbas later stated that he considered the talks very constructive, and advocated the start of 'final status' negotiations with Israel after its disengagement from the Gaza Strip.

In accordance with the agreement reached by Abbas and Sharon in February 2005 at Sharm esh-Sheikh, in late May the Israeli Government approved the release of 400 Palestinian prisoners. (A total of 398 prisoners were released in early June—two had chosen to remain in gaol.) Israel had released 500 prisoners shortly after the February summit meeting, but had delayed further releases, urging the PA to curb terrorism more effectively. Meanwhile, Palestinians in Gaza continued to fire rockets and mortar at Jewish settlements in Gaza, and at targets in Israel, prompting Israeli troops to attack the bases of militants whom they considered to be responsible for the assaults.

In late June 2005, following a series of Palestinian militant attacks on Israeli and Jewish targets (which the militants justified as retaliation for Israeli violations of the cease-fire, and for Israeli arrests of militants), Israel carried out raids across the West Bank and detained around 50 members of Islamic Jihad. The Israeli Minister of Defence, Lt-Gen. Shaul Mofaz, asserted that the PA's incompetence had prompted Israel to carry out the raids. Israel apparently readopted its policy of 'targeted assassinations' of militants (suspended at the February summit between Abbas and Sharon), when it launched a missile strike on Gaza in a failed attempt to kill an Islamic Jihad militant. Palestinian Minister of the Interior and National Security Maj.-Gen. Nasser Yousuf declared a state of emergency in the Gaza Strip, and gave his forces permission to prevent militants from launching rocket and mortar attacks on targets in Israel. Clashes broke out between members of the Palestinian security services and Hamas militants, in which two Palestinians were killed and 30 injured. As confrontations between Palestinian security officials and militants continued, Israel carried out further air attacks on Hamas targets, killing seven fighters. Abbas and Sharon held their second summit meeting since Abbas's election to the presidency in Jerusalem in late July. Sharon again urged Abbas to rein in militants and suppress terrorism. However, the two leaders reportedly failed to make any progress on any matter under discussion.

Islamic Jihad claimed responsibility for a suicide bomb attack near a shopping mall in Netanya in mid-July 2005 that killed four Israelis; President Abbas condemned the attack. Israeli troops re-entered Tulkarm (military control and responsibility for security of which Israel had surrendered to the PA in March—see above), after it was reported that the suicide bomber had come from a nearby village. Meanwhile, Hamas launched a series of rocket attacks from Gaza, killing an Israeli woman and prompting Israel to carry out air-strikes on targets in Gaza used by the militant group; no casualties were reported.

Although Israel's withdrawal from the Gaza Strip was accompanied by relatively little violence (see the chapter on Israel), in late August 2005 Israeli troops raided a refugee camp near Tulkarm, killing five Palestinians. Israel asserted that the five were suspected of involvement in two suicide bombings and had resisted arrest. In response, the Popular Resistance Committees claimed responsibility for firing a rocket that landed near Sderot. Israel completed its withdrawal from the Gaza Strip (according to the terms of its unilateral Disengagement Plan) ahead of schedule on 12 September, when the last Israeli forces left Gaza. Thousands of Palestinians entered the evacuated settlements and started to damage buildings and demolish synagogues. Although in early July Israeli and Palestinian officials had reportedly agreed in principle to establish a 'safe passage' between the West Bank and Gaza Strip following the withdrawal, the status of Gaza's southern crossing into Egypt at Rafah was still disputed. Soon after it had completed the disengagement, Israel declared that the crossing would be closed for six months. Meanwhile, in late August Israel had approved the deployment of 750 Egyptian troops along Egypt's border with the Gaza Strip, having accepted Egypt's offer to deploy the troops in December 2004 (see above). In mid-November 2005, following intervention by US Secretary of State Condoleezza Rice, Israel reached an agreement with Palestinian officials to reopen the Rafah crossing, despite having declared in September that it would not allow it to be reopened for six months (see above). The PA, assisted by European monitors, was to manage the crossing, which Israeli, Palestinian and EU observers were to monitor remotely from a control centre via live television cameras. The crossing was opened in late November.

In late September 2005 21 people were killed and some 80 wounded when a Palestinian truck carrying rockets exploded during a Hamas parade in the Jabalia refugee camp in the Gaza Strip. Hamas accused Israel of having fired a missile at the truck from a remote-controlled drone aircraft; both Israel and the PA denied the accusation. However, Hamas responded by launching mortars into Sderot, injuring five people. The Israeli Government decided at an emergency meeting to permit the army to use any means necessary to suppress militants. Accordingly, the Israeli army stationed tanks and artillery batteries on Gaza's eastern and northern borders, began seizing Hamas and Islamic Jihad activists in the West Bank and readopted its policy of 'targeted killings', using air-strikes to kill militants in Gaza and to destroy a weapons store and weapons-production facilities, despite a pledge from Hamas to end attacks and return to the cease-fire. Abbas condemned the operations as unjustified aggression. Later in the month Israel killed three militants in the West Bank.

The PA released figures in mid-October 2005 showing that more than one-half of the 437 Palestinians killed during the year had been killed by other Palestinians. Meanwhile, earlier in the month Palestinian police clashed with Hamas militants in Gaza City; a police commander and two civilians died as a result of the violence. The following day police-officers forced their way into the Palestinian legislative building in Gaza City and disrupted proceeding for 15 minutes, in order to protest against the poor provision of military equipment to them during their recent clash with Hamas.

Later in October 2005 Israeli soldiers killed two senior Islamic Jihad militants in Tulkarm, and arrested five other members of the Tulkarm cell, which Israel believed to be responsible for the suicide attacks in Tel-Aviv in February 2005 and in Netanya in July, and to be planning further attacks. Islamic Jihad vowed to avenge the killings: later in the month it launched a suicide bomb attack on a market in Hadera, killing five Israelis. Israeli Prime Minister Ariel Sharon declared a 'broad and continuous' offensive against militant Islamist groups, and hours later the Israeli army launched an air-strike on a car carrying two senior Islamic Jihad militants in Gaza: eight Palestinians, mostly civilians, died. Israeli forces killed further militants linked to attacks on Israeli targets throughout November. In early December Islamic Jihad launched a further suicide attack on the shopping mall in Netanya that it had targeted in July, killing a further five Israelis. Israel responded by arresting Palestinians thought to be associated with the bomber, and carrying out air-strikes to target further militants.

Israel reacted to Hamas's victory in the legislative elections held in January 2006 (see below) by declaring that it would not negotiate with a Palestinian authority that included 'an armed terrorist organization' that advocated Israel's destruction; US President Bush announced that his country would also refuse to deal with Hamas, which it considered a terrorist organization, until it renounced its call to destroy Israel, and would consider halting aid to the Palestinians. The Quartet group urged Hamas to renounce violence, respect agreements approved by the Fatah regime and recognize Israel's right to exist, and declared that financial assistance to a future administration would depend on how Hamas responded to such calls. Egypt and Jordan later also demanded that the militant organization reject violence and accept Israel's existence. The head of Hamas's political bureau, Khalid Meshaal, announced that his organization could enter a long-term truce with Israel, under certain conditions, including the return of Israel to its pre-1967 borders. However, Meshaal asserted that violent resistance of the occupation was legal.

In mid-February 2006 Israel announced that, in order to punish the new Palestinian regime until it renounced violence and recognized Israel's right to exist, it would stop collecting customs and tax revenues on Palestinians' behalf, and would ask foreign donors to cease all payments to the PA; however, it would permit the transfer of humanitarian aid to the Palestinians. President Abbas announced that the PA faced a financial crisis, while Hamas asserted that Arab and Islamic countries would compensate for a reduction in aid from Israel and the West. Later in the month the EU, which considered Hamas to be a terrorist organization, announced that it was to give the PA US $140m.-worth of aid to save the interim administration from financial collapse; however, the EU refused to indicate whether it would finance any future Hamas-led administration. In the event, following the installation of the new Cabinet on 28 March, both the USA and the EU announced that they were withdrawing direct aid to the PA until Hamas fulfilled the three conditions placed on it by the Quartet group following Hamas's election victory.

Meanwhile, as Israel continued to kill militants in the Palestinian territories following further missile strikes, it declared that, should Hamas resume attacks on Israel, all members of the organization would be deemed to be legitimate targets for assassinations, including Prime Minister-designate Ismail Haniya and future ministers. In mid-March 2006 Israeli forces stormed the gaol in Jericho in which the Secretary-General of the PFLP, Ahmad Saadat, was being held prisoner, detaining him and other inmates suspected of involvement in attacks on Israel. US and British monitors had left the gaol just prior to the raid, ostensibly to protest against poor security arrangements there. A Palestinian high court had announced in 2002 that there was no evidence that Saadat had been involved in Rechavam Ze'evi's murder, and both President Abbas and Hamas had recently announced plans to release him, as he had been elected to the PLC at the elections in January 2006. Israel, however, still wished to interrogate him in connection with the murder, and therefore resolved to detain him before the Palestinian authorities released him. The raid, in which two Palestinians were killed, provoked unrest throughout the territories. Palestinians set fire to the British Council building in Jericho in protest at perceived British collusion with the Israeli authorities, and gunmen kidnapped 11 foreign workers (they were released the following day). Palestinian factions urged schools and businesses to go on strike, and the PFLP vowed to avenge Saadat's capture, which President Abbas condemned as a crime and a humiliation for Palestinians. In late April the Israeli Ministry of Justice announced that a pre-trial inquiry had not produced enough evidence to try Saadat for Ze'evi's murder, but that he would be tried for other security offences. However, four other militant PFLP members detained with him were charged with the murder, among them the man accused of firing the shot.

Legislative elections took place on 20 January 1996, with the participation of some 79% of the estimated 1m. eligible Palestinian voters, selecting 88 deputies to the 89-seat PLC. (One seat was reserved for the president of the Council's executive body—the Palestinian President.) Although irregularities were reported during voting, these were not regarded as sufficiently serious to compromise the final outcome. At the concurrent election for a Palestinian Executive President, Yasser Arafat defeated his only rival, Samiha Khalil, winning 88.1% of the votes cast, and took office as President on 12 February. Deputies returned to the PLC automatically became members of the PNC, the existing 483 members of which were subsequently permitted to return from exile by the Israeli authorities. The PLC held its first session in Gaza City on 7 March, electing Ahmad Quray as its Speaker.

At the 21st session of the PNC, held in Gaza City on 22–24 April 1996, the PNC voted to amend the Palestinian National Charter (or PLO Covenant) by annulling those clauses that sought the destruction of the State of Israel and those that were inconsistent with the agreement of mutual recognition concluded by Israel and the PLO in September 1993. At the close of its session the PNC elected a new Executive Committee, and in May 1996 President Arafat appointed a Palestinian Cabinet. The appointments were approved by the PLC in July.

In April 1997 Arafat's audit office disclosed evidence of the misappropriation by PA ministers of some US $326m. of public funds. The PA General Prosecutor, Khalid al-Qidram, resigned in response to the findings, and was reportedly placed under house arrest in June. In August the findings of a parliamentary committee appointed by Arafat to investigate the affair led to the resignation of the Cabinet; however, the ministers were to remain in office in a provisional capacity until new appointments were made in early 1998. In March the PLC threatened to hold a vote of 'no confidence' in Arafat's leadership, in protest at alleged corruption within the PA, as well as at the prolonged delay in approval of budget proposals for 1998 and at the failure to hold local government elections. The Cabinet resigned in June, apparently in order to obstruct another 'no confidence' motion. A new Cabinet was appointed by Arafat in August, but soon attracted criticism from officials of the principal international organizations granting funds to the PA. In November donors pledged aid worth more than $3,000m., to be disbursed over the next five years. In October 1998 the PA was again accused of financial mismanagement, after customs revenues amounting to some $70m. allegedly failed to be deposited at the PA treasury.

US officials reportedly confirmed in March 1998 that the CIA was assisting the Palestinian security forces in the spheres of espionage, information-gathering and interrogation, in an attempt to reassure the Israeli Government of the PA's ability to take effective action against groups involved in attacks on Israeli targets. (Under the terms of the Wye Memorandum, the CIA was to monitor the PA's compliance with the security provisions of the accord.) In October the PA detained 11 journalists who had attempted to obtain an interview with the spiritual leader of Hamas, Sheikh Ahmad Yassin (who was subsequently placed under house arrest); Palestinian police also arrested an outspoken cleric and Islamic Jihad's chief spokesman for publicly criticizing the newly signed Wye Memorandum (see above). In subsequent weeks several radio and television stations, as well as press offices, were closed down by the PA, and numerous journalists were imprisoned. There was also a marked increase in self-censorship in the state-controlled and pro-Government media.

In January 1999 the PLC approved a motion urging an end to political detentions and the release of all those imprisoned on exclusively political charges; the motion further demanded the formation of a special committee to assess the case of every political prisoner in the Palestinian territories and to recommend prisoner releases. The committee was duly appointed in February, under the chairmanship of the Minister of Justice. Despite the release of 37 political prisoners by the PA, however, in late January Hamas and Islamic Jihad activists began a hunger strike in Jericho and Nablus, in protest at their continued detention without trial. In early February some 3,000 protesters marched to the headquarters of the PA, whom they accused of 'subservience to Israel and the CIA'. In March a security agent and former member of Hamas's military wing was sentenced to death for the killing of a Palestinian intelligence officer in Rafah. The verdict provoked serious clashes between Palestinian police and protesters in the Gaza Strip, and Arafat was forced to curtail an official visit to Jordan to address the domestic security crisis. In November 20 leading Palestinian intellectuals (including members of the PLC) issued a joint statement in which they criticized alleged corruption, mismanagement and abuse of power within the PA, and accused Palestinian officials of ineffectiveness in the peace talks with Israel. An official crack-down on Arafat's critics was subsequently instigated, during which several of the document's signatories were detained or placed under house arrest (they were later released on bail). The establishment, announced in January 2000, of a Higher Council for Development under Arafat's chairmanship was welcomed by foreign donors as a major step towards ending corruption and mismanagement within the Palestinian administration.

In August 1999 a Palestinian national dialogue conference was held in Cairo, Egypt, between representatives of Fatah and the PFLP. Later in August Arafat and the Secretary-General of the DFLP, Naif Hawatmeh, met, also in Cairo, for the first time since 1993. At the end of the month representatives of nine Palestinian political factions, meeting in Ramallah, agreed on an agenda for a comprehensive national dialogue; Hamas and Islamic Jihad, however, refused to participate. In late September the PFLP's deputy leader, Abu Ali Moustafa, was permitted by the Israeli Government to return to the West Bank from exile in Jordan, in order to participate in reconciliation talks with Arafat. George Habash stepped down as leader of the PFLP in April 2000, and Abu Ali Moustafa was elected to lead the organization in July. (Following Moustafa's assassination in August 2001, Ahmad Saadat assumed the party leadership.)

In February 2000 a controversial visit to the Palestinian Autonomous Areas by the French Prime Minister, Lionel Jospin (who described Hezbollah's resistance in southern Lebanon as 'terrorism'), provoked an outbreak of violent clashes between Palestinian civilians and the security forces in the West Bank. About 120 students were arrested, and the PA declared that henceforth all marches, rallies and public gatherings would require the prior consent of the police. Meanwhile, in late 1999 Human Rights Watch had urged Arafat to take action in order to increase press freedom. In May 2000 the chief news editor at the Voice of Palestine radio station, Fathi Barqawi, was arrested after publicly criticizing the PA's 'secret' talks with Israel in Sweden. During May and June the PA intensified its crack-down on political activists and journalists who criticized Arafat's administration: four television and two radio stations were reportedly shut down by the authorities.

The start of the al-Aqsa *intifada* by Palestinians in September 2000 moved some analysts to suggest that Arafat's influence over Palestinians might be waning, as other Fatah leaders began to pursue their own agendas and to speak out against the President: Marwan Barghouthi, in particular, was said to be attracting considerable support among Palestinians in the West Bank, where he was the regional leader of Fatah. In December a court in Nablus sentenced to death a Palestinian who had been convicted of collaborating with Israeli secret services in the assassination of a Hamas commander. The harsh sentence apparently signalled a change in policy by the PA, which in January 2001 carried out the executions, by firing squad, of two alleged collaborators. The Al-Aqsa Martyrs Brigades claimed responsibility for the assassination in mid-January of Hisham Mekki, the Chairman of Palestinian Satellite Television, director of the state broadcasting corporation and a close associate of Arafat. In August a group of Palestinians were sentenced to death, and at least 100 others arrested, on charges of having collaborated with Israeli security services in recent attacks against Hamas officials. In early October three Palestinians were killed by security forces in Gaza during violent protests in support of Osama bin Laden. Although the al-Qa'ida leader claimed to have launched the previous month's suicide attacks against the USA partly in protest against Israel's occupation of Palestinian territory, the PA sought to distance itself from the atrocities.

A report published by Human Rights Watch at the end of November 2001 accused the PA of systematic abuses of human rights since the start of the al-Aqsa *intifada*, citing incidences of arbitrary arrests and of detention without trial and torture of prisoners. When Sheikh Ahmad Yassin was placed under house arrest in early December, hundreds of Hamas supporters demanded his release, resulting in clashes between Hamas gunmen and security forces. Fierce protests by militants also ensued in mid-January 2002 when Palestinian security services in Ramallah arrested the PFLP leader, Ahmad Saadat. There were also an increasing number of 'vigilante killings': in early February a crowd led by members of the security services entered a military court in Jenin and killed three defendants, two of whom had just been sentenced to death for the murder of a security official; in mid-March a suspected collaborator was hanged in Ramallah; and during one day in early April 2002 11 alleged collaborators were reportedly murdered by Palestinians in Tulkarm, Qalqilya and Bethlehem.

At an emergency meeting of the PA leadership held following Arafat's release from Israeli house arrest in early May 2002, the Minister of Parliamentary Affairs, Nabil Amr, tendered his resignation, reportedly after the President had rejected his proposals for a reorganization of the Cabinet. Arafat implemented major government changes in early June: membership of the Cabinet was reduced from 31 ministers to 21, with several ministries being either merged or abolished. Maj.-Gen. Abd ar-Razzaq al-Yahya was appointed Minister of the Interior—a position previously held by Arafat. Dr Salam Fayyad was named as the new Minister of Finance. The new Government was described as an 'interim' administration, and its main task was to be the preparation and supervision of far-reaching reforms, including the organization of municipal elections towards the end of 2002 and of presidential and legislative elections by early 2003. The planned reforms would also include the streamlining of the Palestinian security services. Perhaps most importantly, draft legislation was being prepared that would create a new post of Prime Minister, to be responsible for the day-to-day administration of the PA. President Bush emphasized in late June 2002 that, if the PA undertook constitutional and judicial reforms, the USA would give its support to the creation of a 'provisional Palestinian state'. On 11 September the entire Palestinian Cabinet resigned in order to prevent a vote of 'no confidence' being brought in the legislature; however, the Cabinet was to remain in place until the appointment of a new administration (which was announced in late October). On the same day the PA President set 20 January 2003 as the day on which legislative and presidential elections were to be held. However, in late December 2002 Arafat announced a postponement of the polls, claiming that it would be untenable to hold elections while Israel continued to occupy PA-controlled population centres in the West Bank and Gaza.

Palestinian representatives participated in a conference on reform of the Palestinian administration, held in London in mid-January 2003, via a video link, after the Israeli Government refused to allow the delegates to attend the talks following a double suicide bombing in Tel-Aviv (in which more than 20 Israelis died). At the conference, which was also attended by officials of the Quartet group (comprising the USA, Russia, the UN and the EU) and representatives from Jordan, Egypt and Saudi Arabia, it was agreed that a new draft Palestinian constitution would be presented within two weeks. In mid-March the PLC endorsed a bill defining the role to be played by a future Palestinian Prime Minister, after having rejected amendments to the legislation proposed by Arafat according to which the President would retain authority over the appointment of Cabinet ministers. In the proposed power-sharing arrangement, the President was reportedly to control security and foreign affairs and would also have the authority to appoint and dismiss a premier, while the Prime Minister would nominate ministers and retain responsibility for domestic affairs. Mahmud Abbas, the Secretary-General of the PLO Executive Committee, formally accepted the post of Prime Minister on 19 March; on 29 April the Palestinian legislature endorsed his appointment. A newly expanded Palestinian Cabinet was announced on that day, comprising 25 ministers under the premiership of Mahmud Abbas (who also became Minister of the Interior). Muhammad Dahlan was confirmed as the Minister of State for Security Affairs, while Dr Nabil Shaath was named as the Minister of External Affairs and Saeb Erakat as the Minister of Negotiation Affairs. Dr Salam Fayyad—who some had believed would become premier—retained the finance portfolio in the new administration. The announcement of the new PA Cabinet prompted the publication of the Quartet-sponsored 'roadmap' peace plan (see above).

Ongoing tensions between Arafat and Abbas appeared to be the principal reason for the resignation of Saeb Erakat in mid-May 2003. Erakat was regarded as an Arafat ally and had traditionally been at the forefront of Palestinian negotiations with Israel; however, his resignation was interpreted as a protest against his omission from the Palestinian delegation, which included Abbas, Muhammad Dahlan and the PLC Speaker, Ahmad Quray, scheduled to hold talks with Ariel Sharon and leading Israeli officials. Immediately following the Aqaba summit (see above), Abbas had engaged in a round of discussions with Hamas and Islamic Jihad to effect a cease-fire in attacks by those groups against Israeli targets; despite an early walk-out by Hamas, a cease-fire was duly brought into effect at the end of June, with the support of Fatah. Abbas and Arafat continued to clash on the issue of security: after a meeting of the Fatah Central Committee on 7 July, Abbas offered to resign, having been criticized for making too many concessions to Israel. On 2 August Palestinian security forces arrested 20 militants, mostly believed to belong to the Al-Aqsa Martyrs Brigades, who were sheltering in Arafat's Ramallah compound. Arafat's appointment of a new National Security Adviser, Brig.-Gen. Jibril Rajoub (who had been dismissed as commander of the Preventive Security Force in the West Bank in 2002), on 25 August, was interpreted as a snub to Abbas and Muhammad Dahlan: as head of the National Security Council, Rajoub would be *de facto* commander in the field of the Palestinian security forces. (Rajoub was reported to have resigned from the post in January 2005.)

Mahmud Abbas resigned as Prime Minister in early September 2003, seemingly representing the culmination of his power struggle with Arafat over control of the Palestinian security apparatus. Arafat nominated the Speaker of the PLC, Ahmad Quray to replace Abbas. Also at that time, Saeb Erakat was reinstated as Minister of Negotation Affairs, and it appeared that Arafat had effectively regained control of the PA. However, on 5 October Yasser Arafat declared a state of emergency in the Palestinian territories, following Israel's continuing construction of the 'security fence' (see above) and the arrest of a key member of Islamic Jihad; he also announced the establishment of an eight-member Emergency Cabinet. However, shortly after the formation of the Emergency Cabinet, Quray reportedly offered his resignation. On 12 November the PLC approved Ahmad Quray's first full Cabinet. Ministers who retained their portfolios from the previous administration under Mahmud Abbas included Dr Nabil Shaath as Minister of Foreign Affairs and Dr Salam Fayyad as Minister of Finance; notable new appointments included Hakam Balawi as Minister of the Interior and Nahid ar-Rayyis as Minister of Justice. Rafiq an-Natsheh was elected Speaker of the PLC.

In late November 2003 the EU initiated an investigation into claims that EU funding for the PA had been channelled to the Al-Aqsa Martyrs Brigades. An audit of the PA's finances carried out by the IMF in 2003 had estimated that in the period 1995–2000 nearly US $900m. had been diverted into accounts controlled by Yasser Arafat. Moreover, documents seized by Israeli forces during the reoccupation of Palestinian areas in 2001 reportedly revealed that some EU funds had been used by the Al-Aqsa Martyrs Brigades. In late February 2004 Israeli soldiers raided banks in Ramallah in an operation to seize funds reputedly belonging to Palestinian militant groups. The Arab Bank and the Cairo-Amman Bank were among those raided, and it was later reported that nearly $9m. had been confiscated.

In early December 2003 Quray held talks in Cairo with the principal militant organizations, including Fatah, Hamas, Islamic Jihad and the PFLP, in order to achieve a full cessation of attacks against Israeli targets. Several of the Palestinian groups rejected a total cease-fire, and a joint statement by all parties at the conclusion of the talks stated that while attacks against civilian targets inside Israel would cease, attacks would continue against Israeli military targets and Jewish settlements in the Palestinian areas. In early February 2004 more than 300 members of Fatah resigned from the group in protest at alleged corruption and the failure to instigate reform, particularly with regard to elections to the leadership of the organization, which had last been held in 1989.

In July 2004 Arafat's authority was further threatened by mass disorder in the Gaza Strip, in protest against PA corruption and incompetence, as well as a threat by Prime Minister Quray to bring about the collapse of the administration if his powers were not increased. In mid-July Arafat took measures against the growing anarchy in Gaza, discharging two senior security commanders, declaring a state of emergency, and sending loyal troops to protect official buildings in Gaza. He also replaced the national police chief and the commander of general security forces in Gaza (the latter with his cousin, Musa Arafat), and amalgamated eight rival security forces into three, following internal pressure on Arafat to combat corruption and to reform the PA and its security services. However, Fatah members demanding reforms rejected those introduced by the President as 'superficial and unconvincing', and pressure on Arafat (especially from the Al-Aqsa Martyrs Brigades) apparently forced him to reverse his decision to appoint his cousin as head of security. In late July Quray reportedly announced his resignation (which was rejected by Arafat) after chaos erupted in Gaza following the kidnapping of the Palestinian police commander, a colonel in the PA security forces and four French aid workers. However, Quray later announced his intention to stay in office as 'caretaker' Prime Minister, having, according to one of his ministers, urged Arafat to forgo some of his powers to prevent the PA from collapsing further. Yet Quray did little to combat the widespread poverty in the Palestinian territories, a principal cause of popular anger, nor to address the power struggle within the Fatah movement, and in early August the Minister of Justice, Nahid ar-Rayyis, resigned, citing the ongoing disorder in Gaza.

It was announced on 11 November 2004 that Yasser Arafat, who had been undergoing treatment at a military hospital in France, had died. In accordance with Palestinian law, the Speaker of the PLC, Rawhi Fattouh, was sworn in as acting President, pending elections due to take place in the territories within 60 days. Mahmud Abbas assumed the chairmanship of the PLO, and Quray was chosen to head the National Security Council in addition to taking charge of the administration of the PA. Farouk Kaddoumi was appointed leader of Fatah.

In late November 2004 Abbas was nominated to contest the elections as Fatah's only candidate. Although the Al-Aqsa Martyrs Brigades supported Abbas, concern was expressed at the possibility of inciting militants' anger, and further fighting within the group, if Abbas conceded too much to the Israelis. In early December Hamas declared that it would not be fielding a candidate for the forthcoming election, which they urged voters to boycott, while Marwan Barghouthi registered as a candidate. Islamic Jihad also announced a boycott of the ballot. Palestinian election officials declared that a total of 10 candidates had qualified for registration, including a human rights activist, Mustafa Barghouthi, who was to stand as an independent. Marwan Barghouthi later withdrew from the campaign, following pressure on him to give Abbas the best chance of securing the presidency; it had been feared that, had Barghouthi won the ballot, Israel would have refused to negotiate with him due to his imprisonment.

The first municipal elections to be held in the West Bank since 1976 began on 23 December 2004, at which Hamas, participating in an election in the Palestinian territories for the first time, won 16 councils and Fatah secured nine, with the two movements to share the control of one municipality. At the local elections held in the Gaza Strip in late January 2005 Hamas secured control of seven of the 10 councils. The lack of support for Fatah was attributed to its association with corruption, while voters were encouraged by Hamas's provision of welfare and educational services and by its opposition to Israel.

The election to appoint a successor to Yasser Arafat was held in the West Bank, Gaza Strip and East Jerusalem on 9 January 2005. The Palestinian Central Elections Commission (CEC) asserted that the presence of Israeli forces in Jerusalem interfered with the voting process, forcing international observers to intervene. Moreover, polling centres remained open for an extra two hours because some citizens had difficulty locating them, and owing to problems with voter registration. However, international observers considered the overall conduct of the election to have been free and fair. Final results showed that, from the seven candidates, Abbas had received 62.5% of votes cast, and Mustafa Barghouthi had taken 19.5%. Abbas was sworn in as Executive President of the PA on 15 January.

In early February 2005 a Hamas militant attack on Israeli army outposts and settlements in the Gaza strip prompted Abbas to dismiss senior security commanders. Later in the month the PLC voted to approve a new Cabinet under Prime Minister Ahmad Quray. Dr Nabil Shaath was appointed Deputy Prime Minister and Minister of Information; Shaath's previous role as Minister of Foreign Affairs was assumed by Dr Nasser al-Kidwa, hitherto the Palestinian representative to the UN. Maj.-Gen. Nasr Yousuf became Minister of the Interior and National Security, while Dr Salam Fayyad retained the finance portfolio. Quray pledged the new administration's determination to heighten security and combat poverty.

In late March 2005, after militants from the Fatah-affiliated Al-Aqsa Martyrs Brigades reportedly shot at the presidential compound in Ramallah, President Abbas removed the military chief in the West Bank and the Ramallah district commander, explaining that the security apparatus had failed and needed to be reorganized. In an effort to consolidate various (often rival) factions into a unified command, in late April Abbas nominated four new heads of security forces in the West Bank and Gaza Strip, and ordered 10 senior officers to resign.

A reported 82% of eligible voters took part in a second round of municipal elections in the West Bank and Gaza Strip on 5 May 2005. According to official results, 45 of the 84 municipal districts contested were to be governed by councils with a majority of Fatah representatives (which took 56% of votes). Hamas, which had not participated in the presidential elections, took 23 councils (33% of votes), and left-wing and independent lists secured 16 councils. Later in the month the CEC declared that elections to the PLC, scheduled for July, would be delayed while the PLC ratified a new elections law, intended to replace the system of simple majority by which the 1996 general elections had been held, with a 'mixed' electoral system (see President and Legislature). The PLC ratified the new law in mid-June 2005. In late August Abbas issued a decree setting 25 January 2006 as the date for the legislative elections. A third round of municipal elections was held in 82 towns and villages in the West Bank on 29 September 2005. Fatah won a reported 54% of the votes, and Hamas took 26%. At local elections in some of the largest cities in the West Bank conducted on 15 December, Fatah won 35% of the 414 contested seats, and Hamas took 26%. However, although Fatah retained control of Ramallah, Hamas notably gained control of Nablus and Jenin.

In accordance with Palestinian elections law (which stipulates that officials intending to contest seats in elections to the PLC must resign their posts two months in advance of the ballot), various ministers were reported to have submitted their resignations in late November 2005, including the Minister of Finance, Dr Salam Fayyad. Prime Minister Ahmad Quray also resigned in mid-December in order to be eligible to take part in the elections. Deputy Prime Minister and Minister of Information Dr Nabil Shaath was appointed to replace him; however, later in the month Quray declared that he would not take part in the poll, and returned to his former post.

In late December 2005 Israel announced that it would not allow Arabs in East Jerusalem to vote if Hamas participated in the forthcoming legislative elections. After PA officials threatened to postpone the elections, in mid-January 2006 Israel declared that it would allow a small number of Arabs in East Jerusalem to vote, and that candidates from groups other than Hamas could campaign there. In the event, Hamas, competing as the Change and Reform list in order to avoid a ban on their direct participation, secured 74 of the 132 seats, and Fatah retained 45. Other groups, including the PFLP (contesting the poll as Martyr Abu Ali Moustafa) and independents, also achieved representation. Quray announced the resignation of his administration on 26 January.

The new PLC was inaugurated on 18 February 2006. Aziz Duweik was appointed to replace Rawhi Fattouh as Speaker, and President Abbas called on Hamas to establish a new administration. Hamas subsequently held discussions with Abbas and with other factions, including Fatah, concerning the possibility of forming a coalition administration of 'national unity', and nominated Ismail Haniya as Prime Minister. Haniya, who had led the organization's national list for the elections, had held senior positions within Hamas, and had actively participated in many of its activities. Imprisoned in Israeli gaols in 1987–89 for his participation in the first *intifada* and leading one of Hamas's security apparatuses, Haniya had survived an Israeli assassination attempt in 2003, five years after assuming control of Sheikh Ahmad Yassin's office.

Hamas began to assert its authority at a PLC session in early March 2006 when it reversed legislation that the Fatah-led parliament had approved immediately prior to its dissolution. Fatah deputies walked out of the session, asserting that Hamas had no right to reverse their decisions. The new laws had given President Abbas further powers, apparently in an attempt to increase his authority and curb that of parliament, in anticipation of Fatah's rival's domination of the legislature. One of the rulings had provided for the establishment of a constitutional court and granted President Abbas the right to elect its members.

Hamas leaders continued their attempts to persuade Fatah to join Hamas in an administration of 'national unity'. However, in late March 2006, after weeks of discussions between the two factions, Fatah rejected Hamas's offer, and Hamas decided to form a cabinet alone. One of the most important matters of dispute had been Hamas's rejection of bilateral Israeli-Palestinian agreements approved by the former legislature: Hamas considered that by recognizing these accords it would be accepting Israeli occupation of Palestinian territory.

The PLC approved Hamas's proposed Cabinet on 28 March 2006, and President Abbas inaugurated the new administration on the following day. Notable appointees included Nasser ash-Shaer as Deputy Prime Minister and Minister of Education and Higher Education, Mahmud az-Zahhar as Minister of Foreign Affairs, Said Siyam as Minister of the Interior and Civil Affairs, and Omar ar-Razik as Minister of Finance. One woman and one Christian were appointed, as Minister of Women's Affairs and Minister of Tourism and Antiquities, respectively.

Government

In accordance with the Declaration of Principles on Palestinian Self-Rule and the Cairo Agreement on the Gaza Strip and Jericho (see Recent History, above), the PLO assumed control of the Jericho area of the West Bank and of the Gaza Strip on 17 May 1994. In November and December 1995, under the terms of the Israeli-Palestinian Interim Agreement on the West Bank and the Gaza Strip concluded in September 1995, Israeli armed forces withdrew from the West Bank towns of Nablus, Ramallah, Jenin, Tulkarm, Qalqilya and Bethlehem. In late December the PLO assumed responsibility in some 17 areas of civil administration in the town of Hebron. The Interim Agreement divided the West Bank into three zones: Areas A, B and C. As of July 1998, the PA had sole jurisdiction and security control in Area A (2% of the West Bank), but Israel retained authority over movement into and out of the area. In Area B (26% of the West Bank) the PA had some limited authority while Israel remained in control of security. Area C, the remaining 72% of the West Bank, was under Israeli military occupation. In accordance with the Wye Memorandum of October 1998 (see Recent History), Israel effected a further redeployment of its armed forces from approximately 500 sq km of West Bank territory in November. Of this, about 400 sq km became Area A territory and the remainder Area B territory. The Sharm esh-Sheikh Memorandum of September 1999 (see Recent History) was intended to facilitate completion of outstanding commitments under agreements previously signed, as well as to enable the resumption of 'final status' negotiations with Israel. By October 2000 approximately 17.2% of the West Bank (Area A) was under sole Palestinian jurisdiction and security control, although Israel retained authority over access to and from the zone; about 23.8% (Area B) was under Israeli military control, with the PA responsible for civil administration and public order; the remaining 59% (Area C) remained under Israeli military occupation. Israel implemented its unilateral Disengagement Plan, according to which it dismantled Israeli military installations and settlements in the Gaza Strip, and withdrew from four settlements in the West Bank, in August–September 2005 (see Recent History). The total area of the territory over which the PA will eventually assume control, and the extent of its jurisdiction there, remain subject to 'final status' talks.

Defence

Paramilitary forces in the Gaza Strip and in the areas of the West Bank where the PA has assumed responsibility for security totalled an estimated 56,000 in August 2005; however, figures for personnel strength in the various forces were unknown. (Security forces in the Palestinian territories were undergoing a major restructuring at this time.) Paramilitary forces of 29,000 in August 2002 included a Public Security Force of 14,000 (Gaza 6,000, West Bank 8,000); a Civil Police Force of 10,000 (Gaza 4,000, West Bank 6,000); a Preventive Security Force of 3,000 (Gaza 1,200, West Bank 1,800); a General Intelligence Force of 1,000; a Military Intelligence Force of 500; and a Presidential Security Force of an estimated 500. In addition, there are small forces belonging to Coastal Police, Civil Defence, Air Force, a Customs and Excise Police Force and a University Security Service. Units of the Palestine National Liberation Army (PNLA) are garrisoned in various countries in the Middle East and North Africa. The public security and order budget of the Palestinian Autonomous Areas was estimated at US $433.9m. in 2004.

Economic Affairs

In 2003, according to estimates by the World Bank, the gross national income (GNI) of the West Bank and the Gaza Strip, measured at average 2001–03 prices, was US $3,771m., equivalent to $1,120 per head. During 1995–2004, it was estimated, the population increased at an average annual rate of 4.3%, while in 1995–2003 gross domestic product (GDP) per head decreased, in real terms, by an average of 6.9% per year. Overall GDP decreased, in real terms, at an average annual rate of 2.8% in 1995–2003; GDP declined by an estimated 19.1% in 2002 and by some 1.7% in 2003.

Agriculture and fishing contributed 10.7% of the GDP of the West Bank and Gaza Strip in 2004, according to official figures. In mid-2005 agriculture (including hunting, forestry and fishing) engaged an estimated 15.6% of the employed Palestinian labour force. Citrus fruits are the principal export crop, and horticulture also makes a significant contribution to trade. Other important crops are tomatoes, cucumbers, olives and grapes. The livestock sector is also significant. According to the World Bank, agricultural GDP decreased at an average annual rate of 4.0% during 1995–2003. Agricultural GDP declined by 19.8% in 2002 and by 2.6% in 2003.

Industry (including mining, manufacturing, electricity and water supply, and construction) contributed 20.6% of Palestinian GDP in 2004. The industrial sector engaged some 26.2% of the employed labour force of the West Bank and Gaza in mid-2005. Construction alone accounted for 5.0% of GDP in 2004 and employed some 13.0% of the working population in mid-2005. During 1995–2003 industrial GDP decreased at an average rate of 9.7% annually. The sector's GDP contracted by 24.8% in 2002 and by 10.0% in 2003.

Mining and quarrying contributed 0.7% of the GDP of the Palestinian territories in 1998, and engaged an estimated 0.4% of the employed labour force in 2001. Two significant gas fields were discovered off the Gazan coast in 1999.

Manufacturing contributed 9.8% of the GDP of the West Bank and Gaza Strip in 2003, according to the World Bank. In 2001 about 13.8% of the employed labour force were engaged in the sector. Palestinian manufacturing is characterized by small-scale enterprises, which typically engage in food-processing and the production of textiles and footwear. The frequent closure of the West Bank and Gaza by the Israeli authorities has prompted the development of free-trade industrial zones on the Palestinian side of the boundaries separating Israel from the territories: Israeli and Palestinian enterprises can continue to take advantage of low-cost Palestinian labour at times of closure, and the zones also benefit from tax exemptions and export incentives. Manufacturing GDP contracted at an average annual rate of 5.1% during 1995–2003. The GDP of the sector decreased by 24.2% in 2002 and by 8.3% in 2003.

The energy sector (comprising electricity and water supply) accounted for an estimated 2.0% of Palestinian GDP in 1998. Electricity, gas and water utilities together employed some 0.2% of the labour force of the West Bank and Gaza in 2001. In the West Bank there is no utility supplying electric power apart from the Jerusalem District Electric Company Ltd, which supplies Jerusalem, Bethlehem, Ramallah and Al-Birah. Most municipalities in the Gaza Strip purchase electricity from the Israel Electric Corporation. However, the Palestine Electric Company (established in 1999) is constructing a power plant in Gaza, while the National Electric Company (created in 2000) plans to build a second power plant in the West Bank.

In 2004 the services sector contributed 68.7% of Palestinian GDP. Services engaged 58.2% of the employed labour force in mid-2005. Although tourism previously contributed more than 10% of the GDP of the West Bank and Gaza, it has been all but halted by the ongoing violence in the territories. The GDP of the services sector decreased at an average rate of 0.1% per year during 1995–2003. Services GDP declined by 16.7% in 2002 and by 3.4% in 2003.

In 2003, according to preliminary estimates, the West Bank and Gaza Strip recorded a visible trade deficit of US $1,499m. and a deficit of $198m. on the current account of the balance of payments. In the absence of seaport facilities and of an airport (Gaza International Airport was opened in November 1998 but has frequently been closed by the Israeli authorities), foreign trade (in terms of value) has been conducted almost exclusively with Israel since occupation. Most Palestinian exports are of agricultural or horticultural products. One notable feature of this trade is that Palestinian goods have often in the past been exported to Israel, and subsequently re-exported as originating in Israel. In 2003 imports (c.i.f.) from Israel alone were valued at $1,800.4m. and exports (f.o.b.) to Israel and elsewhere totalled $276.4m.

In 2003, according to official revised estimates, the PA recorded an overall budget deficit of US $702.5m. Provisional figures for 2004 predicted an estimated budget deficit of $790.1m. The annual rate of inflation in the West Bank and Gaza averaged 4.4% in 1996–2005; consumer prices increased by an average of 3.1% in 2004 and 3.5% in 2005. According to official estimates, some 26.8% of the labour force were unemployed in 2004; however, the British parliamentary International Development Select Committee estimated unemployment to be around 60%–70% in early 2004. Moreover, the World Bank estimated that unemployment was around two-and-a-half times higher than it had been before the start of the *intifada* in 2000.

The prospects for an improvement in economic conditions in the Palestinian Autonomous Areas, which remain highly dependent on Israel, are inextricably linked to the full implementation of the Oslo accords (see Recent History, above) and the outcome of the (currently suspended) 'final status' negotiations between the PA and Israel. Examples of this economic dependency are the large number of Palestinian workers employed in Israel, and the reliance of the trade sector on Israel as a market for exports and source of imports. The underdevelopment of Palestinian agriculture and industry is a consequence of the Israeli occupation, when investment became orientated towards residential construction at the expense of these sectors. Agriculture remains focused mainly on meeting local demand, although the sector supplies the bulk of Palestinian exports and there is proven demand for Palestinian products beyond the Israeli market. The expansion of Palestinian agriculture is also limited by problems with irrigation: access to water supplies is subject to 'final status' discussions. Economic conditions in the West Bank and Gaza have deteriorated markedly since 1993, largely as a result of frequent border closures enforced by the Israeli authorities in reprisal for terrorist attacks by militant Islamist groups opposed to the Oslo accords. Such closures lead to an immediate rise in the rate of unemployment among Palestinians, increase transportation costs for Palestinian goods and, at times, halt trade entirely. The Oslo accords provide for the development of seaport facilities and for the opening of Gaza International Airport and of a safe passage linking the Gaza Strip with the West Bank. However, by early 2006 the provision for a seaport at Gaza had still not been implemented, while the airport and safe passage were both closed by the Israeli authorities.

Since 1998 the PA has aimed to achieve current budget surpluses, and to focus public expenditure on health, education and infrastructural investment. In early 2000 the PA announced the creation of a Palestinian Investment Fund and a Higher Council for Development, charging the latter with the preparation of a comprehensive privatization strategy. However, in the context of the renewed Palestinian *intifada*, in November 2000 Israel imposed a complete economic blockade on the West Bank and Gaza, and halted the payment of tax transfers to the PA. The closure quickly reversed any recent economic successes (such as declining unemployment and strong GDP growth), and by the beginning of 2003 economic losses resulting from the blockade were estimated at US $2,240m., while unemployment remained high. With the economy in a state of paralysis, the PA was effectively bankrupt, largely as a result of the withholding of taxes collected by Israel on behalf of the PA. For this reason, donor support has arguably become the key source of funding for the PA. In 2004 the World Bank estimated that a further 250,000 people would have been living below the poverty line without the annual average of $950m. in aid provided by international donors during 2000–03. A further report, produced jointly with the Palestinian Central Bureau of Statistics, found that around 600,000 Palestinians were unable to meet their basic needs in terms of food, clothing and shelter. The Palestinian economy, despite stabilizing in 2003, continued to suffer from the deep recession that had been affecting it since the start of the latest *intifada*; the World Bank cited closures by the Israeli authorities as a principal factor in the stagnation (see above). In late 2004 the PA sold state-owned assets worth $600m. in an effort to control its budget deficit and to promote the development of a free economy. The opening of the Rafah crossing between the Gaza Strip and Egypt in November 2005 (see Recent History) was considered to significantly improve conditions for the Palestinian export market and opportunities for Palestinians to work abroad. However, the constant closure of the Karni crossing between the Gaza Strip and Israel hindered the Palestinian economy, especially the food-export sector. Shortly after it was reported that the militant Islamic Resistance Movement (Hamas) had secured the highest number of seats at the legislative elections of January 2006, Israel halted payments of tax and customs duties to the PA. Following the installation of the Hamas-led administration in March, the USA and the EU declared that they were withdrawing direct aid to the PA. Every year since the creation of the PA in 1994, the EU had donated an estimated $600m., and the USA some $400m. However, the USA pledged to increase by over 50% the amount of humanitarian aid it donated to the Palestinians via agencies not linked to the administration, to $245m. The EU asserted that its direct humanitarian aid to Palestinians, which included annual donations from individual states of some $262m., would not be affected by its decision to withdraw direct aid to the PA. Meanwhile, the new Cabinet held discussions with other majority-Muslim states on the possibility of future funding. Gulf states pledged aid to the PA of some $80m. and Iran some $50m.; however, none of the countries specified when the aid would be provided. Analysts predicted that the Palestinian economy and its people would suffer grave economic consequences if other donors did not compensate for the withdrawal of aid by the USA and EU. Hamas claimed to require $115m. every month merely to pay the wages of government workers, which constituted about one-quarter of the population under the PA's control.

Education

In the West Bank the Jordanian education system is in operation. Services are provided by the Israeli Civil Administration, the UN Relief and Works Agency for Palestine Refugees in the Near East (UNRWA) and private, voluntary organizations, which provide all university and most community college education. There are 20 community and teacher training colleges in the West Bank, and six universities (including an open university). The Egyptian system of education operates in the Gaza Strip, where there are two universities and one teaching training college. Palestinian education has been severely disrupted since 1987, and more recently as a result of the al-Aqsa *intifada* which began in late 2000. Since May 1994 the PA has assumed responsibility for education in Gaza and parts of the West Bank. In 2004/05 73,119 pupils attended 901 pre-primary schools, 931,260 pupils attended 1,497 primary schools, and 112,675 students were enrolled at 695 secondary institutions. In 2002/03 104,331 students attended universities or equivalent third-level institutions.

Since 1950 UNRWA has provided education services to all Palestinian refugees. The focus of UNRWA's education programme is basic primary and junior secondary schooling, offered free of charge to all refugee children and youth in accordance with local systems. In 2005/06 UNRWA operated 94 schools in the West Bank and 187 in the Gaza Strip, providing education to 59,023 pupils in the West Bank and to 193,662 pupils in Gaza. In addition, UNRWA operated four vocational training centres.

Public Holidays

2006: 1 January (Fatah Day), 10 January*† (Id al-Adha, Feast of the Sacrifice), 23 October* (Id al-Fitr, end of Ramadan), 15 November (Independence Day), 31 December*† (Id al-Adha, Feast of the Sacrifice).

2007: 1 January (Fatah Day), 13 October* (Id al-Fitr, end of Ramadan), 15 November (Independence Day), 20 December* (Id al-Adha, Feast of the Sacrifice).

* These holidays are dependent on the Islamic lunar calendar and may vary by one or two days from the dates given.

† This festival occurs twice (in the Islamic years AH 1426 and 1427) within the same Gregorian year.

Christian holidays are observed by the Christian Arab community.

Weights and Measures

The metric system is in force, although local weights and measures are also used.

Statistical Survey

Source (unless otherwise indicated): Palestinian Central Bureau of Statistics (PCBS), POB 1647, Ramallah; tel. 2-2406340; fax 2-2406343; e-mail diwan@pcbs.gov.ps; internet www.pcbs.gov.ps.

Note: Unless otherwise indicated, data include East Jerusalem, annexed by Israel in 1967.

Area and Population

AREA, POPULATION AND DENSITY

Area (sq km)	6,020*
Population (census of 9 December 1997)†	
Males	1,470,506
Females	1,425,177
Total	2,895,683
Population (official estimates at end of year)	
2002	3,559,999
2003	3,737,895
2004	3,699,767
Density (per sq km) at end of 2004	614.6

* 2,324 sq miles. The total comprises: West Bank 5,655 sq km (2,183 sq miles); Gaza Strip 365 sq km (141 sq miles).

† Figures include an estimate of 210,209 for East Jerusalem and an adjustment of 83,805 for estimated underenumeration. The total comprises 1,873,476 (males 951,693, females 921,783) in the West Bank (including East Jerusalem) and 1,022,207 (males 518,813, females 503,394) in the Gaza Strip. The data exclude Jewish settlers. According to official Israeli estimates, the population of Israelis residing in Jewish localities in the West Bank (excluding East Jerusalem) and Gaza Strip was 243,900 at 31 December 2004 (West Bank 235,700, Gaza Strip 8,200). The withdrawal of Israeli settlers residing in Jewish localities in the Gaza Strip was completed in September 2005—see Recent History.

GOVERNORATES
(official estimates, mid-2004)

	Area (sq km)	Population*	Density (per sq km)
West Bank			
Janin (Jenin)	583	246,685	423.1
Tubas	402	45,168	112.4
Tulkarm	246	162,936	662.3
Qalqilya	166	90,960	548.0
Salfit	204	60,132	294.8
Nabulus (Nablus)	605	317,331	524.5
Ram Allah (Ramallah) and Al-Birah	855	270,678	316.6
Al-Quds (Jerusalem)†	345	389,663	1,129.5
Ariha (Jericho) and Al-Aghwar	593	40,909	69.0
Beit Lahm (Bethlehem)	659	169,190	256.7
Al-Khalil (Hebron)	997	506,641	508.2
Gaza Strip			
North Gaza	61	254,093	4,165.5
Gaza	74	470,605	6,359.5
Deir al-Balah	58	193,648	3,338.8
Khan Yunus (Khan Yunis)	108	259,640	2,404.1
Rafah	64	159,250	2,488.3
Total	**6,020**	**3,637,529**	**604.2**

* Figures exclude Jewish settlers.

† Figures refer only to the eastern sector of the city.

PALESTINIAN AUTONOMOUS AREAS

PRINCIPAL LOCALITIES
(estimated population at mid-2002, excluding Jewish settlers)

West Bank
Al-Quds (Jerusalem)	242,081*	Adh-Dhahiriya		25,348
Al-Khalil (Hebron)	147,291	Ar-Ram and Dahiyat		
Nabulus (Nablus)	121,344	al-Bareed		23,038
		Ram Allah		
Tulkarm	41,109	(Ramallah)		22,493
Qalqilya	39,580	Halhul		19,345
Yattah (Yatta)	38,023	Dura		19,124
Al-Birah	34,920	Ariha (Jericho)		18,239
Janin (Jenin)	32,300	Qabatiya		17,788
Beit Lahm				
(Bethlehem)	26,847			

Gaza Strip
Ghazzah (Gaza)	361,651	Beit Lahya		50,576
Khan Yunus (Khan		Deir al-Balah		43,593
Yunis)	110,677	Bani Suhaylah		28,761
Jabalyah (Jabalia)	104,620	Beit Hanun		27,341
Rafah	62,452	Tel as-Sultan Camp		21,477
An-Nuseirat	56,449	Al-Maghazi Camp		21,278

* The figure refers only to the eastern sector of the city.

BIRTHS AND DEATHS
(official estimates)*

	2002	2003	2004
Live births:			
West Bank	58,954	58,090	57,680
Gaza Strip	43,507	43,981	46,781
Deaths:			
West Bank	5,908	5,719	5,392
Gaza Strip	4,254	4,299	4,241

* Excluding Jewish settlers.

Birth rate (official estimates per 1,000): 240.2 in 2001; 39.6 in 2002; 38.8 in 2003; 38.1 in 2004.

Death rate (official estimates per 1,000): 4.4 in 2001; 4.3 in 2002; 4.2 in 2003; 4.1 in 2004.

MARRIAGES
(number registered)

	2002	2003	2004
West Bank	12,319	14,782	15,551
Gaza Strip	10,292	11,485	12,083

ECONOMICALLY ACTIVE POPULATION
('000 persons aged 15 years and over)*

	2001	2002	2003†
Agriculture, hunting, forestry and fishing	61	72	92
Manufacturing, mining and quarrying	72	65	75
Construction	74	53	78
Wholesale and retail trade	88	88	109
Hotels and restaurants	10	9	10
Transport, storage and communications	28	27	34
Financial intermediation	5	5	4
Real estate, renting and business activities	8	8	9
Public administration and defence	72	68	71
Education	54	52	61
Health	19	21	23
Services	13	13	17
Others	4	5	7
Total employed	508	486	591
Males	430	407	490
Females	78	79	101
Unemployed	174	221	203
Total labour force	682	707	794

* Figures refer to Palestinians only, and include Palestinians employed in Israel and the Jewish settlements.
† Source: ILO.

Economically Active Population (average employment distribution of persons aged 15 years and over in April–June 2005): Agriculture, hunting, fishing and forestry 15.6%; Mining, quarrying and manufacturing 13.2%; Construction 13.0%; Commerce, restaurants and hotels 19.2%; Transport, storage and communications 5.6%; Services and other branches 33.4%.

Health and Welfare

KEY INDICATORS

Total fertility rate (children per woman, 1999)	5.9
Under-5 mortality rate (per 1,000 live births, 2004)	24
Physicians (per 1,000 head, 2001)	0.84
Hospital beds (per 1,000 head, 2000)	1.4
Access to water (% of persons, 2002)	94
Access to sanitation (% of persons, 2002)	76
Human Development Index (2003): ranking	102
Human Development Index (2003): value	0.729

For sources and definitions, see explanatory note on p. vi.

Agriculture

PRINCIPAL CROPS
('000 metric tons)

	2002	2003	2004
Wheat	54.3	44.9	46.3
Barley	21.9	21.4	14.7
Potatoes	59.6	56.6	41.1
Sweet potatoes	7.1	4.9	5.0
Olives	85.0	141.4	90.0*
Cabbages	17.5	17.9	18.1
Tomatoes	192.8	197.9	205.8
Cauliflower	19.8	19.7	21.2
Cucumbers and gherkins	147.6	152.8	138.9
Aubergines (Eggplants)	44.9	41.2	48.7

PALESTINIAN AUTONOMOUS AREAS

—continued

	2002	2003	2004
Dry onions	27.3	18.7	26.1
Watermelons	9.4	11.3	12.4
Grapes	78.2	57.1	56.3
Plums	19.5	7.9	9.8
Oranges	71.1	46.8	41.2
Tangerines, mandarins, clementines and satsumas	10.5	8.4	7.3
Lemons and limes	19.6	14.6	13.5
Grapefruit and pomelos	3.1	2.1	1.9
Bananas	5.4	7.8	9.1
Strawberries	4.0	5.7	7.6

* FAO estimate.
Source: FAO.

LIVESTOCK
('000 head)

	2002	2003	2004
Cattle	30.1	33.2	32.4
Sheep	758.3	828.7	811.9
Goats	355.4	392.1	398.8
Chickens	12.9*	9.8*	12.7
Beehives	47.9	51.4	52.0*

* FAO estimate.
Source: FAO.

Fishing

GAZA STRIP
(metric tons, live weight)

	2001*	2002	2003
Bogue	50	32	33
Jack and horse mackerels	115	125	75
Sardinellas	1,300	1,299	620
Chub mackerel	190	160	124
Cuttlefish and bobtail squids	50	55	80
Total catch (incl. others)	2,500	2,379	1,508

* FAO estimates.
Source: FAO.

Finance

CURRENCY AND EXCHANGE RATES

Monetary Units
At present there is no domestic Palestinian currency in use. The Israeli shekel, the Jordanian dinar and the US dollar all circulate within the West Bank and the Gaza Strip.

BUDGET OF THE PALESTINIAN AUTHORITY
(estimates, US $ million)

Revenue	2002	2003*	2004†
Domestic revenue	185	259	298
Revenue clearances‡	150	442	508
Total	335	701	806

Expenditure	2002	2003*	2004†
Central administration	141.8	128.0	109.2
Public security and order	310.4	392.1	433.9
Financial affairs	292.5	352.2	410.7
Foreign affairs	13.8	17.2	25.6
Economic development	35.8	39.8	43.1
Social services	340.5	432.9	526.6
Cultural and information services	25.4	29.2	32.8
Transport and communication services	10.4	12.1	14.2
Total	1,170.6	1,403.5	1,596.1

* Revised estimates.
† Provisional figures.
‡ Figures refer to an apportionment of an agreed pool of selected tax revenues arising as a result of the *de facto* customs union between Israel and the Palestinian territories. Israel is the collecting agent for these receipts and periodically makes transfers to the Palestinian Authority.

Source: Ministry of Finance, Ramallah.

COST OF LIVING
(Consumer Price Index; base: 1996 = 100)

	2003	2004	2005
Food	129.5	132.3	137.3
Beverages and tobacco	152.0	154.1	162.7
Textiles, clothing and footwear	128.6	127.4	129.5
Housing	147.3	152.0	158.4
All items (incl. others)	137.7	141.9	146.8

NATIONAL ACCOUNTS
(US $ million at current prices, preliminary figures)

Expenditure on the Gross Domestic Product

	2001	2002	2003
Final consumption expenditure	5,697.9	5,507.7	5,376.3
Households	4,222.3	4,140.4	4,131.7
Non-profit institutions serving households	149.5	144.3	116.4
General government	1,326.1	1,223.0	1,128.2
Gross capital formation	1,186.2	727.2	1,127.2
Gross fixed capital formation	1,160.2	698.6	1,118.3
Changes in inventories	26.0	28.6	8.9
Statistical discrepancy*	−8.1	−15.5	—
Total domestic expenditure	6,876.0	6,219.4	6,503.5
Net exports and imports of goods and services	−2,550.3	−2,050.2	−2,338.2
GDP in purchasers' values	4,325.7	4,169.3	4,165.3

* Referring to the difference between the sum of the expenditure components and official estimates of GDP, compiled from the production approach.

Gross Domestic Product by Economic Activity

	2002	2003	2004
Agriculture and fishing	387.1	422.1	403.0
Mining, manufacturing, electricity and water	636.1	489.7	586.0
Construction	111.7	145.2	188.8
Wholesale and retail trade	460.6	378.6	401.1
Transport, storage and communications	454.7	378.5	315.9
Financial intermediation	146.5	139.6	139.5
Public administration and defence	523.9	647.6	653.9
Domestic services of households	8.6	8.7	7.6
Public-owned enterprises	142.9	83.7	—*
Other services	1,005.3	975.5	1,071.5
Sub-total	3,877.4	3,669.2	3,767.3
Financial intermediation services indirectly measured	−109.6	−118.9	−115.6
Customs duties	184.2	144.9	216.7
VAT on imports (net)	217.2	470.3	262.8
GDP in purchasers' values	4,169.3	4,165.3	4,131.2

* Value added by public-owned enterprises in 2004 was distributed by contribution to each activity.

PALESTINIAN AUTONOMOUS AREAS

BALANCE OF PAYMENTS
(preliminary estimates, US $ million)

	2001	2002	2003
Exports of goods f.o.b.	508.7	392.6	326.6
Imports of goods f.o.b.	−2,132.5	−1,606.4	−1,825.8
Trade balance	−1,623.7	−1,213.8	−1,499.3
Exports of services	107.5	128.5	77.9
Imports of services	−747.7	−702.0	−676.1
Balance on goods and services	−2,263.9	−1,787.3	−2,097.5
Other income received (net)	485.9	381.8	481.4
Balance on goods, services and income	−1,778.1	−1,405.6	−1,616.1
Current transfers (net)	971.3	1,109.0	1,417.8
Current balance	−806.7	−296.6	−198.3
Capital account (net)	229.8	160.7	413.7
Direct investment abroad (net)	−359.3	−349.9	−367.8
Portfolio investment (net)	−137.5	−155.7	−177.3
Other investment (net)	864.7	647.7	874.6
Net errors and omissions	170.5	110.0	−402.1
Overall balance	−38.6	116.3	142.7

External Trade

PRINCIPAL COMMODITIES
(US $ million)

Imports c.i.f.*	2001	2002	2003
Food and live animals	408.6	324.6	377.8
Beverages and tobacco	97.2	75.8	90.6
Crude materials (inedible) except fuels	42.1	35.5	40.5
Mineral fuels, lubricants, etc.	377.5	361.3	425.8
Animal and vegetable oils and fats	15.9	15.5	19.6
Chemicals and related products	163.5	139.6	162.7
Basic manufactures	498.4	291.5	351.3
Machinery and transport equipment	248.3	180.8	211.8
Miscellaneous manufactured articles	181.0	90.9	116.3
Commodities not classified elsewhere	1.2	0.0	3.9
Total	2,033.6	1,515.6	1,800.4

Exports f.o.b.	2001	2002	2003
Food and live animals	34.1	27.0	34.1
Beverages and tobacco	13.5	13.7	12.9
Crude materials (inedible) except fuels	12.9	14.4	13.2
Mineral fuels, lubricants, etc.	2.2	2.5	3.8
Animal and vegetable oils and fats	5.8	5.7	7.2
Chemicals and related products	27.6	20.3	25.3
Basic manufactures	120.5	95.0	109.2
Machinery and transport equipment	16.9	12.0	14.4
Miscellaneous manufactured articles	56.5	49.8	50.7
Other commodities and transactions	0.5	0.5	5.7
Total	290.3	240.9	276.4

* Figures refer to imports from Israel only.

Transport

ROAD TRAFFIC
(registered motor vehicles holding Palestinian licence, 2004)

	West Bank	Gaza Strip	Total
Private cars	46,166	39,692	85,858
Taxis	7,911	1,173	9,084
Buses	878	202	1,080
Trucks and commercial cars	13,430	9,842	23,272
Motorcycles and mopeds	24	270	294
Tractors	829	1,111	1,940
Other vehicles	224	323	547
Total	69,504	53,310	122,814

Tourism

ARRIVALS OF VISITORS AT HOTELS*

	2001	2002	2003
Total	60,208	51,357	62,912

* Including Palestinians numbering 17,432 in 2001, 17,924 in 2002 and 26,090 in 2003 (estimate).

Communications Media

	2002	2003	2004
Telephones ('000 main lines in use)	301.6	315.8	357.3
Mobile cellular telephones ('000 subscribers)	320.0	480.0	974.3
Personal computers ('000 in use)	125	125	169
Internet users ('000)	105	145	160

Source: International Telecommunication Union.

Book production (1996): 114 titles; 571,000 copies (Source: UNESCO, *Statistical Yearbook*).

Daily newspapers (titles): 2 in 2004.

Non-daily newspapers (titles): 11 in 2004.

Education

(2004/05)

	Institutions	Teachers	Students
Pre-primary	901	2,860	73,119
Primary	1,497	38,805	931,260
Secondary	695		112,675
Higher:*			
universities, etc.	16	3,384	98,439
other	22	563	5,892

* 2002/03.

Adult literacy rate (official estimates): 91.9% (males 96.3%; females 87.4%) in 2003.

Directory

Administration

PALESTINIAN NATIONAL AUTHORITY

Appointed in May 1994, the Palestinian National Authority (PNA), generally known internationally as the Palestinian Authority (PA), has assumed some of the civil responsibilities formerly exercised by the Israeli Civil Administration in the Gaza Strip and parts of the West Bank.

Executive President: MAHMUD ABBAS (assumed office 15 January 2005).

CABINET
(April 2006)

The sole faction represented in the Cabinet is the Islamic Resistance Movement (Hamas); the Cabinet also comprises technocrats or academics who are not affiliated with any political organization but are supported by Hamas, and independents (Ind.).

Prime Minister and Minister of Youth and Sports: ISMAIL ABD AS-SALAM AHMAD HANIYA (Hamas).
Deputy Prime Minister and Minister of Education and Higher Education: Dr NASSER ED-DIN MUHAMMAD AHMAD ASH-SHAER (Hamas).
Minister of the Interior and Civil Affairs: SAID MUHAMMAD SHABAN SIYAM (Hamas).
Minister of Foreign Affairs: Dr MAHMUD KHALID AZ-ZAHHAR (Hamas).
Minister of Justice: Dr AHMAD ABD AL-HAMID MUBARAK AL-KHALIDI (supported by Hamas).
Minister of Finance: Dr OMAR MAHMUD MATAR ABD AR-RAZIK (Hamas).
Minister of National Economy: Eng. ALA ED-DIN MUHAMMAD HUSSEIN AL-ARAJ (Ind.).
Minister of Agriculture: Dr MUHAMMAD RAMADAN MUHAMMAD AL-AGHA (Hamas).
Minister of Public Works and Housing: Eng. ZIYAD SHUKRI ABD AR-RABBUH AZ-ZAZA (Hamas).
Minister of Planning: Dr SAMIR ABD AS-SALIH ABU AISHA (Hamas).
Minister of Labour: Eng. MUHAMMAD IBRAHIM MUSA AL-BARGHOUTHI.
Minister of Social Affairs: FAKHRI FAHD MUSA TURKUMAN (Ind.).
Minister of Local Government: Eng. ISSA KHAIRI ISSA AL-JABARI.
Minister of Transport: Eng. ABD AR-RAHMAN FAHMI ZEIDAN (Hamas).
Minister of Culture: Dr ATALLAH ABD AL-MUHAMMAD ABU AS-SIBAH (Hamas).
Minister of Information: Dr YOUSUF MUSA MUHAMMAD RIZQA (supported by Hamas).
Minister of Tourism and Antiquities: Eng. JOUDA GEORGE JOUDA MARKOS (Ind.).
Minister of Health: Dr BASSEM NAIM MUHAMMAD NAIM (Hamas).
Minister of Women's Affairs: Dr MARIAM MAHMUD HASSAN SALEH (Hamas).
Minister of Prisoners' Affairs: Eng. WASFI MOUSTAFA IZZAT QABAHA.
Minister of Telecommunications and Information Technology: Eng. JAMAL NAJI SHIHADAH AL-KHUDARI (Ind.).
Minister of Awqaf (Religious Endowments): Sheikh NAYEF MAHMUD MUHAMMAD AR-RAJOUB (Hamas).
Minister of State for Refugees' Affairs: Dr ATIF IBRAHIM MUHAMMAD ADWAN (Hamas).
Minister of State for Jerusalem Affairs: Eng. KHALID IBRAHIM ISHAQ ABU ARAFA (Hamas).

MINISTRIES

Ministry of Agriculture: POB 197, Ramallah; tel. (2) 2961080; fax (2) 2961212; e-mail moa@planet.edu.
Ministry of Awqaf (Religious Endowments): POB 54825, Jerusalem; tel. (2) 6282085; fax (2) 2986401.
Ministry of Civil Affairs: Ramallah; tel. (2) 2987336; fax (2) 2987335.
Ministry of Culture: POB 147, Ramallah; tel. and fax (2) 2986205; e-mail moc@moc.gov.ps; internet www.moc.gov.ps.
Ministry of Education and Higher Education: POB 576, Ramallah; tel. (2) 2983254; fax (2) 2983261; e-mail moe@planet.com; internet www.moe.gov.ps.
Ministry of Environmental Affairs: POB 3841, Ramallah; tel. (2) 2403495; fax (2) 2403494; e-mail menawb@gov.ps; internet www.mena.gov.ps.
Ministry of Finance: POB 795, Sateh Marhaba, Al-Birah/Ramallah; POB 4007, Gaza; tel. (2) 2400650; fax (2) 2400595; tel. (8) 2826188; fax (8) 2820696; e-mail cbomof@palnet.com; internet www.mof.gov.ps.
Ministry of Foreign Affairs: POB 1336, Ramallah; POB 4017, Gaza; tel. (2) 2405040; fax (2) 2403772; tel. (8) 2829260; fax (8) 2868971; e-mail pressmofa@gov.ps; internet www.mopic.gov.ps.
Ministry of Health: POB 14, al-Mukhtar St, Nablus; POB 1035, Abu Khadra Center, Gaza; tel. (9) 2384772; fax (9) 2384777; e-mail moh@gov.ps; internet www.moh.gov.ps; tel. (8) 2829173; fax (8) 2826295; e-mail mohgaza@palnet.com.
Ministry of Industry: POB 2073, Ramallah; POB 4053, Gaza; tel. (2) 2987641; fax (2) 2987640; tel. (8) 2826463; fax (8) 2824884; e-mail industry_wb@gov.ps; internet www.industry.gov.ps.
Ministry of Information: POB 224, Al-Irsal St, Ramallah; Gaza; tel. (2) 2986466; fax (2) 2954043; e-mail minfo@minfo.gov.ps; internet www.minfo.gov.ps.
Ministry of the Interior and Civil Affairs: Gaza; tel. (8) 2829185; fax (8) 2862500.
Ministry of Jerusalem Affairs: POB 20479, Jerusalem; tel. (2) 6273330; fax (2) 6286820.
Ministry of Justice: Gaza; tel. (8) 2822231; fax (8) 2867109.
Ministry of Labour: POB 350, Al-Irsal St, Ramallah; tel. (2) 2967420; fax (2) 2967418; e-mail narman@gov.ps; internet www.mol.gov.ps.
Ministry of Local Government: Jericho; tel. (2) 2321260; fax (2) 2321240; internet www.molg.gov.ps.
Ministry of National Economy: POB 1629, Ramallah; POB 4023, Gaza; tel. (2) 2981218; fax (2) 2981207; tel. (8) 2874146; fax (8) 2874145; e-mail info@met.gov.ps; internet www.met.gov.ps.
Ministry of Public Works and Housing: Gaza; tel. (8) 2829232; fax (8) 2823653; e-mail mopgaza@palnet.com.
Ministry of Social Affairs: POB 3525, Ramallah; tel. (2) 2986181; fax (2) 2985239; e-mail Msa@hally.net; internet www.mosa.gov.ps.
Ministry of Supply: Gaza; tel. (8) 2824324; fax (8) 2826430.
Ministry of Telecommunications and Information Technology: Ramallah; Gaza; tel. (2) 9986555; fax (2) 9986556; tel. (8) 2829171; fax (8) 2824555; e-mail jbakeer@gov.ps; internet www.mtit.gov.ps.
Ministry of Tourism and Antiquities: POB 534, Manger St, Bethlehem; tel. (2) 2741581; fax (2) 2743753; e-mail mota@visit-palestine.com; internet www.visit-palestine.com.
Ministry of Transport: POB 399, Ramallah; tel. (2) 2986945; fax (2) 2986943.
Ministry of Youth and Sports: POB 52, Ramallah; tel. (2) 2985983; fax (2) 2985991; e-mail youth@p-ol.com; internet www.mys.gov.ps.

President and Legislature

PRESIDENT

Election, 9 January 2005

Candidates	Votes	%
Mahmud Abbas (Fatah)	501,448	62.52
Mustafa Barghouthi (Independent)	156,227	19.48
Tayseer Khalid (DFLP)	26,848	3.35
Abd al-Halim al-Ashqar (Independent)	22,171	2.76
Bassam es-Salhi (PPP)	21,429	2.67
As-Said Baraka (Independent)	10,406	1.30
Abd al-Karim Shbeir (Independent)	5,717	0.71
Invalid votes	57,831	7.21
Total	**802,077**	**100.00**

PALESTINIAN LEGISLATIVE COUNCIL

Speaker: AZIZ DUWEIK.

PALESTINIAN AUTONOMOUS AREAS

General Election, 25 January 2006

Parties, Lists and Coalitions	Majority system	Proportional system	Total
Change and Reform*	29	45	74
Fatah	28	17	45
Martyr Abu Ali Moustafa†	3	0	3
The Third Way	2	0	2
The Alternative‡	2	0	2
Independent Palestine§	2	0	2
Independents	0	4	4
Total	**66**	**66**	**132**

* The Islamic Resistance Movement (Hamas) contested the elections as Change and Reform.
† The Popular Front for the Liberation of Palestine contested the elections as Martyr Abu Ali Moustafa.
‡ Electoral list comprising the Palestinian Democratic Union, the Coalition of the Democratic Front (representing the Democratic Front for the Liberation of Palestine) and the Palestinian People's Party.
§ Coalition comprising independents and representatives of the Palestinian National Initiative.

A reported 77.7% of eligible voters participated in the legislative elections conducted on 25 January 2006. On 18 June 2005 the Palestinian Legislative Council (PLC) had approved a new election law, adopting a 'mixed' electoral system for forthcoming legislative polls: the system combined a 'majority system' and a system of proportional representation. Under the majority system, according to which candidates were elected to 66 of the PLC's 132 seats, the Palestinian Autonomous Areas were divided into 16 electoral districts (11 in the West Bank and five in the Gaza Strip), and candidates contested seats allocated to their district in proportion to the size of its population. The remaining 66 deputies were elected to the PLC by the system of proportional representation, under which the Palestinian territories were treated as one electoral district, and voters chose between nation-wide lists of political organizations and coalitions ('party lists'). Six of the seats were reserved for Christians. All deputies elected to the PLC automatically became members of the Palestine National Council (PNC—see the Palestinian Liberation Organization or PLO). Following the signing of the Declaration of Principles on Palestinian Self-Rule in the Occupied Territories (the Oslo Agreement) by Israel and the PLO in September 1993 and of an agreement providing for Palestinian Self-Rule in the Gaza Strip and Jericho in May 1994, the first Palestinian legislative elections had been held on 20 January 1996 (see Recent History). The existing 483 members of the PNC were permitted to return from exile by the Israeli authorities in April, in order, among other things, to amend parts of the Palestinian National Charter (or PLO Covenant), which has largely been superseded by the Oslo accords and other subsequent agreements concluded between Israel and the PLO.

Election Commission

Central Elections Commission (CEC): POB 2319, Qasr al-Murjan Bldg, Al-Balou, nr Jawwal Circle, Ramallah; tel. (2) 2969700; fax (2) 2969712; e-mail info@pal-cec.org; internet www.elections.ps; f. 2002; independent; comprises nine mems, appointed by the Exec. Pres. of the PA; Chair. Dr HANNA NASIR; Sec.-Gen. Dr RAMI HAMDALLAH.

Political Organizations

Alliance of Palestinian Forces: f. 1994; 10 members representing the PFLP, the DFLP, the PLF, the PPSF, the Palestine Revolutionary Communist Party and the PFLP—GC; opposes the Declaration of Principles on Palestinian Self-Rule signed by Israel and the PLO in September 1993, and subsequent agreements concluded within its framework (the 'Oslo accords'). The PFLP and DFLP left the Alliance in 1996. The **Fatah Revolutionary Council**, headed by Sabri Khalil al-Banna, alias 'Abu Nidal', split from Fatah in 1973. Its headquarters were formerly in Baghdad, Iraq, but the office was closed down and its staff expelled from the country by the Iraqi authorities in November 1983; a new base was established in Damascus, Syria, in December. Al-Banna was readmitted to Iraq in 1984, having fled Syria. With 'Abu Musa' (whose rebel Fatah group is called **Al-Intifada**, or 'Uprising'), 'Abu Nidal' formed a joint rebel Fatah command in February 1985, and both had offices in Damascus until June 1987, when those of 'Abu Nidal' were closed by the Syrian Government. Forces loyal to 'Abu Nidal' surrendered to Fatah forces at the Rashidiyeh Palestinian refugee camp near Tyre, northern Lebanon, in 1990. 'Abu Nidal' was reported to have been found dead in Baghdad in August 2002.

Arab Liberation Front (ALF): Ramallah; f. 1969; formerly supported by the Iraqi Baath regime; opposes Oslo accords; Sec.-Gen. RAKAD SALIM (imprisoned in 2002).

Democratic Front for the Liberation of Palestine (DFLP) (Al-Jabha ad-Dimuqratiyya li-Tahrir Filastin): Damascus, Syria; f. 1969 following split with PFLP; Marxist-Leninist; contested Jan. 2006 legislative elections on The Alternative electoral list as the Coalition of the Democratic Front; Sec.-Gen. NAIF HAWATMEH (Damascus).

Fatah (Harakat at-Tahrir al-Watani al-Filastin—Palestine National Liberation Movement): e-mail fateh@fateh.org; internet www.fateh.net; f. 1957; militant group which became the single largest Palestinian organization and strongest faction in both the administration and Palestinian Legislative Council until the legislative elections of Jan. 2006; Leader FAROUK KADDOUMI (Tunis, Tunisia); leadership is nominally shared by the members of the Central Committee, who were elected at Fatah's Fifth General Conference on 8 August 1989; however, some of those elected to the Central Committee have since died.

Islamic Jihad (Al-Jihad al-Islami): Damascus, Syria; f. 1979–80 by Palestinian students in Egypt; militant Islamist; opposed to the Oslo accords; Gen. Sec. RAMADAN ABDULLAH SHALLAH.

Islamic Resistance Movement (Hamas—Harakat al-Muqawama al-Islamiyya): Gaza; Damascus, Syria; f. 1987; originally welfare organization Mujama (f. 1973) led by the late Sheikh AHMAD YASSIN (killed by Israeli forces March 2004); militant Islamist; opposes the Oslo accords and does not recognize the PA as the sole national authority in the Palestinian Autonomous Areas; contested Jan. 2006 legislative elections as Change and Reform; following the killing by Israeli forces of the leader of Hamas in the Gaza Strip, Abd al-Aziz ar-Rantisi, in April 2004, the group announced that it was adopting a policy of 'collective leadership' (see Recent History); Head of Political Bureau KHALID MESHAAL (Damascus); Gen. Commdr of military wing, Izz ad-Din al-Qassam Brigades MUHAMMAD DEIF (in hiding from the Israeli authorities since 1992, though presumed to be in Gaza).

Palestine Liberation Front (PLF): f. 1977 following split with PFLP—GC; the PLF split into three factions in the early 1980s, all of which retained the name PLF; one faction (Leader MUHAMMAD 'ABU' ABBAS) was based in Tunis, Tunisia, and Baghdad, Iraq, and remained nominally loyal to Yasser Arafat; the second faction (Leader TALAAT YAQOUB) belonged to the anti-Arafat National Salvation Front and opened offices in Damascus, Syria, and Libya; a third group derived from the PLF was reportedly formed by its Central Cttee Secretary, ABD AL-FATTAH GHANIM, in June 1986; the factions of Yaqoub and Ghanim were reconciled in early 1985; at the 18th session of the PNC, a programme for the unification of the PLF was announced, with Yaqoub (died November 1988) named as Secretary-General and 'Abu Abbas' appointed to the PLO Executive Committee, while unification talks were held. The merging of the two factions was announced in June 1987, with Abu Abbas becoming Deputy Secretary-General. Abu Abbas was apprehended by US-led coalition forces in Iraq in April 2003, and reportedly died of natural causes in March 2004 while still in US custody.

Palestine Liberation Organization (PLO) (Munazzimat at-Tahrir al-Filastiniyya): Gaza City; f. 1964; the supreme organ of the PLO is the Palestine National Council (PNC; Pres. SALIM AZ-ZA'NUN), while the PLO Executive Committee (Chair. MAHMUD ABBAS; Sec.-Gen. FAROUK KADDOUMI) deals with day-to-day business. Fatah (the Palestine National Liberation Movement) joined the PNC in 1968, and all the guerrilla organizations joined the Council in 1969. In 1973 the Palestinian Central Council (PCC; Chair. SALIM AZ-ZA'NUN) was established to act as an intermediary between the PNC and the Executive Committee. The Council, which had 124 mems at April 1999, meets when the PNC is not in session and approves major policy decisions on its behalf; Chair. MAHMUD ABBAS.

Palestine Revolutionary Communist Party (Al-Hizb ash-Shuyu'i at-Thawri al-Filastini): principally based in Lebanon; Sec.-Gen. ARBI AWAD.

Palestinian Democratic Union (FIDA): POB 247, Ramallah; fax (2) 2954071; e-mail fida@palnet.com; internet www.fida-palestine.org; f. 1990 following split from the DFLP; contested Jan. 2006 legislative elections on The Alternative electoral list; Leader YASSER ABD AR-RABBUH; Sec.-Gen. SALEH RA'FAT.

Palestinian National Initiative (Al-Mubadara): Ramallah; tel. (5) 9293006; e-mail almubadara@almubadara.org; internet www.almubadara.org; f. 2002; seeks peaceful resolution of conflict with Israel through establishment of an independent, viable and democratic Palestinian state, with East Jerusalem as its capital; advocates reform of internal political structures, and aims to fight

PALESTINIAN AUTONOMOUS AREAS

corruption and injustice, and to uphold citizens' rights; contested Jan. 2006 legislative elections as part of the Independent Palestine coalition; Gen. Sec. Dr MUSTAFA BARGHOUTHI.

Palestinian People's Party (PPP) (Hezb ash-Sha'ab): Ramallah; tel. (2) 2960104; fax (2) 2960640; e-mail shaab@palpeople.org; internet www.palpeople.org; f. 1921 as Palestine Communist Party; adopted current name in 1991; admitted to the PNC at its 18th session in 1987; contested Jan. 2006 legislative elections on The Alternative electoral list; Sec.-Gen. BASSAM ES-SALHI.

Palestinian Popular Struggle Front (PPSF) (Jabhat an-Nidal ash-Sha'biyya al-Filastiniyya): f. 1967; has reportedly split into two factions which either support or oppose the PA; the pro-PA faction (Leader SAMIR GHOSHEH) is based in the West Bank; the anti-PA faction (Leader KHALID ABD AL-MAJID) is based in Damascus, Syria.

Popular Front for the Liberation of Palestine (PFLP) (Al-Jabha ash-Sha'biyya li-Tahrir Filastin): Damascus, Syria; e-mail info@pflp.net; internet www.pflp.net; f. 1967; Marxist-Leninist; publ. Democratic Palestine (English; monthly); contested Jan. 2006 legislative elections as Martyr Abu Ali Moustafa; Sec.-Gen. AHMAD SAADAT (imprisoned in 2002).

Popular Front for the Liberation of Palestine—General Command (PFLP—GC): Damascus, Syria; f. 1968 following split from the PFLP; pro-Syrian; Leader AHMAD JIBRIL.

Popular Front for the Liberation of Palestine—National General Command: Amman, Jordan; split from the PFLP—GC in 1999; aims to co-operate with the PA; Leader ATIF YUNUS.

As-Saiqa (Thunderbolt, or Vanguard of the Popular Liberation War): f. 1968; Syrian-backed; pan-Arab; opposed to the Oslo accords; Sec.-Gen. ISSAM AL-QADI.

The formation of the **Right Movement for Championing the Palestinian People's Sons** by former members of Hamas was announced in April 1995. The movement, based in Gaza City, was reported to support the PA. The **Al-Aqsa Martyrs Brigades**, consisting of a number of Fatah-affiliated activists, emerged soon after the start of the al-Aqsa *intifada* in September 2000, and have carried out attacks against Israeli targets in Israel, the West Bank and Gaza Strip.

Diplomatic Representation

Countries with which the PLO maintains diplomatic relations include:

Afghanistan, Albania, Algeria, Angola, Austria, Bahrain, Bangladesh, Benin, Bhutan, Botswana, Brunei, Bulgaria, Burkina Faso, Burundi, Cambodia, Cameroon, Cape Verde, Central African Republic, Chad, China (People's Rep.), Comoros, Congo (Dem. Rep.), Congo (Rep.), Cuba, Cyprus, Czech Republic, Djibouti, Egypt, Equatorial Guinea, Ethiopia, Gabon, Gambia, Ghana, Guinea, Guinea-Bissau, Hungary, India, Indonesia, Iran, Iraq, Jordan, Korea (Dem. People's Rep.), Kuwait, Laos, Lebanon, Libya, Madagascar, Malaysia, Maldives, Mali, Malta, Mauritania, Mauritius, Mongolia, Morocco, Mozambique, Nepal, Nicaragua, Niger, Nigeria, Norway, Oman, Pakistan, Philippines, Poland, Qatar, Romania, Russia, Rwanda, São Tomé and Príncipe, Saudi Arabia, Senegal, Serbia and Montenegro, Seychelles, Sierra Leone, Somalia, Sri Lanka, Sudan, Swaziland, Sweden, Tanzania, Togo, Tunisia, Turkey, Uganda, United Arab Emirates (UAE), Uzbekistan, Vanuatu, the Vatican City, Viet Nam, Yemen, Zambia and Zimbabwe.

The following states, while they do not recognize the State of Palestine, allow the PLO to maintain a regional office: Belgium, Brazil, France, Germany, Greece, Italy, Japan, the Netherlands, Portugal, Spain, Switzerland and the United Kingdom.

A Palestinian passport has been available for residents of the Gaza Strip and the Jericho area only since April 1995. In September of that year the passport was recognized by 29 states, including: Algeria, Bahrain, Bulgaria, China (People's Rep.), Cyprus, Egypt, France, Germany, Greece, India, Israel, Jordan, Malta, Morocco, the Netherlands, Pakistan, Qatar, Romania, Saudi Arabia, South Africa, Spain, Sweden, Switzerland, Tunisia, Turkey, the UAE, the United Kingdom and the USA.

Judicial System

In the Gaza Strip, the West Bank towns of Jericho, Nablus, Ramallah, Jenin, Tulkarm, Qalqilya, Bethlehem and Hebron, and in other, smaller population centres in the West Bank, the PA has assumed limited jurisdiction with regard to civil affairs. However, the situation is confused owing to the various and sometimes conflicting legal systems which have operated in the territories occupied by Israel in 1967: Israeli military and civilian law; Jordanian law; and acts, orders-in-council and ordinances that remain from the period of the British Mandate in Palestine. Religious and military courts have been established under the auspices of the PA. In February 1995 the PA established a Higher State Security Court in Gaza to decide on security crimes both inside and outside the PA's area of jurisdiction; and to implement all valid Palestinian laws, regulations, rules and orders in accordance with Article 69 of the Constitutional Law of the Gaza Strip of 5 March 1962. As of September 2000 the PLC had passed a total of 30 laws.

General Prosecutor of the PA: KHALID AL-QIDRA.

Religion

The vast majority of Palestinians in the West Bank and Gaza are Muslims, while a small (and declining) minority are Christians of the Greek Orthodox and Roman Catholic rites.

ISLAM

The PA-appointed Mufti of Jerusalem is the most senior Muslim cleric in the Palestinian territories.

Mufti of Jerusalem: Sheikh IKRIMAH SA'ID SABRI.

CHRISTIANITY

The Roman Catholic Church

Latin Rite

The Patriarchate of Jerusalem covers Israel and the Occupied Territories, the Palestinian Autonomous Areas, Jordan and Cyprus. At 31 December 2003 there were an estimated 77,000 adherents.

Patriarchate of Jerusalem: Patriarcat Latin, POB 14152, Jerusalem 91141; tel. 2-6282323; fax 2-6271652; e-mail chancellery@latinpat.org; internet www.lpj.org; Patriarch His Beatitude MICHEL SABBAH; Vicar-General for Jerusalem KAMAL HANNA BATHISH (Titular Bishop of Jericho); Vicar-General for Israel GIACINTO-BOULOS MARCUZZO (Titular Bishop of Emmaus Nicopolis).

Melkite Rite

The Greek-Melkite Patriarch of Antioch and all the East, of Alexandria and of Jerusalem (GRÉGOIRE III LAHAM) is resident in Damascus, Syria.

Patriarchal Vicariate of Jerusalem: Patriarcat Grec-Melkite Catholique, POB 14130, Porte de Jaffa, Jerusalem 91141; tel. 2-6271968; fax 2-6286652; e-mail gcpjer@p-ol.com; about 3,300 adherents (31 December 2003); Protosyncellus Archim. MTANIOS HADDAD (resident in Rome).

The Greek Orthodox Church

The Patriarchate of Jerusalem contains an estimated 260,000 adherents in Israel and the Occupied Territories, the Palestinian Autonomous Areas, Jordan, Kuwait, the UAE and Saudi Arabia.

Patriarchate of Jerusalem: POB 19632-633, Greek Orthodox Patriarchate St, Old City, Jerusalem; tel. 2-6274941; fax 2-6282048; internet www.jerusalem-patriarchate.org; Patriarch IRINEOS I (Irineos I was dismissed in May 2005, and a new Patriarch, Theophilos III, was elected by the Greek Orthodox synod in August and inaugurated in November. However, although Jordan and the Palestinian Autonomous Areas approved his appointment, it was not accepted by the Israeli authorities).

The Press

NEWSPAPERS

Al-Ayyam: POB 1987, Ramallah; tel. (2) 2987341; e-mail info@al-ayyam.com; internet www.al-ayyam.com; Arabic; weekly; Editor-in-Chief AKRAM HANIYAH.

Al-Ayyam al-Arabi: Ramallah; f. 1999; Arabic; daily newspaper published by the PA; Editor-in-Chief SALIM SALAMAH.

Filastin ath-Thawra (Palestine Revolution): normally published in Beirut, but resumed publication from Cyprus in November 1982; Arabic; weekly newspaper of the PLO.

Al-Hadaf: organ of the PFLP; Arabic; weekly.

Al-Hayat al-Jadidah: West Bank; e-mail info1@alhayat-j.com; internet www.alhayat-j.com; f. 1994; Arabic; weekly; Editor NADIL AMR.

Al-Hourriah (Liberation): e-mail info@alhourriah.org; internet www.alhourriah.org; organ of the DFLP; Arabic; publ. in Beirut, Lebanon and Damascus, Syria; Editor-in-Chief HAMADEH MUTASIM.

Al-Istiqlal: Gaza City; e-mail alesteqlal@p-i-s.com; organ of Islamic Jihad; Arabic; weekly.

Al-Quds (Jerusalem): Jerusalem; e-mail info@alquds.com; internet www.alquds.com; Arabic; independent; pro-PA; supports peace

PALESTINIAN AUTONOMOUS AREAS

negotiations; reportedly has largest circulation of all Palestinian newspapers; daily.

Ar-Risala (Letter): Gaza City; organ of the Islamist Construction and Democracy Party; Arabic; weekly; Editor-in-Chief GHAZI HAMAD.

Al-Watan: Gaza City; supports Hamas; Arabic; weekly.

PERIODICALS

Filastin (Palestine): Gaza City; e-mail adel@falasteen.com; internet www.falasteen.com; f. 1994; Arabic; weekly.

Palestine Report: Jerusalem Media and Communications Centre, POB 25047, 7 Nablus Rd, Jerusalem; tel. (2) 5819777; fax (2) 5829534; e-mail palreport@palestinereport.org; internet www.palestinereport.org; f. 1990; English; publ. by the Jerusalem Media and Communications Centre; weekly; current affairs; Man. Dir OMAR KARMI; Editor-in-Chief JOHARAH BAKER.

Youth Times: POB 50465, Flat 12, 4th Floor, Julani Bldg, Ar-Ram, Jerusalem; tel. (2) 2343428; fax (2) 2343430; e-mail pyalara@pyalara.org; internet www.pyalara.org; f. 1998; publ. by the Palestinian Youth Association for Leadership and Rights Activation; Arabic and English; monthly; Editor-in-Chief HANIYA BITAR.

NEWS AGENCY

Wikalat Anbaa' Filastiniya (WAFA, Palestine News Agency): Gaza City; tel. (8) 2824056; fax (8) 2824046; e-mail wafa15@palnet.com; internet www.wafa.pna.net; official PLO news agency; Editor ZIAD ABD AL-FATTAH.

Broadcasting and Communications

TELECOMMUNICATIONS

Palestine Telecommunications Co PLC (PalTel): POB 1570, Nablus; tel. (9) 2376225; fax (9) 2376227; e-mail paltel@palnet.net; internet www.paltel.ps; f. 1995; privately owned monopoly; launched cellular telephone service (Palcel, now Jawwal) in 1999; Chair. SABIH T. MASRI; CEO Dr ABD AL-MALEK JABER.

Palestine Cellular Co (Jawal): Rafeedia St, Nablus; tel. (9) 2337370; fax (9) 2337366; e-mail atyourservice@jawwal.ps; internet www.myjawwal.com; f. 1999; 65% owned by PalTel; CEO HAKAM KANAFANI.

BROADCASTING

Palestinian Broadcasting Corpn (PBC): POB 984, Al-Birah/Ramallah; tel. (2) 2959894; fax (2) 2959893; e-mail pbc@palnet.com; internet www.pbc.gov.ps; Chair. BASEM ABU SUMAYA.

Sawt Filastin (Voice of Palestine): c/o Police HQ, Jericho; tel. (2) 921220; internet www.bailasan.com/pinc; f. 1994; official radio station of the PA; broadcasts in Arabic from Jericho and Ramallah; Dir RADWAN ABU AYYASH.

Palestine Television: f. 1994; broadcasts from Ramallah and Gaza City; Dir RADWAN ABU AYYASH.

Finance

(cap. = capital; dep. = deposits; brs = branches; m. = million)

BANKING

The Palestine Monetary Authority (PMA) is the financial regulatory body in the Palestinian Autonomous Areas, and is expected to evolve into the Central Bank of Palestine. Three currencies circulate in the Palestinian economy—the Jordanian dinar, the Israeli shekel and the US dollar—and the PMA currently has no right of issue. According to the PMA, there were 22 banks with a total of 126 branches operating in the West Bank and Gaza in December 2001. In January 2002 the banks' deposit base amounted to US $3,275m.

Palestine Monetary Authority (PMA): Nablus Rd, Ramallah; tel. (2) 2409920; fax (2) 2409922; e-mail info@pma.gov.ps; internet www.pma-palestine.org; f. 1994; began licensing, inspection and supervision of the Palestinian and foreign commercial banks operating in the Gaza Strip and the Jericho enclave in the West Bank in July 1995; assumed responsibility for 13 banks in the Palestinian territories over which the Central Bank of Israel had hitherto exercised control in December 1995; Gov. GEORGE T. ABED.

National Banks

Bank of Palestine Ltd: POB 50, Omar al-Mukhtar St, Gaza City; tel. (8) 2826818; fax (8) 2828973; e-mail info@bankofpalestine.com; internet www.bankofpalestine.com; f. 1960; cap. US $20.3m., res $3.4m., dep. $300.8m., total assets $333.5m. (Dec. 2003); Chair. and Gen. Man. Dr HANI HASHEM SHAWA; 19 brs in West Bank and Gaza.

Directory

Commercial Bank of Palestine PLC: POB 1799, Michael Tanous Bldg, Alawda St, Ramallah; tel. (2) 2954141; fax (2) 2953888; e-mail cbp@cbpal.palnet.com; internet www.cbpal.com; f. 1992; total assets US $73m.; Gen. Man. Dr ANIS AL-HAJJEH; 5 brs.

Palestine International Bank: Al-Birah/Ramallah; tel. (2) 2983300; fax (2) 2983344; e-mail pib@pib.palnet.com; f. 1996; cap. US $20m.; Chair. JARRAR AL-QUDWA; 4 brs.

Investment Banks

Arab Palestinian Investment Bank: POB 1260, Al-Harji Bldg, Ramallah; tel. (2) 2987126; fax (2) 2987125; e-mail apibank@palnet.com; f. 1996; Arab Bank of Jordan has a 51% share; cap. US $15m.

Palestine Investment Bank PLC: POB 3675, Al-Helal St, Al-Birah/Ramallah; tel. (2) 2407880; fax (2) 2407887; e-mail info@pinvbank.com; f. 1995 by the PA; some shareholders based in Jordan and the Gulf states; cap. US $20m.; provides full commercial and investment banking services throughout the West Bank and Gaza; Man. IBRAHIM ABU DAYH; 6 brs.

Al-Quds Bank for Development and Investment: POB 2471, Ramallah; tel. (2) 2961750; fax (2) 2961753; e-mail qudsbkhq@palnet.com; f. 1996; merchant bank; Dirs MUHAMMAD SALMAN, GHAZI A. MUSLEH; 9 brs.

Islamic Banks

Arab Islamic Bank: POB 631, Nablus St, Al-Birah/Ramallah; tel. (2) 2407060; fax (2) 2407065; e-mail aib@aibnk.com; internet www.aibnk.com; f. 1995; cap. US $21m., res $2m., dep. $112m., total assets $145m. (Dec. 2004); Chair. WALID T. FAKHOURI; Gen. Man. ATIYEH A. SHANANIER; 7 brs.

Palestine Islamic Bank: POB 1244, Omar al-Mukhtar St, Gaza City; tel. (8) 2825259; fax (8) 2825269.

Foreign Banks

Arab Bank PLC (Jordan): Regional Management, POB 1476, Ramallah; tel. (2) 2982400; fax (2) 2982444; e-mail arabbank@palnet.com; internet www.arabbank.com; f. 1930; cap. US $146.9m., res $2,691.7m., dep. $20,930.1m. (Dec. 2003); Chair. ABD AL-HAMID SHOMAN; Vice-Chair. MUNIB RASHID MASRI; 14 brs and 5 offices in the West Bank and Gaza.

Bank of Jordan PLC: POB 1829, Ramallah; tel. (2) 2958686; fax (2) 2958684; e-mail boj@bankofjordan.com; internet www.bankofjordan.com; Chair. TAWFIK FAKHOURY; Gen. Man. SHAKER FAKHOURY; 5 brs.

Cairo Amman Bank (Jordan): POB 1870, College St, Ramallah; tel. (2) 2983500; fax (2) 2955437; e-mail cabl@attmail.com; internet www.ca-bank.com; Regional Man. BISHARA DABBAH; 19 brs in the West Bank and Gaza.

Jordan National Bank PLC: POB 550, Al-Quds St, Ramallah; tel. (2) 2959343; fax (2) 2959341; e-mail info@jnbpalestine.com; internet www.ahli.com; f. 1995; cap. US $5m., dep. $100m. (Feb. 2005); Chair. Dr RAJAEE MUASHER; Regional Man. HANNA GHATTAS; 6 brs.

Other foreign banks include Egyptian Arab Land Bank, Housing Bank for Trade and Finance (Jordan), HSBC Bank Middle East (United Kingdom), Jordan Gulf Bank, Jordan Kuwait Bank, Principal Bank for Development and Agricultural Credit (Egypt), Standard Chartered Grindlays Bank Ltd (United Kingdom) and Union Bank for Savings and Investment (Jordan).

STOCK EXCHANGE

Palestine Securities Exchange (PSE): POB 128, 3rd Floor, Al-Qaser Bldg, Nablus; tel. (9) 2376666; fax (9) 2375945; e-mail pse@p-s-e.com; internet www.p-s-e.com; f. 1997; Chair. Dr HASSAN ABU LIBDEH; Gen. Man. Dr HASSAN YASSIN.

INSURANCE

A very small insurance industry exists in the West Bank and Gaza.

Arab Insurance Establishment Co Ltd (AIE): POB 166, Nablus; tel. (9) 2341040; fax (9) 2341033; e-mail aie@palnet.com; f. 1975; Gen. Man. IBRAHIM HIJAZI.

Gaza Ahliea Insurance Co Ltd: POB 1214, Al-Jalaa Tower, Remal, Gaza; tel. (8) 2824035; fax (8) 2824015; e-mail gaicnet@palnet.com; f. 1994; Chair. and Gen. Man. Dr MUHAMMAD SABAWI; 6 brs.

National Insurance Co: POB 1819, 34 Municipality St, Al-Birah/Ramallah; tel. (2) 2983800; fax (2) 2407460; e-mail nic@palnet.com; f. 1992; Chair. MUHAMMAD MAHMOUD MASROUJI; Gen. Man. AZIZ MAHMOUD ABD AL-JAWAD; 8 brs.

DEVELOPMENT FINANCE ORGANIZATIONS

Arab Palestinian Investment Co Ltd: POB 2396, Kharaz Center, Yafa St, Industrial Zone, Ramallah; tel. (2) 2984242; fax (2) 2984243; e-mail apic@palnet.com; internet www.apic-pal.com.

Jerusalem Real Estate Investment Co: POB 1876, Ramallah; tel. (2) 2965215; fax (2) 2965217; e-mail jrei@palnet.com; f. 1996; Man. Dir WALID AL-AHMAD.

Palestine Development & Investment Co (PADICO): POB 316, Nablus; tel. (9) 2384354; fax (9) 2384355; e-mail padico@padico.com; internet www.padico.com; f. 1993; Chair. MUNIB R. AL-MASRI; Vice-Chair. NABIL GHATTAS SARRAF.

Palestine Real Estate Investment Co (Aqaria): POB 4049, Gaza; tel. (8) 2824815; fax (8) 2824845; e-mail aqaria@rannet.com; internet www.aqaria.com; f. 1994; Chair. NABIL SARRAF; Man. MUHAMMAD ISMAEL.

Palestinian Economic Council for Development and Reconstruction (PECDAR): POB 54910, Dahiyat Al-Barid, Jerusalem; tel. (2) 2362300; fax (2) 2347041; e-mail info@pecdar.pna.net; internet www.pecdar.org; privately owned; Dir-Gen. Dr MUHAMMAD SHTAYYEH.

Trade and Industry

CHAMBERS OF COMMERCE

Federation of Chambers of Commerce, Industry and Agriculture: tel. (2) 6280727; fax (2) 6280644; e-mail fpccia@palnet.com; internet www.pal-chambers.org; f. 1989; 14 chambers, 32,000 mems.

Bethlehem Chamber of Commerce and Industry: POB 59, Bethlehem; tel. (2) 2742742; fax (2) 2764402; e-mail bcham@palnet.com; internet www.pal-chambers.org/chambers/bethlehem.html; f. 1952; 2,500 mems.

Gaza Chamber of Commerce, Industry and Agriculture: POB 33, Sabra Quarter, Gaza; tel. (8) 2844047; fax (8) 2821172; e-mail gazacham@palnet.com; internet www.pal-chambers.org/chambers/gaza.html; f. 1954; Chair. MUHAMMAD AL-QUDWAH; 14,000 mems.

Hebron Chamber of Commerce and Industry: POB 272, Hebron; tel. (2) 2228218; fax (2) 2227490; e-mail hebcham@hebronet.com; internet www.pal-chambers.org/chambers/hebron.html; f. 1954; Chair. ABD AN-NABI AN-NATSHEH; 5,500 mems.

Jenin Chamber of Commerce, Industry and Agriculture: Jenin; tel. (4) 2501107; fax (4) 2503388; e-mail jencham@hally.net; internet www.pal-chambers.org/chambers/jenin.html; f. 1953; 3,800 mems.

Jericho Chamber of Commerce, Industry and Agriculture: POB 91, Jericho 00970; tel. (2) 2323313; fax (2) 2322394; e-mail jericho@pal-chambers.org; internet www.pal-chambers.org/chambers/jericho.html; f. 1953; 400 mems; Chair. HAJ MANSOUR SALAYMEH.

Jerusalem Arab Chamber of Commerce and Industry: POB 19151, Jerusalem 91191; tel. (2) 2344923; fax (2) 2344914; e-mail chamber@jerusalemchamber.org; internet www.jerusalemchamber.org; f. 1936; 2,050 mems; Chair. AHMAD HASHEM ZUGHAYAR; Dir AZZAM ABU SAOUD.

Nablus Chamber of Commerce and Industry: POB 35, Nablus; tel. (9) 2380335; fax (9) 2377605; e-mail nablus@palnet.com; internet www.pal-chambers.org/chambers/nablus.html; f. 1941; Pres. MA'AZ NABULSI; Dir TAJ ED-DIN BITAR; 5,900 mems.

Palestinian-European Chamber of Commerce: tel. (2) 894883.

Qalqilya Chamber of Commerce, Industry and Agriculture: POB 13, Qalqilya; tel. (9) 2941473; fax (9) 2940164; e-mail chamberq@hally.net; internet www.pal-chambers.org/chambers/qalqilya.html; f. 1972; 1,068 mems.

Ramallah Chamber of Commerce and Industry: POB 256, Al-Birah/Ramallah; tel. (2) 2955052; fax (2) 2984691; e-mail info@ramallahcci.org; internet www.ramallahcci.org; f. 1950; Chair. MUHAMMAD AHMAD AMIN; Vice-Chair. YOUSUF ASH-SHARIF; 4,100 mems.

Salfit Chamber of Commerce, Industry and Agriculture: Salfit; tel. and fax (9) 2515970; e-mail salfeetchamber@hotmail.com; internet www.pal-chambers.org/chambers/salfeet.html; Chair. NABEEL OZRAIL.

Tulkarm Chamber of Commerce, Industry and Agriculture: POB 51, Tulkarm; tel. (9) 2671010; fax (9) 2675623; e-mail tulkarem@palnet.com; internet www.pal-chambers.org/chambers/tulkarem.html; f. 1945; 625 mems; Chair. SHUKRI AHMAD JALLAD.

TRADE AND INDUSTRIAL ORGANIZATIONS

Palestinian General Federation of Trade Unions (PGFTU): POB 102, Nablus; tel. (9) 2387868; fax (9) 2384374; e-mail pgftu@pgftu.org; internet www.pgftu.org; Sec.-Gen. SHAHER SAED.

Union of Industrialists: POB 1296, Gaza; tel. (8) 2866222; fax (8) 2862013; Chair. MUHAMMAD YAZIJI.

UTILITIES

Electricity

Palestinian Energy Authority (PEA): POB 3591, Nablus St, Al-Birah/Ramallah; POB 3041, Gaza; tel. (2) 2986190; fax (2) 2986191; tel. (8) 2808484; fax (8) 2808488; e-mail pea@palnet.com; internet www.palnet.com/~eigr/index2.htm; f. 1994; Chair. Dr ABD AR-RAHMAN T. HAMAD.

Jerusalem District Electricity Co Ltd (JDECO): internet www.jdeco.net.

National Electric Co (NEC): West Bank; f. 2000.

Palestine Electric Co (PEC): Gaza; f. 1999; 33% state-owned; Chair. SAID KHOURY; Man. Dir SAMIR SHAWWA.

Water

Palestinian Water Authority (PWA): POB 2174, Ramallah; f. 1995; Dir Eng. NABIL ASH-SHARIF.

Transport

CIVIL AVIATION

Palestinian Civil Aviation Authority (PCAA): Yasser Arafat International Airport, POB 8007, Rafah, Gaza; tel. (7) 2134338; fax (7) 2134159; e-mail abuhalib@gaza-airport.org; internet www.arafat-airport.ps; f. 1994; Gaza International Airport (renamed as above after Arafat's death in Nov. 2004) was formally inaugurated in November 1998 to operate services by Palestinian Airlines (its subsidiary), Egypt Air and Royal Jordanian Airline; Royal Air Maroc began to operate services to Amman, Abu Dhabi, Cairo, Doha, Dubai, Jeddah, Istanbul and Larnaca, and intends to expand its network to Europe; the airport was closed by the Israeli authorities in February 2001 and the runway seriously damaged by Israeli air-strikes in late 2001 and early 2002; Dir-Gen. SALMAN ABU HALIB.

Palestinian Airlines: POB 4043, Gaza; tel. (8) 2822800; fax (8) 2821309; e-mail commercial@palairlines.com; internet www.palairlines.com; f. 1994; state-owned; Dir-Gen. Dr BAJES AL-ALI; Exec. Dir YOUSUF SHAATH.

Tourism

Although the tourist industry in the West Bank was virtually destroyed as a result of the 1967 Arab–Israeli War, by the late 1990s the sector was expanding significantly, with a number of hotels being opened or under construction. Much of the tourism in the West Bank centres around the historical and biblical sites of Jerusalem and Bethlehem. However, the renewed outbreak of Israeli–Palestinian conflict in the West Bank and Gaza Strip from late 2000 has prevented the recovery of the tourist industry.

Ministry of Tourism and Antiquities: POB 534, Manger St, Bethlehem; tel. (2) 2741581; fax (2) 2743753; e-mail mota@visit-palestine.com; internet www.visit-palestine.com.

Near East Tourist Agency: POB 19015, 18 Azzahra St, Jerusalem; tel. (2) 5328706; fax (2) 5328701; e-mail jerusalem@netours.com; internet www.netours.com; Pres. HANI ABU DAYYEH.

PANAMA

Introductory Survey

Location, Climate, Language, Religion, Flag, Capital

The Republic of Panama is a narrow country situated at the southern end of the isthmus separating North and South America. It is bounded to the west by Costa Rica and to the east by Colombia in South America. The Caribbean Sea is to the north, and the Pacific Ocean to the south. Panama has a tropical maritime climate (warm, humid days and cool nights). There is little seasonal variation in temperatures, which average 23°C–27°C (73°F–81°F) in coastal areas. The rainy season is from April until December. Spanish is the official language. Almost all of the inhabitants profess Christianity, and some 85% are Roman Catholics. The national flag (proportions 2 by 3) is composed of four equal rectangles: on the top row the quarter at the hoist is white, with a five-pointed blue star in the centre, while the quarter in the fly is red; on the bottom row the quarter at the hoist is blue, and the quarter in the fly is white, with a five-pointed red star in the centre. The capital is Panamá (Panama City).

Recent History

Panama was subject to Spanish rule from the 16th century until 1821, when it became independent as part of Gran Colombia. Panama remained part of Colombia until 1903, when it declared its separate independence with the support of the USA. In that year the USA purchased the concession for construction of the Panama Canal, which was opened in 1914. The 82-km Canal links the Atlantic and Pacific Oceans, and is a major international sea route. Under the terms of the 1903 treaty between Panama and the USA concerning the construction and administration of the Canal, the USA was granted ('in perpetuity') control of a strip of Panamanian territory, known as the Canal Zone, extending for 8 km on either side of the Canal route. The treaty also established Panama as a protectorate of the USA. In exchange for transferring the Canal Zone, Panama was to receive an annuity from the USA. The terms of this treaty and its successors have dominated relations between Panama and the USA since 1903.

In 1939 a revised treaty with the USA ended Panama's protectorate status. A new Constitution for Panama was adopted in 1946. Following a period of rapidly changing governments, the 1952 presidential election was won by Col José Antonio Remón, formerly Chief of Police. During his term of office, President Remón negotiated a more favourable treaty with the USA, whereby the annuity payable to Panama was increased. In January 1955, however, before the treaty came into force, Remón was assassinated. He was succeeded by José Ramón Guizado, hitherto the First Vice-President, but, less than two weeks after assuming power, the new President was implicated in the plot to assassinate Remón. Guizado was removed from office and later imprisoned. Remón's Second Vice-President, Ricardo Arias Espinosa, then completed the presidential term, which expired in 1956, when Ernesto de la Guardia was elected President. The next presidential election was won by Roberto Chiari, who held office in 1960–64, and his successor was Marco Aurelio Robles (1964–68). During this period there were frequent public demands for the transfer to Panama of sovereignty over the Canal Zone.

Presidential and legislative elections took place in May 1968. The presidential contest was won by Dr Arnulfo Arias Madrid, the candidate supported by the coalition Unión Nacional (which included his own Partido Panameñista). Dr Arias had been President in 1940–41 and 1949–51, but both terms had ended in his forcible removal from power. He took office for a third term in October 1968 but, after only 11 days, he was deposed by the National Guard (Panama's only military body), led by Col (later Brig.-Gen.) Omar Torrijos Herrera, who accused him of planning to establish a dictatorship. The Asamblea Nacional (National Assembly) was dissolved, and political activity suspended. Political parties were banned in February 1969.

In August 1972 elections were held to a new legislative body, the 505-member Asamblea Nacional de Corregidores (National Assembly of Community Representatives). In October the Asamblea conferred extraordinary powers on Gen. Torrijos as Chief of Government for six years.

In February 1974 representatives of Panama and the USA concluded an agreement on principles for a new treaty whereby the USA would surrender its jurisdiction over the Canal Zone. Discontent arising from the Government's handling of subsequent protracted negotiations, combined with deteriorating living standards, culminated in student riots in 1976. Intensified talks in 1977 resulted in two new Canal treaties, which were approved by 66% of voters at a referendum in October. The treaties became effective from October 1979. Panama assumed control of the former Canal Zone, which was abolished. Administration of the Canal was placed under the control of a joint Panama Canal Commission until the end of 1999. US military forces in Panama were to remain until 2000, and the USA was to be entitled to defend the Canal's neutrality thereafter.

In August 1978 elections were held to the Asamblea Nacional de Corregidores; in October the new representatives elected Dr Arístides Royo Sánchez, hitherto Minister of Education, to be President for a six-year term. Gen. Torrijos resigned as Chief of Government, but continued in the post of Commander of the National Guard, and effectively retained power until his death in an air crash in July 1981. President Royo failed to gain the support of the National Guard, and in July 1982 he was forced to resign by Col Rubén Darío Paredes, who had ousted Col Florencio Flores as Commander-in-Chief in March. The Vice-President, Ricardo de la Espriella, was installed as President, and, under the direction of Col Paredes, promoted business interests and pursued a foreign policy more favourable to the USA.

In April 1983 a series of amendments to the Constitution were approved by referendum. However, in spite of new constitutional measures to limit the power of the National Guard, de facto power remained with the armed forces, whose position was strengthened by a decision in September to unite all security forces within one organization (subsequently known as the National Defence Forces). In June Paredes was succeeded as Commander-in-Chief by Brig. (later Gen.) Manuel Antonio Noriega Morena. In February 1984 Dr Jorge Illueca, hitherto the Vice-President, became Head of State after the sudden resignation of President de la Espriella, who was believed to have been ousted from power by the National Defence Forces.

Elections to the presidency and the legislature (the new 67-member Asamblea Legislativa—Legislative Assembly) took place in May 1984. Despite allegations of extensive electoral fraud, Dr Nicolás Ardito Barletta, the candidate of the Partido Revolucionario Democrático (PRD) who received the electoral support of the armed forces, was eventually declared President-elect, narrowly defeating Arias Madrid, standing as candidate of the Partido Panameñista Auténtico (PPA). However, as a result of protracted opposition to his economic policies, President Ardito was unable to secure a political base to support his administration, and in September 1985 he resigned. Ardito claimed that his resignation had been prompted by the deterioration in his relations with the legislature and with the National Defence Forces, although there was considerable speculation that he had been forced to resign by Gen. Noriega, to prevent a public scandal over the alleged involvement of the National Defence Forces in the murder of Dr Hugo Spadafora, a former deputy minister under Torrijos and a leading critic of Noriega. Ardito was succeeded as President in September by Eric Arturo Delvalle, formerly First Vice-President.

In June 1986 US sources alleged that Noriega was involved in the trafficking of illegal drugs and weapons and in the transfer of proceeds from these activities through Panamanian banks. In addition, Noriega was implicated in the sale of US national security information and restricted technology to Cuba. There were also renewed allegations of his involvement in the murder of Dr Spadafora and in electoral fraud during the 1984 presidential election. Strikes and demonstrations in support of demands for Noriega's dismissal resulted in violent clashes with the National Defence Forces. Following this outbreak of violence, the US Senate approved a resolution urging the establishment of democracy in Panama, the suspension of Noriega and the holding of an independent investigation into the allegations against him. The Panamanian Government responded by accusing the USA of interfering in Panamanian affairs, and a wave of anti-US sentiment was unleashed, including an attack on the US embassy building by protesters in July 1987. The USA subsequently suspended economic and military aid to Panama and downgraded its official links with the country. Protests against Noriega continued, in an atmosphere of mounting political and economic insecurity.

In February 1988 Noriega was indicted by two US Grand Juries on charges of drugs-smuggling and racketeering. On 25 February President Delvalle dismissed Noriega from his post, following his refusal to resign voluntarily. However, leading members of the ruling coalition and the National Defence Forces united in support of their Commander-in-Chief, and on the following day the Asamblea Legislativa voted to remove President Delvalle from office because of his 'failure to abide by the Constitution'. The Minister of Education, Manuel Solís Palma, was appointed acting President. Delvalle refused to accept his dismissal, and the US Administration affirmed its support for the ousted President by declining to recognize the new leadership. Delvalle, who went into hiding, became the figurehead of the USA's attempts to oust Noriega, and in late February, following Delvalle's demand that the US Government impose an economic boycott on Panama, US courts authorized a 'freeze' on some US $50m. of Panamanian assets held in US banks. This move, coupled with a general strike organized by the Cruzada Civilista Nacional (a broadly based opposition grouping led by the business sector) after Delvalle's dismissal, brought economic chaos to Panama, prompting the closure of all banks for more than two months.

In March 1988 a coup attempt by the chief of police, Col Leónidas Macías, was thwarted by members of the National Defence Forces loyal to Noriega. The attempted coup represented the first indication of opposition to Noriega from within the security forces. The Government announced a state of emergency (which was revoked in April) and the suspension of civil rights. Negotiations between Noriega and a representative of the US Administration, during which the USA was reported to have proposed the withdrawal of charges against Noriega in exchange for his retirement and departure into exile before the elections scheduled for 1989, ended acrimoniously in late March. The US Administration subsequently reinforced economic sanctions against Panamanian interests.

Presidential, legislative and municipal elections were held on 7 May 1989. The presidential candidate of the pro-Government electoral alliance, the Coalición de Liberación Nacional (COLINA), was Carlos Duque Jaén, the leader of the PRD and a close associate of Noriega. Guillermo Endara Galimany of the PPA was the presidential candidate of the opposition alliance, the Alianza Democrática de Oposición Civilista (ADOC). The election campaign was dominated by accusations of electoral malpractice, and, following the voting, both ADOC and COLINA claimed victory, despite indications from exit polls and unofficial sources that ADOC had received between 50% and 75% of votes cast. A group of international observers declared that the election had been conducted fraudulently. A delay in announcing the results was interpreted by the opposition as an attempt by the Government to falsify the outcome. Endara declared himself President-elect; in subsequent demonstrations crowds clashed with the National Defence Forces, and many members of the opposition, including Endara and other leaders, were severely beaten. On 10 May the election results were annulled by the Electoral Tribunal, which cited US interference.

On 31 August 1989, following intervention by the Organization of American States (OAS, see p. 333), Panama's General State Council announced the appointment of a provisional Government and a 41-member Legislative Commission to preserve 'institutional order'. The holding of elections was to be considered within six months, but this was to be largely dependent upon the cessation of US 'hostilities' and the withdrawal of US economic sanctions. On 1 September Francisco Rodríguez, a known associate of Noriega, was inaugurated as President, and Carlos Ozores Typaldos as Vice-President. The USA immediately severed diplomatic relations with Panama and expressed its intention to impose more stringent economic sanctions upon the new Government, including a ban on the use of US ports by Panamanian-registered ships. In October an attempted coup, led by middle-ranking officers seeking to replace Noriega at the head of the *de facto* military dictatorship, was suppressed by forces loyal to Noriega.

In November 1989 the Asamblea Nacional de Corregidores was provisionally restored. This body, now numbering 510 members, was intended to fulfil a consultative and (limited) legislative function. Noriega was elected as its 'national co-ordinator'. In mid-December the Asamblea adopted a resolution declaring Noriega to be Head of State and 'leader of the struggle for national liberation', and announced that a state of war existed with the USA. On 20 December a US military offensive ('Operation Just Cause'), involving some 24,000 troops, was launched against Noriega and the headquarters of the National Defence Forces from US bases within Panama. The objects of the assault were swiftly brought under US control, although sporadic attacks on US bases by loyalist forces continued for several days, and Noriega eluded capture long enough to take refuge in the residence of the Papal Nuncio in Panama. On 21 December Endara, who had been installed as Head of State in a ceremony attended by a Panamanian judge at the Fort Clayton US military base only hours before the invasion, was officially inaugurated as President. President Endara declared that the Panamanian judicial system was inadequate to try Noriega. Following his surrender to US forces on 3 January 1990, Noriega was immediately transported to the USA and arraigned on several charges of involvement in drugs-trafficking and money-laundering operations. (Noriega, who claimed the status of a prisoner of war, refused to recognize the right of jurisdiction of a US court.) In April 1992 Noriega was found guilty on eight charges of conspiracy to manufacture and distribute cocaine; he was sentenced to 40 years' imprisonment.

International criticism of the USA's military operation was widespread, although the Administration cited the right to self-defence, under Article 51 of the UN Charter, as a legal justification for armed intervention, and US President George Bush asserted that military action was necessary for the protection of US citizens, the protection of the Panama Canal, support for Panama's 'democratically elected' officials and the pursuit of an indicted criminal. According to the US Government, 'Operation Just Cause' resulted in about 500 Panamanian casualties, but a total of at least 1,000 Panamanian deaths was estimated by the Roman Catholic Church and other unofficial sources; 26 US troops were killed, and more than 300 wounded, during the invasion.

Following the appointment of a new Cabinet (comprising members of the ADOC alliance) in late December 1989, the Endara administration declared itself to be a 'democratic Government of reconstruction and national reconciliation'. Shortly afterwards the Electoral Tribunal revoked its annulment of the May elections and announced that ADOC had obtained 62% of the votes cast in the presidential election, according to copies of incomplete results (covering 64% of total votes) that had been held in safe keeping by the Bishops' Conference of the Roman Catholic Church. In February 1990 the composition of the Asamblea Legislativa was announced, based on the same documentation, with 51 seats awarded to ADOC and six to COLINA; fresh elections were to be held for nine seats that could not be reliably allocated. The National Defence Forces were officially disbanded, and a new, 'non-political' Public Force was created.

Although the overthrow of Noriega immediately released US $375m. in assets that had previously been withheld by the US Government, the new administration inherited serious economic difficulties. The cost of 'Operation Just Cause', in terms of damage and lost revenues alone, was estimated to be at least $2,000m. Although the Administration of US President George Bush agreed to provide aid amounting to more than $1,000m., the US Congress was slow to approve the appropriation of funds. In April 1990 the USA revoked the economic restrictions that had been imposed two years previously, and in May Congress approved financial assistance to Panama totalling $420m. Disbursement of a substantial tranche was to be dependent upon the successful negotiation of a Mutual Legal Assistance Treaty (MLAT) between the two countries, whereby the US authorities sought to gain greater access to information amassed by Panama City's 'offshore' international finance centre, in order to combat the illegal laundering of money. In August the Endara Government announced its 'Strategy of Development and Economic Modernization', which included provisions for the transfer to private ownership of several state-controlled enterprises. The new economic measures encountered vociferous political opposition from the Partido Demócrata Cristiano (PDC—one of the parties in the ruling coalition) and prompted widespread disaffection among public-sector workers whose jobs were threatened by the short-term divestment programme.

Accusations from public and political opponents that the security forces had not been adequately purged following the ousting of Noriega were seemingly justified by a succession of coup attempts during the early 1990s. Meanwhile, growing public concern at the Government's failure to restore civil and economic order was reflected in the results of elections held in January 1991 for the nine seats in the Asamblea Legislativa that had not been awarded by the Electoral Tribunal following the elections of May 1989 (see above). Member parties of the former electoral alliance COLINA, which had supported the previous regime, secured five of the contested seats, while parties represented in the governing alliance secured only four seats. President Endara's recently formed Partido Arnulfista (PA, formerly a faction of the PPA) failed to secure a single seat. Serious concern had been expressed at the increasing level of influence exerted by the US Government over the President, particularly when it became known that in July 1990 the Government had accepted US funds to establish, by decree, a 100-strong Council for Public Security, which would maintain close links with the US Central Intelligence Agency.

Long-standing political differences within the Government reached a crisis in March 1991, when the PDC initiated proceedings to impeach Endara for involving the US armed forces in suppressing an uprising in December 1990 (a technical violation of the 1977 Panama Canal Treaty). Although the proposal was dismissed by the Asamblea Legislativa, Endara and his supporters strongly criticized leaders of the PDC, accusing them of participating in illegal activities to gather intelligence information and of obtaining armaments in preparation for a coup attempt. In the following month Endara dismissed the five PDC members of his Cabinet and significantly increased the representation of the PA in the Government.

In July 1991 the Asamblea Legislativa approved the terms of the MLAT, following indications in US intelligence documents that drugs-related activities in Panama (and money-laundering in particular) had returned to the levels that had prevailed prior to the removal of Gen. Noriega. The Panamanian Government's urgent need of direct financial aid (the disbursement of which the USA had made dependent on the MLAT) prompted it to sign the treaty with only minor modifications to the terms of the agreement.

In October 1991 and February 1992 two further alleged coup attempts were immediately suppressed, and resulted in the detention of several more members of the former National Defence Forces, and the creation, in March 1992, of a presidential police force to be directly responsible to the Head of State. In November, however, the President suffered a serious political reverse, when proposals for more than 50 reforms (including the constitutional abolition of the armed forces and the creation of the post of ombudsman to protect the rights of Panamanian citizens) were rejected by 64% of voters in a referendum. Opposition groups reiterated demands for the creation of a constituent assembly to draft a new constitution, and stressed popular concerns regarding the future security of the Panama Canal in the absence of an effective Panamanian military force.

The acquittal, in September 1993, of seven former soldiers tried for involvement in the 1985 assassination of Dr Spadafora provoked widespread public outrage. Noriega was tried in connection with the affair *in absentia* and, in October 1993, was found guilty and sentenced to 20 years' imprisonment for ordering his murder. In March 1994 Noriega was also convicted *in absentia* for the 1989 murder of an army major who had led an unsuccessful military coup against him; he was sentenced to a further 20 years' imprisonment for this offence. Furthermore, in August 2001 he was sentenced to a further eight years' imprisonment after being convicted *in absentia* of corruption charges.

A presidential election was held on 8 May 1994. Ernesto Pérez Balladares, the candidate of the Pueblo Unido alliance (that included the PRD), won a narrow victory, gaining 33% of the votes cast, ahead of Mireya Moscoso de Gruber (the widow of former President Arias Madrid), who attracted 30%. Moscoso was the nominee of the Alianza Democrática, a grouping of the PA with the Partido Liberal (PL), the Partido Liberal Auténtico (PLA), the Unión Democrática Independiente and the Partido Nacionalista Popular (PNP). The failure of the Pueblo Unido alliance to secure a majority in the legislature was reflected in the broad political base of Pérez Balladares' proposed Cabinet, announced in May. Post-electoral political manoeuvring resulted in the creation of the Alianza Pueblo Unido y Solidaridad, Pérez Balladares' electoral alliance having secured the additional support of the Partido Solidaridad in the Asamblea. Pérez Balladares assumed the presidency on 1 September 1994. A new Cabinet, installed on the same day, included former members of the PA and the PDC who had been obliged to resign their party membership in order to take up their cabinet posts.

In May 1996 the credibility of the Government was damaged by the discovery that a private Panamanian bank (Banaico, which had collapsed earlier in the year), in whose activities senior PRD members were implicated, had been a centre for money-laundering. In June, moreover, the position of President Pérez Balladares was undermined by reports that an alleged drugs-trafficker had contributed some US $51,000 to his 1994 presidential campaign. Pérez Balladares was forced to admit that his campaign fund had 'unwittingly' received the payment; the Procurator-General subsequently announced a thorough investigation into the origin of the 1994 campaign funds.

At a presidential election conducted on 2 May 1999, Mireya Moscoso de Gruber, the candidate of the Unión por Panamá alliance (comprising the PA, Movimiento Liberal Republicano Nacionalista—MOLIRENA, Movimiento de Renovación Nacional and Cambio Democrático), was elected with 45% of the votes, ahead of Martín Torrijos Espino, son of former dictator Omar Torrijos, the candidate of the Nueva Nación alliance (comprising the PRD, the Partido Solidaridad, the Partido Liberal Nacional—PLN—and the Movimiento Papa Egoró—MPE), who secured 38%, and Alberto Vallarino, the candidate of the Acción Opositora alliance (comprising the PDC, the Partido Renovación Civilista—PRC, the PNP and the PL). However, the Unión por Panamá failed to secure a majority in the concurrent legislative election, obtaining 24 of the 71 contested seats in the Asamblea Legislativa, while Nueva Nación secured 41 seats and Acción Opositora won six seats. Moscoso assumed the presidency on 1 September. A new Cabinet, installed on the same day, included members of the Partido Solidaridad, the PLN, the PDC and the PRC, each of which had abandoned their respective electoral alliances in order to form a 'Government of national unity', thereby giving Moscoso a narrow majority in the legislature.

In July 1999 the Commander-in-Chief of the US Southern Command, Gen. Charles Wilhelm, caused considerable unease in Panama when he indicated that the USA had contingency plans for defending the Panama Canal, following US withdrawal at the end of 1999, should violence spread from Colombia into Panama: according to the 1977 Canal treaties, the USA was entitled unilaterally to intervene if it had reason to suppose that the security of the Canal was threatened. In November the USA completed its withdrawal from Howard air base, and the last of the US military bases, Fort Clayton, was ceded to Panama. In December, the Panamanian Government announced that a national security plan was under negotiation to ensure the security of the Canal and to combat border incursions, drugs-trafficking and international crime. On 31 December 1999 the USA officially relinquished ownership of the Canal to Panama. In early 2000 a five-year canal-modernization project was initiated. In February the Government negotiated a counter-narcotics agreement with the USA.

In August 2000 the governing coalition lost its narrow legislative majority after the PRD and the PDC formed an alliance. The effective legislative impasse was ended in February 2002 following the defection of three opposition deputies.

Following the discovery of human remains in a former military barracks in Tocumen, in December 2000 President Moscoso announced the establishment of a Truth Commission, headed by Alberto Santiago Almanza Henriquez, to investigate 'disappearances' during the military dictatorships of 1968–89. In October 2001 the Commission reported that, following excavations in 12 separate areas, it was able to confirm that 72 of the 189 people believed to have 'disappeared' had been killed or tortured by state forces. In March 2004 the Asamblea approved the establishment of a Special Prosecutor's Office to investigate crimes committed during the military dictatorships; in late February 2006 the Special Prosecutor announced that four officers who served in the military regimes were prepared to offer anonymous testimonies against former colleagues.

Accusations of corruption within the legislature led to public protests in early 2002. In January three PRD members were accused of having received payment in exchange for voting for two Supreme Court candidates not approved by their party, while PRD member Carlos Afú confessed that he had accepted a bribe to vote in favour of a Caribbean port-development project. President Moscoso's administration encountered further problems in the wake of an agreement signed in February 2002, which provided for US authorities to join the Panamanian National Maritime Service in patrolling its territorial waters, in an attempt to control the illegal trade in narcotics. The agreement was strongly criticized by opposition members. However, in September a number of defections from the opposition to the governing coalition gave Moscoso a working majority in the Asamblea for the first time since taking office. At the end of the month the Government was able to make further amendments to the controversial bilateral maritime agreement with the USA, which gave both countries' security forces the right to search vessels and pursue criminals in each other's territorial waters. An additional accord, which provided the USA with increased powers to inspect Panama's financial and tax records as part of its campaign against money-laundering, similarly provoked protests from opposition parties. The Moscoso Government had already introduced legislation aimed at eliminating the abuse of the financial system, which had facilitated the removal of Panama from the USA's blacklist of so-called tax 'havens'. In April 2002 Panama was also removed from the Organisation for Economic Co-operation and Development's (OECD) list of 'uncooperative tax havens', after the Government committed to making its financial sector more transparent. In January 2004 the country's bank auditors, the Unidad de Análisis Financiero, identified 392 bank accounts that it suspected were being used for money-laundering purposes. They included 40 accounts associated with the former President of Nicaragua, Arnoldo Alemán Lacayo, and a further 14 connected to the former Guatemalan President, Alfonso Portillo Cabrera.

Members of a national dialogue forum established by President Moscoso reached agreement on a number of reforms to the tax system in January 2003. Proposed changes included the extension of sales tax to luxury goods and services, although the level of taxation on income and business corporations was to remain unchanged. In March, following a further decline in profits, the US Chiquita Brands company announced that it was to sell its 12 Pafco fruit plantations in Colón to a plantation workers' co-operative. On 28 February 2004 two of these plantations ceased operations as a result of industrial action by over 500 of the plantations' 3,000 employees, in demand of higher wages and improved benefits. A second strike ended after five days in mid-March following the resignation of the Secretary-General of the banana workers union.

On 10 September 2003 President Moscoso dismissed Juan Jované as Director of the social security fund, the Caja de Seguro Social (CSS) after he had refused to agree on a balanced budget with the other members of the CSS board. The CSS had been running at a loss for years, and, according to the Government, would go bankrupt without reform. In a subsequent television appearance, however, Jované alleged that he had been removed to allow for the privatization of the CSS. Furthermore, he claimed that the Government was intending to compel the CSS to purchase US $500m. of government debt, in order to finance the PA's re-election campaign. On 12 September CSS employees, trade union members and students marched through the capital to protest at Jované's dismissal. Faced with public protests, one week later President Moscoso signed a declaration pledging not to sell off the CSS. Nevertheless, a second march was held in the capital on 19 September. Furthermore, an umbrella trade union organization, known as the Frente Nacional por la Defensa de la Seguridad Social (FRENADESSO), held a widely observed 24-hour general strike on 23 September (although only 40% of government workers were estimated to have participated following a threat of dismissal). As well as protesting the dismissal of Jované, the strike was intended to highlight the level of public discontent at the policies of the Moscoso Government. A second, smaller general strike was held on 29 October, in which some 30,000 workers participated.

Presidential and legislative elections took place on 2 May 2004, in which 76.9% of the electorate participated. Martín Torrijos Espino, the candidate of the PRD (which contested the elections as part of the Patria Nueva electoral alliance with the Partido Popular) won the presidential ballot, winning 47.4% of the votes cast. Former President Endara, representing the Partido Solidaridad, came second with 30.9% of the ballot. The PA's presidential candidate, former Minister of Foreign Affairs José Miguel Alemán (officially the representative of the Visión de País electoral alliance, comprising the PA, MOLIRENA and the PLN) attracted only 16.4% of the votes cast. (Alemán's campaign had been undermined by the Government's unpopularity and by accusations that he had received illegal funding from Moscoso.) The Patria Nueva also performed well in the concurrently held elections to the enlarged, 78-seat Asamblea Legislativa: the party won 43.9% of the votes cast and secured a total of 43 seats, 42 of which were won by the PRD. The PA obtained 19.3% of the ballot and 16 seats, while the Partido Solidaridad received 15.7% of the votes cast and nine seats. Torrijos assumed office on 1 September.

In late August 2004, just prior to the end of her mandate, President Moscoso announced she was to pardon and release four prisoners sought by the authorities in Cuba for allegedly plotting to assassinate the Cuban leader Fidel Castro Ruz in 2000. The men had been found guilty by a Panamanian court in April of illegal possession of weapons and sentenced to varying terms of imprisonment. The Venezuelan Government also had been attempting to extradite one of the men in connection with the bombing of a Cuban aeroplane in 1976. The Cuban Government threatened to suspend diplomatic relations with Panama, prompting Moscoso to recall the Panamanian ambassador in Havana and to expel the Cuban representative in Panama. The men were pardoned on 26 August and on the same day Castro's Government severed diplomatic ties. The Venezuelan Government did likewise the following day. Following the inauguration of the administration of President Torrijos in September, the new Minister of Foreign Affairs, Samuel Lewis Navarro, succeeded in restoring diplomatic relations with Venezuela on 6 September. However, relations with Cuba proved more sensitive and full diplomatic ties were not restored until August 2005.

Even before he assumed the presidency, Torrijos was successful in bringing about several constitutional amendments. In late July 2004 his proposed reform of the Asamblea Legislativa received legislative approval. The number of parliamentary seats was to be reduced to 71 (from 78) from 2009. Furthermore, deputies voted to end parliamentary immunity from prosecution and to transfer the authority to ratify constitutional amendments from the Asamblea Legislativa to a constituent assembly. President Torrijos also pledged to address the problem of official corruption. One week after taking office, Panama's ambassador to Cuba, Abraham Bárcenas, who had been recalled at the end of the previous month, was arrested as part of an investigation into the alleged sale of Panamanian visas to Cuban citizens. Bárcenas' predecessor, Oscar Alarcón, was also under investigation for alleged corruption. Then, on 1 November the Government announced that corruption charges had been filed against the former Minister of Finance and the Treasury, Norberto Delgado. His successor, Ricuarte Vázquez Morales, criticized the former administration's fiscal management, and stated that the fiscal deficit was an estimated 5.4% of gross domestic product, rather than the 2.7% announced by his predecessor. In order to reduce the deficit to 1% by 2009, fiscal reform legislation was submitted to the Asamblea Legislativa in January 2005 that proposed, inter alia, to reduce the public-sector work-force by 12% over five years and to revise methods of corporate taxation. Despite opposition from business associations and trade unions, the legislation was approved at the end of the month.

On 12 October 2004 some 5,000 people participated in a protest march organized by the FRENADESSO, the social organization established to resist privatization of the CSS. The new Government denied it intended fully to privatize the CSS, but emphasized the need for reform in light of the institution's estimated deficit of between US $2,500m.–$3,000m. Proposed social security reforms included an increase in the retirement age, a reduction in retirement benefits and the transfer of some pensions into private funds. Teachers, pension-fund employees and construction workers participated in further protests and industrial action co-ordinated by FRENADESSO in late May 2005. The protests culminated in a major demonstration against the reform proposals on 1 June. Nevertheless, the following day the pension reforms were approved by the Asamblea Legislativa. However, they included a number of concessions, including proportional pensions for those who failed to make sufficient contributions, and the reduction in the proposed pensionable retirement age for women from 62 years of age to 60 (hitherto 57). None the less, industrial unrest continued and on 8 June medical workers joined the ongoing strike. On 26 June President Torrijos agreed partially to suspend implementation of the new law for 90 days to allow a dialogue process. Representatives of the Government, trade unions and the Roman Catholic church participated in negotiations during the following months and in December a revised series of measures was presented to the Asamblea Legislativa. The new proposals, which maintained the retirement age for women at 57 years of age and increased the minimum qualifying number of monthly pension contributions from 180 to just 240 (rather than 300 as initially suggested), were voted into law on 21 December.

On 3 September 2005 Torrijos announced a minor cabinet reorganization in which hitherto Deputy Minister of Education, Miguel Angel Cañizales, was appointed Minister of Education, succeeding Juan Bosco Bernal, while María del Carmen Roquebert León replaced Leonor Calderón as Minister of Youth, Women, Family and Childhood. At the end of October Torrijos launched a welfare programme that provided subsidies for the purchase of food to some 4,200 peasant families in the province of Veraguas, conditional upon their children attending school and medical centres.

The Minister of Agricultural Development, Laurentino Cortizo, submitted his resignation on 10 January 2006, the day before the commencement of the ninth round of negotiations towards a free trade agreement with the USA. Cortizo reportedly resigned in protest at US pressure to adopt that country's plant and livestock regulations, which he claimed could compromise Panama's food health standards. He was replaced by Guillermo Augusto Salazar Nicolau.

In April 2006 the Autoridad del Canal de Panamá (ACP) was expected to announce plans to widen the Canal to allow the passage of larger commercial container vessels. President Torrijos promised to hold a national debate and an eventual referendum on the ACP's proposals. While widely considered to be vital to the future of the Canal and therefore the country's commercial sector, concerns were raised relating to the environmental consequences of the expansion and the possible relocation of farmers in communities bordering the Canal.

In July 1997, in the light of the increasing number of incursions by Colombian guerrillas and paramilitary groups into Panamanian territory, the Government deployed more than 1,200 members of the security forces to Darién Province to secure the border with Colombia. In previous months Colombian paramilitary members were reported to have forcibly occupied several settlements in the area while in pursuit of guerrillas who had taken refuge over the border. Following discussions between Pérez Balladares and his Colombian counterpart, Andrés Pastrana Arango, an agreement on improved co-operation concerning border security was reached. In June 1999, following further incursions by Colombian guerrillas into Darién Province, Panama and Colombia reached agreement on the strengthening of military patrols on both sides of the countries' joint border. However, in October 2000 one person was killed and 12 people were injured when Colombian paramilitaries attacked the town of Nazaret. In early 2002 an escalation in the conflict in Colombia led to fears of an influx of refugees into Darién and prompted the Panamanian Government to reinforce its border.

In October 1993 President Endara signed a protocol to establish Panama's membership of the Central American Parliament (Parlacen), a regional political forum with its headquarters in Guatemala. Later in the month Endara, together with the five Presidents of the member nations of the Central American Common Market (CACM, see p. 188), signed a protocol to the 1960 General Treaty on Central American Integration, committing Panama to fuller economic integration in the region. However, at a meeting of Central American Presidents, convened in Costa Rica in August 1994, Pérez Balladares (attending as an observer) stated that his administration considered further regional economic integration to be disadvantageous to Panama, owing to the differences between Panama's services-based economy and the reliance on the agricultural sector of the other Central American states. Negotiations on a free trade agreement with El Salvador were concluded in March 2002. Although Panama was excluded from the negotiations towards a Dominican Republic-Central American Free Trade Agreement (DR-CAFTA) with the USA, discussions regarding a bilateral free trade agreement with the USA were ongoing from 2001, although no accord had been reached by early 2006 and a ninth round of talks collapsed in January over food safety issues (see above). Panama has observer status within the Andean Community of Nations (see p. 158).

Government

Legislative power is vested in the unicameral Asamblea Legislativa (Legislative Assembly), which replaced the Asamblea Nacional de Corregidores (National Assembly of Community Representatives) in 1984 (except for its brief reintroduction in late 1989), with a total of 71 members elected for five years by universal adult suffrage. Executive power is held by the President, also directly elected for a term of five years, assisted by two elected Vice-Presidents and an appointed Cabinet. Panama is divided into nine provinces and three autonomous Indian Reservations. Each province has a governor, appointed by the President.

Defence

In 1990, following the overthrow of Gen. Manuel Noriega, the National Defence Forces were disbanded and a new Public Force was created. This numbered 11,800 men in August 2005, comprising the National Police (11,000 men), the National Air Service (400 men) and the National Maritime Service (an estimated 400 men). Budgeted security expenditure for 2005 was US $158m.

Economic Affairs

In 2004, according to estimates by the World Bank, Panama's gross national income (GNI), measured at average 2002–04 prices, was US $13,467.9m., equivalent to $4,450 per head (or $6,870 on an international purchasing-power parity basis). During 1995–2004, it was estimated, the population increased at an average annual rate of 1.6%, while gross domestic product (GDP) per head increased, in real terms, by an average of 2.4% per year. Overall GDP increased, in real terms, at an average annual rate of 4.0% in 1995–2004; growth was an estimated 7.6% in 2004.

Agriculture (including hunting, forestry and fishing) contributed an estimated 7.4% of GDP and engaged some 19.1% of the employed labour force in 2004. Rice, maize and beans are cultivated as subsistence crops, while the principal cash crops are bananas (which accounted for an estimated 11.5% of total export earnings in 2004), melons, sugar cane and coffee. Cattle-raising, tropical timber and fisheries (particularly shrimps and yellowfin tuna for export) are also important. The banana sector was adversely affected by industrial action and poor weather conditions in the early 2000s. The end of the European Union's (EU, see p. 228) quota system on banana imports from 2006 was expected to boost the sector; however, Panama was expected to appeal against the EU's introduction of a tariff on Latin American bananas of €176 per metric ton. Owing to low world commodity prices, the coffee sector experienced a reversal in 2001–03. In the 1990s, in an attempt to diversify the agricultural sector, new crops such as oil palm, cocoa, coconuts, various winter vegetables and tropical fruits were introduced. Fish exports increased steadily from the 1990s. In 2004 exports of yellowfin tuna and fish fillet accounted for an estimated 30.0% of export revenue. Agricultural GDP increased by an average of 4.5% annually during 1995–2004; the sector increased by 4.5% in 2003 and by 5.0% in 2004.

Industry (including mining, manufacturing, construction and power) contributed an estimated 16.6% of GDP and engaged 17.7% of the employed labour force in 2004. According to World Bank figures, industrial GDP increased at an average annual rate of 2.4% during 1995–2004; the sector's GDP increased by an estimated 7.0% in both 2003 and 2004.

Mining contributed an estimated 1.0% of GDP and engaged 0.1% of the employed labour force in 2004. Panama has significant deposits of copper and coal. The GDP of the mining sector increased by an estimated average of 14.7% per year in 2000–04; the sector expanded by 35.4% in 2003 and by an estimated 12.7% in 2004. This dramatic expansion in the sector was owing to the demand for stone, sand and clay, associated with residential construction and road-building, in particular the ongoing widening of the Pan-American Highway.

Manufacturing contributed an estimated 7.5% of GDP and engaged an estimated 9.4% of the employed labour force in 2004. The most important sectors, measured by output in producers' prices, were refined petroleum products, food-processing, beverages, and cement, lime and plaster. Manufacturing GDP decreased by an average of 1.2% annually during 1995–2004; the sector declined by 1.5% in 2003 before increasing by 2.0% in 2004.

The country's topography and climate make it ideal for hydro-electric power, and in 2004 approximately 71.2% of Panama's total output of electricity was water-generated. Petroleum accounted for the remainder (28.8%) of the country's generating capacity. In the same year imports of mineral products accounted for an estimated 14.4% of the value of merchandise imports.

Panama's economy is dependent upon the services sector, which contributed an estimated 76.1% of GDP and engaged 63.2% of the employed labour force in 2004. The Panama Canal contributed an estimated 4.9% of the country's GDP in 2003. Panama is an important 'offshore' financial centre, and in 2004 financial, property and business services contributed an estimated 27.10% of GDP. Important contributions to the economy are also made by trade in the Colón Free Zone (CFZ—in which some 1,800 companies were situated in 2005, and which contributed an estimated 6.5% of GDP in 2002), and by the registration of merchant ships under a 'flag of convenience' in Panama. The tourism sector also increased steadily from the last decade of the 20th century. In 2003 income from tourism totalled US $809m., compared with $721m. in the previous year. According to the World Bank, the GDP of the services sector increased by an average of 4.4% per year in 1995–2004; the sector grew by 4.1% in 2003 and by 4.4% in 2004.

In 2004 Panama recorded a visible trade deficit of US $1,585.3m., and there was a deficit of $1,104.3m. on the current account of the balance of payments. In 2005 the principal source of imports (27.2%) was the USA, which was also the principal market for exports (43.5%). Other major trading partners are Costa Rica, Japan, Mexico and Spain. The principal exports in 2004 were yellowfin tuna and fish fillet, bananas and melons. The principal imports in that year were primary materials and products for industry, non-durable consumer goods, and transport and telecommunications equipment.

In 2004 there was an estimated overall budgetary deficit of US $768m. (equivalent to 5.4% of GDP). Panama's external debt at the end of 2003 was US $8,770m., of which $8,286m. was long-term debt. In that year the cost of debt-servicing was equivalent to 11.3% of the value of exports of goods and services. Annual inflation averaged 1.1% in 1990–2003; consumer prices increased by 1.4% in 2003 and by 0.5% in 2004. Some 9.6% of the labour force were unemployed in mid-2005.

Panama is a member of the Inter-American Development Bank (IDB, see p. 284). In September 1997 Panama joined the World Trade Organization (WTO, see p. 370). In March 2002 Panama concluded a free trade agreement with El Salvador. In August 2003 a free trade accord between Panama and Taiwan was concluded. In early 2006 negotiations towards a free trade agreement with the USA were ongoing (although a ninth round of talks collapsed in January of that year).

Following the cession to Panamanian control of the Panama Canal at the end of 1999, the waterway was operated as a profit-making venture, providing the Government with a considerable source of funds. (Toll revenues from the Canal totalled $848m. in 2005.) Nevertheless, the administration of President Martín Torrijos Espino, which took office in September 2004, faced the problems of high unemployment and widespread poverty (affecting an estimated 40% of the population), as well as a continuing fiscal deficit, which reached a substantial 5.4% of GDP in 2004. In February 2005 the Asamblea Legislativa approved a fiscal adjustment programme designed to reduce the deficit to 1% of GDP by 2009: this was to be achieved by increasing the tax yield, rationalizing public spending and reducing expenditure on salaries. Tax revenue was particularly low, having declined from the equivalent of 11.4% of GDP in 1995 to an estimated 8.7% of GDP in 2004. The Government intended to reduce business tax evasion and to increase the penalties for non-compliance. The cost of services to businesses in the CFZ was also increased. The legislative approval, in December 2005, of controversial reforms to the Caja de Seguridad Social (see Recent History) was also expected to increase government revenue. In addition, it was hoped that implementation of the much-needed reforms would help the Torrijos Government secure financing, on favourable terms, for the planned widening of the Panama Canal; this project was expected to cost some US $4,500m. It was estimated that the economy grew by 5.0% in 2005 and was forecast to expand by a further 5.2% in 2006.

Education

The education system is divided into elementary, secondary and university schooling, each of six years' duration. Education is free up to university level, and is officially compulsory for six years between six and 15 years of age. In 2003 some 51.0% of children aged 4–5 years were enrolled at pre-primary schools. Primary education begins at the age of six, and secondary education, which comprises two three-year cycles, at the age of 12. The enrolment at primary schools of children in the relevant age-group was 100.0% in 2003, and secondary enrolment was 63.8% in the same year. There are four public universities, with regional centres in the provinces, and 11 private ones, including one specializing in distance learning. Budgetary expenditure on education by the central Government in 2004 totalled 637m. balboas (equivalent to 24.6% of total expenditure).

Public Holidays

2006: 1 January (New Year's Day), 9 January (National Martyrs' Day), 27–28 February (Carnival), 1 March (Ash Wednesday), 13 April (Maundy Thursday), 14 April (Good Friday), 1 May (Labour Day), 14 August (Foundation of Panama City, Panama City only)*, 11 October (Revolution Day), 1 November (National Anthem Day)*, 2 November (Day of the Dead), 3 November (Independence from Colombia), 4 November (Flag Day)*, 5 November (Independence Day, Colón only), 10 November (First Call for Independence), 28 November (Independence from Spain), 8 December (Immaculate Conception, Mothers' Day), 25 December (Christmas).

2007: 1 January (New Year's Day), 9 January (National Martyrs' Day), 19–20 February (Carnival), 21 February (Ash Wednesday), 5 April (Maundy Thursday), 6 April (Good Friday), 1 May (Labour Day), 15 August (Foundation of Panama City, Panama City only)*, 11 October (Revolution Day), 1 November (National Anthem Day)*, 2 November (Day of the Dead), 3 November (Independence from Colombia), 4 November (Flag Day)*, 5 November (Independence Day, Colón only), 10 November (First Call for Independence), 28 November (Independence from Spain), 8 December (Immaculate Conception, Mothers' Day), 25 December (Christmas).

* Official holiday: banks and government offices closed.

Weights and Measures

Both the metric and the imperial systems of weights and measures are in use.

PANAMA

Statistical Survey

Sources (unless otherwise stated): Dirección de Estadística y Censo, Contraloría General de la República, Avda Balboa y Federico Boyd, Apdo 5213, Panamá 5; tel. 210-4800; fax 210-4801; e-mail cgrdec@contraloria.gob.pa; internet www.contraloria.gob.pa; Viceministerio del Comercio Exterior, Plaza Edison, 3°, Avda El Paical, Apdo 55-2359, Panamá; e-mail secomex@mici.gob.pa; internet www.vicomex.gob.pa.

Note: The former Canal Zone was incorporated into Panama on 1 October 1979.

Area and Population

AREA, POPULATION AND DENSITY

Area (sq km)	75,517*
Population (census results)	
13 May 1990	2,329,329
14 May 2000	
Males	1,432,566
Females	1,406,611
Total	2,839,177
Population (official estimates at mid-year)	
2002	3,060,090
2003	3,116,277
2004	3,172,360
Density (per sq km) at mid-2004	42.0

* 29,157 sq miles.

ADMINISTRATIVE DIVISIONS
(population at census of May 2000)

Province	Population	Capital (and population)*
Bocas del Toro	89,269	Bocas del Toro (9,916)
Chiriquí	368,790	David (124,280)
Coclé	202,461	Penonomé (72,448)
Colón	204,208	Colón (42,133)
Comarca Emberá	8,246	—
Comarca Kuna Yala	32,446	—
Comarca Ngöbe-Buglé	110,080	—
Darién	40,284	Chepigana (27,461)
Herrera	102,465	Chitré (42,467)
Los Santos	83,495	Las Tablas (24,298)
Panamá	1,388,357	Panamá (708,438)
Veraguas	209,076	Santiago (74,679)
Total	**2,839,177**	—

* Population of district in which capital is located.

Note: Population figures include the former Canal Zone.

PRINCIPAL TOWNS
(population at 2000 census)

Panamá (Panama City, capital)	463,093	Pacora	57,232
San Miguelito	291,769	Santiago	55,146
Tocumen	81,250	La Chorrera	54,823
David	76,481	Colón	52,286
Nuevo Arraiján	63,753	Changuinola	45,063
Puerto Armuelles	60,102	Pedregal	45,033

BIRTHS, MARRIAGES AND DEATHS

	Registered live births		Registered marriages*		Registered deaths	
	Number	Rate (per 1,000)†	Number	Rate (per 1,000)†	Number	Rate (per 1,000)†
1997	68,009	25.0	10,357	4.1	12,179	4.5
1998	62,351	22.6	10,415	4.1	11,824	4.3
1999	64,248	22.9	10,388	3.9	11,938	4.2
2000	64,839	22.7	10,430	3.9	11,841	4.1
2001	63,900	21.3	9,687	3.6	12,442	4.1
2002	61,671	20.2	9,558	3.1	12,428	4.1
2003	61,753	19.8	10,310	3.3	13,248	4.3
2004	62,743	19.8	10,290	3.2	13,475	4.2

* Excludes tribal Indian population.
† Based on official mid-year population estimates.

Expectation of life (WHO estimates, years at birth): 75 (males 73; females 78) in 2003 (Source: WHO, *World Health Report*).

EMPLOYMENT
('000 persons aged 15 years and over, August of each year)

	2002	2003	2004
Agriculture, hunting and forestry	222.2	228.3	215.1
Fishing	12.4	11.7	13.7
Mining and quarrying	1.6	1.0	0.7
Manufacturing	100.2	105.8	112.7
Electricity, gas and water supply	8.6	8.8	8.3
Construction	71.9	79.9	90.4
Wholesale and retail trade; repair of motor vehicles, motorcycles and personal and household goods	195.6	196.4	209.6
Hotels and restaurants	47.9	53.4	60.8
Transport, storage and communications	81.9	85.9	89.0
Financial intermediation	22.5	21.5	24.8
Real estate, renting and business activities	42.1	44.6	53.8
Public administration and defence; compulsory social service	70.5	74.5	73.9
Education	62.5	65.1	67.8
Health and social work	39.1	38.2	43.8
Other community, social and personal service activities	70.4	65.7	63.2
Private households with employed persons	62.0	64.0	69.2
Extra-territorial organizations and bodies	0.2	1.0	0.7
Total employed	**1,111.7**	**1,146.0**	**1,197.6**
Unemployed	173.3	172.0	159.7
Total labour force	**1,285.0**	**1,318.0**	**1,357.3**

Health and Welfare

KEY INDICATORS

Total fertility rate (children per woman, 2003)	2.7
Under-5 mortality rate (per 1,000 live births, 2004)	24
HIV/AIDS (% of persons aged 15–49, 2003)	0.9
Physicians (per 1,000 head, 2000)	1.68
Hospital beds (per 1,000 head, 1996)	2.21
Health expenditure (2002): US $ per head (PPP)	576
Health expenditure (2002): % of GDP	8.9
Health expenditure (2002): public (% of total)	71.7
Access to water (% of persons, 2002)	91
Access to sanitation (% of persons, 2002)	72
Human Development Index (2003): ranking	56
Human Development Index (2003): value	0.804

For sources and definitions, see explanatory note on p. vi.

Agriculture

PRINCIPAL CROPS
('000 metric tons)

	2002	2003	2004*
Rice (paddy)	245.2	295.4	296.0
Maize	75.6	72.4	80.0†
Sugar cane	1,440.6	1,572.1	1,650.0
Roots and tubers*	79.9	85.3	92.5
Fresh vegetables*	82.0	87.2	89.4
Watermelons	25.3	39.5	40.0
Cantaloupes and other melons	36.0	39.0	39.5
Bananas	521.7	509.0	525.0
Plantains	116.3	120.9	129.0
Oranges	46.6	39.4	40.0
Other fruit (excl. melons)*	58.6	70.2	72.0
Coffee (green)	13.9	10.8	8.7†
Tobacco (leaves)*	2.2	2.2	2.3

* FAO estimates.
† Unofficial figure.
Source: FAO.

LIVESTOCK
('000 head, year ending September)

	2002	2003	2004*
Horses*	170	175	178
Mules*	4	4	4
Cattle	1,533	1,550	1,550
Pigs	303	312	315
Goats	6	6	6
Chickens	13,894	13,143	13,500
Ducks*	215	220	225
Turkeys*	30	33	35

* FAO estimates.
Source: FAO.

LIVESTOCK PRODUCTS
('000 metric tons)

	2002	2003	2004*
Beef and veal	53.7	51.7	53.5
Pig meat	18.2	20.3	20.5
Poultry meat	88.7	82.8	85.0
Cows' milk	178.1	179.7	181.0
Cheese	9.9	10.0	10.0
Hen eggs	26.3	19.9	20.0

* FAO estimates.
Source: FAO.

Forestry

ROUNDWOOD REMOVALS
('000 cubic metres, excluding bark)

	2002	2003	2004*
Sawlogs, veneer logs and logs for sleepers	63	63*	63
Other industrial wood	90	90	90
Fuel wood*	1,248	1,234	1,219
Total*	1,401	1,387	1,372

* FAO estimate(s).
Source: FAO.

SAWNWOOD PRODUCTION
('000 cubic metres, incl. railway sleepers)

	2000	2001	2002
Coniferous (softwood)	2	2*	2*
Broadleaved (hardwood)	46	40	24
Total	48	42*	26*

* FAO estimate.
2003–04: Production as in 2002 (FAO estimates).
Source: FAO.

Fishing

('000 metric tons, live weight)

	2001	2002	2003
Capture	256.4	305.1	223.4
Snappers and jobfishes	22.3	26.6	13.1
Pacific thread herring	29.0	48.2	55.7
Pacific anchoveta	129.1	160.4	78.6
Skipjack tuna	5.8	7.6	11.5
Yellowfin tuna	12.3	20.4	28.7
Marine fishes	52.4	41.5	12.8
Aquaculture	3.1	4.3	6.2
Total catch	259.5	309.4	229.7

Note: Figures exclude crocodiles. The number of spectacled caimans caught was: 11,700 in 2001; 13,298 in 2002; 14,694 in 2003.
Source: FAO.

Industry

SELECTED PRODUCTS
('000 metric tons, unless otherwise indicated)

	2002	2003	2004
Salt	16	13	19
Sugar	152	147	157
Beer (million litres)	135	149	164
Wines and spirits (million litres)	13	13	14
Non-alcoholic, carbonated beverages (million litres)	163	—	—
Evaporated, condensed and powdered milk	28	23	20
Fish oil	10	8	5
Footwear ('000 pairs)	78	73	30
Electricity (million kWh, net)	4,996	5,281	5,475

PANAMA

Finance

CURRENCY AND EXCHANGE RATES

Monetary Units
100 centésimos = 1 balboa (B).

Sterling, Dollar and Euro Equivalents (30 December 2005)
£1 sterling = 1.722 balboas;
US $1 = 1.000 balboas;
€1 = 1.180 balboas;
100 balboas = £58.08 = $100.00 = €84.77.

Exchange Rate: The balboa's value is fixed at par with that of the US dollar.

BUDGET
(million US $)

Revenue	2002	2003	2004
Tax revenue	1,051	1,127	1,209
Income tax	452	435	489
Taxes on foreign trade	184	200	217
Taxes on domestic transactions	359	408	426
Other direct taxes	56	84	77
Other current revenue	926	835	815
Panama Canal	152	145	183
Transfers from balance of public sector	212	207	198
Capital revenue	90	36	18
Total revenue	2,067	1,998	2,042

Expenditure	2002	2003	2004
Current expenditure	1,973	2,081	2,355
Wages and salaries*	696	728	763
Goods and services	147	179	208
Pensions and transfers	568	560	738
Social Security Agency	280	282	376
Interest payments	508	559	593
Other current expenditure	54	54	53
Capital expenditure	332	406	455
Fixed capital formation	284	332	358
Capital transfers	49	74	97
Total	2,305	2,487	2,810

* Including severance payments and payments of wages outstanding.

INTERNATIONAL RESERVES
(US $ million at 31 December*)

	2002	2003	2004
IMF special drawing rights	1.1	0.8	0.9
Reserve position in IMF	16.1	17.6	18.4
Foreign exchange	1,165.7	992.5	611.4
Total	1,182.8	1,011.0	630.6

* Excludes gold, valued at US $476,000 in 1991–93.

Source: IMF, *International Financial Statistics*.

Note: US treasury notes and coins form the bulk of the currency in circulation in Panama.

COST OF LIVING
(Consumer Price Index, Panamá (Panama City); base: 1987 = 100)

	2001	2002	2003
Food (incl. beverages)	112.8	112.1	113.5
Rent, fuel and light	122.1	125.8	129.5
Clothing (incl. footwear)	113.5	113.2	114.5
Medical and health care	126.4	124.5	122.6
Transport and communications	106.6	113.4	114.5
All items (incl. others)	114.3	115.5	117.1

NATIONAL ACCOUNTS
(million balboas at current prices)

National Income and Product

	2002	2003	2004*
Compensation of employees	4,378.8	4,523.6	4,694.4
Operating surplus	4,478.8	4,735.4	5,565.0
Net mixed income	1,518.7	1,619.2	1,802.9
Domestic factor incomes	10,376.3	10,878.2	12,062.3
Consumption of fixed capital	981.7	992.6	1,039.6
Gross domestic product (GDP) at factor cost	11,358.0	11,870.8	13,101.9
Indirect taxes	969.4	1,111.2	1,186.8
Less Subsidies	55.0	48.8	84.5
GDP in purchasers' values	12,272.4	12,933.2	14,204.2
Less Net factor income paid to the rest of the world	565.7	969.7	1,286.0
Gross national product	11,706.7	11,963.5	12,918.2
Less Consumption of fixed capital	981.7	992.6	1,039.6
National income in market prices	10,725.0	10,970.9	11,878.6
Other current transfers from abroad (net)	170.9	180.3	159.4
National disposable income	10,895.9	11,151.2	12,038.0

* Provisional figures.

Expenditure on the Gross Domestic Product

	2002	2003	2004*
Government final consumption expenditure	1,819.3	1,807.0	1,929.7
Private final consumption expenditure	7,885.2	8,015.7	9,061.0
Increase in stocks	268.1	249.4	301.8
Gross fixed capital formation	1,664.8	2,207.3	2,443.1
Total domestic expenditure	11,637.4	12,279.4	13,735.6
Exports of goods and services	8,278.9	8,225.2	9,627.8
Less Imports of goods and services	7,643.9	7,571.4	9,159.1
GDP in purchasers' values	12,272.4	12,933.2	14,204.2
GDP at constant 1996 prices	11,691.1	12,182.8	13,103.8

* Provisional figures.

Gross Domestic Product by Economic Activity

	2002	2003	2004*
Agriculture, hunting, forestry and fishing	887.4	961.1	1,012.4
Mining and quarrying	90.1	127.8	143.3
Manufacturing	973.6	969.4	1,027.4
Electricity, gas and water	350.1	362.9	421.9
Construction	426.4	593.5	677.1
Wholesale and retail trade	1,645.9	1,647.1	1,910.7
Hotels and restaurants	254.0	283.0	319.2
Transport, storage and communications	1,706.0	1,855.4	2,151.0
Financial services	1,184.3	1,155.1	1,193.4
Renting, real estate and business services	2,231.5	2,381.8	2,522.3
Social welfare and health services	461.4	492.2	511.2
Education	535.9	568.0	587.6
Other community, social and personal service activities	407.8	439.1	460.7
Government services	609.2	542.7	645.4
Employed persons in private households	106.0	113.0	121.2
Sub-total	11,869.6	12,492.1	13,704.8
Less Financial intermediation services indirectly measured	370.3	404.0	404.0
Gross value added in basic prices	11,499.3	12,088.1	13,300.8
Import duties and other taxes	828.1	893.9	987.9
Less Grants and subsidies	55.0	48.8	84.5
GDP in market prices	12,272.4	12,933.2	14,204.2

* Provisional figures.

PANAMA

BALANCE OF PAYMENTS
(US $ million)*

	2002	2003	2004
Exports of goods f.o.b.	5,283.8	5,048.9	5,885.6
Imports of goods f.o.b.	−6,460.2	−6,161.6	−7,470.9
Trade balance	−1,176.4	−1,112.7	−1,585.3
Exports of services	2,290.6	2,556.6	2,725.8
Imports of services	−1,263.6	−1,302.5	−1,430.4
Balance on goods and services	−149.4	141.4	−289.9
Other income received	919.5	769.5	786.0
Other income paid	−1,136.3	−1,589.4	−1,828.4
Balance on goods, services and income	−366.2	−678.5	−1,332.3
Current transfers received	242.0	301.8	323.3
Current transfers paid	−29.5	−60.5	−95.3
Current balance	−153.7	−437.2	−1,104.3
Direct investment from abroad	56.9	791.5	1,012.3
Portfolio investment assets	159.7	−59.3	−605.2
Portfolio investment liabilities	367.5	139.6	775.9
Other investment assets	3,342.3	464.1	−889.3
Other investment liabilities	−3,660.0	−1,310.5	713.8
Net errors and omissions	729.8	257.3	−299.4
Overall balance	842.5	−154.5	−396.1

* Including the transactions of enterprises operating in the Colón Free Zone.

Source: IMF, *International Financial Statistics*.

External Trade

PRINCIPAL COMMODITIES
(US $ million)

Imports c.i.f.	2002	2003	2004*
Consumer goods	1,207.3	1,294.0	1,387.3
Non-durable	496.9	545.5	533.8
Semi-durable	297.3	270.9	269.0
Domestic utensils	117.3	117.6	117.1
Fuels, lubricants and related products	295.7	360.0	467.4
Intermediate goods	1,092.2	994.4	1,024.9
Primary materials and products for agriculture	63.2	74.3	83.1
Primary materials and products for industry	837.6	671.3	670.4
Construction materials	158.8	216.0	235.8
Other	32.6	32.8	35.6
Capital goods	735.8	833.8	836.6
Agricultural	20.1	24.0	24.1
For industry, construction and electricity	235.1	254.4	251.7
Transport and telecommunications equipment	407.0	468.0	471.8
Other	73.6	87.4	89.0
Total (incl. others)	3,035.3	3,122.3	3,248.7

* Preliminary figures.

Exports f.o.b.	2002	2003*	2004*
Sugar	15.1	12.8	10.4
Bananas	109.4	1112.8	108.2
Melons	40.7	47.6	70.9
Coffee	9.2	12.2	11.0
Shrimps	58.0	56.5	53.8
Fishmeal	7.6	13.0	9.3
Fresh and frozen fish and fillets (incl. yellowfin tuna)	169.5	262.6	281.8
Clothing	13.3	11.0	8.8
Meat from cattle	14.3	9.6	14.4
Standing cattle	13.3	18.0	13.2
Petroleum	148.7	n.a	n.a
Total (incl. others)	900.6	838.8	938.5

* Preliminary figures.

PRINCIPAL TRADING PARTNERS
(US $ '000)

Imports c.i.f.	2002	2003	2005*
Canada	20,035	20,192	n.a.
Colombia†	179,627	123,191	143,638
Costa Rica	127,822	151,133	194,623
Ecuador	99,116	7,003	n.a.
Germany	45,747	49,211	52,774
Guatemala	62,953,	71,097	83,664
Japan	164,610	193,231	188,157
Korea, Republic	63,536	63,803	102,877
Mexico	112,440	119,155	154,058
Netherlands Antilles‡	52,013	89,613	475,190
Spain	41,617	48,693	63,151
Trinidad and Tobago	38,551	19,550	43,823
United Kingdom	18,590	31,815	n.a.
USA	1,016,191	1,066,132	1,130,661
Venezuela	127,675	84,877	44,789
Total (incl. others)	3,035,737	3,124,885	4,155,293

Exports f.o.b.	2003	2004	2005
Belgium-Luxembourg	24,340	29,684	24,907
China, People's Republic	n.a.	10,817	20,046
Colombia†	8,574	11,892	15,465
Costa Rica	33,466	36,772	38,748
Dominican Republic	8,264	9,744	16,441
Ecuador	3,883	5,696	5,302
El Salvador	9,403	10,591	9,335
Guatemala	13,254	11,612	24,907
Honduras	13,362	15,403	15,620
Hong Kong	5,122	7,656	6,595
India	n.a.	18,125	6,552
Italy	9,517	12,525	15,153
Mexico	12,060	13,916	17,112
Netherlands	n.a.	38,784	47,056
Nicaragua	24,815	18,227	21,380
Portugal	27,469	23,240	12,645
Puerto Rico	12,954	11,894	13,121
Spain	45,593	44,999	85,626
Sweden	48,262	57,994	54,332
Taiwan	6,618	11,390	20,046
United Kingdom	n.a.	6,565	18,430
USA	402,604	433,004	419,412
Total (incl. others)	798,747	891,105	963,764

* Figures for 2004 not available.
† Excluding San Andrés island.
‡ Curaçao only.

Transport

RAILWAYS
(traffic)

	2001	2002
Passenger-km (million)*	24,576	35,693
Freight ton-km (million)†	4,896	20,665

* Panama Railway and National Railway of Chiriquí.
† Panama Railway only.

Source: UN, *Statistical Yearbook*.

ROAD TRAFFIC
(motor vehicles in use)

	2000	2001	2002
Cars	223,433	219,372	224,504
Buses and coaches	16,865	15,558	16,371
Lorries and vans	75,454	73,139	74,247

Source: IRF, *World Road Statistics*.

PANAMA

SHIPPING

Merchant Fleet
(registered at 31 December)

	2002	2003	2004
Number of vessels	6,247	6,302	6,477
Total displacement ('000 grt)	124,729.1	125,721.7	131,451.7

Source: Lloyd's Register-Fairplay, *World Fleet Statistics*.

International Sea-borne Freight Traffic
('000 metric tons)

	2001	2002	2003
Goods loaded	108,456	110,556	99,516
Goods unloaded	84,864	99,288	76,152

Panama Canal Traffic

	2002	2003	2004
Transits	13,185	13,154	14,035
Cargo (million long tons)	187.8	188.3	200.2

Source: Panama Canal Authority.

CIVIL AVIATION
(traffic on scheduled services)

	2001	2002	2003
Kilometres flown (million)	40	38	43
Passengers carried ('000)	1,115	1,048	1,264
Passengers-km (million)	3,004	2,974	3,371
Total ton-km (million)	25	22	20

Source: UN Economic Commission for Latin America and the Caribbean, *Statistical Yearbook*.

Tourism

VISITOR ARRIVALS BY COUNTRY OF ORIGIN

	2001	2002	2003
Argentina	9,403	7,196	9,363
Canada	14,652	15,897	15,167
Chile	6,006	6,444	7,116
Colombia	80,972	88,049	93,821
Costa Rica	56,846	57,550	54,290
Dominican Republic	8,843	7,702	6,291
Ecuador	19,171	22,049	20,357
El Salvador	7,585	7,992	9,837
Germany	4,494	4,441	4,941
Guatemala	12,937	14,205	14,284
Honduras	9,012	8,508	9,846

—continued	2001	2002	2003
Italy	4,510	7,213	5,378
Jamaica	8,491	4,720	4,620
Mexico	20,447	20,784	24,398
Nicaragua	12,905	12,045	11,755
Peru	8,378	10,643	10,789
Puerto Rico	6,666	7,254	7,526
Spain	7,947	9,298	9,549
USA	112,585	116,103	132,898
Venezuela	17,606	14,357	14,827
Total (incl. others)	482,040	499,643	534,208

Tourism receipts (US $ million, incl. passenger transport): 674 in 2001; 721 in 2002; 809 in 2003.

Sources: World Tourism Organization.

Communications Media

	2002	2003	2004
Telephones ('000 main lines in use)	377	387	376
Mobile cellular telephones ('000 subscribers)	475	834	856
Personal computers ('000 in use)	115	n.a.	130
Internet users ('000)	120	192	300

Radio receivers ('000 in use): 815 in 1997.
Television receivers ('000 in use): 550 in 2000.
Daily newspapers: 7 in 1997.

Sources: UNESCO, *Statistical Yearbook*; UN, *Statistical Yearbook*; International Telecommunication Union.

Education

(provisional, 2004, unless otherwise indicated)

	Institutions*	Teachers	Pupils
Pre-primary	1,662	4,155	79,366
Primary	3,116	17,882	429,837
Secondary	442	17,308	254,357
University	24	4,972†	128,863

* 2001/02 figures.
† 2000 figure.

Sources: Ministry of Education; UNESCO, *Statistical Yearbook*.

Adult literacy rate (UNESCO estimates): 91.9% (males 92.5%; females 91.2%) in 2003 (Source: UN Development Programme, *Human Development Report*).

Directory

The Constitution

Under the terms of the amendments to the Constitution, implemented by the adoption of Reform Acts No. 1 and No. 2 in October 1978, and by the approval by referendum of the Constitutional Act in April 1983, the 67 (later 78) members of the unicameral Asamblea Legislativa (Legislative Assembly) are elected by popular vote every five years. Executive power is exercised by the President of the Republic, who is also elected by popular vote for a term of five years. Two Vice-Presidents are elected by popular vote to assist the President. The President appoints the Cabinet. The armed forces are barred from participating in elections. In July 2004 further amendments to the Constitution were adopted, including a reduction (to 71) in the number of members of the Asamblea from 2009, the abolition of parliamentary immunity from prosecution, and the creation of a constitutional assembly to consider future changes to the Constitution.

The Government

HEAD OF STATE

President: MARTÍN TORRIJOS ESPINO (took office 1 September 2004).
First Vice-President: SAMUEL LEWIS NAVARRO.

THE CABINET
(April 2006)

Minister of the Interior and Justice: OLGA GÓLCHER.
Minister of Foreign Affairs: SAMUEL LEWIS NAVARRO.
Minister of Public Works: BENJAMÍN COLAMARCO.
Minister of Finance and the Treasury: CARLOS VALLARINO.
Minister of Agricultural Development: GUILLERMO AUGUSTO SALAZAR NICOLAU.
Minister of Commerce and Industry: ALEJANDRO FERRER.

PANAMA

Minister of Public Health: CAMILO ALLEYNE.
Minister of Labour and Social Welfare: REYNALDO RIVERA.
Minister of Education: MIGUEL ANGEL CAÑIZALES.
Minister of Housing: BALBINA HERRERA.
Minister of the Presidency: UBALDINO REAL.
Minister of Social Development: MARÍA DEL CARMEN ROQUEBERT LEÓN.

MINISTRIES

Office of the President: Palacio Presidencial, Valija 50, Panamá 1; tel. 227-4062; fax 227-0076; internet www.presidencia.gob.pa.

Ministry of Agricultural Development: Edif. 576, Calle Manuel E. Melo, Altos de Curundú, Apdo 5390, Panamá 5; tel. 232-6254; fax 232-5044; e-mail infomida@mida.gob.pa; internet www.mida.gob.pa.

Ministry of Commerce and Industry: El Paical, 3°, Avda Ricardo J. Alfaro, Plaza Edison, Apdo 9658, Panamá 4; tel. 360-0600; fax 360-0663; e-mail uti@mici.gob.pa; internet www.mici.gob.pa.

Ministry of Education: Edif. Poli y Los Rios, Avda Justo Arosemena, Calles 26 y 27, Apdo 2440, Panamá 3; tel. 211-4400; fax 262-9087; e-mail meduc@meduc.gob.pa; internet www.meduc.gob.pa.

Ministry of Finance and the Treasury: Edif. Ogawa, Vía España, Apdo 5245, Panamá 5; tel. 269-4369; fax 264-7755; e-mail mhyt@mhyt.gob.pa; internet www.mef.gob.pa.

Ministry of Foreign Affairs: Altos de Ancón, Complejo Narciso Garay, Panamá 4; tel. 227-0013; fax 227-4725; e-mail prensa@mire.gob.pa; internet www.mire.gob.pa.

Ministry of Housing: Avda Ricardo J. Alfaro, Edif. Plaza Edison, 4°, Apdo 5228, Panamá 5; tel. 279-9200; fax 321-0028; e-mail webmaster@mivi.gob.pa; internet www.mivi.gob.pa.

Ministry of the Interior and Justice: Avda Central, entre calle 2 y 3, San Felipe, Apdo 1628, Panamá 1; tel. 212-2000; fax 212-2126; e-mail informa@gobiernoyjusticia.gob.pa; internet www.gobiernoyjusticia.gob.pa.

Ministry of Labour and Social Welfare: Avda Ricardo J. Alfaro, Plaza Edison, 5°, Apdo 2441, Panamá 3; tel. 260-9087; fax 260-4466; e-mail mitrabs2@sinfo.net; internet www.mitradel.gob.pa.

Ministry of the Presidency: Palacio de Las Garzas, Corregimiento de San Felipe, Apdo 2189, Panamá 1; tel. 227-9663; fax 227-4119; e-mail ofasin@presidencia.gob.pa; internet www.presidencia.gob.pa.

Ministry of Public Health: Apdo 2048, Panamá 1; tel. 225-6080; fax 212-9202; e-mail ministro@minsa.gob.pa; internet www.minsa.gob.pa.

Ministry of Public Works: Edif. 1019, Curundú, Zona 1, Apdo 1632, Panamá 1; tel. 207-9400; fax 232-8776; e-mail info@mop.gob.pa; internet www.mop.gob.pa.

Ministry of Social Development: Avda Ricardo J. Alfaro, 4°, Edison Plaza, Apdo 680-50, El Dorado, Panamá; tel. 279-0702; fax 279-0665; e-mail minjumnfa@sinfo.net; internet www.minjumnfa.gob.pa.

President and Legislature

PRESIDENT

Election, 2 May 2004

Candidate	Votes	% of votes
Martín Torrijos Espino (Patria Nueva*)	711,447	47.44
Guillermo Endara Galimany (Partido Solidaridad)	462,766	30.86
José Miguel Alemán (Visión de País†)	245,845	16.39
Ricardo A. Martinelli Berrocal (Cambio Democrático)	79,595	5.31
Total	1,499,653	100.00

* Electoral alliance comprising the Partido Revolucionario Democrático and the Partido Popular.
† Electoral alliance comprising the Partido Arnulfista (now the Partido Panameñista), the Movimiento Liberal Republicano Nacionalista and the Partido Liberal Nacional.

ASAMBLEA LEGISLATIVA
(Legislative Assembly)

President: ELÍAS A. CASTILLO GONZÁLEZ.

General Election, 2 May 2004

Affiliation/Party	% of votes	Seats
Patria Nueva		
Partido Revolucionario Democrático (PRD)	37.9	42
Partido Popular (PP)	6.0	1
Visión de País		
Partido Arnulfista (PA)	19.3	16
Movimiento Liberal Republicano Nacionalista (MOLIRENA)	8.6	4
Partido Liberal Nacional (PLN)	5.2	3
Partido Solidaridad	15.7	9
Cambio Democrático (CD)	7.4	3
Total	**100.0**	**78**

Election Commission

Tribunal Electoral: Avda Ecuador y Justo Arosemena, Edif. Dirección Superior, Apdo 5281, Panamá 5; tel. 207-8000; e-mail secretaria-general@tribunal-electoral.gob.pa; internet www.tribunal-electoral.gob.pa; f. 1956; independent; Pres. EDUARDO VALDÉS ESCOFFERY.

Political Organizations

Cambio Democrático (CD): Parque Lefevre, Plaza Carolina, arriba de la Juguetería del Super 99, Panamá; tel. 217-2643; fax 217-2645; e-mail cambio.democrático@hotmail.com; formally registered 1998; Pres. RICARDO A. MARTINELLI BERROCAL; Sec.-Gen. GIACOMO TAMBURELLI.

Movimiento Liberal Republicano Nacionalista (MOLIRENA): Calle Venezuela, Casa No 5, entre Vía España y Calle 50, Panamá; tel. 213-5928; fax 265-6004; formally registered 1982; conservative; contested the 2004 elections as part of the Visión de País electoral alliance; Pres. JESÚS L. ROSAS ABREGO; Sec.-Gen. MIGUEL CÁRDENAS SANDOVAL.

Movimiento Nacional por la Defensa de la Soberanía (Monadeso): Panamá; left-wing umbrella group; Leader CONRADO SANJUR.

Partido Panameñista (PP): Avda Perú y Calle 38E, No 37–41, al lado de Casa la Esperanza, Apdo 9610, Panamá 4; tel. 227-1267; f. 1990 by Arnulfista faction of the Partido Panameñista Auténtico as Partido Arnulfista (PA); contested the 2004 elections as part of the Visión de País electoral alliance; name changed as above in Jan. 2005; Pres. MARCO AMEGLIO; Sec.-Gen. CARLOS RAÚL PIAD H.

Partido Liberal Nacional (PLN): Vía Fernandez de Córdoba, Vista Hermosa, Plaza Córdoba, antigua Ersa, Local 6–7, Panamá; tel. 229-7523; fax 229-7524; e-mail pln@sinfo.net; f. 1979; mem. of Liberal International, and founding mem. of Federación Liberal de Centroamérica y el Caribe (FELICA); contested the 2004 elections as part of the Visión de País electoral alliance; 40,645 mems; Pres. ANÍBAL GALINDO; Sec. ABRAHAM WILLIAMS.

Partido Popular (PP): Avda Perú, frente al Parque Porras, Apdo 6322, Panamá 5; tel. 227-3204; fax 227-3944; e-mail pdc@cwpanama.net; f. 1960 as Partido Demócrata Cristiano; name changed as above in Sept. 2001; contested the 2004 elections as part of the Patria Nueva electoral alliance; Pres. RUBÉN AROSEMENA VALDÉS.

Partido Revolucionario Democrático (PRD): Calle 42 Bella Vista, entre Avda Perú y Avda Cuba, bajando por el teatro Bella Vista, Panamá 9; tel. 225-1050; e-mail prdpanama@yahoo.com; f. 1979; supports policies of late Gen. Omar Torrijos Herrera; combination of Marxists, Christian Democrats and some business interests; contested the 2004 elections as part of the Patria Nueva electoral alliance; Pres. HUGO H. GUIRAUD; Sec.-Gen. MARTÍN TORRIJOS ESPINO.

Partido Solidaridad: Edif. Maheli, Avda Ramón Arias, esq. con la Vía Transístmica, Panamá; tel. 261-2966; fax 261-5083; formally registered 1993; Pres. SAMUEL LEWIS GALINDO; Vice-Pres. JOSÉ RAÚL MULINO; Sec.-Gen. JORGE RICARDO FABREGA.

Vanguardia Moral de la Patria: Vía España, esq. con Vía Porras, Panamá; tel. 212-7300; f. 2004; Pres. GUILLERMO ENDARA; Gen. Sec. Dr JOHN HOGER CASTRELLON.

Diplomatic Representation

EMBASSIES IN PANAMA

Argentina: Edif. del Banco de Iberoamérica, 7°, Avda 50 y Calle 53, Apdo 1271, Panamá 1; tel. 264-6561; fax 269-5331; e-mail embargen@c-com.net.pa; Ambassador JORGE ALBERTO ARGUINDEGUI.

Belize: Villa de la Fuente I, POB 205, El Dorado, Panamá; tel. 236-3762; fax 236-4132; e-mail nmusa@cwpanama.net; Ambassador NAIM E. MUSA.

Bolivia: Calle Eric Arturo del Valle, Bella Vista 1, Panamá; tel. 269-0274; fax 264-3868; e-mail emb_bol_pan@cwpanama.net; internet www.emboliviapanama.com.pa; Ambassador CARLOS AGUIRRE BASTOS.

Brazil: Edif. El Dorado, 1°, Calle Elvira Méndez y Avda Ricardo Arango, Urb. Campo Alegre, Apdo 4287, Panamá 5; tel. 263-5322; fax 269-6316; e-mail embrasil@embrasil.org.pa; Ambassador LUÍZ TUPY CALDAS DE MOURA.

Canada: Edif. World Trade Center, Galería Comercial, 1°, Urb. Marbella, Apdo 0832-2446, Panamá; tel. 264-7115; fax 263-8083; e-mail panam@international.gc.ca; internet www.dfait-maeci.gc.ca/panama; Ambassador JOSÉ HERRÁN LIMA.

Chile: Edif. Banco de Boston, 11°, Calle Elvira Méndez y Vía España, Apdo 7341, Panamá 5; tel. 223-9748; fax 263-5530; e-mail echilepa@cw.panama.net; internet www.embachilepanama.com; Ambassador JAIME ROCHA MANRIQUE.

China (Taiwan): Edif. Torre Hong Kong Bank 10°, Avda Samuel Lewis, Panamá; tel. 223-3424; fax 269-8757; e-mail embchina@cableonda.net; Ambassador TOMÁS PING-FU HOU.

Colombia: Edif. World Trade Center, Of. 1802, Calle 53, Urb. Marbella, Panamá; tel. 264-9644; fax 223-1134; e-mail epanama@minrelext.gov.co; Ambassador GINA BENEDETTI DE VELEZ.

Costa Rica: Edif. Plaza Omega, 3°, Calle Samuel Lewis, Apdo 8963, Panamá; tel. 264-2980; fax 264-4057; e-mail embarica@cwp.net.pa; Ambassador VERA VIOLETA CASTRO CASTRO.

Cuba: Avda Cuba y Ecuador 33, Apdo 6-2291, Bellavista, Panamá; tel. 227-5277; fax 225-6681; e-mail embacuba@cableonda.net; Ambassador CARLOS ELOY GARCÍA TRÁPAGA.

Dominican Republic: Casa 40A, Calle 75, Apdo 6250, Panamá 5; tel. 270-3884; fax 270-3886; e-mail embajdom@sinfo.net; Ambassador VIRGILIO AUGUSTO ALVAREZ BONILLA.

Ecuador: Edif. Torre 2000, 6°, Calle 50, Marbella, Bellavista, Panamá; e-mail eecuador@cwpanama.net; tel. 264-2654; fax 223-0159; Ambassador ERNESTO JOUVIN VERNAZA.

Egypt: Calle 55, No 15, El Cangrejo, Apdo 7080, Panamá 5; tel. 263-5020; fax 264-8406; Ambassador SAFIA IBRAHIM AMIEN.

El Salvador: Edif. Metropolis, 4°, Avda Manuel Espinosa Batista, Panamá; tel. 223-3020; fax 264-1433; e-mail embasalva@cwpanama.net; Ambassador GERARDO SOL MIXCO.

France: Plaza de Francia 1, Las Bovedas, San Felipe, Apdo 869, Panamá 1; tel. 211-6200; fax 211-6201; internet www.ambafrance-pa.org; Ambassador CHRISTOPHE PHILBERT.

Germany: Edif. World Trade Center, 20°, Calle 53E, Marbella, Apdo 0832-0536, Panamá 5; tel. 263-7733; fax 223-6664; e-mail germpanama@cwp.net.pa; internet www.panama.diplo.de; Ambassador BORUSSO VON BLÜCHER.

Guatemala: Edif. Altamira, Of. 925, Vía Argentina, El Cangrejo, Corregimiento de Bella Vista, Panamá 9; tel. 269-3475; fax 223-1922; Ambassador GUISELA ATALIDA GODÍNEZ DE GUTIÉRREZ.

Haiti: Edif. Dora Luz, 2°, Calle 1, El Cangrejo, Apdo 442, Panamá 9; tel. 269-3443; fax 223-1767; e-mail ambhaiti@panama.c-com.net; Chargé d'affaires BOCCHIT EDMOND.

Holy See: Punta Paitilla, Avda Balboa y Vía Italia, Apdo 4251, Panamá 5 (Apostolic Nunciature); tel. 269-2102; fax 264-2116; e-mail nuncio@sinfo.net; Apostolic Nuncio Most Rev. GIAMBATTISTA DIQUATTRO (Titular Archbishop of Giru Mons).

Honduras: Edif. Bay Mall, 1°, 112 Avda Balboa, Apdo 8704, Panamá 5; tel. 264-5513; fax 224-5513; e-mail ehpan@cableonda.net; Ambassador RAÚL CARDONA LÓPEZ.

India: Avda Federico Boyd y Calle 51, Bella Vista, Apdo 8400, Panamá 7; tel. 264-3043; fax 264-2855; e-mail indempan@c-com.net.pa; internet www.indempan.org; Ambassador ASHOK TOMAR.

Israel: Panamá; tel. 208-4700; fax 208-4755; Ambassador MENASHE BAR-ON.

Italy: Torre Banco Exterior, 25°, Avda Balboa, Apdo 2369, Panamá 9; tel. 225-8950; fax 227-4906; e-mail panitamb@cwp.net.pa; Ambassador MARCO ROCCA.

Japan: Calle 50 y 60E, Obarrio, Apdo 1411, Panamá 1; tel. 263-6155; fax 263-6019; e-mail taiship2@sinfo.net; internet www.panama.emb-japan.go.jp; Ambassador SHUJI SHIMOKOJI.

Korea, Republic: Edif. Plaza, planta baja, Calle Ricardo Arias y Calle 51E, Campo Alegre, Apdo 8096, Panamá 7; tel. 264-8203; fax 264-8825; e-mail panama@mofat.go.kr; Ambassador TAE YOUNG MOON.

Libya: Avda Balboa y Calle 32 (frente al Edif. Atalaya), Apdo 6-894 El Dorado, Panamá; tel. 227-3342; fax 227-3886; Chargé d'affaires ABDULMAJID MILUD SHAHIN.

Mexico: Edif. Torre ADR, 10°, Avda Samuel Lewis y Calle 58, Urb. Obarrio, Corregimiento de Bella Vista, Panamá; tel. 263-4900; fax 263-5446; e-mail embamexpan@cwpanama.net; internet www.embamexpan.org; Ambassador YANERIT CRISTINA MORGAN SOTOMAYOR.

Nicaragua: Quarry Heights, 16°, Ancon, Apdo 772, Zona 1, Panamá; tel. 211-2113; fax 211-2116; e-mail embapana@sinfo.net; Ambassador XAVIER ENRIQUE SARRIA ABAUNZA.

Peru: Edif. World Trade Center, 12°, Calle 53 Marbella, Apdo 4516, Panamá 5; tel. 223-1112; fax 269-6809; e-mail embaperu@pananet.com; Ambassador JOSÉ ANTONIO BELLINA ACEVEDO.

Russia: Torre IBC, 10°, Avda Manuel Espinosa Batista, Apdo 6-4697, El Dorado, Panamá; tel. 264-1408; fax 264-1588; e-mail emruspan@sinfo.net; Ambassador EVGENY ROSTISLAVOVICH VORONIN.

Spain: Calle 53 y Avda Perú (frente a la Plaza Porras), Apdo 1857, Panamá 1; tel. 227-5122; fax 227-6284; e-mail embespa@cwpanama.net; Ambassador GERARDO ZALDÍVAR MIQUELARENA.

United Kingdom: Torre Swiss Bank, 4°, Urb. Marbella, Calle 53, Apdo 0816-07946, Panamá 1; tel. 269-0866; fax 223-0730; e-mail britemb@cwpanama.net; Ambassador JAMES (JIM) MALCOLM.

USA: Avda Balboa y Calle 38, Apdo 6959, Panamá 5; tel. 207-7000; fax 227-1964; e-mail panamaweb@state.gov; internet panama.usembassy.gov; Ambassador WILLIAM ALAN EATON.

Uruguay: Edif. Los Delfines, Of. 8, Avda Balboa, Calle 50E Este, Apdo 8898, Panamá 5; tel. 264-2838; fax 264-8908; e-mail urupanam@cwpanama.net; Ambassador DOMINGO FRANCISCO SCHIPANI BRIAN.

Venezuela: Torre Hong Kong Bank, 5°, Avda Samuel Lewis, Apdo 661, Panamá 1; tel. 269-1014; fax 269-1916; e-mail embvenp@c-com.net.pa; Ambassador JOSÉ LUIS PERISSE SEOANE.

Viet Nam: 52 Jose Gabriel Duque, La Cresta, Apdo 12434-6A, El Dorado, Panamá; tel. 264-2551; fax 265-6056; e-mail embavinapa@cwpanama.net; Ambassador NGHIEM XUAN LUONG.

Judicial System

The judiciary in Panama comprises the following courts and judges: Corte Suprema de Justicia (Supreme Court of Justice), with nine judges appointed for a 10-year term; 10 Tribunales Superiores de Distrito Judicial (High Courts) with 36 magistrates; 54 Jueces de Circuito (Circuit Judges) and 89 Jueces Municipales (Municipal Judges).

Panama is divided into four judicial districts and has seven High Courts of Appeal. The first judicial district covers the provinces of Panamá, Colón, Darién and the region of Kuna Yala and contains two High Courts of Appeal, one dealing with criminal cases, the other dealing with civil cases. The second judicial district covers the provinces of Coclé and Veraguas and contains the third High Court of Appeal, located in Penonomé. The third judicial district covers the provinces of Chiriquí and Bocas del Toro and contains the fourth High Court of Appeal, located in David. The fourth judicial district covers the provinces of Herrera and Los Santos and contains the fifth High Court of Appeal, located in Las Tablas. Each of these courts deals with civil and criminal cases in their respective provinces. There are two additional special High Courts of Appeal. The first hears maritime, labour, family and infancy cases; the second deals with antitrust cases and consumer affairs.

Corte Suprema de Justicia

Edif. 236, Calle Culebra, Ancón, Apdo 1770, Panamá 1; tel. 262-9833; e-mail prensa@organojudicial.gob.pa; internet www.organojudicial.gob.pa.

President of the Supreme Court of Justice: GRACIELA JOSEFINA DIXON CATON.

Attorney-General: ANA MATILDE GÓMEZ DE RUILOBA.

Religion

The Constitution recognizes freedom of worship and the Roman Catholic Church as the religion of the majority of the population.

CHRISTIANITY

The Roman Catholic Church

For ecclesiastical purposes, Panama comprises one archdiocese, five dioceses, the territorial prelature of Bocas del Toro and the Apostolic Vicariate of Darién. There were an estimated 1,802,175 adherents at 31 December 2003, equivalent to 85% of the population.

Bishops' Conference

Conferencia Episcopal de Panamá, Secretariado General, Apdo 870933, Panamá 7; tel. 223-0075; fax 223-0042; f. 1958; statutes approved 1986; Pres. Rt Rev. OSCAR MARIO BROWN JIMÉNEZ (Bishop of Santiago de Veraguas).

Archbishop of Panamá: Most Rev. JOSÉ DIMAS CEDEÑO DELGADO, Arzobispado Metropolitano, Calle 1a Sur Carrasquilla, Apdo 6386, Panamá 5; tel. 261-0002; fax 261-0820; e-mail asccn4@keops.utp.ac.pa.

The Baptist Church

The Baptist Convention of Panama (Convención Bautista de Panamá): Apdo 6212, Panamá 5; tel. 264-5585; fax 259-5485; e-mail convencionbautistadepanam@hotmail.com; internet www.panamabaptist.com; f. 1959; Pres. JUSTO PASTOR CASTILLO; Exec. Sec. ESMERALDA DE TUY.

The Anglican Communion

Panama comprises one of the five dioceses of the Iglesia Anglicana de la Región Central de América.

Bishop of Panama: Rt Rev. JULIO MURRAY, Edif. 331A, Calle Culebra, Apdo R, Balboa; tel. 212-0062; fax 262-2097; e-mail anglipan@sinfo.net; internet www.panama.anglican.org.

BAHÁ'Í FAITH

National Spiritual Assembly of the Bahá'ís: Apdo 815-0143, Panamá 15; tel. 231-1191; fax 231-6909; e-mail panbahai@cwpanama.net; internet www.pa.bahai.org; mems resident in 529 localities; National Sec. EMELINA RODRÍGUEZ.

The Press

DAILIES

Crítica Libre: Vía Fernández de Córdoba, Apdo B-4, Panamá 9A; tel. 261-0575; fax 230-0132; e-mail esotop@epasa.com; internet www.critica.com.pa; f. 1925; morning; independent; Pres. ROSARIO ARIAS DE GALINDO; Dir JUAN PRITSIOLAS; circ. 40,000.

La Estrella de Panamá: Calle Alejandro Duque, Vía Transistmica y Frangipani, Panamá; tel. 227-0555; fax 227-1026; e-mail laestre@estrelladepanama.com; internet www.estrelladepanama.com; f. 1853; morning; Publr AUGUSTO GARCÍA; Editor JAMES APARICIO; circ. 10,000.

El Panamá América: Vía Ricardo J. Alfaro, al lado de la USMA, Apdo B-4, Panamá 9A; tel. 230-1666; fax 230-1035; e-mail director@epasa.com; internet www.epasa.com; f. 1958; morning; independent; Pres. ROSARIO ARIAS DE GALINDO; Editor OCTAVIO AMAT; circ. 25,000.

La Prensa: Avda 12 de Octubre, Hato Pintado, Apdo 6-4506, El Dorado, Panamá; tel. 222-1222; fax 221-7328; e-mail editor@prensa.com; internet www.prensa.com; f. 1980; morning; independent; closed by Govt 1988–90; Pres. RICARDO ALBERTO ARIAS; Editor GILBERTO SUCRE; circ. 38,000.

La República: Vía Fernández de Córdoba, Apdo B-4, Panamá 9A; tel. 261-0813; evening; circ. 5,000.

El Siglo: Calle 58 Obarrio, Panama; tel. 264-3921; fax 269-6954; e-mail redaccion@elsiglo.com; internet www.elsiglo.com; f. 1985; morning; acquired by Geo-Media, SA in 2001; Pres. Dr NIVIA ROSSANA CASTRELLÓN; Editor OCTAVIO COGLEY; circ. 30,000.

El Universal: Avda Justo Arosemena, entre Calles 29 y 30, Panamá; tel. 225-7010; fax 225-6994; e-mail eluniver@sinfo.net; f. 1995; Pres. TOMÁS GERARDO DUQUE ZERR; Editor MILTON HENRÍQUEZ; circ. 16,000.

PERIODICALS

Análisis: Edif. Señorial, Calle 50, Apdo 8038, Panamá 7; tel. 226-0073; fax 226-3758; e-mail mrognoni@revistaanalisis.com; internet www.revistaanalisis.com; monthly; economics and politics; Dir MARIO A. ROGNONI.

Diálogo Social: Calle 71 Este Bis, Barrio Carrasquilla, Apdo 9A-192, Panamá; tel. 229-1542; fax 261-0215; e-mail ccspanama@cwpanama.net; internet www.hri.ca/partners/ccs; f. 1967; publ. by Centro de Capacitación Social; monthly; religion, economics and current affairs; Pres. CELIA SANJUR; circ. 3,000.

Dirección de Estadística y Censo: Avda Balboa y Federico Boyd, Apdo 0816-01521, Panamá 5; tel. 210-4800; fax 210-4801; e-mail cgrdec@contraloria.gob.pa; internet www.contraloria.gob.pa/dec; f. 1941; published by the Contraloría General de la República; statistical survey in series according to subjects; Controller-General DANI KUZNIECKY; Dir of Statistics and Census LUIS ENRIQUE QUESADA.

FOB Colón Free Zone: Apdo 6-3287, El Dorado, Panamá; tel. 225-6638; fax 225-0466; e-mail focusint@sinfo.net; internet www.colonfreezone.com; annual; bilingual trade directory; publ. by Focus Publications; circ. 35,000.

Focus Panama: Apdo 6-3287, Panamá; tel. 225-6638; fax 225-0466; e-mail focusint@sinfo.net; internet www.focuspublicationsint.com; f. 1970; 2 a year; publ. by Focus Publications; visitors' guide; separate English and Spanish editions; Dir KENNETH J. JONES; circ. 60,000.

Informativo Industrial: Apdo 6-4798, El Dorado, Panamá 1; tel. 230-0482; fax 230-0805; monthly; organ of the Sindicato de Industriales de Panamá; Pres. GASPAR GARCÍA DE PAREDES.

Maga: Avda Edif. 2, Avda Manuel E. Batista, Panamá; tel. 205-6627; e-mail jaramillo.levi@utp.ac.pa; publ. by Universidad Tecnológica de Panamá; 3 a year; literature, art and sociology; Dir ENRIQUE JARAMILLO LEVI.

Revista SIETE: Avda Ricardo J. Alfaro, al lado de la USMA, Apdo B-4, Panamá 9A; tel. 230-7777; fax 230-1033; e-mail revista.siete@epasa.com; internet www.epasa.com/siete; weekly; publ. by Editora Panamá América; Dir GUIDO RODRÍGUEZ.

PRESS ASSOCIATION

Sindicato de Periodistas de Panamá: Avda Gorgas 287, Panamá; tel. 214-0163; fax 214-0164; e-mail sindiperpana@yahoo.com; f. 1949; Sec.-Gen. JAIME BEITIA.

FOREIGN NEWS BUREAUX

Agencia EFE (Spain): Edif. Comosa, 22°, Avda Samuel Lewis y Calle Manuel María Icaza, Apdo 479, Panamá 9; tel. 223-9014; fax 264-8442; e-mail cenaca@sinfo.net; Bureau Chief HUGO FABIÁN ORTIZ DURÁN.

Agenzia Nazionale Stampa Associata (ANSA) (Italy): Edif. Banco de Boston, 17°, Vía España 601, Panamá; tel. 269-6623; e-mail panansa@sinfo.net; Dir LUIS LAMBOGLIA.

Central News Agency (Taiwan): Apdo 6-693, El Dorado, Panamá; tel. 223-8837; Correspondent HUANG KWANG CHUN.

Deutsche Press-Agentur (dpa) (Germany): Panamá; tel. 233-0396; fax 233-5393.

Inter Press Service (IPS) (Italy): Panamá; tel. 225-1673; fax 264-7033; Correspondent SILVIO HERNÁNDEZ.

Reuters (United Kingdom): Edif. Banco de Boston, Of. 504, Calle Elvira, Apdo 2523, Panamá 9; tel. 263-8285.

Xinhua (New China) News Agency (People's Republic of China): Vía Cincuentenario 48, Viña del Mar, Panamá 1; tel. 226-4501; Dir HU TAIRAN.

Publishers

Editora Panamá América (EPASA): Avda Ricardo J. Alfaro, al lado de la USMA, Apdo B-4, Zona 9A, Panamá; tel. 230-7777; fax 230-0136; e-mail gerente.general@epasa.com; internet www.epasa.com; Pres. FRANCISCO ARIAS V.; Gen. Man. RAMÓN R. VALLARINO A.

Editora Sibauste, SA: Panamá; tel. 229-4577; fax 229-4582; e-mail esibauste@cwpanama.net; Dir ENRIQUE SIBAUSTE BARRÍA.

Editorial Universitaria: Vía José de Fábrega, Panamá; tel. 264-2087; f. 1969; history, geography, law, sciences, literature.

Focus Publications: Apdo 6-3287, El Dorado, Panamá; tel. 225-6638; fax 225-0466; e-mail focusint@sinfo.net; internet www.focuspublicationsint.com; f. 1970; guides, trade directories, yearbooks and maps; Gen. Man. KENNETH J. JONES.

Publicar Centroamericana, SA: Edif. Banco de Boston, 7°, Vía España 200 y Calle Elvira Méndez, Apdo 4919, Panamá 5; tel. 223-9655; fax 269-1964.

Ruth Casa Editorial: Edif. Los Cristales, Of. No 6, Apdo 2235, Zona 9A, Panamá; e-mail webmaster@forumdesalternatives.org; internet www.forumdesalternatives.org/Ruth_editorial.htm; Pres. FRANÇOIS HOUTART.

GOVERNMENT PUBLISHING HOUSE

Editorial Mariano Arosemena: Instituto Nacional de Cultura, Apdo 662, Panamá 1; tel. 211-4000; fax 211-4016; e-mail comunicacion@inac.gob.pa; internet www.inac.gob.pa; f. 1974; division of National Institute of Culture (INAC); literature, history, social sciences, archaeology; Dir LESLIE MOCK.

PANAMA

Broadcasting and Communications

REGULATORY AUTHORITY

Ente Regulador de los Servicios Públicos: Vía España, Edif. Office Park, Apdo 4931, Panamá 5; tel. 278-4500; fax 278-4600; e-mail webmaster@ersp.gob.pa; internet www.entereguladror.gob.pa; f. 1996; state regulator with responsibility for television, radio, telecommunications, water and electricity; Pres. JOSÉ GALÁN PONCE; Dirs CARLOS RODRÍGUEZ BETHANCOURT, NILSON ESPINO.

TELECOMMUNICATIONS

Dirección Nacional de Medios de Comunicación Social: Avda 7A Central y Calle 3A, Apdo 1628, Panamá 1; tel. 262-3197; fax 262-9495; Dir EDWIN CABRERA.

Major Service Providers

Cable & Wireless Panama: Apdo 659, Panamá 9A; e-mail cwp@cwpanama.com; internet www.cwpanama.com.pa; 49% govt-owned, 49% owned by Cable & Wireless; major telecommunications provider; lost monopoly in Jan. 2003; Vice-Pres. ENRIQUE GARCÍA.

Movistar: Edif. Magna, Area Bancaria, Calle 51 Este y Manuel M. Icaza, Panamá; tel. 265-0955; f. 1996 as BellSouth Panamá SA; acquired by Telefónica Móviles, SA (Spain) in Oct. 2004; name changed as above in April 2005; mobile telephone services; Gen. Man. CLAUDIO HIDALGO.

Optynex Telecom SA: Calle 40 Bella Vista, Edif. 2-79, Entre Avda México y Avda Chile, Apdo 0832-2650, Panamá; tel. 380-0000; fax 380-0099; e-mail info@optynex.com; internet www.optynex.com; f. 2002; Gen. Man. ERIC MEYER.

BROADCASTING

Radio

Asociación Panameña de Radiodifusión: Apdo 7387, Estafeta de Paitilla, Panamá; tel. 263-5252; fax 226-4396; Pres. ALESSIO GRONCHI; Vice-Pres. RICARDO A. BUSTAMANTE.

In 2004 there were 109 AM (Medium Wave) and 181 FM stations registered in Panama. Most stations are commercial.

La Mega 98.3 FM: Casa 35, Calle 50 y 77 San Francisco, Panamá; tel. 270-3242; fax 226-1021; e-mail ventas@lamegapanama.com; internet www.lamegapanama.com; f. 2000.

Omega Stereo: Calle G, El Cangrejo 3, Panamá; e-mail omegaste@omegastereo.com; internet www.omegastereo.com; f. 1981; Pres. GUILLERMO ANTONIO ADAMES.

RPC Radio: Calle 50, Urb. Obarrio 6, Panamá; e-mail rpcradio@medcom.com.pa; internet www.rpcradio.com; f. 1949; broadcasts news, sports and commentary; Man. LUÍS EDUARDO QUIRÓS.

SuperQ: Calle 45 Este, Bella Vista, Panamá; tel. 227-0366; e-mail exitosa@psi.net.pa; internet www.superqpanama.com; f. 1984; Pres. G. ARIS DE ICAZA.

WAO 97.5: Edif. Plaza 50, 2°, Calle 50 y Vía Brasil, Panamá; tel. 223-8348; fax 223-8351; internet www.wao975.com; Gen. Man. ROGELIO CAMPOS.

Television

Fundación para la Educación en la Televisión—FETV (Canal 5): Vía Ricardo J. Alfaro, Apdo 6-7295, El Dorado, Panamá; tel. 230-8000; fax 230-1955; e-mail comentarios@fetv.org; internet www.fetv.org; f. 1992; Pres. JOSÉ DIMAS CEDEÑO DELGADO; Dir MANUEL SANTIAGO BLANQUER I PLANELLS; Gen. Man. MARÍA EUGENIA FONSECA M.

Medcom: Calle 50, No 6, Apdo 116, Panamá 8; tel. 210-6700; fax 210-6797; e-mail murrutia@medcom.com.pa; internet www.rpctv.com; f. 1998 by merger of RPC Televisión (Canal 4) and Telemetro (Canal 13); commercial; also owns Cable Onda 90, and RPC radio; Pres. FERNANDO ELETA; CEO NICOLÁS GONZÁLEZ-REVILLA.

RTVE_Panama (Canal 11): Curundu, Area Revertida, Avda Omar Torrijos, al lado del MOP, Panamá; tel. 232-8558; fax 223-2921; f. 1978; educational and cultural; Dir-Gen. CARLOS AGUILAR NAVARRO.

Televisora Nacional—TVN (Canal 2): Vía Bolívar, Apdo 6-3092, El Dorado, Panamá; tel. 236-2222; fax 236-2987; e-mail tvn@tvn-2.com; internet www.tvn-2.com; f. 1962; Dir JAIME ALBERTO ARIAS.

In 2005 there were 133 authorized television channels broadcasting in Panama.

Directory

Finance

(cap. = capital; res = reserves; dep. = deposits; m. = million; amounts in balboas, unless otherwise stated)

BANKING

In February 1998 new banking legislation was approved, providing for greater supervision of banking activity in the country, including the creation of a Banking Superintendency. In 2004 a total of 73 banks operated in Panama.

Superintendencia de Bancos (Banking Superintendency): Torre HSBC, 18°, Apdo 2397, Panamá 1; tel. 206-7800; fax 264-9422; internet www.superbancos.gob.pa; f. 1970 as Comisión Bancaria Nacional (National Banking Commission); licenses and controls banking activities within and from Panamanian territory; Comisión Bancaria Nacional superseded by Superintendencia de Bancos in June 1998 with enhanced powers to supervise banking activity; Supt DELIA CÁRDENAS.

National Bank

Banco Nacional de Panamá: Torre BNP, Vía España, Apdo 5220, Panamá 5; tel. 263-5151; fax 269-0091; e-mail bnpvalores@cwp.net.pa; internet www.banconal.com.pa; f. 1904; govt-owned; cap. 500.0m., dep. 2,846.8m., total assets 3,453.2m. (Dec. 2002); Chair. ARTURO MELO SARASQUETA; Gen. Man. JUAN RICARDO DE DIANUOS; 53 brs.

Savings Banks

Banco General, SA: Calle Aquilino de la Guardia, Apdo 4592, Panamá 5; tel. 227-3200; fax 265-0210; e-mail info@bgeneral.com; internet www.bgeneral.com; f. 1955; cap. 300.0m., res 11.3m., dep. 2,057.1m., total assets 2,626.5m. (2004); purchased Banco Comercial de Panamá (BANCOMER) in 2000; Chair. and CEO FEDERICO HUMBERT; Exec. Vice-Pres. and Gen. Man. RAÚL ALEMÁN Z.; 35 brs.

Banco Panameño de la Vivienda (BANVIVIENDA): Casa Matriz-Bella Vista, Avda Chile y Calle 41, Apdo 8639, Panamá 5; tel. 227-4020; fax 227-5433; e-mail bpvger@pty.com; internet www.banvivienda.com; f. 1981; cap. 12.4m., dep. 128.0m., total assets 150.3m. (2004); Pres. ORLANDO SANCHEZ AVILES; Dir MARIO L. FÁBREGA AROSEMENA; 3 brs.

Caja de Ahorros: Vía España y Calle Thays de Pons, Apdo 1740, Panamá 1; tel. 205-1000; fax 269-3674; e-mail atencionalcliente@cajadeahorros.com.pa; internet www.cajadeahorros.com.pa; f. 1934; govt-owned; cap. 129.0m., dep. 671.8m., total assets 1,096.3m. (2004); Pres. ROGELIO ALEMÁN; Gen. Man. EUDORO JAÉN E.; 37 brs.

Domestic Private Banks

Banco Atlántico (Panamá), SA: Edif. Banco Iberóamerica, Calle 50 y Calle 53, Apdo 6553, Panamá 5; tel. 263-5656; fax 269-1616; e-mail ibergeren@pan.gbm.net; internet www.bancoatlantico.com.pa; f. 1975 as Banco de Iberoamerica, SA; current name adopted in 2000; Pres. JOSÉ M. CHIMENO CHILLÓN; Gen. Man. RUBÉN FABREGAT BRACCO; 4 brs.

Banco Continental de Panamá, SA: Calle 50 y Avda Aquilino de la Guardia, Apdo 135, Panamá 9A; tel. 215-7000; fax 215-7134; e-mail bcp@bcocontinental.com; internet www.bbvabancocontinental.com; f. 1972; merged with Banco Internacional de Panamá in 2002; cap. 813.2m., res 189.1m., dep. 11,288.0m. (Dec. 2003); Pres. PEDRO BRESCIA CAFFERATA; Gen. Man. JOSÉ ANTONIO COLOMER GUIU; 7 brs.

Banco Cuscatlán-Panabank: Edif. Panabank, Casa Matriz, Calle 50, Apdo 1828, Panamá 1; tel. 208-8300; fax 269-1537; e-mail gerencia@panabank.com; internet www.bancocuscatlan.com/panama; f. 1983; acquired Banco Panamericano (Panabank) in 2004; Chair. MAURICIO SAMAYOA; Gen Man. GUIDO J. MARTINELLI, Jr.

Banco Mercantil del Istmo, SA: Calle Manuel M. Icaza, Panamá; tel. 205-5306; fax 263-6262; e-mail mguerra@banistmo.com; internet www.banistmo.com; f. 1967 as Banco de Santander y Panamá; current name adopted in 1992; cap. 26.2m., res 0.2m., dep. 308.2m., total assets 378.8m. (Dec. 2002); Pres. SAMUEL LEWIS GALINDO; Gen. Man. MANUEL JOSÉ BARREDO MARTÍNEZ.

Global Bank Corporation: Torre Global Bank, Calle 50, Apdo 55-1843, Paitilla, Panamá; tel. 206-2000; fax 263-3518; e-mail global@pan.gbm.net; internet www.globalbank.com.pa; f. 1994; total assets 458.6m. (June 2001); Pres. JORGE VALLARINO S.

Multi Credit Bank Inc: Edif. Prosperidad, planta baja, Vía España 127, Apdo 8210, Panamá 7; tel. 269-0188; fax 264-4014; e-mail banco@grupomulticredit.com; internet www.grupomulticredit.com; f. 1990; total assets 343.9m. (Dec. 2000); Gen. Man. MOISÉS D. COHEN M.

Primer Banco del Istmo, SA: Edif. Bancoistmo, Calle 50 y 77, San Francisco, Panamá; tel. 270-0015; fax 270-1952; internet www.banistmo.com; f. 1984 as Banco del Istmo; current name adopted in 2000 following merger of Primer Grupo Nacional and Banco del

Istmo; merged with Banco de Latinoamerica in Sept. 2002; cap. US $480m., res $58m., dep. $2,869m. (Dec. 2003); Chair. José Raúl Arias García de Paredes; Gen. Man. L. J. Montague Belanger.

Towerbank International Inc: Edif. Tower Plaza, Calle 50 y Beatriz M. de Cabal, Apdo 6-6039, Panamá; tel. 269-6900; fax 269-6800; e-mail towerbank@towerbank.com; internet www.towerbank.com; f. 1971; cap. 32.0m., res 0.04m., dep. 316.5m. (Dec. 2003); Pres. Sam Kardonski; Gen. Man. Gijsbertus Antonius de Wolf.

Foreign Banks

Principal Foreign Banks with General Licence

BAC International Bank (Panamá), Inc (USA): Avda de la Guardia, planta baja, Apdo 6-3654, Panamá; tel. 213-0822; fax 269-3879; e-mail rcucalon@bacbank.com; internet www.bac.net/panama; Chair. Carlos Pellas; Pres. and CEO Ernesto Castegnaro.

BANCAFE (Panamá), SA (Colombia): Avda Manuel María Icaza y Calle 52E, No 18, Apdo 384, Panamá 9A; tel. 264-6066; fax 263-6115; e-mail bancafe@bancafe-panama.com; internet www.bancafe-pa.com; f. 1966 as Banco Cafetero; current name adopted in 1995; cap. 27.6m., dep. 299.5m. (Dec. 1994); Pres. Jorge Castellanos Rueda; Gen. Man. Jaime de Gamboa Gamboa; 2 brs.

Banco Bilbao Vizcaya Argentaria (Panama), SA (Spain): Torre BBVA, Avda Balboa, Apdo 8673, Panamá 5; tel. 227-0973; fax 227-3663; e-mail fperezp@bbvapanama.com; internet www.bbvapanama.com; f. 1982; cap. 8.7m., res 56.6m., dep. 648.6m. (Dec. 2002); Chair. Manuel Zubiría Pastor; Gen. Man. Francisco Javier Lejarraja.

Banco de Bogotá, SA (Colombia): Avda Aquilino de la Guardia 48, Apdo 4599, Panamá 5; tel. 264-6000; fax 263-8037; e-mail banbogo@sinfo.net; internet www.bancobogota-panama.com; f. 1967; cap. 2,254m., res 858,248m., dep. 4,697,328m. (Dec. 2002); merged with Banco del Comercio, SA (Colombia) in 1994; Gen. Man. Fabio Riaño.

Banco do Brasil, SA: Edif. Interseco, planta baja, Calle Elvira Méndez 10, Apdo 87-1123, Panamá 7; tel. 263-6566; fax 269-9867; e-mail panama@bb.com; internet www.bb.com.br; f. 1973; cap. and res 52.3m., dep. 1,248.1m., total assets 1,320.2m. (Dec. 1993); Gen. Man. Luiz Eduardo Jacobina; 1 br.

Banco Internacional de Costa Rica, SA: Calle Manuel M. Icaza 25, Apdo 600, Panamá 1; tel. 263-6822; fax 263-6393; e-mail informacion@bicaspan.net; internet www.bicsa.com; f. 1976; total assets 15,382m. (1999); Gen. Man. José Francisco Ulate.

Banco Latinoamericano de Exportaciones (BLADEX) (Multinational): Casa Matriz, Calles 50 y Aquilino de la Guardia, Apdo 6-1497, El Dorado, Panamá; tel. 210-8500; fax 269-6333; e-mail infobla@blx.com; internet www.blx.com; f. 1979; groups together 254 Latin American commercial and central banks, 22 international banks and some 3,000 New York Stock Exchange shareholders; cap. US $280.0m., res $153.3m., dep. $1,875.7m. (Dec. 2003); CEO José Castañeda; COO Jaime Rivera.

Bancolombia (Panama), SA: Edif. Comosa, planta baja, Avda Samuel Lewis, Corregimiento de Bella Vista, Panamá; tel. 263-6955; fax 269-1138; e-mail mdebetan.bicpma@mail.bic.com.co; internet www.bancolombiapanama.com; f. 1973; current name adopted in 1999; cap. US $14.0m., res $20.7m., dep. $1,057.5m. (Dec. 2003); Gen. Man. María Isabel Uribe.

Bank of China: Apdo 87-1056, Panamá 7; tel. 263-5522; fax 223-9960; e-mail bocpanama@cwpanama.net; internet www.bank-of-china.com; f. 1994; Gen. Man. Quingbo Wang.

Bank of Nova Scotia (Canada): Edif. P. H. Scotia Plaza, Avda Federico Boyd y Calle 51, Apdo 7327, Panamá 5; tel. 263-6255; fax 263-8636; e-mail scotiabk@cwpanama.net; internet www.scotiabank.com; Gen. Man. Terence S. McCoy.

Bank Leumi Le-Israel, BM (Israel): Edif. Grobman, planta baja, Calle Manuel M. Icaza 10, Apdo 6-4518, El Dorado, Panamá; tel. 263-9377; fax 269-2674; Gen. Man. Uri Rom.

BNP Paribas SA (France): Edif. Omanco, Vía España 200, Apdo 1774, Panamá 1; tel. 263-6600; fax 263-6970; e-mail bnpparibas.panama@americas.bnpparibas.com; internet www.bnpparibas.com; f. 1948; name changed as above in 2002; cap. 10.0m., res 6.7m., dep. 194.9m., total assets 224.0m. (Dec. 1999); Gen. Man. Christian Giraudon.

Citibank NA (USA): Plaza Panama Bldg, Calle 50, Apdo 555, Panamá 9A; tel. 210-5900; fax 210-5901; internet www.citibank.com.pa; f. 1904; Gen. Man. Francisco Conto; 10 brs.

Credicorp Bank, SA: Apdo 833-0125, Panamá; tel. 210-1111; fax 210-0069; e-mail sistemas@plazapan.com; internet www.credicorpbank.com; f. 1993; Gen. Man. Carlos Guevara.

GNB Sudameris Bank, SA (Multinational): Avda Balboa y Calle 41, Apdo 1847, Panamá 9A; tel. 227-2777; fax 227-5828; e-mail banque.sudameris@sudameris.com.pa; internet www.gnbsudameris.com; f. 1971 as Banco de Colombia (Panama); name changed to GNB Bank in 1998; name changed as above in 2004.

HSBC Bank USA: Apdo 9A-76, Panamá 9A; tel. 263-5855; fax 263-6009; e-mail hsbcpnm@sinfo.net; internet www.pa.hsbc.com; dep. 477m. (1999); in 2000 it acquired the 11 branch operations of the Chase Manhattan Bank, with assets of US $752m; Gen. Man. Joseph L. Salterio; 3 brs.

International Commercial Bank of China (Taiwan): Calles 50 y 56E, Apdo 4453, Panamá 5; tel. 263-8565; fax 263-8392; e-mail icbcpmpm@pananet.com; internet www.icbc.com.tw; Chair. Tzong-Yeong Lin; Gen. Man. Show-Loong Hwang.

Korea Exchange Bank (Republic of Korea): Torre Global Bank, Calle 50, Apdo 8358, Panamá 7; tel. 269-9966; fax 264-4224; e-mail koexpa@cwp.net.pa; internet www.keb.co.kr; Gen. Man. Kwang-Suck Koh.

Principal Foreign Banks with International Licence

Atlantic Security Bank: Torre Banco Continental 28° y 29°, Calle 50 y Aquilino de la Guardia, Apdo 6-8934, El Dorado, Panamá; tel. 269-5944; fax 215-7302; internet www.asbnet.com; f. 1984; subsidiary of El Grupo Credicorp, Peru; 'offshore' bank; Chair. Dionisio Romero; Gen. Man. Jorge Ponce Mendoza.

Banco Alemán Platina, SA: Panamá; tel. 269-2666; fax 269-0910; e-mail baplatina@balpa.com; internet www.bancoalemanplatina.com; f. 1965 as Banco Alemán-Panameño; current name adopted in 1993; cap. US $42.0m., res $10.3m., dep. $244.6m. (Aug. 2001); subsidiary of Grupo Financiero Continental; Chair. Stanley A. Motta; Gen. Man. Ralf Fischer.

Banco de la Nación Argentina: Edif. World Trade Center 501, Calle 53, Urb. Marbella, Panamá; tel. 269-4666; fax 269-6719; e-mail bna@panama.phoenix.net; internet www.bna.com.ar; f. 1977; Man. Olga Solís.

Banco de Occidente (Panama), SA: Calle 50 y Aquilino de la Guardia, Apdo 6-7430, El Dorado, Panamá; tel. 263-8144; fax 269-3261; e-mail boccipan@pty.com; internet www.bancoccidente.com.pa; f. 1982; cap. US $6.3m., res $6.0m., dep. $199.0m. (Dec. 2002); Pres. Efraín Otero Alvarez.

Banco del Pacífico (Panama), SA: Calle Aquilino de la Guardia y Calle 52, Apdo 6-3100, El Dorado, Panamá; tel. 263-5833; fax 263-7481; e-mail bpacificopanama@pacifico.fin.ec; internet www.bancodelpacifico.com.pa; f. 1980; Pres. Ana Escobar.

Bancrédito (Panama), SA: Plaza Regency, 22°, Apdo 0832-1700, Panamá; tel. 223-2977; fax 264-6781; f. 1998; Gen. Man. Carlos Humberto Rojas Martínez.

BNP Paribas: Edif. Omanco, Vía España 200, Apdo 0816-07547, Panamá; tel. 264-8555; fax 263-5004; e-mail bnpparibas@americas.bnpparibas.com.pa; internet www.bnpparibas.com.pa; f. 1972; Gen. Man. Thierry Dingreville.

Popular Bank Ltd Inc: Apdo 0816-00265, Panamá; tel. 269-4166; fax 269-1309; e-mail gversari@bpt.com.pa; f. 1983 as Banco Popular Dominicano (Panama), SA; current name adopted in 2003; cap. 24.4m., res 9.3m., dep. 338.8m. (Dec. 2004); Pres. Rafael A. Rodríguez; Gen. Man. Gianni Versari.

UBS (Panama), SA: Calle 53 Este, Edif. Marbella Swiss Tower, Apdo 0834-61, Panamá 9A; tel. 206-7100; fax 206-7100; internet www.ubs.com; f. 1968; acquired Dresdner Bank Lateinamerika in 2004; Chair. Martin Wirz.

Banking Association

Asociación Bancaria de Panamá (ABP): Torre Hong Kong Bank, 15°, Avda Samuel Lewis, Apdo 4554, Panamá 5; tel. 263-7044; fax 223-5800; e-mail abp@orbi.net; internet www.asociacionbancaria.com; f. 1962; 79 mems; Pres. Jorge E. Vallarino S.; Exec. Vice-Pres. Mario de Diego, Jr.

STOCK EXCHANGE

Bolsa de Valores de Panamá: Edif. Vallarino, planta baja, Calles Elvira Méndez y 52, Apdo 87-0878, Panamá; tel. 269-1966; fax 269-2457; e-mail bvp@pty.com; internet www.panabolsa.com; f. 1960; Chair. Dulcidio de la Guardia; Gen. Man. Roberto Brenes Pérez.

INSURANCE

Aseguradora Mundial, SA: Edif. Aseguradora Mundial, Avda Balboa y Calle 41, Apdo 8911, Panamá 5; tel. 207-6600; fax 207-8787; e-mail info@mundial.com; internet www.amundial.com; general; f. 1937; Pres. Manuel José Paredes L.

ASSA Cía de Seguros, SA: Edif. ASSA, Avda Nicanor de Obarrio (Calle 50), Apdo 5371, Panamá 5; tel. 269-0443; fax 263-9623; e-mail assamercadeo@assanet.com; internet www.assanet.com; f. 1973; Pres. Lorenzo Romagosa; Gen. Man. Pablo De La Hoya.

Cía Nacional de Seguros, SA: Edif. No 62, Calle 50, Apdo 5303, Panamá 5; tel. 205-0300; fax 223-1146; e-mail conase@conase.net; f. 1957; Gen. Man. Raúl Morrice.

PANAMA

CONASE (Cía Internacional de Seguros, SA): Avda Cuba y Calles 35 y 36, Apdo 1036, Panamá 1; tel. 227-4000; e-mail conase@conase.net; internet www.conase.com; f. 1910; Pres. RICHARD A. FORD; Gen. Man. MANUEL A. ESKILDSEN.

La Seguridad de Panamá, Cía de Seguros, SA: Edif. American International, Calle 50, esq. Aquilino de la Guardia, Apdo 5306, Panamá 5; tel. 263-6700; f. 1986; Gen. Man. MARIELA OSORIO.

Trade and Industry

Colón Free Zone (CFZ): Avda Roosevelt, Apdo 1118, Colón; tel. 445-1033; fax 445-2165; e-mail zonalibre@zolicol.org; internet www.colonfreezone.com; f. 1948; to manufacture, import, handle and re-export all types of merchandise; some 1,800 companies were established in 2005; well-known international banks operate in the CFZ, where there are also customs, postal and telegraph services; the main exporters to the CFZ are Japan, the USA, Hong Kong, Taiwan, the Republic of Korea, Colombia, France, Italy and the United Kingdom; the main importers from the CFZ are Brazil, Venezuela, Mexico, Ecuador, the Netherlands Dependencies, Bolivia, the USA, Chile, Argentina and Colombia; the total area of the CFZ was 485.3 ha; Gen. Man. DANILO MANUEL CHEN DAVIS.

GOVERNMENT AGENCY

Instituto Panameño de Comercio Exterior (IPCE): 3 Edison Plaza, Avda El Paical, Apdo 55-2339, Paitilla, Panamá; tel. 225-7244; fax 225-2193; f. 1984; foreign trade and investment promotion organization; Dir KENIA JAÉN RIVERA.

CHAMBERS OF COMMERCE

American Chamber of Commerce and Industry of Panama: POB 0843-00152, Panamá; tel. 301-3881; fax 301-3882; e-mail amcham@panamcham.com; internet www.panamcham.com; Pres. GLEN A. CHAMPION; Exec. Dir DAVID HUNT.

Cámara Oficial Española de Comercio: Calle 33E, Apdo 1857, Panamá 1; tel. 225-1487; fax 225-0626; internet www.caespan.com.pa; Pres. EDELMIRO GARCÍA VILLA VERDE; Sec.-Gen. ATILIANO ALFONSO MARTÍNEZ.

Cámara de Comercio, Industrias y Agricultura de Panamá: Avda Cuba y Ecuador 33A, Apdo 74, Panamá 1; tel. 227-1233; fax 227-4186; e-mail infocciap@panacamara.com; internet www.panacamara.com; f. 1915; Pres. AUGUST E. SIMONS; First Vice-Pres. JOSÉ JAVIER RIVERA; 1,300 mems.

INDUSTRIAL AND TRADE ASSOCIATIONS

Cámara Panameña de la Construcción: Calle Aquilino de la Guardia No 19, Apdo 0816-02350, Panamá 5; tel. 265-2500; fax 265-2571; e-mail finanzas@capac.org; internet www.capac.org; represents interests of construction sector; Pres. MANUEL R. VALLARINO.

Codemín: Panamá; tel. 263-7475; state mining org.; Dir JAIME ROQUEBERT.

Corporación Azucarera La Victoria: Transístmica, San Miguelito; tel. 229-4794; state sugar corpn; scheduled for transfer to private ownership; Dir Prof. ALEJANDRO VERNAZA.

Corporación para el Desarrollo Integral del Bayano: Avda Balboa, al lado de la estación del tren, Estafeta El Dorado, Panamá 2; tel. 232-6160; f. 1978; state agriculture, forestry and cattle-breeding corpn.

Dirección General de Industrias: Edif. Plaza Edison, 3°, Apdo 9658, Panamá 4; tel. 360-0720; govt body which undertakes feasibility studies, analyses and promotion; Dir-Gen. LUCÍA FUENTES DE FERGUSON; Nat. Dir of Business Development FRANCISCO DE LA BARRERA.

Sindicato de Industriales de Panamá: Vía Ricardo J. Alfaro, Entrada Urb. Sara Sotillo, Apdo 6-4798, Estafeta El Dorado, Panamá; tel. 230-0169; fax 230-0805; e-mail sip@cableonda.net; internet www.industriales.org; f. 1945; represents and promotes activities of industrial sector; Pres. GASPAR GARCÍA DE PAREDES.

EMPLOYERS' ORGANIZATIONS

Asociación Panameña de Ejecutivos de Empresas (APEDE): Edif. APEDE, Calle 42, Bella Vista y Avda Balboa, Apdo 1331, Panamá 1; tel. 227-3511; fax 227-1872; e-mail apede@sinfo.net; internet www.apede.org; Pres. ENRIQUE DE OBARRIO.

Consejo Nacional para el Desarrollo de la Pequeña Empresa: Ministry of Commerce and Industry, Apdo 9658, Panamá 4; tel. 227-3559; fax 225-1201; f. 1983; advisory and consultative board to the Ministry of Commerce and Industry.

Consejo Nacional de la Empresa Privada (CONEP): Avda Morgan, Balboa, Ancón, Casa 302, Apdo 1276, Panamá 1; tel. 211-2672; fax 211-2964; e-mail www.conep.org.pa; Pres. JUAN F. KIENER.

UTILITIES

Regulatory Authority

Ente Regulador de los Servicios Públicos: Vía España, Edif. Office Park, Apdo 4931, Panamá 5; tel. 278-4500; fax 278-4600; e-mail webmaster@ersp.gob.pa; internet www.enteregulador.gob.pa; f. 1996; state regulator with responsibility for water, electricity, broadcasting and telecommunications; Pres. JOSÉ GALÁN PONCE; Dirs CARLOS RODRÍGUEZ BETHANCOURT, NILSON ESPINO.

Electricity

Instituto de Recursos Hidráulicos y Electrificación (IRHE): Edif. Poli, Avda Justo Arosemena y 26E, Apdo 5285, Panamá 5; tel. 262-6272; state org. responsible for the national public electricity supply; partial divestment of generation and distribution operations completed in Dec. 1998; transmission operations remain under complete state control; Dir-Gen. Dr FERNANDO ARAMBURÚ PORRAS.

Water

Instituto de Acueductos y Alcantarillados Nacionales (IDAAN) (National Waterworks and Sewage Systems Institute): Panamá; Dir-Gen. ELIDA DÍ.

TRADE UNIONS

Central General Autónoma de Trabajadores de Panamá (CGTP): Casa 15, Calle Tercera Perejil, Vía España, Panamá; tel. 269-9741; fax 223-5287; e-mail cgtpan@cwpanama.net; fmrly Central Istmeña de Trabajadores; Sec.-Gen. MARIANO E. MENA.

Confederación Nacional de Unidad Sindical Independiente (CONUSI): 0421B Calle Venado, Ancón, Apdo 830344, Zona 3, Panamá; tel. 212-3865; fax 212-2565; e-mail conusipanama@hotmail.com; Sec.-Gen. GABRIEL E. CASTILLO C.

Confederación de Trabajadores de la República de Panamá (CTRP) (Confederation of Workers of the Republic of Panama): Calle 31, entre Avdas México y Justo Arosemena 3-50, Apdo 8929, Panamá 5; tel. 225-0293; fax 225-0259; e-mail ctrp@sinfo.net; f. 1956; admitted to ICFTU/ORIT; Sec.-Gen. GUILLERMO PUGA; 62,000 mems from 13 affiliated groups.

Consejo Nacional de Trabajadores Organizados (CONATO) (National Council of Organized Labour): Edif. 777, 2°, Balboa-Ancón, Panamá; tel. and fax 228-0224; e-mail conato@cwpanama.net; Co-ordinator PEDRO HURTADO; 150,000 mems.

Convergencia Sindical: Casa 2490, Balboa Corregimiento de Ancón, Calle Bonparte, Apdo 10536, Panamá; tel. and fax 314-1615; e-mail conversind@cwpanama.net; Sec.-Gen. LUIS GONZÁLEZ.

Federación Nacional de Asociaciones de Empleados y Servidores Públicos (FENASEP) (National Federation of Associations of Public Employees): Galerías Alvear, 2°, Of. 301, Vía Argentina, Apdo 66-48, Zona 5, Panamá; tel. and fax 269-1316; e-mail fenasep@sinfo.net; f. 1984; Sec.-Gen. LEANDRO ÁVILA.

A number of unions exist without affiliation to a national centre.

Transport

RAILWAYS

In 1998 there were an estimated 485 km of track in Panama. In 2000 a US $75m. project to modernize the line between the ports at either end of the Panama Canal began. In July 2001 the 83-km trans-isthmian railway, originally founded in 1855, reopened.

Ferrocarril Nacional de Chiriquí: Apdo 12B, David City, Chiriquí; tel. 775-4241; fax 775-4105; 126 km linking Puerto Armuelles and David.

Panama Canal Railway Company: Edif. T-376, Corozal Oeste, Apdo 2669, Balboa Ancón, Panamá; tel. 317-6070; fax 317-6061; e-mail info@panarail.com; internet www.panarail.com; govt-owned; 83 km linking Panama City and Colón, running parallel to Panama Canal; operation on concession by Kansas City Southern (KS, USA) and Mi-Jack Products (IL, USA); modernization programme completed in 2001; operates daily passenger and cargo service; Marketing Dir THOMAS KENNA.

ROADS

In 2004 there were an estimated 11,985 km of roads, of which some 4,387 km were paved. The two most important highways are the Pan-American Highway and the Boyd-Roosevelt or Trans-Isthmian,

PANAMA

linking Panama City and Colón. The Pan-American Highway to Mexico City runs for 545 km in Panama and was being extended towards Colombia. There is also a highway to San José, Costa Rica.

SHIPPING

The Panama Canal opened in 1914. In 1984 more than 4% of all the world's seaborne trade passed through the waterway. It is 82 km long, and ships take an average of eight hours to complete a transit. In 2004 some 14,035 transits were recorded. The Canal can accommodate ships with a maximum draught of 12 m, beams of up to approximately 32.3 m (106 ft) and lengths of up to about 290 m (950 ft), roughly equivalent to ships with a maximum capacity of 65,000–70,000 dwt. In 2000 a five-year modernization project was begun. The project included: a general improvement of facilities; the implementation of a satellite traffic-management system; the construction of a bridge; and the widening of the narrowest section of the Canal, the Culebra Cut (which was completed in 2001). Plans were also announced to construct a 203-ha international cargo-handling platform at the Atlantic end of the Canal, including terminals, a railway and an international airport. Terminal ports are Balboa, on the Pacific Ocean, and Cristóbal, on the Caribbean Sea.

Autoridad del Canal de Panamá (ACP): Administration Bldg, Balboa Heights, Panamá; tel. 272-7602; fax 272-7622; e-mail info@pancanal.com; internet www.pancanal.com; f. 1997; manages, operates and maintains the Panama Canal; succeeded the Panama Canal Commission, a US govt agency, on 31 December 1999, when the waterway was ceded to the Govt of Panama; the ACP is the autonomous agency of the Govt of Panama; there is a Board of 11 mems; Chair. RICAURTE VÁSQUEZ; Administrator ALBERTO ALEMÁN ZUBIETA; Dep. Administrator MANUEL BENITEZ.

Autoridad Marítima de Panamá: Edif. 5534, Diablo Heights, Ancón, Apdo 8062, Panama 7; tel. 232-5528; fax 232-5527; e-mail ampadmin@amp.gob.pa; internet www.amp.gob.pa; f. 1998 to unite and optimize the function of all state institutions with involvement in maritime sector; Administrator RUBÉN AROSEMENA VALDÉS.

Autoridad de la Región Interoceánica (ARI): Panamá; tel. 228-5668; fax 228-7488; e-mail ari@sinfo.net; internet www.ari.gob.pa; f. 1993; administers the land and property of the former Canal Zone following their transfer from US to Panamanian control from 2000; legislation approved in early 1995 transferred control of the ARI to the Pres. of the Republic; Pres. GUSTAVO GARCÍA DE PAREDES.

Panama City Port Authority and Foreign Trade Zone 65: Apdo 15095, Panamá; FL 32406, USA; tel. 767-3220; e-mail wstubbs@portpanamacityusa.com; internet www.portpanamacityusa.com; Exec. Dir WAYNES STUBBS.

There are deep-water ports at Balboa and Cristóbal (including general cargo ships, containers, shipyards, industrial facilities); Coco Solo (general cargo and containers); Bahía Las Minas (general bulk and containers); Vacamonte (main port for fishing industry); Puerto Armuelles and Almirante (bananas); Aguadulce and Pedregal (export of crude sugar and molasses, transport of fertilizers and chemical products); and Charco Azul and Chiriquí Grande (crude oil).

The Panamanian merchant fleet was the largest in the world in December 2004, numbering 6,477 vessels with total displacement of 131.5m. gross registered tons. In November 2000 construction was completed on the largest container terminal in Latin America, in Balboa.

CIVIL AVIATION

Tocumen (formerly Omar Torrijos) International Airport, situated 19 km (12 miles) outside Panamá (Panama City), is the country's principal airport and is served by many international airlines. A project to expand the airport's facilities, at a cost of US $20m., was announced in 2004. The France Airport in Colón and the Rio Hato Airport in Coclé province have both been declared international airports. There are also 11 smaller airports in the country.

Aerolíneas Pacífico Atlántico, SA (Aeroperlas): Apdo 6-3596, El Dorado, Panamá; tel. 315-7500; fax 315-0331; e-mail info@aeroperlas.com; internet www.aeroperlas.com; f. 1970; fmrly state-owned, transferred to private ownership in 1987; operates scheduled regional and domestic flights to 16 destinations; initiated international flights in 2000; Pres. GEORGE F. NOVEY; Gen. Man. EDUARDO STAGG.

Compañía Panameña de Aviación, SA (COPA): Avda Justo Arosemena 230 y Calle 39, Apdo 1572, Panamá 1; tel. 227-2522; fax 227-1952; e-mail proquebert@mail.copa.com.pa; internet www.copaair.com; f. 1947; scheduled passenger and cargo services from Panamá (Panama City) to Central America, South America, the Caribbean and the USA; Chair. ALBERTO MOTTA; Exec. Pres. PEDRO O. HEILBRON.

Tourism

Panama's attractions include Panamá (Panama City), the ruins of Portobelo and 800 sandy tropical islands, including the resort of Contadora, one of the Pearl Islands in the Gulf of Panama, and the San Blas Islands, lying off the Atlantic coast. In 2003 the number of visitors stood at 534,208. Income from tourism was some US $809m. in that year. In 2000 there were some 5,700 hotel rooms in Panama.

Instituto Panameño de Turismo (IPAT): Centro de Convenciones ATLAPA, Vía Israel, Apdo 4421, Panamá 5; tel. 226-7000; fax 226-3483; e-mail ggral@ns.ipat.gob.pa; internet www.ipat.gob.pa; f. 1960; Dir-Gen. RUBÉN BLADES.

Asociación Panameña de Agencias de Viajes y Turismo (APAVIT): Bella Vista Local 24, Calle 51, Apdo 55-1000 Paitilla, Panamá 3; tel. 264-3526; fax 264-5355; e-mail apavit@cableonda.net; internet www.apavitpanama.org; f. 1957; Pres. AIDA QUIJANO J.; Vice-Pres. ERICK GOLDONI.

PAPUA NEW GUINEA

Introductory Survey

Location, Climate, Language, Religion, Flag, Capital

The Independent State of Papua New Guinea lies east of Indonesia and north of the north-eastern extremity of Australia. It comprises the eastern section of the island of New Guinea (the western section being Papua (West Papua), formerly Irian Jaya, which forms part of Indonesia) and about 600 smaller islands, including the Bismarck Archipelago (mainly New Britain, New Ireland and Manus) and the northern part of the Solomon Islands (mainly Bougainville and Buka). The climate is hot and humid throughout the year, with an average maximum temperature of 33°C (91°F) and an average minimum of 22°C (72°F). Rainfall is heavy on the coast but lower inland: the annual average varies from about 1,000 mm (40 ins) to 6,350 mm (250 ins). There are an estimated 742 native languages, but Pidgin and, to a lesser extent, standard English are also spoken, and, together with Motu, are the official languages in Parliament. More than 90% of the population profess Christianity. The national flag (proportions 3 by 4) is divided diagonally from the upper hoist to the lower fly: the upper portion displays a golden bird of paradise in silhouette on a red ground, while the lower portion has five white five-pointed stars, in the form of the Southern Cross constellation, on a black ground. The capital is Port Moresby.

Recent History

Papua New Guinea was formed by the merger of the Territory of Papua, under Australian rule from 1906, with the Trust Territory of New Guinea, a former German possession which Australia administered from 1914, first under a military Government, then under a League of Nations mandate, established in 1921, and later under a trusteeship agreement with the UN. During the Second World War, parts of both territories were occupied by Japanese forces from 1942 to 1945.

A joint administration for the two territories was established by Australia in July 1949. The union was named the Territory of Papua and New Guinea. A Legislative Council was established in November 1951 and was replaced by a House of Assembly, with an elected indigenous majority, in June 1964. The territory was renamed Papua New Guinea in July 1971. It achieved internal self-government in December 1973 and full independence on 16 September 1975, when the House of Assembly became the National Parliament.

Michael Somare, who from 1972 served as Chief Minister in an interim coalition Government, became Prime Minister on independence. He remained in office until 1980, despite widespread allegations of inefficiency in government ministries and of discrimination against the Highland provinces. The first elections since independence were held in June and July 1977, and Somare's Pangu (Papua New Guinea Unity) Pati formed a governing coalition, first with the People's Progress Party (PPP) and later with the United Party (UP).

In March 1980 the Government lost a vote of confidence, the fourth in 15 months, and Sir Julius Chan, the leader of the PPP and a former Deputy Prime Minister, succeeded to the premiership. Somare became Prime Minister again following a general election in June 1982. In 1983 the Somare Government effected a constitutional change to provide the central authorities with greater control of the provincial governments as a means of preventing abuse of their powers. As a result, between 1983 and 1991 a total of nine provincial governments were suspended by the central Government for alleged maladministration.

In March 1985 a motion expressing 'no confidence' in Somare's Government was introduced in Parliament by Chan, who nominated Paias Wingti (hitherto Deputy Prime Minister and a member of the Pangu Pati) as alternative Prime Minister. Somare quickly formed a coalition, comprising the ruling Pangu Pati, the National Party (NP) and the Melanesian Alliance (MA), and the 'no confidence' motion was defeated. Fourteen members of Parliament who had supported the motion were expelled from the Pangu Pati, and subsequently formed a new political party, the People's Democratic Movement (PDM), under the leadership of Wingti.

In August 1985 the NP withdrew from Somare's coalition Government, and in November Chan presented another motion of 'no confidence', criticizing Somare's handling of the economy. Somare was defeated and Wingti took office as Prime Minister of a new five-party coalition Government (comprising the PDM, the PPP, the NP, the UP and the MA), with Chan as Deputy Prime Minister.

At the mid-1987 general election to the National Parliament Somare's Pangu Pati won 26 of the 109 elective seats, while Wingti's PDM obtained 18. However, by forming a coalition with minor parties, Wingti succeeded in securing a parliamentary majority and was re-elected Prime Minister. In July 1988 Wingti was defeated in a 'no confidence' motion, proposed by Rabbie Namaliu, who had replaced Somare as leader of the Pangu Pati. As a result, Namaliu took office as Prime Minister and announced a new coalition Government, comprising members of the Pangu Pati and five minor parties: the People's Action Party (PAP), the MA, the NP, the League for National Advancement (LNA) and the Papua Party. In August Ted Diro, the leader of the PAP, was acquitted on a charge of perjury by the Supreme Court (having been accused of illegally appropriating funds for his party). An amendment to the Constitution, whereby a motion expressing 'no confidence' in the Prime Minister could not be proposed until he or she had completed 18 months in office, was approved by Parliament in August 1990 and incorporated into the Constitution in July 1991.

Apart from the continued unrest on Bougainville (see below), the principal cause for concern in Papua New Guinea's domestic affairs during the 1980s and 1990s was the increase in serious crime. In 1991 the National Parliament approved a programme of severe measures to combat crime, including the introduction of the death penalty and the tattooing of the foreheads of convicted criminals.

In September 1991 a leadership tribunal found Ted Diro, the leader of the PAP, guilty of 81 charges of misconduct in government office. However, the Governor-General, Sir Serei Eri, refused to ratify the tribunal's decision and reinstated Diro as Deputy Prime Minister, despite recommendations that he be dismissed. A constitutional crisis subsequently arose, during which a government envoy was sent to the United Kingdom to request that the monarch dismiss Eri. However, on 1 October the resignation of the Governor-General was announced; this was followed shortly afterwards by that of Diro.

In 1992 the Government continued to be troubled by allegations of corruption and misconduct (notably bribery and misuse of public funds). Campaigning for the 1992 general election began amid serious fighting among the various political factions, which led to rioting, in April, by some 10,000 supporters of rival candidates. At the election in June a total of 59 members of the legislature (including 15 ministers) lost their seats. The final result gave the Pangu Pati 22 of the 109 elective seats, while the PDM secured 15. Independent candidates won a total of 31 seats. Paias Wingti of the PDM was subsequently elected Prime Minister by the National Parliament, defeating Rabbie Namaliu of the Pangu Pati by a single vote. Wingti formed a coalition Government, comprising PDM, PPP and LNA members, as well as several independents. As part of the new administration's anti-corruption policy, Wingti suspended six provincial governments for financial mismanagement in October, and threatened to abolish the entire local government system.

In early 1993 a resurgence of tribal violence, mainly in the Enga Province, resulted in the deaths of more than 100 people. This development, together with a continued increase in violent crime throughout the country (despite the severe measures introduced in 1991), prompted the National Parliament to approve a new internal security act in May 1993. The measures—which included an amendment of the legal system that required defendants accused of serious crimes to prove their innocence, rather than be proven guilty—were criticized by the opposition as oppressive. In May 1994 the Supreme Court nullified six of the 26 sections of the act (most of which concerned the extension of police powers), denouncing them as unconstitutional.

In September 1993 Prime Minister Wingti announced his resignation to Parliament. The Speaker immediately requested nominations for the premiership, and Wingti was re-elected unopposed with 59 of the 109 votes. According to the Constitution (as amended in 1991), a motion of 'no confidence' in the Prime Minister could not be presented for at least 18 months, and Wingti claimed that his action had been necessary in order to secure a period of political stability for the country. Opposition members, however, described the events as an abuse of the democratic process, and several thousand demonstrators gathered in the capital to demand Wingti's resignation. In December the National Court rejected a constitutional challenge from the opposition to Wingti's re-election. However, in August 1994 the Supreme Court declared Wingti's re-election in September 1993 invalid. Wingti did not contest the ensuing parliamentary vote for a new Prime Minister, in which Sir Julius Chan of the PPP defeated the Speaker, Bill Skate, by 66 votes to 32; Chris Haiveta, the leader of the Pangu Pati, was appointed Deputy Prime Minister.

The abolition of the directly-elected provincial government system, as proposed by Wingti, was rejected by Chan's Government. However, there was still considerable support among the opposition for the planned changes, and, as a result, it was decided that Parliament would vote on a series of motions to amend the Constitution accordingly; the first of these was approved in March 1995. However, in June the Pangu Pati withdrew its support for the reforms, and considerable opposition to the proposals was expressed by the provincial governments. Nevertheless, the controversial legislation was approved later that month on condition that Chan lent his support to several opposition amendments to be considered later in the year. Chan subsequently dismissed six ministers for failing to vote for the legislation and effected a major reorganization of portfolios. The new regional authorities, comprising national politicians and selected local councillors and led by appointed governors, were appointed in that month. Wingti resigned as parliamentary leader of the opposition in order to assume the post of Governor in the Western Highlands Province, and was replaced by another PDM member, Roy Yaki.

Meanwhile, the country continued to experience serious problems relating to crime and tribal violence throughout 1995–96, and in November 1996 the Government imposed a nation-wide curfew to combat the increasing lawlessness.

The mercenary affair on Bougainville in early 1997 (see below) led to a period of extreme instability throughout the country, culminating in Chan's temporary resignation and the appointment of John Giheno as acting Prime Minister for about two months. The atmosphere of political uncertainty was exacerbated by serious outbreaks of violence in the weeks preceding the general election (which had been set for mid-June). The Government imposed a dusk-to-dawn curfew and a nation-wide ban on the sale of alcohol, and dispatched security personnel across the country in an attempt to quell the politically-motivated disturbances. Many senior politicians failed to be re-elected in the general election, including Giheno and Wingti. Outbreaks of violence were reported in several Highlands constituencies as the results were declared. A period of intense political manoeuvring followed the election, as various members sought to form coalitions and groupings in an attempt to achieve a majority in Parliament. On 22 July Bill Skate of the People's National Congress (PNC), who was the former Speaker and Governor of the National Capital District, was elected Prime Minister, defeating Sir Michael Somare (who had established a new party—the National Alliance—in 1996) by 71 votes to 35. Skate was supported by a coalition of the PNC, PDM, PPP, Pangu Pati and independent members. A new Government was appointed in late July, and extensive changes in the functional responsibilities of ministries were announced.

In September 1997 the Government declared a national disaster following a prolonged period of drought believed to have been caused by El Niño (a periodic warming of the tropical Pacific Ocean). By December more than 1,000 people had died, and as many as 1.2m. were threatened by starvation, as a result of the drought, which was the most severe in the country's recorded history. Several countries and organizations that had provided relief funds during the disaster were highly critical of the Government's management of the aid it received. The Minister for Finance, Roy Yaki, was dismissed, in part for his role in the affair, and responsibility for the administration of relief funds was subsequently transferred from the Department of Finance to the Department of Provincial Affairs. In March 1998 (when the drought was deemed to have ended following heavy rainfall) it was revealed that less than one-half of the relief aid received had been deployed to help the victims of the disaster.

On 14 November 1997 Silas (later Sir Silas) Atopare was appointed Governor-General, defeating Sir Getake Gam, head of the Evangelical Lutheran Church, by 54 votes to 44 in the legislature.

A serious political scandal erupted in late November 1997, following allegations of corruption against Skate. The accusations centred on a videotape broadcast on Australian television, which appeared to show Skate arranging bribes and boasting of his strong connections with criminal elements in Port Moresby. The Prime Minister dismissed his recorded comments (and the resultant allegations) saying that he had been drunk at the time of filming. Several senior politicians, including Somare, demanded his resignation over the affair. Meanwhile, Skate dismissed the leaders of the Pangu Pati and the PPP (Chris Haiveta and Andrew Baing, respectively), his coalition partners, accusing them of conspiring against him. The situation intensified with the resignation of seven Pangu Pati members from the Government in early December, and the announcement that the Pangu Pati and the PPP would join the opposition. However, the PPP rejoined the Government shortly afterwards, having voted to replace Baing as leader of the party with Michael Nali. Similarly, four Pangu Pati ministers rejoined the Government, thereby restoring Skate's majority in the National Parliament. A major ministerial reorganization was subsequently announced, in which Nali was appointed Deputy Prime Minister.

In April 1998 Skate announced the formation of a new political grouping, the Papua New Guinea First Party (which absorbed the PNC, the Christian Country Party and several other minor parties), and effected a ministerial reorganization. The Government's majority was subsequently undermined, however, following a series of decisions by the Court of Disputed Returns during mid-1998, which declared the election of seven government MPs (at the 1997 general election) null and void. Furthermore, in June the Pangu Pati officially joined the opposition, thereby reducing the Government's representation to 61 members in the National Parliament.

Rumours of a motion expressing 'no confidence' in the Prime Minister prompted the formation of a new pro-Skate coalition in the National Parliament in late July 1998. In the same month Skate announced a number of major reforms in the structure of the Government, including the merging of several ministerial portfolios, the establishment of new departments for Private Enterprise and Rural Development, a series of new appointments to various public bodies and an extensive ministerial reorganization.

In July 1998 a state of national disaster was declared, following a series of tsunamis (huge tidal waves caused by undersea earthquakes) which obliterated several villages on the northwest coast of the country and killed an estimated 3,000 people. An estimated K10m. was subsequently received for disaster relief operations, although widespread concern at the apparently inefficient distribution of the funds was expressed in the following months.

In October 1998 the PPP left the governing coalition and, in a subsequent ministerial reorganization, the party's leader, Nali, was replaced as Deputy Prime Minister by Iairo Lasaro.

In late 1998 there was a series of scandals relating to the various serious misdemeanours of a number of provincial governors. Moreover, outbreaks of tribal fighting continued to cause problems (particularly in the Highlands) in 1998–99. A serious conflict in the Eastern Highlands in early 1999 involved villagers using rocket launchers and grenades, and resulted in numerous deaths. In mid-1999 a state of emergency was declared in the Southern Highlands, following serious disturbances provoked by the death of a former provincial Governor, Dick Mune, in a road accident.

The establishment of a new political party, the PNG Liberal Party (PNGLP), in May 1999 by the Speaker, John Pundari (relaunched in June as the Advance PNG Party—APP), encouraged rumours of a forthcoming vote of 'no confidence' against the Prime Minister. In early June, as part of a government reorganization, Skate dismissed the PDM leader, Sir Mekere Morauta, and three other PDM ministers, replacing them with four Pangu Pati members, including Haiveta. Later that month both the PDM and the United Resource Party (URP) announced their decision to withdraw completely from the coalition Government, following the resignation of nine government ministers. Both parties were expected to support the APP, in an attempt to subject Skate to a vote of 'no confidence'. On 7 July, however, Skate unexpectedly resigned, but declared that he would remain in power, in an acting capacity, until the appointment of a new Prime Minister. The opposition alliance announced Morauta as their candidate for the premiership. On the day before the National Parliament was due to reconvene, Skate claimed that the APP had pledged support for the Government, thereby ensuring that it would have a sufficient majority to defeat any motion of 'no confidence'. At the opening session of the National Parliament in mid-July, Lasaro, the incumbent Prime Minister's nominee, defeated the opposition candidate, Bernard Narokobi of the PDM by 57 votes to 45, to become Speaker. However, on the next day Morauta was elected as new Prime Minister with an overwhelming majority, following his nomination by Pundari, who had transferred his allegiance from Skate, having refused to accept the latter's nomination of himself as candidate for the premiership. Lasaro immediately resigned as Speaker, and Narokobi was elected unopposed to the position. Morauta subsequently appointed a new coalition Government, with Pundari as Deputy Prime Minister.

In early August 1999 Morauta, a former Governor of the central bank, presented a 'mini-budget', in an attempt to combat various economic problems which, he claimed, were a consequence of the previous Government's mismanagement. As part of a series of measures aimed at stabilizing the political situation in the country, legislation was drafted in October 1999 to prevent ministers transferring political allegiances. In early December Prime Minister Morauta expelled the APP from the coalition Government and dismissed Pundari from his post as Deputy Prime Minister, claiming that this constituted a further move towards the restoration of political stability. (Pundari was rumoured to have conspired with the opposition leader, Skate, to oust the Prime Minister.) Pundari was replaced by the former Minister of Works and deputy leader of the PDM, Mao Zeming. Following Pundari's sudden dismissal, four small political parties within the governing coalition—the National Alliance, the People's National Party, the Melanesian Alliance and the Movement for Greater Autonomy—joined to form the People's National Alliance. Also in that month, Skate (who was faced with a charge of attempted fraud during his term in office as Governor of the National Capital District Commission), announced that his party, the People's National Congress (PNC, which had 10 MPs), was to join the coalition Government; in May he assumed leadership of the party. Later in December, the resignation of the Minister of Agriculture and Livestock, Ted Diro, prompted Morauta to carry out a government reshuffle, including the appointment of three new ministers. In February 2000 it was announced that about 25,000 inhabitants of the Duke of York Islands, which are situated in East New Britain Province, were expected to be resettled by the Government, following the publication of a UN report indicating that the islands were becoming uninhabitable owing to rising sea levels resulting from the 'greenhouse effect' (the heating of the earth's atmosphere as a consequence of pollution).

Morauta dismissed three ministers in March 2000, on the grounds that they had allegedly conspired to introduce a parliamentary motion of 'no confidence' in the Prime Minister. The parliamentary strength of the ruling coalition was increased to 76 MPs in April, following the readmission of the APP to government, including the appointment of Pundari, to the post of Minister of Lands and Physical Planning. In an attempt to increase government stability, Morauta proposed legislation in August that would restrict the ability of MPs to change their party allegiance within a parliamentary session. Moreover, Morauta also announced the adjournment of Parliament between January and July 2001, the only period during which votes of 'no confidence' could be tabled. (The Constitution forbids such votes in the 18 months following the election of a Prime Minister, and in the 12 months prior to a general election.) In November, however, a revolt by 25 government MPs (including six cabinet ministers) prevented a vote on the so-called Political Parties Integrity Bill. The rebellion prompted a major cabinet reshuffle, in which all of the ministers involved in the revolt, including the Deputy Prime Minister, Mao Zeming, were dismissed. Further changes to the composition of the cabinet were made in December, notably the dismissal of Michael Somare, the Minister for Foreign Affairs and Trade, following which Morauta secured the parliamentary approval of the bill. The Prime Minister claimed that the introduction of the new legislation represented the most important constitutional change in Papua New Guinea since independence and would greatly enhance the political stability of the country, as it required members of Parliament who wished to change party allegiance to stand down and contest a by-election.

Allegations of corruption and mismanagement resulted in the suspension of four provincial governments (Western Province, Southern Highlands, Enga and the National Capital District—NCD) in late 2000 and early 2001. The central Government claimed that a failure to deliver services had resulted from the misuse of public funds. Moreover, in January 2001 the Minister for Provincial and Local Government, Iairo Lasaro, was arrested for the alleged misappropriation of public funds, and in mid-March Bill Skate was charged with the same crime, having been acquitted earlier in the month of conspiring to defraud an insurance company (the trial was to be abandoned in December 2001 owing to lack of evidence).

A Commonwealth report into the Papua New Guinea Defence Force published in January 2001 recommended reducing the number of army personnel by one-third. Subsequent plans by the Government to make more than 2,000 soldiers redundant (equivalent to some 50% of the entire Defence Force) resulted in a revolt at the Port Moresby barracks in March. It was believed that senior officers had helped to distribute arms to the rebels, who demanded the resignation of the Prime Minister and the transfer of power to a caretaker administration. The rebellion ended some two weeks later with an amnesty for the soldiers involved, during which hundreds of looted weapons were surrendered. In March 2002 another rebellion by soldiers protesting against the proposed reductions in defence personnel took place at the Moem barracks on the northern coast. The leader of the rebellion, Nebare Dege, was sentenced to 15 years' imprisonment in December 2002.

In April 2001 the Advance PNG Party, led by John Pundari, was dissolved and merged with the PDM, led by the Prime Minister. In May, following a minor ministerial reorganization in March, Morauta expelled the National Alliance from the ruling coalition and dismissed the party's ministers (including Bart Philemon, Minister for Foreign Affairs) from the National Executive Council, accusing Somare, its leader, of attempting to destabilize the Government.

In late June, following several days of protests against the Government's economic reforms, police used tear gas to disperse hundreds of demonstrators outside the Prime Minister's office in Port Moresby. In a separate incident, four students were killed and several injured when riot police allegedly entered the premises of the University of Papua New Guinea and opened fire. A temporary curfew was imposed, and a Commission of Inquiry was established; in December relatives of one of the dead students began legal action against the police force.

In October 2001 the Prime Minister effected another reallocation of ministerial portfolios. At the end of the month, furthermore, the Minister for Foreign Affairs, John Pundari, was dismissed. His removal from office followed his criticism of the Government's participation in Australia's 'Pacific Solution', whereby 216 refugees, who had attempted to enter Australia illegally, were being housed in a former military prison on Manus Island. In December negotiations with Australia were under way to accommodate a further 1,000 asylum-seekers, and Australia had requested the Government to hold the refugees for an additional six months, although no formal agreement was made. In January 2002 the Government decided to accept 784 additional asylum-seekers. It was understood that they were to remain only until their asylum claims were processed. The agreement with Australia to accommodate the asylum-seekers on Manus Island was extended for a further 12 months in October 2002 and was to provide for the housing of an additional 1,000 people. The camp remained open, despite the Australian Government's announcement in August 2003 that it intended to close the facility. In early 2004 it was revealed that the sole occupant of the camp was a Palestinian refugee who had been held in solitary confinement for almost seven months at a cost of more than US $3m. Opposition politicians in Australia noted that the amount of money spent maintaining the camp on Manus Island and its one occupant would fund unemployment benefit payments for all the asylum-seekers currently detained in Australian centres.

A general election was held in the latter part of June 2002. Voting commenced on 15 June and was to extend over a two-week period. Many polling stations, however, failed to open as scheduled, amid reports of the theft of ballot papers and subsequent strike action by electoral staff. Some 25 people were killed and dozens injured in election-related violence, much of which occurred in the Highlands provinces as a result of disputes between clan-based candidates. A Commonwealth inquiry was subsequently planned to investigate the events surrounding the election, which was described as the worst in the country's history. In the final results announced in August six seats in the Highlands provinces remained vacant where voting had been unable to proceed. Of the 103 seats determined, Somare's National Alliance won 19 and Morauta's PDM secured 12. Independent candidates won 17 seats, with the remainder divided among a large number of minor parties, many of which had been formed specifically to contest the election.

On 5 August 2002 Sir Michael Somare was elected Prime Minister, with 88 parliamentary votes. No candidates stood against him, and Morauta and his supporters abstained from the vote. Bill Skate, who had played an important part in Somare's campaign, was elected Speaker. After appointing a 28-member Cabinet (which was dominated by 19 newly elected MPs), Somare began his third term as Prime Minister, pledging to restore stability, halt the privatization programme and reduce expenditure. Instability within the parliamentary opposition in late 2002 resulted in the dismissal of Morauta as Leader of the Opposition in December; he was replaced in that role by John Muinepe. Morauta was replaced as PDM leader by Paias Wingti, who had been expelled from the party in the previous August. However, in February 2003 a court ruled that this action had been unlawful and Morauta was subsequently reinstalled as party leader.

In April and May 2003 elections were held for the six Highlands constituencies where voting had failed to take place in the previous year. In June the Government submitted proposals for a number of changes to the political system, including a mandatory general election following the approval of a 'no confidence' motion and stricter rules governing the switching of party allegiances among members of the National Parliament. In late 2003 the Government proposed legislation that would extend the period that a new government should be exempt from votes of 'no confidence' from 18 months to three years. Both attempts to introduce these constitutional changes were unsuccessful, despite government inducements of some US $25,000 for members of Parliament to support the proposals.

On 18 September 2003 Sir Albert Kipalan defeated Sir Paulias Matane by a single vote in the final poll to elect a new Governor-General. Kipalan was expected to take up the position on 13 November when the term of the incumbent Sir Silas Atopare expired. However, questions concerning possible flaws in the procedure arose in the following week, casting doubt on the validity of the election, and the Supreme Court subsequently declared it to be defective and invalid. Speaker Bill Skate was appointed acting Governor-General until a new election could be arranged. At the poll, which was duly held on 4 December, Sir Pato Kakaraya was the successful candidate. However, Kipalan, who had also contested the election, challenged the result and, owing to a number of objections, was granted a legal injunction against Kakaraya's swearing-in, which had been due to take place in late January 2004. Moreover, in early March Bill Skate was obliged to resign briefly as acting Governor-General to stand trial on charges of misappropriating public funds. He resumed the position a few days later having been cleared of the charges. In late March the Supreme Court declared the election of Sir Pato Kakaraya to be null and void. Somare consequently ordered the recall of the National Parliament in order that a new election to the post could be organized. Following four rounds of voting Sir Paulias Matane, a former Minister of Foreign Affairs, was narrowly elected Governor-General in late May and, when the Supreme Court had dismissed an injunction against his appointment by Kakaraya, was duly sworn in in the following month.

In May 2004 Somare dismissed Deputy Prime Minister Moses Maladina together with all the PNC members of the Cabinet who had refused to support proposed government legislation and who were believed to be planning a vote of 'no confidence' in the Government. Meanwhile, ongoing fears about increasing gun ownership were highlighted in early August when the National Parliament was adjourned for a period of three months after both the Government and the opposition expressed concern over the number of members of Parliament who were reported to be bringing firearms into Parliament. In early 2005 Somare announced a reorganization of cabinet portfolios which included the appointment of his son, Arthur, to the role of Minister for National Planning and Monitoring. In February 2006, however, Arthur Somare resigned from his cabinet position following allegations of misappropriation of public funds; he was referred to the Public Prosecutor for failing to submit annual statements on time and to account for financial support grants that had been applied within his district. The Minister for Forestry, Patrick Pruaitch, was appointed to the post in an acting capacity. In a reallocation of portfolios in early April, Pruaitch also assumed responsibility for the finance portfolio, which was removed from Bart Philemon, who nevertheless remained as Minister for Treasury. Mark Maipakai, hitherto Minister of Justice, was appointed Minister for Housing and Urban Resettlement, being replaced in the former position by Bire Kimisopa. Kimisopa had previously served as Minister for Internal Security, a post to which Alphonse Willie was appointed.

Relations with Australia have been affected by various developments. In December 2003, following the apparent success of the intervention in Solomon Islands earlier in the year, Australia announced the deployment of some 250 of its security personnel to different regions of Papua New Guinea, as part of plans for a five-year operation costing US $325m., aimed at restoring order to troubled areas of the country. Moreover, the Australian Government was to send up to 70 officials to Papua New Guinea to take up senior public roles in the spheres of finance, justice, public sector management, immigration, border security and transport safety. The agreement, known as the Enhanced Co-operation Program (ECP), was officially concluded in June 2004 and incorporated a total aid 'package' worth US $690m. Somare had initially been reluctant to accept Australia's expanded role in the country, fearing that it would erode national sovereignty, but had been obliged to reconsider when the Australian Prime Minister, John Howard, implied that aid payments to Papua New Guinea were dependent on the country's co-operation. A report by the Australian Strategic Policy Institute, published in December 2004, claimed that Papua New Guinea was facing economic and social collapse. It urged the Australian Government to intervene further in the country by radically increasing the amount of aid it provided and by taking control of some aspects of government, particularly immigration. Research by the organization indicated that government and state institutions had become too weak to prevent drugs and weapons smuggling, human trafficking and 'money-laundering' activities, operated by international criminal groups, which had relocated to Papua New Guinea from South-East Asia in recent years. Furthermore, an investigation carried out by Australian journalists, the results of which were published in early 2005, alleged that Chinese mafia groups had infiltrated the highest levels of Papua New Guinea's police force. According to the report, the corruption of the country's authorities was facilitating serious criminal activities that posed a threat to the national security of Australia. It was also believed that the criminals had been recruiting Port Moresby's notorious 'raskol' gangs (groups of heavily armed, disaffected young men responsible for much of the violent crime in the capital) to commit armed robberies, assaults and other crimes in support of their activities.

The ECP suffered a serious reversal in May 2005 when Papua New Guinea's Supreme Court ruled that the deployment of Australian security personnel in the country was unconstitutional (principally because they had been given immunity from prosecution). Personnel began to return to Australia shortly after the ruling. Relations between the two countries had deteriorated in March when Prime Minister Sir Michael Somare had been subjected to a security search at Brisbane airport. A demonstration by more than 7,000 people in Lae, demanding an apology from Australia for the incident and accusing that country's authorities of showing contempt and disrespect for Papua New Guinea, took place in the following month. In October, following revisions to the ECP, it was announced that Australia was to commit as many as 40 police officers to assist the local forces in a renewed attempt to curb the increasing levels of violence and crime in the country. The dispatch of the new police component was part of the revised ECP. In February 2006 an internal police investigation that had begun in 2003 revealed that as many as 66 police officers had been implicated in corrupt activities, such as receiving funds from Asian crime syndicates.

Further controversy surrounding the role of foreign interests in the exploitation of the country's natural resources arose in early 2005 when a group representing landowners near the Porgera mine protested at the mysterious deaths of villagers while panning for alluvial gold near the mine. The group claimed that several local people had been shot dead by Porgera security personnel and their bodies removed and that others had been seriously assaulted. Mine officials denied the allegations, stating that most of the deaths had been caused by falling rocks or other accidents, and that any shootings by their security guards had been carried out in self-defence. The opposition leader, Peter O'Neill, demanded an official inquiry into the deaths, which by early May had reached 29, with many others having been seriously assaulted.

Tribal conflicts, principally between the Ujimap and Wagia tribes, broke out near Mendi, the capital of Southern Highlands Province, in December 2001. It was alleged that national and local politicians, along with tribal leaders, had made little effort to end the fighting, which had originated in a dispute over the governorship of the province in 1997; furthermore, many were dissatisfied at the election of Tom Tomiape as Governor, in late November, and at the widespread political corruption and deteriorating public services in the province. Tomiape's election was ruled invalid by the Supreme Court in December, and Wambi Nondi was appointed acting Governor. A brief cease-fire was brokered in early January and an independent peace commission was formed in February, headed by Francis Awesa, a local businessman. By early 2002 more than 120 people had been killed since the onset of the fighting.

Ethnic and tribal violence continued in several regions of the country during 2003. Eight people were killed in fighting near Port Moresby in May, and 17 died during inter-clan violence involving more than 1,000 people in Enga Province in July. Further killings led to rioting in the following month and to an appeal by the Governor of the province for those responsible to be hanged. In early 2004 eight villagers were killed in Enga Province in further tribal conflicts and by mid-2004 ethnic violence in Morobe, Chimbu and East Highlands Provinces had resulted in many more deaths, including those of several children. Concerns regarding the conduct of the national police force in tackling such conflicts intensified following an incident in August when a confrontation between security personnel and a group of youths in Enga Province resulted in police setting fire to an entire village, killing domestic animals and shooting dead a villager and injuring several others. Earlier in the year the former Commander-in-Chief of the Defence Force, Jerry Singirok, stated his belief that the marked increase in ownership of illegal firearms, particularly in the Highlands region, was the single most significant problem in Papua New Guinea. Ethnic violence continued in 2005 with at least 10 people being killed in February in an incident in Enga Province prompted by the incorrect allocation of a village magistrate's allowance. Some 5,000 villagers were left homeless following fighting in Chimbu Province in April, which resulted in damage to property estimated at K1m. Further violence during the year, particularly in the Highlands provinces, resulted in many more deaths. In one outbreak of fighting, resulting from a land dispute, in July an estimated 7,000 guns were believed to have been used and police officers declined to intervene as they were considerably less well-armed. In another incident fuel shortages prevented police from attending a serious tribal conflict in which many people were killed. A report published in July 2005 claimed that the majority of illegal firearms in circulation in the country originated from Papua New Guinea Defence Force or police stocks. Another report released in early 2006 confirmed that many of the weapons used in these inter-tribal conflicts had been bought or stolen from the security forces, who appeared to be unable or unwilling to intervene in such incidents, while home-made shotguns were increasingly being replaced by more sophisticated weaponry.

Fears that rising sea-levels would have very serious consequences for Pacific islanders increased in May 2003 when an emergency operation was undertaken to save the inhabitants of Carteret and Mortlock islands near Bougainville. Food supplies were sent to the islands, the 2,000 inhabitants of which were reported to be suffering from starvation and health problems related to poor diet, since the failure of their crops, which had been flooded by sea water. The islanders, however, were reluctant to accept a government proposal to relocate them to Bougainville, fearing the loss of their distinct Polynesian culture and way of life. In November 2005 it was reported that the proposed relocation of families was finally to commence, with as many as 16 families scheduled to be moved to Bougainville by the end of 2006.

The country was beset by a series of severe floods in late 2003 and early 2004 which affected some 5,000 people in Morobe Province and more than 10,000 in West Highlands Province. Food crops, livestock and entire villages were destroyed by the floods.

Following a series of volcanic eruptions in October 2004 on the island of Manam in Madang Province, the Government undertook a programme of evacuation of the island's more than 9,000 residents to the mainland. Several villages were completely destroyed by volcanic ash and lava, which continued to flow for several weeks. Although no residents were killed in the immediate aftermath of the eruptions, by mid-2005 more than 100 islanders had died from illnesses believed to have resulted from poisoning by volcanic gases. The volcano erupted again in late February 2006, when clouds of ash reportedly reached a height of 2 km. Hundreds of Manam's inhabitants were instructed to leave the island, to be relocated to neighbouring Madang, but many returned to their homes after the eruptions abated.

The status of the province of Bougainville was increasingly questioned in the late 1980s, a problem that developed into civil unrest and a long-term national crisis. In April 1988 landowners on the island of Bougainville submitted compensation claims amounting to K10,000m., for land mined by the Australian-owned Bougainville Copper Ltd since 1972. When no payment was forthcoming, acts of sabotage were perpetrated in late 1988 by the Bougainville Revolutionary Army (BRA), led by Francis Ona, a former mine surveyor and landowner, and the mine was obliged to suspend operations for an initial period of six days. However, when repairs had been completed, the mine's owners refused to resume operations for fear of further attack, and the President, Rabbie Namaliu, was forced to deploy members of the security forces in the area. Production at the mine recommenced in December, but, after further violence in January 1989, a curfew was imposed. In early 1989 it was announced that, in an attempt to appease landowners, their share of mining royalties was to be increased from 5% to 20%.

The BRA's demands increasingly favoured secession from Papua New Guinea for Bougainville (and for North Solomons Province as a whole), together with the closure of the mine until their demands for compensation and secession had been met. In May 1989, as the violent campaign on the island intensified, the mine was forced once more to suspend production, and in June the Papua New Guinea Government declared a state of emergency on Bougainville, sending 2,000 security personnel to the island. In September a minister in the Bougainville provincial government, who had been negotiating an agreement with Bougainville landowners to provide them with financial compensation, was shot dead. The signing of the accord, due to take place the following day, was postponed indefinitely. Diro, who had been reinstated in the Government in May, as Minister of State with responsibility for overseeing the Bougainville crisis, responded by offering a reward for the capture or killing of Ona and seven of his deputies, including the BRA's military commander, Sam Kauona. In January 1990 the owners of the Bougainville mine made redundant 2,000 of the remaining 2,300 staff.

The escalation of violence on Bougainville led the Australian Government to announce plans to send in military forces to evacuate its nationals trapped on the island, and to withdraw the remaining 300 personnel of Bougainville Copper Ltd. Criticism of the Government's failure to resolve the dispute, the rising death toll among the security forces, rebels and civilians and a worsening economic crisis, which was aggravated by the conflict, led the Government to negotiate a cease-fire with the BRA, with effect from the beginning of March 1990. The Government undertook to withdraw its security forces and to release 80 detainees. Bougainville came under the control of the BRA in mid-March, after the sudden departure of the security forces. The premature withdrawal of the troops was seen as an attempt by Paul Tohian, the police commissioner who had been in charge of the state of emergency on Bougainville, to disrupt the peace process, and was followed by an apparent abortive coup, allegedly led by Tohian, who was summarily dismissed from his post.

In late March 1990 the Government imposed an economic blockade on Bougainville; this was intensified in May, when banking, telecommunications and public services on the island were suspended. On 17 May the BRA, apparently in response to the Government's implementation of economic sanctions, proclaimed Bougainville's independence, renaming the island the Republic of Bougainville. The unilateral declaration of independence, made by Ona, who also proclaimed himself interim President, was immediately dismissed by Namaliu as unconstitutional and invalid. In July negotiations between the BRA and the Government finally began on board a New Zealand naval vessel, *Endeavour*. In the resulting 'Endeavour Accord', the BRA representatives agreed to defer implementation of the May declaration of independence and to hold further discussions on the political status of the island. The Government agreed to end the blockade, and to restore essential services to the island. However, despite assurances from Namaliu that troops would not be sent to the island, the first two ships that left for Bougainville with supplies were found to be carrying 100 security personnel, intending to disembark on the island of Buka, north of Bougainville. The BRA accused the Government of violating the accord, and a week later the security forces and the two ships, together with the supplies, withdrew. In mid-September the Government sent armed troops to take control of Buka, stating that this was in response to a petition for help from Buka islanders. Violent clashes ensued between the BRA and the armed forces on Buka, in which many people were reported to have been killed.

In January 1991 further negotiations took place between representatives of the Papua New Guinea Government and of Bougainville in Honiara, the capital of Solomon Islands, which resulted in the 'Honiara Accord'. The agreement stated that the Papua New Guinea Government would not station its security forces on Bougainville if the islanders agreed to disband the BRA and to surrender all prisoners and weapons to a multinational peace-keeping force. The Bougainville secessionists were guaranteed immunity from prosecution. The agreement, however, made no provision for any change in the political status of Bougainville, and by early March it appeared to have failed. Government troops launched a further attack on Bougainville in April 1991. In June Col Leo Nuia was dismissed from his post as Commander of the Papua New Guinea Defence Force, after admitting that his troops had committed atrocities during fighting on Bougainville in early 1990. Further allegations of human rights abuses and summary executions of BRA members and sympathizers by government troops prompted Namaliu to announce plans for an independent inquiry into the claims.

Fighting continued throughout 1991 and the situation deteriorated further in early 1992 when, in an attempt to force the Government to end its economic blockade of the island, the BRA intercepted and set fire to a supply ship, and held its crew hostage. As a result, all shipping and air services to Bougainville were suspended.

In October 1992 government troops began a major offensive against rebel-held areas of Bougainville and, later in the month, announced that they had taken control of the main town, Arawa. The BRA, however, denied the claim and began a campaign of arson against government offices and public buildings in Arawa. Violence on the island intensified in early 1993, and allegations of atrocities and violations of human rights by both sides were widely reported.

Talks between government representatives and secessionists in Honiara during 1994 led to the signing of a cease-fire agreement in September. Under the terms of the agreement, a regional peace-keeping force, composed of troops from Fiji, Vanuatu and Tonga, was deployed in October (with the Governments of Australia and New Zealand in a supervisory role) and the economic blockade of Bougainville was lifted. In the following month Chan and a group of non-BRA Bougainville leaders signed the Charter of Mirigini, which provided for the establishment of a transitional Bougainville government. The BRA declared its opposition to the proposed authority, reiterating its goal of outright secession.

In April 1995, following the suspension of the Bougainville provincial government, 27 members of the 32-member transitional administration were sworn in at a ceremony on Buka Island, attended by the Prime Minister and several foreign dignitaries. Theodore Miriong, a former legal adviser to Ona, was elected Premier of the authority. However, the three seats reserved for the BRA leaders, Ona, Kauona and Joseph Kabui (a former Premier of North Solomons Province), remained vacant, as the rebels urged their supporters to reject the new administration and to continue the violent campaign for independence. An amnesty, declared in May by the transitional administration and the Government, for all who had committed crimes during the conflict, was rejected by the BRA. Violence escalated during July and August, and a campaign of arson against public buildings was conducted by BRA rebels. Meanwhile, the Government denied any involvement in a series of attacks on BRA leaders, including an assassination attempt on Kabui. The murder of several more members of the security forces in March 1996 led the Government to abandon all talks with the secessionists and to reimpose a military blockade on Bougainville. An escalation of violence in mid-1996 culminated in a major military offensive against rebel-held areas in June. Civilians on the island were encouraged to seek refuge in government 'care centres', and by August it was estimated that some 67,000 Bougainvilleans were being accommodated in 59 such centres. In the same month defence forces arrested Miriong, accusing him of incitement regarding the killing of 13 government soldiers at an army camp. The incident, in which Miriong was removed from Bougainville and kept under surveillance on Buka, caused the Government considerable embarrassment, particularly as it followed a number of similar cases in which the security forces had chosen to act independently of government policy. On 12 October Miriong was assassinated at his home in south-west Bougainville by unidentified gunmen. The following month an official inquiry concluded that a group of government soldiers was responsible for the killing, assisted by pro-Government civilians (known as 'resistance fighters'). Meanwhile, Gerard Sinato was elected as the new Premier of the Bougainville Transitional Government.

An apparent deterioration in the situation on Bougainville in late 1996 was characterized by an increase in BRA attacks against civilian targets and a similar escalation in violence by government troops and 'resistance fighters'. The Red Cross temporarily suspended its operations on the island following an attack on one of its vehicles, and human rights organizations repeated demands that observers be allowed to monitor incidents on the island, following a series of attacks on civilians (for which both sides denied responsibility). A report commissioned by the Government and published in late 1996 recommended a thorough reorganization of the country's armed forces. The report identified a number of problems which had contributed to a lack of cohesion and discipline and a marked decline in morale among troops, which had resulted in many soldiers refusing to serve in Bougainville.

In February 1997 unofficial reports suggested that the Government was planning to engage the services of a group of mercenaries on Bougainville. Chan reacted angrily to the reports, which he claimed were inaccurate; however, he confirmed that a company based in the United Kingdom, Sandline International (a subsidiary of Executive Outcomes, a notorious supplier of private armed forces in Africa), had been commissioned to provide military advice and training for soldiers on Bougainville. Subsequent reports of mercenary activity on the island and of the large-scale purchase of military equipment and weapons provoked expressions of condemnation from numerous interests in the region, including the British High Commission in Port Moresby, and, in particular, from the Government of Australia. The situation developed into a major crisis when on 16 March the Commander of the Defence Force, Brig.-Gen. (later Maj.-Gen.) Jerry Singirok, announced on national radio and television that the country's armed forces were refusing to co-operate with the mercenary programme and demanded the immediate resignation of Chan. He explained that the mercenaries (most of whom were from South Africa) had been captured by the armed forces and were being detained while arrangements were made for their deportation. Singirok denied that his actions constituted a coup attempt. The following day Chan dismissed Singirok, replacing him with Col Alfred Aikung. However, the armed forces rejected the new leadership, remaining loyal to Singirok. Popular support for the army's stance became increasingly vocal, as several thousand demonstrators rampaged through the streets of the capital, looting and clashing with security forces. Armed forces in Australia were reported to be prepared for deployment to Papua New Guinea in the event of any worsening of the situation. In view of the escalation in civil unrest, Chan announced the suspension of the contract with Sandline International on 20 March, pending an inquiry into the affair. The following day the remaining mercenaries left the country and Aikung was replaced as Commander of the Defence Force by Col Jack Tuat. Despite these attempts at conciliation, however, demands for Chan's resignation intensified, with military, political and religious leaders, as well as the Governor-General, urging him to leave office. Moreover, four government ministers resigned their posts in an attempt to increase the pressure on Chan to do likewise. On 25 March the National Parliament voted on a motion of 'no confidence' in the Prime Minister. When the vote was defeated protesters laid siege to the parliament building, effectively imprisoning more than 100 members inside the building until the next day, while an estimated 15,000 demonstrators marched on Parliament from across the capital. The following day Chan announced his resignation, along with that of the Deputy Prime Minister and the Minister for Defence. John Giheno, the erstwhile Minister for Mining and Petroleum, was subsequently elected acting Prime Minister.

In April 1997 an inquiry was initiated into the mercenary affair. The chief executive of Sandline International, Col (retd) Tim Spicer, was questioned over his alleged acceptance of bribes and in connection with various firearms offences. During the inquiry it was revealed that the company had requested part-ownership of the Panguna copper mine as payment for its military services. Criminal charges against Spicer were withdrawn within several days. The inquiry concluded in early June that Chan had not been guilty of misconduct in relation to the mercenary affair, and, as a result (despite Giheno's stated intention to continue as acting Prime Minister until a general election had taken place), Chan announced his immediate resumption of his former position. Shortly after resuming office, Chan again provoked controversy by appointing Col Leo Nuia to the position of Commander of the Defence Force. (Nuia had been dismissed from the post in 1991, following an admission that his troops had committed atrocities during fighting on Bougainville.)

Following the election of a new Government, it was announced in August 1997 that a second inquiry into the mercenary affair, based on broader criteria, would be conducted. Meanwhile, government soldiers reacted angrily to the prosecution of military leaders involved in the operation to oust Sandline mercenaries from Bougainville in March. Nuia was imprisoned in his barracks by members of the Defence Force, while Maj. Walter Enuma, who was being held while awaiting trial on charges of 'raising an illegal force', was freed by rebel soldiers. The second inquiry concluded in September 1998 that Chris Haiveta (the former Deputy Prime Minister) had been the beneficiary of corrupt payments from Sandline and upheld the first inquiry's finding that Chan had not been guilty of any wrongdoing in the affair. In the same month an international tribunal ruled that the Government owed $A28m. to Sandline in outstanding payments under the mercenary contract. In May 1999 the Government agreed to pay this debt and the two parties undertook to end all legal action against each other. The Papua New Guinea Defence Force was to be allowed to retain Sandline military equipment stored on Bougainville.

In July 1997 talks were held in New Zealand (at the Burnham army base) between secessionists and representatives of the Bougainville Transitional Government. As a result of the negotiations, Sinato and Kabui signed the 'Burnham Declaration', which recommended the withdrawal of government troops from Bougainville and the deployment of a neutral peace-keeping force. Persistent reports of internal divisions within the BRA were refuted by the leadership, despite Ona's declared opposition to the 'Burnham Declaration'. However, hopes for a significant improvement in the political climate on Bougainville were encouraged by an official visit by the new Prime Minister, Bill Skate, in August (the first such visit since 1994) and by the resumption of talks in New Zealand in the following month. Negotiations concluded on 10 October 1997 with the signing of the 'Burnham Truce', in which representatives from both sides agreed to a series of interim measures, which included refraining from acts of armed confrontation pending a formal meeting of government and secessionist leaders in early 1998. Ona (who appeared to be becoming increasingly marginalized within the BRA) refused to be a party to the truce, however, claiming that similar agreements had not been honoured by government troops and 'resistance fighters' in the past, and indirectly threatened the members of an unarmed group of regional representatives, established to monitor the truce. The Prime Ministers of both Papua New Guinea and Solomon Islands made an extended visit to Bougainville in December 1997 to demonstrate their united support for the truce. Further talks held at Lincoln University in Christchurch, New Zealand, in January 1998 resulted in the 'Lincoln Agreement', providing for an extension to the truce, the initiation of a disarmament process and the phased withdrawal of government troops from the island. Skate also issued a public apology for mistakes made by successive administrations during the conflict, which was estimated to have resulted in the deaths of some 20,000 people and to have cost a total of K200m.

In accordance with the provisions of the 'Burnham Truce', a permanent cease-fire agreement was signed in Arawa on 30 April 1998. The occasion was attended by senior government members from Australia, New Zealand, Solomon Islands and Vanuatu, as well as Papua New Guinea government representatives and secessionist leaders. Ona declined to take part in the ceremony, reiterating his opposition to the peace agreement. In the following month he attracted statements of condemnation from Kabui and Kauona for issuing a 'shoot-to-kill' order against the peace-keeping troops on Bougainville to the small band of rebels who remained loyal to him. In June government troops were withdrawn from Arawa under the terms of the agreement and reconstruction projects on Bougainville, financed by funds from various sources, including an aid package of $NZ1m. from the New Zealand Government, were initiated. An increase in crime and arson attacks, however, was reported in the demilitarized zones in the following months.

In August 1998 more than 2,000 representatives from different groups in Bougainville met in Buin (in the south of the island) to discuss their response to the 'Burnham Truce'. The resultant 'Buin Declaration' stated that the islanders were united in their aspiration for independence through peaceful negotiation. In October the National Parliament voted to amend the Constitution to allow the Bougainville Reconciliation Government to replace the Bougainville Transitional Government. The new authority came into existence on 1 January 1999, following the renewed suspension of the Bougainville provincial government, and at its first sitting elected Sinato and Kabui as its co-leaders. In April an agreement signed by Bougainville and Papua New Guinea government representatives (although not acknowledged by the BRA), known as the Matakana and Okataina Understanding, reaffirmed both sides' commitment to the cease-fire, while undertaking to discuss options for the political future of the island. Elections to the Bougainville People's Congress (BPC, formerly the Bougainville Reconciliation Government) were held in early May 1999, and were reported to have proceeded smoothly. At the first sitting of the BPC, Kabui was elected President by an overwhelming majority, securing 77 of the 87 votes, thus defeating his former co-leader, Sinato, who received only 10 votes. Kabui subsequently appointed 29 members to the Congressional Executive Council, and Linus Konukong was elected Speaker. Ona refused Kabui's offer to join the BPC, stating that he did not wish to co-operate with the Government. At a subsequent session of the Council, Kabui announced his intention to campaign for independence for Bougainville. In response, Prime Minister Bill Skate stated that, although there was no possibility of independence (as this was not provided for in the Constitution), Parliament would consider terms for greater autonomy for the island. Plans for the disposal of weapons on Bougainville were expected to be drafted by the UN under terms agreed upon at a meeting with the Peace Process Consultative Committee in June. In August the suspension of the Bougainville provincial government was extended for a further six months in an attempt to find a peaceful resolution to the issue of autonomy for Bougainville; the decision was confirmed at a parliamentary session the following month. Following a visit to Bougainville, the Minister for Bougainville Affairs and for Foreign Affairs, Sir Michael Somare (as he had become), stated that the Government was willing to grant the island a greater degree of autonomy. Somare proposed that Bougainville be self-governing in all matters except foreign affairs, defence and policing, all of which would remain the responsibility of the central Government. The proposal was welcomed as an important development by members of the BPC, although they also announced their intention not to surrender their weapons until the Government had agreed to the holding of a referendum on independence. Following further talks between Somare and Kabui, the former reiterated Skate's earlier comments that there was no provision for a referendum on independence in the Constitution.

In October 1999 a Supreme Court ruling declared the suspension of the Bougainville provincial government illegal on technical grounds. On 9 December the provincial government was formally recognized, in theory, despite protests by members of the BPC and concerns that this development would hinder the peace process. In effect, however, the provincial government comprised only four members—the Bougainville Regional Member of Parliament, John Momis, who thus became Governor-elect (although he agreed not to exercise his powers for the mean time) and the three other Bougainville parliamentarians. Following talks in mid-December between Somare and members of the BPC, the BRA and elders of the island, Somare declared, in the consequent agreement, to considering the possibility of a referendum on independence for Bougainville. The agreement, known as the Hutjena Record, stated that the highest possible degree of autonomy should be accorded to the island. Further talks regarding the future status of Bougainville commenced in early March 2000. However, following the rejection of an initial proposal on the island's autonomy by secessionist leaders, the talks were suspended. Negotiations resumed in mid-March, and on 23 March an agreement, known as the Loloata Understanding, allowing for the eventual holding of a referendum on independence, once full autonomy had been implemented, and the formal establishment of the Bougainville Interim Provincial Government (BIPG), composed of an Executive Council and a 25-member Provincial Assembly (including the four original members), was signed by Somare and Kabui.

On 30 March 2000 the Provincial Assembly and the Executive Council were sworn in by the Governor-General. Another six seats were left vacant in the Provincial Assembly for other Bougainville officials such as Kabui and Ona; Kabui, however, stated that, rather than joining the BIPG, he would wait until the establishment of a fully autonomous government (which he hoped would be in place by early 2001). In May 2000 the Office of Bougainville Affairs was renamed the Office of Peace and Reconstruction. In July Somare approved an allocation of K200,000, as part of a scheme co-ordinated by the United Nations Development Programme (UNDP), to facilitate the collection and disposal of weapons held by dissident groups. Although an initial deadline of 15 September to determine the form and date of a referendum was not met, a further round of negotiations that month was presented as a significant advance in the peace process. Uncertainties regarding the proposed date of a referendum continued to delay the progress of negotiations; Somare's statement in May that the referendum would be held 15 years hence contradicted a previously-stated deadline of December 2000. Concerns about renewed Australian funding of the Papua New Guinea Defence Force troops stationed on Bougainville and the failure of the BRA to begin disarmament before the implementation of political autonomy, further impeded progress. In October the BRA's commander, Ishmael Toroama, threatened to abandon the organization's cease-fire. Following a further round of peace talks in November, Kabui confirmed that he had secured an agreement from Somare that a future referendum would include a legally-binding option of independence, although disagreement over how soon the vote should be held persisted. In the following month Somare was abruptly dismissed from his ministerial position and replaced by Bart Philemon; Morauta believed Somare was impeding the progress of the Political Parties Integrity Bill.

In February 2001 agreement on the terms of the referendum was finally reached following the intervention of the Australian Minister for Foreign Affairs. The agreement stated that the referendum would be held in 10–15 years' time and would contain the option of independence. In the interim the provincial government was to be granted increased autonomy and the BRA would be expected to disarm. Despite a temporary breakdown in negotiations, in early May commanders of the BRA and the Bougainville Resistance Force (a militia that was allied to the Government during the civil conflict on Bougainville) signed an agreement to surrender their weapons. In the same month, in Port Moresby, the Government and the BPA held negotiations on autonomy for Bougainville. In late June Moi Avei, who had replaced Philemon as Minister for Bougainville Affairs in May, announced that further talks had resulted in a comprehensive agreement on autonomy for the island, with the Government ceding to the BPA's demands that Bougainville be accorded its own system of criminal law and an autonomous police force. It was also agreed that the Papua New Guinea Defence Force's jurisdiction on the island would be strictly limited. On 30 August the Government and island leaders signed the Bougainville peace agreement in Arawa. Although he signed the accord, which was still to be approved by the National Parliament, Toroama stated that the BRA would campaign for the referendum to be held in three–five years' time and would continue to seek full independence. Francis Ona did not attend the signing ceremony.

The weapons disposal process was threatened in late November 2001 when Henry Kiumo, a former commander of the pro-Government Bougainville Resistance Force (BRF) militia, was murdered. However, weapons disposal by the BRA and BRF began in early December, and the UN Observer Mission on Bougainville (UNOMB) formally acknowledged the Bougainville Peace Agreement later in that month. In January 2002 the National Parliament unanimously endorsed the Organic Law enacting the Bougainville peace agreement, along with a bill containing the requisite constitutional amendment. A second vote, held in late March, ratified the legislation, and the Papua New Guinea Defence Force began its withdrawal from Bougainville. The withdrawal of troops was completed in late December. In the same month, however, the peace process was jeopardized by the theft of 360 weapons from containers being used in the weapons disposal process.

In January 2003 it was announced that the BIPG and the BPC would be merged to form the Bougainville Constituent Assembly. The new body, which was expected to be composed of some 90 members, would debate and approve a proposed constitution for the island and complete the weapons disposal process. In late June an Australian-led group of regional representatives, who had been monitoring the truce on Bougainville since its signing in 1997, officially left the island. Joseph Kabui used the opportunity of their departure to appeal to ex-combatants not to endanger the peace process. Meanwhile, members of a group calling itself the Me'ekamui Fighters, loyal to Francis Ona, reiterated their disillusionment with the peace process and stated that they were fighting for independence rather than autonomy. Regional concern for the future of the island was highlighted when, in August 2003, the Pacific Islands Forum urged the UN Security Council to remain involved in the peace process on Bougainville. In the same month the Government of Papua New Guinea formally announced its plan for autonomy in Bougainville, allowing provincial authorities to proceed with the establishment of a constitution and the eventual organization of elections for an autonomous government leader and local assembly. In March 2004 the BIPG passed legislation providing for the establishment of the Bougainville Constituent Assembly (BCA), which was finally convened later that month to consider the third and final draft of the proposed constitution. In June the UN agreed to extend the term of its Observer Mission on the island by six months, but stressed that there would be no further extensions and urged the BCA to organize elections by the end of 2004. In the following month 50 newly trained officers began duty in their role as Bougainville's first police force. They were to be supported by a small team of police officers from Australia under the terms of that country's ECP with Papua New Guinea (see above). In mid-December the Government of Papua New Guinea finally approved Bougainville's Constitution. Elections for the President of the new autonomous Government of Bougainville and for the 39 members of the first local assembly began on 20 May 2005 and continued for two weeks to allow islanders, some of whom had to travel for several days on foot or by canoe, sufficient time to reach the polling stations. Despite some attempts by armed rebels to disrupt the election process, it was deemed to have been largely successful. Joseph Kabui was declared to be Bougainville's first President with 37,928 votes, defeating several other candidates (the closest of whom, former Governor, John Momis, received 23,861 votes). The inauguration of the autonomous assembly took place on 14 June and was attended by most members of the Cabinet, as well as by several foreign dignitaries. Kabui appointed a local 10-member cabinet several days later. In late July rebel leader and self-declared King of Bougainville, Francis Ona, who had opposed the peace process and autonomy for the island, died at the age of 52 after a short illness.

In December 2004 the UN agreed to extend its Observer Mission to the island by another six months to cover the period of the election. The leader of the Observer Mission left Papua New Guinea at the beginning of August 2005. Also in August the Government announced its commitment to ensuring that a referendum on the independence of Bougainville be carried out by 2020. In March 2006 the autonomous Government requested that the UN assist in the ongoing efforts to resolve peacefully the issue of the continued presence of five former Fijian soldiers in Bougainville. It had been reported that the former soldiers had been recruited by an alleged fraudster, Noah Musingku, and in the south-west of the island were training a militia group in the use of powerful weaponry.

In September 2000 a group of landowners from Bougainville initiated legal action in a US court against Rio Tinto, the operator of the Panguna copper mine between 1972 and 1988. The group was reported to be suing the company for the environmental and social damage caused by its activities, including health problems experienced by workers and islanders living near the mine. Moreover, their case alleged that the company had effectively transformed the Papua New Guinea Defence Force into its own private army and was therefore responsible for the deaths of some 15,000 civilians in military action and a further 10,000 as a result of the economic blockade on the island. A committee was established by the provincial Government in late 2005 to work on reopening the mine following an overwhelming vote in favour of the proposal.

In November 2005 it was announced that a trade agreement between Bougainville and Jilin Province in the People's Republic of China had been signed, with the aim of increasing commercial links. The fulfilment of commitments made on behalf of both Governments was to be monitored by the administration of the Bougainville Executive Council. The administration was also to investigate the possibility, through discussions with private-sector representatives, of establishing an international business council. The intention was to move towards a wider agreement between China and Bougainville, with Bougainville advocating the appointment of a Papua New Guinean trade officer in the People's Republic.

In 1984 more than 9,000 refugees crossed into Papua New Guinea from the Indonesian province of Irian Jaya (officially known as Papua from January 2002), as a consequence of operations by the Indonesian army against Melanesian rebels of the pro-independence Organisasi Papua Merdeka (Free Papua Movement—OPM). For many years relations between Papua New Guinea and Indonesia had been strained by the conflict in Irian Jaya, not least because the independence movement drew sympathy from many among the largely Melanesian population of Papua New Guinea. A new border treaty was signed in October 1984, and attempts were made to repatriate the refugees, based on assurances by the Indonesian Government that there would be no reprisals against those who returned. In October 1985 representatives of the Papua New Guinea and Indonesian Governments signed a treaty providing for the settlement of disputes by consultation, arbitration and 'other peaceful means'. The treaty, however, provoked strong criticism among opposition politicians in Papua New Guinea, who claimed that it effectively precluded the censure of any violation of human rights in Irian Jaya. In 1988 the Government condemned the incursions by Indonesian soldiers into Papua New Guinea, in search of OPM members, and the resultant violence and killings as a breach of bilateral accords, and affirmed that Papua New Guinea would not support Indonesia in its attempt to suppress the OPM. In late 1995 the Indonesian consulate in the border town of Vanimo was attacked by OPM rebels and a subsequent increase in Indonesian troops along the border was reported. Violent confrontations resulted in the killing of several rebels and security personnel and the kidnapping by OPM activists of some 200 villagers. Australia urged the Papua New Guinea Government to accept several thousand refugees living in camps along the border, and in May 1996 the Government announced that 3,500 Irian Jayans would be allowed to remain in Papua New Guinea on condition that they were not involved in OPM activities. In mid-1998, on an official visit to Indonesia, the Prime Minister, Bill Skate, signed a memorandum of understanding on bilateral relations, which was expected to provide the basis for closer co-operation in political, economic and defence matters. Under the terms of the agreement, troop numbers along the border were increased in March 1999. In May of that year 11 Javanese people were taken hostage and three people were reported to have been killed by OPM rebels in the West Sepik Province of Papua New Guinea. The hostages were later released as a result of the intervention of Papua New Guinea security forces. The OPM subsequently demanded an inquiry into the operation leading to the release of the hostages, after its communications director was allegedly shot dead at a border post. During 2000 hundreds of refugees were voluntarily repatriated to Indonesia (including more than 600 in a major operation in early September), although approximately 7,000 were believed to remain in Papua New Guinea in September. In late 2000 it was reported that Indonesian security forces had made some 400 incursions into Papua New Guinea in the previous two months while pursuing separatists. In December the border with Irian Jaya was officially closed, while Morauta reaffirmed his recognition of Indonesia's sovereignty over the region.

In January 2003 the Papua New Guinea Government denied a number of security breaches, which were reported to have occurred along its border with Indonesia. Concerns grew following a dramatic increase in the numbers of Indonesian troops along the border, from some 150 in late 2002 to a reported 1,500 in early 2003. In late January the Government of Papua New Guinea ordered its security forces to arrest OPM rebels believed to be staying in refugee camps along the border, following complaints from the Indonesian authorities that rebels based there were carrying out operations in the province of Papua. The Government also confirmed in April that it had been unable to persuade more than 400 Papuans living in a camp near the border town of Vanimo to return to Indonesia, despite assurances that their safety would not be at risk. In July 2004 it was announced that Vanuatu would host a series of negotiations between the Indonesian authorities and Papuan separatists

From 1990 relations with Solomon Islands were overshadowed by the conflict on Bougainville. Solomon Islands (the inhabitants of which are culturally and ethnically very similar to Bougainville islanders) protested against repeated incursions by Papua New Guinea defence forces into Solomon Islands' territorial waters, while the Papua New Guinea Government consistently accused Solomon Islands of harbouring members of the BRA and providing them with supplies. Despite several attempts during the 1990s to improve the situation between the two countries (including an agreement by Solomon Islands in 1993 to close the BRA office in the capital, Honiara), relations remained tense. In April 1997 the Solomon Islands Government announced that it was considering the initiation of proceedings against the Papua New Guinea Government concerning the latter's attempted use of mercenaries on Bougainville. In June of that year Papua New Guinea and Solomon Islands concluded a maritime border agreement, following several years of negotiations. The purpose of the agreement (which came into effect in January 1998) was not only to delineate the sea boundary between the two countries but also to provide a framework for co-operation in matters of security, natural disaster, customs, quarantine, immigration and conservation. In March 2000 relations between Papua New Guinea and Solomon Islands were further strengthened following the opening of a Solomon Islands High Commission in Port Moresby. In March 2004 the two countries signed a number of treaties and agreements relating to the management of their common border area.

Concerns were expressed in mid-2003 that the rebel Solomon Islands leader Harold Keke (responsible for a campaign of terror in Solomon Islands) was recruiting new members for his Guadalcanal Liberation Force in Bougainville and strengthening his links with the BRA. These fears were exacerbated by sightings of Keke in Buka and Bougainville and attacks against journalists who had reported on the activities of Keke's supporters (including the stockpiling of weapons) along the border between Papua New Guinea and Solomon Islands. However, in August the Governor of Bougainville, John Momis, officially stated that he did not believe that any link existed between Keke and the BRA. In that month Keke surrendered and was arrested by the regional peace-keeping force in Solomon Islands.

In March 1988 Papua New Guinea signed an agreement with Vanuatu and Solomon Islands to form the 'Melanesian Spearhead Group', dedicated to the preservation of Melanesian cultural traditions and to achieving independence from the French Overseas Territory of New Caledonia. In 1989 Papua New Guinea increased its links with South-East Asia, signing a Treaty of Amity and Co-operation with the Association of South East Asian Nations (ASEAN, see p. 172).

The growing exploitation of Papua New Guinea's natural resources in the 1990s led to considerable concern over the impact of the activities of numerous foreign business interests on the country's environment. Activity in the forestry sector increased dramatically in the early 1990s, and an official report published in 1994 indicated that the current rate of logging was three times the sustainable yield of the country's forests. Attempts to introduce new regulations to govern the industry, however, were strongly opposed by several Malaysian logging companies with operations in the country. In early 2000, however, environmentalists welcomed a commitment by the Papua New Guinea Government to impose a moratorium on all new forestry licences and to review all existing licences. Concern continued among conservation organizations as the Government failed to enforce laws promoting sustainable forestry activity, which if upheld were deemed sufficient to ensure the long-term survival of the forestry sector. In March 2006 it was reported that if illegal felling continued at present rates Papua New Guinea might lose the majority of its rainforest within a decade. Most of the timber was exported to China for use in its manufacturing industry prior to export to developed nations. Conservationists hoped that pressure from consumers in the destination countries might lead to a reduction in illegal logging.

The exploitation of Papua New Guinea's extensive mineral resources has also resulted in considerable environmental damage. In 1989 the Government gave the operators of the Ok

PAPUA NEW GUINEA

Tedi gold and copper mine permission to discharge 150,000 metric tons of toxic waste per day into the Fly River. In 1994 6,000 people living in the region began a compensation claim against the Australian company operating the mine for damage caused by the resultant pollution. A settlement worth some $A110m. was reached in an Australian court in 1995 (and a further settlement worth $A400m. for the establishment of a containment system was concluded in mid-1996), despite opposition from the Papua New Guinea Government, which feared that such action might adversely affect the country's prospects of attracting foreign investment in the future. Similar claims were initiated by people living near the Australian-controlled Porgera gold-mine in early 1996 for pollution of the Strickland River system, as well as by landowners near the Kutubu oilfield. The results of an independent study into the effects of mining activities by Ok Tedi Mining Ltd (OTML), published in mid-1999, showed that damage to the environment might be greater than originally believed, casting doubts over the future of the mine. The Government, however, announced that it would await the findings of an independent review, carried out by the World Bank. The results of this report, which were published in March 2000, found that closure of the mine was necessary on environmental grounds. However, it also emphasized the potentially damaging impact of the mine's early closure on both the local economy and world copper markets. In October 2001 BHP Billiton, the Australian operator, announced its withdrawal from the OTML venture and in early 2002 transferred its 52% stake in the company to a development fund called the PNG Sustainable Development Programme Ltd. In early 2006 the managing director of OTML acknowledged that mining operations had caused major damage to the environment. It was estimated that over the past 20 years the Ok Tedi mine had deposited as much as 80m. tons of tailings and waste rock annually into the Ok Tedi and Fly River systems, resulting in flooding and forest die-back. Furthermore, the toxic effects of this waste were now believed to be threatening supplies of ground and drinking water.

In February 2004 Prime Minister Sir Michael Somare led a delegation of 80 officials (the largest such group Papua New Guinea had ever sent on a state visit) to China. Almost one-half of the delegates were representatives from the mining sector, who were hoping to secure agreements with Chinese interests relating to petroleum, gas and other mineral developments in Papua New Guinea. China and Papua New Guinea upgraded their military links by exchanging defence attachés in July 2005.

On an official visit to Japan in February 2005 Somare secured significant funding from that country to provide for an upgrade of Port Moresby's sewerage system and to finance his Government's stake in the proposed gas pipeline from Papua New Guinea to Queensland, in eastern Australia.

In February 2006 Papua New Guinea announced plans to improve security in its maritime sector, in an effort to reduce terrorism and cross-border crime. As recommended by the International Maritime Organization (IMO, see p. 117), the Government introduced new regulations governing port security and countering unlawful intervention with maritime transport in Papua New Guinean waters.

Government

Executive power is vested in the British monarch (the Head of State), represented locally by the Governor-General, who is appointed on the proposal of the National Executive Council (the Cabinet) in accordance with the decision of the National Parliament by simple majority vote. The Governor-General acts on the advice of the National Executive Council, which is led by the Prime Minister. The Prime Minister is appointed and dismissed by the Head of State on the proposal of the National Parliament. Legislative power is vested in the unicameral National Parliament, with 109 members elected by universal adult suffrage for a term of five years. The National Executive Council is responsible to the National Parliament. The local government system underwent extensive reform in 1995, when the 19 directly-elected provincial governments were replaced by new regional authorities, composed of members of the National Parliament and local councillors, and led by an appointed Governor. The National Capital District (NCD) has its own governing body.

In January 2005 the National Government approved the final draft of the proposed Constitution for the province of Bougainville, and elections for the President of the new autonomous Government and for the 39 members of the House of Representatives commenced in May (see Recent History). In mid-June the new President was duly sworn in and the House of Representatives was inaugurated.

Defence

In August 2005 Papua New Guinea's national Defence Force numbered an estimated 3,100, comprising an army of 2,500, a navy of 400 and an air force of 200. In addition, 38 troops from Australia were stationed in the country for training purposes. Military service is voluntary. Budget estimates for 2005 allocated K81.8m. to defence.

Economic Affairs

In 2004, according to estimates by the World Bank, Papua New Guinea's gross national income (GNI), measured at average 2002–04 prices, was US $3,262m., equivalent to $580 per head (or $2,300 per head on an international purchasing-power parity basis). During 1995–2004, it was estimated, the population increased at an average annual rate of 2.5%, while gross domestic product (GDP) per head decreased, in real terms, by an average of 1.5% per year. Overall GDP increased, in real terms, at an average annual rate of 0.9% in 1995–2004. According to the Asian Development Bank (ADB), real GDP increased by 2.9% in 2004 and by 3.0% in 2005. GDP was forecast to increase by 3.2% in 2006.

Agriculture (including hunting, forestry and fishing) contributed 25.7% of GDP in 2003, and in that year engaged an estimated 72.6% of the labour force. The principal cash crops are coffee (which accounted for 3.5% of export earnings in 2004), cocoa (2.7%), coconuts (for the production of copra and coconut oil), palm oil (5.4%), rubber and tea. In March 2006 plans for the development of a 4,000-ha oil-palm plantation in Morobe Province were announced, with planting expected to start in September. Vanilla was becoming an important export crop in the early 2000s. Roots and tubers, vegetables, bananas and melons are also grown as food crops. Forestry is an important activity, and Papua New Guinea is one of the world's largest exporters of unprocessed tropical timber. Exports of logs accounted for 5.3% of total export revenue in 2004, compared with 13.0% in 1998. There is serious concern about the environmental damage caused by extensive logging activity in the country, much of which is illegal. The sale of fishing licences to foreign fleets provides a substantial source of revenue, estimated at US $15m. in 1998. However, a report published in 2004 claimed that the tuna industry alone could generate revenue of some $1,000m. per year if the catch was processed locally (see below); some 95% of tuna was estimated to be caught by foreign fleets and shipped directly overseas. During 1995–2004, according to figures from the World Bank, agricultural GDP increased by an average annual rate of 0.5%. According to the ADB, the GDP of the agricultural sector expanded by by 2.8% in 2004 and by 4.1% in 2005.

Industry (including mining, manufacturing, construction and power) contributed an estimated 39.1% of GDP in 2003. During 1995–2004 industrial GDP decreased by an average of 0.2% per year, according to figures from the World Bank. ADB figures indicated that industrial GDP decreased by 10.2% in 2002, but increased by 2.7% in 2003 and by 2.8% in 2004.

Mining and quarrying provided an estimated 16.6% of GDP and 74.7% of total export earnings in 2003. Petroleum (which accounted for 20.8% of export revenue in 2003), gold (35.8% in that year) and copper (18.0%) are the major mineral exports. In 2005 mining production declined by 4.1% due largely to a fall in gold production (21% of total exports by June 2005). Papua New Guinea also has substantial reserves of natural gas, and deposits of silver, chromite, cobalt, nickel and quartz. The country's largest petroleum refinery at Napa Napa began production in mid-2004 and was expected to process some 33,000 barrels per day. In early 2002 plans were concluded for the construction of a gas pipeline to Queensland, Australia, expected to be completed by 2007, in which the Government held a 22.5% stake. The pipeline would be the longest of its kind in the southern hemisphere. The Government secured funding for its share of the project from Japan in early 2005. From the 1980s large gold deposits were discovered at several sites (including the largest known deposit outside South Africa at Lihir, which began operations in 1997), and annual gold production subsequently rose at a steady rate, reaching an estimated 74 metric tons in 2000 and totalling 66 tons in 2004. New discoveries of gold reserves at the Porgera mine in 2005 led to an increase in drilling operations and the extension of the life of the mine from its planned closure in 2009 to 2015. Moreover, the important Ramu cobalt-nickel project was launched in February 2003. In early

2006 the opening of two new gold mines was announced by Ok Tedi. The first, being developed at Mount Sinivit near Kokopo, was to begin production in the second quarter of 2006. The second, located at Kainantu in the Eastern Highlands, began production at the beginning of 2006 and exported some 25,000 tons of pure gold concentrate to Japan in the first three months of the year. Further exploration activities were scheduled to be carried out by New Guinea Gold at the Sehulea and Normanby properties throughout 2006. According to figures from the ADB, the GDP of the mining sector decreased at an average annual rate of 4.8% during 1995–2002. The sector's GDP declined by 15.9% in 2003.

Manufacturing contributed an estimated 9.0% of GDP in 2003, and employed 1.9% of the working population in 1980. Measured by the value of output, the principal branches of manufacturing are food products, beverages, tobacco, wood products, metal products, machinery and transport equipment. Several fish canneries were established in the 1990s and exports of canned tuna were expected to increase significantly, following the signing of a new quota agreement with the European Union (EU) in March 2003. A tuna cannery in Wewak, to be constructed with US $30m. provided by Thai investors, was due to begin production in 2006. The plant was expected to process 120 metric tons of fish per day and to provide direct employment for some 2,000 people. A major new fish-processing plant to enable the export of live fish and lobsters to China began operations in 2004 following the receipt of funding for the project of some US $30m. from a Chinese company. Exports of fresh, frozen and canned fish increased by some 40% to $109m. in 2003, representing the highest revenue ever earned by the industry. According to the World Bank, during 1995–2003 manufacturing GDP increased by an average of 2.0% per year. Compared with the previous year, the sector's GDP contracted by 10.8% in 2002 but expanded by 3.8% in 2003.

Energy is derived principally from hydroelectric power, which in 2000 accounted for more than 50% of electricity supplies. A diesel power station to be constructed by South Korean interests in Port Moresby in 1999 was expected to supply 30% of the capital's electricity needs. Plans to build a new hydroelectric power station at the Yonki Dam on the Ramu River were announced in March 2006. At a cost of some K60m., the station was to be constructed alongside the existing dam wall and was expected to provide an output of at least 16 MW.

The services sector contributed an estimated 35.2% of GDP in 2003. Tourism is an expanding industry, although political instability and reports of widespread violent crime have had a detrimental effect on the sector. According to one source, total foreign visitor arrivals increased by 2,837 in 2004 to reach 59,022. Tourism receipts were worth an estimated US $168m. in 2005, when short-term international visitors totalled 69,250 (of whom 65% were business travellers). The GDP of the services sector declined at an average annual rate of 0.4% in 1995–2004, according to figures from the World Bank. The sector's GDP expanded by 2.7% in 2003, however, and by 1.7% in 2004.

In 2004 Papua New Guinea recorded a visible trade surplus of K3,530m., and a surplus of K393m. on the current account of the balance of payments. According to the ADB, the latter surplus decreased from the equivalent of 3.0% of GDP in 2004 to 1.8% in 2005. In 2004 the principal source of imports (45.2%) was Australia; other major suppliers were Singapore (21.1%), New Zealand (7.5%) and Japan (4.2%). In that year Australia was also the principal market for exports (27.7%), followed by the People's Republic of China (5.8%), Japan (5.7%), and Germany (5.0%). The principal exports in the early 2000s were gold, copper ore and concentrates, petroleum, coffee, cocoa, palm oil and logs. The principal imports were machinery and transport equipment, basic manufactures, food and live animals, miscellaneous manufactured articles, chemicals and mineral fuels.

The 2006 budget, announced in November 2005, envisaged total government revenue of K4,740m., while expenditure was projected to total K4,830m., an increase of K160m. compared with the previous year. The resultant budgetary deficit of K90m. in 2006 was expected to reach the equivalent of 0.6% of the country's GDP, the same level as in 2005. Papua New Guinea receives grants for budgetary aid from Australia. In 2005/06 official development assistance from Australia was projected at $A492.3m. while New Zealand's allocation of aid totalled almost $NZ13.5m. Papua New Guinea's external debt totalled US $2,463.4m. at the end of 2003, of which $1,504m. was long-term public debt. In 2004, according to the ADB, the cost of debt-servicing was equivalent to 1.4% of the value of exports of goods and services. A World Bank report in 2003 estimated that one-half of the work-force was unemployed throughout Papua New Guinea at that time. In urban areas, however, the unemployment rate was estimated at some 70%. In the rural areas underemployment remained a serious problem. According to figures from the National Bank of Papua New Guinea, the annual rate of inflation averaged 10.8% in 1995–2004. The average annual inflation rate declined from 2.2% in 2004 to 1.7% in 2005, but the rate was reported to have risen in the final quarter of 2005, partly as a result of increases in fuel prices.

Papua New Guinea is a member of Asia-Pacific Economic Co-operation (APEC, see p. 164), the Asian Development Bank (ADB, see p. 169), the Colombo Plan (see p. 385), the Pacific Community (see p. 350), the Pacific Islands Forum (see p. 352), the UN Economic and Social Commission for Asia and the Pacific (ESCAP, see p. 33), the International Cocoa Organization (see p. 382) and the International Coffee Organization (see p. 382). Papua New Guinea is also a member of the Melanesian Spearhead Group, which among other benefits provides for free trade among members.

Papua New Guinea has remained dependent on aid from Australia and other international donors for its economic development, and in the early 2000s it was estimated that at least 70% of the population were within the subsistence sector of the economy. The country's difficult terrain, vulnerability to extreme climatic conditions (such as droughts and tidal waves), lack of infrastructure and the limitations of the domestic market have impeded Papua New Guinea's progress. Development has also been constrained by a shortage of skilled workers, and an increase in migration from rural areas to urban centres led to a rise in unemployment. Furthermore, the proportion of the labour force employed in the formal sector remained comparatively low, the difficulties being compounded by the country's exceptionally high rate of population growth. A 'recovery' budget for 2000 included plans for the privatization of government assets, the proceeds of which were to be used to repay a proportion of the national debt. A joint funding programme, valued at US $500m., was agreed upon by the IMF and the World Bank to assist the Government in the implementation of the economic reforms. Australia pledged a total of US $1,000m. in programme aid over a period of three years. Almost 1,500 public servants were made redundant in late 2000, as part of ongoing government retrenchment measures, and in 2002 a further 3,000 civil servants were made redundant. A marked increase in the country's debt, as well as a continued decline in the value of the kina (which fell by some 10% between October and November) resulted in serious financial difficulties for the new Government of Michael Somare, which took office in August 2002, particularly when a request to the Australian Government to help restructure US $180m. of debt was refused. Expenditure in the 2003 budget was significantly reduced in an attempt to control the growing deficit, although a large proportion of this was allocated to major infrastructure projects, such as the Highlands Highway (which, it was hoped, would stimulate the economy, particularly the agricultural sector). The 2004 budget included a temporary tax on imports and reduced personal tax rebates, in an attempt to control the deficit. New agricultural developments were also to receive corporate tax concessions in order to encourage several important projects in the sector, although fears were expressed that export revenue from some of the country's most important commodities might decline upon the expiry in 2007 of a trade agreement allowing free access to the EU market. The Government's success in restoring a measure of economic stability to the country, including a significant reduction in the budget deficit and the achievement of a lower rate of inflation, earned it praise from the IMF in mid-2004. Tax receipts from the mining and petroleum sectors increased substantially in 2005, enabling the Government to exceed its revenue projections in that year. The country's currency also continued to strengthen, partly as a result of higher export earnings from minerals and from agricultural produce. The aims of the 2006 budget included the continued promotion of rural development, reductions in income tax for the majority of workers and significant new incentives for the tourism sector. The priorities of the Government's Medium Term Development Strategy for 2005–10 incorporated the rehabilitation and improved maintenance of the transport network. The plan also emphasized the improvement of the country's basic education and health services.

Education

Education is not compulsory. Primary education, available at community schools, begins at seven years of age and lasts for six

PAPUA NEW GUINEA

years. Secondary education, beginning at the age of 13, lasts for up to six years (comprising two cycles, the first of four years, the second two). Originally, schooling was free; fees and charges for equipment were introduced, although the 2002 budget provided for the reinstatement of free education. In 1995 the total enrolment at primary schools was equivalent to 80% of children in the relevant age-group (87% of boys; 74% of girls). In the same year total secondary enrolment was equivalent to 14% of children in the relevant age-group (boys 17%; girls 11%). Tertiary education is provided by the University of Papua New Guinea and the University of Technology. There are also teacher-training colleges and higher institutions, which cater for specific professional training, such as a medical school, which had a total enrolment of 656 students in early 2005. Budget allocations for 2006 granted K43m. to the education sector. In February 2006 it was announced that the European Union was to grant a total of K156m. over the next six years in support of education and training in Papua New Guinea. The Government hoped that this would enable it to provide universal primary education by 2015 and to eliminate gender disparities.

Public Holidays

2006: 1 January (New Year's Day), 14–17 April (Easter), 12 June (Queen's Official Birthday), 23 July (Remembrance Day), 16 September (Independence Day and Constitution Day), 25 December (Christmas Day), 26 December (Boxing Day).

2007: 1 January (New Year's Day), 6–9 April (Easter), 11 June (Queen's Official Birthday), 23 July (Remembrance Day), 16 September (Independence Day and Constitution Day), 25 December (Christmas Day), 26 December (Boxing Day).

Weights and Measures

The metric system is in force.

Statistical Survey

Source (unless otherwise stated): Papua New Guinea National Statistical Office, POB 337, Waigani, NCD; tel. 3011200; fax 3251869; e-mail pmaime@nso.gov.pg; internet www.nso.gov.pg.

Area and Population

AREA, POPULATION AND DENSITY

Area (sq km)	462,840*
Population (census results)	
11 July 1990†	3,607,954
9 July 2000	
Males	2,661,091
Females	2,469,274
Total	5,130,365
Population (UN estimates at mid-year)‡	
2002	5,538,000
2003	5,772,000
2004	5,887,000
Density (per sq km) at mid-2004	12.7

* 178,704 sq miles.
† Excluding North Solomons Province (estimated population 154,000).
‡ Source: UN, *World Population Prospects: The 2004 Revision*.

PRINCIPAL TOWNS
(census of 9 July 2000)

Port Moresby (capital)	254,158	Mount Hagen		27,782
Lae	78,038	Madang		27,394
Arawa	36,443	Kokopo/Vunamami		20,262

Source: Thomas Brinkhoff, *City Population* (internet www.citypopulation.de).

Mid-2003 (UN estimate, incl. suburbs): Port Moresby 274,872 (Source: UN, *World Urbanization Prospects: The 2003 Revision*).

BIRTHS AND DEATHS
(2003)

Live births 192,817; Deaths 7,054. (Source: UN, *Population and Vital Statistics Report*). *1996* (estimates): Birth rate 32.6 per 1,000; Death rate 10.1 per 1,000.

Expectation of life (WHO estimates, years at birth): 60 (males 59; females 62) in 2003 (Source: WHO, *World Health Report*).

ECONOMICALLY ACTIVE POPULATION
(2000 census, persons aged 10 years and over)

Agriculture, hunting and forestry	1,666,247
Fishing	30,024
Mining and quarrying	9,282
Manufacturing	25,557
Electricity, gas and water	2,208
Construction	48,312
Wholesale and retail trade; repair of motor vehicles, motorcycles and personal and household goods	353,186
Hotels and restaurants	4,395
Transport, storage and communications	24,513
Financial intermediation	3,670
Real estate, renting and business activities	27,459
Public administration and defence; compulsory social security	32,043
Education	27,118
Health and social work	12,341
Other community, social and personal service activities	31,409
Private households with employed persons	15,523
Extra-territorial organizations and bodies	163
Activities not adequately defined	31,284
Total employed	**2,344,734**
Unemployed	68,623
Total labour force	**2,413,357**
Males	1,256,887
Females	1,156,470

Source: ILO.

Mid-2003 (estimates in '000): Agriculture, etc. 1,982; Total 2,730 (Source: FAO).

Health and Welfare

KEY INDICATORS

Total fertility rate (children per woman, 2003)	4.0
Under-5 mortality rate (per 1,000 live births, 2004)	93
HIV/AIDS (% of persons aged 15–49, 2003)	0.6
Physicians (per 1,000 head, 2000)	0.05
Hospital beds (per 1,000 head, 1990)	4.02
Health expenditure (2002): US $ per head (PPP)	136
Health expenditure (2002): % of GDP	4.3
Health expenditure (2002): public (% of total)	88.6
Access to water (% of persons, 2002)	39
Access to sanitation (% of persons, 2002)	45
Human Development Index (2003): ranking	137
Human Development Index (2003): value	0.523

For sources and definitions, see explanatory note on p. vi.

PAPUA NEW GUINEA

Agriculture

PRINCIPAL CROPS
('000 metric tons)

	2002	2003	2004
Sweet potatoes	490*	520	520*
Cassava (Manioc)	130†	120*	120*
Yams*	280	280	280
Taro (Coco yam)*	250	250	256
Other roots and tubers*	300	300	306
Sugar cane*	370	442	442
Coconuts	513*	570†	650*
Oil palm fruit*	1,178	1,161	1,250
Vegetables and melons*	495	495	500
Pineapples*	18	18	18
Bananas*	860	870	870
Other fruit (excl. melons)*	884	894	800
Coffee (green)	63†	65*	65†
Cocoa beans†	42	42	43
Tea (made)	10*	6†	9*
Natural rubber (dry weight)†	4	4	4

* FAO estimate(s).
† Unofficial figure(s).
Source: FAO.

LIVESTOCK
(FAO estimates, '000 head, year ending September)

	2002	2003	2004
Horses	2	2	2
Cattle	89	90	91
Pigs	1,800	1,800	1,700
Sheep	7	7	7
Goats	2.4	2.5	2.6
Chickens	3,800	3,900	3,900

Source: FAO.

LIVESTOCK PRODUCTS
(FAO estimates, '000 metric tons)

	2002	2003	2004
Beef and veal	3.2	3.2	3.2
Pig meat	68	68	64
Poultry meat	6.6	6.7	6.6
Game meat	300	310	320
Poultry eggs	4.9	4.9	4.9

Source: FAO.

Forestry

ROUNDWOOD REMOVALS
('000 cubic metres, excluding bark)

	2000	2001	2002*
Sawlogs, veneer logs and logs for sleepers	2,064	1,611	1,611
Pulpwood	120	97	97
Fuel wood*	5,533	5,533	5,533
Total	7,717	7,241	7,241

* FAO estimates.

2003–04: Production assumed to be unchanged from 2002 (FAO estimates).

Source: FAO.

SAWNWOOD PRODUCTION
('000 cubic metres, including railway sleepers)

	2001	2002	2003
Coniferous (softwood)	—	10	10*
Broadleaved (hardwood)	40	60	50†
Total	40	70	60*

* FAO estimate.
† Unofficial figure.

2004: Production assumed to be unchanged from 2003 (FAO estimates).

Source: FAO.

Fishing

('000 metric tons, live weight of capture)

	2001	2002	2003
Mozambique tilapia*	2.3	2.3	0.3
Other freshwater fishes*	6.7	6.7	6.7
Sea catfishes*	1.9	1.9	1.9
Skipjack tuna	66.7	90.7	121.4
Yellowfin tuna	26.0	28.8	35.4
Total catch (incl. others)*	122.5	150.7	187.9

* FAO estimates.

Note: Figures exclude crocodiles, recorded by number rather than weight. The number of estuarine crocodiles caught was: 10,677 in 2001; 9,332 in 2002; 9,000 in 2003 (estimate). The number of New Guinea crocodiles caught was: 20,668 in 2001; 18,798 in 2002; 18,000 in 2003.

Source: FAO.

Mining

	2000	2001	2002*
Petroleum, crude ('000 barrels)	24,967	20,423	20,000
Copper ('000 metric tons)†	203.1	203.8	204.0
Silver (metric tons)†	79.2	69.4	73.0
Gold (metric tons)†	74.5	67.0	70.0

* Preliminary figures.
† Figures refer to metal content of ore.

Note: Figures for 2003 assumed to be unchanged from 2002 (all estimates).

Source: US Geological Survey.

Industry

SELECTED PRODUCTS
(FAO estimates, '000 metric tons)

	2002	2003	2004
Beer of barley	40	n.a.	39
Palm oil ('000 metric tons)	316	326	345
Raw sugar ('000 metric tons)	51	51	46

Electric energy (million kWh): 2,180 in 2000; 1,390 in 2001.

Sources: mainly FAO, *Production Yearbook*; UN, *Industrial Commodity Statistics Yearbook*.

Finance

CURRENCY AND EXCHANGE RATES

Monetary Units
100 toea = 1 kina (K).

Sterling, Dollar and Euro Equivalents (30 November 2005)
£1 sterling = 5.338 kina;
US $1 = 3.091 kina;
€1 = 3.638 kina;
100 kina = £18.73 = $32.35 = €27.49.

Average Exchange Rate (kina per US $)
2002   3.8952
2003   3.5635
2004   3.2225

Note: The foregoing information refers to the mid-point exchange rate of the central bank. In October 1994 it was announced that the kina would be allowed to 'float' on foreign exchange markets.

BUDGET
(million kina)*

Revenue*	2003	2004	2005†
Taxation	2,678.0	3,220.2	2,985.0
Personal tax	758.3	826.5	865.0
Company tax	731.0	1,071.0	882.1
Other direct tax	297.2	325.8	294.2
Import duties	73.7	75.2	75.4
Excise duties	284.5	326.5	342.4
Export tax	111.8	101.5	76.6
Goods and services tax	311.8	315.7	332.5
Other indirect tax	109.7	178.0	116.8
Non-tax revenue	239.2	240.1	371.6
Dividends	159.7	159.7	183.0
Interest revenue/fees	4.3	2.8	5.0
Other internal revenue	75.2	77.6	183.6
Total	2,917.2	3,460.3	3,356.6

Expenditure‡	2003	2004	2005†
Recurrent expenditure	2,704.9	2,812.3	2,893.1
National departmental	1,192.4	1,556.6	1,586.6
Provincial governments	594.5	672.2	628.1
Interest payments	739.6	375.6	480.5
Foreign	160.8	138.1	133.4
Domestic	578.8	237.5	347.1
Other grants and expenditure	178.4	207.9	197.9
Development expenditure	1,039.0	903.6	1,888.3
National projects	922.0	707.6	1,596.0
Provincial projects	117.0	196.0	292.3
Total	3,743.9	3,715.9	4,781.4

* Excluding grants received from abroad (million kina): 693.0 in 2003; 479.2 in 2004; 1,283.1 in 2005 (forecast).
† Forecasts.
‡ Excluding net lending (million kina): −9.6 in 2003; −10.4 in 2004; −4.0 in 2005 (forecast).

Source: Bank of Papua New Guinea, Port Moresby.

INTERNATIONAL RESERVES
(US $ million at 31 December)

	2002	2003	2004
Gold (national valuation)	21.89	25.83	27.55
IMF special drawing rights	6.06	3.68	0.73
Reserve position in IMF	0.49	0.59	0.66
Foreign exchange	314.96	489.90	631.17
Total	343.40	520.00	660.11

Source: IMF, *International Financial Statistics*.

MONEY SUPPLY
(million kina at 31 December)

	2002	2003	2004
Currency outside banks	379.94	417.93	445.33
Demand deposits at deposit money banks	1,241.13	1,474.95	1,880.69
Total money (incl. others)	1,629.66	1,897.48	2,330.79

Source: IMF, *International Financial Statistics*.

COST OF LIVING
(Consumer Price Index; base: 1977 = 100)

	2002	2003	2004
Food	665.2	753.5	757.4
Clothing and footwear	457.0	478.2	490.4
Rent, fuel and power	265.1	281.1	301.0
All items (incl. others)	667.3	765.4	782.0

Source: Bank of Papua New Guinea, Port Moresby.

NATIONAL ACCOUNTS
(million kina at current prices)

National Income and Product

	2000	2001	2002
Compensation of employees	1,927.3	2,063.5	2,259.7
Operating surplus	6,374.8	6,770.4	7,617.1
Domestic factor incomes	8,302.1	8,833.9	9,876.8
Consumption of fixed capital	549.0	642.2	690.2
Gross domestic product (GDP) at factor cost	8,851.1	9,476.1	10,567.1
Indirect taxes / *Less* Subsidies	884.7	920.2	1,001.4
GDP in purchasers' values	9,735.8	10,396.3	11,568.6
Net factor income from abroad	−391.3	−408.1	−405.3
Gross national product	9,344.5	9,988.2	11,163.3
Less Consumption of fixed capital	549.0	642.2	690.2
National income in market prices	8,795.5	9,346.0	10,473.1

Source: Bank of Papua New Guinea, Port Moresby.

Expenditure on the Gross Domestic Product

	2002	2003	2004
Government final consumption expenditure	1,788	1,917	1,938
Private final consumption expenditure	7,060	6,515	6,891
Increase in stocks	206	222	236
Gross fixed capital formation	2,264	2,281	2,294
Total domestic expenditure	11,318	10,935	11,359
Exports of goods and services	7,100	8,724	9,130
Less Imports of goods and services	6,761	6,790	7,455
Statistical discrepancy	—	−80	827
GDP in purchasers' values	11,657	12,949	13,861
GDP at constant 1998 prices	7,728	7,953	8,183

Source: IMF, *International Financial Statistics*.

PAPUA NEW GUINEA

Gross Domestic Product by Economic Activity

	2000	2001	2002
Agriculture, hunting, forestry and fishing	3,306.9	3,577.5	4,428.0
Mining and quarrying	2,463.5	2,401.1	2,149.6
Manufacturing	1,026.6	1,285.3	1,421.4
Electricity, gas and water	139.6	167.2	194.8
Construction	450.2	687.0	973.0
Wholesale and retail trade	902.5	1,078.6	1,441.1
Transport, storage and communications	439.4	560.9	620.8
Finance, insurance, real estate and business services*	395.6	406.7	407.2
Community, social and personal services (incl. defence)	1,297.3	1,240.6	1,351.8
Sub-total	10,421.6	11,404.9	12,987.5
Import duties, *less* subsidies	299.4	303.3	294.6
Statistical discrepancy	28.9	50.1	92.9
GDP in purchasers' values	10,749.9	11,758.3	13,375.0

* After deducting imputed bank service charge.

Source: Asian Development Bank, *Key Indicators of Developing Asian and Pacific Countries*.

BALANCE OF PAYMENTS
(million kina)

	2002	2003	2004
Exports of goods f.o.b.	6,387	7,842	8,233
Imports of goods f.o.b.	−4,197	−4,231	−4,703
Trade balance	2,190	3,611	3,530
Exports of services	630	829	656
Imports of services	−2,640	−3,092	−3,217
Balance on goods and services	180	1,348	969
Other income received	106	58	64
Other income paid	−894	−1,757	−1,470
Balance on goods, services and income	−608	−351	−437
Current transfers received	334	1,137	1,080
Current transfers paid	−229	−290	−250
Current balance	−502	496	393
Direct investment abroad	3	11	0
Direct investment from abroad	71	360	83
Portfolio investment assets	−5	−166	−336
Portfolio investment liabilities	0	0	−2
Financial derivatives assets	0	83	−32
Other investment assets	381	−788	110
Other investment liabilities	−130	318	97
Net errors and omissions	−57	40	16
Overall balance	−239	353	329

Source: Bank of Papua New Guinea, Port Moresby.

External Trade

PRINCIPAL COMMODITIES
(US $ million)

Imports f.o.b.*	2001	2002	2003
Food and live animals	180.5	176.5	192.4
Meat and meat preparations	38.9	32.9	34.8
Fresh, chilled or frozen meat	36.3	30.2	32.7
Cereals and cereal preparations	83.8	82.8	96.2
Rice	53.0	53.1	61.5
Milled or semi-milled rice	40.1	23.5	20.5
Mineral fuels, lubricants and related materials	294.7	153.8	173.3
Motor spirit (petrol), incl. aviation spirit	230.7	143.0	168.1
Chemicals and related products	94.9	85.7	105.1
Basic manufactures	201.4	239.3	235.6
Iron and steel	44.8	40.9	52.0
Manufactures of other metals	60.8	95.1	70.0

Imports f.o.b.*—continued	2001	2002	2003
Machinery and transport equipment	414.9	398.7	453.0
Power-generating machinery and equipment	38.0	36.1	51.2
Machinery specialized for particular industries	52.3	63.7	56.9
General industrial machinery and equipment	98.3	109.1	125.1
Electrical machinery, apparatus and appliances, etc.†	38.5	40.5	46.6
Road vehicles and parts†	107.6	63.1	68.1
Motor vehicles for goods transport	40.0	22.9	20.8
Other transport equipment and parts†	38.9	27.9	46.4
Miscellaneous manufactured articles	86.0	94.3	104.1
Total (incl. others)	1,309.3	1,184.5	1,302.4

* Figures include migrants' and travellers' dutiable effects, but exclude military equipment and some parcel post.
† Data on parts exclude tyres, engines and electrical parts.

Exports f.o.b.	2002	2003
Food and live animals	206.3	285.1
Coffee, tea, cocoa and spices, etc.	127.9	193.2
Crude materials, inedible, except fuels	847.9	1,107.2
Cork and wood	96.4	54.3
Metalliferous ores and metal scrap	738.0	1,043.4
Ores and concentrates of precious metals	475.9	645.0
Mineral fuels, lubricants and related materials	273.4	459.3
Crude petroleum and oils obtained from bituminous materials	273.2	458.1
Animal and vegetable oils, fats and waxes	107.0	146.5
Palm oil	86.0	122.8
Gold, non-monetary, unwrought or semi-manufactured	113.5	143.9
Total (incl. others)	1,624.7	2,260.2

Source: UN, *International Trade Statistics Yearbook*.

PRINCIPAL TRADING PARTNERS
(US $ million)

Imports c.i.f.	2001	2002	2003
Australia	786.2	701.5	729.8
China, People's Republic	16.5	20.5	57.4
Hong Kong	10.9	9.0	11.3
Indonesia	27.8	24.5	26.7
Japan	111.0	62.2	65.4
Malaysia	24.6	25.8	33.6
New Zealand	43.9	47.4	63.1
Singapore	102.1	68.3	89.2
Thailand	18.9	14.6	24.1
United Kingdom	5.9	38.7	10.2
USA	92.5	103.0	115.7
Total (incl. others)	1,309.3	1,184.5	1,302.4

Exports f.o.b.	2002	2003
Australia	389.9	358.3
China, People's Republic	43.2	28.9
Germany	63.3	76.6
Italy	23.2	28.9
Japan	59.0	96.1
Korea, Republic	15.3	25.0
Philippines	15.6	35.0
Singapore	82.0	27.5
United Kingdom	50.9	78.9
USA	58.4	59.8
Total (incl. others)	1,624.7	2,260.2

Source: UN, *International Trade Statistics Yearbook*.

Transport

ROAD TRAFFIC
('000 vehicles in use)

	1998	1999	2000
Passenger cars	21.7	18.8	24.9
Commercial vehicles	89.7	87.0	87.8

Source: UN, *Statistical Yearbook*.

SHIPPING
Merchant Fleet
(registered at 31 December)

	2002	2003	2004
Number of vessels	111	112	114
Total displacement ('000 grt)	72.4	73.3	74.7

Source: Lloyd's Register-Fairplay, *World Fleet Statistics*.

International Sea-borne Freight Traffic

	1997	1998	1999
Cargo unloaded ('000 metric tons)	2,208.6	2,209.0	2,062.8
Cargo loaded ('000 metric tons)	735.9	823.3	788.1

Source: Papua New Guinea Harbours Board, *Monthly Shipping Register Form*.

CIVIL AVIATION
(traffic on scheduled services)

	1999	2000	2001
Kilometres flown (million)	12	17	17
Passengers carried ('000)	1,102	1,100	1,188
Passenger-km (million)	641	1,036	1,110
Total ton-km (million)	80	118	124

Source: UN, *Statistical Yearbook*.

Tourism

FOREIGN TOURIST ARRIVALS

Country of origin	2001	2002	2003
Australia	27,661	26,562	30,118
Canada	705	848	4,566
Germany	1,148	802	885
Japan	2,686	3,804	3,893
Malaysia	108	140	1,856
New Zealand	2,731	2,351	1,935
Philippines	474	416	2,790
United Kingdom	2,133	1,803	1,469
USA	5,314	6,053	4,566
Total (incl. others)	54,235	53,762	56,282

Receipts from tourism (US $ million, excl. passenger transport): 75 in 2001.

Source: World Tourism Organization.

Communications Media

	2000	2001	2002
Television receivers ('000 in use)	100	110	n.a.
Telephones ('000 main lines in use)	64.8	62.0	62.0
Mobile cellular telephones ('000 subscribers)	8.6	10.7	15.0
Personal computers ('000 in use)	280	300	321
Internet users ('000)	45.0	50.0	75.0

2004 ('000): Internet users 170; Personal computers in use 367.
Daily newspapers (1996): 2 (combined circulation 65,000 copies).
Radio receivers (1997): 410,000 in use.
Facsimile machines (1994): 795 in use.

Sources: UNESCO, *Statistical Yearbook*; International Telecommunication Union.

Education

(2001, unless otherwise indicated)

	Institutions*	Teachers	Students
Pre-primary	29	2,144	62,788
Primary	2,790	18,486	663,170
Secondary	n.a.	7,730	159,846
Tertiary†	n.a.	815	13,761

* 1995 figures.
† 1999 figures.

Sources: National Department of Education, *The state of education in PNG* (March 2001); UN, *Statistical Yearbook for Asia and the Pacific*.

Adult literacy rate (UNESCO estimates): 57.3% (males 63.4%; females 50.9%) in 2003 (Source: UN Development Programme, *Human Development Report*).

Directory

The Constitution

The present Constitution came into effect on 16 September 1975, when Papua New Guinea became independent. The main provisions of the Constitution are summarized below:

PREAMBLE

The national goals of the Independent State of Papua New Guinea are: integral human development, equality and participation in the development of the country, national sovereignty and self-reliance, conservation of natural resources and the environment and development primarily through the use of Papua New Guinean forms of social, political and economic organization.

BASIC HUMAN RIGHTS

All people are entitled to the fundamental rights and freedoms of the individual whatever their race, tribe, place of origin, political opinion, colour, creed or sex. The individual's rights include the right to freedom, life and the protection of the law, freedom from inhuman treatment, forced labour, arbitrary search and entry, freedom of conscience, thought, religion, expression, assembly, association and employment, and the right to privacy. Papua New Guinea citizens also have the following special rights: the right to vote and stand for public office, the right to freedom of information and of movement, protection from unjust deprivation of property and equality before the law.

THE NATION
Papua New Guinea is a sovereign, independent state. There is a National Capital District which shall be the seat of government.

The Constitution provides for various classes of citizenship. The age of majority is 19 years.

HEAD OF STATE
Her Majesty the Queen of the United Kingdom of Great Britain and Northern Ireland is Queen and Head of State of Papua New Guinea. The Head of State appoints and dismisses the Prime Minister on the proposal of the National Parliament and other ministers on the proposal of the Prime Minister. The Governor-General and Chief Justice are appointed and dismissed on the proposal of the National Executive Council. All the privileges, powers, functions, duties and responsibilities of the Head of State may be exercised or performed through the Governor-General.

Governor-General
The Governor-General must be a citizen who is qualified to be a member of Parliament or who is a mature person of good standing who enjoys the respect of the community. No one is eligible for appointment more than once unless Parliament approves by a two-thirds' majority. No one is eligible for a third term. The Governor-General is appointed by the Head of State on the proposal of the National Executive Council in accordance with the decision of Parliament by simple majority vote. He may be dismissed by the Head of State on the proposal of the National Executive Council in accordance with a decision of the Council or of an absolute majority of Parliament. The normal term of office is six years. In the case of temporary or permanent absence, dismissal or suspension he may be replaced temporarily by the Speaker of the National Parliament until such time as a new Governor-General is appointed.

THE GOVERNMENT
The Government comprises the National Parliament, the National Executive and the National Judicial System.

National Parliament
The National Parliament, or the House of Assembly, is a single-chamber legislature of members elected from single-member open or provincial electorates. The National Parliament has 109 members elected by universal adult suffrage. The normal term of office is five years. There is a Speaker and a Deputy Speaker, who must be members of Parliament and must be elected to these posts by Parliament. They cannot serve as government ministers concurrently.

National Executive
The National Executive comprises the Head of State and the National Executive Council. The Prime Minister, who presides over the National Executive Council, is appointed and dismissed by the Head of State on the proposal of Parliament. The other ministers, of whom there shall be not fewer than six nor more than a quarter of the number of members of the Parliament, are appointed and dismissed by the Head of State on the proposal of the Prime Minister. The National Executive Council consists of all the ministers, including the Prime Minister, and is responsible for the executive government of Papua New Guinea.

National Judicial System
The National Judicial System comprises the Supreme Court, the National Court, Local Courts and Village Courts. The judiciary is independent.

The Supreme Court consists of the Chief Justice, the Deputy Chief Justice and the other judges of the National Court. It is the final court of appeal. The Chief Justice is appointed and dismissed by the Head of State on the proposal of the National Executive Council after consultation with the minister responsible for justice. The Deputy Chief Justice and the other judges are appointed by the Judicial and Legal Services Commission. The National Court consists of the Chief Justice, the Deputy Chief Justice and no fewer than four nor more than six other judges.

The Constitution also makes provision for the establishment of the Magisterial Service and the establishment of the posts of Public Prosecutor and the Public Solicitor.

THE STATE SERVICES
The Constitution establishes the following State Services which, with the exception of the Defence Force, are subject to ultimate civilian control.

National Public Service
The Public Service is managed by the Department of Personnel Management which is headed by a Secretary, who is appointed by the National Executive Council on a four-year contract.

Police Force
The Police Force is subject to the control of the National Executive Council through a minister and its function is to preserve peace and good order and to maintain and enforce the law.

Papua New Guinea Defence Force
The Defence Force is subject to the superintendence and control of the National Executive Council through the Minister of Defence. The functions of the Defence Force are to defend Papua New Guinea, to provide assistance to civilian authorities in a civil disaster, in the restoration of public order or during a period of declared national emergency.

The fourth State Service is the Parliamentary Service.

The Constitution also includes sections on Public Finance, the office of the Auditor-General, the Public Accounts Commission and the declaration of a State of National Emergency.

The Government

HEAD OF STATE
Queen: HM Queen Elizabeth II.
Governor-General: Sir Paulias Matane (sworn in 29 June 2004).

NATIONAL EXECUTIVE COUNCIL
(April 2006)

Prime Minister: Sir Michael Somare.
Deputy Prime Minister and Minister for Petroleum and Energy: Sir Moi Avei.
Minister for Agriculture and Livestock: Mathew Siune.
Minister for Communications and Information: Ben Semri.
Minister for Correctional Service: Posi Menai.
Minister for Culture and Tourism: David Basua.
Minister for Defence: Yarka Kappa.
Minister for Education, Science and Technology: Michael Lamo.
Minister for Environment and Conservation: William Duma.
Minister for Finance and Forestry and Acting Minister for National Planning and Monitoring: Patrick Pruaitch.
Minister for Fisheries: Alois King.
Minister for Foreign Affairs and Immigration: Sir Rabbie Namaliu.
Minister for Health and Bougainville Affairs: Sir Peter Barter.
Minister for Housing and Urban Resettlement: Mark Maipakai.
Minister for Inter-Government Relations: Melchior Pep.
Minister for Internal Security: Alphonse Willie.
Minister for Justice: Bire Kimisopa.
Minister for Labour and Industrial Relations: Tom Tomiape.
Minister for Lands and Physical Planning and Minister of State assisting the Prime Minister: Dr Puka Temu.
Minister for Mining: Sam Akoitai.
Minister for Public Services: Sinai Brown.
Minister for Science and Technology: Roy Biyama.
Minister for Trade and Industry: Paul Tiensten.
Minister for Transport and Civil Aviation: Don Polye.
Minister for Treasury: Bart Philemon.
Minister for Welfare and Social Development: Dame Carol Kidu.
Minister for Works: Gabriel Kapris.

GOVERNMENT DEPARTMENTS AND OFFICES

Office of the Prime Minister: POB 639, Waigani, NCD; tel. 3276544; fax 3277380; e-mail primeminister@pm.gov.pg; internet www.pm.gov.pg/pmsoffice/PMsoffice.nsf.

Department of Agriculture and Livestock: POB 2033, Port Moresby 121, NCD; tel. 3202885; fax 3202883; e-mail dalit@daltron.com.pg; internet www.agriculture.gov.pg.

Department of the Attorney-General: POB 591, Waigani, NCD; tel. 3230138; fax 3230241.

Department of Defence: Murray Barracks, Free Mail Bag, Boroko 111, NCD; tel. 3242480; fax 3256117; internet www.defence.gov.pg.

PAPUA NEW GUINEA

Department of Education: POB 446, Waigani, NCD 131, Fin Corp Haus; tel. 3013555; fax 3254648; internet www.education.gov.pg.

Department of Environment and Conservation: POB 6601, Boroko 111, Kamul Ave, Waigani, NCD; tel. 3011607; fax 3011691.

Department of Family and Church Affairs: Ori Lavi Haus, Nita St, POB 7354, Boroko, NCD; tel. 3254566; fax 3251230; internet www.datec.com.pg/government/famchurch/default.htm.

Department of Finance and Treasury: POB 710, Waigani, Vulupindi Haus, NCD; internet www.treasury.gov.pg.

Department of Fisheries and Marine Resources: POB 2016, Port Moresby; tel. 3271799; fax 3202074; internet www.fisheries.gov.pg.

Department of Foreign Affairs: Central Government Offices, Kumul Ave, Post Office, Wards Strip, Waigani, NCD; tel. 3271311; fax 3254467.

Department of Health: POB 3991, Boroko, Aopi Centre, Waigani Drive, Waigani; tel. 3254648; fax 3013555; internet www.health.gov.pg.

Department of Housing and Urban Resettlement: POB 1550, Boroko, NCD; tel. 3247200; fax 3259918.

Department of Inter-Government Relations: Somare Haus, Independence Drive, Waigani, POB 1287, Boroko, NCD; tel. 3011002; fax 3250553; e-mail paffairs@dalton.com.pg; internet www.dplga.gov.pg.

Department of Justice: Port Moresby; internet www.justice.gov.pg.

Department of Labour and Industrial Relations: POB 5644, Boroko, NCD; tel. 3217408; fax 3214085.

Department of Lands and Physical Planning: POB 233, Boroko, NCD; tel. 3013206; fax 3013205; e-mail onnoj@lands.gov.pg; internet www.lands.gov.pg.

Department of Mineral Resources: PMB PO, Konedobu, Port Moresby 121; tel. 3227600; fax 3213701; internet www.mineral.gov.pg.

Department of Mining: Private Mailbag, Port Moresby Post Office; tel. 3227670; fax 3213958.

Department of Personnel Management: POB 519, Wards Strip, Waigani, NCD; tel. 3276422; fax 3250520; e-mail perrtsiamalili@dpm.gov.pg.

Department of Petroleum and Energy: POB 1993, Port Moresby, NCD; tel. 3224200; fax 3224222; e-mail joseph_gabut@petroleum.gov.pg; internet www.petroleum.gov.pg.

Department of Planning and Implementation: POB 710, Waigani 131, Vulupindi Haus, Port Moresby, NCD; tel. 3288302; fax 3288375.

Department of Police: Police Headquarters, POB 85, Konedobu, NCD; tel. 3226100; fax 3226113; internet www.police.gov.pg.

Department of Private Enterprise: Central Government Offices, Kumul Ave, Post Office, Wards Strip, Waigani, NCD.

Department of Social Welfare and Development, Youth and Women: Maori Kiki Bldg, 2nd Floor, POB 7354, Boroko, NCD; tel. 3254967; fax 3213821.

Department of State: Haus To Makala, 5th Floor, Post Office, Wards Strip, Waigani, NCD; tel. 3276758; fax 3214861.

Department of Trade and Industry: Heduru Haus, Waigani Drive, POB 375, Waigani 131, NCD; tel. 3255311; fax 3254482; internet www.trade.gov.pg.

Department of Transport and Civil Aviation: POB 1489, Port Moresby; tel. 3222580; fax 3200236; e-mail dotdirectro@datec.com.pg.

Correctional Service: POB 6889, Boroko, NCD III; tel. 3231437; fax 3230407; e-mail rsikani@hq.cs.gov.pg.

National Forest Authority: POB 5055, Boroko, Frangipani St, Hohola, Port Moresby; tel. 3277800; fax 3254433; internet www.datec.com.pg/government/forest/default.htm.

Office of Civil Aviation: POB 684, Boroko 111, NCD; tel. 3257077; fax 3251919; e-mail dgoca@datec.net.pg; internet www.oca.gov.pg.

Office of Peace and Reconstruction (fmrly Office of Bougainville Affairs): Morauta Haus, POB 343, Waigani 131, NCD; tel. 3276760; fax 3258038; internet www.oba.gov.pg.

Office of Information and Communication: Port Moresby; internet www.communication.gov.pg.

Office of Works: POB 1489, Port Moresby 121, cnr Champion Parade and Musgrave St; tel. 3222500; fax 3200236; internet www.works.gov.pg.

Legislature

NATIONAL PARLIAMENT

The unicameral legislature has 109 elective seats: 89 representing open constituencies and 20 representing provincial constituencies. There is constitutional provision for up to three nominated members.

Speaker: JEFFREY NAPE (acting).

General Election, 15 June–29 July 2002

Party	Seats
National Alliance	19
People's Democratic Movement	12
People's Progress Party	8
Pangu Pati	6
People's Action Party	5
People's Labour Party	4
Christian Democratic Party	3
Melanesian Alliance	3
National Party	3
United Party	3
National Transformation Party	2
Pan-Melanesian Congress Party	2
People's National Congress	2
People's Solidarity Party	2
Pipol First Party	2
Rural Pipol's Pati	2
Others and undeclared	14
Independents	17
Total	**109**

Note: In many cases party affiliations were subject to review in the immediate aftermath of the election.

Autonomous Region

BOUGAINVILLE ASSEMBLY

In late March 2004 the Bougainville Interim Provincial Government (BIPG—see Recent History) approved legislation to establish the Bougainville Constituent Assembly (BCA). The organization, which was composed of the members of both the BIPG and the Bougainville People's Congress (BPC), was convened for the first time on 30 March 2004, to approve the third and final draft of the proposed Constitution for Bougainville. Following its consideration by the Bougainville Constitutional Commission in August, in November the BCA recommended the proposed Constitution to the National Government, which approved the document in January 2005. Elections for the 39 seats of the new autonomous assembly and for the President of the incoming autonomous Government took place over a period of two weeks commencing on 20 May 2005. Joseph Kabui was elected as President of the new Government, winning 54.7% of the total votes cast, defeating his nearest rival, John Momis (34.4%), and three other candidates. Kabui was sworn in and the House of Representatives was inaugurated on 14 June. Nick Peniai was appointed as the assembly's Speaker.

President: JOSEPH KABUI.

Vice-President: JOSEPH WATAWI.

Election Commission

Election Commission of Papua New Guinea: POB 5348, Boroko NCD, Port Moresby; tel. 3254402; fax 3257418; e-mail atrawen@pngec.gov.pg; internet www.pngec.gov.pg; Electoral Commr ANDREW TRAWEN.

Political Organizations

Bougainville Revolutionary Army (BRA): f. 1988; demands full independence for island of Bougainville; Leader ISMAEL TOROAMA.

League for National Advancement (LNA): POB 6101, Boroko, NCD; f. 1986; Leader JOHN NILKARE.

Melanesian Labour Party: Port Moresby; Leader PAUL MONDIA.

Melanesian United Front: Boroko, NCD; f. 1988; fmrly Morobe Independent Group; Leader UTULA SAMANA.

National Alliance: c/o National Parliament, Port Moresby; f. 1996; to combat corruption in public life; Leader Sir MICHAEL SOMARE.

National Party (NP): Private Bag, Boroko, NCD; f. 1979; fmrly People's United Front; Leader MICHAEL MEL.

PAPUA NEW GUINEA

Pangu (Papua New Guinea Unity) Pati: POB 289, Waigani, NCD; tel. 3277628; fax 3277611; f. 1968; urban- and rural-based; Leader CHRIS HAIVETA; Pres. PATE WAMP; Sec.-Gen. MOSES TAIAN.

People's Action Party (PAP): Boroko, NCD; tel. 3251343; f. 1985; Leader TED DIRO.

People's Democratic Movement (PDM): POB 972, Boroko, NCD; f. 1985; merged with Advance PNG Party in 2001; Leader Sir MEKERE MORAUTA.

People's National Alliance (PNA): c/o National Parliament, Port Moresby; f. 1999; by merger of following:

   Melanesian Alliance (MA): Port Moresby; tel. 3277635; f. 1978; socialist; Chair. Fr JOHN MOMIS; Gen. Sec. FABIAN WAU KAWA.

   Movement for Greater Autonomy: Manus Province; Leader STEPHEN POKAWIN.

   People's National Party: Port Moresby.

People's National Congress (PNC): c/o National Parliament, Port Moresby; Leader PETER O'NEILL.

People's Progress Party (PPP): POB 6030, Boroko, NCD; f. 1970; Parliamentary Leader ANDREW BAING; Nat. Pres. ALEX ANISI; Gen. Sec. EMOS DANIELS.

People's Unity Party: c/o National Parliament, Port Moresby; Leader ALFRED KAIABE.

United Resource Party (URP): Port Moresby; f. 1997; aims to secure greater representation in Government for resource owners; Leader MASKET IANGALIO; Chair. PITA IPATAS.

Diplomatic Representation

EMBASSIES AND HIGH COMMISSIONS IN PAPUA NEW GUINEA

Australia: POB 129, Waigani, NCD; tel. 3259333; fax 3259183; internet www.embassy.gov.au/pg.html; High Commissioner MICHAEL POTTS.

China, People's Republic: POB 1351, Boroko, NCD; tel. 3259836; fax 3258247; e-mail chnempng@daltron.com.pg; Ambassador WEI RUIXING.

Fiji: Defence House, 4th Floor, Champion Parade, Port Moresby, NCD; tel. 3211914; fax 3217220; e-mail rakaie@fijihighcom.org.pg; High Commissioner Ratu INOKE KUBUABOLA.

France: Defens Haus, 6th Floor, Cnr of Hunter St and Champion Parade, POB 1155, Port Moresby; tel. 3215550; fax 3215549; internet www.ambafrance-pg.org; Ambassador JACQUES-OLIVIER MANENT.

Holy See: POB 98, Port Moresby; tel. 3256021; fax 3252844; e-mail nunciaturepng@datec.net.pg; Apostolic Nuncio Archbishop ADOLFO TITO YLLANA.

India: Port Moresby; tel. 3254757; fax 3253138; e-mail hcipom@datec.net.pg; High Commissioner H. V. S. MANRAL.

Indonesia: 1-2/410 Kiroki St, Sir John Guise Dr., Waigani, NCD; tel. 3253116; fax 3253544; e-mail kbripom@daltron.com.pg; Ambassador JOHANNES RUDOLF GERSON DJOPARDI.

Japan: Cuthbertson House, Cuthbertson St, POB 1040, Port Moresby; tel. 3211800; fax 3217906; Ambassador KANJI HANAGATA.

Korea, Republic: Pacific View Apts, Lot 1, sec. 84, Pruth St, Korobosea, Port Moresby; tel. 3254755; fax 3259996; Ambassador Dr SEO HYUN-SEOP.

Malaysia: POB 1400, Pacific View Apts, Units 201/203, 2nd floor, Pruth St, Korobosea, Port Moresby; tel. 3252076; fax 3252784; e-mail mwpom@datec.com.pg; High Commissioner Dato' KAMILAN MAKSOM.

New Zealand: Embassy Drive, POB 1051, Waigani, NCD; tel. 3259444; fax 3250565; e-mail nzhcpom@dg.com.pg; High Commissioner LAURIE MARKES.

Philippines: POB 5916, Boroko, NCD; tel. 3256577; fax 3231803; e-mail pomphpem@datec.com.pg; Ambassador BIENVENIDO TEJANO.

Solomon Islands: Port Moresby; e-mail sihicomm@daltron.com.pg; High Commissioner BERNARD BATA'ANISIA.

United Kingdom: Kiroki St, Locked Bag 212, Waigani 131, NCD; tel. 3251677; fax 3253547; e-mail bhcpng@datec.net.pg; internet www.britishhighcommission.gov.uk/papuanewguinea; High Commissioner DAVID GORDON-MACLEOD.

USA: Douglas St, POB 1492, Port Moresby; tel. 3211455; fax 3211593; e-mail png@state.gov; internet www.portmoresby.usembassy.gov; Ambassador ROBERT FITTS.

Judicial System

The Supreme Court is the highest judicial authority in the country, and deals with all matters involving the interpretation of the Constitution, and with appeals from the National Court. The National Court has unlimited jurisdiction in both civil and criminal matters. All National Court Judges (except acting Judges) are Judges of the Supreme Court. District Courts are responsible for civil cases involving compensation, for some indictable offences and for the more serious summary offences, while Local Courts deal with minor offences and with such matters as custody of children under the provision of Custom. There are also Children's Courts, which judge cases involving minors. Appeal from the District, Local and Children's Courts lies to the National Court. District and Local Land Courts deal with disputes relating to Customary land, and Warden's Courts with civil cases relating to mining. In addition, there are other courts with responsibility for determining ownership of government land and for assessing the right of Customary landowners to compensation. Village Courts, which are presided over by Magistrates with no formal legal qualification, are responsible for all Customary matters not dealt with by other courts.

Supreme Court of Papua New Guinea

POB 7018, Boroko, NCD; tel. 3245700; fax 3234492; **Chief Justice:** Sir MARI KAPI.

Attorney-General: FRED TOMO (acting).

Religion

The belief in magic or sorcery is widespread, even among the significant proportion of the population that has adopted Christianity (nominally 97% in 1990). Pantheism also survives. There are many missionary societies.

CHRISTIANITY

Papua New Guinea Council of Churches: POB 1015, Boroko, NCD; tel. 3259961; fax 3251206; f. 1965; seven mem. churches; Chair. EDEA KIDU; Gen. Sec. SOPHIA W. R. GEGEYO.

The Anglican Communion

Formerly part of the Province of Queensland within the Church of England in Australia (now the Anglican Church of Australia), Papua New Guinea became an independent Province in 1977. The Anglican Church of Papua New Guinea comprises five dioceses and had 246,000 members in 2000.

Archbishop of Papua New Guinea and Bishop of Aipo Rongo: Most Rev. JAMES AYONG, POB 893, Mount Hagen, Western Highlands Province; tel. 5421131; fax 5421181; e-mail acpnghgn@global.net.pg.

General Secretary: MARTIN GARDHAM, POB 673, Lae, Morobe Province; tel. 4724111; fax 4721852; e-mail acpng@global.net.pg.

The Roman Catholic Church

For ecclesiastical purposes, Papua New Guinea comprises four archdioceses and 15 dioceses. At 31 December 2003 there were 1,694,588 adherents.

Catholic Bishops' Conference of Papua New Guinea and Solomon Islands
POB 398, Waigani, NCD; tel. 3259577; fax 3232551; e-mail cbc@catholic.org.pg; internet www.catholicpng.org.pg; f. 1959; Pres. Most Rev. FRANCESCO SAREGO (Bishop of Goroka); Gen. Sec. LAWRENCE STEPHENS.

Archbishop of Madang: Most Rev. WILLIAM KURTZ, Archbishop's Residence, POB 750, Madang; tel. 8522946; fax 8522596; e-mail Kurtz_caom@global.net.pg.

Archbishop of Mount Hagen: Most Rev. MICHAEL MEIER, Archbishop's Office, POB 54, Mount Hagen, Western Highlands Province; tel. 5421285; fax 5422128; e-mail archdios@online.net.pg.

Archbishop of Port Moresby: Most Rev. Sir BRIAN BARNES, Archbishop's House, POB 1032, Boroko, NCD; tel. 3251192; fax 3256731; e-mail archpom@daltron.com.pg.

Archbishop of Rabaul: Most Rev. KARL HESSE, Archbishop's House, POB 357, Kokopo, East New Britain Province; tel. 9828369; fax 9828404; e-mail abkhesse@online.net.pg.

Other Christian Churches

Baptist Union of Papua New Guinea Inc: POB 705, Mount Hagen, Western Highlands Province; tel. 5522364; fax 5522402; e-mail bupng@global.net.pg; f. 1976; Gen. Sec. JOHN KAENKI; 48,000 mems.

Evangelical Lutheran Church of Papua New Guinea: Bishop Rt Rev. WESLEY KIGASUNG POB 80, Lae, Morobe Province; tel. 4723711; fax 4721056; e-mail bishop@elcpng.org.pg; f. 1956; Sec. REUBEN KURE; 815,000 mems.

Gutnius Lutheran Church of Papua New Guinea: Bishop Rev. DAVID P. PISO, POB 111, 291 Wabag, Enga Province; tel. 5471280; fax 5471235; e-mail dpisoglc@online.net.pg; f. 1948; Gen. Sec. RICHARD R. MOSES; 138,000 mems.

Papua New Guinea Union Mission of the Seventh-day Adventist Church: POB 86, Lae, Morobe Province 411; tel. 4721488; fax 4721873; Pres. Pastor WILSON STEPHEN; Sec. Pastor BRADLEY RICHARD KEMP; 200,000 adherents.

The United Church in Papua New Guinea: POB 1401, Port Moresby; tel. 3211744; fax 3214930; e-mail ucpng@daltron.com.pg; f. 1968; formed by union of the Methodist Church in Melanesia, the Papua Ekalesia and United Church, Port Moresby; Moderator Rev. SAMSON LOWA; 600,000 mems; Gen. Sec. Rev. SIULANGI KAVORA.

BAHÁ'Í FAITH

National Spiritual Assembly: Private Mail Bag, Boroko, NCD; tel. 3250286; fax 3236474; e-mail nsapng@datec.net.pg.

ISLAM

In 2000 the Muslim community in Papua New Guinea numbered about 1,500, of whom approximately two-thirds were believed to be expatriates. The religion was introduced to the island in the 1970s. The first mosque there was opened in late 2000 at Poreporena Highway, Hohola, Port Moresby; Imam KHALID ARAI (acting).

The Press

There are numerous newspapers and magazines published by government departments, statutory organizations, missions, sporting organizations, local government councils and regional authorities. They are variously in English, Tok Pisin (Pidgin), Motu and vernacular languages.

Ailans Nius: POB 1239, Rabaul, East New Britain Province; weekly.

Foreign Affairs Review: Dept of Foreign Affairs, Central Government Offices, Kumul Ave, Post Office, Wards Strip, Waigani, NCD; tel. 3271401; fax 3254886.

Hailans Nius: Mount Hagen, Western Highlands Province; weekly.

Lae Nius: POB 759, Lae, Morobe Province; 2 a week.

The National: POB 6817, Boroko, NCD; tel. 3246888; fax 3246868; e-mail national@thenational.com.pg; internet www.thenational.com.pg; f. 1993; daily; Editor BRIAN GOMEZ; circ. 20,000.

Niugini Nius: POB 3019, Boroko, NCD; tel. 3252177; e-mail niusedita@pactok.net; internet pactok.net.au/docs/nius/; daily.

Papua and New Guinea Education Gazette: Dept of Education, PSA Haus, POB 446, Waigani, NCD; tel. 3272413; fax 3254648; monthly; Editor J. OBERLENTER; circ. 8,000.

Papua New Guinea Post-Courier: POB 85, Port Moresby; tel. 3091000; fax 3212721; e-mail postcourier@ssp.com.pg; internet www.postcourier.com.pg; f. 1969; daily; English; published by News Corpn; Gen. Man. TONY YIANNI; Editor OSEAH PHILEMON; circ. 25,044.

Sunkamap Times: Bougainville, North Solomons Province; monthly; f. 2004; community newsletter.

Wantok (Friend) Niuspepa: POB 1982, Boroko, NCD; tel. 3252500; fax 3252579; e-mail word@global.net.pg; f. 1970; weekly in New Guinea Pidgin; mainly rural readership; Publr ANNA SOLOMON; Editor YAKAM KELO; circ. 10,000.

Publishers

Gordon and Gotch (PNG) Pty Ltd: POB 107, Boroko, NCD; tel. 3254855; fax 3250950; e-mail ggpng@online.net.pg; f. 1970; books, magazines and stationery; Gen. Man. PETER G. PORTER.

Scripture Union of Papua New Guinea: POB 280, University, Boroko, NCD; tel. and fax 3253987; f. 1966; religious; Chair. RAVA TAVIRI.

Word Publishing Co Pty Ltd: POB 1982, Boroko, NCD; tel. 3252500; fax 3252579; e-mail word@global.net.pg; f. 1982; 60% owned by the Roman Catholic Church, 20% by Evangelical Lutheran, 10% by Anglican and 10% by United Churches; Gen. Man. JEREMY BURGESS.

Broadcasting and Communications

TELECOMMUNICATIONS

Office of Information and Communication: POB 639, Waigani; tel. 3256853; fax 3250412; internet www.communication.gov.pg.

Pacific Mobile Communications Company Ltd: POB 785, Waigani, NCD; tel. 3236336; fax 3258916; e-mail pmc@tiare.net.pg; internet www.pacificmobile.com.pg; Chair. FLORIAN GUBON.

Papua New Guinea Telecommunication Authority (Pangtel): POB 8444, Boroko, NCD; tel. 3258633; fax 3256868; internet www.pangtel.gov.pg; f. 1997; CEO PHILIP AEAVA.

Telikom PNG Pty Ltd: POB 7395, Boroko, NCD; tel. 3005000; fax 3259582; internet www.telikompng.com.pg; Man. Dir GEREA AOPI; Chair. FLORIAN GUBON.

BROADCASTING

Radio

National Broadcasting Corporation of Papua New Guinea: POB 1359, Boroko, NCD; tel. 3257175; fax 3256296; e-mail md.nbc@global.net.pg; f. 1973; commercial and free govt radio programmes services; broadcasting in English, Melanesian, Pidgin, Motu and 30 vernacular languages; Chair. CHRIS RANGATIN; Man. Dir Dr KRISTOFFA NINKAMA.

Kalang Service (FM): POB 1359, Boroko, NCD; tel. 3255233; commercial radio co established by National Broadcasting Commission; Chair. CAROLUS KETSIMUR.

Nau FM/Yumi FM: POB 774, Port Moresby; tel. 3201996; fax 3201995; internet www.naufm.com.pg; f. 1994; Gen. Mans MARK ROGERS, JUSTIN KILI.

Television

EM TV: POB 443, Boroko, NCD; tel. 3257322; fax 3254450; e-mail emtv@emtv.com.pg; internet www.emtv.com.pg; f. 1988; operated by Media Niugini Pty Ltd; Gen. Man. GLENN ARMSTRONG.

Media Niugini Pty Ltd: POB 443, Boroko, NCD; tel. 3257322; fax 3254450; e-mail emtv@emtv.com.pg; internet www.emtv.com.pg; f. 1987; owned by Nine Network Australia; Gen. Man. GLENN ARMSTRONG.

Finance

(cap. = capital; res = reserves; dep. = deposits; m. = million; brs = branches; amounts in kina unless otherwise stated)

BANKING

Central Bank

Bank of Papua New Guinea: Douglas St, POB 121, Port Moresby; tel. 3227200; fax 3211617; e-mail bpng@datec.com.pg; internet www.bankpng.gov.pg; f. 1973; bank of issue since 1975; sold to Bank of South Pacific in 2002; cap. 62.0m., res 680.2m., dep. 1,040.0m. (Dec. 2002); Gov. WILSON KAMIT; Deputy Gov. BENNY POPOITAI.

Commercial Banks

Australia and New Zealand Banking Group (PNG) Limited: Defens Haus, 3rd Floor, cnr of Champion Parade and Hunter St, POB 1152, Port Moresby; tel. 3223333; fax 3223306; f. 1976; cap. 4.7m., res 1.1m., dep. 494.1m. (Sept. 1998); Chair. R. G. LYON; Man. Dir ALLAN MARLIN; 8 brs.

Bank of South Pacific Ltd: Douglas St, POB 173, Port Moresby; tel. 3212444; fax 3200053; e-mail service@bsp.com.pg; internet www.bsp.com.pg; f. 1974; acquired from National Australia Bank Ltd by Papua New Guinea consortium (National Investment Holdings, now BSP Holdings Ltd) in 1993; cap. 182.9m., res 19.8m., dep. 1,629.3m. (Dec. 2003); Chair. NOREO BEANGKE; Man. Dir NOEL R. SMITH; 8 brs and 2 sub-brs.

Maybank (PNG) Ltd: Waigani, NCD; f. 1995.

MBf Finance (PNG) Ltd: Elsa Beach Towers, Ground Floor, cnr of Musgrave St, POB 329, Port Moresby; tel. 3213555; fax 3213480; f. 1989.

Papua New Guinea Banking Corporation: cnr of Douglas and Musgrave Sts, POB 78, Port Moresby; tel. 3229700; fax 3211683; f. 1974; corporatized in 2001; cap. 11.3m., res 72.9m., dep. 978.8m. (Dec. 1997); Chair. ROGER PALME; Man. Dir HENRY FABILA; 34 brs.

Westpac Bank—PNG—Ltd: Mogoru Motu Bldg, 5th Floor, Champion Parade, POB 706, Port Moresby; tel. 3220800; fax 3213367; e-mail westpacpng@westpac.com.au; f. 1910; est. as Bank of New South Wales, present name since 1982; 90% owned by Westpac Banking Corpn, Australia; cap. 5.8m., res 6.1m., dep. 554.7m. (Sept. 1999); Chair. ALAN WALTER; Man. Dir SIMON MILLETT; 15 brs.

Development Bank

Rural Development Bank of Papua New Guinea: Somare Crescent, POB 686, Waigani, NCD; tel. 3247500; fax 3259817; f. 1967; est. as Agriculture Bank of Papua New Guinea; name changed as above in 1994; cap. 32.6m., res 17.1m. (Dec. 1992);

PAPUA NEW GUINEA

statutory govt agency; Chair. RUPA MULINA; Man. Dir ANDREW NAGARI; 10 brs.

Savings and Loan Societies

Registry of Savings and Loan Societies: Financial System Supervision Dept, POB 121, Port Moresby; tel. 3227200; fax 3214548; 21 savings and loan societies; 154,846 mems (2005); total funds 331.6m., loans outstanding 115.2m., investments 123.7m. (Dec. 2005); Man. ELLISON PIDIK.

STOCK EXCHANGE

Port Moresby Stock Exchange (POMSoX) Ltd: Level 4, Defens Haus, POB 1531, Port Moresby; tel. 3201980; fax 3201981; e-mail pomsox@pomsox.com.pg; internet www.pomsox.com.pg; f. 1999; Chair. GEREA AOPI; Gen. Man. VINCENT IVOSA.

INSURANCE

Pacific MMI Insurance Ltd: POB 331, Port Moresby, NCD; tel. 3214077; fax 3214837; e-mail wdorgan@pacificmmi.com; internet www.pacificmmi.com; f. 1998; fmrly Niugini Insurance Corpn Ltd; jt venture; general and life insurance; financial services; Chair. Dr JOHN MUA; Man. Dir WAYNE DORGAN.

Pan Asia Pacific Assurance (PNG) Pty Ltd (PAPA): POB 3757, Boroko, NCD; tel. 3202344; fax 3203443; e-mail pap@daltron.com.pg; f. 1993; Gen. Man. SOMASHEKAR MIRLE.

There are branches of several Australian and United Kingdom insurance companies in Port Moresby, Rabaul, Lae and Kieta.

Trade and Industry

GOVERNMENT AGENCIES

Investment Corporation of Papua New Guinea: Hunter St, POB 155, Port Moresby; tel. 3212855; fax 3211240; f. 1971; as govt body to support local enterprise and to purchase shares in foreign businesses operating in Papua New Guinea; partially transferred to private ownership in 1993.

Investment Promotion Authority (IPA): POB 5053, Boroko, NCD 111; tel. 3217311; fax 3212819; e-mail iepd@ipa.gov.pg; internet www.ipa.gov.pg; f. 1992; following reorganization of National Investment and Development Authority; a statutory body responsible for the promotion of foreign investment; the first contact point for foreign investors for advice on project proposals and approvals of applications for registration to conduct business in the country; contributes to planning for investment and recommends priority areas for investment to the Govt; also co-ordinates investment proposals; Man. Dir SIMON PETER (acting).

Privatization Commission: Port Moresby; f. 1999; to oversee transfer of state-owned enterprises to private ownership; Exec. Chair. BEN MICAH.

DEVELOPMENT ORGANIZATIONS

CDC Capital Partners Ltd: CDC Haus, 2nd Floor, POB 907, Port Moresby; tel. 3212944; fax 3212867; e-mail png@cdc.com.pg; internet www.cdcgroup.com; fmrly Commonwealth Development Corpn; Man. Dir ASHLEY EMBERSON-BAIN.

Industrial Centres Development Corporation: POB 1571, Boroko, NCD; tel. 3232913; fax 3231109; promotes foreign investment in non-mining sectors through establishment of manufacturing facilities.

CHAMBERS OF COMMERCE

Lae Chamber of Commerce and Industry: POB 265, Lae, Morobe Province; tel. 4722340; fax 4726038; e-mail lcci@global.net.pg; internet www.lcci.org.pg; Pres. ALAN MCLAY.

Papua New Guinea Chamber of Commerce and Industry: POB 1621, Port Moresby; tel. 3213057; fax 3210566; e-mail pngcci@global.net.pg; internet www.pngcci.org.pg; Pres. MICHAEL MAYBERRY; CEO SHIRLEY BAQUE.

Papua New Guinea Chamber of Mines and Petroleum: POB 1032, Port Moresby; tel. 3212988; fax 3217107; e-mail ga@pngchamberminpet.com.pg; internet www.pngchamberminpet.com.pg; Exec. Dir GREG ANDERSON; Pres. PETER BOTTEN.

Port Moresby Chamber of Commerce and Industry: POB 1764, Port Moresby; tel. 3213077; fax 3214203; Pres. DAVID CONN.

INDUSTRIAL AND TRADE ASSOCIATIONS

Cocoa Board of Papua New Guinea: POB 532, Rabaul, East New Britain Province; tel. 9829083; fax 9828712; e-mail l.tautea@global.net.pg; f. 1974; Chair. JIMMY SIMITAB; CEO LAUATU TAUTEA.

Coffee Industry Corpn Ltd: POB 137, Goroka, Eastern Highlands Province; tel. 7321266; fax 7321431; e-mail cicgka@daltron.com.pg; internet www.coffeecorp.org.pg; CEO RICKY MITTIO.

Fishing Industry Association (PNG) Inc: POB 2340, Boroko, NCD; e-mail netshop1@daltron.com.pg; Chair. MAURICE BROWNJOHN.

Forest Industries Association: POB 229, Waigani, NCD; internet www.fiapng.com; Pres. STANIS BAI; CEO ROBERT TATE.

Higaturu Oil Palms Pty Ltd: POB 28, Popondetta, Oro Province; tel. 3297177; fax 3297137; f. 1976; jtly owned by the Commonwealth Development Corpn (UK) and the Papua New Guinea Govt; major producer of palm oil and cocoa; Gen. Man. RICHARD CASKIE.

Kokonas Indasrti Korporesen (KIK): POB 81, Port Moresby; tel. 3211133; fax 3214257; e-mail infor@kik.com.pg; regulates and markets all copra and coconut products in Papua New Guinea; consists of a chair. and mems representing producers; formerly known as the Copra Marketing Board of Papua New Guinea; Chair. JOSEPH EKO; CEO TORE OVASURU.

Manufacturers' Council of Papua New Guinea: POB 598, Port Moresby; tel. 3259512; fax 3230199; e-mail pngmade@global.com.pg; internet www.pngmade.org.pg; Chair. WAYNE GOLDING; CEO BRUCE REVILLE.

Mineral Resources Development Corporation: POB 1076, Port Moresby; tel. 3255822; fax 3252633; e-mail info@mrdc.com.pg; Man. Dir FRANCIS KAUPA.

National Contractors' Association: Port Moresby; formed by construction cos for the promotion of education, training and professional conduct in the construction industry; Pres. ROY THORPE.

National Fisheries Authority: POB 2016, Port Moresby; tel. 3212643; fax 3202061; e-mail nfa@fisheries.gov.pg; internet www.fisheries.gov.pg; Man. Dir TONY LEWIS; Dep. Man. Dir MICHAEL BATTY.

National Housing Corpn (NHC): POB 1550, Boroko, NCD; tel. 3247000; fax 3254363; Man. Dir GABRIEL TOVO.

New Britain Palm Oil Ltd: POB 389, Kimbe, West New Britain; tel. 9852177; fax 9852003; e-mail nbpol@nbpol.com.pg; internet www.nbpol.com.pg; f. 1967; 80% owned by Kulim (Malaysia), 20% owned by Govt, employees and local producers; major producer of palm oil, coffee trader and exporter, supplier of high quality oil palm seed; Man. Dir NICK THOMPSON; Sec. HIMSON WANINARA.

Niugini Produce Marketing Pty Ltd: Lae, Morobe Province; f. 1982; govt-owned; handles distribution of fruit and vegetables throughout the country.

Palm Oil Producers Association: Port Moresby; Exec. Sec. ALLAN MAINO.

Papua New Guinea Forest Authority: POB 5055, Boroko, NCD; tel. 3277800; fax 3254433; Man. Dir THOMAS NEN; Chair. VALENTINE KAMBORI.

Papua New Guinea Growers Association: POB 14, Kokopo, East New Britain Province 613; tel. 9829123; fax 9829264; e-mail growers@global.net.pg; Pres. PAUL ARNOLD; Exec. Dir DAVID LOH.

Papua New Guinea Holdings Corpn: POB 131, Port Moresby; fax 3217545; f. 1992; responsible for managing govt privatization programme; Chair. MICHAEL MEL; Man. Dir PETER STEELE.

Papua New Guinea Log Carriers Association: f. 1993.

Pita Lus National Silk Institute: Kagamuga, Mount Hagen, Western Highlands Province; f. 1978; govt silk-producing project.

Rural Industries Council: Chair. PETER COLTON.

UTILITIES

Electricity

PNG Electricity Commission (Elcom): POB 1105, Boroko, NCD; tel. 3243200; fax 3214051; plans to privatize the organization were announced in 1999; Chair. PAUL AISA; Chief Exec. SEV MASO.

Water

Eda Ranu (Our Water): POB 1084, Waigani, NCD; tel. 3122100; fax 3122190; e-mail enquiries@edaranu.com.pg; internet www.edaranu.com.pg; fmrly Port Moresby Water Supply Company; Gen. Man. BILLY IMAR.

PNG Waterboard: POB 2779, Boroko, NCD; tel. 3235700; fax 3236317; e-mail pamini@pngwater.com.pg; f. 1986; govt-owned; operates 12 water supply systems throughout the country; Man. Dir PATRICK AMINI.

TRADE UNIONS

The Industrial Organizations Ordinance requires all industrial organizations that consist of no fewer than 20 employees or four employers to register. In 1977 there were 56 registered industrial organizations, including a general employee group registered as a workers' association in each province and also unions covering a specific industry or profession.

Papua New Guinea Trade Unions Congress (PNGTUC): POB 254, Boroko, NCD; tel. 3212132; fax 3212498; e-mail tucl@daltron.com.pg; Pres. GASPER LAPAN; Gen. Sec. JOHN PASKA; 52 affiliates, 76,000 mems.

The following are among the major trade unions:

Bougainville Mining Workers' Union: POB 777, Panguna, North Solomons Province; tel. 9958272; Pres. MATHEW TUKAN; Gen. Sec. ALFRED ELISHA TAGORNOM.

Central Province Building and Construction Industry Workers' Union: POB 265, Port Moresby.

Central Province Transport Drivers' and Workers' Union: POB 265, Port Moresby.

Employers' Federation of Papua New Guinea: POB 490, Port Moresby; tel. 3214772; fax 3214070; f. 1963; Pres. G. J. DUNLOP; Exec. Dir TAU NANA; 170 mems.

National Federation of Timber Workers: Madang; f. 1993; Gen. Sec. MATHIAS KENUANGI (acting).

Papua New Guinea Communication Workers' Union: Pres. BOB MAGARU; Gen. Sec. EMMANUEL KAIRU.

Papua New Guinea National Doctors' Association: Pres. Dr BOB DANAYA; 225 mems.

Papua New Guinea Teachers' Association: POB 1027, Waigani, NCD; tel. 3262588; fax 321514; f. 1971; Pres. TOMMY HECKO; Gen. Sec. GORDON KAVOP; 18,500 mems.

Papua New Guinea Waterside Workers' and Seamen's Union: Port Moresby; f. 1979; an amalgamation of four unions; Sec. DOUGLAS GADEBO.

Police Association of Papua New Guinea: POB 903, Port Moresby; tel. 3214172; f. 1964; Pres. ROBERT ALI; 4,596 mems.

Port Moresby Council of Trade Unions: POB 265, Boroko, NCD; Gen. Sec. JOHN KOSI.

Port Moresby Miscellaneous Workers' Union: POB 265, Boroko, NCD.

Printing and Kindred Industries Union: Port Moresby.

Public Employees' Association: POB 965, Boroko, NCD; tel. 3252955; fax 3252186; f. 1974; Pres. NAPOLEON LIOSI; Gen. Sec. JACK N. KUTAL; 28,000 mems.

Transport

There are no railways in Papua New Guinea. The capital city, Port Moresby, is not connected by road to other major population centres. Therefore, air and sea travel are of particular importance.

ROADS

In 1999 there were an estimated 19,600 km of roads in Papua New Guinea, of which 3.5% were paved. Japan offered a grant-in-aid in 1998 of 940m. yen for the reconstruction of a bridge on the Highlands Highway. In October 2000 it was announced that this highway was to be upgraded over six years at a cost of 26.3m. kina, financed through a loan negotiated with the Asian Development Bank (ADB). In October 2005 the ADB agreed to provide US $18m. for road improvements during 2006–07, in addition to the $42m. loan already arranged for the same two-year period.

Papua New Guinea Roads Authority: Lae, Morobe Province; f. 2004; statutory authority established to maintain the road network, particularly the Highlands Highway; Chair. ALLAN MCLAY; Deputy Chair. ALPHONSE NIGGINS.

SHIPPING

Papua New Guinea has 16 major ports and a coastal fleet of about 300 vessels. In early 1999 a feasibility study was commissioned to investigate the possible relocation of port facilities in Port Moresby. In February 2006 it was announced that facilities at the port of Lae were to be upgraded. The Asian Development Bank was expected to provide assistance.

Papua New Guinea Harbours Board: POB 671, Port Moresby; tel. 3211400; fax 3211546; Chair. TIMOTHY BONGA.

Port Authority of Kieta: POB 149, Kieta, North Solomons Province; tel. 9956066; fax 9956255; Port Man. SAKEUS GEM.

Port Authority of Lae: POB 563, Lae, Morobe Province; tel. 4422477; fax 4422543; Port Man. JOSHUA TARUNA.

Port Authority of Madang: POB 273, Madang; tel. 8523381; fax 8523097; e-mail gregory.fae@pngharbours.com.pg; internet www.pngharbours.com.pg; owned by PNG Harbours Ltd; Port Man. GREGORY FAE.

Port Authority of Port Moresby: POB 671, Port Moresby; tel. 211400; fax 3211546; Gen. Man. T. AMAO.

Port Authority of Rabaul: POB 592, Rabaul, East New Britain Province; tel. 9821533; fax 9821535.

Shipping Companies

Coastal Shipping Co Ltd: Sulphur Creek Rd, POB 423, Rabaul, East New Britain Province; tel. 9821746; fax 9821734; e-mail coastco@global.net.pg; f. 1967; Man. Dir HENRY CHOW.

Lutheran Shipping: POB 789, Madang; tel. 8522577; fax 8522180; e-mail finance.luship@global.net.pg.

Morehead Shipping Pty Ltd: POB 1908, Lae, Morobe Province; tel. 4423602.

New Guinea Australia Line Pty Ltd: POB 145, Port Moresby; tel. 3212377; fax 3214879; e-mail ngal@daltron.com.pg; f. 1970; operates regular container services between Australia, Papua New Guinea, Singapore, Indonesia, Vanuatu, Tuvalu and Solomon Islands; Chair. (vacant); Gen. Man. GEOFFREY CUNDLE.

P & O PNG Ltd (trading as Century Shipping Agencies): MMI House, 3rd Floor, Champion Parade, POB 1403, Port Moresby; tel. 3229200; fax 3229251; e-mail cgcpom@popng.com.pg; owned by P & O (Australia); Gen. Man. ANDREW CRIDLAND.

Papua New Guinea Shipping Corporation Pty Ltd: POB 634, Port Moresby; tel. 3220290; fax 3212815; e-mail shipping@steamships.com.pg; f. 1977; owned by Steamships Trading Co Ltd; provides a container/break-bulk service to Australia and the Pacific islands; Chair. CHRISTOPHER PRATT; Man. Dir JOHN DUNLOP.

South Sea Lines Proprietary Ltd: POB 5, Lae, Morobe Province; tel. 4423455; fax 4424884; Man. Dir R. CUNNINGHAM.

Western Tug & Barge Co P/L: POB 175, Port Moresby; tel. 3212099; fax 3217950; shipowning arm of P & O PNG; operates 24 vessels.

CIVIL AVIATION

There is an international airport at Port Moresby, Jackson's Airport, and there are more than 400 other airports and airstrips throughout the country. International services from Lae and Mount Hagen airports began in March 1999. A programme to upgrade eight regional airports over three years, with finance of $A30m. from the Australian Government, was initiated in mid-1997. New domestic and international terminal buildings were opened at Jackson's Airport in 1998, following a 13-year project financed with K120m. from the Japanese Government. A project to redevelop Tari airport was announced in late 1999. It was expected that, following redevelopment, the airport would receive international flights.

Air Niugini: POB 7186, Boroko, NCD; tel. 3259000; fax 3273482; e-mail airniugini@airniugini.com.pg; internet www.airniugini.com.pg; f. 1973; govt-owned national airline (plans to privatize the airline were announced in 1999); operates scheduled domestic cargo and passenger services within Papua New Guinea and international services to Australia, Solomon Islands, Philippines, Singapore and Japan; Chair. JOSEPH PHILLIP KAPAL; CEO ROD NELSON; Man. Dir MICHAEL BULEAU (acting).

MBA Pty Ltd: POB 170, Boroko, NCD; tel. 3252011; fax 3252219; e-mail mba@mbapng.com; internet www.mbapng.com; f. 1984; operates domestic scheduled and charter services; Chair. and CEO JOHN R. WILD; Gen. Man. SIMON D. WILD.

National Aviation Services: Boroko, NCD; f. April 2005; provides services between all small airstrips in Central, Oro, Gulf and Western provinces, primarily for the transport of agricultural products from producers to markets; Operations Man. GILBERT YENBARI; Propr and CEO TED DIRO.

Tourism

Despite Papua New Guinea's spectacular scenery and abundant wildlife, tourism makes only a small contribution to the economy. In 1998 there were 4,280 hotel beds. In 2004 visitor arrivals were estimated at 59,022. The industry earned an estimated US $75m. in 2001.

PNG Tourism Promotion Authority: POB 1291, Port Moresby; tel. 3200211; fax 3200223; e-mail tourismpng@dg.com.pg; internet www.paradiselive.org.pg; CEO PETER VINCENT.

PARAGUAY

Introductory Survey

Location, Climate, Language, Religion, Flag, Capital

The Republic of Paraguay is a land-locked country in central South America. It is bordered by Bolivia to the north, by Brazil to the east, and by Argentina to the south and west. The climate is sub-tropical. Temperatures range from an average maximum of 34.3°C (93.7°F) in January to an average minimum of 14°C (51°F) in June. The official language is Spanish, but the majority of the population speak Guaraní, an indigenous Indian language. Almost all of the inhabitants profess Christianity, and some 92% adhere to the Roman Catholic Church, the country's established religion. There is a small Protestant minority. The national flag (proportions 3 by 5) has three equal horizontal stripes, of red, white and blue. It is the only national flag with a different design on each side, having a varying emblem in the centre of the white stripe: the obverse side bears the state emblem (a white disc with a red ring bearing the words 'República del Paraguay', in yellow capitals, framing a blue disc with the five-pointed 'May Star', in yellow, surrounded by a wreath, in green), while the reverse side carries the seal of the Treasury (a white disc with a red ribbon bearing the words 'Paz y Justicia' in yellow capitals above a lion supporting a staff, surmounted by the red 'Cap of Liberty'). The capital is Asunción.

Recent History

Paraguay, ruled by Spain from the 16th century, achieved independence in 1811. In 1865 Paraguay was involved in a disastrous war against Brazil, Argentina and Uruguay (the Triple Alliance), resulting in the loss of more than one-half of its population. Paraguay also suffered heavy losses in the Chaco Wars of 1928–30 and 1932–35 against Bolivia, but won a large part of the disputed territory when the boundary was fixed in 1938. Gen. Higinio Morínigo established an authoritarian regime in 1940, but the return of a number of political exiles in 1947 precipitated a civil war in which supporters of the right-wing Asociación Nacional Republicana (Partido Colorado) defeated the Liberals and the Partido Revolucionario Febrerista, leading to the overthrow of Gen. Morínigo in June 1948. A period of great instability ensued. In May 1954 Gen. Alfredo Stroessner Mattiauda, the Army Commander-in-Chief, assumed power in a military coup. He nominated himself for the presidency, as the Colorado candidate, and was elected unopposed in July to complete the term of office of his predecessor, Federico Chávez. In 1955 Stroessner assumed extensive powers, and established a state of siege. Regular purges of the Partido Colorado membership, together with the mutual co-operation of the ruling party, the armed forces and the business community, enabled Stroessner to become the longest-serving dictator in Latin America: he was re-elected President, by large majorities, at five-yearly elections in 1958–88.

In February 1978 President Stroessner revoked the state of siege in all areas except Asunción. The assassination of the former Nicaraguan dictator, Gen. Anastasio Somoza Debayle, in Asunción in September 1980, however, caused President Stroessner to doubt the security of his own position, and the state of siege was reimposed throughout the country; harassment of leaders of the political opposition and of peasant and labour groups continued. The leader of the Partido Demócrata Cristiano, Luis Alfonso Resck, was expelled from the country in June 1981, and Domingo Laíno, leader of the Partido Liberal Radical Auténtico (PLRA), was deported in December 1982. After Ronald Reagan took office as President of the USA in 1981, Paraguay encountered less pressure from the US Administration to curb abuses of human rights, and the use of torture against detainees reportedly became widespread once more. It was estimated at this time that more than 60% of all Paraguayans resided outside the country.

The majority of opposition parties boycotted the presidential and legislative elections of February 1983, enabling Stroessner to obtain more than 90% of the votes cast in the presidential poll, and in August he formally took office for a further five-year term. In May 1983 the Government instigated a campaign of repression against students and trade unionists. In February 1984 opposition parties organized demonstrations in Asunción for the first time in 30 years.

Divisions over Stroessner's continuance in office led to factionalism within the Partido Colorado in the mid-1980s. In April 1987 Stroessner announced that the state of siege was to be ended, since extraordinary security powers were no longer necessary to maintain peace. (Later in the month Laíno was finally allowed to return to Paraguay.) However, the suppression of civil liberties and of political activity continued under the new penal code that replaced the state of siege. The level of participation in the 1988 presidential election (which took place simultaneously with legislative elections) was reported to be 93% of eligible voters, and it was announced that Stroessner had received 89% of the votes cast. However, opposition leaders (who had urged voters to boycott the elections) complained of electoral malpractice, and denounced Stroessner's re-election as fraudulent.

On 3 February 1989 Gen. Stroessner was overthrown in a coup led by Gen. Andrés Rodríguez, the second-in-command of the armed forces. Stroessner was allowed to leave for exile in Brazil, as Gen. Rodríguez assumed the presidency (in a provisional capacity) and appointed a new Council of Ministers. The interim President pledged to respect human rights and to strengthen links with neighbouring countries. At the presidential election in May Rodríguez, the candidate of the Partido Colorado, was confirmed as President, receiving 74% of the votes cast; his closest rival, Laíno, secured 20% of the votes. The Partido Colorado, having won 73% of the votes in the concurrent congressional election, automatically took two-thirds of the seats in both the Cámara de Diputados (Chamber of Deputies) and the Senado (Senate—48 and 24, respectively). The most successful opposition party was the PLRA, which obtained 19 seats in the Cámara and 10 in the Senado. Despite widespread allegations of electoral fraud, all parties agreed to respect the results.

In July 1989 the Cámara ratified the San José Pact on Human Rights, adopted by the Organization of American States (OAS, see p. 333) in 1978. In August 1989 the Congreso Nacional (National Congress—comprising the Cámara de Diputados and the Senado) initiated judicial proceedings against former government officials for violations of human rights. Following the repeal, in August 1989, of laws that had provided a basis for political repression under the Stroessner regime, the PCP was formally legalized. In November 1990, however, Rodríguez vetoed congressional proposals for the establishment of a legislative commission to investigate alleged violations of human rights.

Divisions within the Partido Colorado became evident at its annual convention in December 1989, when the 'Tradicionalistas' attempted to elect new party officials drawn exclusively from their own membership. The newly emerged Coloradismo Democrático faction, led by Blás Riquelme (a vice-president of the party at that time), succeeded in obtaining a judicial annulment of all decisions of the convention. The political crisis led to the resignation of the entire Council of Ministers. However, Rodríguez subsequently reappointed all but one of the outgoing ministers to their former posts. In February 1990 a new electoral code was adopted; this banned party affiliation for serving members of the armed forces and the police, and reformed procedures for the election of party officials. In March the 'Tradicionalista' President of the Partido Colorado, Juan Ramón Chaves, resigned. In July Dr Luis María Argaña, the acting President of the party, was dismissed from his post as Minister of Foreign Affairs, after having publicly vowed that the Partido Colorado would never relinquish power and would retain control by whatever means possible.

Paraguay's first direct municipal elections took place in May 1991. Although the Partido Colorado secured control of a majority of municipalities, the important post of mayor of Asunción was won by a relatively unknown candidate, Carlos Filizzola, the representative of a new centre-left coalition, Asunción Para Todos (APT). Defeat in the capital precipitated mutual recriminations within the increasingly fragmented Partido Colorado, and, shortly after Filizzola's election, the ruling party's youth wing, Juventud Colorada, organized a demonstration to demand the resignation of Argaña from the party presidency.

In August 1991 the Congreso Nacional approved proposals for a complete revision of the 1967 Constitution. In anticipation of the elections to a National Constituent Assembly, President Rodríguez and military leaders made concerted efforts to forge unity within the Partido Colorado, with the result that the party's three main factions, the 'Renovadores', the 'Democráticos' and the 'Autónomos' were persuaded to present a single list of candidates, under the title 'Tradicionalistas'. In the December elections the Partido Colorado won 55% of the votes cast, thus securing an overwhelming majority of the Assembly's 198 seats. The PLRA won 27% of the votes, while Constitución Para Todos, formed as a result of APT's success in the municipal elections, won 11% of the votes. The new body was convened in January 1992.

In November 1991 new legislation, drafted by President Rodríguez in co-operation with military leaders, was approved by the Congreso Nacional. The law appeared to guarantee the autonomy of the armed forces, and the definition of the role of the military was expanded to include responsibility, at the request of the Head of State, for civil defence and internal order. Apparently in contradiction of the 1990 electoral code, no restrictions were placed on political activities by serving members of the armed forces. Provision was made for the President to delegate the functions of Commander-in-Chief of the Armed Forces to a senior military officer (with the Head of State retaining only ceremonial powers as the military commander). Opposition parties protested that, should the new legislation be entrenched in the new Constitution, the armed forces would remain a 'parallel' political force, following the transition to civilian rule.

On 20 June 1992 the new Constitution was promulgated before the Constituent Assembly. Under the new Constitution, the President and the Vice-President (a new post) were to be elected by a simple majority of votes. The Constituent Assembly had ostensibly disregarded the November 1991 military legislation by confirming the President as Commander-in-Chief of the Armed Forces and excluding officers on active duty from participating directly in politics. Other significant changes in the Constitution included the abolition of the death penalty and the granting of the right to unionize and to strike to public-sector employees (excluding the armed forces and police).

In August 1992, following the party's first direct internal elections, Blás Riquelme was appointed President of the Partido Colorado. However, serious divisions within the party persisted. An internal election, conducted in December, to select the party's presidential candidate was declared to have been won by Argaña (who had resigned the position in 1992), the candidate of the far-right. However, the candidate believed to be favoured by Rodríguez, Juan Carlos Wasmosy, refused to recognize the result, claiming that the vote had been fraudulent. An electoral tribunal failed to resolve the issue, and, following intense pressure and alleged death threats by both factions, several members of the tribunal resigned. Party leaders organized an extraordinary national convention in February 1993, at which a new electoral tribunal was to be chosen. Wasmosy was eventually confirmed as the presidential candidate of the Partido Colorado. The decision was denounced by Argaña, whose supporters threatened to resign en masse from the party.

At the general election of 9 May 1993, Wasmosy was elected President with 40% of the votes cast, ahead of Laíno (32%) and Guillermo Caballero Vargas of Encuentro Nacional (EN) (23%). However, the Partido Colorado failed to gain a majority in either the Cámara or the Senado. Moreover, the faction of the Partido Colorado led by Argaña, the Movimiento de Reconciliación Colorada (MCR), negotiated with the PLRA and the EN to exclude supporters of the President-elect from appointment to important posts in the Congreso Nacional (with the support of the MCR, the overall opposition strength stood at 35 of a total of 45 seats in the Senado and 64 of the 80 seats in the Cámara, sufficient to approve legislation affecting the Constitution).

Wasmosy was inaugurated as President on 15 August 1993. The opposition expressed some concern over the composition of his first Council of Ministers, many of whom had served in the administrations of Rodríguez and Stroessner. Despite Wasmosy's apparent desire to restrict the influence of the military (he notably appointed a civilian to the post of Minister of National Defence), the designation of Gen. Lino César Oviedo Silva as Commander of the Army provoked further criticism, since, prior to the elections, Oviedo had publicly stated that the army would not accept an opposition victory.

A preliminary agreement on a 'governability pact' between the Government and the opposition, initiated in an attempt to facilitate the implementation of a coherent economic and legislative programme, was signed in October 1993, and this, in turn, facilitated an agreement between the Government and the legislature towards resolving the controversial question of judicial reform. Under the latter agreement, the two were to appoint members of the Supreme Court and the Supreme Electoral Tribunal by consensus. (The new members of the Supreme Court, enlarged from five to nine justices in accordance with the 1992 Constitution, were eventually elected in April 1995). In January 1994 Blás Riquelme resigned as President of the Partido Colorado, following disagreements with Wasmosy. By early 1995 speculation concerning unrest in the armed forces, prompted by Wasmosy's recent uncompromising manipulation of the ranks of the military high command, and by a reported clash of interests between the President and Gen. Oviedo, had reached such a level that Wasmosy was forced to issue a public statement discounting the possibility of a military coup. In February Wasmosy announced a further reorganization of the military high command, thus consolidating his position of authority.

In May 1995 an investigation into corruption at the Central Bank revealed the existence of an illegal 'parallel' financial system involving a network of institutions, including the Central Bank. The investigation precipitated the collapse of the system and a severe liquidity crisis. In December the Government issued an emergency decree extending the powers of intervention of the Central Bank, with the aim of resolving the financial crisis and restoring confidence in the banking sector. By late December the Central Bank had disbursed almost $400m. of reserves in order to contain the liquidity crisis, which had resulted in the closure of several financial institutions.

In early March 1996 some 30,000 farm workers conducted a demonstration outside the building of the Congreso Nacional, in support of demands for agrarian reform and improved working conditions, and in protest at government economic policy—in particular the privatization of state assets and Paraguay's membership of Mercosur (see below), which, its opponents maintained, led to excessive competition from agricultural imports. The demonstration prompted the resignation of the Minister of Agriculture and Livestock. In late March labour confederations organized a 24-hour general strike in support of demands for a 31% increase in all salaries, measures to alleviate rural poverty, a referendum on the privatization of state assets and a renegotiation of Paraguay's involvement in Mercosur. The strike was notable for the support it received from the Confederación Paraguaya de Trabajadores, a labour confederation dominated by supporters of the Partido Colorado. The Government's failure to respond to the protesters' demands prompted a further, 48-hour general strike in early May, when additional demands were made for the reversal of government plans to privatize the social security system and for the dismissal of the Minister of Justice and Labour. Violent confrontations between demonstrators and the security forces resulted in numerous injuries and the arrest of several leading labour representatives.

In April 1996 a serious confrontation arose between President Wasmosy and Gen. Oviedo, with the result that a military coup was only narrowly averted. Following an attempt by Oviedo to postpone the internal elections of the Partido Colorado, Wasmosy accused Oviedo of contravening the ban on political activity by serving members of the military, and, on 22 April, demanded his resignation as Commander of the Army. When Oviedo refused to resign, Wasmosy promptly announced his dismissal, naming Gen. Oscar Rodrigo Díaz Delmas as his successor. Oviedo rejected the decision, and installed himself at the army headquarters in Asunción, from where he issued demands for Wasmosy's resignation and threatened, with the support of the army, violently to overthrow the Government. Wasmosy took refuge in the US embassy building. The following day, in a demonstration of popular support for Wasmosy, thousands rallied outside the presidential palace. Declarations of support were also issued by the Commanders of the Navy and the Air Force, and by the Congreso Nacional. External pressure for Wasmosy to resist the overthrow of democratic rule came from the USA, which immediately suspended military aid, and from neighbouring South American countries, and was sufficient to prompt Wasmosy to seek a compromise: in return for his retirement from military service, Oviedo was given the position of Minister of Defence. However, the measure was condemned by the legislature, which threatened to initiate impeachment proceedings against Wasmosy should Oviedo be appointed. Public opinion was also strongly opposed to the appointment, and on 25 April, following Oviedo's retirement from military service and his replacement by Gen. Díaz, Wasmosy withdrew the offer of the defence portfolio. Despite fears of an outright coup, Oviedo accepted the final outcome of the dispute and announced that, as a private citizen, he would now dedicate himself to the political campaign of the Partido Colorado.

In late April 1996 the internal elections of the Partido Colorado resulted in victory for Dr Luis María Argaña, the leader of the Movimiento de Reconciliación Colorada faction, who was appointed President of the party. In May Gen. (retd) Oviedo announced the creation of a new faction of the Partido Colorado, the Unión Nacional de Colorados Eticos (UNACE). In that month, in an effort to purge the armed forces of officers sympathetic to Oviedo, Wasmosy announced the retirement of some 20 high-ranking officers, including the Commander of the First Army Corps and the Chief of Staff of the Army. In June Oviedo was placed under house arrest on charges of insurrection and insubordination with respect to the events of April. In July Oviedo's assets were seized and the order for his detention was revised from house arrest to preventative imprisonment. This development provoked protest by Oviedo's supporters, who rallied outside the Congreso Nacional to demand his release. Wasmosy continued to reorganize the military hierarchy, replacing several senior officers. In August an appeal court acquitted Oviedo of the charge of insurrection, ruling that there was insufficient evidence to suggest that he had made military preparations to overturn the constitutional order. In December 1996 Oviedo was acquitted of the lesser charge of insubordination.

In early January 1997 Wasmosy indicated his willingness to effect a *rapprochement* with Argaña's faction of the Partido Colorado, with a view to uniting in support of a single nominee—the Minister of Education and Culture, Dr Oscar Nicanor Duarte Frutos—as the party's presidential candidate. However, in February Wasmosy announced his intention to support his own nominee—the Minister of Finance, Carlos Facetti Masulli. The decision provoked Duarte's resignation from the Government, as well as those of the Ministers of the Interior and of Integration.

In June 1997 further evidence of illegal 'parallel' operations in the nation's banking sector emerged when the Central Bank was forced to intervene in the operations of three financial institutions (Banco de Ahorros Paraguayos, Banco Unión, and Banco de Inversiones del Paraguay) that were experiencing serious liquidity problems. The crisis prompted the resignation in late June of the Minister of Industry and Commerce, who was a shareholder in Banco Unión and brother of the bank's president.

In August 1997 Juan Carlos Galaverna, a Partido Colorado senator and prominent supporter of Dr Argaña, presented a motion to the Senado seeking the impeachment of President Wasmosy on the grounds that he had contravened the Constitution by attempting to influence the outcome of the forthcoming Partido Colorado primary election; Wasmosy denied the allegations. Although the impeachment motion was unsuccessful, it illustrated the extent of division between rival factions of the Partido Colorado in advance of the forthcoming general election, scheduled for 10 May 1998. In September Gen. Oviedo succeeded in securing the Partido Colorado's presidential nomination, defeating Wasmosy's preferred candidate, Facetti, and Argaña himself, in the party's primary. However, Argaña's faction, which effectively controlled the party's executive board, refused to accept the outcome of the ballot, claiming that it had been fraudulent, and presented a legal challenge to the result.

In early October 1997 Wasmosy issued an executive order for the 'disciplinary arrest', for a period of 30 days, of Gen. Oviedo; the grounds for the detention was contempt of the President and Commander-in-Chief of the Armed Forces, after Oviedo had publicly accused Wasmosy of corruption. An appeal court subsequently issued an injunction suspending the arrest order, prompting Wasmosy to file a petition requesting that the Supreme Court uphold his order. Oviedo, meanwhile, had gone into hiding. In December, following a ruling by the Supreme Court endorsing the arrest order issued by Wasmosy in October, Oviedo surrendered to the military authorities in order to serve the 30-day period of confinement. Later that month the Supreme Electoral Tribunal rejected the petition by Argaña's faction of the Partido Colorado to have the results of the party's primary election annulled, and in early January 1998 it registered Oviedo as the official presidential candidate of the Partido Colorado, without the endorsement of the party's executive board. Oviedo completed his period of confinement on 11 January; however, a special military tribunal, established by Wasmosy to investigate the events of the coup attempt led by Oviedo in April 1996, ordered that he be detained indefinitely pending the results of the investigation. In March the special military tribunal found Oviedo guilty of crimes committed against the order and security of the armed forces, and also of sedition, and sentenced him to 10 years' imprisonment. In the following month the Supreme Court ratified the military tribunal's decision and the Supreme Electoral Tribunal consequently annulled Oviedo's presidential candidacy. In accordance with the law, the candidacy of the Partido Colorado was assumed by Raúl Cubas Grau, hitherto the vice-presidential nominee; Argaña was to be the new candidate for the vice-presidency.

The presidential election of 10 May 1998 resulted in victory for candidate Raúl Cubas Grau, who secured some 55% of the votes cast, ahead of the candidate of the Alianza Democrática (an electoral alliance comprising the PLRA and the EN), Domingo Laíno, who received 44% of the votes. Partido Colorado candidates were also most successful at legislative elections and at elections for provincial administrators held concurrently. The elections were generally considered to have been free and fair, and turn-out was estimated at an impressive 85%. Cubas Grau's election campaign had emphasized his support for his long-time political ally, Oviedo. Prior to the inauguration of the new administration, in July Vice-President-elect Argaña (a staunch opponent of Oviedo) concluded an informal political pact involving his faction of the Partido Colorado and the opposition PLRA and EN, effectively depriving Cubas Grau of a congressional majority, while in early August President Wasmosy implemented a comprehensive reorganization of the military high command, which promoted the interests of many of Oviedo's military opponents.

Cubas Grau duly took office on 15 August 1998, and a new Council of Ministers, largely composed of supporters of Gen. Oviedo, was sworn in on the same day. On 18 August, deliberately circumventing the new law restricting presidential pardons, Cubas Grau issued a decree commuting Oviedo's prison sentence to time already served. On the following day the Congreso Nacional voted to condemn the decree and to initiate proceedings to impeach the President for unconstitutional procedure. (A successful impeachment would result in the elevation of Oviedo's severest critic, Vice-President Argaña, to the presidency.) The new President's confrontational stance (and the release of Oviedo) also provoked dissent among his own supporters and associates; Cubas Grau's brother, Carlos, resigned the industry and commerce portfolio in the new Council of Ministers later that month. On 5 December the Argaña faction-controlled central apparatus of the Partido Colorado expelled Oviedo from the party. While the Congreso Nacional was unable to muster the two-thirds' majority support necessary to impeach President Cubas Grau, the country remained in effective political deadlock, prompting serious concerns in the business community that the country's mounting economic difficulties would not be addressed.

In March 1999, however, the political impasse ended dramatically. On 23 March Vice-President Argaña was assassinated, prompting nation-wide speculation that Oviedo was behind the attack, and galvanizing the Congreso Nacional sufficiently to secure the support of the two-thirds' majority needed to initiate Cubas Grau's impeachment. Increasing tensions were exacerbated three days later, by the killing of seven protesters who were demonstrating in Asunción in support of demands for the resignation of the President, in the light of Argaña's assassination. On 28 March Cubas Grau resigned the presidency and sought refuge in Brazil, while Oviedo crossed the border to Argentina. (In February 2002 Cubas Grau surrendered to the Paraguayan authorities to face trial for the killings of the protesters and was placed under house arrest until June 2003, when he was released without the charges against him having been dismissed.) In early April the judicial authorities ordered the arrest of Oviedo for involvement in the death of Argaña, after three of his close collaborators were identified as the assassins. (In October 2000 Maj.-Gen. Reinaldo Servin, Constantino Rodas and Pablo Vera Esteche were sentenced to long prison terms for their roles in the assassination.) However, the Argentine Government rejected Paraguay's request for extradition, resulting in a rapid deterioration in the relationship between the two countries. When the extradition request was rejected for the second time in early September, the Paraguayan Government recalled its ambassador to Argentina. The Argentine authorities did, however, banish Oviedo to Tierra del Fuego in the extreme south after he repeatedly violated the terms of his asylum by making political statements. However, Oviedo left Argentina in early December in order to avoid being extradited by the new Argentine Government of Fernando de la Rúa. (In April 2004 the Supreme Court upheld the sentences against the alleged perpetrators of the killing.)

Meanwhile, in accordance with the terms of the Constitution, in the absence of the elected President and Vice-President, the President of the Congreso Nacional, the pro-Argaña Partido Colorado senator, Luis González Macchi, was swiftly installed as Head of State. He announced the composition of a multi-party Government of National Unity at the end of March 1999. In late April, following careful scrutiny of the articles of the Constitution, the Supreme Court ruled that González Macchi should serve the remainder of Cubas Grau's presidential term (scheduled to expire in 2003). The Court also ruled that an election to select a new Vice-President should be conducted. Hoping to consolidate the new Government, González Macchi announced that his own party would not present a vice-presidential candidate. However, prominent figures within the Partido Colorado decided to contest the election none the less, precipitating tension with the PLRA (the main opposition and largest coalition partner), which had effectively been promised the post. Meanwhile, factionalism within the PLRA placed increasing strains on the Government of National Unity. Events culminated in February 2000 when PLRA members voted to withdraw from the ruling coalition, depriving the Government of a legislative majority. The Partido Colorado's remaining coalition partner, the EN, was, furthermore, divided over its continuing participation in the Government.

In late May 1999 González Macchi forcibly retired more than 100 army officers, including several high-ranking supporters of Gen. Oviedo. By mid-November another 45 senior commanders, who were thought to be supporters of Oviedo, had been replaced. However, the reorganization did not prevent a coup attempt, in mid-May 2000, by rebellious soldiers thought to be sympathetic to Oviedo. It was swiftly defeated by the Government (most army brigades and the air force remained loyal to the President), which declared a 30-day nation-wide state of emergency, assuming extraordinary powers that resulted in the arrest of more than 70 people, mostly members of the security forces. Oviedo denied any involvement with the coup, but in mid-June he was arrested by Brazilian police in Foz do Iguaçú, near the Brazilian border with Paraguay. In March 2001 the Brazilian Chief Prosecutor ruled that Oviedo could be extradited, but in December the Supreme Court rejected the ruling, stating that Oviedo was a victim of political persecution, and released him from imprisonment.

The initial popularity of the Government of National Unity collapsed as thousands of peasants, assembled by rural organizations, mobilized on several occasions during 1999 to protest against the Government's lack of action on rural issues. In response to the protests, in November the Government offered a US $168m. rescue package for the agricultural and livestock sector, mostly for debt-refinancing schemes. In March 2000 the Government announced a scheme to assist 250,000 small farmers. However, by the end of the month there were an estimated 10,000 smallholders camped outside the Congreso building. (The protests continued until March 2001, when government concessions were eventually secured.) Strikes were undertaken by power and telecommunications workers and by public-sector workers during March and June 2000, respectively. However, the Government insisted it would continue with its 'state restructuring' programme. In mid-November the Congreso Nacional approved legislation allowing for the sale of the state railway, water and telecommunications companies.

In April 2000 the Partido Colorado nominated Félix Argaña, son of the late Vice-President, to be its candidate in the forthcoming vice-presidential ballot. However, at the election, which was finally held on 13 August, the 53-year Colorado monopoly on power was ended when Argaña was narrowly defeated (by less than 1% of the votes cast) by the PLRA candidate, Julio César Franco. The election of Franco, whose candidacy was endorsed by Oviedo, increased the divisions within the Partido Colorado and resulted in the resignation of the Minister of National Defence, Nelson Argaña, another son of the late Vice-President.

In February 2001 the Minister of Education and Culture, Oscar Nicanor Duarte Frutos, resigned in order to campaign for the presidency of the Partido Colorado, which he secured, with almost 50% of the vote, in an election in early May. At the same time, the Government was further undermined by tensions between the President and the Vice-President; Franco, as the most senior elected government official, demanded the resignation of President González Macchi in the name of democratic legitimacy. In mid-March the Government's problems intensified when the three EN representatives in the Council of Ministers threatened to resign in response to allegations that the President's car was a stolen vehicle, illegally smuggled into the country. In an attempt to restore confidence, González Macchi carried out a cabinet reshuffle.

Another corruption scandal emerged in early May 2001, which forced the President of the Central Bank, Washington Ashwell, to resign over his alleged involvement in the fraudulent transfer of US $16m. to a US bank account. An opposition attempt to impeach the President over his alleged involvement in the fraud was defeated by the Cámara de Diputados in August. In September several thousand protesters marched in Asunción to demand the resignation of González Macchi. In April 2002 González Macchi was formally charged with involvement in the corruption scandal.

In late January 2002 the credibility of the Government was further undermined after two leaders of the left-wing party Movimiento Patria Libre (MPL) alleged that they had been illegally detained for 13 days and tortured by the police, with the knowledge of government ministers, as part of an investigation into a kidnapping case. In response to the allegations, in early February the head of the national police force and his deputy, as well as the head of the judicial investigations department, were dismissed. Following sustained public and political pressure the Minister of the Interior, Julio César Fanego, and the Minister of Justice and Labour, Silvio Ferreira Fernández, resigned soon afterwards, although both protested their innocence. In addition, the national intelligence agency, the Secretaría Nacional de Informaciones, was disbanded. The Cámara de Diputados issued a statement assigning some responsibility for the detention of the MPL leaders to the President and the Attorney-General, and describing the event as 'state terrorism'. In April former President Wasmosy was convicted of misuse of public funds and sentenced to four years' imprisonment. (His conviction was quashed, however, in September 2004).

Throughout 2002 an alliance of farmers, trade unions and left-wing organizations staged mass protests throughout the country to call for an end to the Government's free-market policies and to protest at widely perceived government corruption. In response to the mounting opposition, in June the Government suspended its planned privatization of the state telecommunications company, Corporación Paraguaya de Comunicaciones (COPACO). Nevertheless, the protests continued as the economic situation worsened, prompting González Macchi to declare a state of emergency in July, which was lifted two days later after clashes between anti-Government protesters and security forces resulted in two fatalities.

In August 2002 the IMF approved, subject to conditions, a US $200m. stand-by loan to Paraguay. However, in November the Congreso failed to approve the financial reforms necessary to fulfil the Fund's conditions. The congressional impasse prompted the resignation of the Minister of Finance. In early December the lower house of the Congreso voted in favour of the impeachment of President González Macchi on five charges of corruption. In an attempt to avoid the charges, González Macchi offered to step down early from office, immediately following the presidential election that was scheduled to be held in April 2003 (his term of office officially ended in August of that year). However, in February 2003 the Senate voted narrowly against impeachment. Proceedings began against González Macchi in mid-2004 on charges relating to the May 2001 embezzlement scandal; in February 2005 further charges were brought against him for misuse of public funds.

Legislative and presidential elections were held on 27 April 2003. The ruling Asociación Nacional Republicana—Partido Colorado extended its unbroken 56-year hold on power as its candidate, Oscar Nicanor Duarte Frutos, won 37.1% of the votes cast in the presidential ballot, compared with the 24.0% attracted by the PLRA candidate and former Vice-President, Julio César Franco, who had resigned in October 2002 in order to contest the election. A businessman, Pedro Nicolás Fadul Niella, of the Patria Querida (Beloved Fatherland) movement, came third with 21.3% of the votes, while Guillermo Sánchez Guffanti of UNACE attracted 13.5% of the ballot. However, the Colorados secured only 37 of the 80 seats in the Cámara de Diputados, thus losing its majority in the chamber (the PLRA won 21 seats, the Patria Querida 10 seats, UNACE 10 seats and the Partido País Solidario two seats). The Partido Colorado performed better in the upper-house election, winning 16 of the 45 seats in the Senado, followed by the PLRA with 12 seats and the Patria Querida with eight seats.

At his inauguration on 15 August 2003, President Duarte Frutos reiterated his election pledges to reduce corruption, improve the public finances and restore the country's international credibility. A number of well-regarded technocrats were appointed to the Council of Ministers, notably including the new Minister of Finance, Dionisio Borda. On taking office, Duarte Frutos announced his intention to effect wide-ranging judicial reform; to this effect, on 24 October the Congreso reached consensus on impeachment proceedings against six Supreme Court judges suspected of corruption. Four of the judges resigned during the impeachment process, which finally resulted in the indictment of the remaining two judges on 12 December. However, despite hopes that political influence in the selection of new judges might be avoided, two of the six new Supreme Court judges appointed in March 2004 were Colorado supporters. In April cross-party consensus was reached on initiating proceedings against the Attorney-General, Oscar Germán Latorre, following a series of corruption scandals. However, the motion for the impeachment of Latorre was rejected by the Cámara de Diputados, having failed to obtain the necessary two-thirds' majority. (Latorre was replaced as Attorney-General by former Minister of Justice and Labour Rubén Candia Amarilla in August 2005.)

In mid-December 2003 the Duarte Frutos administration's credibility was considerably enhanced by the IMF's decision to grant a US $73m. credit to Paraguay, in support of a series of planned economic reforms. A series of scandals in late 2003, including the discovery of illegal transfers by employees of the Instituto de Previsión Social and the Banco Nacional de Fomento, in addition to widely acknowledged corruption in the operation of the Yacyretá hydroelectric dam, underlined the urgent need for international assistance in the new Government's efforts to revitalize the economy. The Fund approved its first review of the programme in April 2004 (see Economic Affairs).

In June 2004 Oviedo returned voluntarily from Brazil. On arrival, he was taken to military prison to serve a 10-year sentence for organizing an attempted coup in 1996 against the Government of former President Wasmosy (see above). Oviedo was also to be tried on other charges still pending against him (see above). In October, however, Oviedo was provisionally acquitted of having organized the failed coup attempt of May 2000, and in January 2005 charges against him relating to a discovered arms cache were dismissed. In mid-March the Supreme Court ruled that Oviedo would nevertheless have to serve out his prison sentence; Oviedo subsequently announced his intention to appeal to the Inter-American Court of Human Rights (IACHR, see p. 334). Throughout the rest of 2005 demonstrations against his detention were staged by his supporters.

In September 2004 arrest warrants were issued for former President Stroessner and some 30 retired military personnel (including former Chief of Staff Alejandoro Fretes Davalos) The warrants related to three Paraguayan nationals who 'disappeared' in Argentina, allegedly as a result of 'Plan Condor' (an intelligence operation to eliminate opponents of the Latin American military dictatorships in the 1970s).

In October 2004 the kidnap and murder of an 11-year-old child provoked a vociferous public outcry against the perceived deterioration of security in Paraguay. In response, President Duarte dismissed the Minister of the Interior, Orlando Fiorotto Sanchez (who was replaced by Attorney-General Nelson Mora), and the head of the national police, Umberto Nuñez. In February Mora was himself dismissed—in addition to some 50 senior members of the police force—following the discovery on 16 February of the body of Cecilia Cubas under a house in a suburb of Asunción. Cubas, the daughter of former President Raúl Cubas Grau, had been kidnapped in the previous September. In advance of the police inquiry, President Duarte held the MPL responsible for the killing and subsequently supported claims made by the Colombian President, Alvaro Uribe Vélez, that the MPL had been assisted by the Fuerzas Armadas Revolucionarias de Colombia—Ejército del Pueblo (FARC—EP).

There were several changes to the Council of Ministers in 2005. In mid-April President Duarte dismissed Julio César Velázquez from the post of Minister of Public Health and Social Welfare after Velázquez announced his candidacy for the leadership of the Partido Colorado. In May Juan Darío Monges, the Minister of Justice and Labour, resigned, apparently in order also to contest the Colorado leadership election. He was replaced by Rubén Candia Amarilla. In the same month Dionisio Borda resigned as Minister of Finance, ostensibly owing to disagreements with the incoming Central Bank President Mónica Luján Pérez Dos Santos, although Borda later admitted that his primary motivation was his opposition to President Duarte's economic policy, which, Borda argued, aimed at unsustainable growth levels without providing for necessary fiscal and monetary reforms. Borda was succeeded by Ernst Begen, hitherto Minister of Industry and Commerce. That portfolio was given to Raúl José Vera Bogado, a former president of the Central Bank.

In November 2005 President Duarte announced plans to reform the Constitution in order to allow for presidential re-election. At that time, Duarte was also seeking re-election to leadership of the Colorado party, which he had ceded on taking office as President. However, opposition groups argued that it was unconstitutional for the President to hold any additional public office, and, in mid-December, a motion to impeach President Duarte was proposed in the Cámara de Diputados by the opposition Patria Querida. However, the proposal was defeated, receiving only 39 votes in favour (a minimum two-thirds' majority, or 53 votes, was required to pass an impeachment motion). In January 2006 the Electoral Court rejected criminal charges against President Duarte, brought by the leader of the Frente Colorado faction, Luis Talavera, for attempting to hold two public offices, although the Court ruled that it would be unconstitutional for Duarte to hold another office concurrently with the presidency of the Republic.

In February 2006, nevertheless, Duarte won a convincing victory in the Colorado party's leadership election, defeating his rival Osvaldo Domínguez Dibb, who represented the pro-Stroessner ('Stronista') faction of the party. In early March the Supreme Court overturned the Electoral Court's February ruling that forbade the President of the Republic from holding an additional office; as a result, on 13 March Duarte assumed the leadership of his party. On the same day he announced a proposed referendum on whether to amend the Consitution to allow presidential re-election. In response to the Supreme Court's ruling, opposition groups again initiated impeachment proceedings against Duarte, as well as against the five judges of the Court's Constitutional Panel. Faced with such resistance, the following day Duarte stepped down from the party presidency (José Alderete Rodríguez, hitherto Minister of Public Works and Communications, assumed the post in an acting capacity). Although Duarte withdrew his proposal to amend the Constitution, impeachment proceedings were ongoing in early April.

Throughout 2003 and 2004 strikes, roadblocks, marches and illegal land occupations were organized by farmers and indigenous groups in protest at a range of government policies, including agrarian reform and privatizations. In response to the continuing civil unrest, in September 2004 the Government signed an agreement to distribute some 13,000 ha of land in six western departments to landless peasants; the main peasant grouping, the Federación Nacional Campesina de Paraguay (FNC), however, maintained its demand for the redistribution of some 100,000 ha of land. In October President Duarte submitted to the Congreso a proposal for a new tax on landowners that would raise an estimated US $100m.–$125m. in government revenues (intended for poverty reduction rather than agrarian reform). Illegal land occupations and other protests continued in late 2004 and 2005, none the less, resulting in the arrest of hundreds of protesters and several fatalities. In February 2005 Duarte announced the creation of a three-year security plan, which, among other measures, would provide for a greater role of the armed forces in policing rural areas. The plan was publicly opposed in Asunción by some 5,000 rural activists in March. In the same month, following discussions in the Colombian capital with President Uribe, Duarte announced that the Paraguayan and Colombian security services would strengthen bilateral co-operation.

In March 1991 the Presidents and Ministers of Foreign Affairs of Argentina, Brazil, Uruguay and Paraguay signed a formal agreement in Asunción creating a common market of the 'Southern Cone' countries, the Mercado Común del Sur (Mercosur, see p. 363). The agreement allowed for the dismantling of trade barriers between the four countries, and entered into full operation in 1995.

Government

Under the 1992 Constitution, legislative power is held by the bicameral Congreso Nacional (National Congress), whose members serve for five years. The Senado (Senate) has 45 members, and the Cámara de Diputados (Chamber of Deputies) 80 members. Elections to the legislature are by universal adult suffrage. Executive power is held by the President, directly elected for a single term of five years at the same time as the legislature. The President of the Republic governs with the assistance of a Vice-President and an appointed Council of Ministers. Paraguay is divided into 17 departments, each administered by an elected governor.

Defence

The armed forces totalled 10,300 men (including 2,000 conscripts) in August 2005. There was an army of 7,600 men and an air force of 1,100. The navy, which is largely river-based, had 1,600 men, including 900 marines. There is also a 14,800-strong paramilitary police force, including 4,000 conscripts. Military service, which is compulsory, lasts for 12 months in the army and for two years in the navy. The defence budget for 2005 totalled an estimated 359,000m. guaraníes.

Economic Affairs

In 2004, according to estimates by the World Bank, Paraguay's gross national income (GNI), measured at average 2002–04 prices, was US $6,752.4m., equivalent to $1,170 per head (or $4,870 per head on an international purchasing-power parity basis). During 1995–2004, it was estimated, the population increased at an average annual rate of 2.3%, while gross domestic product (GDP) per head decreased, in real terms, by an average of 1.3% per year. Overall GDP declined, in real terms, at an average annual rate of 1.0% in 1995–2004; according to the Central Bank, GDP increased by an estimated 4.1% in 2004.

According to provisional figures, agriculture (including forestry, hunting and fishing) contributed an estimated 23.9% of GDP in 2004. In 2003 an estimated 32.9% of the economically active population were employed in the sector. The principal cash crop is soya bean seeds, which accounted for an estimated 35.4% of total export revenue in 2003. The production of soya had reportedly fallen in 2004, owing to adverse weather conditions. Other significant crops are sugar cane, cassava, sunflowers, cotton, wheat and maize. Timber and wood manufactures provided an estimated 3.5% of export revenues in 2003. The raising of livestock (particularly cattle and pigs) is also important. Meat accounted for an estimated 4.1% of export earnings in 2003. Agricultural GDP increased at an average annual rate of 2.9% in 1995–2004; real agricultural GDP increased by 3.8% in 2003 and by 5.1% in 2004.

According to provisional figures, industry (including mining, manufacturing, construction and power) contributed an estimated 23.3% of GDP in 2004 and employed 16.0% of the working population in 2000. Industrial GDP increased by an average of 0.3% per year in 1995–2004; the sector decreased by 0.3% in 2003, but increased by 2.1% in 2004.

Paraguay has almost no commercially exploited mineral resources, and the mining sector employed only 0.1% of the labour force in 2000 and contributed a provisional 0.1% of GDP in 2004. Production is confined to gypsum, kaolin and limestone. However, foreign companies have been involved in exploration for gold and petroleum deposits, and deposits of natural gas were discovered in 1994.

Manufacturing contributed a provisional 15.6% of GDP in 2004 and employed 11.2% of the working population in 2000. The main branch of manufacturing (in terms of value added) was production of food and beverages. The other principal sectors were wood and wood products, handicrafts, paper, printing and publishing, hides and furs, and non-metallic mineral products. Manufacturing GDP decreased at an average annual rate of 0.2% in 1995–2004. Manufacturing GDP decreased by 0.1% in 2003, but increased by 2.1% in 2004.

Energy is derived almost completely from hydroelectric power. Imports of mineral fuels comprised an estimated 20.5% of the value of total merchandise imports in 2003. Ethyl alcohol (ethanol), derived from sugar cane, is widely used as a component of vehicle fuel.

The services sector contributed a provisional 52.8% of GDP in 2004, and engaged 48.8% of the working population in 2000. Paraguay traditionally serves as an entrepôt for regional trade. The GDP of the services sector increased by an average of 0.3% per year in 1995–2004; the sector decreased by 0.4% in 2003, but increased by 3.9% in 2004.

In 2004 Paraguay recorded a visible trade deficit of US $391.3m., but there was a surplus of $20.4m. on the current account of the balance of payments. According to preliminary figures, in 2003 the principal source of registered imports was Brazil (32.5%); other major suppliers in this year were Argentina, the People's Republic of China and the USA. Brazil was also the principal market for registered exports in that year (a preliminary 34.2% of total exports); other notable purchasers were Uruguay and Argentina. The principal exports in 2003 were, according to preliminary estimates, soya bean seeds and animal feed. The principal imports were mineral fuels, machinery and transport equipment, and chemicals and related products.

In 2005 there was, according to revised projections, an overall general budget deficit of 71m. guaraníes (equivalent to 0.3% of GDP). Paraguay's total external debt was US $3,210m. at the end of 2003, of which $2,658m. was long-term public debt. In that year the cost of debt-servicing was equivalent to 9.9% of the total value of exports of goods and services. Annual inflation averaged 8.9% in 1995–2004; consumer prices increased by an average of 14.3% in 2003 and by 4.4% in 2004. An estimated 8.1% of the labour force were unemployed in 2003.

Paraguay is a member of the Inter-American Development Bank (IDB, see p. 284), of the Latin American Integration Association (ALADI, see p. 305), of the Latin American Economic System (SELA, see p. 386) and of the Mercado Común del Sur (Mercosur, see p. 363). In December 2004 Paraguay was one of 12 countries that were signatories to the agreement, signed in Cusco, Peru, creating the South American Community of Nations (Comunidad Sudamericana de Naciones), intended to promote greater regional economic integration, due to become operational by 2007.

The Government was paralysed by a lack of resources until 1999, when Taiwan agreed to underwrite a $400m. bond issue and when the Government agreed on a long-term structural reform strategy with the IMF and World Bank. However, in May 2002 the Government was again forced to postpone the sale of the state telecommunications company, Corporación Paraguaya de Comunicaciones (COPACO), following mass protests. In that year the economic situation worsened, partly as a result of the continuing financial crisis in neighbouring Argentina. Political instability obliged the Government to postpone the planned sales of state assets, revenues from which had been intended to reduce the fiscal deficit. An IMF stand-by loan of US $200m., approved in August, was conditional on the Government implementing a controversial fiscal reform programme, known as the 'economic transition law' or 'el impuestazo' (the 'tax shock'), but the proposed legislation was rejected by the legislature in November. A series of financial scandals relating to state-owned enterprises in 2003, as well as the collapse of the private bank Multibanco in June of that year, further undermined investor confidence. However, the economic policies set out by the new administration of President Oscar Nicanor Duarte Frutos, which took office in August, resulted in the agreement of a $73m. IMF stand-by loan in December, again on condition of structural reform. Some $44m. was disbursed immediately, and the Fund approved the reviews of its programme in April and December 2004. In March 2005 the IMF, gave a broadly positive assessment of the Government's economic management, while encouraging further reform. In November the IMF released a further $71.2m. in funding. Government revenues increased significantly in both 2004 and 2005, owing to improved tax collection and a widening of the tax base. Nevertheless, in the face of widespread public opposition, the Government still was unable to proceed with its privatization programme in 2005. In September of that year the Government denied persistent reports that it was planning to negotiate a bilateral free trade agreement with the USA or to allow US troops to construct a permanent military base in the country. The Government also denied that it was considering Paraguay's withdrawal from Mercosur. A reduced fiscal deficit of 71m. guaraníes was forecast in 2005. Investor confidence continued to be dampened by perceived widespread public-sector corruption and inefficiency. According to IMF projections, the annual rate of inflation increased in 2005, to 10.0%. Growth in 2005, which was impeded by low world market prices for soya, was put at 3.0%.

Education

Education is, where possible, compulsory for six years, to be undertaken between six and 12 years of age, but there are insufficient schools, particularly in the remote parts of the country. Primary education begins at the age of six and lasts for six years. Secondary education, beginning at 12 years of age, lasts for a further six years, comprising two cycles of three years each. In 2001 91.5% of children in the relevant age-group were enrolled at primary schools, while secondary enrolment included

PARAGUAY

an estimated 50.1% of children in the relevant age-group. There is one state and one Roman Catholic university in Asunción. Expenditure by the Ministry of Education in 1996 amounted to 777,652m. guaraníes, equivalent to some 18.6% of total government spending.

Public Holidays

2006: 1 January (New Year's Day), 3 February (San Blás, Patron Saint of Paraguay), 1 March (Heroes' Day), 13 April (Maundy Thursday), 14 April (Good Friday), 1 May (Labour Day), 14–15 May (Independence Day celebrations), 25 May (Ascension Day), 12 June (Peace of Chaco), 15 June (Corpus Christi), 15 August (Founding of Asunción), 25 August (Constitution Day), 29 September (Battle of Boquerón), 12 October (Day of the Race, anniversary of the discovery of America), 1 November (All Saints' Day), 8 December (Immaculate Conception), 25 December (Christmas Day).

2007: 1 January (New Year's Day), 3 February (San Blás, Patron Saint of Paraguay), 1 March (Heroes' Day), 5 April (Maundy Thursday), 6 April (Good Friday), 1 May (Labour Day), 14–15 May (Independence Day celebrations), 17 May (Ascension Day), 7 June (Corpus Christi), 12 June (Peace of Chaco), 15 August (Founding of Asunción), 25 August (Constitution Day), 29 September (Battle of Boquerón), 12 October (Day of the Race, anniversary of the discovery of America), 1 November (All Saints' Day), 8 December (Immaculate Conception), 25 December (Christmas Day).

Weights and Measures

The metric system is in force.

Statistical Survey

Sources (unless otherwise stated): Dirección General de Estadística, Encuestas y Censos, Naciones Unidas, esq. Saavedra, Fernando de la Mora, Zona Norte; tel. (21) 51-1016; fax (21) 50-8493; internet www.dgeec.gov.py; Banco Central del Paraguay, Avda Federación Rusa y Marecos, Casilla 861, Barrio Santo Domingo, Asunción; tel. (21) 61-0088; fax (21) 60-8149; e-mail ccs@bcp.gov.py; internet www.bcp.gov.py; Secretaría Técnica de Planificación, Presidencia de la República, Iturbe y Eligio Ayala, Asunción.

Area and Population

AREA, POPULATION AND DENSITY

Area (sq km)	406,752*
Population (census results)	
26 August 1992	4,152,588
28 August 2002	
Males	2,627,831
Females	2,555,249
Total	5,183,080
Population (UN estimates at mid-year)†	
2003	5,878,000
2004	6,017,000
Density (per sq km) at mid-2004	14.8

* 157,048 sq miles.
† Source: UN, *World Population Prospects: The 2004 Revision*.

DEPARTMENTS
(census of August 2002)

	Area (sq km)	Population	Density (per sq km)	Capital
Alto Paraguay (incl. Chaco) .	82,349	13,250	0.2	Fuerte Olimpo
Alto Paraná .	14,895	559,769	37.6	Ciudad del Este
Amambay . .	12,933	115,320	8.9	Pedro Juan Caballero
Asunción . .	117	510,910	4,366.8	—
Boquerón (incl. Nueva Asunción) .	91,669	43,480	0.5	Doctor Pedro P. Peña
Caaguazú . .	11,474	443,311	38.6	Coronel Oviedo
Caazapá . .	9,496	139,080	14.6	Caazapá
Canindeyú . .	14,667	140,250	9.6	Salto del Guairá
Central . .	2,465	1,362,650	552.8	Asunción
Concepción . .	18,051	178,900	9.9	Concepción
Cordillera . .	4,948	233,170	47.1	Caacupé
Guairá . .	3,846	178,130	46.3	Villarrica
Itapúa . .	16,525	459,480	27.8	Encarnación
Misiones . .	9,556	102,230	10.7	San Juan Bautista
Ñeembucú . .	12,147	76,730	6.3	Pilar
Paraguarí . .	8,705	224,850	25.8	Paraguarí
Presidente Hayes	72,907	82,030	1.1	Pozo Colorado
San Pedro . .	20,002	319,540	16.0	San Pedro
Total . .	406,752	5,183,080	12.7	—

PRINCIPAL TOWNS
(population at 2002 census, incl. rural environs)

Asunción (capital) .	510,910	Lambaré . . .	119,830
Ciudad del Este* . .	222,109	Fernando de la Mora	113,990
San Lorenzo . .	203,150	Caaguazú . .	100,132
Luque	185,670	Encarnación . .	97,000
Capiatá	154,520	Pedro Juan Caballero . . .	88,530

* Formerly Puerto Presidente Stroessner.

BIRTHS, MARRIAGES AND DEATHS
(UN estimates, annual averages)

	1990–95	1995–2000	2000–05
Birth rate (per 1,000)	34.1	31.3	29.6
Death rate (per 1,000)	6.0	5.4	5.0

Source: UN, *World Population Prospects: The 2004 Revision*.

2002: Registered live births 46,012; Marriages 16,100; Deaths 19,416.

2003: Registered live births 45,669; Marriages 17,717; Deaths 19,593.

Expectation of life (WHO estimates, years at birth): 72 (males 69; females 75) in 2003 (Source: WHO, *World Health Report*).

ECONOMICALLY ACTIVE POPULATION
(household survey, August–December 2000)

	Males	Females	Total
Agriculture, hunting, forestry and fishing	689,825	212,497	902,322
Mining and quarrying	2,500	—	2,500
Manufacturing	186,322	99,864	286,186
Electricity, gas and water . . .	10,432	3,300	13,732
Construction	107,340	—	107,340
Trade, restaurants and hotels .	281,928	306,039	587,967
Transport, storage and communications	62,788	11,461	74,249
Financing, insurance, real estate and business services . .	55,836	28,950	84,786
Community, social and personal services	174,747	326,571	501,318
Activities not adequately described	208	—	208
Total employed	1,571,926	988,682	2,560,608

PARAGUAY

Health and Welfare

KEY INDICATORS

Total fertility rate (children per woman, 2003)	3.8
Under-5 mortality rate (per 1,000 live births, 2004)	24
HIV/AIDS (% of persons aged 15–49, 2003)	0.5
Physicians (per 1,000 head, 2000)	1.17
Hospital beds (per 1,000 head, 1996)	1.34
Health expenditure (2002): US $ per head (PPP)	343
Health expenditure (2002): % of GDP	8.4
Health expenditure (2002): public (% of total)	38.1
Access to water (% of persons, 2002)	83
Access to sanitation (% of persons, 2002)	78
Human Development Index (2003): ranking	88
Human Development Index (2003): value	0.755

For sources and definitions, see explanatory note on p. vi.

Agriculture

PRINCIPAL CROPS
('000 metric tons)

	2002	2003	2004
Wheat	359	500*	715
Rice (paddy)	105	110	125
Maize	867	1,055	1,120
Sorghum	40	27	19
Sweet potatoes	124	106	167
Cassava (Manioc)	4,430	4,669	5,500
Sugar cane	3,210	3,260	3,637
Dry beans	54	65	65
Soybeans (Soya beans)	3,300	4,205	3,584
Oil palm fruit*	126	127	126
Sunflower seed	36	31†	45
Tung nuts	31	27	30*
Cottonseed	74†	112*	192
Tomatoes	58	67	69
Dry onions*	34	30	30
Carrots	29	17	20
Other vegetables*	36	37	37
Watermelons*	115	115	115
Cantaloupes and other melons*	28	30	29
Bananas	61	62	44
Oranges	207	201	200
Tangerines, mandarins, clementines and satsumas	23	19	20
Grapefruit and pomelo	47	41	40
Mangoes*	29	29	29
Pineapples	82	73	52
Maté	137	89	77

* FAO estimate(s).
† Unofficial figure.
Source: FAO.

LIVESTOCK
('000 head, year ending September)

	2002	2003	2004
Cattle	9,260	10,128	9,622
Horses*	358	360	360
Pigs	1,365	1,474	1,507
Sheep	410	423	525
Goats	125	105	159
Chickens	15,351	16,744	17,000
Ducks*	720	725	730
Geese*	85	90	95
Turkeys*	95	100	105

* FAO estimates.
Source: FAO.

LIVESTOCK PRODUCTS
('000 metric tons)

	2002	2003	2004
Beef and veal	205	215	215
Pig meat*	78	93	156
Poultry meat*	37	39	39
Cows' milk	375	380*	362*
Hen eggs*	94	101	100
Cattle hides*	33	34	34

* FAO estimate(s).
Source: FAO.

Forestry

ROUNDWOOD REMOVALS
(FAO estimates, '000 cubic metres, excluding bark)

	2002	2003	2004
Sawlogs, veneer logs and logs for sleepers	3,515	3,515	3,515
Other industrial wood	529	529	529
Fuel wood	5,743	5,843	5,944
Total	9,787	9,887	9,988

Source: FAO.

SAWNWOOD PRODUCTION
('000 cubic metres, including railway sleepers)

	1995	1996	1997
Total (all broadleaved)	400	500	550

1998–2004: Annual production as in 1997 (FAO estimates).
Source: FAO.

Fishing

(FAO estimates, unless otherwise indicated, '000 metric tons, live weight)

	1996	1997	1998
Capture	22.0*	28.0*	25.0
Characins	8.0	10.0	9.0
Freshwater siluroids	10.0	13.0	12.0
Other freshwater fishes	4.0	5.0	4.0
Aquaculture	0.4	0.4	0.1*
Total catch	22.4	28.4	25.1

* Official figure.

Note: Figures exclude crocodiles, recorded by number rather than by weight. The number of spectacled caimans caught was: 503 in 1997; 4,445 in 1998; 0 in 1999; 9,750 in 2000; 3,793 in 2001; 8,373 in 2002; 3,781 in 2003.

1999–2003: Capture data as in 1998 (FAO estimates).
Source: FAO.

Industry

SELECTED PRODUCTS
('000 metric tons, unless otherwise indicated)

	2000	2001	2002
Soya bean oil*	138	177	219
Sugar (raw)†	135	149	170
Hydraulic cement‡	650	650	650§

* Unofficial figures.
† FAO estimates.
‡ Data from US Geological Survey.
§ Estimate.
Source (unless otherwise indicated): FAO.

Finance

CURRENCY AND EXCHANGE RATES

Monetary Units
100 céntimos = 1 guaraní (G).

Sterling, Dollar and Euro Equivalents (30 December 2005)
£1 sterling = 10,538.0 guaraníes;
US $1 = 6,120.0 guaraníes;
€1 = 7,219.8 guaraníes;
100,000 guaraníes = £9.49 = $16.34 = €13.85.

Average Exchange Rate (guaraníes per US dollar)
2003   6,424.3
2004   5,974.6
2005   5,716.3

BUDGET
('000 million guaraníes)

Revenue	2003	2004	2005*
Taxation	3,676	4,929	5,283
Non-tax revenue and grants	2,318	2,696	2,810
Capital revenues	7	12	3
Total	6,001	7,637	8,096

Expenditure	2003	2004	2005*
Current expenditure	4,981	5,363	6,275
Goods and services	408	447	555
Wages and salaries	2,724	2,984	3,321
Interest payments	489	483	568
Transfers	1,334	1,431	1,807
Pensions and benefits	943	940	1,172
Other	26	18	23
Capital expenditure and net lending	1,165	1,625	1,895
Net lending	−88	−29	−17
Statistical discrepancy	−29	151	0
Total	6,117	7,139	8,170

* Revised projections.
Source: IMF, *Paraguay: Sixth Review Under the Stand-By Arrangement—Staff Report; and Press Release on the Executive Board Discussion* (March 2006).

INTERNATIONAL RESERVES
(US $ million at 31 December)

	2002	2003	2004
Gold*	12.14	14.51	n.a.
IMF special drawing rights	113.18	125.75	133.62
Reserve position in IMF	29.20	31.91	33.35
Foreign exchange	486.82	811.19	1,000.17
Total	641.35	983.36	1,167.14

* National valuation $347 per troy ounce at 31 December 2002; $415 per troy ounce at 31 December 2003.

Source: IMF, *International Financial Statistics*.

MONEY SUPPLY
('000 million guaraníes at 31 December)

	2002	2003	2004
Currency outside banks	1,451.20	1,814.57	2,116.69
Demand deposits at commercial banks	1,273.39	1,918.52	2,610.19
Total money (incl. others)	2,759.53	3,788.14	4,784.12

Source: IMF, *International Financial Statistics*.

COST OF LIVING
(Consumer Price Index for Asunción; base: 2000 = 100)

	2002	2003	2004
Food (incl. beverages)	114.4	139.3	149.7
Housing (incl. fuel and light)	125.4	137.8	139.8
Clothing (incl. footwear)	108.4	117.0	122.5
All items (incl. others)	118.5	135.4	141.3

Source: ILO.

NATIONAL ACCOUNTS
('000 million guaraníes at current prices)

National Income and Product

	1999	2000	2001
Compensation of employees	7,764.3	8,340.1	9,030.2
Operating surplus*	12,736.9	14,467.8	14,699.2
Domestic factor incomes	20,501.2	22,807.9	23,729.4
Consumption of fixed capital	1,889.6	2,051.9	2,142.8
Gross domestic product (GDP) at factor cost	22,390.7	24,859.8	25,872.1
Indirect taxes, *less* subsidies	1,753.6	2,061.2	2,246.7
GDP in purchasers' values	24,144.3	26,921.0	28,118.8
Factor income received from abroad, *less* factor income paid abroad	132.2	380.7	164.2
Gross national product	24,276.5	27,301.7	28,283.0
Less Consumption of fixed capital	1,889.6	2,051.9	2,142.8
National income in market prices	22,386.9	25,249.8	26,140.2

* Obtained as a residual.
Source: UN Economic Commission for Latin America and the Caribbean.

Expenditure on the Gross Domestic Product

	2001	2002	2003*
Government final consumption expenditure	2,479.9	2,470.2	2,679.3
Private final consumption expenditure	24,604.3	27,527.0	34,044.8
Increase in stocks	265.5	292.3	315.7
Gross fixed capital formation	5,295.0	5,812.5	7,373.6
Total domestic expenditure	32,644.7	36,102.1	44,413.4
Exports of goods and services	6,170.1	9,822.8	12,524.1
Less Imports of goods and services	10,696.0	13,948.0	18,131.9
GDP in purchasers' values	28,118.8	31,977.0	38,805.5
GDP at constant 1982 prices	1,157.0	1,130.1	1,159.0

* Provisional figures.

PARAGUAY

Gross Domestic Product by Economic Activity

	2002	2003	2004*
Agriculture, hunting, forestry and fishing	7,546.6	10,570.8	9,010.1
Mining and quarrying	87.9	105.2	45.9
Manufacturing	4,475.0	5,274.9	5,898.7
Construction	1,432.8	1,793.1	1,941.5
Electricity and water	2,041.8	2,229.9	915.1
Trade and finance	8,189.4	9,998.8	9,126.8
Transport and communications	1,679.6	1,862.6	2,829.1
Government services	1,570.9	1,714.2	3,446.0
Real estate and housing	695.3	771.7	603.4
Other services	4,257.6	4,484.2	3,912.0
GDP in purchasers' values	31,976.9	38,805.5	37,728.1

* Provisional figures.

BALANCE OF PAYMENTS
(US $ million)

	2002	2003	2004
Exports of goods f.o.b.	1,858.0	2,175.3	2,811.7
Imports of goods f.o.b.	-2,137.9	-2,450.5	-3,203.0
Trade balance	-279.9	-275.2	-391.3
Exports of services	568.4	582.7	585.8
Imports of services	-354.6	-333.1	-336.9
Balance on goods and services	-66.1	-25.5	-142.4
Other income received	195.7	166.3	185.9
Other income paid	-152.9	-172.8	-217.2
Balance on goods, services and income	-23.3	-32.0	-173.8
Current transfers received	117.5	166.1	195.7
Current transfers paid	-1.6	-1.5	-1.5
Current balance	92.6	132.5	20.4
Capital account (net)	4.0	15.0	16.0
Direct investment abroad	-5.5	-5.5	-6.0
Direct investment from abroad	10.0	32.8	92.5
Portfolio investment assets	—	—	—
Portfolio investment liabilities	-0.1	-0.4	-0.1
Other investment assets	-16.1	212.5	-8.5
Other investment liabilities	52.2	-66.3	35.2
Net errors and omissions	-262.8	-87.8	120.5
Overall balance	-125.7	232.8	270.0

Source: IMF, *International Financial Statistics*.

External Trade

(excl. border trade)

PRINCIPAL COMMODITIES
(US $ million)

Imports f.o.b.	2001	2002	2003*
Food and live animals	57.3	30.9	30.7
Beverages and tobacco	111.9	67.8	56.8
Mineral fuels	302.8	239.2	327.0
Chemical products	105.5	141.9	219.3
Pharmaceuticals	53.9	38.1	38.7
Road vehicles	110.7	59.4	58.6
Transport equipment and accessories	66.3	55.4	68.1
Paper, paperboard and pulp	83.4	68.4	67.9
Textiles and textile products	51.8	33.1	67.9
Base metals and metal goods	81.0	60.1	69.4
Motors, general industrial machinery equipment and parts	336.0	281.7	281.6
Agricultural equipment and vehicles	35.0	41.2	91.4
Total (incl. others)	1,590.0	1,251.8	1,598.9

Exports f.o.b.	2001	2002	2003*
Meat and derivatives	65.1	72.7	61.2
Cereals	47.3	35.9	85.9
Oleaginous seeds	364.5	350.4	529.9
Vegetable oils	44.9	79.0	95.3
Feeding stuff for animals	96.2	120.1	129.4
Leather	48.2	47.5	45.1
Wood and wooden products	63.1	49.8	52.9
Cotton fibres	90.5	37.9	64.9
Total (incl. others)	1,167.4	1,132.8	1,496.1

* Preliminary figures.

PRINCIPAL TRADING PARTNERS
(US $ million)

Imports c.i.f.	2001	2002	2003*
Argentina	478.6	309.4	402.7
Bahamas	42.8	28.5	54.4
Brazil	563.6	477.6	605.1
Chile	42.0	19.3	32.7
France (incl. Monaco)	21.3	17.6	15.5
Germany	50.3	45.6	34.2
Italy	25.3	13.6	13.7
Japan	86.2	49.6	65.5
Korea, Republic	24.2	14.6	17.7
Spain	21.0	16.2	33.5
Switzerland-Liechtenstein	36.6	59.1	56.3
Taiwan	18.5	16.8	16.1
United Kingdom	35.1	22.0	33.9
USA	118.4	77.6	71.2
Uruguay	69.3	58.4	59.1
Total (incl. others)	1,988.8	1,510.2	1,862.0

Exports f.o.b.	2001	2002	2003*
Argentina	60.8	34.7	66.4
Brazil	277.9	353.0	424.9
Chile	61.5	49.1	12.6
Colombia	10.5	3.0	1.4
France (incl. Monaco)	4.8	8.0	10.4
Germany	13.1	8.8	7.2
Hong Kong	12.0	11.8	9.2
India	28.5	2.8	0.1
Italy	42.1	34.9	40.4
Japan	11.8	8.1	5.4
Netherlands	29.4	19.2	12.5
Spain	10.8	7.7	8.7
Switzerland-Liechtenstein	34.4	33.4	97.1
Taiwan	11.6	11.0	11.5
United Kingdom	2.6	1.1	1.5
USA	29.3	37.4	44.1
Uruguay	180.0	165.1	243.1
Venezuela	7.4	9.7	6.5
Total (incl. others)	990.2	950.6	1,241.5

* Preliminary figures.

Source: UN, *International Trade Statistics Yearbook*.

Transport

RAILWAYS
(traffic)

	1988	1989	1990
Passengers carried	178,159	196,019	125,685
Freight (metric tons)	200,213	164,980	289,099

Source: UN, *Statistical Yearbook*.

Passenger-kilometres: 3.0 million per year in 1994–96.

Freight ton-kilometres: 5.5 million in 1994.

Source: UN Economic Commission for Latin America and the Caribbean.

PARAGUAY

ROAD TRAFFIC
(vehicles in use)

	1999	2000
Cars	267,587	274,186
Buses	8,991	9,467
Lorries	41,329	42,992
Vans and jeeps	134,144	138,656
Motorcycles	6,872	8,825

Source: Organización Paraguaya de Cooperación Intermunicipal.

SHIPPING

Merchant Fleet
(registered at 31 December)

	2002	2003	2004
Number of vessels	46	44	44
Total displacement ('000 grt)	47.5	45.1	44.3

Source: Lloyd's Register-Fairplay, *World Fleet Statistics*.

CIVIL AVIATION
(traffic on scheduled services)

	2001	2002	2003
Kilometres flown (million)	5.5	5.8	6.5
Passengers carried ('000)	281.0	268.6	313.0
Passenger-km (million)	294.3	278.6	324.5

Source: UN Economic Commission for Latin America and the Caribbean, *Statistical Yearbook*.

Tourism

ARRIVALS BY NATIONALITY

	2001	2002	2003
Argentina	170,575	160,758	177,741
Brazil	60,193	43,134	40,651
Chile	5,964	4,694	6,262
Uruguay	5,351	4,939	5,775
USA	8,695	9,012	9,210
Total (incl. others)	278,672	250,423	268,175

Tourism receipts (US $ million, incl. passenger transport): 87 in 2001; 73 in 2002; 81 in 2003.

Source: World Tourism Organization.

Communications Media

	2002	2003	2004
Telephones ('000 main lines in use)	273.2	273.2	280.8
Mobile cellular telephones ('000 subscribers)	1,667.0	1,770.3	1,767.8
Personal computers ('000 in use)	200	n.a.	356
Internet users ('000)	100	120	150

Television receivers ('000 in use): 1,200 in 1997.

Radio receivers ('000 in use): 925 in 1997.

Facsimile machines (number in use): 1,691 in 1992.

Daily newspapers: 5* in 1996 (average circulation 213,000* copies).

Non-daily newspapers: 2 in 1988 (average circulation 16,000* copies).

Book production: 152 titles (incl. 23 pamphlets) in 1993.
* Estimate.

Sources: UNESCO, *Statistical Yearbook*; UN, *Statistical Yearbook*; International Telecommunication Union.

Education

(2002/03, unless otherwise indicated)

	Institutions*	Teachers	Students
Pre-primary schools	4,071	4,554†	138,913
Primary	7,456	35,709	962,661
Secondary	2,149	43,835	519,054
Tertiary: university level	111	1,844‡	146,892§

* 1999.
† Estimate for 1998/99.
‡ 1999/2000.
§ Estimate.

Source: partly UNESCO Institute for Statistics.

Adult literacy rate: 91.6% (males 93.1%; females 90.2%) in 2003.

Directory

The Constitution

A new Constitution for the Republic of Paraguay came into force on 22 June 1992, replacing the Constitution of 25 August 1967.

FUNDAMENTAL RIGHTS, DUTIES AND FREEDOMS

Paraguay is an independent republic whose form of government is representative democracy. The powers accorded to the legislature, executive and judiciary are exercised in a system of independence, equilibrium, co-ordination and reciprocal control. Sovereignty resides in the people, who exercise it through universal, free, direct, equal and secret vote. All citizens over 18 years of age and resident in the national territory are entitled to vote.

All citizens are equal before the law and have freedom of conscience, travel, residence, expression, and the right to privacy. The freedom of the press is guaranteed. The freedom of religion and ideology is guaranteed. Relations between the State and the Catholic Church are based on independence, co-operation and autonomy. All citizens have the right to assemble and demonstrate peacefully. All public- and private-sector workers, with the exception of the Armed Forces and the police, have the right to form a trade union and to strike. All citizens have the right to associate freely in political parties or movements.

The rights of the indigenous peoples to preserve and develop their ethnic identity in their respective habitat are guaranteed.

LEGISLATURE

The legislature (Congreso Nacional—National Congress) comprises the Senado (Senate) and the Cámara de Diputados (Chamber of Deputies). The Senado is composed of 45 members, the Cámara of 80 members, elected directly by the people. Legislation concerning national defence and international agreements may be initiated in the Senado. Departmental and municipal legislation may be initiated in the Cámara. Both chambers of the Congreso are elected for a period of five years.

GOVERNMENT

Executive power is exercised by the President of the Republic. The President and the Vice-President are elected jointly and directly by the people, by a simple majority of votes, for a period of five years. They may not be elected for a second term. The President and the Vice-President govern with the assistance of an appointed Council of

PARAGUAY

Ministers. The President participates in the formulation of legislation and enacts it. The President is empowered to veto legislation sanctioned by the Congreso, to nominate or remove ministers, to direct the foreign relations of the Republic, and to convene extraordinary sessions of the Congreso. The President is Commander-in-Chief of the Armed Forces.

JUDICIARY

Judicial power is exercised by the Supreme Court of Justice and by the tribunals. The Supreme Court is composed of nine members who are appointed on the proposal of the Consejo de la Magistratura, and has the power to declare legislation unconstitutional.

The Government

HEAD OF STATE

President: Oscar Nicanor Duarte Frutos (took office 15 August 2003).

Vice-President: Luis Alberto Castiglioni Soria.

COUNCIL OF MINISTERS
(April 2006)

Minister of the Interior: Rogelio Raimundo Benítez Vargas.

Minister of Foreign Affairs: Leila Rachid de Cowles.

Minister of Finance: Ernst Ferdinand Bergen Schmidt.

Minister of Industry and Commerce: Raúl José Vera Bogado.

Minister of Public Works and Communications: José Alberto Alderete Rodríguez.

Minister of National Defence: Roberto Eudez González Segovia.

Minister of Public Health and Social Welfare: Dra María Teresa León Mendaro.

Minister of Justice and Labour: Derlis Alcides Céspedes Aguilera.

Minister of Agriculture and Livestock: Nelson Gustavo Ruiz Díaz Roa.

Minister of Education and Culture: Blanca Ovelar de Duarte.

MINISTRIES

Ministry of Agriculture and Livestock: Presidente Franco 472, Asunción; tel. (21) 44-9614; fax (21) 49-7965.

Ministry of Education and Culture: Chile, Humaitá y Piribebuy, Asunción; tel. (21) 44-3078; fax (21) 44-3919; internet www.paraguaygobierno.gov.py/mec.

Ministry of Finance: Chile 128, esq. Palmas, Asunción; tel. (21) 44-0010; e-mail info@hacienda.gov.py; internet www.hacienda.gov.py.

Ministry of Foreign Affairs: Juan E. O'Leary y Presidente Franco, Asunción; tel. (21) 49-4593; fax (21) 49-3910; internet www.mre.gov.py.

Ministry of Industry and Commerce: Avda España 323, Asunción; tel. (21) 20-4638; fax (21) 21-3529; e-mail msalcedo@mic.gov.py; internet www.mic.gov.py.

Ministry of the Interior: Estrella y Montevideo, Asunción; tel. (21) 49-3661; fax (21) 44-6448; internet www.ministeriodelinterior.gov.py.

Ministry of Justice and Labour: G. R. de Francia y Estados Unidos, Asunción; tel. (21) 49-3515; fax (21) 20-8469; e-mail mjt@conexion.com.py.

Ministry of National Defence: Avda Mariscal López y Vice-Presidente Sánchez, Asunción; tel. (21) 20-4771; fax (21) 21-1583.

Ministry of Public Health and Social Welfare: Avda Pettirossi y Brasil, Asunción; tel. (21) 20-7328; fax (21) 20-6700; internet www.mspbs.gov.py.

Ministry of Public Works and Communications: Oliva y Alberdi, Asunción; tel. (21) 44-4411; fax (21) 44-4421; internet www.mopc.gov.py.

President and Legislature

PRESIDENT

Election, 27 April 2003

Candidate	% of votes
Oscar Nicanor Duarte Frutos (Partido Colorado)	37.1
Julio César Ramón Franco Gómez (PLRA)	24.0
Pedro Nicolás Fadul Niella (Patria Querida)	21.3
Guillermo Sánchez Guffanti (UNACE)	13.5
Total (incl. others)	100.0

CONGRESO NACIONAL
(National Congress)

President of the Senado and the Congreso Nacional: Dr Carlos Filizzola.

President of the Cámara de Diputados: Víctor Bogado.

General Election, 27 April 2003

	Seats	
Party	Cámara de Diputados	Senado
Partido Colorado	37	16
Partido Liberal Radical Auténtico	21	12
Patria Querida	10	8
Unión Nacional de Ciudadanos Eticos	10	7
Partido País Solidario	2	2
Total	80	45

Election Commission

Tribunal Superior de Justicia Electoral (TSJE): Eusebio Ayala y Santa Cruz de la Sierra, Asunción; tel. (21) 61-8011; e-mail info@tsje.gov.py; internet www.tsje.gov.py; Pres. Dr Alberto Ramírez Zambonini.

Political Organizations

Asociación Nacional Republicana—Partido Colorado (National Republican Association—Colorado Party): Casa de los Colorados, 25 de Mayo 842, Asunción; tel. (21) 44-4137; fax (21) 49-7857; f. 19th century; principal factions include: Movimiento de Reconciliación Colorada; Coloradismo Unido, led by Dr Angel Roberto Seifart; Coloradismo Democrático, led by Blás Riquelme; Acción Democrática Republicana, led by Carlos Facetti Masulli; Frente Republicano de Unidad Nacional, led by Wálter Bower Montalto; 947,430 mems (1991); Pres. Herminio Cáceres; Vice-Pres. Cándido Aguilera.

Encuentro Nacional (EN): 370 Avda Senador Long, Asunción; tel. (21) 60-3935; fax (21) 61-0699; e-mail parenac@pla.net.py; internet www.quanta.net.py/ifes/partidos/pen.htm; f. 1991; coalition comprising factions of PRF, PDC, Asunción Para Todos and a dissident faction of the Partido Colorado; formed to contest presidential and legislative elections of May 1993; Pres. Luis Torales Kennedy; Vice-Pres. Dr Secundino Núñez.

Movimiento Patria Libre (MPL): 15 de Agosto 1939, Asunción; tel. (21) 37-2384; left-wing; Asst. Sec.-Gen. Anuncio Marti Méndez.

Partido Blanco: Asunción; tel. (21) 55-4068; Pres. Gregorio Segovia Silvera; Vice-Pres. Edgar A. Ortigoza Cardozo.

Partido Comunista Paraguayo (PCP): Asunción; f. 1928; banned 1928–46, 1947–89; Sec.-Gen. Ananías Maidana.

Partido Demócrata Cristiano (PDC): Colón 871, Casilla 1318, Asunción; internet www.pdc.org.py; f. 1960; 20,500 mems; Pres. Dr Luis M. Andrada Nogués; Vice-Pres. Dr José V. Altamirano.

Partido Frente Amplio Paraguayo: Antequera 764, esq. Fulgencio R. Moreno, Asunción; tel. (21) 44-1389; Sec.-Gen. Víctor Bareiro Roa.

Partido Humanista Paraguayo: Fulgencio R. Moreno 584, esq. Paraguari, Asunción; tel. (21) 44-2625; internet www.humanista.org.py; f. 1985; recognized by the Supreme Tribunal of Electoral Justice in March 1989; campaigns for the protection of human rights and environmental issues; Gen. Sec. Nicolás Servín.

PARAGUAY

Partido Independiente: Irrazabal 857, Asunción; tel. (21) 20-1375; e-mail motazu@gmail.com; Pres. MIGUEL OTAZÚ MONTANARO; Sec.-Gen. AURORA ALMADA FLORES.

Partido Liberal Radical Auténtico (PLRA): Azara y General Santos 2486, Asunción; tel. (21) 20-1337; fax (21) 20-4869; e-mail plra-prensa@mmail.com.py; f. 1978; centre party; Pres. BLÁS ANTONIO LLANO.

Partido País Solidario: Avda 5, esq. Méjico, Asunción; tel. (21) 39-1271; Pres. Dr CARLOS FILIZZOLA; Vice-Pres. JORGE GIUCICH.

Partido Revolucionario Febrerista (PRF): Casa del Pueblo, Manduvira 552, Asunción; tel. (21) 49-4041; e-mail partyce@mixmail.com; f. 1951; social democratic party; affiliated to the Socialist International; Pres. OSCAR MONTIEL GALVÁN; Vice-Pres. MIRTA TORRES ANTÚNEZ.

Partido de los Trabajadores (PT): Asunción; f. 1989; Socialist.

Partido Unión Nacional de Ciudadanos Eticos (UNACE): Eusebio Ayala 4135, esq. Corrales, Asunción; e-mail loviedo@unace.org.py; internet www.unace.org.py; f. 2002; left-wing; break-away faction of the Partido Colorado; Pres. ENRIQUE GONZÁLEZ QUINTANA; Vice-Pres. Dr CARLOS ROGER CABALLERO FIORI.

Patria Querida: 469 Padre Cardozo, Asunción; tel. 21-3300; e-mail info@patriaquerida.org; internet www.patriaquerida.org; f. 2002; recognized by the Supreme Tribunal of Electoral Justice in March 2004; Leader PEDRO NICOLÁS FADUL NIELLA.

Unidad Popular: Azara 2843, esq. Rodó, Asunción; tel. (21) 21-5059; recognized by the Supreme Tribunal of Electoral Justice in March 2004; Pres. JUAN DE DIOS ACOSTA MENA.

OTHER ORGANIZATIONS

Federación Nacional Campesina de Paraguay (FNC): Nangariry 1196, esq. Cacique Cará Cará, Asunción; tel. (21) 51-2384; grouping of militant peasants' orgs; Sec.-Gen. ODILÓN ESPÍNOLA; Asst Sec.-Gen. MARCIAL GÓMEZ.

Frente en Defensa de los Bienes Públicos y el Patrimonio Nacional: Asunción; left-wing grouping of orgs opposed to privatization; Co-ordinator GABRIEL ESPÍNOLA.

Frente Nacional de Lucha por la Soberanía y la Vida: Asunción; left-wing grouping of orgs campaigning for agrarian reform and opposed to privatization; Co-ordinator LUIS AGUAYO.

Diplomatic Representation

EMBASSIES IN PARAGUAY

Argentina: Avda España, esq. Avda Perú, Casilla 757, Asunción; tel. (21) 21-2320; fax (21) 21-1029; e-mail embarpy@supernet.com.py; internet www.embajada-argentina.org.py; Ambassador RAFAEL EDGARDO ROMÁ.

Bolivia: América 200 y Mariscal López, Asunción; tel. (21) 22-7213; fax (21) 21-0440; e-mail embolivia-asuncion@webmail.com.py; Ambassador ALFREDO SEOANE FLORES.

Brazil: Col Irrazábal, esq. Eligio Ayala, Casilla 22, Asunción; tel. (21) 21-4466; fax (21) 21-2693; e-mail acesar@embajadabrasil.org.py; internet www.embajadabrasil.org.py; Ambassador WALTER PECLY MOREIRA.

Chile: Capital Emilio Nudelman 351, Asunción; tel. (21) 61-3855; fax (21) 66-2755; e-mail echilepy@conexion.com.py; Ambassador JUAN EDUARDO BURGOS SANTANDER.

China (Taiwan): Avda Mariscal López 1143 y Mayor Bullo, Casilla 503, Asunción; tel. (21) 21-3362; fax (21) 21-2373; e-mail giopy@telesurf.com.py; e-mail emorc@highway.com.py; internet www.roc-taiwan.org.py; Ambassador DAVID HU.

Colombia: Calle Coronel Brizuela, esq. Ciudad del Vaticano, Asunción; tel. (21) 22-9888; fax (21) 22-9703; e-mail easuncio@minrelext.gov.co; Ambassador CARLOS ALBERTO BERNAL ROMÁN.

Costa Rica: Carlos Díaz León 3245, casi Escurra Barrio Herrera, Asunción; tel. and fax (21) 67-5297; e-mail embarica@uninet.com.py; Ambassador FERNANDO JOSÉ GUARDIA ALVARADO.

Cuba: Luis Morales 757, esq. Luis León y Luis Granado, Barrio Jara, Asunción; tel. (21) 22-2763; fax (21) 21-3879; e-mail embacuba@cmm.com.py; Ambassador ADOLFO CURBELO CASTELLANOS.

Ecuador: Justo Román y Julio C. Escobar, esq. Barrio Manorá, Casilla 13162, Asunción; tel. (21) 61-4814; fax (21) 61-4813; e-mail mecuapy@conexion.com.py; Ambassador JULIO CÉSAR PRADO ESPINOSA.

France: Avda España 893, Calle Pucheu, Casilla 97, Asunción; tel. (21) 21-2449; fax (21) 21-1690; e-mail chancellerie@ambafran.gov.py; internet www.ambafran.gov.py; Ambassador DENIS VÈNE.

Germany: Avda Venezuela 241, Casilla 471, Asunción; tel. (21) 21-4009; fax (21) 21-2863; e-mail aaasun@pla.net.py; internet www.pla.net.py/embalem; Ambassador Dr HORST-WOLFRAM KERLL.

Holy See: Calle Ciudad del Vaticano 350, casi con 25 de Mayo, Casilla 83, Asunción (Apostolic Nunciature); tel. (21) 21-5139; fax (21) 21-2590; e-mail nunapos@conexion.com.py; Apostolic Nuncio Most Rev. ANTONIO LUCIBELLO (Titular Archbishop of Thurio).

Italy: Quesada 5871 con Bélgica, Asunción; tel. (21) 61-5620; fax (21) 61-5622; e-mail ambitalia@cmm.com.py; internet www.embajadaitalia.org.py; Ambassador BENEDETTO AMARI.

Japan: Avda Mariscal López 2364, Casilla 1957, Asunción; tel. (21) 60-4616; fax (21) 60-6901; e-mail japoncul@rieder.net.py; internet www.py.emb-japan.go.jp; Ambassador TOSHIHIRO TAKAHASHI.

Korea, Republic: Avda Rep. Argentina Norte 678, esq. Pacheco, Casilla 1303, Asunción; tel. (21) 60-5606; fax (21) 60-1376; e-mail paraguay@mofat.go.kr; Ambassador CHUNG YOUNG-KOO.

Mexico: Avda España, esq. San Rafael, Casilla 1184, Asunción; tel. (21) 616-8200; fax (21) 6-2500; e-mail evamx@embamex.com.py; internet www.embamex.com.py; Ambassador ERNESTO CAMPOS TENORIO.

Panama: Piribeduy 765, casi Ayolas, Casilla 873, Asunción; tel. (21) 44-3522; fax (21) 44-6192; e-mail embapana@conexion.com.py; Ambassador ROBERTO MORENO OLIVARES.

Peru: Feliciano Marecos 441, casi Agustín Barrios y España, Manorá, Casilla 433, Asunción; tel. (21) 60-0226; fax (21) 60-7327; e-mail embperu@embperu.com.py; Ambassador ENRIQUE PALACIOS REYES.

Spain: Edif. S. Rafael, 5° y 6°, Yegros 437, Asunción; tel. (21) 49-0686; fax (21) 44-5394; e-mail embesppy@correo.mae.es; Ambassador EDUARDO DE QUESADA FERNÁNDEZ DE LA PUENTE.

Switzerland: Edif. Parapití, 4°, Ofs 419–423, Juan E. O'Leary 409 y Estrella, Casilla 552, Asunción; tel. (21) 44-8022; fax (21) 44-5853; e-mail vertretung@asu.rep.admin.ch; Ambassador (vacant).

USA: Avda Mariscal López 1776, Casilla 402, Asunción; tel. (21) 21-3715; fax (21) 21-3728; e-mail paraguayusembassy@state.gov; internet asuncion.usembassy.gov; Ambassador JAMES CALDWELL CASON.

Uruguay: Guido Boggiani 5832, 3°, Asunción; tel. (21) 66-4244; fax (21) 60-1335; e-mail embauru@telesurf.com.py; internet www.embajadauruguay.com.py; Ambassador CARLOS ERNESTO ORLANDO BONET.

Venezuela: Mariscal Estigarribia 1023 con Estados Unidos, Asunción; tel. (21) 66-4682; tel. (21) 66-4683; fax (21) 66-4683; e-mail bolivar@pla.net.py; internet www.embaven.com.py; Ambassador JOSÉ HUERTA CASTILLO.

Judicial System

The Corte Suprema de Justicia (Supreme Court of Justice) is composed of nine judges appointed on the recommendation of the Consejo de la Magistratura (Council of the Magistracy).

Corte Suprema de Justicia: Palacio de Justicia, Asunción; Members ANTONIO FRETES (President), VÍCTOR MANUEL NÚÑEZ, MIGUEL O. BAJAC, SINDULFO BLANCO, ALICIA BEATRIZ PUCHETA DE CORREA, WILDO RIENZI GALEANO, JOSÉ V. ALTAMIRANO AQUINO, CÉSAR ANTONIO GARAY ZUCCOLILLO, JOSÉ RAÚL TORRES KIRMSER.

Consejo de la Magistratura

Palacio de Justicia, Asunción; Members RUBÉN DARÍO ROMERO (President), MARIO SOTO ESTIGARRIBIA (Vice-President), GUILLERMO DELMÁS FRESCURA, RODOLFO IRÚN ALAMANNI, RAÚL BATTILANA NIGRA, MARCELINO GAUTO BEJERANO, EUSEBIO RAMÓN AYALA, ANTONIO FRETES.

Attorney-General: RUBÉN CANDIA AMARILLA.

Under the Supreme Court are the Courts of Appeal, the Tribunal of Jurors and Judges of First Instance, the Judges of Arbitration, the Magistrates (Jueces de Instrucción), and the Justices of the Peace.

Religion

The Roman Catholic Church is the established religion, although all sects are tolerated.

CHRISTIANITY

The Roman Catholic Church

For ecclesiastical purposes, Paraguay comprises one archdiocese, 11 dioceses and two Apostolic Vicariates. At 31 December 2003 there were an estimated 5,241,609 adherents in the country, representing about 91.5% of the total population.

PARAGUAY   Directory

Bishops' Conference

Conferencia Episcopal Paraguaya, Calle Alberdi 782, Casilla 1436, 1209 Asunción; tel. (21) 49-0920; fax (21) 49-5115; e-mail cep@infonet.com.py; f. 1977; statutes approved 2000.
Pres. Rt Rev. CATALINO CLAUDIO GIMÉNEZ MEDINA (Bishop of Caacupé).
Archbishop of Asunción: Most Rev. EUSTAQUIO PASTOR CUQUEJO VERGA, Arzobispado, Avda Mariscal López 130 esq. Independencia Nacional, Casilla 654, Asunción; tel. (21) 44-5551; fax (21) 44-4150.

The Anglican Communion

Paraguay constitutes a single diocese of the Iglesia Anglicana del Cono Sur de América (Anglican Church of the Southern Cone of America). The Presiding Bishop of the Church is the Bishop of Northern Argentina.
Bishop of Paraguay: Rt Rev. JOHN ELLISON, Iglesia Anglicana, Avda España casi Santos, Casilla 1124, Asunción; tel. (21) 20-0933; fax (21) 21-4328; e-mail iapar@sce.cnc.una.py; internet www.anglicanos.net.

The Baptist Church

Baptist Evangelical Convention of Paraguay: Casilla 1194, Asunción; tel. (21) 22-7110; Exec. Sec. Lic. RAFAEL ALTAMIRANO.

BAHÁ'Í FAITH

National Spiritual Assembly of the Bahá'ís of Paraguay: Eligio Ayala 1456, Apdo 742, Asunción; tel. (21) 22-0250; fax (21) 22-5747; e-mail bahai@uninet.com.py; Sec. MIRNA LLAMOSAS DE RIQUELME.

The Press

DAILIES

ABC Color: Yegros 745, Apdo 1421, Asunción; tel. (21) 49-1160; fax (21) 415-1310; e-mail azeta@abc.com.py; internet www.abc.com.py; f. 1967; independent; Propr ALDO ZUCCOLILLO; circ. 45,000.
El Día: Avda Mariscal López 2948, Asunción; tel. (21) 60-3401; fax (21) 66-0385; e-mail eldia@infonet.com.py; internet www.infonet.com.py/eldia; Dir HUGO OSCAR ARANDA; circ. 12,000.
La Nación: Avda Zavala Cué entre 2da y 3ra, Fernando de la Mora, Asunción; tel. (21) 51-2520; fax (21) 51-2535; e-mail redaccion@lanacion.com.py; internet www.lanacion.com.py; f. 1995; Dir-Gen. OSVALDO DOMÍNGUEZ DIBB; circ. 10,000.
Noticias: Avda Artigas y Avda Brasilia, Casilla 3017, Asunción; tel. (21) 29-2721; fax (21) 29-2716; e-mail alebluth@diarionoticias.com; internet www.diarionoticias.com.py; f. 1985; independent; Dir ALEJANDRO BLUTH; circ. 20,000.
Popular: Avda Mariscal López 2948, Asunción; tel. (21) 60-3401; fax (21) 60-3400; e-mail popular@mm.com.py; internet www.diariopopular.com.py; Dir JAVIER PIROVANO PEÑA; circ. 28,000.
Ultima Hora: Benjamín Constant 658, Asunción; tel. (21) 49-6261; fax (21) 44-7071; e-mail ultimahora@uhora.com.py; internet www.ultimahora.com; f. 1973; independent; Dir DEMETRIO ROJAS; circ. 30,000.

PERIODICALS

Acción: Casilla 1072, Asunción; tel. (21) 37-0753; e-mail cepag@uninet.com.py; internet www.uninet.com.py/accion; monthly; Dir JOSÉ MARÍA BLANCH.
La Opinión: Boggiani, esq. Luis Alberto de Herrera, Asuncíon; tel. (21) 50-7501; fax (21) 50-2297; weekly; Dir FRANCISCO LAWS; Editor BERNARDO NERI.
TeVeo: Santa Margarita de Youville 250, Santa María, Asunción; tel. (21) 67-2079; fax (21) 21-1236; e-mail sugerencias@teveo.com.py; internet www.teveo.com.py; weekly; society.
Tiempo 14: Mariscal Estigarribia 4187, Asunción; tel. (21) 60-4308; fax (21) 60-9394; weekly; Dir HUMBERTO RUBÍN; Editor ALBERTO PERALTA.

NEWS AGENCIES

Agencia Paraguaya de Noticias (APN): Asunción; e-mail apn@supernet.com.py; internet www.supernet.com.py/usuarios/apn.

Foreign Bureaux

Agence France-Presse (AFP): Herrera 195, 8°, Of. 802, Asunción; tel. (21) 49-4520; fax (21) 44-3725; Correspondent HUGO RUIZ OLAZAR.
Agencia EFE (Spain): Yegros 437, Asunción; tel. (21) 49-2730; fax (21) 49-1268; Bureau Chief LUCIO GÓMEZ-OLMEDO.

Agenzia Nazionale Stampa Associata (ANSA) (Italy): Edif. Interexpress, 4°, Of. 403, Luis Alberto de Herrera 195, Asunción; tel. (21) 44-9286; fax (21) 44-2986; e-mail ansaasu@rieder.net.py.
Associated Press (AP) (USA): Calle Caballero 742, Casilla 264, Asunción; tel. (21) 60-6334.
Deutsche Presse-Agentur (dpa) (Germany): Edif. Segesa, Of. 705, Oliva 309, Asunción; tel. (21) 45-0329; fax (21) 44-8116; Correspondent EDUARDO ARCE.
Inter Press Service (IPS) (Italy): Edif. Segesa, 3°, Of. 5, Oliva 393 y Alberdi, Asunción; tel. and fax (21) 44-6350; Legal Rep. CLARA ROSA GAGLIARDONE.
TELAM (Argentina) is also represented in Paraguay.

Publishers

La Colmena, SA: Asunción; tel. (21) 20-0428; Dir DAUMAS LADOUCE.
Dervish SA, Editorial: Avda Mariscal López 1735, CP 1584, Asunción; tel. (21) 21-1729; fax (21) 22-2580; e-mail dervish@dervish.com.py; f. 1989; Co-ordinator JORGELINA MIGLIORISI; Vice-Pres. and Dir JANINE GIANI PATTERSON.
Ediciones Diálogo: Calle Brasil 1391, Asunción; tel. (21) 20-0428; f. 1957; fine arts, literature, poetry, criticism; Man. MIGUEL ANGEL FERNÁNDEZ.
Ediciones Nizza: Eligio Ayala 1073, Casilla 2596, Asunción; tel. (21) 44-7160; medicine; Pres. Dr JOSÉ FERREIRA MARTÍNEZ.
Editorial Comuneros: Cerro Corá 289, Casilla 930, Asunción; tel. (21) 44-6176; fax (21) 44-4667; e-mail rolon@conexion.com.py; f. 1963; social history, poetry, literature, law; Man. OSCAR R. ROLÓN.
Editorial Quijote: Mall Excelsior, Chile y Manduvirá, Asunción; tel. (21) 49-4445; fax (21) 44-7677; e-mail guasti@quijote.com.py; internet www.quijote.com.py; f. 1983; Gen. Man. GUSTAVO GUASTI.
Librería Intercontinental: Caballero 270, Asunción; tel. (21) 49-6991; fax (21) 48-721; e-mail agatti@pla.net.py; internet www.libreriaintercontinental.com.py; political science, law, literature, poetry; Dir ALEJANDRO GATTI VAN HUMBEECK.
R. P. Ediciones: Eduardo Víctor Haedo 427, Asunción; tel. (21) 49-8040; Man. RAFAEL PERONI.

ASSOCIATION

Cámara Paraguaya del Libro: Nuestra Señora de la Asunción 697, esq. Eduardo Víctor Haedo, Asunción; tel. (21) 44-4104; fax (21) 44-7053; Pres. PABLO LEÓN BURIAN; Sec. EMA DE VIEDMA.

Broadcasting and Communications

TELECOMMUNICATIONS

Comisión Nacional de Telecomunicaciones (CONATEL): Edif. San Rafael, 2°, Yegros 437 y 25 de Mayo, Asunción; tel. (21) 44-0020; fax (21) 49-8982; Pres. VÍCTOR ALCIDES BOGADO.
Corporación Paraguaya de Comunicaciones (COPACO): Edif. Morotí, 1°–2°, esq. Gen. Bruguéz y Teodoro S. Mongelos, Casilla 2042, Asunción; tel. (21) 20-3800; fax (21) 20-3888; internet www.copaco.com.py; fmrly Administración Nacional de Telecomunicaciones (ANTELCO); changed name as above in Dec. 2001 as part of the privatization process; privatization suspended in June 2002; Gen. Man. EDGAR PINEDA.

BROADCASTING

Radio

Radio Arapysandú: Avda Mariscal López y Capitán del Puerto San Ignacio, Misiones; tel. (82) 2374; fax (82) 2206; f. 1982; AM; Dir HECTOR BOTTINO.
Radio Asunción: Avda Artígas y Capitán Lombardo 174, Asunción; tel. (21) 29-5375; fax (21) 29-2718; AM; Dir MIGUEL G. FERNÁNDEZ.
Radio Cáritas: Kubitschek y 25 de Mayo, Asunción; tel. (21) 21-3570; fax (21) 20-4161; f. 1936; station of the Franciscan order; AM; Pres. Most Rev. EUSTAQUIO PASTOR CUQUEJO VERGA (Archbishop of Asunción); Dir MARIO VELÁZQUEZ.
Radio Cardinal: Río Paraguay 1334 y Guariníes, Casilla 2532, Lambaré, Asunción; tel. (21) 31-0555; fax (21) 31-0557; f. 1991; AM and FM; Pres. NÉSTOR LÓPEZ MOREIRA.
Radio City: Edif. Líder III, Antequera 652, 9°, Asunción; tel. (21) 44-3324; fax (21) 44-4367; f. 1950; FM; licence until 2014; Dir GREGORIO RAMAN MORALES.
Radio Concepción: Coronel Panchito López 241, entre Schreiber y Profesor Guillermo A. Cabral, Casilla 78, Concepción; tel. (31) 42318; fax (31) 42254; f. 1963; AM; Dir SERGIO E. DACAK.

PARAGUAY

Radio Emisoras del Paraguay: Avda General Santos 2525 y 18 de Julio, Asunción; tel. (21) 31-0644; FM; licence until 2014; Gen. Man. GUILLERMO HEISECKE.

Radio Guairá: Presidente Franco 788 y Alejo García, Villarica; tel. (541) 42130; fax (541) 42385; f. 1950; AM and FM; Dir LÍDICE RODRÍGUEZ DE TRAVERSI.

Radio Itapirú S.R.L.: Avda San Blás esq. Coronel Julián Sánchez, Ciudad del Este, Alto Paraná; tel. (61) 57-2206; fax (61) 57-2210; f. 1969; AM and FM; Gen. Man. ANTONIO ARANDA ENCINA.

Radio La Voz de Amambay: 14 de Mayo y Cerro León, Pedro Juan Caballero, Amambay; tel. (36) 72537; f. 1959; AM and FM; Gen. Man. DANIEL ROLÓN DANTAS P.

Radio Nacional del Paraguay: Blas Garay 241 y Iturbe, Asunción; tel. (21) 39-0374; fax (21) 39-0376; f. 1957; AM and FM; Dir TEODOSO FERMÍN ESPINOSA.

Radio Ñandutí: Choferes del Chaco y Carmen Soler, Asunción; tel. (21) 60-4308; fax (21) 60-6074; internet www.infonet.com.py/holding/nanduam; f. 1962; FM; Dir HUMBERTO LEÓN RUBÍN.

Radio Nuevo Mundo: Coronel Romero 1181 y Flórida, San Lorenzo, Asunción; tel. (21) 58-6258; fax (21) 58-2424; f. 1972; AM; Dir JULIO CÉSAR PEREIRA BOBADILLA.

Radio Primero de Marzo: Avda General Perón y Concepción, Casilla 1456, Asunción; tel. (21) 31-1564; fax (21) 33-3427; AM and FM; Dir-Gen. ANGEL R. GUERREÑOS.

Radio Santa Mónica FM: Avda Boggiani y Herrera, 3°, Asunción; tel. (21) 50-7501; fax (21) 50-9494; f. 1973; FM; Dir RICARDO FACCETTI.

Radio Uno: Avda Mariscal López 2948, Asunción; tel. (21) 61-2151; f. 1968; as Radio Chaco Boreal; AM; Dir JAVIER MARÍA PIROVANO SILVA.

Radio Venus: Avdas República Argentina y Souza, Asunción; tel. (21) 61-0151; e-mail venus@infonet.com.py; internet www.venus.com.py; f. 1987; FM; Dir ANGEL AGUILERA.

Radio Ysapy: Independencia Nacional 1260, 1°, Asunción; tel. (21) 44-4037; FM; Dir JOSÉ TOMÁS CABRIZA SALVIONI.

Television

Teledifusora Paraguaya—Canal 13: Chile 993, Asunción; tel. (21) 33-2823; fax (21) 33-1695; f. 1980; Gen. Man. NESTOR LÓPEZ MOREIGA.

Televisión Cerro Corá—Canal 9: Avda Carlos A. López 572, Asunción; tel. (21) 42-4222; fax (21) 48-0230; f. 1965; commercial; Dir Gen. ISMAEL HADID.

Televisora del Este: San Pedro, Calle Pilar, Area 5, Ciudad del Este; tel. (61) 8859; commercial; Dir Lic. JALIL SAFUAN; Gen. Man. A. VILLALBA V.

Televisión Itapúa—Canal 7: Encarnación; tel. (71) 20-4450; commercial; Dir Lic. JALIL SAFUAN; Station Man. JORGE MATEO GRANADA.

Finance

(cap. = capital; res = reserves; dep. = deposits; m. = million; amounts in guaraníes, unless otherwise indicated)

BANKING

Superintendencia de Bancos: Edif. Banco Central del Paraguay, Avda Federación Rusa y Avda Marecos, Barrio Santo Domingo, Asunción; tel. (21) 60-8011; fax (21) 60-8149; e-mail eleguiza@bcp.gov.py; internet www.bcp.gov.py/supban/principal.htm; Supt EDGAR ANDRÉS LEGUIZAMON CARMONA.

Central Bank

Banco Central del Paraguay: Avda Federación Rusa y Cabo 1° Marecos, Casilla 861, Barrio Santo Domingo, Asunción; tel. (21) 61-0088; fax (21) 60-8149; e-mail informaciones@bcp.gov.py; internet www.bcp.gov.py; f. 1952; Pres. Dr MÓNICA LUJÁN PÉREZ DOS SANTOS; Gen. Man. DARÍO ROLANDO ARRÉLLAGA YALUK (acting).

Development Banks

Banco Nacional de Fomento: Independencia Nacional y 25 de Mayo, Asunción; tel. (21) 44-4440; fax (21) 44-6056; e-mail correo@bnf.gov.py; internet www.bnf.gov.py; f. 1961; to take over the deposit and private banking activities of the Banco del Paraguay; Pres. Lic. GERMÁN HUGO ROJAS IRIGOYEN; Sec.-Gen. ALFREDO MALDONADO GÓMEZ; 52 brs.

Crédito Agrícola de Habilitación: Caríos 362 y Willam Richardson, Asunción; tel. (21) 56-9010; fax (21) 55-4956; e-mail cah@quanta.com.py; f. 1943; Pres. Ing. WALBERTO FERREIRA.

Fondo Ganadero: Avda Mariscal López 1669 esq. República Dominicana, Asunción; tel. (21) 29-4361; fax (21) 44-6922; internet www.fondogan.gov.py; f. 1969; govt-owned; Pres. GUILLERMO SERRATTI G.

Commercial Banks

Banco Amambay, SA: Avda Aviadores del Chaco, entre San Martín y Pablo Alborno, Asunción; tel. (21) 60-8831; fax (21) 60-8813; e-mail bcoama@bcoamabancoamambay.com.py; internet www.bancoamambay.com.py; f. 1992; Pres. GUIOMAR DE GÁSPERI; Gen. Man. HUGO PORTILLO SOSA.

Banco Continental, SAECA: Estrella 621, Casilla 2260, Asunción; tel. (21) 44-2002; fax (21) 44-2001; e-mail contil@connexion.com.py; f. 1980; cap. US $4.2m., res $2.5m., dep. $44.6m. (Dec. 2001); Chair. GUILLERMO GROSS BROWN; First Vice-Pres. JAVIER GONZÁLEZ PÉREZ.

Banco Finamérica SA: Chile y Oliva, Casilla 1321, Asunción; tel. (21) 49-1021; fax (21) 44-5199; f. 1988; Pres. Dr GUILLERMO HEISECKE VELÁZQUEZ; Gen. Man. ENRIQUE FERNÁNDEZ ROMAY.

Interbanco, SA: Oliva 349, esq. Chile y Alberdi, Asunción; tel. (21) 49-4992; fax (21) 41-71372; e-mail interban@conexion.com.py; internet www.interbanco.com.py; f. 1978; owned by Unibanco (Brazil); cap. 19,000.0m., res 55,864.0m., dep. 812,840.4m. (Dec. 2002); Pres. SERGIO ZAPPA; Gen. Man. CARLOS EDUARDO CASTRO; 5 brs.

Foreign Banks

ABN AMRO Bank NV (Netherlands): Alberdi y Estrella, Casilla 1180, Asunción; tel. (21) 49-0001; fax (21) 49-1734; e-mail clientes@py.abnamro.com; internet www.abnamronet.com; f. 1965; Gen. Man. PETER BALTUSSEN.

Banco Asunción, SA: Palma esq. 14 de Mayo, Asunción; tel. (21) 41-77000; fax (21) 41-77222; e-mail bancoasuncion@bancoasuncion.com.py; internet www.bancoasuncion.com.py; f. 1964; major shareholder Banco Central Hispano (Spain); Exec. Pres. LISARDO PELÁEZ ACERO; 2 brs.

Banco Bilbao Vizcaya Argentaria Paraguaya, SA (Spain): Yegros 435 y 25 de Mayo, Casilla 824, Asunción; tel. (21) 49-2072; fax (21) 44-7874; e-mail bbva.paraguay@bbva.com.py; f. 1961; as Banco Exterior de España, SA; renamed Argentaria Banco Exterior in 1999, name changed to above in 2000; Pres. and Gen. Man. ANGEL SORIA TABUENCA; 5 brs.

Banco do Estado de São Paulo SA (BANESPA) (Brazil): Independencia Nacional, esq. Fulgencio R. Moreno, Casilla 2211, Asunción; tel. (21) 49-4981; fax (21) 49-4985; e-mail banesspa@infonet.com.py; Pres. and Dir GABRIEL JARAMILLO SANINT.

Banco de la Nación Argentina: Chile y Palma, Asunción; tel. (21) 44-8566; fax (21) 44-4365; e-mail bnaasn@bna.com.py; f. 1942; Man. ALDO DARIO PAVIOTTI; 3 brs.

Banco del Paraná, SA: Chile, esq. Eduardo V. Haedo, Apdo 2298, Asunción; tel. (21) 44-6691; fax (21) 49-8909; e-mail banco.parana@bancodelparana.com.py; internet www.bancodelparana.com.py; f. 1980; cap. US $12.6m., dep. $32.3m. (Dec. 2001); 90.79% owned by Banestado (Brazil); Pres. ANTONIO CARLOS GENOVESE; Dir MIRAMAR BOTTINI, Filho; 5 brs.

Banco Sudameris Paraguay, SA: Independencia Nacional y Cerro Corá, Casilla 1433, Asunción; tel. (21) 44-8670; fax (21) 44-4024; e-mail gerencia@sudameris.com.py; internet www.sudameris.com.py; f. 1961; savings and commercial bank; subsidiary of Banque Sudameris; cap. 41,659.1m., res 24,067.3m., dep. 1,033,524.7m. (Dec. 2002); Pres. CARLOS GONZÁLEZ TABOADA; Man. IGNACIO JAQUOTOT; 5 brs.

Citibank NA (USA): Estrella, esq. Chile, Asunción; tel. (21) 494-951; fax (21) 444-820; e-mail citservi.paraguay@citicorp.com; internet www.citibank.com/paraguay; f. 1958; dep. 55,942.2m.; total assets 1,316,258.1m. (Dec. 1997); Gen. Man. HENRY COMBER.

Lloyds Bank PLC (United Kingdom): Palma, esq. Juan E. O'Leary, Apdo 696, Asunción; tel. (21) 491-7000; fax (21) 491-7414; e-mail lbpyitec@conexion.com.py; f. 1920; Man. STUART R. C. DUNCAN.

Banking Associations

Asociación de Bancos del Paraguay: Jorge Berges 229, esq. EEUU, Asunción; tel. (21) 21-4951; fax (21) 20-5050; e-mail abp.par@pla.net.py; mems: Paraguayan banks and foreign banks with brs in Asunción; Pres. CELIO TUNHOLI.

Cámara de Bancos Paraguayos: 25 de Mayo, esq. 22 de Setiembre, Asunción; tel. (21) 22-2373; Pres. MIGUEL ANGEL LARREINEGABE.

STOCK EXCHANGE

Bolsa de Valores y Productos de Asunción SA: Estrella 540, Asunción; tel. (21) 44-2445; fax (21) 44-2446; internet www.bvpasa.com.py; f. 1977; Pres. JORGE DANIEL PECCI MILTOS; Gen. Man. HUGO EUGENIO SALINAS VALDÉS.

PARAGUAY

INSURANCE

Supervisory Authority

Superintendencia de Seguros: Edif. Banco Central del Paraguay, 1°, Federación Rusa y Sargento Marecos, Asunción; tel. (21) 619-2605; fax (21) 619-2637; e-mail gbenitez@bcp.gov.py; internet www.bcp.gov.py/supseg/default.html; Supt MÁXIMO GUSTAVO BENÍTEZ GIMÉNEZ.

Principal Companies

La Agrícola SA de Seguros Generales: Mariscal López 5377 y Consejal Vargas, Asunción; tel. (21) 60-9509; fax (21) 60-9606; e-mail laagricola@rieder.net.py; f. 1982; general; Pres. Dr VICENTE OSVALDO BERGUES; Gen. Man. CARLOS ALBERTO LEVI SOSA.

ALFA SA de Seguros y Reaseguros: Yegros 944, Asunción; tel. (21) 44-9992; fax (21) 44-9991; e-mail alfa.seg@conexion.com.py; Pres. NICOLAS SARUBBI ZAYAS.

América SA de Seguros y Reaseguros: Alberdi 980 esq. Manduvirá, 1°, Asunción; tel. (21) 49-1713; fax (21) 44-8036; e-mail amea@telesurf.com.py; Pres. EDUARDO NICOLÁS BO PEÑA.

Aseguradora del Este SA de Seguros: Edif. Castilla Center, 3°, Carlos A. López esq. Paí Pérez, Ciudad del Este; tel. (61) 51-2941; fax (61) 50-4843; e-mail dcespedes@aesaseguros.com.py; Pres. VÍCTOR ANDRÉS RIBEIRO ESPÍNOLA.

Aseguradora Paraguaya, SA: Israel 309 esq. Rio de Janeiro, Casilla 277, Asunción; tel. (21) 21-5086; fax (21) 22-2217; e-mail asepasa@asepasa.com.py; f. 1976; life and risk; Pres. GERARDO TORCIDA CONEJERO.

Aseguradora Yacyreta SA de Seguros y Reaseguros: Oliva 685, esq. Juan E. O'Leary y 15 de Agosto, Asunción; tel. (21) 45-2374; fax (21) 44-5070; e-mail spalomar@yacyreta.com.py; f. 1980; Pres. OSCAR HARRISON JACQUET.

Atalaya SA de Seguros Generales: Independencia Nacional 565, 1°, esq. Azara y Cerro Corá, Asunción; tel. (21) 49-2811; fax (21) 49-6966; e-mail ataseg@telesurf.com.py; f. 1964; general; Pres. KARIN M. DOLL.

Cenit de Seguros, SA: Ayolas 1082, esq. Ibáñez del Campo, Asunción; tel. (21) 44-4972; fax (21) 44-9502; e-mail cenitsa@rieder.net.py; Pres. Dr FELIPE OSCAR ARMELE BONZI.

Central SA de Seguros: Edif. Betón I, 1° y 2°, Eduardo Víctor Haedo 179, Independencia Nacional, Casilla 1802, Asunción; tel. (21) 49-4654; fax (21) 49-4655; e-mail censeg@conexion.com.py; f. 1977; general; Pres. MIGUEL JACOBO VILLASANTI; Gen. Man. Dr FÉLIX AVEIRO.

El Comercio Paraguayo SA Cía de Seguros Generales: Alberdi 453 y Oliva, Asunción; tel. (21) 49-2324; fax (21) 49-3562; f. 1947; life and risk; Dir Dr BRAULIO OSCAR ELIZECHE.

La Consolidada SA de Seguros y Reaseguros: Chile 719 y Eduardo Víctor Haedo, Casilla 1182, Asunción; tel. (21) 49-5174; fax (21) 44-5795; e-mail info@laconsolidada.com.py; f. 1961; life and risk; Pres. JUAN CARLOS DELGADILLO ECHAGÜE.

Fénix SA de Seguros y Reaseguros: Iturbe 823 y Fulgencio R. Moreno, Asunción; tel. (21) 49-5549; fax (21) 44-5643; e-mail fenix@quanta.com.py; Pres. VÍCTOR MARTÍNEZ YARYES.

Garantía SA de Seguros y Reaseguros: 25 de Mayo 640, Asunción; tel. (21) 44-3748; fax (21) 49-0678; e-mail garantia@rieder.net.py; Pres. GERALDO CRISTALDO JURE.

Grupo General de Seguros y Reaseguros, SA: Edif. Grupo General, Jejuí 324 y Chile, 2°, Asunción; tel. (21) 49-7897; fax (21) 44-9259; e-mail general_de_seguros@ggeneral.com.py; Pres. JORGE OBELAR LAMAS.

La Independencia de Seguros y Reaseguros, SA: Edif. Parapatí, 1°, Juan E. O'Leary 409, esq. Estrella, Casilla 980, Asunción; tel. (21) 44-7021; fax (21) 44-8996; e-mail la_independencia@par.net.py; f. 1965; general; Pres. REGINO MOSCARDA; Gen. Man. JUAN FRANCISCO FRANCO LÓPEZ.

Intercontinental SA de Seguros y Reaseguros: Iturbe 1047 con Teniente Fariña, Altos, Asunción; tel. (21) 49-2348; fax (21) 49-1227; e-mail mvmodica@yahoo.com; f. 1978; Pres. Dr JUAN MÓDICA LUCENTE; Gen. Man. LUIS SANTACRUZ.

Mapfre Paraguay, SA: Avda Mariscal López 910 y General Aquino, Asunción; tel. (21) 44-1983; fax (21) 49-7441; e-mail sac@mapfre.com.py; Pres. LUIS MARÍA ZUBIZARRETA.

La Meridional Paraguaya SA de Seguros: Iturbe 1046, Teniente Fariña, Asunción; tel. (21) 49-8827; fax (21) 49-8826; e-mail meridian@conexion.com.py; Pres. TITO LIVIO MUJICA VARELA.

Mundo SA de Seguros: Estrella 917 y Montevideo, Asunción; tel. (21) 49-2787; fax (21) 44-5486; e-mail mundosa@par.net.py; f. 1970; risk; Pres. JUAN MARTÍN VILLALBA DE LOS RÍOS; Gen. Man. BLAS MARCIAL CABRAL BARRIOS.

La Paraguaya SA de Seguros: Estrella 675, 7°, Asunción; tel. (21) 49-1367; fax (21) 44-8235; e-mail lps@conexion.com.py; f. 1905; life and risk; Pres. JUAN BOSCH BEYNEN.

Patria SA de Seguros y Reaseguros: General Santos 715 esq. Siria, Asunción; tel. (21) 22-5250; fax (21) 21-4001; e-mail patria@conexion.com.py; f. 1968; general; Pres. Dr MARCOS PERERA R.

El Productor SA de Seguros y Reaseguros: Ind. Nacional 811 esq. Fulgencio R. Moreno, 8°, Asunción; tel. (21) 49-1577; fax (21) 49-1599; e-mail ncabanas@elproductor.com.py; Pres. REINALDO PAVÍA MALDONADO.

Real Paraguaya de Seguros, SA: Edif. Banco Real, 1°, Estrella esq. Alberdi, Casilla 1442, Asunción; tel. (21) 49-2221; fax (21) 49-8129; e-mail realseg@pla.net.py; f. 1974; general; Pres. EUCLIDES HUMBERTO VARNIERI RIBEIRO.

Regional SA de Seguros y Reaseguros: Roque González 390 y Dr Hassler, Asunción; tel. (21) 61-0692; fax (21) 22-4447; e-mail regisesa@itacom.com.py; Pres. JUAN A. DIAZ DE VIVAR PRIETO.

Rumbos SA de Seguros: Estrella 851, Ayolas, Casilla 1017, Asunción; tel. (21) 44-9488; fax (21) 44-9492; e-mail rumbos@conexión.com.py; f. 1960; general; Pres. MIGUEL A. LARREINEGAVE LESME; Man. Dir ROBERTO GÓMEZ VERLANGIERI.

La Rural SA de Seguros: Avda Mariscal López 1082, esq. Mayor Bullo, Casilla 21, Asunción; tel. (21) 49-1917; fax (21) 44-1592; e-mail larural@larural.com.py; f. 1920; general; Pres. YUSAKU MATSUMIYA; Gen. Man. EDUARDO BARRIOS PERINI.

Seguros Chaco SA de Seguros y Reaseguros: Mariscal Estigarribia 982, Casilla 3248, Asunción; tel. (21) 44-7118; fax (21) 44-9551; e-mail segucha@conexion.com.py; f. 1977; general; Pres. EMILIO VELILLA LACONICH; Exec. Dir ALBERTO R. ZARZA TABOADA.

Seguros Generales, SA (SEGESA): Edif. SEGESA, 1°, Oliva 393 esq. Alberdi, Casilla 802, Asunción; tel. (21) 49-1362; fax (21) 49-1360; e-mail segesa@conexion.com.py; f. 1956; life and risk; Pres. CÉSAR AVALOS.

El Sol del Paraguay, Cía de Seguros y Reaseguros, SA: Cerro Corá 1031, Asunción; tel. (21) 49-1110; fax (21) 21-0604; e-mail mab@elsol.com.py; f. 1978; Pres. MIGUEL ANGEL BERNI CENTURIÓN; Vice-Pres. CAROLINA VEGA DE ONETTO.

Universo de Seguros y Reaseguros, SA: Edif. de la Encarnación, 9°, 14 de Mayo esq. General Díaz, Casilla 788, Asunción; tel. (21) 44-8530; fax (21) 44-7278; f. 1979; Pres. ZENÓN AGÜERO MIRANDA.

Insurance Association

Asociación Paraguaya de Cías de Seguros: 15 de Agosto, esq. Lugano, Casilla 1435, Asunción; tel. (21) 44-6474; fax (21) 44-4343; e-mail apcs@uninet.com.py; f. 1963; Pres. Dr EMILIO VELILIA LACONICH; Gen. Man. RUBÉN RAPPENECKER.

Trade and Industry

GOVERNMENT AGENCIES

Consejo Nacional para las Exportaciones: Asunción; f. 1986; founded to eradicate irregular trading practices; Dir RAÚL JOSÉ VERA BOGADO (Minister of Industry and Commerce).

Consejo de Privatización: Edif. Ybaga, 10°, Presidente Franco 173, Asunción; fax (21) 44-9157; responsible for the privatization of state-owned enterprises; Exec. Dir RUBÉN MORALES PAOLI.

Instituto Nacional de Tecnología y Normalización (INTN) (National Institute of Technology and Standardization): Avda General Artigas 3973 y General Roa, Casilla 967, Asunción; tel. (21) 29-0160; fax (21) 29-0266; e-mail intn@intn.gov.py; internet www.intn.gov.py; national standards institute; Dir-Gen. LILIAN MARTÍNEZ DE ALONSO.

Instituto de Previsión Social: Constitución y Luis Alberto de Herrera, Casilla 437, Asunción; tel. (21) 22-5719; fax (21) 22-3654; f. 1943; responsible for employees' welfare and health insurance scheme; Pres. PEDRO FERREIRA.

DEVELOPMENT ORGANIZATIONS

Secretaría Técnica de Planificación del Desarrollo Económico y Social: Edif. AYFRA, 3°, Presidente Franco y Ayolas, Asunción; tel. (21) 45-0422; fax (21) 49-6510; e-mail webmarketing@stp.gov.py; govt body responsible for overall economic and social planning; Exec. Sec. CARLOS LUIS FILIPPI SANABRÍA; Sec.-Gen. Lic. OSVALDO MARTINEZ ORTEGA.

Acuerdo Ciudadano (Articulación de la Sociedad Civil): República de Siria 35, Asunción; tel. (21) 20-7757; fax (21) 20-2918; e-mail info@acuerdociudadano.org.py; internet www.acuerdociudadano.org.py; f. 2001; grouping of social devt orgs; Gen. Co-ordinator PASCUAL RUBIANI YANHO.

PARAGUAY

AFS: Azara 2242 con 22 de Setiembre, Asunción; tel. (21) 44-2369; fax (21) 49-3277; e-mail info-paraguay@afs.org; internet www.afs.org.py; educational and social devt; Exec. Dir VICTORIA VILLALBA.

Alter Vida (Centro de Estudios y Formación para el Ecodesarrollo): Itapúa 1372, esq. Primer Presidente y Río Monday, Barrio Trinidad, Asunción; tel. (21) 29-8842; fax (21) 29-8845; e-mail info@altervida.org.py; internet www.altervida.org.py; f. 1985; ecological devt; Dir BEATRÍZ CHASE.

Asociación Rural del Paraguay (ARP): Ruta Transchaco, Km. 14, Asunción; tel. (21) 75-4412; e-mail ania@arp.org.py; internet www.arp.org.py; grouping of agricultural cos and farmers; Dir M. R. ALONSO.

Centro de Información y Recursos para el Desarrollo (CIRD): Asunción; tel. (21) 22-6071; fax (21) 21-2540; e-mail cird@cird.org.py; internet www.cird.org.py; f. 1988; information and resources for devt orgs; Exec. Pres. AGUSTÍN CARRIZOSA.

Consejo Nacional de Coordinación Económica: Presidencia de la República, Paraguayo Independiente y Juan E. O'Leary, Asunción; responsible for overall economic policy; Sec. FULVIO MONGES OCAMPOS.

Consejo Nacional de Desarrollo Industrial (National Council for Industrial Development): Asunción; national planning institution.

Cooperación Empresarial y Desarrollo Industrial (CEDIAL): Edif. UIP, 2°, Cerro Corá 1038, esq. Estados Unidos y Brasil, Asunción; tel. (21) 23-0047; e-mail cedial@cedial.org.py; internet www.cedial.org.py; promotes commerce and industrial devt; Gen. Man. HERNÁN RAMÍREZ.

Instituto de Bienestar Rural (IBR): Tacuary 276, Asunción; tel. (21) 44-0578; fax (21) 44-6534; responsible for rural welfare and colonization; Pres. ANTONIO IBÁÑEZ.

Instituto Paraguayo del Indígena (INDI): Don Bosco 745, Casilla 1575, Asunción; tel. (21) 49-3737; fax (21) 44-7154; f. 1981; responsible for welfare of Indian population; Pres. OLGA ROJAS DE BAEZ.

ProParaguay: Edif. Ayfra, 12°, Presidente Franco y Ayolas, Asunción; tel. (21) 49-3625; fax (21) 49-3862; e-mail ppy@proparaguay.gov.py; internet www.proparaguay.gov.py; f. 1991; responsible for promoting investment in Paraguay and the export of national products; Dir-Gen. LUIS MORINIGO GANCHI.

Red Rural de Organizaciones Privadas de Desarrollo: Manuel Domínguez 1045, Asunción; tel. (21) 22-9740; e-mail redrural@telesurf.com.py; internet www.redrural.org.py; f. 1989; co-ordinating body for rural devt orgs; Gen. Co-ordinator IDALINA GÓMEZ; Sec. HEBE GONZÁLEZ.

CHAMBERS OF COMMERCE

Cámara Nacional de Comercio y Servicios de Paraguay: Estrella 540-550, Asunción; tel. (21) 49-3321; fax (21) 44-0817; e-mail info@ccparaguay.com.py; internet www.ccparaguay.com.py; f. 1898; fmrly Cámara y Bolsa de Comercio; name changed 2002; Pres. RAUL RICARDO DOS SANTOS; Gen. Man. Lic. MIGUEL RIQUELME OLAZAR.

Cámara de Comercio Paraguayo-Americano (Paraguayan-American Chamber of Commerce): Edif. El Faro Internacional, 4°, Of. 1, General Díaz 521, Asunción; tel. and fax (21) 44-2135; e-mail pamchamb@conexion.com.py; internet www.pamcham.com.py; f. 1981; c. 120 mem cos.

Cámara de Comercio Paraguayo-Arabe: Próceres de Mayo 296, esq. Ana Díaz, Asunción; tel. 22-7197; fax 21-3240; Pres. MOHAMED RAHAL.

Cámara de Comercio Paraguayo-Británico: Avda Boggiani 5848, Asunción; tel. 61-2611; fax 60-5007; e-mail britcham@conexion.com.py; Pres. RONALD BURNETT.

Cámara de Comercio Paraguayo-Chileno: Guido Spano 1687, Asunción; tel. and fax 66-3085; e-mail ccpch@quanta.com.py; Pres. GUSTAVO OLMEDO SISUL.

Cámara de Comercio Paraguayo-Francesa (CCPF): Yegros 837, 1°, Of. 12, CP 3009, Asunción; tel. 49-7852; fax 44-6324; e-mail info@ccpf.com.py; internet www.ccpf.com.py; Man. IRIS FELIU DE FLEITAS.

EMPLOYERS' ORGANIZATIONS

Asociación de Empresas Financieras del Paraguay (ADEFI): Edif. Ahorros Paraguayos, Torre II, 6°, Of. 05, General Díaz 471, Asunción; tel. (21) 44-82 98; fax (21) 49-8071; e-mail adefi@conexion.com.py; internet www.adefi.org.py; f. 1975; grouping of financial cos; Pres. BELTRÁN MACCHI SALÍN.

Asociación Paraguaya de la Calidad: Luis Alberto de Herrera 195, 19°, Asunción; tel. (21) 44-7348; fax (21) 45-0705; e-mail apc@apc.org.py; internet www.apc.org.py; f. 1988; grouping of cos to promote quality of goods and services; Pres. MIGUEL ANGEL CASTILLO.

Federación de la Producción, Industria y Comercio (FEPRINCO): Edif. Union Club, Palma 751, 3°, esq. O'Leary y Ayolas, Asunción; tel. (21) 44-6634; fax (21) 44-6638; e-mail feprinco@quanta.com.py; org. of private-sector business execs; Pres. MIGUEL ANGEL CARRIZOSA GALLIANO.

Unión Industrial Paraguaya (UIP): Cerro Corá 1038, entre Estados Unidos y Brasil, Casilla 782, Asunción; tel. (21) 21-2556; fax (21) 21-3360; e-mail uip@uip.org.py; internet www.uip.org.py; f. 1936; org. of business entrepreneurs; Pres. Ing. GUILLERMO STANLEY.

UTILITIES

Electricity

Administración Nacional de Electricidad (ANDE): Avda España 1268, Asunción; tel. (21) 21-1001; fax (21) 21-2371; e-mail ande@ande.gov.py; internet www.ande.gov.py; f. 1949; national electricity board, privatization plans cancelled in June 2002; Pres. MARTÍN GONZÁLEZ GUGGIANI; Sec.-Gen. LUÍS OSVALDO VIVEROS GÓMEZ.

Itaipú Binacional: Centro Administrativo, Ruta Internacional Km 3.5, Avda Señor Rodríguez 150, Ciudad del Este; tel. (61) 57-2600; e-mail itaipu@itaipu.gov.br; internet www.itaipu.gov.br; f. 1974; jtly owned by Paraguay and Brazil; hydroelectric power-station on Brazilian-Paraguayan border; 1.3m. GWh of electricity produced in 2004; Dir-Gen. (Paraguay) Dr VÍCTOR BERNAL GARAY.

Water

Empresa de Servicios Sanitarios del Paraguay (ESSAP): José Berges 516, entre Brasil y San José, Asunción; tel. (21) 21-0319; fax (21) 21-5061; fmrly Corporación de Obras Sanitarias (CORPOSANA); responsible for public water supply, sewage disposal and drainage; privatization plans suspended in 2002; Pres. CARLOS ANTONIO LÓPEZ RODRÍGUEZ.

TRADE UNIONS

Central Nacional de Trabajadores (CNT): Piribebuy 1078, Asunción; tel. (21) 44-4084; fax (21) 49-2154; e-mail cnt@telesurf.com.py; Sec.-Gen. EDUARDO OJEDA; 80,000 mems.

Central de Sindicatos de Trabajadores del Estado Paraguayo (Cesitep): Asunción; Pres. REINALDO BARRETO MEDINA.

Central Unitaria de Trabajadores (CUT): San Carlos 836, Asunción; tel. (21) 44-3936; fax (21) 44-8482; f. 1989; Pres. ALAN FLORES; Sec.-Gen. JORGE ALVARENGA.

Confederación Paraguaya de Trabajadores (CPT) (Confederation of Paraguayan Workers): Yegros 1309–33 y Simón Bolívar, Asunción; tel. (21) 44-4921; fax (21) 20-5070; e-mail sixto10@telesurf.com.py; f. 1951; Pres. SIXTO ALONSO MENDOZA; Sec.-Gen. PATROCINIO CARMONA; 43,500 mems from 189 affiliated groups.

Coordinadora Agrícola de Paraguay (CAP): Asunción; farmers' org.; Pres. HÉCTOR CRISTALDO.

Organización de Trabajadores de Educación del Paraguay (OTEP): Avda del Pueblo 845 con Ybyra Pyta, Barrio Santa Lucía, Lambaré; tel. and fax (21) 55-5525; e-mail otepsn@highway.com.py.

Transport

RAILWAYS

Ferrocarriles del Paraguay: México 145, Casilla 453, Asunción; tel. (21) 44-3273; fax (21) 44-2733; e-mail ferroca@rieder.net.py; internet www.ferrocarriles.com.py; f. 1854; state-owned since 1961; 376 km of track; scheduled for privatization; Pres. LAURO MANUEL RAMÍREZ LÓPEZ.

ROADS

In 1999 there were an estimated 29,500 km of roads, of which 14,986 km were paved. The Pan-American Highway runs for over 700 km in Paraguay and the Trans-Chaco Highway extends from Asunción to Bolivia.

SHIPPING

Administración Nacional de Navegación y Puertos (ANNP) (National Shipping and Ports Administration): Cólon y El Paraguayo Independiente, Asunción; tel. (21) 49-5086; fax (21) 49-7485; e-mail annp@mail.pla.net.py; internet www.annp.gov.py; f. 1965; responsible for ports services and maintaining navigable channels in rivers and for improving navigation on the Rivers Paraguay and Paraná; Pres. MILCIADES RABERY OCAMPOS.

Inland Waterways

Flota Mercante Paraguaya SA (FLOMEPASA): Estrella 672-686, Casilla 454, Asunción; tel. (21) 44-7409; fax (21) 44-6010; boats and barges up to 1,000 tons displacement on Paraguay and Paraná rivers; cold storage ships for use Asunción–Buenos Aires–Montevideo; Pres. Capt. ANÍBAL GINO PERTILE R.; Commercial Dir Dr EMIGDIO DUARTE SOSTOA.

Ocean Shipping

Compañía Paraguaya de Navegación de Ultramar, SA: Presidente Franco 625, 2°, Casilla 77, Asunción; tel. (21) 49-2137; fax (21) 44-5013; f. 1963; to operate between Asunción, US and European ports; 10 vessels; Exec. Pres. JUAN BOSCH B.

Navemar S.R.L.: B. Constant 536, 1°, Casilla 273, Asunción; tel. (21) 49-3122; 5 vessels.

Transporte Fluvial Paraguayo S.A.C.I.: Edif. de la Encarnación, 13°, 14 de Mayo 563, Asunción; tel. (21) 49-3411; fax (21) 49-8218; e-mail tfpsaci@tm.com.py; Admin. Man. DANIELLA CHARBONNIER; 1 vessel.

CIVIL AVIATION

The major international airport, Aeropuerto Internacional Silvio Pettirossi, is situated 15 km from Asunción. A second international airport, Aeropuerto Internacional Guaraní, 30 km from Ciudad del Este, was inaugurated in 1996.

National Airlines

Transportes Aéreos del Mercosur (TAM Mercosur): Aeropuerto Internacional Silvio Pettirossi, Hangar TAM/ARPA, Luque, Asunción; tel. (21) 49-1039; fax (21) 64-5146; e-mail tammercosur@uninet.com.py; internet www.tam.com.py; f. 1963; as Líneas Aéreas Paraguayas (LAP), name changed as above in 1997; services to destinations within South America; 80% owned by TAM Linhas Aéreas (Brazil); Pres. MIGUEL CANDIA.

Aerolíneas Paraguayas (ARPA): Terminal ARPA, Aeropuerto Internacional Silvio Pettirossi, Asunción; tel. (21) 21-5072; fax (21) 21-5111; f. 1994; domestic service; wholly owned by Transportes Aéreos del Mercosur (TAM Mercosur).

Tourism

Tourism is undeveloped, but, with recent improvements in infrastructure, efforts were being made to promote the sector. Tourist arrivals in Paraguay in 2003 totalled 268,175. In that year tourism receipts were US $81m.

Secretaría Nacional de Turismo: Palma 468, Asunción; tel. (21) 49-4110; fax (21) 49-1230; e-mail infosenatur@senatur.gov.py; internet www.senatur.gov.py; f. 1998; Exec. Sec. MARÍA EVANGELISTA TROCHE DE GALLEGOS.

PERU

Introductory Survey

Location, Climate, Language, Religion, Flag, Capital

The Republic of Peru lies in western South America, bordered by Ecuador and Colombia to the north, by Brazil and Bolivia to the east, and by Chile to the south. Peru has a coastline of more than 2,300 km (1,400 miles) on the Pacific Ocean. The climate varies with altitude, average temperatures being about 11°C (20°F) lower in the Andes mountains than in the coastal plain. The rainy season is between October and April, with heavy rainfall in the tropical forests. Temperatures in Lima are usually between 13°C (55°F) and 28°C (82°F). The three official languages are Spanish, Quechua and Aymará. Almost all of the inhabitants profess Christianity, and the great majority are adherents of the Roman Catholic Church. The civil flag (proportions 2 by 3) has three equal vertical stripes, of red, white and red. The state flag additionally has the national coat of arms (a shield divided into three unequal segments: red, with a golden cornucopia spilling coins of yellow and white at the base, blue, with a yellow vicuña in the dexter chief, and white, with a green tree in the sinister chief; all surmounted by a green wreath, and framed by branches of palm and laurel, tied at the bottom with a red and white ribbon) in the centre of the white stripe. The capital is Lima.

Recent History

Since independence from Spain, declared in 1821 and finally achieved in 1824, Peruvian politics have been characterized by alternating periods of civilian administration and military dictatorship. In the early 1920s opposition to the dictatorial regime of President Augusto Bernardino Leguía resulted in the creation of the Alianza Popular Revolucionaria Americana (APRA—also known as the Partido Aprista Peruano), Peru's oldest political party to command mass support. The party, founded as a nationalist revolutionary movement, was formally established in Peru in 1930, when Leguía was deposed and the party's founder (and its leader for more than 50 years), Dr Víctor Raúl Haya de la Torre, returned from enforced exile in Mexico. A long-standing tradition of hostility developed between APRA and the armed forces, and the party was banned in 1931–45, and again in 1948–56.

During 1945–63 political power shifted regularly between the armed forces and elected government. In 1948 Dr José Luis Bustamente y Rivera was deposed by Gen. Manuel Odría, following a right-wing military rebellion. Odría established a military junta which governed until 1950, when the General was elected unopposed to the presidency, and subsequently appointed a cabinet composed of military officers and civilians. In 1956 Odría was succeeded by Dr Manuel Prado y Ugartache (who had been President in 1939–45). An inconclusive presidential election in 1962 precipitated military intervention, and power was assumed by Gen. Ricardo Pérez Godoy, at the head of a military junta. In March 1963, however, Pérez was supplanted by his second-in-command, Gen. Nicolás Lindley López.

Fernando Belaúnde Terry, the joint candidate of his own Acción Popular (AP) party and the Partido Demócrata Cristiano, emerged as the successful contestant at presidential elections conducted in June 1963. An increase in internal disturbances in predominantly Indian areas resulted in the temporary suspension of constitutional guarantees in 1965–66 and an intensive military campaign of counter-insurgency. Although the Belaúnde administration successfully promoted agrarian reform, lack of congressional support for the Government contributed to a succession of ministerial crises which, together with continuing internal unrest, prompted renewed military intervention in October 1968, when Gen. Juan Velasco Alvarado assumed the presidency, dissolved Congress and appointed a military cabinet.

Despite the re-emergence of internal disturbances and dissension within the armed forces, provoked by the introduction of radical reforms and austerity measures, Velasco retained power until August 1975, when he was overthrown and replaced by Gen. Francisco Morales Bermúdez. In July 1977 President Morales announced plans for the restoration of civilian rule. Accordingly, a national election was conducted in June 1978 to select the members of a constituent assembly, which was to draft a new constitution in preparation for presidential and congressional elections. In the election, APRA emerged as the largest party, and in July the assembly elected the 83-year-old Dr Haya de la Torre to be its President. The new Constitution, adopted in July 1979, provided for elections by universal adult suffrage, and extended the franchise to the sizeable illiterate population.

The presidential contest of May 1980 was won decisively by Belaúnde. At the same time, the AP won an outright majority in the Cámara de Diputados (Chamber of Deputies) and also secured the greatest representation in the Senado (Senate). The new organs of state were inaugurated in July, when the new Constitution became fully effective. While Belaúnde sought to liberalize the economy and to reverse many of the agrarian and industrial reforms implemented under Velasco, much of his term of office was dominated by the increasing threat to internal stability posed by the emergence, in the early 1980s, of the Maoist terrorist group, the Sendero Luminoso (SL—Shining Path). The situation deteriorated following the uncompromising response of the armed forces to terrorist activity in a designated emergency zone, which extended to 13 provinces (primarily in the departments of Ayacucho, Huancavelica and Apurímac) by mid-1984, and a dramatic increase in violent deaths and violations of human rights was reported.

At elections in April 1985 Alan Gabriel Ludwig García Pérez (the candidate for APRA) received 46% of the total votes in the presidential poll, while APRA secured a majority in both houses (the Cámara and the Senado) of the Congreso (legislature). García's victory was ensured in May, prior to a second round of voting, when his closest opponent, Dr Alfonso Barrantes Lingán (of the left-wing Izquierda Unida coalition), withdrew his candidature. At his inauguration in July, García announced that his Government's priorities would be to arrest Peru's severe economic decline and to eradicate internal terrorism.

Despite APRA successes at municipal elections in 1986, widespread opposition to the Government's economic programme was manifested in a succession of well-supported general strikes in 1987 and 1988. Government plans in 1987 for the nationalization of Peru's banks and private financial and insurance institutions encountered considerable opposition from the financial sector, and prompted the creation of Libertad, a 'freedom movement' expressing opposition to the plans (which were subsequently modified), which was established under the leadership of a well-known writer, Mario Vargas Llosa. The authority of the García administration was further undermined by persistent rumours of military unrest, allegations of links between members of the Government and the right-wing paramilitary 'death squad', the Comando Rodrigo Franco, and by the continuing terrorist activities of SL and a resurgence of activity by the Movimiento Revolucionario Tupac Amarú (MRTA) guerrilla group, in north-east Peru. In addition, the Government was criticized by international human rights organizations for its methods of combating political violence.

General elections took place on 8 April 1990, despite the attempts of SL to disrupt the elections with another 'armed strike' and a campaign of bombing and looting. In the presidential poll Vargas Llosa, the candidate of the centre-right FREDEMO alliance (established in 1988 by the AP, Libertad and the Partido Popular Cristiano), obtained the largest percentage of the total votes cast, but failed to attain the required absolute majority by only narrowly defeating a hitherto little-known agronomist, Alberto Fujimori, the candidate of the Cambio 90 group of independents. In a second round of voting, conducted on 10 June, Fujimori emerged as the successful candidate, having attracted late support from left-wing parties and from APRA. Following his inauguration in July, Fujimori announced the composition of a new centre-left Council of Ministers, with Juan Carlos Hurtado Miller, a member of the AP, as Prime Minister and Minister of Economy and Finance.

Proposals for economic readjustment announced in August 1990 abolished subsidies for consumers, thereby increasing prices by more than 3,000% for petrol and by as much as 600% for basic foods. Despite the success of these economic reforms in securing Peru's rehabilitation within the international financial community, the adverse consequences to consumers of adjustment provoked widespread opposition and industrial unrest (as well as the resignation of Hurtado from the cabinet). In November 1991, despite public and congressional dissent, Fujimori took advantage of a 150-day period of emergency legislative powers (granted to him in June in order that the country's potentially destabilizing economic and security problems might be addressed) to issue a series of economic decrees that represented a continuation of policies which concerned the elimination of state monopolies of telecommunications, postal networks and railways, the opening to private investment of the power sector, the privatization of schools and a reform of the health and social security services.

The increasing divergence of interests of President Fujimori and the Congreso (which had expressed considerable disaffection with the President's reliance upon emergency legislative powers and his attempts to govern by decree) was exacerbated in January 1992 by congressional approval of that year's draft budget, which Fujimori had opposed on the grounds that it contained provisions for excessive expenditure. On 5 April Fujimori announced the immediate suspension of the 1979 Constitution and the dissolution of the Congreso, pending a comprehensive restructuring of the legislature. The President maintained that the reform of the Congreso was essential in order to eradicate 'corruption and inefficiency', to enable him to implement a programme of 'pacification' of the nation by combating terrorism and drugs-trafficking, and also fully to implement free-market economic policies. In the interim an Emergency and National Reconstruction Government would govern the country, and legislative power would be exercised by the President, with the approval of the Council of Ministers. Fujimori also announced a reform of the judiciary. The constitutional coup (or 'autogolpe') was implemented, without recorded casualties, with the full co-operation and support of the armed forces. On the following day the Prime Minister, Alfonso de los Heros Pérez Albela, resigned in protest, and was replaced by Oscar de la Puente; most government ministers, however, elected to remain in office. Members of the dissolved parliament declared Fujimori to be incapable of continuing in office, although an attempt to establish Máximo San Román, the First Vice-President, as the head of an alternative 'constitutional government' was undermined by a lack of domestic and international support. Moreover, while Fujimori's actions prompted outrage from politicians, the judiciary and the media, popular reaction to the 'autogolpe' was less hostile. Bolstered by demonstrations of public support for his actions, Fujimori dismissed 13 of Peru's 28 Supreme Court judges, whom he accused of corruption, and detained several prominent opposition party figures.

Indications that a return to constitutional government would be undertaken within a 12–18-month period did little to alleviate mounting international pressure upon the Government to take immediate steps to return to full democracy. The Organization of American States (OAS, see p. 333), deplored Fujimori's actions, and dispatched a mission to attempt to effect a reconciliation between the legislature and the executive. Later in April 1992 Fujimori defined a more comprehensive timetable for the restoration of democracy, with congressional elections to be conducted in February 1993. The Minister of Foreign Affairs and the Minister of Industry, Commerce, Tourism and Integration resigned. The President of the Central Bank was also removed from office, as were 134 judges; 12 provisional members of the Supreme Court were later appointed.

The threat posed to Fujimori's programme of radical reform by economic constraints resulting from the suspension of international financial aid to Peru prompted the revision of the timetable for a return to democracy, and in June 1992 Fujimori confirmed that national elections would be conducted in October to a unicameral constituent congress, which would then draft a new constitution (to be submitted for approval in a national referendum at a later date). The President also announced that, pending approval of a new document, the 1979 Constitution would be reinstated without certain articles that might 'impede the progress of the Government'.

A 'National Dialogue for Peace and Development', comprising a series of discussions with representatives of the political opposition and with the public, sought to identify important issues for future consideration by the new Congreso Constituyente Democrático (CCD). Elections to the CCD, conducted on 22 November 1992 and attended by OAS observers, were a qualified success for pro-Government parties. An electoral coalition of Cambio 90 and the Nueva Mayoría (a new independent party supported by many former cabinet ministers), headed by Fujimori's former Minister of Energy and Mines, Jaime Yoshiyama Tanaka (who was subsequently elected President of the CCD), secured 44 of the 80 congressional seats. The only significant opposition party not to boycott the elections, the Partido Popular Cristiano, took eight seats. In December, at the inaugural meeting of the CCD, Yoshiyama identified its immediate aims as the restoration of the autonomy of the judiciary, the eradication of terrorism, the generation of employment and of favourable conditions for foreign investment, and the projection of an enhanced national image abroad. In January 1993, having formally reinstated the 1979 Constitution, the CCD confirmed Fujimori as constitutional Head of State. Following the resignation of de la Puente's Government in July, Alfonso Bustamente y Bustamente was appointed Prime Minister in August.

The final text of the draft Constitution, which enhanced presidential powers and provided for the establishment of a unicameral legislature, was approved by the CCD in September 1993. A national referendum seeking popular approval for the new Constitution was scheduled for 31 October—the first occasion on which such popular consultation had been sought in Peru. Among the text's most controversial articles were the introduction of the death penalty for convicted terrorists and a provision permitting a President of the Republic to be re-elected for a successive five-year term of office. At the referendum the Constitution was narrowly approved, by an overall 52% of the votes cast. The Constitution was promulgated on 29 December, at a ceremony boycotted by opposition members of the CCD.

Presidential and legislative elections were scheduled for April 1995. However, there was little political campaigning, as Peru's border conflict with Ecuador (see below) resulted in cross-party consensus on the need to maintain national unity. In the presidential election, conducted on 9 April, Fujimori secured an unexpected outright victory over his closest opponent, Javier Pérez de Cuéllar de la Guerra (the former UN Secretary-General and the candidate of the Unión por el Perú—UPP), obtaining 64% of the total votes. In the concurrent legislative elections, Fujimori's coalition movement, Cambio 90-Nueva Mayoría (C90-NM), also secured an absolute majority in the unicameral Congreso. The composition of the new Government, installed following Fujimori's inauguration in July, was largely unaltered. Efraín Goldenberg, who had succeeded Bustamente as Prime Minister in February 1994, was replaced by Dante Córdova Blanco.

In mid-June 1995 new legislation was approved by the Congreso granting an amnesty to all members of the military, police and intelligence forces who had been convicted of human rights violations committed since 1980 in the internal conflict against separatist violence; ostensibly the legislation was to promote national reconciliation, although it was also widely thought to have been introduced by the President in order to consolidate his relationship with the military leadership. The legislation attracted broad criticism from opposition parties, and internationally. In August an international warrant was issued for the arrest of former President Alan García, who had been accused of receiving bribes and other corrupt practices during his term of office.

In April 1996 the sudden resignation of the Prime Minister demonstrated the extent of disunity within the Government, particularly over economic policy. Alberto Pandolfi Arbulu was appointed Prime Minister, and the Government's privatization programme was accelerated. Meanwhile, Fujimori was attempting to formulate legislation that would allow him to stand for election for a third presidential term. A congressional committee approved a new 'interpretation' of the Constitution in August (on the grounds that Fujimori was first elected under the 1979 Constitution), and the legislation was approved by the Congreso later in that month (with a boycott of the vote by the majority of opposition politicians). In January 1997 the Constitutional Court ruled the new interpretation of the Constitution to be invalid.

On 17 December 1996 MRTA activists launched an assault on the residence of the Japanese ambassador in Lima, and detained by force more than 500 people attending an evening reception. Among those taken hostage were the Peruvian Ministers of Foreign Affairs and of Agriculture, at least nine foreign ambassadors and other diplomatic personnel, leading police and security officials and representatives of the business community. The MRTA activists' demands included the release of all 458 MRTA prisoners in detention in Peru, safe passage to an area in Peru's central highlands, greater economic assistance to the country's poorest people and payment of a 'war tax'. On 27 December Fujimori declared a state of emergency in Lima. On 22 April 1997 Peruvian troops launched an unexpected assault on the ambassador's residence, ending the MRTA siege. Two soldiers and all 14 of the MRTA activists were killed in the operation, and one of the 72 remaining hostages died of heart failure. President Fujimori presented the assault as a measure of his Government's uncompromising stance against terrorism; however, it was later alleged that some of the MRTA members might have been killed after having surrendered to army officers.

The Fujimori administration came under renewed attack for its authoritarian style of government in mid-1997, following the dismissal, by the Government-dominated Congreso, of three members of the Tribunal Constitucional (Constitutional Tribunal) who had opposed the Congreso's endorsement of Fujimori's attempt to seek a third term of office. The deteriorating popularity of the administration prompted a number of ministerial resignations in July. Meanwhile, the opposition took advantage of the disarray of the Government to announce the creation of a number of new political alliances to contest forthcoming elections, including a revived and reorganized Coordinación Democrática (Code), to be led by the former Minister of the Economy, Carlos Boloña, with support from Renovación and prominent APRA dissidents.

Fujimori's immediate hopes for election to a third presidential term were encouraged in February 1998 by the Supreme Court's announcement that it could foresee no significant obstacle to Fujimori's candidature in 2000. However, a final decision on his eligibility was to be decided by the Jurado Nacional Electoral (JNE—National Electoral Board). The Government was accused of further supporting the subversion of normal judicial processes in March, when the Congreso approved a new law whereby the regulatory powers of the National Council of the Judiciary were severely reduced. The legislation prompted the resignation of all seven members of the Council, and the cancellation, by the World Bank, of a substantial loan to the Peruvian Government, intended for judicial reform projects.

In mid-1998 there was considerable media speculation that political opponents of the Government were being harassed by government agencies with fabricated charges of technical violations of the law. There was further evidence of the President's circumvention of the traditional role of the judiciary in May when Fujimori introduced draconian anti-crime legislation by decree (subsequently approved by the Congreso) seeking to extend the extreme powers and penalties employed in the recent successful anti-terrorism initiatives (see below) to other areas of criminal activity. Among the provisions of the new law were plans to increase the powers of military tribunals to try civilians. Despite calls by international observers and opposition groups for greater judicial independence and respect for human rights, in December the Congreso voted to extend the period of judicial reorganization initiated by Fujimori's administration for a further two-year period.

Fujimori's popularity continued to wane during 1998 (the ruling party chose not to field candidates for local elections conducted in October, as a consequence), and the President's attempts to consolidate his position and reassert his authority resulted in repeated changes to the Council of Ministers. In mid-April 1999 the entire Council of Ministers resigned, amid a rift over corruption allegations against officials at the state customs authority. Another mass cabinet resignation followed in early October, in accordance with the law requiring those public officials intending to stand for election to resign their posts six months before the April 2000 polls. A new cabinet was inaugurated in mid-October, with Alberto Bustamante Belaúnde as Prime Minister.

Meanwhile, Fujimori's continuing efforts to secure support for a third presidential term were encouraged by the defeat in the Congreso, in September 1998, of an opposition proposal to decide the question of Fujimori's eligibility by a national referendum. (In July a 7,000-strong opposition delegation had presented a petition containing 1.4m. signatures in support of this proposal to the JNE.) Opposition to Fujimori's possible re-election was vociferously expressed when a broad range of labour unions and political parties participated in late April 1999 in a one-day general strike. However, this, together with a demonstration involving some 20,000 people in mid-October, failed to prevent the announcement in late December of Fujimori's candidature on behalf of the Perú 2000 alliance (a new movement formed to support the incumbent's re-election campaign). On 1 January 2000 the JNE, which was dominated by Fujimori's supporters, ratified his registration as a candidate in response to a legal challenge issued by the political opposition. The election board's rationale was that although the Constitution did not permit a President to serve three terms, Fujimori had only served one term under the current Constitution, as amended in 1993, and therefore was eligible for re-election. The ruling precipitated further street protests. Allegations of electoral fraud and campaign misconduct were widespread. Accusations by opposition leaders included government manipulation of the media to deny them equal access, the use of state resources (including the military and the intelligence services) to promote Fujimori's campaign, and alleged falsification of more than 1m. signatures by members of Perú 2000 to register Fujimori's candidacy. In December 14 leaders of political parties and political movements signed a 'governability agreement', which contained proposals to guarantee democracy, justice and respect for human rights. However, opposition plans to reach a consensus on a single candidate to challenge Fujimori did not materialize, and in January 2000 seven opposition candidates registered to stand for election to the presidency.

The general election proceeded on 9 April 2000. During the vote count opposition candidates and international observers, including representatives of the OAS and the US-based Carter Center, alleged that the ballot was marred by fraud. There were reports of unexplained delays in counting the votes, discrepancies in early official tallies and ballot tampering. US officials issued increasingly strong statements stressing the need for a second round of voting as the only credible proof of legitimacy. At the final count Fujimori officially received 49.9% of the votes cast and Alejandro Toledo (the first presidential candidate of Amerindian descent) 40.2%. A second round was scheduled for 28 May. In the congressional elections Perú 2000 won 52 of the 120 seats while Perú Posible (PP), which supported Toledo, won 29 seats. The JNE resisted both domestic and external pressure for a postponement of the second round, in order to correct irregularities noted in the first round. In response, Toledo withdrew his candidature one week before the election and urged his supporters to spoil their votes in protest. Violent incidents, including the fire-bombing of the presidential palace, followed the JNE decision. The OAS and Carter Center suspended monitoring of the election, citing difficulties with the computer system for tabulating votes. Amid further mass demonstrations, Fujimori contested the election effectively unopposed (although the JNE ruled that Toledo remained a candidate and refused to remove his name from the ballot papers), taking 51.2% of the total votes; Toledo received 17.7%. Excluding spoilt (29.9%) and blank (1.2%) papers, the incumbent was thus returned to office with 74.3% of the valid votes cast. The result was denounced as invalid by the political opposition and by the US Government (though it later moderated its position, describing the outcome as imperfect). Fujimori's inauguration on 28 July was accompanied by violent protests in Lima.

In September 2000 a major political scandal erupted after the disclosure of a video that allegedly showed Vladimiro Montesinos, the head of the national intelligence service and a close ally of the President, bribing an opposition member of the Congreso. In response, on 16 September Fujimori declared that new elections would be held, in which he would not participate. He also announced that the national intelligence service would be disbanded. At the same time, 10 Perú 2000 deputies defected to the opposition, thus depriving Fujimori of his majority in the legislature. Demonstrations, led by Toledo, demanded the immediate resignation of Fujimori and the arrest of Montesinos, who fled to Panama. On 5 October the Congreso approved OAS-mediated proposals paving the way for power to be transferred from Fujimori to his successor in mid-2001, as well as the disbandment of the Congreso to make way for a newly elected legislature. Later in the month Fujimori announced the replacement of the most senior commanders of the armed forces.

In late October 2000 the political crisis deepened, when Montesinos returned from Panama, after failing to obtain political asylum there. His apparent impunity supported the widely held view that the armed forces were protecting him. At the same time, the first Vice-President, Francisco Tudela, resigned in protest at government attempts to make new elections conditional upon an amnesty for those in the armed forces accused of human rights violations. Further OAS-sponsored negotiations between opposition groups and the Government led to the announcement, at the end of the month, that new elections would be held on 8 April 2001, without any conditions attached.

An investigation into Montesinos' activities was launched, with charges ranging from corruption to torture and murder. In mid-November the Congreso voted to replace its pro-Fujimori President, Martha Hildebrandt Pérez Treviño, with Valentín Paniagua Corazao, effectively giving the opposition control of the legislature. The following day, amid rumours that he was planning to seek political asylum, Fujimori travelled to Japan, from where, on 20 November, he resigned the presidency. The Congreso, however, refused to accept the resignation, and instead voted to dismiss Fujimori.

On 22 November 2000 Paniagua was appointed interim President. A new cabinet was sworn in three days later, which included Javier Pérez de Cuéllar as Prime Minister and Minister of Foreign Affairs. The aims of the interim Government, the mandate of which would last until 28 July 2001, included the achievement of a balanced budget and the strengthening of democracy. Several days later the new Minister of Defence, Walter Ledesma Rebaza, announced the decision to retire 13 generals, who were known to be associates of Montesinos (including Gen. Chacón Málaga, the former armed forces commander). A congressional commission, established in the same month to investigate the activities of Montesinos, uncovered hundreds of secret videotapes that seemed to compromise the integrity of judges, politicians, military officers, businessmen and bishops. In early December it was announced that the commission's investigations were to extend to Fujimori. In mid-December it was announced that Fujimori had taken up Japanese citizenship and was thus, in effect, protected from the threat of extradition from Japan. Nevertheless, in February 2001 corruption charges were formally filed against him. Furthermore, in August the Congreso voted unanimously to lift Fujimori's constitutional immunity and issued an international warrant for his arrest on the charge of dereliction of duty. Further charges of embezzlement and illicit enrichment were subsequently filed against the former President. However, the Japanese Government proved unresponsive to diplomatic pressure and stated that it had no intention of allowing Fujimori's extradition. In mid-June 2005 the Japanese authorities rejected a further extradition request for Fujimori, citing a lack of further evidence to justify its approval. Meanwhile, in February of that year the Constitutional Court ruled that Fujimori was ineligible to stand in the presidential election scheduled for April 2006. In September 2005 the Government submitted to the Japanese authorities a third request for Fujimori's extradition. Then, on 6 November, Fujimori was arrested on his arrival in Santiago, Chile, where he had arrived unannounced from Japan via Mexico. It was believed he had planned to conduct his election campaign from Chile. Immediately following the former President's arrest, the Peruvian authorities informally requested that Chile extradite him to Peru to face charges pending against him. On 10 November Peru withdrew its ambassador to Japan in protest at Japan's perceived opposition to Fujimori being extradited from Chile, following Japanese representations to Chile that he should be treated as a Japanese citizen, not a Peruvian. Three days later the Chilean authorities forbade Fujimori from campaigning for office while in custody. Following amendments to the extradition petition recommended by the Peruvian Supreme Court on 19 November, it was formally submitted to the Chilean Government in early January 2006. Fujimori remained in Chilean custody in mid-April.

In June 2001 Montesinos was arrested in the Venezuelan capital. He was sent back to Peru and, in July 2002, sentenced to nine years' imprisonment on charges relating to 'usurpation of power'. However, investigating judges subsequently brought a further 80 indictments against him, including murder, bribery and the illegal sale of weapons and narcotics. Following his first public trial in February 2003, Montesinos was convicted on corruption charges and sentenced to a further five years' imprisonment. In late June 2004 Montesinos was found guilty of bribing newpaper editors to support Fujimori's re-election attempt in 2000, and was sentenced to a further 15 years' imprisonment. (In January 2005 eight newspaper chiefs were sentenced to five years in gaol after being convicted of receiving payments from Montesinos.) In August 2005 the trial began of Montesinos and 56 alleged members of an assassination squad known as the Colina group (see below), on charges of involvement in the disappearances of 36 people under the administration of President Fujimori.

In January 2001, only a few days after corruption charges against him were ruled to have expired under the statute of limitations, the former President, Alan García Pérez, returned to Peru to launch his campaign for the forthcoming presidential election. The first round of the election was held on 8 April, following a bitter campaign. Toledo won 37% of the votes cast, while García attracted 26% of the ballot and Lourdes Flores Nano of the Unidad Nacional alliance, 24%. In concurrently held elections to the 120-seat Congreso, no party secured a majority: PP gained 45 seats, APRA 27 and the Unidad Nacional 17, while the right-wing Frente Independiente Moralizador won 12 seats. Election monitors declared the election process to have been open and fair. In the second round of the presidential election, held on 3 June, Toledo won with 53% of the vote against García's 47%. Toledo was inaugurated on 28 July. A broad-based 15-member cabinet was appointed, headed by lawyer Roberto Dañino and with Pedro Pablo Kuczynski as Minister of the Economy and Finance. The new Government promised to create more jobs, to reduce poverty and to put an end to the corruption of the Fujimori regime. In the previous month a congressional commission implicated 180 people in corruption scandals that took place during Fujimori's presidencies, including Gen. Walter Chacón Málaga, the recently appointed head of the armed forces.

However, the popularity of the Toledo Government declined sharply after only a few months in power, as high expectations were not matched by an increase in economic prospects. In late September and October 2001 popular protests erupted throughout Peru as workers demanded more jobs and improvements to transport infrastructure and health care. In January 2002 Toledo implemented a partial cabinet reshuffle, in which, notably, Aurelio Loret de Mola replaced David Waisman as the Minister of Defence. The change in government portfolios caused a rift within PP as all three dismissed ministers were from Toledo's own party. Hundreds of former public-sector workers protested in central Lima in January 2002 to demand their jobs back, and in February cotton producers and fishery workers both staged demonstrations to demand more government aid. The protests proliferated, and in late June, following a week of violent demonstrations in protest at government plans to privatize two regional electricity companies in Arequipa, the Minister of the Interior, Fernando Rospigliosi Capurro, resigned and the privatization process was suspended indefinitely. An extensive cabinet reshuffle was carried out in July, in which the Secretary-General of PP, Luis Solari, replaced Dañino as prime minister and Kuczynski was succeeded as Minister of Economy and Finance by Javier Silva Ruete. Nevertheless, popular dissatisfaction continued, and in January 2003 difficulties in the reform of the police service led to the resignation of the Minister of the Interior, Gino Costa Santolaya. He was succeeded by Alberto Sanabría Ortiz, a leading member of PP. In the same month the ruling party's congressional majority was reduced after five PP deputies resigned from the party in order to form a new movement, to be known as Perú Ahora.

In November 2002 the results of the elections to the newly created regional authorities represented a further example of the dramatic decline in popular support for President Toledo. PP secured just one of the 25 new regional presidencies, compared with the 12 secured by APRA (with the majority of the remaining presidencies largely won by independent candidates). The poor result for PP was widely attributed to the Government's inability to translate strong economic growth and an improving fiscal balance into a tangible increase in employment.

In early January 2003 a constitutional tribunal ruled that anti-terrorism legislation passed by the Fujimori administration had violated the Constitution. In order to alleviate the potential pressure on the judiciary, and to prevent the release of large numbers of alleged terrorists, in the same month the Congreso granted President Toledo exceptional temporary powers to legislate by decree on security issues. In February the Government announced that all military sentences passed during Fujimori's presidency were to be annulled. The courts would have 60 days to decide whether to release convicted individuals or commit them for retrial. In March anti-terrorism legislation received congressional approval.

In February 2003 coca growers staged demonstrations to demand the suspension of the Government's coca-eradication policy. The demonstrations escalated after a coca growers' federation leader, Nelson Palomino La Serna, was imprisoned on terrorism charges. At the end of the month the Government announced that some US $3,000m. was to be invested in a coca-eradication plan by 2020. Following 11 days of protests, in early March a temporary truce was declared between the coca growers and the Government, although the Government refused to release Palomino La Serna and pledged to continue with its eradication strategy. Following 20 days of further negotiations, the Government agreed to give $11m. in direct aid to farmers affected by the eradication efforts. In April thousands of coca growers began a protest march towards Lima to demand subsidies for alternative crops and an increase in the amount of coca that could legally be grown. Following a meeting with the coca leaders, on 23 April President Toledo signed into law a decree which pledged that the eradication programme would be gradual and that the Government would discuss policy with the growers. Nevertheless, civil unrest continued; in May public-sector workers began a series of demonstrations in the same month against salary levels and conditions, and farmers also continued to mount protests. Outbreaks of violence during these demonstrations prompted the President to declare a state of emergency in 12 of the country's 25 departments. In June the Government acquiesced to teachers' demands and in July the Congreso approved a series of limited fiscal measures intended to pay for the wage increases.

In 2003 and 2004 a rapid succession of government changes reflected President Toledo's deteriorating public credibility. In June 2003 the entire cabinet resigned; on 28 June the President appointed Beatriz Merino Lucero, previously the head of the tax inspection service, as prime minister. Further appointments were effected in July. Merino Lucero proved popular, although she was obliged to resign in mid-December following reports of nepotistic practices during her previous career and opposition allegations relating to her personal life. Carlos Ferrero Costa, a former President of the Congreso and a leading member of the PP, was appointed to succeed her. In February 2004 Ferrero Costa effected a wide-ranging cabinet reshuffle; a number of independent technocrats were appointed to the Council of Ministers. A notable inclusion in the new cabinet was Pedro Pablo Kuczynski, who was reappointed Minister of the Economy and Finance. Furthermore, the reallocation of portfolios removed members of the Frente Independiente Moralizador (FIM) from the Government; nevertheless, the FIM pledged to continue its legislative alliance with PP.

Throughout 2004 President Toledo, his family and advisers were implicated in several major scandals. In January a purported recording was made public of his former legal adviser, César Almeyda, meeting with an associate of Vladimiro Montesinos. Almeyda was placed under house arrest at the end of January, but was cleared of any wrongdoing in June. Almeyda had been director of the national intelligence service until early April 2003, when he had been forced to resign after being accused of authorizing the illegal use of surveillance technology. He was replaced by Adm. (retd) Alfonso Panizzo; however, in September Panizzo also tendered his resignation after it emerged that the intelligence agency had been spying on journalists investigating corrupt practices in public office. Panizzo's successor, Gen. (retd) Daniel Mora, held the post until March 2004, when the revelation that the agency had been compiling a dossier on Minister of the Interior Fernando Rospigliosi Capurro forced his resignation. Valdivia's successor, Adm. Ricardo Arboccó, was also quickly forced to step down after it was revealed that he was facing trial on corruption charges. In late March Toledo announced that the national intelligence agency was to be abolished. A government committee was immediately formed to oversee the establishment of a successor body, to be known as the Agencia de Inteligencia Estratégica. On 6 May Rospigliosi Capurro himself was forced to resign from the Government following a motion of censure that had narrowly been carried in the Congreso the previous day. Rospigliosi had been held responsible for the authorities' inability to quell violent disturbances in the southern region of Puno, which had culminated in late April in the lynching of a local mayor. Javier Reátegui was named as the new Minister of the Interior on 8 May.

In July 2004 the President's sister, Margarita Toledo, was ordered by a judge not to leave the country pending investigations into an alleged large-scale forging of signatures in 1999 in order to register PP for the 2000 legislative elections. Toledo and her husband were placed under house arrest in January 2005. A special congressional commission was established to investigate the case. Meanwhile, in July 2004 President Toledo granted investigators authority to investigate bank accounts held in Peru and abroad by himself and his wife, Eliane Karp, following media accusations that they had accepted bribes. In mid-July a general strike was held in protest, *inter alia*, at the perceived corruption of the Toledo administration and its failure to fulfil electoral promises, as well as at the proposed free trade agreement with the USA and the Government's failure to act upon the findings of the Truth Commission (see below). Then, on 26 July, PP suffered another major set-back when its candidate for the presidency of the Congreso, Luis Solari, was defeated by Antero Flores-Aráoz of the Unidad Nacional. In early May a congressional committee concluded that Toledo and his associates had violated electoral law by forging signatures to register the PP for the 2000 legislative elections. However, on 20 May Congress decided, by 57 to 47 votes, not to impeach President Toledo. In February 2006 the Supreme Court issued a ruling ending Margarita Toledo's house arrest; however, the charges of electoral fraud against her remained.

Meanwhile, on 1 January 2005 about 200 members of the ultra-nationalist grouping, the Movimiento Etnocacerista (allied to the Movimiento Nacionalista Peruana) forcibly occupied a police station in the southern province of Andahuaylas, taking 21 people hostage. President Toledo immediately declared a state of emergency in the province and troops were dispatched to the region. The uprising, which lasted for two days and resulted in the death of seven people, including four police-officers, was primarily intended to force the resignation of President Toledo, whom the group accused of incompetence, corruption, acquiescence to foreign interests and the debasement of the armed forces. On 3–4 January the insurgents and their leader, Maj. (retd) Antauro Igor Humala Tasso, surrendered to the police; all were arrested on terrorism charges. In response to public dissatisfaction with the authorities' handling of events, on 10 January Reátegui resigned as Minister of the Interior, shortly before he was due to face questioning in the Congreso over the matter; he was succeeded by Félix Murazzo, the former head of the national police.

In mid-August 2005, following the resignation of the Minister of Foreign Affairs, Manuel Rodrígues Cuadros, President Toledo appointed the outspoken FIM leader Fernando Olivera to succeed him. However, Olivera's appointment caused dissent within the Council of Ministers (ostensibly over Olivera's approval of the legalization of coca cultivation for traditional use in the province of Cusco), and prompted the resignation of the prime minister, Carlos Ferrero Costa, as well as the housing minister, Carlos Bruce Montes de Oca. Three days after his appointment, Olivera stepped down as foreign minister. President Toledo was forced to effect a major cabinet reshuffle. Notable among the new appointments was Pedro Pablo Kuczynski, hitherto Minister of the Economy and Finance, who was appointed prime minister, while Marciano Rengifo was appointed Minister of Defence and Oscar Maúrtua de Romaña Minister of Foreign Affairs. The appointment of Kuczynski received broad congressional and popular approval, although President Toledo's approval ratings remained low for the remainder of the year.

Presidential and legislative elections were held on 9 April 2006. According to opinion polls in the months preceding the ballot the leading contender to secure the presidency was the candidate of the conservative Unidad Nacional, Lourdes Flores Nano. Her main rivals were former President García, representing APRA, and a hitherto unknown left-wing nationalist candidate, Lt-Col (retd) Ollanta Moises Humala Tasso of the UPP. However, Humala came first with 30.62% of valid votes, while García secured 24.32% of the ballot and Flores came third with 23.81% of the votes. A second round of voting, between Humala and García, was scheduled to be held in early June. Concern was expressed that militant supporters of Humala, whose imprisoned brother Antauro had led the Movimiento Etnocacerista's uprising in January 2005 (see above), would seek to overthrow the Government were he not elected President. There was also disquiet from moderate parties and foreign Governments, including that of the USA, over Humala's reportedly racist and homophobic views and his proposed policy of legalizing coca cultivation. In the light of preliminary results in the concurrently held legislative elections, the parties likely to secure the most seats in the new Congreso were the UPP APRA, the Unidad Nacional and the Alianza por el Futuro.

In the early 1990s the SL intensified its attacks against government and military targets, strategic power installations, commercial enterprises and rural defence groups. Following Fujimori's 'autogolpe' of April 1992 (effected partly in response to continuing congressional opposition to his efforts to expand the role of the armed forces), considerable concern was expressed by human rights organizations that the security forces would be permitted an increasing degree of autonomy, with unprecedented rights of civil intervention. In September 1992 government forces succeeded in capturing SL's founder and leader, Abimael Guzmán Reynoso, together with 20 prominent SL members. Guzmán was tried by a military court, where he was found guilty of treason and sentenced to life imprisonment. SL, however, remained highly active, and in early 1993 was held responsible for the assassination of 20 candidates campaigning in local elections, and for attacks on rural communities that had formed self-defence militia units. The Government actively pursued its offensive against terrorist organizations in the mid-1990s, and publicized the detention of leading members of SL, the MRTA and the dissident SL 'Sendero Rojo' faction (which advocated a continuation of the armed struggle). In 1999 Oscar Ramírez Durand (alias 'Comrade Feliciano'), the leader of Sendero Rojo, was captured and sentenced to life imprisonment.

The SL emerged again in 2001, with at least 31 deaths attributed to the terrorist organization in that year. In March 2002, three days before the US President, George W. Bush, was due to visit Peru, the first such visit by a serving US head of state, a car bomb killed 10 people and injured at least 40 more near the US embassy in Lima. The attack was attributed to a radical wing of the SL, and did not herald an immediate return to a sustained campaign of terrorism. In April 2003 the Government increased the defence budget by US $203.5m., which included substantial funds to support alternative development strategies, in order to help combat the illegal drugs trade. In June the Government attributed the abduction of 60 pipeline construction workers in the department of Ayacucho to the remnants of the SL; the hostages were subsequently released unharmed. In November the kidnappers' alleged leader, Jaime Zuñiga Córdova, was captured by security forces. In early November 2004 a retrial of Gúzman and 16 other SL militants began in a civilian court after the Constitutional Court ruled that their convictions by military court in 1992 were invalid. The retrial was subsequently suspended for 30 days following the resignation, at the request of the state prosecutor, of two of the three judges. President Toledo's announcement in late November 2004, in advance of the verdict, that none of the defendants would go free also contributed to the collapse of the retrial soon afterwards. In late September 2005, however, the retrial of Guzmán began anew. In December 13 police-officers were killed in ambushes by SL guerrillas in rural provinces known to be centres of coca cultivation and cocaine production. It was believed the SL attacks were motivated by a desire to protect the illegal drugs trade, from which the SL allegedly derived a substantial part of its funding. In mid-January 2006 President Toledo announced the establishment of a new police unit to combat the resurgence of the SL.

The Peruvian Government attracted criticism from human rights organizations for its methods in achieving the apparent subjugation of the terrorist movements in the 1990s. In July 1999 Peru withdrew from the jurisdiction of the Inter-American Court of Human Rights (IACHR, see p. 334), a branch of the OAS, after the court ruled the previous month that new trials should be held for four Chilean MRTA activists who were serving life sentences. However, in January 2001, apparently as part of its effort to improve the country's international image, the Congreso approved Peru's return to the jurisdiction of the IACHR. In March, one week after the IACHR ruled that a military amnesty law approved in 1995 was incompatible with the American Convention on Human Rights, two former intelligence generals were arrested on charges of involvement in the early 1990s with a right-wing death squad, known as the Colina group. In September the Attorney-General charged Fujimori with responsibility for two mass killings by the Colina group that took place in the early 1990s.

In January 2001 a Truth Commission, composed of church leaders and civil and military representatives, was established to investigate the impact of the campaign against the guerrilla groups in the 1980s and 1990s. The Commission conducted some 17,000 interviews, and initially secured the support of the Peruvian army (although the navy refused to co-operate). In August 2003 the body presented its findings, which estimated the number of deaths during the conflict at some 69,000, twice the previous official total, with some 6,000 individuals reported as 'disappeared'. Nevertheless, despite the report's conclusion that SL was responsible for the greater part of the killings, its conclusions were criticized by elements of the Roman Catholic Church, the military and APRA. In November President Toledo publicly apologized for the state's actions during the period and announced a US $817m. plan to improve social conditions in the regions most affected by the violence.

In February 1990, in Cartagena, Colombia, the Presidents of Peru, Colombia, Bolivia and the USA signed the Cartagena Declaration, pledging the intensification of efforts to combat the consumption, production and trafficking of illegal drugs. However, financial commitments to fund subsequent anti-drugs schemes in Peru were suspended by the US Administration as a result of international criticism of the Peruvian Government's record on human rights and its flouting of accepted democratic processes. In January 1996 responsibility for combating the drugs trade was transferred from the military to the national police force, following a series of allegations that army officers had themselves been involved in illegal trafficking. A new bilateral agreement to combat the drugs trade was signed with the USA in July. Following the approval of the Andean Trade Promotion and Drug Eradication Act by the US Congress in August 2002, it was announced that Peru qualified for expanded US benefits and trade preferences under the new legislation. In March 2003 a new $3,000m. development strategy for the regions of Peru affected by coca cultivation was announced; the plans envisaged the reforestation of 1m. hectares of arable land judged to be capable of producing coca, and the replanting of some 500,000 ha with alternative crops. The Government also envisaged that the new initiatives would lead to the creation of some 2.5m. jobs by 2020, with the complete elimination of coca in the area under illegal cultivation (which totalled approximately 24,600 ha). However, in early February 2005 it was reported that US funding to the Andean region for drugs eradication would prioritize Colombia over Bolivia and Peru, which were to receive some 16% less in 2005 (Peru's funding would total some $115m. and $97m. in 2005 and 2006, respectively). There was speculation that the reduction of funding to Peru reflected the US Administration's disappointment with the lack of progress made by the Toledo Government in coca eradication. In that same month Nils Ericsson, head of the Comisión Nacional para el Desarrollo y Vida sin Drogas (Devida—Peru's anti-narcotics agency), announced that some 17,000 ha of coca had been planted in 2004, exceeding the quantities eradicated, and that cocaine production had increased by 13% in the previous year to 160 metric tons. In May 2005 there were violent clashes in the Amazonian town of Puerto Pizana between police and coca growers protesting against a coca-eradication operation there. In mid-October Ericsson announced that international funding for Peru's counter-narcotics operations in 2006 would be some $10m. less than in the previous year.

Meeting in Caracas, Venezuela, in May 1991, the Presidents of the five South American nations comprising the Andean Group (now the Andean Community of Nations, see p. 158) formalized their commitment to the full implementation of an Andean free trade area by the end of 1995, to be achieved by a gradual reduction in tariffs and other trade barriers. An agreement to restructure the Group into the Andean Community, thus strengthening regional integration, was signed in March 1996 in Trujillo. In June 1997 the Peruvian Government announced plans to abolish tariffs on some 2,500 goods entering Peru from within the Community (with immediate effect), and its intention to remove tariffs on a further 3,500 goods (including more than 600 deemed 'sensitive') by 2005. Peru was admitted as an associate member of the Southern Common Market, Mercosur (Mercado Común del Sur, see p. 363) in August 2003 (see Economic Affairs). In August 2002 the US Andean Trade Promotion and Drug Eradication Act (ATPDEA) came into operation, which awarded Peru significant new tariff reductions on exports to the USA, including clothing and manufactures. In September 2005 the ATPDEA was renewed and extended until December 2006. Peru also concluded a free trade agreement with the USA in December 2005, in spite of vociferous opposition from left-wing and indigenous groups.

A long-standing border dispute with Ecuador over the Cordillera del Cóndor descended into armed conflict in January 1981. A cease-fire was declared a few days later, under the auspices of the guarantors (Argentina, Brazil, Chile and the USA) of the Rio de Janeiro Protocol of 1942, which had awarded the area, affording access to the Amazon river basin, to Peru. However, the Protocol has never been recognized by Ecuador, and, despite mutual efforts to achieve a constructive dialogue, the matter continued to be a source of tension and recurrent skirmishes between the two countries. In January 1995 serious fighting broke out. In February representatives of both countries, meeting in Brazil under the auspices of the Rio de Janeiro Protocol guarantors, approved a provisional cease-fire. Following further negotiations, on 17 February both countries signed the Itamaraty Peace Declaration. Foreign affairs ministers from both countries, meeting in Uruguay at the end of the month, signed the Montevideo Declaration, which ratified the Itamaraty agreement. The withdrawal of forces from the disputed border area was achieved by mid-May. None the less, reports of further armed clashes prompted requests from both countries for an extension of the observer mission. Agreement on the delimitation of a demilitarized zone in the disputed Cenepa river region came into effect on 1 August. In September Fujimori agreed to reopen the border with Ecuador for commercial purposes, and in November both countries agreed to pursue further confidence-building measures. In October 1996 the Ministers of Foreign Affairs of both countries, meeting in Chile under the auspices of the guarantor countries, signed the Santiago Agreement, which was to provide a framework for a settlement of the border issue.

Following further negotiations in early 1998 a number of commissions were established to examine specific aspects of a potential agreement between Peru and Ecuador, including a trade and navigation treaty and the fixing of frontier markers on the ground in the Cordillera del Cóndor. Talks culminated in the signing of an accord in Brasília on 26 October by the Ministers of Foreign Affairs of Peru and Ecuador in the presence of the two countries' Presidents and of six other regional leaders. The accord confirmed Peru's claim regarding the delineation of the border, but granted Ecuador navigation and trading rights on the Amazon and its tributaries and the opportunity to establish two trading centres in Peru (although this was not to constitute sovereign access). Moreover, Ecuador was given 1 sq km of territory, as private property, at Tiwintza in Peru where many Ecuadorean soldiers, killed during the conflict in 1995, were buried. Both countries were committed to establish ecological parks along the border where military personnel would not be allowed access. Although considerable opposition to the accord was expressed in Peru, notably in the town of Iquitos, international reaction was very favourable and resulted in several offers of finance from multilateral agencies for cross-border development projects. The Presidents of Peru and Ecuador met in May 1999 at the Peru–Ecuador frontier to mark the placing of the last boundary stone on the border.

In January 1992 the Presidents of Peru and Bolivia concluded an agreement whereby Bolivia would be granted access to the Pacific Ocean via the Peruvian port of Ilo (which would be jointly developed as a free zone). In return, Bolivia agreed to help facilitate Peruvian access to the Atlantic Ocean (through Brazil) by way of the Bolivian town of Puerto Suárez. In August 2004, following negotiations on economic integration, the Presidents of Peru and Bolivia signed a declaration of intent to create a special zone in Ilo for the exportation of Bolivian gas.

Government

A new Constitution, drafted by the Congreso Constituyente Democrático, was approved by a national referendum on 31 October 1993, and was promulgated on 29 December. Under the terms of the Constitution, executive power is vested in the President, who is elected for a five-year term by universal adult suffrage and is eligible for re-election for a successive term of office. Two Vice-Presidents are also elected. The President governs with the assistance of an appointed Council of Ministers. Legislative power is vested in a single chamber Congreso, elected for five years by a single national list system. For administrative purposes, Peru comprises 25 regional presidencies, 278 regional authorities and 12,138 municipal authorities, following amendments to the Constitution approved in December 2002.

Defence

Military service is selective and lasts for two years. At 1 August 2005 the armed forces numbered 80,000 men: an army of 40,000, a navy of 25,000 and an air force of 15,000. There are paramilitary police forces numbering 77,000 men. The 2005 budget allocated 3,600m. new soles for defence and domestic security.

Economic Affairs

In 2004, according to estimates by the World Bank, Peru's gross national income (GNI), measured at average 2002–04 prices, was US $65,042.9m., equivalent to $2,360 per head (or $5,370 per head on an international purchasing-power parity basis). During 1995–2004, it was estimated, the population increased by an average of 1.6% per year, while gross domestic product (GDP) per head increased, in real terms, at an average annual rate of 1.3%. Overall GDP increased, in real terms, at an average annual rate of 2.9% in 1995–2004; growth was 4.8% in 2004.

Agriculture (including forestry and fishing) contributed 7.6% of GDP in 2003 and the sector (including forestry and fishing) engaged 8.8% of the total working population in 2001. Rice, maize and potatoes are the principal food crops. The principal cash crop is coffee. Peru is the world's leading producer of coca, and the cultivation of this shrub, for the production of the illicit drug cocaine, reportedly generated revenue of US $1,500m.–$2,500m. per year. Undeclared revenue from the export of coca is believed to exceed revenue from legal exports. Fishing, particularly for the South American pilchard and the anchoveta, provides another important source of revenue, and the fishing sector contributed an estimated 0.6% of GDP in 2003. Fishing accounted for 2.4% of the total value of exports in 2003. During 1995–2004 agricultural GDP (including fishing) increased at an average annual rate of 4.0%; the sector's GDP increased by 1.5% in 2003 and by 2.0% in 2004.

Industry (including mining, manufacturing, construction and power) provided an estimated 30.7% of GDP in 2003 and the sector employed 17.9% of the working population in 2001. During 1995–2004 industrial GDP increased by an average of 2.5% per year; industrial GDP increased by 5.4% in 2003 and by 6.2% in 2004.

Mining (including hydrocarbon extraction) contributed 6.6% of GDP in 2003 and employed 0.6% of the working population in 2001. Copper (which accounted for 10.4% of total export earnings in 2003), zinc, gold, petroleum and its derivatives, lead and silver are the major mineral exports. It was expected that the sector's contribution to GDP would increase dramatically following the start of operations of the Camisea natural gas export pipeline in August 2004. During 1991–2003 the GDP of the mining and petroleum sector increased at an average annual rate of 7.4%; real GDP growth in the sector was 9.0% in 2002 and 6.5% in 2003.

Manufacturing contributed 15.7% of GDP in 2003 and employed 12.6% of the working population in 2001. The principal branches of manufacturing, measured by gross value of output, were food products, petroleum refineries, non-ferrous metals, beverages and textiles and clothing. During 1995–2004 manufacturing GDP increased by an average of 2.0% per year. The sector's GDP increased by 2.1% in 2003 and by 3.0% in 2004.

Energy is derived principally from domestic supplies of hydroelectric power (82.1% of total electricity production in 2002) and petroleum (10.3%). Imports of mineral fuels and lubricants comprised 17.4% of the value of merchandise imports in 2003.

The services sector contributed an estimated 61.8% of GDP in 2003 and employed 73.3% of the working population in 2001. Tourism is gradually emerging as an important source of foreign revenue (US $959m. in 2003). In 1995–2004 the GDP of the services sector increased by an average annual rate of 4.9%. The sector's GDP grew by 3.1% in 2003 and by an impressive 23.6% in 2004.

In 2004 Peru recorded a visible trade surplus of US $2,792m. and there was a deficit of $10m. on the current account of the balance of payments. In 2003 the principal source of imports (18.6%) was the USA, which was also the principal market for exports (26.5%). Other major trading partners were Argentina, Brazil and the People's Republic of China for imports, and the United Kingdom, the People's Republic of China and Switzerland for exports. In 2004 trade between Peru and the People's Republic of China had increased by reportedly some 51%, to be worth over $2,000m. In January 2005 Peru signed an agreement with China to increase bilateral trade as 'strategic partners'. In December of that year Peru also concluded a free trade agreement with the USA. The principal exports in 2003 were food and live animals and metals (particularly gold and copper). The principal imports in the same year were machinery and transport equipment, mineral fuels and lubricants, and chemicals.

In 2001 there was an estimated budgetary deficit of 5,339m. new soles. Peru's external debt at the end of 2003 was US $29,857m., of which $22,072m. was long-term public debt. In that year the cost of debt-servicing was equivalent to 21.6% of the value of exports of goods and services. The annual rate of inflation averaged 4.7% in 1995–2004. Consumer prices increased by an average of 2.3% in 2003 and by 3.6% in 2004. An estimated 9.6% of the urban labour force were unemployed in 2005.

Peru is a member of the Andean Community of Nations (see p. 158), the Inter-American Development Bank (see p. 284) and the Latin American Integration Association (see p. 305), all of which encourage regional economic development, and of the Rio Group (formerly the Group of Eight, see p. 397), which attempts to reduce regional indebtedness. Peru became a member of the Asia-Pacific Economic Co-operation group (APEC, see p. 164) in 1998. In December 2004 Peru was one of 12 countries that were signatories to the agreement, signed in Cusco, creating the South

American Community of Nations (Comunidad Sudamericana de Naciones), intended to promote greater regional economic integration, due to become operational by 2007.

The administration of Alberto Fujimori achieved considerable success in its reform of the economy in the 1990s, restoring international reserves and reducing the rate of inflation. Tax reforms increased central government revenue and contributed to a reduction of the public-sector deficit, while the implementation of economic liberalization measures and the repayment of arrears improved relations with the international financial community. However, the contraction in domestic demand in the late 1990s led to a widening of the fiscal deficit, and the political crisis in 2000 (see above) led to a sharp decrease in investment as well as consumer demand. As political instability abated and investor confidence gradually increased, following the installation of the Government of Alejandro Toledo in July 2001, a main priority was also the resumption of the privatization process (concentrating on the energy and infrastructure sectors) to reduce the fiscal deficit. However, violent protests led to the suspension of the privatization programme in mid-2002. In November 2003 the Inter-American Development Bank approved US $135m. in financing for the potentially lucrative Camisea natural gas export pipeline, which came onstream in August 2004, despite widespread concerns that construction work was damaging environmentally sensitive Amazonian regions. In June 2004 the IMF approved a 26-month stand-by credit arrangement worth $422.8m., and in November some $191.2m. of this credit was disbursed. Further disbursements, of $220m. and $296m. were made following broadly favourable IMF reviews in June 2005 and January 2006, respectively. From late 2004, meanwhile, efforts were being made towards the reinitiation of privatization programmes. Government tax revenues in 2004 increased by 13.6%, according to official estimates, owing both to the strong growth and to improved tax collection, while Peruvian exports exceeded $12,000m., according to preliminary central bank estimates. Despite the instability of the Toledo administration, investor confidence remained high in 2005, and GDP growth in that year was an estimated 6.7%, partly as a consequence of the pension reform, stricter fiscal controls and investment incentive initiatives introduced by the Government.

Inflation also remained relatively low (at 3.6% in 2004). Growth of 5.2% was forecast for 2006, although economic prospects were dependent on the policies of the new Government, due to take office in mid-2006.

Education

Reforms introduced after the 1968 revolution have instituted a three-level educational system. The first is for children up to six years of age in either nurseries or kindergartens. Basic (primary) education is free and compulsory, and is received between six and 11 years of age. Secondary education, beginning at the age of 12, is divided into two stages, of two and three years, respectively. In 1997 some 91% of children in the relevant age-group were enrolled at primary schools, while secondary enrolment included 55% of the appropriate age-group. Higher education includes the pre-university and university levels. There are 25 national and 10 private universities. There is also provision for adult literacy programmes and bilingual education. Under the new Constitution, adopted in 1993, the principle of free university education was abolished. Total central government expenditure on education was estimated at 2.9% of GDP in 2000. Budget proposals for 2005 included some US $2.6m for education.

Public Holidays

2006: 1 January (New Year's Day), 13 April (Maundy Thursday), 14 April (Good Friday), 1 May (Labour Day), 24 June (Day of the Peasant, half-day only), 29 June (St Peter and St Paul), 28–29 July (Independence), 30 August (St Rose of Lima), 8 October (Battle of Angamos), 1 November (All Saints' Day), 8 December (Immaculate Conception), 25 December (Christmas Day).

2007: 1 January (New Year's Day), 5 April (Maundy Thursday), 6 April (Good Friday), 1 May (Labour Day), 24 June (Day of the Peasant, half-day only), 29 June (St Peter and St Paul), 28–29 July (Independence), 30 August (St Rose of Lima), 8 October (Battle of Angamos), 1 November (All Saints' Day), 8 December (Immaculate Conception), 25 December (Christmas Day).

Weights and Measures

The metric system is in force.

Statistical Survey

Sources (unless otherwise stated): Banco Central de Reserva del Perú, Jirón Antonio Miró Quesada 441–445, Lima 1; tel. (1) 4276250; fax (1) 4275880; e-mail webma; internet www.bcrp.gob.pe; Instituto Nacional de Estadística e Informática, Avda General Garzón 658, Jesús María, Lima; tel. (1) 4334223; fax (1) 4333140; e-mail infoinei@inei.gob.pe; internet www.inei.gob.pe.

Area and Population

AREA, POPULATION AND DENSITY
(excluding Indian jungle population)

Area (sq km)	
Land	1,280,086
Inland water	5,130
Total	1,285,216*
Population (census results)†	
12 July 1981	17,005,210
11 July 1993	
Males	10,956,375
Females	11,091,981
Total	22,048,356
Population (official estimates at mid-year)	
2002	26,748,972
2003	27,148,101
2004	27,546,574
Density (per sq km) at mid-2004	21.5‡

* 496,225 sq miles.
† Excluding adjustment for underenumeration, estimated at 4.1% in 1981 and 2.35% in 1993.
‡ Land area only.

REGIONS
(30 June 2003)

	Area (sq km)	Population (estimates)	Density (per sq km)	Capital
Amazonas	39,249	435,556	11.1	Chachapoyas
Ancash	35,877	1,123,410	31.3	Huaráz
Apurímac	20,896	470,719	22.5	Abancay
Arequipa	63,345	1,113,916	17.6	Arequipa
Ayacucho	43,814	561,029	12.8	Ayacucho
Cajamarca	33,318	1,515,827	45.5	Cajamarca
Callao*	147	799,530	5,439.0	Callao
Cusco	72,104	1,223,248	17.0	Cusco (Cuzco)
Huancavelica	22,131	451,508	20.4	Huancavelica
Huánuco	36,887	822,804	22.3	Huánuco
Ica	21,328	698,437	32.7	Ica
Junín	44,197	1,260,773	28.5	Huancayo
La Libertad	25,500	1,528,448	59.9	Trujillo
Lambayeque	14,231	1,131,467	79.5	Chiclayo
Lima	34,802	7,880,039	226.4	Lima
Loreto	368,852	919,505	2.5	Iquitos

PERU

—continued	Area (sq km)	Population (estimates)	Density (per sq km)	Capital
Madre de Dios	85,183	102,174	1.2	Puerto Maldonado
Moquegua	15,734	160,232	10.2	Moquegua
Pasco	25,320	270,987	10.7	Cerro de Pasco
Piura	35,892	1,660,952	46.3	Piura
Puno	71,999	1,280,555	17.8	Puno
San Martín	51,253	767,890	15.0	Moyabamba
Tacna	16,076	301,960	18.8	Tacna
Tumbes	4,669	206,578	44.2	Tumbes
Ucayali	102,411	460,557	4.5	Pucallpa
Total	1,285,216	27,148,101	21.1	—

* Province.

PRINCIPAL TOWNS
(estimated population of towns and urban environs at 1 July 1998)

Lima (capital)	7,060,600*	Piura	308,155
Arequipa	710,103	Huancayo	305,039
Trujillo	603,657	Chimbote	298,800
Callao	515,200†	Cusco (Cuzco)	278,590
Chiclayo	469,200	Pucallpa	220,866
Iquitos	334,013	Tacna	215,683

* Metropolitan area (Gran Lima) only.
† Estimated population of town, excluding urban environs, at mid-1985.

Mid-2004 (official estimate, metropolitan area): Lima 8,049,619.

BIRTHS AND DEATHS*

	Live births		Deaths	
	Number	Rate (per 1,000)	Number	Rate (per 1,000)
1996	656,435	27.1	160,045	6.6
1997	652,467	26.4	160,830	6.5
1998	648,075	25.8	161,615	6.4
1999	642,874	25.2	162,457	6.4
2000	636,064	24.5	163,263	6.3
2001	630,947	24.0	164,296	6.2
2002	626,714	23.4	165,467	6.2
2003	623,521	23.0	166,777	6.1

* Data are estimates and projections based on incomplete registration, but including an upward adjustment for under-registration.

Marriages: 78,946 in 1997 (marriage rate 3.2 per 1,000); 60,730 in 1998 (marriage rate 2.4 per 1,000) (Source: UN, *Demographic Yearbook*).

Expectation of life (WHO estimates, years at birth): 70 (males 68; females 73) in 2003 (Source: WHO, *World Health Report*).

ECONOMICALLY ACTIVE POPULATION
('000 persons aged 14 and over, urban areas, July–September)

	1999	2000	2001
Agriculture, hunting and forestry	355.0	456.4	620.7
Fishing	65.3	25.8	47.1
Mining and quarrying	31.3	52.5	45.9
Manufacturing	897.6	963.5	956.4
Electricity, gas and water	41.3	28.1	20.4
Construction	378.2	299.5	341.3
Wholesale and retail trade; repair of motor vehicles, motorcycles and personal and household goods	2,077.0	2,060.5	2,124.5
Hotels and restaurants	470.6	431.9	593.8
Transport, storage and communications	618.2	639.0	641.0
Financial intermediation	76.3	66.6	47.9
Real estate, renting and business activities	407.5	413.4	342.6
Public administration and defence; compulsory social security	349.0	346.7	298.1
Education	551.5	479.7	552.1
Health and social work	165.1	169.7	213.5
Other services	372.9	368.2	406.2
Private households	353.8	326.8	366.3
Not classifiable	—	—	1.9
Total employed	7,211.2	7,128.4	7,619.9
Unemployed	624.9	566.5	651.5
Total labour force	7,836.1	7,694.9	8,271.4

Source: ILO.

Health and Welfare

KEY INDICATORS

Total fertility rate (children per woman, 2003)	2.8
Under-5 mortality rate (per 1,000 live births, 2004)	29
HIV/AIDS (% of persons aged 15–49, 2003)	0.5
Physicians (per 1,000 head, 1999)	1.17
Hospital beds (per 1,000 head, 1996)	1.47
Health expenditure (2002): US $ per head (PPP)	226
Health expenditure (2002): % of GDP	4.4
Health expenditure (2002): public (% of total)	49.9
Access to water (% of persons, 2002)	81
Access to sanitation (% of persons, 2002)	62
Human Development Index (2003): ranking	79
Human Development Index (2003): value	0.762

For sources and definitions, see explanatory note on p. vi.

Agriculture

PRINCIPAL CROPS
('000 metric tons)

	2002	2003	2004
Wheat	186.7	190.6	168.7
Rice (paddy)	2,118.6	2,135.7	1,816.6
Barley	199.7	193.7	176.9
Maize	1,292.0	1,356.9	1,180.8
Potatoes	3,298.0	3,151.4	2,996.1
Sweet potatoes	224.5	193.7	183.8
Cassava (Manioc)	891.1	913.8	961.4
Sugar cane*	9,100.0	9,550.0	9,680.0
Dry beans	88.2	88.0	83.2
Oil palm fruit	149.0	180.4	208.5
Cottonseed†	76.5	76.2	100.0
Cabbages	34.6	31.9	29.6
Asparagus	181.2	187.2	190.1
Tomatoes	129.9	148.9	181.2
Pumpkins, squash and gourds	90.9	101.3	88.9
Green chillies and peppers	52.0	54.0*	57.0*
Dry onions	458.2	472.8	492.9
Garlic	62.9	57.9	49.2
Green peas	81.1	83.7	65.5
Green broad beans	66.0	61.9	56.5†
Carrots	155.8	157.2	149.0
Green corn	393.9	395.0	362.4
Other fresh vegetables	204.5	192.9†	173.2†
Plantains	1,570.0	1,618.7	1,660.3
Oranges	292.4	305.8	328.9
Tangerines, mandarins clementines and satsumas	133.2	161.2	175.4

PERU

Statistical Survey

—continued	2002	2003	2004
Lemons and limes	254.3	250.0	209.5
Apples	123.5	134.4	146.1
Grapes	136.1	146.0	146.5
Watermelons	52.7	45.6	46.0
Mangoes	181.1	198.5	238.0†
Avocados	93.8	100.0	107.0
Pineapples	156.4	164.0	175.8
Papayas	173.0	191.0	194.7
Cotton (lint)	42.0†	43.0*	43.0*
Coffee (green)	178.3	169.5	185.0†

* FAO estimate(s).
† Unofficial figure(s).

Source: FAO.

LIVESTOCK
('000 head, year ending September)

	2002	2003	2004
Horses*	710	720	725
Mules*	270	280	285
Asses*	580	600	610
Cattle	4,990	5,046	5,050*
Pigs	2,849	2,851	2,880*
Sheep	14,025	13,995	14,050*
Goats	1,942	1,942	1,950*
Poultry	90,685	91,118	93,000*

* FAO estimate(s).

Source: FAO.

LIVESTOCK PRODUCTS
('000 metric tons)

	2002	2003	2004
Beef and veal	141.5	144.9	151.9
Mutton and lamb	31.8	32.3	33.5
Pig meat	84.9	85.7	87.7
Poultry meat	609.4	636.0	643.1
Cows' milk	1,194.3	1,226.1	1,264.9
Hen eggs	181.6	181.8	172.8
Wool (greasy)	11.6	11.6	11.6

Source: FAO.

Forestry

ROUNDWOOD REMOVALS
('000 cubic metres, excluding bark)

	2002	2003	2004
Sawlogs, veneer logs and logs for sleepers	1,194	1,000	1,300
Other industrial wood	0	0	0
Fuel wood	7,335	7,300	7,300
Total	8529	8,300	8,600

Source: FAO.

SAWNWOOD PRODUCTION
('000 cubic metres, including railway sleepers)

	2002	2003	2004
Coniferous (softwood)	5	6	9
Broadleaved (hardwood)	621	522	662
Total	626	528	671

Source: FAO.

Fishing
('000 metric tons, live weight)

	2001	2002	2003
Capture	7,982.9	8,763.0	6,089.7
Chilean jack mackerel	723.7	154.2	217.7
Anchoveta (Peruvian anchovy)	6,358.2	8,104.7	5,347.2
Aquaculture	7.6	11.6	13.8
Total catch	7,990.5	8,774.6	6,103.5

Note: Figures exclude aquatic plants ('000 metric tons): 5.5 (capture 5.5, aquaculture 0.0) in 2001; 6.2 in 2002 (all capture); 7.9 in 2003 (all capture). Also excluded are aquatic mammals, recorded by number rather than by weight. The number of toothed whales caught was: 26 in 2001; 195 in 2002; 0 in 2003.

Source: FAO.

Mining
('000 metric tons, unless otherwise indicated)*

	2002	2003	2004
Crude petroleum ('000 barrels)	35,355.8	33,342.6	34,448.0
Copper	642.8	625.3	868.6
Lead	273.9	283.2	306.2
Zinc	1,045.4	1,171.0	1,209.0
Iron ore	3,105.0	3,540.7	4,247.2
Gold (metric tons)	152.4	172.9	173.2
Silver (metric tons)	2,528.0	2,611.0	3,059.8

* Figures for metallic minerals refer to metal content only.

Source: Ministry of Energy and Mines.

Industry

SELECTED PRODUCTS
('000 metric tons, unless otherwise indicated)

	1999	2000	2001
Canned fish	63.6	77.2	79.0*
Wheat flour	903	907	1,001*
Raw sugar†	617	747	786
Beer ('000 hectolitres)	6,168	5,706	5,296*
Cigarettes (million)	3,580	3,605	3,310*
Rubber tyres ('000)‡	1,067	1,208	1,351
Motor spirit (petrol, '000 barrels)	9,449	9,299	8,646
Kerosene ('000 barrels)	4,910	5,239	5,441
Distillate fuel oils ('000 barrels)	13,622	12,371	13,476
Residual fuel oils ('000 barrels)	17,437	18,382	19,256
Cement	3,799	3,684	3,589
Crude steel§	510	510	510
Copper (refined)	185.7	193.3	196.4
Lead (refined)	121.1‖	116.4‖	116.0
Zinc (refined)	197.2	199.9	201.8
Electric energy (million kWh)	17,366.2	18,327.7	19,213.3

* Estimate.
† Data from FAO.
‡ Data from UN Economic Commission for Latin America and the Caribbean. Excludes tyres for bicycles and other non-motorized cycles.
§ US Geological Survey estimates.
‖ Includes secondary metal production.

2002 ('000 barrels): Motor spirit 8,414; Kerosene 5,464; Distillate fuel oils 13,706; Residual fuel oils 17,576.

2003 ('000 barrels): Motor spirit 8,408; Kerosene 3,945; Distillate fuel oils 13,866; Residual fuel oils 17,836.

Source (unless otherwise indicated): partly UN, *Industrial Commodity Statistics Yearbook*.

Finance

CURRENCY AND EXCHANGE RATES

Monetary Units
100 céntimos = 1 nuevo sol (new sol).

Sterling, Dollar and Euro Equivalents (30 December 2005)
£1 sterling = 5.91 new soles;
US $1 = 3.43 new soles;
€1 = 4.05 new soles;
100 new soles = £16.93 = $29.15 = €24.71.

Average Exchange Rate (new soles per US $)
2003	3.478
2004	3.413
2005	3.296

Note: On 1 February 1985 Peru replaced its former currency, the sol, by the inti, valued at 1,000 soles. A new currency, the nuevo sol (equivalent to 1m. intis), was introduced in July 1991.

GENERAL BUDGET
(million new soles)

Revenue	1999	2000	2001
Taxation	21,483	22,376	22,626
Taxes on income, profits, etc.	5,072	5,130	5,630
Taxes on payroll and work-force	1,000	1,038	847
Domestic taxes on goods and services	14,475	15,418	15,341
Value-added tax	11,029	11,996	11,808
Excises	3,446	3,421	3,533
Import duties	2,848	2,913	2,740
Other taxes	229	648	902
Adjustment to tax revenue	−2,142	−2,769	−2,834
Other current revenue	3,810	5,038	4,121
Resources of ministries and other non-tax revenues	3,548	4,893	4,088
Interest on privatization funds	262	145	33
Capital revenue	624	530	291
Total (incl. grants)	25,916	27,944	27,039

Expenditure	1999	2000	2001
Current non-interest expenditure	21,797	23,757	23,853
Labour services	11,778	12,394	12,566
Wages and salaries	7,774	8,180	8,385
Pensions	3,281	3,418	3,432
Social security contributions	724	796	750
Goods and non-labour services	6,210	7,068	7,067
Transfers	3,808	4,294	4,219
Private sector	1,095	1,140	821
Non-financial public sector	2,714	3,154	3,397
Interest payments	3,680	4,076	4,059
Capital expenditure	5,900	5,232	4,467
Gross capital formation	5,652	4,749	3,898
Total	31,378	33,065	32,378

Source: IMF, *Peru—Statistical Appendix* (March 2003).

INTERNATIONAL RESERVES
(US $ million at 31 December)

	2003	2004	2005
Gold*	462.7	488.7	575.9
IMF special drawing rights	0.4	0.4	0.5
Foreign exchange	9,776.4	12,176.0	13,598.9
Total	10,239.5	12,665.1	14,175.3

* National valuation $415 per troy ounce at 31 December 2003; $438 per troy ounce at 31 December 2004; $517 per troy ounce at 31 December 2005.

Source: IMF, *International Financial Statistics*.

MONEY SUPPLY
(million new soles at 31 December)

	2003	2004	2005
Currency outside banks	6,370	8,036	10,116
Demand deposits at commercial and development banks	8,193	9,942	11,625
Total money (incl. others)	21,351	23,728	21,741

Source: IMF, *International Financial Statistics*.

COST OF LIVING
(Consumer Price Index, Lima metropolitan area; base: 2000 = 100)

	2002	2003	2004
Food (incl. beverages)	100.2	101.0	106.6
Rent	103.7	110.5	115.5
Clothing (incl. footwear)	103.9	104.6	105.9
All items (incl. others)	102.2	104.5	108.3

Source: ILO.

NATIONAL ACCOUNTS
(million new soles at current prices)

National Income and Product

	2001	2002	2003
Compensation of employees	46,306	47,792	49,949
Operating surplus	110,828	118,880	126,250
Domestic factor incomes	157,134	166,672	176,199
Consumption of fixed capital	14,086	14,409	15,111
Gross domestic product (GDP) at factor cost	171,220	181,081	191,310
Indirect taxes	17,093	17,576	19,437
GDP at market prices	188,313	198,657	210,747

Source: UN Economic Commission for Latin America and the Caribbean.

Expenditure on the Gross Domestic Product

	2002	2003	2004
Government final consumption expenditure	20,234	21,892	23,728
Private final consumption expenditure	143,027	149,824	161,041
Increase in stocks	2,232	2,037	1,101
Gross fixed capital formation	35,128	37,748	42,230
Total domestic expenditure	200,621	211,501	228,100
Exports of goods and services	32,780	37,378	48,968
Less Imports of goods and services	34,530	37,387	42,809
GDP in purchasers' values	198,871	211,492	234,261
GDP at constant 1994 prices	127,086	132,119	138,474

Source: IMF, *International Financial Statistics*.

Gross Domestic Product by Economic Activity

	2001	2002	2003
Agriculture, hunting and forestry	13,218.1	12,731.2	13,315.8
Fishing	1,318.2	1,592.2	1,235.0
Mining and quarrying	10,021.5	11,272.5	12,703.9
Manufacturing	27,230.2	28,658.0	30,065.0
Electricity and water	4,447.7	4,327.6	4,679.7
Construction	9,389.6	10,515.8	11,475.4
Wholesale and retail trade	25,442.7	27,561.0	28,123.7
Restaurants and hotels	7,779.7	8,226.5	8,679.5
Transport and communications	15,386.0	15,768.9	16,819.0
Government services	13,908.1	14,585.2	15,978.3
Finance, insurance, real estate, business and other services	43,208.1	46,368.2	49,025.5
Sub-total	171,349.7	181,606.9	192,100.9
Import duties	2,755.0	14,364.2	2,549.7
Other taxes on products	13,146.3	2,465.8	16,096.8
GDP in purchasers' values	187,251.0	198,436.9	210,747.4

PERU

BALANCE OF PAYMENTS
(US $ million)

	2002	2003	2004
Exports of goods f.o.b.	7,714	9,091	12,616
Imports of goods f.o.b.	−7,422	−8,255	−9,824
Trade balance	292	836	2,792
Exports of services	1,530	1,695	1,914
Imports of services	−2,471	−2,549	−2,756
Balance on goods and services	−649	−18	1,949
Other income received	370	322	332
Other income paid	−1,827	−2,466	−3,753
Balance on goods, services and income	−2,106	−2,162	−1,472
Current transfers received	1,052	1,234	1,467
Current transfers paid	−8	−6	−6
Current balance	−1,062	−934	−10
Capital account (net)	−107	−107	−86
Direct investment abroad	—	−60	—
Direct investment from abroad	2,156	1,335	1,816
Portfolio investment assets	−316	−1,287	−425
Portfolio investment liabilities	1,724	1,211	1,244
Other investment assets	—	127	13
Other investment liabilities	−1,581	−506	−273
Net errors and omissions	197	783	178
Overall balance	1,010	561	2,456

Source: IMF, *International Financial Statistics*.

External Trade

PRINCIPAL COMMODITIES
(distribution by SITC, US $ million)

Imports c.i.f.	2001	2002	2003
Food and live animals	808.0	795.1	810.6
Cereals and cereal preparations	365.2	367.4	401.4
Mineral fuels, lubricants, etc.	973.5	1,037.8	1,461.8
Petroleum, petroleum products, etc.	873.2	919.7	1,298.7
Crude petroleum oils, etc.	595.2	646.4	867.3
Refined petroleum products	268.1	264.2	422.5
Chemicals and related products	1,178.2	1,245.5	1,358.5
Artificial resins and plastics	295.2	318.7	371.9
Polymerization and copolymerization products	206.6	229.1	251.5
Basic manufactures	1,144.8	1,303.9	1,278.9
Paper, paperboard and pulp	235.3	250.2	259.3
Iron and steel	250.2	388.5	309.9
Machinery and transport equipment	2,291.7	2,083.0	2,383.6
Machinery specialized for particular industries	316.1	303.3	341.6
General industrial machinery equipment and parts	351.3	373.1	445.3
Office machines and automatic data-processing equipment	261.5	229.5	266.1
Telecommunications and sound equipment	408.3	371.2	465.0
Parts and accessories for telecommunications and sound equipment	286.7	219.1	268.5
Other electrical machinery apparatus, etc.	336.0	254.7	280.6
Road vehicles and parts (excl. tyres, engines and electrical parts)	461.1	408.7	412.0
Miscellaneous manufactured articles	600.7	685.7	629.3
Total (incl. others)	7,315.9	7,493.0	8,414.1

Exports f.o.b.	2001	2002	2003
Food and live animals	1,631.2	1,693.6	1,714.6
Fish and fish preparations	206.4	172.4	205.9
Vegetables and fruit	292.2	365.6	416.0
Coffee, tea, cocoa and spices	210.0	226.3	227.5
Coffee (not roasted); husks and skins	180.2	187.9	180.7
Feeding stuff for animals (excl. unmilled cereals)	858.9	848.0	769.4
Flours and meals of meat, fish, etc. (unfit for human consumption)	838.3	820.0	740.7
Crude materials (inedible) except fuels	1,020.0	1,277.5	1,420.7
Metalliferous ores and metal scrap	860.0	1,092.8	1,219.3
Ores and concentrates of base metals	725.1	959.1	1,084.4
Copper ores and concentrates	218.9	425.4	422.0
Zinc ores and concentrates	355.7	338.4	430.2
Mineral fuels, lubricants, etc.	414.0	472.0	668.0
Petroleum, petroleum products, etc.	414.0	471.8	667.9
Refined petroleum products	294.1	308.6	401.3
Basic manufactures	1,520.1	1,505.8	1,658.9
Non-ferrous metals	1,213.9	1,209.7	1,339.8
Copper and copper alloys	800.7	829.3	910.9
Unwrought copper and alloys	741.3	759.9	835.6
Refined copper (excl. master alloys)	697.1	710.8	792.6
Zinc and zinc alloys	180.6	131.6	159.0
Miscellaneous manufactured articles	657.9	718.6	862.0
Clothing and accessories	506.3	530.1	652.8
Cotton undergarments, not elastic or rubberized	302.9	317.4	396.1
Non-monetary gold (excl. gold ores and concentrates)	1,166.1	1,467.4	2,021.2
Total (incl. others)	6,825.6	7,490.4	8,749.4

Source: UN, *International Trade Statistics Yearbook*.

PRINCIPAL TRADING PARTNERS
(US $ million)

Imports c.i.f.	2001	2002	2003
Argentina	455.0	593.7	525.5
Brazil	327.7	489.5	549.4
Canada	148.9	123.5	113.1
Chile	428.5	419.0	429.3
China, People's Republic	353.6	463.4	640.0
Colombia	378.6	456.5	498.7
Ecuador	348.2	436.4	650.6
France (incl. Monaco)	137.4	115.8	126.3
Germany	222.9	231.0	242.4
Italy	134.1	140.8	190.3
Japan	429.1	411.1	368.8
Korea, Republic	256.5	228.9	276.2
Mexico	248.1	275.3	278.9
Nigeria	123.3	128.8	156.1
Spain	175.2	165.3	177.8
United Kingdom	90.6	73.4	77.4
USA	1,691.5	1,440.5	1,565.8
Venezuela	372.7	245.6	313.9
Total (incl. others)	7,315.9	7,493.0	8,414.1

Exports f.o.b.	2001	2002	2003
Belgium	107.4	103.1	95.8
Bolivia	97.7	90.3	99.3
Brazil	227.1	193.5	231.3
Canada	143.1	140.2	134.9
Chile	281.9	251.4	416.1
China, People's Republic	426.3	596.9	675.3
Colombia	150.4	156.7	187.2
Ecuador	120.4	135.4	154.3
Germany	207.8	251.3	254.6
Italy	139.5	174.1	187.2
Japan	383.0	372.6	390.2
Korea, Republic	110.6	168.1	176.3

Exports f.o.b.—continued	2001	2002	2003
Mexico	127.9	128.5	108.0
Netherlands	78.4	126.7	139.7
Panama	75.1	48.5	145.4
Spain	202.6	231.4	288.8
Switzerland-Liechtenstein	305.6	563.3	672.0
Thailand	70.3	25.9	26.7
United Kingdom	923.2	864.3	1,082.4
USA	1,693.6	1,917.0	2,318.5
Venezuela	145.2	113.9	108.6
Total (incl. others)	6,825.6	7,490.4	8,749.4

Source: UN, *International Trade Statistics Yearbook*.

Transport

RAILWAYS
(traffic)*

	2000	2001	2002
Passenger-km (million)	107	122	98
Freight ton-km (million)	877	1,148	1,008

* Including service traffic.

Source: UN, *Statistical Yearbook*.

ROAD TRAFFIC
(motor vehicles in use)

	2000	2001	2002
Passenger cars	716,931	750,610	791,862
Buses and coaches	44,820	47,452	45,089
Lorries and vans	372,398	382,664	400,015

Source: IRF, *World Road Statistics*.

SHIPPING

Merchant Fleet
(registered at 31 December)

	2002	2003	2004
Number of vessels	719	718	726
Total displacement ('000 grt)	240.3	223.6	226.8

Source: Lloyd's Register-Fairplay, *World Fleet Statistics*.

International Sea-borne Freight Traffic
('000 metric tons)

	2000*	2001	2002
Goods loaded	6,504	6,616	6,111
Goods unloaded	6,900	7,152	8,260

* Approximate figures extrapolated from monthly averages.

Source: UN, *Monthly Bulletin of Statistics*.

CIVIL AVIATION
(traffic on scheduled services)

	2001	2002	2003
Kilometres flown (million)	38	38	40
Passengers carried ('000)	1,844	2,092	2,233
Passenger-km (million)	2,627	2,340	2,443
Total ton-km (million)	116	100	114

Source: UN Economic Commission for Latin America and the Caribbean, *Statistical Yearbook*.

Tourism

ARRIVALS BY NATIONALITY

	2001	2002	2003
Argentina	36,416	34,912	39,242
Bolivia	47,407	58,356	60,849
Brazil	23,744	24,945	29,016
Canada	19,868	21,572	21,995
Chile	107,994	97,724	138,856
Colombia	26,220	32,022	30,895
Ecuador	33,632	58,255	54,206
France	33,681	37,571	39,820
Germany	30,174	31,558	33,390
Italy	18,623	22,530	21,922
Japan	14,711	17,737	20,823
Spain	26,938	31,224	30,847
United Kingdom	40,743	42,363	46,747
USA	186,459	197,944	203,072
Venezuela	18,408	15,253	12,930
Total (incl. others)	801,334	865,602	933,643

Tourism receipts (US $ million, incl. passenger transport): 818 in 2001; 838 in 2002; 959 in 2003.

Source: World Tourism Organization.

Communications Media

	2002	2003	2004
Telephones ('000 main lines in use)	1,656.6	1,839.2	2,049.8
Mobile cellular telephones ('000 subscribers)	2,306.9	2,908.8	4,092.6
Personal computers ('000 in use)	1,149	n.a.	2,689
Internet users ('000)	2,400	2,850	3,220

Television receivers ('000 in use): 3,800 in 2000.
Radio receivers ('000 in use): 6,650 in 1997.
Facsimile machines ('000 in use, estimate): 15 in 1995.
Book production (titles): 612 in 1996.
Daily newspapers: 74 in 1996.

Sources: UNESCO, *Statistical Yearbook*; International Telecommunication Union.

Education

(2003, incl. adult education, at documented institutions only)

	Institutions	Teachers	Pupils
Nursery	16,211	41,718	763,252
Primary	34,600	182,369	4,225,086
Secondary	10,278	152,047	2,505,956
Higher: universities*	78	33,177	435,637
Higher: other tertiary	1,066	27,478	389,223
Special	407	3,331	24,672
Vocational	1,893	11,438	248,003

* Figures for 2000.

Source: Ministerio de Educación del Perú.

Adult literacy rate (UNESCO estimates): 87.7% (males 93.5%; females 82.1%) in 2003 (Source: UN Development Programme, *Human Development Report*).

Directory

The Constitution

In 1993 the Congreso Constituyente Democrático (CCD) began drafting a new constitution to replace the 1979 Constitution. The CCD approved the final document in September 1993, and the Constitution was endorsed by a popular national referendum that was conducted on 31 October. The Constitution was promulgated on 29 December 1993.

EXECUTIVE POWER

Executive power is vested in the President, who is elected for a five-year term of office by universal adult suffrage; this mandate is renewable once. The successful presidential candidate must obtain at least 50% of the votes cast, and a second round of voting is held if necessary. Two Vice-Presidents are elected in simultaneous rounds of voting. The President is prohibited from serving two consecutive terms. The President is competent to initiate and submit draft bills, to review laws drafted by the legislature (Congreso) and, if delegated by the Congreso, to enact laws. The President is empowered to appoint ambassadors and senior military officials without congressional ratification, and retains the right to dissolve parliament if two or more ministers have been censured or have received a vote of 'no confidence' from the Congreso. In certain circumstances the President may, in accordance with the Council of Ministers, declare a state of emergency for a period of 60 days, during which individual constitutional rights are suspended and the armed forces may assume control of civil order. The President appoints the Council of Ministers.

LEGISLATIVE POWER

Legislative power is vested in a single-chamber Congreso (removing the distinction in the 1979 Constitution of an upper and lower house) consisting of 120 members. The members of the Congreso are elected for a five-year term by universal adult suffrage. The Congreso is responsible for approving the budget, for endorsing loans and international treaties and for drafting and approving bills. It may conduct investigations into matters of public concern, and question and censure the Council of Ministers and its individual members. Members of the Congreso elect a Standing Committee, to consist of not more than 25% of the total number of members (representation being proportional to the different political groupings in the legislature), which is empowered to make certain official appointments, approve credit loans and transfers relating to the budget during a parliamentary recess, and conduct other business as delegated by parliament.

ELECTORAL SYSTEM

All citizens aged 18 years and above, including illiterate persons, are eligible to vote. Voting in elections is compulsory for all citizens aged 18–70, and is optional thereafter.

JUDICIAL POWER

Judicial power is vested in the Supreme Court of Justice and other tribunals. The Constitution provides for the establishment of a National Council of the Judiciary, consisting of nine independently elected members, which is empowered to appoint judges to the Supreme Court. An independent Constitutional Court, comprising seven members elected by the Congreso for a five-year term, may interpret the Constitution and declare legislation and acts of government to be unconstitutional.

The death penalty may be applied by the Judiciary in cases of terrorism or of treason (the latter in times of war).

Under the Constitution, a People's Counsel is elected by the Congreso with a five-year mandate which authorizes the Counsel to defend the constitutional and fundamental rights of the individual. The Counsel may draft laws and present evidence to the legislature.

According to the Constitution, the State promotes economic and social development, particularly in the areas of employment, health, education, security, public services and infrastructure. The State recognizes a plurality of economic ownership and activity, supports free competition, and promotes the growth of small businesses. Private initiative is permitted within the framework of a social market economy. The State also guarantees the free exchange of foreign currency.

The Government

HEAD OF STATE

President: Dr Alejandro Toledo Manrique (took office 28 July 2001).
Vice-President: Dr David Waisman Rjavinsthi.

COUNCIL OF MINISTERS
(April 2006)

President of the Council of Ministers: Pedro Pablo Kuczynski.
Minister of Foreign Affairs: Oscar Maúrtua de Romaña.
Minister of Defence: Marciano Rengifo Ruiz.
Minister of the Interior: Rómulo Pizarro Tomasio.
Minister of Justice: Alejandro Tudela Chopitea.
Minister of Economy and Finance: Fernando Zavala Lombardi.
Minister of Labour and Employment: Juan Sheput.
Minister of International Trade and Tourism: Alfredo Ferrero Diez Canseco.
Minister of Transport and Communications: José Ortiz Rivera.
Minister of Housing, Construction and Sanitation: Rudecindo Vega Carreazo.
Minister of Health: Pilar Mazzetti Soler.
Minister of Agriculture: Manuel Manrique Ugarte.
Minister of Energy and Mines: Glodomiro Sánchez Mejía.
Minister of Production: David Lemor Bezdin.
Minister of Education: Javier Sota Nadal.
Minister for the Advancement of Women and Social Development: Ana María Romero Lozada Lauezzari.

MINISTRIES

Office of the President of the Council of Ministers: 28 de Julio 878, Miraflores, Lima; tel. (1) 4469800; fax (1) 4449168; e-mail webmaster@pcm.gob.pe; internet www.pcm.gob.pe.

Ministry for the Advancement of Women and Social Development: Jirón Camaná 616, Lima 1; tel. (1) 4289800; fax (1) 4261665; e-mail postmaster@mimdes.gob.pe; internet www.mimdes.gob.pe.

Ministry of Agriculture: Avda Salaverry s/n, Jesús María, Lima 11; tel. (1) 4310424; fax (1) 4310109; e-mail postmast@minag.gob.pe; internet www.minag.gob.pe.

Ministry of Defence: Avda Arequipa 291, Lima 1; tel. (1) 4335150; fax (1) 4333636; e-mail webmaster@mindef.gob.pe; internet www.mindef.gob.pe.

Ministry of Economy and Finance: Jirón Junín 339, 4°, Circado de Lima, Lima 1; tel. (1) 4273930; fax (1) 4282509; e-mail postmaster@mef.gob.pe; internet www.mef.gob.pe.

Ministry of Education: Avda Van Develde 160, cuadra 33 Javier Prado Este, San Borja, Lima 41; tel. (1) 4353900; fax (1) 4370471; e-mail postmaster@minedu.gob.pe; internet www.minedu.gob.pe.

Ministry of Energy and Mines: Avda Las Artes Sur 260, San Borja, Apdo 2600, Lima 41; tel. (1) 4752969; fax (1) 4750689; internet www.minem.gob.pe.

Ministry of Foreign Affairs: Jirón Lampa 535, Lima 1; tel. (1) 3112402; fax (1) 3112406; internet www.rree.gob.pe.

Ministry of Health: Avda Salaverry cuadra 8, Jesús María, Lima 11; tel. (1) 4310408; fax (1) 4310093; e-mail webmaster@minsa.gob.pe; internet www.minsa.gob.pe.

Ministry of Housing, Construction and Sanitation: Avda Paseo de la República 3361, San Isidro, Lima; tel. (1) 2117930; e-mail webmaster@vivienda.gob.pe; internet www.vivienda.gob.pe.

Ministry of the Interior: Plaza 30 de Agosto 150, San Isidro, Lima 27; tel. (1) 2242406; fax (1) 2242405; e-mail ofitel@mininter.gob.pe; internet www.mininter.gob.pe.

Ministry of International Trade and Tourism: Calle 1 Oeste 50, Urb. Corpac, San Isidro, Lima 27; tel. (1) 2243345; fax (1) 2243362; e-mail webmaster@mincetur.gob.pe; internet www.mincetur.gob.pe.

Ministry of Justice: Scipión Llona 350, Miraflores, Lima 18; tel. (1) 4222654; fax (1) 4223577; e-mail webmaster@minjus.gob.pe; internet www.minjus.gob.pe.

Ministry of Labour and Employment: Avda Salaverry 655, cuadra 8, Jesús María, Lima 11; tel. (1) 4332512; fax (1) 4230741; e-mail webmaster@mintra.gob.pe; internet www.mintra.gob.pe.

PERU

Ministry of the Presidency: Avda Paseo de la República 4297, Lima 1; tel. (1) 4465886; fax (1) 4470379; internet www.peru.gob.pe.

Ministry of Production: Calle 1 Oeste 60, Urb. Corpac, San Isidro, Lima 27; tel. (1) 2243333; fax (1) 2243237; internet www.produce.gob.pe.

Ministry of Transport and Communications: Avda 28 de Julio 800, Lima 1; tel. (1) 4330010; fax (1) 4339378; internet www.mtc.gob.pe.

Regional Presidents
(April 2006)

Amazonas: MIGUEL REYES CATALINO CONTRERAS (APRA).
Ancash: RICARDO NARVÁEZ SOTO (APRA).
Apurímac: ROSA AURORA SUÁREZ ALIAGA (Ind.).
Arequipa: DANIEL ERNESTO VERA BALLÓN (APRA).
Ayacucho: WERNER OMAR QUEZADA MARTÍNEZ (APRA).
Cajamarca: LUIS FELIPE PITA GASTELUMENDI (APRA).
Callao: ROGELIO CANCHES GUZMAN (PP).
Cusco: CARLOS CUARESMA SÁNCHEZ (FIM).
Huancavelica: SALVADOR CRISANTO ESPINOZA HUAROC (Ind.).
Huánuco: LUZMILA TEMPLO CONDEZO (Ind.).
Ica: MANUEL VICENTE TELLO CÉSPEDES (APRA).
Junín: MANUEL DUARTE VELARDE (Ind.).
La Libertad: HOMERO BENJAMÍN BURGOS OLIVEROS (APRA).
Lambayeque: YEHUDE SIMON MUNARO (UPP).
Lima: MIGUEL ANGEL MUFARECH (APRA).
Loreto: ROBINSON RIVADENEYRA (Ind.).
Madre de Dios: RAFAEL EDWIN RÍOS LÓPEZ (MNI).
Moquegua: MARÍA CRISTALA CONSTANTINIDES (SP).
Pasco: VÍCTOR RAÚL ESPINOZA SOTO (Ind.).
Piura: CÉSAR TRELLES LARA (APRA).
Puno: DANIEL ANÍBAL JIMÉNEZ SARDÓN (Ind.).
San Martín: MAX HENRY RAMÍREZ GARCÍA (APRA).
Tacna: JULIO ANTONIO ALVA CENTURIÓN (APRA).
Tumbes: IRIS MEDINA FEIJOÓ (APRA).
Ucayali: EDWIN VÁSQUEZ LÓPEZ (Ind.).

President and Legislature

PRESIDENT

Presidential Election, First Round, 9 April 2006*

Candidate	Valid votes	% of votes
Lt-Col (retd) Ollanta Moises Humala Tasso (UPP)	3,758,258	30.62
Alan Gabriel Ludwig García Pérez (APRA)	2,985,858	24.32
Lourdes Flores Nano (Unidad Nacional)	2,923,280	23.81
Martha Gladys Chávez Cossío de Ocampo (Alianza por el Futuro)	912,420	7.43
Valentín Paniagua Corazao (Frente de Centro)	706,156	5.75
Humberto Lay Sun (Restauración Nacional)	537,564	4.38
Others	451,849	3.68
Total†	12,275,385	100.00

* A second round of voting between the two leading candidates was scheduled to be held on 4 June 2006.
† Excluding 1,737,045 blank votes and 619,573 spoiled votes.

CONGRESO

President: MARCIAL AYAIPOMA.

General Election, 9 April 2006*

Parties	Votes	% of votes
Unión por el Perú (UPP)	2,063,429	21.93
Alianza Popular Revolucionaria Americana (APRA)	1,930,049	20.51
Unidad Nacional	1,394,580	14.82
Alianza por el Futuro	1,186,111	12.60
Frente de Centro	668,908	7.10
Restauración Nacional	372,782	3.96
Perú Posible (PP)	369,172	3.92
Alianza para el Progreso	225,114	2.39
Fuerza Democrática	144,892	1.54
Partido Justicia Nacional	141,090	1.50
Frente Independiente Moralizador	139,852	1.49
Movimiento Nueva Izquierda	124,541	1.32
Partido Socialista	117,313	1.25
Avanza País (Partido de Integración Social)	110,328	1.17
Others	421,717	4.48
Total†	9,409,878	100.00

* Preliminary results as of 16 May 2006, at which time the allocation of congressional seats was pending.
† Excludes 1,511,791 blank votes, 1,707,505 spoiled votes and 564 rejected votes.

Election Commission

Oficina Nacional de Procesos Electorales (ONPE): Jirón Washington 1894, Lima; tel. (1) 4170630; internet www.onpe.gob.pe; independent; Nat. Dir MAGDALENA CHÚ VILLANUEVA.

Political Organizations

Acción Popular (AP): Paseo Colón 218, Lima 1; tel. (1) 3321965; fax (1) 3321965; e-mail webmaster@accionpopular.org.pe; internet www.accionpopular.org.pe; f. 1956; 1.2m. mems; liberal; contested the presidential and legislative elections of April 2006 as part of the Frente de Centro coalition; Leader FERNANDO BELAÚNDE TERRY; Sec.-Gen. LUIS ALBERTO VELARDE YAÑEZ.

Alianza por el Futuro: Lima; f. 2005 as a coalition of Cambio 90 and Nueva Mayoría in order to contest the presidential and legislative elections of April 2006; Presidential Candidate MARTHA GLADYS CHÁVEZ COSSÍO DE OCAMPO.

Alianza Popular Revolucionaria Americana (APRA): Avda Alfonso Ugarte 1012, Lima 5; tel. (1) 4281736; internet www.apra.org.pe; f. in Mexico 1924, in Peru 1930 as Partido Aprista Peruano (PAP); legalized 1945; democratic left-wing party; Sec.-Gen. JORGE DEL CASTILLO; 700,000 mems.

Alianza para el Progreso: Avda de la Policía 643, Jesús María, Lima; tel. (1) 4601251; e-mail alianzaparaelprogreso2006@hotmail.com; internet www.app-peru.org.pe; f. 2001; Sec.-Gen. CÉSAR ACUÑA PERALTA.

Avanza País (Partido de Integración Social): Huaura 175, Of. 104, Rímac, Lima; tel. (1) 3813250; e-mail info@partidoavanzapais.org; internet www.partidoavanzapais.org; f. 2005; Exec. Pres. PEDRO CENAS CASAMAYOR.

Cambio 90 (C90): Jirón Santa Isabel 590, Urb. Colmenares, Pueblo Libre, Lima; tel. (1) 9441739; internet www.fujimori2006.com; f. 1990; part of Alianza por el Futuro coalition formed with Nueva Mayoría in order to contest the presidential and legislative elections of April 2006; Pres. ANDRÉS REGGIARDO SAYÁN.

Coordinación Democrática (CODE): Lima; f. 1992; by dissident APRA members; Leader JOSÉ BARBA CABALLERO.

Coordinadora Nacional de Independientes (CNI): Domingo Elías 1450, Surquillo, Lima; tel. (1) 2411884; fax (1) 4455968; e-mail info@independientes.org.pe; internet www.independientes.org.pe; f. 2003; contested the presidential and legislative elections of April 2006 as part of the Frente de Centro coalition; Leader DRAGO KISIC.

Frente de Centro: Avda Paseo de la República 3920, Miraflores, Lima; f. 2005 as a coalition of Acción Popular, Somos Perú and the Coordinadora Nacional de Independientes in order to contest the presidential and legislative elections of April 2006; Presidential Candidate VALENTÍN PANIAGUA CORAZAO.

Frente Independiente Moralizador (FIM): Pancho Fierro 133, San Isidro, Lima; tel. (1) 4220583; internet www.congreso.gob.pe/grupo_parlamentario/fim/inicio.htm; f. 1990; right-wing; Pres. LUIS FERNANDO OLIVERA VEGA; Sec.-Gen. GONZALO CARRIQUIRY BLONDET.

PERU

Directory

Frente Nacional de Trabajadores y Campesinos (FNTC/FRENATRACA): Lima; tel. (1) 4272868; f. 1968; left-wing party; Pres. Dr RÓGER CÁCERES VELÁSQUEZ; Sec.-Gen. Dr EDMUNDO HUANQUI MEDINA.

Frente Popular Agrícola del Perú (Frepap): Avda Morro Solar 1234; Santiago de Surco, Lima; tel. (1) 2753847; f. 1989; Leader EZEQUIEL ATAUCUSI GAMONAL.

Fuerza Democrática (FD): Avda La Marina 1520, Pueblo Libre, Lima; tel. (1) 4606335; e-mail editor@fuerzademocratica.net; internet www.fuerzademocratica.info; Leader ALBERTO BOREA ODRÍA.

Movimiento Nueva Izquierda (MNI): Jirón Miró Quesada 360, Lima; tel. (1) 4264640; e-mail mni_peru@yahoo.es; internet www.mni.org.pe; f. 2005; left-wing; Leader RAFAEL EDWIN RÍOS LÓPEZ.

Nueva Mayoría: Lima; internet www.fujimori2006.com; f. 1992; part of Alianza por el Futuro coalition formed with Cambio 90 in order to contest the presidential and legislative elections of April 2006; Pres. MARTHA GLADYS CHÁVEZ COSSÍO DE OCAMPO; Sec.-Gen. DEMETRIO PATSIAS MELLA.

Partido Comunista Peruano (PCP): Plaza Ramón Castilla 67, Lima; tel. and fax (1) 3306106; e-mail unidad@ec-red.com; internet www.pcp.miarroba.com; f. 1928; Pres. JORGE DEL PRADO.

Partido Demócrata Cristiano (PDC): Avda España 321, Lima 1; tel. (1) 4238042; f. 1956; 95,000 mems; Chair. CARLOS BLANCAS BUSTAMANTE.

Partido Democrático Descentralista (PDD): Huancayo; e-mail pddperu@yahoogroups.com; internet www.pddperu.net; f. 2002; left-wing; regionalist; Leader JAVIER DIEZ CANSECO.

Partido Justicia Nacional: Avda Arequipa 1799, Lince, Lima; tel. (1) 4723744; e-mail info@justicianacional.com; internet www.justicianacional.com; f. 2003; Pres. JAIME SALINAS LÓPEZ-TORRES.

Partido Nacionalista Peruano: Lima; tel. (1) 2641738; e-mail pnacionalista@yahoo.com; internet www.partidonacionalistaperuano.com; f. 2005, to support presidential candidacy of Lt-Col. (retd) Ollanta Moises Humala Tasso; contested the 2006 elections in coalition with the Unión por el Perú; Leader Lt-Col (retd) OLLANTA MOISES HUMALA TASSO.

Partido Popular Cristiano (PPC): Avda Alfonso Ugarte 1484, Lima; tel. (1) 4238723; fax (1) 4238721; e-mail estflores@terra.com.pe; f. 1967; splinter group of Partido Demócrata Cristiano; 250,000 mems; Pres. Dr ANTERO LOURDES FLORES-NANO; Vice-Pres RAÚL CASTRO STAGNARO, JAVIER BEDOYA DE VIVIANCO, XAVIER BARRÓN CEBRERROS, ALEJANDRO CASTAGNOLA PINILLOS.

Partido Socialista: Plaza Bolognesi 590, Breña, Lima 5; tel. (1) 3305558; internet www.socialista.org.pe; contested the 2006 election; Presidential Candidate JAVIER DIEZ CANSECO.

Partido Verde del Perú (Movimiento Independiente Verde del Perú en Formación): Avda Jorge Chávez 654, 4°, Lima 33; e-mail allparuna@yahoo.es; internet www.unii.net/allparuna/peruverde.html; ecologist.

Perú Ahora: Plaza Bolognesi 600, Breña, Lima 5; tel. (1) 3309230; e-mail partidopolitico@peruahora.org; internet www.peruahora.org; f. 1998; relaunched in 2003 by fmr mems of Perú Posible; Sec.-Gen. LUIS GUERRERO FIGUEROA.

Perú Posible (PP): Avda Faustino Sánchez Carrión, Lima; tel. (1) 4620303; e-mail sgpp@mixmail.com; internet www.peruposible.org.pe/indice.htm; f. 1994 to support Toledo's candidacy for the 1995 presidential election in alliance with CODE; Leader ALEJANDRO TOLEDO; Sec.-Gen. JAVIER REÁTEGUI ROSELLÓ.

Proyecto País: Nicolás de Piérola 917, Of. 211, Plaza San Martín, Lima; tel. (1) 3312696; fax (1) 2222785; e-mail info@proyectopais.org.pe; internet www.proyectopais.org.pe; f. 1998; Leader MARCO ANTONIO ARRUNATEGUI CEVALLOS.

Renacimiento Andino: Calle Real 583, 2°, Huancayo; tel. (4) 214620; fax (4) 217480; e-mail webmaster@renacimientoandino.org.pe; internet www.renacimientoandino.org.pe; f. 2001; Leader CIRO ALFREDO GÁLVEZ HERRERA.

Renovación: c/o Edif. Complejo 510, Avda Abancay 251, Lima; tel. (1) 4264260; fax (1) 4263023; f. 1992; Leader RAFAEL REY REY.

Restauración Nacional: Avda Arequipa 3750, San Isidro, Lima; tel. (1) 2226525; internet www.restauracionnacional.org; contested the 2006 presidential election as part of the Frente de Centro coalition; f. 2005; Pres. HUMBERTO LAY SUN.

Sí Cumple: Jirón Lampa 974, Lima; tel. (1) 4266451; e-mail sicumple@trincheranaranja.com; internet www.trincheranaranja.com; f. 2003; supporters of fmr President Fujimori; Sec-Gen. LUIS DELGADO APARICIO.

Solidaridad Nacional (SN): Armando Blondet 106, San Isidro, Lima; tel. (1) 2218948; e-mail fsandoval@psn.org.pe; internet www.psn.org.pe; f. 1999; centre-left; Pres. LUIS CASTAÑEDA LOSSIO; Sec.-Gen. MARCO ANTONIO PARRA SÁNCHEZ.

Solución Popular: Avda Guzmán Blanco 240, Of. 1001, Lima; tel. (1) 4263017; Leader CARLOS BOLOÑA.

Somos Perú (SP): Avda Arequipa 3990, Miraflores, Lima; tel. (1) 4219363; e-mail postmaster@somosperu.org.pe; internet www.somosperu.org.pe; f. 1998; contested the April 2006 elections as part of the Frente de Centro coalition; Leader ALBERTO ANDRADE CARMONA; Sec.-Gen. EDUARDO CARHUARICRA MEZA.

Todos por la Victoria: Avda Grau 122, La Victoria, Lima; tel. (1) 4242446; f. 2001; Leader RICARDO MANUEL NORIEGA SALAVERRY.

Unidad Nacional: Calle Ricardo Palma 1111, Miraflores, Lima; tel. (1) 2242773; f. 2000; centrist alliance; Leader LOURDES FLORES NANO.

Unión de Izquierda Revolucionaria (UNIR) (Union of the Revolutionary Left): Jirón Puno 258, Apdo 1165, Lima 1; tel. (1) 4274072; f. 1980; Chair. Sen. ROLANDO BREÑA PANTOJA; Gen. Sec. JORGE HURTADO POZO.

Unión por el Perú (UPP): Pablo de Olavide 270, San Isidro, Lima; tel. (1) 4403227; e-mail ivega@partidoupp.org; internet www.partidoupp.org; independent movt; f. 1994; contested 2006 elections in coalition with Partido Nacionalista Peruano, led by Lt-Col (retd) Ollanta Moises Humala Tasso; Pres. Dr ALDO ESTRADA CHOQUE.

Vamos Vecino: Lima; f. 1998; Leader ABSALON VÁSQUEZ.

ARMED GROUPS

Movimiento Nacionalista Peruano (MNP) (Movimiento Etnocacerista): Pasaje Velarde 188, Of. 204, Lima; tel. (1) 3311074; e-mail movnacionalistaperuano@yahoo.es; internet mnp.tripod.com.pe; ultra-nationalist paramilitary group; Pres. Dr ISAAC HUMALA NÚÑEZ; Leaders of paramilitary wing Maj. (retd) ANTAURO IGOR HUMALA TASSO (arrested Jan. 2005 following an armed uprising in Andahuaylas).

Sendero Luminoso (Shining Path): f. 1970; began armed struggle 1980; splinter group of PCP; based in Ayacucho; advocates the policies of the late Mao Zedong and his radical followers, including the 'Gang of Four' in the People's Republic of China; founder Dr ABIMAEL GUZMÁN REYNOSO (alias 'Comandante Gonzalo'—arrested Sept. 1992); current leaders MARGIE CLAVO PERALTA (arrested March 1995), PEDRO DOMINGO QUINTEROS AYLLÓN (alias 'Comrade Luis'—arrested April 1998).

  Sendero Rojo (Red Path): dissident faction of Sendero Luminoso opposed to leadership of Abimael Guzmán; Leader FILOMENO CERRÓN CARDOSO (alias 'Comrade Artemio').

Movimiento Revolucionario Tupac Amarú (MRTA): f. 1984; began negotiations with the Govt to end its armed struggle in September 1990; Leader VÍCTOR POLAY CAMPOS (alias 'Comandante Rolando'—arrested in 1992).

Diplomatic Representation

EMBASSIES IN PERU

Argentina: Arequipa 121, Lima 1; tel. (1) 4339966; fax (1) 4330769; e-mail embajada@terra.com.pe; Ambassador JORGE ALBERTO VÁZQUEZ.

Austria: Avda Central 643, 5°, San Isidro, Lima 27; tel. (1) 4420503; fax (1) 4428851; e-mail lima-ob@bmaa.gv.at; Ambassador GERHARD DOUJAK.

Bolivia: Los Castaños 235, San Isidro, Lima 27; tel. (1) 4402095; fax (1) 4402298; e-mail jemis@emboli.attla.com.pe; Ambassador ELOY AVILA ALBERDI.

Brazil: Avda José Pardo 850, Miraflores, Lima; tel. (1) 4215660; fax (1)4452421; e-mail embajada@embajadabrasil.org.pe; internet www.embajadabrasil.org.pe; Ambassador LUIZ AUGUSTO DE ARAUJO CASTRO.

Canada: Casilla 18-1126, Correo Miraflores, Lima; tel. (1) 4444015; fax (1) 4444347; e-mail lima@dfait-maeci.gc.ca; internet www.dfait-maeci.gc.ca/peru; Ambassador GENEVIÈVE DES RIVIÈRES.

Chile: Avda Javier Prado Oeste 790, San Isidro, Lima; tel. (1) 6112211; fax (1) 6112223; e-mail embajada@embachileperu.com.pe; internet www.embachileperu.com.pe; Ambassador JUAN PABLO LIRA BIANCHI.

China, People's Republic: Jirón José Granda 150, San Isidro, Apdo 375, Lima 27; tel. (1) 2220841; fax (1) 4429467; e-mail chinaemb_pe@mfa.gov.cn; internet www.embajadachina.org.pe; Ambassador YIN HENGMIN.

Colombia: Avda J. Basadre 1580, San Isidro, Lima 27; tel. (1) 4410954; fax (1) 4419806; e-mail elima@minrelext.gov.co; Ambassador ÁLVARO PAVA CAMELO.

Costa Rica: Calle Baltazar La Torre 828, San Isidro, Lima; tel. (1) 2642999; fax (1) 2642799; e-mail costarica@terra.com.pe; Ambassador JULIO SUÑOL LEAL.

Cuba: Coronel Portillo 110, San Isidro, Lima; tel. (1) 2642053; fax (1) 2644525; e-mail embacuba@ecuperu.minrex.gov.cu; Ambassador ROGELIO SIERRA DÍAZ.

Czech Republic: Baltazar La Torre 398, San Isidro, Lima 27; tel. (1) 2643374; fax (1) 2641708; e-mail lima@embassy.mzv.cz; internet www.mfa.cz/lima; Chargé d'affaires a.i. KAMILA HRABÁKOVÁ.

Dominican Republic: Calle Tudela y Varela 360, San Isidro, Lima; tel. (1) 4219765; fax (1) 421-9763; e-mail embdomperu@terra.com.pe; Ambassador VINICIO ALFONSO TOBAL UREÑA.

Ecuador: Las Palmeras 356 y Javier Prado Oeste, San Isidro, Lima 27; tel. (1) 2124171; fax (1) 4220711; e-mail embajada@mecuadorperu.org.pe; internet www.mecuadorperu.org.pe; Ambassador Dr LUIS VALENCIA RODRÍGUEZ.

Egypt: Avda Jorge Basadre 1470, San Isidro, Lima 27; tel. (1) 4402642; fax (1) 4402547; e-mail emb-egypt@amauta.rcp.net.pe; Ambassador DESOUKY ALI FAYED.

El Salvador: Avda Javier Prado 2108, San Isidro, Lima 27; tel. (1) 4403500; fax (1) 2212561; e-mail embajadasv@terra.com.pe; internet www.embajadaelsalvador.org.pe; Ambassador RAÚL SOTO-RAMÍREZ.

Finland: Avda Víctor Andrés Belaúnde 147, Edif. Real Tres, Of. 502, San Isidro, Lima; tel. (1) 2224466; fax (1) 2224463; e-mail sanomat.lim@formin.fi; internet www.finlandiaperu.org.pe; Ambassador KIMMO PULKKINEN.

France: Avda Arequipa 3415, Lima 27; tel. (1) 2158400; fax (1) 2158410; e-mail france.consulat@ambafrance-pe.org; internet www.ambafrance-pe.org; Ambassador PIERRE CHARRASSE.

Germany: Avda Arequipa 4210, Miraflores, Lima 18; tel. (1) 2125016; fax (1) 4226475; e-mail kanzlei@embajada-alemana.org.pe; internet www.embajada-alemana.org.pe; Ambassador ROLAND ERNEST-AUGUST KLIESOW.

Greece: Avda Principal 190, 6°, Urb. Santa Catalina, Lima 13; tel. (1) 4761548; fax (1) 4761329; e-mail emgrecia@terra.com.pe; Ambassador VASSILOS SIMANTIRAKIS.

Guatemala: Inca Ripac 309, Jesús María, Lima 11; tel. (1) 4602078; fax (1) 4635885; e-mail embperu@minex.gob.gt; Ambassador OLGA MARÍA AGUJA SUÑIGA.

Holy See: Avda Salaverry, 6a cuadra, Apdo 397, Lima 100 (Apostolic Nunciature); tel. (1) 4319436; fax (1) 4315704; e-mail nunciatura@speedy.com.pe; Apostolic Nuncio Most Rev. RINO PASSIGATO (Titular Archbishop of Nova Caesaris).

Honduras: Avda Las Camelias 491, Of. 202, San Isidro, Lima; tel. (1) 4228111; fax (1) 2211677; e-mail embhonpe@speedy.com.pe; Ambassador JUÁN JOSÉ CUEVA.

Hungary: Calle Alfredo Roldán 124, San Isidro, Lima 18; tel. (1) 4223069; fax (1) 4223093; e-mail oficinalima@embajadadehungaria.com; Ambassador JÓZSEF KOSÁRKA.

India: Avda Salaverry 3006, San Isidro, Lima 27; tel. (1) 4602289; fax (1) 4610374; e-mail hoc@indembassy.org.pe; internet www.indembassy.org.pe; Ambassador RIEWAD V. WARJRI.

Indonesia: Avda Las Flores 334, San Isidro, Lima; tel. (1) 222-0308; fax (1) 222-2684; Ambassador GUSTI NGURAH SWETJA.

Israel: Edif. El Pacifico, 6°, Plaza Washington, Natalio Sánchez 125, Santa Beatriz, Lima; tel. (1) 4334431; fax (1) 4338925; e-mail info@lima.mfa.gov.il; internet lima.mfa.gov.il; Ambassador WALID MANSOUR.

Italy: Avda Gregorio Escobedo 298, Apdo 0490, Lima 11; tel. (1) 4632727; fax (1) 4635317; e-mail segretaria@italembperu.org.pe; internet www.italembperu.org.pe; Ambassador FABIO CLAUDIO DE NARDIS.

Japan: Avda San Felipe 356, Apdo 3708, Jesús María, Lima 11; tel. (1) 2181130; fax (1) 4630302; internet www.pe.emb-japan.go.jp; Ambassador HITOHIRO ISHIDA.

Korea, Democratic People's Republic: Los Nogales 227, San Isidro, Lima; tel. (1) 4411120; fax (1) 4409877; e-mail embcorea@hotmail.com; Ambassador YU CHANG UN.

Korea, Republic: Avda Principal 190, 7°, Urb. Santa Catalina, La Victoria, Lima; tel. (1) 4760815; fax (1) 4760950; e-mail korembj-pu@mofat.go.kr; Ambassador CHUNG JIN-HO.

Malaysia: Avda Daniel Hernández 350, San Isidro, Lima 27,; tel. (1) 4220297; fax (1) 2210786; e-mail mwlima@terra.com.pe; Ambassador Datuk MOHD NOR ATAN.

Mexico: Avda Jorge Basadre 710, esq. Los Ficus, San Isidro, Lima; tel. (1) 2211100; fax (1) 4404740; e-mail info@mexico.org.pe; internet www.mexico.org.pe; Ambassador ANTONIO GUILLERMO VILLEGAS VILLALOBOS.

Morocco: Calle Manuel Ugarte y Morosco 790, San Isidro, Lima; tel. (1) 2643323; fax (1) 2640006; e-mail sifamlim@chavin.rcp.net.pe; Ambassador MAHMOUD RMIKI.

Netherlands: Avda Principal 190, 4°, Urb. Santa Catalina, La Victoria, Lima; tel. (1) 4150660; fax (1) 4150689; e-mail info@nlgovlim.com; internet www.nlgovlim.com; Ambassador PAUL W. A. SCHELLEKENS.

Nicaragua: Avda Alvarez Calderón 738, San Isidro, Lima; tel. (1) 4223892; fax (1) 4223895; e-mail embanic@telefonica.net.pe; Chargé d'affaires a.i. MARITZA ROSALES GRANERA.

Panama: Alvarez Calderón 738, San Isidro, Lima 27; tel. (1) 4413652; fax (1) 4419323; e-mail panaemba@amauta.rcp.net.pe; Ambassador ROBERTO DÍAZ HERRERA.

Paraguay: Alcanfores 1286, Miraflores, Lima; tel. (1) 4474762; fax (1) 4442391; e-mail embaparpe@terra.com.pe; Ambassador Dra JULIA VELILLA LACONICH.

Poland: Apdo 180174, Miraflores, Lima 18; tel. (1) 4713920; fax (1) 4714813; e-mail consrplima@amauta.rcp.net.pe; internet www.polonia.org.pe; Ambassador ZDZISLAW SOSNICKI.

Portugal: Avda Central 643, 4°, Lima 27; tel. (1) 4409905; fax (1) 4429655; e-mail limaportugal@hotmail.com; Ambassador MÁRIO ALBERTO LINO DA SILVA.

Romania: Avda Jorge Basadre 690, San Isidro, Lima 27; tel. (1) 4224587; fax (1) 4210609; e-mail ambrom@terra.com.pe; Ambassador STEFAN COSTIN.

Russia: Avda Salaverry 3424, San Isidro, Lima 27; tel. (1) 2640036; fax (1) 2640130; e-mail embrusa@amauta.rcp.net.pe; Ambassador ANATOLY P. KUZNETSOV.

Serbia and Montenegro: Carlos Porras Osores 360, Apdo 18-0392, San Isidro, Lima 27; Apdo 0392, Lima 18; tel. (1) 4212423; fax (1) 4212427; e-mail yugoembperu@amauta.rcp.net.pe; Ambassador GORAN MESIC.

South Africa: POB 27-013 L27, Lima; tel. (1) 4409996; fax 4223881; e-mail saemb@amauta.rcp.net.pe; Ambassador Dr C. J. STREETER.

Spain: Jorge Basadre 498, San Isidro, Lima 27; tel. (1) 2125155; fax (1) 4410084; e-mail embesppe@correo.mae.es; Ambassador JULIO ALBI DE LA CUESTA.

Switzerland: Avda Salaverry 3240, San Isidro, Lima 27; tel. (1) 2640305; fax (1) 2641319; e-mail vertretung@lim.rep.admin.ch; internet www.eda.admin.ch/lima_emb/s/home.html; Ambassador BEAT LOELIGER.

Ukraine: Calle José Dellepiani 470, San Isidro, Lima; tel. (1) 264-2884; fax (1) 264-2892; e-mail emb-pe@mfa.gov.ua; Ambassador IGOR GRUSHKO.

United Kingdom: Torre Parque Mar, 22°, Avda José Larco 1301, Miraflores, Lima; tel. (1) 6173000; fax (1) 6173100; e-mail belima@fco.gov.uk; internet www.britemb.org.pe; Ambassador CATHERINE NETTLETON.

USA: Avda La Encalada 17, Surco, Lima 33; tel. (1) 4343000; fax (1) 6182397; internet usembassy.state.gov/lima; Ambassador JAMES CURTIS STRUBLE.

Uruguay: Calle José D. Anchorena 84, San Isidro, Lima; tel. (1) 2640099; fax (1) 2640112; e-mail uruinca@embajada-uruguay.com; Ambassador JUAN BAUTISTA ODDONE SILVEIRA.

Venezuela: Avda Arequipa 298, Lima; tel. (1) 4334511; fax (1) 4331191; e-mail embavene@millicom.com.pe; internet www.embavenezperu.com; Ambassador CRUZ MANUEL MARTÍNEZ RAMÍREZ (recalled in May 2006).

Judicial System

The Supreme Court consists of a President and 17 members. There are also Higher Courts and Courts of First Instance in provincial capitals. A comprehensive restructuring of the judiciary was implemented during the late 1990s.

SUPREME COURT

Corte Suprema
Palacio de Justicia, 2°, Avda Paseo de la República, Lima 1; tel. (1) 4284457; fax (1) 4269437; internet www.pj.gob.pe.
President: Dr WALTER HUMBERTO VÁSQUEZ VEJARANO.
Attorney-General: FLORA ADELAIDA BOLIVAR ARTEAGA.

Religion

CHRISTIANITY

The Roman Catholic Church

For ecclesiastical purposes, Peru comprises seven archdioceses, 18 dioceses, 11 territorial prelatures and eight Apostolic Vicariates. At

PERU

31 December 2003 92.0% of the country's population (an estimated 29.5m.) were adherents of the Roman Catholic Church.

Bishops' Conference

Conferencia Episcopal Peruana, Jirón Estados Unidos 838, Apdo 310, Lima 100; tel. (1) 4631010; fax (1) 4636125; e-mail sgc@iglesiacatolica.org.pe.
f. 1981; statutes approved 1987, revised 1992 and 2000; Pres. Mgr José Hugo Garaycoa Hawkins (Bishop of Tacna y Moquegua).

Archbishop of Arequipa: José Paulino Ríos Reynoso, Arzobispado, Moral San Francisco 118, Apdo 149, Arequipa; tel. (54) 234094; fax (54) 242721; e-mail arzobispadoaqp@planet.com.pe.

Archbishop of Ayacucho or Huamanga: Luis Abilio Sebastiani Aguirre, Arzobispado, Jirón 28 de Julio 148, Apdo 30, Ayacucho; tel. and fax (64) 812367; e-mail arzaya@mail.udep.edu.pe.

Archbishop of Cusco: Juan Antonio Ugarte Pérez, Arzobispado, Herrajes, Hatun Rumiyoc s/n, Apdo 148, Cusco; tel. (84) 225211; fax (84) 222781; e-mail arzobisp@terra.com.pe.

Archbishop of Huancayo: Pedro Ricardo Barreto Jimeno, Arzobispado, Jirón Puno 430, Apdo 245, Huancayo; tel. (64) 234952; fax (64) 239189; e-mail arzohyo@hotmail.com.

Archbishop of Lima: Cardinal Juan Luis Cipriani Thorne, Arzobispado, Jirón Carabaya, Plaza Mayor, Apdo 1512, Lima 100; tel. (1) 4275980; fax (1) 4271967; e-mail arzolim@terra.com.pe; internet www.arzobispadodelima.org.

Archbishop of Piura: Oscar Rolando Cantuarias Pastor, Arzobispado, Libertad 1105, Apdo 197, Piura; tel. and fax (74) 327561; e-mail ocordova@upiura.edu.pe.

Archbishop of Trujillo: Héctor Miguel Cabrejos Vidarte, Arzobispado, Jirón Mariscal de Orbegozo 451, Apdo 42, Trujillo; tel. (44) 256812; fax (44) 231473; e-mail arztrujillo@terra.com.pe.

The Anglican Communion

The Iglesia Anglicana del Cono Sur de América (Anglican Church of the Southern Cone of America), formally inaugurated in April 1983, comprises seven dioceses, including Peru. The Presiding Bishop of the Church is the Bishop of Northern Argentina.

Bishop of Peru: Rt Rev. Harold William Godfrey, Apdo 18-1032, Miraflores, Lima 18; tel. and fax (1) 4229160; e-mail wgodfrey@amauta.rcp.net.pe.

The Methodist Church

There are an estimated 4,200 adherents of the Iglesia Metodista del Perú.

President: Rev. Jorge Figueroa, Baylones 186, Lima 5; Apdo 1386, Lima 100; tel. (1) 4245970; fax (1) 4318995; e-mail iglesiamp@computextos.com.pe.

Other Protestant Churches

Among the most popular are the Asamblea de Dios, the Iglesia Evangélica del Perú, the Iglesia del Nazareno, the Alianza Cristiana y Misionera and the Iglesia de Dios del Perú.

BAHÁ'Í FAITH

National Spiritual Assembly of the Bahá'ís of Peru: Horacio Urteaga 827, Jesús María, Apdo 11-0209, Lima 11; tel. (1) 4316077; fax (1) 4333005; e-mail bahai@terra.com.pe; mems resident in 220 localities; Nat. Sec. María Loreto Jara de Roeder.

The Press

DAILIES

Lima

El Bocón: Jirón Jorge Salazar Araoz 171, Urb. Santa Catalina, Apdo 152, Lima 1; tel. (1) 4756355; fax (1) 4758780; internet www.elbocon.com.pe; f. 1994; football; Editorial Dir Jorge Estéves Alfaro; circ. 90,000.

El Comercio: Empresa Editora 'El Comercio', SA, Jirón Antonio Miró Quesada 300, Lima; tel. (1) 4264676; fax (1) 4260810; e-mail editorweb@comercio.com.pe; internet www.elcomercioperu.com.pe; f. 1839; morning; Editor Juan Carlos Luján; Dir-Gen. Alejandro Miró Quesada G., Francisco Miró Quesada C.; circ. 150,000 weekdays, 220,000 Sundays.

Expreso: Jirón Antonio Elizalde 753, Lima; tel. (1) 6124000; fax (1) 4447125; e-mail webmaster@expreso.com.pe; internet www.expreso.com.pe; f. 1961; morning; conservative; Pres. Manuel Ulloa; Dir Carlos Espá; circ. 100,000.

Extra: Jirón Libertad 117, Miraflores, Lima; tel. (1) 4447088; fax (1) 4447117; e-mail extra@expreso.com.pe; f. 1964; evening edition of Expreso; Dir Carlos Sánchez; circ. 80,000.

Gestión: Avda Salaverry 156, Miraflores, Lima 18; tel. (1) 4776919; fax (1) 4476569; e-mail gestion@gestion.com.pe; internet www.gestion.com.pe; f. 1990; Gen. Editor Julio Lira; Gen. Man. Oscar Romero Caro; circ. 131,200.

Ojo: Jirón Jorge Salazar Araoz 171, Urb. Santa Catalina, Apdo 152, Lima; tel. (1) 4709696; fax (1) 4761605; internet www.ojo.com.pe; f. 1968; morning; Editorial Dir Agustín Figueroa Benza; circ. 100,000.

El Peruano (Diario Oficial): Avda Alfonso Ugarte 873, Lima 1; tel. (1) 3150400; fax (1) 4245023; e-mail gbarraza@editoraperu.com.pe; internet www.elperuano.com.pe; f. 1825; morning; official State Gazette; Editorial Dir Gerardo Barraza Soto; circ. 27,000.

La República: Jirón Camaná 320, Lima 1; tel. (1) 4276455; fax (1) 2511029; e-mail otxoa@larepublica.com.pe; internet www.larepublica.com.pe; f. 1982; left-wing; Dirs Gustavo Mohme Seminario, Gustavo Gorriti; circ. 50,000.

Perú 21: Jirón Miró Quesada 247, 6°, Lima; tel. (1) 311-6500; fax (1) 311-6391; e-mail director@peru21.com; internet www.peru21.com; independent; Editor Augusto Alvarez Rodrich.

Arequipa

Arequipa al Día: Avda Jorge Chávez 201, IV, Centenario, Arequipa; tel. (54) 223566; fax (54) 217810; f. 1991; Editorial Dir Carlos Meneses Cornejo.

Correo de Arequipa: Calle Bolívar 204, Arequipa; tel. (54) 235150; e-mail diariocorreo@epensa.com.pe; internet www.correoperu.com.pe; Dir Aldo Mariátegui; circ. 70,000.

El Pueblo: Sucre 213, Apdo 35, Arequipa; tel. (54) 211500; fax (54) 213361; f. 1905; morning; independent; Editorial Dir Eduardo Laime Valdivia; circ. 70,000.

Chiclayo

La Industria: Tacna 610, Chiclayo; tel. (74) 237952; fax (74) 227678; internet www.laindustria.com.pe; f. 1952; Dir Julio Alberto Ortiz Cerro; circ. 20,000.

Cusco

El Diario del Cusco: Centro Comercial Ollanta, Avda El Sol 346, Cusco; tel. (84) 229898; fax (84) 229822; e-mail buzon@diariodelcusco.com; internet www.diariodelcusco.com; morning; independent; Exec. Pres. Washinton Alosilla Portillo; Gen. Man. José Fernandez Núñez.

Huacho

El Imparcial: Avda Grau 203, Huacho; tel. (34) 2392187; fax (34) 2321352; e-mail elimparcial1891@hotmail.com; f. 1891; evening; Dir Adán Manrique Romero; circ. 5,000.

Huancayo

Correo de Huancayo: Jirón Cusco 337, Huancayo; tel. (64) 235792; fax (64) 233811; evening; Editorial Dir Rodolfo Orosco.

La Opinión Popular: Huancayo; tel. (64) 231149; f. 1922; Dir Miguel Bernabé Suárez Osorio.

Ica

La Opinión: Avda Los Maestros 801, Apdo 186, Ica; tel. (56) 235571; f. 1922; evening; independent; Dir Gonzalo Tueros Ramírez.

La Voz de Ica: Castrovirreyna 193, Ica; tel. and fax (56) 232112; e-mail lavozdeica1918@infonegocio.net.pe; f. 1918; Dir Atilio Nieri Boggiano; Man. Mariella Nieri de Macedo; circ. 4,500.

Pacasmayo

Diario Ultimas Noticias: Ancash 691, San Pedro de Lloc, Pacasmayo; fax (44) 9651477; e-mail ultimasnoticias@pacasmayo.net; internet www.pacasmayo.net/ultimasnoticias; f. 1973; morning; independent; Editor María del Carmen Ballena Razuri; circ. 3,000.

Piura

Correo: Zona Industrial Manzana 246, Lote 6, Piura; tel. (74) 321681; fax (74) 324881; Editorial Dir Rolando Rodrich Arango; circ. 12,000.

El Tiempo: Ayacucho 751, Piura; tel. (74) 325141; fax (74) 327478; e-mail direccion@eltiempo.com.pe; internet www.eltiempo.com.pe; f. 1916; morning; independent; Dir Luz María Helguero; circ. 18,000.

PERU

Tacna

Correo: Jirón Hipólito Unanue 636, Tacna; tel. (54) 711671; fax (54) 713955; Editorial Dir RUBÉN COLLAZOS ROMERO; circ. 8,000.

Trujillo

La Industria: Gamarra 443, Trujillo; tel. (44) 234720; fax (44) 427761; e-mail industri@united.net.pe; internet www.unitru.edu.pe/eelitsa; f. 1895; morning; independent; Gen. Man. ISABEL CERRO DE BURGA; circ. 8,000.

PERIODICALS AND REVIEWS

Alerta Agrario: Avda Salaverry 818, Lima 11; tel. (1) 4336610; fax (1) 4331744; f. 1987; by Centro Peruano de Estudios Sociales; monthly review of rural problems; Dir BERTHA CONSIGLIERI; circ. 100,000.

The Andean Report: Pasaje Los Pinos 156, Of. B6, Miraflores, Apdo 531, Lima; tel. (1) 4472552; fax (1) 4467888; e-mail egriffis@peruviantimes.com; internet www.perutimes.com; f. 1975; weekly newsletter; economics, trade and commerce; English; Publr ELEANOR GRIFFIS DE ZÚÑIGA; circ. 1,000.

Caretas: Jirón Huallaya 122, Portal de Botoneros, Plaza de Armas, Lima 1; Apdo 737, Lima 100; tel. (1) 4289490; fax (1) 4262524; e-mail info@caretas.com.pe; internet www.caretas.com.pe; weekly; current affairs; Editor ENRIQUE ZILERI GIBSON; circ. 90,000.

Cosas: Calle Recaveren 111, Miraflores, Lima 18; tel. (1) 2411178; fax (1) 4473776; internet www.cosasperu.com; weekly; society; Editor ELIZABETH DULANTO.

Debate: Apdo 671, Lima 100; tel. (1) 2425656; fax (1) 4455946; f. 1980; every 2 months; Editor GONZALO ZEGARRA-HUILANDVICH.

Debate Agrario: Avda Salaverry 818, Lima 11; tel. (1) 4336610; fax (1) 4331744; e-mail cepes@cepes.org.pe; f. 1987; by Centro Peruano de Estudios Sociales; every 4 months; rural issues; Dir FERNANDO EGUREN L.

Gente: Eduardo de Habich 170, Miraflores, Lima 18; tel. (1) 4465046; fax (1) 4461173; e-mail correo@genteperu.com; internet www.genteperu.com; f. 1958; weekly; circ. 25,000.

Hora del Hombre: Lima; tel. (1) 4220208; f. 1943; monthly; cultural and political journal; illustrated; Dir JORGE FALCÓN.

Industria Peruana: Los Laureles 365, San Isidro, Apdo 632, Lima 27; f. 1896; monthly publication of the Sociedad de Industrias; Editor ROLANDO CELI BURNEO.

Lima Times: Pasaje Los Pinos 156, Of. B6, Miraflores, Apdo 531, Lima 100; tel. (1) 4469120; fax (1) 4467888; e-mail perutimes@amauta.rcp.net.pe; internet www.perutimes.com; f. 1975; monthly; travel, cultural events, general news on Peru; English; Editor ELEANOR GRIFFIS DE ZÚÑIGA; circ. 10,000.

Mercado Internacional: Lima; tel. (1) 4445395; business.

Monos y Monadas: Lima; tel. (1) 4773483; f. 1981; fortnightly; satirical; Editor NICOLÁS YEROVI; circ. 17,000.

Oiga: Pedro Venturo 353, Urb. Aurora, Miraflores, Lima; tel. (1) 4475851; weekly; right-wing; Dir FRANCISCO IGARTUA; circ. 60,000.

Ollanta: e-mail ollantaprensa@yahoo.com; internet ollantaprensa.tripod.com.pe; fortnightly; published by the Movimiento Nacionalista Peruano (MNP—'Movimiento Etnocacerista'); Dir Maj. (retd) ANTAURO IGOR HUMALA TASSO (arrested Jan. 2005 following an armed uprising in Andahuaylas).

Onda: Jorge Vanderghen 299, Miraflores, Lima; tel. (1) 4227008; f. 1959; monthly cultural review; Dir JOSÉ ALEJANDRO VALENCIA-ARENAS; circ. 5,000.

Orbita: Parque Rochdale 129, Lima; tel. (1) 4610676; weekly; f. 1970; Dir LUZ CHÁVEZ MENDOZA; circ. 10,000.

Perú Económico: Apdo 671, Lima 100; tel. (1) 2425656; fax (1) 4455946; f. 1978; monthly; Editor GONZALO ZEGARRA-HUILANDVICH.

QueHacer: León de la Fuente 110, Lima 17; tel. (1) 6138300; fax (1) 6138308; e-mail qh@desco.org.pe; internet www.desco.org.pe/qh/qh-in.htm; f. 1979; 6 a year; supported by Desco research and devt agency; Editor MARTÍN PAREDES; Dir MÓNICA PRADEL; circ. 5,000.

Runa: Lima; f. 1977; monthly; review of the Instituto Nacional de Cultura; Dir MARIO RAZZETO; circ. 10,000.

Semana Económica: Apdo 671, Lima 100; tel. (1) 2425656; fax (1) 4455946; f. 1985; weekly; Editor GONZALO ZEGARRA-HUILANDVICH.

Unidad: Jirón Lampa 271, Of. 703, Lima; tel. (1) 4270355; weekly; Communist; Dir GUSTAVO ESTEVES OSTOLAZA; circ. 20,000.

Vecino: Avda Petit Thouars 1944, Of. 15, Lima 14; tel. (1) 4706787; f. 1981; fortnightly; supported by Yunta research and urban publishing institute; Dirs PATRICIA CÓRDOVA, MARIO ZOLEZZI; circ. 5,000.

NEWS AGENCIES

Government News Agency

Agencia de Noticias Peruana (Andina): Jirón Quilca 556, Lima; tel. (1) 3306341; fax (1) 4312849; e-mail webmaster_anidina@editoraperu.com.pe; internet www.andina.com.pe; f. 1981; state-owned news agency; Dir GERARDO BARRAZA SOTO.

Foreign Bureaux

Agence France-Presse (AFP): F. Masías 544, San Isidro, Lima; tel. (1) 4214012; fax (1) 4424390; e-mail yllorca@amautarcp.net.pe; Bureau Chief YVES-CLAUDE LLORCA.

Agencia EFE (Spain): Manuel González Olaechea 207, San Isidro, Lima; tel. (1) 4412094; fax (1) 4412422; Bureau Chief FRANCISCO RUBIO FIGUEROA.

Agenzia Nazionale Stampa Associata (ANSA) (Italy): Avda Gen. Córdoba 2594, Lince, Lima 14; tel. (1) 4225130; fax (1) 4229087; Correspondent ALBERTO KU-KING MATURANA.

Deutsche Presse-agentur (dpa) (Germany): Schell 343, Of. 707, Miraflores, Apdo 1362, Lima 18; tel. (1) 4441437; fax (1) 4443775; Bureau Chief GONZALO RUIZ TOVAR.

Inter Press Service (IPS) (Italy): Daniel Olaechea y Olaechea 285, Lima 11; tel. and fax (1) 4631021; Correspondent ABRAHAM LAMA.

Prensa Latina (Cuba): Edif. Astoria, Of. 303, Avda Tacna 482, Apdo 5567, Lima; tel. (1) 4233908; Correspondent LUIS MANUEL ARCE ISAAC.

Reuters (United Kingdom): Avda Paseo de la República 3505, 4°, San Isidro, Lima 27; tel. (1) 2212111; fax (1) 4418992; Man. EDUARDO HILGERT.

Xinhua (New China) News Agency (People's Republic of China): Parque Javier Prado 181, San Isidro, Lima; tel. (1) 4403463; Bureau Chief WANG SHUBO.

PRESS ASSOCIATIONS

Asociación Nacional de Periodistas del Perú: Jirón Huancavélica 320, Apdo 2079, Lima 1; tel. (1) 4270687; fax (1) 4278493; e-mail anp@amauta.rcp.net.pe; internet ekeko2.rcp.net.pe/anp; f. 1928; 8,800 mems; Pres. ROBERTO MARCOS MEJÍA ALARCÓN.

Federación de Periodistas del Perú (FPP): Avda Abancay 173, Lima; tel. (1) 4284373; f. 1950; Pres. PABLO TRUEL URIBE.

Publishers

Asociación Editorial Bruño: Avda Arica 751, Breña, Lima 5; tel. (1) 4244134; fax (1) 4251248; f. 1950; educational; Man. FEDERICO DÍAZ PINEDO.

Biblioteca Nacional del Perú: Avda Abancay, 4a cuadra, Apdo 2335, Lima 1; tel. (1) 4287690; fax (1) 4277331; e-mail dn@binape.gob.pe; internet www.binape.gob.pe; f. 1821; general non-fiction, directories; Nat. Dir SINESIO LÓPEZ JIMÉNEZ.

Colección Artes y Tesoros del Perú: Calle Centenario 156, Urb. Las Laderas de Melgarejo, La Molina, Lima 12; tel. (1) 3493128; fax (1) 3490579; e-mail acarulla@bcp.com.pe; f. 1971; Dir ALVARO CARULLA.

Ediciones Médicas Peruanas, SA: Lima; f. 1965; medical; Man. ALBERTO LOZANO REYES.

Editora Normas Legales SA: La Santa María 173, San Isidro, Lima; tel. (1) 2212598; fax (1) 2212598; e-mail enormaslegales@terra.com.pe; law textbooks; Man. JAVIER SANTA MARÍA SILVE.

Editorial Book City: Calle José R. Pizarro 1260 (espalda cuadra 11 de La Mar), Pueblo Libre, Lima; tel. (1) 2613266; general interest, juvenile, reference and literature; Man. MIRTHA YI YANG.

Editorial Colegio Militar Leoncio Prado: Avda Costanera 1541, La Perla, Callao; f. 1946; textbooks and official publications; Man. OSCAR MORALES QUINA.

Editorial Cuzco SA: Calle 5 Marzo, Jirón Lote 3, Urb. Las Magnolias, Surco, Lima; tel. (1) 4453261; e-mail ccuzco@camaralima.org.pe; law; Man. SERGIO BAZÁN CHACÓN.

Editorial D.E.S.A.: General Varela 1577, Breña, Lima; f. 1955; textbooks and official publications; Man. ENRIQUE MIRANDA.

Editorial Desarrollo, SA: Ica 242, 1°, Apdo 3824, Lima; tel. and fax (1) 4286628; f. 1965; business administration, accounting, auditing, industrial engineering, English textbooks, dictionaries, and technical reference; Dir LUIS SOSA NÚÑEZ.

Editorial Horizonte: Avda Nicolás de Piérola 995, Lima 1; tel. (1) 4279364; fax (1) 4274341; e-mail damonte@terra.com.pe; f. 1968; social sciences, literature, politics; Man. HUMBERTO DAMONTE.

Editorial Labrusa, SA: Los Frutales Avda 670-Ate, Lima; tel. (1) 4358443; fax (1) 4372925; f. 1988; literature, educational, cultural; Gen. Man. ADRIÁN REUILLA CALVO; Man. FEDERICO DÍAZ TINEO.

Editorial Milla Batres, SA: Lima; f. 1963; history, literature, art, archaeology, linguistics and encyclopaedias on Peru; Dir-Gen. CARLOS MILLA BATRES.

Editorial Navarrete SRL-Industria del Offset: Manuel Tellería 1842, Apdo 4173, Lima; tel. (1) 4319040; fax (1) 4230991; Man. LUIS NAVARRETE LECHUGA.

Editorial Océano Peruana SA: Avda Salaverry 2890, San Isidro, Lima; tel. (1) 2613999; fax (1) 4618628; e-mail ocelibros@oceano.com.pe; general interest and reference.

Editorial Peisa: Avda 2 de Mayo 1285, San Isidro, Lima; tel. (1) 4410473; fax (1) 2215988; e-mail burtech@yahoo.com; fiction and scholarly; Man. BENJAMIN URTECHO.

Editorial Salesiana: Avda Brasil 218, Apdo 0071, Lima 5; tel. (1) 4235225; f. 1918; religious and general textbooks; Man. Dir Dr FRANCESCO VACARELLO.

Editorial Santillana: Avda San Felipe 731, Jesús María, Lima; tel. (1) 4610277; fax (1) 2181014; e-mail santillana@santillana.com.pe; internet www.santillana.com; literature, scholarly and reference; Man. ANA CECILIA HALLO.

Editorial Universo, SA: Lima; f. 1967; literature, technical, educational; Pres. CLEMENTE AQUINO; Gen. Man. Ing. JOSÉ A. AQUINO BENAVIDES.

Fundación del Banco Continental para el Fomento de la Educación y la Cultura (EDUBANCO): Avda República de Panamá 3055, San Isidro, Apdo 4687, Lima 27; tel. (1) 2111000; fax (1) 2112479; f. 1973; Pres. PEDRO BRESCIA CAFFERATA; Man. FERNANDO PORTOCARRERO.

Industrial Gráfica, SA: Jirón Chavín 45, Breña, Lima 5; fax (1) 4324413; f. 1981; Pres. JAIME CAMPODONICO V.

INIDE: Van de Velde 160, Urb. San Borja, Lima; f. 1981; owned by National Research and Development Institute; educational books; Editor-in-Chief ANA AYALA.

Librerías ABC, SA: Avda Paseo de la República 3440, Local B-32, Lima 27; tel. (1) 4422900; fax (1) 4422901; f. 1956; history, Peruvian art and archaeology; Man. Dir HERBERT H. MOLL.

Librería San Pablo: Jirón Callao 198, Lima 1; tel. (1) 3795336; fax (1) 4593842; e-mail admlima@paulinas.org.pe; internet www.paulinas.org.pe; f. 1981; religious and scholastic texts; Man. Sister MARÍA GRACIA CAPALBO.

Librería Studium, SA: Lima; tel. (1) 4326278; fax (1) 4325354; f. 1936; textbooks and general culture; Man. Dir EDUARDO RIZO PATRÓN RECAVARREN.

Pablo Villanueva Ediciones: Lima; f. 1938; literature, history, law, etc.; Man. AUGUSTO VILLANUEVA PACHECO.

Pontificia Universidad Católica del Perú: Fondo Editorial, Plaza Francia 1164, Lima; tel. (1) 330710; fax (1) 3307405; e-mail feditor@pucp.edu.pe; internet www.pucp.edu.pe; Dir of Admin. AUGUSTO EGUIGUREN PRAELI.

Sociedad Bíblica Peruana, AC: Avda Petit Thouars 991, Apdo 14-0295, Lima 100; tel. (1) 4335815; fax (1) 4336389; internet www.members.tripod.com/sbpac; f. 1821; Christian literature and bibles; Gen. Sec. PEDRO ARANA-QUIROZ.

Universidad Nacional Mayor de San Marcos: Of. General de Editorial, Avda República de Chile 295, 5°, Of. 508, Lima; tel. (1) 4319689; f. 1850; textbooks, education; Man. Dir JORGE CAMPOS REY DE CASTRO.

PUBLISHING ASSOCIATION

Cámara Peruana del Libro: Avda Cuba 427, esq. Jesús María, Apdo 10253, Lima 11; tel. (1) 4729516; fax (1) 2650735; e-mail cp-libro@amauta.rep.net.pe; internet www.pl.org.pe; f. 1946; 102 mems; Pres. CARLOS A. BENVIDES AGUIJE; Exec. Dir LOYDA MORÁN BUSTAMANTE.

Broadcasting and Communications

TELECOMMUNICATIONS

Regulatory Authorities

Dirección de Administración de Frecuencias: Ministerio de Transportes y Comunicaciones, Avda 28 de Julio 800, Lima 1; tel. (1) 4331990; e-mail dgcdir@mtc.gob.pe; manages and allocates radio frequencies; Dir JOSÉ VILLA GAMBOA.

Dirección General de Telecomunicaciones: Ministerio de Transportes y Comunicaciones, Avda 28 de Julio 800, Lima 1; tel. (1) 4330752; fax (1) 4331450; e-mail dgtdir@mtc.gob.pe; Dir-Gen. MIGUEL OSAKI SUEMITSU.

Instituto Nacional de Investigación y Capacitación de Telecomunicaciones (INICTEL): Avda San Luis 1771, esq. Bailetti, San Borja, Lima 41; tel. (1) 3461808; fax (1) 3464354; e-mail informes@inictel.gob.pe; internet www.inictel.gob.pe; Pres. MANUEL ADRIANZEN.

Organismo Supervisor de Inversión Privada en Telecomunicaciones (OSIPTEL): Calle de la Prosa 136, San Borja, Lima 41; tel. (1) 2251313; fax (1) 4751816; e-mail sid@osiptel.gob.pe; internet www.ospitel.gob.pe; established by the Peruvian Telecommunications Act to oversee competition and tariffs, to monitor the quality of services and to settle disputes in the sector; Pres. EDWIN SAN ROMÁN ZUBIZARRETA.

Major Service Providers

BellSouth Perú: Edif. Banco Continental, República de Panamá 3055, San Isidro, Lima 27; tel. (1) 9552000; internet www.bellsouth.com.pe; f. 1997; 97% owned by Telefónicas Móviles, SA (Spain); mobile telephone services; Pres. JUAN SACA; Exec. Vice-Pres. FABIO COELHO; 900,000 customers.

Telefónica del Perú, SA: Avda Arequipa 1155, Santa Beatriz, Lima 1; tel. (1) 2101013; fax (1) 4705950; e-mail mgarcia@tp.com.pe; internet www.telefonica.com.pe; Exec. Pres. MANUEL GARCÍA G.

Telefónica MoviStar: Juan de Arona 786, San Isidro, Lima; tel. (1) 9817000; internet www.telefonicamoviles.com.pe; f. 1994, 98% bought by Telefónicas Móviles, SA (Spain) in 2000; mobile telephone services; 1.8m. customers.

BROADCASTING

In 1999 there were 1,425 radio stations and 105 television stations in Peru.

Regulatory Authorities

Asociación de Radio y Televisión del Perú (AR&TV): Avda Roma 140, San Isidro, Lima 27; tel. (1) 4703734; Pres. HUMBERTO MALDONADO BALBÍN; Dir DANIEL LINARES BAZÁN.

Coordinadora Nacional de Radio: Santa Sabina 441, Urb. Santa Emma, Apdo 2179, Lima 100; tel. (1) 5640760; fax (1) 5640059; e-mail postmaster@cnr.org.pe; internet www.cnr.org.pe; f. 1978; Pres. RODOLFO AQUINO RUIZ.

Instituto Nacional de Comunicación Social: Jirón de la Unión 264, Lima; Dir HERNÁN VALDIZÁN.

Unión de Radioemisoras de Provincias del Perú (UNRAP): Mariano Carranza 754, Santa Beatriz, Lima 1.

Radio

Radio Agricultura del Perú, SA—La Peruanísima: Casilla 625, Lima 11; tel. (1) 4246677; e-mail radioagriculturadelperu@yahoo.com; f. 1963; Gen. Man. LUZ ISABEL DEXTRE NÚÑEZ.

Radio América: Montero Rosas 1099, Santa Beatriz, Lima 1; tel. (1) 2653841; fax (1) 2653844; e-mail kcrous@americatv.com.pe; f. 1943; Dir-Gen. KAREN CROUSILLAT.

Radio Cadena Nacional: Los Angeles 129, Miraflores, Lima; tel. (1) 4220905; fax (1) 4221067; Pres. MIGUEL DÍEZ CANSECO; Gen. Man. CÉSAR LECCA ARRIETA.

Cadena Peruana de Noticias: Gral Salaverry 156, Miraflores, Lima; tel. (1) 4461554; fax (1) 4457770; e-mail webmastercpn@gestion.com.pe; internet www.cpnradio.com.pe; f. 1996; Pres. MANUEL ROMERO CARO; Gen. Man. OSCAR ROMERO CARO.

Radio Cutivalú, La Voz del Desierto: Jirón Ignacio de Loyola 300, Urb. Miraflores, Castilla, Piura; tel. (74) 342802; fax (74) 343370; e-mail cutivalu@cipcaorg.pe; f. 1986; Pres. FRANCISCO MUGUIRO IBARRA; Dir RODOLFO AQUINO RUIZ.

Emisoras 'Cruz del Perú': Victorino Laynes 1402, Urb. Elio, Lima 1; tel. (1) 4521028; Pres. FERNANDO CRUZ MENDOZA; Gen. Man. MARCO CRUZ MENDOZA M.

Emisoras Nacionales: León Velarde 1140, Lince, Lima 1; tel. (1) 4714948; fax (1) 4728182; Gen. Man. CÉSAR COLOMA R.

Radio Inca del Perú: Pastor Dávila 197, Lima; tel. (1) 2512596; fax (1) 2513324; e-mail corporacion@corporacionradial.com.pe; f. 1951; Gen. Man. ABRAHAM ZAVALA CHOCANO.

Radio Nacional del Perú: Avda Petit Thouars 447, Santa Beatriz, Lima; tel. (1) 4331712; fax (1) 4338952; Pres. LUIS ALBERTO MARAVÍ SÁENZ; Gen. Man. CARLOS PIZANO PANIAGUA.

Radio Panamericana: Paseo Parodi 340, San Isidro, Lima 27; tel. (1) 4226787; fax (1) 4221182; e-mail mad@radiopanamericana.com; internet www.radiopanamericana.com; f. 1953; Dir RAQUEL DELGADO DE ALCÁNTARA.

Radio Programas del Perú (GRUPORPP): Avda Paseo de la República 38667, San Isidro, Lima; tel. (1) 4338720; Pres. MANUEL DELGADO PARKER; Gen. Man. HUGO DELGADO NACHTIGALL.

Radio Santa Rosa: Jirón Camaná 170, Apdo 206, Lima; tel. (1) 4277488; fax (1) 4269219; e-mail santarosa@viaexpresa.com.pe; f. 1958; Dir P. JUAN SOKOLICH ALVARADO.

Sonograbaciones Maldonado: Mariano Carranza 754, Santa Beatriz, Lima; tel. (1) 4715163; fax (1) 4727491; Pres. HUMBERTO MALDONADO B.; Gen. Man. LUIS HUMBERTO MALDONADO.

Television

América Televisión, Canal 4: Jirón Montero Rosas 1099, Santa Beatriz, Lima; tel. (1) 2657361; fax (1) 2656979; e-mail infoamerica@americatv.com.pe; internet www.americatv.com.pe; Gen. Man. MARISOL CROUSILLAT.

ATV, Canal 9: Avda Arequipa 3570, San Isidro, Lima 27; tel. (1) 2118800; fax (1) 4427636; e-mail andinatelevision@atv.com.pe; internet www.atv.com.pe; f. 1983; Gen. Man. MARCELLO CÚNEO LOBIANO.

Frecuencia Latina, Canal 2: Avda San Felipe 968, Jesús María, Lima; tel. (1) 4707272; fax (1) 4714187; internet www.frecuencialatina.com.pe; Pres. BARUCH IVCHER.

Global Televisión, Canal 13: Gen. Orbegoso 140, Breña, Lima; tel. (1) 3303040; fax (1) 4238202; f. 1989; Pres. GENARO DELGADO PARKER; Gen. Man. RAFAEL LEGUÍA.

Nor Peruana de Radiodifusión, SA: Avda Arequipa 3520, San Isidro, Lima 27; tel. (1) 403365; fax (1) 419844; f. 1991; Dir FRANCO PALERMO IBARGUENGOITIA; Gen. Man. FELIPE BERNINZÓN VALLARINO.

Panamericana Televisión SA, Canal 5: Avda Alejandro Tirado 217, Santa Beatriz, Lima; tel. (1) 4113201; fax (1) 4703001; e-mail fanchorena@pantel.com.pe; internet www.24horas.com.pe; Pres. RAFAEL RAVETTINO FLORES; Gen. Man. FREDERICO ANCHORENA VÁSQUEZ.

Cía Peruana de Radiodifusión, Canal 4 TV: Mariano Carranza y Montero Rosas 1099, Santa Beatriz, Lima; tel. (1) 4728985; fax (1) 4710099; f. 1958; Dir JOSÉ FRANCISCO CROUSILLAT CARREÑO.

RBC Televisión, Canal 11: Avda Manco Cápac 333, La Victoria, Lima; tel. (1) 4310169; fax (1) 4331237; Pres. FERNANDO GONZÁLEZ DEL CAMPO; Gen. Man. JUAN SÁENZ MARÓN.

Radio Televisión Peruana, Canal 7: Avda José Galvez 1040, Santa Beatriz, Lima 1; tel. (1) 4718000; fax (1) 4726799; f. 1957; Pres. LUIS ALBERTO MARAVÍ SÁENZ; Gen. Man. CARLOS ALBERTO PIZZANO P.

Cía de Radiodifusión Arequipa SA, Canal 9: Centro Comercial Cayma, R2, Arequipa; tel. (54) 252525; fax (54) 254959; e-mail crasa@ibm.net; f. 1986; Dir ENRIQUE MENDOZA NÚÑEZ; Gen. Man. ENRIQUE MENDOZA DEL SOLAR.

Uranio, Canal 15: Avda Arequipa 3570, 6°, San Isidro, Lima; e-mail agamarra@atv.com.pe; Gen. Man. ADELA GAMARRA VÁSQUEZ.

Finance

In April 1991 a new banking law was introduced, which relaxed state control of the financial sector and reopened the sector to foreign banks (which had been excluded from the sector by a nationalization law promulgated in 1987).

BANKING
(cap. = capital; res = reserves; dep. = deposits; m. = million; amounts in new soles)

Superintendencia de Banca y Seguros: Los Laureles 214, San Isidro, Lima 27; tel. (1) 2218990; fax (1) 4417760; e-mail mostos@sbs.gob.pe; internet www.sbs.gob.pe; f. 1931; Supt JUAN JOSÉ MARTHANS LEÓN; Sec.-Gen. NORMA SOLARI PRECIADO.

Central Bank

Banco Central de Reserva del Perú: Jirón Antonio Miró Quesada 441-445, Lima 1; tel. (1) 6132000; fax (1) 4275880; e-mail webmaster@bcrp.gob.pe; internet www.bcrp.gob.pe; f. 1922; refounded 1931; cap. 172.0m., res 171.8m., dep. 25,814.9m. (Dec. 2003); Pres. JAVIER SILVA RUETE; Gen. Man. RENZO ROSSINI; 7 brs.

Other Government Banks

Banco de la Nación: Avda Canaval y Moreyra 150, San Isidro, Lima 1; tel. (1) 4405858; fax (1) 4223451; e-mail imagen@bn.com.pe; internet www.bn.com.pe; f. 1966; cap. 674.1m., res 239.3m., dep. 6,673.9m. (Dec. 2003); conducts all commercial banking operations of official govt agencies; Pres. KURT BURNEO FARFÁN; Gen. Man. PEDRO ERNESTO MENÉNDEZ RICHTER; 368 brs.

Corporación Financiera de Desarrollo (COFIDE): Augusto Tamayo 160, San Isidro, Lima 27; tel. (1) 4422550; fax (1) 4423374; e-mail postmaster@cofide.com.pe; internet www.cofide.com.pe; f. 1971; also owners of Banco Latino; Pres. AURELIO LORET DE MOLA BÖHME; Gen. Man. MARCO CASTILLO TORRES; 11 brs.

Commercial Banks

Banco de Comercio: Avda Paseo de la República 3705, San Isidro, Lima; tel. (1) 4229800; fax (1) 4405458; e-mail postmaster@bancomercio.com.pe; internet www.bancomercio.com; f. 1967; fmrly Banco Peruano de Comercio y Construcción; cap. 68.8m., res 0.2m., dep. 445.8m. (Dec. 2003); Chair. OSCAR BALLÓN JARGAS; Gen. Man. CARLOS MUJICA CASTRO; 14 brs.

Banco de Crédito del Perú: Calle Centenario 156, Urb. Las Laderas de Melgarejo, Apdo 12-067, Lima 12; tel. (1) 3132000; internet www.viabcp.com; f. 1889; cap. 1,226.4m., res 698.4m., dep. 18,850.7m., total assets 22,941.2m. (Dec. 2003); Pres. and Chair. DIONISIO ROMERO SEMINARIO; 217 brs.

Banco Interamericano de Finanzas, SA: Avda Rivera Navarrete 600, San Isidro, Lima 27; tel. (1) 2113000; fax (1) 2212489; internet www.bif.com.pe; f. 1991; total assets US $695m. (Dec. 2005); 33 brs; Pres. FRANCISCO ROCHE; Gen. Man. and CEO RAÚL BALTAR.

Banco Sudamericano: Avda Camino Real 815, San Isidro, Lima 27; tel. (1) 6161111; fax (1) 6161112; e-mail e-servicios@bansud.com.pe; internet www.sudamericano.com; f. 1981; cap. 147.9m., res 9.4m., dep. 2,038.7m. (Dec. 2003); Pres. ROBERTO CALDA CAVANNA; Gen. Man. RAFAEL VENEGAS VIDAURRE; 9 brs.

Banco del Trabajo: Avda Paseo de la República 3587, 4°, San Isidro, Lima; tel. (1) 4219000; fax (1) 4212521; e-mail informes@bantra.com.pe; internet www.bantra.com.pe; Chair. CARLOS ENRIQUE CARRILLO QUIÑONES; Gen. Man. MAX JULIO CHION LI; 46 brs.

Banco Wiese Sudameris: Avda Dionisio Derteano 102, San Isidro, Apdo 1235, Lima; tel. (1) 2116000; fax (1) 2116886; e-mail wiesenet@wiese.com.pe; internet www.bws.com.pe; f. 1943; cap. 186.0m., dep. 7,434.4m., total assets 10,531.6m. (Dec. 2003); taken over by Govt in Oct. 1987; returned to private ownership in Oct. 1988 as Banco Wiese Ltdo; 71.11% owned by Banca Intesa SpA (Italy); Chair. RAÚL BARRIOS; Gen. Man. CARLOS GONZÁLEZ TABOADA.

BBVA Banco Continental: Avda República de Panamá 3055, San Isidro, Lima 27; tel. (1) 2111000; fax (1) 2111788; internet www.bbvabancocontinental.com; f. 1951; merged with BBVA of Spain in 1995; 92.01% owned by Holding Continental, SA; cap. 813.2m., res 189.1m., dep. 11,288.0m. (Dec. 2003); Pres. and Chair. PEDRO BESCIA CAFFERATA; Gen. Man. JOSÉ ANTONIO COLOMER GUIU; 190 brs.

INTERBANK (Banco Internacional del Perú): Carlos Villarán 140, Urb. Santa Catalina, Lima 13; tel. (1) 2192000; fax (1) 2192336; e-mail krubin@intercorp.com.pe; internet www.interbank.com.pe; f. 1897; commercial bank; cap. 286.1m., res 84.1m., dep. 4,570.5m. (Dec. 2003); Chair. and Pres. CARLOS RODRÍGUEZ-PASTOR; Gen. Man. ISMAEL BENAVIDES FERREYROS; 90 brs.

Foreign Banks

Banco do Brasil, SA: Avda Camino Real 348, 9°, Torre El Pilar, San Isidro 27, Lima; tel. (1) 2124230; fax (1) 4424208; e-mail bblima@infonegocio.net.pe; closed to public.

Citibank NA (USA): Torre Real, 5°, Avda Camino Real 456, Lima 27; tel. (1) 4214000; fax (1) 4409044; internet www.citibank.com.pe/peru/homepage/index-e-htm; f. 1920; cap. US $47,520m., res $1,936m., dep. $139,627m. (Nov. 1997); Vice-Pres. GUSTAVO MARÍN; 1 br.

Banking Association

Asociación de Bancos del Perú: Calle 41, No 975, Urb. Corpac, San Isidro, Lima 27; tel. (1) 2241718; fax (1) 2241707; e-mail earroyo@asbanc.com.pe; f. 1929; refounded 1967; Pres. JOSÉ NICOLINI LORENZONI; Gen. Man. JUAN KLINGENBERGER LOMELLINI.

STOCK EXCHANGE

Bolsa de Valores de Lima: Pasaje Acuña 106, Lima 100; tel. (1) 4260714; fax (1) 4267650; internet www.bvl.com.pe; f. 1860; Exec. Pres. RAFAEL D'ANGELO SERRA.

REGULATORY AUTHORITY

Comisión Nacional Supervisora de Empresas y Valores (CONASEV): Santa Cruz 315, Miraflores, Lima; tel. (1) 4416620; fax (1) 4428401; internet www.conasev.gob.pe; f. 1968; regulates the securities market; responsible to Ministry of Economy and Finance; Pres. FABIOLA BARRIGA SAN MIGUEL.

INSURANCE
Lima

Altas Cumbres Cía de Seguros de Vida, SA: Avda Paseo de la República 3587, San Isidro, Lima; tel. (1) 4428228; fax (1) 2213313; e-mail asalazar@altascumbres.com.pe; internet www.altascumbres.com.pe; f. 1999; life; Pres. CARLOS CARRILLO QUIÑONES; Gen. Man. ALFREDO SALAZAR DELGADO.

Generali Perú, Cía de Seguros y Reaseguros: Jirón Antonio Miró Quesada 191, Apdo 1751, Lima 100; tel. (1) 3111000; fax (1)

3111004; e-mail borlandini@generali-peru-com.pe; internet www.generali-peru.com.pe; f. 1896; Pres. RAFFAELE TIANO SAMBO; Gen. Man. BRUNO ORLANDINI ALVAREZ-CALDERÓN.

Interseguro Compañía de Seguros de Vida, SA: Avda Pardo y Aliaga 640, 4°, San Isidro, Lima; tel. (1) 2223233; fax (1) 2223222; e-mail juan.vallejo@intercorp.com.pe; f. 1998; life; Pres. FELIPE MORRIS GUERINONI; Gen. Man. JUAN CARLOS VALLEJO BLANCO.

Invita Seguros de Vida, SA: Torre Wiese, Canaval y Moreyra 532, San Isidro, Lima; tel. (1) 2222222; fax (1) 2211683; e-mail dcosta@invita.com.pe; internet www.invita.com.pe; f. 2000; life; fmrly Wiese Aetna, SA; Pres. CARIDAD DE LA PUENTE WIESE; Gen. Man. DULIO COSTA OLIVERA.

Mapfre Perú Cía de Seguros: Avda 28 de Julio 873, Miraflores, Apdo 323, Lima 100; tel. (1) 4444515; fax (1) 4469599; e-mail fmarco@mapfreperu.com; internet www.mapfreperu.com; f. 1994; general; fmrly Seguros El Sol, SA; Pres. Dr FRANCISCO JOSÉ MARCO ORENES.

Pacífico, Cía de Seguros y Reaseguros: Avda Arequipa 660, Lima 100; tel. (1) 4333626; fax (1) 4333388; e-mail arodrigo@pps.com.pe; f. 1943; general; Pres. CALIXTO ROMERO SEMINARIO; Gen. Man. ARTURO RODRIGO SANTISTEVAN.

La Positiva Cía de Seguros y Reaseguros, SA: esq. Javier Prado Este y Francisco Masías 370, San Isidro, Lima; tel. (1) 2110000; fax (1) 2110020; e-mail jaimep@lapositiva.com.pe; internet www.lapositiva.com.pe; f. 1947; Pres. Ing. JUAN MANUEL PEÑA ROCA; Gen. Man. JAIME PÉREZ RODRÍGUEZ.

Rimac Internacional, Cía de Seguros: Las Begonias 475, 3°, San Isidro, Lima; tel. (1) 4218383; fax (1) 4210570; e-mail jortecho@rimac.com.pe; internet www.rimac.com.pe; f. 1896; acquired Seguros Fénix in 2004; Pres. Ing. PEDRO BRESCIA CAFFERATA; Gen. Man. PEDRO FLECHA ZALBA.

SECREX, Cía de Seguro de Crédito y Garantías: Avda Angamos Oeste 1234, Miraflores, Apdo 0511, Lima 18; tel. (1) 4424033; fax (1) 4423890; e-mail ciaseg@secrex.com.pe; internet www.secrex.com.pe; f. 1980; Pres. Dr RAÚL FERRERO COSTA; Gen. Man. JUAN A. GIANNONI MURGA.

Sul América Compañía de Seguros, SA: Jirón Sinchi Roca 2728, Lince, Lima; tel. (1) 2150515; fax (1) 4418730; e-mail lavila@sulamerica.com.pe; internet www.sulamerica.com.pe; f. 1954; part of Sul América, SA (Brazil); Pres. RAÚL BARRIOS ORBEGOSO; Gen. Man. LUIS MIGUEL AVILA MERINO.

Insurance Association

Asociación Peruana de Empresas de Seguros (APESEG): Arias Araguez 146, Miraflores, Lima 100; tel. (1) 4442294; fax (1) 4468538; e-mail rda@apeseg.org.pe; internet www.apeseg.org.pe; f. 1904; Pres. RAÚL BARRIOS ORBEGOSO; Gen. Man. RAÚL DE ANDREA DE LAS CARRERAS.

Trade and Industry

GOVERNMENT AGENCIES

Agencia de Promoción de la Inversión Privada (ProInversión): Avda Paseo de la República 3361, 9°, San Isidro, Lima 27; tel. (1) 6121200; fax (1) 2212942; e-mail gvillegas@proinversion.gob.pe; internet www.proinversion.gob.pe; f. 2002; to promote economic investment; Dir RENÉ CORNEJO DÍAZ; Gen. Sec. ITALO BIZERRA.

Empresa Nacional de la Coca, SA (ENACO): Avda Arequipa 4528, Miraflores, Lima; tel. (1) 4271369; fax (1) 4273071; e-mail lmarin@enaco.com.pe; internet www.enaco.com.pe; f. 1949; agency with exclusive responsibility for the purchase and resale of legally produced coca and the promotion of its derivatives; Pres. LIDA MARIN LOAYZA; Gen. Man. JORGE LUIS TANG CASTRO.

Fondo Nacional de Compensación y Desarrollo Social (FONCODES): Avda Paseo de la República 3101, San Isidro, Lima; tel. (1) 4212102; fax (1) 4218026; e-mail consultas@foncodes.gob.pe; internet www.foncodes.gob.pe; f. 1991; responsible for social development and eradicating poverty; Exec. Dir Dr ALEJANDRO NARVÁEZ LICERAS.

Instituto Nacional de Recursos Forestales (INRENA): Calle Diecisiete 355, Urb. El Palomar, Lima; tel. (1) 225-2113; fax (1) 224-3218; e-mail gerencia.general@inrena.gob.pe; internet www.inrena.gob.pe; f. 1992; promotes sustainable development of Amazon rain forest; Pres. LEONCIO ALVAREZ VÁSQUEZ; Gen. Man. PERCY A. CÁCEDA HURTADO.

Perupetro: Luis Aldana 320, San Borja, Lima; tel. (1) 4759590; fax (1) 4757722; e-mail admweb@perupetro.com.pe; internet www.perupetro.com.pe; f. 1993; responsible for promoting investment in hydrocarbon exploration and exploitation; Chair. ANTONIO CUETO DUTHURBURU; CEO JOSÉ CHAVEZ CÁCERES.

DEVELOPMENT ORGANIZATIONS

Acción Comunitaria del Perú: Avda Domingo Orue 165, Surquillo, Lima 34; tel. (1) 2220202; fax (1) 2224166; e-mail accion@accion.org.pe; internet www.accion.org.pe; f. 1969; promotes economic, social and cultural devt through improvements in service provision; Dir CARLOS CULQUICHICÓN.

Asociación de Exportadores (ADEX): Javier Prado Este 2875, San Borja, Lima 41; Apdo 1806, Lima 1; tel. (1) 3462530; fax (1) 3461879; e-mail prensa@adexperu.org.pe; internet www.adexperu.org.pe; f. 1973; exporters' asscn; Pres. LUIS VEGA MONTEFERRI; Gen. Man. ALVARO BARRENECHEA; 600 mems.

Asociación Kallpa para la Promoción Integral de la Salud y el Desarrollo: Jirón Rospigliosi 105, Barranco, Lima 4; tel. (1) 4455521; fax (1) 2429693; e-mail postmast@kallpa.org.pe; internet www.kallpa.org.pe; health devt for youths; Pres. ARIELA LUNA FLORES.

Asociación Nacional de Centros de Investigación, Promoción Social y Desarrollo: Pablo Bermúdez 234, Jesús María, Lima; tel. (1) 4411063; fax (1) 4411227; e-mail postmaster@anc.org.pe; internet www.anc.org.pe; umbrella grouping of devt orgs; Pres. LUIS SIRUMBAL; Exec. Dir FEDERICO ARNILLAS L.

Asociación para la Naturaleza y Desarrollo Sostenible (ANDES): Calle Ruinas 451, Cusco; tel. (8) 4245021; e-mail andes@andes.org.pe; internet www.andes.org.pe; devt org. promoting the culture, education and environment of indigenous groups.

Sociedad Nacional de Industrias (SNI) (National Industrial Association): Los Laureles 365, San Isidro, Apdo 632, Lima 27; tel. (1) 4218830; fax (1) 4422573; e-mail sni@sni.org.pe; internet www.sni.org.pe; f. 1896; comprises permanent commissions covering various aspects of industry including labour, integration, fairs and exhibitions, industrial promotion; its Small Industry Committee groups over 2,000 small enterprises; Pres. ROBERTO NESTA BRERO; Gen. Man. SERGIO MAZURÉ; 90 dirs (reps of firms); 2,500 mems; 60 sectorial committees.

Centro de Desarrollo Industrial (CDI): Los Laureles 365, San Isidro, Lima; tel. (1) 2158888; fax (1) 2158877; e-mail cdi@sni.org.pe; internet www.cdi.org.pe; f. 1986; supports industrial devt and programmes to develop industrial cos; Exec. Dir LUIS TENORIO PUENTES.

CHAMBERS OF COMMERCE

Cámara de Comercio de Lima (Lima Chamber of Commerce): Avda Gregorio Escobedo 398, Jesús María, Lima 11; tel. (1) 4633434; fax (1) 4632837; e-mail perured@camaralima.org.pe; internet www.camaralima.org.pe; f. 1888; Pres. GRACIELA FERNÁNDEZ-BACA DE VALDEZ; 3,500 mems.

Cámara Nacional de Comercio, Producción y Servicios (PERUCAMARAS): Avda Gregorio Escobedo 396, Jesús María, Lima 11; e-mail administracion@perucam.com; internet www.perucamaras.com; national asscn of chambers of commerce; Pres. SAMUEL GLEISER KATZ; Gen. Man. JOSÉ MARTÍN TELLO.

There are also Chambers of Commerce in Arequipa, Cusco, Callao and many other cities.

EMPLOYERS' ORGANIZATIONS

Asociación Automotriz del Perú: Dos de Mayo 299, Apdo 1248, San Isidro, Lima 27; tel. (1) 4404119; fax (1) 4428865; e-mail aap@terra.com.pe; f. 1926; asscn of importers of motor cars and accessories; 360 mems; Pres. CARLOS BAMBARÉN GARCÍA-MALDONADO; Gen. Man. CÉSAR MARTÍN BARREDA.

Asociación de Ganaderos del Perú (Association of Stock Farmers of Peru): Pumacahua 877, 3°, Jesús María, Lima; f. 1915; Gen. Man. Ing. MIGUEL J. FORT.

Consejo Nacional del Café: Lima; reps of Govt and industrial coffee growers; Pres. ENRIQUE ALDAVE.

Sociedad Nacional de Minería y Petróleo: Francisco Graña 671, Magdalena del Mar, Lima 17; tel. (1) 4601600; fax (1) 4601616; e-mail postmaster@snmpe.org.pe; internet www.snmpe.org.pe; f. 1940; Pres. JOSÉ MIGUEL MORALES DASSO; Sec.-Gen. KLAUS HUYS JACOBI; asscn of cos involved in mining, petroleum and energy.

Sociedad Nacional de Pesquería (SNP): Javier Prado Oeste 2442, San Isidro, Lima 27; tel. (1) 2612970; fax (1) 2617912; e-mail snpnet@terra.com.pe; internet www.snp.org.pe; f. 1952; private-sector fishing interests; Pres. RAÚL ALBERTO SÁNCHEZ SOTOMAYOR.

UTILITIES

Regulatory Authority

Comisión de Tarifas Eléctricas (CTE): Avda Canadá 1470, San Borja, Lima 41; tel. (1) 2240487; fax (1) 2240491; e-mail info@cte.org.pe; internet www.cte.org.pe; 5-mem. autonomous agency controlling tariffs.

Electricity

Electrolima, SA: Jirón Zorritos 1301, Lima 5; tel. (1) 4324153; fax (1) 4323042; internet www.electrolima.com; f. 1906; produces and supplies electricity for Lima and the surrounding districts; state-owned; Gen. Man. Dr DARÍO CUERVO VILLAFAÑE.

ElectroPerú: Prolongación Pedro Miotta 421, San Juan de Miraflores, Lima 29; tel. (1) 4660506; fax (1) 4663448; internet www.electroperu.com; state-owned; Pres. Ing. GUILLERMO CASTILLO JUSTO; Gen. Man. Ing. IVÁN LA ROSA ALZAMORA.

Empresa Regional de Servicio Público de Electricidad Norte (Electronorte, SA): Vicente de la Vega 318, Chiclayo; tel. (74) 231580; fax (74) 227751; Pres. JORGE RODRÍGUEZ RODRÍGUEZ; Gen. Man. RICARDO ARRESE PÉREZ.

Sociedad Eléctrica del Sur-Oeste, SA (SEAL): Consuelo 310, Arequipa; tel. (54) 212946; fax (54) 213296; e-mail seal@sealperu.com; internet www.sealperu.com; f. 1905; Pres. ALFREDO LLOSA BARBER; Gen. Man. AMÉRICO PORTUGAL AMPUERO.

TRADE UNIONS

The right to strike was restored in the Constitution of July 1979. In 1982 the Government recognized the right of public employees to form trade unions.

Central Unica de Trabajadores Peruanos (CUTP): Lima; f. 1992; Pres. JULIO CÉSAR BAZÁN; includes:

Confederación General de Trabajadores del Perú (CGTP): Plaza 2 de Mayo 4, Lima 1; tel. (1) 4314738; e-mail cgtp@cgtp.org.pe; internet www.cgtp.org.pe; f. 1968; Pres. MARIO HUAMÁN RIVERA; Sec.-Gen. JUAN JOSÉ GORRITI VALLE.

Confederación Nacional de Trabajadores (CNT): Avda Iquitos 1198, Lima; tel. (1) 4711385; affiliated to the PPC; 12,000 mems (est.); Sec.-Gen. ANTONIO GALLARDO EGOAVIL.

Confederación de Trabajadores del Perú (CTP): Jirón Ayacucho 173, CP 3616, Lima 1; tel. (1) 4261310; e-mail ctp7319@hotmail.com; affiliated to APRA; Sec.-Gen. ELÍAS GRIJALVA ALVARADO.

Confederación Intersectorial de Trabajadores Estatales (CITE) (Union of Public Sector Workers): Lima; tel. (1) 4245525; f. 1978; Sec.-Gen. ALAVARO COLE; Asst Sec. OMAR CAMPOS; 600,000 mems.

Federación de Empleados Bancarios (FEB) (Union of Bank Employees): Jirón Miró Quesada 260, 7°, Lima; tel. (1) 7249570; e-mail febperu@terra.com.pe; Sec.-Gen. HÉCTOR PÉREZ PÉREZ.

Federación Nacional de Trabajadores Mineros, Metalúrgicos y Siderúrgicos (FNTMMS) (Federation of Peruvian Mineworkers): Jirón Callao 457, Of. 311, Lima; tel. (1) 4277554; Sec.-Gen. PEDRO ESCATE SULCA; 70,000 mems.

Movimiento de Trabajadores y Obreros de Clase (MTOC): Lima.

Sindicato Unitario de los Trabajadores en la Educación del Perú (SUTEP) (Union of Peruvian Teachers): Camaná 550, Lima; tel. (1) 4276677; fax (1) 4268692; e-mail suteperu@yahoo.es; internet www.sutep.org.pe; f. 1972; Sec.-Gen. CARIDAD DEL ROSARIO MONTES REBAZA.

Independent unions, representing an estimated 37% of trade unionists, include the Comité para la Coordinación Clasista y la Unificación Sindical, Confederación de Campesinos Peruanos (CCP) and the Confederación Nacional Agraria (Pres. MIGUEL CLEMENTE ALEGRE).

Confederación Nacional de Comunidades Industriales (CONACI): Lima; co-ordinates worker participation in industrial management and profit-sharing.

The following agricultural organizations exist:

Confederación Nacional de Productores Agropecuarios de las Cuencas Cocaleras del Perú (CONPACCP): Lima; coca-growers' confederation; Leader ELSA MALPARTIDA.

Consejo Unitario Nacional Agrario (CUNA): f. 1983; represents 36 farmers' and peasants' orgs, including:

Confederación Campesina del Perú (CCP): radical left-wing; Pres. ANDRÉS LUNA VARGAS; Sec. HUGO BLANCO.

Organización Nacional Agraria (ONA): organization of dairy farmers and cattle-breeders.

Transport

RAILWAYS

In 2000 there were some 2,123 km of track. A programme to develop a national railway network (Sistema Nacional Ferroviario) was begun in the early 1980s, aimed at increasing the length of track to about 5,000 km initially. The Government also plans to electrify the railway system and extend the Central and Southern Railways.

Ministerio de Transportes y Comunicaciones: see section on The Government (Ministries).

Consorcio de Ferrocarriles del Perú: in July 1999, following the privatization of the state railway company, Enafer, the above consortium won a 30-year concession to operate the following lines:

Empresa Minera del Centro del Perú SA—División Ferrocarriles (Centromín-Perú SA) (fmrly Cerro de Pasco Railway): Edif. Solgas, Avda Javier Prado Este 2175, San Borja, Apdo 2412, Lima 41; tel. (1) 4761010; fax (1) 4769757; 212.2 km; acquired by Enafer-Perú in 1997; Pres. HERNÁN BARRETO; Gen. Man. GUILLERMO GUANILO.

Ferrocarril Central Andino, SA: Jirón Brasil, esq. San Fernando-Chosica, Lima; tel. (1) 3612828; fax (1) 3610380; e-mail ferrocarrilcentral@fcca.com.pe; internet www.ferroviasperu.com.pe; f. 1999.

Ferrocarril del Centro del Perú (Central Railway of Peru): Ancash 201, Apdo 301, Lima; tel. (1) 4276620; fax (1) 4281075; 591 km open; Man. ADRIEL ESTRADA FARFAN.

Ferrocarril del Sur del Perú ENAFER, SA (Southern Railway): Avda Tacna y Arica 200, Apdo 194, Arequipa; tel. (54) 215350; fax (54) 231603; 915 km open; also operates steamship service on Lake Titicaca; Man. C. NORIEGA.

Tacna–Arica Ferrocarril (Tacna–Arica Railway): Avda Aldarracín 484, Tacna; 62 km open.

Ferrocarril Pimentel (Pimentel Railway): Pimentel, Chiclayo, Apdo 310; 56 km open; owned by Empresa Nacional de Puertos; cargo services only; Pres. R. MONTENEGRO; Man. LUIS DE LA PIEDRA ALVIZURI.

Private Railways

Ferrocarril Ilo–Toquepala–Cuajone: Apdo 2640, Lima; 219 km open, incl. five tunnels totalling 27 km; owned by the Southern Peru Copper Corpn for transporting copper supplies and concentrates only; Pres. OSCAR GONZÁLEZ ROCHA; Gen. Man. WILLIAM TORRES.

Ferrocarril Supe–Barranca–Alpas: Barranca; 40 km open; Dirs CARLOS GARCÍA GASTAÑETA, LUIS G. MIRANDA.

ROADS

There were an estimated 78,000 km of roads in Peru, of which approximately 30% was paved or semi-paved. The most important highways are: the Pan-American Highway (3,008 km), which runs southward from the Ecuadorean border along the coast to Lima; Camino del Inca Highway (3,193 km) from Piura to Puno; Marginal de la Selva (1,688 km) from Cajamarca to Madre de Dios; and the Trans-Andean Highway (834 km), which runs from Lima to Pucallpa on the River Ucayali via Oroya, Cerro de Pasco and Tingo María.

SHIPPING

Most trade is through the port of Callao but there are 13 deep-water ports, mainly in northern Peru (including Salaverry, Pacasmayo and Paita) and in the south (including the iron-ore port of San Juan). There are river ports at Iquitos, Pucallpa and Yurimaguas, aimed at improving communications between Lima and Iquitos, and a further port is under construction at Puerto Maldonado.

Empresa Nacional de Puertos, SA (Enapu): Avda Contralmirante Raygada 110, Callao; tel. (1) 4299210; fax (1) 4691010; e-mail enapu@inconet.net.pe; internet www.enapu.com.pe; f. 1970; govt agency administering all coastal and river ports; Gen. Man. ROBERTO COLOMBO MISCHIATTI.

Asociación Marítima del Perú: Avda Javier Prado Este 897, Of. 33, San Isidro, Apdo 3520, Lima 27; tel. and fax (1) 4221904; f. 1957; association of 20 international and Peruvian shipping companies; Pres. LUIS FELIPE VILLENA GUTIÉRREZ.

Consorcio Naviero Peruano, SA: Avda Central 643, San Isidro, Apdo 18-0736, Lima 1; tel. (1) 4116500; fax (1) 4116599; e-mail cnp@cnpsa.com; internet www.cnpsa.com; f. 1959.

Naviera Humboldt, SA: Edif. Pacifico–Washington, 9°, Natalio Sánchez 125, Apdo 3639, Lima 1; tel. (1) 4334005; fax (1) 4337151; e-mail postmast@sorcomar.com.pe; internet www.humbolt.com.pe; f. 1970; cargo services; Pres. AUGUSTO BEDOYA CAMERE; Man. Dir LUIS FREIRE R.

Agencia Naviera Maynas, SA: Avda San Borja Norte 761, San Borja, Lima 41; tel. (1) 4752033; fax (1) 4759680; e-mail lima@navieramaynas.com.pe; f. 1996; Pres. R. USSEGLIO D.; Gen. Man. ROBERTO MELGAR B.

Naviera Universal, SA: Calle 41 No 894, Urb. Corpac, San Isidro, Apdo 10307, Lima 100; tel. (1) 4757020; fax (1) 4755233; Chair. HERBERT C. BUERGER.

Petrolera Transoceánica, SA (PETRANSO): San Isidro, Lima 27; tel. (1) 5139300; fax (1) 5139322; e-mail petranso@petranso.com; internet www.petranso.com; Gen. Man. JUAN VILLARÁN.

A number of foreign lines call at Peruvian ports.

CIVIL AVIATION

Of Peru's 294 airports and airfields, the major international airport is Jorge Chávez Airport near Lima. Other important international airports are Coronel Francisco Secada Vignetta Airport, near Iquitos, Velasco Astete Airport, near Cusco, and Rodríguez Ballón Airport, near Arequipa.

Corporación Peruana de Aeropuertos y Aviación Comercial: Aeropuerto Internacional Jorge Chávez, Callao; tel. (1) 5750912; fax (1) 5745578; internet www.corpac.gob.pe; f. 1943; Pres. LEOPOLDO PFLUCKER LLONA; Gen. Man. ROBERT MCDONALD ZAPFF.

Domestic Airlines

Aero Condor: Juan de Arona 781, San Isidro, Lima; tel. (1) 4425215; fax (1) 2215783; internet www.aerocondor.com.pe; domestic services; Pres. CARLOS PALACÍN FERNÁNDEZ.

LAN Perú, SA: Lima; tel. (1) 2138200; internet www.lan.com; f. 1999; operations temporarily suspended in Oct. 2004; Exec. Vice-Pres. ENRIQUE CUETO P.

Nuevo Continente: Avda José Pardo 605, Lima 18; tel. (1) 2414816; fax (1) 2413074; internet www.aerocontinente.com.pe; f. 1992; domestic services; fmrly Aero Continente; operations suspended in July 2004; acquired by Vuela Perú in Nov. 2004; Pres. LUPE L. Z. GONZALES.

Tourism

Tourism is centred on Lima, with its Spanish colonial architecture, and Cusco, with its pre-Inca and Inca civilization, notably the 'lost city' of Machu Picchu. Lake Titicaca, lying at an altitude of 3,850 m above sea level, and the Amazon jungle region to the north-east are also popular destinations. From the mid-1990s there was evidence of a marked recovery in the tourism sector, which had been adversely affected by health and security concerns. In 2003 Peru received 933,643 visitors. Receipts from tourism generated US $959m. in that year.

Comisión de Promoción del Perú (PromPerú): Edif. Mitinci, Calle Uno Oeste, 13°, Urb. Corpac, San Isidro, Lima 27; tel. (1) 2243279; fax (1) 2243323; e-mail postmaster@promperu.gob.pe; internet www.peru.org.pe; f. 1993; Head of Tourism MARÍA DEL PILAR LAZARTE CONROY; Exec. Sec. MARIELA AUSEJO VIDAL.

THE PHILIPPINES

Introductory Survey

Location, Climate, Language, Religion, Flag, Capital

The Republic of the Philippines lies in the western Pacific Ocean, east of mainland South-East Asia. The island of Borneo is to the south-west, and New Guinea to the south-east. The principal islands of the Philippine archipelago are Luzon, in the north, and Mindanao, in the south. Between these two (which together account for 66% of the country's area) lie the 7,000 islands of the Visayas. The climate is maritime and tropical. It is generally hot and humid, except in the mountains. There is abundant rainfall, and the islands are frequently in the path of typhoons. At the 1995 census there were 102 languages; the most frequently used were Tagalog (by 29.3% of the population), Cebuano (21.2%), Ilocano (9.3%), Hiligaynon (Ilongo—9.1%) and Bicol (5.7%). Filipino, based on Tagalog, is the native national language. English is widely spoken, and Spanish is used in some communities. In 1991 94.2% of the population were Christians (84.1% Roman Catholics, 6.2% belonged to the Philippine Independent Church (Aglipayan) and 3.9% were Protestants). In 1990 an estimated 4.6% of the population were Muslims. The national flag (proportions 1 by 2) has two equal horizontal stripes, of blue and red, with a white triangle, enclosing a yellow 'Sun of Liberty' (with eight large and 16 small rays) and three five-pointed yellow stars (one in each corner), at the hoist. The capital is Manila, on the island of Luzon.

Recent History

The Philippines became a Spanish colony in the 16th century. During the Spanish–American War, the independence of the Philippines was declared on 12 June 1898 by Gen. Emilio Aguinaldo, leader of the revolutionary movement, with the support of the USA. Under the Treaty of Paris, signed in December 1898, Spain ceded the islands to the USA. A new Constitution, ratified by plebiscite in May 1935, gave the Philippines internal self-government and provided for independence after 10 years. During the Second World War the islands were occupied by Japanese forces from 1942, but, after Japan's surrender in 1945, US rule was restored. The Philippines became an independent republic on 4 July 1946, with Manuel Roxas as its first President. A succession of Presidents, effectively constrained by US economic interests and the Filipino land-owning class, did little to help the peasant majority or to curb disorder and political violence.

At elections in November 1965 the incumbent President, Diosdado Macapagal of the Liberal Party (LP), was defeated by Ferdinand Marcos of the Nacionalista Party (NP). Rapid development of the economy and infrastructure followed. President Marcos was re-elected in 1969. His second term was characterized by civil unrest and economic difficulties. During the early 1970s there was also an increase in guerrilla activity, by the New People's Army (NPA), the armed wing of the outlawed (Maoist) Communist Party of the Philippines (CPP), in the north of the country, and by the Moro National Liberation Front (MNLF), a Muslim separatist movement, in the south.

In September 1972, before completing the (then) maximum of two four-year terms of office, Marcos declared martial law in order to deal with subversive activity and to introduce drastic reforms. The bicameral Congress was suspended, opposition leaders were arrested, the private armies of the landed oligarchs were disbanded, stringent press censorship was introduced, and Marcos began to rule by decree. In November a new Constitution was approved by a constitutional convention, and in January 1973 it was ratified by Marcos. It provided for a unicameral National Assembly and a Constitutional President, with executive power held by a Prime Minister, to be elected by the legislature. Transitional provisions gave the incumbent President the combined authority of the presidency (under the 1935 Constitution) and the premiership, without any fixed term of office. Under martial law, the definitive provisions of the new Constitution remained in abeyance.

A referendum in July 1973 approved Marcos's continuation in office beyond his elected term. Referendums in February 1975 and October 1976 approved the continuation of martial law and the adoption of constitutional amendments, including a provision for the formation of an interim assembly. In December 1977 a fourth referendum approved the extension of Marcos's presidential term.

Criticism of Marcos became more widespread after November 1977, when a sentence of death was imposed by a military tribunal on the principal opposition leader, Benigno Aquino, Jr (a former senator and Secretary-General of the LP, who had been detained since 1972), for alleged murder, subversion and the possession of firearms. Marcos allowed a stay of execution, and conceded some relaxation of martial law in 1977. Elections to the interim National Assembly took place in April 1978. Opposition parties were allowed to participate, but the pro-Government Kilusang Bagong Lipunan (KBL—New Society Movement), founded in 1978 by Marcos and former members of the NP, won 151 of the Assembly's 165 elective seats. The Assembly was inaugurated in June, when Marcos was also confirmed as Prime Minister. Martial law remained in force, and Marcos retained the power to legislate by decree. Local elections, the first to be held in eight years, took place in January 1980, resulting in decisive victories for the KBL. In May Aquino was released from prison to undergo medical treatment in the USA, where he renewed his opposition to Marcos's regime.

In January 1981 martial law was ended, although Marcos retained most of his former powers. A referendum in April approved constitutional amendments that permitted Marcos to renew his mandate by direct popular vote and to nominate a separate Prime Minister. In June, amid allegations of electoral malpractice, Marcos was re-elected President for a six-year term. In April 1982 the United Nationalist Democratic Organization (UNIDO), an alliance of opposition groups, formed an official coalition: it included Lakas ng Bayan (the People's Power Movement, founded by Aquino in 1978) and the Pilipino Democratic Party (PDP), which merged to form PDP-Laban in 1983.

In August 1983 Aquino, returning from exile in the USA, was shot dead on arrival at Manila airport. Rolando Galman, the alleged communist assassin, was killed immediately by military guards. A commission of inquiry, nominated by the Government, concluded that Aquino's murder had been a military conspiracy. The Supreme Court announced in December 1985, however, that the evidence submitted to the commission was inadmissible, acquitted the 26 military personnel who had been accused of conspiring to murder Aquino and upheld the Government's assertion that the assassin was Galman.

Aquino's death proved to be a turning-point in Philippine politics, uniting the opposition in its criticism of Marcos. At elections to the National Assembly in May 1984, public participation was high, and, after numerous accusations by the opposition of electoral fraud and corruption by Marcos, the opposition won 59 of the 183 elective seats, compared with 14 in 1978.

In November 1985, in response to US pressure (and after continued appeals for domestic reform), Marcos announced that a presidential election would be held in February 1986, 18 months earlier than scheduled. Corazon Aquino, the widow of Benigno Aquino, was chosen as the UNIDO presidential candidate, in spite of her lack of political experience. More than 100 people were killed in violence during the election campaign. Vote-counting was conducted by the government-controlled National Commission on Elections (Comelec) and by the independent National Citizens' Movement for Free Elections (Namfrel). Allegations of large-scale electoral fraud and irregularities, apparently perpetrated by supporters of Marcos, were substantiated by numerous international observers. On 16 February 1986 the National Assembly declared Marcos the winner of the presidential election, with 10.8m. votes, compared with 9.3m. for Aquino, according to figures from Comelec. According to Namfrel figures (based on 69% of the total votes), Aquino was in the lead. Marcos immediately announced the resignation of the Cabinet, and declared his intention to establish a council of presidential advisers. Aquino rejected an offer to participate in the council, and launched a campaign of non-violent pressure on the Government.

On 22 February 1986 Lt-Gen. (later Gen.) Fidel Ramos, the acting Chief of Staff of the Armed Forces, and Juan Enrile, the Minister of National Defense, along with about 300 troops, established a rebel headquarters in the Ministry of National Defense in Manila (later moving to the police headquarters), stating that they no longer accepted Marcos's authority and asserting that Aquino was the rightful President. Attempts by forces loyal to Marcos to attack the rebels were foiled by large unarmed crowds, which gathered to protect them at the instigation of the Catholic Archbishop of Manila, Cardinal Jaime Sin. Troops supporting Ramos subsequently secured control of the government broadcasting station, with little bloodshed. On 25 February rival ceremonies were held, at which both Marcos and Aquino were sworn in as President. Later the same day, however, under pressure from the USA, Marcos finally agreed to withdraw, and left the Philippines for Hawaii.

President Aquino received world-wide recognition, including that of the US Government, upon her inauguration. She appointed her Vice-President, Salvador Laurel (the President of UNIDO), to be Prime Minister and Minister of Foreign Affairs, while Enrile retained the post of Minister of National Defense. Ramos was appointed Chief of Staff of the Armed Forces. At the end of February 1986 Aquino ordered the controversial release of all political prisoners, including communist leaders. In March the Government announced the restoration of habeas corpus, the abolition of press censorship and the suspension of local government elections (scheduled for May). The Government also secured the resignation of all Justices of the Supreme Court, as well as the resignation of Comelec members. On 25 March Aquino announced that the 1973 Constitution was to be replaced by an interim document, providing for the immediate abolition of the National Assembly and for the inauguration of a provisional government, with the President being granted emergency powers. The post of Prime Minister was temporarily abolished, and in May a commission was appointed to draft a new constitution.

In March 1986 military leaders pledged their loyalty to Aquino as President and Commander-in-Chief of the Armed Forces. The Government then began to implement a programme of military reform, in accordance with the demands of officers of the Rebolusyonaryong Alyansang Makabayan (RAM—Nationalist Revolutionary Alliance—also known as the Reform the Armed Forces Movement), who had supported the February revolution. In September the Supreme Court ordered the retrial of the members of the military who had earlier been acquitted of the murder of Benigno Aquino. In September 1990, following a trial lasting more than three years, a special court convicted 16 members of the armed forces of the murder of both Aquino and Galman; a further 20 defendants were acquitted.

In July 1986 an abortive coup took place in Manila, led by Arturo Tolentino, a former Minister of Foreign Affairs and Marcos's vice-presidential candidate, and a group of 300 pro-Marcos troops. One of the principal reasons for military dissatisfaction was the new Government's conciliatory attitude towards communist insurgents. In June the Government had attempted to bring guerrilla activity by the NPA (estimated to number 25,000–30,000 members at that time) to an end, announcing that formal negotiations for a cease-fire agreement would begin with representatives of the National Democratic Front (NDF—a left-wing group that included the CPP and the NPA). In October, however, increasing pressure from Enrile and the RAM prompted Aquino to threaten the insurgents with open warfare if a solution were not reached by the end of November. In late November a group of army officers attempted to gain control of several military camps and to replace Aquino with Nicanor Yniguez, a former Speaker of the National Assembly. The rebellion was quelled by Ramos and troops loyal to Aquino; Enrile was dismissed from the Cabinet. In January 1987 there was a further coup attempt by 500 disaffected troops; an attempt by Marcos to return to the Philippines was thwarted by US officials, and the two-day rebellion was suppressed by forces loyal to Aquino.

In February 1987 a new Constitution was approved by 76% of voters in a national plebiscite. The new Constitution gave Aquino a mandate to rule until 30 June 1992, and established an executive presidency (see Government, below). All members of the armed forces swore an oath of allegiance to the new Constitution. An order followed disbanding all 'fraternal organizations' (such as the RAM) within the armed forces, because they 'encouraged divisiveness'. Elections to the bicameral Congress of the Philippines took place on 11 May 1987, at which more than 83% of the electorate participated. Aquino's Lakas ng Bayan coalition secured 180 of the 200 elective seats in the House of Representatives and 22 of the 24 seats in the Senate.

In August 1987 Ramos and troops loyal to Aquino averted a serious coup attempt, when rebel officers (led by Col Gregorio Honasan, an officer closely associated with Enrile) occupied the army headquarters, and captured a radio and television station. In the intense fighting that ensued in Manila and Cebu, 53 people were killed. Honasan and his supporters fled the following day, successfully evading capture until December. (Honasan, however, escaped from detention in April 1988.) In December 1990 a military court sentenced 81 members of the armed forces to prison terms of up to 32 years for their part in the rebellion.

In October 1988 Marcos and his wife, Imelda, were indicted in the USA and charged with the illegal transfer into the country of some US $100m. that had allegedly been obtained by embezzlement and racketeering. Marcos was said to be too ill to attend the proceedings. In November thousands of civilian supporters of Marcos entered Manila and distributed leaflets demanding a military rebellion to overthrow Aquino, before being dispersed by the armed forces. In February 1989 Laurel (who had formally dissociated himself from Aquino in August) visited Marcos in hospital in Hawaii, and began to campaign for Marcos to be permitted to return to the Philippines. In May Marcos's NP was revived, with Laurel as President and Enrile as Secretary-General.

In September 1989 the Philippine Government began the first of 35 planned civil suits against Marcos *in absentia* on charges of corruption. After Marcos's death in Hawaii at the end of September, the opposition, particularly Laurel, exerted pressure on Aquino to allow Marcos a funeral in the Philippines. In October the Supreme Court upheld its previous ruling prohibiting the return of Marcos's body, in response to a petition, submitted by the former President's supporters, asking the court to overrule the ban. Imelda Marcos was acquitted of charges of fraud and of the illegal transfer of stolen funds into the USA in New York in July 1990.

In December 1989 an abortive coup was staged by members of two élite military units, in collusion with the now illicit RAM and officers loyal to Marcos. Aquino subsequently addressed a rally of 100,000 supporters, during which she accused Laurel and Enrile (who were both included in an eight-member provisional junta named by the rebels) of involvement in the coup attempt. At the end of August 1990 Aquino expressed willingness to hold discussions with both dissident troops (who had perpetrated a series of bombings of allegedly corrupt businesses owned by US interests or associated with the Aquino Government) and communist rebels (who had unilaterally declared a cease-fire in Manila and in northern areas affected by an earthquake in July), in an effort to achieve a general reconciliation. Opposition leaders, including Enrile (who had been charged with rebellion), were also invited to attend. In early September Aquino belatedly suspended offensives against the NPA in the affected areas. Later that month, however, the NPA ended the truce and threatened to intensify the insurgency. The dissident members of the armed forces also continued their campaign to destabilize the Government: between mid-August and the beginning of October about 40 incendiary devices were planted (allegedly by members of the armed forces) in and around Manila.

In July 1991 Ramos resigned as Secretary of National Defense in order to contest the presidential election (scheduled for 1992). Having failed to secure the nomination of the ruling party, Laban ng Demokratikong Pilipino (LDP, formed in 1988 by members of pro-Government parties), Ramos, with Aquino's endorsement, resigned from the LDP and registered a new party, EDSA-LDP, with the support of 25 former LDP members of Congress. (EDSA was the popular acronym for the Epifanio de los Santos Avenue, the main site of the February 1986 uprising.) The party, which subsequently altered its title to Lakas ng EDSA, formed an alliance with the National Union of Christian Democrats to become Lakas-NUCD. The Roman Catholic Church extended its support to the LDP's candidate, Ramon Mitra, and criticized Ramos, a Protestant, for his involvement in the Marcos regime.

In February 1992 a prominent human rights organization, Amnesty International, published a report accusing the Aquino administration of acquiescence in violations of human rights by the armed forces. The report, which followed previous documents critical of the Aquino Government, alleged that 550 extrajudicial killings had taken place during 1988–91. The armed forces denied the report's findings, and accused Amnesty International of ignoring rebel atrocities. The NPA had killed 563 members of the armed forces between January and April 1991.

On 11 May 1992 elections took place to select the President, Vice-President, 12 senators, 200 members of the House of Representatives and 17,014 local officials. Ramos was elected to the presidency, with 23.6% of the votes cast; his closest rivals were Miriam Defensor Santiago, a former Secretary of Agrarian Reform, (with 19.7%) and Eduardo Cojuangco (Aquino's estranged cousin, whose wing of the NP had been renamed the Nationalist People's Coalition—NPC) (18.2%). The election was relatively free and fair. The success of Ramos and the high level of support for Santiago (whose electoral campaign had emphasized the need to eradicate corruption) was widely regarded as a rejection of traditional patronage party politics, since neither candidate was supported by a large-scale party organization. In the legislative elections, however, the LDP (the only party that had local bases in every province) won 16 of the 24 seats in the Senate and 89 of the 200 elective seats in the House of Representatives.

Following his inauguration on 30 June 1992, Ramos formed a new administration that included six members of the outgoing Government and many senior business executives. Despite his party's poor representation in Congress, Ramos managed to gain the support of Cojuangco's NPC, the LP and 55 defectors (now known as Laban) from the LDP, to form a 'rainbow coalition', comprising 145 of the 200 elected members of the House of Representatives. The Senate remained nominally under the control of the LDP, but Ramos ensured that he maintained good relations with individual senators.

In July 1992 Ramos formed the Presidential Anti-Crime Commission (PACC), to combat organized crime. Joseph Estrada, who was elected Vice-President, following the withdrawal of his presidential candidacy to support that of Cojuangco, was appointed to head the Commission. A principal concern of the PACC was the increase in abduction, mainly of wealthy ethnic Chinese Filipinos, for ransom, owing to its detrimental effect on investment. It emerged that members of the Philippine National Police (PNP) were largely responsible for the abductions, and in August the Chief of Police resigned. In April 1993, following a review of the PNP, Ramos ordered the discharge of hundreds of personnel, including 63 of the 194 senior officers. There was also a serious decline in public respect for the judiciary, following allegations that seven Supreme Court judges were accepting bribes from drugs-dealers and other criminal syndicates. In February Congress adopted legislation (which was signed into law in December) to reinstate the death penalty, which had been banned under the 1987 Constitution with a provision for its reintroduction under extreme circumstances.

On assuming power, Ramos undertook to give priority to the restoration of order by persuading mutinous right-wing soldiers, communist insurgents and Muslim separatists to abandon their armed struggle. In July 1992 two communist leaders were conditionally released, and Ramos submitted to Congress an amnesty proclamation for about 4,500 members of the NPA, the MNLF and renegade former members of the armed forces who had already applied for amnesty. In August the National Unification Commission (NUC) was formed to consult rebel groups and formulate a viable amnesty programme. Later that month Ramos ordered the temporary release from prison of more communist leaders, including the Commander of the NPA, Romulo Kintanar, and the NDF Spokesman, Saturnino Ocampo, and also of 16 rebel soldiers. In the same month the Government began discussions with exiled representatives of the NDF in the Netherlands.

In September 1992 Ramos repealed anti-subversion legislation, in place since 1957, that proscribed the CPP. However, the exiled leadership of the NDF issued a statement to the effect that the CPP would continue its armed struggle, although there was a widening division within the CPP over co-operation with the NUC. Jose Maria Sison, a founder member of the CPP who had been based in the Netherlands since his release from prison in 1986, resumed the party chairmanship in April 1992. However, his election to the leadership was not recognized by all party members. In December Sison, who adopted an intransigent stance towards the Government's peace moves and who initiated a (largely ignored) purge in the CPP of those members who had deviated from Maoist orthodoxy, accused his opponents, including Kintanar, of collusion with the Ramos administration.

In July 1993 the CPP's influential Manila-Rizal regional committee publicly broke away from the CPP Central Committee led by Sison. This followed the attempted dissolution by Sison of the region's leading committee and its armed unit, the Alex Boncayao Brigade (ABB), accused of factionalism and military excesses. The Manila-Rizal organization, which comprised about 40% of CPP members, was subsequently joined by the CPP regional committee of the Visayas. In October four communist leaders, including Kintanar, were expelled from the CPP and the NPA for refusing to recognize the authority of Sison.

Negotiations between the Government and the NDF in 1994–96 were marred by their failure to agree terms for the granting of immunity for NDF members and the arrest and subsequent release of a number of leading members of the organization. In March 1997, however, peace negotiations in the Netherlands were reported to have achieved some success. In March 1998, despite the intensification during 1997 of both attacks by communist rebels and security operations by the Government, the Government and the NDF signed a Comprehensive Agreement on Respect for Human Rights and International Law, the first of four agreements that would complete the peace process.

In September 1992 seven military renegades, including Honasan, were granted passes of safe conduct to enable peace talks to proceed. In December the seven fugitives emerged from hiding to sign a preliminary agreement to take part in talks with the Government. Discussions between the NUC and representatives of the RAM and the Young Officers' Union (YOU—a progressive offshoot of the RAM, which was alleged to have played an important role in the December 1989 coup attempt) began in January 1993, were suspended (owing to disagreement), resumed in February and were subsequently suspended again. In February 1994 it was announced that peace negotiations with the RAM and the YOU would remain suspended, pending the release of six military detainees. The following month Ramos proclaimed a general amnesty for all rebels and for members of the security forces charged with offences committed during counter-insurgency operations, as recommended by the NUC in a report submitted to Ramos in July 1993; the amnesty did not, however, include persons convicted of torture, arson, massacre, rape and robbery. The RAM rejected the amnesty on the grounds that it failed to address the causes of the rebellion, while Ocampo dismissed the proclamation as being biased against the communist rebels. Following agreement between the RAM and the Government during 1994 on certain government programmes and the issue of electoral reform, in 1995 formal negotiations resumed. In October the RAM and the YOU signed a peace agreement with the Government, which provided for the return of the rebels' military weapons within 90 days and the reintegration of members of the two organizations into the armed forces.

In September 1993, with the permission of Ramos, Marcos's remains were returned to the Philippines, and a funeral service was conducted in his native province of Ilocos Norte, attended by only a few thousand supporters. Later that month Imelda Marcos (who had returned to the Philippines in 1991, with Aquino's permission, to stand trial on charges of fraud and tax evasion) was convicted of corruption and sentenced to 18 years' imprisonment; she remained at liberty pending an appeal against the conviction. In February 1994 a district court in Honolulu, Hawaii, awarded US $2,000m. in punitive damages to 10,000 Filipinos tortured under President Marcos's administration, following a court ruling in October 1992 that victims of abuses of human rights under the Marcos regime could sue his estate for compensation. Imelda Marcos announced that she would appeal against the decision. Further charges of embezzlement were filed against her in April and June 1994 and in September 1995.

In March 1995 Imelda Marcos announced that she would seek election to the House of Representatives. Comelec disqualified her candidacy, ruling that she failed to fulfil residency criteria; however, she appealed to the Supreme Court to overturn the disqualification, and was allowed to contest the election pending the outcome of her appeal. Although her candidacy was successful, she was not permitted to take her seat in Congress until November, following a ruling in her favour by the Supreme Court. Marcos's son, Ferdinand 'Bong-Bong' Marcos II, contested (unsuccessfully) a seat in the Senate, and in July was sentenced to nine years' imprisonment following a conviction for tax evasion. However, he was released in August.

On 8 May 1995 elections were held to contest 12 of the 24 seats in the Senate, the 204 elective seats in the House of Representatives, 76 provincial governorships and more than 17,000 local government positions. Prior to the elections, in which an estimated 80% of all eligible voters participated, more than 80 people were killed in campaign violence. The ruling coalition won the vast majority (about 70%) of seats in the House of Representatives and an electoral alliance between Lakas-NUCD and the LDP (Lakas-Laban) won nine of the 12 seats in the Senate. One of the three opposition seats was secured by Honasan, despite a campaign by Aquino against his candidacy.

During 1995–97 Ramos's supporters campaigned to amend the constitutional stipulation that restricted the President to a single term of office; the Senate, however, opposed any such amendment. In September a rally organized by Cardinal Sin (to coincide with the 25th anniversary of the declaration of martial law by Marcos), to protest against any constitutional changes aimed at enabling Ramos to contest the forthcoming presidential election, was attended by more than 500,000 demonstrators. The rally was supported by Aquino as well as opposition politicians and influential business executives, who attributed the rapid decline of the peso, in part, to the insecurity created by speculation regarding Ramos's ambitions for a second term of office. Prior to the rally, in an attempt to defuse negative sentiment, Ramos finally stated categorically that he would not contest the presidential election.

The formation of an opposition grouping, the Laban ng Makabayang Masang Pilipino (LaMMP—Struggle of Nationalist Filipino Masses), to contest the elections scheduled for May 1998 was announced in June 1997. The LaMMP was composed of the Partido ng Masang Pilipino, led by Estrada, the LDP, led by Edgardo Angara (which had withdrawn from its alliance with Lakas-NUCD in February 1996), and the NCP, led by Ernesto Maceda. In December Estrada and Angara were formally endorsed as the LaMMP's presidential and vice-presidential candidates respectively. By the end of the registration period in February 83 candidates had registered to contest the presidential election, of whom 72 were subsequently disqualified by Comelec. Following the withdrawal of Imelda Marcos in April, a total of 10 candidates contested the election. The campaign was characterized by an emphasis on personalities and scandals and failed to address substantive policy issues. Estrada's immense popularity was apparently unaffected by personal attacks, including an unsubstantiated allegation that he had attempted to assassinate Ramos, and by the opposition of the Catholic Church to his candidacy, owing to his reputedly dissolute lifestyle.

Elections to the presidency, the vice-presidency, the Senate, the House of Representatives, provincial governorships and local government positions took place on 11 May 1998; an estimated 80% of the electorate participated in the polls. Although an estimated 51 people were killed in pre-election violence (mostly in the southern province of Mindanao), the elections were considered relatively orderly and free. Estrada was elected to the presidency with 39.9% of the votes cast. His closest rival was the Lakas-NUCD candidate, Jose de Venezia (who was responsible for progress in negotiations with both the Islamist separatists and the NDF), who secured 15.9% of the votes. The vice-presidency was won by Gloria Macapagal Arroyo (the daughter of former President Diosdado Macapagal), who had been second in the opinion polls as a presidential candidate before agreeing to support de Venezia's candidacy. According to Comelec, seven of the victorious senators were members of the LaMMP, while the other five were Lakas-NUCD candidates. However, Lakas-NUCD dominated the House of Representatives, gaining 106 seats compared with only 66 for the LaMMP. In a development indicative of the weakness of the party system, many congressional members subsequently defected to Estrada's party, which was renamed Laban ng Masang Pilipino (Fight of the Filipino Masses).

Estrada's election altered the political climate considerably for the family and former associates of Marcos. In June 1998 the Solicitor-General, Romeo de la Cruz, recommended that the Supreme Court acquit Imelda Marcos of charges of corruption. A ruling by the Supreme Court in January had upheld her appeal against one charge of corruption but dismissed an appeal against her conviction in 1993 on a second corruption charge, which carried a sentence of between nine and 12 years' imprisonment. She remained at liberty pending the reconsideration of the verdict by the court. Ramos, however, dismissed de la Cruz and his appointed successor, Silvestre Bello, and withdrew the Government's petition for acquittal. Marcos was, nevertheless, acquitted in October 1998, although numerous civil suits remained pending against her. In December Marcos announced plans to initiate a legal appeal to recover 500,000m. pesos in assets allegedly belonging to her husband, including shares in the Philippine Long Distance Telephone Co, the San Miguel Corporation and Philippine Airlines (PAL). Marcos claimed her husband had entrusted the money to close associates who had refused to return it. The election of the Marcoses' daughter, Imee, to Congress and of their son, Ferdinand Jr, to the governorship of Ilocos Norte was indicative of the general rehabilitation of the Marcos family. Estrada favoured a negotiated settlement with the Marcos family to resolve the dispute over funds misappropriated by the former President and also gave his support to the burial of Marcos in the cemetery of National Heroes. However, popular outrage and public protests supported by Aquino and Ramos towards the end of June prompted Imelda Marcos to postpone the burial indefinitely in the national interest.

Following a ruling in January 1998 by the Swiss Supreme Court that the total sum of US $560m. of Marcos's wealth in Swiss bank accounts be released (to be disbursed by the Philippine courts), the transfer of $280m. was halted, owing to an appeal by Marcos's lawyers. The final appeal was rejected by the Swiss Supreme Court in June. In February 1999 the Marcos family agreed to pay a total of $150m. in damages to 9,539 victims of human rights abuses. However, the court subsequently ruled against the release of funds from those sequestered by the Government from Swiss bank accounts. In March 1999 the Supreme Court upheld a 1990 decision by the Bureau of Internal Revenue assessing the unpaid inheritance tax owed by the heirs of Ferdinand Marcos at 23,500m. pesos.

Estrada was inaugurated as President on 30 June 1998. In his inaugural address he reiterated campaign pledges to eradicate poverty and corruption, but also assured the business sector that he would continue Ramos's programme of economic reform. His new Cabinet, which elicited widespread approval, comprised members from a wide political and social spectrum, including wealthy ethnic Chinese business executives, former associates of Marcos, and allies from Estrada's career as mayor and senator, as well as former activists from the communist movement and left-wing non-governmental organizations (NGOs). Five members of Lakas-NUCD were allocated portfolios and Ramos accepted a post as Senior Adviser. Estrada was, however, criticized for appointing friends and relatives to lucrative and influential positions. Additional concerns about a reversion to the Marcos era of 'cronyism' were raised by the return to prominence of former Marcos associates, some of whom had made substantial financial contributions to Estrada's presidential campaign fund, while Estrada also dismissed political adversaries.

Estrada's administration was criticized for factionalism, although supporters maintained that the competing aims of several influential groups minimized the risk of corruption and ensured balanced advice. In spite of widespread apprehension regarding his leadership abilities, Estrada was credited with several successes during his first year in office. His creation in July 1998 of the Presidential Anti-Organized Crime Task Force resulted in a dramatic reduction in kidnappings for ransom. The elimination of several large organized syndicates was achieved by granting autonomy from the PNP (which had been implicated in many incidents) to the head of the Task Force, Brig.-Gen. Panfilo Lacson. (Lacson's appointment, however, attracted criticism from human rights organizations, owing to his conviction with other military officers in 1993 for the illegal detention and torture of anti-Government dissidents in the 1970s.) Estrada effectively abolished 'pork barrel' funds (state funds from which congressmen finance projects in their constituencies), which had led to corruption and the reinforcement of patronage politics. Subsequently, however, Estrada became the target of renewed criticism in the media, which he attributed to a conspiracy to discredit his administration. In February 1999 *The Manila Times* described Estrada as an 'unwitting godfather' to an allegedly improper government contract. Estrada sued the newspaper for 101m. pesos and only abandoned his legal complaint after he received an apology. Concerns about the administration's attitude towards the freedom of the press were exacerbated by an effective advertising boycott of the *Philippine Daily Inquirer*, following claims by Estrada in July that the newspaper was biased against him.

The strained relationship between Estrada and Ramos deteriorated in March 1999 when the Senate Blue Ribbon Committee, which had been established to investigate anomalies in government and was led by a member of Estrada's party, Aquilino Pimentel, recommended the prosecution of Ramos and five members of his Cabinet for the misapplication of public funds to celebrate the centennial anniversary of Philippine independence in June 1998. Ramos was issued with a summons to this effect in April 1999 and was obliged to justify his actions before a newly formed Independent Citizens' Committee. Ramos claimed that the accusations were politically motivated and designed to distract attention from investigations into misconduct by Estrada's friends and relatives. The Committee's final report recommended the indictment for graft of the former Vice-President, Salvador Laurel, who had led the centennial celebration committee, and fines for Ramos and his Secretary of Finance, Salvador Enrique, for failing to prevent Laurel's abuses.

In late 1999 Estrada's hitherto excellent popularity ratings began to decline amid increasing concern that 'cronyism' and corruption in his administration were undermining the gains secured by the overthrow of Marcos in 1986. In August 1999 Aquino and Cardinal Sin mobilized 100,000 demonstrators in a Rally for Democracy held in protest against such perceived erosions, in particular government plans to amend the 1987 Constitution. Estrada's stated aim in amending the Constitution was to extend economic deregulation by altering the provisions limiting to 40% foreign ownership of land and public utilities. While in any case opposed to these proposals, critics feared the potential removal from the Constitution of the stipulation limiting the President to a single term of office. Later in August 1999 Estrada relaunched the ruling coalition, restyling it the Lapian ng Masang Pilipino (LAMP—Party of the Filipino Masses).

Estrada's popularity was also adversely affected by his failure to fulfil his pledges to alleviate poverty. Little progress had been made with regard to land redistribution or 'food security' apart from the rehousing of 25,000 poor in Manila in the year to September 1999. The perceived lack of focus in economic policy and Estrada's failure to enact reformist economic legislation attracted further censure.

Following a report by the World Bank in November 1999 alleging that 20% of the Philippine budget was lost to corruption, Estrada pledged to intensify investigations of officials suspected of dishonesty. (The former chief of police, Roberto Lastimoso, and the former Secretary of the Interior and Local Government, Ronaldo Puno, were indicted on charges of graft in February 2000.) In the same month, in a further attempt to dispel criticism, Estrada established the EDSA People Power Commission to promote the ideals of the 1986 uprising; its 15 members included Aquino, Ramos and Estrada. In order to dispel allegations of media censorship, the advertising boycott against the *Philippine Daily Inquirer* was lifted. Also in November, having achieved significant reductions in kidnappings for ransom in his previous post, Lacson was appointed to head the PNP. All of these measures, however, proved inadequate to reverse a trend that was compounded by the unexpected resignation of the respected Secretary of Finance, Edgardo Espiritu, in January 2000 and his subsequent accusations concerning the undue influence exerted by unelected associates of Estrada. Estrada responded to growing public dissatisfaction by announcing the reform of his administration. He dismissed his informal advisers, replacing them with a six-member Economic Co-ordinating Council to promote coherence in economic affairs, and recruited five eminent business leaders to act as an economic advisory council. The proposed constitutional reforms were suspended and replaced by plans to achieve economic liberalization through legislation. Estrada's attempts to improve his popularity were, however, swiftly undermined by the testimony in January of the Chairman of the Securities and Exchange Commission (SEC), Perfecto Yasay, to a Senate Committee investigating possible illegal share trading. Yasay alleged that Estrada had pressed him to exonerate his close associate, Dante Tan, who was suspected of illegally manipulating the share price of BW Resources Corporation. Estrada denied the intervention, although he admitted telephoning Yasay four times in relation to the investigation. Despite frequent rumours of an impending coup attempt and a request for Estrada's resignation from Teofisto Guingona, the President of Lakas-NUCD, an attempt to mobilize anti-Estrada sentiment in a mass protest in April received very little support.

In October 2000 the Philippines was engulfed by a political crisis that arose as a result of allegations, made to an investigative committee of the Senate by the Governor of Ilocos Sur, Luis Singson, that President Estrada had accepted large sums of money as bribes from illegal gambling businesses. Despite the President's denial of these allegations, opposition parties announced their intention to begin the process of impeaching him. Earlier in the month Vice-President Gloria Macapagal Arroyo had announced her resignation from the Cabinet, in which she served as Secretary of Social Welfare and Development. The fact that she did not relinquish the vice-presidency at the same time led to speculation that she was preparing to succeed Estrada in the event of his being forced out of office. Following her resignation from the Cabinet, Arroyo established an alliance of opposition parties.

In early November 2000 anti-Government protests throughout the Philippines intensified. Vice-President Arroyo announced that a transitional government was prepared to assume power should the President resign. On 13 November the House of Representatives endorsed the impeachment of the President after more than one-third of its members signed a petition favouring this action. Supporters of Estrada condemned the impeachment proceedings as unconstitutional since they had not been submitted to a formal vote in the House of Representatives. (The Speaker of the House had ruled that such a vote was unnecessary because more than one-third of its members had signed the petition.) Estrada himself welcomed an impeachment trial in the Senate as an opportunity to prove his innocence and declared that he would not resign. On 20 November the Senate formally summoned the President.

The legal action pursued by Estrada in order to force the Senate to dismiss the charges against him was unsuccessful, and at the beginning of December 2000 he pleaded not guilty to charges of bribery, corruption, betrayal of public trust and violation of the Constitution. The impeachment trial in the Senate was adjourned indefinitely in mid-January 2001, however, after prosecutors failed to obtain the disclosure of bank records as evidence against him. This effective acquittal of the President provoked mass demonstrations against him, although it was notable that the majority of the participants were members of the middle class. Estrada had lost the support of many members of his Cabinet, the police and the armed forces, and, in response to a request by Vice-President Gloria Macapagal Arroyo, the Supreme Court declared the presidency to be vacant. Arroyo was sworn in as the new President on 20 January. Estrada had earlier offered to hold a presidential election in May at which he would not be a candidate. He did not formally resign, however, in response to the Supreme Court's declaration.

By late January 2001 most of the positions in President Arroyo's new Cabinet had been filled. The new administration moved quickly to prevent Estrada, members of his family and his associates from leaving the Philippines and insisted that the former President would be prosecuted for his alleged crimes. The manner in which Arroyo had assumed the presidency, however, exacerbated the continued political crisis and raised fears of an impending military *coup d'état*. Estrada continued to assert that he remained the legitimate Head of State and pledged to take legal action to regain the presidency. In March, however, the Supreme Court affirmed the legitimacy of Arroyo's office. In April Estrada was formally indicted for a number of alleged offences, including one of economic plunder, which was punishable by the death penalty. Estrada was arrested for the first time on 16 April and charged with graft and perjury. At the beginning of May there was violent unrest in Manila when supporters of Estrada attempted to storm the presidential palace. Three members of the Senate were arrested for having allegedly conspired to bring down the Government, and President Arroyo declared a state of rebellion, which permitted her to deploy the armed forces to quell the unrest. Estrada, who had been rearrested on 25 April, was removed to a detention centre outside Manila, having had his application for bail denied.

Legislative and local elections were held on 14 May 2001. Lakas-NUCD secured 87 seats in the House of Representatives, followed by the NPC with 62. The People Power Coalition (PPC)—a coalition of Lakas-NUCD, the LP and several smaller parties, which had been formed by President Arroyo to contest the election—won eight seats in the Senate, while allies of the Laban ng Demokratikong Pilipino-Puwersa ng Masa (LDP-PnM)—the opposition coalition formed to support Estrada— secured four. The remaining seat went to an independent candidate. President Arroyo thus succeeded in securing a majority in both chambers. As a result of violence throughout the election period, 83 people died. The elections were further marred by reports of widespread corruption.

In early October 2001 Estrada's trial on charges of perjury and plunder finally commenced; he had refused to enter a plea to any of the charges against him. Later in the month Estrada won an initial victory when the judge refused to permit the presentation of crucial evidence in the prosecution case for perjury owing to a legal technicality. In November the trial was overshadowed by a feud between two of the judges involved, presiding judge Justice Anacleto Badoy and his senior colleague, Justice Francis Garchitorena. The trial was interrupted further when the chief prosecutor, Aniano Desierto, was accused of corruption. Shortly afterwards the Supreme Court rejected a legal challenge brought by Estrada against his ongoing trial and affirmed the constitutionality of the anti-plunder law under which he was being tried. At the end of November the Supreme Court suspended Justice Garchitorena following complaints that cases under his remit, including that of Estrada, were proceeding too slowly. In December Justice Badoy was also suspended indefinitely, following defence allegations that he lacked impartiality. The trial was subsequently adjourned and resumed in January 2002 in a special anti-graft court. In February Estrada instructed his entire legal team to resign in protest at what he alleged to be a prejudiced court. The Government stated that the trial would proceed once it had appointed new legal representation for the defendant. Estrada's trial continued to proceed, slowly, in 2003, and in December Estrada was permitted to travel to the USA for surgery on his knee, returning to the Philippines in March 2004. In July 2004 the court ruled that Estrada was not guilty of money laundering when he opened a bank account under a different name in 2000. A few days later the court approved Estrada's transfer from military detention to house arrest. His trial on the remaining charges of perjury and plunder continued in early 2006.

In October 2001 Jose Miguel Arroyo, the husband of the President, was investigated by the Senate over allegations that he had diverted funds from a state lottery in order to finance electoral campaigns for prospective senators. In the same month Imelda Marcos was rearrested on four charges of corruption, connected to the suspected plunder of the economy under the regime of her late husband, before being released on bail. In November the widow of President Marcos appeared in court and denied all the charges. She was reported to be seeking huge damages from the Government over the claims that had been made against her. In December the court ruled that Imelda Marcos could leave the country for one month to seek medical treatment in the People's Republic of China.

In June 2002 the Government's control over the legislature was threatened when Senator John Osmeña defected to the opposition, depriving the PPC of its narrow majority in the Senate. Owing to the simultaneous absence abroad of another senator, proceedings in the Senate were suspended for almost two months. The Government was weakened further in July when Vice-President Teofisto Guingona announced his resignation from his concurrent position as Secretary of Foreign Affairs, owing largely to his disagreement with the Government's decision to allow the deployment of US troops in the country. Blas Ople was appointed to the post later in that month.

In October 2002 the Senate gave its assent to the Absentee Voting Bill, which rendered Filipino citizens living and working abroad eligible to vote in future legislative and presidential elections. The bill was enacted in February 2003. In November President Arroyo announced her intention to adopt a strict policy aimed at ending the corruption apparently endemic within the Government. In the following month the Director-General of the National Economic and Development Authority, Dante Canlas, resigned from his post at the request of the President. Later in December the President announced that she did not intend to contest the presidential election scheduled to take place in 2004, claiming that her decision was motivated by a desire to spare the country further political division. She subsequently stated her intention to revive the Council of State, an advisory body originally established by her father, Diosdado Macapagal, during his time in power, whilst holding exploratory talks with leading members of the opposition with the possible aim of forming a 'government of national unity'.

In July 2003 approximately 350 disaffected members of the armed forces staged a mutiny, taking control of a shopping centre in the Manila commercial district of Makati. The rebels, who demanded the resignation of the President and the Secretary of National Defense, finally surrendered peacefully. While the Government claimed that the mutiny constituted an attempted *coup d'état*, those who had participated claimed that they were merely seeking a chance to air their grievances, which included, most notably, allegations that senior military personnel were guilty of systematic collusion with Muslim rebels in the south. Later in that month Ramon Cardenas, a former aide to President Estrada, was arrested and charged in connection with the attempted coup. Shortly afterwards the head of military intelligence, Brig.-Gen. Victor Corpus, who had been accused of misconduct by the rebels, resigned. In the aftermath of the mutiny President Arroyo declared a nation-wide state of rebellion, which was lifted in August. In that month charges were filed against more than 1,000 people in connection with the coup attempt. Senator Gregorio Honasan was charged with involvement, along with six of his associates. Meanwhile, Secretary of National Defense Angelo Reyes resigned, while denying the allegations of corruption. President Arroyo assumed the defence portfolio on an interim basis before appointing Eduardo Ermita to the position in September. In November the criminal charges of *coup d'état* that had been filed against 290 of those who had taken part in the July mutiny were abandoned; it was announced, however, that the 31 officers believed to have led the mutiny would be tried by a civilian court. In addition, all 321 soldiers were to face a court martial on separate charges related to their involvement in the mutiny. Six of the leaders of the uprising publicly apologized to the President in September 2004. In November at least 117 members of Congress signed a resolution urging the granting of amnesty to the accused. None the less, after several delays, both the trial and the court martial were ongoing in 2005.

Meanwhile, in July 2003 the Supreme Court ruled that the sum of approximately US $658m. that had been held by Ferdinand Marcos in several Swiss bank accounts should be released to the Philippine Government. In August the Governor of the Central Bank, Rafael Buenaventura, together with four senior bank officials, was convicted of having neglected his duties regarding the closure of a small commercial bank in 2000 and was suspended from office for one year; he continued in his post pending an appeal. (In June 2004 the charges against all five bank officials were dismissed, and the suspensions lifted.) In September 2003 Cardinal Jaime Sin, Archbishop of Manila, retired. Sin had been notable for his involvement in Philippine politics, having played a significant part in orchestrating the popular uprising that had contributed to the overthrow of President Ferdinand Marcos in 1986. He was succeeded by the former Archbishop of Lipa, Most Rev. Gaudencio B. Rosales.

In October 2003, in a reversal of her statement of December 2002, President Arroyo announced that she did intend to contest the next presidential election, scheduled to take place in May 2004. Vice-President Teofisto Guingona resigned from Lakas-NUCD (which restyled itself as Lakas-Christian Muslim Democrats—Lakas-CMD—in 2003), in advance of the announcement, citing differences of principle. However, he retained his cabinet position. In the same month 80 members of the House of Representatives filed an impeachment complaint against Chief Justice Hilario G. Davide, Jr, alleging that he had misused judicial funds. However, the Supreme Court later prohibited the House of Representatives from referring the complaint to the Senate, on the grounds that it was unconstitutional, owing to a previous failed impeachment attempt earlier in that year brought by former President Joseph Estrada. In November the House of Representatives voted against continuing proceedings against Davide. Nevertheless, the attempted impeachment was widely perceived to be illustrative of increasing tensions between the legislative branch and the judiciary. Meanwhile, Secretary of Finance Jose Isidro Camacho tendered his resignation; Under-Secretary Juanita Amatong was appointed to succeed him. In the same month two armed men, one of whom was the former head of the Air Transportation Office, occupied the air traffic control tower at the Ninoy Aquino International Airport in Manila, protesting against government corruption and prompting speculation of another coup attempt. Both men were shot dead by the police.

In December 2003 Secretary of Foreign Affairs Blas Ople died unexpectedly; Under-Secretary Delia Domingo-Albert was appointed as his successor. Meanwhile, in advance of the legislative and presidential elections to be held in May 2004, Senator Edgardo Angara, President of the opposition LDP, announced that his party had merged with the PDP-Laban Party and Estrada's Puwersa ng Masang Pilipino (PMP) to form the Koalisyon ng Nagkakaisang Pilipino (KNP—Coalition of the United Filipino). The KNP subsequently announced that it had nominated the film actor Fernando Poe, Jr, as its presidential candidate. Later in the same month, however, former chief of police Gen. Panfilo Lacson stated his intention to stand as the official presidential candidate of the LDP, supported by another faction of the party, which was led by its Secretary-General,

Agapito Aquino. The former Secretary of Education, Culture and Sports, Raul Roco, who had resigned in August 2002, secured the presidential nomination of Aksyon Demokratiko. The fifth presidential candidate to emerge was Eduardo Villanueva, the leader of the 'Jesus is Lord' Church, who was to represent the newly established Bangon Pilipinas (Rise Philippines). In January 2004 the candidacy of Poe was brought into doubt by allegations that the actor was not a Philippine citizen, as his father was Spanish and his mother a US citizen. However, Comelec later dismissed a petition founded on these claims, declaring that Poe's father was in fact Filipino, and in March the Supreme Court endorsed the Commission's decision, voting in favour of allowing Poe to contest the election. The incumbent President Arroyo formed a new coalition in support of her candidacy—the Koalisyon ng Katapatan at Karanasan sa Kinabukasan (K-4). The alliance consisted of Lakas-CMD, the LP, Reporma and Probinsya Muna Development Intiatives (PROMDI). The coalition replaced the PPC, which had effectively been disbanded following the withdrawal of its most important members.

On 10 May 2004 elections took place to select the President, Vice-President, 12 members of the Senate and 212 members of the House of Representatives, and also to choose more than 17,000 local officials. Almost 100 people were killed as a result of violence during the campaign period, despite the deployment of some 230,000 police officers and troops at polling stations throughout the country. The full results of the polls were announced six weeks later. Arroyo won a narrow victory in the presidential election, receiving 40.0% of the votes cast, compared with Poe's 36.5%. Poe refused to accept the result, alleging widespread fraud. Noli de Castro, representing Lakas-CMD, was elected to the vice-presidency. Lakas-CMD also performed well in the legislative elections, securing 93 of the 212 elective seats in the House of Representatives, while the NPC won 54 seats and the LP 34. Seven candidates of the K-4 coalition, dominated by Lakas-CMD, were elected to the Senate, with the remaining five seats taken by the KNP.

Having secured an electoral mandate for her presidency, Arroyo was sworn in for a second term of office at the end of June 2004. During her inauguration speech she pledged to curb corruption, to improve basic services and to reform the economy, notably promising to create 6m. new jobs during her six-year term. On the day before the ceremony police had dispersed several thousand supporters of Poe who were demonstrating against the Government in Manila and, in a separate incident, arrested four Muslims suspected of planning a bomb attack in the capital during the inauguration. In early July Angelo Reyes, a close ally of the President, returned to the Government as Secretary of the Interior and Local Government, following the resignation of Jose Lina from that position. Later that month Poe and his defeated vice-presidential candidate, Loren Legarda, lodged separate complaints with the Supreme Court, demanding a recount of votes cast in more than 118,000 voting precincts on the grounds of massive electoral fraud. Poe died in December after suffering a stroke. His burial, attended by thousands of supporters, was held under heightened security in Manila, amid government concerns about an alleged plot to use the funeral march to incite unrest; in the event, however, the procession was largely peaceful. In the following month his widow, Susan Roces, requested that the Supreme Court allow her to pursue her husband's electoral protest.

In mid-August 2004 Arroyo announced a cabinet reshuffle, in which former Executive Secretary Alberto Romulo succeeded Delia Albert as Secretary of Foreign Affairs, while Eduardo Ermita, hitherto Secretary of National Defense, replaced Romulo, and Avelino Cruz, the President's former chief legal adviser, was allocated the defence portfolio. The Government launched a medium-term development plan for 2004–10 in October. As well as setting various economic targets, the plan proposed a number of political reforms, some of which would require the amendment of the Constitution. Major changes envisaged included the introduction of a federal form of government and a unicameral parliamentary system; the revision of restrictive provisions on foreign ownership; and the reform of the electoral system. Discussions on constitutional amendments were not expected to commence before mid-2005.

In late 2004 and early 2005 a number of military officers were charged with corruption, as the authorities demonstrated their commitment to eradicating graft in the armed forces. The most high-profile case was that of Maj.-Gen. Carlos Garcia, the former comptroller of the armed forces, who faced charges relating to 143m. pesos in unexplained wealth that he had allegedly amassed. He went on trial before both a military court and the special anti-graft court in November 2004. Eight people were killed and more than 50 others injured in mid-November when police dispersed several thousand workers who were protesting against low wages and the failure to implement land redistribution laws on a sugar plantation in Tarlac province, owned by the family of former President Corazon Aquino. Two senior police commanders were subsequently dismissed for excessive use of force, and an investigation into the police action was ordered.

In early January 2005 the police claimed to have foiled a plot to bomb a forthcoming Roman Catholic festival in the capital, arresting 16 people. Later that month the Secretary of Finance, Juanita Amatong, and the Secretary of Energy, Vicente Perez, resigned from office. The finance portfolio was allocated to Cesar Purisima, hitherto Secretary of Trade and Industry, who was replaced by Juan Santos. Perez agreed to remain in the post until the end of March, when he was succeeded by Raphael Lotilla.

In June 2005 a major political scandal arose over the issue of a recording of a telephone conversation held between President Arroyo and an election official while votes in the 2004 presidential poll were still in the process being counted. Arroyo acknowledged that she had made an 'error of judgement' by speaking with an election official at that time, but strenuously denied having tried to influence the outcome of the poll. Secretary of Agriculture Arthur Yap tendered his resignation from the Cabinet at the end of the month in order to focus his efforts on contesting tax evasion charges filed against him following the purchase of property in Pasig City. Further resignations from the Cabinet followed in early July, in protest at what the departing ministers, who included Secretary of Finance Cesar A. V. Purisima, perceived to be the illegitimacy of Arroyo's presidency. Later that month Arroyo announced that Purisima's position was to be assumed by Margarito Teves. In early September Congress formally rejected three separate impeachment cases against Arroyo, deeming the complaints too weak to stand up to legislative scrutiny. In January 2006 the influential 120-member Catholic Bishops' Conference urged that investigations into the allegations against Arroyo be continued since previous efforts were perceived to have been undermined by 'acts of evasion and obstruction of truth'. In February the National Bureau of Investigation announced that it had concluded its own investigation into the episode, since (because the recording of the conversation had been adjudged to have been tampered with) there was no longer any sound basis for continuing with the proceedings. In the same month an estimated 20,000 people marched through the capital to demand President Arroyo's resignation as they marked the 20th anniversary of the ousting of President Ferdinand Marcos. In March it was reported that members of the opposition were compiling evidence with which to file another impeachment complaint against Arroyo, regarding not only the vote-manipulation allegations but also accusations concerning the mismanagement of a sum of 728m. pesos that had been intended to fund a fertilizer scheme, which, it was claimed, had been misappropriated by Arroyo and her allies to help fund her presidential election campaign in 2004.

Meanwhile, in February 2006 President Arroyo effected a minor reorganization of the Cabinet. Notable changes included the transfer of the Secretary of the Budget and Management, Romuli Neri, to the position of Director-General of NEDA, and the appointment of Rolando Andaya, Jr, as Neri's replacement. Ronaldo Puno was appointed to the position of Secretary of the Interior and Local Government in place of Angelo Reyes, who was transferred to the Department of the Environment and Natural Resources. In the same month the Presidential Anti-Graft Commission (PGAC) signed an agreement with the NGO Volunteers Against Crime and Corruption (VACC) that was intended to bolster the Government's efforts to address the problem of corruption. The VACC submitted the names of 10 senior government officials, thought to include one minister of cabinet rank, to be investigated through the new joint initiative. In the same month a minor explosion within the presidential palace compound at Malacañang led to rumours of a potential military coup. A statement purporting to be from a rebel military faction, the Young Officers' Union-new generation (YOUng), claimed responsibility for the explosion; however, the YOUng leadership distanced itself from the statement, and, furthermore, Presidential Chief of Staff Michael Defensor stressed that forensic tests had revealed the blast to have been the result of an inadvertent chemical reaction, rather than of terrorist activity. In late February it was reported that an attempted military coup intended to displace the Arroyo Government had been averted after 14 junior army officers had confessed to their involvement in the plot. A few days later President Arroyo issued Presidential Proclamation 1017, the declaration of a state of emergency, in response to the 'clear threat' to the nation, a decision that attracted considerable censure from the opposition, the media and civil liberties groups, which lambasted Arroyo for infringing upon public freedoms. Under the terms of martial law, the authorities were granted the right to arrest people without warrant and to detain suspects without charge for an extended period of time; public protests were also prohibited. Following the military's announcement that the threat had been successfully countered, Arroyo lifted the state of emergency one week later. A Supreme Court hearing into the legality of Proclamation 1017 commenced in March. Only days after start of the proceedings Solicitor-General Alfredo Benipayo tendered his resignation, effective from the beginning of April, amidst rumours that Arroyo was dissatisfied with his efforts. Also in March 25 soldiers, including eight army officers, were detained under suspicion of involvement in the coup plot. In the same month a special task force, comprising élite army units, was created in order to counter any further threats to the Government.

Meanwhile, the Philippines continued to be affected by regional instability, owing to the activities of several insurgent groups, operational particularly in the central and southern areas of the country. Despite President Estrada's inclusion of former communist activists in the Government, including the former head of the proscribed NDF, Horacio Morales, Jr, as Secretary of Agrarian Reform, the leadership of the NDF-CPP-NPA condemned his administration. In July 1998 Estrada approved the human rights agreement that had been reached by the NDF and the Ramos administration, and invited the exiled leadership of the NDF to the Philippines to resume peace negotiations. In February 1999, however, Estrada suspended peace talks with the communists following the NPA's abduction of three hostages. The Government also suspended the Joint Agreement on Safety and Immunity Guarantees, exposing NDF-CPP-NPA members to the risk of arrest. A total of five hostages were released by the NPA in April, although the communists continued to reject other conditions for negotiations.

At the end of May 1999 the NDF withdrew from peace negotiations in response to the Senate's ratification of a defence treaty with the USA (see below). Estrada subsequently adopted a position of outright hostility towards the movement. However, the NDF-CPP-NPA were recruiting increasing numbers of members, who were disillusioned with the Estrada administration and the continued social inequalities in the Philippines. In an attempt to divide the communist movement, Estrada entered into negotiations with several breakaway factions, but failed to make substantial progress. In January 2000 the Government suspended military operations against the communists to facilitate the release of two NPA hostages. In December Estrada announced that a peace agreement had been concluded with the Revolutionary Proletarian Army (RPA)-ABB. The agreement, which applied only to the central Philippines, was accompanied by a presidential amnesty for some political prisoners whose death sentences had been upheld by the Supreme Court, and by the release of an additional 235 political detainees. In the same month the NPA rejected an offer by the Government of a truce and subsequently attacked a police station in Sorsogan province, killing one policeman.

In April 2001 the Government of President Arroyo held peace talks with the NDF in Oslo, Norway. The talks were reported to have made some progress, with both sides agreeing to undertake confidence-building measures, including the release of political prisoners. Further discussions were held at the end of May 2001. However, the negotiations were suspended in June when the NDF was implicated in the assassination of Congressman Rodolfo Aguinaldo. The Government insisted that the NDF was to carry out no further political killings during the peace process. However, the rebels refused, claiming that such actions were integral to their political agenda. In November a total of 28 people were killed on the island of Mindanao when fighting broke out between the NPA and government soldiers. Despite the renewal of violence, however, exiled NDF members announced shortly afterwards that they had agreed to resume peace talks with the Government in Oslo in December. In the same month President Arroyo announced a temporary cease-fire with the NDF, following its offer to suspend hostilities for one month if the Government made a reciprocal gesture. However, the arrival of US troops in the Philippines in 2002 (see below) threatened further peace negotiations, as the NDF continued to oppose any US involvement in the country. In May President Arroyo called off further peace negotiations after a number of political assassinations occurred.

In August 2002 the USA added the CPP and the NPA to its list of international terrorist organizations and requested that the Government of the Netherlands cease benefit payments to all group members resident there. In the same month government representatives met with members of the NDF in Quezon City, with the intention of resuming peace talks. However, the chairman of the CPP, Jose Maria Sison, continued to oppose any negotiations while President Arroyo remained in power. In October the Government formally designated the NDF a terrorist organization, while emphasizing that it remained willing to continue peace negotiations. In December the NPA rejected the Government's offer of a unilateral cease-fire over the Christmas period. In January 2003 police officials announced that they intended to charge Sison with involvement in several murders, including those of Congressman Rodolfo Aguinaldo and former NPA army leader Romulo Kintanar (who was killed by unidentified gunmen in that month), and to seek his extradition to face trial in the Philippines. In June fighting broke out between government troops and NPA rebels on the island of Samar and in July, following continued hostilities by the NPA, the Government announced that it intended to launch a military offensive in order to quell the insurgency. In January 2004 NPA rebels attacked a power station near Manila, causing eight deaths.

Peace negotiations between the Government and the NDF finally recommenced in Oslo in February 2004, despite ongoing clashes between the two sides. A third round of talks took place in Oslo in late June. Negotiations were scheduled to resume in August, but were suspended after the NDF claimed that the Government was failing to meet its demands, including the implementation of measures to secure the removal of the CPP and the NPA from the USA's list of international terrorist organizations. Sporadic violence continued, and at the end of 2004 the armed forces announced that a total of 182 NPA members had been killed in clashes with government troops that year and a further 910 had surrendered or been captured. In February 2005 14 NPA rebels and two government soldiers were killed in skirmishes in the town of Compostela, some 930 km south-east of Manila. Meanwhile, the peace talks remained stalled, as the CPP rejected government calls for a cease-fire. Negotiations between the NDF and the Government resumed during the first half of 2005, but were abandoned by the former in August in response to the political scandal surrounding President Arroyo (see above); the NDF announced that it would not resume talks until Arroyo had been removed from power. Notwithstanding this ultimatum, discussions between the two sides resumed in September. However, hopes for a peaceable resolution to the ongoing conflict suffered a set-back in November, when at least nine soldiers were killed and approximately 20 were injured in an ambush near Calinog, in the province of Iloilo, which was alleged to have been carried out by NPA members. Furthermore, in January 2006 a group of suspected NPA members conducted a raid on a prison in Barangay Cuta, Iloilo, during which they released 14 detainees. Later that month it was reported that Philippine troops had killed at least 18 NPA rebels during fierce clashes in Santa Ignacia, north of Manila.

During 1986 the Aquino Government conducted negotiations to seek a solution to the conflict with Muslim separatists in the south. A cease-fire was established with the MNLF in September, following an announcement by the Government that it would grant legal and judicial autonomy to four predominantly Muslim provinces in Mindanao. Further talks ensued, under the auspices of the Organization of the Islamic Conference (OIC, see p. 340), and on 5 January 1987 the MNLF signed an agreement to relinquish demands for complete independence in Mindanao, and to accept autonomy. In February 1988, however, the MNLF resumed its offensive against the Government, which had attempted to prevent the MNLF from gaining membership of the OIC (which would imply that the MNLF was regarded as representing an independent state). The 1987 Constitution granted eventual autonomy to Muslim provinces in Mindanao, which had been promised by President Marcos in 1976. In November 1989 a referendum was held, in the country's 13 southern provinces and nine cities in Mindanao, on proposed legislation that envisaged the autonomy of these provinces and cities, with direct elections to a unicameral legislature in each province; this contrasted with the MNLF's demand for autonomy in 23 provinces, to be granted without a referendum. Four provinces (Lanao del Sur, Maguindanao, Tawi-Tawi and Sulu) voted in favour of the government proposal, and formed the autonomous region of Muslim Mindanao.

In February 1990 the candidate favoured by Aquino, Zacaria Candao (formerly the legal representative of the MNLF), was elected to the governorship of Muslim Mindanao. In October the autonomous regional government was granted limited executive powers. The MNLF boycotted the election, on the grounds that the provisions for autonomy were more limited than those reached with Marcos in 1976. Under Ramos's programme of reconciliation, the MNLF participated in discussions with the NUC. In October 1992 the leader of the MNLF, Nur Misuari, agreed to return to the Philippines from exile in Libya to facilitate negotiations. In January 1993 talks were suspended, and violence in Mindanao escalated prior to the impending elections for the region's Governor and Assembly. At the elections, which took place on 25 March, a former ambassador, Lininding Pangandaman, won 72% of the votes cast in the gubernatorial contest, with the unofficial support of Ramos; 81% of the electorate voted.

In April 1993 exploratory discussions in Jakarta, Indonesia, between Nur Misuari and representatives of the Philippine Government led to an agreement on the resumption of formal peace talks under the auspices of the OIC. Further exploratory talks took place in Saudi Arabia in June, prior to the first formal negotiations in October in Jakarta, where the MNLF demanded the creation of an autonomous Islamic state in the south, as agreed in 1976. In November 1993 the two sides signed a memorandum of understanding and an interim cease-fire was agreed.

The second round of formal peace negotiations between the Government and the MNLF took place in Jakarta in April. Agreement was subsequently reached on government administration in the proposed autonomous region, Islamic law, education and revenue-sharing between Manila and the autonomous zones. In August 1995 Misuari agreed for the first time to a referendum (which was required under the Constitution) prior to the establishment of an autonomous zone, but demanded the immediate establishment of a provisional MNLF government to ensure that the referendum was conducted fairly.

In June 1996 it was announced that the MNLF and the Government had finally reached agreement on a proposal by Ramos for the establishment of a transitional administrative council, to be known as the Southern Philippines Council for Peace and Development (SPCPD), which was to derive powers from the Office of the President. The five-member SPCPD, which was to be headed by Misuari, was to co-ordinate peace-keeping and development efforts in 14 provinces and 10 cities in Mindanao, with the assistance of an 81-member Consultative Assembly and a religious advisory council. After a period of three years a referendum was to be conducted in each province and city to determine whether it would join the existing Autonomous Region of Muslim Mindanao (ARMM—the MNLF had abandoned its demands for autonomy in 23 provinces in Mindanao). In July 1996 government officials announced that, under the peace agreement, Muslims were to be allocated one cabinet post, and were to be granted representation in state-owned companies and constitutional commissions. In addition, Ramos offered to support the candidacy of Misuari in the forthcoming gubernatorial election in the ARMM. In early September the Government and the MNLF signed a final draft of the peace agreement in Jakarta. In the same month elections took place peacefully in the ARMM for the region's Governor and Assembly; Misuari, who, as agreed, contested the gubernatorial election with the support of Lakas-NUCD, was elected unopposed. In October it was announced that Misuari had been officially appointed Chairman of the SPCPD. In March 1997 more than 1,000 former members of the MNLF were integrated into the armed forces under the terms of the peace accord.

In August 2001, after some delay, the referendum was finally held. As a result, the city of Marawi and the province of Basilan elected to join the ARMM. However, 10 provinces and 13 cities rejected the offer of membership and the electoral turn-out was low. In November around 600 supporters of Governor Misuari (who had been dismissed from the leadership of the MNLF in April owing to his widespread unpopularity) led an armed uprising against military and police outposts on the island of Jolo, resulting in the deaths of more than 100 people. The violence was reportedly intended to prevent an election to the governorship of the ARMM, scheduled for late November, from taking place. By instigating the rebellion Misuari had violated the terms of his five-year peace accord with the Government, although he claimed that by holding an election the Government was itself breaking the terms of the agreement. Shortly afterwards President Arroyo suspended Misuari from his post. Later in November Misuari and six of his supporters were arrested by the Malaysian authorities for attempting to gain illegal entry into the country. On 26 November polls to elect a new governor, vice-governor and 44 regional legislators for the province were conducted. The turn-out was low, a fact partly attributed to the escalating military presence in the region. The next day government forces launched air strikes on MNLF insurgents who remained in Zamboanga City, killing 25 rebels and one civilian. As they attempted to flee, the rebels took several local residents hostage. The next day the hostages were released in return for the rebels' safe passage out of the city, thus bringing an end to the confrontation. In early December the President's favoured candidate, former MNLF member Farouk Hussein, was declared Governor. He immediately urged the establishment of peace in the troubled region and stated that he would seek to open a dialogue with the remaining followers of Misuari and other radical groups in the area, including Abu Sayyaf (see below). Meanwhile, President Arroyo indicated that she would prefer the Malaysian authorities to keep Misuari in custody as the Government feared that he would become a focal point for disaffected Muslims upon his return. In January 2002 Misuari was finally deported from Malaysia to face trial in Manila on charges of inciting a rebellion. Misuari remained in custody, awaiting trial, in early 2004, having refused to enter a plea to the charges against him. Meanwhile, in January 2003 the four factions comprising the MNLF signed a declaration of unity in advance of the election of a new leadership; significantly, Misuari's name was excluded from the statement, preventing him from regaining the chairmanship of the group. In early February 2005 more than 500 MNLF rebels loyal to Misuari attacked government troops in several towns on the island of Jolo, in retaliation for a recent army assault, which military leaders insisted had been targeted at Abu Sayyaf (see below), rather than the MNLF; an estimated 30 soldiers and 70 MNLF fighters were killed in the ensuing clashes. Meanwhile, supporters of Misuari, who remained in custody near Manila, urged the Government either to release the former MNLF leader or to transfer him to a prison in Jolo.

The Moro Islamic Liberation Front (MILF), an Islamist fundamentalist grouping demanding secession for Mindanao, which was formed as a breakaway movement from the MNLF in 1978, was covered by the government cease-fire agreed in January 1994 but was not a party to the peace talks. The grouping was widely suspected of having taken advantage of negotiations between the MNLF and the Government to strengthen its position, both by an accumulation of arms and the recruitment of young militants disaffected with the compliance of the MNLF. During early 1996 the MILF initiated further attacks on villages and churches in Mindanao and was engaged in clashes with government troops. In April the Government and the MILF agreed to a cease-fire in North Cotabato.

In August 1996, for the first time, MILF and government officials met in Davao City for preliminary peace discussions. The MILF had rejected the peace agreement with the MNLF and continued to demand separatism for 23 provinces in Mindanao. Alternating hostilities and short-term cease-fires, together with a high incidence of abductions by the rebels, characterized relations between the Government and the MILF between late 1996 and late 1997. In November 1997 a further cease-fire agreement was signed in which so-called terrorist acts (including abduction and arson) were banned as well as public executions based on Islamic (*Shari'a*) law. However, when the leader of the MILF, Hashim Salamat, returned to the Philippines (after living in Libya for 20 years) in December, he announced that public executions would continue in defiance of the government ban. Despite further clashes between the MILF and the Government in January 1998, with mutual accusations of violations of the cease-fire agreement, peace negotiations continued in February when the MILF demanded recognition of 13 MILF camps in Mindanao as 'legitimate territories'. In March the two sides agreed to create a 'quick response team' to resolve conflicts and confrontations before they escalated into serious clashes. In October the MILF and the Government agreed to disclose the location of their forces to prevent accidental encounters. However, in January 1999, following a statement by the MILF advocating independence for Mindanao, Estrada conducted successive offensives against the MILF, causing the collapse of the 1997 cease-fire agreement. Up to 60 people were estimated to have died in the ensuing fighting and 90,000 residents were displaced. A new cease-fire was implemented at the end of January 1999 and at the beginning of February the Presidential Adviser, Robert Aventajado, was sent to Mindanao to meet Salamat inside an MILF camp. They agreed to the resumption of peace negotiations and to a meeting between Salamat and Estrada to re-establish goodwill between the two sides. However, Estrada cancelled the meeting, as a result of a dispute over its location and security considerations. In March 1999 Salamat and Nur Misuari met for the first time in 20 years in an attempt to promote the peace process.

Estrada continued to vacillate between supporting the economic development of Mindanao to eradicate insurrection and threatening to eliminate the rebels through military action. Negotiations between the Government and the MILF took place in October 1999, despite MILF protests at continued government attacks on MILF camps in Mindanao. Clashes between the Government and the MILF continued despite reports of a renewed cease-fire agreement in November. Formal peace negotiations, originally scheduled for December, finally commenced in January 2000 but failed to achieve substantial progress. In that month Estrada announced a new anti-insurgency programme, the National Peace and Development Plan, which aimed to remove the causes of insurgency in Mindanao, including poverty, injustice and disease. Peace talks resumed in March after negotiations scheduled for February were suspended owing to escalating violence, during which the Government claimed to have captured an important MILF base, Camp Omar. Several incendiary devices planted on buses in Mindanao in February, which resulted in nearly 50 civilian deaths, were attributed by government sources to the MILF. The MILF, however, claimed that the bombings were perpetrated by government agents in an attempt to justify the intensification of the military campaign against the MILF. At a second round of talks in March a protocol was signed with improved cease-fire provisions, whereby the Government agreed to recognize 39 MILF camps as 'safe areas' while the MILF representatives agreed to carry a government identity card during talks (which they had formerly claimed would represent a surrender of sovereignty). However, intense fighting took place between the MILF and government forces in March and April in Lanao del Norte and Maguindanao Provinces. The MILF, which captured a small town in Lanao del Norte, claimed the attacks were designed to pressure government forces into the immediate cessation of its offensive against the MILF in central Mindanao. The escalation of violence in Mindanao prompted Estrada to convene a meeting of the National Security Council in March.

In May 2000 the MILF was reported to have withdrawn from a section of the Narciso Ramos highway, a strategically significant route, which it had controlled for more than five years. The withdrawal appeared to augur well for the resumption of peace negotiations, although the Government held Islamist separatist movements responsible for bomb attacks in Manila and Mindanao in the same month. Peace negotiations between the Government and the MILF resumed later in May, and in June the MILF was reported to be assessing an improved offer of autonomy by the Government. However, the MILF subsequently rejected the extension of the deadline for its acceptance of this offer from 1 July to 15 December, owing to a stipulation that it should meanwhile abandon its pursuit of independence. In late June, following a major offensive, government forces captured the MILF's military headquarters at Abubakar. In December the MILF appeared to have resumed its armed struggle after an attack on government forces on Jolo island was attributed to the movement. Bomb explosions in Manila at the end of the month, in which 22 people died, were also blamed on the group. (In August 2004, however, two Filipino Muslim militants with alleged links to the regional terrorist organization Jemaah Islamiah were arrested in connection with the bombings.)

The new Cabinet appointed by President Arroyo in January 2001 included two members who originated from Mindanao. The incoming President stated that she would seek to resume the peace negotiations with the MILF, and in February the Government's military campaign against the MILF ceased. The MILF welcomed the Government's offer to resume talks, although sporadic clashes between its forces and those of the Government continued throughout February. In late March the Government announced that it had reached an agreement with the MILF to resume peace negotiations, and appeared prepared to accept the MILF's condition that renewed talks should be held in an OIC member state. In April the MILF announced a unilateral cease-fire, declaring its intention to observe this until the conclusion of a peace agreement. In June government representatives initiated talks with the MILF in Libya, leading to the conclusion of a preliminary cease-fire agreement in July. Later in the same month a new round of peace talks commenced, and in August a further cease-fire agreement was signed. In the same month the MILF also reached an accord with the MNLF. In September sporadic fighting between the MILF and army troops on Mindanao, which led to the deaths of 15 rebels, threatened to undermine the peace process. However, in October the MILF signed a pact with the Government to safeguard the recent cease-fire agreement. In November 2001 the Pentagon Gang—formed in 2000 and mainly comprised of renegade members of the MILF—kidnapped an Italian priest, Father Giuseppe Pierantoni, in northern Manila. The leader of the faction, Akiddin Abdusalem, was shot dead as he attempted to escape from custody after being captured by government troops. In January 2002 39 separatist MILF guerrillas surrendered to government forces and relinquished a large cache of weapons. In February the MILF announced that it was to hold a new series of discussions with the Government as the situation had been complicated by the arrival of US troops on the island of Basilan (see below). In April government troops finally secured the release of Father Pierantoni after conducting intensive operations against the Pentagon Gang.

In May 2002 the Government signed several new peace agreements with the MILF in Putrajaya, Malaysia. In December the MILF denied responsibility for an ambush on Mindanao that resulted in the deaths of 12 employees of a Canadian mining company, as well as for a bomb attack that killed 17 people in the same week; the group claimed that it continued to observe the cease-fire agreed upon in 2001. Meanwhile, President Arroyo succeeded in deterring the US Government from classifying the MILF as an international terrorist organization, citing concerns that the ongoing negotiation process might be undermined by such an action. In February 2003 peace negotiations broke down when government troops assumed control of the important MILF base of Pikit, on Mindanao, in violation of the cease-fire arrangement. The Government claimed that it had ordered the military action in an attempt to capture members of the Pentagon Gang, whom it believed were being sheltered by the MILF. Although President Arroyo called for a halt to the operation several days later and proposed a peace agreement, many rebels were believed to have been killed in the fighting that had resulted. Insurgency in the area continued to intensify, as the MILF refused to negotiate unless government troops withdrew from Pikit. A number of attacks occurred, the most serious of which took place in March when a bomb exploded near Davao Airport, resulting in the deaths of 23 people. Although the MILF denied responsibility for the attack, the police subsequently filed charges against 150 of its members; four of the group's leaders were charged with murder and warrants issued for their arrest. (Five alleged members of the MILF were arrested in late 2004 in connection with the bomb attack. One of those detained reportedly claimed to have been trained by a leader of Jemaah Islamiah.) In late March 2003 the MILF sent representatives for preliminary discussions with government officials in Malaysia and, in April, the Government declared that formal peace negotiations would restart, although with the exclusion of those indicted in connection with the March attack on Davao Airport, including MILF leader Hashim Salamat. However, shortly afterwards the MILF was responsible for several further outbreaks of violence in the area and, in May, the Government abandoned peace talks and renewed its military offensive against the organization. Later in that month the MILF declared a 10-day unilateral cease-fire in order, it claimed, to prepare the way for the renewal of negotiations. However, the Government rejected the offer following the perpetration of further attacks by the MILF during the cease-fire period. Nevertheless, at the request of the Malaysian Government, the MILF extended the cease-fire by a further 10 days in June and, later in that month, Salamat announced that the group had renounced terrorism, an important precondition for any peace agreement. Despite this, the Government continued to take military action against the organization. However, in July it was announced that the two sides had finally concluded a peace agreement. In August it was reported that Hashim Salamat had died as a result of a heart attack in the previous month; he was replaced as Chairman by Al Haj Murad.

Following exploratory talks in February 2004, formal peace negotiations were to take place in April, but were postponed owing to the May elections (see above). In late April the MILF protested against the arrest of four of its members on suspicion of collaborating with Jemaah Islamiah, claiming it contravened the cease-fire agreement. In July it was announced that the MILF had agreed to co-operate with the armed forces in operations against kidnapping gangs and Jemaah Islamiah elements based in Mindanao. A 60-member international monitoring team, led by Malaysia, was deployed in Mindanao in October to oversee the ongoing cease-fire between the government forces and the MILF; it was expected to remain on the island for at least one year. Further exploratory talks aimed at restarting the stalled formal peace negotiations were held in December; the two sides reportedly made progress on the contentious issue of ancestral domain. In mid-January 2005 at least six government soldiers were killed in an attack on an army outpost by MILF rebels. The Government stated that it regarded the attack, which had not been sanctioned by the MILF leadership, as an isolated incident. Exploratory talks between the two sides were conducted between February and December. Meanwhile, in March the Government and the MILF finally agreed to resume formal peace negotiations in Malaysia, which commenced in February 2006 at Port Dickson, near Kuala Lumpur. ARMM Governor Zaldy Puti U. Ampatuan called for the holding of a plebiscite to assist the efforts to resolve the contentious issue of ancestral domain. Both the Government and MILF announced that they hoped to have signed an agreement on ancestral domain by the end of the following month, the first time in almost a decade that a time frame for the signing of a peace pact between the two sides had been agreed upon. In early March, however, the Malaysian Government postponed the next round of talks, scheduled for 5–7 March, owing to the state of emergency imposed upon the Philippines by President Arroyo (see above), although negotiations were resumed in late March following the removal of martial law. In the same month rumours circulated of a failed attempt to oust Murad Ebrahim from the MILF leadership, but senior MILF members denied such reports. Also in March it was reported that at least 50 suspected members of MILF had surrendered to the army in advance of the resumption of peace talks with the Government; however, a spokesman for the organization disputed that those who had surrendered were in any way associated with MILF, alleging that they were instead affiliated to MNLF.

In early June 1994 the Government undertook a major offensive against Abu Sayyaf, a Muslim secessionist group held responsible for numerous attacks, principally on the islands of Jolo and Basilan, to the south of Mindanao. In retaliation for the capture by the armed forces of its base on Jolo, the group took a number of Christians hostage on Basilan, killing 15 of them. All but one of the remaining 21 hostages were released in mid-June, following the apparent payment of a ransom and the intercession of the MNLF. Later in June government troops captured the group's main headquarters in Basilan. In early August the group's remaining hostage was released, and the authorities announced that Abu Sayyaf had been 'eliminated'. In April 1995, however, the group was believed to be responsible for an attack on the town of Ipil, in Mindanao, in which as many as 100 people were killed. Some of the assailants were also believed to belong to a splinter group of the MNLF, the Islamic Command Council. Some 14 hostages were reportedly killed as the army pursued the rebels in their retreat from Ipil. Despite intense counter-insurgency measures by government troops, Abu Sayyaf perpetrated a further assault on the Tungawan, in which six civilians were killed. In April 1996 two bomb explosions in Zamboanga City were widely attributed to Abu Sayyaf or to other groups opposed to the peace negotiations between the Government and the MNLF. Abu Sayyaf subsequently denounced the MNLF's peace agreement with the Government. Clashes between government forces and Abu Sayyaf were reported on the island of Basilan in March 1998. In December the leader of Abu Sayyaf, Abdurajat Abubakar Janjalani, was killed in an exchange of fire with government security forces.

In April 2000 armed Abu Sayyaf troops abducted 21 people, including 10 foreign tourists, from the island resort of Sipadan in Malaysia, and held them hostage on Jolo. One month earlier members of a separate Abu Sayyaf group had seized a number of Filipino hostages on the island of Basilan where, demanding the release of convicted Islamist terrorists held in US prisons, they had at the end of April managed to evade capture by government forces by which they had been besieged. The Government's military response to the hostage crisis remained largely ineffective, and a stalemate lasting several months ensued, punctuated by both formal and informal negotiations and a partially successful intervention, involving the payment of ransoms, by Libyan mediators. While sporadic releases were secured, however, some hostages were also killed by their captors. In early April 2001 President Arroyo declared 'all-out war' against Abu Sayyaf.

In May 2001 Abu Sayyaf rebels abducted 20 people, including three US tourists, from a holiday resort off the western island of Palawan. President Arroyo immediately ordered a military response, although the group threatened to kill the hostages if it was attacked. In early June the rebels succeeded in fleeing from under military siege; nine Filipino captives escaped as a result. Later in the same month the Government was forced to bring in a Malaysian mediator in order to avert the threatened execution of the three US hostages still being held. It was reported that one, Guillermo Sobero, had already been beheaded, although his body had not been found. In early July two Filipino hostages were released, but Abu Sayyaf stated that it intended to continue attacking US and European citizens until government forces had been withdrawn from the southern Philippines. Shortly afterwards Nadzmie Sabtulah, the rebel leader alleged to have planned the May abductions, was arrested, together with three other members of the group. However, the arrests failed to bring an end to Abu Sayyaf activities, and in August a group of Abu Sayyaf guerrillas raided the town of Lamitan on the island of Basilan, taking at least 36 hostages and beheading 10. The next day 11 hostages were released and soon afterwards 13 more were freed, following an armed raid by government troops. However, the military failed to capture any members of the Abu Sayyaf leadership and 21 hostages remained in captivity, leading to allegations of collusion between Abu Sayyaf and the Philippine military. Soon afterwards three Chinese nationals were abducted as they tried to negotiate the release of a Chinese engineer who had been held by the group since June 2001. Two of the Chinese hostages were later killed following a clash between the kidnappers and government forces in Sultan Kudurat province. The Chinese embassy in Manila expressed its concern at the incident.

In October 2001 the Abu Sayyaf group was responsible for two explosions in the Zamboanga City. Meanwhile, government soldiers were reported to have cornered the kidnappers and their hostages following two days of fighting, which had resulted in the deaths of 21 guerrillas. Shortly afterwards the group threatened to behead its two US hostages—Martin and Gracia Burnham—prior to President Arroyo's scheduled November visit to the USA unless the military halted its offensive. In late October an explosion in Zamboanga, which killed six people, was attributed to the group. In the following month a Canadian man was abducted by men claiming to be Abu Sayyaf separatists. Shortly afterwards the group released one hostage, followed one week later by a further seven. In December government troops succeeded in rescuing the Canadian man. Three hostages remained—the Burnhams and Ediborah Yap, a Filipino nurse. The military offensive against the guerrilla group was intensified by the arrival of US troops on Basilan in 2002. In April a series of bombs exploded in the southern city of General Santos, killing 15 people and prompting President Arroyo to declare a state of emergency in the area. The police later arrested five men in connection with the attacks. While the suspects were initially thought to be connected to the MILF, Abu Sayyaf claimed responsibility for the bombings. Shortly afterwards four men reported to be members of Abu Sayyaf were killed during a gun battle with police in the area. In June 2002 Gracia Burnham was rescued in a military operation. Her husband and Ediborah Yap, however, were killed. Later in the same month it was reported that Aldam Tilao (alias Abu Sabaya), a senior member of the organization, had died during a gunfight at sea.

In July 2002 the joint US-Philippine military exercises that had been conducted on Basilan were formally concluded; President Arroyo subsequently ordered the redeployment of government forces to combat insurgency elsewhere in the country. Although it was thought that the exercises had achieved some success in defeating Abu Sayyaf, in August the group was responsible for the kidnapping of eight members of a Christian sect on Jolo; although two of the hostages were released, a further two were beheaded. Following the group's threat to perpetrate attacks in retaliation for the military offensive being conducted against it, in early October a bomb exploded in the Zamboanga City, resulting in the deaths of three people, including a US soldier. Responsibility for the attack was attributed to

Abu Sayyaf. Later in the same month two further explosions in Zamboanga, which led to the deaths of seven people, were also suspected to have been carried out by members of Abu Sayyaf, although there was speculation that the regional terrorist organization Jemaah Islamiah might have been involved. The bombings followed the terrorist attack on the island of Bali, Indonesia, several days previously (see the chapter on Indonesia). Meanwhile, a bomb exploded on a bus in the capital, Manila, killing at least three people.

In January 2003 three government soldiers were killed during a battle with Abu Sayyaf rebels on the island of Jolo. In the following month further fighting broke out in advance of the resumption of counter-terrorism exercises between US and Philippine troops in the area. In late February President Arroyo imposed a 90-day deadline upon military commanders for the elimination of the threat posed by Abu Sayyaf. In May the final two members of the Christian sect captured in August 2002 were freed from captivity and, in June, the last hostage to have been taken from Sipadan in April 2000 escaped. Meanwhile, the Government announced the establishment of a commission to investigate claims by former hostage Gracia Burnham that collusion had taken place between Abu Sayyaf and Philippine military forces during her time in captivity. In December 2003 it was announced that government forces had captured Galib Andang, alias 'Commander Robot', a senior Abu Sayyaf figure, following a gun battle in Sulu. Abu Sayyaf claimed responsibility for a bomb explosion in February 2004 that caused a fire on a passenger ferry in Manila Bay in which 116 were presumed to have died. In March the Government announced that it had apprehended six members of Abu Sayyaf, thought to have connections to Jemaah Islamiah, who were believed to have been planning a bomb attack on Manila; one of those detained also allegedly confessed to planting the bomb on the ferry. In April the armed forces claimed to have killed Hamsiraji Sali, a leading member of Abu Sayyaf for whose capture the USA had offered a reward of US $1m., following a gun battle on the island of Basilan. Also in April at least eight members of Abu Sayyaf were among 53 prisoners who escaped from a prison on Basilan, using smuggled firearms; within four days 34 of the prisoners had been killed or recaptured by the security forces. In August 17 members of Abu Sayyaf were sentenced to death, having been convicted of kidnapping Ediborah Yap, two other nurses and a general hospital worker in 2001; four of the defendants were among those who had escaped in April and were sentenced *in absentia*. Sitra Tilao, the sister of Aldam, was arrested in September for her alleged participation in the kidnapping operations of Abu Sayyaf. In October President Arroyo announced that six members of Abu Sayyaf had been charged with murder and attempted murder in connection with the ferry bombing in February; Redendo Dellosa and Alhamser Limbong had been arrested in March, but the other four remained at large. A bomb exploded in a market in General Santos in mid-December, killing 16 people and injuring 52. The police arrested five men in connection with the attack, for which Abu Sayyaf was suspected of being responsible.

In late January 2005 the armed forces commenced a major offensive against Abu Sayyaf. Some 30,000 people fled the heavy fighting that ensued in the following month on the island of Jolo between government troops and Abu Sayyaf members, joined by followers of former MNLF leader Nur Misuari. Meanwhile, in mid-February Abu Sayyaf claimed responsibility for three co-ordinated bomb explosions, in Manila, General Santos and Davao City, in which 12 people were killed and some 150 injured. Amid fears of further attacks, the Government increased security at airports, seaports, bus terminals and shopping centres. In mid-March the security forces quashed an uprising at a prison near Manila, killing at least 22 detainees, including the Abu Sayyaf leaders Nadzmie Sabtulah, Galib Andang and Alhamser Limbong, after the expiry of an ultimatum for the prisoners to surrender weapons that they had seized from guards. Abu Sayyaf subsequently threatened to retaliate for the deaths of its members.

In the southern Philippines in August 2005 three explosive devices were detonated in Zamboanga City, injuring 26 people. In the same month a bomb exploded on a ferry, injuring at least 30 people. The Philippine authorities attributed the attacks to Abu Sayyaf. In October two alleged Abu Sayyaf members were sentenced to death, together with a suspected member of Jemaah Islamiah, for their part in a bomb attack on a bus in Manila's financial district, which had killed four people in February. In November at least 23 alleged Abu Sayyaf members were killed, and dozens more wounded, in violent clashes with government troops on the island of Jolo. In February 2006, in another suspected Abu Sayyaf attack, an explosion near an army base that was being used by US troops killed one person and injured an estimated 28 others.

Meanwhile, at the end of November 1991 the US military formally transferred management of the Clark Air Base to the Philippines, in accordance with the Constitution's stipulation that foreign military bases should not be allowed in the country after 1991. In late December negotiations for an extended withdrawal period of US forces from Subic Bay naval base collapsed, owing principally to the USA's policy of refusing to confirm or deny the presence of nuclear weapons (prohibited from the Philippines under the 1987 Constitution) on board naval vessels. US personnel withdrew from Subic Naval Bay at the end of September 1992, and from the Cubi Point Naval Air Station towards the end of November.

In November 1994 the Philippine Government rejected draft proposals (presented by President Bill Clinton of the USA during a visit to the Philippines earlier in the month) intended to facilitate access for US naval vessels to ports in the Philippines. Relations between the USA and the Philippines improved, however, following the Chinese occupation of a reef in the Spratly Islands claimed by the Philippines (see below). A joint naval exercise between US and Philippine forces took place in July 1995 about 100 km from the Spratly Islands. In January 1998 the Philippine and US Governments signed a Visiting Forces Agreement (VFA), which provided legal status for US military visits to Philippine territory and for the holding of joint military exercises, pending ratification by the Senate. However, the powerful Catholic Church opposed the agreement and the communist guerrillas announced that they would terminate peace talks if the VFA were ratified; in September popular protests against the VFA took place. Owing to the intensification of the dispute with the People's Republic of China concerning the Spratly Islands, the Philippines signed an agreement with the USA in October to allow for the formal resumption of joint military exercises. The Senate ratified the VFA on 27 May. The first phase of joint military exercises between the USA and the Philippines, which took place in January 2000, provoked popular protests outside the US embassy against the return to the Philippines of US troops. In July Estrada visited the USA where he requested financial assistance to combat rebel movements in the Philippines.

Following the terrorist attacks on the USA in September 2001 (see the chapter on the USA) President Arroyo offered President George W. Bush her unqualified support for the US campaign against terrorism. In October the President stated that she had volunteered logistical and intelligence assistance, the use of Philippine airspace, and the former US military bases at Clark and Subic Bay to the US Government. An offer of combat troops had also been made, pending congressional approval. In November President Arroyo left for the USA to address the UN General Assembly and to hold talks with President Bush. In return for the ongoing support of the Philippines in the US anti-terrorist campaign, the US President promised the country US $100m. in military assistance and further development aid for Mindanao. The funds included $39m. to aid the Government in its continuing war against Abu Sayyaf, which had proven links to the al-Qa'ida terrorist network thought to be responsible for the attacks on the USA. President Arroyo declined an offer of direct US military involvement, limiting its role to the provision of technical and financial assistance for the offensive.

In January 2002 it was reported that the US Government had sent 660 soldiers to the southern Philippines. While they would engage in joint training exercises with Philippine troops, they would not participate in any direct combat as this would contravene the Constitution. The deployment marked the first significant extension of the US war on terrorism beyond Afghanistan. Despite some popular opposition to the deployment, President Arroyo's stance was considerably strengthened when she succeeded in winning support for the US military presence from the National Security Council, which accepted that it was authorized under the terms of the VFA. In February more than 20 people died following clashes in the city of Jolo between police and soldiers; a later bomb blast in the city killed a further five people. A second explosion in Zamboanga—serving as a temporary base for US servicemen—occurred on the same day. The incidents were attributed to opponents of the ongoing military exercises. President Arroyo also faced fierce criticism from many members of Congress over her decision to allow the deployment, with several claiming that the exercises were intended to conceal a US offensive against Abu Sayyaf. Her most outspoken critic was the Vice-President and Secretary of Foreign Affairs, Teofisto Guingona, whose stance was a decisive factor in his resignation from the foreign affairs portfolio in July of that year. In April 2002 President Arroyo sanctioned the deployment of hundreds more US troops to the region and extended the deadline for their departure, owing to the apparent success of the exercises in containing terrorist activities in the Philippines. The exercises were formally concluded at the end of July.

In late 2002 the US Government signed a five-year military agreement with the Philippines, pledging to extend co-operation between the armed forces of the two countries and to facilitate the movement of heavy equipment and logistical supplies. In January 2003 an advance deployment of US Special Forces troops arrived in Zamboanga to commence anti-terrorism training exercises. In February the USA announced that it intended to send a new deployment of soldiers to the island of Jolo, a stronghold of Abu Sayyaf; it specified, controversially, that the troops would assume a combat role for the first time. However, the Philippine Government stressed later that US forces would play an entirely non-combative role in any counter-terrorism exercises. In March the President stated that, owing to local opposition, military exercises would not be conducted on Jolo. In April a new joint exercise—'Balikatan 03-1'—was announced, to take place in north Luzon and south-west Sulu.

In May 2003 President Arroyo visited the USA. During her visit, US President George W. Bush designated the country as a Major Non-North Atlantic Treaty Organization (NATO) Ally (MNA), entitling it to increased US military co-operation and supplies of armaments. Later in that month the Government stated that it expected to receive a total of US $356m. in military assistance from the USA. In October President Bush visited the Philippines during a tour of the region and thanked the country for its continued co-operation in the US-led war on terrorism. Relations with the USA were strained in July 2004 by President Arroyo's decision to withdraw the small Philippine contingent from the US-led coalition forces in Iraq a month ahead of schedule in order to comply with the demands of militants who had taken a Filipino civilian hostage in the country. Nevertheless, joint US-Philippine military exercises continued throughout 2004, and in February 2005 officials from both countries met to plan the 28 exercises scheduled to take place in that year. In August bilateral trade discussions were held; issues discussed by the two countries included agriculture, trade and investment, intellectual property rights and telecommunications, with both the Philippines and the USA affirming that the negotiations had generated mutually beneficial results.

Following his inauguration in mid-1992, President Ramos visited Brunei, Thailand, Malaysia, Singapore and Japan, demonstrating an increasing interest in regional relations. The Philippines' commitment to the Association of South East Asian Nations (ASEAN, see p. 172) also deepened. Relations with Malaysia were somewhat strained, owing to the Philippines' claim to the Malaysian state of Sabah, dating from 1962, before Sabah joined the Federation of Malaysia. Sabah was ruled by the Sultan of Sulu, in the southern Philippines, until 1878, when it was leased to what was to become the British North Borneo Company. The Malaysian Government continues to pay a nominal rent to the Sultan. Attempts by both Presidents Marcos and Aquino to abandon the claim were thwarted by the Senate. In August 1993 the Philippine and Malaysian ministers responsible for foreign affairs signed a memorandum creating a commission to address bilateral issues, including the Philippines' claim to Sabah. Following his inauguration in June 1998, Estrada pledged to continue Ramos's commitment to regional relations. At the ASEAN ministerial meeting in Manila in July, Domingo Siazon, Jr, whom Estrada had retained as Secretary of Foreign Affairs, joined his Thai counterpart in expressing support for 'constructive intervention' in member countries' internal affairs, in marked contrast to ASEAN's policy of non-interference hitherto. Later that year relations with Malaysia were strained by Estrada's public condemnation of the arrest and beating of the former Malaysian Deputy Prime Minister, Dato' Seri Anwar Ibrahim. Despite Malaysian opposition, Estrada held a private meeting with Anwar's wife, Wan Azizah Wan Ismail, during her visit to the Philippines in May 1999. In August 2001 President Arroyo visited Malaysia on her first overseas trip since assuming the presidency. In November, however, relations were jeopardized again when the Malaysian authorities detained rebel leader Nur Misuari for attempting to enter the country illegally. After some vacillation, Misuari was finally deported in January 2002 and relations remained cordial. However, in August 2002 the bilateral relationship deteriorated following the implementation of stringent new laws in Malaysia under which all illegal immigrants remaining in the country faced harsh penalties and deportation. Many of those affected were Filipino workers. The Philippine Government filed a formal complaint against Malaysia over its treatment of the immigrants and sent an official delegation to investigate allegations of maltreatment. Malaysia subsequently suspended implementation of the legislation.

In late November 1999 an informal summit meeting took place of the leaders of ASEAN and of the People's Republic of China, Japan and the Republic of Korea (collectively known as ASEAN + 3), the third such meeting in three years. It was formally agreed to hold annual East Asian summit meetings of all 13 nations and to strengthen present economic co-operation with the distant aim of forming an East Asian bloc, with a common market and monetary union. At the annual ASEAN summit meeting held in Laos in November 2004, it was agreed to transform the ASEAN + 3 summit meeting into the East Asia summit, with the long-term objective of establishing an East Asian Community. In March 2006 the Japanese Government pledged 27m. pesos to the Arroyo administration in response to the devastating landslide that in the previous month had engulfed an entire village in the central Philippines killing hundreds, in addition to the provision of relief goods to the value of 11m. pesos.

In August 2001 Indonesian President Megawati Sukarnoputri visited the Philippines on her first overseas trip since assuming power. During her brief stay she met with President Arroyo, and the two leaders promised to assist each other in overcoming the separatist violence endemic in both their countries. In March 2002 bilateral relations threatened to become strained when the Philippine police filed charges against three Indonesian men who had been arrested at Manila Airport for illegal possession of explosives. One of those arrested was believed to be a member of the Majlis Mujahidin Indonesia (MMI—Indonesian Mujahidin Council), an extremist Islamist organization, and to have links to Jemaah Islamiah. The Indonesian Government was reported to have been angered by the arrests and stated that the detentions should not be used as a pretext to portray Indonesia as a haven for Islamist extremists. However, in early 2003 it was reported that Philippine rebels were engaged in smuggling arms to militant groups in Indonesia, despite increased anti-terrorism co-operation between the two countries. In October 2003 Fathur Rohman al-Ghozi, believed to be a senior Indonesian member of Jemaah Islamiah, was shot dead by government forces three months after his escape from a prison in Manila, where he had been detained following his conviction for illegal possession of explosives.

The Philippines contributed 1,000 troops to a UN multinational force to restore peace and security in East Timor (which became Timor-Leste upon its accession to independence in May 2002), following the violence that erupted after the East Timorese voted in a referendum for independence from Indonesia; the International Force for East Timor (Interfet) was deployed in the territory in September 1999. The transfer of military command from Interfet to the newly established UN Transitional Administration in East Timor (UNTAET) took place in February 2000; the military component of UNTAET was commanded by a Filipino, Gen. Jaime de los Santos. The two East Timorese independence leaders, José Alexandre (Xanana) Gusmão and José Ramos Horta, visited the Philippines in that month and held a meeting with President Estrada.

Diplomatic relations were established with the People's Republic of China in 1975, at which time the Philippine Government recognized Taiwan as an 'inalienable' part of the People's Republic. Conflicting claims to the Spratly Islands, in the South China Sea, were, however, a source of tension between the Philippines and the People's Republic of China. (Viet Nam, Brunei, Malaysia and Taiwan also claimed sovereignty over some or all of the islands.) In February 1989 Chinese and Philippine warships exchanged gunfire in the vicinity of the Spratly Islands, although it was later declared that the incident occurred as a result of 'confusion over rules of engagement'. Indonesia hosted six rounds of negotiations over the sovereignty of the Spratly Islands between January 1990 and October 1995; all parties agreed to reach a settlement by peaceful means and to develop jointly the area's natural resources. In December 1993 the Philippines and Malaysia agreed to co-operate on fishing rights for the disputed Spratly Islands in the area not claimed by the other four countries. Following a visit to Viet Nam (the first official visit by a Philippine Head of State to that country) in March 1994, Ramos appealed for the six countries with claims to the Spratly Islands to remove all armed forces from the area.

In May 1994 the People's Republic of China made an official protest after the Philippine Government granted a permit to a US company to explore for petroleum off Palawan, in an area including part of the disputed territory of the Spratly Islands. In February 1995 the Philippine Government formally protested when it was revealed that Chinese armed forces had occupied a reef, Mischief Reef, which lay within the Philippines' 200-mile exclusive economic zone established by a UN Convention on the Law of the Sea. Tensions in the disputed region were exacerbated during March by the arrest, by the Philippine naval forces, of more than 60 Chinese fishermen, as well as the seizure of vessels and the destruction of territorial markers allegedly deployed by the People's Republic of China. (Most of the fishermen were released in October and the remainder in January 1996.) Following two days of consultations in August 1995, however, the Chinese Government agreed for the first time to settle disputes in the South China Sea according to international law, rather than insisting that historical claims should take precedence. The Chinese and Philippine Governments issued a joint statement agreeing on a code of conduct to reduce the possibility of a military confrontation in the area. A similar agreement was signed with Viet Nam in November 1995. In March 1996 the Philippines and China agreed to co-operate in combating piracy, which was also a source of tension between the two countries as pirate vessels in the area often sailed under Chinese flags. Despite these agreements, sporadic tension continued during 1996–98.

In August 1998 the Philippines rejected an offer from China for the joint use of the Chinese structures on Mischief Reef. In the same month Philippine and US warships staged military exercises in the South China Seas. The Philippines lodged a diplomatic protest against the People's Republic of China in November, claiming that China was extending its structures on Mischief Reef, in contravention of the mutually agreed code of conduct. China insisted that it was only reinforcing existing structures. Estrada ordered increased naval and air patrols around the Spratly Islands to block entry and exit to the reef. A further 20 Chinese fishermen were arrested by the Philippine navy in November for violating Philippine waters. In January 1999 the National Security Council was convened for the first time in three years to discuss the Spratly Islands and Muslim unrest in Mindanao. The Philippines favoured a multilateral solution to the problems, whereas China opposed any external intervention. China rebuffed the Philippines' attempts to involve the UN through a meeting with the Secretary-General, Kofi Annan, in the USA and threatened to leave the Asia-Europe meeting in Berlin, Germany, if the Spratly issue were discussed. A meeting in Manila achieved little progress, with the Chinese dismissing a Philippine proposal for joint use of the facility, owing to the allegedly aggressive behaviour of the Philippine armed forces. ASEAN, which had failed to condemn China strongly at its summit meeting in December 1998, supported the proposal by the Philippines to draft a regional code of conduct in the South China Sea to prevent the escalation of conflict in the area. In April 1999 the Philippines and Viet Nam agreed to joint operations and leisure activities to reduce the risk of military confrontation. In October, however, the Philippines lodged a protest at the Vietnamese embassy, following an incident in which Vietnamese forces had fired on a Philippine aircraft patrolling in the area of the Spratly Islands.

In November 1999 ASEAN officials agreed on a regional code of conduct drafted by the Philippines to prevent conflicts in the Spratlys. In the same month the Chinese Premier, Zhu Rongji, visited the Philippines, and he and Estrada agreed to strengthen co-operation between the two countries. However, China rejected the proposed regional code of conduct although it agreed to participate in further discussions on the draft. In early 2000 China proposed a new draft code omitting previous references to a ban on construction on islands or atolls and excluded the Paracel Islands, which China had seized from Viet Nam in 1974. However, China did meet with all the ASEAN representatives to discuss the draft, a departure from its previously exclusively bilateral approach. In May 2000 Estrada made a visit to China where he met President Jiang Zemin and signed a joint statement on the framework for co-operation between China and the Philippines.

In mid-2002 relations with China were jeopardized when the Secretary of Justice, Hernando Perez, demanded that the Chinese ambassador be expelled from the country. His request marked the culmination of a dispute regarding the fate of more than 100 Chinese fishermen, who had been arrested over the preceding months and accused of fishing illegally in Philippine waters. Perez accused the ambassador of reneging on an agreement whereby the fishermen would be freed on condition that they entered guilty pleas and paid fines; he claimed that the ambassador had attempted to coerce the Philippine Government into releasing the fishermen without penalty. Perez subsequently withdrew his expulsion demand and, shortly afterwards, the Chinese Minister of Defence, Chi Haotian, paid a goodwill visit to the country. In November 2002 the improvement in bilateral relations was demonstrated when a high-level delegation from the Chinese Communist Party arrived in the Philippines. Also in that month a 'declaration on the conduct of parties in the South China Sea' was signed by the ministers responsible for foreign affairs of China and the ASEAN member states. In September 2004, during a three-day state visit by President Arroyo to China, her first foreign trip since her election, the two countries signed five bilateral agreements, including one to conduct joint marine research in the South China Sea. It was also agreed to explore the possibility of defence co-operation. In March 2006 the Chinese Government granted the Philippine administration US $3m. with which to establish a Chinese-language military training programme, in return for the Philippines' continued adherence to the 'One China' policy, which recognized Taiwan as an integral part of the People's Republic of China. The Chinese Government also donated engineering equipment and invited the Philippines to participate in joint naval exercises.

Relations between the Philippines and Taiwan deteriorated in October 1999, following Estrada's termination of all flights between Taipei and Manila after a failure to settle a dispute over passenger quotas. The Philippine authorities demanded that two Taiwanese airlines reduce passengers from the previously agreed 9,600 per week to 3,000 per week, in order to protect PAL's share of the market. Following negotiations it was agreed in January 2000 that flights would resume in February. However, a disagreement over the interpretation of the new agreement (the Taiwanese authorities claimed the new quota of 4,800 passengers per week applied only to the Manila–Taipei flights whereas the Philippines sought to include the Manila–Kaohsiung route) led the Philippines to sever air links again after only six weeks, despite Taiwanese threats of an investment boycott and curbs on Filipino workers in Taiwan. The dispute was finally resolved in September 2000 when the Philippines and Taiwan agreed to reinstate a bilateral accord concluded in 1996. The Philippines had reportedly accepted that Taiwanese airlines should be allowed to fly passengers on to other destinations after arrival in the Philippines.

Government

The Constitution, which was approved by a national referendum on 2 February 1987, provides for a bicameral Congress, comprising a Senate, with 24 members directly elected by universal suffrage (for a six-year term, with one-half of the membership being elected every three years), and a House of Representatives (with a three-year mandate), with a maximum of 250 members, one to be directly elected from each legislative district: in addition, one-fifth of the total number of representatives can be elected under a party list system from lists of nominees proposed by minority groups. Elections are supervised by a Commission on Elections, which registers political parties.

The President is Head of State, Chief Executive of the Republic and Commander-in-Chief of the Armed Forces. The President is elected by the people for a six-year term, and is not eligible for re-election. The President cannot prevent the enactment of legislative proposals if they are approved by a two-thirds' majority vote in Congress. The President may declare martial law in times of national emergency, but Congress is empowered to revoke such actions at any time by a majority vote of its members. The President appoints a Cabinet and other officials, with the approval of the Commission on Appointments (drawn from members of both chambers of Congress).

Local government is by Barangays (citizens' assemblies), and autonomy is granted to any region where its introduction is endorsed in a referendum. The Autonomous Region of Muslim Mindanao (ARMM), granted autonomy in November 1989, has its own 24-seat Regional Legislative Assembly (RLA).

Defence

The total strength of the active armed forces in August 2005 was an estimated 106,000, comprising an army of 66,000, a navy of approximately 24,000 and an air force of 16,000. There were also reserve forces of 131,000. Paramilitary forces included the Citizens Armed Forces Geographical Units, which comprised about 40,000 men. The 2005 budget allocated an estimated 46,000m. pesos to defence.

Economic Affairs

In 2004, according to estimates by the World Bank, the Philippines' gross national income (GNI), measured at average 2002–04 prices, was US $96,930m., equivalent to $1,170 per head (or $4,890 per head on an international purchasing-power parity basis). During 1995–2004, it was estimated, the population increased at an average annual rate of 2.2%, while gross domestic product (GDP) per head increased, in real terms, by an average of 1.8% per year. According to figures from the World Bank, overall GDP increased, in real terms, at an average annual rate of 4.1% in 1995–2004. According to official figures, GDP increased by 6.2% in 2004 and by 5.7% in 2005.

Agriculture (including hunting, forestry and fishing) contributed 15.3% of GDP in 2004 and engaged 36.5% of the employed labour force in January 2006. Rice, maize and cassava are the main subsistence crops. The principal crops cultivated for export are coconuts, sugar cane, bananas and pineapples. The sector has been generally constrained by inadequate irrigation infrastructure and distribution facilities and by lack of fertilizer. Livestock (chiefly pigs, buffaloes, goats and poultry) and fisheries are important. Deforestation continues at a high rate, owing to illegal logging and to 'slash-and-burn' farming techniques. According to the World Bank, agricultural GDP increased at an average annual rate of 3.0% during 1995–2004. According to the National Economic Development Authority (NEDA), agricultural GDP increased by 4.9% in 2004 and by 2.0% in 2005.

Industry (including mining, manufacturing, construction and power) contributed 31.8% of GDP in 2004 and engaged 15.1% of the employed labour force in January 2006. According to the World Bank, industrial GDP increased at an average annual rate of 3.3% in 1995–2004. According to NEDA, industrial GDP increased by 5.2% in 2004 and by 5.3% in 2005.

Mining contributed 1.1% of GDP in 2004 and engaged less than 0.4% of the employed labour force in January 2006. Copper is the Philippines' leading mineral product; gold, silver, chromium, nickel and coal are also extracted and there are plans to resuscitate the iron ore industry. Commercial production of crude petroleum began in 1979. A substantial natural gas field and petroleum reservoir, off the island of Palawan, has proven recoverable reserves of 100m. barrels of crude petroleum and an estimated 54,000m.–100,000m. cu m of gas. Production from the deposits began in October 2001. In December 2004, following an appeal, the Supreme Court's ruling of the previous January that a mining act introduced in 1995 to encourage foreign investment in the sector was in violation of the country's Constitution was reversed. According to figures from the Asian Development Bank (ADB), mining GDP increased by an annual average of 14.6% in 2000–04. According to NEDA, the GDP of the mining sector increased by 2.6% in 2004 and by 9.3% in 2005; growth in the latter year was boosted by rising metal prices in the global market.

Manufacturing contributed 23.0% of GDP in 2004, and engaged 9.2% of the employed labour force in January 2006. In the late 1990s the most important branches of manufacturing were food products and beverages, electronic products and components (mainly telecommunications equipment), petroleum refineries and chemicals. According to the World Bank, the GDP of the manufacturing sector increased by an annual average of 3.5% in 1995–2004. According to NEDA, manufacturing GDP increased by 5.1% in 2004 and by 5.6% in 2005.

Energy had been derived principally from oil-fired thermal plants, relying chiefly on imported petroleum. However, by 2003 the energy sector's reliance on petroleum had decreased significantly as new sources of power were exploited. In 2002 coal accounted for 33.3% of the total amount of electrical energy produced, natural gas for 18.1%, hydroelectric power for 14.5% and petroleum for 13.0%. In October 2001 the Malampaya gasfield project, approved in 1998, was completed. A 504-km pipeline had been constructed under the sea, at a cost of US $4,500m., to transport gas to three generating plants (with a combined capacity of 2,700 MW) on Luzon Island. The gasfield was expected to supply 16% of the electricity capacity of the Philippines and would limit its reliance on imported petroleum as a source of energy. It became fully operational in mid-2002. Meanwhile, in June 2001 an Electric Power Industry Reform Act was finally enacted; this provided the legislative framework urgently needed to enable the deregulation of the power industry and the privatization and restructuring of the National Power Corporation. In 2004 imports of petroleum and its products accounted for 9.1% of the value of total merchandise imports.

The services sector contributed 52.8% of GDP in 2004, and engaged 48.4% of the employed labour force in January 2006. Remittances from Filipino workers abroad constitute the Government's principal source of foreign exchange. Compared with the previous year, such remittances increased by an estimated 25% in 2005 to reach US $10,700m. Tourism, although periodically affected by political unrest, remains a significant sector of the economy. Compared with the previous year tourist arrivals rose by 23.6% in 2004 to reach 1.8m. Furthermore, the negative effects of the ongoing terrorist activity were offset by other factors during the first half of 2005, including the destruction caused to neighbouring countries by the tsunami of December 2004, which served to divert a proportion of tourism from resorts elsewhere in the region; in the first six months of 2005 arrivals reached 1.3m., an increase of 12.7% compared with the same period in 2004. It was hoped that the construction of a third international terminal at Ninoy Aquino International Airport, which was approaching completion in early 2006, would further increase the number of visitors to the Philippines. In the early 2000s the provision of call-centre services was of increasing significance to the economy. According to the World Bank, the GDP of the services sector increased at an average annual rate of 5.1% in 1995–2004. According to NEDA, the GDP of the services sector increased by 7.1% in 2004 and by 6.3% in 2005.

In 2004 the Philippines recorded a visible trade deficit of US $6,381m., while there was a surplus of $2,080m. on the current account of the balance of payments. In early 2003 the Government announced that, owing to an understatement of the cost of imports of electronic parts used in manufacturing, it had significantly overestimated the size of the current-account surplus since 2000; the figures were subsequently revised. In 2004 the principal source of imports was Japan (accounting for 20.6% of the total); other significant suppliers were the USA (16.0%) Singapore, the People's Republic of China, Hong Kong and the Republic of Korea. The principal market for exports in that year was the USA (17.4%); other major purchasers were Japan (15.8%), the People's Republic of China, Hong Kong and Singapore. The principal imports in 2004 were machinery and transport equipment (37.7%), mineral fuels, basic manufactures, chemical products and food and live animals. The principal exports in that year were machinery and transport equipment, which accounted for 43.5% of total exports. According to NEDA, by 2004 exports of semiconductors and electronic machinery had recovered from a recent decline in global demand; exports in that year recorded an increase of 13.5% compared with 2003.

The budgetary deficit for 2006 was projected at 124,900m. pesos (compared with 146,500m. pesos in the previous year), equivalent to 2.2% of GDP. According to the ADB, the Philippines' external debt totalled US $54,186m. at the end of 2005; in that year the cost of servicing the debt was equivalent to 13.3% of the value of exports of goods and services. The annual rate of inflation averaged 5.7% in 1995–2004; consumer prices increased by 6.0% in 2004 and by 7.6% in 2005. In January 2006 8.1% of the labour force was unemployed.

The Philippines is a member of the UN Economic and Social Commission for Asia and the Pacific (ESCAP, see p. 33), the Asian Development Bank (ADB, see p. 169), the Association of South East Asian Nations (ASEAN, see p. 172), the Asia-Pacific Economic Co-operation forum (APEC, see p. 164) and the Colombo Plan (see p. 385). In January 1993 the establishment of an ASEAN Free Trade Area (AFTA) commenced; a reduction in tariffs to a maximum of 5% was originally to be implemented over 15 years but this was later advanced to 2003 before being formally initiated on 1 January 2002. In November 1999 the target date for zero tariffs in ASEAN was brought forward from 2015 to 2010.

Following the inauguration of President Gloria Macapagal Arroyo in January 2001 and the inception of the new Government's programme of economic liberalization, the peso stabilized, the rate of inflation declined and interest rates returned to the levels prevailing before the political crisis that had surrounded the departure of the incoming President's predecessor. In June 2001, however, the Paris-based Financial Action Task Force (FATF, see p. 385) urged the Philippine Government to impose effective measures to combat money laundering. An Anti-Money Laundering Act was subsequently approved, although it contained significant deficiencies. In February 2003 further anti-money laundering legislation was enacted, which was considered sufficient to avert the imposition of sanctions by FATF member states before the March deadline, although the Philippines remained on the list of non-co-operative countries and territories (NCCTs). Sustained government efforts to address corruption during the course of 2004, including an agreement with Malaysia concerning the exchange of financial intelligence and documentation to facilitate investigation of money laundering and the financing of terrorists, finally led to the removal of the Philippines from the list of NCCTs in February 2005. High levels of unemployment and of underemployment, the latter estimated at 21.3% of the labour force in January 2006, continued to present a major challenge for the Government. Furthermore, between 1998 and 2003 the budget deficit had increased four-fold (in absolute terms) and remained the most significant obstacle to the pursuit of a more ambitious programme of economic liberalization. The Government's efforts to improve tax collection and curb spending had achieved only limited success. The situation was compounded by the failure to control the country's external debt, which had increased from the equivalent of 24.2% of GDP at the height of the financial crisis of 1998 to 37.9% at the end of 2003. By 2004 the servicing of foreign and domestic debt was reported to be consuming almost one-third of total government expenditure, although the Philippines' total external debt declined moderately in 2005 from the previous year's levels. However, it was hoped that the Excise Tax on Alcohol, Cigarettes, and Tobacco Law (signed into law in December 2004) and the Lateral Attrition Law (signed in January 2005) would generate additional annual revenue of 7,500m. pesos and 15,000m. pesos respectively. In May 2005 the Government secured congressional approval for a proposed increase in the rate of value-added tax (VAT) on consumer goods, from 10% to 12%. The so-called 'expanded value-added tax' (EVAT) also provided for an increase in the number of products on which VAT was to be levied; oil, power and medical and legal services were included among those items no longer to be exempt. EVAT was implemented as planned on 1 July 2005, but was suspended by the Supreme Court later that same day, owing to challenges to the law's legitimacy, since it empowered the President, rather than Congress, to impose future changes. In October the Supreme Court rescinded its order, upholding the constitutionality of the new tax and providing for its implementation on 1 January 2006. Following a subsequent delay intended to allow the Bureaus of Internal Revenue, Customs and Treasury additional time to ready themselves, EVAT came into effect on 1 February 2006. It was hoped that its implementation would raise an estimated additional 34,900m. pesos annually. The Government's Medium-Term Philippine Development Plan (MTPDP) for 2004–10, announced in October 2004, emphasized the reduction of the budget deficit, the creation of new jobs and reforms in the power sector. In January 2006 the Board of Investment, in its annual Investments Priorities Plan (IPP), announced that tax and other incentives were to be offered to new investors venturing into certain sectors, including agribusiness, electronics, infrastructure, tourism and health care. The IPP for 2006 also outlined plans further to promote the growth of micro, small and medium enterprises. The MTPDP envisaged that GDP growth would increase to 7.0%–8.0% by 2009–10. The IMF projected a growth rate of 5.0% for 2006.

Education

Elementary education, beginning at seven years of age and lasting for six years, is officially compulsory, and is provided free of charge at public (government-administered) schools. In 2001 93.0% of all children in the relevant age-group were enrolled at primary schools. Secondary education begins at the age of 13 and lasts for five years: there is a common general curriculum for all students in the first two years, and more varied curricula in the third and fourth years, leading to either college or technical vocational courses. In 2002 enrolment at secondary level was equivalent to 74% of males and 81% of females within the relevant age-group. Instruction is in both English and Filipino. In 1999 total enrolment at tertiary level was equivalent to 13.9% of total students enrolled. According to the UN Development Programme, in 2002 the annual expenditure per pupil was just 7,590 pesos (US $138). In the Government's budget proposals for 2003 106,400m. pesos (13.2% of total expenditure) was allocated to education.

Public Holidays

2006: 1 January (New Year's Day), 9 April (Bataan Day, Araw ng Kagitingan), 13 April (Maundy Thursday), 14 April (Good Friday), 1 May (Labour Day), 12 June (Independence Day, anniversary of 1898 declaration), 24 June (Araw ng Maynila)*, 19 August (Quezon Day)†, 27 August (National Heroes' Day), 1 November (All Saints' Day), 30 November (Bonifacio Day), 25 December (Christmas Day), 30 December (Rizal Day), 31 December (Last Day of the Year).

2007: 1 January (New Year's Day), 5 April (Maundy Thursday), 6 April (Good Friday), 9 April (Bataan Day, Araw ng Kagitingan), 1 May (Labour Day), 12 June (Independence Day, anniversary of 1898 declaration), 24 June (Araw ng Maynila)*, 19 August (Quezon Day)†, 26 August (National Heroes' Day), 1 November (All Saints' Day), 30 November (Bonifacio Day), 25 December (Christmas Day), 30 December (Rizal Day), 31 December (Last Day of the Year).

* Observed only in Metro Manila.
† Observed only in Quezon City.

Weights and Measures

The metric system is in force.

THE PHILIPPINES

Statistical Survey

Source (unless otherwise stated): National Statistics Office, Solicarel 1, R. Magsaysay Blvd, Sta. Mesa, 1008 Metro Manila; tel. (2) 7160807; fax (2) 7137073; internet www.census.gov.ph.

Area and Population

AREA, POPULATION AND DENSITY

Area (sq km)	300,000*
Population (census results)	
1 September 1995	68,616,536
1 May 2000	
Males	38,524,267
Females	37,979,810
Total	76,504,077
Population (official estimates at mid-year)	
2002	80,429,769
2003	82,311,608
2004	84,237,476
Density (per sq km) at mid-2004	280.8

* 115,831 sq miles.

REGIONS
(population at 2000 census)

	Area (sq km)	Population	Density (per sq km)
National Capital Region	636.0	9,932,560	15,617
Ilocos	12,840.2	4,200,478	327
Cagayan Valley	26,837.7	2,813,159	105
Central Luzon	18,230.8	8,030,945	441
Southern Tagalog	46,924.0	11,793,655	251
Bicol	17,632.5	4,686,669	266
Western Visayas	20,223.2	6,211,038	307
Central Visayas	14,951.5	5,706,953	382
Eastern Visayas	21,431.7	3,610,355	173
Western Mindanao	15,997.3	3,091,208	193
Northern Mindanao	14,033.0	2,747,585	196
Southern Mindanao	27,140.7	5,189,335	263
Central Mindanao	14,372.7	2,598,210	179
Cordillera Administrative Region	18,293.7	1,365,412	75
Autonomous Region of Muslim Mindanao	11,608.3	2,412,159	211
Caraga	18,847.0	2,095,367	111
Total*	300,000.3	76,504,077†	255

* Total includes a statistical adjustment.
† Including Filipinos in Philippine embassies, consulates and missions abroad (2,851 persons).

PRINCIPAL TOWNS
(population at 2000 census)

Manila (capital)*	1,581,082	Gen. Santos City	411,822
Quezon City*	2,173,831	Marikina City	391,170
Caloocan City*	1,177,604	Muntinlupa City*	379,310
Davao City	1,147,116	Iloilo City	365,820
Cebu City	718,821	Pasay City*	354,908
Zamboanga City	601,794	Iligan City	285,061
Pasig City*	505,058	Mandaluyong City*	278,474
Valenzuela City	485,433	Butuan City	267,279
Las Piñas City	472,780	Angeles City	263,971
Cagayan de Oro City	461,877	Mandaue City	259,728
Parañaque City	449,811	Baguio City	252,386
Makati City*	444,867	Olongapo City	194,260
Bacolod City	429,076	Cotabato City	163,849

* Part of Metropolitan Manila.

Mid-2003 (UN estimates, incl. suburbs): Metropolitan Manila 10,352,249; Davao City 1,254,388 (Source: UN, *World Urbanization Prospects: The 2003 Revision*).

BIRTHS, MARRIAGES AND DEATHS*

	Registered live births		Registered marriages		Registered deaths	
	Number	Rate (per 1,000)	Number	Rate (per 1,000)	Number	Rate (per 1,000)
1995	1,645,043	24.0	504,300	7.3	324,737	4.7
1996	1,608,468	23.0	525,555	7.5	344,363	4.9
1997	1,653,236	23.1	562,808	7.9	339,400	4.7
1998	1,632,859	22.3	549,265	7.5	352,992	4.8
1999	1,613,335	21.6	551,445	7.4	347,989	4.7
2000	1,766,440	23.1	577,387	7.5	366,931	4.8
2001	1,714,093	22.0	559,162	n.a.	381,834	4.9
2002	1,666,773	n.a.	583,167	n.a.	396,297	n.a.

* Registration is incomplete. According to UN estimates, the average annual rates were: births 31.6 per 1,000 in 1990–95, 28.4 in 1995–2000, 25.7 per 1,000 in 2000–05; deaths 6.3 per 1,000 in 1990–95, 5.5 in 1995–2000; 5.1 per 1,000 in 2000–05 (Source: UN, *World Population Prospects: The 2004 Revision*).

Expectation of life (WHO estimates, years at birth): 68 (males 65; females 71) in 2003 (Source: WHO, *World Health Report*).

ECONOMICALLY ACTIVE POPULATION*
('000 persons aged 15 years and over, January)

	2004	2005	2006†
Agriculture, hunting and forestry	9,775	9,949	10,428
Fishing	1,399	1,410	1,405
Mining and quarrying	123	129	120
Manufacturing	3,104	2,995	2,977
Electricity, gas and water	110	128	133
Construction	1,713	1,725	1,652
Wholesale and retail trade; repair of motor vehicles, motorcycles and personal and household goods	5,823	5,910	5,995
Hotels and restaurants	830	836	866
Transport, storage and communications	2,436	2,526	2,547
Financial intermediation	327	304	341
Real estate, renting and business activities	697	711	755
Public administration and defence; compulsory social security	1,478	1,436	1,443
Education	937	959	1,017
Health and social work	365	382	350
Other community, social and personal services	879	763	781
Private households with employed persons	1,548	1,469	1,571
Extra-territorial organizations and bodies	2	0	1
Total employed	31,547	31,634	32,384
Unemployed	3,900	4,030	2,840
Total labour force	35,447	35,664	35,224

* Figures refer to civilians only and are based on annual household surveys (excluding institutional households).
† Preliminary figures.

3538

THE PHILIPPINES

Health and Welfare

KEY INDICATORS

Total fertility rate (children per woman, 2003)	3.1
Under-5 mortality rate (per 1,000 live births, 2004)	34
HIV/AIDS (% of persons aged 15–49, 2003)	<0.1
Physicians (per 1,000 head, 2002)	1.16
Hospital beds (per 1,000 head, 1993)	1.07
Health expenditure (2002): US $ per head (PPP)	153
Health expenditure (2002): % of GDP	2.9
Health expenditure (2002): public (% of total)	39.1
Access to water (% of persons, 2002)	85
Access to sanitation (% of persons, 2002)	73
Human Development Index (2003): ranking	84
Human Development Index (2003): value	0.758

For sources and definitions, see explanatory note on p. vi.

Agriculture

PRINCIPAL CROPS
('000 metric tons)

	2002	2003	2004
Rice (paddy)	13,271	13,500	14,497
Maize	4,319	4,616	5,413
Potatoes	68	68	69
Sweet potatoes	549	547	544
Cassava (Manioc)	1,626	1,622	1,641
Taro	101	101	100*
Yams	26	28	28*
Sugar cane	27,203	30,000*	28,000*
Dry beans	26	26	27
Other pulses*	28	28	28
Groundnuts (in shell)	26	26	27
Coconuts	14,069	14,294	14,345
Oil palm fruit*	212	218	225
Cabbages	91	92	93
Tomatoes	149	150	171
Pumpkins, squash and gourds*	70	70	70
Aubergines (Eggplants)	180	177	183
Dry onions	96	94	87
Green peas	27	29*	29*
Watermelons	79	92	107
Other vegetables (incl. melons)*	4,385	4,379	4,385
Bananas	5,275	5,369	5,638
Oranges†	28	28	29
Tangerines, mandarins, clementines and satsumas†	55	55	56
Lemons and limes†	51	51	52
Grapefruit and pomelos	45	43	43†
Mangoes	956	1,006	968
Avocados	38	35	31
Pineapples	1,639	1,698	1,759
Papayas	128	131	132
Other fruits*	3,365	3,465	3,465
Coffee (green)	107	106	101
Ginger	23	23	23*
Tobacco (leaves)	50	53	48
Natural rubber†	87	88	96

* FAO estimate(s).
† Unofficial figure(s).
Source: FAO.

LIVESTOCK
('000 head, year ending 30 June)

	2002	2003	2004
Cattle	2,548	2,557	2,593
Pigs	11,653	12,364	12,562
Buffaloes	3,122	3,180	3,270
Horses*	230	230	230
Goats*	6,250	6,300	6,300
Sheep*	30	30	30
Chickens	126,831	128,216	122,010
Ducks*	12,600	12,600	11,000

* FAO estimates.
Source: FAO.

LIVESTOCK PRODUCTS
('000 metric tons)

	2002	2003	2004
Beef and veal	182.8	181.0	179.2
Buffalo meat	76.5	76.4	79.7
Pig meat	1,332.3	1,345.8	1,376.1
Poultry meat	650.9	658.8	681.4
Cows' milk	11.0	11.3	11.6
Hen eggs*	495	500	480
Other poultry eggs*	74.4	74.0	72.0
Cattle hides*	15.6	14.4	15.3
Buffalo hides*	8.7	8.8	9.0

* FAO estimates.
Source: FAO.

Forestry

ROUNDWOOD REMOVALS
('000 cubic metres, excl. bark)

	2002	2003	2004
Sawlogs, veneer logs and logs for sleepers	288	346	325
Pulpwood	106	151	355
Other industrial wood*	2,295	2,295	2,295
Fuel wood*	13,328	13,196	13,070
Total	16,017	15,988	16,045

* FAO estimates.
Source: FAO.

SAWNWOOD PRODUCTION
('000 cubic metres, incl. railway sleepers)

	2002	2003	2004
Total (all broadleaved)	163	246	339

Source: FAO.

Fishing

('000 metric tons, live weight)

	2001	2002	2003
Capture	1,949.0	2,030.5	2,169.2
Scads (Decapterus)	291.8	283.6	310.6
Sardinellas	282.6	244.2	235.3
'Stolephorus' anchovies	100.9	74.1	71.1
Frigate and bullet tunas	111.7	163.1	179.1
Skipjack tuna	105.5	110.0	138.3
Yellowfin tuna	83.9	100.3	129.0
Indian mackerel	62.5	72.6	77.1
Freshwater molluscs	69.0	52.6	49.8
Aquaculture	434.7	443.5	459.6
Nile tilapia	89.5	104.4	111.3
Milkfish	225.3	232.0	246.5
Total catch	2,383.7	2,474.1	2,628.8

Note: Figures exclude aquatic plants ('000 metric tons): 786.4 (capture 0.4, aquaculture 785.8) in 2001; 895.6 (capture 0.7, aquaculture 894.9) in 2002; 989.6 (capture 0.7, aquaculture 988.9) in 2003.

Source: FAO.

THE PHILIPPINES

Mining

('000 metric tons, unless otherwise indicated, estimates)

	2001	2002	2003
Coal	1,230	1,665	2,029
Crude petroleum ('000 barrels)	475	2,020	2,000
Chromium ore (metric tons, gross weight)	1,932	2,000	2,600
Copper ore*	20.3	18.4	20.4
Salt (unrefined)	600	600	429
Nickel ore*	23.1	24.1	27.0
Gold (metric tons)*	33.8	35.9	37.8
Silver (metric tons)*	33.6	8.8	9.6
Limestone†	23,000	20,000	16,432

* Figures refer to the metal content of ores and concentrates.
† Excludes limestone for road construction.

Source: US Geological Survey.

Industry

SELECTED PRODUCTS
('000 metric tons, unless otherwise indicated)

	2000	2001	2002
Raw sugar*†	1,676	1,868	1,956
Plywood ('000 cubic metres)*	326	348	409
Mechanical wood pulp*‡	28	28	28
Chemical wood pulp*	147†	147‡	147
Paper and paperboard*	1,107	1,056	n.a.
Nitrogenous fertilizers (a)§	142.	n.a.	n.a.
Phosphate fertilizers (b)§	82	n.a.	n.a.
Jet fuels ('000 barrels)‡‖	6,500	7,000	29,400
Motor spirit—petrol	2,035	2,196	n.a.
Kerosene ('000 barrels)‡‖	4,500	5,000	21,000
Distillate fuel oils ('000 barrels)‡‖	40,000	40,000	168,000
Residual fuel oils ('000 barrels)‡‖	47,000	47,000	215,000
Liquefied petroleum gas‡‖	5,500	6,000	25,200
Cement‡‖	11,959	11,378	11,396
Smelter (unrefined) copper‡‖	160	189	166
Electric energy (million kWh)‡	45,290	46,236	n.a.

* Source: FAO.
† Unofficial figure(s).
‡ Estimate(s).
§ Production of fertilizers is in terms of (a) nitrogen or (b) phosphoric acid.
‖ Source: US Geological Survey.

Sources: mainly UN, *Industrial Commodity Statistics Yearbook*; UN, *Statistical Yearbook for Asia and the Pacific*.

Finance

CURRENCY AND EXCHANGE RATES

Monetary Units
100 centavos = 1 Philippine peso.

Sterling, Dollar and Euro Equivalents (30 December 2005)
£1 sterling = 91.68 pesos;
US $1 = 53.07 pesos;
€1 = 62.60 pesos;
1,000 Philippine pesos = £10.94 = $18.84 = €15.97.

Average Exchange Rate (pesos per US $)
2003   54.203
2004   56.040
2005   55.086

General Budget
(million pesos)

Revenue*	2003	2004	2005†
Tax revenue	537,684	596,408	677,707
Taxes on net income and profits	243,735	278,848	319,102
Taxes on property	712	798	914
Taxes on domestic goods and services	186,784	203,779	225,041
General sales tax	82,444	93,727	109,094
Excises on goods	56,865	51,433	50,699
Taxes on international trade	106,453	112,983	132,650
Non-tax revenue	87,748	79,491	80,239
Bureau of the Treasury income	56,657	40,735	45,369
Fees and charges	29,375	22,993	24,643
Privatization	1,716	1,000	500
Other non-tax revenue	—	14,763	9,726
Total	**625,432**	**675,898**	**757,945**

Expenditure‡	2003	2004	2005†
Economic services	169,881	155,585	159,158
Agriculture	32,932	25,262	25,941
Natural resources and the environment	6,752	6,776	6,803
Trade and industry	2,722	2,833	3,020
Tourism	1,182	1,200	1,412
Power and energy	1,099	1,999	1,512
Water resources, development and flood control	7,007	6,180	6,471
Transport and communications	67,149	54,908	54,949
Other economic services	1,688	7,077	5,982
Allotment to local government units	49,350	49,350	53,068
Social services	237,532	247,888	254,297
Education, culture and training	128,995	133,321	135,470
Health	12,400	12,880	12,927
Social security, welfare and employment	39,096	38,381	40,080
Housing and community development	3,019	2,577	1,739
Land distribution	907	4,284	4,422
Other social services	945	4,275	3,558
Allotment to local government units	52,170	52,170	56,101
Defense	44,439	43,847	44,193
General public services	141,233	137,278	140,650
General administration	43,442	42,254	40,143
Public order and safety	52,565	53,213	54,290
Other general public services	5,746	2,331	3,763
Allotment to local government units	39,480	39,480	42,454
Interest payments	226,408	271,531	301,692
Total	**819,493**	**856,129**	**899,990**

* Excluding grants received (million pesos): 1,198 in 2003; 511 in 2004; 527 in 2005 (forecast).
† Forecasts.
‡ Excluding net lending (million pesos): 5,620 in 2003; 5,500 in 2004; 7,600 in 2005 (forecast).

INTERNATIONAL RESERVES
(US $ million at 31 December)

	2002	2003	2004
Gold*	3,036	3,408	3,112
IMF special drawing rights	10	2	1
Reserve position in IMF	119	130	136
Foreign exchange	13,201	13,523	12,980
Total	**16,365**	**17,063**	**16,228**

* Valued at market-related prices.

Source: IMF, *International Financial Statistics*.

THE PHILIPPINES

MONEY SUPPLY
(million pesos at 31 December)

	2002	2003	2004
Currency outside banks	220,042	238,614	259,572
Demand deposits at commercial banks	252,769	274,921	300,959
Total money (incl. others)	478,482	519,840	567,737

Source: IMF, *International Financial Statistics*.

COST OF LIVING
(Consumer Price Index, annual averages; base: 1994 = 100)

	2002	2003	2004
Food (incl. beverages and tobacco)	154.4	157.5	166.3
Fuel, light and water	168.4	178.5	191.7
Clothing (incl. footwear)	149.2	152.5	156.0
Rent	195.3	201.0	207.7
Services	213.9	226.9	246.7
Miscellaneous	131.8	134.1	137.1
All items	166.4	171.4	180.9

NATIONAL ACCOUNTS

National Income and Product
(million pesos at current prices)

	2000	2001	2002
Compensation of employees	878,800	934,879	1,028,888
Net operating surplus/mixed income	1,922,435	2,141,791	2,355,748
Domestic primary incomes	2,801,235	3,076,670	3,384,636
Consumption of fixed capital	278,154	318,493	342,364
Gross domestic product (GDP) at factor cost	3,079,389	3,395,163	3,727,000
Taxes on production and imports	289,118	286,097	302,654
Less Subsidies	13,780	7,573	6,960
GDP in market prices	3,354,727	3,673,687	4,022,694
Primary incomes received from abroad	359,961	422,345	441,795
Less Primary incomes paid abroad	148,629	177,353	174,290
Gross national income	3,566,059	3,918,679	4,290,199
Less Consumption of fixed capital	278,154	318,493	342,364
Net national income	3,287,905	3,600,186	3,947,835
Current transfers from abroad	24,408	26,313	30,734
Less Current transfers paid abroad	5,011	3,543	4,706
Net national disposable income	3,307,302	3,622,956	3,973,863

Source: UN, *National Accounts Statistics*.

Expenditure on the Gross Domestic Product
(million pesos at current prices, estimates)

	2002	2003	2004
Government final consumption expenditure	457,521	471,429	488,795
Private final consumption expenditure	2,750,853	2,988,124	3,343,973
Increase in stocks / Gross fixed capital formation	695,147	715,308	825,486
Statistical discrepancy	76,091	237,005	187,412
Total domestic expenditure	3,979,612	4,411,866	4,845,666
Exports of goods and services	1,968,524	2,109,394	2,432,683
Less Imports of goods and services	1,988,488	2,221,328	2,434,899
GDP in purchasers' values	3,959,648	4,299,932	4,843,450
GDP at constant 1985 prices	1,032,969	1,081,497	1,148,003

Source: National Statistical Coordination Board.

Gross Domestic Product by Economic Activity
(million pesos at current prices, estimates)

	2002	2003	2004
Agriculture, hunting, forestry and fishing	597,421	637,764	742,112
Mining and quarrying	33,524	43,566	53,032
Manufacturing	915,185	1,004,004	1,116,163
Electricity, gas and water	124,116	137,172	155,346
Construction	185,660	187,755	217,699
Wholesale and retail trade, restaurants and hotels	556,299	602,772	680,762
Transport, storage and communications	276,886	313,160	370,228
Finance, insurance, real estate and business services	423,350	458,088	508,886
Government services	362,296	377,710	393,503
Private services	484,911	537,941	605,719
GDP in purchasers' values	3,959,648	4,299,932	4,843,450

BALANCE OF PAYMENTS
(US $ million)

	2002	2003	2004
Exports of goods f.o.b.	34,377	35,342	38,728
Imports of goods f.o.b.	−33,970	−40,797	−45,109
Trade balance	407	−5,455	−6,381
Exports of services	3,055	3,299	4,101
Imports of services	−4,072	−5,024	−5,383
Balance on goods and services	−610	−7,180	−7,663
Other income received	7,946	3,340	3,549
Other income paid	−3,456	−3,566	−3,402
Balance on goods, services and income	3,880	−7,406	−7,516
Current transfers received	594	9,009	9,858
Current transfers paid	−91	−207	−262
Current balance	4,383	1,396	2,080
Capital account (net)	−19	23	−23
Direct investment abroad	−59	−197	−412
Direct investment from abroad	1,792	347	469
Portfolio investment assets	−449	−1,458	−1,951
Portfolio investment liabilities	1,571	153	324
Other investment assets	−13,165	737	−1,581
Other investment liabilities	7,911	−1,234	201
Net errors and omissions	−2,076	218	−667
Overall balance	−111	−79	−1,587

Source: IMF, *International Financial Statistics*.

External Trade

PRINCIPAL COMMODITIES
(distribution by SITC, US $ million)

Imports c.i.f.	2001	2002	2003
Food and live animals	2,310.8	2,276.0	2,316.7
Crude materials (inedible) except fuels	1,036.0	805.8	998.2
Mineral fuels, lubricants, etc.	3,593.9	3,281.6	3,999.8
Petroleum, petroleum products, etc.	3,244.4	3,002.1	3,603.5
Crude petroleum oils, etc.	2,822.9	2,262.8	2,632.1
Chemicals and related products	2,678.5	2,467.7	3,072.8
Basic manufactures	3,811.2	3,148.4	3,916.1
Textile yarn, fabrics, etc.	1,153.0	812.6	1,070.7
Iron and steel	928.1	977.8	1,162.9
Machinery and transport equipment	16,351.0	13,624.2	23,011.0

THE PHILIPPINES

Imports c.i.f.—continued	2001	2002	2003
Machinery specialized for particular industries	885.9	809.6	916.3
Office machines and automatic data-processing equipment	3,103.2	3,274.4	4,276.4
Parts and accessories for office machines, etc.	2,912.1	3,129.8	4,022.2
Telecommunications and sound equipment	1,891.5	1,268.0	1,424.9
Other electrical machinery, apparatus, etc.	8,039.3	6,073.9	13,832.2
Thermionic valves, tubes, etc.	6,264.3	4,619.5	11,712.7
Electronic microcircuits	1,036.0	906.9	2,032.4
Road vehicles and parts (excl. tyres, engines and electrical parts)	1,048.4	1,060.8	1,258.5
Miscellaneous manufactured articles	1,287.8	986.7	1,804.8
Total (incl. others)	31,357.9	35,426.5	39,543.5

Exports f.o.b.	2001	2002	2003
Food and live animals	1,301.9	1,380.1	1,518.9
Basic manufactures	1,262.0	1,009.7	1,272.5
Machinery and transport equipment	23,870.7	14,089.6	27,103.7
Office machines and automatic data-processing equipment	7,040.7	6,020.5	6,943.1
Automatic data-processing machines and units	4,134.4	4,495.5	4,108.4
Complete digital central processing units	0.1	2,011.2	0.0
Digital central storage units, separately consigned	2,227.5	2,143.7	2,259.5
Peripheral units	462.2	333.4	411.4
Parts and accessories for office machines, etc.	2,815.5	1,480.0	2,773.2
Telecommunications and sound equipment	1,139.7	1,039.0	933.1
Other electrical machinery, apparatus, etc.	14,384.8	5,876.0	17,349.8
Switchgear, resistors, printed circuits, switchboards, etc.	960.9	315.1	602.7
Thermionic valves, tubes, etc.	12,569.9	4,771.6	15,899.7
Diodes, transistors, etc.	809.6	768.9	1,595.4
Electronic microcircuits	11,060.3	3,549.3	13,370.6
Miscellaneous manufactured articles	4,149.5	2,401.5	4,124.2
Clothing and accessories (excl. footwear)	2,422.9	1,366.1	2,286.6
Total (incl. others)	32,149.9	35,208.2	36,231.2

Source: UN, *International Trade Statistics Yearbook*.

2004 (US $ million): *Imports:* Food and live animals 2,832; Crude materials (inedible) except fuels 1,133; Mineral fuels, lubricants, etc. 5,227; Chemicals and related products 3,557; Basic manufactures 3,933; Machinery and transport equipment 16,630; Miscellaneous manufactured articles 1,295; Total (incl. others) 44,079. *Exports:* Food and live animals 1,541; Animal and vegetable oils, fats and waxes 610; Basic manufactures 1,463; Machinery and transport equipment 17,216; Miscellaneous manufactured articles 2,380; Total (incl. others) 39,587 (Source: Asian Development Bank, *Key Indicators of Developing Asian and Pacific Countries*).

PRINCIPAL TRADING PARTNERS
(US $ million)

Imports f.o.b.	2001	2002	2003
Australia	645.4	575.4	526.0
China, People's Republic	1,051.1	1,251.7	1,932.6
Finland	363.7	98.8	193.6
France (incl. Monaco)	286.6	291.6	298.3
Germany	775.6	708.0	967.9
Hong Kong	1,341.0	1,583.2	1,690.9
India	258.4	428.4	330.7
Indonesia	821.7	764.8	890.9
Iran	795.8	433.3	620.2
Ireland	200.7	372.6	225.9
Israel	199.3	97.0	165.2
Japan	6,450.5	7,232.7	8,070.6
Korea, Republic	2,062.6	2,754.2	2,516.4

Imports f.o.b.—continued	2001	2002	2003
Malaysia	977.9	1,293.2	1,434.6
Netherlands	250.6	234.0	323.8
Saudi Arabia	929.4	999.9	1,248.7
Singapore	1,908.0	2,311.1	2,694.7
Taiwan	1,969.5	1,782.7	n.a.
Thailand	956.7	1,052.1	1,453.4
United Arab Emirates	637.0	368.5	504.5
United Kingdom	426.8	463.7	493.1
USA	5,206.7	7,288.8	7,674.5
Total (incl. others)	31,357.9	35,426.5	39,543.5

Exports f.o.b.	2001	2002	2003
Canada	281.6	377.9	319.0
China, People's Republic	792.8	1,355.8	2,144.6
Germany	1,323.1	1,386.1	1,218.6
Hong Kong	1,579.8	2,358.5	3,093.9
Japan	5,057.3	5,295.5	5,768.9
Korea, Republic	1,044.4	1,338.8	1,313.5
Malaysia	1,111.7	1,652.6	2,462.6
Netherlands	2,976.4	3,054.9	2,921.7
Singapore	2,307.7	2,471.7	2,431.1
Taiwan	2,127.4	2,484.9	n.a.
Thailand	1,358.1	1,083.4	1,234.0
United Kingdom	997.3	946.3	695.3
USA	8,993.5	8,690.5	7,273.4
Total (incl. others)	32,149.9	35,208.2	36,231.2

Source: UN, *International Trade Statistics Yearbook*.

2004 (US $ million): *Imports:* China, People's Republic 3,539; Germany 1,366; Hong Kong 2,542; Japan 9,838; Korea, Republic 2,513; Malaysia 2,093; Saudi Arabia 1,496; Singapore 4,019; Thailand 1,878; USA 7,643; Total (incl. others) 47,865. *Exports:* China, People's Republic 5,342; Germany 1,984; Hong Kong 3,859; Japan 7,361; Korea, Republic 1,499; Malaysia 2,567; Netherlands 2,801; Singapore 3,603; Thailand 1,335; USA 8,150; Total (incl. others) 46,705 (Source: Asian Development Bank, *Key Indicators of Developing Asian and Pacific Countries*).

Transport

RAILWAYS
(traffic)

	2000	2001	2002
Passenger-km (million)	123	110	93
Freight ton-km ('000)	49	67	63

Source: UN, *Statistical Yearbook*.

ROAD TRAFFIC
(registered motor vehicles)

	2004
Passenger cars	798,160
Utility vehicles	1,647,524
Sports utility vehicles (SUVs)	141,447
Buses	35,003
Trucks	267,977
Motorcycles and mopeds*	1,847,361
Trailers	23,121

* Including tricycles.

Source: Land Transportation Office, Manila.

SHIPPING

Merchant Fleet
(registered at 31 December)

	2002	2003	2004
Number of vessels	1,686	1,703	1,730
Total displacement (grt)	5,319,573	5,115,708	5,137,000

Source: Lloyd's Register-Fairplay, *World Fleet Statistics*.

THE PHILIPPINES

International Sea-borne Shipping
(freight traffic)

	1994	1995	1996
Vessels ('000 net registered tons):			
entered	53,453	61,298	n.a.
cleared	53,841	61,313	n.a.
Goods ('000 metric tons):			
loaded	14,581	16,658	15,687
unloaded	38,222	42,418	51,830

CIVIL AVIATION
(traffic on scheduled services)

	1999	2000	2001
Kilometres flown (million)	53	67	69
Passengers carried ('000)	5,004	5,756	5,652
Passenger-km (million)	10,292	13,063	13,454
Total ton-km (million)	1,303	1,661	1,666

Source: UN, *Statistical Yearbook*.

Tourism

FOREIGN TOURIST ARRIVALS

Country of residence	2001	2002	2003
Australia	68,541	70,735	69,846
Canada	54,942	54,563	53,601
Germany	40,605	39,103	38,684
Hong Kong	134,408	155,964	139,753
Japan	343,840	341,867	322,896
Korea, Republic	207,957	288,468	303,867
Malaysia	30,498	31,735	31,161
Singapore	44,155	57,662	51,257
Taiwan	85,231	103,024	92,740
United Kingdom	60,147	48,478	47,447
USA	392,099	395,323	387,879
Total (incl. others)	1,796,893	1,932,677	1,907,226

Tourism receipts (US $ million, incl. passenger transport): 1,822 in 2001; 1,827 in 2002; 1,549 in 2003.

Source: World Tourism Organization.

2004: Total visitor arrivals 2,291,352.

Communications Media

	2002	2003	2004
Telephones ('000 main lines in use)	3,310.9	3,340.0	3,437.5
Mobile cellular telephones ('000 subscribers)	15,201.0	21,860.0	32,935.9
Personal computers ('000 in use)	2,200	n.a.	3,684
Internet users ('000)	3,500	n.a.	4,400

Radio receivers ('000 in use): 11,500 in 1997.
Television receivers ('000 in use): 13,500 in 2001.
Facsimile machines (estimated number in use): 50,000 in 1995.
Book production (titles, excluding pamphlets): 1,380 in 1999.
Daily newspapers: 42 (with average circulation of 4,712,000 copies) in 1997.
Non-daily newspapers: 47 (with average circulation of 199,000 copies) in 1997.

Sources: International Telecommunication Union; UN, *Statistical Yearbook*; UNESCO, *Statistical Yearbook*.

Education
(1998/99)

	Institutions	Teachers	Pupils
Pre-primary	8,647	9,644*	n.a.
Primary schools	39,011	328,517	12,474,886
Secondary schools	7,021	108,981	5,066,190
University level	1,316	66,876†	2,481,809
Other tertiary level institutions	1,033	n.a.	4,134‡

* 1990/91 figure.
† 1993/94 figure.
‡ 1995/96 figure.

Sources: Department of Education, Culture and Sports; UNESCO, *Statistical Yearbook*.

2001/02 (preliminary figures): *Primary schools:* Institutions 40,763; Teachers 331,448; Pupils 12,826,218. *Secondary schools:* Institutions 7,683; Teachers 112,210; Pupils 5,813,879.

2002/03 (preliminary figures): *Primary schools:* Institutions 41,267; Teachers 337,082; Pupils 12,962,745. *Secondary schools:* Institutions 7,893; Teachers 119,235; Pupils 6,032,440.

2003/04 (preliminary figures): *Primary schools:* Institutions 41,688; Teachers 337,597; Pupils 12,982,349. *Secondary schools:* Institutions 8,091; Teachers 120,685; Pupils 6,270,208.

Source: Department of Education, Culture and Sports.

Adult literacy rate (UNESCO estimates): 92.6% (males 92.5%; females 92.7%) in 2003 (Source: UN Development Programme, *Human Development Report*).

Directory

The Constitution

A new Constitution for the Republic of the Philippines was ratified by national referendum on 2 February 1987. Its principal provisions are summarized below:

BASIC PRINCIPLES

Sovereignty resides in the people, and all government authority emanates from them; war is renounced as an instrument of national policy; civilian authority is supreme over military authority.

The State undertakes to pursue an independent foreign policy, governed by considerations of the national interest; the Republic of the Philippines adopts and pursues a policy of freedom from nuclear weapons in its territory.

Other provisions guarantee social justice and full respect for human rights; honesty and integrity in the public service; the autonomy of local governments; and the protection of the family unit. Education, the arts, sport, private enterprise, and agrarian and urban reforms are also promoted. The rights of workers, women, youth, the urban poor and minority indigenous communities are emphasized.

BILL OF RIGHTS

The individual is guaranteed the right to life, liberty and property under the law; freedom of abode and travel, freedom of worship, freedom of speech, of the press and of petition to the Government are guaranteed, as well as the right of access to official information on matters of public concern, the right to form trade unions, the right to assemble in public gatherings, and free access to the courts.

The Constitution upholds the right of habeas corpus and prohibits the intimidation, detention, torture or secret confinement of apprehended persons.

SUFFRAGE

Suffrage is granted to all citizens over 18 years of age, who have resided for at least one year previously in the Republic of the

Philippines, and for at least six months in their voting district. Voting is by secret ballot.

LEGISLATURE

Legislative power is vested in the bicameral Congress of the Philippines, consisting of the Senate and the House of Representatives, with a maximum of 274 members. All members shall make a disclosure of their financial and business interests upon assumption of office, and no member may hold any other office. Provision is made for voters to propose laws, or reject any act or law passed by Congress, through referendums.

The Senate shall be composed of 24 members; Senators are directly elected for six years by national vote, and must be natural-born citizens, at least 35 years of age, literate and registered voters in their district. They must be resident in the Philippines for at least two years prior to election, and no Senator shall serve for more than two consecutive terms. One-half of the membership of the Senate shall be elected every three years. No treaty or international agreement may be considered valid without the approval, by voting, of at least two-thirds of members.

A maximum of 250 Representatives may sit in the House of Representatives. Its members may serve no more than three consecutive three-year terms. Representatives must be natural-born citizens, literate, and at least 25 years of age. Each legislative district may elect one representative; the number of legislative districts shall be determined according to population and shall be reapportioned following each census. Representatives must be registered voters in their district, and resident there for at least one year prior to election. In addition, one-fifth of the total number of representatives shall be elected under a party list system from lists of nominees proposed by indigenous, but non-religious, minority groups (such as the urban poor, peasantry, women and youth).

The Senate and the House of Representatives shall each have an Electoral Tribunal which shall be the sole judge of contests relating to the election of members of Congress. Each Tribunal shall have nine members, three of whom must be Justices of the Supreme Court, appointed by the Chief Justice. The remaining six members shall be members of the Senate or of the House of Representatives, as appropriate, and shall be selected from the political parties represented therein, on a proportional basis.

THE COMMISSION ON APPOINTMENTS

The President must submit nominations of heads of executive departments, ambassadors and senior officers in the armed forces to the Commission on Appointments, which shall decide on the appointment by majority vote of its members. The President of the Senate shall act as ex-officio Chairman; the Commission shall consist of 12 Senators and 12 members of the House of Representatives, elected from the political parties represented therein, on the basis of proportional representation.

THE EXECUTIVE

Executive power is vested in the President of the Philippines. Presidents are limited to one six-year term of office, and Vice-Presidents to two successive six-year terms. Candidates for both posts are elected by direct universal suffrage. They must be natural-born citizens, literate, at least 40 years of age, registered voters and resident in the Philippines for at least 10 years prior to election.

The President is Head of State and Chief Executive of the Republic. Bills (legislative proposals) that have been approved by Congress shall be signed by the President; if the President vetoes the bill, it may become law when two-thirds of members in Congress approve it.

The President shall nominate and, with the consent of the Commission on Appointments, appoint ambassadors, officers of the armed forces and heads of executive departments.

The President is Commander-in-Chief of the armed forces and may suspend the writ of habeas corpus or place the Republic under martial law for a period not exceeding 60 days when, in the President's opinion, public safety demands it. Congress may revoke either action by a majority vote.

The Vice-President may be a member of the Cabinet; in the event of the death or resignation of the President, the Vice-President shall become President and serve the unexpired term of the previous President.

THE JUDICIARY

The Supreme Court is composed of a Chief Justice and 14 Associate Justices, and may sit *en banc* or in divisions comprising three, five or seven members. Justices of the Supreme Court are appointed by the President, with the consent of the Commission on Appointments, for a term of four years. They must be citizens of the Republic, at least 40 years of age, of proven integrity, and must have been judges of the lower courts, or engaged in the practice of law in the Philippines, for at least 15 years.

The Supreme Court, sitting *en banc*, is the sole judge of disputes relating to presidential and vice-presidential elections.

THE CONSTITUTIONAL COMMISSIONS

These are the Civil Service Commission and the Commission on Audit, each of which has a Chairman and two other Commissioners, appointed by the President (with the approval of the Commission on Appointments) to a seven-year term; and the Commission on Elections, which enforces and administers all laws pertaining to elections and political parties. The Commission on Elections has seven members, appointed by the President (and approved by the Commission on Appointments) for a seven-year term. The Commission on Elections may sit *en banc* or in two divisions.

LOCAL GOVERNMENT

The Republic of the Philippines shall be divided into provinces, cities, municipalities and barangays. The Congress of the Philippines shall enact a local government code providing for decentralization. A region may become autonomous, subject to approval by a majority vote of the electorate of that region, in a referendum. Defence and security in such areas will remain the responsibility of the national Government.

ACCOUNTABILITY OF PUBLIC OFFICERS

All public officers, including the President, Vice-President and members of Congress and the Constitutional Commissions, may be removed from office if impeached for, or convicted of, violation of the Constitution, corruption, treason, bribery or betrayal of public trust.

Cases of impeachment must be initiated solely by the House of Representatives, and tried solely by the Senate. A person shall be convicted by a vote of at least two-thirds of the Senate, and will then be dismissed from office and dealt with according to the law.

SOCIAL JUSTICE AND HUMAN RIGHTS

The Congress of the Philippines shall give priority to considerations of human dignity, the equality of the people and an equitable distribution of wealth. The Commission on Human Rights shall investigate allegations of violations of human rights, shall protect human rights through legal measures, and shall monitor the Government's compliance with international treaty obligations. It may advise Congress on measures to promote human rights.

AMENDMENTS OR REVISIONS

Proposals for amendment or revision of the Constitution may be made by:
  i) Congress (upon a vote of three-quarters of members);
  ii) A Constitutional Convention (convened by a vote of two-thirds of members of Congress);
  iii) The people, through petitions (signed by at least 12% of the total number of registered voters).

The proposed amendments or revisions shall then be submitted to a national plebiscite, and shall be valid when ratified by a majority of the votes cast.

MILITARY BASES

Foreign military bases, troops or facilities shall not be allowed in the Republic of the Philippines following the expiry, in 1991, of the Agreement between the Republic and the USA, except under the provisions of a treaty approved by the Senate, and, when required by Congress, ratified by the voters in a national referendum.

The Government

HEAD OF STATE

President: GLORIA MACAPAGAL ARROYO (assumed office 20 January 2001; inaugurated for second term 30 June 2004).
Vice-President: NOLI DE CASTRO.

THE CABINET
(April 2006)

Executive Secretary: EDUARDO ERMITA.
Secretary of Agrarian Reform: NASSER C. PANGANDAMAN (acting).
Secretary of Agriculture: DOMINGO F. PANGANIBAN.
Secretary of the Budget and Management: ROLANDO ABAYA.
Secretary of Education, Culture and Sports: FE A. HIDALGO.
Secretary of Energy: RAPHAEL LOTILLA.
Secretary of the Environment and Natural Resources: ANGELO REYES.
Secretary of Finance: MARGARITO TEVES.
Secretary of Foreign Affairs: ALBERTO G. ROMULO.
Secretary of Health: FRANCISCO T. DUQUE III.
Secretary of the Interior and Local Government: RONALDO PUNO.

THE PHILIPPINES

Secretary of Justice: RAUL GONZALES.
Secretary of Labor and Employment: PATRICIA A. SANTO TOMAS.
Secretary of National Defense: AVELINO J. CRUZ, Jr.
Secretary of Public Works and Highways: HERMOGENES EDBANE, Jr.
Secretary of Science and Technology: ESTRELLA F. ALABASTRO.
Secretary of Social Welfare and Development: ESPERANZA CABRAL.
Secretary of Tourism: JOSEPH 'ACE' DURANO.
Secretary of Trade and Industry: PETER FAVILA.
Secretary of Transportation and Communications: LEANDRO MENDOZA.
Director-General of the National Economic and Development Authority: ROMULO NERI.
Presidential Spokesman and Press Secretary: IGNACIO BUNYE.
Presidential Chief of Staff: MICHAEL DEFENSOR.

There are a further 17 officials of cabinet rank.

MINISTRIES

Office of the President: New Executive Bldg, Malacañang Palace Compound, J. P. Laurel St, San Miguel, Metro Manila; tel. (2) 7356201; fax (2) 9293968; e-mail opnet@ops.gov.ph; internet www.opnet.ops.gov.ph.

Office of the Vice-President: PNB Financial Center, President Diosdado Macapagal Blvd, Pasay City, Metro Manila; tel. (2) 8333311; fax (2) 8312618; e-mail vp@ovp.gov.ph; internet www.ovp.gov.ph.

Department of Agrarian Reform: DAR Bldg, Elliptical Rd, Diliman, Quezon City, Metro Manila; tel. (2) 9287031; fax (2) 9292527; e-mail info@dar.gov.ph; internet www.dar.gov.ph.

Department of Agriculture: DA Bldg, 4th Floor, Elliptical Rd, Diliman, Quezon City, Metro Manila; tel. (2) 9288741; fax (2) 9277152; e-mail admin@da.gov.ph; internet www.da.gov.ph.

Department of the Budget and Management: DBM Bldg, Gen. Solano St, San Miguel, Metro Manila; tel. (2) 7354807; fax (2) 7357814; e-mail dbmtis@dbm.gov.ph; internet www.dbm.gov.ph.

Department of Education, Culture and Sports: DepED Complex, Meralco Ave, Pasig City, 1600 Metro Manila; tel. (2) 6321361; fax (2) 6388634; internet www.deped.gov.ph.

Department of Energy: Energy Center, Merritt Rd, Fort Bonifacio, Taguig, Metro Manila; tel. (2) 8441021; fax (2) 8442495; e-mail v_perez@doe.gov.ph; internet www.doe.gov.ph.

Department of the Environment and Natural Resources: DENR Bldg, Visayas Ave, Diliman, Quezon City, 1100 Metro Manila; tel. (2) 9296626; fax (2) 9204352; e-mail web@denr.gov.ph; internet www.denr.gov.ph.

Department of Finance: DOF Bldg, Roxas Blvd, cnr Pablo Ocampo St, 1004 Metro Manila; tel. (2) 4041774; fax (2) 5219495; e-mail hotline@dof.gov.ph; internet www.dof.gov.ph.

Department of Foreign Affairs: DFA Bldg, 2330 Roxas Blvd, Pasay City, 1330 Metro Manila; tel. (2) 8344000; fax (2) 8321597; e-mail webmaster@dfa.gov.ph; internet www.dfa.gov.ph.

Department of Health: San Lazaro Compound, Rizal Ave, Santa Cruz, 1003 Metro Manila; tel. (2) 7438301; fax (2) 7431829; e-mail info@doh.gov.ph; internet www.doh.gov.ph.

Department of the Interior and Local Government: A. Francisco Gold Condominium II, Epifanio de los Santos Ave, cnr Mapagmahal St, Diliman, Quezon City, 1100 Metro Manila; tel. (2) 9250349; fax (2) 9250386; e-mail dilgmail@dilg.gov.ph; internet www.dilg.gov.ph.

Department of Justice: Padre Faura St, Ermita, Metro Manila; tel. (2) 5216264; fax (2) 5211614; e-mail sechbp@info.com.ph; internet www.doj.gov.ph.

Department of Labor and Employment: DOLE Executive Bldg, 7th Floor, Muralla Wing, Muralla St, Intramuros, 1002 Metro Manila; tel. (2) 5273000; fax (2) 5272121; e-mail osec@dole.gov.ph; internet www.dole.gov.ph.

Department of National Defense: DND Bldg, 3rd Floor, Camp Aguinaldo, Quezon City, 1100 Metro Manila; tel. (2) 9113300; fax (2) 9116213; e-mail webmaster@dnd.gov.ph; internet www.dnd.gov.ph.

Department of Public Works and Highways: DPWH Bldg, Bonifacio Drive, Port Area, Metro Manila; tel. (2) 3043000; fax (2) 5275635; e-mail pid@dpwh.gov.ph; internet www.dpwh.gov.ph.

Department of Science and Technology: DOST Compound, Gen. Santos Ave, Bicutan, Taguig, 1631 Metro Manila; tel. (2) 8372071; fax (2) 8373161; e-mail efa@dost.gov.ph; internet www.dost.gov.ph.

Department of Social Welfare and Development: Batasang Pambansa, Constitution Hills, Quezon City, Metro Manila; tel. (2) 9318101; fax (2) 9318107; e-mail mgmontano@dswd.gov.ph; internet www.dswd.gov.ph.

Department of Tourism: Rm 317, DOT Bldg, T. M. Kalaw St, 1000 Metro Manila; tel. (2) 5251805; fax (2) 5256538; e-mail ejarquejr@tourism.gov.ph; internet www.wowphilippines.com.ph.

Department of Trade and Industry: Industry and Investments Bldg, 385 Sen. Gil J. Puyat Ave, Buendia, Makati City, 1200 Metro Manila; tel. (2) 8953611; fax (2) 8956487; e-mail mis@dti.dti.gov.ph; internet www.dti.gov.ph.

Department of Transportation and Communications: Columbia Tower, 17th Floor, Ortigas Ave, Mandaluyong City, 1555 Metro Manila; tel. (2) 7271710; fax (2) 7238235; e-mail aksyonagad@dotc.gov.ph; internet www.dotc.gov.ph.

National Economic and Development Authority (NEDA—Department of Socio-Economic Planning): NEDA-sa-Pasig Bldg, 12 Blessed Josemaria Escriva St, Pasig City, 1605 Metro Manila; tel. (2) 6313747; fax (2) 6313282; e-mail info@neda.gov.ph; internet www.neda.gov.ph.

Philippine Information Agency (Office of the Press Secretary): PIA Bldg, Visayas Ave, Diliman, Quezon City, Metro Manila; tel. (2) 9204339; fax (2) 9815025; e-mail pia@ops.gov.ph; internet www.pia.gov.ph.

President and Legislature

PRESIDENT

Election, 10 May 2004

Candidate	Votes	% of votes
Gloria Macapagal Arroyo (Lakas-CMD)	12,905,808	39.99
Fernando Poe, Jr (KNP)	11,782,232	36.51
Panfilo Lacson (LDP)	3,510,080	10.88
Raul S. Roco (Aksyon Demokratiko)	2,082,762	6.45
Eduardo Villanueva (Bangon Pilipinas)	1,988,218	6.16
Total*	32,269,100	100.00

* Total may not be equal to sum of components, owing to rounding.

THE CONGRESS OF THE PHILIPPINES

Senate

President of the Senate: FRANKLIN M. DRILON.

Elections for 13 of the 24 seats in the Senate were held on 14 May 2001. The People Power Coalition (PPC) won eight seats and the Laban ng Demokratikong Pilipino-Puwersa ng Masa (LDP-PnM) won four. The remaining seat was taken by an independent candidate. Elections for 12 of the 24 seats took place on 10 May 2004. The Koalisyon ng Katapatan at Karanasan sa Kinabukasan (K-4) won seven seats and the Koalisyon ng Nagkakaisang Pilipino (KNP) won five. The result thus gave President Macapagal Arroyo a majority in the upper house.

House of Representatives

Speaker of the House: JOSE DE VENECIA.
General Election, 10 May 2004

	Seats
Lakas ng EDSA-Christian Muslim Democrats (Lakas-CMD)	93
Nationalist People's Coalition (NPC)	54
Liberal Party (LP)	34
Laban ng Demokratikong Pilipino (LDP)	11
Nacionalista Party (NP)	5
Kabalikat ng Malayang Pilipino (KAMPI)	3
Partido ng Masang Pilipino (PMP)	3
Koalisyon ng Nagkakaisang Pilipino (KNP)	2
PDP-Laban Party	2
Independent	1
Others	4
Total*	235

* Total includes 23 members of minority and cause-orientated groups allocated seats in the House of Representatives under the party list elections, which also took place on 10 May 2004.

Autonomous Region

MUSLIM MINDANAO

The Autonomous Region of Muslim Mindanao (ARMM) originally comprised the provinces of Lanao del Sur, Maguindanao, Tawi-Tawi and Sulu. The Region was granted autonomy in November 1989. Elections took place in February 1990, and the formal transfer of limited executive powers took place in October of that year. In August 2001 a plebiscite was conducted in 11 provinces and 14 cities in Mindanao to determine whether or not they would become members of the ARMM. The city of Marawi and the province of Basilan subsequently joined the Region. Elections for the 21 seats of the Regional Legislative Assembly (RLA) were held on 26 November 2001. Elections for the expanded 24-seat RLA took place on 8 August 2005. A total of six candidates contested the concurrent gubernatorial election; Zaldy Puti U. Ampatuan, the candidate of Lakas ng EDSA-Christian Muslim Democrats (Lakas-CMD), won an estimated 63.7% of the votes cast, defeating Mahid Mutilan of the Ompia Party, a Muslim grouping, and Ibrahim Paglas of the Liberal Party, who received 24.3% and 11.8% of the votes respectively.

Governor: ZALDY PUTI U. AMPATUAN (took office 30 September 2005).
Vice-Governor: ANSARUDDIN-ABDULMALIK A. ADIONG.

Election Commission

Commission on Elections (COMELEC): Postigo St, Intramuros, 1002 Metro Manila; tel. (2) 527-5581; e-mail asd@comelec.gov.ph; internet www.comelec.gov.ph; f. 1940; Chair. BENJAMIN S. ABALOS.

Political Organizations

Akbayan (Citizens' Action Party): 101 Matahimik St, Teacher's Village West, Quezon City, 1101 Metro Manila; tel. (2) 4336933; fax (2) 9252936; e-mail secretariat@akbayan.org; internet www.akbayan.org; f. 1998; left-wing party list; Pres. RONALD LLAMAS; Sec.-Gen. ARLENE SANTOS.

Aksyon Demokratiko (Democratic Action Party): 16th Floor, Strata 2000 Bldg, Emerald Ave, Ortigas Center, Pasig City, 1600 Metro Manila; tel. (2) 6385381; fax (2) 6319530; e-mail senator@raulroco.com; internet www.raulroco.com; f. 1997; est. to support presidential candidacy of RAUL ROCO; joined Alyansa ng Pag-asa in 2003 to contest 2004 elections; Chair. JAIME GALVEZ TAN; Pres. RAUL ROCO.

Alayon: c/o House of Representatives, Metro Manila.

Alyansa ng Pag-asa (AP) (Alliance of Hope): 11th Floor, Aurora Milestone Condominium, 1045 Aurora Blvd, Quezon City, Metro Manila; f. 2003 to support presidential candidacy of RAUL ROCO; coalition of Aksyon Demokratiko, PROMDI and Reporma.

Bangon Pilipinas (Rise Philippines): 8th Floor, Dominion Bldg, 833 Arnaiz Ave, Legaspi Village, Makati City, 1200 Metro Manila; tel. (2) 8113355; fax (2) 8111110; e-mail feedback@bangonpilipinas.org; internet www.broeddie.com; supported candidacy of EDUARDO VILLANUEVA in 2004 presidential election; Pres. EDUARDO VILLANUEVA.

Bayan Muna (People First): 153 Scout Rallos St, Kamuning, Quezon City, 1103 Metro Manila; tel. (2) 4251045; fax (2) 9213473; e-mail information@bayanmuna.net; internet www.bayanmuna.net; f. 1999; Pres. SATUR OCAMPO; Chair. Dr REYNALDO LESACA, Jr.

Gabay ng Bayan (Nation's Guide): Metro Manila; fmrly Grand Alliance for Democracy; Leader FRANCISCO TADAD.

Kabalikat ng Malayang Pilipino (KAMPI): c/o House of Representatives, Metro Manila; f. 1997; Chair. MARGARITA COJUANGCO; Pres. RONALDO PUNO.

Kilusan para sa Pambansang Pagpapanibago (BAGO): Metro Manila; f. 1997; est. to support presidential candidacy of SANTIAGO F. DUMLAO, Jr.

Kilusang Bagong Lipunan (KBL) (New Society Movement): Metro Manila; f. 1978 by Pres. MARCOS and fmr mems of the Nacionalista Party; Sec.-Gen. VICENTE MELLORA.

Koalisyon ng Katapatan at Karanasan sa Kinabukasan (K-4) (Coalition of Dedication and Experience for the Future): c/o House of Representatives, Metro Manila; f. 2003 to support presidential candidacy of GLORIA MACAPAGAL ARROYO; coalition of Lakas-CMD, Liberal Party (LP) and People's Reform Party (PRP); Leader GLORIA MACAPAGAL ARROYO.

Koalisyon ng Nagkakaisang Pilipino (KNP) (Coalition of the United Filipino): c/o House of Representatives, Metro Manila; f. Dec. 2003 to support presidential candidacy of FERNANDO POE, Jr; coalition of Angara faction of Laban ng Demokratikong Pilipino (LDP), PDP-Laban Party and Puwersa ng Masang Pilipino (PMP); Exec. Chair. EDGARDO ANGARA.

Laban ng Demokratikong Pilipino (LDP) (Fight of Democratic Filipinos): c/o House of Representatives, Metro Manila; f. 1987; reorg. 1988 as an alliance of Lakas ng Bansa and a conservative faction of the PDP-Laban Party; mem. of Lapian ng Masang Pilipino (LAMP) until Jan. 2001; split into two factions, led by EDGARDO ANGARA and AGAPITO AQUINO, to contest 2004 elections; Angara faction joined Koalisyon ng Nagkakaisang Pilipino (KNP) in Dec. 2003 to support presidential candidacy of FERNANDO POE, Jr; Aquino faction supported presidential candidacy of PANFILO LACSON; Pres. EDGARDO ANGARA; Sec.-Gen. AGAPITO AQUINO.

Lakas ng EDSA (Power of EDSA)-Christian Muslim Democrats (Lakas-CMD): c/o House of Representatives, Metro Manila; f. 1992; est. as alliance to support the presidential candidacy of Gen. FIDEL V. RAMOS; formed alliance with UMDP to contest 1998 and 2001 elections; fmrly Lakas-National Union of Christian Democrats (Lakas-NUCD); name changed as above in 2003; joined Koalisyon ng Katapatan at Karanasan sa Kinabukasan (K-4) in 2003; Pres. JOSE DE VENECIA; Sec.-Gen. HEHERSON ALVAREZ.

Lapian ng Masang Pilipino (LAMP) (Party of the Filipino Masses): Metro Manila; f. 1997 as Laban ng Makabayang Masang Pilipino (LaMMP, Struggle of Nationalist Filipino Masses); renamed Laban ng Masang Pilipino (LMP, Struggle of Filipino Masses) in 1998; present name adopted in 1999; originally coalition of Laban ng Demokratikong Pilipino (LDP), Nationalist People's Coalition (NPC) and Partido ng Masang Pilipino (PMP) until split in Jan. 2001.

Liberal Party (LP): 4th Floor, J & T Bldg, Magsaysay Blvd, Sta. Mesa, 1016 Metro Manila; tel. (2) 7168187; fax (2) 7168210; e-mail admin@liberalparty.ph; internet www.liberalparty.ph; f. 1946; represents centre-liberal opinion of the fmr Nacionalista Party, which split in 1946; joined Koalisyon ng Katapatan at Karanasan sa Kinabukasan (K-4) in Jan. 2004 to contest 2004 elections; Pres. ATIENZA; Chair. MICHAEL DEFENSOR.

Nacionalista Party (NP): Metro Manila; tel. (2) 854418; fax (2) 865602; Pres. ARTURO TOLENTINO; Sec.-Gen. RENE ESPINA.

Nationalist People's Coalition (NPC): Metro Manila; f. 1991; breakaway faction of the Nacionalista Party led by EDUARDO COJUANGCO; mem. of Lapian ng Masang Pilipino (LAMP) from 1997 until Jan. 2001.

New National Alliance: Metro Manila; f. 1998; left-wing; Dep. Sec.-Gen. TEDDY CASINO.

Partido Bansang Marangal (PBM): Metro Manila; f. 1997; est. to support the presidential candidacy of MANUEL L. MORATO.

Partido Demokratiko Sosyalista ng Pilipinas (PDSP) (Philippine Democratic Socialist Party): 33 Nicanor Reyes Rd, Loyola Heights, Quezon City, Metro Manila; tel. and fax (2) 9287884; e-mail pdspgensec@yahoo.com; internet www.pdsp.mypage.org; f. 1981; formed by mems of the Batasang Pambansa allied to the Nacionalista (Roy faction), Pusyon Visaya and Mindanao Alliance parties; joined People Power Coalition (PPC) in Feb. 2001; Leader NORBERTO GONZALES.

Partido Komunista ng Pilipinas (PKP) (Communist Party of the Philippines): f. 1930; Pres. FELICISIMO MACAPAGAL.

Partido Nacionalista ng Pilipinas (PNP) (Philippine Nationalist Party): Metro Manila; f. 1986 by fmr mems of KBL; Leader BLAS F. OPLE.

Partido ng Bayan (New People's Alliance): f. May 1986; formed by JOSE MARIA SISON (imprisoned in 1977–86), the head of the Communist Party of the Philippines (CPP); militant left-wing nationalist group.

Partido ng Manggagawang Pilipino (PMP) (Filipino Workers' Party): f. 2002; est. by fmr supporters of the CPP (see below).

Partido para sa Demokratikong Reporma-Lapiang Manggagawa Coalition (Reporma): c/o House of Representatives, Metro Manila; joined People Power Coalition (PPC) in Feb. 2001; Leader RENATO DE VILLA.

PDP-Laban Party: c/o House of Representatives, Metro Manila; f. February 1983; est. following merger of Pilipino Democratic Party (f. 1982 by fmr mems of the Mindanao Alliance) and Laban (Lakas ng Bayan—People's Power Movement, f. 1978 and led by BENIGNO S. AQUINO, Jr, until his assassination in August 1983); centrist; formally dissolved in Sept. 1988, following the formation of the LDP, but a faction continued to function as a political movement; Pres. JEJOMAR BINAY; Chair. AQUILINO PIMENTEL.

People's Reform Party (PRP): c/o House of Representatives, Metro Manila; f. 1991; formed by MIRIAM DEFENSOR SANTIAGO to support her candidacy in the 1992 presidential election; joined Koalisyon ng Katapatan at Karanasan sa Kinabukasan (K-4) to contest 2004 elections to Senate; Pres. MIRIAM DEFENSOR SANTIAGO.

Probinsya Muna Development Initiatives (PROMDI): 7 Pasteur St, Lahug, Cebu City; tel. (32) 2326692; fax (32) 2313609; e-mail

THE PHILIPPINES

emro@cebu.pw.net.ph; f. 1997; joined People Power Coalition (PPC) to contest 2001 elections; Leader EMILIO ('LITO') OSMEÑA.

Puwersa ng Masa (PnM): c/o House of Representatives, Metro Manila; f. 2001; est. by ex-President JOSEPH EJERCITO ESTRADA; formed an alliance with Laban ng Demokratikong Pilipino (LDP) to contest the 2001 elections to the Senate.

Puwersa ng Masang Pilipino (PMP): Metro Manila; mem. of Lapian ng Masan Pilipino (LAMP) from 1997 until Jan. 2001; joined Koalisyon ng Nagkakaisang Pilipino (KNP) to contest 2004 elections; Leader JOSEPH EJERCITO ESTRADA; Pres. HORACIO MORALES, Jr.

Sandigan ng Lakas at Demokrasya ng Sambayanan (SANLA-KAS) (Upholder of People's Power and Democracy): 150K 6th St, Barangay East Kamias, Quezon City, Metro Manila; tel. (2) 4338377; fax (2) 4262422; e-mail sanlakas1@yahoo.com; internet www .geocities.com/sanlakasonline; leftist multi-sectoral; Pres. and Chair. WILSON FORTALEZA.

United Muslim Democratic Party (UMDP): Mindanao; moderate Islamic party; formed an electoral alliance with Lakas-NUCD for the election to the House of Representatives in May 2001.

United Negros Alliance (UNA): Negros Occidental.

The following organizations are, or have been, in conflict with the Government:

Abu Sayyaf (Bearer of the Sword): Mindanao; radical Islamic group seeking the establishment of an Islamic state in Mindanao; breakaway grouping of the MILF; est. strength 1,500 (2000); Leader KHADAFI JANJALANI.

Alex Boncayao Brigade (ABB): communist urban guerrilla group, fmrly linked to CPP, formed alliance with Revolutionary Proletarian Party in 1997; est. strength 500 (April 2001); Leader NILO DE LA CRUZ.

Islamic Command Council (ICC): Mindanao; splinter group of MNLF; Leader MELHAM ALAM.

Maranao Islamic Statehood Movement: Mindanao; f. 1998; armed grouping seeking the establishment of an Islamic state in Mindanao.

Mindanao Independence Movement (MIM): Mindanao; claims a membership of 1m; Leader REUBEN CANOY.

Moro Islamic Liberation Front (MILF): Camp Abubakar, Lanao del Sur, Mindanao; aims to establish an Islamic state in Mindanao; comprises a faction that broke away from the MNLF in 1978; its armed wing, the Bangsa Moro Islamic Armed Forces, est. 10,000 armed regulars; Chair. Al-Haj MURAD.

Moro Islamic Reform Group: Mindanao; breakaway faction from MNLF; est. strength of 200 in 2000.

Moro National Liberation Front (MNLF): internet www.mnlf .org; seeks autonomy for Muslim communities in Mindanao; signed a peace agreement with the Govt in Sept. 1996; its armed wing, the Bangsa Moro Army, comprised an est. 10,000 mems in 2000; Chair. and Pres. of Cen. Cttee (vacant); Sec.-Gen. MUSLIMIN SEMA.

Moro National Liberation Front—Islamic Command Council (MNLF—ICC): Basak, Lanao del Sur; f. 2000; Islamist separatist movement committed to urban guerrilla warfare; breakaway faction from MNLF.

National Democratic Front (NDF): a left-wing alliance of 14 mem. groups; Chair. MARIANA OROSA; Spokesman GREGORIO ROSAL.

The NDF includes:

Communist Party of the Philippines (CPP): f. 1968; a breakaway faction of the PKP; legalized Sept. 1992; in July 1993 the Metro Manila-Rizal and Visayas regional committees, controlling 40% of total CPP membership (est. 15,000 in 1994), split from the Central Committee; Chair. JOSE MARIA SISON; Gen. Sec. BENITO TIAMZON.

New People's Army (NPA): f. 1969 as the military wing of the CPP; based in central Luzon, but operates throughout the Philippines; est. strength 9,500; Leader JOVENCIO BALWEG; Spokesman GREGORIO ROSAL.

Revolutionary Proletarian Party: Metro Manila; f. 1996; comprises mems of the Metro Manila-Rizal and Visayas regional committees, which broke away from the CPP in 1993; has a front organization called the Bukluran ng Manggagawang Pilipino (Association of Filipino Workers); Leader ARTURO TABARA.

Diplomatic Representation

EMBASSIES IN THE PHILIPPINES

Argentina: 8th Floor, Liberty Center, 104 H. V. de la Costa St, Salcedo Village, Makati City, 1227 Metro Manila; tel. (2) 8453218; fax (2) 8453220; e-mail embarfil@eastern.com.ph; Ambassador ISMAEL MARIO SCHUFF.

Australia: 23rd Floor, Tower II, RCBC Plaza, 6819 Ayala Ave, Makati City, 1200 Metro Manila; tel. (2) 7578100; fax (2) 7578268; e-mail public-affairs-MNLA@dfat.gov.au; internet www.australia .com.ph; Ambassador ANTHONY JOHN HELY.

Austria: Prince Bldg, 4th Floor, 117 Rada St, Legaspi Village, Makati City, 1200 Metro Manila; tel. (2) 8179191; fax (2) 8134238; e-mail manila-ob@bmaa.gv.at; Ambassador JAGER HERBERT.

Bangladesh: Universal-Re Bldg, 2nd Floor, 106 Paseo de Roxas, Legaspi Village, Makati City, Metro Manila; tel. (2) 8175001; fax (2) 8164941; e-mail bdoot.manila@pacific.net.ph; Ambassador MUHAMMAD ABUL QUASHEM.

Belgium: Multinational Bancorporation Center, 9th Floor, 6805 Ayala Ave, Makati City, Metro Manila; tel. (2) 8451869; fax (2) 8452076; e-mail manila@diplobel.org; Chargé d'affaires a.i. JEROEN VERGEYLEN.

Brazil: 16th Floor, Liberty Center, 104 H. V. de la Costa St, Salcedo Village, Makati City, 1227 Metro Manila; tel. (2) 8453651; fax (2) 8453676; e-mail brasemb@info.com.ph; Ambassador CLAUDIO MARIA HENRIQUE DO COUTO LYRA.

Brunei: Bank of the Philippine Islands Bldg, 11th Floor, Ayala Ave, cnr Paseo de Roxas, Makati City, 1227 Metro Manila; tel. (2) 8162836; fax (2) 8916646; Ambassador EMALEEN ABDUL RAHMAN TEO.

Cambodia: Unit 7A, 7th Floor, Country Space One Bldg, Sen. Gil J. Puyat Ave, Makati City, Metro Manila; tel. (2) 8189981; fax (2) 8189983; e-mail cam.emb.ma@netasia.net; Ambassador OK SOCHEAT.

Canada: Floors 6–8, Tower 2, RCBC Plaza, 6819 Ayala Ave, Makati City, 1200 Metro Manila; tel. (2) 8579000; fax (2) 8431082; e-mail manil@dfait-maeci.gc.ca; internet www.dfait-maeci.gc.ca/manila; Ambassador PETER SUTHERLAND.

Chile: 17th Floor, Liberty Center, 104 H. V. de la Costa St, cnr Leviste St, Salcedo Village, Makati City, 1227 Metro Manila; tel. (2) 8433461; fax (2) 8431976; e-mail echileph@meridiantelekoms.net; Ambassador JORGE MONTERO.

China, People's Republic: 4896 Pasay Rd, Dasmariñas Village, Makati City, Metro Manila; tel. (2) 8443148; fax (2) 8452465; e-mail emb-chn@pacific.net.ph; internet www.china-embassy.org.ph; Ambassador LI JINJUN.

Colombia: Aurora Tower, 18th Floor, Araneta Center, Quezon City, Metro Manila; tel. (2) 9113101; fax (2) 9112846; Chargé d'affaires a.i. STELLA MÁRQUEZ DE ARANETA.

Cuba: 101 Aguirre St, cnr Trasierra St, Cacho-Gonzales Bldg Penthouse, Legaspi Village, Makati City, Metro Manila; tel. (2) 8171192; fax (2) 8164094; Ambassador JORGE REY JIMÉNEZ.

Czech Republic: 30th Floor, Rufino Pacific Tower, Ayala Ave, cnr V. A. Rufino St, Makati City, Metro Manila; tel. (2) 8111155; fax (2) 8111020; e-mail manila@embassy.mzv.cz; internet www.mzv.cz/wwo/?zu=manila; Ambassador JAROSLAV LUDVA.

Egypt: 2229 Paraiso St, cnr Banyan St, Dasmariñas Village, Makati City, Metro Manila; tel. (2) 8439232; fax (2) 8439239; Ambassador SABER ABDEL KADER MANSOUR.

Finland: 21st Floor, BPI Buendia Center, Sen. Gil J. Puyat Ave, Makati City, Metro Manila; tel. (2) 8915011; fax (2) 8914106; e-mail sanomat.mni@formin.fi; internet www.finlandembassy.ph; Ambassador RITTA RESCH.

France: Pacific Star Bldg, 16th Floor, Makati Ave, cnr Sen. Gil J. Puyat Ave, 1200 Makati City, Metro Manila; tel. (2) 8576900; fax (2) 8576951; e-mail consulat@ambafrance-ph.org; internet www .ambafrance-ph.org; Ambassador RENÉE VEYRET.

Germany: 25th Floor, Tower 2, RCBC Plaza, 6819 Ayala Ave, Makati City, Metro Manila; tel. (2) 7023000; fax (2) 7023015; e-mail deboma@pldtdsl.net; internet www.manila.diplo.de; Ambassador Dr AXEL WEISHAUPT.

Holy See: 2140 Taft Ave, POB 3364, 1099 Metro Manila (Apostolic Nunciature); tel. (2) 5210306; fax (2) 5211235; e-mail nuntiusp@info .com.ph; Apostolic Nuncio Most Rev. ANTONIO FRANCO (Titular Archbishop of Gallese).

India: 2190 Paraiso St, Dasmariñas Village, POB 2123, Makati City, Metro Manila; tel. (2) 8430101; fax (2) 8158151; e-mail amb@ embindia.org.ph; internet www.embindia.org.ph; Ambassador PINAK RANJAN CHAKRAVARTY.

Indonesia: 185 Salcedo St, Legaspi Village, Makati City, Metro Manila; tel. (2) 8925061; fax (2) 8925878; e-mail bidpen_manila@ yahoo.com; internet www.kbrimanila.org.ph; Chargé d'affaires a.i. ALEXANDER LATURIUW.

Iran: 2224 Paraiso St, cnr Pasay Rd, Dasmariñas Village, Makati City, Metro Manila; tel. (2) 8884757; fax (2) 8884777; e-mail ambassador@iranembassy.org.ph; Ambassador JALAL KALANTARI.

Israel: Trafalgar Plaza, 23rd Floor, 105 H. V. de la Costa St, Salcedo Village, Makati City, 1227 Metro Manila; tel. (2) 8925330; fax (2)

THE PHILIPPINES

8941027; e-mail info@manila.mfa.gov.il; internet manila.mfa.gov.il; Ambassador YEHOSHUA SAGI.

Italy: Zeta Bldg, 6th Floor, 191 Salcedo St, Legaspi Village, Makati City, Metro Manila; tel. (2) 8924531; fax (2) 8171436; e-mail ambitaly@iname.com; Ambassador UMBERTO COLESANTI.

Japan: 2627 Roxas Blvd, Pasay City, 1300 Metro Manila; tel. (2) 5515710; fax (2) 5515780; e-mail info@embjapan.ph; internet www.ph.emb-japan.go.jp; Ambassador RYUICHIRO YAMAZAKI.

Korea, Republic: Pacific Star Bldg, 10th Floor, Sen. Gil J. Puyat Ave, cnr Makati Ave, Makati City, 1226 Metro Manila; tel. (2) 8116139; fax (2) 8116148; Ambassador SHIN GIL SOU.

Kuwait: 1230 Acacia Rd, Dasmariñas Village, Makati City, Metro Manila; tel. (2) 8876880; fax (2) 8876666; Ambassador BADER NASSER AL-HOUTI.

Laos: 34 Lapu-Lapu St, Magallanes Village, Makati City, Metro Manila; tel. and fax (2) 8525759; Ambassador PHIANE PHILAKONE.

Libya: 1644 Dasmarinas St, cnr Mabolo St, Dasmariñas Village, Makati City, Metro Manila; tel. (2) 8177331; fax (2) 8177337; e-mail lpbmanila@skynet.net; Ambassador SALEM M. ADAM.

Malaysia: 107 Tordesillas St, Salcedo Village, Makati City, 1200 Metro Manila; tel. (2) 8174581; fax (2) 8163158; e-mail mwmanila@indanet.com; Ambassador ISKANDAR SARUDIN.

Malta: 6th Floor, Cattleya Condominium, 235 Salcedo St, Legaspi Village, Makati City, Metro Manila; tel. (2) 8171095; fax (2) 8171089; e-mail syquia@intlaw.com.ph; Ambassador SAVIOUR P. GAUCI.

Mexico: 2157 Paraiso St, Dasmariñas Village, Makati City, Metro Manila; tel. (2) 8122211; fax (2) 8929824; e-mail embmexfil@info.com.ph; Ambassador ERENDIRA ARACELI PAZ CAMPOS.

Myanmar: Gervasia Corporation Center, 8th Floor, 152 Amorsolo St, Legaspi Village, Makati City, Metro Manila; tel. (2) 8931944; fax (2) 8928866; e-mail myanila@mydestiny.net; Ambassador U THAUNG TUN.

Netherlands: King's Court Bldg, 9th Floor, 2129 Chino Roces Ave, POB 2448, Makati City, 1264 Metro Manila; tel. (2) 8125981; fax (2) 8154579; e-mail man@minbuza.nl; internet www.netherlandsembassy.ph; Ambassador ROBERT VORNIS.

New Zealand: BPI Buendia Center, 23rd Floor, Sen. Gil J. Puyat Ave, POB 3228, MCPO, Makati City, Metro Manila; tel. (2) 8915358; fax (2) 8915353; e-mail nzmanila@nxdsl.com.ph; Ambassador ROB MOORE-JONES.

Nigeria: 2211 Paraiso St, Dasmariñas Village, Makati City, 1221 Metro Manila; POB 3174, MCPO, Makati City, 1271 Metro Manila; tel. (2) 8439866; fax (2) 8439867; e-mail embnigmanila@pacific.net.ph; Ambassador SAM AZUBUIKE DADA OLISA.

Norway: Petron Mega Plaza Bldg, 21st Floor, 358 Sen. Gil J. Puyat Ave, Makati City, 1209 Metro Manila; tel. (2) 8863245; fax (2) 8863384; e-mail emb.manila@mfa.no; internet www.norway.ph; Ambassador STALE RISA.

Pakistan: Alexander House, 6th Floor, 132 Amorsolo St, Legaspi Village, Makati City, Metro Manila; tel. (2) 8172776; fax (2) 8400229; e-mail pakrepmanila@yahoo.com; Ambassador IFTIKHAR HUSSAIN KAZMI.

Palau: Splendido Gardens, 146 H. V. de la Costa St, cnr Alfaro St, Makati City, Metro Manila; tel. (2) 8130799; e-mail rop_piembassy@yahoo.com; Ambassador ANITA RECHIREI SUTA.

Panama: 10th Floor, MARC 2000 Tower, 1973 Taft Ave and San Andres St, cnr Quirino Ave, Malate, 1004 Metro Manila; tel. (2) 5212790; fax (2) 5215755; e-mail panaembassy@i-manila.com.ph; Ambassador JUAN CARLOS ESCALONA AVILA.

Papua New Guinea: 3rd Floor, Corinthian Plaza Condominium Bldg, cnr Paseo de Roxas and Gamboa St, Makati City, Metro Manila; tel. (2) 8113465; fax (2) 8113466; e-mail kundumnl@pngembmnl.com.ph; Ambassador DAMIEN DOMINIC GAMIANDU.

Peru: Unit 1604, 16th Floor, Antel Corporate Centre, 139 Valero St, Salcedo Village, Makati City, Metro Manila; tel. (2) 8138731; fax (2) 8929831; e-mail leprumanila@embassyperu.com.ph; Ambassador JORGE CHAVEZ SOTO.

Portugal: 17th Floor, Units C and D, Trafalgar Plaza, 105 H. V. de la Costa St, Salcedo Village, Makati City, Metro Manila; tel. (2) 8483789; fax (2) 8483791; Ambassador JOÃO CAETANO DA SILVA.

Qatar: 2056 Lumbang St, Dasmariñas Village, Makati City, Metro Manila; tel. (2) 8874944; fax (2) 8876406; Ambassador IBRAHIM ABDULRAHMAN AL-MEGHAISEEB.

Romania: 1216 Acacia Rd, Dasmariñas Village, Makati City, Metro Manila; tel. (2) 8439014; fax (2) 8439063; e-mail amaro@skynet.net; Ambassador RADU HOMESCU.

Russia: 1245 Acacia Rd, Dasmariñas Village, Makati City, Metro Manila; tel. (2) 8930190; fax (2) 8109614; e-mail RusEmb@i-manila.com.ph; Ambassador ANATOLY NEBOGATOV.

Saudi Arabia: Saudi Embassy Bldg, 389 Sen. Gil J. Puyat Ave Ext., Makati City, Metro Manila; tel. (2) 8909735; fax (2) 8953493; e-mail phemb@mofa.gov.sa; Ambassador MOHAMMAD AMEEN WALI.

Singapore: Enterprise Center, Tower I, 35th Floor, 6766 Ayala Ave, cnr Paseo de Roxas, Makati City, Metro Manila; tel. (2) 7512345; fax (2) 7512346; Ambassador LIM KHENG HUA.

Spain: ACT Tower, 5th Floor, 135 Sen. Gil J. Puyat Ave, Makati City, 1200 Metro Manila; tel. (2) 8183561; fax (2) 8102885; e-mail embesphh@mail.mae.es; Ambassador IGNACIO SAGAZ TEMPRANO.

Sri Lanka: 2260 Avocado Ave, Dasmariñas Village, Makati City, Metro Manila; tel. and fax (2) 8439813; Ambassador ARIYA BANDARA REKAWA.

Sweden: POB 2322, MCPO 1263, Makati City, Metro Manila; tel. (2) 8191951; fax (2) 8153002; e-mail ambassaden.manila@foreign.ministry.se; internet www.swedenabroad.com/manila; Ambassador ANNIKA MARKOVIC.

Switzerland: Equitable Bank Tower, 24th Floor, 8751 Paseo de Roxas, Makati City, 1226 Metro Manila; tel. (2) 7579000; fax (2) 7573718; e-mail vertretung@man.rep.admin.ch; Ambassador LISE FAVRE.

Thailand: 107 Rada St, Legaspi Village, Makati City, 1229 Metro Manila; tel. (2) 8154220; fax (2) 8154221; e-mail thaimnl@pacific.net.ph; Ambassador ASHA DVITIYANANDA.

Turkey: 2268 Paraiso St, Dasmariñas Village, Makati City, Metro Manila; tel. (2) 8439705; fax (2) 8439702; Ambassador TANJU SUMER.

United Arab Emirates: Renaissance Bldg, 2nd Floor, 215 Sakedo St, Legaspi Village, Makati City, Metro Manila; tel. (2) 8173906; fax (2) 8183577; Ambassador MOHAMMED EBRAHIM ABDULLAH AL-JOWAID.

United Kingdom: Locsin Bldg, 15th–17th Floors, 6752 Ayala Ave, cnr Makati Ave, Makati City, 1226 Metro Manila; tel. (2) 8167116; fax (2) 8197206; e-mail uk@info.com.ph; internet www.britishembassy.gov.uk/philippines; Ambassador PETER BECKINGHAM.

USA: 1201 Roxas Blvd, 1000 Metro Manila; tel. (2) 5286300; fax (2) 5223242; e-mail manila1@pd.state.gov; internet manila.usembassy.gov; Ambassador KRISTIE A. KENNEY.

Venezuela: Unit 17A, Multinational Bancorporation Center, 6805 Ayala Ave, Makati City, Metro Manila 1226; tel. (2) 8452841; fax (2) 8452866; e-mail venezemb@info.com.ph; Chargé d'affaires a.i. JOSÉ CLAVIJO.

Viet Nam: 670 Pablo Ocampo St, Malate, Metro Manila; tel. (2) 5252837; fax (2) 5260472; e-mail sqvnplp@qinet.net; Ambassador DINH TICH.

Judicial System

The February 1987 Constitution provides for the establishment of a Supreme Court comprising a Chief Justice and 14 Associate Justices; the Court may sit *en banc* or in divisions of three, five or seven members. Justices of the Supreme Court are appointed by the President from a list of a minimum of three nominees prepared by a Judicial and Bar Council. Other courts comprise the Court of Appeals, Regional Trial Courts, Metropolitan Trial Courts, Municipal Courts in Cities, Municipal Courts and Municipal Circuit Trial Courts. There is also a special court for trying cases of corruption (the Sandiganbayan). The Office of the Ombudsman (Tanodbayan) investigates complaints concerning the actions of public officials.

SUPREME COURT
Taft Ave, cnr Padre Faura St, Ermita, 1000 Metro Manila; tel. (2) 5268123; e-mail infos@supremecourt.gov.ph; internet www.supremecourt.gov.ph.

Chief Justice: ARTEMIO V. PANGANIBAN.

COURT OF APPEALS
Consists of a Presiding Justice and 68 Associate Justices.

Presiding Justice: CANCIO GARCIA.

Islamic *Shari'a* courts were established in the southern Philippines in July 1985 under a presidential decree of February 1977. They are presided over by three district magistrates and six circuit judges.

Religion

In 1991 94.2% of the population were Christians: 84.1% were Roman Catholics, 6.2% belonged to the Philippine Independent Church (Aglipayan) and 3.9% were Protestants. There is an Islamic community, and an estimated 43,000 Buddhists. Animists and persons professing no religion number approximately 400,000.

THE PHILIPPINES

CHRISTIANITY

Sangguniang Pambansa ng mga Simbahan sa Pilipinas (National Council of Churches in the Philippines): 879 Epifanio de los Santos Ave, Diliman, Quezon City, Metro Manila; tel. (2) 9288636; fax (2) 9267076; e-mail nccp-ga@philonline.com; f. 1963; 11 mem. churches, 10 assoc. mems; publishes NCCP news magazine quarterly and TUGON periodically; Gen. Sec. SHARON ROSE JOY RUIZ-DUREMDES.

The Roman Catholic Church

For ecclesiastical purposes, the Philippines comprises 16 archdioceses, 56 dioceses, six territorial prelatures and seven apostolic vicariates. At 31 December 2003 approximately 83.0% of the population were adherents.

Catholic Bishops' Conference of the Philippines (CBCP) 470 General Luna St, Intramuros, 1076 Metro Manila; tel. (2) 5274141; fax (2) 5279634; e-mail cbcpmedia@cbcpworld.com; internet www.cbcponline.org.

f. 1945; statutes approved 1952; Pres. Most Rev. ANGEL R. LAGDAMEO (Archbishop of Jaro).

Archbishop of Caceres: Most Rev. LEONARDO Z. LEGASPI, Archbishop's House, Elias Angeles St, POB 6085, 4400 Naga City; tel. (54) 4738483; fax (54) 4732800.

Archbishop of Cagayan de Oro: Most Rev. JESUS B. TUQUIB, Archbishop's Residence, POB 113, 9000 Misamis Oriental, Cagayan de Oro City; tel. (8822) 8571357; fax (8822) 726304; e-mail orochan@cdo.weblinq.com.

Archbishop of Capiz: Most Rev. ONESIMO C. GORDONCILLO, Chancery Office, POB 44, 5800 Roxas City; tel. (36) 6215595; fax (36) 6211053.

Archbishop of Cebu: Cardinal RICARDO J. VIDAL, Archbishop's Residence, cnr P. Gomez St and P. Burgos St, POB 52, 6000 Cebu City; tel. (32) 2541861; fax (32) 2530123; e-mail adelito@skynet.net.

Archbishop of Cotabato: Most Rev. ORLANDO B. QUEVEDO, Archbishop's Residence, 154 Sinsuat Ave, POB 186, 9600 Cotabato City; tel. (64) 4212918; fax (64) 4211446.

Archbishop of Davao: Most Rev. FERNANDO R. CAPALLA, Archbishop's Residence, 247 Florentino Torres St, POB 80418, 8000 Davao City; tel. (82) 2275992; fax (82) 2279771; e-mail bishop-davao68@yahoo.com.

Archbishop of Jaro: Most Rev. ANGEL N. LAGDAMEO, Archbishop's Residence, Jaro, 5000 Iloilo City; tel. (33) 3294442; fax (33) 3293197; e-mail abpjaro@skyinet.net.

Archbishop of Lingayen-Dagupan: Most Rev. OSCAR V. CRUZ, Archbishop's House, 2400 Pangasinan, Dagupan City; tel. (75) 5235357; fax (75) 5221878; e-mail oscar@rezcom.com.

Archbishop of Lipa: Most Rev. RAMON C. ARGÜELLES, Archbishop's House, St Lorenzo Ruiz Rd, Lipa City, 4217 Batangas; tel. (43) 7562572; fax (43) 7560005; e-mail chancery@batangas.net.ph.

Archbishop of Manila: Most Rev. GAUDENCIO B. ROSALES, Arzobispado, 121 Arzobispo St, Intramuros, POB 132, 1099 Metro Manila; tel. (2) 5277631; fax (2) 5276159; e-mail rcamaoc@tri-isys.com; internet www.rcam.org.

Archbishop of Nueva Segovia: Most Rev. EDMUNDO M. ABAYA, Archbishop's House, Vigan, 2700 Ilocos Sur; tel. (77) 7222018; fax (77) 7221591.

Archbishop of Ozamis: Most Rev. JESUS A. DOSADO, Archbishop's House, POB 2760, Rizal Ave, Banadero, 7200 Ozamis City; tel. (65) 5212771; fax (65) 5211574.

Archbishop of Palo: Most Rev. PEDRO R. DEAN, Archdiocesan Chancery, Bukid Tabor, Palo, 6501 Leyte; POB 173, Tacloban City, 6500 Leyte; tel. (53) 3232213; fax (53) 3235607; e-mail rcap@mozcom.com.

Archbishop of San Fernando (Pampanga): Most Rev. PACIANO B. ANICETO, Chancery Office, San José, San Fernando, 2000 Pampanga; tel. (45) 9612819; fax (45) 9616772; e-mail rca@pamp.pworld.net.ph.

Archbishop of Tuguegarao: Most Rev. DIOSDADO A. TALAMAYAN, Archbishop's House, Rizal St, Tuguegarao, 3500 Cagayan; tel. (78) 8441663; fax (78) 8462822; e-mail dtalamayan-32@yahoo.com.

Archbishop of Zamboanga: Most Rev. CARMELO DOMINADOR F. MORELOS, Sacred Heart Center, POB 1, Justice R. T. Lim Blvd, 7000 Zamboanga City; tel. (62) 9911329; fax (62) 9932608; e-mail aofzam@jetlink.com.ph.

Other Christian Churches

Convention of Philippine Baptist Churches: POB 263, 5000 Iloilo City; tel. (33) 3290621; fax (33) 3290618; e-mail gensec@iloilo.net; f. 1935; Gen. Sec. Rev. Dr NATHANIEL M. FABULA; Pres. DONATO ENABE.

Episcopal Church in the Philippines: 275 E. Rodriguez Sr Ave, Quezon City, 1102 Metro Manila; POB 10321, Broadway Centrum, Quezon City, 1102 Metro Manila; tel. (2) 7228481; fax (2) 7211923; e-mail sitedeacon@episcopalphilippines.net; internet www.episcopalphilippines.net; f. 1901; six dioceses; Prime Bishop Most Rev. IGNACIO C. SOLIBA.

Iglesia Evangélica Metodista en las Islas Filipinas (Evangelical Methodist Church in the Philippines): Beulah Land, Iemelif Center, Greenfields 1, Subdivision, Marytown Circle, Novaliches, Quezon City, 1123 Metro Manila; tel. (2) 9356519; fax (2) 4185017; e-mail iemelifph@yahoo.com; internet www.iemelif.org; f. 1909; 40,000 mems (2003); Gen. Supt Bishop NATHANAEL P. LAZARO.

Iglesia Filipina Independiente (Philippine Independent Church): 1500 Taft Ave, Ermita, 1000 Metro Manila; tel. (2) 5237242; fax (2) 5213932; e-mail gensec@ifi.ph; internet ifi.ph; f. 1902; 34 dioceses; 6.0m. mems; Obispo Maximo (Supreme Bishop) Most Rev. TOMAS MILLAMENA.

Iglesia ni Cristo: 1 Central Ave, New Era, Quezon City, 1107 Metro Manila; tel. (2) 9814311; fax (2) 9811111; f. 1914; 2m. mems; Exec. Minister Brother ERAÑO G. MANALO.

Lutheran Church in the Philippines: 4461 Old Santa Mesa, 1008 Metro Manila; POB 507, 1099 Metro Manila; tel. (2) 7157084; fax (2) 7142395; f. 1946; Pres. Rev. EDUARDO LADLAD.

Union Church of Manila: cnr Legaspi St and Rada St, Legaspi Village, Makati City, Metro Manila; tel. (2) 8126062; fax (2) 8172386; e-mail ucmweb@unionchurch.ph; internet www.unionchurch.ph; Senior Pastor Rev. DAVID GINTER.

United Church of Christ in the Philippines: 877 Epifanio de los Santos Ave, West Triangle, Quezon City, Metro Manila; POB 718, MCPO, Ermita, 1099 Metro Manila; tel. (2) 9240215; fax (2) 9240207; e-mail uccpnaof@manila-online.net; f. 1948; 900,000 mems (1996); Gen. Sec. Rev. ELMER M. BOLOCON (Bishop).

Among other denominations active in the Philippines are the Iglesia Evangélica Unida de Cristo and the United Methodist Church.

ISLAM

Some 14 different ethnic groups profess the Islamic faith in the Philippines, and Muslims comprised 4.6% of the total population at the census of 1990. Mindanao and the Sulu and Tawi-Tawi archipelago, in the southern Philippines, are predominantly Muslim provinces, but there are 10 other such provinces, each with its own Imam, or Muslim religious leader. More than 500,000 Muslims live in the north of the country (mostly in, or near to, Manila).

Confederation of Muslim Organizations of the Philippines (CMOP): Metro Manila; Nat. Chair. JAMIL DIANALAN.

BAHÁ'Í FAITH

National Spiritual Assembly: 1070 A. Roxas St, cnr Bautista St, Singalong Subdiv., Malate, 1004 Metro Manila; POB 4323, 1099 Metro Manila; tel. (2) 5240404; fax (2) 5245918; e-mail nsaphil@skyinet.net; mems resident in 129,949 localities; Chair. GIL MARVEL TABUCANON; Sec.-Gen. VIRGINIA S. TOLEDO.

The Press

The Office of the President implements government policies on information and the media. Freedom of the press and freedom of speech are guaranteed under the 1987 Constitution.

METRO MANILA

Dailies

Abante: Monica Publishing Corpn, Rooms 301–305, BF Condominium Bldg, 3rd Floor, Solana St, cnr. A. Soriano St, Intramuros, Metro Manila; tel. (2) 5273355; fax (2) 5273382; e-mail abante@abante-tonite.com; internet www.abante.com.ph; morning; Filipino and English; Editor NICOLAS QUIJANO, Jr; circ. 417,000.

Abante Tonite: Monica Publishing Corpn, Rooms 301–305, BF Condominium Bldg, 3rd Floor, Solana St, cnr. A. Soriano St, Intramuros, Metro Manila; tel. (2) 5273355; fax (2) 5273382; e-mail tonite@abante-tonite.com; internet www.abante-tonite.com; afternoon; Filipino and English; Man. Editor NICOLAS QUIJANO, Jr; circ. 277,000.

Ang Pilipino Ngayon: 202 Railroad St, cnr 13th St, Port Area, Metro Manila; tel. (2) 401871; fax (2) 5224998; Filipino; Publr and Editor JOSE M. BUHAIN; circ. 286,452.

Balita: Liwayway Publishing Inc, 2249 China Roces Ave, Makati City, Metro Manila; tel. (2) 8193101; fax (2) 8175167; internet www.balita.org; f. 1972; morning; Filipino; Editor MARCELO S. LAGMAY; circ. 151,000.

THE PHILIPPINES

Daily Tribune: Penthouse Suites, GLC Bldg, T. M. Kalaw St, cnr A. Mabini St, Ermita, Metro Manila; tel. (2) 5215511; fax (2) 5215522; e-mail nco@tribune.net.ph; internet www.tribune.net.ph; f. 2000; English; Publr and Editor-in-Chief NINEZ CACHO-OLIVARES.

Malaya: 371 Bonifacio Drive, Port Area, 1018 Metro Manila; tel. (2) 5277651; fax (2) 5271839; e-mail opinion@malaya.com.ph; internet www.malaya.com.ph; f. 1983; English; Editor JOEY C. DE LOS REYES; circ. 175,000.

Manila Bulletin: Bulletin Publishing Corpn, cnr Muralla and Recoletos Sts, Intramuros, POB 769, Metro Manila; tel. (2) 5271519; fax (2) 5277534; e-mail bulletin@mb.com.ph; internet www.mb.com.ph; f. 1900; English; Publr EMILIO YAP; Editor BEN RODRIGUEZ; circ. 265,000.

Manila Standard: Leyland Bldg, 21st St, cnr Railroad St, Port Area, Metro Manila; tel. (2) 5278351; fax (2) 5272059; e-mail mst@manilastandardtoday.com; internet www.manilastandardtoday.com; f. 1987; morning; English; Editor-in-Chief JULLIE YAP DAZA; circ. 96,000.

Manila Times: 371A Bonifacio Drive, Port Area, Metro Manila; tel. (2) 5245664; fax (2) 5216897; e-mail newsboy1@manilatimes.net; internet www.manilatimes.net; f. 1945; morning; English; Publr and Editor-in-Chief FRED DELA ROSA.

People Tonight: Philippine Journalist Inc, Railroad St, cnr 19th and 20th Sts, Port Area, Metro Manila; tel. (2) 5278421; fax (2) 5274627; f. 1978; English and Filipino; Editor FERDIE RAMOS; circ. 500,000.

People's Bagong Taliba: Philippine Journalist Inc, Railroad St, cnr 19th and 20th Sts, Port Area, Metro Manila; tel. (2) 5278121; fax (2) 5274627; Filipino; Editor MATEO VICENCIO; circ. 229,000.

People's Journal: Philippine Journalist Inc, Railroad St, cnr 19th and 20th Sts, Port Area, Metro Manila; tel. (2) 5278421; fax (2) 5274627; English and Filipino; Editor ROSAURO ACOSTA; circ. 219,000.

Philippine Daily Inquirer: Philippine Daily Inquirer Bldg, Chico Roces Ave, cnr Mascardo St and Yague St, Pasong Tamo, Makati City, 1220 Metro Manila; tel. (2) 8978808; fax (2) 8974793; e-mail feedback@inquirer.com.ph; internet www.inquirer.com.ph; f. 1985; English; Chair. MARIXI R. PRIETO; Editor-in-Chief LETTY JIMENEZ-MAGSANOC; circ. 250,000.

Philippine Herald-Tribune: V. Esguerra II Bldg, 140 Amorsolo St, Legaspi Village, Makati City, Metro Manila; tel. (2) 853711; f. 1987; Christian-orientated; Pres. AMADA VALINO.

Philippine Star: 13th and Railroad Sts, Port Area, Metro Manila; tel. (2) 5277901; fax (2) 5276851; e-mail philippinestar@hotmail.com; internet www.philstar.com; f. 1986; Editor BOBBY DE LA CRUZ; circ. 275,000.

Tempo: Bulletin Publishing Corpn, Recoletos St, cnr Muralla St, Intramuros, Metro Manila; tel. (2) 5278121; fax (2) 5277534; internet www.tempo.com.ph; f. 1982; English and Filipino; Editor BEN RODRIGUEZ; circ. 230,000.

Today: Independent Daily News, 55 Paseo de Roxas, Makati City, 1225 Metro Manila; tel. (2) 8940644; fax (2) 8131417; e-mail today@impactnet.com; f. 1993; Editor-in-Chief TEODORO L. LOCSIN, Jr; Man. Editor LOURDES MOLINA-FERNANDEZ; circ. 106,000.

United Daily News: 812 and 818 Benavides St, Binondo, Metro Manila; tel. (2) 2447171; f. 1973; Chinese; Editor-in-Chief CHUA KEE; circ. 85,000.

Selected Periodicals

Weeklies

Banawag: Liwayway Bldg, 2249 Pasong Tamo, Makati City, Metro Manila; tel. (2) 8193101; fax (2) 8175167; f. 1934; Ilocano; Editor DIONISIO S. BULONG; circ. 42,900.

Bisaya: Liwayway Bldg, 2249 Pasong Tamo, Makati City, Metro Manila; tel. (2) 8193101; fax (2) 8175167; f. 1934; Cebu-Visayan; Editor SANTIAGO PEPITO; circ. 90,000.

Liwayway: Liwayway Bldg, 2249 Pasong Tamo, Makati City, Metro Manila; tel. (2) 8193101; fax (2) 8175167; f. 1922; Filipino; Editor RODOLFO SALANDANAN; circ. 102,400.

Panorama: Manila Bulletin Publishing Corpn, POB 769, cnr Muralla and Recoletos Sts, Intramuros, Metro Manila; tel. and fax (2) 5277509; f. 1968; English; Editor RANDY V. URLANDA; circ. 239,600.

Philippine Starweek: 13th St, cnr Railroad St, Port Area, Metro Manila; tel. (2) 5277901; fax (2) 5275819; e-mail starweek@pacific.net.ph; internet www.philstar.com; English; Publr MAXIMO V. SOLIVEN; circ. 268,000.

SELECTED REGIONAL PUBLICATIONS

The Aklan Reporter: 1227 Rizal St, Kalibo, Panay, Aklan; tel. (33) 3181; f. 1971; weekly; English and Aklanon; Editor ROMAN A. DE LA CRUZ; circ. 3,500.

Baguio Midland Courier: 16 Kisad Rd, POB 50, Baguio City; English and Ilocano; Editor SINAI C. HAMADA; circ. 6,000.

Bayanihan Weekly News: Bayanihan Publishing Co, P. Guevarra Ave, Santa Cruz, Laguna; tel. (645) 1001; f. 1966; Mon.; Filipino and English; Editor ARTHUR A. VALENOVA; circ. 1,000.

Bohol Chronicle: 56 B. Inting St, Tagbilaran City, 6300 Bohol; tel. and fax (32) 4113100; e-mail boholchronicle@gmail.com; internet www.boholchronicle.com; f. 1954; 2 a week; English and Cebuano; Editor and Publr ZOILO DEJARESCO; circ. 5,500.

The Bohol Times: 100 Gallares St, Tagbilaran City, 6300 Bohol; tel. (38) 4112961; fax (38) 4112656; e-mail boholtimes@yahoo.com; internet www.boholtimes.com; Publr Dr LILIA A. BALITE; Editor-in-Chief ATTY SALVADOR D. DIPUTADO.

The Kapawa News: L. V. Moles and Jose Abad Santos Sts, Tangub, POB 365, 6100 Bacolod City; tel. and fax (34) 4441941; e-mail LM-Kapawa@eudoramail.com; f. 1966; weekly; Sat.; Hiligaynon and English; Editor NATALIO V. SITJAR; circ. 2,000.

Mindanao Star: 44 Kolambagohan-Capistrano St, Cagayan de Oro City; weekly; Editor ROMULFO SABAMAL; circ. 3,500.

Mindanao Times: UMBN Bldg, Ponciano Reyes St, Davao City, Mindanao; tel. 2273252; e-mail timesmen@mozcom.com; internet www.mindanaotimes.com.ph; daily; Publr JOSEFINA SAN PEDRO (acting); Editor-in-Chief VIC SUMALINOG; circ. 5,000.

Pagadian Times: 0519 Alano St, Pagadian City, 7016; tel. (62) 2151504; fax (62) 2141721; e-mail pedelu@lasialink.com.ph; f. 1969; weekly; English; Publr PEDRO G. LU; Editor REMAI ALEJADS; circ. 7,000.

Palihan: Diversion Rd, cnr Sanciangco St, Cabanatuan City, Luzon; f. 1966; weekly; Filipino; Editor and Publr NONOY M. JARLEGO; circ. 5,000.

Sorsogon Today: 2903 Burgos St, East District, 4700 Sorsogon; tel. and fax (56) 4215306; fax (56) 2111340; e-mail sortoday@yahoo.com; f. 1977; weekly; Publr and CEO MARCOS E. PARAS, Jr; circ. 2,250.

Sun Star Cebu: Sun Star Bldg, P. del Rosario St, Cebu City; tel. (32) 2546100; fax (32) 2537256; e-mail sunnex@sunstar.com.ph; internet www.sunstar.com.ph/cebu; f. 1982; daily; English; Editor-in-Chief ATTY PACHICO A. SEARES; Gen. Man. ORLANDO P. CARVAJAL.

The Tribune: Maharlika Highway, 2301 Cabanatuan City, Luzon; f. 1960; weekly; English and Filipino; Editor and Publr ORLANDO M. JARLEGO; circ. 8,000.

The Valley Times: Daang Maharlika, San Felipe, Ilagan, Isabela; f. 1962; weekly; English; Editor AUREA A. DE LA CRUZ; circ. 4,500.

The Visayan Tribune: 826 Iznart St, Iloilo City; tel. (33) 75760; f. 1959; weekly; Tue.; English; Editor HERBERT L. VEGO; circ. 5,000.

The Voice of Islam: Davao City; tel. (82) 81368; f. 1973; monthly; English and Arabic; official Islamic news journal; Editor and Publr NASHIR MUHAMMAD AL'RASHID AL HAJJ.

The Weekly Negros Gazette: Broce St, San Carlos City, 6033 Negros Occidental; f. 1956; weekly; Editor NESTORIO L. LAYUMAS, Sr; circ. 5,000.

NEWS AGENCIES

Philippines News Agency: PIA Bldg, 2nd Floor, Visayas Ave, Diliman, Quezon City, Metro Manila; tel. (2) 9206551; fax (2) 9206566; e-mail bert.panganiban@gmail.com; internet www.pna.gov.ph; f. 1973; Gen. Man. VITTORIO V. VITUG; Exec. Editor RUBEN B. CAL.

Foreign Bureaux

Agence France-Presse (AFP): Kings Court Bldg 2, 5th Floor, Pasong Tamo, cnr de la Rosa St, Makati City, Metro Manila; tel. (2) 8112028; fax (2) 8112664; Bureau Chief MONICA EGOY.

Agencia EFE (Spain): Unit 1006, 88 Corporate Center Bldg, 141 Sedeño St, cnr Valero St, Salcedo Village, Makati City, 1227 Metro Manila; tel. (2) 8431986; fax (2) 8431973; e-mail manila@efe.com; Bureau Chief ESTHER REBOLLO.

Associated Press (AP) (USA): S&L Bldg, 3rd Floor, 1500 Roxas Blvd, Ermita, 1000 Metro Manila; tel. (2) 5259217; fax (2) 5212430; Bureau Chief DAVID THURBER.

Deutsche Presse Agentur (dpa) (Germany): Physicians Tower Bldg, 533 United Nations Ave, Ermita 1000, Metro Manila; tel. (2) 5221919; fax (2) 5221447; Representative GIRLIE LINAO.

Jiji Tsushin (Jiji Press) (Japan): Legaspi Tower, Suite 21, 3rd Floor, 2600 Roxas Blvd, Metro Manila; tel. (2) 5211472; fax (2) 5211474; Correspondent IPPEI MIYASAKA.

Kyodo News Service (Japan): Pacific Star Bldg, 4th Floor, Makati Ave, cnr Sen. Gil J. Puyat Ave, Makati City, Metro Manila; tel. (2) 8133072; fax (2) 8133914; Correspondent KIMIO OKI.

Reuters (United Kingdom): L.V. Locsin Bldg, 10th Floor, Ayala Ave, cnr Makati Ave, Makati City, 1226 Metro Manila; tel. (2) 8418900; fax (2) 8176267; Country Man. RAJU GOPALAKRISHNAN.

United Press International (UPI) (USA): Manila Pavilion Hotel, Room 526c, United Nations Ave, Ermita, 1000 Metro Manila; tel. (2) 5212051; fax (2) 5212074; Bureau Chief MICHAEL DI CICCO.

Xinhua (New China) News Agency (People's Republic of China): 705B Gotesco Twin Towers, 1129 Concepcion St, Ermita, Metro Manila; tel. (2) 5271404; fax (2) 5271410; Chief Correspondent CHEN HEGAO.

PRESS ASSOCIATION

National Press Club of the Philippines: National Press Club Bldg, Magallanes Drive, Intramuros, 1002 Metro Manila; tel. (2) 3010521; fax (2) 3010522; e-mail ad-nationalpressclub@yahoo.com; f. 1952; Pres. ANTONIO ANTONIO; Vice-Pres. ALICE H. REYES; 1,405 mems.

Publishers

Abiva Publishing House Inc: Abiva Bldg, 851 Gregorio Araneta Ave, Quezon City, 1113 Metro Manila; tel. (2) 7120245; fax (2) 7320308; e-mail mmrabiva@i-manila.com.ph; internet www.abiva.com.ph; f. 1937; reference and textbooks; Pres. LUIS Q. ABIVA, Jr.

Ateneo de Manila University Press: Bellarmine Bldg, Ateneo de Manila University, Katipunan Ave, Loyola Heights, Quezon City, Metro Manila; tel. (2) 4265984; fax (2) 4265909; e-mail unipress@admu.edu.ph; internet www.ateneopress.org; f. 1972; literary, textbooks, humanities, social sciences, reference books on the Philippines; Dir MARICOR E. BAYTION.

Bookman, Inc: 373 Quezon Ave, Quezon City, 1114 Metro Manila; tel. (2) 7124818; fax (2) 7124843; e-mail bookman@info.com.ph; f. 1945; textbooks, reference, educational; Pres. LINA PICACHE-ENRIQUEZ; Exec. Vice-Pres. MARIETTA PICACHE-MARTINEZ.

Capitol Publishing House, Inc: 13 Team Pacific Bldg, Jose C. Cruz St, cnr F. Legaspi St, Barrio Ugong, Pasig City, Metro Manila; tel. (2) 6712662; fax (2) 6712664; e-mail cacho@mozcom.com; f. 1947; Gen. Man. MANUEL L. ATIENZA.

Heritage Publishing House: 33 4th Ave, cnr Main Ave, Cubao, Quezon City, POB 3667, Metro Manila; tel. (2) 7248114; fax (2) 6471393; e-mail heritage@iconn.com.ph; art, anthropology, history, political science; Pres. MARIO R. ALCANTARA; Man. Dir RICARDO S. SANCHEZ.

The Lawyers' Co-operative Publishing Co Inc: 1071 Del Pan St, Makati City, 1206 Metro Manila; tel. (2) 5634073; fax (2) 5642021; e-mail lawbooks@info.com.ph; f. 1908; law, educational; Pres. ELSA K. ELMA.

Liwayway Publishing Inc: 2249 Chino Roces Ave, Makati City, Metro Manila; tel. (2) 8193101; fax (2) 8175167; magazines and newspapers; Pres. RENE G. ESPINA; Chair. DIONISIO S. BULONG.

Mutual Books Inc: 429 Shaw Blvd, Mandaluyong City, Metro Manila; tel. (2) 7257538; fax (2) 7213056; f. 1959; textbooks on accounting, management and economics, computers and mathematics; Pres. ALFREDO S. NICDAO, Jr.

Reyes Publishing Inc: Mariwasa Bldg, 4th Floor, 717 Aurora Blvd, Quezon City, 1112 Metro Manila; tel. (2) 7221827; fax (2) 7218782; e-mail reyespub@skyinet.net; f. 1964; art, history and culture; Pres. LOUIE REYES.

SIBS Publishing House Inc: Phoenix Bldg, 927 Quezon Ave, Quezon City, Metro Manila; tel. (2) 3764041; fax (2) 3764034; e-mail sibsbook@info.com.ph; internet www.sibs.com.ph; f. 1996; science, language, religion, literature and history textbooks; Pres. CARMEN MIMETTE M. SIBAL.

Sinag-Tala Publishers Inc: GMA Lou-Bel Plaza, 6th Floor, Chino Roces Ave, cnr Bagtikan St, San Antonio Village, Makati City, 1203 Metro Manila; tel. (2) 8971162; fax (2) 8969626; e-mail stpi@info.com.ph; internet www.sinagtala.com; f. 1972; educational textbooks; business, professional and religious books; Man. Dir LUIS A. USON.

University of the Philippines Press: Epifanio de los Santos St, U. P. Campus, Diliman, Quezon City, 1101 Metro Manila; tel. (2) 9252930; fax (2) 9282558; e-mail mricana@eee.upd.edu.ph; internet www.upd.edu.ph/~uppress; f. 1965; literature, history, political science, sociology, cultural studies, economics, anthropology, mathematics; Dir MARIA LUISA T. CAMAGAY.

Vibal Publishing House Inc: 1253 G. Araneta Ave, cnr Maria Clara St, Talayan, Quezon City, Metro Manila; tel. (2) 7122722; fax (2) 7118852; e-mail inquire@vibalpublishing.com; internet www.vibalpublishing.com; f. 1955; linguistics, social sciences, mathematics, religion; Pres. and Publr ESTHER A. VIBAL.

PUBLISHERS' ASSOCIATIONS

Philippine Educational Publishers' Asscn: 84 P. Florentino St, Quezon City, 1104 Metro Manila; tel. (2) 7402698; fax (2) 7115702; e-mail dbuhain@pldtdsl.net; Pres. DOMINADOR D. BUHAIN.

Publishers' Association of the Philippines Inc: 4th Floor, Dominga Bldg, 2113 Pasong Tamo, cnr de la Rosa St, Makati City, Metro Manila; tel. (2) 8191215; fax (2) 8931690; f. 1974; mems comprise all newspaper, magazine and book publrs in the Philippines; Pres. KERIMA P. TUVERA; Exec. Dir ROBERTO M. MENDOZA.

Broadcasting and Communications

TELECOMMUNICATIONS

National Telecommunications Commission (NTC): NTC Bldg, BIR Rd, East Triangle, Diliman, Quezon City, 1104 Metro Manila; tel. (2) 9267722; fax (2) 9217128; e-mail ntc@ntc.gov.ph; internet www.ntc.gov.ph; f. 1979; supervises and controls all private and public telecommunications services; Commr RONALD OLIVAR SOLIS.

BayanTel: BayanTel Corporate Center, Maginhawa St, cnr Malingap St, Teacher's Village East, Quezon City, 1101 Metro Manila; tel. (2) 4493000; fax (2) 4492174; e-mail bayanserve@bayantel.com.ph; internet www.bayantel.com.ph; 359,000 fixed lines (1999); Pres. and CEO EUGENIO L. LOPEZ, III.

Bell Telecommunications Philippines (BellTel): Pacific Star Bldg, 3rd and 4th Floors, Sen. Gil J. Puyat Ave, cnr Makati Ave, Makati City, Metro Manila; tel. (2) 8400808; fax (2) 8915618; e-mail info@belltel.ph; internet www.belltel.ph; f. 1997; Pres. EDRAGDO REYES.

Capitol Wireless Inc: Dolmar Gold Tower, 6th Floor, 107 Carlos Palanca, Jr, St, Legaspi Village, Makati City, Metro Manila; tel. (2) 8159961; fax (2) 8941141; Pres. EPITACIO R. MARQUEZ.

Digital Telecommunications Philippines Inc (DIGITEL): 110 Eulogio Rodriguez, Jr, Ave, Bagumbayan, Quezon City, 1110 Metro Manila; tel. and fax (2) 6330000; e-mail support@digitelone.com; internet www.digitelone.com; provision of fixed line telecommunications services; 484,036 fixed lines (1998); Chief Exec. RICARDO J. ROMULO; Pres. JOHN GOKONGWEI.

Domestic Satellite Philippines Inc (DOMSAT): Solid House Bldg, 4th Floor, 2285 Pasong Tamo Ext., Makati City, 1231 Metro Manila; tel. (2) 8105917; fax (2) 8671677; Pres. SIEGFRED MISON.

Globe Telecom (GMCR) Inc: Globe Telecom Plaza, 57th Floor, Pioneer St, cnr Madison St, 1552 Mandaluyong City, Metro Manila; tel. (2) 7302701; fax (2) 7302586; e-mail custhelp@globetel.com.ph; internet www.globe.com.ph; 700,000 fixed and mobile telephone subscribers (1999); Pres. and CEO GERARDO C. ABLAZA, Jr.

Philippine Communications Satellite Corpn (PhilcomSat): 12th Floor, Telecoms Plaza, 316 Sen. Gil J. Puyat Ave, Makati City, Metro Manila; tel. (2) 8158406; fax (2) 8159287; Pres. MANUEL H. NIETO.

Philippine Global Communications, Inc (PhilCom): 8755 Paseo de Roxas, Makati City, 1259 Metro Manila; tel. (2) 8162851; fax (2) 8162872; e-mail webmaster@philcom.com; internet www.philcom.com; Chair. WILLY N. OCIER; Pres. and CEO VICENTE J. JAYME, Jr.

Philippine Long Distance Telephone Co: Ramon Cojuangco Bldg, Makati Ave, POB 2148, Makati City, Metro Manila; tel. (2) 8168883; fax (2) 8446654; e-mail media@pldt.com.ph; internet www.pldt.com.ph; f. 1928; monopoly on overseas telephone service until 1989; retains 94% of Philippine telephone traffic; 2,516,748 fixed lines (1998); Chair. MANUEL V. PANGILINAN; Pres. and CEO NAPOLEON L. NAZARENO.

Smart Communications, Inc (SCI): SMART Tower, 6799 Ayala Ave, Makati City, 1226 Metro Manila; tel. (2) 8881111; fax (2) 8488830; e-mail customercare@smart.com.ph; internet www.smart.com.ph; 20.8m. subscribers (2005); Pres. and CEO NAPOLEON L. NAZARENO.

Pilipino Telephone Corpn (Piltel): SMART Tower, 25th Floor, 6799 Ayala Ave, Makati City, 1200 Metro Manila; tel. (2) 8913888; fax (2) 8171121; major cellular telephone provider; 400,000 subscribers (1999); Chair. MANUEL V. PANGILINAN; Pres. and CEO NAPOLEON L. NAZARENO.

BROADCASTING

Radio

Banahaw Broadcasting Corpn: Broadcast City, Capitol Hills, Diliman, Quezon City, 3005 Metro Manila; tel. (2) 9329949; fax (2) 9318751; 14 stations; Station Man. BETTY LIVIOCO.

Bureau of Broadcast Services (BBS) (Philippine Broadcasting Service): Office of the Press Sec., Philippine Information Agency Bldg, 4th Floor, Visayas Ave, Diliman, Quezon City, 1100 Metro Manila; tel. (2) 9203931; fax (2) 9212520; e-mail mpangilinan@pbs.ops.gov.ph; internet www.pbs.gov.ph; f. 1952 as Philippine Broadcasting Service; govt-operated; 32 radio stations; Dir RAFAEL DANTE A. CRUZ.

THE PHILIPPINES

Cebu Broadcasting Co: c/o Manila Broadcasting Co, Philippine Information Agency Bldg, 4th Floor, Visayas Ave, Quezon City, 1100 Metro Manila; tel. (2) 9203931; fax (2) 9242745; Chair. HADRIAN ARROYO.

Far East Broadcasting Co Inc: POB 1, Valenzuela, 0560 Metro Manila; 62 Karuhatan Rd, Karuhatan, Valenzuela City, 1441 Metro Manila; tel. (2) 2921152; fax (2) 2925790; e-mail info@febc.org.ph; internet www.febc.org.ph; f. 1948; 18 stations; operates a classical music station, eight domestic stations and an overseas service in 64 languages throughout Asia; Pres. CARLOS L. PEÑA.

Filipinas Broadcasting Network: Legaspi Towers 200, Room 306, Paseo de Roxas, Makati City, Metro Manila; tel. (2) 8176133; fax (2) 8177135; Gen. Man. DIANA C. GOZUM.

GMA Network Inc: GMA Network Center, EDSA cnr Timog Ave, Diliman, Quezon City, 1103 Metro Manila; tel. and fax (2) 9287021; e-mail yourgmafamily@gmanetwork.com; internet www.igma.tv; f. 1950; fmrly Republic Broadcasting System Inc; transmits nation-wide through 44 television stations; Chair., Pres. and CEO FELIPE L. GOZON; Exec. Vice-Pres. GILBERTO R. DUAVIT, Jr.

Manila Broadcasting Co: Philippine Information Agency Bldg, 4th Floor, Visayas Ave, Quezon City, 1100 Metro Manila; tel. (2) 9203931; fax (2) 9242745; internet www.dagupan.com/dwidfm/mbc.htm; f. 1946; affiliate of Philippine Broadcasting Service; 10 stations; Pres. RUPERTO NICDAO, Jr; Gen. Man. EDUARDO L. MONTILLA.

Nation Broadcasting Corpn: NBC Tower, Epifanio de los Santos Ave, Guadelupe, Makati City, 1200 Metro Manila; tel. (2) 8195673; fax (2) 8197234; e-mail radio@philexport.com; internet philexport.org/philradio/network/nbchome.htm; f. 1963; 31 stations; Pres. FRANCIS LUMEN.

Newsounds Broadcasting Network Inc: Florete Bldg, Ground Floor, 2406 Nobel, cnr Edison St, Makati City, 3117 Metro Manila; tel. (2) 8430116; fax (2) 8173631; 10 stations; Gen. Man. E. BILLONES; Office Man. HERMAN BASBANO.

Pacific Broadcasting System: c/o Manila Broadcasting Co, Philippine Information Agency Bldg, 4th Floor, Visayas Ave, Quezon City, 1100 Metro Manila; tel. (2) 9203931; fax (2) 9242745; Pres. RUPERTO NICDAO, Jr; Vice-Pres. RODOLFO ARCE.

PBN Broadcasting Network: Ersan Bldg, 3rd Floor, 32 Quezon Ave, Quezon City, Metro Manila; tel. (2) 7325424; fax (2) 7438162; e-mail pbn@philonline.com.ph; Pres. JORGE D. BAYONA.

Philippine Federation of Catholic Broadcasters: 2307 Pedro Gil, Santa Ana, POB 3169, Metro Manila; tel. (2) 5644518; fax (2) 5637316; e-mail nomm@surfshop.net.ph; 48 radio stations and four TV channels; Pres. Fr FRANCIS LUCAS.

Radio Philippines Network, Inc: Broadcast City, Capitol Hills, Diliman, Quezon City, Metro Manila; tel. (2) 9318627; fax (2) 984322; f. 1969; seven TV stations, 14 radio stations; Pres. EDGAR SAN LUIS; Gen. Man. FELIPE G. MEDINA.

Radio Veritas Asia: Buick St, Fairview Park, POB 2642, Quezon City, Metro Manila; tel. (2) 9390011; fax (2) 9381940; e-mail rveritas-asia@rveritas-asia.org; internet www.rveritas-asia.org; f. 1969; Catholic short-wave station, broadcasts in 17 languages; Pres. and Chair. Archbishop GAUDENCIO B. ROSALES; Gen. Man. Fr CARLOS S. LARIOSA (SVD).

UM Broadcasting Network: cnr P Reyes and Palma Gil Sts, Davao City; tel. (82) 2279535; fax (82) 2217824; e-mail umbndvo@mozcom.com; internet www.radyoukay.com.ph; Exec. Vice-Pres. WILLY TORRES.

Vanguard Radio Network: J & T Bldg, Room 208, Santa Mesa, Metro Manila; tel. (2) 7161233; fax (2) 7160899; Pres. MANUEL GALVEZ.

Television

In July 1991 there were seven originating television stations and 105 replay and relay stations. The seven originating stations were ABS-CBN (Channel 2), PTV4 (Channel 4), ABC (Channel 5), GMA (Channel 7), RPN (Channel 9), IBC (Channel 13) and SBN (Channel 21). The following are the principal operating television networks:

ABC Development Corpn: APMC Bldg, 136 Amorsolo St, cnr Gamboa St, Legaspi Village, Makati City, Metro Manila; tel. (2) 8923801; fax (2) 8128840; CEO EDWARD U. TAN.

ABS-CBN Broadcasting Corpn: ABS-CBN Broadcasting Center, Sgt E. Esguerra Ave, cnr Mother Ignacia Ave, Quezon City, 1103 Metro Manila; tel. (2) 9244101; fax (2) 9215888; internet www.abs-cbn.com; Chair. EUGENIO LOPEZ III; Gen. Man. FEDERICO M. GARCIA.

AMCARA Broadcasting Network: ABS-CBN Broadcasting Centre, Mother Ignacia St, cnr Sgt Esguerra Ave, Quezon City, 1103 Metro Manila; tel. (2) 4152272; fax (2) 4121259; e-mail studio23@abs.pinoycentral.com; internet www.studio23.tv; Man. Dir LEONARDO P. KATIGBAK.

Banahaw Broadcasting Corpn: Broadcast City, Capitol Hills, Quezon City, 3005 Metro Manila; tel. (2) 9329949; fax (2) 9318751; Station Man. BETTY LIVIOCO.

Channel V Philippines: Sagittarius Bldg, 6th Floor, H. V. de la Costa St, Salcedo Village, Makati City, Metro Manila; tel. (2) 8173747; fax (2) 8184192; e-mail channelv@i-next.net; Pres. JOEL JIMENEZ; Gen. Man. MON ALCARAZ.

GMA Network, Inc: GMA Network Center, Timog Ave, cnr Epifanio de los Santos Ave, Diliman, Quezon City, 1103 Metro Manila; tel. and fax (2) 9287021; internet www.igma.tv; f. 1950; transmits nation-wide through 45 VHF and 2 affiliate stations and in Asia, Australia and Hawaii through Measat-2 satellite; Chair., Pres. and CEO FELIPE L. GOZON; Exec. Vice-Pres. GILBERTO R. DUAVIT, Jr.

Intercontinental Broadcasting Corpn: Broadcast City Complex, Capitol Hills, Diliman, Quezon City, Metro Manila; tel. (2) 9318781; fax (2) 9318743; 19 stations; Pres. and Chair. BOOTS ANSON-ROA.

People's Television Network Inc (PTV4): Broadcast Complex, Visayas Ave, Quezon City, Metro Manila; tel. (2) 9206514; fax (2) 9204342; f. 1992; public television network; Chair. LOURDES I. ILLUSTRE.

Radio Mindanao Network: State Condominium, 4th Floor, 1 Salcedo St, Legaspi Village, Makati City, Metro Manila; tel. (2) 8120530; fax (2) 8163680; e-mail sales@rmn.com.ph; internet www.rmn.com.ph; f. 1952; owns and operates 50 radio and television stations; Chair. HENRY CANOY; Pres. ERIC S. CANOY.

Radio Philippines Network, Inc: Broadcast City, Capitol Hills, Diliman, Quezon City, Metro Manila; tel. (2) 9315080; fax (2) 9318627; 7 primary TV stations, 14 relay stations; Pres. EDGAR SAN LUIS; Gen. Man. FELIPE G. MEDINA.

Rajah Broadcasting Network, Inc (RJ TV 29): Save a Lot Bldg, 3rd Floor, 2284 Pasong Tamo Ext., Makati City, Metro Manila; tel. (2) 8932360; fax (2) 8933404; e-mail rjofc@compass.com; f. 1993; Gen. Man. BEA J. COLAMONICI.

Southern Broadcasting Network, Inc: Suite 2901, Jollibee Plaza, Ortigas Center, Emerald Ave, Pasig City, Metro Manila; tel. (2) 6363286; fax (2) 6363288; e-mail genceo@sbnphilippines.net; Pres. and CEO TEOFILO A. HENSON; Vice-Pres. LINNIE MAYORALGO.

United Broadcasting Network: FEMS Tower 1, 11th Floor, 1289 Zobel Roxas, cnr South Superhighway, Malate; tel. (2) 5216138; fax (2) 5221226; Gen. Man. JOSEPH HODREAL.

Broadcasting Association

Kapisanan ng mga Brodkaster sa Pilipinas (KBP) (Association of Broadcasters in the Philippines): LTA Bldg, 6th Floor, 118 Perea St, Legaspi Village, Makati City, 1226 Metro Manila; tel. (2) 8151990; fax (2) 8151989; e-mail kbp@pacific.net.ph; internet www.kbp.org.ph; f. 1973 in order to regulate the broadcasting industry, elevate standards, disseminate govt information and strengthen relations with advertising industry; Chair. RUPERTO S. NICDAO, Jr; Pres. BUTCH S. CANOY.

Finance

(cap. = capital; res = reserves; dep. = deposits; m. = million; brs = branches; amounts in pesos, unless otherwise stated)

BANKING

Legislation enacted in June 1993 provided for the establishment of a new monetary authority, the Bangko Sentral ng Pilipinas, to replace the Central Bank of the Philippines. The Government was thus able to restructure the Central Bank's debt (308,000m. pesos).

In May 1994 legislation was promulgated providing for the establishment in the Philippines of up to 10 new foreign bank branches over the following five years (although at least 70% of the banking system's total resources were to be owned by Philippine entities). Prior to this legislation only four foreign banks (which had been in operation when the law restricting the industry to locally owned banks was enacted in 1948) were permitted to operate. Two other foreign banks were subsequently licensed to organize locally incorporated banks with minority Filipino partners. By the end of 2002 the number of foreign banks had increased to 13; at that time some 44 principal commercial banks were operating in the Philippines.

Central Bank

Bangko Sentral ng Pilipinas (Central Bank of the Philippines): A. Mabini St, cnr Pablo Ocampo St, Malate, 1004 Metro Manila; tel. (2) 5247011; fax (2) 5231252; e-mail bspmail@bsp.gov.ph; internet www.bsp.gov.ph; f. 1993; cap. 10,000m., res 171,350m., dep. 487,608m. (Dec. 2002); Gov. AMANDO M. TETANGCO, Jr; 19 brs.

THE PHILIPPINES

Principal Commercial Banks

Allied Banking Corpn: 6754 Allied Bank Centre, Ayala Ave, cnr Legaspi St, Makati City, 1200 Metro Manila; tel. (2) 8187961; fax (2) 8160921; e-mail info@alliedbank.com.ph; internet www.alliedbank.com.ph; f. 1977; cap. 14,046m., res 145,336m., dep. 113,334m. (Dec. 2004); Chair. PANFILO O. DOMINGO; Pres. REYNALDO A. MACLANG; 285 brs.

Banco de Oro Universal Bank: 12 ADB Ave, Mandaluyong City, 1550 Metro Manila; tel. (2) 6366060; fax (2) 6317810; e-mail investor-relations@bdo.com.ph; internet www.bancodeoro.com.ph; f. 1996; acquired 1st e-Bank June 2003; cap. 10,690m. (Sept. 2005); res 77,880m., dep. 56,617m. (Dec. 2001); Chair. TERESITA T. SY; Pres. NESTOR V. TAN; 185 brs.

Bank of Commerce: Phil First Bldg, 6764 Ayala Ave, Makati City, 1226 Metro Manila; tel. (2) 8120000; fax (2) 8300437; e-mail mscallangan@bankcom.com.ph; internet www.bankcom.com.ph; f. 1983; fmrly Boston Bank of the Philippines; merged with Traders Royal Bank 2001; cap. 4,017m., dep. 41,040m. (Aug. 2005); Chair. ANTONIO COJUANGCO; Pres. and CEO RAUL B. DE MESA; 38 brs.

Bank of the Philippine Islands: BPI Bldg, Ayala Ave, cnr Paseo de Roxas, POB 1827, MCC, Makati City, 0720 Metro Manila; tel. (2) 8910000; fax (2) 8910170; e-mail expressonline@bpi.com.ph; internet www.bpiexpressonline.com; f. 1851; merged with Far East Bank and Trust Co in April 2000; merged with DBS Bank Philippines, Inc, 2001; cap. 18,546m., res 27,921m., dep. 325,129m. (Dec. 2003); Pres. and Dir AURELIO R. MONTINOLA III; Chair. JAIME ZOBEL DE AYALA; 339 local brs; 1 overseas br.

China Banking Corpn: CBC Bldg, 8745 Paseo de Roxas, cnr Villar St, Makati City, 1226 Metro Manila; tel. (2) 8855555; fax (2) 8920220; e-mail online@chinabank.com.ph; internet www.chinabank.com.ph; f. 1920; cap. 3,045m., res 2,902m., dep. 72,112m. (Dec. 2003); Chair. GILBERT U. DEE; Pres. and CEO PETER S. DEE; 141 brs.

Development Bank of the Philippines: DBP Bldg, Makati Ave, cnr Sen. Gil J. Puyat Ave, Makati City, 1200 Metro Manila; tel. (2) 8189511; fax (2) 8128089; e-mail info@devbankphil.com.ph; internet www.devbankphil.com.ph; f. 1947 as the Rehabilitation Finance Corpn; govt-owned; provides medium- and long-term loans for agricultural and industrial development; cap. 22,850m., dep. 50,770m. (Dec. 2005); Chair. ANTONINO L. ALINDOGAN, Jr; Pres. and CEO REYNALDO G. DAVID; 77 brs.

East West Banking Corpn: 20th Floor, PBCOM Tower, 6795 Ayala Ave, cnr Herrera St, Salcedo Village, Makati City, 1226 Metro Manila; tel. (2) 8150233; fax (2) 3250412; e-mail service@eastwestbanker.com; internet www.eastwestbanker.com; f. 1994; cap. 1,341m., dep. 2,857m. (March 1997); Chair. ANDREW L. GOTIANUM; Pres. ELREY T. RAMOS; 20 brs.

Equitable PCI Bank: Equitable PCI Bank Towers, 262 Makati Ave, cnr H. V. de la Costa St, Makati City, 1200 Metro Manila; tel. (2) 8407000; fax (2) 8784413; internet www.equitablepcib.com; f. 1950 as Equitable Banking Corpn; name changed as above 1999 following merger with Philippine Commercial International (PCI) Bank; cap. 7,270m., res 34,995m., dep. 186,654m. (Dec. 2003); Chair. CORAZON S. DELA PAZ; Pres. and Dir RENE J. BUENAVENTURA; 409 brs.

Export and Industry Bank, Inc (Exportbank): Exportbank Plaza, Chino Roces Ave, cnr Sen. Gil J. Puyat Ave, Makati City, 1200 Metro Manila; tel. (2) 8789100; fax (2) 8780000; e-mail expertinfo@exportbank.com.ph; internet www.exportbank.com.ph; merged with Urban Bank, Inc, 2002; cap. 1,638m., dep. 2,767m. (Dec. 1997); Chair. SERGIO R. ORTIZ-LUIS, Jr; Pres. BENJAMIN P. CASTILLO.

Land Bank of the Philippines: LandBank Plaza, 1598 M. H. del Pilar St, cnr J. Quintos St, Malate, 1004 Metro Manila; tel. (2) 5220000; fax (2) 5288580; e-mail landbank@mail.landbank.com; internet www.landbank.com; f. 1963; specialized govt bank with universal banking licence; cap. 22,100m., res 20,100m., dep. 185,200m. (Dec. 2003); Chair. GARY B. TEVES; Pres. and CEO GILDA E. PICO (acting); 342 brs.

Manila Banking Corpn: Manila Bank Bldg, 6772 Ayala Ave, Makati City, 1226 Metro Manila; tel. (2) 7516000; fax (2) 8645016; internet www.manilabank.com; f. 1999; cap. 573m., res 2,433m., dep. 3,361m. (Dec. 2002); Pres. BENJAMIN J. YAMBAO; Chair. LUIS B. PUYAT.

Maybank Philippines Inc: Legaspi Towers 300, Pablo Ocampo St, cnr Roxas Blvd, Malate, 1100 Metro Manila; tel. (2) 5237777; fax (2) 5218514; e-mail mayphil@maybank.com.ph; internet www.maybank2u.com.my/philippines/index.shtml; f. 1961; cap. 1,671m., dep. 2,701m. (Dec. 1997); Chair. Tan Sri MOHAMED BASIR BIN AHMAD; Pres. and CEO LIM HONG TAT; 45 brs.

Metropolitan Bank and Trust Co (Metrobank): Metrobank Plaza, Sen. Gil J. Puyat Ave, Makati City, 1200 Metro Manila; tel. (2) 8988000; fax (2) 8176248; e-mail metrobank@metrobank.com.ph; internet www.metrobank.com.ph; f. 1962; acquired Global Business Bank (Globalbank) 2002; cap. 32,673m., res 9,888m., dep. 377,484m. (Dec. 2003); Chair. GEORGE S. K. TY; Pres. ANTONIO S. ABACAN, Jr; 344 local brs, 6 overseas brs.

Philippine Bank of Communications: PBCOM Tower, 6795 Ayala Ave, cnr V. A. Rufino St, 1226 Makati City; tel. (2) 8307000; fax (2) 8182598; e-mail info@pbcom.com.ph; internet www.pbcom.com.ph; f. 1939; merged with AsianBank Corpn in 1999; cap. 6,400m. (March 2004), res 1,508m., dep. 38,492m. (Dec. 2003); Chair. LUY KIM GUAN; Pres. and CEO CARMELO MARIA LUZA BAUTISTA; 64 brs.

Philippine National Bank (PNB): PNB Financial Center, President Diosdado Macapagal Blvd, Pasay City, 1300 Metro Manila; tel. (2) 8916040; fax (2) 8331245; e-mail cmcd@pnb.com.ph; internet www.pnb.com.ph; f. 1916; partially transferred to the private sector in 1996 and 2000; 10.93% govt-owned; cap. 22,930m., res 3,511m., dep. 146,928m. (Dec. 2003); Chair. FLORENCIA G. TARRIELA; Pres. and CEO OMAR BYRON T. MIER; 324 local brs, 5 overseas brs.

Philippine Veterans Bank: PVB Bldg, 101 V. A. Rufino St, cnr de la Rosa St, Legaspi Village, Makati City, Metro Manila; tel. (2) 8943919; fax (2) 8940625; e-mail corpcomm@veteransbank.com.ph; internet www.veteransbank.com.ph; cap. 2,751.8m., res 417.2m., dep. 4,123.7m. (Dec. 2003); Chair. EMMANUEL DE OCAMPO; Pres. and CEO RICARDO A. BALBIDO, Jr; 38 brs.

Philtrust Bank (Philippine Trust Co): Philtrust Bank Bldg, United Nations Ave, cnr San Marcelino St, Ermita, 1045 Metro Manila; tel. (2) 5249061; fax (2) 5217309; e-mail ptc@bancnet.net; f. 1916; cap. 3,683m., res 695m., dep. 33,001m. (Dec. 2003); Pres. ANTONIO H. OZAETA; Chair. EMILIO T. YAP; 38 brs.

Prudential Bank: Prudential Bank Bldg, 6787 Ayala Ave, Makati City, 1200 Metro Manila; tel. (2) 8178981; fax (2) 8175146; e-mail feedback@prudentialbank.com; internet www.prudentialbank.com.ph; f. 1952; merged with Pilipinas Bank in May 2000; cap. 822m., res 7,791m., dep. 38,526m. (Dec. 2002); Chair. and Pres. JOSE L. SANTOS; 117 brs.

Rizal Commercial Banking Corpn: Yuchengco Tower, RCBC Plaza, 6819 Alaya Ave, Makati City, 0727 Metro Manila; tel. (2) 8949000; fax (2) 8949958; e-mail customercontact@rcbc.com; internet www.rcbc.com; f. 1960; cap. and res 14,985m., dep. 156,089m. (Dec. 2003); Hon. Chair. ALFONSO T. YUCHENGCO; Pres. and Dir FRANCISCO S. MAGSAIO, Jr; 287 brs.

Security Bank Corpn: 6776 Ayala Ave, Makati City, 0719 Metro Manila; tel. (2) 8676788; fax (2) 8911079; e-mail herrera@securitybank.com.ph; internet www.securitybank.com; f. 1951; fmrly Security Bank and Trust Co; cap. 9,626m., dep. 54,897m. (Dec. 2004); Pres. and CEO ALBERTO S. VILLAROSA; Chair. FREDERICK Y. DY; 114 brs.

Union Bank of the Philippines: SSS Makati Bldg, Ayala Ave, cnr V. A. Rufino St, Makati City, 1200 Metro Manila; tel. (2) 8920011; fax (2) 8938593; e-mail online@unionbankph.com; internet www.unionbankph.com; f. 1982; cap. 7,087m., res 6,442m., dep. 55,023m. (Dec. 2002); Chair. JUSTO A. ORTIZ; Pres. and CEO VICTOR B. VALDEPEÑAS; 111 brs.

United Coconut Planters' Bank: UCPB Bldg, 7907 Makati Ave, Makati City, 0728 Metro Manila; tel. (2) 8119000; fax (2) 8119706; e-mail crc@ucpb.com; internet www.ucpb.com; f. 1963; cap. and res 6,671m., dep. 66,776m. (Dec. 2003); Chair. ARMAND V. FABELLA; Pres. and CEO JOSE L. QUERUBIN; 178 brs.

United Overseas Bank Philippines: 17th Floor, Pacific Star Bldg, Sen. Gil J. Puyat Ave, cnr Makati Ave, Makati City, Metro Manila; tel. (2) 8788686; fax (2) 8115917; e-mail crd@uob.com.ph; internet www.uob.com.ph; f. 1999; cap. 2,731m., dep. 15,021m. (Dec. 1999); Pres. and CEO WANG LIAN KHEE (acting); 67 brs.

Rural Banks

Small private banks have been established with the encouragement and assistance (both financial and technical) of the Government in order to promote and expand the rural economy. Conceived mainly to stimulate the productive capacities of small farmers, merchants and industrialists in rural areas, and to combat usury, their principal objectives are to place within easy reach and access of the people credit facilities on reasonable terms and, in co-operation with other agencies of the Government, to provide advice on business and farm management and the proper use of credit for production and marketing purposes. The rural banks numbered 1,942 in 1998; their registered resources totalled 59,970m. pesos at 31 December 1998.

Thrift Banks

Thrift banks mobilize small savings and provide loans to lower income groups. The thrift banking system comprises savings and mortgage banks, stock savings and loan associations and private development banks. In 1998 there were 1,474 thrift banks; their registered resources totalled 216,440m. pesos.

Development Bank

Pampanga Development Bank: MacArthur Highway, Dolores San Fernando, Pampanga, Luzon; tel. (45) 9612786; fax (45) 9633931; e-mail pdb@ag.triasia.net; originally Agribusiness Devel-

THE PHILIPPINES

opment Bank; name changed as above 1995; cap. 75.0m., res 6.6m., dep. 72.9m. (June 2003); Pres. JOSE ERIBERTO H. SUAREZ.

Foreign Banks

ANZ Banking Group Ltd (Australia and New Zealand): 23rd Floor, GT Tower International, 6813 Ayala Ave, cnr H. V. de la Costa St, Makati City, Metro Manila; tel. (2) 8188117; fax (2) 8188112; e-mail labrooyM2@anz.com; internet www.anz.com/philippines; f. 1995; cap. 250m., dep. 2,000m. (Dec. 1999); Pres. JOHNNY L. CO.

Banco Santander Philippines, Inc: Tower One, 27th Floor, Ayala Triangle, Ayala Ave, cnr Paseo de Roxas, Makati City, 1200 Metro Manila; tel. (2) 7594144; fax (2) 7594190; cap. 1,351m., dep. 3,943m. (March 1997); Chair. ANA PATRICIA BOTIN; Dir and Pres. VICENTE B. CASTILLO.

Bangkok Bank Public Company Ltd (Thailand): 25th Floor, BPI Buendia Center, Sen. Gil J. Puyat Ave, Makati City, 1200 Metro Manila; tel. (2) 8914011; fax (2) 8914037; e-mail bangkokbank@unet.net.ph; f. 1995; cap. 266m. (Dec. 1996), dep. 647m. (March 1997); Pres. PRASARN TUNTASOOD.

Bank of America NA (USA): 27th Floor, Philamlife Tower, 8767 Paseo de Roxas, Makati City, 1257 Metro Manila; tel. (2) 8155000; fax (2) 8155895; f. 1947; cap. 210m. (Dec. 1996), dep. 5,015m. (June 1999); Pres. and CEO ISABELITA M. PAPA.

Bank of China: Ground and 36th Floors, Philamlife Tower, 8767 Paseo de Roxas, Makati City, Metro Manila; tel. (2) 8850111; fax (2) 8850532; e-mail boc_mnl@bocgroup.com; Pres. ZHANG BAOXI.

Bank of Tokyo-Mitsubishi UFJ Ltd (Japan): 15th Floor, Sky Plaza Bldg, 6788 Ayala Ave, Makati City, Metro Manila; tel. (2) 8867371; fax (2) 8160413; e-mail btm_edp@philcom.com; f. 1977; cap. 200m. (Dec. 1996), dep. 2,940m. (March 1997); Gen. Man. YUKIO TAKEI.

Chinatrust (Philippines) Commercial Bank Corpn: 3rd Floor, Tower One, Exchange Plaza, Ayala Triangle, Ayala Ave, cnr Paseo de Roxas, Makati City, Metro Manila; tel. (2) 8485519; fax (2) 7594982; e-mail ccbmktg@info.com.ph; internet www.chinatrust.com.ph; Chair. ERIC CHEN; Pres. JOEY A. BERMUDEZ; 18 brs.

Citibank NA (USA): Citibank Plaza, 8741 Paseo de Roxas, Makati City, 1226 Metro Manila; tel. (2) 8947700; fax (2) 8157703; internet www.citibank.com.ph; f. 1948; cap. 2,536m., dep. 30,167m. (March 1997); CEO JAMES F. HUNT; 3 brs.

Deutsche Bank AG (Germany): Ayala Triangle, Tower One, 26th Floor, Ayala Ave, cnr Paseo de Roxas, Makati City, 1226 Metro Manila; tel. (2) 8946900; fax (2) 8946901; f. 1995; cap. 625m. (Dec. 1996), dep. 2,595m. (March 1997); Chief Country Officer ENRICO CRUZ.

Hongkong and Shanghai Banking Corpn (HSBC) (Hong Kong): 7th Floor, Enterprise Center, Tower I, 6766 Ayala Ave, cnr Paseo de Roxas, Makati City, 1200 Metro Manila; tel. (2) 8305300; fax (2) 8865350; e-mail hsbc@hsbc.com.ph; internet www.hsbc.com.ph; cap. HK $113,520m., res HK $42,280m., dep. HK $1,419,076m. (June 2002); CEO WARNER N. MANNING; 21 brs.

ING Bank NV (The Netherlands): Ayala Triangle, Tower One, 21st Floor, Ayala Ave, cnr Paseo de Roxas, Makati City, 1200 Metro Manila; tel. (2) 8408888; fax (2) 8151116; f. 1995; cap. 643m., dep. 2,594m. (March 1997); Country Man. MANUEL SALAK.

International Commercial Bank of China (Taiwan): Pacific Star Bldg, Ground and 3rd Floors, Sen. Gil J. Puyat Ave, cnr Makati Ave, Makati City, 1200 Metro Manila; tel. (2) 8115807; fax (2) 8115774; e-mail icbcphmm@unet.net.ph; cap. 188m., dep. 458m. (March 1997); Gen. Man. CHIA JANG LIU.

JP Morgan Chase Bank: 31st Floor, Philamlife Tower, 8767 Paseo de Roxas, Makati City, Metro Manila; tel. (2) 8857700; fax (2) 7298000; e-mail vannie.w.chu@chase.com; Country Man. ROBERTO L. PANLILIO.

Korea Exchange Bank: Citibank Tower, 33rd Floor, 8741 Paseo de Roxas, Makati City, 1229 Metro Manila; tel. (2) 8481988; fax (2) 8195377; e-mail koexbank@surfshop.net.ph; cap. 257m., dep. 271m. (March 1997); Gen. Man. SEUNG-KWON KIM.

Mizuho Bank Ltd (Japan): Citibank Tower, 26th Floor, Valero St, cnr Villar St, Legaspi Village, Makati City, 1229 Metro Manila; tel. (2) 8480001; fax (2) 8153770; e-mail fujibank@unet.net.ph; f. 1995; cap. 202m. (Dec. 1996), dep. 858m. (March 1997); Gen. Man. TATSUJI TAMAKI.

Standard Chartered Bank (Hong Kong): 6788 Ayala Ave, Sky Plaza Bldg, Makati City, 1226 Metro Manila; tel. (2) 8867888; fax (2) 8866866; f. 1873; cap. 1,500m. (Dec. 1996), dep. 3,770m. (March 1997); CEO SIMON MORRIS.

Islamic Bank

Al-Amanah Islamic Investment Bank of the Philippines: Ground Floor, NDC Bldg, 116 Tordesillas St, Salcedo Village, Makati City, Metro Manila; tel. (2) 8164258; fax (2) 8195249; e-mail islambnk@tri-isys.com; internet www.islamicbank.com.ph; f. 1989; Chair. Dato' ZACARIA A. CANDAO; Pres. ABDUL GAFFOOR ASHROOF.

Major 'Offshore' Banks

ABN AMRO Bank, NV (Netherlands): LKG Tower, 18th Floor, 6801 Ayala Ave, V. A. Rufino St, Makati City, 1200 Metro Manila; tel. (2) 8842000; fax (2) 8843954; e-mail inquire@abnamro.com.ph; Gen. Man. CARMELO MARIA L. BAUTISTA.

American Express Bank Ltd (USA): Ayala Bldg, 11th Floor, 6750 Ayala Ave, Makati City, Metro Manila; tel. (2) 8186731; fax (2) 8172589; f. 1977; Sr Dir and Country Man. VICENTE L. CHUA.

BNP Paribas (France): 30th Floor, Philamlife Tower, 8767 Paseo de Roxas, POB 2265 MCPO, Makati City, 1262 Metro Manila; tel. (2) 8148700; fax (2) 8857076; internet www.bnpparibas.com.ph; f. 1977; Country Man. PETER C. LABRIE.

Crédit Agricole Indosuez (France): Citibank Tower, 17th Floor, 8741 Paseo de Roxas, Makati City, 1200 Metro Manila; tel. (2) 8481344; fax (2) 8481380; f. 1977; Gen. Man. MARC MEULEAU.

Crédit Lyonnais (France): Pacific Star Bldg, 14th Floor, Makati Ave, cnr Sen. Gil J. Puyat Ave, 1200 Makati City, Metro Manila; POB 1859 MCC, 3117 Makati City, Metro Manila; tel. (2) 8171616; fax (2) 8177145; f. 1981; Gen. Man. PIERRE EYMERY.

JP Morgan International Finance Ltd: Corinthian Plaza, 4th Floor, 121 Paseo de Roxas, Makati City, Metro Manila; tel. (2) 8113348; fax (2) 8781290; Man. HELEN S. CIFRA.

KBC Bank, NV (Belgium): 38th Floor, Philamlife Tower, 8767 Paseo de Roxas, Makati City, 1226 Metro Manila; tel. (2) 7573728; fax (2) 7573727; e-mail edwin.yaptangco@kbc.be; internet branches.kbc.com/manila; Gen. Man. EDWIN YAPTANGCO.

Société Générale (France): Antel Corporate Center, 21st Floor, 139 Valero St, Salcedo Village, Makati City, Metro Manila; tel. (2) 8492000; fax (2) 8492940; f. 1980; CEO CLAUDE I. TOUITOU.

Taiwan Co-operative Bank: 26th Floor, Citibank Tower Bldg, 8741 Paseo de Roxas, Makati City, Metro Manila; tel. (2) 8481959; fax (2) 8481952.

Union Bank of California (USA): ACE Bldg, 8th Floor, cnr Rada and de la Rosa Sts, Legaspi Village, Makati City, Metro Manila; tel. (2) 8923056; fax (2) 8170102; f. 1977; Branch Man. TERESITA MALABANAN.

Banking Associations

Bankers Association of the Philippines: Sagittarius Cond. Bldg, 11th Floor, H. V. de la Costa St, Salcedo Village, Makati City, Metro Manila; tel. (2) 8103858; fax (2) 8103860; internet www.bap.org.ph; Pres. CESAR E. A. VIRATA; Exec. Dir LEONILO G. CORONEL.

Bankers Institute of the Philippines, Inc (BAIPhil): TRB Tower, Paseo de Roxas, Makati City, Metro Manila; tel. (2) 8325890; e-mail secretariat@baiphil.org; internet www.baiphil.org; f. 1941 under the name National Asscn of Auditors and Comptrollers; name changed to Bank Administration Institute in 1968, and as above in 2001; Pres. AMELIA S. AMPARADO.

Chamber of Thrift Banks: Cityland 10 Condominium Tower 1, Unit 614, H. V. de la Costa St, Salcedo Village, Makati City, Metro Manila; tel. (2) 8126974; fax (2) 8127203; Pres. DIONISIO C. ONG.

Offshore Bankers' Association of the Philippines, Inc: MCPO 3088, Makati City, 1229 Metro Manila; tel. (2) 8103554; Chair. TERESITA MALABANAN.

Rural Bankers' Association of the Philippines: RBAP Bldg, A. Soriano, Jr, Ave, cnr Arzobispo St, Intramuros, Manila; tel. (2) 5272968; fax (2) 5272980; e-mail info@rbap.org; internet www.rbap.org; Pres. WILLIAM K. HOTCHKISS III.

STOCK EXCHANGES

Securities and Exchange Commission: SEC Bldg, Epifanio de los Santos Ave, Greenhills, Mandaluyong City, Metro Manila; tel. (2) 7260931; fax (2) 7255293; e-mail mis@sec.gov.ph; internet www.sec.gov.ph; f. 1936; Chair. FE B. BARIN.

Philippine Stock Exchange: Philippine Stock Exchange Center, Exchange Rd, Ortigas Center, Pasig City, 1605 Metro Manila; tel. (2) 6887600; fax (2) 6345113; e-mail piac@pse.com.ph; internet www.pse.com.ph; f. 1994 following the merger of the Manila and Makati Stock Exchanges; 237 listed cos (Dec. 2005); Chair. JOSE C. VITUG; Pres. FRANCISCO ED. LIM.

INSURANCE

At the end of 2000 a total of 156 insurance companies were authorized by the Insurance Commission to transact in the Philippines. Foreign companies were permitted to operate in the country.

THE PHILIPPINES

Principal Domestic Companies

Ayala Life Assurance Inc: Ayala Life Bldg, 6786 Ayala Ave, Makati City, Metro Manila; tel. (2) 8885433; fax (2) 8180171; e-mail customer.service@ayalalife.com.ph; internet www.ayalalife.com.ph; Pres. ALFONSO L. SALCEDO, Jr.

BPI/MS Insurance Corpn: Ayala Life-FGU Center, 16th Floor, 6811 Ayala Ave, Makati City, 1226 Metro Manila; tel. (2) 8409000; fax (2) 8409099; e-mail insure@bpims.com; internet www.bpims.com; f. 2002 as result of merger of FGU Insurance Corpn and FEB Mitsui Marine Insurance Corpn; jt venture of Bank of the Philippine Islands and Sumitomo Insurance Co (Japan); cap. 731m. (2003); Chair. AURELIO R. MONTINOLA III; Pres. NORIAKI HAMANAKA.

Central Surety & Insurance Co: UniversalRe Bldg, 2nd Floor, 106 Paseo de Roxas, Legaspi Village, Makati City, 1200 Metro Manila; tel. (2) 8174931; fax (2) 8170006; f. 1945; bonds, fire, marine, casualty, motor car; Pres. FERMIN T. CASTAÑEDA.

Commonwealth Insurance Co: 10th Floor, 1st e-Bank Tower, 8737 Paseo de Roxas, Makati City, Metro Manila; tel. (2) 8187626; fax (2) 8138575; f. 1935; Pres. MARIO NOCHE.

Co-operative Insurance System of the Philippines: CISP Bldg, 80 Malakas St, Diliman, Quezon City, Metro Manila; tel. (2) 9240388; fax (2) 9240471; Chair. DOMINADOR ESTRADA; Pres. AMBROSIO M. RODRIGUEZ.

Domestic Insurance Co of the Philippines: 5th Floor, Champ Bldg, Anda Circle, Bonifacio Drive, Port Area, Manila; tel. (2) 5278181; fax (2) 5273052; e-mail gdicp@skyinet.net; f. 1946; cap. 10m.; Pres. and Chair. MAR S. LOPEZ.

Empire Insurance Co: Prudential Life Bldg, 2nd Floor, 843 Arnaiz Ave, Legaspi Village, Makati City, 1229 Metro Manila; tel. (2) 8159561; fax (2) 8152599; f. 1949; fire, bonds, marine, accident, motor car, extraneous perils; Pres. and CEO JOSE MA G. SANTOS.

Equitable Insurance Corpn: Equitable Bank Bldg, 4th Floor, 262 Juan Luna St, Binondo, POB 1103, Metro Manila; tel. (2) 2430291; fax (2) 2415768; e-mail info@equitableinsurance.com.ph; internet www.equitableinsurance.com.ph; f. 1950; fire, marine, casualty, motor car, bonds; Pres. NORA T. GO; Exec. Vice-Pres. ANTONIO C. OCAMPO.

Insular Life Assurance Co Ltd: Insular Life Corporate Center, Insular Life Drive, Filinvest Corporate City, Alabang, 1781 Muntinlupa City; tel. (2) 7711818; fax (2) 7711717; e-mail headofc@insular.com.ph; internet www.insularlife.com.ph; f. 1910; members' equity 7,251m. (Dec. 2002); Chair. and CEO VICENTE R. AYLLÓN.

Makati Insurance Co Inc: BPI Buendia Center, 19th Floor, Sen. Gil J. Puyat Ave, Makati City, 1200 Metro Manila; tel. (2) 8459576; fax (2) 8915229; f. 1965; non-life; Pres. and Gen. Man. JAIME L. DARANTINAO; Chair. OCTAVIO V. ESPIRITU.

Malayan Insurance Co Inc: Yuchengco Tower, 4th Floor, 484 Quintin Paredes St, Binondo, 1099 Metro Manila; tel. (2) 2428888; fax (2) 2412188; e-mail malayan@malayan.com; internet www.malayan.com; f. 1949; cap. 100m. (1998); insurance and bonds; Pres. YVONNE S. YUCHENGCO; Chair. ADELITA VERGEL DE DIOS.

Manila Surety & Fidelity Co Inc: 66 P. Florentino St, Quezon City, Metro Manila; tel. (2) 7122251; fax (2) 7124129; f. 1945; cap. p.u. 50m., members' equity 85m. (Dec. 2003); Pres. MARIA LOURDES V. PEÑA; Vice-Pres. MARIA EDITHA PEÑA-LIM; 4 brs.

Metropolitan Insurance Co: Ateneum Bldg, 3rd Floor, Leviste St, Salcedo Village, Makati City, Metro Manila; tel. (2) 8108151; fax (2) 8162294; f. 1933; non-life; Pres. JOSE M. PERIQUET, Jr; Exec. Vice-Pres. ROBERTO ABAD.

National Life Insurance Co of the Philippines: National Life Insurance Bldg, 6762 Ayala Ave, Makati City, Metro Manila; tel. (2) 8100251; fax (2) 8178718; f. 1933; Pres. BENJAMIN L. DE LEON; Sr Vice-Pres. DOUGLAS MCLAREN.

National Reinsurance Corpn of the Philippines: AXA Life Center, 18th Floor, Sen. Gil J. Puyat Ave, cnr Tindalo St, Makati City, 1200 Metro Manila; tel. (2) 7595801; fax (2) 7595886; e-mail nrcp@nrcp.com.ph; internet www.nrcp.com.ph; f. 1978; Chair. WINSTON F. GARCIA; Pres. and CEO WILFRIDO C. BANTAYAN.

Paramount Union Insurance Corpn: Sage House, 14th and 15th Floors, 110 V. A. Rufino St, Legaspi Village, Makati City, 1229 Metro Manila; tel. (2) 8127956; fax (2) 8131140; e-mail insure@paramount.com.ph; internet www.paramount.com.ph; f. 1950; fmrly Paramount General Insurance Corpn; name changed as above 2002; fire, marine, casualty, motor car; Chair. PATRICK L. GO; Pres. GEORGE T. TIU.

Philippine American Life and General Insurance Co (Philamlife): Philamlife Bldg, United Nations Ave, Metro Manila; POB 2167, 0990 Metro Manila; tel. (2) 5269258; fax (2) 5269253; e-mail philamwebmaster@aig.com; internet www.philamlife.com.ph; Pres. JOSE CUISIA.

Pioneer Insurance and Surety Corpn: Pioneer House Makati, 108 Paseo de Roxas, Legaspi Village, Makati City, 1229 Metro Manila; tel. (2) 812777; fax (2) 8171461; e-mail info@pioneer.com.ph; internet www.pioneer.com.ph; f. 1954; cap. 172.5m. (1997); Pres. and CEO DAVID C. COYUKIAT.

Rizal Surety and Insurance Co: Prudential Life Bldg, 3rd Floor, 843 Arnaiz Ave, Legaspi Village, Makati City, Metro Manila; tel. (2) 8159561; fax (2) 8152599; e-mail rizalsic@mkt.weblinq.com; f. 1939; fire, bond, marine, motor car, accident, extraneous perils; Chair. and Pres. S. CORPUS.

Standard Insurance Co Inc: Standard Insurance Tower, 999 Pedro Gil St, cnr F. Agoncillo St, Metro Manila; tel. (2) 5223230; fax (2) 5261479; f. 1958; Chair. LOURDES T. ECHAUZ; Pres. ERNESTO ECHAUZ.

Sterling Insurance Co: Zeta II Annex Bldg, 6th Floor, 191 Salcedo St, Legaspi Village, Makati City, Metro Manila; tel. (2) 8925787; fax (2) 8183630; f. 1960; fmrly Dominion Insurance Corpn; name changed as above Nov. 2001; fire, marine, motor car, accident, engineering, bonds; Pres. RAFAEL GALLAGA.

Tico Insurance Co Inc: Trafalgar Plaza, 7th Floor, 105 H. V. de la Costa St, Salcedo Village, Makati City, 1227 Metro Manila; tel. (2) 8140143; fax (2) 8140150; f. 1937; fmrly Tabacalera Insurance Co Inc; Chair. and Pres. CARLOS CATHOLICO.

UCPB General Insurance Co Inc: 25th Floor, LKG Tower, 6801 Ayala Ave, Makati City, Metro Manila; tel. (2) 8841234; fax (2) 8841264; e-mail ucpbgen@ucpbgen.com; internet www.ucpbgen.com; f. 1963; non-life; Pres. ISABELO P. AFRICA; Chair. SERGIO ANTONIO F. APOSTOL.

Universal Reinsurance Corpn: Ayala Life Bldg, 9th Floor, 6786 Ayala Ave, Makati City, Metro Manila; tel. (2) 7514977; fax (2) 8173745; f. 1949; life and non-life; Chair. JAIME AUGUSTO ZOBEL DE AYALA II; Pres. HERMINIA S. JACINTO.

Regulatory Body

Insurance Commission: 1071 United Nations Ave, Metro Manila; tel. and fax (2) 5238461; e-mail oic@i-manila.com.ph; internet www.insurance.gov.ph; regulates the private insurance industry by, among other things, issuing certificates of authority to insurance companies and intermediaries and monitoring their financial solvency; Commr EVANGELINE CRISOSTOMO-ESCOBILLO.

Trade and Industry

GOVERNMENT AGENCIES

Board of Investments: 385 Sen. Gil J. Puyat Ave, Makati City, 1200 Metro Manila; tel. (2) 8901332; fax (2) 8953512; e-mail OSAC@boi.gov.ph; internet www.boi.gov.ph; Chair. PETER B. FAVILA; Gov. JOSE ANTONIO C. LEVISTE.

Bureau of Domestic Trade Promotion (BDT): Trade and Industry Bldg, 2nd Floor, 361 Sen. Gil J. Puyat Ave, Makati City, Metro Manila; tel. (2) 8904877; fax (2) 8904858; e-mail morbeta@yahoo.com; internet www.dti.gov.ph/bdtp; Dir MEYNARD R. ORBETA.

Cagayan Economic Zone Authority: Westar Bldg, 7th Floor, 611 Shaw Blvd, Pasig City, 1603 Metro Manila; tel. (2) 6365776; fax (2) 6313997; e-mail cagayanecozone@vasia.com; Administrator RODOLFO G. ALVARADO.

Clark Development Corpn: Bldg 2122, C. P. Garcia St, cnr E. Quirino St, Clark Field, Pampanga; tel. (2) 5994902; fax (2) 5992507; e-mail info@clark.com.ph; internet www.clark.com.ph; Pres. and CEO Dr ANTONIO R. NG.

Industrial Technology Development Institute: DOST Compound, Gen. Santos Ave, Bicutan, Taguig, 1631 Metro Manila; tel. (2) 8372071; fax (2) 8373167; e-mail adiv@dost.gov.ph; internet mis.dost.gov.ph/itdi; Dir Dr NUNA E. ALMANZOR.

Maritime Industry Authority (MARINA): PPL Bldg, 1000 United Nations Ave, cnr San Marcelino St, Ermita, Metro Manila; tel. (2) 5238651; fax (2) 5242746; e-mail feedback@marina.gov.ph; internet www.marina.gov.ph; f. 1974; development of inter-island shipping, overseas shipping, shipbuilding and repair, and maritime power; Administrator VICENTE T. SUAZO, Jr.

National Tobacco Administration: NTA Bldg, Scout Reyes St, cnr Panay Ave, Quezon City, Metro Manila; tel. (2) 3743987; fax (2) 3742505; e-mail ntamis@ph.inter.net; internet www.geocities.com/miscsdnta; f. 1987; Administrator CARLITOS S. ENCARNACION.

Philippine Coconut Authority (PCA): PCA R & D Bldg, Elliptical Rd, Diliman, Quezon City, 1104 Metro Manila; tel. (2) 9278116; fax (2) 9216173; e-mail pca_cpo@yahoo.com.ph; internet www.pca.da.gov.ph; f. 1972; Chair. DOMINGO F. PANGANIBAN; Administrator JESUS EMMANUEL M. PARAS.

Philippine Council for Advanced Science and Technology Research and Development (PCASTRD): DOST Main Bldg, Gen. Santos Ave, Bicutan, Taguig, 1631 Metro Manila; tel. (2)

8377522; fax (2) 8373168; e-mail pcastrd@dost.gov.ph; internet www.pcastrd.dost.gov.ph; f. 1987; Exec. Dir Dr REYNALDO V. EBORA.

Philippine Economic Zone Authority: Roxas Blvd, cnr San Luis St, Pasay City, Metro Manila; tel. (2) 5513454; fax (2) 8916380; e-mail info@peza.gov.ph; internet www.peza.gov.ph; Dir-Gen. LILIA B. DE LIMA.

Privatization and Management Office: Department of Finance, 104 Gamboa St, Legaspi Village, Makati City, 1229 Metro Manila; tel. (2) 8932383; fax (2) 8933453; e-mail pmo@eastern.com.ph; internet ecommunity.ncc.gov.ph/pmo; f. 2002; formed to handle the privatization of govt assets; succeeded Asset Privatization Trust; Chief Exec. RENATO V. VALDECANTOS.

Subic Bay Metropolitan Authority: SBMA Center, Bldg 229, Waterfront Rd, Subic Bay Freeport Zone, 2222 Zambales; tel. (47) 257262; fax (47) 2524004; e-mail webteam@sbma.com; internet www.sbma.com; Chair. FELICIANO G. SALONGA.

DEVELOPMENT ORGANIZATIONS

Bases Conversion Development Authority: 2nd Floor, Bonifacio Technology Center, 31st St, Crescent Park West, Bonifacio Global City, Taguig, 1634 Metro Manila; tel. (2) 8166666; fax (2) 8160996; e-mail bcda@bcda.gov.ph; internet www.bcda.gov.ph; f. 1992; est. to facilitate the conversion, privatization and development of fmr military bases; Chair. FILADELFO S. ROJAS, Jr; Pres. and CEO NARCISO L. ABAYA.

Bureau of Land Development: DAR Bldg, Elliptical Rd, Diliman, Quezon City, Metro Manila; tel. (2) 9287031; fax (2) 9260971; Dir EUGENIO B. BERNARDO.

Bureau of Small and Medium Business Development: Oppen Bldg, 3rd Floor, 349 Sen. Gil J. Puyat Ave, Makati City, Metro Manila; tel. and fax (2) 8967916; e-mail bsmbd@mnl.sequel.net; initiates and implements programmes and projects addressing the specific needs of SMEs in areas concerning entrepreneurship, institutional development, productivity improvement, organization, financing and marketing; Dir MEYNARDO R. ORBETA.

Capital Market Development Council: Metro Manila; Chair. CONCHITA L. MANABAT.

Co-operatives Development Authority: Benlor Bldg, 1184 Quezon Ave, Quezon City, Metro Manila; tel. (2) 3723801; fax (2) 3712077; Chair. JOSE C. MEDINA, Jr; Exec. Dir CANDELARIO L. VERZONA, Jr.

National Development Co (NDC): NDC Bldg, 8th Floor, 116 Tordesillas St, Salcedo Village, Makati City, Metro Manila; tel. (2) 8404898; fax (2) 8404682; e-mail corplan@info.com; internet www.dti.gov.ph/contentment/66/67/788.jsp; f. 1919; govt-owned corpn engaged in the organization, financing and management of subsidiaries and corpns incl. commercial, industrial, mining, agricultural and other enterprises assisting national economic development, incl. jt industrial ventures with other ASEAN countries; Chair. MANUEL A. ROXAS; Gen. Man. OFELIA V. BULAONG.

Philippine National Oil Co (PNOC): Energy Complex, Bldg 6, 6th Floor, Merritt Rd, Fort Bonifacio, Makati City, Metro Manila; tel. (2) 5550254; fax (2) 8442983; internet www.pnoc.com.ph; f. 1973; state-owned energy development agency mandated to ensure stable and sufficient supply of oil products and to develop domestic energy resources; sales 3,482m. pesos (1995); Chair. VINCENT S. PEREZ, Jr; Pres. and CEO THELMO Y. CUNANAN.

Southern Philippines Development Authority: Basic Petroleum Bldg, 104 Carlos Palanca, Jr, St, Legaspi Village, Makati City, Metro Manila; tel. (2) 8183893; fax (2) 8183907; Chair. ROBERTO AVENTAJADO; Manila Rep. GERUDIO 'KHALIQ' MADUENO.

CHAMBERS OF COMMERCE AND INDUSTRY

American Chamber of Commerce of the Philippines: Corinthian Plaza, 2nd Floor, Paseo de Roxas, Makati City, 1229 Metro Manila; tel. (2) 8187911; fax (2) 8113081; e-mail info@amchamphilippines.com; internet www.amchamphilippines.com; Pres. RICK M. SANTOS.

Cebu Chamber of Commerce and Industry: CCCI Center, cnr 11th and 13th Ave, North Reclamation Area, Cebu City 6000; tel. (32) 2321421; fax (32) 2321422; e-mail m@cebuchamber.com.ph; internet www.cebu-chamber.com; f. 1921; Pres. CARLOS G. GO.

European Chamber of Commerce of the Philippines: AXA Life Center, 19th Floor, Sen. Gil J. Puyat Ave, cnr Tindalo St, Makati City, 1200 Metro Manila; tel. (2) 8451324; fax (2) 8451395; e-mail info@eccp.com; internet www.eccp.com; f. 2000; 900 mems; Pres. WILLIAM BAILEY; Exec. Vice-Pres. HENRY J. SCHUMACHER.

Federation of Filipino-Chinese Chambers of Commerce and Industry Inc: Federation Center, 6th Floor, Muelle de Binondo St, POB 23, Metro Manila; tel. (2) 2419201; fax (2) 2422361; e-mail ffcccii@yahoo.com; internet www.ffcccii.com.ph; Chair. Dr LUCIO C. TAN; Pres. FRANCIS CHUA.

Japanese Chamber of Commerce of the Philippines: Trident Tower, 22nd Floor, 312 Sen. Gil Puyat Ave, Salcedo Village, Makati City, Metro Manila; tel. (2) 8923233; fax (2) 8150317; e-mail jccipi@jccipi.com.ph; internet www.jccipi.com.ph; Pres. RYUKICHI KAWAGUCHI.

Philippine Chamber of Coal Mines (Philcoal): Rm 1007, Princeville Condominium, S. Laurel St, cnr Shaw Blvd, 1552 Mandaluyong City; tel. (2) 5330518; fax (2) 5315513; f. 1980; Exec. Dir BERTRAND GONZALES.

Philippine Chamber of Commerce and Industry: 14th Floor, Multinational Bancorporation Centre, 6805 Ayala Ave, Makati City, Metro Manila; tel. (2) 8445713; fax (2) 8434102; e-mail mis@philippinechamber.com; internet www.philippinechamber.com; f. 1977; Chair. SERGIO R. ORTIZ-LUIS, Jr; Pres. DONALD G. DEE.

Philippine Chamber of Mines: Rm 809, Ortigas Bldg, Ortigas Ave, Pasig City, 1605 Metro Manila; tel. (2) 6354123; fax (2) 6354160; e-mail comp@pldtdsl.net; internet www.chamberofminesphilpines.com; f. 1975; Chair. ARTEMIO F. DISINI; Pres. BENJAMIN PHILIP G. ROMUALDEZ.

FOREIGN TRADE ORGANIZATIONS

Bureau of Export Trade Promotion: New Solid Bldg, 5th–8th Floors, 357 Sen. Gil J. Puyat Ave, Makati City, 1200 Metro Manila; tel. (2) 8990133; fax (2) 8904707; e-mail betpod@dti.gov.ph; internet tradelinephil.dti.gov.ph; Dir FERNANDO P. CALA, II.

Bureau of Import Services: Oppen Bldg, 3rd Floor, 349 Sen. Gil J. Puyat Ave, Makati City, Metro Manila; tel. (2) 8905418; fax (2) 8957466; e-mail bis@dti.gov.ph; internet www.dti.gov.ph/bis; Exec. Dir ALEXANDER B. ARCILLA.

Garments and Textile Export Board (GTEB): New Solid Bldg, 2nd and 3rd Floors, 357 Sen. Gil J. Puyat Ave, Makati City, Metro Manila; tel. (2) 8904810; fax (2) 8904653; e-mail gtebebs@dti.gov.ph; internet www.gteb.gov.ph; manages and supervises the garment textile quota system; Exec. Dir FELICITAS R. AGONCILLO REYES.

Philippine International Trading Corpn (PITC): National Development Company, 5th Floor, 116 Tordesillas St, Salcedo Village, 1227 Metro Manila; tel. (2) 8920425; fax (2) 8920782; e-mail pitc@info.com.ph; internet www.dti.gov.ph/pitc; f. 1973; state trading company to conduct international marketing of general merchandise, industrial and construction goods, raw materials, semi-finished and finished goods, and bulk trade of agri-based products; also provides financing, bonded warehousing, shipping, cargo and customs services; Pres. and CEO ANTHONY ABAD.

INDUSTRIAL AND TRADE ASSOCIATIONS

Beverage Industry Association of the Philippines: SMPC Bldg, 23rd Floor, St Francis St, Mandaluyong City, Metro Manila; tel. (2) 6346840; fax (2) 6318672; e-mail rbkmlo@mnl.sequel.net; Pres. HECTOR GUBALLA.

Chamber of Automotive Manufacturers of the Philippines (CAMPI): Suite 1206, 12th Floor, Jollibee Plaza, San Miguel Ave, Ortigas Center, Pasig City, Metro Manila; tel. (2) 6329733; fax (2) 6315313; e-mail campi@pacific.net.ph; Pres. VICENTE MILLS, Jr; Vice-Pres. ELIZABETH LEE.

Construction Industry Authority of the Philippines (CIAP): Jupiter I Bldg, 4th Floor, Jupiter St, Makati City, Metro Manila; tel. (2) 8979336; e-mail pocb@skynet.net; Officer-in-Charge KATHERINE T. DELA CRUZ.

Cotton Development Administration (CODA): Agricultural Training Institute, 1st Floor, Elliptical Rd, Diliman, Quezon City, 1100 Metro Manila; tel. (2) 9208878; fax (2) 9209238; e-mail coda@da.gov.ph; internet www.coda.da.gov.ph; Administrator Dr EUGENIO D. ORPIA, Jr.

Federation of Philippine Industries (FPI): 308 Sen. Gil J. Puyat Ave, Makati City, Metro Manila; tel. (2) 8440324; fax (2) 8447264; e-mail fpi@philonline.com; internet www.philonline.com/~fpi; f. 1991; Chair. MENELEO J. CARLOS, Jr; Pres. JESUS L. ARRANZA.

Fiber Industry Development Authority: Asiatrust Bank Annex Bldg, 1424 Quezon Ave, Quezon City, Metro Manila; tel. (2) 3737489; fax (2) 3737494; e-mail fibernetwk@yahoo.com; internet www.bar.gov.ph/fiber/fida.htm; Administrator CECILIA GLORIA J. SORIANO.

Philippine Association of Electrical Industries: Banks of the Philippines Bldg, Suite 702, Plaza Cervantes, Binondo, Metro Manila; tel. and fax (2) 2421144; Pres. RICARDO SY.

Philippine Fisheries Development Authority: 2nd Floor, PCA Annex Bldg, 1 Elliptical Rd, Diliman, Quezon City, 1109 Metro Manila; tel. (2) 9258472; fax (2) 9256138; e-mail oagm@pfda.gov.ph; internet pfda.da.gov.ph; f. 1976; Gen. Man. PETRONILO B. BUENDIA.

Philippine Liquified Petroleum Gas Association: 218 San Vicente St, Binondo, Metro Manila; tel. (2) 2412668; fax (2) 6337781; f. 1966; Pres. JOSELITO ASENTERO.

THE PHILIPPINES

Semiconductor and Electronic Industries in the Philippines (SEIPI): Unit 902, RCBC Plaza, Tower 2, Sen. Gil J. Puyat Ave, Makati City, Metro Manila; tel. (2) 8449028; fax (2) 8449037; e-mail philippine.electronics@seipi.org.ph; internet www.seipi.org.ph; Exec. Dir ERNESTO B. SANTIAGO.

EMPLOYERS' ORGANIZATIONS

Employers' Confederation of the Philippines (ECOP): ECC Bldg, 2nd Floor, 355 Sen. Gil J. Puyat Ave, Makati City, Metro Manila; tel. (2) 8904845; fax (2) 8958623; e-mail ecop@webquest.com; internet www.ecop.org.ph; f. 1975; Chair. MIGUEL B. VARELA; Pres. RENE Y. SORIANO.

Filipino Shipowners' Association: Victoria Bldg, Room 503, 429 United Nations Ave, Ermita, 1000 Metro Manila; tel. (2) 5227318; fax (2) 5243164; e-mail filiship@info.com.ph; internet www.filipinoshipowners.com; f. 1950; 24 mems, including 6 assoc. mems; Chair. and Pres. CARLOS C. SALINAS; Exec. Sec. AUGUSTO Y. ARREZA, Jr.

Philippine Cement Manufacturers Corporation (PHILCEMCOR): Corporal Cruz, cnr E. Rodriguez Jr Ave, Bagong Ilog, Pasig City, Metro Manila; tel. (2) 6717585; fax (2) 6717588; e-mail alfiler@info.com.ph; Pres. FELIX ENRICO R. ALFILER.

Philippine Cigar and Cigarette Manufacturers' Association: Unit 508, 1851 Dr Antonio Vasquez St, Malate, Metro Manila; tel. (2) 5249285; fax (2) 5249514; Pres. ANTONIO B. YAO.

Philippine Coconut Producers' Federation, Inc: Wardley Bldg, 2nd Floor, 1991 Taft Ave, cnr San Juan St, Pasay City, 1300 Metro Manila; tel. (2) 5230918; fax (2) 5211333; e-mail cocofed@pworld.net.ph; Pres. MARIA CLARA L. LOBREGAT.

Philippine Retailers' Association: Unit 2610, Jollibee Plaza, Emerald Ave, Ortigas Center, Pasig City; tel. (2) 6874180; fax (2) 6360825; e-mail pra@philretailers.com; internet www.philretailers.com; f. 1976; Pres. BIENVENIDO V. TANTOCO, III.

Philippine Sugar Millers' Association Inc: 1402 Security Bank Centre, 6776 Ayala Ave, Makati City, 1226 Metro Manila; tel. (2) 8911138; fax (2) 8911141; e-mail psma@psma.com.ph; internet www.psma.com.ph; f. 1922; Chair. JULIO O. SY; Pres. V. FRANCISCO VARUA.

Textile Mills Association of the Philippines, Inc (TMAP): Ground Floor, Alexander House, 132 Amorsolo St, Legaspi Village, Makati City, 1229 Metro Manila; tel. (2) 8186601; fax (2) 8183107; e-mail tmap@pacific.net.ph; f. 1956; 11 mems; Pres. HERMENEGILDO C. ZAYCO; Chair. JAMES L. GO.

Textile Producers' Association of the Philippines, Inc: Downtown Center Bldg, Room 513, 516 Quintin Paredes St, Binondo, Metro Manila; tel. (2) 2411144; fax (2) 2411162; Pres. GO CUN UY; Exec. Sec. ROBERT L. TAN.

UTILITIES

Energy Regulatory Commission: Pacific Center Bldg, San Miguel Ave, Ortigas Center, Pasig City, 1600 Metro Manila; tel. (2) 9145000; fax (2) 6315818; e-mail info@erc.gov.ph; internet www.erc.gov.ph; Chair. RODOLFO B. ALBANO, Jr; Exec. Dir TERESA R. CASTAÑEDO.

Electricity

Davao Light and Power Co: 163–5 C. Bangoy, Sr, St, Davao City 8000; tel. (82) 2212191; fax (82) 2212105; e-mail davaolight@davao-online.com; internet www.davaolight.com; the country's third largest electric utility with a peak demand of 175 MW in 2000.

Manila Electric Co (Meralco): Lopez Bldg, 2nd Floor, Meralco Center, Ortigas Ave, Pasig City, 0300 Metro Manila; tel. (2) 6312222; fax (2) 6315591; e-mail finplan.inv.relations@meralco.com.ph; internet www.meralco.com.ph; f. 1903; supplies electric power to Manila and seven provinces in Luzon; largest electricity distributor, supplying 54% of total consumption in 2000; privatized in 1991, 34% govt-owned; cap. and res 54,382m., sales 85,946m. (1998); Chair. and CEO MANUEL M. LOPEZ; Pres. JESUS P. FRANCISCO.

National Power Corpn (NAPOCOR): Quezon Ave, cnr BIR Rd, Quezon City, Metro Manila; tel. (2) 9213541; fax (2) 9212468; e-mail webmaster@napocor.gov.ph; internet www.napocor.gov.ph; f. 1936; state-owned corpn supplying electric and hydroelectric power throughout the country; scheduled for privatization; installed capacity in 1998, 11,810 MW; sales 86,611m. pesos (Dec. 1998); 12,043 employees; chaired by the Secretary of Finance; Pres. CYRIL C. DEL CALLAR.

Gas

First Gas Holdings Corpn: Benpres Bldg, 4th Floor, Exchange Rd, cnr Meralco Ave, Pasig City, Metro Manila; tel. (2) 6343428; fax (2) 6352737; e-mail csamurao@firstgas.com.ph; internet www.firstgas.com.ph; major interests in power generation and distribution; Pres. PETER GARRUCHO.

Directory

Water

Regulatory Authority

Metropolitan Waterworks and Sewerage System: 4th Floor, Administration Bldg, MWSS Complex, 489 Katipunan Rd, Balara, Quezon City, 1105 Metro Manila; tel. (2) 9223757; fax (2) 9212887; e-mail info@mwss.gov.ph; internet www.mwss.gov.ph; govt regulator for water supply, treatment and distribution within Metro Manila; Administrator ORLANDO C. HONDRADE.

Distribution Companies

Davao City Water District: Km 5, Jose P. Laurel Ave, Bajada, 8000 Davao City; tel. (82) 2219400; fax (82) 2264885; e-mail dcwd@davao-water.gov.ph; internet www.davao-water.gov.ph; f. 1973; public utility responsible for the water supply of Davao City; Chair. EDUARDO A. BANGAYAN; Gen. Man. Eng. RODORA N. GAMBOA (acting).

Manila Water: Administration Bldg, 2nd Floor, MWSS Compound, 489 Katipunan Rd, Balara, Quezon City, 1105 Metro Manila; tel. (2) 9281223; fax (2) 9223761; e-mail info@manilawateronline.com; internet www.manilawater.com; f. 1997 following the privatization of Metro Manila's water services; responsible for water supply to Manila East until 2023; Pres. ANTONINO T. AQUINO.

Maynilad Water: MWSS Compound, Katipunan Rd, Balara, Quezon City, Metro Manila; tel. (2) 4353583; fax (2) 9223759; e-mail www.mayniladwater.com.ph; f. 1998 following the privatization of Metro Manila's water services; responsible for water supply, sewage and sanitation services for Manila West until 2021; Pres. FIORELLO R. ESTUAR.

Metropolitan Cebu Water District: Magallanes St, cnr Lapulapu St, 6000 Cebu City; tel. (32) 2560413; fax (32) 2545391; e-mail mcwd@cvis.net.ph; internet www.mcwd.gov.ph; f. 1974; public utility responsible for water supply and sewerage of Cebu City and surrounding towns and cities; Chair. JUAN SAUL F. MONTECILLO; Gen. Man. ARMANDO H. PAREDES.

TRADE UNION FEDERATIONS

In 1986 the Government established the Labor Advisory Consultation Committee (LACC) to facilitate communication between the Government and the powerful labour movement in the Philippines. The LACC granted unions direct recognition and access to the Government, which, under the Marcos regime, had been available only to the Trade Union Congress of the Philippines (KMP-TUCP). The KMP-TUCP refused to join the Committee.

In May 1994 a new trade union alliance, the Caucus for Labor Unity, was established; its members included the KMP-TUCP and three groups that had dissociated themselves from the former Kilusang Mayo Uno.

Katipunang Manggagawang Pilipino (KMP-TUCP) (Trade Union Congress of the Philippines): TUCP Training Center Bldg, TUCP-PGEA Compound, Masaya St, cnr Maharlika St, Diliman, Quezon City, 1101 Metro Manila; tel. (2) 9247551; fax (2) 9219758; e-mail secrtucp@tucp.org.ph; internet www.tucp.org.ph; f. 1975; 1.5m. mems; Pres. DEMOCRITO T. MENDOZA; Gen. Sec. ERNESTO F. HERRERA; 39 affiliates, incl.:

Associated Labor Union for Metalworkers (ALU—METAL): TUCP-PGEA Compound, Diliman, Quezon City, 1101 Metro Manila; tel. (2) 9222575; fax (2) 9247553; e-mail alumla@info.com.ph; 29,700 mems; Pres. DEMOCRITO T. MENDOZA.

Associated Labor Union for Textile Workers (ALU—TEXTILE): TUCP-PGEA Compound, Elliptical Rd, Diliman, Quezon City, 1101 Metro Manila; tel. (2) 9222575; fax (2) 9247553; e-mail alumla@info.com.ph; 41,400 mems; Pres. DEMOCRITO T. MENDOZA.

Associated Labor Unions (ALU—TRANSPORT): 1763 Tomas Claudio St, Baclaran, Parañaque, Metro Manila; tel. (2) 8320634; fax (2) 8322392; 49,500 mems; Pres. ALEXANDER O. BARRIENTOS.

Associated Labor Unions—Visayas Mindanao Confederation of Trade Unions (ALU—VIMCONTU): ALU Bldg, Quezon Blvd, Port Area, Elliptical Rd, cnr Maharlika St, Diliman, Quezon City, 1101 Metro Manila; tel. (2) 9222185; fax (2) 9247553; e-mail alumla@info.com.ph; f. 1954; 350,000 mems; Pres. DEMOCRITO T. MENDOZA.

Associated Professional, Supervisory, Office and Technical Employees Union (APSOTEU): TUCP-PGEA Compound, Elliptical Rd, Diliman, Quezon City, 1101 Metro Manila; tel. (2) 9222575; fax (2) 9247553; e-mail alumla@info.com.ph; Pres. CECILIO T. SENO.

Association of Independent Unions of the Philippines: Vila Bldg, Mezzanine Floor, Epifanio de los Santos Ave, Cubao, Quezon City, Metro Manila; tel. (2) 9224652; Pres. EMMANUEL S. DURANTE.

Association of Trade Unions (ATU): Antwel Bldg, Room 1, 2nd Floor, Santa Ana, Port Area, Davao City; tel. (82) 2272394; 2,997 mems; Pres. JORGE ALEGARBES.

THE PHILIPPINES

Confederation of Labor and Allied Social Services (CLASS): Doña Santiago Bldg, TUCP Suite 404, 1344 Taft Ave, Ermita, Metro Manila; tel. (2) 5240415; fax (2) 5266011; f. 1979; 4,579 mems; Pres. LEONARDO F. AGTING.

Federation of Agrarian and Industrial Toiling Hands (FAITH): Kalayaan Ave, cnr Masigla St, Diliman, Quezon City, Metro Manila; tel. (2) 9225244; 220,000 mems; Pres. RAYMUNDO YUMUL.

Federation of Consumers' Co-operatives in Negros Oriental (FEDCON): Bandera Bldg, Cervantes St, Dumaguete City; tel. (32) 2048; Chair. MEDARDO VILLALON.

Federation of Unions of Rizal (FUR): Suite 307, Buenavista Bldg, 3rd Floor, 82 Quirino Ave, cnr Rivera St, Parañaque City, Metro Manila; tel. and fax (2) 8320110; 10,853 mems; Officer-in-Charge EDUARDO ASUNCION.

Lakas sa Industriya ng Kapatirang Haligi ng Alyansa (LIKHA): 32 Kabayanihan Rd Phase IIA, Karangalan Village, Pasig City, Metro Manila; tel. and fax (2) 6463234; e-mail jbvlikha@yahoo.com; Pres. JESUS B. VILLAMOR.

National Association of Free Trade Unions (NAFTU): Rm 404, San Luis Terrace, T. M. Kalaw St, Ermita, Metro Manila; tel. (2) 598705; 7,385 mems; Pres. JAIME RINCAL.

National Congress of Unions in the Sugar Industry of the Philippines (NACUSIP): 7431 A Yakal St, Barangay San Antonio, Makati City, Metro Manila; tel. and fax (2) 8437284; e-mail nacusip@compass.com.ph; 32 affiliated unions and 57,424 mems; Nat. Pres. ZOILO V. DELA CRUZ, Jr.

National Mines and Allied Workers' Union (NAMAWU): Unit 201, A. Dunville Condominium, 1 Castilla St, cnr Valencio St, Quezon City, Metro Manila; tel. (2) 7265070; fax (2) 4155582; 13,233 mems; Pres. ROBERTO A. PADILLA.

Pambansang Kilusan ng Paggagwa (KILUSAN): TUCP-PGEA Compound, Elliptical Rd, Diliman, Quezon City, 1101 Metro Manila; tel. (2) 9284651; 13,093 mems; Pres. AVELINO V. VALERIO; Sec.-Gen. IGMIDIO T. GANAGANA.

Philippine Agricultural, Commercial and Industrial Workers' Union (PACIWU): 5 7th St, Lacson, Bacolod City; fax (2) 7097967; Pres. ZOILO V. DELA CRUZ, Jr.

Philippine Federation of Labor (PFL): FEMII Bldg, Suite 528, Aduana St, Intramuros, Metro Manila; tel. (2) 5271686; fax (2) 5272838; 8,869 mems; Pres. ALEJANDRO C. VILLAVIZA.

Philippine Federation of Teachers' Organizations (PFTO): BSP Bldg, Room 112, Concepcion St, Ermita, Metro Manila; tel. (2) 5275106; Pres. FEDERICO D. RICAFORT.

Philippine Government Employees' Association (PGEA): TUCP-PGEA Compound, Elliptical Rd, Diliman, Quezon City, Metro Manila; tel. (2) 6383541; fax (2) 6375764; e-mail eso_pgea@hotmail.com; f. 1945; 65,000 mems; Pres. ESPERANZA S. OCAMPO.

Philippine Integrated Industries Labor Union (PIILU): Mendoza Bldg, Room 319, 3rd Floor, Pilar St, Zamboanga City; tel. (992) 2299; f. 1973; Pres. JOSE J. SUAN.

Philippine Labor Federation (PLF): ALU Bldg, Quezon Blvd, Port Area, Cebu City; tel. (32) 71219; fax (32) 97544; 15,462 mems; Pres. CRISPIN B. GASTARDO.

Philippine Seafarers' Union (PSU): TUCP-PGEA Compound, Elliptical Rd, Diliman, Quezon City, 1101 Metro Manila; tel. (2) 9222575; fax (2) 9247553; e-mail psumla@info.com.ph; 10,000 mems; Pres. DEMOCRITO T. MENDOZA; Gen. Sec. ERNESTO F. HERRERA.

Philippine Transport and General Workers' Organization (PTGWO–D): Cecilleville Bldg, 3rd Floor, Quezon Ave, Quezon City, Metro Manila; tel. (2) 4115811; fax (2) 4115812; f. 1953; 33,400 mems; Pres. VICTORINO F. BALAIS.

Port and General Workers' Federation (PGWF): Capilitan Engineering Corpn Bldg, 206 Zaragoza St, Tondo, Manila; tel. 208959; Pres. FRANKLIN D. BUTCON.

Public Services Labor Independent Confederation (PSLINK): 15 Clarion Lily St, Congressional Ave, Quezon City, 1100 Metro Manila; tel. (2) 9244710; fax (2) 9281090; e-mail annie.geron@pslink.org; internet www.pslink.org; f. 1987 as Public Sector Labor Integrative Center; 35,108 mems; Pres. JARAH HAMJAH; Gen. Sec. ANNIE ENRIQUEZ-GERON.

United Sugar Farmers' Organization (USFO): SPCMA Annex Bldg, 3rd Floor, 1 Luzuriaga St, Bacolod City; Pres. BERNARDO M. REMO.

Workers' Alliance Trade Unions (WATU): Delta Bldg, Room 300, Quezon Ave, cnr West Ave, Quezon City, Metro Manila; tel. (2) 9225093; fax (2) 975918; f. 1978; 25,000 mems; Pres. TEMISTOCLES S. DEJON, Sr.

INDEPENDENT LABOUR FEDERATIONS

The following organizations are not affiliated to the KMP-TUCP:

Associated Marine Officers and Seamen's Union of the Philippines (AMOSUP): Seaman's Centre, cnr Cabildo and Sta Potenciana Sts, Intramuros, Metro Manila; tel. (2) 5278491; fax (2) 5273534; e-mail s_center@amosup.org; internet www.amosup.org; f. 1960; 23 affiliated unions with 55,000 mems; Pres. GREGORIO S. OCA.

Federation of Free Workers (FFW): FFW Bldg, 1943 Taft Ave, Malate, Metro Manila; tel. (2) 5219435; fax (2) 4006656; f. 1950; affiliated to the Brotherhood of Asian Trade Unionists and the World Confed. of Labour; 300 affiliated local unions and 400,000 mems; Pres. RAMON J. JABAR.

Lakas ng Manggagawa Labor Center: Rm 401, Femii Bldg Annex, A. Soriano St, Intramuros, Metro Manila; tel. and fax (2) 5280482; a grouping of 'independent' local unions; Chair. OSCAR M. ACERSON.

Manggagawa ng Komunikasyon sa Pilipinas (MKP): 22 Libertad St, Mandaluyong City, Metro Manila; tel. (2) 5313701; fax (2) 5312109; f. 1951; Pres. PETE PINLAC.

National Confederation of Labor: Suite 402, Carmen Bldg, Ronquillo St, cnr Evangelista St, Quiapo, Metro Manila; tel. and fax (2) 7334474; f. 1994 by fmr mems of Kilusang Mayo Uno; Pres. ANTONIO DIAZ.

Philippine Social Security Labor Union (PSSLU): Carmen Bldg, Suite 309, Ronquillo St, Quiapo, Metro Manila; f. 1954; Nat. Pres. ANTONIO B. DIAZ; Nat. Sec. OFELIA C. ALAVERA.

Samahang Manggagawang Pilipino (SMP) (National Alliance of Teachers and Office Workers): Fersal Condominium II, Room 33, 130 Kalayaan Ave, Quezon City, 1104 Metro Manila; tel. and fax (2) 9242299; Pres. ADELISA RAYMUNDO.

Solidarity Trade Conference for Progress: Rizal Ave, Dipolog City; tel. and fax (65) 2124303; Pres. NICOLAS E. SABANDAL.

Trade Unions of the Philippines and Allied Services (TUPAS): Med-dis Bldg, Suites 203–204, Solana St, cnr Real St, Intramuros, Metro Manila; tel. (2) 493449; affiliated to the World Fed. of Trade Unions; 280 affiliated unions and 75,000 mems; Nat. Pres. DIOSCORO O. NUÑEZ; Sec.-Gen. VLADIMIR R. TUPAZ.

Transport

RAILWAYS

The railway network is confined mainly to the island of Luzon.

Light Rail Transit Authority (Metrorail): Adm. Bldg, LRTA Compound, Aurora Blvd, Pasay City, Metro Manila; tel. (2) 8530041; fax (2) 8316449; e-mail lrt.authority@lrta.gov.ph; internet www.lrta.gov.ph; managed and operated by Light Rail Transit Authority (LRTA); electrically-driven mass transit system; Line 1 (15 km, Baclaran to Monumento) began commercial operations in Dec. 1984; construction of Line 1 South Extension (12 km, Baclaran to Bacoot) expected to start in 2006 and Line 2 (13.8 km, Santolan to Recto) scheduled to become fully operational by Oct. 2004; Administrator MELQUIADES A. ROBLES.

Philippine National Railways: PNR Management Center, Torres Bugallon St, Kalookan City, 1408 Metro Manila; tel. (2) 3654716; fax (2) 3620824; internet www.pnr.gov.ph; f. 1887; govt-owned; northern line services run from Manila to Caloocan, 6 km (although the track extends to San Fernando, La Union) and southern line services run from Manila to Legaspi, Albay, 479 km; Chair. and Gen. Man. JOSE M. SARASOLA II.

ROADS

In 2000 there were 201,994 km of roads in the Philippines, of which 30,013 km were highways and 49,992 km were secondary roads; an estimated 42,419 km of the network were paved. Bus services provided the most widely-used form of inland transport.

Department of Public Works and Highways: Bonifacio Drive, Port Area, Metro Manila; tel. (2) 5274111; fax (2) 5275635; e-mail soriquest.florante@dpwh.gov.ph; internet www.dpwh.gov.ph; responsible for the construction and maintenance of roads and bridges; Sec. HERMOGENES E. EBDANE, Jr.

Land Transportation Franchising and Regulatory Board: East Ave, Quezon City, Metro Manila; tel. (2) 4262505; fax (2) 4262515; internet www.ltfrb.gov.ph; f. 1987; Chair. DANTE LANTIN.

Land Transportation Office (LTO): East Ave, Quezon City, 1100 Metro Manila; tel. (2) 9219072; fax (2) 9219071; e-mail ltombox@lto.gov.ph; internet www.lto.gov.ph; f. 1987; plans, formulates and implements land transport rules and regulations, safety measures; registration of motor vehicles; issues licences; Exec. Dir BELLA G. BERMUNDO; Asst Sec. ANNELI R. LONTOC.

SHIPPING

In 2000 there were 102 national and municipal ports, 20 baseports, 58 terminal ports and 270 private ports. The eight major ports are Manila, Cebu, Iloilo, Cagayan de Oro, Zamboanga, General Santos, Polloc and Davao.

Pangasiwaan ng Daungan ng Pilipinas (Philippine Ports Authority): Marsman Bldg, 22 Muelle de San Francisco St, South Harbour, Port Area, 1018 Metro Manila; tel. (2) 5274856; fax (2) 5274853; e-mail info@ppa.gov.ph; internet www.ppa.gov.ph; f. 1977; supervises all ports within the Philippine Ports Authority port system; Gen. Man. OSCAR M. SEVILLA.

Philippine Shippers' Bureau (PSB): Trade and Industry Bldg, 5th Floor, 361 Sen. Gil J. Puyat Ave, Makati City, Metro Manila; tel. and fax (2) 8904880; e-mail psb@dti.gov.ph; shipping facilitator for international and domestic trade; promotes and protects the interests of shippers, exporters, importers and domestic traders; Dir PEDRO VICENTE C. MENDOZA.

Domestic Lines

Albar Shipping and Trading Corpn: 2649 Molave St cnr East Service Road, United Parañaque 1, Parañaque, 1713 Metro Manila; tel. (2) 8232391; fax (2) 8233046; e-mail info@albargroup.com.ph; internet www.albargroup.com.ph; f. 1974; manning agency (maritime), trading, ship husbanding; Chair. AKIRA S. KATO; Pres. JOSE ALBAR G. KATO.

Candano Shipping Lines, Inc: Victoria Bldg, 6th Floor, 429 United Nations Ave, Ermita, 2802 Metro Manila; tel. (2) 5238051; fax (2) 5211309; f. 1953; inter-island and Far East chartering, cargo shipping; Pres. and Gen. Man. JOSE CANDANO.

Carlos A. Gothong Lines, Inc: Quezon Blvd, Reclamation Area, POB 152, Cebu City; tel. (32) 211181; fax (32) 212265; Exec. Vice-Pres. BOB D. GOTHONG.

Delsan Transport Lines Inc: Magsaysay Center Bldg, 520 T. M. Kalaw St, Ermita, Metro Manila; tel. (2) 5219172; fax (2) 2889331; Pres. VICENTE A. SANDOVAL; Gen. Man. CARLOS A. BUENAFE.

Eastern Shipping Lines, Inc: ESL Bldg, 54 Anda Circle, Port Area, POB 4253, 2803 Metro Manila; tel. (2) 5277841; fax (2) 5273006; e-mail eastship@skyinet.net; f. 1957; services to Japan; Pres. ERWIN L. CHIONGBIAN; Exec. Vice-Pres. ROY L. CHIONGBIAN.

Loadstar Shipping Co Inc: Loadstar Bldg, 1294 Romualdez St, Paco, 1007 Metro Manila; tel. (2) 5238381; fax (2) 5218061; Pres. and Gen. Man. TEODORO G. BERNARDINO.

Lorenzo Shipping Corpn: Pier 6, North Harbor Tondo, 1012 Metro Manila; tel. (2) 2457481; fax (2) 2446849; internet www.lorenzoship.com.ph; Pres. Capt. ROMEO L. MALIG.

Luzteveco (Luzon Stevedoring Corpn): Magsaysay Bldg, 520 T.M. Kalaw St, Ermita, Metro Manila; f. 1909; two brs; freight-forwarding, air cargo, world-wide shipping, broking, stevedoring, salvage, chartering and oil drilling support services; Pres. JOVINO G. LORENZO; Vice-Pres. RODOLFO B. SANTIAGO.

National Shipping Corpn of the Philippines: Knights of Rizal Bldg, Bonifacio Drive, Port Area, Metro Manila; tel. (2) 473631; fax (2) 5300169; services to Hong Kong, Taiwan, Korea, USA; Pres. TONY CHOW.

Negros Navigation Co Inc: Pier 2, North Harbor, Metro Manila; tel. and fax (2) 2454395; e-mail gcabalo@negrosnavigation.ph; internet www.negrosnavigation.ph; Chair. DANIEL L. LACSON.

Philippine Pacific Ocean Lines Inc: Delgado Bldg, Bonifacio Drive, Port Area, POB 184, Metro Manila; tel. (2) 478541; Vice-Pres. C. P. CARANDANG.

Philippine President Lines, Inc: PPL Bldg, 1000–1046 United Nations Ave, POB 4248, Metro Manila; tel. (2) 5249011; fax (2) 5251308; trading world-wide; Chair. EMILIO T. YAP, Jr; Pres. ENRIQUE C. YAP.

Sulpicio Lines, Inc: 1st St, Reclamation Area, POB 137, Cebu City; tel. (32) 73839; Chair. ENRIQUE S. GO; Man. Dir CARLOS S. GO.

Sweet Lines Inc: Pier 6, North Harbor, Metro Manila; tel. (2) 201791; fax (2) 205534; f. 1937; Pres. EDUARDO R. LOPINGCO; Exec. Vice-Pres. SONNY R. LOPINGCO.

Transocean Transport Corpn: Magsaysay Bldg, 8th Floor, 520 T. M. Kalaw St, Ermita, POB 21, Metro Manila; tel. (2) 506611; Pres. and Gen. Man. MIGUEL A. MAGSAYSAY; Vice-Pres. EDUARDO U. MANESE.

United Philippine Lines, Inc: UPL Bldg, Santa Clara St, Intramuros, POB 127, Metro Manila; tel. (2) 5277491; fax (2) 5271603; e-mail uplines@skyinet.net; services world-wide; Pres. FERNANDO V. LISING.

WG & A Philippines, Inc: South Harbour Center 2, cnr Railroad St, South Harbour, Metro Manila; tel. (2) 5274605; fax (2) 5360945; internet www.wgasuperferry.com; f. 1996 following the merger of William Lines, Aboitiz Shipping and Carlos A. Gothong Lines; passenger and cargo inter-island services; Pres. ENDICA ABOITIZ; Chair. W. L. CHIONGBIAN.

CIVIL AVIATION

In March 1999 there were 92 national and 103 private airports in the Philippines. In addition to the international airports in Metro Manila (the Ninoy Aquino International Airport), Cebu (the Mactan International Airport), Angeles City (the Clark International Airport), and Olongapo City (the Subic Bay International Airport), there are five alternative international airports: Laoag City, Ilocos Norte; Davao City; Zamboanga City; Gen. Santos (Tambler) City; and Puerto Princesa City, Palawan. Plans to build a third international terminal at Ninoy Aquino Airport were approved in 1997; construction work was expected to be completed in mid-2006, although an ongoing legal dispute between the Government and the project's main contractor over alleged contractual anomalies was threatening to delay proceedings. A new international airport, in Davao City, was opened in December 2003. In March 2004 the Government announced that construction of an international airport in Iloilo City, intended to replace the city's existing airport, would begin in that month.

Air Transportation Office: MIA Rd, Pasay City, Metro Manila; tel. (2) 8799104; fax (2) 8340143; e-mail director_gen@ato.gov.ph; internet www.ato.gov.ph; implements govt policies for the development and operation of a safe and efficient aviation network; Dir-Gen. NILO C. JATICO.

Civil Aeronautics Board: Airport Rd, Pasay City, Metro Manila; tel. (2) 8337266; fax (2) 8336911; e-mail tmanalac@cab.gov.ph; internet www.cab.gov.ph; exercises general supervision and regulation of, and jurisdiction and control over, air carriers, their equipment facilities and franchise; Exec. Dir TOMAS T. MAÑALAC.

Manila International Airport Authority (MIAA): NAIA Complex, Pasay City, Metro Manila; tel. (2) 8322938; fax (2) 8331180; e-mail gm@miaa.gov.ph; Gen. Man. ALFONSO G. CUSI.

Air Philippines: R1 Hangar, APC Gate 1, Andrews Ave, Nichols, Pasay City, Metro Manila; tel. (2) 8517601; fax (2) 8517922; e-mail info@airphilippines.com.ph; internet www.airphils.com; f. 1995; domestic and regional services; Chair. and Pres. WILLIAM GATCHALIAN.

Asian Spirit: G & A Bldg, 3rd Floor, 2303 Don Chino Roces Ave, Makati City, Metro Manila; tel. (2) 8403811; fax (2) 8130183; e-mail info@asianspirit.com; internet www.asianspirit.com; Man. ANTONIO BUENDIA.

Cebu Pacific Air: Robinsons Equitable Tower, 16th Floor, ADB Ave, Cnr Poveda Rd, Ortigas Center, Pasig City, Metro Manila; tel. (2) 7020888; fax (2) 6379170; e-mail feedback@cebupacificair.com; internet www.cebupacificair.com; f. 1995; domestic and international services; Chair. RICARDO J. ROMULO; Pres. and CEO LANCE GOKONGWEI.

Grand Air: Mercure Hotel, Philippines Village Airport Compound, 8th Floor, Pasay City, 1300 Metro Manila; tel. (2) 8313001; fax (2) 8917682; f. 1994; Pres. REBECCA PANLILI.

Philippine Airlines Inc (PAL): PAL Corporate Communications Dept, PAL Center, Ground Floor, Legaspi St, Legaspi Village, Makati City, 0750 Metro Manila; tel. (2) 8171234; fax (2) 8136715; e-mail webmgr@pal.com.ph; internet www.philippineairlines.com; f. 1941; in Jan. 1992 67% of PAL was transferred to the private sector; operates domestic, regional and international services to destinations in the Far East, Australasia, the Middle East, the USA and Canada; Chair. and CEO LUCIO TAN; Pres. and COO JAIME J. BAUTISTA.

Tourism

Tourism, although adversely affected from time to time by political unrest, remains an important sector of the economy. In 2003 arrivals totalled 1,907,226, compared with 1,932,677 in the previous year. Tourist receipts, including passenger transport, totalled US $1,549m. in 2003 (compared with $1,827m. in 2002).

Philippine Convention and Visitors' Corpn: Legaspi Towers, 4th Floor, 300 Roxas Blvd, 1004 Metro Manila; tel. (2) 5259318; fax (2) 5216165; e-mail pcvcnet@dotpcvc.gov.ph; internet www.dotpcvc.gov.ph; Chair. ROBERTO M. PAGDANGANAN; Exec. Dir DANIEL G. CORPUZ.

Philippine Tourism Authority: Department of Tourism Bldg, T. M. Kalaw St, Teodoro F. Valencia Circle, Ermita, 1000 Metro Manila; tel. (2) 5247141; fax (2) 5218113; e-mail info@philtourism.gov.ph; internet www.philtourism.com; Gen. Man. and CEO ROBERT DEAN BARBERS.

POLAND

Introductory Survey

Location, Climate, Language, Religion, Flag, Capital

The Republic of Poland is situated in eastern Europe, bounded to the north by the Baltic Sea and an exclave of the Russian Federation (Kaliningrad Oblast), to the north-east by Lithuania, to the east by Belarus, to the south-east by Ukraine, to the west by Germany and to the south by the Czech Republic and Slovakia. The climate is temperate in the west but continental in the east. Poland has short summers and cold, snowy winters. Temperatures in Warsaw are generally between −6°C (21°F) and 24°C (75°F). Most of the inhabitants profess Christianity: more than 95% are adherents of the Roman Catholic Church, but there are numerous other denominations, the largest being the Polish Autocephalous Orthodox Church. The official language is Polish, spoken by almost all of the population, and there is a small German-speaking community. The national flag (proportions 5 by 8) has two equal horizontal stripes, of white and red. The capital is Warsaw (Warszawa).

Recent History

Poland, partitioned since the 18th century, was declared an independent republic on 11 November 1918, at the end of the First World War. The country was ruled by a military regime from 1926 until 1939, when Poland was invaded by both Germany and the USSR and partitioned between the two powers. After Germany declared war on the USSR in June 1941, its forces occupied the whole of Poland until they were expelled by Soviet troops in March 1945.

At the end of the Second World War a pro-communist 'Polish Committee of National Liberation', established under Soviet auspices in July 1944, was transformed into a Provisional Government. Under the Potsdam Agreement, signed by the major Allied powers in 1945, the former German territories lying east of the rivers Oder and Neisse (which now comprise one-third of Poland's total area) came under Polish sovereignty, while Poland's frontier with the USSR was shifted westward. These border changes were accompanied by a major resettlement of the population in the affected areas.

Non-communist political groups suffered severe intimidation during national elections in January 1947, in which the communist-led 'democratic bloc' claimed victory. A People's Republic was established in February, with the Polish Workers' Party (PWP), led by Władysław Gomułka, as the dominant group. Gomułka's reluctance to implement certain aspects of Soviet economic policies, notably the collectivization of agriculture, led to his dismissal as First Secretary of the PWP in 1948. In December of that year the PWP merged with the Polish Socialist Party to form the Polish United Workers' Party (PZPR). Two other parties, the United Peasants' Party (ZSL) and the Democratic Party (Stronnictwo Demokratyczne—SD), were permitted to remain in existence, but were closely controlled by the PZPR, and Poland effectively became a one-party state.

The PZPR's strict control over public life eased slightly following the death of Stalin, the Soviet leader, in 1953. In 1956 mass demonstrations, provoked by food shortages, were suppressed by security forces. In the ensuing political crisis Gomułka was returned to office, despite Soviet opposition. A period of stability and some liberalization followed, and in 1964–70 limited economic reforms were implemented, although the standard of living remained low. In December 1970 a sharp rise in food prices led to strikes and demonstrations in the Baltic port of Gdańsk and in other cities. Many demonstrators were killed or injured in clashes with the police and army, and Gomułka was forced to resign as First Secretary of the PZPR; he was succeeded by Edward Gierek.

In July 1980 an increase in meat prices prompted widespread labour unrest, and shipyard employees in the Baltic ports, notably at Gdańsk, demanded the right to form free trade unions. Following negotiations, the Government finally granted permission to establish several self-governing trade unions, under the guidance of Solidarity (Solidarność), the organization involved in the Gdańsk strike, which was led by a local worker, Lech Wałęsa. In September, as mass labour unrest continued, Gierek was replaced as First Secretary of the PZPR by Stanisław Kania.

Under the growing influence of Solidarity (which claimed an estimated 10m. members in 1981), strikes continued throughout the country, and in February Józef Pińkowski resigned as Chairman of the Council of Ministers. He was succeeded by Gen. Wojciech Jaruzelski, Minister of Defence (a post he retained) since 1968. Despite further concessions to Solidarity, the crisis persisted, forcing Kania's resignation in October; he was succeeded by Jaruzelski, who thus held the leading posts in both the PZPR and the Government.

On 13 December 1981 martial law was imposed throughout Poland. A governing Military Council of National Salvation, led by Jaruzelski, was established; all trade-union activity was suspended, and Wałęsa and other Solidarity leaders were detained. Violent clashes between workers and security forces ensued, and thousands of protesters were arrested. Sporadic disturbances continued in 1982, particularly in response to legislation (imposed in October) abolishing all trade unions. Wałęsa was released in November, and in December martial law was suspended and some other prisoners were freed. (During 1982 about 10,000 prisoners had been detained, and at least 15 demonstrators killed.) In July 1983 martial law was formally ended; the Military Council of National Salvation was dissolved, and an amnesty was declared for most political prisoners and underground activists. In October Wałęsa was awarded the Nobel Peace Prize.

In July 1984, to mark the 40th anniversary of the Polish communist regime, some 35,000 detainees were granted amnesty. In August US sanctions (imposed following the declaration of martial law) were relaxed. However, the murder, in October, of Fr Jerzy Popiełuszko, a well-known pro-Solidarity Roman Catholic priest, provoked renewed unrest. In February 1985 four officers from the Ministry of Internal Affairs were found guilty of the murder, and received lengthy prison sentences. (The case was subsequently reopened; two generals, accused of directing the murder, were acquitted in August 1994, but the verdict was overturned in March 1996, and it was announced that the case was to be re-examined.)

Legislative elections took place in October 1985. New regulations gave voters a choice of two candidates for 410 of the Sejm's 460 seats, the remaining 50 deputies being elected unopposed on a national list. Solidarity appealed to voters to boycott the poll, and subsequently disputed the Government's claim that 79% of the electorate had participated. In November Jaruzelski resigned as Chairman of the Council of Ministers, in order to become President of the Council of State (Head of State). His former post was taken by Prof. Zbigniew Messner, hitherto a Deputy Chairman of the Council of Ministers.

In December 1986, in an effort to increase support for the regime, Jaruzelski established a 56-member Consultative Council, which was attached to the Council of State and comprised mainly non-PZPR members—among them independent Roman Catholic activists and former members of Solidarity. Nevertheless, public discontent intensified in 1987. Solidarity activists attempted to disrupt the official May Day celebrations in several cities, and in June there were violent clashes between police and protesters during a visit by Pope John Paul II to his native country. Significant price rises were imposed in early 1988, prompting widespread protests, and the May Day celebrations were again disrupted. In August a strike by coal-workers rapidly spread to other sectors, leading to the most serious industrial unrest since 1981.

The Messner Government resigned in September 1988. Dr Mieczysław Rakowski, Deputy Chairman in 1981–85, was appointed Chairman of a new Council of Ministers, which included several non-PZPR members and younger, reformist politicians. However, the Government's announcement that the Lenin Shipyard in Gdańsk was to be closed, ostensibly for economic reasons, provoked further strike action. By April 1989 agreement had been reached on the restoration of legal status to Solidarity, as well as on the holding of elections to a new, bicameral legislature, the Zgromadzenie Narodowe (National Assembly). Solidarity and other non-communist groups were to be permitted to contest all the seats in a new upper chamber, the

Senat, which would have a limited right of veto over the lower chamber, the Sejm. Just 35% of the seats in the Sejm were to be subject to free elections, with the remainder open only to candidates of the PZPR and its associate organizations. A new post of executive President was also to be introduced. The necessary amendments to the Constitution were duly approved by the Sejm. In May the Roman Catholic Church was accorded legal status.

Elections to the new legislature took place on 4 and 8 July 1989, with 62% of eligible voters participating in the first round, but only 25% in the second. In the elections to the Senat, the Solidarity Citizens' Committee, the electoral wing of the trade-union movement, secured all but one of the 100 seats. In the elections to the 460-member Sejm, Solidarity secured all the 161 seats that it was permitted to contest, and the other 299 seats were divided between the PZPR (173 seats), its allied parties—the ZSL (76) and the SD (27)—and members of Roman Catholic organizations (23).

The new legislature narrowly elected Jaruzelski, unopposed, to the post of executive President. He was replaced as First Secretary of the PZPR by Rakowski. Jaruzelski accepted Wałęsa's proposal of a coalition of Solidarity, the SD and the ZSL. The appointment of Tadeusz Mazowiecki, a newspaper editor and moderate member of Solidarity, as Chairman of the Council of Ministers, was approved by the Sejm on 24 August 1989, thus ending almost 45 years of exclusive communist rule in Poland. A Solidarity-dominated administration was formed in September.

The new Government's programme of radical political and economic reforms emphasized the creation of democratic institutions and the introduction of a market economy. In December 1989 the legislature voted to rename the country the Republic of Poland, and the national symbols of pre-communist Poland were reintroduced. In January 1990 the PZPR was dissolved to allow the establishment of a new left-wing party, Social Democracy of the Republic of Poland (SdRP). Local elections held in May were the first entirely free elections in Poland for more than 50 years. Candidates of the Solidarity Citizens' Committee won more than 41% of the seats, while nominally independent candidates secured 38%. However, a low rate of participation (only 42% of the electorate) apparently reflected general disenchantment with the Government's austere economic policies. By mid-1990 tension had developed between Wałęsa, who advocated an acceleration of economic reform and privatization, and the more cautious Mazowiecki.

In September 1990 Jaruzelski agreed to resign, to permit a direct presidential election to take place. In the first round, held on 25 November, Mazowiecki received fewer votes than either Wałęsa or an *émigré* business executive, Stanisław Tymiński. Wałęsa and Tymiński proceeded to a second round of voting on 9 December, at which Wałęsa won 74.3% of the votes cast. Wałęsa resigned the chairmanship of Solidarity (he was replaced in February 1991 by Marian Krzaklewski), and in December 1990 was inaugurated as President for a five-year term. Jan Krzysztof Bielecki, a radical economist, became Prime Minister. Bielecki's Council of Ministers retained only two ministers from the outgoing administration. The new regime rapidly encountered challenges to its reform programme. In May 1991 Solidarity organized a nation-wide day of strikes and demonstrations, in protest at the Government's economic policies.

Legislative elections took place on 27 October 1991, with the participation of only 43.2% of the electorate. A total of 29 parties won representation in the Sejm, but none acquired a decisive mandate. The party with the largest number of deputies (62) was Mazowiecki's Democratic Union (UD). The Democratic Left Alliance (Sojusz Lewicy Demokratycznej—SLD), an electoral coalition of the SdRP and the All Poland Trade Unions Alliance, won 60 seats. The UD was also the largest single party in the Senat, with 21 seats, while Solidarity returned 11 senators. After Bronisław Geremek of the UD failed to form a government, Wałęsa nominated Jan Olszewski of the Centre Alliance (PC) as Prime Minister. Criticism of his economic programme by the President and the withdrawal of two parties from the coalition negotiations caused Olszewski to submit his resignation. This was, however, rejected by the Sejm, which proceeded, in December, to approve a new centre-right Council of Ministers, incorporating members of the PC, the pro-Solidarity Peasant Alliance and the Christian National Union (Zjednoczenie Chrześcijańsko-Narodowe—ZChN).

In June 1992, following controversy regarding government attempts to expose alleged communist conspirators, the Sejm approved a motion of 'no confidence' in the Olszewski Government. After the failure of Waldemar Pawlak, the leader of the Polish People's Party (Polskie Stronnictwo Ludowe—PSL) to form a government, the appointment of Hanna Suchocka of the UD was approved by the Sejm. Her new Government, a seven-party coalition dominated by the UD and the ZChN, was immediately challenged by a month-long strike by 40,000 workers at a copper plant in Legnica, supported by several transport and power workers' unions. In December an interim 'Small Constitution' entered into effect, pending a comprehensive revision of the 1952 Constitution. A motion of 'no confidence' in the Suchocka administration, proposed by the Solidarity group after the failure of negotiations between the Government and striking teachers and health workers, was narrowly approved by the Sejm in May 1993. Wałęsa refused to accept Suchocka's resignation; instead, he dissolved the Sejm, scheduling new elections to both houses of parliament for September. The electoral code was amended, in order to achieve greater political stability, with a new stipulation that a party (with the exception of organizations representing national minorities) must secure at least 5% of the total votes cast (8% in the case of an electoral alliance) in order to achieve parliamentary representation.

The general election resulted in victory for parties of the left, as voters demonstrated their dissatisfaction with the recent economic reforms. The SLD and the PSL, both dominated by former communists and their allies, won, respectively, 171 and 132 seats in the Sejm, and 37 and 36 seats in the Senat. The two parties, which together won 35.8% of the total votes in the elections to the Sejm, benefited from the new law to secure more than 65% of the seats in the lower chamber. The UD took 74 seats in the Sejm (with 10.6% of the votes cast) and four in the Senat, while Solidarity won 10 seats in the Senat (although none in the Sejm). Wałęsa's Non-Party Bloc for Reform, established in June, won 16 seats in the Sejm and two seats in the Senat. Almost 35% of the votes cast in elections to the Sejm were for parties that received fewer than 5% of the total votes, notably the PC and the ZChN, and therefore secured no representation; the rate of participation by voters was 52.1%.

In October 1993 Pawlak formed a coalition Government, dominated by members of his PSL and the SLD. The new Prime Minister expressed his commitment to a continuation of market-orientated reforms, but pledged new measures to alleviate their adverse social effects. In early 1994 the Deputy Prime Minister and Minister of Finance, Marek Borowski (of the SLD), resigned. In February at least 20,000 people took part in a Solidarity-led demonstration in Warsaw, to demand increased government investment in the public sector and improved measures to combat unemployment. Solidarity began a nation-wide programme of strike action in March.

In January 1995 Wałęsa refused to endorse legislation to increase rates of personal income tax; however, he was obliged to approve the legislation after his actions were ruled to be unconstitutional. Relations between the Government and the President deteriorated sharply in February, when Wałęsa threatened to dissolve parliament if the Prime Minister did not resign. Further conflict was averted by Pawlak's departure, and in March Józef Oleksy, a member of the SLD and hitherto Marshal (Speaker) of the Sejm, took office as Prime Minister.

The first round of the 1995 presidential election took place on 5 November. The two leading candidates, Aleksander Kwaśniewski, the Chairman of the SdRP (and formerly a leading member of the PZPR), and Wałęsa proceeded to a second round, on 19 November, when Kwaśniewski achieved a narrow victory, with 51.7% of the votes cast. On taking office on 23 December, Kwaśniewski asserted his commitment to the further integration of Poland into Western institutions and to the continuation of policies of economic liberalization. Following Kwaśniewski's election, the ministers responsible for foreign affairs, the interior and national defence (all effectively presidential appointees) submitted their resignations. The outgoing Minister of Internal Affairs, Andrzej Milczanowski, claimed that Oleksy had acted on behalf of Soviet (and subsequently Russian) espionage agents since the 1980s; although Oleksy vehemently denied the charges, he resigned as Prime Minister in January 1996 (he was fully exonerated in an official report published in October). He was subsequently elected Chairman of the SdRP, replacing Kwaśniewski, who had resigned the post and his party membership following his election as President. Włodzimierz Cimoszewicz (the SLD's deputy leader and hitherto deputy Marshal of the Sejm) was appointed as Prime Minister in February.

In June 1996 the Government's decision to file for bankruptcy for the loss-making Gdańsk shipyard prompted Solidarity-led demonstrations. Also in June some 25 centre-right political parties, including Solidarity, the PC and the ZChN, established Solidarity Electoral Action (AWS) to contest the 1997 parliamentary elections. In September 1996 the Prime Minister dismissed the PSL's Jacek Buchacz as Minister of Foreign Economic Relations, prompting the party's withdrawal from government negotiations on proposed administrative reforms. Talks resumed at the end of September, after Cimoszewicz conceded that he had reneged on the coalition accord. Agreement was subsequently reached on the distribution of ministerial portfolios, whereby the PSL was accorded responsibility for the new Ministry of the Treasury, while the SLD secured the Ministry of Internal Affairs and Administration and the new Ministry of the Economy.

On 2 April 1997, after four years of parliamentary negotiations, the legislature adopted a new Constitution, which was approved by 52.7% of the votes cast by some 42.9% of the electorate in a national referendum on 25 May. Right-wing parties, notably AWS and the Movement for the Reconstruction of Poland (Ruch Odbudowy Polski—ROP), had opposed the Constitution, which slightly reduced presidential powers and committed Poland to a social market economy based on the freedom of economic activity and private ownership. The new Constitution came into force on 17 October.

In the general election of 21 September 1997, AWS secured 201 seats in the Sejm (with 33.8% of the valid votes cast) and 51 in the Senate, while the SLD won 164 seats in the Sejm (with 27.1% of the votes) and 28 in the Senate. The PSL retained only 27 seats in the Sejm and three in the Senate. The rate of voter participation was 48%. Marian Krzaklewski, the leader of AWS, subsequently initiated coalition talks with the Freedom Union (UW) and the ROP, which had won, respectively, 60 and six seats in the Sejm, and eight and five in the Senate. Jerzy Buzek (a member of Solidarity since its formation in 1980) was nominated as Prime Minister in mid-October. Following lengthy negotiations, AWS and the UW signed a coalition agreement later that month, despite some opposition from the ZChN and the PC (both members of AWS), which objected to several of the UW's ministerial nominations. A new Council of Ministers was subsequently appointed, which included Leszek Balcerowicz, leader of the UW, as Deputy Prime Minister, Minister of Finance and Chairman of the Economic Committee. In November the Sejm approved the new Government's programme, which prioritized rapid integration with the North Atlantic Treaty Organization (NATO, see p. 314) and the European Union (EU, see p. 228), and accelerated privatization and government reform. Shortly afterwards the Social Movement of Solidarity Electoral Action, which was to replace Solidarity within AWS, applied for registration as a new political party. In December Wałęsa officially formed the Christian Democratic Party of the Third Republic.

In July 1998 a new structure of local and regional government was approved, which reduced the number of voivodships (provinces) from 48 to 16. Local elections were held in the 16 new voivodships in October. In nine voivodships the opposition SLD was returned as the largest party, although the governing AWS-UW coalition won the largest number of seats overall, and secured control of the seven remaining voivodships. Meanwhile, the Government's programme of industrial restructuring continued to provoke public unrest, as well as discord among the governing parties. In April Solidarity organized a 10-day strike at Poland's largest copper mine at Rudna, in protest at planned redundancies. Government proposals to restructure the coal-mining industry, which contradicted pre-election pledges made by the AWS, were presented to the Sejm in that month. In May the Government agreed to reduce the number of job losses in the sector. Railway workers took industrial action in June, and in July around 10,000 farmers attended a demonstration in Warsaw, to demand increased government protection for the agricultural sector. There was further unrest by farmers in August and December. Farmers' protests continued in February 1999, when it was announced that the leader of the Self-Defence Trade Union (Samoobrona, which had organized the protests), Andrzej Lepper, was to stand trial for having organized illegal road blocks. Meanwhile the approval, in July 1998, of the sale of the Gdańsk shipyard (which was completed in September), had prompted six AWS deputies to withdraw their support from the Government in protest. (In preceding weeks nine other deputies had also left the ruling coalition.) In December a strike by coal miners over imminent changes to the pensions system spread to more than 50 mines, and resulted in government concessions; industrial unrest also affected the steel, armaments and railway sectors.

In June 1998 the Sejm adopted a resolution condemning the communist regime imposed on post-war Poland by the USSR; the resolution, which was opposed by the SLD, held the PZPR responsible for offences committed during the communist period. A new penal code came into effect in early September, in conformity with EU criteria, abolishing capital punishment. In late September the Sejm approved legislation granting access for Polish citizens to files compiled on them by the security services during the communist era.

During March 1999 the Prime Minister undertook a major government reorganization, in preparation for a significant reform of state administration, which took effect in April. The Secretary-General of the UW resigned in protest at the appointment of two ministers. In September a new political organization, the Alliance of Polish Christian Democrats (Porozumienie Polskich Chrzescijanskich Demokratów—PPChD), was officially founded; members included the PC—a member of the governing AWS—and the Party of Christian Democrats (PChD).

During May 1999 farmers resumed their protests against agricultural policy. In June a protest in Warsaw by workers from the Lucznik weapons factory in Radom resulted in violent clashes between the police and demonstrators, and nurses and midwives also held protests in the capital in mid-1999. In August farmers joined demonstrations against the low price of grain; an estimated 80 people were injured when violence erupted between police and farmers in northern Poland. Lepper subsequently announced his intention of forming a new anti-Government coalition with other farmers' organizations and trade unions: the Self-Defence Party of the Republic of Poland (Samoobrona) was formally established in January 2000. Protests against the economic slowdown and the implementation of government reforms in education, health and pensions provision culminated, in September 1999, in a march through Warsaw by some 35,000 agricultural and industrial workers (as well as leaders from the opposition SLD and PSL parties).

During September 1999 Buzek came under growing criticism from leading members of his governing coalition, who accused him of weak leadership. At the beginning of the month the Deputy Prime Minister and Minister of Internal Affairs and Administration, Janusz Tomaszewski, announced his resignation. A minor government reorganization took place in early October, and the AWS and the UW renewed their coalition agreement for a further two years. In late October the Government reached a compromise with miners' representatives from Solidarity regarding the restructuring of the industry, following protests in the capital. It was announced in December that Solidarity was to withdraw from political activities and become an 'organization of employees'; the movement's voting rights within the AWS were transferred to the Social Movement of Solidarity Electoral Action.

In mid-May 2000 the ruling coalition entered its most serious crisis, when the Prime Minister suspended the Government of Warsaw's central commune (a coalition of the UW and the SLD) and replaced it with an AWS-affiliated commissioner. At the end of May the UW announced its withdrawal from the coalition, in protest at the blocking of Balcerowicz's proposals for economic reform by AWS deputies. Negotiations aimed at maintaining the coalition collapsed in early June, and Buzek subsequently formed a minority AWS Government. In August the treasury minister, Emil Wąsacz, was dismissed, following long-standing controversy surrounding his privatization policies.

In the presidential election, held on 8 October 2000, Kwaśniewski was re-elected, with 53.9% of the valid votes cast. The second-placed candidate, an independent former foreign minister, Andrzej Olechowski, secured 17.3% of the votes; Krzaklewski obtained 15.6%, Lepper 3.1% and Wałęsa just 1.0%. The rate of participation by the electorate was 61.1%. Wałęsa subsequently announced that he was to retire from politics (although he remained Honorary Chairman of the ChDTRP). Krzaklewski resigned as leader of the AWS in January 2001, and was succeeded by Prime Minister Buzek. (Krzaklewski remained Chairman of Solidarity until September 2002.) Meanwhile, Balcerowicz resigned the leadership of the UW, and became President of the central bank in December 2000.

In January 2001 Olechowski, together with the Marshal of the Sejm, Maciej Plazyński of the AWS, and a Vice-Marshal of the Senat, Donald Tusk of the UW, founded a new political movement, known as the Civic Platform (Platforma Obywatelska—PO). In March the Conservative Peasant Party, a constituent party of the AWS, announced its intention to form an electoral alliance with the PO, although it was to remain in government until the election. Kwaśniewski signed a new electoral law at the end of April, introducing a new method for the calculation of voting under the system of proportional representation, which was expected to favour small and medium-sized parties. Following the enactment of the law, legislative elections were scheduled for 23 September. Thereafter, significant political realignment took place, and in May the AWS was restructured as Solidarity Electoral Action of the Right (AWSP), in alliance with the ROP. At the end of May the traditionalist Roman Catholic, nationalist League of Polish Families (Liga Polskich Rodzin—LPR), which opposed Polish membership of the EU, was registered as a party. In August the legislature rejected an austerity plan proposed by the Minister of Finance, Jarosław Bauc, in an attempt to address the predicted deficit in the budget for 2002, and in late August Buzek announced Bauc's dismissal.

The legislative elections took place as scheduled, on 23 September 2001, with a rate of voter participation of 46.3%. Neither the AWSP nor the UW received the requisite 8% of the votes to obtain seats in the Sejm, although both parties contested the elections to the Senat as part of the Blok Senat 2001 (also comprising the PO, Law and Justice—Prawo i Sprawiedliwość, PiS and the ROP), which won 15 of the 100 seats. Right-wing support was, instead, divided between the PiS, which obtained 44 seats in the Sejm, and the LPR, which secured 38 seats in the Sejm and two seats in the Senat. Another party elected to the Sejm for the first time was the populist agrarian Self-Defence Party, which took 53 seats in the Sejm (with 10.2% of the votes) and two seats in the Senat, and which also opposed accession to the EU. A leftist electoral coalition of the SLD and the Union of Labour (Unia Pracy—UP) won 216 seats in the Sejm (with 41.0% of the votes) and 75 seats in the Senat, but failed to achieve an overall majority. The PO, which received 65 seats in the Sejm (with 12.7% of the votes), rejected an initial proposal to form a coalition with the SLD-UP. Instead, on 9 October the SLD and the UP signed a coalition agreement with the PSL, which had obtained 42 seats in the elections to the Sejm (with 9.0% of the votes) and four seats in the Senat. The leader of the SLD, Leszek Miller, was sworn in as Prime Minister and Chairman of the European Integration Committee on 19 October; the PSL's leader, Jarosław Kalinowski, and the leader of the UP, Marek Pol, were appointed as Deputy Prime Ministers. Miller pledged to revive economic progress and announced that a referendum on entry to the EU would be held in mid-2003,.

In May 2001 Andrzej Lepper was sentenced to 16 months' imprisonment, after being found guilty of charges associated with the farmers' blockades of 1998–99. In November 2001 Lepper was dismissed as a Vice-Marshal of the Sejm, and in January 2002 he was fined for having insulted the President. In the following month he was charged with seven counts of slander. In March, on appeal, Lepper's prison sentence was reduced to a suspended one-year term. Meanwhile, in January the Conservative Peasant Party and the PChD merged to form the Conservative Peasant Party-New Poland Movement, in an attempt to unite the country's fractured right wing. Government changes in July included the resignation of Marek Belka as Minister of Finance; Grzegorz Kołodko subsequently assumed the post (which he had previously held in 1994–97), and in December survived a vote of 'no confidence' in the Sejm.

Meanwhile, on 27 October 2002 local elections were held, in which the ruling SLD-UP coalition won 33.7% of the votes cast; the Self-Defence Party won 18.0% of the votes and the LPR secured 16.4%. A second round of voting took place on 10 November. In January 2003 the Prime Minister reshuffled the cabinet, consolidating the Ministries of the Economy and of Labour into a new Ministry of the Economy, Labour and Social Policy, under Jerzy Hausner. On 1 March Miller expelled the junior coalition partner, the PSL, from the Government, after it voted with opposition deputies against new tax legislation in the Sejm. In mid-March the Sejm rejected a motion, proposed by the LPR, to dissolve parliament. The following day the SLD-UD coalition formed a parliamentary alliance with the Peasant Democratic Party (Partia Ludowo-Demokratyczna—PLD), although it remained 13 seats short of a majority. Meanwhile, public dissatisfaction at the state of the economy and the high rate of unemployment was expressed by often-violent demonstrations led by the Solidarity trade union; in late April some 20,000 people attended one such gathering.

In June 2003 Miller transferred responsibility for economic policy from the Ministry of Finance to Hausner's Ministry of the Economy, Labour and Social Policy, prompting the resignation of the Deputy Prime Minister and Minister of Finance, Kołodko.

Hausner was then appointed a Deputy Prime Minister (retaining his previous portfolio), and Andrzej Raczko became Minister of Finance. The Government subsequently won a vote of confidence in the Sejm. On 20 January 2004 Miller appointed Deputy Chairman of the SLD and former premier Józef Oleksy as Deputy Prime Minister and Minister of Internal Affairs and Administration, in an apparent attempt to reduce tensions within the party. The following day Miller dismissed Piotr Czyżewski as Minister of the Treasury, reportedly owing to his failure to implement the privatization of state-owned companies; he was replaced by Zbigniew Kaniewski.

In late January 2004 the PLD withdrew its support for the ruling coalition, thereby reducing the Government's majority in parliament. Following increasing divisions within the SLD, in mid-February Miller announced that he was to resign as Chairman of the party, but retain the premiership, to enable him to focus on Poland's planned accession to the EU on 1 May (see below). Following Miller's resignation, at a party congress on 6 March Krzysztof Janik was elected as the new party Chairman. None the less, in late March more than 20 deputies, led by Marek Borowski, announced that they were to defect from the SLD in order to establish a new party, Polish Social Democracy (Socjaldemokracja Polski—SDPL); Borowski subsequently resigned as Marshal of the Sejm. On 26 March Miller acknowledged the loss of support for his leadership and announced that he would resign as Prime Minister on 2 May. Three days later President Kwaśniewski nominated former Minister of Finance Belka (latterly Director of Economic Policy in the US-led Coalition Provisional Authority in Iraq) to head a new government; Belka announced that he intended to retain key ministers, including Hausner, who had devised a controversial economic austerity programme for 2004–07, which some observers believed had contributed to Miller's loss of popular support. The lengthy investigation into a media bribery scandal that had emerged in late 2002 had also eroded the credibility of Miller's Government. (A national newspaper, *Gazeta Wyborcza*, had alleged that the film producer Lew Rywin had attempted to solicit a bribe, on behalf of Miller, in return for the approval of amendments to legislation regulating media ownership, which would have enabled the newspaper's parent company to purchase a private television station.) In early April 2004 Miller, who had consistently denied his involvement, was exonerated by a parliamentary investigative commission; Rywin was sentenced to over two years' imprisonment, having been found guilty of corruption. In late April Oleksy (who had been widely regarded as a potential candidate for the premiership) was elected as the new Marshal of the Sejm.

Miller resigned on 2 May 2004, as planned, and Belka's Government, principally composed of SLD members and independents, took office, pending approval by the Sejm. Isabela Jaruga-Nowacka, who had been elected one week earlier to replace Marek Pol as the leader of the UP, was appointed as a Deputy Prime Minister. In mid-May, however, the Sejm rejected Belka's nomination, forcing the resignation of the new Government. The Sejm failed to propose a new candidate for the premiership within the requisite two weeks, and Kwaśniewski duly renominated Belka. In late June the Sejm approved Belka's appointment by 236 votes to 215, thus averting early elections. In order to secure the support of the SDPL, Belka agreed to hold a further confidence vote in October to confirm his mandate to govern.

In July 2004 the Minister of Finance, Andrzej Raczko, resigned to become Poland's representative at the IMF; he was succeeded by Mirosław Gronicki. In August the Government abandoned some elements of its economic austerity programme in order to secure political support for the majority of its proposals; an estimated 30% of Hausner's measures had already been approved by the Sejm. Andrzej Kalwas, an independent, was appointed as Minister of Justice in September, following the resignation of Marek Sadowski, after media reports suggested that he had abused his position as a judge and later as a government minister (both of which granted him immunity from prosecution) to avoid investigation into a road accident that he had allegedly caused in 1995.

In mid-October 2004 Belka narrowly won the scheduled vote of confidence in the Sejm, by 234 votes to 218. Ahead of the vote Belka had announced to the lower chamber that Poland would begin reducing its 2,500-strong military contingent in Iraq (see below) from early 2005. Krzysztof Pater resigned as Minister of Social Policy in November, after the Sejm rejected draft legislation on corporate social insurance and pensions that was to have generated 1,800m. new złotys in budget savings in 2005. Deputy

Prime Minister Jaruga-Nowacka subsequently assumed additional responsibility for social policy.

In December 2004, at a congress of the SLD, Oleksy was elected Chairman of the party, defeating Krzysztof Janik in a second round of voting. The election increased tension within the SLD, which was suffering a decline in popularity, and Janik and his allies announced plans to form an opposition faction within the party. A few days later, following several years of investigations, the Vetting Court ruled that Oleksy had concealed his collaboration with the communist-era military intelligence services; Oleksy, who strongly refuted the charges against him, announced that he would appeal against the Court's verdict. In response to mounting pressure, Oleksy resigned as Marshal of the Sejm, and in early January 2005 Włodzimierz Cimoszewicz, hitherto Minister of Foreign Affairs, was elected as his replacement. Adam Rotfeld assumed the foreign affairs portfolio.

In early February 2005 Hausner resigned from the SLD, after the party's national council voted against holding early legislative elections in June, but announced his intention to retain his ministerial positions. In early March, however, in response to increasing pressure, particularly from the SLD, Hausner tendered his resignation as Deputy Prime Minister and Minister of the Economy and Labour. Jacek Piechota was appointed to the position of Minister of the Economy and Labour. In late February Hausner and Władysław Frasyniuk, the leader of the UW, announced plans to create a new centrist political organization; the Democratic Party (Partia Demokratyczna—Demokraci) held its founding congress in May. Amid speculation that he was to join the new party, in early March Belka urged the Sejm to dissolve itself to allow early elections to take place, as the minority Government lacked sufficient support in the Sejm to pass legislation and, in particular, important budget reforms. In early May, however, the Sejm voted to reject three motions submitted by opposition parties for its dissolution, and President Kwaśniewski rejected Belka's resignation, tendered on 6 May, stating that the Government should remain in office until the forthcoming legislative elections. Meanwhile, in April the Deputy Prime Minister and Minister of Social Policy, Izabela Jaruga-Nowacka, resigned from the leadership of the UP, but retained her ministerial portfolio. In late May Wojciech Olejniczak was elected as Chairman of the SLD, succeeding Józef Oleksy. Olejniczak was replaced as Minister of Agriculture and Rural Development by Jerzy Pilarczyk. A new Minister of the Environment was appointed in the same month. In June Belka made public his police file, in response to allegations that he had collaborated with the communist security services.

In the legislative elections, which took place on 25 September 2005, with a rate of participation by the electorate of 40.5%, the right-wing PiS obtained the largest number of seats in both the Sejm (taking 155 of the 460 seats, with 27.0% of the votes) and the Senat (with 49 of the 100 available). The centre-right PO won 133 seats in the Sejm (with 24.1% of the votes) and 34 seats in the Senat, whereas the incumbent SLD received just 55 seats in the Sejm (with 11.3% of the votes cast). Two days later the leader of the PiS, Jarosław Kaczyński, announced that he did not intend to lead the new government, and instead proposed Kazimierz Marcinkiewicz for the premiership, in an attempt to avoid possible confusion, as Kaczyński's twin brother, Lech, the PiS Mayor of Warsaw, was a principal candidate for the presidency. After a first round of voting in the presidential election, on 9 October, the two leading candidates were PO leader Donald Tusk (with 36.3% of the votes) and Lech Kaczyński (with 33.1%). A second round of voting was held on 23 October, as a result of which Kaczyński emerged as the winner, with 54.0% of the votes. The rate of participation by the electorate was 49.7% in the first round and 51.0% in the second.

Although the PiS and the PO had been widely expected to negotiate a coalition Government, the two parties were unable to agree on the distribution of senior positions, and on 31 October 2005 Marcinkiewicz was appointed as Prime Minister of a minority Government, comprising nine PiS members and eight independents. Coalition negotiations were to continue, however. Stefan Meller, a career diplomat, became Minister of Foreign Affairs, and unaffiliated ministers were also appointed to the treasury, finance and economy portfolios, apparently in an attempt to reassure international investors. Bogdan Borusewicz was appointed Marshal of the Senat and Marek Jurek became Marshal of the Sejm. On 10 November the Government won a motion of confidence in the Sejm, by 272 to 187 votes, with the support of smaller rightist parties (the Self-Defence Party of the Republic of Poland, the LPR and the PSL). Lech Kaczyński was inaugurated as President on 23 December.

In early January 2006 the Minister of the Treasury, Andrzej Mikosz, resigned, following media allegations that his wife had been involved in financial misdemeanours in 2002; he was replaced by Wojciech Jasinski in mid-February 2006. Also in early January Teresa Lubinska was removed from her position as Minister of Finance; she was succeeded by Zyta Gilowska, an independent (formerly aligned with the PO), who also became Deputy Prime Minister. In mid-February President Kaczyński confirmed that he would not schedule early legislative elections, despite the failure of the Senat to approve the budget by the constitutional deadline of 31 January (it was adopted by the Senat on 1 February). In late April the PiS signed a coalition agreement with the populist Self-Defence Party and LPR. Stefan Meller subsequently resigned as Minister of Foreign Affairs, in protest at the Government's decision to co-operate with the Self-Defence Party. Several new ministers were appointed to the Government on 5 May, giving the Government a legislative majority for the first time. Notably, Andrzej Lepper of the Self-Defence Party was appointed as Deputy Prime Minister and Minister of Agriculture and Rural Development, and Roman Giertych of the LPR became Deputy Prime Minister and Minister of National Education.

After 1991 close relations were retained with the Czech Republic, Hungary and Slovakia through the structures of the Visegrad Group and Central European Free Trade Agreement, and also with other countries of the Baltic region. In 1991–92 Poland established diplomatic relations with the former republics of the USSR, developing particularly strong links with Ukraine. In May 1997 the Polish and Ukrainian Presidents signed a declaration of reconciliation, which included the condemnation of the killing of tens of thousands of Poles by Ukrainian nationalists in 1942–43, and of the 'Wisła Operation' of 1947, in which more than 100,000 Ukrainians were forcibly deported from their homes in south-east Poland. During 1998 and early 1999 Poland sought to reassure Ukraine (as well as Russia) that good relations and mutual co-operation between their two countries would continue following Poland's entry into NATO in March 1999 and its eventual membership of the EU. In November and December 2004 President Kwaśniewski mediated in negotiations in Ukraine (q.v.) aimed at resolving a political crisis that had resulted from a disputed presidential election in that country. Following a new election in December, Kwaśniewski attended the inauguration of the new President of Ukraine, Viktor Yushchenko, in January 2005. The Polish Government later welcomed the new Ukrainian Government's pro-European stance, pledging to assist with Ukraine's efforts to join the EU. Meanwhile, relations with neighbouring Lithuania were initially strained by concerns regarding the status of the Polish minority in that country. Relations improved in 1993–94, and in April 1994 Poland and Lithuania signed a treaty of friendship and co-operation, in which both countries renounced any claims on each other's territory. All former Soviet combat troops had been withdrawn from Poland by November 1992, and the last remaining (non-combat) Russian military presence was withdrawn in September 1994.

Relations between Poland and Russia deteriorated as a result of Poland's decision to join NATO in 1999. However, tensions eased in July 2000, when President Kwaśniewski became the first Polish head of state to pay an official visit to Moscow since the collapse of communist rule. Relations improved further in January 2002, when Russian President Vladimir Putin paid an official visit to Poland, his first to a former Eastern bloc country. However, the Polish Government continued to oppose Russia's plans to construct a natural gas pipeline to Slovakia via Poland, bypassing Ukraine, as it feared that the project threatened adversely to affect Polish-Ukrainian relations. Relations were also perceived to have deteriorated as a result of Poland's potential influence over EU foreign policy, after it became a member of the body in May, and following President Kwaśniewski's mediation in Ukraine in late 2004 (see above). In 2005 Poland expressed concern at plans to construct a North European natural gas pipeline between Russia and Germany, under the Baltic Sea, effectively bypassing Poland.

In May 1996 relations with Belarus became strained, following the arrest and deportation of four Solidarity leaders, who had been invited to Minsk by the Free Trade Union of Belarus. Tension between Poland and Belarus increased in January 1999 when the Sejm sent a 'message to the Belarusian nation', which included the demand that Belarusian deputies serving prison sentences for their opposition to the regime should be released. On 1 October 2003 the Polish Government introduced visa requirements for Belarusian, Moldovan, Russian and Ukrainian citizens, in accordance with EU policy, although simplified visa arrangements had been agreed for residents of the Russian exclave of Kaliningrad. Relations with Belarus continued to deteriorate in 2005. In July the offices of the Union of Poles in Belarus were seized by the Belarusian authorities, and the newly elected leadership replaced, apparently owing to fears that the organization might unite with the domestic opposition in an attempt to overthrow the regime of Belarusian President Alyaksandr Lukashenka. Meanwhile, Polish journalists in Belarus were compelled to pay large fines, after protesting at the suppression by the authorities of the country's main Polish-language newspaper. In late July Poland recalled its ambassador to Belarus, and appealed to the EU for assistance in protecting the Polish minority there. The Polish ambassador returned to Belarus in October. Tensions arose again prior to the presidential election held in Belarus in March 2006. Polish journalists and a number of Polish parliamentarians were refused entry to Belarus, and a former Polish ambassador to Belarus was imprisoned for 15 days after participating in an unauthorized protest demonstration; at the end of March Belarus briefly recalled its ambassador to Poland.

In November 1990 Poland and Germany signed a border treaty confirming their post-1945 borders, and in June 1991 the two countries signed a treaty of 'good neighbourliness and friendly co-operation'. Poland welcomed the announcement made by the German Government in February 1999 of the establishment of a compensation fund for over 2m. Poles who were employed as forced labour in German companies during the Second World War. Following a campaign by Polish veteran groups, in May Polish and German representatives began complex negotiations regarding the payment of compensation by several leading German firms. In mid-December a compensation agreement was signed, whereby DM 10,000m. was to be paid by German companies into a compensation fund; however, payments were subject to delays. The German Chancellor, Gerhard Schröder, attended a ceremony in Warsaw in August 2004 to mark the 60th anniversary of the city's failed uprising against the Nazi occupation, becoming the first German leader to participate in such an event. In September, however, a resolution adopted by the Sejm urging Germany to pay reparations for the Nazi invasion of Poland in 1939 threatened to strain relations between the two countries. Both the German and Polish Governments rejected the resolution, which was regarded as a response to demands from groups of Germans for the restitution of ancestral property lost when Poland's border shifted westward at the end of the Second World War. In November, at a joint press conference following talks in Kraków, Belka and Schröder announced that a joint commission had concluded that there was no legal basis for compensation claims to be filed. At the same time, in an attempt to avert further tensions, the two leaders each appointed a special adviser to co-ordinate bilateral relations. In January 2005 the German President, Horst Köhler, attended a ceremony in Poland to commemorate the 60th anniversary of the liberation of the Nazi concentration camp at Oświęcim (Auschwitz).

Poland joined the Council of Europe (see p. 211) in November 1991. In December Poland signed an association agreement with the European Community (now EU), and in April Poland made a formal application for membership of the EU; accession negotiations began in March 1998. In December 2002 Poland, and nine other countries, were formally invited to join the EU from May 2004. In February 2003 the Government reached agreement with the EU on farm subsidies. A national referendum on EU membership took place on 7–8 June, at which some 77% of the votes cast by 58.9% of the electorate were in favour of accession. Poland became a full member of the EU on 1 May, as scheduled. On 13 June the first elections to the European Parliament to be held in Poland were marked by a very low rate of voter participation, of 20.9%. The PO secured 15 of the 54 seats available, while the LPR won 10 seats, the PiS seven seats and the Self-Defence Party six seats. The ruling SLD-UP coalition took only five seats.

Poland, in common with other central and eastern European countries, regarded membership of NATO as a priority in guaranteeing regional security. In January 1994 Poland announced that it was to join that organization's 'Partnership for Peace' programme, and a defence co-operation agreement was duly signed with NATO in March. In May Poland was granted associate partnership status in Western European Union (see p. 365). In July 1997 Poland, together with the Czech Republic and Hungary, was officially invited to commence negotiations on potential membership of NATO. A protocol providing for the accession of the three states was signed in December, and Poland, the Czech Republic and Hungary secured full membership of NATO on 12 March 1999. The Polish Government strongly supported the US-led military campaign to remove from power the regime of the Iraqi President, Saddam Hussain, in early 2003, and Poland was subsequently offered the opportunity to manage one of three reconstruction zones in Iraq, under overall US command. In September the USA transferred responsibility for security in an area of central Iraq to a 9,500-strong multinational force led by Poland, which contributed some 2,500 troops. In early 2005 Poland reduced its military contingent in Iraq to 1,700 troops, following elections there. Although in April the Polish Minister of Defence announced that the country's troops would be withdrawn from Iraq at the end of 2005, the new Government elected in September 2005 retracted this decision and troops continued to be deployed in Iraq in 2006. Meanwhile, new anti-terrorism legislation came into force in Poland in January 2005, allowing the military to shoot down hijacked aircraft on the orders of the Minister of National Defence or the head of the air force. Poland had received threats of attack from extremist Islamist groups since its deployment of troops in Iraq.

Government

Under the Constitution, which came into force in October 1997, legislative power is vested in the bicameral Zgromadzenie Narodowe (National Assembly), which is elected for a four-year term and comprises the 100-member Senat (upper chamber) and the 460-member Sejm (lower chamber). The Senat reviews the laws adopted by the Sejm and may propose their rejection. Senators and deputies are elected by universal, direct suffrage. In the Sejm deputies are elected under a system of proportional representation. Executive power is vested in the President of the Republic, who is directly elected (a second ballot being held if necessary) for a five-year term, and may be re-elected only once, and in the appointed Council of Ministers, led by the Prime Minister. The Council of Ministers is responsible for its activities to the Sejm. On 1 January 1999 new legislation on local government came into effect, as a result of which Poland was divided into 16 voivodships (provinces) and 308 powiats (districts).

Defence

At 1 August 2005 the strength of Poland's active armed forces was estimated to be 141,500 (including an estimated 67,500 conscripts and 8,200 centrally controlled staff): army 89,000, air force 30,000 and navy 14,300. Paramilitary forces of some 21,400 comprised border guards (14,100) and interior ministry units (7,300). In 1988 legislation was enacted permitting conscientious objectors to perform an alternative community service, and from January 2005 compulsory military service was reduced from one year to nine months. In September 1997 the Government adopted a 15-year programme for the modernization of the armed forces; a further reform plan, providing for an eventual reduction in strength to 150,000, was approved in January 2001. State budget expenditure on defence in 2005 was projected at 17,100m. new złotys. In 1994 Poland joined the North Atlantic Treaty Organization's (NATO, see p. 314) 'Partnership for Peace' programme of military co-operation, and it became a full member of the Alliance in March 1999.

Economic Affairs

In 2004, according to the World Bank, Poland's gross national income (GNI), measured at average 2002–04 prices, was US $232,398m., equivalent to $6,090 per head (or $12,640 per head on an international purchasing-power parity basis). During 1995–2004 the population decreased by 0.1%, while gross domestic product (GDP) per head increased, in real terms, at an average annual rate of 4.2%. Overall GDP increased, in real terms, at an average annual rate of 4.1% in 1995–2004; growth was 3.7% in 2003 and 5.3% in 2004.

Agriculture contributed 3.1% of GDP in 2004, according to the World Bank. In that year the sector engaged 18.0% of the employed labour force. The principal crops are potatoes, sugar beet, wheat, rye and barley. Livestock production is important to the domestic food supply. During 1995–2004 the average annual GDP of the agricultural sector increased, in real terms, by 1.4%; real agricultural GDP increased by 0.7% in 2003 and by 1.0% in 2004.

Industry (including mining, manufacturing, power and construction) accounted for 31.3% of GDP in 2004, according to the World Bank. The sector engaged 28.8% of the employed labour force in 2004. During 1995–2004 industrial GDP increased, in real terms, by an average of 4.2% per year; real industrial GDP increased by 4.8% in 2003 and by 7.4% in 2004.

Mining and quarrying contributed 2.3% of GDP in 2001, and engaged 1.6% of the employed labour force in 2004. Poland is a significant producer of copper, silver and sulphur, and there are also considerable reserves of natural gas. The mining sector experienced a marked decline in the 1990s; however, from 1998 the sector underwent significant restructuring. During 1992–96 mining GDP declined at an average annual rate of 1.5%; the sector's GDP declined by 4.3% in 1997, and by an estimated 4.6% in 1998.

The manufacturing sector contributed 18.2% of GDP in 2004, according to the World Bank. In that year the sector engaged 19.9% of the employed labour force. Measured by the value of sold production, in 1998 the principal branches of manufacturing were food products and beverages (accounting for 24.7% of the total), road motor vehicles, chemicals and chemical products, basic metals and non-electric machinery. In 1995–2004 manufacturing GDP increased, in real terms, at an average annual rate of 6.6%. Manufacturing GDP increased by 7.3% in 2003 and by 10.0% in 2004.

Energy is derived principally from coal, which satisfied 94.5% of the country's total energy requirements in 2002. In 1998 the Government announced plans to reduce Poland's dependence on coal: it was projected that by 2010 15% of power generation would be fuelled by imported natural gas. Mineral fuels and lubricants accounted for 11.5% of the value of merchandise imports in 2005; some 6.5% of electricity generated was exported in 2000.

The services sector contributed 65.6% of GDP in 2004, according to the World Bank. In that year the sector engaged 53.2% of the employed labour force. Services expanded rapidly from the early 1990s, with considerable growth in financial services, retailing, tourism and leisure. The GDP of the services sector increased, in real terms, by an average of 4.1% per year in 1995–2004. Real services GDP increased by 3.1% in 2003 and by 6.7% in 2004.

In 2004 Poland recorded a visible trade deficit of US $5,622m., and there was a deficit of $10,357m. on the current account of the balance of payments. In that year, according to preliminary figures, the principal source of imports was Germany (accounting for 24.2%); other major suppliers were Italy (7.9%), Russia (7.3%) and France (6.7%). Germany was also the principal market for exports (30.0%); other significant purchasers were France (6.1%), Italy (6.0%) and the United Kingdom (5.5%). The principal exports in 2005 were machinery and transport equipment, basic manufactures, miscellaneous manufactured articles, food and live animals, chemicals and related products, and mineral fuels and lubricants. The principal imports in that year were machinery and transport equipment, basic manufactures, chemicals and related products, mineral fuels and lubricants, miscellaneous manufactured articles and food and live animals.

According to government figures, Poland's overall budgetary deficit for 2005 was 27,495m. new złotys (equivalent to some 3.2% of GDP). Poland's external debt totalled US $95,219m. at the end of 2003, of which $34,964m. was long-term public debt. In that year the cost of debt-servicing was equivalent to 25.1% of the value of exports of goods and services. The annual rate of inflation averaged 4.8% in 1998–2004. Consumer prices increased by 3.5% in 2004 and by 2.1% in 2005. In February 2005 19.4% of the labour force were registered as unemployed.

Poland is a member, as a 'Country of Operations', of the European Bank for Reconstruction and Development (EBRD, see p. 224). Poland joined the World Trade Organization (WTO, see p. 370) in 1995 and the Organisation for Economic Co-operation and Development (OECD, see p. 320) in 1996. In May 2004 Poland became a full member of the European Union (EU, see p. 228).

In the 1990s Poland undertook an ambitious, market-orientated programme of economic reform. A devalued 'new złoty', introduced in January 1995, was made freely convertible on international currency markets from May. Poland's economic performance was adversely affected by the Russian financial crisis in August 1998, and a decline in international petroleum prices in 2000 prompted a second economic reverse. However, economic recovery was evident in 2002, and accelerated in 2003 and 2004. The rate of economic growth was 3.2% in 2005, but growth was expected to increase in 2006. Following the election of a right-wing Government, under Kazimierz Marcinkiewicz, in late 2005 (see Recent History), the IMF recommended that it aim to stimulate private investment, increase employment and encourage more rapid growth by: restraining public debt; strengthening domestic institutions; and fully utilizing the opportunities offered by EU membership. In March 2006 the EU initiated new legal proceedings against the Government, which it accused of protectionism, after Poland continued to obstruct attempts by an Italian company to merge two majority foreign-owned banks in Poland, thereby challenging the influence of the leading state-owned Polish bank. Meanwhile, there were government proposals for the reversal of plans by the previous left-wing Government to sell national assets to foreign investors. Instead, there were plans for the creation of so-called 'national champions': consolidated, state-owned groups within important sectors, such as energy. The need to reduce the budgetary deficit to less than 3% of GDP remained the most challenging element of the EU's financial criteria for the adoption of the common European currency, the euro, and it appeared unlikely that Poland could adopt the euro before 2010; indeed, the Marcinkiewicz Government did not favour early entry to the euro zone.

Education

Education is free and compulsory for eight years, between the ages of seven and 14 years. Before the age of seven, children may attend crèches (żłobki) and kindergartens (przedszkola). In 1998/99 49.6% of children between the ages of three and six years attended kindergarten, and in 2001/02 99.7% of six-year-olds attended pre-school educational establishments. A reform of primary and secondary education was undertaken in 1999–2004. Basic schooling begins at seven years of age with primary school (szkoła podstawowa), for which there is a common curriculum throughout the country. Primary education lasts for six years, divided into two equal cycles. Lower secondary education (at the gimnazjum) is compulsory for three years. In 2001/02 net enrolment at primary schools was equivalent to 98.9% of children in the relevant age-group and enrolment in lower secondary schools was equivalent to 94.3% of children in the relevant age-group. Three years of education at general secondary schools (liceum ogólnokształcące) commence at the age of 16 years, for pupils who successfully complete the entrance examination; in 2000/01 enrolment at secondary schools was equivalent to 90.1% of children in the appropriate age-group. At this level, there are general secondary schools (accounting for 34%), vocational technical schools (technika zawodowe—56%) and basic vocational schools (zasadnicze szkoły—20%). The last provide courses consisting of three days' theoretical and three days' practical training per week, and in addition some general education is given. New post-secondary schools (szkoła policealna) were introduced in 1999 to prepare students from technical and vocational schools for skilled jobs. Curricula are standardized throughout Poland. In 2003/04 there were 400 higher education establishments in Poland, including 17 universities and 22 technical universities. In 2003 state budgetary expenditure on basic education amounted to 1,498m. new złotys (0.8% of total expenditure), while 7,071m. złotys (3.7%) were allocated to higher education.

Public Holidays

2006: 1 January (New Year's Day), 17 April (Easter Monday), 1 May (Labour Day), 3 May (Polish National Day, Proclamation of 1791 Constitution), 15 June (Corpus Christi), 15 August (Assumption), 1 November (All Saints' Day), 11 November (Independence Day), 25–26 December (Christmas).

2007: 1 January (New Year's Day), 9 April (Easter Monday), 1 May (Labour Day), 3 May (Polish National Day, Proclamation of 1791 Constitution), 7 June (Corpus Christi), 15 August (Assumption), 1 November (All Saints' Day), 11 November (Independence Day), 25–26 December (Christmas).

Weights and Measures

The metric system is in force.

POLAND　　*Statistical Survey*

Statistical Survey

Source (unless otherwise indicated): Główny Urząd Statystyczny (Central Statistical Office), 00-925 Warsaw, Al. Niepodległości 208; tel. (22) 6083161; fax (22) 6083869; internet www.stat.gov.pl.

Area and Population

AREA, POPULATION AND DENSITY

Area (sq km)	
Land	304,465
Inland water	8,220
Total	312,685*
Population (census results)†	
7 December 1988	37,879,105
20 May 2002	
Males	18,516,403
Females	19,713,677
Total	38,230,080
Population (official estimates at 30 June)†	
2003	38,195,177
2004	38,180,249
Density (per sq km) at 30 June 2004	125.4‡

* 120,728 sq miles.
† Figures exclude civilian aliens within the country and include civilian nationals temporarily outside the country.
‡ Land area only.

VOIVODSHIPS
(2002 census)

	Area (sq km)	Population	Density (per sq km)
Dolnośląskie	19,948	2,907,212	145.7
Kujawsko-Pomorskie	17,970	2,069,321	115.2
Lubelskie	25,114	2,199,054	87.6
Lubuskie	13,984	1,008,954	72.1
Łódzkie	18,219	2,612,890	143.4
Małopolskie	15,144	3,232,408	213.4
Mazowieckie	35,597	5,124,018	143.9
Opolskie	9,412	1,065,043	113.2
Podkarpackie	17,926	2,103,837	117.4
Podlaskie	20,180	1,208,606	59.9
Pomorskie	18,293	2,179,900	119.2
Śląskie	12,294	4,742,874	385.8
Świętokrzyskie	11,672	1,297,477	111.2
Warmińsko-Mazurskie	24,203	1,428,357	59.0
Wielkopolskie	29,826	3,351,915	112.4
Zachodniopomorskie	22,902	1,698,214	74.2
Total	**312,685**	**38,230,080**	**122.3**

PRINCIPAL TOWNS
(2002 census)

Warszawa (Warsaw, the capital)	1,671,670	Bielsko-Biała	178,028
Łódź	789,318	Olsztyn	173,102
Kraków (Cracow)	758,544	Rzeszów	160,376
Wrocław	640,367	Ruda Śląska	150,595
Poznań	578,886	Rybnik	142,731
Gdańsk	461,334	Tychy	132,816
Szczecin	415,399	Dąbrowa Górnicza	132,236
Bydgoszcz	373,804	Wałbrzych	130,268
Lublin	357,110	Opole	129,946
Katowice	327,222	Płock	128,361
Białystok	291,383	Elbląg	128,134
Gdynia	253,458	Gorzów Wielkopolski	125,914
Częstochowa	251,436	Włocławek	121,229
Sosnowiec	232,622	Tarnów	119,913
Radom	229,699	Zielona Góra	118,293
Kielce	212,429	Chorzów	117,430
Toruń	211,243	Kalisz	109,498
Gliwice	203,814	Koszalin	108,709
Zabrze	195,293	Legnica	107,100
Bytom	193,546	Grudziądz	100,376

BIRTHS, MARRIAGES AND DEATHS

	Registered live births		Registered marriages		Registered deaths	
	Number	Rate (per 1,000)	Number	Rate (per 1,000)	Number	Rate (per 1,000)
1997	412,635	10.7	204,850	5.3	380,201	9.8
1998	395,619	10.2	209,430	5.4	375,354	9.7
1999	382,002	9.9	219,398	5.7	381,415	9.9
2000	378,348	9.8	211,150	5.5	368,028	9.5
2001	368,205	9.5	195,122	5.0	363,220	9.4
2002	353,765	9.3	191,935	5.0	359,486	9.4
2003	351,072	9.2	195,446	5.1	365,230	9.6
2004	356,131	9.3	191,800*	5.0	363,522	9.5

* Figure is rounded.

Expectation of life (WHO estimates, years at birth): 75 (males 71; females 79) in 2003 (Source: WHO, *World Health Report*).

IMMIGRATION AND EMIGRATION*

	2001	2002	2003
Immigrants	6,625	6,587	7,048
Emigrants	23,368	24,532	20,813

* Figures refer to immigrants arriving for permanent residence in Poland and emigrants leaving for permanent residence abroad.

ECONOMICALLY ACTIVE POPULATION*
('000 persons aged 15 years and over)

	2002	2003	2004
Agriculture, hunting and forestry	2,652	2,497	2,472
Fishing	12	11	12
Mining and quarrying	258	247	227
Manufacturing	2,575	2,592	2,740
Electricity, gas and water supply	263	250	222
Construction	851	803	789
Wholesale and retail trade; repair of motor vehicles, motorcycles and personal and household goods	1,955	1,962	1,997
Hotels and restaurants	252	229	236
Transport, storage and communications	832	823	832
Financial intermediation	314	281	271
Real estate, renting and business activities	675	694	799
Public administration and defence; compulsory social security	801	853	865
Education	933	1,078	1,060
Health and social work	940	838	824
Other community, social and personal service activities	455	449	436
Private households with employed persons	11	8	15
Total employed	**13,782**	**13,617**	**13,795**
Unemployed	3,431	3,329	3,230
Total labour force	**17,213**	**16,945**	**17,025**

* Excluding regular military personnel living in barracks, and conscripts.

Note: Totals may not be equal to the sum of component parts, owing to rounding.

Source: ILO.

POLAND

Health and Welfare

KEY INDICATORS

Total fertility rate (children per woman, 2003)	1.3
Under-5 mortality rate (per 1,000 live births, 2004)	8
HIV/AIDS (% of persons aged 15–49, 2003)	0.1
Physicians (per 1,000 head, 2002)	2.3
Hospital beds (per 1,000 head, 2000)	4.9
Health expenditure (2002): US $ per head (PPP)	657
Health expenditure (2002): % of GDP	6.1
Health expenditure (2002): public (% of total)	72.4
Human Development Index (2003): ranking	36
Human Development Index (2003): value	0.858

For sources and definitions, see explanatory note on p. vi.

Agriculture

PRINCIPAL CROPS
('000 metric tons)

	2002	2003	2004
Wheat	9,304.0	7,858.2	9,892.5
Barley	3,369.9	2,831.5	3,570.8
Maize	1,962.0	1,883.7	2,344.0
Rye	3,831.0	3,172.2	4,280.7
Oats	1,486.6	1,181.9	1,430.5
Buckwheat	40.0	44.1	71.5
Triticale (wheat-rye hybrid)	3,047.7	2,811.6	3,723.3
Mixed grain	3,836.1	3,607.6	4,321.9
Potatoes	15,523.9	13,731.5	13,998.6
Sugar beet	13,433.9	11,739.5	12,730.4
Pulses*	229.0	238.0	270.0
Rapeseed	952.7	793.0	1,632.9
Cabbages	1,188.5	1,236.7	1,371.0
Tomatoes	221.4	234.1	212.7
Cauliflowers	176.4	188.8	205.7
Cucumbers and gherkins	260.0	290.0	255.9
Dry onions	584.9	678.3	865.7
Carrots	692.1	834.6	927.9
Mushrooms†	120.0	120.0	130.0
Other vegetables†	1,485	1,535	1,331
Apples	2,167.5	2,427.8	2,521.5
Pears	92.1	77.2	87.3
Cherries (incl. sour)	213.9	235.2	250.2
Plums	102.9	109.6	132.6
Strawberries	153.1	131.3	185.6
Currants	157.4	192.5	194.5

* Unofficial figures.
† FAO estimates.
Source: FAO.

LIVESTOCK
('000 head year ending September)

	2002	2003	2004
Horses	330	333	335*
Cattle	5,533	5,489	5,353
Pigs	18,707	18,605	16,988
Sheep	345	338	318
Chickens	50,694	102,656	85,733
Geese	538	698	2,864
Turkeys	778	762	566
Ducks	3,572	3,593	4,406

* FAO estimate.
Source: FAO.

LIVESTOCK PRODUCTS
('000 metric tons)

	2002	2003	2004
Beef and veal	281.3	317.4	310.5
Pig meat	2,023.3	2,209.0	1,956.0
Horse meat	7.9	9.0*	11.5*
Game meat*	6.0	6.0	6.0
Chicken meat†	792.3	859.2	917.1
Duck meat*	13.0	19.0	19.0
Turkey meat*	50.0	34.5	24.5
Cows' milk	11,872.7	11,892.3	11,822.0
Cheese	535.1	548.1	580.1
Butter†	180.0	185.0	180.0
Hen eggs	496.2	509.7	514.3
Honey	9.6	11.6	12.0
Cattle hides (fresh)*	38.0	39.0	39.0

* FAO estimate(s).
† Unofficial figures.
Source: FAO.

Forestry

ROUNDWOOD REMOVALS
('000 cubic metres, excl. bark)

	2002	2003	2004
Sawlogs, veneer logs and logs for sleepers	10,620	11,765	13,076
Pulpwood	12,600	13,250	13,960
Other industrial wood	1,775	2,189	2,301
Fuel wood	2,142	3,632	3,396
Total	27,137	30,836	32,733

Source: FAO.

SAWNWOOD PRODUCTION
('000 cubic metres, incl. railway sleepers)

	2002	2003	2004
Coniferous (softwood)	2,574	2,792	3,102
Broadleaved (hardwood)	606	568	641
Total	3,180	3,360	3,743

Source: FAO.

Fishing

('000 metric tons, live weight)

	2001	2002	2003
Capture	225.1	223.4	180.3
Flatfishes	6.7	9.2	7.3
Atlantic cod	23.3	17.2	17.3
Alaska pollock	16.6	—	—
Atlantic herring	37.6	36.8	30.7
European sprat	85.8	81.2	84.1
Antarctic krill	13.7	16.4	8.9
Aquaculture	35.5	32.7	34.5
Common carp	22.0	19.0	20.5
Rainbow trout	11.0	10.7	11.7
Total catch	260.5	255.2	214.8

Source: FAO.

POLAND

Statistical Survey

Mining

('000 metric tons, unless otherwise indicated)

	2001	2002	2003*
Hard coal	103,992	103,546	103,016†
Brown coal (incl. lignite)	59,557	58,210	60,919
Crude petroleum	767	721	754
Salt (unrefined)	3,476	3,558	4,660
Native sulphur (per 100%)	942	760	762
Copper ore (metric tons)‡	545,000	568,000	570,000
Lead ore (metric tons)‡	69,600	73,500	74,000
Magnesite ore—crude	23,000	24,000	24,000
Silver (metric tons)‡	1,190	1,222	1,237
Zinc ore (metric tons)‡	172,300	171,200	172,000
Natural gas (million cu metres)	5,175	5,259	5,315

* Estimates.
† Government revised figure.
‡ Figures refer to the metal content of ores.

Source: US Geological Survey.

Hard coal: 101,230 in 2004; 98,275 in 2005.
Lignite: 61,197 in 2004; 61,589 in 2005.
Natural gas: 5,630 in 2004; 5,703 in 2005.
Sulphur: 821 in 2004; 802 in 2005.

Industry

SELECTED PRODUCTS

('000 metric tons, unless otherwise indicated)

	2003	2004	2005
Sausages and smoked meat	801	856	688
Refined sugar	1,906	2,000	2,057
Margarine	351	355	345
Wine and mead ('000 hectolitres)	3,304	3,030	1,234
Beer ('000 hectolitres)	28,622	31,851	31,365
Cigarettes (million)	82,300	86,600	102,000
Leather footwear ('000 pairs)	18,100	16,800	11,300
Mechanical wood pulp	100,000	n.a.	n.a.
Chemical wood pulp	783,000	n.a.	n.a.
Newsprint ('000 metric tons)	208	n.a.	n.a.
Synthetic rubber	84,200	n.a.	n.a.
Rubber tyres ('000)[1]	23,354	26,026	27,020
Sulphuric acid—100% ('000 metric tons)	1,861	n.a.	n.a.
Nitric acid—100% ('000 metric tons)	1,689	n.a.	n.a.
Caustic soda—96% ('000 metric tons)	427	452	391
Soda ash—98% ('000 metric tons)	1,114	n.a.	n.a.
Nitrogenous fertilizers (a) ('000 metric tons)[2]	1,626	1,644	1,726
Phosphate fertilizers (b) ('000 metric tons)[2]	553	594	591
Motor spirit—Petrol ('000 metric tons)[3]	4,043	4,086	4,178
Distillate fuel oils ('000 metric tons)	4,785	5,323	6,140
Residual fuel oils ('000 metric tons)	4,545	4,523	3,362
Coke-oven coke ('000 metric tons)	10,232	10,214	8,518
Cement ('000 metric tons)	11,653	12,566	12,429
Pig-iron ('000 metric tons)[4]	5,245	n.a.	n.a.
Crude steel ('000 metric tons)	9,107	10,578	8,444
Rolled steel products ('000 metric tons)	6,595	7,507	6,188
Aluminium—unwrought ('000 metric tons)[5]	45.1	45.8	42.7
Refined copper—unwrought	530	550	560

—continued	2003	2004	2005
Refined lead—unwrought ('000 metric tons)	34.0	n.a.	n.a.
Zinc—unwrought[5]	145,700	n.a.	n.a.
Radio receivers ('000)	10	n.a.	n.a.
Television receivers ('000)	6,818	7,012	6,660
Merchant ships launched (gross reg. tons)	546	n.a.	n.a.
Passenger motor cars ('000)	334	522	540
Lorries and tractors (number)	18,511	59,003	67,658
Domestic washing machines ('000)	915	1,159	1,446
Domestic refrigerators and freezers ('000)	1,001	1,280	1,691
Electric energy (million kWh)	151,597	154,132	153,325

[1] Tyres for passenger motor cars and commercial vehicles, including inner tubes and tyres for animal-drawn road vehicles, and tyres for non-agricultural machines and equipment.
[2] Fertilizer production is measured in terms of (a) nitrogen or (b) phosphoric acid. Phosphate fertilizers include ground rock phosphate.
[3] Including synthetic products.
[4] Including blast-furnace ferro-alloys.
[5] Figures refer to both primary and secondary metal. Zinc production includes zinc dust and remelted zinc.

Finance

CURRENCY AND EXCHANGE RATES

Monetary Units
100 groszy (singular: grosz) = 1 new złoty.

Sterling, Dollar and Euro Equivalents (30 December 2005)
£1 sterling = 5.616 new złotys;
US $1 = 3.261 new złotys;
€1 = 3.847 new złotys;
100 new złotys = £17.81 = $30.66 = €25.99.

Average Exchange Rate (new złotys per US dollar)
2003 3.8891
2004 3.6576
2005 3,2355

Note: On 1 January 1995 Poland introduced a new złoty, equivalent to 10,000 of the former units.

STATE BUDGET
(million new złotys)

Revenue	2003	2004	2005
Indirect taxation	95,443.3	100,991.5	116,200.6
Value-added tax	60,359.5	62,263.2	75,930.4
Excises	34,387.7	37,964.0	39,479.1
Other	696.1	764.3	791.1
Corporate income tax	14,108.0	13,071.7	15,785.2
Personal income tax	25,674.9	21,506.2	24,444.1
Customs duties	3,751.3	2,281.0	1,270.6
Dividends and income from profit	958.4	1,810.4	3,161.3
Other revenue	12,174.7	16,620.4	19,544.8
Total	**152,110.6**	**156,281.2**	**180,406.6**

Expenditure	2003	2004	2005
Budgetary expenditure	34,199.5	37,086.1	40,142.5
Social benefits	54,242.0	48,483.5	44,965.7
Domestic debt service	20,328.3	18,423.8	21,225.1
Foreign debt service	3,722.9	4,141.1	3,585.6
General subsidies	31,731.2	31,386.9	32,486.6
Capital expenditure	8,525.3	11,080.4	10,162.3
Total (incl. others)	**189,153.6**	**197,698.3**	**207,901.2**

POLAND

INTERNATIONAL RESERVES
(US $ million at 31 December)

	2003	2004	2005
Gold (national valuation)	1,380.5	1,448.8	1,697.2
IMF special drawing rights	54.8	70.1	77.8
Reserve position in IMF	799.4	700.9	299.0
Foreign exchange	31,724.9	34,552.8	40,486.9
Total	33,959.6	36,772.6	42,560.9

Source: IMF, *International Financial Statistics*.

MONEY SUPPLY
(million new złotys at 31 December)

	2003	2004	2005
Currency outside banks	49,417	50,776	57,155
Demand deposits at commercial banks	84,142	95,278	117,575
Total money (incl. others)	133,576	146,098	174,834

Source: IMF, *International Financial Statistics*.

COST OF LIVING
(Consumer Price Index; base: 2000 = 100)

	2002	2003	2004
Food (incl. alcoholic beverages)	104.6	103.0	108.6
Electricity, gas and other fuels	117.1	121.1	124.7
Clothing (incl. footwear)	100.7	98.2	94.6
Rent	122.8	128.8	133.4
All items (incl. others)	107.5	108.4	112.2

Source: ILO.

NATIONAL ACCOUNTS
(million new złotys at current prices)

Composition of the Gross National Product

	1998	1999	2000
Compensation of employees	250,314.0	276,363.0	297,820.6
Operating surplus / Consumption of fixed capital	227,649.6	250,783.0	293,518.2
Gross domestic product (GDP) at factor cost	477,963.6	527,146.0	591,338.8
Indirect taxes	82,681.1	94,680.5	100,153.3
Less Subsidies	6,763.1	6,711.2	6,566.0
GDP in purchasers' values	553,881.6	615,115.3	684,926.1
Factor income received from abroad / *Less* Factor income paid abroad	−4,115.6	−4,007.2	−6,350.1
Gross national product	549,766.0	611,108.1	678,576.0

Expenditure on the Gross Domestic Product

	2001	2002	2003
Government final consumption expenditure	137,126	141,227	144,619
Private final consumption expenditure	486,375	511,888	537,989
Changes in stocks	512	−1,070	3,386
Gross fixed capital formation	157,209	148,338	148,962
Total domestic expenditure	781,222	800,383	834,956
Exports of goods and services	210,585	231,409	280,698
Less Imports of goods and services	238,562	257,535	300,956
GDP in purchasers' values	760,595*	781,112*	814,698

* Including adjustment.

Gross Domestic Product by Economic Activity

	2000	2001	2002
Agriculture, hunting, forestry and fishing	22,324.6	24,744.8	21,121.0
Industry	155,501.3	161,211.7	160,988.5
Manufacturing	123,717.9	123,249.1	123,121.3
Construction	47,009.8	45,591.8	42,146.9
Market services	310,007.2	326,445.6	347,415.9
Non-market services	98,248.8	109,200.4	111,188.3
Gross value added in basic prices *	633,091.7	667,194.3	682,860.7
Taxes, *less* subsidies, on products	90,794.6	93,401.0	98,251.7
GDP in market prices	723,886.3	760,595.3	781,112.4

* Financial intermediation services indirectly measured (FISIM) is distributed to uses.

BALANCE OF PAYMENTS
(US $ million)

	2002	2003	2004
Exports of goods f.o.b.	46,742	61,007	81,862
Imports of goods f.o.b.	−53,991	−66,732	−87,484
Trade balance	−7,249	−5,725	−5,622
Exports of services	10,037	11,174	13,471
Imports of services	−9,186	−10,647	−12,451
Balance on goods and services	−6,398	−5,198	−4,602
Other income received	1,948	2,108	2,106
Other income paid	−3,837	−5,745	−13,505
Balance on goods, services and income	−8,287	−8,835	−16,001
Current transfers received	4,181	5,316	8,282
Current transfers paid	−903	−1,080	−2,638
Current balance	−5,009	−4,599	−10,357
Capital account (net)	−7	−46	998
Direct investment abroad	−230	−305	−787
Direct investment from abroad	4,131	4,589	12,613
Portfolio investment assets	−1,157	−1,296	−1,329
Portfolio investment liabilities	3,051	3,740	10,854
Financial derivatives liabilities	−898	−870	206
Other investment assets	1,887	−493	−11,828
Other investment liabilities	396	3,321	−1,525
Net errors and omissions	−1,516	−2,835	1,956
Overall balance	648	1,206	801

Source: IMF, *International Financial Statistics*.

External Trade

PRINCIPAL COMMODITIES
(distribution by SITC, million złotys)

Imports c.i.f.	2003	2004	2005
Food and live animals	12,269.6	15,556.2	17,226.9
Crude materials (inedible) except fuels	7,948.3	11,005.1	9,873.3
Mineral fuels, lubricants, etc.	24,133.2	29,806.2	37,571.6
Chemicals and related products	39,106.7	46,138.1	46,583.4
Basic manufactures	55,739.6	67,624.5	67,666.4
Machinery and transport equipment	100,858.4	125,965.7	116,797.0
Miscellaneous manufactured articles	23,011.2	26,805.1	27,488.4
Total (incl. others)	265,133.5	325,596.3	326,110.3

POLAND

Exports f.o.b.	2003	2004	2005
Food and live animals	15,882.0	21,008.8	25,008.4
Mineral fuels, lubricants, etc.	9,008.6	14,857.3	15,555.9
Chemicals and related products	13,619.1	17,499.6	19,604.2
Basic manufactures	49,584.6	63,620.4	65,023.4
Machinery and transport equipment	78,951.6	105,538.2	112,890.8
Miscellaneous manufactured articles	35,710.0	41,036.5	41,870.8
Total (incl. others)	208,944.3	272,102.4	288,682.3

PRINCIPAL TRADING PARTNERS
(million new złotys)*

Imports c.i.f.	2001	2002	2003
Austria	4,032.1	4,309	5,147
Belgium	5,611.0	6,242	6,949
China, People's Republic	6,649.5	8,473	11,273
Czech Republic	7,132.4	7,296	9,089
Denmark	3,607.2	3,896	3,916
Finland	3,475.0	3,492	3,994
France	14,033.7	15,663	18,730
Germany	49,448.0	54,692	64,669
Hungary	3,262.9	3,785	4,750
Italy	17,013.0	18,812	22,570
Japan	4,044.9	4,237	4,948
Korea, Republic	2,135.8	2,357	n.a.
Netherlands	7,323.3	7,891	8,978
Norway	2,008.7	2,737	4,691
Russia	18,201.3	17,978	20,292
Slovakia	3,102.1	3,310	4,073
Spain	5,255.0	5,948	6,911
Sweden	5,547.2	5,942	6,934
Switzerland	2,691.3	2,946	3,050
Turkey	1,633.7	2,569	3,405
Ukraine	1,840.9	2,003	2,902
United Kingdom	8,574.8	8,746	9,879
USA	6,924.7	7,321	6,877
Total (incl. others)	206,252.8	224,816	265,133

Exports f.o.b.	2001	2002	2003
Austria	3,003.2	3,070	3,552
Belgium	4,567.8	5,425	6,742
Czech Republic	5,878.2	6,692	8,470
Denmark	3,827.3	4,622	4,939
France	8,017.0	10,090	12,730
Germany	50,944.5	54,071	67,416
Hungary	3,102.1	3,783	5,047
Italy	7,975.2	9,195	11,992
Netherlands	7,003.4	7,510	9,384
Norway	1,676.8	2,977	4,423
Russia	4,346.3	5,437	5,900
Slovakia	2,119.2	2,337	3,405
Spain	2,381.3	2,953	4,433
Sweden	4,048.3	5,411	7,548
Ukraine	4,114.9	4,817	6,084
United Kingdom	7,376.9	8,683	10,522
USA	3,493.3	4,490	4,662
Total (incl. others)	148,114.5	167,338	208,944

* Imports by country of purchase; exports by country of sale.

2004 (million złotys, preliminary data): *Imports:* Germany 78,651.4; Italy 25,541.5; Russia 23,586.2; France 21,827.5; China, People's Republic 15,004.6; Czech Republic 11,738.6; Netherlands 11,252.4; United Kingdom 10,740.0; Sweden 8,794.4; Spain 8,527.9; Total (incl. others) 324,663.1. *Exports:* Germany 81,632.3; France 16,475.6; Italy 16,398.3; United Kingdom 14,881.3; Czech Republic 11,714.3; Netherlands 11,648.1; Russia 10,443.9; Sweden 9,572.9; Belgium 8,597.9; Ukraine 7,483.0; Total (incl. others) 272,105.9.

Transport

POLISH STATE RAILWAYS
(traffic)

	2001	2002	2003
Paying passengers ('000 journeys)	332,218	304,144	283,390
Passenger-kilometres (million)	22,469	20,809	19,653
Freight carried ('000 metric tons)	166,856	222,908	241,629
Freight ton-kilometres (million)	47,913	47,756	49,584

2004: Paying passenger journeys 272,162,000; Freight carried 282,919,000 metric tons.

ROAD TRAFFIC
('000 motor vehicles registered at 31 December)

	2001	2002	2003
Passenger cars	10,503	11,029	11,244
Lorries and vans (incl. road tractors)	1,979	2,163	2,313
Buses and coaches	82	83	83
Motorcycles*	803	869	845

* Figures for 2001 and 2002 also include scooters.

INLAND WATERWAYS
(traffic, including coastal transport)

	2001	2002	2003
Passengers carried ('000)	1,637	1,648	1,795
Passenger-kilometres (million)	42	37	34
Freight carried ('000 metric tons)	10,255	7,729	7,976
Freight ton-kilometres (million)	1,264	1,126	872

2004: Freight carried 8,748,000 metric tons.

SHIPPING

Merchant Fleet
(registered at 31 December)

	2002	2003	2004
Number of vessels	383	373	378
Displacement ('000 gross registered tons)	585.6	282.4	162.7

Source: Lloyd's Register-Fairplay, *World Fleet Statistics*.

Sea Transport
(by owned or leased ships)

	2001	2002	2003
Passengers carried ('000)	582	559	526
Passenger-kilometres (million)	154	150	137
Freight carried ('000 metric tons)	22,426	25,222	25,435
Freight ton-kilometres (million)	108,517	104,190	100,455

International Sea-borne Shipping at Polish Ports

	2001	2002	2003
Vessels entered ('000 net reg. tons)	39,594	41,563	50,794
Vessels entered (number)	32,299	30,212	29,771
Passengers ('000): arrivals	2,220	1,718	1,617
Passengers ('000): departures	2,197	1,587	1,572
Cargo ('000 metric tons): loaded*	31,526	33,168	35,848
Cargo ('000 metric tons): unloaded*	14,684	14,943	15,171

* Including ships' bunkers and transhipments.

Source: Centre of Maritime Statistics.

CIVIL AVIATION
(scheduled and non-scheduled flights)

	2001	2002	2003
Passengers carried ('000)	3,436	3,667	3,976
Passenger-kilometres (million)	6,412	6,672	6,870
Cargo ('000 metric tons)	27	28	31
Cargo ton-kilometres (million)	79	80	86

Tourism

FOREIGN TOURIST ARRIVALS
('000, including visitors in transit)

Country of residence	2003	2004	2005
Belarus	3,830	3,523	3,651
Czech Republic	8,827	9,286	7,855
Germany	25,457	34,122	37,436
Lithuania	1,366	1,336	1,344
Russia	1,534	1,420	1,599
Slovakia	2,896	4,048	3,378
Ukraine	4,830	4,523	5,279
Total (incl. others)	52,130	61,918	64,606

Receipts from tourism (US $ million): 4,070 in 2003; 5,785 in 2004; 6,230 in 2005.

Source: Institute of Tourism.

Communications Media

	2001	2002	2003
Radio subscribers ('000)*	9,219	n.a.	n.a.
Television subscribers ('000 in use)*	8,969	n.a.	n.a.
Telephones ('000 main lines in use)*	11,400	11,602	12,300
Mobile cellular telephones ('000 subscribers)*	10,005	13,900	17,401
Personal computers ('000 in use)†	3,300	4,079	5,480
Internet users ('000)†	3,800	8,880	8,970
Book production: titles‡	19,189	19,246	20,686
Book production: copies (million)‡	74.4	67.6	81.5
Daily and non-daily newspapers:			
number	66	67	54
average circulation ('000 copies)	4,438	4,191	4,335
Other periodicals: number	5,771	6,122	5,627
Other periodicals: average circulation ('000 copies)	74,043	71,903	69,409

* At 31 December.
† Source: International Telecommunication Union.
‡ Including pamphlets.

2004: Telephones ('000 main lines in use) 12,293; Internet users ('000) 9,000; Personal computers ('000 in use) 7,362; Mobile cellular telephones ('000 subscribers) 23,096.1.

Facsimile machines (estimate, 1995): 55,000 in use (Source: UN, *Statistical Yearbook*).

Education

(2003/04, unless otherwise indicated)

	Institutions	Teachers ('000)	Students ('000)
Pre-primary*	17,337	62.6	848.5
Primary	15,344	242.4†	2,855.6
Lower secondary	6,927	129.4†	1,681.2
Secondary	10,898	146.4†	1,807.9
General	2,603	52.1†	751.8
Technical, vocational and specialized	8,295	94.3†	1,056.1
Post-secondary	3,171	n.a.	265.7
Tertiary	400	88.5†	1,858.7

* 2001 figures.
† 2002/03 figures.

Adult literacy rate (UNESCO estimates): 99.7% (males 99.8%; females 99.7%) in 2002 (Source: UN Development Programme, *Human Development Report*).

Directory

The Constitution

The Constitution of the Republic of Poland was adopted by the National Assembly on 2 April 1997 and endorsed by popular referendum on 25 May of that year. The following is a summary of the main provisions of the Constitution, which came into force on 17 October 1997:

THE REPUBLIC

The Republic of Poland shall be a unitary, democratic state, ruled by law, and implementing the principles of social justice. The Republic of Poland shall safeguard the independence and integrity of its territory, ensure the freedom and rights of persons and citizens, and safeguard the national heritage. The Constitution shall be the supreme law of the Republic of Poland, which shall respect international law binding upon it. Legislative power shall be vested in the Sejm and the Senat, executive power shall be vested in the President and the Council of Ministers, and judicial power shall be vested in courts and tribunals.

The Republic of Poland shall ensure freedom for the creation and functioning of political parties, trade unions and other voluntary associations. The financing of political parties shall be open to public inspection. Political parties and other organizations whose programmes are based upon totalitarian methods and the modes of activity of nazism, fascism and communism, as well as those whose programmes or activities sanction racial or national hatred, or the application of violence for the purpose of obtaining power or to influence the State's policy, or provide for the secrecy of their own structure or membership, shall be forbidden. The Republic of Poland shall ensure freedom of the press and other means of social communication.

A social market economy, based on the freedom of economic activity, private ownership, and solidarity, dialogue and co-operation between social partners, shall be the basis of the economic system of Poland.

Churches and other religious organizations shall have equal rights. Public authorities shall be impartial in matters of personal conviction, whether religious or philosophical, or in relation to outlooks on life, and shall ensure their freedom of expression within public life. The Armed Forces shall observe neutrality regarding political matters and shall be subject to civil and democratic control.

Polish shall be the official language in the Republic of Poland. The image of a crowned eagle upon a red field shall be the coat-of-arms, and white and red shall be the colours of the Republic of Poland. The national anthem shall be the *Mazurka Dąbrowskiego*. The capital of the Republic of Poland shall be Warsaw.

THE FREEDOMS, RIGHTS AND OBLIGATIONS OF PERSONS AND CITIZENS

All persons shall be equal before the law. Men and women shall have equal rights. The Republic of Poland shall ensure Polish citizens belonging to national or ethnic minorities the freedom to maintain and develop their own language, to maintain customs and traditions, and to develop their own culture.

The Republic of Poland shall ensure the legal protection of the life of every human being; the inviolability of the person and of the home; freedom of movement; freedom of faith and religion; and the freedom to express opinions. The freedom of peaceful assembly and association shall be guaranteed. At the age of 18 every citizen shall have the right to participate in a referendum, and to vote in presidential, legislative and local elections. Everyone shall have the right to own property; the freedom to choose and pursue his occupation; the right to health protection; and the right to education. Everyone shall have the right to compensation for any harm done to him by any action of an organ of public authority contrary to law.

SOURCES OF LAW

The sources of universally binding law of the Republic of Poland shall be the Constitution, statutes, ratified international agreements, and regulations.

THE SEJM AND THE SENAT

The Sejm shall be composed of 460 Deputies. Elections to the Sejm shall be universal, equal, direct and proportional and conducted by secret ballot. The Senat shall be composed of 100 Senators. Elections to the Senat shall be universal, direct and conducted by secret ballot. The Sejm and the Senat shall be elected for a four-year term of office. At the ages of 21 and 30, respectively, every citizen having the right to vote shall be eligible for election to the Sejm and the Senat.

The Sejm shall elect from amongst its members a Marshal and Vice-Marshals. The Sejm adopts laws; may adopt a resolution on a state of war; may order a nation-wide referendum; and may appoint investigative committees to examine particular matters.

The Senat reviews laws adopted by the Sejm; it may adopt amendments or resolve upon complete rejection. The Senat can be overriden by the Sejm by an absolute majority vote in the presence of at least one-half of the statutory number of Deputies.

In instances specified in the Constitution, the Sejm and the Senat, sitting in joint session, shall act as the National Assembly (Zgromadzenie Narodowe). The right to introduce legislation shall belong to Deputies, to the Senat, to the President of the Republic, to the Council of Ministers, and to a group of at least 100,000 citizens having the right to vote in elections to the Sejm.

THE PRESIDENT OF THE REPUBLIC

The President of the Republic of Poland shall be the supreme representative of the Polish State and the guarantor of the continuity of state authority. The President shall ensure observance of the Constitution, safeguard the sovereignty and security of the State, as well as the inviolability and integrity of its territory. The President shall be elected in universal, equal and direct elections by secret ballot. The President shall be elected for a five-year term, and may be re-elected only once. Only a Polish citizen aged over 35 years, with full electoral rights in elections to the Sejm, may be elected President. Any such candidature shall be supported by the signatures of at least 100,000 citizens having the right to vote in elections to the Sejm. If the President of the Republic is unable to discharge the duties of his office, the Marshal of the Sejm shall temporarily assume presidential duties.

The President's duties include the calling of elections to the Sejm and the Senat; heading the Armed Forces; nominating and appointing the Prime Minister; appointing senior public officials; and representing the State in foreign affairs.

Bringing an indictment against the President shall be done by resolution of the National Assembly, passed by a majority of at least two-thirds of the statutory number of members, on the motion of at least 140 members.

THE COUNCIL OF MINISTERS AND GOVERNMENT ADMINISTRATION

The Council of Ministers shall conduct the internal affairs and foreign policy of the Republic of Poland, and shall manage the government administration. The President shall nominate a Prime Minister who shall propose the composition of a Council of Ministers. The Prime Minister shall, within 14 days following his appointment, submit a programme of activity of the Council of Ministers to the Sejm, together with a motion requiring a vote of confidence.

The members of the Council of Ministers shall be responsible to the Sejm, both collectively and individually. The Sejm shall pass a vote of no confidence in the Council of Ministers by a majority of votes of the statutory number of Deputies, on a motion of at least 46 Deputies, specifying the name of a candidate for Prime Minister.

LOCAL SELF-GOVERNMENT

The commune (*gmina*) shall be the basic unit of local self-government. Other units of regional and/or local self-government shall be specified by statute. Public duties aimed at satisfying the needs of a self-governing community shall be the direct responsibility of such units. Units of local self-government shall perform their duties through constitutive and executive organs. Units of local self-government shall be assured public funds for the performance of the duties assigned to them.

COURTS AND TRIBUNALS

The courts and tribunals shall constitute a separate and independent power. The administration of justice in the Republic of Poland shall be implemented by the Supreme Court, the common courts, administrative courts and military courts. Judges, within the exercise of their office, shall be independent and subject only to the Constitution and statutes. A judge shall not belong to a political party or trade union, or perform public activities incompatible with the principles of independence of the courts and judges. The Supreme Court shall exercise supervision over common and military courts.

The Constitutional Tribunal

The Constitutional Tribunal shall adjudicate on the conformity of statutes and other normative acts issued by central state organs to the Constitution. Its judgments shall be universally binding and final. Judges of the Tribunal shall be independent and subject only to the Constitution.

The Tribunal of State

Persons holding high state positions (as specified in the Constitution) shall be accountable to the Tribunal of State for violations of the Constitution or statutes. The First President of the Supreme Court shall be chairperson of the Tribunal. Its members shall be independent and subject only to the Constitution and statutes.

ORGANS OF STATE CONTROL FOR THE DEFENCE OF RIGHTS

The Supreme Chamber of Control shall be the chief organ of state order, and shall be subordinate to the Sejm. It shall audit the activity of the organs of government administration, the National Bank of Poland, state legal persons and other state organizational units. The Commissioner for Citizens' Rights shall safeguard the freedoms and rights of persons and citizens as specified in the Constitution and other normative acts. The National Council of Radio and Television Broadcasting shall safeguard freedom of speech and the right to information, as well as the public interest regarding radio and television broadcasting.

PUBLIC FINANCES

The National Bank of Poland, as the central bank of the State, shall have an exclusive right to issue money as well as to formulate and implement monetary policy. It shall be responsible for the value of the Polish currency.

The Council for Monetary Policy, presided over by the President of the National Bank, shall annually formulate the aims of monetary policy and present them to the Sejm at the same time as the submission of the Council of Ministers' draft Budget.

EXTRAORDINARY MEASURES

In situations of particular danger, if ordinary constitutional measures are inadequate, any of the following appropriate extraordinary measures may be introduced in a part or upon the whole territory of the State: martial law, a state of emergency or a state of natural disaster.

The Government

HEAD OF STATE

President: Lech Kaczyński (inaugurated 23 December 2005).

COUNCIL OF MINISTERS
(May 2006)

A coalition of the Law and Justice party (PiS), the Self-Defence Party of the Republic of Poland and the League of Polish Families (LPR).

Prime Minister: Kazimierz Marcinkiewicz (PiS).
Deputy Prime Minister and Minister of Internal Affairs and Administration: Ludwik Dorn (PiS).
Deputy Prime Minister and Minister of Finance: Prof. Zyta Gilowska (Independent).
Deputy Prime Minister and Minister of Agriculture and Rural Development: Andrzej Lepper (Self-Defence).

POLAND

Deputy Prime Minister and Minister of National Education: ROMAN GIERTYCH (LPR).
Minister of Foreign Affairs: ANNA FOTYGA (PiS).
Minister of National Defence: RADOSŁAW SIKORSKI (PiS).
Minister of the Economy: PIOTR GRZEGORZ WOŹNIAK (Independent).
Minister of the State Treasury: WOJCIECH JASIŃSKI (PiS).
Minister of Justice: ZBIGNIEW ZIOBRO (PiS).
Minister of Science and Higher Education: MICHAŁ SEWERYŃSKI (Independent).
Minister of Labour and Social Policy: ANNA KALATA (Self-Defence).
Minister of Regional Development: GRAŻYNA GĘSICKA (Independent).
Minister of Culture and National Heritage: KAZIMIERZ MICHAŁ UJAZDOWSKI (PiS).
Minister of Health: ZBIGNIEW RELIGA (Independent).
Minister of the Environment: JAN SZYSZKO (PiS).
Minister of Transport: JERZY POLACZEK (PiS).
Minister of Sport: TOMASZ LIPIEC (Independent).
Minister of the Marine Economy: RAFAŁ WIECHECKI (LPR).
Minister of Construction: ANTONI JASZCZAK (Self-Defence).
Minister without Portfolio: ZBIGNIEW WASSERMANN (PiS).

MINISTRIES

Chancellery of the President: 00-902 Warsaw, ul. Wiejska 10; tel. (22) 6952900; fax (22) 6952238; e-mail listy@prezydent.pl; internet www.prezydent.pl.
Chancellery of the Prime Minister: 00-583 Warsaw, Al. Ujazdowskie 1/3; tel. (22) 6946000; fax (22) 6252637; e-mail cirinfo@kprm.gov.pl; internet www.kprm.gov.pl.
Ministry of Agriculture and Rural Development: 00-930 Warsaw, ul. Wspólna 30; tel. (22) 6231000; fax (22) 6232750; e-mail kanceleria@minrol.gov.pl; internet www.minrol.gov.pl.
Ministry of Construction: Warsaw.
Ministry of Culture and National Heritage: 00-71 Warsaw, ul. Krakowskie Przedmieście 15/17; tel. (22) 4210100; fax (22) 8261922; e-mail rzecznik@mkidn.gov.pl; internet www.mkidn.gov.pl.
Ministry of the Economy: 00-507 Warsaw, pl. Trzech Krzyży 3/5; tel. (22) 6935000; fax (22) 6934048; e-mail bpi@mgip.gov.pl; internet www.mgip.gov.pl.
Ministry of the Environment: 00-922 Warsaw, ul. Wawelska 52/54; tel. (22) 5792900; fax (22) 5792511; e-mail info@mos.gov.pl; internet www.mos.gov.pl.
Ministry of Finance: 00-916 Warsaw, ul. Świętokrzyska 12; tel. (22) 6945555; fax (22) 8260180; e-mail biuro.prasowe@mofnet.gov.pl; internet www.mf.gov.pl.
Ministry of Foreign Affairs: 00-580 Warsaw, Al. Szucha 23; tel. (22) 5239000; fax (22) 6290287; e-mail dsi@msz.gov.pl; internet www.msz.gov.pl.
Ministry of Health: 00-952 Warsaw, ul. Miodowa 15; tel. (22) 6349600; fax (22) 6358783; e-mail kancelaria@mz.gov.pl; internet www.mz.gov.pl.
Ministry of Internal Affairs and Administration: 02-591 Warsaw, ul. Stefana Batorego 5; tel. (22) 6014427; fax (22) 6227973; e-mail wp@mswia.gov.pl; internet www.mswia.gov.pl.
Ministry of Justice: 00-950 Warsaw, Al. Ujazdowskie 11; tel. (22) 5212888; fax (22) 6215540; e-mail nagorska@ms.gov.pl; internet www.ms.gov.pl.
Ministry of Labour and Social Policy: 00-513 Warsaw, ul. Nowogrodzka 1/3/5; tel. (22) 6610100; fax (22) 6610709; internet www.mpips.gov.pl.
Ministry of Marine Economy: Warsaw.
Ministry of National Defence: 00-909 Warsaw, ul. Klonowa 1; tel. (22) 6280031; fax (22) 8455378; e-mail bpimon@wp.mil.pl; internet www.wp.mil.pl.
Ministry of National Education: 00-918 Warsaw, Al. Szucha 25; tel. (22) 6280461; fax (22) 6297241; e-mail minister@menis.waw.pl; internet www.men.waw.pl.
Ministry of Regional Development: 00-507 Warsaw, pl. Trzech Krzyży 3/5.
Ministry of Science and Higher Education: Warsaw.
Ministry of Sport: 00-559 Warsaw, Al. Róż 2; tel. (22) 5223399; fax (22) 8262172; e-mail rzecznik@msport.gov.pl; internet www.msport.gov.pl.
Ministry of the State Treasury: 00-522 Warsaw, ul. Krucza 36; tel. (22) 6958000; fax (22) 6280872; e-mail minister@msp.gov.pl; internet www.msp.gov.pl.
Ministry of Transport: 00-928 Warsaw, ul. Chałubińskiego 4/6; tel. (22) 6301000; fax (22) 6301116; e-mail info@mtigm.gov.pl; internet www.mi.gov.pl.

President and Legislature

PRESIDENT

Presidential Election, First Ballot, 9 October 2005

Candidates	Votes	%
Donald Tusk	5,429,666	36.33
Lech Kaczyński	4,947,927	33.10
Andrzej Lepper	2,259,094	15.11
Marek Borowski	1,544,642	10.33
Jarosław Kalinowski	269,316	1.80
Janusz Korwin-Mikke	214,116	1.43
Henryka Bochniarz	188,598	1.26
Others	93,330	0.63
Total	14,946,689	100.00

Second Ballot, 23 October 2005

Candidates	Votes	%
Lech Kaczyński	8,257,468	54.04
Donald Tusk	7,022,319	45.96
Total	15,279,787	100.00

ZGROMADZENIE NARODOWE
(National Assembly)

Senat
(Senate)

00-072 Warsaw, ul. Wiejska 4/6; tel. (22) 6942500; fax (22) 2290968; internet www.senat.gov.pl.
Marshal: BOGDAN BORUSEWICZ.

Election, 25 September 2005

Parties and alliances	Seats
Law and Justice (PiS)	49
Civic Platform (PO)	34
League of Polish Families (LPR)	7
Self-Defence Party of the Republic of Poland	3
Polish People's Party (PSL)	2
Independents	5
Total	100

Sejm
(Assembly)

00-902 Warsaw, ul. Wiejska 4/6; tel. (22) 285927; internet www.sejm.gov.pl.
Marshal: MAREK JUREK.

Election, 25 September 2005

Parties and alliances	% of votes	Seats
Law and Justice Party (PiS)	26.99	155
Civic Platform (PO)	24.14	133
Self-Defence Party of the Republic of Poland	11.41	56
Democratic Left Alliance (SLD)	11.31	55
League of Polish Families (LPR)	7.97	34
Polish People's Party (PSL)	6.96	25
German Minority (MN)	0.29	2
Others	10.93	—
Total	100.00	460

Election Commission

Państwowa Komisja Wyborcza (PKW) (State Election Commission): 00–902 Warsaw, ul. Wiejska 10; tel. (22) 6250617; fax (22) 6293959; internet www.pkw.gov.pl; Pres. FERDYNAND RYMARZ.

POLAND

Political Organizations

By January 1998 the number of registered parties operating in Poland had declined from some 360 to 60, as a result of new regulations, which obliged existing parties to apply for re-registration by the end of 1997, presenting a list of a minimum of 1,000 supporting signatures, instead of the previous 15.

Alliance of Polish Christian Democrats (Porozumienie Polskich Chrzescijanskich Demokratów—PPChD): e-mail biuro@chadecja.org.pl; f. 1999 by merger of the Centre Alliance, the Movement for the Republic of Poland and the Party of Christian Democrats; Chair. ANTONI TOKARCZUK; Head of Political Council PAWEŁ LACZKOWSKI.

Centre Party (Partia Centrum): 00-057 Warsaw, pl. Dąbrowskiego 5; tel. (22) 8278442; fax (22) 8278441; e-mail centrum@centrum.org.pl; internet www.centrum.org.pl; f. 2004; Leader JANUSZ STEINHOFF.

Christian-National Union (Zjednoczenie Chrześcijańsko-Narodowe—ZChN): Warsaw, ul. Mokotowska 555/50; tel. (22) 6227120; e-mail biuro@zchn.waw.pl; internet www.zchn.waw.pl; f. 1989; c. 10,000 mems; Chair. STANISŁAW ZAJAC.

Civic Platform (Platforma Obywatelska—PO): 00-121 Warsaw, ul. Andersa 21; tel. (22) 6357879; fax (22) 6357641; e-mail poczta@platforma.org; internet www.platforma.org; f. 2001 by a popular independent presidential candidate and factions of the UW and the AWS; conservative-liberal; Leader DONALD TUSK.

Confederation for an Independent Poland (Konfederacja Polski Niepodległej—KPN): 00-511 Warsaw, ul. Nowogrodzka 25/37; tel. (22) 8261043; fax (22) 8261400; e-mail kpnwa@poczta.onet.pl; internet www.kpn.pl; f. 1979; centre-right; Chair. LESZEK MOCZULSKI.

Conservative Peasant Party-New Poland Movement (Stronnictwo Konserwatywno Ludowe-Ruch Nowej Polski—SKL-RNP—SKL-Ruch Nowej Polski): 00-065 Warsaw, pl. Dąbrowskiego 5; tel. (22) 8278442; fax (22) 8278441; f. 2002 by merger of the Conservative Peasant Party and right-wing elements of the Alliance of Polish Christian Democrats; Chair. ARTUR BALAZS.

Democratic Left Alliance (Sojusz Lewicy Demokratycznej—SLD): 00-419 Warsaw, ul. Rozbrat 44 A; tel. and fax (22) 6218553; e-mail zecznik@sld.org.pl; internet www.sld.org.pl; f. 1999 by reorganization of electoral coalition of former Social Democracy of the Republic of Poland and the All Poland Trade Unions Alliance; formed electoral and government alliance with the Union of Labour in 2001; Chair. WOJCIECH OLEJNICZAK.

Democratic Party—Demokrats (Partia Demokratyczna—Demokraci): 00-681 Warsaw, ul. Marszałkowska 77/79; tel. (22) 8275047; fax (22) 8277851; e-mail kontakt@demokraci.pl; internet demokraci.pl; f. 2005 to replace Freedom Union (UW); Leader JANUSZ ONYSZKIEWICZ.

Democratic Party (SD) (Stronnictwo Demokratyczne): 00-021 Warsaw, ul. Chmielna 9; tel. (22) 8261001; fax (22) 8274051; e-mail sd@sd.org.pl; internet www.sd.org.pl; f. 1937; 12,000 mems (1999); Chair. ANDRZEJ ARENDARSKI.

German Minority (Mniejszość Niemiecka—MN): Leader HENRYK KRÓL.

Law and Justice (Prawo i Sprawiedliwość—PiS): 02-018 Warsaw, ul. Nowogrodzka 84/86; tel. (22) 6215035; fax (22) 6216767; e-mail biuro@pis.org.pl; internet www.pis.org.pl; f. 2001; conservative; formed co-operation agreement with the Civic Platform in advance of local elections in 2002; Leader JAROSŁAW KACZYŃSKI.

League of Polish Families (Liga Polskich Rodzin—LPR): 00-528 Warsaw, ul. Hoża 9; tel. (22) 6223648; fax (22) 6223138; e-mail biuro@lpr.pl; internet www.lpr.pl; f. 2001 as alliance comprising the National Party, All-Poland Youth, the Polish Accord Party, the Catholic National movement and the Peasant National Bloc; Roman Catholic, nationalist, anti-EU; Leader ROMAN GIERTYCH; Chief of Staff ZYGMUNT WRZODAK.

Movement for the Reconstruction of Poland (Ruch Odbudowy Polski—ROP): 00-549 Warsaw, ul. Piękna 22 lok. 7; tel. and fax (22) 6253282; e-mail biuro@rop.sky.pl; internet www.rop.sky.pl; f. 1995; conservative; Leader JAN OLSZEWSKI.

Peasant Democratic Party (Partia Ludowo-Demokratyczna—PLD): 00-539 Warsaw, ul. Piękna 3A; tel. (22) 6294026; fax 6295367; e-mail pld@org.pl; internet www.pld.pl; f. 1998; Leader ROMAN JAGIELIŃSKI.

Polish People's Party (Polskie Stronnictwo Ludowe—PSL): 00-131 Warsaw, ul. Grzybowska 4; tel. (22) 6206020; fax (22) 6543583; e-mail biuronkw@nkw.psl.org.pl; internet www.psl.org.pl; f. 1990 on basis of United Peasant Party (f. 1949) and Polish Peasant Party—Rebirth (f. 1989); centrist, stresses development of agriculture and social-market economy; Chair. WALDEMAR PAWLAK.

Polish Social Democracy (Socjaldemokracja Polski—SDPL): 02-904 Warsaw, ul. Bernardyńska 14A; tel. (22) 8406008; e-mail sdpl.wybory@onet.pl; internet www.sdpl.pl; f. 2004; Leader MAREK BOROWSKI.

Polish Socialist Party (Polska Partia Socjalistyczna—PPS): 00-325 Warsaw, ul. Krakowskie Przedmieście 6; tel. (22) 8262054; fax (22) 8266908; e-mail info@polskapartiasocjalisticzyna.org; internet www.pps.org.pl; f. 1892; re-established 1987; 5,000 mems; Chair. ANDRZEJ ZIEMSKI.

Self-Defence Party of the Republic of Poland (Self-Defence) (Partia Samoobrona Rzeczypospolitej Polskiej—Samoobrona): 00-024 Warsaw, Al. Jerozolimskie 30; tel. (22) 6250472; fax (22) 6250477; e-mail samoobrona@samoobrona.org.pl; internet www.samoobrona.org.pl; f. 2000; agrarian, populist, anti-EU; Leader ANDRZEJ LEPPER.

Union of Labour (Unia Pracy—UP): 00-513 Warsaw, ul. Nowogrodzka 4; tel. and fax (22) 6256776; e-mail biuro@uniapracy.org.pl; internet www.uniapracy.org.pl; f. 1993; formed electoral and government coalition with the Democratic Left Alliance in 2001; Chair. WALDEMAR WITKOWSKI.

Union of the Left (UL) (Unia Lewicy): Warsaw; e-mail zarzad@unia-lewicy.org; internet www.unia-lewicy.org; f. 2005; Chair. PIOTR MUSIAŁ.

Union of Real Politics (Unia Polityki Realnej—UPR): 00-042 Warsaw, ul. Nowy Świat 41; tel. and fax (22) 2264642; e-mail secretariat@upr.org.pl; internet www.upr.org.pl; f. 1996; Leader STANISŁAW MICHALKIEWICZ.

Diplomatic Representation

EMBASSIES IN POLAND

Afghanistan: 02-954 Warsaw, ul. Goplańska 1; tel. (22) 8855410; fax (22) 8856500; e-mail warsaw@afghanembassy.com.pl; internet www.afghanembassy.com.pl; Ambassador ABDUL H. HAIDAR.

Albania: 02-386 Warsaw, ul. Altowa 1; tel. (22) 8241427; fax (22) 8241426; e-mail alb@atos.warman.com.pl; Ambassador SOKOL GJOKA.

Algeria: 03-932 Warsaw, ul. Dąbrowiecka 21; tel. (22) 6175855; fax (22) 6160081; e-mail ambalgva@zigzag.pl; Ambassador ABDELAZIZ LAHIOUEL.

Angola: 02-635 Warsaw, ul. Balonowa 20; tel. (22) 6463529; fax (22) 8447452; e-mail embaixada@emb-angola.pl; Ambassador LISETH NAWANGA SATUMBO PENA.

Argentina: 03-973 Warsaw, ul. Brukselska 9; tel. (22) 6176028; fax (22) 6177162; e-mail secons@ikp.atm.com.pl; Ambassador CARLOS ALBERTO PASSALACQUA.

Armenia: 02-913 Warsaw, ul. A. Waszkowskiego 11; tel. (22) 8408130; fax (22) 6420643; e-mail main@embarmenia.it.pl; Ambassador ASHOT GALOIAN.

Australia: 00-513 Warsaw, ul. Nowogrodzka 11, Nautilus Bldg, 3rd Floor; tel. (22) 5213444; fax (22) 6273500; e-mail ambasada@australia.pl; internet www.australia.pl; Ambassador IAN K. FORSYTH.

Austria: 00-748 Warsaw, ul. Gagarina 34; tel. (22) 8410081; fax (22) 8410085; e-mail warschau-ob@bmaa.gv.at; internet www.ambasadaaustrii.pl; Ambassador ALFRED LÄNGLE.

Azerbaijan: 03-941 Warsaw, ul. Zwycięców 12; tel. (22) 6162188; fax (22) 6161949; e-mail info@azer-embassy.pl; Ambassador VILAYAT GULIYEV.

Belarus: 02-952 Warsaw, ul. Wiertnicza 58; tel. (22) 7420990; fax (22) 7420980; e-mail poland@belembassy.org; internet www.belembassy.org/poland; Ambassador PAVEL P. LATUSHKA.

Belgium: 00-095 Warsaw, ul. Senatorska 34; tel. (22) 8270233; fax (22) 8285711; e-mail ambabel.warsaw@pol.pl; e-mail warsaw@diplobel.org; Ambassador BRUNO NÈVE DE MÉVERGNIES.

Brazil: 03-931 Warsaw, ul. Poselska 11, Saska Kepa; tel. (22) 6174800; fax (22) 6178689; e-mail brasil@brasil.org.pl; internet www.brasil.org.pl; Ambassador MARCELO ANDRADE DE MORAES JARDIM.

Bulgaria: 00-540 Warsaw, Al. Ujazdowskie 33/35; tel. (22) 6294071; fax (22) 6282271; e-mail office@bgemb.com.pl; Ambassador LATCHEZAR Y. PETKOV.

Cambodia: 03-969 Warsaw, ul. Drezdeńska 3; tel. (22) 6165231; fax (22) 6161836; Ambassador CHAN KY SIM.

Canada: 00-481 Warsaw, ul. Matejki 1/5; tel. (22) 5843100; fax (22) 5843190; e-mail wsaw@international.gc.ca; internet www.canada.pl; Ambassador DAVID PRESTON.

Chile: 02-925 Warsaw, ul. Okrężna 62; tel. (22) 8582330; fax (22) 8582329; e-mail embachile@onenet.pl; Ambassador JOSÉ MANUEL OVALLE BRAVO.

China, People's Republic: 00-203 Warsaw, ul. Bonifraterska 1; tel. (22) 8313836; fax (22) 6354211; e-mail consular@chinaembassy.org.pl; internet www.chinaembassy.org.pl; Ambassador YUAN GUISEN.

POLAND

Colombia: 03-936 Warsaw, ul. Zwycięzców 29; tel. (22) 6177157; fax (22) 6176684; e-mail embcol@medianet.com.pl; Ambassador DORY SÁNCHEZ DE WETZEL.

Congo, Democratic Republic: 02-637 Warsaw, ul. Miączyńska 50; tel. and fax (22) 8496999; fax (22) 8485215; e-mail ambardcvarsovie@yahoo.fr; Ambassador ISIDORE MAVAMBU MATUMONA.

Costa Rica: 02-954 Warsaw, ul. Kubickiego 9, m. 5; tel. (22) 8589112; fax (22) 6427832; e-mail emcoripol@neostrada.pl; Ambassador JACHEVET WEINSTOK WOLFOWIEZ.

Croatia: 02-611 Warsaw, ul. Ignacego Krasickiego 25; tel. (22) 8442393; fax (22) 8444808; e-mail croemb@croatia.pol.pl; Ambassador NEBOJŠA KOHAROVIĆ.

Cuba: 02-516 Warsaw, ul. Rejtana 15, m. 8; tel. (22) 8481715; fax (22) 8482231; e-mail embacuba@medianet.pl; Ambassador JORGE FERNANDO LEFEBRE NICOLÁS.

Cyprus: 02-629 Warsaw, ul. Pilicka 4; tel. (22) 8444577; fax (22) 8442558; e-mail embassyofcyprus@neostrada.pl; Ambassador NAFSIKA C. KROUSTI.

Czech Republic: 00-555 Warsaw, ul. Koszykowa 18; tel. (22) 6287221; fax (22) 6298045; e-mail warsaw@embassy.mzv.cz; internet www.mfa.cz/warsaw; Ambassador BEDŘICH KOPECKÝ.

Denmark: 02-517 Warsaw, ul. Rakowiecka 19; tel. (22) 5652900; fax (22) 5652970; e-mail wawamb@um.dk; internet www.danishembassy.pl; Ambassador KAREN WERMUTH.

Ecuador: 02-516 Warsaw, ul. Rejtana 15, m. 15; tel. (22) 8487230; fax (22) 8488196; e-mail mecuapol@it.com.pl; internet www.mmrree.gov.ec; Ambassador FERNANDO FLORES MACÍAS.

Egypt: 03-972 Warsaw, ul. Alzacka 18; tel. (22) 6176973; fax (22) 6179058; e-mail embassyofegypt@zigzag.pl; Ambassador YEHYA IBRAHIM EL-RAMLAWY.

Estonia: 02-639 Warsaw, ul. Karwińska 1; tel. (22) 6464480; fax (22) 6464481; e-mail saatkond@varssavi.vm.ee; internet www.estemb.pl; Ambassador ANTS FROSCH.

Finland: 00-559 Warsaw, ul. Chopina 4/8; tel. (22) 6294091; fax (22) 6213442; e-mail sanomat.var@formin.fi; Ambassador JAN STORE.

France: 00-477 Warsaw, ul. Piękna 1; tel. (22) 5293000; fax (22) 5293001; e-mail presse@ambafrance-pl.org; internet www.ambafrance-pl.org; Ambassador PIERRE MÉNAT.

Georgia: 03-934 Warsaw, ul. Wąchocka 1s; tel. (22) 3531650; fax (22) 4997752; e-mail geoemb@mfa.gov.ge; Ambassador GIORGI KAVTARADZE.

Germany: 03-932 Warsaw, ul. Dąbrowiecka 30; tel. (22) 5841700; fax (22) 5841739; e-mail info@ambasadaniemiec.pl; internet www.ambasadaniemiec.pl; Ambassador REINHARD SCHWEPPE.

Greece: 00-432 Warsaw, ul. Górnośląska 35; tel. (22) 6229460; fax (22) 6229464; e-mail embassy@greece.pl; internet www.greece.pl; Chargé d'affaires a.i. NIKI KAMBA.

Holy See: 00-582 Warsaw, Al. J. Ch. Szucha 12, POB 163; tel. (22) 6288488; fax (22) 6284556; e-mail nuncjatura@episkopat.pl; Apostolic Nuncio Most Rev. JÓZEF KOWALCZYK (Titular Archbishop of Eraclea).

Hungary: 00-559 Warsaw, ul. Chopina 2; tel. (22) 6284451; fax (22) 6218561; e-mail magyar@optimus.waw.pl; Ambassador MIHÁLY GYŐR.

India: 02-516 Warsaw, ul. Rejtana 15, m. 2–7; tel. (22) 8495800; fax (22) 8496705; e-mail ss-com@it.com.pl; internet www.indianembassy.pl; Ambassador ANIL WADHWA.

Indonesia: 03-903 Warsaw, ul. Estońska 3/, POB 33; tel. (22) 6175179; fax (22) 6178451; e-mail info@indonesianembassy.pl; internet www.indonesianembassy.pl; Chargé d'affaires a.i. HENDRA SATYA PRAMANA.

Iran: 03-928 Warsaw, ul. Królowej Aldony 22; tel. (22) 6174293; fax (22) 6178452; e-mail iranemb@iranemb.warsaw.pl; internet www.iranemb.warsaw.pl; Ambassador MUHAMMAD MEHDI POURMUHAMMADI.

Iraq: 03-932 Warsaw, ul. Dąbrowiecka 9A; tel. (22) 6175773; fax (22) 6177065; e-mail ambasada.irak@neostrada.pl; Ambassador WALID HAMID SHILTAGH.

Ireland: 00-496 Warsaw, ul. Mysia 5; tel. (22) 8496633; fax (22) 8498431; e-mail ambasada@irlandia.pl; internet www.irlandia.pl; Ambassador DECLAN O'DONOVAN.

Israel: 02-078 Warsaw, ul. Krzywickiego 24; tel. (22) 8250923; fax (22) 8251607; e-mail itonut@israel.pl; internet www.israel.pl; Ambassador DAVID ABRAHAM AKIVA PELEG.

Italy: 00-055 Warsaw, pl. Dąbrowskiego 6; tel. (22) 8263471; fax (22) 8278507; e-mail ambasciata@italianembassy.pl; internet www.italianembassy.pl; Ambassador ANNA BLEFARI MELAZZI.

Japan: 00-464 Warsaw, ul. Szwoleżerów 8; tel. (22) 6965000; fax (22) 6965001; e-mail info-cul@emb-japan.pl; internet www.emb-japan.pl; Ambassador MASAKI ONO.

Kazakhstan: 02-954 Warsaw, ul. Królowej Marysieńki 14; tel. (22) 6425388; fax (22) 6423427; e-mail kazdipmis@hot.pl; internet www.kazakhstan.pl; Ambassador ALEKSEI VOLKOV.

Korea, Democratic People's Republic: 00-728 Warsaw, ul. Bobrowiecka 1A; tel. (22) 8405813; fax (22) 8405710; e-mail dprkemb_pl@hotmail.com; Ambassador KIM PYONG IL.

Korea, Republic: 00-464 Warsaw, ul. Szwoleżerów 6; tel. (22) 5592906; fax (22) 5592905; e-mail koremb_waw@mofat.go.kr; Ambassador LEE SANG-CHUL.

Kuwait: 00-486 Warsaw, ul. Franciszka Nullo 13; tel. (22) 6222860; fax (22) 6274314; e-mail embassy@kue.com.pl; Ambassador JAMAL MUHAMMAD ISSA AL-GHUNAIM.

Laos: 02-516 Warsaw, ul. Rejtana 15, m. 26; tel. (22) 8484786; fax (22) 8497122; e-mail embassylaos@yahoo.com; Ambassador SOMPHONE SICHALEUNE.

Latvia: 03-928 Warsaw, ul. Królowej Aldony 19; tel. (22) 6174389; fax (22) 6174289; e-mail embassy.poland@mfa.gov.lv; Ambassador ALBERTS SARKANIS.

Lebanon: 02-516 Warsaw, ul. Starościńska 1B, m. 10–11; tel. (22) 8445065; fax (22) 6460030; e-mail embleban@pol.pl; Ambassador MASSOUD MAALOUF.

Libya: 03-934 Warsaw, ul. Kryniczna 2; tel. (22) 6174822; fax (22) 6175091; e-mail alfath2@ikp.atm.com.pl; Sec. of the People's Bureau (Ambassador) MUHAMMAD IBRAHIM OMER ALBADRI.

Lithuania: 00-580 Warsaw, Al. J. Ch. Szucha 5; tel. (22) 6253368; fax (22) 6253440; e-mail ambasada@lietuva.pl; internet www.lietuva.pl; Ambassador EGIDIJUS MEILŪNAS.

Luxembourg: 00-493 Warsaw, ul. Prusa 2; tel. (22) 6570071; fax (22) 6570340; e-mail ambaluxpol@gmail.com; Ambassador RONALD DOFING.

Macedonia, former Yugoslav republic: 02-954 Warsaw, ul. Królowej Marysieńki 40; tel. (22) 6517291; fax (22) 6517292; e-mail ambrmwar@zigzag.pl; internet www.ambasadarm.zigzag.pl; Ambassador DIMKO KOKAROVSKI.

Malaysia: 03-902 Warsaw, Saska-Kepa, ul. Gruzińska 3; tel. (22) 6174413; fax (22) 6176256; e-mail mwwarsaw@poczta.neostrada.pl; Ambassador Dato MD DAUD M. YUSOFF.

Mexico: 02-516 Warsaw, ul. Starościńska 1B, m. 4/5; tel. (22) 6468800; fax (22) 6464222; e-mail embamex@ikp.pl; Ambassador FRANCISCO JOSÉ CRUZ GONZÁLEZ.

Moldova: 02-634 Warsaw, ul. Miłobędzka 12; tel. (22) 8447278; fax (22) 6462099; e-mail embassy@moldova.pl; internet www.moldova.pl; Ambassador BORIS GAMURARI.

Mongolia: 02-516 Warsaw, ul. Rejtana 15, m. 16; tel. (22) 8482063; fax (22) 8499391; e-mail mongamb@ikp.atm.com.pl; internet www.ambmong.net7.pl; Ambassador TUGALKHUU BAASANSUREN.

Morocco: 02-516 Warsaw, ul. Starościńska 1B, m. 11/12; tel. (22) 8496341; fax (22) 8481840; e-mail info@moroccoembassy.org.pl; internet www.moroccoembassy.org.pl; Ambassador ABDESSELAM ALEM.

Netherlands: 00-468 Warsaw, ul. Kawalerii 10; tel. (22) 5591200; fax (22) 8402638; e-mail nlgovwar@ikp.pl; Ambassador JAN EDWARD CRAANEN.

New Zealand: 00-536 Warsaw, Al. Ujazdowskie 51; tel. (22) 5210500; fax (22) 5210510; e-mail nzwsw@nzembassy.pl; Ambassador PHILIP WALLACE GRIFFITHS.

Nigeria: 02-952 Warsaw, ul. Wiertnicza 94; tel. (22) 8486944; fax (22) 8485379; e-mail info@nigeriaembassy.pl; internet www.nigeriaembassy.pl; Ambassador NUHU NYAM BAJOGA AUDU.

Norway: 00-559 Warsaw, ul. Chopina 2A; tel. (22) 6964030; fax (22) 6280938; e-mail emb.warsaw@mfa.no; internet www.amb-norwegia.pl; Ambassador KNUT HAUGE.

Pakistan: 02-516 Warsaw, ul. Starościńska 1, m. 1/2; tel. (22) 8494808; fax (22) 8491160; e-mail parepwarsaw@wp.pl; internet www.pakembwaw.com.pl; Ambassador FAUZIA NAZREEN.

Peru: 02-516 Warsaw, ul. Starościńska 1, m. 3–4; tel. (22) 6468806; fax (22) 6468617; e-mail embperpl@atomnet.pl; internet www.perupol.pl; Ambassador JUAN ANTONIO VELIT GRANDA.

Portugal: 03-905 Warsaw, ul. Francuska 37; tel. (22) 5111010; fax (22) 5111013; e-mail embaixada@embport.internetdsl.pl; Chargé d'affaires a.i. MANUELA PAULA TEIXERA PINTO.

Romania: 00-559 Warsaw, ul. Chopina 10; tel. (22) 6283156; fax (22) 6285264; e-mail embassy@roembassy.com.pl; Ambassador GABRIEL CONSTANTIN BÂRTAȘ.

Russia: 00-761 Warsaw, ul. Belwederska 49; tel. (22) 6213453; fax (22) 6253016; e-mail ambrus@poczta.fm; internet www.poland.mid.ru; Chargé d'affaires a.i. VLADIMIR SEDYKH.

Saudi Arabia: 00-739 Warsaw, ul. Stępińska 55; tel. (22) 8400000; fax (22) 8406003; e-mail info@saudiembassy.pl; tel. www.saudiembassy.pl; Ambassador NASSER BIN AHMED ALBRAIK.

Serbia and Montenegro: 00-540 Warsaw, Al. Ujazdowskie 23/25; tel. (22) 6285161; fax (22) 6297173; e-mail yuabapl@zigzag.pl; Ambassador RAMIZ BAŠIĆ.

Slovakia: 00-581 Warsaw, ul. Litewska 6; tel. (22) 5258110; fax (22) 5258122; e-mail slovakia@ambasada-slowacji.pl; internet www.ambasada-slovacji.pl; Ambassador FRANTIŠEK RUŽIČKA.

Slovenia: 02-516 Warsaw, ul. Starościńska 1, m. 23–24; tel. (22) 8498282; fax (22) 8484090; e-mail vvr@gov.si; Ambassador JOŽEF DROFENIK.

South Africa: 00-675 Warsaw, ul. Koszykowa 54 IPC Business Centre, 6th floor; tel. (22) 6256228; fax (22) 6256270; e-mail saembassy@supermedia.pl; Ambassador FÉBÉ CHERLENE POTGIETER-GQUBULE.

Spain: 00-459 Warsaw, ul. Myśliwiecka 4; tel. (22) 6224250; fax (22) 6225408; e-mail embesp@medianet.pl; Ambassador RAFAEL MENDÍVIL PEYDRO.

Sri Lanka: 02-665 Warsaw, Al. Wilanowska 313A; tel. (22) 8538896; fax (22) 8435348; e-mail lankaemb@medianet.pl; internet www.srilanka.pl; Ambassador NALLATHAMBY NAVARATNARAJAH.

Sweden: 00-585 Warsaw, ul. Bagatela 3; tel. (22) 6408900; fax (22) 6408983; e-mail ambassaden.warszawa@foreign.ministry.se; internet www.swedishembassy.pl; Ambassador TOMAS BERTELMAN.

Switzerland: 00-540 Warsaw, Al. Ujazdowskie 27; tel. (22) 6280481; fax (22) 6210548; e-mail swiemvar@mailer.cst.tpsa.pl; Ambassador ANDRÉ VON GRAFFENREID.

Syria: 02-536 Warsaw, ul. Narbutta 19A; tel. (22) 8491456; fax (22) 8491847; e-mail embsyria@palmyra.neostrada.pl; internet www.syrian-embassy.com; Ambassador MUHAMMAD ALI HAMOUI.

Thailand: 00-790 Warsaw, ul. Willowa 7; tel. (22) 8492655; fax (22) 8492630; e-mail thaiemb@thaiemb.pol.pl; Ambassador THAKUR PHANIT.

Tunisia: 00-459 Warsaw, ul. Myśliwiecka 14; tel. (22) 6286330; fax (22) 6216298; e-mail at.varsovie@it.com.pl; Ambassador BECHIR CHEBAANE.

Turkey: 02-622 Warsaw, ul. Malczewskiego 32; tel. (22) 6464323; fax (22) 6463757; e-mail turkemb@zigzag.pl; Ambassador KADRI ECVET TEZCAN.

Ukraine: 00-580 Warsaw, Al. J. Ch. Szucha 7; tel. (22) 6250127; fax (22) 6298103; e-mail emb_pl@mfa.gov.ua; internet www.ukraine-emb.pl; Ambassador OLEKSANDR MOTSYK.

United Kingdom: 00-556 Warsaw, Al. Róż 1; tel. (22) 6281001; fax (22) 6217161; e-mail info@britishembassy.pl; internet www.britishembassy.pl; Ambassador CHARLES GRAHAM CRAWFORD.

USA: 00-540 Warsaw, Al. Ujazdowskie 29/31; tel. (22) 6283041; fax (22) 6288298; internet www.warsaw.usembassy.gov; Ambassador VICTOR HENDERSON ASHE.

Uzbekistan: 02-804 Warsaw, ul. Kraski 21; tel. (22) 8946230; fax (22) 8946231; internet www.uzbekistan.pl; Chargé d'affaires a.i. DZHAVHAR IZAMOV.

Uruguay: 02-516 Warsaw, ul. Rejtana 15, m. 12; tel. (22) 8495040; fax (22) 6466887; e-mail uropol@ikp.atm.com.pl; Ambassador Dr LUIS SICA BERGARA.

Venezuela: 02-516 Warsaw, ul. Rejtana 15, m. 10; tel. (22) 6461846; fax (22) 6468761; e-mail embavenez.pl@qdnet.pl; Ambassador FRANKLIN RAMÓN GONZÁLEZ.

Viet Nam: 02-956 Warsaw, ul. Resorowa 36; tel. (22) 6516098; fax (22) 6516095; e-mail office@ambasadawietnamu.org; internet www.ambasadawietnamu.org; Ambassador DINH XUAN LUU.

Yemen: 03-941 Warsaw, ul. Zwycięzców 18; tel. (22) 6176025; fax (22) 6176022; e-mail yemen-embassy@yemen-embassy.pl; internet www.yemen-embassy.pl; Ambassador SHAIF BADR ABDULLAH QAID.

Judicial System

Supreme Court
(Sąd Najwyższy Rzeczpospolitej Polskiej)

00-951 Warsaw, pl. Krasińskich 2/4/6; tel. (22) 5308213; fax (22) 5309065; e-mail press@sn.pl; internet www.sn.pl.

the highest judicial organ; exercises supervision over the decision-making of all other courts; functions include: the examination of final decisions made by courts of appeal; the interpretation of legal provisions; justices of the Supreme Court are appointed by the President of the Republic on motions of the National Council of Judiciary and serve until the age of retirement. The First President of the Supreme Court is appointed (and dismissed) from among the Supreme Court Justices by the President of the Republic, and serves a six-year term. The other presidents of the Supreme Court are appointed by the President of the Republic from among the Supreme Court Justices.

First President: Prof. Dr hab. LECH GARDOCKI.

Supreme Administrative Court
(Naczelny Sąd Administracyjny)

00-013 Warsaw, ul. Jasna 6; tel. (22) 8276031; e-mail informacje@nsa.gov.pl; internet www.nsa.gov.pl.

f. 1980 examines complaints concerning the legality of administrative decisions; 11 regional branches.

President: JANUSZ TRZCIŃSKI.

Religion

CHRISTIANITY

The Roman Catholic Church

The Roman Catholic Church was granted full legal status in May 1989, when three laws regulating aspects of relations between the Church and the State were approved by the Sejm. The legislation guaranteed freedom of worship, and permitted the Church to administer its own affairs. The Church was also granted access to the media, and allowed to operate its own schools, hospitals and other charitable organizations. A Concordat, agreed by the Polish Government and the Holy See in 1993, was ratified in January 1998.

For ecclesiastical purposes, Poland comprises 15 archdioceses (including one for the Catholics of the Byzantine-Ukrainian rite) and 29 dioceses (including one for the Catholics of the Byzantine-Ukrainian Rite), an Ordinariate for the faithful of the Oriental Rite, and a Military Ordinariate. At 31 December 2003 there were some 35.1m. adherents in Poland (94.5% of the population).

Bishops' Conference: 01-015 Warsaw, Skwer Kardynała Stefana Wyszyńskiego 6; tel. (22) 8389251; fax (22) 8380967; f. 1969; statutes approved 1995; Pres. Most Rev. JÓZEF MICHALIK (Latin Rite Archbishop of Przemyśl).

Latin Rite

Archbishop of Warsaw and Primate of Poland: Cardinal JÓZEF GLEMP, 00-246 Warsaw, ul. Miodowa 17/19; tel. (22) 5317200; fax (22) 6354324; e-mail prymas@perytnet.pl.

Archbishop of Białystok: Most Rev. WOJCIECH ZIEMBA, 15-087 Białystok, Pl. Jana Pawła II 1; tel. (85) 7416473; fax (85) 7322213; e-mail kuria@bialystok.opoka.org.pl.

Archbishop of Częstochowa: Most Rev. STANISŁAW NOWAK, 42-200 Częstochowa, Al. Najśw. Maryi Panny 54; tel. (34) 3241044; fax (34) 3651182; e-mail kuria@czestochowa.opoka.org.pl.

Archbishop of Gdańsk: Most Rev. TADEUSZ GOCŁOWSKI, 80-330 Gdańsk, ul. Cystersów 15; tel. (58) 5520051; fax (58) 5522775; e-mail kuria@diecezja.gda.pl.

Archbishop of Gniezno: Most Rev. HENRYK MUSZYŃSKI, 62-200 Gniezno, ul. Kanclerza Jana Łaskiego 7; tel. (61) 4262102; fax (61) 4262105; e-mail kuriagni@gniezno.opoka.org.pl.

Archbishop of Katowice: Most Rev. DAMIAN ZIMOŃ, 40-043 Katowice, ul. Jordana 39; tel. (32) 2512160; fax (32) 2514830; e-mail kuria@katowice.opoka.org.pl.

Archbishop of Kraków: Cardinal STANISŁAW DZIWISZ, 31-004 Kraków, ul. Franciszkańska 3; tel. (12) 6288100; fax (12) 4294617; e-mail kuria@diecezja.krakow.pl.

Archbishop of Łódź: Most Rev. WŁADYSŁAW ZIÓŁEK, 90-458 Łódź, ul. Ks Ignacego Skorupki 1; tel. (42) 6375844; fax (42) 6361696; e-mail kuria@archidiecezja.lodz.pl.

Archbishop of Lublin: Most Rev. JÓZEF MIROSŁAW ŻYCIŃSKI, 20-950 Lublin, ul. Ks Prymasa Stefana Wyszyńskiego 2; tel. (81) 5321058; fax (81) 5346141; e-mail kanclerz@kuria.lublin.pl.

Archbishop of Poznań: Most Rev. STANISŁAW GĄDECKI, 61-109 Poznań ul. Ostrów Tumski 2; tel. (61) 8524282; fax (61) 8519748; e-mail kuria@archpoznan.org.pl.

Archbishop of Przemyśl (Latin Rite): Most Rev. JÓZEF MICHALIK, 37-700 Przemyśl, Pl. Katedralny 4A; tel. (16) 6786694; fax (16) 6782674; e-mail kuria@przemysl.opoka.org.pl.

Archbishop of Szczecin-Kamień: Most Rev. ZYGMUNT KAMIŃSKI, 71-459 Szczecin, ul. Papieża Pawła VI 4; tel. (91) 4542292; fax (91) 4536908; e-mail kuria@szczecin.opoka.org.pl.

Archbishop of Warmia: Most Rev. EDMUND MIHAŁ PISZCZ, 10-006 Olsztyn, ul. Pieniężnego 22; tel. (89) 5272291; fax (89) 5351431; e-mail kuria@olsztyn.opoka.org.pl.

Archbishop of Wrocław: Most Rev. MARIAN GOŁĘBIEWSKI, 50-328 Wrocław, ul. Katedralna 13; tel. (71) 3271111; fax (71) 3228269; e-mail kuria@archidiecezja.wroc.pl.

POLAND   *Directory*

Byzantine-Ukrainian Rite

Archbishop of Przemyśl-Warsaw: Most Rev. IVAN MARTYNIAK, 37-700 Przemyśl, ul. Basztowa 13; tel. and fax (16) 6787868; e-mail sobor@przemyslgr.opoka.pl.

Old Catholic Churches

Old Catholic Mariavite Church (Kościół Starokatolicki Mariawitów): 09-400 Płock, ul. Wielkiego 27; tel. and fax (24) 2623086; f. 1906; 25,250 mems (1992); Chief Bishop ZDZISŁAW WŁODZIMIERZ JAWORSKI.

Polish Catholic Church in Poland (Kościół Polskokatolicki w RP): 02-635 Warsaw, ul. Balonowa 7; tel. (22) 8484617; e-mail polskokatolicki@pnet.pl; internet www.polskokatolicki.pl; f. 1920; 21,299 mems (2003); Prime Bishop Most Rev. WIKTOR WYSOCZAŃSKI.

The Orthodox Church

Polish Autocephalous Orthodox Church (Polski Autokefaliczny Kościół Prawosławny): 03-402 Warsaw, Al. Solidarności 52; tel. (22) 6190886; internet www.orthodox.pl; comprises five archbishoprics and three bishoprics; 509,500 mems (2001); Archbishop of Warsaw and Metropolitan of All Poland SAWA (MICHAŁ HRYCUNIAK).

Protestant Churches

In 1999 there were an estimated 148,738 Protestants in Poland.

Baptist Union of Poland (Kościół Chrześcijan Baptystów w RP): 00-865 Warsaw, ul. Waliców 25; tel. and fax (22) 6242783; e-mail baptist@hsn.com.pl; f. 1844; 4,000 mems; Pres. Rev. Dr GRZEGORZ BEDNARCZYK; Gen. Sec. RYSZARD GUTKOWSKI.

Evangelical Augsburg (Lutheran) Church in Poland (Kościół Ewangelicko-Augsburski w RP): 00-246 Warsaw, ul. Miodowa 21; tel. (22) 8870200; fax (22) 8870218; e-mail biskup@luteranie.pl; internet www.luteranie.pl; 77,500 mems, 134 parishes (2005); Bishop and Pres. of Consistory JANUSZ JAGUCKI.

Evangelical-Reformed Church (Kościół Ewangelicko-Reformowany): 00-145 Warsaw, Al. Solidarności 76A; tel. (22) 8314522; fax (22) 8310827; e-mail reformowani@reformowani.pl; internet www.reformowani.pl; f. 16th century; 3,583 mems (2001); Bishop MAREK IZDEBSKI; Pres. of the Consistory WITOLD BRODZINSKI.

Pentecostal Church (Kościół Zielonoświątkowy): 00-825 Warsaw, ul. Sienna 68/70; tel. (22) 6248575; fax (22) 6204073; e-mail nrk@kz.pl; f. 1910; 20,000 mems (2000); Pres. Bishop MIECZYSŁAW CZAJKO.

Seventh-day Adventist Church in Poland (Kościół Adwentystów Dnia Siódmego): 00-366 Warsaw, ul. Foksal 8; tel. (22) 3131431; fax (22) 3131500; e-mail ads@advent.pl; f. 1921; 8,215 mems, 71 preachers (2004); Pres. PAWEŁ LAZAR; Sec. ROMAN CHALUPKA.

United Methodist Church (Kościół Ewangelicko-Metodystyczny w RP): 00-561 Warsaw, ul. Mokotowska 12; tel. and fax (22) 6285328; e-mail kancelaria@metodysci.pl; internet www.metodysci.pl; f. 1921; 5,000 mems; Gen. Supt/Bishop Rev. Dr EDWARD PUŚLECKI.

There are also several other small Protestant churches, including the Church of Christ, the Church of Evangelical Christians, the Evangelical Christian Church and the Jehovah's Witnesses.

ISLAM

In 1999 there were about 5,125 Muslims, principally of Tartar origin, in Białystok Voivodship (Prefecture), in eastern Poland, and smaller communities in Warsaw, Gdańsk and elsewhere.

Religious Union of Muslims in Poland (Muzułmański Związek Religijny): 15-426 Białystok, Rynek Kosciuszki 26, m. 2; tel. (85) 414970; Chair. STEFAN MUCHARSKI.

JUDAISM

The overwhelming majority of the Jewish population of Poland were killed during the occupation by Nazi Germany and the Second World War (1939–45). In the early 2000s there were believed to be between 5,000 and 10,000 Jews in Poland, with the majority living in Warsaw, Wrocław, Kraków and Łódź.

Union of Jewish Communities in Poland (Związek Gmin Wyznaniowych Żydowskich w Rzeczypospolitej Polskiej): 00-950 Warsaw, ul. Twarda 6; tel. (22) 6204324; fax (22) 6201037; e-mail union@jewish.org.pl; 14 synagogues and about 2,500 registered mems; Pres. PIOTR KADLČIK.

The Press

Legislation to permit the formal abolition of censorship and to guarantee freedom of expression was approved in April 1990. In 2003 there were 54 newspapers in Poland, with a total circulation of 4,335,000. In that year there were 5,627 periodicals, with a combined circulation of 69.4m. copies.

PRINCIPAL DAILIES

Białystok

Gazeta Współczesna: 15-950 Białystok, POB 193, ul. Suraska 1; tel. (85) 420935; f. 1951; Editor JERZY KOSTRZEWSKI; circ. 35,000.

Bydgoszcz

Gazeta Pomorska: 85-063 Bydgoszcz, ul. Zamoyskiego 2; tel. (52) 3263100; fax (52) 3221542; e-mail gp.redakcja@gpmedia.pl; internet www.pomorska.pl; f. 1948; independent; Editor MACIEJ KAMIŃSKI; circ. 100,000 (weekdays), 300,000 (weekends).

Gdańsk

Dziennik Bałtycki (Baltic Newspaper): 80-886 Gdańsk, Targ Drzewny 3/7; tel. (58) 3012651; fax (58) 3013560; f. 1945; non-party; Editor KRZYSZTOF KRUPA; circ. 180,000.

Głos Wybrzeża: 80-750 Gdańsk, ul. Stągiewna 13; tel. (58) 3249501; fax (58) 3249500; e-mail glosrek@glos.gda.pl; internet www.glos.gda.pl; f. 1991; Editor-in-Chief ZBIGNIEW ŻUKOWSKI; circ. 50,000.

Katowice

Dziennik Zachodni (Western Daily): 40-092 Katowice, ul. Młyńska 1; tel. (32) 1539084; fax (32) 1538196; e-mail dziennik@dz.com.pl; internet www.dz.com.pl; f. 1945; non-party; Chief Editor MAREK CHYLIŃSKI; circ. 510,000.

Trybuna Śląska (Silesian Tribune): 40-092 Katowice, ul. Młyńska 1; tel. (32) 2537822; fax (32) 2537997; e-mail tsl@trybuna-slaska.com.pl; internet www.trybuna-slaska.com.pl; f. 1945; fmrly *Trybuna Robotnicza*; independent; Editor ROMUALD ORZET; circ. 180,000 (weekdays), 800,000 (weekends).

Kielce

Słowo Ludu (Word of the People): 25-363 Kielce, ul. Wesoła 47/49; tel. (41) 3442480; fax (41) 3446979; e-mail redakcja@slowoludu.com.pl; internet www.slowoludu.com.pl; f. 1949; independent; Editor GRZEGORZ ŚCIWIARSKI; circ. 50,000 (weekdays), 130,000 (weekends).

Koszalin

Głos Pomorza (Voice of Pomerania): 75-604 Koszalin, ul. Zwycięstwa 137/139; tel. (94) 422693; fax (94) 423309; f. 1952; Editor-in-Chief WIESŁAW WIŚNIEWSKI; circ. 60,000 (weekdays), 130,000 (weekends).

Kraków

Czas Krakowski (Kraków Time): Kraków; tel. (12) 4225355; fax (12) 4217502; f. 1848; reactivated 1990; independent; Editor JAN POLKOWSKI; circ. 150,000 (weekdays), 260,000 (weekends).

Dziennik Polski (Polish Daily): 31-072 Kraków, ul. Wielopole 1; tel. (12) 6199200; fax (12) 6199276; e-mail redakcja@dziennik.krakow.pl; internet www.dziennik.krakow.pl; Editor PIOTR ALEKSANDROWICZ.

Echo Krakowa (Kraków Echo): Kraków; tel. (12) 4224678; f. 1946; independent; evening; Editor WITOLD GRZYBOWSKI; circ. 60,000 (weekdays), 90,000 (weekends).

Gazeta Krakowska (Kraków Gazette): 31-548 Kraków, Al. Pokoju 3; tel. (12) 6888000; fax (12) 6888109; e-mail sekretariat@gk.pl; internet www.gk.pl; f. 1949; Editor-in-Chief MAREK ZALEJSKI; circ. 60,000 (weekdays), 150,000 (weekends).

Łódź

Dziennik Łódzki (Łódz Daily): 90-532 Łódź, ul. Ks. Skorupki 17/19; tel. (42) 6303565; fax (42) 6377364; e-mail dziennik@dziennik.lodz.pl; internet www.dziennik.lodz.pl; f. 1945; non-party; Editor JULIAN BECK; circ. 50,000 (weekdays), 110,000 (weekends).

Lublin

Dziennik Lubelski (Lublin Daily): 20-601 Lublin, ul. Zana 38C; tel. (81) 558000; f. 1990; fmrly Sztandar Ludu; Editor ALOJZY LESZEK GZELLA; circ. 45,000 (weekdays), 210,000 (weekends).

Dziennik Wschodni (Eastern Daily): 20-081 Lublin, ul. Staszica 20; tel. (81) 5340600; fax (81) 5340601; e-mail redakcja@dw.lublin.pl; internet www.dw.lublin.pl; Editor STANISŁAW SOWA.

Kurier Lubelski (Lublin Courier): 20-950 Lublin, POB 176; tel. (81) 5326634; fax (81) 5326835; e-mail redakcja@kurierlubelski.pl; internet www.kurier.lublin.pl; f. 1830; independent; evening; Editor PAWEŁ CHROMCEWICZ; circ. 40,000 (weekdays), 100,000 (weekends).

Olsztyn

Gazeta Olsztyńska (Olsztyn Gazette): 10-417 Olsztyn, ul. Towarowa 2; tel. (889) 330277; fax (889) 332691; f. 1886; renamed 1970;

POLAND

independent; Editor-in-Chief TOMASZ ŚRUTKOWSKI; circ. 45,000 (weekdays), 90,000 (weekends).

Opole

Nowa Trybuna Opolska (New Opole Tribune): 45-086 Opole, ul. Powstańców Śląskich 9; tel. (77) 4567041; fax (77) 4543737; e-mail nto@nto.com.pl; internet www.nto.com.pl; f. 1952; independent; Editor WOJCIECH POTOCKI; circ. 80,000.

Poznań

Gazeta Poznańska (Poznań Gazette): 60-782 Poznań, ul. Grunwaldzka 19; tel. (61) 8665568; e-mail gp@gp.pl; internet www.gp.pl; f. 1991; part of the Polskapresse group; Editor JAROSŁAW GOJTOWSKI; circ. 80,000 (weekdays), 320,000 (weekends).

Głos Wielkopolski (Voice of Wielkopolska): 60-782 Poznań, ul. Grunwaldzka 19; tel. (61) 8694100; fax (61) 8659672; e-mail glosmar@sylaba.poznan.pl; internet www.glos.com; f. 1945; independent; Editor-in-Chief MAREK PRZYBYLSKI; circ. 110,000 (weekdays), 160,000 (weekends).

Rzeszów

Noviny—Gazeta Codzienna (News—Daily Gazette): 35-016 Rzeszów, ul. Kraszewskiego 2; tel. (17) 8672200; fax (17) 628836; e-mail nowiny@gcnowiny.pl; internet www.gcnowiny.pl; f. 1949; evening; Editor-in-Chief JANUSZ PAWLAK; circ. 100,000.

Szczecin

Głos Szczeciński (Voice of Szczecin): 70-550 Szczecin, pl. Hołdu Pruskiego 8; tel. (91) 4341306; fax (91) 4345472; e-mail glos@dragon.com.pl; internet www.glosszczecinski.com.pl; f. 1947; Editor-in-Chief ROBERT CIEŚLAK; circ. 30,000 (weekdays), 100,000 (weekends).

Kurier Szczeciński (Szczecin Courier): 70-550 Szczecin, pl. Hołdu Pruskiego 8; tel. and fax (91) 4345741; e-mail redakcja@kurier.szczecin.pl; internet www.kurier.szczecin.pl; Editor ANDRZEJ ŁAPCIEWICZ.

Warsaw

Express Wieczorny (Evening Express): Warsaw; tel. (22) 6285231; fax (22) 6284929; f. 1946; non-party; circ. 140,000 (weekdays), 400,000 (weekends).

Fakt (Fact): 02-222 Warsaw, Al. Jerozolimskie 181; tel. (22) 6085554; fax (22) 6085508; e-mail redakcja@efakt.pl; internet www.efakt.pl; f. 2003; owned by Axel Springer Polska Sp. zo.o.; Editor GRZEGORZ JANKOWSKI; circ. 700,000.

Gazeta Wyborcza: 00-732 Warsaw, ul. Czerska 8/10; tel. (22) 415513; fax (22) 416920; e-mail listy@gazeta.pl; internet wyborcza.gazeta.pl; f. 1989; non-party; national edn and 20 local edns; weekend edn: *Gazeta Świąteczna*; special supplements; Editor-in-Chief ADAM MICHNIK; circ. 516,000 (daily); 686,000 (weekends).

Nasz Dziennik (Our Daily): 04-476 Warsaw, ul. Żeligowskiego 16/20; tel. (22) 6734819; fax (22) 6734817; e-mail redakcja@naszdziennik.pl; internet www.naszdziennik.pl; national; Editor EWA SOŁOWIEJ; circ. 250,000.

Nowa Europa (A New Europa): Warsaw; tel. (22) 6200966; fax (22) 6209145; Editorial Dir ANDRZEJ WROBLEWSKI.

Polska Zbrojna (Military Poland): 00-950 Warsaw, ul. Grzybowska 77; tel. (22) 6204293; fax (22) 6242273; internet www.polska-zbrojna.pl; f. 1943; fmrly *Żolnierz Wolności*, name changed 1990; Editor JERZY ŚLĄSKI; circ. 50,000.

Przegląd Sportowy (Sports Review): 02-017 Warsaw, Al. Jerozolimskie 125/127, POB 181; tel. (22) 6289116; fax (22) 218697; f. 1921; Editor MACIEJ POLKOWSKI; circ. 110,000.

Rzeczpospolita (The Republic): 02-015 Warsaw, pl. Starynkiewicza 7; tel. (22) 6283401; fax (22) 6280588; e-mail p.aleksandrowicz@rzeczpospolita.pl; internet www.rzeczpospolita.pl; f. 1982; 51% owned by Orkla (Norway); Editor-in-Chief GRZEGORZ GAUDEN; circ. 275,000.

Super Express: 00-939 Warsaw, ul. Jubilerska 10; tel. (22) 5159000; fax (22) 5159010; e-mail listy@superexpress.com.pl; internet www.se.com.pl; f. 1991; Editor-in-Chief MARIUSZ ZIOMECKI; circ. 371,106.

Trybuna (Tribune): 00-835 Warsaw, ul. Miedziana 11; tel. (22) 6253015; fax (22) 6204100; e-mail redakcja@trybuna.com.pl; f. 1990; fmrly *Trybuna Ludu* (Peoples' Tribune); organ of Polish Social Democracy; Editor-in-Chief ANDRZEJ URBAŃCZYK; circ. 110,000 (weekdays), 150,000 (weekends).

Wprost (To The Point): 02-017 Warsaw, Al. Jerozolimskie 123, Reform Plaza; tel. (22) 5291100; fax (22) 8529016; e-mail redakcja@wprost.pl; internet www.wprost.pl; Editor MAREK KRÓL.

Życie Warszawy (Warsaw Life): 00-175 Warsaw, Al. Jana Pawła II 80; tel. (22) 3348855; fax (22) 3348863; e-mail zycie@zw.com.pl; internet www.zw.com.pl; f. 1944; independent; Editor-in-Chief ANDRZEJ ZAŁUCKI; circ. 250,000 (weekdays), 460,000 (weekends).

Wrocław

Gazeta Robotnicza (Workers' Gazette): 50-010 Wrocław, ul. Podwale 62; tel. (71) 335756; fax (71) 335756; f. 1948; Editor ANDRZEJ BUŁAT; circ. 30,000 (weekdays), 315,000 (weekends).

Słowa Polskie—Gazeta Wrocławska (Polish Words—Wrocław Gazette): 53-611 Wrocław, ul. Strzegomska 42A; tel. (71) 3748151; fax (71) 3748175; e-mail redakcja@gazeta.wroc.pl; internet gazeta.naszemiasto.pl; Editor-in-Chief AGNIESZKA NICZEWSKA.

Zielona Góra

Gazeta Lubuska: 65-042 Zielona Góra, POB 120, Al. Niepodległości 25; tel. (68) 3254661; fax (68) 3253555; e-mail redakcja@gazetalubuska.pl; internet www.gazetalubuska.pl; f. 1952; independent; Editor MIROSŁAW RATAJ; circ. 60,000 (weekdays), 150,000 (weekends).

PERIODICALS

Computerworld Polska: 04-204 Warsaw, ul. Jordanowska 12, POB 73; tel. (22) 3217810; fax (22) 3217888; e-mail cw@idg.com.pl; internet www.computerworld.pl; weekly; Editor-in-Chief WOJCIECH RADUCHA.

Dobre Rady (Good Advice): 54-432 Wrocław, ul. Strzegornska 236A; tel. (71) 3517758; fax (71) 3737288; e-mail a.sokolowska@burda.pl; f. 2002; published by Burda Polska.

Dom i Wnętrze (House and Interior): 00-480 Warsaw, ul. Wiejska 19; tel. (22) 5842332; fax (22) 5842318; e-mail info@domiwnetrze.pl; internet www.domiwnetrze.pl; f. 1991; illustrated monthly; Editor-in-Chief WIESŁAW KĘDZIERSKI.

Dziecko (Child): 00-732 Warsaw, ul. Czerska 8/10; tel. (22) 5556882; fax (22) 5556669; e-mail dziecko@agora.pl; internet kobieta.gazeta.pl/ edziecko; f. 1995; monthly; women's magazine concerning children's affairs; Editor JUSTYNA DĄBROWSKA; circ. 95,000.

Dziewczyna (Girl): 02-222 Warsaw, Al. Jerozolimskie 181, Axel Springer Polska; tel. (22) 6363681; fax (22) 6365281; e-mail redakcja@dziewczyna.pl; internet www.dziewczyna.pl; f. 1990; monthly; lifestyle magazine for young women; Editor DONATA CIESLIK; circ. 420,000.

Les Echos de Pologne: 02-536 Warsaw, ul. Narbutta 15A/6; tel. (22) 6464212; fax (22) 6462369; e-mail echos@echos.pl; internet www.echos.pl; f. 2003; fortnightly; in French; Editor-in-Chief SYLWIA KAMIŃSKA.

Elle: 02-119 Warsaw, ul. Pruszkowska 17; tel. (22) 6689083; fax (22) 6689183; e-mail elle@elle.com.pl; f. 1994; monthly; women's fashion; Editor-in-Chief MARZENA WILKANOWICZ DEVOUD; circ. 190,000 (1998).

Filipinka: 04-035 Warsaw, ul. Motorowa 1; tel. (22) 5170461; fax (22) 5170469; e-mail filipinka@bauer.pl; internet www.filipinka.pl; f. 1957; fortnightly; illustrated for teenage girls; Editor-in-Chief DOROTA GÓRNICKA-URBAN; circ. 125,600.

Film: Warsaw; tel. (22) 455325; fax (22) 454651; f. 1946; monthly; illustrated magazine; Editor-in-Chief LECH KURPIEWSKI; circ. 105,000.

Forum: 02-309 Warsaw, ul. Słupecka 6; tel. (22) 4516096; fax (22) 4516164; e-mail redakcja@tygodnikforum.pl; internet tygodnikforum.onet.pl; f. 1965; weekly; political, social, cultural and economic; Editor-in-Chief JACEK MOJKOWSKI; circ. 33,000.

Gazeta Bankowa (Banking Gazette): 03-715 Warsaw, ul. Okrzei 1A; tel. (22) 3338887; fax (22) 3338899; e-mail redakcja@wtrendy.pl; internet www.gazetabankowa.pl; f. 1988; weekly; business and finance; Editor-in-Chief ANDRZEJ S. NARTOWSKI.

Gazeta Targowa: 61-707 Poznań, ul. Libelta; tel. (61) 8528582; fax (61) 8526108; e-mail gazetarg@soho.online.com; finance; Editor-in-Chief SŁAWOMIR ERKIERT.

Głos Nauczycielski (Teachers' Voice): 00-389 Warsaw, ul. Smulikowskiego 6/8; tel. (22) 8263420; fax (22) 8281355; e-mail glos@glos.pl; internet www.glos.pl; f. 1917; weekly; organ of the Polish Teachers' Union; Editor WOJCIECH SIERAKOWSKI; circ. 40,000.

Gromada-Rolnik Polski: Warsaw; tel. (22) 278815; fax (22) 278815; f. 1951; 3 a week; agricultural; Editor ZBIGNIEW LUBAK; circ. 281,800.

Kobieta i Życie (Woman and Life): Warsaw; tel. and fax (22) 6283030; f. 1946; weekly; women's; Editor ZOFIA KAMIŃSKA; circ. 400,000.

Lubie Gotować (I Love Cooking): 00-732 Warsaw, ul. Czerska 8–10; tel. (22) 5556606; fax (22) 5556668; e-mail kuchnia@pagora.pl; internet www.lubiegotowac.pl; f. 1997; monthly; cookery; Editor-in-Chief JOANNA NOWICKA.

POLAND

Nie (No): 00-789 Warsaw, ul. Słoneczna 25; tel. (22) 8484420; fax (22) 8497258; e-mail nie@redakija.nie.com.pl; internet www.nie.com.pl; f. 1990; satirical weekly; Editor JERZY URBAN; circ. 500,000.

Nowa Fantastyka (New Fantasy): 02-651 Warsaw, ul. Garażowa 7; tel. (22) 6077790; fax (22) 8494060; e-mail nowafantastyka@fantastyka.pl; internet www.fantastyka.pl; f. 1982; monthly; science fiction and fantasy; Editor ARDIUSZ NAKONIECZNIK; circ. 57,000.

Nowe Życie Gospodarcze (New Economic Life): 00-549 Warsaw, ul. Piękna 24/26; tel. (22) 6280628; fax (22) 6288392; e-mail nzg@nzg.pl; internet www.nzg.pl; f. 1945 as *Życie Gospodarcze* (Economic Life); weekly; economic; Chair. and Editor-in-Chief ADAM CYMER; circ. 35,700.

Panorama: Katowice; tel. (32) 1538595; f. 1960; weekly; socio-cultural magazine; Editor ADAM JAZWIECKI; circ. 150,000.

Państwo i Prawo (State and Law): 00-330 Warsaw, ul. Nowy Świat 72; tel. (22) 6288296; f. 1946; monthly organ of the Polish Academy of Sciences; Editor Dr LESZEK KUBICKI; circ. 3,000.

Polityka (Politics): 02-309 Warsaw, ul. Słupecka 6, POB 13; tel. (22) 4516133; fax (22) 4516135; e-mail polityka@polityka.com.pl; internet polityka.onet.pl; f. 1957; weekly; political, economic, cultural; Editor JERZY BACZYŃSKI; circ. 340,000.

Poradnik Gospodarski (Farmers' Guide): 60-163 Poznań, ul. Sieradzka 29; tel. and fax (61) 8685492; e-mail pg@neostrada.pl; internet www.poradnik.wodr.poznan.pl; f. 1889; monthly; agriculture; Editor-in-Chief TADEUSZ SZALCZYK; circ. 10,000.

Prawo i Gospodarka: Warsaw; tel. (22) 6727961; fax (22) 6727976; e-mail z.maciag@pg.com.pl; Editor ZBIGNIEW MACIĄG.

Przegląd Tygodniowy (Weekly Review): Warsaw; tel. (22) 6207290; fax (22) 6544711; e-mail przegtyg@medianet.pl; internet www.przeglad-tygodniowy.pl; f. 1981; weekly; political, economic, social, historical, cultural, scientific and artistic; Editor-in-Chief JERZY DOMAŃSKI; circ. 35,000.

Przekrój (Review): 00-490 Warsaw, ul. Wiejska 16; tel. (22) 6272306; fax (22) 6272305; e-mail nowy.przekroj@edipresse.pl; internet www.przekroj.pl; f. 1945; weekly; illustrated; cultural; Editor-in-Chief JACEK RAKOWIECKI; circ. 77,500.

Przyjaciółka (Friend): 00-490 Warsaw, ul. Wiejska 16; tel. (22) 6280583; fax (22) 6285866; internet www.przyjaciolka.pl; f. 1948; weekly; women's magazine; Editor EWA NIEZBECKA; circ. 720,000.

Res Publica Nowa (The New Republic): 02-309 Warsaw 1, ul. Słupecka 6, POB 856; tel. (22) 4516180; fax (22) 4516109; e-mail respublica@pro.onet.pl; internet respublica.onet.pl; f. 1987; monthly; political and cultural; Editor MARCIN KRÓL; circ. 5,000.

Sport: 40-082 Katowice, ul. Sobieskiego 11, POB 339; tel. (3) 1539995; fax (3) 1537138; f. 1945; 5 a week; Editor ADAM BARTECZKO; circ. 135,000.

Spotkania (Experiences): Warsaw; tel. (22) 399022; fax (22) 241423; f. 1990; weekly; illustrated; political, social, economic, cultural and scientific magazine; Editor MACIEJ IŁOWIECKI; circ. 80,000.

Sprawy Międzynarodowe (International Affairs): 02-630 Warsaw, ul. Tyniecka 15/17; tel. (22) 5239086; fax (22) 5239027; e-mail aleksandra.zieleniec@msz.gov.pl; internet www.sprawymiedzynarodowe.pl; f. 1948; quarterly; published by the Diplomatic Academy of the Ministry of Foreign Affairs; also English edition, *The Polish Quarterly of International Affairs* (f. 1992); Editor HENRYK SZLAJFER; circ. 800.

Swiat Nauki (World of Science): 00-965 Warsaw, Al. Jerozolimskie 136, p. 9; tel. (22) 5762700; fax (22) 6077645; e-mail swiatnauki@wsip.com.pl; internet www.swiatnauki.pl; f. 1991; monthly; Polish edn of *Scientific American*; Editor-in-Chief JOANNA ZIMAKOWSKA; circ. 45,000.

Szpilki (Needles): Warsaw; tel. (22) 6280429; f. 1935; weekly; illustrated satirical; Editor JACEK JANCZARSKI; circ. 100,000.

Teatr (Theatre): 03-902 Warsaw, ul. Jakubowska 14; tel. (22) 6175594; fax (22) 6174298; f. 1945; monthly; illustrated; theatrical life; Editor JANUSZ MAJCHEREK; circ. 4,000.

Tygodnik Gospodarczy (Economic Weekly): 00-511 Warsaw, ul. Nowogrodzka 31; tel. (22) 6280593; fax (22) 6299614; e-mail redakcja@tygodnikgospodarczy.pl; internet www.waw.pdi.net/sigma; f. 1991; weekly; international business and economics; Publr TADEUSZ JACEWICZ; circ. 52,000.

Tygodnik Solidarność (Solidarity Weekly): 00-019 Warsaw, ul. Jasna 7, POB 2; tel. (22) 8292950; e-mail redakcja@tygodniksolidarnosc.com.pl; internet www.tygodniksolidarnosc.com.pl; f. 1981; reactivated 1989; weekly; Editor-in-Chief JERZY KŁOSIŃSKI; circ. 60,000.

The Warsaw Voice: 00-950 Warsaw, POB 28; tel. (22) 8375138; fax (22) 8371995; e-mail voice@warsawvoice.com.pl; internet www.warsawvoice.com.pl; f. 1988; weekly; economic, political, social, cultural and economic; in English; Editor ANDRZEJ JONAS; Gen. Dir JULIUSZ KŁOSOWSKI; circ. 15,000.

Wiedza i Życie (Knowledge and Life): 02-651 Warsaw, ul. Garażowa 7; tel. (22) 6077630; fax (22) 6077645; e-mail wiedza@proszynski.com.pl; internet www.proszynski.com.pl/wiedzaizycie; f. 1926; monthly; popular science; Editor ANDRZEJ GORZYM; circ. 112,000.

Żołnierz Polski (Polish Soldier): 00-844 Warsaw, ul. Grzybowska 77, POB 68; tel. (22) 6204286; fax (22) 6242273; e-mail ireneusz.czyzewski@bellona.pl; internet www.zolnierz-polski.pl; f. 1945; monthly; illustrated magazine primarily about the armed forces; Editor IRENEUSZ CZYŻEWSKI; circ. 40,000.

NEWS AGENCY

Polska Agencja Prasowa (PAP) (Polish Press Agency): 00-950 Warsaw, Al. Jerozolimskie 7; tel. (22) 6280001; fax (22) 6286407; e-mail webmaster@pap.com.pl; internet www.pap.com.pl; f. 1944; brs in 28 Polish towns and 22 foreign capitals; 274 journalist and photojournalist mems; Pres. ROBERT BOGDAŃSKI.

Foreign Bureaux

Agence France-Presse (AFP): 00-582 Warsaw, Al. Szucha 16, m. 34; tel. (22) 6272409; fax (22) 6223499; e-mail afpwaw@pol.pl; Correspondent PIERRE-ANTOINE DONNET.

Agencia EFE (Spain): 00-656 Warsaw, ul. Śniadeckich 18, Lokal 16; tel. (22) 6282567; fax (22) 6215989; Bureau Chief JORGE RUIZ LARDIZÁBAL.

Agenzia Nazionale Stampa Associata (ANSA) (Italy): 00-672 Warsaw, ul. Piękna 68, p. 301; tel. (22) 298413; fax (22) 299843; Bureau Chief MAURIZIO SALVI.

Associated Press (AP) (USA): 00-433 Warsaw, ul. Profesorska 4; tel. (22) 6287231; fax (22) 6295240; internet www.ap.org; Correspondent ANDRZEJ STYLIŃSKI.

Bulgarska Telegrafna Agentsia (BTA) (Bulgaria): Warsaw; tel. (22) 278059; Correspondent WESELIN JANKOW.

Česká tisková kancelář (ČTK) (Czech Republic): 03-946 Warsaw, ul. Brazylioska 14 A/9; tel. and fax (22) 6728780; e-mail ctk@ctk.if.pl; Correspondent JAN MELICHAR.

Deutsche-Presse Agentur (dpa) (Germany): 03-968 Warsaw, ul. Saska 7A; tel. (22) 6171058; fax (22) 6178481; Correspondent DANIEL BRÖSSLER.

Dow-Jones News Service: 00-433 Warsaw, ul. Profesorska 4; tel. (22) 6222766; fax (22) 6222768; Gen. Dir DAVID MCQUAID.

ITAR—TASS (Information Telegraph Agency of Russia—Telegraphic Agency of the Sovereign Countries (Russia): Warsaw; tel. (22) 292192; fax (22) 296131; Correspondent ALEKSANDR L. POTEMKIN.

Kyodo News Service (Japan): 05-220 Warsaw, Zielonka Prosta 14; tel. and fax (22) 7810246; Chief JUN IWAWAKI.

Reuters (United Kingdom): 00-854 Warsaw, Al. Jana Pawła II 23; tel. (22) 6539700; fax (22) 6539780; internet www.reuters.com.pl; Correspondent ANTHONY BARKER.

RIA—Novosti (Russian Information Agency—News) (Russia): Warsaw; tel. (22) 6283092; 6 correspondents.

Tlačová agentúra Slovenskej republiky (TASR) (Slovakia): Warsaw; tel. and fax (22) 6780399; Correspondent IGOR RABATIN.

Xinhua (New China) News Agency (People's Republic of China): 00-203 Warsaw, ul. Bonifraterska 1; tel. (22) 313876; Correspondents TANG DEQIAO, DONG FUSHENG, SCHAO JIN.

PRESS ASSOCIATION

Stowarzyszenie Dziennikarzy Polskich (SDP) (Polish Journalists' Association): 00-366 Warsaw, ul. Foksal 3/5; tel. and fax (22) 8278720; e-mail sdp@sdp.pl; internet www.sdp.pl; f. 1951; dissolved 1982, legal status restored 1989; 2,320 mems; Pres. KRYSTYNA MOKROSIŃSKA; Gen. Sec. STEFAN TRUSZCZYŃSKI.

Publishers

Bertelsmann Media Sp. z o.o.: 02-786 Warsaw, ul. Rosoła 10; tel. (22) 6458200; fax (22) 6484732; e-mail poczta@swiatksiazki.com.pl; internet www.swiatksiazki.com.pl; f. 1994 as Bertelsmann Publishing Swiat Książki Sp. z o.o.; belles-lettres, science-fiction, popular science, albums, books for children and teenagers; Pres. ANDRZEJ KOSTARCZYK; Editor-in-Chief BOGUSŁAW DĄBROWSKI.

Dom Wydawniczy ABC Sp. z o.o.: 01-231 Warsaw, ul. Płocka 5A; tel. (22) 5358000; fax (22) 5358001; e-mail info@abc.com.pl; internet www.abc.com.pl; f. 1989; legal, business and financial books; part of Polskie Wydawnictwa Profesjonalne Sp. z o.o; owned by Wolters Kluwer (Netherlands); Owners WŁODZIMIERZ ALBIN, KRZYSZTOF BRZESKI.

POLAND

Dom Wydawniczy Bellona: 00-844 Warsaw, ul. Grzybowska 77; tel. (22) 6204291; fax (22) 6522695; e-mail bellona@bellona.pl; internet www.bellona.pl; f. 1947; fiction, history and military; Pres. Col JÓZEF SKRZYPIEC; Dir ZBIGNIEW CZERWIŃSKI.

Dom Wydawniczy Rebis Sp. z o.o.: 60-171 Poznań, ul. Żmigrodzka 41/49; tel. (61) 8678140; fax (61) 8673774; e-mail rebis@rebis.com.pl; internet www.rebis.com.pl; f. 1990; psychology, self-help books and parental guides; Pres. and Man. Dir TOMASZ SZPONDER.

Drukarnia i Księgarnia św. Wojciecha (St Adalbert—Wojciech Printing and Publishing Co): 60-967 Poznań, Pl. Wolności 1; tel. (61) 8529186; fax (61) 8523746; e-mail wydawnictwo@ksw.com.pl; internet www.ksw.com.pl; f. 1895; textbooks and Catholic publications; Dir Rev. BOGDAN REFORMAT; Editor-in-Chief BOŻYSŁAW WALCZAK.

Egmont Sp. z o.o.: 01-029 Warsaw, ul. Dzielna 60; tel. (22) 8384100; fax (22) 8384200; e-mail kluby@egmont.pl; internet www.egmont.pl; f. 1990; books and comics for children and teenagers; Man. Dir JACEK BEŁDOWSKI; Editor-in-Chief HANNA BALTYN.

Instytut Wydawniczy Pax (Pax Publishing Institute): 00-390 Warsaw, ul. Wybrzeże Kościuszkowskie 21A; tel. (22) 6253398; fax (22) 6251378; e-mail iwpax@iwpax.com.pl; internet sklep.iwpax.com.pl; f. 1949; theology, philosophy, religion, history, literature; Dir KRZYSZTOF PRZESTRZELSKI; Editor-in-Chief ZBIGNIEW BOROWIK.

Ludowa Spółdzielnia Wydawnicza (People's Publishing Co-operative): 00-131 Warsaw, ul. Grzybowska 4/8; tel. (22) 6205718; fax (22) 6207277; f. 1949; fiction, poetry and popular science; Chair. and Editor-in-Chief JAN RODZIM.

Muchomor Publishers: 01-552 Warsaw, pl. Inwalidów 10/29; tel. and fax (22) 8394968; e-mail muchomor@muchomor.pl; internet www.muchomor.pl; f. 2002; childrens, illustrated; Editorial Dir MARIA DESKUR.

Muza SA: 00-590 Warsaw, ul. Marszałkowska 8; tel. (22) 6211776; fax (22) 6292349; e-mail muza@muza.com.pl; internet www.muza.com.pl; f. 1991; albums, encyclopedias, lexicons, handbooks, dictionaries, belles-lettres, books for children and youth; Man. Dir MARCIN GARLINSKI.

Niezależna Oficyna Wydawnicza NOWA (Independent Publishing House NOWA): 00-251 Warsaw, ul. Miodowa 10; tel. and fax (22) 6359994; f. 1972; belles-lettres, memoirs, essays, recent history, politics; Pres. GRZEGORZ BOGUTA; Editor-in-Chief MIROSŁAW KOWALSKI.

Oficyna Literacka: 31-436 Kraków, ul. A. Sokołowskiego 19; tel. (12) 4117365; fax (12) 4127599; f. 1982 clandestinely, 1990 officially; belles-lettres, poetry, including débuts, essays; Editor-in-Chief HENRYK KARKOSZA.

Oficyna Wydawnicza Volumen: 00-354 Warsaw, ul. Dynasy 2A; tel. and fax (22) 8260501; e-mail oficyna@poland.com; f. 1984 (working clandestinely as WERS), 1989 officially; science, popular history, anthropology and socio-political sciences; Dir ADAM BOROWSKI.

Pallottinum—Wydawnictwo Stowarzyszenia Apostolstwa Katolickiego: 60-959 Poznań, Al. Przybyszewskiego 30, POB 23; tel. (61) 8675233; fax (61) 8675238; e-mail pallottinum@pallottinum.pl; internet www.pallottinum.pl; f. 1947; religious and philosophical books; Dir STEFAN DUSZA.

Państwowe Wydawnictwo Rolnicze i Leśne (State Agricultural and Forestry Publishers): 02-272 Warsaw, ul. Malownicza 14; tel. and fax (22) 8684529; e-mail pwril@pwril.com; internet www.pwril.com; f. 1947; professional publications on agriculture, forestry, health and veterinary science; Dir and Editor-in-Chief JOLANTA KUCZYŃSKA.

Państwowy Instytut Wydawniczy (State Publishing Institute): 00-372 Warsaw, ul. Foksal 17; tel. (22) 8260201; fax (22) 8261536; e-mail piw@piw.pl; internet www.piw.pl; f. 1946; Polish and foreign classical and contemporary literature, fiction, literary criticism, biographies, performing arts, culture, history, popular science and fine arts; Dir and Editor-in-Chief TADEUSZ NOWAKOWSKI.

Polskie Przedsiębiorstwo Wydawnictw Kartograficznych im. E. Romera SA (Romer Polish Cartographical Publishing House Co): 00-410 Warsaw, ul. Solec 18; tel. (22) 5851800; fax (22) 5851801; e-mail ppwk@ppwk.com.pl; internet www.ppwk.com.pl; f. 1951; maps, atlases, travel guides, books on geodesy and cartography; Man. Dir JACEK BŁASCZYŃSKI.

Polskie Wydawnictwa Profesjonalne (Polish Professional Publishers): 01-231 Warsaw, ul. Płocka 5A; tel. (22) 5358000; fax (22) 5358001; e-mail poczta@pwp.pl; internet www.pwp.pl; country's largest legal publisher, produces CD-rom databases and periodicals; online; Pres. ALBIN WŁODZIMIERZ.

Polskie Wydawnictwo Ekonomiczne SA (Polish Publishing House for Economic Literature): 00-099 Warsaw, ul. Canaletta 4; tel. (22) 8264182; fax (22) 8275567; e-mail pwe@pwe.com.pl; internet www.pwe.com.pl; f. 1949; economics books and magazines; Man. Dir ALICJA RUTKOWSKA; Editor MARIOLA ROMUS.

Polskie Wydawnictwo Muzyczne (Polish Publishing House for Music): 31-111 Kraków, Al. Krasińskiego 11A; tel. (12) 4227044; fax (12) 4220174; e-mail pwm@pwm.com.pl; internet www.pwm.com.pl; f. 1945; music and books on music; Chair. and Man. Dir Dr SŁAWOMIR J. TABKOWSKI; Editor-in-Chief ANDRZEJ KOSOWSKI.

Prószyński i S-ka Publishing House: 02-651 Warsaw, ul. Garazowa 7; tel. (22) 6077700; fax (22) 6077704; e-mail wydawnictwo@proszynski.pl; internet www.proszynski.pl; f. 1990; poetry, fiction, non-fiction, educational text and reference books, popular science etc.; Pres. MIECZYSŁAW PRÓSZYŃSKI; 110 employees.

Spółdzielnia Wydawnicza Czytelnik (Reader Co-operative Publishing House): 00-490 Warsaw, ul. Wiejska 12A; tel. (22) 6289508; fax (22) 6283178; e-mail sekretariat@czytelnik.pl; internet www.czytelnik.pl; f. 1944; general, especially fiction and contemporary Polish literature; Pres. MAREK ŻAKOWSKI; Editor-in-Chief ANNA BRZOZOWSKA.

Spółdzielnia Wydawniczo-Handlowa 'Książka i Wiedza' ('Books and Knowledge' Trade Co-operative Publishing House): 00-375 Warsaw, ul. Smolna 13; tel. (22) 8275401; fax (22) 8279423; e-mail publisher@kiw.com.pl; internet www.kiw.com.pl; f. 1948; philosophy, religion, linguistics, literature and history; Chair. WŁODZIMIERZ GAŁĄSKA; Editor-in-Chief ELŻBIETA KONECKA.

Wydawnictwa Artystyczne i Filmowe (Art and Film Publications): 02-595 Warsaw, ul. Puławska 61; tel. (22) 8455301; fax (22) 8455584; f. 1959; theatre, cinema, photography and art publications and reprints; Pres. and Dir JANUSZ FOGLER.

Wydawnictwa Komunikacji i Łączności (Transport and Communications Publishing House): 02-546 Warsaw, ul. Kazimierzowska 52; tel. (22) 8492314; fax (22) 8492322; e-mail wkl@wkl.com.pl; internet www.wkl.com.pl; f. 1949; technical books on motorization, electronics, radio engineering, television and telecommunications, road, rail and air transport; Dir JERZY KOZŁOWSKI; Editor-in-Chief BOGUMIŁ ZIELIŃSKI.

Wydawnictwa Naukowo-Techniczne (Scientific-Technical Publishers): 00-048 Warsaw, ul. Mazowiecka 2/4, POB 359; tel. (22) 8267271; fax (22) 8268293; e-mail wnt@pol.pl; internet www.wnt.com.pl; f. 1949; scientific and technical books on mathematics, physics, chemistry, foodstuffs industry, electrical and electronic engineering, computer science, automation, mechanical engineering, light industry; technological encyclopedias and dictionaries; Man. Dir and Editor Dr ANIELA TOPULOS.

Wydawnictwa Normalizacyjne Alfa-Wero (Alfa-Wero Standardization Publishing House): 00-820 Warsaw, ul. Sienna 63; tel. (22) 6204500; fax (22) 6207131; e-mail ckn@alfawero.pl; internet www.normy.pl; f. 1956; standards, catalogues and reference books on standardization, periodicals, political and historical literature, science fiction, general; Man. Dir ANDRZEJ ŚWIĘCICKI.

Wydawnictwa Polskiej Agencji Ekologicznej SA (Polish Ecological Publishing House): 02-078 Warsaw, ul. Krzywickiego 34; tel. (22) 3130400; fax (22) 3130446; e-mail ekologia@pae.com.pl; internet www.pae.com.pl; f. 1953; geology; Dir JERZY CHODKOWSKI.

Wydawnictwa Szkolne i Pedagogiczne (WSiP) (School and Pedagogical Publishers): 00-965 Warsaw, Al. Jerozolimskie 136, p. 9; tel. (22) 5762510; fax (22) 5762509; e-mail wsip@wsip.com.pl; internet www.wsip.pl; f. 1945; partially privatized in 1998; further privatized in Nov. 2004; school textbooks and popular science books, scientific literature for teachers, visual teaching aids, periodicals for teachers and youth; Chair. (vacant).

Wydawnictwo Amber Sp. z o.o.: 00-060 Warsaw, ul. Królewska 27; tel. (22) 6204061; fax (22) 6201393; e-mail media@amber.sm.pl; internet www.amber.sm.pl; reference books, fiction, biography and autobiography; Dir ZBIGNIEW FONIOK; Editor MAŁGORZATA CEBO-FONIOK.

Wydawnictwo Arkady: 00-959 Warsaw, ul. Dobra 28, POB 137; tel. (22) 8269316; fax (22) 8274194; e-mail arkady@arkady.com.pl; internet www.arkady.com.pl; f. 1957; publications on building, town planning, architecture and art; Dir and Pres. JANINA KRYSIAK.

Wydawnictwo C. H. Beck.: 01-518 Warsaw, ul. Gen. Zajączka 9; tel. (22) 3377600; fax (22) 3377601; e-mail redakcja@beck.pl; internet www.beck.pl; f. 1993; law and economics; Man. Dir PAWEŁ ESSE.

Wydawnictwo Dolnośląskie Sp. z o.o.: 50-010 Wrocław, ul. Podwale 62; tel. (71) 7859040; fax (71) 7859066; e-mail sekretariat@wd.wroc.pl; internet www.wd.wroc.pl; f. 1986; belles-lettres, essays, memoirs, translations, general non-fiction; Pres. of Bd ANDRZEJ ADAMUS.

Wydawnictwo Infor: 01-042 Warsaw, ul. Okopowa 58/72; tel. (22) 5304050; fax (22) 5304054; e-mail sekretariat.dg@infor.pl; internet www.infor.pl; f. 1987; law, economics, marketing, management; Pres. RYSZARD PIEŃKOWSKI.

Wydawnictwo Iskry (Sparks Publishing House Ltd): 00-375 Warsaw, ul. Smolna 11; tel. and fax (22) 8279415; e-mail iskry@iskry.com.pl; internet www.iskry.com.pl; f. 1952; travel, Polish and foreign

POLAND

fiction, science fiction, essays, popular science, history, memoirs; Chair. Dr Wiesław Uchański; Editor-in-Chief Magdalena Słysz.

Wydawnictwo Kurpisz: 01-341 Poznań, ul. Przemysława 46; tel. (61) 8331517; fax (61) 8351294; e-mail kurpisz@kurpisz.pl; internet www.kurpisz.pl; f. 1991; belles-lettres, reprints, dictionaries, encyclopedias, periodicals; Dir Kazimierz Grzesiak.

Wydawnictwo Lekarskie PZWL (PWSL Medical Publishers): 00-251 Warsaw, ul. Miodowa 10; tel. (22) 6954033; fax (22) 6954486; e-mail promocja@pzwl.pl; internet www.pzwl.pl; f. 1945; medical literature and manuals, lexicons, encyclopedias; Pres. Krystyna Regulska.

Wydawnictwo Literackie (Literary Publishing House): 31-147 Kraków, ul. Długa 1; tel. (12) 4232254; fax (12) 4225423; e-mail redakcja@wl.net.pl; internet www.wl.net.pl; f. 1953; works of literature and belles-lettres; Dir Barbara Drwota; Editor-in-Chief Małgorzata Nycz.

Wydawnictwo Nasza Księgarnia (Our Booksellers' Publishing House): 02-868 Warsaw, ul. Sarabandy 24c; tel. (22) 6439389; fax (22) 6437028; e-mail naszaksiegarnia@nk.com.pl; internet www.nk.com.pl/nasza; f. 1921; books and periodicals for children and young readers; educational publications; Pres. Agnieszka Tokarczyk; Editor Jolanta Sztuczyńska.

Wydawnictwo Naukowe PWN (PWN Scientific Publishers): 00-251 Warsaw, ul. Miodowa 10; tel. (22) 6954153; fax (22) 6954288; e-mail international@pwn.com.pl; internet www.pwn.pl; f. 1951; works of reference, academic publications, multimedia; Pres. Barbara Jozwiak.

Wydawnictwo Nowa Era Sp. z o. o.: 02-305 Warszaw, Al. Jerozolimskie 146d; tel. (22) 5702580; fax (22) 5702581; e-mail nowaera@nowaera.com.pl; internet www.nowaera.com.pl; school textbooks; Chair. Mariusz Koper.

Wydawnictwo Ossolineum (Ossolineum Publishing House): 50-062 Wrocław, pl. Solny 14a; tel. (71) 3436961; fax (71) 3448103; e-mail wydawnictwo@ossolineum.pl; internet www.ossolineum.pl; f. 1817; publishing house of the Polish Academy of Sciences; academic publications in humanities and sciences; Man. Dir Wojciech Karwacki; Editor-in-Chief Stanisław Rościcki.

Wydawnictwo Prawnicze LexisNexis—LexPolonia (LexPolonia—LexisNexis Legal Publishing House): 02-520 Warsaw, ul. Gen. K. Sosnkowskiego 1; tel. (22) 5729500; fax (22) 5729508; e-mail biuro@lexisnexis.pl; internet www.lexisnexis.pl; f. 1952 as Wydawnictwo Prawnidze; present name adopted 2003; Exec. Dir Olga Dymkowska-Pulchny.

Wydawnictwo Publicat: 61-003 Poznań, ul. Chlebowa 24; tel. (61) 8679546; fax (61) 6529200; e-mail office@publicat.pl; internet www.najlepszyprezent.pl; f. 1990 as Wydawnictwo Podsiedlik-Raniowski Sp. z o.o.; popular and children's literature, poetry, prose, classical works, educational books; Pres. Michał Kaik.

Wydawnictwo RTW (RTW Publishers): 01-780 Warsaw, ul. Broniewskiego 9a; tel. (22) 6337010; fax (22) 6637474; f. 1992; education, geography, geology, history, science, atlases, dictionaries, encyclopedias and audio books.

Wydawnictwo Śląsk Sp. z o.o. (Silesia Publishing House Ltd): 40-161 Katowice, Al. W. Korfantego 51; tel. (32) 580756; fax (32) 583229; e-mail biuro@slaskwn.com.pl; internet www.slaskwn.com.pl; f. 1952; social, popular science, technical and regional literature; Chair. and Editor-in-Chief Dr Tadeusz Sierny.

Wydawnictwo W.A.B. (WAB Publishers): 02-502 Warsaw, ul. Łowicka 31; tel. (22) 6460510; fax (22) 6460511; e-mail wab@wab.com.pl; internet www.wab.com.pl; f. 1991; contemporary Polish fiction, historical and cultural essays, and literature for children; Editor Angelika Sasin.

Wydawnictwo Wam (For You Publishers): 31-501 Kraków, ul. Kopernika 26; tel. (12) 4291888; fax (12) 4295003; e-mail wam@wydawnictwowam.pl; internet www.wydawnictwowam.pl; f. 1872; textbooks, encyclopedias, non-fiction, fiction and children's books; Dir Henryk Pietras.

Wydawnictwo Wiedza Powszechna (General Knowledge Publishers): 00-054 Warsaw, ul. Jasna 26; tel. and fax (22) 8270799; e-mail info@wiedza.pl; internet www.wiedza.pl; f. 1952; popular science books, Polish and foreign language dictionaries, foreign language textbooks, encyclopedias and lexicons; Dir Teresa Korsak.

Wydawnictwo Wilga (Yellow Thrush Publishers): 00-389 Warsaw, ul. Smulikowskiego 1/3; tel. (22) 8260882; fax (22) 8260643; e-mail wilga@wilga.com.pl; internet www.wilga.com.pl; f. 1993; education and fiction; Pres. Jan Wojnitko; Editor-in-Chief Olga Wojnitko.

Wydawnictwo Zysk i S-ka (Zysk Publishers): 61-744 Poznań, ul. Wielka 10; tel. (61) 8532767; fax (61) 8526326; e-mail sekretariat@zysk.com.pl; internet www.zysk.com.pl; f. 1994; belles-lettres, popular, scientific and religious literature; Pres. Tadeusz Zysk.

Zakład Wydawnictw Statystycznych (Statistical Publishing Establishment): 00-925 Warsaw, Al. Niepodległości 208; tel. (22) 6083210; fax (22) 6083867; f. 1971; statistics and theory of statistics, economics, social sciences, periodicals; Dir Andrzej Stasiun.

Znak Społeczny Instytut Wydawniczy (Znak Social Publishing Institute): 30-105 Kraków, ul. Kościuszki 37; tel. (12) 6199500; fax (12) 6199502; e-mail redakcja@znak.com.pl; internet www.znak.com.pl; f. 1959; religion, philosophy, belles-lettres, essays, history; Chief Exec. Henryk Woźniakowski; Editor-in-Chief Jerzy Illg.

PUBLISHERS' ASSOCIATION

Polskie Towarzystwo Wydawców Książek (Polish Society of Book Editors): 00-048 Warsaw, ul. Mazowiecka 2/4; tel. and fax (22) 8260735; f. 1921; Pres. Janusz Fogler; 500 mems.

Broadcasting and Communications

TELECOMMUNICATIONS

Regulatory Authority

Telecommunications Regulatory Office (URT): 00-582 Warsaw, ul. Kasprzaka 18/20; tel. (22) 6088270; e-mail prasowy@urt.gov.pl; internet www.urt.gov.pl; f. 2001; Chair. Marek Zdrojewski.

Service Providers

Polkomtel: 02-001 Warsaw, Al. Jerozolimskie 81; tel. (22) 4261000; fax (22) 4261902; internet www.polkomtel.com.pl; f. 1996; provides mobile cellular telecommunications services as Plus GSM, Simplus-Team and mixPlus; 3G network commenced operations Sept. 2004; Pres. Władysław Bartoszewicz.

Polska Telefonia Cyfrowa (PTC) (Polish Digital Telephone): 02-222 Al. Jerozolimskie 181, Warsaw; tel. (22) 4136000; fax (22) 4134949; e-mail biznes@era.pl; internet www.era.pl; f. 1996; provides mobile cellular telecommunications as Era, Heyah and Blue Connect; Pres. Piotr Nurowski.

PTK Centertel (Polish Cellular Telecommunications Co 'Centertel'): 01-230 Warsaw, ul. Skierniewicka 10a; tel. (22) 6342882; fax (22) 5887883; e-mail info@idea.pl; internet www.orange.pl; f. 1998; provides mobile cellular telecommunications services as Orange; 66% owned by TP, 34% by France Telecom (France).

TP—Telekomunikacja Polska (Polish Telecommunications): 00-105 Warsaw, ul. Twarda 18; tel. (22) 5270000; internet www.tp.pl; f. 1992; mem. of France Telecom group (France); Chair. Jan Kulczyk.

BROADCASTING

Regulatory Authority

National Broadcasting Council (Krajowa Rada Radiofonii i Telewizji—KRRiTV): 00-015 Warsaw, Skwer Kardinala Wyszyńskiego, Prymasa Polski 9; tel. (22) 5973001; fax (22) 5973054; internet www.krrit.gov.pl; f. 1993; Chair. Danuta Waniek.

Radio

Polskie Radio (Polish Radio): 00-977 Warsaw, Al. Niepodległości 77/85; tel. (22) 6459259; fax (22) 6455924; e-mail polskie.radio@radio.com.pl; internet www.radio.com.pl; Home Service: four national channels broadcasting 90 hours per day; one long-wave transmitter (600 kW) broadcasting on 225 kHz; 11 medium-wave transmitters and 18 relay stations; 137 VHF transmitters covering all four programmes and 17 local programmes; Foreign Service: five transmitters broadcast on 10 frequencies on short-wave, one transmitter broadcasting on medium-wave; programmes in Polish, English, Esperanto, German, Russian, Belarusian, Ukrainian, Lithuanian, Slovak and Czech; Pres. Krzysztof Michalski.

Radio Maryja: 87-100 Toruń, ul. Żwirki i Wigury 80; tel. (56) 6552361; fax (56) 6552362; e-mail radio@radiomaryja.pl; internet www.radiomaryja.pl; traditionalist Roman Catholic; Dir Tadeusz Rydzyk.

Radio Musyka Fakty (RMF FM): 30-204 Kraków, Al. Waszyngtona 1, Kopiec Kosciuszki; tel. (12) 4219696; fax (12) 4217895; e-mail redakcja@rmf.pl; internet www.rmf.pl; Pres. Stanisław Tyczynski; Dir Jolanta Wiśniewska.

Radio Zet: 00-503 Warsaw, ul. Żurawia 8; tel. (22) 5833382; fax (22) 5833356; e-mail radiozet@radiozet.com.pl; internet www.radiozet.com.pl; f. 1990; independent; 24 hours; national broadcasts commenced 1994; wholly owned by the Eurozet media group; Pres. and Editor-in-Chief Robert Kozyra.

Television

Poland's first private (commercial) TV station began operating in Wrocław in early 1990. Broadcasting is regulated by the Broadcasting Bill, enacted in 1993. Poland's first digital television service was launched in April 1998.

POLAND

Telewizja Polska (Polish Television): 00-999 Warsaw, ul. J. P. Woronicza 17, POB 211; tel. (22) 5476550; fax (22) 5477719; e-mail pr@tvp.pl; internet www.tvp.pl; f. 1952; Chair. JAN DWORAK.

PolSat: 04-028 Warsaw, Al. Stanów Zjednoczonyck 53; tel. (22) 104001; fax (22) 134295; internet www.polsat.com.pl; f. 1992; Polish satellite company, awarded Poland's first national, private television licence in 1994; Propr ZYGMUNT SOLORZ.

TVN SA: 02-952 Warsaw, ul. Wiertnicza 166; tel. (22) 8566060; fax (22) 8566666; e-mail widzowie@tvn.pl; internet www.tvn.pl; f. 1997; TVN Group owns and operates seven television channels: TVN, TVN 7, TVN 24, TVN Meteo, TVN Turbo, ITVN and TVN Style; Pres. PIOTR WALTER.

Finance

(cap. = capital; res = reserves; dep. = deposits; m. = million; amounts in new złotys unless otherwise indicated; brs = branches)

BANKING

Foreign banks were permitted to operate freely in the country from 1997. In 2005 there were 55 domestic commercial banks, 592 co-operative banks and five branches of credit institutions operating in Poland.

National Bank

Narodowy Bank Polski—NBP (National Bank of Poland): 00-919 Warsaw, ul. Świętokrzyska 11/21, POB 1011; tel. (22) 6531000; fax (22) 6208518; e-mail nbp@nbp.pl; internet www.nbp.pl; f. 1945; state central bank; cap. 1,845m. new złotys, res US $34,000m., dep. 23,579m. new złotys (Dec. 2003); Pres. LESZEK BALCEROWICZ; First Deputy Pres. JERZY PRUSKI; 16 brs.

Other Banks

ABN Amro Bank (Polska) SA: 02-134 Warsaw, ul. 1-go Sierpnia 8A, Wisniowy Business Park, POB 417; tel. (22) 5730500; fax (22) 5730501; internet www.abnamro.pl; f. 1994; 100% owned by ABN AMRO Bank, NV (Netherlands); cap. 188.4m., total assets 4,672.7m. (Dec. 2004); Man. H. KESSELER.

Bank Gospodarki Żywnościowej—BGZ (BGZ) (Bank of Food Economy): 01-211 Warsaw, ul. Kasprzaka 10/16; tel. (22) 8604000; fax (22) 8605000; e-mail info@bgz.pl; internet www.bgz.pl; f. 1919; present name adopted 1994; universal commercial bank; finances agriculture, forestry and food processing; 44.5% state-owned; 35.3% owned by Rabobank, Netherlands; cap. 23.4m., res 751.9m., dep. 14,050.4m. (Dec. 2003); Exec. Pres. JACEK BARTKIEWICZ; Man. Dir JACEK RATAJCZYK; 270 brs and sub-brs.

Bank Gospodarstwa Krajowego—BGK (National Economy Bank): 00-955 Warsaw, Al. Jerozolimskie 7, POB 41; tel. (22) 5229127; fax (22) 6270378; e-mail bgk@bgk.com.pl; internet www.bgk.com.pl; f. 1924; state-owned; cap. 678.0m., res 3,391.2m., dep. 3,580.8m. (Dec. 2003); Pres. of Bd ANDRZEJ DOROSZ; 7 brs.

Bank Inicjatiw Społeczno-Economiczynich (Bank for Socio-Economic Initiatives—BISE SA): 00-184 Warsaw, ul. Dubois 5A; tel. (22) 8601100; fax (22) 8601103; e-mail bos@bosbank.pl; internet www.bise.pl; f. 1990; cap. 61.2m., res 49.6m., dep. 1,719.2m.; Pres. WŁODZIMIERZ GRUDZINSKI; Chair. JACEK KOCHANOWICZ; 44 brs.

Bank Millennium: 00-924 Warsaw, ul. Kopernika 36/40; tel. (22) 6575720; fax (22) 8267180; e-mail wojciech.kaczorowski@bankmillennium.pl; internet www.bankmillennium.pl; f. 1989 as Bank Inicjatyw Gospodarczych (BIG); present name adopted 2003; 50.0% owned by Banco Comercial Português SA (Portugal); cap. 849.2m., res 844.8m., dep. 16,081.1m. (Dec. 2003); Chair. of Bd BOGUSŁAW KOTT; 172 brs.

Bank Ochrony Środowiska—BOS (Environmental Protection Bank): 00-950 Warsaw 1, Al. Jana Pawła II 12, POB 150; tel. (22) 8508735; fax (22) 8508891; e-mail bos@bosbank.pl; internet www.bosbank.pl; f. 1991; 47.0% owned by SEB Group (Sweden), 44.36% by Polish National Fund for the Protection of the Environment and Water; cap. 132.0m., res 416.4m., dep. 5,053.2m. (Dec. 2003); Pres. of Exec. Bd JÓZEF KOZIOL; 48 brs.

Bank BPH: 31-548 Kraków, Al. Pokoju 1; tel. (12) 6186888; fax (12) 6186863; e-mail bank@bphpbk.pl; internet www.bph.pl; f. 1989; fmrly Bank Przemysłowo-Handlowy PBK SA—Bank BPH-BPK; 52.1% owned by Bank Austria Creditanstalt AG (HVB Group, Austria); cap. 143.6m., total assets 57,922.2m. (Dec. 2005); Chair. of Sup. Bd ALICJA KORNASIEWICZ; Pres. JÓZEF WANCER; 468 brs and sub-brs.

Bank Polska Kasa Opieki—Bank Pekao: 00-950 Warsaw, ul. Grzybowska 53/57; tel. (22) 6560000; fax (22) 6560004; e-mail info@pekao.com.pl; internet www.pekao.com.pl; f. 1929; universal bank; 53.2% owned by UniCredito Italiano SpA (Italy); cap. 166.1m., res 6,070.1m., dep. 51,471.8m. (Dec. 2003); Chair. ALESSANDRO PROFUMO; 720 brs and sub-brs.

Bank Polskiej Spółdzielczości: 01-231 Warsaw, ul. Plocka 9/11B; tel. (22) 5396224; fax (22) 5395133; e-mail sekretariat_bps@bankbps.pl; internet www.bankbps.pl; f. 1992; present name adopted 2002; cap. 133.2m., res 81.4m., dep. 4,263.1m. (Dec. 2003); Pres. PAWEŁ SIANO.

Bank Zachodni WBK SA (Western Bank): 50-950 Wrocław, Dolnośląskie Rynek 9/11; tel. (71) 3701000; fax (71) 3702771; e-mail dorota.bernatowicz@bzwbk.pl; internet www.bzwbk.pl; f. 1989; present name adopted 2001; 70.5% owned by AIB European Investments Ltd (Ireland); cap. 729.6m., res 1,684.2m., dep. 20,349.3m. (Dec. 2003); Pres. JACEK KSEN; 433 brs.

BNP Paribas Bank Polska SA: 00-078 Warsaw, pl. Pilsudskiego 1; tel. (22) 6972308; fax (22) 6972309; e-mail warsaw.office@bnpparibas.com; internet www.bnpparibas.pl; f. 1994; 100% owned by BNP Paribas (France); present name adopted 2006; commercial and investment bank; cap. 193.4m., res 67.9m., dep. 2,591.7m. (Dec. 2004); Gen. Man JEAN-CLAUDE CHAVAL.

BRE Bank SA: 00-950 Warsaw, ul. Senatorska 18, POB 728; tel. (22) 8290000; fax (22) 8290033; e-mail info@brebank.com.pl; internet www.brebank.com.pl; f. 1987 as Bank Rozwoju Eksportu; 50% owned by Commerzbank AG (Germany); present name adopted 1999; specializes in corporate banking; cap. 91.9m., res 1,179.5m., dep. 23,027.6m. (Dec. 2003); Chair. of Supervisory Bd MACIEJ LESNY; Pres., Chief Exec. and Gen. Man. WOJCIECH KOSTRZEWA; 12 brs.

Citibank Handlowy: 00-923 Warsaw, ul. Senatorska 16; tel. (22) 6904000; fax (22) 6925023; e-mail listybh@citicorp.com; internet www.citibank.pl; f. 1870; trade and finance bank; specializes in corporate and investment banking; fmrly Bank Handlowy w Warszawie (Trade Bank in Warsaw); 89.3% owned by Citibank Overseas Investment Corpn (USA); cap. 522.6m., res 5,181.8m., dep. 25,734.0m. (Dec. 2003); Pres. SŁAWOMIR SIKORA; Chair. STANISŁAW SOŁTYSIŃSKI; 149 brs.

Deutsche Bank PBC SA: 31-047 Kraków, ul. Józefa Sarego 2/4, POB 234; tel. (12) 6182116; fax (12) 6219652; e-mail info@db-pbc.pl; internet www.deutsche-bank-pbc.pl; f. 1991; fmrly Bank Wspolpracy Regionalnej SA w Krakowie; present name adopted 2003; 95.0% owned by Deutsche Bank Privat- und Geschäftskunden Aktiengesellschaft (Germany); cap. 336.1m., res −145.0m., dep. 1,796.2m. (Dec. 2003); Chair. of Supervisory Bd ULRICH KISSING; Pres. MAREK KULCZYCKI.

Deutsche Bank Polska SA: 00-609 Warsaw, Al. Armii Ludowej 26; tel. (22) 5799000; fax (22) 5799001; e-mail public.relations@db.com; internet www.deutsche-bank.pl; f. 1995; 100% owned by Deutsche Bank AG (Germany); cap. 336.3m., res −145.2m., dep. 1,860.9m. (Dec. 2003); Pres. KRZYSZTOF KALICKI; Chair. TESSEN VON HEYDEBRECK.

DZ Bank Polska SA: 00-078 Warsaw, Pl. Piłsudskiego 3; tel. (22) 5057000; fax (22) 5057442; e-mail info@dzbank.pl; internet www.dzbank.pl; f. 1989; fmrly known as Bank Amerykański w Polsce SA—AmerBank; 97.4% owned by DZ Bank AG Deutsche Zentral-Genossenschaftsbank (Germany); commercial bank; Chair. of Bd RAINER FUHRMANN; 3 brs.

Fortis Bank Polska SA: 02-676 Warsaw, ul. Postępu 15; tel. (22) 5669000; fax (22) 5669010; e-mail info@fortisbank.com.pl; internet www.fortisbank.com.pl; f. 1990; present name adopted 2000; 99.1% owned by Fortis Bank (Belgium); cap. 30.2m., res 450.0m., dep. 3,894.9m. (Dec. 2003); Pres. RONNIE RICHARDSON; Chair. LUC DELVAUX.

Getin Bank: 40-479 Katowice, ul. Pszczyńska 10; tel. (32) 2008500; fax (32) 2008685; e-mail gbg@getinbank.pl; internet www.getinbank.pl; f. 1990; fmrly Górnośląski Bank Gospodarczy (GBG Bank); cap. 139.3., res 59.9m., dep. 2,707.0m. (Dec. 2003); Pres. TADEUSZ CYPCAR; Chair. WOJCIECH SOBIERAJ; 44 brs.

Gospodarczy Bank Wielkopolski SA: 61-725 Poznań, ul. Mielzyńskiego 22; tel. (61) 8562434; fax (61) 8517981; e-mail dewizy@gbw.com.pl; internet www.sgb.pl; f. 1990; 97.7% owned by Banki Spółdzielcze (Co-operative Banks); cap. 51.4m., res 107.5m., dep. 2,093.2m. (Dec. 2003); Pres. and Gen. Man. ANDRZEJ CHMIELECKI.

ING Bank Śląski: 40-086 Katowice, ul. Sokolska 34; tel. (32) 3577000; fax (32) 588308; e-mail info@ing.pl; internet www.ing.pl; f. 1989; present name adopted 2001; 87.8% owned by ING Bank NV (Netherlands); cap. 130.1m., res 2,543.5m., dep. 24,590.7m. (Dec. 2003); Chair. ANDRZEJ WROBLEWSKI; Pres. BRUNON BARTKIEWICZ; 332 brs and sub-brs.

Kredyt Bank: 01-211 Warsaw, ul. Kasprzaka 2/8, POB 93; tel. (22) 6345400; fax (22) 6345335; e-mail bew@kredytbank.com.pl; internet www.kredytbank.com.pl; f. 1997; present name adopted 1999; 76.5% owned by KBC Bank NV (Belgium), 18.4% by Deutsche Bank Trust Co Americas (USA); cap. 1,056.5m., res 1,169.7m., dep. 20,926.1m. (Dec. 2003); Chair. ANDRZEJ WITKOWSKI; Pres. MALGORZATA KROKER-JACHIEWICZ; 75 brs.

POLAND

Nordea Bank Polska: 81-308 Gdynia, ul. Kielecka 2, POB 11; tel. (22) 5213640; fax (22) 5213635; e-mail nordea@nordea.pl; internet www.nordeabank.pl; f. 1991; present name adopted 2001; 98% owned by Nordea Bank AB (Sweden); cap. 168.1m., res 342.2m., dep. 3,321.6m. (Dec. 2003); Pres. WLODZIMIERZ KICINSKI; Chair. WOJCIECH RYBOWSKI.

PKO Bank Polski SA—Powszechna Kasa Oszczędności Bank Państwowy—PKO (State Savings Bank): 00-975 Warsaw, ul. Pulawska 15, POB 183; tel. (22) 5218067; fax (22) 5218068; internet www.pkobp.pl; f. 1919; 51% state-owned; cap. 1,000.0m., res 4,164.5m., dep. 72,765.4m. (Dec. 2003); Pres. of Management Bd ANDRZEJ PODSIADLO; Chair. of Supervisory Bd BAZYL SAMOJLIK; 1,153 brs and sub-brs.

Raiffeisen Bank Polska SA: 00-549 Warsaw, ul. Piekna 20, POB 53; tel. (22) 5852000; fax (22) 5852585; internet www.raiffeisen.pl; f. 1991; present name adopted 2000; 100% owned by Raiffeisen Zentralbank Österreich AG (Austria); cap. 407.0m., res 146.2m., dep. 7,844.9m. (Dec. 2003); Pres. PIOTR CZARNECKI; Chair. HERBERT STEPIC; 29 brs.

WestLB Bank Polska SA: 00-688 Warsaw, ul. Emilii Plater 28; tel. (22) 6530500; fax (22) 6530501; e-mail westlb@westlb.pl; internet www.westlb.pl; f. 1995; present name adopted 2003; 100% owned by WestLB AG (Germany); cap. 183.6m., res 7.8m., dep. 1,771.4m. (Dec. 2003); Pres. MACIEJ STANCZUK.

STOCK EXCHANGE

The Warsaw Stock Exchange was re-established in April 1991. In March 1999 it had 37 member companies and listed shares in 205 firms, in addition to 43 issues of Treasury bonds. In January 1998 a derivatives market was launched.

Polish Securities and Exchange Commission (Komisja Papierów Wartościowych i Giełd): Warsaw, Pl. Powstańców Warszawy 1; tel. (22) 3326600; fax (22) 3326602; e-mail kpwig@kpwig.gov.pl; internet www.kpwig.gov.pl; Pres. JAROSŁAW KOZLOWSKI; Dir JERZY WALCZAK.

Warsaw Stock Exchange: 00-498 Warsaw, ul. Książęca 4; tel. (22) 6283232; fax (22) 6281754; e-mail gielda@wse.com.pl; internet www.wse.com.pl; opened for trading in 1991; Pres. and Chief Exec. Dr WIESŁAW ROZUCKI.

INSURANCE

In early 2005 there were 32 insurance companies operating in Poland. The largest companies were Polish National Insurance (Państwowy Zakład Ubezpieczeń—PZU), which dominated the property insurance market, and Warta Insurance and Reinsurance, which specialized in vehicle insurance, and foreign business. PZU's subsidiary, PZU Life, was the largest life insurance company.

Grupa Powszechny Zakład Ubezpieczeń (PZU) (Polish National Insurance Group): 00-133 Warsaw, Al. Jana Pawła II 24; tel. (22) 5823400; fax (22) 5823401; e-mail poczta@pzu.pl; internet ww.pzu.pl; f. 1803; insurance group comprising two principal companies dealing in various areas of insurance (PSU SA—property insurance, and PZU Życie SA—life insurance), and six support companies; 55% state-owned; further privatization scheduled; Pres. CEZARY STYPUŁKOWSKI; 400 brs; 14,000 employees.

Warta—Towarzystwo Ubezpieczeń i Reasekuracji Warta SA (Warta Insurance and Reinsurance Co): 00-805 Warsaw, ul. Chmielna 85/87; tel. (22) 5810100; fax (22) 5811374; e-mail info@warta.pl; internet www.warta.pl; f. 1920; marine, air, motor, fire, luggage and credit; Pres. AGENOR JAN GAWRZYAL; 25 brs.

Trade and Industry

GOVERNMENT AGENCIES

Departments I and II of Privatization (Ministry of the State Treasury): 00-522 Warsaw, ul. Krucza 36; tel. (22) 6959000; fax (22) 6213361; both divisions oversee indirect privatizations of state enterprises and cos; Division I additionally oversees and analyses privatization processes and is responsible for retention of data; Division II additionally manages the direct privatization of state enterprises and the privatization of research and development entities; Dir (Dept I) JACEK GRABARCZUK; Dir (Dept II) MIROSŁAW SKOWERSKI.

Polska Agencja Rozwoju Przedsiębiorczości (PARP) (Polish Agency for Enterprise Development): 00-834 Warsaw, ul. Pańska 81/83; tel. (22) 4328080; fax (22) 4328620; e-mail biuro@parp.gov.pl; internet www.parp.gov.pl; f. 2000; government agency; manages funds assigned from the state budget and the European Union for the support of entrepreneurship and the development of human resources, giving particular consideration to the needs of small and medium-sized enterprises; Pres. MIROSŁAW MAREK.

Polish Information and Foreign Investment Agency (Polska Agencja Informacji i Inwestycji Zagranicznych SA—PAIiIZ): 00-585 Warsaw, ul. Bagatela 12; tel. (22) 3349800; fax (22) 3349999; e-mail post@paiz.gov.pl; internet www.paiz.gov.pl; f. 2003; Pres. ADAM ZOŁNOWSKI.

CHAMBERS OF COMMERCE

Polish Chamber of Commerce (National Economic Chamber—Krajowa Izba Gospodarcza): 00-074 Warsaw, ul. Trębacka 4, POB 361; tel. (22) 6309600; fax (22) 8274673; internet www.kig.pl; f. 1990; Pres. ANDRZEJ ARENDARSKI; Chair. KAZIMIERZ PAZGAN; 150 mems.

Foreign Investors' Chamber of Industry and Trade in Poland (Izba Przemysłowo-Handlowa Inwestorów Zagranicznych—IPHIZ): 00-071 Warsaw, ul. Krakowskie Przedmieście 47/51; tel. (22) 8261822; fax (22) 8268593; e-mail biuro@iphiz.com.pl; internet www.iphiz.com.pl; f. 1990; Pres. ZDZISŁAW JAGODZIŃSKI.

UTILITIES

Energy Regulatory Authority (Urząd Regulacji Energetyki): 00-872 Warsaw, ul. Chłodna 64; tel. (22) 6616107; fax (22) 6616152; e-mail ure@ure.gov.pl; internet www.ure.gov.pl; Pres. Dr LESZEK JUCHNIEWICZ.

Electricity

The electricity sector has been reorganized into separate generation, transmission and distribution entities. Poland's distribution companies were consolidated as follows, to aid privatization: ENEA (comprising five companies in the north-west, around Poznań), ENERGA (G8—covering central and northern Poland), G4 (southern Poland), ENiON (K7—around Kraków), L6 (Lublin and eastern Poland), Energia Pro (W5—around Wrocław).

BOT Górnictwo i Energetyka SA (BOT GiE SA): f. 2004; holding 69% ownership of the power plants and lignite mines: BOT Elektrownia Turów SA, BOT Kopalnia Węgla Brunatnego Turów SA, BOT Elektrownia Bełchatów SA (Europe's largest lignite-powered power plant), BOT Kopalnia Węgla Brunatnego Bełchatów SA and BOT Elektrownia Opole SA; Chief Exec. ZBIGNIEW BICKI.

Koncern Energetyczny ENERGA SA: 80-557 Gdańsk, ul. Marynarki Polskiej 130; tel. (58) 3473013; fax (58) 3010152; e-mail centrala@energa.pl; internet www.energa.pl; f. 2004; renamed as above 2005; group of eight regional electricity distributors in central and northern Poland, known as G8; holds 16% share of electricity-distribution market; partial privatization suspended in 2004; Chief Exec. WALDEMAR BARTELIK; 7,500 employees.

Polish Power Exchange (Towarowa Giełda Energii SA): 02-822 Warsaw, ul. Poleczki 23, bud. H; tel. (27) 2229922; fax (27) 2229910; e-mail polpx@polpx.pl; internet www.polpx.pl; f. 1999; 22.4% state-owned; Pres. GRZEGORZ ONICHIMOWSKI.

Polish Power Grid Company JSC (Polskie Sieci Elektroenergetyczne SA—PSE): 00-496 Warsaw, ul. Mysia 2; tel. (22) 6931580; fax (22) 6285964; internet www.pse.pl; f. 1990; national transmission-system operator; state-owned; Pres. Prof. Dr hab. STANISŁAW DOBRZAŃSKI.

Południowy Koncern Energetyczny SA (PKE): 40-389 Katowice, ul. Lwowska 23; tel. (32) 7312000; fax (32) 7312102; internet www.pke.pl; f. 2000; largest electricity-generation group, a consortium of coal-powered plants in the south of Poland; 30% scheduled for privatization.

State Atomic Energy Agency (Państwowa Agencja Atomistyki): 00-921 Warsaw, ul. Krucza 36; tel. (22) 6282722; fax (22) 6290164; e-mail niewodniczanski@paa.gov.pl; internet www.paa.gov.pl; f. 1982; responsible for the development and safe application of nuclear technologies, as well as for nuclear research and radiation protection; Pres. Prof. JERZY NIEWODNICZAŃSKI.

STOEN Stołeczny Zakład Energetyczny SA (STOEN Capital-City Power Distribution Co): 00-347 Warsaw, Wybrzeże Kopciuszkowskie 41; tel. (22) 8213387; fax (22) 8213122; e-mail rzecznik.prasowy@stoen.pl; internet www.stoen.pl; f. 1993; transmits and distributes electric energy; privatized in 2002; 85% owned by RWE Energie AG (Germany); 15% state-owned; Chief Exec. HARRY SCHUR; Chair. of Supervisory Bd Dr ANDREAS RADMACHER.

Gas

EuRoPol GAZ SA: 04-028 Warsaw, Al. Stanów Zjednoczonych 61; tel. (22) 5174000; fax (22) 5174040; e-mail konto@europolgaz.com.pl; internet www.europolgaz.com.pl; f. 1993; jt venture between PGNiG and Gazprom (Russia); Pres. KAZIMIERZ ADAMCZYK.

Polish Oil and Gas Co (Polskie Górnictwo Naftowe i Gazownictwo SA—PGNiG): 00-537 Warsaw, ul. Krucza 6/14; tel. (22) 5835000; fax (22) 5835856; e-mail pr@pgnig.pl; internet www.pgnig.pl; f. 1982; divided into 6 regional distribution subsidiaries in 2003; state-owned natural-gas producer and supplier; scheduled for partial privatization; Pres. of Bd MAREK KOSSOWSKI; 47,300 employees.

POLAND

TRADE UNIONS

All Poland Trade Unions Alliance (Ogólnopolskie Porozumienie Związków Zawodowych—OPZZ): 00-924 Warsaw, ul. Kopernika 36/40; tel. (22) 8267106; fax (22) 8265102; e-mail opzz@opzz.org.pl; internet www.opzz.org.pl; f. 1984; 2.3m. mems (2000); Chair. JAN GUZ.

Independent Self-governing Trade Union—Solidarity (NSZZ Solidarność): 80-855 Gdańsk, ul. Wały Piastowskie 24; tel. (58) 3016737; fax (58) 3010143; e-mail zagr@solidarnosc.org.pl; internet www.solidarnosc.org.pl; f. 1980; outlawed 1981–89; 1.2m. mems; Chair. JANUSZ SNIADEK.

Private Farmers' Solidarity (Solidarności Rolników Indywidualnych): Leader ROMAN WIERZBICKI.

Transport

RAILWAYS

At the end of 2002 there were 21,073 km of railway lines making up the state network, of which 12,207 km were electrified.

General Railway Inspectorate (Główny Inspektorat Kolejnictwa): 00-928 Warsaw, ul. Chałubinskiego 4/6; e-mail gik@gik.gov.pl; internet www.gik.gov.pl; Gen. Inspector BOLESŁAW MUSIAŁ; Dir-Gen. LIDIA OSTROWSKA.

Polish State Railways Plc (Polskie Koleje Państwowe Spółka Akcyjna—PKP SA): 00-973 Warsaw, ul. Szczęśliwicka 62; tel. (22) 5249000; fax (22) 5249020; e-mail infopkp@pkp.com.pl; internet www.pkp.com.pl; f. 1926; freight and passenger transport; freight company PKP Cargo and PKP Intercity were scheduled for privatization in 2004–05; PKP Gp comprises 12 cos; from January 2004 Regional Services Ltd (WKD), a principal subsidiary, was to be operated by local governments; Polskie Koleje Państwowe Polskie Linie Kolejowe (PKP PLK) operates the railway network; Pres. ADAM FRANCISZEK WIELĘDEK; Gen. Dir MACIEJ MECLEWSKI; 152,586 employees.

ROADS

In 2001 there were 364,697 km of roads, of which 399 km were motorways; 68.3% of the road network was paved. Poland launched a road construction scheme in mid-2002, partly funded by the European Union (EU), which aimed to enhance the country's position as a major transit route between western Europe and the countries of the former USSR. The project, which was to concentrate on road construction, also aimed to modernize some 1,500 km of existing roads. The EU was to provide funding of €2,300m. for road construction in Poland in 2004–06.

General Directorate of Public Roads and Motorways (Generalna Dyrekcja Dróg Krajowych i Autostrad): 00-921 Warsaw, ul. Żelazna 59; tel. (22) 4558602; fax (22) 4558600; e-mail kancelaria@gddkia.gov.pl; internet www.gddkia.gov.pl; Dir DARIUSZ SKOWROŃSKI.

Państwowa Komunikacja Samochodowa (PKS) (Polish Motor Communications): Warsaw; tel. (22) 363594; fax (22) 366733; internet www.pks.pl; f. 1945; state enterprise organizing inland road transport for passengers and goods; bus routes cover a total of 121,000 km; passengers carried 1,039,409 (1995).

INLAND WATERWAYS

Poland has 6,850 km of waterways, of which 3,640 km were navigable in 2002. The main rivers are the Wisła (Vistula, 1,047 km), Odra (Oder, 742 km in Poland), Bug (587 km in Poland), Warta (808 km), San, Narew, Noteć, Pilica, Wieprz and Dunajec. There are some 5,000 lakes, the largest being the Sniardwy, Mamry, Łebsko, Dąbie and Miedwie. In addition, there is a network of canals (approximately 348 km).

About 1,795,000 passengers and 8.0m. metric tons of freight were carried on inland water transport in 2003.

SHIPPING

Poland has three large harbours on the Baltic Sea: Gdynia, Gdańsk and Szczecin. At 31 December 2004 the Polish merchant fleet had 378 vessels, with a total displacement of 162,700 grt.

Authority of Szczecin and Świnoujście Authority SA: 70-603 Szczecin, ul. Bytomska 7; tel. (91) 4308240; fax (91) 4624842; e-mail info@port.szczecin.pl; internet www.port.szczecin.pl; f. 1950; Pres. and Man. Dir DARIUSZ RUTKOWSKI.

Port of Gdańsk Authority Co: 80-955 Gdańsk, ul. Zamknięta 18; tel. (58) 3439300; fax (58) 3439485; e-mail info@portgdansk.pl; internet www.portgdansk.pl; f. 1997; management of land and port infrastructure; Pres. of Bd ANDRZEJ KASPRZAK.

Port of Gdynia Authority SA (ZPMG SA): 81-337 Gdynia, ul. Rotterdamska 9; tel. (58) 6274002; fax (58) 6203191; e-mail marketing@port.gdynia.pl; internet www.port.gdynia.pl; f. 1922; Pres. JERZY WIELIŃSKI.

Principal shipping companies:

Polskie Linie Oceaniczne (PLO) (Polish Ocean Lines): 81-364 Gdynia, ul. 10 Lutego 24, POB 265; tel. (58) 6278222; fax (58) 6278480; e-mail pol@pol.com.pl; internet www.pol.com.pl; f. 1951; holding co for six shipping cos operating within PLO group; Dir-Gen. KRZYSZTOF KREMKY.

Polska Żegluga Bałtycka SA—Polferries (Polish Baltic Shipping Co—POLFERRIES): 78-100 Kołobrzeg, ul. Portowa 41; tel. (94) 3552102; fax (94) 3526612; e-mail info@polferries.pl; internet www.polferries.pl.

Polska Żegluga Morska (PZM) (Polish Steamship Co): 70-419 Szczecin, Pl. Rodła 8; tel. (91) 3595595; fax (91) 4340574; e-mail pzmmanagement@polsteam.com.pl; internet www.polsteam.com.pl; f. 1951; world-wide tramping; fleet of 103 vessels for bulk cargoes totalling nearly 3m. dwt; Gen. Dir PAWEŁ BRZEZICKI.

CIVIL AVIATION

Fryderyka Chopin—Okęcie international airport is situated near Warsaw. In addition, there are international airports at Kraków, Gdańsk and Katowice. Domestic flights serve Gdańsk, Gołeniow, Katowice, Kraków, Poznań, Rzeszów, Szczecin, Warsaw and Wrocław. In 2005 low-cost airlines also commenced international flights from Bydgoszcz airport.

General Inspectorate of Civil Aviation (Główny Inspektorat Lotnictwa Cywilnego): 00-928 Warsaw, ul. Chałubinskiego 4/6; tel. and fax (22) 6298689; e-mail gilc@polbox.pl; internet www.gilc.gov.pl; Gen. Inspector ZBIGNIEW MĄCKA.

Centralwings: 90-312 Łódź, Pl. Zwyciestwa 2; e-mail comments@centralwings.com; internet www.centralwings.com; f. 2004; low-cost subsidiary of LOT (q.v.), in association with Germanwings, a low-cost subsidiary of Lufthansa (Germany); operates flights to 11 European destinations from Warsaw, Katowice and Kraków; Pres. PIOTR KOCIOŁEK.

LOT—Polskie Linie Lotnicze (Polish Airlines): 00-906 Warsaw, ul. 17 Stycznia 39; tel. (22) 6066111; fax (22) 8460909; e-mail lot@lot.com; internet www.lot.com; f. 1929; 67.96% state-owned; 90 air routes, domestic services and international services to the Middle East, Africa, Asia, Canada, USA, and throughout Europe; operates low-cost subsidiary Eurolot (f. 1996) and is a parent co of Centralwings (q.v.); Pres. and CEO MAREK GRABAREK.

Tourism

Poland is rich in historic cities, such as Gdańsk, Wrocław, Kraków, Poznań and Warsaw. There are 30 health and climatic resorts, while the mountains, forests and rivers provide splendid scenery and excellent facilities for touring and sporting holidays. In 2005 Poland was visited by some 64.6m. foreign tourists, 57.9% of whom were from Germany. Receipts from tourism amounted to US $6,230m. in that year.

Institute of Tourism (Instytut Turystyki): 02-511 Warsaw, ul. Merliniego 9A; tel. (22) 8446347; fax (22) 8441263; e-mail it@intur.com.pl; internet www.intur.com.pl; f. 1972; Dir KRZYSZTOF ŁOPACZIŃSKI.

Polish Tourist Organization (Polska Organizacja Turystyczna—POT): 00-613 Warsaw, ul. Chałubskińego 8XIX piętro; tel. (22) 5367070; fax (22) 5367004; e-mail pot@pot.gov.pl; internet www.pot.gov.pl; Pres. TOMASZ WILCZAK.

PORTUGAL

Introductory Survey

Location, Climate, Language, Religion, Flag, Capital

The mainland portion of the Portuguese Republic lies in western Europe, on the Atlantic side of the Iberian peninsula, bordered by Spain to the north and east. The country also includes two archipelagos in the Atlantic Ocean, the Azores and the Madeira Islands. The climate is mild and temperate, with an annual average temperature of 16°C (61°F). In the interior the weather is drier and hotter. Almost all of the inhabitants speak Portuguese and are Christians of the Roman Catholic Church. The national flag (proportions 2 by 3) has two vertical stripes, of green and red, the green occupying two-fifths of the total area; superimposed on the stripes (half on the green, half on the red) is the state coat of arms: a white shield, containing five small blue shields (each bearing five white roundels) in the form of an upright cross, with a red border containing seven yellow castles, all superimposed on a yellow armillary sphere. The capital is Lisbon (Lisboa).

Recent History

The monarchy that had ruled Portugal from the 11th century was overthrown in 1910, when the King was deposed in a bloodless revolution, and a republic was proclaimed. A period of great instability ensued until a military coup installed the regime of the Estado Novo (New State) in 1926. Dr António de Oliveira Salazar became Minister of Finance in 1928 and Prime Minister in 1932, establishing a right-wing dictatorial regime, influenced by Italian Fascism. A new Constitution, establishing a corporate state, was adopted in 1933. Only one political party was authorized, and suffrage was limited. Portugal remained neutral during the Second World War. The Government strove to achieve international acceptance, but Portugal was not admitted to the UN until 1955. Unlike the other European colonial powers, Portugal insisted on maintaining its overseas possessions, regarding them as 'inalienable'. In 1961 Portuguese enclaves in India were successfully invaded by Indian forces, and in the same year a rebellion against Portuguese rule began in Angola. Similar rebellions followed, in Portuguese Guinea (1963) and Mozambique (1964), and protracted guerrilla warfare ensued in the three African provinces. Salazar remained in power until illness forced his retirement in September 1968. He was succeeded by Dr Marcello Caetano, who had been Deputy Prime Minister in 1955–58. Caetano pursued slightly more liberal policies. Opposition parties were legalized for elections to the Assembléia Nacional in October 1969, but the União Nacional, the government party, won all 130 seats. Immediately after the elections, the opposition groups were outlawed again. The government party, renamed Acção Nacional Popular in February 1970, also won every seat at the next elections to the Assembléia, in October 1973, following the withdrawal of all opposition candidates.

The drain on Portugal's economy by the long wars against nationalist forces in the overseas provinces contributed to the overthrow of Caetano in a bloodless coup on 25 April 1974, initiated by the Movimento das Forças Armadas (MFA), a group of young army officers. Gen. António Ribeiro de Spínola, head of the Junta da Salvação Nacional (Junta of National Salvation) which had then assumed power, became President in May and promised liberal reforms. In July Brig.-Gen. Vasco dos Santos Gonçalves replaced Prof. Adelino da Palma Carlos as Prime Minister. The new Government recognized the right of Portugal's overseas territories to self-determination. The independence of Guinea-Bissau (formerly Portuguese Guinea), proclaimed in September 1973, was recognized by Portugal in September 1974. The remaining African territories were all granted independence in 1975. Portugal also withdrew from Portuguese (East) Timor in 1975.

Following a split between the Junta's right and left wings, President Spínola resigned in September 1974 and was replaced by Gen. Francisco da Costa Gomes. An abortive counter-coup by senior officers in March 1975 resulted in a move to the left. All existing organs of the MFA were dissolved, a Supreme Revolutionary Council (SRC) was created, and six of the country's political parties agreed that the SRC would stay in power for five years. On 25 April, the first anniversary of the overthrow of the Caetano regime, a general election was held for a Constituent Assembly. Of the 12 parties contesting the election, the Partido Socialista (PS) obtained the largest share of the votes cast and won 116 of the Assembly's 250 seats. Disputes between Socialists and Communists, however, provoked withdrawals from the new coalition Government, and Gen. Vasco Gonçalves was dismissed from the premiership. Admiral José Pinheiro de Azevedo became Prime Minister in August. In September the provisional Government resigned and a new Government of 'united action' was formed, including members of the armed forces, the PS, the Partido Popular Democrático (PPD) and the Partido Comunista Português (PCP). In November the Government suspended its activities, owing to a lack of support from the armed forces. An abortive leftist military coup resulted from the political turmoil. Changes took place within the SRC, and in December the armed forces announced a plan to reduce their political power.

A new Constitution, committing Portugal to make a transition to socialism, took effect on 25 April 1976. The SRC was renamed the Council of the Revolution, becoming a consultative body, headed by the President, with powers to delay legislation and the right of veto in military matters. At the general election for the new Assembléia da República (Assembly of the Republic), the PS won 107 of the Assembléia's 263 seats. In June the Army Chief of Staff, Gen. António Ramalho Eanes, a non-party candidate supported by the PS, the PPD and the Centro Democrático Social (CDS), was elected President. He took office in July, when a minority Socialist Government was formed under Dr Mário Lopes Soares, who had been Minister of Foreign Affairs in 1974–75. The Government resigned in December 1977, but the President again invited Dr Soares to take office as Prime Minister. A new PS-CDS coalition was established in January 1978, but it collapsed after only six months. A new Government was formed in November under Prof. Carlos Mota Pinto, but he resigned in July 1979.

President Eanes appointed Dr Maria de Lourdes Pintasilgo to head a provisional Government. In September 1979 the President dissolved the Assembléia da República and announced that an early general election would be held in December. The centre-right alliance, Aliança Democrática (AD), which included the Partido Social Democrata (PSD, formerly the PPD) and the CDS, won 128 of the 250 seats in the Assembléia. Dr Francisco Sá Carneiro, the leader of the PSD, was appointed Prime Minister. At the general election held in October 1980, the AD increased its majority of seats in the Assembléia. In December Dr Sá Carneiro and his Minister of Defence, Adelino Amaro da Costa, were killed in an apparent air accident. (In 2004 tests revealed that a bomb had exploded on board the aircraft, and the eighth commission of inquiry into the crash cited Amaro da Costa's attempt to stop the illegal sale of arms to Iran as a possible motive for the bombing.) The presidential election took place as planned, however, and President Eanes won a clear victory, receiving 56.4% of the valid votes cast. Dr Francisco Pinto Balsemão, co-founder of the PSD, was appointed Prime Minister. In March 1981 the offices of the President of the Republic and the Chief of Staff of the Armed Forces were formally separated.

In August 1982 the Assembléia da República approved the final draft of the new Constitution, which abolished the Council of the Revolution and reduced the powers of the President, thus completing the transition to full civilian government. Following divisions within the PSD, and losses at local elections in December 1982, Dr Balsemão resigned as Prime Minister. In addition, the Deputy Prime Minister and leader of the CDS, Prof. Diogo Freitas do Amaral, announced his resignation from all party and political posts. President Eanes dissolved the Assembléia, and announced that a general election would be held. In February 1983 Dr Balsemão was replaced as leader of the PSD by Prof. Carlos Mota Pinto. At the general election, held in April, the PS, led by the former Prime Minister, Dr Mário Soares, won 101 of the Assembléia's 250 seats. Dr Soares formed a coalition Government with the PSD (the AD having been dissolved), which took office in June.

In February 1985 Prof. Carlos Mota Pinto resigned as leader of the PSD, and subsequently as Deputy Prime Minister and Minister of Defence, and was replaced by Rui Machete, the Minister of Justice. In May Machete was replaced as leader of the PSD by Prof. Aníbal Cavaco Silva, a former Minister of Finance. In June 1985, on the day after Portugal signed its treaty of accession to the European Community (EC—now European Union—EU, see p. 228), the PS-PSD coalition disintegrated. Dr Mário Soares resigned as Prime Minister, and Eanes called a general election for October, at which the PSD won 88 of the 250 seats in the Assembléia da República, while the PS won 57 seats and the Partido Renovador Democrático (PRD, a new party founded in early 1985 by supporters of President Eanes) won 45 seats. Cavaco Silva was able to form a minority Government acceptable to President Eanes.

In January 1986 four candidates contested the presidential election. As no candidate achieved the requisite 50% majority, a second round of voting was held in February: Dr Mário Soares narrowly defeated Freitas do Amaral, former leader of the CDS, to become Portugal's first civilian President for 60 years, taking office in March.

The Government of Cavaco Silva hoped to embark on a reformist programme, but, lacking a majority, encountered difficulties in securing the adoption of legislation. In April 1987 Cavaco Silva resigned, following his defeat in a motion of censure. President Soares dissolved the Assembléia da República, prior to the holding of an early general election in July. The election resulted in a decisive victory for the PSD, which secured 148 of the 250 seats in the Assembléia and thus became the first party since 1974 to win an absolute majority. The PS won 60 seats, and the Coligação Democrático Unitária (CDU, a new left-wing coalition comprising mainly the PCP) won 31 seats. The PRD won only seven seats. Eanes resigned from the presidency of the party. Cavaco Silva was reappointed as Prime Minister.

Upon his return to the office of Prime Minister, Cavaco Silva announced a programme of radical economic reform. The gradual partial privatization of state industries was to continue, and fundamental changes in the sectors of agriculture, education and the media were proposed. The most controversial aspect of the programme, however, was the Government's renewed attempt to reform the restrictive labour laws. In March 1988 an estimated 1.5m. workers, fearing for the security of their jobs, took part in a 24-hour general strike to protest against the Government's proposed legislation. Nevertheless, in April the labour laws were approved by the Assembléia da República; the following month, however, the Constitutional Court ruled that the new legislation violated the Constitution. The legislation was approved by President Soares in February, although labour unrest persisted.

In October 1988 the PSD and the opposition PS reached agreement on removing Marxist elements from the Constitution. Having gained the approval of the requisite two-thirds' majority of the Assembléia da República, and also the agreement of President Soares, the constitutional amendments entered into force in August 1989. At municipal elections, held in December, the PS, supported by the PCP and the Greens, took control of Lisbon; Jorge Sampaio, the new Secretary-General of the PS, became Mayor of the capital. The PSD also lost other major cities.

Soares was re-elected President at an election held in January 1991, defeating three other candidates to secure an outright victory. Supported by both the PS and the PSD, the incumbent President received more than 70% of the votes cast.

At legislative elections held in early October 1991 the PSD renewed its absolute majority, winning 135 of the 230 seats in the Assembléia da República. The PS secured 72 seats, the CDU 17 and the CDS five. A new Government was appointed in late October. Following the electorate's clear endorsement of the PSD's policies, Freitas do Amaral resigned from the leadership of the CDS (a post to which he had returned in 1988), not being succeeded until March 1992, upon the appointment of Manuel Monteiro. In February of that year the Secretary-General of the PS, Jorge Sampaio, was replaced by António Guterres. During 1992 tension between President Soares and Cavaco Silva became more evident, owing to the President's increasingly frequent use of his power of veto in order to obstruct the passage of legislation.

In January 1995 Cavaco Silva announced his intention to resign as leader of the PSD. At the party congress in the following month the Minister of Defence, Joaquim Fernando Nogueira, narrowly defeated his principal rival, the Minister of Foreign Affairs, José Manuel Durão Barroso, in the contest for the leadership. In March Fernando Nogueira resigned as Minister of Defence, following the President's veto of the former's proposed appointment as Deputy Prime Minister. At legislative elections held in October the PS won 112 of the 230 seats in the Assembléia da República. The PSD won 88 seats, the Partido Popular (PP, formerly the CDS) 15 and the CDU also 15. António Guterres was appointed Prime Minister, heading a minority administration that incorporated several non-party ministers.

In November 1995 Jorge Sampaio, former Secretary-General of the PS, announced his resignation as Mayor of Lisbon, and declared his candidacy for the forthcoming presidential election. At the election, held in January 1996, Sampaio secured 53.9% of the votes cast, defeating Cavaco Silva. President Sampaio took office in March. Following the presidential election, Fernando Nogueira resigned from the leadership of the PSD, and was replaced by Marcelo Rebelo de Sousa.

In August 1996 the Prime Minister announced proposals for radical reform of the country's political system. A reduction in the number of deputies in the legislature, the opening of electoral lists to independent citizens (thus ending the monopoly of the major parties) and provision for the holding of referendums on issues of national interest were among the changes envisaged. In early 1997 the ruling PS and the opposition PSD reached a broad consensus on these proposals, also agreeing upon the gradual establishment of a professional army and a reduction in compulsory military service. In September the Assembléia da República gave its approval to the various constitutional reforms.

In February 1997, in a free vote, the Assembléia da República narrowly rejected proposals to liberalize the country's restrictive abortion law. The issue aroused bitter controversy, and created a deep division within the ruling PS. The Prime Minister, a practising Catholic, expressed his strong opposition, while certain PS veterans supported the proposed change in the legislation. In February 1998 the legislature voted by a narrow margin to relax the law on abortion. A referendum on the issue was held in June. Although 51% of those casting a vote favoured the liberalization of the law, only 31% (compared with the requisite minimum of 50%) of the electorate participated in the country's first referendum, thereby rendering the result null and void.

At local elections in December 1997 the PS consolidated its position, receiving more than 38% of the votes cast and retaining control of Lisbon and Porto. The PSD obtained 33% of the votes, while the PCP lost considerable support.

In October 1998 the Prime Minister announced the establishment of an anti-corruption unit and various other measures, in response to repeated accusations that political parties and public officials had been in receipt of illicit payments in return for the awarding of public-works contracts. Meanwhile, as an atmosphere of impunity continued to prevail (many serious corruption and other criminal cases taking up to 15 years to reach the courts), both the Government and the opposition reiterated their concerns over the extraordinarily tardy procedures of the country's judicial system.

The Prime Minister suffered a reverse in November 1998 when a referendum on the question of regional devolution resulted in an overwhelming rejection (by 63.6% of voters) of the Government's proposals to divide mainland Portugal into eight administrative regions (each with a proposed elected local assembly and regional president). However, owing to the high abstention rate (over 50%), the referendum result was declared invalid.

In March 1999 Rebelo de Sousa announced his resignation as leader of the opposition PSD and the termination of the party's recently established electoral alliance with the PP, citing disloyalty on the part of the President of the PP, Paulo Portas.

The general election conducted on 10 October 1999 was partially overshadowed by the crisis in the former Portuguese colony of East Timor (now Timor-Leste, see below). Nevertheless, the PS won 44.0% of the votes cast, thus securing 115 of the 230 seats in the Assembléia da República. The PSD, with 32.3% of the votes, was allocated 81 seats. The left-wing CDU won 17 seats (including two seats allocated to the 'green' Partido Ecologista 'Os Verdes'—PEV), while the recently established Bloco Esquerda (BE), a militant left-wing grouping, unexpectedly obtained two seats. Thus, one seat short of an absolute majority, António Guterres was returned to office and a new Council of Ministers was subsequently appointed. In November the incoming Government announced a programme of reforms aimed at narrowing the disparity between Portugal and the more developed member countries of the EU.

During the mid-1980s terrorist attacks were perpetrated by the radical left-wing group Forças Populares de 25 Abril (FP-25) and other groups, targets including both Portuguese and foreign business interests, installations of the North Atlantic Treaty Organization (NATO) and the US embassy in Lisbon. In July 1985 the trial of more than 70 alleged members of FP-25 (including Lt-Col Otelo Saraiva de Carvalho, the former revolutionary commander) opened, but was adjourned, owing to the fatal shooting of a key prosecution witness. However, the trial later resumed and, upon its conclusion in May 1987, Saraiva de Carvalho was found guilty of subversion and sentenced to 15 years' imprisonment (subsequently increased to 18 years). In March 1996, following a personal initiative by President Soares, the Assembléia da República approved a pardon for Saraiva de Carvalho and other members of FP-25. However, in December 1999 Saraiva de Carvalho was placed on trial on renewed charges of terrorism relating to his alleged leadership of FP-25. More than 60 other defendants also faced charges. Saraiva de Carvalho was acquitted in 2001.

The Government came under increasing pressure in late 2000, although a motion of 'no confidence', presented by the PSD in September, was defeated by 117 votes to 96, following the PCP's decision to abstain from voting. In October the Government failed to gain the support of at least one opposition deputy in the Assembléia da República, required to obtain a majority, to ensure the approval of the 2001 budget. Guterres subsequently announced that, rather than accept the amendments to the budgetary proposals demanded by the opposition, he would resign. In the event, however, an independent deputy abstained from the vote, thereby assuring that the budget was passed.

At a presidential election held on 14 January 2001 Sampaio was re-elected for a second term, obtaining 55.8% of the votes cast and defeating four other candidates; his nearest rival, the PSD candidate, Joaquim Ferreira do Amaral, secured 34.5% of the votes.

A major government reorganization was effected in June 2001, in an apparent attempt to appease opposition members who were demanding an early general election. Significantly, the Minister of Finance, Joaquim Augusto Nunes de Pina Moura, was replaced by Guilherme Waldemar Pereira D'Oliveira Martins.

In October 2001 the Assembléia da República ratified the Treaty of Nice, which aimed to reform the institutions of the EU in anticipation of its forthcoming enlargement. The PS, the PSD and the PP voted in favour of the ratification, while the BE and the PCP rejected the Treaty. Earlier that month the Government had excluded the PCP's suggestion of altering the Constitution to ensure that all future treaties on the EU be subject to approval by referendum. A number of constitutional amendments were approved by the Assembléia; these included the incorporation of reciprocal political rights for citizens of lusophone countries, a ban on strike action by police trade unions, and official recognition of the UN International Criminal Court.

The PS was overwhelmingly defeated at municipal elections held in December 2001, at which the party lost control of Lisbon and Porto to the PSD. In response, Guterres resigned as Prime Minister and relinquished the leadership of the PS. The poor electoral results were widely attributed to a decline in the economy, as well as to discontent with public services, which had been adversely affected by reductions in government expenditure. President Sampaio announced that legislative elections would be held in early 2002. Guterres, who remained Prime Minister in an interim capacity pending the elections, was replaced as Secretary-General of the PS in January 2002 by Eduardo Ferro Rodrigues. At the elections, held on 17 March, the PSD, whose campaign had featured reductions in corporate taxation and public expenditure and the privatization of state services, emerged victorious, winning 40.2% of the votes cast and securing 105 seats in the Assembléia da República, although the party did not obtain an overall majority. The PS secured 37.8% of the votes and 96 seats, the PP 8.8% and 14 seats, the PCP-PEV coalition 7.0% and 12 seats, and the BE 2.8% and three seats. The leader of the PSD, José Manuel Durão Barroso, was appointed Prime Minister and formed a centre-right coalition Government with the PP.

Durão Barroso's Government expressed its intention to introduce austerity measures to counter the large public deficit created by the previous left-wing administration in contravention of the country's obligations under the regulations for the EU single currency (see Economic Affairs). In July 2002 a new labour code was proposed that would clarify in a single document 80 previously independent laws. The code was designed to combat low productivity by increasing the ease of recruitment and dismissal of staff and limiting power to the unions; it aroused protests over the possibility of employers being able to prosecute unions responsible for a strike. In November and December two public-sector one-day general strikes, involving up to 500,000 workers, were organized to protest against the introduction of the labour legislation and other recent austerity measures.

In April 2003 the publication of an article in O Independente alleging tax evasion by the Minister of Towns, Territorial Planning and the Environment, Isaltino Morais, led to his immediate resignation, although he denied the accusations. Luís Valente de Oliveira, the Minister of Public Works, Transport and Housing, also resigned, citing health reasons, precipitating the first cabinet reshuffle of the administration. In October the Minister of Foreign Affairs and Portuguese Communities Abroad, António Martins da Cruz, and the Minister of Science and Higher Education, Pedro Lynce de Faría, resigned following allegations that Martins da Cruz's daughter had been inappropriately admitted to university. Martins da Cruz was replaced by Teresa Patricio Gouveia.

In November 2003 many public-sector workers observed a one-day strike to demand higher wages and in protest at government proposals to reform the public sector. Following the extension for a second consecutive year of a freeze on certain public-sector salaries as part of the Government's economic austerity programme, in January 2004 the public-sector unions organized a further one-day strike. In March the Assembléia da República rejected legislation, proposed by the PS and the PEV, aimed at liberalizing abortion laws, currently among the strictest in the EU, although opinion polls suggested popular support for the decriminalization of abortion in February 2004.

In early 2003 a number of establishment figures, including a former ambassador, Jorge Ritto, and a television presenter, Carlos Cruz, were arrested in connection with a paedophilia scandal surrounding the Casa Pía children's home in Lisbon. In May of that year Paolo Pedroso, the deputy leader and parliamentary spokesman of the PS, was also arrested. Throughout his custody he maintained that the allegations against him were part of a PSD plot to discredit him and requested that his parliamentary immunity be lifted to enable him to be questioned. Pedroso was released in October and permitted to resume his former role. However, he was charged in December (with nine other prominent figures) on 23 counts of sexual abuse, although the charges against him were later dropped. The investigation was concluded in May 2004, and seven people, including Cruz and Ritto, went on trial in late November. The trial was ongoing in March 2006.

At elections to the European Parliament, which took place on 13 June 2004, the ruling coalition performed poorly, winning only 33.3% of the votes cast, compared with the 48.9% it had achieved in the 2002 legislative elections. The PS, however, made significant gains, winning 44.5% of the votes cast, compared with 37.8% in the previous legislative elections. Unexpectedly, Durão Barroso was invited in late June 2004 to take over the role of President of the European Commission from Romano Prodi, on the completion of the latter's mandate in October. In order to accept this appointment, Durão Barroso resigned as leader of the PSD, and subsequently as Prime Minister on 5 July. On 1 July the populist Mayor of Lisbon and Secretary-General of the PSD, Pedro Santana Lopes, was elected leader of the PSD.

In early July 2004 President Sampaio held a series of talks with political leaders on whether to hold early legislative elections. In the wake of the PS victory in the European elections, and the disarray caused by Durão Barroso's resignation, the Secretary-General of the PS, Eduardo Ferro Rodrigues, strongly advocated new elections. On 11 July, however, Sampaio invited Santana Lopes to form a new Government, which was inaugurated on 17 July. Only six members of the previous administration remained in the Government. Ferro Rodrigues subsequently resigned his post in the PS, citing the left-wing Sampaio's betrayal of the party's interests. José Sócrates, a moderate and a former Minister of the Environment, was elected Secretary-General of the PS in September. The PS increased its majority in elections to the legislative regional assembly held in the Azores on 17 October, while the PSD retained Madeira in parallel elections held on the same day.

Santana Lopes's Government was beset by problems, including a delay to the start of the school year and claims that it was trying to control the media; in November 2004 directors and a prominent newscaster resigned from the state broadcasting company, Radiotelevisão Portuguesa (RTP), in protest at pressure from the Government, and the state media authority criticized the Government for attempting to limit RTP's freedom.

A series of cabinet reorganizations took place, culminating in the resignation of Henrique Chaves, formerly a close associate of the Prime Minister, as Minister for Youth and Sport. Chaves, who had been moved from the position of Minister in Assistance to the Prime Minister days earlier, cited Santana Lopes's disloyalty. At the end of November President Sampaio informed Santana Lopes of his decision to dissolve parliament and call legislative elections. Prior to the dissolution, the President permitted time for the adoption of the 2005 budget, in order to protect economic stability. However, the expansionary budget, which was approved by the Assembléia da República in early December, proved controversial as it contained tax reductions and increases in the state pension that were likely to cause Portugal to breach the 3% budget deficit limit specified in the EU's Stability and Growth Pact. Sampaio formally dissolved the legislature on 10 December, citing a loss of confidence in the Government, and announced that legislative elections would be held on 20 February 2005.

In December 2004 Santana Lopes was chosen as the PSD's prime-ministerial candidate. It was subsequently announced that the PSD and the PP would not be jointly contesting the elections. The PSD's electoral agenda included pledges not to increase taxes, and to reduce public expenditure. In the elections, which took place as scheduled on 20 February 2005, the PS, which had advocated institutional reform and policies to increase economic growth during the campaign, achieved an overwhelming victory, winning an outright majority for the first time since the restoration of democracy in 1974; voter participation was 64.3%. The PS won 121 of the 230 seats in the Assembléia da República, with 45.0% of the votes cast; the PCP-PEV coalition and the BE also performed well at the expense of the right. The PSD won 75 seats, with 28.8% of the votes cast, while its junior partner in the previous Government, the PP, won 12 seats (7.2%). Santana Lopes and Paulo Portas, the leader of the PP, subsequently resigned their party positions. The new legislature was inaugurated on 10 March. In April 2005 Luís Marques Mendes was elected leader of the PSD, while José Ribeiro e Castro became President of the PP.

José Sócrates was asked by President Sampaio to form a new Government. The new 16-member Council of Ministers was sworn in on 12 March 2005. It included an equal number of members of the PS and independents, most notably, Diogo Freitas do Amaral, the former leader of the right-wing CDS (later restyled as the PP) and an outspoken critic of the US-led invasion of Iraq in 2003, as Minister of Foreign Affairs. Another independent, and former deputy governor of the Banco de Portugal, Luís Campos e Cunha, was allocated the finance portfolio.

On taking office the new Government adopted a policy of strict economic austerity in an effort to reduce the budget deficit, which was forecast to be considerably higher than the EU limit of 3% of GDP. Disagreements arose between Campos e Cunha and Sócrates, however, and the Minister of Finance resigned in July 2005; he was replaced by Fernando Teixeira dos Santos of the PS. Plans to increase value-added tax and reduce government expenditure, notably on social security, led to a series of protests and strikes by public-sector employees. A one-day strike in July, observed by an estimated 500,000 workers, was followed, in September and October, by protests and industrial action staged by employees in various sectors, including health, education and the judiciary. The Government announced a ban on military personnel participating in demonstrations in September, but family of military staff later proceeded with a planned protest. The ruling PS performed poorly in local elections in October, with the PSD retaining control over a majority of municipalities. In November, and again in February 2006, public-sector workers participated in large-scale protests against the reduction in social welfare benefits, a wage freeze and the raising of the retirement age.

In early November 2005 President Sampaio announced that a presidential election would take place on 22 January 2006. Sampaio, who was serving his second term, was not eligible to stand again. Six candidates contested the election, including former President Soares and former Prime Minister Cavaco Silva. The latter was the only candidate representing the centre-right parties, while the centre-left vote was largely split between Soares and Manuel Alegre, also a member of the PS, who was standing as an independent. Cavaco Silva narrowly won the election in a first round of voting, securing 50.5% of the valid votes cast. Alegre won 20.7% of the vote, while Soares took 14.3%. Some 62.6% of the electorate participated in the ballot. Although the result was a setback for Sócrates, who had supported Soares, it was predicted that the relationship between the President and the Prime Minister would be a harmonious one, as both were proponents of economic reform. Cavaco Silva, the first centre-right President since the coup of 1974, took office on 9 March 2006.

The EU Treaty establishing a Constitution for Europe was signed by the EU Heads of State and of Government in October 2004. It required ratification by all 25 EU member states, either through a referendum or by a vote in the national legislature, before it could come into force. In March 2005 the new PS administration announced its intention to hold a referendum on the EU constitutional treaty in October, at the same time as local elections, after seeking the necessary constitutional amendment. However, following the rejection of the treaty in referendums in France and the Netherlands, and the extension by EU leaders of the deadline for ratification until at least mid-2007, in June 2005 the Portuguese Government postponed its own national referendum.

Portugal's leaders were deeply divided over the issue of the proposed US-led military campaign to remove the regime of Saddam Hussain in Iraq in early 2003. Despite domestic popular opposition to a proposed US-led military response and general support for a diplomatic solution to the Iraqi problem, Durão Barroso was a vocal supporter of the US stance on Iraq. In January Barroso announced that his Government had authorized the USA to use an airbase in the Portuguese mid-Atlantic archipelago of the Azores in the event of war. The left-wing President Sampaio was, however, resolutely opposed to any military action in Iraq without a UN mandate and clashed publicly with the Prime Minister over the issue (although under the Constitution foreign policy is the responsibility of the Government, the President is empowered to veto decisions by the Council of Ministers). In early March Durão Barroso affirmed Portuguese support for US-led military action without UN endorsement and subsequently hosted an emergency summit on Iraq between leaders of the USA, the United Kingdom and Spain, at which it was announced that they would launch a military strike with or without UN support. However, following the failure of the coalition to gain support for a second UN Security Council resolution endorsing military action, President Sampaio announced a compromise agreed between himself and Durão Barroso: Portuguese armed forces would not participate in the conflict, although Portugal would render transit facilities to their allies. At the end of March all four left-wing opposition parties, reflecting public discontent with the Government's handling of the crisis, submitted censure motions against the Government for hosting the Azores summit, claiming that Durão Barroso had linked Portugal to a war and had contributed to the weakening of international institutions; the Government defeated the motions owing to its majority in the Assembléia da República. Durão Barroso announced in April that Portugal was prepared to deploy military forces in Iraq for humanitarian and peace-keeping purposes. The opposition subsequently affirmed its support for the deployment only if it took place under the auspices of the UN. In November a contingent of 120 members of the paramilitary National Republican Guard was sent to Iraq. The mission ended in February 2005, following democratic elections in Iraq. In November 2004 Portugal confirmed its participation in one of 13 European Union (see p. 228) battle groups (with Italy, Spain and Greece), which were to be ready for deployment to crisis areas by 2007. In mid-2005 Portuguese troops were deployed in Afghanistan as part of a NATO-led security force; by the end of the year the Portuguese contingent numbered around 200.

In early 1988 Portugal announced that it was to review the terms of the 1983–91 agreement permitting the continued use by the USA of the Portuguese air base at Lajes in the Azores, in return for US economic and military aid. In February 1989 the USA agreed to increase its level of compensation for its use of the base. In June 1995 the two countries signed a five-year accord whereby the USA undertook to supply to Portugal weapons and military equipment worth US $173m. In January 2003 Portugal agreed to US use of the Azores base in the event of war against Iraq, but only if action was ratified by the UN. This was later modified and use was granted without a UN resolution.

Relations with Spain improved in the late 1980s, and in May 1989 King Juan Carlos became the first Spanish monarch to address the Portuguese Assembléia da República. Both Portugal and Spain were admitted to Western European Union (see p. 365) in November 1988. By the mid-1990s the principal bilateral issue had become that of the division of water resources. (However, in November 1998 Portugal and Spain signed an historic accord relating to the sharing of river resources.) In 1997 bilateral relations were severely strained by the Portuguese authorities' decision to release a Basque terrorist suspect, despite the Spanish Government's request for the prisoner's extradition. In June 2002 Spanish border police refused entry to two representatives of the Portuguese legislature attending an anti-globalization conference in Seville. Although the Spanish Government apologized for the incident, in which the representatives claimed they were assaulted by the police, relations between the Governments deteriorated (they had already been strained by the Portuguese refusal to extradite a suspected Basque terrorist and the exclusion of Spanish companies from a motorway-construction project). In the aftermath of the sinking of the oil-tanker *Prestige* in November, off the coast of Galicia, Spain, the Governments disputed responsibility for the disaster after both countries refused to allow the boat to dock. The Spanish administration was additionally accused of irresponsibility in dealing with the wreck and of concealing the possibility of further spills from the sunken tanker; Portuguese authorities claimed their own studies showed leakage, which was subsequently confirmed. In December 2003 the two Governments reached a reciprocal agreement, to last 10 years, defining access to fishing waters.

Negotiations with the People's Republic of China on the question of the Portuguese overseas territory of Macao commenced in June 1986, and in April 1987 Portugal and China signed an agreement whereby Portugal would transfer the administration of Macao to China in December 1999. At midnight on 19 December 1999 the sovereignty of Macao was duly transferred.

The former Portuguese territory of East Timor was unilaterally annexed by Indonesia in 1976. UN-sponsored negotiations between Portugal and Indonesia began in 1983 but proved inconclusive. Under UN auspices, talks between Portugal and Indonesia on the East Timor issue were resumed in December 1992, but again ended without agreement. In January 1995 Portugal and Indonesia agreed to the holding of discussions, under UN auspices, between the factions of East Timor. In early 1996, the UN-sponsored discussions having continued, Portugal offered to re-establish a diplomatic presence in Jakarta in return for the release of the East Timorese resistance leader, Xanana Gusmão, who had been sentenced to life imprisonment in 1993. In August 1998, following President Suharto's replacement in May and the subsequent implementation of a series of Indonesian troop withdrawals from the disputed region, the UN Secretary-General announced that Portugal and Indonesia had agreed to hold discussions on the possibility of autonomy for East Timor. In March 1999 it was announced that Portugal and Indonesia had reached an accord providing for the holding of a referendum in the territory on the question of either autonomy or independence. In late August, following two postponements and despite continuing intimidation and violence, the referendum on the future of East Timor finally proceeded, and resulted in an overwhelming endorsement of proposals for full independence for the territory. The announcement of the result, however, precipitated a rapid decline in the security situation, leading to the declaration of martial law in the territory. In mid-September a multinational peace-keeping force, led by Australia, was deployed in the territory. Following the restoration of order in East Timor and the Indonesian Government's acceptance of the result of the referendum, in December 1999 Portugal and Indonesia resumed full diplomatic relations, which had remained severed since 1975, and in January 2001 a new Indonesian ambassador to Portugal was appointed. Meanwhile, Portugal committed an initial 700 troops to the UN peace-keeping force that was to replace the Australian-led multinational force in early 2000. The Portuguese Government also pledged an annual sum of US $75m. towards the reconstruction of East Timor. Official diplomatic relations with East Timor, now officially known as Timor-Leste, were established with the creation of an embassy in Lisbon in 2002.

Portugal played a significant role in the peace process in Angola, a former Portuguese overseas possession. Several meetings between representatives of the Angolan Government and the rebel group UNITA were held in Lisbon, culminating in the signing of a peace accord in 1991. In June 1993, following the resumption of hostilities in January, UNITA rejected Portugal's status as an observer in the new peace process; however, in May 1994 a UNITA spokesman welcomed the possibility of further Portuguese mediation. A new peace agreement was signed in November of that year. In early 1995, however, the neutrality of the Portuguese Government was undermined by allegations that it had given technical assistance to the Angolan Government. In July 1998, following renewed hostilities in Angola, Portugal requested the intervention of the UN Secretary-General. In August UNITA severed its links with Portugal and the other observers in the peace process, accusing them of bias towards the Angolan Government. In March 2000 tensions between Angola and Portugal increased, following comments by the Angolan Minister of Social Communication, accusing the former Portuguese President, Mario Soares, and his son, João Soares, of benefiting from UNITA's illegal trade in diamonds. The allegations were strongly denied by UNITA. However, in May it was announced that military co-operation between Portugal and the government forces was to be increased. Following the cessation of hostilities in Angola in April 2002, Portugal was one of three states with representatives observing the peace process according to the Lusaka Protocol. Portugal was to continue with military support, including overseeing the integration of UNITA soldiers into a new armed forces and the establishment of a military academy.

Portugal was also active in the quest for peace in Mozambique. Relations with Mozambique, however, deteriorated in March 1989, when a Mozambican diplomat was expelled from Portugal, following his implication in the assassination, in April 1988, of a Mozambican resistance leader. Nevertheless, in January 1992 Portugal received a formal invitation to attend the peace talks as an observer, and in October a peace treaty was signed in Italy.

In July 1996 Portugal hosted the inaugural meeting of the Comunidade dos Países de Língua Portuguesa (CPLP, see p. 395), a grouping of lusophone countries (including Angola, Brazil, Mozambique and Guinea-Bissau), which aimed to promote closer political and economic co-operation. In late 1998, as part of a CPLP initiative, Portugal played a major role in the implementation of a peace agreement in Guinea-Bissau, ending several months of conflict between government and rebel forces in the former colony (q.v.). In the aftermath of a coup in May 1999, the deposed President of Guinea-Bissau, João Vieira, was granted asylum in Portugal. Following the peaceful coup in Guinea-Bissau in September 2003, the Portuguese Government provided US $1.5m. in aid to the new Government.

Government

A new Constitution, envisaging the construction of a socialist society in Portugal, was promulgated in 1976 and revised in 1982. Subsequent revisions included the provision in 1997 for the holding of referendums on issues of national interest. The organs of sovereignty are the President, the Assembléia da República and the Government. The President, elected by popular vote for a five-year term, appoints the Prime Minister and, on the latter's proposal, other members of the Government, principally the Council of Ministers. The Council of State (Conselho de Estado) is a consultative body. Following the election of October 1995, the unicameral Assembléia had 230 members, including four representing Portuguese abroad, elected by universal adult suffrage for four years (subject to dissolution). The mainland comprises 18 administrative districts. The Azores and Madeira (integral parts of the Portuguese Republic) were granted autonomy in 1976. The overseas territory of Macao was governed by special statute until December 1999, when it reverted to Chinese sovereignty.

Defence

Compulsory military service was abolished in 2004. Portugal is a member of the North Atlantic Treaty Organization (NATO, see p. 314) and of Western European Union (see p. 365). In August 2005 the total strength of the armed forces was 44,900 (including 9,100 conscripts), comprising: army 26,700, navy 10,950 (including 1,890 marines) and air force 7,250. There were reserves of 210,930. The paramilitary National Republican Guard and the Public Security Police totalled 26,100 and 21,600, respectively. In August 2005 a total of 1,008 US troops were stationed in Portugal, mainly at the air force base at Lajes in the Azores. In November 2004 Portugal confirmed its participation in one of 13 European Union (see p. 228) battle groups (with Italy, Spain and Greece), which were to be ready for deployment to crisis areas by 2007. The 2005 state budget allocated €1,920m. to defence.

Economic Affairs

In 2004, according to estimates by the World Bank, Portugal's overall gross national income (GNI), measured at average 2002–04 prices, was US $149,790m., equivalent to $14,350 per head (or

$19,250 on an international purchasing-power parity basis). During 1995–2004, it was estimated, the population increased at an average rate of 0.4% per year, while gross domestic product (GDP) per head increased, in real terms, by an average of 1.9% per year. Overall GDP expanded, in real terms, at an average annual rate of 2.3% in 1995–2005; GDP increased by 1.1% in 2004 and by 0.3% in 2005.

Agriculture (including forestry and fishing) contributed 2.8% of GDP in 2005, and the sector engaged 12.1% of the employed labour force in 2004, according to estimates. The principal crops are wheat, maize, potatoes, olives, tomatoes, oranges, grapes and sugar beets. The production of wine, particularly port, is significant. The European Union (EU, see p. 228) imposed a ban on Portuguese beef exports in late 1998 as a result of the detection of bovine spongiform encephalopathy (BSE) in Portuguese cattle. Although the United Kingdom had many more individual cases, Portugal had the highest incidence rate of the disease in the EU in 2003, with 157 BSE cases per million head of cattle, compared with 154 in the United Kingdom. However, EU member states, with the exception of France, agreed to lift the ban on Portuguese beef exports in September 2004. Farm income was expected to decline by some 35% in 2005 as a result of a particularly severe drought (reported to be the worst since 1945) and forest fires, which had become an increasing problem in recent years. It was estimated that over 325,000 ha of forest had been affected by fires in 2005. The fishing industry is important, the sardine catch, at 66,600 metric tons in 2003, being by far the largest. Agricultural GDP decreased, in real terms, by an estimated average of 1.9% per year during 1995–2005, agricultural GDP increased by 0.8% in 2004, but declined by 8.5% in 2005.

Industry (comprising mining, manufacturing, construction and power) contributed 24.6% of GDP in 2005, and engaged 31.2% of the employed labour force in 2004, according to estimates. The GDP of the industrial sector increased, in real terms, by an estimated 1.7% per year during 1995–2005; industrial GDP increased by 0.3% in 2004, but declined by 1.8% in 2005. The mining and quarrying industry makes a minimal contribution to GDP, employing, together with electricity, gas and water, an estimated 0.9% of the employed labour force in 2004. Limestone, granite, marble, copper pyrites, gold and uranium are the most significant products.

Manufacturing provided 15.8% of GDP in 2005, and engaged 19.6% of the employed labour force in 2004, according to estimates. Manufacturing GDP grew by an estimated annual average of 1.8% in 1995–2005; manufacturing GDP declined by 1.6% in 2005. The textile industry is the most important branch of manufacturing, accounting for 21.3% of total export earnings in 2003. Other significant manufactured products include cork items, chemicals, electrical appliances, ceramics and paper pulp.

In 2002 33.3% of electricity production was derived from coal, 25.0% from petroleum, 19.8% from natural gas and 17.1% from hydroelectric power. Total electricity production was 41,346m. kWh in 2004. In 2004 imports of fuel and oil accounted for 10.8% of total import costs. Portugal's heavy dependence on petroleum was reduced in 1997 when a pipeline carrying natural gas from Algeria (via Morocco and Spain) was inaugurated. In 2005 plans were announced for the construction of solar and wind power plants.

Services provided 72.6% of GDP in 2005, and engaged 56.8% of the employed labour force in 2004, according to estimates. The tourism industry remained a significant source of foreign exchange earnings in 2004, when receipts totalled an estimated €6,260.6m. In 2003 there were 11.7m. tourist arrivals in Portugal. Emigrants' remittances are also important to the Portuguese economy, reaching €1,277m. in 2005. The GDP of the services sector increased, in real terms, by an estimated average of 2.6% per year during 1995–2005; services GDP rose by 1.5% in 2004 and by 0.9% in 2005.

In 2004 Portugal recorded a visible trade deficit of US $18,666m., and there was a deficit of $13,158m. on the current account of the balance of payments. Most of Portugal's trade is with other members of the EU. In 2004 Spain, Germany and France supplied 30.0%, 14.2% and 9.3%, respectively, of total imports. The principal export markets were also Spain (which purchased 25.5% of the total), France (13.8%) and Germany (13.4%). The main exports in 2003 were textiles, clothing and footwear (21.3%), machinery (19.7%), transport equipment (15.3%) and mineral products and base metals (9.9%). The principal imports were machinery, transport equipment, food and agricultural products, mineral fuels, and mineral products and base metals.

The budget deficit for 2005 was estimated at €8,866.7m., equivalent to 6.0% of GDP, compared with 3.2% in 2004 and 2.9% in 2003. In 2005 Portugal's general government debt was estimated at €94,070.9m., equivalent to 63.9% of GDP. In 1995–2004 the annual rate of inflation averaged 3.0%. The average rate of inflation was 2.3% in 2004 and 2005. The unemployment rate reached 8.0% in the final quarter of 2005.

Portugal became a member of the European Community (EC—now EU) in January 1986. The Maastricht Treaty on European Union was ratified by the Portuguese legislature in December 1992. In April 1992 Portugal joined the Exchange Rate Mechanism of the European Monetary System (see p. 265). Portugal is also a member of the Organisation for Economic Co-operation and Development (OECD, see p. 320) and of the Comunidade dos Países de Língua Portuguesa (CPLP, see p. 395), which was established in Lisbon in 1996.

From 1997 developments in the economy were strongly influenced by Portugal's participation in the single European currency, the euro, under Economic and Monetary Union (EMU, see p. 265). Portugal adopted the euro at its inception in January 1999 as a single currency unit for transactions throughout the euro zone and as an internationally traded currency, and as legal tender in cash from 1 January 2002. Preparations for entry included a reduction in interest rates in order to achieve European integration, which had a strong positive effect on the growth of domestic demand. Since its entry into the EU in 1986, Portugal has been a net recipient of large-scale financial transfers from the EU. (However, EU funds to Portugal, which accounted for almost 3% of GDP in 2003, were to be reduced from 2006, following the enlargement of the EU from 15 to 25 members in May 2004.) Furthermore, a period of strong growth, full employment, low inflation and inexpensive credit ended in 2000, as a result of rising interest rates and an increase in inflation owing to high international petroleum prices. Economic growth slowed considerably in the early 2000s, and as a consequence, government revenue from taxes declined substantially. The budget deficit in 2001 was 4.1% of GDP, exceeding the 3% stipulated in the EU's Stability and Growth Pact (SGP) and thus contravening the regulations for the single currency. The new administration responded with the announcement in May 2002 of severe austerity measures. The deficit was reduced to 2.9% in 2002, but Portugal became the first country in the euro zone to enter into recession, with a 1.3% decline in GDP in the last quarter of 2002 relative to the same period in 2001. The recession continued through 2003, when GDP declined by 1.1%, but there was a modest recovery in 2004, when growth of 1.1% was achieved. However, growth slowed to only 0.3% in 2005. The Government narrowly succeeded in maintaining the budget deficit below 3% of GDP in 2003, at 2.9%, but a deficit of 3.2% was recorded in 2004. Following the election of the new socialist Government in February 2005, a four-year economic programme, which included the promotion of private investment in infrastructure and the reversal of the previous administration's policy of tax cuts, was introduced. In July the Government announced plans for a four-year programme of infrastructural development, including improving transport links and investing in wind energy. In September EU leaders agreed to allow the Government until 2008 to reduce the budget deficit to less than 3% of GDP. The size of the deficit (which reached 6.0% in 2005) provoked criticism from the European Commission, which reported that it was not the result of exceptional events outwith the Government's control (and therefore did not meet the SGP's criteria for leniency). The budget for 2006 anticipated a budget deficit of 4.8% of GDP, growth of 1.1% and an inflation rate of 2.3%. Notably, exports were expected to rise by 5.7%. In an effort to reduce the fiscal deficit, the budget envisaged the privatization of state-owned companies, particularly in the energy sector, an increase in income tax and a reduction in expenditure of almost €2,000m. Demonstrations against the Government's austerity measures, which particularly affected public-sector workers and included a salary freeze, a reduction in benefits and the raising of the retirement age, took place in late 2005 and early 2006. In early 2006 the Banco de Portugal forecast that growth in that year would be 0.8%.

Education

Formal education at all levels is provided at both public and private institutions. Pre-school education, for three- to six-year olds, is not compulsory, and is available free of charge. Basic education is compulsory for nine years, between the ages of six and 15, and is provided free of charge in public schools. It is divided into three cycles: the first lasts for four years, the second

PORTUGAL

for two years and the third for three years. Secondary education, which is not compulsory, lasts for three years, and comprises a single three-year cycle, with two types: general and vocational. In 2002/03 100% of children in the relevant age-group were enrolled in primary schools (males 100%; females 99%), while 85% of children in the relevant age-group were enrolled in secondary schools (males 81%; females 89%).

Higher education comprises two systems—education provided in universities, which award the following academic degrees: the *licenciatura*, after four to six years of study, the *mestrado*, after one or two years of study and research work, and the *doutoramento* (doctorate); the second system is provided in regional polytechnic institutes, grouping technical, management, educational and fine arts schools, which offer three-year courses leading to the *bacharel*, and specialized studies leading to a diploma after one to two years. New curricula were introduced in 2003/04 and 2004/05. Expenditure on education in 2002 was €5,548.2m.

Public Holidays

2006: 1 January (New Year's Day), 28 February (Carnival Day), 13 April (Maundy Thursday*), 14 April (Good Friday), 25 April (Liberty Day), 1 May (Labour Day), 10 June (Portugal Day), 13 June (St Anthony—Lisbon only), 15 June (Corpus Christi), 24 June (St John the Baptist—Porto only), 15 August (Assumption), 5 October (Proclamation of the Republic), 1 November (All Saints' Day), 1 December (Restoration of Independence), 8 December (Immaculate Conception), 24 December (Christmas Eve), 25 December (Christmas Day).

2007: 1 January (New Year's Day), 20 February (Carnival Day), 5 April (Maundy Thursday*), 6 April (Good Friday), 25 April (Liberty Day), 1 May (Labour Day), 7 June (Corpus Christi), 10 June (Portugal Day), 13 June (St Anthony—Lisbon only), 24 June (St John the Baptist—Porto only), 15 August (Assumption), 5 October (Proclamation of the Republic), 1 November (All Saints' Day), 1 December (Restoration of Independence), 8 December (Immaculate Conception), 24 December (Christmas Eve), 25 December (Christmas Day).

* Afternoon only.

Weights and Measures

The metric system is in force.

Statistical Survey

Source (unless otherwise stated): Instituto Nacional de Estatística (INE), Av. António José de Almeida 2, 1000-043 Lisbon; tel. (21) 8426100; fax (21) 8426380; e-mail ine@ine.pt; internet www.ine.pt.

Area and Population

AREA, POPULATION AND DENSITY

Area (sq km)	
Land	91,906
Inland water	439
Total	92,345*
Population (census results)	
15 April 1991	9,862,540
1 March 2001	
Males	5,000,141
Females	5,355,976
Total	10,356,117
Population (official estimates at 31 December)	
2002	10,368,400
2003	10,474,700
2004	10,529,255
Density (per sq km) at 31 December 2004	114.6

* 35,655 sq miles.

REGIONS
(2001 census)

	Area (sq km)*	Population	Density (per sq km)
Continental Portugal	88,796	9,869,343	111.1
Norte	21,278	3,687,293	173.3
Centro	23,668	2,348,397	99.2
Lisboa e Vale do Tejo	11,931	2,661,850	223.1
Alentejo	26,931	776,585	28.8
Algarve	4,988	395,218	79.2
Autonomous Region: Açores (Azores)	2,330	241,763	103.8
Autonomous Region: Madeira	779	245,011	314.5
Total	91,905	10,356,117	112.7

* Excluding river estuaries (439 sq km).

PRINCIPAL TOWNS
(population at 2001 census)

Lisboa (Lisbon, the capital)	564,657		Vila Nova de Gaia	69,698
Porto (Oporto)	263,131		Guimarães	63,058
Amadora	151,486		Alguierão-Mem Martins	62,557
Braga	112,039		Parede	61,821
Coimbra	104,489		Odivelas	53,449
Funchal	103,961		Amora	50,991
Setúbal	96,776		Leiria	50,167
Aqualva-Cacém	81,845			

Source: Thomas Brinkhoff, *City Population* (internet www.citypopulation.de).

BIRTHS, MARRIAGES AND DEATHS

	Registered live births Number	Rate (per 1,000)	Registered marriages Number	Rate (per 1,000)	Registered deaths Number	Rate (per 1,000)
1997	113,047	11.4	65,770	6.6	105,157	10.5
1998	116,038	11.6	68,710	6.9	108,268	10.8
1999	116,002	11.6	68,710	6.9	108,268	10.8
2000	120,008	12.0	63,752	6.4	105,813	10.6
2001	112,774	11.0	58,390	5.7	105,092	10.2
2002	114,456	11.0	56,457	5.5	106,690	10.3
2003	112,589	n.a.	53,735	n.a.	109,148	n.a.
2004	109,356	10.4	49,178	n.a.	102,371	9.7

Expectation of life (WHO estimates, years at birth): 77 (males 74; females 81) in 2003. (Source: WHO, *World Health Report*).

PORTUGAL

ECONOMICALLY ACTIVE POPULATION
(estimates, ISIC major divisions, '000 persons aged 15 years and over)

	2002	2003	2004
Agriculture, hunting, forestry and fishing	636.9	642.1	618.1
Mining and quarrying	17.4	14.3	} 45.8
Electricity, gas and water supply	39.8	36.1	
Manufacturing	1,052.0	1,018.8	1,002.2
Construction	618.4	583.6	548.0
Wholesale and retail trade; repair of motor vehicles, motorcycles and personal and household goods	774.3	774.7	782.0
Hotels and restaurants	267.5	259.5	265.4
Transport, storage and communications	204.7	213.7	214.5
Financial intermediation	84.1	87.0	96.6
Real estate, renting and business activities	242.7	262.1	292.2
Public administration and defence; compulsory social security	332.7	329.4	331.7
Education	291.4	286.6	306.6
Health and social work	255.7	294.1	313.0
Other community, social and personal service activities*	162.6	156.0	} 306.7
Private households with employed persons	155.7	158.1	
Unallocated	1.3	1.9	
Total employed*	**5,137.3**	**5,118.0**	**5,122.8**
Unemployed	270.5	342.3	365.0
Total labour force	**5,407.8**	**5,460.3**	**5,487.8**

* Including regular members of the armed forces, but excluding persons on compulsory military service.

Source: partly ILO.

Health and Welfare

KEY INDICATORS

Total fertility rate (children per woman, 2003)	1.4
Under-5 mortality rate (per 1,000 live births, 2004)	5
HIV/AIDS (% of persons aged 15–49, 2003)	0.4
Physicians (per 1,000 head, 2001)	3.2
Hospital beds (per 1,000 head, 1998)	4.0
Health expenditure (2002): US $ per head (PPP)	1,702
Health expenditure (2002): % of GDP	9.3
Health expenditure (2002): public (% of total)	70.5
Human Development Index (2003): ranking	27
Human Development Index (2003): value	0.904

For sources and definitions, see explanatory note on p. vi.

Agriculture

PRINCIPAL CROPS
('000 metric tons)

	2002	2003	2004
Wheat	413	150	293
Rice (paddy)	146	148	149
Barley	20	13	26
Maize	797	798	789
Rye	34	27	27
Oats	61	39	61
Triticale (wheat-rye hybrid)	25	11	17
Potatoes*	1,300	1,200	1,250
Sweet potatoes*	22	22	22
Sugar beets	644	484	627
Olives*	240	260	270
Sunflower seeds	21	18	14
Other oilseeds*	20	24	24
Cabbages	209	212	140*
Lettuce*	95	95	95
Tomatoes	867	894	1,201
Cauliflower*	35	35	35

Statistical Survey

—continued	2002	2003	2004
Onions (dry)*	110	110	110
Broad beans (green)*	30	30	30
Beans (green)	16	14	15*
Carrots*	150	150	150
Carobs*	20	20	20
Chestnuts	31	33	31
Other fresh vegetables*	580	580	580
Bananas*	30	30	30
Oranges	277	277	250
Tangerines, mandarins, clementines and satsumas	56	60	60
Apples	300	286	277
Pears	125	90	188
Peaches and nectarines	60	57	52
Grapes	1,039	890	1,000*
Cantaloupes and other melons*	20	20	20

* FAO estimate(s).

Source: FAO.

LIVESTOCK
('000 head, year ending September)

	2002	2003	2004
Horses*	17	17	17
Mules*	45	40	40
Asses*	130	125	125
Cattle	1,404	1,395	1,389
Pigs	2,389	2,344	2,249
Sheep	5,478	5,500*	5,500*
Goats	561	538	502
Chickens*	35,000	35,000	35,000
Turkeys*	7,000	6,000	7,000

* FAO estimates.

Source: FAO.

LIVESTOCK PRODUCTS
('000 metric tons)

	2002	2003	2004
Beef and veal	106	105	118
Mutton and lamb	24	22	22
Pig meat	330	329	315
Poultry meat	251	217	236
Cows' milk	2,040	1,893	1,950
Sheep's milk	97	98	99
Goats' milk	29	29	29
Cheese	76	75	75
Butter	27	26	26
Hen eggs	125	126	132
Cattle hides*	11	11	12

* FAO estimates.

Source: FAO.

Forestry

ROUNDWOOD REMOVALS
('000 cubic metres, excluding bark)

	2002	2003	2004
Sawlogs, veneer logs and logs for sleepers	2,294	2,553	1,890
Pulpwood	5,668	6,340	8,883
Other industrial wood*	180	180	180
Fuel wood*	600	600	600
Total	**8,742**	**9,673**	**11,553**

* FAO estimates.

Source: FAO.

PORTUGAL

SAWNWOOD PRODUCTION
('000 cubic metres, including railway sleepers)

	2002	2003	2004
Coniferous (softwood)	859	910	726
Broadleaved (hardwood)	439	473	374
Total	1,298	1,383	1,100

Source: FAO.

Fishing

('000 metric tons, live weight)

	2001	2002	2003
Capture	193.3	202.8	212.9
Atlantic horse mackerel	15.3	20.7	18.7
European pilchard (sardine)	71.9	68.8	66.6
Black scabbardfish	6.7	6.6	6.5
Atlantic redfishes	8.3	9.7	11.8
Chub mackerel	4.9	5.8	8.9
Octopuses	8.2	8.4	10.2
Aquaculture	8.2	8.3	7.8
Total catch	201.5	211.1	220.8

Note: Figures exclude aquatic plants ('000 metric tons): 1.2 in 2001; n.a. in 2002; 0.4 in 2003.
Source: FAO.

Mining

('000 metric tons, unless otherwise indicated)

	2001	2002	2003*
Iron ore: gross weight	14.5	14.0	14.0
Iron ore: metal content	11.0	10.0	10.0
Copper ore†	83.0	77.2‡	77.9‡
Tin ore (metric tons)†	1,174	574‡	345‡
Tungsten ore (metric tons)†	698	693‡	715‡
Silver ore (metric tons)†	23.1	19.5	21.1‡
Uranium ore (metric tons)†	5.0	2.0	0.0
Marble	835	802	800
Granite (crushed and ornamental)	30,155	29,545	30,900
Kaolin	146.4	148.7‡	150.0
Salt (rock)	625.8	604.0‡	602.0‡
Gypsum and anhydrite	787.6	579.1	580.0
Talc (metric tons)	8,362	8,916‡	5,459‡

* Estimated production.
† Figures refer to the metal content of ores.
‡ Reported figures.

Source: US Geological Survey.

Industry

SELECTED PRODUCTS
('000 metric tons, unless otherwise indicated)

	2000	2001	2002
Frozen fish	34.9	37.8	43.1
Tinned fish	38.7	43.9	44.7
Wheat flour	583	678	686
Refined sugar	344	412	317
Prepared animal feeds	3,781	3,936	3,909
Distilled alcoholic beverages ('000 hectolitres)	300	247	288
Wine ('000 hectolitres)	4,915	5,310	5,397
Beer ('000 hectolitres)	7,090	6,830	7,125
Cigarettes (million units)	21,377	23,479	25,261
Wool yarn (pure and mixed)	5.6	5.7	5.3
Cotton yarn (pure and mixed)	119.4	106.5	95.9
Woven cotton fabrics (million sq metres)	394	398	350

—continued	2000	2001	2002
Woven woollen fabrics (million sq metres)	11.5	11.7	8.9
Knitted fabrics	87.6	88.4	68.1
Footwear, excl. rubber ('000 pairs)	75,716	76,815	73,003
Wood pulp (sulphate and soda)	1,681	1,710	1,826
Caustic soda (Sodium hydroxide)	94	97	91
Soda ash (Sodium carbonate)*	150	150	150
Nitrogenous fertilizers	117	n.a.	n.a.
Jet fuels	798	618	n.a.
Motor spirit (petrol)	2,296	2,615	n.a.
Naphthas	996	986	n.a.
Distillate fuel oils	3,794	4,533	n.a.
Residual fuel oils	3,000	2,703	n.a.
Liquefied petroleum gas	277	371	n.a.
Coke	371	67	n.a.
Gas from cokeries (terajoules)	2,930	548	n.a.
Household ware of porcelain or china (metric tons)	23,010	23,203	29,223
Household ware of other ceramic materials (metric tons)	110,731	111,046	113,431
Clay building bricks	5	5	4
Cement	10,343	10,162	9,761
Pig-iron*	382	82	100
Crude steel (ingots)*	1,097	728	800
Refrigerators for household use ('000)	308	257	281
Radio receivers ('000)	6,848	8,627	8,559
Electric energy (million kWh)	42,736	41,765	n.a.
Gas from gasworks (terajoules)	2,073	219	n.a.

* Figure(s) from the US Geological Survey.

Source: UN, *Industrial Commodity Statistics Yearbook*.

2003 ('000 metric tons, unless otherwise indicated): Wheat flour 692; Refined sugar 370; Animal feeds 3,990; Beer ('000 hectolitres) 7,125; Soft drinks ('000 hectolitres) 6,133; Cigarettes (million units) 25,294; Gasoline 2,625; Cement 8,486; Concrete 23,638.

2004 ('000 metric tons, unless otherwise indicated): Wheat flour 677; Refined sugar 402; Animal feeds 4,411; Cigarettes (million units) 25,912; Gasoline 2,625; Cement 8,769; Concrete 23,739.

Finance

CURRENCY AND EXCHANGE RATES

Monetary Units
100 cent = 1 euro (€).

Sterling and Dollar Equivalents (30 December 2005)
£1 sterling = 1.4596 euros;
US $1 = 0.8477 euros;
€100 = £68.51 = $117.97.

Average Exchange Rate (euros per US dollar)
2003   0.8860
2004   0.8054
2005   0.8041

Note: The national currency was formerly the Portuguese escudo. From the introduction of the euro, with Portuguese participation, on 1 January 1999, a fixed exchange rate of €1 = 200.482 escudos was in operation. Euro notes and coins were introduced on 1 January 2002. The euro and local currency circulated alongside each other until 28 February, after which the euro became the sole legal tender.

BUDGET
(€ million)*

Revenue	2002	2003†	2004‡
Current revenue	53,473	54,328	55,829
Direct taxes	12,575	11,989	11,700
Indirect taxes	19,387	20,575	15,856
Social contributions	15,856	16,564	17,278
Sale of goods and services	3,154	3,188	6,208
Other current revenue	2,502	2,010	
Capital revenue	2,535	4,366	3,807
Total	56,008	58,694	59,636

PORTUGAL

Statistical Survey

Expenditure	2002	2003†	2004‡
Current expenditure	53,549	55,402	57,192
Wages and salaries	19,951	19,442	19,557
Social transfers	19,214	22,114	22,533
Intermediate consumption	5,512	4,912	5,551
Interest payments	3,869	3,795	3,990
Subsidies	1,776	1,926	2,395
Other current expenditure	3,227	3,214	3,166
Capital expenditure	5,929	6,993	6,319
Gross capital formation	4,398	5,103	4,089
Other	1,531	1,890	2,230
Total	**59,478**	**62,395**	**63,511**

* Figures refer to the consolidated accounts of the central Government, excluding assets and liabilities.
† Estimates.
‡ Preliminary figures.

Source: Direcção-Geral do Orçamento, Ministério das Finanças.

INTERNATIONAL RESERVES
(US $ million at 31 December)*

	2003	2004	2005
Gold†	6,938	6,510	6,885
IMF special drawing rights	91	103	103
Reserve position in IMF	536	440	202
Foreign exchange	5,249	4,631	3,173
Total	**12,814**	**11,684**	**10,364**

* Reserves are defined in accordance with the Eurosystem's statistical definition.
† Valued at $417.2 per troy ounce in 2003, $438.1 per ounce in 2004 and $513.0 in 2005.

Source: IMF, *International Financial Statistics*.

MONEY SUPPLY
(€ million at 31 December)

	2003	2004	2005
Currency in circulation*	9,870	1,180	1,327
Demand deposits at banking institutions	49,000	49,740	55,980

* Currency put into circulation by the Banco de Portugal was €5,710m. in 2003, €5,420m. in 2004 and €5,450m. in 2005.

Source: IMF, *International Financial Statistics*.

COST OF LIVING
(Consumer Price Index; base: 2002 = 100)

	2000	2001	2003
Food and non-alcoholic beverages	92.5	98.5	102.6
Alcoholic beverages and tobacco	92.4	95.4	104.6
Clothing and footwear	96.2	97.6	101.4
Housing, utilities, etc.	93.5	97.2	104.0
Furnishings, household equipment and routine maintenance	94.0	97.0	102.6
Health	92.1	95.4	101.9
Transport	90.8	95.2	104.3
Communications	101.5	93.3	98.7
Recreation and culture	97.5	97.8	101.7
Education	89.8	94.5	105.7
Hotels, cafés and restaurants	90.7	94.6	105.7
Other goods and services	89.6	94.5	104.0
All items	**92.5**	**96.5**	**103.3**

All items (base: 2002 = 100): 105.7 in 2004; 108.1 in 2005.

NATIONAL ACCOUNTS
(preliminary figures, € million at current prices)

Composition of the Gross National Product

	2003	2004	2005
Gross domestic product at market prices	137,522.8	142,843.2	147,249.0
Primary incomes received from abroad	6,527.5	7,379.8	7,298.7
Less Primary incomes paid abroad	8,140.3	9,132.3	9,751.2
Gross national income (GNI)	135,910.0	141,090.7	144,796.5
Less Consumption of fixed capital	22,683.2	23,628.5	24,497.9
Net national income	113,226.8	117,462.2	120,298.6
Current transfers from abroad	4,318.0	4,673.9	4,605.4
Less Current transfers paid abroad	2,268.0	2,691.1	3,058.4
Net national disposable income	115,276.8	119,445.0	121,845.6

Expenditure on the Gross Domestic Product

	2003	2004	2005
Final consumption expenditure	115,481.8	121,465.8	127,455.7
Households	85,173.5	89,433.2	93,544.7
Non-profit institutions serving households	2,680.0	2,832.0	2,999.0
General government	27,628.3	29,200.6	30,912.0
Gross capital formation	30,951.2	31,932.8	31,765.7
Changes in stocks	412.0	834.3	1,050.8
Total domestic expenditure	146,845.0	154,232.9	160,272.2
Exports of goods and services	38,563.6	40,786.7	42,060.3
Less Imports of goods and services	47,885.8	52,176.4	55,083.5
GDP in market prices	137,522.8	142,843.2	147,249.0
GDP at constant 2000 prices	124,279.2	125,623.6	126,045.5

Gross Domestic Product by Economic Activity

	2003	2004	2005
Agriculture, hunting, forestry and fishing	4,058.1	4,053.7	3,622.5
Electricity, gas and water	3,029.2	3,170.7	3,177.4
Industry	19,336.4	19,848.3	20,120.8
Construction	7,996.1	8,091.8	7,996.4
Trade, restaurants and hotels	20,877.8	21,771.6	22,716.6
Transport, storage and communications	8,341.9	8,716.6	8,725.7
Finance, insurance and real estate	16,940.6	17,533.1	18,083.9
Other services	38,848.5	40,894.2	42,830.9
Gross value added in basic prices	119,428.6	124,080.1	127,274.2
Taxes on products (net)	18,094.1	18,752.2	20,467.1
Statistical discrepancy	0.1	10.9	−492.3
GDP in market prices	137,522.8	142,843.2	147,249.0

BALANCE OF PAYMENTS
(US $ million)

	2002	2003	2004
Exports of goods f.o.b.	26,087	32,055	37,108
Imports of goods f.o.b.	−39,276	−46,233	−55,774
Trade balance	**−13,189**	**−14,178**	**−18,666**
Exports of services	10,357	12,318	14,791
Imports of services	−7,146	−8,294	−9,637
Balance on goods and services	**−9,979**	**−10,153**	**−13,512**
Other income received	4,901	6,243	6,608
Other income paid	−7,322	−7,995	−9,703
Balance on goods, services and income	**−12,400**	**−11,906**	**−16,607**
Current transfers received	5,445	6,443	7,161
Current transfers paid	−2,641	−3,191	−3,711
Current balance	**−9,596**	**−8,654**	**−13,158**
Capital account (net)	1,906	3,010	2,805

PORTUGAL

—continued	2002	2003	2004
Direct investment abroad	−76	−6,508	−6,121
Direct investment from abroad	1,713	6,610	825
Portfolio investment assets	−7,034	−21,246	−11,466
Portfolio investment liabilities	10,249	15,795	13,246
Financial derivatives assets	3,796	4,590	3,998
Financial derivatives liabilities	−3,802	−4,518	−4,069
Other investment assets	−6,152	−9,170	−596
Other investment liabilities	9,032	14,018	14,095
Net errors and omissions	982	−381	−1,421
Overall balance	1,017	−6,455	−1,863

Source: IMF, *International Financial Statistics*.

External Trade

PRINCIPAL COMMODITIES
(€ million)

Imports c.i.f.	2001	2002	2003
Food and agricultural products	5,389.6	5,341.9	5,334.2
Mineral fuels	4,303.0	4,809.4	4,222.4
Mineral products and base metals	4,027.5	4,041.1	3,936.7
Chemicals	3,568.8	3,813.5	3,887.0
Wood, cork, cellulose pulp, and paper	1,876.4	1,831.9	1,769.5
Leather, leather manufactures and textiles	2,900.5	2,645.1	1,607.7
Clothing and footwear	1,444.6	1,530.4	1,524.4
Machinery	9,675.2	8,917.7	8,817.4
Transport equipment	6,538.6	5,779.0	5,476.6
Total (incl. others)	44,093.9	42,466.3	41,753.7

Exports f.o.b.	2001	2002	2003
Food and agricultural products	1,878.5	2,058.4	2,100.5
Mineral fuels	505.3	538.2	684.9
Mineral products and base metals	2,505.8	2,634.7	2,772.1
Cork and wood and straw manufactures (excl. furniture)	2,602.9	2,446.5	2,698.1
Textiles, leather and leather manufactures	2,133.1	2,112.4	1,704.4
Clothing and footwear	4,746.4	4,513.9	4,292.2
Chemical products	2,002.6	2,206.3	2,453.0
Machinery	5,217.9	5,402.7	5,544.3
Transport equipment	4,224.3	4,102.4	4,301.9
Total (incl. others)	26,918.3	27,398.3	28,092.3

2004 (€ million): *Imports:* Food and beverages 4,975.9; Fuel and oil 4,956.0; Transport equipment 7,454.0; Total (incl. others) 45,861.5. *Exports:* Food and beverages 2,121.4; Fuel and oil 745.9; Transport equipment 6,327.9; Total (incl. others) 29,576.4.

PRINCIPAL TRADING PARTNERS
(€ million)

Imports c.i.f.	2002	2003	2004
Belgium	1,297.9	1,211.0	1,324.1
France	4,348.1	4,085.8	4,278.9
Germany	6,352.6	6,106.0	6,504.9
Italy	2,857.3	2,675.7	2,761.2
The Netherlands	1,938.9	1,957.3	2,116.7
Spain	12,264.9	12,544.6	13,749.9
United Kingdom	2,207.1	2,041.0	2,109.0
USA	883.5	789.9	1,058.1
Total (incl. others)	42,466.3	41,753.7	45,861.5

Exports f.o.b.	2002	2003	2004
Belgium	1,180.4	1,244.3	1,242.0
France	3,706.2	3,702.5	4,083.7
Germany	4,843.7	4,152.2	3,954.5
Italy	1,248.6	1,334.3	1,280.9
The Netherlands	1,053.0	1,057.3	1,194.6
Spain	5,738.0	6,687.3	7,541.0
United Kingdom	2,845.7	2,887.6	2,803.2
USA	1,570.6	1,599.9	1,746.5
Total (incl. others)	27,398.3	28,092.3	29,576.4

Transport

RAILWAYS
(traffic)

	2002	2003	2004
Passenger journeys (million)	161	151	153
Passenger-kilometres (million)	3,926	3,585	3,693
Freight ('000 metric tons)	10,739	8,718	11,151
Freight ton-kilometres (million)	2,583	2,073	2,589

ROAD TRAFFIC
(motor vehicles registered at 31 December)

	2001	2002	2003
Light and heavy vehicles	7,361,572	7,690,019	7,910,572
Motorcycles	371,114	390,209	402,759
Tractors	309,775	322,283	329,761
Trailers and semi-trailers	363,722	376,719	377,552

SHIPPING

Merchant Fleet
(registered at 31 December)

	2002	2003	2004
Number of vessels	449	452	456
Total displacement (grt)	1,099,683	1,156,334	1,336,480

Source: Lloyd's Register-Fairplay, *World Fleet Statistics*.

International Sea-borne Freight Traffic
(Figures exclude the Azores)

	2002	2003	2004
Vessels entered ('000 gross registered tons)	119,009	121,240	118,449
Goods loaded ('000 metric tons)	12,841	14,676	16,000
Goods unloaded ('000 metric tons)	42,758	42,807	43,624

Passengers (2004): Embarked 324,954; Disembarked 324,606.

CIVIL AVIATION
(million)

	2001	2002	2003
Passenger-kilometres	12,857	14,244	16,421
Freight ton-kilometres	218	206	217
Mail ton-kilometres	20	20	21

2004: 18,591m. passenger-kilometres.

PORTUGAL

Tourism

FOREIGN TOURIST ARRIVALS BY COUNTRY OF RESIDENCE

Country of origin	2001	2002	2003
Belgium	270,998	262,253	271,078
France	875,855	844,905	843,762
Germany	908,625	851,596	843,339
Italy	297,279	367,185	333,809
The Netherlands	494,603	482,613	479,271
Spain	5,668,903	5,396,310	5,431,288
United Kingdom	1,976,870	1,858,177	1,873,999
USA	274,412	246,199	252,581
Total (incl. others)	12,167,200	11,644,231	11,707,228

Source: Direcção-Geral do Turismo.

Receipts from tourism (€ million): 5,812.2 in 2003; 6,260.6 in 2004 (provisional figure). (Source: Banco de Portugal).

Communications Media

	2002	2003	2004
Telephones ('000 main lines in use)	4,354.6	4,278.8	4,237.7
Mobile cellular telephones ('000 subscribers)	8,528.9	9,350.5	10,300.0
Personal computers ('000 in use)	1,394	1,398	1,402
Internet users ('000)	2,000	n.a.	2,951

Source: International Telecommunication Union.

Facsimile machines ('000 in use): 70 in 1997.
Radio receivers ('000 in use): 3,020 in 1997.
Television receivers ('000 in use): 6,319 in 2000.
Books published (titles): 2,186 in 1998.
Daily newspapers (number of titles, 2000): 28 (total distribution 1,026,000 in 2000).
Non-daily newspapers (1999): Number 242; Average circulation 1,152,000.

Sources: mainly UN, *Statistical Yearbook*; UNESCO Institute for Statistics; UNESCO, *Statistical Yearbook*.

Education

(preliminary, continental Portugal only, 2005/06, unless otherwise indicated)

	Institutions	Teachers	Students
Pre-school	6,312	15,315	261,090*
Basic: 1st cycle	7,780	33,179	467,061
Basic: 2nd cycle	1,043	32,582	240,218
Basic: 3rd cycle	1,373	43,193	369,081
Secondary	740	36,262	292,841
Professional	210	16,999	33,341
Higher	317†	514‡	395,063*†

* Including the Azores and Madeira.
† 2003/04.
‡ 2001/02.

Source: partly Ministry of Education.

Adult literacy rate (UNESCO estimates): 92.5% (males 95.2%; females 90.3%) in 2002. (Source: UN Development Programme, *Human Development Report*).

Directory

The Constitution

The Constitution of the Portuguese Republic was promulgated on 2 April 1976, and came into force on 25 April. It was revised in 1982, when ideological elements were diminished and the Council of the Revolution was abolished; in 1989, to permit economic reforms and a greater role for the private sector; in 1992, prior to the ratification of the Treaty on European Union (also known as the Maastricht Treaty); in 1997 when changes included provision for the holding of referendums on questions of national interest; and in 2001 to incorporate reciprocal political rights for citizens of lusophone countries, to impose a ban on strike action by police trade unions and officially to recognize the UN International Criminal Court. The following is a summary of the Constitution's main provisions:

FUNDAMENTAL PRINCIPLES

Portugal is a sovereign Republic based on the dignity of the individual and the will of the people, which strives to create a just, caring and free society and to realize economic, social and cultural democracy. It comprises the territory defined by history on the European continent and the archipelagos of the Azores and Madeira. The Azores and Madeira shall constitute autonomous regions.

The fundamental duties of the State include the following: to safeguard national independence; to guarantee fundamental rights and freedoms; to defend political democracy and to encourage citizens' participation in the solving of national problems; and to promote the welfare, quality of life and equality of the people.

FUNDAMENTAL RIGHTS AND DUTIES

All citizens are equal before the law. Rights, freedoms and safeguards are upheld by the State and include the following: the right to life; of habeas corpus; to the inviolability of the home and of correspondence; to freedom of expression and of conscience; to freedom of movement, emigration and of assembly. Freedom of the press is guaranteed.

Rights and duties of citizens include the following: the right and the duty to work; the right to vote (at 18 years of age); the right to form and participate in political associations and parties; the freedom to form trade unions and the right to strike; the right to set up co-operatives; the right to private property; the right to social security and medical services; the duty of the State and of society to protect the family and the disabled; the right to education, culture and sport; consumer rights.

ECONOMIC ORGANIZATION

The economic and social organization of Portugal shall be based on the subordination of economic power to political power, the co-existence of the public, private, co-operative and social sectors of ownership, and the public ownership of the means of production and land, in accordance with the public interest, as well as natural resources; and on the democratic planning of the economy, and democratic intervention by the workers. Enterprises nationalized after 25 April 1974 may be reprivatized. The aims of economic and social development plans include the promotion of economic growth, the harmonious development of sectors and regions, the fair individual and regional distribution of the national product and the defence of the environment and of the quality of life of the Portuguese people. The consultative Economic and Social Council participates in the formulation of development plans. It comprises representatives of the Government, workers' organizations, economic enterprises and representatives of autonomous regions and local organizations.

The aims of agrarian policy are to improve the situation of farm workers and to increase agricultural production and productivity. *Latifúndios* (large estates) will be adjusted in size, and property which has been expropriated, with compensation, shall be handed over to small farmers or co-operatives for exploitation. *Minifúndios* (small estates) will be adjusted in size, through the granting of incentives to integrate or divide. The aims of commercial policy include the development and diversification of foreign economic relations. The aims of industrial policy include an increase in production in the context of modernization and adjustment, greater competition, the support of small and medium enterprises and the support of industrial and technological innovation. The financial and fiscal system aims at encouraging savings and achieving the equal distribution of wealth and incomes. The State Budget shall be supervised by the Accounts Court and the Assembly of the Republic (Assembléia da República). Economic policy includes the stimulation of competition, the protection of consumers and the combating of speculative activities and restrictive trade practices.

POLITICAL ORGANIZATION

Political power shall lie with the people. The organs of sovereignty shall be: the President of the Republic, the Assembly of the Republic, the Government and the Courts. Direct, secret and regular elections shall be held. No-one shall hold political office for life.

PRESIDENT OF THE REPUBLIC

The President of the Republic shall represent the Republic. The President guarantees national independence, the unity of the State, and the proper working of democratic institutions. The President shall be elected by direct and secret universal adult suffrage. The candidate who obtains more than one-half of the valid votes will be elected President. The President shall hold office for five years. The President may not be re-elected for a third consecutive term of office.

The duties of the President include the following: to preside over the Council of State; to set dates for elections; to convene extraordinary sessions of the Assembly of the Republic; to dissolve the Assembly; to appoint and dismiss the Prime Minister; to appoint and dismiss the members of the Government at the proposal of the Prime Minister; to promulgate laws; to veto laws; to apply to the Constitutional Court; to nominate ambassadors, upon the proposal of the Government; to accredit diplomatic representatives; to ratify international treaties, after they have been duly approved; to dismiss the Government if and when the normal functioning of institutions is at stake.

COUNCIL OF STATE

The Council of State (Conselho de Estado) is the political consultative organ of the President of the Republic. It is presided over by the President of the Republic and comprises the President of the Assembly of the Republic, the Prime Minister, the President of the Constitutional Court, the Superintendent of Justice, the Presidents of the Regional Governments, certain former Presidents of the Republic, five citizens nominated by the President of the Republic and five citizens elected by the Assembly.

ASSEMBLY OF THE REPUBLIC

The Assembly of the Republic (Assembléia da República) represents all Portuguese citizens, and shall have a minimum of 180 and a maximum of 230 members, elected under a system of proportional representation by the electoral constituencies. The duties of the Assembly include the following: to present and approve amendments to the Constitution and to approve the political and administrative statutes of the Autonomous Regions; to enact legislation; to confer legislative authority on the Government; to approve plans and the Budget; to approve international conventions and treaties; to propose to the President of the Republic that questions of national interest be submitted to referendum; to supervise the fulfilment of the Constitution and laws. The Assembly supports the participation of Portugal in the process of building the European Union. Each legislative period shall last four years. The legislative session shall run from 15 September to 15 June each year.

GOVERNMENT

The Government formulates the general policy of the country and is the highest organ of public administration. It shall comprise the Prime Minister, Ministers, Secretaries and Under-Secretaries of State and may include one or more Deputy Prime Ministers. The Prime Minister is appointed and dismissed by the President. Other members of the Government are appointed by the President at the proposal of the Prime Minister. The Government shall be responsible to the President and the Assembly. The Government's programme shall be presented to the Assembly of the Republic for scrutiny within 10 days of the appointment of the Prime Minister.

JUDICIARY

The courts are independent organs of sovereignty with competence to administer justice. There shall be Courts of First Instance (District Courts), Courts of Second Instance (Courts of Appeal), the Supreme Administrative Court and the Supreme Court of Justice, in addition to the Constitutional Court. There shall also be military courts (when the State is at war) and an Accounts Court. There may be maritime courts and courts of arbitration.

The jury shall comprise the judges of the plenary court and the jurors. People's judges may be created. It is the duty of the Ministério Público to represent the State. Its highest organ is the Procuradoria-Geral which is presided over by the Procurador-Geral, who is appointed and dismissed by the President of the Republic.

AUTONOMOUS REGIONS

The special political and administrative arrangements for the archipelagos of the Azores and Madeira shall be based on their geographical, economic and social conditions and on the historic aspirations of the people to autonomy. The State is represented in each of the Autonomous Regions by a Minister of the Republic.

The organs of government in the Autonomous Regions (which are subject to dissolution by the President of the Republic if a major breach of the Constitution occurs) are: the Regional Legislative Assembly, elected by direct and secret universal adult suffrage, and the Regional Government which shall be politically responsible to the Regional Legislative Assembly. Its Chairman is appointed by the Minister of the Republic. The Minister shall appoint or dismiss members of the Regional Government on the proposal of its Chairman.

LOCAL GOVERNMENT

The local authorities shall be territorial bodies corporate with representative organs serving the particular interests of the local population. The local authorities on the mainland shall be the parishes, municipal authorities and administrative regions. The Autonomous Regions of the Azores and Madeira shall comprise parishes and municipal authorities.

PUBLIC ADMINISTRATIVE AUTHORITIES

The public administrative authorities shall seek to promote the public interest whilst respecting the legal interests and rights of all citizens. Citizens shall have the right to be informed of, and to have redress against, the public administrative authorities when the matter directly concerns them.

ARMED FORCES

The President of the Republic is Supreme Commander-in-Chief of the Armed Forces, and appoints and dismisses the Chiefs of Staff. The defence forces shall safeguard national independence and territorial integrity. Military service shall be compulsory. The right to conscientious objection is recognized.

SAFEGUARDS AND REVISION OF THE CONSTITUTION

Changes in the Constitution shall be approved by a majority of two-thirds of the members of the Assembly of the Republic present, provided that the number of such members exceeds an absolute majority of the members entitled to vote. Constitutional revisions must comply with the independence, unity and secularism of the State; the rights, freedoms and safeguards of citizens; universal, direct and secret suffrage and the system of proportional representation, etc.

The Government

HEAD OF STATE

President: ANÍBAL CAVACO SILVA (took office 9 March 2006).

COUNCIL OF MINISTERS
(April 2006)

The Government comprises the Partido Socialista (PS) and independents (Ind.).

Prime Minister: JOSÉ SÓCRATES CARVALHO PINTO DE SOUSA (PS).

Minister of State and of Internal Administration: ANTÓNIO COSTA (PS).

Minister of State and of Foreign Affairs: DIOGO FREITAS DO AMARAL (Ind.).

Minister of State and of Finance: FERNANDO TEIXEIRA DOS SANTOS (PS).

Minister of the Presidency: PEDRO SILVA PEREIRA (PS).

Minister of National Defence: LUÍS AMADO (PS).

Minister of Justice: ALBERTO COSTA (PS).

PORTUGAL

Minister of the Environment, Territorial Planning and Regional Development: Francisco Nunes Correia (Ind.).
Minister of the Economy and Innovation: Manuel Pinho (Ind.).
Minister of Agriculture, Rural Development and Fisheries: Jaime Silva (Ind.).
Minister of Public Works, Transport and Communications: Mário Lino (PS).
Minister of Labour and Social Solidarity: José António Vieira da Silva (PS).
Minister of Health: António Correia de Campos (PS).
Minister of Education: Maria de Lurdes Rodrigues (Ind.).
Minister of Science, Technology and Higher Education: Mariano Gago (Ind.).
Minister of Culture: Isabel Pires de Lima (Ind.).
Minister of Parliamentary Affairs: Augusto Santos Silva (PS).
There are also 35 secretaries of state.

MINISTRIES

Office of the President: Presidência da República, Palácio de Belém, Calçada da Ajuda, 1349-022 Lisbon; tel. (21) 3614600; fax (21) 3614611; e-mail presidente@presidenciarepublica.pt; internet www.presidenciarepublica.pt.

Office of the Prime Minister, Presidency of the Council of Ministers: Rua da Imprensa à Estrela 4, 1200-888 Lisbon; tel. (21) 3923500; e-mail pm@pm.gov.pt; internet www.portugal.gov.pt.

Ministry of Agriculture, Rural Development and Fisheries: Praça do Comércio, 1149-010 Lisbon; tel. (21) 3234600; fax (21) 3234601; e-mail geral@min-agricultura.pt; internet www.min-agricultura.pt.

Ministry of Culture: Rua D. Francisco Manuel de Melo 15, 1070-085 Lisbon; tel. (21) 3848400; fax (21) 3848439; e-mail infocultura@min-cultura.pt; internet www.min-cultura.pt.

Ministry of the Economy and Innovation: Rua da Horta Seca 15, 1200-221 Lisbon; tel. (21) 3245400; fax (21) 3245440; e-mail gmei@mei.gov.pt; internet www.min-economia.pt.

Ministry of Education: Av. 5 de Outubro 107, 1069-018 Lisbon; tel. (21) 7811690; fax (21) 7978020; e-mail cirep@min-edu.pt; internet www.min-edu.pt.

Ministry of the Environment, Territorial Planning and Regional Development: Rua de O Século 51, 1200-433 Lisbon; tel. (21) 3232500; fax (21) 3232531; e-mail gsea@maotdr.gov.pt; internet www.mcalhdr.gov.pt.

Ministry of Finance and Public Administration: Rua da Alfândega 5, 1149-006 Lisbon; tel. (21) 8846600; fax (21) 8846651; e-mail relacoes.publicas@sgmf.pt; internet www.min-financas.pt.

Ministry of Foreign Affairs: Palácio das Necessidades, Largo do Rilvas, 1399-030 Lisbon; tel. (21) 3946000; fax (21) 3946053; e-mail gii@mne.gov.pt; internet www.min-nestrangeiros.pt.

Ministry of Health: Av. João Crisóstomo 9, 1049-062 Lisbon; tel. (21) 3305000; fax (21) 3305003; e-mail gms@ms.gov.pt; internet www.min-saude.pt.

Ministry of Internal Administration: Praça do Comércio, 1149-015 Lisbon; tel. (21) 3233000; fax (21) 3468031; e-mail dirp@sg.mai.gov.pt; internet www.mai.gov.pt.

Ministry of Justice: Praça do Comércio, 1149-019 Lisbon; tel. (21) 3222300; fax (21) 3479208; e-mail gmj@mj.gov.pt; internet www.mj.gov.pt.

Ministry of Labour and Social Solidarity: Praça de Londres 2, 1049-056 Lisbon; tel. (21) 8441100; fax (21) 8441322; e-mail portal@sg.mtss.gov.pt; internet www.mtss.gov.pt.

Ministry of National Defence: Av. Ilha de Madeira 1, 1400-204 Lisbon; tel. (21) 3038528; fax (21) 3020284; e-mail gcrp@sg.mdn.gov.pt; internet www.mdn.gov.pt.

Ministry of Parliamentary Affairs: Palácio de São Bento, 1249-068 Lisbon; tel. (21) 3920500; fax (21) 3920515; e-mail map@map.gov.pt.

Ministry of the Presidency: Rua Prof. Gomes Teixeira, 1399-265 Lisbon; tel. (21) 3923600; fax (21) 3927860; e-mail gab.mp@mp.gov.pt; internet www.mp.gov.pt.

Ministry of Public Works, Transport and Communications: Palácio do Conde de Penafiel, Rua de São Mamede (ao Caldas) 21, 1149-050 Lisbon; tel. (21) 8815100; fax (21) 8867622; e-mail gmoptc@moptc.gov.pt; internet www.moptc.pt.

Ministry of Science, Technology and Higher Education: Palácio de Laranjeiras, Estrada de Laranjeiras 197–205, 1649-018 Lisbon; tel. (21) 7231000; fax (21) 7231160; e-mail mctes@mctes.gov.pt; internet www.mctes.pt.

COUNCIL OF STATE

The Council of State (Conselho de Estado) is a consultative body, presided over by the President of the Republic (see The Constitution).

President and Legislature

PRESIDENT

Election, 22 January 2006

Candidate	Votes	% of votes
Aníbal Cavaco Silva (PSD)	2,773,431	50.54
Manuel Alegre de Melo Duarte (Ind.)	1,138,297	20.74
Mário Lopes Soares (PS)	785,355	14.31
Jeronimo Carvalho de Sousa (PCP)	474,083	8.64
Francisco Anacleto Louçã (BE)	292,198	5.32
António Pestana Garcia Pereira (PCTP/MRPP)	23,983	0.44
Total	5,487,347*	100.00

* Excluding 59,636 blank and 43,149 spoiled votes.

ASSEMBLÉIA DA REPÚBLICA

Assembléia da República: Palácio de São Bento, 1249-068 Lisbon; tel. (21) 3919625; fax (21) 3917458; e-mail cic.rp@ar.parlamento.pt; internet www.parlamento.pt.

President: Jaime José Matos da Gama.

General Election, 20 February 2005

Party	Votes	% of votes	Seats
Partido Socialista (PS)	2,588,312	45.03	121
Partido Social Democrata (PSD)	1,653,425	28.77	75
Partido Comunista Português (PCP)-Partido Ecologista 'Os Verdes' (PEV)	433,369	7.54	14
Partido Popular (PP)	416,415	7.24	12
Bloco de Esquerda (BE)	364,971	6.35	8
Total (incl. others)	5,747,834	100.00	230

Autonomous Regions

THE AZORES

President of the Regional Government: Carlos Manuel do Vale César (PS).

Assembléia Legislativa da Região Autónoma dos Açores: 9900-858 Horta, Los Açores; tel. (292) 207600; fax (292) 293798; e-mail secgeral@alra.pt; internet www.alra.pt; Pres. Fernando Manuel Machado Menezes (PS).

MADEIRA

President of the Regional Government: Dr Alberto João Jardim (PSD).

Assembléia Legislativa da Região Autónoma da Madeira: Av. do Mar e das Comunidades Madeirenses, 9004-506 Funchal, Madeira; tel. (291) 210500; fax (291) 232977; e-mail presidencia@alrm.pt; internet www.alrm.pt; Pres. José Miguel Jardim d'Olival Mendonça (PSD).

Election Commission

Comissão Nacional de Eleições (CNE): Av. D. Carlos I 128, 7°, 1249-065 Lisbon; tel. (21) 3923800; fax (21) 3953543; e-mail cne@cne.pt; internet www.cne.pt; mems appointed by the judiciary, the Assembleia da República, and the Govt; Pres. António de Sousa Guedes.

Political Organizations

Bloco de Esquerda (BE): Av. Almirante Reis 131, 2° andar, 1150-015 Lisbon; tel. (21) 3510510; fax (21) 3510519; e-mail bloco.esquerda@bloco.org; internet www.bloco.org; Leader Miguel Portas.

Coligação Democrática Unitária (CDU): coalition of left-wing parties; led by PCP:

PORTUGAL

Partido Comunista Português (PCP) (Portuguese Communist Party): Rua Soeiro Pereira Gomes 3, 1600-196 Lisbon; tel. (21) 7813800; fax (21) 7969126; e-mail pcp@pcp.pt; internet www.pcp.pt; f. 1921; legalized 1974; theoretical foundation is Marxism-Leninism; aims are the defence and consolidation of the democratic regime and the revolutionary achievements, and ultimately the building of a socialist society in Portugal; 140,000 mems (1996); Sec.-Gen. Jeronimo de Sousa.

Partido Ecologista 'Os Verdes' (PEV) (The Greens): Rua da Boavista 83, 3°D, 1200-066 Lisbon; tel. (21) 3960291; fax (21) 3960424; e-mail osverdes@mail.telepac.pt; internet www.osverdes.pt; f. 1982; ecological party.

Frente da Esquerda Revolucionária (FER): Rua de Terreirinho 4, 2°, 1100 Lisbon; tel. (21) 8850450; internet www.rupturafer.org; f. 2000; revolutionary Marxist party, affiliated with Workers International League; part of Bloco de Esquerda.

Movimento O Partido da Terra (MPT) (The Earth Party Movement): Av. Eng. Arantes Oliveira 11, 1° A, 1900-221, Lisbon; tel. (21) 8438021; fax (21) 8438029; e-mail terra@mpt.pt; internet www.partidodaterra.org; Pres. Paolo António Rodrigues de Noronha Trancoso.

Novo Democracia: Lisbon; internet www.pnd.pt; f. 2003; by disaffected members of the PP; right-wing, nationalist and eurosceptic; Pres. Manuel Monteiro.

Partido Comunista dos Trabalhadores Portugueses/Movimento Revolucionário Português do Proletariado (PCTP/MRPP) (Communist Workers' Party/Proletarian Portuguese Revolutionary Movement): Rua Palma 159, 2°D, 1000-391 Lisbon; e-mail pctp@pctpmrpp.org; internet www.pctpmrpp.org; f. 1970; as Movimento Reorganizativo do Partido do Proletariado; name changed in 1976; Leader Garcia Pereira.

Partido da Solidariedade Nacional (Party of National Solidarity): Rua João Deus 1, 9050-027 Funchal; tel. (291) 223131.

Partido Democrático do Atlântico (PDA) (Democratic Party of the Atlantic): Largo 2 Março 65, 2500-152 Ponta Delgada; tel. (296) 284033.

Partido Opérario de Unidade Socialista (POUS) (Workers' Party of Socialist Unity): Rua de Santo António da Glória 52, B-C, 1250-217 Lisbon; tel. (21) 3159284; fax (21) 3257811; e-mail pous_pt@hotmail.com; internet pous.no.sapo.pt.

Partido Popular (PP) (Popular Party): Largo Adelino Amaro da Costa 5, 1149-063 Lisbon; tel. (21) 8814700; fax (21) 8860454; e-mail cds@cds.pt; internet www.partido-popular.pt; f. 1974; fmrly Centro Democrático Social; also known as the CDS-PP; centre-right; mem. of International Democratic Union; supports social market economy and reduction of public-sector intervention in the economy; defended revision of 1976 Constitution; Pres. José Ribeiro e Castro.

Partido Social Democrata (PSD) (Social Democratic Party): Rua de São Caetano 9, 1249-087 Lisbon; tel. (21) 3952140; fax (21) 3976967; e-mail psd@psd.pt; internet www.psd.pt; f. 1974; fmrly Partido Popular Democrático—PPD; aims to promote market economy, taking into account the welfare of the community; encourages European integration; 60,000 mems; Leader Luís Manuel Gonçalves Marques Mendes; Sec.-Gen. Miguel Macedo.

Partido Socialista (PS) (Socialist Party): Largo do Rato 2, 1269-143 Lisbon; tel. (21) 3822000; fax (21) 3822016; e-mail info@ps.pt; internet www.ps.pt; f. 1973; from former Acção Socialista Portuguesa (Portuguese Socialist Action); affiliate of the Socialist International and Party of European Socialists; advocates a society of greater social justice and co-operation between public, private and co-operative sectors, while respecting public liberties and the will of the majority attained through free elections; 100,000 mems; Pres. António de Almeida Santos; Sec.-Gen José Sócrates Carvalho Pinto de Sousa; 84,000 mems.

Partido Socialista Revolucionário (PSR) (Revolutionary Socialist Party): Rua da Palma 268, 1100-394 Lisbon; tel. (21) 8864643; fax (21) 8882736; f. 1978; through merger of two Trotskyist groups.

União Democrática Popular (UDP) (People's Democratic Union): Rua de São Bento 698, 1°, 1250-223 Lisbon; tel. (21) 3826110; fax (21) 3885035; e-mail udp@netcabo.pt; internet www.udp.pt; f. 1974; Marxist-Leninist; comprises various political groups of the revolutionary left; Leader Luís Fazenda.

Diplomatic Representation

EMBASSIES IN PORTUGAL

Algeria: Rua Duarte Pacheco Pereira 58, 1400-140 Lisbon; tel. (21) 3041520; fax (21) 3010393; e-mail embaixada-argelia@clix.pt; internet www.emb-argelia.pt; Ambassador Sabri Boukadoum.

Andorra: Rua do Possolo 76, 2350-251 Lisbon; tel. (21) 3913740; fax (21) 3913749; Chargé d'affaires Jaume Gaytan.

Angola: Av. da República 68, 1069-213 Lisbon; tel. (21) 7961830; fax (21) 7971238; e-mail emb.angola@mail.telepac.pt; internet www.embaixadadeangola.org; Ambassador Assunção Afonso Sousa dos Anjos.

Argentina: Av. João Crisóstomo 8, r/c esq., 1000-178 Lisbon; tel. (21) 7977311; fax (21) 7959225; e-mail embargpi@mail.telepac.pt; Ambassador Jorge Marcelo Faurie.

Australia: Av. da Liberdade 200, 2°, 1250-147 Lisbon; tel. (21) 3943900; fax (21) 3101555; e-mail austemb.lisbon@dfat.gov.au; internet www.portugal.embassy.gov.au; Ambassador Ewald Jäger.

Austria: Av. Infante Santo 43, 4°, 1399-046 Lisbon; tel. (21) 3958220; fax (21) 3958224; e-mail lissabon.ob@bmaa.gv.at; Ambassador Dr Ferdinand Trauttmansdorff.

Belgium: Praça Marquês de Pombal 14, 6°, 1269-024 Lisbon; tel. (21) 3170510; fax (21) 3561556; e-mail lisbon@diplobel.org; internet www.diplobel.org/portugal; Ambassador Paul Ponjaert.

Brazil: Quinta de Milflores, Estrada das Laranjeiras 144, 1649-021 Lisbon; tel. (21) 7248510; fax (21) 7267623; e-mail geral@emb-brasil.pt; internet www.emb-brasil.pt; Ambassador António Paes de Andrade.

Bulgaria: Rua do Sacramento à Lapa 31, 1200-792 Lisbon; tel. (21) 3976364; fax (21) 3979272; e-mail ebul@mail.telepac.pt; Ambassador Maksin Gregoriev Gaytandzhiev.

Canada: Av. da Liberdade 196–200, 3°, 1269-121 Lisbon; tel. (21) 3164600; fax (21) 3164691; e-mail lisbon@dfait-maeci.gc.ca; internet www.dfait-maeci.gc.ca/lisbon; Ambassador Patrick Parisot.

Cape Verde: Av. do Restelo 33, 1449-025 Lisbon; tel. (21) 3041440; fax (21) 3041466; e-mail emb.caboverde@netcabo.pt; Chargé d'affaires Daniel Pereira.

Chile: Av. Miguel Bombarda 5, 1°, 1000-207 Lisbon; tel. (21) 3148054; fax (21) 3150909; e-mail echile.pt@mail.telepac.pt; internet www.emb-chile.pt; Ambassador Manuel José Matta.

China, People's Republic: Rua do Pau de Bandeira 11–13, 1200-756 Lisbon; tel. (21) 3928440; fax (21) 3975632; e-mail chinaemb_pt@mfa.gov.cn; internet www.chineseembassy.org/pot; Ambassador Ma Enhan.

Colombia: Palácio Sottomayor, 6°, Av. Fontes Pereira de Melo 16, 1050-121 Lisbon; tel. (21) 3188480; fax (21) 3188499; e-mail elisboa@minrelex1.gov.co; Ambassador Plínio Apuleyo Mendoza.

Congo, Democratic Republic: Av. Fontes Pereira de Melo 31, 7°, 1050-117 Lisbon; tel. (21) 3522895; fax (21) 3544862; Chargé d'affaires Lokosu N'Kulufa.

Croatia: Rua D. Lourenço de Almeida 24, 1400-126 Lisbon; tel. (21) 3021033; fax (21) 3021251; e-mail croemblis@sapo.pt; Ambassador Zelimir Brala.

Cuba: Rua Pero da Covilhã 14 (Restelo), 1400-297 Lisbon; tel. (21) 3015317; fax (21) 3011895; e-mail embaixada.cuba@netcabo.pt; Ambassador Jorge Castro Benitéz.

Cyprus: Av. da Liberdade 229, 1°, 1250-142 Lisbon; tel. (21) 3194180; fax (21) 3194189; e-mail chipre@netcabo.pt; Ambassador Nearchos Palas.

Czech Republic: Rua Pero de Alenquer 14, 1400-294 Lisbon; tel. (21) 3010487; fax (21) 3010629; e-mail lisbon@embassy.mzv.cz; internet www.mfa.cz/lisbon; Ambassador Ladislav Skeřík.

Denmark: Rua Castilho 14, 3°C, 1269-077 Lisbon; tel. (21) 3512960; fax (21) 3570124; e-mail lisamb@um.dk; internet www.amblissabon.um.dk; Ambassador Lars Vissing.

Dominican Republic: Av. das Forças Armadas 133, Bloco B 3, 1600-081 Lisbon; tel. (21) 7247030; fax (21) 7247039; e-mail embajadom@mail.telepac.pt; Ambassador Marina Isabel Cáceres Estévez.

Egypt: Av. D. Vasco da Gama 8, 1400-128 Lisbon; tel. (21) 3018301; fax (21) 3017909; e-mail egiptembassy@ip.pt; Ambassador Ibrahim Salamah.

Estonia: Rua Filipe Folque 10, 2° J esq., 1050-113 Lisbon; tel. (21) 3194150; fax (21) 3194155; e-mail embest@embest.pt; Ambassador Aino Lepik von Wirén.

Finland: Rua do Possolo 76, 1°, 1350-251 Lisbon; tel. (21) 3933040; fax (21) 3904758; e-mail sanomat.lis@formin.fi; internet www.finlandia.org.pt; Ambassador Sauli Erik Feodorow.

France: Rua de Santos-o-Velho 5, 1249-079 Lisbon; tel. (21) 3939100; fax (21) 3939150; e-mail ambafrance@hotmail.com; internet www.ambafrance-pt.org; Ambassador Patrick Gautrat.

Germany: Campo dos Mártires da Pátria 38, 1169-043 Lisbon; tel. (21) 8810210; fax (21) 8853846; e-mail embaixada.alemanha@clix.pt; internet www.lissabon.diplo.de; Ambassador Dr Hans-Bodo Bertram.

Greece: Rua do Alto do Duque 13, 1449-026 Lisbon; tel. (21) 3031260; fax (21) 3011205; e-mail ambagrelis@mail.telepac.pt; Ambassador Jean C. Vavvas.

PORTUGAL

Guinea-Bissau: Rua de Alcolena 17, 1400-004 Lisbon; tel. (21) 3030440; fax (21) 3019653; Ambassador JOÃOZINHO VIEIRA CÓ.
Holy See: Av. Luís Bivar 18, 1069-147 Lisbon; tel. (21) 3171130; fax (21) 3171149; e-mail nunap@ip.pt; Apostolic Nuncio Most Rev. ALFIO RAPISARDA (Titular Archbishop of Canne).
Hungary: Calçada de Santo Amaro 85, 1349-042 Lisbon; tel. (21) 3630395; fax (21) 3632314; e-mail huemblis@mail.telepac.pt; Ambassador ATTILA GECSE.
India: Rua Pêro da Covilhã 16, 1400-297 Lisbon; tel. (21) 3041090; fax (21) 3016576; e-mail main@indembassy-lisbon.org; internet www.indembassy-lisbon.org; Ambassador VIJAYA LATHA REDDY.
Indonesia: Rua Miguel Lupi 12, 1°, 1249-080 Lisbon; tel. (21) 3932070; fax (21) 3932079; e-mail kbrilisabon@iol.pt; Ambassador FRANCISCO LOPES DA CRUZ.
Iran: Rua do Alto do Duque 49, 1400-009 Lisbon; tel. (21) 3010871; fax (21) 3010777; e-mail 2191@info.gov.ir; internet www.emb-irao.pt; Ambassador MOHAMMAD TAHERI.
Iraq: Rua do Arriaga à Lapa 9, 1200-608 Lisbon; tel. (21) 3908215; fax (21) 3977052; e-mail lisemb@iraqmofa.net; Ambassador HUSSAIN MUAALA.
Ireland: Rua da Imprensa à Estrela 1, 4°, 1200-684 Lisbon; tel. (21) 3929440; fax (21) 3977363; e-mail lisbon@iveagh.irlgov.ie; Ambassador JIM BRENNAN.
Israel: Rua António Enes 16, 4°, 1050-025 Lisbon; tel. (21) 3553640; fax (21) 3553658; e-mail israemb@lisboa.mfa.gov.il; internet www.lisbon.mfa.gov.il; Ambassador AHARON RAM.
Italy: Largo Conde de Pombeiro 6, 1150-100 Lisbon; tel. (21) 3515320; fax (21) 3154926; e-mail amblisb@embital.pt; internet www.embital.pt; Ambassador EMILIO BARBARANI.
Japan: Av. da Liberdade 245–6, 1269-033 Lisbon; tel. (21) 3110560; fax (21) 3534802; e-mail bunka@ip.pt; internet www.pt.emb-japan.go.jp; Ambassador SATOSHI HARA.
Korea, Republic: Edif. Presidente 7°, Av. Miguel Bombarda 36, 1051-802 Lisbon; tel. (21) 7937200; fax (21) 7977176; e-mail emb.pt@mofat.go.kr; Ambassador SHIM YOON-JOE.
Latvia: Travessa da Palmeira 31A, 1200-315 Lisbon; tel. (21) 3407170; fax (21) 3469045; e-mail embassy.portugal@mfa.gov.lv; Ambassador INTS UPMACIS.
Libya: Av. das Descobertas 24, 1400-092 Lisbon; tel. (21) 3016301; fax (21) 3012378; Chargé d'affaires ALI EMDORED.
Lithuania: Av. 5 de Outubro 81, 1° esq., 1050-050 Lisbon; tel. (21) 7990110; fax (21) 7996363; e-mail emb.lituania@mail.telepac.pt; Chargé d'affaires HILDA GRIŠKEVIČIUNE.
Luxembourg: Rua das Janelas Verdes 43, 1200-690 Lisbon; tel. (21) 3931940; fax (21) 3901410; e-mail lisbonne.amb@mae.etat.lu; Ambassador ALAIN DE MUYSER.
Malta: Lisbon; Ambassador SALV STELLINI.
Mexico: Estrada de Monsanto 78, 1500-462 Lisbon; tel. (21) 7621290; fax (21) 7620045; e-mail embamex.port@mail.telepac.pt; internet www.sre.gob.mx/portugal; Ambassador MAURICIO TOUSSAINT RIBOT.
Morocco: Rua Alto do Duque 21, 1400-099 Lisbon; tel. (21) 3020842; fax (21) 3020935; e-mail cifmar@emb-maroccos.pt; internet www.emb-maroccos.pt; Ambassador SAMIR ARROUR.
Mozambique: Av. de Berna 7, 1050-036 Lisbon; tel. (21) 7961672; fax (21) 7932720; Ambassador MIGUEL DA COSTA MKAIMA.
Netherlands: Av. Infante Santo 43, 5°, 1399-011 Lisbon; tel. (21) 3914900; fax (21) 3966436; e-mail nlgovlis@mail.telepac.pt; internet www.emb-paisesbaixos.pt; Ambassador HERMAN R. R. V. FROGER.
Nigeria: Av. D. Vasco da Gama 3, 1400-127 Lisbon; tel. (21) 3016189; fax (21) 3018152; e-mail nigerlis@mail.telepac.pt; Ambassador AKAFU A. ELLA.
Norway: Av. D. Vasco da Gama 1, 1400-127 Lisbon; tel. (21) 3015344; fax (21) 3016158; e-mail emb.lisbon@mfa.no; internet www.noruega.org.pt; Ambassador ARNT MAGNE RINDAL.
Pakistan: Av. da República 20, 1°, 1050-192 Lisbon; tel. (21) 3150000; fax (21) 3155805; e-mail parep.lisbon.1@mail.telepac.pt; Ambassador FAUSIA M. SANA.
Panama: Av. Helen Keller 15, Lote C 4° esq., 1400-197 Lisbon; tel. (21) 3642899; fax (21) 3644589; e-mail panemblisboa@netcabo.pt; Ambassador MINERVA LARA BATISTA.
Paraguay: Campo Grande 4, 7° dto, 1700-092 Lisbon; tel. (21) 7965907; fax (21) 7965905; e-mail embaparlisboa@mail.telepac.pt; Chargé d'affaires a.i. ANTONIO RIVAS PALÁCIOS.
Peru: Rua Castilho 50, 4° dto, 1250-071 Lisbon; tel. (21) 3827470; fax (21) 3827479; e-mail embperuport@mail.telepac.pt; Ambassador MANUEL VERAMENDI I SERRA.
Poland: Av. das Descobertas 2, 1400-092 Lisbon; tel. (21) 3041410; fax (21) 3010202; e-mail brh.lizbona@mail.telepac.pt; Ambassador JANUSZ RYDZKOWSKI.

Romania: Rua de São Caetano a Lapa 5, 1200-828 Lisbon; tel. (21) 3960866; fax (21) 3960984; e-mail ambrom@mail.telecim.pt; Ambassador GABRIEL GAFITA.
Russia: Rua Visconde de Santarém 59, 1000-286 Lisbon; tel. (21) 8462423; fax (21) 8463008; e-mail mp71fm@telepac.pt; internet www.portugal.mid.ru; Ambassador BAKHTIER KHAKIMOV.
São Tomé and Príncipe: Edif. EPAC 6°, Av. Gago Coutinho 26, 1000-017 Lisbon; tel. (21) 8461917; fax (21) 8461895; e-mail embstp@mail.telepac.pt; Ambassador ALDA ALVES DE MELO DOS SANTOS.
Saudi Arabia: Av. do Restelo 42, 1400-315 Lisbon; tel. (21) 3041750; fax (21) 3014209; e-mail saudiembassy@netcabo.pt; Ambassador MUHAMMAD AR-RASHID.
Serbia and Montenegro: Av. das Descobertas 12, 1400-092 Lisbon; tel. (21) 3015311; fax (21) 3015313; e-mail yuemba@netcabo.pt; Ambassador DUSAN KOVACEVIC.
Slovakia: Av. Fontes Pereira de Melo 19, 7° dto, 1050-116 Lisbon; tel. (21) 3583300; fax (21) 3583309; e-mail emslovak@mail.telepac.pt; Ambassador RADOMIR BOHAC.
Slovenia: Av. da Liberdade 49, 6° esq., 1250-139 Lisbon; tel. (21) 3423301; fax (21) 3423305; e-mail vli@mzz-dkp.gov.si; Ambassador BOGDAN BENKO.
South Africa: Av. Luís Bivar 10, 1269-124 Lisbon; tel. (21) 3192200; fax (21) 3192211; e-mail embsa@embaixada-africadosul.pt; Ambassador THANDIWE JANUARY-MCLEAN.
Spain: Rua do Salitre 1, 1296-052 Lisbon; tel. (21) 3472381; fax (21) 3472384; e-mail embesppt@correo.mae.es; Ambassador ENRIQUE PANÉS CALPE.
Sweden: Rua Miguel Lupi 12, 2°, 1249-077 Lisbon; tel. (21) 3942260; fax (21) 3942261; e-mail ambassaden.lissabon@foreign.ministry.se; internet www.embsuecia.pt; Ambassador MARIE GABRIELLA LINDHOLM.
Switzerland: Travessa do Jardim 17, 1350-185 Lisbon; tel. (21) 3944090; fax (21) 3955945; e-mail vertretung@lis.rep.admin.ch; Ambassador CATHERINE KREIG POLEJACK.
Thailand: Rua de Alcolena 12, 12A, 1400-005 Lisbon; tel. (21) 3014848; fax (21) 3018181; e-mail thai.lis@mail.telepac.pt; Ambassador PENSAK CHALARAK.
Timor Leste: Av. Infante Santo 17, 6°, 1350-175 Lisbon; tel. (21) 3933730; fax (21) 3933739; e-mail embaixada.rdtl@mail.telepac.pt; Ambassador PASCOELA BARRETO.
Tunisia: Rua Rodrigo Rebelo 16, 1400-318 Lisbon; tel. (21) 3010330; fax (21) 3016817; e-mail atlisbon@netcabo.pt; Ambassador MOHAMED RIDHA FARHAT.
Turkey: Av. das Descobertas 22, 1400-092 Lisbon; tel. (21) 3003110; fax (21) 3017934; e-mail info-turk@mail.telepac.pt; internet turquia.planetaclix.pt; Ambassador ZERGUN KORUTURK.
Ukraine: Av. das Descobertas 18, 1400-092 Lisbon; tel. (21) 3010043; fax (21) 3010059; e-mail emb_pt@mfa.gov.ua; Ambassador ROSTYSLAV TRONENKO.
United Kingdom: Rua de São Bernardo 33, 1249-082 Lisbon; tel. (21) 3924000; fax (21) 3924021; e-mail ppa@fco.gov.uk; internet www.uk-embassy.pt; Ambassador JOHN BUCK.
USA: Av. das Forças Armadas (Sete Rios), 1600-081 Lisbon; tel. (21) 7273000; fax (21) 7269109; e-mail ref@american-embassy.pt; internet www.american-embassy.pt; Ambassador ALFRED HOFFMAN.
Uruguay: Rua Sampaio Pina 16, 2°, 1070-249 Lisbon; tel. (21) 3889265; fax (21) 3889245; e-mail urulusi@sapo.pt; Ambassador GASTON LASARTE.
Venezuela: Av. Duque de Loulé 47, 4°, 1050-086 Lisbon; tel. (21) 3573803; fax (21) 3527421; e-mail embavenez@mail.telepac.pt; Ambassador MANUEL QUIJADA.

Judicial System

The judicial system of the Portuguese Republic comprises several categories of courts which, according to the Constitution, are sovereign bodies. The country is divided into four judicial districts, which are, in turn, divided into 37 judicial circuits. The principle of habeas corpus is recognized. Citizens who have been unjustly convicted are entitled to a review of their sentence and to compensation. The death penalty is prohibited by the Constitution. The jury system, reintroduced for certain types of crime in 1976, operates only at the request of the Public Prosecutor or defendant.

Judges are appointed for life and are irremovable. Practising judges may not hold any other office, whether public or private, except a non-remunerated position in teaching or research in the legal field. The Conselho Superior da Magistratura controls their appointment, transfer and promotion and the exercise of disciplinary action.

PORTUGAL

PUBLIC PROSECUTION

The State is represented in the courts by the Public Prosecution, whose highest organ is the Procuradoria-Geral da República (Attorney-General's Office).

Procuradoria-Geral da República: Rua da Escola Politécnica 140, 1269-269 Lisbon; tel. (21) 3921900; fax (21) 3975255; e-mail mailpgr@pgr.pt; internet www.pgr.pt; Attorney-General Dr JOSÉ ADRIANO MACHADO SOUTO DE MOURA.

Gabinete de Documentação e Direito Comparado: Rua Vale de Pereiro 2, 1269-113 Lisbon; tel. (21) 3820300; fax (21) 3820301; e-mail mail@gddc.pt; internet www.gddc.pt; Dir JOANA GOMES FERRERIA.

SUPREME COURT

Supremo Tribunal de Justiça

Praça do Comércio, 1149-012 Lisbon; tel. (21) 3218900; fax (21) 3474919; e-mail correio@lisboa.stj.mj.pt; internet www.stj.pt.

The highest organ of the judicial system; has jurisdiction over Metropolitan Portugal, the Azores and Madeira; it consists of 60 judges, incl. the President.

President: JOSÉ MOURA NUNES DA CRUZ.

COURTS OF SECOND INSTANCE

There are four Courts of Second Instance (or Courts of Appeal):

Tribunal da Relação de Coímbra: Palácio da Justiça, 3049 Coimbra; tel. (239) 852950; fax (239) 824310; e-mail trc@netcabo.pt; internet www.trc.pt; 46 judges, incl. the President; Pres. Dr CARLOS MANUEL GASPAR LEITÃO.

Tribunal da Relação de Évora: Largo das Alterações 1, 7034 Évora; tel. (266) 724147; fax (266) 721529; internet www.tre.pt; 39 judges, incl. the President; Pres. Dr ARMINDO RIBEIRO LUIS.

Tribunal da Relação de Lisboa: Rua Arsenal Letra G, 1100-038 Lisbon; tel. (21) 3222900; fax (21) 3222934; internet www.trl.pt; 108 judges, incl. the President; Pres. Dr LUÍS MARIA VAZ DAS NEVES.

Tribunal da Relação de Porto: Campo Mártires de Pátria, 4099-012 Porto; tel. (22) 2008531; fax (22) 2000715; e-mail info@trp.pt; internet www.trp.pt; 91 judges, incl. the President; Pres. Dr JOSÉ FERREIRA CORREIA DE PAIVA.

COURTS OF FIRST INSTANCE

There are 258 courts of first instance within Portuguese territory: 195 *comarca* hear cases of a general nature, while 46 labour courts hear specific matters. There are five family courts and two courts for the enforcement of sentences. Circuit Courts total 33.

CONSTITUTIONAL COURT

Tribunal Constitucional

Palácio Ratton, Rua de O Século 111, 1249-117 Lisbon; tel. (21) 3233600; fax (21) 3233669; e-mail tribunal@tribconstitucional.pt; internet www.tribunalconstitucional.pt.

Rules on matters of constitutionality according to the terms of the Constitution of the Portuguese Republic; exercises jurisdiction over all Portuguese territory; consists of 13 judges.

President: ARTUR JOAQUIM DE FARIA MAURICIO.

SUPREME ADMINISTRATIVE COURT

Supremo Tribunal Administrativo

Rua de S. Pedro de Alcântara 73–79, 1269-137 Lisbon; tel. (21) 3216200; fax (21) 3466129; e-mail correio@lisboa.sta.mj.pt; internet www.sta.mj.pt.

The highest organ of the administrative system; has jurisdiction over metropolitan Portugal, the Azores and Madeira; consists of 46 judges, incl. the President.

President: MANUEL FERNANDO DOS SANTOS SERRA.

Religion

There is freedom of religion in Portugal. The dominant Christian denomination is Roman Catholicism, but a number of Protestant Churches have been established. In the 2001 census, of the 8,699,515 respondents to the question regarding religion, 7,353,548 identified themselves as Roman Catholic, 17,443 as Orthodox, 48,301 as Protestant and 122,745 as other Christian. A further 1,773 were Jewish, 12,014 were Muslim and 13,882 followed another religion.

CHRISTIANITY

Conselho Português de Igrejas Cristãs (COPIC) (Portuguese Council of Christian Churches): Apto 392, 4430-003 Vila Nova de Gaia; tel. (233) 754018; fax (233) 752016; e-mail igreja@lusitana.org; f. 1971; three mem. churches, two observers; Gen. Sec. (vacant).

The Roman Catholic Church

For ecclesiastical purposes, Portugal comprises 17 dioceses, grouped into three metropolitan sees (the patriarchate of Lisbon and the archdioceses of Braga and Évora). At 31 December 2003 some 9.4m. Portuguese were adherents of the Roman Catholic Church, representing 90.4% of the population.

Bishops' Conference

Conferência Episcopal Portuguesa, Campo dos Mártires da Pátria 43, 1° esq., 1150-225 Lisbon; tel. (21) 8855460; fax (21) 8855461; e-mail webmaster@ecclesia.pt; internet www.ecclesia.pt.

f. 1932; Pres. Most Rev. JORGE FERREIRA DA COSTA ORTIGA (Archbishop of Braga); Sec. TOMAZ PEDRO DA SILVA NUNES.

Patriarch of Lisbon: Cardinal JOSÉ DA CRUZ POLICARPO, Casa Patriarcal Seminário dos Olivais, Quinta do Cabeço, 1800 Lisbon; tel. (21) 9457310; fax (21) 9457329; e-mail vigararia.geral@patriarcado-lisboa.pt; internet www.patriarcado-lisboa.pt.

Archbishop of Braga: Most Rev. JORGE FERREIRA DA COSTA ORTIGA, Paço Arquiepiscopal, Rua de Santa Margarida 181, 4710-306 Braga; tel. (253) 203180; fax (253) 203198; e-mail diocese@diocese-braga.pt; internet www.diocese-braga.pt.

Archbishop of Évora: Most Rev. MAURÍLIO JORGE QUINTAL DE GOUVEIA, Cúria Arquiepiscopal, Largo Marquês de Marialva 6, 7000-809 Évora; tel. (266) 748850; fax (266) 748851; e-mail diocese@diocese-evora.pt; internet www.diocese-evora.pt.

The Anglican Communion

The Lusitanian Catholic Apostolic Evangelical Church was established by the American Episcopal Church in 1880. After integration in 1980, the church became an extraprovincial diocese under the metropolitan authority of the Archbishop of Canterbury (United Kingdom).

Church of England: Rua João de Deus 5, Alcoitão, 2645-128 Alcabideche; tel. and fax (21) 4692303; e-mail gl-chaplaincy@clix.pt; internet www.lisbonanglicans.org; Chaplain Canon MICHAEL BULLOCK.

Igreja Lusitana Católica Apostólica Evangélica (Lusitanian Catholic Apostolic Evangelical Church): Apdo 392, 4431-905 Vila Nova de Gaia; tel. (22) 3754018; fax (22) 3752016; e-mail centrodiocesano@igreja-lusitana.org; internet www.igreja-lusitana.org; f. 1880; Bishop Rt Rev. FERNANDO LUZ SOARES.

Other Christian Churches

Associação de Igrejas Baptistas Portuguesas (Asscn of Portuguese Baptist Churches): Rua da Escola 18, Maceira, 2715 Pero Pinheiro; tel. (21) 9271150; f. 1955; Pres. Rev. JOÃO S. REGUEIRAS.

Convenção das Assembleias de Deus em Portugal (Assembly of God): Av. Almirante Gago Coutinho 158, 1170-033 Lisbon; tel. (21) 8464317; e-mail geral@convencao-assembleia-deus.org; internet www.convencao-assembleias-deus.org; Pres. Pastor ANTÓNIO VIEITO ANTUNES, Pastor DINIS RODRIGUES.

Convenção Baptista Portuguesa (Portuguese Baptist Convention): Queluz; tel. (21) 4343370; fax (21) 4343379; e-mail convbaptport@mail.telepac.pt; f. 1920; Pres. Dr JOSÉ P. DE SOUSA; Sec. MARIA HERCÍLIA MELO; 4,338 mems (2003).

Igreja Evangélica Alemã de Lisboa (German Evangelical Church in Lisbon): Av. Columbano Bordalo Pinheiro 48, 1070-064 Lisbon; tel. (21) 7260976; fax (21) 7274839; e-mail dekl@deutsche-kirche-portugal.org; internet www.deutsche-kirche-portugal.org; Pastor Rev. HILDEGARD JUSEK.

Igreja Evangélica Metodista Portuguesa (Portuguese Evangelical Methodist Church): Praça Coronel Pacheco 23, 4050-453 Porto; tel. (22) 2007410; fax (22) 2086961; e-mail sede-geral@igreja-metodista.pt; internet www.igreja-metodista.pt; Bishop SIFREDO TEIXEIRA.

Igreja Evangélica Presbiteriana de Portugal (Presbyterian Church of Portugal): Rua Tomás da Anunciação, 56, 1° dto, 1350-328 Lisbon; tel. (21) 3974959; fax (21) 3956326; e-mail office@iepp.org; internet www.iepp.org; f. 1952; Pres. EUNICE LEITE; Gen. Sec. DAVID VALENTE.

ISLAM

Comunidade Islamica de Lisboa: Mesquita Central de Lisboa, Av. José Malhoa, 1070 Lisbon; tel. (21) 3874142; fax (21) 3872230; Pres. ABDUL KARIM VAKIL.

JUDAISM

There are Jewish communities in Lisbon, Oporto, Belmonte and Faro.

PORTUGAL
Directory

Comunidade Israelita de Lisboa: Rua do Monte Olivete 16, r/c, 1200-280 Lisbon; tel. (1) 3931130; fax (1) 3931139; e-mail administrativo@cilisboa.org; internet www.cilisboa.org; Pres. Dr José Oulman Carp.

The Press

Under the 1976 Constitution, the freedom of the press is guaranteed. In 2003 754 newspapers and 773 magazines were published. The daily newspapers had an average circulation of 727,625 per edition.

PRINCIPAL DAILIES

Aveiro

Diário de Aveiro: Av. Dr Lourenço Peixinho 15-1°G, 3800-801 Aveiro; tel. (234) 000031; fax (234) 000032; e-mail diarioaveiro@netcabo.pt; internet www.diarioaveiro.pt; f. 1985; morning; Dir Adriano Callé Lucas; circ. 4,500.

Braga

Correio do Minho: Praçeta Escola do Magisterio 34 Maximinos, Apdo 2290, 4700-236 Braga; tel. (253) 309500; fax (253) 309525; e-mail redaccao@correiodominho.com; internet www.correiodominho.com; morning; Dir A. Costa Guimarães; circ. 1,573.

Diário do Minho: Rua de Santa Margarida 4, 4710-306 Braga; tel. (253) 609460; fax (253) 609465; e-mail geral@diariodominho.pt; internet www.diariodominho.pt; f. 1919; morning; Dir João Aguiar Campos; circ. 4,000.

Coímbra

Diário as Beiras: Rua 25 de Abril, Apdo 44, 3040-935 Taveiro, Coímbra; tel. (239) 980280; fax (239) 983574; internet beirastexto@asbeiras.pt; internet www.asbeiras.pt; Dir António Abrantes.

Diário de Coímbra: Rua Adriano Lucas, 3020-264 Coímbra; tel. (239) 492133; fax (239) 492128; e-mail redac@diariocoimbra.pt; internet www.diariocoimbra.pt; f. 1930; morning; Domingo publ. on Sun. (f. 1974; circ. 8,000); Dir Eng. Adriano Mário da Cunha Lucas; circ. 9,000.

Évora

Diário do Sul: Travessa de Santo André 8, Apdo 2037, 7021 Évora; tel. (266) 703144; fax (266) 741252; f. 1969; morning; Dir Manuel Madeira Piçarra; circ. 8,500.

Leiria

Diário de Leiria: Edif. Maringá, Rua S. Franciso 7, 4° esq., 2400-232 Leiria; tel. (244) 000031; fax (244) 000032; e-mail jornaldl@esoterica.pt; internet www.diarioleiria.pt; f. 1987; morning; Dir Adriano Callé Lucas; circ. 3,500.

Lisbon

A Bola: Travessa da Queimada 23, 2°D r/c esq., 1294 Lisbon; tel. (21) 3463981; fax (21) 3432275; internet www.abola.pt; f. 1945; sport; Dir Victor Serpa; circ. 180,000.

A Capital: Rua Basílio Teles 24, 1070-021 Lisbon; tel. (21) 7248000; fax (21) 7248001; e-mail acapital@acapital.pt; internet www.acapital.pt; f. 1968; evening; Dir Luís Osorio.

Correio da Manhã: Av. João Crisóstomo 72, 1069-043 Lisbon; tel. (21) 3185200; fax (21) 3156146; e-mail luisbcm@mail.telepac.pt; internet www.correiomanha.pt; f. 1979; morning; independent; Dir Agostinho de Azevedo; circ. 85,000.

Diário Económico: Rua de Oliveira ao Carmo 8, 1200-309 Lisbon; tel. (21) 3236768; fax (21) 3236775; e-mail deconomico@economica.iol.pt; internet www.diarioeconomico.com; Dir Miguel Coutinho.

Diário de Notícias: Av. da Liberdade 266, 1250-149 Lisbon; tel. (21) 3187500; fax (21) 3187515; e-mail webmaster@dn.pt; internet www.dn.pt; f. 1864; morning; Dir Antonio José Teixeira; Exec. Editor Paulo Baldaia; circ. 75,561.

Jornal de O Dia: Rua Rodrigo da Fonseca 204, 1070-245 Lisbon; tel. (21) 3864203; fax (21) 3864198; e-mail jornalodia@mail.pt; internet odia.no.sapo.pt; f. 1975; as O Dia; morning; right-wing; Dir Adelino Alves.

Público: Rua Agostinho Neto 16c, Quinta do Lambert, 1769-010 Lisbon; tel. (21) 7501075; fax (21) 7587638; e-mail publico@publico.pt; internet www.publico.pt; f. 1990; morning; Dir José Manuel Fernandes; circ. 75,000.

Record: Av. Conde Valbom 30, 4-5°, 1050-068 Lisbon; tel. (21) 0124900; fax (21) 3476279; e-mail record@record.pt; internet www.record.pt; f. 1949; sport; Dir João Marcelino; Editor-in-Chief João Manha; circ. 132,000.

24 Horas: Av. 5 de Outubro 17, 2b, 1050-047 Lisbon; tel. (21) 3186500; fax (21) 3155787; e-mail 24horas@mail.prodiario.pt; Dir Jorge Alberto Monteiro Morais.

Porto

O Comércio do Porto: Rua Fernandes Tomás 352, 7°, 4000 Porto; tel. (22) 563571; fax (22) 575095; f. 1854; morning; Dir Luís de Carvalho; circ. 30,295.

O Jogo: Rua de Gil Vicente 129, 1°, 4000-814 Porto; tel. (22) 5071900; fax (22) 5504550; e-mail ojogo@mail.telepac.pt; internet www.ojogo.pt; sporting news; Dir Manuel Tavares.

Jornal de Notícias: Rua Gonçalo Cristóvão 195–219, 4049-011 Porto; tel. (22) 2096111; fax (22) 2006330; e-mail noticias@jn.pt; internet www.jn.pt; f. 1888; morning; Dir Frederico Martins Mendes; circ. 105,000.

O Primeiro de Janeiro: Rua Coelho Neto 65, 4000 Porto; tel. (22) 0109100; fax (22) 5103291; e-mail geral@oprimeirodejaneiro.pt; internet www.oprimeirodejaneiro.pt; f. 1868; independent; morning; Dir Nassalete Miranda; circ. 20,200.

Setúbal

Correio de Setúbal: Rua Camilo Castelo Branco 163, f–h, Apdo 549, 2900 Setúbal; tel. (265) 538818; fax (265) 538819.

Viseu

Diário Regional Viseu: Rua Alexandre Herculano 198, 1° esq., 3510-033 Viseu; tel. (232) 000031; fax (232) 000032; e-mail diario-viseu@clix.pt; internet www.diarioregional.pt; Dir Adriano Callé Lucas.

Notícias de Viseu: Av. do Convento 1, Apdo 3115, 3511-689 Viseu; tel. (232) 410410; fax (232) 410418; e-mail geral@noticiasdeviseu.com; internet www.noticiasdeviseu.com; f. 1974; Dir Fernando Abreu.

Madeira
(Funchal)

Diário de Notícias: Rua Dr Fernão de Ornelas 56, 3°, 9054-514 Funchal; tel. (291) 202300; fax (291) 202306; e-mail dnmad@dnoticias.pt; internet www.dnoticias.pt; f. 1876; morning; independent; Dir José Bettencourt da Câmara; circ. 19,000.

Jornal da Madeira: Rua Dr Fernão de Ornelas 35, 4°, 9001-905 Funchal; tel. (291) 210400; fax (291) 210401; e-mail editorial@jornaldamadeira.pt; internet www.jornaldamadeira.pt; f. 1927; morning; Catholic; Dir Silva Velosa; circ. 8,000.

The Azores

Açoriano Oriental: Rua Dr Bruno Tavares Carreiro 36, 9500-055 Ponta Delgada; tel. (296) 202800; fax (296) 202826; e-mail pub.ao@acorianooriental.pt; internet www.acorianooriental.pt; f. 1835; morning; Dir Paolo Simões; circ. 6,000.

O Correio da Horta: Rua Ernesto Rebelo 5, 9900 Horta; tel. (292) 292821; fax (292) 392234; e-mail correiodahorta@ciberacores.net; internet www.ciberacores.net/correiodahorta; f. 1930; evening; Dir Rúben Rodrigues; circ. 1,410.

Correio dos Açores: Rua Dr João Francisco de Sousa 14, 9500 Ponta Delgada; tel. (296) 201060; fax (296) 286119; e-mail redaccao@correiodosazores.com; internet www.correiodosazores.com; f. 1920; morning; Dir Américo Natalino Viveiros; circ. 4,460.

Diário dos Açores: Rua do 'Diário dos Açores' 5, 9500-178 Ponta Delgada; tel. (296) 286902; fax (296) 284840; e-mail diario@virtualazores.net; internet www.virtualazores.net/diario; f. 1870; morning; Dir Paulo Hugo Viveiros; circ. 2,380.

Diário Insular: Av. Infante D. Henrique 1, 9700-098 Angra do Heroísmo, Terceira; tel. (295) 401050; fax (295) 214246; e-mail diarioins@mail.telepac.pt; internet www.diarioinsular.com; f. 1946; morning; Dir José Lourenço; circ. 3,400.

O Telégrafo: Rua Conselheiro Medeiros 30, 9902 Horta; tel. (292) 22245; fax (292) 22245; f. 1893; morning; Dir Ruben Rodrigues; circ. 3,200.

A União: Rua da Palha 11–17, 9700-144 Angra do Heroísmo; tel. (295) 214275; fax (295) 214062; e-mail auniao@auniao.com; internet www.auniao.com; f. 1893; morning; Dir Tómas Detinho; circ. 1,500.

PRINCIPAL PERIODICALS

Activa: Rua Calvet de Magalhães 242, Laveiras, 2770-022 Paço de Arcos; tel. (21) 4143078; fax (21) 4107050; e-mail acj@acj.pt; internet www.acj.pt; f. 1991; monthly; for women; Editor-in-Chief Clara Marques; circ. 90,000.

Africa Hoje: Rua Joaquim António de Aguiar 45, 5° esq., 1070 Lisbon; tel. (21) 557175; fax (21) 3557667; e-mail geral@lucidus.pt;

PORTUGAL

internet africa.sapo.pt; f. 1985; monthly; African affairs; circ. 30,000; Dir ALBÉRICO CARDOSO.

Anglo-Portuguese News: Apdo 113, 2766-902 Estoril, Lisbon; tel. (21) 4661471; fax (21) 4660358; e-mail apn@mail.telepac.pt; f. 1937; every Thursday; English language newspaper; Publr and Editor NIGEL BATLEY; circ. 30,000.

Autosport: Edif. São Francisco de Sales, Rua Calvet de Magalhães 242, 2770-022 Paço de Arcos; tel. (21) 4698197; fax (21) 4698552; e-mail autosport@autosport.pt; internet www.autosport.pt; weekly; motoring; Dir RUI FREIRE; circ. 23,000.

Avante: Av. Almirante Gago Coutinho 121, 1700-029 Lisbon; tel. (21) 7817190; fax (21) 7817193; e-mail avante.pcp@mail.telepac.pt; internet www.avante.pt; weekly; organ of the Communist Party; Dir JOSÉ CASANOVA.

Brotéria—Revista de Cultura: Rua Maestro António Taborda 14, 1249-094 Lisbon; tel. (21) 3961660; fax (21) 3956629; e-mail broteria@clix.pt; internet www.broteria.pt; f. 1902; monthly; review of culture; Dir HERMÍNIO RICO; circ. 1,400.

Casa e Decoração: Av. Duque d'Avila 26, 3°, 1049-042 Lisbon; tel. (21) 3168500; fax (21) 3168578; e-mail casadeco@meriberica.pt; internet www.meriberica.pt; f. 1981; 12 a year; home and interior decoration; Dir URSULA BASTOS; circ. 35,000.

Casa & Jardim: Rua da Misericórdia 137, s/loja, 1249-037 Lisbon; tel. (21) 3472127; fax (21) 3421490; e-mail direccao@casajardim.pt; internet www.casajardim.net; f. 1978; monthly; home, interior and exterior design, fine arts, exhibitions and antique fairs; Dir EDUARDO FORTUNATO DE ALMEIDA; circ. 20,000.

Colecções Moda & Beleza: Rua Dona Filipa de Vilhena 4, 5° esq., 1000-135 Lisbon; tel. (21) 3105300; fax (21) 3105309; e-mail bdesenhada@meriberica.pt; internet www.meriberica.pt; 5 a year; fashion and beauty; Editor CRISTINA COSTA; circ. 240,000.

Colóquio/Letras: Av. de Berna 45A, 1067-001 Lisbon; tel. (21) 7823000; fax (21) 7823021; e-mail info@gulbenkian.pt; internet www.gulbenkian.pt/educacao/revista.asp; f. 1971; 4 a year; literary; Dir Dra JOANA VARELA; circ. 3,600.

Correio da Madeira: Rua do Carmo 19, 3° dto, 9000 Funchal; tel. (291) 20738; f. 1987; weekly newspaper; Dir JOSÉ CAMPOS; circ. 5,000.

Cosmopolitan: Rua Calvet de Magalhães 242, Laveiras, 2770-022 Paço de Arcos; tel. (21) 4698861; e-mail cosmopolitan@acj.pt; internet www.acj.pt; f. 1992; monthly; women's magazine; Editor MARIA SERINA.

O Diabo (The Devil): Rua Alexandre Herculano 7, 5° esq., 1100 Lisbon; tel. (21) 572367; fax (21) 570263; e-mail diabo@esoterica.pt; f. 1976; weekly newspaper; Dir VERA LAGOA; circ. 46,000.

Eles e Elas: Praça Luiz de Camões 36, 2°D, 1200-243 Lisbon; tel. (21) 3224660; fax (21) 3224679; e-mail gabinete1@gabinete1.pt; internet www.gabinete1.pt; f. 1983; monthly; fashion, culture, social events; Dir MARIA DA LUZ DE BRAGANÇA.

Elle: Rua Filipe Folque 40, 4°, 1050 Lisbon; tel. (21) 3156907; fax (21) 3164205; e-mail elle@hachette.pt; f. 1988; monthly; women's magazine; Dir FÁTIMA COTTA; circ. 48,916.

Expresso: Rua Duque de Palmela 37, 3° dto, 1296 Lisbon; tel. (21) 3114000; fax (21) 3543858; e-mail info@mail.expresso.pt; internet www.expresso.pt; weekly newspaper; Dir JOSÉ ANTÓNIO PAULA SARAIVA; Vice-Dir NICOLAU SANTOS; circ. 160,000.

Gente e Viagens: Rua Joaquim António de Aguiar 45, 1099-058 Lisbon; tel. (21) 3839810; fax (21) 862746; e-mail lucidus@mail.telepac.pt; internet genteviagens.sapo.pt; f. 1980; monthly; tourism; Dir ALBÉRICO CARDOSO; circ. 30,000.

Guia—Revista Prática: Av. Almirante Gago Coutinho 113, 1749-087 Lisbon; tel. (21) 8474410; fax (21) 8474396; e-mail mpcorreia@tvguia.pt; weekly women's magazine; fashion and housekeeping; Dir MARGARIDA PINTO CORREIA; Editor-in-Chief PALMIRA SIMÕES; circ. 40,000.

O Independente: Av. Almirante Reis 113, sala 802, 1150-014 Lisbon; tel. (21) 3116500; fax (21) 3116502; e-mail correio@oindependente.pt; internet www.oindependente.pt; f. 1988; weekly; Propr SOCI; Dir PAULO PORTAS; circ. 103,500.

JL (Jornal de Letras, Artes e Ideias): Rua Calvet de Magalhães 242, Laveiras, 2770-022 Paço de Arcos; tel. (21) 574520; e-mail jl@acj.pt; internet www.acj.pt; weekly; Dir JOSÉ CARLOS DE VASCONCELOS; Editor MANUEL BECA MURIAS; circ. 80,000.

Manchete: Rua das Flores 105, 1° esq., 1200-194 Lisbon; tel. (21) 3224660; fax (21) 3224679; e-mail gabinete1@gabinete1.pt; internet www.gabinete1.pt; f. 1992; monthly; national and international events; Dir MARIA DA LUZ DE BRAGANÇA.

Maria: Av. Miguel Bombarda 33, 2745 Queluz; tel. 4364401; fax 4365001; internet www.impala.pt/maria; f. 1977; weekly; women's magazine; Dir JACQUES RODRIGUES; Editor-in-Chief PAULA RODRIGUES; circ. 392,000.

Máxima: Av. João Crisóstemo 72, 3°, 1069-043 Lisbon; tel. (21) 3309400; fax (21) 3540410; e-mail maximaonline@edimoda.pt; internet www.maxima.pt; f. 1989; women's magazine; Dir LAUZA LUZES TORRES; circ. 45,000.

Moda & Moda: Rua Braamcamp 12, r/c esq., 1250-050 Lisbon; tel. (21) 3886068; fax (21) 3862426; e-mail modaemoda@netcabo.pt; f. 1984; 5 a year; fashion, beauty and art; Dir MARIONELA GUSMÃO; circ. 20,000.

Mulher Moderna: Av. Miguel Bombarda 33, 2745 Queluz; tel. 4364401; fax 4365001; f. 1988; weekly; women's magazine; Dir JACQUES RODRIGUES; Editor-in-Chief PAULA RODRIGUES; circ. 60,000.

Nova Gente: Av. Miguel Bombarda 33, 2745 Queluz; tel. 4364388; fax 4365001; f. 1979; weekly; popular; Dir JACQUES RODRIGUES; Editor-in-Chief ANTÓNIO SIMÕES; circ. 200,000.

Portugal Socialista: Largo do Rato 2, 1269-143 Lisbon; tel. (21) 3822000; f. 1967; quarterly; organ of the Socialist Party; Dir AUGUSTO SANTOS SILVA; circ. 5,000.

Povo Livre: Rua S. Caetano 9, 1249-087 Lisbon; tel. (21) 3952140; fax (21) 3976967; weekly; organ of the Social Democratic Party; Dir LUÍS ALVARO CAMPOS FERREIRA.

Revista ACP: Rua Rosa Araújo 24, 1250-195 Lisbon; tel. (21) 3180100; fax (21) 3180170; internet www.acp.pt; f. 1908; monthly; motoring and tourism; Propr Automóvel Club de Portugal; Editor ANTÓNIO RAPOSO DE MAGALHÃES; circ. 190,000.

Revista Exame: Rua Calvet de Magalhães 242, Laveiras, 2770-022 Paço de Arcos; e-mail exame@acj.pt; tel. (21) 4143078; fax (21) 4107050; monthly; finance; circ. 21,000.

Revista Negócios: Rua do Norte 14, 2°, 1200 Lisbon; tel. (21) 3471259; monthly; business and finance; circ. 10,000.

Segredos de Cozinha: Edif. do Grupo Impala, Ranholas, 2710-460 Sintra; tel. (21) 92398033; fax (21) 9238044; e-mail gracamorais@impala.pt; f. 1985; weekly; cookery; Dir GRAÇA MORAIS; Editor-in-Chief PAULA RODRIGUES; circ. 40,000.

Selecções do Reader's Digest: Rua D. Francisco Manuel de Melo 21, 1070 Lisbon; tel. (21) 3810000; fax (21) 3859203; internet www.looksmart.com; monthly magazine; Dir ISABEL BIVAR; circ. 200,000.

Semanário: Rua S. Cabral 26–30, 1495 Lisbon; tel. (21) 4198065; fax (21) 4243328; weekly newspaper; Dir Dr ALVARO MENDONÇA; circ. 55,000.

Semanário Económico: Rua da Oliveira ao Carmo 8, 5° andar, 1200-309 Lisbon; tel. (21) 3236900; fax (21) 3236901; e-mail seconomico@economica.iol.pt; internet www.semanarioeconomico.iol.pt; weekly; economy, business and finance; Dir JOÃO VIEIRA PEREIRA; circ. 20,000.

Tal & Qual: Av. 5 de Outubro 17, 1200 Lisbon; tel. (21) 3115200; fax (21) 3155793; weekly; popular newspaper; Editor JOÃO FERREIRA; circ. 61,000.

TV Guia: Av. Almirante Gago Coutinho 113, 1749-087 Lisbon; tel. (21) 8474410; fax (21) 8474395; e-mail jgobern@tvguia.pt; weekly; TV programmes and general features; Dir JOÃO GOBERN; circ. 108,500.

TV 7 Dias: Av. Miguel Bombarda 33, 2745 Queluz; tel. 4364401; fax 4365001; f. 1985; weekly; television magazine; Dir VENTURA MARTINS; Editor-in-Chief FREDERICO VALARINHO; circ. 100,000.

Vida Económica: Rua Gonçalo Cristovão 111, 5°–7°, 4049-037 Porto; tel. (22) 3399400; fax (22) 2058098; e-mail redaccao@vidaeconomica.pt; internet www.vidaeconomica.pt; weekly; financial; Dir JOÃO PEIXOTO DE SOUSA; Editor-in-Chief JOÃO LUÍS DE SOUSA.

Visão: Rua Calvet de Magalhães 242, Laveiras, 2770-022 Paço de Arcos; tel. (22) 4698000; fax (22) 8347557; e-mail visao@ajc.pt; internet www.visaoonline.pt; f. 1993; weekly magazine; Dir-Gen. PEDRO CAMAHO; circ. 58,172.

NEWS AGENCIES

Agência Europeia de Imprensa, Lda (AEI): Largo da Rosa 6, 1149-054 Lisbon; tel. (21) 0307860; fax (21) 8875725; e-mail aei@mail.aei.pt; internet www.aei.pt; f. 1962; Man. Dir Dr ALEXANDRE CORDEIRO.

Agência de Representações Dias da Silva, Lda (ADS): Av. Almirante Reis 82, 6° dto, 1169-163 Lisbon; tel. (21) 8110270; fax (21) 8154542; e-mail adspress@mail.telepac.pt; f. 1964; pictorial news, features, photographic reports, news, comic strips, literary material, etc.; Dir JÚLIO CALDERON DIAS DA SILVA.

Lusa (Agência de Notícias de Portugal, SA): Rua Dr João Couto, Lote C, 1500 Lisbon; tel. (21) 7144099; fax (21) 7145443; e-mail dinformacao@lusa.pt; internet www.lusa.pt; f. 1987; Chair. MARIA ROSA SIMÕES.

Foreign Bureaux

Agence France-Presse (AFP) (France): Rua Rosa Araújo 34, 3°, 1250-195 Lisbon; tel. (21) 3556939; fax (21) 3520866; e-mail lisboa@afp.com; internet www.afp.com/portugues; Dir ISABELLE HOURCADE.

PORTUGAL

Directory

Agencia EFE (Spain): Rua Castilho 13D, 5°A, Lisbon; tel. (21) 8875712; fax (21) 8875713; e-mail agencia.efe@mail.telepac.pt; Dir NEMESIO RODRÍGUEZ LÓPEZ.

Angola Press (ANGOP) (Angola): Rua Luciano Cordeiro 89, 4°, 1150-213 Lisbon; tel. (21) 3139706; e-mail angop@mail.telepac.pt.

Associated Press (AP) (USA): P. Duque de Saldanha 1, 10°B, 1050-094 Lisbon; tel. (21) 3191860; fax (21) 3191885; Admin. Dir EMMA E. A. GILBERT.

Deutsche Presse-Agentur (dpa) (Germany): Praça da Alegria 58, 5°B, 1200 Lisbon; tel. (21) 3469837; Bureau Chief ARTUR MARGALHO.

Maghreb Arabe Presse (Morocco): Rua Chagas 20, 2°D, 1200-107 Lisbon; tel. (21) 3257982.

Reuters Europe—Portugal Brance (UK): Av. da Liberdade 190, 2° A, 1050-197 Lisbon; tel. (21) 3509200; fax (21) 3150036; e-mail lisbon.newsroom@reuters.com; Chief Correspondent IAN SIMPSON.

Rossiyskoye Informatsionnoye Agentstvo—Novosti (RIA—Novosti) (Russia): Praça Andrade Caminha 3, 1700-039 Lisbon; tel. (21) 7934700; fax (21) 7934717; e-mail rialisboa@mail.telepac.pt; Dir VITALI MIRNYI.

Xinhua (New China) News Agency (People's Republic of China): Rua Gonçalo Velho Cabral 11A, Restelo, Lisbon 3; tel. (21) 615783; e-mail xinhua@mail.telepac.pt; Chief Correspondent XIAO ZIAOQUAN.

PRESS ASSOCIATIONS

Associação da Imprensa (AIND) (Portuguese Press Association): Rua Gomes Freire 183, 4° esq., 1169-041 Lisbon; tel. (21) 3555092; fax (21) 3142191; e-mail geral@aind.pt; internet www.aind.pt; f. 1960; represents 450 publications, both local and national; Pres. JOÃO PALMEIRO; Sec.-Gen. JOANA RAMADA CURTO.

Associação da Imprensa Diária (Association of the Daily Press): Rua de Artilharia Um 69, 2°, 1297 Lisbon; tel. (21) 3857584; fax (21) 3873541; f. 1976; 27 mems; Pres. ANTÓNIO FREITAS CRUZ; Sec. JORGE MOURA.

Associação da Imprensa Estrangeira em Portugal (AIEP): Sala da Imprensa, Palácio Foz, Praça dos Restauradores, 1250-187 Lisbon; fax (21) 3464145; e-mail aieportugal@sapo.pt; f. 1976; Pres. RAMÓN FONT BOVÉ; Exec. Sec. ANNE GOVERNO.

Publishers

Ancora Editora: Av. Infante Santo 52, 3° esq., 1350-179 Lisbon; tel. (21) 3951223; fax (21) 3951222; e-mail ancora.editora@ancora-editora.pt; internet www.ancora-editora.pt; f. 1998; Portuguese literature and culture, factual and educational works.

Areal Editores: Av. da Boavista 1471, Loja 10 r/c, 4100-131 Porto; tel. (22) 3393900; fax (22) 2005708; e-mail areal@arealeditores.pt; internet www.arealeditores.pt; educational.

Assírio & Alvim: Rua Passos Manuel 67B, 1150-258 Lisbon; tel. (21) 3583030; fax (21) 3583039; e-mail assirio@assirio.com; internet www.assirio.pt; f. 1972; poetry, fiction, essays, gastronomy, photography, art, children's literature, history, social science; Man. VASCO DAVID.

Bertrand Editora, SA: Rua Anchieta 319, 1°, 1249-060 Lisbon; tel. (21) 3420085; fax (21) 3479728; e-mail editora@bertrand.pt; internet www.bertrand.pt; literature, arts, humanities, educational; Man. MARIO CORREIA.

Campo das Letras: Rua D. Manuel II 33, 5°, 4050-345 Porto; tel. (22) 6080870; fax (22) 6080880; e-mail campo.letras@mail.telepac.pt; internet www.campo-letras.pt; f. 1994; literature, juvenile, current affairs.

Circulo de Leitores: Rua Prof. Jorge da Silva Horta 1, 1500-499 Lisbon; tel. (21) 7626100; fax (21) 7607149; e-mail correio@circuloleitores.pt; internet www.circuloleitores.pt; fiction and non-fiction.

Coímbra Editora, Lda: Rua do Armado, Apdo 101, 3001-951 Coímbra; tel. (239) 8526540; fax (239) 852651; e-mail info@mail.coimbraeditora.pt; internet www.coimbraeditora.pt; f. 1920; law, education, linguistics; Man. Dr JOÃO CARLOS A. OLIVEIRA SALGADO.

Contexto Editora, Lda: Largo D. Estfânia, 01000 Lisbon; tel. (21) 1570082; fax (21) 3520208; fiction, poetry, children's literature; Dir MANUEL DE BRITO.

Edições Afrontamento, Lda: Rua de Costa Cabral 859, 4200-225 Porto; tel. (22) 5074220; fax (22) 5074229; e-mail editorial@edicoesafrontamento.pt; internet www.edicoesafrontamento.pt; f. 1963; fiction, poetry, cinema, children's books, history, sociology, philosophy, economics, politics, etc.; Dirs J. SOUSA RIBEIRO, A. SOUSA LUÍS.

Edições Almedína, SA: Arco de Almedína 15, 3004-509 Coímbra; tel. (239) 851903; e-mail editora@almedina.net; internet www.almedina.net; law, education; Dir JOAQUIM MACHADO.

Edições Asa: Edif. Oceanus, Sala 4.1, Av. de Boavista 3625, 4100-138 Porto; tel. (22) 6166030; fax (22) 6155346; e-mail edicoes@asa.pt; internet www.asa.pt; f. 1951; literature, arts, schoolbooks, children's books, educational equipment; Gen. Man. AMÉRICO A. AREAL.

Edições Caixotim: Rua dos Clérigos 23, 4050-205 Porto; tel. (22) 3390831; fax (22) 3390833; e-mail edicoescaixotim@caixotim.pt; internet www.caixotim.pt; f. 2001; literature, history, criticism etc.; Dir PAULO SAMUEL.

Edições João Sá da Costa, Lda: Av. do Brasil 120, 1° esq., 1700-074 Lisbon; tel. (21) 8400428; fax (21) 8401056; e-mail edijsc@mail.telepac.pt; f. 1984; linguistics, poetry, dictionaries, geography, history, reference books; Man. Dirs IDALINA SÁ DA COSTA, JOÃO SÁ DA COSTA.

Edições 70, Lda: Rua Luciano Cordeiro 123, 1° esq., 1069-157 Lisbon; tel. (21) 3190240; fax (21) 3190249; e-mail edi.70@mail.telepac.pt; internet www.edicoes70.pt; f. 1970; history, linguistics, anthropology, philosophy, psychology, education, art, architecture, science, reference books; Dir JOAQUIM JOSÉ SOARES DA COSTA.

Editora Educação Nacional, Lda: Rua do Almada 125, 4050 Porto; tel. (22) 2005351; fax (22) 2080742; e-mail contacto@editoraeducnacional.pt; internet www.editoraeducnacional.pt; school textbooks and review, Educação Nacional.

Editora Livros do Brasil, SA: Rua dos Caetanos 22, 1200-079 Lisbon; tel. (21) 3462621; fax (21) 3428487; e-mail geral@livrosdobrasil.com; internet www.livrosdobrasil.com; f. 1944; literature, history, politics, science, management, health, children's books; Dir ANTÓNIO LUIS DE SOUZA PINTO.

Editora Pergaminho, Lda: Rua de Alegria 486, 2645-167 Alcabideche; tel. (21) 4680083; fax (21) 4674000; e-mail pergaminho.mail@netcabo.pt; internet www.editorapergaminho.pt; f. 1991; cinema, music, humour, fiction; Dir MÁRIO MENDES DE MOURA.

Editora Portugalmundo, Lda: Rua Gonçalves Crespo 47, r/c, 1150-184 Lisbon; tel. (21) 3304685; fax (21) 3304687; e-mail editorportugalmundo@gmail.com; internet membros.aveiro-digital.net/portugalmundo; children's books, poetry, biographies, law, music, fiction, theatre; Dir MARIA HELENA MATOS.

Editora Replicação, Lda: Av. Infante Santo 343, r/c, 1350-277 Lisbon; fax (21) 3969808; e-mail replic@mail.telepac.pt; f. 1982; textbooks, children's books, dictionaries, language materials; Dir JOSÉ CARLOS ANAIA CRISTO.

Editorial Bizancia, Lda: Largo Luis Chaves 11-11A, 1600-487 Lisbon; tel. (21) 7550228; fax (21) 7520072; e-mail bizancio@editorial-bizancio.pt; internet www.editorial-bizancio.pt; f. 1998; general fiction and non-fiction.

Editorial Confluência: Calçada do Combro 99, 1200-112 Lisbon; tel. and fax (21) 3466917; e-mail livroshorizonte@mail.telepac.pt; f. 1945; dictionaries; Man. ROGÉRIO MENDES DE MOURA.

Editorial Estampa, Lda: Rua da Escola do Exército 9, r/c dto, 1169-090 Lisbon; tel. (21) 3555663; fax (21) 3141911; e-mail estampa@mail.telepac.pt; internet www.editorialestampa.pt; sociology, economics, occult, fiction, sport, history, art, alternative medicine, children's; Dir ANTÓNIO CARLOS MANSO PINHEIRO.

Editorial Futura: Rua General Morais Sarmento 9, c/v esq., 1500-310 Lisbon; tel. and fax (21) 7155848; e-mail editorialfutura@netcabo.pt; literature, comics.

Editorial Minerva: Rua da Alebria 30, 1250-007 Lisbon; tel. (21) 3224950; fax (21) 3224952; e-mail minerva_dna@netcabo.pt; internet www.editorialminerva.com; f. 1927; literature, politics, children's; Man. NARCISA FERNANDES.

Editorial Notícias: Rua Bento de Jesus Caraça 17, 1495-684 Cruz Quebrada; tel. (21) 0052350; fax (21) 0052340; e-mail geral@editorialnoticias.pt; internet www.editorialnoticias.pt; fiction, politics, religion, history, economics, biographies, linguistics, law, management, education, dictionaries, ethnology.

Editorial Nova Ática, SA: Calçado Nova de S. Francisco, 10, 1° esq., 1200-300 Lisbon; tel. (21) 3420557; fax (21) 3420305; e-mail editorialnovaatica@sapo.pt; f. 1935; poetry, literature, essays, theatre, history, philosophy; Chief Execs VASCO SILVA, JOSÉ RODRIGUES.

Editorial Presença, Lda: Estrada das Palmeiras 59, Queluz de Baixo, 2730-132 Barcarena; tel. (21) 4347000; fax (21) 4346502; e-mail info@presenca.pt; internet www.presenca.pt; f. 1960; social sciences, fiction, textbooks, computer books, business, leisure, health, children's books, etc.; Dir FRANCISCO ESPADINHA.

Editorial Verbo SA: Av. António Augusto de Aguiar 148, 2B, 1069-019 Lisbon; tel. (21) 3801100; fax (21) 3865397; e-mail comerciais@editorialverbo.pt; internet www.editorialverbo.pt; f. 1958; imprints include Editora Ulisseia; encyclopedias, dictionaries, reference, history, general science, textbooks, education and children's books; Dir FERNANDO GUEDES.

Europress—Editores e Distribuidores de Publicações, Lda: Praceta da República, Loja A, 2620-162 Póvoa de Santo Adrião; tel.

PORTUGAL

(21) 9381450; fax (21) 9381452; e-mail europress@mail.telepac.pt; internet www.europress.pt; f. 1982; academic, children's, law, poetry, health, novels, history, social sciences, medicine, etc.; Man. ANTÓNIO BENTO VINTÉM.

FCA (Editora de Informática, Lda): Rua D. Estefânia 183, 1° esq., 1000-154 Lisbon; tel. (21) 3532735; fax (21) 3577827; e-mail fca@fca.pt; internet www.fca.pt; f. 1991; computer science.

Gradiva—Publicações, Lda: Rua Almeida e Sousa 21, r/c esq., 1399-041 Lisbon; tel. (21) 3974067; fax (21) 3953471; e-mail geral@gradiva.mail.pt; internet www.gradiva.pt; f. 1981; philosophy, education, history, fiction, science, social science, children's books, cartoons; Man. Dir GUILHERME VALENTE.

Guimarães Editores Lda: Rua da Misericórdia 68-70, 1200-273 Lisbon; tel. (21) 3243120; fax (21) 3243129; e-mail geral@guimaraes-ed.pt; internet www.guimaraes-ed.pt; f. 1899; literature, philosophy, history, etc.

Impala Editores, SA: Edif. Grupo Impala, Ranholas, 2710-460 Sintra; tel. (21) 9238218; fax (21) 9238463; e-mail assinaturas@impala.pt; internet www.impala.pt; f. 1983; magazines and children's books; Dir JACQUES RODRIGUES.

Imprensa Nacional—Casa da Moeda, SA (INCM): Edif. Casa da Moeda, Av. António de José de Almeida, 1000-042 Lisbon; tel. (21) 7810700; e-mail comercial@incm.pt; internet www.incm.pt; f. 1972 as Imprensa Nacional—Casa da Moeda, EP; changed status as above in 1999; Portuguese literature, arts, philosophy, history, geography, sociology, economics, encyclopedias, dictionaries, and the *Diário da República*; Dir Dr ALCIDES GAMA.

Lello Editores, Lda: Rua Arquitecto Nicolau Nazoni 31, 2° 4050-423 Porto; tel. (22) 3326084; fax (22) 3326086; internet www.lelloeditores.com; fiction, poetry, history, reference, biography, religion; Man. JOSÉ MANUEL BERNARDES PEREIRA LELLO.

Lidel Edições Técnicas, Lda: Rua D. Estefânia 183, r/c dto, 1049-057 Lisbon; tel. (21) 3511440; fax (21) 3577827; e-mail lidel@lidel.pt; internet www.lidel.pt; f. 1963; Portuguese as a foreign language, management, technology, computer science; Man. Dir FREDERICO CARLOS DA SILVA ANNES.

Lisboa Editora, Lda: Av. dos Estados Unidos da América 1B, 1700-163 Lisbon; tel. (21) 8430910; fax (21) 8430911; e-mail geral@lisboaeditora.pt; internet www.lisboaeditora.pt; textbooks; Editorial Dirs MARIA DE LOURDES PAIXÃO, BRIGITTE THUDICHUM.

Livraria Civilização Editora: Av. Almirante Reis 102, r/c D, 1150-022 Lisbon,; tel. (21) 8123388; fax (21) 8123389; f. 1920; social sciences, politics, economics, history, art, medicine, fiction, children's; Man. Dir MOURA BESSA.

Livraria Editora Figueirinhas, Lda: Rua do Almada 47, 4050-036 Porto; tel. (22) 3325300; fax (22) 3325907; e-mail figueirinhas.lda@clix.pt; f. 1898; literature, school textbooks; Dir FRANCISCO GOMES PIMENTA.

Livraria Multinova: Av. Santa Joana Princesa 12E, 1700-357 Lisbon; tel. (21) 8421820; fax (21) 8483436; e-mail geral@multinova.pt; internet www.multinova.pt; f. 1970; schoolbooks, general, religion, Brazilian works; Dir CARLOS SANTOS.

Livraria Romano Torres: Rua João de Paiva 9A e B, 1400-225 Lisbon; tel. (21) 3014914; fax (21) 3015625; e-mail info@estudodidactico.pt; f. 1885; fiction; Dir FRANCISCO NORONHA DE ANDRADE.

Livros Cotovia: Rua Nova da Trindade 24, 1200-303 Lisbon; tel. (21) 3471447; fax (21) 3470467; e-mail livroscotovia@mail.telepac.pt; internet www.livroscotovia.pt; f. 1988; literature, drama, poetry, etc.

Livros Horizonte, Lda: Rua das Chagas 17, 1° dto, 1200-106 Lisbon; tel. (21) 3466917; fax (21) 3159259; e-mail livroshorizonte@mail.telepac.pt; f. 1953; art, pedagogy, history; Chair. ROGÉRIO MENDES DE MOURA.

Lusodidacta (Sociedade Portuguesa de Materia Didáctico, Lda): Rua Darío Cannas 5A, 2670-427 Loures; tel. (21) 9839840; fax (21) 9839847; e-mail loures1@lusodidacta.pt; internet www.lusodidacta.pt; f. 1976; textbooks, dictionaries, medicine.

McGraw-Hill de Portugal: Edif. Castilho 5, r/c A, Rua Barata Salgueiro, 51A, 1250-043 Lisbon; tel. (21) 3553180; fax (21) 3553189; e-mail servico_clientes@mcgraw-hill.com; internet www.mcgraw-hill.pt; scientific, technical and medical; Gen. Man. ANTÓNIO DE MARCO.

PAULUS Editora: Rua Dom Pedro de Cristo 10, 1749-092 Lisbon; tel. (21) 8437621; fax (21) 8437629; e-mail editor@paulus.pt; internet www.paulus.pt; religion, theology, psychology, etc.; Dir JOHN FREDY.

Plátano Editora, SARL: Av. de Berna 31, 2° esq., 1069-054 Lisbon; tel. (21) 7979278; fax (21) 7954019; e-mail geral@platanoeditora.pt; internet www.platanoeditora.pt; f. 1972; literature, educational, science, technical, dictionaries, etc.; Dir FRANCISCO PRATA GINJA.

Porto Editora, Lda: Rua da Restauração 365, 4099-023 Porto; tel. (22) 6088300; fax (22) 6088301; e-mail pe@portoeditora.pt; internet www.portoeditora.pt; f. 1944; general literature, school books, dictionaries, children's books, multimedia; Dirs VASCO TEIXEIRA, JOSÉ ANTÓNIO TEIXEIRA, ROSÁLIA TEIXEIRA.

Publicações Dom Quixote: Edif. Anas, 2°, Rua Ivan Silva 6, 1050-124 Lisbon; tel. (21) 1203010; fax (21) 1209030; e-mail editorial@dquixote.pt; internet www.dquixote.pt; f. 1965; general fiction, poetry, history, philosophy, psychology, politics, didactics and sociology; university text books; children's books.

Publicações Europa-América, Lda: Estrada Nacional 249 (Lisboa–Sintra), Km 14, Apdo 8, 2725-397 Mem Martins; tel. (21) 9267700; fax (21) 9267771; e-mail secretariado@europa-america.pt; internet www.europa-america.pt; f. 1945; imprints include Edições CETOP, Editorial Inquerito, Livros de Vida Editores, Lyon Edições and Publicações Alfa; fiction, current affairs, economics, reference, history, technical, children's; Dir TITO LYON DE CASTRO.

Quimera Editores Lda: Rua do Vale Formoso 37, 1949-013 Lisbon; tel. (21) 8455950; fax (21) 8455951; e-mail quimera@quimera-editores.com; internet www.quimera-editores.com; f. 1987; literature, art, history, photography, etc.; Dirs JOSÉ ALFARO, LUÍS VEIGA.

Rés—Editora, Lda: Praça Marquês de Pombal 78, 4000-390 Porto; tel. (22) 5024174; fax (22) 5026098; e-mail res-editora@res-editora.pt; internet www.res-editora.pt; f. 1975; economics, philosophy, law, sociology; Dir REINALDO DE CARVALHO.

Texto Editora, Lda: Estrada de Paço de Arcos 66 e 66A, 2735-336 Cacém; tel. (21) 4272200; fax (21) 4272201; e-mail info@textoeditora.com; internet www.textoeditora.com; f. 1977; school textbooks, management, pedagogy, health, beauty, cooking, children's books, multimedia; Man. Dir MANUEL JOSÉ DO ESPÍRITO SANTO FERRÃO.

PUBLISHERS' ASSOCIATION

Associação Portuguesa de Editores e Livreiros: Av. dos Estados Unidos da América 97, 6° esq., 1700-167 Lisbon; tel. (21) 8435180; fax (21) 8489377; e-mail apel@apel.pt; internet www.apel.pt; f. 1927; Pres. ANTÓNIO BAPTISTA LOPES; Sec.-Gen. FÁTIMA CORDEIRO.

Broadcasting and Communications

TELECOMMUNICATIONS

Portugal Telecom, SA (PT): Av. Fontes Pereira de Melo 40, 6°, 1069-300 Lisbon; tel. (21) 5002000; fax (21) 3562624; e-mail geral@telecom.pt; internet www.telecom.pt; f. 1994; by merger of three regional telecommunications operators; state holding reduced to 25% in 1997; relinquished monopoly on fixed-line operations in Jan. 2000; Pres. and CEO HENRIQUE GRANADEIRO.

Jazztel Portugal, SA: Edif. Diogo Cão, Doca de Alcântara Norte, 1350-352 Lisbon; tel. 16300; fax 808 301030; e-mail 16300@jazztel.pt; internet www.jazztel.pt; f. 2000; fixed-line operator.

Netvoice, SA: Cais da Rocha, Conde d'Óbidos, Pavilhão 1, Doca de Alcântara Norte, 1350-352 Lisbon; tel. (21) 8452050; fax (21) 8452051; e-mail info@netvoice.pt; internet www.netvoice.pt; f. 2000; fixed-line operator.

Novis Telecom, SA: Edif. Novis, Estrada da Outurela 118, Carnaxide, 2790-114 Lisbon; tel. (21) 0100000; fax (21) 0129210; e-mail wholesale.geral@novis.pt; internet www.novis.pt; fixed-line operator.

Oni Telecom, SA: Edif. 12, Lagoas Park, 2740-269 Porto Salvo; tel. (21) 0005300; fax (21) 0007175; e-mail info@oninet.pt; internet www.oni.pt; f. 2000; fixed-line operator; Pres. PEDRO NORTON DE MATOS.

Optimus Telecomunicações, SA: Edif. Green Park, 13° e 14°A, Av. do Combatentes 43, 1600 Lisbon; tel. (21) 7233600; fax (21) 7546275; e-mail contacto@optimus.pt; internet www.optimus.pt; f. 1998; provides mobile telephone services.

TMN (Telecomunicações Móveis Nacionais), SA: Av. Álvaro Pais 2, 1649-041 Lisbon; tel. (21) 7914400; fax (21) 7914500; e-mail 1696@tmn.pt; internet www.tmn.pt; commenced mobile telephone services in 1989; part of Portugal Telecom.

Vodafone—Comunicações Pessoais, SA: Parque das Nações, Av. D. João II, Lote 10401, 8°, 1998-017 Lisbon; tel. (21) 0915252; fax (21) 0915480; e-mail ir.pt@vodafone.com; internet www.vodafone.pt; f. 1992; fmrly Telecel-Comunicações Pessoais; provides mobile and fixed-line telephone services; Exec. Officer A. RUI DE LACERDA CARRAPATOSO.

UZO: Av. Alvaro Pais 2, 1649-041 Lisbon; e-mail info@uzo.pt; internet www.uzo.com.pt; f. 2005; part of Portugal Telecom; mobile operator; Exec. Dir JOÃO MENDES.

Other fixed-line operators included Cabovisão, Coltel, Refer Telecom and Telemilénio.

PORTUGAL

Regulatory Authority

Autoridade Nacional de Comunicações (ANACOM): Av. José Malhoa 12, 1009-017 Lisbon; tel. (21) 7211000; fax (21) 7211001; e-mail info@icp.pt; internet www.icp.pt; formerly known as the Instituto das Comunicações de Portugal (ICP); Pres. PEDRO DUARTE NEVES.

BROADCASTING

In early 2006 there were around 350 radio stations in operation.

Radio

State Radio Network

Radiodifusão Portuguesa, SA (RDP): Av. Marechal Gomes da Costa 37, Lisbon; tel. (21) 7947000; fax (21) 7947669; e-mail ruimartins@rdp.pt; internet www.rdp.pt; f. 1975; created after the nationalization of nine radio stations and their merger with the existing national broadcasting company; Pres. ALMERINDO MARQUES.

Domestic Services:

Antena 1: tel. (21) 3820000; fax (21) 3873977; Dir JOÃO COELHO; broadcasts 24 hours daily on medium-wave and FM; news, sport, music, etc.

Antena 2: tel. (21) 3820000; fax (21) 3873986; Dir JOÃO PEREIRA BASTOS; broadcasts classical music 24 hours daily on FM.

Antena 3: tel. (21) 3820000; fax (21) 3873977; Dir JORGE ALEXANDRE LOPES; broadcasts 24 hours daily on FM; music and entertainment for young people.

Private Stations

National Stations

RR (Rádio Renascença): Rua Capelo 5, 1294-108 Lisbon; tel. (21) 3239200; fax (21) 3239220; e-mail info@rr.pt; f. 1937; Roman Catholic station; broadcasts 24 hours a day on Rádio Renascença (FM, medium-wave and satellite; internet www.rr.pt; Dir RUI PÊGO), on RFM (FM and satellite; internet www.rfm.pt; Dir António Mendes) and on MEGA FM (FM and satellite; internet www.mega.fm.pt; Dir Nelson Ribeiro); Chair. FERNANDO MAGALHÃES CRESPO.

Rádio Comercial, SA: Rua Sampaio e Pina 24/26, 1000 Lisbon; tel. (21) 3821500; fax (21) 3821559; e-mail geral@radiocomercial.pt; internet www.radiocomercial.pt; f. 1979; as RDP-3, transferred to private ownership in 1993; broadcasts music, news and sport 24 hours daily on Rádio Comercial: (FM); and since March 1998 on Rádio Nacional on MW to central and southern Portugal, also music, news and sport; Head LUÍS MONTEZ; Dir of Programmes MIGUEL CRUZ.

Regional Stations

Rádio Nostalgia: Rua Sampaio e Pina 26, 1099-044 Lisbon; tel. (21) 3821500; fax (21) 3821559; e-mail internet@radiocomercial.pt; f. 1992; fmrly Radio Commercial; broadcasts music 24 hours daily on FM; Head LUÍS MONTEZ; Dir of Programmes MIGUEL CRUZ.

TSF-Press: Rua das Mercês 58/62, 4200 Porto; tel. (22) 5573500; fax (22) 557352; f. 1990; fmrly Radiopress; broadcasts news, sport, music, etc. 24 hours daily on FM; Dir CARLOS ANDRADE.

Local Stations

TSF—Rádio Jornal: Edif. Altejo, Sala 301, Rua 3 da Matinha, 1900-823 Lisbon; tel. (21) 8612500; fax (21) 8612510; e-mail tsfnoticias@lusomundo.net; internet www.tsf.pt; broadcasts news and sport 24 hours daily on FM; Dir JOSÉ FRAGOSO.

Other Stations

The first 'thematic' radio stations were classified in November 1997: 13 as musical programming and three as news programming.

Music Channels

Memória FM: Rua João de Barros 265, 4000 Porto; tel. (22) 6101390; fax (22) 6101421; internet www.memoria.esoterica.pt; one FM transmitter; broadcasts 24 hours a day.

Orbital FM: Av. S. José 20, 4° esq., 2686 Sacavém; tel. (21) 9414311; fax (21) 9414302; one FM transmitter; broadcasts 24 hours a day.

Rádio Activa: Rua das Mercês 58–62, 4200 Porto; tel. (22) 5573500; fax (22) 5505567; one FM transmitter; broadcasts 24 hours a day.

Rádio Capital: Rua Torcato José Clavine 17D, Piso 02, Pragal, 2804-526 Almada; tel. (21) 2721380; fax (21) 2740781; one FM transmitter; broadcasts 24 hours a day.

Rádio Cidade: Praceta Notícias da Amadora, Loja 2, 2700 Amadora; tel. (21) 4922972; fax (21) 490789; internet www.rcidade.pt; one FM transmitter; broadcasts 24 hours a day.

Rádio Cidade de Vila Nova de Gaia—Rádio Satélite: Rua Álvares Cabral 54, 1° sala 18, 4400 Vila Nova de Gaia; tel. (22) 3701031; one FM transmitter; broadcasts 24 hours a day.

Rádio Clube de Gondomar: Rua Cosme Ferreira de Castro 527, 4420 Gondomar; tel. (22) 4837134; fax (22) 4837134; one FM transmitter; broadcasts 24 hours a day.

Rádio Juventude: Edif. Plátano, Loja A, Rua Prof. Hugo Correia Pardal, 6000-267 Castelo Branco; tel. (272) 341758; fax (272) 347660; e-mail radiojuventude@netvisao.pt; internet www.radiojuventude.com; one FM transmitter; broadcasts 24 hours a day.

Rádio Paris Lisboa: Rua Latino Coelho, 50, 1°, 1050-137 Lisbon; tel. (21) 3510580; fax (21) 3510598; e-mail geral@rpl.fm; internet www.rpl.fm; one FM transmitter; broadcasts 24 hours a day.

Rádio 7 FM: Av. Visconde Barreiros 89, 5°, 4470 Maia; tel. (22) 9439380; fax (22) 9439381; one FM transmitter; broadcasts 18 hours a day.

News Channels

Rádio Santa Maria: Rua Sotto Mayor 7, 3° dto, 8000 Faro; tel. (289) 21115; one FM transmitter; broadcasts 17 hours a day.

Rádio Viriato: Complexo Conventurispress, Orgens, Apdo 3115, 3511-689 Viseu; tel. (232) 410416; fax (232) 410418; e-mail inforadio@viriato.fm.com; internet www.viriatofm.com; f. 1987; one FM transmitter; broadcasts 24 hours a day; Dir ANABELA ABREU.

TSF—Rádio Jornal: see Local Stations.

Radio Associations

Associação Portuguesa de Radiodifusão (APR) (Portuguese Radio Association): Av. das Descobertas, 17, 1400-091 Lisbon; tel. (21) 3015453; fax (21) 3016536; e-mail apr@apradiodifusao.pt; internet www.apradiodifusao.pt; fmrly Instituto das Rádios Locais; f. 1987; Pres. JOSÉ FAUSTINO; 220 mem. radio stations.

Associação das Rádios de Inspiração Cristã (ARIC) (Christian Radio Association): Rua da Prata 224, 2° esq., 1100 Lisbon; tel. (21) 8873723; fax (21) 8873903.

Television

State Television Network

Radiotelevisão Portuguesa, SA (RTP): Av. Marechal Gomes da Costa 37, 1849-030 Lisbon; tel. (21) 7947000; fax (21) 7947570; e-mail rtp@rtp.pt; internet www.rtp.pt; f. 1956; nationalized in 1975; became joint-stock co (with 100% public capital) in August 1992; 12 studios incl. Lisbon, Porto, Ponta Delgada and Funchal; Pres. ALMERINDO MARQUES; Dir of Programmes MARIA ELISA DOMINGUES.

Regional Centres:

RTP/Porto: Rua Conceição Fernandes, Apdo 174, 4402 Vila Nova de Gaia; tel. (22) 7156000; fax (22) 7110963; Dir DJALME NEVES.

RTP/Açores: Rua Ernesto Canto 40, 9500 Ponta Delgada, São Miguel; tel. (296) 202700; fax (296) 202771; e-mail rtpa@rtp.pt; internet www.rtp.pt; Dir OSVALDO CABRAL.

RTP/Madeira: Sítio da Madalena, Caminho Santo António 145, 9000 Funchal; tel. (291) 709100; fax (291) 741859; Dir CARLOS ALBERTO FERNANDES.

RTP/Internacional (RTPi): e-mail rtpi@rtp.pt; internet rtpi.rtp.pt; commenced satellite transmissions in June 1992; broadcasts in Portuguese 24 hours a day; Dir FERNANDO BALSINHA.

RTP/Africa: commenced transmissions to lusophone countries of Africa in 1997; broadcasts 24 hours a day; Dir AFONSO RATO.

Private Stations

SIC (Sociedade Independente de Comunicação, SA): Estrada da Outurela, Carnaxide, 2795 Linda-a-Velha; tel. 4173111; fax 4173118; e-mail atendimento@sic.pt; internet www.sic.pt; commenced transmissions in 1992; news and entertainment; Head FRANCISCO PINTO BALSEMÃO; Dir of Programmes EMÍDIO RANGEL.

TVI (Televisão Independente, SA): Rua Mário Castelhano 40, 2740-502 Barcarena; tel. (21) 4347500; fax (21) 434756; internet www.tvi.pt; commenced transmissions in 1993; Pres. MIGUEL PAÍS DO AMARAL; Gen. Man. JOSÉ EDUARDO MONIZ.

Cable Television

By 2003 cable television subscribers totalled 3,487,000.

Regional Companies

Cabo TV Açoreana: Av. Antero de Quental 9C, 1°, 9500-160 Ponta Delgada; tel. (296) 302400; fax (296) 302405.

Cabo TV Madeirense: Av. Estados Unidos da América, Nazaré, 9000-090 Funchal; tel. (291) 700800; fax (291) 766132; e-mail tvcabo@cavotvm.pt; internet www.cabotvm.pt.

PORTUGAL

TV Cabo: Rua Adelina Abranches Ferrão 10, 1600 Lisbon; tel. 808 200400; e-mail cliente@netcabo.pt; internet www.tvcabo.pt; 17 regional companies, including ones listed below.

Regional Centres:

TV Cabo Douro: Av. da Liberdade 424, 8°, 4700 Braga; tel. (253) 215870; fax (253) 215851.

TV Cabo Guadiana: Rua do Sol 24, 2°, 8000 Faro; tel. (89) 807070; fax (89) 807077.

TV Cabo Lisboa: Rua Adelina Abranches Ferrão, 10, 1600 Lisbon; tel. (21) 7956768; fax (21) 7956769.

TV Cabo Mondego: Rua do Carmo 82, 3000 Coímbra; tel. (239) 851050; fax (239) 832932.

TV Cabo Porto: Edif. Mundial Confiança, Centro Comercial Brasília, Av. da Boavista 253–267, 9°, 4000 Porto; tel. (22) 6006050; fax (22) 6006075.

TV Cabo Sado: Rua Galileu Saúde Correia 13, 2800 Almada; tel. (21) 2725555; fax (21) 2730238.

TV Cabo Tejo: Edif. Inovação II, Sala 414, Taguspark, 2780 Oeiras; tel. (21) 4227700; fax (21) 4211828; e-mail mafalda.soares@tvcabo.pt; internet www.tvcabo.pt; f. 1994; CEO JOSÉ GRAÇA BAU.

Other licensed cable television enterprises are:

Bragatel—Companhia de Televisão por Cabo de Braga, SA: Av. 31 de Janeiro 177, Apdo 17, 4715-052 Braga; tel. (253) 616600; fax (253) 616998; e-mail mail@bragatel.pt; f. 1993; authorized to operate in Braga, Barceios and Espsende.

Cabovisão—Sociedade de Televisão por Cabo, SA: Lugar de Poços, Vale do Outeiro, 2950-425 Palmela; tel. (21) 0801080; fax (21) 0801000; e-mail info@cabovisao.pt; internet www.cabovisao.pt; authorized to operate in 156 municipalities (4.5m. homes).

Pluricanal Leiria: Av. General Humberto Delgado 2, 2400 Leiria; tel. (244) 824925; fax (244) 824943.

Pluricanal Santarém: Edif. Ribatel, Estrada Nacional 3, S. Pedro, 2000 Santarém; tel. (244) 824925; fax (244) 824943.

PT Multimédia—Serviços de Telecomunicações e Multimédia, SGPS, SA: Av. 5 de Outubro 208, 1069-203 Lisbon; tel. (21) 7824725; fax (21) 7824735; e-mail ir@pt-multimedia.pt; internet www.pt-multimedia.pt; 54% owned by Portugal Telecom; CFO LUÍS PACHECO DE MELO; 1.7m. customers.

Finance

(cap. = capital; res = reserves; dep. = deposits; m. = million; brs = branches)

BANKING

Central Bank

Banco de Portugal: Rua do Ouro 27, 1100-150 Lisbon; tel. (21) 3213200; fax (21) 3464843; e-mail info@bportugal.pt; internet www.bportugal.pt; f. 1846; reorganized 1931 with the sole right to issue notes; nationalized Sept. 1974; cap. €1.0m., res €1,988.2m., dep. €14,924.9m. (Dec. 2003); Gov. VÍTOR CONSTÂNCIO; 10 brs.

Locally Incorporated Banks

Banco Activobank (Portugal), SA: Rua Augusta 84, 1100-053 Lisbon; tel. (21) 4232502; fax (21) 4233939; e-mail backoffice@activobank7.pt; internet www.activobank7.com; f. 1969 as Sociedade Financeira Portuguesa; nationalized 1975, privatized 1991 and name changed to Banco Mello, SA; 2001 name changed to above; 100% owned by Banco Comercial Português, SA; cap. €23.5m., res €–1.6m., dep. €126.2m. (Dec. 2002); Chair. JORGE JARDIM GONÇALVES.

Banco Bilbao Vizcaya Argentaria (Portugal), SA: Av. da Liberdade 222, 1250-148 Lisbon; tel. (21) 3117200; fax (21) 3117500; e-mail helpdesk@bbva.pt; internet www.bbva.pt; f. 1991; as Banco Bilbao Vizcaya; name changed 2000; cap. €125.0m., res €9.8m., dep. €1,732.9m. (Dec. 2004); Pres. JOSÉ VERA JARDIN; Gen Man. SEGUNDO HUARTE MARTIN; 110 brs.

Banco BPI, SA: Rua Tenente Valadim 284, 4100-476 Porto; tel. (22) 6073100; fax (22) 6002954; e-mail bpionline@bpi.pt; internet www.bancobpi.pt; f. 1998; founded following the absorption of Banco Fonsecas e Burnay and Banco Borges e Irmão by Banco de Fomento e Exterior; cap. €760m., res €303.4m., dep. €22,850.4m. (Dec 2003); Chair. FERNANDO ULRICH; 483 brs.

Banco Comercial dos Açores: Edif. BCA, Rua Dr José Bruno Tavares Carreiro, 9500-119 Ponta Delgada, São Miguel, Azores; tel. (296) 629070; fax (296) 629657; e-mail bca@mail.telepac.pt; internet www.bca.pt; f. 1912; fmrly Banco Micaelense; 100% owned by Banif Comercial SGPS, SA; cap. €51.9m., res €29.9m., dep. €798.3m. (Dec. 2003); Chair. HORÁCIO DA SILVA ROQUE; Pres. and CEO Dr JOAQUIM MARQUES DOS SANTOS; 44 brs.

Banco Comercial Português (Millennium BCP): Praça D. João I 28, 4000-295 Porto; tel. (22) 2064000; fax (22) 2064139; internet www.millenniumbcp.pt; f. 1985; merged with Banco Pinto e Sotto Mayor in 2000; cap. €3,257.4m., res €–406.2m., dep. €55,879.1m. (Dec. 2003); Chair and CEO JORGE JARDIM GONÇALVES; 1,048 brs.

Banco Efisa SA: Av. Antonio Augusto de Aguiar 134, 4°, 1050-020 Lisbon; tel. (21) 3117800; fax (21) 3117908; e-mail dcb@bancoefisa.pt; internet www.bancoefisa.it; f. 1994; by merger, 99.8% owned by BPN Participações Financeiras SGPS, Lisbon; cap. €18.2m., res €4.4m., dep. €83.6m. (Dec. 2001); Pres. and Chair. ADBOOL VAKIL.

Banco Espírito Santo, SA: Av. da Liberdade 195, 1250-142 Lisbon; tel. (21) 3501000; fax (21) 3501033; e-mail info@bes.pt; internet www.bes.pt; f. 1884; nationalized in 1975; transfer to private sector completed in Feb. 1992; fmrly Banco Espírito Santo e Comercial de Lisboa; 42% owned by BESPAR SGPS Lisbon; cap. €1,500m., res €345.9m., dep. €37,510.9m. (Dec. 2003); Pres. RICARDO ESPÍRITO SANTO SILVA SALGADO; Chair. ANTÓNIO LUIS ROQUETTE RICCIARDI; 463 brs.

Banco Finantia: Rua General Firmino Miguel 5, 1600-100 Lisbon; tel. (21) 7202000; fax (21) 7202030; e-mail finantia@finantia.com; internet www.finantia.com; f. 1987; investment bank; 60% owned by Finantipar SGPS SA; cap. €75.0m., res €43.7m., dep. €939.0m. (Dec. 2003); Pres. ANTÓNIO MANUEL AFONSO GUERREIRO.

Banco Internacional de Crédito (BIC), SA: Av. Fontes Pereira de Melo 27, 1050-117 Lisbon; tel. (21) 3157135; fax (21) 3146165; e-mail mkt@bic.pt; internet www.bic.pt; f. 1986; wholly owned by Banco Espírito Santo, SA; cap. €150.0m., res €103.4m., dep. €6.8m. (Dec. 2004); Pres. and Chair. Dr JOSÉ MANUEL FERREIRA NETO; 121 brs.

Banco Itaú Europa, SA: Centro Comercial Amoreiras, Torre 3, 11°, Rua Tierno Galvan, 1099-048 Lisbon; tel. (21) 3811000; fax (21) 3887219; e-mail bie.global@itaueuropa.pt; internet www.itaueuropa.pt/itaueuropa; f. 1994; 100% owned by Itaúsa Portugal SGPS, Lisbon; cap. €317.9m., res €34.0m., dep. €1,575.6m. (Dec. 2003); Pres. and Chair. ROBERTO EGYDIO SETUBAL; Chief Exec. ALMIR VIGNOTO.

Banco Privado Português, SA: Rua Mouzinho da Silveira 12, 1250-167 Lisbon; tel. (21) 3137000; fax (21) 3137092; internet www.bpp.pt; f. 1996; cap. €125.0m., res €11.3m., dep. €250.7m. (Dec. 2003); Chair. Dr JOÃO OLIVEIRA RENDEIRO.

Banco Santander Totta: Rua do Ouro 88, 1100-061 Lisbon; tel. (21) 3262000; fax (21) 3262271; e-mail superlinha@santander.pt; internet www.santandertotta.pt; f. 2004 by merger of Banco Totta & Açores, Banco Santander Portugal and Crédito Predial Português; cap. €529.1m., res €536.0m., dep. €23,099.4m. (Dec. 2002); Chair. EURICO DE MELO; CEO ANTÓNIO HORTA OSÓRIO; 640 brs.

BANIF (Banco Internacional do Funchal): Rua de João Tavira 30, Rua Câmara Pestana, 9000-509 Funchal, Madeira; tel. (291) 207700; fax (291) 224822; e-mail info@banif.pt; internet www.banif.pt; f. 1988; cap. €240.0m., res €5.1m., dep. €3,612.0m. (Dec. 2003); Chair. HORÁCIO DA SILVA ROQUE; CEO Dr JOAQUIM FILIPE MARQUES DOS SANTOS; 149 brs.

BNC—Banco Nacional de Crédito, SA: Rua Ramalho Ortigão 51, 1099-090 Lisbon; tel. (21) 0071000; fax (21) 0071982; e-mail dri@bnc.pt; internet www.bnc.pt; f. 1991; 100% owned by Banco Popular Español; mortgage institution; cap. €175.9m., res €89.9m., dep. €4,071.0m. (Dec. 2004); Pres. Dr FILIPE DE LIMA MAYER; 137 brs.

BPN (Banco Português de Negócios, SA): Av. António Augusto de Aguiar 132, 1050-020 Lisbon; tel. (21) 3598000; fax (21) 3598669; e-mail marketing@banco.bpn.pt; internet www.bpn.pt; f. 1993; 100% owned by BPN-SGPS SA; cap. €280m., res €–16.6m., dep. €4,319.5m. (Dec. 2003); Chair. Dr JOSÉ DE OLIVEIRA COSTA; 189 brs.

Caixa-Banco de Investimento, SA: Rua Barata Salgueiro 33, 1269-057 Lisbon; tel. (21) 3137300; fax (21) 3522905; f. 1984 as Manufacturers Hanover Trust Co.; name changed to above in 2000; 99.6% owned by Caixa Geral de Depósitos, SA; cap. €81.2m., res €45.9m., dep. €678.4m. (Dec. 2002); Pres. and Chair. Dr ANTÓNIO DE SOUSA; CEO JORGE TOMÉ; 2 brs.

Caixa Central de Crédito Agrícola Mútuo CRL: Rua Castilho 233–233A, 1099-004 Lisbon; tel. (21) 3860006; e-mail dint.cccam@creditoagricola.pt; internet www.creditoagricola.pt; f. 1984; co-operative bank; cap. €559.4m., res €–77.8m., dep. €7,289.0m. (Dec. 2003); Chair. and Pres. ADRIANO DIEGUES; Chief Exec. JOÃO COSTA PINTO; 606 brs.

Caixa Económica Montepio Geral: Rua Áurea 219–241, POB 2882, 1100-062 Lisbon; tel. (21) 3248220; fax (21) 3248228; internet www.montepiogeral.pt; f. 1844; cap. €405.0m., res €169.2m., dep. €10,945.2m. (Dec. 2003); Chair. JOSÉ SILVA LOPES; 55 brs.

Caixa Geral de Depósitos (CGD): Av. João XXI 63, 1000-300 Lisbon; tel. (21) 7953000; fax (21) 7905050; e-mail cgd@cgd.pt; internet www.cgd.pt; f. 1876; wholly state-owned; grants credit for agriculture, industry, building, housing, energy, trade and tourism; cap. €2,450.0m., res €184.2m., dep. €59,001.5m. (Dec. 2002); Chair. ANTÓNIO DE SOUSA; CEO LUIS FERNANDO MIRA AMARAL; 513 brs.

Crédibanco—Banco de Crédito Pessoal, SA: Rua Agusta 62–74, 1100-053 Lisbon; tel. (21) 8427200; fax (21) 8427372; f. 1992; as Banco Central Hispano; owned by Banco Comercial Português Empresas; Pres. JORGE JARDIM GONÇALVES.

Finibanco SA: Rua Júlio Dinis 157, 4050-323 Porto; tel. (22) 6084500; fax (22) 6084501; e-mail finibanco.online@finibanco.pt; internet www.finibanco.pt; f. 1993; cap. €80m., res €15.1m., dep. €1,367.0m. (Dec. 2003); Pres. ALVARO COSTA LEITE; 80 brs.

Foreign Banks

ABN-AMRO Bank NV (Netherlands): Av. da Liberdade 131, 5°, POB 10070, 1269-036 Lisbon; tel. (21) 3211810; fax (21) 3211890; Country Man. Dr JAN C. PANMAN.

Banco BAI Europa, SA: Av. Antonio Augusto de Aguiar 130, 1050-020 Lisbon; tel. (21) 3513750; fax (21) 3513756; e-mail geral@bailisboa.pt; f. 2002; 100% owned by Banco Africano de Investimentos, SA, Angola; cap. €17.5m., res €2.2m., dep. €111.2m. (Dec. 2002); Pres. MARIO ABILIO PALHARES; Exec. Dir Dr ANTÓNIO PINTO DUARTE.

Banco do Brasil: Praça Marquês de Pombal 16, 1269-134 Lisbon; tel. (21) 3585000; fax (21) 3585022; Gen. Man. Dr LUIZ CARLOS DE BRITO LOURENÇO.

Bank of Tokyo-Mitsubishi UFJ Ltd (Japan): Av. da Liberdade 180, E6 esq., 1250-146 Lisbon; tel. (21) 3514550; Man. Dir MIKIHIKO OHIRA.

Barclays Bank PLC (UK): Av. da República 50, 2°, 1050-196 Lisbon; tel. (21) 7911100; fax (21) 7911123; e-mail barclays.pt@barclays.co.uk; internet www.barclays.pt; f. 1987; Gen. Man. Dr RUI SEMEDO.

BNP Paribas, SA (France): Edif. BNP, Av. 5 de Outubro 206, 1050-065 Lisbon; tel. (21) 7910203; fax (21) 7955630; internet www.bnpparibas.pt; f. 1985; Dir-Gen. BENOIT MONSAINGEON.

Deutsche Bank (Portugal) SA: Rua Castilho 20, 1250-069 Lisbon; tel. (21) 3111200; fax (21) 3535241; f. 1990; as Deutsche Bank de Investimento; name changed 1999; cap. €42.2m., res €16.4m., dep. €7,105.9m. (Dec. 2001); Pres. Dr HOMERO JOSÉ DE PINHO COUTINHO.

Fortis Bank NV (Belgium): Rua Alexandre Herculano 50, 6°, 1250 Lisbon; tel. (21) 3139300; fax (21) 3139350; f. 1986; Dir-Gen. YVES DE CLERCK.

Banking Association

Associação Portuguesa de Bancos (APB): Av. da República 35, 5°, 1050-186 Lisbon; tel. (21) 3510070; fax (21) 3579533; Pres. Dr JOÃO SALGUEIRO; Sec.-Gen. Dr JOÃO MENDES RODRIGUES.

STOCK EXCHANGE

Euronext Lisbon: Av. da Liberdade 196, 1250-147 Lisbon; tel. (21) 7900000; fax (21) 7952021; e-mail marketing@euronext.pt; internet www.euronext.pt; f. 1769 as Bolsa de Valores de Lisboa e Porto; merged with Euronext in 2002 and adopted current name; Chair. and CEO JEAN-FRANÇOIS THÉODORE.

Regulatory Authority

Comissão do Mercado de Valores Mobiliários (CMVM): Av. Liberdade 252, 1056-801 Lisbon; tel. (21) 3177000; fax (21) 3537077; e-mail cmvm@cmvm.pt; internet www.cmvm.pt; f. 1991; independent securities exchange commission; Pres. CARLOS TAVARES.

INSURANCE

The Portuguese insurance market is developing in accordance with EU regulations and practices. At the end of 2004 there were 358 insurance companies in operation, of which 14 specialized in life insurance and 31 were foreign. Net profits in that year were €425.4m.

Supervisory Authority

Instituto de Seguros de Portugal (ISP): Av. de Berna 19, 1050-037 Lisbon; tel. (21) 7903100; fax (21) 7938568; e-mail isp@isp.pt; internet www.isp.pt; f. 1982; office in Porto; Pres. Dr RUI LEÃO MARTINHO.

Representative Bodies

Associação das Empresas Gestoras de Fundos de Pensões (AEGFP): Rua da Misericórdia 76, 1200-273 Lisbon; tel. (21) 3210147; fax (21) 3210264; e-mail aegfp.pensoes@mail.telepac.pt; f. 1990; pension funds; Pres. Dr RUI PEDRAS; Sec.-Gen. Dr FRANCISCO J. DE MEDEIROS CORDEIRO.

Associação Nacional dos Agentes e Corretores de Seguros (ANACS): Rua da Xabregas, Lote A, Sala 138, 1900-440 Lisbon; tel. (21) 8688013; fax (21) 8688014; e-mail anacsegur@netc.pt; Pres. MANUEL GASPAR DA CUNHA.

Associação Portuguesa de Seguradores (APS): Rua Rodrigo da Fonseca 41, 1250-190 Lisbon; tel. (21) 3848100; fax (21) 3831422; e-mail aps@apseguradores.pt; internet www.apseguradores.pt; f. 1982; Pres. JAIME D'ALMEIDA.

Associação Portuguesa dos Produtores Profissionais de Seguros (APROSE): Praça da República 93, Sala 301, 4050-497 Porto; tel. (22) 2003000; fax (22) 3322519; e-mail aprose@aprose.pt; internet www.aprose.pt; f. 1976; Pres. ANTÓNIO VILELA; Exec. Dir PAULO CORVACEIRA GOMES.

Principal Companies

Axa-Portugal—Companhia de Seguros, SA: Praça Marquês de Pombal 14, Apdo 1953, 1058-801 Porto; tel. (21) 3506100; fax (21) 3506136; e-mail contacto@axa-seguros.pt; internet www.axa.pt; non-life; net profits €20.0m. (2004); Pres. Dr JOÃO LEANDRO.

Axa-Portugal—Companhia de Seguros de Vida, SA: Praça Marquês de Pombal 14, Apdo 1953, 1250-162 Lisbon; tel. (21) 3506100; fax (21) 3506136; e-mail contacto@axa-seguros.pt; internet www.axa.pt; life and pension funds; net profits €9.6m. (2004); Pres. Dr CARLOS PEDRO BRANDÃO DE MELO DE SOUSA E BRITO.

BPI Vida—Companhia de Seguros de Vida, SA: Rua Braamcamp 11, 8°, 1250-049 Lisbon; tel. (21) 3111020; fax (21) 3111082; internet www.bpiinvestimentos.pt; life and pension funds; net profits €11.7m. (2004); Pres. Dr FERNANDO MARIA COSTA DUARTE ULRICH.

Companhia de Seguros Açoreana, SA: Largo da Matriz 45–52, 9500-094 Ponta Delgada, S. Miguel, Azores; tel. (296) 653521; fax (296) 653516; e-mail acoreana@csanet.pt; internet www.acornet.pt; f. 1892; life and non-life; net profits €10.9m. (2004); Pres. Dr HORÁCIO DA SILVA ROQUE.

Companhia de Seguros Allianz Portugal, SA: Rua Andrade Corvo 32, 1069-014 Lisbon; tel. (21) 3165300; fax (21) 3193125; e-mail info@allianz.pt; internet www.allianz.pt; f. 1907; fmrly Allianz Portugal; life, non-life and pension funds; net profits €21.4m. (2004); Pres. Dr FRANCISCO JOSÉ PEREIRA PINTO BALSEMÃO.

Companhia de Seguros Fidelidade–Mundial, SA: Largo do Calhariz 30, 1249-001 Lisbon; tel. (21) 3238000; fax (21) 3238001; internet www.fidelidade.pt; f. 1980 from merger of four companies; life, non-life and pension funds; net profits €89.6m. (2004); Pres. Dr VITOR MANUEL LOPES FERNANDES.

Companhia de Seguros Tranquilidade, SA: Av. da Liberdade 242, 1250-149 Lisbon; tel. (21) 3503500; fax (21) 3156062; e-mail infogeral@tranquilidade.pt; internet www.tranquilidade.pt; f. 1871; non-life; net profits €25.0m. (2004); 100% privatized in 1990; Pres. PETER DE BRITO E CUNHA.

Companhia de Seguros Tranquilidade Vida, SA: Av. da Liberdade 230, 1250-148 Lisbon; tel. (21) 3167500; fax (21) 3153194; e-mail correio@tranquilidade-vida.pt; life and pension funds; net profits €21.2m. (2004); Pres. Dr LUÍS FREDERICO REDONDO LOPES.

Cosec (Companhia de Seguro de Créditos, SA): Av. da República 58, 1069-057 Lisbon; tel. (21) 7913700; fax (21) 7913720; e-mail cosec@cosec.pt; internet www.cosec.pt; f. 1969; domestic and export credit insurance; bond insurance; net profits €2.5m. (2004); Chair. Eng. JOSÉ MIGUEL GOMES DA COSTA.

Crédito Agrícola Vida, SA: Rua Castilho 233A, 1050-185 Lisbon; tel. (21) 3805510; fax (21) 3859695; e-mail linhadirecta@creditoagricola.pt; internet www.credito-agricola.pt; life; net profits €3.4m. (2004).

Eurovida, SA: Av. da República 571, 1050-189 Lisbon; tel. (21) 7924700; fax (21) 7924701; e-mail seguros@eurovida.pt; internet www.eurovida.pt; net profits €1.9m. (2004); Pres. Dr LUÍS BARBOSA.

GAN Portugal Vida, SA: Av. de Berna 24D, 1069-170 Lisbon; tel. (21) 7923100; fax (21) 7923232; e-mail gan.portugal@mail.telepac.pt; internet www.gan.pt; net profits €0.6m. (2004).

Global—Companhia de Seguros, SA: Av. Duque de Avila 171, 1069-031 Lisbon; tel. (21) 3137500; fax (21) 3559060; internet www.global-seguros.pt; non-life; net profits €7.9m. (2004); Pres. DIAMANTINO PEREIRA PEREIRA MARQUES.

Império Bonança—Companhia de Seguros, SA: Av. José Malhoa 9, 1070-157 Lisbon; tel. (21) 7216000; fax (21) 7216112; by merger of Companhia de Seguros Bonança, SA and Companhia de Seguros Império, SA; net profits €26.4m. (2004); Chair. Dr CARLOS SANTOS FERREIRA.

Liberty Seguros, SA: Av. Fontes Pereira de Melo 6, 1069-001 Lisbon; tel. (21) 3124300; fax (21) 3183800; e-mail contact_center@libertyseguros.pt; internet www.libertyseguros.pt; f. 1922; life and non-life; formerly Companhia Europeia de Seguros, SA; net profits €10.9m. (2004).

Lusitânia—Companhia de Seguros, SA: Rua São Domingos à Lapa 35–41, 1200-833 Lisbon; tel. (21) 3926970; fax (21) 3973099; internet www.lusitania-cs.pt; life and non-life; net profits €2.6m. (2004); Pres. Dr ANTÓNIO DE SEIXAS DA COSTA LEAL.

Mapfre Seguros Gerais, SA: Rua Castilho 52, 1250-071 Lisbon; tel. (21) 3819700; fax (21) 3819799; e-mail marketing@mapfre.pt;

PORTUGAL

internet www.mapfre.pt; non-life; net profits €3.3m., cap. €33.1m. (2004); Pres. AGUSTIN BERNAL DE LA CUESTA.

Ocidental—Companhia Portuguesa de Seguros, SA/Ocidental—Companhia Portuguesa de Seguros de Vida, SA/Seguros y Pensões: Av. da República 26, 1069-058 Lisbon; tel. (21) 3121300; fax (21) 3121313; non-life; net profits €63.0m. (2004); Pres. Eng. JOÃO LUÍS RAMALHO DE CARVALHO TALONE.

Real Seguros, SA: Edif. Capitólio, Av. de França 316, 4050-276 Porto; tel. (22) 8330100; fax (22) 8301670; e-mail info@realseguros.pt; internet www.realseguros.pt; f. 1988; non-life; net profits €5.9m. (2004); Pres. Eng. FERNANDO SOARES FERREIRA.

Totta Seguros—Companhia de Seguros de Vida, SA: internet www.totta.pt; life; net profits €6.8m. (2004).

Victoria—Seguros de Vida, SA/Victoria—Seguros, SA: Edif. Victoria, Av. da Liberdade 200, 1250-147 Lisbon; tel. (21) 3134450; fax (21) 3477823; e-mail victoria@victoria-seguros.pt; internet www.victoria-seguros.pt; f. 1930/1981; transferred to private sector in 1993; life and pensions; non-life; net profits €4.3m. (2004); Pres. Dr MICHAEL ROSENBERG.

Zurich—Companhia de Seguros, SA: Rua Barata Salgueiro 41, 1269-058 Lisbon; tel. (21) 3133100; fax (21) 3133111; internet www.zurichportugal.com; f. 1918; fmrly Companhia de Seguros Metrópole; non-life; net profits €20.7m. (2004); Pres. Dr NUNO MARIA SERRA SOARES DA FONSECA; Chief Exec. JOSÉ M. COELHO.

Mutual Companies

Mútua dos Armadores da Pesca do Arrasto: Av. António Augusto de Aguiar 7, 1°, 1069-145 Lisbon; tel. (21) 3561051; fax (21) 3561058; f. 1942; marine and workers' compensation, personal accident, sickness, fire, etc.; Pres. Dr ANTÓNIO ALBERTO CARVALHO DA CUNHA.

Mútua dos Pescadores—Mútua dos Seguros, C.R.L.: Edif. Vasco da Gama, Bloco C 1°, Rua General Gomes de Araújo, 1399-005 Lisbon; tel. (21) 3936300; fax (21) 3936310; e-mail isawra.costao@mutuap.pt; internet www.mutuapescadores.pt; f. 1942; privately owned; personal accident, marine, fire, workers' compensation, etc; net profits €–0.3m. (2004).

Trade and Industry

DEVELOPMENT ORGANIZATIONS

Centro para o Desenvolvimento e Inovação Tecnológicos (CEDINTEC): Rua de São Domingos à Lapa 117, 2° dto, 1200-834 Lisbon; tel. (21) 3955302; fax (21) 3961203; e-mail geral@cedintec.pt; internet www.cedintec.pt; f. 1982; supports the creation of technological infrastructures; Pres. Eng. JOÃO PEDRO DE SALDANHA VERSCHNEIDER GONÇALVES.

Cotec Portugal: Rua de Salazares 842, 4149-002 Porto; tel. (22) 6192910; fax (22) 6192919; e-mail secretariado@cotec.pt; internet www.cotec.pt; f. 2003; co-ordinates research and innovation between public and private bodies; Pres. Dr FRANCISCO MURTEIRA NABO; Dir-Gen. Prof. RUI CAMPOS GUIMARÃES.

Gabinete de Estudos e Prospectiva Económica (GEPE): Rua José Estevão 83A, 4° dto, 1169-153 Lisbon; tel. (21) 3110770; fax (21) 3110773; e-mail gep@mail.telepac.pt; internet www.gepe.pt; economic studies and analyses (Ministry of the Economy and Innovation); Dir JOÃO ABEL DE FREITAS.

ICEP Portugal—Investimentos, Comércio e Turismo: Av. 5 de Outubro 101, 1050-051 Lisbon; tel. (21) 7909500; fax (21) 7935028; e-mail icep@icep.pt; internet www.icep.pt; f. 1982; promotes Portuguese exports of goods and services; Pres. Dr JOÃO MANUEL MARQUES DA CRUZ.

Instituto de Apoio às Pequenas e Médias Empresas e ao Investimento (IAPMEI): Rua Rodrigo da Fonseca 73, 1269-158 Lisbon; tel. (21) 3836000; fax (21) 3836283; internet www.iapmei.pt; financial and technical support to small and medium-sized enterprises; Pres. JAIME SERRÃO ANDREZ; Sec.-Gen. ANTÓNIO BRANCO.

Instituto de Financiamento e Apoio ao Desenvolvimento da Agricultura e Pescas (IFADAP): Rua Castilho 45–51, 1269-163 Lisbon; tel. (21) 3846000; fax (21) 3846170; e-mail ifadap.site@ifadap.min-agricultura.pt; internet www.ifadap.min-agricultura.pt; f. 1977; provides loans for agriculture and fisheries, acts as intermediary with the European Agricultural Guidance and Guarantee Fund (EAGGF) and the Financing Instrument for Fisheries Guidance (FIFG); Chair. CARLOS FIGUEIREDO.

Instituto Nacional de Engenharia Tecnologia e Inovação (INETI): Estrada do Paço do Lumiar, 1649-038 Lisbon; tel. (21) 0924602; fax (21) 71619211; internet www.ineti.pt; f. 1977; industrial and technological research; Pres. Dr ALCIDES PEREIRA.

Instituto Português de Apoio ao Desenvolvimento (IPAD): Av. da Liberdade 192, 2°, 1250-147 Lisbon; tel. (21) 3176700; fax (21) 3147897; e-mail cooperacao.portuguesa@ipad.mne.gov.pt; internet www.mne.gov.pt; part of Ministry of Foreign Affairs; f. 2003; supports international development.

Instituto Português da Qualidade (IPQ): Rua António Gião 2, 2829-513 Caparica; tel. (21) 2948100; fax (21) 2948101; e-mail ipq@mail.ipq.pt; internet www.ipq.pt; manages and develops the Portuguese Quality System (SPQ); Pres. JOSÉ MANUEL DIOGO MARQUES DOS SANTOS.

Instituto do Vinho do Douro e do Porto (IVDP): Rua dos Camilos 90, 5050 Peso da Régua; tel. (25) 4320130; fax (25) 4320149; e-mail ivdp@ivdp.pt; internet www.ivdp.pt; an official body dealing with quality control and the promotion of port and Douro wines; also gives technical advice to exporters; Pres. Eng. JORGE NICOLAU DA COSTA MONTEIRO.

Sociedade de Desenvolvimento da Madeira (SDM): Rua da Mouraria 9, 1°, 9000-047 Funchal, Madeira; tel. (291) 201333; fax (291) 201399; e-mail sdm@sdm.pt; internet www.sdm.pt; concessionaire of Madeira's International Business Centre; Chair. Dr FRANCISCO COSTA.

Sociedade Nacional de Empreendimentos e Desenvolvimento Económico, SA (SNEDE): Av. Fontes Pereira de Melo 35, 19A, 1050-118 Lisbon; tel. (21) 3139889; fax (21) 3139889; e-mail snede@mail.telepac.pt; internet www.snede.pt; f. 1976; private consultancy co in economy and management; Pres. Dr ALFREDO GONZALEZ ESTEVES BELO.

CHAMBERS OF COMMERCE AND TRADE ASSOCIATIONS

Associação Comercial e Industrial do Funchal (ACIF)/Câmara de Comércio e Indústria da Madeira (ACIF/CCIM): Rua dos Aranhas 24–26, 9000-044 Funchal; tel. (291) 206800; fax (291) 206868; e-mail geral@acif-ccim.pt; internet www.acif-ccim.pt; f. 1836; Pres. LUÍS SOTERO GOMES.

Associação Comercial de Lisboa/Câmara de Comércio e Indústria Portuguesa (ACL/CCIP): Palácio do Comércio, Rua das Portas de Santo Antão 89, 1169-022 Lisbon; tel. (21) 3224050; fax (21) 3224051; e-mail geral@port-chambers.com; internet www.port-chambers.com; f. 1834; Pres. Eng. VASCO PINTO BASTO; Gen. Sec. ANTÓNIO MONICA; 2,100 mems.

Associação Comercial do Porto/Câmara de Comércio e Indústria do Porto (ACP/CCIP): Palácio da Bolsa, Rua Ferreira Borges, 4050-253 Porto; tel. (22) 3399000; fax (22) 3399090; e-mail cciporto@mail.telepac.pt; internet www.cciporto.com; f. 1834; Pres. Dr RUI MOREIRA; 800 mems.

Associação Industrial Portuguesa/Câmara de Comércio e Indústria (AIP/CCI): Praça das Indústrias, Apdo 3200, 1300-907 Lisbon; tel. (21) 3601000; fax (21) 3641301; e-mail info@aip.pt; internet www.aip.pt; f. 1837; CEO ANTÓNIO MANUEL VINAGRE ALFAIATE; 3,900 mems.

Câmara de Comércio e Indústria de Ponta Delgada/Associação Empresarial das Ilhas de São Miguel e Santa Maria (CCIPD): Rua Ernesto do Canto 13–15, 9504-531 Ponta Delgada, Azores; tel. (296) 305000; fax (296) 305050; e-mail ccipd@ccipd.pt; internet www.ccipd.pt; f. 1979; Dir CARLOS ALBERTO DA COSTA MARTINS; 800 mems.

OTHER INDUSTRIAL AND TRADE ASSOCIATIONS

Associação dos Comerciantes e Industriais de Bebidas Espirituosas e Vinhos (ACIBEV): Largo do Carmo 15, 1°, 1200-095 Lisbon; tel. (21) 3462318; fax (21) 3427517; e-mail acibevmail@acibev.pt; internet www.acibev.pt; f. 1975; spirit and wine traders and manufacturers; Chair. Eng. JOÃO CALLEYA SERRA; Pres. Dr ANTÓNIO SOARES FRANCO.

Associação Empresarial de Portugal: Av. da Boavista 2671, 4100-135 Porto; tel. (22) 6158500; fax (22) 6176840; e-mail aep@aeportugal.com; internet www.aeportugal.pt; f. 1849; represents industry in northern Portugal in all sectors; organizes trade fairs, exhibitions, congress, etc.; Pres. Eng. ANGELO LUDGERO MARQUES; 2,500 mems.

Associação dos Industriais e Exportadores de Cortiça (AIEC): Av. Duque de Avila 169, 2° esq., 1050-081 Lisbon; tel. (21) 3158506; fax (21) 570878; e-mail aiecortica@mail.telepac.pt; internet www.aiec.pt; f. 1993; national asscn of cork manufacturers and exporters; Pres. EDMUNDO PEREIRA.

Associação Nacional de Comerciantes e Industriais de Produtos Alimentares (ANCIPA): Largo de São Sebastião da Pedreira 31, 1050-205 Lisbon; tel. (21) 3528803; fax (21) 3154665; e-mail ancipa@netcabo.pt; internet www.ancipa.pt; f. 1975; national asscn of food products manufacturers and traders; Pres. MANUEL FULGÉNCIO TARRÉ FERNANDES; Gen. Sec. DOMITÍLIA LOPES DE ALMEIDA.

Associação Nacional das Indústrias de Vestuário e Confecção (ANIVEC/APIV): Av. da Boavista 3523, 7°, 4100-139 Porto; tel. (22) 6165470; fax (22) 6100049; e-mail geral@anivec.com; internet www

.anivec.com; clothing manufacturers' asscn; Exec. Dir ALEXANDRE PINHEIRO.

Associação Portuguesa da Indústria de Cerâmica (APICER): Edif. C, Rua Col Veiga Simão, 3020-053 Coimbra; tel. (239) 497600; fax (239) 497601; e-mail info@apicer.pt; internet www.apicer.pt; ceramics asscn; Chair. Eng. BERNARDO VASCONCELOS E SOUSA; Pres. Eng. A. GALVÃO LUCAS.

Associação Portuguesa de Cortiça (APCOR) (Portuguese Cork Association): Av. Comendador Henrique Amorim 580, 4536-904 Sta Maria de Lamas; tel. (22) 7474040; fax (22) 7474049; e-mail realcork@apcor.pt; internet www.corkmasters.com; www.apcor.pt; f. 1956; asscn of cork manufacturers and exporters; Pres. ANTÓNIO RIOS DE AMORIM.

Associação Portuguesa dos Industriais de Calçado, Componentes, e Artigos de Pele e seus Sucedâneos (APICCAPS): Rua Alves Redol 372, 4011-001 Porto; tel. (22) 5074150; fax (22) 5074179; e-mail apiccaps@mail.telepac.pt; internet www.apiccaps.pt; f. 1975; footwear and leather goods manufacturers' asscn; Pres. FORTUNATO FREDERICO.

Associação Têxtil e Vestuário de Portugal (ATP): Rua Guillhermina Suggia 224, 1°, sala 8, 4200-318 Porto; tel. (22) 5074250; fax (22) 5074259; e-mail atp@atp.pt; internet www.atp.pt; knitwear and ready-to-wear clothing industries; Pres. Dr PAULO NUNES DE ALMEIDA.

Confederação dos Agricultores de Portugal (CAP): Av. do Colégio Militar, Lote 1786, 1549-012 Lisbon; tel. (21) 7100000; fax (21) 7166122; e-mail cap@cap.pt; internet www.cap.pt; farmers' confederation; Pres. JOÃO PEDRO GORJÃO CIRYLLO MACHADO.

Confederação do Comércio e Serviços de Portugal (CCP): Av. D. Vasco da Gama 29, 1449-032 Lisbon; tel. (21) 3031380; fax (21) 3031400; e-mail ccp@ccp.pt; internet www.ccp.pt; f. 1976; Pres. VASCO SOUSA DA GAMA; Gen. Sec. JOSÉ ANTÓNIO CORTEZ; c. 100 mem. trade asscns.

Confederação da Indústria Portuguesa (CIP): Av. 5 de Outubro 35, 1°, 1069-193 Lisbon; tel. (21) 3164700; fax (21) 3579986; e-mail geral@cip.org.pt; internet www.cip.org.pt; f. 1974; represents employers; Pres. FRANCISCO VAN ZELLER; over 35,000 mems.

Gabinete Portex: Porto; tel. (22) 6068758; fax (22) 600058; textile manufacturers; Pres. ALEXANDRE PINHEIRO; Gen. Sec. Dr JOSÉ LUÍS SOARES BARBOSA.

UTILITIES

In 2001 Spain and Portugal signed an agreement on the establishment of an integrated electricity market, the *Mercado Ibérico de Electricidade* (MIBEL), which was inaugurated in May 2004. It was scheduled to be fully operational by 2008. In mid-2005 it was announced that the energy sector would be restructured. Some 22 wind farms would be constructed by 2007 in a project partly funded by the European Investment Bank, and a solar power station sited in Alentejo, expected to be the biggest in the world, was due to begin operating in 2007.

Regulatory Authority

Entidade Reguladora dos Serviços Energéticos (ERSE): Rua Dom Cristovão da Gama 1, 1400-113 Lisbon; tel. (21) 3033200; fax (21) 3033201; e-mail erse@erse.pt; internet www.erse.pt; regulator of electricity and natural gas in Portugal; Chair. JORGE VASCONCELOS.

Electricity

Rede Eléctrica Nacional, SA (REN): Av. Estados Unidos da América 55, 1749-061 Lisbon; tel. (21) 0013500; fax (21) 0013950; e-mail secretariaren@ren.pt; internet www.ren.pt; f. 1994; concessionaire of the Portuguese Transmission Grid and Transmission System Operator in mainland Portugal; since Jan. 2002, it has also been a Public Telecommunications Network Operator through its subsidiary company REN TELECOM—Comunicações SA; Pres. JOSÉ RODRIGUES PEREIRA DOS PENEDOS.

Energias de Portugal—EDP, SA: Praça Marquês de Pombal 12, 1250-162 Lisbon; tel. (21) 0012500; fax (21) 0021403; internet www.edp.pt; fmrly Electricidade de Portugal; production, purchase, transport, distribution and sale of electrical energy in Portugal and Spain (via Hidrocantábrico); partially privatized in 2004; Pres. ANTÓNIO MEXIA.

EDP Comercial—Comercialização de Energia, SA: Rua Camilo Castelo Branco 46, 5°, 1050-045 Lisbon; tel. (21) 0015462; fax (21) 0015492; internet www.edpcorporate.pt; Pres. Eng. ARNALDO PEDRO FIGUERÒA NAVARRO MACHADO.

EDP Distribuição: Praça Marquês de Pombal 12, 1250-162 Lisbon; tel. (21) 0012500; fax (21) 0021403; internet www.edp.pt; electricity distribution.

EDP Produção—Gestãoda Produção de Energia, SA: Praça Marquês de Pombal 12, 1250-162 Lisbon; tel. (21) 0012680; fax (21) 0012910; e-mail geral@edpproducao.edp.pt; internet www.edp.pt; production and sale of electrical energy; in 2005 the Govt reduced its stake from 30% to 10%; Pres. Eng. JOÃO TALONE; Vice-Pres. Eng. JORGE RIBEIRINHO MACHADO.

Gas

Galp Energia, SGPS, SA: Edif. Galp Energia, Rua Tomás de Fonseca, 1600-209 Lisbon; tel. (21) 7242500; fax (21) 7242965; e-mail comunicacao.corporativa@galpenergia.com; internet www.galpenergia.com; partially privatized in 2000; comprises the companies listed below, plus Petróleos de Portugal (Petrogal), SA, a petroleum refining company, and Gás de Portugal (GDP), SA, a gas distribution company; Chair. FRANCISCO LUÍS MURTEIRA NABO; CEO JOSÉ ANTÓNIO MARQUES GONÇALVES.

Lisboagás GDL—Sociedade Distribuidora de Gás Natural de Lisboa, SA: Av. Marechal Gomes da Costa, Cabo Ruivo, 1800-253 Lisbon; tel. (21) 6855400; fax (21) 8681161; regional natural gas distribution; there are five other regional distributors operating in Portugal: Portgás, Lusitâniagás, Setgás, Tagusgás, and Beiragás; Pres. RITA DE ANDRADE LOPES PICÃO FERNANDES CAMPOS CARVALHO.

Transgás—Sociedade Portuguesa de Gás Natural, SA: EN 116, Vila de Rei, 2674-505 Bucelas; tel. (21) 9688200; fax (21) 9693810; natural gas transport; also operates public telecommunications network; Pres. MARIA HELENA CLARO GOLDSCHMIDT.

Water

Aguas de Portugal (AdP): Av. da Liberdade 110, 7°, 1269-042 Lisbon; tel. (21) 3230700; fax (21) 3472642; e-mail geral@adp.pt; internet www.adp.pt; f. 1993; scheduled for partial privatization in 2005; Pres. PEDRO CUNHA SERRA.

LABOUR ORGANIZATIONS

Confederação Geral dos Trabalhadores Portugueses-Intersindical Nacional (CGTP-IN): Rua Victor Cordon 1, 2°, 1249-102 Lisbon; tel. (21) 3236500; fax (21) 3236695; e-mail cgtp@cgtp.pt; internet www.cgtp.pt; f. 1970; reorganized 1974; 107 affiliated unions; 704,048 mems; Gen. Sec. MANUEL CARVALHO DA SILVA.

União Geral dos Trabalhadores de Portugal (UGTP): Rua Buenos Aires 11, 1249-067 Lisbon; tel. (21) 3931200; fax (21) 3974612; e-mail ugt@mail.telepac.pt; internet www.ugt.pt; f. 1978; pro-socialist; c. 0.9m. mems; Pres. JOÃO DIAS DA SILVA; Sec.-Gen. JOÃO PROENÇA.

Transport

RAILWAYS

In 2004 the total length of the railtrack totalled 3,612.9 km, of which 1,358.9 km was electrified. In 2005 the Government announced plans to develop two high-speed rail links connecting Lisbon and Oporto with the Spanish capital, Madrid. Construction was scheduled to begin in 2008 and be completed by 2014.

Rede Ferroviária Nacional—REFER, E.P.: Estação de Santa Apolónia, Largo dos Caminhos de Ferro, 1100-105 Lisbon; tel. (21) 1022000; fax (21) 1022439; internet www.refer.pt; f. 1997; assumed responsibility for rail infrastructure in 1999; Pres. LUÍS FILIPE MELO E SOUSA PARDAL.

Caminhos de Ferro Portugueses, EP (CP): Calçada do Duque 20, 1249-109 Lisbon; tel. (21) 3215700; fax (21) 3473093; e-mail webmaster@mail.cp.pt; internet www.cp.pt; f. 1856; nationalized in 1975; incorporated Sociedade Estoril Caminhos de Ferro from Cais do Sodré to Cascais in 1977; Pres. ERNESTO JORGE SANCHEZ MARTINS DE BRITO.

Metropolitano de Lisboa, EP (ML): Av. Fontes Pereira de Melo 28, 1069-095 Lisbon; tel. (21) 3558457; fax (21) 3574908; e-mail relacoes.publicas@metrolisboa.pt; internet www.metrolisboa.pt; opened 1959; operates the 30-km underground system; Pres. CARLOS ALBERTO MINEIRO AIRES.

ROADS

The country is divided into 18 road districts and 4 regions: North, Centre, Lisbon and South. In 2004 there were 12,689 km of roads in continental Portugal, of which 2,125 km were motorway.

Brisa—Auto-Estradas de Portugal, SA: Edif. Brisa, Quinta da Torre da Aguilha, 2785-599 São Domingos de Rana; tel. (21) 4448500; fax (21) 4448773; e-mail contacto@brisa.pt; internet www.brisa.pt; f. 1972; responsible for construction, maintenance and operation of motorways; Pres. Eng. MANUEL VAN HOOF RIBEIRO.

Instituto das Estradas de Portugal (IEP): Praça da Portagem, 2804-534 Almada; tel. (21) 2947100; fax (21) 2951997; internet www

PORTUGAL

.iestradas.pt; f. 1999; merged with Instituto para a Conservação e Exploração da Rede Rodoviária (ICERR) and Instituto para a Construção Rodoviária (ICOR) in 2002; road infrastructure policy, construction and maintenance of the road network; Pres. Eng. JOSÉ RIBEIRO DOS SANTOS.

SHIPPING

The principal Portuguese ports are Lisbon, Leixões (Porto), Setúbal and Funchal (Madeira), and the Viana do Castelo port is being developed. The ports of Portimão (Algarve) and the Azores regularly receive international cruise liners. At December 2004 Portugal's registered merchant fleet comprised 456 vessels, totalling 1,336,480 grt.

Principal Shipping Companies

Portline—Transportes Marítimos Internacionais, SA: Av. Infante D. Henrique 332, 3°, 1849-025 Lisbon; tel. (21) 8391800; fax (21) 8376680; e-mail mail@portline.pt; internet www.portline.pt; f. 1984; marine transport; Gen. Man. MANUEL PINTO DE MAGALHÃES.

Sacor Marítima, SA: Rua do Açúcar 86, 1950-010 Lisbon; tel. (21) 8625500; fax (21) 8687548; tanker transport; Chair. LUÍS MARTINS CARNEIRO.

Soponata (Sociedade Portuguesa de Navios Tanques, SA): Largo Rafael Bordalo Pinheiro 20, 5°, 1249-050 Lisbon; tel. (21) 3224440; fax (21) 3476772; e-mail soponata@soponata-sa.pt; internet www.soponata.pt; f. 1947; oil tankers; CEO Eng. PEDRO DE MELLO.

CIVIL AVIATION

There are international airports at Lisbon, Porto, Faro (Algarve), Funchal (Madeira), Santa Maria (Azores) and São Miguel (Azores). Construction of a second international airport serving Lisbon was to be completed by 2017.

TAP Portugal: Aeroporto de Lisboa, CP 50194, 1704-801 Lisbon; tel. (21) 8415000; fax (21) 8415881; e-mail gcrp.com@tap.pt; internet www.flytap.com; f. 1945; due to be partially privatized in 2007; national airline serving destinations in Europe, Africa, North, Central and South America; scheduled, international, domestic, passenger and cargo services; joined Star Alliance in 2005; Pres. MANUEL PINTO BARBOSA; CEO FERNANDO PINTO.

Air Luxor: Av. da República 26, 1050-192 Lisbon; tel. (21) 0062200; fax (21) 0062361; e-mail airluxor@airluxor.com; internet www.airluxor.com; f. 1988; regional, European and African flights; Chair. PAULO MIRIPIRI.

PGA—Portugália Airlines (Companhia Portuguesa de Transportes Aéreos) SA: Edif. 70, Aeroporto de Lisboa, Rua C, 1749-078 Lisbon; tel. (21) 8425500; fax (21) 8425623; e-mail pga@mail.telepac.pt; internet www.pga.pt; f. 1988; regional airline operating scheduled and charter, international and domestic flights from Lisbon; Chair. JOÃO RIBEIRO DA FONSECA.

SATA (Air Açores—Serviço Açoreano de Transportes Aéreos—EP): Av. Infante D. Henrique 55, 9505-528 Ponta Delgada, São Miguel, 9500 Azores; tel. (296) 209727; fax (296) 209722; e-mail pdlsd@sata.pt; internet www.sata.pt; f. 1941; owned by the regional government of the Azores; inter-island services in the Azores archipelago; Pres. and Chief Exec. ANTÓNIO CANSADO.

TRANSPORT ASSOCIATION

Federação Portuguesa dos Transportes: Rua Viriato 5, 1°, 1000 Lisbon; tel. (21) 577562; fax (21) 574104; Pres. Eng. JOSÉ CARLOS GONÇALVES VIANA.

Tourism

Portugal is popular with visitors because of its mild and clement weather. Apart from Lisbon and the Algarve on the mainland, Madeira and the Azores are much favoured as winter resorts. Earnings from tourism totalled an estimated €6,260.6m. in 2004; in 2003 the number of tourist arrivals totalled 11.7m., compared with 7.0m. in 1980. In 2004 there were 1,954 hotels and guesthouses, etc., with 112,659 beds.

Direcção-Geral do Turismo: Av. António Augusto de Aguiar 86, 1069-021 Lisbon; tel. (21) 3586400; fax (21) 3586666; e-mail dgturismo@dgturismo.pt; internet www.dgturismo.pt; Dir-Gen. Dr CRISTINA SIZA VIEIRA.

Fundo de Turismo: Rua Ivone Silva, Lote 6, 1050 Lisbon; tel. (21) 7937490; fax (21) 524221; Pres. Eng. RUI MIL HOMENS.

ICEP Portugal—Comércio, Investimento e Turismo: Tourism Promotion Dept: Av. Duque d'Avila 185, 4°, 1050-082 Lisbon; tel. (21) 7909500; fax (21) 3556896; e-mail turismo@icep.pt; internet www.portugalinsite.pt; Exec. Vice-Pres. responsible for Tourism Dr CARLOS COSTA.

Instituto de Formação Turística: Escola de Hotelaria e Turismo de Lisboa, Av. Eng° Arantes e Oliveira 7, 1900-221 Lisbon; tel. (21) 8426900; fax (21) 8493130; e-mail ehtlisboa@inftur.min-economia.pt; internet www.inftur.pt; Dir Dra CLARA FREITAS.

QATAR

Introductory Survey

Location, Climate, Language, Religion, Flag, Capital

The State of Qatar occupies a peninsula, projecting northwards from the Arabian mainland, on the west coast of the Persian (Arabian) Gulf. It is bordered, to the south, by Saudi Arabia and the United Arab Emirates. The archipelago of Bahrain lies to the north-west. On the opposite side of the Gulf lies Iran. The climate is exceptionally hot in the summer, when temperatures may reach 49°C (120°F), with high humidity on the coast; conditions are relatively mild in the winter. Rainfall is negligible. The official language is Arabic. Almost all of the inhabitants are adherents of Islam. Native Qataris, who comprise less than one-third of the total population, belong mainly to the strictly orthodox Wahhabi sect of Sunni Muslims. The national flag (proportions 11 by 28) is maroon, with a broad vertical white stripe at the hoist, the two colours being separated by a serrated line. The capital is Doha.

Recent History

Qatar was formerly dominated by the Khalifa family of Bahrain. The peninsula became part of Turkey's Ottoman Empire in 1872, but Turkish forces evacuated Qatar at the beginning of the First World War (1914–18). The United Kingdom recognized Sheikh Abdullah ath-Thani as Ruler of Qatar, and in 1916 made a treaty with him, providing British protection against aggression in return for supervision of Qatar's external affairs. A 1934 treaty extended fuller British protection to Qatar.

In October 1960 Sheikh Ali ath-Thani, Ruler of Qatar since 1949, abdicated in favour of his son, Sheikh Ahmad. In 1968 the British Government announced its intention to withdraw British forces from the Persian (Arabian) Gulf area by 1971. Qatar thus attempted to associate itself with Bahrain and Trucial Oman (now the United Arab Emirates—UAE) in a proposed federation. In April 1970 Sheikh Ahmad announced a provisional Constitution, providing for a partially elected Consultative Assembly, although he retained effective power. In May the Deputy Ruler, Sheikh Khalifa ath-Thani (a cousin of Sheikh Ahmad), was appointed Prime Minister. After the failure of attempts to agree terms for union with neighbouring Gulf countries, Qatar became fully independent on 1 September 1971, whereupon the Ruler took the title of Amir. The 1916 treaty was replaced by a new treaty of friendship with the United Kingdom.

In February 1972 the Amir was deposed in a bloodless coup. Claiming support from the royal family and the armed forces, Sheikh Khalifa proclaimed himself Amir. Sheikh Khalifa, who retained the premiership, adopted a policy of wide-ranging social and economic reform, and the previous extravagance and privileges of the royal family were curbed. In accordance with the 1970 Constitution, the Amir appointed an Advisory Council in April 1972 to complement the ministerial Government. The Council was expanded from 20 to 30 members in 1975 and to 35 members in 1988. Its term was extended for four years in 1978, and for further terms of four years in 1982, 1986, 1990, 1994 and 1998.

On 27 June 1995 the Deputy Amir, Heir Apparent, Minister of Defence and Commander-in-Chief of the Armed Forces, Maj.-Gen. Sheikh Hamad bin Khalifa ath-Thani, deposed his father in a bloodless coup. Sheikh Hamad proclaimed himself Amir, claiming the support of the royal family and the Qatari people. Sheikh Khalifa, who was in Switzerland at the time of the coup, immediately denounced his son's actions, and vowed to return to Qatar. Although Sheikh Khalifa had effectively granted Sheikh Hamad control of the emirate's affairs (with the exception of the treasury) in 1992, a power struggle was reported to have emerged between the two in the months prior to the coup: Sheikh Khalifa was particularly opposed to his son's independent foreign policy (notably the strengthening of relations with both Iran and Iraq, and with Israel), and had attempted to regain influence in policy-making. Sheikh Hamad, however, reputedly enjoyed widespread support both nationally and internationally, and his domestic reforms were perceived as having contributed to Qatar's stability at a time when social unrest and Islamic extremism were emerging in the region. The United Kingdom, the USA and Saudi Arabia swiftly recognized the new Amir. In July 1995 Sheikh Hamad reorganized the Council of Ministers and appointed himself Prime Minister, while retaining the posts of Minister of Defence and Commander-in-Chief of the Armed Forces.

Meanwhile, the deposed Amir took residence in the UAE, and visited several other countries of the region in an apparent attempt to assert his legitimacy as ruler of Qatar. In January 1996 it was confirmed that Sheikh Khalifa had gained control of a substantial part of Qatar's financial reserves. In the following month security forces in Qatar were reported to have foiled an attempted coup. As many as 100 people were arrested, and a warrant was issued for the arrest of Sheikh Hamad bin Jasim bin Hamad ath-Thani, a former government minister and a cousin of the Amir. Sheikh Khalifa denied any involvement, although he was quick to imply that the alleged plot indicated popular support for his return. In July legal proceedings were initiated in Qatar, Europe and the USA in an attempt to recover some US $3,000m.–$8,000m. in overseas assets that were asserted by the new Amir to have been amassed by his father from state oil and investment revenues. In October, however, it was reported that Sheikh Hamad and Sheikh Khalifa had been reconciled and had reached an out-of-court settlement regarding the return of state funds. By early 1997 all lawsuits issued against the former Amir had been withdrawn. In November 1997, meanwhile, the trial began of 110 people (40 of whom were charged *in absentia*) accused of involvement in the attempted coup of February 1996. Hearings were immediately adjourned. A number of those being tried *in absentia* were apprehended during 1998, including Qatar's former deputy head of intelligence, who was extradited from Yemen.

In October 1996 Sheikh Hamad named the third of his four sons, Sheikh Jasim bin Hamad bin Khalifa ath-Thani, as Heir Apparent. The Amir subsequently appointed his younger brother, Sheikh Abdullah bin Khalifa ath-Thani (the Minister of the Interior), as Prime Minister. Further to the ending of media censorship earlier in the year, the post of Minister of Information and Culture was abolished. (The relevant ministry was dissolved in March 1998.) In November 1996 Sheikh Hamad announced the creation of a new Defence Council, over which he would preside. The Council, to be comprised of senior ministers and armed forces and security personnel, was expected to function in an advisory and consultative capacity. It was also reported that the Amir had appointed the Gulf region's first female member of government (as Under-Secretary of State for Education and Culture).

Elections to Qatar's new central Municipal Council, held by universal suffrage on 8 March 1999, were the first in the country's history. Announced by Sheikh Hamad in November 1997 and provided for by law in July 1998, the Municipal Council was to have a consultative role in the operations of the Ministry of Municipal Affairs and Agriculture. The rate of participation by voters reportedly exceeded 90% in Doha, and was estimated at 60%–70% of the registered electorate in rural areas. However, only about 22,000 voters of an eligible 40,000 actually participated in the elections.

In July 1999 a 32-member constitutional committee was established to draft a permanent constitution; this was to include provision for the creation of a new National Assembly. The committee produced a draft constitution in July 2002, which provided for a separation of the executive, the judiciary and the legislature, but which would retain executive power in the hands of the Amir and the Council of Ministers. The draft constitution also guaranteed freedom of expression, religion and association, and provided for the establishment of an independent judiciary and of a new 45-member Consultative Council (to replace the Advisory Council), comprising 30 elected and 15 appointed members. Under the proposed constitution the Amir would be obliged to provide reasons for rejecting draft laws adopted by the Council. The Amir would be required to approve such legislation sent to him a second time by the Council with two-thirds' majority support, although he would have a discretionary right to halt implementation of laws in question on a temporary basis if he deemed this to be in the greater interests of the country. The parliament was to have a four-year mandate, and suffrage was to be extended to all citizens, including women, aged 18 years and above. On 29 April 2003 a referendum open to all citizens of 18 years of age or above was held to determine whether or not the Amir should approve the new document. An overwhelming majority (96.6%) of the 71,406 voters approved the new Constitution, and it was expected that the affirmative vote would lead to legislative elections being conducted in 2004. These were delayed, however, and in late March 2005 the Amir announced that the elections would take place between June 2005 and June 2006. In late December 2005 the First Deputy Prime Minister and Minister of Foreign Affairs, Sheikh Hamad bin Jasim bin Jaber ath-Thani, stated that preparations were now directed at holding the elections in early 2007. The delay was apparently related partly to the controversy over the legal status of the Murra tribe, whose Qatari citizenship had been revoked after it had been discovered that some members of the tribe also held Saudi citizenship. Dual nationality is not recognized under Qatari law and some members of the tribe were expelled to Saudi Arabia over the issue; in addition, it was alleged that severe punishments were extended to individuals who expressed sympathy for the victims. It was reported in February 2006, however, that the tribe were expected to have their Qatari citizenship returned.

Meanwhile, Sheikh Hamad bin Jasim bin Hamad ath-Thani was arrested in July 1999 for his alleged role in the coup plot of 1996 (see above). The trial of those accused of involvement in the coup ended in February 2000, with the former minister and 32 co-defendants sentenced to life imprisonment; 85 others were acquitted. Appeal proceedings were subsequently lodged by all 33 who had been convicted. In May 2001 the Court of Appeal overruled the previous sentences of life imprisonment, sentencing to death 19 of the defendants (including Sheikh Hamad bin Jasim bin Hamad); the court was also reported to have sentenced 26 defendants to terms of life imprisonment, and acquitted two others.

In early January 2002 it was reported that a group styling itself the General Congress of the Qatari Opposition had emerged to demand that the Amir stand down in favour of his son, Crown Prince Jasim. The group, which claimed to include former members of the armed forces, tribal chiefs, businessmen, students and officials who had served under the previous regime, accused the Amir of pursuing 'reckless' policies, of corruption and of alienating Qatar's Gulf neighbours. This last charge was interpreted as possibly referring not only to Qatar's pursuit of an increasingly independent foreign policy but also to the activities of Al-Jazeera, a satellite television station linked to the ath-Thani family with a wide audience throughout the region. Al-Jazeera's reporting style and scope of coverage had on occasions caused several governments to threaten to restrict its freedom to operate in their country: notably, in May 2002 authorities in Bahrain announced that the station was to be banned from reporting there, apparently in response to its recent unauthorized coverage of anti-US demonstrations in Bahrain, and in June the Jordanian Government ordered the closure of Al-Jazeera's Amman office after the station broadcast programmes considered unfavourable to Jordan. In January 2005 it was announced that Al-Jazeera was to be privatized; the sale was regarded as a means of distancing the Qatari Government from Al-Jazeera's more controversial broadcasts and was a further indication of the closeness of the relationship between Qatar and the US Government, which had allegedly considered launching a military attack on the station.

The second elections to the Municipal Council were held on 7 April 2003. A turn-out of about 50% was estimated for the country as a whole, but the rate of participation was reportedly as low as 25%–35% of the registered electorate at several polling stations, including in the largest constituency, al-Kharitaat. A female candidate was elected unopposed after the competing candidates stood aside, and thus became the first woman in the Gulf region to hold elected office, but none of the five other women who contested the elections was successful. Three further candidates were also elected unopposed, and the remaining 25 seats were contested by 85 candidates, including 18 incumbents. In early May the Amir appointed Sheikha bint Ahmad al-Mahmoud as Minister of Education; she replaced Dr Ahmad bin Khalifa Busherbak al-Mansouri and became the first woman to join the Council of Ministers. Further government changes were affected in late December, when Sheikh Muhammad bin Ahmad bin Jassim ath-Thani replaced Sheikh Hamad bin Faisal ath-Thani as Minister of Economy and Trade, and in March 2004 when the Amir appointed Sultan bin Hassan adh-Dhabit ad-Dousary as Minister of Municipal Affairs and Agriculture in place of Ali bin Saad al-Kawari. In July the Amir made two further minor changes to the Council of Ministers.

Meanwhile, in February 2004 the Government approved an anti-terrorism law, which included the provision of the death penalty for anyone who killed 'through a terror act' and for anyone 'founding, organizing or managing a group or organization to commit a terror act'. In addition, the crime of assisting a terrorist group was to be punishable by a life sentence. In May a law permitting the formation of trade unions was approved. In addition, the legislation granted workers the right to strike, banned children aged under 16 years from employment and set a maximum eight-hour working day.

In December 2004 Sheikh Hamad bin Nasser bin Jasim ath-Thani was demoted from the position of Minister of State for the Interior to that of Minister of State without Portfolio; Sheikh Abdullah bin Nasser bin Khalifa ath-Thani, whose background was in the intelligence services, was appointed to the interior ministry as his replacement in February 2005. In April the Amir removed from their posts his Chief of Staff, Abdullah bin Muhammad bin Sa'ud ath-Thani, and two recently appointed ministers—Muhammad bin Abd al-Latif bin Abd ar-Rahman al-Mana, the Minister of Awqaf (Religious Endowments) and Islamic Affairs, and Muhammad bin Isa Hamad al-Mehannadi, the Minister of State for Council of Ministers' Affairs—amid allegations that three cabinet members and several businessmen had been questioned by officials over their connections to fraudulent activities relating to the sale of the state-owned Qatar Gas Transport Co (Nakilat) in early 2005. Faisal bin Abdullah al-Mahmud was named as the new religious affairs minister, ad-Dousary received the position of Minister of State for Council of Ministers' Affairs in addition to his existing responsibilities and Sheikh Abd ar-Rahman bin Sa'ud ath-Thani was appointed as the new Chief of Staff.

A bomb exploded outside a theatre frequented by Western expatriates in Doha on 19 March 2005. One British citizen was killed in the suicide attack and 12 people were injured. The bomber was reported to be an Egyptian citizen, Omar Ahmad Abdullah Ali, and Jund ash-Sham (the Army of the Levant), a previously little known militant grouping, claimed responsibility for the attack. Although the bombing was the first of its kind in Qatar, Western embassies had previously issued warnings to expatriates that the threat from terrorism in the emirate was high.

On 28 March 2006 the Minister of Economy and Trade, Sheikh Muhammad, was unexpectedly dismissed from the Council of Ministers. No reason was given for his removal and the ministerial portfolio was immediately added to the responsibilities of the Minister of Finance, Yousuf bin Hussain Kamal.

In July 1991 Qatar instituted proceedings at the International Court of Justice (ICJ) regarding sovereignty of the Hawar islands (in 1939 a British judgment had awarded sovereignty of the islands to Bahrain), the shoals of Fasht ad-Dibal and Qit'at Jaradah (over which the British had recognized Bahrain's 'sovereign rights' in 1947), together with the delimitation of the maritime border between Qatar and Bahrain. Bahrain's insistence that the two countries seek joint recourse to the ICJ was rejected by Qatar. The matter was further confused in April 1992, when the Government of Qatar issued a decree redefining its maritime borders to include territorial waters claimed by Bahrain. Furthermore, Bahrain attempted to widen the issue to include its long-standing claim to the area around Zubarah, in mainland Qatar. In February 1994 a hearing of the ICJ opened in The Hague, Netherlands, in order to determine whether the court was competent to rule on the dispute. In July the ICJ requested that Qatar and Bahrain resubmit their dispute by 30 November, either jointly or separately. The two countries failed to reach agreement on joint presentation to the court, and at the end of November Qatar submitted a unilateral request to pursue its case through the ICJ. In February 1995, while the ICJ declared that it would have authority to adjudicate in the dispute (despite Bahrain's refusal to accept the principle of an ICJ ruling), Saudi Arabia also proposed to act as mediator between the two countries. Qatar subsequently indicated its willingness to withdraw the case from the ICJ if Saudi arbitration proved successful.

Relations with Bahrain subsequently deteriorated, and in December 1996 Bahrain boycotted the annual summit meeting of the Co-operation Council for the Arab States of the Gulf (Gulf

Co-operation Council—GCC, see p. 205), which took place in Doha. The meeting none the less decided to establish a quadripartite committee, comprising those GCC countries not involved in the dispute, to mediate between Qatar and Bahrain. The committee's efforts achieved a degree of success, and meetings between senior Qatari and Bahraini representatives in London, United Kingdom, and Manama, Bahrain, in early 1997 resulted in the announcement that diplomatic relations at ambassadorial level were to be established. In September, however, Bahrain challenged the authenticity of documents presented to the ICJ by Qatar in support of its territorial claim; the ICJ subsequently directed Qatar to produce a report on the authenticity of the documents by September 1998. Following the submission of the report, in which four experts differed in their opinion of the documents, Qatar announced its decision to disregard them, to enable the case to proceed 'without further procedural complications'. In December 1999 the Amir made his first official visit to Manama, during which it was agreed that a joint committee, headed by the Crown Princes of Bahrain and Qatar, would be established to encourage bilateral co-operation. Qatar also agreed to withdraw its petition from the ICJ in the event of the joint committee's reaching a solution to the territorial disputes. A second senior-level meeting was held in January 2000, when the new Amir of Bahrain made his first visit to Qatar. The two countries agreed to expedite the opening of embassies in Manama and Doha. In February, following the first meeting of the Bahrain-Qatar Supreme Joint Committee, it was announced that the possibility of constructing a causeway to link the two states was to be investigated. In May Bahrain announced its decision to suspend the activities of the Supreme Joint Committee pending the ICJ ruling on the dispute. Hearings at the ICJ, which began later that month, ended in June. The final verdict, issued in mid-March 2001, was virtually identical to the British judgment of 1939. Bahrain was found to have sovereignty over the Hawar islands and Qit'at Jaradah, while Qatar held sovereignty over Zubarah, Janan island and the low-tide elevation of Fasht ad-Dibal; the Court drew a single maritime boundary between the two states. Both Qatar and Bahrain accepted the ICJ ruling, and declared that their territorial dispute was ended. Later in March 2001 it was announced that meetings of the Supreme Joint Committee would resume. In August 2002 a Danish consortium completed a feasibility study for the construction of the planned causeway linking Qatar to Bahrain (the Friendship Bridge). Both Governments had approved the US $2,000m. project by May 2004, and international companies were invited to present bids for the contract in late 2004. Bahrain and Qatar were, by this time, reportedly discussing co-operation on gas projects and on other economic issues.

Following the multinational military operation to liberate Kuwait from Iraq in early 1991, Qatar resumed tentative contact with Iraq in 1993. In March 1995, during the first official visit to the country by a senior Iraqi official since the Gulf War, Iraq's Minister of Foreign Affairs met with his Qatari counterpart to discuss the furtherance of bilateral relations; the Qatari Minister subsequently indicated Qatar's determination to pursue a foreign policy independent from that of its GCC neighbours when he announced his country's support for the ending of UN sanctions against Iraq. In early 1998, as the crisis deepened regarding UN weapons inspections in Iraq (see the chapter on Iraq), Qatar urged a diplomatic solution, and appealed to Iraq to comply with all pertinent UN Security Council resolutions. With Qatar continuing to advocate an end to sanctions against Iraq, in December 2001 a meeting took place in Doha between the new Iraqi Minister of Foreign Affairs, Naji Sabri, and Qatari and Omani officials. In June 2003, after the removal of Saddam Hussain's regime by the US-led coalition, Qatar Airways became the first airline for 12 years to operate commercial air services to Iraq, after the scheduling of a bi-weekly service to Basra. Meanwhile, in September the US-appointed interim Cabinet in Iraq voted to expel Al-Jazeera reporters for one month, pending a review of their broadcasts, after the station was accused of inciting violence against US and Iraqi authorities. In early 2006 negotiations had yet to take place with the new Iraqi administration regarding the cancellation of the estimated US $4,000m. worth of debt owed to Qatar by Iraq.

In September 1992 tension arose with Saudi Arabia (with which Qatar has generally enjoyed close ties) when Qatar accused Saudi forces of attacking a Qatari border post, killing two border guards and capturing a third in the process. In protest, in October Qatar suspended a 1965 border agreement with Saudi Arabia (which had never been fully ratified) and temporarily withdrew its 200-strong contingent from the Saudi-based GCC 'Peninsula Shield' force (at the time stationed in Kuwait). The Saudi Government denied the involvement of its armed forces, claiming that the incident had been caused by fighting between rival Bedouin tribes within Saudi territory. Relations between the two countries reportedly improved as a result of Kuwaiti mediation, and the Qatari hostage was released later in October 1992; Qatar nevertheless registered its disaffection by not attending meetings of GCC ministers which took place in Abu Dhabi and Kuwait in November. In December, after mediation by Egypt, Sheikh Khalifa and King Fahd of Saudi Arabia signed an agreement whereby a committee was to be established formally to demarcate the border between the two states. In November 1994, however, Qatar boycotted a GCC ministerial meeting in Saudi Arabia, in protest at what it alleged to have been armed incidents on the border with Saudi Arabia in March and October. Bilateral relations appeared to improve in August 1995, when the new Amir held talks with King Fahd in Saudi Arabia. In December, nevertheless, Qatar boycotted the closing session of the annual GCC summit, following the appointment of a Saudi national as the next GCC Secretary-General (in preference to a Qatari candidate). In March 1996 the dispute was reported to have been settled, after mediation by Oman, and in April Qatar and Saudi Arabia agreed to establish a joint committee to complete the demarcation of their mutual border. Officials from both countries met in Saudi Arabia in June 1999 to sign the border demarcation maps. In late March 2001, at a ceremony in Doha, Saudi and Qatari officials signed a final agreement concerning the land and maritime demarcation of their joint border; the accord included provision for a joint Saudi-Qatari committee, whose task was to ensure that all provisions of the 1965 accord were implemented. In October 2002 relations between Saudi Arabia and Qatar worsened, however, when the Saudi ambassador to Qatar was recalled following the airing of a television programme via the Al-Jazeera network that was deemed to be critical of the Saudi regime. Relations had already been strained by the expansion of US military facilities in Qatar and by the relocation, in late April, of the main US air operations in the Gulf region from Saudi Arabia to Doha (see the chapter on Saudi Arabia).

In January 1994 Qatar was reported to have commenced discussions with Israel regarding the supply of natural gas to that country, in apparent disregard for the Arab economic boycott of Israel. Following pressure from its GCC allies, Qatar subsequently announced that the proposed sale would depend on Israel's withdrawal from all Arab territories occupied in 1967. In September 1994, however, Qatar, along with the other GCC states, revoked aspects of the economic boycott of Israel. In November 1995 Israel signed a memorandum of intent to purchase Qatari liquefied natural gas (LNG). Relations between the two countries were consolidated further in April 1996, when Shimon Peres made the first official visit to Qatar by an Israeli Prime Minister. However, in late 1996 Israel declared that the memorandum of intent had expired, although negotiations would continue, and in November Qatar stated that any deal would be dependent on progress in the peace process. The fourth Middle East and North Africa economic summit was scheduled to take place in Doha in November 1997. However, in protest at the intended presence of representatives of Israel, which was regarded by the Arab states as failing to comply with its obligations with regard to the Middle East peace process, most of Qatar's fellow members of the League of Arab States (the Arab League, see p. 306) and the GCC refused to attend. As a result of the boycott, the summit was downgraded to a conference, and was attended by representatives of only seven Arab states; a 'low-level' Israeli delegation attended, as did the US Secretary of State, Madeleine Albright.

In March 1998 the Qatari Government stated that it was reviewing its relations with Israel, given the severe difficulties in the Middle East peace process. Nevertheless, Qatar was criticized by other Arab states in September 2000 following a meeting in New York at the UN Millennium Summit between the Amir and the Israeli Prime Minister, Ehud Barak. Prior to the ninth conference of the Organization of the Islamic Conference (OIC, see p. 340), held in Doha in November, several Arab states (notably Saudi Arabia and Iran) threatened to boycott the summit unless Qatar agreed to sever its low-level diplomatic relations with Israel. (Arab states were keen to demonstrate support for the Palestinians in their renewed uprising against Israeli occupation from late September.) The Qatari leadership apparently bowed to regional pressure when, in early November, it announced that the Israeli trade office in Doha was to be closed, although there were subsequent reports that the office was still functioning. An emergency session of the OIC was convened in Doha in December 2001 to demonstrate solidarity with the Palestinians as the crisis deepened still further; Sheikh Hamad proposed the establishment of a panel comprising prominent representatives of the Islamic community to lobby Western governments to support an independent Palestinian state. In March 2002 Qatar's Minister of Foreign Affairs travelled to the Palestinian territories for talks with the leader of the Palestinian (National) Authority, Yasser Arafat, who at that time remained under Israeli siege in Ramallah. In late 2002 it was again reported that the Israeli trade office in Doha was still functioning; Qatar's continuing refusal to close the establishment exacerbated tensions with Saudi Arabia in particular.

An emergency summit meeting of the OIC was convened in Doha in October 2001, in response to the previous month's suicide attacks against New York and Washington, DC, and the subsequent commencement of US-led military action against targets in Afghanistan linked to the Taliban regime and to the al-Qa'ida (Base) organization of Osama bin Laden, the Saudi-born fundamentalist Islamist held principally responsible for the attacks in the USA.

Despite Qatar's active support for an end to UN sanctions against Iraq, and its pursuit of contacts with the incumbent regime of Saddam Hussain (see above), by the time US Vice-President Dick Cheney visited Qatar in mid-March 2002—as part of a tour of the Gulf aimed at garnering support for a potential extension of the US-led 'war on terror' to target the Iraqi regime, Qatar was apparently alone among the Gulf states in indicating that it would allow the use of its territory as a base for action against Saddam Hussain. During the decade after the Gulf War the Government had signed a number of defence agreements with the USA and there was reported to have been a significant increase in the amount of US military personnel and equipment positioned in Qatar since September 2001; some 5,000 US troops had arrived at a military base south of Doha in late 2001 for what a Qatari official had described as 'routine' exercises. Furthermore, the construction of a major air facility at the Al-Udaid military base enhanced its strategic importance within the US military network in the region; in December 2002 the US Department of Defense dispatched more than 600 personnel from the US military command centre to the base, which was to act as the main US command post in the Gulf. None the less, Qatar, concerned about the popular reaction to a US-led war in Iraq and the regional implications such a conflict might have, continued to advocate a diplomatic solution to the crisis. By the time of the commencement of hostilities in March 2003 the USA had stationed some 3,000 air force personnel and 36 tactical jets at Al-Udaid. In April, following the removal of Saddam Hussain's regime by the US-led coalition, Qatar's Minister of Foreign Affairs, Sheikh Hamad bin Jasim bin Jaber ath-Thani, urged the USA to reject the possibility of pursuing its 'war on terror' to target the Syrian regime of President Bashar al-Assad. In March 2004 the US military invited bids for a project to expand the Al-Udaid base, at a cost of US $30m.–$100m.

The assassination in mid-February 2004 of an exiled Chechen militant, Zelimkhan Yandarbiyev, apparently with the involvement of the Russian military, brought into question the emirate's security regime and disrupted its relationship with Russia. Yandarbiyev was acting President of Chechnya in 1996–97, but had been sheltered with his family by Qatar since 2000. Despite Qatar's close ties with the USA and Russia, both of which accused Yandarbiyev of being involved in international terrorism (with alleged links to al-Qa'ida), the Qatari Government had refused to extradite the Chechen. Later in February 2004 three Russians were arrested by Qatari security agents; although one of the men was subsequently released and deported following the intervention of the Russian foreign ministry, the other two were charged with involvement in Yandarbiyev's murder. The two defendants reportedly admitted, under interrogation, to being members of Russian special security forces; Russia, however, demanded their immediate release. At the end of June a Qatari court sentenced the two Russian intelligence officers to terms of life imprisonment. An appeal against their sentences was rejected in late July, but the officers were allowed to return to Russia in December.

In October 2005 Qatar was elected to a non-permanent seat on the UN Security Council. The two-year term commenced on 1 January 2006.

Government

According to the provisional Constitution that took effect in 1970, Qatar is an absolute monarchy, with full powers vested in the Amir as Head of State. Executive power is exercised by the Council of Ministers, appointed by the Head of State. An Advisory Council was formed in April 1972, with 20 nominated members (expanded to 30 in 1975 and to 35 in 1988). The Advisory Council's constitutional entitlements include the power to debate legislation drafted by the Council of Ministers before ratification and promulgation. It also has the power to request ministerial statements on matters of general and specific policy, including the draft budget. In March 1999 elections took place, by universal adult suffrage, for a 29-member Municipal Council, which was to have a consultative role in the operations of the Ministry of Municipal Affairs and Agriculture; further elections were held in April 2003. The Amir formally adopted a new Constitution following its approval at a referendum held on 29 April. Under the Constitution, the Amir is to remain head of the executive, while a 45-member unicameral parliament, of which two-thirds are to be directly elected (the remainder being appointed by the Amir), is to have the powers, *inter alia*, to legislate, review the state budget and monitor government policy. It was expected that elections to the new legislature, after which the Advisory Council was to be abolished, would take place in 2007.

Defence

In August 2005 the armed forces comprised an estimated 12,400 men: army 8,500; navy an estimated 1,800 (including Marine Police); air force 2,100. Government expenditure on defence was budgeted at an estimated QR 8,000m. in 2005.

Economic Affairs

In 1997, according to estimates by the World Bank, Qatar's gross national income (GNI), measured at average 1995–97 prices, was US $11,627m., equivalent to $22,147 per head. According to unofficial sources, GNI totalled $17,150m. in 2001 and $17,490m. in 2002 (equivalent to some $28,300 per head). During 1995–2004, it was estimated, the population increased at an average annual rate of 2.6%, while gross domestic product (GDP) per head increased, in real terms, by an average of 5.1% per year. Non-Qataris accounted for some 80% of the total population by the beginning of the 21st century. Overall GDP was estimated to have increased, in real terms, at an average rate of 9.8% per year in 1995–2004; growth was estimated at 8.6% in 2003 and at 9.3% in 2004.

Agriculture (including fishing) contributed an estimated 0.2% of GDP in 2004, and employed some 2.7% of the economically active population in that year. All agricultural land is owned by the Government, and most farm managers are immigrants employing a largely expatriate work-force. The main crops are cereals (principally barley), vegetables and dates. Qatar is self-sufficient in winter vegetables and nearly self-sufficient in summer vegetables. Some vegetables are exported to other Gulf countries. The Government has prioritized education in agricultural techniques and experimentation with unconventional methods of cultivation (including the use of sea water and solar energy to produce sand-based crops). Livestock-rearing and fishing are also practised. The GDP of the agricultural sector was estimated to have declined at an average annual rate of 4.5% during 1993–2002. However, real agricultural GDP increased by an estimated 6.4% in 2002.

Industry (including mining, manufacturing, construction and power) contributed an estimated 75.8% of GDP and employed 41.0% of the economically active population in 2004. Industrial GDP was estimated to have increased by an average of 9.8% per year during 1993–2002. Growth in the sector's real GDP was estimated at 7.6% in 2002.

The mining and quarrying sector (comprising principally the extraction and processing of petroleum and natural gas) provided an estimated 61.0% of GDP in 2004, and employed 4.1% of the economically active population in that year. Petroleum is currently the major mineral export. Proven recoverable petroleum reserves at the end of 2004 were 15,200m. barrels, sufficient to maintain production for 42 years at 2004 levels—averaging some 990,000 barrels per day (b/d). With effect from July 2005 Qatar's production quota within the Organization of the Petroleum Exporting Countries (OPEC, see p. 344) was 726,000 b/d. Proven gas reserves were 25,780,000m. cu m at the end of 2004 (representing 14.4% of known world reserves at that date—behind only the Russia and Iran), primarily located in the North Field, the world's largest gas reserve not associated with petroleum. The real GDP of the mining and quarrying sector was estimated to have increased at an average annual rate of 11.7% in 1993–2002. Growth was estimated at 8.5% in 2002.

Manufacturing contributed an estimated 7.5% of GDP in 2004 (excluding activities related to petroleum and natural gas), and the sector employed 9.2% of the economically active population in that year. The principal manufacturing activities are linked to the country's oil and gas resources—petroleum refining and the production of liquefied natural gas (LNG—developed as part of the North Field project), together with industrial chemicals (particularly fertilizers), and steel production. Manufacturing GDP (excluding hydrocarbons) was estimated to have increased by an average of 4.5% per year in 1993–2002. The sector's real GDP increased by an estimated 7.1% in 2002.

Electrical energy is derived almost exclusively from Qatar's natural gas resource. Solar energy is being developed in conjunction with desalination.

The services sector contributed an estimated 24.0% of GDP in 2004, and engaged 56.2% of the employed labour force in that year. The establishment of the Qatar Financial Centre in January 2005, which was to provide a hub for the emirate's financial services sector, had reportedly proved popular with investors by early 2006 and was expected to stimulate further activity in the sector. The GDP of the services sector was estimated to have increased by an average of 6.1% per year in 1993–2002. Services GDP increased by an estimated 3.9% in 2002.

Preliminary figures indicate that in 2004 Qatar recorded a visible trade surplus of QR 43,944m., while there was a surplus of QR 29,426m. on the current account of the balance of payments. In 2004 the principal source of imports (26.7%) was France; other important suppliers in that year were the USA, Saudi Arabia, the UAE, Germany, Japan and the United Kingdom. In the same year Japan took 42.2% of Qatar's exports. The principal exports are petroleum and gas and their derivatives (mineral fuels and lubricants provided 87.6% of domestic export revenues in 2004). In that year LNG exports alone were estimated to have accounted for 35.0% of export revenues. The principal imports in 2004 were machinery and transport equipment, basic manufactures, food and live animals, and chemicals and related products.

In the financial year ending 31 March 2005 Qatar recorded a budget surplus of QR 14,294m. The annual rate of inflation averaged 3.0% in 1995–2004; consumer prices increased by an average of 8.8% in 2005. The Qatari economy is heavily dependent on immigrant workers, owing to a shortage of indigenous labour; 88.5% of the employed population were non-Qataris at the census of March 2004.

Other than its membership of OPEC, Qatar is a member of the Organization of Arab Petroleum Exporting Countries (OAPEC, see p. 338), the Co-operation Council for the Arab States of the Gulf (GCC, see p. 205), the Arab Fund for Economic and Social Development (AFESD, see p. 161), the Arab Monetary Fund (see p. 163) and the Islamic Development Bank (see p. 303). GCC member states created a unified regional customs tariff in January 2003, and have undertaken to establish a single market and currency no later than January 2010. The economic convergence criteria for the monetary union were agreed at a GCC summit in Abu Dhabi, the UAE, in December 2005.

A priority following the assumption of power by Sheikh Hamad in 1995 was the maximizing of Qatar's energy-derived wealth so as to replenish state reserves, much of which were under the control of the deposed Amir. The development of the North Field gas project has been of prime importance, with the aim that Qatar should become a major regional and international supplier of gas and associated products. One of the most notable recent generators of income has been LNG, exports of which began in 1997 and by 2004, with related products, were valued at some US $6,912m.: LNG was expected to outstrip petroleum as Qatar's principal export commodity in 2005. In the petroleum sector, meanwhile, efforts have been made to expand production capacity (which was expected to reach 1m. b/d by the end of 2009—considerably in excess of Qatar's recent OPEC production quotas). The investment of over $30,000m. in oil and gas projects during 1995–2003, which led to a succession of budgetary deficits, entailed the accumulation of an external debt equivalent to some 90% of GDP by the end of 2002. In addition, a further $80,000m. was scheduled to be invested in the sector during 2004–10. However, there was confidence both within Qatar and in the international financial community that revenue from the gas industry (particularly sales of LNG under long-term sales contracts with companies in the Far East and Europe) would be sufficient to ensure the prompt dispatch of debt; since the 2000/01 financial year five successive fiscal surpluses have been recorded. (Although a small deficit was forecast for the 2004/05 budget, a considerable surplus was recorded in the out-turn figures.) Meanwhile, the divestment of a 45% holding in the state telecommunications company in 1998 was to be followed by the sale of shares in several other state-owned companies. The recently formed Qatar Gas Transport Co (Nakilat) was partially privatized in February 2005. In addition, the Government was expected to break the monopoly of the partially divested Qatar Telecommunications Corpn in 2006–08. However, despite the enactment in 2002 of legislation allowing 100% foreign ownership of companies involved in areas of agriculture, manufacturing, education, health and tourism, and the inauguration in early 2002 of Qatar's first semi-private company in the energy sector (engaged in the sale of liquefied petroleum gas), the state retained responsibility for some 75% of GDP. Alongside measures to increase the size of the private sector, the Government's priority for the early part of the 21st century was the development of the emirate's infrastructure: the budget for 2005/06 provided for a 32% rise in overall expenditure, and spending on infrastructure projects alone was projected to reach $2,742m. In particular, Doha's status as the venue for the 2006 Asian Games tournament entailed huge expenditure; among non-energy sector projects scheduled to be completed by the start of the Games were the Museum of Islamic Arts, a new broadcasting complex, the Hamad Medical City (to be used as the athletes' village), an expansion of the City Centre Doha shopping mall and the construction of numerous hotels—at least 41 were scheduled to be constructed by 2008. The recently established Public Works Authority (Ashgal) reportedly aimed to spend some $27,000m. on construction projects by 2011. Despite the sharp rise in budgeted expenditure, a small fiscal surplus was forecast for 2005/06; this was almost certain again to be a conservative estimate, with petroleum prices projected to increase further. Bolstered by huge petroleum and gas revenues, economic growth was estimated at 9.3% in 2004, and rates of 7.9% and 6.5% were forecast for 2005 and 2006, respectively. The downside of this robust expansion, however, was a strain on the emirate's infrastructure, resources and housing stock and a significant increase in inflation, in particular in costs associated with the construction industry.

Education

A state education system was introduced in 1956. Education is free at all levels, although not compulsory. In 2004 there was a combined total of around 74,000 students at the primary, intermediate and secondary levels of government-funded education in Qatar; in addition, there were about 44,000 students in private schools in the 1999/2000 academic year. Primary education begins at six years of age and lasts for six years. The next level of education, beginning at the age of 12, is divided into two cycles of three years (preparatory and secondary). In 2002/03 the equivalent of 94% of children in the relevant age-group (boys 95%; girls 94%) were enrolled at primary schools, while the comparable ratio for secondary enrolment was equivalent to 82% (boys 80%; girls 85%). In late 2004 12 government-funded schools were leased to private operators in an attempt to improve educational standards. There are specialized religious, industrial, commercial and technical secondary schools for boys; the technical school admitted its first students in 1999/2000, as did two scientific secondary schools (one for girls). In 2004 there were 7,867 undergraduate students and a teaching staff of 691 at the University of Qatar. The Qatar Foundation for Education, Science and Community Development, established in 1995, is involved in programmes including the development of a faculty of medicine, in association with a US university, and a technology college, in association with a Canadian educational body and an international university, as part of its Education City complex, which opened in October 2003 and was scheduled for completion in 2008. The 2005/06 budget allocated QR 486m. to expenditure on education.

Public Holidays

2006: 10 January*† (Id al-Adha, Feast of the Sacrifice), 31 January* (Islamic New Year), 27 June (Anniversary of the Amir's Accession), 21 August* (Leilat al-Meiraj, Ascension of the Prophet), 3 September (National Day), 24 September* (Ramadan begins), 23 October* (Id al-Fitr, end of Ramadan), 31 December*† (Id al-Adha, Feast of the Sacrifice).

QATAR

2007: 20 January* (Islamic New Year), 27 June (Anniversary of the Amir's Accession), 10 August* (Leilat al-Meiraj, Ascension of the Prophet), 3 September (National Day), 13 September* (Ramadan begins), 13 October* (Id al-Fitr, end of Ramadan), 20 December* (Id al-Adha, Feast of the Sacrifice).

*These holidays are dependent on the Islamic lunar calendar and may differ by one or two days from the dates given.

† This festival occurs twice (in the Islamic years AH 1426 and 1427) within the same Gregorian year.

Weights and Measures

The metric system has been adopted legally, but imperial measures are still used.

Statistical Survey

Sources (unless otherwise stated): Press and Publications Dept, Ministry of Education, POB 80, Doha; tel. 4333444; fax 4413886; internet www.moe.edu.qa; Dept of Economic Policies, Qatar Central Bank, POB 1234, Doha; tel. 4456456; fax 4413650; e-mail elzainys@qcb.gov.qa; internet www.qcb.gov.qa; Planning Council, POB 1855, Doha; tel. 4381222; fax 4445573; e-mail statistics@planning.gov.qa; internet www.planning.gov.qa.

AREA AND POPULATION

Area: 11,493 sq km (4,437 sq miles).

Population: 522,023 (males 342,459, females 179,564) at census of 1 March 1997; 744,029 (males 496,382, females 247,647) at census of 1 March 2004.

Density (at 2004 census): 64.7 per sq km.

Principal Towns (population of municipalities, 2004 census): Ad-Dawhah (Doha, the capital) 339,847; Ar-Rayyan 272,860; Umm Salal 31,605; Al-Khawr (Al-Khor) 31,547; Al-Wakrah 31,441.

Births and Deaths (2004): Registered live births 12,856 (birth rate 17.3 per 1,000); Registered marriages 2,550 (marriage rate 3.4 per 1,000); Registered deaths 1,311 (death rate 1.8 per 1,000).

Expectation of Life (years at birth): 74 (males 75; females 74) in 2003. Source: WHO, *World Health Report*.

Economically Active Population (persons aged 15 years and over, 2004 census): Agriculture and fishing 12,025; Mining and quarrying 17,997; Manufacturing 40,039; Electricity, gas and water 4,364; Construction 117,049; Trade, restaurants and hotels 64,718; Transport and communications 15,218; Finance, insurance and real estate 16,625; Community, social and personal services 149,526; *Total employed* 437,561 (Qatari nationals 50,282, non-Qataris 387,279).

HEALTH AND WELFARE

Key Indicators

Total Fertility Rate (children per woman, 2003): 3.2.

Under-5 Mortality Rate (per 1,000 live births, 2004): 21.

Physicians (per 1,000 head, 1998): 0.09.

Hospital Beds (per 1,000 head, 1997): 1.65.

Health Expenditure (2002): US $ per head (PPP): 894.

Health Expenditure (2002): % of GDP: 3.1.

Health Expenditure (2002): public (% of total): 78.2.

Access to Water (% of persons, 2002): 100.

Access to Sanitation (% of persons, 2002): 100.

Human Development Index (2003): ranking: 40.

Human Development Index (2003): value: 0.849.

For sources and definitions, see explanatory note on p. vi.

AGRICULTURE, ETC.

Principal Crops (FAO estimates, '000 metric tons, 2004): Barley 4.7; Maize 1.7; Cabbages 2.3; Tomatoes 7.0; Cauliflowers 1.0; Pumpkins, squash and gourds 8.5; Cucumbers and gherkins 4.0; Aubergines (Eggplants) 3.5; Chillies and green peppers 0.9; Dry onions 4.0; Green corn (maize) 1.0; Cantaloupes and other melons 4.3; Other vegetables (incl. melons) 9.3; Dates 16.5; Other fruit 1.5.

Livestock (FAO estimates, '000 head, year ending September 2004): Horses 3; Cattle 10; Camels 37; Sheep 200; Goats 180; Poultry 4,500.

Livestock Products (FAO estimates, '000 metric tons, 2004): Mutton and lamb 8.2; Camel meat 1.1; Poultry meat 4.2; Other meat 1.0; Cows' milk 11.2; Camels' milk 13.3; Sheep's milk 5.1; Goats' milk 5.7; Hen eggs 5.0.

Fishing (metric tons, live weight, 2003): Groupers 1,804; Grunts and sweetlips 745; Emperors—Scavengers 3,421; King soldier bream 560; Spinefeet—Rabbitfishes 469; Narrow-barred Spanish mackerel 1,945; Jacks and crevalles 351; Carangids 456; *Total catch* 11,000.

Source: FAO.

MINING

Production (estimates, 2004): Crude petroleum ('000 barrels) 287,000; Natural gas (million cu m) 50,000. Source: US Geological Survey.

INDUSTRY

Production (estimates, 2004): Wheat flour (including bran, '000 metric tons) 26; Ammonia (nitrogen content, '000 metric tons) 1,428; Urea (nitrogen content, '000 metric tons) 1,000; Motor spirit (petrol, '000 barrels) 15,000; Kerosene ('000 barrels) 7,400; Gas-diesel (Distillate-fuel) oils ('000 barrels) 7,400; Residual fuel oils ('000 barrels) 2,900; Other refinery products ('000 barrels) 9,600; Liquefied natural gas ('000 barrels) 28,000; Cement ('000 metric tons) 1,400; Crude steel ('000 metric tons) 1,046; Electric energy (million kWh) 12,993. Sources: mainly US Geological Survey, and UN, *Industrial Commodity Statistics Yearbook*.

FINANCE

Currency and Exchange Rates: 100 dirhams = 1 Qatar riyal (QR). *Sterling, Dollar and Euro Equivalents* (30 December 2005): £1 sterling = 6.268 riyals; US $1 = 3.640 riyals; €1 = 4.294 riyals; 100 Qatar riyals = £15.95 = $27.47 = €23.29. *Exchange Rate*: Since June 1980 the official mid-point rate has been fixed at US $1 = QR 3.64.

Budget (preliminary, QR million, 2004/05, year ending 31 March): *Revenue:* Petroleum and natural gas revenue 30,932; Investment revenue 13,878; Total (incl. others) 49,550. *Expenditure:* Recurrent expenditure 27,516 (Salaries and wages 7,535, Interest payments 1,571, Supplies and services 1,521, Other current expenditure 16,889), Capital expenditure 7,740; Total 35,256.

International Reserves (US $ million at 31 December 2004): Gold 18.3; IMF special drawing rights 36.4; Reserve position in IMF 134.1; Foreign exchange 3,225.4; Total 3,414.2. Source: IMF, *International Financial Statistics*.

Money Supply (QR million at 31 December 2004): Currency outside banks 2,594; Demand deposits at commercial banks 12,004; Total money 14,599. Source: IMF, *International Financial Statistics*.

Cost of Living (Consumer Price Index; base: 2001 = 100): 102.51 in 2003; 109.48 in 2004; 119.13 in 2005.

Expenditure on the Gross Domestic Product (estimates, QR million at current prices, 2003): Government final consumption expenditure 13,405; Private final consumption expenditure 13,094; Increase in stocks 640; Gross fixed capital formation 22,707; *Total domestic expenditure* 49,846; Exports of goods and services 44,192 *Less* Imports of goods and services 19,687; *GDP in purchasers' values* 74,351.

Gross Domestic Product by Economic Activity (preliminary, QR million at current prices, 2004): Agriculture and fishing 202; Mining and quarrying 64,365; Manufacturing 7,922; Electricity, gas and water 2,324; Construction 5,414; Trade, restaurants and hotels 4,350; Transport and communications 2,907; Finance, insurance, real estate and business services 6,910; Community, social and personal services 653; Government services 9,938; Domestic services of households 607; *Sub-total* 105,592; *Less* Imputed bank service charge 2,654; *GDP at factor cost* 102,938; Import duties 625; *GDP in purchasers' values* 103,563.

Balance of Payments (estimates, QR million, 2004): Exports f.o.b. 61,505; Imports f.o.b. −17,561; *Trade balance* 43,944; Exports of ser-

QATAR

vices 6,110; Imports of services -9,587; *Balance on goods and services* 40,467; Other income received 4,633; Other income paid -7,469; *Balance on goods, services and income* 37,631; Transfers (net) -8,205; *Current balance* 29,426; Capital account (net) -2,004; Financial account (net) -2,857; New errors and omissions -10,271; *Overall balance* 14,294.

EXTERNAL TRADE

Principal Commodities (distribution by SITC, QR million, 2004): *Imports c.i.f.:* Food and live animals 1,387.2; Chemicals and related products 1,251.9; Basic manufactures 3,859.0; Machinery and transport equipment 12,283.7 (Road vehicles 1,375.1); Miscellaneous manufactured articles 2,134.9; Total (incl. others) 21,856.2. *Exports f.o.b.:* Mineral fuels and lubricants 58,835.2 (Crude petroleum 35,317.6; Natural and manufactured petroleum gases 23,517.6); Chemicals and related products 6,440.0; Total (incl. others) 67,162.3.

Principal Trading Partners (QR million, 2004): *Imports c.i.f.:* Australia 250.3; Bahrain 289.2; People's Republic of China 668.3; France 5,846.1; Germany 1,148.9; India 513.7; Italy 740.3; Japan 1,141.4; Republic of Korea 408.9; Netherlands 275.6; Saudi Arabia 2,079.0; Switzerland 391.3; United Arab Emirates 1,381.3; United Kingdom 1,119.3; USA 2,102.0; Total (incl. others) 21,856.2. *Exports f.o.b.:* People's Republic of China 751.3; India 3,655.0; Japan 28,312.8; Republic of Korea 10,676.8; Philippines 782.5; Saudi Arabia 706.2; Spain 1,257.8; Singapore 6,167.1; Taiwan 921.8; Thailand 1,153.3; United Arab Emirates 1,974.0; USA 854.6; Total (incl. others) 67,162.3.

TRANSPORT

Road Traffic (motor vehicles in use, 2002): Private cars 230,155; Buses and coaches 104,341; Lorries and vans 14,344; Motor cycles and mopeds 4,061. Source: IRF, *World Road Statistics*.

Shipping (international sea-borne freight traffic, '000 metric tons, 1994): *Goods loaded:* 5,853; *Goods unloaded:* 2,500. *Merchant Fleet* (registered at 31 December 2004): 79 vessels; 575,300 gross registered tons (Source: Lloyd's Register-Fairplay, *World Fleet Statistics*).

Civil Aviation (scheduled services, 2001): Kilometres flown (million) 50; Passengers carried ('000) 2,778; Passenger-km (million) 6,510; Total ton-km (million) 876. Figures include an apportionment (one-quarter) of the traffic of Gulf Air, a multinational airline with its headquarters in Bahrain. Source: UN, *Statistical Yearbook*.

TOURISM

Tourist Arrivals: 375,954 in 2001; 586,645 in 2002; 556,965 in 2003.

Tourist Receipts (US $ million, incl. passenger transport): 272 in 2001; 285 in 2002; 369 in 2003.

Source: World Tourism Organization.

COMMUNICATIONS MEDIA

Radio Receivers ('000 in use, 1997): 256*.
Television Receivers ('000 in use, 2000): 520†.
Telephones ('000 main lines in use, 2004): 190.9†.
Facsimile Machines ('000 in use, 1996): 10.4‡.
Mobile Cellular Telephones ('000 subscribers, 2003): 490.3†.
Personal Computers ('000 in use, 2004): 133†.
Internet Users ('000, 2004): 165†.
Daily Newspapers (2001): 5 (circulation 90,000 copies, 1996*).
Weekly Newspapers (2001): 2 (circulation 7,000 copies, 1995*).
Book Production (titles, 1996): 209*.

* Source: UNESCO, *Statistical Yearbook*.
† Source: International Telecommunication Union.
‡ Source: UN, *Statistical Yearbook*.

EDUCATION

Pre-primary (1995/96): 64 schools; 321 teachers; 7,018 pupils.
Primary (2004, government schools only): 112 schools; 3,953 teachers; 38,070 pupils.
Intermediate (2004, government schools only): 54 schools; 1,795 teachers; 19,231 pupils.
Secondary (2004, government schools only): 46 schools; 1,854 teachers; 16,720 pupils.
University (2004): 1 institution; 691 teaching staff; 9,452 students (incl. 1,585 graduate students).

Source: partly UNESCO, *Statistical Yearbook*.

Adult Literacy Rate (UNESCO estimates): 89.2% in 1995–99.
Source: UN Development Programme, *Human Development Report*.

Directory

The Constitution

According to the provisional Constitution adopted on 2 April 1970, executive power was vested in the Amir, as Head of State, and exercised by the Council of Ministers, appointed by the Head of State. The Amir was assisted by the appointed Advisory Council of 20 members (increased to 30 in 1975 and to 35 in 1988), whose term was extended for six years in 1975, for a further four years in 1978, and for further terms of four years in 1982, 1986, 1990, 1994 and 1998. All fundamental democratic rights were guaranteed. In 1975 the Advisory Council was granted the power to summon individual ministers to answer questions on legislation before promulgation. In March 1999 elections took place, by universal adult suffrage, for a 29-member Municipal Council, which was to have a consultative role in the operations of the Ministry of Municipal Affairs and Agriculture. The Amir formally adopted a new Constitution following a referendum held on 29 April 2003. Under the new Constitution, the Amir is to remain head of the executive, while a 45-member unicameral parliament, of which two-thirds are to be directly elected (the remainder being appointed by the Amir), is to have the powers to legislate, review the state budget, monitor government policy and hold ministers accountable for their actions. The parliament is to have a four-year mandate. Elections to the new legislature, after which the Advisory Council was to be abolished, were expected to be conducted by 2007, with suffrage extended to all citizens, including women, aged 18 years and above. The Constitution also guarantees freedom of association, expression and religious affiliation and provides for the establishment of an independent judiciary; however, it does not authorize political parties.

The Government

HEAD OF STATE

Amir: Maj.-Gen. Sheikh HAMAD BIN KHALIFA ATH-THANI (assumed power 27 June 1995).

Crown Prince and Commander-in-Chief of the Armed Forces: Sheikh TAMIM BIN HAMAD BIN KHALIFA ATH-THANI.

COUNCIL OF MINISTERS
(April 2006)

Amir and Minister of Defence: Maj.-Gen. Sheikh HAMAD BIN KHALIFA ATH-THANI.

Prime Minister and Minister of the Interior: Sheikh ABDULLAH BIN KHALIFA ATH-THANI.

First Deputy Prime Minister and Minister of Foreign Affairs: Sheikh HAMAD BIN JASIM BIN JABER ATH-THANI.

Second Deputy Prime Minister and Minister of Energy and Industry: ABDULLAH BIN HAMAD AL-ATTIYA.

Minister of Finance, and of Economy and Trade: YOUSUF BIN HUSSAIN KAMAL.

Minister of Awqaf (Religious Endowments) and Islamic Affairs: FAISAL BIN ABDULLAH AL-MAHMUD.

Minister of Municipal Affairs and Agriculture and Minister of State for Council of Ministers' Affairs: SULTAN BIN HASSAN ADH-DHABIT AD-DOUSARY.

Minister of Justice: HASSAN BIN ABDULLAH AL-GHANIM.

Minister of Education: Sheikha BINT AHMAD AL-MAHMOUD.

Minister of Civil Service Affairs and Housing: Sheikh FALAH BIN JASIM ATH-THANI.

Minister of State for Foreign Affairs: AHMAD BIN ABDULLAH AL-MAHMOUD.

QATAR

Minister of State for the Interior: Sheikh ABDULLAH BIN NASSER BIN KHALIFA ATH-THANI.

Minister of State without Portfolio: Sheikh MUHAMMAD BIN KHALID ATH-THANI.

MINISTRIES

Ministry of Amiri Diwan Affairs: POB 923, Doha; tel. 4367575; fax 4361212; e-mail adf@diwan.gov.qa; internet www.diwan.gov.qa.

Ministry of Awqaf (Religious Endowments) and Islamic Affairs: POB 422, Doha; tel. 4470777; fax 4327383; e-mail minister@islam.gov.qa; internet www.islam.gov.qa.

Ministry of Civil Service Affairs and Housing: POB 36, Doha; tel. 4335335; fax 4446298; internet www.mcsah.gov.qa.

Ministry of Defence: Qatar Armed Forces, POB 37, Doha; tel. 4404111.

Ministry of Economy and Trade: Doha.

Ministry of Education: POB 80, Doha; tel. 4333444; fax 4413886; internet www.moe.edu.qa.

Ministry of Energy and Industry: POB 2599, Doha; tel. 4832121; fax 4832024; internet www.kahramaa.com.

Ministry of Finance: POB 3322, Doha; tel. 4461444; fax 4431177.

Ministry of Foreign Affairs: POB 250, Doha; tel. 4334334; fax 4442777; e-mail webmaster@mofa.gov.qa; internet www.mofa.gov.qa.

Ministry of the Interior: POB 115, Doha; tel. 4330000; fax 4429565; e-mail info@moi.gov.qa; internet www.moi.gov.qa.

Ministry of Justice: POB 917 (Dept of Legal Affairs), Doha; tel. 4835200; fax 4832868.

Ministry of Municipal Affairs and Agriculture: POB 820, Doha; tel. 4336336; fax 4430239; e-mail mmaa@mmaa.gov.qa; internet www.mmaa.gov.qa.

ADVISORY COUNCIL

The Advisory or *Shura* Council was established in 1972, with 20 nominated members. It was expanded to 30 members in 1975, and to 35 members in 1988. Under the terms of the new Constitution, which was promulgated in 2003, the Advisory Council is to be replaced by a 45-member unicameral parliament.

Speaker: MUHAMMAD BIN MUBARAK AL-KHOLAIFI.

Diplomatic Representation

EMBASSIES IN QATAR

Afghanistan: POB 22104, Doha; tel. 4930821; fax 4930819; e-mail afgembqatar@hotmail.com; Ambassador NASIR AHMAD NOOR.

Algeria: POB 2494, Doha; tel. 4831186; fax 4836452; Ambassador MOHAMED BOUROUBA.

Bahrain: POB 24888, 5846 As-Siedari St, Sq. 31, Doha New Area, Doha; tel. 4839360; fax 4839360; Ambassador ABD AR-RAHMAN MUHAMMAD AL-FATHEL.

Bangladesh: POB 3080, Doha; tel. 4671927; fax 4671190; e-mail bdootqat@qatar.net.qa; Ambassador AHSEN N. AMIN.

Bosnia and Herzegovina: POB 876, Doha; tel. 4670194; fax 4670595; e-mail ambasada@qatar.net.qa; internet www.bhembassyqatar.org; Ambassador HUSEIN PANJETA.

Brunei: POB 22772, Doha; tel. 4854444; fax 4832703; e-mail bruemb@qatar.net.qa; Chargé d'affaires HAJ NORDIN HAJ AHMAD.

China, People's Republic: POB 17200, Doha; tel. 4824200; fax 4873959; e-mail chinashi@qatar.net.qa; Ambassador LI JIANYING.

Cuba: POB 12017, Doha; tel. 4672072; fax 4672074; e-mail enbacuba@qatar.net.qa; Ambassador ENRIQUE ENRÍQUEZ RODRÍGUEZ.

Egypt: POB 2899, Doha; tel. 4832555; fax 4832196; e-mail info@egyptembqatar.com; internet www.egyptembqatar.com; Ambassador AHDY KHAIRAT.

Eritrea: POB 4309, Doha; tel. 4667934; fax 4664139; Ambassador ALI IBRAHIM AHMED.

France: POB 2669, Doha; tel. 4832283; fax 4832254; e-mail ambadoha@qatar.net.qa; internet www.ambafrance-qa.org.qa; Ambassador ALAN AZOUAOU.

Gambia: POB 22377, Doha; tel. 4651429; fax 4651705; Chargé d'affaires BASSIROU DRAMMEH.

Germany: POB 3064, Doha; tel. 4876959; fax 4876949; e-mail germany@qatar.net.qa; Ambassador RAINOLD FRICKHINGER.

Hungary: POB 23525, Doha; tel. 4932531; fax 4932537; e-mail huembdoh@qatar.net.qa; Ambassador FERENC CSILLAG.

India: POB 2788, Doha; tel. 4672021; fax 4670448; e-mail indembdh@qatar.net.qa; internet www.indianembassy.gov.qa; Ambassador GEORGE JOSEPH.

Indonesia: POB 22375, Al-Maheed St, Doha; tel. 4657945; fax 4657610; e-mail inemb@qatar.net.qa; internet www.kbridoha.com; Ambassador ABDUL WAHID MAKTUB.

Iran: POB 1633, Doha; tel. 4835300; fax 4831665; tel. embiriqr@qatar.net.qa; Ambassador DHABEEH ALLAH NOUVERSTI.

Iraq: POB 1526, Doha; tel. 4672237; fax 4673347; e-mail dohemb@iraqmofamail.net; Ambassador SADIQ HAMEEDI AR-RAKAWI.

Italy: POB 4188, Doha; tel. 4436842; fax 4446466; e-mail ambasciata.doha@esteri.it; internet sedi.esteri.it/doha; Ambassador GIUSEPPE BUCCINO GRIMALDI.

Japan: POB 2208, Doha; tel. 4831224; fax 4832178; Ambassador KATZUYA IKEDA.

Jordan: POB 2366, Doha; tel. 4832202; fax 4832173; e-mail jordand@qatar.net.qa; Ambassador OMAR AL-AHMAD.

Korea, Democratic People's Republic: POB 799, Doha; tel. 4417614; fax 4424735; Ambassador KIM HYONG JUN.

Korea, Republic: POB 3727, Doha; tel. 4832238; fax 4833264; e-mail koemb_ga@mofa.go.kr; Ambassador KIM JAE-GOUK.

Kuwait: POB 1177, Doha; tel. 4832111; fax 4832042; e-mail kuwaitembassy@qatar.net.qa; Ambassador DHARI AL-AJRAN.

Lebanon: POB 2411, Doha; tel. 4933330; fax 4933331; e-mail embleb@qatar.net.qa; Ambassador HASSAN SAAD.

Libya: POB 574, Doha; tel. 4429546; fax 4429548; Chargé d'affaires AL-MABROUK MUHAMMAD AL-MUADANE.

Malaysia: POB 23760, Doha; tel. 4836463; fax 4836453; e-mail maldoha@kln.gov.my; Ambassador KU JAAFAR B. KU SHAARI.

Mauritania: POB 3132, Doha; tel. 4836003; fax 4836015; Ambassador MUHAMMAD AL-AMIN AS-SALEM WALD DADA.

Morocco: POB 3242, Doha; tel. 4831885; fax 4833416; e-mail moroccoe@qatar.net.qa; Ambassador ABDELADIM TABIR.

Nepal: POB 23002, Doha; tel. 4675681; fax 4675680; e-mail rnedoha@qatar.net.qa; internet www.rnedoha.org.qa; Ambassador SHYAMANANDA SUMAN.

Oman: POB 1525, Doha; tel. 4670744; fax 4670747; e-mail oman_e126@hotmail.com; Ambassador NASSER BIN KHALFAN AL-KHAROOSI.

Pakistan: POB 334, Doha; tel. 4832525; fax 4832227; e-mail parepqat@qatar.net.qa; Ambassador KAMAL ARIF.

Philippines: POB 24900, Doha; tel. 4831585; fax 4831595; e-mail dohape@qatar.net.qa; Ambassador WENCESLAO J. O. QUIROLGICO.

Romania: POB 22511, Doha; tel. 4934848; fax 4934747; e-mail romamb@qatar.net.qa; Ambassador NICOLAE ROPOTEAN.

Russia: POB 15404, Doha; tel. 4329117; fax 4329118; e-mail rusemb@qatar.net.qa; Ambassador VIKTOR KUDRYAVTSEV.

Saudi Arabia: POB 1255, Doha; tel. 4832030; fax 4832720; Ambassador HAMAD BIN SALEH AT-TUAIMI (recalled Sept. 2002).

Senegal: POB 8291, Doha; tel. 4676587; fax 4676589; Ambassador PAPA ALIOUNE NDIAYE.

Somalia: POB 1948, Doha; tel. 4832200; fax 4832182; Ambassador SHARIF MUHAMMAD OMAR.

South Africa: Al-Dafna St 523, House 91, Doha; tel. 4366480; fax 4366468; Ambassador LUNGILI PEPANI.

Sri Lanka: 4 Al-Kharja St, POB 19705, Doha; tel. 4677627; fax 4674788; e-mail lankaemb@qatar.net.qa; Ambassador MEERA SAHIB MAHROOF.

Sudan: POB 2999, Doha; tel. 4423007; fax 4351366; Ambassador MUHAMMAD AHMAD MUSTAFA AD-DABY.

Syria: POB 1257, Doha; tel. 4831844; fax 4832139; Chargé d'affaires HAJEM ABD AL-HAMED IBRAHIM.

Thailand: POB 22474, Doha; tel. 4550715; fax 4550835; Ambassador VORAVEE WIRASAMBAN.

Tunisia: POB 2707, Doha; tel. 4832645; fax 4832649; e-mail at.doha@qatar.net.qa; Ambassador MUHAMMAD SAAD.

Turkey: POB 1977, Doha; tel. 4835553; fax 4835206; e-mail tcdohabe@qatar.net.qa; Ambassador NACI SARIBAS.

United Arab Emirates: POB 3099, Doha; tel. 4838880; fax 4836186; e-mail emarat@qatar.net.qa; Ambassador ABD AR-REDHA ABDULLAH KHORI.

United Kingdom: POB 3, Doha; tel. 4421991; fax 4438692; e-mail bembcomm@qatar.net.qa; internet www.britishembassy.gov.uk/qatar; Ambassador SIMON COLLIS.

USA: POB 2399, Doha; tel. 4884101; fax 4884298; e-mail pasdoha@state.gov; internet qatar.usembassy.gov; Ambassador CHASE UNTERMEYER.

Yemen: POB 3318, Doha; tel. 4432555; fax 4429400; Ambassador YAHYA HUSSAIN AL-AARASHI.

Judicial System

Independence of the judiciary is guaranteed by the provisional Constitution. All aspects pertaining to the civil judiciary are supervised by the Ministry of Justice, which organizes courts of law through its affiliated departments. The *Shari'a* judiciary hears all cases of personal status relating to Muslims, other claim cases, doctrinal provision and crimes under its jurisdiction. Legislation adopted in 1999 unified all civil and *Shari'a* courts in one judicial body, and determined the jurisdictions of each type of court. The law also provided for the establishment of a court of cassation; this was to be competent to decide on appeals relating to issues of contravention, misapplication and misinterpretation of the law, and on disputes between courts regarding areas of jurisdiction. The law also provided for the establishment of a supreme judiciary council, to be presided over by the head of the court of cassation and comprising, *inter alia*, the heads of the *Shari'a* and civil courts of appeal. The establishment of a judicial inspection system was also envisaged. An amiri decree published in June 2002 sought to establish an independent public prosecution system. Further elaboration of provisions for the creation of an independent judiciary were contained in the Constitution formally adopted by the Amir in April 2003.

Chief Justice: MUBARAK BIN KHALIFA AL-ASARI.

Public Prosecutor: Col ABDULLAH AL-MAL.

Presidency of Shari'a Courts: POB 232, Doha; tel. 4452222; Pres. Sheikh ABD AR-RAHMAN BIN ABDULLAH AL-MAHMOUD.

Religion

The indigenous population are Muslims of the Sunni sect, most being of the strict Wahhabi persuasion.

CHRISTIANITY

The Anglican Communion

Within the Episcopal Church in Jerusalem and the Middle East, Qatar forms part of the diocese of Cyprus and the Gulf. The Anglican congregation in Qatar is entirely expatriate. The Bishop in Cyprus and the Gulf is resident in Cyprus, while the Archdeacon in the Gulf is resident in Qatar.

Archdeacon in the Gulf: POB 3, Doha; Archdeacon Ven. IAN YOUNG.

The Roman Catholic Church

An estimated 60,000 adherents in Qatar, mainly expatriates, form part of the Apostolic Vicariate of Arabia. The Vicar Apostolic is resident in the United Arab Emirates.

The Press

Al-'Arab (The Arabs): POB 6334, Doha; tel. 4325874; fax 4440016; f. 1972; daily; Arabic; publ. by Dar al-Ouroba Printing and Publishing; Editor-in-Chief KHALID NAAMA; circ. 25,000.

Ad-Dawri (The Tournament): POB 310, Doha; tel. 4328782; fax 4447039; f. 1978; weekly; Arabic; sport; publ. by Abdullah Hamad al-Atiyah and Ptnrs; Editor-in-Chief Sheikh RASHID BIN OWAIDA ATH-THANI; circ. 6,000.

Gulf Times: POB 2888, Doha; tel. 4350478; fax 4350474; e-mail edit@gulf-times.com; internet www.gulf-times.com; f. 1978; daily and weekly editions; English; political; publ. by Gulf Publishing and Printing Co; Editor-in-Chief ABD AR-RAHMAN SAIF AL-MADHADI; circ. 15,000 (daily).

Al-Jawhara (The Jewel): POB 2531, Doha; tel. 4414575; fax 4671388; f. 1977; monthly; Arabic; women's magazine; publ. by al-Ahd Establishment for Journalism, Printing and Publications Ltd; Editor-in-Chief ABDULLAH YOUSUF AL-HUSSAINI; circ. 8,000.

Nada (A Gathering): POB 4896, Doha; tel. 4445564; fax 4433778; f. 1991; weekly; social and entertainment; publ. by Akhbar al-Usbou'; Editor-in-Chief ADEL ALI BIN ALI.

Al-Ouroba (Arabism): POB 663, Doha; tel. 4325874; fax 4429424; f. 1970; weekly; Arabic; political; publ. by Dar al-Ouroba Printing and Publishing; Editor-in-Chief YOUSUF NAAMA; circ. 12,000.

The Peninsula: POB 3488, Doha; tel. 4663945; fax 4663965; e-mail penqatar@qatar.net.qa; f. 1996; daily; English; political; publ. by Dar ash-Sharq Printing, Publishing and Distribution; Editor-in-Chief ABD AL-AZIZ AL-MAHMOUD; Man. Editor GEORGE ABRAHAM; circ. 8,000.

Qatar Lil Inshaa (Qatar Construction): POB 2203, Doha; tel. 4424988; fax 4432961; f. 1989; publ. by Almaha Trade and Construction Co; Gen. Man. MUHAMMAD H. AL-MIJBER; circ. 10,000.

Ar-Rayah (The Banner): POB 3464, Doha; tel. 4466555; fax 4350476; e-mail www.edit@raya.com; internet www.raya.com; f. 1979; daily and weekly editions; Arabic; political; publ. by Gulf Publishing and Printing Co; Editor NASSER AL-OTHMAN; circ. 25,000.

Saidat ash-Sharq: POB 3488, Doha; tel. 4662445; fax 4662450; f. 1993; monthly; Arabic; women's magazine; publ. by Dar ash-Sharq Printing, Publishing and Distribution; Editor NASSER AL-OTHMAN; circ. 15,000.

Ash-Sharq (The Orient): POB 3488, Doha; tel. 4662444; fax 4662450; e-mail webmaster@al-sharq.com; internet www.al-sharq.com; f. 1985; daily; Arabic; political; publ. by Dar ash-Sharq Printing, Publishing and Distribution; Gen. Supervisor NASSER AL-OTHMAN; circ. 45,018.

At-Tarbiya (Education): POB 9865, Doha; tel. 4861412; fax 4880911; e-mail netcom@qatar.net.qa; f. 1971; quarterly; publ. by Qatar National Commission for Education, Culture and Science; Editor-in-Chief YOUSUF BIN ALI AL-KHATER; circ. 2,000.

This is Qatar and What's On: POB 4015, Doha; tel. 4413813; fax 4413814; f. 1978; quarterly; English; tourist information; publ. by Oryx Publishing and Advertising Co; Editor-in-Chief YOUSUF J. AD-DARWISH; circ. 10,000.

Al-Ummah: POB 893, Doha; tel. 4447300; fax 4447022; e-mail m_dirasat@islam.gov.qa; internet www.islam.gov.qa; f. 1982; bi-monthly; Islamic thought and affairs, current cultural issues, book serializations.

Al-Watan: POB 22345, Doha; tel. 4652244; fax 4660440; e-mail feedback@al-watan.com; internet www.al-watan.com; f. 1995; daily; Arabic; political; publ. by Dar al-Watan Printing, Publishing and Distribution; Editor-in-Chief AHMAD ALI AL-ABDULLAH; circ. 25,000.

NEWS AGENCY

Qatar News Agency (QNA): POB 3299, Doha; tel. 4450319; fax 4438316; e-mail info@qnaol.com; internet www.qnaol.com; f. 1975; affiliated to Ministry of Foreign Affairs; Dir and Editor-in-Chief AHMAD JASSIM AL-HUMAR.

Publishers

Ali bin Ali Media and Publishing: POB 75, Doha; tel. 4313245; fax 4411251; e-mail publishing@alibinali.com; internet www.alibinali.com; publishers of *Qatar Telephone Directory* and *Yellow Pages*.

Dar al-Ouroba Printing and Publishing: POB 52, Doha; tel. 4423179.

Dar ash-Sharq Printing, Publishing and Distribution: POB 3488, Doha; tel. 4662444; fax 4662450; e-mail alsharq1@qatar.net.qa; Editor-in-Chief ABDULLATIF AL-MAHMOUD; circ. 22,000.

Gulf Publishing and Printing Co: POB 533, Doha; tel. 4466555; fax 4424171; e-mail gm@gulftimes.com; internet www.gulf-times.com; Gen. Man. MUHAMMAD ALLAM ALI.

Oryx Publishing and Advertising Co: POB 405, Doha; tel. 4672139; fax 4550982.

Qatar National Printing Press: POB 355, Doha; tel. 4448453; fax 4449550; Man. ABD AL-KARIM DEEB.

Broadcasting and Communications

TELECOMMUNICATIONS

Supreme Council for Communications and Information Technology (SCCIT): Doha; f. 2005 to oversee the deregulation of the telecommunications sector; Chair. Sheikh TAMIM BIN HAMAD BIN KHALIFA ATH-THANI.

Qatar Telecommunications Corpn—Qatar Telecom (Q-Tel): POB 217, Doha; tel. 4400400; fax 4413904; e-mail webmaster@qtel.com.qa; internet www.qtel.com.qa; f. 1987; majority state-owned; provides telecommunications services within Qatar; Chair. Sheikh ABDULLAH BIN MUHAMMAD ATH-THANI; CEO Dr NASSER MARAFIH.

BROADCASTING

Regulatory Authority

Qatar Radio and Television Corpn (QRTC): Doha; f. 1997; autonomous authority reporting directly to the Council of Ministers.

Radio

Qatar Broadcasting Service (QBS): POB 3939, Doha; tel. 4894444; fax 4882888; f. 1968; govt service transmitting in Arabic, English, French and Urdu; programmes include Holy Quran Radio and Doha Music Radio; Dir MUHAMMAD A. AL-KUWARI.

Television

Al-Jazeera Satellite Channel: POB 23123, Doha; tel. 4896000; fax 4885333; internet www.aljazeera.net; f. 1996; 24-hr broadcasting; Arabic; English-language service planned; Pres. HAMAD BIN THAMER ATH-THANI; Editor-in-Chief AHMAD SHEIKH.

Qatar Television Service (QTV): POB 1944, Doha; tel. 4894444; fax 4874170; f. 1970; operates two channels; Dir AHMAD AR-RASHID; Asst Dir ABD AL-WAHAB MUHAMMAD AL-MUTAWA'A.

Finance

(cap. = capital; res = reserves; dep. = deposits; m. = million; brs = branches; amounts in Qatar riyals unless otherwise stated)

BANKING

Central Bank

Qatar Central Bank: POB 1234, Doha; tel. 4456456; fax 4413650; e-mail webmaster@qcb.gov.qa; internet www.qcb.gov.qa; f. 1966 as Qatar and Dubai Currency Board; became Qatar Monetary Agency in 1973; renamed Qatar Central Bank in 1993; cap. 1,000m., res 558.8m., dep. 1,732.6m., currency in circulation 2,266.6m. (Dec. 2002); Gov. ABDULLAH BIN SAID ABD AL-AZIZ ATH-THANI.

Commercial Banks

Ahlibank QSC: POB 2309, Ahli Bank Bldg, Salwa Rd, Ramada Intersection, Doha; tel. 4326611; fax 4444652; e-mail abarrage@ahlibank.com.qa; f. 1984 as Al-Ahli Bank of Qatar QSC; name changed as above in 2004; cap. 182.8m., res 78.5m., dep. 2,092.5m. (July 2004); Gen. Man. QASIM M. QASIM; 8 brs.

Commercial Bank of Qatar QSC: POB 3232, Grand Hamad Ave, Doha; tel. 4900000; fax 4438182; e-mail info@cbq.com.qa; internet www.cbq.com.qa; f. 1975; owned 35% by board of directors and 65% by Qatari citizens and organizations; cap. 747.5m., res 2,158.9m., dep. 7,206.3m. (June 2005); Chair. ABDULLAH BIN KHALIFA AL-ATTIYA; Gen. Man. ANDREW C. STEVENS; 17 brs.

Doha Bank: POB 3818, Grand Hamad Ave, Doha; tel. 4456600; fax 4416631; e-mail international@dohabank.com.qa; internet www.dohabank.com.qa; f. 1979; cap. 407.9m., res 712.1m., dep. 7,426.7m. (Dec. 2003); Chair. Sheikh FAHAD BIN MUHAMMAD BIN JABER ATH-THANI; Dep. CEO R. SEETHARAMAN; 16 brs.

International Bank of Qatar QSC (IBQ): POB 2001, Suhaim bin Hamad St, Doha; tel. 4473700; fax 4473710; e-mail qatarenq@ibq.com.qa; internet www.ibq.com; f. 2000 as Grindlays Qatar Bank QSC; previously a branch of ANZ Grindlays Bank, f. 1956; name changed as above in 2004, after National Bank of Kuwait SAK assumed management of the bank; cap. 75.0m., res 45.4m., dep. 1,131.3m. (Dec. 2003); Gen. Man. DESMOND HOLMES.

Qatar Industrial Development Bank: POB 22789, Doha; tel. 4421600; fax 4350433; e-mail contact@qidb.com; internet www.qidb.com.qa; f. 1996; inaugurated Oct. 1997; state-owned; provides long-term low-interest industrial loans; cap. 200m.; Chair. Sheikh ABDULLAH BIN SAUD ATH-THANI.

Qatar International Islamic Bank QSC (QIIB): POB 664, Grand Hamad St, Doha; tel. 4385555; fax 4444101; e-mail qiibit@qatar.net.qa; internet www.qiibonline.com; f. 1990; cap. 125.0m., res 186.4m., dep. 3,509.4m. (Dec. 2003); Chair. THANI BIN ABDULLAH ATH-THANI; Gen. Man. ABD AL-BASIT ASH-SHAIBEI; 3 brs.

Qatar Islamic Bank SAQ: POB 559, Doha; tel. 4409409; fax 4412700; e-mail qibt@qatar.net.qa; internet www.qib.com.qa; f. 1983; cap. 250.0m., res 285.7m., dep. 4,821.6m. (Dec. 2003); Chair., Man. Dir and Pres. KHALID BIN AHMAD AS-SUWAIDI; Gen. Man. SALEH MUHAMMAD JAIDAH; 9 brs.

Qatar National Bank SAQ: POB 1000, Doha; tel. 4407407; fax 4413753; e-mail ccsupport@qnb.com.qa; internet www.qnb.com.qa; f. 1964; owned 50% by Govt of Qatar and 50% by Qatari nationals; cap. 1,038.2m., res 3,596.6m., dep. 25,621.1m. (Dec. 2002); Chair. YOUSUF BIN HUSSAIN KAMAL (Minister of Finance, and of Economy and Trade); Chief Exec. ALI SHARIF AL-EMADI (acting); 32 brs.

Foreign Banks

Arab Bank PLC (Jordan): POB 172, 119 Hamad al-Kabeer St, Doha; tel. 4427979; fax 4410774; e-mail arabbank@qatar.net.qa; internet www.arabbank.com; f. 1957; total assets 1,100m. (Dec. 1996); Regional Man. GHASSAN A. BUNDAKJI; Dep. Man. WALDI SHATARA; 2 brs.

Bank Saderat Iran: POB 2256, Doha; tel. 4414646; fax 4430121; e-mail bsiiran@qatar.net.qa; internet www.bank-saderat-iran.com/gulf.htm; f. 1970; Man. MUHAMMAD ZAMANI.

BNP Paribas (France): POB 2636, Al-Istiqal St, Doha; tel. 4433844; fax 4410861; e-mail qatar.paribas@paribas.com; internet www.qatar.bnpparibas.com; f. 1973; Gen. Man. CHRISTIAN DE LA TOUCHE.

HSBC Bank Middle East (UK): POB 57, 810 Abdullah bin Jassim St, Doha; tel. 4382222; fax 4416353; e-mail hsbcqa@qatar.net.qa; internet www.middleeast.hsbc.com; f. 1954; fmrly British Bank of the Middle East; total assets US $550m. (1999); CEO MATTHEW SMITH; 3 brs.

Mashreq Bank PSC (UAE): POB 173, Al-Murqab St, Doha; tel. 4413213; fax 4413880; f. 1971; Gen. Man. NASIR AHMAD KHAN.

Standard Chartered PLC (UK): POB 29, Abdullah bin Jassim St, Doha; tel. 4414252; fax 4413739; e-mail arifmansoor@qa.standardchartered.com; internet www.standardchartered.com/qa; f. 1950; total assets 1,241m.; Country CEO KRIS BABICCI.

United Bank Ltd (Pakistan): POB 242, Doha; tel. 4424400; fax 4424600; e-mail ubldoha@qatar.net.qa; internet www.ubl.com.pk; f. 1970; Gen. Man. and Vice-Pres. RAI MUHAMMAD ASIF KHAN.

STOCK EXCHANGE

Doha Securities Market (DSM): POB 22114, Doha; tel. 4333666; fax 4326497; e-mail dsm@dsm.com.qa; internet www.dsm.com.qa; f. 1997; 32 cos listed in Oct. 2005; Gen. Man. Dr GHANIM AL-HAMMADI.

INSURANCE

Doha Insurance Co: POB 7171, Doha; tel. 4335000; fax 4657777; e-mail dohainsco@qatar.net.qa; f. 1999 as public shareholding co; cap. 127.2m. (2003); Chair. Sheikh NAWAF BIN NASSER BIN KHALID ATH-THANI; Gen. Man. BASSAM HUSSAIN.

Al-Khaleej Insurance Co (SAQ): POB 4555, Doha; tel. 4414151; fax 4430530; e-mail alkhalej@qatarnet.qa; internet www.alkhaleej.com; f. 1978; cap. 29.0m. (2003); all classes except life; Chair. ABDULLAH BIN MUHAMMAD JABER ATH-THANI; Gen. Man. AYED HIKMAT ABU AISHEH.

Qatar General Insurance and Reinsurance Co SAQ: POB 4500, A Ring Road, Al-Asmakh Area, Doha; tel. 4357000; fax 4437302; e-mail qgirc-tec@qatar.net.qa; internet www.qgirc.com.qa; f. 1979; cap. 50m. (July 2004); all classes; Chair. and Man. Dir Sheikh NASSER BIN ALI ATH-THANI; Gen. Man. GHAZI ABU NAHL.

Qatar Insurance Co SAQ: POB 666, Tamin St, West Bay, Doha; tel. 4838520; fax 4831569; e-mail qatarins@qatar.net.qa; internet www.qatarinsurance.com; f. 1964; cap. 127.8m. (2003); all classes; the Govt has a majority share; Chair. Sheikh KHALID BIN MUHAMMAD ALI ATH-THANI; Gen. Man. KHALIFA A. AS-SUBAY'I; brs in Doha, Khalifa Town, Dubai (UAE) and Malta.

Qatar Islamic Insurance Co: POB 12402, Doha; tel. 4413413; fax 4447277; e-mail qiic@qatar.net.qa; internet www.qiic.net; f. 1993; cap. 20m. (2003); Chair. Sheikh THANI BIN ABDULLAH ATH-THANI; Gen. Man. IZZAT M. AR-RASHID.

Trade and Industry

DEVELOPMENT ORGANIZATIONS

Department of Industrial Development: POB 2599, Doha; tel. 4846444; fax 4832024; e-mail did@qatar.net.qa; govt-owned; conducts research, licensing, development and supervision of new industrial projects; Dir-Gen. SAID MUBARAK AL-KUWAIRI.

Public Works Authority (Ashgal): Doha; f. 2004; Man. Dir ZAYED MANSOOR AL-KHAYARIN.

CHAMBER OF COMMERCE

Qatar Chamber of Commerce and Industry: POB 402, Doha; tel. 4621131; fax 4622538; e-mail qcci@qatar.net.qa; internet www.qatar.net.qa/qcci; f. 1963; 17 elected mems; Pres. MUHAMMAD BIN KHALID AL-MANA; Dir-Gen. Dr MAJID ABDULLAH AL-MALKI.

STATE HYDROCARBONS COMPANIES

Qatar Petrochemical Co (QAPCO) SAQ: POB 756, Doha; tel. 4242444; fax 4324700; e-mail information@qapco.com.qa; internet www.qapco.com; f. 1974; Industries Qatar (IQ) has an 80% share; 20% is held by TOTAL Petrochemicals (France); total assets QR 3,547.9m. (2004); operation of petrochemical plant at Mesaieed; produced 494,205 metric tons of ethylene, 372,825 tons of low-density polyethylene, and 42,839 tons of solid sulphur in 2004; Vice-Chair. and Gen. Man. Eng. HAMAD RASHID AL-MOHANNADI; 879 employees (2004).

Qatar Petroleum (QP): POB 3212, Doha; tel. 4491491; fax 4831125; e-mail webmaster@qp.com.qa; internet www.qp.com.qa;

f. 1974 as the Qatar General Petroleum Corpn (QGPC), name changed 2001; cap. QR 20,000m.; the State of Qatar's interest in companies active in petroleum and related industries has passed to QP; has responsibility for all phases of oil and gas industry both on shore and off shore, including exploration, drilling, production, refining, transport and storage, distribution, sale and export of oil, natural gas and other hydrocarbons; Chair. ABDULLAH BIN HAMAD AL-ATTIYA; Vice-Chair. HUSSAIN KAMAL; 5,500 employees.

Qatar Petroleum wholly or partly owns: Industries Qatar (IQ) and its subsidiaries, Qatar Gas Transport Co (Nakilat), Ras Laffan LNG Co Ltd (Rasgas), Gulf Helicopters Co Ltd (GHC), Qatar Vinyl Co (QVC), Qatar Chemical Co (Q-Chem), Qatar Clean Energy Co (QACENCO), Qatar Electricity and Water Co (QEWC), Qatar Shipping Co (Q-Ship), Arab Maritime Petroleum Transport Co (AMPTC), Arab Petroleum Pipelines Co (SUMED), Arab Shipbuilding and Repair Yard Co (ASRY), Arab Petroleum Services Co (APSC) and Arab Petroleum Investments Corpn (APICORP); and also the following:

Qatar Liquefied Gas Co (QATARGAS): POB 22666, Doha; tel. 4736000; fax 4736666; e-mail webmaster@qatargas.com.qa; internet www.qatargas.com; f. 1984 to develop the North Field of unassociated gas; cap. QR 500m.; QP has a 65% share; ExxonMobil and Total hold 10% each; the Marubeni Corpn and Mitsui and Co of Japan hold 7.5% each; Chair. ABDULLAH BIN HAMAD AL-ATTIYA (Minister of Energy and Industry); Vice-Chair. and Man. Dir FAISAL MUHAMMAD AS-SUWAIDI.

UTILITIES

Qatar General Electricity and Water Corpn (Kahramaa): POB 41, Doha; tel. 4845484; fax 4845496; e-mail pr@kahramaa.com.qa; internet www.kahramaa.com.qa; f. 2000; state authority for planning, implementation, operation and maintenance of electricity and water sectors; Chair. ABDULLAH BIN HAMAD AL-ATTIYA.

Qatar Electricity and Water Co (QEWC): POB 22046, Doha; tel. 4858585; fax 4831116; e-mail qewc@qatar.net.qa; internet www.qewc.com; f. 1990; 57% privately owned; has responsibility for adding new generating capacity in Qatar; Gen. Man. FAHAD HAMAD AL-MOHANNADI.

Transport

ROADS

In 1991 there were some 1,191 km of surfaced road linking Doha and the petroleum centres of Dukhan and Umm Said with the northern end of the peninsula. The total road network in 1999 was estimated to be 1,230 km. A 105-km road from Doha to Salwa was completed in 1970, and joins one leading from Al-Hufuf in Saudi Arabia, giving Qatar land access to the Mediterranean. A 418-km highway, built in conjunction with Abu Dhabi, links both states with the Gulf network. A major upgrading of the national road network was planned for the first years of the 21st century. In August 2002 a Danish consortium completed a feasibility study for the construction of a planned causeway (the Friendship Bridge) linking Qatar with Bahrain. The project, expected to cost some US $2,000m., was approved by both Governments in 2004. In addition, provisional plans for the construction of a causeway between Qatar and the United Arab Emirates were announced in December.

SHIPPING

Doha Port has nine general cargo berths of 7.5 m–9.0 m depth. The total length of the berths is 1,699 m. In addition, there is a flour mill berth, and a container terminal (with a depth of 12.0 m and a length of 600 m) with a roll-on, roll-off berth at the north end is currently under construction. Cold storage facilities exist for cargo of up to 500 metric tons. At Umm Said Harbour the Northern Deep Water Wharves consist of a deep-water quay 730-m long with a dredged depth alongside of 15.5-m, and a quay 570-m long with a dredged depth alongside of 13.0 m. The General Cargo Wharves consist of a quay 400-m long with a dredged depth alongside of 10.0 m. The Southern Deep Water Wharves consist of a deep water quay 508 m long with a dredged depth alongside of 13.0 m. The North Field gas project has increased the demand for shipping facilities. A major new industrial port was completed at Ras Laffan in 1995, providing facilities for LNG and condensate carriers and roll-on, roll-off vessels. Qatar Petroleum initiated a US $1,000m. expansion of Ras Laffan port in mid-2005. A proposal to move Doha port to a fresh site, near Doha International Airport, was approved in the same year; upon completion of the new facility, the existing port was to be decommissioned.

Customs and Ports General Authority: POB 81, Doha; tel. 4457457; fax 4413563; Dir of Ports G. A. GENKEER.

Qatar National Navigation and Transport Co Ltd (QNNTC): 60 Al-Tameen St, West Bay, POB 153, Doha; tel. 4468666; fax 4468777; e-mail navigation@qnntc.com; internet www.qnntc.com; f. 1957; 100%-owned by Qatari nationals; shipping agents, stevedoring, chandlers, forwarding, shipowning, repair, construction, etc.; Chair. SALEH MUBARAK AL-KHOLEILI; Vice-Chair. and Chair. of Exec. Cttee Sheikh ABDULLAH MUHAMMAD JABER ATH-THANI.

Qatar Shipping Co QSC (Q-Ship): POB 22180, Al-Muntazah St, Doha; tel. 4315500; fax 4315565; e-mail qshipops@qship.com; internet www.qship.com; f. 1992; oil and bulk cargo shipping; Chair. SALEM BIN BUTTI AN-NAIMI; Gen. Man. NASSER SAID AR-ROMAIHI.

CIVIL AVIATION

Doha International Airport is equipped to receive all types of aircraft. In 2001 some 2.7m. passengers used the airport. In 2004 Bechtel, a US engineering company, won the contract to manage the redevelopment of the airport (to be known upon completion of the project as New Doha International Airport), 4 km to the east of the existing site. Phase one of the project, which was expected to cost some US $2,800m., was set to increase annual passenger-handling capacity to around 12m. by 2008. Upon completion of phase three of the expansion, scheduled for 2015, passenger-handling capacity was to reach 50m.

Civil Aviation Authority: POB 3000, Doha; tel. 4428177; fax 4429070; Chair. and Man. Dir ABD AL-AZIZ MUHAMMAD AN-NOAIMI.

Doha International Airport: POB 73, Doha; tel. 4622222; fax 4622044; internet www.dohaairport.com; CEO AKBAR AL-BAKER.

Gulf Helicopters Co Ltd (GHC): POB 811, Doha; tel. 4333888; fax 4411004; e-mail mohd@gulfhelicopters.com; internet www.gulfhelicopters.com; f. 1974; owned by QP; Chair. ABDULLAH BIN HAMAD AL-ATTIYA.

Qatar Airways: POB 22550, Doha; tel. 4621717; fax 4621533; e-mail infodesk@qatarairways.com; internet www.qatarairways.com; f. 1993; services to more than 20 international destinations; CEO AKBAR AL-BAKER.

Tourism

Qatar's tourism industry is small, owing to its limited infrastructure. There were 556,965 tourist arrivals in 2003. Since 2000 tourism has been actively promoted, and Qatar's reputation as a venue for international conferences and sporting events has grown. The 2006 Asian Games, to be held in Doha, provided an impetus for increased hotel construction from 2004.

Qatar Tourism Authority (QTA): POB 24624, Doha; tel. 4411555; fax 4411550; e-mail info@experienceqatar.com; internet www.experienceqatar.com; f. 2002; affiliated with Council of Ministers; Chair. AKBAR AL-BAKER; Dir-Gen. JAN DE BOER (acting).

ROMANIA

Introductory Survey

Location, Climate, Language, Religion, Flag, Capital

Romania lies in south-eastern Europe, bounded to the north and east by Ukraine, to the north-east by Moldova, to the north-west by Hungary, to the south-west by Serbia and to the south by Bulgaria. The south-east coast is washed by the Black Sea. Romania has hot summers and cold winters, with a moderate rainfall. The average summer temperature is 23°C (73°F) and the winter average is −3°C (27°F). The official language is Romanian, although minority groups speak Hungarian (Magyar), German and other languages. Most of the inhabitants profess Christianity, and about 87% of believers are adherents of the Romanian Orthodox Church. The national flag (proportions 3 by 5) consists of three equal vertical stripes, of blue, yellow and red. The capital is Bucharest (București).

Recent History

Formerly part of Turkey's Ottoman Empire, Romania became an independent kingdom in 1881. During the dictatorship of the Fascist 'Iron Guard' movement, Romania entered the Second World War as an ally of Nazi Germany. However, Soviet forces entered Romania in 1944, when the pro-Nazi regime was overthrown. Under Soviet pressure, King Michael accepted the appointment of a communist-led coalition Government in March 1945. At elections in November 1946 a communist-dominated bloc claimed 89% of the votes cast, but the results were widely believed to have been fraudulent. In 1947 the small Romanian Communist Party (RCP) merged with the Social Democratic Party to become the Romanian Workers' Party (RWP). King Michael was forced to abdicate on 30 December 1947, when the Romanian People's Republic was proclaimed. The republic's first Constitution was adopted in 1948, and in the same year the nationalization of the main industrial and financial institutions was begun. In 1949 private landholdings were expropriated and amalgamated into state and collective farms. The implementation of Soviet-style economic policies was accompanied by numerous arrests of non-communists and the establishment of full political control by the RWP.

In 1952, following a purge of the RWP membership, a new Constitution, closer to the Soviet model, was adopted. Gheorghe Gheorghiu-Dej, the First Secretary of the RWP, became Romania's unchallenged leader and proceeded to implement large-scale plans for industrialization, despite the Soviet leadership's preference for Romania to remain as a supplier of agricultural goods. Gheorghiu-Dej died in 1965; he was succeeded as First Secretary of the RWP by Nicolae Ceaușescu, a Secretary of the RWP Central Committee since 1954. In June 1965 the RWP again became the RCP, and Ceaușescu's post of First Secretary was restyled General Secretary. A new Constitution, adopted in August, changed the country's name to the Socialist Republic of Romania.

Ceaușescu continued his predecessor's relatively independent foreign policy, criticizing the invasion of Czechoslovakia by troops of the Warsaw Pact (the defence grouping of the Soviet bloc) in 1968, and establishing links with Western states and institutions. However, the use of foreign loans for investment led to severe economic problems by the early 1980s. In order to strengthen his position, Ceaușescu (who had become President of the Republic in 1974) implemented frequent changes in the RCP leadership and the Government. In March 1980 his wife, Elena, became a First Deputy Chairman of the Council of Ministers, and numerous other family members held government and party posts.

Legislative elections were held in March 1985, when only 2.3% of the total number of voters were reported to have voted against the candidates approved by the RCP. In October an energy crisis resulted in a declaration of a state of emergency in the electric-power industry and the dismissal of ministers and senior officials. Shortages led to strict energy rationing in early 1987, and strikes were organized in provincial factories. In November thousands of people marched through the city of Brașov and stormed the local RCP headquarters, protesting against the decline in living standards and in working conditions. Hundreds of arrests were made, and similar protests followed in other cities. Ceaușescu announced improvements in food supplies and increases in wages, but continued to oppose reform. In March he announced details of a rural urbanization programme, to entail the demolition of some 8,000 villages, and the resettlement of their residents (mostly ethnic Hungarians) in new 'agro-industrial centres'. The plan attracted much domestic and international criticism, but Ceaușescu maintained that the programme would raise living standards and ensure social equality.

During 1988 and 1989 Romania became increasingly isolated from the international community. Romania continued to obstruct progress at the Vienna Conference on Security and Co-operation in Europe (begun in November 1986); on adoption of the final document by the Conference in January 1989, Romania declared that it did not consider itself bound by certain provisions relating to human rights, considering them to constitute the right of interference in a country's internal affairs. In early 1989 France and the Federal Republic of Germany recalled their ambassadors from Bucharest.

There were also signs of increasing criticism of the regime within Romania. In March 1989, in an open letter to the President, six retired RCP officials accused Ceaușescu of disregard for the Constitution and economic mismanagement, and were particularly critical of the rural urbanization programme. It was subsequently reported that the signatories had been detained. In December there was unrest in Timișoara as supporters of a Protestant clergyman (an ethnic Hungarian who had repeatedly criticized the Government's policies) demonstrated their opposition to his eviction from his church. A further protest, at which considerable criticism of the regime was expressed, was attended by thousands of local residents. Security forces opened fire on the crowd, reportedly killing several hundred people. There were reports of protests in other towns, and the country's borders were closed.

On 21 December 1989 President Ceaușescu attended a mass rally in Bucharest, intended to demonstrate popular support. Instead, his address was interrupted by hostile chanting, and anti-Government demonstrations followed later in the day, leading to clashes between protesters and members of the Securitate (the secret police force), during which many civilians were killed. The disturbances quickly spread to other parts of the country, and on the following day Ceaușescu declared a state of emergency; however, soldiers of the regular army declared their support for the protesters. Nicolae and Elena Ceaușescu escaped by helicopter from the roof of the RCP Central Committee headquarters as demonstrators stormed the building. They were captured near Târgoviște and, on 25 December, after a summary trial, were executed by firing squad. Fighting continued for several days, mainly between Securitate forces and regular soldiers.

Meanwhile, a revolutionary, 145-member National Salvation Front (NSF) was formed, and a provisional Government, comprising liberal communists, intellectuals and members of the armed forces, was established. Ion Iliescu, a former Secretary of the RCP Central Committee, became interim President, and Petre Roman, an academic, was appointed Prime Minister. The new Government immediately decreed an end to the RCP's constitutional monopoly of power, and cancelled the rural urbanization programme. The RCP was banned, it was announced that free elections would be held in 1990, and the designation of Socialist Republic was abandoned. By early January 1990 the army had restored order, and the Securitate was abolished. According to official figures, 689 people were killed during the revolution.

Special military tribunals were established to try Ceaușescu's former associates. In February 1990 four senior RCP officials were found guilty of responsibility for the shootings in Timișoara and Bucharest and were sentenced to life imprisonment. Numerous other former government and RCP members were similarly charged. In September Ceaușescu's son, Nicu, who was found to have ordered security forces to open fire on demonstrators in Sibiu in December 1989, received a 20-year prison sentence. (He was released in 1992 on the grounds of ill health, and died in 1996.) Gen. Iulian Vlad, the former head of the Securitate, was sentenced to 12 years' imprisonment in 1991; in January 1994, however, he was released as part of a general amnesty. In December 1991 eight associates of the former President were sentenced to prison terms of up to 25 years for their part in the shootings in Timișoara.

Despite the widespread jubilation that followed the downfall of Ceaușescu, the NSF did not enjoy total public support. Many citizens believed that the Front's leadership was too closely linked with the Ceaușescu regime, and were particularly critical of the NSF's control of the media. Furthermore, the NSF's announcement, in January 1990, that it was to contest the forthcoming elections, and its reversal of a decision to abolish the RCP, increased fears that members of the disgraced regime were attempting to regain power. In January the offices of two opposition parties, the National Liberal Party (NLP) and the National Peasants' Party, were attacked by NSF supporters. In February, after negotiations among representatives of 29 political parties, the NSF agreed to share power with the opposition, pending the elections, in a 180-member Provisional National Unity Council (PNUC). Each of the political parties represented in the talks was allocated three seats on the Council, and the PNUC was subsequently expanded to 253 members to permit representation by other political parties; nevertheless, NSF members and supporters occupied 111 seats in the Council. The PNUC elected an Executive Bureau, with Ion Iliescu as its President. Opposition to the NSF persisted, particularly in the armed forces. The Minister of National Defence was replaced in compliance with demands from within the military, but shortly afterwards thousands of anti-Government demonstrators demanded the resignation of Iliescu, and some 250 protesters forcibly entered the NSF headquarters.

As the elections approached there were mass anti-communist demonstrations daily in central Bucharest. The election campaign was acrimonious, and there were widespread accusations of systematic intimidation and harassment of the NSF's opponents. At the presidential and legislative elections, held on 20 May 1990, the NSF achieved an overwhelming victory. Allegations of irregularities were, however, confirmed by international observers. According to official figures, Iliescu won 85.1% of the valid votes cast in the presidential poll. In the elections to the bicameral legislature, the NSF won 65% of the votes cast, securing 263 of the 387 seats in the Camera Deputaților (Chamber of Deputies) and 91 of the 119 seats in Senatul (the Senate).

Unrest continued, and in mid-June 1990 a protest in central Bucharest was forcibly broken up by the police. The brutal treatment of the demonstrators provoked renewed clashes, in which the armed forces opened fire on rioters. Following an appeal for support by Iliescu, some 7,000 miners and other workers were transported to the capital, where they swiftly seized control of the streets. The disturbances resulted in several deaths and hundreds of injuries. Following President Iliescu's inauguration in late June, Roman was reappointed Prime Minister, and a new Council of Ministers was formed, in which nearly all the members of the interim administration were replaced.

In August 1990 there were further anti-Government demonstrations in Bucharest and Brașov. In the following months, as popular discontent at the deteriorating economic situation intensified, there was widespread strike action. In October Roman announced extensive economic reforms. In the following month price increases led to demonstrations in Bucharest, including a protest march by some 100,000 people, organized by a new opposition grouping, the Civic Alliance. Nevertheless, the Government proceeded with its (slightly modified) reform programme, resulting in further large price rises in April. At the end of that month Roman allocated three government portfolios to opposition politicians.

In September 1991 miners, by this time opposed to President Iliescu, began a strike in support of demands for pay increases and the resignation of the Government. Thousands of miners travelled to Bucharest, where they attacked government offices and ransacked the parliament building. Four people were killed and hundreds injured during violent clashes with the security forces, as a result of which the Council of Ministers was obliged to resign. Theodor Stolojan, a former Minister of Finance, was appointed as Prime Minister, leading a coalition Government formed in October, comprising members of the NSF, the NLP, the Agrarian Democratic Party of Romania (ADPR) and the Romanian Ecological Movement.

A new Constitution, enshrining a multi-party system, a free-market economy and guarantees of the respect of human rights, was approved by the legislature in November 1991 and was endorsed by some 77.3% of voters in a referendum in December. The results of local elections, which took place between February and April 1992, confirmed the decline in support for the NSF. Many seats were won by the centre-right Democratic Convention of Romania (DCR), an alliance of 18 parties and organizations, including the Christian Democratic National Peasants' Party (CDNPP) and the Party of the Civic Alliance. The NSF divided into two factions, and in April the faction loyal to Iliescu was registered as the Democratic National Salvation Front (DNSF), a moderate left-wing party that favoured only limited reforms.

Against a background of renewed labour unrest, legislative and presidential elections took place on 27 September 1992. The DNSF won 117 of the 328 elective seats in the Camera Deputaților and 49 of the 143 seats in Senatul, making it the largest party in the new Parlamentul (Parliament). Its closest rival was the DCR, with 82 seats in the Camera Deputaților and 34 in Senatul. The NSF secured only 43 and 18 seats, respectively. In the presidential election, the two leading candidates, Iliescu and Emil Constantinescu, representing the DCR, proceeded to a second round of voting on 11 October, at which Iliescu won 61.4% of the votes cast. In November Nicolae Văcăroiu, an economist with no professed political party affiliation, formed a Government comprising equal numbers of DNSF members and independents.

In February 1993 thousands of people protested in Bucharest against rising prices, low wages and unemployment. The abolition of price subsidies for many basic commodities and services, from the beginning of May, precipitated renewed labour unrest, and there were subsequently further strikes and demonstrations across the country. The Government's position was also undermined by successive confidence motions, and by allegations of high-level corruption. Meanwhile, the DNSF had changed its name to the Party of Social Democracy of Romania (PSDR) in July and absorbed three other left-wing parties. In May, in an apparently similar attempt to distance itself from the events of 1989–90, Roman's NSF had renamed itself the Democratic Party—National Salvation Front (DP—NSF). By late 1993 Văcăroiu's administration appeared increasingly unstable. In November a protest march in Bucharest, demanding rapid economic reforms, was the largest public demonstration in the country since the overthrow of the Ceaușescu regime. In February 1994 renewed industrial unrest led to a general strike. A government reshuffle in March continued the pattern of single-party (PSDR) rule supplemented by independent 'technocrats' (although later in the year two members of the Romanian National Unity Party—RNUP—were appointed to the Council of Ministers). In November 1995 Iliescu approved legislation providing for the restitution of property confiscated by the communist regime in the late 1940s and 1950s.

In May 1996 the PSDR terminated its parliamentary co-operation with the RNUP. Although the PSDR secured the largest number of mayoral and council seats at the local elections in June, the results indicated a decline in support for the party. The DCR and the Social Democratic Union (SDU), formed by the DP—NSF and the Romanian Social Democratic Party (RSDP) in January, won control of many major cities, including Bucharest, where the DCR's Victor Ciorbea (a former trade unionist) achieved election. In September the RNUP ministers were dismissed from the Government: the breakdown in relations with the PSDR had been exacerbated by the RNUP's opposition to the signing of a treaty with Hungary (see below).

Legislative and presidential elections took place on 3 November 1996. The DCR won the largest number of parliamentary seats, with 122 of the 328 seats in the Camera Deputaților and 53 of the 143 seats in Senatul. The PSDR took 91 and 41 seats in the respective chambers, and the SDU 53 and 23. The DCR and the SDU subsequently reached agreement on political co-operation. In the first round of the presidential election, which was contested by 16 candidates, Iliescu won 32.3% of the valid votes cast, and Constantinescu took 28.2%. With the support of nearly all the opposition parties, Constantinescu was duly elected in a second round on 17 November, with 54.4% of the votes cast. Constantinescu pledged to combat corruption and accelerate economic reform, and had asserted his commitment to the integration of Romania into Western political, economic and defence institutions. At the end of November Ciorbea was nominated as Prime Minister, and in mid-December a new coalition Government, comprising the DCR, the SDU and the Democratic

Alliance of Hungarians in Romania (DAHR), was officially sworn in.

In January 1997 Romania's Alternative Party (RAP—a member of the DCR alliance), apparently dissatisfied with the positions that it had been allocated in the Government and local administration, withdrew its unconditional support for government policy. Despite protests from opposition parties, the Government restored citizenship to former King Michael, who visited Romania in February. Meanwhile, in January a National Council for Action against Corruption and Organized Crime, headed by Constantinescu, was established; a number of leading bankers were subsequently arrested, principally on charges of fraud, and several senior members of the security forces were dismissed. The arrest of Miron Cozma, the leader of the miners' demonstrations in Bucharest in June 1990 and September 1991, prompted protests from miners and their trade-union leaders. In November 1997 an estimated 40,000 people attended a rally in Bucharest to protest against increasing poverty.

Meanwhile, several prominent members of the PSDR resigned from the party in June 1997, and formed a new centre-left party, the Alliance for Romania (AFR), which claimed, by August, to hold 13 seats in the Camera Deputaţilor, and two in Senatul. A government reshuffle in December, which included the appointment of a number of technocrats to principal portfolios, failed to ease mounting tensions within the coalition, and the DAHR temporarily suspended its participation in the Government in protest at the rejection of amendments to legislation on education by DCR senators.

Adrian Severin, Minister of State and Minister of Foreign Affairs, and a member of the DP (formerly DP—NSF), resigned in December 1997, after a judicial investigation failed to confirm his allegations that certain political leaders and newspaper editors were working with foreign intelligence services. In January 1998 the resignation of the Minister of Transport, Traian Băsescu of the DP, owing to his criticism of Ciorbea's Government, led the DP to demand his reinstatement, and DP ministers eventually withdrew from the Government. However, the DP agreed to remain in the coalition, and to give parliamentary support to a minority DCR-DAHR Government, provided that the economic reform programme was accelerated. Social unrest continued to mount, however, and large anti-Government rallies took place in Bucharest and Braşov.

At the end of March 1998, in response to increasing pressure within the coalition, Ciorbea and his Government resigned. Radu Vasile, the Secretary-General of the CDNPP and a Deputy Chairman of Senatul, was designated Prime Minister in April. A new Council of Ministers was appointed, which was endorsed by Parlamentul in mid-April. A new coalition protocol was designed to strengthen the authority of the Prime Minister and improve co-operation between government members. In June the approval of legislation by Senatul that debarred former secret police agents from holding public office led to the resignation of the Minister of Health, Francis Baranyi.

As Romania's economic situation worsened, the Minister of Finance, Daniel Dăianu, was dismissed in September 1998; he was replaced by Decebal Trăian Remes. In October Sorin Dimitriu resigned as Minister of Privatization and head of the State Ownership Fund, and shortly afterwards the RAP withdrew from the governing coalition and from the DCR, apparently in protest at the slow pace of reform. Meanwhile, in early September the DAHR threatened to leave the ruling coalition unless Parlamentul adopted legislation providing for the establishment of a minority-language university. At the end of the month the Government duly agreed to create an independent university in Cluj-Napoca for Hungarian and German minorities.

Protests against austerity measures, which had begun the previous month, intensified in December 1998. In January 1999 a strike by miners escalated when Vasile refused to negotiate with Cozma, who had been released from prison in July 1998, after serving an 18-month sentence for the possession of firearms and ammunition. Encouraged by nationalist politicians (notably from the Greater Romania Party—GRP), 10,000–20,000 miners marched towards Bucharest, and in Costeşti, some 190 km north-west of Bucharest, violent clashes broke out with the security forces. Following emergency talks between the Prime Minister and miners' leaders, a temporary agreement was reached. The Minister of the Interior, Gavril Dejeu, resigned, amid severe criticism of the security forces' failure to halt the march; he was replaced by Constantin Dudu Ionescu. In February the Supreme Court of Justice sentenced Cozma, in absentia, to 18 years' imprisonment for undermining state authority.

In protest, some 2,000–4,000 miners, led by Cozma, again marched towards Bucharest. The miners were stopped by the security forces some 160 km west of Bucharest, where more than 100 people were injured and one miner died during the violence that ensued; Cozma and several hundred miners were arrested. Labour unrest continued throughout the first half of 1999.

In early June 1999 the Camera Deputaţilor approved amendments to the electoral law, increasing the threshold for parliamentary representation from 3% to 5%, with alliances required to secure a further 3% for each member party. Later that month the Camera Deputaţilor voted in favour of providing public access to the files of the Securitate (although many documents were already believed to have been destroyed); the President promulgated the legislation in December. Also in June legislation was approved by Parlamentul, providing for minority-language education at every level of the education system. In July Gen. Victor Stănculescu and Gen. Mihai Chiţac were sentenced to 15 years' imprisonment, having been found guilty of the murders of 72 people, by ordering the security forces to open fire on protesters during the Timişoara uprising in December 1989. The ruling was severely criticized by a number of senior politicians, including Victor Babiuc, the Minister of National Defence, whose ministry, together with Stănculescu and Chiţac, was ordered to pay damages to those wounded in the shootings and the relatives of the dead.

In November 1999 students undertook strike action and some 10,000 trade union members participated in protest rallies to demand the resignation of the Government. In mid-December, as labour unrest continued, Constantinescu dismissed Vasile, after all seven CDNPP government ministers, followed by the three NLP ministers, resigned from the Government and withdrew their support for the Prime Minister. Constantinescu nominated Mugur Isărescu, hitherto Governor of the National Bank of Romania (and without affiliation to any political party), as Prime Minister. The legislature subsequently approved the appointment of Isărescu and his Council of Ministers, which remained largely unchanged, although Roman joined the new Government as Minister of State and Minister of Foreign Affairs. Vasile was expelled from the CDNPP later that month. In March 2000 Sorin Frunzaverde of the DP was appointed to replace Babiuc, who had resigned from both the party and the Government, as Minister of National Defence.

In the local elections, held on 4 June 2000, the PSDR won the majority of votes cast (36.7%), followed by the DP, with 12.7%. Anca Boagiu replaced Băsescu as Minister of Transport in June, following Băsescu's election as Mayor of Bucharest. In July President Constantinescu unexpectedly announced that he would not stand for re-election at the forthcoming presidential election. In August Remes, who supported Isărescu's presidential candidacy, resigned from the NLP, when the party nominated former Prime Minister Theodor Stolojan as its presidential candidate. Meanwhile, a number of alliances were formed in the weeks preceding legislative elections, to be held concurrently with the presidential election in late November. In early September the RSDP withdrew from the governing coalition, announcing that it was to merge with the main opposition party, the PSDR.

Legislative and presidential elections took place on 26 November 2000. The PSDR secured 155 seats in the Camera Deputaţilor and 65 in Senatul, while the GRP obtained 84 and 37 seats, respectively. The rate of voter participation was the lowest recorded since the collapse of communism, at 57.5%. Representatives of the PSDR and the GRP were also the principal candidates in the presidential election, in which the former President, Iliescu, obtained 36.4% of the votes cast and Corneliu Vadim Tudor of the GRP achieved 28.3%. As neither candidate secured an overall majority, a 'run-off' election was held on 10 December, in which Iliescu won 66.8% of the votes cast. Iliescu immediately rejected the possibility of forming a coalition government with the GRP. The increased support for the right wing was thought to reflect popular disillusionment with economic hardship and high unemployment.

In late December 2000 President Iliescu nominated Adrian Năstase of the PSDR as Prime Minister. Năstase subsequently signed a joint statement on priorities for the development of Romania with the leaders of the DAHR, the NLP and the DP. Although Năstase insisted that the declaration did not represent a coalition agreement, the support of those parties enabled the PSDR to form a minority Government, and ensured the isolation of the GRP. The new, expanded Council of Ministers was sworn in on 28 December. Despite their shared objective of implementing reform with a view to attaining membership of the European Union (EU, see p. 228), the new President and Prime Minister came from different ideological backgrounds.

In mid-January 2001 the Camera Deputaţilor approved a law, which aimed to return some 300,000 properties nationalized during the communist era to their original owners. President Iliescu endorsed the law in early February; it was to supersede the law on the restitution of property that had been approved in 1995. In late February 2001 the Supreme Court convicted two military officers of manslaughter for their roles in the deaths of dozens of people at Bucharest airport during the 1989 revolution. In June 2001 a five-month labour strike in western Romania ended with a mass protest against the planned privatization of the Reşiţa steel factory, which was cancelled later that month.

Meanwhile, the outcome of the general election led to political restructuring and the appointment of new leaders to several parties. Ciorbea became Chairman of the CDNPP (which had failed to obtain any parliamentary representation) in July 2001, following the resignation of Andrei Marga (who had assumed the position in January). In May Băsescu replaced Roman as leader of the DP. In mid-June the PSDR and the RSDP formally merged, creating the Social Democratic Party (SDP), under the leadership of Prime Minister Năstase. In November the NLP and the AFR agreed to merge under the name of the former party, a process that was finalized in late January 2002. Meanwhile, in November 2001 some 15,000 people took part in a demonstration in Bucharest against poverty and the Government's austerity programme. A further large-scale protest took place in December.

In March 2002 attempts to tackle corruption led the Government to announce the establishment, with effect from September, of a new National Anti-corruption Prosecution office. Also in March the Government sought to moderate the power of labour organizations through the signature of a 'social pact' with three of the five largest trade unions, which provided for an increased minimum wage and the creation of 10,000 jobs. Meanwhile, the Supreme Court sentenced Tudor Postelnicu, a former chief of the Securitate, and Gheorghe Homostean, a former Minister of the Interior, to 14 years' imprisonment for their role in the deaths of a group of escaped prisoners in 1981; the case formed part of an ongoing investigation of crimes committed during the communist era.

In August 2002 Stolojan was elected as the new Chairman of the NLP. In September Senatul approved a new law on political parties, which required all parties to re-register by 31 December, and to be composed of a minimum of 10,000 members from at least 21 of Romania's 41 counties. On 10 November local elections took place in 21 counties, in which the SDP was the most successful party. In early 2003 a number of prominent CDNPP members were expelled from the party after participating in the foundation of the new Popular Action civic movement, led by former President Constantinescu; in February it was confirmed that the movement was to become a political party.

In June 2003 Năstase reorganized the Council of Ministers, reducing the number of portfolios from 23 to 14 and introducing three new ministers. In a referendum held on 18–19 October, some 90% of votes cast by 55.7% of the electorate approved 79 proposed amendments to the Constitution, which aimed to bring it into conformity with EU requirements (by, *inter alia*, guaranteeing the right to private property, strengthening legal rights for ethnic minorities and limiting the powers of the executive branch of government). The revised Constitution entered into force on 29 October.

In mid-February 2004 Parlamentul approved legislation providing for a further restructuring of the Council of Ministers. In the following month Năstase announced the appointment of three new Ministers of State (effectively deputy prime ministers). Three existing ministers also assumed the additional positions of Minister of State. In March the Camera Deputaţilor approved legislation banning the adoption of Romanian children by the residents of other countries (following criticism of the practice by the EU, and prompting protests from the USA). In July Nicolae Popa was appointed as President of the High Court of Cassation and Justice (which replaced the Supreme Court). In mid-August charges of abuse of office and embezzlement were brought against 79 people, including Băsescu (in his former capacity as Minister of Transport in 1991–92 and 1997–2000), relating to the alleged illegal sale of 16 ships from the national maritime fleet in 1991–2000. Some commentators suggested that the charge was an attempt to discredit the opposition prior to national legislative and presidential elections; Băsescu had been re-elected as Mayor of Bucharest two months previously. In local elections held on 6 and 20 June 2004 the PSD received the greatest number of mayoral mandates, closely followed by the NLP. Following the poor performance of the CDNPP in the local elections, in August Ciorbea resigned as party Chairman; he was replaced by Gheorghe Ciuhandu, the only party member to have won a mayoral post.

In September 2004 the SDP and the Humanist Party of Romania (PUR) formed an electoral alliance, known as the National Union. In the same month President Iliescu accepted an invitation to rejoin the SDP in order to stand for election to Senatul. Meanwhile, the NLP and the DP announced their intention to contest the forthcoming legislative elections as the Justice and Truth Alliance. In October Stolojan, the presidential candidate of the Justice and Truth Alliance, withdrew from the contest and the chairmanship of the NLP owing to ill health; Călin Popescu-Tăriceanu was nominated as his successor as party leader and Băsescu replaced him as the Alliance's candidate for the presidency.

On 28 November 2004 presidential and legislative elections were held concurrently, as scheduled. The National Union emerged as the largest bloc in both legislative chambers, with 132 seats (of a total of 332) in the Camera Deputaţilor and 57 (of a total of 137) in Senatul. The Justice and Truth Alliance received 112 seats in the Camera Deputaţilor and 49 in Senatul. The representation of the GRP was markedly reduced in both chambers, to 48 deputies in the lower chamber, and 21 senators. In the presidential ballot no candidate secured an absolute majority of votes cast, and Năstase (with 40.9%) and Traian Băsescu (with 33.9%) proceeded to a second round of voting on 12 December (Tudor was the third-placed candidate, with only 12.6% of the votes). In the 'run-off' election, Băsescu achieved a narrow victory, with 51.2% of the votes cast. (As President, Băsescu was immune from prosecution.) On 18 December Băsescu resigned from the DP, in compliance with constitutional requirements, and he was inaugurated as President two days later. Năstase was elected as Chairman of the Camera Deputaţilor, and a Deputy Chairman of the SDP, Nicolae Văcăroiu, was elected as Chairman of Senatul in a vote that was boycotted by senators of the Justice and Truth Alliance and the DAHR.

Băsescu nominated Călin Popescu-Tăriceanu of the Justice and Truth Alliance to form a Government, but the approval of a cabinet was dependent upon its ability to achieve a majority in Parlamentul; ultimately, the grouping that would hold the majority in the legislature was to be determined by the allegiance of the PUR (as the DAHR did not possess a sufficient number of mandates to decide the issue). The PUR was persuaded to abandon its electoral partner, the SDP, but even collectively, the coalition of the NLP, the DP, the DAHR and the PUR only amounted to one more than the requisite quorum in the bicameral legislature. On 28 December 2004 the new Council of Ministers was approved by both chambers of the legislature; it was to comprise 25 ministers: nine from the NLP, eight from the DP, four from the DAHR and three from the PUR. However, in late January 2005 Sorin Vicol of the PUR resigned as Minister-delegate for the National Control Authority, after many of the portfolio's responsibilities were transferred to the Ministry of Finance. In February Popescu-Tăriceanu was elected as Chairman of the NLP. In March Tudor, the founder of the GRP, resigned as party leader; he was succeeded by Corneliu Ciontu. In the same month, the CDNPP absorbed the Union for the Reconstruction of Romania and changed its name to the Popular Christian-Democratic Party of Romania. Meanwhile, on 16 February the leaders of the Justice and Truth Alliance, the DAHR and the PUR signed a coalition agreement.

The PUR was renamed the Conservative Party in May 2005. In June Ion Iliescu reportedly became the subject of an investigation into the deaths of six people during the demonstrations by miners in 1990 (see above); however, as a member of Senatul and a former Head of State, Iliescu was immune from prosecution. In late June 2005 Emil Boc was confirmed as President of the DP (he had hitherto occupied the post in an acting capacity). In early July the Constitutional Court rejected a programme for judicial reform that had been proposed by the Government in order to satisfy requirements for membership of the EU, prompting Prime Minister Popescu-Tăriceanu to announce that he intended to submit the resignation of his administration, in an attempt to precipitate early elections. However, on 13 July an emergency session of Parlamentul approved amendments to the legislation on judicial reform, in conformity with the Court's objections. Meanwhile, central and eastern parts of the country were affected by severe flooding, which resulted in more than 20 deaths, and on 19 July Popescu-Tăriceanu announced that his Government would remain in place in order to respond to the emergency situation. In late August Popescu-Tăriceanu reorganized the Council of Ministers. Sebastian Vlădescu was appointed as Minister of Public Finance, and Anca Boagiu as Minister of European Integration. Adrian Iorgulescu replaced Mona Octavia Muscă, who had resigned as Minister of Culture and Religious Affairs in the previous month, and Eugen Nicolăescu assumed the health portfolio; Gheorghe Pogea became Minister of State responsible for the Co-ordination of Activities in the Economic Field. In October Romania became the first country in Europe to report a case of avian influenza, leading to widespread concern that the virus was spreading from Asia, along migratory routes. In November Mihai Hărdău was appointed as Minister of Education and Research, following the resignation of Mircea Miclea in protest at inadequate funding; a general strike was staged by teachers over the same issue.

Meanwhile, in October 2005 the EU Commissioner responsible for Enlargement, Olli Rehn, warned Romania that its objective of acceding to the EU in 2007 could be subject to delay if measures were not taken to combat corruption and accelerate the pace of judicial reform. In early 2006 a number of political figures duly came under investigation as a result of allegations of fraud, and in January Adrian Năstase resigned from the leadership of the SDP, following concerns about the legitimacy of an inheritance received by his wife. In early February Năstase was indicted on charges of bribery, pertaining to the acquisition of land in 1998. However, Senatul rejected legislation that would have permitted officials from the National Anti-corruption Prosecution office increased powers to facilitate the investigation of senior politicians and members of the judiciary (and subsequently restricted prosecutors from searching Năstase's property). Năstase resigned as Chairman of the Camera Deputaţilor in mid-March, following a vote of 'no confidence' by the SDP; he was succeeded by Bogdan Olteanu of the NLP, erstwhile Minister-delegate for Relations with Parliament. Meanwhile, in late February the Government survived a parliamentary motion of 'no confidence' prompted by its proposed health-care reforms, submitted by the opposition SDP and GRP.

Romania experienced frequent occurrences of ethnic unrest after the fall of Ceauşescu. In 1991 there were organized attacks on Roma (Gypsy) communities throughout Romania, resulting in the emigration of many Roma to Germany. In September 1992 Germany repatriated 43,000 Romanian refugees, more than one-half of whom were Roma, having agreed to provide financial assistance for their resettlement in Romania. The migration of Roma to the member countries of the EU strained relations with Romania throughout the remainder of the 1990s. In May 2001 the GRP unexpectedly proposed new legislation to improve the rights and integration of the Roma population. However, in January 2002 the Council of Europe (see p. 211) published a report condemning police brutality and widespread discrimination against Roma communities in Romania, and the EU made the improvement of the treatment of the Roma minority a requirement for Romania to be declared eligible to accede to the Union. In February 2005 Romania was one of eight countries in the region to announce its adherence to a World Bank-financed 10-year plan to assist the Roma community.

Following the overthrow of Ceauşescu, ethnic Hungarians (a sizeable minority, numbering more than 7% of the total population at the 1992 census) sought to increase their cultural and linguistic autonomy in Transylvania. In March 1990 demonstrations by ethnic Hungarians demanding such rights were attacked by Romanian nationalists in Târgu Mureş. Tanks and troops were deployed to quell the unrest, in which several people were killed, and a state of emergency was declared in the town. In mid-1992 there was renewed tension when the Mayor of Cluj-Napoca, Gheorghe Funar (later head of the right-wing RNUP), ordered the removal of Hungarian-language street signs in the city, and ethnic Hungarian prefects in Covasna and Harghita were replaced by ethnic Romanians. The Government attempted to calm the situation by appointing 'parallel' prefects of ethnic Hungarian background, but further controversy was caused by the removal, in September, of the only ethnic Hungarian State Secretary in the Government. An agreement on Hungarian minority rights was signed in July 1993, which included guarantees of the training of Hungarian-speaking schoolteachers and bilingual street signs in areas with Hungarian populations of at least 30%. In August Bela Marko, the President of the DAHR, insisted that any Hungarian-Romanian state treaty should enshrine a 'special status' for ethnic Hungarians in Romania. Marko's proposals included the equal status of the Hungarian and Romanian languages in predominantly Hungarian-populated areas and greater control for the minority over educational and cultural affairs. However, the DAHR became increasingly isolated from the other opposition parties. In May Romania ratified the Framework Convention of the Council of Europe on the general protection of national minorities. In September 1996 Romania and Hungary signed a treaty of friendship, as a result of which Romania agreed to safeguard the rights of ethnic Hungarians, and Hungary relinquished any claim to territory in Transylvania. In December two DAHR leaders were appointed to the new Government. Relations between Romania and Hungary improved further in February 1997 with the signature of a defence co-operation agreement. Proposals to amend legislation on education, in favour of ethnic minorities, provoked controversy in Romania in 1997 and 1998; however, the amendments were finally approved in June 1999.

In January 2001 the Camera Deputaţilor approved a new public administration law, which made compulsory bilingual place names and signs, and the use of a given minority's language in local administration, in towns where that minority formed at least 20% of the population. In June the Government condemned Hungary's intention to introduce a new 'status law', which was to grant education, employment and medical rights to ethnic Hungarians living in neighbouring countries (including Romania) from January 2002. The Romanian Government feared that Hungary was seeking to increase its influence in Romania and other countries with large Hungarian communities, thereby bypassing the Treaty of Trianon of 1920, which had awarded large parts of Hungary to its neighbours. In December 2001 the Prime Ministers of the two countries signed a memorandum of understanding, which extended the short-term employment rights offered to ethnic Hungarians under the terms of the status law to all Romanian citizens. Finally, in September 2003 Prime Minister Năstase and his Hungarian counterpart, Péter Medgyessy, signed a bilateral agreement on the implementation of the status law in Romania. Hungary proved to be a staunch supporter of Romania's candidacy for EU membership. In October 2005 the first joint Romanian-Hungarian inter-governmental meeting was held in Bucharest, at which a treaty was concluded on the border regime, co-operation and mutual assistance.

Diplomatic relations with the former Soviet republic of Moldova (much of which formed part of Romania in 1918–40, and where a majority of the population are ethnic Romanians) were established in August 1991, and some political groups began to advocate the unification of the two states. The Romanian leadership opposed unification, but encouraged the development of closer cultural and economic ties with Moldova. The support of the Russian military in Moldova for the secessionist movement in the self-proclaimed 'Transdnestrian Moldovan Soviet Socialist Republic' damaged relations between Romania and Russia. In March 1994 a plebiscite was held in Moldova on the question of reunification with Romania; more than 95% of those who took part in the referendum voted for an independent state, effectively signalling the demise of the pro-unification movement. In 2000, as formal negotiations on Romania's accession to the EU commenced, hundreds of Moldovans applied for Romanian citizenship, in anticipation of the eventual tightening of border regulations. Relations with Moldova deteriorated from late 2001. In October Năstase cancelled a planned visit to Moldova, after President Vladimir Voronin of Moldova accused Romania of 'expansionism'. The communist-dominated Government elected in Moldova in that year also accused Romania of interfering in Moldova's internal affairs by supporting protests against the perceived 'russification' of that country in early 2002; in February the Russian State Duma also adopted a resolution condemning Romanian involvement in Moldova's domestic concerns. Romania, for its part, denied the accusations, and warned that Moldova was threatening the stability of the region. Relations had improved by 2003, following a meeting between the respective Presidents at a conference in Beirut, Lebanon, in September 2002, and inter-ministerial co-operation was restored in April 2003; Romania confirmed that it would not require Moldovan citizens to possess entry visas until its accession to the EU, anticipated in 2007–08. However, in late 2003 Năstase indicated that Romania no longer considered a basic political treaty with Moldova, which had been initialled in April 2000 (but never signed), to be relevant to the existing political situation. None the less, relations improved further over the course of 2004, with the apparent reorientation of Moldovan foreign policy towards the West. Moldova was the first country to which newly elected President Traian Băsescu paid a state visit in January 2005, and Romania offered support for Moldova's objective of securing eventual membership of the EU, as its relations with Russia deteriorated in 2005–06 (see the chapter on Moldova).

A basic treaty between Romania and Ukraine, signed in early June 1997, guaranteed the inviolability of their joint border, and provided for separate treaties to be established regarding the administration of the frontier and the disputed ownership of the Black Sea continental shelf. In January 2002 Anatoliy Kinakh became the first Ukrainian Prime Minister officially to visit Romania, where talks on economic co-operation and border delimitation took place. In June 2003 President Iliescu and President Leonid Kuchma of Ukraine signed an accord confirming their mutual land border, as it was delineated in 1961, with the exception of the continental shelf. No further progress was made in resolving the disagreement over the disputed area (known as Serpent's Island). In late 2003 Romania accused Ukraine of populating the area in an attempt to claim exclusive rights over petroleum and gas reserves, and in 2004 submitted a formal complaint over the matter to the International Court of Justice. A further dispute arose between the two countries in that year over the construction by Ukraine of a canal through the environmentally sensitive Danube delta. However, the election of a new President in Ukraine in late 2004 was expected to lead to improved relations. In February 2006, during a visit to Ukraine by President Traian Băsescu, the Presidents of Romania and Ukraine announced the establishment of a bilateral commission, with responsibility for the resolution of the border dispute. The commission was also to recommend joint policies on security, humanitarian issues and economic development. It was hoped that the two countries could reach agreement on the joint development of mineral resources in the disputed area.

Following the overthrow of President Ceaușescu in 1989, President François Mitterrand of France visited Romania in April 1991, and in April 1992 Romania and Germany signed a treaty of friendship and co-operation. Relations with other western European countries took longer to develop, but an association agreement with the European Community (now EU) was signed in February 1993; in June 1995 Romania formally applied for full membership of the EU. Romania applied for membership of the Council of Europe in May 1993, but was initially rejected, owing to its poor record on civil liberties. In October, however, Romania was admitted to the organization. In July 1997 the European Commission recommended that negotiations on Romania's accession to the EU should be deferred. However, in December 1999 Romania was one of six countries invited to begin negotiations on possible entry to the EU, and formal accession talks finally commenced in February 2000. In December the EU decided to impose conditions on Romania before granting its citizens the right to visa-free travel in Europe, partly in response to Romania's failure to combat illegal immigration. In March 2004 the European Parliament adopted a pre-accession report on Romania, which stated that accession, which had been anticipated for 2007, would be deferred unless the Government implemented measures to combat corruption, reform the judiciary, ensure media freedom and revise legislation on the protection and adoption of children. In December 2004 Romania concluded accession negotiations, but with a cautionary clause whereby the country's accession could be delayed by one year if it failed to meet its reform commitments. (In March 2005 the Government presented a two-year plan to combat corruption and implement judicial reform. Romania's success in carrying out remaining administrative and economic reforms was to be monitored closely during the two years prior to accession.) In mid-April members of the European Parliament voted to approve 2007 as the anticipated accession date for Romania and Bulgaria (despite the concerns remaining among some existing members). Formal accession agreements were signed by both Bulgaria and Romania on 25 April 2005. In mid-May both chambers of the legislature unanimously ratified the EU accession treaty. The new Government elected at the end of 2004 was perceived to have implemented reform at a more rapid rate than the previous Government. The European Commission was due to publish a report in October 2006, recommending a final accession date of either 2007 or 2008.

In the early 1990s attempts by the Romanian Government to enforce the UN embargo on Yugoslavia (Serbia and Montenegro), by preventing the passage of vessels to or from that country via the Danube, encountered strong opposition from the Yugoslav authorities. In January 1993 Yugoslavia impounded 22 Romanian ships in retaliation for the detention of 40 Yugoslav vessels by Romania. Romania reiterated its commitment to upholding the UN embargo in February 1993, but proceeded to sign a treaty with Yugoslavia on bilateral political relations in April 1994. A further treaty of friendship was signed in May 1996. In 1998 the Romanian Government expressed its support for international efforts to find a diplomatic solution to hostilities between the Serbian authorities and ethnic Albanian separatists in the Yugoslav province of Kosovo, and in October the legislature approved Romania's participation in the Kosovo Verification Mission of the Organization for Security and Co-operation in Europe (OSCE, see p. 327). In March 1999, however, following the failure of peace negotiations, the North Atlantic Treaty Organization (NATO, see p. 314) launched a campaign of air-strikes against Serb military and strategic targets; in April Romania approved a NATO request for unrestricted access to its airspace, but did not become militarily involved in the conflict. In late November 2001 the Danube Commission declared the river safe for navigation for the first time since the NATO airstrikes.

In June 1992 Romania, together with 10 other countries (including six of the former Soviet republics), established what became known as the Organization of the Black Sea Economic Co-operation (see p. 339), which aimed to encourage regional trade and co-operation in developing transport and infrastructure. In May 1994 Romania was granted associate partnership status of Western European Union (see p. 365).

In early 1997 Romania appealed directly to NATO member countries to support its candidacy for admittance to the Alliance. Following the large-scale suicide attacks against the USA on 11 September 2001, attributed by the USA to the Saudi-born Islamist fundamentalist, Osama bin Laden (see the US chapter), Romania immediately pledged full co-operation with US efforts to assemble a coalition of allied countries to combat global terrorism, and opened its airspace to US military flights to and from Afghanistan, the Taliban regime of which was harbouring militants of bin Laden's al-Qa'ida (Base) organization. As the strategic importance of the Black Sea increased, Romania also made available basing facilities in the port city of Constanța, and offered the USA the use of its airbases. None the less, concerns remained about the presence in the Romanian intelligence services of former members of the communist-era Securitate, and there were doubts about Romania's economic preparedness for NATO membership. However, the intelligence services were restructured in January 2002, and Romania secured an invitation to join NATO at a summit meeting held in Prague, Czech Republic, in November, after which US President George W. Bush paid a visit to the country. Romania was forthright in its support for US-led military action in Iraq in early 2003 (despite some criticism from within the EU, notably France), opening its airspace and offering other resources to the coalition, particularly following Turkey's refusal to allow US troops the use of its territory. Romania was officially admitted to NATO on 29 March 2004, together with six other countries. In 2005 a parliamentary commission was established to investigate allegations that Romania had permitted US aircraft transporting possible terrorist suspects to use one of its airbases, without due attention to international law; the Council of Europe also launched an investigation. In December 2005 the US Secretary of State signed an agreement with the Romanian Minister of Foreign Affairs, Mihai-Răzvan Ungureanu, in Bucharest, granting US troops access to military bases under the command of the Romanian army; this was the first instance of the USA committing to station troops permanently in a former Warsaw Pact country.

Government

Following approval by plebiscite of 79 proposed amendments to the Constitution, the amendments came into force on 29 October 2003. Under the Constitution, legislative power is vested in the bicameral Palamentul (Parliament), comprising the Camera Deputaților (Chamber of Deputies, lower house) and Senatul (the Senate, upper house). Parlamentul is elected by universal adult suffrage on the basis of proportional representation for a term of four years. Executive power is vested in the President of the Republic, who may serve a maximum of two five-year terms and who is directly elected by universal adult suffrage. The President appoints the Prime Minister, who in turn appoints the Council of Ministers.

For administrative purposes, Romania comprises 40 administrative divisions (counties) and the municipality of Bucharest.

Defence

In January 1994 Romania became the first former Warsaw Pact state to join the North Atlantic Treaty Organization's (NATO) 'Partnership for Peace' (see p. 316) programme. Romania became a full member of NATO on 29 March 2004. In mid-2003 the headquarters of the international peace-keeping force SEEBRIG (comprising troops from Albania, Bulgaria, Greece, Italy, the former Yugoslav republic of Macedonia, Romania and Turkey) was relocated from Plovdiv, Bulgaria, to Constanța. In November 2005 the establishment of an EU rapid reaction combat force between Bulgaria, Cyprus, Greece and Romania was agreed; the force was to be operational from mid-2007 to address any requirements in the Balkan area.

Military service is compulsory, although it was intended to be gradually abolished by 2007. In 2003 the term of service was reduced from 12 to eight months. At 1 August 2005 active forces totalled 97,200 (including an estimated 29,600 conscripts and 10,000 in centrally controlled units): army 66,000 (including 18,500 conscripts), navy 7,200 and air force 14,000. There were also 22,900 border guards and a gendarmerie of an estimated 57,000 (under the control of the Ministry of the Interior and Public Administration). The defence budget for 2005 was an estimated 60,600,000m. lei.

Economic Affairs

In 2004, according to the World Bank, Romania's gross national income (GNI), measured at average 2002–04 prices, totalled US $63,910m., equivalent to $2,920 per head (or $8,190 per head on an international purchasing-power parity basis). During 1995–2004, it was estimated, the population decreased at an average annual rate of 0.4%, while gross domestic product (GDP) per head increased, in real terms, at an average annual rate of 2.0%. Overall GDP increased, in real terms, by an average of 1.6% annually during 1995–2004. Real GDP increased by 4.9% in 2003 and by 8.3% in 2004.

Agriculture (including hunting, forestry and fishing) contributed 12.8% of GDP in 2004, according to the World Bank. The sector employed 31.6% of the employed labour force in that year. The principal crops are maize, wheat, potatoes, sugar beet, barley, apples and grapes. Wine production plays a significant role in Romanian agriculture. Forestry, the cropping of reeds (used as a raw material in the paper and cellulose industry) and the breeding of fish are also important. By 1999, according to the IMF, some 97.2% of agricultural land was privately owned. During 1995–2004, according to the World Bank, agricultural GDP increased, in real terms, by an average of 0.7% per year. Real agricultural GDP increased by 3.0% in 2003 and by 19.7% in 2004.

According to the World Bank, industry (including mining, manufacturing, construction, power and water) accounted for 40.2% of GDP in 2004, when the sector employed 31.2% of the working population. According to the World Bank, industrial GDP increased, in real terms, by an average of 1.7% annually in 1995–2004. Real industrial GDP increased by 4.6% in 2003 and by 6.2% in 2004.

The mining sector employed 1.5% of the employed labour force in 2004. Brown coal, hard coal, salt, iron ore, bauxite, copper, lead and zinc are mined. Onshore production of crude petroleum began to increase in the early 1990s, and in 2004 Romania had proven reserves of 500m. barrels of petroleum, remaining the largest producer in central and eastern Europe, despite a dramatic decline in production. At the beginning of the 1990s seven offshore platforms were operating in the Romanian sector of the Black Sea, accounting for more than 10% of annual hydrocarbons production. Methane gas is also extracted. In April 1996 Romania launched an international invitation to tender for exploration and production rights on 15 new blocks in the Black Sea. Mining output indices (at 1998 prices) increased by 2.1% in 2001, but decreased by 1.9% in 2002.

Manufacturing employed 22.4% of the employed labour force in 2004, when it accounted for some 33.4% of GDP, according to the World Bank. The sector is based mainly on the metallurgical, mechanical engineering, chemical and timber-processing industries. However, many industries (particularly iron and steel) have been hampered by shortages of electricity and raw materials. According to the World Bank, manufacturing GDP increased, in real terms, by an average of 0.1% annually in 1994–2001. Real sectoral GDP increased by some 6.2% in 2000 and by 8.0% in 2001.

According to the World Bank, in 2002 37.6% of gross electricity production was derived from coal, 29.2% from hydroelectric power, 16.7% from natural gas and 10.0% from nuclear power. The initial unit of Romania's first nuclear power station, at Cernavoda, became operational in December 1996; the second (700 MW) unit was scheduled to enter into operation in 2007 (when it was expected to supply some 19% of total power); the construction of a third unit was scheduled to commence in 2006, and was to be completed by 2011. A programme of rehabilitation for 10 thermal power stations was completed in 2005. In 2006 an agreement was reached with the Turkish power grid operator TEIAȘ on the construction of a 400-km under-sea transmission cable, which was to be completed by 2009. A natural gas pipeline to connect the country with Hungary, and ultimately with a 'corridor' between Austria and Turkey (the Nabucco project), was also under construction. According to official data, 32.3% of energy resources were imported in 2003. In 2003 mineral fuels accounted for 10.9% of total imports.

In 2004 the services sector contributed 47.0% of GDP, according to the World Bank. The sector engaged 37.2% of the working labour force in that year. According to the World Bank, the GDP of the services sector increased, in real terms, by an average of 2.0% per year in 1995–2004; the real GDP of the sector increased by 5.2% in 2003 and by 6.0% in 2004.

In 2004 Romania recorded a visible trade deficit of US $6,665m., while there was a deficit of $6,382m. on the current account of the balance of payments. In 2004, according to preliminary figures, the principal source of imports was Italy, which provided 17.2% of the total. Germany was also a major supplier, as were Russia and France. The main market for exports in that year was Italy (accounting for 21.2%); other important purchasers were Germany, France, Turkey and the United Kingdom. In 2003 the principal imports were machinery and transport equipment, basic manufactures (particularly textiles), miscellaneous manufactured articles, mineral fuels and lubricants, chemicals, and food and live animals. The major exports in that year were miscellaneous manufactured articles, machinery and transport equipment, basic manufactures, mineral fuels and crude materials.

The overall budget deficit for 2003 was 28,898m. lei (equivalent to some 1.5% of GDP). Romania's total external debt at the end of 2003 was US $21,281m., of which $11,730m. was long-term public debt. In that year the cost of debt-servicing was equivalent to 17.3% of revenue from exports of goods and services. The annual rate of inflation averaged 43.2% in 1995–2004; the rate of inflation was 11.9% in 2004 and 9.0% in 2005. In February 2006 6.3% of the labour force were registered as unemployed.

Romania is a member (as a 'Country of Operations') of the European Bank for Reconstruction and Development (EBRD, see p. 224). In February 1993 Romania signed an association agreement with the European Union (EU, see p. 228). Romania formally applied for full membership of the EU in June 1995; accession negotiations commenced in February 2000. The country was expected to secure membership of the EU in 2007–08.

During the 1990s Romania's progress towards the development of a market economic system was considerably slower than that of many other post-communist states of central and eastern Europe. An extensive programme, announced in 2001, for the privatization of 63 large state-owned enterprises, encountered strong opposition, although in October the Government succeeded in divesting the Sidex steel works at Galați, in what was Romania's most significant privatization to date. Overall, Romania's economic prospects were regarded as more positive, and in late October the IMF, which had been withholding further assistance pending substantive progress on reform, approved a stand-by credit of some US $383m. None the less, many observers considered membership of the EU by 2007 to be a difficult objective. During 2003 the process of privatization accelerated, and inflation continued to decline as macroeconomic stability increased. In October the EU stated that Romania could be considered to have achieved the status of a functioning market economy, provided it continued to consolidate the progress that it had made. Further reforms remained necessary in the public-administration and judicial sectors if a more efficient business environment was to be created. Growth in 2004 was the result, in particular, of large-scale foreign investment and financial assistance from the EU, but concerns remained over the size of the country's current-account deficit and the high (if considerably reduced) rate of inflation. In January 2005 a uniform rate of corporate and personal income tax, of 16%, was introduced, greatly diminishing budgetary revenue and against the advice of international organizations. Further uncomfortable reforms remained to be implemented in preparation for EU membership and in conformity with a two-year IMF stand-by agreement (finalized in July 2004); for example, the Government committed to making some 7,000 redundancies in the mining sector in 2005, as part of a national restructuring plan that also encompassed the iron, steel and railway industries. The Romanian currency (the leu) was redenominated from 1 July 2005, but was subject to strong appreciation pressures thereafter (compounded by the inflow of emigrants' remittances from abroad). The IMF arrangement was suspended in October owing to disagreements over the economic programme for 2006 (the Government was reluctant to increase value-added tax or the price of natural gas, and also hoped to avoid restricting wage increases for public-sector workers). In 2005 GDP increased by 4.1%, although the economy was adversely affected by both severe flooding and an outbreak of avian influenza. International financial organizations emphasized the importance of increasing tax revenue in order to reduce the budgetary and external deficits, which left the Government with insufficient resources to fund planned infrastructural developments and social reforms. (The attraction of foreign investment was to become increasingly important, as large-scale privatization was completed.) There was international concern that the country was becoming less competitive prior to EU membership and that it was failing to make full use of EU funds. The European Commission was due to make a final decision on Romania's accession date in October 2006. Real GDP was expected to expand by some 5% in 2006/07, and the rate of inflation was expected to reach 6.5%.

Education

Children under the age of six years may attend crèches (creşe), and kindergartens (grădiniţe de copii). In 2002/03 76.5% of pre-school age children were attending kindergarten. Between the ages of six and 16 years children are obliged to attend the general education school (şcoală de cultură generală de zece ani). The general secondary school (liceul), for which there is an entrance examination, provides a specialized education suitable for entering college or university. There are also specialized secondary schools, where the emphasis is on industrial, agricultural and teacher training, and art schools, which correspond to secondary schools, but cover several years of general education. Vocational secondary schools (şcoli profesionale de ucenici) train pupils for a particular career. Tuition in minority languages, particularly Hungarian and German, is available. In 2002/03 primary enrolment included 96.5% of children in the relevant age-group, while the comparable ratio for secondary education was 94.1% for the 11–14 year old age group and 73.7% (males 71.4%; females 76.1%) for children of 15–18 years. There are 122 higher education establishments in Romania; enrolment in tertiary education was equivalent to 40.7% in 2002/03. Expenditure on education by the state budget in 2003 amounted to 15,561m. lei (representing 5.5% of total expenditure).

Public Holidays

2006: 1–2 January (New Year), 6 January (Epiphany), 23–24 April (Orthodox Easter), 1 May (Labour Day), 1 December (National Day), 25–26 December (Christmas).

2007: 1–2 January (New Year), 6 January (Epiphany), 1 May (Labour Day), 8–9 April (Orthodox Easter), 1 December (National Day), 25–26 December (Christmas).

Weights and Measures

The metric system is in force.

Statistical Survey

Source (unless otherwise indicated): Institutul National de Statistică (National Institute of Statistics), Bucharest, Bd. Libertăţii 16; tel. (21) 3124875; fax (21) 3124873; e-mail romstat@insse.ro; internet www.insse.ro/indexe.htm.

Area and Population

AREA, POPULATION AND DENSITY

Area (sq km)	238,391*
Population (census results)	
7 January 1992	22,810,035
18–27 March 2002	
Males	10,568,741
Females	11,112,233
Total	21,680,974
Population (official estimates at mid-year)	
2003	21,734,000
2004	21,673,000
Density (per sq km) at mid-2004	90.9

*92,043 sq miles.

POPULATION BY ETHNIC GROUP
(2002 census)

	Number	% of total
Romanian	19,399,597	89.5
Hungarian	1,431,807	6.6
Gypsy (Roma)	535,140	2.5
Ukrainian	61,098	0.3
German	59,764	0.3
Carpathio-Rusyn	35,791	0.2
Turkish	32,098	0.1
Others and unknown	125,679	0.6
Total	**21,680,974**	**100.0**

ADMINISTRATIVE DIVISIONS
(at mid–2003)

	Area (sq km)	Population	Density (per sq km)	Administrative capital
Alba	6,242	385,514	61.8	Alba Iulia
Arad	7,754	461,744	59.5	Arad
Argeş	6,826	650,502	95.3	Piteşti
Bacău	6,621	725,005	109.5	Bacău
Bihor	7,544	600,262	79.6	Oradea
Bistriţa-Năsăud	5,355	319,090	59.6	Bistriţa
Botoşani	4,986	460,825	92.4	Botoşani
Brăila	4,766	374,318	78.5	Brăila
Braşov	5,363	595,777	111.1	Braşov
Buzău	6,103	498,085	81.6	Buzău
Călăraşi	5,088	319,701	62.8	Călăraşi
Caraş-Severin	8,520	333,860	39.2	Reşiţa
Cluj	6,674	684,383	102.5	Cluj-Napoca
Constanţa	7,071	713,563	100.9	Constanţa
Covasna	3,710	224,922	60.6	Sfântu Gheorghe
Dâmboviţa	4,054	539,322	133.0	Târgovişte
Dolj	7,414	725,342	97.8	Craiova
Galaţi	4,466	622,936	139.5	Galaţi
Giurgiu	3,526	289,484	82.1	Giurgiu
Gorj	5,602	386,890	69.1	Târgu Jiu
Harghita	6,639	329,344	49.6	Miercurea-Ciuc
Hunedoara	7,063	489,872	69.3	Deva
Ialomiţa	4,453	293,969	66.0	Slobozia
Iaşi	5,476	816,003	149.0	Iaşi
Ilfov*	1,593	276,864	173.8	Bucharest
Maramureş	6,304	519,057	82.3	Baia Mare
Mehedinţi	4,933	307,288	62.3	Drobeta-Turnu-Severin
Mureş	6,714	585,990	87.3	Târgu Mureş
Neamţ	5,896	572,255	97.1	Piatra-Neamţ
Olt	5,498	491,359	89.4	Slatina
Prahova	4,716	832,558	176.5	Ploieşti
Sălaj	3,864	249,194	64.5	Zalău
Satu Mare	4,418	372,933	84.4	Satu Mare

ROMANIA

—continued	Area (sq km)	Population	Density (per sq km)	Administrative capital
Sibiu	5,432	423,724	78.0	Sibiu
Suceava	8,553	705,547	82.5	Suceava
Teleorman	5,790	432,856	74.8	Alexandria
Timiş	8,697	661,171	76.0	Timişoara
Tulcea	8,499	254,455	29.9	Tulcea
Vâlcea	5,765	418,463	72.6	Râmnicu Vâlcea
Vaslui	5,318	464,184	87.3	Vaslui
Vrancea	4,857	395,330	81.4	Focşani
Bucharest Municipality*	228	1,929,615	8,463.2	Bucharest
Total	238,391	21,733,556	91.2	

* The Bucharest Municipality is a separate administrative division, but the city is also the capital of the adjacent Ilfov region. The area and population of Bucharest are included only in figures for the municipality.

PRINCIPAL TOWNS
(at mid-2003)

Bucureşti (Bucharest, the capital)	1,929,615	Arad		171,330
Iaşi	313,444	Sibiu		156,092
Constanţa	309,965	Târgu Mureş		149,467
Timişoara	308,019	Baia Mare		142,651
Craiova	300,843	Buzău		138,458
Galaţi	300,211	Satu Mare		117,698
Cluj-Napoca	294,906	Botoşani		117,184
Braşov	286,371	Râmnicu-Vâlcea		111,980
Ploieşti	236,724	Piatra-Neamţ		111,488
		Drobeta-Turnu-Severin		109,941
Brăila	221,369			
Oradea	208,805	Suceava		108,144
Bacău	183,484	Focşani		102,197
Piteşti	173,739			

BIRTHS, MARRIAGES AND DEATHS

	Registered live births		Registered marriages		Registered deaths	
	Number	Rate (per 1,000)	Number	Rate (per 1,000)	Number	Rate (per 1,000)
1996	231,348	10.2	150,388	6.7	286,158	12.7
1997	236,891	10.5	147,105	6.5	279,315	12.4
1998	237,297	10.5	145,303	6.5	269,166	12.0
1999	234,600	10.4	140,014	6.2	265,194	11.8
2000	234,521	10.5	135,808	6.1	255,820	11.4
2001	220,368	9.8	129,930	5.8	259,603	11.6
2002	210,529	9.7	129,018	5.9	269,666	12.4
2003	212,459	9.8	133,953	6.2	266,575	12.3

Expectation of life (WHO estimates, years at birth): 71 (males 68; females 75) in 2003 (Source: WHO, *World Health Report*).

ECONOMICALLY ACTIVE POPULATION
(labour force surveys, '000 persons aged 15 years and over)

	2002	2003	2004
Agriculture, hunting and forestry	3,356.8	3,285.8	2,892.8
Fishing	4.7	6.6	3.4
Mining and quarrying	144.2	138.2	134.5
Manufacturing	1,971.7	1,999.1	2,051.3
Electricity, gas and water	194.8	187.1	191.8
Construction	412.8	425.9	478.5
Wholesale and retail trade; repair of motor vehicles, motorcycles and personal and household goods	859.3	861.3	943.4
Hotels and restaurants	112.0	119.4	147.9
Transport, storage and communications	457.7	461.4	454.1
Financial intermediation	75.5	82.9	86.2

—continued	2002	2003	2004
Real estate, renting and business services	135.2	149.9	231.5
Public administration	548.8	529.9	538.2
Education	410.8	406.0	402.7
Health and social assistance	350.4	350.3	361.7
Other services	199.6	218.9	239.6
Total employed	9,234.2	9,222.5	9,157.6
Unemployed	845.3	691.8	799.5
Total labour force	10,079.5	9,914.3	9,957.1
Males	5,525.6	5,464.7	5,470.8
Females	4,553.8	4,449.5	4,486.3

Registered unemployed ('000 persons, at end of year): 760.6 in 2002; 658.9 in 2003; 557.9 in 2004.

Source: ILO.

Health and Welfare

KEY INDICATORS

Total fertility rate (children per woman, 2003)	1.3
Under-5 mortality rate (per 1,000 live births, 2004)	20
HIV/AIDS (% of persons aged 15–49, 2003)	<0.1
Physicians (per 1,000 head, 2001)	1.89
Hospital beds (per 1,000 head, 2001)	7.49
Health expenditure (2002): US $ per head (PPP)	469
Health expenditure (2002): % of GDP	6.3
Health expenditure (2002): public (% of total)	65.9
Access to water (% of persons, 2002)	57
Access to sanitation (% of persons, 2002)	51
Human Development Index (2003): ranking	64
Human Development Index (2003): value	0.792

For sources and definitions, see explanatory note on p. vi.

Agriculture

PRINCIPAL CROPS
('000 metric tons)

	2002	2003	2004
Wheat	4,421.0	2,479.1	7,812.4
Barley	1,160.4	540.8	1,406.0
Maize	8,399.8	9,577.0	14,541.6
Rye	20.1	17.4	55.0
Oats	327.4	323.1	447.1
Potatoes	4,077.6	3,947.2	4,230.2
Sugar beet	954.6	764.5	672.7
Dry beans	33.6	36.7	53.5
Dry peas	20.5	23.5	58.0
Walnuts	37.5	50.8	15.6
Soybeans (Soya beans)	145.9	224.9	298.5
Sunflower seed	1,002.8	1,506.4	1,557.8
Rapeseed	35.9	8.1	98.7
Cabbages	821.4	1,019.2	919.1
Lettuce	5.0*	4.0†	3.6
Tomatoes	658.8	818.9	1,330.1
Pumpkins, squash and gourds	170.0*	200.0*	290.8
Cucumbers and gherkins	140.8	151.3	199.5
Chillies and green peppers	197.4	249.1	237.2
Dry onions	340.8	350.4	332.8
Garlic	72.4	76.5	65.9
Green beans	49.9	52.5	52.2
Green peas	19.6	20.2	17.4
Other vegetables*	377.0	475.5	304.1

ROMANIA

—continued	2002	2003	2004
Apples	491.5	811.1	1,097.8
Pears	68.1	103.8	45.9
Cherries	66.3	98.5	51.0
Apricots	18.3	42.6	20.6
Plums	220.6	909.6	475.8
Grapes	1,076.7	1,078.0	1,230.4
Cantaloupes and other melons	651.3	764.6	765.1
Other fruits*	87.2	122.9	116.9
Pimento†	30.0	30.0	30.0
Tobacco (leaves)	16.0	7.9	7.5

* Unofficial figure(s).
† FAO estimate(s).
Source: FAO.

LIVESTOCK
('000 head, year ending September)

	2002	2003	2004
Horses	860	879	897
Cattle	2,800	2,878	2,808
Pigs	4,447	5,058	6,495
Sheep	7,251	7,312	7,425
Goats	525	633	661
Chickens	71,413	77,379	87,014

Source: FAO.

LIVESTOCK PRODUCTS
('000 metric tons)

	2002	2003	2004
Beef and veal	156.1	185.4	161.6
Mutton and lamb	51.0	62.1	66.7
Goat meat	3.5	5.4	6.3
Pig meat	476.2	532.5	374.1
Horse meat*	9.0	9.9	9.9
Poultry meat	339.9	344.2	153.5
Cows' milk	4,637.4	4,852.1	5,716.2
Sheep's milk	267.7	271.9	342.2
Cheese	35.6	39.4	37.9*
Butter	6.0	6.0	7.1
Hen eggs	321.6	332.1	369.0
Other poultry eggs	33.0	30.6	35.6
Honey	13.4	17.4	19.2
Wool: greasy	16.7	16.9	17.5
Wool: scoured	10.0	10.1	10.6
Cattle hides (fresh)*	27.2	24.3	22.3
Sheepskins (fresh)*	10.3	15.9	13.7

* FAO estimate(s).
Source: FAO.

Forestry

ROUNDWOOD REMOVALS
('000 cubic metres, excluding bark)

	2002	2003	2004
Sawlogs, veneer logs and logs for sleepers	7,062	7,952	8,166
Pulpwood	2,463	2,486	2,500
Other industrial wood	2,567	2,099	2,096
Fuel wood	3,062	2,903	3,015
Total	15,154	15,440	15,777

Source: FAO.

SAWNWOOD PRODUCTION
('000 cubic metres, including railway sleepers)

	2002	2003	2004
Coniferous (softwood)	2,264	2,696	2,808
Broadleaved (hardwood)	1,432	1,550	1,780
Total	3,696	4,246	4,588

Source: FAO.

Fishing
(metric tons, live weight)

	2001	2002	2003
Capture	7,637	6,989	10,050
Freshwater bream	800	918	2,018
Common carp	566	486	342
Goldfish	1,149	1,097	2,348
Silver carp	644	411	3
Pontic shad	128	266	651
European sprat	1,792	1,617	1,219
Aquaculture	10,818	9,248	9,042
Common carp	2,432	2,675	2,309
Goldfish	1,744	1,545	1,705
Silver carp	3,316	2,186	1,970
Bighead carp	2,215	1,650	1,400
Rainbow trout	500	620	606
Total catch	18,455	16,237	19,092

Source: FAO.

Mining
('000 metric tons, unless otherwise indicated)

	2001	2002	2003
Brown coal (incl. lignite)	30,750	28,015	31,121
Crude petroleum	6,011	5,810	5,651
Iron ore*	221	248	244
Copper concentrates†	19.2	19.0	21.3
Lead concentrates†	19.7	15.1	18.1
Zinc concentrates†	29.8	21.2	23.5
Salt (unrefined)	2,225	2,258	2,417
Natural gas (million cu metres)	14,090	13,647	13,174

* Figures refer to gross weight.
† Figures refer to the metal content of concentrates.
Source: partly US Geological Survey.

Industry

SELECTED PRODUCTS
('000 metric tons, unless otherwise indicated)

	2001	2002	2003
Refined sugar	493	514	460
Margarine	45.6	60.0	68.2
Wine ('000 hectolitres)	5,463	5,488	5,457
Beer ('000 hectolitres)	12,663	11,627	13,292
Tobacco products	39	35	36
Cotton yarn—pure and mixed	31	32	31
Cotton fabrics—pure and mixed (million sq metres)	159	170	177
Woollen yarn—pure and mixed	12	22	23
Woollen fabrics—pure and mixed (million sq metres)	18	14	12
Silk fabrics—pure and mixed (million sq metres)*	32	31	35
Flax and hemp yarn—pure and mixed	4	3	3
Linen, hemp and jute fabrics—pure and mixed (million sq metres)	4	4	4

ROMANIA

—continued

	2001	2002	2003
Chemical filaments and fibres	30	26	22
Footwear (million pairs)	67	74	80
Chemical wood pulp	215	243	260
Paper and paperboard	418	456	489
Synthetic rubber	23	15	12
Rubber tyres ('000)	3,933	7,290	11,242
Sulphuric acid	59	58	65
Caustic soda (sodium hydroxide)	346	353	382
Soda ash (sodium carbonate)	448	454	406
Nitrogenous fertilizers (a)†	814	806	1,207
Phosphatic fertilizers (b)†	82	78	102
Pesticides	5	3	2
Plastics and resins	359.2	473.0	n.a.
Motor spirit (petrol)	3,394	4,404	3,841
Kerosene and white spirit	340	186	443
Distillate fuel oils	3,842	4,305	3,721
Residual fuel oils	1,797	2,050	1,558
Petroleum bitumen (asphalt)	184	169	204
Liquefied petroleum gas	325	344	327
Coke	1,413	1,866	1,638
Cement	5,702	5,680	5,992
Pig-iron	3,243	3,979	4,101
Crude steel	4,935	5,490	5,693
Aluminium—unwrought	185	191	205
Refined copper—unwrought	9	9	4
Television receivers ('000)	29	60	90
Merchant ships launched ('000 deadweight tons)	158	349	160
Passenger motor cars ('000)	72	66	76
Motor tractors, lorries and dump trucks (number)	352	476	257
Tractors (number)	5,272	n.a.	n.a.
Domestic refrigerators ('000)	313	390	522
Domestic washing and drying machines ('000)	24	29	35
Domestic vacuum cleaners ('000)	157	127	108
Domestic cookers ('000)	445	487	598
Electric energy (million kWh)	53,866	54,935	56,645

* Including fabrics of artificial silk.
† Production in terms of (a) nitrogen or (b) phosphoric acid.

Finance

CURRENCY AND EXCHANGE RATES

Monetary Units
100 bani (singular: ban) = 1 Romanian leu (plural: lei).

Sterling, Dollar and Euro Equivalents (30 December 2005)
£1 sterling = 53.51 lei;
US $1 = 31.08 lei;
€1 = 36.66 lei;
100 Romanian lei = £1.87 = $3.22 = €2.73.

Average Exchange Rate (lei per US $)
2003   33,200.1
2004   32,636.6
2005   2.9137

Note: On 1 July 2005 the leu was revalued at a rate of 10,000 old lei = 1 new leu. Some figures given in the survey are in terms of the former valuation.

STATE BUDGET
('000 million lei)

Revenue*	2001	2002	2003
Current revenue	146,852	178,649	251,845
Tax revenue	137,277	167,752	236,023
Direct taxes	41,146	41,851	50,193
On profits	21,991	29,979	43,681
On income	36,749	41,323	53,269
Indirect taxes	96,131	125,901	185,830
Value-added tax	51,793	72,644	95,469
Customs duties	9,038	9,362	12,882
Excises	27,293	32,434	60,408
Other indirect taxes	8,007	11,462	17,071
Non-tax revenue	9,574	10,897	15,822
Capital revenue	86	212	496
Total	**146,938**	**178,862**	**252,447**

Expenditure†	2001	2002	2003
General public services	11,050	13,580	19,621
Defence	17,579	23,759	29,166
Public order and safety	20,017	25,331	33,133
Education	9,884	12,633	15,561
Health	6,775	9,429	11,091
Social security and welfare	23,657	27,013	35,602
Services and public development, dwellings, environment and water	4,009	6,499	8,599
Recreational, cultural and religious affairs	3,702	4,211	5,913
Economic affairs	32,737	42,639	68,283
Agriculture	10,680	11,729	17,725
Industry	5,893	8,684	16,525
Transport and communications	14,107	18,486	28,277
Other	3,926	4,991	6,651
Expenditure from funds at government disposal	422	302	232
Transfers	3,807	3,265	7,752
Total	**137,565**	**173,651**	**241,604**

* Excluding grants and donations received ('000 million lei): 1,272 in 2001; 344 in 2002; 106 in 2003.
† Excluding lending minus repayments ('000 million lei): 46,447 in 2001; 53,173 in 2002; 39,847 in 2003.

INTERNATIONAL RESERVES
(US $ million at 31 December)

	2003	2004	2005
IMF special drawing rights	—	1	1
Foreign exchange	8,040	14,616	19,872
Total (excl. gold)	**8,040**	**14,617**	**19,873**

Source: IMF, *International Financial Statistics*.

MONEY SUPPLY
('000 million lei at 31 December)

	2003	2004	2005
Currency outside banks	5.80	7.46	11.39
Demand deposits at deposit money banks	4.96	6.97	11.78
Total money	**10.76**	**14.44**	**23.17**

Source: IMF, *International Financial Statistics*.

COST OF LIVING
(Consumer Price Index; base: 2000 = 100)

	2002	2003	2004
Food	160.5	184.1	201.5
Fuel and light	200.9	244.9	297.8
Clothing	148.2	163.8	175.4
Rent	140.4	162.1	187.8
All items (incl. others)	**164.8**	**189.9**	**212.5**

Source: ILO.

NATIONAL ACCOUNTS
('000 million lei at current prices)

Expenditure on the Gross Domestic Product

	2001	2002	2003
Final consumption expenditure	994,737.1	1,272,692.1	1,615,021.5
Households	917,185.7	1,169,404.2	1,483,480.7
Government	77,551.4	103,287.9	131,540.8
Gross capital formation	263,448.4	328,397.1	436,686.5
Gross fixed capital formation	241,153.6	322,836.0	422,535.1
Change in stocks	22,294.8	5,561.1	14,151.4
Total domestic expenditure	**1,258,185.5**	**1,601,089.2**	**2,051,708.0**
Exports of goods and services	389,147.4		
Less Imports of goods and services	479,645.9	−86,338.3	−148,354.1
GDP in purchasers' values	**1,167,687.0**	**1,514,750.9**	**1,903,353.9**

ROMANIA

Gross Domestic Product by Economic Activity

	2001	2002	2003
Agriculture, hunting, fishing and forestry	156,128.6	173,012.2	223,084.5
Fishing	50.6	63.8	82.5
Mining and quarrying			
Manufacturing	323,046.8	426,098.2	518,924.9
Electricity, gas and water			
Construction	62,333.7	87,888.8	114,261.3
Trade	106,640.7	130,334.0	162,784.3
Hotels and restaurants	24,590.0	32,337.6	40,484.5
Transport, storage and communications	116,813.2	146,708.4	181,775.9
Financial intermediation	23,006.5	35,243.8	43,593.1
Real estate transactions, renting and service activities	156,554.4	211,375.9	251,227.7
Public administration and defence	42,486.9	58,047.8	78,934.8
Education	31,087.6	42,102.5	54,452.6
Health and social assistance	18,082.9	29,788.7	37,358.8
Sub-total	1,060,821.9	1,373,001.7	1,706,964.9
Less Financial intermediation services indirectly measured	17,984.6	16,810.0	25,240.7
Gross value added in basic prices	1,042,837.3	1,356,191.7	1,681,724.2
Taxes on products	121,857.7	157,694.9	220,720.3
Import duties	9,038.2	9,361.5	13,296.8
Less Subsidies) on products	6,046.2	8,497.2	12,387.4
GDP in market prices	1,167,687.0	1,514,750.9	1,903,353.9

BALANCE OF PAYMENTS
(US $ million)

	2002	2003	2004
Exports of goods f.o.b.	13,876	17,618	23,485
Imports of goods f.o.b.	−16,487	−22,155	−30,150
Trade balance	−2,611	−4,537	−6,665
Exports of services	2,347	3,028	3,614
Imports of services	−2,338	−2,958	−3,879
Balance on goods and services	−2,602	−4,467	−6,930
Other income received	413	372	433
Other income paid	−872	−1,077	−3,582
Balance on goods, services and income	−3,061	−5,172	−10,079
Current transfers received	1,808	2,200	4,188
Current transfers paid	−272	−339	−491
Current balance	−1,525	−3,311	−6,382
Capital account (net)	93	213	643
Direct investment abroad	−16	−39	−70
Direct investment from abroad	1,144	1,844	6,443
Portfolio investment assets	—	9	−559
Portfolio investment liabilities	382	569	28
Other investment assets	692	72	−212
Other investment liabilities	1,877	1,945	5,131
Net errors and omissions	−856	−289	1,167
Overall balance	1,791	1,013	6,189

Source: IMF, *International Financial Statistics*.

External Trade

PRINCIPAL COMMODITIES
(distribution by SITC, € million)

Imports c.i.f.	2001	2002	2003
Food and live animals	1,060	905	1,204
Crude materials (inedible) except fuels	578	597	631
Mineral fuels, lubricants, etc.	2,195	2,103	2,312
Petroleum, petroleum products, etc.	1,506	1,402	1,306
Gas, natural and manufactured	398	447	724
Chemicals and related products	1,721	2,032	2,186
Basic manufactures	4,861	5,496	5,492
Textiles and textile articles	2,254	2,512	2,537
Iron and steel	589	627	705
Manufactures of metals	428	529	672
Machinery and transport equipment	4,848	5,323	6,251
Machinery specialized for particular industries	608	655	718
General industrial machinery and parts	706	809	945
Telecommunications, sound recording and reproducing equipment	646	582	629
Electric machinery, apparatus, etc.	1,274	1,545	1,778
Road vehicles	783	913	1,058
Miscellaneous manufactured articles	1,892	2,171	2,415
Total (incl. others)	17,383	18,881	21,201

Exports f.o.b.	2001	2002	2003
Crude materials (inedible) except fuels	778	801	974
Cork and wood	395	418	424
Mineral fuels, lubricants, etc.	794	1,160	1,023
Petroleum, petroleum products, etc.	693	1,019	926
Chemicals and related products	659	686	746
Basic manufactures	2,400	2,756	3,019
Iron and steel	905	1,066	1,149
Non-ferrous metals	420	357	296
Machinery and transport equipment	2,525	3,106	3,356
Telecommunications, sound recording and reproducing equipment	384	516	427
Electrical machinery, apparatus, etc.	632	903	1,095
Other transport equipment	387	445	451
Miscellaneous manufactured articles	5,120	5,734	6,071
Furniture and parts	558	653	699
Clothing and accessories (excl. footwear)	3,107	3,442	3,606
Footwear	1,091	1,229	1,262
Total (incl. others)	12,722	14,675	15,614

ROMANIA

PRINCIPAL TRADING PARTNERS
(€ million)*

Imports c.i.f.	2001	2002	2003
Austria	493	628	749
Belgium	287	301	313
Brazil	242	204	226
China, People's Republic	283	392	583
Czech Republic	307	368	433
France (incl. Monaco)	1,093	1,206	1,542
Germany	2,644	2,805	3,145
Greece	365	281	287
Hungary	671	675	766
Italy	3,470	3,911	4,140
Japan	171	230	265
Kazakhstan	168	358	211
Korea, Republic	188	238	219
Netherlands	360	412	413
Poland	308	368	491
Russia	1,320	1,349	1,751
Slovakia	156	171	213
Spain	245	306	383
Sweden	174	190	199
Switzerland-Liechtenstein	189	163	190
Turkey	421	592	815
Ukraine	359	366	487
United Kingdom	603	722	702
USA	552	571	493
Total (incl. others)	17,383	18,881	21,201

Exports f.o.b.	2001	2002	2003
Austria	382	446	502
Belgium	216	233	248
Bulgaria	226	186	254
China, People's Republic	100	216	248
France (incl. Monaco)	1,025	1,121	1,145
Germany	1,988	2,293	2,458
Greece	353	413	379
Hungary	414	456	545
Israel	136	159	88
Italy	3,172	3,670	3,774
Netherlands	432	461	555
Spain	200	216	279
Turkey	503	611	798
United Kingdom	654	849	1,046
USA	404	627	551
Serbia and Montenegro	172	135	135
Total (incl. others)	12,722	14,675	15,614

* Imports by country of production; exports by country of last consignment.

Transport

RAILWAYS
(traffic)

	2001	2002	2003
Passenger journeys (million)	113.7	95.6	94.8
Passenger-km (million)	10,966	8,502	8,529
Freight transported (million metric tons)	72.6	70.7	71.4
Freight ton-km (million)	16,102	15,218	15,039

ROAD TRAFFIC
(motor vehicles in use at 31 December)

	2001	2002	2003
Passenger cars	2,881,191	2,973,390	3,087,628
Buses and coaches	40,791	40,780	41,947
Lorries and vans	437,968	447,299	463,099
Motorcycles and mopeds	237,901	238,480	235,850

INLAND WATERWAYS
(traffic)

	2001	2002	2003
Passenger journeys ('000)	165	155	174
Passenger-km (million)	19	18	16
Freight transported ('000 metric tons)	11,342	13,946	12,848
Freight ton-km (million)	2,746	3,641	3,521

SHIPPING

Merchant Fleet
(registered at 31 December)

	2002	2003	2004
Number of vessels	237	232	221
Total displacement ('000 grt)	622.0	563.1	426.7

Sources: Lloyd's Register-Fairplay, *World Fleet Statistics*.

International Sea-borne Freight Traffic
('000 metric tons)

	1999	2000	2001
Goods loaded	14,376	12,648	13,788
Goods unloaded	11,100	12,828	15,120

Source: UN, *Monthly Bulletin of Statistics*.

2003 ('000 metric tons): Goods loaded 28,149; Goods unloaded 29,669.

CIVIL AVIATION
(traffic)

	2001	2002	2003
Passenger journeys ('000)	1,278	1,193	1,172
Passenger-km (million)	2,020	1,843	1,760
Freight transported ('000 metric tons)	7	7	6
Freight ton-km (million)	12	11	9

Tourism

FOREIGN VISITOR ARRIVALS
('000)*

Country of origin	2001	2002	2003
Bulgaria	392	363	340
Germany	328	359	380
Hungary	1,131	1,153	1,537
Italy	219	230	259
Moldova	1,033	857	1,059
Poland	106	113	109
Serbia and Montenegro	127	175	271
Slovakia	84	103	84
Turkey	230	191	205
Ukraine	324	289	349
Total (incl. others)	4,938	4,794	5,595

* Figures refer to arrivals at frontiers of visitors from abroad, including same day visitors (excursionists).

Tourism receipts (US $ million, incl. passenger transport): 500 in 2001; 400 in 2002; 523 in 2003.

Source: World Tourism Organization.

Communications Media

	2001	2002	2003
Telephones ('000 main lines in use)	4,116.0	4,215.2	4,333.4
Mobile cellular telephones ('000 subscribers)	3,845.1	5,110.6	7,046.4
Personal computers ('000 in use)	800	1,800	2,100
Internet users ('000)	1,000	2,200	4,000
Book production (incl. pamphlets):			
titles	10,478	11,571	12,864
copies ('000)	10,426	11,189	8,350
Daily newspapers	98	94	69
Other periodicals	1,824	1,853	1,944

1997: Radio receivers ('000 in use) 7,200.

2000: Television receivers ('000 in use) 8,500.

2004: Telephones ('000 main lines in use) 4,389; Mobile cellular telephones ('000 subscribers) 10,215; Internet users ('000) 4,500; Personal computers ('000) 2,450.

Source: partly International Telecommunication Union.

Education

(2003/04)

	Institutions	Pupils	Teachers
Kindergartens	7,616	636,709	34,585
Primary and gymnasium schools	8,714	2,122,226	150,510
Secondary schools	1,397	758,917	58,925
Vocational schools	79	279,124	5,782
Specialized technical schools	84	54,732	1,333
Higher education	122	620,785	30,137

Adult literacy rate (UNESCO estimates): 97.3% (males 98.4%; females 96.3%) in 2003 (Source: UN Development Programme, *Human Development Report*).

Directory

The Constitution

Following its assumption of power in December 1989, the National Salvation Front decreed radical changes to the Constitution of 1965. The name of the country was changed from the Socialist Republic of Romania to Romania. The leading role of a single political party was abolished, a democratic and pluralist system of government being established.

The combined chambers of the legislature elected in May 1990, working as a constituent assembly, drafted a new Constitution (based on the Constitution of France's Fifth Republic), which was approved in a national referendum on 8 December 1991. A plebiscite held on 18–19 October 2003 approved 79 amendments to the Constitution, bringing it into conformity with EU legislation. The amendments entered into force on 29 October.

Under the amended Constitution, political power in Romania belongs to the people and is exercised according to the principles of democracy, freedom and human dignity, of inviolability and inalienability of basic human rights. Romania is governed on the basis of a multi-party democratic system and of the separation of the legal, executive and judicial powers. Romania's legislature, consisting of the Camera Deputaților (Chamber of Deputies—the lower house) and Senatul (the Senate—the upper house), and Romania's President are elected by universal, free, direct and secret vote, the President serving a maximum of two terms. The term of office of the legislature is four years and five years for the President, with effect from the elections held in late 2004. The number of Deputies and Senators is established under the election law, in proportion to Romania's overall population. Citizens have the right to vote at the age of 18, and may be elected at the age of 21 to the Camera Deputaților and at the age of 30 to Senatul, with no upper age limit. Those ineligible for election include former members of the Securitate (the secret police of President Ceaușescu) and other former officials guilty of repression and abuses. Independent candidates are eligible for election to the Camera Deputaților and to Senatul if supported by at least 251 electors and to the Presidency if supported by 100,000 electors. Once elected, the President may not remain a member of any political party. The President appoints the Prime Minister, who in turn appoints the Council of Ministers.

The Government

HEAD OF STATE

President: TRAIAN BĂSESCU (elected 12 December 2004; inaugurated 14 December 2004).

COUNCIL OF MINISTERS
(April 2006)

A coalition of the Justice and Truth Alliance (DA—principally comprising the National Liberal Party, the Democratic Party and Independents), the Democratic Alliance of Hungarians in Romania (DAHR) and the Conservative Party.

Prime Minister: CĂLIN CONSTANTIN ANTON POPESCU-TĂRICEANU (DA).

Minister of State, responsible for the Co-ordination of Activities in the Economic Field: GHEORGHE POGEA (DA).

Minister of State, responsible for Co-ordination of Activities in the Fields of Culture, Education and European Integration: BELA MARKO (DAHR).

Minister of State, responsible for Co-ordination of Activities in the Fields of Business and Small and Medium-Sized Entreprises: GHEORGHE COPOS (Conservative Party).

Minister of Foreign Affairs: MIHAI-RĂZVAN UNGUREANU (DA).

Minister of European Integration: ANCA BOAGIU (DA).

Minister of Public Finance: SEBASTIAN VLĂDESCU (DA).

Minister of Justice: MONICA LUISA MACOVEI (DA).

Minister of the Interior and Public Administration: VASILE BLAGA (DA).

Minister of Economy and Commerce: IOAN-CODRUȚ ȘEREȘ (Conservative Party).

Minister of National Defence: TEODOR ATANASIU (DA).

Minister of Labour, Social Solidarity and Family: GHEORGHE BARBU (DA).

Minister of Agriculture, Forestry and Rural Development: GHEORGHE FLUTUR (DA).

Minister of Transport, Construction and Tourism: GHEORGHE DOBRE (DA).

Minister of Education and Research: MIHAIL HĂRDĂU (DA).

Minister of Culture and Religious Affairs: ADRIAN IORGULESCU (DA).

Minister of Health: EUGEN NICOLĂESCU (DA).

Minister of Communications and Information Technology: ZSOLT NAGY (DAHR).

Minister of the Environment and Water Management: SULFINA BARBU (DA).

Minister-delegate, responsible for Co-ordinating the Government General Secretariat: MIHAI ALEXANDRU VOICU (DA).

Minister-delegate, responsible for the Process of Implementation of Internationally Financed Programmes and the European Union's *acquis communautaire*: CRISTIAN DAVID (DA).

Minister-delegate, responsible for the Co-ordination of Public Works and Territory Management: LÁSZLÓ BORBELY (DAHR).

Minister-delegate for Commerce: IULIU WINKLER (DAHR).

MINISTRIES

Office of the President: 060116 Bucharest, Palatul Cotroceni, str. Geniuliu 1–3, Sector 5; tel. (21) 4100581; fax (21) 4103858; e-mail presedinte@presidency.ro; internet www.presidency.ro.

ROMANIA

Office of the Prime Minister: 71201 Bucharest, Piaţa Victoriei 1; tel. (21) 3131450; fax (21) 3122436; e-mail prim.ministru@guv.ro; internet www.cancelarie.ro.

Ministry of Agriculture, Forestry and Rural Development: 70312 Bucharest, Bd. Carol I 24; tel. (21) 6144020; fax (21) 3124410; internet www.maap.ro.

Ministry of Communications and Information Technology: 70060 Bucharest 5, Bd. Libertăţii 14; tel. (21) 3361961; e-mail office@mcti.ro; internet www.mcti.ro.

Ministry of Culture and Religious Affairs: 71341 Bucharest, Piaţa Presei Libere 1; tel. (21) 2228479; fax (21) 2245440; e-mail tudor.maruntelu@cultura.ro; internet www.ministerulculturii.ro.

Ministry of the Economy and Commerce: 010096 Bucharest 1, Calea Victoriei 152; tel. (21) 2129437; fax (21) 3120321; e-mail linia-cetateanului@minind.ro; internet www.minind.ro.

Ministry of Education and Research: 70738 Bucharest, Str. Gen. Berthelot 28–30, Sector 1; tel. (21) 6133315; fax (21) 3124719; internet www.edu.ro.

Ministry of the Environment and Water Management: 76106 Bucharest 5, Bd. Libertăţii 12; tel. (1) 4100482; fax (1) 3124227; internet www.mappm.ro.

Ministry of European Integration: 050741 Bucharest 5, Str. Apolodor 17, Latura Nord; tel. (21) 3011502; fax (21) 3368509; e-mail andreea.vaida@mie.ro; internet www.mie.ro.

Ministry of Foreign Affairs: 71274 Bucharest, Al. Alexandru 33; tel. (21) 2302071; fax (21) 2314090; e-mail maero@mae.kappa.ro; internet www.mae.ro.

Ministry of Health: 70109 Bucharest, Str. Cristian Popisteanu 1–3; tel. (21) 3072690; fax (21) 3124916; e-mail ministru@ms.ro; internet www.ms.ro.

Ministry of the Interior and Public Administration: 70622 Bucharest, Sector 6, Str. Mihai Vodă 6; tel. (21) 3158616; fax (21) 3149718; e-mail drp@mi.ro; internet www.mi.ro.

Ministry of Justice: 70663 Bucharest 5, Str. Apolodor 17; tel. (21) 3112266; fax (21) 3155389; e-mail relatiipublice@just.ro; internet www.just.ro.

Ministry of Labour, Social Solidarity and Family: 010026 Bucharest, Str. Demetru I. Dobrescu 2B, Sector 1; tel. (21) 3156563; fax (21) 3122768; e-mail ministrummssf@mmssf.ro; internet www.mmssf.ro.

Ministry of National Defence: 77303 Bucharest, Str. Izvor 13–15, Sector 5; tel. (21) 4106876; fax (21) 3120863; e-mail drp@mapn.ro; internet www.mapn.ro.

Ministry of Public Finance: 70663 Bucharest 5, Str. Apolodor 17; tel. (21) 4103400; fax (21) 3122077; e-mail presa@mail.mfinante.ro; internet www.mfinante.ro.

Ministry of Transport, Construction and Tourism: 010873 Bucharest, Bd. Dinicu Golescu 38; tel. (21) 4101933; fax (21) 4111138; internet www.mt.ro.

President

Presidential Election, First Ballot, 28 November 2004

Candidates	Votes	%
Adrian Năstase (National Union*)	4,278,864	40.94
Traian Băsescu (Justice and Truth Alliance†)	3,545,236	33.92
Corneliu Vadim Tudor (Greater Romania Party)	1,313,714	12.57
Bela Marko (Democratic Alliance of Hungarians in Romania)	533,446	5.10
Gheorghe Ciuhandu (Christian Democratic National Peasants' Party of Romania)	198,394	1.90
Gheorghe Becali (New Generation Party)	184,560	1.77
Petre Roman (Democratic Force of Romania)	140,702	1.35
Gheorghe Dinu (Independent)	113,321	1.08
Others	143,968	1.38
Total	**10,452,205**	**100.00**

Second Ballot, 12 December 2004

Candidates	Votes	%
Traian Băsescu (Justice and Truth Alliance†)	5,126,794	51.23
Adrian Năstase (National Union*)	4,881,520	48.77
Total	**10,008,314**	**100.00**

* An alliance of the Social Democratic Party and the Humanist Party of Romania (Social-Liberal).
† An alliance of the National Liberal Party and the Democratic Party.

Legislature

PARLAMENTUL ROMÂNIEI
(The Romanian Parliament)

The bicameral Parlamentul României comprises the 346-member lower chamber, the Camera Deputaţilor (Chamber of Deputies) and the 140-member upper chamber, Senatul (the Senate). Members of both chambers are directly elected, for a term of four years.

Camera Deputaţilor
(Chamber of Deputies)
50563 Bucharest, Palatul Parlamentului, Str. Izvor 2–4, Sector 5; tel. (21) 4021444; fax (21) 4022149; e-mail secretar.general@cdep.ro; internet www.cdep.ro.

Chairman: BOGDAN OLTEANU.

General Election, 28 November 2004

Parties	Seats
National Union*	132
Justice and Truth Alliance†	112
Greater Romania Party	48
Democratic Alliance of Hungarians in Romania	22
Minority parties	18
Total	**332**

* An alliance of the Social Democratic Party and the Humanist Party of Romania (Social-Liberal).
† An alliance of the National Liberal Party and the Democratic Party.

Senatul
(The Senate)
050711 Bucharest 5, Calea 13 Septembrie 1–3; tel. (21) 4021111; fax (21) 3121184; e-mail csava@senat.ro; internet www.senat.ro.

Chairman: NICOLAE VĂCĂROIU.

General Election, 28 November 2004

Parties	Seats
National Union*	57
Justice and Truth Alliance†	49
Greater Romania Party	21
Democratic Alliance of Hungarians in Romania	10
Others	—
Total	**137**

* An alliance of the Social Democratic Party and the Humanist Party of Romania (Social-Liberal).
† An alliance of the National Liberal Party and the Democratic Party.

Election Commission

Central Electoral Office (Biroul Electoral Central): Bucharest 3, Str. Zborului 10; tel. (21) 3268427; fax (21) 3268430; internet www.bec2004.ro; Pres. EMIL GHERGUT.

Political Organizations

Civic Alliance (Alianţa Civică): 70174 Bucharest, Piaţa Amzei 13, etaj 2, Sector 1; tel. (21) 2127542; fax (21) 2127541; e-mail aliantacivica@fx.ro; internet www.aliantacivica.ro; f. 1990; as alliance of opposition groupings outside legislature; Pres. SERBAN RADULESCU-ZONER.

Conservative Party (Partidul Conservator): 010093 Bucharest 1, Calea Victoriei 118, etaj 5, Sector 1; tel. (21) 3170614; fax (21) 3170613; e-mail secretariat@partidulconservator.ro; internet www.partidulconservator.ro; f. 1991 as the Humanist Party of Romania;

ROMANIA

contested legislative and presidential elections in 2004 in alliance with the SDP, as the National Alliance; renamed in May 2005; absorbed the Romanian National Unity Party in Feb. 2006; Pres. DAN VOICULESCU.

Democratic Alliance of Hungarians in Romania (DAHR) (Uniunea Democrată Maghiară din România—UDMR): 024015 Bucharest, Str. Avram Iancu 8; tel. and fax (21) 3144356; e-mail elhivbuk@rmdsz.rdsnet.ro; internet www.rmdsz.ro; f. 1990; supports the rights of Hungarians in Romania; Pres. BELA MARKO; Exec. Pres. CSABA TAKÁCS.

Democratic Force of Romania (Forţa Democrăta din România—FDR): Bucharest 3, Calea Călăraşi 76; e-mail contact@fortademocratatimis.ro; internet www.fotademocratatimis.ro; f. 2004; Chair. PETRE ROMAN.

Democratic Party (DP) (Partidul Democrat—PD): 71274 Bucharest, Al. Modrogan 1; tel. and fax (21) 2301332; e-mail office@pd.ro; internet www.pd.ro; f. 1993; fmrly Democratic Party—National Salvation Front; centre-left; social-democratic; contested legislative and presidential elections in 2004 in alliance with the NLP, as the Justice and Truth Alliance; Pres. EMIL BOC; Exec. Chair. ADRIAN VIDEANU.

Greater Romania Party (Partidul România Mare—PRM): 70101 Bucharest, Str. G. Clemenceau 8–10; tel. (21) 3130967; fax (21) 3126182; e-mail prm@prm.org.ro; internet www.prm.org.ro; f. 1991; known as the Popular Greater Romania Party (under the chairmanship of Corneliu Ciontu) in March–June 2005; nationalist; splinter group formed under Ciontu in mid-2005 (People's Party); Chair. CORNELIU VADIM TUDOR.

National Liberal Party (NLP) (Partidul Naţional Liberal—PNL): 70112 Bucharest, Bd. Aviatorilor 86; tel. (21) 2310795; fax (21) 2317511; e-mail dre@pnl.ro; internet www.pnl.ro; f. 1990 as revival of party originally founded in 1869 and banned in 1947; merged with Liberal Party in 1993, and with Party of the Civic Alliance and Liberal Party of Romania in 1998, absorbed Alliance for Romania in 2002 and the Union of Rightist Forces in 2003; supports the integration of Romania into the European Union and the North Atlantic Treaty Organizaton, advocates freedom of expression and religion, a market economy and the decentralization of state powers; contested legislative and presidential elections in 2004 in alliance with the Democratic Party, as the Justice and Truth Alliance; Pres. CĂLIN POPESCU-TĂRICEANU; Sec.-Gen. MIHAI VOICU.

New Generation Party (Partidul Noua Generatie—PNG): 030061 Bucharest 3, Str. Blănari 21–23; tel. (21) 3149360; fax (21) 3149361; e-mail contact@png.ro; internet www.png.ro; f. 2003; Chair. GHEORGHE BECALI.

Popular Action (Actiunea Populara): 050093 Bucharest 5, Splaiul Independenţei 17/101; tel. (21) 3353040; fax (21) 3354014; e-mail office@actiunea.ro; internet www.actiunea.ro; f. 2003 by mems of the Christian Democratic National Peasant's Party of Romania; merged with the Popular Christian Party in Nov. 2003; Chair. EMIL CONSTANTINESCU.

Popular Christian-Democratic Party of Romania (Partidul Popular Creştin-Democrat din România—PPCD): 73231 Bucharest, Bd. Carol I 34; tel. (21) 6154533; fax (21) 6143277; internet www.pntcd.ro; f. 1989 by merger of centre-right Christian Democratic Party and traditional National Peasant Party, as revival of party originally founded in 1869 and banned in 1947; changed name as above from Christian Democratic National Peasants' Party of Romania (CDNPP) in 2005; absorbed the Union for the Reconstruction of Romania in March 2005; supports pluralist democracy and the restoration of peasant property; Chair. GHEORGHE CIUHANDU; Sec.-Gen. ADRIAN BOC.

Romanian Ecological Federation (REF) (Federaţia Ecologistă din România—FER): 73226 Bucharest, Str. Matei Voievod 102; tel. (21) 6352743; alliance incl. the Romanian Ecological Movement; Leader EDWARD GUGUI.

Romanian Ecological Party (Partidul Ecologist Român): Bucharest; tel. (21) 6158285; merged with the Green Alternative Party of Ecologists and the Ecologist Convention in 2003; Chair. CORNELIU PROTOPOPESCU.

Social Democratic Party (SDP) (Partidul Social Democrat—PSD): 71271 Bucharest 2, Str. Kiseleff 10; tel. (21) 2222958; fax (21) 2223272; internet www.psd.ro; f. 2001 by the merger of the Romanian Social Democratic Party and the Party of Social Democracy of Romania; contested legislative and presidential elections in 2004 in alliance with the HPR, as the National Alliance; Pres. MIRCEA DAN GEOANĂ; Sec.-Gen. MIRON MITREA.

Diplomatic Representation

EMBASSIES IN ROMANIA

Albania: 71274 Bucharest, Str. Duiliu Zamfirescu 7, Sector 1; tel. (21) 2118743; fax (21) 2108039; e-mail albemb@mailbox.ro; Ambassador LEONIDHA MËRTIRI.

Algeria: 71111 Bucharest, Bd. Lascar Catargiu 29; tel. (21) 2115150; fax (21) 2115695; Ambassador ABDEL HAMID SENOUCI BEREKSI.

Argentina: 10031 Bucharest, Union Internacional Centre, Str. Ion Campineanu 11; tel. (21) 3122626; fax (21) 3120116; e-mail eruma@mrecic.gov.ar; Ambassador ADRIÁN GUILLERMO MIRSON.

Armenia: 030593 Bucharest 3, Str. Calotesti 1, ap. 2; tel. (21) 3215930; fax (21) 3125679; e-mail armembro@starnets.ro; Ambassador YEGISHE SARKISSIAN.

Austria: 70254 Bucharest, Str. Dumbrava Roşie 7; tel. (21) 2104354; fax (21) 2100885; e-mail bukarest-ob@bmaa.gv.at; Ambassador Dr CHRISTIAN ZEILEISSEN.

Azerbaijan: 711492 Bucharest I, Str. Ion Caragea Voda 23; tel. (21) 2113044; fax (21) 2110513; e-mail azsefroman@pcnet.ro; internet www.azembassy.ro; Ambassador ELDAR HASANOV.

Belarus: 011343 Bucharest 1, Şos. Pavel Kiseleff 55, Vila 6; tel. (21) 2233510; fax (21) 2231763; e-mail romania@belembassy.org; Ambassador VIKTAR SHYKH.

Belgium: 70256 Bucharest, Bd. Dacia 58, Sector 2; tel. (21) 2102970; fax (21) 2102803; e-mail ambabuc@ines.ro; internet www.diplobel.org/romania; Ambassador PHILIPPE ROLAND.

Brazil: 011802 Bucharest I, Str. Praga 11; tel. (21) 2301130; fax (21) 2301599; e-mail braembuc@starnets.ro; internet www.brazil.as.ro; Ambassador TADEU VALADARES.

Bulgaria: 71272 Bucharest, Str. Rabat 5; tel. (21) 2302150; fax (21) 2307654; e-mail bulembasy@pcnet.ro; internet www.bgembassy-romania.org; Ambassador KONSTANTIN ANDREEV.

Canada: 010436 Bucharest, Str. Nicolae Iorga 36; tel. (21) 3075000; fax (21) 3075015; e-mail bucst@dfait-maeci.gc.ca; internet www.dfait-maeci.gc.ca/Bucharest; Ambassador FRANCO D. PILLARELLA.

Chile: 71113 Bucharest, Str. Sevastopol 13–17; tel. (21) 3127239; fax (21) 3127246; e-mail embachile@consuladochile.ro; Ambassador MANUEL ENRIQUE HINOJOSA MUÑOZ.

China, People's Republic: 71512 Bucharest, Şos. Nordului 2; tel. (21) 2328858; fax (21) 2330684; Ambassador XU JIAN.

Congo, Democratic Republic: 711471 Bucharest, Str. Mihai Eminescu 50–54/15/7, Sector 1; tel. (21) 2105498; e-mail ambardcbuc@yahoo.fr; Chargé d'affaires a.i. PHOBA KI KUMBU.

Congo, Republic: 703122 Bucharest 2, Bd. Pache Protopopescu 14; tel. and fax (21) 3153371; e-mail ambacobuc@yahoo.fr; Chargé d'affaires GEORGES AMBARA.

Croatia: 73102 Bucharest, Str. Dr Burghelea 1, Sector 2; tel. (21) 3130457; fax (21) 3130384; e-mail croemb.bucharest@mvp.hr; Ambassador ŽELJKO KUPRESAK.

Cuba: 71148 Bucharest, Str. Mihai Eminescu 44–48, etaj 2, ap. 5; tel. and fax (21) 2118916; e-mail embacuba@kappa.ro; Ambassador MANUEL ISMAEL HERMIDA MEDINA.

Czech Republic: 70418 Bucharest, Str. Ion Ghica 11, Sector 3; tel. (21) 3039230; fax (21) 3122539; e-mail bucharest@embassy.mzv.cz; internet www.mzv.cz/bucharest; Ambassador Dr RADEK PECH.

Denmark: 73102 Bucharest, Str. Dr Burghelea 3; tel. (21) 3120352; fax (21) 3120358; e-mail buhamb@um.dk; internet www.ambbukarest.um.dk; Ambassador ERIK BOM.

Egypt: 70185 Bucharest, Bd. Dacia 21; tel. (21) 2110938; fax (21) 2100337; e-mail egyptemb@canad.ro; Ambassador MUHAMMAD AL-SAYYID GOHAR.

Finland: 71217 Bucharest, Str. Atena 2 bis; tel. (21) 2307504; fax (21) 2307505; e-mail sanomat.buk@formin.fi; internet www.finlandia.ro; Ambassador TAPIO SAARELA.

France: 70172 Bucharest, Str. Biserica Amzei 13–15; tel. (21) 3120217; fax (21) 3120200; e-mail chancellerie.bucarest-amba@diplomatie.gouv.fr; internet www.ambafrance-ro.org; Ambassador HERVÉ BOLOT.

Georgia: 010516 Bucharest 1, Str. Mihai Eminescu 44–48, ap. 8; tel. (21) 2100602; fax (21) 2100502; Ambassador ZURAB BERIDZE.

Germany: 011849 Bucharest, Str. Capt. Aviator Gh. Demetriade 6–8; tel. (21) 2029830; fax (21) 2305846; e-mail botschaft@deutschebotschaft-bukarest.ro; internet www.bukarest.diplo.de; Ambassador WILFRIED GRUBER.

Greece: 71108 Bucharest, Bd. Pache Protopopescu, Sector 2; tel. (21) 2094170; fax (21) 2094175; e-mail grembassy@grembassy.ro; internet www.grembassy.ro; Ambassador ATHANASIOS DENDOULIS.

Holy See: 010187 Bucharest, Str. Pictor C. Stahi 5–7 (Apostolic Nunciature); tel. (21) 3139490; fax (21) 3120316; e-mail nuntius@fx

ROMANIA

.ro; Apostolic Nuncio Most Rev. JEAN-CLAUDE PÉRISSET (Titular Archbishop of Iustiniana prima).

Hungary: 70202 Bucharest, Str. Jean-Louis Calderon 63; tel. (21) 3120073; fax (21) 3120467; e-mail hunembro@ines.ro; internet hungaryemb.ines.ro; Ambassador JÁNOS TERÉNYI.

India: 712663 Bucharest, Str. Uruguay 11; tel. (21) 2225451; fax (21) 2232681; e-mail office@embassyofindia.ro; internet www.embassyofindia.ro; Ambassador RAM MOHAN.

Indonesia: 71108 Bucharest, Str. Orlando 10; tel. (21) 3120742; fax (21) 3120214; e-mail indo.bucharest@itcnet.ro; Ambassador NUNI TURNIATI JOKO.

Iran: 71112 Bucharest, Bd. Lascar Catargiu 39, Sector 1; tel. (21) 3120495; fax (21) 3120496; e-mail office@iranembassy.ro; internet www.iranembassy.ro; Ambassador ALI AKBAR FARAZI.

Iraq: 70189 Bucharest, Str. Polonă 8; tel. (21) 2110835; fax (21) 2100477; Ambassador ADIL MURAD.

Ireland: 020492 Bucharest, Str. Vasile Lascar 42–44; tel. (21) 2122088; fax (21) 2122089; e-mail embassybucharest@yahoo.ie; f. 2005; Ambassador PÁDRAIC CRADOCK.

Israel: 751211 Bucharest 4, Bd. Dimitrie Cantemir 1, Bl. B2, etaj 5; tel. (21) 3304149; fax (21) 3300750; e-mail israel.embassy@algoritma.ro; Ambassador RODICA RADIAN GORDON.

Italy: 711192 Bucharest, Str. Henri Coandă 7–9; tel. (21) 3113465; fax (21) 3124269; e-mail primosegretario@ambitalia.ro; internet www.ambitalia.ro; Ambassador STEFANO RONCA.

Japan: 70189 Bucharest 1, Str. Polonă 4; tel. (21) 2100790; fax (21) 2100272; e-mail embjpn@mb.roknet.ro; internet www.ro.emb-japan.go.jp; Ambassador KANJI TSUSHIMA.

Jordan: 702542 Bucharest, Str. Dumbrava Roşie 1; tel. (21) 2104705; fax (21) 2100320; e-mail jordan.embassy@pcnet.ro; Ambassador MAZEN KHAIR.

Korea, Democratic People's Republic: 715145 Bucharest, Şos. Nordului 6; tel. and fax (21) 2329665; Ambassador JO SUNG JU.

Korea, Republic: 71293 Bucharest, Bd. Mircea Eliade 14; tel. (21) 2307198; fax (21) 2307629; e-mail koerom@mofat.go.kr; Ambassador KIM EUN-KI.

Lebanon: 71249 Bucharest 1, Str. Paris 46, ap.1; tel. (21) 2309205; fax (21) 2307534; e-mail emblebanon@k.ro; Ambassador MUHAMMAD EL-DIB.

Libya: 71111 Bucharest, Bd. Lascar Catargiu 15; tel. (21) 2127832; fax (21) 3120232; Chargé d'affaires NASSRADIN S. ELKWELDY.

Macedonia, former Yugoslav Republic: 712182 Bucharest, Str. Mihai Eminescu 144; tel. (21) 2100880; fax (21) 2117295; e-mail ammakbuk@rdsmail.ro; Ambassador TIHOMIR ILIEVSKI.

Malaysia: 020025 Bucharest 2, Str. Pta Cantacuzino 1, etaj 3, ap. 8; tel. (21) 2113801; fax (21) 2100270; e-mail mwbucrst@itcnet.ro; Chargé d'affaires JAMALUDDIN SABEH.

Mexico: 702281 Bucharest, Str. Mihai Eminescu 124C, ap. 13, Sector 2; tel. (21) 2104417; fax (21) 2104713; e-mail embamex@xnet.ro; internet www.embamex.ro; Chargé d'affaires a.i. MIGUEL ANGEL OROZCO GUZMÁN.

Moldova: 71273 Bucharest 1, Al. Alexandru 40; tel. (21) 2300474; fax (21) 2307790; e-mail ambasadamoldova@zappmobile.ro; Ambassador LIDIA GUTU.

Morocco: 70256 Bucharest, Bd. Dacia 75, Sector 2; tel. (21) 2102945; fax (21) 2102767; e-mail ambamarbuc@ambasadamaroc.ro; internet www.ambasadamaroc.ro; Ambassador LAHCEN AZOULY.

Netherlands: 011823 Bucharest, Al. Alexandru 20; tel. (21) 2086030; fax (21) 2307620; e-mail bkr@minbuza.nl; internet www.olanda.ro; Ambassador PIETER JAN WOLTHERS.

Nigeria: 010449 Bucharest, POB 1–305, Str. Gina Patrichi 9; tel. (21) 3128685; fax (21) 3120622; e-mail nigeremb@canad.ro; Ambassador UMAR ILIYA DAMAGUM.

Norway: 70254 Bucharest, Str. Dumbrava Roşie 4; tel. (21) 2100274; fax (21) 2100275; e-mail emb.bucharest@mfa.no; internet www.norvegia.ro; Ambassador LEIF ARNE ULLAND.

Pakistan: 71304 Bucharest 1, Str. Barbu Delavrancea 22; tel. (21) 2225736; fax (21) 2225737; e-mail parepbuc@k.ro; Ambassador SANAULLAH.

Peru: 011346 Bucharest 1, Şos. Pavel Kiseleff 18; tel. (21) 2231956; fax (21) 2231088; e-mail embaperu@pcnet.ro; Ambassador ELARD ESCALA SANCHEZ-BARRETO.

Philippines: 71039 Bucharest, Str. Carol Davila 107, et. 5, ap. 10–11; tel. (21) 2248058; fax (21) 2233500; e-mail daciafil@dnt.ro; Ambassador NOEL C. CABRERA.

Poland: 71273 Bucharest, Al. Alexandru 23; tel. (21) 2302330; fax (21) 2307832; e-mail ampolemb@mail.flamingo.ro; Ambassador MICHAL KLINGER.

Portugal: 011815 Bucharest 1, Str. Paris 55; tel. (21) 2304136; fax (21) 2304117; e-mail secretariat@embportugal.ro; internet www.embportugal.ro; Ambassador ALEXANDRE VASSALO.

Qatar: 011834 Bucharest, Str. Venezuela 10A; tel. (21) 2304741; fax (21) 2305446; e-mail qtr_ambassador@b.astral.ro; Ambassador ALI SULTAN AL-ZAMAN.

Russia: 71269 Bucharest, Şos. Kiseleff 6; tel. (21) 2223170; fax (21) 2229450; e-mail rab@mb.roknet.ro; Ambassador ALEKSANDR A. TOLKACH.

Saudi Arabia: 010501 Bucharest 1, Str. Polonă 6; tel. (21) 2109109; fax (21) 2107093; Chargé d'affaires AHMAD M. AL-ZUGHAIBI.

Serbia and Montenegro: 71132 Bucharest, Calea Dorobanţilor 34; tel. (21) 2119871; fax (21) 2100175; e-mail ambiug@ines.ro; Ambassador DUŠAN CRNOGORCEVIĆ.

Slovakia: 20977 Bucharest 2, Str. Oţetari 3; tel. (21) 3126822; fax (21) 3122435; e-mail slovakembassy@b.astral.ro; internet www.bucharest.mfa.sk; Ambassador JAN SOTH.

Spain: 71274 Bucharest, Str. Tirana 1; tel. (21) 2339190; fax (21) 2307626; e-mail embespro@mail.mae.es; Ambassador JESÚS ATIENZA SERNA.

Sudan: 70256 Bucharest, Bd. Dacia 71; tel. (21) 2114967; fax (21) 2111217; e-mail sudanbuc@mb.roknet.ro; Ambassador BASHIR MOHAMED EL-HASSAN.

Sweden: 71276 Bucharest, Str. Sofia 5, POB 63–11; tel. (21) 4067100; fax (21) 4067124; e-mail ambassaden.bukarest@foreign.ministry.se; internet www.swedishembassy.ro; Ambassador SVANTE KILANDER.

Switzerland: 010626 Bucharest, Str. Grigore Alexandrescu 16–20; tel. (21) 2061600; fax (21) 2061620; e-mail vertretung@buc.rep.admin.ch; internet www.eda.admin.ch/bucarest; Ambassador FRANÇOIS CHAPPUIS.

Syria: 71114 Bucharest, Bd. Lascar Catargiu 50; tel. (21) 2124186; fax (21) 3129554; e-mail embsyrom@yahoo.com; Chargé d'affaires a.i. MUHAMMAD ABBAS.

Thailand: 020953 Bucharest, Str. Vasile Conta 12; tel. (21) 3110031; fax (21) 3110044; e-mail thaibuh@speedmail.ro; Ambassador Dr WARAWIT KANITHASEN.

Turkey: 71142 Bucharest, Calea Dorobanţilor 72; tel. (21) 2100279; fax (21) 2100407; e-mail bozkir@easynet.ro; Ambassador AHMERT RIFAT OKCUN.

Ukraine: 71132 Bucharest, Calea Dorobanţilor 16; tel. (21) 2116986; fax (21) 2116949; e-mail emb_ro@mfa.gov.ua; Ambassador TEOFIL Y. BAUER.

United Kingdom: 70154 Bucharest, Str. Jules Michelet 24; tel. (21) 2017200; fax (21) 2017299; e-mail press.bucharest@fco.gov.uk; internet www.britishembassy.gov.uk/romania; Ambassador QUINTON QUAYLE.

USA: 70132 Bucharest, Str. Tudor Arghezi 7–9; tel. (21) 2104042; fax (21) 2100395; e-mail infobuch@pd.state.gov; internet bucharest.usembassy.gov; Ambassador NICHOLAS TAUBMAN.

Venezuela: 71312 Bucharest 1, Str. Pictor G.D. Mirea 18; tel. (21) 2225874; fax (21) 2226183; e-mail embavero@kappa.ro; Chargé d'affaires a.i. WOLFGANG GONZALES.

Viet Nam: 73112 Bucharest, Str. C. A. Rosetti 35; tel. (21) 3111604; fax (21) 3121626; e-mail vietrom2005@hotmail.com; Ambassador LE MANH HUNG.

Yemen: 71279 Bucharest, Bd. Aviatorilor 50; tel. (21) 2313272; fax (21) 2307679; Ambassador ALI AHMED M. ALKHALEDI.

Judicial System

In the mid-2000s, in preparation for its anticipated entry into the European Union, Romania was in the process of implementing a programme of judicial reform, with a particular emphasis on guaranteeing the independence of the judiciary.

High Court of Cassation and Justice
(Înalte Curte de Casaţie şi Justiţie a României)

70503 Bucharest 2, Str. Batistei 2; tel. (21) 3137656; fax (21) 3137655; internet www.scj.ro.

The High Court of Cassation and Justice, which was reorganized in June 2004, exercises control over the judicial activity of all courts. It ensures the correct and uniform application of the law. The Court includes sections dealing with: civil and intellectual property law; criminal law; commercial law; and administrative and fiscal regulations.

President: NICOLAE POPA.

ROMANIA

Constitutional Court of Romania
(Curtea Constituţională a României)
76112 Bucharest, Palatul Parlamentului, Calea 13 Septembrie 2, Sector 5; tel. (21) 4022121; fax (21) 3124359; e-mail ccr@ccr.ro; internet www.ccr.ro; f. 1992

President: IOAN VIDA.

COUNTY COURTS AND LOCAL COURTS

The judicial organization of courts at the county and local levels was established by Law 92 of 4 August 1992. In each of the 40 counties of Romania there is a county court and between three and six local courts. The county courts also form 15 circuits of appeal courts, where appeals against sentences passed by local courts are heard, which are generally considered courts of first instance. There is also a right of appeal from the appeal courts to the Supreme Court. In both county courts and local courts the judges are professional magistrates.

Office of the Prosecutor-General
76105 Bucharest 5, Bd. Libertăţii 14; tel. (21) 4102727; fax (21) 3113939; e-mail pg@kappa.ro.

The General Prosecuting Magistracy functions under Law 92 of 4 August 1992. There are prosecuting magistracies operating through each court, under the authority of the Minister of Justice.

Prosecutor-General: ILIE BOTAS.

Religion

In Romania there are 15 religious denominations and more than 400 religious associations recognized by the state. According to census figures, about 87% of the population belonged to the Romanian Orthodox Church in January 1992.

State Secretariat for Religious Affairs: 70136 Bucharest, Str. Nicolae Filipescu 40; tel. (21) 2118116; fax (21) 2109471; e-mail ssc@mediasat.ro; f. 1990; State Sec. LAURENŢIU TĂNASE.

CHRISTIANITY

The Romanian Orthodox Church

The Romanian Orthodox Church is the major religious organization in Romania (with more than 19m. believers) and is organized as an autocephalous patriarchate, led by the Holy Synod and headed by a patriarch. The Patriarchate comprises five metropolitanates, 10 archdioceses and 13 dioceses.

Romanian Patriarchate
(Patriarhia Română)
040163 Bucharest, Al. Dealul Mitropoliei 25; tel. (21) 3374035; fax (21) 3370097; e-mail externe@patriarhia.ro; internet www.patriarhia.ro.

Patriarch, Metropolitan of Munténia and Dobrogea and Archbishop of Bucharest: TEOCTIST (ARĂPAŞU), 70526 Bucharest, Str. Patriarhiei 21; tel. (21) 3372776.

Metropolitan of Banat and Archbishop of Timişoara and Caransebeş: Dr NICOLAE (CORNEANU), 300021 Timişoara, Bd. Constantin Diaconovici Loga 7; tel. (256) 190960; internet www.mitropolia-banatului.home.ro.

Metropolitan of Moldova and Bucovina and Archbishop of Iaşi: Dr DANIEL (CIOBOTEA), 700064 Iaşi, Bd. Ştefan cel Mare şi Sfânt 16; tel. (232) 214771; fax (232) 212656; e-mail iecum@mail.dntis.ro; internet www.mmb.ro.

Metropolitan of Oltenia and Archbishop of Craiova: TEOFAN, 200381 Craiova, Str. Mitropolit Firmilian 3; tel. (251) 415054; fax (251) 418369; e-mail mitrop_teofan@m-ol.ro; internet www.m-ol.ro.

Metropolitan of Transylvania, Crişana and Maramureş and Archbishop of Sibiu: Dr ANTONIE (PLĂMĂDEALĂ), 550179 Sibiu, Str. Mitropoliei 24; tel. (269) 412867.

Archbishop of Alba Iulia: ANDREI , Alba Iulia, Str. Mihai Viteazul 6; tel. (258) 811690; internet www.reintegrare.ro/arhiepiscopie.

Archbishop of Suceava and Rădăuti: PIMEN (ZAINEA), 720034 Suceava, Str. Ion Vodă Viteazul 2; tel. (230) 215796; internet www.arhiepiscopia.assist.ro.

Archbishop of Târgovişte: Dr NIFON (MIHAITA), 130004 Târgovişte, Str. Mihai Bravu 5-8; tel. (245) 211588; e-mail ips-nifon@k.ro.

Archbishop of Tomis: LUCIAN (FLOREA), 900732 Constanţa, Str. Arhiepiscopiei 23; tel. (241) 614257; internet www.arhiepiscopiatomisului.ro.

Archbishop of Vad, Feleac and Cluj: BARTOLOMEU (ANANIA), 400117 Cluj-Napoca, Piaţa Avram Iancu 18; tel. (264) 559010; e-mail nemes@arhiepiscopia-ort-cluj.org; internet www.arhiepiscopia-ort-cluj.org.

The Roman Catholic Church

Roman Catholics in Romania include adherents of the Armenian, Latin and Romanian (Byzantine) Rites.

Bishops' Conference: 10804 Bucharest, via Popa Tatu 68; tel. (21) 3111289; fax (21) 3111591; e-mail b_cazmir@pcnet.ro; f. 1993; Pres. Most Rev. LUCIAN MUREŞAN (Archbishop of Făgăraş and Alba Iulia).

Latin Rite

There are two archdioceses (including one directly subordinate to the Holy See) and four dioceses. At 31 December 2003 there were 1,141,389 adherents of the Latin Rite (about 5.3% of the total population).

Archbishop of Alba Iulia: Most Rev. GYÖRGY-MIKLÓS JAKUBÍNYI, 510010 Alba Iulia, Str. Mihai Viteazul 21; tel. (258) 811689; fax (258) 811454; e-mail albapress@apulum.ro.

Archbishop of Bucharest: Most Rev. IOAN ROBU, 010164 Bucharest, Str. Gen. Berthelot 19; tel. (21) 3158349; fax (21) 3121208.

Romanian Rite

There is one archdiocese and four dioceses. At 31 December 2003 there were 736,606 adherents of the Romanian Rite.

Archbishop of Făgăraş and Alba Iulia: Most Rev. LUCIAN MUREŞAN, 515400 Blaj, Str. Petru Pavel Aron 2; tel. (258) 712057; fax (258) 713602; e-mail mitropoliablaj@albacomp.ro.

Protestant Churches

Baptist Union of Romania: 78152 Bucharest 1, Str. Dîmbovitei 9–11, Sector 6; tel. (21) 2205053; fax (21) 4302942; 1,450 churches; Pres. Pastor VASILE ALEXANDRU TALOŞ.

Evangelical Church of the Augsburg (Lutheran) Confession in Romania: 550185 Sibiu, Str. General Magheru 4; tel. and fax (269) 217864; e-mail ev.landeskon@artelecom.net; founded in the 16th century; comprises some 14,770 mems (2004); mainly of German nationality; Bishop of Sibiu Dr CHRISTOPH KLEIN; Gen. Sec. FRIEDRICH GUNESCH.

Reformed (Calvinist) Church

The Reformed (Calvinist) Church has some 700,000 mems. There are two bishoprics.

Bishop of the Transylvanian Reformed Church District: Rev. GÉZA PAP, 400079 Cluj-Napoca, Str. I. C. Brătianu 51; tel. (264) 197472; fax (264) 195104; e-mail office@reformatus.ro.

Bishop of Oradea: LÁSZLÓ TŐKÉS, 410210 Oradea, Str. J. Calvin 1; tel. (259) 432837; e-mail partium@rdsor.ro; internet www.kiralyhagomellek.ro.

Evangelical-Lutheran Church in Romania: 400105 Cluj-Napoca, Bd. 21 Decembrie 1989, nr 1; tel. (264) 596614; fax (264) 593897; e-mail ph@lutheran.ro; internet www.lutheran.ro; comprises about 27,100 Hungarians, 4,600 Slovaks and 340 Romanians; Superintendent Bishop ZOLTÁN ADORJANI DEZSŐ.

Romanian Evangelical Church (Biserica Evanghelica România): 76207 Bucharest, Str. Carol Davila 68; tel. (21) 4119622; fax (21) 4103652; e-mail ber@fx.ro; internet www.ber.ro.

Unitarian Church in Transylvania: 400105 Cluj-Napoca, Str. 21 Decembrie 9; tel. (264) 593236; fax (264) 595927; e-mail ekt@unitarius.com; internet www.unitarius.com; f. 1568; comprises about 75,000 mems of Hungarian nationality; 125 churches and 30 fellowships; Bishop ÁRPÁD SZABÓ.

Other Christian Churches

Armenian-Gregorian Church: 021042 Bucharest, Str. Armenească 9; tel. (21) 3139070; fax (21) 3121083; e-mail paulbogdan@armenia.com; 3,000 mems; Archbishop TIRAIR MARTICHIAN.

Bulgarian Church: 70014 Bucharest, Str. Doamnei 18, Sector 4; tel. (21) 6135881.

Jehovah's Witnesses: 021468 Bucharest, Str. Teleajen 84, Sector 2; tel. (21) 3027500; fax (21) 3027501; e-mail ormi@zappmobile.ro.

Old Believers' Orthodox Church (Belaya Krinitsa) (Russian Orthodox Old-Rite Church): 810140 Brăila, Str. Zidari 5; tel. (239) 647023; Eastern Orthodox Church of the Old Believers' tradition; 50,000 mems of Russian nationality; Metropolitan LEONTY IZOTOV.

Pentecostal Church: 76252 Bucharest, Str. Carol Davila 81; tel. (21) 2126419; fax (21) 2204303; e-mail cuvadev@fx.ro; f. 1922; 2,455 churches, 525 pastors (Dec. 2001); 450,000 mems; Pres. Rev. RIVIS TIPEI PAVEL; Gen. Sec. Rev. IOAN GURĂU.

Serbian Orthodox Church (Vicariatul Ortodox Sarb): 300085 Timişoara, Piaţa Unirii 4; tel. and fax (256) 130426; some 22,000 adherents; Administrator Bishop LUKIJAN.

ROMANIA

Seventh-day Adventist Church: 72900 Voluntari, Ilfov, Str. Erou Iancu Nicolae 38; tel. (21) 4908590; fax (21) 4908570; e-mail communicatii@adventist.ro; internet www.adventist.ro; f. 1920; 67,000 mems; Pres. of the Union Rev. ADRIAN BOCANEANU; Sec.-Gen. TEODOR HUTANU.

Ukrainian Orthodox Church (Vicariatul Ortodox Ucrainean): 435500 Sighetu Marmației, Str. Bogdan Vodă 12; tel. (262) 511879; some 52,000 adherents.

Union of Brethren Assemblies: 72461 Bucharest, Andronache 60A; tel. and fax (21) 2407865; f. 1925; Pres. MIRCEA CIOATĂ.

BAHA'I FAITH

Baha'i Community: Bucharest.

ISLAM

The Muslim Community comprises some 55,000 members of Turkish-Tatar origin.

Muftiatul Cultului Musulman din Romania: Grand Mufti OSMAN NEGEAT, 900742 Constanța, Bd. Tomis 41; tel. (241) 611390.

JUDAISM

In 1999 there were about 14,000 Jews, organized in some 70 communities, in Romania.

Federation of Jewish Communities: 030202 Bucharest 3, Str. Sf. Vineri 9–11; tel. (21) 3132538; fax (21) 3120869; e-mail asivan@jewish.ro; Chief Rabbi MENACHEM HACOHEN.

The Press

The Romanian press is highly regionalized, with newspapers and periodicals appearing in all of the administrative districts. In 2003 there were a total of 69 daily newspapers and 1,944 periodicals in circulation. In 2002 some 10 newspapers and 207 periodicals were published in the languages of ethnic minorities in Romania, including Hungarian, German, Serbian, Ukrainian, Armenian and Yiddish.

The publications listed below are in Romanian, unless otherwise indicated.

PRINCIPAL DAILY NEWSPAPERS

Adevărul (The Truth): 71341 Bucharest, Piața Presei Libere 1; tel. (21) 2240067; fax (21) 2243612; e-mail redactia@adevarul.kappa.ro; internet www.adevarulonline.ro; f. 1888; daily except Sun.; independent; Dir CHRISTIAN TUDOR POPESCU; circ. 200,000.

Azi (Today): 70101 Bucharest, Calea Victoriei 39A, CP 45–49; tel. (21) 3144215; fax (21) 3120128; e-mail redactie@azi.ro; internet www.azi.ro; f. 1990; independent; Editor-in-Chief ANA MOD.

Cotidianul (The Daily): 020922 Bucharest 2, Bd Carol I 34–36; tel. (21) 3173192; fax (21) 3173124; e-mail rhpress@cotidianul.ro; internet www.cotidianul.ro; f. 1991; daily except Sun.; Editorial Dir DORU BUSCU; Editor-in-Chief CAROL SEBASTIAN; circ. 120,000.

Cronica Română: 013701 Bucharest 1, POB 33, Piața Presei Libere 1, corp. C, etaj 1, camera 31; tel. and fax (21) 3179165; fax (21) 3179169; e-mail webmaster@cronicaromana.ro; internet www.cronicaromana.ro; f. 1992; daily; Dir HORIA ALEXANDRESCU; Editor-in-Chief DAN OLTEANU; circ. 29,000.

Curierul Național (The National Courier): 010024 Bucharest, Str. Cristian Popișteanu 2–4; tel. (21) 3159512; fax (21) 3121300; e-mail curiernational@yahoo.com; internet www.curierulnational.ro; f. 1991; Editor-in-Chief CRISTINA OROVEANU; circ. 55,000.

Dimineață (Morning): Bucharest, Str. Roma 48; tel. (21) 2120337; fax (21) 2120496; e-mail dimineata@kappa.ro; f. 1990; Dir SORIN STEFAN STANCIU.

Evenimentul Zilei (The Event of the Day): 71341 Bucharest, Piața Presei Libere 1; tel. (21) 2226381; fax (21) 2226382; internet www.expres.ro; f. 1991; tabloid; Editor-in-Chief RAZVAN IONESCU; circ. 200,000.

Gazeta Sporturilor (Sports Gazette): Bucharest 1, Șos. Bucuresti—Ploiești 17; tel. (21) 2087460; fax (21) 2087484; e-mail gazeta@gsp.ro; internet www.gazetasporturilor.ro; f. 1924; daily except Sun.; independent; Editor-in-Chief CATALIN TOLONTAN; circ. 50,000.

Jurnalul National (The National Journal): Bucharest 1, Piața Presei Libere 1, Corp. D, etaj 8; tel. (21) 2243701; fax (21) 2243351; e-mail off@jurnalul.ro; internet www.jurnalul.ro; f. 1993; Editor-in-Chief MARIUS TUCĂ; circ. 70,000.

Libertatea (Freedom): 70711 Bucharest, Șos. Fabrica de Glucoza Nr. 5, Sector 2; tel. (21) 2035646; fax (21) 2030830; internet www.libertatea.ro; f. 1989; daily except Sun.; morning paper; Editor-in-Chief ADRIAN HALPERT; circ. 140,000.

România Libera (Free Romania): 71341 Bucharest, Piața Presei Libere 1, Corp. C, etaj 4; tel. (21) 2224770; fax (21) 2232071; e-mail redactia@romanialibera.ro; internet www.romanialibera.ro; f. 1877; daily except Sun.; independent; Editor-in-Chief BOGDAN FICEAC; circ. 100,000.

Ziarul Financiar: 030195 Bucharest, Str. Bărăției 31; tel. (31) 8256235; fax (31) 8256285; e-mail zf@zf.ro; internet www.zf.ro.

Ziua (The Day): 010036 Bucharest, Str. Ion Câmpineanu 4; tel. and fax (21) 3113155; e-mail ziua@ziua.ro; internet www.ziua.net; f. 1930; Dir SORIN ROSCA STANESCU.

DISTRICT NEWSPAPERS

Alba

Unirea (The Union): 510093 Alba Iulia, Str. Decebal 27; tel. and fax (258) 811420; e-mail unirea@unirea-pres.ro; internet www.ziarulunirea.ro; f. 1891; independent; daily except Sun.; Gen. Man. GHEORGHE CIUL; Editor-in-Chief MARIA LUCIA MUNTEANU; circ. 32,000.

Arad

Adevărul (The Truth): 310130 Arad, Bd. Revoluției 81; tel. (257) 213302; fax (257) 280904; e-mail adevarul@arad.ro; f. 1989; independent; daily; Dir DOREL ZAVOIANU; circ. 53,000.

Argeș

Argeșul Liber (Free Argeș): 110177 Pitești, Str. Republicii 88; tel. (276) 30490; e-mail argesul@rdspt.ro; internet www.cotidianul-argesul.ro; f. 1990; independent; daily; Editor-in-Chief MARIN MANOLACHE.

Bacău

Deșteptarea (The Awakening): 600010 Bacău, Str. Vasile Alecsandri 41; tel. (234) 511272; fax (234) 524927; e-mail dsa@desteptarea.ro; internet www.desteptarea.ro; f. 1989; Editor-in-Chief DORIAN POCOVNICU; circ. 50,000.

Bihor

Erdélyi Napló: 400750 Oradea, POB 1320, Of. p. 1.; tel. (264) 420773; fax (259) 417126; e-mail erdelyinaplo@cluj.astral.ro; internet www.hhrf.org/erdelyinaplo; in Hungarian; weekly; Editor-in-Chief LÁSZLÓ DÉNES.

Bistrița-Năsăud

Mesagerul de Bistrița-Năsăud: Str. Ursului 14; tel. (402) 63234688; fax (402) 63234689; e-mail mesagerul@mesagerul.ro; internet www.mesagerul.ro; daily.

Răsunetul (Sound): 420087 Bistrița, Str. Bistricioarei 6; tel. (290) 11684; f. 1990; journal of the National Salvation Front, Bistrița-Năsăud County; Editor-in-Chief VASILE TABĂRĂ.

Botoșani

Monitorul de Botoșani: 710210 Botoșani, Str. Mihail Kogălniceanu 4; tel. (231) 515053; fax (231) 515130; e-mail monitorul@monitorulbt.ro; internet www.monitorulbt.ro; Editor-in-Chief CATALIN MORARU.

Brăila

Libertatea (Freedom): Brăila; tel. (294) 635946; f. 1989; independent; daily; Editor-in-Chief RODICA CANĂ.

Brașov

Bună Ziua Brașov (Good Afternoon Brașov): Brașov, Str. Mihai Kogalniceanu 19, etaj 7; tel. (268) 411073; fax (268) 314692; e-mail bzb@bzb.ro; internet www.bzb.ro; f. 1995; Dir OVIDIU FODOR; circ. 30,000.

Gazeta de Transilvania (Transylvanian Gazette): 2200 Brașov, Str. M. Sadoveanu 3; tel. (268) 8142029; fax (268) 8152927; f. 1838; ceased publication 1946, re-established 1989; daily except Mon.; independent; Editor-in-Chief EDUARD HUIDAN.

Buzău

Opinia (Opinion): Buzău; tel. (238) 412764; fax (238) 711063; internet opinia.buzau.ro; f. 1990; independent; daily; Editor-in-Chief CALIN BOSTAN.

Călărași

Pământul (Free Earth): 8500 Călărași, Str. București 187; tel. (2911) 15840; fax (2911) 313630; f. 1990; socio-political; weekly; Editor-in-Chief GHEORGHE FRANGULEA.

ROMANIA

Caraş-Severin

Timpul (The Times): 1700 Reşiţa, Piaţa Republicii 7; tel. (55) 212739; fax (55) 216709; e-mail redactia@timpul-cs.ro; internet www.timpul-cs.ro; f. 1990; independent daily; Editor-in-Chief GHEORGHE JURMA.

Cluj

Adevărul de Cluj (Truth of Cluj): 401050 Cluj-Napoca, Str. Napoca 16; tel. and fax (264) 597418; e-mail adevcjr@adevarul.cluj.astral.ro; internet adevarul.cluj.astral.ro; f. 1989; daily; independent; Editor-in-Chief ILIE CĂLIAN; circ. 200,000.

Szabadság (Freedom): 400009 Cluj-Napoca, Str. Napoca 16, POB 340; tel. (264) 598985; fax (264) 597206; e-mail szabadsag@szabadsag.dntcj.ro; internet www.szabadsag.ro; f. 1989; Minerva Cultural Assocn (non-governmental organization); daily except Sun.; in Hungarian; online edition in parallel since 1995 (up to 5,000 readers); covers five counties; Editor-in-Chief ÁRON BALLÓ; circ. 10,000.

Constanţa

Cuget Liber (Free Thinking): 900711 Constanţa, Şos. I. C. Brătianu 5; tel. (241) 582120; fax (241) 619524; e-mail office@cugetliber.ro; internet www.cugetliber.ro; f. 1989; independent; daily; Editor-in-Chief ION ŢIŢA CĂLIN.

Covasna

Cuvântul nou (New Word): 4000 Sfântu Gheorghe, Str. Pieţei 8; tel. (240) 2311388; f. 1968; new series 1990; daily except Mon.; Editor-in-Chief DUMITRU MÂNOLĂCHESCU.

Háromszék (Three Chairs): 4000 Sfântu Gheorghe, Str. Presei 8A; tel. (240) 67351504; fax (240) 67351253; e-mail hpress@3szek.ro; internet www.3szek.ro; f. 1989; socio-political; daily; in Hungarian; Editor-in-Chief FARKAS ÁRPÁD.

Dâmboviţa

Dâmboviţa: 0200 Târgovişte, Str. Unirii 32; f. 1990; independent; daily; Editor-in-Chief ALEXANDRU ILIE.

Dolj

Cuvântul Libertăţii (Word of Liberty): 1100 Craiova, Str. Lyon 8; tel. (251) 2457; fax (251) 4141; f. 1989; daily except Sun.; Editor-in-Chief DAN LUPESCU; circ. 40,000.

Galaţi

Viaţa Libera (Free Life): 6200 Galaţi, Str. Domnească 68; tel. (23) 460620; fax (23) 471028; e-mail redactie@viata-libera.galati.ro; internet www.vlg.sisnet.ro; f. 1990; independent; daily; Dir RADU MACOVEI.

Giurgiu

Cuvântul Liber (Free Word): 8375 Giurgiu, Str. 1 Decembrie 1918 60A; tel. (2912) 21227; f. 1990; weekly; Editor-in-Chief ION GAGHII; circ. 10,000.

Gorj

Gorjanul: 1400 Târgu Jiu, Str. Constantin Brâncuşi 15; tel. (2929) 17464; f. 1990; socio-political; daily; Editor-in-Chief NICOLAE BRÎNZAN.

Harghita

Adevărul Harghitei (Truth of Harghita): 4100 Miercurea-Ciuc, Str. Leliceni 45; tel. (266) 171805; fax (266) 172065; e-mail adevarulhr@kabelkon.ro; f. 1990; independent; daily; Editor-in-Chief MIHAI GROZA.

Hargita Népe: Miercurea-Ciuc, Str. Leliceni 45; tel. and fax (266) 171322; e-mail hargitanepe@topnet.to; internet www.topnet.ro/hargitanepe; daily; in Hungarian; Dir LÁSZLÓ BORBELY.

Hunedoara

Cuvântul Liber (The Free Word): 2700 Deva, Str. 22 Decembrie 37A; tel. (256) 211275; fax (256) 218061; e-mail cuvlib@rdslink.ro; internet cuvlibdeva.recep.ro/ziar.htm; f. 1949; daily except Mon.; Editor-in-Chief CORNEL POENAR; circ. 25,000.

Ialomiţa

Tribuna Ialomiţei (Ialomiţa Tribune): 8400 Slobozia, Str. Dobrogeanu-Gherea 2; f. 1969; weekly; Editor-in-Chief TITUS NIŢU.

Iaşi

Evenimentul: 6600 Iaşi, Str. Ştefan cel Mare 4; tel. (232) 112023; fax (232) 112025; e-mail evenimentul@mail.dntis.ro; f. 1991; daily; Editor-in-Chief CONSTANTIN PALADUTA.

Opinia (Opinion): Iaşi 8; tel. (232) 452105; f. 1990; social, political and cultural; daily; Editor-in-Chief VASILE FILIP.

Ziarul de Iaşi: 6600 Iaşi, Str. Smârdan 5; tel. (232) 271271; fax (232) 270415; e-mail ziaruldeiasi@ziaruldeiasi.ro; internet www.ziaruldeiasi.ro; daily.

Maramureş

Bányavidéki Új Szó (Miner's New Word): 4800 Baia Mare, Bd. Bucureşti 25; tel. (262) 274465; fax (262) 432585; e-mail genius@sintec.ro; f. 1989; weekly; in Hungarian; Editor-in-Chief MARIA SZILVESZTER.

Graiul Maramureşului (The Voice of Maramureş): 4800 Baia Mare, Bd. Bucureşti 25; tel. (262) 221017; fax (262) 224871; e-mail graiul@graiul.ro; internet www.graiul.ro; f. 1989; independent; daily except Sun.; Editor-in-Chief AUGUSTIN COZMUŢA; circ. 10,000.

Mehedinţi

Datina (Tradition): 1500 Drobeta-Turnu-Severin, Str. Trâian 89; tel. (2978) 119950; f. 1990; independent; daily; Editor-in-Chief GHEORGHE BUREŢEA.

Mureş

Cuvântul Liber (The Free Word): 4300 Târgu Mureş, Str. Gh. Doja 9; tel. (265) 36636; f. 1990; independent; daily; Editor-in-Chief LAZĂR LADARIU.

Népújság (People's Journal): 540015 Târgu Mureş, Str. Gh. Doja 9; tel. (265) 266780; fax (265) 266270; e-mail nepujsag@e-nepujsag.ro; internet www.hhrf.org/nepujsag; f. 1990; daily; in Hungarian; Editor-in-Chief JÁNOS MAKKAI.

Neamţ

Ceahlăul: 5600 Piatra-Neamţ, Al. Tiparului 14; tel. and fax (233) 625282; f. 1989; daily; Editor-in-Chief VIOREL TUDOSE; circ. 20,000.

Olt

Olt Press: 0500 Slatina, Str. G. Poborau 5; tel. (244) 439441; e-mail oltpress@yahoo.com; f. 1990; fmrly *Glasul Adevărului* (Voice of Truth); 5 a week.

Prahova

Prahova: 2000 Ploieşti, Bd. Republicii 2; tel. (244) 141245; fax (244) 111206; internet www.ziarulprahova.ro; f. 1870; Editor-in-Chief DUMITRU CÂRSTEA; circ. 17,000.

Sălaj

Graiul Sălajului (Voice of Sălaj): 4700 Zalău, Piaţa Unirii 7; tel. (299) 614120; f. 1990; daily; Editor-in-Chief IOAN LUPA.

Szilágyaság (Word from Sălaj): 4700 Zalău, Piaţa Libertăţii 9, POB 68; tel. (299) 633736; f. 1990; organ of Hungarian Democratic Union of Romania; weekly; Editor-in-Chief JÁNOS KUI.

Satu Mare

Ardealul: 3900 Satu Mare; tel. (261) 730661; f. 1990; organ of Christian Democratic National Peasants' Party; weekly; Dir NAE ANTONESCU.

Szatmári Friss Újság: 3900 Satu Mare, Str. M. Viteazu 32; tel. (261) 712024; fax (261) 714654; e-mail szfu@multiarea.ro; internet www.hhrf.org/frissujsag; f. 1990; daily except Sun.; in Hungarian; Editor-in-Chief VERES ISTVÁN.

Sibiu

Tribuna: 550013 Sibiu, Str. Gheorghe Coşbuc 38; tel. (269) 2113333; fax (269) 216603; e-mail red@tribuna.ro; internet www.tribuna.ro; f. 1884; daily; independent; Editor-in-Chief MIRCEA BITU; circ. 17,000.

Suceava

Crai nou: 5800 Suceava, Str. Mihai Viteazul 32; tel. (230) 214723; fax (230) 530285; e-mail redactie@crainou.ro; internet www.crainou.ro; f. 1990; daily; Editor-in-Chief TEODORESCU DUMITRU.

Teleorman

Teleormanul Liber (Free Teleorman): 0700 Alexandria, Str. Ion Creangă 63, jud. Teleorman; tel. (247) 311950; fax (247) 323871;

ROMANIA

e-mail etl@starnets.ro; f. 1990; daily; Editor-in-Chief GHEORGHE FILIP.

Timiş

Renaşterea Bănăţeană: Timişoara, Bd. Revoluţiei 8; tel. (256) 490145; fax (256) 495317; e-mail renasterea@renasterea.ro; internet www.renasterea.ro; f. 1990; daily; independent; tabloid; Editor-in-Chief ADRIAN POP; circ. 19,000.

Timişoara: 1900 Timişoara, Str. Brediceanu 37A; tel. (56) 264546; fax (56) 146170; e-mail timisoara@rdstm.ro; internet www.cotidianultimisoara.ro; f. 1990; daily; Editor-in-Chief OSCAR BERGER.

Tulcea

Delta (The Delta): 8800 Tulcea, Str. Spitalului 4; tel. (2405) 12406; fax (2405) 16616; f. 1885; new series 1990; daily except Mon.; Editor-in-Chief NECULAI AMIHULESEI.

Vaslui

Adevărul (The Truth): 6500 Vaslui, Str. Ştefan cel Mare 79; tel. (2983) 12203; socio-cultural publication; twice weekly; f. 1990; Editor-in-Chief TEODOR PRAXIU.

Vâlcea

Curierul de Vâlcea (Courier of Vâlcea): 1000 Râmnicu Vâlcea, Calea lui Traian 127; tel. (250) 702942; fax (250) 702941; e-mail office@curierul.ro; internet www.curierul.ro; f. 1990; independent; daily except Mon.; commerce; Dir IOAN BARBU.

Vrancea

Milcovul Liber (Free Milcov): 5300 Focşani, Bd. Unirii 18; tel. (237) 614579; fax (237) 613588; f. 1989; weekly; Dir OVIDIU BUTUC.

PRINCIPAL PERIODICALS

Bucharest

22: 70179 Bucharest, Calea Victoriei 120; tel. (21) 3141776; fax (21) 3112208; e-mail r22@r22.sfos.ro; f. 1990; weekly; published by the Group for Social Dialogue; Editor-in-Chief GABRIELA ADAMEŞTEANU; circ. 13,000.

Academia Caţavencu (Dubious Academy): Bucharest 2, Bd. Regina Elisabeta 7–9, et. 6; tel. (21) 4209459; fax (21) 3140258; internet www.catavencu.ro; f. 1991; weekly; satirical; Dir MIRCEA DINESCU; circ. 85,000.

Auto Pro: Bucharest; tel. (21) 4113225; fax (21) 4111043; f. 1994; monthly; motor-vehicles; Editor-in-Chief DAN VARDIE; circ. 50,000.

Bursa: 010804 Bucharest 1, Str. Popa Tatu 7; tel. (21) 3154356; fax (21) 3124556; e-mail marketing@bursa.ro; internet www.bursa.ro; f. 1990; finance; Editor-in-Chief FLORIAN GOLDSTEIN; circ. 35,000.

Capital: Bucharest, Şos. Fabrica de Glucoza 5, Sector 2; tel. (21) 2030802; fax (21) 2425259; e-mail office@capital.ro; internet www.capital.ro; f. 1990; weekly; Editor-in-Chief IONUT POPESCU; circ. 60,000.

Doina: 71341 Bucharest, Piaţa Presei Libere 1; tel. (21) 2223346; fax (21) 2244801; f. 1991; monthly; Dir VASILE TINCU.

Economistul (The Economist): Bucharest, Calea Grivitei 21; tel. (21) 6507820; fax (21) 3129717; f. 1990; daily; Editor-in-Chief IOAN ERHAN.

Contemporanul—Ideea Europeană: 71341 Bucharest, Piaţa Presei Libere 1; tel. (21) 177316; f. 1881; weekly; cultural, political and scientific review, published by the Ministry of Culture and Religious Affairs; Dir NICOLAE BREBAN.

Expres Magazin: Bucharest; tel. (21) 2225119; fax (21) 3128381; independent; weekly; Dir CORNEL NISTORESCU; circ. 98,000.

Familia Moderna (Modern Family): 71341 Bucharest, Piaţa Presei Libere 1; tel. (21) 2223209; fax (21) 2227810; f. 1995; Dir VASILE TINCU.

Femeia Moderna (Modern Woman): 71341 Bucharest, Piaţa Presei Libere 1, Corp. C, etaj 4, Rm 405–408; tel. (21) 2029194; fax (21) 2224801; e-mail redactia@femeia.ro; internet www.femeia.ro; f. 1868; monthly; Dir VASILE TINCU.

Flacăra (The Flame): 71341 Bucharest 1, Piaţa Presei Libere 1; tel. (21) 2243688; fax (21) 2273713; e-mail redactia@flacara21.ro; internet www.flacara21.ro; f. 1911; monthly; Editor-in-Chief ALEXANDRU ARION; circ. 30,000.

Jurnalul Afacerilor (Business Journal): Bucharest, Piaţa Presei Libere 1; tel. (21) 2223760; fax (21) 2230691; f. 1990; Dir MARCEL BARBU; circ. 25,000.

Luceafărul (The Morning Star): 71102 Bucharest, Calea Victoriei 133; tel. (21) 596760; f. 1958; weekly; published by the Writers' Union; Dir LAURENTIU ULICI.

Magazin (The Magazine): Bucharest, Piaţa Presei Libere 1; tel. (21) 2225111; fax (21) 2230866; f. 1958; Dir FILIP DUMITRU.

Magazin istoric (Historical Magazine): 70711 Bucharest, Piaţa Valter Mărăcineanu 1–3; tel. (21) 3126877; fax (21) 3150991; e-mail mistoric@itcnet.ro; internet magazinistoric.itcnet.ro; f. 1967; monthly; review of historical culture; owned by the Cultural Foundation Magazin Istoric; Chief Editor DORIN MATEI; circ. 30,000.

Meridian: Bucharest 2, Laurentiu Claudian 9; tel. (21) 2500030; fax (21) 2501261; e-mail office@libripress.ro; internet www.libripress.ro; f. 1993; monthly; tourism.

Panoramic Radio-TV: 79757 Bucharest, Str. Molière 2–4; tel. (21) 2307501; fax (21) 156992; e-mail micara.dumutrescu@tvr.ro; f. 1990; weekly; Dir STEFAN DIMITRIU; Editor-in-Chief ADRIAN IONESCU; circ. 50,000.

PC World Romania: 71316 Bucharest, Bd. Mareşal Averescu 8–10, Sector 1; tel. and fax (21) 2241132; e-mail pcworld@idg.ro; internet www.pcworld.ro; f. 1993; monthly; computing; Editor-in-Chief BOGDAN LEARSCHI; circ. 15,000.

Revista Română de Statistică (Romanian Review of Statistics): 70542 Bucharest, Bd. Libertăţii 16; tel. (21) 4106744; fax (21) 3124873; e-mail munteanu@cns.kappa.ro; f. 1952; monthly; organ of the National Statistics Commission; Editor-in-Chief NICOLAE GÂRCEAG.

România Literară (Literary Romania): 71102 Bucharest, Calea Victoriei 133; tel. (21) 6506286; fax (21) 6503369; e-mail romlit@romlit.ro; internet www.romlit.ro; f. 1968; as successor to *Gazeta Literară*; weekly; literary, artistic and political magazine; published by the Fundation România Literară (Writers' Union); Dir NICOLAE MANOLESCU; Editor-in-Chief ALEX ŞTEFĂNESCU.

România Mare (Greater Romania): 70101 Bucharest, Calea Victoriei 39A; tel. (21) 6156093; fax (21) 3125396; f. 1990; weekly; independent nationalist; Editor-in-Chief CORNELIU VADIM TUDOR; circ. 90,000.

Romanian Panorama: Bucharest; tel. (21) 2242162; e-mail rps@dial.kappa.ro; f. 1955; monthly; in English, French, German, Russian and Spanish; economy, politics, social affairs, science, history, culture, sport, etc; published by the Foreign Languages Press Group; Dir NICOLAE ŞARAMBEI; circ. 166,000.

Super Magazin: Bucharest, Piaţa Presei Libere 1; tel. (21) 2223323; fax (21) 2226382; f. 1993; Editor-in-Chief GHEORGHE VOICU; circ. 200,000.

Tehnium: 79784 Bucharest, Piaţa Presei Libere 1; tel. (21) 2223374; f. 1970; monthly; hobbies; Editor-in-Chief Ing. ILIE MIHĂESCU; circ. 100,000.

Telecom Romania: Bucharest; tel. (21) 2120340; f. 1994; bi-monthly; networking and telecommunications; Editor-in-Chief ANDREI SAVU.

Tribuna economică (Economic Tribune): 010336 Bucharest, Bd. Magheru 28–30; tel. (21) 2127938; fax (21) 3102934; e-mail tribunae@tribunaeconomica.ro; internet www.tribunaeconomica.ro; f. 1899; weekly; Editor-in-Chief EMILIAN STANCU; circ. 10,000.

Vânătorul şi Pescarul Român (The Romanian Hunter and Angler): 70344 Bucharest, Calea Moşilor 128; tel. (21) 3133863; fax (21) 3136804; e-mail agvpsrom@yahoo.com; f. 1948; monthly review; published by the General Association of Hunters and Anglers; Editor-in-Chief GABRIEL CHEROIU.

Cluj-Napoca

Korunk (Our Time): 400105 Cluj-Napoca, Str. Iaşilor 14; tel. and fax (264) 432154; e-mail korunk@mail.dntcj.ro; internet www.korunk.org; f. 1926; monthly; social review; in Hungarian; Editor-in-Chief LAJOS KÁNTOR; circ. 1,500.

Napsugár (Sun Ray): 401050 Cluj-Napoca, Str. L. Rebreanu 58/28, POB 137; tel. and fax (264) 541323; e-mail napsugar@mail.dntcj.ro; internet www.dntcj.ro/ngos/napsugar; f. 1956; monthly illustrated literary magazine for children aged 7–12 years; in Hungarian; Editor-in-Chief EMESE ZSIGMOND; circ. 17,500.

Szivárvány (Rainbow): 401050 Cluj-Napoca, Str. L. Rebreanu 58/28, POB 137; tel. and fax (264) 541323; e-mail napsugar@mail.dntcj.ro; f. 1980; monthly illustrated literary magazine for children aged 3–6 years; in Hungarian; Editor-in-Chief EMESE ZSIGMOND; circ. 21,000.

Tribuna: 3400 Cluj-Napoca, Str. Universităţii 1; tel. (264) 117548; f. 1884; weekly; cultural review; Editor-in-Chief AUGUSTIN BUZURA.

Iaşi

Cronica: 700037 Iaşi, Str. I. C. Brătianu 22; tel. and fax (232) 262140; e-mail cronica_iasi@yahoo.com; f. 1966; monthly; cultural review; Editor-in-Chief VALERIU STANCU; circ. 5,000.

Timişoara

Orizont (Horizon): 1900 Timişoara, Piaţa Sf. Gheorghe 3; tel. and fax (256) 133376; f. 1949; weekly; review of the Writers' Union (Timişoara branch); Editor-in-Chief MIRCEA MIHAIES.

Târgu Mureş

Erdélyi Figyelö (Transylvanian Observer): 4300 Târgu-Mureş, Str. Primăriei 1; tel. (265) 166910; fax (265) 168688; f. 1958; fmrly Uj Élet; trimestrial; illustrated magazine; in Hungarian; Editor-in-Chief JÁNOS LÁZOK.

Látó (Visionary): Târgu Mureş, Str. Tuşnad 5; tel. (265) 540027; fax (265) 267087; e-mail lato@rdslink.ro; internet epa.oszk.hu/lato; f. 1953; fmrly Igaz Szó; monthly; in Hungarian; literature; circ. 1,000.

NEWS AGENCIES

Mediafax: Bucharest 2, Str. Tudor Arghezi 3 B; tel. (31) 8256100; fax (31) 8256140; e-mail customer@mediafax.ro; internet www.mediafax.ro; f. 1991; largest independent news agency in Romania; Editor-in-Chief CRISTIAN DIMITRIU.

Rompres (Romanian National News Agency): 71341 Bucharest, Piaţa Presei Libere 1; tel. (21) 2228340; fax (21) 2220089; e-mail webmaster@rompres.ro; internet www.rompres.ro; f. 1949; fmrly Agerpres; provides news and photo services to more than 110 subscribers in Romanian media and 40 overseas news agencies; daily news released in English and French; publs news and feature bulletins in English and French; Chamber of Deputies reassumed control in Feb. 2002; Gen. Man. CONSTANTIN BADEA.

Foreign Bureaux

Agence France-Presse (AFP): Bucharest 1, Str. Muzeul Zambaccian 22B, ap. 1; tel. (21) 2312002; fax (21) 2300178; e-mail afp.buc@afp.com; Dir YVES-CLAUDE LLORCA.

Agenzia Nazionale Stampa Associata (ANSA) (Italy): Bucharest; tel. and fax (21) 6335325; f. 1970; Chief Correspondent GIAN MARCO VENIER.

Bulgarska Telegrafna Agentsia (BTA) (Bulgaria): Bucharest; tel. (21) 191880; Correspondent PETYO PETKOV.

Deutsche Presse-Agentur (dpa) (Germany): Bucharest; tel. (21) 121481; fax (21) 123079; Correspondent JOACHIM SONNENBERG.

Dow-Jones News Service: Bucharest 1, Str. Gheorghe Manu 12, etaj 2, Apt 5; tel. (21) 2108197; fax (21) 2103125; Gen. Dir CRISTI CRETZAN.

ITAR—TASS (Information Telegraph Agency of Russia—Telegraphic Agency of the Sovereign Countries) (Russia): Bucharest, Str. Armeneasca 41; tel. (21) 2106050; fax (21) 2107490; e-mail itartass@mb.roknet.ro; Correspondent NIKOLAI N. MOROZOV.

Magyar Távirati Iroda (MTI) (Hungary): 72238 Bucharest, Al. Alexandru 10, ap. 1; tel. and fax (21) 2307741; e-mail mtibuc@pcnet.ro; internet www.mti.hu; Correspondent ISTVÁN GOZON.

Polska Agencja Prasowa (PAP) (Poland): Bucharest; tel. (21) 206870; Correspondent STANISŁAW WOJNAROWICZ.

Reuters (UK): Bucharest; tel. (21) 3158772; fax (21) 6158448.

RIA—Novosti (Russian Information Agency—News) (Russia): 76100 Bucharest, Pandur Hw. 15, Block P18, ap. 6, Sector 5; tel. (21) 4108855; fax (21) 4115812; Correspondent VYACHESLAV SAMOSHIN.

Xinhua (New China) News Agency (People's Republic of China): 71512 Bucharest, Şos. Nordului 2; tel. (21) 2329675; fax (21) 2320258; e-mail xinhua@dial.kappa.ro; Correspondent CHEN JIN.

PRESS ASSOCIATIONS

Society of Romanian Journalists—Federation of All Press Unions (Societatea Ziariştilor din România—Federaţia Sindicatelor din Întreaga Presă): Bucharest, Piaţa Presei Libere 1; tel. (21) 2228351; fax (21) 2224266; f. 1990; affiliated to International Organization of Journalists and to International Federation of Journalists; Pres. RADU SORESCU; 5,000 mems.

The Union of Professional Journalists (Pres. ŞTEFAN MITROI) was established in 1990, as was the Democratic Journalists' Union (Pres. P. M. BACANU). There is also an Association of Hungarian Journalists of Romania (Pres. LAJOS KANTOR).

Publishers

Editura Academiei Române (Publishing House of the Romanian Academy): 050711 Bucharest, Calea 13 Septembrie 13; tel. (21) 4119008; fax (21) 4103983; e-mail edacad@ear.ro; internet www.ear.ro; f. 1948; books and periodicals on original scientific work, 80 periodicals in Romanian and foreign languages; Gen. Man. DUMITRU RADU POPESCU.

Editura Albatros: 013701 Bucharest, Piaţa Presei Libere 1, Of. 33; tel. and fax (21) 2228493; e-mail editura_albatros@yahoo.com; f. 1969; Romanian literature and culture; Editor-in-Chief GEORGETA DIMISIANO.

Editura Artemis (Artemis Publishing House): 71341 Bucharest, Piaţa Presei Libere 1; tel. (21) 2226661; f. 1991; fine arts, fiction, children's literature, history; Dir MIRELLA ACSENTE.

Editura Cartea Românească (Publishing House of the Romanian Book): Bucharest 1, Calea Victoriei 115; tel. (21) 2315237; fax (21) 2244829; e-mail ecr@cartearomaneasca.ro; internet www.cartearomaneasca.ro; f. 1969; Romanian contemporary literature; Dir DAN CRISTEA.

Editura Ceres: 71341 Bucharest, Piaţa Presei Libere 1; tel. (21) 2224836; f. 1953; books on agriculture and forestry; Dir MARIA DAMIAN.

Editura Dacia (Dacia Publishing House): 3400 Cluj-Napoca, Str. Ospatarului 4; tel. and fax (264) 429675; e-mail office@edituradacia.ro; internet www.edituradacia.ro; f. 1969; classical and contemporary literature, science fiction, academic, technical, philosophical and scientific books in Romanian and Hungarian; Gen. Man. IOAN VĂDAN.

Editura Didactică şi Pedagogică (Educational Publishing House): 70738 Bucharest, Str. Spiru Haret 12; tel. and fax (21) 3122885; e-mail edp@totalnet.ro; internet www.edituradp.ro; f. 1951; school, university, technical and vocational textbooks; pedagogic literature and methodology; teaching materials; Gen. Man. Prof. MIHAELA ZĂRNESCU-ENCEANU.

Editura Eminescu (Eminescu Publishing House): Bucharest 2, Intr. Pictor Vermont 1; tel. and fax (21) 3153588; e-mail info@edituraeminescu.com; internet www.edituraeminescu.com; f. 1969; contemporary original literary works and translations of world literature; Dir SILVIA CINCA.

Editura Enciclopedică (Encyclopedic Publishing House): 71341 Bucharest, Piaţa Presei Libere 1; tel. and fax (21) 2243667; f. 1968; merged with Scientific Publishing House, as Editura Ştiinţifică şi Enciclopedică, 1974–90; encyclopedias, dictionaries, bibliographies, chronologies, monographs, reference books and children's books; popular and informational literature; provides photographs and encyclopedic and statistical data about Romania for publishing houses abroad; Dir MARCEL POPA.

Editura Humanitas (Humanitas Publishing House): 79734 Bucharest, Piaţa Presei Libere 1; tel. (21) 2228546; fax (21) 2243632; e-mail editors@agora.humanitas.ro; internet www.humanitas.ro; f. 1990; philosophy, religion, political and social sciences, economics, history, fiction, textbooks, art, literature, practical books; Dir GABRIEL LIICEANU.

Editura Junimea (Junimea Publishing House): 6600 Iaşi, Str. Cuza Vodă 29, POB 28; tel. (232) 117290; f. 1969; Romanian literature, art books, translations, scientific and technical books; Dir CONSTANTIN DRAM.

Editura Kriterion (Kriterion Publishing House): 70002 Bucharest, str. Franceža 6/1; tel. (21) 3146246; e-mail krit@dnt.ro; internet www.kriterion.ro; f. 1969; classical and contemporary literature, reference books in science and art in Hungarian, German, Romanian, Russian, Serbian, Slovak, Tatar, Turkish, Ukrainian and Yiddish; translations in Romanian, Hungarian and German; Dir GYULA H. SZABÓ.

Editura Litera Internaţional (The International Letter Publishing House): Bucharest; tel. (21) 3310660; fax (21) 3303502; e-mail info@litera.ro; internet www.litera.ro; f. 1989; original literature; Dir DAN VIDRASCU.

Editura Medicală SA (Medical Publishing House): Bucharest 2, Bd. Pache Protopescu 131; tel. (21) 2525188; fax (21) 3124879; e-mail ed-medicala@b.astral.ro; internet www.ed-medicala.ro; f. 1954; medical literature; Dir Prof. AL. C. OPROIU.

Editura Meridiane (Meridiane Publishing House): 71341 Bucharest, Piaţa Presei Libere 1; tel. (21) 2243623; fax (21) 2223037; f. 1952; arts, history, biographies, religion, social sciences, cultural studies, media, anthropology, essays, medicine, travel, archaeology, linguistics; Dir ELENA-VICTORIA JIQUIDI; Senior Editors LIVIA SZASZ CÂMPEANU, ANDREI NICULESCU.

Editura Militară (Military Publishing House): 70764 Bucharest, Str. Gen. Constantin Cristescu 3–5; tel. and fax (21) 3112191; f. 1950; military history, theory, science, technics, medicine and fiction; Dir LUCIAN JUMĂTATE.

Editura Minerva (Minerva Publishing House): 041833 Bucharest 4, Bd. Metalurgiei 45–46, OP 42, CP 38; tel. and fax (21) 4610808; f. 1969; Romanian classical literature, world literature, original literary works, literary criticism and history; Dir ONDINE DASCĂLIŢA.

Editura Muzicală (Musical Publishing House): 71102 Bucharest, Calea Victoriei 141; tel. and fax (21) 3129867; e-mail

ROMANIA

editura_muzicala@hotmail.com; f. 1957; books on music, musicology and musical scores; Dir MARIUS VASILEANU.

Editura pentru Turism (Tourism Publishing House): 70161 Bucharest 1, Bd. Gh. Magheru 7; tel. (21) 6145160; f. 1990; tourism; Dir VICTOR CRĂCIUN.

Editura Porto-Franco (Porto-France Publishing House): 6200 Galați, Bd. George Coșbuc 223A; tel. (236) 464602; fax (236) 461204; f. 1990; literary and scientific books, translations; Dir ADRIANA ALDEA.

Editura Scrisul Românesc (Romanian Writing Publishing House): 1100 Craiova, Str. Mihai Viteazul 4; tel. (241) 413763; fax (251) 419506; e-mail scrisulromanesc@topedge.ro; f. 1922; socio-political, technical, scientific and literary works; Dir MARIUS GHICA.

Editura Sport-Turism (Sport-Tourism Publishing House): 79736 Bucharest, Str. Vasile Conta 16; tel. (21) 107480; f. 1968; sport, tourism, monographs, translations, postcards, children's books; Dir MIHAI CAZIMIR.

Editura Științifică (Scientific Publishing House): Bucharest 5, Șos. Panduri 31; tel. and fax (21) 2244014; f. 1990; fmrly Editura Științifică și Enciclopedică; language dictionaries, bibliographies, monographs, chronologies, reference books, popular and informational literature; Dir DINU GRAMA.

Editura Tehnică (Technical Publishing House): 71341 Bucharest, Piața Presei Libere 1; tel. (21) 2228348; fax (21) 2242164; e-mail tehnica@edituratehnica.ro; internet www.tehnica.ro; f. 1950; technical and scientific books, technical dictionaries; Dir ROMAN CHIRILĂ.

Editura Univers: 010209 Bucharest, Str. Ionel Perlea 8; tel. (21) 3110201; fax (21) 2243765; e-mail univers@rnc.ro; f. 1961; translations from world literature, criticism, essays, literary history, philosophy of culture, educational; Dir DIANA CRUPENSCHI.

Editura de Vest (West Publishing House): 1900 Timișoara, Piața Sfântul Gheorghe 2; tel. (256) 18218; fax (256) 14212; f. 1972; as Editura Facla; socio-political, technical, scientific and literary works in Romanian, Hungarian, German and Serbian; Dir VASILE POPOVICI.

Rao International Publishing: 78217 Bucharest, Bd. 1 Mai 125; tel. (21) 2104588; fax (21) 2228059; educational books.

PUBLISHERS' ASSOCIATIONS

Cultura Națională: Bucharest; tel. (21) 6181255; state organization attached to Ministry of Culture; administration, production and distribution of literary magazines and books of national interest; organization of imports and exports.

Romanian Publishers' Assocn (Asociația Editorilor din România): 010326 Bucharest, Bd. Magheru 35, etaj 4, Ap. 42; tel. (21) 2125162; fax (21) 2125178; e-mail info@aer.ro; internet www.aer.ro; f. 1993; 57 mems; Pres. GABRIEL LIICEANU.

WRITERS' UNION

Romanian Writers' Union (Uniunea Scriitorilor din România): 71102 Bucharest, Calea Victoriei 115; tel. (21) 6507245; fax (21) 3129634; f. 1949; Dir NICOLAE BREBAN (acting).

Broadcasting and Communications

TELECOMMUNICATIONS

Regulatory Authority

National Regulatory Authority for Communications (Autoritatea Naționala de Reglementare in Comunicații—ANRC): 050706 Bucharest 5, Bd. Libertății 14; tel. (21) 3075400; fax (21) 3075402; e-mail anrc@anrc.ro; internet www.anrc.ro; f. 2002.

Service Providers

Connex (MobiFon SA): 061344 Bucharest 6, Bd. Vasile Milea 4A; tel. (21) 3021111; fax (21) 3021413; e-mail contact@connex.ro; internet www.connex.ro; f. 1996; operates mobile cellular telephone network and third-generation (GSM) services and provides internet services; in 2005 Vodafone Group Plc (United Kingdom) acquired 79% of MobiFon SA from Telesystem Intl Wireless Inc. (Canada); 99% owned by Vodafone Group Plc; 5.2m. customers (June 2005); Pres. AL TOLSTOY.

Cosmote SA: Bucharest 6, str. Drumul Taberei 47; tel. (21) 4041234; fax (21) 4137530; e-mail info@cosmorom.ro; internet www.cosmorom.ro; f. 2000; fmrly CosmoROM; owned by COSMOTE (Greece); mobile cellular telecommunications services.

Orange Romania SA: Bucharest 1, Bd. Lascar Catargiu 51–53, Europe House; tel. (21) 2033030; fax (21) 2033413; e-mail infocorporate@orange.ro; internet www.orange.ro; f. 1996; fmrly Mobil-Rom; mobile cellular telecommunications services; owned by Orange (France); Exec. Dir PIERRE MATTEI; 5m. subscribers (2005).

Romtelecom SA: 70060 Bucharest 5, Bd. Libertății 14–16; tel. (21) 4001212; fax (21) 4105581; e-mail contact@romtelecom.ro; internet www.romtelecom.ro; f. 1933; joint-stock co; former state monopoly; 54% owned by Hellenic Telecommunications Organization (Greece); Dir-Gen. FLORIN ANGHEL.

Telemobil SA (Zapp): Bucharest, 2B Bis, Balotesti, Jud. Ilfov; tel. (21) 4024444; fax (21) 4024456; internet www.telemobil.ro; f. 1999; operates mobile cellular telephone network; Man. Dir and Chief Exec. DIWAKER SINGH.

BROADCASTING

Radio

Societatea Romăna de Radiodifuziune (SRR) (Romanian Radio Corpn): 70747 Bucharest, Str. Gen. Berthelot 60–64, POB 63-1200; tel. (21) 3031432; fax (21) 3121057; e-mail mesaje@rornet.ro; internet www.srr.ro; f. 1928; 39 transmitters on medium-wave, 69 transmitters on VHF; 114 relays; operates the Radio Romania and Radio Romania International stations: news, cultural, youth and music programmes, plus two local and six regional programmes; foreign broadcasts on one medium-wave and eight short-wave transmitters in Arabic, Bulgarian, Chinese, English, German, Greek, Hungarian, Italian, Portuguese, Romanian, Russian, Serbian, Spanish, Turkish and Ukrainian; Pres. MARIA TOGHINA.

Kiss FM: Bucharest 6, Spl. Independenței 202A; tel. (21) 3188000; fax (21) 3125346; e-mail kissfm@kissfm.ro; internet www.kissfm.ro; owned by SBS Broadcasting Sa.r.l..

Pro FM: Bucharest 2, Bd. Pache Protopopescu 109, etaj 6; tel. (21) 250143O; internet www.profm.ro; f. 1993; owned by Central European Media Enterprises Ltd (CME), Bermuda; Gen. Dir ADRIAN SARBU.

Radio Europa FM: Bucharest 1, Intr. Camil Petrescu 5; tel. (21) 2010500; fax (21) 2010519; e-mail europafm@europafm.ro; internet www.europafm.ro; Gen. Dir ILIE NĂSTASE.

Radio Nord-Est: 6600 Iași, Str. Codrescu 1; tel. and fax (232) 211570; e-mail rneiasi@dntis.ro; f. 1992; independent; Man. MIHAI GRETY.

Societatea Națională de Radiocommunicații, SA (National Radiocommunications Co): 050706 Bucharest 5, Bd. Libertății 14; tel. (21) 3073007; fax (21) 3149798; e-mail info@snr.ro; internet www.snr.ro; f. 1991 through the reorganization of Rom Post Telecom; state-owned; radio and television broadcasting (including digital), high-speed internet and broadband services, video conferencing, satellite communications; 2,445 employees.

Television

Televiziunea Romănă (TVR) (Romanian Television): 015089 Bucharest, Calea Dorobanților 191, POB 63-1200; tel. (21) 2312704; fax (21) 2307514; e-mail tvr@tvr.ro; internet www.tvr.ro; f. 1956; state-owned; public broadcasting service; four channels broadcasting 24 hrs; Pres. and Dir-Gen. TUDOR GIURGIU.

Channel 2 TV Romănă (TVR 2): Bucharest; f. 1992; as a jt venture; 80% owned by Atlantic Television Ltd (UK-Canada), 20% by Radioteleviziunea Romănă; independent commercial channel; Man. Dir ROBIN EDWARDS.

Antena 1: 71561 Bucharest, Șos. București-Ploiești 25–27; tel. (21) 2121844; internet www.antena1.ro; f. 1993; first independent commercial television station.

Prima TV: Bucharest 4, Calea Serban Voda 95–101; tel. (21) 3359341; e-mail focus@primatv.ro; internet www.primatv.ro; f. 1997; owned by SBS Broadcasting SA.

Pro TV: Bucharest 2, Bd. Pache Protopopescu 109, etaj 6; tel. (21) 2505063; fax (21) 2501951; e-mail info@protv.ro; internet www.protv.ro; f. 1995; owned by Central European Media Enterprises Ltd (CME), Bermuda; commercial station; Gen. Dir ADRIAN SARBU.

Realitatea TV: Bucharest, Șos. Dudesti Pantelimon 1–3; tel. and fax (21) 2552665; e-mail office@realitatea.tv; internet www.realitatea.tv; f. 2001; 24 hours; primarily news content.

Finance

(cap. = capital; res = reserves; dep. = deposits; m. = million; amounts in lei, unless otherwise indicated; brs = brs)

BANKING

In April 1997 legislation providing for the privatization of state-owned banks was approved; Banca Romănă Pentru Dezvoltare SA was the first to be sold, in December 1998.

Central Bank

National Bank of Romania (Banca Națională a României): 70421 Bucharest 3, Str. Lipscani 25; tel. (21) 3130410; fax (21) 3123831;

internet www.bnro.ro; f. 1880; central bank and bank of issue; manages monetary policy; supervises commercial banks and credit business; cap. and res 56,247,100m., dep. 243,466,400m. (Dec. 2003); Gov. MUGUR CONSTANTIN ISĂRESCU; 22 brs.

Other Banks

Alpha Bank Romania SA: 712811 Bucharest 1, Calea Dorobanților 237B; tel. (21) 2092100; fax (21) 2316570; e-mail bbr@alphabank.ro; internet www.alphabank.ro; f. 1994; as Banca București SA, present name since 2000; 53.9% owned by Alpha Romanian Holdings AE (Greece), 41.5% owned by Alpha Bank AE (Greece); cap. 1,452,415m., res 1,100,868m., dep. 19,348,005m. (Dec. 2003); Pres. CHRISTOS GIAMPANAS.

Banc Post SA: 761062 Bucharest 5, Bd. Libertății 18–20–22, Bl. 102–103–104; tel. (21) 3361124; fax (21) 3360772; e-mail bpt@bancpost.ro; internet www.bancpost.ro; f. 1991; 36.3% owned by EFG Eurobank Ergasias SA (Greece), 17.0% by Banco Portugues de Investimento SA (Portugal); cap. 2,460,509m., dep. 17,011,789m. (Dec. 2002); Pres., Chair. and Chief Exec. ELENA PETCULESCU.

Banca Comercială Carpatica SA: 550135 Sibiu, Sibiu, Bd. Autogarii 1; tel. (269) 233815; fax (269) 233371; e-mail extern@carpatica.ro; internet www.carpatica.ro; f. 1999; cap. 475,106m., res 248,016m., dep. 1,864,504m. (Dec. 2003); Pres. and Chair. NICOLAE HOANTA.

Banca Comercială 'Ion Tiriac'—Banca Tiriac: 74228 Bucharest, Str. Nerva Traian 3, Complex M101; tel. (21) 302600; fax (21) 3025700; e-mail secrgen@cbit.ro; internet www.bancatiriac.ro; f. 1991; cap. 6,681,832m., res 484,748m., dep. 12,039,495m. (Dec. 2002); Chair. and CEO GHEORGHE MUCIBABICI; 44 brs and sub-brs.

Banca Comercială Robank—Robank SA: 741382 Bucharest 3, Bd. Unirii 59; tel. (21) 3225700; fax (21) 3226885; e-mail office@robank.ro; internet www.robank.ro; f. 1995; cap. 425,904m., res 427,507m., dep. 4,178,567m. (Dec. 2003); Pres. and Chair. MUSTAFA AYAN; 5 brs.

Banca Comercială Română SA—BCR (Romanian Commercial Bank): 70348 Bucharest 3, Bd. Regina Elisabeta 5; tel. (21) 3126185; fax (21) 3122096; e-mail bcr@bcr.ro; internet www.bcr.ro; f. 1990; absorbed operations of Banca Română de Comerț Exterior (BANCOREX) in Oct. 1999; 61.88% owned by Erste Bank (Austria) from Dec. 2005; commercial banking services for domestic and foreign customers; cap. 21,196,925m., res 6,932,592m., dep. 158,187,857m. (Dec. 2003); Pres. and Chair. NICOLAE DĂNILĂ; 372 brs and agencies.

Banca Daewoo (Romania) SA: Bucharest 2, 1/F, International Business Centre, Bd. Carol I 34–36; tel. (21) 2505711; fax (21) 2505831; e-mail daewoo@fx.ro; f. 1996; 99.99% owned by Daewoo Securities Co Ltd (Rep. of Korea); cap. US $11.4m., dep. US $31.7m., total assets US $49.3m. (Dec. 2002); Pres. BUM-SHIK BAE.

Banca de Credit și Dezvoltare (ROMEXTERRA) SA (Bank of Credit and Development): 540447 Târgu Mureș, Mureș, Bd. 1 Decembrie 1918 93; tel. (265) 266640; fax (265) 266047; e-mail info@romexterra.ro; internet www.romexterra.ro; f. 1993; cap. 600,000m., res 378,569m., dep. 3,346,809m. (Dec. 2003); Pres. VASILE IFRIM; 31 brs.

Banca de Export-Import a României—Eximbank SA: 050092 Bucharest 5, Str. Splaiul Independenței 15; tel. (21) 3364185; fax (21) 3366380; e-mail pr@eximbank.ro; internet www.eximbank.ro; f. 1992; 87.4% owned by State Privatization Agency; cap. 9,437,532m., res 7,895,123m., dep. 6,256,782m. (Dec. 2003); Chair. and Chief Exec. CARMEN RADU; 7 brs.

Banca Pentru Mică Industrie și Liberă Inițiativă SA—MINDBANK (Bank for Small Industry and Free Enterprise—MINDBANK SA): 010732 Bucharest 1, Calea Grivitei 24; tel. (21) 3030700; fax (21) 3030732; e-mail mindbank@mindbanksa.ro; internet www.mindbanksa.ro; f. 1990; cap. 370,000m., res 575,101m., dep. 1,300,472m. (Dec. 2004); privately owned; Chair. IOAN PRUNDUS; 12 brs.

Banca Română Pentru Relansare Economica—Libra Bank SA (Romanian Bank for Economic Revival–Libra Bank): 712791 Bucharest 1, Bd. Aviatorilor 46; tel. (21) 2303333; fax (21) 2306565; e-mail libra.bank@librabank.ro; internet www.librabank.ro; f. 1996; cap. 365,000m., dep. 532,960m., total assets 913,755m. (Dec. 2003); Vice-Pres. CRISTINA MAHIKA VOICONI; Vice-Pres. EMILIAN BITULEANU.

Banca Românească SA (Romanian Bank): 70401 Bucharest 3, Bd. Unirii 35, Bloc A3; tel. (21) 3211602; fax (21) 3213624; e-mail office@brom.ro; internet www.brom.ro; f. 1993; 90.9% owned by National Bank of Greece SA (NBG); cap. 1,193,054m., res 84,181m., dep. 4,681,893m. (Dec. 2003); Gen. Man. PETRU RAREŞ.

Banca Transilvania SA (Transylvanian Bank): 400027 Cluj-Napoca, Str. G. Baritiu 8; tel. (264) 407150; fax (264) 407179; e-mail bancatransilvania@bancatransilvania.ro; internet www.bancatransilvania.ro; f. 1994; res. 682,159m. (Dec. 2002); cap.1,869,825m., dep. 10,602,725m. (Dec. 2003); Chief Exec. ROBERT C. REKKERS; 32 brs.

BRD-Groupe Société Générale SA (Romanian Bank for Development): 011171 Bucharest 1, Bd. Ion Mihalache 1–7; tel. (21) 3016100; fax (21) 3016636; e-mail communication@brd.ro; internet www.brd.ro; f. 1990 to replace Investment Bank of Romania (f. 1923); name changed in 2004 from Banca Română Pentru Dezvoltare SA-Groupe Société Générale (BRD); financial and banking services and operations to individual and private and small cos, etc; 51.9% owned by Société Générale (France); cap. 3,484,507m., res 16,628,892m., dep. 51,465,181m. (Dec. 2002); Chair. BOGDAN BALTAZAR; Chief Exec. PATRICK GELIN; 191 brs.

Casa de Economii și Consemnațiuni—CEC SA (Savings and Consignation Bank): 79104 Bucharest 3, Calea Victoriei 13; tel. (21) 3122895; fax (21) 3143970; e-mail office@rsb.ro; internet www.rsb.ro; f. 1864; state-owned; scheduled for privatization; handles private savings, loans for the inter-banking market and mortgages; cap. 1,497,000m., res 1,454,858m., dep. 34,900,455m. (Dec. 2003); Chair. and Chief Exec. EUGEN RADULESCU; 42 brs.

Citibank Romania SA: 011742 Bucharest 1, Bd. Lancu de Hunedoara 8, POB 63-5; tel. (21) 2101850; fax (21) 2101854; internet www.citibank.ro; f. 1996; 99.6% owned by Citigroup Overseas Investment Corpn (USA); cap. 995,039m., dep. 14,763,627m. (Dec. 2003); Pres. and Chair. WITOLD ZIELINSKI.

Finansbank (Romania) SA: 040034 Bucharest 4, Str. Splaiul Unirii 12, Bl. B6; tel. (21) 3017100; fax (21) 3310970; e-mail hoffice@finansbank.ro; internet www.finansbank.ro; f. 1993; adopted present name 2000; 63.6% owned by Finansbank AS (Turkey); cap. 1,118,516m., dep. 3,571,888m., total assets 4,320,209m. (Dec. 2003); Pres. TAMER OZATAKUL.

HVB Bank Romania SA: 011857 Bucharest 1, Piața Charles de Gaulle 15; tel. (21) 2032222; fax (21) 2308485; e-mail contact@ro.hvb-cee.com; internet www.hvb.ro; f. 1997 as Creditanstalt SA; present name adopted 2001; wholly owned by Bank Austria Creditanstalt AG; cap. 362,733.9m., res 325,504.2m., dep. 18,001,740.0m. (Dec. 2002); Pres. and Chair. DAN PASCARIU.

Nova Bank SA: 040231 Bucharest 24, Bd. D. Cantemir 2, Bl. P3, T II; tel. (21) 3363125; fax (21) 3362414; e-mail office@nova-bank.ro; internet www.nova-bank.ro; f. 1997; as Banca Comercială Unirea; cap. 879,539m., res 449,493m., dep. 88,534m. (Dec. 2003); Pres. ANATOLY PATRON; Gen. Man. VALERY TOKSIN.

Piraeus Bank Romania SA: Bucharest 2, Bd. Carol I 34–36, International Business Centre; tel. (21) 3036900; fax (21) 3036900; e-mail cristian.radu@piraeusbank.ro; internet www.piraeusbank.ro; f. 1995; present name adopted 2000; 99.99% owned by Piraeus Bank (Greece); cap. €22.1m., dep. €84.3m., total assets €105.3m. (Dec. 2002); Pres., Chief Exec. and Chair. EMANUEL ODOBESCU; Dir-Gen. SOFRONIS STRINOPOULOS; 3 brs.

Raiffeisen Bank SA: 742141 Bucharest 3, Bd. Mircea Voda 44; tel. (21) 3230031; fax (21) 3236027; e-mail centrala@rzb.ro; internet www.raiffeisen.ro; f. 2002 by merger of Banca Agricola-Raiffeisen SA and Raiffeisenbank (Romania) SA; 99.4% owned by Raiffeisen International Beteiligungs AG (Austria); cap. 6,961,479m., res 11,088m., total assets 26,827,294m.; Pres. STEVEN VAN GRONIGEN.

Romanian International Bank: 70401 Bucharest 3, Bd. Unirii 68, Bloc K2; tel. (21) 3227005; fax (21) 3237272; e-mail office@roib.ro; internet www.roib.ro; f. 1998; privately owned; cap. 320,000m. (Dec. 2003), dep. US $11.4m. (Dec. 2002); Chair. of Bd ION GHICA; 10 brs.

Sanpaolo IMI Bank Romania SA: 310025 Arad, Bd. Revoluției 88; tel. (257) 284888; fax (257) 285998; e-mail headoffice@sanpaoloimi.ro; f. 1996; as Banca Comercială West Bank SA; present name adopted Sept. 2003; 98.4% owned by Sanpaolo IMI SpA (Italy); cap. 748,850m., res 1,888,002m., dep. 23,471m. (Dec. 2002); Pres. GIOVANNI RAVASIO; Gen. Man. MARCO CAPELLINI.

UniCredit Romania SA: 70401 Bucharest 4, Bd. Splaiul Unirii 16; tel. (21) 3015555; fax (21) 3303992; e-mail office@unicredit.ro; internet www.unicredit.ro; f. 1997 as DEMiRBANK Romania SA; name changed as above in 2002; 99.87% owned by UniCredito Italiano SpA (UCI); cap. 1,067,062m., res 149,149m., dep. 5,874,029m. (Dec. 2003); Pres. of Management Bd FAUSTO PETTENI; Chief Exec. SELÇUK SALDIRAK; 15 brs.

BANKING ASSOCIATION

Romanian Banking Association (Asociația Română a Băncilor): Bucharest 3, Str. Sfanta Vineri 34, bl. A6; tel. (21) 3212078; fax (21) 3212095; e-mail arb@arexim.ro; internet www.arb.ro; f. 1991; 40 mems; Chair. RADU GRAȚIAN GHEȚEA; Sec.-Gen. RADU NEGREA.

STOCK EXCHANGE

Bucharest Stock Exchange (Bursa de Valori București): 020922 Bucharest 2, Bd. Carol I 34–36, et. 14; tel. (21) 3079500; fax (21) 3079519; e-mail bvb@bvb.ro; internet www.bvb.ro; f. 1882; reopened 1995 (ceased operations 1948); 128 listed cos; Pres. SERGIU OPRESCU; Gen. Man. STERE FARMACHE.

ROMANIA

COMMODITIES EXCHANGE

Romanian Commodities Exchange (Bursa Română de Mărfuri): 013701 Bucharest 1, Piaţa Presei Libere 1; tel. (21) 2244560; fax (21) 2242878; e-mail bursa@brm.ro; internet www.brm.ro; Pres. MIRCEA FILIPOIU.

INSURANCE

In 2003 there were 46 insurance companies.

Allianz-Tiriac Asigurări: 71139 Bucharest, Cáderea Bastiliei 80–84; tel. (21) 2082222; fax (21) 2082211; e-mail office@allianztiriac.ro; internet www.allianztiriac.ro.

Asigurarea Românéasca SA (ASIROM) (Romanian Insurance): 70332 Bucharest 2, Bd. Carol I 31–33; tel. (21) 2504271; fax (21) 2504145; internet www.asirom.com.ro; f. 1991; following the restructuring of the state insurance monopoly ADAS into three JSCs; 40.55% owned by InterAgro (Romania–UK); all types of insurance, including life insurance; Dir-Gen. ION GHEORGHE BRATULESCU; 41 brs.

Astra SA: 71291 Bucharest 1, Str. Puşkin 10–12; tel. (21) 2318080; fax (21) 2305248; e-mail info@astrasig.ro; internet www.astrasig.ro; f. 1991; following the restructuring of the state insurance monopoly ADAS into three JSCs; Gen. Man. DAN ADAMESCU.

Certasig SA: Bucharest 1, Str. Buzesti 75, et. 1; tel. (21) 3133375; fax (21) 3133376; e-mail office@certasig.ro; internet www.certasig.ro; formerly Fortuna SA, merged with Romanian-Canadian Insurance Co (AROCA) in 2003; insurance and reinsurance; Pres. ROBERT-SARBINIU SERBAN.

ING Asigurări de Viaţa SA: Bucharest 3, Str. Costache Negri 1–5, Opera Centre; tel. (21) 4028580; fax (21) 4028581; e-mail client@ingasigurari.ro; internet www.ingasigurari.ro; f. 1997; life insurance; Gen. Man. BRAM BOON.

Omniasig SA: Bucharest 1, Bd. Aviatorilor 28; tel. (21) 2315040; fax (21) 2315029; e-mail secretary@omniasig.ro; internet www.omniasig.ro; f. 1994; insurance and reinsurance co; 70.7% owned by TBI Financial Services Group (Netherlands); Chair. CONSTANTIN TOMA.

Unita: Bucharest 1, Bd. Dacia 30; tel. (21) 2120852; fax (21) 2120843; e-mail unita@unita.ro; internet www.unita.ro; f. 1990; mem. of Wiener Stadtische Group (Austria); Dir DAN ODOBESCU.

Insurance Association

Uniunea Naţională a Societăţilor de Asigurare şi Reasigurare din România (National Association of Insurance and Reinsurance Companies of Romania): Bucharest 4, Bd. Libertăţii 12, bl. 114, sc. 3, et. 4, ap. 68; tel. (21) 3351269; fax (21) 3372243; e-mail unsar@dnt.ro; internet www.unsar.ro; f. 1994; 22 mems; Pres. CRISTIAN CONSTANTINESCU; Gen. Sec. FLORENTINA ALMAJANU.

Trade and Industry

GOVERNMENT AGENCIES

Agency for Small and Medium Enterprises and Co-operatives (Agenţia Naţionala pentru Întreprinderi Mici şi Mijlocii şi Cooperaţie): Bucharest 4, Str. Poteraşi 11; tel. (21) 3352620; fax (21) 3361843; e-mail mariana.spranceana@mimmc.ro; internet www.mimmc.ro; Pres. EUGEN OVIDIU CHIROVICI.

Authority for the Capitalization of State Assets (Autoritatea pentru Valorificarea Activelor Statului—AVAS): 715151 Bucharest 1, Str. Capt. A. Şerbănescu 50; tel. (21) 3036122; fax (21) 3036521; e-mail infopublic@avas.gov.ro; internet www.apaps.ro; created by merger of the Banking Assets Resolution Agency (AVAB) and the Authority for Privatization and Management of State Ownership (APAPS); successor org. to the State Ownership Fund; Gen. Dir GILIOLA CIORTEANU (acting).

Romanian Agency for Foreign Investment: Bucharest 1, Bd Primaverii 22; tel. (21) 2339103; fax (21) 2339104; e-mail aris@arisinvest.ro; internet www.arisinvest.ro; f. 2002; Pres. ANA-MARIA CRISTINA; Sec.-Gen. FLORIN VASILACHE.

Romanian Development Agency (Agenţia Română de Dezvoltare): 70161 Bucharest, Bd. Magheru 7; tel. (21) 3122886; fax (21) 3120371; f. 1991; promotes foreign investment in Romanian industry; Pres. SORIN FODOREANU.

CHAMBER OF COMMERCE

Chamber of Commerce and Industry of Romania and the Municipality of Bucharest: Bucharest 3, Bd. Octavian Goga 2; tel. (21) 3229536; fax (21) 3229542; e-mail ccir@ccir.ro; internet www.ccir.ro; f. 1868; non-governmental organization; Pres. GHEORGHE COJOCARU.

EMPLOYERS' ASSOCIATIONS

Alliance of Employers' Confederations of Romania (ACPR) (Alianţa Confederaţiilor Patronale din România): Bucharest 3, Str. Octavian Goga 2, floor 10; tel. (21) 3211381; fax (21) 3211443; e-mail office@acpr.ro; internet www.acpr.ro; f. 2004; includes the National Confederation of Romanian Employers (CNPR) and the Employer Confederation of Romanian Industry (CONPIROM) and four others; Pres. GHEORGHE COPOS.

National Confederation of Romanian Employers (Confederaţia Naţională a Patronatului Roman—CNPR): 020982 Bucharest 3, Bd. Octavian Goga 2; tel. (21) 3212074; fax (21) 3212075; e-mail cnpr@untrr.ro; internet www.cnpr.org.ro; Pres. DINU PATRICIU; Dir-Gen. CRISTIAN PARVAN.

Romanian Private Farmers' Federation (Federaţia agricultorilor privatizaţi din România): 70111 Bucharest 1, Bd. Nicolae Bălcescu 17–19; tel. (21) 6131869; fax (21) 6133043; f. 1991; represents 4,000 farming co-operatives and 41 district unions; Pres. GHEORGHE PREDILA.

Union of Romanian Employers (Uniunea Patronatelor din România—UPR): Bucharest; f. 2004; consists of 6 nationally representative employers' organizations; Pres. GHEORGHE CONSTANTIN PĂUNESCU.

UTILITIES

Regulatory Authority

National Energy Regulatory Authority (Autoritatea Nationala de Reglementare in domeniul Energiei—ANRE): 020995 Bucharest 2, Str. Constantin Nacu 3; tel. (21) 3112244; fax (21) 3124365; e-mail anre@anre.ro; internet www.anre.ro; f. 1999; Pres. NICOLAE OPRIS.

National Regulatory Authority for the Natural Gas Sector (Autoritatea Nationala de Reglementare in domeniul Gazelor Naturala—ANRGN): Bucharest 6, Şos. Cotroceni 4; tel. (21) 3033800; fax (21) 3033808; e-mail anrgn@anrgn.ro; internet www.anrgn.ro; f. 2000; Pres. STEFAN COSMEANU.

Electricity

Electrica SA: Bucharest, Str. Grigore Alexandrescu 9, Sector 1; tel. (21) 2085999; fax (21) 2085998; internet www.electrica.ro; f. 2002; following the reorganization of the National Electricity Company CONEL; electricity distributor and supplier; 8 regional branches; two regional branches, Electrica Banat and Electrica Dobrogea, divested to ENEL (Italy) in 2005; 51% of Electric Oltenia was acquired by CEZ (Czech Republic) and 51% in Electric Moldova by E.ON Energie (Germany) in 2005; Electrica Muntenia Sud was scheduled for privatization in 2006; Chair. CRISTIAN ISTODORESCU.

Hidroelectrica SA: 70219 Bucharest, Str. Constantin Nacu 3, Sector 2; tel. (21) 3112231; fax (21) 3111174; e-mail generala@hidroelectrica.ro; internet www.hidroelectrica.ro; state-owned; administers 120 hydropower plants and 4 pumping stations through 10 regional subsidiaries; Gen. Man. EUGEN PENA.

Nuclearelectrica SA: 010494 Bucharest 1, POB 22–102, Str. Polonă 65; tel. (21) 2038200; fax (21) 2119400; e-mail office@nuclearelectrica.ro; internet www.nuclearelectrica.ro; f. 1998; electrical and thermal power generation; production of nuclear fuel; Gen. Dir Dr IOAN ROTARU; 2,308 employees (2003).

Termoelectrica SA: Bucharest, Bd. Lacul Tei 1–3; tel. (21) 3037303; fax (21) 3037503; e-mail office@termoelectrica.ro; internet www.termoelectrica.ro; f. 2000.

Transelectrica SA: 010325 Bucharest 1, Bd Gen. Gh. Magheru 33; tel. (21) 3035600; fax (21) 3035820; e-mail office@transelectrica.ro; internet www.transelectrica.ro; f. 2000; formerly part of the National Electricity Company CONEL; state-owned; transmission system operator of the Romanian power system; includes 8 subsidiaries and OPCOM SA power market operator; Chair. DORIN MUCEA; Gen. Dir JEAN CONSTANTINESCU; 2,140 employees.

Gas

SC DistriGaz Nord SA: 540049 Mureş, Târgu Mureş, Piaţa Trandafirilor 21; tel. and fax (265) 267229; e-mail dgnm@distrigaznord.ro; internet www.distrigaznord.ro; f. 1975; privatized in 2004/05; 51% owned by E.On Ruhrgas (Germany); natural gas distributor.

SC DistriGaz Sud SA: Bucharest 4, Bd. Maraşesti 4–6; tel. (21) 3012000; fax (21) 3012151; e-mail dgnb@distrigazsud.ro; internet www.distrigazsud.ro; privatized 2004/05; 30% owned by Gaz de France (France); natural gas distributor.

SNGN Romgaz SA: 3125 Mediaş, Str. Unirii 4; tel. (269) 801014; fax (269) 841769; e-mail contact@exprogaz.ro; internet www.exprogaz.ro; gas exploration, storage and production; also operates under the name Exprogaz.

SNTGN Transgaz SA: 3125 Mediaş, Str. Unirii 4; tel. (269) 842262; fax (269) 839031; e-mail cabinet@romgaz.ro; internet www.transgaz

.ro; state-owned; exploration, transmission and distribution of natural gas; Pres. and Gen. Dir GABRIEL COCONEA.

TRADE UNIONS

The regulations governing trade unions were liberalized in early 1990. The Uniunea Generală a Sindicatelor din România (UGSR) was dissolved. Several new trade union organizations were established.

National Trade Union Confederation Cartel Alfa (Confederaţia Naţionala Sindicală Cartel Alfa—CNS Cartel Alfa): 060041 Bucharest 6, Spl. Independenţiei 202A, et. 2; tel. (21) 3171040; fax (21) 3123481; e-mail alfa@cartel-alfa.ro; internet www.cartel-alfa.ro; f. 1990; 1m. mems; 38 professional affiliations; Pres. BOGDAN IULIU HOSSU.

Confederation of Democratic Trade Unions of Romania (Confederaţia Sindicatelor Democratice din România—CSDR): Bucharest 1, Piaţa Walter Maracineanu 1–3; tel. (21) 3156542; e-mail csdr@b.astral.ro; f. 1994; 20 professional federations; 640,000 mems; Pres. IACOB BACIU.

National Confederation of Free Trade Unions of Romania 'Brotherhood' (Confederaţia Naţională a Sindicatelor Libere din România Frăţia—CNSLR Frăţia): 010024 Bucharest 1, Str. Cristian Popisteanu 1–3; tel. and fax (21) 3151632; e-mail biroupresa@cnslr-fratia.ro; internet www.cnslr-fratia.ro; merged with the National Trade Union Bloc (Blocul Naţional Sindical—f. 1991) in 2004; 800,000 mems; 44 professional federations; Pres. MARIUS PETCU.

Meridian National Trade Union Confederation (MNTUC) (Confederaţia Sindicala Nationala Meridian): 010366 Bucharest 1, Str. D. I. Mendeleev 36–38; tel. (21) 3168017; fax (21) 3168018; e-mail csnmeridian@csnmeridian.ro; internet www.csnmeridian.ro; f. 1994; 27 br. federations; Gen. Sec. ION ALBU.

Transport

RAILWAYS

In 2003 there were 11,077 km of track in operation (of which 3,965 km were electrified). In September 1998 the Societatea Nationale a Căilor Ferate Române (SNCFR—National Romanian Railway Company) was divided into five companies.

Romanian Railway Authority (Autoritatea Feroviara Româna—AFER): Bucharest 1, Calea Grivitei 393; tel. (21) 3077900; fax (21) 2241832; e-mail secretariat@afer.ro; internet www.afer.ro; f. 1998; under the jurisdiction of the Ministry of Transport, Construction and Tourism; Gen. Dir VASILE BELIBOU.

Company for Railways Assets Management (SAAF): 77113 Bucharest, Bd. Dinicu Golescu 38; tel. (21) 6373252; fax (21) 2227877; Gen. Man. MIRCEA DINU.

National Railways Company for Freight Traffic (CFR Marfa SA): 77113 Bucharest, Bd. Dinicu Golescu 38; tel. (21) 2249336; fax (21) 3124700; e-mail vtulbure@marfa.cfr.ro; f. 1988; after the reorganization of the SNCFR; main railway freight transport operator in Romania; Gen. Man. VASIK TULBURE.

National Passenger Railway Transport Co (CFR Calatori): 77113 Bucharest, Bd. Dinicu Golescu 38; tel. (21) 3190322; fax (21) 4112054; e-mail irina.vlad@cfr.ro; internet www.cfr.ro; f. 1998; divided into eight regional administrations since 1999; reorganized in Feb. 2001 and merged with eight regional companies; operates all local, regional, long-distance and international passenger rail services; Chair. and Chief Exec. ALEXANDRU NOAPTES.

National Railways Company (CFR SA): 010873 Bucharest, Bd. Dinicu Golescu 38; tel. (21) 2223637; fax (21) 3123200; e-mail virgil.daschievici@cfr.ro; internet www.cfr.ro; management of railway infrastructure; Gen. Dir TRAIAN PREOTEASA; 28,936 employees.

Rail Management Services Company (SMF): 77113 Bucharest, Bd. Dinicu Golescu 38; tel. (21) 2233560; fax (21) 6384530; e-mail spopeanga@central.cfr.ro; provides financial, judicial and accounting services; Gen. Man. SILVIA POPEANGA.

City Underground Railway

The Bucharest underground railway network totals 63.5 km in length.

Metrorex SA—Societatea Comercială de Transport cu Metroul Bucureşti: 010873 Bucharest 1, Bd. Dinicu Golescu 38; tel. (21) 2248975; fax (21) 3125149; e-mail contact@metrorex.ro; internet www.metrorex.ro; f. 1977; Gen. Man. MARIUS IONEL LĂPĂDAT.

ROADS

At the end of 2003 there were 79,001 km of public roads, of which 15,122 km were national roads and 63,879 km secondary roads. Under the 1991–2005 road development programme, more than 3,000 km of motorways were to be built and 4,000 km of existing roads were to be modernized (by 2003 20,368 km of roads had been modernized). The Bucharest–Constanţa motorway was to be completed by the end of 2006, as part of the pan-European Corridor IV project, the 800-km Romanian stretch of which (connecting Nadlac on the western border with the Black Sea coast) was scheduled to be completed by 2011, at a cost of some €5,000m. A project to construct the Braşov–Bors motorway was also under way.

National Administration of Roads (Regia Autonomă Administraţia Naţională a Drumurilor—AND): Ministerul Transporturilor, 77113 Bucharest 1, Bd. Dinicu Golescu 38, Rm 55; tel. (21) 2232606; fax (21) 3120984; Dir-Gen. Dr Ing. DANILA BUCSA.

INLAND AND OCEAN SHIPPING

Navigation on the River Danube is open to shipping of all nations. The Danube–Black Sea Canal was officially opened to traffic in 1984, and has an annual handling capacity of 80m. metric tons. The first joint Romanian-Yugoslav Iron Gates (Porţile de Fier) power and navigation system on the Danube was completed in 1972, and Iron Gates-2 opened to navigation in 1984. Romania's principal ports are at Constanţa, on the Black Sea; and Tulcea, Galaţi, Brăila and Giurgiu, on the Danube. In 1995 Romania launched its first ferry service to Turkey, operating between Constanţa and Samsun. In 2004 Romania's merchant fleet had 221 vessels, with a combined aggregate displacement of 426,700 grt. Of the River Danube, 1,075 km flowed through Romanian territory, with 524 km of secondary branches and 64km of canals; the total length of canals in the country was some 132 km.

Galaţi Corpn for the Administration of the Lower Danube (Regia Autonomă Administraţia Fluvială a Dunării de Jos Galaţi): 6200 Galaţi, Str. Portului 28–30; tel. (236) 460812; fax (236) 460847; Gen. Man. MIHAI OCHIALBESCU.

National Co for the Administration of the Maritime Port of Constanţa SA: 8700 Constanţa, Portului Incinta, Gara Maritima; tel. (241) 611540; fax (241) 619512; e-mail apmc@constantza-port.ro; internet www.constantza-port.ro; f. 1991; also administrates Midia, Mangalia and Tomis ports; Gen. Man. GHEORGHE MOLDOVEANU.

National Co for the Administration of Maritime Ports on the Danube: 6200 Galaţi, Str. Portului 34; tel. (236) 460660; fax (236) 460140; Gen. Man. ALEXANDROS GALIATATOS.

National Co for the Administration of Navigable Canals SH: 8700 Constanţa, Str. Ecluzei Agigea 1, POB 93; tel. (241) 738505; fax (241) 639402; e-mail compania@acn.ro; internet www.acn.ro; fmrly Constanţa Corpn for Navigable Channels; Gen. Man. SEVASTIAN STEFAN.

National Co for the Administration of River Ports on the Danube: 8375 Giurgiu, Şos. Portului 1; tel. (246) 213003; fax (246) 3110521; e-mail apdf@infogrup.pcnet.ro; internet www.intelsev.ro/apdf; f. 1998; Gen. Man. CRISTIAN NEMTESCU.

NAVROM—Romanian Shipping Co: 8700 Constanţa, Portului Incinta; tel. (241) 615166; fax (241) 618413; organizes sea transport; operates routes to most parts of the world; Gen. Man. MANEA GHIOCEL.

Petromin Shipping Co: Constanţa, Portului Incinta, Poarta 2; tel. (241) 617802; fax (241) 619690; e-mail office@petromin.cunet.ro; merchant fleet of 30 ships and tankers; Chair. ANDREI CARAIANI.

Romline: 8700 Constanţa, Poarta 2 Hostel; tel. (241) 617285; fax (241) 615647; f. 1990; merchant shipping company.

CIVIL AVIATION

There are two international airports at Bucharest: Aurel Vlaicu International (at Băneasa, renamed in 2004) and the largest, Henri Coandă International (at Otopeni, also renamed in 2004). There are other international airports at M. Kogălniceanu-Constanţa (which is also a military airbase), Timişoara, Sibiu and Cluj-Napoca. Airports at Arad, Oradea, Bacau and elsewhere provide domestic connections for international flights.

Romanian Civil Aeronautic Authority (Regia Autonomă Autoritatea Aeronautică Civilă Română): 715621 Bucharest, District 1, Şos. Bucureşti-Ploieşti 38–40; tel. (21) 2081508; fax (21) 2081572; internet www.caa.ro; Gen. Man. AURELIAN BOTEZATU.

Angel Airlines: 712961 Bucharest, Str. 18 Amiral Constantin Basescu; tel. (21) 2315944; fax (21) 2315947; internet www.angelairlines.ro; f. 2001; scheduled domestic flights; Chair. and Chief Exec. KHOSRO AZAD.

Carpatair: Bucharest, 1 Dr Iacob Felix 55; tel. (21) 3130308; fax (21) 3130500; internet www.carpatair.com; f. 1998; as Veg Air, assumed present name in 1999; scheduled domestic and regional flights to Hungary, Italy and Moldova; Pres. NICOLAE PETROV.

Jaro International: Bucharest, Str. Batistei 11; tel. (21) 2123013; fax (21) 2115820; f. 1990; private charter airline; Pres. and Dir-Gen. MIRICA DIMITRESCU.

ROMANIA

Liniile Aeriene Române (LAR) (Romanian Airlines): 70733 Bucharest, Şos. Ştirbei Vodă 2–4; tel. (21) 3153206; fax (21) 3120148; e-mail dorin@baneasa.biz; f. 1975; by Tarom to operate passenger charter services; re-established as independent airline in 1990; Man. Dir DORIN IVAŞCU.

Romavia Romanian Aviation Co: 75121 Bucharest, Bd. Dimitrie Cantemir 1; tel. (21) 3301160; fax (21) 3301049; f. 1991; owned by Ministry of National Defence; state VIP and chartered and scheduled passenger and cargo flights; Man. Dir IULIU-ADRIAN GOLEANU.

Tarom—Compania Nationala de Transporturi Aeriene Române SA: 79154 Bucharest, Şos. Bucureşti–Ploieşti, km 16.5, Otopeni Airport; tel. (21) 2322494; fax (21) 3125686; e-mail secrgen@tarom.ro; internet www.tarom.ro; f. 1954; joint-stock company; services throughout Europe, the Middle East, Asia and the USA and domestically; Pres. GHEORGHE RACARU.

Tourism

The Carpathian Mountains, with their numerous painted monasteries, the Danube delta and the Black Sea resorts (Mamaia, Eforie, Mangalia and others) are the principal attractions. In 2003 there were 5.6m. foreign tourist arrivals, and receipts from tourism totalled US $523m.

National Tourism Authority: 70663 Bucharest 1, Bd. Dinicu Golescu 38; tel. (21) 3149957; fax (21) 3149960; e-mail promovare@mturism.ro; internet www.romaniatravel.com; govt org.; Pres. IULIU MARIAN OVIDIU.

THE RUSSIAN FEDERATION

Introductory Survey

Location, Climate, Language, Religion, Flag, Capital

The Russian Federation, or Russia, constituted the major part of the USSR, providing some 76% of its area and approximately 51% of its population in 1989. It is bounded by Norway, Finland, Estonia and Latvia to the north-west and by Belarus and Ukraine to the west. The southern borders of European Russia are with the Black Sea, Georgia, Azerbaijan, the Caspian Sea and Kazakhstan. The Siberian and Far Eastern regions have southern frontiers with the People's Republic of China, Mongolia and the Democratic People's Republic of Korea. The eastern coastline is on the Sea of Japan, the Sea of Okhotsk, the Pacific Ocean and the Barents Sea, and the northern coastline is on the Arctic Ocean. The region around Kaliningrad (formerly Königsberg in East Prussia), on the Baltic Sea, became part of the Russian Federation in 1945. Separated from the rest of Russia by Lithuania and Belarus, it borders Poland to the south, Lithuania to the north and east and has a coastline on the Baltic Sea. The climate of Russia is extremely varied, ranging from extreme Arctic conditions in northern areas and much of Siberia to generally temperate weather in the south. The average temperature in Moscow in July is 19°C (66°F); the average for January is –9°C (15°F). Average annual rainfall in Moscow is 575 mm (23 ins). The official language is Russian, but many other languages are also used. Christianity is the major religion, mostly adhered to by ethnic Russians and other Slavs, with the Russian Orthodox Church (Moscow Patriarchate) the largest denomination. The main concentrations of adherents of Islam are among the Tatar, Bashkir and Chuvash peoples of the Middle Volga, and the peoples of the northern Caucasus, including the Chechen, Ingush, Kabardins and the peoples of Dagestan. Buddhism is the main religion of the Buryats, the Tyvans and the Kalmyks. The large pre-1917 Jewish population has been depleted by war and emigration, but there remained some 230,000 Jews in the Russian Federation in 2002, according to provisional results of the census. The national flag (proportions 2 by 3) consists of three equal horizontal stripes of (from top to bottom) white, blue and red. The capital is Moscow (Moskva).

Recent History

By the late 19th century the Russian Empire extended throughout vast territories in eastern Europe, and included much of northern and central Asia, a result of the territorial expansionism of the Romanov dynasty, which had ruled Russia as an autocracy since 1613. Growing dissatisfaction with economic conditions in urban areas, combined with the adverse effect of defeats in the Russo–Japanese War (1904–05) led Tsar Nicholas (Nikolai) II (1894–1917) to issue a manifesto in October 1905, which promised respect for civil liberties and the introduction of some constitutional order, although the ensuing attempt at reforms failed to placate the increasingly restive workers and peasants. In 1917 there were strikes and demonstrations in the capital, Petrograd (as St Petersburg had been renamed in 1914). In March 1917 the Tsar was forced to abdicate and a liberal Provisional Government, composed mainly of landowners, took power. However, most real authority lay with the soviets (councils), composed largely of workers and soldiers, which were attracted to socialist ideas.

The inability of the Provisional Government, led first by Prince Georgii Lvov and then by the moderate socialist Aleksandr Kerenskii, to implement land reforms, or to effect a withdrawal from the First World War, allowed more extreme groups, such as the Bolshevik faction of the Russian Social Democratic Labour Party (RSDLP), led by a prominent interpreter of Marxist theory, Vladimir Ulyanov (Lenin), to foster support among disaffected soldiers and workers. On 7 November 1917 (25 October in the Old Style calendar, which remained in use until February 1918) the Bolsheviks, who had come to dominate the Petrograd Soviet, seized power in the capital, with minimal use of force, and proclaimed the Russian Soviet Federative Socialist Republic (RSFSR or Russian Federation). The Bolsheviks subsequently adopted the name All-Russian Communist Party (Bolsheviks).

The Bolsheviks asserted that they would respect the self-determination of the former Empire's many nations. Poland, Finland and the Baltic states (Estonia, Latvia and Lithuania) achieved independence, but other independent states established in 1917–18 were forced, militarily, to declare themselves Soviet Republics. These were proclaimed as 'independent' socialist republics, in alliance with the RSFSR, but the laws, Constitution and Government of the Federation were supreme in all of them. This recentralization of power was recognized as politically damaging by the Bolsheviks. Thus, in 1922 the RSFSR joined the Belarusian, Ukrainian and Transcaucasian republics as constitutionally equal partners in a Union of Soviet Socialist Republics (USSR, or Soviet Union), and institutions of the RSFSR were re-formed as institutions of the new Union. The USSR eventually numbered 15 constituent Soviet Socialist Republics (SSRs). Moscow, the RSFSR's seat of government since 1918, became the capital of the USSR.

The RSFSR, in common with the other republics, experienced hardship as a result of the collectivization campaign of the early 1930s and the widespread repression under Iosif Dzhugashvili (Stalin), who established a brutal dictatorship after the death of Lenin in 1924. The Five-Year Plans, introduced in the late 1920s, effected rapid industrialization, a process that was reinforced by the removal of strategic industries from the west of the republic to the Ural regions during the Second World War (or 'Great Patriotic War'), which the USSR entered in 1941. Under the Nazi-Soviet Treaty of Non-Aggression (the 'Molotov-Ribbentrop Pact') of August 1939, the USSR annexed the Baltic states as well as other territories. Victory in the war in 1945 led to further territorial gains for the Russian Federation. In the west it gained part of East Prussia around Königsberg (now Kaliningrad) from Germany, a small amount of territory from Estonia and Latvia and those parts of Finland annexed during the Soviet–Finnish War (1939–40). In the east it acquired the Kurile Islands from Japan. The nominally independent People's Republic of Tuva (Tyva), situated between the USSR and Mongolia, was annexed in 1944. In 1954 the peninsula of Crimea was ceded by the Russian Federation to the Ukrainian SSR.

Shortly after the death of Stalin in 1953, Nikita Khrushchev took over the post of First Secretary of the Communist Party of the Soviet Union (CPSU—as the Communist Party had been renamed in 1952), and gradually assumed predominance over his rivals. The most brutal aspects of the regime were ended, and in 1956 Khrushchev admitted the existence of large-scale repression under Stalin. Khrushchev was dismissed in 1964. He was replaced as First Secretary (later General Secretary) of the CPSU by Leonid Brezhnev. During the 1970s relations with the West, which had, since the late 1940s, been generally characterized by the intense mutual hostility of the 'Cold War', experienced a considerable *détente*; however, this was ended by the Soviet invasion of Afghanistan in 1979. Brezhnev's successor as CPSU General Secretary, following his death in 1982, was Yurii Andropov. He was succeeded upon his death, in February 1984, by Konstantin Chernenko, who, however, died in March 1985.

Chernenko's successor as General Secretary was Mikhail Gorbachev, a proponent of gradual political and economic reform. A policy of *glasnost* (openness) provided a greater degree of freedom for the mass media. In November 1987, however, supporters of *perestroika* (restructuring), as Gorbachev's reform programme was known, seemed to suffer a reverse, with the dismissal from the Politburo (the executive committee of the CPSU) of Boris Yeltsin, after he severely criticized the apparent conservatism of senior members of the leadership. In June 1988 Gorbachev announced plans for the introduction of a two-tier legislature, elected largely by competitive elections. In elections to the new USSR Congress of People's Deputies, held in March 1989, many reformist politicians, including Yeltsin, were successful in achieving election. In May the Congress elected Gorbachev to the new post of executive President of the USSR.

Within the USSR the RSFSR was clearly pre-eminent, both economically and politically, and ethnic Russians dominated the Soviet élite. However, this prominence meant that Russia developed few autonomous institutions. The initial stage in the process of instituting Russian sovereignty was the election of the RSFSR Congress of People's Deputies in March 1990 by largely free and competitive elections. In May the Congress elected Yeltsin to the highest state post in the RSFSR, the Chairman of the Supreme Soviet (the permanent working body of the Congress). On 12 June the Congress adopted a declaration asserting the sovereignty of the RSFSR in which the federation laws had primacy over all-Union legislation. Thereafter, the political, cultural and scientific institutions that Russia had lacked began to be established.

In March 1991, when a referendum was held in nine republics to determine whether a restructured USSR should be retained, voters in the RSFSR also approved an additional question on the introduction of a Russian presidency. A direct presidential election, held in June, was won by Yeltsin and his Vice-President, Aleksandr Rutskoi, with 57.3% of the votes cast.

On 19 August 1991, one day before the new union treaty was due to be signed, the conservative communist 'State Committee for the State of Emergency' (SCSE), led by the Soviet Vice-President, Gennadii Yanayev, seized power in Moscow, taking advantage of Gorbachev's absence from the city. The coup d'état collapsed within three days, and Yeltsin asserted control over all-Union bodies, appointing RSFSR ministers to head central institutions.

In October 1991 Yeltsin announced a programme of radical economic reforms. In November a new Government was announced, with Yeltsin as Chairman (Prime Minister). The CPSU was banned. In November 1991 the Congress granted Yeltsin special powers for one year, including the right to issue decrees with legislative force and to appoint government ministers without parliamentary approval, and elected Ruslan Khasbulatov, hitherto First Deputy Chairman of the Supreme Soviet, to succeed Yeltsin as Chairman.

On 8 December 1991 the leaders of Belarus, Ukraine and Russia announced the annulment of the 1922 Union Treaty creating the USSR; the Commonwealth of Independent States (CIS, see p. 201), defined as a co-ordinating organization, was created in its place. The CIS was formally established by the Alma-Ata (Almaty) Declaration, signed on 21 December 1991. Of the former Soviet republics, only Georgia, Estonia, Latvia and Lithuania remained outside the new body. (Georgia acceded to the CIS in December 1993.) On 25 December 1991 Gorbachev resigned as President of the USSR, and the Russian Supreme Soviet formally changed the name of the RSFSR to the Russian Federation.

Politics in the Russian Federation in the early 1990s was characterized by heightened tensions between the legislature and the executive. In June 1992 Yeltsin appointed Yegor Gaidar, an advocate of radical economic reform, as acting Chairman, and in the same month the Supreme Soviet adopted legislation permitting large-scale privatization. In December the Congress of People's Deputies refused to endorse Gaidar's nomination, and Yeltsin was forced to appoint a new, substantially less reformist premier, Viktor Chernomyrdin. Following the annulment, in March 1993, of an agreement on constitutional reform by the Congress, Yeltsin announced that he would rule by decree prior to the holding of a referendum on a draft constitution, which was held on 25 April 1993. A question on confidence in Yeltsin as President received a positive response from 57.4% of voters, while 53.7% of voters expressed support for Yeltsin's socio-economic policies. Support for early presidential elections was only 49.1%, but 70.6% of voters favoured early elections to the Congress of People's Deputies.

By mid-1993 Vice-President Rutskoi, while nominally remaining Vice-President, had been divested of his official responsibilities by Yeltsin. In July the Constitutional Conference approved a draft that provided for a presidential system with a bicameral parliament—the Federalnoye Sobraniye (Federal Assembly)—comprising a lower chamber (Gosudarstvennaya Duma—State Duma) and an upper chamber (Sovet Federatsii—Federation Council); however, the Congress of People's Deputies rejected this draft. The long-standing impasse between the presidential administration and the legislature eventually resulted in violent confrontation. On 21 September Yeltsin suspended the Congress of People's Deputies and the Supreme Soviet, and scheduled elections to the Federalnoye Sobraniye for December. The Supreme Soviet consequently voted to dismiss Yeltsin as President, announcing the appointment of Rutskoi in his place; an emergency session of the Congress of People's Deputies confirmed this appointment, and voted to impeach Yeltsin. On 27 September government troops surrounded the parliament building: some 180 deputies remained inside, with armed supporters. Conflict erupted in early October, as supporters of the rebel deputies attempted to seize control of strategic buildings in Moscow, and Yeltsin declared a state of emergency in the capital. On 4 October army tanks bombarded the parliament building, forcing the surrender of the rebels. The leaders of the rebellion were imprisoned, and subsequently charged with inciting 'mass disorder'. According to official figures, 160 people were killed in the fighting.

In the immediate aftermath of the rebellion, Yeltsin briefly suspended several parties that had supported the conflict, including the Communist Party of the Russian Federation (CPRF), which had been founded in early 1993. Yeltsin cancelled a proposed presidential election in 1994, announcing that he would remain in office for the duration of his mandate, until June 1996.

The new draft constitution, which strengthened the powers of the President, was submitted to a referendum on 12 December 1993, held concurrently with elections to the Federalnoye Sobraniye. Of the 54.8% of the registered electorate that participated in the plebiscite, 58.4% endorsed the draft. In the elections to the Gosudarstvennaya Duma, Vladimir Zhirinovskii's nationalist Liberal Democratic Party of Russia (LDPR) secured a total of 64 seats, the largest number obtained by any single party or alliance. (Of the 450 members of the lower chamber, 225 were elected by proportional representation on the basis of party lists, and 225 within single-member constituencies.) Russia's Choice, an alliance of pro-reform groups, led by Gaidar, secured 58 seats. The CPRF took 48 seats, while the Agrarian Party of Russia (APR) won 33 seats. With the ensuing alignment of parties and the 130 independents into parliamentary factions, Russia's Choice emerged as the largest group in the Duma, although no coherent pro-Government majority was established. The Sovet Federatsii was to comprise two representatives from each of Russia's 89 federal subjects (as the constituent territories of the Federation were known), although in December representatives were not elected in the separatist republics of Tatarstan and Chechnya, owing to a voter boycott. The majority of the Council's members were non-partisan republican or regional leaders. A new Government was appointed in January 1994. In February the Duma voted in favour of granting amnesties to Rutskoi, Khasbulatov and other leaders of the 1993 rebellion, as well as to the SCSE.

In October 1994 a sudden decline in the value of the rouble prompted the resignation or dismissal of government members and the Chairman of the Central Bank, Viktor Gerashchenko. In November the reformist Anatolii Chubais, who had hitherto been responsible for the privatization programme, was promoted to the post of First Deputy Chairman, although other government appointments appeared to advance those opposed to further economic liberalization.

In late 1994 Russia commenced military intervention in the separatist Chechen Republic (Chechnya); an apparent lack of progress there, together with the continued deterioration of the economy, were instrumental in the approval by the Duma, in June 1995, of a motion expressing 'no confidence' in the Government. Yeltsin subsequently dismissed a number of ministers, and in July a second vote of 'no confidence' (as required by the Constitution) failed to secure the necessary majority.

Elections to the Duma took place on 17 December 1995. In accordance with a new electoral law, which introduced a minimum requirement of 5% of the votes cast for seats allocated on the basis of party lists, only four parties (the CPRF, the LDPR, Chernomyrdin's Our Home is Russia—OHR and the liberal Yabloko) secured representation on this basis, while an additional 10 parties and 77 independent candidates obtained seats through voting in single-member constituencies. Overall, the CPRF emerged as the largest single party in the Duma, with 157 of the 450 deputies, although its ability to achieve a majority in the legislature depended on the support of the APR and of smaller parties and independent deputies. OHR won 55 seats, the LDPR 51 and Yabloko 45.

In January 1996 Yeltsin dismissed Chubais as First Deputy Chairman. In the same month the Duma elected Gennadii Seleznev, a CPRF deputy, as its Chairman. In the first round of presidential voting, held on 16 June, and contested by 10 candidates, Yeltsin, with 35.8% of the votes cast, narrowly defeated Gennadii Zyuganov (of the CPRF), with 32.5%. Gen. Aleksandr Lebed, who had until recently commanded Russian forces in the separatist Transnistria region of Moldova, was placed third, with 14.7%. Since neither had received the 50% of the votes required for outright victory, Yeltsin and Zyuganov proceeded to a second round of voting. Yeltsin subsequently appointed Lebed as Secretary of the Security Council and National Security Adviser, and granted him particular responsibility for resolving the crisis in Chechnya. Despite increasingly infrequent public appearances, apparently a result of poor health, Yeltsin was re-elected as President in the second ballot, on 3 July, with 54% of the total votes cast. Chernomyrdin was subsequently re-appointed as premier, and Chubais was promoted to head the Presidential Administration. Despite the successful negotiation of a cease-fire agreement in Chechnya in August, in October Yeltsin dismissed Lebed. In November Yeltsin underwent heart surgery, re-assuming full presidential duties in late December, although he was again hospitalized shortly afterwards, and there was growing pressure for his resignation.

Although Yeltsin delivered a vehement criticism of the Government in his annual address to the Federalnoye Sobraniye in March 1997, in a subsequent government reorganization Chernomyrdin retained his post, thereby avoiding the need to seek parliamentary approval of the new, broadly reformist, cabinet. Chubais was appointed First Deputy Chairman and Minister of Finance, and Boris Nemtsov was appointed as First Deputy Chairman, with responsibility for dismantling state monopolies, particularly in the areas of fuel and energy; a priority of reforms was to increase tax revenue in order to settle wages' and pensions' arrears. (In March some 2m. people had participated in demonstrations protesting at the non-payment of wages and pensions.) In November Nemtsov lost the fuel and energy portfolio, and Chubais was dismissed as Minister of Finance, although both retained their posts as First Deputy Chairmen.

A cabinet reshuffle in January 1998 significantly consolidated Chernomyrdin's authority. Yeltsin, whose erratic behaviour during several overseas tours had again given rise to concerns about his health, had been absent from public life in late 1997. In late March 1998 Yeltsin removed Chernomyrdin from office. The Duma confirmed the appointment of Sergei Kiriyenko, the hitherto Minister of Fuel and Energy, as Chairman in mid-April. Several ministers, including Nemtsov, retained their portfolios in the new Government formed during April–May. Chubais, meanwhile, was appointed Chairman of the electricity monopoly, Unified Energy System of Russia. An attempt by the CPRF to initiate impeachment charges against Yeltsin was ruled unconstitutional by a parliamentary commission in late July. In mid-August, however, the Duma succeeded in approving a resolution demanding the voluntary resignation of Yeltsin.

In August 1998 mounting political instability was exacerbated by severe economic difficulties. The value of the rouble declined rapidly. Yeltsin dismissed Kiriyenko and his Government, re-appointing Chernomyrdin as Chairman. However, Chernomyrdin's candidacy to the premiership was twice rejected by the Duma. In mid-September Yeltsin (aware that should his candidate be rejected for a third time he would be constitutionally obliged to dissolve the Duma) nominated Yevgenii Primakov (Minister of Foreign Affairs since 1996, and a former Director of the Foreign Intelligence Service) as Chairman, a candidacy that was endorsed by a large majority.

In May 1999 Yeltsin dismissed Primakov. Sergei Stepashin, hitherto First Deputy Chairman and Minister of Internal Affairs, was appointed as Chairman, and a new Government was formed later in the month. However, Yeltsin dismissed Stepashin in August. Later in the month the Duma endorsed his replacement by Vladimir Putin, a former colonel in the Soviet Committee for State Security (KGB), First Deputy Chairman of St Petersburg City Government in 1994–96, and hitherto head of the Federal Security Service (FSB) and Secretary of the Security Council.

Following a number of incursions by Chechen militants into the neighbouring Republic of Dagestan in August 1999, tensions resurfaced relating to the unresolved status of Chechnya and the emergence there, from the mid-1990s, of militant Islamist groups. Moreover, Putin attributed to Chechen militant groups a series of bomb explosions in Moscow, in Dagestan and in Rostov Oblast, which took place in August–September, killing more than 300 people. Citing the threat posed by militants in the separatist republic, Putin announced that military action was to recommence and, prior to the large-scale deployment of ground troops, the aerial bombardment of Chechnya began on 23 September.

In the months preceding Duma elections in December 1999 several new political alliances were formed; in August Fatherland-All Russia (FAR) was formed by the merger of the centrist party of the Mayor of Moscow, Yurii Luzhkov, with a grouping of regional governors. In September a pro-Government bloc, Unity, was formed under the leadership of Sergei Shoigu, the civil defence and emergencies minister, while Kiriyenko and Nemtsov were among the leaders of a new pro-market bloc, the Union of Rightist Forces (URF).

Some 29 parties and blocs contested the elections to the Gosudarstvennaya Duma on 19 December 1999, in which 62% of the electorate participated. Six parties obtained representation on the basis of party lists; a further eight parties and blocs, and 106 independent candidates, secured representation from single-member constituency ballots. The CPRF, with 24.3% of the votes, again obtained the largest number of seats, although its quota of 113 deputies was significantly smaller than that achieved in the 1995 elections. Unity, which received 23.3% of the votes cast, was the second largest party in the Duma, with 72 seats. FAR won 67 seats, the URF 29, the Zhirinovskii bloc (chiefly comprising the LDPR) won 17 seats, and Yabloko 21.

On 31 December 1999 Boris Yeltsin unexpectedly resigned as President. Putin assumed the presidency in an acting capacity. He granted Yeltsin immunity from prosecution, and removed from office principal members of Yeltsin's administration. When the new Duma convened in mid-January 2000, the CPRF and Unity factions formed an alliance; thus, for the first time since the dissolution of the USSR, pro-Government forces held a majority in the legislature.

Putin received 52.9% of the votes cast in the presidential election held on 26 March 2000, having received the support of FAR, as well as Unity. His closest rival was Zyuganov, of the CPRF, with 29.2%. Putin was inaugurated as President on 7 May. In mid-May Mikhail Kasyanov, hitherto First Deputy Chairman and Minister of Finance, was approved as Chairman of the Council of Ministers, and a new Government was appointed shortly afterwards.

Concerns regarding the freedom of the media in Russia were heightened following the presidential approval in September 2000 of a new information doctrine and by the severe restrictions imposed over coverage of the conflict in Chechnya. Meanwhile, Vladimir Gusinskii, the owner of the Mediya-Most holding company (which included Russia's only wholly independent national television broadcaster, NTV), was arrested in June and charged with fraud. Although all charges were withdrawn in late July, ostensibly owing to a lack of evidence, Gusinskii fled to Spain. In September the state-controlled gas monopoly, Gazprom (to which Mediya-Most was heavily indebted), brought charges of criminal embezzlement against Mediya-Most's management. Gusinskii lost control of the company in November, and the deal reached with Alfred Kokh, the head of the Gazprom subsidiary, Gazprom-Mediya, effectively gave the State a controlling stake in all Mediya-Most enterprises, with the exception of NTV. In December the Moscow fiscal authorities demanded that Mediya-Most be closed, on grounds of insolvency, and Gusinskii, for the arrest of whom an international warrant had been issued, was detained in Spain in the same month. Following the refusal of the Spanish authorities to extradite Gusinskii to Russia, in April 2001 he took up residence in Israel (where he held dual citizenship), purportedly in an attempt to complicate extradition procedures. None the less, Russia issued a fresh warrant for Gusinskii's arrest, on charges of money 'laundering' (the processing of illegally obtained funds into legitimate accounts). In October 2003, following Gusinskii's arrest in Greece, a Greek court ruled against his extradition to Russia.

Meanwhile, other prominent businessmen were subjected to examinations of their business affairs, in what was interpreted as an attempt by the Government to reduce the powers of the 'oligarchs', as a number of wealthy businessmen, who in many cases had acquired control of formerly nationalized industries in the 1990s, were widely known. (Unconfirmed reports alleged that an informal agreement had been reached between Putin and several leading 'oligarchs', in accordance with which possible past irregularities in business activities would not be investigated by the authorities, subject to the condition that the business executives concerned refrained from overt political activity.) In July 2000 Boris Berezovskii, a prominent business executive and former Deputy of the Security Council and Executive Secretary of the CIS (who had played a major role in promoting Putin's candidacy as President), relinquished his seat in the Duma and, therefore, his immunity from prosecution, accusing Putin of having adopted an increasingly authoritarian style of governance. (Berezovskii later resigned from Unity.) In

September Berezovskii announced his intention to relinquish his 49% of shares in the state-controlled television station, ORT, claiming that he had received an ultimatum that he should surrender his holding to the state or risk imprisonment; the sale finally took place in February 2001. None the less, a warrant for Berezovskii's arrest was issued in November 2000, after he failed to return to Russia from France to answer questions relating to charges of money laundering and illegal entrepreneurship in a case which, having been closed in late 1999, had recently been reopened.

Putin introduced significant changes to regional governance during 2000. In May, as part of measures intended to promote structures of 'vertical power', seven Federal Okrugs (Districts) were created, each of which was headed by a presidential appointee, to whom regional governments and governors were to be answerable. A new consultative body, the State Council, comprising the heads of the federal subjects, was created by presidential decree in September; participation in the Council was, however, to be voluntary.

In mid-March 2001 the Duma rejected a motion of 'no confidence' in the Government, proposed by Zyuganov. In late March Putin implemented a minor ministerial reshuffle, appointing Boris Gryzlov, the head of the Unity faction in the Duma, as Minister of Internal Affairs, and Sergei Ivanov (hitherto Secretary of the Security Council and a former deputy head of the FSB) as Minister of Defence. In April it was announced that the Unity faction in the Duma was, henceforth, to form an alliance with FAR, in preference to the CPRF; it was subsequently announced that Unity and FAR were to merge.

Meanwhile, in early April 2001 NTV was acquired by Gazprom-Mediya. Following the dismissal of NTV's management, Yevgenii Kiselyev, the company's former Director-General and Editor-in-Chief, was appointed to head a small television channel owned by Berezovskii, TV6, to which the majority of the former NTV journalists transferred. Moreover, the staff at the two newspapers published by Mediya-Most were dismissed and the publications closed. Later in the year Berezovskii, who remained outside Russia, announced the formation of a political party, Liberal Russia. Meanwhile, in July the legislature approved a new law, which banned foreign citizens, as well as those Russians holding dual citizenship, from acquiring a majority stake in Russian television channels.

In July 2001 Putin signed a law imposing new conditions on political parties; henceforth, parties would be required to have a minimum of 10,000 members, including no fewer than 100 members in at least 50 of the 89 federal subjects, in order to be permitted to participate in elections. At the beginning of December the first congress of Unity and Fatherland-United Russia (subsequently known simply as United Russia—UR), the successor to FAR and Unity, marked the formal establishment of the party, which held a majority of seats in both parliamentary houses. Although not a member of that party or of any other, Putin attended the founding congress.

In January 2002 TV6 ceased transmissions, following a court case brought by a minority shareholder, a subsidiary of the state-controlled petroleum company LUKoil, which had demanded the television company's liquidation on the grounds of unprofitability. Suggestions that the ruling may have been at least partly motivated by political considerations were heightened at the beginning of January by the repeal of the law under which the case had been brought. In late March it was announced that a new, non-profit organization, Mediya-Sotsium, associated with Primakov, had been awarded the contract to broadcast formerly held by TV6; Kiselyev and many journalists from that station transferred to the new channel, which commenced operations under the name TVS. Meanwhile, Berezovskii presented a video-recording in London, United Kingdom, which purported to demonstrate the FSB's involvement, and Putin's acquiescence, in the apartment block bombings of mid-1999; although 100 copies of the recording were confiscated by Russian customs authorities in March, the programme was broadcast at meetings held by Liberal Russia (support for which remained negligible) in several cities.

Meanwhile, in January 2002 a new session of the Sovet Federatsii opened, with a reformed composition. In place of regional leaders and chairmen of regional legislative assemblies, the Council comprised their full-time appointees, who were obliged to surrender their commercial interests during their term of office; the formation of political factions and groups in the Council was to be prohibited. (Sergei Mironov, an ally of Putin, had been elected as Chairman of the Council in December 2001.)

In March 2002 the Duma voted to remove the deciding vote in the governing body of the chamber, the Duma Council, from the Chairman, CPRF deputy Seleznev. In early April the Duma voted to revoke seven of the nine committee chairmanships held by the CPRF.

In October 2002 Berezovskii was charged, *in absentia*, with defrauding the state. In November the Russian authorities requested Berezovskii's extradition from the United Kingdom, where he was resident. (In March 2003 Berezovskii was arrested in London, in response to the extradition request. In September of that year he was granted political asylum, and the extradition proceedings were dismissed.) Meanwhile, in mid-October 2002, following the publication of an interview in a nationalist journal in which Berezovskii appeared to support the formation of a united opposition front by liberal and left-wing forces, he was suspended from Liberal Russia; one week later the Ministry of Justice agreed to register the party, which had hitherto been denied registration on several occasions.

Meanwhile, in late October 2002, following the deaths of at least 129 people as the result of an armed siege at a Moscow theatre by heavily armed militants, linked to Chechen extremists (see below), the Government implemented a number of personnel changes in Chechnya, and in mid-November Stanislov Ilyasov, hitherto the Prime Minister of Chechnya, was appointed to the federal Government as Minister without Portfolio, responsible for the Social and Economic Development of the Chechen Republic.

On 11 March 2003 presidential decrees provided for a reorganization of the federal security agencies, as a result of which additional powers were transferred from various other organs of state to the FSB and to the Ministry of Internal Affairs. In mid-April one of the co-chairmen of Liberal Russia, Sergei Yushenkov, was assassinated in Moscow (another deputy of the party, Vladimir Golovlev, had been murdered in August 2002); in June 2003 a party member, Mikhail Kodanev, was arrested on suspicion of involvement in the killing of Yushenkov, along with three others. (In late March 2004 Kodanev was sentenced to 20 years' imprisonment for organizing the assassination; the three other suspects each received custodial sentences of between 11 and 20 years.) Concerns about press freedom were heightened by the closure, in late June, of TVS by the Ministry of the Press, Broadcasting and Mass Media, purportedly as a result of financial difficulties experienced by the station, the broadcasts of which were replaced by a newly established, state-controlled sports channel.

Meanwhile, on 18 June 2003 the Duma failed to approve a motion of 'no confidence' in the Government that had been presented by the CPRF and Yabloko factions. Meanwhile attacks against civilian targets by militants associated with Chechen separatist, or Islamist, rebels continued to occur, particularly in regions of southern Russia near Chechnya and in Moscow. In July at least 18 people were killed following two suicide bombings at a music festival near Moscow. In early September two bombs exploded under a passenger train in southern Russia, killing at least six people and injuring 40 others, and a suicide bombing, in early December, on another train killed at least 42 people, and injured some 200 others. On 9 December, two days after the legislative elections (see below), a suicide bombing in central Moscow resulted in at least six deaths. In early February 2004 at least 39 people were killed and more than 100 injured in a further bomb attack on a train on the Moscow Metro.

During the latter half of 2003 several court cases and judicial investigations were instigated against senior officials of the prominent privately owned petroleum company, Yukos, and its subsidiary companies. Speculation mounted that the investigations into the company were, at least in part, politically motivated, as the chief executive of the company, Mikhail Khodorkovskii (who was believed to be the wealthiest person in Russia) had recently announced that he was providing financial support to Yabloko and the URF. On 25 October Khodorkovskii was arrested by FSB officers; he was subsequently charged with tax evasion and fraud, and imprisoned pending further investigations. At the end of the month it was announced that a significant stake in the company had been 'frozen' by the authorities. (In early November Khodorkovskii resigned as head of Yukos, and at the end of the month it was announced that the proposed merger of Yukos with another prominent petroleum company, Sibneft, had been suspended.) On 30 December 2003 charges of tax evasion worth US $3,300m. were brought against Yukos.

Elections to the Duma, held on 7 December 2003, were contested by 32 parties and blocs. Only four of these groupings received the minimum 5% share of votes cast required to obtain representation on the basis of federal party lists: UR obtained an absolute majority of seats in the new legislature, with 226 seats, while the representation of the CPRF, with 53 seats, was considerably less than in the outgoing chamber. The LDPR obtained 38 seats, while a recently formed electoral bloc, Motherland—People's Patriotic Union (Motherland), which comprised several communist and nationalist groups, received 37 seats. Nine other groups and 57 independent deputies achieved representation in the new Duma on the basis of constituency voting. The failure of the URF and Yabloko to obtain representation on the basis of proportional representation (the two parties obtained around 8% of the votes between them, and a total of seven deputies) was regarded as a serious reverse for the parliamentary representation of pro-Western reformists. The URF, Yabloko and the CPRF alleged that electoral fraud had been perpetrated, and electoral observers of the Organization for Security and Co-operation in Europe (OSCE, see p. 327) expressed concern that UR, which had become increasingly identified with the presidential administration, had benefited from the use of state administrative resources, including the state-controlled media, in support of the party. Moreover, several members of the Government held senior positions in UR, in apparent defiance of a constitutional clause prohibiting ministers from holding membership of political parties, and the party had effectively received the endorsement of Putin on several occasions. Gryzlov, the Chairman of the Supreme Council of UR, was elected as the Chairman of the Duma on 24 December. (He was replaced as Minister of Internal Affairs by Col-Gen. Rashid Nurgaliyev.) UR rapidly consolidated its position in the Duma, obtaining the chairmanship and first deputy chairmanship of every parliamentary committee.

Campaigning for the presidential election held on 14 March 2004 was characterized by an absence of credible challengers to Putin, who contested the election as an independent candidate, and refused to participate in televised debates with other candidates. The CPRF nominated Nikolai Kharitonov, a relatively obscure figure, as its candidate, while the LDPR candidate was Oleg Malyshkin, who had limited political experience or support. The URF's refusal to endorse the presidential candidacy of one of its leading members, Irina Khakamada, obliged her to campaign as an independent candidate; Khakamada and Nemtsov both subsequently announced their resignations from the URF. Meanwhile, the presidential candidacy of Sergei Glazyev, an economist who had been regarded as the principal instigator of the Motherland electoral bloc, failed to obtain the support of any of its constituent parties, and he was therefore obliged to campaign as an independent candidate. Mironov also contested the election, as the candidate of his party, the Russian Party of Life, but none the less expressed support for Putin's candidacy. (A further candidate, Ivan Rybkin, an ally of Berezovskii, withdrew his candidacy in early March, after he had apparently been taken hostage in Ukraine for several days, in circumstances that remained obscure.) Meanwhile, the leader of Yabloko, Grigorii Yavlinskii, announced that his party was to boycott the presidential election. On 24 February Putin dismissed the Government, and on 1 March Putin announced the nomination of Mikhail Fradkov, hitherto the permanent representative of Russia to the European Communities, as the new Chairman of the Government. The appointment of Fradkov, widely regarded as a 'technocrat', without significant political support of his own, was subsequently approved by the Duma, and on 9 March the formation of a new Government was announced; the number of ministers was significantly reduced to 17, compared with 31 in the outgoing administration. Although most of the principal positions within the Government remained unchanged, a new Minister of Foreign Affairs, Sergei Lavrov, hitherto ambassador to the UN, was appointed.

On 14 March 2004 Putin was re-elected, as had been widely anticipated, for a second, and, in accordance with the Constitution, final term of office, receiving 71.3% of the votes cast. His nearest rival, Kharitonov, received 13.7%, while Glazyev, the third-placed candidate, obtained just 4.1% of the votes. The rate of participation was 64.4%. Putin's inauguration took place on 7 May.

Violent attacks on Russian civilians, attributed to extremist Chechen separatists, culminated in a series of incidents in mid-2004, which intensified following the assassination of the President of the Republic in May (see below). On 24 August two passenger planes, both flying from Moscow's Domodedovo airport, crashed within minutes of each other, killing all 89 people on board. Both crashes were subsequently attributed to Chechen suicide bombers. On 31 August, two days after a presidential election in Chechnya, an explosion outside a Moscow Metro station killed 10 people. On 1 September, the first day of the school year, armed militants occupied a school in Beslan, in the Republic of North Osetiya—Alaniya, taking at least 1,100 children, parents and teachers hostage. On 3 September troops stormed the building, reportedly in reaction to a series of explosions. Some 350 hostages, including 186 children, died in the ensuing battle, according to official figures. The siege was characterized by conflicting information and uncertainty regarding the number of hostages, the number of casualties, the sequence of events leading to the storming of the school, and the number, ethnicity and demands of the hostage takers, although the militant Chechen leader, Shamil Basayev, subsequently claimed responsibility for the hostage-taking operation.

Apparently in reaction to this event, President Putin announced a series of proposed political reforms, which he argued would serve further to unify and strengthen the country. Chief among these reforms was the introduction of a system whereby all regional governors would be appointed by the federal president, subject to the approval of the appropriate regional legislature. (Directly elected governors had become almost universal across the subjects of the Russian Federation in the second half of the 1990s.) Moreover, in the event that the regional legislature rejected the candidate, the president could submit another, or re-submit the original candidate; if the candidate were once more rejected, the federal president would have the power to dissolve that regional legislature and appoint an interim head of administration. Putin signed legislation to this end on 12 December, following its approval by both chambers of the Federalnoye Sobraniye. The final scheduled gubernatorial election in the Federation took place on 6 February 2005, and during 2005 numerous regional governors were appointed in accordance with the new system, several governors having resigned in order to seek an expression of confidence from the federal President; by the end of the year the majority of incumbent governors reaching the expiry of their mandate or seeking a new mandate had been approved for a further term, although, notably, several new regional leaders were appointed in several of the ethnic republics of the North Caucasus, which had been subject to increasing insecurity in the previous months (see below). Putin also announced proposals that all 450 members of the Duma be elected on the basis of proportional representation and party lists. Moreover, the minimum membership required of a political party for it to be eligible for registration was to be increased from 10,000 to 50,000; this requirement was to take effect from January 2006. The quota for representation in the Duma on the basis of federal party lists was also to be increased from 5% of the total votes cast to 7%. Putin also announced plans to establish a new public body with recommendatory powers, the Civil Chamber, which was to be composed of 126 representatives of civil society; the first 42 members of this body (those appointed directly by the President) took up office when the Chamber was inaugurated, in early October 2005. Draft legislation providing for extraordinary powers to be granted to the state and security services in the event of the declaration of a 'state of terrorist danger' was also approved by the Duma in December, pending further discussions.

Meanwhile, in June 2004 the trial of Khodorkovskii and his business associate Platon Lebedev, chairman of the Menatep financial group, began in Moscow, on seven charges, which included tax evasion, forgery and fraud. While the trial was in progress, the Russian authorities presented Yukos with a series of demands for unpaid taxes for 2000–03, totalling some US $27,500m. In order that this sum be paid, the authorities demanded that the principal production subsidiary of Yukos, Yuganskneftegaz, be brought to auction. Yuganskneftegaz was sold for $9,350m. to a previously unknown company, Baikalfinansgrup, which was acquired by Rosneft shortly after the auction. Yukos protested that its subsidiary had been sold for one-half of its true value, and sought to obtain damages for this allegedly illegal sale in the USA; a court in Houston, Texas (in which state Yukos had a subsidiary company, and where the company had filed for bankruptcy protection), however, rejected the case in February, ruling that it did not possess jurisdiction in the matter. Meanwhile, in closing statements in late March, the prosecution in the trial of Lebedev and Khodorkovskii demanded sentences of 10 years' imprisonment for the accused; defence

THE RUSSIAN FEDERATION

lawyers began their closing statements on 1 April. At the end of May both Khodorkovskii and Lebedev were sentenced to nine years' imprisonment, having each been found guilty of six charges, including tax evasion and embezzlement. (These sentences were confirmed on appeal in September.)

Meanwhile, in January 2005 a series of demonstrations took place across Russia in protest at the introduction of social welfare reforms, most notably the replacement of pensioners' entitlements to free public transport and medicine with a system of monetary payments. Opposition parties attempted to use this expression of public unrest to their advantage, and CPRF leader Zyuganov launched an unsuccessful vote of 'no confidence' in the Government in the Duma in mid-February. Putin subsequently stated that mistakes had been made in the implementation of the reforms, and several conciliatory measures were announced.

In mid-March 2005 it was announced that an assassination attempt against Chubais had been thwarted; the suspected instigator of the attack, who was reported to be a radical nationalist, was brought to trial later in the year. In late June two men received long custodial sentences for their roles in the murder in 1998 of Galina Starovoitova, a prominent liberal deputy and human rights activist; however, it was not established whether the killing had been motivated on political grounds, or in relation to Starovoitova's investigations into corruption and corporate crime. In mid-July 2005 a criminal investigation, on charges of corruption related to the illicit acquisition of a state property, was opened against former Chairman of the Government Kasyanov, amid widespread speculation that the charges were politically motivated, as Kasyanov had become an increasingly outspoken critic of various policies recently implemented by Putin; in mid-September Kasyanov announced that he intended to contest the presidential election scheduled for early 2008. Meanwhile, liberal-democratic and pro-Western opposition to the Putin administration was increasingly expressed by the '2008 Free Choice Committee', led by the former international chess champion, Garri Kasparov, which sought to ensure that the election held in that year would be free and fair. (Putin repeatedly rejected speculation that he intended to seek a third term of office, in defiance of the Constitution, or that he would amend the Constitution to ensure that he retained substantial powers after 2008.)

On 14 November 2005 President Putin announced a government reshuffle. Dmitrii Medvedev, the Chairman of the Board of Directors of Gazprom and hitherto Chief of the Presidential Staff, was appointed to the newly created post of First Deputy Chairman (Medvedev was, additionally, to retain his position at Gazprom). Sergei Ivanov, while retaining his responsibilities as Minister of Defence, was additionally to serve as one of two Deputy Chairmen of the Government. Medvedev was replaced as Chief of the Presidential Staff by Sergei Sobyanin, hitherto Governor of Tyumen Oblast, one of the principal natural resource-producing regions of Russia. New appointments were also made to two of the seven presidential representatives to the federal okrugs; notably, former premier Sergei Kiriyenko was dismissed as the representative in the Volga Federal Okrug.

A major focus of parliamentary activity during the second half of 2005 was the development of measures intended to result in greater government supervision and regulation of civil society and non-governmental organizations (NGOs); at least in part, demands for increased control in these areas (which would further be promoted by the establishment of the Civil Chamber, inaugurated in October) had evolved in response to apparent concern that the so-called 'colour revolutions' that had taken place in Georgia in 2003, Ukraine in 2004 and Kyrgyzstan earlier in 2005 had been, to a large extent, facilitated by externally financed NGOs. (Despite the evidence of fraudulent practice in the subsequently annulled second round of presidential voting in Ukraine in late 2004, Putin described the protests in Kyiv that resulted in the election being repeated, and in the defeat of Putin's favoured candidate, as unconstitutional acts.) After several months of discussions, new legislation that, *inter alia*, permitted the authorities to close NGOs deemed to infringe Russia's sovereignty, unity or cultural heritage, was signed into law by President Putin in mid-January 2006. Meanwhile, in late December 2005 a principal economic adviser to the President, Andrei Illarionov, resigned, issuing a statement that strongly criticized the increased state intervention in the economy in recent years and declared that he no longer regarded Russia as a 'free country'.

In the early 1990s the Russian Federation encountered difficulties in attempting to satisfy the aspirations of its many nationalities for self-determination. In March 1992 some 18 of Russia's 20 nominally autonomous republics signed a federation treaty. The two dissenters, both predominately Islamic and petroleum-producing regions, were Tatarstan, which had voted for self-rule earlier in the month, and the Checheno-Ingush Republic, which had declared independence from Russia in November 1991 (as the Chechen Republic—Chechnya). The new treaty granted the republics greater authority, including control of natural resources and formal borders, and allowed them to conduct their own foreign trade. An agreement signed with the Russian Government in February 1994 accorded Tatarstan a considerable measure of sovereignty. Other power-sharing agreements, granting varying degrees of sovereignty, were eventually signed by some 42 of the 89 federal subjects during Yeltsin's presidency, although from 2000 Putin implemented a number of measures intended to curtail the power of regional governors, which led to the rescission of the vast majority of the power-sharing treaties by mid-2002. In May 2000 the Gosudarstvennaya Duma approved legislation intended to strengthen 'vertical' power relationships within the Federation, according the President the right to dismiss regional governors, a prerogative that was extended to governors with regard to those elected officials subordinate to them; however, by 2004 these powers had been seldom used, although as a result of legislation approved in December (see above), the appointment of regional governors (the election of whom had become almost universal across the Federation by the late 1990s) by the federal President, subject to the approval of regional legislatures, became the norm from early 2005; during that year the majority of regional leaders reaching the end of their elective mandate, or who had resigned in order to seek an expression of confidence from the federal authorities, were re-appointed, although there were some notable exceptions.

In March 1992, in response to the unilateral declaration of independence by Chechnya, the Ingush inhabitants of the former Checheno-Ingush Republic demanded the establishment of a separate republic. The formation of the new republic, Ingushetiya, was approved by the federal Supreme Council in June. Additionally, Ingush activists claimed territories in neighbouring North Osetiya—Alaniya, which had formed part of the Ingush Republic prior to the Second World War, when the Ingush (and Chechens, in common with several other nationalities of the USSR) were deported *en masse* to Central Asia. In October 1992 violent conflict broke out in the disputed Prigorodnyi district in North Osetiya. By November more than 300 people had died in the conflict and some 50,000 Ingush had fled the region. In September 1997, following mediation by Yeltsin, a treaty on normalizing relations was signed by the republican Governments of North Osetiya and Ingushetiya.

In late 1993 armed hostilities commenced in Chechnya between forces loyal to the republican authorities and those of the separatist leader, Gen. Dzhokhar Dudayev (who had been elected President of the Republic in October 1991, following a *coup d'état* against the republic's communist Government, led by Doku Zavgayev). Chechnya boycotted the Russian general election and referendum of December 1993; in August 1994 an unsuccessful attempt to overthrow the Dudayev regime was reputedly aided by the federal security services. Following the defeat of a further offensive in November, federal troops entered Chechnya in December, with the stated aim of reintroducing constitutional rule in the republic. The troops rapidly gained control of the lowland area of northern Chechnya, where support for Dudayev was weakest. Dudayev's forces, estimated to number some 15,000 irregular troops, were concentrated in the Chechen capital, Groznyi, a city upon which federal troops launched an assault in late December, following heavy bombardment from the air. Despite sustaining significant casualties, federal troops gradually took control of the city and seized the presidential palace (the headquarters of Dudayev's forces) in January 1995. Groznyi suffered great devastation during the assault, and there were reported to be thousands of civilian casualties. In June 1995 Chechen gunmen engaged local security forces in Budennovsk, in Stavropol Krai, some 200 km from the border with Chechnya, and took hostage more than 1,000 people in the city hospital. The rebels demanded that the Russian Government initiate talks with Dudayev on the immediate withdrawal of troops from Chechnya. Following the failure of attempts by federal army units to free the hostages, telephone negotiations were conducted between the rebel leader, Shamil Basayev, and federal premier Chernomyrdin, by which time some 100 people had reportedly been killed. Subsequently, as a cease-fire took effect in Chechnya, the rebels (who were permitted to re-enter Chechnya) began gradually to release hostages. Peace talks between a delegation from the federal Government and the Chechen leadership commenced in Groznyi in late June, and a cease-fire agreement was formalized in July.

In October 1995, following an assassination attempt on the commander of the federal forces in Chechnya, the federal Government announced a temporary suspension of the July agreement. In response, the Chechen leadership announced its complete rejection of the accord. Meanwhile, the Russian Government sought to establish a viable administration in Chechnya. In December elections took place in the Republic, both to the Duma and to the Chechen presidency. Zavgayev was elected republican President, reportedly receiving some 93% of the votes cast in elections that Dudayev rejected as invalid. (Some 74.8% of the electorate were reported to have voted.)

In January 1996 Chechen militants seized about 2,000 civilians in Kizlyar, Dagestan, and held them hostage in a hospital. Following negotiations, most were released, and the rebels departed, accompanied by some 150 hostages, for Chechnya. Federal troops halted the rebels in the border village of Pervomaiskoye and demanded the release of the remaining hostages. After further negotiations failed, federal forces attacked and captured the village. Although the rebels' leader, Salman Raduyev, escaped to Chechnya with some of his forces and around 40 hostages, some 150 rebels, and a number of their captives, were reportedly killed in the assault. In April Dudayev was killed in a missile attack. He was succeeded as leader of the separatists by Zemlikhan Yandarbiyev, who subsequently developed an association with the Islamist Taliban regime in Afghanistan, which, in return, announced its recognition of Chechnya's independence. Sporadic fighting persisted, but a new cease-fire agreement between the federal authorities and Yandarbiyev was reached in May. A formal military agreement, concluded in June, envisaged a withdrawal of the federal troops by the end of August and the disarmament of the separatist fighters. In August separatist forces, led by Basayev, launched a sustained offensive against Groznyi, routing many of the federal troops stationed in the city and trapping thousands of civilians. Yeltsin granted Gen. Lebed, the recently appointed Secretary of the Security Council, extensive powers to co-ordinate federal operations in the republic and to conduct a negotiated settlement. Following discussions involving Yandarbiyev and the Chechen military leader, Gen. Khalid ('Aslan') Maskhadov, a fresh cease-fire was brokered in mid-August. Following further negotiations, the withdrawal of troops commenced, and on 31 August Lebed and Maskhadov signed a conclusive peace agreement (known as the Khasavyurt Accords) in Dagestan, according to which any decision regarding Chechnya's future political status was to be deferred until December 2001. The withdrawal of federal troops and the exchange of prisoners of war began, and the cease-fire was largely respected. In September 1996 a Chechen Government was created, with Maskhadov as Prime Minister, and Yandarbiyev as Chairman of the cabinet. Nevertheless, sporadic violence continued: by early 1997 it was estimated that the conflict had caused some 80,000 deaths, and resulted in the displacement of 415,000 civilians.

All federal troops were withdrawn before the republican presidential and legislative elections, held on 27 January 1997. Maskhadov was elected President, with some 59.3% of the total votes cast. Of the 12 opposing candidates, Basayev won 23.5% of the votes, and Yandarbiyev 10.1%. The rate of voter participation was reported to be 79.4%, and international observers reported no serious discrepancies in the electoral process. Maskhadov declined his seat in the Sovet Federatsii, and affirmed his support for Chechen independence. Elections to the Chechen legislature were inconclusive and, after a second round of voting, only 45 of the 63 seats had been filled; further rounds were held in May and June. On 12 May Yeltsin and Maskhadov signed a formal peace treaty, defining the principles of future relations between Chechnya and the Russian Federation, and renouncing the use of violence as a means of resolving differences. The treaty, however, did not address the issue of Chechnya's constitutional status and, moreover, was refused ratification by the Gosudarstvennaya Duma.

Attacks and, in particular, hostage-taking, continued to be perpetrated by rebels opposed to the peace agreement (Russia claimed that some 800 hostages had been captured during 1997). Meanwhile, Chechnya's introduction of elements of *Shari'a* (Islamic religious) law in 1997, in particular the holding of public executions, was strongly opposed by the federal authorities. In January 1998 Maskhadov dismissed his cabinet and entrusted Basayev (who had been indicted by the federal authorities on charges of terrorism), hitherto Chechen First Deputy Prime Minister, but now appointed acting Prime Minister, with the formation of a new government. In late March the republican parliament announced that the territory was henceforth to be known as the 'Chechen Republic of Ichkeriya'. Increasing lawlessness and militancy was reported in the republic. In May 1998 Chechen rebels kidnapped Yeltsin's special representative to Chechnya, Vladimir Vlasov; he was freed in November by interior ministry troops. Four employees of a British telecommunications company were kidnapped in Chechnya in October; their decapitated bodies were found several weeks later. As disorder increased, Maskhadov dismissed the entire Chechen administration in October, and declared a further state of emergency in December. It became apparent that militant Islamist groups, including a faction led in Chechnya by Omar ibn al-Khattab (believed to be of Saudi or Jordanian origin) were increasingly implicated in the violence in Chechnya, as Maskhadov's authority apparently became more restricted.

In August–September 1999 Islamist factions associated with Basayev launched a series of attacks on Dagestan from Chechnya, with the aim of protecting and extending the jurisdiction of a 'separate Islamic territory' in Dagestan, over which rebels had obtained control in the previous year. (The territory was returned to federal rule in mid-September.) Federal troops were dispatched to the area, and after two weeks of fighting and aerial bombardment the rebels withdrew. However, there were renewed incursions and fighting in September. Meanwhile, in mid-August Maskhadov declared a one-month state of emergency in Chechnya, following threats by the federal authorities to bomb alleged terrorist bases in the republic. A series of bomb explosions in August and September in Moscow, Dagestan and Volgodonsk (Rostov Oblast), including two that destroyed entire apartment blocks, officially attributed by the Government to Chechen separatists, killed almost 300 people, prompting the redeployment of federal armed forces in the Republic from late September; the recently inaugurated premier, Vladimir Putin, described the deployment as an 'anti-terrorist operation'. Allegations persisted that sources associated with the FSB had ordered the attacks, in order to justify a renewed military campaign in Chechnya; notably, the discovery of an apparent attempt to initiate a further bombing in an apartment block in Ryazan heightened concerns of FSB involvement, although the authorities insisted that the incident was simply an exercise designed to ensure a heightened state of public vigilance. (In January 2004 two men were sentenced to life imprisonment for their part in the attacks; the Russian authorities stated that two suspects remained at large and that several others had been killed in the conflict in Chechnya.) Following air and ground offensives, federal troops had advanced to within 10 km of Groznyi by late October 1999, and both sides claimed to have inflicted heavy losses on the other. In December the federal Government issued an ultimatum, urging citizens to leave Groznyi immediately, or face death; many republican and federal administrative bodies were relocated to Gudermes, the Republic's second city. In February 2000 federal forces obtained control of Groznyi and proceeded to destroy much of the city.

In May 2000 President Putin decreed that, henceforth, Chechnya would be governed fed erally. Mufti Akhmad haji Kadyrov was inaugurated as administrative leader (Governor) of the republic in June. Kadyrov, a former ally of Maskhadov, was to be directly responsible to the federal authorities. In January 2001 Putin signed a decree transferring control of operations in Chechnya from the Ministry of Defence to the FSB, and announced the intention of withdrawing the majority of the 80,000-strong federal forces from the region, in order to leave a 15,000-strong infantry division and 7,000 interior ministry troops. The local administration in Chechnya was restructured, and Stanislav Ilyasov, a former Governor of Stavropol Krai, was appointed as the Chechen premier. Despite claims that federal military operations had effectively ended, guerrilla attacks showed no sign of abating, and concern escalated among international human rights organizations about the conduct of 'cleansing' operations by federal troops, in which entire towns or areas were searched for rebels; in 2001–02 the discovery of a number of mass graves, containing severely mutilated corpses, prompted outrage internationally.

In early 2001 a number of violent incidents outside Chechnya were staged by rebels, with the intention of drawing attention to the ongoing conflict. In mid-March three armed Chechen rebels hijacked a passenger aeroplane en route from İstanbul, Turkey, to Moscow, causing it to be diverted to Medina, Saudi Arabia. The rebels demanded that federal forces withdraw from Chechnya. Following the intervention of Saudi security forces, three hijackers were detained; three people, including one of the hijackers, were killed in the struggle. Later in the month 23 people were killed, and more than 140 were injured in three simultaneous bomb attacks in southern Russia, which were attributed to associates of Khattab.

In early May 2001 the continuing disorder in Chechnya was demonstrated by the announcement that the withdrawal of troops from the province had been terminated; by this time only 5,000 federal troops had left Chechnya. Meanwhile, tensions increased between federal forces and the Governor of Chechnya, and in August, writing in the federal parliamentary journal, *Parlamentskaya Gazeta*, Kadyrov called for an expedited end to the Government's campaign.

In early September 2001 a bomb was detonated in the offices of the republican Government, which had, by this time, returned to Groznyi; both Kadyrov and Ilyasov escaped unharmed. However, at the end of September Putin announced his willingness to participate in negotiations, for the first time since the beginning of the renewed conflict in 1999. He urged the rebels to 'halt all contacts with international terrorists' and to establish contact with the federal authorities, citing a 72-hour period during which arms could be surrendered without charge; however, only a negligible quantity of weapons was surrendered. (The authorities persistently issued reports purporting that Chechen militants were associated with the al-Qa'ida—Base—organization of the Saudi-born militant Islamist, Osama bin Laden, which had organized devastating attacks in the USA earlier that month.)

In October 2001 Kadyrov reformed the Chechen administration; although Ilyasov (who remained resident in Stavropol) was maintained as republican Prime Minister, a new, more senior position, the Chief of Staff of the Chechen Administration, was assigned to Lt-Gen. Yakov Sergunin, hitherto responsible for the judicial system in Chechnya. On 18 November the first direct negotiations between the warring factions since the renewal of hostilities in 1999, held in Moscow between the presidential representative to the Southern Federal Okrug, Col-Gen. Viktor Kazantsev and Maskhadov's deputy, Akhmed Zakayev, reached no substantive agreement, and no further high-level meetings took place. In late December Raduyev, the only prominent Chechen rebel leader to have been captured by federal forces, was sentenced to life imprisonment, having been guilty of 10 charges, including murder, terrorism and hostage-taking. (Raduyev died in prison in December 2002.)

In April 2002 Khattab was killed by federal forces. However, rebel activity increased markedly in the months that followed; although the political authority of Maskhadov had dwindled, his military leadership of what was known as the State Defence Committee became increasingly prominent as a focus for resistance to the federal troops. In July it was reported that Basayev had been appointed to a senior position on the Committee. Meanwhile, on 9 May, during celebrations in Kaspiisk, Dagestan, to mark 'Victory Day', some 45 people were killed and more than 130 injured in an explosion, which the federal authorities attributed to Chechen rebels. In mid-August federal forces experienced their single largest loss of life since the recommencement of operations in 1999, when a military helicopter was shot down by rebels in Groznyi, killing some 118 troops; at the end of the month a second federal helicopter was attacked, killing its two crew members, and two further helicopters had been shot down by early November. Meanwhile, in late September rebels staged incursions into Ingushetiya; at least 17 deaths were reported in fighting. Moreover, an explosion outside a police station in Groznyi in mid-October resulted in the deaths of at least 24 people.

On 23–26 October 2002 over 40 heavily armed rebels, led by Movsar Barayev, the cousin of a Chechen rebel leader who had been killed by federal troops in 2001, held captive more than 800 people in a Moscow theatre, and demanded the withdrawal of federal troops from the republic. The rebels described themselves as members of a 'suicide battalion'. The siege ended when élite federal forces stormed the theatre, having initially filled the building with an unidentified incapacitating gas. The rebels were killed, and it subsequently emerged that at least 129 hostages had also died, in almost all cases owing to the toxic effects of the gas. Putin stated that the siege had been planned outside Russia, by international terrorist groups, citing evidence that the hostage-takers had communicated with their purported sponsors in Qatar, Saudi Arabia and the United Arab Emirates during the course of the siege. Maskhadov issued a statement condemning the rebels' use of terrorist methods, but, despite denials by the rebel Chechen leadership of their involvement in the incident, Zakayev was arrested in late October, reportedly on the orders of the federal Government, in Denmark. In early December the Danish authorities refused to extradite Zakayev to Russia, citing a lack of credible evidence of his involvement in terrorist activities. Zakayev's presence in Denmark resulted in the relocation to Brussels, Belgium, of the EU-Russia summit that had been scheduled to take place in Copenhagen in November. Zakayev subsequently fled to the United Kingdom, where extradition proceedings commenced in late January 2003. (However, it was announced in late November that Zakayev had been granted political asylum in the United Kingdom, following the dismissal of the Russian request for his extradition.)

In mid-November 2002 Ilyasov was removed from his position as Prime Minister of Chechnya and, in what was widely perceived as a promotion, appointed as a minister in the federal Government, in which capacity he was to be responsible for the social and economic development of Chechnya; Ilyasov was succeeded as the premier of Chechnya by Capt (retd) Mikhail Babich, who had previously held senior positions in two regional administrations elsewhere in Russia. In late November Ilyasov announced that a referendum on a new draft Chechen constitution, which would, *inter alia*, determine the status of the republic within the Russian Federation, was to be held in March 2003. At the end of December at least 83 people died, and more than 150 others were injured, when suicide bombers detonated bombs in two vehicles stationed outside the headquarters of the republican Government in Groznyi; no senior officials were killed. (Basayev subsequently claimed responsibility for the attack.) By late December 2002 federal losses during the campaign, according to official figures, were put at 4,572 dead and 15,549 wounded, with 29 missing, although Chechen estimates were considerably higher. (It was also estimated that more than 14,000 rebel fighters had been killed since September 1999.) In late January 2003 Babich resigned as premier. On 10 February Anatolii Popov, the hitherto deputy chairman of the state commission for the reconstruction of Chechnya, was appointed as the new republican premier.

The referendum on the draft constitution for Chechnya, describing the republic (referred to as the Chechen—Nokchi Republic) as both a sovereign entity, with its own citizenship, and as an integral part of the Russian Federation proceeded, as scheduled, on 23 March 2003, despite concerns that the instability of the republic would prevent the poll from being free and fair. The draft constitution also provided for the holding of fresh elections to a strengthened republican presidency and legislature. According to the official results, some 88.4% of the electorate participated in the plebiscite, of whom 96.0% supported the draft constitution. Two further questions, on the method of electing the President and the Parliament of the Republic of Chechnya, were supported by 95.4% and 96.1% of participants, respectively. However, independent observers challenged the results, reporting that the rate of participation by the electorate had been much lower than officially reported. (According to official results, an identical number of valid votes had been cast in response to all three questions, while it was reported that the total number of votes cast had, in fact, been in excess of the registered electorate.)

Political violence continued to dominate Chechen affairs after the referendum; in early April 2003 at least 22 people were killed in two separate incidents when their vehicles detonated landmines. In early May at least 59 people were killed when suicide bombers attacked government offices in the north of Chechnya. Two days later another suicide bombing at a religious festival attended by Kadyrov in Ilishkan-Yurt, near Gudermes, resulted in at least 14 deaths, although Kadyrov escaped unhurt; Basayev claimed responsibility for the organization of both attacks. On 21 June Kadyrov inaugurated an interim legislative body, the State Council, comprising the head of, and an appointed representative of, each administrative district. In early July Putin announced that presidential elections in Chechnya would be held in early October. None the less, clashes continued, and in early August at least 50 people were killed in an attack on a military hospital in the neighbouring Republic of North Osetiya—Alaniya.

From 1 September 2003 control of military operations in Chechnya was transferred from the FSB to the federal Ministry of Internal Affairs; such operations were no longer regarded as having an 'anti-terrorist' character but were, rather, to form part of an 'operation to protect law and constitutional order'. Meanwhile, campaigning for the presidential election commenced, and by 20 August 11 valid applications for candidacies had been made. However, the subsequent withdrawal of Aslanbek Aslakhanov, a representative of Chechnya in the Gosudarstvennaya Duma, and the debarring of a business executive, Malik Saidullayev, effectively removed any major challenges to Kadyrov's candidacy. As had been widely anticipated, on 5 October Kadyrov was elected as President, receiving 87.7% of the votes cast, according to official figures. The rate of participation by the electorate was stated to be 82.6%. In mid-December at least 12 people were killed in clashes that followed incursions by heavily armed Chechen rebels into Dagestan, resulting in the imposition of a state of emergency in the region. An explosion in a Moscow Metro train on 6 February 2004, which resulted in the deaths of at least 39 people, was attributed to Chechen militants. In mid-February Yandarbiyev was killed by a car bomb in Doha, Qatar (two Russian intelligence agents were subsequently tried for Yandarbiyev's murder by a Qatari court, and sentenced to life imprisonment; however, they were returned to Russia to serve out their sentences in December, and in early 2005 it was reported that they were no longer being held in detention). In early March 2004 another influential rebel leader, Ruslan Gelayev, was reported to have been killed in clashes with federal troops in Dagestan. In mid-March Popov was formally dismissed as premier of Chechnya, following a period of ill health; he was replaced by Sergei Abramov, who had previously served in the republican Ministry of Finance in Ilyasov's Government. In accordance with the provisions of the constitutional referendum held in the previous year, his appointment required, and duly obtained, the endorsement of the republican State Council.

An explosion in Groznyi on 9 May 2004, at a celebration to mark 'Victory Day', resulted in the deaths of several senior officials, including Kadyrov and Khusain Isayev, the head of the republican legislature. (Basayev subsequently claimed responsibility for the attack.) Abramov assumed presidential responsibilities in an acting capacity, pending elections, while Ramzan Kadyrov, the son of the assassinated President and the leader of the presidential security service (often known as the *Kadyrovtsi* and which was widely believed to have been implicated in several unexplained 'disappearances'), was appointed as First Deputy Prime Minister. Chechen militants were suspected of involvement in a series of raids on interior ministry targets in the neighbouring republic of Ingushetiya, which took place in June. In the presidential election held on 29 August, Maj.-Gen. Alu Alkhanov, an officer in the interior ministry troops, and generally acknowledged to be the candidate favoured by the federal Government, was elected President, receiving 73.7% of the votes cast, according to official figures, which evaluated the rate of participation at 85.3%. The Council of Europe described the elections as undemocratic. Alkhanov retained Abramov as Prime Minister, while Ramzan Kadyrov was retained both as First Deputy Prime Minister and as head of the presidential security service. (Meanwhile, proposed elections to the republican legislature were postponed.) In the period immediately before and after the election, attacks on Russian civilians, attributed to extremist Chechen separatists, intensified, with the destruction, apparently by suicide bombers, of two passenger planes on 24 August, the explosion of a bomb outside a Moscow Metro station on 31 August, and the occupation of a school in Beslan, in the Republic of North Osetiya—Alaniya, on 1–3 September (see above). Basayev subsequently released a statement claiming that the attacks had occurred under his orchestration, and describing the demands of the Beslan hostage-takers as the complete withdrawal of federal troops from Chechnya and the resignation of President Putin.

In February 2005 Maskhadov announced that he had ordered separatist fighters to observe a unilateral one-month cease-fire, in what he described as a 'goodwill gesture' towards the Russian authorities (reports were varied as to the success of the order). On 8 March Russian media reported that Maskhadov had been killed during a special operation by FSB forces in the village of Tolstoi-Yurt, north of Groznyi. Footage of what appeared to be Maskhadov's corpse was broadcast on national television later that day. The federal authorities subsequently refused to return Maskhadov's body to his relatives, stating that this was prohibited by anti-terrorist legislation. Maskhadov was replaced as leader of the State Defence Committee by his chosen successor, Abdul-Khalim Sadulayev. Sadulayev, like Maskhadov before

him, announced his willingness to enter into negotiations with the federal authorities, but maintained that the use of force was legitimate in the absence of such negotiations. In June Sadulayev issued a decree appointing Doku Umarov (who had, earlier in the year, stated that Chechen militants would launch large-scale operations in other regions of Russia as part of a so-called 'Caucasus Front') as vice-president of the rebel leadership; he also issued a statement to the effect that the expulsion of Russian forces from Chechnya would not constitute an end to the conflict, as the Chechens would be obligated to take vengeance against 'unbelievers' (i.e. non-Muslims) for their actions in Chechnya. In mid-July at least 15 people were killed following the detonation of a car bomb in Znamenskoye. In mid-August Sadulayev dismissed the rebel Chechen 'parliament-in-exile' and a network of 'ambassadors', which he collectively accused of financial malpractice and incompetence; he also appointed a new rebel 'Government' at the end of the month, to which, notably, Basayev was appointed as 'First Deputy Prime Minister', while Zakayev was appointed to represent the rebel authorities internationally. In early September Basayev was interviewed by a US television station, and stated that he accepted his designation as a 'terrorist', but that he regarded his use of violence as justified. In early October a co-ordinated series of attacks by some 100 militants against law-enforcement bodies in Nalchik, the capital of the Kabardino-Balkar Republic, in the western North Caucasus, resulted in the deaths of at least 130 people; Basayev claimed responsibility for the organization of the attack. An Islamist group active in the Kabardino-Balkar Republic, the Dzhamaat Yarmuk, also claimed to have participated in the attacks, as part of the 'Caucasus Front'. Meanwhile, tensions between Chechens and the most numerous ethnic group in neighbouring Dagestan, the Avars, were also heightened on several occasions from the first half of 2005, as a result of security forces associated with the Chechen authorities (most notably members of the *Kadyrovtsi*) making incursions into Dagestan, apparently in response to Chechen rebels taking refuge in the neighbouring Republic. Relations with Dagestan were further strained after 11 villagers were abducted during a 'cleansing' operation in the eastern village of Borozdinovskaya in early June; some 400 people, principally ethnic Avars, subsequently fled to Dagestan and remained there for several weeks; the operation was condemned by both the Chechen and federal authorities, and Alkhanov dismissed the administrator of the district in which the village was located. Clashes were also reported between those troops loyal to Ramzan Kadyrov and those loyal to the federal authorities.

On 27 November 2005 elections were held in Chechnya to a new, bicameral legislature, comprising the 18-seat Council of the Republic (the upper chamber) and the 40-seat People's Assembly (the lower chamber). The federal Government cited the ballot as evidence that normality was returning to Chechnya, although no candidates advocating Chechen independence were allowed to stand. The rate of participation by the electorate was estimated as some 60%, well above the 25% required to validate the election; however, international observers expressed doubt that the vote was free and fair. As predicted, the majority of deputies in the new parliament (33 out of 58) were from UR. The CPRF, the pro-market URF and the Eurasian Union also obtained representation, as did 14 deputies with no party affiliation. Thus the position of Kadyrov, a member of UR and for a long time perceived as *de facto* leader of the Chechen Government, was consolidated; furthermore, Kadyrov at this time held the position of acting premier, after Abramov sustained injuries in an automobile accident earlier in the month.

In December 2005 four men arrested at the house in Tolstoi-Yurt where Maskhadov was killed were sentenced to between six and 15 years' imprisonment, on charges that included unlawful possession of weapons and membership of an illegal armed group. It emerged that Maskhadov had been shot by his bodyguards at his own request, in order to avoid capture and trial.

On 28 February 2006 Abramov resigned as Prime Minister of Chechnya. On 4 March the republican legislature unanimously approved the appointment of Kadyrov as his successor. Although this appointment effectively confirmed the distribution of power that had been in place in the Republic for several months, it was not without controversy. As acting Prime Minister, Kadyrov had spoken in favour of permitting men to marry up to four women (although this would be in clear breach of the family code, he stated that no change to legislation would be required for this to be permitted); moreover, before being overruled by Alkhanov, Kadyrov had prohibited a Danish humanitarian relief organization from operating in Chechnya, as part of international protests by Muslims that followed the publication of cartoons depicting the Prophet Muhammad, initially in a Danish newspaper (and their circulation, by a group of imams, in various countries of the Middle East), which were deemed to be offensive towards Islam.

Following the dissolution of the USSR in December 1991, Russia's most immediate foreign policy concerns were with the other former Soviet republics, generally referred to in Russia as the 'near abroad'. Relations with Ukraine were, initially, dominated by a dispute over the division of the former Soviet Black Sea Fleet, based mainly in Sevastopol, on the Crimean peninsula (Ukraine). Russia and Ukraine signed an agreement on the division of the Fleet in June 1995, but Russia subsequently refused to implement the accord, owing to continued disagreement concerning the status of Sevastopol. In May 1997 an agreement was concluded with Ukraine, whereby Russia was to lease part of the city's naval base for a period of 20 years, and was to provide financial compensation for ships and equipment received from Ukraine. (Upon expiry, the treaty could be renewed for five years, should both parties agree, but would then be subject to renegotiation.) A Treaty on Friendship, Cooperation and Partnership was signed by the two countries in that month. In 1999 Ukraine's inability to pay for Russian energy supplies, and accusations that Ukraine had diverted gas from Russia's export pipelines, temporarily caused difficulties between the two countries. In March 2000, despite Ukraine having 'frozen' the accounts of the Black Sea Fleet and having detained officials of the company, as part of an investigation into alleged fiscal malpractice, the two countries signed seven agreements relating to payment for the operation and services of jointly used facilities. An agreement was reached in December permitting the payment of Ukraine's energy debts to Russia over a period of 10 years. In February 2001 Putin visited Ukraine to mark the signature of a number of accords, including an agreement to reconnect the Russian and Ukrainian power grids. In May former premier Viktor Chernomyrdin was appointed as ambassador to Ukraine, in what was interpreted as an indication of strengthening ties between the two countries. In January 2003 a treaty delineating the land boundary between Russia and Ukraine (which remained largely unmarked and unregulated) was signed by Putin and President Leonid Kuchma of Ukraine, although discussions on the status of the Sea of Azov, which lies between the two countries, remained unresolved. Work on the construction of a dam in the Sea, which commenced, apparently at the instigation of the regional authorities in Krasnodar Krai, in September, precipitated considerable controversy, and raised concerns that the territorial integrity of Ukraine was being violated. Putin reportedly ordered the Krasnodar authorities to halt the construction work, and Ukrainian border guards were dispatched to Tuzla island, near the westernmost end of the dam. (A permanent border post was opened on the island later in the year.) In late December the Presidents of the two countries signed an agreement on the use of the Sea of Azov, the entirety of which was defined as comprising the internal waters of both countries. Agreement was also reached on the maritime state boundary of Russia and Ukraine in the region.

Relations with Ukraine were jeopardized by the circumstances of the disputed 2004 presidential election in that country (see the chapter on Ukraine), as Putin openly supported the candidacy of the incumbent Prime Minister, Viktor Yanukovych, whose reported victory in the second round was subsequently overturned following large public protests over the conduct of the poll. Notably, Putin visited Ukraine twice during the campaign, appearing publicly with Yanukovych on both occasions, and telephoned Yanukovych to congratulate him on his victory before the official (and later discredited) results had been announced. Putin also described the protests that led to the election being repeated, and which became known as the 'orange revolution', as a violation of constitutional order. In a move widely interpreted as acknowledging the necessity of continued co-operation between the two countries (and reflecting the substantial ethnic Russian and Russian-speaking population of Ukraine), the newly elected President, Viktor Yushchenko, visited Moscow the day after his inauguration in late January 2005. However, relations between the two countries were again strained later in 2005, following the announcement by the Russian state-controlled company, Gazprom, that it intended to charge Ukraine market prices (US $230 per 1,000 cu m) for the supply of natural gas, which had, hitherto, been supplied at the subsidized rate of $50 per 1,000 cu m. After an agreement failed to be reached, on 1 January 2006 Gazprom halted supplies to Ukraine, a measure that resulted in a reduced output of gas in several countries in central and western Europe supplied by pipelines crossing Ukraine. Later in January the Ukrainian Government reached an agreement with Gazprom that would result in Ukraine paying $95 per 1,000 cu m for a mixture of Russian and Turkmenistani natural gas; a new, Swiss-registered company, Ukrtransgaz, was to be established to that end. However, this agreement was to be subject to renegotiation.

In April 1996 Russia and Belarus signed an agreement creating a 'Community of Russia and Belarus', according to which the two countries would pursue economic integration and close co-ordination of foreign and defence policies. In May 1997 a 'Charter of the Union of Belarus and Russia' was concluded, which, while promoting greater co-operation between the two countries, moved away from advocating full union, although in June the first official session of the Union's joint Parliamentary Assembly was convened. During 1998 the Union was strengthened by the decision to grant joint citizenship to residents, and the establishment of a joint legislative and representative body to deal with union issues. The bicameral assembly was to comprise an upper chamber, the Council of the Union, to which members would be delegated by the Russian Federalnoye Sobraniye and the Belarusian Natsionalnoye Sobraniye (National Assembly), and a lower chamber, the Council of Representatives, elected on the basis of universal suffrage, with 25 deputies from Belarus and 75 from Russia. A treaty on unification, which came into force on 26 January 2000, when the President of Belarus, Alyaksandr Lukashenka, was appointed Chairman of the High State Council of the Union, did not satisfy the Belarusian President's wishes for the formation of a single state. Although a union budget was passed at a session of the Parliamentary Assembly (established under the 1996 Treaty, and comprising 36 members from the legislature of each country) in May, President Putin remained more reticent than Lukashenka, in particular with regard to the formation of joint armed forces. Although agreement was reached in March 2002 on the harmonization of the two countries' customs and tax laws, and on the removal of trade barriers, Putin was increasingly dismissive of Lukashenka's proposals for a closer union of the two states. In August Putin presented Lukashenka with a new unification plan, which effectively provided for the absorption of Belarus' seven oblasts (regions) into the Russian Federation and, following referendums on unification in May 2003, for parliamentary and presidential elections to the new state to be held in late 2003 and early 2004, respectively, at the same time as the elections to the Russian Gosudarstvennaya Duma and presidency; the plan also provided for the introduction of the Russian rouble as the currency of Belarus from January 2004. The proposals were, however, rejected by Lukashenka, who stated that the introduction of such measures would undermine Belarusian sovereignty.

Concern at the treatment and status of ethnic Russians in the three Baltic states remained a particular source of tension, and the demarcation of mutual frontiers also created difficulties. In the early 2000s Russia expressed particular concern for its citizens in the Russian exclave of Kaliningrad, which is separated from the remainder of the Russian Federation by Belarus and Lithuania. Russian premier Kasyanov attempted to ensure that residents of the exclave would be exempted from visa requirements that were to be imposed by Lithuania and Poland prior to the two countries' accession to the EU (which took effect from 1 May 2004). In November 2002, at an EU-Russia summit meeting, held in Brussels, Russia finally agreed to an EU proposal for simplified visa arrangements. According to the compromise accord, multiple-transit travel documentation would be made available to residents of the exclave travelling by motor vehicle; the new regulations came into effect on 1 July 2003.

Following the dissolution of the USSR, Russia maintained significant political and military influence in many former Soviet republics, especially in those areas involved in civil or ethnic conflicts. Russian troops were deployed in Tajikistan to support the Tajikistani Government against rebel forces during the civil war of 1992–97, and remained thereafter to ensure the security of the Tajikistani–Afghan border. In 2004 it was announced that Russian troops were to transfer responsibility for border security to the Tajikistani military, although it was envisaged that Russia would continue to assist Tajikistan to defend its border through the provision of military equipment and training; in October, meanwhile, it was announced that Russia had been formally granted a permanent military base in Tajikistan. In

October 2003 a Russian military base commenced operations in Kyrgyzstan, the first to be established outside Russia subsequent to the dissolution of the USSR; the base was intended to meet the requirements of the Collective Security Treaty Organization (comprising Armenia, Belarus, Kazakhstan, Kyrgyzstan, Russia and Tajikistan), inaugurated in April to succeed the CIS Collective Security Treaty. Following the resignation of President Askar Akayev in early 2005, in the wake of protests against the results of parliamentary elections, the Russian Government stated that it would continue to co-operate with Kyrgyzstan's new leadership. In November Putin and President Islam Karimov of Uzbekistan signed a defence pact, which provided for mutual support in the event that one of the countries came under attack; this measure followed the departure of US troops from a base in Uzbekistan, on the orders of Karimov, following US (and widespread international) criticism of the use of violence by Uzbekistani troops against demonstrators in the city of Andijon in May of that year (see the chapter on Uzbekistan).

Considerable controversy arose throughout the 1990s and the first half of the 2000s because of the Russian Government's provision of support for separatist factions in Moldova and Georgia. In 1999 it was announced that all Russian troops in the separatist Transnistria region of Moldova were to be withdrawn by the end of 2002, although the proposed withdrawal was subsequently postponed until December 2003. However, the withdrawal was further delayed, and in February 2004 the Russian Minister of Defence, Sergei Ivanov, indicated that Russia intended to maintain a military presence in the region. Meanwhile, in December 1998 Russia and Georgia signed an agreement that provided for the incremented transfer of the control of their mutual frontiers, from Russian to Georgian guards. (Control of the frontier was, however, complicated by the existence of separatist and rebel-controlled regions on both sides of the border—Chechnya within Russia, and Abkhazia and South Ossetia within Georgia—see the chapter on Georgia). In November 1999 it was agreed that two of the four Russian bases on Georgian territory would be withdrawn by mid-2001. Russian troops left the two bases in Georgia by November 2001; the Russian authorities stated that the two remaining bases would be vacated by 2015, instead of the deadline of 2005 requested by Georgia. (In mid-2005, however, it was announced that the departure of Russian troops from Georgia would be completed by the end of 2008.) In October 2001, as the conflict in Abkhazia intensified, Chechen rebels made incursions into the Kodori Gorge, on the Abkhazia–Georgia border, and into the Pankisi Gorge, south of Chechnya. Following the aerial bombardment of villages in the Kodori Gorge by unmarked aircraft at the end of the month, Russia and Georgia each accused the other of having commanded the bombings. In September 2002 the Russian authorities accused Georgia of permitting Chechen rebels to operate from bases within its territory, and declared that Russia reserved the right to instigate 'pre-emptive' military action, in self-defence, should the situation persist. However, in early October tensions abated somewhat, when Russia and Georgia agreed to commence joint patrols of their common border. Putin attended talks in Moscow with the recently inaugurated President of Georgia, Mikheil Saakashvili, in February 2004, when progress was reportedly made towards the planned signature of a framework agreement between the two countries on matters of concern, including, notably, co-operation on measures to combat terrorism. Relations between the two countries continued to be complicated, however, by Russian support for the secessionist regimes in Abkhazia and South Ossetia and, in particular, by the granting of Russian citizenship to those resident in the separatist regions. The presence of Russian peace-keeping troops in South Ossetia caused tension when a series of armed clashes took place after Georgian forces were deployed to the region in mid-2004.

In September 2003, meeting in Yalta, Crimea (Ukraine), the Presidents of Belarus, Kazakhstan, Russia and Ukraine announced their intention of forming a 'single economic zone', to include a trade and customs union, which would be introduced incrementally.

After December 1991 the Russian Federation was recognized as the successor to the USSR. It was granted the USSR's permanent seat on the UN Security Council and, additionally, was to be responsible for the receipt and destruction of all nuclear weapons of the former USSR located in other newly independent republics (Belarus, Kazakhstan and Ukraine), a process that was successfully completed by the mid-1990s. In January 1993 Russia and the USA signed the second Strategic Arms' Reduction Treaty (START II), which envisaged a reduction in the strategic nuclear weapons of both powers. The Russian legislature ratified START II in April 2000. Following the first meeting of President Putin and President George W. Bush of the USA, in Ljubljana, Slovenia, in June 2001, relations appeared to improve markedly. Putin assumed a notably measured approach towards the proposed abrogation by the USA of the Anti-Ballistic Missile (ABM) treaty (signed with the USSR in 1972), which formed a principal part of the Bush Administration's foreign defence policy.

Russia offered assistance and gave support to the USA in its attempts to form a global coalition against militant Islamist terrorism, after the suicide air attacks against the USA of 11 September 2001 (see the chapter on the USA). Although Russia refused to commit troops to participate in the military campaign against targets of the Taliban regime in Afghanistan, which commenced on 7 October, it provided military intelligence, and allowed the coalition access to its airspace. Russia also increased logistical and military support to the anti-Taliban forces of the United Islamic Front for the Salvation of Afghanistan.

In mid-November 2001, at a meeting in Crawford, Texas, Bush and Putin announced that significant reductions would be made to their countries' nuclear arsenals over the following decade; Putin did not specify how many weapons would be destroyed, and emphasized his desire to formalize the agreement by means of a treaty, together with clear verification procedures, in contrast to the more informal measures envisaged by Bush. In mid-December, following the USA's announcement that it was to withdraw unilaterally from the ABM treaty, with effect from June 2002, Putin reiterated earlier claims that, while he did not support the abrogation of the treaty, its abandonment did not pose a security threat to Russia. In mid-May 2002 Russia and the USA announced that agreement had been reached on the reduction of their nuclear arsenals by approximately two-thirds, and a nuclear accord and a declaration on strategic partnership were duly signed by Presidents Putin and Bush on 24 May. The USA withdrew from the ABM treaty on 13 June, and the following day Russia withdrew from START II, which had been superseded by the treaty signed with the USA in the previous month.

The Russian Government consistently condemned intermittent US-led missile attacks on Iraq during the 1990s and early 2000s; additionally, in 1996, in contravention of a UN embargo, Russia concluded an agreement with Iraq on the development of petroleum fields in that country. In late 1997, following Iraq's refusal to permit weapons inspectors of the UN Special Commission (UNSCOM) access to contentious sites, the Russian Government intervened in an attempt to avert a renewal of hostilities, and the conclusion of an agreement between the UN and Iraq in late February 1998 was regarded by Russia as a significant diplomatic success. Russia resumed scheduled flights to Iraq in late 2000, in contravention of UN sanctions. In mid-2001 Russia, which supported Iraq in its demands that the sanctions regime in force since 1990 should be revoked, effectively obstructed a British-drafted proposal before the Security Council for the introduction of a new, US-advocated, programme of 'smart' sanctions. As the US Administration of George W. Bush, from the second half of 2002, utilized increasingly bellicose rhetoric against Iraq, Russia urged the USA to avoid the use of unilateral force, and encouraged Iraq's compliance with UN demands regarding weapons inspections, so as to facilitate the lifting of sanctions. Although Russia voted to support UN Security Council Resolution 1441, approved in November 2002, which provided for the expedited return of weapons inspectors to Iraq under the auspices of the UN Monitoring, Verification and Inspection Commission (UNMOVIC), it was a leading opponent, with France and Germany, of attempts, led by the USA and the United Kingdom in February–March 2003, to approve a further Security Council resolution explicitly to endorse military action in Iraq, and President Putin described the conflict, which commenced in mid-March, as a 'political mistake'. Although senior members of the US Government criticized various aspects of Russian policy (including, notably, progress towards establishing democratic governance and the rule of law in Russia) during 2003, Putin, in particular, emphasized the importance of maintaining co-operative relations with the USA. Observers speculated that Russia's commitment to renew exports of nuclear fuel to Iran in early 2005 (see below), and seeming pursuit of closer ties with Syria (with reports in 2005 suggesting that Russia was to sell missiles to Syria), could be harmful to relations with the USA, the foreign policy of which was notably hostile towards those countries.

In June 1994 Russia joined the North Atlantic Treaty Organization's (NATO) 'Partnership for Peace' (see p. 314) programme of military co-operation with former Eastern bloc states. A 'Founding Act on Mutual Relations, Co-operation and Security between NATO and the Russian Federation' was signed in May 1997. The Act provided for enhanced Russian participation in all NATO decision-making activities, equal status in peace-keeping operations and representation at the Alliance headquarters at ambassadorial level. A NATO-Russian Permanent Joint Council was established. Russia's relations with NATO became increasingly strained in 1999, in particular after the failure of Russian attempts to achieve a diplomatic solution to the situation in the province of Kosovo (Kosovo and Metohija), in the republic of Serbia, Yugoslavia (subsequently Serbia and Montenegro) precipitated the aerial bombardment of Yugoslav targets to be initiated by NATO forces later in March (see the chapter on Serbia and Montenegro). Russia condemned the air offensive, and suspended its relations with the Alliance. Following the capitulation of Yugoslav forces in mid-June, and their withdrawal from Kosovo, Russian troops were the first to enter the province, before NATO forces. Contacts were resumed between Russia and NATO in February 2000. In July 2001 Putin called for a pan-European security pact to be established in place of NATO, to incorporate Russia. On 28 May 2002 Putin and the heads of state and of government of the 19 NATO member states, meeting in Italy, signed the Rome Declaration, inaugurating a new NATO-Russia Council to replace the Permanent Joint Council. The new Council would enable Russia to enter into negotiations with its members on a range of issues, including terrorism, non-proliferation, defence and peace-keeping. Although Russia had expressed concern at the expansion of NATO to include seven eastern European countries, including the three Baltic states, from early 2004, Putin emphasized that the expansion would not have negative consequences for the Alliance's relations with Russia.

In January 1996 Russia was admitted as a member of the Council of Europe (see p. 211). As a condition of membership, Russia was to abolish the death penalty by the end of February 1999. By mid-2004, however, the Duma had yet to approve its abolition, although capital punishment had been subject to a moratorium since Russia's admission to the organization. Russia's voting rights were suspended between April 2000 and January 2001, as a result of allegations of human rights abuses committed during Russia's renewed military campaign in Chechnya. In April 2003 the Parliamentary Assembly of the Council of Europe voted, by a large majority, in favour of the establishment of an international tribunal to try those suspected of war crimes in the republic. In February 2005 the European Court of Human Rights, a subsidiary institution of the Council of Europe, ruling on cases brought by six Chechen citizens, concluded that serious human rights abuses had been committed by the Russian military in Chechnya and ordered the Russian Government to pay compensation to the victims' relatives.

In 2006 Russia became the rotating chairman of the Group of Eight leading industrialized nations (G-8), to which it had been admitted in 2000.

In November 2004, following approval by both chambers of the legislature, President Putin signed a bill ratifying the Kyoto Protocol to the United Nations Framework Convention on Climate Change, thereby bringing the Protocol into force for its signatories. Observers suggested that the decision to approve the protocol may have been motivated by the Russian Government's ongoing pursuit of membership of the World Trade Organization (WTO, see p. 370), which some predicted would be achieved in 2006.

Russia's relations with Iran in the late 1990s and early 2000s were a cause of concern for the USA. In mid-1997 Iran and Russia held discussions on nuclear co-operation, primarily focusing on the development of a nuclear power plant in Bushehr, Iran. In December 2000 Igor Sergeyev, the Russian Minister of Defence, paid the first official visit to Iran by a Russian official since 1979, with a view to increasing military and technical co-operation. In March 2001, during a visit to Moscow by the Iranian President, Muhammad Khatami, Russia agreed to resume the sale of conventional weapons to Iran and to assist with the construction of the Bushehr power plant; an agreement for arms sales worth some US $300m., the first such agreement between the two countries since 1995, was signed in October. Although in December 2002 it was announced that Russia was to increase its nuclear co-operation with Iran, the Russian Minister of Foreign Affairs, Igor Ivanov, reiterated that this co-operation was of a civilian nature and that Russia remained opposed to Iran's potential development of nuclear weapons. In mid-2003 Russia announced that it was to suspend exports of nuclear fuel to Iran; however, in February 2005 a new agreement was reached between the two countries on the provision of nuclear fuel (which would, however, be returned to Russia, once it was spent). In February 2006 Russia was one of 27 countries represented on the 35-member Board of Governors of the International Atomic Energy Agency (IAEA) to vote in favour of Iran's referral to the UN Security Council, after it was discovered not to have complied with the conditions of an agreement reached with the IAEA; none the less, Russia remained opposed to the use of military force against Iran to bring it into compliance.

Relations with Japan were complicated by a continuing dispute over the status of the Kurile Islands (in Sakhalin Oblast, and known in Japan as the Northern Territories), which became part of the USSR at the end of the Second World War; Japan maintained its long-standing demand that four of the islands be returned to Japanese sovereignty. Despite discussions on the territorial dispute between the leaderships of Russia and Japan from the late 1990s, by late 2006 the signature of any peace treaty (or the terms thereof) remained in abeyance.

Relations with the People's Republic of China improved significantly during the 1990s, and in April 1996 several bilateral agreements were concluded during a visit by Yeltsin to China. Following a visit to Russia by the Chinese President, Jiang Zemin, in April 1997, a joint declaration that envisaged a heightened strategic partnership between the two countries was issued. In 1999 several agreements on bilateral economic and trade co-operation, and a final accord on the demarcation of a common border between the two countries, were signed. Meanwhile, negotiations in the mid-1990s that initially focused on defining the mutual borders of China, Kazakhstan, Kyrgyzstan, Russia and Tajikistan appeared to be instrumental in bringing about closer co-operation between these countries, which in 1996 formed the so-called Shanghai Five group. The group subsequently broadened its areas of activity to include trade, cultural, military and security co-operation; in June 2001 Uzbekistan joined the grouping, which was renamed the Shanghai Co-operation Organization (see p. 398). In September 2003 the Organization announced its intention to establish a joint anti-terrorism centre, to be located in Tashkent, Uzbekistan, and a secretariat, in the Chinese capital, Beijing. Kasyanov visited Beijing in August 2002, to discuss strategic issues, and Putin visited China in December, when he met President Jiang and his appointed successor, Hu Jintao. The two countries issued a joint declaration on a number of global strategic issues, particularly urging a peaceful resolution to the USA's diplomatic crisis with Iraq. Russia also participated in multilateral negotiations in China in mid-2003, attended by representatives of the Governments of China, the Democratic People's Republic of Korea (DPRK—North Korea), Japan, the Republic of Korea (South Korea) and the USA, which were intended to encourage the DPRK to abandon its nuclear weapons programme. In October 2004 a treaty was signed by Presidents Putin and Hu settling a long-running dispute over the course of the border between the two states, particularly with regard to a number of islands in the Amur river. The decision, announced in early 2005, to build a long-planned petroleum export pipeline from eastern Siberia to the Pacific coast, rather than south to China, was perceived as a potential reverse in Sino-Russian relations; however, an accord was reached in April regarding the continuation of Russian petroleum supplies to China, with the possibility of an additional branch of the pipeline being constructed to accommodate Chinese needs. In mid-2005 Russia and China conducted joint military manoeuvres for the first time.

Government

Under the Constitution of December 1993, the Russian Federation is a democratic, federative, multi-ethnic republic, in which state power is divided between the legislature, executive and judiciary, which are independent of one another. The President of the Russian Federation is Head of State and Commander-in-Chief of the Armed Forces, and also holds broad executive powers. The President, who is elected for a term of four years, renewable once, by universal direct suffrage, appoints the Chairman of the Government (Prime Minister). Supreme legislative power is vested in the bicameral Federalnoye Sobraniye (Federal Assembly). The upper chamber is the 176-member Sovet Federatsii (Federation Council), which comprises two representatives from each of the country's federal territorial units (appointed by the legislature and the executive in each region); its lower chamber is the 450-member Gosudarstvennaya Duma (State Duma), which is elected by direct universal suffrage for a period of four years.

For much of the 1990s and the first half of the 2000s the Russian Federation comprised 89 federal territorial units ('federal subjects'). Following the formation of Perm Krai by the merger of Perm Oblast with the Komi-Permyak Autonomous Okrug, which took effect from 1 December 2005, the number of federal subjects was reduced to 88, comprising 21 republics, seven krais (provinces), 48 oblasts (regions), two cities of federal status, one autonomous oblast and nine autonomous okrugs (districts). Further mergers were expected to take place in 2007 and 2008. The republics and the autonomous oblast and okrugs are nominally representative of ethnic groups, and the administrative oblasts and krais of geographic regions. The cities of Moscow and St Petersburg have special administrative status. In May 2000 the federal subjects were grouped into seven federal okrugs, each headed by a presidential appointee. In December 2004 the federal legislature approved proposals, initially presented by President Putin, in accordance with which governors of all federal subjects were henceforth to be appointed by the federal authorities, subject to approval by regional legislatures (the direct election of regional leaders had become almost universal across the Federation by the late 1990s); the election of a Governor in the Nenets Autonomous Okrug in January–February 2005 was expected to represent the final such poll. During the course of 2005 the appointment of governors became widespread, sometimes occurring when an incumbent regional leader's mandate expired, but also taking place when a leader requested an expression of confidence from the federal President. During that year only a small number of incumbent leaders were not returned to office as a result of these procedures.

Defence

In May 1992 the Russian Federation established its own armed forces, on the basis of former Soviet forces on the territory of the Russian Federation, and former Soviet forces outside its territory not subordinate to other former republics of the USSR. In August 2005 the total Russian active armed forces numbered an estimated 1,037,000, with an estimated 20,000,000 reserves. These included an estimated 129,000 permanent members of the Strategic Deterrent Forces, an estimated 395,000 in the army (including some 190,000 conscripts), 142,000 in the navy, and an estimated 170,000 in the air force, following its merger with the air defence troops. There were a further estimated 415,000 paramilitary troops. Conscription is compulsory for males over the age of 18 years, and lasts for 18–24 months. However, the rate of conscription evasion is reported to be extremely high. In November 2005 President Putin announced that the duration of service by conscription was to be reduced to 12 months by January 2008. The defence budget for 2005 allocated 529,000m. roubles to defence.

Economic Affairs

In 2004, according to estimates by the World Bank, Russia's gross national income (GNI), measured at average 2002–04 prices, was US $487,335m., equivalent to $3,410 per head (or $9,620 per head on an international purchasing-power parity basis). Between 1995 and 2004, it was estimated, the population declined by an annual average of 0.4%, while gross domestic product (GDP) per head increased, in real terms, at an average annual rate of 4.0%. According to the World Bank, overall GDP increased, in real terms, at an average annual rate of 3.6% in 1995–2004. Real GDP increased by 7.2% in 2004 and by 6.4% in 2005.

Agriculture contributed 5.4% of GDP in 2005. In 2003, according to the ILO, 10.0% of the employed labour force were engaged in the agricultural sector. The principal agricultural products are grain, potatoes and livestock. In 1990 the Russian Government began a programme to encourage the development of private farming, to replace the state and collective farms. Legislation to permit the sale and purchase of agricultural land from 2003 was approved by the Gosudarstvennaya Duma in June 2002. According to World Bank estimates, real agricultural GDP increased at an average annual rate of 2.6% in 1995–2003; the GDP of the sector increased by 3.4% in 2002 and by 2.7% in 2003.

Industry contributed 37.1% of GDP in 2005. In 2003 the industrial sector (including mining, manufacturing, construction and utilities) provided 45.9% of employment. According to estimates by the World Bank, industrial GDP declined, in real terms, by an annual average of 3.6% in 1995–2003. Industrial GDP increased by 3.8% in 2002 and by 8.5% in 2003.

Mining and quarrying contributed 10.5% of GDP in 2005 and employed 1.7% of the employed labour force in 2003. Russia has considerable reserves of energy-bearing minerals, including one-third of the world's natural gas reserves and substantial deposits of petroleum, coal and peat. It also has large supplies of palladium, platinum and rhodium. Other minerals exploited include bauxite, cobalt, copper, diamonds, gold, iron ore, mica, nickel and tin.

The manufacturing sector contributed 17.4% of GDP in 2005, and the sector provided 19.8% of employment in 2003.

Electric energy is derived from petroleum-, gas- and coal-fired power stations, nuclear power stations and hydroelectric installations. In 2002 Russia's 29 nuclear reactors supplied some 15.9% of total electricity generation, while coal accounted for some 19.2% of Russia's generating capacity; hydroelectric power accounted for 18.2% of electricity production, and 43.3% of the country's generating capacity originated from natural gas. Russia is a major exporter of natural gas and crude petroleum, and Russia's largest company, Gazprom, is also the world's largest producer of natural gas. Countries of the CIS remain highly dependent on Russia for imports of these fuels. However, owing to high levels of non-payment from certain countries, from the late 1990s Russia sought, with some success, to increase its exports of mineral fuels to other countries, particularly to the countries of central and western Europe. The construction of the 'Blue Stream' pipeline, which was to carry natural gas from Novorossiisk, Krasnodar Krai, in southern Russia, to Ankara, Turkey, was completed in October 2002, and was expected to facilitate further growth in Russia's energy exports. In early 2005 it was announced that a pipeline would be constructed from eastern Siberia to the port of Nakhodka on the Pacific Coast, enabling exports to Japan and the wider Pacific region; this route was chosen in favour of a long-discussed alternative route to the People's Republic of China (see above). Imports of fuel comprised just 2.3% of the value of Russia's total merchandise imports in 2003.

The services sector contributed 57.5% of GDP in 2005, and provided 44.1% of employment in 2003. According to estimates by the World Bank, the GDP of the services sector increased, in real terms, at an average annual rate of 3.0% in 1995–2003. The GDP of the sector increased by 5.5% in 2002 and by 7.1% in 2003.

In 2004 Russia recorded a visible trade surplus of US $85,825m., and there was a surplus of $58,563m. on the current account of the balance of payments. In 2003 the most significant source of imports was Germany (accounting for 14.1% of the total), followed by Belarus (8.5%), Ukraine (7.7%), the People's Republic of China (5.7%) and the USA (5.2%). The largest market for Russian exports in 2003 was the Netherlands (purchasing 6.2% of the total), followed by China (5.8%) and Belarus (5.7%). The principal exports in 2003 were mineral fuels and lubricants (comprising 52.8% of Russia's total exports), followed by basic manufactures (14.4%), and machinery and transport equipment (6.9%). The principal imports in that year were machinery and transport equipment (accounting for 31.6% of total imports), followed by food and live animals (15.2%), basic manufactures (13.4%), and chemicals and related products (12.0%).

In 2004 Russia recorded a surplus on the federal budget of 342,099.2m. roubles, equivalent to 2.0% of GDP. At the end of 2003 the country's total external debt was US $175,257m., of which $98,264m. was long-term public debt. In that year the cost of debt-servicing was equivalent to 11.8% of the value of exports of goods and services. In 1995–2004 the average annual rate of inflation was 27.0%. Following the collapse of the rouble in 1998, the rate of inflation was 85.7% in 1999, but it declined thereafter. The rate of inflation was 12.0% in 2003 and 11.7% in 2004. In November 2004 some 6.1m. people (8.3% of the labour force) were unemployed.

Russia became a member of the World Bank and the IMF in 1992. Russia is also a member (as a 'Country of Operations') of the European Bank for Reconstruction and Development (EBRD, see p. 224). In 1994 Russia signed an agreement of partnership and co-operation with the European Union (EU, see p. 228). Russia is also pursuing membership of the World Trade Organization (WTO, see p. 370). Russia joined the Asia-Pacific Economic Co-operation forum (APEC, see p. 164) in 1998.

After the dissolution of the USSR, a programme of economic reforms was initiated to effect the transition from a centrally planned economy to a market-orientated system. Following a severe financial crisis in August 1998, Russia recorded sustained growth in subsequent years, although analysts expressed concern that this growth was largely attributable to high international prices for petroleum, natural gas and metals, Russia's principal exports, rather than the result of structural reforms or technological or industrial innovations. The Government of President Vladimir Putin, from 2000, initially appeared to implement economic reforms more consistently than had the Yeltsin administration in the 1990s, with significant reforms in the areas of land ownership, fiscal procedure and banking being introduced in 2001–03. Moreover, in mid-2003 Russia was removed from the list of 'non-compliant' countries and territories of the Financial Action Task Force on Money Laundering (FATF), following the introduction of measures intended to hinder money 'laundering'. In early 2003 Putin announced that a priority of his administration was to increase Russia's GDP two-fold over a period of 10 years, while a decline in both the rate of inflation and the unemployment rate in the early 2000s appeared to mark the onset of relative stability. None the less, surveys by the German-based NGO Transparency International indicated that Russia continued to be perceived as a highly corrupt country in 2005, and a report by the Russian Ministry of Internal Affairs, published in late 2005, stated that the 'shadow' economy continued to account for more than 40% of GDP. The merger in early 2003 of two Russian petroleum companies, Sidanco and Tyumen Oil Co (TNK), with the Russian interests of BP (United Kingdom), to form TNK-BP, represented an unprecedented level of co-operation between Russian and foreign investors in the Russian petroleum sector. (Although in late 2005 BP sold a substantial proportion of its interests in Russia to various Russian firms, the company emphasized that it remained committed to operations in Russia.) However, the dismantling, in late 2004, of the privately owned petroleum company Yukos, and the effective renationalization of its most productive subsidiary, Yuganskneftegaz, through its effective acquisition by the state-owned petroleum company Rosneft (see Recent History), was widely regarded as a reverse from the principles of privatization that the Putin administration had previously appeared to endorse. This, together with the approval in late 2005 of legislation that limited the degree of involvement permitted to foreign companies in the exploitation of Russian sub-soil natural resources in certain designated regions and projects, raised concerns that Russia was becoming less hospitable to foreign investors, although only three large petroleum fields were to be subject to these restrictions, which were considerably less rigorous than had initially been anticipated. However, in early 2005 Putin emphasized that the Government had no intention of reversing the privatizations conducted in the mid-1990s. Concerns that the Government was seeking to restrict foreign involvement in the Russian economy were further alleviated in early 2006, when it was announced that, henceforth, foreign investors were to be permitted to own up to 49% of the natural gas monopoly, Gazprom (hitherto, foreigners had not been permitted to own more than 20% of the company; the remaining 51% was to remain under state control). In the mid-2000s Gazprom contributed around 8% of GDP and was increasingly regarded as playing an important role in Russia's international relations; indeed, the construction of a new natural gas pipeline from Russia to Germany, under the Baltic Sea, which was expected to commence operations in 2010, was regarded with considerable concern by the Governments of the Baltic states and Poland, which were effectively by-passed by the pipeline. (The appointment of the former German Chancellor, Gerhard Schröder, to a senior position in relation to this project, further heightened concerns.) Nevertheless, high demand in Europe and East Asia for Russian fossil fuels, together with the potential mineral wealth of vast, as yet unexploited areas of the country's territory, meant there was potential for continued economic success in the late 2000s, although corruption and a continuing demographic crisis remained serious obstacles to sustained growth.

Education

Education is compulsory for nine years, to be undertaken between the ages of six and 15 years. State education is generally provided free of charge, although in 1992 some higher education establishments began charging tuition fees. Students of selected courses in higher education receive a small stipend from the state. Primary education usually begins at seven years of age and lasts for three years. Secondary education, beginning at 10 years of age, lasts for seven years, comprising a first cycle of five years and a second of two years. In 1997 the total enrolment at primary schools was equivalent to 99.9% of the school-age population. Secondary enrolment in that year was equivalent to 87.6% of children in the appropriate age-group.

The level of education in the Russian Federation is relatively high, and 6.9m. students were enrolled at institutes of higher education in 2004/05. Although Russian is the principal language used in educational establishments, a number of local languages are also in use. Budgetary expenditure on education (excluding scientific research and technology) in 2004 was an estimated 117,791.9m. roubles (representing 4.9% of total federal government expenditure).

All educational institutions were state-owned under Soviet rule, but a wide range of independent schools and colleges commenced operations in the early 1990s. In 2000/01 there were some 635 independent schools and 358 independent higher education institutions. In the early 1990s there were extensive changes to the curriculum in all branches of the education system, including an end to the study of politically-inspired subjects, a new approach to the study of Soviet and Russian history, and the introduction of study of previously prohibited literary works.

Public Holidays

2006: 1–5 January (for New Year), 7 January (Orthodox Christmas), 23 February (Defenders of the Fatherland Day), 8 March (International Women's Day), 1 May (Spring Holiday and Labour Day), 9 May (Victory Day), 12 June (Russia Day), 4 November (National Unity Day).

2007: 1–5 January (for New Year), 7 January (Orthodox Christmas), 23 February (Defenders of the Fatherland Day), 8 March (International Women's Day), 1 May (Spring Holiday and Labour Day), 9 May (Victory Day), 12 June (Russia Day), 4 November (National Unity Day).

Weights and Measures

The metric system is in force.

THE RUSSIAN FEDERATION

Statistical Survey

Statistical Survey

Source (unless otherwise indicated): Federal Service of State Statistics 103450 Moscow, ul. Myasnitskaya 39; tel. (495) 207-49-02; fax (495) 207-40-87; e-mail stat@gks.ru; internet www.gks.ru.

Area and Population

AREA, POPULATION AND DENSITY

Area (sq km)	17,075,400*
Population (census results)	
12 January 1989	147,021,869
9–16 October 2002	
Males	67,605,133
Females	77,561,598
Total	145,166,731
Population (official estimates at 1 January)	
2003	144,963,700
2004	144,168,200
2005	143,474,200
Density (per sq km) at 1 January 2005	8.4

* 6,592,850 sq miles.

POPULATION BY ETHNIC GROUP
(census of 9–16 October 2002)

	'000	%
Russian[1]	115,889.1	79.83
Tatar[2]	5,554.6	3.83
Ukrainian	2,943.0	2.03
Bashkir	1,673.4	1.15
Chuvash	1,637.1	1.13
Chechen[3]	1,360.2	0.94
Armenian	1,130.5	0.78
Mordovian[4]	843.4	0.58
Avar[5]	814.5	0.56
Belarusian	808.0	0.56
Kazakh	654.0	0.45
Udmurt	636.9	0.44
Azeri	621.8	0.43
Mari[6]	604.3	0.42
German	597.2	0.41
Kabardin	520.1	0.36
Osetiyan[7]	514.9	0.35
Dargin[8]	510.2	0.35
Others[9]	7,853.5	5.41
Total	145,166.7	100.00

[1] Including Cossacks (140,028) and Pomors (6,571).
[2] Including Astrakhan Tatars (2,003), Kryashens (Christian Tatars, 24,668) and Siberian Tatars (9,611), but excluding Crimean Tatars (4,131).
[3] Including Chechen-akkintsy (218).
[4] Including Erzya-Mordovians (84,407) and Moksha-Mordovians (49,624).
[5] Including Akhvakhtsy (6,376), Andiitsy (21,808), Archintsy (89), Bagulaly (40), Bezhtintsy (6,198), Botlikhtsy (16), Chamalaly (12), Didoitsy (15,256), Ginukhtsy (531), Godoberintsy (39), Gunzibtsy (998), Karatintsy (6,052), Khvarshiny (128) and Tindaly (44).
[6] Including Lugovo-Vostochnye Mari (56,119) and Mountain Mari (18,515).
[7] Including Digor-Osetiyans (607) and Irontsy-Osetiyans (97).
[8] Including Kaitagtsy (5) and Kubachintsy (88).
[9] Including 1,460,751 respondents (1.01% of the total) who did not state their nationality or ethnic group.

ADMINISTRATIVE DIVISIONS
(census of 9–16 October 2002, except where otherwise stated)

Territory	Area ('000 sq km)	Population ('000)	Density (per sq km)	Capital (with population, '000)*
Central Federal Okrug	650.7	38,000.7	58.4	Moscow
City of Federal Status				
Moscow City	1.0	10,382.7	10,382.7	Moscow (10,407)
Oblasts				
Belgorod	27.1	1,511.6	55.8	Belgorod (341)
Bryansk	34.9	1,378.9	39.5	Bryansk (424)
Ivanovo	21.8	1,148.3	52.7	Ivanovo (418)
Kaluga	29.9	1,041.6	34.8	Kaluga (329)
Kostroma	60.1	736.6	12.3	Kostroma (276)
Kursk	29.8	1,235.1	41.4	Kursk (406)
Lipetsk	24.1	1,213.5	50.3	Lipetsk (503)
Moscow	46.0	6,618.5	143.9	Moscow†
Orel Oblast	24.7	860.3	34.8	Orel (329)
Ryazan	39.6	1,227.9	31.0	Ryazan (516)
Smolensk	49.8	1,049.6	21.1	Smolensk (319)
Tambov	34.3	1,178.4	34.3	Tambov (287)
Tula	25.7	1,675.8	65.2	Tula (466)
Tver	84.1	1,471.5	17.5	Tver (407)
Vladimir	29.0	1,524.0	52.6	Vladimir (310)
Voronezh	52.4	2,378.8	45.4	Voronezh (849)
Yaroslavl	36.4	1,367.3	37.6	Yaroslavl (605)
North-Western Federal Okrug	1,677.9	13,974.5	8.3	St Petersburg
City of Federal Status				
St Petersburg	0.6	4,661.2	7,768.3	St Petersburg (4,600)
Republics				
Kareliya	172.4	716.3	4.2	Petrozavodsk (266)
Komi	415.9	1,018.7	2.4	Syktyvkar (229)
Oblasts				
Archangel	587.4	1,336.5	2.3	Archangel (352)
Nenets AOk	176.7	41.5	0.2	Naryn-Mar (19‡)
Kaliningrad	15.1	955.3	63.2	Kaliningrad (426)
Leningrad	85.3	1,669.2	19.6	St Petersburg†
Murmansk	144.9	892.5	6.2	Murmansk (325)
Novgorod	55.3	694.4	12.5	Velikii Novgorod (219)
Pskov	55.3	760.8	13.8	Pskov (200)
Vologda	145.7	1,269.6	8.7	Vologda (288)
Southern Federal Okrug	589.2	22,907.1	38.9	Rostov-on-Don
Republics				
Adygeya	7.6	447.1	58.8	Maikop (157)
Chechen (Nokhchi)§	n.a.	1,103.7	n.a.	Groznyi (216)
Dagestan	50.3	2,576.5	51.2	Makhachkala (465)
Ingushetiya§	n.a.	467.3	n.a.	Magas (0‡)
Kabardino-Balkar	12.5	901.5	72.2	Nalchik (273)
Kalmykiya	75.9	292.4	3.8	Elista (103)
Karachai-Cherkess	14.1	439.5	31.2	Cherkessk (117)
North Osetiya—Alaniya	8.0	710.3	88.8	Vladikavkaz (314)

THE RUSSIAN FEDERATION

Statistical Survey

Territory—*continued*	Area ('000 sq km)	Population ('000)	Density (per sq km)	Capital (with population, '000)*
Krais				
Krasnodar	76.0	5,125.2	67.4	Krasnodar (715)
Stavropol	66.5	2,735.1	41.1	Stavropol (356)
Oblasts				
Astrakhan	44.1	1,005.3	22.8	Astrakhan (501)
Rostov	100.8	4,404.0	43.7	Rostov-on-Don (1,058)
Volgograd	113.9	2,699.2	23.7	Volgograd (999)
Volga Federal Okrug	1,038.0	31,155.5	30.0	Nizhnii Novgorod
Republics				
Bashkortostan	143.6	4,104.3	28.6	Ufa (1,036)
Chuvash	18.3	1,313.8	71.8	Cheboksary (443)
Marii-El	23.2	728.0	31.4	Yoshkar-Ola (253)
Mordoviya	26.2	888.8	33.9	Saransk (299)
Tatarstan	68.0	3,779.3	55.6	Kazan (1,110)
Udmurt	42.1	1,570.3	37.3	Izhevsk (623)
Krai				
Perm¶	160.6	2,819.4	17.6	Perm (989)
Oblasts				
Kirov	120.8	1,503.5	12.5	Kirov (449)
Nizhnii Novgorod	76.9	3,524.0	45.8	Nizhnii Novgorod (1,289)
Orenburg	124.0	2,180.0	17.6	Orenburg (539)
Penza	43.2	1,452.9	33.6	Penza (513)
Samara	53.6	3,239.7	60.4	Samara (1,133)
Saratov	100.2	2,668.3	26.6	Saratov (858)
Ulyanovsk	37.3	1,382.5	37.1	Ulyanovsk (623)
Urals Federal Okrug	1,788.9	12,373.9	6.9	Yekaterinburg
Oblasts				
Chelyabinsk	87.9	3,603.3	41.0	Chelyabinsk (1,095)
Kurgan	71.0	1,019.5	14.4	Kurgan (334)
Sverdlovsk	194.8	4,486.2	23.0	Yekaterinburg (1,304)
Tyumen	1,435.2	3,264.8	2.3	Tyumen (538)
Khanty-Mansii AOk—Yugra	523.1	1,432.8	2.7	Khanty-Mansiisk (41‡)
Yamalo-Nenets AOk	750.3	507.0	0.7	Salekhard (37‡)
Siberian Federal Okrug	5,114.8	20,062.9	3.9	Novosibirsk
Republics				
Altai	92.6	202.9	2.2	Gorno-Altaisk (54‡)
Buryatiya	351.3	981.2	2.8	Ulan-Ude (353)
Khakasiya	61.9	546.1	8.8	Abakan (165)
Tyva	170.5	305.5	1.8	Kyzyl (108)
Krais				
Altai	169.1	2,607.4	15.4	Barnaul (631)
Krasnoyarsk	2,339.7	2,966.0	1.3	Krasnoyarsk (917)
Evenk AOk	767.6	17.7	0.0	Tura (6‡)
Taimyr (Dolgano-Nenets) AOk	862.1	39.8	0.0	Dudinka (25‡)
Oblasts				
Chita	431.5	1,155.3	2.7	Chita (308)
Aga-Buryat AOk	19.0	72.2	3.8	Aginskoye (12‡)
Irkutsk	767.9	2,581.7	3.4	Irkutsk (583)
Ust-Orda Buryat AOk	22.4	135.3	6.0	Ust-Ordynskii (30‡)
Kemerovo	95.5	2,899.1	30.4	Kemerovo (523)
Novosibirsk	178.2	2,692.3	15.1	Novosibirsk (1,406)
Omsk	139.7	2,079.2	14.9	Omsk (1,143)
Tomsk	316.9	1,046.0	3.3	Tomsk (487)
Far Eastern Federal Okrug	6,215.9	6,692.9	1.1	Khabarovsk
Republic				
Sakha (Yakutiya)	3,103.2	949.3	0.3	Yakutsk (236)
Krais				
Khabarovsk	788.6	1,436.6	1.8	Khabarovsk (579)
Maritime (Primorskii)	165.9	2,071.2	12.5	Vladivostok (587)
Oblasts				
Amur	363.7	902.8	2.5	Blagoveshchensk (218)
Kamchatka	472.3	358.8	0.8	Petropavlovsk-Kamchatskii (196)
Koryak AOk	301.5	25.2	0.1	Palana (4‡)
Magadan	461.4	182.7	0.4	Magadan (99‡)
Sakhalin	87.1	546.7	6.3	Yuzhno-Sakhalinsk (174)
Autonomous Oblast				
Jewish	36.0	190.9	5.3	Birobidzhan (77‡)
Autonomous Okrug (AOk)				
Chukot	737.7	53.8	0.1	Anadyr (11‡)
Russian Federation	17,075.4	145,166.7	8.5	Moscow

* Official estimates of population at 1 January 2005, except where otherwise stated.
† Although Moscow and St Petersburg are the administrative centres of Moscow and Leningrad Oblasts, respectively, the cities themselves do not form part of the oblasts.
‡ Population at the 2002 census (preliminary result).
§ Before 1992 the territories of the Chechen (Nokchi) Republic and the Republic of Ingushetiya were combined in the Checheno-Ingush Autonomous Republic (area 19,300 sq km).
¶ Perm Krai was formed on 1 December 2005 by the merger of Perm Oblast and the Komi-Permyak Autonomous Okrug.

THE RUSSIAN FEDERATION

Statistical Survey

PRINCIPAL TOWNS
(1 January 2005, official estimates, rounded figures)

Town	Population	Town	Population
Moskva (Moscow, the capital)	10,407,000	Naberezhnye Chelnyi	508,000
Sankt-Peterburg (St Petersburg)*	4,600,000	Lipetsk	503,000
Novosibirsk	1,406,000	Astrakhan	501,000
Yekaterinburg*	1,304,000	Tomsk	487,000
Nizhnii Novgorod*	1,289,000	Tula	466,000
Omsk	1,143,000	Makhachkala	465,000
Samara*	1,133,000	Kirov*	449,000
Kazan	1,110,000	Cheboksary	443,000
Chelyabinsk	1,095,000	Kaliningrad	426,000
Rostov-na-Donu (Rostov-on-Don)	1,058,000	Bryansk	424,000
Ufa	1,036,000	Ivanovo	418,000
Volgograd	999,000	Magnitogorsk	417,000
Perm	989,000	Tver*	407,000
Krasnoyarsk	917,000	Kursk	406,000
Saratov	858,000	Nizhnii Tagil	383,000
Voronezh	849,000	Stavropol	356,000
Krasnodar	715,000	Ulan-Ude	353,000
Tolyatti	705,000	Arkhangelsk (Archangel)	352,000
Barnaul	631,000	Belgorod	341,000
Izhevsk*	623,000	Kurgan	334,000
Ulyanovsk*	623,000	Kaluga	329,000
Yaroslavl	605,000	Orel	329,000
Vladivostok	587,000	Sochi	329,000
Irkutsk	583,000	Murmansk	325,000
Khabarovsk	579,000	Smolensk	319,000
Novokuznetsk	563,000	Vladikavkaz*	314,000
Orenburg	539,000	Vladimir	310,000
Tyumen	538,000	Cherepovets	309,000
Kemerovo	523,000	Volzhskii	309,000
Ryazan	516,000	Chita	309,000
Penza	513,000		

* Some towns that were renamed during the Soviet period have reverted to their former names: St Petersburg (Leningrad); Nizhnii Novgorod (Gorkii); Yekaterinburg (Sverdlovsk); Samara (Kuibyshev); Izhevsk (Ustinov); Naberezhnye Chelny (Brezhnev); Tver (Kalinin); Vladikavkaz (Ordzhonikidze). The towns of Ulyanovsk and Kirov, which retained their Soviet-era names in the mid-2000s, are sometimes unofficially referred to by their pre-Soviet designations, of Simbirsk and Vyatka, respectively.

BIRTHS, MARRIAGES AND DEATHS

	Registered live births Number	Rate (per 1,000)	Registered marriages Number	Rate (per 1,000)	Registered deaths Number	Rate (per 1,000)
1997	1,259,943	8.6	928,411	6.3	2,015,779	13.7
1998	1,283,292	8.8	848,691	5.8	1,988,744	13.6
1999	1,214,689	8.3	911,162	6.2	2,144,316	14.7
2000	1,266,800	8.7	897,327	6.2	2,225,332	15.3
2001	1,311,604	9.0	1,001,589	6.9	2,254,856	15.6
2002	1,396,967	9.7	1,019,762	7.1	2,332,272	16.2
2003	1,477,301	10.2	1,091,778	7.6	2,365,826	16.4
2004	1,502,500*	10.4	979,700*	6.8	2,295,400*	16.0

* Rounded figure.

Expectation of life (WHO estimates, years at birth): 65 (males 58; females 72) in 2003 (Source: WHO, *World Health Report*).

IMMIGRATION AND EMIGRATION

	2002	2003	2004
Immigrants	184,612	129,144	119,157
Emigrants	106,685	94,018	79,795

ECONOMICALLY ACTIVE POPULATION
(sample surveys, '000 persons aged 15 to 72 years, at November, excl. Chechen Republic)

	2001	2002	2003
Agriculture, hunting and forestry	6,866	6,872	6,474
Fishing	190	172	177
Mining and quarrying	1,299	1,313	1,109
Manufacturing	12,663	12,721	13,166
Electricity, gas and water supply	1,643	1,882	2,193
Construction	3,363	3,621	4,316
Wholesale and retail trade; repair of motor vehicles and motorcycles and personal and household goods	8,833	9,298	9,765
Restaurants and hotels	1,005	1,114	1,259
Transport, storage and communications	5,931	5,809	5,957
Financial intermediation	828	842	755
Real estate, renting and business activities	2,594	2,535	3,775
Public administration and defence; compulsory social security	4,893	4,583	4,622
Education	5,729	6,030	6,043
Health and social work	4,649	4,690	4,790
Other community, social and personal service activities	4,158	4,270	2,066
Private households with employed persons	14	11	16
Extra-territorial organizations and bodies	6	3	13
Total employed	**64,664**	**65,766**	**66,496**
Males	33,435	33,615	34,023
Females	31,229	32,151	32,473
Unemployed	6,303	6,154	n.a.
Total labour force	**70,968**	**71,919**	**n.a.**

Source: mostly ILO.

2002 (sample surveys, '000 persons aged 15 to 72 years, at November, revised figures, incl. Chechen Republic): Total employed 65,858 (males 33,653, females 32,205); Unemployed 6,268; Total labour force 72,127.

2003 (sample surveys, '000 persons aged 15 to 72 years, at November, revised figures, incl. Chechen Republic): Total employed 67,247 (males 34,229, females 33,018); Unemployed 5,951; Total labour force 73,198.

2004 (sample surveys, '000 persons aged 15 to 72 years, at November, incl. Chechen Republic): Total employed 67,244 (males 34,227, females 33,017); Unemployed 6,116; Total labour force 73,359.

Health and Welfare

KEY INDICATORS

Total fertility rate (children per woman, 2003)	1.1
Under-5 mortality rate (per 1,000 live births, 2004)	21
HIV/AIDS (% of persons aged 15–49, 2003)	1.1
Physicians (per 1,000 head, 2001)	4.17
Hospital beds (per 1,000 head, 2001)	10.83
Health expenditure (2002): US $ per head (PPP)	535
Health expenditure (2002): % of GDP	6.2
Health expenditure (2002): public (% of total)	55.8
Access to water (% of persons, 1999)	99
Human Development Index (2003): ranking	62
Human Development Index (2003): value	0.795

For sources and definitions, see explanatory note on p. vi.

THE RUSSIAN FEDERATION

Agriculture

PRINCIPAL CROPS
('000 metric tons)

	2002	2003	2004
Wheat	50,609.1	34,104.3	45,412.7
Rice (paddy)	490.0	450.8	471.1
Barley	18,738.9	18,003.3	17,179.7
Maize	1,562.9	2,121.9	3,515.7
Rye	7,126.7	4,151.9	2,871.9
Oats	5,694.2	5,183.4	4,954.8
Millet	292.9	975.2	1,117.2
Sorghum	27.3	33.4	43.7
Buckwheat	302.5	525.4	649.6
Potatoes	32,870.8	36,746.5	35,914.2
Sugar beet	15,664.8	19,383.7	21,848.3
Dry peas	1,267.5	1,052.1	1,242.5
Soybeans (Soya beans)	422.8	393.3	555.3
Sunflower seed	3,684.4	4,870.6	4,800.7
Rapeseed	115.0	192.1	275.9
Cabbages	3,651.9	4,442.2	4,067.7
Tomatoes	1,979.5	2,021.1	2,017.9
Cucumbers and gherkins	1,173.7	1,312.0	1,321.9
Dry onions	1,402.2	1,564.7	1,673.4
Garlic	230.2	219.6	236.2
Carrots	1,474.1	1,735.8	1,762.0
Other vegetables*	3,122.4	3,484.9	3,508.6
Watermelons	857.2	932.4	920.4
Apples*	1,950	1,690	2,030
Cherries (incl. sour cherries)*	260	290	325
Plums*	152	160	178
Strawberries*	200	205	215
Raspberries*	165	150	170
Currants*	347	345	396
Grapes	217.4	348.3	318.3
Other fruits*	270.5	263.0	308.5

* Unofficial figures.
Source: FAO.

LIVESTOCK
('000 head at 1 January)

	2002	2003	2004
Horses	1,578	1,499	1,500*
Cattle	27,107	26,524	24,935
Pigs	16,047	17,337	15,980
Sheep	13,035	13,728	14,669
Goats	2,292	2,322	2,361
Chickens	335,356	337,027	328,338
Turkeys	3,000†	2,500†	2,500*
Geese	4,000†	2,950†	2,800*

* FAO estimate.
† Unofficial figure.
Source: FAO.

LIVESTOCK PRODUCTS
('000 metric tons)

	2002	2003	2004
Beef and veal	1,957.3	1,989.5	1,951.2
Mutton and lamb	115.3	114.0	125.6
Pig meat	1,583.3	1,706.3	1,643.9
Poultry meat	937.6	1,030.4	1,152.2
Other meat	106.6	104.6	107.6
Cows' milk	33,208.9	33,085.3	31,664.3
Goats' milk	294.4	287.1	268.2
Cheese*	496.2	528.7	517.9
Butter	279.1	284.8	276.2
Hen eggs	2,022.5	2,032.5	1,991.5
Honey	49.4	48.0	52.8
Wool: greasy	41.4	43.4	45.6
Wool: scoured	20.7	21.7	22.8
Cattle hides*	224.4	229.1	222.7

* FAO estimates.
Source: FAO.

Forestry

ROUNDWOOD REMOVALS
('000 cubic metres, excl. bark)

	2002	2003	2004
Sawlogs, veneer logs and logs for sleepers	57,100	54,574	58,758
Pulpwood	51,400	50,886	54,171
Other industrial wood	10,100	21,140	21,071
Fuel wood	46,400	47,400	48,000
Total	**165,000**	**174,000**	**182,000**

Source: FAO.

SAWNWOOD PRODUCTION
('000 cubic metres, incl. railway sleepers)

	2002*	2003	2004
Coniferous (softwood)	16,931	17,736	18,900
Broadleaved (hardwood)	2,309	2,419	2,600
Total	**19,240**	**20,155**	**21,500**

* Unofficial figures.
Source: FAO.

Fishing

('000 metric tons, live weight)

	2001	2002	2003
Capture	3,628.5	3,232.3	3,281.2
Pink (humpback) salmon	167.6	117.6	188.1
Atlantic cod	188.9	188.2	186.2
Alaska (Walleye) pollock	1,145.0	826.7	1,055.9
Blue whiting (Poutassou)	315.6	298.4	360.2
Atlantic herring	127.4	128.1	144.2
Pacific herring	278.5	203.4	190.8
Capelin	181.6	250.9	96.0
Aquaculture	89.9	101.3	108.7
Total catch	**3,718.4**	**3,333.6**	**3,389.9**

Note: Figures exclude seaweeds and other aquatic plants ('000 metric tons): 28.0 (capture 27.5, aquaculture 0.5) in 2001; 55.5 (capture 55.4, aquaculture 0.1) in 2002; 38.9 (capture 38.8, aquaculture 0.1) in 2003. Also excluded are aquatic mammals, recorded by number rather than weight. The number of whales caught was: 120 in 2001; 153 in 2002; 195 in 2003. The number of seals (incl. walrus) caught was: 47,544 in 2001; 46,819 in 2002; 48,412 in 2003.

Source: FAO.

Mining

('000 metric tons, unless otherwise indicated)

	2000	2001	2002
Hard coal	172,060	155,721	164,520
Lignite	83,740	100,100	74,200
Crude petroleum	324,000	348,000	379,000
Natural gas (million cu metres)*	584,000	581,000	595,000
Iron ore: gross weight	86,630	82,850†	84,236
Iron ore: metal content	50,000	48,000†	49,000†
Copper ore†‡	570	600	695
Nickel ore†‡	315	325	310
Bauxite†	4,200	4,000	3,800
Lead ore‡	13.3	12.3†	13.5†
Zinc ore‡	136§	124	130
Tin (metric tons)†‡	5,000	4,500	2,900
Manganese ore†‡	23	23	23
Chromium ore	92.0	69.9	70.0†
Tungsten concentrates (metric tons)†‡	3,500	3,500	3,400
Molybdenum (metric tons)†	2,400	2,600	2,900
Antimony ore (metric tons)†‡	4,500	4,500	n.a.

THE RUSSIAN FEDERATION

—continued	2000	2001	2002
Cobalt ore (metric tons)[†][‡]	4,000	4,600	4,600
Mercury (metric tons)[†]	50	50	50
Silver (metric tons)[†][‡]	370	380	400
Uranium concentrate (metric tons)[†][‡]	2,500	2,500	2,900
Gold (metric tons)[†][‡]	142.7	152.5	158.0
Platinum (metric tons)[†]	34	35	34
Palladium (metric tons)[†]	71	72	69
Kaolin (concentrate)	45.0	45.0[†]	45.0[†]
Magnesite[†]	1,000	1,000	1,000
Phosphate rock (Apatite)[§][‖]	4,150[§]	3,900[§]	4,100
Potash[†][¶]	3,700	4,300	4,400
Native sulphur[†]	50	50	50
Fluorspar (concentrate)	187.6	190.0[†]	200.0[†]
Barite (Barytes)[†]	60	60	60
Salt (unrefined)	3,200[†]	2,800	2,800[†]
Diamonds: gems ('000 metric carats):			
gem[†]	11,600	11,600	11,500
industrial[†]	11,600	11,600	11,500
Gypsum (crude)[†]	700	700	700
Graphite[†]	6	6	6
Asbestos[†]	750	750	750
Mica[†]	100	100	100
Talc[†]	100	100	100
Feldspar[†]	45	45	45
Peat (fuel use)	2,100	2,100	2,100[†]

* Marketed production.
† Estimated production.
‡ Figures refer to the metal content of ores.
§ Reported figure.
‖ Figures refer to the phosphoric acid content. The data exclude sedimentary rock (estimates, '000 metric tons): 300 per year in 2000–02.
¶ Figures refer to the potassium oxide content.

Source: US Geological Survey.

Industry

SELECTED PRODUCTS
('000 metric tons, unless otherwise indicated)

	2000	2001	2002
Margarine	319	373	396
Wheat flour	10,388	10,399	9,568
Raw sugar	6,077	6,590	6,165
Vodka and other spirits (million hectolitres)	12.3	13.1	14.0
Wine ('000 hectolitres)	2,410	2,740	3,329
Beer ('000 hectolitres)	51,563	63,780	70,266
Cigarettes (million)	333,953	355,632	382,503
Wool yarn (pure and mixed)	31.1	30.2	24.2
Cotton yarn (pure and mixed)	271.8	296.0	296.3
Flax, ramie and hemp yarn	19.8	22.0	23.2
Cotton fabrics (million sq metres)	2,026	2,209	2,173
Woollen fabrics (million sq metres)	67.2	67.5	55.2
Linen fabrics (million sq metres)	91.6	101.3	101.2
Leather footwear ('000 pairs)	32,935	36,794	41,860
Plywood ('000 cubic metres)	1,484	1,590	1,808
Particle board ('000 cubic metres)	2,335	2,545	2,732
Mechanical wood pulp	1,196	1,215	1,202
Chemical and semi-chemical wood pulp	4,646	4,937	5,212
Newsprint	1,694	1,732	1,713
Other printing and writing paper	575	639	659
Other paper and paperboard	6,251	6,112	5,673
Sulphuric acid	8,258	8,209	8,458
Caustic soda (sodium hydroxide)	1,241	1,197	1,146
Soda ash (sodium carbonate)	2,201	2,339	2,385
Nitrogenous fertilizers (a)[1,2]	5,818	5,890	5,968
Phosphate fertilizers (b)[1,2]	2,379	2,391	2,513
Potassic fertilizers (c)[1,2]	4,017	4,745	5,080
Synthetic rubber	836.8	919.3	920.1
Aviation gasoline	34	35	n.a.
Jet fuels	8,718	8,966	n.a.
Motor spirit (petrol)	27,152	27,610	n.a.
Kerosene	82	63	n.a.
Gas-diesel (distillate fuel) oils	49,249	50,161	n.a.
Residual fuel oils	53,347	55,575	n.a.
Lubricating oils	2,647	2,811	n.a.

—continued	2000	2001	2002
Petroleum wax (paraffin)	196	210	n.a.
Petroleum coke	1,123	874	n.a.
Petroleum bitumen (asphalt)	4,896	4,928	n.a.
Liquefied petroleum gas	7,329	7,903	n.a.
Coke	29,216	29,919	n.a.
Rubber tyres ('000)[3]	27,819	31,121	33,041
Rubber footwear ('000 pairs)	18,526	17,125	14,023
Cement	32,389	35,271	37,706
Pig-iron: foundry	1,140	1,306	1,415
Pig-iron: steel-making	43,352	43,634	45,199
Crude steel: for castings	3,633	3,718	3,755
Crude steel: ingots	55,517	55,312	56,128
Copper (refined, unwrought)[4]	840.0[5]	894.5[5]	870.0
Aluminium (unwrought): primary[4]	3,245.0	3,300.0	3,347.0
Tractors (number)[6]	19,231	14,193	9,174
Domestic refrigerators ('000)	1,151	1,542	1,733
Domestic washing machines ('000)	954	1,039	1,369
Television receivers ('000)	1,116	1,024	1,980
Radio receivers ('000)	390	281	253
Passenger motor cars ('000)	969	1,022	981
Buses and motor coaches (number)	54,040	56,506	66,692
Lorries (number)	184,489	172,597	172,552
Cameras: photographic ('000)	137	136	77
Watches ('000)[7]	7,438	7,024	6,047
Electric energy (million kWh)	877,766	891,284	n.a.

[1] Total production.
[2] Official figure(s).
[3] Tyres for road motor vehicles, excluding bicycles and motorcycles.
[4] Data from US Geological Survey.
[5] Estimated production.
[6] Tractors of 10 horse-power and over, excluding industrial tractors and tractors for tractor-trailer combinations.
[7] Household watches and clocks.

Source: mainly UN, *Industrial Commodity Statistics Yearbook*.

Finance

CURRENCY AND EXCHANGE RATES

Monetary Units
100 kopeks = 1 Russian rubl (ruble or rouble).

Sterling, Dollar and Euro Equivalents (30 December 2005)
£1 sterling = 49.561 roubles;
US $1 = 28.783 roubles;
€1 = 33.955 roubles;
1,000 roubles = £20.18 = $34.74 = €29.45.

Average Exchange Rate (roubles per US dollar)
2003   30.6920
2004   28.8137
2005   28.2844

Note: On 1 January 1998 a new rouble, equivalent to 1,000 of the former units, was introduced. Figures in this Survey are expressed in terms of new roubles, unless otherwise indicated.

THE RUSSIAN FEDERATION

Statistical Survey

FEDERAL BUDGET
(million roubles)

Revenue	2002	2003	2004
Tax revenue	1,726,310.1	1,892,363.7	2,071,384.5
Taxes on corporate profit and capital gains	207,443.7	179,550.5	164,587.4
Taxes on goods and services	n.a.	1,178,971.2	1,088,389.6
Value added tax	773,508.0	946,218.5	988,389.6
Excise duties	221,259.8	227,708.8	94,357.7
Natural gas	134,153.5	133,112.1	20,000.0
Taxes on the use of natural resources	183,715.7	183,129.5	279,381.1
Taxes on international trade and transactions	324,108.9	335,975.5	532,538.2
Customs duties on imports	118,669.0	150,355.9	180,613.5
Customs duties on exports	205,439.9	185,619.6	351,924.7
Non-tax revenue	104,284.2	145,721.8	219,194.4
Income from state property and activities	50,472.5	83,158.8	165,612.1
Special budgetary funds	13,893.9	14,066.3	14,061.5
Contribution of unified social tax to federal budget	281,230.0	365,640.0	438,210.0
Total	2,125,718.2	2,417,791.8	2,742,850.4

Expenditure	2002	2003	2004
State administration	56,745.6	66,506.9	76,967.2
Judicial system	19,112.0	25,481.9	33,250.8
International organizations, etc.	42,858.8	33,447.7	32,589.2
National defence	284,157.8	219,884.6	255,390.2
Public order and state security	173,863.3	190,080.1	250,025.3
Scientific and technical research	30,318.0	40,206.0	46,200.0
Industry, energy and construction	57,707.7	63,304.5	67,422.2
Agriculture and fisheries	26,821.5	31,167.7	29,578.7
Education	80,088.3	97,672.0	117,791.9
Health and sport	31,908.1	39,344.8	47,097.8
Highways and road infrastructure	68,519.4	79,111.7	79,133.3
Social security and welfare	430,350.5	150,685.0	161,193.5
Servicing of government debt	285,009.3	277,510.1	287,570.6
Federal transfers	265,406.6	714,600.2	813,969.8
Special budgetary funds	13,893.9	14,066.3	14,061.5
Total (incl. others)	1,947,386.3	2,123,424.9	2,400,751.2

Source: Ministry of Finance, Moscow.

INTERNATIONAL RESERVES
(US $ million at 31 December)

	2003	2004	2005
Gold (national valuation)	3,763.4	3,732.4	6,349.0*
IMF special drawing rights	0.7	0.9	5.6
Reserve position in IMF	2.1	2.8	195.9
Foreign exchange	73,172.1	120,805.1	175,689.9
Total	76,938.3	124,541.2	182,240.4

*Valued at current quotations fixed by the Central Bank of the Russian Federation; previously gold was valued at US $300 per fine troy oz.

Source: IMF, *International Financial Statistics*.

MONEY SUPPLY
(million roubles at 31 December)

	2003	2004	2005
Currency outside banks	1,147,039	1,534,755	2,009,240
Demand deposits at banks	1,003,198	1,277,488	1,805,708
Total money (incl. others)	2,181,933	2,848,345	3,858,515

Source: IMF, *International Financial Statistics*.

COST OF LIVING
(Consumer Price Index; base: previous year = 100)

	2002	2003	2004
Food and beverages	111.0	110.2	112.3
Other consumer goods	110.9	109.2	107.4
Services	136.2	122.3	117.7
All items	115.1	112.0	111.7

NATIONAL ACCOUNTS
('000 million roubles at current prices)

Expenditure on the Gross Domestic Product

	2003	2004	2005
Final consumption expenditure	9,024.8	11,114.0	13,850.0
Households	6,540.2	8,132.2	10,161.1
Non-profit institutions serving households	154.0	180.3	230.9
General government	2,330.6	2,801.5	3,458.0
Gross capital formation	2,755.0	3,532.5	4,512.0
Gross fixed capital formation. Acquisitions, less disposals, of valuables	2,432.2	3,106.5	3,296.1
Changes in inventories	322.8	426.0	585.9
Total domestic expenditure	11,779.8	14,646.5	18,362.0
Exports of goods and services (net)	1,502.0	2,116.1	2,989.7
Sub-total	13,281.8	16,762.6	21,351.7
Statistical discrepancy*	−38.6	245.8	313.3
GDP in market prices	13,243.2	17,008.4	21,665.0
GDP at constant 2003 prices	13,243.2	14,190.8	15,100.7

*Referring to the difference between the sum of the expenditure components and official estimates of GDP, compiled from the production approach.

Gross Domestic Product by Economic Activity

	2003	2004	2005
Agriculture, hunting, etc.	730.1	843.7	950.9
Forestry, logging, etc.	61.0	66.7	77.3
Mining and quarrying	785.0	1,441.3	2,000.3
Manufacturing	1,976.3	2,641.7	3,319.3
Electricity, gas and water supply	428.0	530.4	651.4
Construction	716.2	833.3	1,082.7
Wholesale and retail trade; repair of motor vehicles, motorcycles and personal and household goods	2,589.5	3,129.6	3,923.1
Hotels and restaurants	95.1	130.2	179.7
Transport, storage and communication	1,261.6	1,670.8	1,943.6
Financial intermediation	397.6	509.1	698.7
Real estate, renting and business activities	1,259.3	1,370.8	1,762.6
Public administration and defence; compulsory social security	651.3	764.2	973.1
Education	318.5	402.5	497.8
Health and social work	376.7	466.2	589.5
Other community, social and personal services	220.0	302.2	377.6
Sub-total	11,866.2	15,102.7	19,027.6
Less Financial intermediation services indirectly measured	211.5	307.1	436.8
Gross value added in basic prices	11,654.8	14,795.7	18,590.6
Taxes, *less* subsidies, on products	1,588.5	2,212.6	3,074.3
GDP in market prices	13,243.2	17,008.4	21,665.0

BALANCE OF PAYMENTS
(US $ million)

	2002	2003	2004
Exports of goods f.o.b.	107,301	135,929	183,207
Imports of goods f.o.b.	−60,966	−76,070	−97,382
Trade balance	46,335	59,860	85,825
Exports of services	13,611	16,229	20,290
Imports of services	−23,497	−27,122	−33,732
Balance on goods and services	36,449	48,996	72,383
Other income received	5,677	11,057	10,381
Other income paid	−12,260	−24,228	−23,524
Balance on goods, services and income	29,866	35,795	59,240
Current transfers received	1,352	2,537	3,640
Current transfers paid	−2,103	−2,922	−4,317
Current balance	29,116	35,410	58,563
Capital account (net)	−12,396	−995	−1,626

THE RUSSIAN FEDERATION

—continued	2002	2003	2004
Direct investment abroad	−3,533	−9,727	−10,346
Direct investment from abroad	3,461	7,958	12,824
Portfolio investment assets	−796	−2,180	−4,257
Portfolio investment liabilities	3,756	−2,329	4,406
Financial derivatives assets	80	1,017	758
Financial derivatives liabilities	−67	−377	−857
Other investment assets	2,120	−15,352	−24,853
Other investment liabilities	−3,676	24,049	19,083
Net errors and omissions	−6,502	−9,713	−7,054
Overall balance	11,563	27,762	46,640

Source: IMF, *International Financial Statistics*.

External Trade

PRINCIPAL COMMODITIES
(distribution by SITC, US $ million)*

Imports c.i.f.	2001	2002	2003
Food and live animals	6,704.8	7,359.7	8,741.9
Meat and meat preparations	1,755.9	2,293.1	2,181.9
Fresh, chilled or frozen meat and edible offal	1,690.4	2,229.2	2,123.9
Vegetables and fruit	1,201.4	1,494.3	2,063.0
Sugar, sugar preparations and honey	1,362.3	995.3	1,038.7
Sugar and honey	1,266.2	936.6	965.7
Beverages and tobacco	1,273.2	1,380.7	1,645.8
Crude materials (inedible) except fuels	2,334.3	2,082.3	2,285.4
Metalliferous ores and metal scrap	1,461.6	1,228.4	1,309.3
Chemicals and related products	5,022.8	5,342.0	6,911.8
Medicinal and pharmaceutical products	1,867.0	1,627.1	2,369.9
Medicaments (incl. veterinary medicaments)	1,579.0	1,362.2	2,042.4
Basic manufactures	5,585.7	5,804.1	7,670.3
Iron and steel	1,471.4	1,181.5	1,849.4
Machinery and transport equipment	11,410.2	14,070.2	18,118.2
Machinery specialized for particular industries	1,894.0	2,177.2	2,690.1
General industrial machinery, equipment and parts	2,466.8	2,868.4	3,499.1
Telecommunications, sound recording and reproducing equipment	1,432.7	1,805.1	1,885.1
Electrical machinery, apparatus and appliances, etc	1,795.0	2,322.2	3,077.4
Road vehicles	1,869.3	2,321.2	3,953.9
Passenger motor vehicles (excl. buses)	947.4	1,281.6	2,452.1
Miscellaneous manufactured articles	3,533.6	3,930.5	4,779.8
Total (incl. others)†	41,527.9	46,173.4	57,415.2

Exports f.o.b.	2001	2002	2003
Crude materials (inedible) except fuels	4,100.6	4,693.1	5,927.0
Mineral fuels, lubricants, etc.	53,477.7	55,736.7	70,859.2
Petroleum, petroleum products, etc.	34,071.7	38,688.5	50,900.3
Crude petroleum oils, etc.	24,562.6	27,445.4	36,841.0
Refined petroleum products	9,412.5	11,144.3	13,932.7
Natural and manufactured gas	17,881.6	15,472.8	17,580.0
Petroleum gases, etc., in the gaseous state	17,766.0	15,358.8	17,388.5
Chemicals and related products	4,802.4	4,633.9	5,795.5
Basic manufactures	15,648.9	15,956.1	19,237.0
Iron and steel	5,582.0	6,408.8	8,220.7
Non-ferrous metals	6,764.9	6,465.1	7,548.6
Aluminium	4,267.0	3,495.7	3,937.3
Aluminium and aluminium alloys, unwrought	3,632.4	2,893.0	3,317.6
Machinery and transport equipment	6,234.9	6,208.3	9,247.3
Total (incl. others)†	100,653.0	106,711.7	133,716.8

*Figures are provisional. Including adjustments (e.g. for barter trade), the revised totals (in US $ million) are: Imports c.i.f. 58,992 in 2001, 66,243 in 2002, and 81,654 in 2003; Exports f.o.b. 103,139 in 2001, 107,110 in 2002 and 134,377 in 2003 (Source: IMF, *International Financial Statistics*).
† Including commodities not classified according to kind (US $ million): Imports 4,165.7 in 2001, 4,327.9 in 2002 and 5,313.9 in 2003; Exports 13,009.2 in 2001, 15,820.7 in 2002 and 18,414.3 in 2003.

Source: UN, *International Trade Statistics Yearbook*.

PRINCIPAL TRADING PARTNERS
(US $ million)*

Imports	2001	2002	2003
Austria	540.1	606.5	790.2
Belarus	3,941.0	3,977.1	4,898.7
Belgium	642.7	763.1	889.9
Brazil	920.6	1,303.9	1,478.7
China, People's Republic	1,616.9	2,394.7	3,300.9
Cuba	434.8	288.0	181.0
Czech Republic	463.0	558.4	698.0
Denmark	496.0	512.8	610.9
Finland	1,273.8	1,514.5	1,846.4
France (incl. Monaco)	1,520.6	1,891.7	2,342.1
Germany	5,753.6	6,583.9	8,104.9
Hungary	443.5	511.6	590.3
India	542.3	512.9	583.6
Italy	1,691.1	2,216.8	2,397.7
Japan	814.5	978.7	1,879.7
Kazakhstan	1,815.6	1,795.3	2,210.7
Korea, Republic	788.9	926.5	1,330.3
Netherlands	846.8	1,056.2	1,255.9
Poland	952.3	1,296.7	1,706.1
Spain	488.3	576.0	760.6
Sweden	713.6	1,015.2	1,204.5
Turkey	512.4	727.3	924.9
Ukraine	3,779.4	3,190.5	4,397.8
United Kingdom	984.2	1,117.3	1,428.8
USA	3,208.0	2,974.9	2,964.5
Uzbekistan	581.3	342.8	426.2
Total (incl. others)	41,527.9	46,173.4	57,415.2

Exports	2001	2002	2003
Belarus	5,249.0	5,922.3	7,559.3
British Virgin Islands	3,006.9	2,538.1	2,512.3
China, People's Republic	3,878.3	5,309.9	7,815.1
Cyprus	1,397.1	1,507.4	4,242.5
Czech Republic	1,586.7	1,468.0	1,035.2
Estonia	1,251.1	1,700.6	1,332.0
Finland	3,164.9	2,930.9	3,726.8
France (incl. Monaco)	1,995.0	2,381.4	1,686.2
Germany	8,375.6	7,599.9	6,344.9
Hungary	2,203.4	2,059.5	1,452.9
India	704.4	731.3	1,562.0
Italy	6,972.6	7,066.8	5,787.6
Japan	2,020.7	1,743.0	2,250.3
Kazakhstan	2,671.5	2,569.4	3,096.1
Korea, Republic	733.8	1,153.3	1,227.1

THE RUSSIAN FEDERATION

Exports—continued	2001	2002	2003
Lithuania	1,782.7	1,745.5	1,932.4
Netherlands	4,469.6	6,934.8	8,253.0
Poland	4,106.0	3,692.3	3,718.7
Slovakia	2,092.7	1,948.0	1,394.8
Spain	890.7	1,098.7	1,308.0
Sweden	1,623.6	967.8	918.9
Switzerland-Liechtenstein	1,473.1	3,088.6	3,561.1
Turkey	3,027.5	3,136.2	3,130.8
Ukraine	6,853.6	6,788.3	6,265.9
United Kingdom	3,115.3	2,944.1	3,905.0
USA	2,876.3	3,026.1	3,074.2
Total (incl. others)	100,653.0	106,711.7	133,716.8

* The figures are compiled on the basis of reporting by Russia's trading partners. Adjusted totals (in US $ million) are: Imports c.i.f. 58,992 in 2001, 66,243 in 2002 and 81,654 in 2003; Exports f.o.b. 103,139 in 2001, 107,110 in 2002 and 134,377 in 2003 (Source: IMF, *International Financial Statistics*).

Source: UN, *International Trade Statistics Yearbook*.

2004 (US $ million): Total imports c.i.f. 104,006; Total exports f.o.b. 181,529 (Source: IMF, *International Financial Statistics*).

Transport

RAILWAYS
(traffic)

	2002	2003	2004
Paying passengers ('000 journeys)	1,271,000	1,304,000	1,335,000
Freight carried ('000 metric tons)	1,084,000	1,161,000	1,221,000
Passenger-km (million)	152,900	157,600	164,300
Freight ton-km (million)	1,510,000	1,669,000	1,804,000

ROAD TRAFFIC
(motor vehicles in use)

	1998	1999	2000
Passenger cars	18,819,600	19,717,800	20,353,000
Buses and coaches	627,500	633,200	640,100
Lorries and vans	4,260,000	4,387,800	4,400,600
Motorcycles and mopeds	7,165,900	6,328,600	n.a.

Source: IRF, *World Road Statistics*.

SHIPPING
Merchant Fleet
(registered at 31 December)

	2002	2003	2004
Number of vessels	4,943	4,950	3,802
Total displacement ('000 grt)	10,380.0	10,430.8	8,638.9

Source: Lloyd's Register-Fairplay, *World Fleet Statistics*.

International Sea-borne Freight Traffic
('000 metric tons)

	2002	2003	2004
Goods loaded	10,164	9,204	8,208
Goods unloaded	1,044	1,056	1,128

Source: UN, *Monthly Bulletin of Statistics*.

CIVIL AVIATION
(traffic on scheduled services)

	1999	2000	2001
Kilometres flown (million)	550	534	568
Passengers carried ('000)	18,600	17,688	20,301
Passenger-km (million)	45,863	42,950	48,321
Total ton-km (million)	5,036	4,948	5,292

Source: UN, *Statistical Yearbook*.

Tourism

FOREIGN VISITOR ARRIVALS
('000, incl. excursionists)

Country of origin	2001	2002	2003
Armenia	316.5	309.0	331.9
Azerbaijan	842.4	844.3	826.0
Belarus	188.9	197.5	149.0
China, People's Republic	461.2	725.8	679.6
Estonia	358.7	386.5	406.0
Finland	1,290.7	1,161.2	1,154.1
Georgia	974.6	988.2	737.9
Germany	415.0	493.3	516.2
Kazakhstan	2,539.5	2,956.0	2,674.9
Latvia	245.3	292.6	345.0
Lithuania	1,058.7	950.6	873.8
Moldova	657.7	695.0	751.6
Poland	884.6	1,209.8	1,232.9
Tajikistan	332.2	358.5	366.9
Ukraine	7,924.8	8,299.8	7,686.2
USA	210.1	235.7	280.8
Uzbekistan	497.1	507.0	554.0
Total (incl. others)	21,570.0	23,296.0	22,521.1

Tourism receipts (US $ million, incl. passenger transport): 4,726 in 2001; 5,428 in 2002; 5,879 in 2003.

Source: World Tourism Organization.

Communications Media

	2001	2002	2003
Telephones ('000 main lines in use)	33,278.2	35,500.0	36,993.0
Mobile cellular telephones ('000 subscribers)	7,750.5	17,608.8	36,500.0
Personal computers ('000 in use)	11,000	13,000	n.a.
Internet users ('000)	4,300	6,000	n.a.

Source: International Telecommunication Union.

Television receivers ('000 in use): 79,000 in 2000.

Radio receivers ('000 in use): 61,500 in 1997.

Facsimile machines (number in use): 52,900 in 1998.

Book production (including pamphlets): 36,237 titles in 1996 (421,387,000 copies).

Daily newspapers: 285 in 1996 (average circulation 15,517,000 copies); 333 in 2000.

Non-daily newspapers: 4,596 in 1996 (average circulation 98,558,000 copies); 10,188 in 2000.

Other periodicals: 2,751 in 1996 (average circulation 387,832,000 copies).

2004: Mobile cellular telephone subscribers 74,420,000; Personal computers in use 19,010,000; Internet users 16,000,000.

Sources: UNESCO, *Statistical Yearbook*; and UN, *Statistical Yearbook*.

Education

(2004/05, except where otherwise specified)

	Institutions	Students*	Teachers
Pre-primary	47,185	4,442,600	605,320†
Primary and general secondary	63,182	16,561,000	1,596,000*
Vocational secondary	3,686	1,604,000	n.a.
Higher	1,071	6,884,200	364,300*

* Rounded figure(s).
† 2001/02 figure (Source: UNESCO Institute of Statistics).

Adult literacy rate (UNESCO estimates): 99.4% (males 99.7%; females 99.2%) in 2003 (Source: UN Development Programme, *Human Development Report*).

Directory

The Constitution

The current Constitution of the Russian Federation came into force on 12 December 1993, following its approval by a majority of participants in a nation-wide plebiscite. It replaced the Constitution originally adopted on 12 April 1978, but amended many times after 1990.

THE PRINCIPLES OF THE CONSTITUTIONAL SYSTEM

Chapter One of Section One declares that the Russian Federation (Russia) is a democratic, federative, law-based state with a republican form of government. Its multi-ethnic people bear its sovereignty and are the sole source of authority. State power in the Russian Federation is divided between the legislative, executive and judicial branches, which are independent of one another. Ideological pluralism and a multi-party political system are recognized. The Russian Federation is a secular state and all religious associations are equal before the law. All laws are made public and in accordance with universally acknowledged principles and with international law.

HUMAN AND CIVIL RIGHTS AND FREEDOMS

Chapter Two states that the basic human rights and freedoms of the Russian citizen are guaranteed regardless of sex, race, nationality or religion. It declares the right to life and to freedom and personal inviolability. The principles of freedom of movement, freedom of expression and freedom of conscience are upheld. Censorship is prohibited. Citizens are guaranteed the right to vote and stand in state and local elections and to participate in referendums. Individuals are to have equal access to state employment, and the establishment of trade unions and public associations is permitted. The Constitution commits the State to protection of motherhood and childhood and to granting social security, state pensions and social benefits. Each person has the right to housing. Health care and education are free of charge. Basic general education is compulsory. Citizens are guaranteed the right to receive qualified legal assistance. Payment of statutory taxes and levies is obligatory, as is military service.

THE ORGANIZATION OF THE FEDERATION

Chapter Three names the members (federal territorial units) of the Russian Federation. Russian is declared the state language, but all peoples of the Russian Federation are guaranteed the right to preserve their native tongue. The state flag, emblem and anthem of the Russian Federation are established by a federal constitutional law. The Constitution defines the separate roles of the authority of the Russian Federation, as distinct from that of the joint authority of the Russian Federation and the members of the Russian Federation. It also establishes the relationship between federal laws, federal constitutional laws and the laws and other normative legal acts of the subjects of the Russian Federation. The powers of the federal executive bodies and the executive bodies of the members of the Russian Federation are defined.

THE PRESIDENT OF THE RUSSIAN FEDERATION

Chapter Four describes the powers and responsibilities of the Head of State, the President of the Russian Federation. The President is elected to office for a term of four years by universal, direct suffrage. The same individual may be elected to the office of President for no more than two consecutive terms. The President may appoint the Chairman of the Government (Prime Minister) of the Russian Federation, with the approval of the Gosudarstvennaya Duma, and may dismiss the Deputy Chairmen and the federal ministers from office. The President is entitled to chair sessions of the Government. The President's responsibilities include scheduling referendums and elections to the Gosudarstvennaya Duma, dissolving the Gosudarstvennaya Duma, submitting legislative proposals to the Gosudarstvennaya Duma and promulgating federal laws. The President is responsible for the foreign policy of the Russian Federation. The President is Commander-in-Chief of the Armed Forces and may introduce martial law or a state of emergency under certain conditions.

If the President is unable to carry out the presidential duties, these will be assumed by the Chairman of the Government. The acting President, however, will not possess the full powers of the President, such as the right to dissolve the Gosudarstvennaya Duma or to order a referendum. The President may only be removed from office by the Sovet Federatsii on the grounds of a serious accusation by the Gosudarstvennaya Duma.

THE FEDERALNOYE SOBRANIYE

Chapter Five concerns the Federalnoye Sobraniye, which is the highest representative and legislative body in the Russian Federation. It consists of two chambers: the Sovet Federatsii (Federation Council—upper chamber) and the Gosudarstvennaya Duma (State Duma—lower chamber). The Sovet Federatsii comprises two representatives from each member of the Russian Federation, one appointed by its legislative and one by its executive body (178 senators in total). The Gosudarstvennaya Duma, which is composed of 450 deputies, is elected for a term of four years. The procedures for forming the Sovet Federatsii and for electing the Gosudarstvennaya Duma are determined by federal legislation. The deputies of the Russian Federation must be over 21 years of age and may not hold government office or any other paid job. The Federalnoye Sobraniye is a permanent working body.

Both chambers of the Federalnoye Sobraniye may elect their Chairman and Deputy Chairmen, who preside over parliamentary sessions and supervise the observance of their regulations. Each chamber adopts its code of procedure. The powers of the Sovet Federatsii include the approval of the President's decrees on martial law and a state of emergency, the scheduling of presidential elections and the impeachment of the President. The Gosudarstvennaya Duma has the power to approve the President's nominee to the office of Chairman of the Government. Both chambers of the Federalnoye Sobraniye adopt resolutions by a majority vote of the total number of members. All federal and federal constitutional laws are adopted by the Gosudarstvennaya Duma and submitted for approval first to the Sovet Federatsii and then to the President. If the Sovet Federatsii or the President reject proposed legislation it is submitted for repeat consideration to one or both chambers of the Federalnoye Sobraniye.

The Gosudarstvennaya Duma may be dissolved by the President if it rejects all three candidates to the office of Chairman of the Government or adopts a second vote of 'no confidence' in the Government. However, it may not be dissolved during a period of martial law or a state of emergency or in the case of charges being lodged against the President. A newly elected Gosudarstvennaya Duma should be convened no later than four months after dissolution of the previous parliament.

THE GOVERNMENT OF THE RUSSIAN FEDERATION

The executive authority of the Russian Federation is vested in the Government, which is comprised of the Chairman, the Deputy Chairmen and federal ministers. The Chairman is appointed by the President and his nomination approved by the Gosudarstvennaya Duma. If the Gosudarstvennaya Duma rejects three candidates to the office of Chairman, the President will appoint the Chairman, dissolve the Gosudarstvennaya Duma and order new elections. The Government's responsibilities are to submit the federal budget to the Gosudarstvennaya Duma and to supervise its execution, to guarantee the implementation of a uniform state policy, to carry out foreign policy and to ensure the country's defence and state security. Its duties also include the maintenance of law and order.

Regulations for the activity of the Government are determined by a federal constitutional law. The Government can adopt resolutions and directives, which may be vetoed by the President. The Government must submit its resignation to a newly elected President of the Russian Federation, which the President may accept or reject. A vote of 'no confidence' in the Government may be adopted by the Gosudarstvennaya Duma. The President can reject this decision or demand the Government's resignation. If the Gosudarstvennaya Duma adopts a second vote of 'no confidence' within three months, the President will announce the Government's resignation or dissolve the Gosudarstvennaya Duma.

JUDICIAL POWER

Justice is administered by means of constitutional, civil, administrative and criminal judicial proceedings. Judges in the Russian Federation must be aged 25 or over, have a higher legal education and have a record of work in the legal profession of no less than five years. Judges are independent, irremovable and inviolable. Proceedings in judicial courts are open. No criminal case shall be considered in the absence of a defendant. Judicial proceedings may be conducted with the participation of a jury.

The Constitutional Court comprises 19 judges. The Court decides cases regarding the compliance of federal laws and enactments, the constitutions, statutes, laws and other enactments of the members of the Russian Federation, state treaties and international treaties that have not yet come into force. The Constitutional Court settles disputes about competence among state bodies. Enactments or their individual provisions that have been judged unconstitutional by the Court are invalid. At the request of the Sovet Federatsii, the Court will pronounce its judgment on bringing an accusation against the President of the Russian Federation.

The Supreme Court is the highest judicial authority on civil, criminal, administrative and other cases within the jurisdiction of the common plea courts. The Supreme Arbitration Court is the

THE RUSSIAN FEDERATION

highest authority in settling economic and other disputes within the jurisdiction of the courts of arbitration.

The judges of the three higher courts are appointed by the Federation Council on the recommendation of the President. Judges of other federal courts are appointed by the President.

The Prosecutor's Office is a single centralized system. The Prosecutor-General is appointed and dismissed by the Sovet Federatsii on the recommendation of the President. All other prosecutors are appointed by the Prosecutor-General.

LOCAL SELF-GOVERNMENT

Chapter Eight provides for the exercise of local self-government through referendums, elections and through elected and other bodies. The responsibilities of local self-government bodies include: independently managing municipal property; forming, approving and executing the local budget; establishing local taxes and levies; and maintaining law and order.

CONSTITUTIONAL AMENDMENTS AND REVISION OF THE CONSTITUTION

Chapter Nine states that no provision contained in Chapters One, Two and Nine of the Constitution is to be reviewed by the Federalnoye Sobraniye, while amendments to the remaining Chapters may be passed in accordance with the procedure for a federal constitutional law. If a proposal for a review of the provisions of Chapters One, Two and Nine wins a three-fifths majority in both chambers, a Constitutional Assembly will be convened.

CONCLUDING AND TRANSITIONAL PROVISIONS

Section Two states that the Constitution came into force on the day of the nation-wide vote, 12 December 1993. Should the provisions of a federal treaty contravene those of the Constitution, the constitutional provisions will apply. All laws and other legal acts enforced before the Constitution came into effect will remain valid unless they fail to comply with the Constitution. The President of the Russian Federation will carry out the presidential duties established by the Constitution until the expiry of his term of office. The Council of Ministers will acquire the rights, duties and responsibility of the Government of the Russian Federation established by the Constitution and henceforth be named the Government of the Russian Federation. The courts will administer justice in accordance with their powers established by the Constitution and retain their powers until the expiry of their term.

The Government

HEAD OF STATE

President of the Russian Federation: VLADIMIR V. PUTIN (elected 26 March 2000; re-elected 14 March 2004; inaugurated 7 May 2004).

THE GOVERNMENT
(April 2006)

Chairman (Prime Minister): MIKHAIL YE. FRADKOV.
First Deputy Chairman: DMITRII A. MEDVEDEV.
Deputy Chairman, Minister of Defence: SERGEI B. IVANOV.
Deputy Chairman: ALEKSANDR D. ZHUKOV.
Head of the Government Staff, Minister: SERGEI YE. NARYSHKIN.
Minister of Agriculture: ALEKSEI V. GORDEYEV.
Minister of Civil Defence, Emergencies and Clean-up Operations: Col-Gen. SERGEI K. SHOIGU.
Minister of Culture and the Mass Media: ALEKSANDR S. SOKOLOV.
Minister of Economic Development and Trade: GERMAN O. GREF.
Minister of Education and Science: ANDREI A. FURSENKO.
Minister of Finance: ALEKSEI L. KUDRIN.
Minister of Foreign Affairs: SERGEI V. LAVROV.
Minister of Health and Social Development: MIKHAIL YU. ZURABOV.
Minister of Industry and Energy: VIKTOR B. KHRISTENKO.
Minister of Information and Communications Technologies: LEONID D. REIMAN.
Minister of Internal Affairs: Col-Gen. RASHID G. NURGALIYEV.
Minister of Justice: YURII YA. CHAIKA.
Minister of Natural Resources: YURII P. TRUTNEV.
Minister of Regional Development: VLADIMIR A. YAKOVLEV.
Minister of Transport: IGOR YE. LEVITIN.

MINISTRIES

Office of the President: 103132 Moscow, Staraya pl. 4; tel. (495) 925-35-81; fax (495) 206-07-66; e-mail president@gov.ru; internet www.kremlin.ru.
Office of the Government: 103274 Moscow, Krasnopresnenskaya nab. 2; tel. (495) 205-57-35; fax (495) 205-42-19; internet www.government.ru.
Ministry of Agriculture: 107139 Moscow, Orlikov per. 1/11; tel. (495) 207-83-86; fax (495) 207-95-80; e-mail info@mcx.ru; internet www.mcx.ru.
Ministry of Civil Defence, Emergencies and Clean-up Operations: 109012 Moscow, Teatralnyi proyezd 3; tel. (495) 926-39-01; fax (495) 923-57-45; e-mail info@mchs.gov.ru; internet www.mchs.gov.ru.
Ministry of Culture and the Mass Media: 109074 Moscow, Kitaigorodskii proyezd 7; tel. (495) 928-38-72; internet www.mkmk.ru.
Ministry of Defence: 105175 Moscow, ul. Myasnitskaya 37; tel. (495) 293-38-54; fax (495) 296-84-36; internet www.mil.ru.
Ministry of Economic Development and Trade: 125993 Moscow, ul. 1–ya Tverskaya-Yamskaya 1/3; tel. (495) 200-03-47; e-mail presscenter@economy.gov.ru; internet www.economy.gov.ru.
Ministry of Education and Science: 103905 Moscow, ul. Tverskaya 11; tel. (495) 237-97-63; internet www.mon.gov.ru.
Ministry of Finance: 109097 Moscow, ul. Ilinka 9; tel. (495) 298-91-01; fax (495) 925-08-89; internet www.minfin.ru.
Ministry of Foreign Affairs: 119200 Moscow, Smolenskaya-Sennaya pl. 32/34; tel. (495) 244-16-06; fax (495) 230-21-30; e-mail ministry@mid.ru; internet www.mid.ru.
Ministry of Health and Social Development: 127994 Moscow, Rakhmanovskii per. 3/25; tel. (495) 927-28-48; fax (495) 928-58-15; internet www.mzsrrf.ru.
Ministry of Industry and Energy: 109074 Moscow, Kitaigorodskii pr. 7; tel. (495) 710-55-00; fax (495) 710-57-22; e-mail info@mte.gov.ru; internet www.minprom.gov.ru.
Ministry of Information and Communications Technologies: 125375 Moscow, ul. Tverskaya 7; tel. (495) 771-81-00; fax (495) 771-87-18; internet www.minsvyaz.ru.
Ministry of Internal Affairs: 119049 Moscow, ul. Zhitnaya 16; tel. (495) 239-69-71; fax (495) 293-59-98; e-mail mvd12@mvdrf.ru; internet www.mvd.ru.
Ministry of Justice: 119991 Moscow, Zhitnaya 14; tel. (495) 955-59-99; fax (495) 916-29-03; internet www.minjust.ru.
Ministry of Natural Resources: 123242 Moscow, ul. B. Gruzinskaya 4/6; tel. (495) 254-48-00; fax (495) 254-43-10; e-mail admin@mnr.gov.ru; internet www.mnr.gov.ru.
Ministry of Regional Development: 103051 Moscow, ul. Sadovaya-Samotechnaya 10/23/1; tel. (495) 200-25-65; fax (495) 299-38-41; e-mail info@minregion.ru; internet www.minregion.ru.
Ministry of Transport: 109012 Moscow, ul. Rozhdestvenka 1/1; tel. (495) 926-10-00; fax (495) 200-33-56; e-mail mcc@morflot.ru; internet www.mintrans.ru.

President and Legislature

PRESIDENT

Presidential Election, 14 March 2004

Candidates	Votes	%
Vladimir V. Putin	49,565,238	71.31
Nikolai M. Kharitonov	9,513,313	13.69
Sergei Yu. Glazyev	2,850,063	4.10
Irina M. Khakamada	2,671,313	3.84
Oleg A. Malyshkin	1,405,315	2.02
Sergei M. Mironov	524,324	0.75
Against all candidates	2,396,219	3.45
Total (incl. invalid votes)	69,504,609	100.00

LEGISLATURE

The Federalnoye Sobraniye (Federal Assembly) is a bicameral legislative body, comprising the Sovet Federatsii (Federation Council) and the Gosudarstvennaya Duma (State Duma).

Sovet Federatsii
(Federation Council)

103426 Moscow, ul. B. Dmitrovka 26; tel. (495) 203-90-74; fax (495) 203-46-17; e-mail post_sf@gov.ru; internet www.council.gov.ru.

THE RUSSIAN FEDERATION

The Sovet Federatsii is the upper chamber of the Federalnoye Sobraniye. It comprises 178 deputies, two appointed from each of the constituent members (federal territorial units) of the Russian Federation, representing the legislative and executive branches of power in each republic and region.

Chairman: SERGEI M. MIRONOV.

Gosudarstvennaya Duma
(State Duma)

103265 Moscow, Okhotnyi ryad 1; tel. (495) 292-83-10; fax (495) 292-94-64; e-mail www@duma.ru; internet www.duma.ru.

Chairman: BORIS V. GRYZLOV.

General Election, 7 December 2003

Parties and blocs	Federal party lists % of votes	Seats	Total seats*
Unity and Fatherland—United Russia	37.57	120	226
Communist Party of the Russian Federation	12.61	40	53
Liberal Democratic Party of Russia	11.45	36	38
Motherland—People's Patriotic Union†	9.02	29	37
People's Party of the Russian Federation	1.18	—	19
Yabloko Russian Democratic Party	4.30	—	4
Union of Rightist Forces	3.97	—	3
Agrarian Party of Russia	3.64	—	3
Party of the Rebirth of Russian-Russian Party of Life electoral bloc	1.88	—	3
Russian Pensioners' Party-Party of Social Justice electoral bloc	3.01	—	1
Others‡	5.09	—	—
Independents	—	—	57
Against all lists	4.70	—	—
Total	**100.00§**	**225**	**447‖**

* Including 225 seats filled by voting in single-member constituencies.
† An electoral bloc, comprising the Party of National Rebirth—People's Will, the Party of the Russian Regions and the Socialist United Party of Russia—Spiritual Heritage.
‡ There were 13 other groups.
§ Including spoilt ballot papers (1.58% of the total).
‖ Repeat elections were scheduled to be held in March 2004 in three constituencies where the electorate had voted against all candidates.

Election Commission

Central Electoral Commission of the Russian Federation (Tsentralnaya izbiratelnaya komissiya Rossiiskoi Federatsii): 109012 Moscow, B. Cherkassii per. 9; tel. (495) 206-79-57; internet www.cikrf.ru; Chair. ALEKSANDR A. VESHNYAKOV.

Political Organizations

Legislation approved by President Vladimir Putin in July 2001 required each political party to have at least 10,000 members, including no fewer than 100 members in at least 50 of the 89 subjects of the Russian Federation, in order to register and to function legally. The elections to the Gosudarstvennaya Duma (State Duma), held on 7 December 2003, were contested by 27 electoral associations (parties) and five electoral blocs. In December 2004 President Putin signed into law a series of amendments to the legislation of 2001, notably increasing the minimum membership required for registration of a political party to 50,000, with the additional requirement that at least 500 members of the party must be resident in more than one-half of the subjects (territorial units) of the Federation, with at least 250 members in each of the remaining regions. Parties previously registered under the original legislation were obliged to meet the new membership requirements by 1 January 2006. In July 2005 new legislation increased the threshold for parties to obtain representation in the Gosudarstvennaya Duma from 5% to 7%, while single-mandate constituencies (which hitherto provided one-half of deputies) were to be abolished. By May 2005 there were 47 political parties registered with the Ministry of Justice, of which the following were among the most important:

Agrarian Party of Russia (APR) (Agrarnaya partiya Rossii): 107045 Moscow, per. B. Golovin 20/1; tel. (495) 207-99-51; fax (495) 207-99-01; e-mail press@agroparty.ru; internet www.agroparty.ru; f. 1993; left-wing, supports the agricultural sector; Chair. VLADIMIR N. PLOTNIKOV; 41,477 mems (2002).

Communist Party of the Russian Federation (CPRF) (Kommunisticheskaya partiya Rossiiskoi Federatsii—KPRF): 103051 Moscow, per. M. Sukharevskii 3/1; tel. (495) 928-71-29; fax (495) 292-90-50; e-mail kprf2005@yandex.ru; internet www.kprf.ru; f. 1993; claims succession to the Russian Communist Party, which was banned in 1991; membership of the People's Patriotic Union of Russia (Narodno-patrioticheskii soyuz Rossii—NPSR) in dispute following split in party between factions headed by Zyuganov and Gennadii Semigin at 10th Party Congress in July 2004; Chair. of Central Committee GENNADII A. ZYUGANOV; 19,013 mems (2002).

Greens—Russian Ecological Party (Rossiiskaya ekologicheskaya partiya–Zelenye): 107045 Moscow, Poslednyi per. 26; tel. (495) 207-10-39; fax (495) 737-54-29; e-mail info@greenparty.ru; internet www.greenparty.ru; f. 2002 on the basis of the Cedar Tree—Ecological Party of Russia (Ekologicheskaya partiya Rossii—Kedr); Chair. of the Presidium ANATOLII A. PANFILOV; Chair. of the Central Council ANDREI N. NAGIBIN; 21,243 mems (2005).

Liberal Democratic Party of Russia (LDPR) (Liberalno-demokraticheskaya partiya Rossii): 103045 Moscow, Lukov per. 9; tel. (495) 692-11-95; fax (495) 692-92-42; e-mail pressldpr@list.ru; internet www.ldpr.ru; f. 1988; nationalist; generally supportive of Pres. Putin; Chair. VLADIMIR V. ZHIRINOVSKII; 19,098 mems (2002).

Motherland (Rodina): 107031 Moscow, ul. B. Dmitrovka 32/1; tel. (495) 221-15-15; e-mail info@rodina-nps.ru; internet www.rodina-nps.ru; f. 1998 as Party of the Russian Regions; 'national-patriotic' party, associated with the Congress of Russian Communities; participated in the 2003 Gosudarstvennaya Duma elections as part of the Motherland—People's Patriotic Union electoral bloc; present name adopted Feb. 2004; absorbed People's Will—Party of National Rebirth (led by SERGEI BABURIN) in 2004; Chair. ALEKSANDR M. BABAKOV; 25,000 mems (2003).

Party of the Rebirth of Russia (Partiya vozrozhdeniya Rossii): c/o 103625 Moscow, Okhotnyi ryad 1, State Duma; internet seleznev.on.ru/party; f. 2002 on the basis of the Russia (Rossiya) movement; socialist, aims to re-establish Russia as a great power; contested 2003 elections to the Gosudarstvennaya Duma in electoral bloc with Russian Party of Life; Leader GENNADII N. SELEZNEV; 20,282 mems (2002).

Party of Social Justice (Partiya Sotsialnoi Spravedlivosti): 115054 Moscow, ul. Bakhrushina 32/2; tel. (495) 959-14-06; e-mail region@nasled.ru; internet pp-pss.ru; f. 2002; nationalist, statist; contested 2003 elections to the Gosudarstvennaya Duma in electoral bloc with Russian Pensioners' Party (q.v.); Leader ALEKSEI I. PODBEREZKIN; 60,446 mems (2005).

People's Party of the Russian Federation (Narodnaya partiya Rossiiskoi Federatsii—NPRF): 107066 Moscow, ul. Nizhnyaya Krasnoselskaya 39/2; tel. (495) 799-93-40; fax (495) 292-29-32; e-mail press@narod-party.ru; internet www.narod-party.ru; f. 2001 on the basis of the People's Deputy movement; supports nationalization of natural monopolies and a centrally planned economy; generally supportive of President Putin; Chair. of the Central Committee GENNADII V. GUDKOV; 39,293 mems (2002).

Russian Party of Life (Rossiiskaya partiya zhizni): 101000 Moscow, B. Spasoglinishchevskii per. 4/2; tel. (495) 787-85-15; fax (495) 787-85-20; e-mail info@rpvita.ru; internet www.rpvita.ru; f. 2002; supports the restoration of Russia as a great power, and to prolong and improve the quality of life of its citizens; supports presidency of Vladimir Putin; contested 2003 elections to the Gosudarstvennaya Duma in electoral bloc with Party of the Rebirth of Russia; Chair. SERGEI M. MIRONOV; 11,642 mems (2002).

Russian Pensioners' Party (Rossiiskaya partiya pensionerov): 127493 Moscow, 1-yi Volkonskii per. 13/2; tel. and fax (495) 221-73-88; f. 1998; aims to achieve prosperity, health protection and respect for pensioners; contested 2003 elections to the Gosudarstvennaya Duma in electoral bloc with the Party of Social Justice (Partiya sotsialnoi spravedlivosti—f. 2002); Chair. VALERII K. GARTUNG; 18,415 mems (2002).

Social-Democratic Party of Russia (Sotsial-demokraticheskaya partiya Rossii): 109240 Moscow, Moskvoretskaya nab. 7; tel. (495) 921-29-15; fax (495) 921-28-88; e-mail int_dep2002@mail.ru; internet www.sdpr.ru; f. 2001 by merger; Chair. VLADIMIR N. KISHENIN; 49,000 mems (2005).

Union of Rightist Forces (URF) (Soyuz pravykh sil—SPS): 109544 Moscow, ul. M. Andronyevskaya 15; tel. and fax (495) 956-29-09; e-mail edit@sps.ru; internet www.sps.ru; f. 1998 as alliance of nine movements, which merged to form one party in 2001; pro-

THE RUSSIAN FEDERATION

market, economically liberal; Chair. of the Federal Political Council NIKITA YU. BELYKH; 36,189 mems (March 2005).

Unification—Conceptual Party (Unification) (Kontseptualnaya partiya—Yedineniye—Yedineniye—KPYe): 119296 Moscow, Leninskii pr. 68/10/90; tel. (495) 930-35-71; e-mail mera@kpe.ru; internet www.kpe.ru; f. 2002 on the basis of the Towards God's Rule (K bogoderzhaviyu) movement; extreme right-wing, mystical, opposed to liberalism; Leader Maj.-Gen. KONSTANTIN PETROV.

United Russia (Yedinaya Rossiya): 129110 Moscow, Pereyaslavnskii per. 4; tel. and fax (495) 788-44-93; e-mail press@edinros.ru; internet www.edinros.ru; f. 2001 as Unity and Fatherland—United Russia, on the basis of Unity (f. 1999, incorporating Our Home is Russia), Fatherland (f. 1999, and led by Mayor of Moscow YURII LUZHKOV) and the All Russia grouping of regional governors; pragmatic centrist grouping that promotes moderate economic reforms and a strong state; strongly supportive of President Putin; Chair BORIS V. GRYZLOV; more than 860,000 mems (Nov. 2004).

Yabloko Russian Democratic Party (Rossiisskaya demokraticheskaya partiya 'Yabloko'): 119034 Moscow, per. M. Levshinskii 7/3; tel. (495) 201-43-79; fax (495) 292-34-50; e-mail admin@yabloko.ru; internet www.yabloko.ru; f. 1993 on the basis of the Yavlinskii-Boldyrev-Lukin electoral bloc; democratic, politically and socially liberal; Chair. GRIGORII A. YAVLINSKII; 26,500 mems (2003).

Diplomatic Representation

EMBASSIES IN RUSSIA

Afghanistan: 101000 Moscow, Sverchkov per. 3/2; tel. (495) 923-94-19; fax (495) 924-04-78; e-mail afghanem@online.ru; Ambassador (vacant).

Albania: 119049 Moscow, ul. Mytnaya 3/8; tel. (495) 230-77-32; fax (495) 230-76-35; e-mail embassy@ent.ru; Chargé d'affaires a.i. HALIT FURRIKU.

Algeria: 103051 Moscow, Krapivinskii per. 1A; tel. (495) 200-66-42; fax (495) 923-02-98; e-mail algamb@ntl.ru; internet www.algerianembassy.ru; Ambassador AMAR ABBA.

Angola: 119590 Moscow, ul. U. Palme 6; tel. (495) 939-95-18; fax (495) 956-18-80; e-mail angomosc@col.ru; Ambassador (vacant).

Argentina: 119017 Moscow, ul. B. Ordynka 72; tel. (495) 502-10-20; fax (495) 502-10-21; e-mail efrus@co.ru; Chargé d'affaires a.i. ALEJANDRO JULIO PIÑEIRO ARAMBURU.

Armenia: 101990 Moscow, Armyanskii per. 2; tel. (495) 924-12-69; fax (495) 924-45-35; e-mail info@armen.ru; internet www.armenianembassy.ru; Ambassador ARMEN B. SMBATIAN.

Australia: 109028 Moscow, Podkolokolii per. 10A/2; tel. (495) 956-60-70; fax (495) 956-61-70; e-mail postmaster@australianembassy.ru; internet www.australianembassy.ru; Ambassador ROBERT TYSON.

Austria: 119034 Moscow, Starokonyushennyi per. 1; tel. (495) 502-95-12; fax (495) 937-42-69; e-mail moscau-ob@bmaa.qv.at; internet www.aussenministerium.at/moskau; Ambassador Dr MARTIN VUKOVICH.

Azerbaijan: 103009 Moscow, Leontyevskii per. 16; tel. (495) 229-16-49; fax (495) 202-50-72; e-mail azerirus@cnt.ru; Ambassador RAMIZ G. RIZAYEV.

Bahrain: 109017 Moscow, ul. B. Ordynka 18/1; tel. (495) 230-00-13; fax (495) 230-24-01; e-mail moscowbah@yahoo.com; Ambassador ABDULHAMEED ALI HASAN ALI.

Bangladesh: 119121 Moscow, Zemledelcheskii per. 6; tel. (495) 246-78-04; fax (495) 248-31-85; e-mail moscow.bangla@com2com.ru; internet www.bangladeshembassy.ru; Ambassador AMIR HUSSAIN SIKDER.

Belarus: 101990 Moscow, ul. Maroseika 17/6; tel. (495) 777-66-44; fax (495) 777-66-33; e-mail mail@embassybel.ru; internet www.embassybel.ru; Ambassador VLADIMIR V. GRIGORYEV.

Belgium: 121069 Moscow, ul. M. Molchanovka 7; tel. (495) 780-03-31; fax (495) 780-03-32; e-mail moscow@diplobel.org; internet www.diplomatie.be/moscowfr; Ambassador VINCENT MERTENS DE WILMARS.

Benin: 127006 Moscow, Uspenskii per. 7; tel. (495) 299-23-60; fax (495) 200-02-26; e-mail ambabeninmoscou@hotmail.com; Ambassador VISSINTO AYI D'ALMEIDA.

Bolivia: 115191 Moscow, ul. Serpukhovskii Val 8/135–137; tel. (495) 954-06-30; fax (495) 958-07-55; e-mail embolrus@online.ru; Ambassador SERGIO SÁNCHEZ BALLIVIÁN.

Bosnia and Herzegovina: 119590 Moscow, ul. Mosfilmovskaya 50/1/484; tel. (495) 147-64-88; fax (495) 147-64-89; e-mail embassybih@mail.cnt.ru; Ambassador ENVER HALILOVIĆ.

Brazil: 121069 Moscow, ul. B. Nikitskaya 54; tel. (495) 363-03-66; fax (495) 363-03-67; e-mail brasrus@brasemb.ru; internet www.brasemb.ru; Ambassador CARLOS AUGUSTO REGO SANTOS-NEVES.

Brunei: 121059 Moscow, Berezhkovskaya nab. 2, Radisson-Slavyanskaya Hotel, kom. 440–441; tel. (495) 941-82-16; fax (495) 941-82-14; e-mail brumos@mosbusiness.ru; Ambassador JANIN BIN ERIH.

Bulgaria: 119590 Moscow, ul. Mosfilmovskaya 66; tel. (495) 143-67-00; fax (495) 232-33-02; e-mail bulemrus@bolgaria.ru; internet www.bolgaria.ru; Ambassador ILIYAN D. VASSILEV.

Burundi: 119049 Moscow, Kaluzhskaya pl. 1/226–227; tel. (495) 230-25-64; fax (495) 230-20-09; e-mail bdiam@mail.cnt.ru; Ambassador EMMANUEL TUNGAMWESE.

Cambodia: 119002 Moscow, Starokonyushennyi per. 11; tel. (495) 201-21-15; fax (495) 956-65-73; e-mail camemru@mail.cnt.ru; Ambassador CHUM SOUNRY.

Cameroon: 121069 Moscow, ul. Povarskaya 40, BP 136; tel. (495) 290-65-49; fax (495) 290-61-16; Ambassador ANDRÉ NGONGANG OUANDJI.

Canada: 119002 Moscow, Starokonyushennyi per. 23; tel. (495) 105-60-00; fax (495) 105-60-25; e-mail mosco@international.gc.ca; internet www.dfait-maeci.gc.ca/canada-europa/russia; Ambassador CHRISTOPHER WESTDAL.

Central African Republic: 117571 Moscow, ul. 26-i Bakinskikh Kommissarov 9/124–125; tel. (495) 434-45-20; fax (495) 933-28-99; Ambassador CLAUDE BERNARD BELOUM.

Chad: 117393 Moscow, ul. A. Pilyugina 14/3/895–896; tel. (495) 936-17-63; fax (495) 936-11-01; Ambassador DJIBRINE ABDOUL.

Chile: 119002 Moscow, Denezhnii per. 7/1; tel. (495) 241-01-45; fax (495) 241-68-67; e-mail echileru@col.ru; internet www.embachilerusia.cl; Ambassador MARIO SILBERMAN GUROVICH.

China, People's Republic: 119330 Moscow, ul. Druzhby 6; tel. (495) 938-20-06; fax (495) 938-21-32; Ambassador LIU GUCHANG.

Colombia: 119121 Moscow, ul. Burdenko 20/2; tel. (495) 248-30-42; fax (495) 248-30-25; e-mail emrusia@colombia.ru; Ambassador MIGUEL ANTONIO SANTAMARÍA DAVILA.

Congo, Democratic Republic: 117556 Moscow, Simferopolskii bulv. 7A/49-50; tel. and fax (495) 113-83-48; e-mail rdcambamoscou@yahoo.fr; Ambassador RAPHAËL MUTOMBO TSHITAMBWE.

Congo, Republic: 119034 Moscow, Kropotinskii per. 12; tel. (495) 236-33-68; fax (495) 236-41-16; Ambassador JEAN-PIERRE LOUYÉBO.

Costa Rica: 121615 Moscow, Rublevskoye shosse 26/1/23; tel. (495) 415-40-42; fax (495) 415-40-14; e-mail embaric2@rol.ru; Ambassador PLUTARCO ELIAS HERNÁNDEZ SANCHO.

Côte d'Ivoire: 119034 Moscow, Korobeinikov per. 14/9; tel. (495) 201-24-00; fax (495) 230-20-45; e-mail ambacimow@hotmail.com; internet ambaci-russie.org; Ambassador JEAN-CLAUDE KALOU-DJE.

Croatia: 119034 Moscow, per. Korobeinikov 16/10; tel. (495) 201-38-68; fax (495) 201-46-24; e-mail croemb.russia@mvp.hr; internet ru.mvp.hr; Ambassador BOŽO KOVAČEVIĆ.

Cuba: 1025009 Moscow, Leontiyevskii per. 9; tel. (495) 290-28-82; fax (495) 290-38-04; e-mail embajador@ecurusia.minrex.gov.cu; Ambassador JORGE MARTÍ MARTINEZ.

Cyprus: 121069 Moscow, ul. Povarskaya 9; tel. (495) 744-29-44; fax (495) 744-29-35; e-mail moscowembassy@mfa.gov.cy; Ambassador LEONIDAS PANTELIDES.

Czech Republic: 123056 Moscow, ul. Yu. Fuchika 12/14; tel. (495) 251-05-40; fax (045) 250-15-23; e-mail moscow@embassy.mzv.cz; internet www.mfa.cz/moscow; Ambassador MIROSLAV KOSTELKA.

Denmark: 119034 Moscow, Prechistenskii per. 9; tel. (495) 775-01-90; fax (495) 775-01-91; e-mail mowamb@um.dk; internet www.ambmoskva.um.dk; Ambassador PER CARLSEN.

Ecuador: 103064 Moscow, Gorokhovskii per. 12; tel. (495) 261-27-39; fax (495) 267-70-79; e-mail embajada@ecuaemb.ru; internet www.ecuaemb.ru; Ambassador ROBERTO PONCE ALVARADO.

Egypt: 119034 Moscow, Kropotkinskii per. 12; tel. (495) 246-30-96; fax (495) 246-10-64; e-mail egyemb_moscow@yahoo.com; Ambassador RAOUF ADLY SAAD ELKHARAT.

Equatorial Guinea: 119017 Moscow, Pogorelskii per. 7/1; tel. (495) 953-27-66; Ambassador FAUSTO ABESO FUMA.

Eritrea: 129090 Moscow, ul. Meshchanskaya 17; tel. (495) 631-06-20; fax (495) 631-37-67; Ambassador TEKLAY MINASSIE ASGEDOM.

Estonia: 125009 Moscow, M. Kislovskii per. 5; tel. (495) 737-36-40; fax (495) 737-36-46; e-mail embassy.moskva@mfa.ee; internet www.estemb.ru; Ambassador MARINA KALJURAND.

Ethiopia: 129041 Moscow, Orlovo-Davydovskii per. 6; tel. (495) 280-16-16; fax (495) 280-66-08; e-mail eth-emb@col.ru; Ambassador Brig.-Gen. ASAMINEW BEDANIE AREGGIE.

THE RUSSIAN FEDERATION   *Directory*

Finland: 119034 Moscow, Kropotkinskii per. 15/17; tel. (495) 787-41-74; fax (495) 247-33-80; e-mail sanomat.mos@formin.fi; internet www.finemb-moscow.fi; Ambassador Harry Gustaf Helenius.

France: 119049 Moscow, ul. B. Yakimanka 45; tel. (495) 937-15-00; fax (495) 937-14-46; e-mail amba@ambafrance.ru; internet www.ambafrance.ru; Ambassador Jean Cadet.

Gabon: 119002 Moscow, Denezhnyi per. 16; tel. (495) 241-00-80; fax (495) 244-06-94; Ambassador Paul Bié Eyené.

Georgia: 121069 Moscow, M. Rzhevskii per. 6; tel. (495) 291-13-59; fax (495) 291-21-36; e-mail ineza@got.mmtel.ru; Ambassador Irakli Chubinashvili.

Germany: 119285 Moscow, ul. Mosfilmovskaya 56; tel. (495) 937-95-00; fax (495) 938-23-54; e-mail germanmo@aha.ru; internet www.moskau.diplo.de; Ambassador Dr Walter Schmid.

Ghana: 121069 Moscow, Skatertnyi per. 14; tel. (495) 202-18-71; fax (495) 916-54-28; e-mail embghmos@astelit.ru; Ambassador Air Vice-Marshall Edward A. Mantey.

Greece: 103009 Moscow, Leontiyevskii per. 4; tel. (495) 290-14-46; fax (495) 771-65-10; e-mail gremb.mow@mfa.gr; internet www.hellas.ru; Ambassador Dimitrios Paraskevopoulos.

Guatemala: 119049 Moscow, ul. Korovii Val 7/92; tel. (495) 238-22-14; fax (495) 238-14-46; e-mail embguarus@minex.gob.gt; Ambassador Luis Alberto Padilla Menendez.

Guinea: 119034 Moscow, Pomerantsev per. 6; tel. (495) 201-36-01; fax (502) 220-21-38; Ambassador Lt-Col Amara Bangoura.

Guinea-Bissau: 117556 Moscow, Simferopolskii bulv. 7a/183; tel. and fax (495) 317-95-82; Ambassador Rogerio Araujo Adolpho Herbert.

Holy See: 127055 Moscow, Vadkovskii per. 7/37; tel. (495) 726-59-30; fax (495) 726-59-32; e-mail nuntius@cityline.ru; Apostolic Nuncio Most Rev. Antonio Mennini (Titular Archbishop of Ferrento).

Hungary: 119590 Moscow, ul. Mosfilmovskaya 62; tel. (495) 796-93-70; fax (495) 796-93-80; e-mail aszekely@huembmow.macomnet.ru; internet www.huembmow.macomnet.ru; Ambassador Árpád Székely.

Iceland: 101000 Moscow, Khlebnyi per. 28; tel. (495) 956-76-05; fax (495) 956-76-12; e-mail emb.moscow@mfa.is; Ambassador Benedikt Jónsson.

India: 101000 Moscow, ul. Vorontsovo Pole 6/8; tel. (495) 783-75-35; fax (495) 917-42-09; e-mail india@online.ru; internet www.indianembassy.ru; Ambassador Kanval Sibal.

Indonesia: 109017 Moscow, ul. Novokuznetskaya 12; tel. (495) 951-95-50; fax (495) 230-64-31; e-mail kbrimos@online.ru; Ambassador Susanto Pujomartono.

Iran: 117292 Moscow, Pokrovskii bulv. 7; tel. (495) 917-72-82; fax (495) 230-28-97; Ambassador Gholmreza Shafehee.

Iraq: 119121 Moscow, ul. Pogodinskaya 12; tel. (495) 246-55-07; fax (495) 230-29-22; e-mail mosemb@iraqmofamail.net; Ambassador Dr Abdul-Karim Hashim.

Ireland: 129010 Moscow, Grokholskii per. 5; tel. (495) 937-59-11; fax (495) 975-20-66; e-mail ireland@co.ru; Ambassador Justin Harman.

Israel: 115095 Moscow, ul. B. Ordynka 56; tel. (495) 230-67-00; fax (495) 238-13-46; e-mail moscow@israel.org; Ambassador Arkady Mil-Man.

Italy: 119002 Moscow, Denezhnyi per. 5; tel. (495) 241-10-29; fax (495) 253-92-89; e-mail embitaly@ambmosca.ru; internet www.ambmosca.ru; Ambassador Gianfranco Facco Bonetti.

Japan: 125009 Moscow, Kalashnyi per. 12; tel. (495) 291-85-00; fax (495) 200-12-40; e-mail embjapan@mail.cnt.ru; internet www.embjapan.ru; Ambassador Issei Nomura.

Jordan: 123001 Moscow, Mamonovskii per. 3; tel. (495) 299-12-42; fax (495) 299-43-54; e-mail emjordan@dol.ru; Ambassador Abdelilah Muhammad Ali al-Kurdi.

Kazakhstan: 101000 Moscow, Chistoprudnyi bulv. 3a; tel. (495) 927-17-15; fax (495) 208-26-50; e-mail kazembassy@kazembassy.ru; internet www.kazembassy.ru; Ambassador Zhanseit K. Tuimebayev.

Kenya: 131000 Moscow, ul. B. Ordynka 70; tel. (495) 237-47-02; fax (495) 230-23-40; e-mail kenrepru@yahoo.com; Ambassador Matthew Kathurima M'Ithiri.

Korea, Democratic People's Republic: 107140 Moscow, ul. Mosfilmovskaya 72; tel. (495) 143-62-49; fax (495) 143-63-12; Ambassador Pak Ui Chun.

Korea, Republic: 131000 Moscow, ul. Plyushchikha 56/1; tel. (495) 783-27-27; fax (495) 783-27-77; e-mail info@koreaemb.ru; internet www.koreaemb.ru; Ambassador Kim Jae-Sup.

Kuwait: 119285 Moscow, ul. Mosfilmovskaya 44a; tel. (495) 147-00-40; fax (495) 956-60-32; Ambassador Suleiman Ibrahim al-Morjan.

Kyrgyzstan: 119017 Moscow, ul. B. Ordynka 64; tel. (495) 237-48-82; fax (495) 237-44-52; e-mail 3235.g23@g23.relcom.ru; Ambassador Apas Jumagulov.

Laos: 131940 Moscow, ul. M. Nikitskaya 18; tel. (495) 290-25-60; fax (495) 203-49-24; e-mail thingsavanh_ph@yahoo.com; Ambassador Thongsavanh Phomvihane.

Latvia: 105062 Moscow, ul. Chaplygina 3; tel. (495) 925-27-03; fax (495) 623-92-95; e-mail embassy.russia@mfa.gov.lv; internet www.am.gov.lv/lv/moscow; Ambassador Andris Teikmanis.

Lebanon: 103051 Moscow, ul. Sadovaya-Samotechnaya 14; tel. (495) 200-00-22; fax (495) 200-32-22; Ambassador Dr Assem Jaber.

Libya: 131940 Moscow, ul. Mosfilmovskaya 38; tel. (495) 143-03-54; fax (495) 938-21-62; Secretary of Peoples' Bureau (Ambassador) Abdul-Adim Khimali.

Lithuania: 121069 Moscow, Borisoglebskii per. 10; tel. (495) 785-86-05; fax (495) 785-86-00; e-mail amb.ru@urm.lt; internet ru.urm.lt; Ambassador Rimantas Sidlauskas.

Luxembourg: 119034 Moscow, Khrushchevskii per. 3; tel. (495) 203-53-81; e-mail moscou.amb@mae.etat.lu; Ambassador Carlo Krieger.

Macedonia, former Yugoslav republic: 117292 Moscow, ul. D. Ulyanova 16/2/509–510; tel. (495) 124-33-57; fax (495) 982-36-34; e-mail mkambmos@mail.tascom.ru; Ambassador Risto Nikovski.

Madagascar: 119034 Moscow, Kursovoi per. 5; tel. (495) 290-02-14; fax (495) 202-34-53; e-mail info@ambamadagascar.ru; internet www.ambamadagascar.ru; Ambassador Eloi Maxime Dovo.

Malaysia: 119192 Moscow, ul. Mosfilmovskaya 50; tel. (495) 147-15-14; fax (495) 937-96-02; e-mail malmoscow@kln.gov.my; Ambassador Dato Muhammad Khalis al-Hamani.

Mali: 113184 Moscow, ul. Novokuznetskaya 11; tel. (495) 951-06-55; fax (495) 230-28-89; e-mail amaliru@mail.ru; Ambassador Gen. Bréhima Siré Traoré.

Malta: 119049 Moscow, ul. Korovii Val 7/219; tel. (495) 237-19-39; fax (495) 237-21-58; e-mail maltaembassy.moscow@gov.mt; Ambassador Dr Mario Costa.

Mauritania: 119049 Moscow, ul. B. Ordynka 66; tel. (495) 237-37-92; fax (495) 237-28-61; e-mail m_embassy@oss.ru; Ambassador Muhammad Mahmoud Ould Dahi.

Mexico: 119034 Moscow, B. Levshinskii per. 4; tel. (495) 201-48-48; fax (495) 230-20-42; e-mail embmxru@online.ru; Ambassador Luciano Eduardo Joublanc Montaño.

Moldova: 107031 Moscow, ul. Kuznetskii most 18; tel. (495) 924-53-53; fax (495) 924-95-90; e-mail info@moldembassy.ru; internet www.moldembassy.ru; Ambassador Vasile Sturza.

Mongolia: 121069 Moscow, Borisoglebskii per. 11; tel. (495) 290-67-92; fax (495) 291-46-36; e-mail mongolia@online.ru; Ambassador Luvsandandaryn Khangai.

Morocco: 119034 Moscow, Prechistenskii per. 8; tel. (495) 201-73-51; fax (495) 230-20-67; e-mail sifmamos@df.ru; Ambassador Noureddine Sefiani.

Mozambique: 129090 Moscow, ul. Gilyarovskogo 8/25; tel. (495) 684-40-07; fax (495) 684-36-54; e-mail embamocru@hotmail.com; Ambassador Bernardo Marcelino Cherinda.

Myanmar: 119049 Moscow, ul. Korovii Val 7/135; tel. (495) 230-24-26; fax (495) 730-96-46; e-mail mofa.aung@mptmail.net.mm; Ambassador U Tin Soe.

Namibia: 113096 Moscow, 2-i Kazachii per. 7; tel. (495) 230-32-75; fax (495) 230-22-74; e-mail namembrf@online.ru; Ambassador Dr Sam K. Mbambo.

Nepal: 119121 Moscow, 2-i Neopalimovskii per. 14/7; tel. (495) 244-02-15; fax (495) 244-00-00; e-mail nepalemb@mtu-net.ru; internet www.nepalembassyrus.org; Ambassador (vacant).

Netherlands: 125009 Moscow, Kalashnyi per. 6; tel. (495) 797-29-00; fax (495) 797-29-04; e-mail mos@minbuza.nl; internet www.netherlands-embassy.ru; Ambassador Jan-Paul Dirkse.

New Zealand: 121069 Moscow, ul. Povarskaya 44; tel. (495) 956-35-79; fax (495) 956-35-83; e-mail nzembmos@umail.ru; internet www.nzembassy.msk.ru; Ambassador Christopher J. Elder.

Nigeria: 121069 Moscow, ul. M. Nikitskaya 13; tel. (495) 290-37-83; fax (495) 956-28-25; e-mail ngrmosco@online.ru; internet www.nigerianembassy.ru; Ambassador Air Cdre (retd) Dan Suleiman.

Norway: 131940 Moscow, ul. Povarskaya 7; tel. (495) 933-14-10; fax (495) 933-14-11; e-mail emb.moscow@mfa.no; internet www.norvegia.ru; Ambassador Øyvind Nordsletten.

Oman: 109180 Moscow, Staromonetnii per. 14/1; tel. (495) 230-15-87; fax (495) 230-15-44; e-mail amoman@ipc.ru; Ambassador Muhammad bin Said bin Muhammad al-Lawati.

Pakistan: 123001 Moscow, ul. Sadovaya-Kudrinskaya 17; tel. (495) 254-97-91; fax (495) 956-90-97; e-mail chancery@interanet.ru; Ambassador MUSTAFA KAMAL KAZI.

Panama: 119590 Moscow, ul. Mosfilmovskaya 50/1; tel. (495) 956-07-29; fax (495) 956-07-30; e-mail empanrus@aha.ru; Ambassador (vacant).

Peru: 121002 Moscow, Smolenskii bulv. 22/14; tel. (495) 248-27-66; fax (495) 230-20-00; e-mail leprumoscu@mtu-net.ru; internet www.embperu.ru; Ambassador Dr HUMBERTO UMERES ALVARES.

Philippines: 121099 Moscow, Karmanitskii per. 6; tel. (495) 241-05-63; fax (495) 241-26-30; e-mail moscowpe@utsmail.ru; internet www.phil-embassy.ru; Ambassador ERNESTO VILLARIKA LLAMAS.

Poland: 123557 Moscow, ul. Klimashkina 4; tel. (495) 231-15-00; fax (495) 231-15-15; e-mail embassy@polandemb.ru; internet www.polandemb.ru; Chargé d'affaires a.i. WIKTOR ROSS.

Portugal: 129010 Moscow, Botanicheskii per. 1; tel. (495) 981-34-10; fax (495) 981-34-16; e-mail embptrus@moscovo.dgaccp.pt; Ambassador MANUEL MARCELO MONTIERO CURTO.

Qatar: 119049 Moscow, ul. Korovii Val 7/196–198; tel. (495) 230-15-77; fax (495) 935-76-70; e-mail moscow@mofa.gov.qa; Ambassador SAAD MUHAMMAD SAAD AL-KOBAISI.

Romania: 119590 Moscow, ul. Mosfilmovskaya 64; tel. (495) 143-04-24; fax (495) 143-04-49; e-mail ambasada@orc.ru; Ambassador IOAN DONCA.

Saudi Arabia: 119121 Moscow, 3-i Neopalimovskii per. 3; tel. (495) 245-23-10; fax (495) 246-94-71; e-mail saudimoscow@yahoo.com; internet www.mofa.gov.sa/detail.asp?InServiceID=238; Ambassador MOHAMMED HASSAN ABDULWALI.

Senegal: 119049 Moscow, ul. Korovii Val 7/193–194; tel. (495) 230-21-02; fax (495) 230-20-63; Ambassador Maj.-Gen. MOUNTAGA DIALLO.

Serbia and Montenegro: 119285 Moscow, ul. Mosfilmovskaya 46; tel. (495) 147-41-06; fax (495) 147-41-04; e-mail ambasada@co.ru; Ambassador MILAN ROCEN.

Sierra Leone: 121615 Moscow, Rublevskoye shosse 26/1/58–59; tel. (495) 415-41-66; fax (495) 415-29-85; Ambassador MELROSE BEYOH KAI-BANYA.

Singapore: 121099 Moscow, per. Kamennoi Slobody 5; tel. (495) 241-39-13; fax (495) 241-72-91; e-mail singemb_mow@sgmfa.gov.sg; internet www.mfa.gov.sg/moscow; Ambassador MICHAEL TAY CHEOW ANN.

Slovakia: 123056 Moscow, ul. Yu. Fuchika 17/19; tel. (495) 250-10-70; fax (495) 973-20-81; e-mail embassy@moskva.mfa.sk; internet www.moscow.mfa.sk; Ambassador Dr AUGUSTÍN ČISÁR.

Slovenia: 127006 Moscow, ul. M. Dmitrovka 14/1; tel. (495) 737-33-98; fax (495) 200-15-68; e-mail vmo@gov.si; internet www.gov.si/mzz-dkp/vmo; Ambassador ANDREJ BENEDEJČIČ.

Somalia: 117556 Moscow, Simferopolskii bulv. 7A /145; tel. and fax (495) 317-06-22; e-mail somemb@nabad.org; Chargé d'affaires a.i. MOHAMED MOHAMED HANDULLE.

South Africa: 123001 Moscow, Granatnyi per. 1/9; tel. (495) 540-11-77; fax (495) 540-11-78; e-mail southafrica@embassy-moscow.ru; internet saembassy.ru; Ambassador Dr MOCHUBELA JACOB SEEKOE.

Spain: 121069 Moscow, ul. B. Nikitskaya 50/8; tel. (495) 202-21-61; fax (495) 291-91-71; e-mail embespru@mail.mae.es; internet www.ispania.aha.ru; Ambassador FRANCISCO JAVIER ELORZA CAVENGT.

Sri Lanka: 129090 Moscow, ul. Shchepkina 24; tel. (495) 688-16-20; fax (495) 688-17-57; e-mail lankaemb@com2com.ru; Ambassador NEVILLE R. B. RANASURIYA.

Sudan: 127006 Moscow, Uspenskii per. 4A; tel. (495) 299-54-61; fax (495) 299-33-42; e-mail sudmos@cityline.ru; Ambassador CHOL DENG ALAK.

Sweden: 119590 Moscow, ul. Mosfilmovskaya 60; tel. (495) 937-92-00; fax (495) 937-92-02; e-mail moscow.sweinfo@foreign.ministry.se; internet www.swedenabroad.com/moscow; Ambassador JOHAN MOLANDER.

Switzerland: 101000 Moscow, per. Ogorodnoi Slobody 2/5; tel. (495) 258-38-30; fax (495) 200-17-28; e-mail vertretung@mos.rep.admin.ch; internet www.eda.admin.ch/moscow_emb/e/home.html; Ambassador ERWIN H. HOFER.

Syria: 119034 Moscow, Mansurovskii per. 4; tel. (495) 203-15-21; fax (495) 956-31-91; Ambassador WAHIB AL-FADEL.

Tajikistan: 123001 Moscow, Granatnyi per. 13; tel. (495) 290-38-46; fax (495) 291-89-98; e-mail embassy_moscow@tajikistan.ru; internet www.tajikistan.ru; Ambassador SAFAR G. SAFAROV.

Tanzania: 109017 Moscow, ul. Pyatnitskaya 33; tel. (495) 953-82-21; fax (495) 956-61-30; e-mail tzmos@wm.west.call.com; Ambassador PATRICK SEGEJA CHOKALA.

Thailand: 129090 Moscow, ul. B. Spasskaya 9; tel. (495) 208-08-17; fax (495) 207-53-43; e-mail thaiemb@nnt.ru; Ambassador SORAYOUTH PROMPOJ.

Tunisia: 113105 Moscow, ul. M. Nikitskaya 28/1; tel. (495) 291-28-58; fax (495) 291-75-88; Ambassador MUHAMMAD BELLAGI.

Turkey: 119121 Moscow, 7-i Rostovskii per. 12; tel. (495) 956-55-95; fax (495) 956-55-97; e-mail turemb@co.ru; Ambassador KURTULUŞ TAŞKENT.

Turkmenistan: 119019 Moscow, Filippovskii per. 22; tel. (495) 291-66-36; fax (495) 291-09-35; Ambassador KHALNAZAR A. AGAKHANOV.

Ukraine: 103009 Moscow, Leontiyevskii per. 18; tel. (495) 229-19-88; fax (495) 924-84-69; e-mail ukremb@online.ru; internet www.ukremb.ru; Ambassador OLEH O. DYOMIN.

United Arab Emirates: 101000 Moscow, ul. U. Palme 4; tel. (495) 147-00-66; fax (495) 234-40-70; e-mail uae@col.ru; Ambassador MUHAMMAD ALI AL-OSAIMI.

United Kingdom: 121099 Moscow, Smolenskaya nab. 10; tel. (495) 956-72-00; fax (495) 956-72-01; e-mail moscow@britishembassy.ru; internet www.britaininrussia.ru; Ambassador ANTHONY BRENTON.

USA: 121099 Moscow, B. Devyatinskii per. 8; tel. (495) 728-50-00; fax (495) 728-50-90; e-mail pamoscow@pd.state.gov; internet www.usembassy.ru; Ambassador WILLIAM J. BURNS.

Uruguay: 119330 Moscow, Lomonosovskii pr. 38; tel. (495) 143-04-01; fax (495) 938-20-45; e-mail ururus.uruguay.org.ru; internet www.uruguay.org.ru; Ambassador ALBERTO LEOPOLDO FAJARDO KLAPPENBACH.

Uzbekistan: 109017 Moscow, Pogorelskii per. 12; tel. (495) 230-00-76; fax (495) 238-89-18; e-mail info@uzembassy.ru; internet www.uzembassy.ru; Ambassador BAKHTIYER A. ISLAMOV.

Venezuela: 127051 Moscow, B. Karetnyi per. 13/15; tel. (495) 299-40-42; fax (495) 956-61-08; e-mail info@embaven.ru; internet www.embaven.ru; Ambassador Dr ALEXIS RAFAEL NAVARRO ROJAS.

Viet Nam: 119021 Moscow, ul. B. Pirogovskaya 13; tel. (495) 245-09-25; fax (495) 246-31-21; e-mail dsqvn@com2com.ru; Ambassador NYUGEN VAN NGANG.

Yemen: 119121 Moscow, 2-i Neopalimovskii per. 6; tel. (495) 246-15-40; fax (495) 230-23-05; Ambassador ABDULWAHAB MUHAMMAD ALI AL-RAWHANI.

Zambia: 129041 Moscow, pr. Mira 52A; tel. (495) 688-50-01; fax (495) 975-20-56; Ambassador Rev. Dr PETER L. CHINTALA.

Zimbabwe: 119121 Moscow, per. Serpov 6; tel. (495) 248-43-67; fax (495) 230-24-97; e-mail zimbabwe@rinet.ru; Ambassador Brig. (retd) AGRIPPAH MUTAMBARA.

Judicial System

In January 1995 the first section of a new code of civil law came into effect. It included new rules on commercial and financial operations, and on ownership issues. The second part of the code was published in January 1996. The Constitutional Court rules on the conformity of government policies, federal laws, international treaties and presidential enactments with the Constitution. Following its suspension in October 1993, the Court was reinstated, with a new membership of 19 judges, in April 1995. The Supreme Arbitration Court rules on disputes between commercial bodies. The Supreme Court oversees all criminal and civil law, and is the final court of appeal from lower courts. A system of Justices of the Peace, to deal with certain civil cases, and with criminal cases punishable by a maximum of two years' imprisonment, was established in 1998. In December 2001 President Putin approved several reforms to the judicial system, including the introduction of trials by jury across the Russian Federation, and procedures to guarantee the independence of judges. The majority of Russia's administrative regions introduced jury trials, in many cases only for the most serious crimes, during 2003.

Constitutional Court of the Russian Federation (Konstitutsionnyi Sud Rossiiskoi Federatsii): 103132 Moscow, ul. Ilinka 21; tel. (495) 206-18-82; fax (495) 206-19-78; e-mail ksrf@ksmail.rfnet.ru; internet www.ksrf.ru; f. 1991; Chair. VALERII D. ZORKIN; Sec.-Gen. YURII V. KUDYAVTSEV.

Office of the Prosecutor-General: 103793 Moscow, ul. B. Dmitrovka 15A; tel. (495) 292-88-69; fax (495) 292-88-48; Prosecutor-General VLADIMIR V. USTINOV.

Supreme Arbitration Court of the Russian Federation (Vysshii Arbitrazhnyi Sud Rossiiskoi Federatsii): 101000 Moscow, M. Kharitonevskii per. 12; tel. (495) 208-11-19; fax (495) 208-11-62; internet www.arbitr.ru; f. 1993; Chair. ANTON A. IVANOV.

Supreme Court of the Russian Federation (Verkhovnyi Sud Rossiiskoi Federatsii): 103289 Moscow, ul. Ilinka 7/3; tel. (495) 924-23-47; fax (495) 202-71-18; e-mail gastello@ilinka.supcourt.ru; internet www.supcourt.ru; Chair. VYACHESLAV M. LEBEDEV.

Religion

The majority of the population of the Russian Federation are adherents of Christianity, but there are significant Islamic, Buddhist and Jewish minorities.

In September 1997 legislation concerning the regulation of religious organizations was approved, whereby only those religious groups able to prove that they had been established in Russia for a minimum of 15 years were to be permitted to operate. Russian Orthodoxy, Islam, Buddhism and Judaism, together with some other Christian denominations, were deemed to comply with the legislation. Religious organizations failing to satisfy this requirement were, henceforth, obliged to register annually for 15 years, before being permitted to publish literature, hold public services or invite foreign preachers into Russia. Moreover, foreign religious groups were additionally obliged to affiliate themselves to Russian organizations. An extension of this law, announced in August 1998, decreed that foreign religious workers were permitted to remain in Russia for a maximum of three months per visit. In March 2000 President Putin signed a decree that required all non-registered religious groups to be dissolved by the end of the year; however neither this decree nor the legislation passed in 1997 was applied consistently across the Russian Federation, and some constituent regions introduced legislation that was more restrictive than the 1997 law.

CHRISTIANITY

The Russian Orthodox Church (Moscow Patriarchate)

The Russian Orthodox Church (Moscow Patriarchate) is the dominant religious organization in the Russian Federation, with an estimated 75m. adherents. In 2004 there were 12,638 parishes, 189 monasteries and 205 convents operating under the auspices of the Patriarchate in Russia. The Patriarchate's jurisdiction is mainly challenged by the Russian Orthodox Church Abroad (operating in Russia as the Free Russian Orthodox Church, which itself split with the overseas hierarchy and established the Russian Autonomous Orthodox Church in 1998), the jurisdiction of which was established in 1921 in the Kingdom of Serbs, Croats and Slovenes (Yugoslavia) and which primarily operated in the USA, rejecting the canonical legitimacy of the Moscow Patriarchate. It re-established operations in Russia after 1988.

The Russian Orthodox Church (Moscow Patriarchate) is governed by the Holy Synod, consisting of six bishops (permanent members), the Patriarch, and several temporary member bishops. The supreme ruling organ of the Church is the Local Synod, which comprises representatives of bishops, clergy, monks and laity and convenes once every five years.

Moscow Patriarchate: 115191 Moscow, Danilov Monastery, ul. Danilovskii Val 22; tel. (495) 230-24-39; fax (495) 230-26-19; e-mail commserv@mospatr.ru; internet www.mospat.ru; Patriarch of Moscow and all Rus ALEKSEI II (Ridiger).

The Roman Catholic Church

At 31 December 2003 there were an estimated 787,000 Roman Catholics in the Russian Federation. In 1991 administrative structures of the Roman Catholic Church in Russia were restored, with the establishment of two apostolic administratures. In 1999 each administrature was sub-divided, establishing two additional administratures. In February 2002 the administratures were replaced by: one archdiocese, the Archdiocese of the Mother of God at Moscow; and three dioceses, the Diocese of St Clement at Saratov, of the Transfiguration at Novosibirsk, and of St Joseph at Irkutsk. There is also one apostolic prefecture, and an apostolic exarchate for adherents of the Byzantine Rite.

Bishops' Conference

Conference of Catholic Bishops of the Russian Federation, 101031 Moscow, ul. Petrovka 19/5/35; tel. and fax (495) 923-16-97; e-mail ostastop@glasnet.ru; internet www.catholic.ru.
f. 1999; Pres. Most. Rev. TADEUSZ KONDRUSIEWICZ (Archbishop of the Archdiocese of the Mother of God at Moscow).

Archbishop of the Archdiocese of the Mother of God at Moscow: Most Rev. TADEUSZ KONDRUSIEWICZ, 107078 Moscow, POB 116, ul. N. Basmannaya 16/31; tel. and fax (495) 261-67-14; e-mail cathmos@dol.ru.

Protestant Churches

In 2001 there were more than 3,000 religious organizations registered with the Ministry of Justice. Among these were 1,323 Pentecostal groups, 975 Baptist groups, 784 other evangelical or charismatic organizations, 563 Seventh Day Adventist groups, 213 Lutheran churches, 192 Presbyterian churches and 330 branches of the Jehovah's Witnesses. There were also a small number of groups registered representing sects which had broken away from the Russian Orthodox Church, including the Old Believers (with a total of 278 organizations), the Molokane ('Milk-drinkers'—19 organizations) and Dubkhovory ('Spirit-wrestlers'—one organization). Some of these are regarded as having similar doctrines and practices to churches of the Western reformed traditions.

Russian Church of Christians of the Evangelical Faith: 123363 Moscow, ul. Fabritsiusa 31A; tel. (495) 493-57-88; e-mail rzti@comail.ru; internet hve.ru; f. 1907, re-established 1990; fmrly known as Union of Christians of the Evangelical Faith-Pentecostalists in Russia; 1,600 parishes and more than 300,000 adherents in 2005; Elder NAZAR P. RESHCHIKOVETS.

Russian Union of Evangelical Christians-Baptists: 117015 Moscow, Varshavskoye shosse 29/2; tel. (495) 958-13-36; fax (495) 975-23-67; e-mail bapt.un@g23.relcom.ru; internet baptist.org.ru; affiliated to the Euro-Asiatic Federation of Evangelical Christians-Baptists; Exec. Sec. YURII APATOV.

Other Christian Churches

Armenian Apostolic Church: 123022 Moscow, ul. S. Makeyeva 10; tel. (495) 255-50-19.

Russian Orthodox Old Belief (Old Ritual) Church (Russkaya Pravoslavnaya Staroobryadcheskaya Tserkov): 109052 Moscow, ul. Rogozhskii pos. 29; tel. (495) 361-51-92; e-mail expers2rpsc.ru; internet www.rpsc.ru; f. 1666 by separation from the Moscow Patriarchate; some 300 groups registered in 2005; divided into two main branches: the *popovtsi* (which have priests) and the *bespopovtsi* (which reject the notion of ordained priests and the use of all sacraments, other than that of baptism). Both branches are further divided into various groupings. The largest group of *popovtsi* are those of the Belokrinitskii Concord, under the Archbishop of Novozybkov, Moscow and All Rus, KORNILII (TITOV); c. 250 parishes, seven bishops in Russia, Ukraine and Moldova; a further significant group of *popovtsi* Old Believers are those of the Beglopopovtsyi Concord.

Russian Autonomous Orthodox Church: 125212 Moscow, Church of the New Martyrs and Confessors of Russia, Golovinskoye shosse 13 A; tel. (495) 152-50-76; formally established in 1990 as the Free Russian Orthodox Church; re-registered in 1998 under above name following opposition by local, 'catacomb' priests to moves of reconciliation between the Russian Orthodox Church Abroad and the Moscow Patriarchate; 100 parishes in 2001; First Hierarch Metropolitan of Suzdal and Vladimir VALENTIN (RUSANTSOV).

ISLAM

Most Muslims in the Russian Federation are adherents of the Sunni sect. Islam is the predominant religion among many peoples of the North Caucasus, such as the Chechens, the Ingush and many smaller groups, and also in the Central Volga region, among them the Tatars, Chuvash and Bashkirs. In 2000 there were some 7,000 mosques in Russia, and there were estimated to be between 19m. and 20m. Muslims in Russia in 2001. There were 3,048 Islamic religious organizations registered with the Ministry of Justice in January 2001. In November 2003 President Putin announced that Russia was to apply for observer status at the Organization of the Islamic Conference.

Central Muslim Spiritual Board for Russia and European Countries of the CIS: 450057 Bashkortostan, Ufa, ul. Tukaya 50; tel. (3472) 50-80-86; f. 1789; 27 regional branches in the Russian Federation, and one branch in Ukraine; Chair. (vacant).

Council of Muftis of Russia: 129090 Moscow, per. Vypolzov 7; tel. and fax (495) 681-49-04; e-mail mufty@muslim.ru; internet www.muslim.ru; Chair. Mufti Sheikh RAVIL KHAZRAT GAINUTDIN.

JUDAISM

At the beginning of the 20th century approximately one-half of the world's Jews lived in the Russian Empire (primarily in those regions that form part of present-day Ukraine, Belarus, Moldova and Lithuania). Although many Jews emigrated from the USSR in the 1970s and 1980s, there is still a significant Jewish population (230,000 in late 2002, according to the official results of the census, although some estimates were considerably higher) in the Russian Federation, particularly in the larger cities. In January 2001 there were 197 Jewish religious organizations registered with the Ministry of Justice, of which 176 were Orthodox and 21 Reform.

Congress of Jewish Religious Communities and Organizations of Russia: 101000 Moscow, B. Spasoglinishevskii per. 10, Moscow Choral Synagogue; tel. (495) 917-95-92; fax (495) 740-12-18; e-mail keroor@mail.ru; f. 1996; co-ordinates activities of 120 Jewish communities throughout Russia; Chief Rabbi ADOLF SHAYEVICH; Dir ZINOVY KOGAN.

Federation of the Jewish Communities of Russia: 121099 Moscow, ul. Novyi Arbat 36/9/2; tel. (495) 290-75-18; fax (495) 290-86-19; e-mail office@fjc.ru; internet www.fjc.ru; unites 179 communities in Russia; affiliated to Federation of the Jewish Communities of the CIS and the Baltic States; Chief Rabbi of Russia, Chair. of Rabbinical Alliance of Russia and the CIS BEREL LAZAR.

Russian Jewish Congress: 101000 Moscow, B. Spasoglinishchevskii per. 9/1/936; tel. (495) 780-61-00; fax (495) 780-60-90; e-mail rjc@rjc.ru; internet www.rjc.ru; Pres. VYACHESLAV KANTOR.

BUDDHISM

Buddhism (established as an official religion in Russia in 1741) is most widespread in the Republic of Buryatiya, where the Traditional Buddhist Sangkha of Russia has its seat, the Republics of Kalmykiya and Tyva and in Irkutsk and Chita Oblasts. There are also newly established communities in Moscow and St Petersburg. Before 1917 there were more than 40 datsans (monasteries) in Buryatiya, but in 1990 only two of these remained in use. By December 1999 19 datsans had been built or restored. There were believed to be 1m. Buddhists in Russia in 1997. There were 193 Buddhist organizations registered with the Ministry of Justice in January 2001.

Buddhist Traditional Sangkha of Russia (Buddiiskaya Traditsionnaya Sangkha Rossii): 670000 Buryatiya, Ulan-Ude, Ivolginskii datsan; e-mail buddhism@buryatia.ru; internet buddhism.buryatia.ru; Head Pandito Khambo Lama DAMBA AYUSHEYEV.

Permanent Representation of the Buddhist Traditional Sangkha of Russia in Moscow: 119034 Moscow, ul. Ostozhenka 49; tel. (495) 245-09-39.

BAHÁ'Í FAITH

National Office of the Bahá'ís of Russia: 129515 Moscow, POB 55; tel. and fax (495) 956-24-96; e-mail secretariat@bahai.ru; internet www.bahai.ru; over 3,800 adherents in more than 410 locations; 19 registered orgs in January 2001; Sec. ANKE GROSSMANN.

The Press

In 2004 there were 46,000 officially registered printed media, including some 26,000 newspapers. However, the number of titles in circulation was only around one-half of the total. The total print run of Russian newspapers in that year was 8,500m. copies, and that of magazines was around 600m. copies. At that time *Moskovskii Komsomolets*, with a circulation of 2.2m., was the best-selling daily, while the weekly, *Argumenty i Fakty*, which had a circulation of 2.9m. in 2000, was the best-selling newspaper overall.

Federal Agency for the Press and the Mass Media (Federalnoye Agentstvo po pechati i massovym kommunikatsiyam): 127994 Moscow, Strastnoi bulv. 5; tel. (495) 209-39-86; fax (495) 200-22-81; e-mail first@mptr.ru; internet www.fapmc.ru; f. 2004; Chair. MIKHAIL V. SESLAVINSKII.

PRINCIPAL NEWSPAPERS

Moscow

Argumenty i Fakty (Arguments and Facts): 101000 Moscow, ul. Myasnitskaya 42; tel. (495) 923-35-41; fax (495) 925-61-82; e-mail n-boris@aif.ru; internet www.aif.ru; f. 1978; weekly; Editor VLADISLAV A. STARKOV; circ. 2,880,000 (2000).

Gazeta (Newspaper): 123242 Moscow, ul. Zoologicheskaya 4; tel. (495) 787-39-99; fax (495) 787-39-98; e-mail info@gzt.ru; internet www.gzt.ru; f. 2001; Editor-in-Chief PETR YE. FADEYEV; circ. 726,000 (2005).

Gazeta.ru: 117152 Moscow, Zagorodnoye shosse 1/1; tel. (495) 785-09-76; internet www.gazeta.ru; online only; has no asscn with the newspaper *Gazeta*; Editor-in-Chief ALEKSANDR PISAREV.

Grani.ru: Moscow; tel. (495) 363-36-08; e-mail info@grani.ru; internet grani.ru; f. 2000; online only; Dir-Gen. YULIYA BEREZOVSKAYA; Editor-in-Chief VLADIMIR KORSUNSKII.

Gudok (The Horn): 105066 Moscow, ul. Staraya Basmannaya 38/2/3; tel. (495) 262-26-53; fax (495) 262-45-74; e-mail admin@gudok.info; internet www.gudok.ru; f. 1917 as newspaper of railway workers; daily; Editor-in-Chief IGOR T. YANIN.

Izvestiya (News): 127994 Moscow, ul. Tverskaya 18/1, POB 4; tel. (495) 209-05-81; fax (495) 933-64-62; e-mail info1@izvestia.ru; internet www.izvestia.ru; f. 1917; 50.19% owned by Gazprom Mediya, 49.81% by Prof-Mediya; Editor-in-Chief VLADIMIR BORODIN; circ. 234,500 (2002).

Kommersant (Businessman): 125080 Moscow, ul. Vrubelya 4/1; tel. (495) 943-97-71; fax (495) 195-96-36; e-mail kommersant@kommersant.ru; internet www.kommersant.ru; f. 1989; daily; Editor VLADISLAV BORDULIN; circ. 117,340 (2002).

Komsomolskaya Pravda (Young Communist League Truth): 125866 Moscow, ul. Pravdy 24, POB A-137; tel. (495) 257-51-39; fax (495) 200-22-93; e-mail kp@kp.ru; internet www.kp.ru; f. 1925; fmrly organ of the Lenin Young Communist League (Komsomol); independent; weekly supplements KP-Tolstushka (KP-Fat volume), KP-Ponedelnik (KP-Monday); managed by Prof-Mediya; Editor VLADIMIR SUNGORKIN; circ. 785,000 (2001).

Krasnaya Zvezda (Red Star): 123007 Moscow, Khoroshevskoye shosse 38; tel. (495) 941-21-58; fax (495) 941-40-66; e-mail redstar@mail.cnt.ru; internet www.redstar.ru; f. 1924; organ of the Ministry of Defence; Editor N. N. YEFIMOV; circ. 80,000 (2000).

Krestyanskaya Rossiya (Peasant Russia): 123022 Moscow, ul. 1905 Goda 7; tel. and fax (495) 259-41-49; weekly; f. 1906; Editor-in-Chief KONSTANTIN LYSENKO; circ. 94,000 (2000).

Megapolis-Ekspress (Megalopolis-Express): 115184 Moscow, ul. B. Tatarskaya 29; tel. (495) 721-40-84; fax (495) 959-36-98; e-mail id@megapolis.ru; internet www.megapolis.ru; f. 1990; 2 a week; popular; Editor-in-Chief LEV KULAKOV; circ. 500,000 (2003).

Moskovskaya Pravda (The Moscow Truth): 123846 Moscow, ul. 1905 Goda 7, POB D-22; tel. (495) 259-82-33; fax (495) 259-63-60; e-mail newspaper@mospravda.ru; internet www.mospravda.ru; f. 1918; fmrly organ of the Moscow city committee of the CPSU and the Moscow City Council; 5 a week; independent; Editor SHOD S. MULADZHANOV; circ. 325,000 (2000).

Moskovskii Komsomolets (MK): 123995 Moscow, ul. 1905 Goda 7; tel. (495) 259-50-36; fax (495) 259-46-39; e-mail letters@mk.ru; internet www.mk.ru; f. 1919 as Moskovskii Komsomolets (The Moscow Young Communist); 6 a week; independent; circ. 800,000 in Moscow, 2.2m. nation-wide (2004); Editor-in-Chief PAVEL GUSEV.

Moskovskiye Novosti/The Moscow News: 117152 Moscow, ul. Zagorodnoye shosse 5; tel. (495) 540-99-22; fax (495) 209-17-28; e-mail info@mn.ru; internet www.mn.ru; f. 1930; weekly; in English and in Russian; democratic, liberal; Editor-in-Chief OLGA TIMOFEYEVNA (acting); circ. 63,000 (2005).

Moscow Times: 125212 Moscow, ul. Vyborgskaya 16/4; tel. (495) 937-33-99; fax (495) 937-33-93; e-mail webeditor@imedia.ru; internet www.themoscowtimes.com; f. 1992; daily; in English; independent; Publr STEPHAN GROOTENBOER; Editor LYNN BERRY.

Nezavisimaya Gazeta (NG) (Independent Newspaper): 101000 Moscow, ul. Myasnitskaya 13; tel. (495) 928-48-50; fax (495) 975-23-46; e-mail info@ng.ru; internet www.ng.ru; f. 1990; 5 a week; regular supplements include NG-Nauka (NG-Science), NG-Regiony (NG-Regions), NG-Politekonomiya (NG-Political Economy), NG-Dipkuryer (NG-Diplomatic Courier); Gen. Man. RUSTAM NARZIKULOV; Editor-in-Chief TATIANA KOSHKAREVA; circ. 53,000 (2005).

Novaya Gazeta (New Newspaper): 101000 Moscow, Potapovskii per. 3; tel. (495) 921-57-39; fax (495) 923-68-88; e-mail gazeta@novayagazeta.ru; internet www.novayagazeta.ru; f. 1993; weekly; Editor DMITRII A. MURATOV; circ. 670,000 (2001).

Novye Izvestiya (New News): 125315 Moscow, Leningradskii pr. 68; tel. (495) 783-06-36; fax (495) 783-06-37; e-mail webmaster@newizv.ru; internet www.newizv.ru; f. 2003 following the closure of the fmr *Novye Izvestiya* (f. 1997); daily; Editor-in-Chief VALERII YAKOV.

Parlamentskaya Gazeta (Parliamentary Newspaper): 125190 Moscow, ul. Pravdy 24; tel. (495) 257-50-90; fax (495) 257-50-82; e-mail pg@pnp.ru; internet www.pnp.ru; f. 1998; 5 a week; organ of the Federal Assembly of the Russian Federation; Editor-in-Chief PETR A. KOTOV; circ. 50,000 (2005).

Polit.ru: 101000 Moscow, Krivokolennyi per. 10/6A; tel. (495) 924-80-09; e-mail edit@polit.ru; internet www.polit.ru; f. 1998; independent; online only; Chair. DMITRII ITSKOVICH; Editor-in-Chief VITALII LEIBIN.

Pravda (Truth): 125867 Moscow, ul. Pravdy 24; tel. (495) 257-31-00; fax (495) 251-26-97; e-mail pravda@cnt.ru; internet www.gazeta-pravda.ru; f. 1912; fmrly organ of the Cen. Cttee of the CPSU; independent; communist; Editor-in-Chief ALEKSANDR ILYIN; circ. 70,200 (2001).

Pravda.ru: Moscow; tel. (495) 631-6273; e-mail post@pravda.ru; internet pravda.ru; f. 1999; online only, in Russian, English and Portuguese; has no asscn with the newspaper *Pravda*; Editor-in-Chief DMITRII LITVINOVICH.

Rossiiskaya Gazeta (Russian Newspaper): 125993 Moscow, ul. Pravdy 24, POB 40; tel. (495) 257-52-52; fax (495) 973-22-56; e-mail sekretar@rg.ru; internet www.rg.ru; f. 1990; organ of the Russian Govt; 6 a week; Gen. Man. ALEKSANDR N. GORBENKO; Editor-in-Chief VLADISLAV A. FRONIN; circ. 373,820 (2004).

Rossiiskiye Vesti (Russian News): 119034 Moscow, ul. Prechistenka 28; tel. (495) 933-06-47; fax (495) 201-51-02; e-mail mail@rosvesty.ru; internet www.rosvesty.ru; f. 1991; weekly; Editor-in-Chief ALEKSEI TITKOV; circ. 50,000 (2000).

Rossiya (Russia): 103811 Moscow, Kostyanskii per. 13; e-mail agalakov@rgz.ru; internet www.rgz.ru; f. 2000; controlled by Sistema Mass-Mediya; weekly supplement Gubernskaya Rossiya—Regions of Russia (Mondays), of news from the territories of the Russian Federation; circ. 50,000 (2001).

Russkii Zhurnal (Russian Journal): 125009 Moscow, per. M. Gnezdnikovskii 9/8/3A; tel. (495) 230-17-15; e-mail russ@russ.ru;

THE RUSSIAN FEDERATION

internet www.russ.ru; f. 1997; online only; culture, politics, society; Editor-in-Chief and Publr GLEB PAVLOVSKII.

Selskaya Zhizn (Country Life): 125869 Moscow, ul. Pravdy 24, POB 137; tel. (495) 257-51-51; fax (495) 257-58-39; e-mail sg@sgazeta.ru; internet www.sgazeta.ru; f. 1918 as *Bednota* (Poverty), present name adopted in 1960; 2 a week; fmrly organ of the Cen. Cttee of the CPSU; independent; Editor-in-Chief and Gen. Man. SHAMUN M. KAGERMANOV; circ. 102,000 (2002).

Sovetskaya Rossiya (Soviet Russia): 125868 Moscow, ul. Pravdy 24; tel. (495) 257-53-00; fax (495) 200-22-90; e-mail sovross@aha.ru; internet www.rednews.ru; f. 1956; fmrly organ of the Cen. Cttee of the CPSU and the Russian Federation Supreme Soviet and Council of Ministers; 3 a week; reflects views of left-wing of Communist Party; Editor VIKTOR CHIKIN; circ. 300,000 (2002).

Tribuna (Tribune): 125993 Moscow, ul. Pravdy 24, POB A-40; tel. (495) 257-59-13; fax (495) 973-20-02; e-mail tribuna@tribuna.ru; internet www.tribuna.ru; f. 1969; national industrial daily; Editor-in-Chief OLEG KUZIN; circ. 201,943 (2000).

Trud (Labour): 103792 Moscow, Nastasinskii per. 4; tel. (495) 299-39-06; fax (495) 299-47-40; e-mail letter@trud.ru; internet www.trud.ru; f. 1921; 5 a week; owned by Promsvyazkapital; Editor ALEKSANDR S. POTAPOV.

Vechernyaya Moskva (Evening Moscow): 123849 Moscow, ul. 1905 Goda 7; tel. (495) 256-20-11; fax (495) 259-05-26; e-mail post@vm.ru; internet www.vm.ru; f. 1923; independent; Editor-in-Chief VALERII YEVSEYEV; circ. 300,000 (2001).

Vedomosti (Gazette): 125212 Moscow, ul. Vyborgskaya 16; tel. (495) 232-32-00; fax (495) 956-07-16; e-mail vedomosti@media.ru; internet www.vedomosti.ru; f. 1999; independent business newspaper, publ. jointly with the *Financial Times* (United Kingdom) and the *Wall Street Journal* (USA); Editor LEONID BERSHIDSKII; circ. 42,000 (2001).

Vremya-MN (Time-Moscow News): 103829 Moscow, ul. Tverskaya 16/2; tel. (495) 209-05-20; fax (495) 209-17-28; e-mail vremya@mn.ru; f. 1995; Pres. ALEKSANDR VAINSHTEIN; Editor VLADIMIR V. UMNOV; circ. 54,000 (2001).

Vremya Novosti (Time News): 115326 Moscow, ul. Pyatniyskaya 25; tel. (495) 231-18-77; fax (495) 231-23-04; e-mail vremya@vremya.ru; internet www.vremya.ru; f. 2000; 5 a week; Editor-in-Chief VLADIMIR GUREVICH; circ. 51,000.

Zhizn (Life): 101970 Moscow, ul. Maroseika 13/3; tel. (495) 206-88-56; fax (495) 206-85-48; e-mail info@zhizn.ru; weekly; Editor-in-Chief VLADIMIR TOPORKOV; circ. 1,068,000 (2002).

St Petersburg

Peterburgskii Chas Pik (Petersburg Rush Hour): 191040 St Petersburg, Nevskii pr. 81; tel. (812) 579-25-65; fax (812) 579-19-12; e-mail nabor@chaspik.spb.ru; internet www.chaspik.spb.ru; f. 1990; weekly; owned by Gazprom-Mediya; Editor-in-Chief LARISA AFONINA; circ. 30,000 (2005).

Novosti Peterburga (Petersburg News): 191044 St Petersburg, ul. Novgorodskaya 5/56; tel. (812) 274-30-90; fax (812) 271-06-88; e-mail pr@novosti.sp.ru; f. 1997; Editor-in-Chief VLADIMIR KUZNETSOV; circ. 22,000 (2004).

Sankt-Peterburgskiye Vedomosti (St Petersburg Gazette): 191025 St Petersburg, ul. Marata 25; tel. (812) 325-31-00; fax (812) 164-48-40; e-mail post@spbvedomosti.ru; f. 1728; re-established 1991; Editor-in-Chief ANATOLII A. AGRAFENIN; circ. 90,000 (2002).

Smena (The Rising Generation): 191119 St Petersburg, ul. Marata 69; tel. (812) 315-04-76; fax (812) 315-03-53; e-mail info@smena.ru; internet www.smena.ru; f. 1919; 6 a week, controlled by Sistema Mass-Mediya; Editor-in-Chief LEONID DAVYDOV; circ. 80,000 (2002).

The St Petersburg Times: 190000 St Petersburg, Isaakevskaya pl. 4; tel. and fax (812) 325-60-80; e-mail letters@sptimesrussia.com; internet www.sptimes.ru; f. 1993; 2 a week; in English; independent; Publr TATYANA SHALYGINA; Editor THOMAS RYMER.

Vechernii Peterburg (Evening Petersburg): 191023 St Petersburg, ul. Fontanka 59; tel. (812) 311-88-75; fax (812) 314-31-05; e-mail gazeta@vspb.spb.ru; f. 1992; Editor VLADIMIR GRONSKII; circ. 20,000 (2001).

PRINCIPAL PERIODICALS
Agriculture, Forestry, etc.

Agrarnyi Zhurnal (Agrarian Journal): Moscow; tel. (495) 204-49-80; fax (495) 207-44-78; e-mail mobilecenter@mtu-net.ru; f. 2000; monthly; Editor-in-Chief ALEKSANDR MORGACHEV.

Agrokhimiya (Agrochemistry): 119991 Moscow, Maronovskii per. 26; tel. (495) 238-24-00; e-mail admaron@mail.ru; f. 1964; monthly; journal of the Russian Academy of Sciences; results of theoretical and experimental research work; Editor V. N. KUDEYAROV; circ. 400 (2002).

Doklady Rossiiskoi Akademii Selskokhozyaistvennykh Nauk (Reports of the Russian Academy of Agricultural Sciences): 117218 Moscow, ul. Krzhizhanovskii 15, POB B-2; tel. and fax (495) 977-84-31; f. 1936; 6 a year; developments in agriculture; Editor-in-Chief N. S. MARKOVA; circ. 1,000.

Ekologiya i Promlyshlennost Rossii (The Ecology and Industry of Russia): 119911 Moscow, Leninskii pr. 4; tel. (495) 955-00-58; fax (495) 247-23-08; e-mail ecip@online.ru; internet kalvis.ru; f. 1996; monthly; environmental protection; Editor-in-Chief V. D. KALNER.

Ekonomika Selskokhozyaistvennykh i Pererabatyvayushchikh Predpriyatii (Economics of Agricultural and Processing Enterprises): 107996 Moscow, ul. Sadovaya-Spasskaya 18/423; tel. (495) 207-15-80; fax (495) 207-16-50; internet www.reason.ru/economy; f. 1926; monthly; publ. by Ministry of Agriculture; Editor S. K. DEVIN; circ. 4,500 (1998).

Lesnaya Promyshlennost (Forest Industry): 101934 Moscow, Arkhangelskii per. 1/234; tel. (495) 207-91-53; f. 1926; 3 a week; publ. by the state forest industrial company, Rosleprom; Editor V. G. ZAYEDINOV; circ. 250,000.

Mezhdunarodnyi Selskokhozyaistvennyi Zhurnal (International Agricultural Journal): 107996 Moscow, ul. Sadovaya-Spasskaya 18; tel. and fax (495) 207-23-11; f. 1957; 6 a year; Editor-in-Chief VIKTOR P. KOROVKIN; circ. 4,000.

Molochnoye i Myasnoye Skotovodstvo (Dairy and Meat Cattle Breeding): 107996 Moscow, ul. Sadovaya-Spasskaya 18; tel. (495) 207-19-46; f. 1956; 6 a year; Editor V. V. KORGENEVSKII; circ. 791 (1996).

Selskokhozyaistvennaya Biologiya (Agricultural Biology): 117218 Moscow, ul. Krzhizhanovskogo 15; tel. (495) 921-93-88; f. 1966; 6 a year; publ. by the Russian Academy of Agricultural Sciences; Editor E. M. BORISOVA; circ. 1,000.

Tekhnika v Selskom Khozyaistve (Agricultural Technology): 117218 Moscow, ul. Krzhizhanovskogo 15/2; tel. (495) 207-37-62; fax (495) 207-28-70; e-mail jurali@mail.ru; internet www.tehnvsh.by.ru; f. 1941; 6 a year; journal of the Ministry of Agriculture and the Russian Academy of Agricultural Sciences; Editor-in-Chief PETR S. POPOV; circ. 2,000 (1998).

Veterinariya (Veterinary Science): 107996 Moscow, ul. Sadovaya-Spasskaya 18; tel. (495) 207-10-60; fax (495) 207-28-12; f. 1924; monthly; Editor V. A. GARKAVTSEV; circ. 4,860 (2000).

Zashchita i Karantin Rastenii (The Protection and Quarantine of Plants): 107996 Moscow, ul. Sadovaya-Spasskaya 18, GSB-6, B-78; tel. (495) 207-21-30; fax (495) 207-21-40; e-mail fitopress@ropnet.ru; internet www.z-i-k-r.ru; f. 1932; monthly; Editor YURII N. NEIPERT; circ. 5,000 (2005).

Zemledeliye (Farming): 127434 Moscow, POB 9; tel. and fax (495) 976-11-93; e-mail zemledelie@mtu-net.ru; f. 1939; 6 a year; publ. by Ministry of Agriculture, Russian Academy of Agricultural Sciences, Russian Scientific Research Institute of Farming; Editor M. LOGVINOVA; circ. 2,500 (2005).

For Children

Koster (Campfire): 193024 St Petersburg, ul. Mytninskaya 1/20; tel. (812) 274-15-72; fax (812) 274-46-26; e-mail root@kostyor.spb.org; internet www.kostyor.ru; f. 1936; monthly; journal of the International Union of Children's Organizations (UPO-FCO); fiction, poetry, sport, reports and popular science; for ages 10–14 years; Editor-in-Chief N. B. KHARLAMPIYEV; circ. 7,500 (2000).

Murzilka: 125015 Moscow, ul. Novodmitrovskaya 5A; tel. and fax (495) 285-18-81; e-mail documents@mtu-net.ru; internet www.murzilka.km.ru; f. 1924; monthly; illustrated; for first grades of school; Editor TATYANA ANDROSENKO; circ. 115,000 (2000).

Pioner (Pioneer): 101459 Moscow, Bumazhnyi proyezd 14; tel. (495) 257-34-27; f. 1924; monthly; fmrly journal of the Cen. Cttee of the Lenin Young Communist League (Komsomol); fiction; illustrated; for children of fourth–eighth grades; Editor A. S. MOROZ; circ. 7,000 (2000).

Pionerskaya Pravda (Pioneers' Truth): 127994 Moscow, ul. Sushchevskaya 21; tel. and fax (495) 787-62-43; e-mail info@pionerka.ru; internet www.pionerka.ru; f. 1925; 3 a week; fmrly organ of the Union of Pioneer Organizations (Federation of Children's Organizations) of the USSR; Editor O. I. GREKOVA; circ. 60,000 (2000).

Veselye Kartinki (Merry Pictures): 127015 Moscow, POB 60, ul. Pravdy 24/830; tel. (495) 257-49-06; fax (495) 257-32-01; e-mail info@merrypictures.ru; internet www.merrypictures.ru; f. 1956; monthly; humorous, illustrated; for pre-school and first grades; Editor R. A. VARSHAMOV; circ. 140,000 (1999).

Yunyi Naturalist (Young Naturalist): 125015 Moscow, ul. Novodmitrovskaya 5A; tel. (495) 285-89-67; f. 1928; monthly; fmrly journal of the Union of Pioneer Organizations (Federation of Children's Organizations) of the USSR; popular science for children of fourth–

10th grades, who are interested in biology; Editor B. A. Chashcharin; circ. 16,350 (2000).

Yunyi Tekhnik (Young Technician): 125015 Moscow, ul. Novodmitrovskaya 5A; tel. (495) 285-44-80; e-mail yt@got.mmtel.ru; f. 1956; monthly; publ. by the Molodaya Gvardiya (Young Guard) Publishing House; popular science for children and youth; Editor Boris Cheremisinov; circ. 13,050 (2000).

Culture and Arts

Dekorativnoye Iskusstvo (Decorative Art): 103009 Moscow, ul. Tverskaya 9; tel. (495) 229-19-10; fax (495) 229-68-75; f. 1957; 4 a year; all aspects of visual art; illustrated; Editor A. Kurchi; circ. 1,500 (1999).

Iskusstvo Kino (The Art of the Cinema): 125319 Moscow, ul. Usiyevicha 9; tel. (495) 151-56-51; fax (495) 151-02-72; e-mail filmfilm@mtu-net.ru; internet www.kinoart.ru/main.html; f. 1931; monthly; journal of the Russian Film-makers' Union; Editor Daniil Dondurei; circ. 5,000 (2004).

Knizhnoye Obozreniye (The Book Review): 129272 Moscow, ul. Sushchevskii Val 64; tel. (495) 681-62-66; fax (495) 681-51-45; internet www.knigoboz.ru; f. 1966; weekly; publ. of the Ministry of the Press, Broadcasting and Mass Media; summaries of newly published books; Editor-in-Chief Aleksandr F. Gavrilov; circ. 10,500 (2003).

Kultura (Culture): 127055 Moscow, ul. Novoslobodskaya 73; tel. (495) 285-06-40; fax (495) 200-32-25; e-mail kultura@dol.ru; internet www.kulturagz.ru; f. 1929; controlled by Sistema Mass-Mediya; weekly; Editor Yurii I. Belyavskii; circ. 29,200 (2002).

Literaturnaya Gazeta (Literary Newspaper): 103811 Moscow, Kostyanskii per. 13; tel. (495) 208-96-60; fax (495) 206-62-25; e-mail litera@nettaxi.com; internet www.lgz.ru; f. 1831; publ. restored 1929; weekly; literature, politics, society; controlled by Sistema Mass-Mediya; Editor-in-Chief Lev Gushin; circ. 57,000 (2002).

Literaturnaya Rossiya (Literary Russia): 103051 Moscow, Tsvetnoi bulv. 30; tel. (495) 200-50-10; fax (495) 921-40-00; f. 1958; weekly; essays, verse, literary criticism, political reviews; Editor Vladimir V. Yeremenko; circ. 24,000 (2000).

Muzykalnaya Akademiya (Musical Academy): 103006 Moscow, ul. Sadovaya-Triumfalnaya 14/12; tel. (495) 209-23-84; f. 1933; quarterly; publ. by the Kompozitor (Composer) Publishing House; journal of the Union of Composers of the Russian Federation and the Ministry of Culture; Editor Yu. S. Korev; circ. 1,000 (1998).

Muzykalnaya Zhizn (Musical Life): 103006 Moscow, ul. Sadovaya-Triumfalnaya 14/12; tel. (495) 209-75-24; f. 1957; fortnightly; publ. by the Kompozitor (Composer) Publishing House; journal of the Union of Composers of the Russian Federation and the Ministry of Culture; development of music; Editor J. Platek; circ. 10,000 (2000).

Neva (The River Neva): 191186 St Petersburg, Nevskii pr. 3; tel. and fax (812) 312-65-37; fax (812) 312-65-37; e-mail office@nevajournal .spb.ru; internet www.nevajournal.spb.ru; f. 1955; monthly; journal of the St Petersburg Writers' Organization; fiction, poetry, literary criticism; Editor B. N. Nikolskii; circ. 4,000 (2000).

Oktyabr (October): 125040 Moscow, ul. Pravdy 11/13; tel. (495) 214-62-05; fax (495) 214-50-29; internet magazines.russ.ru/october; f. 1924; monthly; independent literary journal; new fiction and essays by Russian and foreign writers; Editor-in-Chief Irina N. Barmetova; circ. 4,500 (2002).

Sem Dnei (7 Days): 125871 Moscow, Leningradskoye shosse 5A; tel. (495) 195-92-76; fax (495) 753-41-32; e-mail 7days@7days.ru; internet www.7days.ru; f. 1967; celebrity news and television listings magazine; Editor V. V. Orlova; circ. 937,000 (2000).

Teatr (Theatre): 121835 Moscow, ul. Arbat 35; tel. and fax (495) 248-07-45; monthly; publ. by the Izvestiya (News) Publishing House; journal of the Theatrical Workers' Union and the Russian Federation Union of Writers; new plays by Russian and foreign playwrights; Editor V. Semenovski; circ. 5,000 (2000).

Znamya (Banner): 103001 Moscow, ul. B. Sadovaya 2/46; tel. (495) 299-52-38; e-mail info@znamlit.ru; internet magazines.russ.ru/znamia; f. 1931; monthly; independent; novels, poetry, essays; Editor-in-Chief Sergei Chuprinin; circ. 5,300 (2004).

Economics and Finance

Deloviye Lyudi (Business People): 129010 Moscow, pr. Mira 39/1, Russia; tel. (495) 250-77-40; fax (495) 250-77-46; e-mail dl@mk.ru; internet www.dl.mk.ru; f. 1990; monthly; business, management and economics; Editor-in-Chief Andrei I. Lapik.

Dengi (Money): 123308 Moscow, Khoroshevskoye shosse 41; tel. (495) 943-91-17; fax (495) 956-18-13; e-mail dengi@kommersant.ru; internet www.kommersant.ru/k-money; weekly; publ. by the Kommersant Publishing House; Editor Sergei Yakovlev; circ. 85,500 (2002).

Dengi i Kredit (Money and Credit): 103016 Moscow, ul. Neglinnaya 12; tel. (495) 771-99-87; fax (495) 771-99-85; e-mail ggv@cbr.ru; f. 1927; monthly; publ. by the Central Bank; all aspects of banking and money circulation; Editor Y. G. Dmitriyev; circ. 5,430 (2002).

Ekonomika i Matematicheskiye Metody (Economics and Mathematical Methods): 117418 Moscow, Nakhimovskii pr. 47; tel. (495) 332-46-39; internet www.cemi.rssi.ru/emm; f. 1965; 4 a year; publ. by the Nauka (Science) Publishing House; theoretical and methodological problems of economics, econometrics; Editor V. L. Makarov; circ. 796 (2000).

Ekonomika i Zhizn (Economics and Life): 127994 Moscow, Bumazhnyi proyezd 14; tel. (495) 250-57-93; fax (495) 200-22-97; e-mail gazeta@ekonomika.ru; internet www.ekonomika.ru; f. 1918; weekly; fmrly Ekonomicheskaya gazeta; news and information about the economy and business; Editor Tatiana Ivanova; circ. 150,000 (2005).

Ekspert (Expert): 125866 Moscow, ul. Pravdy 24, Novyi Gazetnyi kor.; tel. (495) 257-47-27; fax (495) 250-52-09; e-mail ask@expert.ru; internet www.expert.ru; weekly; business and economics; financial and share markets; policy and culture; owned by Prof-Mediya; Editor-in-Chief Valerii Fadeyev; circ. 60,000 (2002).

Finansovaya Rossiya (Financial Russia): 103051 Moscow, B. Sukharevskii per. 19/1; tel. (495) 207-57-55; e-mail fr@fr.ru; internet www.fr.ru; f. 1996; weekly; economics, business, finance, society; Editor-in-Chief Andrei A. Miroshnichenko; circ. 103,000 (2001).

Finansy (Finances): 125009 Moscow, ul. Tverskaya 22B; tel. (495) 299-44-27; fax (495) 299-96-16; e-mail finance@df.ru; internet www .df.ru/~finance; f. 1926; monthly; publ. by the Finansy (Finances) Publishing House; fmrly journal of the Ministry of Finance; theory and information on finances; compilation and execution of the state budget, insurance, lending, taxation etc.; Editor Yu. M. Artemov; circ. 10,000 (2004).

Kompaniya (The Firm): 125047 Moscow, ul. Usachyeva 11; tel. (495) 755-87-88; fax (495) 755-87-21; e-mail info@ko.ru; internet www.ko.ru; f. 1998; weekly; politics, economics, finance; Editor-in-Chief Andrei Grigoryev; circ. 50,000 (2004).

Mirovaya Ekonomika i Mezhdunarodniye Otnosheniya (World Economy and International Relations): 117859 Moscow, ul. Profsoyuznaya 23; tel. (495) 128-08-83; fax (495) 310-70-27; e-mail memojour@imemo.ru; internet www.imemo.ru; f. 1957; monthly; publ. by the Nauka (Science) Publishing House; journal of the Institute of the World Economy and International Relations of the Russian Academy of Sciences; problems of theory and practice of world socio-economic development, international policies, international economic co-operation, the economic and political situation in Russia and different countries of the world, etc.; Editor A. V. Ryabov; circ. 4,000 (2002).

Profil (Profile): 109544 Moscow, ul. B. Andronyevskaya 17; tel. (495) 745-94-01; fax (495) 278-72-05; e-mail profil@orc.ru; internet www .profil.orc.ru; f. 1997; weekly; Editor-in-Chief Vladimir A. Zmeyushchenko; circ. 103,000 (2001).

Rossiiskii Ekonomicheskii Zhurnal (Russian Economic Journal): 109542 Moscow, Ryazanskii pr. 99; tel. and fax (495) 377-25-56; f. 1958; monthly; fmrly Ekonomicheskiye Nauki (Economic Sciences); theory and practice of economics and economic reform; Editor A. Yu. Melentev; circ. 6,100 (2004).

Vek (The Age): 125124 Moscow, ul. Pravdy 24, POB 35; tel. (495) 257-30-38; fax (495) 251-72-00; f. 1992; Editor-in-Chief Aleksandr Kolodnyi.

Voprosy Ekonomiki (Questions of Economics): 117218 Moscow, Nakhimovskii pr. 32; tel. and fax (495) 124-52-28; e-mail mail@vopreco.ru; internet www.vopreco.ru; f. 1929; monthly; journal of the Institute of Economics of the Russian Academy of Sciences; theoretical problems of economic development, market relations, social aspects of transition to a market economy, international economics, etc.; Editor L. Abalkin; circ. 6,500 (2005).

Education

Pedagogicheskii Vestnik (Pedagogical Herald): 117393 Moscow, ul. Profsoyuznaya 62; tel. (495) 125-95-01; weekly; Editor-in-Chief Leonid Ruvinskii; circ. 120,000 (2002).

Pedagogika (Pedagogy): 119905 Moscow, ul. Pogodinskaya 8; tel. (495) 248-51-49; f. 1937; monthly; publ. by Academy of Education; Chief Editor V. P. Borisenkov; circ. 4,550 (2000).

Semya (Family): 107996 Moscow, Orlikov per. 5; tel. (495) 975-05-29; fax (495) 975-00-76; e-mail mail@semya.ru; internet www.semya .ru; f. 1988; weekly; Editor-in-Chief Sergei A. Abramov; circ. 50,000 (2004).

Semya i Shkola (Family and School): 129278 Moscow, ul. P. Korchagina 7; tel. (495) 283-82-21; fax (495) 283-86-14; e-mail semia_i_shkola@mtu-net.ru; f. 1871; monthly; for parents and children; Gen. Man. V. F. Smirnov; Editor-in-Chief P. I. Gelazoniya; circ. 5,000 (2002).

Shkola i Proizvodstvo (School and Production): 127254 Moscow, ul. Sh. Rustaveli 10/3; tel. and fax (495) 219-83-80; e-mail sip@schoolpress.ru; internet www.schoolpress.ru; f. 1957; 8 a year; publ. by the Shkola-Press (School-Press) Publishing House; Editor Yu. Ye. Rives-Korobkov; circ. 17,000 (2005).

Uchitelskaya Gazeta (Teachers' Gazette): 107045 Moscow, Ananyevskii per. 4/2/1; tel. (495) 928-82-53; fax (495) 928-82-53; e-mail ug@ug.ru; internet www.ug.ru; f. 1924; weekly; independent; Editor Petr Polozhevets; circ. 95,000 (2005).

Vospitaniye Shkolnikov (The Upbringing of Schoolchildren): 129278 Moscow, ul. P. Korchagina 7; tel. (495) 283-86-96; f. 1966; 6 a year; publ. by Pedagogika (Pedagogics) Publishing House; Editor L. V. Kuznetsova; circ. 41,000 (2000).

International Affairs

Ekho Planety (Echo of the Planet): 103860 Moscow, Tverskoi bulv. 10/12; tel. (495) 202-67-48; fax (495) 290-59-11; e-mail echotex@itar-tass.com; internet www.explan.ru; f. 1988; weekly; publ. by ITAR—TASS; international affairs, economic, social and cultural; Editor-in-Chief Valentin Vasilets; circ. 29,000 (2002).

Mezhdunarodnaya Zhizn (International Life): 105064 Moscow, Gorokhovskii per. 14; tel. (495) 265-37-81; fax (495) 265-37-71; e-mail inter_affairs@mid.ru; f. 1954; monthly; Russian and English; publ. by the Pressa Publishing House; problems of foreign policy and diplomacy of Russia and other countries; Editor-in-Chief B. D. Pyadyshev; circ. 70,530 (2002).

Novoye Vremya/New Times: 127994 Moscow, M. Putinkovskii per. 1/2, POB 4; tel. and fax (495) 980-87-20; e-mail contact@newtimes.ru; internet www.newtimes.ru; f. 1943; weekly; Russian, English; publ. by the Moskovskaya Pravda Publishing House; foreign and Russian affairs; Editor-in-Chief Aleksandr Pumpyanskii; circ. 25,000 (2002).

Language and Literature

Ex Libris-NG: 113935 Moscow, ul. Myasnitskaya 13; tel. (495) 928-48-50; fax (495) 975-23-46; e-mail info@ng.ru; internet exlibris.ng.ru; weekly; literature; Editor-in-Chief Igor Zotov.

Filologicheskiye Nauki (Philological Sciences): Moscow; tel. (495) 203-36-23; f. 1958; 6 a year; publ. by the Vysshaya Shkola (Higher School) Publishing House; reports of institutions of higher learning on questions of literary studies and linguistics; Editor P. A. Nikolayev; circ. 900 (1999).

Russkaya Literatura (Russian Literature): 199034 St Petersburg, nab. Makarova 4; tel. (812) 328-16-01; fax (812) 328-16-01; e-mail musliter@mail.ru; f. 1958; quarterly; journal of the Institute of Russian Literature of the Russian Academy of Sciences; development of Russian literature from its appearance up to the present day; Editor N. N. Skatov; circ. 1,099 (2004).

Russkaya Rech (Russian Speech): 121019 Moscow, ul. Volkhonka 18/2; tel. (495) 290-23-78; f. 1967; 6 a year; publ. by the Nauka (Science) Publishing House; journal of the Institute of Russian Language of the Academy of Sciences; popular; history of the development of the literary Russian language; Editor V. G. Kostomarov; circ. 1,135 (2004).

Voprosy Literatury (Questions of Literature): 125009 Moscow, B. Gnezdnikovskii per. 10; tel. (495) 629-49-77; fax (495) 629-64-71; internet magazines.russ.ru/voplit; f. 1957; 6 a year; publ. by Foundation for Literary Criticism; theory and history of modern literature and aesthetics; Editor L. I. Lazarev; circ. 2,550 (2005).

Voprosy Yazykoznaniya (Questions of Linguistics): 121019 Moscow, ul. Volkhonka 18/2; tel. (495) 201-25-16; f. 1952; 6 a year; publ. by the Nauka (Science) Publishing House; journal of the Department of Literature and Language of the Russian Academy of Sciences; Editor T. M. Nikolayeva; circ. 1,448 (2000).

Leisure and Sport

Afisha (Poster): 103009 Moscow, per. B. Gnezdnikovskii 7/28/1; tel. (495) 785-17-00; fax (495) 785-17-01; e-mail info@afisha.net; internet www.afisha.ru; f. 1999; every 2 weeks; listings and reviews of events in Moscow; Editor-in-Chief Ilya Oskolkov-Tsentsiper; circ. 82,000 (2003).

Avtopilot (Autopilot): 123308 Moscow, Khoroshevskoye shosse 41; tel. (495) 493-91-44; fax (495) 493-91-64; e-mail autopilot@kommersant.ru; internet autopilot.kommersant.ru; cars; publ. by the Kommersant Publishing House; Editor-in-Chief Aleksandr Fedorov; circ. 96,500 (2002).

Dosug v Moskve (Leisure in Moscow): 101000 Moscow, Potapovskii per. 3; tel. and fax (495) 924-09-27; weekly; Thursday; listings and reviews of events in Moscow; circ 70,000.

Filateliya (Philately): 121069 Moscow, Khlebnyi per. 6; tel. (495) 291-14-32; fax (495) 291-14-32; e-mail office@marka-art.ru; internet www.marka-art.ru; f. 1966; monthly; journal of the Publishing and Trading Centre 'Marka' (Stamps); Editor-in-Chief Y. G. Bekhterev; circ. 2,100 (2004).

Fizkultura i Sport (Exercise and Sport): 125130 Moscow, per. 6-i Novopodmoskovnii 3, POB 198; tel. (495) 786-60-62; fax (495) 786-61-39; e-mail fisemail@mtu-net.ru; internet www.fismag.ru; f. 1922; monthly; activities and development of Russian sports, health; Editor I. Sosnovskii; circ. 37,600 (2001).

Rossiiskaya Okhotnichya Gazeta (Russian Hunters' Magazine): 123848 Moscow, ul. 1905 Goda 7; tel. (495) 256-94-74; e-mail rog@mk.ru; internet www.mk.ru/rog.asp; weekly; hunting, shooting, fishing; Editor-in-Chief Oleg Malov.

Sport Ekspress (Sport Express): 123056 Moscow, ul. Krasina 27/2; tel. (495) 254-47-87; fax (495) 733-93-08; e-mail sport@sport-express.ru; internet www.sport-express.ru; f. 1991; daily; sport; Dir-Gen. Ivan Rubin; Editor-in-Chief Vladimir Kuchmii; circ. in Moscow and St Petersburg 190,000 (2004).

Sovetskii Sport (Soviet Sport): 101913 Moscow, B. Spasoglinishchevskii per. 8; tel. (495) 925-88-75; fax (495) 925-36-26; e-mail sport@sovsport.ru; internet www.sovsport.ru; f. 1924; weekly; majority share owned by Prof-Mediya; Editor-in-Chief Igor Kots; circ. 135,000 (2002); also *Sovetskii Sport Futbol* (Soviet Sport Football), weekly, circ. 230,000.

Teoriya i Praktika Fizicheskoi Kultury (Theory and Practice of Exercise): 105122 Moscow, Sirenevyi bulv. 4; tel. and fax (495) 166-37-74; e-mail tpfk@infosport.ru; internet www.infosport.ru/press/tpfk; f. 1925; monthly; Editor Lyudmila I. Lubysheva; circ. 1,500 (1999).

Turist (Tourist): 107078 Moscow, B. Kharitonevskii per. 14; tel. (495) 923-64-23; fax (495) 959-23-36; f. 1929; every two months; publ. by the Intour Central Council for Tourism; articles, photo-essays, information, recommendations about routes and hotels for tourists, natural, cultural and historical places of interest; Editor Boris V. Moskvin; circ. 3,000 (2000).

Za Rulem (Behind The Wheel): 103045 Moscow, per. Selivyerstov 10; tel. (495) 207-23-82; e-mail stas@zr.ru; internet www.zr.ru; f. 1928; monthly; cars and motorsport; Gen. Man. Viktor Panyarskii; Editor-in-Chief Petr S. Menshikh; circ. 580,000 (2001).

Politics and Military Affairs

Litsa (People): 121099 Moscow, Smolenskaya pl. 13/21, POB 99; tel. (495) 241-37-92; e-mail litsa@aha.ru; f. 1996; monthly; Editor-in-Chief Artem Borovik; circ. 100,000 (2002).

Na Dne (The Lower Depths): 191025 St Petersburg, POB 110; tel. (812) 310-54-12; fax (812) 310-52-09; f. 1994; current affairs; social issues; 2 a month.

Nezavisimoye Voyennoye Obozreniye (Independent Military Review): 101000 Moscow, ul. Myasnitskaya 13; tel. and fax (495) 925-88-29; internet nvo.ng.ru; f. 1995; Editor Vadim Solovyev; circ. 20,140 (2004).

NZ—Neprikosnovennyi Zapas: Debaty o politike i kulture (Reserve Stock: Debates on Politics and Culture): 129626 Moscow, ul. Kostyakova 10, POB 55; tel. (495) 976-47-88; fax (495) 977-08-28; e-mail nz@nlo.magazine.ru; internet www.nz-online.ru; f. 1998; 6 a year; politics, economics, culture and society; Editor-in-Chief Irina Prokhorova.

Rossiya v Globalnoi Politike/Russia in Global Affairs: 103873 Moscow, ul. Mokhovaya 11/3v; tel. (495) 980-73-53; fax (495) 937-76-11; e-mail info@globalaffairs.ru; internet www.globalaffairs.ru; f. 2002; co-founded by the Russian Union of Industrialists and Entrepreneurs, the Council for Foreign and Defence Politics and the newspaper *Izvestiya*, in collaboration with the US journal, *Foreign Affairs*; 6 a year (Russian); 4 a year (English); Chair. of Editorial Bd Sergei A. Karaganov; Editor-in-Chief Fedor A. Lukyanov.

Rossiiskaya Federatsiya Segodnya (The Russian Federation Today): 103800 Moscow, ul. M. Dmitrovka 3/10; tel. (495) 299-40-55; fax (495) 200-30-80; e-mail rfs@rfnet.ru; f. 1994; journal of the Gosudarstvennaya Duma; Editor Yurii A. Khrenov; circ. 50,000 (1999).

The Russia Journal: 113054 Moscow, nab. Ozerkovskaya 50/451; e-mail info@russiajournal.com; internet www.russiajournal.com; f. 1998; published by Norasco Publishing; Editor Jon Wright.

Russia Profile: 119021 Moscow, Zubovskii bulv. 4; tel. (495) 981-64-86; fax (495) 201-30-71; e-mail info@russiaprofile.org; f. 1966; monthly; in English; publ. by Independent Media for RIA-Novosti in association with the International Relations and Security Network (Zurich, Switzerland) and the Center for Defense Information (Washington, DC, USA); Editor Andrei Zolotov Jr.

Shchit i Mech (Shield and Sword): 127434 Moscow, ul. Ivanovskaya 24/18; tel. (495) 976-66-44; fax (495) 977-21-72; e-mail ormvd@itar-tass.com; f. 1989; weekly; military, security, geopolitical concerns; publ. by the Ministry of Internal Affairs; Editor-in-Chief Valerii Kulik; circ. 50,000 (2004).

Sovershenno Sekretno (Top Secret): 121099 Moscow, Smolenskaya pl. 13/21, POB 255; tel. (495) 241-68-73; fax (495) 241-75-55; e-mail velekhov@topsecret.cnt.ru; internet sovsekretno.ru; f. 1989; monthly; Editor-in-Chief GALINA SIDOROVA; circ. 2,300,000 (2002).

Svobodnaya Mysl (Free Thought): 107140 Moscow, ul. Mosfilmovskaya 40; tel. (495) 788-65-00; f. 1924; fmrly Kommunist (Communist); monthly; politics, philosophy, economics; Editor-in-Chief Dr VLADISLAV INOZEMTSEV; circ. 4,600 (2002).

Vlast (Power): 123308 Moscow, Khoroshevskoye shosse 41; tel. (495) 195-96-36; fax (495) 234-16-60; e-mail vlast@kommersant.ru; internet www.kommersant.ru/k-vlast; f. 1997; weekly; publ. by the Kommersant Publishing House; Editor MAKSIM KOVALSKII; circ. 73,500 (2002).

Yezhenedelnyi Zhurnal (Weekly Magazine): 129110 Moscow, Pereyaslavskii per. 4; tel. (495) 785-82-50; fax (495) 785-82-51; e-mail info@ej.ru; internet www.ej.ru; f. 2001; Editor-in-Chief SERGEI PARKHOMENKO.

Zakon (Law): 127994 Moscow, ul. Tverskaya 18/1; tel. (495) 209-75-60; e-mail zakon@izvestia.ru; f. 1992; monthly; publ. by the editorial board of Izvestiya jt-stock co; publishes thematic legislation and commentaries relating to business and commerce; legal issues for businessmen; Editor-in-Chief NIKOLAI KAPINUS; circ. 8,000 (2002).

Zavtra (Tomorrow): 119146 Moscow, Komsomolskii pr. 13; tel. (495) 247-13-37; fax (495) 245-37-10; e-mail zavtra@zavtra.ru; internet zavtra.ru; extreme left, nationalist; Editor-in-Chief ALEKSANDR A. PROGANOV; circ. 100,000 (2002).

Popular, Fiction and General

Akh! (Ah!): 129090 Moscow, ul. Novyi Arbat 21, POB 36; f. 1998; monthly; general; Editor LARISA BORUZDNIA.

Alfavit (Alphabet): 129090 Moscow, ul. Novyi Arbat 21, POB 36; e-mail alphabet@alphabet.ru; internet www.alphabet.ru; f. 1998; weekly; general; Editor-in-Chief MIKHAIL POLYACHEK; circ. 25,000 (2002).

Druzhba Narodov (The Friendship of Peoples): 121827 Moscow, ul. Povarskaya 52; tel. (495) 291-62-27; fax (495) 291-63-54; e-mail dn@mail.sitek.ru; internet magazines.russ.ru/druzhba; f. 1939; monthly; independent; prose, poetry and literary criticism; Editor A. EBANOIDZE; circ. 7,000 (2000).

Geo: 123056 Moscow, per. Krasina 16; tel. (495) 937-60-90; fax (495) 937-60-91; e-mail geo@gjrussia.com; f. 1998; monthly; travel magazine; Editor YEKATERINA SEMINA; circ. 175,000 (2000).

Inostrannaya Literatura (Foreign Literature): 109017 Moscow, ul. Pyatnitskaya 41; tel. (495) 953-51-47; fax (495) 953-50-61; e-mail inolit@rinet.ru; internet magazines.russ.ru/inostran; f. 1891; monthly; independent; Russian translations of modern foreign authors and literary criticism; Editor-in-Chief ALEKSEI SLOVESNII; circ. 10,000 (2002).

Molotok (Little Hammer): 125080 Moscow, vul. Vrubelya 4; tel. (495) 209-11-32; fax (495) 200-40-55; e-mail molotok@unity.kommersant.ru; internet www.zabey.ru; f. 2000; weekly; popular culture.

Moskva (Moscow): 119002 Moscow, ul. Arbat 20; tel. (495) 291-71-10; fax (495) 291-07-32; e-mail jurmos@cityline.ru; f. 1957; monthly; fiction; Editor LEONID I. BORODIN; circ. 7,100 (2002).

Nash Sovremennik (Our Contemporary): 127994 Moscow, Tsvetnoi bulv. 32/2; tel. (495) 200-24-24; fax (495) 200-24-12; f. 1956; monthly; publ. by the Union of Writers of Russia; contemporary prose and 'patriotic polemics'; Editor STANISLAV KUNAYEV; circ. 13,000 (1999).

Novaya Rossiya (New Russia): 103772 Moscow, Petrovskii per. 8; tel. (495) 229-14-19; fax (495) 232-37-99; f. 1930; monthly; in Russian and English; illustrated; Editor A. N. MISHARIN; circ. 15,000 (1999).

Novyi Krokodil (New Crocodile): 129090 Moscow, Potapovskii per. 3, POB 94; tel. (495) 956-71-71; e-mail crocodile@vf-m.ru; internet www.crocodile.su; f. 2005 to replace Krokodil (Crodocile—founded 1922); monthly; satirical; Editor SERGEI MOSTOVSHCHIKOV.

Novyi Mir (New World): 103806 Moscow, M. Putinkovskii per. 1/2; tel. and fax (495) 200-08-29; e-mail nmir@aha.ru; internet magazines.russ.ru/novyi_mi; f. 1925; monthly; publ. by the Izvestiya (News) Publishing House; new fiction and essays; Editor ANDREI V. VASILEVSKII; circ.c. 8,000 (2005).

Ogonek (Beacon): 127055 Moscow, ul. Lesnaya 55/1/2; tel. (495) 647-10-03; fax (495) 973-14-30; e-mail ogoniok@ogoniokpress.ru; internet www.ogoniok.ru; f. 1899; weekly; politics, popular science, economics, literature; Editor VIKTOR LOSHAK; circ. 48,000 (2005).

Rodina (Motherland): 127025 Moscow, ul. Novyi Arbat 19; tel. (495) 203-73-98; fax (495) 203-75-98; e-mail rodina@istrodina.ru; f. 1989; monthly; popular historical; supplement Istochnik (Source), every two months, documents state archives; Editor V. P. DOLMATOV; circ. 20,000 (2003).

Rodnaya Gazeta (Native Gazette): 125137 Moscow, ul. Pravdy 24/2; tel. (495) 789-44-00; fax (495) 789-44-01; e-mail info@rodgaz.ru; internet www.rodgaz.ru; f. 2003; weekly; politics, culture, nationalist, left-wing; Editor-in-Chief ALEKSANDR KOLODNYI.

Rossiiskii Kto Yest Kto (Russian Who's Who): 117335 Moscow, POB 81; tel. (495) 234-46-92; e-mail zhurnal@whoiswho.ru; internet www.whoiswho.ru; 2 a year; biographical and directory material; Editor-in-Chief SVYATOSLAV RYBAS; circ. 10,000.

Sobesednik (Interlocutor): 101484 Moscow, ul. Novoslobodskaya 73, POB 4; tel. (495) 285-56-65; fax (495) 973-20-54; e-mail info@sobesednik.ru; internet www.sobesednik.ru; f. 1984; weekly; Editor-in-Chief YURII PILIPENKO; circ. 227,500 (2002).

SPID-Info: 125284 Moscow, POB 42; tel. (495) 255-02-99; fax (495) 252-09-20; e-mail mail@si.ru; internet www.s-info.ru; f. 1991; two a month; popular; Editor-in-Chief OLGA BELAN; circ. 1,200,000 (2005).

Versiya (Possibility): Smolenskaya pl. 13/21, POB 255; tel. (495) 291-23-76; e-mail versia@topsecret.cnt.ru; internet www.versiasovsek.ru; f. 1998; weekly; Editor-in-Chief A. V. BOKSHITSKAYA.

Vokrug Sveta (Around the World): 125015 Moscow, ul. Argunovskaya 12/1/6A; tel. and fax (495) 215-01-65; e-mail vokrugsveta_g@onlin.ptt.ru; f. 1861; monthly; geographical, travel and adventure; illustrated; Editor A. DMITRII ZAKHAROV; circ. 145,000 (2002).

Zvezda (Star): 191028 St Petersburg, ul. Mokhovaya 20; tel. (812) 272-89-48; fax (812) 273-52-56; e-mail arjev@zvezda.spb.su; internet magazines.russ.ru/zvezda; f. 1923; monthly; publ. by the Zvezda Publishing House; novels, short stories, poetry and literary criticism; Editors A. YU. ARYEV, YA. A. GORDIN; circ. 10,000 (2003).

Popular Scientific

Meditsinskaya Gazeta (Medical Gazette): 129090 Moscow, B. Sukharevskaya pl. 1/2; tel. (495) 208-86-95; fax (495) 208-69-80; e-mail mggazeta@online.ru; internet www.medgazeta.rusmedserv.com; f. 1938; 2 a week; professional international periodical; Editor ANDREI POLTORAK; circ. 52,000 (2002).

Modelist-Konstruktor (Modelmaker-Designer): 125015 Moscow, ul. Novodmitrovskaya 5A; tel. (495) 285-80-46; fax (495) 285-27-57; f. 1962; monthly; information about amateur cars, planes, cross-country vehicles; designs of cars, planes, ships, tanks, garden furniture etc.; Editor A. RAGUZIN; circ. 22,000 (1999).

Nauka i Zhizn (Science and Life): 101990 Moscow, ul. Myasnitskaya 24; tel. (495) 924-18-35; fax (495) 200-22-59; e-mail mail@nauka.relis.ru; internet nauka.relis.ru; f. 1890, resumed 1934; monthly; recent developments in all branches of science and technology; Chief Editor I. K. LAGOVSKII; circ. 42,000 (2004).

PC Week: 109047 Moscow, ul. Marksistskaya 34/10; tel. (495) 974-22-60; fax (495) 974-22-63; e-mail editorial@pcweek.ru; internet www.pcweek.ru; f. 1995; 48 a year; Editor-in-Chief EDUARD PROYDAKOV; circ. 35,000 (2000).

Priroda (Nature): 117810 Moscow, Maronovskii per. 26; tel. (495) 238-24-56; fax (495) 238-26-33; f. 1912; monthly; publ. by the Nauka (Science) Publishing House; journal of the Presidium of the Academy of Sciences; natural sciences; Editor A. F. ANDREYEV; circ. 2,500 (1999).

Radio: 103045 Moscow, per. Seliverstov 10; tel. (495) 207-31-18; fax (495) 208-77-13; f. 1924; monthly; audio, video, communications, practical electronics, computers; Editor Y. I. KRYLOV; circ. 70,000 (2000).

Tekhnika-Molodezhi (Engineering—For Youth): 125015 Moscow, ul. Novodmitrovskaya 5A; tel. (495) 285-16-87; fax (495) 234-16-78; f. 1933; monthly; engineering and science; Editor A. N. PEREVOZCHIKOV; circ. 50,000 (1999).

Vrach (Physician): 119881 Moscow, ul. B. Pirogovskaya 2/6; tel. (495) 248-57-27; fax (495) 248-02-14; e-mail rvrach@mmascience.ru; internet www.rusvrach.ru; f. 1990; monthly; medical, scientific and socio-political; illustrated; Editor-in-Chief I. N. DENISOV; circ. 3,700 (2004).

Zdorovye (Health): 127994 Moscow, Bumazhnyi proyezd 14/1; tel. (495) 250-58-28; fax (495) 257-32-51; e-mail zdorovie@zdr.ru; internet www.zdr.ru; f. 1955; monthly; Editor T. YEFIMOVA; circ. 170,000 (2006).

Zemlya i Vselennaya (The Earth and The Universe): 117810 Moscow, Maronovskii per. 26; tel. (495) 238-42-32; f. 1965; 6 a year; publ. by the Nauka (Science) Publishing House; jt edition of the Academy of Sciences and the Society of Astronomy and Geodesy; current hypotheses of the origin and development of the earth and the universe; astronomy, geophysics and space research; Chief Editor V. K. ABALAKIN; circ. 1,000 (2000).

The Press, Printing and Bibliography

Bibliografiya (Bibliography): 119019 Moscow, Kremlevskaya nab. 1/9; tel. and fax (495) 298-25-85; e-mail raaygistov@mtu-net.ru;

internet www.bookchamber.ru; f. 1929; 6 a year; publ. by the Book Chamber International Publishing House; theoretical, practical and historical aspects of bibliography; Editor K. M. Sukhorukov; circ. 2,300 (2005).

Poligrafist i Izdatel (Printer and Publisher): 129272 Moscow, ul. Sushchevskii Val 64/105; tel. (495) 288-93-17; fax (495) 288-94-44; e-mail pub@online.ru; f. 1994; monthly; Editor A. I. Ovsyannikov; circ. 5,000 (2000).

Poligrafiya (Printing): 129272 Moscow, ul. Sushchevskii Val 64; tel. (495) 281-74-81; fax (495) 288-97-66; e-mail polimag@aha.ru; internet www.aha.ru/~polimag; f. 1924; 6 a year; equipment and technology of the printing industry; Dir N. N. Kondratiyeva; circ. 5,000 (1999).

Slovo (Word): 121069 Moscow, ul. Povarskaya 11/2; tel. and fax (495) 202-50-51; f. 1936; monthly; fmrly V Mire Knig (In the World of Books); reviews of new books, theoretical problems of literature, historical and religious; Editor A. V. Larionov; circ. 4,000 (1999).

Zhurnalist (Journalist): 101453 Moscow, Bumazhnyi proyezd 14; tel. (495) 257-30-58; fax (495) 257-31-27; f. 1920; monthly; publ. by Ekonomicheskaya Gazeta Publishing House; Editor G. P. Maltsev; circ. 6,200 (2002).

Religion

Bratskii Vestnik (Herald of the Brethren): 109028 Moscow, M. Vuzovskii per. 3; tel. (495) 917-96-26; f. 1945; 6 a year; organ of the Russian Union of Evangelical Christians-Baptists; Chief Editor Yu. Agapov; circ. 10,000 (1998).

Istina i Zhizn (Truth and Life): 105264 Moscow, ul. 7-aya Parkovaya 26/1/303; tel. and fax (495) 786-35-89; e-mail istina@aha.ru; internet istina.religare.ru; f. 1990; inter-confessional magazine of Christian culture; monthly; Editor Fr Aleksandr Khmelnitskii.

Mezhdunarodnaya Yevreyskaya Gazeta (International Jewish Newspaper): 107005 Moscow, Pleteshkovskii per. 3A; tel. and fax (495) 225-44-84; e-mail meg@spacenet.ru; internet www.jig.ru; f. 1989; weekly; Dir-Gen. Yakov Polischuk; circ. 15,000 (2002).

NG-Religii (The Independent-Religions): 101000 Moscow, ul. Myasnitskaya 13; tel. (495) 923-42-40; fax (495) 921-58-47; e-mail ngr@ng.ru; internet religion.ng.ru; f. 1997; analysis of religious affairs and their social and political implications both within Russia and worldwide; 2 a month; Editor-in-Chief Maksim Shevchenko; circ. 50,000 (2002).

Tserkovnyi Vestnik (Church Herald): 119435 Moscow, ul. Pogodinskaya 20/2; tel. and fax (495) 246-01-65; e-mail letters@rop.ru; internet www.tserkov.info; f. 1989; 24 a year; organ of the Russian Orthodox Church (Moscow Patriarchate); Editor-in-Chief Very Rev. Vladimir Silovyev; circ. 30,000 (2005).

Yevreiskoye Slovo (The Jewish Word): 127018 Moscow, 2-i Vysheslavtsev per. 5A; tel. (495) 792-31-13; e-mail redaktor@e-slovo.ru; internet e-slovo.ru; f. 2000; Editor-in-Chief Vladimir Podolnii.

Zhurnal Moskovskoi Patriarkhii (Journal of the Moscow Patriarchate): 119435 Moscow, ul. Pogodinskaya 20/2; tel. (495) 246-98-48; fax (495) 246-21-41; e-mail pressmp@jmp.ru; internet www.jmp.ru; f. 1934; monthly; official publication of the Russian Orthodox Church (Moscow Patriarchate); Editor Archpriest Vladimir (Silovyev); circ. 6,000 (1999).

Trade, Trade Unions, Labour and Social Security

Chelovek i Trud (Man and Labour): 105064 Moscow, Yakovoapostolskii per. 6/3; tel. and fax (495) 917-76-36; e-mail chelt@yandex.ru; internet www.chelt.ru; monthly; f. 1956 as Sotsialisticheskii trud (Socialist Labour); present name adopted 1992; employment issues and problems of unemployment, social policy, pensions, personnel management, labour law, etc.; Editor-in-Chief M. A. Barinova; circ. 10,000 (2005).

Profsoyuzy (Trade Unions): 101000 Moscow, ul. Myasnitskaya 13/18/231; tel. (495) 924-57-40; fax (495) 975-23-29; e-mail iidprof@cityline.ru; f. 1917; monthly; fmrly publ. by the General Confederation of Trade Unions of the USSR; Editor Y. I. Korobko; circ. 3,200 (1999).

Vneshnyaya Torgovlya (External Trade): 121108 Moscow, ul. Minskaya 11; tel. (495) 145-68-94; fax (495) 145-51-92; e-mail vneshtorg@mtu-net.ru; internet www.trade-point.ru/vt; f. 1921; monthly; Russian and English; organ of the Ministry of Economic Development and Trade; Editor-in-Chief Yurii Deomidov; circ. 7,000 (1999).

Transport and Communication

Grazhdanskaya Aviyatsiya (Civil Aviation): 125993 Moscow, Leningradskii pr. 37; tel. (495) 155-59-23; fax (495) 155-51-64; f. 1931; monthly; journal of the Union of Civil Aviation Workers; development of air transport; utilization of aviation in construction, agriculture and forestry; Editor A. M. Troshin; circ. 10,000 (2003).

Radiotekhnika (Radio Engineering): 103031 Moscow, Kuznetskii most 20/6/31; tel. (495) 921-48-37; fax (495) 925-92-41; e-mail iprzhr@online.ru; internet www.webcenter.ru/~iprzhr/; f. 1937; monthly; publ. by the Svyaz (Communication) Publishing House; journal of the A. S. Popov Scientific and Technical Society of Radio Engineering, Electronics and Electrical Communication; theoretical and technical problems of radio engineering; other publications include Advances in Radio Science, Radio Systems and Antennae; Editor Yu. V. Gulyayev; circ. 1,500 (1999).

Radiotekhnika i Elektronika (Radio Engineering and Electronics): 103907 Moscow, ul. Mokhovaya 11; tel. (495) 203-47-89; f. 1956; monthly; journal of the Russian Academy of Sciences; theory of radio engineering; Editor Y. V. Gulyayev; circ. 468 (2000).

Vestnik Svyazi (Herald of Communication): 101000 Moscow, Krivokolennyi per. 14/1; tel. (495) 925-42-57; fax (495) 921-27-97; e-mail irais@vestnik-sviazy.ru; internet www.vestnik-sviazy.ru; f. 1917; monthly; publ. by the IRIAS Agency; telecommunications; Editor E. B. Konstantinov; circ. 10,000 (2002).

Women's Interest

Domovoi (House-Sprite): 113035 Moscow, ul. B. Ordynka 16; tel. (495) 956-77-02; fax (495) 956-22-09; e-mail dom@kommersant.ru; internet www.domovoy.ru; monthly; Editor-in-Chief Kseniya Makhnenko; circ. 105,000 (2000).

Elle: 101959 Moscow, ul. Myasnitskaya 35; tel. (495) 204-17-77; fax (495) 795-08-15; e-mail elle@hfm.ru; f. 1996; monthly; fashion; Editor-in-Chief Yelena Sotnikova; circ. 180,000 (1998).

Krestyanka (Peasant Woman): 127994 Moscow, Bumazhnyi proyezd 14; tel. (495) 257-39-39; fax (495) 257-39-63; e-mail mail@krestyanka.ru; internet www.krestyanka.ru; f. 1922; monthly; publ. by the Krestyanka Publishing House; popular; supplements Khozyayushka (Dear Hostess), On i ona (He and She), Moda v dome (Fashion at Home), Samochuvstvie (Health), Nasha Usadba (Our Garden), Pyatnashki (Game of Tag); Pres and Editor-in-Chief Anastasiya V. Kupriyanova; circ. 85,000 (2004).

Mir Zhenshchiny (Woman's World): 101999 Moscow, Glinishchevskii per. 6; tel. and fax (495) 209-95-33; f. 1945; monthly; fmrly Zhenshchina (Woman); in Russian, Chinese, English, French, German and Spanish; fmrly publ. by the Soviet Women's Committee and the General Confederation of Trade Unions; popular; illustrated; Editor-in-Chief V. I. Fedotova; circ. 50,000 (2000).

Modeli Sezona (Models of the Season): 103031 Moscow, Kuznetskii most 7/9; tel. (495) 921-73-93; fax (495) 928-77-93; f. 1957; 4 a year; Editor-in-Chief N. A. Kasatkina; circ. 45,000 (1999).

Rabotnitsa (Working Woman): 101458 Moscow, Bumazhnyi proyezd 14; tel. (495) 257-36-49; fax (495) 956-90-94; e-mail webmaster@rabotnitsa.ru; internet www.rabotnitsa.ru; f. 1914; monthly; publ. by the Pressa Publishing House; popular; Editor Zoya P Krylova; circ. 223,000 (2000).

Zhurnal Mod (Fashion Journal): 103031 Moscow, Kuznetskii most 7/9; tel. (495) 921-73-93; f. 1945; 4 a year; illustrated; Editor-in-Chief N. A. Kasatkina; circ. 45,000 (1999).

Youth

Molodaya Gvardiya (Young Guard): 125015 Moscow, ul. Novodmitrovskaya 5A; tel. (495) 285-88-29; fax (495) 285-56-90; f. 1922; monthly; fiction, poetry, criticism, popular science; Editor Y. Yushin; circ. 6,000 (2000).

Rovesnik (Contemporary): 125015 Moscow, ul. Novodmitrovskaya 5A; tel. (495) 285-89-20; fax (495) 285-06-27; e-mail rovesnik@rovesnik.ru; internet www.rovesnik.ru/dom/rovesnik.asp; f. 1962; fmrly journal of the Cen. Cttee of the Leninist Young Communist League; popular illustrated monthly of fiction, music, cinema, sport and other aspects of youth culture; Editor I. A. Chernyshkov; circ. 100,000 (2000).

Selskaya Molodezh (Rural Youth): 125015 Moscow, ul. Novodmitrovskaya 5A; tel. (495) 285-80-04; fax (495) 285-08-30; f. 1925; monthly; publ. by the Molodaya Gvardiya (Young Guard) Publishing House; supplements Podvigi (Heroic Deeds) and Detektivy selskoy molodezhi (Rural Youth Detective Stories); popular illustrated, fiction, verses, problems of rural youth; Editor-in-Chief Michael Massur; circ. 10,000 (1999).

Smena (The Rising Generation): 101457 Moscow, Bumazhnyi proyezd 14; tel. (495) 212-15-07; fax (495) 250-59-28; e-mail smena@garnet.ru; internet www.smena-id.ru; f. 1924; monthly; publ. by the Pressa Publishing House; popular illustrated, short stories, essays and problems of youth; Editor-in-Chief M. G. Kizilov; circ. 50,000 (2001).

Yunost (Youth): 101524 Moscow, ul. Tverskaya-Yamskaya 8/1; tel. (495) 251-31-22; fax (495) 251-74-60; f. 1955; monthly; novels, short stories, essays and poems by beginners; Editor V. Lipatov; circ. 15,000 (2000).

THE RUSSIAN FEDERATION

NEWS AGENCIES

ANP—Agentstvo novostei i prognozy (News and Forecasting Agency): 103009 Moscow, Kalashnyi per. 10/2; tel. (495) 782-33-71; fax (495) 153-57-45; e-mail aninons@online.ru; f. 2001 on basis of ANI News and Information Agency (f. 1991); Editor-in-Chief ALEKSEI SHCHAVELEV.

Federal News Service (FNS): 119992 Moscow, per. Obolenskyi 10; tel. (495) 245-58-00; fax (495) 245-58-23; e-mail commerce@fednews.ru; internet www.fednews.ru; f. 1992; Bureau Chief VYACHESLAV NEMODRUK.

Interfax: 127006 Moscow, ul. 1-aya Tverskaya-Yamskaya 2; tel. (495) 250-98-40; fax (495) 250-97-27; e-mail info@interfax.ru; internet www.interfax.ru; f. 1989; independent information agency; Chief Exec. MIKHAIL KOMISSAR.

ITAR—TASS (Information Telegraphic Agency of Russia—Telegraphic Agency of the Sovereign Countries): 125993 Moscow, Tverskoi bulv. 10/12; tel. (495) 202-29-81; fax (495) 202-54-74; e-mail worldmarket@itar-tass.com; internet www.itar-tass.com; f. 1904; state information agency; 74 bureaux in Russia and the states of the former USSR, 65 foreign bureaux outside the former USSR; Dir-Gen. VITALII N. IGNATENKO.

Prima Human Rights News Agency: 111399 Moscow, POB 5; tel. and fax (495) 455-30-11; e-mail prima@prima-news.ru; internet www.prima-news.ru; f. 2000; Editor-in-Chief ALEKSANDR PODRABINEK.

RIA—Novosti (Russian Information Agency—News): 103786 Moscow, Zubovskii bulv. 4; tel. (495) 201-82-09; fax (495) 201-45-45; e-mail marketing@rian.ru; internet www.rian.ru; f. 1961; collaborates by arrangement with foreign press and publishing organizations in 110 countries; provider of Russian news features and photographs; Chair. SVETLANA MIRONYUK.

RosBalt Information Agency: 190000 St Petersburg, Konnogvardeiskii bulv. 7; tel. (812) 320-50-30; fax (812) 320-50-31; e-mail rosbalt@rosbalt.ru; internet www.rosbalt.ru; news coverage of European Russia and other countries in northern Europe; bureau in Moscow; Chair. NATALIYA CHERKESOVA; Gen. Man. ALEKSANDR KADYROV.

Rossiiskoye Informatsionnoye Agentstvo 'Oreanda' (RIA 'Oreanda'): 117342 Moscow, POB 21; tel. (495) 330-98-50; fax (495) 23-04-39; e-mail info@oreanda.ru; internet www.oreanda.ru; f. 1994.

Strana.Ru (Country-Russia): 119021 Moscow, Zubovskii bulv. 4, podyezd 8; tel. (495) 981-62-52; fax (495) 981-62-53; e-mail mail@strana.ru; internet www.strana.ru; f. 2000; news agency; central bureau in Moscow, regional bureaux in Groznyi (Chechen—Nokchi Republic) and in Kyiv, Ukraine; controlled by the All-Russian State Television and Radio Broadcasting Company (VGTRK); Editor-in-Chief YULIYA PANFILOVA.

Foreign Bureaux

Agence France-Presse (AFP): 127006 Moscow, ul. Dolgorukovskaya 18/3; tel. (495) 726-59-69; fax (495) 931-95-85; e-mail desk.moscou@afp.com; internet www.afp.com; Dir MICHEL VIATTEAU.

Agencia EFE (Spain): 103051 Moscow, ul. Sadovaya-Samotechnaya 12/24/23; tel. (495) 200-15-32; fax (495) 956-37-38; e-mail efemos@co.ru; internet www.efe.es; Bureau Chief MANUEL VELASCO.

Agenzia Nazionale Stampa Associata (ANSA) (Italy): 121248 Moscow, Kutuzovskii pr. 9/1/12–14; tel. (495) 243-73-93; fax (495) 243-06-37; e-mail ansamos@online.ru; internet www.ansa.it; Bureau Chief GIULIO GELIBTER.

Anadolu Ajansı (Anatolian News Agency) (Turkey): 121248 Moscow, Kutuzovskii pr. 9/2A; tel. (495) 514-11-92; fax (495) 243-67-97; tel. rtual.

Associated Press (AP) (USA): 121248 Moscow, Kutuzovskii pr. 7/4, kor. 5, kv. 33; tel. (495) 234-43-53; fax (495) 974-18-45; e-mail mosed@ap.org; internet www.ap.org; Bureau Chief DEBORAH SEWARD.

Athens News Agency (Greece): 121148 Moscow, Kutuzovskii pr. 13/91; tel. and fax (495) 243-73-73; internet www.ana.gr; Correspondent DIMITRIOS KONSTANTA KOPOULOS.

Baltic News Service (Estonia, Latvia and Lithuania): 121069 Moscow, ul. Povarskaya 24/15; tel. and fax (495) 202-38-05; e-mail juri@bns.ee; internet www.bns.ee; f. 1990; Bureau Chief JÜRI MALOVERJAN; also maintains bureau in Kaliningrad.

Česká tisková kancelář (ČTK) (Czech Republic): 125047 Moscow, ul. 3-aya Tverskaya-Yamskaya 31-35/5/106; tel. and fax (495) 251-71-63; e-mail bwanamar@glas.apc.org; internet www.ctk.cz; Correspondent ALEXANDRA MALACHOVSKA.

Deutsche Presse-Agentur (dpa) (Germany): 121248 Moscow, Kutuzovskii pr. 7/4/210; tel. (495) 243-97-90; fax (495) 243-14-46; internet www.dpa.de; Bureau Chief GÜNTHER CHALUPA.

Iraqi News Agency: 119121 Moscow, ul. Pogodinskaya 12; tel. (495) 316-99-75; fax (495) 246-77-76.

Islamic Republic News Agency (IRNA) (Iran): 121609 Moscow, Rublevskoye shosse 36/2/264; tel. (495) 415-43-62; fax (495) 415-42-88; e-mail irna@garnet.ru; Bureau Chief MAHMOUD HIDAJI.

Jiji Tsushin (Jiji Press) (Japan): 117049 Moscow, ul. Korovii Val 7/35; tel. (495) 564-81-02; fax (495) 564-81-13; Bureau Chief KITAGATA KAZUYA.

Korea Central News Agency (KCNA) (Democratic People's Republic of Korea): 119590 Moscow, ul. Mosfilmovskaya 72; tel. (495) 143-62-31; fax (495) 143-63-12; Bureau Chief KAN CHU MIN.

Kuwait News Agency (KUNA): 117049 Moscow, ul. Korovii Val 7/52; tel. (495) 230-25-10; fax (495) 956-99-06; Correspondent ADIB AL-SAYYED.

Kyodo News (Japan): 121059 Moscow, B. Dorogomilovskaya 12; tel. (495) 956-60-22; fax (495) 956-60-26; Bureau Chief YOSHIDA SHIGEYUKI.

Magyar Távirati Iroda (MTI) (Hungary): 129010 Moscow, ul. B. Spasskaya 12/46; tel. (495) 280-04-25; fax (495) 280-04-21; Bureau Chief SÁNDOR TAMASSY.

Middle East News Agency (MENA) (Egypt): 107113 Moscow, ul. Sokolnicheskii Val 24/2/176; tel. (495) 264-82-76; fax (495) 269-60-93; Correspondent Dr MAMDOUH MUSTAFA.

Mongol Tsahilgaan Medeeniy Agentlag (Montsame) (Mongolia): 117333 Moscow, ul. Vavilova 79/52; tel. (495) 950-55-16; fax (495) 229-98-83; Bureau Chief SHAGDAR.

News Agencies of Sweden, Norway, Denmark and Finland: 121248 Moscow, Kutuzovskii pr. 7/4/5/30; tel. (495) 956-60-50; fax (495) 974-81-52; Correspondent THOMAS HAMBERG.

Notimex News Agency (Mexico): 123182 Moscow, ul. Akademika Bochvara 5/2/30–1; tel. and fax (495) 196-47-75; Correspondent FERNANDO OROZCO LLOREDA.

Polska Agencja Prasowa (PAP) (Poland): 117334 Moscow, Leninskii pr. 45/411; tel. and fax (495) 135-11-06; e-mail papmos@online.ru; Chief Correspondent ANDRZEJ LOMANOWSKI.

Prensa Latina (Cuba): 123182 Moscow, ul. Akademika Bochvara 5/2/30–1; tel. and fax (495) 196-47-75; Chief Correspondent ANTONIO RONDÓN.

Press Trust of India: 129041 Moscow, ul. B. Pereyaslavskaya 7/133–134; tel. and fax (495) 437-43-60; Correspondent VINAY KUMAR SHUKLA.

Reuters (United Kingdom): 121059 Moscow, Radisson-Slavyanskaya Hotel, Berezhkovskaya nab. 2; tel. (495) 941-85-20; fax (495) 941-88-01; Man. MICHAL BRONIATOWSKI.

Rompres (Romania): Moscow, 121248 Kutuzovskii pr. 14/21; tel. (495) 243-67-96; Bureau Chief NICOLAE CRETU.

Schweizerische Depeschenagentur (Switzerland): 121059 Moscow, B. Dorogomilovskaya 8/19; tel. and fax (495) 240-90-78; Bureau Chief CHRISTOPH GÜDEL.

Syrian Arab News Agency (SANA): 121248 Moscow, Kutuzovskii pr. 7/4/184–185; tel. (495) 243-13-00; fax (495) 243-75-12; Dir FAHED KAMNAKESH.

Tlačová agentúra Slovenskej republiky (TASR) (Slovakia): 123056 Moscow, ul. Yu. Fuchika 17–19/43; tel. and fax (495) 250-24-89; Correspondent BLAZEJ PÁNIK.

United Press International (UPI) (USA): 119334 Moscow, Leninskii pr. 45/426; tel. (495) 135-32-55; fax (495) 564-86-61; e-mail newsdesk@unitedpress.ru; internet www.upi.com; Bureau Chief ANTHONY LOUIS.

Viet Nam News Agency (VNA) (Viet Nam): 117334 Moscow, Leninskii pr. 45/326–327; tel. (495) 135-11-08; fax (495) 137-38-67; e-mail pxmoscow@online.ru; Bureau Chief NGO GIA SON.

Xinhua (New China) News Agency (People's Republic of China): 109029 Moscow, ul. M. Kalitnikovskaya 9A; tel. (495) 270-47-41; fax (495) 270-44-85; Dir WEI ZHENGQIANG.

Yonhap (United) News Agency (Republic of Korea): 103009 Moscow, Tverskoi bulv. 10/425; tel. and fax (495) 290-65-75; Correspondent CHI IL-WOO.

PRESS ASSOCIATIONS

Russian Guild of Publishers of Periodical Press: 125047 Moscow, ul. Lesnaya 20/6-211; tel. and fax (495) 978-41-89.

Union of Journalists of Russia: 119021 Moscow, Zubovskii bulv. 4; tel. (495) 201-51-01; fax (495) 201-35-47; f. 1991; Sec.-Gen. IGOR YAKOVENKO.

Publishers

Ad Marginem-Ad Patres: Moscow; f. 1994; fiction, philosophy, artistic and literary criticism; Dir ALEKSANDR IVANOV.

THE RUSSIAN FEDERATION

Aleteiya (Aletheia): 193019 St Petersburg, pr. Obukhovskoi oborony 13; tel. (812) 567-22-39; e-mail aletheia@rol.ru; internet www.orthodoxia.org/aletheia; f. 1992; classics, ancient and medieval history, social sciences; Dir-Gen. I. A. SAVKIN.

AST: 129085 Moscow, Zvezdnyi bulv. 21; tel. (495) 215-01-01; fax (495) 215-51-10; e-mail astpub@aha.ru; internet www.ast.ru; original and translated fiction and non-fiction, children's and schoolbooks.

Avrora (Aurora): 191186 St Petersburg, Nevskii pr. 7/9; tel. (812) 312-37-53; fax (812) 312-54-60; f. 1969; fine arts; published in foreign languages; Dir ZENOBIUS SPETCHINSKII.

Azbuka (Alphabet): 196105 St Petersburg, ul. Reshetnikova 15, POB 192; tel. (812) 327-04-55; fax (812) 327-01-60; e-mail post@azbooka.spb.ru; internet www.azbooka.ru; literary fiction, including translations; f. 1995; Dir-Gen. MAKSIM I. KRYUTCHENKO.

Bolshaya Rossiiskaya Entsiklopediya (The Great Russian Encyclopedia): 109028 Moscow, Pokrovskii bulv. 8; tel. (495) 917-90-00; fax (495) 917-35-62; e-mail secretar@greatbook.ru; f. 1925; universal and specific encyclopedias; Dir N. S. KRAVETS.

Detskaya Entsiklopediya (Children's Encyclopedia): 107042 Moscow, ul. Bakuninskaya 55; tel. (495) 269-52-76; f. 1933; science fiction, literature, poetry, biographical and historical novels.

Detskaya Literatura (Children's Literature): 103720 Moscow, M. Cherkasskii per. 1; tel. (495) 928-08-03; e-mail detlit@detlit.ru; f. 1933; State Publishing House of Children's Literature (other than school books); Dir E. A. NORTSOVA.

Drofa: 127018 Moscow, ul. Sushchevskii Val. 49; tel. (495) 795-05-50; fax (495) 795-05-44; e-mail info@drofa.ru; internet www.drofa.ru; f. 1991; school textbooks, children's fiction; Dir-Gen. ALEKSANDR F. KISELEV.

Ekonomika (Economy): 123955 Moscow, Berezhkovskaya nab. 6; tel. (495) 240-58-18; fax (495) 240-48-178; e-mail info@economizdat.ru; internet www.economizdat.ru; f. 1963; various aspects of economics, management and marketing; Dir YELIZABETA V. POLIYEVKTOVA.

Eksmo: 127299 Moscow, ul. K. Tsetkina 18/5; tel. and fax (495) 411-68-86; e-mail info@eksmo.ru; internet www.eksmo.ru; f. 1991; fiction; Gen. Dir OLEG YE. NOVIKOV.

Energoatomizdat (Atomic Energy Press): 113114 Moscow, Shluzovaya nab. 10; tel. (495) 925-99-93; f. 1981; different kinds of energy, nuclear science and technology; Dir A. P. ALESHKIN.

Finansy i Statistika (Finance and Statistics): 101000 Moscow, ul. Pokrovka 7; tel. (495) 925-47-08; fax (495) 925-09-57; e-mail mail@finstat.ru; internet www.finstat.ru; f. 1924; education, economics, tourism, finance, statistics, banking, insurance, accounting, computer science; Dir Dr A. N. ZVONOVA.

Fizkultura i Sport (Exercise and Sport): 101421 Moscow, ul. Dolgorukovskaya 27; tel. (495) 978-26-90; fax (495) 200-12-17; f. 1923; books and periodicals relating to all forms of sport, chess and draughts, etc.; Gen. Dir T. BALYAN.

Forum: 101831 Moscow, Kolpachnyi per. 9A; tel. and fax (495) 925-01-97; e-mail forum-books@mail.ru; internet www.infra-m.ru/forum.htm; f. 2001; general and professional educational textbooks; Gen. Man. IRINA S. MONAKHOVA.

Galart: 125319 Moscow, ul. Chernyakhovskogo 4; tel. and fax (495) 151-25-02; e-mail galart@m9com.ru; f. 1969; fmrly Sovetskii Khudozhnik (Soviet Artist); art reproduction, art history and criticism; Gen. Dir A. D. SARABYANOV.

Gorodets: 117419 Moscow, 2-i Roshchinskii pr. 8/7/1201; tel. (495) 955-71-28; fax (495) 234-39-67; e-mail info@gorodets.com; internet www.gorodets.com; law, politics, international relations, economics.

INFRA-M: 127282 Moscow, ul. Polyarnara 31B; tel. (495) 380-05-40; fax (495) 363-92-12; e-mail books@infra-m.ru; internet www.infra-m.ru; f. 1992; economics, law, computing, history, reference works, encyclopedias; Man.Dir VYACHESLAV ILYUKHIN.

Iskusstvo (Art): 103009 Moscow, M. Kislovskii per. 3; tel. (495) 203-58-72; f. 1936; fine arts, architecture, cinema, photography, television and radio, theatre; Dir O. A. MAKAROV.

Izobrazitelnoye Iskusstvo (Fine Art): 129272 Moscow, ul. Sushchevskii Val 64; tel. (495) 681-65-48; fax (495) 681-41-11; e-mail iskusstvo@id.ru; reproductions of pictures, pictorial art, books on art, albums, calendars, postcards; Dir G. SH. YERITSYAN.

Khimiya (Chemistry): 107976 Moscow, ul. Strominka 21/2; tel. (495) 268-29-76; f. 1963; chemistry and the chemical industry; Dir BORIS S. KRASNOPEVTSEV.

Khudozhestvennaya Literatura (Fiction): 107078 Moscow, ul. Novobasmannaya 19; tel. (495) 261-88-65; fax (495) 261-83-00; fiction and works of literary criticism, history of literature, etc.; Dir A. N. PETROV; Editor-in-Chief V. S. MODESTOV.

Kniga and Business (Books and Business): 125047 Moscow, ul. 1-aya Tverskaya-Yamskaya 22; tel. (495) 251-60-03; fax (495) 250-04-89; fiction, biographies, history, commerce, general; Dir VIKTOR N. ADAMOV.

Kolos (Ear of Corn): 107807 Moscow, ul. Sadovaya-Spasskaya 18; tel. (495) 207-29-92; fax (495) 207-28-70; f. 1918; all aspects of agricultural production; Dir ANATOLII M. ULYANOV.

Kompozitor (Composer): 127006 Moscow, ul. Sadovaya-Triumfalnaya 12–14; tel. (495) 209-41-05; fax (495) 209-54-98; e-mail komp@kompubl.com; f. 1957; established by the Union of Composers of the USSR; music and music criticism; Dir GRIGORII A. VORONOV.

Malysh (Dear Little One): 121352 Moscow, ul. Davydkovskaya 5; tel. (495) 443-06-54; fax (495) 443-06-55; f. 1958; books, booklets and posters for children aged three to 10 years; Dir V. A. RYBIN.

Meditsina (Medicine): 101838 Moscow, Petroverigskii per. 6/8; tel. (495) 924-87-85; fax (495) 928-60-03; e-mail meditsina@iname.com; internet www.medlit.ru; f. 1918; state-owned; imprint of Association for Medical Literature; books and journals on medicine and health; Dir A. M. STOCHIK; Editor-in-Chief Prof. NIKOLAI R. PALEYEV.

Metallurgiya (Metallurgy): 119034 Moscow, 2-i Obydenskii per. 14; tel. (495) 202-55-32; f. 1939; metallurgical literature; Dir A. G. BELIKOV.

Mezhdunarodnye Otnosheniya (International Relations): 107078 Moscow, ul. Sadovaya-Spasskaya 20; tel. (495) 207-67-93; fax (495) 200-22-04; e-mail info@inter-rel.ru; internet www.inter-rel.ru; f. 1957; international relations, economics and politics of foreign countries, foreign trade, international law, foreign language textbooks and dictionaries, translations and publications for the UN and other international organizations; Dir B. P. LIKHACHEV.

Mir (The World): 107996 Moscow, l-i Rizhskii per. 2; tel. (495) 686-17-83; fax (495) 683-20-58; e-mail akhp@mir-publishers.net; internet www.mir-publishers.net; f. 1946; Russian translations of foreign scientific, technical and science fiction books; translations of Russian books on science and technology into foreign languages; Dir KHABIB P. ABDULLAYEV.

Molodaya Gvardiya (The Young Guard): 127994 Moscow, ul. Sushchevskaya 21; tel. (495) 972-05-46; fax (495) 972-05-82; e-mail dsel@gvardiya.ru; internet www.mg.gvardiya.ru; f. 1922; fmrly publishing and printing combine of the Lenin Young Communist League (Komsomol); joint-stock co; books, magazines, polygraphic services; Gen. Dir V. F. YURKIN.

Moscow University Press: 119899 Moscow, ul. Khokhlova 11; tel. and fax (495) 939-33-23; e-mail kd_mgu@df.ru; f. 1756; more than 200 titles of scientific, educational and reference literature annually, 19 scientific journals; Dir N. S. TIMOFEYEV.

Moskovskii Rabochii (Moscow Worker): 101854 Moscow, Chistoprudnyi bulv. 8; tel. (495) 921-07-35; f. 1922; Dir D. V. YEVDOKIMOV.

Muzyka (Music): 127051 Moscow, ul. Petrovka 26; tel. (495) 921-51-70; fax (495) 928-33-04; e-mail muz-sekretar@yandex.ru; internet www.muzykaizd.ru; f. 1861; sheet music, music scores and related literature; Dir MARK ZILBERWQUIT.

Mysl (Thought): 119071 Moscow, Leninskii pr. 15; tel. (495) 952-50-65; fax (495) 955-04-58; f. 1963; science, popular science, philosophy, history, political science, geography; Dir YE. A. TIMOFEYEV.

Nauka (Science): 117997 Moscow, ul. Profsoyuznaya 90; tel. (495) 334-71-51; fax (495) 420-22-20; e-mail secret@naukaran.ru; internet www.naukaran.ru; f. 1923; publishing house of the Academy of Sciences; general and social science, mathematics, physics, chemistry, biology, earth sciences, oriental studies, books in foreign languages, university textbooks, scientific journals, translation, export, distribution, typesetting and printing services; Dir-Gen. V. VASILIYEV.

Nauka i Tekhnologiya (Science and Technology): 107076 Moscow, Stromynskii per. 4; tel. (495) 269-51-96; fax (495) 269-49-96; e-mail admin@nauka-technologiy.ru; f. 2000; journals on chemistry, electronics and telecommunications; Gen. Dir MAKSIM A. KOVALEVSKII.

Nedra Biznestsentr (Natural Resources Business Centre): 125047 Moscow, pl. Tverskoi Zastavy 3; tel. (495) 251-31-77; fax (495) 250-27-72; e-mail business@nedrainform.ru; internet www.nedrainform.ru; f. 1964; geology, natural resources, mining and coal industry, petroleum and gas industry; Dir V. D. MENSHIKOV.

Nezavisimaya Gazeta ('Independent Newspaper' Publishing House): 101000 Moscow, ul. Myasnitskaya 13/10; tel. and fax (495) 981-61-53; e-mail ngbooks@ng.ru; internet www.ng.ru/izdatelstvo; f. 1991; books on history, literary essays, poetry, history of literature and of art, biography, dictionaries, encyclopaedias; Dir VIKTOR A. OBUKHOV.

Norma (The Norm): 101990 Moscow, Kolpachnyi per. 9A; tel. and fax (495) 925-45-05; e-mail norma@norma-verlag.com; internet www.infra-m.ru/norma.htm; f. 1995; law and jurisprudence, philosophy, psychology, sociology, economics; Gen. Man. EDUARD I. MACHULSKII.

Novosti (News): 105082 Moscow, ul. B. Pochtovaya 7; tel. (495) 265-63-35; fax (495) 975-20-65; f. 1964; politics, economics, fiction, translated literature; Dir ANTON POPOV.

Olma Press: 129075 Moscow, Zvezdnyi bulv. 23/12; tel. (495) 784-67-74; fax (495) 215-80-53; e-mail info@olmapress.ru; internet www.olmapress.ru; f. 1991; fiction, history, reference; children's books, popular science; general; Pres. VLADIMIR I. UZUN; Gen. Man. OLEG P. TKACH.

Pedagogika Press (Pedagogy Press): 119034 Moscow, Smolenskii bulv. 4; tel. and fax (495) 246-59-69; f. 1969; scientific and popular books on pedagogics, didactics, psychology, developmental physiology; young people's encyclopaedia, dictionaries; Dir I. KOLESNIKOVA.

Planeta (Planet): 103779 Moscow, ul. Petrovka 8/11; tel. (495) 923-04-70; fax (495) 200-52-46; f. 1969; postcards, calendars, guidebooks, brochures, illustrated books; co-editions with foreign partners; Dir V. G. SEREDIN.

Pressa (The Press): 125993 Moscow, ul. Pravdy 24; tel. (495) 257-46-22; fax (495) 250-52-05; e-mail jurkevich@media-pressa.ru; f. 1934 as Pravda (Truth) Publishing House; publishes booklets, newspapers and periodicals; Dir I. V. POLTAVTSEV.

Profizdat (Professional Publishers): 101000 Moscow, ul. Myasnitskaya 13/18; tel. (495) 924-57-40; fax (495) 975-23-29; e-mail profizdat@profizdat.ru; f. 1930; books and magazines; Gen. Dir VLADIMIR SOLOVYEV.

Progress (Progress): 119992 Moscow, Zubovskii bulv. 17; tel. (495) 246-90-32; fax (495) 230-24-03; e-mail progress@mcn.ru; f. 1931; translations of Russian language books into foreign languages and of foreign language books into Russian; political and scientific, fiction, literature for children and youth; encyclopedias; Dir-Gen. SARKIS V. OGANIAN.

Prosveshcheniye (Enlightenment): 127521 Moscow, 3-i proyezd M. Roshchi 41; tel. (495) 789-30-40; fax (495) 789-30-41; e-mail prosv@prosv.ru; internet www.prosv.ru; f. 1930; school textbooks, dictionaries, atlases, reference and scientific books, educational materials; Dir A. M. KONDAKOV.

Radio i Svyaz (Radio and Communication): 127473 Moscow, 2-i Shchemilovskii per.5/4/1; tel. (495) 978-68-17; fax (495) 978-53-51; e-mail radsv@garnet.ru; internet www.radiosv.ru; f. 1981; radio engineering, electronics, communications, computer science; Dir YURII G. IVASHOV.

Raduga (Rainbow): 121839 Moscow, per. Sivtsev Vrazhek 43; tel. (495) 241-68-15; fax (495) 241-63-53; e-mail raduga@pol.ru; f. 1982; translations of Russian fiction into foreign languages and of foreign authors into Russian; Dir TANYANA ZIMINA.

Respublika (Republic): 125811 Moscow, Miusskaya pl. 7; tel. (495) 251-42-44; fax (495) 200-22-54; e-mail respublik@dataforce.net; f. 1918; fmrly Politizdat (Political Publishing House); dictionaries, books on politics, human rights, philosophy, history, economics, religion, fiction, arts, reference; Dir ALEKSANDR P. POLYAKOV.

Rosmen (Rosman): 127018 Moscow, ul. Oktyabskaya 4/2; tel. (495) 933-70-70; fax (495) 933-71-36; e-mail rosman@rosman.ru; internet www.rosman.ru; children's literature, general, popular science; Dir-Gen. OLEG V. ZHIVYKH.

Rosspen Publishing House—Russian Political Encylopedia: 117393 Moscow, ul. Profsoyuznaya 82; tel. and fax (495) 334-81-62; e-mail alena@rosspen.com; internet www.rosspen.com; f. 1992; politics, history, other academic and reference publishing; Dir-Gen. A. K. SOROKIN.

Russkaya Kniga (Russian Book): 123557 Moscow, Tishinskii per. 38; tel. (495) 205-33-77; fax (495) 205-34-27; f. 1957 as Sovetskaya Rossiya; fiction, politics, history, social sciences, health, do-it-yourself, children's; Dir M. F. NENASHEV.

Russkii Yazyk (Russian Language): 117303 Moscow, ul. M. Yushunski 1; tel. (495) 319-83-14; fax (495) 319-83-12; e-mail russlang@mtu-net.ru; f. 1974; textbooks, reference, dictionaries; Dir IRINA KAINARSKAYA.

Shkola-Press (School-Press): 127254 Moscow, ul. Sh. Rustaveli 10/3; tel. and fax (495) 219-83-80; e-mail marketing@schoolpress.ru; internet www.schoolpress.ru; books on psychology, pedagogy, magazines.

Slovo (Word): 109147 Moscow, ul. Vorontsovskaya 41; tel. and fax (495) 911-61-33; internet www.slovo-online.ru; f. 1989; illustrated books on art, world literature in translation; Gen-Dir. NATALIYA AVETISYAN.

Sovremennyi Pisatel (The Contemporary Writer): 121069 Moscow, ul. Povarskaya 11; tel. (495) 202-50-51; f. 1934; fiction and literary criticism, history, biography; publ. house of the International Confederation of Writers' Unions and the Union of Russian Writers; Dir A. N. ZHUKOV.

Stroyizdat (Construction Publishing House): 101442 Moscow, ul. Kalyayevskaya 23A; tel. (495) 251-69-67; f. 1932; building, architecture, environmental protection, fire protection and building materials; Dir V. A. KASATKIN.

Sudostroyeniye (Shipbuilding): 191186 St Petersburg, ul. M. Morskaya 8; tel. (812) 312-44-79; fax (812) 312-08-21; e-mail izdsud@peterlink.ru; f. 1940; shipbuilding, ship design, navigation, marine research, underwater exploration, international marine exhibitions; produces quarterly publications *Maritime Journal* and *Marine Radio Electronics*; Dir and Editor-in-Chief A. A. ANDREYEV.

Tekst (Text): 127299 Moscow, ul. Kosmonavta Volkova 7; tel. and fax (495) 150-0472; e-mail textpubl@yandex.ru; internet www.textpubl.ru; f. 1988; foreign poetry and prose fiction in translation, Russian poetry and prose, children's literature, social sciences, history, law; Dir OLGET M. Libkin.

Transport (Transport): 103064 Moscow, Basmannyi tupik 6A; tel. (495) 262-67-73; fax (495) 261-13-22; f. 1923; publishes works on all forms of transport; Dir V. G. PESHKOV.

Vagrius: 129090 Moscow, ul. Troitskaya 7/1; tel. (495) 785-09-62; fax (495) 785-09-69; e-mail vagrius@vagrius.com; internet www.vagrius.com; f. 1992; fiction, politics, history; Pres. and Dir-Gen. GLEB USPENSKII.

Ves Mir (The Whole World): 101831 Moscow, Kolpachnyi per. 9A; tel. (495) 923-68-39; fax (495) 925-42-69; e-mail info@vesmirbooks.ru; internet www.vesmirbooks.ru; f. 1994; university textbooks, scholarly works in social sciences and humanities; Dir Dr OLEG ZIMARIN; Editor-in-Chief TATYANA KOMAROVA.

Vneshtorgizdat (External Trade Printing and Publishing Association): 125047 Moscow, ul. Fadeyev 1; tel. (495) 250-51-62; fax (495) 253-97-94; f. 1925; publishes foreign technical material translated into Russian, and information on export goods, import and export firms, joint ventures; in several foreign languages; Dir-Gen. V. I. PROKOPOV.

Voyenizdat (Military Publishing House): 103160 Moscow, ul. Zorge 1; tel. (495) 195-25-95; fax (495) 195-24-54; military theory and history, general fiction; Dir YURII I. STADNYUK.

Vysshaya Shkola (Higher School): 127994 Moscow, ul. Neglinnaya 29/14; tel. (495) 200-04-56; fax (495) 200-34-86; e-mail info_vshkola@mail.ru; internet www.vshkola.ru; f. 1939; textbooks for higher-education institutions; Dir MIKHAIL L. ZORIN.

Yuridicheskaya Literatura (Legal Literature): 121069 Moscow, ul. M. Nikitskaya 14; tel. (495) 203-83-84; fax (495) 291-98-83; f. 1917; law subjects; official publishers of enactments of the Russian President and Govt; Dir I. A. BUNIN.

Znaniye (Knowledge): 101835 Moscow, proyezd Serova 4; tel. (495) 928-15-31; f. 1951; popular books and brochures on politics and science; Dir V. K. BELYAKOV.

Broadcasting and Communications

TELECOMMUNICATIONS

Golden Telecom: 115114 Moscow, Kozhevnicheskii proyezd 1; tel. (495) 787-10-00; fax (495) 258-78-28; e-mail info@goldentelecom.ru; internet www.goldentelecom.ru; f. 1994 as Teleross; operates mobile cellular telecommunications network in 16 cities in the Russian Federation, and in Almaty (Kazakhstan) and Kyiv (Ukraine); subsidiary of the Golden TeleSystems Group (USA); Pres. and Chief Exec. ALEKSANDR VINOGRADOV.

Megafon: 119435 Moscow, Savvinskaya nab. 15; tel. (495) 504-50-20; fax (495) 504-50-21; e-mail aklimov@megafon.ru; internet www.megafon.ru; f. 2002 by merger; operates mobile cellular communications networks across the territory of the Russian Federation; 6 regional cos; 15.6m. subscribers (March 2005).

Mobile TeleSystems (MTS): 109147 Moscow, ul. Marksistskaya 4; tel. (495) 766-01-77; e-mail info@mts.ru; internet www.mts.ru; f. 1993; 776,000 subscribers (Dec. 2000); provides mobile cellular telecommunications services in 25 regions of Russia; majority-owned by Sistema Telecom; 35.1% owned by Deutsche Telekom (Germany); Pres. M. A. SMIRNOV; 9.5m. subscribers (March 2003).

Moscow City Telephone Network (MGTS—Moskovskaya Gorodskaya Telefonnaya Set): 127994 Moscow, Petrovskii bulv. 12/3; tel. (495) 950-00-00; fax (495) 950-06-18; e-mail mgts@mgts.ru; internet www.mgts.ru; f. 1882; provides telecommunications services to over 4.2m. subscribers (2001) in Moscow City; 56% owned by Sistema Telecom; Gen. Man. VLADIMIR S. LAGUTIN.

Petersburg Telephone Network (PTS—Peterburgsskaya Telefonnaya Set): 119186 St Petersburg, ul. B. Morskaya 24; tel. (812) 314-15-50; fax (812) 110-68-34; e-mail office@ptn.ru; internet www.ptn.ru; f. 1993; subsidiary of Severo-Zapadnyi Telekom (North-Western Telecom); Dir IGOR N. SAMYLIN.

Rostelekom (Rostelecom): 125047 Moscow, ul.1-aya Tverskaya-Yamskaya 14; tel. (495) 787-28-49; fax (495) 972-82-83; e-mail info@rostelecom.ru; internet www.rt.ru; 50.7% owned by Svyazinvest;

dominant long-distance and international telecommunications service provider; seven regional cos based in St Petersburg, Samara, Novosibirsk, Yekaterinburg, Khabarovsk, Moscow and Rostov-on-Don; Dir DMITRII YEROKHIN.

Svyazinvest: 119121 Moscow, ul. Plyushchikha 55/2; tel. (495) 248-24-71; fax (495) 248-24-53; e-mail dms@svyazinvest.ru; internet www.sinvest.ru; f. 1995; 75%-state-owned telecommunications co; holds controlling stakes in 7 'mega-regional' telecommunications operators, 1 international and domestic long–distance operator, and 2 local telecommuncations cos, and non-controlling stakes in 2 city telecommunications cos; Gen. Dir VALERII N. YASHIN.

VympelKom-Bilain (Vympelcom-Beeline): 125083 Moscow, ul. 8 Marta 10/14; tel. and fax (495) 725-07-00; e-mail info@beeline.ru; internet www.beeline.ru; operates mobile cellular telecommunications networks in Moscow City and Moscow Oblast, and in Yaroslavl, Nizhnii Novgorod, Novosibirsk, Omsk, Ufa, Rostov-on-Don and Volgograd; 25% owned by Telenor (Norway), 25% owned by Alfa-Bank; 1,800,000 subscribers (Nov. 2001); Chief Exec. JO LUNDER; Pres. DMITRII B. ZIMIN.

BROADCASTING

In 1995 there was extensive reorganization of Russian broadcasting, and a new organization, Public Russian Television (ORT), was formed to take over the broadcasting responsibilities of the Ostankino Russian State Television and Radio Broadcasting Company. Pervyi Kanal (First Channel), as ORT's Channel 1 was renamed in 2002, is received throughout Russia and many parts of the CIS. The All-Russian State Television Company (VGTRK) broadcasts Telekanal 'Rossiya', which reaches some 92% of the Russian population and Telekanal 'Kultura', founded for the purpose of broadcasting Russian-made programmes. In mid-2003 the VGTRK also began broadcasting a new channel, Telekanal 'Sport', on the frequency vacated by the independent channel, TVS, which had recently ceased operations. In addition to the nation-wide television channels, there are local channels, and the Independent Television (NTV) channel (65% owned by the gas utility, Gazprom, in which the Government holds a majority stake) is broadcast in most of Russia. In the regions, part of Rossiya's programming is devoted to local affairs, with broadcasts in minority languages. In late 2001 there were some 550 television stations in the Russian Federation, of which approximately 150 were state-owned. In 2005 proposals to launch a state-supported international English-language TV station, to be known as Russia Today, were announced. In mid-2005 there were four nation-wide radio stations, as well as 11 urban radio networks and more than 200 regional stations. At that time Radio Rossiya had more listeners than any other state-run channel, but the commercial music station, Russkoye Radio, established in 1995, was the most popular station overall.

Association of Regional State Television and Radio Broadcasters: 113326 Moscow, ul. Pyatnitskaya 25/226; tel. and fax (495) 950-60-28; e-mail fstratyv@rzn.rosmail.com; Chair. of Bd ALEKSANDR N. LEVCHENKO.

Regulatory Authority

Russian Television and Radio Broadcasting Network: 113326 Moscow, ul. Pyatnitskaya 25; tel. (495) 233-66-03; fax (495) 233-28-93; f. 2001; Gen. Man. GENNADII I. SKLYAR.

Radio

All-Russian State Television and Radio Broadcasting Company (VGTRK): 125040 Moscow, ul. 5-aya Yamskogo Polya 19/21; tel. (495) 745-39-78; fax (495) 975-26-11; e-mail rtrinterdep@rfn.ru; internet www.tvradio.ru; f. 1991; broadcasts 'Rossiya' 'Kultura', 'Sport' and 'Planeta' television channels, 89 regional television and radio cos, and national radio stations 'Radio Rossiya', 'Radio Mayak' and 'Radio Nostalzhi'; Chair. OLEG DOBRODEYEV.

Radio Mayak (Radio Beacon): 113326 Moscow, ul. Pyatnitskaya 25; tel. (495) 950-67-67; fax (495) 959-42-04; e-mail inform@radiomayak.ru; internet www.radiomayak.ru; f. 1964; state-owned; Chair. IRINA A. GERASIMOVA.

Radio Nostalzhi (Radio Nostalgia): 113162 Moscow, ul. Shabolovka 37; tel. (495) 955-84-00; e-mail nostalgie@vimain.vitpc.com; f. 1993; Gen. Man. IRINA A. GERASIMOVA.

Radio Rossiya (Radio Russia): 125040 Moscow, ul. 5-aya Yamskogo Polya 19/21; tel. (495) 234-85-94; fax (495) 730-42-77; e-mail direction@radiorus.ru; internet www.radiorus.ru; f. 1990; broadcasts information, social, political, musical, literary and investigate progamming; Dir-Gen. ALEKSEI V. ABAKUMOV.

Ekho Moskvy (Moscow Echo): 119992 Moscow, ul. Novyi Arbat 11; tel. (495) 202-92-29; e-mail info@echo.msk.ru; internet www.echo.msk.ru; f. 1990; stations in Moscow, St Petersburg, Rostov-on-Don and Vologda; also broadcasts from Moscow to Chelyabinsk, Krasnoyarsk, Novosibirsk, Omsk, Perm, Saratov and Yekaterin-burg; 66% -owned by Gazprom-Mediya, 34% staff-owned; Gen. Man. YURII FEDUTINKOV.

Golos Rossii (The Voice of Russia): 113326 Moscow, ul. Pyatnitskaya 25; tel. (495) 950-64-40; fax (495) 230-28-28; e-mail letters@vor.ru; internet www.vor.ru; fmrly Radio Moscow International; international broadcasts in 31 languages; Man. Dir ARMEN G. OGANESIAN.

Russkoye Radio (Russian Radio): 105064 Moscow, ul. Kazakova 16; tel. (495) 232-16-36; fax (495) 956-13-60; internet www.rusradio.ru; f. 1995; owned by Russkaya Mediyagruppa (Russian Media Group); nation-wide commercial music station; broadcasts to more than 700 towns in Russia, Ukraine, Kazakhstan, Moldova, Kyrgyzstan, the Baltic Republics and the USA; also *Russkoye Radio 2*, principally news and talk programming, broadcast to Moscow; Dir-Gen. SERGEI KOZHEVNIKOV.

Serebryanyi Dozhd (Silver Rain): 125083 Moscow, Petrovsko-Razumovskaya alleya 12; tel. (495) 191-97-87; internet www.silver.ru; f. 1995; commercial station broadcasting information and entertainment programming; broadcasts to 98 cities in Russia and the 'near abroad'; Dir-Gen. DMITRII SAVITSKII.

Yevropa Plyus (Europa Plus): 127427 Moscow, ul. Akademika Koroleva 19; tel. (495) 217-82-57; fax (495) 956-35-08; e-mail main@europaplus.ru; internet www.europaplus.ru; FM station, broadcasting music, entertainment and information programmes to 500 cities; Pres. ZHORZH POLINSKI; Gen. Man. ALEKSANDR POLESITSKII.

Television

All-Russian State Television and Radio Broadcasting Company (VGTRK): 125040 Moscow, ul. 5-aya Yamskogo Polya 19/21; tel. (495) 745-39-78; fax (495) 975-26-11; e-mail rtrinterdep@rfn.ru; f. 1991; broadcasts 'Rossiya' 'Kultura', 'Sport' and 'Planeta' television channels, 89 regional television and radio cos, and national radio stations 'Radio Rossiya', 'Radio Mayak' and 'Radio Nostalzhi'; Chair. OLEG DOBRODEYEV.

Telekanal 'Kultura' (Television Channel 'Culture'): 123995 Moscow, ul. M. Nikitskaya 24; e-mail kultura@tvkultura.ru; internet www.tvkultura.ru; f. 1997; Gen. Dir ALEKSANDR S. PONOMAREV.

Telekanal 'Rossiya' (Television Channel 'Russia'): 115162 Moscow, ul. Shabolovka 37; tel. (495) 924-63-74; fax (495) 234-87-71; e-mail info@rutv.ru; internet www.rutv.ru; fmrly RTR-TV; name changed as above in 2002; Dir-Gen. ALEKSANDR S. PONAMAREV.

Telekanal 'Sport' (Television Channel 'Sport'): 113162 Moscow, ul. Shabolovka 37; e-mail info@rtr-sport.ru; internet www.rtr-sport.ru; f. 2003 to assume broadcasting frequencies of TVS; Dir-Gen. VASILII KIKNADZE.

Telekanal 'Zvezda' (Television Channel 'Star'): 129110 Moscow, Suvorovskaya pl. 2; tel. (495) 631-58-83; internet www.tvzvezda.ru; f. 2005; Gen. Dir SERGEI V. SABUSHKIN.

NTV—Independent Television: 127427 Moscow, ul. Akademika Koroleva 12; tel. (495) 725-51-03; fax (495) 725-51-01; e-mail info@ntv.ru; internet www.ntv.ru; f. 1993; 65% owned by Gazprom-Mediya; also NTV World (NTV Mir), broadcasting to Russian communities in Israel, Europe and the USA; Dir-Gen. NIKOLAI YU. SENKEVICH.

Pervyi Kanal—First Channel (Channel One): 127000 Moscow, ul. Akademika Koroleva 12; tel. (495) 215-82-47; fax (495) 215-82-47; e-mail ort_int@ortv.ru; internet www.1tv.ru; f. 1995; fmrly ORT—Public Russian Television; name changed as above in 2002; 51% state-owned; 49% owned by private shareholders; broadcasts Russia's main television channel; Chair. MIKHAIL PYATKOVSKII; Dir-Gen. KONSTANTIN ERNST.

Ren-TV Network: 119843 Moscow, Zubovskii bulv. 17/510; tel. (495) 246-25-06; fax (495) 245-09-98; e-mail site@rentv.dol.ru; internet www.ren-tv.com; f. 1991; network of more than 100 television stations in the Russian Federation and 60 stations in republics of the CIS; 35% owned by Severstal, 35% owned by Surgutneftegaz, 30% owned by RTL Group (Germany); Pres. IRENA LESNEVSKAYA; Gen. Man. DMITRII A. LESNEVSKII.

STS—Network of Television Stations: 123298 Moscow, ul. 3-aya Khoroshevskaya 12; tel. (495) 797-41-73; fax (495) 797-41-01; e-mail www@ctc-tv.ru; internet www.ctc-tv.ru; f. 1996; owned by StoryFirst Communications (USA); broadcasts programmes of popular entertainment to 350 cities in Russia; Dir-Gen. ALEKSANDR YE. RODNYANSKII.

TNT—Territory of Our Viewers—TV Network: 127427 Moscow, ul. Akademika Koroleva 19; tel. (495) 217-81-88; fax (495) 748-14-90; e-mail info@tnt-tv.ru; internet www.tnt-tv.ru; f. 1997; cable television network broadcasting to 582 cities in Russia; Chief Exec. ALEKSANDR DYBAL; Dir-Gen. ROMAN PETRENKO.

TV-Tsentr (TVTs—TV-Centre): 113184 Moscow, ul. B. Tatarskaya 33/1; tel. (495) 959-39-87; fax (495) 959-39-66;

e-mail info@tvc.ru; internet www.tvc.ru; f. 1997; broadcasting consortium for terrestrial cable and satellite television; receives funding from Govt of Moscow City; Pres. OLEG M. POPTSOV; Dir PAVEL V. KASPAROV.

Finance

(cap. = capital; res = reserves; dep. = deposits; m. = million; brs = branches; amounts in new roubles, unless otherwise stated)

BANKING

Following the dissolution of the USSR in 1991, the majority of state-owned banks were privatized and the establishment of private banks was permitted. The Central Bank of the Russian Federation, founded in 1991, replaced the Gosbank (State Bank). Under the 1993 Constitution, responsibility for bank licensing, regulation and supervision was accorded to the Central Bank.

The number of commercial banks increased considerably in the early 1990s, reaching more than 2,500 in 1994. Consolidation of the banking sector, begun in 1995, meant that there were some 1,641 private banks registered in April 1998; at 1 September 2004 there were reported to be 1,318 credit institutions, with a total of 3,210 branches and agencies, in Russia.

Central Bank

Bank Rossii—Central Bank of the Russian Federation: 107016 Moscow, ul. Neglinnaya 12; tel. (495) 771-91-00; fax (495) 921-91-47; e-mail webmaster@www.cbr.ru; internet www.cbr.ru; f. 1990; cap. 298,233m., res 300,489m., dep. 194,937m. (2003); Chair. SERGEI M. IGNATIYEV; 78 brs.

State-owned Banks

Bank Rossiiskii Kredit (Russian Credit Bank): 121002 Moscow, Smolenskii bulv. 26/9; tel. (495) 967-34-48; fax (495) 247-39-39; e-mail cat@roskredit.ru; internet www.roscredit.ru; f. 1990; cap. 391.9m., res −22,325.9m., dep. 34,087.2m. (Dec. 2001); Pres. YURII ISAYEV; Chair. ALEKSANDR LIVSHITS.

Vneshtorgbank (Bank for Foreign Trade): 119992 Moscow, ul. Plyushchka 37; tel. (495) 739-77-99; fax (495) 258-47-81; e-mail info@vtb.ru; internet www.vtb.ru; f. 1990; cap. US $2,153m., res $220m., dep. $7,809m. (Dec. 2003); Chair. and Chief Exec. ANDREI L. KOSTIN; 39 brs.

Major Commercial and Co-operative Banks

AK BARS Bank: 420066 Tatarstan, Kazan, ul. Dekabristov 1; tel. (843) 219-38-02; fax (843) 219-39-76; e-mail kanc@akbars.ru; internet www.akbars.ru; f. 1993; merged with Tatinfrabank in 1997; cap. 2,015.4m., res 819.8m., dep. 18,743.0m. (Dec. 2003); Chair. of Bd ROBERT MINNEGALIYEV; 22 brs.

Alfa-Bank: 107078 Moscow, ul. M. Poryvayevoi 9; tel. (495) 974-25-15; fax (495) 745-57-84; e-mail mail@alfabank.ru; internet www.alfabank.ru; f. 1991; cap. US $160.8m., res $386.2m., dep. $5,115.6m. (Dec. 2003); Chair. of Exec. Bd RUSHAN KHVESYUK; Pres. PETR AVEN; Chief Exec. PETR SMIDR; 45 brs.

Avtobank-Nikoil: 127055 Moscow, ul. Lesnaya 41; tel. (495) 978-00-00; fax (495) 978-66-23; e-mail info@avtobank.ru; internet www.avtobank.ru; f. 1988; present name adopted 2003; 22.7% owned by Ingosstrakh Insurance Co Ltd; cap. US $43m., res $0.9m., dep. $240m. (Sept. 2002); Chair. NATALIYA A. RAYEVSKAYA; 25 brs.

Bank of Khanty-Mansiisk: 628012 Tyumen obl., Khanty-Mansii AOk—Yugra, Khanty-Mansiisk, ul. Mira 38; tel. (34671) 302-10; fax (34671) 302-19; e-mail hmbank@khmb.ru; internet www.khmb.ru; f. 1992; absorbed East European Siberian Bank in 2003; cap. 2,005.0m., res 351.3m., dep. 2,100.0m. (Oct. 2003); 1,270 employees; Pres. DMITRII MIZGULIN; 16 brs.

Bank Petrocommerce (Bank Petrokommertz): 127051 Moscow, ul. Petrovka 24; tel. (495) 925-95-65; fax (495) 923-36-07; e-mail welcome@petrocommerce.ru; internet www.petrocommerce.ru; f. 1992; 77.9% owned by LUKoil; cap. 5,000.0m., res 986.9m., dep. 35,542.4m. (Dec. 2003); Pres. and Chair. of Bd VLADIMIR N. NIKITENKO.

Bank TsentroKredit (CentroCredit Bank): 119017 Moscow, ul. Pyatinitskaya 31/2; tel. (495) 956-86-26; fax (495) 959-02-85; e-mail info@ccb.ru; internet www.ccb.ru; f. 1989; cap. 820.0m., res 169.9m., dep. 8,739.7m. (Dec. 2002); Pres. PAVEL N. KOSOLOBOV; Chair. ANDREI I. TARASOV.

Bank Zenit: 129100 Moscow, Bannyi per. 9; tel. (495) 937-07-37; fax (495) 777-57-06; e-mail info@zenit.ru; internet www.zenit.ru; f. 1994; 50% owned by Tatneft; cap. US $107.1m., res $44.6m., dep. $850.1m. (Dec. 2003); Chair. of Bd ALEKSEI A SOKOLOV; 4 brs.

BIN Bank: 121471 Moscow, ul Grodnenskaya 5A; tel. (495) 755-50-60; fax (495) 440-09-75; e-mail binbank@binbank.ru; internet www.binbank.ru; f. 1993; cap. 2,040.0m., res 1,034m., dep. 9,633.6m. (July 2005); Chair. of Bd SERGEI YE. YEGOROV; Pres. and Chief Exec. MIKHAIL O. SHISHKHANOV; 18 brs.

Evrofinance Mosnarbank: 121099 Moscow, ul. Novyi Arbat 29; tel. (495) 967-81-82; fax (495) 967-81-33; e-mail info@evrofinance.ru; internet www.evrofinance.ru; f. 1990; 19.9% owned by Moscow Narodny Bank Ltd (UK), 16% owned by Vneshekonombank; cap. 3,510.3m., res 2,075.1m, dep. 23,423.2m. (Dec. 2003); Pres. and Chair. of Bd VLADIMIR M. STOLYARENKO; CEO ILYA LOMAKIN; 6 brs.

Gazprombank: 117420 Moscow, ul. Nametkina 16/1; tel. (495) 719-17-63; fax (495) 913-73-19; e-mail mailbox@gazprombank.ru; internet www.gazprombank.ru; f. 1990; 87.5% owned by Gazprom; cap. US $907.1m., res $100.4m., dep. $5,823m. (Dec. 2003); Chair. of Council ALEKSEI B. MILLER; Chair. of Management Bd ANDREI I. AKIMOV; 32 brs.

Globex Commercial Bank (GlobexBank): 121069 Moscow, ul. B. Nikitskaya 60/1; tel. (495) 202-24-82; fax (495) 290-56-08; e-mail post@globexbank.ru; internet www.globexbank.ru; f. 1992; cap. 10,084.4m., res 4.6m., dep. 17,029.0m. (Dec. 2003); Chair. ANDREI F. DUNAYEV; Pres. ANATOLII L. MOTYLEV.

Impexbank (Import-Export Bank): 125252 Moscow, ul. Novopeschanaya 20/10/1A; tel. and fax (495) 752-52-32; e-mail mail@impexbank.ru; internet www.impexbank.ru; f. 1993; cap. US $90.2m., dep. $655.0m. (Dec. 2003), total assets $976.4m. (June 2004); Chair. of Bd PAVEL I. LYSENKO; more than 180 brs in Moscow and regions (2005).

Industry and Construction Bank (ICB) (Promyshlenno-Stroitelnyi Bank): 191014 St Petersburg, ul. Kovenskii 17/18; tel. (812) 329-84-51; fax (812) 310-61-73; e-mail lider@icbank.ru; internet www.icbank.ru; f. 1870 as Volga-Kama Bank; present name adopted 1990; cap. 1,122.1m., res 2,557.3m., dep. 60,571.0m. (Dec. 2003); Chair. ALEKSANDR PUSTOVALOV; 52 brs.

International Bank of St Petersburg (Mezhdunarodnyi Bank Sankt-Peterburga): 194044 St Petersburg, Krapivnyi per. 5; tel. (812) 541-82-17; fax (812) 541-83-93; e-mail mail@ibsp.ru; internet www.ibsp.ru; f. 1989; present name adopted 1999; cap. 14.8m., res 2.2m., dep. 8,170.5m. (Jan. 2005); Pres. SERGEI V. BAZHANOV; 2 brs.

International Moscow Bank (Mezhdunarodnyi Moskovskii Bank): 119034 Moscow, Prechistenskaya nab. 9; tel. (495) 258-72-00; fax (495) 258-72-72; e-mail imbank@imbank.ru; internet www.imb.ru; f. 1989; 47.4% owned by Bayerische Hypo- und Vereinsbank AG (Germany), 22.4% by Nordea Bank Finland, 20% by Banque Commerciale pour l'Europe du Nord—EUROBANK (France), 10.2% owned by European Bank for Reconstruction and Development—EBRD (UK); finances joint ventures, investments and projects of domestic and foreign customers and international trade deals; absorbed Bank Austria Creditanstalt (Russia ZAO) in 2001; cap. US $156.3m., res $117.7m., dep. $263.8m. (Dec. 2004); Chair. of Bd of Dirs PETER O. KOELLE; Chair. of Bd of Management ILKKA SALONEN; 15 brs.

MDM Financial Group (MDM-Bank): 115172 Moscow, Kotelnicheskaya nab. 33/1; tel. (495) 797-95-00; fax (495) 797-95-01; e-mail pr@mdmfinancialgroup.com; internet www.mdmfinancialgroup.com; f. 1993; fmrly Moscow Business World Bank (MDM Bank); cap. US $760.3m., res $95.4m., dep. $2,353.1m. (June 2005); Chief Exec. ANDREI SAVELIYEV; 98 brs and sub-brs.

Mezhdunarodnyi Promyshlennyi Bank (International Industrial Bank): 125009 Moscow, ul. B. Dmitrovka 23–8/1–2; tel. (495) 926-44-46; fax (495) 292-82-84; e-mail mail@iib.ru; internet www.iib.ru; f. 1992; cap. 25,000m., res 354.9m., dep. 99,731.4m. (Dec. 2003); Pres. SERGEI A. VEREMEYENKO; 5 brs.

Moscow Municipal Bank—Bank of Moscow: 107996 Moscow, ul. Rozhdestvenka 8/15/3; tel. (495) 745-80-00; fax (495) 795-26-00; e-mail info@mmbank.ru; internet www.mmbank.ru; f. 1995; 62.7% owned by Govt of Moscow City; cap. 10,476.7m., res 646.0m., dep. 105,989.1m. (Dec. 2003); Pres. and Chief Exec. ANDREI BORODIN; 40 brs.

NIKoil IBG Bank: 119048 Moscow, ul. Yefremova 8; tel. (495) 705-90-39; fax (495) 745-70-10; e-mail pr@nikoil.ru; internet www.nikoil.ru; f. 1990 as Rodina Joint-Stock Bank; present name adopted 1998; cap. 7,360.9m., res 425.8m., dep. 17,204.9m. (Dec. 2002); Chair. MAARTEN LEO PRONK (acting); 6 brs.

Nomos-Bank: 109240 Moscow, ul. V. Radishchevskaya 3/1; tel. (495) 737-73-55; fax (495) 797-32-50; e-mail nmosmail@online.ru; internet www.nomos.ru; f. 1992; fmrly Novaya Moskva (Nomos Bank); cap. 3,678.1m., res 4,674.4m., dep. 8,164.4m. (June 2004); Pres. IGOR FINOGENOV; 8 brs.

Promsvyazbank (Industry and Communications Bank): 109052 Moscow, ul. Smirnovskaya 10/2–3/22; tel. (495) 733-96-20; fax (495) 777-10-20; e-mail postmaster@psbank.ru; internet www.psbank.ru; f. 1995; owned by a consortium of communications cos; cap. 2,272.8m., res 2,085.0m., dep. 35,359.7m. (Dec. 2003); Chair. of Council DMITRII N. ANANIEV; Pres. ALEKSANDR A. LEVKOVSKII; 11 brs.

Rosbank: 107078 Moscow, ul. M. Poryvayevoi 11, POB 208; tel. (495) 725-05-95; fax (495) 725-05-11; e-mail mailbox@rosbank.ru; internet www.rosbank.ru; f. 1998 by merger of Menatep, Most-Bank and Oneximbank, merged with UNEXIMbank in 2000; 91.4% owned by Interros; cap. 5,478.2m., res 2,858.2m., dep. 82,194.0m. (Dec. 2003); Pres. and Chair. of Bd of Dirs ANDREI KLISHAS; Chief. Exec. ALEXANDER POPOV; 11 brs.

Sberbank Rossii—Savings Bank of the Russian Federation (Sberbank): 117997 Moscow, ul. Vavilova 19; tel. (495) 957-57-58; fax (495) 747-37-58; e-mail sbrf@sbrf.ru; internet www.sbrf.ru; f. 1841 as a deposit-taking institution, reorganized as a joint-stock commercial bank in 1991; 60.6% owned by Bank Rossii—Central Bank of the Russian Federation; cap. 148,400m., res 44,600m., dep. 1,178,100m. (Jan. 2004); Chair. of Bd and Chief Exec. ANDREI I. KAZMIN; 17 regional head offices, 1,028 brs and 19,143 sub-brs.

Sobinbank: 123022 Moscow, ul. Rochdelskaya 15/56; tel. (495) 725-25-25; fax (495) 937-99-23; e-mail mail@sobin.ru; internet www.sobinbank.ru; f. 1990; cap. 500.0m., res 3,110.2m., dep. 49.4m. (Dec. 2002); Chair. of Bd SERGEI A KIRILENKO; 17 brs.

Surgutneftegazbank (SNGB): 628400 Tyumen obl., Khanty-Mansii AOk—Yugra, Surgut, ul. Kukuyevitskogo 19; tel. (3462) 39-86-00; fax (3462) 39-87-11; e-mail telex@sngb.ru; internet www.sngb.ru; f. 1965; reorganized as a commercial bank in 1990; 91.6% owned by Surgutneftegaz; cap. 3,553.5m., dep. 29,112.3m., total assets 31,050.4m. (Dec. 2002); Pres. VLADIMIR BOGDANOV; Chair. of Bd YEVGENIYA NEPOMNYASHIKHA.

TransKreditBank (TransCreditBank): 119034 Moscow, Soimonovskii proyezd 5; tel. (495) 788-08-80; fax (495) 788-08-79; e-mail info@bnk.ru; internet www.tcb.ru; f. 1992; 75.0% state-owned; cap. 3,373.6m., res −954.9m., dep. 28,424.9m. (Dec. 2003); Pres. YURII V. KRASOVSKII.

Trust Investment Bank (Investitsisnnyi Bank 'Trast'): 115035 Moscow, ul. Sadovnicheskaya 84/3/7; tel. (495) 247-25-83; fax (495) 956-99-65; e-mail office@trust.ru; internet www.trust.ru; f. 1994; fmrly Doveritelnyi i Investitsionnyi Bank (Trust and Investment Bank); present name adopted 2003; cap. 3,044.6m., res 2,411.2m., dep. 31,805.8m. (Dec. 2003); Chair. and Chief Exec. SERGEI BELYAYEV.

UralSib (Ural-Siberian Bank): 450015 Bashkortostan, Ufa, ul. Revolutsionnaya 41; tel. (3472) 51-94-70; fax (3472) 23-58-35; e-mail ufa@uralsibbank.ru; internet www.uralsibbank.ru; f. 1993 as BashCreditBank, present name adopted 2001; 66% owned by the Government of the Republic of Bashkortostan; cap. 14,887.8m., res −4,924.0m., dep. 48,653.3m. (Dec. 2003); Pres. and Chief Exec. AZAT T. KURMANAYEV; Chair. RAFAEL I. BAIDAVLETOV.

Vneshekonombank (Bank for Foreign Economic Affairs): 107996 Moscow, pr. Sakharova 9; tel. (495) 207-10-37; fax (495) 975-21-43; e-mail info@veb.ru; internet www.veb.ru; f. 1924; total assets US $4,725m. (Dec. 2003); Chair. VLADIMIR A. DMITRIYEV.

Vozrozhdeniye—V-Bank (Rebirth—Moscow Jt-Stock Commercial Bank Vozrozdeniye): 101999 Moscow, per. Luchnikov 7/4/1, POB 9; tel. (495) 929-18-88; fax (495) 929-19-99; e-mail vbank@co.voz.ru; internet www.vbank.ru; f. 1991; cap. 200.4m., res 2,199.5m., dep. 22,612.1m. (Dec. 2003); Chair of Supervisory Bd YURII M. MARINITCHEV; Chair. of Managing Bd DMITRII L. ORLOV; 59 brs.

Foreign Banks

ABN AMRO Bank AO (Netherlands): 103009 Moscow, ul. B. Nikitskaya 17/1; tel. (495) 931-91-41; fax (495) 931-91-40; internet www.abnamro.com; f. 1993 as ABN AMRO Bank; name changed to above in 1997; cap. 677.5m., res 429.4m., dep. 12,497.9m. (Dec. 2002); Dir R. M. SCHWARZ.

Calion Rusbank (France): 191186 St Petersburg, Nevskii pr. 12, POB 139; tel. (812) 313-31-00; fax (812) 313-33-90; f. 1991; fmrly Crédit Lyonnais Rusbank; cap. and res 1,362.1m., dep. 5,078.3m. (Dec. 2002); Chair. BERNARD MIGNUCCI.

Crédit Suisse First Boston (Switzerland): 125009 Moscow, Nikitskii per. 5; tel. (495) 967-82-00; fax (495) 967-82-10; f. 1993; cap. 460.0m., res 1,172.3m., dep. 7,685.7m. (Dec. 2001); Pres. DIANA GINDIN.

Deutsche Bank (Germany): 129090 Moscow, ul. Shepkina 4; tel. (495) 797-50-00; fax (495) 797-50-17; e-mail db.moscow@db.com; internet www.deutsche-bank.ru; f. 1998; cap. 1,237.5m., res 1,108.7m., dep. 9,487.8m. (Dec. 2002); Chair. of Bd ALEXIS RODZIANKO.

Dresdner Bank ZAO (Germany): 190000 St Petersburg, ul. M. Morskaya 23; tel. (812) 118-51-51; fax (812) 324-32-81; e-mail zao@drkw.com; internet www.dresdner-bank.ru; f. 1993 as BNP-Dresdner Bank (ZAO); present name adopted 2001; cap. 727.3m., res 1,222.2m., dep. 4,932.3m. (Dec. 2003); Chair. of Bd CHLODWIG REUTER; Pres. WARNIG MATTHIAS.

ING Bank (Eurasia) ZAO—ING Bank (Netherlands): 127473 Moscow, ul. Krasnoproletarskaya 36; tel. (495) 755-54-00; fax (495) 755-54-99; e-mail russia@ingbank.com; internet www.ing.ru; f. 1993; wholly owned subsidiary of ING Group; present name adopted 1997; cap. US $6.6m., res $84.9m., dep. $1,000.0m. (Dec. 2005); Dir-Gen. HENDRICK WILLEM TEN BOSCH.

Raiffeisenbank Austria ZAO: 129090 Moscow, ul. Troitskaya 17/1; tel. (495) 721-99-00; fax (495) 721-99-01; e-mail common@raiffeisen.ru; internet www.raiffeisen.ru; f. 1996; cap. 1,004.0m., res 780.5m., dep. 39,452.5m. (Dec. 2002); Chair. of Man. Bd MICHEL P. PERHIRIN; 7 brs and sub-brs.

Bankers' Association

Association of Russian Banks (Assostiatsiya Rossiiskikh Bankov): 121069 Moscow, Skaternyi per. 20/1; tel. (495) 291-66-30; fax (495) 291-66-66; e-mail arb@arb.ru; internet www.arb.ru; f. 1991; unites some 500 private banks; Pres. GAREGIN A. TOSUNYAN.

INSURANCE

Agroinvest Insurance Co: 127422 Moscow, ul. Timiryazevskaya 26; tel. (495) 976-94-56; fax (495) 977-05-88; health, life and general insurance services; Pres. YURII I. MORDVINTSEV.

AIG Russia: 103009 Moscow, ul. Tverskaya 16/2; tel. (495) 935-89-50; fax (495) 935-89-52; e-mail aig.russia@aig.com; internet www.aigrussia.ru; f. 1994; mem. of the American International GroupInc; personal and business property insurance, also marine, life, financial etc.; Pres. GARY COLEMAN.

Ingosstrakh Insurance Co: 115998 Moscow, ul. Pyatnitskaya 12/2; tel. (495) 232-32-11; fax (495) 959-45-18; e-mail ingos@ingos.ru; internet www.ingos.ru; f. 1947; undertakes all kinds of insurance and reinsurance; Chair. NATALIYA A. RAYEVSKAYA; Gen. Dir YEVGENII TUMANOV.

Medstrakh—Medical Insurance Fund of the Russian Federation: 107076 Moscow, pl. Preobrazhenskaya 7A /1; tel. (495) 964-84-27; fax (495) 964-84-21; e-mail mz@mcramn.ru; internet www.medstrah.ru; f. 1991; health, life, property, travel, liability; also provides compulsory medical insurance; Pres. PETR KUZNETSOV.

Ost-West Allianz Insurance Co: 127473 Moscow, 3-i Samotechnii per. 3; tel. (495) 937-69-96; fax (495) 937-69-80; e-mail allianz@allianz.ru; internet www.allianz.ru; engineering, professional liability, life, medical, property, marine and private; Man. Dir ERHARD JOERCHEL.

RESO-Garantiya Insurance Co: 125047 Moscow, ul. Gasheka 12/1; tel. (495) 730-30-00; fax (495) 956-25-85; e-mail reso@orc.ru; internet www.reso.ru; f. 1991; Dir-Gen. DMITRII G. RAKOVSHCHIK.

Rosgosstrakh—Russian State Insurance: 127994 Moscow, ul. Novoslobodskaya 23; tel. (495) 781-24-00; fax (495) 978-27-64; e-mail admin@rgs.ru; internet www.gosstrah.ru; majority state-owned; 49% stake transferred to private ownership in 2001; undertakes domestic insurance; subsidiary cos in 80 federal subjects (territorial units) of the Russian Federation; Chair. VLADISLAV REZNIK; Gen. Dir RUBEN VARDANIAN.

ROSNO—Russian National Society Insurance Co: 115184 Moscow, Ozerkovskaya nab. 30; tel. (495) 232-33-33; fax (495) 232-00-14; e-mail info@rosno.ru; internet www.rosno.ru; f. 1992; 100 brs and 186 agencies; 47% owned by AFK Sistema; 45.3% owned by Allianz AG (Germany); CEO LEONID MELAMED.

Russkiye Strakhovye Traditsii (Russian Traditions Insurance Co): 129366 Moscow, Raketnyi bulv. 13/2; tel. (495) 283-88-03; fax (495) 283-88-05; e-mail info@rustrad.ru; internet www.rustrad.ru; f. 1992; Pres. IVAN I. DAVYDOV.

SOGAZ—Insurance Co of the Gas Industry: 117997 Moscow, ul. Nametkina 16; tel. (495) 782-09-17; fax (495) 432-90-05; e-mail sogaz@sogaz.ru; internet www.sogaz.ru; f. 1993; owned by gas industry interests; Chair. of Bd of Dirs SERGEI A. LUKASH.

Soglasiye (Agreement) Insurance Co: 109017 Moscow, M. Tolmachevskii per. 8–11/3; tel. and fax (495) 959-46-32; e-mail official@soglasie.ru; internet www.soglasie.ru; f. 1993 as Interros-Soglasiye; owned by Interros; Gen. Man. IGOR ZHUK.

STOCK EXCHANGES

Moscow Stock Exchange (MSE) (Moskovskaya Fondovaya Birzha): 125047 Moscow, Miusskaya pl. 2/2; tel. (495) 771-35-80; fax (495) 250-17-34; e-mail mse@mse.ru; internet www.mse.ru; f. 1997; Pres. ROMAN N. MYLTSEV.

Siberian Stock Exchange: 630104 Novosibirsk, ul. Frunze 5, POB 233; tel. (3832) 21-60-67; fax (3832) 21-06-90; e-mail sibex@sibex.nsk.su; f. 1991; Pres. ALEKSANDR V. NOVIKOV.

COMMODITY EXCHANGES

Asiatic Commodity Exchange: 670000 Buryatiya, Ulan-Ude, ul. Sovetskaya 23/37; tel. and fax (3012) 22-26-81; f. 1991; Chair. ANDREI FIRSOV.

THE RUSSIAN FEDERATION

European-Asian Exchange (EAE): 101000 Moscow, ul. Myasnitskaya 26; tel. and fax (495) 787-58-93; e-mail info@eae.ru; internet www.eae.ru; f. 2000; Chair. of Council TATYANA S. SOKOLOVA; Gen. Man. ALEKSANDR B. YEREMIN.

Khabarovsk Commodity Exchange (KhCE): 680000 Khabarovsk; tel. and fax (4212) 33-65-60; f. 1991; Pres. YEVGENII V. PANASENKO.

Komi Commodity Exchange (KoCE): 167610 Komi, Syktyvkar, Oktyabrskii pr. 16; tel. (8212) 22-32-86; fax (8212) 23-84-43; f. 1991; Pres. PETR S. LUCHENKOV.

Kuzbass Commodity and Raw Materials Exchange (KECME): 650090 Kemerovo, ul. Novgorodskaya 19; tel. (3842) 23-45-40; fax (3842) 23-49-56; f. 1991; Gen. Man. FEDOR MASENKOV.

Moscow Commodity Exchange (MCE): 129223 Moscow, pr. Mira, Russian Exhibition Centre, Pavilion 69 (4); tel. (495) 187-86-14; fax (495) 187-88-76; f. 1990; organization of exchange trading (cash, stock and futures market); Pres. and Chair. of Bd YURII MILYUKOV.

Petrozavodsk Commodity Exchange (PCE): 185028 Kareliya, Petrozavodsk, ul. Krasnaya 31; tel. and fax (8142) 7-80-57; f. 1991; Gen. Man. VALERII SAKHAROV.

Russian Exchange (RE): 101000 Moscow, ul. Myasnitskaya 26; tel. (495) 787-84-34; fax (495) 262-57-57; e-mail ic@ci.re.ru; internet www.re.ru; f. 1990; Pres. PAVEL PANOV.

Russian Commodity Exchange of the Agro-Industrial Complex (RosAgroBirzha): 125080 Moscow, Volokolamskoye shosse 11; tel. (495) 209-52-25; f. 1990; Chair. of Exchange Cttee ALEKSANDR VASILIYEV.

St Petersburg Exchange: 199026 St Petersburg, Vasilyevskii Ostrov, 26-aya liniya 15; tel. (812) 322-44-11; fax (812) 322-73-90; e-mail spbex@spbex.ru; internet www.spbex.ru; f. 1991; Pres. and Chief Exec. VIKTOR V. NIKOLAYEV.

Udmurt Commodity Universal Exchange (UCUE): 426075 Udmurt Rep., Izhevsk, ul. Soyuznaya 107; tel. (3412) 37-08-88; fax (3412) 37-16-57; e-mail iger@udmnet.ru; f. 1991; Pres. N. F. LAZAREV.

Yekaterinburg Commodity Exchange (UCE): 620012 Sverdlovsk obl., Yekaterinburg, pr. Kosmonavtov 23; tel. (343) 234-43-01; fax (343) 251-53-64; f. 1991; Chair. of Exchange Cttee KONSTANTIN ZHUZHLOV.

Trade and Industry

GOVERNMENT AGENCY

Russian Federal Property Fund (Rossiiskii Fond Federalnogo Imushchestva): 119049 Moscow, Leninskii pr. 9; tel. (495) 236-71-15; fax (495) 956-27-80; e-mail rffi@dol.ru; internet www.fpf.ru; f. 1992 to ensure consistency in the privatization process and to implement privatization legislation; Chair. KIRILL TOMASHCHUK (acting).

NATIONAL CHAMBER OF COMMERCE

Chamber of Commerce and Industry of the Russian Federation (Torgovo-Promyshlennaya Palata RF): 109012 Moscow, ul. Ilinka 6; tel. (495) 929-00-09; fax (495) 929-03-60; e-mail dios-inform@tpprf.ru; internet www.tpprf.ru; f. 1991; Pres. YEVGENII M. PRIMAKOV.

REGIONAL CHAMBERS OF COMMERCE

In early 2002 there were a total of 148 regional chambers of commerce in the Russian Federation.

Astrakhan Chamber of Commerce: 414040 Astrakhan, ul. Zhelyabova 50; tel. (8512) 25-58-44; fax (8512) 28-14-42; e-mail cci@mail.astrakhan.ru; internet astrcci.astrakhan.ru; f. 1992; Pres. ALEKSEI D. KANTEMIROV.

Bashkortostan Chamber of Commerce: 450007 Bashkortostan, Ufa, ul. Vorovskogo 22; tel. (3472) 23-23-80; fax (3472) 51-70-79; e-mail office@tpprb.ru; internet www.tpprb.ru; f. 1990; Chair. BORIS A. BONDARENKO.

Bryansk Chamber of Commerce: 241035 Bryansk, ul. Komsomolskaya 11; tel. (483) 256-68-06; fax (483) 256-44-24; e-mail tpp@online.bryansk.ru; internet www.bryansk.ru/btpp; Pres. TATYANA F. SUVOROVA.

Buryat Chamber of Commerce: 670047 Buryatiya, Ulan-Ude, ul. Sakhyanovoi 5, POB 4284; tel. (3012) 37-56-26; fax (3012) 37-34-34; e-mail tpprb@buryatia.ru; f. 1993; Pres. GENNADII M. BERBIDAYEV; 85 mems.

Central Siberian Chamber of Commerce: 660049 Krasnoyarsk, ul. Kirova 26; tel. (3912) 23-96-13; fax (3912) 23-96-83; e-mail cstp@krasmail.ru; internet www.cstpp.ru; f. 1985; Chair. VALERII A. KOSTIN.

Dagestan Chamber of Commerce: 367012 Dagestan, Makhachkala, pl. Lenina 2; tel. (8722) 67-04-61; fax (8722) 67-04-62; e-mail tpprd@dagestan.ru; internet tpp.dagestan.ru; f. 1991; Chair. SAID G. GAZIYEVIG.

Eastern Siberian Chamber of Commerce: 664003 Irkutsk, ul. Sukhe-Batora 16; tel. (3952) 33-50-60; fax (3952) 33-50-66; e-mail info@ccies.ru; internet www.ccies.ru; f. 1974; Pres. KONSTANTIN S. SHAVRIN.

Far East Chamber of Commerce: 680670 Khabarovsk, ul. Sheronova 113; tel. (4210) 30-47-70; fax (4210) 30-54-58; e-mail dvtpp@fecci.khv.ru; f. 1970; Pres. MIKHAIL V. KRUGLIKOV.

Kaliningrad Chamber of Commerce: 236010 Kaliningrad, ul. Vatutina 20; tel. (401) 295-68-01; fax (401) 295-47-88; e-mail kaliningrad_cci@baltnet.ru; internet www.kaliningrad-cci.ru; f. 1990; Pres. IGOR V. TSARKOV.

Kamchatka Chamber of Commerce: 683000 Kamchatka obl., Petropavlovsk-Kamchatskii, ul. Leninskaya 38/208; tel. and fax (4152) 12-35-10; e-mail kamtpp@iks.ru; Pres. ALLA V. PARKHOMCHUK.

Krasnodar Chamber of Commerce: 350063 Krasnodar, ul. Kommunarov 8; tel. and fax (861) 268-22-13; e-mail tppkk@tppkuban.ru; internet www.tppkuban.ru; f. 1969; Chair. YURII N. TKACHENKO.

Kursk Chamber of Commerce and Industry: 305000 Kursk, ul. Kirova 7; tel. and fax (471) 256-25-94; e-mail kcci@kcci.ru; internet www.kcci.ru; f. 1994; Pres. VALENTINA G. ORDYNETS.

Kuzbass Chamber of Commerce: 650099 Kemerovo, pr. Sovetskii 63/407; tel. and fax (3842) 58-77-64; e-mail ktpp@mail.kuzbass.net; internet city.info.kuzbass.net/ktpp; f. 1991; Pres. TATYANA O. IVLEVA.

Lipetsk Chamber of Commerce: 398600 Lipetsk, ul. Pervomaiskaya 78; tel. (474) 222-60-04; fax (474) 222-29-57; e-mail star@cci.lipetsk.su; internet lcci.lipetsk.ru; f. 1992; Pres. LILIYA D. POGUDINA.

Magnitogorsk Chamber of Commerce: 455002 Chelyabinsk obl., Magnitogorsk, ul. Kirova 70; tel. (3519) 24-82-16; fax (3519) 24-82-17; e-mail mtpp@mdv.ru; Pres. GERMAN I. ZAPYANTSEV.

Maritime (Primorskii) Krai Chamber of Commerce: 690600 Maritime Krai, Vladivostok, Okeanskii pr. 13A; tel. (4232) 26-96-30; fax (4232) 22-72-26; e-mail palata@online.vladivostok.ru; internet www.ptpp.ru; f. 1964; Pres. VLADIMIR B. BREZHNEV.

Moscow Chamber of Commerce: 117393 Moscow, ul. Akademika Pilyugina 22; tel. (495) 132-07-33; fax (495) 132-75-03; e-mail extern@mtpp.org; internet www.mtpp.org; f. 1991; Chair. YURII I. KOTOV; Pres. LEONID V. GOVOROV.

Naberezhnye Chelny Chamber of Commerce: 423826 Tatarstan, Naberezhnye Chelny, ul. Sh. Usmanova 122; tel. (8552) 54-79-08; fax (8552) 54-76-31; e-mail tpp@tpp.chelny.ru; f. 1994; Pres. YURII I. PETRUSHIN.

Nizhnii Novgorod Chamber of Commerce: 603005 Nizhnii Novgorod, pl. Oktyabrskaya 1; tel. (8312) 19-42-10; fax (8312) 19-40-09; e-mail tpp@rda.nnov.ru; internet www.tpp.nnov.ru; f. 1990; Pres. GENNADII M. KHODYRYEV.

North Osetiya—Alaniya Chamber of Commerce: 362002 North Osetiya—Alaniya, Vladikavkaz, ul. Avgustovskikh sobytii 10; tel. (8672) 53-15-84; fax (8672) 54-21-61; e-mail tpprso-a@osetia.ru; f. 1993; Pres. KAZBEK KH. TUGANOV.

Northern Chamber of Commerce and Industry: 183766 Murmansk, per. Rusanova 10; tel. (8152) 47-29-99; fax (8152) 47-39-78; e-mail ncci@online.ru; internet www.ncci.ru; f. 1990; Pres. ANATOLII M. GLUSHKOV.

Novgorod Chamber of Commerce: 173002 Velikii Novgorod, ul. Germana 1A; tel. (8162) 13-69-00; fax (8162) 13-20-46; e-mail ncci@ncci.novline.ru; internet nbp.natm.ru/~ncci; Pres. VIKTOR A. BYKOV.

Novosibirsk Chamber of Commerce: 630064 Novosibirsk, pr. K. Marksa 1; tel. and fax (383) 346-41-50; e-mail org@ntpp.ru; internet www.ntpp.ru; f. 1991; Chair. BORIS V. BRUSILOVSKII; 315 mems (2002).

Omsk Chamber of Commerce: 644099 Omsk, ul. Krasnyi Put 18; tel. (3812) 23-05-23; fax (3812) 23-52-48; e-mail omtpp@omsknet.ru; internet www.omsknet.ru/cci; f. 1992; Pres. TATYANA A. KHOROSHAVINA.

Orenburg Chamber of Commerce: 460356 Orenburg, Parkovyi pr. 6; tel. and fax (3532) 77-73-29; e-mail cci@orenburg-cci.ru; internet www.orenburg-cci.ru; f. 1995; Pres. VIKTOR A. SYTYEZHEV.

Perm Chamber of Commerce: 614000 Perm, ul. Sovetskaya 24B; tel. (3422) 12-28-11; fax (3422) 12-41-12; e-mail permttp@permttp.ru; internet www.permtpp.ru; f. 1991; Pres. VIKTOR A. ZAMARAYEV.

Rostov Chamber of Commerce: 344022 Rostov-on-Don, ul. Pushkinskaya 176; tel. and fax (836) 264-45-47; e-mail tpp@rost.ru; internet www.tpp.tis.ru; f. 1992; Pres. NIKOLAI I. PRISYAZHNYUK.

Ryazan Chamber of Commerce: 390023 Ryazan, ul. Gorkovo 14; tel. (491) 277-20-67; fax (491) 228-99-02; e-mail ryazancci@rtpp.ryazan.su; f. 1993; Pres. TATYANA V. GUSEVA; 44 mems.

Sakha (Yakutiya) Chamber of Commerce: 677000 Sakha (Yakutiya), Yakutsk, ul. Lenina 22/214; tel. (4112) 26-64-96; e-mail palata91@mail.ru; f. 1991; Chair. SERGEI G. BAKULIN.

Samara Chamber of Commerce: 443099 Samara, ul. A. Tolstogo 6; tel. (8462) 32-11-59; fax (8462) 70-48-96; e-mail ccisr@samara.ru; internet www.cci.samara.ru; f. 1988; Pres. BORIS V. ARDALIN.

Saratov Regional Chamber of Commerce and Industry: 410600 Saratov, ul. B. Kazachya 30; tel. (8452) 27-70-78; fax (8452) 27-70-82; e-mail srcci@sgtpp.ru; internet www.sgtpp.ru; f. 1986; Pres. MAKSIM A. FATEYEV.

Smolensk Chamber of Commerce: 214000 Smolensk, ul. K. Marksa 12; tel. (481) 255-41-42; fax (481) 223-74-50; e-mail smolcci@keytown.com; internet www.keytown.com/users/Torgpal; f. 1993; Pres. OLEG V. LUKIRICH.

South Urals Chamber of Commerce: 454080 Chelyabinsk, ul. Vasenko 63; tel. (3512) 66-18-16; fax (3512) 68-90-28; e-mail mail@uralreg.ru; internet www.uralreg.ru; f. 1992; Pres. FEDOR L. DEGTYAREV; 365 mems.

St Petersburg Chamber of Commerce: 191123 St Petersburg, ul. Chaikovskogo 46–48; tel. (812) 273-48-96; fax (812) 273-48-96; e-mail spbcci@spbcci.ru; internet www.spbcci.ru; f. 1921; Pres. VLADIMIR I. KATENEV.

Stavropol Chamber of Commerce and Industry: 355003 Stavropol, ul. Lenina 384; tel. (8652) 94-53-34; fax (8652) 34-05-10; e-mail stcci@statel.stavropol.ru; f. 1991; Pres. VITALII S. NABATNIKOV.

Tatarstan Republic Chamber of Commerce and Industry: 420503 Tatarstan, Kazan, ul. Pushkina 18; tel. (843) 264-62-07; fax (843) 236-09-66; e-mail tpp@i-set.ru; internet www.tpprt.ru; f. 1992; Gen. Dir SHAMIL R. AGEYEV; 800 mems.

Tolyatti Chamber of Commerce: 445009 Samara obl., Tolyatti, ul. Pobedy 19A; tel. (8482) 22-46-21; fax (8482) 22-47-45; e-mail tpp@infopac.ru; internet www.ccitogliatti.ru; Pres. VLADIMIR A. ZHUKOV.

Tula Chamber of Commerce: 300600 Tula, Krasnoarmeiskii pr. 25/1001–1007; tel. (487) 231-17-28; fax (487) 236-02-16; e-mail tulacci@tula.net; internet www.ccitula.ru; f. 1993; Pres. YURII M. AGAFONOV.

Udmurt Chamber of Commerce: 426034 Udmurt Republic, Izhevsk, ul. Lenina 101; tel. (3412) 49-02-10; fax (3412) 49-02-13; e-mail udmtpp@udmtpp.ru; internet izhtpp.udmweb.ru; f. 1993; Pres. YEVGENII YU. VYLEGZHANIN.

Ulyanovsk Chamber of Commerce: 432600 Ulyanovsk, ul. Engelsa 19; tel. (8422) 31-45-23; fax (8422) 32-93-73; e-mail ultpp@mv.ru; f. 1992; Pres. YEVGENII S. BALANDIN.

Urals Chamber of Commerce and Industry: 620027 Sverdlovsk obl., Yekaterinburg, ul. Vostochnaya 6; tel. (343) 353-04-49; fax (343) 353-58-63; e-mail ucci@dialup.mplik.ru; internet ucci.ur.ru; f. 1959; Pres. YURII P. MATUSHKIN.

Volgograd Chamber of Commerce: 400005 Volgograd, ul. 7-aya Gvardeiskaya 2; tel. (8442) 93-61-35; fax (8442) 34-22-02; e-mail cci@volgogradcci.ru; internet www.volgogradcci.ru; f. 1990; Pres. ALEKSANDR D. BELITSKII.

Vologda Chamber of Commerce and Industry: 160600 Vologda, ul. Lermontova 15; tel. (8172) 72-14-80; fax (8172) 72-32-58; e-mail grant@vologda.ru; f. 1992; Pres. GALINA D. TELEGINA.

Voronezh Chamber of Commerce: 394030 Voronezh, 'Voronezhvnesh-servis', POB 63; tel. and fax (473) 252-49-38; e-mail mail@ooctpp.vm.ru; f. 1991; fmrly Central-Black Earth Chamber of Commerce and Industry; Pres. VYACHESLAV A. KONDRATYEV.

Vyatka (Kirov) Chamber of Commerce: 610020 Kirov, ul. Engelsa 29/2; tel. and fax (8332) 35-06-06; e-mail iac@vtpp.kirov.ru; internet www.vtpp.kirov.ru; f. 1993; Pres. NIKOLAI M. LIPATNIKOV.

Yaroslavl Chamber of Commerce: 150000 Yaroslavl, Sovetskaya pl. 1/19; tel. (485) 232-88-85; fax (485) 232-88-85; e-mail tpp@adm.yar.ru; internet yartpp.ru; f. 1992; Pres. VALERII A. LAVROV.

EMPLOYERS' ORGANIZATIONS

Co-ordinating Council of Employers' Unions of Russia (Koordinatsionnyi Sovet Obyedinenii Rabotodatelei Rossii—KSORR): 109017 Moscow, per. M. Tolmachevskii 8–11; tel. (495) 232-55-77; fax (495) 959-46-06; e-mail official@ksorr.ru; internet www.ksorr.ru; f. 1994; co-ordinates and represents employers in relations with government bodies and trade unions, and represents Russian employers in the ILO and the International Organization of Employers (IOE); Chair. OLEG V. YEREMEYEV; Gen. Dir (vacant); unites 35 major employers' unions, including the following:

Agro-Industrial Union of Russia: 107139 Moscow, POB 139; tel. (495) 204-41-04; fax (495) 207-83-62; e-mail sva@gvs.aris.ru; Pres. VASILII A. STARODUBTSEV.

All-Russian Social Organization of Small and Medium-sized Businesses (OPORA Rossii) (Obshcherossiiskaya Obshchestvennaya Organizatsiya Malogo i Srednego Predprinimatelstva): 125047 Moscow, ul. 4-ya Tverskaya-Yamskaya 21/22/3; tel. (495) 775-81-11; fax (495) 775-81-91; e-mail id@opora.ru; internet www.opora.ru; f. 2002; Pres. SERGEI BORISOV.

Russian Union of Industrialists and Entrepreneurs (Employers) (RSPPR) (Rossiiskii Soyuz Promyshlennikov i Predprinimatelei): 103070 Moscow, Staraya pl. 10/4; tel. (495) 748-42-37; fax (495) 206-11-29; e-mail pr_dep@rspp.net; internet www.rspp.ru; f. 1991; Pres. ALEKSANDR SHOKHIN; Exec. Sec. NIKOLAI TONKOV.

Union of Russian Shipowners (SOROSS): 121002 Moscow, per. Sivtsev Vrazhek 44/28/10; tel. (495) 241-56-75; fax (495) 248-29-66; e-mail murashovaiv@morflot.ru; internet www.morflot.ru/info/soross.asp; Pres. MIKHAIL A. ROMANOVSKII.

UTILITIES

Electricity

Federal Energy Commission: 103074 Moscow, Kitaigorodskii proyezd 7; tel. (495) 220-40-15; fax (495) 206-81-08; e-mail fecrf@orc.ru; regulatory authority for natural energy monopolies; sole responsibility for establishing tariff rates for energy, transportation, shipping, postal and telecommunications industries in the Russian Federation from Sept. 2001; Chair. ANDREI ZADERNYUK.

Irkutskenergo (Irkutsk Energy Co): 664000 Irkutsk, ul. Sukhe-Batora 3; tel. (3952) 21-73-00; fax (3952) 21-78-99; e-mail idkan@irkutskenergo.ru; internet www.irkutskenergo.ru; f. 1954; generation and transmission of electrical and thermal energy; Dir-Gen. VLADIMIR V. KOLMOGOROV.

Mosenergo (Moscow Energy Co): 113035 Moscow, Raushskaya nab. 8; tel. (495) 957-35-30; fax (495) 957-34-70; e-mail press-centre@mosenergo.ru; internet www.mosenergo.ru; f. 1887; 49% owned by Unified Energy System of Russia; power generator and distributor; Gen. Man. (vacant).

Rosenergoatom (Russian Atomic Energy Concern): 101000 Moscow, POB 912; tel. (495) 239-47-40; fax (495) 239-27-24; e-mail info@rosatom.ru; internet www.rosatom.ru; f. 1992; electricity generating co; Pres. OLEG SARAYEV.

Sverdlovenergo (Sverdlovsk Energy Co): 620219 Sverdlovsk obl., Yekaterinburg, pr. Lenina 38; tel. (343) 259-13-99; fax (343) 259-12-22; e-mail post@energo.pssr.ru; internet www.po.pssr.ru; f. 1942; Chair. of Bd ALEKSANDR V. CHIKUNOV; Gen. Man. VLADIMIR V. KALSIN.

Unified Energy System of Russia (RAO EES Rossii): 119526 Moscow, pr. Vernadskogo 101/3; tel. (495) 710-40-01; fax (495) 927-30-07; e-mail rao@elektra.ru; internet www.rao-ees.ru; f. 1992; operates national electricity grid; 52% state-owned; controls about 2.5m. km of transmission lines, holds shares in 43 power plants 72 regional power cos, including Mosenergo and Lenenergo, accounting for more than 70% of Russia's electricity output; sales 797,300m. (2004). cap. 21,558,000m. (Dec. 2004); Chair. ALEKSANDR S. VOLOSHIN; Chief Exec. ANATOLII B. CHUBAIS; 496,300 employees (2004).

Uralenergo (Ural Energy): 454006 Chelyabinsk, ul. Rossiiskaya 17; tel. (3512) 67-59-54; fax (3512) 67-59-48; e-mail info@uralenergo.com; internet www.uralenergo.com; manages 22 joint-stock cos; oversees 55 thermal power stations and 6 hydroelectric stations; total installed capacity of over 28,500m. kW; Dir ALEKSANDR S. NEMTSEV.

Gas

Gazprom: 117997 Moscow, ul. Nametkina 16; tel. (495) 719-30-01; fax (495) 719-83-33; e-mail gazprom@gazprom.ru; internet www.gazprom.ru; f. 1989 from assets of Soviet Ministry of Oil and Gas; became independent joint-stock co in 1992, privatized in 1994; 51% state-owned; Russia's biggest co. and world's largest natural gas producer, owning 16% of proven global natural gas reserves, or 28,000,000m. cubic metres (December 2003); annual production: 540,000m. cubic metres (2003); Exec. Chair. ALEKSEI B. MILLER; Chair. of Bd of Dirs DMITRII A. MEDVEDEV.

Mezhregiongaz (Inter-Regional Gas Co): 113324 Moscow, ul. Sadovnicheskaya 46/1; tel. and fax (495) 953-08-24; internet www.mrg.ru; f. 1997; gas marketing co, founded by Gazprom; brs in more than 60 federal subjects; Dir-Gen. NIKOLAI GORNOVSKII.

Water

MosVodoKanal: 105005 Moscow, per. Pleteshkovskii 2; tel. (495) 742-96-96; e-mail post@mosvodokanal.ru; internet www.mosvodokanal.ru; provides water and sewerage services to Moscow and the surrounding region; Dir-Gen. STANISLAV KHRAMENKOV.

Vodokanal: 191015 St Petersburg, ul. Kavalergardskaya 42; tel. (812) 274-16-79; fax (812) 274-13-61; e-mail office@vodokanal.spb.ru; internet www.vodokanal.spb.ru; water and sewerage utility; Gen. Man. FELIKS V. KARMAZINOV.

TRADE UNIONS

In 1990, in response to the growing independent labour movement, several branch unions of the All-Union Central Council of Trade Unions (ACCTU) established the Federation of Independent Trade Unions of the Russian Federation (FITUR), which took control of part of the property and other assets of the ACCTU. The ACCTU was reformed as the General Confederation of Trade Unions of the USSR, which was, in turn, renamed the General Confederation of Trade Unions—International Organization in 1992. In November of that year, in an attempt to challenge the influence of the FITUR, the ITUM and several other independent trade unions established a consultative council to co-ordinate their activities.

All-Russian Labour Confederation: 103031 Moscow, ul. Rozhdestvenka 5/7; tel. (495) 785-21-30; fax (495) 915-83-67; e-mail vktrussia@online.ru; internet www.trud.org/guide/VKT.htm; f. 1995; unites five national trade unions and 40 regional orgs with 1,270,900 mems; Pres. ALEKSANDR N. BUGAYEV.

General Confederation of Trade Unions (VKP): 119119 Moscow, Leninskii pr. 42; tel. (495) 952-27-82; fax (495) 938-21-55; e-mail inter@vkp.ru; internet www.vkp.ru; f. 1992 to replace General Confederation of Trade Unions of the USSR; co-ordinating body for trade unions in CIS member states; unites ten national trade union organizations and 32 regional orgs with 52m. mems; publishes *Profsoyuzy* (Trade Unions), weekly, *Vestnik profsoyuzov* (Herald of the Trade Unions), every two weeks, and *Inform-Contact*, in English and French, quarterly; Pres. MIKHAIL SHMAKOV; Sec.-Gen. VLADIMIR SCHERBAKOV.

Federation of Independent Trade Unions of Russia (FITUR) (Federatsiya Nezavisimykh Profsoyuzov Rossii—FNPR): 119119 Moscow, Leninskii pr. 42; tel. (495) 938-73-12; fax (495) 137-06-94; e-mail korneev@fnpr.ru; internet www.fnpr.ru; f. 1990; Pres. MIKHAIL V. SHMAKOV.

FITUR unites 48 national trade unions and 78 regional orgs (with c. 40m. mems), including the following::

All-Russian 'Electroprofsoyuz': 117119 Moscow, Leninskii pr. 42/3; tel. (495) 938-83-78; fax (495) 930-98-62; f. 1990; electrical workers; Pres. VALERII P. KUZICHEV.

Automobile and Farm Machinery Construction Industries Workers' Union: 117119 Moscow, Leninskii pr. 42/3; tel. (495) 938-76-13; fax (495) 938-86-15; Pres. YULII G. NOVIKOV.

Civil Aviation Workers' Union: 117218 Moscow, ul. Krzhizhanovskogo 20/30/5; tel. and fax (495) 125-18-39; Pres. BORIS A. KREMNEV.

Communication Workers' Union of Russia: 117119 Moscow, Leninskii pr. 42/3; tel. (495) 938-72-06; fax (495) 930-22-86; f. 1905; Pres. ANATOLII G. NAZEIKIN.

Construction and Building Materials Industry Workers' Union of the Russian Federation: 117119 Moscow, Leninskii pr. 42/1; tel. (495) 930-71-74; fax (495) 952-55-47; f. 1991; Pres. BORIS A. SOSHENKO.

Geological, Survey and Cartographical Workers' Union of the Russian Federation: 119119 Moscow, Leninskii pr. 42/5; tel. (495) 137-64-37; f. 1954; Chair. of Central Committee NIKOLAI K. POPKOV.

Health Workers' Union of the Russian Federation: 117119 Moscow, Leninskii pr. 42/3; tel. (495) 938-84-43; fax (495) 938-81-34; e-mail ckprz@online.ru; f. 1990; Chair. MIKHAIL M. KUZMENKO.

Moscow Trade Unions Federation: 121205 Moscow, ul. Novyi Arbat 36/9; tel. (495) 290-82-62; fax (495) 202-92-70; e-mail main@mtuf.ru; f. 1990; largest regional branch of FITUR; Chair. MIKHAIL D. NAGAITSEV; 2.2m. mems.

Motor Transport and Road Workers' Union of Russia: 117218 Moscow, ul. Krzhizhanovskogo 20/30/5; tel. (495) 125-23-30; fax (495) 125-07-98; e-mail profavtodor@mtu.ru; f. 1990; Pres. VIKTOR I. MOKHNACHEV.

National Educational and Scientific Workers' Union of the Russian Federation: 117119 Moscow, Leninskii pr. 42/3; tel. (495) 938-87-77; fax (495) 930-68-15; f. 1990; Pres. VLADIMIR M. YAKOVLEV.

Oil, Gas and Construction Workers' Union: 119119 Moscow, Leninskii pr. 42/4; tel. (495) 930-69-74; fax (495) 930-11-24; e-mail rogwu@rogwu.ru; internet www.rogwu.ru; f. 1990; Pres. LEV A. MIRONOV.

Russian Chemical Industry Workers' Union: 117119 Moscow, Leninskii pr. 42/3; tel. (495) 930-69-93; fax (495) 938-21-55; e-mail rcwu@fnpr.ru; f. 1990; Pres. ALEKSANDR SITNOV (acting).

Russian Fishing Industry Workers' Union: 117119 Moscow, Leninskii pr. 42/3; tel. (495) 938-77-82; fax (495) 930-77-26; e-mail bfish@fnpr.ru; f. 1991; Pres. YURII V. SHALONIN.

Russian Independent Trade Union of Coal-industry Workers (Rosuglerof): 109004 Moscow, ul. Zemlyanoi Val 64/2; tel. (495) 915-28-52; fax (495) 915-30-77; e-mail rosugleprof@mail.exline.ru; Chair. IVAN I. MOKHNACHUK.

Russian Radio and Electronics Industry Workers Union: 109180 Moscow, 1-i Golutvinskii per. 3; tel. (495) 238-08-02; fax (495) 238-17-31; Pres. VALERII YE. MARKOV.

Russian Textiles and Light Industry Workers' Union: 117119 Moscow, Leninskii pr. 42/3; tel. (495) 938-78-24; fax (495) 938-84-05; f. 1990; Pres. TATYANA I. SOSNINA.

Russian Trade Union of Railwaymen and Transport Construction Workers (Rosprofzhel): 103064 Moscow, ul. Staraya Basmannaya 11; tel. (495) 262-58-73; fax (495) 923-88-31; e-mail iturr@orc.ru; Pres. ANATOLII B. VASILIYEV.

Russian Union of Aviation Engineering Workers: Moscow; tel. and fax (495) 938-81-07; f. 1934; Pres. ANATOLII F. BREUSOV.

Russian Union of Cultural Workers: 109004 Moscow, ul. Zemlyanoi Val 64/1; tel. (495) 915-06-30; fax (495) 915-09-43; Pres. GENNADII P. PAROSHIN.

Russian Union of Workers in Small and Entrepreneurial Enterprises: 117119 Moscow, Leninskii pr. 42/1; tel. (495) 930-67-71; fax (495) 938-75-85; Pres. VLADIMIR I. KUZNETSOV.

Shipbuilding Workers' Union: 117119 Moscow, Leninskii pr. 42/5; tel. (495) 938-88-72; fax (495) 938-84-74; Pres. VLADIMIR YE. MAKAVCHIK.

Timber Industry Workers' Union of the Russian Federation: 117119 Moscow, Leninskii pr. 42/1; tel. (495) 938-89-03; fax (495) 137-06-81; Pres. VALERII N. OCHEKUROV.

Union of Agro-industrial Workers of the Russian Federation: 117119 Moscow, Leninskii pr. 42/3; tel. (495) 938-77-35; fax (495) 930-68-27; f. 1919; Pres. ALEKSANDR S. DAVYDOV; 37m. mems.

Union of Engineering Workers of the Russian Federation: 127486 Moscow, ul. Deguninskaya 1/2; tel. (495) 487-3507; fax (495) 487-56-37; Pres. YURII S. SPICHENOK.

Union of Food Industry and Production Co-operative Workers of the Russian Federation: 117119 Moscow, Leninskii pr. 42/3; tel. (495) 938-75-03; fax (495) 930-10-56; Pres. VALERII K. ZHOVTERIK.

Union of Security Services Workers of the Russian Federation: 101000 Moscow, ul. M. Lubyanka 5/12; tel. (495) 928-99-76; fax (495) 923-72-36; Pres. YURII N. SIRESHCHIKOV.

Union of State and Community Service Workers of the Russian Federation: 117119 Moscow, Leninskii pr. 42/2; tel. (495) 938-74-44; fax (495) 952-56-24; Pres. VLADIMIR P. SAVCHENKO.

Union of Workers in Enterprises with Foreign Investment of the Russian Federation: 117119 Moscow, Leninskii pr. 42/1; tel. (495) 938-84-62; fax (495) 938-81-95; Pres. VLADIMIR F. BAZAYEV.

Independent Trade Unions

Federation of Air Traffic Controllers' Unions of Russia (FPAR): 125993 Moscow, Leningradskii pr. 37/472, POB 3; tel. (495) 155-57-01; fax (495) 155-59-17; e-mail postmaster@fatcurus.ru; internet www.fatcurus.ru; f. 1989; Pres. SERGEI A. KOVALEV.

Metallurgical Industry Workers' Union: Moscow, ul. Pushkinskaya 5/6; left the FITUR in 1992 to form independent organization; Pres. BORIS MISNIK.

Transport

RAILWAYS

In 2000 the total length of railway track in use was 86,660 km, of which 40,800 km were electrified. The railway network is of great importance in the Russian Federation, owing to the poor road system, and the relatively few private vehicles outside the major cities. The Trans-Siberian Railway, the electrification of which began in 1998, provides the main route connecting European Russia with Siberia and the Far East. A new joint-stock company, Russian Railways, was formed in September 2003 to assume the management of the railways network from the Ministry of Railways, which was subsequently abolished.

Russian Railways OAO (RZhD) (Rossiiskiye zheleznyye dorogi): 107174 Moscow, ul. Novobasmannaya 2; tel. (495) 262-16-28; fax (495) 975-24-11; e-mail info@rzd.ru; internet www.rzd.ru; f. 2003; Pres. VLADIMIR YAKUNIN.

City Underground Railways

Moscow Metro: 129110 Moscow, pr. Mira 41/2; tel. (495) 222-10-01; fax (495) 631-37-44; e-mail info@mosmetro.ru; f. 1935; 11 lines (275.6 km) with 170 stations; the first stage of a suburban light railway extension opened in Dec. 2003; Gen. Man. DMITRII V. GAYEV.

THE RUSSIAN FEDERATION

Nizhnii Novgorod Metro: 603002 Nizhnii Novgorod, pl. Revolutsii 7; tel. (8312) 44-17-60; fax (8312) 44-20-86; e-mail metro@sandy.ru; f. 1985; 15 km with 13 stations; Gen. Man. A. KUZMIN.

Novosibirsk Metro: 630099 Novosibirsk, ul. Serebrennikovskaya 34; tel. (3832) 90-81-10; fax (3832) 46-56-82; e-mail nsk@metro.snt.su; internet www.nsk.su/~metro; f. 1986; 2 lines (13.2 km) with 11 stations, and a further 6 km under construction; Gen. Man. V. I. DEMIN.

St Petersburg Metro: 198013 St Petersburg, Moskovskii pr. 28; tel. (812) 251-66-68; fax (812) 316-14-41; f. 1955; 4 lines (103 km) with 58 stations; Gen. Man. V. A. GARYUGIN.

Short underground railways began to operate Samara, Yekaterinburg and Kazan in 1987, 1991 and 2005, respectively. In 2005 construction of underground railways was under way in Chelyabinsk, Krasnoyarsk and Omsk.

ROADS

In 2001 the total length of roads was 537,289 km (46,254 km of highways and 491,035 km of other roads); 67.4% of roads were paved in 1999. In Siberia and the Far East there are few roads, and they are often impassable in winter, while the *rasputitsa*, or spring thaw, notoriously impedes rural road traffic, even in European Russia. In 1999 the World Bank granted Russia a loan of US $400m. to finance the construction and repair of roads in Siberia and the Far East of Russia. A new highway, linking Vladivostok with St Petersburg, was due for completion in 2004. In August 2003 proposals were announced by the Government of Moscow Oblast for the construction of the first toll-motorway in Russia.

SHIPPING

The seaports of the Russian Federation provide access to the Pacific Ocean, in the east, the Baltic Sea and the Atlantic Ocean, in the west, and the Black Sea, in the south. Major eastern ports are at Vladivostok, Nakhodka, Vostochnyi, Magadan and Petropavlovsk. In the west St Petersburg and Kaliningrad provide access to the Baltic Sea, and the northern ports of Murmansk and Archangel (Arkhangelsk) have access to the Atlantic Ocean, via the Barents Sea. Novorossiisk and Sochi are the principal Russian ports on the Black Sea.

Principal Shipowning Companies

Baltic Shipping Co: 198035 St Petersburg, Mezhevoi kanal 5; tel. (812) 251-33-97; fax (812) 186-85-44; freight and passenger services; Chair. MIKHAIL A. ROMANOVSKII.

Baltic Transport Systems: 199106 St Petersburg, pl. Morskoi Slavy 1; tel. (812) 303-99-14; fax (812) 380-34-76; e-mail bts@baltics.ru; internet www.baltics.ru; f. 1994; freight and passenger services; Gen. Dir ALEKSEI E. SHUKLETSOV.

Far Eastern Shipping Co: 690019 Maritime (Primorskii) Krai, Vladivostok, ul. Aleutskaya 15; tel. (4232) 41-14-32; fax (4232) 52-15-51; e-mail 41401@41.fesco.ru; internet www.fesco.ru; f. 1880; Gen. Man. YEVGENII N. AMBROSOV.

Kamchatka Shipping Co: 683600 Kamchatka obl., Petropavlovsk-Kamchatskii, ul. Radiosvyazi 65; tel. (41522) 2-82-21; fax (41522) 2-19-60; f. 1949; freight services; Pres. NIKOLAI M. ZABLOTSKII.

Murmansk Shipping Co: 183038 Murmansk, ul. Kominterna 15; tel. (8152) 48-10-48; fax (8152) 48-11-48; e-mail postmaster@msco.ru; f. 1939; shipping and icebreaking services; Gen. Dir VYACHESLAV RUKSHA.

Northern Shipping Co (NSC Arkhangelsk) (Severnoye morskoye parokhodstvo OAO—SMP): 163000 Archangel, nab. Severnoi Dviny 36; tel. (8182) 63-72-03; fax (8182) 63-71-95; e-mail nsosnina@ansc.ru; internet www.ansc.ru; f. 1870; dry cargo shipping, liner services; Gen. Dir VIKTOR A. IZBITSKII.

Novorossiisk Shipping Co: 353900 Krasnodar Krai, Novorossiisk, ul. Svobody 1; tel. (8617) 25-31-26; fax (8617) 25-11-43; e-mail novoship@novoship.ru; internet www.novoship.ru; f. 1992; Chair. V. I. YAKUNIN.

Primorsk Shipping Corpn: 692900 Maritime (Primorskii) Krai, Nakhodka-4, Administrativnyi Gorodok; tel. (4236) 69-45-05; fax (4236) 69-45-75; e-mail psc@prisco.ru; internet www.prisco.ru; f. 1972, tanker shipowner; Dir-Gen. ALEKSANDR MIGUNOV.

Sakhalin Shipping Co: 694620 Sakhalin obl., Kholmsk, ul. Pobedy 16; tel. (42433) 6-62-07; fax (42433) 6-60-20; e-mail chief@sasco.sakhalin.ru; internet www.sasco.org; f. 1945; shipowners and managers, carriage of cargo and passengers; Pres. YAKUB ZH. ALEGEDPINOV.

Sovfrakht: 127944 Moscow, Rakhmanovskii per. 4, Morskoi Dom; tel. (495) 258-27-41; fax (495) 230-26-40; e-mail general@sovfracht.ru; internet www.sovfracht.ru; f. 1929; jt-stock co; chartering and broking of tanker, cargo and other ships; forwarding, booking and insurance agency; ship management; Dir-Gen. D. YU. PURIM; 120 employees (2003).

White Sea and Onega Shipping Co (Belomorsko-Onezhskoye parokhodstvo): 185005 Kareliya, Petrozavodsk, ul. Rigachina 7; tel. (8142) 71-12-01; fax (8142) 71-12-67; e-mail dir@bop.onego.ru; internet bop.onego.ru; f. 1940; cargo shipping, cargo-ship construction and repair; Gen. Dir STANISLAV ROZOLINSKII; Pres. ALEKSANDR LYALLYA.

CIVIL AVIATION

Until 1991 Aeroflot—Soviet Airlines was the only airline operating on domestic routes in the former USSR. In 1992–94 some 300 different independent airlines emerged on the basis of Aeroflot's former regional directorates. Several small private airlines were also established. In 1992 Aeroflot—Soviet Airlines became a joint-stock company, Aeroflot—Russian Airlines. The Government retained 51% of the shares, and company personnel own 49%. A reorganization of Russia's civil aviation industry was proposed in 1998. By 2003 there were 451 airports in Russia, compared with 1,302 in 1992.

Aeroflot—Russian Airlines: 125167 Moscow, Leningradskii pr. 37/9; tel. and fax (495) 155-66-43; internet www.aeroflot.ru; f. 1923; 51% state-owned; operates flights to 108 destinations in 54 countries, and to 26 destinations in Russia; Gen. Dir VALERII M. OKULOV.

Bashkir Airlines (BAL): 450056 Bashkortostan, Ufa, Ufa Airport; tel. (3472) 22-75-12; fax (3472) 23-37-36; e-mail interdep@airbal.ufanet.ru; internet www.bal.ufanet.ru; f. 1933; owned by the Govt of the Republic of Bashkortostan; privatization proposed in 2004; flights between Ufa and 24 destinations in Russia, and to the countries of the CIS and Turkey; Dir-Gen. VINER V. SHAKIROV.

Domodedova Airlines: 142045 Moscow, Domodedova Airport; tel. (495) 504-03-00; fax (495) 787-86-18; e-mail ak_e3@tch.ru; internet www.akdal.ru; f. 1964; scheduled passenger flights to domestic and CIS destinations; chartered passenger and freight flights to domestic, CIS and international destinations; Gen. Dir ANDREI MASLOV.

Gazpromavia: 117997 Moscow, ul. Nametkina 16; tel. (495) 719-18-32; fax (495) 719-11-85; e-mail gazpromavia@gazprom.ru; internet www.gazpromavia.com; f. 1995; Dir-Gen. ANDREI S. OVCHARENKO.

Kuban Airlines (Kubanskiye Avialinii): 350026 Krasnodar, Krasnodar—Pashkovskaya Airport; tel. (861) 237-06-00; fax (861) 237-38-11; e-mail info@kuban-airlines.com; internet www.kuban-airlines.de; f. 1932; regional and international flights; 51% owned by Base Element.

Pulkovo Airlines: 196210 St Petersburg, ul. Pilotov 18/4; tel. (812) 324-36-34; fax (812) 104-37-02; internet www.pulkovo.ru; operates regular, direct flights from St Petersburg to 26 destinations in Russia and 10 further destinations in the CIS, as well as destinations in the Middle East; Gen. Dir B. G. DEMCHENKO.

S7 Airlines (Siberia Airlines): 633115 Novosibirsk obl., gorod Ob-4; tel. (3832) 59-90-11; fax (3832) 59-90-64; e-mail pr@s7.ru; internet www.s7.ru; fmrly Sibir Airlines; scheduled and charter flights to domestic, CIS, Asian, European and Middle Eastern destinations; Gen. Dir VLADISLAV FILEV.

Transaero Airlines: 121099 Moscow, 2-i Smolenskii per. 3/4; tel. (495) 937-84-71; fax (495) 937-84-64; e-mail info@transaero.ru; internet www.transaero.ru; f. 1991; Russia's largest privately owned airline; operates scheduled and charter passenger services to the CIS, Europe, Asia and Central America; Chief Exec. OLGA PLESHAKOVA.

Tsentr-Avia: 140150 Moscow obl., pos. Bykovo, ul. Sovetskaya 19; tel. (495) 558-44-07; fax (495) 974-59-32; e-mail marat@at-alliance.ru; internet www.centreavia.ru; f. 1999; flights from Moscow to domestic destinations, and to Austria and Germany.

Ural Airlines (Uralskiye Aviyalinii): 620910 Sverdlovsk obl., Yekaterinburg, ul. Sputnikov 6; tel. (343) 226-81-26; fax (343) 226-82-49; e-mail margarita@uralairlines.ru; internet www.uralairlines.ru; f. 1993; flights from Yekaterinburg to 17 destinations in Russia, and to destinations in the CIS, Europe and the Middle East; Gen. Dir SERGEI SKURATOV.

Vladivostok Avia: 692756 Maritime (Primorskii) Krai, Artem, ul. Portovaya 41, Vladivostok Airport; tel. (4232) 30-73-33; fax (4232) 30-73-43; e-mail office@vladavia.ru; internet www.vladavia.ru; f. 1994; freight and scheduled passenger services to 30 destinations in Russia, and to the People's Republic of China, Japan, the Republic of Korea and Viet Nam; Gen. Dir VLADIMIR SAIBEL.

Tourism

In 2003 there were 22,521,100 tourist arrivals in Russia, and receipts from tourism totalled US $5,879.

Intourist: 129366 Moscow, pr. Mira 150; tel. (495) 956-42-07; fax (495) 730-19-57; e-mail info@intourist.ru; internet www.intourist.ru; f. 1929; brs throughout Russia and abroad; Pres. NIKOLAI KAKORA.

RWANDA

Introductory Survey

Location, Climate, Language, Religion, Flag, Capital

The Rwandan Republic is a land-locked country in eastern central Africa, just south of the Equator, bounded by the Democratic Republic of the Congo to the west, by Uganda to the north, by Tanzania to the east and by Burundi to the south. The climate is tropical, although tempered by altitude. It is hot and humid in the lowlands, but cooler in the highlands. The average annual rainfall is 785 mm (31 ins). The main rainy season is from February to May. The population is composed of three ethnic groups: Hutu (85%), Tutsi (14%) and Twa (1%). French, English and Kinyarwanda, the native language, are all in official use, and Kiswahili is widely spoken. About one-half of the population adhere to animist beliefs. Most of the remainder are Christians, mainly Roman Catholics. There are Protestant and Muslim minorities. The national flag (proportions 1 by 2) has three unequal horizontal stripes, of blue, yellow and green, with a blue-ringed yellow disc (framed by 24 yellow rays) depicted near the fly end of the top stripe. The capital is Kigali.

Recent History

Rwanda, with the neighbouring state of Burundi, became part of German East Africa in 1899. In 1916, during the First World War, it was occupied by Belgian forces from the Congo. From 1920 Rwanda was part of Ruanda-Urundi, administered by Belgium under a League of Nations mandate and later as a UN Trust Territory. Long-standing dissension between the majority Hutu tribe and their former overlords, the Tutsi, caused a rebellion and the proclamation of a state of emergency in 1959. In September 1961 it was decided by referendum to abolish the monarchy and to establish a republic. Full independence followed on 1 July 1962. Serious tribal conflict erupted in December 1963, and massacres (of an estimated 20,000) were perpetrated by the Hutu against the Tutsi. During 1964–65 large numbers of displaced Rwandans were resettled in neighbouring countries. In 1969 Grégoire Kayibanda, the new Republic's first President, was re-elected, and all 47 seats in the legislature were retained by the governing party, the Mouvement démocratique républicain (MDR), also known as the Parti de l'émancipation du peuple Hutu (Parmehutu).

Tension between Hutu and Tutsi escalated again at the end of 1972 and continued throughout February 1973. In July the Minister of Defence and head of the National Guard, Maj.-Gen. Juvénal Habyarimana, led a bloodless coup against President Kayibanda, proclaimed a Second Republic and established a military administration. In August a new Council of Ministers, with Habyarimana as President, was formed. All political activity was banned until July 1975, when a new ruling party, the Mouvement révolutionnaire national pour le développement (MRND), was formed.

A national referendum in December 1978 approved a new Constitution, which was intended to return the country to democratically elected government (in accordance with an undertaking made by Habyarimana in 1973 to end the military regime within five years). Elections to the legislature, the Conseil national de développement (CND), took place in December 1981 and in December 1983; also in December 1983 Habyarimana was re-elected President. In December 1988 Habyarimana was again elected (unopposed) to the presidency, securing 99.98% of the votes cast. Elections to the CND were conducted in the same month.

In September 1990 a Commission was appointed to compile recommendations for a draft national charter, which was to provide for the establishment of a multi-party system. In April 1991, following the CND's revision of the Commission's proposals, a draft constitution were presented to an extraordinary congress of the MRND, at which the party was renamed the Mouvement républicain national pour la démocratie et le développement (MRNDD). On 10 June the reforms were promulgated by Habyarimana, and legislation regulating the formation of political parties was adopted; parties were to be non-tribal and independent, while members of the security forces and the judiciary were to be banned from political activity. (By June 1992 15 parties, among them the MRNDD and a revived MDR, had officially registered.) In October 1991 Sylvestre Nsanzimana, hitherto Minister of Justice, was appointed to the new post of Prime Minister, and in December he formed a transitional Government, in which all but two portfolios (assigned to the Parti démocratique chrétien—PDC) were allocated to members of the MRNDD. Opposition parties, which had been excluded from participation in the transitional Government for their rejection of a MRNDD Prime Minister, organized anti-Government demonstrations in late 1991 and early 1992, demanding the removal of Nsanzimana and the convening of a national conference. A series of negotiations between the Government and the major opposition parties was initiated in February 1992, and in April a protocol agreement was signed, providing for the establishment of a new transitional administration, with Dismas Nsengiyaremye of the MDR as Prime Minister. Habyarimana announced that multi-party elections would be conducted within one year of the installation of the new Government.

Relations with neighbouring Uganda were frequently strained, owing mainly to the presence of some 250,000 Rwandan refugees in Uganda (mainly members of Rwanda's Tutsi minority), who had fled their homeland following successive outbreaks of persecution by the Hutu regime in 1959, 1963 and 1973. In October 1990 rebel forces, based in Uganda, invaded northern Rwanda, occupying several towns. The 4,000-strong rebel army, known as the Front patriotique rwandais (FPR), which mainly comprised Rwandan Tutsi refugees, aimed to overthrow the Habyarimana regime and secure the repatriation of all Rwandan refugees. The Rwandan Government accused the Ugandan leadership of supporting the rebel forces (many of whom had served in the Ugandan armed forces), although this accusation was strenuously denied. With the assistance of French, Belgian and Zairean troops, the Rwandan army succeeded in repelling the FPR before it could reach Kigali. In late October the Government declared a cease-fire, although hostilities continued in northern Rwanda.

Unsuccessful negotiations took place during 1991 and early 1992, but further talks held in Arusha, Tanzania, in July resulted in an agreement on the implementation of a new cease-fire, effective from the end of that month, and the creation of a military observer group (GOM), sponsored by the Organization of African Unity (OAU—now the African Union, see p. 153), to comprise representatives from both sides, together with officers from the armed forces of Nigeria, Senegal, Zimbabwe and Mali. However, subsequent negotiations failed to resolve outstanding problems concerning the creation of a proposed 'neutral zone' between the Rwandan armed forces and the FPR, the incorporation of the FPR in a future combined Rwandan national force, the repatriation of refugees, and FPR demands for full participation in a transitional government and legislature.

A resurgence in violence followed the breakdown of negotiations in February 1993. An estimated 1m. civilians fled southwards and into neighbouring Uganda and Tanzania, as the FPR advanced as far as Ruhengeri. France dispatched reinforcements to join a small military contingent that had been stationed in Kigali since October 1990 to protect French nationals. Meanwhile, the commander of the 50-member GOM declared that the group had inadequate manpower and resources to contain the FPR, and requested the deployment of an additional 400 troops from the OAU. In late February 1993 the Government accepted FPR terms for a cease-fire, in return for an end to attacks against FPR positions and Tutsi communities, and the withdrawal of foreign troops. Although fighting continued with varying intensity, fresh peace negotiations were convened in Arusha in March, and France subsequently began to withdraw its troops. Negotiations conducted during April failed to produce a solution to the crucial issue of the structure of a future single armed Rwandan force. In the same month the five participating parties in the ruling coalition agreed to a three-month extension of the Government's mandate, in order to facilitate the successful conclusion of a peace accord. Significant progress was made during renewed talks between the Government and the FPR during May, when a timetable for the demobilization of the 19,000-

strong security forces was agreed. In June the UN Security Council approved the creation of the UN Observer Mission Uganda-Rwanda (UNOMUR), to be deployed on the Ugandan side of the border, for an initial period of six months, in order to prevent the maintenance of a military supply line for the FPR.

In July 1993 President Habyarimana met with delegates from those political parties represented in the Government to seek a further extension of the coalition's mandate. However, the Prime Minister's insistence that the FPR should be represented in any new government exacerbated existing divisions within the MDR, prompting Habyarimana to conclude the agreement with a conciliatory group of MDR dissidents, including the Minister of Education, Agathe Uwilingiyimana, who was elected to the premiership.

In August 1993 a peace accord was formally signed in Arusha by Habyarimana and Col Alex Kanyarengwe of the FPR. A new transitional government, to be headed by a mutually approved Prime Minister, would be installed by 10 September, and multi-party elections would be conducted after a 22-month period. Failure to establish the transitional institutions by the stipulated deadline was attributed by the Government and the FPR to an increasingly precarious national security situation, and both sides urged the prompt dispatch of a neutral UN force to facilitate the implementation of the accord. In October the UN Security Council adopted Resolution 872, providing for the establishment of the UN Assistance Mission to Rwanda (UNAMIR), to be deployed in Rwanda for an initial period of six months, with a mandate to monitor observance of the cease-fire, to contribute to the security of the capital and to facilitate the repatriation of refugees. UNAMIR, which was to incorporate UNOMUR and GOM and to comprise some 2,500 personnel, was formally inaugurated on 1 November. In December the UN expressed the opinion that conditions had been sufficiently fulfilled to allow the inauguration of the transitional institutions.

On 5 January 1994 Juvénal Habyarimana was invested as President of a transitional administration, for a 22-month period, under the terms of the Arusha accord. The inauguration of the transitional government and legislature was, however, repeatedly delayed, owing to political opposition to the proposed Council of Ministers, and to the insistence of Habyarimana that the list of proposed legislative deputies, presented in March, should be modified to include representatives of additional political parties, including the reactionary Coalition pour la défense de la République (CDR). Meanwhile, political frustration had erupted into violence in February, with the murder of the Minister of Public Works and Energy, Félicien Gatabazi of the Parti social-démocrate (PSD), who had been a prominent supporter of the Arusha accord and of the transitional administration. Within hours the CDR leader, Martin Bucyana, was killed in a retaliatory attack by PSD supporters, and a series of violent confrontations ensued.

On 6 April 1994 the presidential aircraft was fired on, above Kigali airport, and exploded, killing all 10 passengers, including Habyarimana. (The President of Burundi, Cyprien Ntaryamira, two Burundian cabinet ministers and the Chief of Staff of the Rwandan armed forces were among the other victims.) In Kigali the presidential guard immediately initiated a campaign of retributive violence against Habyarimana's political opponents, although it remained unclear who had been responsible for the attack on the aircraft, and UNAMIR officials attempting to investigate the site of the crash were obstructed by the presidential guard. As politicians and civilians fled the capital, the brutality of the political assassinations was compounded by attacks on the clergy, UNAMIR personnel and members of the Tutsi tribe. Many Hutu civilians were reportedly forced to murder their Tutsi neighbours, and the mobilization of the Interahamwe unofficial militias (allegedly affiliated to the MRNDD and the CDR), committed to the massacre of Tutsi civilians and opponents of the Government, was encouraged by the presidential guard (with support from some factions of the armed forces) and by inflammatory broadcasts from Radio Télévision Libre des Mille Collines in Kigali. The Prime Minister, the President of the Constitutional Court, the Ministers of Labour and Social Affairs and of Information, and the Chairman of the PSD were among the prominent politicians murdered (or declared missing and presumed dead) within hours of Habyarimana's death. On 8 April the Speaker of the CND, Dr Théodore Sindikubwabo, announced that he had assumed the office of interim President of the Republic, in accordance with the provisions of the 1991 Constitution. The five remaining participating political parties and factions of the Government selected a new Prime Minister, Jean Kambanda, and a new Council of Ministers (drawn largely from the MRNDD) from among their ranks. The legality of the new administration was immediately challenged by the FPR, which claimed that the terms of the Constitution regarding succession had been superseded by the terms of the Arusha accord. The legitimacy of the Government (which had fled south to Gitarama to escape escalating violence in the capital) was subsequently rejected by several political parties and factions.

In mid-April 1994 the FPR resumed operations from its northern stronghold, with the stated aim of relieving its beleaguered battalion in Kigali, restoring order there and halting the massacre of civilians. The UN mediated a fragile 60-hour cease-fire, during which small evacuation forces from several countries escorted foreign nationals out of Rwanda. Belgium's UNAMIR contingent of more than 400 troops was also withdrawn, having encountered increasing hostility as a result of persistent rumours of Belgian complicity in the attack on President Habyarimana's aircraft, and accusations that Belgian troops were providing logistical support to the FPR.

Members of the Rwandan Government embarked on a diplomatic offensive throughout Europe and Africa, seeking to enhance the credibility of the administration through international recognition of its legal status. However, this initiative achieved only limited success, and the FPR's refusal to enter into dialogue with the 'illegal' administration proved a major obstacle to attempts, undertaken by the UN and the Presidents of Tanzania and of Zaire, to sponsor a new cease-fire agreement in late April and early May 1994.

As the violent campaign initiated by the presidential guard and the estimated 30,000 Interahamwe gathered national momentum, the militia's identification of all Tutsi as political opponents of the State provoked tribal polarization and an effective pogrom. Reports of mass Tutsi graves and of unprovoked attacks on fleeing Tutsi refugees and those sheltering in schools, hospitals and churches provoked unqualified international outrage, and promises were made of financial and logistical aid for an estimated 2m. displaced Rwandans. By late May attempts to assess the full scale of the humanitarian catastrophe in Rwanda were complicated by reports that the FPR (who claimed to control more than one-half of the territory) was perpetrating retaliatory atrocities against Hutu civilians.

In view of the deteriorating security situation, in late April 1994 the UN Security Council approved a resolution to reduce UNAMIR to just 270 personnel. This was condemned by the Rwandan authorities, and in mid-May, following intense international pressure and the disclosure of the vast scale of the humanitarian crisis in the region, the Security Council approved Resolution 917, providing for the eventual deployment of some 5,500 UN troops with a revised mandate, including the protection of refugees in designated 'safe areas'. Further UN-sponsored attempts to negotiate a cease-fire failed in late May and early June, and the FPR made significant territorial gains in southern Rwanda, forcing the Government to flee Gitarama and seek refuge in the western town of Kibuye. In early June the UN Security Council extended the mandate of what was designated UNAMIR II until December. However, the UN Secretary-General continued to encounter considerable difficulty in securing equipment and armaments requested by those countries that had agreed to participate.

By mid-June 1994 the emergence of confirmed reports of retributive murders committed by FPR members and the collapse of an OAU-brokered truce prompted the French Government to announce its willingness to lead an armed police action, endorsed by the UN, in Rwanda. Despite French insistence that its force (expected to total 2,000 troops) would maintain strict political neutrality, and operate, from the border regions, in a purely humanitarian capacity pending the arrival of a multinational UN force, the FPR was vehemently opposed to its deployment, citing the French Government's maintenance of high-level contacts with representatives of the self-proclaimed Rwandan Government as an indication of political bias. The UN Secretary-General welcomed the French initiative; however, the OAU expressed serious reservations as to the appropriateness of the action. In late June a first contingent of 150 French marine commandos launched 'Operation Turquoise', entering the western town of Cyangugu, in preparation for a large-scale operation to protect refugees in the area. By mid-July the French had relieved several beleaguered Tutsi communities, and had established a temporary 'safe haven' for the displaced population in the south-west, through which a massive exodus of Hutu refugees began to flow, prompted by fears that the advancing FPR forces were seeking violent retribution against the Hutu. An estimated 1m. Rwandans sought refuge in the Zairean border town of Goma, while a similar number attempted to cross the border elsewhere in the south-west. The FPR, meanwhile, swiftly secured all major cities and strategic territorial positions, but halted its advance several kilometres from the boundaries of the French-controlled neutral zone, requesting the apprehension and return for trial of those responsible for the recent atrocities. (In early July the UN announced the creation of a commission of inquiry to investigate allegations of genocide, following an initial report that as many as 500,000 Rwandans had been killed since April.)

On 19 July 1994 Pasteur Bizimungu, a Hutu, was inaugurated as President for a five-year term. On the same day the FPR announced the composition of a new Government of National Unity, with the leader of the MDR moderate faction, Faustin Twagiramungu, as Prime Minister. The majority of cabinet posts were assigned to FPR members (including the FPR military chief, Maj.-Gen. Paul Kagame, who became Minister of Defence and also assumed the newly created post of Vice-President), while the remainder were divided among the MDR, the PSD, the Parti libéral (PL) and the Parti démocratique chrétien (PDC). The new administration urged all refugees to return to Rwanda, and issued assurances that civilian Hutus could return safely to their homes. Identity cards bearing details of ethnic origin were to be abolished forthwith. The new Government declared its intention to honour the terms of the Arusha accord within the context of an extended period of transition. In August, however, Twagiramungu declared the country to be effectively bankrupt, claiming that members of the former Government, who had fled abroad, had appropriated all exchange reserves. The claims to legitimacy of the exiled former administration were seriously undermined by recognition by the European Union (EU, see p. 228) of the new Government of National Unity in September.

Amid persistent rumours that the Rwandan armed forces were attempting to regroup and rearm in Zaire, in preparation for a counter-offensive against the FPR, in late August 1994 the UN initiated the deployment of some 2,500 UNAMIR II forces, largely drawn from Ghana and Ethiopia, in the security zone (redesignated 'zone four'). French troops began to withdraw from the area (the final contingent departed in late September), prompting hundreds of thousands of internally displaced Hutu refugees within the zone to move to Zairean border areas. An estimated 500,000 refugees remained at camps in the former security zone at the end of August. The UNAMIR II mandate was extended for a further six months. (In June 1995, at the request of the Rwandan Government, the six-month mandate of the force, which was reduced from 5,586 to 2,330 personnel, was again renewed.)

In November 1994 a number of amendments to the terms of the August 1993 Arusha accord were adopted under a multi-party protocol of understanding. The most notable of the new provisions was the exclusion from the legislative process of those parties implicated in alleged acts of genocide during 1994. A 70-member National Transitional Assembly was formally inaugurated in December, with a composition including five representatives of the armed forces and one member of the national police force. On 5 May 1995 this legislature adopted a new Constitution, which was based on selected articles of the 1991 Constitution, the terms of the Arusha accord, the FPR's victory declaration of July 1994 and the November multi-party protocol.

A political crisis emerged in August 1995, after the Prime Minister expressed dissatisfaction with the Government's lack of adherence to the provisions of the Arusha accord regarding power-sharing, and with the security forces' repeated recourse to violence in their management of the refugee crisis. Twagiramungu and four other disaffected ministers were subsequently replaced. Pierre Célestin Rwigyema of the MDR, also Hutu and the former Minister of Primary and Secondary Education, was named as the new Prime Minister at the end of the month. The new Council of Ministers included representatives of both major ethnic groups and four political parties.

In late 1994 Hutu refugees within Rwanda and in neighbouring countries were continuing to resist the exhortations of the UN and the new Rwandan administration to return to their homes, despite the deteriorating security situation in many camps (which had, moreover, forced the withdrawal of a number of relief agencies). Hutu militias were reported to have assumed control of several camps, notably Katale in Zaire and Benaco in Tanzania. Reports also emerged that Hutu civilians intending to return to their homes had been subjected to violent intimidation by the Interahamwe. It was further alleged that male Hutu refugees were being forced to undergo military training in preparation for a renewed conflict. The reluctance of many refugees to return to their homes was also attributed to persistent allegations that the Tutsi-dominated FPR armed forces (the Armée patriotique rwandaise—APR) were conducting a systematic campaign of reprisal attacks against returning Hutus.

International scepticism regarding the Government's programme of refugee resettlement increased in early 1995, following a series of uncompromising initiatives to encourage the return of internally displaced Rwandans (including the interruption of food supplies to refugee camps), culminating in the forcible closure of the camps through military intervention. An attempt in April to dismantle the Kibeho camp in southern Rwanda provoked widespread international condemnation, after APR troops opened fire on refugees, amid confusion arising from the actions of some hostile elements within the camp and a sudden attempt by large numbers of anxious refugees to break the military cordon; independent sources estimated as many as 5,000 fatalities.

In August 1995, in response to requests made by the Rwandan Government, the UN Security Council voted to suspend the arms embargo to Rwanda (imposed in May 1994) for one year, in order to allow the Government to safeguard against the threat of a military offensive by Hutu extremists encamped in neighbouring countries. Meanwhile, the security situation in refugee camps along the Zairean border had deteriorated to such an extent that the Zairean Government initiated a programme of forcible repatriation, attracting widespread international concern. Despite a formal agreement between the office of the UN High Commissioner for Refugees (UNHCR) and the Zairean Government for a more regulated approach to the refugee crisis, APR attacks near the border with Zaire further deterred refugees. At a conference of the Great Lakes countries, convened in Cairo, Egypt, in late November, and attended by the Presidents of Burundi, Rwanda, Uganda and Zaire and by a Tanzanian presidential envoy, President Mobutu of Zaire indicated that the forcible return of remaining refugees in early 1996 was no longer a realistic objective. The conference also accepted the Rwandan President's assertion that the participation of UNAMIR forces in peace-keeping operations in Rwanda was no longer necessary, but urged the Rwandan Government to accept the extension of a revised, three-month mandate for the forces to provide assistance in the refugee repatriation process. (A three-month mandate for a 1,200-strong force was thus renewed in December 1995, and the mission was formally terminated in April 1996.)

In February 1995 the UN Security Council adopted Resolution 977, whereby Arusha was designated the seat for the International Criminal Tribunal for Rwanda (ICTR). The six-member Tribunal, to be headed by a Senegalese lawyer, Laïty Kama, was inaugurated in June for a four-year term. It was reported that the ICTR intended to investigate allegations made against some 400 individuals (many of them by this time resident outside Rwanda) of direct involvement in the planning and execution of crimes against humanity perpetrated in Rwanda during 1994. In October 1995 a Supreme Court was established by the Transitional National Assembly.

The ICTR began formal proceedings in November 1995. The first court session of the ICTR was convened in September 1996, but hearings concerning the first two (of 21) individuals indicted on charges of crimes against humanity were almost immediately postponed. Tribunal officials attributed the virtual collapse of proceedings to the escalating conflict in eastern Zaire, but widespread concern was expressed at the high number of administrative errors committed. In contrast, in January 1997 regional courts within Rwanda passed death sentences on five individuals accused of acts of genocide. (Whereas capital punishment would not be invoked by the ICTR, legislation published by the Rwandan authorities in September 1996 regarding penalties for crimes committed during 1994 made provision for the application of the death penalty.) In February 1997 the report of an internal UN investigation of the ICTR was highly critical of many aspects of administrative structure and procedure, prompting the resignation of two senior Tribunal officials. In July seven suspects in the 1994 genocide were arrested in Kenya and transferred for trial to Arusha. Among those arrested were former Prime Minister Jean Kambanda, two senior armed forces officers and a former government minister. Later in July a Belgian journalist, who had worked for the extremist Radio

Télévision Libre des Mille Collines at the time of the massacres, was arrested by the Kenyan authorities and similarly transferred for trial (becoming the first foreign national to be indicted by the ICTR).

Meanwhile, some 300 genocide suspects were tried by Rwandan courts during 1997, and an estimated 125,000 defendants were in detention awaiting trial; arrests reportedly continued at a rate of 1,000 per month. In late 1997, in an attempt to address the problem of severe overcrowding in prisons, the release was authorized of elderly, infirm or juvenile detainees. (This policy was denounced by organizations representing survivors of the 1994 massacres, and there were reports of attacks on freed genocide suspects.) The announcement that 23 people convicted of acts of genocide were to be publicly executed provoked international condemnation. Amnesty International and other human rights organizations expressed serious concerns that those convicted had been denied adequate opportunity to prepare a defence. The Rwandan authorities refuted such claims, and dismissed pleas for clemency. The public executions proceeded in April 1998.

In August 1996, during a visit to Kigali by the Zairean Prime Minister, a bilateral agreement for the organized and unconditional repatriation of all Rwandan refugees in Zaire was concluded (without the participation of UNHCR officials). During September, however, relations between the two countries were placed under renewed strain, when the attempts of the Interahamwe and the Zairean armed forces to displace large numbers of Zairean Banyamulenge (ethnic Tutsis) from eastern Zaire encountered large-scale armed resistance from the Banyamulenge, resulting in Zairean accusations of Rwandan support for the Banyamulenge, and culminating in a cross-border exchange of fire later that month. Throughout October, as the rebels made significant gains in the region, the Rwandan Government continued to deny Zairean allegations of its involvement in the Banyamulenge insurrection, and at the end of the month admitted that Rwandan troops had been deployed in eastern Zaire in response to an artillery attack on the Rwandan town of Cyangugu, allegedly made by the Zairean armed forces.

Meanwhile, there was renewed international concern for the estimated 1m. refugees previously encamped in eastern Zaire, following reports that the regional conflict had resulted in the sudden exodus of some 250,000 refugees, and the interruption of food aid distribution. The rebel army in Zaire (known as the Alliance des forces démocratiques pour la libération du Congo-Zaïre—AFDL) declared a cease-fire for returning refugees, and later in the month announced the creation of a humanitarian corridor to the Rwandan border, with the intention that the estimated 700,000 Rwandan refugees now seeking shelter at the Mugunga camp, west of Goma, would return to Rwanda. The large-scale return of refugees was finally prompted by an AFDL attack on Interahamwe units operating from the camp. In April 1997 the AFDL leader, Laurent-Désiré Kabila, demanded that the UN complete full repatriation of the refugees within 60 days, after which time their return would be undertaken unilaterally by the rebels. The Rwandan authorities, meanwhile, expressed concern that the UN was delaying the rapid repatriation of refugees from eastern Zaire. (By the end of May the AFDL had gained control of most of Zaire, which was renamed the Democratic Republic of Congo—DRC, and Kabila assumed power as Head of State.) Continuing ethnic unrest and violence, particularly in north-west Rwanda, throughout 1997 were exacerbated by the return from the DRC of large numbers of Hutus (see also the chapter on the DRC). Both the office of the UN High Commissioner for Human Rights and Amnesty International published reports in August, alleging that as many as 3,000 civilians had been killed by government troops in counter-insurgency operations since May. The Government denied having perpetrated massacres of civilians, and claimed that those killed had been Interahamwe militia. An extensive demobilization programme was undertaken from September, with the aim of reintegrating former combatants into civil society; some 57,500 personnel were to be demobilized over a three-year period.

By late 1997 there was evidence that Hutu rebel forces, estimated to number some 10,000–15,000 Interahamwe and former soldiers, were becoming increasingly confident of their military potential, as a series of raids was launched to free prisoners awaiting trial on genocide charges. More than 300 deaths were reported in an abortive attack by 1,200 rebels on a prison in the north-west in November. In early December, however, rebels successfully released more than 500 inmates from a prison in central Rwanda. Genocide survivors and student groups organized demonstrations in several towns in late 1997 and early 1998 to protest against the Government's failure to suppress the militias and prevent what they regarded as the continuation of the genocide.

The trial of genocide suspects continued in 1998, both in Rwanda and at the ICTR, and in early September the ICTR reached its first verdict. A former mayor of Taba, Jean-Paul Akayesu, was convicted and sentenced to life imprisonment; Kambanda, who had pleaded guilty to six charges of genocide and crimes against humanity, was also given a life sentence. Both appealed against their sentences, and Akayesu later began a hunger strike, claiming he had been denied the lawyer of his choice; a further 25 detainees joined his protest. Rwandan courts, meanwhile, convicted and sentenced some 1,000 genocide suspects during 1998 (the authorities had aimed to hear 5,000 cases during the year). By June about 5,000 suspects in Rwandan prisons had pleaded guilty to acts of genocide in order to lessen their sentences, apparently in response to the public executions in April. In June Maj. Augustine Cyiza, the Vice-President of the Supreme Court and President of the Court of Cassation, resigned (he had been suspended for misconduct in March), and in October some controversy was caused by the decision to release at least 10,000 genocide suspects owing to lack of evidence against them. It was announced in November that 34,000 suspects had been freed since 1994.

In October 1998 the Transitional National Assembly approved the establishment of a fund to assist survivors of the genocide, and in the following month the Council of Ministers approved the establishment of two commissions, for human rights and for unity and reconciliation (both had been established by mid-1999). Between February and May 1999 some 16 deputies resigned, or were expelled, from the Transitional National Assembly for misconduct, incompetence or allegations of involvement in the genocide. In June the period of political transition, originally set at five years in 1994, was extended by a further four years, following agreement between the major political parties.

In January 1999 the Minister of Justice resigned his portfolio and left the country. In a reorganization in the following month the Government was expanded to comprise 21 ministers (compared with the previous 17). New ministers included Jean de Dieu Mucyo (the first Tutsi to be appointed Minister for Justice since 1994). Voting in local elections (the first elections to be held since 1988) were conducted on a non-party basis on 29–31 March 1999. Voter participation was estimated to have been 95%, and at the end of the month the EU special envoy to the Great Lakes region commended the manner in which the elections were conducted. In June the Transitional National Assembly approved draft legislation establishing a commission that was to prepare a new constitution. In July the Minister of Foreign Affairs, Amri Sued, was removed from his post, reportedly for dereliction of duty and embezzlement; he was replaced by the Minister of Information, and that ministry was subsequently dissolved. Legislation establishing a national police force (which was to unify the existing national gendarmerie, and the communal and judicial police) was adopted in August.

During 1999 a number of prominent Hutu, including three former government ministers, were arrested on suspicion of involvement in the 1994 genocide and extradited to the ICTR. In May a former Rwandan mayor (the first Rwandan to be tried abroad for genocide) was convicted by a Swiss court on charges of inciting the killing of Tutsi civilians, and sentenced to life imprisonment. In June Navanethem Pillay succeeded Kama as President of the ICTR, and in September Carla del Ponte became UN Chief Prosecutor. In November the Rwandan Government suspended co-operation with the ICTR, following the Tribunal's decision to release Jean Bosco Barayagwiza, a former government official who was accused of participation in the genocide, owing to his prolonged detention without trial. The Minister of Justice later refused del Ponte authorization to enter Rwanda, and the newly appointed Rwandan representative to the ICTR announced he would not assume his office until the issue had been resolved. In December the Government announced that it would allow del Ponte to enter Rwanda, following her official request for a review of the decision to release Barayagwiza. Full co-operation was resumed with the ICTR in February 2000, after a three-month suspension, and in March, following the examination of fresh evidence, the Appeals Chamber of the ICTR announced its decision that Barayagwiza should stand trial. Further arrests were made in early 2000. In February legislation introducing a traditional system of justice, known as *gacaca* (on the grass), was adopted; certain categories of genocide crimes were to be tried under this system (by council in local communities), while the most serious genocide crimes would continue to be tried under the existing judicial system. It was hoped that the creation of the *gacaca* courts would alleviate the large number of cases awaiting trial and aid the process of national reconciliation.

In February 2000 the National Assembly voted in favour of investigating alleged abuses of power by Rwigyema. On 28 February he resigned from the office of Prime Minister, citing differences with the legislature. Bernard Makuza, hitherto the Rwandan ambassador in Germany, was appointed Prime Minister in March, and subsequently announced a government reorganization, in which six ministers were replaced. The new Government was the first since 1994 in which the parties were not represented in accordance with the 1993 Arusha peace accords. At its inauguration, Kagame (who remained Vice-President and Minister of Defence and National Security) failed to swear allegiance to the President. On 23 March Bizimungu resigned from office, owing to disagreement over the composition of the new Government, in particular the exclusion of Mazimhaka. Kagame was subsequently appointed interim President by the Supreme Court. On 17 April he was formally elected President of Rwanda by members of the Transitional National Assembly and the Government, securing 81 of 86 votes cast. He was inaugurated on 22 April (becoming the first Tutsi Head of State since 1959).

At the end of July 2000 Rwigyema was removed from the leadership of the MDR by the party's political bureau, which accused him of acting contrary to its interests; he subsequently left the country. In October the International Court of Justice (ICJ) at The Hague, Netherlands, upheld the life sentence imposed on Kambanda by the ICTR in 1998. In December 2000 del Ponte announced that the Tribunal was to commence investigations into members of the FPR for involvement in massacres of Hutu (having previously only instigated proceedings against Hutu supporters who had participated in the 1994 genocide of Tutsi). In April 2001 elections to district councils were conducted on a non-party basis throughout the country. Human Rights Watch subsequently criticized the manner in which the local government elections were conducted, however, claiming that only one candidate contested the poll in nearly half of the municipalities.

In April 2001 an international warrant was issued for the arrest of Rwigyema, who had taken refuge in the USA, on suspicion of participating in the genocide of 1994. The trial of four Hutus (including two nuns), on charges of complicity in massacres in the southern Butare prefecture, commenced in Belgium later that month (under Belgian legislation permitting foreign nationals to be arraigned there for war crimes). In early June all four were sentenced to terms of imprisonment. Also in early June a former mayor became the first defendant to be acquitted by the ICTR (which at this time had convicted eight people on charges of involvement in the genocide). In July four Hutus, including a close associate of former President Habyarimana, Protais Zigiranyirazo, were arrested in western Europe and subsequently transferred to the ICTR (increasing the number of suspects held in detention there to more than 50). In the same month a Tribunal of First Instance officially banned the MRNDD and CDR for inciting violence in 1994.

On 4 October 2001 some 250,000 judges for the *gacaca* courts were elected in a national ballot. With the number of prisoners awaiting trial having increased to some 115,000, those suspected of lesser crimes relating to the genocide were henceforth to be tried by the *gacaca* system. In December a new national flag, emblem and anthem officially replaced those adopted at independence in 1962. In April 2002 the trial of Col Theoneste Bagosora, who was considered to be the principal organizer of the genocide, commenced at the ICTR. Bagosora, who had been in custody since his arrest in Cameroon in 1996, had allegedly planned the massacre of Tutsi civilians by the militia and had personally ordered the assassination of prominent politicians. He, and a further three former senior army officers on trial, refused to attend the initial session of the ICTR, on the grounds that their right to defence had been violated. Later in April security forces arrested former President Bizimungu (who had attempted to form an opposition political party in May 2001), and searched his residence. The authorities subsequently announced that Bizimungu had continued to engage in illegal political activity, and would be charged with endangering state security.

In early August 2002 Gen. Augustin Bizimungu, the army Chief of Staff in 1994, who had been indicted by the ICTR jointly with four other former military commanders, was arrested in Angola and transferred to the Tribunal. Later that month he pleaded not guilty to 10 charges, including that of genocide. In November trials by the *gacaca* court system officially commenced in large parts of the country. In the same month several principal ministers, including those responsible for the portfolios of foreign affairs and defence, were replaced in a government reorganization.

In January 2003, in an effort to reduce numbers in prisons, Kagame issued a decree providing for the provisional release of some 40,000 of those held in detention, including many who had pleaded guilty to charges related to the 1994 genocide. Although the Ministry of Justice maintained that legal proceedings against the released prisoners would continue, organizations representing survivors of the genocide criticized the measure. Most of the prisoners due for release were to be dispatched to 'solidarity camps', where they were to be prepared for reintegration into society. (By the end of 2003 some 25,000 suspects had been released.) In February a senior Hutu pastor and his son were convicted by the ICTR of active participation in the massacre of Tutsis in the west of the country in 1994; they were sentenced to 10 and 25 years' imprisonment, respectively.

On 23 April 2003 the Transitional National Assembly adopted a new Constitution, which was to be submitted for approval at a national referendum. The draft Constitution provided for the establishment of a bicameral legislature (comprising an 80-member Chamber of Deputies and a 26-member Senate) and a President, who was to be elected by universal suffrage. In mid-May the former Minister of Information in the Government of April 1994, Eliézer Niyitegeka, was sentenced to life imprisonment by the ICTR, after being convicted on six charges of involvement in the genocide. At the national referendum, which took place on 26 May 2003, the draft Constitution was endorsed by 93.4% of the electorate. The new Constitution entered into effect on 4 June; under its provisions, political associations formed on the basis of ethnicity, tribal or regional affiliation, religion or any other grounds for discrimination were prohibited. (Some existing political organizations were restructured to end such affiliations.) The presidential election was subsequently scheduled for 25 August, and was to be followed by legislative elections in late September. Kagame announced his intention to seek re-election, while former Prime Minister Twagiramungu returned to Rwanda from exile in Belgium in order to contest the presidency. (Twagiramungu of the MDR and Jean-Népomuscène Nayinzira, a former minister and President of the PDC, were both obliged to participate as independent candidates, owing to the dissolution of their political parties under the terms of the new Constitution.)

The first presidential election to take place in Rwanda since the single candidate poll of 1988 was conducted on 25 August 2003 (thereby marking the end of the nine-year transitional period). Kagame was returned to power, with about 95.1% of votes cast, while Twagiramungu won 3.6%, and Nayinzira 1.3% of the votes. However, Twagiramungu accused the authorities of electoral malpractice, and submitted a challenge against the official results at the Supreme Court. EU monitors confirmed that irregularities had been noted, although a South African observer mission declared that the poll had been 'free and fair'. In early September the Supreme Court rejected Twagiramungu's appeal, and he announced that he would not pursue the claim further. Kagame was officially inaugurated on 12 September. Four political parties subsequently agreed to contest the forthcoming legislative elections in alliance with the FPR. Following the dissolution of the MDR, many of its former members joined the newly emerged Parti du progrès et de la concorde. In addition to the FPR-led coalition, the PSD, the PL and a number of independent candidates registered to contest the legislative elections. Elections to the Chamber of Deputies commenced on 29 September, with voting for seats allocated to one disabled and two youth representatives. The poll for the 53 seats contested by political parties and independent candidates followed on 30 September; the FPR-led coalition, with 73.8% of votes cast, secured 40 seats, while the PSD (12.3% of votes) won seven seats, and the PL (10.6%) six seats. The remaining 24 female representatives were selected at provincial level on 2 October. Kagame formed a new Council of Ministers on 19 October; Makuza was reappointed to the office of Prime Minister and most principal ministers retained their portfolios. Twagiramungu left the country in early November, after claiming that he faced detention owing to his opposition to Kagame's Government.

In August 2003, following a two-day mass trial, a *gacaca* court in the prefecture of Butare convicted 105 people of participation in the 1994 genocide, of whom 11 were sentenced to death. In early September a Gambian judge, Hassan Bubacar Jallow, was appointed Chief Prosecutor of the ICTR, replacing del Ponte. In early December the owners of Radio Télévision Libre des Mille Collines and the Hutu extremist newspaper *Kangura* were sentenced to life imprisonment at the ICTR, on charges relating to public incitement to commit genocide. A further former public official connected to the radio station received a sentence of 35 years' imprisonment. In January 2004 a former minister who had served in the April 1994 Government was sentenced to life imprisonment on two of eight charges (of genocide and extermination as a crime against humanity). In February a former commander of an army barracks in Cyangugu, in the south-west of the country, was sentenced to 27 years' imprisonment on six counts relating to the 1994 genocide. (At this time the ICTR had convicted 18 and acquitted three defendants.) In the same month the Rwandan authorities urged those prisoners awaiting trial in connection with the genocide to qualify for a general amnesty by confessing to the charges against them. Meanwhile, at the ongoing trial of Bagosora at the ICTR, the testimony of a principal witness, a former Canadian UN commander, Gen. (retd) Romeo Dallaire, implicated French forces in failing to prevent the genocide.

In June 2004 former President Bizimungu (who had remained in detention since April 2002) was sentenced to a term of 15 years' imprisonment, after being convicted of corruption, inciting civil disobedience and criminal association; he was, however, acquitted of the principal charge of endangering state security through anti-Government activities. A former minister and associate of Bizimungu received a custodial term of 10 years on similar charges. In July the Minister of Finance of the 1994 Government, Emmanuel Ndindabahizi, who had been arrested in Belgium on July 2001, received a sentence of life imprisonment at the ICTR on charges of genocide and two counts of crimes against humanity for his participation in the massacre of Tutsi refugees during that period. In September the trial of a Roman Catholic priest, also for involvement in the organized massacres of Tutsis, commenced at the ICTR. Proceedings for some of the large number of cases to be transferred from the ICTR to the *gacaca* courts commenced in early 2005. In February the Minister of Family and Women's Affairs of the 1994 Government became the first woman to be charged with genocide in connection with organized killings in the Butare prefecture. At the end of March the serving Minister of Defence, Gen. Marcel Gatsinzi, appeared before a *gacaca* court, where he pleaded not guilty to charges of failing to prevent troops under his command from perpetrating massacres in Butare.

In September 2005 a Belgian priest and former missionary was arrested on suspicion of having incited genocidal acts in 1994 (by republishing material from the Hutu extremist newspaper *Kangura*) and was initially arraigned before a *gacaca* court; following a request by the Belgian Government, his trial was transferred to Belgium in November. In early October the trial began of Zigiranyirazo (who had been extradited to the ICTR in October 2001); he pleaded not guilty to all charges relating to the genocide. (By late 2005 it was reported that some 4,162 cases, including those of several former officials, had been tried by the *gacaca* system.)

In October 2005 both legislative chambers approved a number of constitutional amendments, which principally provided for the reorganization of local government structures (reducing the number of provinces, formerly prefectures, from 12 to five) to allow greater decentralization; the territorial reforms entered into effect at the beginning of 2006. In February the Supreme Court upheld the 15-year sentence imposed on Bizimungu (who had submitted an appeal against the charges in October 2005). Also in February 2006 the Rwandan Government denied a request by Jallow for the transfer of the trial of a suspected Interahamwe military leader to Norway. In March a new Minister of Finance was appointed in a government reorganization, which was designed to assist efforts to reconstruct the economy; a new portfolio of science, information technology and research was also created.

At the end of July 1998 Laurent-Désiré Kabila (the President of the DRC since 31 May 1997) announced that military co-operation with both Rwanda and Uganda was to end, and demanded that all foreign forces leave the DRC. Relations between Rwanda and the DRC subsequently deteriorated. Kabila claimed that a rebellion, which commenced in the east of the DRC in August, constituted a Rwandan invasion; the Rwandan Government denied any involvement, but in late 1998 conceded that Rwandan troops were present in the DRC to provide logistical support to the rebel-led action. The Rwandan Government participated in a series of regional peace negotiations, at which Kabila refused to negotiate directly with the rebels. Rwanda later denied reports that it was maintaining a joint military command with Uganda in the DRC (see also the chapter on the DRC).

Rwandan action in the DRC continued in 1999, although Rwanda's alliance with Uganda became increasingly unstable during that year. At the end of April Uganda temporarily recalled its ambassador to Rwanda, following an incident in the DRC, in which Rwandan troops killed a number of members of the Ugandan armed forces. A split within the rebel movement in the DRC, the Rassemblement congolais pour la démocratie (RCD), resulted in the creation of two factions, one supported by Rwanda and one by Uganda. Following further clashes in the DRC between Rwandan and Ugandan troops in Kisangani in August, both armies agreed to leave the city. In June the DRC instituted proceedings against Burundi, Rwanda and Uganda at the ICJ, accusing these countries of acts of armed aggression. (In early February 2001, however, the DRC abandoned proceedings against Burundi and Rwanda.)

In May 2000 Rwandan and Ugandan forces again clashed in the town of Kisangani (despite a cease-fire agreement, which had been reached by all forces involved in the conflict in April). After meeting a UN Security Council delegation, the Rwandan and Ugandan contingents agreed to the demilitarization of the town, and its transfer to the control of the UN Mission in the Democratic Republic of the Congo (MONUC, see p. 77) deployed in the country. Despite further fighting, it was confirmed at the end of June that all Rwandan and Ugandan forces had withdrawn from Kisangani. In December, however, the principal RCD faction, supported by Rwandan troops, succeeded in gaining control of the south-eastern town of Pweto. The Rwandan Government denied any involvement in the assassination of Kabila in January 2001 (see the chapter on the DRC). In February Kagame met the new DRC President, Joseph Kabila (the son of Laurent-Désiré), in Washington, DC, USA, to discuss the ongoing conflict. Later that month the groups involved in the conflict, under the aegis of the UN Security Council, agreed to a disengagement of their forces by mid-March, followed by a complete withdrawal of foreign troops from the DRC by mid-May. Although some military disengagement of forces took place accordingly in March, factions subsequently refused to continue until MONUC guaranteed security in the region. In April the Governments of Burundi, Rwanda and Uganda rejected the claims of a UN report that the forces of these countries had exploited the natural resources of the DRC. In June it was reported that Interahamwe militia, led by former members of the Rwandan army, had intensified incursions into north-western Rwanda from the DRC. Despite continued pressure from the UN Security Council, in August Kagame insisted that Kabila fulfil pledges to demobilize the Interahamwe (who were supporting DRC government forces), as a precondition to the withdrawal of Rwandan forces from the DRC.

At the end of July 2002, after further discussions mediated by the South African Government, a peace agreement was signed by Kabila and Kagame in Pretoria. Under the accord, Kabila pledged to arrest and disarm the Interahamwe militia in the DRC, while the Rwandan Government agreed to withdraw all troops from the country. In October it was announced that all 23,400 Rwandan troops had been withdrawn from the DRC. The Rwandan authorities denied reports that they planned to redeploy forces in the DRC, in response to the continued Ugandan involvement in hostilities there. In September 2003 the Governments of Rwanda and the DRC agreed to re-establish diplomatic links, and the improvement in relations between the two countries was further demonstrated by the visit to Rwanda of the DRC Minister of Foreign Affairs in October. In July 2004, however, a report by a UN commission contained accusations, which were denied by the Rwandan Government, of Rwandan support for an insurrection by dissident members of the armed forces in eastern DRC (see chapter on the DRC). Following a massacre of Banyamulenge refugees from the DRC at a border camp in Burundi in August, the Governments of Rwanda and Burundi claimed that the Interahamwe militia operating within the DRC were implicated and threatened to resume military engagement in the country. Repeated reports (confirmed by MONUC) that Rwandan troops had re-entered DRC territory ensued.

In November 2001 Kagame and the Ugandan Head of State, Lt-Gen. Yoweri Kaguta Museveni, met in London, United Kingdom, in an effort to resolve the increasing tension between the two nations, following the repeated clashes in the DRC. The Ugandan Government had accused Rwanda of supporting dissidents who intended to overthrow Museveni's administration, while Kagame claimed that Ugandan troops were amassing on the joint border between the two countries. In February 2002 further discussions between Kagame and Museveni, with mediation by the British Secretary of State for International Development, were conducted in Uganda. It was agreed that both Governments would urge the dissidents based in their respective countries to take refuge elsewhere, and the adoption of a mutual extradition treaty was envisaged. In July 2003 the Rwandan Government signed a tripartite agreement with the Ugandan authorities and UNHCR, providing for the voluntary repatriation of some 26,000 Rwandans resident in refugee camps in western Uganda. (Similar accords were signed between Rwanda and the Governments of Malawi, Togo, Zambia and Tanzania.) In February 2004 an improvement in diplomatic relations between Rwanda and Uganda (following progress in the situation in the DRC) was demonstrated by a bilateral agreement to strengthen co-operation in several fields.

Since 1994 the role of the international community in failing to avert the genocide has come under frequent scrutiny. In late 1997 the report of a Belgian Senate investigation concluded that the international community, and more specifically the UN and the Belgian authorities, was directly or indirectly responsible for certain aspects of the developments arising from the political violence from April 1994. Testifying before the ICTR in February 1998, the former UNAMIR commander stated that he had warned the UN in early 1994 of the impending ethnic catastrophe in Rwanda, but that the international community had lacked the will to intervene adequately. Suggestions that Kofi Annan, the head of UN peace-keeping operations at the time of the conflict, had failed to respond to such warnings prompted tensions between the UN Secretary-General (as Annan had subsequently become) and the Rwandan authorities in May 1998, as government officials refused to receive the Secretary-General in the course of a visit to Rwanda. Meanwhile, in February the OAU announced the establishment of a committee to investigate the genocide; the committee held its first meeting in October. In December a French parliamentary committee, established in March, presented its report on French involvement in events prior to and at the time of the genocide. (Despite evidence to the contrary, the French authorities have persistently denied allegations that France continued to supply military equipment and support to Rwanda after the imposition of the UN arms embargo in May 1994.) The report cleared France of any direct complicity in the genocide, although it conceded that 'Operation Turquoise' both delayed the accession to power of the FPR, and facilitated the escape of Hutu extremist forces into the DRC. The report attributed responsibility for the genocide to the international community as a whole, particularly to the USA (which had failed to support UN peace-keeping operations in Rwanda).

In March 1999 the UN Security Council approved a proposal for the establishment of a commission of inquiry into the actions of the UN prior to and during the genocide. The three-member commission of inquiry presented its report in December after a six-month investigation. The report criticized the UN for failing in its mission to prevent the genocide and for ignoring the warnings of the head of the peace-keeping mission. It also cited the UN Security Council's failure to deploy a sufficient peace-keeping force at the end of 1993. Following the report, Kofi Annan issued a personal apology for UN inaction at the time. In January 2000 it was announced that two Rwandan genocide survivors were to sue the UN for its 'complicity' in the genocide. In March a Canadian newspaper published a UN memorandum, stating that the FPR was responsible for the attack on the aircraft on 6 April 1994, which killed President Juvénal Habyarimana, and that Kagame had been in overall command of the force that carried out the attack. Kagame subsequently dismissed the allegations, claiming that the report was part of a UN attempt to absolve itself of blame for the genocide of 1994.

In August 2001 the French Minister of Foreign Affairs made an official visit to Rwanda (the first by a senior French official since 1994), in an effort to normalize bilateral relations. (Diplomatic links were restored in 2002.) In March 2002 the French Government (which, within the UN Security Council, had placed increasing pressure on Rwanda to withdraw forces from the DRC) protested that Rwandan troops had launched a major offensive in the east of that country. In March 2004 the results of an official French investigation into the destruction of President Habyarimana's aircraft alleged that Kagame, as leader of the FPR, had ordered the missile attack. Kagame again denied any responsibility, and claimed that French forces had, by training and arming the Hutu militia, supported the mass killings. In early April the French Secretary of State for Foreign Affairs curtailed his visit to Rwanda, after Kagame repeated these accusations at an official ceremony in Kigali commemorating the 10th anniversary of the genocide. On the following anniversary in April 2005 the Rwandan Government reiterated demands that the UN instigate legal proceedings against French officials for complicity in the genocide. In December a French military tribunal began to investigate claims by survivors of the genocide that French forces had facilitated attacks against Tutsi in 1994 (by failing to prevent massacres and then by allowing the perpetrators of the genocide to evade capture).

Government

Under the terms of the Constitution, which entered into force on 4 June 2003, legislative power is vested in a bicameral Parliament, comprising a Chamber of Deputies and a Senate. The Chamber of Deputies has 80 deputies, who are elected for a five-year term. In addition to 53 directly elected deputies, 27 seats are allocated, respectively, to two youth representatives, one disabilities representative, and 24 female representatives, who are indirectly elected. The Senate comprises 26 members, of whom 12 are elected by local government councils in the 12 provinces, and two by academic institutions, while the remaining 12 are nominated (eight by the President and four by a regulatory body, the Parties' Forum). Members of the Senate serve for eight years. Executive power is exercised by the President (Head of State), assisted by an appointed Council of Ministers. The President is elected by universal suffrage for a seven-year term, and is restricted to two mandates.

Following territorial reforms, which entered into effect at the beginning of 2006, the country is divided into five provinces and subdivided into 30 districts, each administered by an elected mayor. Local government elections took place on a non-party basis in April 2001.

Defence

In August 2005 the total strength of the armed forces was estimated at 51,000: army 40,000, air force 1,000, and national police 10,000. In addition, there were local defence forces of about 2,000. Defence expenditure for 2004 was budgeted at 25,800m. Rwanda francs (equivalent to 2.6% of total central government expenditure).

Economic Affairs

In 2004, according to estimates by the World Bank, Rwanda's gross national income (GNI), measured at average 2002–04 prices, was US $1,875m., equivalent to $220 per head (or $1,300 per head on an international purchasing-power parity basis). During 1995–2004, it was estimated, the population increased at an average annual rate of 4.4%, while gross domestic product (GDP) per head rose, in real terms, by an average of 3.1% per year. Overall GDP increased, in real terms, at an average annual rate of 7.7% in 1995–2004; growth in 2004 was 3.7%.

Agriculture (including forestry and fishing) contributed 41.3% of GDP in 2003. An estimated 87.6% of the employed labour force were engaged in the sector (mainly at subsistence level) in 2002. The principal food crops are plantains, sweet potatoes, cassava, sorghum and dry beans. The principal cash crops are coffee (which provided 27.6% of total export earnings in 2003), tea (23.6%), pyrethrum and quinquina. Goats and cattle are traditionally the principal livestock raised. Agricultural GDP increased by an average of 7.7% per year during 1995–2004, but declined by 0.6% in 2004.

Industry (including mining, manufacturing, power and construction) accounted for 21.3% of GDP in 2003, while industrial activities engaged 2.8% of the employed labour force in 2002. Industrial GDP declined at an average annual rate of 8.6% during 1995–2004; however, GDP in the industrial sector increased by 4.3% in 2004.

Mining and quarrying, it was estimated, contributed 0.6% of GDP in 2003. Cassiterite (a tin-bearing ore) is Rwanda's principal mineral resource. There are also reserves of wolframite (a tungsten-bearing ore), columbo-tantalite, gold and beryl, and work has begun on the exploitation of natural gas reserves beneath Lake Kivu, which are believed to be among the largest in the world. Mining GDP declined at an estimated average annual rate of 0.4% in 1990–2002, according to the Banque Nationale du Rwanda. Mining GDP increased by 16.6% in 2001, but declined by an estimated 5.7% in 2002.

Manufacturing accounted for 8.9% of GDP in 2003, while production activities engaged 1.3% of the employed labour force in 2002. The principal branches of manufacturing are beverages and tobacco, food products and basic consumer goods, including soap, textiles and plastic products. Manufacturing GDP declined by an average of 5.9% per year during 1995–2004; however, GDP in the manufacturing sector increased by 5.8% in 2004.

Electrical energy is derived almost entirely from hydroelectric power. In 1999 Rwanda imported 35.5% of its electricity, but subsequently benefited from the completion of the Ruzizi-II plant (a joint venture with Burundi and the Democratic Republic of the Congo). Imports of fuels and lubricants comprised 15.5% of the total value of merchandise imports in 2003.

The services sector contributed 37.4% of GDP in 2003, and engaged 8.6% of the employed labour force in 2002. The GDP of the services sector increased at an average annual rate of 7.3% during 1995–2004; growth in the services sector was 8.6% in 2004.

In 2004 Rwanda recorded a visible trade deficit of US $160.0m., and there was a deficit of $6.2m. on the current account of the balance of payments. In 2003 the principal source of imports (28.4%) was Kenya; other major suppliers were Belgium, Uganda, the United Arab Emirates and Tanzania. In the same year the principal market for exports was also Kenya (40.9%); other significant purchasers were Uganda, Tanzania and the United Kingdom. The principal exports in 2004 were coffee, tea, crude materials, and metalliferous ores (particularly ores and concentrates of tin, molybdenum, niobium and titanium). The main imports in that year were machinery and transport equipment, manufactured goods, mineral fuels (particularly petroleum products) and chemicals.

An overall budgetary deficit of 30,660m. Rwanda francs (equivalent to 3.2% of GDP) was recorded in 2003. At the end of 2003 Rwanda's external debt totalled US $1,540m., of which $1,418m. was long-term public debt. The cost of debt-servicing in that year was equivalent to 14.4% of the value of exports of goods and services. In 1992–2004 the average annual rate of inflation was 11.4%. Consumer prices increased by 7.2% in 2003 and 12.0% in 2004.

Rwanda is a member of the Organization for the Management and Development of the Kagera River Basin (see p. 387), and, with Burundi and the Democratic Republic of the Congo, is a founding member of the Economic Community of the Great Lakes Countries (see p. 385) and of the Common Market for Eastern and Southern Africa (see p. 191). The country is also a member of the International Coffee Organization (see p. 382).

Rwanda has traditionally relied heavily on foreign aid, owing to an economic development impeded by ethnic and political unrest. The genocide of early 1994 (see Recent History) resulted in the destruction of the country's economic base and of prospects of attracting private and external investment. With assistance from the international financial community, the new Government, which was established in July, initiated measures to resettle more than 2m. displaced civilians and to reconstruct the economy. In 1998 a three-year Enhanced Structural Adjustment Facility was approved by the IMF. By the end of 1999 Rwanda had made considerable progress in rehabilitating and stabilizing the economy; government revenue (negligible in 1994) had recovered, and a reduced rate of inflation had been sustained, while an extensive privatization programme had been initiated with the support of the World Bank. In late 2000, following a meeting with international financial donor institutions, Rwanda qualified for debt relief, under the initiative of the IMF and World Bank for heavily indebted poor countries (HIPCs). In October 2001 the IMF approved credit to Rwanda, under a Poverty Reduction and Growth Facility (PRGF). In August 2002 the IMF approved a further three-year credit arrangement under the PRGF, and extended additional assistance to enable the Government to meet its debt-servicing obligations. Economic growth in 2003 was at its lowest level since 1994 (following strong recovery in previous years), owing mainly to poor rainfall and lower agricultural production, which also created additional inflationary pressures. In November the IMF suspended the PRGF arrangement, after the Government failed to meet its principal fiscal targets. Following some improvement in performance criteria, in June 2004 the IMF renewed the PRGF arrangement and granted a further disbursement under the enhanced HIPC initiative. Despite a severe electricity shortage and poor agricultural production, growth recovered significantly in 2004, supported by the construction, transport and communication sectors. However, inflation increased further, with a rise in food and energy prices. In that year the Government developed an emergency action plan to reform the energy sector, which was to be partially financed by the World Bank, and approved a new policy at the end of that year. The Government also announced a number of measures to benefit the coffee and tea sectors, as part of its export strategy. International donor contributions continued to account for about one-half of the national budget. In April 2005 Rwanda reached the completion point of the enhanced HIPC initiative, enabling the Government to save some US $48m. each year in debt-servicing for the subsequent 10 years. Higher growth in 2005 was generated by an rise in the international price of coffee and expansion in the construction industry; the budget for the following fiscal year projected a substantial increase in expenditure. Following a series of investment reforms, which was initiated in 2002, the Government continued progress in privatization of state enterprises, with the divestment of one of the country's largest telecommunications companies in mid-2005. New territorial reform legislation facilitating the private acquisition of land, which entered into effect at the beginning of 2006, was expected further to encourage essential investment in the agriculture, infrastructure and mining sectors.

Education

Primary education, beginning at seven years of age and lasting for six years is officially compulsory. Secondary education, which is not compulsory, begins at the age of 14 and lasts for a further six years. In 2003, however, the Government announced plans to introduce a nine-year system of basic education, including three years of attendance at lower secondary schools. Schools are administered by the state and by Christian missions. In 2003/04 93.0% of children in the relevant age-group (males 91.5%, females 94.5%) were enrolled in primary schools, according to official estimates, while secondary enrolment was equivalent in 1999/2000 to only 12.1% of children in the appropriate age-group (males 12.4%, females 11.8%). Secondary enrolment was equivalent to 13.9% of children in that age-group in 2002. The Ministry of Education established 94 new secondary schools in 2003, and a further 58 in 2005. Rwanda has a university, with campuses at Butare and Ruhengeri, while some students attend universities abroad, particularly in Belgium, France or Germany. In 2003 the number of students at the six public higher education institutions was 12,211, with a further 8,182 attending about seven private higher institutions. Estimated total expenditure by the central Government in 2003/04 represented 23.0% of total public expenditure.

Public Holidays

2006: 1 January (New Year), 28 January (Democracy Day), 7 April (National Mourning Day), 17 April (Easter Monday), 1 May (Labour Day), 25 May (Ascension Day), 1 July (Independence Day), 1 August (Harvest Festival), 15 August (Assumption), 8 September (Culture Day), 25 September (Kamarampaka Day, anniversary of 1961 referendum), 1 October (Armed Forces Day), 1 November (All Saints' Day), 25 December (Christmas).

2007: 1 January (New Year), 28 January (Democracy Day), 7 April (National Mourning Day), 9 April (Easter Monday), 1 May (Labour Day), 17 May (Ascension Day), 1 July (Independence Day), 1 August (Harvest Festival), 15 August (Assumption), 8 September (Culture Day), 25 September (Kamarampaka Day, anniversary of 1961 referendum), 1 October (Armed Forces Day), 1 November (All Saints' Day), 25 December (Christmas).

Weights and Measures

The metric system is in force.

RWANDA

Statistical Survey

Source (unless otherwise stated): Office rwandais d'information, BP 83, Kigali; tel. 75724.

Area and Population

AREA, POPULATION AND DENSITY

Area (sq km)	26,338*
Population (census results)	
15 August 1991	7,142,755
16 August 2002†	
Males	3,879,448
Females	4,249,105
Total	8,128,553
Population (UN estimate at mid-year)‡	
2003	8,882,000
2004	9,038,000
Density (per sq km) at mid-2004	343.2

* 10,169 sq miles.
† Provisional results.
‡ Source: UN, *World Population Prospects: The 2004 Revision*.

PREFECTURES
(1991 census)

	Area (sq km)	Population*	Density (per sq km)
Butare	1,830	765,910	418.5
Byumba	4,987	779,365	159.2
Cyangugu	2,226	517,550	232.5
Gikongoro	2,192	462,635	211.1
Gisenyi	2,395	728,365	304.1
Gitarama	2,241	849,285	379.0
Kibungo	4,134	647,175	156.5
Kibuye	1,320	472,525	358.0
Kigali	3,251	921,050	355.2
Kigali-Ville		233,640	
Ruhengeri	1,762	765,255	434.3
Total	26,338	7,142,755	271.2

* Source: UN, *Demographic Yearbook*.

PRINCIPAL TOWNS
(population at 1978 census)

Kigali (capital)	117,749	Ruhengeri	16,025
Butare	21,691	Gisenyi	12,436

Mid-2003 (UN estimate, incl. suburbs): Kigali 656,153 (Source: UN, *World Urbanization Prospects: The 2003 Revision*).

BIRTHS AND DEATHS
(UN estimates, annual averages)

	1990–95	1995–2000	2000–05
Birth rate (per 1,000)	43.7	41.4	41.0
Death rate (per 1,000)	41.9	23.4	18.3

Source: UN, *World Population Prospects: The 2004 Revision*.

Expectation of life (WHO estimates, years at birth): 45 (males 43; females 46) in 2003 (Source: WHO, *World Health Report*).

ECONOMICALLY ACTIVE POPULATION
(persons aged 14 years and over, at census of August 2002)

	Males	Females	Total
Agriculture	1,218,181	1,731,411	2,949,592
Fishing	3,374	94	3,468
Industrial activities	3,692	1,636	5,328
Production activities	32,994	10,649	43,643
Electricity and water	2,390	277	2,667
Construction	41,641	1,244	42,885
Trade reconstruction	56,869	32,830	89,699
Restaurants and hotels	4,525	2,311	6,836
Transport and communications	29,574	1,988	31,562
Financial intermediaries	1,560	840	2,400
Administration and defence	22,479	5,585	28,064
Education	22,688	17,046	39,734
Health and social services	7,521	7,054	14,575
Activities not adequately defined	69,042	39,458	108,500
Total employed	1,516,530	1,852,423	3,368,953

Source: IMF, *Rwanda: Selected Issues and Statistical Appendix* (December 2004).

Health and Welfare

KEY INDICATORS

Total fertility rate (children per woman, 2003)	5.7
Under-5 mortality rate (per 1,000 live births, 2004)	203
HIV/AIDS (% of persons aged 15–49, 2003)	5.1
Physicians (per 1,000 head, 1993)	0.04
Hospital beds (per 1,000 head, 1990)	1.65
Health expenditure (2002): US $ per head (PPP)	48
Health expenditure (2002): % of GDP	5.5
Health expenditure (2002): public (% of total)	57.2
Access to water (% of persons, 2002)	73
Access to sanitation (% of persons, 2002)	41
Human Development Index (2003): ranking	159
Human Development Index (2003): value	0.450

For sources and definitions, see explanatory note on p. vi.

Agriculture

PRINCIPAL CROPS
('000 metric tons)

	2002	2003	2004
Maize	91.7	78.9	88.2
Sorghum	184.4	171.6	163.8
Potatoes	1,038.9	1,099.5	1,072.8
Sweet potatoes	1,292.4	868.2	908.3
Cassava (Manioc)	1,031.1	1,003.1	765.7
Taro (Coco yam)	122.8	138.8	136.4
Sugar cane*	70.0	70.0	70.0
Dry beans	246.9	239.4	198.2
Dry peas	16.0	17.7	16.8
Groundnuts (in shell)	10.4	10.3	10.8
Pumpkins, squash and gourds*	210.0	210.0	210.0
Plantains	2,784.9	2,407.8	2,469.7
Coffee (green)	19.4	13.8	20.0
Tea (made)	14.9	15.5	14.5

* FAO estimates.

Source: FAO.

RWANDA

LIVESTOCK
('000 head, year ending September)

	2002	2003	2004
Cattle	815.5	991.7	1,003.7
Pigs	207.8	211.9	326.7
Sheep	300.6	371.8	470.0
Goats	919.8	941.1	1,264.0
Rabbits	489	500*	520
Chickens	1,600*	1,800*	2,042

* FAO estimate.
Source: FAO.

LIVESTOCK PRODUCTS
(FAO estimates, '000 metric tons)

	2002	2003	2004
Beef and veal	19.8	23.6	23.0
Goat meat	3.2	3.3	4.5
Pig meat	3.9	3.9	6.0
Poultry meat	1.8	2.0	2.3
Game meat	11.0	11.0	11.0
Other meat	2.8	3.1	3.4
Cows' milk	112.0	112.5	121.4
Sheep's milk	1.6	1.8	1.9
Goats' milk	16.0	17.9	24.0
Poultry eggs	2.3	2.3	2.3
Cattle hides	2.9	3.4	3.3

Source: FAO.

Forestry

ROUNDWOOD REMOVALS
('000 cubic metres, excluding bark)

	2002	2003*	2004*
Sawlogs, veneer logs and logs for sleepers	245	245	245
Other industrial wood*	250	250	250
Fuel wood*	5,000	5,000	5,000
Total	5,495	5,495	5,495

* FAO estimates.
Source: FAO.

SAWNWOOD PRODUCTION
('000 cubic metres, including railway sleepers)

	1997	1998	1999
Coniferous (softwood)	20	21	22
Non-coniferous (hardwood)	54	55	57
Total	74	76	79

Source: FAO.
2000–04: FAO estimates as for 1999.

Fishing
(metric tons, live weight)

	2001	2002*	2003
Capture	6,828	7,000	7,400
Nile tilapia	2,650	2,750	2,800
Aquaculture	435	612	1,027
Nile tilapia	381	542	1,000
Total catch	7,263	7,612	8,427

* FAO estimates.
Source: FAO.

Mining
(metric tons, unless otherwise indicated)

	2001	2002	2003
Tin concentrates*	169	197	427
Tungsten concentrates*	142	153	57
Columbo-tantalite†	241	96	65
Gold (kilograms)*	10‡	10‡	10
Natural gas (million cubic metres)§	800	900	1,000‡

* Figures refer to the metal content of ores and concentrates.
† Figures refer to the estimated production of mineral concentrates. The metal content (estimates, metric tons) was: Niobium (Columbium) 75.8 in 2001, 43.2 in 2002, 29.0 in 2003; Tantalum 50.9 in 2001, 24.0 in 2002, 16.0 in 2003.
‡ Estimate.
§ Figures refer to gross output.
Source: US Geological Survey.

Industry

SELECTED PRODUCTS

	2001	2002	2003
Beer ('000 hectolitres)	479	539	412
Soft drinks ('000 hectolitres)	228	n.a.	n.a.
Cigarettes (million)	278	391	402
Soap (metric tons)	7,056	5,571	4,456
Cement (metric tons)	83,024	100,568	105,105
Electric energy (million kWh)	89.3	n.a.	n.a.

Source: IMF, *Rwanda: Statistical Annex* (August 2002) and IMF, *Rwanda: Selected Issues and Statistical Appendix* (December 2004).

Finance

CURRENCY AND EXCHANGE RATES

Monetary Units
100 centimes = 1 franc rwandais (Rwanda franc).

Sterling, Dollar and Euro Equivalents (30 November 2005)
£1 sterling = 956.101 Rwanda francs;
US $1 = 553.620 Rwanda francs;
€1 = 651.555 Rwanda francs;
10,000 Rwanda francs = £10.46 = $18.06 = €15.35.

Average Exchange Rate (Rwanda francs per US $)
2002 476.327
2003 537.658
2004 574.622

Note: Since September 1983 the currency has been linked to the IMF special drawing right (SDR). Until November 1990 the mid-point exchange rate was SDR 1 = 102.71 Rwanda francs. In November 1990 a new rate of SDR 1 = 171.18 Rwanda francs was established. This remained in effect until June 1992, when the rate was adjusted to SDR 1 = 201.39 Rwanda francs. The latter parity was maintained until February 1994, since when the rate has been frequently adjusted. In March 1995 the Government introduced a market-determined exchange rate system.

RWANDA

BUDGET
('000 million Rwanda francs)

Revenue*	1999	2000	2001†
Tax revenue	60.4	65.3	79.5
Taxes on income and profits	15.2	17.9	23.9
Company profits tax	7.4	10.0	14.4
Individual income tax	6.1	7.5	9.0
Domestic taxes on goods and services	33.6	35.2	41.0
Excise taxes	17.9	18.8	14.2
Turnover tax	12.9	13.8	24.2
Road fund	2.7	2.5	2.6
Taxes on international trade	11.0	11.6	14.0
Import taxes	8.4	9.3	11.1
Non-tax revenue	3.2	3.3	6.7
Total	**63.6**	**68.7**	**86.2**

Expenditure‡	1999	2000	2001†
Current expenditure	86.0	89.2	107.4
General public services	31.5	35.7	53.7
Defence	27.0	25.8	28.6
Social services	21.9	30.5	36.2
Education	17.2	24.0	29.8
Health	3.3	3.8	5.1
Economic services	2.6	2.1	4.9
Energy and public works	0.7	0.4	2.3
Interest on public debt	4.0	1.8	2.8
Adjustment	−1.1	−6.7	−18.8
Capital expenditure	40.8	42.0	50.0
Sub-total	**126.8**	**131.2**	**157.5**
Adjustment for payment arrears§	2.0	−1.2	31.7
Total	**128.8**	**130.0**	**189.2**

* Excluding grants received ('000 million Rwanda francs): 38.5 in 1999; 63.7 in 2000; 63.3† in 2001.
† Estimates.
‡ Excluding lending minus repayments ('000 million Rwanda francs): −0.4 in 1999; 0.5 in 2000; 0.6 in 2001†.
§ Minus sign indicates increase in arrears.

Source: IMF, *Rwanda: Statistical Annex* (August 2002).

2002 (estimates, '000 million Rwanda francs): *Revenue:* Tax revenue 94.6; Non-tax revenue 6.6; Total 101.2, excl. grants received (70.8). *Expenditure:* Current 123.7; Capital 56.4; Total 180.1, excl. net lending (11.5) (Source: IMF, *Rwanda: First Review Under the Three-Year Arrangement Under the Poverty Reduction and Growth Facility and Request for Waiver of Performance Criteria—Staff Report; Staff Statement; Press Release on the Executive Board Discussion; and Statement by the Executive Director for Rwanda*—June 2003).

INTERNATIONAL BANK RESERVES
(US $ million at 31 December)

	2003	2004	2005
IMF special drawing rights	29.77	30.20	25.91
Foreign exchange	184.93	284.44	379.85
Total	**214.70**	**314.64**	**405.76**

Source: IMF, *International Financial Statistics*.

MONEY SUPPLY
(million Rwanda francs at 31 December)

	2002	2003	2004
Currency outside banks	386,942	412,155	458,587
Demand deposits at deposit money banks	503,870	577,664	728,552
Total money (incl. others)	**946,253**	**1,225,559**	**1,330,658**

Source: IMF, *International Financial Statistics*.

COST OF LIVING
(Consumer Price Index for Kigali; base: 1995 = 100)

	2002	2003	2004
All items	105.3	112.8	126.3

Source: IMF, *International Financial Statistics*.

NATIONAL ACCOUNTS
('000 million Rwanda francs at current prices)

Expenditure on the Gross Domestic Product

	2001	2002	2003
Government final consumption expenditure	69.6	75.8	82.6
Private final consumption expenditure	} 696.3	781.2	868.6
Increase in stocks			
Gross fixed capital formation	127.8	146.2	173.7
Total domestic expenditure	**893.7**	**1,003.2**	**1,124.9**
Exports of goods and services	63.9	60.9	61.1
Less Imports of goods and services	190.8	225.6	235.9
GDP in purchasers' values	**766.3**	**838.5**	**950.1**
GDP at constant 1995 prices	**580.2**	**635.6**	**650.8**

Source: IMF, *International Financial Statistics*.

Gross Domestic Product by Economic Activity

	2001	2002	2003
Agriculture, hunting, forestry and fishing	305.2	341.6	373.9
Mining and quarrying	14.5	9.1	5.7
Manufacturing	73.9	80.5	80.3
Electricity, gas and water	3.4	3.4	3.6
Construction	71.2	82.9	103.1
Trade, restaurants and hotels	75.2	82.0	91.7
Transport, storage and communications	55.1	60.7	61.7
Public administration	54.2	55.8	64.8
Other services	101.6	109.0	120.4
GDP at market prices	**754.3**	**825.0**	**905.3**

Source: IMF, *Rwanda: Selected Issues and Statistical Appendix* (December 2004).

BALANCE OF PAYMENTS
(US $ million)

	2002	2003	2004
Exports of goods f.o.b.	67.2	59.2	97.9
Imports of goods f.o.b.	−233.3	−217.8	−257.9
Trade balance	**−166.1**	**−158.7**	**−160.0**
Exports of services	65.2	76.5	102.7
Imports of services	−201.5	−201.1	−235.4
Balance on goods and services	**−302.4**	**−283.3**	**−292.8**
Other income received	8.4	6.2	5.6
Other income paid	−27.2	−34.1	−32.9
Balance on goods, services and income	**−321.1**	**−311.3**	**−320.1**
Current transfers received	215.3	246.4	332.2
Current transfers paid	−20.4	−19.9	−18.3
Current balance	**−126.2**	**−84.8**	**−6.2**
Capital account (net)	65.9	41.1	60.6
Direct investment from abroad	2.6	4.7	7.7
Other investment assets	8.0	19.6	5.4
Other investment liabilities	70.4	14.4	76.1
Net errors and omissions	−41.5	17.4	−42.9
Overall balance	**−20.8**	**12.5**	**100.5**

Source: IMF, *International Financial Statistics*.

RWANDA

External Trade

PRINCIPAL COMMODITIES
(US $ million)

Imports c.i.f.	2001	2002	2003
Food and live animals	46.5	31.7	24.5
Cereals and cereal preparations	24.0	13.5	10.6
Rice	12.2	4.1	3.2
Vegetables and fruit	5.9	6.2	4.2
Sugar, sugar preparations and honey	8.6	5.9	5.0
Crude materials, inedible, except fuels	12.5	12.8	15.2
Textile fibres and their wastes	7.7	8.3	10.3
Mineral fuels, lubricants and related materials	39.7	40.7	40.6
Petroleum, petroleum products and related materials	39.5	40.6	40.5
Motor spirit, incl. aviation spirit	17.0	16.5	15.5
Gas oils	9.7	9.6	10.1
Animal and vegetable oils, fats and waxes	8.7	6.7	4.3
Chemicals and related products	23.8	33.8	30.4
Medicinal and pharmaceutical products	8.5	13.7	12.8
Basic manufactures	36.3	37.3	43.8
Iron and steel	11.3	8.9	12.9
Machinery and transport equipment	60.0	63.2	75.0
Telecommunications, sound recording and reproducing equipment	19.2	7.2	10.9
Electric machinery, apparatus and appliances, and parts	8.3	8.6	10.2
Road vehicles	18.4	24.8	31.2
Miscellaneous manufactured articles	46.2	22.4	25.7
Total (incl. others)	276.1	251.2	261.2

Exports f.o.b.	2001	2002	2003
Food and live animals	31.6	25.9	26.2
Coffee	15.0	14.0	13.9
Tea	16.6	11.8	11.9
Crude materials, inedible, except fuels	22.7	18.8	15.4
Metalliferous ores and metal scrap	20.9	16.3	11.7
Tin ores and concentrates	2.2	1.4	5.1
Ores and concentrates of other non-ferrous base metals	18.7	14.9	6.0
Ores of molybdenum, niobium, titanium	9.5	14.5	5.6
Total (incl. others)	55.5	46.0	50.4

Source: UN, *International Trade Statistics Yearbook*.

PRINCIPAL TRADING PARTNERS
(US $ million)

Imports	2001	2002	2003
Belgium	55.3	32.9	31.9
Canada	2.4	2.9	4.1
China	6.3	5.0	5.0
Denmark	1.9	5.8	2.8
France (incl. Monaco)	6.1	6.4	7.4
Germany	6.6	7.2	11.2
India	6.4	6.8	9.0
Israel	4.8	2.9	2.0
Italy	7.5	3.1	3.0
Japan	7.2	6.4	8.4
Kenya	61.9	66.7	74.1
Netherlands	7.4	5.7	4.5
Singapore	1.6	0.8	0.6

Imports—continued	2001	2002	2003
South Africa	12.5	11.0	12.9
Switzerland-Liechtenstein	1.3	1.3	1.5
Tanzania	9.6	13.2	14.7
Uganda	8.1	11.1	20.0
UAE	19.5	22.0	19.9
United Kingdom	8.0	6.5	4.3
USA	10.4	6.1	2.0
Viet Nam	4.8	0.9	0.2
Zambia	3.4	2.2	0.5
Total (incl. others)	276.1	251.2	261.2

Exports	2001	2002	2003
Belgium	2.1	2.3	0.8
Germany	2.4	0.3	0.2
Hong Kong	1.3	4.6	0.3
Kenya	24.0	18.1	20.6
Netherlands	1.2	6.5	0.0
Pakistan	0.2	1.3	0.6
Russia	1.4	0.0	0.0
South Africa	6.2	0.3	0.5
Switzerland-Liechtenstein	4.2	7.1	0.8
Tanzania	4.8	0.3	4.1
Uganda	2.5	1.0	13.4
United Kingdom	0.3	0.8	3.1
USA	3.0	1.4	0.1
Total (incl. others)	55.5	46.0	50.4

Source: UN, *International Trade Statistics Yearbook*.

Transport

ROAD TRAFFIC
(estimates, motor vehicles in use at 31 December)

	1995	1996
Passenger cars	12,000	13,000
Lorries and vans	16,000	17,100

Source: IRF, *World Road Statistics*.

CIVIL AVIATION
(traffic on scheduled services)

	1992	1993	1994
Passengers carried ('000)	9	9	9
Passenger-km (million)	2	2	2

Source: UN, *Statistical Yearbook*.

Tourism

(by country of residence)

	2000	2001*
Africa	93,058	99,928
Burundi	20,972	9,455
Congo, Democratic Republic	10,450	28,514
Kenya	2,050	2,243
Tanzania	18,320	18,697
Uganda	38,897	38,472
Americas	2,250	2,785
Europe	6,412	8,395
Belgium	1,866	2,057
Total (incl. others)	104,216	113,185

*January–November.

Tourism receipts (US $ million, excl. passenger transport): 23 in 2000; 25 in 2001; 31 in 2002.

Source: World Tourism Organization.

RWANDA

Communications Media

	2002	2003	2004
Telephones ('000 main lines in use)	23.2	n.a.	n.a.
Mobile cellular telephones ('000 subscribers)	110.8	134.0	150.0
Internet users ('000)	25	n.a.	38

Radio receivers ('000 in use): 601 in 1997.
Facsimile machines (number in use): 900 in 1998.
Daily newspapers: 1 in 1996.

Sources: International Telecommunication Union; UN, *Statistical Yearbook*; UNESCO, *Statistical Yearbook*.

Education

(1998)

	Teachers	Students Males	Females	Total
Primary	23,730	644,835	643,834	1,288,669
Secondary: general	} 3,413 {	39,088	38,337	77,425
technical and vocational		6,859	6,935	13,794
Tertiary	412	n.a.	n.a.	5,678

Source: mainly UNESCO Institute for Statistics.

Adult literacy rate (UNESCO estimates): 64.0% (males 70.5%; females 58.8%) in 2003 (Source: UN Development Programme, *Human Development Report*).

Directory

The Constitution

A new Constitution was approved at a national referendum on 26 May 2003 and entered into effect on 4 June. The main provisions are summarized below:

PREAMBLE

The state of Rwanda is an independent sovereign Republic. Fundamental principles are: the struggle against the ideology of genocide and all its manifestations; the eradication of all ethnic and regional divisions; the promotion of national unity; and the equal sharing of power. Human rights and personal liberties are protected. All forms of discrimination are prohibited and punishable by law. The state recognizes a multi-party political system. Political associations are established in accordance with legal requirements, and may operate freely, providing that they comply with democratic and constitutional principles, without harm to national unity, territorial integrity and state security. The formation of political associations on the basis of race, ethnicity, tribal or regional affiliation, sex, religion or any other grounds for discrimination is prohibited.

LEGISLATURE

Legislative power is vested in a bicameral Parliament, comprising a Chamber of Deputies and a Senate. The Chamber of Deputies has 80 deputies, who are elected for a five-year term. In addition to 53 directly elected deputies, 27 seats are allocated, respectively, to two youth representatives, one disabilities representative, and 24 female representatives, who are indirectly elected. The Senate comprises 26 members, of whom 12 are elected by local government councils in the 12 provinces, and two by academic institutions, while the remaining 12 are nominated (eight by the President and four by a regulatory body, the Parties' Forum). Members of the Senate serve for eight years.

PRESIDENT

The President of the Republic is the Head of State, protector of the Constitution, and guarantor of national unity. He is the Commander-in-Chief of the armed forces. Presidential candidates are required to be of Rwandan nationality and aged a minimum of 35 years. The President is elected by universal suffrage for a seven-year term, and is restricted to two mandates. He signs into law presidential decrees in consultation with the Council of Ministers.

GOVERNMENT

The President nominates the Prime Minister, who heads the Council of Ministers. Ministers are proposed by the Prime Minister and appointed by the President.

JUDICIARY

The judiciary is independent and separate from the legislative and executive organs of government. The judicial system is composed of the Supreme Court, the High Court of the Republic, and provincial, district and municipal Tribunals. In addition, there are specialized judicial organs, comprising *gacaca* and military courts. The *gacaca* courts try cases of genocide or other crimes against humanity committed between 1 October 1990 and 31 December 1994. Military courts (the Military Tribunal and the High Military Court) have jurisdiction in military cases. The President and Vice-President of the Supreme Court and the Prosecutor-General are elected by the Senate two months after its installation.

The Government

HEAD OF STATE

President: Maj.-Gen. PAUL KAGAME (took office 22 April 2000; re-elected 25 August 2003).

COUNCIL OF MINISTERS
(April 2006)

Prime Minister: BERNARD MAKUZA.
Minister of Defence: Gen. MARCEL GATSINZI.
Minister of Local Government, Rural Development and Social Affairs: PROTAIS MUSONI.
Minister of Internal Affairs: MUSSA SHEIKH HERERIMANA.
Minister of Foreign Affairs and Co-operation: Dr CHARLES MURIGANDE.
Minister of Finance and Economic Planning: JAMES MUSONI.
Minister of Agriculture and Livestock: ANASTASE MUREKEZI.
Minister of Education, Science, Technology and Research: JEANNE D'ARC MUJAWAMARIYA.
Minister of Infrastructure: STANISLAS KAMANZI.
Minister of Commerce, Industry, Investment Promotion, Tourism and Co-operatives: PROTAIS MITALI.
Minister of Lands, Environment, Forestry, Water and Mines: CHRISTOPHE BAZIVAMO.
Minister of Justice: EDDA MUKABAGWIZA.
Minister of Public Service, Skills Development and Labour: MANASSEH NSHUTI.
Minister of Health: Dr JEAN-DAMASCÈNE NTAWUKURIRYAYO.
Minister of Gender and the Promotion of Women: VALÉRIE NYIRAHABINEZA.
Minister of Youth, Sports and Culture: JOSEPH HABINEZA.
Minister in the Office of the President: SOLINA NYIRAHABIMANA.
Minister in the Office of the President, in charge of Science, Information Technology and Research: ROMAIN MURENZI.
Minister in the Office of the Prime Minister, in charge of Information: Prof. LAURENT NKUSI.
Minister of State for Rural Development and Social Affairs: CHRISTINE NYATANYI.
Minister of State for Skills Development and Labour: ANGELINA MUGANZA.
Minister of State for Primary and Secondary Education: JOSEPH MUREKERAHO.
Minister of State for Lands and the Environment: PATRICIA HAJABAKIGA.
Minister of State for Water and Natural Resources: Prof. BIKORO MUNYANGANIZI.

RWANDA

Minister of State for Economic Planning: MONIQUE NSANZABAGANWA.
Minister of State for HIV/AIDS and Other Infectious Diseases: Dr INNOCENT NYARUHIRIRA.
Minister of State for Energy and Communications: ALBERT BUTARE.
Minister of State for Agriculture: DAPHROSE GAHAKWA.
Minister of State for Regional Co-operation: ROSEMARY MUSEMINARI.
Minister of State for Industry and Industrial Promotion: VINCENT KAREGA.

MINISTRIES

Office of the President: BP 15, Kigali; tel. 59062000; fax 572431; e-mail info@presidency.gov.rw; internet www.presidency.gov.rw.

Office of the Prime Minister: Kigali; tel. 585444; fax 583714; e-mail primature@gov.rw; internet www.primature.gov.rw.

Ministry of Agriculture and Livestock: BP 621, Kigali; tel. 585008; fax 585057; internet www.minagri.gov.rw.

Ministry of Commerce, Industry, Investment Promotion, Tourism and Co-operatives: BP 2378, Kigali; tel. 574725; tel. 574734; fax 575465; internet www.minicom.gov.rw.

Ministry of Defence: Kigali; tel. 577942; fax 576969; internet www.minadef.gov.rw.

Ministry of Education, Science, Technology and Research: BP 622, Kigali; tel. 583051; fax 582161; e-mail info@mineduc.gov.rw; internet www.mineduc.gov.rw.

Ministry of Finance and Economic Planning: BP 158, Kigali; tel. 575756; fax 577581; e-mail mfin@rwanda1.com; internet www.minecofin.gov.rw.

Ministry of Foreign Affairs and Co-operation: blvd de la Révolution, BP 179, Kigali; tel. 574522; fax 572904; internet www.minaffet.gov.rw.

Ministry of Gender and the Promotion of Women: Kigali; tel. 577626; fax 577543.

Ministry of Health: BP 84, Kigali; tel. 577458; fax 576853; e-mail info@moh.gov.rw; internet www.moh.gov.rw.

Ministry of Infrastructure: tel. 585503; fax 585755; e-mail webmaster@mininfra.gov.rw; internet www.mininfra.gov.rw.

Ministry of Internal Affairs: BP 446, Kigali; tel. 86708.

Ministry of Justice: BP 160, Kigali; tel. 586561; fax 586509; e-mail mjust@minijust.gov.rw; internet www.minijust.gov.rw.

Ministry of Lands, Environment, Forestry, Water and Mines: Kigali; tel. 582628; fax 582629; internet www.minitere.gov.rw.

Ministry of Local Government, Rural Development and Social Affairs: BP 790, Kigali; tel. 585406; fax 582228; e-mail webmaster@minaloc.gov.rw; internet www.minaloc.gov.rw.

Ministry of Public Service, Skills Development and Labour: BP 403, Kigali; tel. 585714; fax 583621; e-mail mifotra@mifotra.gov.rw; internet www.mifotra.gov.rw.

Ministry of Youth, Sports and Culture: BP 1044, Kigali; tel. 583527; fax 583518.

President and Legislature

PRESIDENT

Presidential Election, 25 August 2003

Candidate	Votes	% of votes
Paul Kagame	3,544,777	95.05
Faustin Twagiramungu	134,865	3.62
Jean-Népomuscène Nayinzira	49,634	1.33
Total*	3,729,274	100.00

*Excluding 49,634 invalid votes.

CHAMBER OF DEPUTIES

Speaker: ALFRED MUKEZAMFURA.

General Election, 29 September–3 October 2003

Party	Votes	% of votes	Seats
Front patriotique rwandais*	2,774,661	73.78	40
Parti social-démocrate	463,067	12.31	7
Parti libéral	396,978	10.56	6
Others	125,896	3.35	—
Total	3,760,602	100.00	80†

* Contested the elections in alliance with the Parti démocrate centriste, Parti démocratique idéal, Union démocratique du peuple rwandais and Parti socialiste rwandais.
† In addition to the 53 directly elected deputies, 27 seats are allocated, respectively, to two youth representatives, one disabilities representative, and 24 female representatives, who are indirectly elected.

SENATE

Speaker: Dr VINCENT BIRUTA.

The Senate comprises 26 members, of whom 12 are elected by local government councils in the 12 provinces, and two by academic institutions, while the remaining 12 are nominated (eight by the President and four by a regulatory body, the Parties' Forum).

Election Commission

Commission électorale nationale du Rwanda: BP 6449, Kigali; tel. 501136; fax 501045; e-mail comelena@rwanda1.com; internet www.comelena.gov.rw; f. 2000; independent; Chair. Prof. CHRYSOLOGUE KARANGWA.

Political Organizations

Under legislation adopted in June 2003, the formation of any political organization based on ethnic groups, religion or sex was prohibited.

Front patriotique rwandais (FPR): f. 1990; also known as Inkotanyi; comprises mainly Tutsi exiles, but claims multi-ethnic support; commenced armed invasion of Rwanda from Uganda in Oct. 1990; took control of Rwanda in July 1994; Chair. Maj.-Gen. PAUL KAGAME; Vice-Chair. CHRISTOPHE BAZIVAMO; Sec.-Gen. CHARLES MURIGANDE.

Parti démocrate centriste (PDC): BP 2348, Kigali; tel. 576542; fax 572237; f. 1990; fmrly Parti démocrate chrétien; Leader ALFRED MUKEZAMFURA.

Parti démocratique idéal (PDI): Kigali; f. 1991; fmrly Parti démocratique islamique; Leader ANDRÉ BUMAYA HABIB.

Parti démocratique rwandais (Pader): Kigali; f. 1992; Sec. JEAN NTAGUNGIRA.

Parti libéral (PL): BP 1304, Kigali; tel. 577916; fax 577838; f. 1991; restructured 2003; Chair. PROSPER HIGORO; Sec.-Gen. Dr ODETTE NYIRAMIRIMO.

Parti du progrès et de la concorde (PPC): f. 2003; Hutu; incl. fmr mems of Mouvement démocratique républicain; Leader Dr CHRISTIAN MARARA.

Parti progressiste de la jeunesse rwandaise (PPJR): Kigali; f. 1991; Leader ANDRÉ HAKIZIMANA.

Parti républicain rwandais (Parerwa): Kigali; f. 1992; Leader AUGUSTIN MUTAMBA.

Parti social-démocrate (PSD): Kigali; f. 1991 by a breakaway faction of fmr Mouvement révolutionnaire national pour le développement; Leader Dr VINCENT BIRUTA.

Parti socialiste rwandais (PSR): BP 827, Kigali; tel. 576658; fax 83975; f. 1991; workers' rights; Leader Dr MEDARD RUTIJANWA.

Rassemblement travailliste pour la démocratie (RTD): BP 1894, Kigali; tel. 575622; fax 576574; f. 1991; Leader EMMANUEL NIZEYIMANA.

Union démocratique du peuple rwandais (UDPR): Kigali; f. 1992; Leader ADRIEN RANGIRA.

Other political organizations have been formed by exiled Rwandans and operate principally from abroad; these include:

Rassemblement pour le retour des réfugiés et la démocratie au Rwanda (RDR): Mandenmakerstraat 14, 3841 Harderwijk, Netherlands; fax (32) 10455111; e-mail info@rdrwanda.org; internet www.rdrwanda.org; f. 1995 by fmr supporters of Pres. Habyarimana; prin. org. representing Hutu refugees; Chair. VICTOIRE UMUHOZA INGABIRE.

RWANDA

Union du peuple rwandais (UPR): Brussels, Belgium; f. 1990; Hutu-led; Pres. SILAS MAJYAMBERE; Sec.-Gen. EMMANUEL TWAGILIMANA.

Diplomatic Representation

EMBASSIES IN RWANDA

Belgium: rue Nyarugenge, BP 81, Kigali; tel. 575554; fax 573995; e-mail kigali@diplobel.be; Ambassador MARC GEDOPT.
Burundi: rue de Ntaruka, BP 714, Kigali; tel. 575010; Chargé d'affaires a.i. CHARLES NSABIMANA.
Canada: rue Akagera, BP 1177, Kigali; tel. 573210; fax 572719; Ambassador BERNARD DUSSAULT.
Egypt: BP 1069, Kigali; tel. 82686; fax 82686; Ambassador SAMEH SAMY DARWISH.
France: rue du Député Kamunzinzi, BP 53, Kigali; tel. 591800; fax 591806; Ambassador DOMINIQUE DECHERF.
Germany: 8 rue de Bugarama, BP 355, Kigali; tel. 575222; fax 577267; Ambassador Dr HÜBERT ZIEGLER.
Holy See: 49 ave Paul VI, BP 261, Kigali (Apostolic Nunciature); tel. 575293; fax 575181; e-mail nuntrw@rwandatel1.rwanda1.com; Apostolic Nuncio Most Rev. ANSELMO GUIDO PECORARI (Titular Archbishop of Populonia).
Kenya: BP 1215, Kigali; tel. 82774; Ambassador PETER KIHARA G. MATHANJUKI.
Korea, Democratic People's Republic: Kigali; Ambassador KIM PONG GI.
Libya: BP 1152, Kigali; tel. 576470; Secretary of the People's Bureau MOUSTAPHA MASAND EL-GHAILUSHI.
Russia: 19 ave de l'Armée, BP 40, Kigali; tel. 575286; fax 574818; e-mail ambruss@rwandatel1.rwanda1.com; Ambassador ALEKSEI DULYYAN.
South Africa: 1370 blvd de l'Umuganda, POB 6563, Kacyiru-Sud, Kigali; tel. 583185; fax 511760; e-mail saemkgl@rwanda1.com; internet www.saembassy-kigali.org.rw; Ambassador Dr A. M. MBERE.
United Kingdom: Parcelle 1131, Blvd de l'Umuganda, Kacyiru, BP 576, Kigali; tel. 584098; fax 582044; e-mail embassy.kigali@fco.gov.uk; internet www.britishembassykigali.org.rw; Ambassador JEREMY MACADIE.
USA: blvd de la Révolution, BP 28, Kigali; tel. 505601; fax 572128; e-mail amembkigali@hotmail.com; internet usembkigali.net; Ambassador MICHAEL RAY ARIETTI.

Judicial System

The judicial system is composed of the Supreme Court, the High Court of the Republic, and provincial, district and municipal Tribunals. In addition, there are specialized judicial organs, comprising *gacaca* and military courts. The *gacaca* courts were established to try cases of genocide or other crimes against humanity committed between 1 October 1990 and 31 December 1994. Trials for categories of lesser genocide crimes were to be conducted by councils in the communities in which they were committed, with the aim of alleviating pressure on the existing judicial system. Trials under the *gacaca* court system formally commenced on 25 November 2002. Military courts (the Military Tribunal and the High Military Court) have jurisdiction in military cases. The President and Vice-President of the Supreme Court and the Prosecutor-General are elected by the Senate.

Supreme Court

Kigali; tel. 87407.
The Supreme Court comprises five sections: the Department of Courts and Tribunals; the Court of Appeals; the Constitutional Court; the Council of State; and the Revenue Court.
President of the Supreme Court: ALOYSIA CYANZAYIRE.
Vice-President: Prof. SAM RUGEGE.
Prosecutor-General: JEAN DE DIEU MUCYO.

Religion

AFRICAN RELIGIONS
About one-half of the population hold traditional beliefs.

CHRISTIANITY
Union des Eglises Rwandaises: BP 79, Kigali; tel. 85825; fax 83554; f. 1963; fmrly Conseil Protestant du Rwanda.

The Roman Catholic Church
Rwanda comprises one archdiocese and eight dioceses. At 31 December 2003 the estimated number of adherents represented about 48.0% of the total population.

Bishops' Conference
Conférence Episcopale du Rwanda, BP 357, Kigali; tel. 575439; fax 578080; e-mail cerwanda@rwanda1.com.
f. 1980; Pres. Rt Rev. ALEXIS HABIYAMBERE (Bishop of Nyundo).
Archbishop of Kigali: Most Rev. THADDÉE NTIHINYURWA, Archevêché, BP 715, Kigali; tel. 575769; fax 572274; e-mail kigarchi@yahoo.fr.

The Anglican Communion
The Church of the Province of Rwanda, established in 1992, has nine dioceses.
Archbishop of the Province and Bishop of Kigali: Most Rev. EMMANUEL MUSABA KOLINI, BP 61, Kigali; tel. and fax 573213; e-mail sonja914@compuserve.com.
Provincial Secretary: Rt Rev. JOSIAS SENDEGEYA (Bishop of Kigali), BP 2487, Kigali; tel. and fax 514160; e-mail peer@rwandatel1.rwanda1.

Other Protestant Churches
Eglise Baptiste: Nyantanga, BP 59, Butare; Pres. Rev. DAVID BAZIGA; Gen. Sec. ELEAZAR ZIHERAMBERE.
There are about 250,000 other Protestants, including a substantial minority of Seventh-day Adventists.

BAHÁ'Í FAITH
National Spiritual Assembly: BP 652, Kigali; tel. 575982.

ISLAM
There is a small Islamic community.

The Press

Bulletin Agricole du Rwanda: OCIR—Café, BP 104, Kigali-Gikondo; f. 1968; quarterly; French; Pres. of Editorial Bd Dr AUGUSTIN NZINDUKIYIMANA; circ. 800.
L'Ere de Liberté: BP 1755, Kigali; fortnightly.
Etudes Rwandaises: Université Nationale du Rwanda, Rectorat, BP 56, Butare; tel. 30302; f. 1977; quarterly; pure and applied science, literature, human sciences; French; Pres. of Editorial Bd CHARLES NTAKIRUTINKA; circ. 1,000.
Hobe: BP 761, Kigali; f. 1955; monthly; children's interest; circ. 95,000.
Inkingi: BP 969, Kigali; tel. 577626; fax 577543; monthly.
Inkoramutima: Union des Eglises Rwandaises, BP 79, Kigali; tel. 85825; fax 83554; quarterly; religious; circ. 5,000.
Kinyamateka: 5 blvd de l'OUA, BP 761, Kigali; tel. 576164; f. 1933; fortnightly; economics; circ. 11,000.
La Lettre du Cladho: BP 3060, Kigali; tel. 74292; monthly.
The New Times: BP 635, Kigali; tel. 573409; fax 574166; monthly.
Nouvelles du Rwanda: Université Nationale du Rwanda, BP 117, Butare; every 2 months.
Nyabarongo—Le Canard Déchaîné: BP 1585, Kigali; tel. 576674; monthly.
Le Partisan: BP 1805, Kigali; tel. 573923; fortnightly.
La Patrie—Urwatubyaye: BP 3125, Kigali; tel. 572552; monthly.
La Relève: Office Rwandais d'Information, BP 83, Kigali; tel. 75665; f. 1976; monthly; politics, economics, culture; French; Dir CHRISTOPHE MFIZI; circ. 1,700.
Revue Dialogue: BP 572, Kigali; tel. 574178; f. 1967; bi-monthly; Christian issues; Belgian-owned; circ. 2,500.
Revue Médicale Rwandaise: Ministry of Health, BP 84, Kigali; tel. 576681; f. 1968; quarterly; French.
Revue Pédagogique: Ministry of Education, Science, Technology and Research, BP 622, Kigali; tel. 85697; quarterly; French.
Rwanda Herald: Kigali; f. Oct. 2000; owned by Rwanda Independent Media Group.
Rwanda Libération: BP 398, Kigali; tel. 577710; monthly; Dir and Editor-in-Chief ANTOINE KAPITENI.

RWANDA

Rwanda Renaître: BP 426, Butare; fortnightly.

Rwanda Rushya: BP 83, Kigali; tel. 572276; fortnightly.

Le Tribun du Peuple: BP 1960, Kigali; tel. 82035; bi-monthly; Owner JEAN-PIERRE MUGABE.

Ukuli Gacaca: BP 3170, Kigali; tel. 573327; monthly; Dir CHARLES GAKUMBA.

Umucunguzi: Gisenyi; f. 1998; organ of Palir; Kinyarwanda and French; Chief Editor EMILE NKUMBUYE.

Umuhinzi-Mworozi: OCIR—Thé, BP 1334, Kigali; tel. 514797; fax 514796; f. 1975; monthly; circ. 1,500.

Umusemburo—Le Levain: BP 117, Butare; monthly.

Umuseso: Kigali; independent Kinyarwanda language weekly newspaper; Editor CHARLES KABONERO.

Urunana: Grand Séminaire de Nyakibanda, BP 85, Butare; tel. 530793; e-mail wellamahoro@yahoo.fr; f. 1967; 3 a year; religious; Pres. WELLAS UWAMAHORO; Editor-in-Chief DAMIEN NIYOYIREMERA.

NEWS AGENCIES

Agence Rwandaise de Presse (ARP): 27 ave du Commerce, BP 83, Kigali; tel. 576540; fax 576185; e-mail cbohizi@yahoo.fr; f. 1975.

Office Rwandais d'Information (Orinfor): BP 83, Kigali; tel. 575724; Dir JOSEPH BIDERI.

Foreign Bureau

Agence France-Presse (AFP): BP 83, Kigali; tel. 572997; Correspondent MARIE-GORETTI UWIBAMBE.

Publishers

Editions Rwandaises: Caritas Rwanda, BP 124, Kigali; tel. 5786; Man. Dir Abbé CYRIAQUE MUNYANSANGA; Editorial Dir ALBERT NAMBAJE.

Implico: BP 721, Kigali; tel. 573771.

Imprimerie de Kabgayi: BP 66, Gitarama; tel. 562252; fax 562345; f. 1932; Dir THOMAS HABIMANA.

Imprimerie de Kigali, SARL: 1 blvd de l'Umuganda, BP 956, Kigali; tel. 582032; fax 584047; e-mail impkig@rwandatel1.rwanda1.com; f. 1980; Dir ALEXIS RUKUNDO.

Imprimerie URWEGO: BP 762, Kigali; tel. 86027; Dir JEAN NSENGIYUNVA.

Pallotti-Presse: BP 863, Kigali; tel. 574084.

GOVERNMENT PUBLISHING HOUSES

Imprimerie Nationale du Rwanda: BP 351, Kigali; tel. 576214; fax 575820; f. 1967; Dir JUVÉNAL NDISANZE.

Régie de l'Imprimerie Scolaire (IMPRISCO): BP 1347, Kigali; tel. 85818; fax 85695; e-mail imprisco@rwandatel1.rwanda1.com; f. 1985; Dir JEAN DE DIEU GAKWANDI.

Broadcasting and Communications

TELECOMMUNICATIONS

Rwandatel: BP 1332, Kigali; tel. 576777; fax 573110; e-mail info@rwandatel.rw; internet www.rwandatel.rw; national telecommunications service; privatized mid-2005.

MTN Rwandacell: Telecom House, blvd de l'Umuganda, Kigali; f. 1998; provides mobile cellular telephone services; CEO FRANÇOIS DU PLESSIS.

BROADCASTING

Radio

Radio Rwanda: BP 83, Kigali; tel. 575665; fax 576185; f. 1961; state-controlled; daily broadcasts in Kinyarwanda, Swahili, French and English; Dir of Programmes DAVID KABUYE.

Deutsche Welle Relay Station Africa: Kigali; daily broadcasts in German, English, French, Hausa, Swahili, Portuguese and Amharic.

Television

Télévision rwandaise (TVR): Kigali; fax 575024; transmissions reach more than 60% of national territory.

Finance

(cap. = capital; res = reserves; dep. = deposits; m. = million; brs = branches; amounts in Rwanda francs)

BANKING

Central Bank

Banque Nationale du Rwanda: ave Paul VI, BP 531, Kigali; tel. 575249; fax 572551; e-mail info@bnr.rw; internet www.bnr.rw; f. 1964; bank of issue; cap. 2,000m., res 8,256.6m., dep. 171,952.3m. (Dec. 2002); Gov. FRANÇOIS KANIMBA.

Commercial Banks

Following the privatization of two commercial banks, government control of the banking section was reduced from 45% in 2003 to 22% in 2005, although the three largest banks continued to control two-thirds of the system's assets, valued at US $365m. (equivalent to 34% of GDP).

Banque de Commerce, de Développement et d'Industrie (BCDI): ave de la Paix, BP 3268, Kigali; tel. 574437; fax 573790; e-mail info@bcdi.co.rw; internet www.bcdi.co.rw; cap. and res 3,158.4m., total assets 45,950.9m. (Dec. 2003); Pres. and Dir-Gen. ALFRED KALISA.

Banque Commerciale du Rwanda, SA: BP 354, Kigali; tel. 575591; fax 573395; e-mail bcr@rwandatel1.rwanda1.com; internet www.bc-rwanda.com; f. 1963; privatized Sept. 20004; cap. 2,000m., res 881.2m., dep. 31,151.6m. (Dec. 2000); Pres. THACIEN MUNYANEZA; Gen. Man. JOHN MADDER; 5 brs.

Banque à la Confiance d'Or (BANCOR): ave du Commerce, BP 2509, Kigali; tel. and fax 575763; fax 575761; e-mail bancor@rwanda1.com; internet www.bancor.co.rw; f. 1995; cap. and res 2,289.0m., total assets 20,840.4m. (Dec. 2005); Pres. NICHOLAS WATSON.

Banque Continentale Africaine (Rwanda), SA (BACAR): 20 blvd de la Révolution, BP 331, Kigali; tel. 574456; fax 573486; e-mail bacar@rwandatel.rwanda.com; f. 1983; cap. 1,500m., total assets 17,354.0m. (Dec. 2000); privatized; Pres. CÉLESTIN KAYITARE; 3 brs.

Banque de Kigali, SA: 63 ave du Commerce, BP 175, Kigali; tel. 593100; fax 573461; e-mail bkig10@rwanda1.com; f. 1966; cap. 1,500.0m., res 1,553.1m., dep. 48,222.0m. (Dec. 2003); Pres. FRANÇOIS NGARAMBE; 6 brs.

Caisse Hypothécaire du Rwanda (CHR): BP 1034, Kigali; tel. 576382; fax 572799; cap. 778.2m., total assets 6,966.8m. (Dec. 2003); Pres. FRANÇOIS RUTISHASHA; Dir-Gen. PIPIEN HAKIZABERA.

Compagnie Générale de Banque: blvd de l'Umuganda, BP 5230, Kigali; tel. 503343; fax 503336; e-mail cogebank@rwanda1.com; cap. and res 1,210.8m., total assets 7,297.4m. (Dec. 2003); Pres. ANDRÉ KATABARWA.

Development Banks

Banque Rwandaise de Développement, SA (BRD): blvd de la Révolution, BP 1341, Kigali; tel. 575079; fax 573569; e-mail brd@brd.com.rw; internet www.brd.com.rw; f. 1967; 56% state-owned; cap. and res 4,104.6m., total assets 13,920.7m. (Dec. 2003); Pres. GASTON MPATSWE KAGABO.

Union des Banques Populaires du Rwanda (Banki z'Abaturage mu Rwanda): BP 1348, Kigali; tel. 573559; fax 573579; e-mail ubpr@rwandatel1.rwanda1.com; f. 1975; cap. and res 1,180.5370m., total assets 20,433.8m. (Dec. 2002); Pres. INNOCENT KAYITARE; 145 brs.

INSURANCE

Société Nationale d'Assurances du Rwanda (SONARWA): BP 1035, Kigali; tel. 573350; fax 572052; e-mail sonarwa@rwandatel1.rwanda1.com; f. 1975; cap. 500m.; Pres. FRANÇOIS NGARAMBE; Dir-Gen. HOPE MURERA.

Société Rwandaise d'Assurances, SA (SORAS): BP 924, Kigali; tel. 573716; fax 573362; e-mail sorasinfo@rwanda1.com; f. 1984; cap. 501m. (2003); Pres. CHARLES MHORANYI; Dir-Gen. MARC RUGENERA.

Trade and Industry

GOVERNMENT AGENCIES

Centre for Investment Promotion: Kigali; f. 1998.

National Tender Board: ave de la Paix, POB 4276, Kigali; tel. 501403; fax 501402; e-mail ntb@rwanda1.com; internet www.ntb.gov.rw; f. 1998 to organize and manage general public procurement.

Rwanda Revenue Authority: Kigali; f. 1998 to maximize revenue collection; Commissioner-Gen. EDWARD LARBI SIAW.

RWANDA

DEVELOPMENT ORGANIZATIONS

Coopérative de Promotion de l'Industrie Minière et Artisanale au Rwanda (COOPIMAR): BP 1139, Kigali; tel. 82127; fax 72128; Dir DANY NZARAMBA.

Institut de Recherches Scientifiques et Technologiques (IRST): BP 227, Butare; tel. 30396; fax 30939; Dir-Gen. CHRYSOLOGUE KARANGWA.

Institut des Sciences Agronomiques du Rwanda (ISAR): BP 138, Butare; tel. 30642; fax 30644; for the development of subsistence and export agriculture; Dir MUNYANGANIZI BIKORO; 12 centres.

Office des Cultures Industrielles du Rwanda—Café (OCIR—Café): BP 104, Kigali; tel. 575600; fax 573992; e-mail ocircafe@rwandatel1.rwanda1.com; f. 1978; development of coffee and other new agronomic industries; operates a coffee stabilization fund; Dir ANASTASE NZIRASANAHO.

Office des Cultures Industrielles du Rwanda—Thé (OCIR—Thé): BP 1344, Kigali; tel. 514797; fax 514796; e-mail ocirthé@rwanda1.com; development and marketing of tea; Dir CÉLESTIN KAYITARE.

Office National pour le Développement de la Commercialisation des Produits Vivriers et des Produits Animaux (OPROVIA): BP 953, Kigali; tel. 82946; fax 82945; privatization pending; Dir DISMAS SEZIBERA.

Régie d'Exploitation et de Développement des Mines (REDEMI): BP 2195, Kigali; tel. 573632; fax 573625; e-mail ruzredem@yahoo.fr; f. 1988 as Régie des Mines du Rwanda; privatized in 2000; state org. for mining tin, columbo-tantalite and wolfram; Man. Dir JEAN-RUZINDANA MUNANA.

Société de Pyrèthre au Rwanda (SOPYRWA): BP 79, Ruhengeri; tel. and fax 546364; e-mail sopyrwa@rwanda1.com; f. 1978; cultivation and processing of pyrethrum; post-war activities resumed in Oct. 1994; current production estimated at 80% pre-war capacity; Dir SYLVAIN NZABAGAMBA.

CHAMBER OF COMMERCE

Chambre de Commerce et d'Industrie de Rwanda: rue de l'Umuganda, POB 319, Kigali; tel. 83534; fax 83532; Pres. T. RUJUGIRO.

INDUSTRIAL ASSOCIATIONS

Association des Industriels du Rwanda: BP 39, Kigali; tel. and fax 575430; Pres. YVES LAFAGE; Exec. Sec. MUGUNGA NDOBA.

Federation of the Rwandan Private Sector Associations: POB 319, Kigali; tel. 83538; fax 83532; e-mail frsp@rwanda1.com; f. 1999 to represent interests of private sector; Exec. Sec. EUGÈNE BITWAYIKI.

UTILITIES

Electrogaz: POB 537, Kigali; tel. 572392; fax 573802; state-owned water, electricity and gas supplier; Dir JOSEPH MUJENGA.

TRADE UNIONS

Centrale d'Education et de Coopération des Travailleurs pour le Développement/Alliance Coopérative au Rwanda (CECOTRAD/ACORWA): BP 295, Kigali; f. 1984; Pres. ELIE KATABARWA.

Centrale Syndicale des Travailleurs du Rwanda: BP 1645, Kigali; tel. 85658; fax 84012; e-mail cestrav@rwandatel1.rwanda1.com; Sec.-Gen. FRANÇOIS MURANGIRA.

Transport

RAILWAYS

There are no railways in Rwanda, although plans exist for the eventual construction of a line passing through Uganda, Rwanda and Burundi, to connect with the Kigoma–Dar es Salaam line in Tanzania. Rwanda has access by road to the Tanzanian railways system.

ROADS

In 1999 there were an estimated 12,000 km of roads, of which 996 km were paved. There are road links with Uganda, Tanzania, Burundi and the Democratic Republic of the Congo. Internal conflict during 1994 caused considerable damage to the road system and the destruction of several important bridges. In 1997 Rwanda received a US $45m. loan to be used for road improvement.

Office National des Transports en Commun (ONATRACOM): BP 609, Kigali; tel. 575564; Dir (vacant).

INLAND WATERWAYS

There are services on Lake Kivu between Cyangugu, Gisenyi and Kibuye, including two vessels operated by ONATRACOM.

CIVIL AVIATION

The Kanombe international airport at Kigali can process up to 500,000 passengers annually. There is a second international airport at Kamembe, near the border with the Democratic Republic of the Congo. There are airfields at Butare, Gabiro, Ruhengeri and Gisenyi, servicing internal flights.

Alliance Express Rwanda (ALEX): BP 1440, Kigali; tel. 82409; fax 82417; e-mail aev@aev.com.rw; fax 572562; f. 1998 to succeed fmr Air Rwanda as national carrier; 51% owned by Alliance Air (jtly owned by Govts of Uganda and South Africa and by South African Airways), 49% state-owned; domestic and regional passenger and cargo services; Chair. GERALD ZIRIMWABAGABO.

Rwandair Express: BP 3246, Kigali; tel. 577564; fax 577669; f. 1998; privately-owned; operates two passenger aircraft; regional services; CEO PIERRE CLAVER KABERA (acting).

Tourism

Attractions for tourists include the wildlife of the national parks (notably mountain gorillas), Lake Kivu and fine mountain scenery. Since the end of the transitional period in late 2003, the Government has increased efforts to develop the tourism industry. In 1998 there were only an estimated 2,000 foreign visitors to Rwanda, but by 2001 the number of tourist arrivals had increased to 113,185. Total receipts from tourism were estimated at US $31m. in 2002.

Office Rwandais du Tourisme et des Parcs Nationaux (ORTPN): blvd de la Révolution 1, BP 905, Kigali; tel. 576514; fax 576515; e-mail webmaster@rwandatourism.com; internet www.rwandatourism.com; f. 1973; govt agency.

SAINT CHRISTOPHER* AND NEVIS

Introductory Survey

Location, Climate, Language, Religion, Flag, Capital

The Federation of Saint Christopher and Nevis is situated at the northern end of the Leeward Islands chain of the West Indies, with Saba and St Eustatius (both in the Netherlands Antilles) to the north-west, Barbuda to the north-east and Antigua to the south-east. Nevis lies about 3 km (2 miles) to the south-east of Saint Christopher, separated by a narrow strait. The tropical heat, varying between 17°C (62°F) and 33°C (92°F), is tempered by constant sea winds, and annual rainfall averages 1,400 mm (55 ins) on Saint Christopher and 1,220 mm (48 ins) on Nevis. English is the official language. The majority of the population are Christians of the Anglican Communion, and other Christian denominations are represented. The national flag (proportions 2 by 3) comprises two triangles, one of green (with its base at the hoist and its apex in the upper fly) and the other of red (with its base in the fly and its apex in the lower hoist), separated by a broad, yellow-edged black diagonal stripe (from the lower hoist to the upper fly) bearing two five-pointed white stars. The capital is Basseterre, on Saint Christopher.

Recent History

Saint Christopher, settled in 1623, was Britain's first colony in the West Indies. The French settled part of the island a year later, and conflict over possession continued until 1783, when Saint Christopher was eventually ceded to Britain under the Treaty of Versailles. Nevis was settled by the British in 1628, and remained one of the most prosperous of the Antilles until the middle of the 19th century. The island of Anguilla was first joined to the territory in 1816. The St Kitts-Nevis-Anguilla Labour Party, formed in 1932, campaigned for independence for the islands. In 1958 Saint Christopher-Nevis-Anguilla became a member of the West Indies Federation, remaining so until the Federation's dissolution in 1962. A new Constitution, granted to each of the British territories in the Leeward Islands in 1960, provided for government through an Administrator and an enlarged Legislative Council. After an abortive attempt to form a smaller East Caribbean Federation, Saint Christopher-Nevis-Anguilla attained Associated Statehood in February 1967, as part of an arrangement that gave five of the colonies full internal autonomy, while the United Kingdom retained responsibility for defence and foreign relations. The House of Assembly replaced the Legislative Council, the Administrator became Governor, and the Chief Minister, Robert Bradshaw, leader of the Labour Party, became the state's first Premier. Three months later Anguilla rebelled against government from Saint Christopher, and in 1971 reverted to being a *de facto* British dependency. Anguilla was formally separated from the other islands in 1980.

A general election in 1971 returned Robert Bradshaw to the premiership. In the 1975 election the Labour Party again won the largest number of seats, while the Nevis Reformation Party (NRP) again took both the Nevis seats. Bradshaw died in May 1978 and was succeeded as Premier by Paul Southwell, hitherto Deputy Premier (and a former Chief Minister). Southwell died in May 1979, and was replaced by the party's leader, Lee L. Moore (hitherto the Attorney-General).

In February 1980 the Labour Party was removed from government for the first time in nearly 30 years: the Labour Party secured four seats in the legislative election, while the People's Action Movement (PAM) took three and the NRP retained the two Nevis seats. Although the Labour Party had won 58% of the popular vote, a PAM-NRP coalition Government was formed under PAM leader, Dr Kennedy A. Simmonds. The change of government led to the suspension of a timetable for independence, which had been scheduled for June 1980. In 1982 proposals for a greater degree of autonomy for Nevis and for independence for the whole state were approved by the House of Assembly, although the Labour Party opposed the plans, arguing that the coalition Government did not have a mandate for its independence policy. Disagreements concerning the content of the proposed independence constitution led to civil disturbances in 1982 and 1983. Nevertheless, Saint Christopher and Nevis became an independent state, under a federal Constitution, on 19 September 1983. The Labour Party denounced the special provisions for Nevis in the Constitution (see below) as giving the island a powerful role in government that was disproportionate to its size and population. Elections to the Nevis Island Assembly were held in August, at which the NRP, led by Simeon Daniel, won all five elective seats. Upon independence Saint Christopher and Nevis became a full member of the Commonwealth (see p. 193).

Early elections to an enlarged National Assembly (now with 11 elective seats) took place in June 1984, at which the ruling PAM-NRP coalition was returned to power. The PAM, which won a clear majority of the popular vote on Saint Christopher, secured six seats, while the NRP no longer held the balance of power in the National Assembly. The three Nevis seats were won by the NRP.

At an election to the Nevis Island Assembly in December 1987, the NRP retained four seats and the Concerned Citizens' Movement (CCM) secured one. At the general election of March 1989, however, the CCM took one of the three Nevis seats from the NRP. The PAM retained its six seats, and the Labour Party its two. Moore resigned as leader of the Labour Party and was succeeded by Denzil Douglas. The electoral success of the coalition Government under the leadership of Simmonds was attributed to its economic policies, and was achieved despite persistent rumours of official connivance in drugs-trafficking activities on the islands.

The CCM secured a majority in the Nevis Island Assembly at an election in June 1992, with three seats, while the NRP retained two. The leader of the CCM, Vance Amory, became Premier of the Nevis Island Administration.

At a general election in November 1993 neither the PAM nor the Labour Party managed to secure a majority in the National Assembly, with both parties winning four seats. On Nevis the CCM secured two seats, and the NRP one. Following the refusal of Amory to form a coalition government with either the PAM or the Labour Party, the Governor-General, Sir Clement Arrindell, invited Simmonds to form a minority government with the support of the NRP. Douglas protested against the decision and appealed for a general strike to support his demands for a further general election. Serious disturbances ensued, and in early December the Governor-General declared a 21-day state of emergency. Meanwhile, Simmonds withdrew from negotiations with Douglas, although an initial agreement to hold a further general election had been reached, in protest at Douglas's premature public revelation of the agreement.

In October 1994 six people were charged in connection with the murder, in Basseterre, of the head of the Saint Christopher special investigations police unit, Jude Matthew, who had been conducting an investigation into the recent disappearances of William Herbert, the country's Permanent Representative to the UN, and Vincent Morris, a son of the Deputy Prime Minister Sidney Morris. Preliminary investigations suggested that these events were connected to the discovery, at the same time as Morris's disappearance, of a large consignment of cocaine in Saint Christopher. In November Sidney Morris resigned, following the arrest of two other sons on charges related to drugs and firearms offences.

A 'forum for national unity' was convened in November 1994, at which representatives of all political parties, church organizations and tourism, trade, labour and law associations agreed to seek closer political co-operation in the months preceding an early general election, in order to halt the advance of drugs-related crime and the attendant erosion of investor confidence in the islands. None the less, fierce electoral campaigning culminated, in June 1995, in a violent clash between rival PAM and Labour Party supporters, which resulted in a number of serious injuries. The general election, conducted on 3 July, was won decisively by the Labour Party, which secured seven of the elective seats in the National Assembly, and Denzil Douglas became Prime Minister. The CCM won two seats, while the PAM and the NRP each won one. Simmonds was among prominent PAM politicians who lost their seats. Douglas resolved to address

---

*While this island is officially called Saint Christopher as part of the state, the name is usually abbreviated to St Kitts.

SAINT CHRISTOPHER AND NEVIS

promptly the problems of increasingly violent crime and of deteriorating prison conditions. The Prime Minister also announced plans to draft proposals for constitutional reform that would provide for the establishment of separate governments for the two islands.

On 1 January 1996 Sir Cuthbert Montroville Sebastian succeeded Sir Clement Arrindell as Governor-General.

In July 1997 the National Assembly approved legislation to restore a full-time defence force, to include the coastguard, with the principal aim of strengthening the islands' anti-drugs operations. (The Simmonds administration had disbanded the army in 1981.) The Nevis administration and the PAM accused the Labour Government of seeking to enhance its authority by recruiting party loyalists to the force. In July 1998 a convicted murderer was executed—the first implementation of the death penalty in the country since 1985. The Attorney-General, Delano Bart, defended the reintroduction of capital punishment, against criticism from the Roman Catholic Church and the human rights organization Amnesty International, as part of the Government's strategy to reduce crime rates.

The Government established a commission of inquiry in July 1997 to investigate allegations of corruption within the PAM during its period in government. Simmonds and Hugh Heyliger (the former agriculture minister, who had succeeded Morris as Deputy Prime Minister, now the sole PAM member of, and Leader of the Opposition in, the National Assembly) were summoned to answer charges of financial impropriety. Both former ministers denied the allegations. In September Simmonds appealed to the High Court to declare the commission invalid. In December Heyliger was charged (and subsequently released on bail) with contempt of court, after failing to testify before the commission. The High Court dismissed applications made by former members of the PAM administration in 1998 and 1999 to have the commission terminated on the grounds of political bias. In July 1999 concerns were expressed by the High Court that the commission of inquiry might have been unduly influenced against Simmonds by his efforts to have the inquiry terminated. The Government therefore established a second commission which was specifically to investigate allegations against Simmonds, while the initial commission was to continue to investigate general allegations of corruption relating to his administration. The second commission's report, published in February 2000, made 10 specific accusations of negligence, improper behaviour and irresponsible action against Simmonds, who was described as having failed 'to achieve the standards required' of a Prime Minister of a sovereign state. Simmonds, however, vehemently rejected the commission's conclusions; he noted that the treasury had not suffered, as the loan had not been honoured, nor had any member of his Government benefited from the agreement.

In June 1996 Amory announced that the Nevis Island Assembly was initiating proceedings (as detailed in the Constitution—see below) for the secession of Nevis from the federation with Saint Christopher. The announcement was made as plans proceeded for the establishment of a federal government office on Nevis (which Amory considered to be unconstitutional) and as the National Assembly considered a financial services bill that proposed referring all potential investors in Nevis to the federal administration for approval. The Nevis Island Assembly was reported to have interpreted both measures as serious infringements of its administrative rights. Despite the prompt intervention of a number of regional diplomatic initiatives to preserve the Federation, a secession bill for Nevis received its preliminary reading in the National Assembly in July. In October the NRP, while supportive of the right to secede, expressed concern at the precipitant nature of Amory's secession timetable, and in November the NRP representative in the National Assembly boycotted a second reading of the bill, forcing a postponement of the debate.

At elections to the Nevis Island Assembly in February 1997 Amory's CCM retained three of the five elective seats, while the NRP retained the remaining two. In October the Nevis Assembly voted unanimously in favour of secession; a referendum on the issue was held in August 1998, in which 61.7%, less than the two-thirds' majority required by the Constitution, voted for secession. The leaders of the two islands immediately announced that they would work to improve relations, and Douglas pledged to implement the principal recommendations of a constitutional review commission intended to augment inter-island affairs. In September a CARICOM mission, led by the Prime Ministers of Dominica and Saint Vincent and the Grenadines, visited Saint

Introductory Survey

Christopher and Nevis as part of a regional initiative to find a lasting solution to the secession issue.

In March 1999 a Constitutional Task Force, chaired by former Governor Sir Fred Phillips, began work on the drafting of a new constitution. In August the Task Force submitted its report to the Prime Minister, who appointed a seven-member select committee, comprising representatives of all the major parties, to review its recommendations and to draft proposals for constitutional change.

At a general election on 6 March 2000 the Labour Party won all eight seats available on Saint Christopher (with 65% of the votes cast), gaining the seat previously held by the PAM, which won 36% of the votes. There was no change in the position on Nevis, where the CCM retained its two seats and the NRP its one. In October Lindsay Grant, a lawyer, was elected the new leader of the PAM, replacing Simmonds.

The Government sought to address the increasing crime rate on the islands in 2001, which was affecting the tourism industry. In February a curfew for all children under 15 was introduced in an effort to reduce youth crime, and in June the Government sought to persuade the US Navy to relocate one of its bases to Saint Christopher. Douglas stated his hope that the country would derive 'economic, social and financial' benefits from the US presence. The per-head murder rate in 2004 (22 murders per 100,000 people) was the third highest of the Caribbean Community and Common Market (CARICOM, see p. 183) countries, behind Jamaica and Belize, but ahead of both Guyana and Trinidad and Tobago. There was, however, a 16.5% decrease in the number of serious crimes in that year, according to police statistics.

In elections to the Nevis Island Assembly in September 2001 the CCM, led by Amory, strengthened its control of the legislature, gaining a total of four elective seats. The NRP, under the leadership of Joseph Parry, took the remaining one seat.

In October 2002 Douglas, pronouncing on the recurring issue of greater autonomy for Nevis, said that, while he supported the constitutional right of Nevis to secede from the federation, the federal Government was willing to discuss ways to increase the autonomy of the Nevis Island Administration and Assembly. Amory, however, remained convinced that full autonomy and separate membership of the Organisation of Eastern Caribbean States (OECS, see p. 397) would be a better option for Nevis. In January 2004 a meeting between the federal Government and the Nevis administration took place at which Amory continued to press for political independence; in the same month, however, an OECS Heads of Government meeting urged the Nevis administration to review its intention to campaign for independence in favour of preserving the *status quo*. CARICOM, in 2003, and the US Government, earlier in January 2004, also indicated their support for the existing federation.

The Labour Party was returned to office for a third consecutive term at a general election held on 25 October 2004. The incumbent administration, which campaigned on its social development record, won seven of the eight seats on Saint Christopher (with 60.4% of the votes cast—slightly fewer than in 2000); the PAM, whose leader, Lindsay Grant, narrowly failed to get elected, secured the other seat and attracted 37.8% of Saint Christopher's votes. The balance of power remained the same on Nevis where the CCM secured two seats (with 54% of the votes cast on Nevis) and the NRP secured one seat (and the remaining 46% of the island's votes). Turn-out on Saint Christopher was 62.2%, but was less than 50% overall, reflecting the dissatisfaction of many Nevisians with the current system. Although the voter-registration process was regarded as imperfect (not least because of a long-standing failure of the authorities to remove the names of dead or migrated people from the electoral list), the team of CARICOM observers monitoring the election reported the contest to be generally free and fair. In November Douglas announced a slightly reorganized Cabinet featuring two new Ministers of State in the Prime Minister's Office: Senator Nigel Carty was given responsibility for finance, technology and sustainable development; and Senator Roy Skerrit was to be in charge of the tourism, sports and culture portfolios. Among the other changes was the creation of a new Ministry of National Security, Justice, Immigration and Labour, headed by Dwyer Astaphan, the erstwhile Minister of Tourism, Commerce and Consumer Affairs. In April 2005 Grant was re-elected unopposed to the leadership of the PAM.

Saint Christopher and Nevis is a member of CARICOM and of the OECS. In the late 1980s regional discussions were held on the issue of political unity in the East Caribbean. Saint Christopher

SAINT CHRISTOPHER AND NEVIS

and Nevis expressed interest in political unity only if the proposed merger included its Leeward Island neighbours and the Virgin Islands, where an estimated 10,000 Kittitians and Nevisians reside. From January 1990 the OECS agreed to relax restrictions on travel between member states. Moreover, in February 2002 it was agreed, with effect from March, to allow nationals of member states to travel freely within the OECS area and to remain in the territory of any other member state for up to six months. In early 2006 the Prime Minister indicated that Saint Christopher and Nevis would join CARICOM's Caribbean Single Market and Economy (CSME), which was established by six founding member states on 1 January, later in that year. The CSME was intended to enshrine the free movement of goods, services and labour throughout the CARICOM region, although no OECS countries were signatories to the new project from its inauguration.

In September 2005 Douglas reiterated the Government's commitment to its lucrative diplomatic relationship with Taiwan. Saint Christopher and Nevis, along with Saint Vincent and the Grenadines, remained the only Caribbean countries still to recognize the statehood of Taiwan, which was losing a contest of so-called 'dollar diplomacy' in the region with the People's Republic of China.

Government

Saint Christopher and Nevis is a constitutional monarchy. Executive power is vested in the British monarch, as Head of State, and is exercised locally by the monarch's personal representative, the Governor-General, who acts in accordance with the advice of the Cabinet. Legislative power is vested in Parliament, comprising the monarch and the National Assembly. The National Assembly is composed of the Speaker, three (or, if a nominated member is Attorney-General, four) nominated members, known as Senators (two appointed on the advice of the Premier and one appointed on the advice of the Leader of the Opposition), and 11 elected members (Representatives), who are chosen from single-member constituencies for up to five years by universal adult suffrage. The Cabinet comprises the Prime Minister, who must be able to command the support of the majority of the members of the National Assembly, the Attorney-General (ex officio) and four other ministers. The Prime Minister and the Cabinet are responsible to Parliament.

The Nevis Island legislature comprises the Nevis Island Assembly and the Nevis Island Administration, headed by the British monarch (who is represented on the island by the Deputy Governor-General). It operates similarly to the Saint Christopher and Nevis legislature but has power to secede from the Federation, subject to certain restrictions (see Constitution, below).

Defence

The small army was disbanded by the Government in 1981, and its duties were absorbed by the Volunteer Defence Force and a special tactical unit of the police. In July 1997 the National Assembly approved legislation to re-establish a full-time defence force. Coastguard operations were to be brought under military command; the defence force was also to include cadet and reserve forces. Saint Christopher and Nevis participates in the US-sponsored Regional Security System, comprising police, coastguards and army units, which was established by independent East Caribbean states in 1982. Budgetary expenditure on national security in 1998 was approximately EC $23.8m.

Economic Affairs

In 2004, according to estimates by the World Bank, Saint Christopher and Nevis's gross national income (GNI), measured at average 2002–04 prices, was US $357.0m., equivalent to $7,600 per head (or $11,190 per head on an international purchasing-power parity basis). During 1995–2004 the population increased by an average of 1.5% per year, while over the same period, it was estimated, gross domestic product (GDP) per head increased, in real terms, at an average annual rate of 1.8%. Overall GDP increased, in real terms, by an average of 3.3% annually in 1995–2004; according to the Eastern Caribbean Central Bank (ECCB, see p. 388), growth was 7.3% in 2004.

Agriculture (including forestry and fishing) contributed 2.9% of GDP in 2004. Some 14.7% of the working population were employed in the agriculture sector (including sugar manufacturing) in 1994. Major crops include coconuts and sea-island cotton, although some vegetables are also exported. Sugar and sugar products had dominated the economy since the 1960s, but the industry, which had accumulated a debt of US $141.5m. (mainly with the St Kitts-Nevis-Anguilla National Bank and the Development Bank of St Kitts and Nevis), closed after the 2005 harvest and workers at the St Kitts Sugar Manufacturing Corporation received their final payments in March 2006. In spite of a guaranteed European Union (EU, see p. 228) sugar price, which was well above world market levels, the sugar industry had survived only as a result of government subsidies, which were equivalent to 3.5% of GDP in 2001. Large areas formerly used for sugar have been redesignated for tourism and the Government was expected to make provision for the retraining of sugar industry employees. Other important crops include yams, sweet potatoes, groundnuts, onions, sweet peppers, cabbages, carrots and bananas. In July 2004 the Government entered into a partnership with a Canadian corporation to cultivate Stevia—a herb used as a sweetener or dietary supplement. In addition, fishing is an increasingly important commercial activity. Agricultural GDP increased by an annual average of 1.1% in 1996–2004. According to the ECCB, the real value of agricultural GDP decreased by 11.8% in 2004.

Industry (including mining, manufacturing, construction and public utilities) provided 25.7% of GDP in 2004. Excluding sugar manufacturing, the sector employed 21.0% of the working population in 1994. Activity is mainly connected with the construction industry (the real GDP of which expanded by 1.3% in 2004). Real industrial GDP increased by an annual average of 5.1% in 1996–2004. In 2004 the GDP of the sector expanded by 4.5%.

Manufacturing provided 9.5% of GDP in 2004, and non-sugar manufacturing employed 7.8% of the working population in 1994. Apart from the sugar industry (the production of raw sugar and ethyl alcohol), the principal manufactured products are garments, electrical components, food products, beer and other beverages. The sector recorded average annual growth of 5.5% during 1996–2004. In 2004, according to the ECCB, real manufacturing GDP increased by 7.6%.

The islands are dependent upon imports of fuel and energy (7.5% of total imports in 2001) for their energy requirements. In September 2005 the Government became one of 13 Caribbean administrations to sign the PetroCaribe accord, under which Saint Christopher and Nevis would be allowed to purchase petroleum from Venezuela at reduced prices.

The services sector contributed 71.3% of GDP in 2004, and employed 64.4% of the working population in 1994. Tourism is a major contributor to the economy. In 2002, mainly as a result of a contraction in the US tourism market and hurricane damage to the hotel stock, the number of stop-over arrivals fell by 10.1% and the number of cruise-ship passengers decreased by 34.0%. However, the sector stabilized in 2003 when a further 12.5% decrease in the number of cruise-ship passengers was more than outweighed by a 13.5% increase in the number of stop-over tourists, who contribute far more revenue to the economy than cruise-ship passengers. In 2004 the sector built strongly on its recovery when the number of stop-over tourists increased by 32.6% (to 120,088), the number of cruise-ship passengers increased by 77.8% (to 260,121). In that year the volume of receipts totalled EC £288.7m., compared with $154.3m. in 2003 and $203.4m. in 2004. In March 2003 a new 900-room resort at Frigate Bay, Saint Christopher opened, increasing the number of hotel rooms on the island by some 60%; further expansion was expected before the 2007 Cricket World Cup, which was partly to be hosted by Saint Christopher and Nevis. The real GDP of the services sector increased at an average annual rate of 2.8% in 1996–2004; growth was 7.3% in 2004.

In 2004 Saint Christopher and Nevis recorded an estimated visible trade deficit of EC $294.6m. and there was a deficit of some $211.2m. on the current account of the balance of payments. The USA was the islands' principal trading partner in 2001, supplying 50.5% of imports and purchasing 71.5% of exports. Trade with the United Kingdom and with other Caribbean states is also important. The sugar industry is the country's leading exporter (accounting for a 21.0% of total export revenues in 2001), and the principal imports are machinery and transport equipment, basic manufactures and food and live animals.

In 2004 the central Government of Saint Christopher and Nevis recorded an estimated budgetary deficit of EC $79.9m., equivalent to 8.8% of GDP. The country's total external debt was estimated to be US $310.3m. at the end of 2003, of which US $308.8m. was long-term public debt. In that year the cost of debt-servicing was equivalent to 34.9% of the value of exports of goods and services. The annual rate of inflation averaged 2.4%

SAINT CHRISTOPHER AND NEVIS

in 1998–2004; consumer prices increased by 2.3% in both 2003 and 2004. There is, however, a recurring problem of labour shortages in the agricultural sector (which will be eased by the collapse of the sugar industry) and the construction industry, and the rate of unemployment (reported to be around 10% in early 2003) is mitigated by mass emigration, particularly from Nevis: remittances from abroad provide an important source of revenue.

Saint Christopher and Nevis is a member of the Caribbean Community and Common Market (CARICOM, see p. 183), and of the Organisation of Eastern Caribbean States (OECS, see p. 397). The ECCB is based in Basseterre. In 2001 a regional stock exchange, the Eastern Caribbean Securities Exchange, opened in Basseterre. Saint Christopher and Nevis is a party to the Cotonou Agreement (see p. 277), the successor agreement to the Lomé Convention, signed in June 2000 between the EU and a group of developing countries.

Successive Governments attempted to reduce economic dependence on the cultivation and processing of sugar cane, the traditional industry of the islands, and in 2005 the state-run industry was finally closed and its assets dismantled and recycled. The most rapidly developing industry has been tourism, which was estimated by the World Travel and Tourism Council to provide some 28.6% of the country's GDP and 29.1% of employment in 2005. The development of light manufacturing, particularly of electronic components and textiles, has also helped to broaden the islands' economic base. In addition, a small 'offshore' financial sector on Nevis, which, by 2004, had registered 15,000 International Business Companies and 950 trusts, has been developed. Unfortunately, the division of regulatory powers between the island administration on Nevis and the federal Government has at times been unclear. Partly for this reason, Saint Christopher and Nevis was, in June 2000, listed as a 'non-co-operative jurisdiction' by the Financial Action Task Force on Money Laundering (FATF—based at the Secretariat of the Organisation for Economic Co-operation and Development in Paris, France); however, the island was removed from this list in 2002, after instituting stricter regulatory controls. In April 2003 a report indicated that the islands' 'offshore' banking operations had been halved as a result of the FATF action and the subsequent financial reforms. In his December 2005 budget speech, the Prime Minister introduced several new taxation measures designed to strengthen government revenue in the near term, particularly in the period before the 2007 Cricket World Cup, to be jointly hosted by Saint Christopher and Nevis and several other Caribbean countries and territories. Following the announcement of the closure of the sugar industry in March 2005, the EU provided grants worth US $14.6m. to assist economic reform and retraining for sugar industry employees. The total cost of the transition to a non-sugar-producing economy was estimated at some $50m. Economic growth in 2005 was estimated at 3.5%, stimulated by another strong year for the crucial tourism sector.

Education

Education is compulsory for 12 years between five and 17 years of age. Primary education begins at the age of five, and lasts for seven years. Secondary education, from the age of 12, generally comprises a first cycle of four years, followed by a second cycle of two years. In 1993 enrolment at all levels of education was estimated to be equivalent to 78% of the school-age population. There are 30 state, eight private and five denominational schools. There is also a technical college. Budgetary expenditure on education by the central Government in 1998 was projected to be EC $25m. (6.7% of total government expenditure). In September 2000 a privately financed 'offshore' medical college, the Medical University of the Americas, opened in Nevis with 40 students registered. The Ross University of School of Veterinary Medicine and the International University of Nursing also operated on Saint Christopher. A Basic Education Project funded by the Caribbean Development Bank, was in 2003 complemented by a $18.8m. Secondary Education Project, which was to include the construction of a new secondary school in Saddlers.

Public Holidays

2006: 1 January (New Year's Day), 2 January (Carnival Last Lap), 14 April (Good Friday), 17 April (Easter Monday), 1 May (May Day), 5 June (Whit Monday), 12 June (Queen's Official Birthday), 7 August (August Monday), 8 August (Nevis only: Culturama Last Lap), 16 September (Heroes Day), 19 September (Independence Day), 25–26 December (Christmas).

2007: 1 January (New Year's Day), 2 January (Carnival Last Lap), 6 April (Good Friday), 9 April (Easter Monday), 7 May (May Day), 28 May (Whit Monday), 11 June (Queen's Official Birthday), 6 August (August Monday), 7 August (Nevis only: Culturama Last Lap), 16 September (Heroes Day), 19 September (Independence Day), 25–26 December (Christmas).

Weights and Measures

The imperial system is used.

Statistical Survey

Source (unless otherwise stated): St Kitts and Nevis Information Service, Government Headquarters, Church St, POB 186, Basseterre; tel. 465-2521; fax 466-4504; e-mail skninfo@caribsurf.com; internet www.stkittsnevis.net.

AREA AND POPULATION

Area (sq km): 269.4 (Saint Christopher 176.1, Nevis 93.3).

Population: 40,618 (males 19,933, females 20,685) at census of 12 May 1991; 45,841 (males 22,784, females 23,057) at census of 14 May 2001 (provisional results). *2004:* 47,928 (mid-year estimate). Sources: UN, *Population and Vital Statistics Report* and Eastern Caribbean Central Bank.

Density (mid-2004): 177.9 per sq km.

Principal Town (estimated population incl. suburbs, mid-2003): Basseterre (capital) 13,262. Source: UN, *World Urbanization Prospects: The 2003 Revision*.

Births and Deaths (2000): Registered live births 838 (estimated birth rate 20.7 per 1,000); Registered deaths 356 (estimated death rate 8.8 per 1,000). *2003:* Crude birth rate 15.6 per 1,000; Crude death rate 7.6 per 1,000 (Source: Caribbean Development Bank, *Social and Economic Indicators*).

Expectation of life (years at birth): 70 (males 69; females 72) in 2003. Source: WHO, *World Health Report*.

Employment (labour force survey, 1994): Sugar cane production/manufacturing 1,525; Non-sugar agriculture 914; Mining and quarrying 29; Manufacturing (excl. sugar) 1,290; Electricity, gas and water 416; Construction 1,745; Trade (except tourism) 1,249; Tourism 2,118; Transport and communications 534; Business and general services 3,708; Government services 2,738; Other statutory bodies 342; *Total* 16,608 (Saint Christopher 12,516, Nevis 4,092). Source: IMF, *St Kitts and Nevis: Recent Economic Developments* (August 1997).

HEALTH AND WELFARE

Key Indicators

Total Fertility Rate (children per woman, 2003): 2.3.

Under-5 Mortality Rate (per 1,000 live births, 2004): 21.

Physicians (per 1,000 head, 1997): 1.17.

Hospital Beds (per 1,000 head, 1996): 6.36.

Health Expenditure (2002): US $ per head (PPP): 667.

Health Expenditure (2002): % of GDP: 5.5.

Health Expenditure (2002): public (% of total): 62.1.

Access to Water (% of persons, 2002): 99.

Access to Sanitation (% of persons, 2002): 96.

Human Development Index (2003): ranking: 49.

Human Development Index (2003): value: 0.834.

For sources and definitions, see explanatory note on p. vi.

AGRICULTURE, ETC.

Principal Crops (FAO estimates, '000 metric tons, 2004): Roots and tubers 1.0; Sugar cane 193.0; Coconuts 1.0; Vegetables and melons 0.6; Fruits and berries 1.4.

SAINT CHRISTOPHER AND NEVIS

Livestock (FAO estimates, '000 head, year ending September 2004): Cattle 4.3; Sheep 14.0; Goats 14.4; Pigs 4.0; Poultry 60.

Livestock Products (FAO estimates, '000 metric tons, 2004): Beef and veal 0.1; Pig meat 0.3; Poultry meat 0.1; Hen eggs 0.2.

Fishing (FAO estimates, metric tons, live weight, 2003): Snappers 16; Tuna-like fishes 13; Needlefishes, etc. 34; Flyingfishes 42; Bigeye scad 41; Common dolphinfish 40; Stromboid conchs 36; *Total catch* 370.

Source: FAO.

INDUSTRY

Production: Raw sugar 21,000 metric tons in 2002; Electric energy 199.5 million kWh in 2004 (preliminary). Sources: UN, *International Commodity Statistics Yearbook* and Eastern Caribbean Central Bank.

FINANCE

Currency and Exchange Rates: 100 cents = 1 Eastern Caribbean dollar (EC $). *Sterling, US Dollar and Euro Equivalents* (30 December 2005): £1 sterling = EC $4.649; US $1 = EC $2.700; €1 = EC $3.185; EC $100 = £21.51 = US $37.04 = €31.40. *Exchange Rate:* Fixed at US $1 = EC $2.70 since July 1976.

Budget (preliminary, EC $ million, 2004): *Revenue:* Revenue from taxation 281.9 (of which, Taxes on income and profits 80.4; Taxes on domestic goods and services 56.0; Taxes on international trade and transactions 140.5); Other current revenue 83.5; Capital revenue 4.6; Foreign grants 4.1; Total 374.2. *Expenditure:* Current expenditure 376.0 (Personal emoluments 159.7, Goods and services 95.8, Interest payments 76.1, Transfers and subsidies 44.3); Capital expenditure and net lending 78.1; Total 454.1. Source: Eastern Caribbean Central Bank.

International Reserves (US $ million at 31 December 2004): Reserve position in IMF 0.13; Foreign exchange 78.34; Total 78.47. Source: IMF, *International Financial Statistics*.

Money Supply (EC $ million at 31 December 2004): Currency outside banks 44.61; Demand deposits at deposit money banks 162.41; Total money (incl. others) 207.21. Source: IMF, *International Financial Statistics*.

Cost of Living (Consumer Price Index; base: 2000 = 100): 104.2 in 2002; 106.6 in 2003; 109.0 in 2004. Source: IMF, *International Financial Statistics*.

Gross Domestic Product (EC $ million at current factor cost): 802.1 in 2002; 821.5 in 2003; 908.4 in 2004 (preliminary). Source: Eastern Caribbean Central Bank.

Expenditure on the Gross Domestic Product (preliminary, EC $ million at current prices, 2004): Government final consumption expenditure 217.42; Private final consumption expenditure 537.90; Gross fixed capital formation 472.29; *Total domestic expenditure* 1,227.61; Exports of goods and services 534.66; *Less* Imports of goods and services 670.05; *GDP in purchasers' values* 1,092.22. Source: Eastern Caribbean Central Bank.

Gross Domestic Product by Economic Activity (preliminary, EC $ million at current factor cost, 2004): Agriculture, hunting, forestry and fishing 28.63; Mining and quarrying 2.56; Manufacturing 92.12; Electricity and water 24.41; Construction 130.98; Wholesale and retail trade 101.35; Restaurants and hotels 77.21; Transport 75.68; Communications 51.46; Finance and insurance 143.99; Real estate and housing 23.54; Government services 176.64; Other community, social and personal services 42.99; *Sub-total* 971.56; *Less* Imputed bank service charge 63.21; *Total in basic prices* 908.35. Source: Eastern Caribbean Central Bank.

Balance of Payments (EC $ million, 2003): Exports of goods f.o.b. 169.08; Imports of goods f.o.b. −383.62; *Trade balance* −214.54; Exports of services 259.22; Imports of services −203.85; *Balance on goods and services* −159.17; Other income received (net) −117.91; *Balance on goods, services and income* −277.08; Current transfers received (net) 44.65; *Current balance* −232.43; Capital account (net) 14.14; Direct investment from abroad (net) 138.43; Portfolio investment (net) 120.95; Other investment (net) −66.53; Net errors and omissions 22.85; *Overall balance* −2.59. Source: Eastern Caribbean Central Bank.

EXTERNAL TRADE

Principal Commodities (US $ million, 2001): *Imports c.i.f.:* Food and live animals 27.3; Mineral fuels, lubricants, etc. 14.2 (Refined petroleum products 12.1); Chemicals 13.0; Basic manufactures 42.5 (Iron and steel manufactures 6.8); Machinery and transport equipment 51.9 (Road vehicles 9.5); Total (incl. others) 189.2. *Exports f.o.b.:* Food and live animals 7.2 (Raw sugar 6.5); Basic manufactures 0.9 (Metal manufactures 0.9); Machinery and transport equipment 20.2 (Telecommunications equipment 1.3; Other electrical machinery 18.2); Miscellaneous manufactures 2.0 (Printed matter 1.0); Total (incl. others) 31.0. Source: UN, *International Trade Statistics Yearbook*.

Principal Trading Partners (US $ million, 2001): *Imports:* Barbados 4.1; Canada 21.6; France 2.1; Japan 4.7; Netherlands 2.5; Trinidad and Tobago 23.4; United Kingdom 15.6; USA 95.6; Total (incl. others) 189.2. *Exports* (excl. re-exports): Dominica 0.4; United Kingdom 7.3; USA 22.1; Total (incl. others) 30.9. Source: UN, *International Trade Statistics Yearbook*.

TRANSPORT

Road Traffic (registered motor vehicles): 11,352 in 1998; 12,432 in 1999; 12,917 in 2000.

Shipping: *Arrivals* (2000): 1,981 vessels. *International Sea-borne Freight Traffic* ('000 metric tons, 2000): Goods loaded 24.7; Goods unloaded 234.2.

Civil Aviation (aircraft arrivals): 24,800 in 1998; 23,500 in 1999; 19,400 in 2000.

TOURISM

Visitor Arrivals: 246,364 (68,998 stop-over visitors, 3,853 excursionists, 6,283 yacht passengers, 167,230 cruise-ship passengers) in 2002; 246,789 (90,563 stop-over visitors, 4,054 excursionists, 5,855 yacht passengers, 146,317 cruise-ship passengers) in 2003; 389,867 (120,088 stop-over visitors, 4,052 excursionists, 5,606 yacht passengers, 260,121 cruise-ship passengers) in 2004 (preliminary).

Tourism Receipts (EC $ million): 154.3 in 2002; 203.4 in 2003; 288.7 in 2004 (preliminary).

Source: Eastern Caribbean Central Bank.

COMMUNICATIONS MEDIA

Radio Receivers ('000 in use, 1997): 28.

Television Receivers ('000 in use, 1999): 10.

Telephones ('000 main lines in use, 2004): 23.5.

Facsimile Machines (1996): 450.

Mobile Cellular Telephones (subscribers, 2004): 10,000.

Personal Computers (2004): 11,000.

Internet Users (2004): 10,000.

Non-daily Newspapers (2000): Titles 4; Circulation 34,000 (1996).

Sources: mainly UNESCO, *Statistical Yearbook*; UN, *Statistical Yearbook*; International Telecommunication Union.

EDUCATION

Pre-primary (2000/01): 77 schools; 170 teachers; 2,819 pupils.

Primary (2000/01): 23 schools; 302 teachers; 5,608 pupils (2001).

Secondary (2000/01): 7 schools; 365 teachers; 4,445 pupils (2001).

Tertiary (2000/01): 1 institution; 64 teachers (1999/2000); 1,235 students.

Adult Literacy Rate: 97.8% in 2003. Source: UN Development Programme, *Human Development Report*.

Directory

The Constitution

The Constitution of the Federation of Saint Christopher and Nevis took effect from 19 September 1983, when the territory achieved independence. Its main provisions are summarized below

FUNDAMENTAL RIGHTS AND FREEDOMS

Regardless of race, place of origin, political opinion, colour, creed or sex, but subject to respect for the rights and freedoms of others and for the public interest, every person in Saint Christopher and Nevis is entitled to the rights of life, liberty, security of person, equality before

SAINT CHRISTOPHER AND NEVIS

the law and the protection of the law. Freedom of conscience, of expression, of assembly and association is guaranteed, and the inviolability of personal privacy, family life and property is maintained. Protection is afforded from slavery, forced labour, torture and inhuman treatment.

THE GOVERNOR-GENERAL

The Governor-General is appointed by the British monarch, whom the Governor-General represents locally. The Governor-General must be a citizen of Saint Christopher and Nevis, and must appoint a Deputy Governor-General, in accordance with the wishes of the Premier of Nevis, to represent the Governor-General on that island.

PARLIAMENT

Parliament consists of the British monarch, represented by the Governor-General, and the National Assembly, which includes a Speaker, three (or, if a nominated member is Attorney-General, four) nominated members (Senators) and 11 elected members (Representatives). Senators are appointed by the Governor-General; one on the advice of the Leader of the Opposition, and the other two in accordance with the wishes of the Prime Minister. The Representatives are elected by universal suffrage, one from each of the 11 single-member constituencies.

Every citizen over the age of 18 years is eligible to vote. Parliament may alter any of the provisions of the Constitution.

THE EXECUTIVE

Executive authority is vested in the British monarch, as Head of State, and is exercised on the monarch's behalf by the Governor-General, either directly or through subordinate officers. The Governor-General appoints as Prime Minister that Representative who, in the Governor-General's opinion, appears to be best able to command the support of the majority of the Representatives. Other ministerial appointments are made by the Governor-General, in consultation with the Prime Minister, from among the members of the National Assembly. The Governor-General may remove the Prime Minister from office if a resolution of 'no confidence' in the Government is passed by the National Assembly and if the Prime Minister does not resign within three days or advise the Governor-General to dissolve Parliament.

The Cabinet consists of the Prime Minister and other Ministers. When the office of Attorney-General is a public office, the Attorney-General shall, by virtue of holding that office, be a member of the Cabinet in addition to the other Ministers. The Governor-General appoints as Leader of the Opposition in the National Assembly that Representative who, in the Governor-General's opinion, appears to be best able to command the support of the majority of the Representatives who do not support the Government.

CITIZENSHIP

All persons born in Saint Christopher and Nevis before independence who, immediately before independence, were citizens of the United Kingdom and Colonies automatically become citizens of Saint Christopher and Nevis. All persons born in Saint Christopher and Nevis after independence automatically acquire citizenship, as do those born outside Saint Christopher and Nevis after independence to a parent possessing citizenship. There are provisions for the acquisition of citizenship by those to whom it is not automatically granted.

THE ISLAND OF NEVIS

There is a Legislature for the island of Nevis which consists of the British monarch, represented by the Governor-General, and the Nevis Island Assembly. The Assembly consists of three nominated members (one appointed by the Governor-General in accordance with the advice of the Leader of the Opposition in the Assembly, and two appointed by the Governor-General in accordance with the advice of the Premier) and such number of elected members as corresponds directly with the number of electoral districts on the island.

There is a Nevis Island Administration, consisting of a premier and two other members who are appointed by the Governor-General. The Governor-General appoints the Premier as the person who, in the Governor-General's opinion, is best able to command the support of the majority of the elected members of the Assembly. The other members of the Administration are appointed by the Governor-General, acting in accordance with the wishes of the Premier. The Administration has exclusive responsibility for administration within the island of Nevis, in accordance with the provisions of any relevant laws.

The Nevis Island Legislature may provide that the island of Nevis is to cease to belong to the Federation of Saint Christopher and Nevis, in which case this Constitution would cease to have effect in the island of Nevis. Provisions for the possible secession of the island contain the following requirements: that the island must give full and detailed proposals for the future Constitution of the island of Nevis, which must be laid before the Assembly for a period of at least six months prior to the proposed date of secession; that a two-thirds majority has been gained in a referendum which is to be held after the Assembly has passed the motion.

The Government

HEAD OF STATE

Monarch: HM Queen ELIZABETH II.

Governor-General: Sir CUTHBERT MONTROVILLE SEBASTIAN (took office 1 January 1996).

CABINET
(April 2006)

Prime Minister and Minister of Finance, Sustainable Development, Information Technology, Tourism, Sports and Culture: Dr DENZIL LLEWELLYN DOUGLAS.

Deputy Prime Minister and Minister of Education, Youth, Social and Community Development and Gender Affairs: SAM TERRENCE CONDOR.

Minister of Public Works, Utilities, Transport and Posts: Dr EARL ASIM MARTIN.

Minister of National Security, Justice, Immigration and Labour: GERALD ANTHONY DWYER ASTAPHAN.

Minister of Health: RUPERT EMMANUEL HERBERT.

Minister of Foreign Affairs, International Trade, Industry and Commerce: TIMOTHY SYLVESTER HARRIS.

Minister of Housing, Agriculture, Fisheries and Consumer Affairs: CEDRIC ROY LIBURD.

Attorney-General and Minister of Legal Affairs: DELANO FRANK BART.

Minister of State in the Office of the Prime Minister with responsibility for Finance, Technology and Sustainable Development: Sen. NIGEL ALEXIS CARTY.

Minister of State in the Office of the Prime Minister with responsibility for Tourism, Sports and Culture: Sen. RICHARD SKERRITT.

MINISTRIES

Office of the Governor-General: Government House, Basseterre; tel. 465-2315.

Government Headquarters: Church St, POB 186, Basseterre; tel. 465-2521; fax 465-1001; e-mail infocom@caribsurf.com; internet www.gov.kn.

Prime Minister's Office and Ministry of Finance, Sustainable Development, Information Technology, Tourism, Sports and Culture: Church St, POB 186, Basseterre; tel. 465-2521; fax 465-1001; e-mail sknpmoffice@caribsurf.com; internet www.cuopm.com.

Attorney-General's Office and Ministry of Legal Affairs: Church St, POB 164, Basseterre; tel. 465-2521; fax 465-5040; e-mail attnygenskn@caribsurf.com.

Ministry of Education, Youth, Social and Community Development and Gender: Church St, POB 186, Basseterre; tel. 465-2521; fax 465-2556; e-mail minelsc@caribsurf.com.

Ministry of Foreign Affairs, International Trade, Industry and Commerce: Church St, POB 186, Basseterre; tel. 465-2521; fax 465-1778; e-mail mintica@thecable.net.

Ministry of Health: Church St, POB 186, Basseterre; tel. 465-2521; fax 465-1316; e-mail minhwa@caribsurf.com.

Ministry of Housing, Agriculture, Fisheries and Consumer Affairs: Church St, POB 186, Basseterre; tel. 465-2521; fax 465-2635; e-mail minafclh@caribsurf.com.

Ministry of National Security, Justice, Immigration and Labour: Church St, POB 186, Basseterre; tel. 465-2521; fax 465-8244; e-mail mwaskn@caribsurf.com.

Ministry of Public Works, Utilities, Transport and Posts: Church St, POB 186, Basseterre; tel. 466-7032; fax 465-9475; e-mail scaspail@caribsurf.com.

NEVIS ISLAND ADMINISTRATION

Premier: VANCE W. AMORY.

There are also two appointed members.

Administrative Centre: Bath Hotel, Nevis; tel. 469-5521; fax 469-1207; e-mail nevisinfo@nevisweb.kn; internet www.nevisweb.kn.

SAINT CHRISTOPHER AND NEVIS

Legislature

NATIONAL ASSEMBLY

Speaker: Marcella Liburd.
Elected members: 11. Nominated members: 3. *Ex-officio* members: 1.

Election, 25 October 2004

Party	% of votes	Seats
St Kitts-Nevis Labour Party	50.6	7
Concerned Citizens' Movement	8.8	2
People's Action Movement	31.7	1
Nevis Reformation Party	7.5	1
Total (incl. others)	100.0	11

NEVIS ISLAND ASSEMBLY

Elected members: 5. Nominated members: 3.
Elections to the Nevis Island Assembly took place in September 2001. The Concerned Citizens' Movement took four seats, and the Nevis Reformation Party retained one seat.

Political Organizations

Concerned Citizens' Movement (CCM): Charlestown, Nevis; alliance of four parties; Leader Vance W. Amory.

Nevis Reformation Party (NRP): Government Rd, POB 480, Charlestown, Nevis; tel. 469-0630; f. 1970; Leader Joseph Parry; Sec. Levi Morton.

People's Action Movement (PAM): POB 1294, Basseterre; tel. 466-2726; fax 465-0857; e-mail pamdemocrat@pamdemocrat.org; internet www.pamdemocrat.org/party; f. 1965; Political Leader Lindsay Grant; Deputy Leaders Shawn Richards, Eugene Hamilton.

St Kitts-Nevis Labour Party (SKNLP): Masses House, Church St, POB 239, Basseterre; tel. 465-5347; fax 465-8328; internet www.sknlabourparty.org; f. 1932; socialist party; Chair. Timothy Harris; Leader Dr Denzil Llewellyn Douglas.

Diplomatic Representation

EMBASSIES IN SAINT CHRISTOPHER AND NEVIS

China (Taiwan): Taylor's Range, POB 119, Basseterre; tel. 465-2421; fax 465-7921; e-mail rocemb@caribsurf.com; Ambassador John J. K. Liu.

Cuba: 34 Bladen Housing Devt, POB 600, Basseterre; tel. 466-3374; fax 465-8072; e-mail cubaask@thecable.net; Ambassador Orlando Alvarez.

Venezuela: Delisle St, POB 435, Basseterre; tel. 465-2073; fax 465-5452; e-mail frontado@caribsurf.com; Ambassador Miriam Troconis Luzardo.

Diplomatic relations with other countries are maintained at consular level, or with ambassadors and high commissioners resident in other countries of the region, or directly with the other country.

Judicial System

Justice is administered by the Eastern Caribbean Supreme Court, based in Saint Lucia and consisting of a Court of Appeal and a High Court. One of the nine puisne judges of the High Court is responsible for Saint Christopher and Nevis and presides over the Court of Summary Jurisdiction. The Magistrates' Courts deal with summary offences and civil offences involving sums of not more than EC $5,000. In 1998 the death penalty was employed in Saint Christopher and Nevis for the first time since 1985.

Puisne Judge: Neville Smith.

Magistrates' Office: Losack Rd, Basseterre; tel. 465-2926.

Religion

CHRISTIANITY

St Kitts Christian Council: Victoria Rd, POB 48, Basseterre; tel. 465-2167; e-mail stgeorgessk@hotmail.com; Chair. Archdeacon Valentine Hodge.

St Kitts Evangelical Association: Princess St, Basseterre.

The Anglican Communion

Anglicans in Saint Christopher and Nevis are adherents of the Church in the Province of the West Indies. The islands form part of the diocese of the North Eastern Caribbean and Aruba. The Bishop is resident in The Valley, Anguilla.

The Roman Catholic Church

The diocese of Saint John's-Basseterre, suffragan to the archdiocese of Castries (Saint Lucia), includes Anguilla, Antigua and Barbuda, the British Virgin Islands, Montserrat and Saint Christopher and Nevis. At 31 December 2003 the diocese contained an estimated 15,423 adherents. The Bishop participates in the Antilles Episcopal Conference (currently based in Port of Spain, Trinidad and Tobago).

Bishop of Saint John's-Basseterre: Rt Rev. Donald James Reece (resident in St John's, Antigua).

Other Churches

There are also communities of Methodists, Moravians, Seventh-day Adventists, Baptists, Pilgrim Holiness, the Church of God, Apostolic Faith and Plymouth Brethren.

The Press

The Democrat: Cayon St, POB 30, Basseterre; tel. 466-2091; fax 465-0857; e-mail thedemocrat@caribsurf.com; internet www.pamdemocrat.org/Newspaper; f. 1948; weekly on Saturdays; organ of PAM; Dir Capt. J. L. Wigley; Editor Fitzroy P. Jones; circ. 3,000.

The Labour Spokesman: Masses House, Church St, POB 239, Basseterre; tel. 465-2229; fax 466-9866; e-mail skn.union@caribsurf.com; internet www.sknlabourparty.org/spokesman; f. 1957; Wednesdays and Saturdays; organ of St Kitts-Nevis Trades and Labour Union; Editor Dawud Byron; Man. Walford Gumbs; circ. 6,000.

The Leeward Times: Old Hospital Rd, Charlestown, POB 535, Nevis; tel. 469-1409; fax 469-0662; e-mail hbramble@caribsurf.com; Editor Howell Bramble.

The St Kitts and Nevis Observer: Cayon St, POB 657, Basseterre; tel. 466-4994; fax 466-4995; e-mail observsk@caribsurf.com; internet www.stkittsnevisobserver.com; weekly; Publr and Editor-in-Chief Kenneth Williams.

FOREIGN NEWS AGENCIES

Associated Press (USA) and Inter Press Service (IPS) (Italy) are represented in Basseterre.

Publishers

Caribbean Publishing Co (St Kitts-Nevis) Ltd: Dr William Herbert Complex, Frigate Bay Rd, POB 745, Basseterre; tel. 465-5178; fax 466-0307; e-mail sbrisban@caribpub.com; internet www.caribpub.com.

MacPennies Publishing Co: 10A Cayon St East, POB 318, Basseterre; tel. 465-2274; fax 465-8668; e-mail mcpenltd@macpennies.com; internet www.macpennies.com; f. 1969.

Broadcasting and Communications

TELECOMMUNICATIONS

Regulatory Authority

Eastern Caribbean Telecommunications Authority: based on Castries, Saint Lucia; f. 2000; to regulate telecommunications in Saint Christopher and Nevis, Dominica, Grenada, Saint Lucia and Saint Vincent and the Grenadines.

Service Providers

Cable & Wireless St Kitts and Nevis: Cayon St, POB 86, Basseterre; tel. 465-1000; fax 465-1106; internet www.c.com/stkitts_nevis; f. 1985; fmrly St Kitts and Nevis Telecommunications Co Ltd (SKANTEL); 65% owned by Cable & Wireless plc; 17% state-owned; CEO Pat Walters.

UTS-CariGlobe: Basseterre; owned by United Telecom Services—UTS, of Curaçao, the Netherlands Antilles, and CariGlobe, a local operator that was granted a licence in May 2002 to provide mobile telecommunications network; CEO Clecton Phillip.

Digicel St Kitts and Nevis: Wireless Ventures (Saint Kitts and Nevis) Ltd, The Cable Bldg, cnr Cayon and New Sts, POB 1033, Basseterre; e-mail customercarestkittsandnevis@digicelgroup.com; internet www.digicelstkittsandnevis.com; acquired Cingular Wireless' Caribbean operations and licences in 2005; owned by an Irish consortium; Chair. DENIS O'BRIEN; Eastern Caribbean CEO KEVIN WHITE.

BROADCASTING
Radio

Choice FM: Wellington Rd, Needsmust, Basseterre; tel. 466-1891; fax 466-1892; e-mail choicefm@caribsurf.com; Man. VINCENT HERBERT.

Goodwill Radio FM 104.5: POB 98, Lodge Project; tel. 465-7795; fax 465-9556; Gen. Man. DENNIS HUGGINS-NELSON.

Radio One (SKNBC): Bakers Corner, POB 1773, Basseterre; tel. 466-0941; fax 465-0406; e-mail radio1941fm@yahoo.com; owned by St Kitts & Nevis Broadcasting Corpn; music and commentary; Man. Dir GUS WILLIAMS.

Radio Paradise: Bath Plain, POB 423, Nevis; tel. 469-1994; fax 469-1642; owned by US co (POB A, Santa Ana, CA 92711); religious; Man. ARTHUR GILBERT.

Sugar City Rock FM: Greenlands, Basseterre; tel. 466-1113; e-mail sugarcityrock@hotmail.com; Gen. Man. VAL THOMAS.

Trinity Broadcasting Ltd: Bath Plain Rd, Charlestown, Nevis; tel. 469-0285; fax 469-1723; Dir ARTHUR GILBERT.

Voice of Nevis (VON) Radio 895 AM: Bath Plain, Bath Village, POB 195, Charlestown, Nevis; tel. 469-1616; fax 469-5329; e-mail vonradio@caribsurf.com; internet www.vonradio.com; f. 1988; Nevis Broadcasting Co Ltd; Gen. Man. HERBERT EVERED.

WINN FM: Unit C24, The Sands, Newtown Bay Rd, Basseterre; tel. 466-9586; fax 466-7904; e-mail info@winnfm.com; internet www.winnfm.com; owned by Federation Media Group; Chair. MICHAEL KING.

ZIZ Radio and Television: Springfield, POB 331, Basseterre; tel. 465-2622; fax 465-5624; e-mail info@zizonline.com; internet www.zizonline.com; f. 1961; television from 1972; commercial; govt-owned; Gen. Man. WINSTON MCMAHON.

Television

ZIZ Radio and Television: see Radio.

Finance
(cap. = capital; res = reserves; dep. = deposits; brs = branches)

BANKING
Central Bank

Eastern Caribbean Central Bank (ECCB): Headquarters Bldg, Bird Rock, POB 89, Basseterre; tel. 465-2537; fax 465-9562; e-mail eccbinfo@caribsurf.com; internet www.eccb-centralbank.org; f. 1965 as East Caribbean Currency Authority; expanded responsibilities and changed name 1983; responsible for issue of currency in Anguilla, Antigua and Barbuda, Dominica, Grenada, Montserrat, Saint Christopher and Nevis, Saint Lucia and Saint Vincent and the Grenadines; res EC $121.7m., dep. EC $1,041.9m., total assets EC $1,740.5m. (March 2004); Gov. and Chair. Sir K. DWIGHT VENNER; Country Dir WENDELL LAWRENCE.

Local Banks

Bank of Nevis Ltd: Main St, POB 450, Charlestown, Nevis; tel. 469-5564; fax 469-5798; e-mail bon@caribsurf.com; internet www.bankofnevis.com.

RBTT Bank (SKN) Ltd: Main and Chappel Sts, POB 673, Charlestown, Nevis; tel. 469-5277; fax 469-1493; internet www.rbtt.com; f. 1955 as Nevis Co-operative Banking Co Ltd; acquired by Royal Bank of Trinidad and Tobago (later known as RBTT) in 1996; Group Chair. PETER J. JULY.

St Kitts-Nevis Anguilla National Bank Ltd: Central St, POB 343, Basseterre; tel. 465-2204; fax 466-1050; e-mail national_bank@sknanb.com; internet www.sknanb.com; f. 1971; Govt of St Kitts and Nevis owns 51%; cap. EC $81.0m., res EC $92.8m., dep. EC $1,109.0m. (June 2005); Chair. WALFORD GUMBS; Man. Dir EDWIN W. LAWRENCE; 5 brs.

Foreign Banks

Bank of Nova Scotia: Fort St, POB 433, Basseterre; tel. 465-4141; fax 465-8600; Man. W. A. CHRISTIE.

FirstCaribbean International Bank (Barbados) Ltd: Basseterre; internet www.firstcaribbeanbank.com; f. 2002 following merger of Caribbean operations of Barclays Bank PLC and CIBC; Exec. Chair MICHAEL MANSOOR; CEO CHARLES PINK.

Royal Bank of Canada: cnr Bay and Fort St, POB 91, Basseterre; tel. 465-2259; fax 465-1040.

Development Bank

Development Bank of St Kitts and Nevis: Church St, POB 249, Basseterre; tel. 465-2288; fax 465-4016; e-mail dbskn@caribsurf.com; internet www.skndb.com; f. 1981; cap. EC $8.0m., res EC $1.8m., dep. EC $2.5m.; Chair. JOSEPH LLEWELYN EDMEADE; Gen. Man. AUCKLAND HECTOR.

STOCK EXCHANGE

Eastern Caribbean Securities Exchange Ltd: Bird Rock, POB 94, Basseterre; tel. 466-7192; fax 465-3798; e-mail info@ecseonline.com; internet www.ecseonline.com; f. 2001; regional securities market designed to facilitate the buying and selling of financial products for the eight member territories—Anguilla, Antigua and Barbuda, Dominica, Grenada, Montserrat, Saint Christopher and Nevis, Saint Lucia and Saint Vincent and the Grenadines; Gen. Man. TREVOR BLAKE.

INSURANCE

National Caribbean Insurance Co Ltd: Central St, POB 374, Basseterre; tel. 465-2694; fax 465-3659; f. 1973; subsidiary of St Kitts-Nevis Anguilla National Bank Ltd.

St Kitts-Nevis Insurance Co Ltd (SNIC): Central St, POB 142, Basseterre; tel. 465-2845; fax 465-5410; internet www.tdclimited.com/snic; St Kitts-Nevis Anguilla Trading & Devt Co Ltd (TDC).

Several foreign companies also have offices in Saint Christopher and Nevis.

Trade and Industry
GOVERNMENT AGENCIES

Central Marketing Corpn (CEMACO): Pond's Pastire, Basseterre; tel. 465-2326; fax 465-2326; Man. MAXWELL GRIFFIN.

The Department of Planning and Development: The Cotton House, Market St, Charlestown, Nevis; tel. 469-5521; fax 469-1273; e-mail planevis@caribsurf.com.

Frigate Bay Development Corporation (FBDC): Frigate Bay, POB 315, Basseterre; tel. 465-8339; fax 465-4463; promotes tourist and residential developments; Chair. JANET HARRIS.

Investment Promotion Agency: Pelican Mall, Bay Rd, POB 132, Basseterre; tel. 465-4040; fax 465-6968; f. 1987.

Social Security Board: Bay Rd, POB 79, Basseterre; tel. 465-2535; fax 465-5051; e-mail ssbdirof@caribsurf.com; f. 1977; Dir SEPHLIN LAWRENCE.

CHAMBER OF COMMERCE

St Kitts-Nevis Chamber of Industry and Commerce: Horsford Rd, Fortlands, POB 332, Basseterre; tel. 465-2980; fax 465-4490; e-mail sknchamber@caribsurf.com; internet www.stkittsnevischamber.org; incorporated 1949; 140 mems; Pres. ANTHONY ABOURIZK; Exec. Dir WENDY PHIPPS.

EMPLOYERS' ORGANIZATIONS

Building Contractors' Association: Anthony Evelyn Business Complex, Paul Southwell Industrial Park, POB 1046, Basseterre; tel. 465-6897; fax 465-5623; e-mail sknbca@caribsurf.com; Pres. ANTHONY E. EVELYN.

Nevis Cotton Growers' Association Ltd: Charlestown, Nevis; Pres. IVOR STEVENS.

Small Business Association: Anthony Evelyn Business Complex, Paul Southwell Industrial Park, POB 367, Basseterre; tel. 465-8630; fax 465-6661; e-mail sb-association@caribsurf.com; Pres. EUSTACE WARNER.

UTILITIES

Nevis Electricity Company Ltd (Nevlec): Charlestown, Nevis; Gen. Man. EDGAR WIGGINS.

TRADE UNIONS

St Kitts-Nevis Trades and Labour Union: Masses House, Church St, POB 239, Basseterre; tel. 465-2229; fax 466-9866; e-mail sknunion@caribsurf.com; f. 1940; affiliated to Caribbean Maritime and Aviation Council, Caribbean Congress of Labour, International Federation of Plantation, Agricultural and Allied Workers and International Confederation of Free Trade Unions; associated with St Kitts-Nevis Labour Party; Pres. LEE L. MOORE; Gen. Sec. STANLEY R. FRANKS; about 3,000 mems.

SAINT CHRISTOPHER AND NEVIS

United Workers' Union (UWU): Market St, Basseterre; tel. 465-4130; associated with People's Action Movement.

Transport

RAILWAYS

There are 58 km (36 miles) of narrow-gauge light railway on Saint Christopher, serving the sugar plantations. The railway, complete with new trains and carriages, was restored and developed for tourist excursions and opened in late 2002.

St Kitts Scenic Railway: Basseterre; tel. 465-7263; e-mail scenicreservations@caribsurf.com; internet www.stkittsscenicrailway.com; f. 2002.

St Kitts Sugar Railway: St Kitts Sugar Manufacturing Corpn, POB 96, Basseterre; tel. 465-8099; fax 465-1059; e-mail agronomy@caribsurf.com; Gen. Man. J. E. S. ALFRED.

ROADS

In 1999 there were 320 km (199 miles) of road in Saint Christopher and Nevis, of which approximately 136 km (84 miles) are paved. In July 2001 the Caribbean Development Bank loaned US $3.75m. to the Nevis Government for a road improvement scheme.

SHIPPING

The Government maintains a commercial motor-boat service between the islands, and numerous regional and international shipping lines call at the islands. A deep-water port, Port Zante, was opened at Basseterre in 1981. In June 2003 Government of Kuwait agreed to provide a loan of EC $15m. to help fund the development of the cruise-ship facilities at Port Zante.

St Kitts Air and Sea Ports Authority: Bird Rock, POB 693, Basseterre; tel. 465-8121; fax 465-8124; e-mail scaspail@caribsurf.com; f. 1993 to combine St Kitts Port Authority and Airports Authority; Gen. Man. SIDNEY OSBORNE; Airport Man. EDWARD HUGHES; Sea Port Man. CARL BRAZIER-CLARKE.

Shipping Companies

Delisle Walwyn and Co Ltd: Liverpool Row, POB 44, Basseterre; tel. 465-2631; fax 465-1125; e-mail delwal@caribsurf.com; internet www.delisleco.com.

Sea Atlantic Cargo Shipping Corpn: Main St, POB 556, Charlestown, Nevis.

Tony's Ltd: Main St, POB 564, Charlestown, Nevis; tel. 469-5953; fax 469-5413.

CIVIL AVIATION

Robert Llewellyn Bradshaw (formerly Golden Rock) International Airport, 4 km (2½ miles) from Basseterre, is equipped to handle jet aircraft and is served by scheduled links with most Caribbean destinations, the United Kingdom, the USA and Canada. Saint Christopher and Nevis is a shareholder in the regional airline, LIAT (see chapter on Antigua and Barbuda). Vance W. Amory International Airport (formerly Newcastle Airfield), 11 km (7 miles) from Charlestown, Nevis, has regular scheduled services to St Kitts and other islands in the region. A new airport, Castle Airport, was opened on Nevis in 1998. In September 2002 a US $5.9m. project to construct a new passenger terminal at Vance W. Amory Airport was completed.

St Kitts Air and Sea Ports Authority: see Shipping.

Private Airlines

Air St Kitts-Nevis: Vance W. Amory International Airport, Newcastle, Nevis; tel. 469-9241; fax 469-9018.

Caribbean Star Airlines: Robert Llewellyn Bradshaw International Airport; f. 2000; relocated from Antigua in 2003; operates regional services; Pres. and CEO PAUL MOREIRA.

Nevis Express Ltd: Vance W. Amory International Airport, Newcastle, Nevis; tel. 469-9756; fax 469-9751; e-mail reservations@nevisexpress.com; internet www.nevisexpress.com; passenger and cargo charter services to all Caribbean destinations; St Kitts–Nevis shuttle service.

Tourism

The introduction of regular air services to the US cities of Miami and New York has opened up the islands as a tourist destination. Visitors are attracted by the excellent beaches on Saint Christopher and the spectacular mountain scenery of Nevis, the historical Brimstone Hill Fortress National Park on Saint Christopher and the islands' associations with Lord Nelson and Alexander Hamilton. In 2004 there were an estimated 260,121 cruise-ship passengers and 120,088 stop-over visitors. Receipts from tourism were estimated at EC $288.7m. in that year. There were 1,508 rooms in hotels and guest houses in Saint Christopher and Nevis in 1999. In 2005 the National Assembly approved the Cricket World Cup 2007 (Tourism Accommodation Incentives) Act; the Act was designed to encourage the construction and refurbishment of hotels and other tourist accommodation for the 2007 Cricket World Cup, hosted by several Caribbean nations, including St Kitts.

Nevis Tourism Authority: Main St, POB 917, Charlestown; tel. 469-7550; fax 469-7551; e-mail nta2001@caribsurf.com; internet www.nevisisland.com; Dir HELEN KIDD.

St Kitts Tourism Authority: Pelican Mall, Bay Rd, POB 132, Basseterre; tel. 465-4040; fax 465-8794; e-mail stkitts@stkittstourism.kn; internet www.stkittstourism.kn; Permanent Sec. LLOYD LAZAR.

St Kitts-Nevis Hotel and Tourism Association: Liverpool Row, POB 438, Basseterre; tel. 465-5304; fax 465-7746; e-mail stkitnevhta@caribsurf.com; f. 1972; Pres. SAM NG'ALLA; Exec. Dir VAL HENRY.

SAINT LUCIA

Introductory Survey

Location, Climate, Language, Religion, Flag, Capital

Saint Lucia is the second largest of the Windward Islands group of the West Indies, lying 40 km (25 miles) to the south of Martinique and 32 km (20 miles) to the north-east of Saint Vincent, in the Caribbean Sea. The island is volcanic, with spectacular mountain scenery—the Pitons, the island's twin, jungle-clad volcanic mountains were designated a UNESCO (see p. 127) World Heritage Site in June 2004. The average annual temperature is 26°C (79°F), with a dry season from January to April, followed by a rainy season from May to August. The average annual rainfall is 1,500 mm (60 ins) in the low-lying areas, and 3,500 mm (138 ins) in the mountains. The official language is English, although a large proportion of the population speak a French-based patois. Almost all of the island's inhabitants profess Christianity, and 68% are adherents of the Roman Catholic Church. The national flag (proportions 1 by 2) is blue, bearing in its centre a white-edged black triangle partly covered by a gold triangle rising from a common base. The capital is Castries.

Recent History

British settlers made an unsuccessful attempt to colonize the island (originally inhabited by a Carib people) in 1605. A further British party arrived in 1638 but were killed by the indigenous Carib population. France claimed sovereignty in 1642, and fighting between French and Caribs continued until 1660, when a peace treaty was signed. Control of Saint Lucia was transferred 14 times before it was ceded by the French and became a British colony in 1814. It remained under British rule for the next 165 years.

Representative government was introduced in 1924. The colony was a member of the Windward Islands, under a federal system, until December 1959. It joined the newly formed West Indies Federation in January 1958, and remained a member until the Federation's dissolution in May 1962. From January 1960 Saint Lucia, in common with other British territories in the Windward Islands, was given a new Constitution, with its own Administrator and an enlarged Legislative Council.

In 1951 the first elections under adult suffrage were won by the Saint Lucia Labour Party (SLP), which retained power until 1964, when John (later Sir John) Compton, of the newly formed conservative United Workers' Party (UWP), became Chief Minister. In March 1967 Saint Lucia became one of the West Indies Associated States, gaining full autonomy in internal affairs, with the United Kingdom retaining responsibility for defence and foreign relations only. The Legislative Council was replaced by a House of Assembly, the Administrator was designated Governor, and the Chief Minister became Premier.

In 1975 the Associated States agreed that they would seek independence individually. After three years of negotiations, Saint Lucia became independent on 22 February 1979, remaining within the Commonwealth. Compton became the country's first Prime Minister.

A general election in July 1979 returned the SLP to government with a clear majority, and its leader, Allan Louisy, succeeded Compton as Prime Minister. In February 1980 a new Governor-General, Boswell Williams, was appointed. This led to disputes within the Government and contributed to a split in the SLP. Louisy's resignation was demanded by 12 SLP members of the House of Assembly, who favoured his replacement by George Odlum, the Deputy Prime Minister. The controversy continued until April 1981, when Odlum and three other SLP members of the House voted with the opposition against the Government's budget, and Louisy was forced to resign. In May Winston Cenac, the Attorney-General in the Louisy Government, took office as Prime Minister, with a parliamentary majority of one. (Odlum and two other SLP members had broken away to form the Progressive Labour Party—PLP.) In September the Cenac administration defeated by one vote a motion of 'no confidence', introduced jointly by UWP and PLP members of the House, who accused the Government of political and economic mismanagement. In January 1982 a government proposal to alter legislation regarding the expenses of members of Parliament produced widespread accusations of corruption and provoked a series of strikes. Demands for the Government's resignation increased from all sectors of the community, culminating in a general strike. Cenac resigned, and an all-party interim administration was formed, under the deputy leader of the PLP, Michael Pilgrim, pending a general election that was scheduled for May. At the election the UWP was returned to power, and John Compton was re-elected Prime Minister. In December Sir Allen Lewis was reappointed Governor-General, following the dismissal of Boswell Williams because of his previous close association with the SLP.

In 1984 the opposition parties began to reorganize in order to present a more effective opposition to the UWP Government. At a general election to the 17-member House of Assembly in early April 1987, the UWP secured nine seats and the SLP eight. A further election took place at the end of the month, in the hope of a more decisive result, but the distribution of seats remained unchanged. In June the UWP's majority in the House was increased to three seats, when Cenac defected from the SLP. He was subsequently appointed Minister of Foreign Affairs.

In late October 1988 the Government introduced legislation whereby it assumed control of the banana industry for one year. Subsequently, the 1988 annual convention of the Saint Lucia Banana Growers' Association (SLBGA) was cancelled, and the Government dismissed the association's board of directors. The opposition parties alleged that these actions had been motivated by the fact that prominent supporters of the ruling UWP were the SLBGA's principal debtors. Despite continued protests, particularly by banana producers and the SLP, Government control was extended until July 1990.

At a general election in April 1992 the UWP won secured 11 seats and the SLP took the remaining six seats. The SLP attributed its defeat largely to a redefinition of constituency boundaries by the Government prior to the election. In October 1993 a three-day strike was organized by a new pressure group, the Banana Salvation Committee (BSC), in support of demands for an increase in the minimum price paid to local producers for bananas and for the dismissal of the board of directors of the SLBGA. Following recommendations made by a government appointed committee, the Government implemented price increases and dismissed the board of directors of the SLBGA, who were replaced by an interim board including representatives of the BSC. An announcement by the Government, in January 1994, that the SLBGA was to be placed into receivership provoked a strike by the BSC in March. The BSC organized further strikes by banana farmers in December and in February and July 1995, in support of demands for an extraordinary meeting of the SLBGA, and for an inquiry into the deaths of two demonstrators during the October 1993 strike. Further industrial action was undertaken by the BSC in February 1996, in protest at the monopoly on banana exports exercised by the state-run Windward Islands Banana Development and Exporting Co (Wibdeco), in the context of higher prices for produce being offered to banana growers by a US distributor. In September the House of Assembly approved a bill to revise the selection procedure for members of the SLBGA and the responsibilities of its general manager. The new legislation effectively transferred control of the Association from the Government to the banana growers, who would henceforth elect six members of the board of directors (while the Government would continue to nominate the remaining five). In October the BSC co-ordinated industrial action by banana growers in support of renewed demands for an end to the Wibdeco monopoly, and for reform of the industry's management and payment systems. Attempts by a number of farmers who opposed the strike to transport produce to ports resulted in violent clashes. Subsequent negotiations with a parliamentary review committee and with the Government (which promised to transfer some responsibility for the industry to the private sector) failed to appease the farmers.

In August 1995 the report of a commission of inquiry into allegations of the Government's involvement in the misappropriation, for electoral purposes, of some US $100,000 in UN contributions concluded that the former Permanent Representative to the UN, Charles Flemming, had been the sole perpetrator of the fraud. Flemming, who insisted that he had acted with the knowledge and endorsement of senior members of the UWP (including the Prime Minister), failed to return from a visit to the USA undertaken during the commission's hearings. The Minister of State with Responsibility for Financial Services and the National Development Corporation, Rufus Bousquet (who claimed to have been an unwitting recipient of the funds), had been dismissed in May, after he publicly questioned whether it was appropriate that the Government remain in office pending investigation of the affair.

A UWP party conference, convened in January 1996, endorsed the appointment of Vaughan Lewis, the former Director-General of the Organisation of Eastern Caribbean States (OECS, see p. 397), to the vacancy created by the Prime Minister's retirement from the party leadership. Lewis contested and won the Central Castries parliamentary by-election in February, and was subsequently appointed Minister without Portfolio. SLP leader Julian Hunte resigned later in the month, following criticism of the party's poor performance at the by-election; Kenny Anthony, a former SLP education and culture minister, replaced him. In late March Compton resigned the premiership, and was succeeded in early April by Lewis.

A general election on 23 May 1997 was won decisively by the SLP, which was returned to power after 15 years, securing 16 of the 17 seats in the House of Assembly (with 61% of the votes cast). Kenny Anthony was sworn in as the new Prime Minister. Among the nine ministers in his first Cabinet was George Odlum (as Minister of Foreign Affairs and International Trade), who had rejoined the SLP in July 1996. Following his electoral defeat, Lewis announced his intention to resign the leadership of the UWP; Sir John Compton (as he had become), the former UWP leader and former Prime Minister, replaced him in June 1998.

In August 1997 the Governor-General, Sir George Mallet resigned. His appointment, in June 1996, had been opposed by the SLP, on the grounds that the post's tradition of neutrality would be compromised—Mallet had previously been Deputy Prime Minister, and his portfolio had included several influential ministries. Saint Lucia's first female Governor-General, Dr Pearlette Louisy, was appointed in mid-September 1997.

In December 1997, in an attempt to address the proliferation in violent crime, the House of Assembly approved an amendment to the Firearms Act whereby persons in possession of unlicensed guns or ammunition would be liable to up to five years' imprisonment. In March 1998 Anthony announced further measures to ensure public security, including the recruitment of additional police-officers and the denial of bail to suspects in cases involving firearms.

In September 1997 the inquiry into allegations of corruption under the UWP, which had been promised by the SLP Government after its election, began, but hearings were effectively stalled in subsequent months by complaints by lawyers representing Sir John Compton and Vaughan Lewis that the sole commissioner, Monica Joseph, would not be impartial in her judgment. Despite a high court ruling in November that Joseph was competent to judge, further legal challenges were initiated, and Joseph finally withdrew from the inquiry in March 1998. Sir Louis Blom-Cooper, a prominent British jurist, was appointed in her place. In August 1999 Blom-Cooper submitted his report to the Government. The report cleared Compton and Lewis of corruption, but noted instances of impropriety and a 'high degree of maladministration' in their Governments.

In mid-September 1997 the directors of the SLBGA resigned, at Anthony's request: the Government was reportedly concerned that divisions at boardroom level were damaging the association's operations. Such divisions became increasingly pronounced as plans proceeded for the privatization of the SLBGA, one of the stated aims of the SLP Government. The Concerned Farmers Group (CFG), formed in December and led by the ousted Chairman, Rupert Gajadhar, which grouped larger farmers, expressed concern that the more numerous smaller producers in the BSC (whose secretary, Patrick Joseph, was also a government senator) would unduly dominate the new company, since decision-making was to be on the basis of one-member-one-vote. Members of the CFG threatened to establish their own company unless their concerns were addressed.

In July 1998 the SLBGA was privatized and the Saint Lucia Banana Corpn (SLBC) was created in its place. The Government agreed to assume the debts incurred by the dissolved SLBGA, equivalent to EC $44m. The CFG, which had refused to participate in the process, subsequently established a rival company, the Tropical Quality Fruit Co (TQF). In October 1998 a court judgment ruled that the SLBC did not enjoy monopoly rights in the banana trade. This ruling followed complaints from the TQF that Wibdeco had been refusing to accept its fruit for shipment. The TQF alleged that this refusal was owing to pressure exerted by the SLBC Chairman, Patrick Joseph, in his capacity as a member of the Wibdeco board.

In January 1999 the SLBC announced that it had incurred losses of EC $6m. in 1998 and would therefore be forced to reduce the price paid to farmers. The SLBC blamed its operating deficit primarily on the fact that, because banana production had been underestimated, Wibdeco had failed to obtain sufficient European Union (EU, see p. 228) licences, meaning that much of the fruit produced did not reach high-paying markets. The TQF also announced a deficit, but claimed that its lower operating costs had reduced its losses. The TQF further suggested that the SLBC had damaged its own profitability by keeping prices deliberately high in an attempt to force the TQF out of business.

In July 1999 the Government founded a Banana Industry Trust, which was to oversee the improvement of farming practices in the banana sector and manage the financial resources available to the industry, including EC $21m. in funds provided by the EU. In the same month the Government announced that it was to make official loans of $7m. to the SLBC and $1.9m. to the TQF. However, falling prices and the ongoing lack of confidence among growers led the Government to announce that it was to hold senior-level talks with representatives of Wibdeco and Geest Bananas in order to discuss future pricing arrangements, while the Chairman of the SLBC urged Wibdeco and Geest to release money from their emergency funds to farmers threatened with bankruptcy. In August Wibdeco agreed to finance a temporary subsidy on prices in order to alleviate hardship among growers. In late 1999, however, the company encountered increasing pressure from the SLBC and from the Government to deliver increased returns to farmers, and in January 2000, following the expiry of its agreement to sell through Wibdeco, the SLBC announced plans to sell directly to Geest, despite criticism from its other regional partners in Wibdeco. In March Wibdeco announced that it would not contest the SLBC's decision, although it suggested that it might itself bypass the SLBC by buying directly from farmers.

Disbursement of a £1m. bonus fund to banana growers became the centre of a dispute between Wibdeco and the SLBC in April 2000, when the SLBC refused to submit a list of its banana growers and suppliers to Wibdeco, stating instead that it would provide a breakdown of the total payments from either Wibdeco or Geest to the individual growers. SLBC accused Wibdeco of attempting to use SLBC's money to compete directly with growers aligned to the Corporation by making payments directly to the growers. In late May the dispute was resolved when Wibdeco decided to pay the monies to the growers through the local banana associations in the four Windward Islands to whom the growers had sold their bananas in 1999. In October Patrick Joseph resigned as chairman of the SLBC, stating that differences had arisen between himself and the SLBC board. In the following month the SLBC board of directors was dismissed and a three-member management committee was instituted to run the Corporation until the election of a new board.

In January 2001, following an increase in tourist cancellations, Prime Minister Anthony announced a series of measures intended to reduce the crime rate in Saint Lucia. These included the establishment of a National Anti-Crime Commission, the creation of a 10-member police 'rapid response unit', a review of the penal code, and reforms to the police service. In June Anthony announced the creation of four more rapid response units, a special task force to target known criminals, plans for more severe penalties for gun crimes, an increase in police patrols and an amnesty for holders of illegal firearms. A special joint session of Parliament convened in the following month to debate the increase in violent crime.

In March 2001 the Minister of Foreign Affairs and International Trade, George Odlum, left the Government and the SLP to join a new opposition grouping, the National Alliance (NA). The former premier, Sir John Compton, and the UWP leader, Morella Joseph, had founded the NA in advance of legislative elections due in 2002, but widely expected to be held in late 2001. Prime Minister Anthony stated that he had dismissed Odlum from his ministerial post, although Odlum himself claimed that he had resigned from the Government. Julian Hunte, a former Permanent Representative to the UN, replaced Odlum as foreign minister.

In October 2001 the NA's assembly elected Compton to head the party. However, Odlum rejected the decision and claimed the voting process was flawed. Later the same month the UWP withdrew from the Alliance and announced it would contest the elections as a single party. Odlum chose to retain the National Alliance name for his group.

As expected, the ruling SLP achieved another convincing victory at the 3 December 2001 general election, winning 14 of the 17 parliamentary seats (and 54.2% of the valid votes cast). The remaining seats were taken by the UWP (which received 36.6% of the ballot). Joseph and Odlum, leader of the UWP and the NA, respectively, both lost their seats. Nevertheless, the UWP regained two seats in the troubled 'banana belt' region, including that previously held by the Minister of Agriculture, Forestry and Fisheries, Cassius Elias. The voter turn-out rate decreased to 53%, from 67% in the 1997 election. Following the heavy electoral defeat of the UWP, Joseph resigned as the party's leader and was replaced by Vaughan Lewis. Marius Wilson became the new parliamentary leader of the opposition in December 2001. Meanwhile, in the same month, Prime Minister Anthony announced a new 15-member cabinet.

In January 2003 the UWP replaced Wilson as parliamentary leader with Arsene James. In the light of the decision, Wilson, whose 18-month tenure as opposition leader was blighted by controversy and allegations of improper conduct, announced his intention to resign from the party and take up a new position as an independent member of parliament.

Responding to the threat of war in the Middle East, widespread concerns about international terrorism and an increase in the number of people applying for visas to enter Saint Lucia, in March 2003 the Government introduced stricter controls on the processing of passports and visas, and strengthened security measures at air and sea ports.

In July 2003 Parliament approved a constitutional amendment abolishing the oath of allegiance to the British monarch; instead, elected members were to pledge loyalty to the Saint Lucian people. In November the Government announced the establishment of a Constitutional Review Commission. The development, which was supported by the opposition, was designed to expand public particpation in Saint Lucia's democracy. Meanwhile, also in November the Government passed a new Criminal Code, which included two particularly controversial clauses. The first, Section 361, provided for a two-year prison sentence for anyone convicted of spreading 'false news'. The clause provoked consternation among local media representatives and the UWP, whose MPs absented themselves from the vote. The second controversial element of the Code, Section 166, allowed for the legalization of abortions, previously illegal in all circumstances, in cases of rape, incest and medical danger to the mother. The law prompted trenchant criticism from anti-abortion and religious groups, and in January 2004 led to the dismissal of Sarah Flood-Beaubrun from her post as Minister of Home Affairs and Gender Relations, following a vehement disagreement with her fellow ministers over the new legislation; in March she resigned from the SLP and later established a new political party—the Organization for National Empowerment.

Flood-Beaubrun's dismissal from the Government was part of a wider cabinet realignment in early 2004, which included the appointment of the erstwhile Minister of Agriculture, Forestry and Fisheries, Calixte George, as head of a new Ministry of Home Affairs and Internal Security. The new department was to oversee the police service, previously the responsibility of the Attorney-General's Office, and was charged with finding a solution to the island's spiralling crime rate. Nevertheless, in 2004 the number of murders reached a record level, 37, compared with 33 recorded in both 2003 and 2002, and by early November 2005 there had already been 35 murders in that year. In April 2005 the Government announced it would introduce an Interception of Communication bill to Parliament, granting extra powers to law enforcement authorities; the proposed legislation, which attracted trenchant criticism from opposition parties, received senate approval in November. In the first 10 months of that year 154 illegal guns were recovered through police raids and under a new 'amnesty' scheme, compared with 48 in the whole of 2004. Meanwhile, the island's increasing drugs-use problem, which George had, in October, blamed partly on the immigration of Venezuelan drugs-dealers, led the Government to consider in November the establishment of a specialist court, designed both to sentence and to plan the rehabilitation of convicted users. In January 2006 Anthony pledged to make greater use of the death penalty as a weapon against the increasing problem of crime.

In November 2003 the High Court ruled that the Government's approval of the refinancing of the construction of the Hyatt Hotel in 1997 was 'void and illegal'. The opposition criticized the Government for not having sought parliamentary approval for the authorization of the loan and called for the resignation of the Attorney-General, Petrus Compton, whose actions, it claimed, were particularly implicated by the judgment. In October 2004 the much-criticized Compton was moved to the Ministry of Foreign Affairs, International Trade and Civil Aviation. His predecessor, Julian Hunte, had been reappointed ambassador of Saint Lucia to the UN. Victor La Corbiniere was given the vacant role of Attorney-General and Minister of Justice. Meanwhile, in December 2004 Prime Minister Anthony announced his intention to stand for a third term in office at the forthcoming elections, constitutionally due in 2006.

Meanwhile, in early April 2004 Marcus Nicholas, a UWP deputy, withdrew his support for Arsene James, whose popularity had fallen in recent months. With the support of Marius Wilson, Nicholas became the new leader of a four-member opposition. Nicholas criticized the UWP leadership and, in response, the UWP hierarchy cancelled his party membership. In addition to James being the party's sole loyal supporter in the House of Assembly, the UWP remained unable to develop a strong party executive and in March 2005 elected the veteran politician Sir John Compton as its leader, in preference to the incumbent candidate, Vaughan Lewis.

In March 2006 the SLP candidate, Victor La Corbinere, was defeated in a by-election by an independent candidate, Richard Frederick, who was supported by the UWP. A mere 34% of registered voters participated in the election, although some observers regarded the poll as an accurate indication of the SLP's standing before the general election, which was scheduled to be held by December.

Saint Lucia's most important export market is the United Kingdom, which receives most of the banana crop under the terms of the Cotonou Agreement (see p. 277), the successor agreement to the Lomé Convention, which expired in 2000. In July 1993 new regulations came into effect governing the level of imports of bananas by the European Community (now EU, of which the United Kingdom is a member). The regulations were introduced to protect traditional producers covered by the Lomé Convention from competition from the expanding Latin American producers. At the instigation of the Latin American producers, consecutive dispute panels were appointed by the General Agreement on Tariffs and Trade (which was succeeded by the World Trade Organization—WTO, see p. 370) to rule on whether the EU's actions contravened GATT rules. Although the dispute panels ruled in favour of the Latin American producers, the rulings were not enforceable. In February 1996, with support from Ecuador, Guatemala, Mexico and Honduras, the USA renewed consultations, begun in September 1995, with the WTO concerning the EU's banana import quota regime. In March 1997 a WTO interim report appeared to uphold many of the charges of unfair discrimination brought by the plaintiffs. The WTO Appellate Body rejected representations by the EU against the ruling in September, and the EU was informed that it must formulate a new system for banana imports by early 1998. This ruling was accepted by the EU, which in January 1998 proposed new arrangements under which it would apply a system of quotas and tariffs to both groups of producers, while retaining an import-licensing system.

The EU's new banana import regime was implemented on 1 January 1999 in compliance with the WTO ruling, though the USA criticized the reforms as negligible. Further discussions on the issue broke down in late January 1999 when Saint Lucia, backed by other countries, objected to any discussion of US demands for sanctions on EU goods. On 1 February the USA introduced punitive import duties on various EU goods, and in March the WTO disputes panel was asked to consider whether the EU had done enough to amend its import regime and whether the USA could legally impose retaliatory import tariffs of up to 100% on certain EU goods. In retaliation against this move, the banana-exporting countries threatened to withdraw their co-operation with the US campaign against drugs-trafficking, while banana-producers warned that they might switch to growing marijuana if they were forced out of business. On 6 April WTO arbitrators awarded damages against the EU, although at a lower level than the USA had been claiming. On 12 April the

WTO again delivered a ruling criticizing aspects of the EU banana-importing regime, and which gave the USA permission to impose retaliatory tariffs on certain European goods. In April 2001 the USA agreed to suspend these sanctions from 1 July, after the dispute was resolved: following a transition period, a new, tariff-only regime was introduced from 2006.

Saint Lucia is a member of the OECS, and, since May 1987, has been a prominent advocate of the creation of a unitary East Caribbean state. In 1988 however, Antigua and Barbuda expressed opposition to political union, thereby discouraging any participation by Montserrat or Saint Christopher and Nevis. The four English-speaking Windward Islands countries (Saint Lucia, Dominica, Grenada and Saint Vincent and the Grenadines) thus announced plans to proceed independently towards a more limited union. In 1990 the leaders of the four countries established a Regional Constituent Assembly. Following a series of discussions, the Assembly issued its final report in late 1992, in which it stated that the four countries were committed to the establishment of economic and political union under a federal system. In February 2006 the House of Assembly approved legislation allowing Saint Lucia to join the Caribbean Single Market and Economy in June (see Economic Affairs).

The new Government effected a significant reorientation of foreign policy in August 1997, when it was announced that diplomatic relations were to be established with the People's Republic of China; it was reported that China was to provide educational materials valued at US $1m. immediately, and was to finance the construction of a new national sports stadium, a cultural centre, a new highway and a free-trade zone. Taiwan subsequently severed relations with Saint Lucia. By 2004 it was estimated that China had provided Saint Lucia with funds worth US $100m. throughout the seven years of their association. In late 2005 the Prime Minister accused the UWP of jeopardizing Saint Lucia's profitable relationship with China after allegations emerged that Sir John Compton had secretly met the President of Taiwan in Saint Vincent and the Grenadines and sought to develop a relationship between the UWP and Taiwan.

On 19 November 2003 Parliament passed legislation enabling the Government to pledge US $2.5m. towards the establishment of the Caribbean Court of Justice (CCJ), to be headquartered in Trinidad. The CCJ, which replaced the Privy Council in the United Kingdom as the region's highest court, was inaugurated in April 2005.

Government

Saint Lucia is a constitutional monarchy. Executive power is vested in the British monarch, as Head of State, and is exercisable by the Governor-General, who represents the monarchy and is appointed on the advice of the Prime Minister. Legislative power is vested in Parliament, comprising the monarch, the 17-member House of Assembly, elected from single-member constituencies for up to five years by universal adult suffrage, and the Senate, composed of 11 members appointed by the Governor-General, including six appointed on the advice of the Prime Minister and three on the advice of the Leader of the Opposition. Government is effectively by the Cabinet. The Governor-General appoints the Prime Minister and, on the latter's recommendation, the other Ministers. The Prime Minister must have majority support in the House, to which the Cabinet is responsible.

Defence

The Royal Saint Lucia Police Force, which numbers about 300 men, includes a Special Service Unit for purposes of defence. Saint Lucia participates in the US-sponsored Regional Security System, comprising police, coastguards and army units, which was established by independent East Caribbean states in 1982. There are also two patrol vessels for coastguard duties.

Economic Affairs

In 2004, according to estimates by the World Bank, Saint Lucia's gross national income (GNI), measured at average 2002–04 prices, was US $705.5m., equivalent to $4,310 per head (or $5,560 per head on an international purchasing-power parity basis). During 1995–2004, it was estimated, the population increased by an annual average rate of 1.3%, while gross domestic product (GDP) per head remained almost constant, in real terms. Overall GDP increased, in real terms, at an average annual rate of 1.3% in 1995–2004; according to the Eastern Caribbean Central Bank (ECCB, see p. 388), real GDP increased 5.8% in 2004.

In 2004 agriculture (including hunting, forestry and fishing) accounted for 5.1% of GDP and employed some 19.5% of the active working population in 2000. Despite the decline in banana industry, the fruit remains Saint Lucia's principal cash crop, and in 2003 accounted for 40.6% of the total value of domestic merchandise exports (compared with 80.9% in 2000). Other important crops include coconuts, mangoes, citrus fruit, cocoa and spices. Commercial fishing was being developed and in August 2001 Japan granted US $10.6m. towards the rehabilitation and improvement of fishery facilities in the Choiseul and Soufrière districts. During 1996–2004 real agricultural GDP decreased by an annual average of 8.9%, largely as a result of a 12.3% decline in the banana sector. The sector's real GDP decreased by 13.2% in 2004, but expanded by some 5.1% in 2004.

Industry (including mining, manufacturing, public utilities and construction) accounted for 16.5% of GDP in 2004 and the sector engaged an estimated 21.1% of the active working population in 2000. During 1996–2004 industrial GDP increased by an estimated annual average of 1.3%. In 2004 the sector's real GDP increased by only 0.6%. Construction contributed 6.5% to GDP in 2004. The sector demonstrated strong growth in the 1990s, but the real GDP of construction decreased in 2001–03 (by 3.8% in the latter year), before increasing by some 3.1% in 2004.

Manufacturing accounted for 5.0% of GDP in 2004, and employed 10.3% of the employed population in 2000. The principal manufacturing industries, which have been encouraged by the establishment of 'free zones', include the processing of agricultural products, the assembly of electronic components and the production of garments, plastics, paper and packaging (associated with banana production), beer, rum and other beverages. During 1996–2004 the sector's real GDP decreased by an annual average of 0.3%. Real manufacturing GDP, however, increased by 2.5% in 2004.

Energy is traditionally derived from imported hydrocarbon fuels (mineral fuels and lubricants comprised 10.4% of total imports in 2003). There is a petroleum storage and transhipment terminal on the island. In early 2006 the Government was considering signing the PetroCaribe accord, under which Saint Lucia would be allowed to purchase petroleum from Venezuela at reduced prices.

The services sector contributed 78.5% of GDP in 2004 and engaged an estimated 56.9% of those employed in 2000. Tourism is the most important of the service industries, and in 2004 tourist receipts of EC $879.3m. were equivalent to some 74.1% of the value of total exports of goods and services. The number of visitor arrivals increased by 4.5% in 2003 and by 15.5% in 2004, as the sector recovered from a contraction in arrivals of 12.1% in 2002, caused by the effects of the global economic slowdown and the US-led 'war on terror'. Having declined in 2001 and 2002, the real GDP of the hotels and restaurants sector increased by 16.6% in 2003 and by a further 5.9% in 2004. The planned establishment of the island's first casino in December 2006 was expected further to stimulate the sector. During 1996–2004 the real GDP of the services sector increased by an annual average of 2.5%. The sector increased by 4.8% in 2004.

In 2004 Saint Lucia recorded an estimated visible trade deficit of EC $781.7m., and a deficit of some EC $324.0m. on the current account of the balance of payments. The principal source of imports in 2003 was the USA (39.3% of the total); other important markets in that year were Trinidad and Tobago (15.1%) and the United Kingdom (8.1%). The principal market for exports is the United Kingdom, which received 37.6% of total exports in 2003; other major export markets were the USA (20.0%), Trinidad and Tobago (11.7%) and Barbados (9.6%). The Caribbean Community and Common Market (CARICOM, see p. 183) member states accounted for 21.9% of imports and 37.3% of exports in 2003. Food and live animals (comprised mainly of bananas sent to the United Kingdom) was the principal export commodity in 2003, ahead of beverages and tobacco (mainly beer) and miscellaneous manufactured articles. The principal imports were machinery and transport equipment, food and basic manufactures.

In 2004 there was an overall budgetary deficit of EC $52.5m., equivalent to 3.1% of GDP. Saint Lucia's total external debt at the end of 2004 was US $368.3m., of which US $235.0m. was long-term public debt. In that year the cost of debt-servicing was equivalent to 8.7% of the value of exports of goods and services. The annual rate of inflation averaged 2.4% in 1998–2004; inflation averaged 1.0% in 2003 and 4.6% in 2004. In 2004 the average rate of unemployment was 21%.

Saint Lucia is a member of CARICOM, the ECCB, and of the Organisation of Eastern Caribbean States (OECS, see p. 397). Saint Lucia is also a member of the regional stock exchange, the

SAINT LUCIA

Eastern Caribbean Securities Exchange (based in Saint Christopher and Nevis), established in 2001. Saint Lucia has been a strong advocate of closer political and economic integration within the Caribbean region and was scheduled to join CARICOM's Caribbean Single Market and Economy (CSME) in June 2006. The CSME, which was established by six founding member states on 1 January 2006, was to enshrine the free movement of goods, services and labour throughout most of the CARICOM region. Saint Lucia is party to the Caribbean Basin Initiative (CBI) and to the Cotonou Agreement (see p. 277), the successor accord to the Lomé Convention.

The Saint Lucian economy, which traditionally relied on the production of bananas for export, underwent considerable structural change at the end of the 20th century, with the emergence of service industries as the most important sectors of the economy, while investment in the islands' infrastructure also benefited the tourism industry, which became the island's principal source of foreign exchange. In 2005 the World Travel and Tourism Council estimated that the tourism sector accounted for about 43% of Saint Lucia's GDP and employment. However, the agricultural sector remained a significant source of employment and the erosion of Saint Lucia's preferential access to European markets was of considerable concern. Banana production declined dramatically from the 1990s as a result of poor climatic conditions and the retrenchments in the industry caused by increased international competition and lower market prices. Following the devastating effects of 'Hurricane Lili' in September 2002, which destroyed about 50% of the banana crop, the beleaguered industry received assistance worth some US $8.5m. from the Caribbean Development Bank and the EU. Further damage was caused to the sector by 'Hurricane Ivan' and outbreaks of the leafspot fungus in 2004. As part of its efforts to diversify the economy, the Government also attempted to establish Saint Lucia as a centre for international financial services; Saint Lucia's first 'offshore' bank opened in 2001. The economy grew by some 5.8% in 2004, stimulated by a 15.5% increase in visitor arrivals, and was forecast to expand by a further 4.0% in 2005. Strong growth in the tourism industry was expected to continue in the latter year after stop-over arrivals (the highest-spending variety of tourist) in January–June increased by some 14.0%, compared with January–June 2004. The island's hosting of the 2007 Cricket World Cup (along with several other Caribbean countries and territories) was certain further to stimulate the economy. The positive outlook was questioned, however, when Air Jamaica, which operated 14 flights per week to the island, announced it was temporarily suspending its service in early 2005—over 25% of Saint Lucia's 110,000 tourists from North America in 2004 travelled with the airline. Negotiations to resume the service had not been concluded by the end of that year. The Government's stated economic priorities in 2006 included reducing the high rate of unemployment, accelerating the implementation of a universal health-care system, planning entry into the CSME and preparing to host the cricket tournament, which required increasing by some 75% the number of hotel rooms on the island.

Education

Education is compulsory for 10 years between five and 15 years of age. Primary education begins at the age of five and lasts for seven years. Secondary education, beginning at 12 years of age, lasts for five years, comprising a first cycle of three years and a second cycle of two years. Free education is provided in more than 90 government-assisted schools. Facilities for industrial, technical and teacher-training are available at the Sir Arthur Lewis Community College at Morne Fortune, which also houses an extra-mural branch of the University of the West Indies. In May 2002 it was announced that additional US $19m. was to be invested in the education system during September 2002–September 2006. The project, to build two new secondary schools and renovate existing ones, was to be partially funded by the World Bank and UNESCO. The implementation of universal secondary education was a stated aim of the Saint Lucia Labour Party Government. Some EC $132.7m. was allocated to the Ministry of Education, Human Resource Development, Youth and Sports in the 2004/05 budget.

Public Holidays

2006: 1–2 January (New Year), 22 February (Independence Day), 14 April (Good Friday), 17 April (Easter Monday), 1 May (Labour Day), 5 June (Whit Monday), 15 June (Corpus Christi), 1 August (Emancipation Day), 6 October (Thanksgiving Day), 1 November (All Saints' Day), 2 November (All Souls' Day), 22 November (Feast of St Cecilia), 13 December (Saint Lucia Day), 25–26 December (Christmas).

2007: 1–2 January (New Year), 22 February (Independence Day), 6 April (Good Friday), 9 April (Easter Monday), 1 May (Labour Day), 28 May (Whit Monday), 7 June (Corpus Christi), 2 August (Emancipation Day), 5 October (Thanksgiving Day), 1 November (All Saints' Day), 2 November (All Souls' Day), 22 November (Feast of St Cecilia), 13 December (Saint Lucia Day), 25–26 December (Christmas).

Weights and Measures

The imperial system is in use.

Statistical Survey

Source (unless otherwise indicated): St Lucian Government Statistics Department, Block A, Government Bldgs, Waterfront, Castries; tel. 452-6653; fax 451-8254; e-mail statsdept@candw.lc; internet www.stats.gov.lc.

AREA AND POPULATION

Area: 616.3 sq km (238 sq miles).

Population: 135,685 (males 65,988, females 69,697) at census of 12 May 1991; 158,147 (males 77,264, females 80,883) at census of 22 May 2001. *2004:* 162,300 (mid-year estimate). *By District* (2001 census, preliminary figures): Castries 60,390; Anse La Raye 5,954; Canaries 1,741; Soufrière 7,337; Choiseul 5,993; Laborie 7,329; Vieux-Fort 14,561; Micoud 15,892; Dennery 12,537; Gros Islet 19,409. Source: partly Caribbean Development Bank, *Social and Economic Indicators*.

Density (mid-2004): 263.3 per sq km.

Principal Town (estimated population incl. suburbs, mid-2003): Castries (capital) 13,687. Source: UN, *World Urbanization Prospects: The 2003 Revision*.

Births, Marriages and Deaths (2001): Registered live births 2,729 (birth rate 17.3 per 1,000); Registered marriages 449 (marriage rate 2.8 per 1,000); Registered deaths 980 (death rate 6.2 per 1,000). *2003:* Crude birth rate 14.7 per 1,000; Crude death rate 6.5 per 1,000 (Source: Caribbean Development Bank, *Social and Economic Indicators*).

Expectation of Life (years at birth): 72 (males 69; females 75) in 2003. Source: WHO, *World Health Report*.

Economically Active Population (persons aged 15 years and over, labour survey for July–December 2000): Agriculture, hunting and forestry 11,660; Fishing 900; Manufacturing 6,610; Electricity, gas and water 530; Construction 6,460; Wholesale and retail trade; repair of motor vehicles, motorcycles and personal and household goods 11,090; Hotels and restaurants 6,140; Transport, storage and communications 4,540; Financial intermediation 870; Real estate, renting and business activities 1,450; Public administration and defence; compulsory social security 8,180; Education 1,390; Health and social work 450; Other community, social and personal service activities 1,130; Private households with employed persons 1,390; Activities not adequately defined 1,580; *Total employed* 64,370 (males 35,620, females 28,750); Unemployed 13,630; *Total labour force* 78,000.

HEALTH AND WELFARE

Key Indicators

Total Fertility Rate (children per woman, 2003): 2.3.
Under-5 Mortality Rate (per 1,000 live births, 2004): 14.
Physicians (per 1,000 head, 1998): 5.18.
Hospital Beds (per 1,000 head, 1996): 3.38.
Health Expenditure (2002): US $ per head (PPP): 306.
Health Expenditure (2002): % of GDP: 5.0.

SAINT LUCIA

Statistical Survey

Health Expenditure (2002): public (% of total): 68.4.
Access to Water (% of persons, 2002): 98.
Access to Sanitation (% of persons, 2002): 89.
Human Development Index (2003): ranking: 76.
Human Development Index (2003): value: 0.772.

For sources and definitions, see explanatory note on p. vi.

AGRICULTURE, ETC.

Principal Crops (FAO estimates, '000 metric tons, 2004): Cassava 1.0; Yams 4.5; Other roots and tubers 5.7; Coconuts 14.0; Vegetables 1.0; Bananas 120.0; Plantains 1.3; Grapefruit 3.0; Mangoes 28.0; Other fruits 5.7.

Livestock (FAO estimates, '000 head, year ending September 2004): Cattle 12.4; Sheep 12.5; Goats 9.8; Pigs 15.0; Horses 1.0; Asses 0.5; Mules 1.0; Poultry 240.

Livestock Products (FAO estimates, '000 metric tons, 2004): Beef and veal 0.5; Pig meat 0.7; Poultry meat 1.2; Cows' milk 1.0; Hen eggs 0.5.

Fishing (metric tons, live weight, 2003): Capture 1,462 (Snappers 57; Wahoo 169; Skipjack tuna 132; Blackfin tuna 169; Yellowfin tuna 139; Flyingfishes 75; Common dolphinfish 286; Stromboid conches 48); Aquaculture 2 (estimate); Total catch 1,464 (estimate). Figures exclude aquatic plants and mammals.

Source: FAO.

INDUSTRY

Production (preliminary, 2003 unless otherwise stated): Electric energy 199.5 million kWh (preliminary, 2004); Copra 1,162 metric tons; Coconut oil (unrefined) 734,000 litres (2002); Coconut oil (refined) 2,288,000 litres; Coconut meal 829,000 kg; Rum 9,000 hectolitres (revised figure, 1999). Sources: IMF, *St Lucia: Statistical Appendix* (December 2004), Eastern Caribbean Central Bank and UN, *International Commodity Statistics Yearbook*.

FINANCE

Currency and Exchange Rates: 100 cents = 1 Eastern Caribbean dollar (EC $). *Sterling, US Dollar and Euro Equivalents* (30 December 2005): £1 sterling = EC $4.649; US $1 = EC $2.700; €1 = EC $3.185; EC $100 = £21.51 = US $37.04 = €31.40. *Exchange Rate:* Fixed at US $1 = EC $2.70 since July 1976.

Budget (preliminary, EC $ million, 2004): *Revenue:* Tax revenue 494.6 (Taxes on income and profits 116.4; Taxes on domestic goods and services 93.3; Taxes on international trade and transactions 281.0); Other current revenue 40.6; Capital revenue 1.0; Total 536.2 (excl. grants 6.0). *Expenditure:* Current expenditure 481.8 (Personal emoluments 221.8; Goods and services 92.4; Interest payments 62.0; Transfers and subsidies 105.6); Capital expenditure and net lending 112.9; Total 594.7. Source: Eastern Caribbean Central Bank.

International Reserves (US $ million at 31 December 2004): IMF special drawing rights 2.34; Foreign exchange 130.19; Total 132.53. Source: IMF, *International Financial Statistics*.

Money Supply (EC $ million at 31 December 2004): Currency outside banks 99.16; Demand deposits at deposit money banks 407.67; Total money (incl. others) 506.84. Source: IMF, *International Financial Statistics*.

Cost of Living (Consumer Price Index; base: 2000 = 100): 101.7 in 2002; 102.7 in 2003; 107.4 in 2004. Source: IMF, *International Financial Statistics*.

Gross Domestic Product (EC $ million at current factor cost): 1,539.6 in 2002; 1,614.0 in 2003; 1,689.7 in 2004 (preliminary). Source: Eastern Caribbean Central Bank.

Expenditure on the Gross Domestic Product (preliminary, EC $ million at current prices, 2004): Government final consumption expenditure 481.89; Private final consumption expenditure 1,361.98; Gross capital formation 434.31; *Total domestic expenditure* 2,278.18; Exports of goods and services 1,231.52; *Less* Imports of goods and services 1,445.06; *GDP at market prices* 2,064.65. Source: Eastern Caribbean Central Bank.

Gross Domestic Product by Economic Activity (preliminary, EC $ million at current factor cost, 2004): Agriculture, hunting, forestry and fishing 92.70; Mining and quarrying 5.90; Manufacturing 92.20; Electricity and water 84.77; Construction 119.02; Wholesale and retail trade 215.26; Restaurants and hotels 237.25; Transport 211.13; Communications 147.71; Banking and insurance 178.87; Real estate and housing 103.57; Government services 261.22; Other services 84.97; *Sub-total* 1,834.57; *Less* Imputed bank service charge 144.87; *Total in basic prices* 1,689.70. Source: Eastern Caribbean Central Bank.

Balance of Payments (EC $ million, 2003): Exports of goods f.o.b. 189.05; Imports of goods f.o.b. −932.90; *Trade balance* −743.85; Exports of services 907.07; Imports of services −363.53; *Balance on goods and services* −200.31; Other income received (net) −127.46; *Balance on goods, services and income* −327.77; Current transfers received 78.64; Current transfers paid −43.01; *Current balance* −292.14; Capital account (net) 51.12; Direct investment from abroad (net) 268.89; Portfolio investment (net) 168.99; Other investment (net) −193.38; Net errors and omissions 32.52; *Overall balance* 36.00. Source: Eastern Caribbean Central Bank.

EXTERNAL TRADE

Principal Commodities (US $ million, 2003): *Imports c.i.f.:* Food and live animals 74.7 (Meat 16.3; Cereals 16.3); Beverages and tobacco 15.3 (Beverages 13.0); Mineral fuels, lubricants, etc. 42.0 (Refined petroleum products 38.0); Chemicals 26.7; Basic manufactures 61.4 (Metal manufactures 12.1); Machinery and transport equipment 102.7 (Telecommunications equipment 35.9; Road vehicles 20.1); Miscellaneous manufactured articles 60.7; Total (incl. others) 392.8. *Exports f.o.b.:* Food and live animals 18.0 (Bananas and plantains 16.3); Beverages and tobacco 10.7 (Beer 8.5); Mineral fuels, lubricants, etc. 5.9 (Refined petroleum products 5.9); Basic manufactures 5.5 (Paper products 3.5); Machinery and transport equipment 13.9 (Telecommunications equipment 5.7; Electric machinery, etc. 2.4; Road vehicles 2.0); Miscellaneous manufactured articles 5.6 (Clothing 2.5); Total (incl. others) 61.8.

Principal Trading Partners (US $ million, 2003): *Imports c.i.f.:* Barbados 8.9; Canada 10.3; China, People's Republic 8.2; France 7.3; Germany 4.4; Grenada 4.5; Japan 11.8; Netherlands 5.4; Saint Vincent and the Grenadines 4.2; Sweden 5.4; Trinidad and Tobago 51.4; United Kingdom 31.6; USA 182.0; Total (incl. others) 392.8. *Exports f.o.b.:* Antigua and Barbuda 0.7; Barbados 5.2; Dominica 3.6; France 0.8; Germany 1.0; Grenada 2.4; Guyana 0.6; Saint Christopher and Nevis 0.8; Saint Vincent and the Grenadines 2.9; Trinidad and Tobago 10.1; United Kingdom 18.8; USA 12.2; Total (incl. others) 61.8.

Source: UN, *International Trade Statistics Yearbook*.

TRANSPORT

Road Traffic (registered motor vehicles, 2001): Goods vehicles 8,972; Taxis and hired vehicles 1,894; Motorcycles 757; Private vehicles 22,453; Passenger vans 3,387; Total (incl. others) 39,416.

Shipping: *Arrivals* (1999): 2,328 vessels. *International Sea-borne Freight Traffic* ('000 metric tons, 1999): Goods loaded 117; Goods unloaded 666.

Civil Aviation (aircraft movements): 41,798 in 2003; 43,754 in 2004. Source: Saint Lucia Air and Sea Ports Authority.

TOURISM

Visitor Arrivals: 673,871 (253,463 stop-over visitors, 7,712 excursionists, 25,516 yacht passengers, 387,180 cruise-ship passengers) in 2002; 704,236 (276,948 stop-over visitors, 12,817 excursionists, 21,209 yacht passengers, 393,262 cruise-ship passengers) in 2003; 813,681 (298,431 stop-over visitors, 11,441 excursionists, 22,530 yacht passengers, 481,279 cruise-ship passengers) in 2004 (preliminary).

Tourism Receipts (EC $ million): 567.0 in 2002; 761.6 in 2003; 879.3 in 2004 (preliminary).

Source: Eastern Caribbean Central Bank.

COMMUNICATIONS MEDIA

Radio Receivers ('000 in use, 1997): 111.
Television Receivers ('000 in use, 1999): 56.
Telephones ('000 main lines in use, 2004): 51.1.
Mobile Cellular Telephones (subscribers, 2004): 93,000.
Personal Computers ('000 in use, 2004): 26.
Internet Users ('000, 2004): 55.
Non-daily Newspapers (1996): Titles 5; Circulation 34,000.

Sources: UN, *Statistical Yearbook*; UNESCO, *Statistical Yearbook*; International Telecommunication Union.

EDUCATION

Pre-primary (state institutions only, 2000/01): 106 schools; 359 teachers; 4,275 pupils.

Primary (state institutions only, 2000/01): 82 schools; 1,052 teachers; 27,175 pupils (2002).

SAINT LUCIA

General Secondary (state institutions only, 2000/01): 18 schools; 678 teachers; 12,655 pupils (2002).

Special Education (state institutions only, 2000/01): 5 schools; 39 teachers; 227 students.

Adult Education (state institutions only, 2000/01): 19 centres; 80 facilitators; 729 learners.

Tertiary (state institutions, including part-time, 2000/01): 127 teachers; 1,403 students.

Source: partly Caribbean Development Bank, *Social and Economic Indicators*.

Adult Literacy Rate (UNESCO estimates): 90.1% (males 89.5%; females 90.6%) in 2003. Source: UN Development Programme, *Human Development Report*.

Directory

The Constitution

The Constitution came into force at the independence of Saint Lucia on 22 February 1979. Its main provisions are summarized below:

FUNDAMENTAL RIGHTS AND FREEDOMS

Regardless of race, place of origin, political opinion, colour, creed or sex but subject to respect for the rights and freedoms of others and for the public interest, every person in Saint Lucia is entitled to the rights of life, liberty, security of the person, equality before the law and the protection of the law. Freedom of conscience, of expression, of assembly and association is guaranteed and the inviolability of personal privacy, family life and property is maintained. Protection is afforded from slavery, forced labour, torture and inhuman treatment.

THE GOVERNOR-GENERAL

The British monarch, as Head of State, is represented in Saint Lucia by the Governor-General.

PARLIAMENT

Parliament consists of the British monarch, represented by the Governor-General, the 11-member Senate and the House of Assembly, composed of 17 elected Representatives. Senators are appointed by the Governor-General: six on the advice of the Prime Minister, three on the advice of the Leader of the Opposition and two acting on his own deliberate judgement. The life of Parliament is five years.

Each constituency returns one Representative to the House who is directly elected in accordance with the Constitution.

At a time when the office of Attorney-General is a public office, the Attorney-General is an *ex-officio* member of the House.

Every citizen over the age of 21 is eligible to vote.

Parliament may alter any of the provisions of the Constitution.

THE EXECUTIVE

Executive authority is vested in the British monarch and exercisable by the Governor-General. The Governor-General appoints as Prime Minister that member of the House who, in the Governor-General's view, is best able to command the support of the majority of the members of the House, and other Ministers on the advice of the Prime Minister. The Governor-General may remove the Prime Minister from office if the House approves a resolution expressing 'no confidence' in the Government, and if the Prime Minister does not resign within three days or advise the Governor-General to dissolve Parliament.

The Cabinet consists of the Prime Minister and other Ministers, and the Attorney-General as an *ex-officio* member at a time when the office of Attorney-General is a public office.

The Leader of the Opposition is appointed by the Governor-General as that member of the House who, in the Governor-General's view, is best able to command the support of a majority of members of the house who do not support the Government.

CITIZENSHIP

All persons born in Saint Lucia before independence who immediately prior to independence were citizens of the United Kingdom and Colonies automatically become citizens of Saint Lucia. All persons born in Saint Lucia after independence automatically acquire Saint Lucian citizenship, as do those born outside Saint Lucia after independence to a parent possessing Saint Lucian citizenship. Provision is made for the acquisition of citizenship by those to whom it is not automatically granted.

The Government

HEAD OF STATE

Monarch: HM Queen ELIZABETH II.

Governor-General: Dame PEARLETTE LOUISY (took office 17 September 1997).

CABINET
(April 2006)

Prime Minister, Minister of Finance, International Financial Services and Economic Affairs and of Information: Dr KENNY DAVIS ANTHONY.

Deputy Prime Minister and Minister of Education, Human Resource Development, Youth and Sports: MARIO F. MICHEL.

Minister of Commerce, Tourism, Investment and Consumer Affairs: PHILLIP J. PIERRE.

Minister of Agriculture, Forestry and Fisheries: IGNATIUS JEAN.

Minister of Health, Human Services, Family Affairs and Gender Relations: DAMIAN E. GREAVES.

Minister of Physical Development, Environment and Housing: THEOPHILUS FERGUSON JOHN.

Minister of Communications, Works, Transport and Public Utilities: FELIX FINNISTERRE.

Minister of Labour Relations, Public Service and Co-operatives: VELON L. JOHN.

Minister of Home Affairs and Internal Security: Sen. CALIXTE GEORGE.

Minister of Foreign Affairs, International Trade and Civil Aviation: Sen. PETRUS COMPTON.

Minister of Social Transformation, Culture and Local Government: MENISSA RAMBALLY.

Attorney-General and Minister of Justice: Sen. VICTOR PHILIP LA CORBINIERE.

MINISTRIES

Office of the Prime Minister: Greaham Louisy Administrative Bldg, 5th Floor, Waterfront, Castries; tel. 468-2111; fax 453-7352; e-mail pmoffice@candw.lc; internet www.stlucia.gov.lc.

Ministry of Agriculture, Forestry and Fisheries: NIS Bldg, 5th Floor, Waterfront, Castries; tel. 468-4210; fax 453-6314; e-mail adming@candw.lc; internet www.slumaffe.org.

Ministry of Commerce, Tourism, Investment and Consumer Affairs: Ives Heraldine Rock Bldg, 4th Floor, Block B, Waterfront, Castries; tel. 468-4202; fax 451-6986; e-mail mitandt@candw.lc; internet www.commerce.gov.lc.

Ministry of Communications, Works, Transport and Public Utilities: Williams Bldg, Bridge St, Castries; tel. 468-4300; fax 453-2769; e-mail min_com@candw.lc.

Ministry of Education, Human Resource Development, Youth and Sports: Francis Compton Bldg, Waterfront, Castries; tel. 468-5203; fax 453-2299; e-mail mineduc@candw.lc; internet www.education.gov.lc.

Ministry of Finance, International Financial Services and Economic Affairs: Financial Centre, Bridge St, Castries; tel. 468-5503; fax 452-6700; e-mail minfin@gosl.gov.lc.

Ministry of Foreign Affairs, International Trade and Civil Aviation: Conway Business Centre, Waterfront, Castries; tel. 468-4501; fax 452-7427; e-mail foreign@candw.lc.

Ministry of Health, Human Services, Family Affairs and Gender Relations: Chaussee Rd, Castries; tel. 452-2859; fax 452-5655; e-mail health@candw.lc.

Ministry of Home Affairs and Internal Security: Erdiston's Pl., Manoel St, Castries; tel. 452-3772; fax 453-6315.

Ministry of Labour Relations, Public Service and Co-operatives: Greaham Louisy Administrative Bldg, 2nd Floor, Waterfront, Castries; tel. 468-2202; fax 453-1305.

Ministry of Physical Development, Environment and Housing: Greaham Louisy Administrative Bldg, 3rd Floor, Waterfront, Castries; tel. 468-4402; fax 452-2506; e-mail sde@planning.gov.lc.

SAINT LUCIA

Ministry of Social Transformation, Culture and Local Government: Greaham Louisy Administrative Bldg, 4th Floor, Waterfront, Castries; tel. 468-5101; fax 453-7921.

Attorney-General's Office and Ministry of Justice: Francis Compton Bldg, Waterfront, Castries; tel. 468-3200; fax 458-1131; e-mail atgen@candw.lc.

Legislature

PARLIAMENT

Senate

The Senate has nine nominated members and two independent members.

President: HILFORD DETERVILLE.

House of Assembly

Speaker: JOSEPH BADEN ALLAIN.
Clerk: DORIS BAILEY.

Election, 3 December 2001

Party	% of votes	Seats
Saint Lucia Labour Party	54.2	14
United Workers' Party	36.6	3
National Alliance	3.5	—
Others	5.7	—
Total	100.0	17

Election Commission

Election Commission: High St, POB 1074, Castries; tel. 451-6339; e-mail electoral@candw.lc; Chair. CARSON RAGGIE.

Political Organizations

Committee for Meaningful Change and Reconstruction: Castries; f. 2004.

National Alliance (NA): Castries; f. 2001; opposition electoral alliance.

National Development Movement (NDM): Castries; f. 2004; Leader AUSBERT D'AUVERGNE.

Organization for National Empowerment (ONE): Castries; f. 2004; Leader SARAH FLOOD-BEAUBRUN; Chair. THOMAS ROSERIE (acting).

Saint Lucia Freedom Party: Castries; f. 1999; campaigns against the political establishment; Spokesman MARTINUS FRANÇOIS.

Saint Lucia Labour Party (SLP): Tom Walcott Bldg, 2nd Floor, Jeremie St, POB 427, Castries; tel. 451-8446; fax 451-9389; e-mail slp@candw.lc; internet www.geocities.com/~slp; f. 1946; socialist party; Leader Dr KENNY DAVIS ANTHONY; Chair. TOM WALCOTT.

United Workers' Party (UWP): 9 Coral St, POB 1550, Castries; tel. 451-9103; fax 451-9207; e-mail unitworkers@netscape.net; internet www.uwpstlucia.org; f. 1964; right-wing; Chair. STEPHENSON KING; Leader Sir JOHN COMPTON.

Diplomatic Representation

EMBASSIES AND HIGH COMMISSION IN SAINT LUCIA

China, People's Republic: Cap Estate, Gros Islet, POB GM 999, Castries; tel. 452-0903; fax 452-9495; e-mail chinaemb_lc@mfa.gov.cn; Ambassador GU HUAMING.

Cuba: Rodney Heights, Gros Islet, POB 2150, Castries; tel. 458-4665; fax 458-4666; e-mail embacubasantalucia@candw.lc; Ambassador VÍCTOR DANIEL RAMÍREZ PEÑA.

France: French Embassy to the OECS, POB 937, Vigie, Castries; tel. 455-6060; fax 455-6056; e-mail frenchembassy@candw.lc; Ambassador BERNARD VENZO.

United Kingdom: Francis Compton Bldg, Waterfront, POB 227, Castries; tel. 452-2484; fax 453-1543; e-mail britishhc@candw.lc; High Commissioner DUNCAN TAYLOR (resident in Barbados).

Venezuela: Vigie, POB 494, Castries; tel. 452-4033; fax 453-6747; e-mail vembassy@candw.lc; Ambassador CARMEN MAIGUALIDA APONTE.

Judicial System

SUPREME COURT

Eastern Caribbean Supreme Court: Waterfront, Government Bldgs, POB 1093, Castries; tel. 452-2574; fax 452-5475; e-mail appeal@candw.lc; the West Indies Associated States Supreme Court was established in 1967 and was known as the Supreme Court of Grenada and the West Indies Associated States from 1974 until 1979, when it became the Eastern Caribbean Supreme Court. Its jurisdiction extends to Anguilla, Antigua and Barbuda, the British Virgin Islands, Dominica, Grenada (which rejoined in 1991), Montserrat, Saint Christopher and Nevis, Saint Lucia and Saint Vincent and the Grenadines. It is composed of the High Court of Justice and the Court of Appeal. The High Court is composed of the Chief Justice and 13 High Court Judges. The Court of Appeal is presided over by the Chief Justice and includes three other Justices of Appeal. Jurisdiction of the High Court includes fundamental rights and freedoms, membership of the parliaments, and matters concerning the interpretation of constitutions. Following the inauguration of the Caribbean Court of Justice in April 2005, appeals from the Court of Appeal would no longer be made to the Judicial Committee of the Privy Council, based in the United Kingdom, but to the new regional court.

Chief Justice: C. M. DENNIS BYRON.

Religion

CHRISTIANITY

The Roman Catholic Church

Saint Lucia forms a single archdiocese. The Archbishop participates in the Antilles Episcopal Conference (currently based in Port of Spain, Trinidad and Tobago). At 31 December 2003 there were an estimated 100,243 adherents, equivalent to some 68% of the population.

Archbishop of Castries: KELVIN EDWARD FELIX, Archbishop's Office, POB 267, Castries; tel. 452-2416; fax 452-3697; e-mail archbishop@candw.lc.

The Anglican Communion

Anglicans in Saint Lucia are adherents of the Church in the Province of the West Indies, comprising eight dioceses. The Archbishop of the West Indies is the Bishop of Nassau and the Bahamas. Saint Lucia forms part of the diocese of the Windward Islands (the Bishop is resident in Kingstown, Saint Vincent).

Other Christian Churches

Seventh-day Adventist Church: St Louis St, POB 117, Castries; tel. 452-4408; e-mail adventist@candw.lc; Pastor THEODORE JARIA.

Trinity Evangelical Lutheran Church: Gablewoods Mall, POB 858, Castries; tel. 458-4638; fax 450-3382; e-mail spiegelbergs@candw.lc; Rev. TOM SPIEGELBERG.

Baptist, Christian Science, Methodist, Pentecostal and other churches are also represented in Saint Lucia.

The Press

The Catholic Chronicle: POB 778, Castries; f. 1957; monthly; Editor Rev. PATRICK A. B. ANTHONY; circ. 3,000.

The Crusader: 19 St Louis St, Castries; tel. 452-2203; fax 452-1986; f. 1934; weekly; circ. 4,000.

The Mirror: Bisee Industrial Estate, Castries; tel. 451-6181; fax 451-6197; e-mail mirror@candw.lc; internet www.stluciamirroronline.com; f. 1994; weekly on Fridays; Man. Editor GUY ELLIS.

One Caribbean: POB 852, Castries; e-mail dabread@candw.lc; weekly; Editor D. SINCLAIR DABREO.

She Caribbean: Rodney Bay Industrial Estate, Massade, Gros Islet, POB 1146, Castries; tel. 450-7827; fax 450-8694; e-mail waynem@candw.lc; internet www.shecaribbean.com; quarterly; Publr and Editor-in-Chief MAE WAYNE.

The Star: Rodney Bay Industrial Estate, Gros Islet, POB 1146, Castries; tel. 450-7827; fax 450-8694; e-mail starpub@candw.lc; internet www.stluciastar.com; 3 issues a week (Monday, Wednesday and weekend edns); Propr RICK WAYNE.

Tropical Traveller: Rodney Bay Industrial Estate, Massade, Gros Islet, POB 1146, Castries; tel. 450-7827; fax 450-8694; e-mail staceystar@candw.lc; internet www.tropicaltraveller.com; f. 1989; monthly; Editorial Dir MAE WAYNE.

SAINT LUCIA

The Vanguard: Hospital Rd, Castries; weekly; Editor ANDREW SEALY; circ. 2,000.

Visions of St Lucia Tourist Guide: 7 Maurice Mason Ave, Sans Souci, POB 947, Castries; tel. 453-0427; fax 452-1522; e-mail visions@candw.lc; internet www.stlucia.com/visions; f. 1989; official tourist guide; published by Island Visions Ltd; annual; Chair. and Man. Dir ANTHONY NEIL AUSTIN; circ. 100,000.

The Voice of St Lucia: Odessa Bldg, Darling Rd, POB 104, Castries; tel. 452-2590; fax 453-1453; f. 1885; 2 a week; circ. 8,000.

The Weekend Voice: Odessa Bldg, Darling Rd, POB 104, Castries; tel. 452-2590; fax 453-1453; weekly on Saturdays; circ. 8,000.

PRESS ORGANIZATION

Eastern Caribbean Press Council (ECPC): Castries; f. 2003; independent, self-regulating body designed to foster and maintain standards in regional journalism, formed by 14 newspapers in the Eastern Caribbean and Barbados; Chair. Lady MARIE SIMMONS.

NEWS AGENCY

Caribbean Media Corporation: Bisee Rd, Castries; tel. 453-7162; e-mail admin@cananews.com; internet www.cananews.com; f. by merger of Caribbean News Agency and Caribbean Broadcasting Union.

Publishers

Caribbean Publishing Co Ltd: American Drywall Bldg, Vide Boutielle Highway, POB 104, Castries; tel. 452-3188; fax 452-3181; e-mail publish@candw.lc; f. 1978; publishes telephone directories and magazines.

Crusader Publishing Co Ltd: 19 St Louis St, Castries; tel. 452-2203; fax 452-1986.

Island Visions: 7 Maurice Mason Ave, Sans Soucis, POB 947, Castries; tel. 453-0427; fax 452-1522; e-mail visions@candw.lc; internet www.stlucia.com/visions; Chair. and Man. Dir ANTHONY NEIL AUSTIN.

Mirror Publishing Co Ltd: Bisee Industrial Estate, POB 1782, Castries; tel. 451-6181; fax 451-6503; e-mail mirror@candw.lc; internet www.stluciamirroronline.com; f. 1994; Man. Editor GUY ELLIS.

Star Publishing Co: Rodney Bay Industrial Estate, Massade, Gros Islet, POB 1146, Castries; tel. 450-7827; fax 450-8694; e-mail starpub@candw.lc; internet www.stluciastar.com; Propr RICK WAYNE.

Voice Publishing Co Ltd: Odessa Bldg, Darling Rd, POB 104, Castries; tel. 452-2590; fax 453-1453.

Broadcasting and Communications

TELECOMMUNICATIONS

Regulatory Authorities

Eastern Caribbean Telecommunications Authority (ECTEL): Castries; internet ectel.int; f. 2000 to regulate telecommunications in Saint Lucia, Dominica, Grenada, Saint Christopher and Nevis and Saint Vincent and the Grenadines; Dir (Saint Lucia) EMBERT CHARLES.

National Telecommunications Regulatory Commission (NTRC): Global Tile Bldg, Bois d'Orange, Gros Islet, POB 690, Castries; tel. 458-2035; fax 453-2558; e-mail ntrc_slu@candw.lc; internet www.ectel.int/lca; f. 2000; regulates the sector in conjunction with ECTEL; Chair. ELDON MATHURIN.

Major Service Providers

Cable & Wireless St Lucia: Bridge St, POB 111, Castries; tel. 453-9000; fax 453-9700; e-mail talk2us@candw.lc; internet www.candw.lc; provides fixed-line, mobile, internet and cable-television services; CEO COLIN JAMES.

Digicel St Lucia: Rodney Bay, Gros Islet, POB 791, Castries; tel. 456-3400; fax 450-3872; e-mail slucustomercare@digicelgroup.com; internet www.digicelstlucia.com; f. 2003; owned by an Irish consortium; Chair. DENIS O'BRIEN; Eastern Caribbean CEO KEVIN WHITE.

Saint Lucia Boatphone Ltd: POB 2136, Gros Islet; tel. 452-0361; fax 452-0394; e-mail boatphone@candw.lc.

BROADCASTING

Radio

Gem Radio Network: POB 1146, Castries; tel. 459-0609.

Radio Caribbean International: 11 Mongiraud St, POB 121, Castries; tel. 452-2636; fax 452-2637; e-mail rci@candw.lc; internet www.rcistlucia.com; operates Radio Caraïbes; English and Creole services; broadcasts 24 hrs; Pres. H. COQUERELLE; Station Man. WINSTON FOSTER.

Saint Lucia Broadcasting Corporation: Morne Fortune, POB 660, Castries; tel. 452-2337; fax 453-1568; govt-owned; Man. KEITH WEEKES.

Radio 100-Helen FM: Morne Fortune, POB 621, Castries; tel. 451-7260; fax 453-1737; e-mail hts@candw.lc; internet www.htsstlucia.com; Gen. Man. STEPHENSON ANIUS.

Radio Saint Lucia (RSL): Morne Fortune, POB 660, Castries; tel. 452-2337; fax 453-1568; e-mail rsl@candw.lc; internet www.rslonline.com; English and Creole services; Chair. VAUGHN LOUIS FERNAND; Man. KEITH WEEKES.

Television

Cablevision: George Gordon Bldg, Bridge St, POB 111, Castries; tel. 453-9311; fax 453-9740.

Catholic Broadcasting TV Network (CBTN): Micoud St, Castries; tel. 452-7050.

Daher Broadcasting Service Ltd (DBS): Vigie, POB 1623, Castries; tel. 453-2705; fax 452-3544; Man. Dir LINDA DAHER.

Helen Television System (HTS): National Television Service of St Lucia, POB 621, The Morne, Castries; tel. 452-2693; fax 454-1737; e-mail hts@candw.lc; internet www.htsstlucia.com; f. 1967; commercial station; Gen. Man. STEPHENSON ANIUS.

National Television Network (NTN): Castries; f. 2001; operated by the Government Information Service; provides information on the operations of the public sector.

Finance

(cap. = capital; dep. = deposits; m. = million; brs = branches)

BANKING

The Eastern Caribbean Central Bank, based in Saint Christopher, is the central issuing and monetary authority for Saint Lucia.

Eastern Caribbean Central Bank—Saint Lucia Office: Financial Centre, 3rd Floor, Bridge St, POB 295, Castries; tel. 452-7449; fax 453-6022; e-mail eccbslu@candw.lc; Country Dir TREVOR BRAITHWAITE.

Local Banks

Bank of Saint Lucia Ltd: Financial Centre, 5th Floor, 1 Bridge St, POB 1862, Castries; tel. 456-6000; fax 456-6720; e-mail bankofstlucia@candw.lc; f. 2001 by merger of National Commercial Bank of St Lucia Ltd and Saint Lucia Development Bank; dep. EC $480.6m., total assets EC $556.4m. (Dec. 2000); 31.3% state-owned; parent co is East Caribbean Holding Co Ltd; Chair. VICTOR A. EUDOXIE; Man. Dir MARIUS ST ROSE; 7 brs.

First National Bank Saint Lucia Ltd: 21 Bridge St, POB 168, Castries; tel. 452-2880; fax 453-1630; e-mail coopbank@candw.lc; internet www.coopbank.com; inc. 1937 as Saint Lucia Co-operative Bank Ltd; name changed as above Jan. 2005; commercial bank; share cap. EC $4.2m., total assets EC $154.4m. (Dec. 1999); Pres. FERREL CHARLES; Man. Dir C. CARLTON GLASGOW; 3 brs.

RBTT Bank Caribbean (SLU) Ltd: 22 Micoud St, POB 1531, Castries; tel. 452-2265; fax 452-1668; e-mail rbttslu.isd@candw.lc; internet www.rbtt.com/caribbean.htm; f. 1985 as Caribbean Banking Corpn Ltd, in March 2002 name changed as above; owned by R and M Holdings Ltd; Chair. PETER JULY; Country Man. EARL P. CRICHTON; 4 brs.

Foreign Banks

Bank of Nova Scotia Ltd (Canada): 6 William Peter Blvd, POB 301, Castries; tel. 456-2100; fax 456-2130; e-mail bns@candw.lc; Man. S. COZIER; 3 brs.

FirstCaribbean International Bank (Barbados) Ltd: Castries; internet www.firstcaribbeanbank.com; f. 2002 following merger of Caribbean operations of Barclays Bank PLC and CIBC; Exec. Chair. MICHAEL MANSOOR; CEO CHARLES PINK.

Royal Bank of Canada: Laborie St and William Peter Blvd, POB 280, Castries; tel. 452-2245; fax 452-7855; Man. JOHN MILLER.

SAINT LUCIA

'Offshore' Bank

Bank Crozier International Ltd: Crozier Bldg, 21 Brazil St, Castries; e-mail stlucia@bankcrozier.com; internet www.bankcrozier.com; tel. 455-7600; fax 455-6009; f. 2001; CEO and Chair. PETER JOHANSSON; Gen. Man. PATRICK HOLMES.

STOCK EXCHANGE

Eastern Caribbean Securities Exchange: based in Basseterre, Saint Christopher and Nevis; e-mail info@ecseonline.com; internet www.ecseonline.com; f. 2001; regional securities market designed to facilitate the buying and selling of financial products for the eight member territories—Anguilla, Antigua and Barbuda, Dominica, Grenada, Montserrat, Saint Christopher and Nevis, Saint Lucia and Saint Vincent and the Grenadines; Gen. Man. TREVOR BLAKE.

INSURANCE

Local companies include the following:

Caribbean General Insurance Ltd: Laborie St, POB 290; Castries; tel. 452-2410; fax 452-3649.

Eastern Caribbean Insurance Ltd: Laborie St, POB 290, Castries; tel. 452-2410; fax 452-3649; e-mail gci.ltd@candw.lc.

Saint Lucia Insurances Ltd: 48 Micoud St, POB 1084, Castries; tel. 452-3240; fax 452-2240.

Saint Lucia Motor and General Insurance Co Ltd: 38 Micoud St, POB 767, Castries; tel. 452-3323; fax 452-6072.

Trade and Industry

DEVELOPMENT ORGANIZATION

National Development Corporation (NDC): First Floor, Heraldine Rock Bldg, The Waterfront, POB 495, Castries; tel. 452-3614; fax 452-1841; e-mail devcorp@candw.lc; internet www.stluciandc.com; f. 1971 to stimulate, facilitate and promote investment opportunities for foreign and local investors and to promote the economic devt of Saint Lucia; owns and manages four industrial estates; br. in New York, USA; Chair. MICHAEL CHASTANET; CEO WAYNE VITALIS.

CHAMBER OF COMMERCE

Saint Lucia Chamber of Commerce, Industry and Agriculture: Vide Bouteille, POB 482, Castries; tel. 452-3165; fax 453-6907; e-mail chamber@candw.lc; internet www.stluciachamber.org; f. 1884; 150 mems; Pres. LAURIE BARNARD; Exec. Dir BRIAN LOUISY.

INDUSTRIAL AND TRADE ASSOCIATIONS

Saint Lucia Banana Corporation (SLBC): Castries; f. 1998 following privatization of Saint Lucia Banana Growers' Asscn (f. 1967); Chair. (vacant); Sec. FREEMONT LAWRENCE.

Saint Lucia Industrial and Small Business Association: 2nd Floor, Ivy Crick Memorial Bldg, POB 312, Castries; tel. 453-1392; Pres. LEO CLARKE; Exec. Dir Dr URBAN SERAPHINE.

EMPLOYERS' ASSOCIATIONS

Saint Lucia Agriculturists' Association Ltd: Mongiraud St, POB 153, Castries; tel. 452-2494; fax 453-2693; e-mail kseverin@slaa.net; internet www.slaa.net; distributor and supplier of agricultural, industrial and organic products; exporter of cocoa; Chair. CUTHBERT PHILLIPS; CEO KERDE M. SEVERIN.

Saint Lucia Coconut Growers' Association Ltd: Palmiste Rd, POB 269, Castries; tel. 459-7227; fax 459-7216; e-mail slcga1@candw.lc; Chair. EZEKIEL JOSEPH; Man. KENNETH CAZAUBON.

Saint Lucia Employers' Federation: Morgan's Bldg, Maurice Mason Ave, POB 160, Castries; tel. 452-2190; fax 452-7335.

Saint Lucia Fish Marketing Corpn: POB 91, Castries; tel. 452-1341; fax 451-7073; e-mail slfmc@candw.lc.

Saint Lucia Marketing Board (SLMB): Conway, POB 441, Castries; tel. 452-3214; fax 453-1424; e-mail slmb@candw.lc; Chair. DAVID DEMAQUE; Man. MICHAEL WILLIAMS.

Windward Islands Banana Development and Exporting Co (Wibdeco): POB 115, Castries; tel. 452-2651; f. 1994 in succession to the Windward Islands Banana Growers' Asscn (WINBAN); regional org. dealing with banana devt and marketing; jtly owned by the Windward govts and island banana asscns; Chair. EUSTACE MONROSE.

UTILITIES

Electricity

Caribbean Electric Utility Services Corpn (CARILEC): Desir Ave, Sans Souci; tel. 452-0140; fax 452-0142; e-mail admin@carilec.org; internet www.carilec.com; f. 1989.

St Lucia Electricity Services Ltd (LUCELEC): Lucelec Bldg, John Compton Highway, POB 230, Castries; tel. 457-4400; fax 457-4409; e-mail lucelec@candw.lc; internet www.lucelec.com; f. 1964; Chair. MARIUS ST ROSE; Man. Dir TREVOR LOUISY.

Water

Water and Sewerage Authority (WASA): L'Anse Rd, POB 1481, Castries; tel. 452-5344; fax 452-6844; e-mail wasco@candw.lc; f. 1999; legislation to privatize WASA was approved by Parliament in Feb. 2005; Chair. GORDON CHARLES; Man. Dir JOHN C. JOSEPH.

TRADE UNIONS

National Farmers' Union (NFU): St Louis St, Castries; Pres. PETER JOSIE; 3,500 mems.

National Workers' Union: POB 713, Castries; tel. 452-3664; represents daily-paid workers; affiliated to World Federation of Trade Unions; Pres. TYRONE MAYNARD; Gen. Sec. GEORGE GODDARD; 3,000 mems (1996).

Saint Lucia Civil Service Association: POB 244, Castries; tel. 452-3903; fax 453-6061; e-mail csa@candw.lc; f. 1951; Pres. FRANCIS RAPHAEL; Gen. Sec. JAMES PERINEAU; 2,381 mems.

Saint Lucia Media Workers' Association: Castries; provides training for media workers in partnership with the Govt.

Saint Lucia Nurses' Association: POB 819, Castries; tel. 452-1403; fax 453-0960; f. 1947; Pres. LILIA HARRACKSINGH; Gen. Sec. ESTHER FELIX.

Saint Lucia Seamen, Waterfront and General Workers' Trade Union: 24 Chaussee Rd, POB 166, Castries; tel. 452-1669; fax 452-5452; e-mail seamen@candw.lc; f. 1945; affiliated to International Confederation of Free Trade Unions (ICFTU), International Transport Federation (ITF) and Caribbean Congress of Labour; Pres. MICHAEL HIPPOLYTE; Sec. CRESCENTIA PHILLIPS; 1,000 mems.

Saint Lucia Teachers' Union: POB 821, Castries; tel. 452-4469; fax 453-6668; e-mail sltu@candw.lc; internet www.findsltu.org; f. 1934; Pres. URBAN DOLOR; Gen.-Sec. KENTRY D. J. PIERRE.

Saint Lucia Workers' Union: Reclamation Grounds, Conway, Castries; tel. 452-2620; f. 1939; affiliated to ICFTU; Pres. GEORGE LOUIS; Sec. TITUS FRANCIS; 1,000 mems.

Vieux Fort General and Dock Workers' Union: New Dock Rd, POB 224, Vieux Fort; tel. 454-6193; fax 454-5128; f. 1954; Pres. JOSEPH GRIFFITH; 846 mems (1996).

Transport

RAILWAYS

There are no railways in Saint Lucia.

ROADS

In 2000 there was an estimated total road network of 910 km, of which 150 km were main road and 127 km were secondary roads. In that year only 5.2% of roads were paved. The main highway passes through every town and village on the island. The construction of a coastal highway, to link Castries with Cul de Sac Bay, was completed in February 2000. Internal transport is handled by private concerns and controlled by Government.

SHIPPING

The ports at Castries and Vieux Fort have been fully mechanized. Castries has six berths with a total length of 2,470 ft (753 m). The two dolphin berths at the Pointe Seraphine cruise-ship terminal have been upgraded to a solid berth of 1,000 ft (305 m) and one of 850 ft (259 m). A project to upgrade the port at Vieux Fort to a full deep-water container port was completed in 1993. The port of Soufrière has a deep-water anchorage, but no alongside berth for ocean-going vessels. There is a petroleum transhipment terminal at Cul de Sac Bay. In 2004 481,279 cruise-ship passengers called at Saint Lucia. Regular services are provided by a number of shipping lines, including ferry services to neighbouring islands.

Saint Lucia Air and Sea Ports Authority (SLASPA): Manoel St, POB 651, Castries; tel. 452-2893; fax 452-2062; e-mail info@slaspa.com; internet www.slaspa.com; f. 1983; Chair. TREVOR BRAITHWAITE; Gen. Man. VINCENT HIPPOLYTE.

SAINT LUCIA

Saint Lucia Marine Terminals Ltd: POB 355, Vieux Fort; tel. 454-8742; fax 454-8745; e-mail slumarterm@candw.lc; f. 1995; private port management co.

CIVIL AVIATION

There are two airports in use: Hewanorra International (formerly Beane Field near Vieux Fort), 64 km (40 miles) from Castries, which is equipped to handle large jet aircraft; and George F. L. Charles Airport, which is at Vigie, in Castries, and which is capable of handling medium-range jets. Saint Lucia is served by scheduled flights to the USA, Canada, Europe and most destinations in the Caribbean. The country is a shareholder in the regional airline LIAT (see chapter on Antigua and Barbuda).

Saint Lucia Air and Sea Ports Authority: see Shipping.

Air Antilles: Laborie St, POB 1065, Castries; f. 1985; designated as national carrier of Grenada in 1987; flights to destinations in the Caribbean, the United Kingdom and North America; charter co.

Caribbean Air Transport: POB 253, Castries; f. 1975; as Saint Lucia Airways; local shuttle service, charter flights.

Eagle Air Services Ltd: George F. L. Charles Airport, POB 838, Castries; tel. 450-1326; fax 452-9683; e-mail eagleairslu@candw.lc; internet www.eagleairslu.com; charter flights; Man. Dir Capt. EWART F. HINKSON.

Helenair Corpn Ltd: POB 253, Castries; tel. 452-1958; fax 451-7360; e-mail helenair@candw.lc; internet www.stluciatravel.com.lc/helenair.htm; f. 1987; charter and scheduled flights to major Caribbean destinations; Man. ARTHUR NEPTUNE.

Tourism

Saint Lucia possesses spectacular mountain scenery, a tropical climate and sandy beaches. Historical sites, rich birdlife and the sulphur baths at Soufrière are other attractions. Visitor arrivals totalled 813,681 in 2004. Tourist receipts in the same year were an estimated EC $879.3m. North America is the principal market (38.9% of total stop-over visitors in 2003), followed by the United Kingdom (with 29.1%). There were some 3,600 hotel rooms in October 2005; increasing this figure by about 1,100 before the 2007 Cricket World Cup, hosted by several Caribbean states, including Saint Lucia, was a government priority.

Saint Lucia Tourist Board: Sureline Bldg, Top Floor, Vide Bouteille, POB 221, Castries; tel. 452-4094; fax 453-1121; e-mail slutour@candw.lc; internet www.stlucia.org; 2 brs overseas; Chair. COSTELLO MICHEL; Dir PETER HILARY MODESTE.

Saint Lucia Hotel and Tourism Association (SLHTA): POB 545, Castries; tel. 452-5978; fax 452-7967; e-mail slhta@candw.lc; internet www.stluciatravel.com.lc; f. 1963; Pres. ANTHONY BOWEN; Exec. Vice-Pres. ALLEN CHASTANET.

SAINT VINCENT AND THE GRENADINES

Introductory Survey

Location, Climate, Language, Religion, Flag, Capital

Saint Vincent and the Grenadines is situated in the Windward Islands group, approximately 160 km (100 miles) west of Barbados, in the West Indies. The nearest neighbouring countries are Saint Lucia, some 34 km (21 miles) to the northeast, and Grenada, to the south. As well as the main volcanic island of Saint Vincent, the state includes the 32 smaller islands and cayes known as the Saint Vincent Grenadines, the northerly part of an island chain stretching between Saint Vincent and Grenada. The principal islands in that part of the group are Bequia, Canouan, Mustique, Mayreau, Isle D'Quatre and Union Island. The climate is tropical, with average temperatures of between 18°C and 32°C (64°F–90°F). Annual rainfall ranges from 1,500 mm (60 ins) in the extreme south, to 3,750 mm (150 ins) in the mountainous interior of the main island. English is the official language. Most of the inhabitants profess Christianity and are adherents of the Anglican, Methodist or Roman Catholic Churches. The national flag (proportions 2 by 3) has three unequal vertical stripes, of blue (at the hoist), yellow and green (at the fly), with three lozenges in green, in a 'V' formation, superimposed on the broad central yellow stripe. The capital is Kingstown, on the island of Saint Vincent.

Recent History

The islands were first settled by an Arawak people, who were subsequently conquered by the Caribs. The arrival of shipwrecked and escaped African slaves resulted in the increase of a so-called 'Black Carib' population, some of whose descendants still remain. Under the collective name of Saint Vincent, and despite the opposition of the French and the indigenous population, the islands finally became a British possession during the 18th century. With other nearby British territories, the Governor of the Windward Islands administered Saint Vincent, under a federal system, until December 1959. The first elections under universal adult suffrage took place in 1951. The islands participated in the West Indies Federation from its foundation in January 1958 until its dissolution in May 1962. From January 1960, Saint Vincent, in common with the other Windward Islands, had a new Constitution, with its own Administrator and an enlarged Legislative Council.

After the failure of negotiations to form a smaller East Caribbean Federation, most of the British colonies in the Leeward and Windward Islands became Associated States, with full internal self-government, in 1967. This change of status was delayed in Saint Vincent because of local political differences. At controversial elections to the Legislative Council in 1966, the ruling People's Political Party (PPP) was returned with a majority of only one seat. Further elections took place in May 1967, when the Saint Vincent Labour Party (SVLP) secured six of the nine seats in the Council. Milton Cato, leader of the SVLP, became Chief Minister, in succession to Ebenezer Joshua of the PPP. On 27 October 1969, despite objections from the PPP, Saint Vincent became an Associated State, with the United Kingdom retaining responsibility for defence and foreign relations only. The Legislative Council was renamed the House of Assembly, the Administrator was designated Governor, and the Chief Minister became Premier.

Elections were held in April 1972 for an enlarged, 13-seat House of Assembly. The PPP and the SVLP each obtained six seats, while James Mitchell, formerly a minister in the SVLP Government and standing as an independent, secured the remaining one. The PPP agreed to form a Government with Mitchell as Premier and Joshua as Deputy Premier and Minister of Finance. In September 1974 Joshua resigned after policy disagreements with the Premier. A motion expressing 'no confidence' in Mitchell's Government was approved, and the House was dissolved. In the ensuing election, which took place in December, the PPP and SVLP campaigned in a 'unity agreement'. The SVLP secured 10 of the 13 seats, and the PPP two. (Mitchell was again elected as an independent.) Cato became Premier again, at the head of a coalition with the PPP, and committed his Government to attaining full independence from the United Kingdom.

After a constitutional conference in September 1978, the colony became fully independent, within the Commonwealth, as Saint Vincent and the Grenadines, on 27 October 1979. The Governor became Governor-General, while Cato took office as the country's first Prime Minister.

Cato's position was reinforced in the general election of December 1979, when the SVLP obtained 11 of the 13 elective seats in the 19-member House of Assembly. In 1982 the leader of the opposition United People's Movement (UPM), Dr Ralph Gonsalves, resigned, accusing the UPM of harbouring Marxist tendencies, and founded a new party, the Movement for National Unity (MNU). In June 1984 Cato announced an early general election, hoping to take advantage of divisions within the opposition. However, the repercussions of scandals surrounding the Cato Government, and the economic and taxation policies of the SVLP, contributed to an unexpected victory for the centrist New Democratic Party (NDP) at the election in July. The NDP's leader, James Mitchell, became Prime Minister. Cato subsequently retired from politics and in the ensuing by-election the NDP gained another seat. Hudson Tannis replaced Cato as leader of the SVLP in January 1985; Vincent Beache succeeded him as party leader in August 1986.

At a general election conducted in May 1989 the NDP won all 15 elective seats in the newly-enlarged House of Assembly. Mitchell remained as Prime Minister and formed a new Cabinet.

The NDP secured its third consecutive term of office at a general election in February 1994, obtaining 12 seats in the House of Assembly. An electoral alliance formed by the SVLP and the MNU and headed by Vincent Beache won the three remaining elective seats. In September 1994 the MNU and the SVLP announced their formal merger as the Unity Labour Party (ULP).

Opposition charges that the Government had failed to address problems presented by a marked decline in banana production, a crisis in the health and education sectors and persistent allegations that drugs-related activities were being conducted on the islands culminated in the defeat, by 10 votes to three, of a motion of 'no confidence' in the Government, brought by the opposition in August 1994. The execution, by hanging, of three convicted murderers in February 1995 provoked outrage from international human rights organizations, who expressed concern at the alacrity and secrecy with which the sentences had been implemented.

At the general election of 15 June 1998 the NDP lost four seats, retaining eight, while the ULP obtained the remaining seven. The reverse sustained by the NDP was attributed to voter dissatisfaction with the state of the economy. Although the ULP had obtained around 55% of the vote, Mitchell claimed that the result was a mandate for his Government to undertake a record fourth term of office. The ULP leader, Vincent Beache, called on the NDP to hold fresh elections within nine months, and not to govern on the basis of a minority vote. The ULP also claimed to have obtained evidence of irregularities during the elections, particularly in the four seats won by the NDP with margins of between 27 and 109 votes. On 9 July, at the opening of the first session of the House of Assembly, several hundred protesters demonstrated against the new Government and two ministers were attacked as they tried to drive through the crowd.

In mid-November 1998 members of the public and of the opposition demonstrated outside government offices to call for the resignation of Mitchell and Arnhim Eustace, the Minister of Finance and Public Services. The protests followed the announcement of the details of an agreement reached by the Government with the Government of Italy and a consortium of European financial institutions on the repayment of US $67m., incurred because the Government had guaranteed a loan of $50m. made to a company of Italian developers that subsequently went into liquidation. The loan had been made to finance the failed Ottley Hall marina and shipyard project, valued at only $5m. The new agreement stipulated that the shipyard should be sold and that repayments of $32m. of debt should begin immediately, with the remaining $30m. to be set aside.

In December 1998 Dr Ralph Gonsalves, the deputy leader of the ULP, was elected leader at the ULP party congress, following the resignation of Beache, who was to remain leader of the opposition in the House of Assembly.

In late November 1998 marijuana growers demonstrated outside the Prime Minister's office against plans to use regional and US troops to destroy the marijuana crop in the highlands of Saint Vincent. Mitchell refused to meet representatives of the protesters, telling them to take advantage of government schemes to promote economic diversification. In December US marines and troops provided by the Regional Security System destroyed crops during a two-week operation, despite opposition from growers. Mitchell subsequently warned the USA that, if Saint Vincent's banana producers were bankrupted by the US initiative to challenge the preferential treatment accorded by the European Union (EU, see p. 228) to banana exports from Caribbean and African states, it was likely that producers would turn instead to the cultivation of marijuana. In March 1999 Saint Vincent and the Grenadines was one of a number of Caribbean states to warn that, if the USA continued to threaten their economic stability by pursuing its case against the EU banana import regime at the World Trade Organization (see p. 370), they would withdraw co-operation with US-sponsored anti-drugs initiatives. (See the Recent History of Saint Lucia for further details of the trade dispute over bananas between the USA and the EU.) In December, however, a large-scale marijuana eradication exercise took place in Saint Vincent with backing from US marines.

In December 1999 a committee chaired by Dwight Venner, the Governor of the Eastern Caribbean Central Bank, recommended that members of the House of Assembly should receive increased salaries. The committee, however, suggested that the increases should not be awarded until legislation on political integrity had been implemented, and reforms of the public sector had been effected. The proposed increases were opposed by the ULP, which in late January 2000 threatened to introduce a motion of 'no confidence' in the Government, accusing it of corruption, excessive expenditure on development projects, a failure to reduce crime levels and of neglecting education. The Government's subsequent introduction in April of legislation increasing the salaries and benefits of members of the House of Assembly provoked protests throughout the islands, which were directed by the ULP and by public-sector trade unions, who accused the Government of 'disregard and contempt' for ordinary workers. Members of the Saint Vincent Union of Teachers undertook industrial action in protest at the Government's behaviour and to demand wage increases, while the protesters, who were grouped under an 'umbrella' Organization in Defence of Democracy (ODD), demanded the resignation of the Government and fresh elections. Despite appeals for dialogue from the Government, employers' associations and the Chamber of Industry and Commerce, the ODD undertook several days of public demonstrations at the end of April, culminating in a mass rally in Kingstown. In early May the Government and the ODD reached an agreement, known as the Grand Beach accord, whereby fresh legislative elections were to be called before March 2001; the accord also allowed for a national dialogue on constitutional reform.

In August 2000 Mitchell relinquished the post of NDP President in favour of the Minister of Finance and Public Services, Arnhim Eustace, who defeated Jeremiah Scott, the Minister of Agriculture and Labour, in a leadership election. On 27 October Eustace also succeeded Mitchell as Prime Minister, following the latter's retirement as Head of Government. Mitchell stayed on in the Cabinet as Senior Minister.

A general election was held on 28 March 2001. The ULP secured an overwhelming victory, winning 12 of the 15 parliamentary seats and 57% of the votes cast. The NDP, which had been in power since 1984, secured 41% of the votes cast and the remaining three House of Assembly seats. The new Government took office in mid-April, led by Gonsalves. In December 2002 Gonsalves established a 25-member Constitutional Review Commission, the first report of which was presented in late March 2004. Among the issues to be addressed were local government organization and finance, civil service reform and the electoral system.

In June 2002 the Governor-General, Sir Charles Antrobus, died. Sir Frederick Ballantyne was appointed as his successor in September.

In March 2004 the parliamentary opposition boycotted the House of Assembly and established an 'alternative parliament' at the NDP's headquarters; Eustace claimed that the parliamentary Speaker, Hendrick Alexander, had consistently demonstrated a pro-Government bias. In late February Eustace had led NDP members out of Parliament after the Prime Minister was allowed to present an amendment to a motion on a day when opposition business should have taken precedence. The opposition again boycotted the House of Assembly and re-established its 'alternative parliament' in March 2005. On this occasion, the NDP was particularly unhappy about constituency boundaries and the registration of voters before the next elections, which were due by March 2006.

Despite the concerns of the opposition, Gonsalves' Government maintained its popularity; however, in 2004–05 the issue of violent crime was increasingly prominent and it was widely held that the Government had devoted insufficient funds to attempting to resolve the problem. Moreover, Saint Vincent remained one of the largest cultivators of marijuana in the region and in 2003 the Government reported that 40% of prison inmates were jailed for drugs-related offences. In November 2004 Gonsalves, who had previously expressed severe reservations about capital punishment, claimed that the use of the death penalty was necessary to reduce the influence of criminal gangs in the country. The comments were made in the House of Assembly, during the passage of the Firearm Amendment Act, which was to introduce stricter penalties for illegal possession of weapons.

At legislative elections, held on 7 December 2005, the ULP secured 12 of the 15 seats in the House of Assembly (the same figure as in the election of 2001), from 55% of the popular vote (compared with 57% in 2001). The NDP again secured the remaining three legislative seats, although the party increased its share of the vote to 45%, compared with 41% in 2001. A third party, the Saint Vincent and the Grenadines Green Party, garnered just 34 votes from the four constituencies in which it competed. Registered votes were cast by 63.7% of the electorate. Monitoring teams from various international organizations described the contest as free and fair; none the less, the NDP claimed there had been electoral 'irregularities', such as missing ballots and people voting in constituencies in which they did not reside, and pledged to take legal and political action against the results in three closely fought constituencies.

Following the ULP's re-election Gonsalves reorganized and expanded the Cabinet: among other changes, Louis Straker, the Deputy Prime Minister, was given his former portfolio of foreign affairs, commerce and trade. The previous holder of that post, Michael Browne, meanwhile, was placed in charge of a wide-ranging new Ministry of National Mobilization, Social Development, NGO Relations, Family, Gender Affairs and Persons with Disabilities, and Julian Francis was appointed Minister of Housing, Informal Human Settlements, Physical Planning, Lands and Surveys. The Prime Minister also pledged to use the Government's new mandate to introduce constitutional reform, after popular consultation via referendums. In addition, Gonsalves announced his intention to ask the House of Assembly to approve legislation making the Caribbean Court of Justice (which had been inaugurated in Trinidad and Tobago in April 2005) the country's senior court of appeal, in place of the Privy Council in the United Kingdom.

Saint Vincent and the Grenadines is a member of the Caribbean Community and Common Market (CARICOM, see p. 183), of the Organisation of Eastern Caribbean States (OECS, see p. 397), and is a signatory of the Cotonou Agreement (see p. 277), the successor agreement to the Lomé Convention. In 1992 the Regional Constituent Assembly, created two years earlier by the leaders of Saint Vincent and the Grenadines, Dominica, Grenada and Saint Lucia, stated that the four countries were committed to the establishment of economic and political union under a federal system. In September 2001 Gonsalves appointed Joseph Bonadie, an NDP senator, as his adviser on issues related to further OECS integration and in February 2003 proposed that a union of Caribbean states should take the form of a confederal political arrangement similar to that of the EU. In February 2004 parliament passed legislation allowing nationals of OECS member states to travel freely within the OECS area and to remain in a foreign territory within the area for up to six months. During the election campaign of December 2005 Gonsalves described regional integration as the 'bedrock' of his Government's foreign policy. In early 2006 the Government announced that Saint Vincent and the Grenadines would join CARICOM's Caribbean Single Market and

Economy (CSME), which was established by six founding member states on 1 January, later in that year. The CSME was intended to enshrine the free movement of goods, services and labour throughout the CARICOM region, although no OECS countries were signatories to the new project from its inauguration.

In 1992 the islands established diplomatic relations with Cuba. The two countries signed accords pledging further co-operation in a number of areas, including health and education, in September 2001 and November 2002. Diplomatic relations are maintained with Taiwan.

In 2001 Libya granted the islands, in common with other eastern Caribbean countries, access to a US $2,000m. development fund. It was also reported in September that Libya had agreed to provide Saint Vincent and the Grenadines with a grant of $4.5m. (including an immediate disbursement of $1.5m), following Gonsalves' controversial visit to the Libyan capital, Tripoli, earlier in the month. Further controversy arose after Japan pledged to provide $6m. for the construction of a fish market. It was claimed that, in return for Japanese financial aid, Saint Vincent and the Grenadines would support the pro-whaling bloc at meetings of the International Whaling Commission; Gonsalves refuted the allegation, pointing out that the Government had abstained on crucial votes relating to the provision of whale sanctuaries in the South Atlantic and the Pacific.

In February 2003 Saint Vincent and the Grenadines was admitted to the Non-Aligned Movement (see p. 397).

Government

Saint Vincent and the Grenadines is a constitutional monarchy. Executive power is vested in the British monarch, as Head of State, and is exercisable by the Governor-General, who represents the British monarch locally and who is appointed on the advice of the Prime Minister. Legislative power is vested in Parliament, comprising the Governor-General and the House of Assembly (composed of 21 members: six nominated Senators and 15 Representatives, elected for up to five years by universal adult suffrage). Senators are appointed by the Governor-General: four on the advice of the Prime Minister and two on the advice of the Leader of the Opposition. Government is effectively by the Cabinet. The Governor-General appoints the Prime Minister and, on the latter's recommendation, selects the other Ministers. The Prime Minister must be able to command the support of the majority of the House, to which the Cabinet is responsible.

Defence

Saint Vincent and the Grenadines participates in the US-sponsored Regional Security System, comprising police, coastguards and army units, which was established by independent East Caribbean states in 1982. Since 1984, however, the paramilitary Special Service Unit has had strictly limited deployment. Government total expenditure on national security was estimated at EC $36.6m. (6.3% of total current expenditure) in 2006.

Economic Affairs

In 2004, according to estimates by the World Bank, Saint Vincent and the Grenadines' gross national income (GNI), measured at average 2002–04 prices, was US $395.8m., equivalent to $3,650 per head (or $6,250 per head on an international purchasing-power parity basis). During 1995–2004, it was estimated, the population decreased by an annual average rate of 0.3%, while gross domestic product (GDP) per head increased, in real terms, by an average of 2.9% per year. Overall GDP increased, in real terms, by an average annual rate of 2.6% in 1995–2004; according to preliminary figures by the Eastern Caribbean Central Bank (ECCB, see p. 388), real GDP increased by 5.0% in 2004.

Agriculture (including forestry and fishing) contributed an estimated 7.8% of GDP in 2004. The sector employed 25.1% of the working population at the census of 1991, and agricultural products account for the largest share of export revenue. The principal cash crop is bananas, which contributed 33.1% of the value of total domestic exports in 2003. Other important crops are arrowroot, sweet potatoes, tannias, taro, plantains and coconuts. According to the ECCB, during 1996–2004 real agricultural GDP (growth of which is heavily reliant on weather conditions and banana production) decreased by an annual average of 1.8%. A decline of 5.2% was recorded in 2004.

Industry (including mining, manufacturing, electricity, water and construction) employed 21.1% of the working population in 1991, and contributed an estimated 23.5% of GDP in 2004. During 1996–2004 real industrial GDP increased by an annual average of 3.1%; the sector expanded by 9.3% in 2004. In September 2005 the Prime Minister announced that a Canadian company was conducting preliminary petroleum-exploration work in Saint Vincent and the Grenadines' territorial waters.

The manufacturing sector contributed an estimated 5.2% of GDP in 2004, and engaged 8.5% of the employed labour force in 1991. Apart from a garment industry and the assembling of electrical components, the most important activities involve the processing of agricultural products, including flour- and rice-milling, brewing, rum distillation, and processing dairy products. During 1996–2004 real manufacturing GDP decreased by an annual average of 1.8%. However, the sector's real GDP expanded by 2.9% in 2004.

Energy is derived principally from the use of hydrocarbon fuels (mineral fuels and lubricants accounted for 9.8% of total imports in 2003). The islands imported most of their energy requirements. There is, however, an important hydroelectric plant in Cumberland. In September 2005 the Government became one of 13 Caribbean administrations to sign the PetroCaribe accord, under which Saint Vincent and the Grenadines would be allowed to purchase petroleum from Venezuela at reduced prices.

The services sector contributed an estimated 68.9% of GDP in 2004 and engaged 53.8% of the employed population at the time of the 1991 census. Tourism is the most important activity within the sector, but is smaller in scale than in most other Caribbean islands; estimated tourism receipts were equivalent to some 28.3% of GDP in 2004. Tourist activity remains concentrated in the Grenadines and caters for the luxury market. Visitors aboard yachts have traditionally been the most important sector, although the numbers of stop-over and cruise-ship visitors have increased in recent years. In 2001 visitor arrivals declined by 0.8%, partly as a result of repercussions of the terrorist attacks on the USA in September of that year. In response to the downturn, the Hotel and Tourism Association announced in October that room rates would be reduced by 33%. None the less, the number of visitor arrivals decreased by a further 2.6% in 2002 and 2.4% in 2003, although the number of stop-over tourists (the highest-spending sector) recovered slightly in the latter year. The industry was fully rejuvenated in 2004 when the number of visitor arrivals increased by 8.3% (the equivalent increase in the number of stop-over tourists was 10.4%). Aside from tourism, a small 'offshore' financial sector also contributes to the services sector. During 1996–2004 the real GDP of the services sector as a whole increased by an annual average of 4.6%; an increase of 5.6% was recorded in 2004.

In 2004 Saint Vincent and the Grenadines recorded an estimated visible trade deficit of EC $781.7m., while there was a deficit of $324.0m. on the current account of the balance of payments. The principal source of imports is the USA (accounting for 41.2% of the total in 2003). Other important suppliers in that year were Trinidad and Tobago (20.7%) and the United Kingdom (7.2%). The United Kingdom is the principal market for exports (accounting for 29.4% of total exports in 2003). Other important markets in that year were the USA (13.4%), Barbados (11.3%), Trinidad and Tobago (11.0%) and Saint Lucia (10.2%). The principal exports in 2003 were bananas (accounting for 33.1% of exports), machinery and transport equipment (13.6%), wheat flour (12.3%) and rice (7.9%), while the principal imports were machinery and transport equipment (24.7%), basic manufactures (20.2%) and food and live animals (18.8%).

In 2004 there was an estimated overall budget deficit of EC $32.8m., equivalent to 3.6% of GDP. Saint Vincent and the Grenadines' total external debt was US $229.5m. at the end of 2003, of which US $196.0m. was long-term public debt. The cost of debt-servicing was equivalent to 7.3% of the value of exports of goods and services in 2002. The average annual rate of inflation was 1.0% in 1998–2004, and consumer prices increased by an estimated average of 0.3% in 2003 and by 2.9% in 2004. At the 1991 census 20.0% of the labour force were unemployed. In February 2002 the IMF estimated that the rate of unemployment remained at a similar level.

In May 2000 the Financial Stability Forum categorized Saint Vincent and the Grenadines' banking supervision in the lowest group. In June the Organisation for Economic Co-operation and Development (OECD) included Saint Vincent and the Grenadines in a report on countries with harmful tax policies and in the same month it was also included on a list of 'non-co-operative' governments in the fight against money-laundering, by the Financial Action Task Force (FATF—based at the Secretariat of OECD). In July the International Financial Services Authority revoked the licences of six 'offshore' banks in an immediate

SAINT VINCENT AND THE GRENADINES

response to an advisory by the US Department of the Treasury. Following further government commitments to improving the transparency of its tax and regulatory systems, Saint Vincent and the Grenadines was removed from OECD's harmful tax policy list in February 2002. In May 2002 the Government established a Financial Intelligence Unit to counter money-laundering and in June 2003 Saint Vincent and the Grenadines was finally removed from the FATF's blacklist. Only 11 licensed 'offshore' banks remained in mid-2005, compared with a peak of 30 in 2002. Some 6,276 International Business Companies were also registered at the end of 2004. In September 2004 the IMF noted significant improvements in the regulation of the sector; however, questions were raised over 'political involvement with licensing'.

Saint Vincent and the Grenadines is a member of the ECCB, the Caribbean Community and Common Market (CARICOM, see p. 183), which seeks to encourage regional development, particularly by increasing trade between member states, and of the Organisation of Eastern Caribbean States (OECS, see p. 397). The country is also a member of the regional stock exchange, the Eastern Caribbean Securities Exchange (based in Saint Christopher and Nevis), established in 2001. Saint Vincent and the Grenadines was expected to join CARICOM's Caribbean Single Market and Economy (CSME) in mid-2006.

Traditionally the dominant sector of the economy, agriculture declined in importance in the 1990s. The introduction of other crops reduced dependence on the vulnerable banana harvest, although performance is significantly affected by weather conditions. Notably, in October 2002 Prime Minister Gonsalves announced that 'Hurricane Lili' had cost the country's economy some EC $50m., destroying an estimated 45% of the crop. The passage of 'Hurricane Ivan', which struck the islands in September 2004, also proved disastrous for the sector, destroying 20% of the banana crop. The erosion of the islands' preferential access to European markets, together with lower prices and poor climatic conditions, contributed to a decline in banana production after 1992. In addition, exports of bananas decreased to just 33.1% of the total value of merchandise exports in 2003 (compared with 52.2% in 1990). The continued decline of the industry, and a related increase in unemployment and poverty, appeared inevitable. Therefore, the prospects for long-term growth were dependent on economic diversification and a prolonged stabilization of the increasingly important tourism sector. The 2006 budget, presented to Parliament in January of that year, announced no new taxes, but Gonsalves emphasized that revenue-collection procedures would be tightened. The Prime Minister also noted the need to reduce the heavy burden of national debt, which stood at 85.2% of GDP at the end of 2005, according to official figures. The construction by 2011 of a new international airport, at Argyle on Saint Vincent's east coast, was described by Gonsalves in August 2005 as the most expensive project in the country's history. The planned airport, for which the Government was to receive significant international assistance, was expected to cost some $480m., equivalent to about 140% of public revenue in 2005. Another priority for the ULP administration was the upgrading of tourism infrastructure, including the partial reconstruction of the Arnos Vale sports stadium, before the 2007 Cricket World Cup, to be hosted by Saint Vincent and the Grenadines and several other Caribbean countries. According to preliminary ECCB figures, economic growth of 5.0% was achieved in 2004, compared with 3.6% in 2003. The Government forecast that real growth in 2005 would be around 5.5%, although this was widely believed to be an optimistic projection.

Education

Free primary education, beginning at five years of age and lasting for seven years, is available to all children in government schools, although it is not compulsory and attendance is low. There are 60 government, and five private, primary schools. Secondary education, beginning at 12 years of age, comprises a first cycle of five years and a second, two-year cycle. However, government facilities at this level are limited, and much secondary education is provided in schools administered by religious organizations, with government assistance. There are also a number of junior secondary schools. There is a teacher-training college and a technical college. In 1994/95 76% and 24% of children in the relevant age-groups were attending primary and secondary schools, respectively. Total expenditure on education by the central Government was a projected EC $92.5m. in 2006 (15.9% of total current expenditure). The Goverment announced in 2005 that it had succeeded in instituting universal secondary education.

Public Holidays

2006: 1 January (New Year's Day), 14 April (Good Friday), 17 April (Easter Monday), 1 May (Labour Day/Fisherman's Day), 5 June (Whit Monday), 3 July (CARICOM Day), 4 July (Carnival Tuesday), 7 August (Emancipation Day), 27 October (Independence Day), 25–26 December (Christmas).

2007: 1 January (New Year's Day), 6 April (Good Friday), 9 April (Easter Monday), 7 May (Labour Day/Fisherman's Day), 28 May (Whit Monday), 2 July (CARICOM Day), 3 July (Carnival Tuesday), 6 August (Emancipation Day), 27 October (Independence Day), 25–26 December (Christmas).

Weights and Measures

The imperial system is used.

Statistical Survey

Sources (unless otherwise stated): Statistical Office, Ministry of Finance, Planning, Economic Development, Labour and Information, Government Bldgs, Kingstown; tel. 456-1111; e-mail statssvg@vincysurf.com.

AREA AND POPULATION

Area: 389.3 sq km (150.3 sq miles). The island of Saint Vincent covers 344 sq km (133 sq miles).

Population: 97,845 at census of 12 May 1980; 106,499 (males 53,165, females 53,334) at census of 12 May 1991; 109,022 at preliminary census count of May 2001. *2004:* 118,000 (mid-year estimate). Source; partly UN, *World Population Prospects: The 2004 Revision*.

Density (mid-2004): 303.1 per sq km.

Principal Town: Kingstown (capital), population 13,526 at preliminary census count of May 2001. *Mid-2003* (UN estimate, incl. suburbs): Kingstown 29,382 (Source: UN, *World Urbanization Prospects: The 2003 Revision*).

Births and Deaths (registrations, 2000): Live births 2,149 (birth rate 19.2 per 1,000); Deaths 698 (death rate 6.2 per 1,000). *2003:* Birth rate 18.5 per 1,000; Death rate 7.6 per 1,000 (Source: Caribbean Development Bank, *Social and Economic Indicators*).

Expectation of Life (years at birth): 70 (males 68; females 72) in 2003. Source: WHO, *World Health Report*.

Economically Active Population (persons aged 15 years and over, 1991 census): Agriculture, hunting, forestry and fishing 8,377; Mining and quarrying 98; Manufacturing 2,822; Electricity, gas and water 586; Construction 3,535; Trade, restaurants and hotels 6,544; Transport, storage and communications 2,279; Financing, insurance, real estate and business services 1,418; Community, social and personal services 7,696; *Total employed* 33,355 (males 21,656, females 11,699); Unemployed 8,327 (males 5,078, females 3,249); *Total labour force* 41,682 (males 26,734, females 14,948). Source: ILO, *Yearbook of Labour Statistics*.

HEALTH AND WELFARE

Key Indicators

Total Fertility Rate (children per woman, 2003): 2.2.

Under-5 Mortality Rate (per 1,000 live births, 2004): 22.

Physicians (per 1,000 head, 1997): 0.88.

Hospital Beds (per 1,000 head, 1996): 1.85.

Health Expenditure (2002): US $ per head (PPP): 340.

Health Expenditure (2002): % of GDP: 5.9.

Health Expenditure (2002): public (% of total): 65.5.

Access to Water (% of persons, 2000): 93.

Access to Sanitation (% of persons, 2000): 96.

SAINT VINCENT AND THE GRENADINES

Human Development Index (2003): ranking: 87.
Human Development Index (2003): value: 0.755.
For sources and definitions, see explanatory note on p. vi.

AGRICULTURE, ETC.

Principal Crops ('000 metric tons, 2004): Maize 0.7; Cassava 0.7; Sweet potatoes 1.2; Yams 2.2; Other roots and tubers 9.8*; Sugar cane 18.0*; Coconuts 2.6; Vegetables 4.3*; Bananas 45.0; Plaintains 3.5*; Oranges 1.6; Lemons and limes 1.2; Apples 1.2*; Mangoes 1.5*; Other fruits 0.8*.
*FAO estimate.

Livestock ('000 head, year ending September 2004): Cattle 5.0; Sheep 12.0; Goats 7.0; Pigs 9.2; Asses 1.3 (FAO estimate); Poultry 125.

Livestock Products ('000 metric tons, 2004): Pig meat 0.6 (FAO estimate); Cows' milk 1.2; Hen eggs 0.6.

Fishing (metric tons, live weight, 2003): Albacore 1,555; Yellowfin tuna 568; Other tuna-like fishes 1,682; *Total catch* (incl. others) 4,782.

Source: FAO.

INDUSTRY

Selected Products ('000 metric tons, 2004, unless otherwise stated): Copra 2 (FAO estimate); Raw sugar 2 (FAO estimate); Rum 1,000 hectolitres (2001); Electric energy 121.4 million kWh (preliminary). Sources: FAO, Eastern Caribbean Central Bank and UN, *International Commodity Statistics Yearbook*.

FINANCE

Currency and Exchange Rates: 100 cents = 1 Eastern Caribbean dollar (EC $). *Sterling, US Dollar and Euro Equivalents* (30 December 2005): £1 sterling = EC $4.649; US $1 = EC $2.700; €1 = EC $3.185; EC $100 = £21.51 = US $31.33 = €31.40. *Exchange rate:* Fixed at US $1 = EC $2.70 since July 1976.

Budget (preliminary, EC $ million, 2004): *Revenue:* Revenue from taxation 272.1 (Taxes on income 79.3, Taxes on goods and services 51.8, Taxes on international trade and transactions 138.5); Other current revenue 46.6; Capital revenue 3.9; Foreign grants 7.8; Total 330.4. *Expenditure:* Current expenditure 288.1 (Personal emoluments 144.8; Other goods and services 66.6; Interest payments 27.6; Transfers and subsidies 49.1); Capital expenditure and net lending 75.1; Total 363.2. Source: Eastern Caribbean Central Bank.

International Reserves (US $ million at 31 December 2004): Reserve position in IMF 0.78; Foreign exchange 74.20; Total 74.98. Source: IMF, *International Financial Statistics*.

Money Supply (EC $ million at 31 December 2004): Currency outside banks 64.39; Demand deposits 257.46; Total money 321.85. Source: IMF, *International Financial Statistics*.

Cost of Living (Consumer Price Index; base: 2000 = 100): 101.6 in 2002; 101.9 in 2003; 104.9 in 2004. Source: IMF, *International Financial Statistics*.

Gross Domestic Product (EC $ million at current factor cost): 817.2 in 2002; 845.1 in 2003; 911.6 in 2004 (preliminary). Source: Eastern Caribbean Central Bank.

Expenditure on the Gross Domestic Product (preliminary, EC $ million at current prices, 2004): Government final consumption expenditure 216.62; Private final consumption expenditure 749.55; Gross capital formation 384.29; *Total domestic expenditure* 1,350.46; Exports of goods and services 472.51; *Less* Imports of goods and services 721.75; *GDP at market prices* 1,101.22. Source: Eastern Caribbean Central Bank.

Gross Domestic Product by Economic Activity (preliminary, EC $ million at current factor cost, 2004): Agriculture, hunting, forestry and fishing 75.98; Mining and quarrying 2.29; Manufacturing 51.06; Electricity and water 58.81; Construction 117.24; Wholesale and retail trade 176.96; Restaurants and hotels 20.34; Transport 127.22; Communications 57.80; Banking and insurance 78.72; Real estate and housing 20.59; Government services 171.94; Other services 19.67; *Sub-total* 977.62; *Less* Imputed bank service charge 65.99; *Total in basic prices* 911.63. Source: Eastern Caribbean Central Bank.

Balance of Payments (EC $ million, 2003): Exports of goods f.o.b. 105.59; Imports of goods f.o.b. −477.68; *Trade balance* −372.09; Exports of services 369.97; Imports of services −172.93; *Balance on goods and services* −175.05; Other income received (net) −42.23; *Balance on goods, services and income* −217.28; Current transfers received 65.41; Current transfers paid −32.33; *Current balance* −184.20; Capital account (net) 14.10; Direct investment from abroad (net) 118.21; Portfolio investment (net) 53.24; Other investment (net) −35.16; Net errors and omissions 20.47; *Overall balance* −13.34. Source: Eastern Caribbean Central Bank.

EXTERNAL TRADE

Principal Commodities (US $ million, 2003): *Imports c.i.f.:* Food and live animals 37.8 (Meat 8.7; Cereals 10.9); Inedible crude materials 6.4; Mineral fuels, lubricants, etc. 19.8 (Refined petroleum products 17.4); Chemicals and related products 16.3; Basic manufactures 40.7 (Iron and steel 6.4; Other metal manufactures 9.4); Machinery and transport equipment 49.7 (Telecommunications equipment 16.2; Road vehicles 10.0); Miscellaneous manufactures 24.8; Total (incl. others) 201.1. *Exports f.o.b.:* Food and live animals 26.3 (Rice 3.0; Wheat flour 4.7; Roots and tubers 2.6; Bananas 12.6) Beverages 1.6 (Non-alcoholic beverages 1.4); Basic manufactures 2.8 (Iron and steel 1.1); Machinery and transport equipment 5.2 (Road vehicles 2.0); Miscellaneous manufactures 2.1; Total (incl. others) 38.1.

Principal Trading Partners (US $ million, 2003): *Imports c.i.f.:* Australia 2.3; Barbados 7.6; Brazil 2.2; Canada 6.0; Colombia 2.9; Japan 6.6; Saint Lucia 2.3; Sweden 3.5; Trinidad and Tobago 41.6; United Kingdom 14.5; USA 82.9; Total (incl. others) 201.1. *Exports f.o.b.:* Antigua and Barbuda 2.7; Barbados 4.3; British Virgin Islands 0.4; Dominica 1.4; Grenada 1.3; Jamaica 1.0; Netherlands Antilles 0.4; Saint Christopher and Nevis 1.0; Saint Lucia 3.9; Trinidad and Tobago 4.2; United Kingdom 11.2; USA 5.1; Total (incl. others) 38.1.

Source: UN, *International Trade Statistics Yearbook*.

TRANSPORT

Road Traffic (motor vehicles in use, 2002): Private cars 10,504; Buses and coaches 1,150; Lorries and vans 3,019; Road tractors 89. Source: International Road Federation, *World Road Statistics*.

Shipping: *Arrivals* (2000): Vessels 1,007. *International Sea-borne Freight Traffic* ('000 metric tons, 2000): Goods loaded 54; Goods unloaded 156. *Merchant Fleet* (vessels registered at 31 December 2004): Number 1,182; Total displacement 6,324,289 grt (Source: Lloyd's Register-Fairplay, *World Fleet Statistics*).

Civil Aviation (visitor arrivals): 94,030 in 2000; 85,735 in 2001 (preliminary); 90,879 in 2002 (estimate). Source: IMF, *St Vincent and the Grenadines: Statistical Appendix* (February 2003).

TOURISM

Visitor Arrivals: 247,449 (77,622 stop-over visitors, 13,062 excursionists, 86,451 yacht passengers, 70,314 cruise-ship passengers) in 2002; 241,526 (78,535 stop-over visitors, 13,696 excursionists, 84,330 yacht passengers, 64,965 cruise-ship passengers) in 2003; 261,469 (86,721 stop-over visitors, 12,936 excursionists, 84,227 yacht passengers, 77,585 cruise-ship passengers) in 2004 (preliminary).

Tourism Receipts (EC $ million): 245.7 in 2002; 246.2 in 2003; 258.0 in 2004 (preliminary).

Source: Eastern Caribbean Central Bank.

COMMUNICATIONS MEDIA

Radio Receivers ('000 in use, 2000): 100.
Television Receivers ('000 in use, 2000): 50.
Telephones ('000 main lines in use, 2004): 19.
Facsimile Machines (1996): 1,500.
Mobile Cellular Telephones (subscribers, 2003): 57,000.
Personal Computers ('000 in use, 2004): 16.
Internet Users ('000, 2004): 8.
Non-daily Newspapers (2000): Titles 8; Circulation 50,000.

Sources: mainly UNESCO, *Statistical Yearbook*; UN, *Statistical Yearbook*; and International Telecommunication Union.

EDUCATION

Pre-primary (1993/94): 97 schools; 175 teachers; 2,500 pupils.
Primary (2000): 60 schools; 987 teachers; 18,299 pupils (2003).
Secondary (2000): 21 schools; 406 teachers; 8,629 pupils (2003).
Teacher Training (2000): 1 institution; 10 teachers; 107 students.
Technical College (2000): 1 institution; 19 teachers; 187 students.
Community College (2000): 1 institution; 13 teachers; 550 students.
Nursing College (2000): 1 institution; 6 teachers; 60 students.

Source: partly Caribbean Development Bank, *Social and Economic Indicators*.

Adult Literacy Rate: 88.1% in 2003. Source: UN Development Programme, *Human Development Report*.

SAINT VINCENT AND THE GRENADINES

Directory

The Constitution

The Constitution came into force at the independence of Saint Vincent and the Grenadines on 27 October 1979. The following is a summary of its main provisions

FUNDAMENTAL RIGHTS AND FREEDOMS

Regardless of race, place of origin, political opinion, colour, creed or sex, but subject to respect for the rights and freedoms of others and for the public interest, every person in Saint Vincent and the Grenadines is entitled to the rights of life, liberty, security of the person and the protection of the law. Freedom of conscience, of expression, of assembly and association is guaranteed and the inviolability of a person's home and other property is maintained. Protection is afforded from slavery, forced labour, torture and inhuman treatment.

THE GOVERNOR-GENERAL

The British Monarch is represented in Saint Vincent and the Grenadines by the Governor-General.

PARLIAMENT

Parliament consists of the British monarch, represented by the Governor-General, and the House of Assembly, comprising 15 elected Representatives (increased from 13 under the provisions of an amendment approved in 1986) and six Senators. Senators are appointed by the Governor-General—four on the advice of the Prime Minister and two on the advice of the Leader of the Opposition. The life of Parliament is five years. Each constituency returns one Representative to the House who is directly elected in accordance with the Constitution. The Attorney-General is an *ex-officio* member of the House. Every citizen over the age of 18 is eligible to vote. Parliament may alter any of the provisions of the Constitution.

THE EXECUTIVE

Executive authority is vested in the British monarch and is exercisable by the Governor-General. The Governor-General appoints as Prime Minister that member of the House who, in the Governor-General's view, is the best able to command the support of the majority of the members of the House, and selects other Ministers on the advice of the Prime Minister. The Governor-General may remove the Prime Minister from office if a resolution of 'no confidence' in the Government is passed by the House and the Prime Minister does not either resign within three days or advise the Governor-General to dissolve Parliament.

The Cabinet consists of the Prime Minister and other Ministers and the Attorney-General as an *ex-officio* member. The Leader of the Opposition is appointed by the Governor-General as that member of the House who, in the Governor-General's view, is best able to command the support of a majority of members of the House who do not support the Government.

CITIZENSHIP

All persons born in Saint Vincent and the Grenadines before independence who, immediately prior to independence, were citizens of the United Kingdom and Colonies automatically become citizens of Saint Vincent and the Grenadines. All persons born outside the country after independence to a parent possessing citizenship of Saint Vincent and the Grenadines automatically acquire citizenship, as do those born in the country after independence. Citizenship can be acquired by those to whom it would not automatically be granted.

The Government

HEAD OF STATE

Monarch: HM Queen Elizabeth II.
Governor-General: Sir Frederick Nathaniel Ballantyne (took office 2 September 2002).

CABINET
(April 2006)

Prime Minister and Minister of Finance and Economic Planning, National Security, Legal Affairs and Grenadines Affairs: Dr Ralph E. Gonsalves.
Deputy Prime Minister and Minister of Foreign Affairs, Commerce and Trade: Louis Straker.
Minister of Tourism, Youth and Sports: Glen Beache.
Minister of National Mobilization, Social Development, Non-Governmental Organization (NGO) Relations, Family, Gender Affairs and Persons with Disabilities: Michael Browne.
Minister of Education: Girlyn Miguel.
Minister of Rural Transformation, Information, Public Service and Ecclesiastical Affairs: Selmon Walters.
Minister of Health and the Environment: Dr Douglas Slater.
Minister of Telecommunications, Science, Technology and Industry: Dr Jerrol Thompson.
Minister of Urban Development, Labour, Culture and Electoral Affairs: René Mercedes Baptiste.
Minister of Transport and Works: Clayton Burgin.
Minister of Agriculture, Forestry and Fisheries: Montgomery Daniel.
Minister of Housing, Informal Human Settlements, Physical Planning, Lands and Surveys: Sen. Julian Everard Francis.
Minister of State in the Office of the Prime Minister: Conrad Sayers.
Attorney-General: Judith S. Jones-Morgan.

MINISTRIES

Office of the Governor-General: Government House, Kingstown; tel. 456-1401; fax 457-9701.
Office of the Prime Minister: Administrative Centre, Bay St, Kingstown; tel. 456-1703; fax 457-2152; e-mail office.pmoffice@mail.gov.vc.
Office of the Attorney-General and Ministry of Legal Affairs: Grandby St, Kingstown; tel. 456-1762; fax 457-2898; e-mail office.ageneral@mail.gv.vc.
Ministry of Agriculture, Forestry and Fisheries: Richmond Hill, Kingstown; tel. 457-1410; fax 457-1688; e-mail office.agriculture@mail.gov.vc.
Ministry of Education: Halifax St, Kingstown; tel. 456-1877; fax 457-1114; e-mail minedsvg@vincysurf.com.
Ministry of Finance and Economic Planning: Administrative Centre, Bay St, Kingstown; tel. 456-1111.
Ministry of Foreign Affairs, Commerce and Trade: Administrative Centre, Bay St, Kingstown; tel. 456-2060; fax 456-2610; e-mail minister.foreignaffairs@mail.gov.vc.
Ministry of Health and the Environment: Administrative Centre, Bay St, Kingstown; tel. 457-2586; fax 457-2684.
Ministry of Housing, Informal Human Settlements, Physical Planning, Lands and Surveys: Administrative Centre, Bay St.
Ministry of National Security: Halifax St, Kingstown; tel. 451-2707; fax 451-2820; e-mail office.natsec@mail.gov.vc.
Ministry of National Mobilization, Social Development, Non-Governmental Organization (NGO) Relations, Family, Gender Affairs and Persons with Disabilities: Egmont St, Kingstown; tel. 456-1111; fax 457-2476; e-mail office.socialdevelopment@mail.gov.vc.
Ministry of Rural Transformation, Information, Public Service and Ecclesiastical Affairs: Halifax St, Kingstown; tel. 456-1600; e-mail office.api@mail.gov.vc.
Ministry of Telecommunications, Science, Technology and Industry: Administrative Centre, Bay St, Kingstown; tel. 456-1223; fax 457-2880; e-mail webunit.telecom@mail.gov.vc.
Ministry of Tourism, Youth and Sports: Administrative Centre, Bay St, Kingstown; tel. 457-1502; fax 451-2425; e-mail tourism@caribsurf.com.
Ministry of Transport and Works: Grenville St, Kingstown; tel. 457-2039; fax 456-2168; e-mail office.transport@mail.gov.vc.
Ministry of Urban Development, Labour, Culture and Electoral Affairs: Administrative Centre, Bay St, Kingstown; tel. 457-1762; fax 485-6844; e-mail office.elections@mail.gov.vc.

Legislature

HOUSE OF ASSEMBLY

Senators: 6.
Elected Members: 15.
Speaker: Hendrick Alexander.

SAINT VINCENT AND THE GRENADINES

Election, 7 December 2005

Party	Votes	% of votes	Seats
Unity Labour Party	31,848	55.26	12
New Democratic Party	25,748	44.68	3
Saint Vincent and the Grenadines Green Party	34	0.06	—
Total	57,630	100.00	15

Election Commission

Electoral Office: Administrative Centre, Bay St, Kingstown; tel. 457-1762; fax 485-6844; e-mail office.elections@mail.gov.vc; Supervisor of Elections RODNEY ADAMS.

Political Organizations

Canouan Progressive Movement: Kingstown; Leader TERRY BYNOE.

New Democratic Party (NDP): Murray Rd, POB 1300, Kingstown; tel. 457-2647; f. 1975; democratic party supporting political unity in the Caribbean, social development and free enterprise; Pres. ARNHIM EUSTACE; Chair. Dr LINDON LEWIS; 7,000 mems.

Saint Vincent and the Grenadines Green Party: POB 1707, Kingstown; tel. 456-9579; fax 455-6156; e-mail mail@svggreenparty.org; internet www.svggreenparty.org; f. 2005; Leader IVAN O'NEAL.

Unity Labour Party (ULP): Beachmont, Kingstown; tel. 457-2761; fax 456-2811; e-mail ulpweb@aol.com; internet www.ulp.org; f. 1994 by merger of Movement for National Unity and the Saint Vincent Labour Party; moderate, social-democratic party; Leader Dr RALPH E. GONSALVES.

Diplomatic Representation

EMBASSIES AND HIGH COMMISSION IN SAINT VINCENT AND THE GRENADINES

China (Taiwan): Murray Rd, POB 878, Kingstown; tel. 456-2431; fax 456-2913; e-mail rocemsvg@caribsurf.com; Ambassador ELIZABETH Y. F. CHU.

United Kingdom: Granby St, POB 132, Kingstown; tel. 457-1701; fax 456-2750; e-mail bhcsvg@caribsurf.com; High Commissioner resident in Barbados; High Commissioner DUNCAN TAYLOR (resident in Barbados).

Venezuela: Baynes Bros Bldg, Granby St, POB 852, Kingstown; tel. 456-1374; fax 457-1934; e-mail lvccsvg@caribsurf.com; Ambassador TIBISAY URDANETA.

Judicial System

Justice is administered by the Eastern Caribbean Supreme Court, based in Saint Lucia and consisting of a Court of Appeal and a High Court. Two Puisne Judges are resident in Saint Vincent and the Grenadines. There are five Magistrates, including the Registrar of the Supreme Court, who acts as an additional Magistrate.

Puisne Judges: FREDERICK BRUCE-LYLE, LOUISE ESTHER BLENMAN.

Office of the Registrar of the Supreme Court

Registry Dept, Court House, Kingstown; tel. 457-1220; fax 457-1888; Registrar COLEEN MCDONALD.

Chief Magistrate: SIMONE CHURAMAN.

Magistrates: SHARON MORRIS-CUMMINGS, CARL JOSEPH, HILARY SAMUEL.

Director of Public Prosecutions: COLIN WILLIAMS.

Religion

CHRISTIANITY

Saint Vincent Christian Council: Melville St, POB 445, Kingstown; tel. 456-1408; f. 1969; four mem. churches; Chair. Mgr RENISON HOWELL.

The Anglican Communion

Anglicans in Saint Vincent and the Grenadines are adherents of the Church in the Province of the West Indies, comprising eight dioceses. The Archbishop of the West Indies is the Bishop of Nassau and the Bahamas, and is resident in Nassau. The diocese of the Windward Islands includes Grenada, Saint Lucia and Saint Vincent and the Grenadines.

Bishop of the Windward Islands: Rt Rev. SEHON GOODRIDGE, Bishop's Court, POB 502, Kingstown; tel. 456-1895; fax 456-2591; e-mail diocesewi@vincysurf.com.

The Roman Catholic Church

Saint Vincent and the Grenadines comprises a single diocese (formed when the diocese of Bridgetown-Kingstown was divided in October 1989), which is suffragan to the archdiocese of Castries (Saint Lucia). The Bishop participates in the Antilles Episcopal Conference, currently based in Port of Spain, Trinidad and Tobago. At 31 December 2003 there were an estimated 10,073 adherents in the diocese, comprising about 8% of the population.

Bishop of Kingstown: Rt Rev. ROBERT RIVAS, Bishop's Office, POB 862, Edinboro, Kingstown; tel. 457-2363; fax 457-1903; e-mail rcdok@caribsurf.com.

Other Christian Churches

The Methodists, Seventh-day Adventists, Baptists and other denominations also have places of worship.

BAHÁ'Í FAITH

National Spiritual Assembly: POB 1043, Kingstown; tel. 456-4717.

The Press

DAILY

The Herald: Blue Caribbean Bldg, Kingstown; tel. 456-1242; fax 456-1046; e-mail info@heraldsvg.com; internet www.heraldsvg.com; daily; internationally distributed.

SELECTED WEEKLIES

Justice: Kingstown; weekly; organ of the United People's Movement; Editor RENWICK ROSE.

The New Times: POB 1300, Kingstown; f. 1984; Thursdays; organ of the New Democratic Party.

The News: Frenches Gate, POB 1078, Kingstown; tel. 456-2942; fax 456-2941; e-mail thenews@caribsurf.com; weekly; Man. Dir SHELLEY CLARKE.

Searchlight: Interactive Media Ltd, POB 152, Kingstown; tel. 456-1558; fax 457-2250; e-mail search@caribsurf.com; internet www.searchlight.vc; weekly on Fridays; Chair. CORLETHA OLIVERRE.

The Star: POB 854, Kingstown.

The Vincentian: St George's Pl., Kingstown; tel. 456-1123; fax 457-2821; e-mail info@thevincentian.com; internet www.thevincentian.com; f. 1919; weekly; owned by the Vincentian Publishing Co; Man. Dir EGERTON M. RICHARDS; Editor-in-Chief TERRANCE PARRIS; circ. 6,000.

The Westindian Crusader: Kingstown; tel. 458-0073; fax 456-9315; e-mail crusader@caribsurf.com; weekly; Man. Editor LINA CLARKE.

SELECTED PERIODICALS

Caribbean Compass: POB 175, Bequia; tel. 457-3409; fax 457-3410; e-mail compass@caribsurf.com; internet www.caribbeancompass.com; marine news; monthly; free distribution in Caribbean from Puerto Rico to Panama; circ. 12,000; Editor SALLY ERDLE-HOPMANN.

Government Bulletin: Government Information Service, Kingstown; tel. 456-3410; circ. 300.

Government Gazette: POB 12, Kingstown; tel. 457-1840; f. 1868; Govt Printer HAROLD LLEWELLYN; circ. 492.

Unity: Middle and Melville St, POB 854, Kingstown; tel. 456-1049; fortnightly; organ of the United Labour Party.

Publishers

CJW Communications: Frenches Gate, Kingstown; tel. 456-2942; fax 456-2941.

Great Works Depot: Commission A Bldg, Granby St, POB 1849, Kingstown; tel. 456-2057; fax 457-2055; e-mail gwd@caribsurf.com.

The Vincentian Publishing Co Ltd: St George's Pl., Kingstown; tel. 456-1123; fax 457-2821; e-mail info@thevincentian.com; internet www.thevincentian.com; Man. Dir EGERTON M. RICHARDS.

Broadcasting and Communications

TELECOMMUNICATIONS

Regulatory Authority

Eastern Caribbean Telecommunications Authority: based in Castries, Saint Lucia; f. 2000 to regulate telecommunications in Saint Vincent and the Grenadines, Dominica, Grenada, Saint Christopher and Nevis and Saint Lucia.

Major Service Providers

Cable & Wireless (WI) Ltd: Halifax St, POB 103, Kingstown; tel. 457-1901; fax 457-2777; e-mail svdinfo@caribsurf.com; CEO DARYL JACKSON.

Cable & Wireless Caribbean Cellular: Halifax St, Kingstown; tel. 457-4600; fax 457-4940; cellular telephone service.

Digicel: Suite KO59, cnr Granby and Sharpe Sts, Kingstown; tel. 453-3000; fax 453-3010; e-mail customercaresvg@digicelgroup.com; internet www.digicelsvg.com; f. 2003; mobile cellular phone operator; owned by an Irish consortium; Chair. DENIS O'BRIEN; Eastern Caribbean CEO KEVIN WHITE.

BROADCASTING

National Broadcasting Corporation of Saint Vincent and the Grenadines: Richmond Hill, POB 705, Kingstown; tel. 457-1111; fax 456-2749; e-mail nbcsvgadmin@nbcsvg.com; internet www.nbcsvg.com; govt-owned; Chair. KENNETH BROWNE; Gen. Man. CORLETHA OLIVERRE.

Radio

NBC Radio: National Broadcasting Corpn, Richmond Hill, POB 705, Kingstown; tel. 457-1111; fax 456-2749; e-mail nbcsvgadmin@nbcsvg.com; internet www.nbcsvg.com; commercial; broadcasts BBC World Service (United Kingdom) and local programmes.

Television

National Broadcasting Corporation of Saint Vincent and the Grenadines: see Broadcasting

SVG Television: Dorsetshire Hill, POB 617, Kingstown; tel. 456-1078; fax 456-1015; e-mail svgbc@caribsurf.com; internet www.svgbc.com/svgtv.htm; f. 1980; broadcasts US and local programmes; Chief Engineer R. PAUL MACLEISH.

Television services from Barbados can be received in parts of the islands.

Finance

(cap. = capital; res = reserves; dep. = deposits; m. = million; brs = branches)

BANKING

The Eastern Caribbean Central Bank, based in Saint Christopher, is the central issuing and monetary authority for Saint Vincent and the Grenadines.

Eastern Caribbean Central Bank—Saint Vincent and the Grenadines Office: Granby St, POB 839, Kingstown; tel. 456-1413; fax 456-1412; e-mail eccbsvg@caribsurf.com; Country Dir MAURICE EDWARDS.

Regulatory Authority

Financial Intelligence Unit (FIU): POB 1826, Kingstown; tel. 451-2070; fax 457-2014; e-mail svgfiu@vincysurf.com; internet www.stvincentoffshore.com/fin_intl_unit.htm; f. 2002; Dir SHARDA SINANAN-BOLLERS.

Principal Banks

First Saint Vincent Bank Ltd: Lot 112, Granby St, POB 154, Kingstown; tel. 456-1873; fax 456-2675; f. 1988; fmrly Saint Vincent Agricultural Credit and Loan Bank; Man. Dir O. R. SYLVESTER.

National Commercial Bank (SVG) Ltd: Bedford St, POB 880, Kingstown; tel. 457-1844; fax 456-2612; e-mail info@ncbsvg.com; internet www.ncbsvg.com; f. 1977; govt-owned; share cap. EC $14.0m., dep. EC $338.4m., total assets EC $366.4m. (June 2000); Chair. RICHARD JOACHIM; Man. DIGBY AMBRIS; 8 brs.

RBTT Bank Caribbean Ltd: 81 South River Rd, POB 81, Kingstown; tel. 456-1501; fax 456-2141; internet www.rbtt.com; f. 1985 as Caribbean Banking Corpn Ltd; Chair. PETER J. JULY.

Saint Vincent Co-operative Bank: Cnr Long Lane (Upper) and South River Rd, POB 886, Kingstown; tel. 456-1894; fax 457-2183.

Foreign Banks

Bank of Nova Scotia Ltd (Canada): 76 Halifax St, POB 237, Kingstown; tel. 457-1601; fax 457-2623; Man. S. K. SUBRAMANIAM.

FirstCaribbean International Bank (Barbados) Ltd: Kingstown; internet www.firstcaribbeanbank.com; f. 2002 following merger of Caribbean operations of Barclays Bank PLC and CIBC; Exec. Chair. MICHAEL MANSOOR; CEO CHARLES PINK.

STOCK EXCHANGE

Eastern Caribbean Securities Exchange: e-mail info@ecseonline.com; internet www.ecseonline.com; based in Basseterre, Saint Christopher and Nevis; f. 2001; regional securities market designed to facilitate the buying and selling of financial products for the eight mem. territories—Anguilla, Antigua and Barbuda, Dominica, Grenada, Montserrat, Saint Christopher and Nevis, Saint Lucia and Saint Vincent and the Grenadines; Gen. Man. TREVOR BLAKE.

INSURANCE

A number of foreign insurance companies have offices in Kingstown. Local companies include the following:

Abbott's Insurance Co: Cnr Sharpe and Bay St, POB 124, Kingstown; tel. 456-1511; fax 456-2462.

BMC Agencies Ltd: Sharpe St, POB 1436, Kingstown; tel. 457-2041; fax 457-2103.

Durrant Insurance Services: South River Rd, Kingstown; tel. 457-2426.

Haydock Insurances Ltd: Granby St, POB 1179, Kingstown; tel. 457-2903; fax 456-2952.

Metrocint General Insurance Co Ltd: St George's Pl., POB 692, Kingstown; tel. 456-1821.

Saint Hill Insurance Co Ltd: Bay St, POB 1741, Kingstown; tel. 457-1227; fax 456-2374.

Saint Vincent Insurances Ltd: Lot 69, Grenville St, POB 210, Kingstown; tel. 456-1733; fax 456-2225; e-mail vinsure@caribsurf.com.

'OFFSHORE' FINANCIAL SECTOR

Legislation permitting the development of an 'offshore' financial sector was introduced in 1976 and revised in 1996 and 1998. International banks are required to have a place of business on the islands and to designate a licensed registered agent. International Business Companies registered in Saint Vincent and the Grenadines are exempt from taxation for 25 years. Legislation also guarantees total confidentiality. By December 2004 the 'offshore' financial centre comprised 6,276 International Business Companies and 11 banks; in addition, by May 2003 there were five mutual funds, 413 trusts, six mutual-fund managers and three international insurance companies.

International Financial Services Authority (IFSA): Browne's Business Centre, 2nd Floor, Grenville St, POB 356, Kingstown; tel. 456-2577; fax 457-2568; e-mail info@stvincentoffshore.com; internet www.stvincentoffshore.com; f. 1996; Chair. CHRISTIAN IVOR MARTIN; Offshore Finance Inspector and CEO S. LOUISE MITCHELL.

Saint Vincent Trust Service: Trust House, 112 Bonadie St, POB 613, Kingstown; tel. 457-1027; fax 457-1961; e-mail trusthouse@saint-vincent-trust.com; internet www.saint-vincent-trust.com; br. in Liechtenstein; Pres. BRYAN JEEVES.

Trade and Industry

DEVELOPMENT ORGANIZATION

Saint Vincent Development Corporation (Devco): Grenville St, POB 841, Kingstown; tel. 457-1358; fax 457-2838; e-mail devco@caribsurf.com; f. 1970; finances industry, agriculture, fisheries, tourism; Chair. SAMUEL GOODLUCK; Man. CLAUDE M. LEACH.

CHAMBER OF COMMERCE

Saint Vincent and the Grenadines Chamber of Industry and Commerce (Inc): POB 134, Kingstown; tel. 457-1464; fax 456-2944;

SAINT VINCENT AND THE GRENADINES

e-mail svgcic@caribsurf.com; f. 1925; Pres. MARTIN LABORDE; Exec. Dir LEROY ROSE.

INDUSTRIAL AND TRADE ASSOCIATION

Saint Vincent Marketing Corporation: Upper Bay St, POB 872, Kingstown; tel. 457-1603; fax 456-2673; f. 1959; Man. M. DE FREITAS.

EMPLOYERS' ORGANIZATIONS

Saint Vincent Arrowroot Industry Association: Upper Bay St, Kingstown; tel. 457-1511; f. 1930; producers, manufacturers and sellers; 186 mems; Chair. GEORGE O. WALKER.

Saint Vincent Banana Growers' Association: Sharpe St, POB 10, Kingstown; tel. 457-1605; fax 456-2585; f. 1955; over 7,000 mems; Chair. LESLINE BEST; Gen. Man. HENRY KEIZER.

Saint Vincent Employers' Federation: Middle St, POB 348, Kingstown; tel. 456-1269; e-mail svef@caribsurf.com; Pres. DON PROVIDENCE.

UTILITIES

Electricity

Saint Vincent Electricity Services Ltd (VINLEC): Paul's Ave, POB 856, Kingstown; tel. 456-1701; fax 456-2436; internet www.vinlec.com; Chair. CLAUDE SAMUEL; CEO THORNLEY MYERS.

Water

Central Water and Sewerage Authority (CWSA): New Montrose, POB 363, Kingstown; tel. 456-2946; fax 456-2552; e-mail cwsa@caribsurf.com; f. 1961.

CO-OPERATIVES

There are 26 Agricultural Credit Societies, which receive loans from the Government, and five Registered Co-operative Societies.

TRADE UNIONS

Commercial, Technical and Allied Workers' Union (CTAWU): Lower Middle St, POB 245, Kingstown; tel. 456-1525; fax 457-1676; e-mail ctawu@vincysurf.com; f. 1962; affiliated to CCL, ICFTU and other international workers' orgs; Pres. ALICE MANDEVILLE; Gen. Sec. LLOYD SMALL; 2,500 mems.

National Labour Congress: POB 875, Kingstown; tel. 457-101; fax 457-1705; five affiliated unions; Pres. CECIL JACK.

National Workers' Movement: Burkes Bldg, Grenville St, POB 1290, Kingstown; tel. 457-1950; fax 456-2858; e-mail natwok@caribsurf.com; Gen. Sec. NOEL C. JACKSON.

Public Services Union of Saint Vincent and the Grenadines: McKies Hill, POB 875, Kingstown; tel. 457-1950; fax 456-2858; e-mail psuofsvg@caribsurf.com; f. 1943; Gen. Sec. HARVEY FARRELL; 738 mems.

Saint Vincent and the Grenadines Teachers' Union: POB 304, Kingstown; tel. 457-1062; e-mail svgtu@caribsurf.com; f. 1952; mems of Caribbean Union of Teachers affiliated to FISE; Pres. OSWALD ROBINSON; 1,250 mems.

Transport

RAILWAYS

There are no railways in the islands.

ROADS

In 2002 there was an estimated total road network of 829 km (515 miles), of which 580 km (360 miles) was paved.

SHIPPING

The deep-water harbour at Kingstown can accommodate two ocean-going vessels and about five motor vessels. There are regular motor-vessel services between the Grenadines and Saint Vincent. Geest Industries, formerly the major banana purchaser, operated a weekly service to the United Kingdom. Numerous shipping lines also call at Kingstown harbour. Some exports are flown to Barbados to link up with international shipping lines. A new marina and shipyard complex at Ottley Hall, Kingstown, was completed during 1995. A new container port at Campden Park, near Kingstown, was opened in the same year. A new dedicated Cruise Terminal opened in 1999, permitting two cruise ships to berth at the same time.

Saint Vincent and the Grenadines Port Authority: POB 1237, Kingstown; tel. 456-1830; fax 456-2732; e-mail svgport@caribsurf.com; internet www.svgpa.com.

CIVIL AVIATION

There is a civilian airport, E. T. Joshua Airport, at Arnos Vale, situated about 3 km (2 miles) south-east of Kingstown, that does not accommodate long-haul jet aircraft. The island of Canouan has a small airport with a recently upgraded runway and passenger terminal. Mustique island has a landing strip for light aircraft only.. In August 2005 Prime Minister Gonsalves pledged to build an international airport on Saint Vincent by 2011. The facility was to be constructed at Argyle, 13 miles east of Kingstown, at an estimated cost of EC $480m. Cuba and Venezuela were committed to providing funding for the project, and several other countries had been approached for assistance.

American Eagle: POB 1232, E. T. Joshua Airport, Arnos Vale; tel. 456-5555; fax 456-5616.

Mustique Airways: POB 1232, E. T. Joshua Airport, Arnos Vale; tel. 458-4380; fax 456-4586; e-mail info@mustique.com; internet www.mustique.com; f. 1979; charter and scheduled flights; Chair. JONATHAN PALMER.

Saint Vincent and the Grenadines Air Ltd (SVG Air): POB 39, Arnos Vale; tel. 457-5124; fax 457-5077; e-mail fltops@svgair.com; internet www.svgair.net; f. 1990; charter and scheduled flights; CEO J. E. BARNARD.

Tourism

The island chain of the Grenadines is the country's main tourism asset. There are superior yachting facilities, but the lack of major air links with countries outside the region has resulted in a relatively slow development for tourism. In 2004 Saint Vincent and the Grenadines received 77,585 cruise-ship passengers and 86,721 stop-over tourists. Tourism receipts were estimated to total EC $258.0m. in that year. There were 1,762 hotel rooms on the islands in 2001.

Department of Tourism: Cruise Ship Terminal, POB 834, Kingstown; tel. 457-1502; fax 451-2425; e-mail tourism@caribsurf.com; internet www.svgtourism.com; Dir VERA-ANN BRERETON.

Saint Vincent and the Grenadines Hotel and Tourism Association (SVGHTA): E. T. Joshua Airport; tel. 458-4379; fax 456-4456; e-mail office@svghotels.com; internet www.svghotels.net; f. 1968 as Saint Vincent Hotel Assscn; renamed as above in 1999; Exec. Dir DAWN SMITH.

SAMOA

Introductory Survey

Location, Climate, Language, Religion, Flag, Capital

The Independent State of Samoa (formerly Western Samoa) lies in the southern Pacific Ocean, about 2,400 km (1,500 miles) north of New Zealand. Its nearest neighbour is American Samoa, to the east. The country comprises two large and seven small islands, of which five are uninhabited. The climate is tropical, with temperatures generally between 23°C (73°F) and 30°C (86°F). The rainy season is from November to April. The languages spoken are Samoan (a Polynesian language) and English. Almost all of the inhabitants profess Christianity, and the major denominations are the Congregational, Roman Catholic and Methodist Churches. The national flag (proportions 1 by 2) is red, with a rectangular dark blue canton, containing five differently-sized white five-pointed stars in the form of the Southern Cross constellation, in the upper hoist. The capital is Apia.

Recent History

The islands became a German protectorate in 1899. During the First World War (1914–18) they were occupied by New Zealand forces, who overthrew the German administration. In 1919 New Zealand was granted a League of Nations mandate to govern the islands. In 1946 Western Samoa (as it was known until July 1997) was made a UN Trust Territory, with New Zealand continuing as the administering power. From 1954 measures of internal self-government were gradually introduced, culminating in the adoption of an independence Constitution in October 1960. This was approved by a UN-supervised plebiscite in May 1961, and the islands became independent on 1 January 1962. The office of Head of State was held jointly by two traditional rulers but, upon the death of his colleague in April 1963, Malietoa Tanumafili II became sole Head of State for life, performing the duties of a constitutional monarch.

Fiame Mata'afa Mulinu'u, Prime Minister since 1959, lost the general election in 1970, and a new Cabinet, led by Tupua Tamasese Lealofi, was formed. Mata'afa regained power in 1973, following another general election, and remained in office until his death in May 1975. He was again succeeded by Tamasese, who, in turn, lost the general election in March 1976 to his cousin, Tupuola Taisi Efi. The previously unorganized opposition members formed the Human Rights Protection Party (HRPP) in 1979, and won the elections in February 1982, with 24 of the 47 seats in the Fono (Legislative Assembly). Va'ai Kolone was appointed Prime Minister, but in September he was removed from office as a result of past electoral malpractice. His successor, Tupuola Efi, with much popular support, sought to nullify an earlier agreement between Kolone and the New Zealand Government which, in defiance of a ruling by the British Privy Council, denied automatic New Zealand citizenship to all Western Samoans except those already living in New Zealand. However, Tupuola Efi resigned in December 1982, after the Fono had rejected his budget, and was replaced by the new HRPP leader, Tofilau Eti Alesana. At elections in February 1985 the HRPP won 31 of the 47 seats, increasing its majority in the Fono from one to 15 seats; the newly-formed Christian Democratic Party (CDP), led by Tupuola Efi, obtained the remaining 16 seats. In December Tofilau Eti resigned, following the rejection of the proposed budget by the Fono and the Head of State's refusal to call another general election. Va'ai Kolone, with the support of a number of CDP members and HRPP defectors, was appointed Prime Minister of a coalition Government in January 1986.

At the February 1988 general election the HRPP and an alliance composed of independents and the CDP (later known as the Samoa National Development Party—SNDP) both initially gained 23 seats, with votes in the remaining constituency being tied. After two recounts proved inconclusive, a judge from New Zealand presided over a third and declared the CDP candidate the winner. However, before a new government could be formed, a newly-elected member of the Legislative Assembly defected from the SNDP alliance to the HRPP. In April Tofilau Eti was re-elected Prime Minister, and a new Government, composed of HRPP members, was appointed.

Legislation proposed in early 1990 which would permit local village councils to fine or to impose forced labour or exile on individuals accused of offending communal rules was widely perceived as an attempt by the Government to ensure the support of the Matai (elected clan chiefs) at the next general election. Of the 47 seats in the Fono, 45 were traditionally elected by holders of Matai titles. However, the political importance of the Matai had been increasingly diminished by the procurement of Matai titles by people seeking to be elected to the Fono. This practice was believed to have undermined the system of chief leadership to such an extent that universal suffrage would have to be introduced to decide all of the seats in the Fono. A referendum was conducted in October 1990, at which voters narrowly accepted government proposals for the introduction of universal suffrage. A second proposal, to create an upper legislative chamber composed of the Matai, was rejected. A bill to implement universal adult suffrage was approved by the Fono in December 1990, despite strong opposition from the SNDP.

A general election was held in April 1991 (the election had been postponed from February, owing to the need to register an estimated 80,000 newly-enfranchised voters). In the following weeks petitions were filed with the Supreme Court against 11 newly-elected members of the Fono who were accused of corrupt or illegal electoral practices. Moreover, subsequent political manoeuvring resulted in the HRPP increasing its parliamentary representation from an initial 26 to 30 seats, while the SNDP ultimately secured only 16 seats in the Fono, and the remaining seat was retained by an independent. At the first meeting of the new Fono, convened in early May, Tofilau Eti was re-elected for what, he later announced, would be his final term of office as Prime Minister.

In November 1991 the Fono approved legislation to increase the parliamentary term from three to five years and to create an additional two seats in the Fono. These seats were contested in early 1992 and won by the HRPP.

The introduction of a value-added tax on goods and services in January 1994 (which greatly increased the price of food and fuel in the country) provoked a series of demonstrations and protest rallies, as well as demands for the resignation of the Prime Minister. As a result of overwhelming opposition to the new regulations, the Government agreed, in March, to amend the most controversial aspects of the tax. Meanwhile, four members of the Fono (including three recently-expelled HRPP members), who had opposed the financial reforms, established a new political organization, the Samoa Liberal Party, under the leadership of the former Speaker, Nonumalo Leulumoega Sofara.

In May 1994 treasury officials warned the Government that a financial crisis at Polynesian Airlines, the national carrier, was threatening the country's economic stability. It was estimated that the company's debts totalled more than 45m. tala. A report by the Chief Auditor, Tom Overhoff, accused the Government of serious financial mismanagement relating to a series of decisions to commit public funds to the airline, and charged seven cabinet ministers with fraud and negligence in their handling of government resources. An inquiry into the allegations conducted in late 1994 cleared the ministers in question of all the charges, although its findings were harshly criticized by Overhoff, who claimed that the inquiry had been neither independent nor impartial. (In 2005 Polynesian Airlines established a joint venture with Australia's Virgin Blue to form Polynesian Blue—see Economic Affairs.)

Protests against the value-added tax on goods and services continued in early 1995, following the Government's decision to charge two prominent members of the Tumua ma Pule group of traditional leaders and former members of the Fono, with sedition, for organizing demonstrations against the tax during 1994. In March 1995 3,000 people delivered a petition to the Prime Minister, bearing the signatures of 120,000 people (some 75% of the population), that demanded that the tax be revoked. The Prime Minister questioned the authenticity of the signatures and appointed a 14-member committee to investigate the matter. In late June the case against the two members of Tumua ma Pule, which had attracted attention from several international non-governmental organizations (including the World

Council of Churches and Amnesty International) was dismissed on the grounds of insufficient evidence.

The announcement in mid-1995 by the French Government that it was to resume nuclear-weapons testing in the South Pacific provoked large-scale demonstrations in Apia and statements of condemnation by the Government, which imposed an indefinite ban on visits to Western Samoa by French warships and aircraft. The tests were concluded in January 1996.

In December 1995 the HRPP unanimously re-elected Tofilau Eti as the leader of the party, despite concern over the Prime Minister's deteriorating health, as well as a previous declaration that he would retire from politics upon completion of his current term in office.

In March 1996 one of the two female members of the Fono, Matatumua Naimoaga, left the HRPP in order to form the Samoa All-People's Party. The formation of the new party, in preparation for the forthcoming general election, was reportedly a result of dissatisfaction with the Government's alleged mismanagement of public assets together with concern over corruption. Legislation was introduced in April, which attempted to distinguish between the traditional Samoan practice of exchanging gifts and acts of bribery, amid numerous reports that voters were demanding gifts and favours from electoral candidates in return for their support.

A general election took place on 26 April 1996. The opposition was highly critical of the delay in the counting of votes (which took some three weeks in total), claiming that the length of time involved allowed the HRPP to recruit successful independent candidates in an attempt to gain a majority of seats in the Fono. It was eventually announced in mid-May that the HRPP had secured a total of 28 seats (with the recruitment of several independent members to their ranks), the SNDP had won 14 seats and independent candidates had secured seven. Tofilau Eti was subsequently re-elected as Prime Minister, defeating the Leader of the Opposition, Tuiatua Tupua Tamasese, with 34 votes to 14.

The strength of traditional religious beliefs among Samoans and resistance to foreign influences on their culture was illustrated in early 1997. In March a member of the Church of Jesus Christ of Latter-day Saints (Mormon—the fastest-growing denomination in the country) was tied to a stake surrounded by kindling when he refused to obey a banishment order for criticizing the village council's decision to prevent the construction of a Mormon church in the village. The intended victim was rescued by police-officers and church leaders, who negotiated his release from the villagers. A request by the Samoa Council of Churches to impose a ban on the establishment of new churches in the country was refused by the Government as incompatible with the principle of freedom of religion, as guaranteed in the Constitution. The organization was also highly critical of a US religious television channel due to begin operating in the islands in April, claiming that the evangelical style of religion depicted would undermine traditional Samoan Christianity. In mid-2003 US officials arrived in Samoa to investigate the burning of a Mormon church.

In May 1997 the Prime Minister proposed a constitutional amendment in the Fono to change the country's name to Samoa. (The country has been known simply as Samoa at the UN since its admission to the organization in 1976.) On 3 July the Fono voted by 41 votes to one to approve the change, which came into effect on the next day when the legislation was signed by the Head of State. The neighbouring US territory of American Samoa, however, expressed dissatisfaction with the change (which was believed to undermine the Samoan identity of its islands and inhabitants), and in September introduced legislation to prohibit recognition of the new name within the territory. In March 1998 the House of Representatives in American Samoa voted against legislation that proposed not to recognize Samoan passports (thereby preventing Samoans from travelling to the territory), but decided to continue to refer to the country as Western Samoa and to its inhabitants as Western Samoans. Nevertheless, in January 2000 Samoa and American Samoa signed a memorandum of understanding, increasing co-operation in areas including health, trade and education.

A series of reports in *The Samoa Observer* in mid-1997 alleged that a serious financial scandal involving the disappearance of some 500 blank passports, and their subsequent sale to Hong Kong Chinese for up to US $26,000 each, had occurred. The Government refused to comment on the newspaper's allegations, stating only that several senior immigration officials had been suspended pending the outcome of an investigation into the affair. Moreover, the Government subsequently brought charges of defamatory libel against the editor, Savea Sano Malifa, for publishing a letter criticizing the Prime Minister (who was reported to have told the Fono of his intention to change legislation governing business licences, such that publications could have their licences withdrawn for publishing dissenting material). The regional Pacific Islands News Association also condemned the Prime Minister's comments as an attack on freedom of information and expression. The continued existence of the newspaper was placed in jeopardy when Savea Sano Malifa was found guilty of defaming the Prime Minister in two libel cases in July and September 1998, and was ordered to pay a total of some US $17,000 in costs. The newspaper had alleged that public funds had been used to construct a hotel owned by the Prime Minister and had criticized the allocation of $0.25m. in the 1998 budget to Tofilau Eti's legal costs. The Government's increasingly autocratic style, its apparent intolerance of dissent and the perceived lack of accountability of its members, coupled with its poor economic record, resulted in frequent expressions of popular discontent during 1997. These culminated in a series of protest marches in late 1997 and early 1998, organized by the Tumua ma Pule group of chiefs and attended by several thousand people, which aimed to increase pressure on the Prime Minister to resign.

A long-standing dispute over land rights near Faleolo airport appeared to be the cause of violent activity in June 1998, when villagers shot a government official, burnt buildings and slaughtered or stole hundreds of cattle on a government estate. It was subsequently revealed, however, that the incidents had been perpetrated by members of a gang styling themselves as Japanese Ninja warriors, who were believed to be involved in the cultivation of marijuana and cattle theft. Some 38 men, thought to be members of the gang, were later arrested. The dispute, which originated in a land survey carried out in 1871, re-emerged in January 2003 when villagers presented the Government with a petition and a list of demands relating to land rights and revenue from the airport. In July 2005 the Government stated that it wanted all families living on the disputed land to vacate the area (covering some 22 acres) and move to a nearby and larger plot of government land. One of the official reasons given for the request was in order to comply with health and safety regulations. The villagers, however, resolved to resist the Government's request, restating their original demand for the return of 6,000 acres close to the airport, which they claimed had been wrongfully taken from them at the end of the 19th century. They were led in their resistance by senior Matai and former Minister of Civil Aviation, Toalepaiali'i Toeolesulusulu Suafaiga Siueva Pose Salesa III, who claimed that during his tenure in the Cabinet the Government had revealed its desire to remove the villagers' coconut trees in order to create a clearer flight path for aircraft and that this remained their motivation for moving the families.

In November 1998 Tofilau Eti Alesana resigned as Prime Minister, owing to ill health. He was replaced by the Deputy Prime Minister, Tuila'epa Sailele Malielegaoi, and, at the same time, the Cabinet was reshuffled. Tofilau Eti Alesana died in March 1999.

In July 1999 the Minister of Public Works, Luagalau Levaula Kamu, was shot dead while attending an event commemorating the 20th anniversary of the foundation of the ruling HRPP. Speculation followed that the killer's intended target had been the Prime Minister, but this was denied both by Tuila'epa Sailele and by the New Zealand police officers sent to the island to assist in the investigation. A man identified as Eletise Leafa Vitale (son of the Minister of Women's Affairs, Leafa Vitale) was arrested and charged with the murder. Eletise Leafa Vitale was later convicted of the murder and sentenced to death (subsequently commuted to a life sentence). Leafa Vitale was subsequently also charged with the murder of Luagalau, together with the former Minister for Telecommunications, Toi Akuso, who faced additional charges of inciting others to murder Luagalau and the Prime Minister, Tuila'epa Sailele. In mid-April 2000 the two former ministers were found guilty of murdering Luagalau and were sentenced to life (which was similarly commuted to life imprisonment; no death sentence had been carried out since Samoa's independence). It subsequently emerged that Luagalau had been killed in an attempt to prevent him from uncovering cases of corruption and bribery in which the two ministers had become involved.

Meanwhile, in November 1999 the ruling HRPP increased its number of seats in the Fono to 34 (out of a possible 49) following

SAMOA

the defection of an independent candidate to the HRPP. By-elections for the two imprisoned former ministers' seats were held in June 2000, and HRPP candidates were successful in both constituencies.

In August 2000 a supreme court ruling ordered the Government to allow opposition politicians access to the state-controlled media. For several years the opposition had been denied free access to the media.

At a general election on 2 March 2001 the HRPP won 22 seats, the SNDP secured 13 seats and independent candidates took 14 seats. On 16 March Tuila'epa Sailele won 28 votes in the Fono, after securing the support of six independents, to be re-elected Prime Minister. However, the opposition mounted a number of legal challenges to his election. In August eight elected members of Parliament, including the Deputy Prime Minister, the Minister of Health and the Minister of Internal Affairs, Women's Affairs and Broadcasting, faced charges of electoral malpractice in the Supreme Court. None of the Cabinet Ministers was found guilty, and by-elections for the vacant parliamentary seats were held in October and November. The HRPP won all four contested seats.

An Electoral Commission, established shortly after the March elections, published its recommendations in October 2001, urging the replacement of the two Individual Voters Roll seats with two Urban Seats and that government employees who wished to stand for Parliament should first be obliged to resign from their offices.

In mid-2003 members of the medical profession expressed alarm at the increasing numbers of qualified medical staff choosing to emigrate or to leave the profession altogether. It was estimated that one-third of Samoa's nurses had left the profession between 2002 and 2003, while half of all doctors' positions remained vacant. Low pay was blamed for the situation: doctors' salaries were reported to be five times higher in American Samoa and three times higher in New Zealand. Nurses in Samoa, who had not received a pay increase since 1999, complained of similar conditions. In September 2005 Samoan doctors went on strike in protest against entry-level rates of pay and working conditions. When doctors refused to return to work, the Government was forced to recruit temporary staff from overseas. In late November some 1,500 people marched through the streets of Apia in support of 23 doctors who had resigned earlier that month as part of the continuing protest. A petition was presented to the Prime Minister's Department, whereupon two cabinet ministers stated that the issue would be addressed. A commission of inquiry made recommendations for changes, to which the Government then agreed, but no increase in doctors' starting salaries, as demanded by protesters, was forthcoming. By January 2006 four of the doctors involved in the protests had relocated overseas, having found new positions; 11 others returned to government employment. However, the majority remained unemployed and were awaiting licences to open private medical practices.

The general election held on 31 March 2006 was contested by a total of 211 candidates, including 18 women; a total of 79,284 people had registered to vote. The ruling HRPP regained power, securing 33 of the 49 parliamentary seats, thus decisively defeating the Samoa Democratic United Party (formerly the SNDP), which won 10 seats. The remaining seats were taken by independent candidates. As the election results were announced, however, a school was destroyed and a man was shot and wounded. Violence ensued when it was declared that the Minister for Public Works, Faumui Liuga, had defeated Letagaloa Pita, a senior-ranking Matai, in the constituency of Savai'i.

In January 2004, meanwhile, the Fono approved legislation, introduced by the Prime Minister, that abolished the death penalty in Samoa. Capital punishment had not been carried out in the islands for 52 years, and the motion was widely supported by government and opposition members alike.

Samoa was struck by Cyclone Heta in early January 2004. The storm killed one person and caused considerable damage to housing, roads and power supplies on the islands.

Concern was expressed in early 2005 that the proliferation of Matai titles was leading to village councils making hasty and undesirable decisions. A senior village chief and member of the Fono, Leva'a Sauaso, claimed that many of the new title-holders were lacking in knowledge and experience of village affairs and that these clan leaders were consequently making decisions that were detrimental to Samoan society.

Despite independence, Samoa maintains strong links with New Zealand, where many Samoans live and many more receive secondary and tertiary education. In June 2002 New Zealand formally apologized for injustices it had committed against its former colony during its administration between 1914 and 1962. These included carelessness in allowing the 1918 influenza pandemic to kill 22% of Samoa's population (the virus having been brought in on a ship from New Zealand); the murder of a Samoan paramount chief and independence leader, Tupua Tamasese Lealofi III, and the killing of nine other supporters of the pacifist Mau movement during a non-violent protest in 1929; and the banishment of native leaders, who were also stripped of their chiefly titles. The apology, while accepted, attracted mixed reactions from Samoans, many of whom were more concerned with the issue of the restoration of their rights to New Zealand citizenship (which had been severely curtailed by the Citizenship Western Samoa Act of 1982). Moreover, in March 2003 large protest marches took place in Samoa and New Zealand demanding the repeal of the 1982 law, which ended Samoans' automatic right to New Zealand citizenship. In May 2004 a parliamentary select committee rejected a 100,000-signature petition seeking a repeal of the law and upheld the principles of the 1982 ruling. In 2004 the number of Samoans applying for New Zealand citizenship under the quota scheme increased by more than 50% to some 8,600.

In March 2003, in common with many other island nations in the region, large demonstrations were organized in Samoa to protest against the US-led military assault against Iraq. The Samoan Government expressed support for the demonstrations, which were attended by some 2,000 people.

In September 2004 the Samoan Government announced that it was seeking to formalize its maritime boundary with American Samoa, owing to a number of recent, unspecified incidents. Discussions began in Apia in March 2005. In January 2006 the Samoan Government announced that it was to open a consulate in the American Samoan capital of Pago Pago, the functions of which were to include the provision of assistance with immigration issues for Samoan citizens and the encouragement of American Samoans to visit Samoa. In February it was announced that Samoa had established diplomatic relations with Brunei.

Government

The Constitution provides for the Head of State to be elected by the Legislative Assembly for a term of five years. The present Head of State, however, holds the office for life. The Legislative Assembly is composed of 49 members, all of whom are elected by universal suffrage. A total of 47 members are elected from among holders of Matai titles (elected clan chiefs), and two are selected from non-Samoan candidates. Members hold office for five years. Executive power is held by the Cabinet, comprising the Prime Minister and other selected members of the Assembly. The Prime Minister is appointed by the Head of State with the necessary approval of the Assembly.

Defence

In August 1962 Western Samoa and New Zealand signed a Treaty of Friendship, whereby the New Zealand Government, on request, acts as the sole agent of the Samoan Government in its dealings with other countries and international organizations.

Economic Affairs

In 2004, according to estimates by the World Bank, Samoa's gross national income (GNI), measured at average 2001–2003 prices, was US $333.2m., equivalent to US $1,860 per head (or $5,670 per head on an international purchasing-power parity basis). During 1995–2004, it was estimated, the population increased at an average annual rate of 0.9%, while during the same period gross domestic product (GDP) per head increased, in real terms, by an average of 2.3% per year. Overall GDP increased, in real terms, by an average annual rate of 3.2% in 1995–2004. According to the Asian Development Bank (ADB), growth reached 3.7% in 2004 and 5.5% in 2005.

Agriculture (including hunting, forestry and fishing) accounted for 13.6% of GDP in 2004 and engaged some 33% of the labour force in 2003. The principal cash crops are coconuts (in total, coconut oil, cream and copra accounted for 15.0% of total exports in 2000, although coconut cream provided only 8.9% of export revenue in 2004) and taro (also the country's primary staple food). Following a devastating outbreak of taro leaf blight in 1994, a campaign to revive the taro industry was launched in mid-2000. Exports of taro accounted for 3.0% of total exports in 2003, rising to 4.4% in 2004. Breadfruit, yams, maize, passion fruit and mangoes are also cultivated as food crops. Exports of breadfruit and papaya to New Zealand increased significantly following the installation in early 2003 of a treatment facility to eradicate fruit fly from the produce. Plans to expand fresh fruit exports to include pineapples, mangoes and limes were announced in early 2005. Pigs, cattle, poultry and goats are raised, mainly for local consumption. Some 1,800 head of cattle were brought to Samoa from Australia in early 2003, in an attempt to boost stocks and increase beef production. The country's commercial fishing industry expanded considerably in the late 1990s, with export revenues rising from some US $4.8m. in 1997 (33.0% of domestic export earnings) to $29.0m. (62.7%) in 2002. Significant reductions in fishing taxes announced by the Government in March 2003 were expected to stimulate the country's fishing industry. Exports of fresh fish subsequently declined and contributed only 41.5% of total export earnings in 2004. Between 1995 and 2003, according to figures from the World Bank, the GDP of the entire agricultural sector decreased, in real terms, at an average annual rate of 1.9%. In real terms, compared with the previous year, agricultural GDP decreased by 3.5% in 2003 and by a further 6.5% in 2004, according to the ADB.

Industry (comprising manufacturing, mining, construction and power) employed 5.5% of the labour force in 1986 and provided 27.0% of GDP in 2000. According to World Bank figures, between 1995 and 2003 industrial GDP increased, in real terms, at an average annual rate of 2.4%. The GDP of the industrial sector expanded by 6.5% in 2003 and by 6.0% in 2004, according to the ADB.

Manufacturing provided 14.5% of GDP in 2004 and, together with mining, employed 3.5% of the labour force in 1986. The manufacturing sector expanded considerably in the early 1990s with the establishment of a Japanese-owned factory, producing electrical components for road motor vehicles. By 1996 the Yazaki Samoa factory, which assembles wire harnessing systems that are exported to car-manufacturing plants in Australia, engaged about 2,500 workers, making it the largest private-sector employer in the country. Shipments from the Yazaki factory, however, have been generally excluded from official statistics for visible (merchandise) exports. Instead, the value added by the plant has been recorded as part of 'invisible' trade, in the services account of the balance of payments. The initial success of the venture, combined with the availability of government incentives for export-processing activities, encouraged further investment in the manufacturing sector. The other products of the manufacturing sector include beverages (beer—which accounted for 13.1% of exports in 2004—and soft drinks), coconut-based products and cigarettes. The coconut oil mill, however, remained closed for much of 2000, but the opening of a new coconut-processing plant in early 2005 prompted renewed hopes for the regeneration of the industry. The clothing industry has expanded, and in 2004 garments accounted for 40.1% of total export earnings. Between 1995 and 2003, according to the World Bank, manufacturing GDP increased, in real terms, at an average annual rate of 1.6%.

Energy is derived principally from hydroelectric power and thermal power stations. A grant of US $0.3m. was received from the ADB in early 2003 to establish a hydroelectric project on Savai'i island. However, the Government was forced to seek an alternative location for the power plant following the refusal of local chiefs to allow its construction in their village. Chiefs representing the people of Sili village rejected the scheme, which they claimed would pollute local water supplies and harm the environment. Imports of mineral fuels accounted for 17.8% of the value of total imports in 2004. In mid-2005 a US company announced plans to begin conducting exploration activity in Samoan waters, hoping to find new sources of petroleum and natural gas.

The services sector provided 59.4% of GDP in 2004. Between 1995 and 2003, according to World Bank figures, the sector's GDP increased at an average annual rate of 6.7%. Compared with the previous year, the GDP of the services sector expanded by 3.9% in 2003 and by 5.0% in 2004, according to the ADB. Tourism makes a significant contribution to the economy, and tourist revenues, including the proportion of international travel credited to carriers based in Samoa, totalled an estimated 133.1m. tala in 2000, compared with 125.8m. tala in 1999. The number of tourist arrivals rose from 92,313 in 2003 to 98,024 in 2004. The tourist industry was expected ultimately to benefit from the establishment of Polynesian Blue, a joint venture between Polynesian Airlines and Virgin Blue, in 2005 (see below). Offshore banking was introduced to the islands in 1989, and by July of that year more than 30 companies had registered in Apia. A large proportion of the islands' revenue is provided by remittances from nationals working abroad, estimated at 150.7m. tala in 2000 and equivalent to some 19.5% of GDP in that year (more than three times the value of merchandise exports and, for the first time, exceeding tourist remittances). Such remittances remained at the equivalent of about 20% of GDP in 2005.

In 2004 the country recorded a visible trade deficit of US $156.9m., and a surplus of US $10.8m. on the current account of the balance of payments. In that year, when imports totalled 219.0m. tala and exports reached $84.7m., Australia was Samoa's principal trading partner, providing 23.1% of imports and purchasing 71.5% of exports, while New Zealand provided 36.2% of imports and purchased 2.7% of exports. Other important trading partners were the USA (13.6% of imports and 6.3% of exports) and Japan (5.8% of imports). The principal exports are fish, garments, coconut cream, copra and beer. The main imports are food and beverages, industrial supplies and fuels. From 2006 agricultural exports were expected to increase as a result of an expansion in the market for organic produce.

The large budget deficits of the early 2000s reflected an increase in development spending financed by external borrowing and a decrease in lending to the domestic banking system. In the year ending 30 June 2006 the overall budget deficit was projected at 59.3m. tala. This deficit was to be financed by means of concessionary loans to the value of 32.8m. tala, with the remainder being provided through the issuance of government securities. Aid from Australia and New Zealand is a major source of revenue. An estimated $A21.5m. was to be provided by Australia in 2005/06, with a further $NZ8.2m. to be supplied by New Zealand for the same year. At the end of 2003 the country's total external debt was US $365.2m., of which $169.5m. was long-term public debt. In 2004, according to the ADB, the cost of debt-servicing was equivalent to 7.9% of total revenue from exports of goods and services, compared with 8.7% in the previous year. In 1995–2004 the annual rate of inflation averaged 3.7%. Consumer prices increased by 16.3% in 2004 and by 8.0% in 2005, according to the ADB.

Samoa is a member of the Pacific Islands Forum (see p. 352), the Pacific Community (see p. 350), the Asian Development Bank (ADB, see p. 169) and the UN Economic and Social Commission for Asia and the Pacific (ESCAP, see p. 33), and is a signatory to the Lomé Conventions and the successor Cotonou Agreement (see p. 277) with the European Union (EU).

Following the achievement of high rates of GDP growth in 2000–01 (with the construction sector recording particularly strong expansion), Samoa's rate of economic growth decelerated in 2002. The tourism sector, however, continued to perform well, following the completion of new facilities, and was also well placed to benefit from the intermittent political instability in neighbouring Fiji and Solomon Islands. Construction of new tourist facilities was further facilitated by the entry into force of the Tourism and Hotel Development Incentive Act of 2003, which granted various tax concessions. The Government reaffirmed its policies in the Strategy for the Development of Samoa 2002–2004, and in April 2003 the number of government departments and ministries was reduced from 27 to 14 (largely through mergers) as part of the reforms. The document stressed the importance of opportunities for all through sustained economic growth and improvements in health and education. Sound GDP growth was resumed in 2003, but the islands were adversely affected by Cyclone Heta, which struck in January 2004, causing damage to buildings, infrastructure and the agricultural sector. Economic growth in 2004 resulted largely from increased activity in the construction industry, mainly rehabilitation projects in the aftermath of Cyclone Heta, continued private-sector hotel development and the construction of facilities in preparation for the South Pacific Games, which Samoa was to host in 2007. By May 2005 a total of 14m. tala had been allocated to the building of these new sports facilities. GDP growth in 2005 resulted largely from momentum in the areas of tourism, agriculture, transport, communications and construction. The establishment of a joint venture between Polynesian Airlines and Virgin Blue, the Australian carrier, to form Polynesian Blue in 2005, however, resulted in many job losses among the employees of Polynesian Airlines, with the majority of redundancies reportedly involving administrative staff. The new airline, in which the Samoan Government retained a shareholding of 49%, began operations at the end of October. A decrease in production at the Yazaki

SAMOA

Samoa factory (see above) in 2005 was largely responsible for the decline in the country's manufacturing output in that year. In mid-2005 the Samoa's foreign-exchange reserves totalled an estimated 231.6m. tala, deemed sufficient to cover the cost of almost six months of imports. The ADB envisaged overall GDP growth of 2.2% in 2006.

Education

The education system is based on that of New Zealand. About 97% of the adult population are literate in Samoan. In 1988 a national university was established, with an initial intake of 328 students. Faculties of arts and commerce, science, nursing and education exist. A project to upgrade the university campus was completed in early 1997. In 1992 the Government decided to reintroduce bonds for students awarded government scholarships for overseas study. Expenditure on education by the central Government in 2005 was an estimated 52.0m. tala (20.8% of total budgetary expenditure).

Public Holidays

2006: 1 January (Independence Day), 2 January (for New Year), 4 January (Head of State's birthday), 14–17 April (Easter), 25 April (ANZAC Day), 5 June (Whit Monday), 1–3 June (Independence Celebrations), 9 October (White Monday), 3 November (Arbor Day), 19 November (National Women's Day), 25 December (Christmas Day), 26 December (Boxing Day).

2007: 1 January (Independence Day), 2 January (for New Year), 4 January (Head of State's birthday), 6–9 April (Easter), 25 April (ANZAC Day), 5 June (Whit Monday), 1–3 June (Independence Celebrations), 15 October (White Monday), 2 November (Arbor Day), 19 November (National Women's Day), 25 December (Christmas Day), 26 December (Boxing Day).

Statistical Survey

AREA AND POPULATION

Area: Savai'i and adjacent small islands 1,708 sq km, Upolu and adjacent small islands 1,123 sq km; Total 2,831 sq km (1,093 sq miles).

Population: 161,298 (males 84,601, females 76,697) (Savai'i 45,050, Upolu and adjacent small islands 116,248) at census of 3 November 1991; 176,710 (males 92,050, females 84,660) at census of 5 November 2001. *Mid-2004* (UN estimate): 184,000 (Source: UN, *World Population Prospects: The 2004 Revision*).

Density (mid-2004): 65.0 per sq km.

Principal Town: Apia (capital), population 34,126 at census of 3 November 1991. *Mid-2003* (UN estimate, incl. suburbs): Apia 39,666 (Source: UN, *World Urbanization Prospects: The 2003 Revision*).

Births and Deaths (2001): Birth rate 29.0 per 1,000; Death rate 4.4 per 1,000. Source: UN, *Statistical Yearbook for Asia and the Pacific*.

Expectation of Life (WHO estimates, years at birth): 68 (males 67; females 70) in 2003. Source: WHO, *World Health Report*.

Economically Active Population (census of 3 November 1986): Agriculture, hunting, forestry and fishing 29,023; Manufacturing and mining 1,587; Electricity, gas and water 855; Construction 62; Trade, restaurants and hotels 1,710; Transport, storage and communications 1,491; Financing, insurance, real estate and business services 842; Community, social and personal services 9,436; Activities not adequately defined 629; *Total labour force* 45,635 (males 37,054, females 8,581). *1991 Census* (persons aged 15 years and over, excluding armed forces): Total labour force 57,142 (males 38,839, females 18,303) (Source: ILO, *Yearbook of Labour Statistics*). *Mid-2003* (estimates): Agriculture, etc. 21,000; Total labour force 64,000 (Source: FAO).

HEALTH AND WELFARE
Key Indicators

Total Fertility Rate (children per woman, 2003): 4.1.

Under-5 Mortality Rate (per 1,000 live births, 2004): 30.

Physicians (per 1,000 head, 1999): 0.70.

Health Expenditure (2002): US $ per head (PPP): 238.

Health Expenditure (2002): % of GDP: 6.2.

Health Expenditure (2002): public (% of total): 75.9.

Access to Water (% of persons, 2002): 88.

Access to Sanitation (% of persons, 2002): 100.

Human Development Index (2003): ranking 74.

Human Development Index (2003): value 0.776.

For sources and definitions, see explanatory note on p. vi.

AGRICULTURE, ETC.

Principal Crops (FAO estimates, '000 metric tons, 2004): Taro 17; Yams 2.6; Other roots and tubers 3; Coconuts 140; Copra 11; Bananas 21.5; Papayas 3.6; Pineapples 4.6; Mangoes 4; Avocados 1; Other fruits 9; Cocoa beans 0.5.

Livestock (FAO estimates, '000 head, year ending September 2004): Pigs 201; Cattle 29; Horses 1.8; Chickens 450.

Livestock Products (FAO estimates, '000 metric tons, 2004): Beef and veal 1; Pigmeat 3.8.

Forestry (FAO estimates, '000 cubic metres, 2004): *Roundwood Removals* (excl. bark): Sawlogs and veneer logs 58; Other industrial roundwood 3; Fuel wood 70; Total 131. *Sawnwood Production* (incl. sleepers): 21.

Fishing (metric tons, live weight, 2003): Albacore 2,253; Yellowfin tuna 293; Marine molluscs 1,607; Total catch (incl. others, all capture) 10,267.

Source: FAO.

INDUSTRY

Electric Energy (million kWh): 123.8 in 2002; 124.6 in 2003; 123.3 in 2004. Source: Treasury Department of Samoa.

FINANCE

Currency and Exchange Rates: 100 sene (cents) = 1 tala (Samoan dollar). *Sterling, US Dollar and Euro Equivalents* (30 December 2005): £1 sterling = 4.7593 tala; US $1 = 2.7640 tala; €1 = 3.2606 tala; 100 tala = £21.014 = US $36.18 = €30.67. *Average Exchange Rate* (tala per US $): 2.9732 in 2003; 2.7807 in 2004; 2 7103 in 2005.

Budget (provisional, million tala, year ending 30 June 2005): *Revenue:* Tax revenue 239.5 (Income tax 44.9, Excise tax 64.5, Taxes on international trade 38.0, Value-added gross receipts and services tax (VAGST) 85.5, Other taxes 6.6); Other revenue 28.5 (Fees, service charges, etc. 16.3, Departmental enterprises 0.9, Rents, royalties and international investments 11.3); Total 268.0, excl. external grants received (158.3). *Expenditure:* Current expenditure 232.2 (General administration 61.8, Law and order 16.8, Education 52.0, Health 37.6, Social security and pensions 11.5, Agriculture 11.0, Public works 39.2, Natural resources 9.8, Other economic services 1.8, Interest on public debt 4.7, Other purposes (residual) 3.8, *Sub-total* 249.9, *Less* VAGST payable by government 17.7); Development expenditure 176.4; Total 408.6, excl. net lending (26.2).

International Reserves (US $ million at 31 December 2004): IMF special drawing rights 3.77; Reserve position in IMF 1.08; Foreign exchange 90.67; Total 95.51. Source: IMF, *International Financial Statistics*.

Money Supply (million tala at 31 December 2004): Currency outside banks 38.94; Demand deposits at banks 85.99; Total money 124.93. Source: IMF, *International Financial Statistics*.

Cost of Living (Consumer Price Index, excluding rent; base: 2000 = 100): 112.2 in 2002; 112.3 in 2003; 130.7 in 2004. Source: IMF, *International Financial Statistics*.

Gross Domestic Product at Constant 2002 Prices (million tala): 885.0 in 2002; 916.0 in 2003; 951.4 in 2004. Source: Asian Development Bank, *Key Indicators of Developing Asian and Pacific Countries*.

Gross Domestic Product by Economic Activity (million tala at current prices, 2004): Agriculture and fishing 144.3; Manufacturing 153.8; Electricity and water 45.7; Construction 86.2; Trade 225.0; Transport and communications 128.7; Finance 101.0; Housing 40.0; Public administration 76.5; Other services 58.5; *Sub-total* 1,059.6; *Less* Imputed bank service charges 16.0; *Total* 1,043.6. Source: Treasury Department of Samoa.

Balance of Payments (estimates, US $ million, 2004): Exports of goods f.o.b. 11.9; Imports of goods f.o.b. –168.8; *Trade balance*

−156.9; Services and other income (net) 50.9; *Balance on goods, services and income* −106.0; Private remittances (net) 73.7; Official transfers (net) 43.1; *Current balance* 10.8; Capital transactions (incl. net errors and omissions) −15.6; *Overall balance* −4.8. Source: Asian Development Bank, *Key Indicators of Developing Asian and Pacific Countries*.

EXTERNAL TRADE

Principal Commodities ('000 tala, 2004): *Imports c.i.f.*: Food and live animals 90,418; Mineral fuels, etc. 83,222; Basic manufactures 145,811; Machines, transport equipment 111,589; Total (incl. others) 468,271. *Exports f.o.b.*: Coconut cream 2,950; Fish (fresh) 13,738; Beer 4,337; Taro 1,455; Garments 13,284; Total (incl. others) 33,127. Source: Asian Development Bank, *Key Indicators of Developing Asian and Pacific Countries*. Note: The trade data above exclude purchases and sales by the Yazaki car components factory.

Principal Trading Partners (US $ million, 2004): *Imports*: American Samoa 3.25; Australia 25.41; China, People's Republic 5.01; Fiji 47.47; Indonesia 8.85; Japan 21.49; Republic of Korea 4.80; New Zealand 61.21; Singapore 24.22; USA 14.19; Total (incl. others) 265.51. *Exports*: American Samoa 2.87; Australia 63.01; Germany 1.43; Indonesia 17.73; Japan 1.06; New Zealand 1.67; USA 5.09; Total (incl. others) 103.78. Source: Asian Development Bank, *Key Indicators of Developing Asian and Pacific Countries*.

TRANSPORT

Road Traffic (motor vehicles registered, 1998): Private cars 2,100; Pick-ups 2,080; Taxis 804; Trucks 261; Buses 159; Motorcycles 40; Tractors 6; Total (incl. others) 5,813.

International Shipping (freight traffic, '000 metric tons, 2004): Goods loaded 195.1; Goods unloaded 44.4. *Merchant Fleet* (total displacement, '000 grt at 31 December 2004): 10.5; vessels 10 (Source: Lloyd's Register-Fairplay, *World Fleet Statistics*).

Civil Aviation (traffic on scheduled services, 2001): Passengers carried 173,000; Passenger-kilometres 291 million; Total ton-kilometres 29 million. Source: UN, *Statistical Yearbook*.

TOURISM

Visitor Arrivals: 88,960 in 2002; 92,313 in 2003; 98,024 in 2004.

Visitor Arrivals by Country (2002): American Samoa 31,803; Australia 11,438; Fiji 1,928; New Zealand 23,790; USA 8,720. Source: World Tourism Organization, *Yearbook of Tourism Statistics*.

Tourism Receipts (million tala*): 139.58 in 2001; 152.58 in 2002; 158.63 in 2003.

* Includes the proportion of international travel credited to Samoan carriers.

COMMUNICATIONS MEDIA

Telephones (2004): 13,300 main lines in use*.

Facsimile Machines (1999): 500 in use*.

Personal Computers (2002): 1,000*.

Internet Users (2004): 572.5*.

Mobile Cellular Telephones (2004): 10,500 subscribers*.

Radio Receivers (1997): 410,000 in use†.

Television Receivers (2001): 26,000 in use*.

Non-daily Newspapers (1988): 5 (estimated circulation 23,000)†.

* Source: International Telecommunication Union.
† Source: UNESCO, *Statistical Yearbook*.

EDUCATION

Primary (2002 unless otherwise indicated): 155 schools (1996); 1,446 teachers; 38,946 pupils.

Secondary (2001): 1,064 teachers; 22,185 pupils.

Universities and other Higher (2001): 140 teachers; 1,179 students.

Source: mostly UN, *Statistical Yearbook for Asia and the Pacific*.

Adult Literacy Rate (UNESCO estimates): 98.7% (males 98.9%; females 98.4%) in 2003. Source: UN Development Programme, *Human Development Report*.

Directory

The Constitution

A new Constitution was adopted by a constitutional convention on 28 October 1960. After being approved by a UN-supervised plebiscite in May 1961, the Constitution came into force on 1 January 1962, when Western Samoa became independent. A constitutional amendment adopted in July 1997 shortened the country's name to Samoa. The main provisions of the Constitution are summarized below:

HEAD OF STATE

The office of Head of State is held (since 5 April 1963, when his co-ruler died) by HH Malietoa Tanumafili II, who will hold this post for life. After that the Head of State will be elected by the Fono (Legislative Assembly) for a term of five years.

EXECUTIVE

Executive power lies with the Cabinet, consisting of the Prime Minister, supported by the majority in the Fono, and ministers selected by the Prime Minister. Cabinet decisions are subject to review by the Executive Council, which is made up of the Head of State and the Cabinet.

LEGISLATURE

The Fono consists of 49 members. It has a five-year term and the Speaker is elected from among the members. Beginning at the election of 5 April 1991, members are elected by universal adult suffrage: 47 members of the Assembly are elected from among the Matai (elected clan leaders) while the remaining two are selected from non-Samoan candidates.

The Government

HEAD OF STATE

O le Ao o le Malo: HH Malietoa Tanumafili II (took office as joint Head of State 1 January 1962; became sole Head of State 5 April 1963).

CABINET
(April 2006)

Prime Minister and Minister of Foreign Affairs: Tuila'epa Sailele Malielegaoi.

Deputy Prime Minister and Minister of Commerce, Industry and Labour: Misa Telefoni.

Minister of Women, Community and Social Development: Fiame Naomi Mata'afa.

Minister of Police, Prisons and Fire Services: Toleafoa Apulu Faafisi.

Minister of Works, Transport and Infrastructure: Tuisugaletaua Sofara Aveau.

Minister of Natural Resources and Environment: Faumuina Tiatia Liuga.

Minister of Finance: Niko Lee Hang.

Minister of Revenue: Tuu'u Anasi'i.

Minister of Health: Gatoloaifaana Amataga Alesana Gidlow.

Minister of Communications and Information Technology: Mulitalo Sealiimalietoa Siafausa Vui.

Minister of Education, Sports and Culture: Toomata Alapati Poese Toomata.

Minister for Justice and Courts Administration: Unasa Mesi Galo.

Minister of Agriculture: Taua Tavaga Kitiona Seuala.

MINISTRIES AND MINISTERIAL DEPARTMENTS

Prime Minister's Department: POB L 1861, Apia; tel. 63122; fax 21339; e-mail pmdept@ipasifika.net.

Ministry of Agriculture, Forestry, Fisheries and Meteorology: POB 1874, Apia; tel. 22561; fax 21865; e-mail maffm@lesamoa.net.

Broadcasting Department: POB 200, Apia; tel. 21420.

SAMOA

Ministry of Commerce, Industry and Labour: Apia; tel. 20471; fax 21312; e-mail mpal@mcil.gov.ws; internet www.tradeinvestsamoa.ws.
Ministry of Communications and Information Technology: Private Bag, Apia; tel. 26117; fax 24671; e-mail mcit@mcit.gov.ws; internet www.mcit.gov.ws.
Customs Department: POB 44, Apia; tel. 21561.
Economic Affairs Department: POB 862, Apia; tel. 20471.
Ministry of Education, Sports and Culture: POB 1869, Apia; tel. 21911; fax 21917; e-mail samoamesc@lesamoa.net.
Ministry of Finance: PMB, Apia; tel. 34333; fax 21312; e-mail treasury@samoa.ws; internet www.mof.gov.ws.
Ministry of Foreign Affairs: POB L 1859, Apia; tel. 63333; fax 21504; e-mail mfa@mfa.gov.ws.
Health Department: Private Bag, Apia; tel. 21212; fax 21440; e-mail DG@health.gov.ws.
Inland Revenue Department: POB 209, Apia; tel. 20411.
Justice Department: POB 49, Apia; tel. 22671; fax 21050.
Lands, Survey and Environment Department: Private Bag, Apia; tel. 22481; fax 23176.
Public Works Department: Private Bag, Apia; tel. 20865; fax 21927; e-mail pwdir@lesamoa.net.
Statistics Department: POB 1151, Apia; tel. 21371; fax 24675.
Ministry of Transport: POB 1607, Apia; tel. 23701; fax 21990; e-mail mvnofo@mot.gov.ws.

Legislature

FONO
(Legislative Assembly)

The Assembly has 47 Matai members, representing 41 territorial constituencies, and two individual members. Elections are held every five years. At a general election on 31 March 2006, the Human Rights Protection Party (HRPP) won 33 seats, the Samoa Democratic United Party won 10 seats and independent candidates secured six seats.

Speaker: TOLOFUAIVALELEI FALEMOE LEIATAUA.

Political Organizations

Human Rights Protection Party (HRPP): c/o The Fono, Apia; f. 1979; Western Samoa's first formal political party; Leader TUILA'EPA SAILELE MALIELEGAOI; Gen. Sec. LAULU DAN STANLEY.
Samoa All-People's Party: Apia; f. 1996; Leader MATATUMUA NAIMOAGA.
Samoa Democratic United Party (SDUP): POB 1233, Apia; tel. 23543; fax 20536; f. 1988; est. as Samoa National Development Party (SNDP); coalition party comprising the Christian Democratic Party (CDP) and several independents; assumed present name after the 2001 election following merger of the SNDP and the Samoa Independent Party; Leader Hon. LEMAMEA R. MUALIA; Sec. VALASI TAFITO.
Samoa Liberal Party: Apia; f. 1994; Leader NONUMALO LEULUMOEGA SOFARA.
Samoa Mo Taeao (Samoans for a Better Tomorrow): Apia; Chair. TUIFA'ASISINA MEAOLE KEIL.
Samoa National Party: Apia; f. 2001; Sec. FETU TIATIA.

Diplomatic Representation

EMBASSIES AND HIGH COMMISSIONS IN SAMOA

Australia: Beach Rd, POB 704, Apia; tel. 23411; fax 23159; internet www.embassy.gov.au/ws.html; High Commissioner PHILLIP ALLARS.
China, People's Republic: Private Bag, Vailima, Apia; tel. 22474; fax 21115; e-mail tce@samoa.ws; Ambassador LIU GUANREN.
New Zealand: Beach Rd, POB 1876, Apia; tel. 21711; fax 20086; e-mail nzhcapia@samoa.ws; High Commissioner JOHN ADANK.
USA: POB 3430, Apia; tel. 21631; fax 22030; e-mail usembassy@samoa.net; Chargé d'affaires TIMOTHY W. HARLEY.

Judicial System

Attorney-General: BRENDA HEATHER.

The Supreme Court
Is presided over by the Chief Justice. It has full jurisdiction for both criminal and civil cases. Appeals lie with the Court of Appeal.
Chief Justice: TIAVAASUE FALEFATU MAKA SAPOLU.
Secretary for Justice: FAAITAMAI P. F. MEREDITH.
The Court of Appeal: consists of the President (the Chief Justice of the Supreme Court), and of such persons possessing qualifications prescribed by statute as may be appointed by the Head of State. Any three judges of the Court of Appeal may exercise all the powers of the Court.

The District Courts
Replaced the Magistrates' Court in 1998.
Judges: LESATELE RAPI VAAI, TAGALOA ENOKA FERETI PUNI.

The Land and Titles Court
Has jurisdiction in respect of disputes over Samoan titles. It consists of the President (who is also a judge of the Supreme Court) and three Deputy Presidents, assisted by Samoan judges and Assessors.
President of The Land and Titles Court: TIAVAASUE FALEFATU MAKA SAPOLU.

Religion

Almost all of Samoa's inhabitants profess Christianity.

CHRISTIANITY

Fono a Ekalesia i Samoa (Samoa Council of Churches): POB 574, Apia; f. 1967; four mem. churches; Sec. Rev. EFEPAI KOLIA.

The Anglican Communion
Samoa lies within the diocese of Polynesia, part of the Church of the Province of New Zealand. The Bishop of Polynesia is resident in Fiji, while the Archdeacon of Tonga and Samoa is resident in Tonga.
Anglican Church: POB 16, Apia; tel. 20500; fax 24663; Rev. PETER E. BENTLEY.

The Roman Catholic Church
The islands of Samoa constitute the archdiocese of Samoa-Apia. At 31 December 2003 there were an estimated 35,452 adherents in the country. The Archbishop participates in the Catholic Bishops' Conference of the Pacific, based in Fiji.
Archbishop of Samoa-Apia: Cardinal ALAPATI L. MATA'ELIGA, Cardinal's Residence, Fetuolemoana, POB 532, Apia; tel. 20400; fax 20402; e-mail archdiocese@samoa.ws.

Other Churches
Church of Jesus Christ of Latter-day Saints (Mormon): Samoa Apia Mission, POB 1865, Apia; tel. 64210; fax 64222; f. 1888; Pres. RENDAL V. BROOMHEAD; f. 1888; 65,000 mems.
Congregational Christian Church in Samoa: Tamaligi, POB 468, Apia; tel. 22279; fax 20429; e-mail cccsgsec@lesamoa.net; f. 1830; 100,000 mems; Gen. Sec. Rev. MAONE F. LEAUSA.
Congregational Church of Jesus in Samoa: 505 Borie St, Honolulu, HI 96818, USA; Rev. NAITULI MALEPEAI.
Methodist Church in Samoa (Ekalesia Metotisi i Samoa): POB 1867, Apia; tel. 22282; f. 1828; 36,000 mems; Pres. Rev. SIATUA LEULUAIALII; Sec. Rev. FAATOESE AUVAA.
Seventh-day Adventist Church: POB 600, Apia; tel. 20451; f. 1895; covers Samoa and American Samoa; 5,000 mems; Pres. Pastor SAMUELU AFAMASAGA; Sec. UILI SOLOFA.

BAHÁ'Í FAITH

National Spiritual Assembly: POB 1117, Apia; tel. 23348; fax 21363.

The Press

Newsline: POB 2441, Apia; tel. 24216; fax 23623; twice a week.
Samoa News: POB 1160, Apia; daily; merged with the weekly *Samoa Times* (f. 1967) in Sept. 1994; Publr LEWIS WOLMAN.
The Samoa Observer: POB 1572, Apia; tel. 21099; fax 21195; f. 1979; five times a week; independent; English and Samoan; also publ. in New Zealand twice a week; Editor AUMA'AGAOLU ROPETA'ALI; circ. 4,500.
Samoa Weekly: Saleufi, Apia; f. 1977; weekly; independent; bilingual; Editor (vacant); circ. 4,000.

SAMOA

Savali: POB L1861, Apia; publ. of Lands and Titles Court; monthly; govt-owned; Samoan edn f. 1904; Editor FALESEU L. FUA; circ. 6,000; English edn f. 1977; circ. 500; bilingual commercial edn f. 1993; circ. 1,500; Man. Editor (vacant).

South Seas Star: POB 800, Apia; tel. 23684; weekly.

Broadcasting and Communications

TELECOMMUNICATIONS

Samoa Communications Ltd: Samoa Communications Bldg, Private Bag, Apia; tel. 23456; fax 24000; corporatized in July 1999; telecommunications and postal services provider; Gen. Man. MARK YEOMAN.

BROADCASTING

Radio

Samoa Broadcasting Service: Broadcasting Department, POB 1868, Apia; tel. 21420; fax 21072; f. 1948; govt-controlled with commercial sponsorship; operates Radio 2AP; broadcasts on two channels in English and Samoan for 24 hours daily; Dir J. K. BROWN.

Magik 98 FM: POB 762, Apia; tel. 25149; fax 25147; e-mail magic98fm@samoa.net; f. 1989; privately-owned; operates on FM wavelengths 98.1 and 99.9 MHz; Man. COREY KEIL.

Graceland Broadcasting Network: POB 3444, Apia; tel. 20107; fax 25487; e-mail gbn@lesamoa.net; f. 1992; broadcasts gospel music.

Television

Televise Samoa Corporation: POB 3691, Apia; tel. 26641; fax 24789; e-mail ceotvsamoa@samoa.net; f. 1993; govt-owned national television broadcasting service; locally produced programmes and programmes supplied by Australian Television (ATV); in mid-2003 the Govt announced plans to merge its television and radio stations after failing to sell Televise Samoa Corpn; CEO LEOTA UELESE PETAIA.

Finance

(cap. = capital; res = reserves; dep. = deposits; m. = million; brs = branches; amounts in tala, unless otherwise indicated)

BANKING

Central Bank

Central Bank of Samoa: Private Bag, Apia; tel. 34100; fax 20293; e-mail cbs@lesamoa.net; internet www.cbs.gov.ws; f. 1984; cap. 10.0m., res 18.1m., dep. 68.2m. (June 2003); Gov. and Chair. PAPALI'I TOMMY SCANLAN.

Commercial Banks

ANZ Bank (Samoa) Ltd: Beach Rd, POB L 1885, Apia; tel. 22422; fax 24595; e-mail anz@samoa.ws; internet www.anz.com/samoa; f. 1959; est. as Bank of Western Samoa, name changed 1997; owned by ANZ Banking Group Ltd; cap. 1.5m., res 28.4m., dep. 246.1m. (Sept. 2001); Dir R. G. LYON; Man. Dir G. R. TUNSTALL; 1 br.

Industrial Bank Inc: POB 3271, Lotemau Centre, Vaea St, Apia; tel. 21878; fax 21869; f. 1995; owned by Industrial Pacific Investments Ltd; cap. US $0.3m., res US $1.9m. (1995); Chair. and Pres. IAN BYSTROV.

International Business Bank Corporation Ltd: Chandra House, Convent St, Apia; tel. 20660; fax 23253; e-mail ibb@samoa .net; f. 1991; 46.7% owned by ELECS Investment Ltd, 22.5% by Tidal Funds Co Ltd; cap. US $25.5m., res US $0.8m., dep. US $22.2m. (Jan. 1997); Chair. ILIA KARAS; Exec. Dir SERGUEI GREBELSKI.

National Bank of Samoa: POB 3047L, Apia; tel. 26766; fax 23477; e-mail info@nationalbanksamoa.com; internet www .nationalbanksamoa.com; f. 1995; owned by consortium of private interests in Samoa, American Samoa and the USA; Chair. TERENCE BETHAM; CEO ANNE BONISCH; 5 agencies; 1 sub-br.

Samoa Commercial Bank: Apia; tel. 31233; fax 30250; e-mail info@scbl.ws; internet www.scbl.ws; f. 2003; CEO RAY AH LIKI.

Westpac Bank Samoa Ltd: Beach Rd, POB 1860, Apia; tel. 20000; fax 22848; e-mail samoa@westpac.com.ws; f. 1977; est. as Pacific Commercial Bank Ltd, current name adopted 2001; first independent bank; 93.5% owned by Westpac Banking Corpn (Australia); cap. 1.2m., res 5.5m., dep. 96.5m. (Sept. 2002); Chair. ALAN WALTER; Gen. Man. STEVE BAKER; 3 brs.

Development Bank

Development Bank of Samoa: POB 1232, Apia; tel. 22861; fax 23888; internet www.dbsamoa.ws; f. 1974; est. by Govt to foster economic and social development; cap. 12.9m. (1992); Gen. Man. FALEFA LIMA.

INSURANCE

National Pacific Insurance Ltd: NPF Bldg, Private Bag, Apia; tel. 20481; fax 23374; f. 1977; 30% govt-owned; Gen. Man. RICKY WELCH.

Progressive Insurance Company: POB 620, Lotemau Centre, Apia; tel. 26110; fax 26112; e-mail progins@samoa.ws; f. 1993; Gen. Man. I. O. FILEMU.

Western Samoa Life Assurance Corporation: POB 494, Apia; tel. 23360; fax 23024; f. 1977; Gen. Man. A. S. CHAN TING.

Trade and Industry

CHAMBER OF COMMERCE

Chamber of Commerce and Industry: Level one, Lotemau Centre, Convent St, POB 2014, Apia; tel. 31090; fax 31089; e-mail info@samoachamber.com; internet www.samoachamber.com; f. 1938; Pres. NORMAN WETZELL; Vice-Pres. SALA EPA'TUIOTI; Sec. JOHN F. BOYLE.

INDUSTRIAL AND TRADE ASSOCIATIONS

Samoa Coconut Products: Apia.

Samoa Forest Corporation: Apia.

UTILITIES

Electricity

Electric Power Corporation: POB 2011, Apia; tel. 22261; fax 23748; e-mail epcgm@samoa.ws; internet www.epc.ws; f. 1972; autonomous govt-owned corpn; part of Public Works Dept, known as Electric Power Scheme, until 1972; Gen. Man. MUAAUSA JOSEPH WALTER.

Water

Samoa Water Authority: POB 245, Apia; tel. 20409; fax 21298; e-mail taputoa@swa.gov.ws; Man. Dir MAFAA'UO TAPUTOA TITIMAEA.

TRADE UNIONS

Journalists' Association of Samoa: Apia; Pres. APULU LANCE POLU.

Samoa Manufacturers' Association (SMA): Apia; Pres. EDDIE WILSON.

Samoa Nurses' Association (SNA): POB 3491, Apia; Pres. FAAMANATU NIELSEN; 252 mems.

Samoa Trade Union Congress (STUC): POB 1515, Apia; tel. 24134; fax 20014; f. 1981; affiliate of ICFTU; Pres. FALEFATA TUANIU PETAIA; Dir MATAFEO R. MATAFEO; 5,000 mems.

Transport

Public Works Department: see under The Government; Dir of Works ISIKUKI PUNIVALU.

ROADS

In 1999 there were 790 km of roads on the islands, of which some 42% were paved. In mid-2004 the Government announced a programme of road-building, including new roads from Apia to the airport and to the inter-island wharves. New four-lane roads were also to be constructed in the capital in response to increased vehicle numbers, estimated to have risen by some 7% annually in the previous 10 years.

SHIPPING

There are deep-water wharves at Apia and Asau. A programme of improvements to port facilities at Apia, funded by Japanese aid, was completed in 1991. Regular cargo services link Samoa with Australia, New Zealand, American Samoa, Fiji, New Caledonia, Solomon Islands, Tonga, US Pacific coast ports and various ports in Europe.

Samoa Ports Authority: POB 2279, Apia; tel. 23552; fax 25870; e-mail spa@lesamoa.net; f. 1999.

Samoa Shipping Services Ltd: POB 1884, Apia; tel. 20790; fax 20026; e-mail sss@lesamoa.net.

Samoa Shipping Corporation Ltd: Private Bag, Shipping House Matautu-tai, Apia; tel. 20935; fax 22352; e-mail ssc@samoa.net; internet www.samoashippingcorporation.com; Gen. Man. OLOIALII KOKI TUALA.

CIVIL AVIATION

There is an international airport at Faleolo, about 35 km from Apia and an airstrip at Fagali'i, 4 km east of Apia Wharf, which receives light aircraft from American Samoa. In mid-1999 US $19.4m. was allocated by the World Bank to improve facilities at Faleolo airport.

Polynesian Blue: NPF Bldg, Beach Rd, POB 599, Apia; tel. 21261; fax 20023; e-mail enquiries@polynesianairlines.ws; internet www.polynesianblue.com; f. 2005 following establishment of jt venture between Samoa's national airline Polynesian Airlines (f. 1959) and the Australian carrier Virgin Blue; 49% owned by the Samoan Govt, 49% owned by Virgin Blue, 2% owned by an independent Samoan shareholder; international services to American Samoa, Rarotonga (Cook Islands), Nadi (Fiji), Tonga, Sydney and Melbourne (Australia), Auckland and Wellington (New Zealand) and Hawaii and Los Angeles (USA); Domestic Poly Link, also formed in 2005, manages domestic services between islands of Upolu and Savai'i; Chair. TUILA'EPA SAILELE MALIELEGAOI; CEO JOHN FITZGERALD.

Samoa Air: tel. 22901; operates local shuttle services between Pago Pago and Apia; CEO ANDRE LAVIGNE.

Tourism

Samoa has traditionally maintained a cautious attitude towards tourism, fearing that the Samoan way of life might be disrupted by an influx of foreign visitors. The importance of income from tourism has, however, led to some development, including the expansion of hotel facilities and improvements to the road network and airport. A major project to construct a 400-room resort on Taumeasina island, off Apia, began in September 2004. Some 87,688 tourists arrived in 2000, and revenue from the tourist industry totalled 133.1m. tala in that year. In 2000 34.3% of tourists came from American Samoa, 26.0% from New Zealand, 12.5% from Australia and 10.3% from the USA. Visitor arrivals totalled 92,313 in 2003. The principal attractions are the scenery and the pleasant climate.

Samoa Hotel Association: POB 3973, Apia; tel. 30160; fax 30161; e-mail administration@samoahotels.ws; internet www.samoa-hotels.ws; f. 1999; owned by Asscn of Accommodation Providers; Pres. STEVE YOUNG.

Samoa Visitors' Bureau: POB 2272, Apia; tel. 26500; fax 20886; e-mail info@visitsamoa.ws; internet www.visitsamoa.ws; f. 1986; Gen. Man. SONJA HUNTER; Marketing Man. ALISE FAULALO-STUNNENBERG.

SAN MARINO

Introductory Survey

Location, Climate, Language, Religion, Flag, Capital

The Republic of San Marino lies in southern Europe. The country is situated on the slopes of Mount Titano, in the Apennines, bordered by the central Italian region of Emilia-Romagna to the north, and the Marches region to the south. San Marino has cool winters and warm summers, with temperatures generally between −2°C (28°F) and 30°C (86°F). Average annual rainfall totals 880 mm (35 ins). The language is Italian. Almost all of the inhabitants profess Christianity, and the state religion is Roman Catholicism. The civil flag (proportions 3 by 4) has two equal horizontal stripes, of white and light blue. The state flag has, in addition, the national coat of arms (a shield, framed by a yellow cartouche, bearing three green mountains—each with a white tower, surmounted by a stylized ostrich feather, at the summit—the shield being surmounted by a bejewelled crown and framed by branches of laurel and oak, and surmounting a white ribbon bearing, in black, the word 'libertas') in the centre. The capital is San Marino.

Recent History

San Marino evolved as a city-state in the early Middle Ages and is the sole survivor of the numerous independent states that existed in Italy prior to its unification in the 19th century. A treaty of friendship and co-operation with Italy was signed in 1862, renewed in March 1939 and revised in September 1971.

From 1945 to 1957 San Marino was ruled by a left-wing coalition of the Partito Comunista Sammarinese (PCS) and the Partito Socialista Sammarinese (PSS). Defections from the PCS in 1957 led to a bloodless revolution, after which a coalition of the Partito Democratico Cristiano Sammarinese (PDCS) and the Partito di Democrazia Socialista came to power. In early 1973 an internal dispute over economic policy led to the resignation of the Government, and a new Government was formed by an alliance between the PDCS and the PSS. The PSS withdrew from the coalition in November 1975, resulting in the collapse of the Government. The Captains-Regent took over the administration until March 1976, when a new coalition between the PDCS and the PSS was formed. This Government collapsed in late 1977 but continued in an interim capacity until a new administration was formed. Attempts by the PCS to form a government were frustrated by the lack of a clear majority in the unicameral legislature, the Consiglio Grande e Generale (Great and General Council). Eventually the Consiglio agreed to a dissolution and elections were held in May 1978, when the PDCS secured 26 of the 60 seats. However, they were still unable to form an administration and the three left-wing parties, the PCS, PSS and the Partito Socialista Unitario, which together held 31 seats, agreed to form a coalition Government led by the PCS. San Marino thus became the only Western European country with a communist-led government. A left-wing coalition again formed the administration following the May 1983 elections.

In 1986 a political crisis, resulting from a financial scandal which allegedly involved several prominent PSS members, led to the formation of a new coalition Government, the first to be composed of the PDCS and the PCS. At the general election of May 1988, the PDCS and the PCS obtained 27 and 18 seats, respectively, and in June the two parties agreed to form a coalition Government. In 1990 the PCS was renamed the Partito Progressista Democratico Sammarinese (PPDS). In 1992 the PDCS negotiated the formation of a coalition Government with the PSS. The PDCS, with the majority of government members, had decided not to maintain an alliance with the PPDS in view of the demise of communism in Europe.

At the general election of May 1993 the PDCS and the PSS obtained 26 and 14 seats, respectively. The election was regarded as a defeat for the PPDS, which secured only 11 seats, and was also notable for the success of three recently formed parties, the Alleanza Popolare dei Democratici Sammarinese (APDS—also known as the Alleanza Popolare), the Movimento Democratico and the Rifondazione Comunista Sammarinese (RCS). In June the PDCS and the PSS agreed to form a coalition Government. The PDCS and the PSS were again dominant at the general election of 31 May 1998, winning 25 and 14 seats, respectively.

The PPDS won 11 seats, the APDS six, and the RCS two. The remaining two seats were secured by a new grouping, Socialisti per le Riforme, which had been founded in 1997. A coalition Government was formed by the PDCS and the PSS in July 1998. In February 2000 the PSS left the Government, and in March a new coalition Government was formed, with six members of the PDCS, three members of the PPDS and one member of the Socialisti per le Riforme; it also had parliamentary support from Idee in Movimento (as the Movimento Democratico had been renamed in 1998). In March 2001 the Partito dei Democratici Sammarinese (PdD) was formed, following an alliance between Idee in Movimento, the PPDS and the Socialisti per le Riforme; the PPDS Secretary-General, Claudio Felici, was appointed as the PdD's Secretary-General.

At legislative elections, held on 10 June 2001, the PDCS secured 25 seats and 41.5% of the votes cast, and the PSS obtained 15 seats and 24.2% of the votes. The two parties subsequently formed a coalition Government. The PdD won 12 seats (with 20.8% of the votes), while the APDS secured five seats (8%), the RCS two seats (3.4%) and the Alleanza Nazionale Sammarinese one seat (1.9%).

In June 2002 the PDCS-PSS coalition Government collapsed after the PSS withdrew its support, ending the long-term domination of Sammarinese politics by the PDCS. A new coalition Government was formed on 25 June, incorporating five members of the PSS, three of the PdD and two members of the APDS. By December, however, the alliance between the PSS and the PDCS had been renewed, and a new coalition Government was instituted on 17 December, with five members from each party. In January 2003 a new political party, the Sammarinese per la Libertà, was formed. In December the coalition Government collapsed owing to disagreements between the two ruling parties, and a new coalition comprising four PDCS members and two each from the PSS and the PdD was installed.

In early 2005 the PSS and the PdD voted to merge and form the Partito dei Socialisti e dei Democratici. Former members of the PSS founded a new party, the Nuovo Partito Socialista, in November. In March 2006 two new Captains-Regent, Gian Franco Terenzi and Loris Francini, both representing the PDCS, were elected.

San Marino became a member of the UN in 1992. In early 2006 San Marino was represented at a conference of small European states held in Monaco.

Government

San Marino is divided into nine 'Castles' (Castelli) corresponding to the original parishes of the Republic. Each 'Castle' is governed by a Castle-Captain (Capitano di Castello), who holds office for two years, and a Castle Board (Giunte di Castello), which holds office for five years.

Legislative power is vested in the unicameral Consiglio Grande e Generale (Great and General Council), with 60 members elected by universal adult suffrage, under a system of proportional representation, for five years (subject to dissolution). The Consiglio elects two of its members to act jointly as Captains-Regent (Capitani Reggenti), with the functions of Head of State and Government, for six months at a time (ending in March and September). Executive power is held by the Congress of State (Congresso di Stato), with 10 members elected by the Council for the duration of its term. The Congresso is presided over by the Captains-Regent.

Defence

There are combined Voluntary Military Forces. There is no obligatory military service but citizens between 16 and 55 years may be enlisted, in certain circumstances, to defend the state.

Economic Affairs

San Marino's GDP was €995.3m. in 2003, which equated to €26,350 per head. Annual GDP growth averaged 4.2% in 1998–2003; GDP increased by 0.3% in 2002 and by 3.9% in 2003.

Agriculture contributed only 0.1% of GDP in 2003 and engaged 0.2% of the employed population (excluding the self-employed) in 2004. The principal crops are wheat, barley, maize, olives and grapes. Livestock-rearing and dairy farming are also important. Olive oil and wine are produced for export. In 2004 there were 89 agricultural businesses, including 11 co-operatives, in San Marino, compared with 115 in 2001 and 96 in 1998.

Industry (including manufacturing and construction) contributed 48.4% of GDP in 2003 and engaged 41.4% of the employed population (excluding the self-employed) in 2004. Stone-quarrying is the only mining activity in San Marino, and is an important export industry. Manufacturing contributed 41.6% of GDP in 2003 and engaged 33.4% of the employed population (excluding the self-employed) in 2004. The most important branches of manufacturing are the production of cement, synthetic rubber, leather, textiles and ceramics. The sector is largely export orientated, owing to integration with firms in Italy.

Energy is derived principally from gas (more than 75%). San Marino is dependent on the Italian state energy companies for much of its energy requirements.

The services sector contributed 51.5% of GDP in 2003 and engaged 58.4% of the employed population (excluding the self-employed) in 2004. Tourism is the main source of income, contributing about 60% of government revenue. In 2004 the number of visitor arrivals was 2,812,488; however, of that number, only 41,546 stayed at least one night. Receipts from tourism were estimated at US $252.5m. in 1994, equivalent to 41.6% of GDP in that year. Tourism is stimulated by the country's annual hosting of a motor-racing Grand Prix. The sale of coins and postage stamps, mainly to foreign collectors, is also a significant source of foreign exchange. San Marino, along with the Vatican and Monaco, was granted special dispensation to mint its own euro coins in 2002, with a view to providing for this specialist market. The sale of uncirculated minted coins to collectors plays a significant role in San Marino's economy and it was permitted to continue to mint gold scudi as a legal tender for San Marino only.

In 1996, according to IMF estimates, San Marino recorded a trade surplus of US $22.6m., and there was a surplus of $10.7m. on the current account of the balance of payments. (In 2002, according to official figures, San Marino recorded a trade deficit of €96.2m.) Data concerning imports and exports are included in those of Italy, with which San Marino maintains a customs union. A customs union is also maintained with the European Union—EU (see p. 228). The principal source of imports (estimated at 87%) is Italy, upon which the country is dependent for its supply of raw materials. The major exports are wine, woollen goods, furniture, ceramics, building stone and artisan- and hand-made goods.

San Marino receives a subsidy from the Italian Government, under the *Canone Doganale*, amounting to about €11m. annually, in exchange for the Republic's acceptance of Italian rules concerning exchange controls and the renunciation of customs duties.

No consolidated general government accounts are published by San Marino, and separate accounts and budgets are prepared by the central administration, the Social Security Institute, and each of the public enterprises, on an accrual basis. Figures published by the IMF, on a cash basis, for the budget of the central administration indicated a surplus of €15.6m. for 2003 (equivalent to some 1.6% of GDP). The annual rate of inflation averaged 4.3% in 1990–2000; consumer prices increased by an average of 2.1% in 2003 and 1.1% in 2004. In 2004 510 people were unemployed—equivalent to 2.5% of the total labour force. An increasingly large proportion of the work-force (29.8% of the employed labour force in 2004, compared with 10.8% in 1991) are cross-border workers, mainly Italians from the surrounding regions.

Tourism has become increasingly important to San Marino's economy since the 1960s, when an increase in tourist activity in nearby Italian resorts resulted in the arrival of large numbers of excursionists. San Marino is currently dependent on the revenues generated by almost 3m. visitors each year, although the expansion of light industries, based on imported materials from Italy, has been encouraged in order to reduce this dependence. In the 1990s political uncertainty in Italy, together with alternative taxation and regulation structures available in San Marino, resulted in the inflow to the banking sector of a large amount of non-resident deposits, and the development of dynamic financial and commercial sectors, which contributed to remarkable economic growth. In January 1999 San Marino adopted the euro, which became the sole currency in circulation at the start of 2002. In 1999–2000 the budget deficit of the central administration increased to an estimated 2.8% of GDP, compared with an average of some 1.0% of GDP during the 1990s. In 2001 the deficit increased to 3.6%, before falling to 2.2% in 2002. A budget surplus of 1.6% was achieved in 2003. Growth in the financial sector has been stimulated by advantageous banking confidentiality, which aroused some concern from the Organisation for Economic Co-operation and Development (OECD) with respect to money-laundering. However, commitment was expressed in 2000 to adherence to OECD guidelines on 'harmful tax competition'. In 2003 the Istituto di Credito Sammarinese and the Ispettorato per il Credito e le Valute merged to create a new central bank, the Banca Centrale della Repubblica di San Marino. In 2004 the maximum rate of personal income tax in San Marino stood at 12%, compared with 33% in Italy, while the highest rate of corporate tax was 24%, compared with 55% in Italy. In November 2004 the EU reached an agreement with San Marino on the adoption by the latter of measures equivalent to those contained in the EU's savings tax directive, which aimed to prevent EU citizens from avoiding taxes on savings by keeping their money in foreign bank accounts. Under the agreement, which took effect in July 2005, the Sammarinese authorities were to levy a withholding tax on interest payments made to residents of the EU, part of which was to be transferred to investors' states of residence. As an alternative, tax-payers could opt to permit the disclosure of the income to their member states of residence for tax purposes. In late 2005 the Government announced a plan to invest €4.5m. over three years in tourism and commerce.

Education

Education is compulsory for 10 years between the ages of six and 16 years. Primary education begins at six years of age and lasts for five years. Secondary education begins at the age of 11 and may last for up to eight years: a first cycle of three years, a second of two years and a third, non-compulsory, cycle of three years. A state-administered university was inaugurated in 1987. Government expenditure on education was €33.9m. in 2004, equivalent to 6.3% of public spending.

Public Holidays

2006: 1 January (New Year's Day), 6 January (Epiphany), 5 February (Liberation Day and St Agatha's Day), 19 March (St Joseph's Day), 25 March (Anniversary of the Arengo), 1 April (Investiture of the new Captains-Regent), 17 April (Easter Monday), 1 May (Labour Day), 15 June (Corpus Christi), 28 July (Fall of Fascism), 15 August (Assumption of the Virgin), 3 September (San Marino Day and Republic Day), 1 October (Investiture of the new Captains-Regent), 1 November (All Saints' Day), 2 November (Commemoration of the Dead), 8 December (Immaculate Conception), 25 December (Christmas), 26 December (St Stephen's Day).

2007: 1 January (New Year's Day), 6 January (Epiphany), 5 February (Liberation Day and St Agatha's Day), 19 March (St Joseph's Day), 25 March (Anniversary of the Arengo), 1 April (Investiture of the new Captains-Regent), 9 April (Easter Monday), 1 May (Labour Day), 7 June (Corpus Christi), 28 July (Fall of Fascism), 15 August (Assumption of the Virgin), 3 September (San Marino Day and Republic Day), 1 October (Investiture of the new Captains-Regent), 1 November (All Saints' Day), 2 November (Commemoration of the Dead), 8 December (Immaculate Conception), 25 December (Christmas), 26 December (St Stephen's Day).

Weights and Measures

The metric system is in force.

Statistical Survey

Source (unless otherwise stated): Ufficio Programmazione Economica e Centro Elaborazione Dati e Statistica, Viale Antonio Onofri 109, 47890 San Marino; tel. 0549 885150; fax 0549 885154; e-mail statistica.upeceds@pa.sm; internet www.upeceds.sm.

AREA AND POPULATION

Area: 61.2 sq km (23.6 sq miles).

Population: 29,673 (males 14,546, females 15,127) at 31 December 2004 (*of which* Sammarinese 26,176, Italian 3,111, Others 386).

Density (2004): 484.9 per sq km.

Principal Towns (population at 31 December 2004): Serravalle/Dogano 9,543; Borgo Maggiore 6,083; San Marino (capital) 4,464.

Births, Marriages and Deaths (registrations, 2004 unless otherwise indicated): Live births 306 (birth rate 10.6 per 1,000, 2000–04); Marriages 207 (marriage rate 7.0 per 1,000, 2000–04); Deaths 185 (death rate 6.9 per 1,000, 2000–04).

Expectation of Life (WHO estimates, years at birth): 81 (males 78; females 84) in 2003. Source: WHO, *World Health Report*.

Economically Active Population (2004): Agriculture 43; Manufacturing 5,926; Construction 1,417; Trade and hospitality 2,571; Communication and transport 363; Finance 714; Real estate, information technology and business services 1,671; Other services 903; Public sector 4,148; Self-employed 2,207; *Total employed* 19,963 (males 11,757, females 8,206); Unemployed 510 (males 128, females 382); *Total labour force* 20,473 (males 11,885, females 8,588).

HEALTH AND WELFARE
Key Indicators

Total Fertility Rate (children per woman, 2003): 1.2.

Under-5 Mortality Rate (per 1,000 live births, 2004): 4.

Physicians (per 1,000 head, 1990): 2.51.

Hospital Beds (per 1,000 head, 1990): 7.16.

Health Expenditure (2002): US $ per head (PPP): 3,094.

Health Expenditure (2002): % of GDP: 7.7.

Health Expenditure (2002): public (% of total): 79.2.

For sources and definitions, see explanatory note on p. vi.

FINANCE

Currency and Exchange Rates: Italian currency: 100 cent = 1 euro (€). *Sterling and Dollar Equivalents* (30 December 2005): £1 sterling = 1.4596 euros; US $1 = 0.8477 euros; €100 = £68.51 = $111.80. *Average Exchange Rates* (euros per US $): 0.8860 in 2003; 0.8054 in 2004; 0.8041 in 2005. Note: The local currency was formerly the Italian lira (plural = lire). From the introduction of the euro, with Italian participation, on 1 January 1999, a fixed exchange rate of €1 = 1,936.27 lire was in operation. Euro notes and coins were introduced on 1 January 2002. The euro and local currency circulated alongside each other until 28 February, after which the euro became the sole legal tender.

Cash Balance of Central Administration (preliminary figures, € million, 2003): *Revenue*: Tax revenue 219.7 (Taxation on income 100.0, Tax on imports 94.9, Other indirect taxes 24.9); Capital revenue 68.3; Total revenue 288.0. *Expenditure*: Current expenditure 250.6 (Wages and salaries 91.2; Transfers to the public sector 123.7; Transfers to the private sector 8.0; Interest payments 2.2); Capital expenditure 21.8 (Capital transfers 7.9; Other 13.9); Total expenditure 272.4. Source: IMF, *San Marino: Selected Issues and Statistical Appendix* (August 2004).

International Reserves (US $ million at 31 December 2005): IMF special drawing rights 0.87; Reserve position in IMF 6.37; Foreign exchange 348.34; *Total* 355.58. Source: IMF, *International Financial Statistics*.

Money Supply (€ '000 at 31 December 2004): Demand deposits at banks 693,647. Source: IMF, *International Financial Statistics*.

Cost of Living (Consumer Price Index; base: 2002 = 100): All items 102.1 in 2003; 103.2 in 2004. Source: ILO.

Expenditure on the Gross Domestic Product (€ million at current prices, 2003): Final consumption expenditure 494.8; Increase in stocks 13.9; Gross fixed capital formation 570.1; *Total domestic expenditure* 1,078.8; Exports of goods and services 1,763.1; *Less* Imports of goods and services 1,846.6; *GDP in purchasers' values* 995.3.

Gross Domestic Product by Economic Activity (€ million at current prices, 2003): Agriculture 1.1; Manufacturing 413.9; Construction 67.7; Services 512.6 (Trade 96.5, Transport and communications 14.9, Finance and insurance 163.2, Public sector 144.3, Other services 93.6); Total 995.3.

Balance of Payments (estimates, US $ million, 1996): Merchandise exports f.o.b. 1,741,9; Merchandise imports c.i.f. −1,719.3; *Trade balance* 22.6; Exports of services 120.4; Imports of services −102.2; *Balance on goods and services* 40.9; Interest payments 63.5; Net labour income −57.9; Other capital income −45.5; *Balance on goods, services and income* 1.0; Net transfers 9.7; *Current balance* 10.7; Capital account (net) 218.5; Errors and omissions −219.8; *Overall balance* 9.4. Source: IMF, *San Marino: Recent Economic Developments* (April 1999).

EXTERNAL TRADE

Data concerning imports and exports are included in those of Italy, with which San Marino maintains a customs union.

TRANSPORT

Road Traffic (registered motor vehicles, 2004): Motorcycles 9,831; Passenger cars 30,517; Buses and coaches 3,252; Agricultural vehicles 911; Total (incl. others) 45,955.

TOURISM

Visitor Arrivals (incl. excursionists): 3,102,453 in 2002; 2,882,207 in 2003; 2,812,488 in 2004.

Tourist Arrivals (staying at least one night): 45,508 in 2002; 40,686 in 2003; 41,546 in 2004.

COMMUNICATIONS MEDIA

Radio Receivers (1998): 35,100 in use.

Television Receivers (1999): 23,000 in use.

Telephones (2000): 20,302 main lines in use.

Facsimile Machines (1998): 5,800 in use.

Mobile Cellular Telephones (subscribers, 2000): 14,503.

Daily Newspapers (1998): 3 titles; 2,000 copies circulated.

Non-Daily Newspapers (1998): 8 titles; 12,000 copies circulated.

Periodicals (1998): 17 titles; 10,000 copies circulated.

Sources: Direzione Generale Poste e Telecomunicazioni; International Telecommunication Union.

EDUCATION

Pre-primary (2004/05): 14 schools, 139 teachers, 1,060 pupils.

Primary (2004/05): 14 schools, 234 teachers, 1,445 pupils.

Secondary (Scuola Media) (2004/05): 3 schools, 157 teachers, 782 pupils.

Secondary (Scuola Secondaria Superiore) (2004/05): 4 schools, 77 teachers, 534 pupils (a further 493 pupils were studying outside San Marino).

University (2004/05): 1 university, 27 students (a further 1,580 students were attending courses outside San Marino).

There is also a vocational training school (30 pupils 2004/05).

Directory

The Constitution

San Marino, founded in 310 AD, is reputed to be the world's oldest surviving republic. In 1243 the first two Capitani Reggenti (Captains-Regent) were elected to serve as Heads of State by the Consiglio Grande e Generale (Great and General Council). The *Leges Statutae Sancti Marini* date back to 1600 and outline the main administrative posts and legal basis of the state. Electoral legislation dates from 1926.

San Marino is divided into nine Castelli ('Castles') corresponding to the original parishes of the Republic. Each Castello is governed by a Capitano di Castello (Castle-Captain), who holds office for two years, and a Giunte di Castello (Castle Board), which holds office for five years. Legislative power is vested in the unicameral Consiglio Grande e Generale, with 60 members elected by universal adult suffrage, under a system of proportional representation, for five years (subject to dissolution). The Consiglio elects two of its members to act jointly as Capitani Reggenti, with the functions of Head of State and Government, for six months at a time (ending in March and September). Executive power is held by the Congresso di Stato (Congress of State), with 10 members elected by the Consiglio for the duration of its term. The Congresso is presided over by the Capitani Reggenti.

The Government

HEADS OF STATE

Capitani-Reggenti (Captains-Regent): GIAN FRANCO TERENZI (PDCS), LORIS FRANCINI (PDCS) (April–September 2006).

CONGRESS OF STATE
(April 2006)

A coalition of the Partito Democratico Cristiano Sammarinese (PDCS) and the Partito dei Socialisti e dei Democratici (PSD).

Secretary of State for Foreign and Political Affairs, Economic Planning and Justice: FABIO BERNARDI (PSD).

Secretary of State for Internal Affairs, Public Education and the University: ROSA ZAFFERANI (PDCS).

Secretary of State for Finance, the Budget, Transport, Research and Relations with the Azienda Autonoma di Stato Filatelica e Numismatica (AASFN): PIER MARINO MULARONI (PDCS).

Secretary of State for Industry, Handicrafts, Trade, Telecommunications and Economic Co-operation: CLAUDIO FELICI (PSD).

Secretary of State for Territory, Environment, Agriculture and Relations with the Azienda Autonoma di Stato di Produzione (AASP): GIAN CARLO VENTURINI (PDCS).

Secretary of State for Labour and Co-operation, Tourism, Sport and Post: PARIDE ANDREOLI (PSD).

Secretary of State for Health, Social Security, Social Affairs and Equal Opportunities: MASSIMO ROBERTO ROSSINI (PSD).

Secretary of State for Information, Cultural Institutions, Civil Protection, Relations with the Azienda Autonoma di Stato per i Servizi Pubblici (AASS) and Relations with the Castle Boards: GIOVANNI LONFERNINI (PDCS).

MINISTRIES

Secretariat of State for Finance, the Budget, Transport, Research and Relations with the Azienda Autonoma di Stato Filatelica e Numismatica (AASFN): Palazzo Begni, Contrada Omerelli, 47890 San Marino; tel. 0549 882293; fax 0549 882814; e-mail segr.finanze@omniway.sm.

Secretariat of State for Foreign and Political Affairs, Economic Planning and Justice: Palazzo Begni, Contrada Omerelli, 47890 San Marino; tel. 0549 882293; fax 0549 882814; e-mail segretariadistato@esteri.sm; internet www.esteri.sm.

Secretariat of State for Health, Social Security, Social Affairs and Equal Opportunities: Via V. Scialoia, 47895 Cailungo; tel. 0549 883040; fax 0549 883044; e-mail dic.sanita@omniway.sm; internet www.sanita.segreteria.sm.

Secretariat of State for Industry, Handicrafts, Trade, Telecommunications and Economic Co-operation: Palazzo Mercuri, Contrada del Collegio, 47890 San Marino; tel. 0549 882528; fax 0549 882529.

Secretariat of State for Information, Cultural Institutions, Civil Protection, Relations with the Azienda Autonoma di Stato per i Servizi Pubblici (AASS) and Relations with the Castle Boards: Contrada Omerelli, 47890 San Marino; tel. 0549 882550.

Secretariat of State for Internal Affairs, Public Education and the University: Parva Domus, Piazza della Libertà, San Marino; tel. 0549 882196; fax 0549 882261; e-mail segr.pub-istr@omniway.sm; internet www.interni.segreteria.sm.

Secretariat of State for Labour and Co-operation, Tourism, Sport and Post: Palazzo del Turismo, Contrada Omagnano, 47890 San Marino; tel. 0549 882420; fax 0549 992998; e-mail segr.lavoro@omniway.sm; internet www.lavoro.segreteria.sm.

Secretariat of State for Territory, Environment, Agriculture and Relations with the Azienda Autonoma di Stato di Produzione (AASP): Contrada Omerelli, 47890 San Marino; tel. 0549 882470; fax 0549 882473; e-mail segr.territorio@omniway.sm.

Legislature

**Consiglio Grande e Generale
(Great and General Council)**

Palazzo Pubblico, Piazza della Libertà, 47890 San Marino; tel. 0549 882259; fax 0549 882389; e-mail seg.istituzionale@omniway.sm; internet www.consigliograndeegenerale.sm.

Election, 10 June 2001

Party	Votes	%	Seats
PDCS	9,031	41.45	25
PSS*	5,296	24.18	15
PdD*	4,535	20.81	12
APDS	1,974	8.23	5
RCS	738	3.39	2
ANS	421	1.93	1
Total	21,995	100.00	60

* In early 2005 the PSS and the PdD merged to form the PSD.

Political Organizations

Alleanza Nazionale Sammarinese (ANS) (San Marino National Alliance): Via Ventotto Luglio 187, 47893 Borgo Maggiore; tel. 0549 907815; fax 0549 875203; internet www.alleanzanazionalersm.sm; Pres. VITTORIO ENNIO PELLANDRA; Sec. LORENZ BERTI.

Alleanza Popolare dei Democratici Sammarinesi (AP) (Popular Alliance of Sammarinese Democrats): Via Luigi Cibrario 25, 47893 Borgo Maggiore; tel. 0549 907080; fax 0549 907082; e-mail ap@alleanzapopolare.net; internet www.alleanzapopolare.net; f. 1993; also known as Alleanza Popolare (AP); advocates a constitution and institutional reform; Leader ROBERTO GIORGETTI.

Nuovo Partito Socialista (NPS) (New Socialist Party): San Marino; f. 2005 by fmr mems of the Partito Socialista Sammarinese (PSS); Pres. ANTONIO VOLPINARI; Sec.-Gen. AUGUSTO CASALI.

Partito Democratico Cristiano Sammarinese (PDCS) (San Marino Christian Democrat Party): Via delle Scalette 6, 47890 San Marino; tel. 0549 991193; fax 0549 992694; e-mail pdcs@omniway.sm; internet www.pdcs.sm; f. 1948; Political Sec. PIER MARINO MENICUCCI; 2,400 mems.

Partito Progressista Democratico Sammarinese (PPDS) (San Marino Progressive Democratic Party): e-mail info@ppds.sm; internet www.ppds.sm; Pres. CLAUDIO FELICI; Sec.-Gen. MAURIZIO TOMASSONI.

Partito dei Socialisti e dei Democratici (PSD) (Party of Socialists and Democrats): San Marino; e-mail info@democratici.sm; internet www.socialistiedemocratici.sm; f. 2005 by merger of the Partito dei Democratici (PdD) and the Partito Socialista Sammarinese (PSS); Pres. EMMA ROSSI; Sec.-Gen. MAURO CHIARUZZI.

Rifondazione Comunista Sammarinese (RCS) (Sammarinese Communist Refoundation): Via Ca' dei Lunghi 70/A, 47893 Borgo Maggiore, San Marino; tel. 0549 906682; fax 0549 944397; e-mail rcs@omniway.sm; internet www.rifondazionecomunista-rsm.org; f. 1992; communist; Leader IVAN FOSCHI.

Sammarinesi per la Libertà (Sammarinese for Liberty): Via Ca' dei Lunghi 16, 47893 Borgo Maggiore; tel. 0549 902909; fax 0549 944634; e-mail info@sammarinesiperlaliberta.sm; internet www.sammarinesiperlaliberta.sm; f. 2002; Pres. GIUSEPPE ROSSI.

SAN MARINO

Diplomatic Representation

EMBASSIES IN SAN MARINO

Italy: Via del Voltone 55, 47890 San Marino; tel. 0549 991146; fax 0549 992229; e-mail ambsmar@omniway.sm; Ambassador FABRIZIO SANTURRO.

Holy See: Domus Plebis 1, 47890 San Marino; tel. 0549 992448; Apostolic Nuncio Most Rev. PAOLO ROMEO (Titular Archbishop of Vulturia).

Judicial System

The administration of justice is entrusted to foreign judges, with the exception of the Justice of the Peace, who must be of San Marino nationality, and who judges minor civil suits. The major legislative institutions are as follows:

Civil and Criminal Commissionary Tribunal (Tribunale Commissariale Civile e Penale): Salita alla Rocca 44, San Marino; tel. 0549 882626; fax 0549 8825980; e-mail tribunale@omniway.sm.

Law Commissioner (Commissario della Legge): deals with civil and criminal cases where the sentence does not exceed three years' imprisonment.

Criminal Judge of the Primary Court of Claims: deals with criminal cases that are above the competence of the Law Commissioner.

Court of Appeal: two judges, who deal with civil and criminal proceedings.

Council of Twelve (Consiglio dei XII): has authority as a Supreme Court of Appeal, for civil proceedings only.

Religion

CHRISTIANITY

The Roman Catholic Church

Roman Catholicism is the official state religion of San Marino. The Republic forms part of the diocese of San Marino-Montefeltro (comprising mainly Italian territory), suffragan to the archdiocese of Ravenna-Cervia.

Bishop of San Marino-Montefeltro: Rt Rev. LUIGI NEGRI, Curia Vescovile, Via del Seminario 5, 61016 Pennabilli, Pesaro, Italy; tel. (0541) 928415; fax (0541) 928766; e-mail segreteriacuria@libero.it.

The Press

Argomenti: c/o CSdL, Via Cinque Febbraio 17, Fiorina C-3, 47895 Domagnano; tel. 0549 962060; fax 0549 962075; organ of the Confederazione Sammarinese del Lavoro (CSdL); periodical; Dir ANDREA LEARDINI; circ. 5,000.

Corriere di Informazione Sammarinese: Via Piana, 47890 San Marino; tel. 0549 995147; fax 0549 879021; e-mail corriere@rimini.com; daily.

Fixing: Via G. Giacomini 37, 47890 San Marino; e-mail fixing@omniway.sm; periodical.

Il San Marino: Via delle Scalette 6, 47890 San Marino; tel. 0549 991193; fax 0549 992694; e-mail pdcs@omniway.sm; internet www.pdcs.sm; periodical; organ of the PDCS; quarterly; Dir LORENZO LONFERMINI.

San Marino Oggi: Via dei Boschetti 53, 47893 Borgo Maggiore; tel. 0549 906607; fax 0549 906556; e-mail sanmarinooggi@omniway.sm; internet www.omniway.sm/omni_smo; f. 1997; daily; circ. 750; Dir. RENATO CORNACCHIA.

La Tribuna Sammarinese: Via Gino Giacomini 86/A, 47890 San Marino; tel. 0549 990420; fax 0549 990398; e-mail info@latribunasammarinese.net; internet www.latribunasammarinese.net; daily; Dir DAVIDE GRAZIOSI.

Publishers

AIEP Editore: Via Benedetto di Giovanni 12, 47899 San Marino; tel. 0549 941457; fax 0549 973164; e-mail info@aiepeditore.net; f. 1986; general book publishing; Man. GIUSEPPE MARIA MORGANTI.

Guardigli Editore: Via Istriani 94, 47890 San Marino; tel. 0549 995144; fax 0549 990454; e-mail edititano@omniway.sm; internet www.edizionititano.sm; f. 1991; book publishing; Man. Dir PIER PAOLO GUARDIGLI.

Broadcasting and Communications

TELECOMMUNICATIONS

Direzione Generale Poste e Telecomunicazioni: Contrada Omerelli 17, 47890 San Marino; tel. 0549 882555; fax 0549 992760; e-mail poste.dirposte@pa.sm; state body responsible for telecommunications; Dir-Gen. CINZIA CESARINI.

The national telecommunications network is provided by Telecom Italia (see the chapter on Italy).

Intelcom San Marino, SpA: Strada degli Angariari 3, 47031 Falciano; tel. 0549 886303; fax 0549 908654; e-mail secretary@intelcom.sm; internet www.intelcom.sm; f. 1992; provides international telecommunications services; Pres. and CEO ANDREA CENDALI PIGNATELLI.

Telefonia Mobile Sammarinese (TMS): Via Ventotto Luglio 148, 47893 Borgo Maggiore; tel. 0549 980222; fax 0549 980044; e-mail info@tms.sm; internet www.tms.sm; f. 1999; mobile services.

BROADCASTING

In 1987 a 1939 co-operation agreement with Italy, preventing San Marino from operating its own broadcasting services, was abrogated, and a joint venture between San Marino and the Italian state-owned radio and television corporation, Radiotelevisione Italiana (RAI), was established in order to operate an independent broadcasting station for 15 years. RAI (see the chapter on Italy) broadcasts a daily information bulletin about the Republic under the title 'Notizie di San Marino'. San Marino RTV, established in 1991, began broadcasting in mid-1993.

Radio

San Marino RTV (Radiotelevisione della Repubblica de San Marino): Viale Kennedy 13, 47890 San Marino; tel. 0549 882000; fax 0549 882840; e-mail redazione@sanmarinortv.sm; internet www.sanmarinortv.sm; f. 1991; Pres. STEFANO VALENTINO PIVA; Dir-Gen. MICHELE MANGIAFICO.

Radio San Marino: San Marino; tel. 0549 995013; e-mail redazione@radiosanmarino.sm; internet www.radiosanmarino.sm.

Radio Titano: Via delle Carrare 35, Frazione Murata, 47890 San Marino; tel. 0549 997251; Dir P. FAETANINI.

Television

San Marino RTV (Radiotelevisione della Repubblica de San Marino): (see Radio).

Finance

(cap. = capital; res = reserves; dep. = deposits; m. = million; brs = branches; amounts in euros)

In 2004 there were 77 financial institutions operating in San Marino. In September 2005 there were 12 banks.

BANKING

Central Bank

Banca Centrale della Repubblica di San Marino: Via del Voltone 120, 47890 San Marino; tel. 0549 882325; fax 0549 882328; e-mail info@bcsm.sm; internet www.bcsm.sm; f. 2003; formed by a merger between the Istituto di Credito Sammarinese and the Ispettorato per il Credito e le Valute; manages both state and public-sector deposits; cap. 12.9m., res 9.2m., dep. 219.1m. (Dec. 2004); Chair. ANTONIO VALENTINI; Dir-Gen. LUCA PAPI.

Commercial Banks

Banca Agricola Commerciale della Repubblica di San Marino SA: Piazza Marino Tini 26, 47891 Dogana; tel. 0549 871111; fax 0549 871222; internet www.bac.sm; f. 1920; cap. 16.8m., res 65.7m. (Dec. 2001); Pres. LUIGI LONFERNINI; Dir PIER PAOLO FABBRI; 8 brs.

Banca di San Marino, SpA: Strada della Croce 39, 47896 Faetano; tel. 0549 873411; fax 0549 873401; e-mail info@bsm.sm; internet www.bsm.sm; f. 1920 as Cassa Rurale Depositi e Prestiti di Faetano, Scrl; changed name as above in 2001; cap. 114.7m., res 38.6m., dep. 1,150.4m. (Dec. 2004); Chair. MARIO MAIANI; Gen. Man. CESARE RICHELDI; 9 brs.

Cassa di Risparmio della Repubblica di San Marino: Piazzetta del Titano 2, 47890 San Marino; tel. 0549 872311; fax 0549 872700; e-mail info@carisp.sm; internet www.carisp.sm; f. 1882; cap. 350m., res 49.4m. dep. 1,970.4m. (Dec. 2002); Pres. Dott. GILBERTO GHIOTTI; CEO MARIO FANTINI; 16 brs.

Credito Industriale Sammarinese: Piazza Bertoldi 8, 47899 Serravalle; tel. 0549 8740; fax 0549 874116; e-mail cis@omniway.sm; f. 1933; owned by Banca Carim, Italy; cap. 35m., res 38m., dep.

SAN MARINO

399m. (Dec. 2005); Chair. FRANCO CAPICCHIONI; Man. Dir GIOVANNI PACCAPELO; 2 brs.

Euro Commercial Bank SpA: Strada dei Censiti 21, 47891 Rovereta; tel. 0549 943711; fax 0549 943737; e-mail info@ecb.sm; internet www.ecb.sm; f. 2000; cap. 25.0m., res 1.0m.; Dir-Gen. GUISEPPE GUIDI; 1 br.

Istituto Bancario Sammarinese SpA: Via III Settembre 99, 47891 Dogana; tel. 0549 872011; fax 0549 872050; e-mail direzione@ibs.sm; internet www.ibs.sm; f. 2000 as Merchant Bank di San Marino SpA; changed name in 2001 following expansion into commercial banking; Pres. and Man. Dir Dott. GIOVANNI MERCADINI; 3 brs.

INSURANCE

Several major Italian insurance companies have agencies in San Marino.

Trade and Industry

GOVERNMENT AGENCIES

Azienda Autonoma di Stato Filatelica e Numismatica (AASFN): Piazza Garibaldi 5, 47890 San Marino; tel. 0549 882365; fax 0549 882363; e-mail aasfn@omniway.sm; internet www.aasfn.sm; autonomous public enterprise; responsible for production and distribution of postage stamps and coins; Pres. PIGNATTA ORAZIO; Dir Gen. Dott. OTTAVIANO ROSSI.

Azienda Autonoma di Stato di Produzione (AASP): Via Ventotto Luglio 50, 47031 Borgo Maggiore; tel. 0549 883111; fax 0549 883600; e-mail aasp@omniway.sm; civil engineering works, road works, land reclamation; Pres. Ing. PAOLO RONDELLI; Dir FABIO BERARDI.

Azienda Autonoma di Stato per la gestione della Centrale del Latte: Strada Genghe di Atto 71, 47031 Acquaviva; tel. 0549 999207; fax 0549 999606; operates state monopoly in production and distribution of dairy products; Pres. TIZIANO CANINI; Dir PAOLO MUSCI.

CHAMBER OF COMMERCE

Camera di Commercio, Industria, Artigianato e Agricoltura di San Marino (CCIAA): Piazza Mercatale 29, 47893 Borgo Maggiore; tel. 0549 980389; fax 0549 944544; e-mail info@cc.sm; internet www.cc.sm; f. 2004; Dir MASSIMO GHIOTTI.

INDUSTRIAL AND TRADE ASSOCIATIONS

Associazione Nazionale dell'Industria Sammarinese (ANIS) (National Association for Industry): Via Gino Giacomini 39, 47890 San Marino; tel. 0549 991128; fax 0549 992832; e-mail anis@omniway.sm; internet www.anis.sm; Pres. SIMONA MICHELOTTI; Sec.-Gen. CARLO GIORGI.

Associazione Sammarinese Coltivatori Diretti, Affituari e Mezzadri (ASCDAM): San Marino; tel. 0549 998222; farmers' association.

Associazione Sammarinese Produttori Agricoli (ASPA): Serrabolino 42, 47893 Borgo Maggiore; tel. 0549 902617; agricultural producers' association.

Consorzio San Marino 2000 s.r.l.: Via Piana 103, 47890 San Marino; tel. 0549 995031; fax 0549 990573; e-mail info@sanmarino2000.sm; internet www.sanmarino2000.sm; f. 1998; fmrly Unione Sammarinese Operatori Turistici (USOT); hotels and restaurants association.

Organizzazione Sammarinese degli Imprenditori (OSLA): Via N. Bonaparte 75, 47890 San Marino; tel. 0549 992885; fax 0549 992620; e-mail osla@omniway.sm; internet www.osla.sm; f. 1985; organization for the self-employed; Pres. PARIDE BUGLI.

Unione Nazionale Artigiani di San Marino (UNAS): Piazzale M. Giangi 2, San Marino; tel. 0549 992148; e-mail unas@omniway.sm; artisans' association; Pres. GIANFRANCO TERENZI.

Unione Sammarinese Commercianti (USC): Via Piana 111, San Marino; tel. 0549 992892; shopkeepers' association.

UTILITIES

All utilities are imported from Italy.

Azienda Autonoma di Stato per i Servizi Pubblici (AASS): Via Andrea di Superchio 16, 47031 Cailungo; tel. 0549 883700; fax 0549 883720; e-mail aass@omniway.sm; internet www.aass.sm; f. 1981; autonomous state service company; distributes electricity, gas and water within San Marino; Dir-Gen. Ing. MARINO MAIANI.

TRADE UNIONS

Centrale Sindacale Unitaria: Via Cinque Febbraio 12, 47895 Domagnano; tel. 962011; fax 962055; e-mail csu@omniway.sm; internet www.csu.sm; f. 1976; Pres. LUCIANO NICOLINI.

Confederazione Democratica dei Lavoratori Sammarinesi (CDLS): Via Cinque Febbraio 17, Domagnano, 47895 San Marino; tel. 0549 962011; fax 0549 962095; e-mail boss@cdls.sm; internet www.cdls.sm; f. 1957; affiliated to ICFTU; Sec.-Gen. MARCO BECCARI; 4,960 mems.

Confederazione Sammarinese del Lavoro (CSdL): Via Cinque Febbraio 17, 47895 Domagnano; tel. 0549 962060; fax 0549 962075; e-mail info@csdl.sm; internet www.csdl.sm; f. 1943; Sec.-Gen. GIOVANNI GHIOTTI; 5 mem. federations; 4,500 mems.

Transport

The capital, San Marino, is connected with Borgo Maggiore, about 1.5 km away, by funicular. There is also a bus service, and a highway down to the Italian coast at Rimini, about 24 km away. San Marino has an estimated 104 km of motorways. The nearest airport to the Republic is at Rimini. There are no frontier or customs formalities.

Azienda Autonoma di Stato per i Servizi Pubblici (AASS): (see Utilities); numerous responsibilities include public transport and funicular railway.

Tourism

The mild climate attracts many visitors to San Marino each year, as does the annual motor-racing Grand Prix. The contrasting scenery and well-preserved medieval architecture are also attractions. In 2004 San Marino received 2.8m. visitors (including excursionists).

Ufficio di Stato per il Turismo (State Tourist Board): Contrada Omagnano 20, 47890 San Marino; tel. 0549 882914; fax 0549 882575; e-mail info@visitsanmarino.com; internet www.visitsanmarino.com; Dir ANTONIO MACINA.

SÃO TOMÉ AND PRÍNCIPE

Introductory Survey

Location, Climate, Language, Religion, Flag, Capital

The Democratic Republic of São Tomé and Príncipe lies in the Gulf of Guinea, off the west coast of Africa. There are two main islands, São Tomé and Príncipe, and the country also includes the rocky islets of Caroço, Pedras and Tinhosas, off Príncipe, and Rôlas, off São Tomé. The climate is warm and humid, with average temperatures ranging between 22°C (72°F) and 30°C (86°F). The rainy season extends from October to May, and average annual rainfall varies from 500 mm (20 ins) in the southern highlands to 1,000 mm (39 ins) in the northern lowlands. Portuguese is the official language, and native dialects are widely spoken. Almost all of the inhabitants profess Christianity, and the overwhelming majority (some 83%) are adherents of the Roman Catholic Church. The national flag (proportions 1 by 2) has three horizontal stripes, of green, yellow (one-half of the depth) and green, with a red triangle at the hoist and two five-pointed black stars on the yellow stripe. The capital is the town of São Tomé, on São Tomé island.

Recent History

A former Portuguese colony, São Tomé and Príncipe became an overseas province of Portugal in 1951 and received local autonomy in 1973. A nationalist group, the Comissão de Libertação de São Tomé e Príncipe, was formed in 1960 and became the Movimento de Libertação de São Tomé e Príncipe (MLSTP) in 1972, under the leadership of Dr Manuel Pinto da Costa. Based in Libreville, Gabon, the MLSTP was recognized by the Organization of African Unity (now the African Union—AU, see p. 153) in 1973.

Following the military coup in Portugal in April 1974, the Portuguese Government recognized the right of the islands to independence. Negotiations began in November, at which Portugal recognized the MLSTP as the sole representative of the people. On 12 July 1975 independence was achieved, with da Costa as the country's first President and Miguel dos Anjos da Cunha Lisboa Trovoada as Prime Minister. In December a legislative Assembléia Popular Nacional (National People's Assembly) was elected.

In March 1978 the Prime Minister stated that an attempted coup by foreign mercenaries, orchestrated from Gabon by Carlos Alberto Monteiro Dias da Graça, an exiled former Minister of Health, had been suppressed. Angolan troops were called in to support the Government, and in March 1979 the alleged conspirators were sentenced to terms of imprisonment. President da Costa took over the post of Prime Minister, and Trovoada was arrested in September and charged with complicity in the coup attempt. He was released and allowed to go into exile in 1981.

In March 1986 two externally based opposition groups, the União Democrática Independente de São Tomé e Príncipe and da Graça's more radical Frente de Resistência Nacional de São Tomé e Príncipe (FRNSTP), announced that they had formed a coalition and demanded the holding of democratic elections. In May da Graça resigned as President of the FRNSTP and expressed his willingness to co-operate with the Government.

Worsening economic conditions, following a severe drought in 1982, prompted the Government to review the country's close ties with communist regimes and its consequent isolation from major Western aid sources. In late 1984 da Costa declared São Tomé and Príncipe to be politically non-aligned.

In October 1987 the Central Committee of the MLSTP announced major constitutional reforms, including the election by universal adult suffrage of the President of the Republic and of members of the Assembléia Popular Nacional. The amended Constitution also allowed 'independent' candidates to contest legislative elections, although the President of the MLSTP, chosen by the MLSTP Congress from two candidates proposed by the Central Committee, would continue to be the sole candidate for the presidency of the Republic. In January 1988 the premiership was restored, and Celestino Rochas da Costa, hitherto Minister of Education, Labour and Social Security, was appointed as Prime Minister. Rochas da Costa formed a new Council of Ministers, appointing da Graça as Minister of Foreign Affairs.

In March 1990 a joint meeting of the Assembléia Popular Nacional and the MLSTP Central Committee approved a new draft Constitution, which provided for the establishment of a multi-party system, limited the President's tenure of office to two five-year terms, and permitted independent candidates to participate in legislative elections. In May 1990 Trovoada returned from exile to contest the forthcoming presidential election. On 22 August, in a national referendum, 72% of the electorate endorsed the new Constitution. In the following month new legislation on the formation of political parties came into effect. Delegates to the MLSTP Congress in October voted to replace da Costa as party President, appointing da Graça to the new post of Secretary-General. The party's name was amended to the Movimento de Libertação de São Tomé e Príncipe—Partido Social Democrata (MLSTP—PSD). In November da Graça resigned the foreign affairs portfolio. In the same month several thousands took part in a demonstration over election postponements led by the newly registered opposition parties, notably the Partido de Convergência Democrática—Grupo de Reflexão (PCD—GR).

On 20 January 1991 elections to the new Assembléia Nacional resulted in defeat for the MLSTP—PSD, which secured only 21 seats in the 55-member legislature, while the PCD—GR won 33 seats. The Partido Democrático de São Tomé e Príncipe—Coligação Democrático da Oposição (PDSTP—CODO) took the remaining seat. In February a transitional Government, headed by the Secretary-General of the PCD—GR, Daniel Lima dos Santos Daio, was installed. In the same month President da Costa announced that he would not be contesting the presidential election, to be held in March. The MLSTP—PSD did not present an alternative candidate. In late February two of the three remaining presidential candidates withdrew from the election. Miguel Trovoada, who stood as an independent candidate (with the support of the PCD—GR), was thus the sole contender, and on 3 March he was elected President with the support of 81% of those who voted. He took office on 3 April. The transitional Government resigned in mid-April, and was reappointed shortly afterwards.

In April 1992, following demonstrations demanding the resignation of the Daio Government due to the unpopular imposition of stringent austerity measures, Trovoada dismissed the Daio administration. The PCD—GR was invited to designate a new Prime Minister, and in May Norberto Costa Alegre (hitherto Minister of Economy and Finance) was chosen as Prime Minister. A new Government was named shortly afterwards. At the first local elections since independence, held in December, the PCD—GR suffered a considerable reverse, failing to secure control of any of the seven districts. Conversely, the opposition MLSTP—PSD gained control of five districts. In February 1993 Daio resigned as Secretary-General of the PCD—GR; he was succeeded by the more moderate João do Sacramento Bonfim.

In April 1994 the Assembléia Nacional adopted legislation, drafted by the MLSTP—PSD, reinforcing the rights of the parliamentary opposition. All opposition parties represented in the legislature were to be consulted on major political issues, including defence, foreign policy and the budget. In the same month deputies began discussion of a draft bill providing for a degree of autonomy for the island of Príncipe, to include the creation of a regional council. The proposed legislation was prompted by concern among inhabitants of Príncipe that the island had been neglected by the central administration.

Meanwhile, relations between the Government and the presidency deteriorated, and in April 1994 Trovoada publicly dissociated himself from government policy. Political tension increased in June, when the PCD—GR accused Trovoada of systematic obstruction of the government programme. In that month opposition parties petitioned the President to dismiss the Government, conduct early legislative elections and appoint foreign auditors to investigate the management of public finances under the PCD—GR administration. In July Trovoada dismissed the Alegre Government, citing 'institutional conflict' as justification for his action, following a dispute concerning the control of the budget. Trovoada appointed Evaristo do Espírito Santo de Carvalho (the Minister of Defence and Security in the

SÃO TOMÉ AND PRÍNCIPE

outgoing administration) as Prime Minister. The PCD—GR, refusing to participate in an administration formed on presidential initiative, subsequently expelled Carvalho from the party. An interim Government, comprising principally technocrats and senior civil servants, was appointed. Shortly afterwards Trovoada dissolved the Assembléia Nacional, thus preventing the PCD—GR from using its parliamentary majority to declare the new Government unconstitutional.

Legislative elections were held on 2 October 1994, at which the MLSTP—PSD secured 27 seats, one short of an absolute majority. The PCD—GR and Acção Democrática Independente (ADI) each obtained 14 seats; da Graça was subsequently appointed Prime Minister. Despite initial efforts to involve opposition parties in a government of national unity, his Council of Ministers was dominated by members of the MLSTP—PSD.

In March 1995 the first elections to a new seven-member regional assembly and five-member regional government were conducted on Príncipe, which had been granted local autonomy by the Assembléia Nacional in 1994. The elections resulted in an absolute majority for the MLSTP—PSD; the ADI and the PCD—GR did not present candidates, supporting instead a local opposition group. The new regional Government began functioning in April 1995.

In February 1995 the Government announced a general salary increase of 64%–90% in an effort to assuage increasing social tension caused by the high rate of inflation, however unrest continued. In mid-August a group of some 30 soldiers, led by five junior officers, seized control of the presidential palace in a bloodless coup. Trovoada was detained at the headquarters of the armed forces, and da Graça was placed under house arrest. The legislature was disbanded, the Constitution suspended and a curfew imposed. Following talks mediated by an Angolan delegation, the insurgents and the Government signed a 'memorandum of understanding', providing for the reinstatement of Trovoada and the restoration of constitutional order. In return, the Government gave an undertaking to restructure the armed forces, and the Assembléia Nacional granted a general amnesty to all those involved in the coup.

In late December 1995 Armindo Vaz d'Almeida was appointed Prime Minister, by presidential decree, to head a Government of National Unity. The new administration included six members of the MLSTP—PSD, four members of the ADI and one of the PDSTP—CODO. The three parties had signed a political pact, with the aim of ensuring political stability. The PCD—GR refused to participate in the new Government. In February 1996, at the request of the Commissão Eleitoral Nacional (National Electoral Commission), the forthcoming presidential election, which had been set for March, was postponed, pending the satisfactory completion of the electoral rolls. The date of the election was subsequently rescheduled for 30 June. In March Pinto da Costa was selected as the presidential candidate of the MLSTP—PSD, while Francisco Fortunato Pires was appointed Secretary-General of the party, replacing the more moderate da Graça. In April Trovoada declared his candidacy for the presidential election, supported by the ADI and the PDSTP—CODO.

At the presidential election of 30 June 1996 no candidate secured an absolute majority. The two leading candidates thus proceeded to a second round of voting on 21 July, at which Trovoada won 52.7% of the votes, defeating Pinto da Costa. In late July da Costa, who had initially acknowledged Trovoada's victory, claimed that irregularities had occurred in the registration process. In early August the Supreme Court declared that it was unable to adjudicate on the appeal made by da Costa, and recommended that the Government seek international legal arbitration. However, on 20 August da Costa withdrew his challenge, and Trovoada was confirmed as President. Although he did not command majority support in the Assembléia Nacional, Trovoada dismissed the possibility of new legislative elections, announcing instead his intention to seek a broadly based government of national consensus. In September the Vaz d'Almeida administration was dissolved, following its defeat in a confidence motion in the Assembléia Nacional. The motion had been proposed by Vaz d'Almeida's own party, the MLSTP—PSD, which accused the Government of inefficiency and corruption, and had received the support of the PCD—GR. Vaz d'Almeida remained as Prime Minister in an interim capacity until November, when Raul Wagner da Conceição Bragança Neto, Assistant Secretary-General of the MLSTP—PSD, was appointed Prime Minister. A new coalition Government, including five members of the MLSTP—PSD, three members of the PCD—GR and one independent, was inaugurated later that month.

At an extraordinary congress of the MLSTP—PSD in May 1998, Pinto da Costa was elected unopposed as President of the party. (The ruling party of Angola, the Movimento Popular de Libertação de Angola (MPLA), had made the resumption of financial support for the MLSTP—PSD conditional on da Costa's election; following his defeat in the 1996 presidential election, the MPLA had ceased payments, creating serious problems for the MLSTP—PSD.) New party statutes were approved, creating the position of party President, together with three vice-presidential posts.

At legislative elections held on 8 November 1998 the MLSTP—PSD secured a majority, with 31 seats, while the ADI won 16 seats and the PCD—GR obtained the remaining eight seats. In December Guilherme Pósser da Costa (a Vice-President of the MLSTP—PSD and former Minister of Foreign Affairs and Cooperation) was appointed Prime Minister. However, the MLSTP—PSD accused Trovoada of interfering in areas outside his jurisdiction when, later that month, he vetoed Pósser da Costa's initial nominations for the Council of Ministers. A revised Council of Ministers was finally installed on 5 January 1999.

In March 1999 the Governor of the Central Bank, Carlos Quaresma, was dismissed for his alleged involvement in corrupt financial practices. The accusations arose following the detention in Brussels, Belgium, two months earlier of three men who had attempted to sell falsified Santomean treasury bonds worth US $500m. The bonds bore the signature of Quaresma, who was alleged to have links with the men concerned. The Government subsequently appointed a commission to conduct an inquiry into the case; its report, released in mid-March, concluded that the bonds had been issued illegally, and the case was referred to the Attorney-General for investigation. Quaresma, meanwhile, denied all allegations of corruption and declared that the deal had been intended to finance development projects in the country and that former Prime Ministers Vaz d'Almeida and Bragança, as well as President Trovoada, had been completely aware of the proceedings. Trovoada denied these allegations. In May the Assembléia Nacional suspended Quaresma's parliamentary immunity to allow him to be questioned by the Office of the Attorney-General. Quaresma was detained in October. However, in March 2000 he was released, following the discovery of a document signed by Vaz d'Almeida, ordering the treasury bonds to be issued. Vaz d'Almeida denied any involvement, claiming that the documents had been falsified.

In August 2000 the parliamentary leader of the PCD—GR, Sebastião Santos, accused Prime Minister Pósser da Costa of giving preferential treatment to a construction company, Solar Construções, that had been awarded a public tender for road repairs. Santos revealed that da Costa owned 5% of the company's shares, and a parliamentary inquiry into the affair was instigated. However, when the results of the inquiry were presented to the Assembléia Nacional in January 2001, the MLSTP—PSD members of the commission refused to sign the document, rejecting the conclusion that the Prime Minister had acted improperly.

A presidential election took place on 29 July 2001. Among the five candidates hoping to succeed Trovoada were former President Manuel Pinto da Costa, the leader of the MLSTP—PSD, and Fradique de Menezes, a businessman standing for the ADI. In the event, de Menezes was elected to the presidency, winning 56.3% of the votes cast, while da Costa secured 38.7% and the remaining three candidates each gained less than 5%. De Menezes was inaugurated as President on 3 September. Following the dissolution by de Menezes of Pósser da Costa's administration (owing to disagreements over the distribution of ministerial positions), a new Government of 'presidential initiative', which did not include any members of the MLSTP—PSD, was appointed in late September. The new Council of Ministers, led by Évaristo de Carvalho as Prime Minister, was composed of members of the ADI, the PCD (which had voted to remove the suffix Grupo de Reflexão from its official name at a recent congress) and one independent. In early December de Menezes dissolved the Assembléia Nacional and announced that legislative elections would be held in March 2002, after which a new, more broadly based Government would be formed, according to an agreement reportedly signed by the President and representatives of political parties. In January 2002 the PCD formed an electoral alliance with the Movimento Democrático Força da Mudança (MDFM), which had been created in December by supporters of de Menezes.

At legislative elections, held on 3 March 2002, no party obtained an absolute majority in the Assembléia Nacional.

SÃO TOMÉ AND PRÍNCIPE

Provisional results indicated that the MLSTP—PSD and the MDFM-PCD alliance had each secured 23 of the 55 seats, while the remaining nine seats had been won by Uê Kédadji (UK), an alliance of the ADI and four minor parties. However, following a rerun of voting in one district, the MLSTP—PSD secured an extra seat, to the cost of the UK alliance, and was proclaimed victorious. Gabriel da Costa, the former ambassador to Portugal, was subsequently appointed as the nominally independent Prime Minister, and in April a new coalition Government of National Unity, which included representatives of the MLSTP—PSD, the MDFM-PCD and UK, as well as a number of independents, was installed.

In late September 2002 the controversial promotion of the Minister of Defence and Internal Affairs, Victor Tavares Monteiro, to the rank of Lt-Col by President de Menezes was quickly followed by Monteiro's resignation over personal differences with the President. Da Costa's Government was subsequently dismissed by de Menezes, who appointed Maria das Neves de Souza, of the MLSTP—PSD, hitherto Minister of Trade, Industry and Tourism, as Prime Minister in early October. A new Government of National Unity, with six representatives from the MLSTP—PSD, five from the MDFM-PCD alliance, two from the UK alliance and one independent, was formed. Dismissed Prime Minister da Costa accused de Menezes of acting unconstitutionally, particularly in his assumption of control over petroleum affairs. Da Costa was subsequently sentenced to 30 days' imprisonment for defamation of the President. In December the first MDFM congress elected Tomé Vera Cruz as Secretary-General of the party.

Meanwhile, in November 2002 the Assembléia Nacional approved a resolution for constitutional reform, altering the structure of the semi-presidential system to reduce presidential power. However, the draft revisions caused a political crisis over President de Menezes' delays in their promulgation and his repeated threats to veto them, according to powers vested in him by the Constitution of 1990; de Menezes also threatened to dismiss the Government if limitations were imposed on presidential power. An apparent consensus was reached in December 2002, but the situation deteriorated further in early 2003, and in mid-January the President vetoed the new draft Constitution, on the grounds that it should be endorsed by public referendum before coming into force. De Menezes dissolved the Assembléia Nacional by presidential decree later that month and called early elections for 13 April. However, Prime Minister das Neves vowed to continue working and transferred the Government of National Unity to the island of Príncipe. Following swift negotiations between the Government and the President, de Menezes reversed his decree, reinstating the Government, and a 'memorandum of understanding' was signed by de Menezes and the Assembléia Nacional, which provided for the immediate promulgation of the new Constitution, but called for a referendum to take place in March–April 2006 on the system of government.

The new Constitution, which took effect in March 2003, provided for the establishment of an advisory Council of State and a Constitutional Tribunal, with jurisdiction over issues of constitutionality. The President's right to veto constitutional amendments was removed. The changes were regarded as significantly reducing the executive power of the President, although maintaining a semi-presidential system pending the referendum.

On 16 July 2003, while de Menezes was in Nigeria, Maj. Fernando Pereira 'Cobo', together with Sabino dos Santos and Alércio Costa, the leaders of a small political party, the Frente Democrata Cristã (FDC), took power in a bloodless *coup d'état*. Citing ongoing government corruption and widespread poverty as their motivation, they formed a Junta Militar de Salvação Nacional and detained government ministers. It was claimed that the FDC had connections with the former 'Buffalo Battalion', a group of South African-trained mercenaries who were believed to have participated in several regional conflicts. The coup was condemned by the international community, which demanded a return to civilian rule. Following successful regional mediation efforts, co-ordinated by Rodolphe Adada, the Republic of the Congo's Minister of Foreign Affairs, Co-operation and Francophone Affairs, on 22 July de Menezes returned to São Tomé, accompanied by President Olusegun Obasanjo of Nigeria. On the same day de Menezes, Pereira and Adada signed a 'memorandum of understanding', which provided for the restoration of de Menezes to the presidency, an amnesty for the coup leaders, a more transparent system of government finance, and the formation of a new government. The army was also to be privy to government information on the petroleum sector. A commission to monitor the implementation of these measures was created. In accordance with the conditions of the memorandum, Prime Minister das Neves resigned. She was subsequently reappointed by de Menezes to head a new Government of National Unity, comprising representatives of the MLSTP—PSD, the MDFM and the ADI. Vera Cruz was appointed to the increasingly significant post of Minister of Natural Resources and the Environment, and Lt-Col Oscar Sousa, an independent reportedly with close ties to de Menezes, became Minister of Defence and Internal Affairs.

In March 2004 tension increased between das Neves and de Menezes. Das Neves had repeatedly requested the dismissal of Vera Cruz and of Mateus Rita, the Minister of Foreign Affairs and Co-operation, claiming that she had not been appropriately consulted by either minister on government decisions. The subsequent resignation of Rita and Vera Cruz—both members of the MDFM—prompted the remaining two MDFM ministers, responsible for health and justice, to resign in protest. Agreements that Vera Cruz had signed with Canadian and South African mining companies were subsequently annulled. Later that month members of the ADI were appointed to head the ministries of health and of natural resources and the environment, while Elsa Pinto of the MLSTP—PSD became Minister of Justice, State Reform and Public Administration, and an independent, Ovídio Manuel Barbossa Pequeno, was appointed Minister of Foreign Affairs and Co-operation.

In April 2004 Leonel Mário d'Alva was elected President of the PCD, while later that month Vera Cruz was re-elected as Secretary-General of the MDFM, which was renamed the MDFM—Partido Liberal (PL), although it subsequently reverted to its original name. The following month Patrice Trovoada was elected Secretary-General of the ADI, a position that had been vacant since 2001. Also in May 11 presidential advisors, holding positions corresponding to government ministries, were appointed by de Menezes. The President denied claims that he had formed a shadow executive, insisting that the advisors would improve his capacity to evaluate government policies.

In early September 2004 a report issued by the Auditor-General, Adelino Pereira, accused the das Neves Government of the embezzlement of funds provided by foreign donors and also revealed a series of financial irregularities during 2001–04, including illicit transfers of funds to the Ministry of Finance. Following requests by the MDFM and UK (the latter resigned from the Government in mid-September) for the removal of the das Neves Government, President de Menezes held a series of meetings with the main political parties in an attempt to establish a consensus. Das Neves and her Council of Ministers were dismissed on 14 September, and Damião Vaz de Almeida, hitherto Minister of Labour, Employment and Security and Vice-President of the MLSTP—PSD, was asked to form a new administration. The new 14-member Government installed days later was a coalition of the MLSTP—PSD, the ADI and independents and comprised six members of the previous administration. Pequeno retained the foreign affairs and co-operation portfolio, and Adelino Castelo David became Minister of Planning and Finance. Vaz de Almeida identified the improvement of basic social services as a priority for his administration.

In late September 2004 Diógenes Moniz, the former Director of the Gabinete de Gestão das Ajudas (GGA—a department attached to the Ministry of Trade, Industry and Tourism responsible for the administration of food aid counterpart funds) was arrested on charges of embezzlement. In October das Neves was among a number of former ministers questioned by the Public Prosecutor about their involvement with the GGA.

In January 2005 an attempt by de Menezes to sue das Neves for libel—in September 2004, following her dismissal from the premiership, she had accused de Menezes and other members of the Government of corruption—was rejected by the Assembléia Nacional, on the grounds that das Neves enjoyed parliamentary immunity. However, in February 2005 the Assembléia voted to remove parliamentary immunity from the former Prime Minister, Guilherme Pósser da Costa, in order that he be questioned regarding an alleged assault on Pereira in November 2004. (Pósser da Costa received a suspended sentence in March 2005.) A further four members of the Assembléia, including das Neves, also had their immunity lifted, thus providing for the possibility of them being tried in connection with the GGA case. In May das Neves and Arzemiro dos Prazeres, a former Minister of Trade, Industry and Tourism, were charged with embezzlement. Meanwhile, in late February Pósser da Costa was elected President of the MLSTP—PSD.

In April 2005 trade unions representing public-sector workers demanded a significant increase in the minimum salaries of their members. The Government, however, citing budgetary constraints, was unable to accede to the unions' demands and in late May the unions commenced a five-day general strike. Following declarations by de Menezes that the Government was responsible for the action, Prime Minister Vaz de Almeida abruptly resigned, accusing the President of a lack of institutional solidarity with the Government. On 9 June a new MLSTP—PSD Council of Ministers, led by Maria do Carmo Silveira, hitherto the Governor of the central bank, took office, and in late July the Assembléia Nacional approved the new Government's budget, and a preliminary agreement on a pay rise for public-sector workers was reached. Relations between de Menezes and the Government remained strained, however, and further tension arose when the President suggested holding the referendum on constitutional reform first proposed in 2003, a move that was strongly opposed by the Assembléia and the Government.

In early 2006 allegations arose that Pequeno had illegally transferred abroad funds donated by Morocco. Pequeno, who enjoyed close relations with de Menezes, claimed that the money had been a gift from the King of Morocco directly to de Menezes, while the President accused the Government of seeking to discredit him, and rejected a request by the Prime Minister to dismiss Pequeno. In mid-January, however, Pequeno resigned. The Minister of Defence and Internal Order, Lt-Col Óscar Sousa, was allocated the foreign affairs portfolio on a temporary basis. An official investigation subsequently revealed that Pequeno and his predecessor, Mateus Meira Rita, had been responsible for irregularities in their dealings with aid donations from Morocco.

Meanwhile, in October 2005, in preparation for the legislative elections due in early 2006, the MDFM and the PCD announced that they would renew their electoral alliance. On 10 February President de Menezes confirmed that the elections would take place on 26 March; by late February a total of eight parties and two coalitions had registered to contest the elections.

Voting in the legislative elections began as scheduled on 26 March 2006, however, owing to boycotts and protests against continuing poor living conditions, voting at 26 polling stations was rescheduled for 2 April when it proceeded without incident. According to results released by the Constitutional Court on 18 April, the MDFM-PCD alliance won 23 seats in the Assembléia Nacional, the MLSTP—PSD took 20 and the ADI 11, while a newly formed party, the Novo Rumo, secured the remaining seat. Tomé Vera Cruz, Secretary-General of the MDFM, was subsequently appointed Prime Minister (also assuming the information and regional integration portfolios) and the new 12-member Government took office on 21 April. Maria dos Santos Tebus Torres of the PCD, became Deputy Prime Minister, with responsibility for finance and planning.

In late April 2006 President de Menezes announced that a presidential election would be held on 30 July, with local elections on the island of Príncipe scheduled to take place on 9 July.

São Tomé and Príncipe maintains cordial relations with the other former Portuguese African colonies and with Portugal. In July 1996 São Tomé and Príncipe was among the five lusophone African countries that, together with Portugal and Brazil, formed the Comunidade dos Países de Língua Portuguesa (CPLP, see p. 395), a Portuguese-speaking commonwealth seeking to achieve collective benefits from co-operation in technical, cultural and social matters. Following the *coup d'état* in July 2003, an group of regional mediators, including representatives from the CPLP and the AU, successfully negotiated a return to civilian rule. In February 2004 Angola and São Tomé and Príncipe signed an agreement on the creation of a permanent joint commission on parliamentary co-operation.

São Tomé and Príncipe has important trade links with the nearby mainland states of Gabon, Cameroon and Equatorial Guinea. In November 1999 São Tomé and Príncipe was a founder of the seven-member Gulf of Guinea Commission; it was hoped that the commission would assist in solving inter-state conflicts within the region.

In 2000 São Tomé and Príncipe and Nigeria agreed to establish a joint development zone (JDZ) for the exploitation of petroleum resources. A further accord, on the joint exploitation of a variety of mineral resources, was signed in February 2001; Nigeria was to receive 60% of revenues and São Tomé and Príncipe 40%. In January 2002 the Presidents of both countries inaugurated a development authority to oversee the affairs of the JDZ. Disagreements developed during 2002, however, over Nigeria's commitment to provide São Tomé and Príncipe with 60,000 barrels of petroleum per day (reduced to 40,000 in September, and to 10,000 in October) and the relative lack of Santomean representation in the development authority. In November de Menezes refused to continue with the proposed sale of oil blocs until the issue was resolved; he was supported in this by a report from the World Bank, which suggested that the division of profits was unfair to São Tomé and Príncipe. By 2003, however, issues had been resolved sufficiently for bids for exploration rights in the first nine of the 25 blocs in the JDZ to open in October.

Government

Under the 2003 Constitution, legislative power is vested in the Assembléia Nacional, which comprises 55 members, elected by universal adult suffrage for a term of four years. No limit is placed on the number of political parties permitted to operate. Executive power is vested in the President of the Republic, who is Head of State, and who governs with the assistance of an appointed Council of Ministers, led by the Prime Minister. The Council of State acts as an advisory body to the President, who is elected by universal suffrage for a term of five years. The President's tenure of office is limited to two successive terms. The Prime Minister, who is appointed by the President, is, in theory, nominated by the deputies of the Assembléia Nacional.

In 1994 the Assembléia Nacional granted political and administrative autonomy to the island of Príncipe. Legislation was adopted establishing a seven-member regional assembly and a five-member regional government; both are accountable to the Government of São Tomé and Príncipe.

Defence

In 1992 a reorganization was initiated of the islands' armed forces (estimated to comprise some 600 men in 1995) and the police into two separate police forces, one for public order and another for criminal investigation. In the budget for 2000 expenditure on defence amounted to 1,100m. dobras.

Economic Affairs

In 2004, according to estimates by the World Bank, São Tomé and Príncipe's gross national product (GNI), measured at average 2002–04 prices, was US $60m., equivalent to $370 per head. During 1995–2004, it was estimated, the population increased at an average annual rate of 2.2%, while gross domestic product (GDP) per head, in real terms, increased at an average annual rate of 0.8%. Overall GDP increased, in real terms, at an average annual rate of 3.1% in 1995–2004; growth was 4.5% in 2004.

Agriculture (including fishing) contributed an estimated 15.6% of GDP in 2004, and accounted for 62.2% of the employed population in 2003. The principal cash crop is cocoa, which accounted for 91.4% of export earnings in 2004. Secondary cash crops include coconuts and coffee. Staple crops for local consumption include bananas, taro, tomatoes and cassava. Agricultural production is principally concentrated on export commodities, although smallholder agriculture has become increasingly important. An agricultural policy charter, the Carta de Política e Desenvolvimento Rural, which was introduced in 2000, aimed to emphasize private-sector involvement and diversification into areas such as ylang ylang, pepper, vanilla, fruits, vegetables and flowers. Fishing is also a significant activity. The sale of fishing licences to foreign fleets is an important source of income. According to the World Bank, agricultural GDP increased at an average annual rate of 3.6% in 1995–2004; growth in 2004 was 2.9%.

Industry (including manufacturing, construction and power) contributed an estimated 13.4% of GDP in 2004, and employed 17.0% of the employed population in 2001. According to the World Bank, industrial GDP increased by an average of 2.8% per year in 1995–2003; growth in 2003 was 4.7%.

There are no mineral resources on the islands, but offshore prospecting for hydrocarbons resulted in the discovery of significant quantities of petroleum in 1998, including an estimated 4,000m. barrels in the joint development zone (JDZ) with Nigeria (see Recent History), as well as higher-risk resources in São Tomé's exclusive economic zone (EEZ). More than 20 companies lodged bids for exploration rights in the first nine of the 25 blocs in the JDZ in October 2003. In February 2005 a consortium led by ChevronTexaco was awarded a concession to exploit the first section of the JDZ. However negotiations regarding the granting of concessions for a further five blocs in the JDZ were delayed by

SÃO TOMÉ AND PRÍNCIPE

conflict and allegations of corruption within the Government, and a preliminary agreement was not reached until August. It was anticipated that revenue generated from the first bloc would amount to US $49.4m. and some $113.2m. from the other five blocs. Negotiations were also taking place with Galp Energia (Portugal) in late 2005 in connection with the exploitation of São Tomé's EEZ.

The manufacturing sector consists solely of small processing factories, producing soap, soft drinks, textiles and beer. Manufacturing, including electricity, gas and water, contributed an estimated 3.9% of GDP in 2004. According to the World Bank, manufacturing GDP increased at an average annual rate of 2.2% in 1995–2003; growth in 2003 was 4.5%.

In 2000 some 74% of electricity generation was derived from thermal sources, and 26% from hydroelectric sources. Imports of petroleum products comprised 15.0% of the value of merchandise imports in 2004. In late 2004 the national utility company was privatized. In early 2006 it was announced that a thermal power plant, which would increase São Tomé's energy production by 70%, was to be built by a Nigerian company.

The services sector contributed an estimated 71.1% of GDP in 2004, and engaged 51.5% of the employed population in 2001. According to the World Bank, the GDP of the services sector increased by an average of 2.4% per year in 1995–2003; growth in 2003 was 5.3%.

In 2002 São Tomé and Príncipe recorded a trade deficit of US $22.8m. and a deficit of $22.8m. on the current account of the balance of payments. In 2004 the principal source of imports (60.5%) was Portugal; other major suppliers were Angola, Belgium and Japan. The principal market for exports in that year were Portugal (62.3%), the Netherlands, Belgium and the USA. The principal export in 2004 was cocoa. The principal imports in that year were foodstuffs, and petroleum and petroleum products, beverages, equipment, beverages, transport equipment and construction materials.

In 2003 there was a budgetary deficit of 95,100m. dobras (equivalent to 17.1% of GDP). São Tomé's total external debt was US $337.5m. at the end of 2003, of which $326.1m. was long-term public debt. In that year the cost of debt-servicing was equivalent to 31.2% of the total value of exports of goods and services. Annual inflation averaged 23.5% in 1996–2003. Consumer prices increased by an average of 10.0% in 2003. According to official figures, 27.4% of the labour force were unemployed in 1993.

São Tomé and Príncipe is a member of the International Cocoa Organization (see p. 382) and of the Communauté économique des états de l'Afrique centrale (see p. 385).

São Tomé and Príncipe's economy has traditionally been dominated by cocoa production, and is therefore vulnerable to adverse weather conditions and to fluctuations in international prices for that commodity. While the discovery of petroleum in Santomean waters, and the anticipated increase in government revenues the sale of that commodity would provide, was a welcome development, concerns were raised by international institutions regarding the lack of transparency and accountability in the petroleum sector. Thus, in mid-2004 the Government agreed to establish a National Petroleum Fund into which all petroleum earnings were to be deposited, and which was to be subject to annual independent audits; it was also announced that 65% of the total revenue from petroleum was to be allocated to the upgrading of infrastructure and to improvements in the health care and education sectors. Despite ongoing investigations into the misappropriation of donor funds São Tomé and Príncipe continued to be a major recipient of external assistance. In 2005 the Group of Eight leading industrial nations (G-8) announced that São Tomé and Príncipe was among nine 'second wave' countries deemed eligible for the cancellation of their debts owed to the IMF, the World Bank and the ABD. The Government hoped that some US $300m. of international debt would be pardoned in 2006. In late 2005 the construction of a free trade zone was begun on the island of Príncipe, while in August, following a series of missions since the suspension of the Poverty Reduction and Growth Facility (PRGF) arrangement in 2000, the IMF announced a new three-year PRGF, worth $4.3m. In December 2004 the Central Bank reported that economic growth in 2004 had been below 4%, while inflation was recorded at 15%.

Education

Primary education is officially compulsory for a period of four years between six and 14 years of age. Secondary education lasts for a further seven years, comprising a first cycle of four years and a second, pre-university cycle of three years. In 2001 the country had 73 primary schools, with a total enrolment of 20,858 pupils. There were 13 secondary schools (including two devoted to vocational training) in that year, with a total enrolment of 13,874 pupils. There was one polytechnic institute (with an enrolment of 117 in 2000/01). In 2000 public investment in education (including culture and sport) amounted to US $1.3m., equivalent to 6.7% of total public investment.

Public Holidays

2006: 1 January (New Year), 4 January (King Amador Day), 3 February (Martyrs' Day), 1 May (Labour Day), 12 July (Independence Day), 6 September (Armed Forces Day), 30 September (Agricultural Reform Day), 21 December (São Tomé Day), 25 December (Christmas Day).

2007: 1 January (New Year), 4 January (King Amador Day), 3 February (Martyrs' Day), 1 May (Labour Day), 12 July (Independence Day), 6 September (Armed Forces Day), 30 September (Agricultural Reform Day), 21 December (São Tomé Day), 25 December (Christmas Day).

Weights and Measures

The metric system is in force.

Statistical Survey

Source (unless otherwise stated): Instituto Nacional de Estatística, CP 256, São Tomé; tel. 221982.

AREA AND POPULATION

Area: 1,001 sq km (386.5 sq miles); São Tomé 859 sq km (331.7 sq miles), Príncipe 142 sq km (54.8 sq miles).

Population: 117,504 at census of 4 August 1991; 137,599 (males 68,236, females 69,363) at census of September 2001; 153,000 in 2004 (UN estimate at mid-year. Source: UN *World Population Prospects: The 2004 Revision*).

Density (mid-2004): 152.8 per sq km.

Population by District (census of 2001): Água-Grande 51,886, Mé-Zochi 35,105, Cantagolo 13,258, Caué 5,501, Lembá 10,696, Lobata 15,157, Pagué (Príncipe) 5,966; Total 137,599.

Principal Towns (population at census of 1991): São Tomé (capital) 42,300; Trindade 11,400; Santana 6,200; Santo Amaro 5,900; Neves 5,900. Source: Stefan Helders, *World Gazetteer* (internet www.world-gazetteer.com). *Mid-2003* (incl. suburbs): São Tomé (capital) 53,570 (Source: UN, *World Urbanization Prospects: The 2003 Revision*).

Births, Marriages and Deaths (2000): Registered live births 4,078 (birth rate 29.20 per 1,000); Registered marriages 210 (marriage rate 1.5 per 1,000); Registered deaths 1,030 (death rate 7.51 per 1,000). *2003:* Birth rate 32.6 per 1,000; Death rate 5.7 per 1,000 (Source: African Development Bank).

Expectation of Life (years at birth, estimates): 59 (males 58; females 60) in 2003.

Economically Active Population (census of 2001): Agriculture and fishing 13,518; Industry, electricity, gas and water 2,893; Public works and civil construction 4,403; Trade, restaurants and hotels 8,787; Transport, storage and communications 792; Public administration 3,307; Health 776; Education 1,373; Other activities 7,088; *Total employed* 42,937. *Mid-2003* (estimates in '000): Agriculture, etc. 46; Total labour force 74. (Source: FAO).

HEALTH AND WELFARE

Key Indicators

Total Fertility Rate (children per woman, 2003): 3.9.

Under-5 Mortality Rate (per 1,000 live births, 2004): 118.

Physicians (per 1,000 head, 1996): 0.47.

Hospital Beds (per 1,000 head, 1991): 4.74.

SÃO TOMÉ AND PRÍNCIPE

Statistical Survey

Health Expenditure (2002): US $ per head (PPP): 108.
Health Expenditure (2002): % of GDP: 11.1.
Health Expenditure (2002): public (% of total): 87.7.
Access to Water (% of persons, 2002): 79.
Access to Sanitation (% of persons, 2002): 24.
Human Development Index (2003): ranking: 126.
Human Development Index (2003): value: 0.604.

For sources and definitions, see explanatory note on p. vi.

AGRICULTURE, ETC.

Principal Crops (FAO estimates, metric tons, 2004): Bananas 27,900; Maize 2,500; Cassava (Manioc) 5,800; Taro 28,000; Yams 1,500; Cocoa beans 3,500; Coconuts 28,500; Oil palm fruit 40,000; Coffee (green) 20; Cinnamon 30. Source: FAO.

Livestock (FAO estimates, head, 2004): Cattle 4,600; Sheep 2,800; Goats 5,000; Pigs 2,500; Poultry 381,000. Source: FAO.

Livestock Products (FAO estimates, metric tons, 2004): Beef and veal 122; Pig meat 92; Sheep and goat meat 25; Poultry meat 636; Hen eggs 385; Cows' milk 145. Source: FAO.

Forestry ('000 cubic metres, 1988): Roundwood removals 9; Sawnwood production 5. *1989–2004:* Annual output assumed to be unchanged since 1988. Source: FAO.

Fishing (metric tons, live weight, 2003): Total catch 3,283 (Pandoras 135; Threadfins and tasselfishes 102; Halfbeaks 156; Flyingfishes 800; Jacks and crevalles 152; Sharks, rays and skates 165). Source: FAO.

INDUSTRY

Production (metric tons, unless otherwise indicated): Bread and biscuits 3,768 (1995); Soap 261.1 (1995); Beer (litres) 529,400 (1995); Palm oil 2,000 (2004, FAO estimate); Electric energy (million kWh) 31.2 (2002). Sources: IMF, *São Tomé and Príncipe: Statistical Appendix* (September 1998, February 2002 and April 2004), and FAO.

FINANCE

Currency and Exchange Rates: 100 cêntimos = 1 dobra (Db). *Sterling, Dollar and Euro Equivalents* (30 November 2005): £1 sterling = 20,238.36 dobras; US $1 = 11,718.80 dobras; €1 = 13,791.85 dobras; 100,000 dobras = £4.94 = $8.53 = €7.25. *Average Exchange Rate* (dobras per US $): 9,088.3 in 2002; 9,347.6 in 2003; 9,825.7 in 2004.

Budget ('000 million dobras, 2003): *Revenue:* Taxation 114.2; Oil revenue 3.3; Other current revenue 26.2; Total 143.8, excl. grants (137.1). *Expenditure:* Current expenditure 170.8 (Personnel costs 55.0, *of which* Wages and salaries 50.5; Goods and services 43.9; Interest on external debt 34.3; Interest on internal debt 1.9; Transfers 13.4; Other current expenditure 20.1; Redeployment fund 2.2); Capital expenditure 163.1; HIPC-related social expenditure 28.0; Net lending 0.0; Total 361.9. Note: Expenditure excludes adjustment for net change in arrears (14.1). Source: IMF, *São Tomé and Príncipe: Statistical Appendix* (April 2004).

International Reserves (US $ million at 31 December 2004): Total 19.76 (all foreign exchange). Source: IMF, *International Financial Statistics*.

Money Supply (million dobras at 31 December 2004): Currency outside banks 60,003; Demand deposits at commercial banks 112,687; Total money (incl. others) 172,817. Source: IMF, *International Financial Statistics*.

Cost of Living (Consumer Price Index; base: 1996 = 100): 364.6 in 2001; 397.5 in 2002; 437.2 in 2003. Source: IMF, *São Tomé and Príncipe: Statistical Appendix* (April 2004).

Expenditure on the Gross Domestic Product ('000 million dobras at current prices, 2003, estimates): Government final consumption expenditure 220.8; Private final consumption expenditure 388.5; Gross capital formation 169.4; *Total domestic expenditure* 778.8; Exports of goods and services 209.8; *Less* Imports of goods and services 431.7; *GDP in purchasers' values* 556.9. Source: IMF, *São Tomé and Príncipe: Statistical Appendix* (April 2004).

Gross Domestic Product by Economic Activity ('000 million dobras at current prices, 2003, estimates): Agriculture 77.3; Fishing 17.2; Manufacturing, electricity, gas and water 24.7; Construction 56.5; Trade and transport 150.0; Public administration 156.8; Financial institutions 59.1; Other services 15.3; *Total* 556.9. Source: IMF, *São Tomé and Príncipe: Statistical Appendix* (April 2004).

Balance of Payments (US $ million, 2002): Exports of goods f.o.b. 5.1; Imports of goods f.o.b. −28.0; *Trade balance* −22.8; Exports of services 13.4; Imports of services −13.4; *Balance on goods and services* −22.9; Other income (net) −4.7; *Balance on goods, services and income* −27.6; Current transfers (net) 4.9; *Current balance* −22.8; Capital account (net) 12.1; Direct investment (net) 3.0; Other investment liabilities (net) 0.9; *Overall balance* −7.0. Source: IMF, *International Finance Statistics*.

EXTERNAL TRADE

Principal Commodities (US $ million, 2004): *Imports f.o.b.:* Foodstuffs 10.3; Beverages 5.0; Petroleum and petroleum products 6.2; Equipment 4.9; Transport equipment 4.4; Construction materials 2.9; Total (incl. others) 41.4. *Exports f.o.b.:* Cocoa 3.2; Coconuts 0.1; Total (incl. others) 3.5.

Principal Trading Partners (US $ million, 2004): *Imports c.i.f.:* Angola 6.6; Belgium 3.6; Gabon 0.6; Japan 2.5; Netherlands 0.4; Portugal 25.0; Total (incl. others) 41.3. *Exports f.o.b.:* Belgium 0.3; Gabon 0.1; Netherlands 1.8; Portugal 2.2; USA 0.2; Total (incl. others) 3.5. Source: Banco Central de São Tomé e Príncipe.

TRANSPORT

Road Traffic (registered vehicles, 1996, estimates): Passenger cars 4,000; Lorries and vans 1,540. Source: International Road Federation, *World Road Statistics*.

Shipping: *International Freight Traffic* (estimates, metric tons, 1992): Goods loaded 16,000; Goods unloaded 45,000. *Merchant Fleet* (registered at 31 December 2004): Number of vessels 42; Total displacement 57,809 grt (Source: Lloyd's Register-Fairplay, *World Fleet Statistics*).

Civil Aviation (traffic on scheduled services, 2001): Passengers carried ('000) 35; Passenger-km (million) 14; Total ton-km (million) 1. Source: UN, *Statistical Yearbook*.

TOURISM

Foreign Tourist Arrivals: 5,584 in 1998; 5,710 in 1999; 7,137 in 2000. Source: Tourism and Hotels Bureau.

Arrivals by Country of Residence (2001): Angola 660; Cape Verde 179; France 1,233; Gabon 371; Nigeria 472; Portugal 1,886; Spain 280; USA 330; Total (incl. others) 7,569. Source: World Tourism Organization.

Tourism Receipts (US $ million, excl. passenger transport): 10 in 2000; 10 in 2001; 10 in 2002. Source: World Tourism Organization.

COMMUNICATIONS MEDIA

Radio Receivers (1998): 45,000 in use. Source: UNESCO, *Statistical Yearbook*.

Television Receivers (1999): 33,000 in use. Source: UNESCO, *Statistical Yearbook*.

Newspapers and Periodicals (2000): Titles 14 (1997); Average circulation 18,500 copies.

Telephones ('000 main lines, 2003): 7.0 in use. Source: International Telecommunication Union.

Mobile Cellular Telephones ('000 subscribers, 2003): 4.8. Source: International Telecommunication Union.

Facsimile Machines (2000): 372 in use.

Internet Users (2004): 20,000. Source: International Telecommunication Union.

EDUCATION

Pre-primary (2001): 18 schools; 2,376 pupils.

Primary (2001): 73 schools; 623 teachers; 20,858 pupils.

General Secondary and Pre-university (2001): 11 schools; 630 teachers; 13,874 (including vocational education) pupils. There are also 2 vocational secondary schools.

Tertiary (2000/01): 1 polytechnic; 29 teachers; 117 pupils.

Source: mainly *Carta Escolar de São Tomé e Príncipe,* Ministério de Educação de Portugal.

Adult Literacy Rate (official estimate, 2001): 83.1%. Source: UN Development Programme, *Human Development Report*.

Directory

The Constitution

A new Constitution came into force on 4 March 2003, after the promulgation by the President of a draft approved by the Assembléia Nacional (National Assembly) in December 2002. A 'memorandum of understanding', which was signed in January 2003 by the President and the Assembléia Nacional, provided for the scheduling of a referendum on the system of governance for March–April 2006, to coincide with the expiry of the current presidential mandate and with legislative elections. The following is a summary of the main provisions of the Constitution:

The Democratic Republic of São Tomé and Príncipe is a sovereign, independent, unitary and democratic state. Sovereignty resides in the people, who exercise it through universal, equal, direct and secret vote, according to the terms of the Constitution. There shall be complete separation between Church and State. There shall be freedom of thought, expression and information and a free and independent press, within the terms of the law.

Executive power is vested in the President of the Republic, who is elected for a period of five years by universal adult suffrage. The President's tenure of office is limited to two successive terms. He is the Supreme Commander of the Armed Forces and is accountable to the Assembléia Nacional. In the event of the President's death, permanent incapacity or resignation, his functions shall be assumed by the President of the Assembléia Nacional until a new President is elected.

The Council of State acts as an advisory body to the President and comprises the President of the Assembléia Nacional, the Prime Minister, the President of the Constitutional Tribunal, the Attorney-General, the President of the Regional Government of Príncipe, former Presidents of the Republic who have not been dismissed from their positions, three citizens of merit nominated by the President and three elected by the Assembléia Nacional. Its meetings are closed and do not serve a legislative function.

Legislative power is vested in the Assembléia Nacional, which comprises 55 members elected by universal adult suffrage. The Assembléia Nacional is elected for four years and meets in ordinary session twice a year. It may meet in extraordinary session on the proposal of the President, the Council of Ministers or of two-thirds of its members. The Assembléia Nacional elects its own President. In the period between ordinary sessions of the Assembléia Nacional its functions are assumed by a permanent commission elected from among its members.

The Government is the executive and administrative organ of State. The Prime Minister is the Head of Government and is appointed by the President. Other ministers are appointed by the President on the proposal of the Prime Minister. The Government is responsible to the President and the Assembléia Nacional.

Judicial power is exercised by the Supreme Court and all other competent tribunals and courts. The Supreme Court is the supreme judicial authority, and is accountable only to the Assembléia Nacional. Its members are appointed by the Assembléia Nacional. The right to a defence is guaranteed.

The Constitutional Tribunal, comprising five judges with a mandate of five years, is responsible for jurisdiction on matters of constitutionality. During periods prior to, or between, the installation of the Constitutional Tribunal, its function is assumed by the Supreme Court. The Constitution may be revised only by the Assembléia Nacional on the proposal of at least three-quarters of its members. Any amendment must be approved by a two-thirds' majority of the Assembléia Nacional. The President does not have right of veto over constitutional changes.

Note: In 1994 the Assembléia Nacional granted political and administrative autonomy to the island of Príncipe. Legislation was adopted establishing a seven-member Regional Assembly and a five-member Regional Government; both are accountable to the Government of São Tomé and Príncipe.

The Government

HEAD OF STATE

President and Commander-in-Chief of the Armed Forces: FRADIQUE DE MENEZES (took office 3 September 2001).

COUNCIL OF MINISTERS
(April 2006)

The Government comprises members of the Movimento Democrático Força da Mudança (MDFM) and the Partido de Convergência Democrática (PCD).

Prime Minister and Minister of Information and Regional Integration: TOMÉ VERA CRUZ (MDFM).
Deputy Prime Minister and Minister of Planning and Finance: MARIA DOS SANTOS TEBUS TORRES (PCD).
Minister of Foreign Affairs, Co-operation and Communities: CARLOS GUSTAVO DOS ANJOS.
Minister of Defence and Internal Order: Lt-Col ÓSCAR AGUÍAR SACRAMENTO E SOUSA (Ind.).
Minister of Natural Resources: MANUEL DE DEUS LIMA.
Minister of the Economy: CRISTINA MARIA FERNANDES DIAS.
Minister of Public Works and Infrastructure: DELFIM NEVES (PCD).
Minister of Education, Culture, Youth and Sport: MARIA DE SOUSA ALMEIDA.
Minister of Health: ARLINDO CARVALHO.
Minister of Justice and Parliamentary Affairs: JUSTINO VEIGA.
Minister of Labour, Solidarity, Women and the Family: MARIA DE CARVALHO.
Minister of Public Administration, State Reform and Territorial Administration: ARMINDO AGUIAR.

MINISTRIES

Office of the President: Palácio Presidêncial, São Tomé; internet www.presidencia.st.
Office of the Prime Minister: Rua do Município, CP 302, São Tomé; tel. 223913; fax 224679; e-mail gpm@cstome.net.
Ministry of Defence and Internal Order: Av. 12 de Julho, CP 427, São Tomé; tel. 222041; e-mail midefesa@cstome.net.
Ministry of the Economy: São Tomé.
Ministry of Education, Culture, Youth, and Sport: Rua Misericórdia, CP 41, São Tomé; tel. 222861; fax 221466; e-mail mineducal@cstome.net.
Ministry of Foreign Affairs, Co-operation and Communities: Av. 12 de Julho, CP 111, São Tomé; tel. 221017; fax 222597; e-mail minecoop@cstome.net.
Ministry of Health: Av. Patrice Lumumba, CP 23, São Tomé; tel. 241200; fax 221306; e-mail msaude@cstome.net.
Ministry of Information and Regional Integration: São Tomé.
Ministry of Justice and Parliamentary Affairs: Av. 12 de Julho, CP 4, São Tomé; tel. 222318; fax 222256; e-mail emilioma@cstome.net.
Ministry of Labour, Solidarity, Women and the Family: Rua Município, Edif. Ministério do Trabalho, São Tomé; tel. 221466.
Ministry of Natural Resources: CP 1093, São Tomé; tel. 225272; fax 226262; e-mail mirecurna@cstome.net.
Ministry of Planning and Finance: Largo Alfândega, CP 168, São Tomé; tel. 224173; fax 222683; e-mail mpfc@cstome.net.
Ministry of Public Administration, State Reform and Territorial Administration: Av. Kwame Nkrumah, CP 136, São Tomé; tel. 224750; fax 222824; e-mail mirna@cstome.net.
Ministry of Public Works and Infrastructure: São Tomé.

President and Legislature

PRESIDENT

Presidential Election, 29 July 2001

Candidate	Votes	% of votes
Fradique de Menezes	21,149	56.31
Manuel Pinto da Costa	14,544	38.73
Carlos Tiny	1,237	3.29
Victor Monteiro	381	1.02
Francisco Fortunato Pires	244	0.65
Total	**37,555**	**100.00**

ASSEMBLÉIA NACIONAL

Assembléia Nacional: Palácio dos Congressos, CP 181, São Tomé; tel. 222986; fax 222835; e-mail garepi@cstome.net; internet www.anstp.st.
President: FRANCISCO DA SILVA.

SÃO TOMÉ AND PRÍNCIPE

General Election, 26 March and 2 April 2006

	% of valid votes	Seats
Movimento Democrático Força da Mudança-Partido de Convergência Democrática	36.79	23
Movimento de Libertação de São Tomé e Príncipe—Partido Social Democrata	29.47	20
Acção Democrática Independente (ADI)	20.00	11
Novo Rumo (NR)	4.71	1
Others	9.03	—
Total	100.00	55

Election Commission

Commissão Eleitoral Nacional (CEN): São Tomé; Pres. José Carlos Barreiro.

Political Organizations

Acção Democrática Independente (ADI): Av. Marginal 12 de Julho, Edif. C. Cassandra, São Tomé; tel. 222201; f. 1992; Sec.-Gen. Patrice Trovoada.

Frente Democrata Cristã—Partido Social da Unidade (FDC—PSU): São Tomé; f. 1990; Pres. Arlécio Costa; Vice-Pres. Sabino dos Santos.

Geração Esperança (GE): São Tomé; f. 2005; Leader Edmilza Bragança.

Movimento Democrático Força da Mudança (MDFM): São Tomé; f. 2001; formed alliance with PCD to contest legislative elections in 2006; Sec.-Gen. Tomé Vera Cruz.

Movimento de Libertação de São Tomé e Príncipe—Partido Social Democrata (MLSTP—PSD): Estrada Riboque, Edif. Sede do MLSTP, São Tomé; tel. 222253; f. 1972 as MLSTP; adopted present name in 1990; sole legal party 1972–90; Pres. Guilherme Pósser da Costa; Sec.-Gen. Homéro Salvaterra.

Novo Rumo: São Tomé; f. 2006 by citizens disaffected by current political parties; Leader João Gomes.

Partido de Convergência Democrática (PCD): Av. Marginal 12 de Julho, CP 519, São Tomé; tel. and fax 223257; f. 1990 as Partido de Convergência—Grupo de Reflexão; formed alliance with MDFM to contest legislative elections in 2006; Pres. Leonel Mário d'Alva; Sec.-Gen. Marcelino Costa.

Partido de Coligação Democrática (CÓDÓ): São Tomé; f. 1990 as Partido Democrático de São Tomé e Príncipe—Coligação Democrática da Oposição; renamed as above June 1998; Leader Manuel Neves e Silva.

Partido Social e Liberal (PSL): São Tomé; f. 2005; promotes development and anti-corruption; Leader Agostinho Rita.

Partido Popular do Progresso (PPP): São Tomé; f. 1998; Leader Francisco Silva.

Partido de Renovação Democrática (PRD): São Tomé; f. 2001; Pres. Armindo Graça.

Partido Social Renovado (PSR): São Tomé; f. 2004; Leader Hamilton Vaz.

Uê Kédadji (UK): electoral coalition comprising the CÓDÓ, the PPP, the PRD, the PSR and the UNDP.

Partido Trabalhista Santomense (PTS): CP 254, São Tomé; tel. 223338; fax 223255; e-mail pascoal@cstome.net; f. 1993 as Aliança Popular; Leader Anacleto Rolin.

União para a Democracia e Desenvolvimento (UDD): São Tomé; f. 2005; Leader Manuel Diogo.

União Nacional para Democracia e Progresso (UNDP): São Tomé; f. 1998; Leader Paixão Lima.

Diplomatic Representation

EMBASSIES IN SÃO TOMÉ AND PRÍNCIPE

Angola: Av. Kwame Nkrumah 45, CP 133, São Tomé; tel. 222376; fax 221362; e-mail embang@cstome.net; Ambassador Pedro Fernando Mavunza.

Brazil: Av. Marginal de 12 de Julho 20, São Tomé; tel. 226060; fax 226895; e-mail brasembstome@cstome.net; Ambassador Paulo Dyrceu Pinheiro.

China (Taiwan): Av. Marginal de 12 de Julho, CP 839, São Tomé; tel. 223529; fax 221376; e-mail rocstp@cstome.net; Ambassador Ching-yuen Yang.

Equatorial Guinea: Rua Ex-Adriano Moreira, São Tomé; tel. 225427.

Gabon: Rua Damão, CP 394, São Tomé; tel. 224434; fax 223531; e-mail ambagabon@cstome.net; Ambassador Bekalé Michel.

Nigeria: Av. Kwame Nkrumah, CP 1000, São Tomé; tel. 225404; fax 225406; e-mail nigeria@cstome.net; Ambassador Saidu S. Pindar.

Portugal: Av. Marginal de 12 de Julho, CP 173, São Tomé; tel. 224974; fax 221190; e-mail eporstp@sol.stome.net; Ambassador Américo Madeira Bárbara.

Judicial System

Judicial power is exercised by the Supreme Court of Justice and the Courts of Primary Instance. The Supreme Court is the ultimate judicial authority. There is also a Constitutional Court, which rules on election matters.

Supreme Court: Av. Marginal de 12 de Julho, São Tomé; tel. and fax 222329; e-mail tsupremo@cstome.net; Pres. Alice Vera Cruz de Carvalho.

Religion

According to the 2001 census more than 80% of the population are Christians, almost all of whom are Roman Catholics.

CHRISTIANITY

The Roman Catholic Church

São Tomé and Príncipe comprises a single diocese, directly responsible to the Holy See. At 31 December 2003 an estimated 88.0% of the population were adherents. The bishop participates in the Episcopal Conference of Angola and São Tomé (based in Luanda, Angola).

Bishop of São Tomé and Príncipe: Rt Rev. Abílio Rodas de Sousa Ribas, Centro Diocesano, CP 104, São Tomé; tel. and fax 223455; e-mail diocese@cstome.net.

Other Churches

Igreja Adventista do 7° Dia (Seventh-Day Adventist Church): Rua Barão de Agua Izé, São Tomé; tel. 223349.

Igreja Evangélica: Rua 3 de Fevereiro, São Tomé; tel. 221350.

Igreja Evanélica Assembléia de Deus: Rua 3 de Fevereiro, São Tomé; tel. and fax 222442; e-mail iead@cstome.net.

Igreja Maná: Av. Amílcar Cabral, São Tomé; tel. and fax 224654; e-mail imana@cstome.net.

Igreja do Nazareno: Vila Dolores, São Tomé; tel. 223943; e-mail nszst@cstome.net.

Igreja Nova Apostólica: Fruta Fruta, São Tomé; tel. and fax 222406; e-mail inasaotome@cstome.net.

Igreja Universal do Reino de Deus: Travessa Imprensa, São Tomé; tel. 224047.

The Press

Correio da Semana: Av. Amílcar Cabral 382, São Tomé; tel. 225299; f. 2005; weekly; Publr Rafael Branco; Dir Nelson Mendes; circ. 3,000.

Diário da República: Cooperativa de Artes Gráficas, Rua João Devs, CP 28, São Tomé; tel. 222661; internet dre.pt/stp; f. 1836; official gazette; Dir Oscar Ferreira.

O País: Av. Amílcar Cabral, CP 361, São Tomé; tel. 223833; fax 221989; e-mail iucai@cstome.net; f. 1998; Dir Francisco Pinto da Silveira Rita.

O Parvo: CP 535, São Tomé; tel. 221031; f. 1994; weekly; Publr Ambrósio Quaresma; Editor Armindo Cardoso.

Piá: Edif. Centro Cultural Português 1c, CP 600, São Tomé; tel. 226332; e-mail doriadesign@hotmail.com; f. 2002; monthly; Dir Nilton Dória.

O Semanário: Av. Marginal de 12 de Julho, CP 112, São Tomé; tel. 222629; fax 221784; e-mail jsemanario@cstome.net; f. 2001; Dir Adelino Lucas.

Téla Nón: Largo Água Grande, Edif. Complexo Técnico da CST, São Tomé; tel. 225099; e-mail diario_digital@cstome.net; internet www.cstome.net/diario; f. 2000; provides online daily news service; Chief Editor Abel Veiga.

SÃO TOMÉ AND PRÍNCIPE

Tribuna: Praça Yon Gato, CP 19, São Tomé; tel. and fax 223295; e-mail tribuna@clix.pt; f. 1998; Dir NELSON MENDES.

A Vitrina: Rua do Município, CP 628, São Tomé; tel. 224688; fax 224966; e-mail diario_vitrina@cstome.net; internet www.cstome.net/vitrina; f. 1999; online newspaper; Dir PETTER LEAL BOUÇAS.

Online newspapers include the Jornal de São Tomé e Príncipe (www.jornal.st). Periodicals include the bi-monthly Ecuador.

PRESS ASSOCIATION

Associação Nacional de Imprensa (ANI): São Tomé; Pres. MANUEL BARRETO.

NEWS AGENCY

STP-Press: Av. Marginal de 12 de Julho, CP 112, São Tomé; tel. 223431; fax 221365; e-mail stp_press@cstome.net; f. 1985; operated by the radio station in asscn with the Angolan news agency ANGOP; Dir MANUEL DÊNDE.

Lusa—Agência de Notícias de Portugal has a correspondent, Ricardo Neto, in São Tomé.

Broadcasting and Communications

TELECOMMUNICATIONS

Companhia Santomense de Telecomunicações, SARL (CST): CP 141, São Tomé; tel. 222226; fax 222500; e-mail cst@cstome.net; internet www.cstome.net; f. 1989 by Govt of São Tomé (49%) and Rádio Marconi SA (Portugal, 51%) to facilitate increased telecommunications links and television reception via satellite; in March 1997 CST introduced internet services; Rádio Marconi's shares subsequently assumed by Portugal Telecom SA; introduced mobile cellular telephone service in 2001; Pres. of Admin. Bd JOSÉ MANUEL BRIOSA E GALA; Administrator-Delegate MANUEL JOAQUIM CAPITÃO AMARO.

BROADCASTING

Portuguese technical and financial assistance in the establishment of a television service was announced in May 1989. Transmissions commenced in 1992, and the service currently broadcasts seven days a week. In 1995 Radio France Internationale and Rádio Televisão Portuguesa Internacional began relaying radio and television broadcasts, respectively, to the archipelago. In 1997 Voice of America, which had been broadcasting throughout Africa since 1993 from a relay station installed on São Tomé, began local transmissions on FM. In 2004 there were plans for Televisão Pública de Angola to begin transmitting by the end of the year. The liberalization of the sector was approved by the Government in early 2005 and Rádio Jubilar, Rádio Tropicana (operated by the Roman Catholic Church) and Rádio Viva FM subsequently began broadcasting.

Radio

Rádio Nacional de São Tomé e Príncipe: Av. Marginal de 12 de Julho, CP 44, São Tomé; tel. 223293; fax 221973; e-mail rnstp@cstome.net; f. 1958; state-controlled; home service in Portuguese and Creole; Dir MÁXIMO CARLOS.

Rádio Jubilar: Rua Padre Martinho Pinto da Rocha, São Tomé; tel. 223455; f. 2005; operated by the Roman Catholic Church; Dir FERNANDO CORREIA.

Rádio Tropicana: Travessa João de Deus, CP 709, São Tomé; tel. 226856; f. 2005; Dir AGUINALDO SALVATERRA.

Television

Televisão Santomense (TVS): Bairro Quinta de Santo António, CP 393, São Tomé; tel. 221041; fax 221942; state-controlled; Dir VICTOR CORREIA.

Finance

(cap. = capital; res = reserves; dep. = deposits; m. = million; br. = branch)

BANKING

Central Bank

Banco Central de São Tomé e Príncipe (BCSTP): Praça da Independência, CP 13, São Tomé; tel. 221966; fax 222777; e-mail bcentral@sol.stome.telepac.st; internet www.bcstp.st; f. 1992 to succeed fmr Banco Nacional de São Tomé e Príncipe; bank of issue; Gov. MARIA DO CARMO SILVEIRA.

Commercial Banks

Afriland First Bank/STP: Praça da Independência, CP 202, São Tomé; tel. 226749; fax 226747; e-mail firstbank@cstome.net; internet www.afrilandfirstbank.com; f. 2003; private bank; owned by Afriland First Bank, SA, Cameroon; cap. US $1.8m.; Dir PIERRE MARIE NOUNAMO; Administrator-Delegate JOSEPH TINDJOU.

Banco Equador: Rua Moçambique, 3, CP 361, São Tomé; tel. 226150; fax 226149; e-mail banco_equador@cstome.net; internet www.bce.st; f. 1995 as Banco Comercial do Equador; restructured and name changed to above in 2003; owned by Monbaka (Angola) (40%) and Grupo António Mbakassi (40%); cap. US $3m.; Dir RUI ALEXANDRE R. CARVALHO MENDONÇA; 1 br..

Banco Internacional de São Tomé e Príncipe (BISTP) (International Bank of São Tomé and Príncipe): Praça da Independência, CP 536, São Tomé; tel. 243100; fax 222427; e-mail bistp@cstome.net; f. 1993; 48% govt-owned, 30% owned by Banco Totta e Açores, SA (Portugal), 22% by Caixa Geral de Depósitos (Portugal); cap. US $3.0m., res $3.1m., dep. $22.2m. (2004); Pres. MANUEL FERNANDO MONTEIRO PINTO; 3 brs.

Island Bank, SA: Rua de Guiné, CP 1044, São Tomé; tel. 222521; f. 2005; cap. US $1.8m. (2005); Pres. MARC WABARA; Dir CHRIS U. MMEJE.

Other banks active in 2005 were the Ocean Offshore Bank, SA and the Banco Comercial do Equador.

INVESTMENT BANK

National Investment Bank: Rua de Angola, São Tomé; tel. 908221; f. 2004; owned by Air Luxor (Portugal, 90%); cap. US $2.5m..

INSURANCE

Instituto de Segurança Social: Rua Soldado Paulo Ferreira, São Tomé; tel. 221382; e-mail inss@cstome.net; f. as Caixa de Previdência dos Funcionários Públicos, adopted present name 1994; insurance fund for civil servants; Pres. of Admin. Bd ALBINO GRAÇA DA FONSECA; Dir JUVENAL DO ESPÍRITO SANTO.

SAT INSURANCE: Av. 12 de Julho, CP 293, São Tomé; tel. 226161; fax 226160; e-mail satinsuran@cstome.net; f. 2001; general insurance; cap. US $0.5m.; Dir MICHEL SOBGUI.

Trade and Industry

DEVELOPMENT ORGANIZATION

Instituto para o Desenvolvimento Económico e Social (INDES): Travessa do Pelourinho, CP 408, São Tomé; tel. 222491; fax 221931; e-mail indes@cstome.net; f. 1989 as Fundo Social e de Infrastructuras; adopted present name 1994; channels foreign funds to local economy; Dir HOMERO JERÓNIMO SALVATERRA.

CHAMBER OF COMMERCE

Câmara do Comércio, Indústria, Agricultura e Serviços (CCIAS): Av. Marginal de 12 de Julho, CP 527, São Tomé; tel. 222723; fax 221409; e-mail ccias@cstome.net; Pres. ABÍLIO AFONSO HENRIQUES.

UTILITIES

Electricity and Water

Empresa de Água e Electricidade (EMAE): Av. Água Grande, CP 46, São Tomé; tel. 222096; fax 222488; e-mail emae@cstome.net; f. 1979; Synergie Investments (UK); state electricity and water co; privatized in 2004; Dir ANDRE GOMES.

TRADE UNIONS

Federação Nacional dos Pequenos Agricoltores (FENAPA): Rua Barão de Água Izé, São Tomé; tel. 224741; Pres. TEODORICO CAMPOS.

Organizacão Nacional de Trabalhadores de São Tomé e Príncipe (ONTSTP): Rua Cabo Verde, São Tomé; tel. 222431; e-mail ontstpdis@cstome.net; Sec.-Gen. JOÃO TAVARES.

Sindicato de Jornalistas de São Tomé e Príncipe (SJS): São Tomé; Pres. AMBRÓSIO QUARESMA.

Sindicato dos Trabalhadores Estatales (Sintresp): São Tomé; Sec.-Gen. AURÉLIO SILVA.

União Geral dos Trabalhadores de São Tomé e Príncipe (UGSTP): Av. Kwame Nkrumah, São Tomé; tel. 222443; e-mail ugtdis@cstome.net; Sec.-Gen. COSTA CARLOS.

Transport

RAILWAYS

There are no railways in São Tomé and Príncipe.

ROADS

In 1999 there were an estimated 320 km of roads, of which 218 km were asphalted. In 2005 the European Union granted €930,000 towards upgrading the road network.

SHIPPING

The principal ports are at São Tomé city and at Neves on São Tomé island. At December 2004 São Tomé and Príncipe's registered merchant fleet comprised 42 vessels, totalling 57,809 grt.

Agência de Navegação e Turismo, Lda (AGENTUR): Rua Cabo Verde, São Tomé; tel. 224866; fax 221894.

Companhia Santomense de Navegação, SA (CSN): CP 49, São Tomé; tel. 222657; fax 221311; e-mail csn@setgrcop.com; internet www.navegor.pt; shipping and freight forwarding.

Empresa Nacional de Administração dos Portos (ENAPORT): Largo Alfândega, São Tomé; tel. 221841; fax 224949; e-mail enaport@cstome.net; Dir-Gen. CELESTINO ANDRADE.

Navetur-Equatour, Navegação e Turismo, Lda: Rua Viriato da Curz, CP 277, São Tomé; tel. 222122; fax 221748; e-mail navequatur@cstome.net; internet www.navetur-equatour.st; shipping and tourism.

Transportes e Serviços, Lda (TURIMAR): Rua Patrice Lumumba, CP 48, São Tomé; tel. 221869; fax 222162; e-mail turimar@cstome.net.

CIVIL AVIATION

The international airport is at São Tomé.

Empresa Nacional de Aeroportos e Segurança Aérea (ENASA): Aeroporto, CP 703, São Tomé; tel. 221878; fax 221154; e-mail enasa@cstome.net.

Air Luxor STP: Av. Kwame Nkrumah, São Tomé; f. 2002; 49% owned by Air Luxor, Portugal; operates weekly direct service to Lisbon.

Air São Tomé e Príncipe: Av. Marginal de 12 de Julho, CP 45, São Tomé; tel. 221976; fax 221375; e-mail astp@cstome.net; f. 1993; owned by Govt of São Tomé (35%), TAP-Air Portugal, SA (40%), Golfe International Air Service (France, 24%) and Mistral Voyages (France, 1%); operates domestic service between the islands of São Tomé and Príncipe and international connection to Libreville (Gabon); Pres. RAÚL BRAGANÇA WAGNER NETO; Man. Dir ALCINO BARROS PINTO.

Linhas Aéreas São-tomenses (LAS): São Tomé; f. 2002.

Tourism

The islands benefit from spectacular mountain scenery, unspoilt beaches and unique species of flora and wildlife. Although still largely undeveloped, tourism is currently the sector of the islands' economy attracting the highest level of foreign investment. However, the high level of rainfall during most of the year limits the duration of the tourist season, and the expense of reaching the islands by air is also an inhibiting factor. There were 7,569 tourist arrivals in 2001, and receipts totalled some US $10m. in 2002. In 2000 there were seven hotels, seven boarding houses (pensões) and four guest houses (residências), with a total of 495 beds.

SAUDI ARABIA
Introductory Survey

Location, Climate, Language, Religion, Flag, Capital

The Kingdom of Saudi Arabia occupies about four-fifths of the Arabian peninsula, in south-western Asia. It is bordered by Jordan, Iraq and Kuwait to the north, by Yemen to the south, by Oman to the south and east, and by Qatar and the United Arab Emirates to the north-east. Saudi Arabia has a long western coastline on the Red Sea, facing Egypt, Sudan and Eritrea, and a shorter coastline (between Kuwait and Qatar) on the Persian (Arabian) Gulf, with the Bahrain archipelago just off shore and Iran on the opposite coast. Much of the country is arid desert, and some places are without rain for years. In summer average temperatures in coastal regions range from 38°C to 49°C, and humidity is high. Temperatures sometimes reach 54°C in the interior. Winters are mild, except in the mountains. Annual rainfall averages between 100 mm and 200 mm in the north, and is even lower in the south. The official language is Arabic, which is spoken by almost all of the population. Except for the expatriate community (estimated to represent some 27% of the total population in 2004), virtually all of the inhabitants are adherents of Islam, the official religion. About 85% of the population are Sunni Muslims, and most of the indigenous inhabitants belong to the strictly orthodox Wahhabi sect. About 15% of the population are Shi'a Muslims, principally in the east of the country. The national flag (proportions 2 by 3) is green and bears, in white, an Arabic inscription ('There is no God but Allah and Muhammad is the Prophet of Allah') above a white sabre. The capital is Riyadh.

Recent History

The whole of the Arabian peninsula became part of Turkey's Ottoman Empire in the 16th century. Under the suzerainty of the Ottoman Sultan, the local tribal rulers enjoyed varying degrees of autonomy. The Wahhabi movement, dedicated to the reform of Islam, was launched in the Najd (Nejd) region of central Arabia in the 18th century. A Wahhabi kingdom, ruled by the House of Sa'ud from its capital at Riyadh, quickly expanded into the Hedjaz region on the west coast of Arabia. In 1890 the rival Rashidi family seized control of Riyadh, but in 1902 a member of the deposed Sa'udi family, Abd al-Aziz ibn Abd ar-Rahman, expelled the Rashidi dynasty and proclaimed himself ruler of Najd. In subsequent years he recovered and consolidated the outlying provinces of the kingdom, defeating Turkish attempts to subjugate him. Having restored the House of Sa'ud as a ruling dynasty, Abd al-Aziz became known as Ibn Sa'ud. In order to strengthen his position, he instituted the formation of Wahhabi colonies, known as Ikhwan ('Brethren'), throughout the territory under his control.

During the First World War, in which Turkey was allied with Germany, the Arabs under Ottoman rule rebelled. In 1915 the United Kingdom signed a treaty of friendship with Ibn Sa'ud, who was then master of central Arabia, securing his co-operation against Turkey. Relations subsequently deteriorated as a result of the British Government's decision to support Hussein ibn Ali, who proclaimed himself King of the Hedjaz in 1916, as its principal ally in Arabia. Hussein was also Sharif of Mecca (the holiest city of Islam), which had been governed since the 11th century by his Hashimi (Hashemite) family, rivals of the House of Sa'ud. At the end of the war, following Turkey's defeat, the Ottoman Empire was dissolved. Continuing his conquests, Ibn Sa'ud successfully campaigned against the rulers of four Arabian states (the Hedjaz, Asir, Hayil and Jauf) between 1919 and 1925. In September 1924 his forces captured Mecca, forcing Hussein to abdicate, and in 1925 they overran the whole of the Hedjaz. In January 1926 Ibn Sa'ud was proclaimed King of the Hedjaz and Sultan of Najd. On 23 September 1932 the dual monarchy ended when the two areas were merged as the unified Kingdom of Saudi Arabia.

Commercially exploitable deposits of petroleum (the basis of Saudi Arabia's modern prosperity) were discovered in the Eastern Province in 1938, and large-scale exploitation of the kingdom's huge reserves of petroleum began after the Second World War. Petroleum royalties were used to develop and modernize the country's infrastructure and services.

Ibn Sa'ud remained in power until his death in November 1953; all subsequent rulers of Saudi Arabia have been sons of Ibn Sa'ud. The kingdom has remained an absolute monarchy and a traditional Islamic society. The King is the supreme religious leader as well as the Head of State, and governs by royal decree. In foreign affairs, Saudi Arabia has historically allied itself with the USA and other Western countries.

Ibn Sa'ud was succeeded by the Crown Prince, Sa'ud ibn Abd al-Aziz. Another of the late King's sons, Faisal ibn Abd al-Aziz, replaced Sa'ud as Crown Prince and Prime Minister. In 1958, bowing to pressure from the royal family, King Sa'ud conferred on Crown Prince Faisal full powers over foreign, internal and economic affairs. In March 1964 King Sa'ud relinquished power to Crown Prince Faisal, and in November was forced by the royal family to abdicate in his favour. The new King Faisal retained the post of Prime Minister, and appointed his half-brother, Khalid ibn Abd al-Aziz, to be Crown Prince in 1965. In the Six-Day War of June 1967 Saudi Arabian forces collaborated with Iraqi and Jordanian troops in action against Israel. As a result of the Arab–Israeli War of October 1973, Saudi Arabia led a movement by Arab petroleum producers to exert pressure on Western countries by reducing supplies of crude oil.

In March 1975 King Faisal was assassinated by one of his nephews, and was immediately succeeded by Crown Prince Khalid. The new King also became Prime Minister, and appointed his brother, Fahd ibn Abd al-Aziz (Minister of the Interior since 1962), as Crown Prince and First Deputy Prime Minister.

The religious fervour that the Middle East experienced in the wake of the Iranian Revolution also arose in Saudi Arabia in late 1979, when an armed group of about 250 Sunni Muslim extremists attacked and occupied the Grand Mosque in Mecca, the most important centre of pilgrimage for Muslims. There was also a riot by Shi'a Muslims in the Eastern Province. In response to the unrest, Crown Prince Fahd announced in early 1980 that a consultative assembly would be formed to act as an advisory body, although the assembly was not inaugurated until December 1993 (see below).

King Khalid died in June 1982 and was succeeded by Crown Prince Fahd, who, following precedent, became Prime Minister and appointed a half-brother, Abdullah ibn Abd al-Aziz (Commander of the National Guard since 1962), to be Crown Prince and First Deputy Prime Minister.

As a result of its position as the world's leading exporter of petroleum, Saudi Arabia is a dominant member of the Organization of the Petroleum Exporting Countries (OPEC, see p. 344) and one of the most influential countries in the Arab world. In May 1981 the kingdom joined five neighbouring states in establishing the Co-operation Council for the Arab States of the Gulf (the Gulf Co-operation Council—GCC, see p. 205). In August Crown Prince (subsequently King) Fahd announced an eight-point plan for the settlement of the Arab–Israeli conflict. His proposals, by implication, recognized Israel as a legitimate state. At a summit conference of Arab states in September 1982, the so-called 'Fahd Plan' formed the basis of an agreed proposal for the achievement of peace in the Middle East, and during 1983 Saudi Arabia sponsored repeated diplomatic initiatives within the region. In November 1987 Saudi Arabia resumed full diplomatic relations with Egypt. Relations had been severed in 1979, following the signing of the peace treaty between Egypt and Israel.

Relations with Iran, already strained as a result of Saudi Arabia's support for Iraq in the Iran–Iraq War, deteriorated further in July 1987 following fierce clashes between Iranian pilgrims and Saudi security forces during the *Hajj*, in which 402 people, including 275 Iranians, were killed. Mass demonstrations took place in Tehran, where the Saudi Arabian embassy was sacked, and Iranian leaders vowed to avenge the pilgrims' deaths by overthrowing the Saudi ruling family. In March 1988 the Government announced its intention to limit the number of foreign pilgrims during the *Hajj* season by allocating national quotas. Saudi Arabia severed diplomatic relations with Iran, which subsequently refused to send pilgrims on that year's *Hajj*.

SAUDI ARABIA

In July 1988, after the US Congress had refused to sanction an agreement to supply military equipment to Saudi Arabia (following the delivery of an unspecified number of medium-range missiles from the People's Republic of China to Saudi Arabia earlier that year), the Government signed a large-scale defence procurement agreement with the United Kingdom, which as a result superseded the USA as Saudi Arabia's main supplier of military equipment.

Widely held misgivings regarding national defence capabilities, and fears of Iraqi expansionist policy (a pact of non-aggression was signed with Iraq in March 1989), were exacerbated in August 1990, when Iraq invaded and annexed Kuwait and proceeded to deploy armed forces along the Kuwaiti–Saudi Arabian border. King Fahd requested that US forces be deployed in Saudi Arabia, as part of a multinational force, in order to deter a possible attack by Iraq. The dispatch of US combat troops and aircraft to Saudi Arabia signified the beginning of 'Operation Desert Shield' for the defence of Saudi Arabia, in accordance with Article 51 of the UN Charter. By the beginning of 1991 some 30 countries had contributed ground troops, aircraft and warships to the US-led multinational force based in Saudi Arabia and the Gulf region. The entire Saudi Arabian armed forces (numbering about 67,500 men) were mobilized. In January, following the failure of international diplomatic efforts to secure Iraq's withdrawal from Kuwait, the multinational force launched a military campaign ('Operation Desert Storm') to liberate Kuwait. As part of its response to the initial aerial bombardment, Iraq launched *Scud* missiles against targets in Saudi Arabia. However, fighting on Saudi Arabian territory was confined to a few minor incidents. In February Iraq formally severed diplomatic relations with Saudi Arabia.

Following the liberation of Kuwait in February 1991, the ministers responsible for foreign affairs of the GCC met their Syrian and Egyptian counterparts in Damascus, Syria, in March in order to discuss regional security issues. The formation of an Arab peace-keeping force, comprising mainly Egyptian and Syrian troops, was subsequently announced. In May, however, following the endorsement by the GCC member states of US proposals for an increased Western military presence in the Gulf region, Egypt announced its decision to withdraw all of its forces from the region, casting doubt on the future of joint Arab regional security arrangements. Diplomatic relations between Saudi Arabia and Iran were re-established in March, and Iranian pilgrims resumed attendance of the *Hajj*, their numbers regulated in accordance with the quota system.

In March 1992 King Fahd announced by royal decree the imminent creation of an advisory Consultative Council (Majlis ash-Shoura), with 60 members to be selected by the King every four years. Two further decrees provided for the establishment of regional authorities, and a 'basic law of government', equivalent to a written constitution. In September Sheikh Muhammad al-Jubair, hitherto Minister of Justice, was appointed Chairman of the Majlis. In November a major reorganization of the 18-member Council of Ulema (Saudi Arabia's most senior Islamic authority) was instigated by royal decree. The Majlis was inaugurated by King Fahd at the end of 1993. (Its membership was increased to 90 in July 1997, and to 120 in May 2001.)

In September 1992 Qatar accused a Saudi force of attacking a Qatari border post, killing two border guards and capturing a third. As a result, Qatar suspended a 1965 border agreement with Saudi Arabia, which had never been fully ratified. In December 1992, following mediation by President Hosni Mubarak of Egypt, the Qatari Amir, Sheikh Khalifa, signed an agreement in Medina with King Fahd to establish a committee to demarcate the disputed border. In June 1999 officials of the two countries met in Riyadh to sign the maps defining their joint border, and a final land and maritime demarcation agreement was signed in Doha, Qatar, in March 2001. The border agreement provided for a joint Saudi-Qatari committee, charged with ensuring full implementation of the 1965 accord. In October 2002 the Saudi ambassador to Qatar returned to Riyadh for unspecified 'consultations', apparently following broadcasts by the Qatari television news channel Al-Jazeera that were deemed to be critical of the Saudi regime. Saudi-Qatar relations were also reported to be strained over competition to influence the USA in its plans to attack the regime of Saddam Hussain in Iraq.

In May 1993 the Saudi authorities disbanded the Committee for the Defence of Legitimate Rights (CDLR), recently established by a group of six prominent Islamist scholars and lawyers. The organization's founders were also dismissed from their positions, and their spokesman, Muhammad al-Masari, was arrested. In April 1994 it was reported that members of the CDLR, including al-Masari (who had recently been released from custody), had relocated their organization to the United Kingdom. In January 1996 the British authorities ordered the deportation of al-Masari to Dominica: prominent British defence and aerospace companies were believed to have exerted pressure on their Government to concede to Saudi Arabia's demands that al-Masari be expelled in order to secure the continuation of lucrative trade agreements with Saudi Arabia. However, the Chief Immigration Adjudicator in the United Kingdom rejected the deportation order, recommending that the Government should reconsider al-Masari's application for political asylum, and in April al-Masari was granted exceptional leave to remain in the United Kingdom for a period of at least four years, although he was not granted asylum.

In September 1994 the CDLR was among organizations to report the arrest of more than 1,000 people, including clerics and academics, most of whom had attended a demonstration in Buraidah, north-west of Riyadh, to protest at the arrest of two religious leaders who had allegedly been agitating for the stricter enforcement of *Shari'a* (Islamic) law. The Government announced in October that 130 of the 157 people arrested in September had since been released. Also in October the King approved the creation of a Higher Council for Islamic Affairs, under the chairmanship of Prince Sultan ibn Abd al-Aziz, the Second Deputy Prime Minister and Minister of Defence and Civil Aviation, in a measure apparently aimed at limiting the influence of militant clerics and at diminishing the authority of the powerful Council of Ulema. In mid-1995 King Fahd replaced six of the seven University chancellors and more than one-half of the members of the Council of Ulema, in an attempt to counter the perceived spread of Islamist fundamentalism.

In June 1995 an opposition activist, Abdullah Abd ar-Rahman al-Hudaif, was sentenced to 20 years' imprisonment for his part in an attack on a security officer and for maintaining links with the CDLR in the United Kingdom. In August al-Hudaif was reported to have been executed; no explanation was given for the alteration of his sentence, nor were details of his trial revealed. A further nine opposition activists reportedly received prison sentences ranging from three to 18 years; according to prominent human rights organization Amnesty International, as many as 200 'political suspects' remained in detention in Saudi Arabia.

In August 1995 the King announced the most far-reaching reorganization of the Council of Ministers for two decades, although no changes were made to the portfolios held by members of the royal family. The strategic portfolios of finance and national economy and of petroleum and mineral resources were allocated to younger, though highly experienced, officials.

A Supreme Economic Council, established by royal decree, convened for the first time in October 1997 under the chairmanship of the Crown Prince. A Supreme Petroleum and Minerals Council was established by royal decree in January 2000. In April the Government approved broad guide-lines for the issuing of tourist visas, and the creation of a supreme commission to promote foreign tourism in Saudi Arabia was announced. The Government declared in May that ministers were to lose their right to hold company posts while in office, with the exception of employees of the state-owned Saudi Aramco petroleum corporation. In June the inaugural session was held of the newly formed Royal Family Council, an officially apolitical body to be chaired by Crown Prince Abdullah.

King Fahd announced a restructured 27-member Council of Ministers at the end of April 2003; this was only the third reorganization of the Government in almost 30 years. Reformists were disappointed that most of the key positions were unchanged, and that all the senior ministers belonging to the ruling as-Sa'ud family remained in post.

Following reports in the early part of 2003 that the Saudi Government intended to follow the example of Bahrain and hold elections to the Majlis ash-Shoura in 2005, on 13 October 2003, at a human rights conference in Riyadh, the Government disclosed plans to create municipal councils and hold local elections by October 2004. The news was received with some scepticism among Saudi reformists, who noted that one-half of the councillors would be centrally appointed and that there had been no suggestion in the official announcement that suffrage would be extended to women. The decision by the authorities to introduce a degree of democracy to the kingdom came amid huge pressure both from inside and outside the country to implement social, economic, political and constitutional reforms. On 30 November 2003 King Fahd issued a decree widening the legislative power of the Majlis. Under the new regulations, the Majlis was to be allowed to propose new laws and amendments to existing legislation without first asking permission from the King. In addition, the Council of Ministers was to be obliged to return laws to the Majlis for amendment should there be disagreement on an issue. (Under the previous system, whereby the Majlis was a purely advisory body, the matter would be resolved by the King.) In April 2005 a royal decree increased the membership of the Majlis to 150; the expansion prompted renewed demands for the introduction of a partially elected membership.

In February 2004 a reported 251 *Hajj* pilgrims died and some 244 others were injured in a stampede near the Jamarat Bridge in Mina, near Mecca. Some 345 pilgrims were killed and a further 289 were injured in another stampede near the foot of the bridge in January 2006. Earlier in the same month 76 people had died when a hostel servicing the *Hajj* collapsed. Around 2.5m. pilgrims were estimated to have attended the *Hajj* in that year. The Jamarat Bridge area was scheduled to be restructured, at a cost of US $1,400m., by 2009.

On 9 July 2004 Prince Mutaib ibn Abd al-Aziz as-Sa'ud, the Minister of Municipal and Rural Affairs, announced that elections for 178 municipal authorities in all 13 of the kingdom's provinces would be held, slightly earlier than expected, in September; however, it was announced in September that the elections would be delayed until early 2005. The first stage of the municipal elections eventually took place on 10 February 2005 in Riyadh; disappointingly for reformists, suffrage was not extended to women. In excess of 1,800 candidates stood for the 592 contested seats in the 178 councils; however, reportedly only about one-quarter of eligible voters in the capital had registered for the elections. Some analysts blamed this apathy on public dissatisfaction with the magnitude of the legislative reforms, which were widely seen merely as token measures. The second phase of the elections took place in the Eastern, Aseer, Jazan, Najran and al-Baha provinces on 3 March. According to the local chamber of commerce, only around 12% of the local male population in the Eastern province had registered to vote. The final phase, in the northern border provinces, was held on 21 April. Nationally, Islamist candidates secured a comfortable majority of the council seats. Meanwhile, later in the year women were allowed to campaign openly for elected positions on the 18-member board of the Jeddah Chamber of Commerce and Industry; two women secured seats on the board. In December a female candidate secured an elected position on the 10-member board of the Saudi Engineers' Council.

In late May 2005 the increasingly frail King Fahd was declared to have been admitted to hospital in Riyadh suffering from pneumonia. The King died on 1 August and was succeeded by his half-brother, Crown Prince Abdullah, also aged 84, who had been the *de facto* ruler of the kingdom since King Fahd suffered a stroke in 1995. The Second Deputy Prime Minister, Minister of Defence and Civil Aviation and Inspector General, Prince Sultan, a full brother of King Fahd and also in his eighties, was named as the new Crown Prince. The Council of Ministers remained essentially unchanged; in accordance with the Constitution, King Abdullah assumed the role of Prime Minister and the Crown Prince was appointed Deputy Prime Minister. No replacement was named for the position of Second Deputy Prime Minister, however, which increased the speculation surrounding the succession to the throne after Crown Prince Sultan. Some observers believed that the succession would miss a generation and that one of King Ibn Sa'ud's many grandsons would emerge as a viable heir, but the mostly likely candidates to succeed Sultan, should he become King, remained another of King Fahd's full brothers. In October 2005 it was announced that a National Security Council (NSC), chaired by King Abdullah, was to be established. Among its extensive powers, the NSC was to: have the power to declare states of emergency and war; be given control over diplomatic relations; and be tasked with combating public corruption and mismanagement. Meanwhile, in December the Crown Prince announced that popular elections to the Majlis were not necessary on the basis that its existing members were highly capable; he claimed, however, not to be opposed to legislative elections in principle.

Saudi Arabia's human rights record has for many years been the focus of international scrutiny, particularly regarding the use of public beheading in the Saudi judicial system. A report issued by Amnesty International in March 2000 alleged that Saudi Arabia was guilty of widespread human rights abuses, including use of torture and refusal to allow prisoners access to family members and lawyers. A document published by Amnesty International in September accused the Saudi authorities of widespread discrimination against women and cited serious abuses of their human rights, including arbitrary detention and torture. The organization also reiterated its criticism of the Saudi judiciary for failing to conduct trials in compliance with internationally recognized standards. However, it was reported in late 2000 that Saudi Arabia had agreed to sign the UN Convention on the Elimination of All Forms of Discrimination against Women, although it stated that it would lodge reservations regarding any section deemed to contravene *Shari'a* law. In October 2003 Saudi Arabia held its first human rights conference in Riyadh; Western human rights bodies, however, such as Amnesty International, were not invited. Several hundred protesters took part in an illegal demonstration, organized by the London-based Movement for Islamic Reform, outside the conference on 14 October, demanding widespread reforms including the removal of the House of Sa'ud. Reports indicated that around 150 people were arrested the following day in connection with the demonstration. In January 2005 15 people were sentenced to short prison sentences and 150–200 lashes each after having taken part in an anti-monarchy demonstration in December 2004. In May 2005 three Saudi reformists were sentenced to terms of imprisonment ranging from six to nine years for having called for the establishment of a constitutional monarchy; however, the three dissidents were pardoned in October. In the same month the Government announced the establishment of a human rights watchdog headed by Turki ibn Khalid as-Sudairi, who would be given the equivalent rank to that of a government minister. Nevertheless, pressure for real liberalization, from both inside and outside the administration, was limited.

Numerous bombings and terrorist attacks, often targeted against foreign civilians, have taken place in recent years. In November 1995 a car bomb exploded outside the offices of the Saudi Arabian National Guard in Riyadh, which was being used by US civilian contractors to train Saudi personnel. Seven foreign nationals (including five US citizens) were killed in the explosion, and a further 60 were injured. Responsibility for the bomb was claimed by several organizations, including the Islamic Movement for Change, which earlier in the year had warned that it would initiate attacks if non-Muslim Western forces did not withdraw from the Gulf region. In May 1996 four Saudi nationals were executed, having been convicted of involvement in the attack.

In June 1996 19 US military personnel were killed, and as many as 400 others (including 147 Saudi, 118 Bangladeshi and 109 US citizens) were injured, when an explosive device attached to a petroleum tanker was detonated outside a military housing complex in al-Khobar, near Dhahran. By late 1996 there was speculation that the investigating authorities were holding Saudi Shi'a groups with possible links to Iran responsible for the atrocity, rather than the same Sunni extremist factions that were widely blamed for the November 1995 bombing. The Iranian Government, however, repeatedly denied any involvement in the incident. In March 1997 the Canadian intelligence service announced the detention, in Ottawa, of Hani Abd ar-Rahim as-Sayegh, a Saudi Shi'a Muslim implicated in the al-Khobar attack and who was alleged to have links with the militant Hezbollah. In June as-Sayegh was extradited from Canada to stand trial in the USA, but in September US officials announced that there was insufficient evidence to secure a conviction and that as-Sayegh would not be tried in the USA. Saudi Arabia subsequently applied for as-Sayegh's extradition. In May 1998 Saudi Arabia's Minister of the Interior stated that there was no indication of a foreign role in the bombing, despite continuing US assertions of Iranian involvement. There were reports in June that US investigations into the bombing had collapsed and that the USA had withdrawn the majority of its investigators from Saudi Arabia. In October 1999, however, as-Sayegh was extradited from the USA to Saudi Arabia, shortly after the Saudi Minister of the Interior stated that the country's security services possessed information regarding as-Sayegh's involvement in the attack. Several Saudi nationals were arrested in January 2001 in connection with the bombing. In June US investigators indicted 14 individuals on charges relating to the explosion, although three of them remained at large in June 2002 when the Saudi authorities announced that sentences had been imposed on a number of the detainees. Meanwhile, as-Sayegh remained in custody in Saudi Arabia.

In October 2000 a Saudi Arabian Airlines passenger flight, en route from Jeddah to the United Kingdom and carrying some 40

British citizens, was hijacked by two armed Saudi nationals. The aircraft finally landed in the Iraqi capital, Baghdad, where the hijackers (who were reportedly protesting against human rights abuses in Saudi Arabia and the presence of US and British troops on Saudi territory) were detained by the Iraqi authorities. Saudi Arabia initially demanded the men's extradition; however, in December Saudi officials announced that they would not be pursuing such a demand. Meanwhile, one British national died and three were injured in November, as a result of two separate car bomb attacks in Riyadh. No group claimed responsibility for the blasts, although they were initially believed to have been perpetrated by militant Islamists in protest at the role of Western states in the Israeli–Palestinian crisis. In December it was reported that a US citizen was among several foreign nationals arrested for questioning in relation to the bombings; Saudi officials suggested that the attacks may not have been politically motivated. A third bomb was detonated in al-Khobar in that month, and was followed by several more attacks throughout 2001. In February of that year four expatriates (three British nationals and a Belgian) were detained by the Saudi authorities. Saudi television subsequently broadcast alleged confessions by the three British men relating to their involvement in the November bomb explosions, an admission punishable by the death penalty. By August three more expatriates (all Britons) had been detained and their alleged confessions broadcast on Saudi television. The confessions, however, were later withdrawn amid allegations that the accused had been tortured. In December 2002 one of four British nationals who had in December 2000 been sentenced to 12 years' imprisonment for the al-Khobar bombing admitted responsibility for the attack as part of a wider bombing campaign, which was said to be related to gang warfare over illegal trade in alcohol. (The man's family claimed that his confession had been extracted under torture and that Islamist dissidents were responsible for the bombings.) Meanwhile, another Briton was detained (but not charged) in November 2002 for the alleged murder of a German national in a car bomb attack in September. A total of six Britons were convicted in connection with the bombing campaign (two were sentenced to death; the remainder were given prison terms of between eight and 18 years), although in February 2003 a report by the Special Rapporteur of the UN Commission on Human Rights on the independence of judges and lawyers, which cited 'substantial procedural irregularities' and noted that the men's descriptions of torture were 'consistent', cast considerable doubt on the validity of their trials. (In May one of the men was released from his eight-year sentence.) In early August the six Britons, the Belgian and the British expatriate arrested in November 2002 for the killing of the German national were released, having been granted a royal pardon; the decision was seen as a tacit admission by the authorities that terrorists were the more likely perpetrators of the recent wave of bombings. Following the murders of a British defence contractor in February 2003 and of two North Americans in March, fears of intensified attacks against Westerners proved well-founded when a series of co-ordinated suicide attacks devastated an expatriate housing compound in Riyadh on 12 May (see below).

In late 1997, as the crisis developed regarding access to sites in Iraq by weapons inspectors of the UN Special Commission (UNSCOM, see p. 101), Saudi Arabia firmly advocated a diplomatic solution. In February 1998 Saudi Arabia stated that it would not allow the USA to use Saudi territory as a base for air-strikes against Iraq, and reiterated its desire for a diplomatic solution. As relations deteriorated between Iraq and UNSCOM in late 1998, Saudi Arabia again refused to allow its territory to be used as a base for US-led air-strikes against Iraq, although it was later claimed that discreet support had been given which included the use of its bases. In September 2000 Iraq accused Saudi Arabia and Kuwait of inflicting (through the maintenance of the sanctions regime) suffering on the Iraqi population, and alleged that Saudi Arabia was appropriating Iraqi petroleum transported under the oil-for-food programme. Saudi Arabia, encouraged by the mediation of the League of Arab States (the Arab League, see p. 306), indicated at the beginning of 2002 that it was ready for a cautious *rapprochement* with Iraq. In October the border crossing from Saudi Arabia to Iraq was reopened, providing a fifth land route for Iraqi trade under the UN oil-for-food arrangement. Following the US-led military campaign to remove Saddam Hussain's regime in Iraq in 2003 (see below), Saudi Arabia announced in September 2005 that it was planning to reopen its embassy in Baghdad. Diplomatic relations between Iraq and Saudi Arabia had been severed in 1991, following Iraq's invasion of Kuwait.

Relations between Saudi Arabia and Iran, which were particularly strained by suspicions of Iranian involvement in the 1996 al-Khobar bombing (see above), improved considerably following the election of Muhammad Khatami to the Iranian presidency in 1997. Co-operation was notably strengthened following the September 2001 attacks on New York and Washington, DC, for which the USA held the al-Qa'ida (Base) organization of the Saudi-born militant Islamist Osama bin Laden to be principally responsible, as Saudi Arabia and Iran sought to counter the emergence of anti-Islamic sentiment in the West.

In December 1994 Yemen accused Saudi Arabia of erecting monitoring posts and constructing roads on Yemeni territory. Relations had been strained as a result of Saudi Arabia's apparent support for secessionist forces in Yemen earlier in the year (q.v.). There was a further deterioration in January 1995, when the two countries failed to renew the 1934 Ta'if agreement (renewable every 20 years), delineating their *de facto* frontier. Following military clashes between Saudi and Yemeni forces, and intense mediation by Syria, a joint statement was issued in mid-January 1995 in which the two sides undertook to halt all military activity in the disputed border area; it was subsequently agreed to pursue demarcation of the border by a joint committee. In February the Saudi and Yemeni Governments signed a memorandum of understanding that reaffirmed their commitment to the legitimacy of the Ta'if agreement and provided for the establishment of six joint committees to delineate the land and sea borders and to develop economic and commercial ties. The two countries signed a border security agreement in July 1996. In May 1998, however, Saudi Arabia invaded the disputed island of Huraym in the Red Sea and was reported to have sent a memorandum to the UN stating that it did not recognize the 1992 border agreement between Yemen and Oman, claiming that parts of the area involved were Saudi Arabian territory. The Saudi objection to the accord was widely believed to be related to its attempts to gain land access to the Arabian Sea, via a corridor between Yemen and Oman, which it had thus far been denied in its negotiations with Yemen. In July 1998 Yemen submitted a memorandum to the Arab League, refuting the Saudi claim to the land and stating that the Saudi protests contravened the Ta'if agreement signed by that country. Further clashes were reported close to the land and sea border between Yemen and Saudi Arabia in June, and in July three Yemeni troops were killed during fighting with a Saudi border patrol on the disputed island of Duwaima in the Red Sea; Saudi Arabia claimed its actions there were in self-defence and that, under the Ta'if agreement, three-quarters of the island was Saudi territory. In January 2000 both countries denied further reports of armed confrontations in the border area, and a meeting of a joint military committee began in San'a in February. Talks on the border issue continued meanwhile, and in June, during a visit to Saudi Arabia by President Saleh, a final agreement delineating land and sea borders was signed. As part of the accord, which incorporated the 1934 Ta'if agreement and much of the 1995 memorandum of understanding, both sides agreed to promote economic, commercial and cultural relations, and each undertook not to permit on its territory activities against the other by opposition groups. The agreement did not demarcate sections of the eastern border, and in August 2000 three Saudi border guards and one Yemeni soldier were reportedly killed in border clashes. Nevertheless, the first meeting of the Saudi-Yemen Co-operation Council for more than a decade took place in December; a further meeting followed in June 2001. Meanwhile, it was reported that the withdrawal from the border region of troops of both countries, in accordance with the border agreement, was almost complete. However, relations deteriorated again in early 2004 after the Saudi Government began construction of a 'security fence' along the border that risked violating the border demarcation treaty signed in June 2000. The construction of the barrier reflected a profound lack of trust on the part of the Saudi authorities in Yemen's ability to prevent weapons smugglers from infiltrating Saudi territory.

In July 1995 officials from Saudi Arabia and Oman signed documents to demarcate their joint border. In March 1999 Saudi Arabia held talks with Iran in an effort to mediate in its dispute with the United Arab Emirates (UAE) over the Tunb islands. Following a statement by the GCC condemning both Iran's recent military exercises near the islands and its claim to them and emphasizing UAE sovereignty of the islands, the Iranian President cancelled a planned visit to Saudi Arabia (the visit proceeded in May). Saudi Arabia's *rapprochement* with

Iran had resulted in a deterioration in its relations with the UAE, and in March the UAE boycotted a meeting of GCC ministers responsible for petroleum production in protest at Saudi exploration of an oilfield in disputed territory prior to an agreement being reached. In September 2000 the Saudi Government approved an agreement, signed in July, which ended the long-standing dispute with Kuwait regarding their mutual sea border. Final maps delineating that border were signed by officials from both sides in January 2001.

Saudi Arabia severed diplomatic relations with the Taliban regime in Afghanistan in late September 2001, in response to the suicide attacks on the mainland USA. Saudi Arabia was only one of three countries (along with Pakistan and the UAE) to have recognized the Taliban administration in Afghanistan. Although the USA's principal suspect in the attacks, Osama bin Laden (who was at that time based in Afghanistan), was born to a wealthy Saudi Arabian family, the Saudi authorities emphasized that bin Laden had been exiled since 1991 and his nationality revoked because of his subversive activities against the royal family. It was later revealed that 15 of the 19 hijackers were also of Saudi descent (although many of the identities were forged or stolen). Visiting Washington shortly after the attacks, Saudi Arabia's Minister of Foreign Affairs stated that he had conveyed to the US Secretary of State, Colin Powell, the support of the Saudi people for efforts to eliminate terrorism. Saudi Arabia also agreed to investigate alleged Saudi funding of bin Laden's al-Qa'ida network, said to be raised through certain charitable organizations and individual donations. However, the Saudi regime, under pressure from internal Islamist groups implacably opposed to the US military presence on Saudi territory and to any military action against another Islamic state, subsequently refused permission for the use of its airbases for military action against Afghanistan (although an air 'command and control' base in the kingdom was made available to support the military operation). Following the launch of military attacks against Afghanistan by the US-led 'coalition against terror' in October, the USA briefly closed its embassy in Saudi Arabia because of fear of reprisals. Later that month Crown Prince Abdullah accused the US media of conspiring to damage Saudi Arabia's reputation following the publication of articles highly critical of Saudi Arabia's perceived lack of co-operation after the September attacks. Although official statements by the US Administration continued to praise the Saudi regime, rumours of a deterioration in the relationship between the two countries persisted, and in January 2002 there was speculation that Saudi Arabia was considering demanding the withdrawal of all US forces from its territory. Both Governments denied that a formal request had been issued. In the same month the Saudi authorities asked for the return of all Saudi citizens (reported to number more than 100 detainees), captured in Afghanistan while apparently fighting for the Taliban, who were imprisoned at Camp X-Ray, Guantánamo Bay (Cuba). This request was denied by the US authorities, but in June a delegation of officials of the Saudi Ministries of the Interior and of Foreign Affairs was reported to have been allowed access to the Saudi prisoners.

Relations between Saudi Arabia and the USA were placed under renewed strain in August 2002 after a group representing 900 relatives of victims of the September 2001 attacks filed a civil suit in Washington, DC, against senior Saudi ministers and institutions (and the Government of Sudan) seeking compensation amounting to US $1,000,000m. for their alleged funding of al-Qa'ida activities. Saudi investors reacted angrily to the suit, threatening in response to withdraw from the USA some $750,000m. in Saudi investments. In late 2002 Saudi Arabia was criticized by the USA for ignoring the funding of alleged terrorist organizations by Saudi nationals, and in November US media reports claimed that a charitable donation from the Saudi royal family had assisted two hijackers responsible for the suicide attacks on the USA. The allegations were strenuously denied by the Saudi authorities, and the US Administration was swift to defend the role Saudi Arabia had played in President George W. Bush's 'war on terror'. Nevertheless, in the same month a senior US presidential spokesman asserted that Saudi Arabia could take further action to fight terrorism, and it emerged that US authorities were investigating the affairs of a number of wealthy Saudis in connection with alleged sponsorship of Islamist extremists, including al-Qa'ida. Saudi Arabia countered that it was being unfairly maligned, reiterating that it had begun auditing all charitable organizations operating in the country and that it had frozen three bank accounts allegedly linked to radical Islamist groups. Also in November the Saudi authorities, hitherto reluctant to admit to an al-Qa'ida presence in the country, conceded that some 100 Saudis had been detained under suspicion of involvement with the organization and that a further 700 people had been questioned. The Minister of the Interior, Prince Nayef ibn Abd al-Aziz as-Sa'ud, subsequently confirmed that 90 suspects were referred for trial in February 2003, while 250 people remained under investigation in that month; he added that some 150 Saudis had been released after investigations proved they had no links with al-Qa'ida.

Despite the tensions between Saudi Arabia and the USA, in September 2002, following intense pressure from the USA and the United Kingdom, the Saudi Minister of Foreign Affairs indicated that Saudi Arabia might be prepared to approve the use of military bases in Saudi Arabia for a future US-led attack on the regime of Saddam Hussain in Iraq. However, he emphasized that Saudi co-operation would only be forthcoming if the Iraqi authorities continued to reject UN resolutions demanding the unconditional return of weapons inspectors to Iraq and if such a military undertaking was to be conducted under UN auspices. In late December it was reported that the USA would be allowed to use Saudi airbases. It was later established that the highly equipped Prince Sultan airbase would be made available to the US military, and, although combat aircraft would not be allowed to fly offensive missions from the base with the primary aim of bombing Iraqi targets, aircraft launched from Iraqi soil would be permitted to open fire or release bombs in self-defence. In January 2003 Saudi Arabia attempted to secure support for a plan to persuade Saddam Hussain to relinquish power and go into exile in order to avert a US-led war to oust his regime. In the following month, however, as conflict appeared increasingly inevitable, the Saudi authorities deployed warships, troops and military helicopters to Kuwait, in order to strengthen the emirate's defences. In late April, after most of the USA's principal military objectives in Iraq had been achieved, it was announced that all but 400 of the 5,000 US military personnel in the country were to be withdrawn from Saudi Arabia by the end of August. Those troops that remained were to assist in training the Saudi armed forces.

On 12 May 2003 suicide bomb attacks on three expatriate residential compounds in Riyadh killed 34 people. The Minister of Foreign Affairs indicated that 19 people, including 17 Saudis, were believed to have been responsible for the attacks. The bombings, widely held to be the work of al-Qa'ida, provoked further US criticism of Saudi security measures, and led to the withdrawal of most of the US diplomats stationed in the kingdom. It emerged after the attacks that the Saudi authorities had made an unsuccessful attempt to apprehend the perpetrators in the week prior to 12 May. In response to the bombings, and to the US reaction, the Saudi leadership acknowledged more openly than before that the threat presented by al-Qa'ida was indeed serious and pledged to take effective action against the terrorist network, including those fundamentalist Islamic figures suspected of converting Saudis to al-Qa'ida's cause. In August the Crown Prince announced that the kingdom was engaged in a 'decisive battle' against terrorism, and throughout mid-2003 security forces intensified their campaign against militants, in particular against those linked to the 12 May suicide bombings.

In total, between 12 May 2003 and late October, at least 600 suspected militant Islamists were arrested, 70–90 of whom were charged, and more than 2,000 people were interrogated. In addition, in June some 1,000 Muslim clergy were suspended and ordered to undergo retraining aimed at eliminating Islamist militancy from the profession. Despite these measures, the terrorist violence reached new levels of intensity from late 2003. On 8 November al-Qa'ida apparently struck again when 17 people were killed and more than 120 people were injured in a suicide attack on a housing complex, mostly populated by Arab expatriates, in Riyadh. It remained unclear as to why the housing complex had been targeted, although bin Laden's organization was blamed for the attack. At a human rights conference held in Riyadh in October, delegates from the US, German and British embassies had warned that their intelligence agencies had received evidence of a planned terrorist attack on Riyadh's two main skyscrapers; Western governments issued further warnings against non-essential travel to Riyadh later in the same month. In December the Government stated that, according to DNA evidence, two Saudi nationals, both of whom had been pursued by the authorities on security charges, had carried out the 8 November suicide bombing.

On 21 April 2004 a car bomb exploded near one of the headquarters of Riyadh's security services, killing five people and wounding up to 150. A militant Islamist group called the al-Haramain Brigades (alleged to have links to al-Qa'ida) claimed responsibility for the attack, which was regarded as the first direct assault on the Saudi regime. On 1 May gunmen in the Red Sea port of Yanbu killed at least one Saudi and five Western petroleum industry workers. Later in the same month, on 29 May, an attack by a minimum of four militants against a compound housing oil workers at al-Khobar resulted in the deaths of three Saudis and 19 expatriate workers. The compound was eventually surrounded by Saudi police, which resulted in a 25-hour siege. Despite an attempt by security forces to storm the compound, three of the attackers managed to escape. It was alleged that the militants had struck a deal with police-officers sympathetic to al-Qa'ida, an accusation that was angrily denied by the Saudi ambassador to the United Kingdom, Prince Turki al-Faisal. It was reported on 2 June that two of those responsible for the atrocity had been killed by Saudi forces near Mecca. One of the men was believed to be Abd ar-Rahman Muhammad Yazji, one of the kingdom's most wanted militants. On 23 June, during a public address broadcast on Saudi television, the Crown Prince announced that a dozen named individuals with alleged ties to al-Qa'ida would not face the death penalty should they surrender to the security forces within one month. The Saudi authorities were particularly keen to obtain the surrender of Saleh Muhammad al-Oufi, regarded as the overall leader of al-Qa'ida in the kingdom following the death of Abd al-Aziz al-Muqrin in a police raid in June. It was, however, reported on 1 November that al-Qa'ida had appointed Saud bin Hamoud al-Otaibi as the new leader of its Saudi network; some commentators presumed that this confirmed suspicions that al-Oufi had been killed by security forces in July. In December seven expatriates and five Saudis died when gunmen attacked the US consulate in Jeddah. Significant militant activity and regular reprisals from security forces continued into early 2006, including an attempted suicide bombing on 24 February at the strategically important Abqaiq oil facility, which produces some 4% of the kingdom's petroleum output. Four suspected al-Qa'ida operatives were killed in government reprisals three days later. Meanwhile, in February 2005 the Government launched a national awareness campaign to mobilize people against militant activity.

Although relations remained cool, Saudi Arabia was keen to improve its ties with the USA. On 28 July 2004, during a visit to Jeddah by Secretary of State Powell, Crown Prince Abdullah raised the possibility of Saudi Arabia taking a leading role in the formation of a Muslim security force for Iraq. Meanwhile, Saudi Arabia and Iraq announced that their embassies in Baghdad and Riyadh, respectively, would be reopened for the first time since 1990. The move attracted predictable criticism from Islamist groups. In mid-2004 the deteriorating domestic security situation reportedly led some US companies to scale back their operations in the kingdom. The December attack by militants on the US consulate in Jeddah led to a further decline in bilateral relations. In September 2005 a US envoy to Saudi Arabia, having commended the Saudi Government for its counter-terrorism actions, again strongly criticized the protection of human rights in the kingdom. King Abdullah visited China in January 2006 and signed an agreement to co-operate in the petroleum and natural gas sectors. With the deterioration in Saudi–US relations, the kingdom was keen to diversify its international trade and China, as the world's second largest petroleum consumer, was an ideal candidate for partnership. In February, following the victory of the Islamic Resistance Movement (Hamas) in the Palestinian legislative elections of the previous month, the Saudi Government incurred further US displeasure when it refused to support a US-led plan to deny regional aid to the new Hamas-led administration.

Meanwhile, at a summit meeting of the Arab League Council in March 2003, Libya was strongly critical of Saudi Arabia for hosting US forces on its territory. Relations deteriorated further when, in late July 2004, allegations were made in the Saudi-owned pan-Arab daily al-Sharq al-Aswat concerning a Libyan plot to assassinate Crown Prince Abdullah. On 22 December Saudi Arabia recalled its ambassador to Tripoli over the alleged conspiracy and expelled the Libyan ambassador, Dr Muhammad Sa'id al-Qashshat, to Riyadh from the kingdom. However, the Libyan embassy in Riyadh and the Saudi embassy in Tripoli remained open during the dispute, and relations were normalized in late 2005. Al-Qashshat duly resumed his position as ambassador in the Saudi capital in January 2006.

In February 2002 Crown Prince Abdullah put forward a proposal, based on the 1981 'Fahd Plan', to end the escalating conflict between Israel and the Palestinians based on the principle of 'land-for-peace'. In return for a collective Arab recognition of the State of Israel, the plan insisted on Israel's complete withdrawal from Arab territories occupied since 1967. The Crown Prince also urged the US Administration to exert pressure on Israel to withdraw its forces from the West Bank. The Saudi peace initiative was unanimously endorsed at a summit conference of the Arab League Council held in late March 2002 in Beirut (see the Recent History of Lebanon), but was categorically rejected by Israel. During a summit meeting with US President George W. Bush in Crawford, Texas, in late April, Crown Prince Abdullah reiterated his call for the USA to restrain Israel's actions against the Palestinians. In 2006 Saudi Arabia's accession to the World Trade Organization (WTO, see p. 370) was expected to lead to a reconsideration of the kingdom's boycott of trade with Israel (in line with the Arab League).

In 2005 relations deteriorated between Saudi Arabia and three of its Gulf neighbours: Bahrain, Oman and the UAE. Bahrain and Oman had signed free-trade agreements with the USA in September 2004 and October 2005, respectively, and in April 2006 the UAE was involved in negotiations with a view to signing a similar accord. Saudi Arabia, which argued that the GCC should negotiate a trade deal as a single body, claimed that the agreements contravened the GCC's external tariff treaty. In December relations with the UAE were further strained by a border dispute relating to the Shaybah oilfield in the Rub al-Khali desert region.

In January 2006 Saudi Arabia recalled its ambassador to Denmark in protest at a series of cartoons regarded as extremely offensive to Muslims that were published in a Danish newspaper in late 2005. In addition, a recently established Saudi newspaper, ash-Shams, had its licence to operate revoked in February 2006, after it reprinted some of the controversial cartoons.

Government

Saudi Arabia is an absolute monarchy, with no legislature or political parties. Constitutionally, the King rules in accordance with the Shari'a, the sacred law of Islam. He appoints and leads a Council of Ministers, which serves as the instrument of royal authority in both legislative and executive matters. Decisions of the Council are reached by majority vote, but require royal sanction. A Consultative Council (Majlis ash-Shoura) was officially inaugurated in December 1993. Members of the Majlis are chosen by the King. The membership of the Majlis was increased from 60 to 90 in July 1997, at the beginning of the council's second four-year term, to 120 in May 2001 and to 150 in April 2005.

The organs of local government are the General Municipal Councils and the tribal and village councils. A General Municipal Council is established in the towns of Mecca, Medina and Jeddah. Its members are proposed by the inhabitants and must be approved by the King. Functioning concurrently with each General Municipal Council is a General Administration Committee, which investigates ways and means of executing resolutions passed by the Council. Every village and tribe has a council composed of the sheikh, who presides, his legal advisers and two other prominent personages. These councils have power to enforce regulations. A system of provincial government was announced in late 1993 by royal decree: this defined the nature of government for 13 newly created regions, as well as the rights and responsibilities of their governors, and appointed councils of prominent citizens for each region to monitor development and advise the government. Each council was to meet four times a year under the chairmanship of a governor, who would be an emir with ministerial rank. A royal decree, issued in April 1994, further divided the 13 regions into 103 governorates. In October 2003 it was announced that new municipal councils, of which one-half of the membership would be elected by universal suffrage and one-half appointed by the central Government, would be introduced. Municipal elections took place in early 2005.

Defence

In August 2005 the active armed forces totalled an estimated 124,500 men: army 75,000, air force 18,000, navy 15,500 (including 3,000 marines); air defence forces 16,000. There were also paramilitary forces totalling more than 15,500 men, which included a frontier force of 10,500 and a 4,500-strong coastguard. There was a National Guard with 75,000 active personnel and 25,000 tribal levies. The GCC's Peninsula Shield Force, based in Saudi Arabia, comprised some 9,000 troops. Military service is voluntary. The allocation for defence and security in the budget for 2005 was SR 95,146m., equivalent to an estimated 34.0% of total expenditure for that year.

Economic Affairs

In 2004, according to estimates by the World Bank, Saudi Arabia's gross national income (GNI), measured at average 2002–04 prices, was US $242,180m., equivalent to $10,430 per head (or $14,010 per head on an international purchasing-power parity basis). During 1995–2004, it was estimated, the population increased by an average annual rate of 2.7%, while gross domestic product (GDP) per head increased, in real terms, by an average of 0.2% per year. Overall GDP increased, in real terms, at an average annual rate of 2.9% in 1995–2004; real GDP increased by 7.7% in 2003 and by 5.2% in 2004.

Agriculture (including forestry and fishing) contributed an estimated 3.9% of GDP in 2004, and employed 4.7% of the economically active population in 2002. The principal crop is wheat; from the late 1980s a large wheat surplus was exported. Barley, dates, tomatoes, watermelons and potatoes are also significant crops. Saudi Arabia is self-sufficient in many dairy products, and in eggs and broiler chickens. Agricultural GDP increased by an average of 1.8% per year in 1998–2004; the sector's real GDP increased by 1.8% in 2004.

Industry (including mining, manufacturing, construction and power) employed 21.0% of the active labour force in 2002, and provided an estimated 58.4% of GDP in 2004. During 1998–2004, it was estimated, industrial GDP increased at an average annual rate of 2.5%; the sector expanded by 6.2% in 2004.

Mining and quarrying engaged only 1.6% of the employed population in 2002, but contributed an estimated 41.9% of GDP in 2004. The sector is dominated by petroleum and natural gas, which provided an estimated 41.6% of GDP in that year. Saudi Arabia remained the largest petroleum producer in the world in 2004, and mineral products provided an estimated 88.0% of total export revenue in the same year. At the end of 2004 Saudi Arabia's proven recoverable reserves of petroleum were 262,700m. barrels, sufficient to maintain production at 2004 levels for almost 68 years, and equivalent to 22.1% of the world's proven oil reserves. Crude petroleum production averaged 10.58m. barrels per day (b/d) in 2004; the kingdom has a production capacity of some 11m. b/d. With effect from July 2005, Saudi Arabia's production quota within the Organization of the Petroleum Exporting Countries (OPEC, see p. 344) was 9,099,000 b/d. Gas reserves, mostly associated with petroleum, totalled 6,750,000m. cu m at the end of 2004. In October 2002 the world's largest natural gas plant was opened at Hawiya; the plant, which was the first Saudi project to produce gas not associated with petroleum, was expected to increase the country's production of gas by more than 30%. Further non-associated gas reserves are yet to be fully exploited. Other minerals produced include limestone, gypsum, marble, clay and salt, while there are substantial deposits of phosphates, bauxite, gold and other metals. The GDP of the mining sector increased at an average annual rate of 1.2% in 1998–2004; the rate of growth was 5.8% in 2004.

Manufacturing contributed an estimated 10.0% of GDP in 2004, and provided 7.6% of employment in 2002. The most important activity is the refining of petroleum. The production of petrochemicals, fertilizers, construction materials (particularly steel and cement), and food- and drink-processing are also important activities. Manufacturing GDP increased by an estimated average of 5.2% per year in 1998–2004; the GDP of the sector increased by 7.1% in 2004.

Electrical energy is generated by thermal power stations, using Saudi Arabia's own petroleum resources, although an increasing amount of electricity is now produced in association with sea-water desalination. Electricity expansion projects were planned in the early part of the 21st century to satisfy increased demand.

The services sector contributed an estimated 37.7% of GDP in 2004, and engaged 74.4% of the employed labour force in 2002. The GDP of the services sector increased by an estimated average of 4.7% per year in 1998–2004; the rate of growth was 5.5% in 2004.

In 2004 Saudi Arabia recorded a visible trade surplus of US $85,222m., and a surplus of $51,488m. on the current account of the balance of payments. In 2004 the principal source of imports (15.3%) was the USA; other important suppliers were Japan, Germany, the People's Republic of China and the United Kingdom. The USA was also the principal market for exports (17.2%) in 2004; other major markets were Japan, the Republic of Korea, India, China and Singapore. In 2004 the dominant exports were mineral products, chemicals products and plastic products. The principal imports in the same year were electrical machines, equipment and tools, transport equipment and spare parts, base metals and metal products, and chemical products.

A budgetary deficit of SR 30,000m. was forecast for 2004; however, revised figures indicated a surplus of SR 107,091m. A balanced budget was forecast for 2005. Consumer prices decreased by an annual average of 0.4% in 1998–2004; however, they increased by 0.3% in 2004. Unemployment was estimated to stand at around 20% of Saudi nationals in 2005; the rate was higher among Saudi women. In 2001 non-Saudi nationals comprised 52.1% of the labour force, although the *Middle East Economic Digest* indicated that the total was 65.4% in 2002. The Government approved legislation in 2005 to reduce the number of foreign workers to 20% of the population by 2015; the new law was also to provide maternity-leave rights and childcare facilities, in order to boost female participation in the work-force.

In addition to its membership of OPEC, Saudi Arabia is a member of the Islamic Development Bank (see p. 303), and the Organization of Arab Petroleum Exporting Countries (OAPEC, see p. 338). Saudi Arabia is the major aid donor in the region, disbursing loans to developing countries through the Arab Fund for Economic and Social Development (AFESD, see p. 161), the Arab Bank for Economic Development in Africa (BADEA, see p. 307) and other organizations. The kingdom acceded to the World Trade Organization (WTO, see p. 370) in December 2005. Saudi Arabia is also a member of the Co-operation Council for the Arab States of the Gulf (GCC, see p. 205), which created a unified regional customs tariff in January 2003, and has undertaken to establish a single market and currency no later than January 2010. The economic convergence criteria for the monetary union were agreed at a GCC summit in Abu Dhabi, the UAE, in December 2005.

Saudi Arabia's prosperity is based on exploitation of its petroleum reserves. Although the country remained the world's largest oil producer at the beginning of the 21st century, and continued to play a crucial role in determining OPEC production levels and thus world prices, the decline in the price of petroleum in the early 1990s caused the Government to seek alternative sources of revenue. The 2000–05 economic plan aimed to increase private investment and growth in the private and non-oil sectors, and envisaged the expansion of employment opportunities for the rapidly expanding Saudi population. The Manpower Development Fund, partly financed by more expensive expatriate work permits and visas, was launched in April 2002 to subsidize skills training for Saudi nationals and to promote the 'Saudiization' of the work-force. The anticipated involvement of international companies in Saudi hydrocarbons and utilities industries was expected to contribute to private-sector growth. As part of a process of structural and administrative reform, two new policy-making bodies, the Supreme Economic Council and the Supreme Petroleum and Minerals Council, have been established (the latter accompanied by the creation of the Saudi Electricity Company), and, as part of the deregulation process, two independent supervisory authorities for the electricity and telecommunications sectors were created in 2001. A successful public offering of 20% of the Saudi Telecommunications Company in January 2002 preceded the liberalization of the telecommunications sector in 2004, when a consortium led by Etisalat, of the UAE, was awarded the kingdom's second GSM licence. Tenders for the third such licence were scheduled to be issued in 2006. It was announced in October 2003 that local and international airports (excluding security operations) were also to be privatized; in preparation for this, the Presidency of Civil Aviation was to be restructured as the General Aviation Authority. In addition, plans to deregulate the water sector and to introduce elements of competition into the reorganized electricity industry were in progress in 2006. Tourism, regarded as hugely underdeveloped in the kingdom, was another sector that the authorities sought to stimulate. To this end, a Supreme Commission for Tourism was established in 2001 with the primary aim of increasing the number of visitors to the kingdom to 21m. by 2020. Plans for the construction of the new King Abdullah Economic City, situated on the west coast between Jeddah and Rabigh, were also in progress in 2006. The project was projected to cost US $27,000m. and was intended to provide improved facilities for the financial sector, in particular. Saudi Arabia failed to achieve a planned balanced budget for 2001 because of the sharp fall in world petroleum prices following the September attacks on the USA and the resulting fears of a global recession. Despite the introduction of strict spending limits for the 2002 and 2003 budgets, further deficits were planned in 2002–04. As petroleum prices rallied, however, the planned deficit of SR 39,000m. in 2003

SAUDI ARABIA

was turned into a surplus of SR 36,000m., and, following impressive economic growth of 5.2%, the planned deficit of SR 30,000m. in 2004 was converted into a surplus of SR 107,091m. A balanced budget was announced for 2005, but, despite an increase in expenditure of some 22%, much of which was earmarked for development projects, this too was estimated to have been transformed into a very healthy surplus of SR 214,000m. (Economic growth, meanwhile, was estimated at about 6.5% for that year.) The 2006 budget, announced in December 2005, forecast a further 19.6% increase in expenditure, but, owing to an apparently more realistic forecast of future petroleum prices, revenue was projected to increase by 39%, leading to an estimated surplus of SR 55,000m. Due to sustained high oil prices and continued expansion in many of the non-petroleum sectors, the IMF predicted that strong growth (of some 6.2%) would continue in 2006.

Education

Elementary, secondary and higher education are available free of charge, but education is not compulsory. Primary education begins at six years of age and lasts for six years. From the age of 12 there are three years of intermediate education, followed by three years of secondary schooling. According to UNESCO estimates, primary enrolment included 54% of children in the relevant age-group (boys 55%; girls 54%) in 2002/03. In the same year enrolment at the secondary level was equivalent to 53% of children (boys 54%; girls 52%). The proportion of females enrolled in Saudi Arabian schools increased from 25% of the total number of pupils in 1970 to 47.7% in 2004. In 2004 573,736 students were enrolled in higher education. Tertiary institutions in that year included 108 university colleges and 87 colleges exclusively for women. Construction of the first private university, King Faisaliyah University, in partnership with a US technology institute, was under way in 2006. Education was reportedly allocated 24.5% of total expenditure in the 2006 budget, equivalent to SR 87,300m.

Public Holidays

2006: 7–15 January*† (Id al-Adha, Feast of the Sacrifice), 23 September (National Day), 18–28 October* (Id al-Fitr, end of Ramadan), 28 December 2006–05 January 2007*† (Id al-Adha, Feast of the Sacrifice).

2007: 23 September (National Day), 8–18 October* (Id al-Fitr, end of Ramadan), 17–25 December* (Id al-Adha, Feast of the Sacrifice).

* These holidays are dependent on the Islamic lunar calendar and may vary by one or two days from the dates given.

† This festival occurs twice (in the Islamic years AH 1426 and 1427) within the same Gregorian year.

Weights and Measures

The metric system is in force.

Statistical Survey

Sources (unless otherwise indicated): Central Department of Statistics, Ministry of Economy and Planning, POB 358, University St, Riyadh 11182; tel. (1) 401-3333; fax (1) 401-9300; e-mail info@cds.gov.sa; internet www.planning.gov.sa/statistic/sindexe.htm; Saudi Arabian Monetary Agency, *Annual Report* and *Statistical Summary*.

Area and Population

AREA, POPULATION AND DENSITY

Area (sq km)	2,240,000*
Population (census results)	
9–14 September 1974	7,012,642
27 September 1992†	
Males	9,479,973
Females	7,468,415
Total	16,948,388
Population (official estimates at mid-year)	
2002	22,043,861
2003	22,670,014
2004	22,673,538‡
Density (per sq km) at mid-2004	10.1

* 864,869 sq miles.

† Of the total population at the 1992 census, 12,310,053 (males 6,215,793, females 6,094,260) were nationals of Saudi Arabia, while 4,638,335 (males 3,264,180, females 1,374,155) were foreign nationals.

‡ Comprising an estimated 16,529,302 Saudi nationals and 6,144,236 foreign nationals.

SAUDI ARABIA-IRAQ NEUTRAL ZONE: The Najdi (Saudi Arabian) frontier with Iraq was defined in the Treaty of Mohammara in May 1922. Later a Neutral Zone of 7,044 sq km was established adjacent to the western tip of the Kuwait frontier. No military or permanent buildings were to be erected in the zone and the nomads of both countries were to have unimpeded access to its pastures and wells. A further agreement concerning the administration of this zone was signed between Iraq and Saudi Arabia in May 1938. In July 1975 Iraq and Saudi Arabia signed an agreement providing for an equal division of the diamond-shaped zone between the two countries, with the border following a straight line through the zone.

SAUDI ARABIA-KUWAIT NEUTRAL ZONE: A Convention signed at Uqair in December 1922 fixed the Najdi (Saudi Arabian) boundary with Kuwait. The Convention also established a Neutral Zone of 5,770 sq km immediately to the south of Kuwait in which Saudi Arabia and Kuwait held equal rights. The final agreement on this matter was signed in 1963. Since 1966 the Neutral Zone, or Partitioned Zone as it is sometimes known, has been divided between the two countries and each administers its own half, in practice as an integral part of the State. However, the petroleum deposits in the Zone remain undivided and production from the onshore oil concessions in the Zone is shared equally between the two states' concessionaires.

ADMINISTRATIVE REGIONS
(population at mid-2000)

Riyadh	4,730,330	Ha'il	519,984
Makkah	5,448,773	Northern Borders	249,544
Al-Madinah	1,378,870	Jazan	1,083,022
Qassim	979,858	Najran	385,588
Eastern	3,008,913	Al-Baha	476,382
Aseer	1,637,464	Al-Jouf	354,450
Tabouk	593,706		

PRINCIPAL TOWNS
(population at 1992 census)

Riyadh (royal capital)	2,776,096	Khamis-Mushait	217,870
Jeddah (administrative capital)	2,046,251	Ha'il (Hayil)	176,757
Makkah (Mecca)	965,697	Al-Kharj	152,071
Al-Madinah (Medina)	608,295	Al-Khubar	141,683
Dammam	482,321	Jubail	140,828
At-Ta'if	416,121	Hafar al-Batin	137,793
Tabouk	292,555	Yanbu	119,819
Buraidah	248,636	Abha	112,316
Hufuf	225,847	Ar Ar	108,055
Al-Mobarraz	219,123	Al-Qatif	98,920

Mid-2003: (UN estimates, incl. suburbs) Jeddah 3,556,556; Mecca 1,446,419; Riyadh 5,125,753 (Source: UN, *World Urbanization Prospects: The 2003 Revision*).

BIRTHS AND DEATHS
(UN estimates, annual averages)

	1990–95	1995–2000	2000–05
Birth rate (per 1,000)	34.6	31.2	28.5
Death rate (per 1,000)	4.6	4.1	3.9

Source: UN, *World Population Prospects: The 2004 Revision*.

Expectation of life (WHO estimates, years at birth): 71 (males 68; females 74) in 2003 (Source: WHO, *World Health Report*).

SAUDI ARABIA

EMPLOYMENT
('000 persons aged 15 years and over)

	2000	2001	2002
Agriculture, hunting and forestry	341.5	340.2	263.4
Fishing	7.9	9.1	12.2
Mining and quarrying	101.9	87.9	95.4
Manufacturing	440.7	467.8	448.3
Electricity, gas and water	76.0	77.3	65.6
Construction	515.9	585.3	629.6
Wholesale and retail trade	901.5	837.2	861.7
Restaurants and hotels	164.6	154.6	170.3
Transport and communications	242.3	247.9	265.3
Financial intermediation	42.5	58.5	49.8
Real estate, renting and business activities	139.5	144.3	143.2
Public administration and defence	1,116.2	1,157.5	1,212.9
Education	713.0	720.1	751.5
Health and social work	217.6	278.1	224.0
Other community and personal services	133.0	101.9	115.4
Private households with employed persons	551.0	521.4	595.9
Extra-territorial organizations	5.3	6.8	8.4
Activities not adequately defined	3.0	12.5	—
Total employed	5,713.3	5,808.6	5,913.0
Males	4,943.5	5,027.7	5,115.8
Females	769.8	780.9	797.2
Unemployed	273.6	281.2	328.6
Males	194.3	202.6	225.0
Females	79.3	78.6	103.7
Total labour force	5,986.9	6,089.8	6,239.6
Males	5,137.8	5,230.3	5,340.8
Females	849.1	859.5	900.8

Source: ILO.

Health and Welfare

KEY INDICATORS

Total fertility rate (children per woman, 2003)	4.5
Under-5 mortality rate (per 1,000 live births, 2004)	27
Physicians (per 1,000 head, 2001)	1.40
Hospital beds (per 1,000 head, 1997)	2.3
Health expenditure (2002): US $ per head (PPP)	534
Health expenditure (2002): % of GDP	4.3
Health expenditure (2002): public (% of total)	77.1
Access to water (% of persons, 2000)	95
Access to sanitation (% of persons, 2000)	100
Human Development Index (2003): ranking	77
Human Development Index (2003): value	0.772

For sources and definitions, see explanatory note on p. vi.

Agriculture

PRINCIPAL CROPS
('000 metric tons)

	2002	2003	2004
Wheat	2,436	2,524	2,358
Barley	138	138	138
Maize	30	36	44
Millet	9	9	8
Sorghum	240	242	244
Potatoes	315	318	321
Pulses*	8	8	8
Tomatoes	409	424	440
Pumpkins, squash and gourds	99	101	103
Cucumbers and gherkins	176	180	183
Aubergines (Eggplants)	76	74	73

—continued	2002	2003	2004
Dry onions	86	92	97
Carrots	59	63	67
Okra	46	48	46*
Other vegetables	378	400*	400*
Watermelons	272	283	295
Cantaloupes and other melons	221	233	246
Citrus fruit	140	151	140*
Grapes	93	97	102
Dates	830	884	901
Other fruit	179	180*	180*

* FAO estimate(s).

Source: FAO.

LIVESTOCK
('000 head, year ending September)

	2002	2003	2004
Asses	100	100*	100*
Camels	253	260*	260*
Cattle	322	332*	342*
Sheep	7,010	7,000*	7,000*
Goats	2,214	2,200*	2,200*
Poultry*	130,000	135,000	137,000

* FAO estimate(s).

Source: FAO.

LIVESTOCK PRODUCTS
('000 metric tons)

	2002	2003	2004
Beef and veal*	21.9	22.3	22.8
Mutton and lamb†	75.6	76.0	76.0
Goat meat	22.3*	22.5†	22.5†
Poultry meat	467.0	468.0	480.7
Camel meat†	40.0	40.0	41.3
Cows' milk	826.0	830.0†	900.0†
Sheep's milk†	82.0	82.5	82.5
Goats' milk†	76.5	76.5	76.5
Camels' milk†	89.5	90.0	90.0
Hen eggs	138.4	137.4	140.0
Wool: greasy†	10.6	10.8	10.8
Cattle hides (fresh)†	3.1	3.1	3.1
Sheepskins (fresh)†	32.0	32.0	32.0
Goatskins (fresh)†	3.9	3.9	3.9

* Unofficial figure.
† FAO estimate(s).

Source: FAO.

Fishing

(metric tons, live weight)

	2001	2002	2003
Capture	49,167	55,330	52,929
Groupers and seabasses	5,273	6,838	5,233
Snappers and jobfishes	2,092	1,988	1,802
Emperors (Scavengers)	7,448	8,902	8,803
Porgies and seabreams	2,646	3,252	3,869
Spinefeet (Rabbitfishes)	1,822	1,998	2,018
Narrow-barred Spanish mackerel	5,532	6,399	4,800
Carangids	5,943	6,287	3,997
Indian mackerel	1,803	1,921	3,279
Penaeus shrimps	4,761	3,996	6,474
Aquaculture	8,218	6,744	11,824
Nile tilapia	3,918	1,854	2,400
Indian white prawn	4,150	4,650	9,160
Total catch	57,385	62,074	64,753

Source: FAO.

SAUDI ARABIA

Mining

(estimates, '000 metric tons, unless otherwise indicated)

	2002	2003	2004
Crude petroleum (million barrels)*	2,589	3,000	3,151
Natural gas (million cu metres)*†	57,314	60,060	68,000
Silver (kilograms)‡	14,000	13,000	6,000
Gold (kilograms)‡	4,192	8,769	9,000
Salt (unrefined)	220	220	230
Gypsum (crude)	350	350	350
Pozzolan	150	160	160

* Including 50% of the total output of the Neutral or Partitioned Zone, shared with Kuwait.
† On a dry basis.
‡ Figures refer to the metal content of concentrate and bullion.

Source: US Geological Survey.

Industry

SELECTED PRODUCTS
(including 50% of the total output of the Neutral Zone; estimates, '000 barrels, unless otherwise indicated)

	2002	2003	2004
Phosphatic fertilizers ('000 metric tons)*	150	150	295
Nitrogenous fertilizers†	1,241	1,247	1,242
Motor spirit (petrol) and naphtha	153,000	171,720	185,000
Jet fuel and kerosene	59,702	65,550	70,000
Gas-diesel (distillate fuel) oils	193,000	215,590	225,000
Residual fuel oils	158,000	169,380	190,000
Petroleum bitumen (asphalt)	9,180	10,240	10,000
Liquefied petroleum gas	10,340	10,150	12,000
Cement ('000 metric tons)	22,000	23,000	23,200
Crude steel ('000 metric tons)	3,570	3,944	3,902
Electric energy (million kWh)	128,629	142,000	145,469

* Production in terms of phosphoric acid.
† Production in terms of nitrogen.

Source: mainly US Geological Survey.

Finance

CURRENCY AND EXCHANGE RATES

Monetary Units
100 halalah = 20 qurush = 1 Saudi riyal (SR).

Sterling, Dollar and Euro Equivalents (30 December 2005)
£1 sterling = 6.449 riyals;
US $1 = 3.750 riyals;
€1 = 4.418 riyals;
100 Saudi riyals = £15.51 = $26.67 = €22.63.

Exchange Rate: Since June 1986 the official mid-point rate has been fixed at US $1 = 3.75 riyals.

BUDGET ESTIMATES
(million riyals)

Revenue	2003	2004	2005
Petroleum revenues	110,000	145,000	220,000
Other revenues	60,000	55,000	60,000
Total	170,000	200,000	280,000

Expenditure	2003	2004	2005
Human resource development	49,609	55,832	69,899
Transport and communications	5,634	6,352	8,629
Economic resource development	6,927	7,020	10,516
Health and social development	16,767	17,971	23,057
Infrastructure development	2,544	2,620	3,292
Municipal services	5,393	6,192	8,976
Defence and security	70,303	78,414	95,146
Public administration and other government spending	44,848	49,936	51,665
Government lending institutions*	375	387	502
Local subsidies	6,600	5,276	8,318
Total	209,000	230,000	280,000

* Including transfers to the Saudi Fund for Development (SFD).

2003 (revised figures, million riyals): Total revenue 293,000 (Petroleum revenue 231,000, Other revenue 62,000); Total expenditure 257,000.

2004 (revised figures, million riyals): Total revenue 392,291 (Petroleum revenue 330,000, Other revenue 62,291); Total expenditure 285,200.

INTERNATIONAL RESERVES
(US $ million in December)

	2002	2003	2004
Gold*	219	239	250
IMF special drawing rights	332	431	519
Reserve position in IMF	3,564	4,527	3,499
Foreign exchange	16,715	17,662	23,273
Total	20,830	22,859	27,541

* Valued at US $ 54 per troy ounce at 31 December 2004.

Source: IMF, *International Financial Statistics*.

MONEY SUPPLY
('000 million riyals in December)

	2002	2003	2004
Currency outside banks	52.33	55.44	60.13
Demand deposits at commercial banks	150.24	167.78	203.81
Total money	202.57	223.22	263.94

Source: IMF, *International Financial Statistics*.

COST OF LIVING
(Consumer Price Index for all cities; base: 1999 = 100)

	2002	2003	2004
Food and beverages	98.0	98.6	103.4
Housing, fuel and water	100.0	100.0	100.3
Textiles and clothing (incl. footwear)	92.3	91.8	89.6
House furnishing	96.8	96.2	94.5
Medical care	100.8	101.0	101.4
Transport and communications	96.4	94.8	94.2
Entertainment and education	99.3	98.7	98.1
All items (incl. others)	98.0	98.6	98.9

SAUDI ARABIA

NATIONAL ACCOUNTS
(million riyals at current prices)

Expenditure on the Gross Domestic Product
(figures rounded to nearest 10 million riyals)

	2002	2003	2004
Government final consumption expenditure	184,520	198,150	218,370
Private final consumption expenditure	260,400	269,980	282,450
Increase in stocks	11,040	11,370	14,860
Gross fixed capital formation	128,070	148,100	163,020
Total domestic expenditure	584,030	627,600	678,700
Exports of goods and services	291,160	371,090	494,700
Less Imports of goods and services	168,110	194,040	233,810
GDP in purchasers' values	707,070	804,650	939,590
GDP at constant 1999 prices	637,230	686,040	721,940

Source: IMF, *International Financial Statistics*.

Gross Domestic Product by Economic Activity

	2002	2003	2004*
Agriculture, forestry and fishing	36,101	36,454	37,187
Mining and quarrying:			
crude petroleum and natural gas	234,206	291,326	393,672
other	2,720	2,785	2,886
Manufacturing:			
petroleum refining	20,434	29,732	31,570
other	52,541	56,535	63,392
Electricity, gas and water	9,303	9,870	10,406
Construction	44,739	47,137	51,141
Trade, restaurants and hotels	51,735	53,856	58,132
Transport, storage and communications	31,934	33,224	35,667
Finance, insurance, real estate and business services:			
ownership of dwellings	44,989	45,979	47,950
other	37,082	39,863	43,268
Government services	124,486	139,929	144,952
Other community, social and personal services	24,124	25,114	26,478
Sub-total	714,394	811,804	946,701
Import duties	7,386	8,087	8,838
Less Imputed bank service charge	14,714	15,244	15,950
GDP in purchasers' values	707,067	804,648	939,591

* Preliminary figures.

BALANCE OF PAYMENTS
(US $ million)

	2002	2003	2004
Exports of goods f.o.b.	72,464	93,244	126,063
Imports of goods f.o.b.	−29,624	−33,868	−40,841
Trade balance	42,840	59,376	85,222
Exports of services	5,177	5,713	5,858
Imports of services	−19,980	−20,857	−25,677
Balance on goods and services	28,037	44,232	65,403
Other income received	3,714	2,977	3,863
Other income paid	−3,925	−4,277	−4,123
Balance on goods, services and income	27,827	42,931	65,143
Current transfers paid	−15,954	−14,883	−13,655
Current balance	11,873	28,048	51,488
Direct investment from abroad	−614	−587	−1,933
Portfolio investment assets	7,552	−18,738	−26,654
Other investment assets	−11,644	−6,333	−19,919
Other investment liabilities	−4,431	−783	1,516
Overall balance	2,736	1,608	4,498

Source: IMF, *International Financial Statistics*.

External Trade

PRINCIPAL COMMODITIES
(million riyals)

Imports c.i.f.	2002	2003	2004
Live animals and animal products	6,550	7,181	8,397
Vegetable products	6,908	7,723	8,266
Prepared foodstuffs, beverages, spirits, vinegar and tobacco	5,690	6,710	7,484
Chemical products	14,493	17,987	15,285
Textiles and textile articles	6,932	7,513	8,052
Base metals and articles of base metal	9,962	12,533	16,552
Electrical machines, equipment and tools	26,593	30,210	36,707
Transport equipment and spare parts	26,723	29,299	35,862
Total (incl. others)	121,088	138,435	166,398

Exports*	2002	2003	2004
Mineral products	239,973	308,993	415,696
Chemical products	19,421	23,211	31,128
Plastic products	5,717	7,011	12,455
Total (incl. others)	271,741	349,664	472,491

* Including re-exports (million riyals): 4,077 in 2002; 4,928 in 2003; 9,229 in 2004.
† Provisional and excl. petroleum exports.

PRINCIPAL TRADING PARTNERS
(million riyals)

Imports c.i.f.	2002	2003	2004
Australia	4,223	3,708	4,786
Belgium	2,089	2,309	2,226
Brazil	2,074	2,349	2,930
Canada	1,321	1,388	1,866
China	6,441	8,199	11,092
France	4,350	5,062	5,853
Germany	10,217	12,377	13,449
India	3,307	4,093	5,306
Indonesia	1,355	1,326	1,539
Italy	5,203	5,508	5,704
Japan	13,405	14,316	16,347
Korea, Republic	3,989	5,099	6,268
Malaysia	1,124	1,391	1,668
Netherlands	2,045	2,771	2,987
Spain	1,540	1,834	2,239
Sweden	1,490	2,099	2,789
Switzerland	2,012	2,675	3,168
Syria	2,020	1,510	1,526
Thailand	1,222	1,496	2,070
Turkey	1,471	2,095	2,245
United Arab Emirates	3,068	3,597	4,380
United Kingdom	7,240	8,120	9,477
USA	19,737	20,077	25,491
Total (incl. others)	121,088	138,435	166,938

Exports (incl. re-exports)	2002	2003	2004
Bahrain	6,577	8,105	11,507
China	10,820	15,367	22,787
France	7,738	n.a.	n.a.
Greece	3,382	n.a.	n.a.
India	14,742	20,804	27,625
Indonesia	4,088	5,917	6,871
Italy	6,746	8,865	12,553
Japan	38,974	49,325	67,006
Jordan	753	4,029	6,852
Korea, Republic	25,813	31,816	40,382
Netherlands	6,989	10,338	18,216
Pakistan	4,474	4,828	7,979

SAUDI ARABIA

Exports (incl. re-exports)—*continued*	2002	2003	2004
Philippines	3,694	n.a.	n.a.
Singapore	13,905	15,940	22,147
South Africa	5,370	7,331	8,876
Spain	5,539	n.a.	n.a.
Taiwan	7,674	12,279	15,396
Thailand	4,085	n.a.	n.a.
United Arab Emirates	6,460	9,812	12,230
United Kingdom	2,740	n.a.	n.a.
USA	53,511	65,385	81,360
Total (incl. others)	271,741	349,664	472,491

Transport

RAILWAYS (traffic)

	1999	2000	2001
Passenger journeys ('000)	770.4	853.8	790.4
Freight carried ('000 metric tons)	1,800	1,600	1,500

ROAD TRAFFIC (motor vehicles in use at 31 December)

	1989	1990	1991
Passenger cars	2,550,465	2,664,028	2,762,132
Buses and coaches	50,856	52,136	54,089
Goods vehicles	2,153,297	2,220,658	2,286,541
Total	4,754,618	4,936,822	5,103,205

1996 (estimates): Passenger cars 1,744,000; Buses and coaches 23,040; Goods vehicles 1,169,000; Total 2,935,000.

Source: IRF, *World Road Statistics*.

SHIPPING

Merchant Fleet (vessels registered at 31 December)

	2002	2003	2004
Oil tankers:			
vessels	29	28	30
displacement ('000 grt)	664	585	907
Others:			
vessels	251	257	262
displacement ('000 grt)	808	779	771
Total vessels	280	285	292
Total displacement ('000 grt)	1,472	1,364	1,678

Source: Lloyd's Register-Fairplay, *World Fleet Statistics*.

International Sea-borne Freight Traffic ('000 metric tons)*

	1988	1989	1990
Goods loaded	161,666	165,989	214,070
Goods unloaded	42,546	42,470	46,437

* Including Saudi Arabia's share of traffic in the Neutral or Partitioned Zone.

Source: UN, *Monthly Bulletin of Statistics*.

2001 ('000 metric tons, excluding crude oil): Goods loaded 68,894; Goods unloaded 31,668.

CIVIL AVIATION (traffic on scheduled services)

	1999	2000	2001
Kilometres flown (million)	128	133	126
Passengers carried ('000)	12,328	12,566	12,836
Passenger-kilometres (million)	19,618	20,229	20,217
Total ton-km (million)	2,738	2,836	2,633

Source: UN, *Statistical Yearbook*.

Tourism

Country of nationality	2001	2002	2003
Bahrain	235,415	252,697	281,875
Bangladesh	195,400	221,447	209,560
Egypt	957,764	1,015,078	787,277
India	313,131	373,636	362,609
Indonesia	371,962	418,704	396,709
Iran	309,687	376,774	618,897
Jordan	247,719	263,592	240,356
Kuwait	903,017	1,010,943	971,341
Pakistan	446,748	529,842	539,471
Qatar	342,155	363,345	388,239
Sudan	139,760	156,342	108,742
Syria	533,105	564,776	541,894
Turkey	159,593	175,988	177,467
United Arab Emirates	172,196	177,581	189,471
Yemen	184,036	255,054	212,292
Total (incl. others)	6,726,620	7,511,299	7,332,233

Tourism receipts (US $ million, incl. passenger transport): 3,418 in 2002.

Source: World Tourism Organization, *Yearbook of Tourism Statistics*.

PILGRIMS TO MECCA FROM ABROAD*

	2001/02	2002/03	2003/04
Total	1,354,184	1,431,012	1,419,706

* Figures relate to Islamic lunar years. The equivalent dates in the Gregorian calendar are: 25 March 2001 to 14 March 2002; 15 March 2002 to 4 March 2003; 5 March 2003 to 22 February 2004.

Communications Media

	2002	2003	2004
Telephones ('000 main lines in use)	3,317.5	3,502.6	3,695.1
Mobile cellular telephones ('000 subscribers)	5,008.0	7,238.2	9,175.8
Personal computers ('000 in use)	3,003	n.a.	8,476
Internet users ('000)	1,418.9	1,500.0	1,586.0

1995 (estimate): 150,000 facsimile machines in use.

1996: 13 daily newspapers; 185 non-daily newspapers.

1997: 6,250,000 radio receivers in use; Book titles published 3,780.

Sources: UNESCO, *Statistical Yearbook*; International Telecommunication Union.

Education

(2004)

	Institutions	Teachers	Students
Pre-primary*	893	7,703	85,484
Primary	12,994	206,036	2,389,310
Intermediate	6,852	101,103	1,058,314
Secondary (general)	3,970	74,721	874,981
Teacher training†	18	2,215	29,989
Technical and vocational	92	6,216	75,860
University colleges†	108	11,627	211,430

* Figures refer to 1996/97 (Source: UNESCO, *Statistical Yearbook*).
† 2003 figures.

Adult literacy rate (UNESCO estimates): 79.4% (males 87.1%; females 69.3%) in 2003 (Source: UNDP, *Human Development Report*).

Directory

The Constitution

The Basic Law of Government was introduced by royal decree in 1992.

Chapter 1 defines Saudi Arabia as a sovereign Arab, Islamic state. Article 1 defines God's Book and the Sunnah of his prophet as the constitution of Saudi Arabia. The official language is Arabic. The official holidays are Id al-Fitr and Id al-Adha. The calendar is the Hegira calendar.

Chapter 2 concerns the system of government, which is defined as a monarchy, hereditary in the male descendants of Abd al-Aziz ibn Abd ar-Rahman al-Faisal as-Sa'ud. It outlines the duties of the Heir Apparent. The principles of government are justice, consultation and equality in accordance with Islamic law (*Shari'a*).

Chapter 3 concerns the family. The State is to aspire to strengthen family ties and to maintain its Arab and Islamic values. Article 11 states that 'Saudi society will be based on the principle of adherence to God's command, on mutual co-operation in good deeds and piety and mutual support and inseparability'. Education aims to instil the Islamic faith.

Chapter 4 defines the economic principles of the State. All natural resources are the property of the State. The State protects public money and freedom of property. Taxation is only to be imposed on a just basis.

Chapter 5 concerns rights and duties. The State is to protect Islam and to implement the *Shari'a* law. The State protects human rights in accordance with the *Shari'a*. The State is to provide public services and security for all citizens. Punishment is to be in accordance with the *Shari'a*. The Royal Courts are open to all citizens.

Chapter 6 defines the authorities of the State as the judiciary, the executive and the regulatory authority. The judiciary is independent, and acts in accordance with *Shari'a* law. The King is head of the Council of Ministers and Commander-in-Chief of the Armed Forces. The Prime Minister and other ministers are appointed by the King. It provides for the establishment of a Consultative Council (Majlis ash-Shoura).

Chapter 7 concerns financial affairs. It provides for the annual presentation of a state budget. Corporate budgets are subject to the same provisions.

Chapter 8 concerns control bodies. Control bodies will be established to ensure good financial and administrative management of state assets.

Chapter 9 defines the general provisions pertaining to the application of the Basic Law of Government.

The Government

HEAD OF STATE

King: HM King ABDULLAH IBN ABD AL-AZIZ AS-SA'UD (acceded to the throne 1 August 2005).
Crown Prince: SULTAN IBN ABD AL-AZIZ AS-SA'UD.

COUNCIL OF MINISTERS
(April 2006)

Prime Minister and Commander of the National Guard: King ABDULLAH IBN ABD AL-AZIZ AS-SA'UD.
Deputy Prime Minister, Minister of Defence and Civil Aviation and Inspector General: Crown Prince SULTAN IBN ABD AL-AZIZ AS-SA'UD.
Minister of Municipal and Rural Affairs: Prince MUTAIB IBN ABD AL-AZIZ AS-SA'UD.
Minister of the Interior: Prince NAYEF IBN ABD AL-AZIZ AS-SA'UD.
Minister of Foreign Affairs: Prince SA'UD AL-FAISAL AS-SA'UD.
Minister of Petroleum and Mineral Resources: Eng. ALI IBN IBRAHIM AN-NUAIMI.
Minister of Labour: GHAZI AL-GOSAIBI.
Minister of Social Affairs: Dr ABD AL-MOHSEN IBN ABD AL-AZIZ AL-AKKAS.
Minister of Agriculture: Dr FAHD IBN ABD AR-RAHMAN IBN SULAIMAN BALGHUNAIM.
Minister of Water and Electricity: ABDULLAH AL-HUSSEIN.
Minister of Education: Dr ABDULLAH IBN SALIH IBN UBAYD.
Minister of Higher Education: Dr KHALID IBN MUHAMMAD AL-ANGARI.
Minister of Communications and Information Technology: MUHAMMAD IBN JABIL IBN AHMAD MULLA.
Minister of Finance: Dr IBRAHIM IBN ABD AL-AZIZ AL-ASSAF.
Minister of Economy and Planning: KHALED IBN MUHAMMAD AL-QUSAIBI.
Minister of Information and Culture: Dr IYAD IBN AMIN MADANI.
Minister of Commerce and Industry: Dr HASHEM IBN ABDULLAH YAMANI.
Minister of Justice: Dr ABDULLAH IBN MUHAMMAD IBN IBRAHIM ASH-SHEIKH.
Minister of Pilgrimage (Hajj) Affairs: FOUAD IBN ABD AS-SALAM IBN MUHAMMAD FARSI.
Minister of Awqaf (Religious Endowments), Dawa, Mosques and Guidance Affairs: SALEH IBN ABD AL-AZIZ MUHAMMAD IBN IBRAHIM ASH-SHEIKH.
Minister of Health: Dr HAMAD IBN ABDULLAH AL-MANE.
Minister of the Civil Service: MUHAMMAD IBN ALI AL-FAYEZ.
Minister of Transport: Dr JUBARAH IBN EID AS-SURAISERI.
Ministers of State: Dr MUTLIB IBN ABDULLAH AN-NAFISA, Dr MUSAID IBN MUHAMMAD AL-AYBAN, Dr ABD AL-AZIZ AL-ABDULLAH AL-KHUWAITER, Prince ABD AL-AZIZ IBN FAHD AS-SA'UD, ABDULLAH IBN AHMAD IBN YOUSUF ZAINAL, NIZAR MADANI.

MINISTRIES

Most ministries have regional offices in Jeddah.

Council of Ministers: Murabba, Riyadh 11121; tel. (1) 488-2444.
Ministry of Agriculture: Airport Rd, Riyadh 11195; tel. (1) 401-6666; fax (1) 404-4592; e-mail info@agrwat.gov.sa; internet www.agrwat.gov.sa.
Ministry of Awqaf (Religious Endowments) Dawa, Mosques and Guidance Affairs: Riyadh 11232; tel. (1) 473-0401; internet www.islam.org.sa.
Ministry of the Civil Service: POB 18367, Riyadh 11114; tel. (1) 402-6900; fax (1) 403-4998; internet www.mcs.gov.sa.
Ministry of Commerce and Industry: POB 1774, Airport Rd, Riyadh 11162; tel. (1) 401-2222; fax (1) 403-8421.
Ministry of Communications and Information Technology: Airport Rd, Riyadh 11178; tel. (1) 404-3000; fax (1) 403-1401.
Ministry of Defence and Civil Aviation: POB 26731, Airport Rd, Riyadh 11165; tel. (1) 476-9000; fax (1) 405-5500; internet www.pca.gov.sa.
Ministry of Economy and Planning: POB 358, University St, Riyadh 11182; tel. (1) 401-3333; fax (1) 404-9300; e-mail info@planning.gov.sa; internet www.planning.gov.sa.
Ministry of Education: POB 3734, Airport Rd, Riyadh 11481; tel. (1) 402-9500; fax (1) 404-1391; e-mail webmaster@moe.gov.sa; internet www.moe.gov.sa.
Ministry of Finance: Airport Rd, Riyadh 11177; tel. (1) 405-0000; fax (1) 401-0583; e-mail info@mof.gov.sa; internet www.mof.gov.sa.
Ministry of Foreign Affairs: POB 55937, Riyadh 11544; tel. (1) 405-5000; fax (1) 403-0645; internet www.mofa.gov.sa.
Ministry of Health: Airport Rd, Riyadh 11176; tel. (1) 401-5555; fax (1) 402-9876; internet www.moh.gov.sa.
Ministry of Higher Education: King Faisal Hospital St, Riyadh 11153; tel. (1) 441-9849; fax (1) 441-9004; internet www.mohe.gov.sa.
Ministry of Information and Culture: POB 570, Nasseriya St, Riyadh 11161; tel. (1) 406-8888; fax (1) 404-4192; internet www.saudinf.com.
Ministry of the Interior: POB 2933, Airport Rd, Riyadh 11134; tel. (1) 401-1111; fax (1) 403-1185.
Ministry of Justice: University St, Riyadh 11137; tel. (1) 405-7777.
Ministry of Labour: Omar bin al-Khatab St, Riyadh 11157; tel. (1) 477-8888; fax (1) 478-9175; internet www.mol.gov.sa.
Ministry of Municipal and Rural Affairs: Nasseriya St, Riyadh 11136; tel. (1) 441-8888; fax (1) 441-7368; internet www.momra.gov.sa.
Ministry of Petroleum and Mineral Resources: POB 247, King Abd al-Aziz Rd, Riyadh 11191; tel. (1) 478-1661; fax (1) 478-1980; internet www.mopm.gov.sa.
Ministry of Pilgrimage (Hajj) Affairs: Omar bin al-Khatab St, Riyadh 11183; tel. (1) 404-3003; fax (1) 402-2555.
Ministry of Social Affairs: Omar bin al-Khatab St, Riyadh 11157; tel. (1) 477-8888; fax (1) 478-9175.
Ministry of Transport: Riyadh.
Ministry of Water and Electricity: Riyadh.

SAUDI ARABIA

MAJLIS ASH-SHOURA
(Consultative Council)

In March 1992 King Fahd issued a decree to establish a Consultative Council of 60 members, whose powers include the right to summon and question ministers. The composition of the Council was announced by King Fahd in August 1993, and it was officially inaugurated in December of that year. Each member is to serve for four years. The Council's membership was increased to 90 when its second term began in July 1997; it was increased further, to 120, in May 2001, and to 150 in April 2005. King Fahd issued a decree extending the legislative powers of the Council in November 2003, including the right to propose new legislation.

Chairman: SALIH IBN HUMAYD.

Vice-Chairman: ABDULLAH IBN UMAR IBN MUHAMMAD IBN NASIF.

Secretary-General: SALIH MALIK.

Diplomatic Representation

EMBASSIES IN SAUDI ARABIA

Afghanistan: POB 93337, Riyadh 11673; tel. (1) 480-3459; fax (1) 480-3451; e-mail afgembriyad@hotmail.com; Ambassador KABIR FARAHI.

Algeria: POB 94388, Riyadh 11693; tel. (1) 488-7171; fax (1) 482-1703; Ambassador ABD AL-KARIM GHARIB.

Argentina: POB 94369, Riyadh 11693; tel. (1) 465-2600; fax (1) 465-3057; e-mail earab@nesma.net.sa; Ambassador ENRIQUE ANTONIO PAREJA.

Australia: POB 94400, Riyadh 11693; tel. (1) 488-7788; fax (1) 488-7973; internet www.saudiarabia.embassy.gov.au; Ambassador IAN BIGGS.

Austria: POB 94373, Riyadh 11693; tel. (1) 480-1217; fax (1) 480-1526; e-mail riyadh-ob@bmaa.gov.at; internet www.aussenministerium.at/riyadh; Ambassador Dr FRIEDRICH STIFT.

Azerbaijan: 59 Al-Worood Quarter St, off Amir Failsal bin Sa'ud Abd ar-Rahman, Aloroba Rd, Riyadh; tel. (1) 419-2382; fax (1) 419-2260; e-mail asim67@awalnet.net.sa; Ambassador ELMAN ARASLI.

Bahrain: POB 94371, Riyadh 11693; tel. (1) 488-0044; fax (1) 488-0208; Ambassador RASHID SAAD AD-DOSERI.

Bangladesh: POB 94395, Riyadh 11693; tel. (1) 419-6665; fax (1) 419-3555; e-mail bdootriyadh@zajil.net; Ambassador MUHAMMAD AKRAM UL-HAQ.

Belgium: POB 94396, Riyadh 11693; tel. (1) 488-2888; fax (1) 488-2033; e-mail ambelriyad@nesma.net.sa; Ambassador RUDI SCHELLINCK.

Bosnia and Herzegovina: POB 94301, Riyadh 11693; tel. (1) 456-7914; fax (1) 454-4360; e-mail baembsaruh@awalnet.net.sa; Ambassador RAZIM ČOLIĆ.

Brazil: POB 94348, Riyadh 11693; tel. (1) 488-0018; fax (1) 488-1073; e-mail arabras@shabakah.net.sa; Ambassador LUÍS SÉRGIO GAMA FIGUEIRA.

Brunei: POB 94314, al-Warood, Area 29, al-Fujairah St, Riyadh 11693; tel. (1) 456-0814; fax (1) 456-1594; e-mail brunei@shabakah.net.sa; Ambassador Pengiran Haji JABARUDDIN BIN Pengiran Haji MUHAMMAD SALLEH.

Burkina Faso: POB 94330, Riyadh 11693; tel. (1) 465-2244; fax (1) 465-3397; e-mail burkinafaso.ksa@arab.net.sa; Ambassador OUMAR DIAWARA.

Cameroon: POB 94336, Riyadh 11693; tel. (1) 488-0022; fax (1) 488-1463; e-mail ambacamriyad@ifrance.com; Ambassador MOHAMADOU LABARANG.

Canada: POB 94321, Riyadh 11693; tel. (1) 488-2288; fax (1) 488-1997; e-mail ryadh@dfait-maeci.gc.ca; Ambassador RODERICK BELL.

Chad: POB 94374, Riyadh 11693; tel. and fax (1) 465-7702; Ambassador al-Hajji DJIME TOUGOU.

China, People's Republic: POB 75231, Riyadh 11578; tel. (1) 482-4246; fax (1) 482-1123; e-mail chinaemb_sa@mfa.gov.cn; internet www.chinaembassy.org.sa; Ambassador WU CHUNHUA.

Côte d'Ivoire: POB 94303, Riyadh 11693; tel. (1) 482-5582; fax (1) 482-9629; e-mail ambciryd@digi.net.sa; Ambassador LANCINA DOSSO.

Denmark: POB 94398, Riyadh 11693; tel. (1) 488-0101; fax (1) 488-1366; e-mail ruhamb@um.dk; internet www.ambriyadh.um.dk; Ambassador HANS KLINGENBERG.

Djibouti: POB 94340, Riyadh 11693; tel. (1) 454-3182; fax (1) 456-9168; e-mail dya_bamakhrama@hotmail.com; Ambassador DYA-EDDINE SAID BAMAKHRAMA.

Egypt: POB 94333, Riyadh 11693; tel. (1) 481-0464; fax (1) 481-0463; Ambassador MUHAMMAD ABD AL-HAMID KASSEM.

Ethiopia: POB 94341, Riyadh 11693; tel. (1) 477-5285; fax (1) 476-8020; e-mail ethiopian@naseej.com.sa; Ambassador Ato MUHAMMAD ALI.

Finland: POB 94363, Riyadh 11693; tel. (1) 488-1515; fax (1) 488-2520; e-mail finemb@nesma.net.sa; Ambassador MARTTI ISOARO.

France: POB 94367, Riyadh 11693; tel. (1) 488-1255; fax (1) 488-2882; e-mail diplomatie@ambafrance.org.sa; internet www.ambafrance.org.sa; Ambassador CHARLES HENRI D'ARAGON.

Gabon: POB 94325, Riyadh 11693; tel. (1) 456-7173; fax (1) 470-0669; Ambassador NABIL KOUSSOU INAMA.

Gambia: POB 94322, Riyadh 11693; tel. (1) 205-2158; fax (1) 456-2024; e-mail gamextriyadh@yahoo.com; Ambassador LAMIN BAJO.

Germany: POB 94001, Riyadh 11693; tel. (1) 488-0700; fax (1) 488-0660; e-mail info@riad.diplo.de; internet www.riad.diplo.de; Ambassador Dr GERHARD ENVER SCHRÖMBGENS.

Ghana: POB 94339, Riyadh 11693; tel. (1) 454-5122; fax (1) 450-9819; e-mail ghanaemb@naseej.com; Ambassador ALHAJI RASHID BAWA.

Greece: POB 94375, Riyadh 11693; tel. (1) 480-1975; fax (1) 480-1969; e-mail gremb.ria@mfa.gr; Ambassador IOANNIS-THEODOROS ECONOMOU.

Guinea: POB 94326, Riyadh 11693; tel. (1) 488-1101; fax (1) 482-6757; Ambassador el-Hadj ABOUL KARIM DIOUBATÉ.

Hungary: POB 94014, al-Waha District, Ahmad Tonsy St 23, Riyadh 11693; tel. (1) 454-6707; fax (1) 456-0834; e-mail huemb.ryd@nournet.com.sa; Ambassador ISTVÁN TÖLLI.

India: POB 94387, Riyadh 11693; tel. (1) 488-4144; fax (1) 488-4189; e-mail com@indianembassy.org.sa; internet www.indianembassy.org.sa; Ambassador M. O. H. FAROUK.

Indonesia: POB 94343, Riyadh 11693; tel. (1) 488-2800; fax (1) 488-2966; e-mail contact@kbri-riyadh.org.sa; internet www.kbri-riyadh.org.sa; Ambassador Dr ISMAIL SUNY.

Iran: POB 94394, Riyadh 11693; tel. (1) 488-1916; fax (1) 488-1890; Ambassador HOSSEIN SADEQI.

Ireland: POB 94349, Riyadh 11693; tel. (1) 488-2300; fax (1) 488-0927; e-mail irishembassy@awalnet.net.sa; Ambassador TOM RUSSELL.

Italy: POB 94389, Riyadh 11693; tel. (1) 488-1212; fax (1) 488-1951; e-mail segreteria1.riad@esteri.it; internet www.ambriad.esteri.it; Ambassador EUGENIO D'AURIA.

Japan: POB 4095, Riyadh 11491; tel. (1) 488-1100; fax (1) 488-0189; e-mail cultural@jpn-emb-sa.com; internet www.ksa.emb-japan.go.jp; Ambassador YASUO SAITO.

Jordan: POB 94316, Riyadh 11693; tel. (1) 488-0051; fax (1) 488-0072; e-mail jordan.embassy@nesma.net.sa; Ambassador HANI KHALIFAH.

Kazakhstan: POB 94012, Riyadh 11693; tel. (1) 470-1839; fax (1) 454-7781; e-mail office@kazembgulf.net; Ambassador ASKAR MUSINOV.

Kenya: POB 94358, Riyadh 11693; tel. (1) 488-1238; fax (1) 488-2629; Ambassador YUSUF ABDULRAHMEN NZIBO.

Korea, Republic: POB 94399, Riyadh 11693; tel. (1) 488-2211; fax (1) 488-1317; Ambassador KANG GWANG-WON.

Kuwait: POB 94304, Riyadh 11693; tel. (1) 488-3401; fax (1) 488-3682; Ambassador ABD AR-RAHMAN AHMAD AL-BAKR.

Lebanon: POB 94350, Riyadh 11693; tel. (1) 488-4060; fax (1) 480-4703; Ambassador AHMAD CHAMMAT.

Libya: POB 94365, Riyadh 11693; tel. (1) 454-4511; fax (1) 456-7513; Ambassador MUHAMMAD SA'ID AL-QASHSHAT.

Malaysia: POB 94335, Riyadh 11693; tel. (1) 488-7100; fax (1) 482-4177; e-mail mwriyadh@awalnet.net.sa; Ambassador Datuk ISMA'IL IBRAHIM.

Mali: POB 94331, Riyadh 11693; tel. (1) 464-5640; fax (1) 419-5016; Ambassador MOHAMED MAHMOUD OULD BOUYA.

Malta: POB 94361, Riyadh 11693; tel. (1) 463-2345; fax (1) 463-3993; e-mail maltaembassy.riyadh@gov.mt; Ambassador GODWIN MONTANARO.

Mauritania: POB 94354, Riyadh 11693; tel. (1) 464-6749; fax (1) 465-8355; Ambassador MUHAMMAD WALAD MUHAMMAD FAL.

Mexico: POB 94391, Riyadh 11693; tel. (1) 480-8822; fax (1) 480-8833; e-mail embasaudita@sre.gob.mx; Ambassador RAÚL LÓPEZ LIRA NAVA.

Morocco: POB 94392, Riyadh 11693; tel. (1) 481-1858; fax (1) 482-7016; e-mail moembassy@hotmail.com; Ambassador ABD AL-KRIM SEMMAR.

Nepal: POB 94384, Riyadh 11693; tel. (1) 461-1108; fax (1) 464-0690; e-mail info@rneksa.org; internet www.rneksa.org; Ambassador ABU ALLAITH TAKWARI.

SAUDI ARABIA

Netherlands: POB 94307, Riyadh 11693; tel. (1) 488-0011; fax (1) 488-0544; e-mail riy@minbuza.nl; internet www.holland.org.sa; Ambassador NICHOLAS BEETS.
New Zealand: POB 94397, Riyadh 11693; tel. (1) 488-7988; fax (1) 488-7912; e-mail nzembassy@awalnet.net.sa; Ambassador JAMES HOWELL.
Niger: POB 94334, Riyadh 11693; tel. and fax (1) 464-2931.
Nigeria: POB 94386, Riyadh 11693; tel. (1) 482-3024; fax (1) 482-4134; e-mail nigeria@sbm.net.sa; internet www.nigeriariyadh.com; Ambassador IBRAHIM MUSA KAZAURE.
Norway: POB 94380, Riyadh 11693; tel. (1) 488-1904; fax (1) 488-0854; e-mail emb.riyadh@mfa.no; internet www.al-norwige.org.sa; Ambassador SVEIN ANDREASSEN.
Oman: POB 94381, Riyadh 11693; tel. (1) 482-3120; fax (1) 482-3738; Ambassador HAMAD H. AL-MO'AMARY.
Pakistan: POB 94007, Riyadh 11693; tel. (1) 488-7272; fax (1) 488-7953; Ambassador Adm. (retd) ADUL AZIZ MIRZA.
Philippines: POB 94366, Riyadh 11693; tel. (1) 488-0835; fax (1) 488-3945; Ambassador BAHNAREM GENOMLA.
Portugal: POB 94328, Riyadh 11693; tel. (1) 462-2115; fax (1) 462-2105; e-mail portriade@nesma.net.sa; Ambassador Dr HENRIQUE M. V. DE SILVEIRA BORGES.
Qatar: POB 94353, Riyadh 11461; tel. (1) 482-5544; fax (1) 482-5394; Ambassador ALI ABDULLAH AL-MAHMOUD.
Russia: POB 94308, Riyadh 11693; tel. (1) 481-1875; fax (1) 481-1890; Ambassador IGOR A. MELIKHOV.
Rwanda: POB 94383, Riyadh 11693; tel. (1) 454-0808; fax (1) 456-1769; Ambassador SIMON INSONERE.
Senegal: POB 94352, Riyadh 11693; tel. (1) 488-0146; fax (1) 488-3804; Ambassador MODOU DIA.
Sierra Leone: POB 94329, Riyadh 11693; tel. (1) 464-3982; fax (1) 464-3662; e-mail slembrdh@zajil.net; Ambassador Alhaji AMADU DEEN TEJAN-SIE.
Singapore: POB 94378, Riyadh 11693; tel. (1) 480-3855; fax (1) 483-0632; e-mail ang_chay_chuan@mfa.gov.sg; internet www.mfa.gov.sg/riyadh; Chargé d'affaires a.i. ANG CHAY CHUAN.
Somalia: POB 94372, Riyadh 11693; tel. (1) 464-3456; fax (1) 464-9705; Ambassador ABD AR-RAHMAN A. HUSSEIN.
South Africa: POB 94006, Riyadh 11693; tel. (1) 456-2982; fax (1) 454-3727; e-mail info@southafrica.com.sa; internet www.southafrica.com.sa; Ambassador ABD AL-HAMID KHUBAIR.
Spain: POB 94347, Riyadh 11693; tel. (1) 488-0606; fax (1) 488-0420; e-mail embespsa@mail.mae.es; Ambassador MANUEL ALBERT FERNANDEZ KABAD.
Sri Lanka: POB 94360, Riyadh 11693; tel. (1) 460-8689; fax (1) 460-8846; e-mail lankaemb@shabakah.net.sa; Ambassador ADAM JAAFAR SADIQ.
Sudan: POB 94337, Riyadh 11693; tel. (1) 488-7979; fax (1) 488-7729; Ambassador Dr MUHAMMAD AMIN ABDULLAH AL-KARB.
Sweden: POB 94382, Riyadh 11693; tel. (1) 488-3100; fax (1) 488-0604; e-mail ambassaden.riyadh@foreign.ministry.se; internet www.swedemb.org.sa; Ambassador AKE KARLSSON.
Switzerland: POB 94311, Riyadh 11693; tel. (1) 488-1291; fax (1) 488-0632; e-mail vertretung@rya.rep.admin.ch; Ambassador DOMINIK M. ALDER.
Syria: POB 94323, Riyadh 11693; tel. (1) 482-6191; fax (1) 482-6196; Ambassador MUHAMMAD KHALID AT-TALL.
Tanzania: POB 94320, Riyadh 11693; tel. (1) 454-2839; fax (1) 454-9660; e-mail tzriyad@deltasa.com; Ambassador Prof. A. A. SHAREEF.
Thailand: POB 94359, Riyadh 11693; tel. (1) 488-1174; fax (1) 488-1179; e-mail thaiemry@awalnet.net.sa; internet www.thaiembassy.org/riyadh; Chargé d'affaires a.i. SUVAT CHIRAPANT.
Tunisia: POB 94368, Riyadh 11693; tel. (1) 488-7900; fax (1) 488-7641; Ambassador KACEM BOUSNINA.
Turkey: POB 94390, Riyadh 11693; tel. (1) 482-0101; fax (1) 488-7823; e-mail turkishembassy@sps.net.sa; Ambassador UGUR DOGAN.
Uganda: POB 94344, Riyadh 11693; tel. (1) 454-4910; fax (1) 454-9264; e-mail ugariyadh@hotmail.com; Ambassador IBRAHIM MUKAIBI.
United Arab Emirates: POB 94385, Riyadh 11693; tel. (1) 482-9652; fax (1) 482-7504; Ambassador ISSA K. AL-HURAIMIL.
United Kingdom: POB 94351, Riyadh 11693; tel. (1) 488-0077; fax (1) 488-2373; e-mail information.riyadh@fco.gov.uk; internet www.britishembassy.gov.uk/saudiarabia; Ambassador Sir SHERARD COWPER-COLES.
USA: POB 94309, Riyadh 11693; tel. (1) 488-3800; fax (1) 488-7360; e-mail usisriyadh@yahoo.com; internet riyadh.usembassy.gov; Ambassador JAMES C. OBERWETTER.
Uruguay: POB 94346, Riyadh 11693; tel. (1) 462-0739; fax (1) 462-0648; e-mail ururia@nesma.net.sa; Ambassador CARLOS A. CLULOW.
Uzbekistan: POB 94008, Riyadh 11693; tel. (1) 263-5223; Ambassador ISROILOV ULUGBEK ABDUKAYUMOVICH.
Venezuela: POB 94364, Riyadh 11693; tel. (1) 476-7867; fax (1) 476-8200; e-mail embvenar@embvenar.org.sa; Ambassador RAMON HERRERA NAVARRO.
Yemen: POB 94356, Riyadh 11693; tel. (1) 488-1769; fax (1) 488-1562; Ambassador MUHAMMAD ALI MOHSEN AL-AHWAL.

Judicial System

Judges are independent and governed by the rules of Islamic *Shari'a*. The following courts operate:

Supreme Council of Justice: consists of 11 members and supervises work of the courts; reviews legal questions referred to it by the Minister of Justice and expresses opinions on judicial questions; reviews sentences of death, cutting and stoning; Chair. Sheikh SALIH BIN MUHAMMAD AL-LUHAIDAN.
Court of Cassation: consists of Chief Justice and an adequate number of judges; includes department for penal suits, department for personal status and department for other suits.
General (Public) Courts: consist of one or more judges; sentences are issued by a single judge, with the exception of death, stoning and cutting, which require the decision of three judges.
Summary Courts: consist of one or more judges; sentences are issued by a single judge.
Specialized Courts: Article 26 of the judicial system stipulates that the setting up of specialized courts is permissible by Royal Decree on a proposal from the Supreme Council of Justice.

Religion

ISLAM

Arabia is the centre of the Islamic faith, and Saudi Arabia includes the holy cities of Mecca and Medina. Except in the Eastern Province, where a large number of people follow Shi'a rites, the majority of the population are Sunni Muslims, and most of the indigenous inhabitants belong to the strictly orthodox Wahhabi sect. The Wahhabis originated in the 18th century but first became unified and influential under Abd al-Aziz (Ibn Sa'ud), who became the first King of Saudi Arabia. They are now the keepers of the holy places and control the pilgrimage to Mecca. In 1986 King Fahd adopted the title of Custodian of the Two Holy Mosques; the title passed to King Abdullah upon his accession to the throne in August 2005. The country's most senior Islamic authority is the Council of Ulema.

Mecca: Birthplace of the Prophet Muhammad, seat of the Grand Mosque and Shrine of Ka'ba, visited by 1,419,706 Muslims in the Islamic year 1424 (2003/04).
Medina: Burial place of Muhammad, second sacred city of Islam.

Grand Mufti and Chairman of Council of Ulema: Sheikh ABD AL-AZIZ IBN ABDULLAH ASH-SHEIKH.

CHRISTIANITY

The Roman Catholic Church

A small number of adherents, mainly expatriates, form part of the Apostolic Vicariate of Arabia. The Vicar Apostolic is resident in the United Arab Emirates.

The Anglican Communion

Within the Episcopal Church in Jerusalem and the Middle East, Saudi Arabia forms part of the diocese of Cyprus and the Gulf. The Anglican congregations in the country are entirely expatriate. The Bishop in Cyprus and the Gulf is resident in Cyprus, while the Archdeacon in the Gulf is resident in Qatar.

Other Denominations

The Greek Orthodox Church is also represented.

The Press

Since 1964 most newspapers and periodicals have been published by press organizations, administered by boards of directors with full autonomous powers, in accordance with the provisions of the Press Law. These organizations, which took over from small private firms,

SAUDI ARABIA

are privately owned by groups of individuals experienced in newspaper publishing and administration (see Publishers).

There are also a number of popular periodicals published by the Government and by the Saudi Arabian Oil Co, and distributed free of charge. The press is subject to no legal restriction affecting freedom of expression or the coverage of news.

DAILIES

Arab News: POB 10452, Jeddah 21433; tel. (2) 639-1888; fax (2) 639-3223; e-mail arabnews@arabnews.com; internet www.arabnews.com; f. 1975; English; publ. by Saudi Research and Marketing Co; Editor-in-Chief KHALED AL-MAEENA; circ. 110,000.

Al-Bilad (The Country): POB 6340, Jeddah 21442; tel. (2) 672-3000; fax (2) 671-2545; f. 1934; Arabic; publ. by Al-Bilad Publishing Organization; Editor-in-Chief QUINAN AL-GHOMDI; circ. 66,210.

Al-Jazirah (The Peninsula): POB 354, Riyadh 11411; tel. (1) 487-0000; fax (1) 487-1201; e-mail chief@al-jazirah.com; internet www.al-jazirah.com; Arabic; Gen. Man. ABD AR-RAHMAN BIN FAHD AR-RASHAD; Editor-in-Chief KHALID IBN HAMAD AL-MALIK; circ. 94,000.

Al-Madina al-Munawara (Medina—The Enlightened City): POB 807, Makkah Rd, Jeddah 21421; tel. (2) 671-2100; fax (2) 671-1877; f. 1937; Arabic; publ. by Al-Madina Press Establishment; Chief Editor USAMA AS-SIBA'IE; circ. 46,370.

An-Nadwah (The Council): Jarwal Sheikh Sayed Halabi Bldg, POB 5803, Mecca; tel. (2) 520-0111; fax (2) 520-3055; f. 1958; Arabic; publ. by Mecca Printing and Information Establishment; Editor Dr ABD AR-RAHMAN AL-HARTHI; circ. 35,000.

Okaz: POB 1508, Seaport Rd, Jeddah 21441; tel. (2) 672-2630; fax (2) 672-4297; e-mail 104127.266@compuserve.com; f. 1960; Arabic; Editor-in-Chief HASHIM ABDU HASHIM; circ. 107,614.

Ar-Riyadh: POB 2943, Riyadh 11476; tel. (1) 442-0000; fax (1) 441-7417; internet www.alriyadh.com.sa; f. 1965; Arabic; publ. by Al-Yamama Publishing Establishment; Editor TURKI A. AS-SUDARI; circ. 150,000 (Sat.–Thurs.), 90,000 (Fri.).

Riyadh Daily NP: POB 2943, Riyadh 11476; tel. (1) 441-7544; fax (1) 441-7116; English; publ. by Yamama Publishing Establishment; Editor-in-Chief TALA'T WARFA.

Saudi Gazette: POB 5576, Jeddah 21432; tel. (2) 676-0000; fax (2) 672-7621; e-mail news@saudigazette.com.sa; internet www.saudigazette.com.sa; f. 1976; English; publ. by Okaz Organization for Press and Publication; Editor-in-Chief Dr AHMAD AL-YOUSUF; circ. 60,000.

Al-Watan: POB 15156, Airport Road, Abha; tel. (7) 227-3333; fax (7) 227-3590; internet www.alwatan.com.sa; f. 1998; publ. by Assir Establishment for Press and Publishing; Asst Man. Dir Dr MAMDOUH A. BA-OWAIDAN; Editor (vacant).

Al-Yaum (Today): POB 565, Dammam 31421; tel. (3) 858-0800; fax (3) 858-8777; e-mail admin@alyaum.com; internet www.alyaum.com; f. 1965; Editor-in-Chief MUHAMMAD AL-WAEEL; circ. 80,000.

WEEKLIES

Al-Muslimoon (The Muslims): POB 13195, Jeddah 21493; tel. (2) 669-1888; fax (2) 669-5549; f. 1985; Arabic; cultural and religious affairs; publ. by Saudi Research and Marketing Co; Editor-in-Chief Dr ABDULLAH AR-RIFA'E; circ. 68,665.

Saudi Arabia Business Week: POB 2894, Riyadh; English; trade and commerce.

Saudi Economic Survey: POB 1989, Jeddah 21441; tel. (2) 651-4952; fax (2) 652-2680; e-mail info@saudieconomicsurvey.com; internet www.saudieconomicsurvey.com; f. 1967; English; review of Saudi Arabian economic and business activity; Publr S. A. ASHOOR; Gen. Man. WALID S. ASHOOR; circ. 6,000.

Sayidati (My Lady): POB 4556, Madina Rd, Jeddah 21412; tel. (2) 639-1888; fax (2) 669-5549; Arabic; women's magazine; publ. by Saudi Research and Marketing Co; Editor-in-Chief MATAR AL-AHMADI.

Ash-Shams (The Sun): Riyadh; f. 2005; tabloid format; sports, culture, entertainment; publishing licence revoked by the Govt in Feb. 2006.

Al-Yamama: POB 851, Riyadh 11421; tel. (1) 442-0000; fax (1) 441-7114; f. 1952; literary magazine; Editor-in-Chief ABDULLAH AL-JAHLAN; circ. 35,000.

OTHER PERIODICALS

Ahlan Wasahlan (Welcome): POB 8013, Jeddah 21482; tel. (2) 686-2349; fax (2) 686-2006; monthly; flight journal of Saudi Arabian Airlines; Gen. Man. and Editor-in-Chief YARUB A. BALKHAIR; circ. 150,000.

Al-Faysal: POB 3, Riyadh 11411; tel. (1) 465-3027; fax (1) 464-7851; monthly; f. 1976; Arabic; culture, education, health, interviews; Man. Editor ABDULLAH Y. AL-KOWAILEET.

Al-Manhal (The Spring): POB 2925, Jeddah; tel. (2) 643-2124; fax (2) 642-8853; f. 1937; monthly; Arabic; cultural, literary, political and scientific; Editor NABIH ABD AL-QUDOUS ANSARI.

Majallat al-Iqtisad wal-Idara (Journal of Economics and Administration): King Abd al-Aziz University, POB 9031, Jeddah 21413; twice a year; Chief Editor Prof. ABD AL-AZIZ A. DIYAB.

The MWL Journal: Press and Publications Department, Rabitat al-Alam al-Islami, POB 537, Mecca; fax (2) 544-1622; monthly; English; Dir MURAD SULAIMAN IRQISOUS.

Ar-Rabita: POB 537, Mecca; tel. (2) 560-0919; fax (2) 543-1488; e-mail info@themwl.org; internet www.themwl.org; Arabic; Chief Editor Dr OSMAN ABUZAID.

Saudi Review: POB 4288, Jeddah 21491; tel. (2) 651-7442; fax (2) 653-0693; f. 1966; English; monthly; newsletter from Saudi newspapers and broadcasting service; publ. by International Communications Co; Chief Editor SAAD AL-MABROUK; circ. 5,000.

Ash-Sharkiah-Elle (Oriental Elle): POB 6, Riyadh; monthly; Arabic; women's magazine; Editor SAMIRA M. KHASHAGGI.

As-Soqoor (Falcons): POB 2973, Riyadh 11461; tel. (1) 476-6566; f. 1978; 2 a year; air-force journal; cultural activities; Editor HAMAD A. AS-SALEH.

At-Tadhamon al-Islami (Islamic Solidarity): Ministry of Pilgrimage (*Hajj*) Affairs, Omar bin al-Khatab St, Riyadh 11183; monthly; Editor Dr MUSTAFA ABD AL-WAHID.

At-Tijarah (Commerce): POB 1264, Jeddah 21431; tel. (2) 651-5111; fax (2) 651-7373; e-mail jcci@mail.gcc.com.bh; f. 1960; monthly; publ. by Jeddah Chamber of Commerce and Industry; Chair. Sheikh ISMAIL ABU DAUD; circ. 8,000.

NEWS AGENCIES

International Islamic News Agency (IINA): POB 5054, Jeddah 21422; tel. (2) 665-2056; fax (2) 665-9358; e-mail iina@islamicnews.org.sa; internet www.islamicnews.org.sa; f. 1972; operates under OIC auspices; Dir-Gen. ABD AL-WAHAB KASHIF.

Islamic Republic News Agency (IRNA) (Iran): Riyadh; f. 2001; Dir-Gen. ABDOLLAH NASIRI.

Saudi Press Agency (SPA): c/o Ministry of Information and Culture, POB 570, Nasseriya St, Riyadh 11161; tel. (1) 462-3333; fax (1) 462-6747; e-mail wass@spa.gov.sa; internet www.spa.gov.sa; f. 1970; the Government planned to transform the SPA into a public corpn; Dir-Gen. BADI KUIAYYEM.

Publishers

Assir Establishment for Press and Publishing: POB 15156, Abha; tel. (7) 227-3333; fax (7) 227-3590; f. 1998; publishes *Al-Watan*; cap. 200m.; Chair. and Acting Dir-Gen. FAHD AL-HARITHI.

Al-Bilad Publishing Organization: POB 6340, As-Sahafa St, Jeddah 21442; tel. (2) 672-3000; fax (2) 671-2545; publishes *Al-Bilad* and *Iqra'a*; Dir-Gen. AMIN ABDULLAH AL-QARQOURI.

Dar ash-Shareff for Publishing and Distribution: POB 58287, Riyadh 11594; tel. (1) 403-4931; fax (1) 405-2234; f. 1992; fiction, religion, science and social sciences; Pres. IBRAHIM AL-HAZEMI.

Dar al-Yaum Press, Printing and Publishing Ltd: POB 565, Dammam 31421; tel. (3) 858-0800; fax (3) 858-8777; e-mail salhumaidan@alyaum.com; f. 1964; publishes *Al-Yaum*.

International Publications Agency (IPA): POB 70, Dhahran 31942; tel. (3) 895-4925; fax (3) 895-4925; publishes material of local interest; Man. SAID SALAH.

Al-Jazirah Corpn for Press, Printing and Publishing: POB 354, Riyadh 11411; tel. (1) 441-9999; fax (1) 441-2536; e-mail marketing@al-jazirah.com; f. 1964; 42 mems; publishes *Al-Jazirah* and *Al-Masaeyah* (both dailies); Dir-Gen. SALAH AL-AJROUSH; Editor-in-Chief KHALID EL-MALEK.

Al-Madina Press Establishment: POB 807, Jeddah 21421; tel. (2) 671-2100; fax (2) 671-1877; f. 1937; publishes *Al-Madina al-Munawara*; Gen. Man. AHMAD SALAH JAMJOUM.

Makkah Printing and Information Establishment: POB 5803, Jarwal Sheikh Sayed Halabi Bldg, Mecca; tel. (2) 542-7868; publishes *An-Nadwah* daily newspaper.

Okaz Organization for Press and Publication: POB 1508, Jeddah 21441; tel. (2) 672-2630; fax (2) 672-8150; publishes *Okaz*, *Saudi Gazette* and *Child*.

Saudi Publishing and Distributing House: Umm Aslam District, nr Muslaq, POB 2043, Jeddah 21451; tel. (2) 629-4278; fax (2) 629-4290; e-mail info@spdh-sa.com; internet www.spdh-sa.com; f. 1966; publishers, importers and distributors of English and Arabic books; Chair. MUHAMMAD SALAHUDDIN.

SAUDI ARABIA

Saudi Research and Publishing Co: POB 4556, Jeddah 21412; tel. (2) 669-1888; fax (2) 669-5549; e-mail arabnews@arabnews.com; internet www.arabnews.com; publishes 17 titles incl. *Arab News, Asharq al-Awsat, Al-Majalla, Al-Muslimoon* and *Sayidati*; Chair. Prince AHMAD IBN SALMAN.

Yamama Publishing Establishment: POB 2943, Riyadh 11476; tel. (1) 442-0000; fax (1) 441-7116; publishes *Ar-Riyadh* and *Al-Yamama*; Dir-Gen. SAKHAL MAIDAN.

Broadcasting and Communications

TELECOMMUNICATIONS

Saudi Communications Commission (SCC): Riyadh; f. 2001; ind. regulatory authority; Gov. MUHAMMAD JAMIL MULLA.

Ettihad Etisalat: Al-Malaka Trade Centre 23088, Riyadh 11321; tel. (1) 211-8015; fax (1) 211-8029; e-mail admin@nic.ae; internet www.etisalat.co.ae; f. 2004; owned by a consortium led by Emirates Telecommunications Corpn (United Arab Emirates); awarded the second licence to provide mobile phone services in 2004; operates under the brand name Mobily (launched 2005); CEO KHALID AL-KAF.

Saudi Telecommunications Co—Saudi Telecom (STC): Riyadh; internet www.stc.com.sa; f. 1998; provides telecommunications services in Saudi Arabia; partially privatized in 2002; cap. 12,000m. riyals; Chair. ABD AL-AZIZ BIN RASHID BIN IBRAHIM AR-RASHID; Pres. Eng. SA'UD BIN MAJID AD-DOWAISH.

BROADCASTING

Radio

Saudi Arabian Broadcasting Service: c/o Ministry of Information and Culture, POB 60059, Riyadh 11545; tel. (1) 401-4440; fax (1) 403-8177; 24 medium- and short-wave stations, including Jeddah, Riyadh, Dammam and Abha, broadcast programmes in Arabic and English; 23 FM stations; overseas service in Bengali, English, Farsi, French, Hausa, Indonesian, Somali, Swahili, Turkestani, Turkish and Urdu; Dir-Gen. MUHAMMAD AL-MANSOOR.

Saudi Aramco FM Radio: Bldg 3030 LIP, Dhahran 31311; tel. (3) 876-1845; fax (3) 876-1608; f. 1948; English; private; for employees of Saudi Aramco; Man. ESSAM Z. TAWFIQ.

Television

Saudi Arabian Government Television Service: POB 7971, Riyadh 11472; tel. (1) 401-4440; fax (1) 404-4192; began transmission 1965; 112 stations, incl. six main stations at Riyadh, Jeddah, Medina, Dammam, Qassim and Abha, transmit programmes in Arabic and English; Dir-Gen. ABD AL-AZIZ AL-HASSAN (Channel 1).

Saudi Arabian Government Television Service Channel 2: POB 7959, Riyadh 11472; tel. (1) 442-8400; fax (1) 403-3826; began transmission 1983; Dir-Gen. ABD AL-AZIZ S. ABU ANNAJA.

Finance

(cap. = capital; res = reserves; dep. = deposits; m. = million; brs = branches; amounts in Saudi riyals unless otherwise stated)

BANKING

At the end of February 2006 the Saudi Arabian banking system consisted of: the Saudi Arabian Monetary Agency, as central note-issuing and regulatory body; 14 commercial banks (three national and eleven foreign banks); and five specialist banks. There is a policy of 'Saudiization' of the foreign banks.

Central Bank

Saudi Arabian Monetary Agency (SAMA): POB 2992, Riyadh 11169; tel. (1) 463-3000; fax (1) 466-2963; e-mail info@sama.ksa.org; internet www.sama.gov.sa; f. 1952; functions include stabilization of currency, administration of monetary reserves, regulation of banking and issue of notes and coins; res 1,417.4m., dep. 74,887.5m., total assets 163,179.6m. (June 2003); Gov. Sheikh HAMAD SA'UD AS-SAYARI; 10 brs.

National Banks

National Commercial Bank (NCB): POB 3555, King Abd al-Aziz St, Jeddah 21481; tel. (2) 649-3333; fax (2) 644-6468; e-mail contact@alahli.com; internet www.alahli.com; f. 1950; 69.3% government-owned; cap. 6,000m., res 4,331.7m., dep. 102,754.4m. (Dec. 2003); Chair. and Man. Dir Sheikh ABDULLAH SALIM BAHAMDAN; Gen. Man. ABD AL- KAREEM ABU AN-NASIR; 258 brs.

Ar-Rajhi Bank: POB 28, Al-Akariya Bldg, Oleya St, Riyadh 11411; tel. (1) 460-1000; fax (1) 460-0922; e-mail contactus@alrajhibank.com.sa; internet www.alrajhibank.com.sa; f. 1988; operates according to Islamic financial principles; cap. 2,250.0m., res 3,650.0m., dep. 49,907.7m. (Dec. 2003); Chair. and Man. Dir Sheikh SULAYMAN BIN ABD AL-AZIZ AR-RAJHI; Gen. Man. ABDULLAH SULAIMAN AR-RAJHI; 379 brs.

Riyad Bank Ltd: POB 22601, King Abd al-Aziz St, Riyadh 11416; tel. (1) 401-3030; fax (1) 404-2707; internet www.riyadbank.com.sa; f. 1957; cap. 4,000m., res 4,090.6m., dep. 59,793.7m. (Dec. 2003); Chair. RASHED A. AR-RASHED; Pres. and CEO TALAL I. AL-QUDAIBI; 180 brs.

Specialist Bank

Arab Investment Co SAA (TAIC): POB 4009, King Abd al-Aziz St, Riyadh 11491; tel. (1) 476-0601; fax (1) 476-0514; e-mail taic@taic.com; internet www.taic.com; f. 1974 by 17 Arab countries for investment and banking; cap. US $400.0m., res $86.3m., dep. $1,682.1m. (Dec. 2003); Chair. Dr MUHAMMAD SULAYMAN AL-JASSER; Dir-Gen. Dr SALIH AL-HUMAIDAN; 1 br.

Banks with Foreign Interests

Arab National Bank (ANB): POB 56921, King Faisal St, North Murabba, Riyadh 11564; tel. (1) 402-9000; fax (1) 402-7747; e-mail info@anb.com.sa; internet www.anb.com.sa; f. 1980; ownership: Arab Bank plc, Jordan, 40%, Saudi shareholders 60%; cap. 2,000.0m., res 2,776.7m., dep. 56,136.0m. (Dec. 2004); Chair. ABDULLATIF H. AL-JABR; Man. Dir and CEO NEMEH SABBAGH; 117 brs.

Bank al-Jazira: POB 6277, Khalid bin al-Waleed St, Jeddah 21442; tel. (2) 651-8070; fax (2) 653-2478; e-mail info@baj.com.sa; internet www.baj.com.sa; 94.17% Saudi-owned; cap. 600.0m., res 246.9m., dep. 7,981.3m. (Dec. 2003); Chair. ABD AL-MOHEM AR-RASHID; Gen. Man. and CEO MISHARI I. AL-MISHARI; 16 brs.

Banque Saudi Fransi (Saudi French Bank): POB 56006, Ma'ather Rd, Riyadh 11554; tel. (1) 404-2222; fax (1) 404-2311; e-mail communications@alfransi.com.sa; internet www.alfransi.com.sa; f. 1977, name changed as above 2002; Saudi shareholders 68.9%, Crédit Agricole Indosuez 31.1%; cap. 2,250.0m., res 2,791.0m., dep. 46,308.3m. (Dec. 2003); Chair. IBRAHIM A. AT-TOUQ; Man. Dir BERTRAND P. VIRIOT; 59 brs.

Gulf International Bank (Bahrain): POB 93413, Riyadh 11673; tel. (1) 218-0888; fax (1) 218-0888; f. 2000; Man. ALAA AL-JABRI.

SAMBA Financial Group: POB 833, Riyadh 11421; tel. and fax (1) 477-4770; internet www.samba.com.sa; f. 1980; 74% owned by Saudi nationals; merged with United Saudi Bank in 1999; cap. 4,000.0m., res 4,484.8m., dep. 67,623.6m. (Dec. 2003); Chair. ABD AL-AZIZ IBN HAMAD AL-GOSAIBI; Man. Dir EISA AL-EISA; 43 brs.

Saudi British Bank: POB 9084, Prince Abdulaziz bin Mossaid bin Jalawi St, Riyadh 11413; tel. (1) 405-0677; fax (1) 405-0660; e-mail info@sabb.com.sa; internet www.sabb.com.sa; f. 1978; 60% owned by Saudi nationals, 40% by HSBC Holdings BV; cap. 2,000.0m., res 2,176.8m., dep. 39,510.1m. (Dec. 2003); Chair. Sheikh ABDULLAH MUHAMMAD AL-HUGAIL; Man. Dir JOHN COVERDALE; 78 brs.

Saudi Hollandi Bank (Saudi Dutch Bank): POB 1467, Head Office Bldg, al-Dhabab St, Riyadh 11431; tel. (1) 401-0288; fax (1) 403-1104; e-mail csc@shb.com.sa; internet www.saudihollandibank.com; f. 1977 to assume activities of Algemene Bank Nederland NV in Saudi Arabia; a joint-stock co; ownership: ABN AMRO Bank (Netherlands) 40%, Saudi citizens 60%; cap. 945.0m., res 1,600.2m., dep. 23,868.2m. (Dec. 2003); Chair. Sheikh SULEYMAN A. R. AS-SUHAIMI; Man. Dir GIEL-JAN VAN DER TOL; 40 brs.

Saudi Investment Bank (SAIB): POB 3533, Riyadh 11481; tel. (1) 477-8433; fax (1) 477-6781; e-mail info@saib.com.sa; internet www.saib.com.sa; f. 1976; provides a comprehensive range of traditional and specialized banking services; cap. 1,375.0m., res 1,329.1m., dep. 20,181.2m. (March 2004); Chair. Dr ABD AL-AZIZ O'HALI; Pres. and Gen. Man. SA'UD AS-SALEH; 14 brs.

Government Specialized Credit Institutions

Real Estate Development Fund (REDF): POB 5591, Riyadh 11139; tel. (1) 479-2222; fax (1) 479-0148; f. 1974; provides interest-free loans to Saudi individuals and cos for private or commercial housing projects; cap. 70,841m. (1993); loans granted amounted to 1,900m. in 2000; Gen. Dir AHMAD AL-AKEIL; 25 brs.

Saudi Arabian Agricultural Bank (SAAB): POB 1811, Riyadh 11126; tel. (1) 402-3911; fax (1) 402-2359; f. 1963; cap. 10,000m. (1982); loans disbursed amounted to 803.9m. in 2000; Controller-Gen. ABDULLAH SAAD AL-MENGASH; Gen. Man. ABD AL-AZIZ MUHAMMAD AL-MANQUR; 70 brs.

Saudi Credit Bank: POB 3401, Riyadh 11471; tel. (1) 402-9128; f. 1973; provides interest-free loans for specific purposes to Saudi citizens of moderate means; loans disbursed amounted to 321.3m. in 2000; Chair. SAID IBN SAIED; Dir-Gen. MUHAMMAD AD-DRIES; 24 brs.

SAUDI ARABIA   *Directory*

STOCK EXCHANGE

The Saudi Arabian Monetary Agency (see Central Bank, above) operates the Electronic Securities Information System. In mid-2005 shares in 75 companies were being traded. A total of 12,291m. shares were traded in that year, amounting to 4,138,695m. riyals.

INSURANCE

In 2004 22 insurance companies operated in Saudi Arabia.

Amana Gulf Insurance Co (E.C.): POB 6559, Jeddah 21452; tel. and fax (2) 665-5692.

Arabia Ace Insurance Co Ltd (E.C.): POB 276, Dammam 31411; tel. (3) 832-4441; fax (3) 834-9389; cap. US $1m.; Chair. Sheikh ABD AL-KARIM AL-KHEREIJI; Man. Dir TAJUDDIN HASSAN.

Independent Insurance Co of Saudi Arabia Ltd: POB 1178, Jeddah 21431; tel. (2) 651-7732; fax (2) 651-1968; f. 1977; all classes of insurance; cap. US $1m.; Pres. KHALID TAHER; Man. JULIAN D. SHARPE.

Insaudi Insurance Co (E.C.): POB 3984, Riyadh 11481; tel. (1) 476-7711; fax (1) 476-1213.

Islamic Arab Insurance Co: POB 122392, Jeddah 21332; tel. (2) 664-7877; fax (2) 664-7387; e-mail iaic.ksa@islamicarab.com.

Al-Jazira Insurance Co Ltd: POB 153, al-Khobar 31952; tel. and fax (3) 895-3445.

National Co for Co-operative Insurance (NCCI): POB 86959, Riyadh 11632; tel. (1) 218-0100; fax (1) 218-0102; e-mail ncci@ncci.com.sa; internet www.ncci.com.sa; f. 1985 by royal decree; owned by three govt agencies; proposed privatization approved by the Supreme Economic Council in May 2004; initial public offering of shares in Jan. 2005; auth. cap. 500m.; Chair. SULAYMAN AL-HUMMAYYD; Man. Dir and Gen. Man. MOUSA AR-RUBAIAN; 13 brs and sales offices.

Ar-Rajhi Insurance Co: POB 22073, Jeddah 21495; tel. (2) 651-1017; fax (2) 651-1797.

Ar-Rajhi Islamic Co for Co-operative Insurance: POB 42220, Jeddah 21541; tel. (2) 651-4514; fax (2) 651-3185.

Red Sea Insurance Group of Cos: POB 5627, Jeddah 21432; tel. (2) 660-3538; fax (2) 665-5418; e-mail redsea@anet.net.sa; internet www.redsains.com; f. 1974; insurance, development and reinsurance; cap. US $9m. (1998); Chair. KHALDOUN B. BARAKAT.

Royal & Sun Alliance Insurance (Middle East) Ltd (E.C.): POB 2374, Jeddah 21451; tel. (2) 671-8851; fax (2) 671-1377; internet www.royalsun-me.com; managed by Royal & Sun Alliance Insurance Group, London; total assets US $73.0m. (2002); Chair. WAHIB S. BINZAGR; Man. Dir P. W. HEAD; Country Man. W. J. DAVIES.

Saudi Continental Insurance Co: POB 2940, Riyadh; tel. (1) 479-2141; fax (1) 476-9310; f. 1983; all classes of insurance; cap. US $3m.; Chair. OMAR A. AGGAD; Gen. Man. J. A. MCROBBIE.

Saudi National Insurance Co (E.C.): POB 5832, Jeddah 21432; tel. (2) 660-6200; fax (2) 667-4530; Gen. Man. OMAR S. BILANI.

Saudi Union National Insurance Corpn: POB 2357, Jeddah 21451; tel. (2) 667-0648; fax (2) 667-2084.

Saudi United Insurance Co Ltd: POB 933, al-Khobar 31952; tel. (3) 894-9090; fax (3) 894-9428; f. 1976; all classes of insurance and reinsurance except life; majority shareholding held by Ahmad Hamad al-Gosaibi & Bros; cap. US $5m.; Chair. and Man. Dir Sheikh ABD AL-AZIZ HAMAD AL-GOSAIBI; Dir and Gen. Man. ABD AL-MOHSIN AL-GOSAIBI; 6 brs.

U.C.A. Insurance Co (E.C.): POB 5019, Jeddah 21422; tel. (2) 653-0068; fax (2) 651-1936; e-mail uca@uca.com; f. 1974 as United Commercial Agencies Ltd; all classes of insurance; cap. US $14m.; Chair. ABU BAKER AL-HAMED; Senior Vice-Pres. MACHAAL A. KARAM.

Al-Yamamah Insurance Co Ltd: POB 41522, Riyadh 11531; tel. (1) 477-4498; fax (1) 477-4497.

Trade and Industry

(Figures for weight are in metric tons)

DEVELOPMENT ORGANIZATIONS

Arab Petroleum Investments Corpn: POB 1547, al-Khobar 31932; tel. (3) 887-0555; fax (3) 887-0404; f. 1975; affiliated to the Organization of Arab Petroleum Exporting Countries; specializes in financing petroleum and petrochemical projects and related industries in the Arab world and in other developing countries; shareholders: Kuwait, Saudi Arabia and the United Arab Emirates (17% each), Libya (15%), Iraq and Qatar (10% each), Algeria (5%), Bahrain, Egypt and Syria (3% each); auth. cap. US $1,200m.; subs. cap. $460m. (Dec. 1996); Chair. ABDULLAH A. AZ-ZAID; Gen. Man. RASHEED AL-MARAJ.

General Investment Fund: c/o Ministry of Finance, Airport Rd, Riyadh 11177; tel. (1) 405-0000; f. 1970; provides government's share of capital to mixed capital cos; 100% state-owned; cap. 1,000m. riyals; Chair. Dr IBRAHIM IBN ABD AL-AZIZ AL-ASSAF; Sec.-Gen. SULAYMAN MANDIL.

National Agricultural Development Co (NADEC): POB 2557, Riyadh 11461; tel. (1) 404-0000; fax (1) 405-5522; e-mail info@nadec-sa.com; internet www.nadec.com.sa; f. 1981; interests include four dairy farms, 40,000 ha for cultivation of wheat, barley, forage and vegetables and processing of dates; the Govt has a 20% share; chief agency for agricultural development; cap. 400m. riyals; Chair. SULAYMAN ABD AL-AZIZ ALRAJHI; Pres. and Gen. Man. ABD AL-AZIZ AL-BABTAIN.

National Industrialization Co (NIC): POB 26707, Riyadh 11496; tel. (1) 476-7166; fax (1) 477-0898; e-mail general@nic.com.sa; internet www.nic.com.sa; f. 1985 to promote and establish industrial projects in Saudi Arabia; cap. 785m. riyals; 100% owned by Saudi nationals; CEO MOAYYED AL-QURTAS.

Saudi Arabian General Investment Authority (SAGIA): POB 1267, Riyadh 11431; tel. 448-4533; fax 448-1234; e-mail alshareef@sagia.org; internet www.sagia.gov.sa; f. 2000 to promote foreign investment; Gov. AMIR BIN ABDULLAH AD-DABBAGH.

Saudi Fund for Development (SFD): POB 50483, Riyadh 11523; tel. (1) 464-0292; fax (1) 464-7450; e-mail info@sfd.gov.sa; internet www.sfd.gov.sa; f. 1974 to help finance projects in developing countries; cap. 31,000m. riyals (1991); had financed 344 projects by 2002; total commitments amounted to 23,150.6m. riyals; Chair. Dr IBRAHIM IBN ABD AL-AZIZ AL-ASSAF; Vice-Chair. and Man. Dir E. YOUSUF I. AL-BASSAM.

Saudi Industrial Development Fund (SIDF): POB 4143, Riyadh 11149; tel. (1) 477-4002; fax (1) 479-0165; f. 1974; supports and promotes local industrial development, providing medium-term interest-free loans; also offers marketing, technical, financial and administrative advice; cap. 7,000m. riyals (1996); loans disbursed amounted to 1,100m. riyals in 2000; Chair. HAMAD BIN SAUD AS-SAYYARI; Dir-Gen. SALEH ABDULLAH AN-NAIM.

CHAMBERS OF COMMERCE

Council of Saudi Chambers of Commerce and Industry: POB 16683, Riyadh 11474; tel. (1) 405-3200; fax (1) 402-4747; e-mail council@saudichambers.org.sa; internet www.saudichambers.org.sa; comprises one delegate from each of the chambers of commerce in the kingdom; Chair. ABD AR-RAHMAN ALI AL-JERAISY; Sec.-Gen. Dr FAHD AS-SULTAN.

Abha Chamber of Commerce and Industry: POB 722, Abha; tel. (7) 227-1818; fax (7) 227-1919; e-mail bhachamber@arab.net.sa; Pres. ABDULLAH SAEED AL-MOBTY; Sec.-Gen. Dr MUHAMMAD Y. AL-MIZHIR.

Al-Ahsa Chamber of Commerce and Industry: POB 1519, al-Ahsa 31982; tel. (3) 852-0458; fax (3) 857-5274; Pres. ABD AL-AZIZ SULAYMAN AL-AFALIQ.

Ar'ar Chamber of Commerce and Industry: POB 440, Ar'ar; tel. (4) 662-6544; fax (4) 662-4581; Sec.-Gen. MATAB MOZIL AS-SARRAH.

Al-Baha Chamber of Commerce and Industry: POB 311, al-Baha; tel. (7) 727-0291; fax (7) 828-0146; Pres. SAID ALI AL-ANGARI; Sec.-Gen. YAHYA AZ-ZAHRANI.

Eastern Province Chamber of Commerce and Industry: POB 719, Dammam 31421; tel. (3) 857-1111; fax (3) 857-0607; e-mail info@chamber.org.sa; internet www.chamber.org.sa; f. 1952; Chair. ABD AR-RAHMAN RASHID AR-RASHID; Sec.-Gen. IBRAHIM ABDULLAH AL-OLAYAN.

Federation of Gulf Co-operation Council Chambers (FGCCC): POB 2198, Dammam 31451; tel. (3) 826-5943; fax (3) 826-6794; e-mail fgccc@zajil.net; Pres. SALIM H. ALKHALILI; Sec.-Gen. MUHAMMAD A. AL-MULLA.

Ha'il Chamber of Commerce and Industry: POB 1291, Ha'il; tel. (6) 532-1060; fax (6) 533-1366; e-mail info@hail_chamber.org.sa; internet www.hail_chamber.org.sa; Pres. MANSOUR AGEEL AL-AMAR; Sec.-Gen. MUBARAK A. AR-RABAH (acting).

Jeddah Chamber of Commerce and Industry: POB 1264, Jeddah 21431; tel. (2) 651-5111; fax (2) 651-7373; e-mail customerservice@jcci.org.sa; internet www.jcci.org.sa; f. 1946; 26,000 mems; Chair. ABEL MUHAMMAD FAKEIH; Sec.-Gen. Dr MAJED A. AL-KASSABI.

Jizan Chamber of Commerce and Industry: POB 201, Jizan; tel. (7) 322-5155; fax (7) 322-3635; Pres. Dr SALEH AZ-ZAIDAN.

Al-Jouf Chamber of Commerce and Industry: POB 585, al-Jouf; tel. (4) 624-9060; fax (4) 624-0108; Pres. MA'ASHI DUKAN AL-ATTIYEH; Sec.-Gen. AHMAD KHALIFA AL-MUSALLAM.

Al-Majma' Chamber of Commerce and Industry: POB 165, al-Majma' 11952; tel. (6) 432-0268; fax (6) 432-2655; Pres. FAHD MUHAMMAD AR-RABIAH; Sec.-Gen. ABDULLAH IBRAHIM AL-JAAWAN.

SAUDI ARABIA

Mecca Chamber of Commerce and Industry: POB 1086, Mecca; tel. (2) 534-3838; fax (2) 534-2904; f. 1947; Pres. ADEL ABDULLAH KA'AKI; Sec.-Gen. ABDULLAH ABD AL-GAFOOR TOUJAR-ALSHAHI.

Medina Chamber of Commerce and Industry: POB 443, King Abd al-Aziz Rd, Medina; tel. (4) 838-8909; fax (4) 838-8905; e-mail info@mcci.org.sa; internet www.mcci.org.sa; Sec.-Gen. Dr LOUI BAKUR AT-TAYAR.

Najran Chamber of Commerce and Industry: POB 1138, Najran; tel. (7) 522-2216; fax (7) 522-3926; Sec.-Gen. MAKHFOOR ABDULLAH AL-BISHER.

Al-Qassim Chamber of Commerce and Industry: POB 444, Buraydah, Qassim; tel. (6) 381-4000; fax (6) 381-2231.

Al-Qurayat Chamber of Commerce and Industry: POB 416, al-Qurayat; tel. (4) 642-6200; fax (4) 642-3172; Pres. OTHMAN ABDULLAH AL-YOUSEF; Sec.-Gen. JAMAL ALI AL-GHAMDI.

Riyadh Chamber of Commerce and Industry: POB 596, Riyadh 11421; tel. (1) 404-0044; fax (1) 402-1103; e-mail rdchamber@rdcci.org.sa; f. 1961; acts as arbitrator in business disputes, information centre; Chair. Sheikh ABD AR-RAHMAN AL-JERAISY; Sec.-Gen. HUSSEIN ABD AR-RAHMAN AL-AZAL; 23,000 mems.

Tabouk Chamber of Commerce and Industry: POB 567, Tabouk; tel. (4) 422-2736; fax (4) 422-7387; Pres. ABD AL-AZIZ M. OWADEH; Sec.-Gen. AWADH AL-BALAWI.

Ta'if Chamber of Commerce and Industry: POB 1005, Ta'if; tel. (2) 736-6800; fax (2) 738-0040; Pres. IBRAHIM ABDULLAH KAMAL; Sec.-Gen. Eng. YOUSUF MUHAMMAD ASH-SHAFI.

Yanbu Chamber of Commerce and Industry: POB 58, Yanbu; tel. (4) 322-7878; fax (4) 322-6800; f. 1979; produces quarterly magazine; 5,000 members; Pres. Dr TALAL ALI ASH-SHAIR; Sec.-Gen. OSMAN NAIM AL-MUFTI.

STATE HYDROCARBONS COMPANIES

General Petroleum and Mineral Organization (PETROMIN JET): POB 7550, 21472 Jeddah; tel. (2) 685-7666; fax (2) 685-7545; works in conjunction with the Ministry of Petroleum and Mineral Resources to oversee petroleum industry; Chair. and Exec. Asst ABDULLAH O. ATTAS (acting).

Arabian Drilling Co: POB 708, Dammam 31421; tel. (3) 887-2020; fax (3) 882-6588; e-mail adcgen@al-khobar.oilfield.slb.com; f. 1964; PETROMIN shareholding 51%, remainder French private cap.; undertakes contract drilling for oil (on shore and off shore), minerals and water both inside and outside Saudi Arabia; Chair. SULAYMAN J. AL-HERBISH; Man. Dir SAAD ABDULLAH SAAB.

Arabian Geophysical and Surveying Co (ARGAS): POB 535, al-Khobar 31952; tel. (3) 882-9122; fax (3) 882-9060; f. 1966; PETROMIN shareholding 51%; remainder provided by Cie Générale de Géophysique; geophysical exploration for petroleum, other minerals and groundwater, as well as all types of land, airborne and marine surveys; Chair. AHMAD MUHAMMAD GHAZZAWI; Man. Dir HABIB M. MERGHELANI.

Petromin Marketing (PETMARK): POB 50, Dhahran Airport 31932; tel. (3) 890-3883; f. 1967; operates the installations and facilities for the distribution of petroleum products in the Eastern, Central, Southern and Northern provinces of Saudi Arabia; Pres. and CEO HUSSEIN A. LINJAWI.

Saudi Arabian Oil Co (Saudi Aramco): POB 5000, Dhahran 31311; tel. (3) 875-4915; fax (3) 873-8490; e-mail webmaster@aramco.com.sa; internet www.saudiaramco.com; f. 1933; previously known as Arabian-American Oil Co (Aramco); in 1993 incorporated the Saudi Arabian Marketing and Refining Co (SAMAREC, f. 1988) by merger of operations; holds the principal working concessions in Saudi Arabia; operates five wholly owned refineries (at Jeddah, Rabigh, Ras Tanura, Riyadh and Yanbu) with total capacity of more than 1m. barrels per day; Pres. and CEO ABDULLAH S. JAMA'AH; Exec. Vice-Pres. (Exploration and Production) SADAD AL-HUSSEINI.

Saudi Arabian Lubricating Oil Co (PETROLUBE): POB 1432, Jeddah 21431; tel. (2) 661-3333; fax (2) 661-3322; e-mail info@petrominoils.com; internet www.petrominoils.com; f. 1968; 71% owned by Saudi Aramco, 29% by Mobil; for the manufacture and marketing of lubricating oils and other related products; production 140m. litres (2002); cap. 110m. riyals; Pres. SALEM H. SHAHEEN.

Saudi Aramco Lubricating Oil Refining Co (LUBEREF): POB 5518, Jeddah 21432; tel. (2) 638-5040; fax (2) 636-6932; f. 1975; owned 70% by Saudi Aramco and 30% by Mobil; production 3,800,000 barrels; Chair. SALIM S. AL-AYDH; Pres. and CEO MUHAMMAD ALI AL-HARAZY.

Saudi Aramco Mobil Refinery Co Ltd (SAMREF): POB 30078, Yanbu; tel. (4) 396-4000; fax (4) 396-0942; f. 1981; operated by Saudi Aramco and Mobil, capacity 360,000 b/d; Pres. and CEO MUHAMMAD A. MISFER.

Saudi Aramco Shell Refinery Co (SASREF): POB 10088, Jubail 31961; tel. (3) 357-2000; fax (3) 358-9667; e-mail k.al-buainain@pr.sasrefalj.simis.com; internet www.shell.com; operated by Saudi Aramco and Shell; capacity 300,000 b/d; exports began in 1985; Chair. ABD AL-AZIZ M. AL-HOKAIL.

Saudi Basic Industries Corpn (SABIC): POB 5101, Riyadh 11422; tel. (1) 401-2033; fax (1) 401-2045; internet www.sabic.com; f. 1976 to foster the petrochemical industry and other hydrocarbon-based industries through jt ventures with foreign partners, and to market their products; 70% state-owned; production 38.79m. tons (2002); Vice-Chair. and CEO MUHAMMAD AL-MADY.

Projects include:

Al-Jubail Petrochemical Co (Kemya): POB 10084, Jubail 31961; tel. (3) 357-6000; fax (3) 358-7858; f. 1980; began production of linear low-density polyethylene in 1984, of high-density polyethylene in 1985, and of high alfa olefins in 1986, capacity of 330,000 tons per year of polyethylene; jt venture with Exxon Corpn (USA) and SABIC; Pres. ABD AL-AZIZ I. AL-AUDAH; Exec. Vice-Pres. CLAY LEWIS.

Arabian Petrochemical Co (Petrokemya): POB 10002, Jubail 31961; tel. (3) 358-7000; fax (3) 358-4480; e-mail otaibifr@petrokemya.sabic.com; produced 2.4m. tons of ethylene, 135,000 tons of polystyrene, 100,000 tons of butene-1; 570,000 tons of propylene, 100,000 tons of butadiene and 150,000 tons of benzene in 2001; wholly-owned subsidiary of SABIC; owns 50% interest in ethylene glycol plant producing 610,000 tons per year of monoethylene glycol, 65,000 tons per year of diethylene glycol and 3,900 tons per year of triethylene glycol; Chair. HOMOOD AT-TUWAIJRI; Pres. KHALID S. AR-RAWAF.

Eastern Petrochemical Co (Sharq): POB 10035, Jubail 31961; tel. (3) 357-5000; fax (3) 358-0383; f. 1981 to produce linear low-density polyethylene, ethylene glycol; total capacity 660,000 tons of ethylene glycol and 280,000 tons of polyethylene per year; a SABIC jt venture; Pres. IBRAHIM S. ASH-SHEWEIR.

National Industrial Gases Co (Gas): POB 10110, Jubail 31961; tel. (3) 357-5700; fax (3) 358-5542; total capacity of 876,000 tons of oxygen and 492,750 tons of nitrogen per year; jt venture with Saudi private sector; Pres. ABDULLAH MUJBEL AL-JALAWI.

National Plastic Co (Ibn Hayyan): POB 10002, Jubail 31961; tel. (3) 358-7000; fax (3) 358-4736; f. 1984; produces 390,000 tons per year of vinylchloride monomer and 324,000 tons per year of polyvinylchloride; jt venture with Lucky Group (Republic of Korea), SABIC and three other cos; Pres. KHALED AR-RAWAF.

Saudi-European Petrochemical Co (Ibn Zahr): POB 10330, Jubail 31961; tel. (3) 341-5060; fax (3) 341-2966; f. 1985; annual capacity 1.4m. tons of methyl-tertiary-butyl ether (MTBE), 0.3m. tons of propylene; SABIC has a 70% share, Ecofuel, Nesté Corpn and APICORP each have 10%; Pres. SAMI AS-SUWAIGH.

Saudi Methanol Co (ar-Razi): POB 10065, Jubail Industrial City 31961; tel. (3) 357-7820; fax (3) 358-0838; e-mail emt@arrazi.com; f. 1979; capacity of 3,158,000 tons per year of chemical-grade methanol; total methanol exports in 2001 were 3,248,000 tons; jt venture with a consortium of Japanese cos; Pres. NABIL A. MANSOURI; Exec. Vice-Pres. H. MIZUNO.

Saudi Petrochemical Co (Sadaf): POB 10025, Jubail 31961; tel. (3) 357-3000; fax (3) 357-3142; f. 1980 to produce ethylene, ethylene dichloride, styrene, crude industrial ethanol, caustic soda and methyl-tertiary-butyl-ether (MTBE); total capacity of 4,710,000 tons per year; Shell (Pecten) has a 50% share; Pres. MOSAED S. AL-OHALI.

Saudi Yanbu Petrochemical Co (Yanpet): POB 30139, Yanbu; tel. (4) 396-5000; fax (4) 396-5006; f. 1980 to produce 820,000 tons per year of ethylene, 600,000 tons per year of high-density polyethylene and 340,000 tons per year of ethylene glycol; total capacity 1,692,200 tons per year by 1990; Mobil and SABIC each have a 50% share; Pres. ALI AL-KHURAIMI; Exec. CEO P. J. FOLEY.

Foreign Concessionaires

Arabian Oil Co Ltd (AOC): POB 256, Ras al-Khafji 31971; tel. (3) 766-0555; fax (3) 766-2001; f. 1958; holds concession (2,200 sq km at Dec. 1987) for offshore exploitation of Saudi Arabia's half-interest in the Saudi Arabia-Kuwait Neutral Zone; Pres. KEIICHI KONAGA; Chief Exec. General Affairs AHMAD IBRAHIM AL-ASFOUR.

Saudi Arabian Texaco Inc: POB 363, Riyadh; tel. (1) 462-7274; fax (1) 464-1992; also office in Kuwait; f. 1928; fmrly Getty Oil Co; holds concession (5,200 sq km at Dec. 1987) for exploitation of Saudi Arabia's equal share in the Saudi Arabia-Kuwait Neutral Zone.

UTILITIES

Utilities Co (Uco): Jubail; f. 1999; owned equally by Royal Commission for Jubail and Yanbu, Public Investment Fund, Saudi Aramco and SABIC; cap. 2,000m. riyals; provides utilities in industrial cities of Jubail and Yanbu.

SAUDI ARABIA

Electricity

Electricity Services Regulatory Authority (ESRA): Riyadh; f. 2001 to regulate the power industry and to recommend tariffs for the sector; Gov. FAREED ZEDAN.

Saudi Electricity Co (SEC): POB 57, Riyadh 11411; tel. (1) 403-2222; fax (1) 405-1191; f. 2000 following merger of 10 regional companies, to organize the generation, transmission and distribution of electricity into separate operating companies; joint-stock co; cap. 33,758m.; Chair. GHAZI AL-GOSAIBI; CEO SULAYMAN A. AL-QADI.

Water

Saline Water Conversion Corpn (SWCC): POB 4931, 21412 Jeddah; tel. (2) 682-1240; fax (2) 682-0415; privatization under consideration in 2006; provides desalinated water; 24 plants; capacity 2m. cu m per day (1994); Gov. FAHID ASH-SHARIF; Dir-Gen. ABD AL-AZIZ OMAR NASSIEF.

TRADE UNIONS

Trade unions are illegal in Saudi Arabia.

Transport

RAILWAYS

Saudi Arabia has the only rail system in the Arabian peninsula. The Saudi Government Railroad comprises 719 km of single and 157 km of double track. In addition, the total length of spur lines and sidings is 348 km. The main line, which was opened in 1951, is 578 km in length; it connects Dammam port, on the Gulf coast, with Riyadh, and passes Dhahran, Abqaiq, Hufuf, Harad and al-Kharj. A 310-km line, linking Hufuf and Riyadh, was inaugurated in May 1985. New 950-km and 115-km lines, connecting Riyadh with Jeddah and Dammam with Jubail, respectively, known as the Saudi Landbridge Project, were planned in 2006. The revamped network was to connect the Red Sea with the Persian (Arabian) Gulf and was to be closely linked with Jeddah Islamic Port and King Abd al-Aziz Port (at Dammam). The scheme was presented to potential investors in January 2005. Concessions to build a 570-km 'Western Region' line, connecting the west-coast centres of Jeddah, Mecca, Medina and Yanbu, and a 1,300-km 'North–South' line, connecting Riyadh, Qassim, Ha'il, az-Zubayrah and al-Jalamid, were to be tendered at a later stage. A US $400m.-project to construct two light urban lines in Riyadh was also planned in 2006. The project was scheduled for completion in 2013. A total of 1.3m. passengers travelled by rail in the kingdom in 2004.

Saudi Railways Organization (SRO): POB 36, Dammam 31241; tel. (3) 871-3000; fax (3) 827-1130; e-mail sro@sro.org.sa; internet www.saudirailways.org; Pres. KHALED H. AL-YAHYA.

ROADS

Asphalted roads link Jeddah to Mecca, Jeddah to Medina, Medina to Yanbu, at-Ta'if to Mecca, Riyadh to al-Kharj, and Dammam to Hufuf, as well as the principal communities and certain outlying points in Saudi Aramco's area of operations. The trans-Arabian highway links Dammam, Riyadh, at-Ta'if, Mecca and Jeddah. The construction of a 810-km road connecting Qassim, Medina, Yanbu, Rabigh and Thuwal, at a cost of some SR 5,350m., was under way in 2006, and in February 2006 the long-considered project to build a road bridge between Saudi Arabia and Egypt across the Straits of Tiran was revived. Construction of the latter project was likely to commence in 2007. In 2004 there were 170,796 km of roads, of which 14,936 km were main roads (including motorways), 11,161 km were secondary roads and 25,845 km were asphalted agricultural roads. Metalled roads link all the main population centres.

Saudi Public Transport Co (SAPTCO): POB 10667, Riyadh 11443; tel. (1) 454-5000; fax (1) 454-2100; f. 1979; operates a public bus service throughout the country and to neighbouring countries; the Govt holds a 30% share; Chair. Dr NASIR AS-SALOOM; CEO Dr ABD AL-AZIZ AL-OHALY.

National Transport Co of Saudi Arabia: Queen's Bldg, POB 7280, Jeddah 21462; tel. (2) 643-4561; specializes in inward clearance, freight forwarding, general and heavy road haulage, re-export, charter air freight and exhibitions; Man. Dir A. D. BLACKSTOCK; Operations Man. I. CROXSON.

SHIPPING

Responsibility for the management, operation and maintenance of the commercial ports of Jeddah, Dammam, Yanbu, Dhiba and Jizan, the King Fahd Industrial Ports of Jubail and Yanbu, and the oil port of Ras Tanura, as well as a number of minor ports, began to be transferred to the private sector after 1997, but all ports remain subject to regulation and scrutiny by the Ports Authority. Some 98% of Saudi Arabia's imports and exports passed through the country's sea ports, which received 10,163 vessels, in 2004. In 2002 there were 183 mechanized and organized berths. In 2004 the total cargo handled by Saudi Arabian ports, excluding crude petroleum, was 119.9m. metric tons, compared with 68.2m. tons in 1990/91. Some 2.1m. passengers were also embarked and disembarked in that year.

Jeddah is the principal commercial port and the main point of entry for pilgrims bound for Mecca. It has berths for general cargo, container traffic, 'roll on, roll off' (ro-ro) traffic, livestock and bulk grain shipments, with draughts ranging from 8 m to 16 m. The port also has a 200-ton floating crane, cold storage facilities and a fully-equipped ship-repair yard. In 2004 a total of 4,654 vessels called at Jeddah Islamic Port, and some 33.5m. tons of cargo, excluding crude petroleum, were handled and 1.1m. passengers were processed.

Dammam is the second largest commercial port and has general cargo, container, ro-ro, dangerous cargo and bulk grain berths. Draughts at this port range from 8 m to 13.5 m. It has a 200-ton floating crane and a fully-equipped ship-repair yard. In 2004 a total of 2,028 vessels called at King Abd al-Aziz Port in Dammam and some 14.0m. tons of cargo, excluding crude petroleum, were handled.

Jubail has one commercial and one industrial port. The commercial port has general cargo, bulk grain and container berths with ro-ro facilities, and a floating crane. Draughts at this port range from 12 m to 14 m. In 2004 a total of 157 vessels called at Jubail Commercial Port, and 2.1m. tons of goods, excluding crude petroleum, were handled. The industrial port has bulk cargo, refined and petrochemical and ro-ro berths, and an open sea tanker terminal suitable for vessels up to 300,000 dwt. Draughts range from 6 m to 30 m. In 2004 a total of 1,284 vessels called at King Fahd Industrial Port in Jubail; 36.4m. tons of cargo, excluding crude petroleum, were handled in that year.

Yanbu, which comprises one commercial and one industrial port, is Saudi Arabia's nearest major port to Europe and North America, and is the focal point of the most rapidly growing area, in the west of Saudi Arabia. The commercial port has general cargo, ro-ro and bulk grain berths, with draughts ranging from 10 m to 12 m. It also has a floating crane, and is equipped to handle minor ship repairs. A total of 113 vessels called at Yanbu Commercial Port, and less than 1.0m. tons of cargo, excluding crude petroleum, were handled in 2004. The industrial port has berths for general cargo, containers, ro-ro traffic, bulk cargo, crude petroleum, refined and petrochemical products and natural gas liquids, and a tanker terminal on the open sea. In 2004 a total of 1,447 vessels called at King Fahd Industrial Port in Yanbu; the port handled 32.0m. tons of cargo, excluding crude petroleum, in that year.

Jizan is the main port for the southern part of the country. It has general cargo, ro-ro, bulk grain and container berths, with draughts ranging from 8 m to 11 m. It also has a 200-ton floating crane. In 2004 a total of 31 vessels called at Jizan Port; 0.6m. tons of cargo, excluding crude petroleum, were handled in the same year.

Dhiba port, on the northern Red Sea coast, serves the Tabouk region. It has three general cargo berths with a ro-ro ramp, and passenger-handling facilities. Maximum draught is 10.5 m. In 2004 a total of 899 vessels called at Dhiba; 0.4m. tons of cargo, excluding crude petroleum, were handled in that year.

In addition to these major ports, there are a number of minor ports suitable only for small craft, including Khuraiba, Haql, al-Wajh, Umlujj, Rabigh, al-Lith, Qunfoudah, Farasan and al-Qahma on the Red Sea coast and al-Khobar, al-Qatif, Uqair, Darin and Ras al-Khafji on the Gulf coast. Ras Mishab, on the Gulf coast, is operated by the Ministry of Defence and Civil Aviation.

Saudi Ports Authority: POB 5162, Riyadh 11422; tel. (1) 405-0005; fax (1) 405-3508; internet www.ports.gov.sa; f. 1976; regulatory authority; Chair. Dr FAYEZ I. BADR; Vice-Chair. and Dir-Gen. MUHAMMAD IBN ABD AL-KARIM BAKR.

Dammam: POB 28062, Dammam 31188; tel. (3) 858-3900; fax (3) 857-1727; e-mail kaap@ports.gov.sa; internet www.ports.gov.sa; Dir-Gen. NAEEM IBRAHIM AN-NAEEM.

Dhiba: POB 190, Dhiba; tel. (4) 432-1060; fax (4) 432-2679; Dir-Gen. MUHAMMAD ASH-SHAREEF.

Jeddah: POB 9285, Jeddah 21188; tel. (2) 647-1200; fax (2) 647-7411; Dir-Gen. SAHIR M. TAHLAWI.

Jizan: POB 16, Jizan; tel. (7) 317-1000; fax (7) 317-0777; Dir-Gen. ALI HAMOUD BAKRI.

Jubail: POB 547, Jubail 31951; tel. (3) 357-8000; fax (3) 357-8011; Dir-Gen. MUTHANNA ISA AL-QURTAS.

Yanbu: POB 30325, Yanbu; tel. (4) 396-7000; fax (4) 396-7037; Dir-Gen. Dr HUMOOD SAADI.

Arabian Petroleum Supply Co Ltd: POB 1408, Al-Qurayat St, Jeddah 21431; tel. (2) 637-1120; fax (2) 636-2366; Chair. Sheikh MUHAMMAD YOUSUF ALI REZA; Gen. Man. E. D. CONNOLLY.

Baaboud Trading and Shipping Agencies: POB 7262, Jeddah 21462; tel. (2) 642-1468; fax (2) 644-0912; Chair. AHMAD M. BAABOUD; Man. Dir ABOUD M. BAABOUD.

SAUDI ARABIA

Bakry Navigation Co Ltd: POB 3757, Jeddah 21481; tel. (2) 651-9995; fax (2) 651-2908; Chair. Sheikh A. K. AL-BAKRY; Man. Dir G. A. K. AL-BAKRY.

National Shipping Co of Saudi Arabia (NSCSA): POB 8931, Riyadh 11492; tel. (1) 478-5454; fax (1) 477-8036; e-mail prmail@nscsa.com.sa; internet www.nscsa.com; f. 1979; transportation of crude petroleum and petrochemical products; routes through Red Sea and Mediterranean to USA and Canada; operates a fleet of 37 ships; Chair. SULEIMAN J. AL-HERBISH; CEO KHALIL I. AL-GANNAS.

Saudi Lines: POB 66, Jeddah 21411; tel. (2) 642-3051; regular cargo and passenger services between Red Sea and Indian Ocean ports; Pres. M. A. BAKHASHAB PASHA; Man. Dir A. M. BAKHASHAB.

Saudi Shipping and Maritime Services Co Ltd (TRANSHIP): POB 7522, Jeddah 21472; tel. (2) 642-4255; fax (2) 643-2821; e-mail tranship@tri.net.sa; Chair. Prince SA'UD IBN NAYEF IBN ABD AL-AZIZ; Man. Dir Capt. MUSTAFA T. AWARA.

Shipping Corpn of Saudi Arabia Ltd: POB 1691, Arab Maritime Center, Malik Khalid St, Jeddah 21441; tel. (2) 647-1137; fax (2) 647-8222; Pres. and Man. Dir ABD AL-AZIZ AHMAD ARAB.

CIVIL AVIATION

King Abd al-Aziz International Airport (KAIA), in Jeddah, which was opened in 1981, has three terminals, one of which is specifically designed to cope with the needs of the many thousands of pilgrims who visit Mecca and Medina each year. The airport handled 12.1m. passengers in 2001. Construction work on two new terminals and improvements at KAIA commenced in late 2004. The project was to cost US $600m. and was due to be completed by late 2010. King Khalid International Airport, in Riyadh, opened in 1983 with four terminals. It handled 8.7m. passengers in 2001. A third major airport, King Fahd International Airport (with an initial handling capacity of 5.2m. passengers per year), opened in the Eastern Province in 1994. Some 2.7m. passengers used the airport in 2001. Overall, the country's airports were used by 32.2m. passengers in 2004. There are 27 commercial airports in the kingdom. Plans to privatize the kingdom's airports were announced in October 2003. In March 2005 British Airways (BA) suspended its London–Jeddah and London–Riyadh services, stating that the routes were unprofitable. (In 2003 BA had suspended its services to Saudi Arabia for three weeks due to fears of terrorist activity.) However, another British company, British Midland Airways, began operating three weekly London–Riyadh flights from September.

Presidency of Civil Aviation (PCA): POB 887, Jeddah 21165; tel. (2) 640-5000; fax (2) 640-2444; internet www.pca.gov.sa; pending approval by the Council of Ministers, the PCA was to be restructured as the General Aviation Authority; Pres. Dr ALI ABD AR-RAHMAN AL-KHALAF.

National Air Services Co: Riyadh; f. 1998; privately owned; cap. 60m. riyals; Chair. YOUSUF AL-MAIMANI.

Saudi Arabian Airlines: POB 620, Jeddah 21231; tel. (2) 686-0000; fax (2) 686-4552; internet www.saudiairlines.com; f. 1945; began operations in 1947; carried 15.4m. passengers in 2004; regular services to 25 domestic and 52 international destinations; scheduled for privatization; Chair. Prince SULTAN IBN ABD AL-AZIZ; Dir-Gen. KHALED A. IBN AL-BAKR; Exec. Vice-Pres. (operations) ADNAN AD-DABBAGH.

Tourism

All devout Muslims try to make at least one visit to the holy cities of Medina, the burial place of Muhammad, and Mecca, his birthplace. In 2000 there were 518 hotels in the kingdom, with a total of more than 50,000 rooms. Tourist numbers decreased to 7.3m. in 2003 (compared with 7.5m. in 2002), and receipts from tourism amounted to US $3,418m. riyals in 2002. A total of 1,419,706 foreign pilgrims visited Mecca in the Islamic year ending in February 2004.

In 2000 the Government decided to issue tourist visas for the first time. A Supreme Commission for Tourism (SCT), to develop the tourism industry in Saudi Arabia, was subsequently established. In 2005 the SCT announced plans to increase the kingdom's supply of hotel rooms to 150,000 by 2013 (from the present 95,000).

Saudi Hotels and Resort Areas Co (SHARACO): POB 5500, Riyadh 11422; tel. (1) 481-6666; fax (1) 480-1666; f. 1975; Saudi Govt has 40% interest; Chair. MUSAAD AS-SENANY; Dir-Gen. ABD AL-AZIZ AL-AMBAR.

Supreme Commission for Tourism (SCT): POB 66680, Riyadh 11586; tel. and fax (2) 480-8855; e-mail hamidiw@sct.gov.sa; internet www.sct.gov.sa; f. 2001; Sec-Gen. Prince SULTAN IBN SALMAN IBN ABD AL-AZIZ AS-SA'UD.

SENEGAL

Introductory Survey

Location, Climate, Language, Religion, Flag, Capital

The Republic of Senegal lies on the west coast of Africa, bordered to the north by Mauritania, to the east by Mali, and to the south by Guinea and Guinea-Bissau. In the southern part of the country The Gambia forms a narrow enclave extending some 320 km (200 miles) inland. The climate is tropical, with a long dry season followed by a short wet season—from June to September in the north, and from June to October in the south. Average annual temperatures range from 22°C (72°F) to 28°C (82°F). French is the official language; the most widely spoken national languages at the time of the 1988 census were Wolof (spoken by 49.2% of the population), Peul (22.2%), Serer (12.8%) and Diola (5.1%). At the 1988 census almost 94% of the population were Muslims, and some 4% Christians, mostly Roman Catholics; a small number followed traditional beliefs. The national flag (proportions 2 by 3) has three equal vertical stripes, of green, yellow and red, with a five-pointed green star in the centre of the yellow stripe. The capital is Dakar. In July 2005 the Assemblée nationale approved legislation providing for the creation of a new administrative capital, near Kébèmer, on the Atlantic littoral.

Recent History

After 300 years as a French colony, Senegal became a self-governing member of the French Community in November 1958. The formation in April 1959 of the Mali Federation, linking Senegal with Soudan (later the Republic of Mali), had only two months of independence before being dissolved when Senegal seceded, to become a separate independent state, on 20 August 1960. The Republic of Senegal was proclaimed on 5 September, with Léopold Sédar Senghor, leader of the Union progressiste sénégalaise (UPS), as the country's first President.

In late 1962, following the discovery of a coup attempt led by the Prime Minister, Mamadou Dia, Senghor assumed the premiership. Following the victory of the UPS at elections to the Assemblée nationale in 1963, other political parties were gradually absorbed into it or outlawed, effectively creating a one-party state by 1966. In 1970 the office of Prime Minister was restored and assigned to a provincial administrator, Abdou Diouf, who in 1976 was made Senghor's constitutional successor. In 1973 Senghor, the sole candidate, was re-elected President. Senghor amended the Constitution in March 1976 to allow three parties to contest elections—the UPS, renamed the Parti socialiste (PS), the Parti démocratique sénégalais (PDS) and the Parti africain de l'indépendance (PAI). The first national elections under the three-party system took place in February 1978; the PS won 83 of the 100 seats in the Assemblée nationale, the remainder being won by the PDS. In the concurrent presidential election, Senghor overwhelmingly defeated the leader of the PDS, Abdoulaye Wade.

Senghor was succeeded as President by Diouf in January 1981. An amnesty was declared for political dissidents, and the Constitution was amended to allow the existence of an unlimited number of political parties. At elections in February 1983 Diouf received 83.5% of the presidential vote (compared with 14.8% for his nearest rival, Wade), while in legislative elections the PS won 111 of the 120 seats. Disputing the results, the opposition boycotted the Assemblée nationale for several months. In April Diouf abolished the post of Prime Minister, which had latterly been held by Habib Thiam.

When preliminary results of the February 1988 presidential and legislative elections indicated clear victories for both Diouf and the PS, opposition parties alleged fraud on the part of the ruling party, and, following the outbreak of rioting in Dakar, a state of emergency was imposed. Various opposition members, including Wade and Amath Dansokho, the leader of the Parti de l'indépendance et du travail (PIT), were arrested. According to the official results of the presidential election, contested by four candidates, Diouf obtained 73.2% of the votes cast, and Wade 25.8%. In the legislative elections, the PS won 103 seats, and the PDS the remaining 17. Wade, Dansokho and other opposition activists were tried on charges of incitement to violence and attacks on the internal security of the State; Dansokho and five others were acquitted, but in May Wade received a one-year suspended prison sentence. Later in the month, however, Diouf announced an amnesty for all those who had been condemned in the aftermath of the elections.

In October 1989 changes to the electoral code were approved by PS representatives in the Assemblée nationale (PDS deputies had begun a boycott of legislative sessions in mid-1989, in protest against what they perceived as the unsatisfactory media coverage of parliamentary debates); a partial system of proportional representation was to be introduced for legislative elections, and access to the state-owned media was to be granted to opposition parties. The opposition boycotted municipal and rural elections in November 1990, claiming that the modified electoral code permitted widespread electoral malpractice.

In March 1991 the legislature approved several amendments to the Constitution, notably the restoration of the post of Prime Minister, to which post Thiam was again named in the following month. Thiam's Government included four representatives of the PDS (including Wade, as Minister of State, effectively the most senior post in the Government other than the Prime Minister); Dansokho, the PIT leader, became Minister of Town Planning and Housing. In September 1991 the Assemblée nationale adopted amendments to the electoral code. Presidential elections would henceforth take place, in two rounds if necessary (to ensure that the President would be elected by an absolute majority of votes cast), every seven years, with a mandate that would be renewable only once. Legislative voting would, however, continue to take place at five-yearly intervals.

In October 1992 Wade and his three PDS colleagues resigned from the Council of Ministers, protesting that they had been excluded from the governmental process. Eight candidates contested the presidential election, which took place in February 1993. Despite some irregularities, voting was reported to be orderly in most areas, outwith Casamance (see below). The opposition denounced the preliminary results, which indicated that Diouf had won a clear majority. In March the Constitutional Council announced that Diouf had been re-elected with 58.4% of the votes cast (51.6% of the electorate had voted); Wade secured 32.0% of the votes.

Elections to the Assemblée nationale took place in May 1993, in which the PS won 84 of the 120 elective seats; the PDS took 27 seats. The rate of participation by voters was 40.7%. Shortly after the announcement of the results the Vice-President of the Constitutional Council, Babacar Sèye, was assassinated. Wade and three other PDS leaders were detained for three days in connection with the killing. Thiam formed a new Government in June. Dansokho, who had supported Diouf's presidential campaign, retained his portfolio, while Abdoulaye Bathily, the leader of the Ligue démocratique—Mouvement pour le parti du travail (LD—MPT), who had also contested the presidency, received a ministerial post. In October Wade was charged with complicity in the assassination of Sèye; Wade's wife and a PDS deputy were also charged in connection with the killing. In November Ousmane Ngom, the PDS parliamentary leader, and Landing Savané, the leader of And Jëf—Parti africain pour la démocratie et le socialisme (AJ—PADS), were among those detained following a protest in Dakar to demand the cancellation of austerity measures. Ngom, Savané and some 87 others were convicted of participating in an unauthorized demonstration, and received suspended prison sentences.

Following the devaluation of the CFA franc, in January 1994, emergency measures were adopted to offset the immediate adverse economic effects and consequent hardship. In February a demonstration in Dakar to denounce the devaluation, degenerated into serious rioting, as a result of which eight people were killed. Wade and Savané were among those subsequently charged in association with the unrest. Charges against Wade and his opposition associates in connection with the murder of Sèye were dismissed in May 1994, although Wade and Savané, remained in custody until July, in connection with the post-devaluation violence. In October three of Sèye's alleged assassins were convicted and sentenced to 18–20 years' imprisonment.

Five members of the PDS, including Wade, as Minister of State at the Presidency, were appointed to a new Council of Ministers in March 1995. Djibo Kâ, a long-serving government member who, as Minister of the Interior, had been associated with the legal proceedings against Wade and other opposition leaders, left the Government. In September Dansokho and another PIT member were dismissed from the Council of Ministers. In January 1996 Diouf announced that a second legislative chamber, the Sénat, was to be established.

In January 1998 Maj.-Gen. Lamine Cissé retired as the armed forces Chief of Staff, prior to his appointment as Minister of the Interior. In February Wade appealed to the Constitutional Council to reject an amendment to the electoral code whereby the number of deputies in the Assemblée nationale was to be increased to 140; later in the month the Council annulled the proposed increase, the first occasion on which the Council had ruled against a decision of the legislature. In March, however, the Assemblée nationale again voted to increase the number of deputies. In early April Wade, stating that he was no longer a member of the Government, refused an invitation to the presidential palace to meet President Bill Clinton of the USA. At the same time Kâ resigned from the PS to present his own list of candidates, as the Union pour le renouveau démocratique (URD).

Some 18 parties and coalitions contested the legislative elections on 24 May 1998. Outwith Casamance, voting was reported to have taken place generally in an atmosphere of calm. The PS obtained 93 seats in the enlarged assembly, with 50.2% of the valid votes cast, while the number of PDS deputies was reduced to 23; Kâ's URD, in alliance with the Alliance pour le progrès et la justice—Jëf-Jël (APJ—JJ), secured 11 seats. The rate of participation by voters was 39% of the registered electorate. In July Thiam resigned as Prime Minister, and was replaced by Mamadou Lamine Loum. A new Council of Ministers was named shortly afterwards, in which most ministers in the outgoing administration, with the notable exception of Moustapha Niasse, hitherto Minister of Foreign Affairs and Senegalese Abroad, retained their portfolios. Serigne Diop, the leader of the Parti démocratique sénégalais—Rénovation (which had broken away from the PDS in 1997) was the only non-PS member of the Government.

In August 1998 the Assemblée nationale voted to revise the Constitution to remove the clause restricting the Head of State to a maximum of two terms of office, thus permitting Diouf to contest the next presidential election, in 2000. A requirement that the President be elected by more than 25% of all registered voters was also abandoned. The opposition parties, condemning the amendments, boycotted the vote.

The PS won all 45 elective seats in the first, indirect, elections to the Sénat in January 1999; these 45 members were chosen by an electoral college of deputies, local, municipal and regional councillors. Only the PS, the Parti libéral du Sénégal (formed in 1998 by Ngom, leading a breakaway movement from the PDS), and a coalition of the PIT and AJ—PADS contested the elections; the PDS and other opposition parties were opposed to the introduction of an additional parliamentary chamber. A further 12 senators were appointed by the President of the Republic, including two opposition figures, and three were elected by Senegalese resident abroad. One of the 12 senators nominated by Diouf, Abdoulaye Diack, a prominent member of the PS, was elected President of the new body.

In March 1999 an alliance of AJ—PADS, the PIT, the PDS and the LD—MPT agreed to nominate Wade, who had resigned from the Assemblée nationale in mid-1998, as their joint candidate in the presidential election scheduled for 2000. Also in March 1999 Talla Sylla, the leader of the APJ—JJ, was sentenced to six months' imprisonment for having denounced the Head of State at an unauthorized rally held in October 1998. Sylla, who had been planning to stand in the presidential election, was also banned from voting or participating in elections for a period of five years. In April 1999 the PDS began a boycott of the Assemblée nationale, accusing the Government of seeking to manipulate the voters' register for the presidential election. In June Niasse announced his intention of contesting the presidential election, and published a document accusing Diouf and the PS of corruption; Niasse was consequently expelled from the PS and subsequently formed the Alliance des forces de progrès (AFP).

Shortly before the election, held on 27 February 2000 and was contested by eight candidates, violent incidents were recorded following visits to Saint-Louis by Diouf and Wade, in which 10 people were injured in clashes and the headquarters of two parties loyal to Diouf were set on fire, while in the town of Ndofane, in the Kaolack region, two people were reportedly killed, and others injured, during clashes between supporters of the PS and of the opposition. Although Diouf won the largest proportion of votes cast (41.3%), his failure to secure an absolute majority of votes cast meant that a second round of voting, between Diouf and Wade (who had secured 31.0% of votes cast), would be necessary. Of the remaining candidates, Niasse received 16.8% of votes cast, while Kâ took 7.1%. Prior to the second round of voting, Wade received the endorsement of Niasse, and of the majority of the candidates defeated in the first round, with the notable exception of Kâ, who defied the wishes of his party and gave public support to Diouf. At the second round, on 19 March, Wade won 58.5% of the total votes cast, thus taking the presidency from the PS for the first time. Turn-out in the second round was estimated at 60.1%, marginally lower than in the first round.

Wade was sworn in as President on 1 April 2000, at a public ceremony attended by seven African Heads of State. Niasse was named Prime Minister in the 29-member Council of Ministers appointed later in the month, and several other opposition leaders, including Savané of AJ—PADS and Bathily of the LD—MPT, and representatives of civil society received ministerial portfolios. Wade announced that he did not envisage governing alongside an Assemblée nationale dominated by the PS, and that he therefore intended to hold fresh legislative elections, following a constitutional referendum initially scheduled for 27 November 2000. Among the proposed changes, the President would gain the power to dissolve the Assemblée nationale, while other presidential powers would be transferred to the Prime Minister, and the presidential mandate would again be reduced from seven to five years, renewable only once. Furthermore, the Sénat was to be abolished.

The constitutional referendum was held, following several postponements, on 7 January 2001. Some 94.0% of votes cast in the plebiscite supported the new Constitution; 65.8% of the registered electorate voted. Most provisions of the Constitution, including the abolition of the Sénat and the Economic and Social Council, took immediate effect, following its promulgation by the President, with only those sections relating to the legislature necessitating new elections before their implementation. Future presidential mandates would be reduced from seven to five years, and the number of deputies in the Assemblée nationale was reduced from 140 to 120.

In February 2001, following student disorder, in which one student had died in clashes with police, a new Minister of Higher Education was appointed. The President dissolved the Assemblée nationale in mid-February and announced that the new legislature, which was to be elected in April, would consist of 65 seats elected by majority voting in departments, and 55 by proportional representation using national lists. In March Wade appointed Mame Madior Boye, a magistrate and member of no political party, and hitherto Minister of Justice, as Prime Minister. In the ensuing reshuffle Niasse and other members of the AFP were removed from office, in what was regarded as an attempt by Wade to create a more unified Government, which incorporated greater representation for the PDS and its allies, prior to the legislative elections.

The legislative elections duly took place on 29 April 2001, in conditions that were widely praised for their democracy and transparency; outbreaks of violence in Casamance were none the less reported. Apart from the pro-Wade Sopi (Change) coalition (comprising 40 parties, led by the PDS), a further 24 parties contested the polls. The Sopi coalition won 49.6% of votes cast, and 89 of the 120 seats in the Assemblée nationale. The AFP obtained 11 seats, with 16.1% of the vote. The PS, despite receiving a slightly larger share of the vote than the AFP (17.4%), secured only 10 seats. The rate of electoral participation was 67.5%. Boye was reappointed as Prime Minister on 10 May. The new 24-member Government comprised 11 members of the PDS (who obtained most principal posts), nine representatives of civil society, and two members each of AJ—PADS and the LD—MPT.

Following the elections, nine parties, including the AFP, the APJ—JJ and the URD, announced that they were to join the PS in an informal opposition alliance. In late 2001 the Minister of the Economy and Finance, Mamadou Seck, resigned and was replaced by Abdoulaye Diop. Seck's resignation followed reports, which he denied, that he had previously received a suspended prison sentence on charges of embezzlement. In August 2001 some 25 parties, led by the PDS, formed a pro-presidential electoral alliance, the Convergence des actions autour du Président en perspective du 21ième siècle (CAP-21), in advance of local and municipal elections (initially scheduled for November, but subsequently postponed); meanwhile, opposition groups also formed an electoral alliance, the Cadre permanent de concertation. In February 2002 the three men convicted of the assassination of Babacar Sèye in 1993 were granted presidential pardons and subsequently released from prison, provoking renewed controversy about the case, as the three recipients of the pardon continued to protest their innocence. In the delayed local and municipal elections, which were eventually held on 12 May 2002, CAP-21 won control of nine of the 11 regional governments, as well as a majority of municipal and communal seats. In June Youssou Diagne tendered his resignation as President of the Assemblée nationale, and from his position of a deputy; he was subsequently appointed as ambassador to the Republic of China (Taiwan). Meanwhile, Pape Diop, a PDS deputy who had recently been elected as Mayor of Dakar, was elected as the new President of the legislature. In mid-October Diouf resigned from the chairmanship of the PS, in order to assume the elected position of Secretary-General of La Francophonie.

The sinking of a state-owned passenger ferry, the MV *Joola*, in late September 2002, *en route* from Ziguinchor, the principal city of Casamance, to Dakar led to a national political crisis, even before the final death toll of the accident, subsequently enumerated at more than 1,800 people, became apparent. In early October the Minister of Equipment and Transport, Youssouph Sakho, and the Minister of the Armed Forces, Yoba Sambou, resigned in response to the tragedy, as it became clear that the vessel had been severely overloaded; only 64 survivors were reported. Later in the month the head of the navy was dismissed, and Wade announced that the Government accepted responsibility for the disaster. In early November Wade dismissed Boye and her Government; although no official reason for the dismissal was given, it was widely believed to have been prompted by the Government's response to the disaster. Shortly after Boye's dismissal, an inquiry into the incident found that safety regulations had been widely violated on the *Joola*, and that the dispatch of rescue equipment and staff to the ship by the armed forces had been inexplicably delayed. Idrissa Seck, the Mayor of Thiès, a close ally of Wade and previously a senior official in the PDS, was appointed as the new Prime Minister; several principal posts in the new Government remained unchanged. In mid-December the Government announced that a new capital city was to be constructed at Mékhé-Pékesse, 120 km from Dakar.

During 2003 the consequences of the sinking of the *Joola* continued to be of political significance; in July the relatives of those killed accepted an offer of compensation made by the Government, having rejected three previous offers. In August the Court of Cassation closed an investigation into the incident, stating that no further public action was feasible, as the commander of the ship, whom the court described as the sole person responsible for the overloading of the vessel, had died in the accident. However, later in the month the Chief of Staff of the Armed Forces and the Chief of Staff of the Air Force were dismissed as a result of disciplinary action related to the response to the sinking of the *Joola*.

In late August 2003 Seck announced the resignation of his Government. Wade reappointed Seck as premier and expressed his preference that a broadly based government administration, including representatives of opposition parties, be formed. However, opposition parties declined to nominate candidates, and many of the senior positions in the new Government, formed at the end of the month, remained unchanged.

In late 2003 opposition figures, including the Executive Secretary of the PS, Ousmane Tanor Dieng, identified several arson attacks that had occurred since 2000 against premises occupied by a trade union, a small opposition party and a publishing and broadcasting company as evidence of an apparent increase in politically motivated violence in Senegal during recent years. An attack on Sylla in Dakar in October 2003, by unknown individuals armed with a hammer, which resulted in the President of the APJ—JJ seeking medical treatment in France, prompted a large demonstration in Dakar against political violence. Members of the opposition described the assault on Sylla as an assassination attempt, and alleged that the attackers were associates of President Wade; although these claims remained unproven, several associates of Wade were apparently questioned during the police investigation into the attack, and Wade reportedly refused to condemn what he referred to as an 'incident'.

Political tensions intensified further in early 2004 as several parties that had supported Wade's candidacy in the presidential election of 2000 and had ministerial representation in the Government, including the LD—MPT and AJ—PADS, declined to participate in celebrations organized to mark the fourth anniversary of Wade's accession to power. Moreover, while the President continued to announce his intention of forming a broadly based Government, most opposition parties reiterated their reluctance to participate in any such administration. In late April Wade dismissed Seck's Government, appointing Macky Sall, hitherto Minister of State, Minister of the Interior and Local Communities, Government Spokesperson, as the new premier. Although the allocation of most strategic portfolios in the new Council of Ministers, formed on the following day, remained largely unchanged, Cheikh Sadibou Fall was accorded the post of Minister of the Interior, and two new ministers of state were appointed to the Government: Aminata Tall, as Minister of State, Minister of Local Communities and Decentralization, and the URD's Kâ, as Minister of State, Minister of the Maritime Economy. In November Wade reorganized his Government, dismissing Fall from his position as Minister of the Interior and replacing him with Ngom (who had been appointed as Minister of Trade in July). In December the Assemblée nationale approved legislation abolishing the death penalty in Senegal (the bill had previously been unanimously adopted by the Government in July).

In January 2005 the Assemblée nationale approved controversial legislation granting amnesty from prosecution to those suspected of 'politically motivated' offences committed between 1 January 1983 and 31 December 2004, and specifically those implicated in the murder, in 1993, of Babacar Sèye. The Constitutional Council ruled, in response to an appeal by opposition legislators, that the proposed amnesty did not contradict the Constitution, although its ruling did invalidate the separate article granting amnesty to those involved in the Sèye case. The law was subsequently promulgated by President Wade on 17 February 2005. In March Wade effected a further government reshuffle, replacing two members of the LD—MPT with affiliates of the PDS leaving AJ—PADS as the only party (other than the PDS) to retain ministerial representation from the alliance that supported Wade's presidential candidacy in 2000. The dismissals followed several months of discord between the PDS and the LD—MPT over the latter's criticism of Wade's presidency and its opposition to the amnesty legislation. In late April 12 PDS deputies, who were reported to be close to former Prime Minister Seck, resigned from the majority parliamentary group, and formed their own group within the Assemblée nationale, the Forces de l'alternance (FAL), led by Oumar Sarr. Amid ongoing tensions within the PDS, a further reorganization of the Government in May was interpreted as an attempt to strengthen support for the President. New appointees included Awa Fall Diop, of AJ—PADS, as Minister of Relations with the Institutions, while both the party's leader, Landing Savané, hitherto Minister of State, Minister of Industry and Crafts, and Serigne Diop, hitherto Minister of State, Keeper of the Seals, Minister of Justice, became Ministers of State at the Presidency (however, in July, Serigne Diop left the Government to become an adviser to the President); Cheikh Tidiane Sy assumed responsibility for the justice portfolio, and Abdoulaye Diop, Minister of the Economy and Finance, additionally received the designation of Minister of State.

In late May 2005 opposition leaders condemned the detention of Abdourahim Agne, the Secretary-General of a minor opposition party, the Parti de la réforme, who was charged with threatening state security after he called for street demonstrations against the President. Meanwhile, following a meeting between Wade and the 12 dissident PDS deputies, at which the President promised to address their grievances, the FAL was disbanded. Wade appointed members to a new Commission électorale nationale autonome in early June. However, the opposition expressed concern at the composition of the commission, particularly the new Chairman, Mamadou Moustapha Touré, whose wife was said to be an influential member of the PDS. Further minor reorganizations of the Government took place in June, July and August.

Seck was questioned by police in mid-July 2005, after he was accused by President Wade of overspending on work to upgrade roads in Thiès, where he served as mayor. The former Prime Minister, whose house had been attacked in May, refuted any suggestion that he had embezzled government funds from the project. Later that month Seck was formally charged with endangering national security; there was no immediate explanation of the charges, which Seck's defence lawyers claimed to be politically motivated. In early September the Assemblée nationale ruled that Seck should be brought to trial on charges of embezzlement at the High Court of Justice, which was reserved for cases concerning crimes committed by members of the Government in the exercise of their duties. Widely regarded as a potential successor to Wade, Seck had made clear his presidential ambitions, although he had pledged not to stand against Wade if the President decided to seek a second term in the election due in 2007. Meanwhile, the Assemblée nationale adopted legislation providing for the eventual creation of a new administrative and political capital some 150 km north-east of Dakar, near Kébèmer (rather than at Mékhé-Pékesse, which had been the location proposed in December 2002).

In mid-December 2005 the Assemblée nationale approved legislation, supported by President Wade, that delayed the legislative elections, which had been scheduled for mid-2006, until 2007, when they were to be held concurrently with presidential voting. Wade justified this postponement (which was condemned by the parliamentary opposition) on financial grounds, stating that the Government had recently been obliged to make unplanned spending on mitigating the effects of flooding. Further minor governmental reorganizations took place in early February and mid-March 2006.

Meanwhile, in early February 2006 Seck was released from detention, following the partial dismissal of the charges of corruption and embezzlement against him (some minor charges remained against him, however); the charges of endangering state security had been dropped in the previous month.

Long-standing resentment against the Government of Senegal in the southern province of Casamance (which is virtually cut off from the rest of the country by the enclave of The Gambia) was embodied from the early 1980s by the separatist Mouvement des forces démocratiques de la Casamance (MFDC). The MFDC initiated a new offensive from April 1990. The Senegalese Government dispatched military reinforcements, and in September 1990 a military governor was appointed for Casamance. By April 1991 at least 100 people had reportedly died as a result of violence in the region, while more than 300 Casamançais were awaiting trial for sedition. The announcement in May 1991 of the imminent release of more than 340 detainees (including the Secretary-General and executive leader of the MFDC, Fr Augustin Diamacouné Senghor) who had been arrested in connection with unrest in Casamance facilitated the conclusion, shortly afterwards in Guinea-Bissau, of a cease-fire agreement by representatives of the Senegalese Government and of the MFDC. In June the region's military Governor was replaced by a civilian. An amnesty was approved by the Assemblée nationale later in June, and some 400 detainees were released. A period of relative calm ensued.

In January 1992 a peace commission, comprising government representatives and members of the MFDC, was established, with mediation by Guinea-Bissau. A resurgence of violence in Casamance from July prompted the Government to redeploy armed forces in the region, giving rise to MFDC protests that the 'remilitarization' of Casamance contravened the truce. Contradictory statements made by MFDC leaders regarding their commitment to the peace accord evidenced a split within the movement. The 'Front nord' and the MFDC Vice-President, Sidi Badji, appealed to the rebels to lay down their arms; meanwhile, the 'Front sud', led by Diamacouné Senghor (who was now based in Guinea-Bissau), appeared determined to continue the armed struggle. After an escalation of the conflict in late 1992 and early 1993, in which more than 500 people were killed, hundreds injured and tens of thousands forced to leave their homes, a new round of negotiations resulted in the signing, in July 1993, of a cease-fire agreement, known as the Ziguinchor Accord, between the Government and Diamacouné Senghor (who had returned to Ziguinchor in March). Guinea-Bissau was to act as a guarantor of the agreement, and the Government of France was to be asked to submit an historical arbitration regarding the Casamance issue. In December France issued its judgment that Casamance had not existed as an autonomous territory prior to the colonial period, and that independence for the region had been neither demanded nor considered at the time of decolonization.

From early 1995, renewed violence indicated a re-emergence of divisions between the two factions of the MFDC. Rebels in the south accused the Senegalese armed forces of violating the provisions of the 1993 cease-fire accord. A major military operation was instigated following the disappearance, in April, of four French tourists in Basse-Casamance. More than 1,000 élite Senegalese troops were assisted in their search by French reconnaissance aircraft; although they failed to locate the missing tourists, the aim of the operation appeared increasingly to be to dislodge MFDC dissidents from the border region. Although both factions of the MFDC denied any involvement in the apparent kidnap of the tourists, who were never found, Diamacouné Senghor was placed under house arrest in late April, and the other members of the MFDC 'political bureau' were detained. In June MFDC rebels announced an end to the cease-fire, again accusing government forces of having violated the 1993 accord. Although Diamacouné Senghor appealed to the rebels not to break the truce, renewed violence in the south-west resulted in some 60 deaths.

In September 1995 a Commission nationale de paix (CNP) was established, headed by a Casamance-born former Minister of State for Foreign Affairs (in 1973–78), Assane Seck. Members of the commission reportedly sought a dialogue with Diamacouné Senghor and the MFDC's four other political leaders (all of whom remained under house arrest). During October, renewed rebel attacks on government forces were accompanied by a major army offensive in the south-west. By the end of the November it was reported that about 150 separatists and 15 members of the armed forces had been killed in clashes. In December Diamacouné Senghor made a televised appeal to the rebels to lay down their arms. He proposed that preliminary talks between the MFDC and the CNP take place in January 1996, to be followed by peace negotiations, in a neutral country, three months later. The members of the MFDC 'political bureau' were released from house arrest at the end of December 1995; it was also reported that the CNP had secured the release of 50 of some 150 suspected separatists detained in recent months. Peace talks, scheduled to begin in Ziguinchor in April, were postponed indefinitely, following the refusal of Diamacouné Senghor and other MFDC leaders to attend, citing the failure of the Government to meet a number of their conditions, and renewed violence was reported in the region. During a visit to Ziguinchor in May, Diouf expressed his commitment to the pursuit of peace, stating that the ongoing process of administrative decentralization would afford greater autonomy to the region, but as an integral part of Senegal.

There was renewed optimism regarding the possible resumption of negotiations between a united MFDC and the authorities, following discussions in July 1996 between Diamacouné Senghor and Diouf's personal Chief of Staff in Ziguinchor. However, in March 1997 more than 40 rebels and two members of the armed forces were killed in clashes near the border with Guinea-Bissau. The MFDC denied that it had ended its cease-fire, stating that it would investigate these incidents. In that month four representatives of the MFDC had been permitted to travel to France, where they had spent three weeks meeting with representatives of the movement based in Europe.

While both the Senegalese authorities and the MFDC leadership appeared committed to reviving the peace process, the deaths of 25 soldiers in August 1997 near Ziguinchor prompted fears of a revival of the conflict. In September the armed forces launched a new offensive, in which rebel forces were reported to have sustained heavy losses. A further armed forces offensive in October, the largest such operation in Casamance since the 1995 cease-fire, involved as many as 3,000 soldiers and resulted in the deaths of 12 soldiers and 80 rebels in clashes near the border with Guinea-Bissau, according to Senegalese military sources. Salif Sadio, the MFDC's military leader, stated that the organization remained committed to the peace process, but maintained that its forces were justified in defending themselves against armed attack.

In January 1998 Diamacouné Senghor appealed for a cease-fire, indicating that his organization would be prepared to abandon its demand for independence, subject to the Government instituting measures to ensure greater economic and social development in Casamance. Security operations in advance of the legislative elections resulted in the deaths of some 30 rebels in May, and six civilians were killed by separatists on the day before the election. There was further violence as voting proceeded, and two soldiers who were transporting voting results were reportedly killed. In August the Senegalese army bombarded rebel positions on both sides of the border with Guinea-Bissau. The armed forces reported that seven soldiers and 43 rebels had been killed in the clashes, although the MFDC claimed that the majority of the victims were civilians. Rebel violence continued intermittently throughout the second half of 1998.

In June 1999 talks between several MFDC factions began in Banjul, The Gambia, although several leaders of military and exiled factions of the MFDC did not attend, claiming that Diamacouné Senghor was effectively a hostage of the Senegalese Government. Some 50 observers attended the talks, including Gen. Ansumane Mané, the leader of the rebels in Guinea-Bissau, and two Senegalese ministers. At the meeting, Léopold Sagna was confirmed as the head of the armed forces of the MFDC, replacing Salif Sadio, who was reportedly less prepared to compromise with government demands. The Senegalese authorities subsequently acceded to the MFDC's demand that Diamacouné Senghor be released from house arrest; his movements were, however, to remain restricted.

In November 1999 Diamacouné Senghor agreed to recommence negotiations with the Senegalese Government, demanding, however, that the safety of MFDC negotiators be guaranteed, and that representatives of Casamançais civil society be included in the negotiations. At the meeting, held in Banjul in late December, the Senegalese Government and the MFDC agreed to an immediate cease-fire and to create the conditions necessary to bring about lasting peace; the Governments of The Gambia and of Guinea-Bissau were to monitor the situation in the region. A further meeting between the two parties took place in January 2000.

In early February 2000 a joint mission of the Senegalese Government and the MFDC was established to oversee the cease-fire. Despite the presence of the mission and of increased security designed to prevent the disturbance of the Senegalese presidential election, violent incidents, in which three soldiers and two civilians were killed, were reported in February. Following his election as President in early March, Abdoulaye Wade announced that he was to continue the process of negotiations, but that his preference was to conduct direct dialogue with the MFDC. Wade further announced that Diamacouné Senghor would be permitted total freedom of movement. However renewed clashes were subsequently reported. In August Senegal and Guinea-Bissau announced that they would undertake joint military border patrols in order to restrict rebel activities in the region.

In November 2000 members of a peace commission, headed by the Minister of the Interior, Maj.-Gen. Mamadou Niang, and by Diamacouné Senghor, signed a joint statement that envisaged a series of official meetings between the Senegalese Government and the MFDC, the first of which would convene on 16 December. The Government simultaneously warned that full legal action would be taken against any person promoting or distributing speeches in favour of separatism. The discussions in mid-December were boycotted by representatives of the Front sud of the MFDC, led by Ali Badji. However, a senior MFDC official present at the onset of negotiations, Alexandre Djiba (who had long been resident outside Senegal), subsequently reportedly met Ali Badji's representatives in Guinea-Bissau. The Senegalese Minister of the Armed Forces, Yoba Sambou, himself a native of Casamance, meanwhile stated that the Government preferred the rebels to unite into a single faction, so that more militant factions within the MFDC would not dispute the peace talks. As a result of renewed unrest, however, the MFDC postponed a proposed meeting in Banjul, to be held in January 2001, which had been intended to establish a common position between its various factions.

The overwhelming support in Casamance for the new Constitution, which was endorsed by 96% of voters in the region at the referendum in January 2001, prompted Wade to announce that Casamance had definitively voted to remain part of Senegal. In mid-January the Guinea-Bissau armed forces reportedly destroyed all the Casamance rebel bases in that country, in response to clashes between rival MFDC factions there. Continued unrest in the region south-west of Ziguinchor further delayed the signature of a cease-fire agreement, originally intended to take place at the meeting of mid-December, which had been rescheduled to occur in Dakar in early February.

In February 2001 Diamacouné Senghor announced that, in order to accelerate the peace process in Casamance, several senior members of the MFDC, including Sidi Badji and Djiba, had been removed from their positions. However, Sidi Badji, who had served as Military Affairs Adviser to Diamacouné Senghor, rejected the legitimacy of his dismissal. Also in mid-February, in what was reportedly the most serious attack on civilian targets in Casamance for several years, separatist rebels killed some 13 civilians in an ambush. Both Sidi Badji and Diamacouné Senghor denied any knowledge of their supporters' involvement and condemned the attack, into which Wade announced the opening of a judicial inquiry. Later in February a Senegalese soldier was killed in an attack on an army supply convoy, and two people were killed and 13 others injured in two further ambushes, attributed to separatist rebels, in late February and early March. In early March Diamacouné Senghor accused Sadio of being implicated in the recent killings of civilians; in mid-March the Senegalese Government issued an international arrest warrant for Sadio, who had recently been removed from Guinea-Bissau, and announced that a reward of some US $200,000 would be paid for his capture.

In mid-March 2001 Niang and Diamacouné Senghor signed a cease-fire agreement at a meeting in Ziguinchor, which provided for the release of detainees, the return of refugees, the removal of landmines (which had been utilized in the region since 1998) and for economic aid to reintegrate rebels and to ameliorate the infrastructure of Casamance. Some 16 prisoners were released several days after the accord was signed. The Gambian Government issued a communiqué in mid-March, in which it promised to prevent armed rebel groups from operating on Gambian territory; it was suspected that the renewed violence had been co-ordinated by groups based in The Gambia. Later in March Niang and Diamacouné Senghor signed a further agreement, which provided for the disarmament of rebel groups and the confinement to barracks of military forces in Casamance. In April Wade and Sambou participated in negotiations with Diamacouné Senghor, at which other MFDC leaders, including Sidi Badji, were also present.

As a result of the renewed conflict, Diamacouné Senghor announced, in late May 2001, that a proposed reconciliation forum, intended to unite the various factions of the MFDC, had been postponed indefinitely, and a number of members of the movement, including Djiba, were reportedly expelled. None the less, Diamacouné Senghor and Sidi Badji attended a meeting convened by the Gambian Government in Banjul in early June, in an attempt to overcome the impasse. As tensions between factions within the MFDC intensified, with further clashes reported in June and July, Diamacouné Senghor was removed from the position of Secretary-General of the MFDC in August, at the much-delayed reconciliation forum, and appointed as honorary President. Jean-Marie François Biagui, who had previously been involved in the French-based section of the MFDC, became Secretary-General and *de facto* leader. Sidi Badji, who continued to question the tactics of Diamacouné Senghor, was appointed as the organization's head of military affairs. Biagui not only demonstrated considerable reluctance to play a leadership role, but was also apparently unable to prevent Sadi Badji, who was reputed to have support from the authorities in The Gambia, from becoming the dominant force in the movement.

Despite these personnel changes within the MFDC, President Wade met Diamacouné Senghor at the presidential palace in Dakar in September 2001; both leaders reiterated the importance of implementing the cease-fire agreement. In response to this meeting, it was reported that the new leadership of the MFDC had suspended all further negotiations with the Government. Following further attacks by rebels, Biagui resigned as Secretary-General in early November. Sidi Badji was announced as Biagui's successor, in an acting capacity, although Diamacouné Senghor rejected this appointment, and reappointed Biagui as Secretary-General. In November MFDC rebels launched numerous attacks on civilians in Casamance. Diamacouné Senghor led a rally in Ziguinchor in mid-November to demand an immediate cease-fire; the rally was boycotted by supporters of Sidi Badji. Violence in the province intensified in December; several civilians were killed during attacks on villages. In an attempt to quell the rebellion, Diamacouné Senghor appointed an envoy, his nephew, Laurent Diamacouné, to seek negotiations with Sidi Badji, but with only limited success. In mid-December Diamacouné Senghor's position was further undermined, when an episcopal conference declared that his leadership of a movement that was using armed struggle to attain its ends was incompatible with his role as a Roman Catholic priest.

In mid-January 2002 Niang held talks with Diamacouné Senghor and Sidi Badji, although no date for the resumption of peace negotiations with the Government was forthcoming. In March further incidents of looting and robbery by MFDC militants were reported, with several attacks notably occurring in the hitherto largely peaceful region around Bignona, where Sadio was now believed to be based. In late March mediators from The Gambia and Guinea-Bissau met with MFDC representatives, with the intention of establishing a timetable for the resumption of peace talks. Following continued fighting, some 9,000 Casamançais were reported to have fled to The Gambia by the end of June.

In late August 2002, following a joint declaration signed by Diamacouné Senghor and Sidi Badji urging the resumption of peace talks between the rebels and the Government, Wade appointed an official delegation, chaired by the Second Vice-President of the Assemblée nationale and President of Ziguinchor Regional Council, Abdoulaye Faye, and including among its membership Niang and Sambou, to undertake negotiations with the MFDC. Meanwhile, the holding of an intra-Casamance conference, in early September, appeared to indicate a decline in support for separatist aspirations, as the conference produced a declaration, signed by representatives of 10 ethnic groups resident in the region, in favour of a 'definitive peace in Casamance', and which referred to the region as 'belonging to the great and single territory of Senegal'. Moreover, the absence from the meeting of the MFDC faction loyal to Sidi Badji appeared to refute reports that the various wings of the MFDC had effectively reunited. In mid-September a further meeting between Faye and Niang, representing the Government, and Diamacouné Senghor and Sidi Badji, for the MFDC, was held in Ziguinchor. In late September five civilians, including the brother of Sambou, were killed in an attack attributed to separatist rebels north of Ziguinchor. The internal disunity of the MFDC was emphasized in mid-October, when Biagui, announcing that the conflict had definitively ended, publicly demanded forgiveness from the people of Casamance and Senegal for the actions of the organization and acknowledged that the MFDC was responsible for causing suffering to the populace; this statement was emphatically rejected by Sidi Badji. In spite of further discussions between the government commission and Diamacouné Senghor and Sidi Badji in January 2003, intermittent conflict and banditry continued to be reported in Casamance in early 2003, although by the end of April all members of the MFDC who had been imprisoned on charges other than murder had been released on bail.

In early May 2003 President Wade, meeting with a delegation of MFDC leaders, including Diamacouné Senghor, at the republican palace in Dakar, announced that several substantive measures towards the normalization of the political and economic situation in Casamance were to be implemented, notably major infrastructural projects and the rehabilitation of damaged villages. The Assemblée nationale was to consider an amnesty for all those implicated in crimes related to the conflict, following a convention of the MFDC, to be held, at an unspecified date, in Guinea-Bissau, prior to the conclusion of final peace talks between the MFDC and the Government. Wade also announced that the Government intended to accede to a further MFDC demand, by dismissing those implicated in the failed attempt to rescue the passengers of the stricken *Joola* ferry in September 2002 (see above), and arranging the provision of a replacement for the vessel, which had provided a key transport link between the Casamance region and Dakar. Mine-clearing operations, to involve both regular members of the army and former rebel fighters, were also to commence. (Sidi Badji had been a notable absentee from the delegation present at the meeting; his absence was attributed to ill health.) Meanwhile, Diamacouné Senghor reiterated on several occasions that the Casamance conflict had concluded; reports suggested that the apparent death of Sadio, regarded as a leading opponent of compromise within the MFDC, had been a major factor in facilitating the improved relationship between the organization and the Government. (However, no clear proof of Sadio's death was presented.)

In late May 2003 Diamacouné Senghor announced that the MFDC convention, comprising 460 participants from the various factions of the organization, was to be held in Guinea-Bissau in early June, although it was reported that factions opposed to the proposed peace agreement would refuse to attend the gathering. Following the death of Sidi Badji, from natural causes, in late May, the convention was postponed, initially to late July. However, the Guinea-Bissau authorities announced that they would be unable to provide sufficient guarantees of security for participants, and the meeting was again postponed, until early October, when the gathering was held in Ziguinchor. On this occasion, which was not attended by hardline factions of the MFDC loyal to Djiba, both Diamacouné Senghor and Biagui issued statements confirming that the conflict had ended, and announced that what was termed the emancipation of Casamance did not, as a matter of course, necessarily entail its independence from Senegal. Following the restoration of peace in Casamance, it was anticipated that some 15,000 displaced persons would return to their home villages in the Ziguinchor administrative region, while demining operations commenced in July.

In mid-March 2004 unconfirmed reports suggested that Diamacouné Senghor had removed Biagui from the post of Secretary-General of the MFDC. In early April three members of the armed forces were reported to have been killed and a further five injured in an attack attributed to the MFDC. Later that month Diamacouné Senghor attended official celebrations in Dakar to mark the 44th anniversary of Senegal's independence, at the invitation of President Wade. The MFDC held a convention in Ziguinchor in early May, at which it proposed the cantonment of its combatants while observing a unilateral one-month cease-fire, in return for the withdrawal of government troops deployed in Casamance since 1982. In July the Assemblée nationale adopted legislation providing for an amnesty for all MFDC combatants; however, MFDC leaders claimed that their members had done nothing from which they required amnesty and urged the Government to engage in negotiations with the organization.

In September 2004 it was reported that an extraordinary general assembly of the MFDC had dismissed Diamacouné Senghor as the organization's leader and, as in 2001, appointed him Honorary President, while Biagui was reappointed Secretary-General and *de facto* leader. Biagui subsequently announced that the MFDC intended to transform itself into a legitimate political party and contest national elections; however, his status as leader was rejected by the MFDC's military wing, which issued a statement declaring its continuing recognition of Diamacouné Senghor as the movement's leader, while also reaffirming its commitment to full independence for Casamance. (The Senegalese Government was also reported to regard Diamacouné Senghor as remaining the MFDC's legitimate leader for the purposes of negotiations.) Following talks in Paris between representatives of the Government and the external wing of the MFDC, plans were announced for the signing of a cease-fire between the two parties in late December 2004, to be followed by detailed negotiations towards a peaceful political settlement, although the Government's representatives insisted that there would be no concessions offered on the issue of independence for the region. Concerns persisted, however, over internal divisions within the MFDC: Diamacouné Senghor's appeal for a general assembly of the movement in late November, intended to reconcile the various factions in advance of the signing of the cease-fire, was reportedly rejected by his rivals in the movement's political wing, while Abdoulaye Diedhiou, leader of the military wing Atika ('arrow'), insisted that independence remained the MFDC's primary aim and criticized Diamacouné Senghor for making excessive concessions to the Senegalese Government. On 30 December a 'General Peace Accord' was signed in Ziguinchor by the Minister of the Interior, on behalf of the Government, and Diamacouné Senghor, representing the MFDC. President Wade also signed the accord, which was, however, rejected by several factions of the MFDC, including Atika, the Front nord and elements of the movement's international wing. Negotiations aimed at achieving a definitive resolution of the conflict in Casamance were opened by Prime Minister Sall on 1 February 2005 in the town of Foundiougne, some 160 km south-east of Dakar, but were boycotted by Biagui and Diédhiou, who reportedly favoured further dialogue within the MFDC before engaging in talks with the Government. Both sides agreed to establish joint technical commissions to address reconstruction, economic and social development, and disarmament, demobilization and demining. In June a number of attacks in Casamance were variously attributed to dissident members of the MFDC or to bandits. Meanwhile, Diamacouné Senghor appointed Ansoumana Badji, formerly the MFDC's representative in Portugal, as Secretary-General of the movement; Badji stated that he aimed to persuade as many MFDC members as possible to join the peace process. Biagui rejected the legitimacy of Badji's appointment.

From 1989 Senegal's regional relations underwent a period of considerable strain. A long-standing border dispute with Mauritania, which also involved ethnic and economic rivalries, was exacerbated by the deaths, in April of that year, of two Senegalese farmers, who had been involved in a dispute regarding grazing rights with Mauritanian livestock-breeders. Mauritanian nationals residing in Senegal were attacked, and their businesses looted, while Senegalese nationals in Mauritania suffered similar aggression. By early May it was believed that several hundred people, mostly Senegalese, had been killed. Operations to repatriate nationals of both countries commenced, with international assistance. Diplomatic relations, which had been suspended in August 1989, were fully restored in April 1992, and the process of reopening the border began in May, although the contentious issues that had hitherto impeded the normalization of relations remained largely unresolved. In December 1994, however, the Governments of Senegal and Mauritania agreed new co-operation measures, including efforts to facilitate the free movement of goods and people between the two countries.

In January 1995 the Governments of Senegal, Mauritania and Mali undertook to co-operate in resolving joint border issues and in combating extremism, arms-smuggling and drugs-trafficking. In July the office of the UN High Commissioner for Refugees (UNHCR) began a census of Mauritanian refugees in Senegal, estimated to number some 66,000, as part of initiatives for their eventual repatriation. In May 1998 the Ministers of the Interior of Mauritania, Mali and Senegal met to discuss border security, following reports of increased cross-border banditry, particularly in eastern Senegal. The unrest in the region was blamed by the Senegalese press on the continued presence there of Mauritanian refugees; in September it was reported that the Senegalese authorities had ceased to issue the refugees with travel documents. In May 1999 the two countries signed a further agreement on the joint exploitation of fisheries. In mid-2000, however, a dispute over water rights resulted in a period of substantial tension between Senegal and Mauritania. Following renewed negotiations, the visit of President Taya of Mauritania to Dakar in April, as the guest of honour at a ceremony to commemorate the 41st anniversary of the independence of Senegal, was widely regarded as indicating an improvement in relations between the countries. Presidents Taya and Wade met again in July 2003, when negotiations were conducted on a range of bilateral and international issues; Wade reiterated his support for Taya's administration, following an attempted *coup d'état* in Mauritania in the previous month. The extradition of one of the suspected coup plotters from Senegal to Mauritania was also interpreted as an indication of improved relations between the countries, as was the Mauritanian Government's decision to accord 270 temporary fishing licences to Senegalese fishermen in June 2004. According to provisional figures, 19,778 UNHCR-assisted Mauritanian refugees remained in Senegal at the end of 2004.

In October 1993 Senegal and Guinea-Bissau signed an agreement regarding the joint exploitation and management of fishing and petroleum resources in their maritime zones. This treaty was ratified in December 1995, to the effect that fishing resources were to be shared equally between the two countries, while Senegal was to benefit from an 85% share of revenue obtained from petroleum deposits. During bilateral contacts in 1995–97 Senegal and Guinea-Bissau pledged co-operation in matters of joint defence and security. It was hoped that the movement of refugees from the conflict in Casamance to Guinea-Bissau, which began, under the auspices of UNHCR, in February 1996, would expedite efforts to restore security in the border region between the countries. In January 1998 it was announced that the authorities in Guinea-Bissau had intercepted a consignment of armaments destined for MFDC rebels, and that some 15 officers of the Guinea-Bissau armed forces had been arrested and suspended from duty, including the head of the armed forces, Brig. (later Gen.) Ansumane Mané. In June, however, troops loyal to Mané rebelled against President Commdr João Vieira of Guinea-Bissau, and civil war broke out in that country. Senegalese troops intervened in support of the armed forces loyal to Vieira. By the end of the month refugees from the conflict were crossing into Casamance, exacerbating security concerns in the province, while it was also reported that members of the MFDC were fighting alongside the rebels against the Government of Guinea-Bissau and Senegalese forces. From December, as a result of a peace-keeping agreement brokered by the Economic Community of West African States (ECOWAS, see p. 217), Senegalese troops began to depart from Guinea-Bissau, but strengthened their presence in the border area, while the ECOWAS peace-keeping force, ECOMOG (see p. 220), assumed positions on the Guinea-Bissau side of the frontier with Casamance.

In May 1999 fighting again broke out in Guinea-Bissau, and Vieira was overthrown. Tensions between the two countries resurfaced in April 2000, when an armed group, reportedly composed of members of the MFDC operating from within Guinea-Bissau, attacked a Senegalese border post, killing three soldiers, and later that month the border between the two countries was temporarily closed. In August the terms of the agreement concerning the joint exploitation of maritime resources by the two countries was revised; henceforth, Guinea-Bissau was to receive 20% rather than 15% of the revenue generated from petroleum deposits. In early September, following clashes near the border in Guinea-Bissau, attributed to an armed faction of the MFDC, the Senegalese Government closed all border posts between the two countries. Following the killing of Mané in November 2000, during an attempted *coup d'état*, relations between Senegal and Guinea-Bissau improved significantly. In January 2001 Guinea-Bissau forces launched a new offensive against MFDC rebel bases, while heightened security in the border regions during 2001 was regarded as a significant factor in restricting rebel activity and funding.

In August 1989 Diouf announced the withdrawal of Senegalese troops from The Gambia, in protest at a request by President Jawara of that country that The Gambia be accorded more power within the confederal agreement of Senegambia that had been formed by the two countries in 1982. Diouf subsequently stated that, in view of The Gambia's reluctance to proceed towards full political and economic integration with Senegal, the functions of the Confederation would be suspended. The Confederation was dissolved in September. In January 1991 the two countries signed a bilateral treaty of friendship and co-operation. Senegal's abrupt decision to close the Senegalese–Gambian border in September 1993, apparently to reduce smuggling between the two countries, again strained relations, although subsequent negotiations sought to minimize the adverse effects of the closure on The Gambia's regional trading links. Since the *coup d'état* in The Gambia in July 1994 Senegal has fostered cordial relations with the Government of President Jammeh and in June 1996 the two countries agreed to take joint measures to combat insecurity, illegal immigration, arms-trafficking and drugs-smuggling. In early 1998 Jammeh offered to act as a mediator between the Senegalese Government and the MFDC, and subsequently held regular meetings with MFDC representatives. None the less, intermittent disputes relating to transportation issues between the two countries have occurred, and in July 2002 the Gambian Secretary of State for Foreign Affairs, Blaise Baboucar Jagne, was prevented from entering Senegal by demonstrators protesting at the recent increase in fees for the transportation of foreign-registered vehicles on the ferry across the Gambia river, a principal trade route from the south of Senegal; the increase was revoked later in the month, following a meeting between Senegalese and Gambian officials. In April 2003 the Governments of the two countries announced that preliminary agreement had been reached on the construction of a road bridge between the northern and southern parts of Senegal. Tensions between the two countries again heightened in mid-2005, following a 100% increase in transportation fees on the ferry across the Gambia river by the Gambian port authorities. Senegalese trade unionists blockaded border crossings between Senegal and The Gambia to protest at the increase, and the Senegalese Government granted fuel subsidies to drivers who used a longer, alternative route between the southern and northern parts of Senegal, avoiding The Gambia. Although tensions lessened later in the year, when the port authority reduced the ferry charges by 15%, in what was described as a gesture of goodwill, there was increasing speculation that the Senegalese authorities were considering the construction of a tunnel to link the southern and northern parts of Senegal.

Since his election in March 2000, President Wade has on several occasions promoted greater democratization in other West African countries and encouraged an expansion in the international political engagement of African countries. Notably, Wade's well-publicized condemnation, at an international conference on racism and xenophobia held under the auspices of the office of the UN High Commissioner for Human Rights in Dakar in January 2001, of the increasing importance of ethnically based politics in Côte d'Ivoire prompted violent demonstrations across Côte d'Ivoire. At the UN World Conference against Racism, Racial Discrimination, Xenophobia and Related Intolerance, held in Durban, South Africa, in August–September, Wade, notably among African leaders, condemned the notion that reparations should be paid by Western nations to the descendants of slaves. Following the disputed presidential election in Madagascar in December 2001, Wade hosted peace talks between the two rival candidates in Dakar, which led to the signing of an accord, in April 2002, between the two parties.

Further negotiations, which ended without a resolution of the dispute, were held in Dakar in June, and in July Senegal recognized Marc Ravalomanana as President of Madagascar, to which position he had been inaugurated in early May, in spite of objections by the Organization of African Unity (OAU, now the African Union, see p. 153) and other African states.

President Wade was one of the four African leaders most closely involved in the initial development of the New Partnership for Africa's Development (NEPAD, see p. 157), a long-term plan for socio-economic recovery in Africa that was launched in October 2001 in accordance with a decision of the OAU summit of heads of state and government held in Lusaka, Zambia, in July of that year.

Relations with France have remained particularly strong since independence, and the existing defence arrangements between France and Senegal remained substantially unaltered following the major restructuring of the French armed forces undertaken by the administration of Jacques Chirac in the late 1990s and early 2000s. Closer relations with the USA were also established from the late 1990s. In 1998 US President Bill Clinton visited Senegal and met President Diouf; their respective successors, George W. Bush and Wade, met in Senegal in July 2003.

In late 2005 Senegal announced that it was to terminate its diplomatic relations with Taiwan in order to resume relations with the People's Republic of China. The respective embassies in Dakar and Beijing were re-opened, and ambassadors were exchanged between the two countries in early 2006.

Senegal is an active participant in regional and international peace-keeping operations. In February 1998 Senegal, with Mali and Mauritania, was among the principal participants in multinational military exercises conducted in eastern Senegal under the auspices of the UN and the OAU, as part of efforts to establish a regional crisis-intervention force. The exercise was organized by France and involved almost 3,500 troops from eight West African countries, as well as units from the USA, the United Kingdom and Belgium. Senegal is a member of the Accord de Non-agression et d'assistance en matière de défense, which in April 1999 adopted a draft protocol on the setting up of a peace-keeping force in the region. In September 1999 a Senegalese contingent joined the international peace-keeping operation in the Kosovo and Metohija province of Yugoslavia (now Serbia and Montenegro). In April 2001 more than 500 Senegalese soldiers joined UN observer missions in the Democratic Republic of the Congo. In early 2003 it was announced that Senegal was to contribute some 650 troops to the ECOWAS military mission in Côte d'Ivoire (ECOMICI); Senegalese troops were also expected to play a prominent role in the UN Operation in Côte d'Ivoire (UNOCI, see p. 80) that assumed the responsibilities of ECOMICI from April 2004. Meanwhile, in August 2003 some 260 Senegalese troops were dispatched to serve in the ECOWAS Mission in Liberia (ECOMIL), which was replaced by the UN Mission in Liberia (UNMIL, see p. 76) in October.

Government

Under the terms of the Constitution, approved by popular referendum in January 2001, executive power is held by the President, who is directly elected for a mandate of five years, which is renewable only once. (President Wade will, however, complete the seven-year mandate to which he was elected in March 2000 by the terms of the former Constitution). Legislative power rests with the Assemblée nationale, with 120 members elected for five years by universal adult suffrage. (In late 2005 the existing legislature voted to extend its mandate, exceptionally, by one further year.) The formation of parties on an ethnic, religious or geographical basis is prohibited. The President appoints the Prime Minister, who, in consultation with the President, appoints the Council of Ministers. Senegal comprises 11 regions, each with an appointed governor, an elected local assembly and a separate budget.

Defence

In August 2005 Senegal's active armed forces totalled 13,620 men: army 11,900, navy 950, air force 770. There was also a 5,000-strong paramilitary gendarmerie. Military service is by selective conscription and lasts for two years. France and the USA provide technical and material aid, and in August 2005 there were 1,100 French troops stationed in Senegal. The defence budget for 2005 was 52,000m. francs CFA.

Economic Affairs

In 2004, according to estimates by the World Bank, Senegal's gross national income (GNI), measured at average 2002–04 prices, was US $6,967m., equivalent to $670 per head (or $1,720 on an international purchasing-power parity basis). During 1995–2004, it was estimated, the population increased at an average annual rate of 2.6%, while gross domestic product (GDP) per head increased by an average of 2.4% per year. Overall GDP increased, in real terms, at an average annual rate of 5.1% per year in 1995–2004; growth in 2004 was 6.0%.

Agriculture (including forestry and fishing) contributed 17.0% of GDP in 2004; in 2003 some 72.8% of the labour force were engaged in the sector. The principal cash crops are groundnuts and cotton. In the late 1990s Senegal began to export mangoes, melons, asparagus and green beans to European markets. Groundnuts, millet, sorghum, rice, maize and vegetables are produced for domestic consumption, although Senegal has yet to achieve self-sufficiency in basic foodstuffs. In 2004 Senegal's agricultural output was decreased by the swarms of locusts that invaded the Sahel region of Africa from mid-year; however, the swarms only affected crops in the north of the country, while the primary crop-growing regions of the south were undamaged. The fishing sector makes an important contribution to both the domestic food supply and export revenue: fish and fish products had become Senegal's principal export commodity by the mid-1980s, and provided 24.5% of export earnings in 2003. The sale of fishing licences to the European Union (EU, see p. 228) was an important source of revenue from the late 1990s. Senegalese concerns at the dwindling fish stocks in its waters were addressed in an agreement signed with the EU in 2002, with an annual two-month moratorium on fishing. According to the World Bank, during 1995–2004 agricultural GDP increased by an average of 3.1% per year; agricultural GDP increased by 8.4% in 2004.

Industry (including mining, manufacturing, construction and power) contributed 21.2% of GDP in 2004. The principal activities are the processing of fish and agricultural products and of phosphates, while the production of cement is of increasing importance. According to the World Bank, during 1995–2004 industrial GDP increased at an average annual rate of 6.6%. Industrial GDP increased by 6.9% in 2004.

Mining contributed 1.4% of GDP in 2003. The principal mining activity is the extraction of calcium phosphates (aluminium phosphates are also mined in smaller quantities). Deposits of salt, fuller's earth (attapulgite), clinker and natural gas are also exploited, and there are currently investigations under way into the feasibility of mining copper, alluvial diamonds and iron ore. Explorations at Sabodala have revealed gold reserves estimated at 30 metric tons. Offshore deposits of petroleum are also to be developed, in co-operation with Guinea-Bissau. According to IMF estimates, the GDP of the mining sector declined by an average of 4.0% per year in 1992–99; the GDP of the sector fell by 2.0% in 1998, but increased by 20.8% in 1999.

Manufacturing contributed 12.6% of GDP in 2004. The most important manufacturing activities are food-processing (notably fish, groundnuts and sugar), chemicals, textiles and petroleum-refining (using imported crude petroleum). According to the World Bank, manufacturing GDP increased at an average annual rate of 5.3% in 1995–2004; growth in 2004 was 5.9%.

Electrical energy was wholly derived from petroleum in 2002. The Manantali hydroelectric power installation (constructed under the auspices of the Organisation pour la Mise en Valeur du Fleuve Sénégal—OMVS) commenced operations in December 2001; it was anticipated that Senegal would receive approximately one-third of the energy generated by the installation. Imports of fuels accounted for 18.6% of the value of merchandise imports in 2003.

The services sector contributed 61.8% of GDP in 2004. Tourism is a major source of foreign exchange, generating some US $184,000m. in 2002 and about 4,500 people are directly employed (and some 15,000 indirectly employed) in the sector. Dakar's port is of considerable importance as a centre for regional trade. According to the World Bank, the GDP of the services sector increased by an average of 5.2% per year in 1995–2004. The GDP of the sector increased by 5.0% in 2004.

In 2003 Senegal recorded a visible trade deficit of 470,000m. francs CFA, while there was a deficit of 244,000m. francs CFA on the current account of the balance of payments. In 2003 the principal source of imports (24.6%) was France; other major suppliers were Nigeria and Thailand. India and France were the principal market for exports in that year (taking 12.8% and

11.9% of the total, respectively); Mali, Italy, Côte d'Ivoire and Guinea were also important purchasers. The principal exports in 2003 were food and live animals (accounting for 29.8% of the total, and principally comprising fish), chemicals and chemical products (22.4%) and mineral fuels and lubricants (20.1%, chiefly refined petroleum products). The principal imports in that year were food and live animals (amounting to 23.6% of total imports), machinery and transport equipment (20.3%), mineral fuels and lubricants, basic manufactures and chemicals and related products.

Senegal recorded an overall budget deficit of 52,300m. francs CFA (equivalent to 1.4% of GDP) in 2003. Total external debt was US $4,418m. at the end of 2003, of which $4,023m. was long-term public debt. In that year the cost of debt-servicing was equivalent to 10.4% of the value of exports of goods and services. In 1990–93 consumer prices declined by an annual average of 0.8%. However, following the 50% devaluation of the CFA franc, inflation averaged 32.3% in 1994; inflation subsequently slowed to an annual average of 1.3% in 1996–2004. Consumer prices decreased by 0.1% in 2003, but increased by 0.5% in 2004. In early 1999 some 157,063 people were registered as unemployed.

Senegal is a member of the Economic Community of West African States (ECOWAS, see p. 217), of the West African organs of the Franc Zone (see p. 282), of the African Groundnut Council (see p. 381), of the West Africa Rice Development Association (see p. 383), of the Gambia River Basin Development Organization (see p. 386) and of the OMVS (see p. 387).

The attainment of sustained economic growth has been impeded by Senegal's dependence on revenue from a narrow export base, and by its consequent vulnerability to fluctuations in international prices for its principal commodities. Several important state-owned companies were privatized from the late 1990s, although the divestiture programme was subject to delays and difficulties. The transfer of the groundnut-oil production company, the Société Nationale de Commercialisation des Oléagineux du Sénégal (SONACOS), to majority private ownership, which had been unsuccessfully attempted in both 1997 and 1999, was finally completed in mid-2005. Meanwhile, the perceived under-performance of the electricity company, the Société Nationale d'Electricité (SENELEC), led the Government, in 2001, to reacquire those shares in the company that had previously been sold to private investors; its reprivatization, initially scheduled for 2003, was repeatedly delayed. Senegal has generally enjoyed good relations with the IMF; following an agreement under the Poverty Reduction and Growth Facility (PRGF) between 1998 and 2002, in April 2003 a further PRGF arrangement, amounting to some US $33m., was concluded with the IMF in support of the Government's economic reform programme for 2003–06. In 2000 Senegal was declared eligible for assistance under the initiative for heavily indebted poor countries; the country reached 'completion point' under the terms of the initiative in April 2004, resulting in debt relief of $850m. in nominal terms, or $488m. in net present value terms. In July 2005 Senegal was among 18 countries to be granted 100% debt relief on multilateral debt agreed by the Group of Eight leading industrialized nations (G-8), subject to the approval of the lenders. The involvement of President Wade in the creation and promotion of the New Partnership for Africa's Development (NEPAD) has served to increase Senegal's international profile as a country committed to thorough economic reform and transparency, although concerns were expressed, in late 2003, by the President of the European Commission, Romano Prodi, at the pace of reform in areas such as administration and good governance. (Indeed, in mid-2005 Wade himself criticized the operations of the NEPAD secretariat as inefficient.) The Government was keen to develop Senegal's considerable potential for tourism, planning to double receipts from that sector by 2010. However, the continued prosperity of the fishing sector—traditionally Senegal's primary source of foreign currency income—was endangered by ageing equipment and the depletion of stocks as a result of unregulated overfishing. GDP growth of around 5% was predicted for both 2005 and 2006.

Education

Primary education, which usually begins at seven years of age, lasts for six years and is officially compulsory. In 2000/01 primary enrolment included 63% of children in the relevant age-group (males 66%; females 60%), according to UNESCO estimates. The 1995–2008 Educational and Training Plan places special emphasis on increasing levels of female enrolment, and is intended to raise overall levels of pupil enrolment by 5% annually. Secondary education usually begins at the age of 13, and comprises a first cycle of four years (also referred to as 'middle school') and a further cycle of three years. In 2000/01 secondary enrolment was equivalent to only 18% of children in the relevant age-group (males 21%; females 14%), according to UNESCO estimates. There are two universities in Senegal, the Université Cheikh Anta Diop in Dakar and the Université Gaston Berger in Saint-Louis. Since 1981 the reading and writing of national languages has been actively promoted, and is expressly encouraged in the 2001 Constitution. Current government expenditure on education in 2000 was some 100,400m. francs CFA (representing 24.4% of total current expenditure). Some 40% of the Senegalese budget for 2005 was designated for the educational sector.

Public Holidays

2006: 1 January (New Year's Day), 10 January*† (Tabaski, Feast of the Sacrifice), 9 February* (Ashoura), 4 April (National Day), 10 April* (Mouloud, Birth of the Prophet), 14 April (Good Friday), 17 April (Easter Monday), 1 May (Labour Day), 25 May (Ascension Day), 5 June (Whit Monday), 14 July (Day of Association), 15 August (Assumption), 23 October* (Korité, end of Ramadan), 1 November (All Saints' Day), 25 December (Christmas), 31 December*† (Tabaski, Feast of the Sacrifice).

2007: 1 January (New Year's Day), 30 January* (Ashoura), 31 March* (Mouloud, Birth of the Prophet), 4 April (National Day), 6 April (Good Friday), 9 April (Easter Monday), 1 May (Labour Day), 17 May (Ascension Day), 28 June (Whit Monday), 14 July (Day of Association), 15 August (Assumption), 13 October* (Korité, end of Ramadan), 1 November (All Saints' Day), 20 December* (Tabaski, Feast of the Sacrifice), 25 December (Christmas).

* These holidays are determined by the Islamic lunar calendar and may vary by one or two days from the dates given.

† This festival occurs twice (in the Islamic years AH 1426 and 1427) within the same Gregorian year.

Weights and Measures

The metric system is in force.

SENEGAL

Statistical Survey

Source (unless otherwise stated): Direction de la Prévision et de la Statistique, Ministère de l'Economie et des Finances, rue René Ndiaye, BP 4017, Dakar; tel. 821-96-99; fax 822-41-95.

Area and Population

AREA, POPULATION AND DENSITY

Area (sq km)	196,722*
Population (census results)†	
16 April 1976	5,085,388
27 May 1988	
Males	3,353,599
Females	3,543,209
Total	6,896,808
Population (UN estimates at mid-year)‡	
2002	10,856,000
2003	11,119,000
2004	11,386,000
Density (per sq km) at mid-2004	57.9

* 75,955 sq miles.
† Figures refer to the *de jure* population. The *de facto* population at the 1976 census was 4,907,507, and at the 1988 census was 6,773,417.
‡ Source: UN, *World Population Prospects: The 2004 Revision*.

POPULATION BY ETHNIC GROUP
(at 1988 census)

Ethnic group	Number	%
Wolof	2,890,402	42.67
Serere	1,009,921	14.91
Peul	978,366	14.44
Toucouleur	631,892	9.33
Diola	357,672	5.28
Mandingue	245,651	3.63
Rural-Rurale	113,184	1.67
Bambara	91,071	1.34
Maure	67,726	1.00
Manjaag	66,605	0.98
Others	320,927	4.74
Total	**6,773,417**	**100.00**

Source: UN, *Demographic Yearbook*.

REGIONS
(official estimates, 1 January 2001)

	Area (sq km)	Population	Density (per sq km)
Dakar (capital)	550	2,411,528	4,834.6
Diourbel	4,359	930,008	213.4
Fatick	7,935	639,075	86.4
Kaolack	16,010	1,128,128	70.5
Kolda	21,011	834,753	39.7
Louga	29,188	559,268	19.2
Matam	25,083	291,555	11.6
Saint-Louis	19,044	571,885	30.0
Tambacounda	59,602	530,332	8.9
Thiès	6,601	1,348,637	204.3
Ziguinchor	7,339	557,606	76.0
Total	**196,722**	**9,802,775**	**49.8**

PRINCIPAL TOWNS
(estimated population at mid-1996)

Dakar (capital)*	1,770,068	Mbour	109,317
Thiès	228,017	Diourbel	99,437
Kaolack	199,023	Louga	59,745
Rufisque†	185,142	Tambacounda	56,173
Ziguinchor	180,555	Richard Toll	53,105
Saint-Louis	132,425	Mbacké	51,859

* Including Pikine and Guediawaye.
† Including Bargny.

Mid-2003 (UN estimate, incl. suburbs): Dakar 2,166,861 (Source: UN, *World Urbanization Prospects: The 2003 Revision*).

BIRTHS AND DEATHS
(UN estimates, annual averages)

	1990–95	1995–2000	2000–05
Birth rate (per 1,000)	42.2	39.6	37.4
Death rate (per 1,000)	13.1	12.4	11.7

Source: UN, *World Population Prospects: The 2004 Revision*.

Expectation of life (WHO estimates, years at birth): 56 (males 54; females 57) in 2003 (Source: WHO, *World Health Report*).

ECONOMICALLY ACTIVE POPULATION
('000 persons, ILO estimates, 1990)

	Males	Females	Total
Agriculture, hunting, forestry and fishing	1,319	1,190	2,508
Industry	195	51	246
Manufacturing	177	50	227
Services	370	145	516
Total	**1,884**	**1,386**	**3,269**

Source: ILO.

Mid-2003 (estimates in '000): Agriculture, etc. 3,296; Total labour force 4,530 (Source: FAO).

Unemployed (general survey, February–March 1999): 157,063 (males 99,892, females 57,171).

Health and Welfare

KEY INDICATORS

Total fertility rate (children per woman, 2003)	4.9
Under-5 mortality rate (per 1,000 live births, 2004)	137
HIV/AIDS (% of persons aged 15–49, 2003)	0.8
Physicians (per 1,000 head, 1998)	0.10
Hospital beds (per 1,000 head, 1998)	0.40
Health expenditure (2002): US $ per head (PPP)	62
Health expenditure (2002): % of GDP	5.1
Health expenditure (2002): public (% of total)	45.2
Access to water (% of persons, 2002)	72
Access to sanitation (% of persons, 2002)	52
Human Development Index (2003): ranking	157
Human Development Index (2003): value	0.458

For sources and definitions, see explanatory note on p. vi.

SENEGAL

Agriculture

PRINCIPAL CROPS
('000 metric tons)

	2002	2003	2004
Rice (paddy)	172.4	231.8	264.5*
Maize	80.4	400.9	422.6*
Millet	414.8	628.4	379.2*
Sorghum	116.9	189.8	132.4*
Cassava (Manioc)	107.0	181.7	180.0†
Sugar cane†	890	850	850
Pulses†	13.1	35.0	40.3
Cashew nuts†	4.5	4.5	4.5
Groundnuts (in shell)	265.3	440.7	465.0*
Oil palm fruit†	65	70	70
Cottonseed	19.0†	30.0*	30.0*
Tomatoes†	15	15	15
Dry onions†	90	90	90
Other vegetables†	53.0	63.5	63.5
Watermelons	220.9	398.5	398.5†
Oranges†	31	35	35
Mangoes†	73	75	75
Other fruit†	27.8	29.5	29.5
Cotton (lint)	14.2	22.0*	22.0*

* Unofficial figure.
† FAO estimate(s).
Source: FAO.

LIVESTOCK
('000 head, year ending September)

	2002	2003	2004*
Cattle	2,997	3,018	3,100
Sheep	4,540	4,613	4,700
Goats	3,900	3,969	4,000
Pigs	291	303	315
Horses	496	500	505
Asses	400	400	406
Camels	4	4	4
Poultry	45,000*	45,000*	46,000

* FAO estimate(s).
Source: FAO.

LIVESTOCK PRODUCTS
('000 metric tons)

	2002	2003	2004*
Beef and veal	45.1	43.3	47.8
Mutton and lamb	14.9	14.8	15.5
Goat meat	16.3*	16.5*	16.6
Pig meat	11.2	9.9	10.0
Horse meat	6.8*	6.9*	6.9
Poultry meat	64.1*	64.1*	65.3
Other meat	6.5*	6.5*	7.0
Cows' milk	86.0	92.3	96.1
Sheep's milk	15.6*	15.9*	16.2
Goats' milk	16.4*	16.7*	16.8
Poultry eggs	33*	33*	34
Cattle hides	9.0*	8.7*	9.6

* FAO estimate(s).
Source: FAO.

Forestry

ROUNDWOOD REMOVALS
(FAO estimates, '000 cubic metres, excl. bark)

	2002	2003	2004
Sawlogs, veneer logs and logs for sleepers*	40	40	40
Other industrial wood†	754	754	754
Fuel wood	5,178	5,210	5,243
Total	5,972	6,004	6,037

* Annual output assumed to be unchanged since 1986 (FAO estimates).
† Annual output assumed to be unchanged since 1999 (FAO estimates).
Source: FAO.

SAWNWOOD PRODUCTION
('000 cubic metres, incl. railway sleepers)

	1989	1990	1991
Total (all broadleaved)	15	22	23

1992–2004: Annual production as in 1991 (FAO estimates).
Source: FAO.

Fishing

('000 metric tons, live weight)

	2001	2002	2003
Capture*	403.2	375.8	448.2
Freshwater fishes*	22.0	22.1	21.9
Round sardinella	112.1	78.2	107.6
Madeiran sardinella	99.9	105.8	149.0
Bonga shad	31.7	26.2	23.6
Octopuses	3.0	12.8	10.9
Aquaculture	0.1	0.1	0.1
Total catch*	403.3	375.9	448.3

* FAO estimates.
Source: FAO.

Mining

('000 metric tons, unless otherwise stated)

	2002	2003	2004
Cement, hydraulic	1,653	1,694	1,700
Gold (kg)*	600	600	600
Calcium phosphates	1,547	1,761	1,800
Aluminium phosphates	4	4	4
Fuller's earth (attapulgite)	138	195	200
Salt (unrefined)	172	235	240

* Government estimate of unreported production of artisanal gold.
Source: US Geological Survey.

SENEGAL

Industry

PETROLEUM PRODUCTS
('000 metric tons, estimates)

	1999	2000	2001
Jet fuels	48*	66*	56
Motor gasoline (petrol)	135*	145*	111
Kerosene	25	21	22
Gas-diesel (distillate fuel) oils	385	390	392
Residual fuel oils*	230	237	231
Lubricating oils*	3	5	5
Liquefied petroleum gas	8	9	7

* Estimate.

Source: UN, *Industrial Commodity Statistics Yearbook*.

SELECTED OTHER PRODUCTS
('000 metric tons, unless otherwise indicated)

	2001	2002	2003
Raw sugar	95.0*	95.0†	95.0†
Sugar cubes	27.2	19.8	23.2
Tobacco products (tons)	2,132	2,245	2,218
Groundnut oil—crude	125.3	98.1	39.2
Vegetable oil—refined	70.6	78.5	75.7
Canned tuna	12.1	10.7	6.9
Footwear (million pairs)	0.6	n.a.	n.a.
Cotton yarn (tons)	411	n.a.	n.a.
Soap	38.6	34.8	33.4
Paints and varnishes	4.6	4.3	4.6
Cement	1,539.0	1,653.2	1,693.9
Metal cans (million)	113.2	185.2	182.2
Electricity (million kWh)	1,651.2	1,557.3	1,855.5

* Unofficial figure.
† FAO estimate.

Source: mainly IMF, *Senegal: Selected Issues and Statistical Appendix* (May 2005).

Nitrogenous fertilizers (nitrogen content, '000 metric tons, unofficial figures): 38.8 in 1998; 24.5 in 1999; 19.4 in 2000 (Source: FAO).

Phosphate fertilizers (phosphoric acid content, '000 metric tons, unofficial figures): 67.5 in 1998; 45.0 in 1999; 32.4 in 2000 (Source: FAO).

Source: IMF, *Senegal: Statistical Appendix* (June 2003).

Cement ('000 metric tons): 1.0 annually in 2001–03 (Source: US Geological Survey).

Finance

CURRENCY AND EXCHANGE RATES

Monetary Units
100 centimes = 1 franc de la Communauté financière africaine (CFA).

Sterling, Dollar and Euro Equivalents (30 December 2005)
£1 sterling = 957.440 francs CFA;
US $1 = 556.037 francs CFA;
€1 = 655.957 francs CFA;
10,000 francs CFA = £10.44 = $17.98 = €15.24.

Average Exchange Rate (francs CFA per US $)
2003   581.20
2004   528.29
2005   527.47

Note: An exchange rate of 1 French franc = 50 francs CFA, established in 1948, remained in force until January 1994, when the CFA franc was devalued by 50%, with the exchange rate adjusted to 1 French franc = 100 francs CFA. This relationship to French currency remained in effect with the introduction of the euro on 1 January 1999. From that date, accordingly, a fixed exchange rate of €1 = 655.957 francs CFA has been in operation.

BUDGET
('000 million francs CFA)

Revenue*	2001	2002	2003
Tax revenue	576.8	629.2	677.0
Taxes on income and property	130.6	145.9	159.3
Individual	58.8	74.7	80.8
Corporate	48.9	54.2	55.9
Taxes on goods and services (excl. petroleum)	254.8	258.3	308.9
Value-added tax on domestic goods	90.5	114.6	128.7
Value-added tax on imported goods	112.7	86.4	119.8
Taxes on imports (excl. petroleum)	107.3	107.7	107.9
Taxes on petroleum products	84.1	115.4	100.9
Value-added tax	38.6	64.4	37.3
Excises	44.7	44.8	56.4
Non-tax revenue	25.9	35.4	43.1
Total	**602.7**	**664.6**	**720.1**

* Excluding grants received ('000 million francs CFA): 61.7 in 2001; 62.1 in 2002; 77.7 in 2003.

Expenditure*	2001	2002	2003
Current expenditure	516.6	478.2	529.5
Wages and salaries	177.3	199.4	203.7
Other operational expenses	189.9	309.0	
Interest payments on public debt	30.3	39.8	44.6
External	23.7	35.4	40.0
Capital expenditure	232.3	275.9	338.5
Treasury special accounts and correspondents (net)	3.8	−18.2	−11.1
Total	**752.7**	**735.9**	**856.9**

* Excluding net lending ('000 million francs CFA): −4.6 in 2001; −5.6 in 2002; −6.8 in 2003.

Source: IMF, *Senegal: Selected Issues and Statistical Appendix* (May 2005).

INTERNATIONAL RESERVES
(excluding gold, US $ million at 31 December)

	2002	2003	2004
IMF special drawing rights	9.1	10.6	7.3
Reserve position in IMF	2.0	2.2	2.4
Foreign exchange	626.3	1,098.2	1,376.7
Total	**637.4**	**1,110.9**	**1,386.4**

Source: IMF, *International Financial Statistics*.

MONEY SUPPLY
('000 million francs CFA at 31 December)

	2002	2003	2004
Currency outside banks	191.9	337.5	342.3
Demand deposits at deposit money banks	366.1	484.7	532.5
Checking deposits at post office	5.3	8.5	12.8
Total money (incl. others)	**563.9**	**832.2**	**887.9**

Source: IMF, *International Financial Statistics*.

COST OF LIVING
(Consumer Price Index, Dakar; base: 1996 = 100)

	2002	2003	2004
Food, beverages and tobacco	113.9	113.2	114.1
Clothing	92.1	90.3	87.4
Housing, water, electricity and gas	114.7	116.4	117.1
All items (incl. others)	**110.0**	**109.9**	**110.5**

Source: Banque centrale des états de l'Afrique de l'ouest.

SENEGAL

NATIONAL ACCOUNTS
('000 million francs CFA at current prices)

Expenditure on the Gross Domestic Product

	2001	2002	2003
Final consumption expenditure	3,052.6	3,278.6	3,433.8
Households Non-profit institutions serving households	2,566.3	2,840.2	2,948.9
General government	486.3	438.4	484.9
Gross capital formation	613.3	581.3	727.2
Gross fixed capital formation	762.1	798.7	851.9
Changes in inventories Acquisitions, less disposals, of inventories	−148.8	−217.4	−124.7
Total domestic expenditure	3,665.9	3,859.9	4,161.0
Exports of goods and services	1,027.1	1,061.4	1,082.1
Less Imports of goods and services	1,350.3	1,448.6	1,513.4
GDP in purchasers' values	3,342.7	3,472.7	3,729.7

Gross Domestic Product by Economic Activity

	2001	2002	2003
Agriculture, hunting, forestry and fishing	582.8	472.0	568.2
Mining and quarrying	39.1	38.4	46.0
Manufacturing	391.0	440.8	446.3
Electricity, gas and water	69.2	70.6	84.5
Construction	137.6	155.0	172.9
Trade, restaurants and hotels	597.3	641.0	679.9
Transport, storage and communications	228.0	245.8	265.9
Non-market services	266.7	296.5	298.7
Other services	622.2	670.4	706.5
Sub-total	2,933.9	3,030.5	3,268.9
Import taxes and duties	408.8	442.3	460.8
GDP in purchasers' values	3,342.7	3,472.7	3,729.7

Source: Banque centrale des états de l'Afrique de l'ouest.

BALANCE OF PAYMENTS
('000 million francs CFA)

	2001	2002	2003
Exports of goods f.o.b.	735	743	731
Imports of goods f.o.b.	−1,047	−1,118	−1,201
Trade balance	−312	−375	−470
Services and income: credit	341	365	400
Services and income: debit	−408	−456	−487
Balance on goods, services and income	−379	−466	−557
Unrequited private transfers (net)	173	192	241
Unrequited public transfers (net)	50	68	72
Current balance	−155	−206	−244
Capital account (net)	64	66	67
Direct investment (net)	29	31	29
Portfolio investment (net)	10	2	13
Other investment (net)	88	163	153
Net errors and omissions	26	53	32
Overall balance	62	109	50

Source: IMF, *Senegal: Selected Issues and Statistical Appendix* (May 2005).

External Trade

PRINCIPAL COMMODITIES
(distribution by SITC, US $ million)

Imports c.i.f.	2001	2002	2003
Food and live animals	386.3	527.3	563.5
Cereals and cereal preparations	229.0	344.3	327.1
Rice, broken	142.0	240.0	216.0
Crude materials (inedible) except fuels	54.5	63.9	87.5
Mineral fuels, lubricants, etc.	291.1	1,002.9	445.3
Petroleum, petroleum products, etc.	250.4	941.7	399.9
Crude petroleum oils, etc.	168.6	592.7	276.3
Petroleum products, refined	77.8	341.6	118.3
Gasoline and other light oils	0.5	7.2	117.8
Motor spirit, incl. aviation spirit	0.1	0.7	117.8
Kerosene and other medium oils	29.1	262.3	—
Kerosene (incl. kerosene type jet fuel)	23.9	249.1	—
Animal and vegetable oils, fats and waxes	46.8	43.4	86.7
Fixed vegetable oils and fats	44.5	35.3	74.2
Chemicals and related products	190.6	246.3	250.8
Medicinal and pharmaceutical products	56.9	68.2	79.7
Basic manufactures	252.1	287.4	306.4
Iron and steel	55.2	62.9	72.6
Machinery and transport equipment	392.1	474.3	486.3
General industrial machinery, equipment and parts	73.9	96.4	98.1
Electrical machinery, apparatus, etc.	56.5	54.5	67.8
Road vehicles and parts (excl. tyres, engines and electrical parts)	126.5	161.3	160.9
Passenger motor vehicles (excl. buses)	63.5	77.2	83.1
Miscellaneous manufactured articles	86.8	91.6	107.1
Total (incl. others)	1,730.2	2,779.9	2,391.5

Exports f.o.b.	2001	2002	2003
Food and live animals	287.3	50.6	343.0
Fish, crustaceans and molluscs, and preparations thereof	246.5	0.4	282.0
Fish, fresh, chilled or frozen	126.2	0.2	104.1
Fish, fresh or chilled, excl. fillets	25.0	—	14.5
Fish, frozen, excl. fillets	53.2	—	62.0
Fish fillets, frozen	37.9	—	16.0
Crustaceans and molluscs, fresh, chilled, frozen, salted, etc	94.6	—	142.0
Feeding stuff for animals (excl. unmilled cereals)	22.3	22.7	13.0
Crude materials (inedible) except fuels	53.4	63.6	77.1
Crude fertilizers and crude minerals	30.5	36.0	31.3
Mineral fuels, lubricants, etc.	140.1	157.8	231.6
Petroleum, petroleum products, etc.	139.3	157.1	230.8
Crude petroleum and oils obtained from bituminous materials	16.5	21.2	43.5
Refined petroleum products	121.6	133.9	184.4
Gasolene and other light oils	9.0	8.9	184.4
Motor spirit, incl. aviation spirit	5.2	5.2	184.4
Kerosene and other medium oils	98.8	111.7	—
Kerosene (incl. kerosene-type jet fuel)	97.6	110.4	—

SENEGAL

Statistical Survey

Exports f.o.b.—*continued*	2001	2002	2003
Animal and vegetable oils, fats and waxes	71.6	53.6	37.4
Fixed vegetable oils and fats	71.6	53.5	36.9
Groundnut (peanut) oil	71.3	53.2	36.5
Chemicals and related products	138.2	266.2	257.9
Inorganic chemicals	75.7	171.5	139.9
Phosphorus pentoxide and phosphoric acids	74.7	170.6	138.0
Oils and perfume materials; toilet and cleansing preparations	23.9	28.9	39.0
Manufactured fertilizers	20.1	37.5	49.7
Nitrogen-phosphorus-potassium fertilizer	18.3	35.2	48.0
Basic manufactures	35.9	42.7	57.1
Machinery and transport equipment	34.9	24.3	48.2
Miscellaneous manufactured articles	18.7	25.2	33.4
Total (incl. others)	785.1	696.0	1,151.2

Source: UN, *International Trade Statistics Yearbook*.

PRINCIPAL TRADING PARTNERS
(US $ million)

Imports c.i.f.	2001	2002	2003
Argentina	10.5	40.4	26.1
Belgium	57.6	86.7	67.2
Brazil	27.7	36.7	70.9
China, People's Republic	42.3	48.2	64.2
Côte d'Ivoire	49.4	81.1	86.1
France (incl. Monaco)	480.6	553.4	588.9
Germany	82.8	77.1	82.4
India	20.2	50.3	52.6
Ireland	26.3	28.6	28.7
Italy	68.8	125.5	86.1
Japan	46.6	58.1	57.8
Netherlands	57.0	107.0	71.4
Nigeria	169.5	549.6	280.7
Russia	31.3	43.6	42.4
Saudi Arabia	9.9	34.0	14.3
South Africa	22.7	26.0	24.1
Spain	74.4	95.7	103.5
Thailand	132.5	201.3	173.9
United Kingdom	23.8	39.2	49.3
USA	72.1	79.2	86.1
Viet Nam	24.5	25.8	21.9
Total (incl. others)	1,730.2	2,779.9	2,391.5

Exports f.o.b.	2001	2002	2003
Belgium	17.3	2.6	7.8
Benin	6.8	21.8	32.7
Burkina Faso	3.0	6.3	29.5
Cameroon	9.2	3.5	10.3
China, People's Republic	8.1	0.6	15.3
Congo, Republic	9.8	3.4	7.0
Côte d'Ivoire	25.9	28.2	61.4
France (incl. Monaco)	131.5	53.6	137.5
Gabon	9.5	4.3	4.2
The Gambia	26.9	33.9	42.8
Germany	7.4	3.1	5.7
Greece	57.3	—	16.6
Guinea	30.9	17.7	59.9
Guinea-Bissau	—	21.3	
India	97.5	196.4	147.2
Italy	46.8	22.6	95.6
Mali	54.4	86.3	114.9
Mauritania	30.4	30.9	33.3
Netherlands	21.3	14.5	9.8
Portugal	8.1	3.9	8.6
Spain	31.4	2.2	56.3
Togo	6.4	8.5	14.9
United Kingdom	9.8	1.6	2.7
Total (incl. others)	785.1	696.0	1,151.2

Source: UN, *International Trade Statistics Yearbook*.

Transport

RAILWAYS
(traffic)

	1997	1998	1999
Passengers ('000)	5,065	4,029	4,789
Freight carried ('000 metric tons)	2,088	1,992	2,017

Passenger-km (million): 74 in 2000; 88 in 2001; 105 in 2002 (Source: UN, *Statistical Yearbook*).

Net ton-km (million): 361 in 2000; 321 in 2001; 345 in 2002 (Source: UN, *Statistical Yearbook*).

ROAD TRAFFIC
(motor vehicles in use)

	1997	1998	1999
Passenger cars	76,971	85,805	98,260
Buses and coaches	9,236	9,974	10,477
Lorries and vans	21,693	23,851	25,276
Road tractors	2,110	2,278	2,458
Motorcycles and mopeds	3,624	4,155	4,515

Source: IRF, *World Road Statistics*.

SHIPPING

Merchant Fleet
(vessels registered at 31 December)

	2002	2003	2004
Number of vessels	190	187	178
Total displacement ('000 grt)	46.6	45.8	40.8

Source: Lloyd's Register-Fairplay, *World Fleet Statistics*.

International Sea-borne Freight Traffic
('000 metric tons)

	2000	2001	2002
Goods loaded	2,060	2,282	2,622
Goods unloaded	5,301	5,983	6,440

Source: Port Autonome de Dakar.

CIVIL AVIATION
(traffic on scheduled services)*

	1999	2000	2001
Kilometres flown (million)	3	3	4
Passengers carried ('000)	103	98	176
Passenger-km (million)	241	222	319
Total ton-km (million)	37	32	116

* Including an apportionment of the traffic of Air Afrique.

Source: UN, *Statistical Yearbook*.

Tourism

FOREIGN TOURIST ARRIVALS BY NATIONALITY*

	2001	2002	2003
Belgium, Luxembourg and the Netherlands	18,786	15,628	17,025
France	209,641	230,088	181,470
Germany	10,847	8,458	7,985
Italy	15,616	19,496	9,279
Spain	23,499	23,224	12,680
USA	9,180	8,241	8,518
Total (incl. others)	396,254	426,825	353,539

* Figures refer to arrivals at hotels and similar establishments.

Tourism receipts (US $ million, excl. passenger transport): 174 in 2000; 190 in 2001; 184 in 2002.

Source: World Tourism Organization.

Communications Media

	2002	2003	2004
Telephones ('000 main lines in use)	224.6	228.8	n.a.
Mobile cellular telephones ('000 subscribers)	455.6	575.9	1,028.1
Personal computers ('000 in use)	200	220	242
Internet users ('000)	105.0	225.0	482.0

Television receivers: ('000 in use) 380 in 2000.

Radio receivers: ('000 in use) 1,240 in 1997.

Daily newspapers: 1 (average circulation 45,000 copies) in 1996; 4 in 1997; 5 in 1998.

Non-daily newspapers: 6 (average circulation 37,000 copies) in 1995.

Source: mainly International Telecommunication Union; UNESCO, *Statistical Yearbook*, UNESCO Institute for Statistics.

Education

(2002/03, unless otherwise indicated)

	Males	Females	Total
Pre-primary	18,285	20,057	38,342
Primary	675,471	611,622	1,287,093
Middle	140,356	99,057	239,413
Secondary:			
general	41,525	25,089	66,613
technical	2,795	1,630	4,425

Source: Ministry of Education, Dakar.

Institutions (2002/03, unless otherwise indicated): Pre-primary 460, Primary 5,670, Middle *and* Secondary (general) 579, Secondary (technical, 1999/2000) 12.

Teachers (2002/03, unless otherwise indicated): Pre-primary 1,413, Primary 29,216, Middle *and* Secondary (general) 7,601, Secondary (technical, 1999/2000) 384.

Tertiary: 29,303 students in 1998/99 (Source: UNESCO Institute for Statistics).

Adult literacy rate (UNESCO estimates): 39.3% (males 51.1%; females 29.2%) in 2003 (Source: UN Development Programme, *Human Development Report*).

Directory

The Constitution

The Constitution of the Republic of Senegal was promulgated following its approval by popular referendum on 7 January 2001, and entered into force thereafter, with the exception of those sections relating to the Assemblée nationale and the relations between the executive and legislative powers (articles 59–87), which took effect following legislative elections on 29 April 2001. The main provisions are summarized below:

PREAMBLE

The people of Senegal, recognizing their common destiny, and aware of the need to consolidate the fundaments of the Nation and the State, and supporting the ideals of African unity and human rights, proclaim the principle of national territorial integrity and a national unity respecting the diverse cultures of the Nation, reject all forms of injustice, inequality and discrimination, and proclaim the will of Senegal to be a modern democratic State.

THE STATE AND SOVEREIGNTY

Articles 1–6: Senegal is a secular, democratic Republic, in which all people are equal before the law, without distinction of origin, race, sex or religion. The official language of the Republic is French; the national languages are Diola, Malinké, Pular, Sérère, Soninké, Wolof and any other national language that may be so defined. The principle of the Republic is 'government of the people, by the people and for the people'. National sovereignty belongs to the people who exercise it, through their representatives or in referenda. Suffrage may be direct or indirect, and is always universal, equal and secret. Political parties and coalitions of political parties are obliged to observe the Constitution and the principles of national sovereignty and democracy, and are forbidden from identifying with one race, one ethnic group, one sex, one religion, one sect, one language or one region. All acts of racial, ethnic or religious discrimination, including regionalist propaganda liable to undermine the security or territorial integrity of the State are punishable by law. The institutions of the Republic are: the President of the Republic; the Assemblée nationale; the Government and the Constitutional Council; the Council of State; the Final Court of Appeal (Cour de Cassation); the Revenue Court (Cour de Comptes); and Courts and Tribunals.

PUBLIC LIBERTIES AND THE HUMAN PERSON; ECONOMIC AND SOCIAL RIGHTS AND COLLECTIVE RIGHTS

Articles 7–25: The inviolable and inalienable rights of man are recognized as the base of all human communities, of peace and justice in the world, and are protected by the State. All humans are equal before the law. The Republic protects, within the rule of law, the right to free opinion, free expression, a free press, freedom of association and of movement, cultural, religious and philosophical freedoms, the right to organize trade unions and businesses, the right to education and literacy, the right to own property, to work, to health, to a clean environment, and to diverse sources of information. No prior authorization is required for the formation of an organ of the press. Men and women are guaranteed equal rights to possess property.

Marriage and the family constitute the natural and moral base of the human community, and are protected by the State. The State is obliged to protect the physical and moral health of the family, in particular of the elderly and the handicapped, and guarantees to alleviate the conditions of life of women, particularly in rural areas. Forced marriages are forbidden as a violation of individual liberty. The State protects youth from exploitation, from drugs, and from delinquency.

All children in the Republic have the right to receive schooling, from public schools, or from institutions of religious or non-religious communities. All national educational institutions, public or private, are obliged to participate in the growth of literacy in one of the national languages. Private schools may be opened with the authorization of, and under the control of, the State.

Freedom of conscience is guaranteed. Religious communities and institutions are separate from the State.

All discrimination against workers on grounds of origins, sex, political opinions or beliefs are forbidden. All workers have the right to join or form trade or professional associations. The right to strike is recognized, under legal conditions, as long as the freedom to work is not impeded, and the enterprise is not placed in peril. The State guarantees sanitary and human conditions in places of work.

THE PRESIDENT OF THE REPUBLIC

Articles 26–52: The President of the Republic is elected, for a term of five years, by universal direct suffrage. The mandate may be renewed once. Candidates for the presidency must be of solely Senegalese nationality, enjoy full civil and political rights, be aged 35 years or more on the day of elections, and must be able to write, read and speak the official language fluently. All candidates must be presented by a political party or a legally constituted coalition of political parties, or be accompanied by a petition signed by at least 10,000 electors, including at least 500 electors in each of six administrative regions. Candidates may not campaign predominately on ethnic or regional grounds. Each political party or coalition of political parties may present only one candidate. If no candidate receives an absolute majority of votes cast in the first round, representing the support of at least one-quarter of the electorate, a second round of elections is held between the two highest-placed candidates in the first round. In the case of incapacity, death or resignation, the President's position is assumed by the President of the Assemblée nationale, and in the case

SENEGAL

of his or her incapacity, by one of the Vice-Presidents of the Assemblée nationale, in all cases subject to the same terms of eligibility that apply to the President. The President presides over the Council of Ministers, the Higher Council of National Defence, and the National Security Council, and is the Supreme Chief of the Armed Forces. The President appoints a Prime Minister, and appoints ministers on the recommendation of the Prime Minister.

THE GOVERNMENT
Articles 53–57: The head of the Government is the Prime Minister. In the event of the resignation or removal from office of a Prime Minister, the entire Government is obliged to resign.

THE OPPOSITION
Article 58: The Constitution guarantees the right to oppose to political parties that are opposed to Government policy, and recognizes the existence of a parliamentary opposition.

THE ASSEMBLÉE NATIONALE
Article 59–66: Deputies of the Assemblée nationale are elected by universal direct suffrage, for a five-year mandate, subject only to the dissolution of the Assemblée nationale. Any serving deputy who resigns from his or her party shall have his or her mandate removed. Deputies enjoy immunity from criminal proceedings, except with the authorization of the bureau of the Assemblée nationale. The Assemblée nationale votes on the budget. Deputies vote as individuals and must not be obligated to vote in a certain way. Except in exceptional and limited circumstances, sessions of the Assemblée nationale are public.

RELATIONS BETWEEN THE EXECUTIVE AND LEGISLATIVE POWERS
Articles 67–87: The Assemblée nationale is the sole holder of legislative power, votes on the budget and authorizes a declaration of war. The President of the Republic may, having received the opinion of the Prime Minister and the President of the Assemblée nationale, pronounce by decree the dissolution of the Assemblée nationale, except during the first two years of any Assemblée.

INTERNATIONAL TREATIES
Articles: 88–91: The President of the Republic negotiates international engagements, and ratifies or approves them with the authorization of the Assemblée nationale. The Republic of Senegal may conclude agreements with any African State that would comprise a partial or total abandonment of national sovereignty in order to achieve African unity.

JUDICIAL POWER
Articles 92–98: The judiciary is independent of the legislature and the executive power. The judiciary consists of the Constitutional Council, the Council of State, the Court of Final Appeal, the Revenue Court and Courts and Tribunals. The Constitutional Council comprises five members, including a President, a Vice-President and three judges. Each member serves for a mandate of six years (which may not be renewed) with partial renewals occurring every two years. The President of the Republic appoints members of the Constitutional Council, whose decisions are irreversible.

THE HIGH COURT OF JUSTICE
Articles 99–101: A High Court of Justice, presided over by a magistrate and comprising members elected by the Assemblée nationale, is instituted. The President of the Republic can only be brought to trial for acts accomplished in the exercise of his duties in the case of high treason. The High Court of Justice tries the Prime Minister and other members of the Government for crimes committed in the exercise of their duties.

LOCAL GOVERNMENT
Article 102: Local government bodies operate independently, by means of elective assemblies, in accordance with the law.

ON REVISION
Article 103: Only the President of the Republic or the deputies of the Assemblée nationale, of whom a three-quarters' majority must be in favour, may propose amending the Constitution. Amendments may be approved by referendum or, at the initiative of the President of the Republic, solely by approval by the Assemblée nationale, in which case a three-fifths' majority must be in favour.

The Government

HEAD OF STATE
President: ABDOULAYE WADE (took office 1 April 2000).

COUNCIL OF MINISTERS
(April 2006)

Prime Minister: MACKY SALL.
Minister of State at the Presidency: LANDING SAVANÉ.
Minister of State at the Presidency: SERIGNE DIOP.
Minister of State at the Presidency: CHRISTIAN SINA DIATTA.
Minister of State at the Presidency: AMINATA TALL.
Minister, Director of the President's Cabinet: SOULEYMANE NDÉNÉ NDIAYE.
Minister of State, Minister of Foreign Affairs: CHEIKH TIDIANE GADIO.
Minister of State, Minister of the Economy and Finance: ABDOULAYE DIOP.
Minister of State, Keeper of the Seals, Minister of Justice: CHEIKH TIDIANE SY.
Minister of State, Minister of the Maritime Economy: DJIBO LEÏTY KÂ.
Minister of State, Minister of Infrastructure, Capital Works, Land Transport and Internal Maritime Transport: HABIB SY.
Minister of the Armed Forces: BÉCAYE DIOP.
Minister of the Interior and Local Communities: OUSMANE NGOM.
Minister of Education: MOUSTAPHA SOURANG.
Minister of Tourism and Air Transport: OUSMANE MASSECK NDIAYE.
Minister of Energy and Mining: MADICKÉ NIANG.
Minister of Trade: MAMADOU DIOP.
Minister of Health and Preventative Medicine: ABDOU FALL.
Minister of the Civil Service, Labour, Employment and Professional Organizations: ADAMA SALL.
Minister of International Co-operation and Decentralized Co-operation: LAMINE BÂ.
Minister of Women, the Family and Social Development: AÏDA MBODJ.
Minister of Agriculture, Rural Water Resources and Food Security: FARBA SENGHOR.
Minister of Town Planning and Territorial Management: ASSANE DIAGNE.
Minister of Posts, Telecommunications and New Information and Communication Technologies: JOSEPH NDONG.
Minister of Sports: El Hadj DAOUDA FAYE.
Minister of Industry and Crafts: BINETA BÂ SAMB.
Minister of Preventive Care, Public Hygiene, Decontamination and Urban Water Resources: Dr ISSA MBAYE SAMB.
Minister of the Environment and the Protection of Nature: THIERNO LO.
Minister of Culture and Protected National Heritage: MAME BIRAME DIOUF.
Minister of Property, Housing and Construction: OUMAR SARR.
Minister of Information, Government Spokesperson: BACAR DIA.
Minister of the New Partnership for Africa's Development (NEPAD), African Economic Integration and the Politics of Good Governance: ABDOU AZIZ SOW.
Minister of Small- and Medium-sized Enterprises, Female Entrepreneurship and Micro-finance: MARIE-PIERRE SARR TRAORÉ.
Minister of Scientific Research: YAYE KENE GASSAMA DIA.
Minister of Planning and Sustainable Development: MAMADOU SIDIBÉ.
Minister of Youth: ALIOU SOW.
Minister of Senegalese Nationals Abroad: ABDOUL MALAL DIOP.
Minister of Stockbreeding: OUMY KHAÏRY GUÈYE SECK.
Minister of Technical and Professional Training: GEORGES TENDENG.
Minister of Relations with the Institutions: AWA FALL DIOP.
Minister of the Quality of Life and Leisure: MAÏMOUNA SOURANG NDIR.
Minister-delegate at the Office of the Prime Minister, responsible for Local Development: SOKHNA TOURÉ FALL.

SENEGAL

Minister-delegate at the Office of the Minister of State, Minister of the Economy and Finance, responsible for the Budget: CHEIKH HADJIBOU SOUMARÉ.

Minister-delegate at the Ministry of Education, responsible for Pedagogical Affairs: IBRAHIMA FALL.

Minister-delegate at the Ministry of Education, responsible for Literacy, National Languages and Francophone Affairs: DIÉGANE SÈNE.

MINISTRIES

Office of the President: ave Léopold Sédar Senghor, BP 168, Dakar; tel. 823-10-88; internet www.gouv.sn/institutions/president.html.

Office of the Prime Minister: Bldg Administratif, ave Léopold Sédar Senghor, BP 4029, Dakar; tel. 849-70-00; fax 822-55-78; internet www.gouv.sn.

Ministry of Agriculture, Rural Water Resources and Food Security: Bldg Administratif, BP 4005; Dakar; tel. 823-39-74; fax 821-32-68; e-mail agric@agric.gouv.sn; internet www.agriculture.gouv.sn.

Ministry of the Armed Forces: Bldg Administratif, ave Léopold Sédar Senghor, BP 4041, Dakar; tel. 823-56-13; fax 823-63-38; internet www.forcesarmees.gouv.sn.

Ministry of the Civil Service, Labour, Employment and Professional Organizations: Bldg Administratif, BP 4007, Dakar; tel. 849-72-48; fax 823-74-29; internet www.fonctionpublique.gouv.sn.

Ministry of Culture and Protected National Heritage: Bldg Administratif, ave Léopold Sédar Senghor, BP 4001, Dakar; tel. 822-95-49; fax 822-16-38.

Ministry of the Economy and Finance: rue René Ndiaye, BP 4017, Dakar; tel. 822-11-06; fax 822-41-95; e-mail i_diouf@minfinances.sn; internet www.finances.gouv.sn.

Ministry of Education: rue Docteur Calmette, BP 4025, Dakar; tel. 849-54-54; fax 821-12-28; internet www.education.gouv.sn.

Ministry of Energy and Mining: 4e étage, Bldg Administratif, BP 4029, Dakar; tel. 849-70-00; fax 823-44-70.

Ministry of the Environment and the Protection of Nature: Bldg Administratif, BP 4019, Dakar; tel. 889-02-34; fax 822-21-80; e-mail mepn@sentoo.sn; internet www.environnement.gouv.sn.

Ministry of Foreign Affairs: place de l'Indépendance, BP 4044, Dakar; tel. 823-42-84; fax 823-84-88; internet www.diplomatie.gouv.sn.

Ministry of Health and Preventative Medicine: Bldg Administratif, ave Léopold Sédar Senghor, BP 4022, Dakar; tel. 823-10-88; fax 822-26-90; e-mail spmin@sante.gouv.sn; internet www.sante.gouv.sn.

Ministry of Industry and Crafts: 122 bis ave Peytavin, BP 4037, Dakar; tel. 822-96-26; fax 822-55-94; e-mail mmai@sentoo.sn; internet www.industrie.gouv.sn.

Ministry of Information: 58 blvd de la République, Dakar; tel. 823-10-65; fax 821-45-04; internet www.information.gouv.sn.

Ministry of Infrastructure, Capital Works, Land Transport and Internal Maritime Transport: Ex-Camp Lat Dior, Corriche, Dakar; tel. 849-07-59; fax 823-82-79; internet www.equipement.gouv.sn.

Ministry of the Interior and Local Communities: blvd de la République, Dakar; tel. 842-67-90; fax 821-05-42; e-mail mint@primature.sn; internet www.interieur.gouv.sn.

Ministry of International Co-operation and Decentralized Co-operation: Dakar; tel. 842-58-47; fax 860-16-05; e-mail mcdpr@primature.sn; internet www.mcdpr.gouv.sn.

Ministry of Justice: Bldg Administratif, ave Léopold Sédar Senghor, BP 4030, Dakar; tel. 849-70-00; fax 823-27-27; e-mail justice@justice.gouv.sn.

Ministry of the Maritime Economy: Bldg Administratif, BP 4050, Dakar; tel. 823-34-26; fax 823-87-20; e-mail abdoumbodj@yahoo.fr; internet www.ecomaritime.gouv.sn.

Ministry of NEPAD, African Economic Integration and the Politics of Good Governance: 94 rue Félix Faure, Dakar; tel. 889-11-60; fax 842-42-65; e-mail dgnepad@sentoo.sn; internet www.nepad.gouv.sn.

Ministry of Planning and Sustainable Development: 8 rue du Dr Guillet, BP 4010, Dakar; tel. 823-29-93; fax 823-14-37; e-mail xadijabousso@hotmail.com; internet www.plan.gouv.sn.

Ministry of Posts, Telecommunications and New Information and Communication Technologies: 2 rue Béranger Ferraud, angle ave Assane Ndoye, Dakar; tel. 887-17-15; fax 842-87-24; internet www.telecom.gouv.sn.

Ministry of Preventive Care, Public Hygiene, Decontamination and Urban Water Resources: 2 rue Béranger Ferraud, angle ave Assane Ndoye, Dakar; tel. 889-17-04; fax 842-84-25; e-mail mphpa@sentoo.sn; internet www.prevention.gouv.sn.

Ministry of Property, Housing and Construction: blvd Dial Diop, place de l'ONU, BP 11552, Dakar; tel. 869-15-42; fax 869-59-32.

Ministry of the Quality of Life and Leisure: Dakar.

Ministry of Relations with the Regional and National Parliamentary Institutions, and with those of the African Union: Bldg Administratif, ave Léopold Sédar Senghor, BP 49, Dakar; tel. 821-80-60; fax 821-88-50; e-mail mmbodj@sentoo.sn; internet www.mri.gouv.sn.

Ministry of Scientific Research: Bldg Administratif, ave Léopold Sédar Senghor, BP 36005, Dakar; tel. 849-75-52; fax 822-45-63; internet www.recherche.gouv.sn.

Ministry of Senegalese Nationals Abroad: Immeuble ROES, face station Mobil VDN, Dakar; tel. 864-50-87; fax 864-50-89.

Ministry of Small- and Medium-sized Enterprises, Female Entrepreneurship and Micro-finance: Bldg Administratif, 6e étage, ave Léopold Sédar Senghor, BP 36008, Dakar; tel. 822-36-94; fax 842-02-92; e-mail contact@pme.gouv.sn; internet www.pme.gouv.sn.

Ministry of Sports: place de l'Indépendance, Dakar; tel. 821-65-04; fax 822-48-31; internet www.sports.gouv.sn.

Ministry of Stockbreeding: VDN, BP 45677, Dakar-Fann; tel. 864-50-91; fax 864-50-90.

Ministry of Tourism and Air Transport: rue Calmette, BP 4049, Dakar; tel. 821-11-26; fax 822-94-13; internet www.tourisme.gouv.sn.

Ministry of Town Planning and Territorial Management: Ex-Camp Lat Dior, Dakar; tel. 842-08-13; fax 842-08-12; e-mail muat@sentoo.sn; internet www.muat.gouv.sn.

Ministry of Trade: Bldg Administratif, ave Léopold Sédar Senghor, BP 4029, Dakar; tel. 849-70-00; fax 821-91-32; internet www.commerce.gouv.sn.

Ministry of Women, the Family and Social Development: Bldg Administratif, Dakar; tel. 849-70-63; fax 822-94-90; internet www.famille.gouv.sn.

Ministry of Youth: 2 rue Emile Zola, angle rue Mohamed V, BP 4055, Dakar; tel. 849-59-00; fax 822-97-64; e-mail jeunesse@jeunesse.gouv.sn; internet www.jeunesse.gouv.sn.

President and Legislature

PRESIDENT

Presidential Election, First Ballot, 27 February 2000

Candidate	Votes	% of votes
Abdou Diouf (PS)	690,886	41.33
Abdoulaye Wade (PDS)	517,642	30.97
Moustapha Niasse (AFP)	280,085	16.76
Djibo Kâ (URD)	118,487	7.09
Others	64,343	3.85
Total	1,671,443	100.00

Second Ballot, 19 March 2000

Candidate	Votes	% of votes
Abdoulaye Wade (PDS)	969,332	58.49
Abdou Diouf (PS)	687,969	41.51
Total	1,657,301	100.00

LEGISLATURE

Assemblée nationale

pl. Soweto, BP 86, Dakar; tel. 823-10-99; fax 823-67-08; e-mail assnat@assemblee-nationale.sn; internet www.assemblee-nationale.sn.

President: PAPE DIOP.

SENEGAL

General Election, 29 April 2001

Party	Votes	% of votes	Seats
Sopi Coalition*	931,144	49.59	89†
Alliance des forces de progrès (AFP)	303,012	16.14	11‡
Parti socialiste du Sénégal (PS)	325,979	17.36	10
Union pour le renouveau démocratique (URD)	68,956	3.67	3§
And Jëf—Parti africain pour la démocratie et le socialisme (AJ—PADS)	76,083	4.05	2
Parti libéral sénégalais (PLS)	17,232	0.92	1
Parti pour le progrès et la citoyenneté (PPC)	17,119	0.91	1
Alliance pour le progrès et la justice—Jëf-Jël (APJ—JJ)	15,041	0.80	1
Rassemblement national démocratique (RND)	13,279	0.71	1
Parti de l'indépendance et du travail (PIT)	10,854	0.58	1
Others	99,137	5.28	—
Total	**1,877,836**	**100.00**	**120**

* A coalition of some 40 parties and movements, led by the PDS.
† Including 62 seats won by majority voting within departments.
‡ Including two seats won by majority voting within departments.
§ Including one seat won by majority voting within departments.

Election Commission

Commission électorale nationale autonome (CENA): Dakar; f. 2005; Pres. MAMADOU MOUSTAPHA TOURÉ.

Political Organizations

In early 2006 there were more than 70 political parties registered in Senegal, of which the following were among the most important:

Alliance des forces de progrès (AFP): rue 1, angle rue A, point E, BP 5825, Dakar; tel. 825-40-21; fax 864-07-07; e-mail admin@afp-senegal.org; internet www.afp-senegal.org; f. 1999; mem. of opposition Cadre permanent de concertation (f. 2001); Sec.-Gen. MOUSTAPHA NIASSE.

Alliance pour le progrès et la justice—Jëf-Jël (APJ—JJ): BP 7838, Dakar; tel. 682-60-55; fax 630-44-51; e-mail tallasylla@hotmail.com; mem. of opposition Cadre permanent de concertation (f. 2001); Pres. TALLA SYLLA.

And Jëf—Parti africain pour la démocratie et le socialisme (AJ—PADS): Villa 1, Zone B, BP 12136, Dakar; tel. 825-76-67; fax 823-58-60; e-mail webmaster@ajpads.org; internet x.ajpads.org; f. 1992; Sec.-Gen. LANDING SAVANÉ.

Bloc des centristes Gaïndé (BCG): Villa no 734, Sicap Baobabs, Dakar; tel. 825-37-64; e-mail jpdias@sentoo.sn; f. 1996; Pres. and First Sec. JEAN-PAUL DIAS.

Ligue démocratique—Mouvement pour le parti du travail (LD—MPT): ave Bourguiba, Dieuppeul 2, Villa 2566, BP 10172, Dakar Liberté; tel. 825-67-06; fax 827-43-00; regd 1981; social-democrat; Sec.-Gen. ABDOULAYE BATHILY.

Mouvement pour la démocratie et le socialisme—Naxx Jarinu (MDS—NJ): Unité 20, Parcelles Assainies, Villa no 528, Dakar; tel. 869-50-49; f. 2000; Leader OUMAR KHASSIMOU DAI.

Mouvement de la réforme pour le développement social (MRDS): HLM 4, Villa 858, Dakar; tel. 644-31-70; f. 2000; Pres. IBRAHIMA DIENG; Sec.-Gen. Imam BABACAR NIANG.

Mouvement pour le socialisme et l'unité (MSU): HLM 1, Villa 86, Dakar; tel. 825-85-44; f. 1981 as Mouvement démocratique populaire; mem. of opposition Cadre permanent de concertation (f. 2001); National Co-ordinator-Gen. MOUHAMADOU BAMBA N'DIAYE.

Mouvement républicain sénégalais (MRS): Résidence du Cap-Vert, 10e étage, 5 pl. de l'Indépendance, BP 4193, Dakar; tel. 822-03-19; fax 822-07-00; e-mail agaz@omnet.sn; Sec.-Gen. DEMBA BA.

Parti africain de l'indépendance (PAI): Maison du Peuple, Guediewaye, BP 820, Dakar; tel. 837-01-36; f. 1957; reorg. 1976; Marxist; Sec.-Gen. MAJMOUT DIOP.

Parti démocratique sénégalais (PDS): blvd Dial Diop, Immeuble Serigne Mourtada Mbacké, Dakar; tel. 823-50-27; fax 823-17-02; e-mail cedobe@aol.com; internet www.sopionline.com; f. 1974; liberal democratic; Sec.-Gen. Me ABDOULAYE WADE.

Parti de l'indépendance et du travail (PIT): route front de terre, BP 10470, Dakar; tel. 827-29-07; fax 820-90-00; e-mail pit@telecomplus.sn; regd 1981; Marxist-Leninist; mem. of opposition Cadre permanent de concertation (f. 2001); Sec.-Gen. AMATH DANSOKHO.

Parti libéral sénégalais (PLS): 13 ave Malick Sy, BP 28277, Dakar; tel. and fax 823-15-60; f. 1998 by breakaway faction of PDS; Leader Me OUSMANE NGOM.

Parti populaire sénégalais (PPS): Quartier Escale, BP 212, Diourbel; tel. 971-11-71; regd 1981; populist; mem. of opposition Cadre permanent de concertation (f. 2001); Sec.-Gen. Dr OUMAR WANE.

Parti pour le progrès et la citoyenneté (PPC): Quartier Merina, Rufique; tel. 836-18-68; absorbed Rassemblement pour le progrès, la justice et le socialisme in 2000; Sec.-Gen. Me MBAYE JACQUES DIOP.

Parti pour la renaissance africaine—Sénégal (PARENA): Sicap Dieuppeul, Villa no 2685/B, Dakar; tel. 636-87-88; fax 823-57-21; e-mail mariamwane@yahoo.fr; f. 2000; Sec.-Gen. MARIAM MAMADOU WANE LY.

Parti de la renaissance et de la citoyenneté: Liberté 6, Villa 7909, Dakar; tel. 827-85-68; f. 2000; supports Pres. Wade; Sec.-Gen. SAMBA DIOULDÉ THIAM.

Parti socialiste du Sénégal (PS): Maison du Parti Socialiste Léopold Sédar Senghor, Colobane, BP 12010, Dakar; tel. and fax 824-77-44; e-mail partisocialiste@sentoo.sn; internet www.partisocialiste.sn; f. 1958; as Union progressiste sénégalaise, reorg. 1978; democratic socialist; mem. of opposition Cadre permanent de concertation (f. 2001); First Sec. OUSMANE TANOR DIENG.

Rassemblement des écologistes du Sénégal—Les verts (RES): rue 67, angle rue 52, Gueule Tapée, BP 25226, Dakar-Fann; tel. and fax 842-34-42; e-mail lesverts@arc.sn; f. 1999; Sec.-Gen. OUSMANE SOW HUCHARD.

Rassemblement national démocratique (RND): Sacré-Coeur III, Villa no 972, Dakar; tel. 827-50-72; e-mail wourydiouf@hotmail.com; f. 1976; legalized 1981; mem. of opposition Cadre permanent de concertation (f. 2001); Sec.-Gen. MADIOR DIOUF.

Rassemblement des travailleurs africains—Sénégal (RTA-S): Villa 999, HLM Grand Yoff, BP 13725, Dakar; tel. 827-15-79; e-mail sambmomar@hotmail.com; f. 1997; Co-ordinator El Hadj MOMAR SAMBE.

Union pour le renouveau démocratique (URD): Bopp Villa 234, rue 7, Dakar; tel. 820-55-98; fax 820-73-17; f. 1998 by breakaway faction of PS; mem. of opposition Cadre permanent de concertation (f. 2001); Sec.-Gen. DJIBO LEÏTY KÂ.

In August 2001 some 25 pro-Government parties, which were formerly members of the Sopi (Change) Coalition that contested the legislative elections in April 2001, formed an electoral alliance, the **Convergence des actions autour du Président en perspective du 21ième siècle (CAP-21)**, to contest municipal and local elections in May 2002. In May 2001 several opposition parties (numbering 16 in January 2002 and led by the AFP) formed an opposition consultative framework, the **Cadre permanent de concertation (CPC)**, which was also to operate as an electoral alliance in the municipal and local elections.

The **Mouvement des forces démocratiques de la Casamance (MFDC)** was founded in 1947; it had paramilitary and political wings and formerly sought the independence of the Casamance region of southern Senegal. The MFDC is not officially recognized as a political party (the Constitution of 2001 forbids the formation of parties on a geographic basis) and waged a campaign of guerrilla warfare in the region from the early 1980s. Representatives of the MFDC have participated in extensive negotiations with the Senegalese Government on the restoration of peace and the granting of greater autonomy to Casamance, and in December 2004 a cease-fire agreement was signed between the two sides, pending further peace negotiations. The Honorary President of the MFDC is Fr AUGUSTIN DIAMACOUNÉ SENGHOR and the post of Secretary-General was disputed between JEAN-MARIE FRANÇOIS BIAGUI and ANSOUMANA BADJI.

Diplomatic Representation

EMBASSIES IN SENEGAL

Algeria: 5 rue Mermoz, Plateau, Dakar; tel. 822-35-09; fax 821-16-84; Ambassador Dr ABDELHAMID CHEBCHOUB.

Austria: 18 rue Emile Zola, BP 3247, Dakar; tel. 849-40-00; fax 849-43-70; e-mail dakar-ob@bmaa.gv.at; Ambassador GERHARD WEINBERGER.

Belgium: ave des Jambaars, BP 524, Dakar; tel. 821-25-24; fax 821-63-45; e-mail ambelda@sentoo.sn; internet www.diplomatie.be/dakar; Ambassador LUC DE WILLEMARCK.

SENEGAL

Brazil: Immeuble Fondation Fahd, 4e étage, blvd Djily Mbaye, angle rue Macodou Ndiaye, BP 136, Dakar; tel. 823-14-92; fax 823-71-81; e-mail embdakar@sentoo.sn; Ambassador Ricardo Carvahlo do Nascimento Borges.
Burkina Faso: Sicap Sacré Coeur III, Extension VDN No. 10628B, BP 11601, Dakar; tel. 864-58-24; fax 864-58-23; e-mail ambabf@sentoo.sn; Ambassador Salamata Sawadogo.
Cameroon: 157–9 rue Joseph Gomis, BP 4165, Dakar; tel. 849-02-92; fax 823-33-96; Ambassador Emmanuel Mbonjo-Ejangue.
Canada: Rue Galliéni, angle Brière de l'Isle, BP 3373, Dakar; tel. 889-47-00; fax 889-47-20; e-mail dakar@international.gc.ca; internet www.dakar.gc.ca; Ambassador Louise R. Marchand.
Cape Verde: 3 blvd El-Hadji Djilly M'Baye, BP 11269, Dakar; tel. (221) 22-42-85; fax (221) 21-06-97; e-mail acvc.sen@metissacana.sn; Ambassador Raúl Jorge Vera Cruz Barbosa.
China, People's Republic: Dakar; Ambassador Lu Shaye.
Congo, Democratic Republic: Fenêtre Mermoz, Dakar; tel. 825-12-80; Chargé d'affaires Fataki Nicolas Lunguele Musambya.
Congo, Republic: Statut Mermoz, BP 5242, Dakar; tel. 634-50-22; fax 825-78-56; Chargé d'affaires Joseph Ngoubéli.
Côte d'Ivoire: ave Birago Diop, BP 359, Dakar; tel. 869-02-70; fax 825-21-15; e-mail cmrci@ambaci-dakar.org; internet www.ambaci-dakar.org; Ambassador Fatimata Tanoe Touré.
Cuba: 43 rue Aimé Césaire, BP 4510, Dakar-Fann; tel. 869-02-40; fax 864-10-63; e-mail embacubasen@sentoo.sn; Ambassador Llusif Sadin Tassé.
Egypt: 22 ave Brière de l'Isle, Plateau, BP 474, Dakar; tel. 889-24-74; fax 821-89-93; e-mail ambegydk@telecomplus.sn; Ambassador Sanaa Ismail Atta allah.
Ethiopia: 18 blvd de la République, BP 379, Dakar; tel. 821-98-96; fax 821-98-95; e-mail ethembas@sentoo.sn; Ambassador Atu Dinberu Alemu.
France: 1 rue El Hadj Amadou Assane Ndoye, BP 4035, Dakar; tel. 839-51-00; fax 839-51-81; e-mail webmestre.dakar-amba@diplomatie.gouv.fr; internet www.ambafrance-sn.org; Ambassador André Parant.
Gabon: 12 ave Albert Sarraut, BP 436, Dakar; tel. 865-28-34; fax 864-31-45; Ambassador Patrice Tonda.
The Gambia: 11 rue de Thiong, BP 3248, Dakar; tel. 821-44-16; fax 821-62-79; Ambassador Ebou Momar Taal.
Germany: 20 ave Pasteur, angle rue Mermoz, BP 2100, Dakar; tel. 889-48-84; fax 822-52-99; e-mail reg1@daka.auswaertiges-amt.de; internet www.dakar.diplo.de; Ambassador Doretta Loschelder.
Ghana: Dakar; Ambassador Fred Amartey Laryea.
Guinea: rue 7, angle B&D, point E, BP 7123, Dakar; tel. 824-86-06; fax 825-59-46; Ambassador Keita Kobélé Hadja Makelé Camara.
Guinea-Bissau: rue 6, angle B, point E, BP 2319, Dakar; tel. 823-00-59; fax 825-29-46; Ambassador Lansana Touré.
Holy See: rue Aimé Césaire, angle Corniche-Ouest, Fann Résidence, BP 5076, Dakar; tel. 824-26-74; fax 824-19-31; e-mail vatemb@sentoo.sn; Apostolic Nuncio Most Rev. Giuseppe Pinto (Titular Archbishop of Anglona).
India: 5 rue Carde, BP 398, Dakar; tel. 822-58-75; fax 822-35-85; e-mail indiacom@sentoo.sn; internet www.ambassadeinde.sn; Ambassador (vacant).
Indonesia: ave Cheikh Anta Diop, BP 5859, Dakar; tel. 825-73-16; fax 825-58-96; e-mail kbri@sentoo.sn; internet www.indonesia-senegal.org; Ambassador Ahzam Bahdari Razif.
Iran: rue AX8, point E, BP 735, Dakar; tel. 825-25-28; fax 824-23-14; e-mail ambiiran@telecomplus.sn; Ambassador Mohammad Hoseini.
Israel: Immeuble SDIH, 3 pl. de l'Indépendance, BP 2096, Dakar; tel. 823-79-65; fax 823-64-90; e-mail info@dakar.mfa.gov.il; internet dakar.mfa.gov.il; Ambassador Daniel Pinhasi.
Italy: rue Alpha Achamiyou Tall, BP 348, Dakar; tel. 822-05-78; fax 821-75-80; e-mail ambasciata.dakar@esteri.it; internet sedi.esteri.it/dakar; Ambassador Agostino Mathis.
Japan: blvd Martin Luther King, Corniche-Ouest, BP 3140, Dakar; tel. 849-55-00; fax 849-55-55; Ambassador Akira Nakajima.
Korea, Republic: 4e étage, Immeuble Fayçal, 3 rue Parchappe, BP 3338, Dakar; tel. 822-58-22; fax 821-66-00; e-mail senegal@mofat.go.kr; internet www.mofat.go.kr/senegal; Ambassador Jae Chol Hahn.
Kuwait: blvd Martin Luther King, Dakar; tel. 824-17-23; fax 825-08-99; Ambassador Muhammad az-Zuwaikh.
Lebanon: 56 ave Jean XXIII, BP 234, Dakar; tel. 822-02-55; fax 823-58-99; e-mail ambaliban@sentoo.sn; Ambassador Michel Haddad.
Libya: route de Ouakam, Dakar; tel. 824-57-10; fax 824-57-22; Ambassador Al Hady Salem Hammad.
Madagascar: 4 rue de Oukham, Sotrac Mermoz, BP 25395 Dakar; tel. 860-29-87; fax 860-29-95; e-mail ambadak@yahoo.fr; internet www.ambamad.sn; Ambassador Lila Hanitra Ratsifandrihamanana.
Malaysia: 7 (VDN) Fann Mermoz, BP 15057, Dakar; tel. 825-89-35; fax 825-47-19; e-mail mwdakar@sentoo.sn; Ambassador (vacant).
Mali: Fann Résidence, Corniche-Ouest, rue 23, BP 478, Dakar; tel. 824-62-52; fax 825-94-71; e-mail ambamali@sentoo.sn; Ambassador N'Tji Laïco Traoré.
Mauritania: 37 blvd Charles de Gaulle, Dakar; tel. 823-53-44; fax 823-53-11; Ambassador Mohamed el-Moctar Ould Mohamed Yahya.
Morocco: 73 ave Cheikh Anta Diop, BP 490, Dakar; tel. 824-69-27; fax 825-70-21; e-mail ambmadk@sentoo.sn; Ambassador Moha Ouali Tagma.
Netherlands: 37 rue Kléber, BP 3262, Dakar; tel. 849-03-60; fax 821-70-84; e-mail dak@minbuza.nl; internet www.nlambassadedakar.org; Ambassador Dr J. W. G. Jansing.
Nigeria: 8 ave Cheikh Anta Diop, BP 3129, Dakar; tel. 824-43-97; fax 825-81-36; Ambassador Aisha Margaret Eyo Jimeta.
Pakistan: Stèle Mermoz, Villa no 7602, BP 2635, Dakar; tel. 824-61-35; fax 824-61-36; e-mail parepdakar@sentoo.sn; Ambassador Iftikhar A. Arian.
Poland: Villa 'Les Ailes', Fann Résidence, angle Corniche-Ouest, BP 343, Dakar; tel. 824-23-54; fax 824-95-26; e-mail ambassade.pl@sentoo.sn; internet www.ambassade-pologne.sn; Ambassador Andrzej Michal Lupina.
Portugal: 5 ave Carde, BP 281, Dakar; tel. 864-03-17; fax 864-03-22; e-mail ambportdakar@sentoo.sn; Ambassador António Montenegro.
Qatar: 25 blvd Martin Luther King, BP 5150, Dakar; tel. 820-95-59; fax 869-10-12; Ambassador Khamees Butti al-Sahouti.
Romania: rue A prolongée, Point E, BP 3171, Dakar; tel. 825-20-68; fax 824-91-90; e-mail romania@sentoo.sn; Ambassador Vlad Galin-Corini.
Russia: ave Jean Jaurès, angle rue Carnot, BP 3180, Dakar; tel. 822-48-21; fax 821-13-72; e-mail ambrus@sentoo.sn; Ambassador Aleksandr A. Romanov.
Saudi Arabia: route Corniche-Ouest, face Olympique Club, BP 3109, Dakar; tel. 864-01-41; fax 864-01-30; e-mail snemb@mofa.gov.sa; Ambassador Ahmed bin Mohamed Bayari.
South Africa: Memoz SUD, Lotissement Ecole de Police, BP 21010, Dakar-Ponty; tel. 865-19-59; fax 864-23-59; e-mail ambafsud@sentoo.sn; internet www.saesenegal.info; Ambassador O. Rantobeng William Mokou.
Spain: 18–20 ave Nelson Mandela, BP 2091, Dakar; tel. 821-11-78; fax 821-68-45; e-mail ambespsn@mail.mae.es; Ambassador Fernando Morán Calvo-Soleto.
Sudan: 31 route de la Pyrotechnie, Mermoz, BP 15033, Dakar-Fann; tel. 824-98-53; fax 824-98-52; e-mail sudembse@sentoo.sn; internet www.ambassade-soudan-senegal.org; Ambassador Mahmoud Hassan el-Amin.
Sweden: 18 rue Emile Zola, BP 6087, Dakar; tel. 849-03-33; fax 849-03-40; e-mail ambassaden.dakar@foreign.ministry.se; internet www.swedenabroad.com/dakar; Ambassador Annika Magnusson.
Switzerland: rue René N'Diaye, angle rue Seydou, BP 1772, Dakar; tel. 823-05-90; fax 822-36-57; e-mail vertretung@dak.rep.admin.ch; internet www.eda.admin.ch/dakar; Ambassador Livio Hürzeler.
Syria: rue 1, point E, angle blvd de l'Est, BP 498, Dakar; tel. 824-62-77; fax 825-17-55; Chargé d'affaires Nadim Jabar.
Thailand: 10 rue Léon Gontran Damas, BP 3721, Dakar-Fann; tel. 824-30-76; fax 824-84-58; e-mail thaidkr@sentoo.sn; Ambassador Kanya Chaiman.
Tunisia: rue El Hadj Seydou Nourou Tall, BP 3127, Dakar; tel. 823-47-47; fax 823-72-04; Ambassador Jalel Lakhdar.
Turkey: ave des Ambassadeurs, Fann Résidence, BP 6060, Etoile, Dakar; tel. 869-25-42; fax 825-69-77; e-mail trambdkr@sentoo.sn; Ambassador Yalçın Kaya Erensoy.
United Kingdom: 20 rue du Dr Guillet, BP 6025, Dakar; tel. 823-73-92; fax 823-27-66; e-mail britemb@sentoo.sn; internet www.britishembassy.gov.uk/senegal; Ambassador Peter Newall.
USA: ave Jean XXIII, angle rue Kleber, BP 49, Dakar; tel. 823-42-96; fax 823-51-63; e-mail usadakar@state.gov; internet dakar.usembassy.gov; Ambassador Janice L. Jacobs (designate).

Judicial System

In 1992 the Supreme Court was replaced by three judicial bodies. The Constitutional Council verifies that legislation and international agreements are in accordance with the Constitution. It decides disputes between the Executive and the Legislature, and determines the relative jurisdictions of the Council of State and the Court of Cassation. The Council of State judges complaints brought against the Executive. It also resolves electoral disputes. The Court of Cassation is the highest court of appeal, and regulates the activities of subordinate courts and tribunals. The Revenue Court supervises the public accounts.

Constitutional Council: Fann Résidence, Ex-Musée Dynamique, Dakar; tel. 822-52-52; internet www.gouv.sn/institutions/conseil_const.html; 5 mems; Pres. MIREILLE NDIAYE.

Council of State: rue Béranger Ferraut, Dakar; tel. 822-47-86; internet www.gouv.sn/institutions/conseil_etat.html; Pres. ABDOU AZIZ BA.

Court of Cassation: blvd Martin Luther King, BP 15184, Dakar-Fann; tel. 889-10-10; fax 821-18-90; e-mail courdecass@sentoo.sn; internet www.gouv.sn/institutions/cour_cassation.html; First Pres. GUIBRIL CAMARA; Procurator-Gen. MAISSA DIOUF; Sec.-Gen. MAMADOU BADIO CAMARA.

Revenue Court (Cour des Comptes): 15 ave Franklin Roosevelt, BP 9097, Peytavin, Dakar; tel. 849-40-01; fax 849-43-62; e-mail askonte@courdescomptes.sn; internet www.courdescomptes.sn; Pres. ABDOU BAME GUEYE; Sec.-Gen. El Hadji MALICK KONTE; Pres. of Chambers ABBA GOUDIABY, MOUSTAPHA GUEYE, MAMADOU HADY SARR; Chief Administrator ABDOURAHMANE DIOUKNANE.

High Court of Justice: Dakar; competent to try the Prime Minister and other members of the Government for crimes committed in the exercise of their duties; The President of the Republic may only be brought to trial in the case of high treason; mems elected by the Assemblée nationale.

Religion

At the time of the 1988 census almost 94% of the population were Muslims, while some 4% professed Christianity (the dominant faith being Roman Catholicism); a small number, mostly in the south, followed traditional beliefs.

ISLAM

There are four main Islamic brotherhoods active in Senegal: the Tidjanes, the Mourides, the Layennes and the Qadiriyas.

Association pour la coopération islamique (ACIS): Dakar; f. 1988; Pres. Dr THIERNAO KÂ.

Grande Mosquée de Dakar: Dakar; tel. 822-56-48; Grand Imam El Hadj BAYE DAME DIÈNE.

CHRISTIANITY

The Roman Catholic Church

Senegal comprises one archdiocese and six dioceses. At 31 December 2003 there were an estimated 677,426 adherents of the Roman Catholic Church, representing about 6.5% of the total population.

Bishops' Conference

Conférence des Evêques du Sénégal, de la Mauritanie, du Cap-Vert et de Guinée-Bissau, BP 941, Dakar; tel. 836-33-09; fax 836-16-17; e-mail archevchedkr@sentoo.sn; f. 1973; Pres. Most Rev. THÉODORE-ADRIEN SARR (Archbishop of Dakar).

Archbishop of Dakar: Most Rev. THÉODORE-ADRIEN SARR, Archevêché, ave Jean XXIII, BP 1908, Dakar; tel. 823-69-18; fax 823-48-75; e-mail archevechedkr@sentoo.sn.

The Anglican Communion

The Anglican diocese of The Gambia, part of the Church of the Province of West Africa, includes Senegal and Cape Verde. The Bishop is resident in Banjul, The Gambia.

Protestant Church

Eglise Protestante du Sénégal: 65 rue Wagane Diouf, BP 22390, Dakar; tel. 821-55-64; fax 821-71-32; f. 1862; Pastor ETITI YOMO DJERIWO.

BAHÁ'Í FAITH

National Spiritual Assembly: Point E, rue des Ecrivains, 2è impasse à droite après la Direction de la statistique, BP 1662, Dakar; tel. 824-23-59; e-mail bahai@sentoo.sn; internet www.sn.bahai.org; regd 1975; Sec. SHAHNAZ R. ARDEKANI.

The Press

DAILY NEWSPAPERS

L'Actuel: route du Front de Terre, angle ave Bourguiba, Immeuble Dramé, BP 11874, Dakar; tel. 864-26-01; fax 864-26-02; e-mail lactuel@sentoo.sn.

Dakar Soir: Dakar; tel. and fax 832-10-93; e-mail dakar-soir@telecomplus.sn; f. 2000.

Dekeu Bi: Quartier Casier, Thiès; tel. 557-29-15.

L'Evénement du Soir: Fann Résidence, rue A, angle rue 4, point E, BP 16060, Dakar; tel. 864-34-30; fax 864-36-00; evenings.

Frasques Quotidiennes: 51 rue du Docteur Thèze, BP 879, Dakar; tel. 842-42-26; fax 842-42-77; e-mail frasques@arc.sm.

L'Info 7: Sicap rue 10, BP 11357, Dakar; tel. and fax 864-26-58; e-mail comsept@sentoo.sn; f. 1999.

Le Matin: route de l'Aéroport Léopold Sédar Senghor, BP 6472, Dakar; tel. 825-73-59; fax 825-73-58; e-mail lematin@metissacana.sn; daily; independent; Dir MAME LESS CAMARA; Editor-in-Chief ALIOUNE FALL.

La Pointe: Dakar; tel. 820-50-35; fax 820-50-43.

Le Populaire: 114 ave Peytavin, Immeuble Serigne Massamba Mbacké, Dakar; tel. 822-79-77; fax 822-79-27; e-mail populaire@sentoo.sn; f. 2000; Editor-in-Chief MAMADOU THIERNO TALLA.

Scoop: route du Service Géographique, BP 92, Dakar; tel. 859-59-59; fax 859-60-50.

Le Soleil: Société sénégalaise de presse et de publications, route du Service géographique, Hann, BP 92, Dakar; tel. 859-59-40; fax 859-60-50; e-mail lesoleil@lesoleil.sn; internet www.lesoleil.sn; f. 1970; Dir-Gen.and Dir of Publication MAMADOU SEYE; Editors-in-Chief HABIB DEMBA FALL, IBRAHIMA MBODJ; circ. 25,000 (2005).

Sud Quotidien: Immeuble Fahd, BP 4130, Dakar; tel. 821-33-38; fax 822-52-90; e-mail info@sudonline.sn; internet www.sudonline.sn; independent; Dir ABDOULAYE NDIAGA SYLLA; circ. 30,000.

Tract: 13 rue de Thann, BP 3683, Dakar; tel. and fax 823-47-25; e-mail tract.sn@laposte.net; f. 2000.

Le Volcan: Dakar; tel. 820-50-35; fax 820-50-43.

Wal Fadjri/L'Aurore (The Dawn): Sicap Sacré-Coeur no 8542, BP 576, Dakar; tel. 824-23-43; fax 824-23-46; e-mail walf@walf.sn; internet www.walf.sn; f. 1984; Exec. Dir MBAYE SIDY MBAYE; circ. 15,000.

PERIODICALS

Afrique Médicale: 10 rue Abdou Karim Bourgi, BP 1826, Dakar; tel. 823-48-80; fax 822-56-30; f. 1960; 11 a year; review of tropical medicine; Editor P. CORREA; circ. 7,000.

Afrique Nouvelle: 9 rue Paul Holle, BP 283, Dakar; tel. 822-51-22; f. 1947; weekly; development issues; Roman Catholic; Dir RENÉ ODOUN; circ. 15,000.

Afrique Tribune: Dakar; tel. and fax 821-15-92; monthly.

Amina: BP 2120, Dakar; e-mail amina@calva.net; monthly; women's magazine.

Le Cafard Libéré: 10 rue Tolbiac, angle Autoroute, Soumédioune, BP 7292, Dakar; tel. 822-84-43; fax 822-08-91; e-mail caflibere@sentoo.sn; f. 1987; weekly; satirical; Editor PAPE SAMBA KANE; circ. 12,000.

Construire l'Afrique: Dakar; tel. 823-07-90; fax 824-19-61; f. 1985; six a year; African business; Dir and Chief Editor CHEIKH OUSMANE DIALLO.

Le Courrier du Sud: BP 190, Ziguinchor; tel. 991-11-66; weekly.

Démocratie: Liberté V, 5375 M, 71 rue du rond-point Liberté V et VI; tel. 824-86-69; fax 825-18-79.

Eco Hebdo: 22 x 19 rue Médina, BP 11451, Dakar; tel. and fax 837-14-14; weekly.

L'Equipe Sénégal: Dakar; tel. 824-00-13; e-mail lequipesenegal@yahoo.fr; weekly; sports.

Ethiopiques: BP 2035, Dakar; tel. and fax 821-53-55; f. 1974; literary and philosophical review; publ. by Fondation Léopold Sédar Senghor.

Le Journal de l'Economie: 15 rue Jules Ferry, BP 2851, Dakar; tel. 823-87-33; fax 823-60-07; weekly.

Journal Officiel de la République du Sénégal: Rufisque; f. 1856; weekly; govt journal.

Momsareew: BP 820, Dakar; f. 1958; monthly; publ. by PAI; Editor-in-Chief MALAMINE BADJI; circ. 2,000.

Nord Ouest: Immeuble Lonase, BP 459, Louga; tel. 680-79-43; e-mail lenordouest@yahoo.fr; regional monthly; Dir of Publication PAPE MOMAR CISSÉ.

Nouvel Horizon: Dakar; tel. and fax 822-74-14; weekly.

Nuit et Jour: Dakar; tel. 832-15-70; weekly.

Le Politicien: Dakar; tel. and fax 827-63-96; f. 1977; weekly; satirical.

Promotion: BP 1676, Dakar; tel. 825-69-69; fax 825-69-50; e-mail giepromo@telecomplus.sn; f. 1972; fortnightly; Dir BOUBACAR DIOP; circ. 5,000.

République: BP 21740, Dakar; tel. 822-73-73; fax 822-50-39; e-mail republike@yahoo.fr; f. 1994.

Sénégal d'Aujourd'hui: Dakar; monthly; publ. by Ministry of Culture; circ. 5,000.

Sopi (Change): 5 blvd Dial Diop, Dakar; tel. 824-49-50; fax 824-47-00; f. 1988; weekly; publ. by PDS; Dir of Publishing JOSEPH NDONG; Editor CHEIKH KOUREYSSI BA.

Le Témoin: Gibraltar II, Villa no 310, Dakar; tel. 822-32-69; fax 821-78-38; f. 1990; weekly; Editor-in-Chief MAMADOU OUMAR NDIAYE; circ. 5,000.

Unir Cinéma: 1 rue Neuville, BP 160, Saint Louis; tel. 861-10-27; fax 861-24-08; f. 1973; quarterly African cinema review; Editor PIERRE SAGNA.

Vive La République: Sicap Amitié III, Villa no 4057, Dakar; tel. 864-06-31; weekly.

Xareli (Struggle): BP 12136, Dakar; tel. 822-54-63; fortnightly; publ. by AJ—PADS; circ. 7,000.

NEWS AGENCIES

Agence Panafricaine d'Information—PANA-Presse SA: ave Bourjuiba, BP 4056, Dakar; tel. 824-13-95; fax 824-13-90; e-mail panapress@panapress.com; internet www.panapress.com; f. 1979 as Pan-African News Agency (under the auspices of the Organization of African Unity), restructured as 75% privately-owned co in 1997; Co-ordinator-Gen. BABACAR FALL.

Agence de Presse Sénégalaise: 58 blvd de la République, BP 117, Dakar; tel. 823-16-67; fax 822-07-67; e-mail aps@aps.sn; internet www.aps.sn; f. 1959; govt-controlled; Dir AMADOU DIENG.

Foreign Bureaux

Agence France-Presse (AFP): Immeuble Maginot, 7e étage, BP 363, Dakar; tel. 823-21-92; fax 822-16-07.

Xinhua (New China) News Agency (People's Republic of China): Villa 1, 2 route de la Pyrotechnie, Stèle Mermoz, BP 426, Dakar; tel. 823-05-38.

ANSA (Italy), ITAR—TASS (Russia) and UPI (USA) are also represented in Dakar.

PRESS ORGANIZATION

Syndicat des Professionnels de l'Information et de la Communication du Sénégal (SYNPICS): BP 21722, Dakar; tel. 822-36-25; fax 822-17-61.

Publishers

Africa Editions: BP 1826, Dakar; tel. 823-48-80; fax 822-56-30; f. 1958; general, reference; Man. Dir JOËL DECUPPER.

Agence de Distribution de Presse: km 2.5, blvd du Centenaire de la Commune de Dakar, BP 374, Dakar; tel. 832-02-78; fax 832-49-15; e-mail adpresse@telecomplus.sn; f. 1943; general, reference; Man. Dir PHILIPPE SCHORP.

Centre Africain d'Animation et d'Echanges Culturels Editions Khoudia: BP 5332, Dakar-Fann; tel. 21-10-23; fax 21-51-09; f. 1989; fiction, education, anthropology; Dir AISSATOU DIA.

Editions Clairafrique: 2 rue El Hadji Mbaye Guèye, BP 2005, Dakar; tel. 822-21-69; fax 821-84-09; f. 1951; politics, law, sociology, anthropology, literature, economics, development, religion, school books.

Editions des Ecoles Nouvelles Africaines: ave Cheikh Anta Diop, angle rue Pyrotechnie, Stèle Mermoz, BP 581, Dakar; tel. 864-05-44; fax 864-13-52; e-mail eenas@sentoo.sn; youth and adult education, in French.

Editions Juridiques Africaines (EDJA): 18 rue Raffenel, BP 22420, Dakar-Ponty; tel. 821-66-89; fax 823-27-53; e-mail edja.ed@sentoo.sn; f. 1986; law; Dir SALIMATA NGOM DIOP.

Editions des Trois Fleuves: blvd de l'Est, angle Cheikh Anta Diop, BP 123, Dakar; tel. 825-79-23; fax 825-59-37; f. 1972; general non-fiction; luxury edns; Dir GÉRARD RAZIMOWSKY; Gen. Man. BERTRAND DE BOISTEL.

Enda—Tiers Monde Editions (Environmental Development Action in the Third World): 54 rue Carnot, BP 3370, Dakar; tel. 822-98-90; fax 823-51-57; e-mail editions@enda.sn; internet www .enda.sn; f. 1972; third-world environment and development; Dir GIDEON PRISLER OMOLU; Exec. Sec. JACQUES BUGNICOURT.

Grande imprimerie africaine (GIA): 9 rue Amadou Assane Ndoye, Dakar; tel. 822-14-08; fax 822-39-27; f. 1917; law, administration; Man. Dir CHEIKH ALIMA TOURÉ.

Institut fondamental d'Afrique noire (IFAN)—Cheikh Anta Diop: BP 206, Campus universitaire, Dakar; tel. 825-98-90; fax 824-49-18; e-mail bifan@telecomplus.sn; internet www.afrique-ouest.auf .org; f. 1936; scientific and humanistic studies of Black Africa, for specialist and general public.

Nouvelles éditions africaines du Sénégal (NEAS): 10 rue Amadou Assane Ndoye, BP 260, Dakar; tel. 822-15-80; fax 822-36-04; e-mail neas@telecomplus.sn; f. 1972; literary fiction, schoolbooks; Dir-Gen. SAYDOU SOW.

Per Ankh: BP 2, Popenguine; history.

Société africaine d'édition: 16 bis rue de Thiong, BP 1877, Dakar; tel. 821-79-77; f. 1961; African politics and economics; Man. Dir PIERRE BIARNES.

Société d'édition 'Afrique Nouvelle': 9 rue Paul Holle, BP 283, Dakar; tel. 822-38-25; f. 1947; information, statistics and analyses of African affairs; Man. Dir ATHANASE NDONG.

Société nationale de Presse, d'édition et de publicité (SONAPRESS): Dakar; f. 1972; Pres. OBEYE DIOP.

Sud-Communication: BP 4100, Dakar; operated by a journalists' co-operative; periodicals.

Xamal, SA: BP 380, Saint-Louis; tel. 961-17-22; fax 961-15-19; e-mail xamal@sentoo.sn; general literature, social sciences, in national languages and in French; Dir ABOUBAKAR DIOP.

GOVERNMENT PUBLISHING HOUSE

Société sénégalaise de presse et de publications—Imprimerie nationale (SSPP): route du Service géographique, BP 92, Dakar; tel. 832-46-92; fax 832-03-81; f. 1970; 62% govt-owned; Dir SALIOU DIAGNE.

Broadcasting and Communications

TELECOMMUNICATIONS

Regulatory Authority

Agence de Régulation des Télécommunications (ART): rue 3, angle rue F, Fann Résidence, BP 14130, Dakar-Peytavin; tel. 869-03-69; fax 869-03-70; e-mail contact@art.sn; internet www .art-telecom-senegal.org; f. 2001; Chair. of Bd Prof. ABDOULAYE SAKHO; Dir-Gen. DANIEL G. GOUMALO SECK.

Service Providers

Excaf Telecom: Domaine Industriel SODIDA, rue 14 Prolongée, BP 1656, Dakar; tel. 824-24-24; fax 824-21-91.

Sentel Sénégal GSM: ave Nelson Mandela, angle ave Moussé Diop. BP 146, Dakar; tel. 675-42-02; fax 823-18-73; mobile cellular telephone operator in Dakar, most western regions, and in selected localities nation-wide; 75% owned by Millicom International Cellular (Luxembourg), 25% by Senegalese private investors; Gen. Man. YOUVAL ROSH; 250,000 subscribers (2003).

Société Nationale des Télécommunications du Sénégal (SONATEL): 46 blvd de la République, BP 69, Dakar; tel. 839-11-18; fax 823-60-37; e-mail webmaster@sonatel.sn; internet www .sonatel.sn; f. 1985; 42% owned by France Câbles et Radio; Pres. MICHEL HIRSCH; Man. Dir CHEIKH TIDIANE MBAYE; 1,673 employees (2003).

Alizé: 46 blvd de la République, BP 2352, Dakar; tel. 839-17-00; fax 839-17-54; e-mail webmaster@alize.sn; internet www.alize.sn; f. 1996 as Sonatel Mobiles.

Télécom Plus SARL: 20 rue Amadou Assane Ndoye, BP 21100, Dakar; tel. 839-97-00; fax 823-46-32; telecommunications products and services.

BROADCASTING

Regulatory Authority

Haut Conseil de l'Audiovisuel: Immeuble Fahd, Dakar; tel. and fax 823-47-84; f. 1991; Pres. AMINATA CISSÉ NIANG.

Radio

Société nationale de la Radiodiffusion-Télévision Sénégalaise (RTS): Triangle sud, angle ave Malick Sy, BP 1765, Dakar; tel. 849-12-12; fax 822-34-90; e-mail rts@rts.sn; internet www .rts.sn; f. 1992; state broadcasting co; broadcasts two national and eight regional stations; Dir-Gen. DAOUDA NDIAYE.

Radio Sénégal Internationale: Triangle sud, angle ave El Hadj Malick Sy, BP 1765, Dakar; tel. 849-12-12; fax 822-34-90; f. 2001; broadcasts news and information programmes in French, English, Arabic, Portuguese, Spanish, Italian, Soninké, Pulaar and Wolof from 14 transmitters across Senegal and on cable; Dir CHÉRIF THIAM.

RST1: Triangle sud, angle ave El Hadj Malick Sy, BP 1765, Dakar; tel. 849-12-12; fax 822-34-90; f. 1992; broadcasts in French, Arabic and six vernacular languages from 16 transmitters across Senegal; Dir MANSOUR SOW.

JDP FM (Jeunesse, Développement, Paix): BP 17040, Dakar; tel. 827-20-97; fax 824-07-41; e-mail sarrabdou@sentoo.sn.

Radio Nostalgie Dakar: BP 21021, Dakar; tel. 821-21-21; fax 822-22-22; e-mail nostafric@globeaccess.net; f. 1995; music; broadcasts in French and Wolof; Gen. Man. SAUL SAVIOTE.

Oxy-Jeunes: Fojes BP 18303, Pikine, Dakar; tel. 834-49-19; fax 827-32-15; e-mail cheikh_seck@eudoramail.com; f. 1999; youth and community radio station supported by the World Assn of Community Radio Stations and the Catholic Organization for Development and Peace.

Radio PENC-MI: BP 51, Khombole; tel. 957-91-03; fax 824-58-98; e-mail rdoucoure@oxfam.org.uk.

Radio Rurale FM Awagna de Bignona: BP 72, Bignona; tel. 994-10-21; fax 994-19-09; e-mail mksonko2000@yahoo.fr.

Sud FM: Immeuble Fahd, 5e étage, BP 4130, Dakar; tel. 822-53-93; fax 822-52-90; e-mail info@sudonline.sn; f. 1994; operated by Sud-Communication; regional stations in Saint-Louis, Kaolack, Louga, Thiès, Ziguinchor and Diourbel; Man. Dir CHERIF EL-WAHIB SEYE.

Wal Fadjri FM: Sicap Sacré-Coeur no 8542, BP 576, Dakar; tel. 824-23-43; fax 824-23-46; f. 1997; Islamic broadcaster; Exec. Dir MBAYE SIDY MBAYE.

Broadcasts by the Gabonese-based Africa No. 1, the British Broadcasting Corporation and Radio France Internationale are received in Dakar.

Television

Radiodiffusion-Télévision Sénégalaise (RTS): see Radio; Dir of Television DAOUDA NDIAYE.

Canal Horizons Sénégal: 31 ave Albert Sarrault, BP 1390, Dakar; tel. 823-25-25; fax 823-30-30; e-mail canalh@sonatel.sn; internet www.canalhorizons.com; f. 1990; private encrypted channel; 18.8% owned by RTS and Société Nationale des Télécommunications du Sénégal, 15% by Canal Horizons (France); Man. Dir JACQUES BARBIER DE CROZES.

Réseau MMDS-EXCAF Télécom: rue 14 prolongée, HLM 1, Domaine Industriel SODIDA, BP 1656, Dakar; tel. 824-24-24; fax 824-21-91; broadcasts selection of African, US, European and Saudi Arabian channels.

The French television stations, France-2, TV5 and Arte France, are also broadcast to Senegal.

Finance

(cap. = capital; res = reserves; dep = deposits; m. = million; brs = branches; amounts in francs CFA)

BANKING

Central Bank

Banque Centrale des Etats de l'Afrique de l'Ouest (BCEAO): National HQ: blvd du Général de Gaulle, angle Triangle Sud, BP 3159, Dakar; tel. 823-53-84; fax 823-57-57; e-mail akangni@bceao.int; internet www.bceao.int; f. 1962; bank of issue for mem. states of the Union économique et monétaire ouest africaine (UEMOA, comprising Benin, Burkina Faso, Côte d'Ivoire, Guinea-Bissau, Mali, Niger, Senegal and Togo); cap. and res 859,313m., total assets 5,671,675m. (Dec. 2002); Gov. CHARLES KONAN BANNY; Dir in Senegal SEYNI NDIAYE; brs at Kaolack and Ziguinchor.

Commercial Banks

Attijariwafa Bank Sénégal: 5 rue Victor Hugo, angle ave Léopold Sédar Senghor, Dakar; f. 2004; 100% owned by Attijariwafa Bank Maroc (Morocco); Pres. and Dir-Gen. SAÏD RAKI.

Bank of Africa—Sénégal: Résidence Excellence, 4 ave Léopold Sédar Senghor, BP 1992, Dakar; tel. 849-62-40; fax 842-16-67; e-mail boadg@sentoo.sn; internet www.bkofafrica.net/senegal.htm; f. 2001; 59.32% owned by African Financial Holding, 15.00% by Bank of Africa—Benin; cap. and res 1,661.2m., total assets 20,588.0m. (Dec. 2003); Pres. MAMADOU AMADOU AW; Dir-Gen. BERNARD PUECHALDOU; 1 br.

Banque Internationale pour le Commerce et l'Industrie du Sénégal (BICIS): 2 ave Léopold Sédar Senghor, BP 392, Dakar; tel. 839-03-90; fax 823-37-07; e-mail bicis@bicis.sn; internet www.bicis.sn; f. 1962; 54.09% owned by Groupe BNP Paribas (France); cap. and res 15,638m., total assets 227,702m. (Dec. 2003); Pres. LANDING SANÉ; Dir-Gen. AMADOU KANE; 17 brs.

Citibank Dakar: Immeuble SDIH, 4e étage, 2 pl. de l'Indépendance, BP 3391, Dakar; tel. 849-11-11; fax 823-88-17; e-mail thioro.ba@citicorp.com; f. 1975; wholly-owned subsidiary of Citibank NA (USA); cap. 1,626m., total assets 84,864m. (Dec. 2001); Pres. JOHN REED; Dir-Gen. MICHAEL GROSSMAN; 1 br.

Compagnie Bancaire de l'Afrique Occidentale (CBAO): 1 pl. de l'Indépendance, BP 129, Dakar; tel. 839-96-96; fax 823-20-05; e-mail cbaonet@sentoo.sn; f. 1853; 76% owned by Groupe Mimran; cap. 5,253m., res 9,000m., dep. 213,067m. (Dec. 2003); Pres. JEAN CLAUDE MIMRAN; Dir-Gen. PATRICK MESTRALLET; 24 brs.

Compagnie Ouest Africaine de Crédit Bail (LOCAFRIQUE): Immeuble Coumaba Castel, 11 rue Galandou Diouf, BP 292, Dakar; tel. 822-06-47; fax 822-08-94; e-mail locafrique@are.sn; cap. 579m., total assets 1,241m. (Dec. 2003); Pres. and Dir-Gen. PATRICIA CISSÉ.

Crédit Lyonnais Sénégal (CLS): blvd El Hadji Djily Mbaye, angle rue Huart, BP 56, Dakar; tel. 849-00-00; fax 823-84-30; e-mail cl_senegal@creditlyonnais.fr; internet www.creditlyonnais.sn; f. 1989; 95% owned by Crédit Lyonnais (France); 5% state-owned; cap. 2,000m., res 7,077m., dep. 101,764m. (Dec. 2003); Pres. and Chair. BAUDOUIN MERLET; Dir-Gen. JEAN PAUL VERU; 1 br.

Crédit National du Sénégal (CNS): 7 ave Léopold Sédar Senghor, BP 319, Dakar; tel. 823-34-86; fax 823-72-92; f. 1990 by merger; 87% state-owned; cap. 1,900m., total assets 2,032m. (Dec. 1996); Pres. ABDOU NDIAYE.

Ecobank Sénégal: 8 ave Léopold Sédar Senghor, BP 9095, Dakar; tel. 849-20-00; fax 823-47-07; e-mail ecobank.sn@ecobank.com; internet www.ecobank.com; 41.45% owned by Ecobank Transnational Inc (Togo), operating under the auspices of the Economic Community of West African States), 17.0% by Ecobank Bénin, 12.43% by Ecobank Côte d'Ivoire, 4.56% by Ecobank Niger, 4.56% by Ecobank Togo; cap. and res 3,181m., total assets 48,591m. (Dec. 2003); Pres. MAHENTA BIRIMA FALL; Dir-Gen. EVELYNE TALL.

Société Générale de Banques au Sénégal (SGBS): 19 ave Léopold Sédar Senghor, BP 323, Dakar; tel. 839-55-00; fax 823-90-36; e-mail sgbs@sentoo.sn; internet www.sgbs.sn; f. 1962; 57.72% owned by Société Générale (France), 35.23% owned by private Senegalese investors; cap. and res 35,352.6m., total assets 345,230.5m. (Dec. 2003); Pres. PAPA-DEMBA DIALLO; Dir-Gen. SANDY GILLIOT; 30 brs and sub-brs.

Development Banks

Banque de l'Habitat du Sénégal (BHS): 69 blvd du Général de Gaulle, BP 229, Dakar; tel. 839-33-33; fax 823-80-43; e-mail bdld10@calva.com; internet www.bhs.sn; f. 1979; 9.09% state-owned, 9.09% owned by BCEAO; cap. and res 19,661.0m., total assets 132,554.6m. (Dec. 2003); Pres. AHMED YÉRO DIALLO; Dir-Gen. SOULEYMANE LY; 2 brs.

Banque Sénégalo-Tunisienne (BST): Immeuble Kebe, 97 ave André Peytavin, BP 4111, Dakar; tel. 849-60-60; fax 823-82-38; e-mail bst@bst.sn; internet www.banquesenegalotunisienne.com; f. 1986; 56.6% owned by Compagnie Africaine pour l'Investissement; cap. 4,200m., res 1,509m., dep. 74,897m. (Dec. 2003); Pres. and Chair. MAMADOU TOURÉ; Dir-Gen. ABDOUL MBAYE; 7 brs.

Caisse Nationale de Crédit Agricole du Sénégal (CNCAS): pl. de l'Indépendance, Immeuble ex-Air Afrique, 31–33 rue El Hadji Asmadou Assane Ndoye, angle ave Colbert, Dakar; tel. 839-36-36; fax 821-26-06; e-mail cncas@cncas.sn; internet www.cncas.sn; f. 1984; 23.8% state-owned; cap. and res 4,991.8m., total assets 74,227.9m. (Dec. 2003); Pres. ABDOULAYE DIACK; Dir-Gen. ARFANG BOUBACAR DAFFE; 13 brs.

Société Financière d'Equipement (SFE): 2e étage, Immeuble Sokhna Anta, rue Dr Thèze, BP 252, Dakar; tel. 823-66-26; fax 823-43-37; e-mail sfe@telecomplus.sn; 59% owned by Compagnie Bancaire de l'Afrique Occidentale; cap. and res 388m., total assets 6,653m. (Dec. 1999); Pres. ARISTIDE ORSET ALCANTARA; Dir-Gen. MOHAMED A. WILSON.

Islamic Bank

Banque Islamique du Sénégal (BIS): Immeuble Abdallah Fayçal, rue Huart, angle rue Amadou Ndoye, BP 3381, 18524 Dakar; tel. 849-62-62; fax 822-49-48; e-mail contact@bis-bank.com; internet www.bis-bank.com; f. 1983; 44.5% owned by Dar al-Maal al-Islami (Switzerland), 33.3% by Islamic Development Bank (Saudi Arabia), 22.2% state-owned; cap. 2,706m., dep. 33,592m. (Dec. 2004); Pres. of Bd of Administration BADER EDDINE NOUIOUA; Dir-Gen. AZHAR S. KHAN; 3 brs.

SENEGAL

Banking Association

Association Professionnelle des Banques et des Etablissements Financiers du Sénégal (APBEF): 5 pl. de l'Indépendance, BP 6403, Dakar; tel. 823-60-93; fax 823-85-96; e-mail apbef@sentoo.sn; Pres. EVELYNE TALL (Dir-Gen of Ecobank Sénégal).

STOCK EXCHANGE

Bourse Régionale des Valeurs Mobilières (BRVM): BP 22500, Dakar; tel. 821-15-18; fax 821-15-06; e-mail osane@brvm.org; internet www.brvm.org; f. 1998; national branch of BRVM (regional stock exchange based in Abidjan, Côte d'Ivoire, serving the member states of UEMOA); Man. OUSMANE SANE.

INSURANCE

AGF Sénégal Assurances: rue de Thann, angle ave Abdoulaye Fadiga, Dakar; tel. 849-44-00; fax 823-10-78; Dir-Gen. BERNARD GIRARDIN.

Les Assurances Conseils Dakarois A. Gueye et cie: 20 rue Mohamed V, BP 2345, Dakar; tel. 822-69-97; fax 822-86-80.

Assurances Générales Sénégalaises (AGS): 43 ave Albert Sarraut, BP 225, Dakar; tel. 839-36-00; fax 823-37-01; e-mail ags@metissacana.sn; f. 1977; cap. 2,990m.; Dir-Gen. IBRAHIM GUEYE.

AXA Assurances Sénégal: 5 pl. de l'Indépendance, BP 182, Dakar; tel. 849-10-10; fax 823-46-72; e-mail info@axa.sn; f. 1977; fmrly Csar Assurances; 51.5% owned by AXA (France); cap. 1,058m. (Mar. 2004); Pres. MOUSTAPHA CISSÉ; Dir-Gen. ALIOUNE NDOUR DIOUF.

V. Capillon Assurances: BP 425, Dakar; tel. 821-13-77; fax 822-24-35; f. 1951; cap. 10m.; Pres. and Man. Dir GILLES DE MONTALEMBERT.

Compagnie d'Assurances-Vie et de Capitalisation (La Nationale d'Assurances-Vie): 7 blvd de la République, BP 3853, Dakar; tel. 822-11-81; fax 821-28-20; f. 1982; cap. 80m.; Pres. MOUSSA DIOUF; Man. Dir BASSIROU DIOP.

Compagnie Sénégalaise d'Assurances et de Réassurances (CSAR): 5 pl. de l'Indépendance, BP 182, Dakar; tel. 823-27-76; fax 823-46-72; f. 1972; cap. 945m.; 49.8% state-owned; Pres. MOUSTAPHA CISSÉ; Man. Dir MAMADOU ABBAS BA.

Gras Savoye Sénégal: 15 blvd de la République, BP 9, Dakar; tel. 823-01-00; fax 821-54-62; e-mail olivier.destriau@grassavoye.sn; affiliated to Gras Savoye (France); Man. OLIVIER DESTRIAU.

Intercontinental Life Insurance Co (ILICO): BP 1359, Dakar; tel. 821-75-20; fax 822-04-49; f. 1993; life insurance; fmrly American Life Insurance Co; Pres. and Dir-Gen. MAGATTE DIOP.

Mutuelles Sénégalaises d'Assurance et de Transport (MSAT): Dakar; tel. 822-29-38; fax 823-42-47; f. 1981; all branches; Dir MOR ATJ.

La Nationale d'Assurances: 5 ave Albert Sarrault, BP 3328, Dakar; tel. 822-10-27; fax 821-28-20; f. 1976; fire, marine, travel and accident insurance; privately owned; Pres. AMSATA DIOUF; also La Nationale d'Assurances—Vie; life insurance.

La Sécurité Sénégalaise (ASS): BP 2623, Dakar; tel. 849-05-99; e-mail ass.dk@sentoo.sn; f. 1984; cap. 500m. (2002); Pres. MOUSSA SOW; Man. Dir MBACKE SENE.

Société Africaine d'Assurances: ave Léopold Sédar Senghor, angle Victor Hugo, BP 508, Dakar; tel. 823-64-75; fax 823-44-72; f. 1945; cap. 9m.; Dir CLAUDE GERMAIN.

Société Nationale d'Assurances Mutuelles (SONAM): 6 ave Léopold Sédar Senghor, BP 210, Dakar; tel. 823-10-03; fax 820-70-25; f. 1973; cap. 1,464m.; Pres. ABDOULAYE FOFANA; Man. Dir DIOULDÉ NIANE.

Société Nouvelle d'Assurances du Sénégal (SNAS): rue de Thann, BP 2610, Dakar; tel. 823-41-76; fax 823-10-78; e-mail snas@telecomplus.sn; Dir-Gen. FRANÇOIS BURGUIERRE.

Société Sénégalaise de Courtage et d'Assurances (SOSECODA): 16 ave Léopold Sédar Senghor, BP 9, Dakar; tel. 823-54-81; fax 821-54-62; f. 1963; cap. 10m.; 55% owned by SONAM; Man. Dir A. AZIZ NDAW.

Société Sénégalaise de Réassurances SA (SENRE): 6 ave Léopold Sédar Senghor, angle Carnot, BP 386, Dakar; tel. 822-80-89; fax 821-56-52; cap. 600m.

Insurance Association

Syndicat Professionel des Agents Généraux d'Assurances du Sénégal: 43 ave Albert Sarraut, BP 1766, Dakar; Pres. URBAIN ALEXANDRE DIAGNE; Sec. JEAN-PIERRE CAIRO.

Trade and Industry

GOVERNMENT AGENCIES

Agence de Développement et d'Encadrement des Petites et Moyennes Entreprises (ADEPME): BP 333, Dakar-Fann; tel. 860-13-63; e-mail adepme@sentoo.sn; f. 2001; assists in the formation and operation of small and medium-sized enterprises; Dir MARIE THÉRÈSE DIEDHIOU.

Agence nationale pour la promotion des investissements et des grands travaux (APIX): BP 430, 52–54 rue Mohamed V, BP 430, 18524 Dakar; tel. 849-05-55; fax 823-94-89; e-mail contact@apix.sn; internet www.investinsenegal.com; promotes investment and major projects; f. 2000; Dir-Gen. AMINATA NIANE.

Agence Sénégalaise de Promotion des Exportations (ASEPEX): Dakar; f. 2005; promotes exports; Dir-Gen. MAIMOUNA SAVANÉ.

Société de Développement Agricole et Industriel (SODAGRI): BP 222, Dakar; tel. 821-04-26; fax 822-54-06; cap. 120m. francs CFA; agricultural and industrial projects; Pres. and Dir-Gen. AMADOU TIDIANE WANE.

Société de Gestion des Abattoirs du Sénégal (SOGAS): BP 14, Dakar; tel. 854-07-40; fax 834-23-65; e-mail sogas@sentoo.sn; f. 1962; cap. 619.2m. francs CFA; 28% state-owned; livestock farming; Dir-Gen. SOW SADIO.

Société Nationale d'Aménagement et d'Exploitation des Terres du Delta du Fleuve Sénégal et des Vallées du Fleuve Sénégal et de la Falémé (SAED): 200 ave Insa Coulibaly-Sor, BP 74, Saint-Louis; tel. 961-15-33; fax 961-14-63; e-mail saed@refer.sn; internet www.saed.sn; f. 1965; cap. 2,500m. francs CFA; 100% state-owned; controls the agricultural development of more than 40,000 ha around the Senegal river delta; Dir-Gen. MAMOUDOU DEME.

Société Nationale d'Etudes et de Promotion Industrielle (SONEPI): Domaine Industriel SODIDA, BP 100, Dakar; tel. 825-21-30; fax 824-654-65; f. 1969; cap. 150m. francs CFA; 28% state-owned; promotion of small- and medium-sized enterprises; Chair. and Man. Dir HADY MAMADOU LY.

Société Nouvelle des Etudes de Développement en Afrique (SONED—AFRIQUE): 22 rue Moussé Diop, BP 2084, Dakar; tel. 823-94-57; fax 823-42-31; e-mail sonedaf@telecomplus.sn; f. 1974; cap. 150m. francs CFA; Pres. ABDOU WAHAB TALLA; Man. Dir El Hadj AMADOU WONE.

DEVELOPMENT ORGANIZATIONS

Agence Française de Développement (AFD): 15 ave Mandela, BP 475, Dakar; tel. 849-19-99; fax 823-40-10; e-mail afddakar@groupe-afd.org; Country Dir JEAN-MARC GRAVELLINI.

Association Française des Volontaires du Progrès (AFVP): BP 1010, route de la VDN, Sacré coeur 3, Villa no 9364, Dakar; tel. 827-40-75; fax 827-40-74; e-mail afvp@telecomplus.sn; internet www.afvp.org; f. 1972; Regional Delegate for Senegal, Cape Verde, Guinea, Guinea-Bissau, Mali and Mauritania JEAN-LOUP CAPDEVILLE; Nat. Delegate KARIM DOUMBIA.

Centre International du Commerce Extérieur du Sénégal: route de l'Aéroport, BP 8166, Dakar-Yoff; tel. 827-54-66; fax 827-52-75; e-mail cices@metissacana.sn; Sec.-Gen. AMADOU SY.

Service de Coopération et d'Action Culturelle: BP 2014, Dakar; tel. 839-53-05; administers bilateral aid from France; fmrly Mission Française de Coopération et d'Action Culturelle; Dir XAVIN ROZE.

CHAMBERS OF COMMERCE

Union Nationale des Chambres de Commerce, d'Industrie et d'Agriculture du Sénégal: 1 pl. de l'Indépendance, BP 118, Dakar; tel. 823-71-69; fax 823-93-63; f. 1888; restructured 2002; Pres. MAMADOU LAMINE NIANG.

  Chambre de Commerce, d'Industrie et d'Agriculture de Dakar: 1 pl. de l'Indépendance, BP 118, Dakar; tel. 823-71-89; fax 823-93-63; e-mail cciad@sentoo.sn; internet www.cciad.sn; f. 1888; Pres. MAMADOU LAMINE NIANG; Sec.-Gen. ALY MBOUP (acting).

  Chambre de Commerce, d'Industrie et d'Agriculture de Diourbel: BP 7, Diourbel; tel. 971-12-03; fax 971-38-49; e-mail ccdiour@cyg.sn; f. 1969; Pres. MOUSTAPHA CISSÉ LO; Sec.-Gen. MAMADOU NDIAYE.

  Chambre de Commerce de Fatick: BP 66, Fatick; tel. and fax 949-14-25; e-mail ccfatick@cosec.sn; Pres. BABOUCAR BOP; Sec.-Gen. SEYDOU NOUROU LY.

  Chambre de Commerce et d'Industrie de Kaolack: BP 203, Kaolack; tel. 941-20-52; fax 941-22-91; e-mail cciak@netcourrier.com; internet www.cciak.fr.st; Pres. IDRISSA GUÈYE; Sec.-Gen. SALIMATA S. DIAKHATE.

SENEGAL

Directory

Chambre de Commerce d'Industrie et d'Agriculture de Kolda: BP 23, Quartier Escale, Kolda; tel. 996-12-30; fax 996-10-68; Pres. AMADOU MOUNIROU DIALLO; Sec.-Gen. YAYA CAMARA.

Chambre de Commerce, d'Industrie et d'Agriculture de Louga: BP 26, Louga; tel. 967-11-14; fax 967-08-25; e-mail ccial@sentoo.sn; Pres. CHEIKH MACKÉ FAYE; Sec.-Gen. DOUDOU NIANG.

Chambre de Commerce, d'Industrie et d'Agriculture de Matam: BP 95, Matam; tel. and fax 966-65-91; Pres. MAMADOU NDIADE; Sec.-Gen. MOUSSA NDIAYE.

Chambre de Commerce, d'Industrie et d'Agriculture de Saint-Louis: 10 rue Blanchot, BP 19, Saint-Louis; tel. 961-10-88; fax 961-29-80; f. 1879; Pres. El Hadj ABIBOU DIEYE; Sec.-Gen. MOUSSA NDIAYE.

Chambre de Commerce, d'Industrie et d'Agriculture de Tambacounda: BP 127, Tambacounda; tel. 981-10-14; fax 981-29-95; e-mail cham.comm.tamba@sentoo.sn; Pres. DJIBY CISSÉ; Sec.-Gen. TENGUELLA BA.

Chambre de Commerce, d'Industrie et d'Agriculture de Thiès: 96 ave Lamine Guèye, BP 3020, Thiès; tel. 951-10-02; fax 952-13-97; e-mail ccthies@cosec.sn; f. 1883; 38 mems; Pres. ATTOU NDIAYE; Sec.-Gen. ABDOULKHADRE CAMARA.

Chambre de Commerce, d'Industrie et d'Artisanat de Ziguinchor: rue du Gen. de Gaulle, BP 26, Ziguinchor; tel. 991-13-10; fax 991-52-38; f. 1908; Pres. MAMADOU DIALLO; Sec.-Gen. ALASSANE NDIAYE.

EMPLOYERS' ASSOCIATIONS

Chambre des Métiers de Dakar: route de la Corniche-Ouest, Soumbedioune, Dakar; tel. 821-79-08; Sec.-Gen. MBAYE GAYE.

Confédération Nationale des Employeurs du Sénégal: Dakar; tel. 821-76-62; fax 822-96-58; e-mail cnes@sentoo.sn; Pres. MANSOUR CAMA.

Conseil National du Patronat du Sénégal (CNP): 70 rue Jean Mermoz, BP 3537, Dakar; tel. 821-58-03; fax 822-28-42; e-mail cnp@sentoo.sn; Pres. YOUSSOUPHA WADE; Sec.-Gen. MABOUSSO THIAM.

Groupement Professionnel de l'Industrie du Pétrole du Sénégal (GPP): rue 6, km 4.5, blvd du Centenaire de la Commune de Dakar, BP 479, Dakar; tel. and fax 832-52-12; e-mail noeljp@sentoo.sn; Sec.-Gen. JEAN-PIERRE NOËL.

Organisation des Commerçants, Agriculteurs, Artisans et Industriels: Dakar; tel. 823-67-94.

Rassemblement des Opérateurs Economiques du Sénégal (ROES): Dakar; tel. 825-57-17; fax 825-57-13.

Syndicat des Commerçants Importateurs, Prestataires de Services et Exportateurs de la République du Sénégal (SCIMPEX): 2 rue Parent, angle ave Abdoulaye Fadiga, BP 806, Dakar; tel. and fax 821-36-62; e-mail scimpex@sentoo.sn; f. 1943; Pres. PAPE ALSASSANE DIENG.

Syndicat Patronal de l'Ouest Africain des Petites et Moyennes Entreprises et des Petites et Moyennes Industries: Dakar; tel. 821-35-10; fax 823-37-32; f. 1937; Pres. BABACAR SEYE; Sec.-Gen. MOCTAR NIANG.

Syndicat Professionnel des Entrepreneurs de Bâtiments et de Travaux Publics du Sénégal: ave Abdoulaye Fadiga, BP 593, Dakar; tel. 823-43-73; f. 1930; 130 mems; Pres. CHRISTIAN VIRMAUD.

Syndicat Professionnel des Industries du Sénégal (SPIDS): BP 593, Dakar; tel. 823-43-24; fax 822-08-84; e-mail spids@syfed.refer.sn; f. 1944; 110 mems; Pres. CHRISTIAN BASSE.

Union des Entreprises du Domaine Industriel de Dakar: BP 10288, Dakar-Liberté; tel. 825-07-86; fax 825-08-70; e-mail snisa@sentoo.sn; Pres. ARISTIDE TINO ADEDIRAN.

Union Nationale des Chambres de Métiers: Domaine Industriel SODIDA, ave Bourguiba, BP 30040, Dakar; tel. 825-05-88; fax 824-54-32; f. 1981; Pres. El Hadj SEYNI SECK; Sec.-Gen. BABOUCAR DIOUF.

Union Nationale des Commerçants et Industriels du Sénégal (UNACOIS): BP 11542, 3 rue Valmy, Dakar; tel. 826-15-19.

UTILITIES

Electricity

Société Nationale d'Electricité (SENELEC): 28 rue Vincent, BP 93, Dakar; tel. 839-30-00; fax 823-82-46; e-mail senelec@senelec.sn; internet www.senelec.sn; f. 1983; 100% state-owned; Dir-Gen. SAMUEL SARR.

Gas

Société Sénégalaise des Gaz: Dakar; tel. 832-82-12; fax 823-59-74.

Water

Société Nationale des Eaux du Sénégal (SONES): route de Front de Terre, BP 400, Dakar; tel. 839-78-00; fax 832-20-38; e-mail sones@sones.sn; internet www.sones.sn; f. 1995; water works and supply; state-owned; Pres. ABDOUL ALY KANE; Dir-Gen. AMADOU NDIAYE.

Sénégalaise des Eaux (SDE): BP 224, Dakar; tel. 839-37-37; fax 839-37-05; e-mail bdtt@sde.sn; f. 1996; subsidiary of Groupe Saur International (France); water distribution services; Pres. ABDOULAYE BOUNA FALL; Dir-Gen. BERNARD DEBENEST.

TRADE UNIONS

Confédération Nationale des Travailleurs du Sénégal (CNTS): 7 ave du Président Laminé Gueye, BP 937, Dakar; tel. 821-04-91; fax 821-77-71; e-mail cnts@sentoo.sn; f. 1969; affiliated to PS; Sec.-Gen. MODY GUIRO.

Confédération Nationale des Travailleurs du Sénégal—Forces de Changement (CNTS—FC): Dakar; f. 2002; following split from CNTS; Sec.-Gen CHEIKH DIOP; 31 affiliated asscns.

Confédération des Syndicats Autonomes (CSA): Dakar; organization of independent trade unions; Sec.-Gen. IBA NDIAYE DIADJI.

Union Démocratique des Travailleurs du Sénégal (UDTS): BP 7124, Médina, Dakar; tel. 835-38-97; fax 854-10-70; 18 affiliated unions; Sec.-Gen. ALIOUNE SOW.

Union Nationale des Syndicats Autonomes du Sénégal (UNSAS): BP 10841, HLM, Dakar; fax 824-80-13; Sec.-Gen. MADEMBA SOCK.

Transport

RAILWAYS

There are 922 km of main line including 70 km of double track. One line runs from Dakar north to Saint-Louis (262 km), and the main line runs to Bamako (Mali). All the locomotives are diesel-driven. In late 1995 the Governments of Senegal and Mali agreed to establish a joint company to operate the Dakar–Bamako line. Tenders were invited from private interests to operate the company in early 2001.

Société Nationale des Chemins de Fer du Sénégal (SNCS): BP 175A, Thiès; tel. 951-10-13; fax 951-13-93; e-mail siamoncs@telecomplus.sn; f. 1905; state-owned; operates passenger and freight services on Dakar–Thiès and Djourbel–Kaoulack lines, following transfer of principal Dakar–Bamako (Mali) line to private management in 2003; suburban trains operate on Dakar–Thiès route as 'Le Petit Train Bleu', pending their proposed transfer to private management by 2006; Pres. DRAME ALIA DIENE; Man. Dir DIOUF MBAYE.

ROADS

In 1996 there were 14,576 km of roads, of which 3,361 km were main roads and 1,194 km were secondary roads. Some 4,265 km of the network were paved. A 162.5 km road between Dialakoto and Kédougou, the construction of which (at a cost of some 23,000m. francs CFA) was largely financed by regional donor organizations, was inaugurated in March 1996. The road is to form part of an eventual transcontinental highway linking Cairo (Egypt) with the Atlantic coast, via N'Djamena (Chad), Bamako (Mali) and Dakar. In 1999 new highways were completed in the east of Senegal, linking Tambacounda, Kidira and Bakel.

Comité Executif des Transports Urbains de Dakar (CETUD): Résidence Fann, route du Front de Terre, Dakar; tel. 832-47-42; fax 832-47-44; e-mail cetud@telecomplus.sn; f. 1997; regulates the provision of urban transport in Dakar; Pres. OUSMANE THIAM.

Dakar-Bus: Dakar; f. 1999; operates public transport services within the city of Dakar; owned by RATP (France), Transdev (France), Eurafric-Equipment (Senegal), Mboup Travel (Senegal) and Senegal Tours (Senegal).

INLAND WATERWAYS

Senegal has three navigable rivers: the Senegal, navigable for three months of the year as far as Kayes (Mali), for six months as far as Kaédi (Mauritania) and all year as far as Rosso and Podor, and the Saloun and the Casamance. Senegal is a member of the Organisation de mise en valeur du fleuve Gambie and of the Organisation pour la mise en valeur du fleuve Sénégal, both based in Dakar. These organizations aim to develop navigational facilities, irrigation and hydroelectric power in the basins of the Gambia and Senegal rivers, respectively.

SHIPPING

The port of Dakar is the second largest in West Africa, after Abidjan (Côte d'Ivoire), and the largest deep sea port in the region, serving

SENEGAL

Directory

Senegal, Mauritania, The Gambia and Mali. It handled more than 7m. metric tons of international freight in 1999. The port's facilities include 40 berths, 10 km of quays, and also 53,000 sq m of warehousing and 65,000 sq m of open stocking areas. There is also a container terminal with facilities for vessels with a draught of up to 11 m. In March 2005 the Governments of Mauritania, Morocco and Senegal agreed that a shipping line linking the three countries and to transport merchandise was to commence operations, following the completion of a tendering process.

Compagnie Sénégalaise de Navigation Maritime (COSENAM): Dakar; tel. 821-57-66; fax 821-08-95; f. 1979; 26.1% state-owned, 65.9% owned by private Senegalese interests, 8.0% by private French, German and Belgian interests; river and ocean freight transport; Pres. ABDOURAHIM AGNE; Man. Dir SIMON BOISSY.

Conseil Sénégalais des Chargeurs (COSEC): BP 1423, Dakar; tel. 849-07-07; fax 823-11-44; e-mail cosec@cyg.sn; Dir-Gen. AMADOU KANE DIALLO.

Dakarnave: Dakar; tel. 823-82-16; fax 823-83-99; e-mail commercial@dakarnave.sn; internet www.dakarnave.com; responsible for Senegalese shipyards; owned by Chantier Navals de Dakar, SA (Dakarnave), a subsidiary of Lisnave International, Portugal; Dir-Gen. JOSÉ ANTÓNIO FERREIRA MENDES.

Maersk Sénégal: route de Rufisque, BP 3836, Dakar; tel. 859-11-11; fax 832-13-31; e-mail senmkt@maersk.com; internet www.maersksealand.com/senegal; f. 1986.

SDV Sénégal: 47 ave Albert Sarrault, BP 233, Dakar; tel. 839-00-00; fax 839-00-69; e-mail sdvdir@sentoo.sn; f. 1936; 51.6% owned by Groupe Bolloré (France); shipping agents, warehousing; Pres. ANDRÉ GUILLABERT; Dir-Gen. BERNARD FRAUD.

Société pour le Développement de l'Infrastructure de Chantiers Maritimes du Port de Dakar (Dakar-Marine): Dakar; tel. 823-36-88; fax 823-83-99; f. 1981; privately-controlled; operates facilities for the repair and maintenance of supertankers and other large vessels; Man. YORO KANTE.

Société Maritime de l'Atlantique (SOMAT): c/o Port Autonome de Dakar, BP 3195, Dakar; f. 2005; 51% owned by Compagnie Marocaine de Navigation, COMANAV (Morocco), 24.5% by Conseil Sénégalais des Chargeurs, COSEC, 24.5% by Société Nationale de Port Autonome de Dakar, PAD; operates foot passenger and freight ferry service between Dakar and Ziguinchor (Casamance).

Société Nationale de Port Autonome de Dakar (PAD): 21 blvd de la Libération, BP 3195, Dakar; tel. 823-45-45; fax 823-36-06; e-mail pad@sonatel.senet.net; internet www.portdakar.sn; f. 1865; state-owned port authority; Pres. and Dir-Gen. BARA SADY.

SOCOPAO-Sénégal: BP 233, Dakar; tel. 823-10-01; fax 823-56-14; f. 1926; warehousing, shipping agents, sea and air freight transport; Man. Dir GILLES CUCHE.

TransSene: 1 blvd de l'Arsenal, face à la gare ferroviaire, Dakar; tel. 821-81-81; e-mail transsen@telecomplus.sn; internet www.transsene.sn.

Yenco Shipping: Fondation Fahd, blvd Djily Mbaye, Dakar; tel. 821-27-26; fax 822-07-81; e-mail yencoshi@sentoo.sn; f. 1988; Dir of Finance M. DIANKA; Dir of Shipping M. DIOKHANE.

CIVIL AVIATION

The international airport is Dakar-Léopold Sédar Senghor. There are other major airports at Saint-Louis, Ziguinchor and Tambacounda, in addition to about 15 smaller airfields. Facilities at Ziguinchor and Cap-Skirring were upgraded during the mid-1990s, with the aim of improving direct access to the Casamance region. In 1998 the Islamic Development Bank agreed to fund a new international airport at Tobor, Casamance. In 2000 work began to extend the runway at Saint-Louis in order to accommodate larger aircraft. The construction of a new international airport, at Ndiass, commenced in 2003.

Agence nationale de l'aviation civile (DAC): BP 8184, Dakar; fax 820-39-67; civil aviation authority; Dir-Gen. MATHIACO BESSANE.

Aeroservices: Dakar; f. 1996; charter flights; Sec.-Gen. El Hadj OMAR BA.

African West Air: Dakar; tel. 822-45-38; fax 822-46-10; f. 1993; services to western Europe and Brazil; Man. Dir J. P. PIEDADE.

Air Sénégal International (ASI): 45 ave Albert Serraut, Dakar; tel. 842-41-00; e-mail siege@airsenegalinternational.sn; internet www.air-senegal-international.com; f. 2000; 51% owned by Royal Air Maroc, 43% state-owned; domestic, regional and international services; Dir-Gen. MOHAMED FATTAHI.

Tourism

Senegal's attractions for tourists include six national parks (one of which, Djoudj, is listed by UNESCO as a World Heritage Site) and its fine beaches. The island of Gorée, near Dakar, is of considerable historic interest as a former centre for the slave-trade. In 1993 the number of foreign tourist arrivals declined dramatically, largely as a result of the suspension of tourist activity in the Casamance region in that year. The sector recovered strongly from 1995 onwards, and in 2003 visitor arrivals of 353,539 were recorded; receipts from tourism in 2002 were US $184m.

Ministry of Tourism and Air Transport: rue Calmette, BP 4049, Dakar; tel. 821-11-26; fax 822-94-13; internet www.tourisme.gouv.sn.

SERBIA AND MONTENEGRO

Introductory Survey

Location, Climate, Language, Religion, Flag, Capital

The State Union of Serbia and Montenegro (formerly the Federal Republic of Yugoslavia) lies in south-eastern Europe. Serbia and Montenegro is bordered to the north by Hungary, to the east by Romania and Bulgaria, and by the former Yugoslav republic of Macedonia and Albania to the south; Montenegro, in the south-west, has a coastline on the Adriatic Sea, and the Union's inland western border is with Bosnia and Herzegovina and with Croatia. The climate is continental in the hilly interior and Mediterranean on the coast, with steady rainfall throughout the year. The average summer temperature in Belgrade is 22°C (71°F), the winter average being 0°C (32°F). The principal language is Serbian of the *ekavian* and *ijekavian* variants. In Serbia these are written mainly in the Cyrillic script, while in Montenegro the Cyrillic and Latin scripts are both in equal official use. Orthodox Christianity is predominant, the Serbian Orthodox Church being the largest denomination. There is a significant Muslim population, principally in the south of the country, and Roman Catholicism is especially strong in the Vojvodina province of Serbia. There is a small Jewish community. The national flag (proportions 1 by 2) has three equal horizontal stripes, of blue, white and red. Belgrade (Beograd) is the capital of the State Union of Serbia and Montenegro, and of Serbia, and Podgorica is the capital of Montenegro. On 21 May 2006 a referendum on independence was conducted in Montenegro. Official preliminary results confirmed that voters had narrowly endorsed independence, with 55.5% of participants voting in favour.

Recent History

A movement for the union of the South Slav peoples, despite long-standing ethnic rivalries and cultural diversity, began in the early 19th century. However, it was not until the end of the First World War, and the collapse of the Austro-Hungarian empire (which ruled Croatia, Slovenia and Bosnia and Herzegovina), that the project for a Yugoslav ('south Slav') state could be realized. A pact between Serbia (which was under Ottoman Turkish rule until the 19th century) and the other South Slavs was signed in July 1917, declaring the intention to merge all the territories in a united state under the Serbian monarchy. Accordingly, when the First World War ended and Austria-Hungary was dissolved, the Kingdom of Serbs, Croats and Slovenes was proclaimed on 4 December 1918.

Prince Aleksandar, Regent of Serbia since 1914, accepted the regency of the new state, becoming King in August 1921. Following bitter disputes between Serbs and Croats, King Aleksandar assumed dictatorial powers in January 1929. He formally changed the country's name to Yugoslavia in October. Aleksandar's regime was Serb-dominated, and in October 1934 he was assassinated in France by Croatian extremists. His brother, Prince Pavle, assumed power as Regent on behalf of King Petar II. Pavle's regime retained power with the support of the armed forces, despite internal unrest, particularly in Croatia. Among the anti-Government groups was the Communist Party of Yugoslavia (CPY), which had been officially banned in 1921, but continued to operate clandestinely. In 1937 the CPY appointed a new General Secretary, Josip Broz (Tito).

In March 1941 the increasingly pro-German regime of Prince Pavle was overthrown in a coup, and a Government that supported the Allied Powers was installed, with King Peter as Head of State. In April, however, German and Italian forces invaded, forcing the royal family and Government into exile. Resistance to the occupation forces was initially divided between two rival groups. The Yugoslav Army of the Fatherland (Cetniks) operated mainly in Serbia and represented the exiled Government, while the National Liberation Army (Partisans), led by the CPY, under Gen. (later Marshal) Tito, recruited supporters from Bosnia, Croatia, Montenegro and Slovenia. Rivalry between the two groups led to civil war, eventually won by the communist Partisans. On 29 November 1943 the Partisans proclaimed their own government in liberated areas. Attempts to reconcile the Tito regime with the exiled Government proved unsuccessful, and King Petar II was deposed in 1944.

After the war ended, elections were held, under communist supervision, for a Provisional Assembly. The Federative People's Republic of Yugoslavia was proclaimed on 29 November 1945, with Tito as Prime Minister. A Soviet-style Constitution, establishing a federation of six republics (Serbia, Montenegro, Croatia, Slovenia, Macedonia and Bosnia and Herzegovina) and two autonomous provinces (Kosovo—with a large Albanian population, but also the location of the seat of the Serbian Orthodox Patriarchate, and Vojvodina—with a large Hungarian population, both within Serbia), was adopted in January 1946.

In 1948 Yugoslavia was expelled from the Soviet-dominated Cominform. The CPY was renamed the League of Communists of Yugoslavia (LCY) in November 1952, by which time it had established exclusive political control. A new Constitution was adopted in January 1953, with Tito becoming President of the Republic. Another Constitution, promulgated in April 1963, changed the country's name to the Socialist Federal Republic of Yugoslavia (SFRY). Links with the USSR were resumed in 1955, but Yugoslavia largely pursued a policy of non-alignment, the first conference of the Non-aligned Movement (see p. 397) being held in the Serbian and federal capital, Belgrade, in 1961.

In July 1971 President Tito introduced a system of collective leadership and regular rotation of personnel between posts, in an attempt to unify the various nationalities. A collective State Presidency, headed by Tito, was established. The two autonomous provinces within Serbia obtained substantially the same powers, with regard to representation at federal level, as the six republics, as a result of which three of the eight members of the rotating collective presidency represented Serbia and its provinces. A new Constitution, introduced in February 1974, granted Tito the presidency for an unlimited term of office, and in May he became Life President of the LCY. Tito died in 1980, and his responsibilities were transferred to the collective State Presidency and to the Presidium of the LCY.

Subsequently, inter-ethnic tensions, largely suppressed during Tito's period in power, became evident. In early 1981 there were widespread demonstrations in Kosovo by Albanian nationalists, demanding that the province receive full republican status. A state of emergency was declared, and the riots resulted in several deaths. Further demonstrations took place in March 1982, and hundreds of Albanian nationalists were convicted and imprisoned. Tensions were exacerbated in April 1987, when thousands of Serbs and Montenegrins gathered at Kosovo Polje (the site of a famous military defeat of Serbian forces by Ottoman Turkish troops in 1389) to protest at alleged harassment by the Albanian majority population clashed violently with the security forces. The perceived failure of the Serbian and federal leadership to curb Albanian nationalism led to the dismissal in September of the First Secretary of the League of Communists of Serbia (LCS—the Serbian branch of the LCY), Ivan Stambolić, and his replacement by Slobodan Milošević. Milošević had denounced the Serbian leadership's policy on Kosovo and promised to reverse the emigration of Serbs from the area and halt the activities of Albanian nationalists.

During 1988 and 1989 ethnic unrest increased. Proposals to amend the Serbian Constitution to reduce the level of autonomy of the two provinces were supported by regular demonstrations by Serbs. Demonstrations against the local party leadership were organized by Milošević and his supporters in Vojvodina. In October 1988 protests by some 100,000 demonstrators in Novi Sad, the administrative centre of Vojvodina, forced the resignation of the Presidium of the League of Communists of Vojvodina, which had opposed some of the proposed constitutional amendments. Tension between the respective party leaderships of Kosovo and Serbia increased, and in November, following the resignation of several members of the Kosovo leadership, some 100,000 ethnic Albanians demonstrated in Priština (the administrative capital of Kosovo) to demand their reinstatement. In Belgrade a further mass rally was staged by Serbs in protest at alleged discrimination by the Albanian population in Kosovo. Public demonstrations in Kosovo were banned in late November. In Montenegro continuing unrest resulted in the resignations of the members of the Montenegrin Presidency and of the republican party leadership in January 1989, and their replacement by leaders more sympathetic to Milošević.

In February 1989 the dismissal from the LCY Central Committee of Azem Vlasi, a popular Kosovan Albanian, and the adoption by the Assembly of the Serbian Republic of the constitutional amendments limiting provincial autonomy, led to renewed unrest in Kosovo. Rioting was precipitated by the arrest of Vlasi in early March, and the approval of the new constitutional arrangements by the Kosovo Provincial Assembly later that month. Unrest persisted throughout the year, and protests escalated again in January 1990. The situation was further exacerbated when Milošević (who had been elected President of the Serbian State Presidency in May 1989) urged the Serbs to begin a campaign of mass settlement in Kosovo (some 50,000 Serbs and Montenegrins were reported to have left the province since 1981). A curfew was imposed in Priština, and units of the federal army were deployed to quell the disturbances. In April 1990 the state of emergency was ended, and Vlasi and other defendants were acquitted and released.

Meanwhile, in May 1988 an emergency conference of the LCY took place. Radical economic and political reforms, including the separation of the powers of the LCY and the State, and greater democracy within the LCY, were proposed. At the end of December, having been defeated in a vote of 'no confidence' (based on the Government's economic policy), Branko Mikulić, the President of the Federal Executive Council (Prime Minister), and his Government were obliged to resign. In January 1989 Ante Marković, a member of the Croatian Presidency, was appointed to head a new Government. In September the Slovene Assembly voted to adopt radical amendments to the Constitution of Slovenia, affirming its sovereignty and its right to secede from the SFRY. Relations with the leadership of Serbia and the other constituent republics deteriorated sharply, and in Serbia and Montenegro demonstrations were staged in response to the perceived threat to the unity of Yugoslavia. In early December Serbia imposed economic sanctions on Slovenia. In January 1990 the abolition of the LCY's constitutional monopoly of power and the introduction of a multi-party system were formally approved, but a proposal by Slovenia to award greater autonomy to the republican branches of the LCY was defeated. As a result, the Slovene delegation left the Congress, which was then adjourned. It resumed its work in May, but was not attended by delegations from Croatia, Slovenia or Macedonia, where the local communist parties had effectively seceded from the LCY. The LCY was reconstituted in November as the League of Communists—Movement for Yugoslavia.

Multi-party elections took place in Slovenia and Croatia in April and May 1990, respectively; in both cases opponents of Serbian nationalism and the regime of Milošević were elected to senior positions. In May, under the system of rotating leadership, Dr Borisav Jović of Serbia replaced Janez Drnovšek of Slovenia as President of the Federal Presidency. Jović promised to uphold national integrity and advocated the introduction of a stronger federal constitution. In early July a referendum in Serbia resulted in approval for proposed amendments to the republic's Constitution, effectively removing the autonomous status of the provinces of Kosovo (which was renamed Kosovo and Metohija) and Vojvodina. The Kosovo Provincial Assembly and Government were dissolved by the Serbian authorities. In response, a group of 114 ethnic Albanian deputies to the Assembly attempted to declare Kosovo's independence from Serbia. Unrest continued, and in September a general strike was organized to protest against the mass dismissals of ethnic Albanian officials by the Serbian authorities. Criminal charges were brought against more than 100 members of the Provincial Assembly who attempted to re-establish the body, and several former ministers in the Government of Kosovo were charged with establishing an illegal separatist organization.

During November and December 1990 multi-party elections were held in four republics. In Bosnia and Herzegovina (where tension between Serbs and Muslims—Bosniaks—had led to clashes) and in Macedonia nationalist parties were successful. In Montenegro the League of Communists was able to retain the Presidency and secure a majority of seats in the republican Assembly. In Serbia, amid allegations of widespread irregularities, Milošević was re-elected President, overcoming a challenge by Vuk Drašković of the nationalist and anti-communist Serbian Renewal Movement (SRM). In the Narodna skupština Republike Srbije (National Assembly of the Republic of Serbia—Serbian Assembly) 194 of the 250 seats were won by the Socialist Party of Serbia (SPS—led by Milošević), which had been formed in July 1990 by the LCS and a smaller left-wing faction.

In October 1990 Croatia and Slovenia had proposed the transformation of the Yugoslav federation into a looser confederation, in which constituent republics would have the right to maintain armed forces and enter into diplomatic relations with other states. Serbia and Montenegro, however, advocated a centralized federal system, while Macedonia and Bosnia and Herzegovina supported the concept of a federation of sovereign states. Tension increased in December, when Croatia adopted a new Constitution, giving the republic the right to secede from Yugoslavia, while in Slovenia a majority voted in favour of secession at a referendum. In January 1991 Macedonia declared its sovereignty and right to secede from the SFRY.

In March 1991 mass demonstrations, led by Drašković's SRM, demanding the resignation of Milošević, were violently suppressed by the security forces. Jović resigned as President of the Federal Presidency, following his failure to secure approval from other members of the Presidency for emergency measures; his resignation was withdrawn following an appeal from the Narodna skupština Republike Srbije

Meanwhile, in February 1991 Slovenia formally initiated its process of 'dissociation' from Yugoslavia, and Croatia asserted the primacy of its Constitution and laws over those of the federation; both Republics declared their willingness to engage in negotiations. Later that month the self-proclaimed 'Serb Autonomous Region (SAR) of Krajina' (which subsequently formed part of a self-styled 'Republic of the Serb Krajina'—RSK) declared its separation from Croatia and the intention to unite with Serbia. In Croatia in May the population voted in favour of independence at a referendum that was largely boycotted by the Serb minority, and armed clashes between Serbs and Croats ensued. Relations between Serbia and Croatia deteriorated further in that month, when Serbian representatives in the Federal Presidency refused to sanction the scheduled transfer of the Presidency to Stipe Mesić of Croatia. On 25 June, following the failure of negotiations to consider a compromise, Slovenia and Croatia declared independence. In response, federal troops (largely Serb-dominated) attacked a number of targets in Slovenia, including Ljubljana airport, resulting in 79 deaths, according to official figures. A cease-fire agreement, mediated by the European Community (EC—now European Union—EU, see p. 228), resulted in Serbia's acceptance of Mesić as President of the Federal Presidency. In early July agreement was reached on the immediate cessation of hostilities and on a three-month suspension in the implementation of dissociation by Croatia and Slovenia. The withdrawal of federal troops from Slovenia (which had a negligible Serb population) began almost immediately, but fighting intensified in Croatia, where federal troops increasingly identified openly with local Serb forces. By September Serb forces controlled almost one-third of Croatia's territory, and successive cease-fire agreements failed to end the conflict. In the same month, at a referendum in Macedonia, voters approved the establishment of an independent republic.

In late September 1991 the UN Security Council adopted Resolution 713, which imposed an armaments embargo on all governments within the territories that had formed part of the SFRY and urged that all hostilities end immediately. However, sporadic fighting continued in Croatia. In October Croatia and Slovenia formally ended their association with Yugoslavia, the moratoriums on independence (agreed in July) having expired. In the same month the Assembly of Bosnia and Herzegovina declared the republic's sovereignty, despite the objections of ethnic Serb deputies. The EC continued its negotiation efforts, and the UN also become directly involved. In Yugoslavia the Federal Prime Minister, Ante Marković, resigned, having been defeated in a vote of 'no confidence' in the bicameral Savezna skupština (Federal Assembly, comprising the directly elected Veće građana—Chamber of Citizens—and the indirectly elected Veće Republika—Chamber of Republics). In December, declaring that Yugoslavia had ceased to exist, Stipe Mesić resigned as President of the Federal Presidency. In January 1992 Slovenia and Croatia were recognized as independent states by the EC; numerous other countries followed. The deployment in Croatia of a UN contingent of 14,000 peace-keeping troops, the UN Protection Force, UNPROFOR (agreed by the Federal Presidency in December 1991) commenced in February 1992.

Following the international recognition of the independence of Croatia and Slovenia, Serbia and Montenegro agreed to uphold the Yugoslav state, Montenegrin commitment being endorsed at a referendum in March 1992 (which was boycotted by the ethnic

Albanian and Muslim minorities). Macedonia's representative to the Federal Presidency had resigned in January, but EC recognition of Macedonian independence was delayed, owing to opposition from Greece (see the chapter on the former Yugoslav republic of Macedonia). In March Bosnia and Herzegovina declared its independence from the SFRY, the decision having been approved by the electorate in a referendum that had been largely boycotted by the large ethnic Serb population, some of whom had established several SARs during 1991. Later that month the 'Serb Republic (Republika Srpska) of Bosnia and Herzegovina' (renamed Republika Srpska in August 1992) was proclaimed, and a severe escalation in the Bosnian conflict ensued, as troops from Republika Srpska launched military action against Bosniaks and besieged several cities, including the capital of Bosnia and Herzegovina, Sarajevo.

In April 1992 the Savezna skupština adopted a new Constitution, formally establishing the Federal Republic of Yugoslavia (FRY), which comprised Serbia (including the two provinces of Kosovo and Metohija, and of Vojvodina) and Montenegro, thereby effectively acknowledging the secession of the other four republics. In late May elections to the Savezna skupština were held, the SPS enjoying considerable success as a result of an opposition boycott. In June Dobrica Ćosić became President of the FRY, and the collective Federal Presidency ceased to exist. In that month an alliance of opposition parties formed the Democratic Movement of Serbia (Depos), led by Drašković, and mass anti-Milošević demonstrations took place at the end of June.

In May 1992 elections, declared to be illegal by the Serbian authorities, were held in Kosovo to establish a 130-member provincial Assembly. The Democratic Alliance of Kosovo (DAK) secured most seats in the elections, and the movement's leader, Dr Ibrahim Rugova, was elected 'President' of the self-proclaimed 'Republic of Kosovo'. In July Milan Panić was elected Federal Prime Minister by the Savezna skupština. Following a visit to Albania in August (the first by a Yugoslav leader since 1948), Panić revoked the state of emergency in Kosovo, which had been in effect since the unrest of 1989–90. At a conference on the former Yugoslavia, which took place in London, United Kingdom, in August 1992, Panić condemned the policy of 'ethnic cleansing', following the discovery of Serb-run concentration camps in Bosnia and Herzegovina, and reiterated the claim that there was no federal military involvement in the republic. In an attempt to force Milošević's removal from office, presidential and legislative elections were scheduled for December. In October Milošević retaliated by using Serbian police forces to seize control of the federal police headquarters in Belgrade, blockading the building for several weeks. In November Panić narrowly survived a second vote of 'no confidence' in the Savezna skupština. The Federal Minister of Foreign Affairs resigned in September, in protest at Panić's policies; in November three more federal ministers resigned.

Presidential and parliamentary elections, at both federal and republican levels, took place on 20 December 1992. Ćosić was re-elected Federal President, with some 85% of the votes cast. Milošević was re-elected President of Serbia, receiving 57.5% of the votes cast, and the SPS secured 47 of the 138 seats in the Veće građana. Panić, who contested the Serbian presidency, winning some 35% of the votes, subsequently demanded that new elections be held, alleging widespread electoral malpractice on the part of the SPS. However, he was removed from the office of Federal Prime Minister on 29 December, after losing a third vote of 'no confidence'. The SPS won 101 seats in the elections to the 250-member Narodna skupština Republike Srbije, while the extreme nationalist Serbian Radical Party (SRP) secured 73. In early February 1993 a new Federal Government, comprising the SPS and the DPMS, was established, with Radoje Kontić as Federal Prime Minister. In the same month the SPS formed a new Serbian Government, headed by Nikola Sainović. Depos, which had obtained 49 seats in the Serbian legislature, commenced a legislative boycott, claiming that the elections had been fraudulent. In Montenegro Predrag Bulatović of the ruling Democratic Party of Montenegrin Socialists (DPMS—the former League of Communists of Montenegro) failed to win an overall majority in the first round of the presidential election. He was re-elected President in a second round of voting on 10 January 1993, defeating the nationalist Branko Kostić. A new coalition Government, headed by Milo Đukanović, was established in Montenegro in March.

On 1 June 1993 Ćosić (who was accused of conspiring with army generals to overthrow Milošević) was removed from office by a vote of 'no confidence' in the Savezna skupština; the motion had been initiated by deputies of the SPS and the SRP, in what was widely regarded as an attempt by Milošević to consolidate his power. Ćosić's dismissal was followed by a large anti-Government demonstration in Belgrade, at which Drašković and his wife were arrested; they were released in July. In late June the Savezna skupština appointed Zoran Lilić of the SPS, regarded as sympathetic to Milošević, as Federal President, and a reorganization of the Serbian Government in July followed. In August it was announced that the Supreme Defence Council was to assume responsibility for all military and defence duties, and that the republican defence ministries were to be abolished (a measure that was opposed by the Montenegrin Government).

By the second half of 1993 it appeared that the co-operation between Milošević and the SRP had ended; in October an attempt by the SRP to force a parliamentary vote expressing 'no confidence' in the Sainović Government prompted Milošević to dissolve the Narodna skupština Republike Srbije. In response to SRP allegations that the Serbian leadership was betraying national interests by its involvement in attempts to end the conflict in Bosnia and Herzegovina, the party's leader, Dr Vojislav Šešelj, and his associates were accused of involvement in atrocities, and prominent members connected with its paramilitary wing were arrested.

In the elections to the 250-member Narodna skupština Republike Srbije, which took place on 19 December 1993, the SPS increased its representation to 123 deputies, winning 36.7% of the votes cast. Depos secured 45 seats (with 16.6% of the votes), and the SRP took 39 (with 13.9%). Prolonged negotiations to form a government between the SPS and opposition parties ensued, and in late February 1994 a new Serbian Government was formed, with the support of the six members of the New Democracy (ND) party, which had campaigned in the elections as a member of the Depos coalition. Mirko Marjanović, a pro-Milošević business executive, was appointed Prime Minister, replacing Sainović, who became a Deputy Prime Minister in the Federal Government. In September a smaller, 14-member Federal Government, which included six new ministers, was appointed. Radoje Kontić retained the post of Federal Prime Minister. The results of the elections in Serbia and the defection of the ND to the Government permitted Milošević to distance himself further from his erstwhile allies in the nationalist opposition, notably the SRP, and to consolidate his political control in the FRY. Šešelj's personal position was further discredited by his being sentenced to a short term of imprisonment in September for assaulting the parliamentary Speaker.

In August 1994, in a controversial vote that was boycotted by the opposition, the Narodna skupština Republike Srbije endorsed a peace plan, sponsored by the five-nation 'Contact Group' on the conflict in Bosnia and Herzegovina, which the authorities of Republika Srpska had recently rejected. The SRP, the Democratic Party (DP) and the Democratic Party of Serbia (DPS) continued to oppose the peace proposals. A decision by the Serbian leadership to impose a blockade on Republika Srpska in September was strongly opposed by the SRP (which retained close links with the Bosnian Serb leadership) and other opposition movements.

In early August 1995, in a military offensive, Croatian troops took control of the RSK, prompting a mass exodus of ethnic Serbs from the region. The Yugoslav leadership protested strongly against the Croatian action, demanding UN intervention and a withdrawal of Croatian troops from the area. However, President Milošević also blamed the leadership of the RSK, accusing it of intransigence, and criticizing its reluctance to comply with international peace proposals. Some opposition groups, notably the SRP, condemned the Yugoslav leadership for failing to provide military support for the Serbs in Croatia, and organized protest rallies in Belgrade. The Croatian offensive against the RSK resulted in the exodus of some 150,000 Serb refugees to Yugoslavia and Serb-controlled areas of Bosnia and Herzegovina. Many were settled in Vojvodina, prompting protests from ethnic Hungarians in that region.

In early November 1995 peace negotiations were convened in Dayton, Ohio, USA, with the aim of resolving the conflict in the former Yugoslavia. The conference, at which Milošević represented not only Yugoslavia, but also the Bosnian Serbs, resulted in an agreement on the future territorial and constitutional structure of Bosnia and Herzegovina, including the recognition of Republika Srpska as one of two constituent entities within Bosnia and Herzegovina. In response to Yugoslav acceptance of the plan, all UN sanctions against the FRY were revoked in late November. The SRP denounced the Dayton agreement, which was also criticized by the DP, the DPS and the increasingly nationalist leadership of the Serbian Orthodox Church. However, the SRM supported the agreement. In late November Milošević dismissed several leading members of the SPS, who were known to be critical of the Dayton accord and supportive of militant factions within Republika Srpska. In June 1996 the Serbian Government was reorganized. All the new ministers appointed were members of the increasingly influential Yugoslav United Left (YUL), led by Milošević's wife, Mirjana Marković.

In August 1996 Rugova announced that ethnic Albanians in Kosovo would boycott forthcoming federal parliamentary elections. Prior to the elections, a number of new coalitions were formed, notably a grouping known as Together (Zajedno), which comprised the SRM, the DP, the DPS and the Civic Alliance of Serbia. The SPS established an alliance with the YUL and the ND, which became known as the United List.

On 3 November 1996 municipal elections, elections to the federal Veće građana and the Skupština Republike Crne Gore (Assembly of the Republic of Montenegro—Montenegrin Assembly) were held. At the elections to the Veće građana, the United List secured 64 seats, Together took 22, the DPMS 20 and the SRP 16; of the 138 elected deputies, 108 were from Serbia and 30 from Montenegro. At the concurrent elections to the Skupština Republike Crne Gore, the DPMS won 45 seats (with the total number of seats reduced from 85 to 71). The DPMS also secured control of the majority of the municipal assemblies in Montenegro. Following a second round of voting in the Serbian municipal elections, provisional results indicated that Together had obtained control of 14 principal towns, including Belgrade. After the SPS challenged the results, however, most of the opposition victories were annulled by (SPS-dominated) municipal courts and electoral commissions, precipitating mass demonstrations.

In December 1996 opposition supporters continued to organize daily demonstrations (which had developed into general protests against the Milošević Government) in Belgrade and other towns. The Serbian Minister of Information resigned in protest at the Government's temporary closure of two independent radio stations, which had reported the demonstrations. Milošević denied government involvement in electoral malpractice and condemned the protests. In late December the hitherto peaceful demonstrations degenerated into violent clashes with members of the security forces in Belgrade; it was reported that two people had been killed and 58 injured. The Ministry of Internal Affairs subsequently ordered a ban on demonstrations, which the security forces attempted to enforce; nevertheless, anti-Government rallies continued. At the end of December a delegation from the Organization for Security and Co-operation in Europe (OSCE, see p. 327), which earlier that month had been invited by the Federal Minister of Foreign Affairs to visit Serbia, issued a report upholding the results of the municipal elections that had been invalidated. The international community consequently increased pressure on Milošević to comply with the OSCE ruling. In early February 1997 the violent suppression of anti-Government demonstrations attracted further international criticism. Shortly afterwards Milošević publicly instructed Marjanović to prepare emergency legislation providing for the official recognition of the results of the municipal elections, in accordance with the OSCE ruling. However, the leader of the DP, Zoran Đinđić, urged his supporters to continue protests until the election results were officially verified, further demanding that the electoral code and legislation governing the media be reformed and that members of the security forces involved in the violence earlier that month be charged. On 11 February the Narodna skupština Republike Srbije voted in favour of reinstating the annulled results (with deputies from the opposition and extreme nationalist parties boycotting the session); Together consequently obtained control of the municipal assemblies in Belgrade and 13 other towns. At the same time seven ministers were replaced in a reorganization of the Serbian Cabinet. Later in February Đinđić was elected Mayor of Belgrade by Together members, who controlled 69 of the 110 seats in the city's municipal council.

In February 1997 an interview with Đukanović, in which he pronounced Milošević to be unfit to hold public office, prompted criticism from the Serbian state-owned press. In March Đukanović was obliged to resign from the post of Deputy Chairman of the DPMS, owing to opposition within the party. Meanwhile, a number of additional DPMS representatives were included in the Federal Government, following a ministerial reorganization. In April a Montenegrin Deputy Prime Minister, Slavko Drljević, was obliged to resign, after stating that a separate Montenegrin currency might be introduced in the event of further 'hyperinflation' in the FRY. (In the event, Montenegro adopted the German currency, the Deutsche Mark—DM, as its official currency in November 1999, and the European common currency, the euro, when that replaced the DM in January 2002.)

In June 1997 it was announced that the SRM had withdrawn from Together. The SPS nominated Milošević as a candidate for the federal presidency and proposed constitutional amendments for the direct election of the President. Later that month a DPMS committee declared its support for Milošević's candidature (which was, however, strongly opposed by elements within the party, including Đukanović), but rejected the proposed amendments. On 25 June Lilić relinquished office; the Speaker of the Veće Republika, Srđan Bozović, was to act as interim President for one month, pending an election. In early July Dušan Vlatković, hitherto the Serbian Minister of Finance, was appointed as Governor of the National Bank of Yugoslavia. In the same month supporters of Đukanović within the DPMS voted to remove Bulatović from the leadership of the party, on the grounds that he was too closely associated with the Serbian Government. In mid-July Milošević was elected to the federal presidency by the Savezna skupština (having arranged for the parliamentary session to take place earlier than scheduled, owing to concern that the division within the DPMS would undermine his support). Opposition deputies boycotted the vote in the Veće građana, which they subsequently declared to be invalid. On 23 July Milošević formally resigned from the office of President of Serbia and was inaugurated as Federal President.

In September 1997 students demonstrated in Belgrade in support of Đinđić, who, following the dissolution of Together, urged a boycott of the forthcoming Serbian presidential and legislative elections, on the grounds that they would be biased in favour of the incumbent administration. At the elections to the Narodna skupština Republike Srbije, held on 21 September, the United List coalition won 110 seats (thereby failing to secure an outright majority); the SRP increased its representation to 82 seats and the SRM obtained 45 seats. In the concurrent presidential election, which was contested by 17 candidates, Lilić (the candidate of the United List) received 35.7% of the votes cast, while Šešelj, who contested the poll on behalf of the SRP, won 27.3% of the votes and Drašković 20.6%. Despite the boycott implemented by supporters of a number of opposition parties and ethnic Albanians in Kosovo, some 62% of the electorate participated in the poll. Since none of the candidates had secured the requisite majority of more than one-half of the votes cast, a second round was scheduled to take place on 5 October. In early October SPS and SRP councillors in the Belgrade municipal assembly voted in support of an SRM initiative to remove Đinđić from the office of Mayor of Belgrade. Security forces subsequently suppressed protests in Belgrade by supporters of the DP, who demanded that further legislative and municipal elections be conducted. In the second round of voting in the Serbian presidential election on 5 October Šešelj won 49.1% and Lilić 47.9% of the votes cast. However, owing, in part, to the boycott organized by Đinđić, less than 50% of the electorate participated in the poll, which was consequently declared to be invalid. The Serbian authorities announced that a new presidential election would take place on 7 December.

In the first round of the election to the presidency of Montenegro, which was contested by a total of eight candidates on 5 October 1997, Bulatović secured 48.2% of the votes cast, narrowly defeating Đukanović, with 47.4%, but failed to obtain the requisite majority of the votes. At a second round of voting, on 19 October, Đukanović was elected to the Montenegrin presidency, with 50.8% of the votes cast. Although the OSCE declared the conduct of the elections to be generally satisfactory, Bulatović subsequently claimed that Đukanović's supporters had falsified voting lists prior to the second round. The Montenegrin Constitutional Court rejected an appeal by Bulatović that the results of the presidential election be annulled.

Following his appointment as a federal Deputy Prime Minister in November 1997, Lilić withdrew his candidacy to the Serbian presidency. In the Serbian presidential election, which was contested by seven candidates on 7 December, the United List coalition was represented by the federal Minister of Foreign Affairs, Milan Milutinović, who secured 43.7% of the votes cast; Šešelj received 32.2% of the votes. In the ensuing second round, which took place on 21 December, Milutinović won 59.2% of the votes cast, while Šešelj obtained 37.5% of the votes. The Serbian electoral commission announced that about 50.1% of the electorate had participated in the poll, which was consequently pronounced to be valid. However, Šešelj claimed that the Serbian authorities had perpetrated electoral malpractice, particularly in Kosovo, where ethnic Albanians had again boycotted the polls. Later in December OSCE observers issued a report indicating that severe irregularities had taken place. On 29 December Milutinović was inaugurated as President of Serbia.

In January 1998 protests by supporters of Bulatović against the election of Đukanović to the Montenegrin presidency resulted in increasing violence. Two members of the security forces were killed in clashes with demonstrators, who had attempted to seize government buildings in Podgorica. After continued violent protests in response to Đukanović's inauguration, the Montenegrin authorities prohibited further demonstrations. Following mediation by the Federal Prime Minister, Radoje Kontić, however, the authorities agreed that early legislative elections would take place in Montenegro in May; supporters of Bulatović were to refrain from staging new protests. In early February the Skupština Republike Crne Gore approved the establishment of a transitional Montenegrin Government, pending legislative elections (scheduled for 31 May). The new administration comprised 17 representatives of Đukanović's faction of the DPMS, seven members of opposition parties and four ministers without party affiliation. (Bulatović's faction of the DPMS and the Liberal Alliance of Montenegro refused to participate in the Government.) It was announced that criminal proceedings were to be initiated against Bulatović and three of his prominent supporters, who were accused of inciting the unrest in January. Later in February the Skupština Republike Crne Gore adopted new electoral legislation, which increased the number of seats in the chamber to 78 (of which five were to be allocated to representatives of the ethnic Albanian minority).

In February 1998 Milutinović reappointed Marjanović to the office of Serbian Prime Minister. Following protracted negotiations, the SPS formed an alliance with the SRP in March. Marjanović subsequently formed a new coalition Government, comprising 15 representatives of the SRP (including Šešelj, who became a Deputy Prime Minister), 13 representatives of the SPS, and four of the YUL. In May the Savezna skupština adopted a motion expressing 'no confidence' in Kontić, which had apparently been initiated by DPMS deputies. Milošević's subsequent nomination of Bulatović to the office of Federal Prime Minister was approved by the Savezna skupština, and a new Federal Government was established. Đukanović, however, declared Bulatović's Government to be illegitimate. At the legislative elections in Montenegro on 31 May a coalition (known as 'For a Better Life'), headed by Đukanović, secured 42 seats in the Skupština Republike Crne Gore, while the Socialist People's Party of Montenegro (SNP), led by Bulatović, obtained 29 seats. In June the new Montenegrin legislature withdrew the 20 deputies representing the Republic from the Veće Republika and replaced them with members of Đukanović's coalition, to ensure that Milošević would not command the requisite two-thirds' majority for constitutional amendments. (Milošević, however, refused to allow deputies from Đukanović's coalition to assume seats in the Veće Republika.) In July a new Montenegrin Government, headed by Filip Vujanović of the DPMS, was installed. In early August the Montenegrin administration announced that it had suspended links with the Federal Government until Bulatović agreed to resign from the office of federal Prime Minister in favour of a supporter of Đukanović.

In May 1999 the International Criminal Tribunal for the former Yugoslavia (ICTY, see p. 17) indicted Milošević, together with Milutinović, Šainović, the former Serbian Minister of the Interior, Vlajko Stojiljković, and the Yugoslav Army Chief of Staff, Gen. Dragoljub Ojdanić, for crimes against humanity. In June SRP ministers and legislative deputies temporarily suspended participation in the Serbian Government, in protest at Milošević's acceptance of the peace plan for Kosovo, whereby forces of the North Atlantic Treaty Organization (NATO, see p. 314) were to be deployed in the province under a peace-keeping mandate. During July a series of demonstrations was conducted by a loose grouping of opposition associations, known as Alliance for Change, in support of Milošević's resignation. In early August Milošević reorganized the Federal Government. Also in August the Montenegrin Government presented proposals for the dissolution of the FRY, and its replacement with an 'Association of States of Serbia and Montenegro', and announced that a referendum on independence for the republic would be conducted if Milošević failed to agree to the demands. In September the Alliance for Change initiated a campaign against Milošević; however, Drašković refused to endorse the protest rallies. In January 2000, following inter-party discussions, leaders of the Alliance for Change presented unified demands for elections to be conducted in Serbia by the end of April.

In mid-January 2000 a notorious Serbian paramilitary leader and war crimes suspect, Zeljko Raznatović ('Arkan'), was shot and killed in Belgrade. It was suggested that, following his indictment by the ICTY in 1997, he had been prepared to implicate Milošević in war crimes. In February 2000 the Federal Minister of Defence, Pavle Bulatović, was also killed. Milošević subsequently appointed Gen. Ojdanić to the post. In July the Savezna skupština approved constitutional amendments removing limits on the President's tenure of office, providing for direct election to the presidency and the Veće Republika, and reducing Montenegro's status within the FRY. The amendments attracted immediate criticism from Serbian opposition parties and the international community. The Skupština Republike Crne Gore subsequently voted to reject the amendments, which Vujanović condemned as an attempt by Milošević to retain power. At the end of July Milošević announced that federal presidential and legislative elections were to take place on 24 September. The Montenegrin Government announced that the republic would not participate in the forthcoming elections, in protest at the amendments. In early August an alliance of 18 opposition parties, known as the Democratic Opposition of Serbia (DOS), presented the leader of the DPS, Dr Vojislav Koštunica, as their joint candidate to oppose Milošević in the presidential election.

Numerous allegations of electoral malpractice and intimidation emerged, both prior to and following the voting to the federal presidency and legislature on 24 September 2000. Preliminary results, released by the Federal Election Commission, indicated that Koštunica had won about 48% of the votes cast, compared with the 40% of the votes received by Milošević, and thereby failed to obtain the 50% majority required to secure the presidency. Milošević subsequently insisted that a second round of voting be conducted on 8 October, while Koštunica rejected the results of the Commission as fraudulent, and claimed to have won the election outright. The international community declared its support for Koštunica and urged Milošević to accept defeat. The Yugoslav army announced that it would not intervene on Milošević's behalf, while the SRP and Serbian parties in Montenegro also acknowledged Koštunica's victory. Opposition supporters commenced a campaign of peaceful protest in Serbia (including a widely observed general strike from the beginning of October), in an effort to compel Milošević to resign. On 5 October protesters, who had gathered to stage a mass rally in Belgrade, overpowered security forces and seized control of the parliament building, the state television station and the official news agency, subsequently declaring Koštunica to be the elected President. On the following day, amid increasing international pressure, Milošević finally relinquished the presidency. Koštunica was officially inaugurated as President on 7 October. According to the final official results, Koštunica received 51.7% of the votes cast and Milošević 38.2%; in the concurrent legislative elections, the DOS secured 58 seats in the 138-member Veće građana, and the SPS 44. After the DOS negotiated an agreement with the SPS in mid-October, the Narodna skupština Republike Srbije was dissolved, and a transitional Government, in which the SPS retained the premiership, was installed later that month, pending legislative elections, which were brought forward to December. Since only about 30% of the Montenegrin electorate had participated in the voting, as a result of Đukanović's boycott, Koštunica was obliged to form an administration with the SNP (the only Montenegrin party to be represented in the legislature). A member of that party, Zoran Zizic, was nominated to the post of Prime Minister, and a new Federal Government, comprising representatives of the DOS and the Socialist People's Party, was established in early November. Following the installation of the new Government, the normalization of relations between the FRY and the international community proceeded rapidly, and the country was readmitted to the UN on 1 November. In December Koštunica reorganized the armed forces, removing officers loyal to Milošević.

In the elections to the 250-member Narodna skupština Republike Srbije, held on 23 December 2000, the DOS secured a substantial majority, with 176 seats, while the SPS won 37 seats and the SRP 23. Later that month Đukanović announced proposals that the FRY become a loose union of two internationally recognized, separate states. At the end of December the People's Party of Montenegro, which supported a continued federation, withdrew from the governing coalition. Đukanović subsequently announced that elections to the Skupština Republike Crne Gore would take place in April 2001. In January Đinđić was elected to the Serbian premiership, and a new Government, comprising members of the DOS, was installed later that month.

In early 2001 the Federal Government came under increasing pressure from the EU and USA to arrest Milošević and other war crimes suspects (following their indictment in May 1999); Koštunica maintained that their extradition would contravene the Constitution. Following a warning by the USA that it would end financial aid to the FRY unless the new administration fully cooperated with the ICTY by the end of March 2001, Milošević was taken into custody on 1 April. The federal Public Prosecutor issued a series of charges against Milošević for abuses of power during his term of office (principally extensive embezzlement from state funds, and involvement in political assassinations, electoral malpractice and organized crime). Later that month Milošević, who was in detention in Belgrade, received the ICTY indictment. At the end of April Serbian courts authorized the extension of Milošević's period of detention for a further two months, despite an appeal that he be released on grounds of ill health. Koštunica, however, refused to comply with international demands that Milošević be dispatched for trial at the ICTY (apparently owing to concern that his extradition might prompt political unrest).

Meanwhile, elections to the 78-member Skupština Republike Crne Gore were conducted on 22 April 2001. The pro-independence alliance, led by the DPMS, won 36 seats, while the coalition opposing independence, led by the SNP, won 33 seats, and the Liberal Alliance of Montenegro (LAM) six seats. Despite having failed to secure a decisive majority in the legislature, Đukanović announced that he would continue to pursue his aim of organizing a referendum on independence. In May an agreement was signed between the DPMS, the Social Democratic Party of Montenegro (SDP) and the LAM, whereby a LAM representative was to become Speaker of the Skupština Republike Crne Gore. In late June Vujanović formed a new coalition Government, comprising representatives of the DPMS, the SDP and a junior member of the DPMS alliance, the Democratic Union of Albanians.

In late June 2001, following continued international pressure for the authorities to co-operate with the ICTY, the Serbian Government approved a decree, providing for the extradition of Milošević and other indicted war criminals to the ICTY. Supporters of Milošević subsequently staged a large demonstration in Belgrade. The Serbian Government refused to comply with a ruling by the federal Constitutional Court that the decree was invalid, and on 29 June (shortly before an important international donor conference was to take place) Milošević was extradited to the ICTY. On the following day Zizić resigned from the office of federal Prime Minister, in protest at Milošević's extradition (which had been strongly opposed by the SNP). In July Koštunica appointed Dragiša Pešić, also a member of the SNP and hitherto federal Minister of Finance, to the post. Later that month a reorganized Federal Government, proposed by Pešić, was approved in the legislature. In August the division between Koštunica and Đinđić resulting from the Serbian Government's decision to extradite Milošević was further exacerbated by the killing in Belgrade of a security agent, who had reportedly been investigating alleged connections of prominent state officials to organized crime. Koštunica accused Đinđić's administration of failing to address widespread crime, and withdrew the DPS ministers from the Government (although the party officially remained within the DOS coalition).

In October 2001 the initial indictment against Milošević relating to Kosovo was amended, henceforth alleging that he had organized security-force operations against Kosovan Albanians, which had resulted in the expulsion of 80,000 civilians from the province. Also in October Milošević was further indicted in connection with war crimes perpetrated in Croatia in 1991–92; he was accused of ordering the forcible removal of the majority of the non-Serb population from one-third of the territory of Croatia, with the aim of incorporating the region into a Serb-dominated state. Four former naval officers were also indicted for participation in an offensive by the Yugoslav People's Army against the Dubrovnik region of Croatia in late 1991. The former Commander of the Yugoslav Navy, Pavle Strugar, surrendered to the ICTY later in October 2001. In November Milošević (hitherto indicted for crimes against humanity, breaches of the 1949 Geneva Convention, and violations of the laws or customs of war) was charged with genocide, in connection with the atrocities perpetrated by Serb forces in Bosnia and Herzegovina in 1992–95. He continued to refuse to recognize the authority of the ICTY, and 'not guilty' pleas were submitted on his behalf for all three indictments. The trial of Milošević, who had decided to conduct his own defence, officially commenced on 12 February 2002.

In December 2001 the Speaker of the Narodna skupština Republike Srbije, who was the deputy leader of the DPS and a close associate of Koštunica, resigned, having accused parties belonging to the DOS coalition of electoral malpractice. In January 2002 the federal Minister of Finance also tendered his resignation. In March one of the Serbian Deputy Prime Ministers, Momčilo Perišić, was arrested, and subsequently resigned, after military intelligence sources claimed to have evidence that he had given classified information to a US diplomat. Đinđić rejected demands by Koštunica that he submit his resignation over the issue, and requested the dismissal of the head of the military security service responsible for Perišić's arrest. Perišić claimed that the charges had been fabricated, in an attempt to cause the dissolution of Đinđić's Government. In June the DPS withdrew from the Narodna skupština Republike Srbije, in protest at the expulsion of 21 DPS deputies. (The party was formally expelled from the ruling DOS coalition in the following month.) The Serbian Government was reorganized in the same month.

Following protracted negotiations on the issue of Montenegro's independence (which were mediated by the EU from November 2001), the government leaders of the FRY and the two republics signed a framework agreement on 14 March 2002, providing for the establishment of a State Union of Serbia and Montenegro. Under the accord, the two republics were to maintain separate economies, but have joint foreign and defence ministries, and elect a new, joint presidency and legislature. (However, Montenegro was to retain the right to refer the issue of independence to a referendum after a period of three years.) It was envisaged that, following endorsement of the agreement by the Savezna skupština and the legislatures of the two republics, a new constitution would be adopted, and elections to the new joint parliament would take place later that year. Later in March the LAM withdrew from Đukanović's coalition (thereby ending its narrow majority in the Skupština Republike Crne Gore), in protest at the agreement, which prompted widespread criticism from pro-independence supporters. In early April the legislatures of Serbia and Montenegro both approved the accord, which was submitted for ratification in the Savezna skupština. However, four principal pro-independence ministers, belonging to the LAM and the SDP, subsequently resigned from the Montenegrin Government. On 19 April Vujanović submitted his resignation. He was subsequently reappointed to office by Đukanović, but proved unable to secure majority support in the legislature for a new government.

Meanwhile, the USA renewed pressure on the Federal Government to demonstrate co-operation with the ICTY. Following the expiry of a deadline for Yugoslav compliance with these demands, economic aid to the FRY was suspended at the end of March 2002. On 11 April the Savezna skupština finally approved legislation providing for the extradition of indicted war crimes suspects, and the issue of arrest warrants for those who did not surrender to the ICTY. Shortly afterwards Stojiljković (the former Serbian Minister of the Interior who had been indicted in May 1999), committed suicide. Of 10 former Yugoslav state officials indicted, six (including Gen. Ojdanić and Šainović) agreed to surrender to the Tribunal. In early May 2002 Šainović was voluntarily transferred to the ICTY.

In late May 2002 the Savezna skupština officially approved the agreement on the creation of a State Union (which had been ratified by the legislatures of both republics in April). In July Lilić was arrested and extradited to the ICTY, having been subpoenaed as a prosecution witness in the trial of Milošević. He refused to testify unless he was guaranteed immunity from prosecution. It was announced that the presidential election in Serbia would be brought forward to 29 September, to allow the extradition of Milutinović to the ICTY. In mid-July 2002, following the failure of Vujanović to secure majority support for a new government, the Skupština Republike Crne Gore was dissolved; further legislative elections were scheduled for 6 October.

At the Serbian presidential election, held on 29 September 2002, Koštunica won some 30.9% of the votes cast, while Miroljub Labus (the incumbent federal Deputy Prime Minister and Minister of Foreign Trade, who was supported by Đinđić) received 27.4% and Šešelj 23.2%; 55.5% of the registered electorate voted. A second round of voting took place on 13 October between Koštunica and Labus, at which Koštunica secured some 68.4% of the votes cast. However, the election was declared invalid, owing to the participation of only 44.0% of the electorate, lower than the required minimum level of 50%. (Šešelj had urged his supporters not to participate in the poll, and it was reported that Đinđić had also unofficially supported a boycott).

Elections to the Skupština Republike Crne Gore took place on 20 October 2002: Đukanović's pro-independence coalition, now known as Democratic List for a European Montenegro, secured 39 of the 75 seats, with the SNP-led Together for Change coalition, which had opposed the planned creation of a looser union with Serbia, receiving 30 seats. In November Đukanović resigned from the office of President (prior to becoming the new Prime Minister), and a presidential election in Montenegro was scheduled for 22 December. On 6 December a 27-member commission on constitutional reform, comprising representatives of the principal parties of the two republics, submitted a draft of the new Constitutional Charter for the proposed State Union. A third presidential poll in Serbia on 8 December (in which Koštunica won just 57.7% of the votes) was again annulled, owing to a rate of participation of just 45.0%. On 30 December Milutinović was replaced, on an interim basis, by the President of the Narodna skupština Republike Srbije, Nataša Micić. The presidential election in Montenegro on 22 December was also invalidated by a participation level of 45.9%, following a boycott organized by the SNP and the LAM; Vujanović (representing the Democratic List for European Montenegro) had secured 83.7% of the votes cast in the ballot. Following protracted disagreement in the Skupština Republike Crne Gore between the DPMS and the allied SDP over the allocation of ministerial portfolios, a new Cabinet, headed by Đukanović, was approved by the Montenegrin legislature on 8 January 2003.

On 20 January 2003 Milutinović was voluntarily transferred to the ICTY, where he subsequently pleaded not guilty to charges relating to crimes perpetrated during the 1999 conflict in Kosovo. The new Constitutional Charter, which provided for the creation of the State Union of Serbia and Montenegro, was approved by the Narodna skupština Republike Srbije on 27 January 2003 and by the Skupština Republike Crne Gore on 29 January. On 4 February both chambers of the Savezna skupština approved the Constitutional Charter, thereby officially replacing the FRY with the State Union of Serbia and Montenegro. Ethnic Albanians in Kosovo expressed their opposition to the province's inclusion in the new Union as part of Serbia, and continued to demand independence.

A further presidential ballot in Montenegro on 9 February 2003 (at which Vujanović secured 82.0% of votes cast) was again declared invalid, with a rate of participation of 46.6%. Later in February Šešelj surrendered to the ICTY, where he was charged in connection with the forcible removal of the non-Serb population from various regions of Bosnia and Herzegovina, Croatia and Serbia (Vojvodina) in 1991–95. On 25 February 2003, in accordance with the Constitutional Charter, the existing federal and republican legislatures elected a 126-member Skupština Srbije i Crne Gore (Assembly of Serbia and Montenegro), comprising 91 Serbian and 35 Montenegrin deputies. On 7 March a former parliamentary Speaker, Svetozar Marović, was elected unopposed as President of Serbia and Montenegro by the Skupština Srbije i Crne Gore. The President was also to chair a five-member Council of Ministers (with portfolios that included foreign affairs, defence, and human and minority rights), which was approved by the Skupština Srbije i Crne Gore on 18 March.

On 12 March 2003 Đinđić, having survived an apparent assassination attempt in February, was shot dead outside government buildings in Belgrade. Micić immediately imposed a state of emergency in Serbia, and some 1,200 suspects, including a former Serbian Minister of Security, were arrested in connection with the assassination. The former federal Minister of Internal Affairs, Zoran Živković, was nominated by the DP to replace Đinđić, and was approved by the Narodna skupština Republike Srbije as new Serbian Prime Minister on 18 March. At the end of March security forces discovered the remains of Ivan Stambolić, who had been abducted in August 2000. The Serbian authorities issued an international arrest warrant for Mirjana Marković and her son (who were in hiding in Russia), in connection with the killing of Stambolić; Milošević was subsequently also charged. In mid-April the Skupština Srbije i Crne Gore voted in favour of extending the state's co-operation with the ICTY, ending a stipulation that all war crimes suspects indicted by the Tribunal from that month be tried by domestic courts. Later that month the state of emergency in Serbia was ended and some 45 suspects, including Šešelj, were charged with alleged involvement in the assassination of Đinđić. Two former senior security advisers of Koštunica were also charged with conspiring to overthrow the Government in a coup, which, according to the Serbian authorities, was to have followed Đinđić's killing, with the aim of reinstating an administration opposed to co-operation with the ICTY. In early May two former heads of the Serbian security services and close associates of Milošević, already in detention in Belgrade in connection with Đinđić's assassination, were also indicted by the ICTY for war crimes.

On 11 May 2003 Vujanović was elected to the presidency of Montenegro, with 63.3% of the votes cast. (Although only about 48% of the electorate had participated in the ballot, regulations had been amended to remove the 50% minimum requirement.) Vujanović was officially inaugurated on 13 June. He subsequently pledged that a referendum on the issue of independence would be conducted in Montenegro within three years.

In early June 2003 the former Serbian Minister of State Security, Jovica Stanišić, and his deputy, Franko Simatović, were extradited to the ICTY, having been indicted in May. Stanišić and Simatović had been arrested in connection with Đinđić's assassination. In August a senior naval officer, Vice-Adm. Miodrag Jokić, reached a compromise agreement with ICTY prosecutors, according to which he pleaded guilty to six charges relating to the bombardment of Dubrovnik. In the same month the Serbian Government issued arrest warrants for 44 people suspected of involvement in Đinđić's assassination, principally Milorad 'Legija' Luković (also known as Ulemek), the leader of an organized criminal group and a prominent member of a 'Red Beret' paramilitary unit of Milošević's regime. In September the Serbian Government announced that Milošević would be arraigned at a special court on charges of ordering the killing of Stambolić. In October the ICTY issued indictments against four senior Serbian military and security officials, including the former Chief of General Staff of the Yugoslav Army, Col-Gen. Nebojsa Pavković (who had been removed from his post by Koštunica in June 2002), for war crimes perpetrated against the civilian population of Kosovo in 1998–99. Serbian leaders, including Zivković, condemned the measure, claiming that they had been implicitly assured of indemnity from prosecution.

In November 2003 the Montenegrin Minister of the Interior, Milan Filipović, resigned, reportedly in connection with allegations that a judge presiding over a sex-trafficking case involving government officials had been placed under clandestine state surveillance. Also in November, following long-standing dissension within the DOS, two small parties withdrew from the coalition, thereby ending its parliamentary majority. The DOS subsequently dissolved, and Živković scheduled fresh elections to the Narodna skupština Republike Srbije. Meanwhile, on 16 November a further presidential poll in Serbia (at which Tomislav Nikolić of the SRP secured 47.9% of the votes cast) was declared invalid, owing to a rate of electoral participation of some 38.8%. In December the trial began of 36 suspects charged in connection with Đinđić's assassination (15 of them, including Luković, in absentia). At the elections to the Narodna skupština Republike Srbije, held on 28 December, the SRP, with 28.0% of the votes cast, secured 82 seats, the DPS (18.0%) 53 seats, the DP (12.8%) 37 seats, a newly emerged reformist grouping known as G17 Plus (11.6%) 34 seats, an alliance of the SRM and New Serbia (NS—7.8%) 22 seats, and the SPS (7.7%) 22 seats. Candidates contesting parliamentary seats notably included four indicted war crimes suspects, two of whom (Milošević and Šešelj) were in detention at The Hague. (Despite the electoral success of their parties, Milošević and Šešelj were denied parliamentary representation.) Following lengthy inter-party discussions, the DPS formed a minority coalition with G17 Plus and the SRM-NS alliance, which was also, to the concern of the international community, reliant on the support of the SPS. On 4 February 2004 the DPS Vice-President, Dragan Maršićanin, was elected President of the Narodna skupština Republike Srbije, thereby replacing Micić as the Republic's acting President. In that month the Serbian Assembly voted to abolish the minimum rate of participation for elections to the republican presidency, as a means of ending the protracted political impasse. A new Council of Ministers, headed by Koštunica, was formed in March; owing to Maršićanin's inclusion in the administration as Minister of the Economy, he was replaced as President of the Narodna skupština Republike Srbije (and therefore acting President of Serbia) by the hitherto deputy speaker, Predrag Marković. In mid-April the Skupština Srbije i Crne Gore approved a reorganization of the state union Council of Ministers; Drašković received the foreign affairs portfolio, Prvoslav Davinić of G17 Plus replaced Tadić as Minister of Defence, and Predrag Ivanović of the DPMS became Minister of Foreign Economic Relations. The principal suspect in the assassination of Đinđić, Luković, surrendered to the Serbian authorities in early May, subsequently denying all charges.

Some 15 candidates contested the elections to the presidency of Serbia, held on 13 June 2004. Nikolić secured 30.1% of the votes cast, and Boris Tadić, the state Minister of Defence, won 27.7% of the votes. Bogoljub Karić, who was considered to be one of the most wealthy businessmen in Serbia, won 18.5% of the votes, and Maršićanin (having resigned his ministerial post) 13.5%. Nikolić's narrow victory in the first round was attributed to the failure of the reformist parties to agree on a common candidate. A second round between Nikolić and Tadić was conducted on 27 June; Tadić, who benefited from the transferred support of the governing coalition parties, was elected to the presidency, receiving 54.0% of the votes. At his inauguration on 17 July, Tadić pledged commitment to the continuation of economic reforms and for the eventual integration of Serbia into the EU. At the end of November it was reported that Tadić had been the subject of an apparent assassination attempt in Belgrade.

In early December 2004 a former Yugoslav Army officer, Gen. Dragoljub Milošević, surrendered to the Serbian authorities and was extradited to the ICTY, where he was charged with crimes relating to the blockade and bombardment of Sarajevo in 1994. In January 2005, however, the USA expressed dissatisfaction with the failure of Serbia and Montenegro to co-operate with the ICTY, and announced a reduction in financial aid and the withdrawal of US technical advisers from Serbian ministries. The EU subsequently indicated that the prospects for Serbia and Montenegro's eventual accession would be dependent on the extradition of the four former Serbian military and security officials who had been indicted in October 2003 for crimes committed during the conflict in Kosovo. Representatives of the international community repeatedly accused the Serbian authorities of aiding the continuing evasion from the Tribunal of the Bosnian Serb indictee, Ratko Mladić, and also cited his extradition as essential for Serbia and Montenegro's accession to NATO's Partnership for Peace programme. In early February 2005 one of those indicted, a former military commander in Priština, Gen. Vladimir Lazarević, agreed to surrender to the ICTY after meeting with Koštunica, and was subsequently extradited. (The other three indictees were, however, believed to be in hiding.) Later in February Koštunica rejected a proposal by the Montenegrin Government for a greater separation of powers between the two republics in the State Union.

Amid increasing concern over the future of the State Union, in February 2005 Koštunica and Đukanović met for discussions on the scheduling of elections to the Skupština Srbije i Crne Gore. On 7 April, following mediation by the EU High Representative for Common Foreign and Security Policy, Javier Solana Madriaga, the Presidents agreed that the election of representatives to the Skupština Srbije i Crne Gore would take place concurrently with elections to the two republican legislatures; the Constitutional Charter was to be amended to allow the extension of the mandates of the incumbent deputies. The Montenegrin Government favoured the organization of a referendum on independence prior to elections, while supporters of the continuation of the State Union insisted that such a measure would require adherence to EU conditions and arbitration. Solana welcomed the agreement and commended Serbia's improved co-operation with the ICTY (following the transfer, between late 2004 and mid-2005, of 13 Serbian and Bosnian Serb war crime suspects, in surrenders mediated by the Koštunica Government). Shortly afterwards the European Commission indicated that sufficient progress had been made for Serbia and Montenegro to commence negotiations on a Stabilization and Association Agreement with the EU. The surrender of Pavković to the ICTY in late April demonstrated further progress towards improved relations between Serbia and the EU.

At the end of June 2005 the head of Milošević's secret service, Radomir Marković, together with Milorad Luković and three other former paramilitary members, were sentenced to terms of imprisonment for involvement in an assassination attempt against Drašković in 1999. In July 2005 Luković was sentenced to 40 years' and Marković to 15 years' imprisonment for the killing of Stambolić in August 2000; six former secret service officers also received custodial terms. In September 2005 a further international arrest warrant was issued for Mirjana Marković, who had failed to fulfil pledges to return from exile in Russia. On 10 October negotiations officially commenced between the Government of Serbia and Montenegro and the EU on a Stabilization and Association Agreement. In early October five members of a former Serb paramilitary unit were charged in Serbia with the massacre of six Muslims at Srebrenica, Bosnia and Herzegovina, following the release of video evidence of the killings; their trial commenced in December. Also in December some 14 members of a former Serb militia were sentenced by a Serbian court to terms of between five and 20 years for killing 200 Croat prisoners near the Croatian town of Vukovar in November 1991.

In November 2005 Milošević's trial at the ICTY was again adjourned on grounds of ill health; he subsequently rejected an attempt by the Tribunal to expedite proceedings. On 27 February 2006 a case submitted by Bosnia and Herzegovina against Serbia in 1993, demanding reparations for the genocide of the Bosnian Muslim population in 1992–95, finally commenced at the International Court of Justice (ICJ) at the Hague. Proceedings were expected to continue until May 2006, with a ruling by the end of the year. At the end of February the Montenegrin Government and opposition agreed that the planned referendum would take place on 21 May, and that, in accordance with EU stipulations, a vote in favour of independence would require the approval of 55% of the votes cast, with 50% of the electorate participating. On 1 March legislation providing for the organization of the referendum was approved by 60 of the 75 deputies in the Skupština Republike Crne Gore.

On 11 March 2006 Milošević died while in custody at the ICTY. Preliminary autopsy results concluded that the cause of death was a heart attack, but supporters of Milošević immediately criticized the medical treatment that he had received in detention and the Tribunal's refusal in late February to grant a request for his transfer to hospital in Russia. (It emerged that shortly before his death Milošević had written to the Russian Minister of Foreign Affairs, claiming that he was being poisoned in detention.) ICTY officials expressed regret that his trial had not been concluded. The Serbian authorities refused to organize a state funeral, and members of Milošević's family, including Mirjana Marković (despite the temporary suspension of the international arrest warrant against her), failed to attend the ceremony, which took place at his family residence in the Serbian town of Pozarevac; although there were scenes of public mourning, former nationalist supporters at the funeral were reported to number only a few hundred. In early April an independent investigation by Dutch pathologists confirmed that Milošević's death was the result of a heart attack.

In early 2006 the Serbian authorities came under increasing pressure from the EU to effect Mladić's extradition to the ICTY, with frequent speculation that his capture was imminent. At the end of March the ICTY Prosecutor, Carla Del Ponte, visited Belgrade, with the aim of securing assurances that Mladić would be apprehended, and the EU issued an ultimatum that failure to arrest Mladić by 5 April would result in the suspension of the negotiations on the Stabilization and Association Agreement. Discussions continued during that month, but were, however, suspended, after the Serbian Government failed to meet a further deadline, of 30 April, for Mladić's extradition. In early May Labus resigned from the post of Deputy Prime Minister of Serbia in protest at the failure of the authorities to apprehend Mladić. Labus subsequently resigned from the leadership of G17 Plus, after the party refused to withdraw other representatives from the Government. In the referendum held in Montenegro on 21 May some 55.5% of votes were cast in favour of independence, narrowly exceeding the minimum requirement of 55% stipulated by the EU; the rate of participation was about 86.3%. Parties opposed to independence subsequently demanded that the results of the ballot be recounted.

With the imposition by the UN, from May 1992, of economic sanctions against the FRY, in an attempt to force Serbia to exert its influence to bring about an end to the conflict in Bosnia and Herzegovina, and the FRY's exclusion from the UN and other major multilateral organizations, Yugoslavia was largely isolated from the international community. In September 1994, after the Yugoslav Government imposed an embargo against Bosnia and Herzegovina in response to Bosnian Serb opposition to a peace plan, the UN suspended certain sanctions against the FRY. All UN sanctions against the FRY were suspended in November 1995, and the Yugoslav authorities ended the blockade of Bosnian Serb territories (Republika Srpska, Bosnia and Herzegovina) in February 1996. In early April Yugoslavia and the former Yugoslav republic of Macedonia (FYRM) signed an agreement on mutual diplomatic recognition. This was one of the major conditions imposed by the EU for wider recognition of Yugoslavia, and during April most EU countries proceeded to recognize the FRY as one of the successor states of the SFRY, and to upgrade their diplomatic relations to ambassadorial level. In August the FRY and Croatia signed a treaty of mutual recognition, providing for the establishment of full diplomatic relations; remaining issues of contention, notably the territorial dispute over the Prevlaka Peninsula, on the Adriatic coast, were to be resolved by further negotiations. In October the UN Security Council officially ended sanctions against the FRY; however, some punitive measures imposed by the USA remained in place, effectively preventing the FRY Government access to the international financial institutions.

In October 1997 students demonstrated in Priština in support of demands that the Serbian authorities implement an agreement, reached in 1996, which provided for the restoration of an Albanian language curriculum in the education system in Kosovo. In late December the Serbian security forces violently suppressed further student protests in the province. In early January 1998 the Kosovo Liberation Army (KLA), a paramilitary movement that had claimed responsibility for a number of attacks against members of the Serbian security forces in 1997, announced its intention to achieve independence for the province through armed resistance. Later in January 1998 special Serbian security forces were dispatched to Kosovo with the aim of quelling KLA activity. In late February four members of the Serbian security forces were killed by KLA troops, prompting a retaliatory operation, in which some 24 ethnic Albanians were killed in central Kosovo. Although the Serbian authorities claimed that those killed had been members of the KLA, they were accused of instigating massacres of civilians. In early March Serbian security forces staged an offensive against KLA bases in central Kosovo, subsequently claiming to have killed the movement's leader and capturing a number of its troops. Ethnic Albanians staged a number of mass protests in response to the violence in the province. Despite international condemnation (see below), the Serbian security forces continued to instigate reprisals for KLA attacks; by the end of March it was reported that about 80 ethnic Albanians had been killed. The UN Preventive Deployment Force in Macedonia (UNPREDEP) increased its presence at the border with the FRY, amid international concern that the violence would escalate into a regional conflict.

In early March 1998 a Serbian government delegation was dispatched to Priština to enter into discussions with the 'government' of the self-proclaimed 'Republic of Kosovo', headed by Ibrahim Rugova (which supported the achievement of autonomy for the province through peaceful means). However, Rugova rejected the offer of negotiations, on the grounds that it had been made in an effort to reduce international pressure on the FRY Government. Elections to the 'Kosovo Assembly' took place later in March, and Rugova was elected 'President' with more than 90% of the votes cast. (The Serbian authorities declared the elections to be illegal.) In early April Milošević announced that a referendum was to be conducted in Serbia to determine whether the authorities should accept the mediation urged by the international community to resolve the conflict in Kosovo; at the referendum, which took place later that month, the refusal of mediation was endorsed by 94.7% of votes cast. In May the Serbian authorities dispatched large numbers of security forces to western Kosovo, following reports that the KLA was receiving illicit supplies of armaments from Albania.

In February 1998 the US Government announced a relaxation of its remaining sanctions against the FRY. In early March, however, the USA and EU issued statements condemning the violent measures taken by the Serbian security forces to suppress the activities of the KLA in Kosovo, while also criticizing the violence employed by the KLA. The US Government announced that it was to withdraw the concessions that it had granted to the FRY in February, and threatened possible military intervention in Kosovo. The 'Contact Group' comprising representatives of five governments, which had been established in response to the conflict in Bosnia and Herzegovina, was convened in London; member nations envisaged the imposition of further sanctions against the FRY, including an embargo on armaments, unless the Serbian authorities acceded to a number of demands, including the withdrawal of security forces from Kosovo and the initiation of negotiations regarding the future status of the province. The British Government subsequently submitted a draft resolution to the UN Security Council for the imposition of an embargo on armaments against the FRY. Following a further meeting of the 'Contact Group', which took place in Bonn, Germany, later in March a statement was issued conceding that the Serbian authorities had achieved progress in reaching an agreement on education (see above), but continued to demand that they engage in negotiations regarding the future status of Kosovo. At the end of March the UN Security Council officially imposed an embargo on armaments against the FRY; of the member nations of the Council, only the People's Republic of China failed to endorse the resolution. The members of the 'Contact Group' (apart from Russia) announced in April that Yugoslav assets abroad were to be 'frozen' and in May imposed a ban on foreign investment in Serbia.

In early July 1998 Milošević agreed that diplomatic observers from the EU, the USA and Russia would be allowed access to all regions of Kosovo to report on the activities of Serbian security forces. The 'Contact Group', which met in Bonn to discuss a peace settlement for Kosovo, recognized for the first time that it would be necessary to include KLA representatives in future negotiations on the status of the province. Meanwhile, Serbian security forces continued to initiate attacks against the KLA. Violence in the province continued during August, with further Serbian offensives against the KLA and killings of ethnic Albanian civilians (including a massacre at the southern town of Orahovac).

In September 1998 the UN Security Council adopted Resolution 1199 (with the People's Republic of China abstaining), which demanded the immediate cessation of hostilities in Kosovo, the withdrawal of Serbian forces from the province, unrestricted access for humanitarian aid organizations, and the continuation of negotiations to determine the status of the province. NATO subsequently authorized its Supreme Allied Commander, Gen. Wesley Clark, to request member states to provide forces for possible military intervention. Despite an announcement by Marjanović at the end of September that Serbian security forces had suspended hostilities against the KLA, intensive fighting south of Priština was reported. NATO officially approved air bombardments against the FRY, and issued an ultimatum to Milošević that attacks would commence unless he complied with UN demands by a stipulated date later that month. (Russia continued to oppose military intervention against the FRY and had indicated that it would veto a further UN Security Council resolution authorizing such action.) Following intensive discussions with the US special envoy, Richard Holbrooke, Milošević agreed to the presence in Kosovo of a 2,000-member OSCE 'verification force' (to be known as the Kosovo Diplomatic Observer Mission), and to NATO surveillance flights in FRY airspace, to monitor the implementation of the UN Security Council's demands. Serbian leaders in Kosovo criticized Milošević's acceptance of the peace settlement, while the KLA considered the deployment of the OSCE monitors to be inadequate and continued to urge NATO military intervention. It was subsequently reported that the majority of federal army units had been withdrawn from Kosovo, but that some 11,600 members of the special Serbian security forces remained in the province. NATO urged further progress in the withdrawal of Serbian forces from Kosovo, but at the end of October suspended indefinitely the implementation of military action against the FRY.

In November 1998 the deployment of OSCE observers in Kosovo commenced; however, intermittent violations of the cease-fire were reported. Following the outbreak of heavy fighting between the KLA and Serbian forces in northern Kosovo in December, it became evident that the OSCE monitoring force was inadequate (and had no mandate) for peace-keeping operations. A 2,300-member NATO 'extraction force' was deployed in the FYRM, near the border with Kosovo, to effect the evacuation of the OSCE monitors in the event of attacks against them. In early January 1999 further clashes between Serbian and KLA forces were reported. In mid-January the discovery that some 45 ethnic Albanian civilians had been killed at the village of Račak prompted international condemnation of the Serbian authorities. OSCE observers dismissed claims by the Federal Government that those killed had been members of the KLA. At the end of January the 'Contact Group', meeting in London, decided that a peace conference should be convened at the French town of Rambouillet in early February. The British Secretary of State for

Foreign and Commonwealth Affairs, Robin Cook, visited Belgrade to present the demands of the 'Contact Group' (which he chaired) that Serbian, DAK and KLA leaders attend the negotiations on a draft peace agreement. Following international pressure, the KLA agreed that representatives of the movement would attend the conference, while in early February the Serbian legislature voted in favour of participation.

In early February 1999 the peace conference was convened in Rambouillet, as scheduled. Under the proposed peace plan, which was presented by the 'Contact Group' to the delegations, the Serbian authorities would be required to withdraw most of the 14,000 armed and security forces in Kosovo, while the KLA would disarm within a period of three months. It was envisaged that NATO troops would be deployed in Kosovo to enforce the peace agreement. Negotiations at Rambouillet were extended, owing to the opposition of the Serbian delegation to the proposed deployment of the NATO force, and to the reluctance of elements of the KLA to accept the provisions in the agreement for disarmament. At the end of February, however, the ethnic Albanian delegation, including the KLA representatives, agreed, in principle, to accept the peace plan. Meanwhile, in early March it was reported that Serbian troops had forced several thousand ethnic Albanian civilians to flee from southern Kosovo, amid continued heavy fighting in the province. The peace conference was reconvened at Rambouillet in mid-March. The ethnic Albanian representatives signed the agreement; however, the Serbian delegation continued to present objections and proposed amendments to the peace plan, which were rejected by the 'Contact Group'. It was subsequently reported that the Federal Government had deployed a further 30,000 Serbian forces in, or near, Kosovo. NATO reiterated threats of imminent air bombardments, despite continued opposition from the Russian Government, which attempted unsuccessfully to persuade Milošević to accept the peace plan. In the absence of a negotiated settlement to the conflict, the NATO Secretary-General ordered the commencement of air attacks against the FRY, in a campaign, codenamed Operation Allied Force, which was designed to force Milošević's capitulation to the demands of the 'Contact Group'.

On 24 March 1999 NATO forces commenced an aerial bombardment of air defences and military installations, notably in Belgrade, Novi Sad, Priština and Podgorica. The Federal Government declared a state of war (which, however, the Montenegrin administration refused to recognize), suspended diplomatic relations with the USA, France, Germany and the United Kingdom (the countries directly involved in the attacks), and ordered foreign journalists to leave the country. The People's Republic of China and Russia immediately condemned the air offensive (which NATO justified on humanitarian grounds, despite the lack of endorsement by a UN Security Council resolution), while the Italian and Greek Governments expressed reservations, and urged further diplomatic efforts. Serbian security forces in Kosovo subsequently intensified the campaign of mass expulsions and large-scale massacres of the ethnic Albanian civilian population (which was condemned by the international community as genocidal), precipitating a continued exodus of refugees from the province. By early April some 140,000 ethnic Albanians had fled to the FYRM, 300,000 to Albania, and 32,000 to Montenegro. Some 12,000 NATO troops were stationed at the FYRM border with Kosovo, after the reinforcement of the 'extraction force'.

During April 1999 the NATO air offensive intensified, with the extension of targets to include those of political and economic significance, including the Serbian state television station. The increasing number of civilian casualties was condemned by opponents of the air offensive; notably, NATO aircraft bombarded a convoy of ethnic Albanian refugees in Kosovo in mid-April, killing about 64, apparently owing to confusion over Serbian military targets. Đukanović refused to comply with an order from Milošević to place Montenegrin security forces under federal military command (following warnings by NATO that Milošević intended to overthrow the Montenegrin Government). In late April Drašković was removed from his office of Federal Deputy Prime Minister, after he publicly opposed Milošević's refusal to comply with NATO demands.

From April 1999 the Russian special envoy to the Balkans, Viktor Chernomyrdin, was engaged in intensive mediation efforts with the Federal Government, but urged a suspension of the NATO air offensive. NATO, however, continued to demand the full withdrawal of Serbian forces from Kosovo, and the return of refugees with an international military presence, as a precondition to the suspension of air attacks. In early May the Group of Eight (G-8—comprising the seven Western industrialized nations and Russia), meeting in Bonn, agreed on general principles for a political solution to the conflict (which was referred to the UN Security Council), although differences over the composition of the international military force for Kosovo remained. Shortly afterwards, apparently owing to faulty military information, NATO forces bombarded the embassy of the People's Republic of China in Belgrade. Violent anti-NATO protests ensued in the Chinese capital, Beijing, and the Chinese Government, supported by Russia, demanded a cessation of the air offensive as a precondition to the discussion of the settlement at the UN Security Council. The Federal Government protested to the International Court of Justice (ICJ) that the NATO air offensive was an illegal act of aggression, on the grounds that it had not received UN authorization. (The ICJ subsequently rejected the legal appeal.) At mid-May it was estimated that the NATO air campaign had resulted in the deaths of 1,200 civilians; about 600,000 ethnic Albanian refugees from Kosovo had fled to neighbouring countries.

At the beginning of June 1999 the Federal Government announced that it had accepted the G-8 principles for a solution to the conflict. On 3 June, following mediation by the President of Finland, Martti Ahtisaari, the Narodna skupština Republike Srbije formally approved a peace plan presented to the Federal Government by EU and Russian envoys. The peace agreement provided for the withdrawal of Serbian forces from Kosovo, and the deployment of a joint NATO-Russian peace-keeping force of about 50,000 personnel. Ethnic Albanian refugees were to be allowed to return to Kosovo, and the province was to be granted some autonomy under an interim administration. On 9 June, following discussions between NATO and Yugoslav military commanders, which were conducted in the FYRM, a Military Technical Agreement, providing for the complete withdrawal of Serbian forces within 11 days, was signed. On the following day the UN Security Council adopted Resolution 1244 (with the People's Republic of China abstaining) approving the peace plan for Kosovo, and NATO announced the suspension of the air offensive, after it had been verified that the withdrawal of Serbian forces had commenced. NATO formally approved the establishment of the Kosovo Force (KFOR), and divided the province into five sectors (which were to be under the respective control of the United Kingdom, Germany, France, the USA and Italy). Shortly before NATO troops commenced deployment in Kosovo, however, about 200 Russian forces unexpectedly entered the province, and assumed control of the airport at Priština. Following discussions between the US Secretary of Defense, William Cohen, and his Russian counterpart, Igor Sergeyev, an agreement was reached whereby a Russian contingent, numbering about 3,600, would participate in KFOR (without controlling a separate sector as the Russian Government had previously demanded). Under the terms of the UN Resolution, the UN Interim Administration Mission in Kosovo (UNMIK, see p. 72) was established as the supreme legal and executive authority in Kosovo, with responsibility for civil administration, and for facilitating the reconstruction of the province as an autonomous region. A 3,100-member international police unit (which constituted part of UNMIK) was to supervise the creation of a new security force in Kosovo. The OSCE was allocated primary responsibility for installing democratic institutions, organizing elections in 2000 and monitoring human rights in the province. On 20 June 1999 NATO announced that the air campaign had officially ended, following the completion of the withdrawal of Serbian forces from Kosovo in accordance with the peace plan. The KLA subsequently signed an agreement with NATO, whereby the paramilitary organization was to disarm within a period of 90 days. On 24 June the Narodna skupština Republike Srbije formally ended the state of war in Serbia. Meanwhile, following the deployment of KFOR troops, nearly one-half of the ethnic Albanian refugees in neighbouring countries had returned to Kosovo by the end of the month, while an estimated 70,000 Serbian civilians had fled from the province, following reprisal attacks from KLA forces and members of the returning Albanian community. Investigators from the ICTY discovered increasing forensic evidence of large-scale massacres perpetrated by the Serbian forces against ethnic Albanian civilians during the conflict.

In early July 1999 the UN Secretary-General appointed Bernard Kouchner, the French Secretary of State for Health, as his permanent Special Representative to head UNMIK. Later that month the Kosovo Transitional Council (KTC), comprising representatives of the principal political parties and ethnic groups in Kosovo, was created as a consultative body to UNMIK. In August Rugova, who had initially boycotted the KTC, owing to the exclusion of other parties formerly represented in the DAK 'government' of Kosovo, agreed to join the Council (which also included four members of the KLA). Meanwhile, despite the efforts of the KFOR troops to enforce order in Kosovo, the increasing incidence of bomb attacks and killings of Serbian civilians, particularly in Priština, prompted most of the remaining Serbian residents to flee from the city. In September attempts to resettle ethnic Albanian refugees in the province were impeded by increased violence, with armed clashes between Serbs and Albanians, in which KFOR troops also became involved. Later that month, following protracted negotiations prior to the expiry of the stipulated date for the disarmament of the KLA, NATO acceded to demands that the paramilitary organization be reconstituted as a 5,000-member civil emergency security force, the Kosovo Protection Corps. The Serbian representatives in the KTC subsequently withdrew from the Council in protest at the agreement.

In October 1999 KFOR troops intervened to suppress violent rioting by ethnic Albanians in the northern town of Kosovska Mitrovica (Mitrovice), which, following the conflict, had become divided into separate ethnic Albanian and Serb regions. In the same month a UN official was killed in Priština by ethnic Albanians, who reportedly believed him to be a local Serb. Later that month the UN Secretary-General recommended that the Security Council increase the strength of the UNMIK police force to 4,718, in response to a request from Kouchner. However, KFOR and UNMIK forces attracted increasing criticism for failing to protect the Serbian minority in Kosovo. In February 2000 five ethnic Albanians were killed in clashes with KFOR troops in Kosovska Mitrovica. Additional peace-keeping forces were dispatched to the town, and later that month NATO approved a reinforcement of KFOR (which at that time numbered 30,000). In the same month the 'Republic of Kosovo' was dissolved, and Rugova established the Democratic League of Kosovo (DLK) as a successor organization to the DAK. In April Serbian representatives announced that they were to resume participation in the KTC and another multi-ethnic body established by UNMIK. (By the end of April some 200,000 Serbs were estimated to have fled Kosovo in response to attacks by KLA supporters, while about 822,000 of the estimated 900,000 ethnic Albanian refugees had returned to the province.)

Following the completion of a voter registration process, local government elections took place in Kosovo on 28 October 2000. Rugova's DLK secured 58% of the votes cast to 30 municipal councils, while the Democratic Party of Kosovo (DPK), led by a former KLA Commander, Hashim Thaçi, won 27% of the votes. In late November members of an ethnic Albanian separatist movement, the Army of Preševo, Medveđa and Bujanovac (believed to be related to the former KLA) launched an offensive in the Preševo region in southern Serbia, near the border with Kosovo. Serbian authorities threatened to dispatch troops to the region (which formed part of the demilitarized zone under the June 1999 agreement), if KFOR troops failed to suppress the rebel activity. In January 2001 the Danish Minister of Defence, Hans Hækkerup, was nominated by the UN to replace Kouchner as head of UNMIK. Violence continued in the province between the KFOR and ethnic Albanian separatists, who staged numerous attacks against Serb civilians. In early March the ethnic Albanian rebels signed a cease-fire agreement, after NATO agreed for the first time to allow Serbian forces to enter the demilitarized zone; the troops were to provide support to KFOR in suppressing separatist activity in the province and to deter infiltration into Macedonia by ethnic Albanian militants (see the chapter on the FYRM). In September the UN Security Council finally ended the embargo on armaments that had been imposed against the FRY in March 1998.

In May 2001 UNMIK presented a plan granting provisional self-government for Kosovo, and announced that elections to a legislative assembly would take place in the province on 17 November. (However, the head of UNMIK was to retain ultimate executive authority, and control over the province's finances and judiciary.) Elections to 100 seats of the 120-member Kosovo Assembly were conducted peacefully, as scheduled. (The remaining 20 seats were allocated proportionally to Serbs and other ethnic groups.) Rugova's DLK secured 47 seats, while the DPK won 26 seats and an alliance of Serb parties, known as the Return Coalition (Koalicija Povratak), 22 seats. A seven-member presidency for the legislature was established in December. However, repeated attempts to elect Rugova as President of Kosovo proved unsuccessful, owing to a boycott of the vote by the other parties represented in the legislature. In January 2002 the Narodna skupština Republike Srbije voted in favour of restoring the autonomy of Vojvodina. In the same month a German diplomat, Michael Steiner, replaced Hækkerup as head of UNMIK. On 4 March, following protracted inter-party discussions, Rugova was finally elected President of Kosovo, after it was agreed that a member of the DPK, Bajram Rexhepi, would become Prime Minister. A 10-member Cabinet (in which the LDK held four and the DPK two portfolios) was subsequently established. In April the Return Coalition finally agreed to join the Government. On 28 July, under an agreement reached by the Serbian authorities and ethnic Albanian separatists, elections to new multi-ethnic local governments in the municipalities of Preševo, Medveđa and Bujanovac were conducted peacefully. In August KFOR troops arrested a former KLA commander, Rustem Mustafa; he and a further three KLA members were subsequently charged with war crimes perpetrated against ethnic Albanians who had been perceived as co-operating with the Serbian authorities. The LDK won control of most municipalities at local government elections in Kosovo, which were conducted on 26 October.

In February 2003 KFOR arrested three prominent members of the KLA, who were subsequently extradited to the ICTY and pleaded not guilty to crimes committed at a detention camp during the Kosovo conflict. A fourth suspect evaded arrest in Kosovo, but was detained in Slovenia and transferred to the Tribunal later in February. The inclusion of Kosovo in the new State Union of Serbia and Montenegro prompted protests among the ethnic Albanian population in Kosovo, who continued to demand independence for the province. Steiner, however, declared that the issue of Kosovo's future status could not be resolved at that time. (Only about 7,000 refugees had returned to the province since 2000.) In July a Kosovo court established by UNMIK (in the first war crimes trial in the province) convicted and imposed custodial terms on four former KLA members, including Rustem Mustafa, who received a sentence of 17 years. The final contingent of Russian forces withdrew from Kosovo later that month, as part of a progressive reduction in the size of KFOR. On 25 July the UN Secretary-General appointed a former Finnish Prime Minister, Harri Holkeri, to replace Steiner as head of UNMIK. In early August, following an increase in anti-UN sentiment in Kosovo, in response to the conviction of the former KLA members, an UNMIK police officer was killed in an attack near Kosovska Mitrovica (the first fatality suffered by the UN Mission since 1999). Later that month Serbs staged protests throughout the province, after two Serb civilians were killed in an attack. In October Serbian and Kosovan leaders met for the first time since 1999, under the aegis of the UN, in Vienna, Austria. The conference failed to result in direct dialogue on the future status of Kosovo, but the two leaderships agreed to establish joint commissions to discuss issues such as energy and transport links, the return of some 230,000 Kosovan refugees from elsewhere in Serbia and Montenegro and missing civilians. In March 2004 a former member of a Serb paramilitary unit was sentenced to 20 years' imprisonment for participating in the killing of 14 Kosovan Albanians in March 1999 (the first major trial for war crimes committed against Kosovans).

In March 2004 the deaths of three ethnic Albanian boys, who had allegedly been pursued by a group of Serbs into the Ibar River, precipitated rioting in Kosovska Mitrovica, which escalated into several days of clashes between the Serbian and Albanian communities throughout the province. NATO deployed some 2,000 KFOR reinforcements in the province to quell the violence (increasing the size of the contingent to some 21,000). At the end of the month it was reported that 19 civilians had been killed (11 ethnic Albanians and eight Serbs), while some 4,000 Serbs and Roma had been forced to flee from their residences, after being attacked by ethnic Albanian rioters. The Kosovo authorities had detained some 180 in connection with the violence. Also in late March two members of UNMIK were killed in an attack by unidentified militia near Priština. At the beginning of April the UN announced a plan (drafted jointly by UNMIK and the Kosovo Government) to restore stability to the province, prior to a review of its status in 2005. The programme was designed to guarantee minority rights and establish conditions to allow the return of Serbian refugees through a measure of decentralization and the redelineation of municipal boundaries in Kosovska Mitrovica; the continuation of dialogue between Serbian and Kosovan leaders was envisaged.

In June 2004 Søren Jessen-Petersen was appointed new head of UNMIK, following the resignation of Holkeri, officially on grounds of ill health, in May. In June the shooting of a Serb youth near Priština increased concerns of further ethnic violence in the province. Elections to the Kosovo Assembly were conducted on 23 October. Rugova's DLK retained a majority of 47 seats in the 120-member legislature, while the DPK increased its representation to 30 seats. Despite a widely observed Serb boycott of the elections (with only an estimated 0.3% of the community voting), Serbs retained an allocation of 10 seats in the Assembly. In mid-November the trial of three former members of the KLA, who had been extradited in February 2003 on charges relating to crimes committed during the conflict in Kosovo, commenced at the ICTY. Following protracted discussions between the parties represented in the Assembly, a coalition agreement was reached between the DLK and the Alliance for the Future of Kosovo (AFK), which had secured nine seats, whereby the leader of the AFK, Ramush Haradinaj, was elected Prime Minister on 3 December 2004. Serb parties strongly opposed the appointment of Haradinaj, who was under investigation by the ICTY for alleged war crimes perpetrated while serving as a senior KLA member in 1997–99. The Serbian Government announced the suspension of the informal UN-mediated discussions with Kosovan officials, which had commenced in October 2003 in the Austrian capital, Vienna.

On 8 March 2005 Haradinaj submitted his resignation from the post of Prime Minister, after the ICTY issued an indictment against him for alleged war crimes perpetrated while serving as a senior KLA member in 1997–99; he surrendered to the Tribunal on the following day, causing widespread protests in the province (prompting the dispatch of some 500 British military reinforcements). On 23 March 2005 a new Kosovo Government, led by Bajram Kosumi, also of the AFK, was formed.

After the European Commission released a favourable report on Serbia and Montenegro in early April 2005, the resolution of Kosovo's future status became an increasingly pressing issue. The European Commission pledged to continue support for the eventual integration of Kosovo into European institutions, provided that the Kosovo Government demonstrated progress in meeting UN-endorsed standards of reform and democratic principles in eight areas. The process towards an agreement on a future status for Kosovo was expected to be problematic, since the Serbia and Montenegro authorities strongly favoured conditions of increased autonomy, but less than total independence, while the Kosovan Albanian population insisted on unconditional independence; any final settlement was also to exclude any partition or border changes. In early June UN Secretary-General Kofi Annan appointed the Norwegian ambassador to NATO, Kai Eide, as the special envoy responsible for assessing standards in Kosovo, who was to undertake a comprehensive review of the Government's commitment to democracy, good governance and human rights. A positive review would allow negotiations on the final status of the province to proceed; following their conclusion, a draft settlement (the 'Kosovo Accord'), would, together with a draft constitution prepared by the Kosovo Assembly, be submitted for endorsement by a UN-sponsored international conference. In early July three bombs exploded in the province, near UN offices, the OSCE headquarters and the Kosovo Assembly building, causing minor damage; Rugova condemned the attacks as an attempt to undermine negotiations on the future status of Kosovo with Serbian officials. Later that month Eide conducted further discussions with leading members of the Serbian Government, including Tadić, to urge Serb participation in Kosovo's provisional institutions of government. In August two Serbs were killed and a third injured in a shooting near a predominantly Serbian part of the province.

In September 2005 delegations from the Governments of Serbia and Kosovo met in Vienna for preliminary discussions on decentralization and other technical issues. On 4 October Eide officially submitted the review on Kosovo to Annan; the report stated that the Government had made significant progress in establishing executive, legislative and judicial institutions, although efforts to maintain the rule of law and reduce the incidence of multi-ethnic attacks, violence and organized crime remained limited. On 24 October the UN Security Council endorsed the initiation of final status negotiations on Kosovo. In November the Serbian Government adopted a unanimous resolution rejecting independence in Kosovo, while the Kosovo Assembly approved a motion stating that it would only accept independence as final status. Later that month a former Finnish President, Martti Ahtisaari, who had been appointed by Annan as the special envoy for the negotiations on Kosovo's future status, commenced separate discussions with Serbian and Kosovan leaders.

At the end of November 2005 the ICTY imposed a sentence (the first relating to crimes committed in Kosovo) of 13 years' imprisonment on a former KLA Commander who had been convicted of human rights abuses; a further two defendants were acquitted. In December UNMIK established Ministries of the Interior and Justice (increasing the total number of ministries to 14), to which powers formerly under UN control were to be transferred.

On 21 January 2006 Rugova died after an illness, prompting concerns of renewed ethnic unrest in the province. Final status negotiations, scheduled to commence in Vienna on 25 January, under the auspices of Ahtisaari, were rescheduled for February. Later in January the DLK nominated Fatmir Sejdiu as the new party candidate to succeed Rugova. Sejdiu was elected unopposed as the new President by the Kosovo Assembly on 10 February. The first round of final status negotiations on Kosovo was subsequently conducted in Vienna on 20–21 February, and was followed by a second on 17 March. Discussions focused on issues related to decentralization, particularly the financing of Serb municipalities, which the Serbian delegation insisted be from the Serbian state budget, while the Kosovan Albanians maintained that they be funded from the Kosovo budget. Serbia submitted a formal objection to the participation in the negotiations of the former KLA leader, Hashim Thaçi, accusing him of having committed crimes during the conflict in Kosovo. A third round of negotiations between the Kosovan Albanian and Serbian delegations again ended without agreement on 3 April; it was reported that the Kosovan Albanian officials continued to oppose Serbian insistence on autonomous funding as an attempt to create a Serb entity in the province. A further round of discussions on 28 April also resulted in little progress.

Government

On 4 February 2003 the legislature of the Federal Republic of Yugoslavia (FRY—comprising the two republics of Serbia and Montenegro) approved a Constitutional Charter, thereby officially reconstituting the FRY as the State Union of Serbia and Montenegro. On 25 February, in accordance with the Constitutional Charter, the existing federal and republican legislatures elected a 126-member Skupština Srbije i Crne Gore (Assembly of Serbia and Montenegro), comprising 91 deputies from Serbia, and 35 from Montenegro, for a four-year term. On 7 March the Skupština elected a joint President of Serbia and Montenegro, who was also to chair the Council of Ministers of the Union, for a four-year term. A five-member joint Council of Ministers was approved by the Skupština on 18 March. At republican level legislative power continued to be vested, respectively, in the 250-member Narodna skupština Republike Srbije (National Assembly of the Republic of Serbia) and the 75-member Skupština Republike Crne Gore (Assembly of the Republic of Montenegro), both of which were directly elected. Each member state had its own elected President and Government. Under the Constitutional Charter, the armed forces of Serbia and Montenegro were under the command of the Supreme Defence Council, which comprised the Presidents of the two republics, and the President of the State Union. The Constitutional Charter was to be amended to allow the extension of the mandate of parliamentary deputies, who were to be elected concurrently with the separate elections to the state legislatures.

In June 1999 the UN Interim Administration Mission in Kosovo (UNMIK, see p. 72) was established as the supreme executive and legal authority in the province of Kosovo and Metohija (see Recent History). (Kosovo remained part of Serbia under the Constitutional Charter of February 2003.) Elections to 100 seats of a 120-member Kosovo Assembly were conducted on 17 November 2001. (The remaining 20 seats were allocated proportionally to Serbs and other ethnic groups.) A seven-member presidency for the legislature was subsequently established. In March 2002 the Assembly elected a President, and a Government, headed by a Prime Minister, for the province.

For administrative purposes, Montenegro is divided into 21 municipalities. Serbia comprises 29 administrative regions, including the territories of Kosovo and the formerly autonomous province of Vojvodina (which have five and seven districts respectively).

Defence

Military service is compulsory for men, and lasts for six months. Voluntary military service for women was introduced in 1983. In

August 2005 the estimated total strength of the armed forces was 65,300, including an army of 55,000 (including 25,000 conscripts), a navy of 3,800 and an air force of 6,500. Projected budgetary expenditure on defence by the Government in 2005 was an estimated 45,700m. dinars.

Under an agreement between the North Atlantic Treaty Organization (NATO, see p. 314) and the Federal Government, reached in June 1999 (see Recent History), and a subsequent UN resolution, the Kosovo Force (KFOR), led by NATO, was deployed in the province of Kosovo and Metohija. The UN Security Council established the UN Interim Administration Mission in Kosovo (UNMIK, see p. 72) as the supreme legal and executive authority in the province. In September, following the disarmament of the insurgent paramilitary organization, the Kosovo Liberation Army, the movement became reconstituted as a 5,000-member civil emergency security force, known as the Kosovo Protection Corps. At the end of February 2006 UNMIK comprised 2,221 police, 38 military personnel, and an additional 797 international civilian personnel and 2,277 local civilian personnel. KFOR (which had originally reached its maximum authorized strength of 50,000 personnel) had been gradually reduced in size, and in early 2006 about 17,000 troops were deployed in Kosovo, although the contingent was frequently reinforced on a temporary basis, when necessitated by renewed violence in the province.

Economic Affairs

In 2004, according to estimates by the World Bank, the gross national income (GNI) of the State Union of Serbia and Montenegro (as the Federal Republic of Yugoslavia had been reconstituted in February of that year), measured at 2002–04 prices, was US $21,715m., equivalent to $2,620 per head. During 1995–2004, it was estimated, the population declined by an annual average of 2.8%, while gross domestic product (GDP) per head increased, in real terms, by 5.1%. Overall GDP increased, in real terms, at an average annual rate of 2.1% in 1995–2004; growth was 2.7% in 2003 and 7.2% in 2004.

Agriculture (including hunting, forestry and fishing) contributed an estimated 16.3% of GDP in 2002. In 2004 3.3% of the total employed labour force were engaged in the sector. Serbia and Montenegro's principal crops are maize, wheat, sugar beet and potatoes. The cultivation of fruit and vegetables is also important. Agricultural production in Serbia and Montenegro declined by 13.0% in 2000, increased by 17.2% in 2001, decreased by 2.1% in 2002 and by 6.9% in 2003, but rose by an estimated 18.2% in 2004.

Industry (including mining, manufacturing, construction and power) contributed an estimated 31.8% of GDP in 2002, and engaged 31.6% of the employed labour force in 2004. Industrial production increased by an estimated 18.9% in 1996–2000. According to the IMF, industrial output increased by 11.1% in 2000, remained constant in 2001 and rose by an estimated 1.7% in 2002, declining by 2.7% in 2003 but increasing by an estimated 7.5% in 2004.

The mining and quarrying sector contributed an estimated 4.3% of GDP in 2002, and engaged 1.7% of the employed labour force in 2004. The principal minerals extracted are coal (mainly brown coal), copper ore and bauxite. Iron ore, crude petroleum, lead and zinc ore and natural gas are also produced. Mining has been less severely affected in recent years than other sectors. Production in the mining and quarrying sector increased by 6.0% in 2000, declined by 12.7% in 2001, rose by 2.2% in 2002 and by 0.8% in 2003, but decreased by 1.1% in 2004.

The manufacturing sector contributed an estimated 19.5% of GDP in 2002, and engaged 23.2% of the employed labour force in 2004. In 2003 the principal branches of manufacturing were building materials, metalworking and electrical equipment, chemicals and paper, textiles, leather and rubber, woodworking, and food products and tobacco. Manufacturing production increased by 14.0% in 2000, by 0.8% in 2001, by 2.7% in 2002, declining by 4.4% in 2003, but rising by 9.8% in 2004.

Energy in Serbia and Montenegro is derived principally from coal (which provided about 66.1% of total electricity generated in 2002) and hydroelectric power (31.5%). Imports of mineral fuels accounted for 15.2% of the value of total imports in 2003.

Services contributed an estimated 51.8% of GDP in 2002. Some 65.0% of the employed labour force were employed in the sector in 2004. Total foreign tourist arrivals increased from 151,650 in 1999 to 481,070 in 2003.

In 2004 Serbia and Montenegro recorded a trade deficit of US $7,344m., and there was a deficit of $3,597m. on the current account of the balance of payments. In 2003 the principal source of imports was Germany (13.6%); other major sources were Russia and Italy. The principal market for exports in that year was Bosnia and Herzegovina (15.0%); other important purchasers were Italy, Germany, the former Yugoslav republic of Macedonia and Switzerland. (These figures excluded trade to or from Kosovo and Metohija.) The main exports in 2003 were basic manufactures, food and live animals, miscellaneous manufactured articles, machinery and transport equipment, chemicals and crude materials. The principal imports in that year were machinery and transport equipment, basic manufactures, mineral fuels and lubricants, chemicals, miscellaneous manufactured articles, and food and live animals.

In 2004, according to preliminary figures, the overall budgetary deficit was 108,300m. dinars (equivalent to some 0.3% of GDP). At the end of 2003 the country's total external debt was $14,885m., of which $9,679m. was long-term public debt. In that year the cost of debt-servicing was equivalent to 13.6% of the value of exports of goods and services. In 1995–2004 the rate of inflation increased by an annual average of 40.8%. Consumer prices increased by 9.4% in 2003 and by an estimated 9.5% in 2004. The rate of unemployment was estimated at 18.5% in 2004.

Owing to armed conflict in parts of the former SFRY and the imposition by the UN of sanctions on the FRY in May 1992, the country's membership of numerous international organizations was suspended. Following the political changes in the FRY in September 2000, the country was readmitted to the UN on 1 November. It was readmitted to the Organization for Security and Co-operation in Europe (OSCE, see p. 327) later in November, to the IMF in December and to the World Bank in May 2001. Serbia and Montenegro officially became a member of the Council of Europe (see p. 211) in April 2003.

Following the election of a new Federal Government in September 2000, the FRY's integration into international institutions progressed rapidly. In October the European Union (EU, see p. 228) ended all sanctions against the FRY, and it was agreed that the country would receive aid under the EU's programme for Balkan reconstruction, development and stabilization. In December the FRY was readmitted to the IMF, and was granted emergency post-conflict assistance. The US Government officially ended economic sanctions against the FRY in January 2001; however, subsequent financial support from the USA was made conditional on the Yugoslav authorities' co-operation with the International Criminal Tribunal for the former Yugoslavia (ICTY, see p. 17). Economic activity continued to increase from very low levels, but real GDP remained at less than one-half of its 1989 level. In May 2002 the IMF approved a credit arrangement to support the Government's economic programme for 2002–05. It was hoped that the establishment of the State Union of Serbia and Montenegro in February 2003 would further the normalization of economic relations between the two republics, with the harmonization of trade, customs and tax systems in accordance with EU standards. Economic growth and the level of international reserves remained strong (with particularly high GDP growth recorded in Serbia), but inflation and the already high current-account deficit continued to increase, as a result of a sharp rise in domestic demand. In January 2005, however, the USA expressed dissatisfaction with Serbia and Montenegro's failure to co-operate with the ICTY, and announced punitive measures, including a reduction in financial aid. However, following the extradition of a number of Serb war crimes suspects to the Tribunal, the European Commission indicated, in April, that sufficient progress had been made for Serbia and Montenegro to commence negotiations on a Stabilization and Association Agreement later in the year, subject to continued reforms and ongoing co-operation with the ICTY. Further IMF reviews on economic development were conducted in July and October. Negotiations between the Government of Serbia and Montenegro and the EU on a Stabilization and Association Agreement officially commenced in October. Meanwhile, in February 2006 the IMF approved the completion of its extended three-year stand-by credit arrangement with Serbia and Montenegro, allowing the country to secure a final cancellation of outstanding debt, under the terms of an agreement made in 2001 with the 'Paris Club' of international creditors. The IMF's decision followed a December 2005 agreement with Serbia, which approved the Government's policies for 2006, including measures to reduce the rate of inflation (which had far exceeded 2005 targets) and restrict salary increases in state enterprises. In early 2006, however, the EU made the continuation of negotiations on the Stabilization and Association Agreement increasingly conditional on the extradition of the Bosnian Serb war crimes suspect,

SERBIA AND MONTENEGRO

Ratko Mladić, to the ICTY (see Recent History). At the end of April discussions were suspended, after the Serbian Government failed to meet a deadline to comply with this demand.

Education

The educational system of Serbia and Montenegro is organized at republican level. Elementary education is free and compulsory for all children between the ages of seven and 15, when children attend the 'eight-year school'. Various types of secondary education are available to all who qualify, but the vocational and technical schools are the most popular. Alternatively, children may attend a general secondary school (gymnasium) where they follow a four-year course, prior to university entrance. At the secondary level there are also a number of art schools, apprentice schools and teacher-training schools. In 2000/01 some 96% of children in the appropriate age-group (males 96%; females 96%) were enrolled in primary schools, while secondary education was equivalent to 89% (males 88%; females 89%) in the relevant age-group. In 2002/03 207,082 students were enrolled in 150 institutes of higher education (including six universities).

Public Holidays

2006: 1–2 January (New Year), 7–8 January (Christmas), 15 February (National Day, Serbia only), 21–24 April (Orthodox Easter), 27 April (Statehood Day), 1–2 May (Labour Days), 9 May (Victory Day), 13 July (National Day, Montenegro only), 29–30 November (Republic Days).

2007: 1–2 January (New Year), 7–8 January (Christmas), 15 February (National Day, Serbia only), 6–9 April (Orthodox Easter), 27 April (Statehood Day), 1–2 May (Labour Days), 9 May (Victory Day), 13 July (National Day, Montenegro only), 29–30 November (Republic Days).

Weights and Measures

The metric system is in force.

Statistical Survey

Sources: Savezni zavod za statistiku (Federal Statistical Office), 11000 Belgrade, Kneza Miloša 20; tel. (11) 681999; fax (11) 642368; internet www.szs.sv.gov.yu; Jugoslovenski Pregled (Yugoslav Survey), Dečanska 8, POB 677, Belgrade; tel. (11) 3233610; internet www.yusurvey.co.yu.

Note: Unless otherwise indicated, figures in this Survey refer to the territory of the State Union of Serbia and Montenegro, formerly the Federal Republic of Yugoslavia (FRY).

Area and Population

AREA, POPULATION AND DENSITY

Area (sq km)	102,173*
Population (census results)	
31 March 1991	10,120,209
31 March 2002†	
Males	3,960,684
Females	4,173,933
Total	8,134,617
Population (official estimates at mid-year)‡	
2002	8,113,900
2003	8,152,700
2004§	8,146,800
Density (per sq km) at mid-2004‡	89.2

* 39,449 sq miles.
† Comprising the results of a population census held in Serbia (excluding Kosovo) in 2002 and estimates for Montenegro in that year—7,498,001 and 636,616, respectively).
‡ Excluding Kosovo.
§ Provisional.

REPUBLICS
(census of 31 March 1991; revised figures)

Republic	Area (sq km)	Population	Density (per sq km)	Capital (with population)
Serbia	88,361	9,505,174	108	Belgrade (1,130,241)
Vojvodina*	21,506	1,966,367	91	Novi Sad (177,005)
Kosovo*†	10,887	1,956,196	180	Priština (155,499)
Montenegro†	13,812	615,035	45	Podgorica‡ (117,875)
Total	102,173	10,120,209	99	—

* Provinces within Serbia.
† Data not revised.
‡ Formerly Titograd.

PRINCIPAL TOWNS
(population at 1991 census, revised figures)

Beograd (Belgrade, the capital)	1,130,241	Podgorica*†	117,875
Novi Sad	177,005	Subotica	98,873
Niš	173,250	Zrenjanin	80,174
Kragujevac	144,606	Pančevo	71,668
Priština†	155,409	Čačak	69,625

* Formerly Titograd.
† Data not revised.

2002 (census of Serbia—excluding Kosovo, 1 March, preliminary figures): Belgrade 1,119,020; Novi Sad 190,602; Niš 173,390; Kragujevac 145,890; Subotica 99,471; Zrenjanin 79,545; Pančevo 71,668; Čačak 73,152.

POPULATION BY ETHNIC GROUP
(1991 census, unrevised data)

Ethnic group	Population ('000)	%
Serbs	6,504	62.6
Albanians	1,715	16.5
Montenegrins	520	5.0
Yugoslavs	350	3.4
Hungarians	344	3.3
Muslims	336	3.2
Total (incl. others)	10,394	100.0

SERBIA AND MONTENEGRO

BIRTHS, MARRIAGES AND DEATHS

	Registered live births Number	Rate (per 1,000)	Registered marriages Number	Rate (per 1,000)	Registered deaths Number	Rate (per 1,000)
1995	140,504	13.3	60,325	5.7	107,535	10.2
1996	137,312	13.0	56,719	5.4	111,146	10.5
1997*	131,400	12.4	56,200	5.3	111,800	10.5
1998*	128,500	12.1	54,800	5.3	113,300	10.5
1999*	124,000	11.7	53,000	5.0	115,500	10.9
2000*	125,900	11.8	58,300	5.5	118,100	11.1
2001*	130,200	12.2	57,200	5.4	113,100	10.6
2002*	132,200	12.4	57,800	5.4	119,100	11.2

* Rounded figures. Data for Kosovo are estimates (Source: Federal Statistical Office, Belgrade).

Source: UN, *Demographic Yearbook*.

Expectation of life (WHO estimates, years at birth): 73 (males 70; females 75) in 2003 (Source: WHO, *World Health Report*).

ECONOMICALLY ACTIVE POPULATION
('000 employees, annual averages)*

	2002	2003	2004
Agriculture, forestry, fishing and water works	84	78	73
Mining and quarrying	38	37	37
Manufacturing	594	552	510
Public utilities	53	53	52
Construction	97	95	95
Wholesale and retail trade	222	220	232
Hotels and restaurants	43	37	37
Transport, storage and communications	136	131	133
Financial intermediation	35	32	33
Real estate and property	58	58	64
Public administration and social security	74	77	80
Education	141	141	144
Health and social care	174	173	176
Other community, social and personal services	55	55	57
Private shop workers and owners	401	440	471†
Total employed	2,207	2,179	2,194
Unemployed	923	1,019	n.a.
Total labour force	3,130	3,198	n.a.

* Excluding Kosovo.
† Excluding 7,000 entrepreneurial staff from Montenegro, distributed according to activities.

Health and Welfare

KEY INDICATORS

Total fertility rate (children per woman, 2002)	1.6
Under-5 mortality rate (per 1,000 live births, 2004)	15
HIV/AIDS (% of persons aged 15–49, 2003)	0.2
Physicians (per 1,000 head, 1999)	2.13
Hospital beds (per 1,000 head, 1995)	5.31
Health expenditure (2001): US $ per head (PPP)	305
Health expenditure (2001): % of GDP	8.1
Health expenditure (2001): public (% of total)	62.8
Access to water (% of persons, 2002)	93
Access to sanitation (% of persons, 2002)	87

For sources and definitions, see explanatory note on p. vi.

Agriculture

PRINCIPAL CROPS
('000 metric tons)

	2002	2003	2004
Wheat	2,245.0	1,369.2	2,746.0
Barley	354.5	196.6	410.0
Maize	5,597.2	3,825.5	6,575.0*
Oats	109.7	135.0	119.4
Potatoes	1,030.0	803.0	1,098.0
Sugar beet	2,098.1	1,738.0	2,643.0
Dry beans	58.5	47.2	61.0*
Soybeans (Soya beans)	244.3	226.0	317.8
Sunflower seed	279.8	353.8	437.6
Cabbages	354.7	278.6	380.0*
Tomatoes	223.6	186.4	205.0*
Chillies and green peppers	161.5	158.4	160.0*
Dry onions	132.6	97.7	145.9*
Carrots	60.8	44.4	52.0†
Watermelons and melons	342.6	320.0	305.0*
Apples	101.6	251.1	188.0
Pears	35.9	70.8	60.0*
Sour cherries	49.8	86.9	112.3
Peaches and nectarines	45.6	59.2	62.0*
Plums	205.4	577.4	567.0
Raspberries	94.4	79.5	91.7
Grapes	429.8	485.3	497.0
Tobacco (leaves)	18.4	11.9	13.0

* Unofficial figure.
† FAO estimate.

Source: FAO.

LIVESTOCK
('000 head, year ending 30 September)

	2002	2003	2004
Horses	39	34	35
Cattle	1,306	1,294	1,276
Pigs	3,608	3,656	3,463
Sheep	1,691	1,756	1,838
Goats	226	245	195
Chickens*	17,452	16,344	15,000

* Unofficial figures.

Source: FAO.

LIVESTOCK PRODUCTS
('000 metric tons)

	2002	2003	2004
Beef and veal*	166.0	164.0	161.0
Mutton and lamb	19.4	21.3	20.0
Pig meat*	616.7	573.9	538.5
Poultry meat	88.9	81.0	85.6
Cows' milk	1,821.6	1,822.8	1,807.0*
Sheep's milk	27.6	24.3	25.0
Cheese	14.2	15.4	15.2
Butter	2.4	2.5†	2.5†
Hen eggs	69.9	76.5	76.0
Honey	2.9	3.6	4.0
Wool: greasy	2.5	2.6	2.5
Wool: scoured	1.5	1.6	1.5
Cattle hides†	19.0	17.7	16.5
Sheep skins†	3.9	4.0	4.2

* Unofficial figure(s).
† FAO estimate(s).

Source: FAO.

Forestry

ROUNDWOOD REMOVALS
('000 cubic metres, excl. bark)

	2002	2003	2004
Sawlogs, veneer logs and logs for sleepers	1,040	1,082	1,138
Pulpwood	164	106	196
Other industrial roundwood	82	66	89
Fuel wood	1,650	1,901	2,097
Total	2,936	3,155	3,520

Source: FAO.

SAWNWOOD PRODUCTION
('000 cubic metres, incl. railway sleepers)

	2002	2003	2004
Coniferous (softwood)	122	158	207
Non-coniferous (hardwood)	310	356	368
Total	432	514	575

Source: FAO.

Fishing

('000 metric tons, live weight)

	2001	2002	2003
Capture	1.0	1.4	1.1
Freshwater fishes	0.6	0.9	0.6
Aquaculture	2.7	2.4	2.6
Rainbow trout	2.7	2.4	2.6
Total catch	3.7	3.8	3.7

Source: FAO.

Mining

('000 metric tons, unless otherwise indicated)

	2000	2001	2002
Coal	32,275	33,382	33,488
Crude petroleum	805	746	682
Lead and zinc ore*	1,302	926	577
Lead content of ore†	26	19	12
Zinc content of ore†	29	20	9
Bauxite	630	610	612
Natural gas (million cubic metres)	160	111	107

* Figures refer to gross weight of ores extracted.
† Estimates.
Source: US Geological Survey.

Industry

SELECTED PRODUCTS
('000 metric tons, unless otherwise indicated; excluding Kosovo)

	2001	2002	2003
Edible oils	85.0	83.3	87.6
Wine ('000 hectolitres)	664	589	912
Beer ('000 hectolitres)	6,063	5,764	6,049
Cotton yarn	8.6	5.9	2.0
Wool yarn	6.2	6.0	5.0
Leather footwear ('000 pairs)	4,278	2,971	2,329
Cement	2,418	2,396	2,075
Sulphuric acid	68.5	73.9	24.8
Gas-diesel (distillate fuel) oil	559	728	884
Residual fuel oil	633	848	766

—continued	2001	2002	2003
Pig-iron	461	485	635
Crude steel	598	596	722
Aluminium—unwrought	100.2	111.7	116.7
Refined copper—unwrought	32.4	35.9	14.0
Zinc—unwrought	13.5	1.5	0.1
Stoves, furnaces and cookers ('000)	267.0	294.3	297.8
Electric light bulbs ('000)	16,868	9,890	5,489
Lorries (number)	590	595	487
Motor cars (number)	7,197	11,354	11,234
Bicycles (number)	20,201	24,708	n.a.
Household furniture ('000 pieces)	849	762	725
Complete furniture suites ('000 sets)	20.1	21.9	23.6
Electric energy (million kWh)	34,583	33,877	34,994

Finance

CURRENCY AND EXCHANGE RATES (Serbia)

Monetary Units
100 para = 1 Yugoslav dinar.

Sterling, Dollar and Euro Equivalents (30 November 2005)
£1 sterling = 123.19 dinars;
US $1 = 71.33 dinars;
€1 = 83.95 dinars;
1,000 Yugoslav dinars = £8.12 = $14.02 = €11.91.

Average Exchange Rate (new dinars per US $)
1989   2.876
1990   11.318
1991   19.638

Note: On 1 January 1990 the new dinar, equivalent to 10,000 old dinars, was introduced in the Socialist Federal Republic of Yugoslavia (SFRY). After the disintegration of the SFRY, the Federal Republic of Yugoslavia (FRY) continued to use the Yugoslav dinar as its currency. Meanwhile, the other republics of the former SFRY introduced their own currencies to replace (initially at par) the Yugoslav dinar. As a result of rapid inflation in the FRY, the value of the Yugoslav dinar depreciated sharply. By the end of May 1993 the exchange rate was about 89,000 dinars per US dollar. After further devaluations, the currency was redenominated from 1 October, with the introduction of another new dinar, worth 1,000,000 of the former units. However, the depreciation of the currency continued, and on 30 December the new dinar was replaced by a further dinar, worth 1,000 million of its predecessors. In January 1994 there was another currency reform, with the establishment of a dinar officially valued at 1 Deutsche Mark (DM, equivalent to 13 million former dinars). In November 1999 Montenegro, one of the two constituent republics of the FRY, announced the introduction of the DM as its official currency. In September of that year the UN had decided to adopt the DM as the currency for official transactions in the Serbian province of Kosovo. Euro notes and coins were introduced on 1 January 2002, replacing the DM, at an exchange rate of €1 = 1.95583 DM.

SERBIA AND MONTENEGRO

Statistical Survey

CURRENCY AND EXCHANGE RATES (Montenegro and Kosovo)

Monetary Units
100 cent = 1 euro (€).

Sterling, Dollar and Euro Equivalents (31 May 2005)
£1 sterling = 1.4744 euros;
US $1 = 0.8110 euros;
€100 = £67.82 = $123.31.

Average Exchange Rate (euros per US $)
2002 1.0626
2003 0.8860
2004 0.8054

CONSOLIDATED BUDGET*
('000 million dinars)

Revenue†	2003	2004‡	2005§
Current revenue	503.0	589.2	685.8
Tax revenue	461.0	534.3	624.6
Personal income tax	74.3	79.5	88.8
Social security contributions	126.1	147.3	176.2
Corporate income tax	6.8	8.7	8.8
Retail sales tax	135.3	153.6	194.3
Excises	62.1	81.3	88.8
Taxes on international trade and operations	31.4	36.4	43.0
Other current revenue	42.1	54.9	61.2
Capital revenue	4.9	0.8	0.6
Total	**507.9**	**590.0**	**686.4**

Expenditure‖	2003	2004‡	2005§
Current expenditure	508.8	570.7	654.8
Expenditure on goods and services	216.3	241.2	283.3
Wages and salaries	123.3	143.6	163.7
Interest payments	12.2	15.4	24.4
Subsidies and other current transfers	274.0	307.4	343.4
Transfers to households	232.1	258.8	299.3
Capital expenditure	29.3	39.8	37.3
General reserves	0.6	5.1	3.8
Total	**538.7**	**615.5**	**695.9**

* Comprising a consolidation of the Federal Budget, and the budgets of the Republic of Serbia and the Republic of Montenegro.
† Excluding grants received ('000 million dinars): 2.7 in 2003; 3.6 in 2004 (preliminary); 0.7 in 2005 (projected).
‡ Preliminary figures.
§ Projected figures.
‖ Excluding lending minus repayments ('000 million dinars): 8.7 in 2003; 6.0 in 2004 (preliminary); 3.1 in 2005 (projected).

Source: IMF, *Serbia and Montenegro: Fourth Review Under the Extended Arrangement, Financing Assurances Review, and Request for Waiver of Performance Criteria and Modification of End-December Performance Criterion—Staff Report; Staff Statement; Press Release on the Executive Board Discussion; and Statement by the Executive Director for Serbia and Montenegro* (January 2005).

INTERNATIONAL RESERVES
(former SFRY*, US $ million at 31 December)

	1989	1990	1991
Gold†	80	81	81
IMF special drawing rights	—	13	—
Foreign exchange	4,136	5,461	2,682
Total	**4,216**	**5,555**	**2,763**

* The Socialist Federal Republic of Yugoslavia (SFRY) comprised six republics.
† Valued at US $42.22 per troy ounce.

Source: IMF, *International Financial Statistics*.

Foreign exchange (FRY, US $ million at 31 December): 663.0 in 1999; 890.0 in 2000; 1,808.6 in 2001.

MONEY SUPPLY
(million dinars at 31 December)

	2003	2004*
Currency in circulation	42,979	44,913
Demand deposits	55,244	63,531
Total money	**98,223**	**108,444**

* Projected figures.

Source: IMF, *Serbia and Montenegro: Fourth Review Under the Extended Arrangement, Financing Assurances Review, and Request for Waiver of Performance Criteria and Modification of End-December Performance Criterion—Staff Report; Staff Statement; Press Release on the Executive Board Discussion; and Statement by the Executive Director for Serbia and Montenegro* (January 2005).

COST OF LIVING
(Consumer Price Index; base: previous year = 100)

	2001	2002	2003
Food	188.2	106.5	100.8
Clothing and footwear	184.0	116.7	108.5
Rent	226.8	145.6	135.7
Fuel and light	220.4	152.2	126.7
All items (incl. others)	**189.2**	**116.5**	**109.4**

NATIONAL ACCOUNTS

Gross Domestic Product by Economic Activity
(million dinars at current prices)*

	2001	2002
Agriculture, hunting, forestry and fishing	146,969	140,210
Mining and quarrying	28,225	36,773
Manufacturing	153,182	166,925
Electricity, gas and water	17,943	36,311
Construction	26,170	32,978
Wholesale and retail trade; and repairs	69,305	69,937
Restaurants and hotels	8,917	11,430
Transport, storage and communications	54,867	78,032
Financial intermediation	39,719	55,580
Real estate, renting and business activities	61,567	95,217
Public administration and defence; compulsory social security	27,662	38,931
Education	19,431	31,301
Health and social work	27,370	39,804
Other community, social and personal services	20,149	23,458
Private households with employed persons	926	1,081
Gross value added in basic prices †	**702,402**	**857,968**
Taxes, less subsidies, on products‡	80,032	140,238
GDP in market prices	**782,434**	**998,206**

* Excluding Kosovo.
† Deduction for financial intermediation services indirectly measured assumed to be distributed by sector.
‡ Figure obtained as a residual.

BALANCE OF PAYMENTS
(US $ million)

	2003	2004*
Exports of goods f.o.b.	3,054	4,044
Imports of goods c.i.f.	−7,941	−11,388
Trade balance	**−4,886**	**−7,344**
Exports of services	1,130	1,646
Imports of services	−795	−1,046
Balance on goods and services	**−4,552**	**−6,744**
Factor income received from abroad	70	81
Factor income paid abroad	−291	−352
Balance on goods, services and income	**−4,773**	**−7,015**
Private remittances and other transfers received from abroad	2,661	4,035
Private remittances and other transfers paid abroad	−422	−598
Adjustment	—	−19

SERBIA AND MONTENEGRO

—continued	2003	2004*
Current balance (excl. grants)	−2,543	−3,597
Official grants	538	562
Foreign direct investment (net)	1,405	1,031
Medium- and short-term loans: disbursements	974	2,119
Medium- and long-term loans: amortization	−218	−513
Short-term loans and deposits (net)	66	393
Other capital inflows	281	58
Commercial banks (net)	31	88
Net errors and omissions	409	505
Overall balance	943	646

* Estimates.

Source: IMF, *Serbia and Montenegro: Sixth Review Under the Extended Arrangement, Financing Assurances Review, Request for Waivers of Non-observance of Performance Criteria, and Proposed Post-Program Monitoring—Staff Report; Press Release on the Executive Board Discussion; and Statement by the Executive Director for Serbia and Montenegro* (February 2006).

External Trade

PRINCIPAL COMMODITY GROUPS
(distribution by SITC, US $ million)*

Imports c.i.f.	2001	2002	2003
Food and live animals	441	527	568
Crude materials (inedible) except fuels	188	208	227
Mineral fuels, lubricants, etc.	1,001	1,070	1,210
Chemicals and related products	698	856	1,066
Basic manufactures	948	1,270	1,598
Machinery and transport equipment	1,029	1,629	2,270
Miscellaneous manufactured articles	356	553	766
Total (incl. others)	4,837	6,320	7,952

Exports f.o.b.	2001	2002	2003
Food and live animals	275	482	498
Crude materials (inedible) except fuels	101	118	141
Mineral fuels, lubricants, etc.	50	78	59
Chemicals and related products	132	169	246
Basic manufactures	653	713	839
Machinery and transport equipment	243	254	310
Miscellaneous manufactured articles	363	369	457
Total (incl. others)	1,903	2,275	2,650

* Excluding figures for Kosovo.

PRINCIPAL TRADING PARTNERS
(US $ million)*

Imports c.i.f.	2001	2002	2003
Austria	147	194	256
Bosnia and Herzegovina	135	231	224
Bulgaria	153	111	134
China, People's Republic	134	193	324
France	129	182	289
Germany	589	829	1,081
Greece	218	169	217
Hungary	194	276	277
Italy	500	653	806
Romania	175	150	144
Russia	685	787	1,033
Slovenia	145	n.a.	253
Total (incl. others)	4,837	6,320	7,952

Exports f.o.b.	2001	2002	2003
Bosnia and Herzegovina	249	331	397
France	43	62	115
Germany	231	243	288
Greece	63	83	61
Hungary	65	79	76
Italy	312	330	358
Macedonia, former Yugoslav republic	176	207	220
Russia	80	91	127
Slovenia	41	82	93
Switzerland	160	170	162
Total (incl. others)	1,903	2,275	2,650

* Excluding figures for Kosovo.

Transport

RAILWAYS
(traffic)

	2000	2001	2002
Passengers carried ('000)	12,221	10,985	10,060
Passenger-kilometres (million)	1,436	1,263	1,146
Freight carried ('000 metric tons)	9,278	9,376	10,334
Freight ton-kilometres (million)	1,970	2,042	3,728

ROAD TRAFFIC
(motor vehicles in use at 30 June)

	1999	2000	2001
Passenger cars	1,712,128	1,406,949	1,498,802
Buses and coaches	12,520	9,760	9,895
Goods vehicles	141,968	123,135	130,293
Motorcycles and mopeds	35,952	13,687	13,477

Source: IRF, *World Road Statistics*.

INLAND WATERWAYS

Traffic
('000 metric tons, excluding Kosovo)

	2000	2001
Goods carried	3,729	3,609

SHIPPING

Merchant Fleet
(registered at 31 December)

	2002	2003	2004
Number of vessels	6	6	8
Displacement ('000 gross registered tons)	1.1	1.1	6.1

Source: Lloyd's Register-Fairplay, *World Fleet Statistics*.

International Sea-borne Freight Traffic
('000 metric tons, unless otherwise indicated)

	1998	1999	2000
Goods loaded	40	30	16
Goods unloaded	61	81	94

CIVIL AVIATION
(traffic)

	1999	2000	2001
Passengers carried ('000)	489	1,122	1,211
Passenger-kilometres (million)	332	978	997
Cargo carried ('000 tons)	1,091	3,053	3,773
Ton-kilometres (million)	1.6	7.6	4.2

Tourism

FOREIGN TOURIST ARRIVALS
(at accommodation establishments)

Country of origin	2001	2002	2003
Austria	10,059	13,999	15,507
Bosnia and Herzegovina	73,533	62,646	63,403
Bulgaria	10,562	14,334	18,149
Croatia	13,775	19,341	23,191
Czech Republic and Slovakia	21,186	40,712	34,326
Germany	18,650	33,454	38,644
Greece	8,299	12,453	15,582
Hungary	9,743	14,205	14,343
Italy	16,813	23,410	24,795
Macedonia, former Yugoslav republic	25,846	32,150	32,162
Poland	7,818	14,448	15,871
Romania	10,931	12,322	11,360
Russia	18,393	20,898	18,606
Slovenia	20,851	29,829	36,382
Total (incl. others)	351,333	448,223	481,070

Tourism receipts (US $ million, excl. passenger transport): 54 in 2001; 97 in 2002; 201 in 2003.

Source: World Tourism Organization.

Communications Media

	2002	2003	2004
Telephones ('000 main lines in use)	2,493.0	2,611.7	2,685.4
Mobile cellular telephones ('000 subscribers)	2,750.4	3,634.6	4,729.6
Personal computers ('000 in use)	290	n.a.	389
Internet users ('000)	640	847	1,200

Television receivers ('000 in use): 3,000 in 2000.

Radio receivers ('000 in use): 3,150 in 1997.

Facsimile machines (number in use): 19,860 in 1999.

Books (titles published): 5,367 in 1996.

Daily newspapers (provisional data): 27 in 2001 (total annual circulation 287,703,000).

Non-daily newspapers (provisional data): 580 in 2001 (total annual ciculation 81,374,000).

Periodicals (provisional data): 491 in 2001 (total annual circulation 3,818,000).

Source: partly International Telecommunication Union; UNESCO Institute for Statistics; UN *Statistical Yearbook*.

Education

(2002/03, excluding Kosovo, unless otherwise indicated)

	Institutions	Teachers	Students
Pre-primary*	1,748	17,198	182,125
Primary	4,063	49,212	771,772
Secondary:			
general	534	28,711	336,927
teacher training*	n.a.	n.a.	327
vocational*	n.a.	n.a.	265,749
Higher†	150	11,320	207,082

* 1996/97 figures, including Kosovo.
† Including high schools.

Adult literacy rate: 96.4% (males 98.9%; females 94.1%) in 2003 (Source: UN, *Human Development Report*).

Directory

The Constitution

The Constitutional Charter of the State Union of Serbia and Montenegro was adopted by the Federal Assembly and entered into force on 4 February 2003, following its ratification by the Narodna skupština Republike Srbije (National Assembly of the Republic of Serbia) and the Skupština Republike Crne Gore (Assembly of the Republic of Montenegro). The following is a summary of the main articles of the Constitutional Charter:

INTRODUCTION

Serbia and Montenegro is based on the equality of the two member states, the state of Serbia and the state of Montenegro. The aims of Serbia and Montenegro are: respect for human rights of all persons under its jurisdiction; the preservation and promotion of human dignity, equality and the rule of law; integration into European structures, particularly the European Union (EU); harmonization of regulations and practices with European and international standards; the development of a market economy based on free enterprise, competition and social justice; and the establishment and smooth operation of a common market on its territory, through co-ordination and harmonization of the economic systems of the member states with the principles and standards of the EU. The symbols of Serbia and Montenegro are its flag, anthem and coat-of-arms, which are determined by the law of Serbia and Montenegro. The territory of Serbia and Montenegro is composed of the territories of the member states of Serbia and Montenegro. The border of Serbia and Montenegro is inviolable. The border between the member states is unalterable, except by mutual consent. Belgrade is the administrative centre of Serbia and Montenegro. The seat of the Skupština Srbije i Crne Gore (Assembly of Serbia and Montenegro) and the Council of Ministers is in Belgrade, Serbia, and the seat of the Court of Serbia and Montenegro is in Podgorica, Montenegro. A citizen of a member state is also a citizen of Serbia and Montenegro. A citizen of a member state has equal rights and duties in the other member state, except for the right to vote and be elected.

HUMAN AND MINORITY RIGHTS AND CIVIL LIBERTIES

The Charter on Human and Minority Rights and Civil Liberties is an integral part of the Constitutional Charter. The member states regulate, ensure and protect human and minority rights and civil liberties in their respective territories. The attained level of such liberties may not be reduced. Serbia and Montenegro monitors the exercise of human and minority rights and civil liberties and ensures their protection, in the case where such protection has not been provided in the member states. The provisions of international treaties on human and minority rights and civil liberties in force in the territory of Serbia and Montenegro are applicable directly.

ECONOMIC RELATIONS

Economic relations in Serbia and Montenegro are based on the market economy, supported by free enterprise, competition, a liberal foreign trade policy and the protection of property. Serbia and Montenegro co-ordinates and harmonizes the economic systems of the member states. Serbia and Montenegro has a common market, and member states are responsible for its smooth operation. Obstruction of the free flow of people, goods, services and capital between the state of Serbia and the state of Montenegro is prohibited.

SERBIA AND MONTENEGRO

PERSONALITY IN INTERNATIONAL LAW

Serbia and Montenegro is a single personality in international law and a member of international global and regional organizations that make international personality a requirement for membership. The member states may be members only of international global and regional organizations that do not make international personality a requirement for membership. Serbia and Montenegro may establish international relations with other states and international organizations and conclude international treaties and agreements. The member states may maintain international relations, conclude international agreements and establish their representative offices in other states, if that is not contrary to the authority of Serbia and Montenegro and the interests of the other member state. The ratified international treaties and generally accepted rules of international law shall have precedence over the law of Serbia and Montenegro and the laws of the member states.

LEGISLATURE

The Skupština Srbije i Crne Gore enacts laws and other instruments relating to the following: the institutions established in accordance with the Constitutional Charter and their operation; the enforcement of international law and the conventions obligating Serbia and Montenegro to co-operate with international courts; the declaration and abolition of the state of war, subject to the preliminary approval of the Assemblies of the member states; military issues and defence; membership of Serbia and Montenegro as a personality of international law in international organizations and the rights and duties arising from that membership, subject to preliminary approval of the competent bodies of the member states; the delimitation of the borders of Serbia and Montenegro, subject to the preliminary approval of the Skupština of the member state in which the border in question is located; issues pertaining to standardization, intellectual property, measurements and precious metals and statistics; policy of immigration, granting of asylum, the visa regime and integrated border management, in accordance with the standards of the EU; ratification of international treaties and agreements of Serbia and Montenegro; the annual revenues and expenditures, required for financing the authorities vested in Serbia and Montenegro at the proposal of the competent bodies of the member states and the Council of Ministers; the prevention and removal of obstacles to the free movement of persons, goods, services and capital within Serbia and Montenegro; the election of the President of Serbia and Montenegro and the Council of Ministers; the flag, anthem and coat-of-arms of Serbia and Montenegro. The Skupština Srbije i Crne Gore also performs other duties within the authorities of Serbia and Montenegro, as determined by the Constitutional Charter.

The Skupština Srbije i Crne Gore is unicameral and comprises 126 deputies, of whom 91 are from Serbia and 35 from Montenegro. The deputies of the Skupština Srbije i Crne Gore are elected from every member state in accordance with European and democratic standards on the basis of the laws of the member states. During the first two years after the adoption of the Constitutional Charter the deputies are elected indirectly, in proportion to the representation in the Narodna skupština Republike Srbije and the Skupština Republike Crne Gore. At the first elections the deputies are to be elected from the membership of the Narodna Republike skupština Srbije, the Skupština Republike Crne Gore and the Savezna skupština (Federal Assembly). If a member state holds parliamentary elections in that period, the membership of its delegation in the Skupština Srbije i Crne Gore is to be modified to reflect the outcome of the election. After this initial period, the deputies of the Skupština Srbije i Crne Gore are to be elected by direct ballot. The deputies shall have a four-year term of office. The Skupština elects from among its deputies its President and Vice-President, who may not be from the same member state. The President of the Skupština Srbije i Crne Gore and the President of Serbia and Montenegro may not be from the same member state. The Skupština Srbije i Crne Gore takes decisions by a majority vote of the total number of deputies. For a decision to be taken, the majority of the total number of deputies from each member state also have to vote for it. Deputies shall enjoy freedom of expression at the Skupština Srbije i Crne Gore and shall have immunity for the words uttered and for other acts he performs in his capacity as deputy. Deputies may not be called to answer, detained or punished without the approval of the Skupština Srbije i Crne Gore, except if found committing a criminal offence punishable by more than five years in prison. Apart from deputies, the President of Serbia and Montenegro, the members of the Council of Ministers and the judges of the Court of Serbia and Montenegro also have immunity. The Council of Ministers, a deputy and the Skupština of the member state may submit a draft law to the Skupština Srbije i Crne Gore.

PRESIDENT

The authority vested in the President of Serbia and Montenegro is as follows: representing Serbia and Montenegro at home and abroad; chairing the Council of Ministers and administering its work; proposing to the Skupština Srbije i Crne Gore the members of the Council of Ministers and the relief of duty of its members; being a member of the Supreme Command Council; issuing decrees on the appointment and dismissal of heads of diplomatic consular missions of Serbia and Montenegro, and receiving foreign diplomatic representatives' credentials and letters of recall; conferring awards and other honours; proclaiming laws approved by the Skupština Srbije i Crne Gore and the regulations approved by the Council of Ministers; scheduling elections for the Skupština Srbije i Crne Gore; and performing other duties determined by the Constitutional Charter. The President and the Vice-President of the Skupština Srbije i Crne Gore proposes to the Skupština a candidate for the President of Serbia and Montenegro. If the proposed candidate fails to win the requisite number of votes, the President and the Vice-President of the Skupština shall, within 10 days, propose a new candidate. If that candidate, too, fails to poll the requisite number of votes, the Skupština shall be dissolved and elections shall be called. If the elected President of Serbia and Montenegro is from the same member state as the President of the Skupština Srbije i Crne Gore, the President and the Vice-President of the Skupština Srbije i Crne Gore shall exchange posts. The President of Serbia and Montenegro may not be from the same member state for two consecutive terms. The procedure for the election and relief of duty of the President of Serbia and Montenegro shall be determined by law. The President of Serbia and Montenegro shall answer to the Skupština Srbije i Crne Gore. The term of office of the President of Serbia and Montenegro shall last four years. The President of the State Union's term of office may cease prematurely by his resignation, relief of duty and the dissolution of the Skupština Srbije i Crne Gore. The President of the State Union's term of office shall cease by his resignation when the Assembly takes note of it. The Skupština may relieve the President of Serbia and Montenegro of his duty if it is established that he has infringed the Constitutional Charter. The procedure to establish the infringement of the Constitutional Charter is initiated by the Skupština Srbije i Crne Gore, and the infringement is established by the Court of Serbia and Montenegro. The President of Serbia and Montenegro whose term of office has ceased owing to the dissolution of the Assembly of Serbia and Montenegro shall continue to carry out his duty pending the election of a new President. If the President of Serbia and Montenegro tenders his resignation or is relieved of his duty, his office shall, pending the election of a new President of Serbia and Montenegro, be assumed on a provisional basis by the Vice-President of the Skupština.

COUNCIL OF MINISTERS

The authority of the Council of Ministers is as follows: determining and conducting the policy of Serbia and Montenegro in conformity with the jointly agreed policy and interests of the member states; co-ordinating the work of the ministries; proposing to the Skupština Srbije i Crne Gore the laws and other acts falling within the competence of the ministries; appointing and dismissing the heads of diplomatic consular missions of Serbia and Montenegro and other officials in accordance with the law; approving regulations, decisions and other general enactments for enforcement of the laws of Serbia and Montenegro; and performing other executive duties in accordance with the Constitutional Charter. The member states are to be represented on a parity basis and by rotation in the missions of Serbia and Montenegro to international organizations. The manner of representation of the member states in international financial organizations is determined by the Council of Ministers, subject to the approval of the competent institutions of the member states. The representation of the member states in diplomatic consular missions of Serbia and Montenegro is determined by the Council of Ministers, subject to the approval of the competent institutions of the member states. The President of Serbia and Montenegro proposes to the Skupština Srbije i Crne Gore candidates for ministers of the Council of Ministers and candidates for the Deputy Minister of Foreign Affairs and Deputy Minister of Defence. Two candidates for ministers should be from the same member state as the President of Serbia and Montenegro and three from the other member state. The candidates for the Minister of Foreign Affairs and the Minister of Defence should be from different member states and this should also apply to their deputies. The list of candidates for the Council of Ministers is submitted to a vote at the Skupština. If the list does not obtain the requisite number of votes, the President may propose two more lists of candidates. If a list of candidates does not obtain the requisite number of votes within 60 days from the proposal of the first list of candidates, the Skupština Srbije i Crne Gore should be dissolved and elections scheduled. The procedure for the election and the termination of the term of office of the Council of Ministers is determined by law. The Council of Ministers approves decisions by a majority vote. If both proposals win the same number of votes, the vote of the President shall be decisive if at least one minister from the other member state has voted in favour of the decision. The Council of Ministers is answerable to the Skupština Srbije i Crne Gore. The Council of Ministers has a four-year term of office. The term of office of the Ministers and their Deputies may cease prematurely by their resignation, by a vote of 'no confidence' or by the dissolution of the Skupština Srbije i Crne Gore. The ministers and deputy ministers whose term of office has been terminated are to continue performing their duties pending the election of new ones.

The Minister of Foreign Affairs conducts and is responsible for the foreign policy of Serbia and Montenegro, negotiates international agreements and proposes to the Council of Ministers candidates for heads of diplomatic consular missions of Serbia and Montenegro. The Minister of Foreign Affairs co-ordinates the charting of foreign policy with the competent bodies of the member states. The Minister of Defence co-ordinates and implements the charted defence policy and commands the military, in accordance with the law and the powers of the Supreme Command Council. The Minister of Defence proposes to the Supreme Command Council candidates for posts and appoints, promotes and relieves of duty military officers in accordance with the law. The Minister of Defence should be a civilian. After a period of two years, the Ministers of Foreign Affairs and of Defence should exchange offices with their deputies. The Minister of Foreign Economic Relations is responsible for negotiations and co-ordination of the implementation of international agreements, including treaty relations with the EU and co-ordination of relations with international economic and financial institutions, following the consultation with the competent ministers of the member states. The Minister for Internal Economic Relations is responsible for the co-ordination and harmonization of the member states' economic systems in order to establish and ensure the smooth operation of the common market, including the free movement of people, goods, services and capital. The Minister of Human and Minority Rights monitors the exercise of human and minority rights and, together with the competent bodies of the member states, co-ordinates the implementation and compliance with international conventions for the protection of human and minority rights.

JUDICIARY

The Court of Serbia and Montenegro has authority to adjudicate the following: settlement of disputes between the institutions of Serbia and Montenegro concerning the issues within their competence under the Constitutional Charter; cases between Serbia and Montenegro and one or both member states, or between the two member states, concerning issues within their competence; appeals submitted by citizens if no other legal remedies have been stipulated, in the case that an institution of Serbia and Montenegro has interfered with the rights and liberties that are guaranteed to them by the Constitutional Charter; compatibility of the Constitutions of the member states with the Constitutional Charter; compatibility of the laws of Serbia and Montenegro with the Constitutional Charter; compatibility of the laws of the member states with the law of the Serbia and Montenegro; legality of final administrative acts of the institutions of Serbia and Montenegro. The Court takes legal positions and gives legal opinions on matters relating to the unification of court practices. The Court of Serbia and Montenegro comprises an equal number of judges from both member states. The judges of the Court of Serbia and Montenegro are elected by the Skupština Srbije i Crne Gore on the proposal of the Council of Ministers for a period of six years, and are restricted to one term. The judges are independent in their work and may not be relieved of duty prior to the expiry of the period for which they have been elected, except in cases stipulated by law. The decisions of the Court of Serbia and Montenegro are binding and without the right of appeal. The Court is authorized to put in abeyance the laws, other regulations and acts of the institutions of Serbia and Montenegro that are in conflict with the Constitutional Charter and with the laws of Serbia and Montenegro. When assessing whether the laws or competences of the member states are in accordance with the laws and responsibilities of Serbia and Montenegro, or whether this is the case between the member states, the deliberations at the meeting of the Court of Serbia and Montenegro should also be attended by the judges of the Constitutional Courts of the member states who should take part in decision-making. When assessing whether the Constitution, laws or competences of a member state are in accordance with the Constitutional Charter, the laws and competences of Serbia and Montenegro, the meeting of the Court of Serbia and Montenegro is also to be attended by the judges of the Constitutional Court of that particular member state, who should take part in decision-making. The Constitutional Charter, laws and the competences of Serbia and Montenegro and the Constitutions, laws and competences of the member states should be harmonized.

ARMED FORCES

Serbia and Montenegro has an Army, which is under democratic and civilian control. The duty of the Army is to defend Serbia and Montenegro in accordance with the Constitutional Charter and the principles of international law that regulate the use of force. The defence strategy is adopted by the Skupština Srbije i Crne Gore, in accordance with the law. The Supreme Commander of the Army is the Supreme Command Council, which decides on the use of the Army of Serbia and Montenegro. The Supreme Command Council comprises the President of Serbia and Montenegro and the Presidents of the member states. The Supreme Command Council takes decisions by consensus.

WITHDRAWAL FROM THE STATE UNION

After the expiry of a three-year period, each member state has the right to initiate the proceedings for the change in its status or for breaking away from the State Union of Serbia and Montenegro. The decision on breaking away from the State Union of Serbia and Montenegro may be taken following a referendum. Legislation on referendums should be adopted by member states, taking into account internationally recognized democratic standards. In the event that Montenegro breaks away from the State Union of Serbia and Montenegro, the international documents pertaining to the Federal Republic of Yugoslavia would concern and apply in their entirety to Serbia as the successor state. A member state that implements this right may not inherit the right to international personality and all disputable issues should be separately regulated between the successor state and the newly independent state. In the event that both member states vote for a change in their respective state status or for independence in a referendum procedure, all disputable issues should be regulated in a succession procedure, as was the case with the former Socialist Federal Republic of Yugoslavia.

The Government

HEAD OF STATE

President of the State Union of Serbia and Montenegro: SVETOZAR MAROVIĆ (elected 7 March 2003).

COUNCIL OF MINISTERS
(April 2006)

Minister of International Economic Relations: Prof. PREDRAG IVANOVIĆ.
Minister of Foreign Affairs: VUK DRAŠKOVIĆ.
Minister of Defence: ZORAN STANKOVIĆ.
Minister of Internal Economic Relations: AMIR NURKOVIĆ.
Minister of Human and Minority Rights: RASIM LJAJIĆ.

Note: The Council of Ministers is chaired by the President of the State Union of Serbia and Montenegro.

MINISTRIES

Office of the President of the State Union of Serbia and Montenegro: 11070 Belgrade, Palata Federacije, Bulevar Mihaila Pupina 2; tel. (11) 3118363; fax (11) 3015055; internet www.predsednik.gov.yu.

Office of the Council of Ministers: 11070 Belgrade, Palata Federacije, Bulevar Mihaila Pupina 2; tel. (11) 3114350; fax (11) 3111818; e-mail office@info.gov.yu; internet www.gov.yu.

Ministry of Defence: 11000 Belgrade, Birčaninova 5; tel. (11) 3616170; fax (11) 3117809; e-mail kabinetmo@ptt.yu; internet www.mod.gov.yu.

Ministry of Foreign Affairs: 11000 Belgrade, Kneza Miloša 26; tel. (11) 3615666; fax (11) 3618366; e-mail mfa@smip.sv.gov.yu; internet www.mfa.gov.yu.

Ministry of Human and Minority Rights: 11070 Belgrade, Bulevar Mihaila Pupina 2; tel. (11) 3114240; fax (11) 3113432; e-mail office@humanrights.gov.yu; internet www.humanrights.gov.yu.

Ministry of Internal Economic Relations: 11070 Belgrade, Bulevar Mihaila Pupina 2; tel. (11) 3111312; fax (11) 142088; e-mail kabinet@smput.sv.gov.yu.

Ministry of International Economic Relations: 11070 Belgrade, Bulevar Mihaila Pupina 2; tel. (11) 698389; fax (11) 3112780; internet www.umier.gov.yu.

President and Legislature of the State Union

PRESIDENT

The President of the State Union of Serbia and Montenegro is elected for a four-year term by the Skupština Srbije i Crne Gore.

SERBIA AND MONTENEGRO

Skupština Srbije i Crne Gore
(Assembly of Serbia and Montenegro)

11000 Belgrade, Trg Nikole Pasica 13; tel. (11) 3026200; fax (11) 3220880; e-mail lucicm@yubc.net; internet www.parlament.gov.yu..

The Skupština Srbije i Crne Gore comprises 126 deputies (91 from Serbia and 35 from Montenegro), who each serve for a term of four years. The Skupština was elected on 25 February 2003 by the existing federal and republican legislatures.

Speaker: ZORAN SAMI.

Election, 25 February 2003

Party	Seats
Democratic Opposition of Serbia*	37
Democratic List for European Montenegro†	19
Democratic Party	17
Together for Changes‡	14
Socialist Party of Serbia	12
Serbian Radical Party	8
Social Democratic Party of Montenegro	5
Party of Serbian Unity	5
Christian Democratic Party of Serbia	2
Democratic Alternative	2
Others	5
Total	**126**

* Alliance of 18 political parties.
† Coalition principally comprising the Democratic Party of Montenegrin Socialists, the Social-Democratic Party of Montenegro and the Citizens' Party of Montenegro.
‡ Coalition comprising the Socialist People's Party of Montenegro, the Serbian People's Party of Montenegro and the People's Party of Montenegro.

The Republics of Serbia and Montenegro

REPUBLICAN GOVERNMENT OF MONTENEGRO

Republican President

President of the Republic of Montenegro: FILIP VUJANOVIĆ (elected 11 May 2003; took office 13 June 2003).

Ministers
(April 2006)

A coalition of the Democratic Party of Montenegrin Socialists (DPMS), the Social Democratic Party of Montenegro (SDP) and the Democratic Union of Albanians (DUA).

Prime Minister: MILO ĐUKANOVIĆ (DPMS).
Deputy Prime Minister, with responsibility for the Political System and Internal Policy: DRAGAN ĐUROVIĆ (DPMS).
Deputy Prime Minister, with responsibility for the Financial System and Public Spending: MIROSLAV IVANIŠEVIĆ (SDP).
Deputy Prime Minister, with responsibility for Economic Policy and Development: BRANIMIR GVOZDENOVIĆ (DPMS).
Minister of Justice: ŽELJKO ŠTURANOVIĆ (DPMS).
Minister of Finance: IGOR LUKŠIĆ (DPMS).
Minister of Foreign Affairs: MIODRAG VLAHOVIĆ (SDP).
Minister of Education and Science: Prof. SLOBODAN BACKOVIĆ (DPMS).
Minister of Culture: Prof. VESNA KILIBARDA (Independent).
Minister of Economic Affairs: PREDRAG BOŠKOVIĆ (DPMS).
Minister of Maritime Affairs and Transportation: Dr ANDRIJA LOMPAR (SDP).
Minister of Agriculture, Forestry and Water Management: MILUTIN SIMOVIĆ (DPMS).
Minister of Tourism: PREDRAG NENEZIĆ (DPMS).
Minister of Internal Affairs: JUSUF KALAMPEROVIĆ.
Minister of Environmental Protection and Town Planning: BORO VUCINIĆ (DPMS).
Minister of Health: Dr MIODRAG PAVLIČIĆ (SDP).
Minister of Labour and Social Welfare: SLAVOLJUB STIJEPOVIĆ (DPMS).
Minister of International Economic Relations and European Integration: Dr GORDANA ĐUROVIĆ (Independent).
Minister for the Protection of the Rights of Minorities: GEZIM HAJDINAGA (DUA).
Minister without Portfolio: SUAD NUMANOVIĆ (DPMS).

Ministries

Office of the President: 81000 Podgorica, Sveti Petar Cetinjski 3; tel. (81) 242388; fax (81) 246608; e-mail predsjednik@cg.yu; internet www.predsjednik.cg.yu.
Office of the Prime Minister: 81000 Podgorica, Jovana Tomaševića bb; tel. (81) 52833; fax (81) 52246; internet www.vlada.cg.yu.
Ministry of Agriculture, Forestry and Water Management: 81000 Podgorica, Poslovni centar Vektra, Cetinjski put bb; tel. (81) 482109; fax (81) 234306; e-mail milutins@mn.yu; internet www.minpolj.vlada.cg.yu.
Ministry of Culture: 81000 Podgorica, Vuka Karadžića 3; tel. (81) 231540; fax (81) 231541; e-mail min.kulture.rcg@cg.yu; internet www.ministarstvokulture.vlada.cg.yu.
Ministry of Education and Science: 81000 Podgorica, Rimski trg bb; tel. (81) 405301; fax (81) 405343; e-mail mpin@cg.yu; internet www.mpin.vlada.cg.yu.
Ministry of the Environmental Protection and Town Planning: 81000 Podgorica, Poslovni centar Vektra I 2; tel. (81) 482211; fax (81) 234131; e-mail milenaz@mn.yu; internet www.mepp.vlada.cg.yu.
Ministry of Finance: 81000 Podgorica, Stanka Dragojevića 2; tel. (81) 242835; fax (81) 224450; e-mail mf@mn.yu; internet www.ministarstvo-finansija.vlada.cg.yu.
Ministry of Foreign Affairs: 81000 Podgorica, Stanka Dragojevića 2; tel. (81) 224609; fax (81) 224670; e-mail mip@mn.yu; internet www.mip.vlada.cg.yu.
Ministry of Health: 81000 Podgorica, Rimski trg bb; tel. (81) 242276; fax (81) 242762; e-mail caro@cg.yu; internet www.mzdraveja.vlada.cg.yu.
Ministry of Internal Affairs: 81000 Podgorica, Bulevar Svetog Petra Cetinjskog 22; tel. (81) 241252; fax (81) 9820; internet www.mup.vlada.cg.yu.
Ministry for International Economic Relations and European Integration: 81000 Podgorica, Stanka Dragojevića 2; tel. (81) 225568; fax (81) 225591; e-mail mierei@mn.yu; internet www.minevrint.vlada.cg.yu.
Ministry of Justice: 81000 Podgorica, Vuka Karadžića 3; tel. and fax (81) 248541; e-mail zeljkos@cg.yu; internet www.pravda.vlada.cg.yu.
Ministry of Labour and Social Welfare: 81000 Podgorica, Cetinjski put bb; tel. and fax (81) 234252; fax (81) 482443; e-mail tanjas@mn.yu; internet www.minrada.vlada.cg.yu.
Ministry of Maritime Affairs and Transportation: 81000 Podgorica, Cetinjski put bb; tel. (81) 234179; fax (81) 234331; e-mail angelinaz@mn.yu; internet www.minsaob.vlada.cg.yu.
Ministry for the Protection of the Rights of Minorities: 81000 Podgorica, Cetinjski put bb; tel. (81) 482126; fax (81) 234198; e-mail min.manj@cg.yu; internet www.minmanj.vlada.cg.yu.
Ministry of Tourism: 81000 Podgorica, Cetinjski put bb; tel. (81) 482329; fax (81) 234168; e-mail zeljkar@mn.yu; internet www.mturizma.vlada.cg.yu.

REPUBLICAN PRESIDENT OF MONTENEGRO

The presidential elections of 22 December 2002 and 9 February 2003 had a participation rate of 45.9% and 46.6%, respectively, and were consequently declared invalid (under electoral regulations requiring a minimum voter turn-out of 50%). On both occasions, FILIP VUJANOVIĆ, the candidate of the Democratic List for a European Montenegro, obtained the largest share of the votes cast, receiving 83.7% and 82.0% in the first and second elections, respectively. The requirement for a minimum rate of participation of 50% was subsequently abolished, and new elections, in which around 48% of the electorate participated, were held on 11 May 2003.

Presidential Election, 11 May 2003

Candidate	Votes*	% of votes
Filip Vujanović (Democratic List for European Montenegro)†	141,000	63.3
Dragan Hajduković (Independent)	69,000	30.8
Miodrag Zivković (Liberal Alliance of Montenegro)	8,000	3.9
Total‡	**218,000**	**100.0**

* Estimated number of votes cast.
† Coalition, principally comprising the Democratic Party of Montenegrin Socialists, the Social Democratic Party of Montenegro and the Citizens' Party of Montenegro.
‡ Total excludes an estimated 4,500 invalid votes. Percentage of votes is based on total votes cast.

SERBIA AND MONTENEGRO

REPUBLICAN LEGISLATURE OF MONTENEGRO

Skupština Republike Crne Gore
(Assembly of the Republic of Montenegro)

81000 Podgorica; e-mail ranko.krivokapic@skupstina.cg.yu; internet www.skupstina.cg.yu.

Speaker: RANKO KRIVOKAPIĆ.

Election, 20 October 2002

Party	Votes	% of votes	Seats
Democratic List for European Montenegro*	167,166	47.97	39
Together for Changes†	133,900	38.43	30
Liberal Alliance of Montenegro	20,365	5.83	4
Albanians Together‡	8,498	2.44	2
Total (incl. others)§	330,199	100.00	75

* Coalition, principally comprising the Democratic Party of Montenegrin Socialists, the Social Democratic Party of Montenegro and the Citizens' Party of Montenegro.
† Coalition, comprising the Socialist People's Party of Montenegro, the Serbian People's Party of Montenegro and the People's Party of Montenegro.
‡ Coalition, principally comprising the Democratic Union of Albanians and the Democratic Alliance of Albanians in Montenegro.
§ Excluding 9,851 invalid votes.

REPUBLICAN GOVERNMENT OF SERBIA

Republican President

President of the Republic of Serbia: BORIS TADIĆ (inaugurated 11 July 2004).

Ministers
(May 2006)

A coalition comprising representatives of the Democratic Party of Serbia (DPS), G17 Plus, and an alliance of the Serbian Renewal Movement and New Serbia (SRM/NS).

Prime Minister: Dr VOJISLAV KOŠTUNICA (DPS).
Deputy Prime Minister, in charge of European Integration: (vacant).
Minister of Internal Affairs: DRAGAN JOČIĆ (DPS).
Minister of Finance: MLAĐAN DINKIĆ (G17 Plus).
Minister of Justice: ZORAN STOJKOVIĆ (DPS).
Minister of Public Administration and Local Self-Government: ZORAN LONCAR (DPS).
Minister of Agriculture, Forestry and Water Management: IVANA DULIĆ-MARKOVIĆ (G17 Plus).
Minister of the Economy: PREDRAG BUBALO (DPS).
Minister of Energy and Mining: RADOMIR NAUMOV (DPS).
Minister of Capital Investment: VELIMIR ILIĆ (SRM/NS).
Minister of Trade, Tourism and Services: BOJAN DIMITRIJEVIĆ (SRM/NS).
Minister of International Economic Relations: MILAN PARIVODIĆ (DPS).
Minister of Labour, Employment and Social Affairs: SLOBODAN LALOVIĆ (G17 Plus).
Minister of Science and Environmental Protection: ALEKSANDAR POPOVIĆ (DPS).
Minister of Education and Sport: SLOBODAN VUKSANOVIĆ (DPS).
Minister of Culture: DRAGAN KOJADINOVIĆ (SRM/NS).
Minister of Health: TOMICA MILOSAVLJEVIĆ (G17 Plus).
Minister of Religious Affairs: MILAN RADULOVIĆ (DPS).
Minister of the Diaspora: VOJISLAV VUKCEVIĆ (SRM/NS).

Ministries

Office of the President: 11000 Belgrade, Andrićev venac 1; tel. (11) 3030866; fax (11) 3030868; e-mail kprs@ptt.yu.
Office of the Prime Minister: 11000 Belgrade, Nemanjina 11; tel. (11) 3617719; fax (11) 3617609; e-mail predsednikvladesrbije@srbija.sr.gov.yu.
Ministry of Agriculture, Forestry and Water Management: 11000 Belgrade, Nemanjina 22–26; tel. (11) 3065038; fax (11) 3616272; e-mail office@minpolj.sr.gov.yu; internet www.minpolj.sr.gov.yu.
Ministry of Capital Investment: 11000 Belgrade, Nemanjina 22–26; tel. (11) 3065038; fax (11) 3617486; e-mail cabinet@mki.sr.gov.yu.
Ministry of Culture: 11000 Belgrade, 11 Nikola Pasic Sq; tel. (11) 3346330; fax (11) 3346100; e-mail kabinet@min-cul.sr.gov.yu; internet www.min-cul.sr.gov.yu.
Ministry of the Diaspora: 11000 Belgrade, Svetozara Markovica 42; tel. (11) 687775; e-mail info@mzd.sr.gov.yu.
Ministry of the Economy: 11000 Belgrade, Srpskih vladara 16; tel. tel. (11) 3617599; fax (11) 3617640; e-mail officemprov@mpriv.sr.gov.yu; internet www.mpriv.sr.gov.yu.
Ministry of Education and Sport: 11000 Belgrade, Nemanjina 22–26; tel. (11) 3616489; fax (11) 3616491; e-mail webmaster.mps@mps.sr.gov.yu; internet www.mps.sr.gov.yu.
Ministry of Energy and Mining: 11000 Belgrade, Kralja Milana 36; tel. (11) 3346755; fax 3616603; e-mail kabinet.mem@mem.sr.gov.yu; internet www.mem.sr.gov.yu.
Ministry of Finance: 11000 Belgrade, Nemanjina 22–26; tel. (11) 3616361; fax (11) 3616535; e-mail bdjelsc@mfin.sr.gov.yu; internet www.mfin.sr.gov.yu.
Ministry of Health: 11000 Belgrade, Nemanjina 22–26; tel. (11) 3616251; fax (11) 3616596; e-mail kabinet.zdravlje@zdravlije.sr.gov.yu; internet www.zdravlje.sr.gov.yu.
Ministry of Internal Affairs: 11000 Belgrade, Kneza Miloša 103; tel. (11) 3612589; fax (11) 3617814; e-mail muprs@mup.sr.gov.yu; internet www.mup.sr.gov.yu.
Ministry of International Economic Relations: 11000 Belgrade, Gračanička 8; tel. (11) 3617628; fax (11) 3633142; e-mail office@mier.sr.gov.yu; internet www.mier.sr.gov.yu.
Ministry of Justice: 11000 Belgrade, Nemanjina 22–26; tel. (11) 3616548; fax (11) 3616419; e-mail kabinet@mpravde.sr.gov.yu; internet www.mpravde.sr.gov.yu.
Ministry of Labour, Employment and Social Affairs: 11000 Belgrade, Nemanjina 22; tel. (11) 3616253; fax (11) 3617498; e-mail minrzs@minrzs.sr.gov.yu; internet www.minrzs.sr.gov.yu.
Ministry of Public Administration and Local Self-Government: 11000 Belgrade, Bircaninova 6; tel. (11) 2685387; fax (11) 2685315; e-mail info.mpalsg.sr.gov.yu; internet www.mpalsg.sr.gov.yu.
Ministry of Religious Affairs: 11000 Belgrade, Nemanjina 11; tel. and fax (11) 3633446; e-mail kabinet.mv@mv.sr.gov.yu.
Ministry of Science and Environmental Protection: 11000 Belgrade, Nemanjina 22–26; tel. (11) 3616516; fax (11) 3616584; e-mail info@mntr.sr.gov.yu.
Ministry of Trade, Tourism and Services: 11000 Belgrade, Nemanjina 22–26; tel. (11) 3618852; fax (11) 3610258; e-mail kabinet@minttu.sr.gov.yu; internet www.minttu.sr.gov.yu.

REPUBLICAN PRESIDENT OF SERBIA

Presidential Election, First Ballot, 13 June 2004

Candidate	Votes	% of votes
Tomislav Nikolić (Serbian Radical Party)	954,339	30.97
Boris Tadić (Democratic Party)	853,584	27.70
Bogoljub Karić (Independent)	568,691	18.46
Dragan Maršićanin (Democratic Party of Serbia/G17 Plus/Serbian Renewal Movement–New Serbia)	414,971	13.47
Ivica Dačić (Socialist Party of Serbia)	125,952	4.09
Others	163,503	5.31
Total	3,081,040	100.00

Second Ballot, 27 June 2004

Candidate	Votes	% of votes
Boris Tadić (Democratic Party)	1,681,528	53.97
Tomislav Nikolić (Serbian Radical Party)	1,434,068	46.03
Total	3,115,596	100.00

REPUBLICAN LEGISLATURE OF SERBIA

Narodna skupština Republike Srbije
(National Assembly of the Republic of Serbia)

11000 Belgrade, Kralja Milana 14; tel. (11) 3222001; e-mail webmaster@parlament.sr.gov.yu; internet www.parlament.sr.gov.yu.

President: PREDRAG MARKOVIĆ.

SERBIA AND MONTENEGRO

Election, 28 December 2003

Party	Votes	% of votes	Seats
Serbian Radical Party	1,056,256	27.97	82
Democratic Party of Serbia	678,031	17.96	53
Democratic Party	481,249	12.75	37
G17 Plus	438,422	11.61	34
Serbian Renewal Movement/New Serbia	293,082	7.76	22
Socialist Party of Serbia	291,341	7.72	22
Others	537,335	14.23	—
Total	**3,775,716**	**100.00**	**250**

PROVINCES OF SERBIA

Kosovo

Until 1990 Kosovo (subsequently officially known as Kosovo and Metohija) was an autonomous province within Serbia, with its own provincial assembly and government; following the adoption of amendments to the Yugoslav Constitution, the province's autonomous status was removed, and the provincial assembly and government dissolved. Most ethnic Albanian deputies in the assembly opposed its dissolution, and formed a 'Kosovo assembly-in-exile', which proclaimed Kosovo a 'republic'. They also established an interim 'government', based in Zagreb, Croatia, which organized a referendum among the ethnic Albanian population in September 1991, which was overwhelmingly in favour of Kosovo's becoming a sovereign republic. The Assembly-in-Exile also arranged elections to a new 130-seat provincial assembly on 24 May 1992 (the Democratic Alliance of Kosovo won the most seats and its leader, Dr IBRAHIM RUGOVA, was declared the President of the 'Republic of Kosovo'). The referendum and the elections were declared illegal by the Serbian and federal authorities. Further presidential and legislative elections, again declared illegal, took place in the province in March 1998. In May 2001 the UN Interim Administration Mission in Kosovo agreed to grant the province provisional self-government. Elections to a new, 120-member legislative Assembly took place on 17 November (10 seats were allocated proportionally to Serbs and 10 to other ethnic groups). On 4 March 2002 Rugova was elected President of Kosovo. Further elections to the Assembly were conducted on 23 October 2004. Rugova's Democratic League of Kosovo retained the highest number of seats (47), while the Democratic Party of Kosovo increased its representation to 30 members. Despite a widely observed Serb boycott of the elections, Serbs retained the allocation of 10 seats in the Assembly. Following Rugova's death in January 2006, the Kosovo Assembly elected FATMIR SEJDIU to succeed him in February.

Vojvodina

The Province of Vojvodina has an elected Provincial Assembly, based at Novi Sad. Elections to the Provincial Assembly took place on 24 September and 8 October 2000. The President of the Provincial Assembly is BOJAN KOSTREŠ. The Prime Minister is BOJAN PAJTIĆ. In January 2002 the Narodna škupstine Republike Srbije voted in favour of restoring partial autonomy to Vojvodina.

Election Commissions

Central Election Commission: 11000 Belgrade, 13 trg Nikole Pasica; tel. (11) 3026340; fax (11) 3248985; e-mail drgranic@yubc.net; Chair. NOVICA KULIĆ.

Kosovo Central Election Commission: OSCE Mission in Kosovo, Rruga Belgrade 32, 38000 Priština; tel. (38) 500162; fax (38) 500188; e-mail press@omik.org; internet www.osce.org/kosovo; f. 2000; Chair. WERNER WNENDT.

Montenegrin Republican Election Commission: Podgorica; Chair. BRANISLAV RADULOVIĆ.

Serbia Republic Electoral Commission: Belgrade, Kralja Milana 14; tel. (11) 3222001; fax (11) 3617839; e-mail rik@parlament.sr.gov.yu; internet www.rik.parlament.sr.gov.yu; Chair. RADOSLAV BACOVIĆ.

Political Organizations

Alliance for the Future of Kosovo (Aleanca për Ardhmërinë e Kosovës—AAK): Priština, Kodra e Trimave; tel. (44) 219080.

Alliance of Vojvodina Hungarians (Vajdasági Magyar Szövetség/Savez Vojvođanskih Madara): 24000 Subotica, Age Mamuzica 13; tel. (24) 553801; e-mail office@vmsz.org.yu; internet www.vmsz.org.yu; f. 1994; supports autonomous status for Vojvodina; Chair. JOŽEF KASZA.

Christian Democratic Party of Serbia (Demohriščanska Stranka Srbije) (DHSS): 11000 Belgrade, Hadži Nikole Živkovića 2; tel. 3032272; e-mail dhss@net.yu; internet www.dhss.org.yu; Pres. Dr VLADAN BATIĆ.

Civic Alliance of Serbia (CAS) (Građanski savez Srbije—GSS): 11000 Belgrade, Dušana Bogdanovića 10; tel. (11) 3443481; fax (11) 2434244; e-mail gss@gradjanskisavez.org.yu; internet www.gradjanskisavez.org.yu; f. 1992; Pres. NATAŠA MIĆIĆ.

Democratic League of Kosovo (DLK) (Lidhja Demokratike e Kosovës—LDK): Priština, Kompleksi 'Qafa'; tel. (38) 242242; fax (38) 245305; e-mail ldk@ldk-kosova.org; internet www.ldk-kosova.org; f. 2000 as successor to the Democratic Alliance of Kosovo; party with largest representation in Kosovo Assembly after Oct. 2004 elections; Chair. FATMIR SEJDIU.

Democratic Party (DP) (Demokratska Stranka): 11000 Belgrade, Krunska 69; tel. (11) 3443003; fax (11) 2444864; e-mail info@ds.org.yu; internet www.ds.org.yu; f. 1990; Pres. BORIS TADIĆ.

Democratic Party of Kosovo (DPK) (Partia Demokratike e Kosovës—PDK): Priština, N. Tereze 20; tel. (44) 156774; fmrly Party for the Democratic Party of Kosovo; represented in Kosovo Assembly after Oct. 2004 elections; Chair. HASHIM THAÇI.

Democratic Socialist Party of Montenegro (Demokratska Partija Socijalista Crne Gore): 81000 Podgorica, Jovana Tomaśevića 33; tel. (81) 225830; fax (81) 242101; e-mail webmaster@dps.cg.yu; internet www.dps.cg.yu; name changed from League of Communists of Montenegro in 1991; supports the independence of Montenegro; Chair. MILO ĐUKANOVIĆ.

Democratic Party of Serbia (DPS) (Demokratska stranka Srbije—DSS): 11000 Belgrade, Pariska 13; tel. (11) 3204719; fax (11) 3204743; e-mail info@dss.org.yu; internet www.dss.org.yu; f. 1992 following split from Democratic Party; Leader Dr VOJISLAV KOŠTUNICA.

G17 Plus: 11000 Belgrade, trg Republike 5; tel. and fax (11) 3344930; e-mail office@g17plus.org.yu; internet www.g17plus.org.yu; f. 2003; Pres. (vacant).

League for Šumadija—Šumadija Coalition (Koalicija Šumadija—Liga za Šumadiju): 34000 Kragujevac, Lole Ribara 9A; tel. and fax (34) 337227; e-mail sumadija@infosky.net; internet www.sumadija.org.yu; supports a decentralization of powers within Serbia; Pres. BRANISLAV KOVACEVIĆ.

League of Social-Democrats of Vojvodina (Liga Socijaldemokrata Vojvodine—LSV): 21000 Novi Sad, trg Mladenaca 10; tel. (21) 29139; e-mail office@lsv.org.yu; internet www.lsv.org.yu; Pres. NENAD ČANAK.

Liberal Alliance of Montenegro (LAM) (Liberalni Savez Crne Gore—LSCG): 81000 Podgorica, Bratstva i jedinstva 57; tel. (81) 625245; fax (81) 601506; e-mail lscg@cg.yu; internet www.lscg.cg.yu; pro-independence; Leader VESNA PEROVIĆ; Pres. DŽEMAL PEROVIĆ.

Liberal Democratic Party (Liberalno-demokratska Stranka): 11000 Belgrade, Njegoševa 1; tel. (11) 3233930; e-mail abv@ptt.yu; internet www.lds-serbia.org.yu; f. 1989; favours the restoration of a Serbian Monarchy, a free-market economy, and integration of Serbia with European and Atlantic institutions; Leader PREDRAG M. VULETIĆ.

Liberals of Serbia (Liberali Srbije): Belgrade, Krunska 76; tel. (11) 4440677; fax (11) 3444230; e-mail mail@liberali-srbije.org.yu; internet www.liberali-srbije.org.yu; f. 1990 as New Democracy—Movement for Serbia; Chair. DUŠAN MIHAILOVIĆ; Sec.-Gen. VESELIN ŽIVKOVIĆ.

New Serbia: 11000 Belgrade, Dragoslava Jovanovića 7; tel. and fax (11) 3238225; e-mail info@nova-srbija.org.yu; internet www.nova-srbija.org.yu; Pres VELIMIR ILIĆ, MIHAJLO MARKOVIĆ.

Party of Serb Unity (Stranka Srpskog Jedinstva—SSJ): 11000 Belgrade, Beogradska 23; tel. (11) 3345579; fax (11) 3346302; e-mail stranka@strankasrpskogjedinstva.org; internet www.strankasrpskogjedinstva.org; f. 1993 by Żeliko Ražnatovič ('Arkan'); extreme nationalist; Leader BORISLAV PELEVIĆ.

People's Party of Montenegro (Narodna Stranka Crne Gore): 11000 Belgrade, Srpskih Vladara 14; e-mail narodna@cg.yu; internet www.narodnastranka.cg.yu; Chair. DRAGAN SOC.

Return Coalition (Koalicija Povratak—KP): Priština; coalition of Serb parties in Kosovo and Metohija; Leader DRAGIŠA KRSTOVIĆ.

Serb People's Party of Montenegro (Srpska Narodna Stranka Crne Gore): 81000 Podgorica, Vojislava Grujića 4; tel. (81) 652149; e-mail sns@cg.yu; internet www.sns.cg.yu; seeks to represent the interests of ethnic Serbs in Montenegro; Pres. ANDRIJA MANDIĆ.

Serb Radical Party (SRP) (Srpska Radikalna Stranka—SRS): 11080 Belgrade, Zemun, Magistratski trg 3; tel. (11) 3164621; e-mail info@srs.org.yu; internet www.srs.org.yu; f. 1991; extreme nationalist; advocates a 'Greater Serbian' state of territories inhabited by

Serbs within and outside Serbia; Leader TOMISLAV NIKOLIĆ; Gen. Sec. ALEKSANDAR VUCIĆ.

Serb Renewal Movement (SRM) (Srpski pokret obnove—SPO): Belgrade, Krez Mihajlovna 48; tel. (11) 635281; fax (11) 628170; internet www.spo.org.yu; f. 1990; right-wing; nationalist; Pres. VUK DRAŠKOVIĆ.

Social Democracy (Socijal demokratija—SD): 11000 Belgrade, Terazije 3/I; tel. (11) 3225771; fax (11) 3226521; e-mail info@socijaldemokratija.org.yu; internet www.socijaldemokratija.org.yu; f. 1997; Pres. Dr VUK OBRADOVIĆ.

Social Democratic Party (Socijaldemokratska Partija—SDP): 11000 Belgrade, Ruzveltova 45; tel. (11) 3290820; fax 911) 3294507; e-mail internacional@sdp.org.yu; internet www.sdp.org.yu; f. 1997; Pres. Dr NEBOJŠA ČOVIĆ.

Social Democratic Party of Montenegro (Socijaldemokratska Partija Crne Gore—SDP): 81000 Podgorica, Jovana Tomasévića bb; tel. (81) 248648; fax (81) 612133; e-mail sdp@cg.yu; internet www.sdp.cg.yu; Pres. RANKO KRIVOKAPIĆ.

Social Democratic Union (Socijaldemokratska Unija): 11000 Belgrade, Masarikova 5; tel. and fax (11) 3061394; e-mail info@sdu.org.yu; internet www.sdu.org.yu; Pres. ŽARKO KORAĆ.

Socialist Party of Serbia (SPS) (Socijalistička partija Srbije): 11000 Belgrade, bul. Lenjina 6; tel. (11) 634921; fax (11) 628642; internet www.sps.org.yu; f. 1990 by merger of League of Communists of Serbia and Socialist Alliance of Working People of Serbia; Pres. IVICA DAČIĆ.

Socialist People's Party of Montenegro (Socijalistička Narodna Partija Crne Gore—SNP): Vaka Djurovica 5, 81000 Podgorica; tel. (81) 272421; fax (81) 272430; e-mail snp@cg.yu; internet www.snp.cg.yu; Leader PREDRAG BULATOVIĆ.

Vojvodina Coalition (Koalicija Vojvodina): Pančevo, trg Slobode 3; tel. and fax (13) 353629; e-mail info@koalicijavojvodina.org.yu; internet www.koalicijavojvodina.org.yu; support a tolerant, decentralized system of Government in Serbia; Pres. Dr DRAGAN VESELINOV.

Diplomatic Representation

EMBASSIES IN SERBIA AND MONTENEGRO

Albania: 11000 Belgrade, Bulevar Mira 25 A; tel. (11) 3065350; fax (11) 665439; e-mail albembassy_belgrade@hotmail.com; Ambassador PETRIT BUSHATI.

Algeria: 11000 Belgrade, Maglajska 26 B; tel. (11) 3671211; e-mail ambalg@eunet.yu; Ambassador BOUDJEMAA DELMI.

Angola: 11000 Belgrade, Vase Pelagića 32 51; tel. (11) 3690241; fax (11) 3690191; Ambassador FILIPE FELISBERTO MONIMAMBU.

Argentina: 11000 Belgrade, Knez Mihajlova 24/I; tel. (11) 2623569; fax (11) 2622630; e-mail embaryu@eunet.yu; Ambassador MARIO EDUARDO BOSSI DE EZCURRA.

Australia: 11000 Belgrade, Čika Ljubina 13; tel. (11) 3303400; fax (11) 3303409; e-mail belgrade.embassy@dfat.gov.au; internet www.serbiamontenegro.embassy.gov.au; Ambassador JOHN G. W. OLIVER.

Austria: 11000 Belgrade, Kneza Sime Markovića 2; tel. (11) 635955; fax (11) 635500; e-mail belgrad-ob@bmaa.gv.at; internet www.aussenministerium.at/belgrad; Ambassador GERHARD JANDL.

Belarus: 11000 Belgrade, Deligradska 13; tel. (11) 3616836; fax (11) 3616938; e-mail sam@belembassy.org; Ambassador VLADIMIR MATSKEVICH.

Belgium: 11000 Belgrade, Krunska 18; tel. (11) 3230018; fax (11) 3244394; e-mail belgrade@diplobel.org; Ambassador DENISE DE HAUWERE.

Bosnia and Herzegovina: Milana Tankosića 8; tel. (11) 766507; fax (11) 3291277; e-mail ambasadabih@yubc.net; Ambassador TOMISLAV LEKO.

Brazil: 11000 Belgrade, Krunska 14; tel. (11) 3239781; fax (11) 3230653; e-mail brasbelg@eunet.yu; Ambassador DANTE COELHO DE LIMA.

Bulgaria: 11000 Belgrade, Birčaninova 26; tel. (11) 3613980; fax 3611136; e-mail bulgamb@eunet.yu; Ambassador GEORGI DIMITROV.

Canada: 11000 Belgrade, Kneza Miloša 75; tel. (11) 3063000; fax (11) 3063042; e-mail bgrad@international.gc.ca; internet www.canada.org.yu; Ambassador ROBERT MCDOUGALL.

China, People's Republic: 11000 Belgrade, Lackovićeva 6; tel. (11) 662737; fax (11) 653538; e-mail chinaemb_yu@mail.mfa.gov.cn; Ambassador LI GUOBANG.

Congo, Democratic Republic: 11000 Belgrade, Diplomatska kolonija 3; tel. (11) 664131; Chargé d'affaires a.i. PAUL EMILE TSHINGA AHUKA.

Croatia: 11000 Belgrade, Kneza Miloša 62; tel. (11) 3610535; fax (11) 3610032; e-mail croambg@eunet.yu; Ambassador TONČI STANIĆIĆ.

Cuba: 11000 Belgrade, Vasilija Gaćeše 9 B; tel. (11) 3692441; fax (11) 3692442; e-mail emcubayu@eunet.yu; Ambassador JULIO CÉSAR CANCIO FERRER.

Cyprus: 11040 Belgrade, Diplomatska Kolonija 9; tel. (11) 3672725; fax (11) 3671348; e-mail cyprus@eunet.yu; Chargé d'affaires CHARIS MORITSIS.

Czech Republic: 11000 Belgrade, bul. Kralja Aleksandra 22; tel. (11) 3230133; fax (11) 3236448; e-mail belgrade@embassy.mzv.cz; internet www.mzv.cz/belgrade; Ambassador IVAN JESTŘÁB.

Denmark: 11040 Belgrade, Neznanog Junaka 9A; tel. (11) 3670443; fax (11) 2660759; e-mail begamb@um.dk; internet www.ambbeograd.um.dk; Ambassador RUBEN MADSEN.

Egypt: 11000 Belgrade, Andre Nikolića 12; tel. (11) 651225; fax (11) 652036; Ambassador ADEL AHMED NAGUIB.

Finland: 11001 Belgrade, Birčaninova 29, POB 926; tel. (11) 3065400; fax (11) 3065375; e-mail sanomat.beo@formin.fi; Ambassador ANNA-MARIJA KORPI.

France: 11000 Belgrade, Pariska 11, POB 283; tel. (11) 3023500; fax (11) 3023510; e-mail amba_fr@eunet.yu; internet www.ambafrance-yu.org; Ambassador HUGUES PERNET.

Germany: 11000 Belgrade, Kneza Miloša 76; tel. (11) 3064300; fax (11) 3064303; e-mail germemba@eunet.yu; internet www.belgrad.diplo.de; Ambassador ANDREAS ZOBEL.

Ghana: 11000 Belgrade, Đorđa Vajferta 50; tel. (11) 3440856; fax (11) 3440071; e-mail ghana@eunet.yu; Ambassador Dr NYAHO NYAHO-TAMAKLOE.

Greece: 11000 Belgrade, Francuska 33; tel. (11) 3226523; fax 3344746; e-mail office@greekemb.co.yu; internet www.greekemb.co.yu; Ambassador CHRISTOS PANAGOPOULOS.

Guinea: 11000 Belgrade, Ohridska 4; tel. (11) 431830; fax (11) 451391; Ambassador El Hadj MUHAMMAD ISSIAGA KOUROUMA.

Holy See: 11000 Belgrade, Svetog Save 24; tel. (11) 3085356; fax (11) 3085216; e-mail nunbel@eunet.yu; Apostolic Nuncio Most Rev. EUGENIO SBARBARO (Titular Archbishop of Tiddi).

Hungary: 11000 Belgrade, ul. Ivana Milutinovica 74; tel. (11) 4440472; fax (11) 3441876; e-mail hunemblg@eunet.yu; internet www.hunemblg.hu; Ambassador SÁNDOR PAPP.

India: 11070 Belgrade, B06-07 Genex International Centre, Vladimira Popovica 6,; tel. (11) 2223306; fax (11) 2223357; e-mail indemb@eunet.yu; Ambassador LAVANYA PRASAD.

Indonesia: 11000 Belgrade, bul. Mira 18; tel. (11) 3674062; fax (11) 3672984; e-mail kombeojo@eunet.yu; Chargé d'affaires a.i. SUTADI HADIWIYOTO.

Iran: 11000 Belgrade, Krunska 9; tel. (11) 338782; fax (11) 3223676; Ambassador SEYED MIR HEYDARI.

Israel: 11000 Belgrade, bul. Mira 47; tel. (11) 3672400; fax (11) 3670304; e-mail embisr@eunet.yu; Ambassador YAFFA BEN-ARI.

Italy: 11000 Belgrade, ul. Birčaninova 11; tel. (11) 3066100; fax (11) 3249413; e-mail office@italy.org.yu; internet www.italy.org.yu; Ambassador ALESSANDRO MEROLA.

Japan: 11070 Novi Belgrade, Vladimira Popovica 6; tel. (11) 3012800; fax (11) 3118258; Ambassador TADASHI NGAI.

Korea, Republic: 11070 Belgrade, Hyatt Regency, Milentija Popovića 5; tel. (11) 3011194; fax (11) 3011195; Ambassador Dr KIM YOUNG-HEE.

Lebanon: 11000 Belgrade, Vase Pelagića 38; tel. (11) 3691178; fax (11) 3690155; e-mail ambaleb@eunet.yu; Ambassador CHÉHADÉ MOUALLEM.

Libya: 11000 Belgrade, Mirka Tomića 6; tel. (11) 663445; fax (11) 3670805; e-mail libyaamb@eunet.yu; Chargé d'affaires a.i. HAMAU KHALED ZOGHBIA.

Macedonia, former Yugoslav republic: 11000 Belgrade, Gospodar Jevremova 34; tel. (11) 3284924; fax (11) 3285076; e-mail macemb@eunet.yu; Ambassador VIKTOR DIMOVSKI.

Mexico: 11000 Belgrade, Ljutice Bogdana 5, Savski venac; tel. (11) 3674170; fax (11) 3675013; e-mail embamex@net.yu; internet www.mexican-embassy.org.yu; Chargé d'affaires a.i. EDUARDO HÉCTOR MOGUEL FLORES.

Morocco: 11000 Belgrade, Sanje Živanović 4; tel. (11) 3691866; fax (11) 3690499; e-mail sifamabe@eunet.yu; Ambassador KAMAL FAQIR BENAISSA.

Myanmar: 11000 Belgrade, Kneza Miloša 72; tel. (11) 645420; fax (11) 3614968; e-mail mebel@eunet.yu; Chargé d'affaires a.i. U THIHA HAN.

Netherlands: 11000 Belgrade, Simina 29, POB 489; tel. (11) 2023900; fax (11) 2023999; e-mail info@nlembassy.org.yu; internet www.nlembassy.org.yu; Ambassador BAREND C. A. F. VAN DER HEIJDEN.

SERBIA AND MONTENEGRO

Norway: 11000 Belgrade, Kablarska 30; tel. (11) 3690154; fax (11) 3690158; Ambassador HAAKON BLANKENBORG.

Pakistan: 11000 Belgrade, bul. Mira 62; tel. (11) 661676; fax (11) 661667; e-mail parepbeograd@vubc.net; Ambassador RASHED SALEEM KHAN.

Peru: 11000 Belgrade, Terazije 1/II; tel. (11) 3221197; fax (11) 3228694; e-mail leprubelgrado@b92.net; Ambassador WALTER NEGREIROS PORTELLA.

Poland: 11000 Belgrade, Kneza Miloša 38; tel. (11) 2065318; fax (11) 3616939; e-mail ambrpfrj@eunet.yu; Ambassador MACIEJ SZYMAŃSKI.

Portugal: 11040 Belgrade, Vladimira Gaćinovića 4; tel. (11) 2662895; fax (11) 2662892; e-mail embporbg@yubc.net; Ambassador PAULO TIAGO JERÓNIMO DA SILVA.

Romania: 11000 Belgrade, Kneza Miloša 70; tel. (11) 3618327; fax (11) 3618339; e-mail ambelgro@infosky.net; Chargé d'affaires a.i. ALEXANDRU MURESAN.

Russia: 11000 Belgrade, ul. Deligradska 32; tel. (11) 3611323; fax (11) 3611900; e-mail ambarusk@eunet.yu; Ambassador ALEKSANDR N. ALEKSEYEV.

Slovakia: 11070 Belgrade, bul. Umetvosti 18; tel. (11) 3010000; fax (11) 3010020; e-mail embassy@belehrad.mfa.sk; Ambassador IGOR FURDÍK.

Slovenia: Belgrade, ul. Zmaj Jovina 33 A; tel. (11) 3282610; fax (11) 2625884; e-mail vbg@mzz-dkp.gov.si; Ambassador MIROSLAV LUCI.

Spain: 11000 Belgrade, Prote Mateje 45; tel. (11) 3440231; fax (11) 3444203; e-mail embespyu@mail.mae.es; internet www.spanija.org.yu; Ambassador JOSÉ RIERA SIQUIER.

Sweden: 11040 Belgrade, Ledi Pedzet 2, POB 5; tel. (11) 2069200; fax (11) 2069250; e-mail ambassaden.belgrad@foreign.ministry.se; internet www.swedenabroad.se/belgrad; Ambassador LARS-GÖRAN ENGFELDT.

Switzerland: 11000 Belgrade, Birčaninova 27; tel. (11) 3065820; fax (11) 657253; e-mail vertretung@bel.rep.admin.ch; Chargé d'affaires a.i. WILHELM MEIER.

Syria: 11000 Belgrade, Aleksandra Stamboliskog 13; tel. (11) 2666124; fax (11) 2660221; e-mail syremb@net.yu; Chargé d'affaires a.i. Dr ABDUL MAJID RIFAI.

Tunisia: 11000 Belgrade, Vase Pelagića 19; tel. (11) 3691961; fax (11) 3690642; e-mail at.belgr@eunet.yu; Chargé d'affaires a.i. ABDELWAHED BOUZOUITA.

Turkey: 11000 Belgrade, Krunska 1; tel. (11) 3235431; fax (11) 3235433; e-mail turem@eunet.yu; Ambassador HASAN SERVET ÖKTEM.

Ukraine: 11000 Belgrade, Josipa Slavenskog 27; tel. (11) 3671516; fax (11) 36781; e-mail emb_sm@mfa.gov.ua; internet www.ukrembassy.org.yu; Ambassador ANATOLIY OLYNYK.

United Kingdom: 11000 Belgrade, Resavska 46; tel. (11) 2645055; fax (11) 659651; e-mail belgrade.man@fco.gov.uk; internet www.britishembassy.gov.uk/serbiaandmontenegro; Ambassador DAVID GOWAN.

USA: 11000 Belgrade, Kneza Miloša 50; tel. (11) 3619344; fax (11) 3615489; internet www.belgrade.usembassy.gov; Ambassador MICHAEL C. POLT.

Zimbabwe: 11000 Belgrade, Tolstojeva 51; tel. (11) 3672996; fax (11) 3671218; e-mail zimbegd@eunet.yu; Ambassador LLOYD GUNDU.

Judicial System

The judicial system comprises courts of general jurisdiction, organized in accordance with individual republican legislation. In general, the courts are entitled to proceed in criminal, civil and administrative matters. Military courts, headed by the Supreme Military Court, proceed in criminal and administrative matters connected with military service or national defence. Economic or trade matters are under the jurisdiction of economic courts. Judges are elected or replaced by the republican assemblies or the Skupština Srbije i Crne Gore (see below).

The Federal Court and Constitutional Court were to continue functioning under the Constitutional Charter, adopted on 4 February 2003, until otherwise specified by this law. The Skupština Srbije i Crne Gore, which was established on 25 February, approved legislation providing for the creation of the Court of the State Union of Serbia and Montenegro. Unfinished cases before the existing federal Constitutional Court and Federal Court within the remit of the Court of the State Union of Serbia and Montenegro were to be transferred to that Court. The Court was to have both constitutional administrative functions, and was to decide on the harmonization of court practice between the two republics.

THE COURT OF THE STATE UNION OF SERBIA AND MONTENEGRO

The Court of Serbia and Montenegro comprises an equal number of judges from both member states. The judges of the Court of Serbia and Montenegro are elected by the Skupština Srbije i Crne Gore on the proposal of the Council of Ministers for a period of six years, and are restricted to one term.

Court of the State Union of Serbia and Montenegro (Sud državne zajednice Srbije i Crne Gore): 81000 Podgorica; f. 2004; Pres. Prof. BLAGOTA MITRIĆ; Judges Prof. SLOBODAN PEROVIĆ, LJUBOMIR POPOVIĆ, KATARINA MANOJLOVIĆ-ANDRIĆ, MIHAJLO RULIĆ, MIODRAG LATKOVIĆ, EMILIJA DURUTOVIĆ.

THE REPUBLICAN JUDICIARIES

Montenegro

The courts in Montenegro are supervised by the republican Ministry of Justice. The highest courts in the republican judicial system are the Supreme Court and the Constitutional Court.

Constitutional Court of the Republic of Montenegro: 81000 Podgorica, Lenjina 3; tel. (81) 41846; Pres. RADOJE KORAĆ.

Supreme Court: 81000 Podgorica, Njegoševa 6; tel. (81) 43070; Pres. STEVAN DAMJANOVIĆ.

Office of the Public Prosecutor: 81000 Podgorica, Njegoševa 6; tel. (81) 43053; Public Prosecutor VESNA MEDENICA.

Serbia

All courts in Serbia are within the jurisdiction of the republican Ministry of Justice. The Supreme Court and the Constitutional Court are the highest courts in the republican judicial system.

Constitutional Court of Serbia (Ustavni Sud Srbije): 11000 Belgrade, Nemanjina 22–26; tel. (11) 3613734; Pres. SLOBODAN VUCETIĆ.

Supreme Court of Serbia: 11000 Belgrade, Nemanjina 22–26; tel. (11) 658755; Pres. VIDA PETROVIĆ-SKERO.

Office of the Public Prosecutor of Serbia: 11000 Belgrade, Nemanjina 24–26; tel. (11) 658755; Public Prosecutor MILOMIR JAKOVLJEVIĆ.

Religion

Most of the inhabitants of Serbia and Montenegro are, at least nominally, Christian, but there is a significant Muslim minority. The main Christian denomination is Eastern Orthodox, but there is a strong Roman Catholic presence. There are also small minorities of Old Catholics, Protestants and Jews.

CHRISTIANITY

The Eastern Orthodox Church

Serbian Orthodox Church (Srpska Pravoslavna Crkva): 11001 Belgrade, Kralja Petra 5, POB 182; tel. (11) 3283997; fax (11) 182780; e-mail pravoslavlje@spc.yu; internet www.spc.yu; 11m. adherents; Patriarch of Serbia, Archbishop of Peć and Metropolitan of Belgrade-Karlovci PAVLE.

Orthodox Metropolitanate of Montenegro and the Littoral—Serbian Orthodox Church (Pravoslavna Mitropolitija Crnogorsko Primorska—Srpska Pravoslavna Crkva): Cetinje; e-mail mitropolija@cg.yu; internet www.mitropolija.cg.yu; Metropolitan of Montenegro and the Littoral (Primorje) AMFILOHIJE (RADOVIĆ).

Montenegrin Orthodox Church (Crnogorska Pravoslavna Crkva): 81250 Cetinje, Gruda bb; tel. and fax (86) 31310; e-mail crkva@moc-cpc.org; internet www.moc-cpc.org; autocephalous until 1920, when it was dissolved and annexed to the Serbian Orthodox Church; restored 1993; Archbishop of Cetinje and Metropolitan of Montenegro His Excellency MIHAILO (DEDEIĆ).

The Roman Catholic Church

Serbia and Montenegro and the former Yugoslav republic of Macedonia together comprise two archdioceses (including one, Bar, directly responsible to the Holy See) and four dioceses. At 31 December 2003 adherents of the Roman Catholic Church represented about 5.2% of the total population.

Archbishop of Bar: Most Rev. JOSIP ZEF GASHI, 85000 Bar, Popovići 98; tel. (85) 344236; fax (85) 344233; e-mail zega_bar@cg.yu.

Archbishop of Belgrade: Most Rev. STANISLAV HOČEVAR, 11000 Belgrade, Svetozara Markovića 20; tel. (11) 3234846; fax (11) 3344613; e-mail nadbisbg@eunet.yu.

SERBIA AND MONTENEGRO

Old Catholic Church

Old Catholic Church in Serbia and Vojvodina: 11000 Belgrade; Dir of Diocese JOVAN AJHINGER.

Protestant Churches

Christian Nazarene Community (Hrišćanska nazarenska zajednica): 21000 Novi Sad, Vodnikova 12; tel. (21) 401049; Pres. KAROL HRUBIK VLADIMIR.

Christian Reformed Church: 24323 Feketic, Bratsva 26; tel. and fax (24) 738070; f. 1919; 22,000 mems; Bishop ISTVAN CSETE-SZEMESI.

Evangelical Christian Church of the Augsburg (Lutheran) Confession in Serbia-Vojvodina (Ágostai Hitvallású Evangélikus Keresztyén Egyház Szerbiában-Vajdaságban—AHEKESZ-V/ Evangelische Christliche Kirche A.B. in Serbien-Wojwodina): 24000 Subotica, Brace Radiča 17; tel. and fax (24) 721048; e-mail dolinsky@stcable.co.yu; internet www.lutheran.org.yu; Superintendent DOLINSKY ÁRPÁD.

Seventh-Day Adventist Church (Hrišćanska adventistička crkva): 11000 Belgrade, Radoslava Grujića 4; tel. (11) 2448824; e-mail hacbg@eunet.yu; internet www.hac-beograd.org; Pres. RADIŠA ANTIĆ.

Slovak Evangelical Church of the Augsburg (Lutheran) Confession: 21000 Novi Sad, Karadžićeva 2; tel. (21) 6611882; e-mail secav@eunet.yu; 50,000 mems (2002); Bishop Dr SAMUEL VRBOVSKY.

Union of Baptist Churches in Serbia: 11000 Belgrade, Slobodanke D. Savic 33; tel. and fax (11) 410964; f. 1992; Gen. Sec. Rev. AVRAM DEGA.

ISLAM

Almost 20% of the Montenegrin population profess Islam as their faith, many being ethnic Slav Muslims of the Sandžak region (which was partitioned between Montenegro and Serbia in 1913). Most Muslims in Serbia are ethnic Albanians, mainly resident in the province of Kosovo, but there are also ethnic Slav Muslims in the part of Sandžak located in south-west Serbia. Serbian Islam is predominantly Sunni, although a Dervish sect, introduced in 1974, is prominent among the Albanian population (with some 50,000 adherents, mainly in Kosovo).

Islamic Community: 38000 Priština; Pres. of the Mesihat Dr REDZEP BOJE.

JUDAISM

Federation of Jewish Communities in Serbia and Montenegro: Belgrade, Kralja Petra 71A/III, POB 512; tel. (11) 624359; fax (11) 2621837; e-mail office@savezscg.net; f. 1919, revived 1944; Pres. ACA SINGER.

The Press

In 2001 some 607 newspapers and 491 periodicals were published in Serbia and Montenegro.

PRINCIPAL DAILIES
(In Serbian, except where otherwise stated)

Belgrade

Blic: 11000 Belgrade, Masarikova 5; tel. (11) 3619471; fax (11) 3619326; e-mail redakcija@blic.co.yu; internet www.blic.co.yu; f. 1996; Editor-in-Chief VESLIN SIMONOVIĆ; circ. 230,000.

Borba: 11000 Belgrade, trg Nikole Pasica 7; tel. (11) 334531; fax (11) 344913; e-mail borba@bits.net; internet www.borba.co.yu; f. 1922; morning; Editor-in-Chief SRDJAN PETKOVIĆ.

Politika: 11000 Belgrade, Makedonska 29; tel. (11) 3373111; fax (11) 3373164; e-mail redakcija@politika.co.yu; internet www.politika.co.yu; f. 1904; Dir-Gen. DARKO RIBNIKOR; Editor-in-Chief MILON MIŠIĆ; circ. 130,000.

Politika Ekspres: 11000 Belgrade, Makedonska 29; tel. (11) 325630; evening; Editor-in-Chief MILE KORDIĆ; circ. 76,000.

Pregled: 11000 Belgrade, Toplicin venac 21/I; tel. and fax (11) 3282405; e-mail info@pregled.com; internet www.pregled.com; f. 1950; business and economics; Dir and Chief Editor SANDRA LABUDOVIĆ.

Večernje novosti (Evening News): 11000 Belgrade, trg Nikole Pašića 7; tel. (11) 3028000; e-mail internet@novosti.co.yu; internet www.novosti.co.yu; f. 1953; Dir and Editor-in-Chief MANOJLO MANJO VUKOTIĆ; circ. 270,000.

Niš

Narodne Novine (The People's News): 18000 Niš, Vojvode Gojka 14; internet www.narodne.com; morning.

Novi Sad

Dnevnik (Daily News): 21000 Novi Sad, Bulevar oslobođenja 81; tel. (21) 421493; e-mail redakcija@dnevnik.co.yu; internet www.dnevnik.co.yu; f. 1942 as *Slobodna Vojvodina* (Free Vojvodina); morning; Editor-in-Chief PETAR PETROVIĆ.

Magyar Szó (Hungarian Word): 21000 Novi Sad, V. Mišića 1; tel. (21) 456066; fax (21) 456482; e-mail foszerk@magyar-szo.co.yu; internet www.magyar-szo.co.yu; f. 1944; morning; in Hungarian; Editor-in-Chief PETER KOKAI; circ. 25,590.

Podgorica

Pobjeda (Victory): 81000 Podgorica, Bulevar Revolucije 11, POB 101; tel. (81) 245955; fax (81) 224901; e-mail direktor@pobjeda.cg.yu; internet www.pobjeda.co.yu; f. 1944; morning; Editor-in-Chief ANDRIJA RACKOVIĆ; circ. 18,000 (2003).

Publika (The Public): 81000 Podgorica, Crnogorskih serdara 8; tel. (81) 601430; fax (81) 625123; e-mail info.publika@cg.yu; internet www.publika.co.yu.

Priština

Koha Ditore: Priština; e-mail koha@magnet.ch; internet www.koha.net; in Albanian; Editor VETON SURROI.

PERIODICALS

Belgrade

Ekonomist: Belgrade, Kneza Mihaila 2–4; tel. (11) 3284034; e-mail office@ekonomist.co.yu; internet www.ekonomist.co.yu; f. 1948; quarterly; journal of the Yugoslav Association of Economists; Editor Dr HASAN HADŽIOMEROVIĆ.

Ekonomska Politika (Economic Policy): 11000 Belgrade, trg Nikole Pašića 7; tel. (11) 3398298; fax (11) 3398300; e-mail office@ekopol.co.yu; internet www.ekopol.co.yu; f. 1952; weekly; Dir CEDOMIR SOŠKIĆ; Editor-in-Chief SLAVKA KOVAČ.

Glas Javnosti (Voice of the Public): 11000 Belgrade, Vlajkovićeva 8; tel. (11) 3249125; fax (11) 3225095; e-mail webmaster@glas-javnosti.co.yu; internet www.glas-javnosti.co.yu; f. 1874; Dir and Editor-in-Chief PETAR LAZIĆ.

Ilustrovana Politika: 11000 Belgrade, 29. novembra 24; tel. (11) 3301442; fax (11) 3373346; f. 1958; weekly illustrated review; Gen. Dir DARKO RIBNIKAR; Editor-in-Chief GORDANA KNEŽEVIĆ; circ. 90,000.

Jisa Info: 11000 Belgrade, Zmaj Jovina 4; tel. (11) 620374; fax (11) 626576; e-mail jisa@jisa.org.yu; internet www.jisa.org.yu; f. 1993; publ by Jisa (Jedinstveni informatički savez Srbije i Crne Gore—Union of ICT Societies of Serbia and Montenegro); computing, technology; Dir and Editor-in-Chief DUBRAVKA ĐURIĆ.

Međunarodni Problemi/International Problems: 11000 Belgrade, Institute of International Politics and Economics, Makedonska 25; tel. (11) 3373633; fax (11) 3373835; e-mail branam@gmail.com; internet www.diplomacy.bg.ac.yu/mpro.htm; f. 1949; quarterly; in Serbian and English; Editor BRANA MARKOVIĆ; circ. 1,000.

Mikro/PC World: 11030 Belgrade, Požeška 81A; tel. (11) 5447971; fax (11) 542397; e-mail pisma@mikro.co.yu; internet www.mikro.co.yu; f. 1997; 11 a year; computing; Editorial Dir ALEKSANDAR SPASIĆ; circ. 23,000.

Nezavisna Svetlost: 34000 Kragujevac, Branka Radicevica 9; tel. and fax (34) 334746; e-mail nsvet@eunet.yu; internet www.svetlost.co.yu; f. 1995; weekly news; Editor-in-Chief MIROSLAV JOVANOVIĆ.

NIN—Nedeljne informativne novine (Weekly Informative News): 11000 Belgrade, Cetinjska 1, POB 208; tel. (11) 3373111; fax (11) 3373171; e-mail redakcija@nin.co.yu; internet www.nin.co.yu; f. 1935; politics, economics, culture; Dir DRAŠKO TANKOSIĆ; Editor-in-Chief SLOBODAN RELJIĆ; circ. 35,000.

Novi Glasnik (New Messenger): 11002 Belgrade, Balkanska 53; tel. (11) 645795; e-mail genstaffinfo@vj.yu; internet www.vj.yu/english/en_publikacije/glasnik.htm; f. 1993; 6 a year; publ. by Military Publishing Institute for the Armed Forces of Serbia and Montenegro; in Serbian and English; Editor-in-Chief Col MILAN SUMONJA.

Ošišani Jež: 11000 Belgrade, Resavska 28; tel. (11) 3232211; fax (11) 3232423; internet www.jez.co.yu; f. 1935 as *Jež* (Hedgehog); fortnightly; satirical; Editor RADIVOJE BOJIČIĆ; circ. 50,000.

Politikin Zabavnik: Belgrade, 11000 Makedonska 29; f. 1939; weekly; comic; Editor RADOMIR SOŠKIĆ; circ. 41,000.

Pravoslavlje (Orthodoxy): 11000 Belgrade, Kralja Petra 5; tel. (11) 3282596; fax (11) 630865; e-mail pravoslavlje@spc.yu; internet www.pravoslavlje.com; f. 1967; fortnightly; Orthodox Christian.

Survey Serbia & Montenegro/Pregled SCG: 11000 Belgrade, Dečanska 8, POB 677; tel. (11) 3233610; fax (11) 3240291; e-mail info@yusurvey.co.yu; internet www.yusurvey.co.yu; f. 1960 as

Yugoslav Survey / Jugoslovenski pregled; quarterly; general reference publication of basic documentary information about Serbia and Montenegro in English and Serbian; Editor-in-Chief ILE KOVAČEVIĆ.

Svet Kompjutera (The World of the Computer): 11000 Belgrade, Cetinjska 1; tel. (11) 3301498; fax (11) 3373358; e-mail editors@sk.co.yu; internet www.sk.co.yu; f. 1984; monthly; computing; Editor ZORAN MOŠORINSKI.

Viva: 11000 Belgrade, Cetinjska 1V; tel. (11) 3220132; fax (11) 3220552; e-mail viva@politika.co.uk; monthly; health; Editor DRAGUTIN GREGORIĆ; circ. 25,000.

Vojska (Soldier): 11002 Belgrade, Katanicveva 16; internet www.vj.yu/english/en_publikacije/vojska.htm; tel. and fax (11) 644042; f. 1945; weekly; publ. by Military Publishing Institute for the Armed Forces of Serbia and Montenegro; weekly; Editor-in-Chief Col SLAVOLJUB RANĐELOVIC.

Vreme (Time): Belgrade, Mišarska 12–14; tel. (11) 3234774; fax (11) 3238662; internet www.vreme.com; Editor-in-Chief DRAGOLJUB ŽARKOVIĆ.

Yugoslav Journal of Operations Research: 11000 Belgrade, Faculty of Organizational Sciences, University of Belgrade, Jove Ilica 154; tel. (11) 3972383; fax (11) 461221; e-mail yujor@fon.fonbg.ac.yu; internet yujor.fon.bg.ac.yu; 2 a year; systems science and management science; Editor RADIVOJ PETROVIĆ; circ. 700.

Novi Sad

Letopis Matice Srpske: 21000 Novi Sad, Matice srpske 1; tel. (21) 27622; fax (21) 528901; e-mail ms@maticasrpska.org.yu; internet www.maticasrpska.org.yu/pages/izdanja/letopis.htm; f. 1824; monthly; literary review; Editor Prof. Dr SLAVKO GORDÍC.

Podgorica

Koha (Time): Podgorica; f. 1978; Albanian-language magazine; circ. 2,000.

Stvaranje: Podgorica, Revolucije 78; f. 1946; monthly; literary review; publ. by the Literary Asscn of Montenegro; Man. RANKO JOVOVIĆ.

Priština

Koha (Time): Priština; f. 1994; Albanian-language magazine; Editor-in-Chief VETON SUROI.

Zeri: Priština; political weekly; in Albanian; Editor-in-Chief BLERIM SHALA.

NEWS AGENCIES

Beta News Agency: 11000 Belgrade, Kraljana Milana 4; tel. (11) 3602400; fax (11) 642551; e-mail marketing@beta.co.yu; internet www.beta.co.yu; f. 1992; regional independent news service; Dir LJUBICA MARKOVIĆ; Editor-in-Chief DRAGAN JANJIĆ.

Tanjug News Agency (Novinska Agencija Tanjug): 11001 Belgrade, Obilićev Venac 2, POB 439; tel. (11) 3281608; fax (11) 633550; e-mail direkcija@tanjug.co.yu; internet www.tanjug.co.yu; f. 1943; press and information agency; in Serbian, English, French and Spanish; Dir and Editor-in-Chief DUŠAN ĐORĐEVIĆ.

Foreign Bureaux

Agence France-Presse (AFP) (France): 11000 Belgrade, trg Nikole Pasica 2; tel. (11) 3232622; fax (11) 620638; e-mail afpbgd@eunet.yu; Bureau Chief JEAN-EUDES BARBIER.

Agenzia Nazionale Stampa Associata (ANSA) (Italy): 11000 Belgrade, Braće Jugovića 5; tel. (11) 3281232; fax (11) 3281609; e-mail ansa@eunet.yu; Bureau Chief LUCIANO CAUSA.

Allgemeiner Deutschen Nachrichtendienst (ADN) (Germany): 11000 Belgrade, Šiva Stena 1A; tel. (11) 461752; Correspondent Dr WILLFRIED MUCH.

Associated Press (AP) (USA): 11000 Belgrade, Dositejeva 12; tel. (11) 631553; Correspondent IVAN STEFANOVIĆ.

Bulgarska Telegrafna Agentsia (BTA) (Bulgaria): Belgrade; tel. (11) 636361; fax (11) 636361; Correspondent NIKOLA KITSEVSKI.

Česká tisková kancelář (ČTK) (Czech Republic): 11070 Belgrade, 190/Stan. 6/III, Blok 37; tel. (11) 134892; Correspondent MIROSLAV JILEK.

ITAR—TASS (Information Telegraph Agency of Russia—Telegraphic Agency of the Sovereign Countries (Russia): Belgrade, Ognjena Price 17; tel. (11) 4446928; Correspondent MIKHAIL ABELEV.

Korean Central News Agency (KCNA) (Democratic People's Republic of Korea): Belgrade, Dr Milutina Ivkovića 9; tel. (11) 668426; Bureau Chief KIM JONG SE.

Magyar Távirati Iroda (MTI) (Hungary): 11030 Belgrade, Vladimira Rolovica 176; tel. (11) 506508; Correspondent GYÖRGY WALKO.

RIA—Novosti (Russian Information Agency—News) (Russia): Belgrade, Strahinjića Bana 50; tel. (11) 629419; Bureau Chief SERGEI GRIZUNOV.

United Press International (UPI) (USA): 11000 Belgrade, Generala Zdanova 19; tel. (11) 342490; Correspondent NESHO DJURIĆ.

Xinhua (New China) News Agency (People's Republic of China): Belgrade; tel. (11) 493789; Correspondent YANG DAZHOU.

PRESS ASSOCIATIONS

Association of Professional Journalists of Montenegro: 81000 Podgorica, 13 Jul 25; tel. and fax (81) 243169; e-mail publika.cg.yu; Pres. DANILO BURZAN, RADOVAN MILJANIĆ.

Independent Association of Journalists of Serbia: 11000 Belgrade, Resavska 28/II; tel. (11) 3343255; fax (11) 3343136; e-mail ijas@eunet.yu; internet www.nuns.org.yu; Pres. NEBOJŠA BUGARINOVIĆ.

Publishers

Alfa-Narodna knjiga (Alfa-People's Book): 11000 Belgrade, Šafarikova 11; tel. (11) 3227426; fax (11) 3227946; e-mail tea@eunet.yu; internet www.narodnaknjiga.co.yu; f. 1950; fiction, non-fiction, children's books and dictionaries; Gen. Man. MILIČKO MIJOVIĆ.

BIGZ (Beogradski izdavačko-grafički zavod) Publishing a.d. (Belgrade Publishing and Graphics Cp): 11000 Belgrade, bulevar vojvode Mišića 17/III; tel. (11) 3691259; fax (11) 3690519; e-mail office@bigz-publishing.co.yu; internet www.bigz-publishing.co.yu; f. 1831; privately owned; literature and criticism, children's books, pocket books, popular science, philosophy, politics; Dir MIRJANA MILORADOVIĆ.

Dečje novine: 32300 Gornji Milanovac, T. Matijevića 4; tel. (32) 711759; fax (32) 711248; general literature, children's books, science, science fiction, textbooks; Gen. Dir MIROSLAV PETROVIĆ.

Forum Publishing House: 21000 Novi Sad, Vojvode Mišića 1, POB 200; tel. (21) 611300; f. 1957; newspapers, periodicals and books in Hungarian; Dir GYULA GOBBY.

Građevinska Knjiga (Citizens' Books) Publishing House: 11000 Belgrade, trg Nikole Pašića 8/II; tel. (11) 3233565; fax (11) 3233563; f. 1948; technical, scientific and educational textbooks; Dir LJUBINKO ANĐELIĆ.

Jedinstvo (Unity) Publishing House: 38000 Priština, Dom štampe bb, POB 81; tel. (38) 27549; fax (38) 29809; poetry, novels, general literature, science, children's books; Dir JORDAN RISTIĆ.

Jugoslovenska knjiga (Yugoslav Books) Publishing House: 11000 Belgrade, trg Republike 5, POB 36; tel. (11) 621992; fax (11) 625970; art, economics and culture; Dir ZORAN NIKODIJEVIĆ.

Vuk Karadžič Publishing House: 11000 Belgrade, Kraljevića Marka 9, POB 762; tel. (11) 628066; fax (11) 623150; scientific and academic literature, popular science, children's books, general; Gen. Man. VOJIN ANČIĆ.

Matice srpske Publishing House: 21000 Novi Sad, trg Toze Markovića 2; tel. (21) 420199; fax (21) 27281; e-mail m.grujic@sezampro.yu; internet www.maticasrpska.org.yu; f. 1826; domestic and foreign fiction and humanities; Man. Dir MILORAD GRUJIĆ.

Medicinska knjiga (Medical Books) Publishing House: 11001 Belgrade, Mata Vidakovića 24–26; tel. (11) 458165; f. 1947; medicine, pharmacology, stomatology, veterinary; Dir MILE MEDIĆ.

Minerva Publishing House: 24000 Subotica, trg 29 novembra 3; tel. (24) 25712; fax (24) 23208; novels and general; Dir LADISLAV ŠEBEK.

Naučna knjiga (Scientific Books) Publishing House: 11000 Belgrade, Uzun Mirkova 5; tel. (11) 637220; f. 1947; school, college and university textbooks, publications of scientific bodies; Dir Dr BLAŽO PEROVIĆ.

Nolit: 11000 Belgrade, Terazije 27; tel. (11) 3245017; fax (11) 627285; f. 1928; belles-lettres, philosophy and fine art; scientific and popular literature; Dir-Gen. RADIVOJE NESIĆ; Editor-in-Chief RADIVOJE MIKIĆ.

Obod: 81250 Cetinje, Njegoševa 3; tel. (86) 21331; fax (86) 21953; general literature; Dir VASKO JANKOVIĆ.

Panorama: Priština; f. 1994; publishes newspapers and journals in Serbian, Albanian and Turkish; Dir JORDAN RISTIĆ.

Pobjeda (Victory) Publishing House: 81000 Podgorica, Južni bul. bb; tel. (81) 44433; f. 1974; poetry, fiction, lexicography and scientific works.

Prosveta (Education) Publishing House: 11000 Belgrade, Čika Ljubina 1; tel. (11) 629843; fax (11) 182581; f. 1944; general literature, art books, dictionaries, encyclopaedias, science, music; Dir BUDIMIR RUDOVIĆ.

SERBIA AND MONTENEGRO   Directory

Rad (Labour) Publishing House: 11000 Belgrade, Dečanska 12; tel. (11) 3239998; fax (11) 3230923; e-mail rad@radbooks.co.yu; internet www.radbooks.co.yu; f. 1949; politics, economics, sociology, psychology, literature, biographies; Man. Dir SIMON SIMONOVIĆ; Editor-in-Chief NOVICA TADIĆ.

Rilindja Publishing House: 38000 Priština, Dom štampe bb; tel. (38) 23868; popular science, literature, children's fiction and travel books, textbooks in Albanian; Dir NAZMI RRAHMANI.

Savremena administracija (Contemporary Administration) Publishing House: 11000 Belgrade, Crnotravska 7–9; tel. (11) 667633; fax (11) 667277; f. 1954; economy, law, science university textbooks; Dir TOMISLAV JOVIĆ.

Sportska knjiga (Sports Books) Publishing House: 11000 Belgrade, Makedonska 19; tel. (11) 320226; f. 1949; sport, chess, hobbies; Dir BORISLAV PETROVIĆ.

Srpska književna zadruga (Serb Publishing Collective): 11000 Belgrade, Srpskih Vladara 19/I; tel. (11) 330305; fax (11) 626224; f. 1892; works of classical and modern Serb writers, and translations of works of foreign writers; Pres. RADOVAN SAMARDŽIĆ; Editor RADOMIR RADOVANAC.

Svetovi: 21000 Novi Sad, Arse Teodorovića 11; tel. (21) 28032; fax (21) 28036; general; Dir JOVAN ZIVLAK.

Tehnička Knjiga (Technical Books) Publishing House: 11000 Belgrade, Vojvode Stepe 89; tel. (11) 468596; fax (11) 473442; f. 1948; technical works, popular science, reference books, hobbies; Dir RADIVOJE GRBOVIĆ.

Zavod za udžbenike i nastavna sredstva (Institute for School Books and Teaching Aids): 11000 Belgrade, Obilićev Venac 5; tel. (11) 638463; fax (11) 637426; e-mail press@zavod.co.yu; internet www.zavod.co.yu; fax (11) 630014; f. 1957; textbooks and teaching aids; Dir RADOSLAV PETKOVIĆ.

PUBLISHERS' ASSOCIATIONS

Asscn of Publishers and Booksellers of Serbia and Montenegro (Udruženje izdavača i knjižara Srbije i Crne Gore): 11000 Belgrade, Kneza Miloša 25, POB 570; tel. (11) 642533; fax (11) 646339; e-mail ognjenl@eunet.yu; f. 1954; organizes Belgrade International Book Fair; Dir OGNJEN LAKIĆEVIĆ; 116 mem. organizations.

Asscn of Publishers and Booksellers of Vojvodina (Poslovno udruženje izdavača i knjižara Vojvodine): 21000 Novi Sad; tel. and fax (21) 4720452; e-mail info@knjigavoj.co.yu; internet www.knjigavoj.co.yu; f. 2001; Dir ROMAN VEHOVEC; Chair. of Council ĐEZE BORDAS.

Broadcasting and Communications

TELECOMMUNICATIONS

063 Mobtel Srbija: 11070 Belgrade, Bulevar Nikole Tesle 42A; tel. (11) 3013267; e-mail pr@mobtel.co,yu; internet www.mobtel.co.yu; f. 1994; 51% owned by BK Trade Moscow (Russia), 49% by Telekom Srbija; provides mobile cellular telecommunications in Serbia.

Monet: 81000 Podgorica, Bulevar svetog Petra cetinjskog bb; tel. (81) 400801; fax (81) 225752; e-mail office@monetcg.com; internet www.monetcg.com; f. 2000; provides mobile cellular telecommunications services in Montenegro.

ProMonte: 81000 Podgorica, Bulevar Džordža Vašingtona 83; tel. (81) 235000; fax (81) 235035; e-mail info@promonte.com; internet www.promonte.com; f. 1996; 100% owned by Telenor (Norway); provides mobile cellular telecommunications services in Montenegro; Gen. Dir IVAR SLIPER.

Telekom Srbija (Telecom Serbia): 11000 Belgrade, Takovska 7; tel. (11) 3229991; e-mail webmaster@telekom.yu; internet www.telekomsrbija.com; 20% owned by OTE (Greece; provides fixed line and mobile cellular telecommunications services in Serbia; Dir-Gen. DRAŠKO PETROVIĆ.

BROADCASTING

Association of Independent Electronic Media: 11000 Belgrade, Marsala Birjuzova 3/IV; tel. and fax (11) 3034807; e-mail anem@anem.org.yu; internet www.anem.org.yu; f. 1993; comprises 16 television and 28 radio stations, and 70 affiliated orgs; Chair. SLOBODAN STOJSIĆ.

Radio

Međunarodni Radio Srbija i Crna Gora (International Radio Serbia and Montenegro): 11000 Belgrade, Hilandarska 2, POB 200; tel. (11) 3244455; e-mail radioyu@bitsyu.net; internet www.radioyu.org; f. 1951; fmrly Radio Jugoslavija (Radio Yugoslavia); state-owned short-wave station; broadcasts daily in Serbian, English, French, German, Russian and Spanish; Dir MILENA JOKIĆ.

Radio B92: 11000 Belgrade, Bulevar Avnoja 64; tel. (11) 3012000; fax (11) 3012001; internet www.b92.net; f. 1989; independent; Dir VERAN MATIĆ; Dir of Radio Programming GORICA NEŠOVIĆ.

Radio D: 81000 Podgorica, 13 jula bb; tel. (81) 238909; e-mail mladenm@cg.yu; f. 2000; independent; Dir SVETLANA VUČELJIĆ.

Radio JAT: 11000 Belgrade, Svetog Save 1/XVI; tel. (11) 2440142; e-mail radio_jat@jat.com; internet www.radiojat.co.yu.

Radiotelevizija Crne Gore (Radio and Television of Montenegro): 81000 Podgorica, Cetinjski put bb; tel. (81) 225607; fax (81) 245595; internet www.rtcg.org; f. 1944; 2 radio channels—Prvi program (Channel 1) and Radio 98; Dir-Gen. RADOVAN MILJANIĆ; Dir of Radio BUDIMIR RAIČEVIĆ.

Radiotelevizija Košava: 11000 Belgrade, Masarikova 5; tel. (11) 3061491; fax (11) 3612135; e-mail office@kanal1.co.yu; internet www.kosava.co.yu; f. 1994; radio station broadcasting popular music and talk programmes to most regions of Serbia.

Radiotelevizija Srbije (RTS) (Radio-Television of Serbia): 11000 Belgrade, Takovska 10; tel. (11) 3212200; fax (11) 3212211; e-mail rtstv@rts.co.yu; internet www.rts.co.yu; f. 1929; 5 radio programmes; comprises Radiotelevizija Beograd (Radio-Television of Belgrade), Radiotelevizija Novi Sad (Radio-Television of Novi Sad, Vojvodina) and Radiotelevizija Priština (Radio-Television of Priština, Kosovo and Metohija); Dir-Gen. ALEKSANDAR TIJANIĆ.

Radio TV Bajina Basta: 31250 Bajina Basta, Svetosavska 34; tel. (31) 851688; fax (31) 853162; e-mail office@bajinabasta.org; internet www.bajinabasta.org; f. 1986; independent radio and television station; Dir BOBAN TOMIĆ.

Television

B92 Televizija: 11000 Belgrade, Bulevar Avnoja 64; tel. (11) 3012000; fax (11) 3012001; internet www.b92.net; f. 2000; independent; Dir VERAN MATIĆ; Dir of Programming IVA IVANIŠEVIĆ.

BK Telecom (BK): 1070 Belgrade, Nikole Tesle 42A; tel. (11) 3013555; fax (11) 3013526; e-mail office@bktv.com; internet www.bktv.com; f. 1994; independent television station; Dir-Gen. Dr TIMOHIR SIMIĆ; Editor-in-Chief MILOMIR MARIĆ.

Radiotelevizija Crne Gore (Radio and Television of Montenegro): 81000 Podgorica, Cetinjski put bb; tel. (81) 225602; fax (81) 225108; internet www.rtcg.org; f. 1971; 2 terrestrial television channels and 1 satellite channel; Dir-Gen. RADOVAN MILJANIĆ; Dir of Television VELJO JAUKOVIĆ.

Radiotelevizija Srbije: 11000 Belgrade, Takovska 10; tel. (11) 3212200; fax (11) 3212211; e-mail rtstv@rts.co.yu; internet www.rts.co.yu; f. 1929; 5 radio programmes; comprises Radiotelevizija Beograd (Radio-Television of Belgrade), Radiotelevizija Novi Sad (Radio-Television of Novi Sad, Vojvodina) and Radiotelevizija Priština (Radio-Television of Priština, Kosovo); Dir-Gen. ALEKSANDAR TIJANIĆ.

Finance

(cap. = capital; res = reserves; dep. = deposits; m. = million; amounts in convertible Yugoslav dinars unless otherwise stated; br. = branch)

BANKING

Central Banking System

In 2003, following the reconstitution of the Federal Republic of Yugoslavia as the State Union of Serbia and Montenegro, the National Bank of Yugoslavia became Serbia's central bank, and was renamed the National Bank of Serbia. Its functions include the issue of money, provision of credit to banks and government authorities, control of credits and bank activities, recommendation of legislation relating to the activities, recommendation of legislation relating to the foreign exchange system and its implementation, management of gold and foreign exchange reserves, control of foreign exchange operations and other special activities. A Central Bank of Montenegro was established in 2001.

Central Bank of Montenegro (Centralna Banka Crne Gore—CBCG): 81000 Podgorica, Bulevar Petra Cetinjskog 6; tel. (81) 225150; fax (81) 248801; e-mail info@cb-cg.org; internet www.cb-mn.org; f. 2001; cap. 2.6m., res 29.9m., dep. 40.8m. (2003); Gov. LJUBISA KRGOVIĆ.

National Bank of Serbia (Narodna banka Srbije): 11000 Belgrade, Kralja Petra 12, POB 1010; tel. (11) 3027100; fax (11) 3027113; e-mail kabinet@nbs.yu; internet www.nbs.yu; f. 1884; fmrly National Bank of Yugoslavia; cap. 2,278m., dep. 114,565m., total assets 273,436m. (Dec. 2003); Gov. RADOVAN JELAŠIĆ; 4 brs.

Other Banks

A Banka: 11030 Belgrade, Požeška 65B; tel. (11) 3050300; fax (11) 3540930; e-mail banka@alcoyu.co.yu; internet www.alcobanka.co.yu; f. 1996 as Alco Banka; present name adopted 2004; cap. 535.9m., res 162.0m., dep. 1,203.7m. (Dec. 2002); Chair. MIROLJUB ALEKSIĆ.

Continental Banka a.d.: 21000 Novi Sad, trg Mladenaca 1–3; tel. (21) 615500; fax (21) 616560; e-mail cont@cont.co.yu; internet www.cont.co.yu; f. 1991; cap. 3,772.8m., dep. 4,975.9m. (Dec. 2003); Chair. ĐORĐE ĐUKIĆ.

Delta Banka a.d. Beograd: 11070 Belgrade, Milentija Popovica St 7B; tel. (11) 2011213; fax (11) 2011207; e-mail dbanka@deltabanka.co.yu; internet www.deltabanka.co.yu; f. 1991; cap. 3,553.1m., res 1,338.8m., dep. 36,718.3m. (Dec. 2003); Pres. MIROSLAV MIŠKOVIĆ; 160 brs.

Hypo Alpe-Adria-Bank a.d. Beograd: 11070 Novi Beograd, Goce Delčeva 44; tel. (11) 671531; fax (11) 672873; e-mail office@hypo-alpe-adria.co.yu; internet www.hypo-alpe-adria.co.yu; f. 1991 as Depozitno-Kreditna Banka; merged with Hypo Alpe-Adria-Bank 2002; cap. 1,654.1m., res 32.8m., dep. 4,796.9m. (Dec. 2003); Gen. Man. MARKUS FERSTL.

Jubanka a.d. Beograd: 11000 Belgrade, Kralja Milana 11; tel. (11) 3234931; fax (11) 3246840; e-mail jubanka@jubanka.com; internet www.jubanka.com; f. 1956; cap. 6,277.9m., res 60.4m., dep. 8,755.1m. (Dec. 2003); Dir-Gen. BORISLAV ĐOKIĆ; 17 brs.

Jubmes Banka—Jugoslovenska Banka Za Medjunarodnu Ekonomsku Saradnju (Yugoslav Bank for International Economic Co-operation): 11000 Belgrade, Bulevar Avnoja 121, POB 219; tel. (11) 3115270; fax (11) 3110217; e-mail jubmes@jubmes.co.yu; internet www.jubmes.co.yu; f. 1979; focuses on the financing of export-orientated and development projects; cap. 849m., res 182m., dep. 1,111m. (Dec. 2003); Pres. DARKO ČUKIĆ.

Komercijalna Banka a.d. Beograd: 11000 Belgrade, Svetog Save 14; tel. (11) 3080100; fax (11) 3441335; e-mail posta@kombank.com; internet www.kombank.com; cap. 5,036.7m., res 474.4m., dep. 36,969.1m. (Dec. 2003); Pres. IVICA SMOLIĆ.

Metals Banka a.d. Novi Sad: 21000 Novi Sad, Bulevar Cara Lazara 7A; tel. (21) 450695; fax (21) 350611; e-mail metalsb@eunet.yu; internet www.metals-banka.co.yu; f. 1990; cap. 818.9m., res 12.3m., dep. 1,097.9m. (2003); Gen. Man. ANANIJE PAVIĆEVIĆ.

Novosadska Banka a.d.: 21000 Novi Sad, Bulevar Mihajla Pupina 3; tel. (21) 27733; fax (21) 29507; e-mail info@novban.co.yu; internet www.novban.co.yu; f. 1864; cap. 2,777.5m., res 86.7m., dep. 7,422.2m. (Dec. 2003); Gen. Man. VOJIN BJELICA.

Panonska Banka a.d.: 21001 Novi Sad, 76 Bulevar Oslobodjenja, POB 351; tel. (21) 4887100; fax (21) 6611977; e-mail office@panban.co.yu; internet www.panban.co.yu; f. 1974 as branch of Vojvodjanska Banka-Centrala; cap. 3,153.3m., res 113.5m., dep. 4,382.2m. (Dec. 2003); Gen. Man. SRĐAN PETROVIĆ; 12 brs.

Privredna Banka Beograd a.d.: 11000 Belgrade, Bulevar Vojske Jugoslavije 4; tel. (11) 641255; fax (11) 641894; internet www.pbbad.com; f. 1973; cap. 854.1m., res 36.0m., dep. 2,501.2m. (Dec. 2003); Gen. Man. MILOVAN KVRGIĆ.

ProCredit Bank a.d. Serbia: 11000 Belgrade, 29 novembra 68c; tel. (11) 2077906; fax (11) 2077905; e-mail info@procreditbank.co.yu; internet www.procreditbank.co.yu; f. 2001 as Micro Finance Banka; present name adopted 2003; cap. 720.0m., res 54.7m., dep. 4,225.8m. (Dec. 2003); Chair. Dr KLAUS GLAUBITT.

ProCredit Bank Kosova: Priština, Skenderbeu, Kosovo; tel. (39) 248778; fax (38) 248777; e-mail payment@mebkosovo.com; internet www.mebkosovo.com; f. 2000 as Micro Enterprise Bank; present name adopted 2003; cap. €10.1m., res €0.5m., dep. €254.8m. (Dec. 2003); Gen. Man. FRIEDER WÖHRMANN.

Vojvodjanska Banka, a.d. Novi Sad: 21000 Novi Sad, POB 391, Trg Slobode 7; tel. (21) 4886600; fax (21) 624859; e-mail office@voban.co.yu; internet www.voban.co.yu; f. 1962; cap. 6,863.0m., res 187.9m., dep. 21,372.6m. (Dec. 2003); Gen. Man. ZORAN RADONJIĆ; 200 brs.

Zepter Banka a.d. Beograd: 11070 Belgrade, Bulevar Mihaila Pupina 117; tel. (11) 3113233; fax (11) 138603; e-mail office@banka.zepter.co.yu; internet www.banka.zepter.co.yu; cap. 662.9m., res 122.2m., dep. 3,689.1m. (Dec. 2002); Pres. PHILIP ZEPTER.

Banking Association

Association of Banks of Serbia (Udruženje banaka Srbije): 11001 Belgrade, Bulevar kralja Aleksandra 86; tel. (11) 3020760; fax (11) 3370179; e-mail ubs@finnet.co.yu; internet www.finnet.co.yu; f. 1955; association of business banks; works on improving inter-bank co-operation, organizes agreements of mutual interest for banks, gives expert assistance, establishes co-operation with foreign banks, other financial institutions and their associations, represents banks in relations with the Government and the National Bank of Serbia; Sec.-Gen. VEROLJUB DUGALIĆ.

STOCK EXCHANGES

Belgrade Stock Exchange (Beogradska Berza): 11070 Belgrade, Omladinskih brigada 1, POB 50; tel. (11) 3117297; fax (11) 3117304; e-mail marketing@belex.co.yu; internet www.belex.co.yu; Chair. of Bd DARKO ČUKIĆ.

Montenegro Stock Exchange (Montenegroberza): 81000 Podgorica, Zgrada Vektre 2A; tel. (81) 235051; fax (81) 205940; e-mail mberza@cg.yu; internet www.montenegroberza.com; f. 1993; Pres. of Board of Dirs Dr ŠALETA ĐUROVIĆ; Dir-Gen. DEJANA ŠUŠKAVČEVIĆ.

INSURANCE

Dunav Osiguranje (Danube Insurance Co): 11001 Belgrade, Makedonska 4, POB 624; tel. (11) 3224001; fax (11) 624652; e-mail info@dunav.com; internet www.dunav.com; f. 1974; all types of insurance and reinsurance.

Lovćen Osiguranje a.d. Podgorica (Lovćen Insurance Co Podgorica): 81000 Podgorica, ul. Slobode 13 A; tel. (81) 404400; fax (81) 245482; e-mail lovosig@cg.yu; internet www.lovcenosiguranje.cg.yu; insurance and reinsurance; Sec. PURIĆ RADENKO.

Trade and Industry

GOVERNMENT AGENCIES

Foreign Trade Institute (Institut za Spoljnu Trgovinu): 11000 Belgrade, Moše Pijade 8; tel. (11) 3235391; fax (11) 3235306; e-mail radovank@eunet.yu; Dir Dr SLOBODAN MRKŠA.

Kosovo Trust Agency: Green Bldg, Rruga Vellusha II, Priština; tel. (38) 400255; fax (38) 248076; e-mail soetenders@eumik.org; internet www.kta-kosovo.org; Kosovo's privatization agency, supervised by UN mission in the province.

Serbian Investment and Export Promotion Agency (Agencija za strana ulaganja i promociju izvoza—SIEPA): 11000 Belgrade, Vlajkovićeva 3; tel. (11) 3398550; fax (11) 3398814; e-mail office@siepa.sr.gov.yu; internet www.siepa.sr.gov.yu.

CHAMBERS OF COMMERCE

Chamber of Commerce and Industry of Serbia and Montenegro (Privredna Komora Srbije i Crne Gore): 11000 Belgrade, Terazije 23, POB 1003; tel. (11) 3248123; fax (11) 3248754; e-mail info@pkj.co.yu; internet www.pkj.co.yu; f. 1990; independent organization affiliating all domestic economic organizations; Pres. Dr SLOBODAN KORAĆ.

Chamber of Commerce of Montenegro (Privredna Komora Crne Gore): 81000 Podgorica, Novaka Miloševa 29; tel. (81) 31071; fax (81) 34926; e-mail pkcg@cg.yu; internet www.pkcg.org; Pres. VOJIN ĐUKANOVIĆ.

Chamber of Commerce of Serbia (Privredna Komora Srbije): 11000 Belgrade, Gen. Zdanova 13–15; tel. (11) 3240611; fax (11) 3230949; e-mail pksrbije@pks.co.yu; internet www.pks.co.yu; Pres. RADOSLAV VESELINOVIĆ.

UTILITIES

Electricity

Elektroprivreda Crne Gore a.d. Nicšić (Montenegro Electricity Corpn): 81400 Nicšić, ul. Vuka Karadžića 2; tel. and fax (83) 214252; e-mail Listepcg@cg.yu; internet www.epcg.cg.yu; production, transmission and distribution of electric power in Montenegro.

Elektroprivreda Srbije (EPS) (Serbia Electricity Corpn): 11000 Belgrade, Balkanska 13; tel. (11) 3610580; fax (11) 3611908; e-mail momcilo.cebalovic@eps.co.yu; internet www.eps.co.yu; state-owned; production, transmission and distribution of electric power in Serbia (incl. Kosovo and Metohija); Dir-Gen. VLADIMIR ĐORĐEVIĆ.

Gas

NIS-Energogas: 11070 Belgrade, Autoput 11; tel. (11) 2672033; fax (11) 602200; e-mail energogas@energogas.co.yu; internet www.energogas.co.yu; subsidiary of Naftna Industrija Srbije (Petroleum Industry of Serbia); transportation and distribution of natural gas and liquid petrol gas, civil engineering.

TRADE UNIONS

Association of Free and Independent Trade Unions: 11000 Belgrade, Karađorđeva 71; tel. and fax (11) 2623671; e-mail asns@asns.org.yu; internet www.asns.org.yu; Pres. RANKA SAVIĆ.

Confederation of Autonomous Trade Unions of Serbia and Montenegro (Savez Samostalnih Sindikata Srbije i Crne Gore):

SERBIA AND MONTENEGRO

11000 Belgrade, trg Nikola Pašić 5; tel. (11) 3230922; fax (11) 3241911; e-mail sssj@ptt.yu; 600,000 mems.

Agricultural, Food and Tobacco Industry Workers' Union (Sindikat radnika poljprivrede, prehrambene i duvanske industrije): Pres. Federal Cttee ERNE KIČI.

Building Workers' Union (Sindikat radnika gradjevinarstva): Pres. Federal Cttee MILOŠ ŽORIĆ.

Catering and Tourism Workers' Union (Sindikat radnika u ugostiteljstvu i turizmu): Pres. Federal Cttee MILAN FRKOVIĆ.

Chemistry and Non-Metallic Industry Workers' Union (Sindikat radnika hemije i nemetala): Pres. Federal Cttee STOJMIR DOMAZETOVSKI.

Commerce Workers' Union (Sindikat radnika u trgovini): Pres. Federal Cttee LJUBICA BRAČKO.

Education, Science and Culture Workers' Union (Sindikat radnika delatnosti vaspitanja, obrazovanja, nauke i kulture): Pres. Federal Cttee BORIS LIPUŽIĆ.

Energy Workers' Union (Sindikat radnika energetike): Pres. Federal Cttee VASKRSIJE SAVIČIĆ.

Forestry and Wood Industry Workers' Union (Sindikat radnika šumarstva i prerade drveta): Pres. Federal Cttee DRAGOLJUB OBRADOVIĆ.

Health and Social Care Workers' Union (Sindikat radnika delatnosti zdravstva i socijalne zaštite): Pres. Federal Cttee LJILJANA MILOŠEVIĆ.

Metal Production and Manufacturing Workers' Union (Sindikat radnika proizvodnje i prerade metala): Pres. Federal Cttee SLAVKO URŠIĆ.

Public Utilities and Handicrafts Workers' Union (Sindikat radnika u komunalnoj privredi i zanatstvu): Pres. Federal Cttee JOSIP KOLAR.

Printing, Newspaper, Publishing and Information Workers' Union (Sindikat radnika grafičke, novinsko-izdavačke i informativne delatnosti): Pres. Federal Cttee BORIS BIŠĆAN.

State Administration and Finance Workers' Union (Sindikat radnika državne uprave i finansijskih organa): Pres. Federal Cttee RAM BUĆAJ.

Textile, Leather, and Footwear Workers' Union (Sindikat radnika industrije tekstila, kože i obuće): Pres. Federal Cttee JOZEFINA MUSA.

Transport and Communications Workers' Union (Sindikat radnika saobraćaja i veza): Belgrade; tel. (11) 646321; Pres. Federal Cttee HASAN HRNJIĆ.

Transport

In 2000 it was announced that the Federal Republic of Yugoslavia (FRY—Serbia and Montenegro) was to receive aid from the Stability Pact for South Eastern Europe for transport projects. The construction of the road and railway bridge across the River Danube in Novi Sad was completed in May. Work on the construction of the Belgrade–Novi Sad highway began in June.

RAILWAYS

In 2004 there were 4,347 km of railway track in use in Serbia, excluding Kosovo, of which 1,387 km were electrified. In 2005 a major infrastructure project for the relocation of the central railway station in Belgrade was near completion and the rehabilitation of the capital's rail system was also under way.

Željeznica Crne Gore: 81000 Podgorica, Trg Golootočkih žrtava 13; tel. (81) 633498; fax (81) 633957; e-mail zcg-uprava@cg.yu; internet www.zeljeznica.cg.yu; fmrly Montenegrin branch of Zajednica Jugoslovenskih Železnica (Union of Yugoslav Railways); 60.1% state-owned; Chair. of Bd of Dirs RANKO MEDENIĆA; Gen. Man. REŠAD NUHODŽIĆ.

Železnice Srbije (Serbian Railways): 11000 Belgrade, Nemanjina 6, POB 553; tel. (11) 3616722; fax (11) 3616797; e-mail posta@yurail.co.yu; internet www.yurail.co.yu; fmrly Serbian branch of Zajednica Jugoslovenskih Železnica (Union of Yugoslav Railways); Chair. of Management Bd Dr PAVLE POPOVIĆ; Gen. Man. PREDRAG NIKOLIĆ.

ROADS

In 2001 there were an estimated 44,993 km of roads, of which 28,031 km were paved.

INLAND WATERWAYS

About 3.7m. metric tons of freight were carried on inland water transport in 2000.

SHIPPING

The principal coastal outlet is the Montenegrin port of Bar, which is linked to the Italian ports of Ancona and Bari by a regular ferry service.

Jugoagent Pomorska—rečna Agencija (Yugo Maritime and Rivers Shipping Agency): 11070 Belgrade, bul. Mihaila Pupina 165A, POB 210; tel. (11) 2018700; fax (11) 3112070; e-mail office@jugoagent.net; internet www.jugoagent.net; f. 1947; fmrly Jugoslovenska Pomorska Agencija (Yugoslav Maritime Agency); charter services, liner and container transport, port agency, passenger service, air cargo service; Gen. Man. ZORAN NETKOVIĆ.

Jugooceanija: 85330 Kotor, Njegoseva bb; tel. (82) 325121; fmrly Jugoslovenska Oceanska Plovidba (Yugoslav Ocean Lines); 51% transfer to private ownership proposed in 2005.

CIVIL AVIATION

There are international airports at Belgrade (Serbia), Podgorica (Montenegro) and Priština (Kosovo, Serbia), as well as several domestic airports, including those at Niš (Serbia) and Tivat (Montenegro).

Jat Airways: 11070 Belgrade, Bulevar umetnosti 16; tel. (11) 3114222; fax (11) 3112853; e-mail pr@jat.com; internet www.jat.com; f. 1927 as Aeroput; fmrly Jugoslovenski Aerotransport (JAT—Yugoslav Airlines); 51% owned by Govt of Serbia; flights between Serbia and Montenegro and destinations in Central, Western, Eastern and Southern Europe and the Middle East; Dir-Gen. PREDRAG VUJOVIĆ.

Montenegro Airlines: 81000 Podgorica, Beogradska 10; tel. (81) 405501; fax (81) 623762; e-mail contact@mgx.cg.yu; internet www.montenegroairlines.com; f. 1994; operations commenced 1997; direct flights between Podgorica and: Tivat (Montenegro); Belgrade and Niš (Serbia); Frankfurt (Germany); Ljubljana (Slovenia); Paris (France); Rome (Italy); Vienna (Austria) and Zurich (Switzerland); Pres. ZORAN DURIŠIĆ.

Tourism

Notable tourist attractions include Serbia's mountain scenery and monasteries, the great lake of Scutari, in Montenegro and Montenegro's Adriatic coastline. In 2003 tourist arrivals totalled 481,070 (compared with 448,223 in 2002), and tourism receipts amounted to US $201m.

National Tourism Organization of Montenegro: 81000 Podgorica, Omladinskih brigada 7; tel. (81) 230959; fax (81) 230979; e-mail tourism@cg.yu; internet www.visit-montenegro.com; Man. Dir PREDRAG JELUSIĆ.

National Tourism Organization of Serbia (Turistička Organizacija Srbije): 11000 Belgrade, POB 433, Dobrinska 11; tel. (11) 3612754; fax (11) 686804; e-mail ntos@eunet.yu; internet www.serbia-info.com/ntos; f. 1953; produces information and conducts market research and promotion in the field of tourism; Dir JOVAN POPESKU.

SEYCHELLES

Introductory Survey

Location, Climate, Language, Religion, Flag, Capital

The Republic of Seychelles comprises about 115 islands, widely scattered over the western Indian Ocean. Apart from the Seychelles archipelago, the country includes several other island groups, the southernmost being about 210 km (130 miles) north of Madagascar. The climate is tropical, with small seasonal variations in temperature and rainfall. The average temperature in Victoria is nearly 27°C (80°F) and average annual rainfall 236 cm (93 ins). In 1981 Seselwa, a creole spoken by virtually all Seychellois, replaced English and French as the official language. Almost all of the inhabitants are Christians, of whom more than 90% belong to the Roman Catholic Church. The national flag (proportions 1 by 2) has five rays, extending from the lower hoist corner, of blue, yellow, red, white and green. The capital is Victoria, on the island of Mahé.

Recent History

Seychelles was uninhabited until colonized by France in 1770. It was ceded to the United Kingdom in 1814 and administered as a dependency of Mauritius until 1903, when it became a Crown Colony.

During the 1960s political activity was focused on the centre-right Seychelles Democratic Party, led by James (later Sir James) Mancham, and the socialist-orientated Seychelles People's United Party (SPUP), led by Albert René. A ministerial system of government was introduced in 1970, and Seychelles proceeded to full independence, as a sovereign republic within the Commonwealth, on 29 June 1976, under a coalition Government with Mancham as President and René as Prime Minister. Under the independence agreement, the United Kingdom returned to Seychelles the islands of Aldabra, Farquhar and Desroches, detached in 1965 to form part of the British Indian Ocean Territory (q.v.) and subsequently leased to the USA. In 1982 the Aldabra group, which (including its lagoon) represents about one-third of Seychelles' total area, was designated by UNESCO as a world heritage site.

In June 1977 the SPUP staged an armed coup while Mancham was absent from the islands. René was declared President, the National Assembly was dissolved and the Constitution suspended. In May 1978 the SPUP was renamed the Seychelles People's Progressive Front (SPPF). A new Constitution, proclaimed in March 1979, established a one-party state. In June elections for a new National Assembly were held. René was the sole candidate in the concurrent presidential election and was re-elected in June 1984 and, again in 1989 as sole candidate, for a third term of office, the maximum period permitted under the 1979 Constitution. During this period opponents of René's socialist Government made a number of attempts to overthrow the regime, with the use of foreign-backed mercenaries. The most serious assault took place in November 1981, when about 50 mercenaries, mainly South Africans posing as tourists, flew to join insurgents already on the islands. When the rebellion collapsed, most of the mercenaries escaped to South Africa, where several of their number were later tried and imprisoned. Further plots, discovered in October 1982 and November 1983, were ascribed to the same Seychellois exiles who had planned the 1981 coup attempt. In November 1985 Gérard Hoareau, the leader of an exiled opposition group, was shot dead in the United Kingdom. The incident formed one of a series of attacks on, and disappearances of, anti-René activists.

Until the early 1990s exiled opposition to René remained split among a number of small groups based principally in London, United Kingdom. In July 1991 five of these parties formed a coalition, the United Democratic Movement (UDM), under the leadership of Dr Maxime Ferrari, a former political associate of René, while ex-President Mancham established a 'Crusade for Democracy'. René, meanwhile, came under increasing pressure from France and the United Kingdom, the islands' principal aid donors, to restore a democratic political system. Internally, open opposition to the SPPF was fostered by the newly formed Parti Seselwa, or Parti Seychellois (PS), led by an Anglican clergyman, Wavel Ramkalawan. In August 1991 Ferrari returned from exile to organize support for the UDM, and in November the Government invited all political dissidents to return to the islands. In the following month the Minister of Tourism and Transport, Jacques Hodoul, left the Government; he subsequently formed the Seychelles Movement for Democracy.

In December 1991 the SPPF agreed to surrender the party's monopoly of power. It was announced that, from January 1992, political groups numbering at least 100 members would be granted official registration, and that multi-party elections would take place in July for a constituent assembly, whose proposals for constitutional reform would be submitted to a national referendum, with a view to holding multi-party parliamentary elections before the end of 1992. In April Mancham returned from exile to lead the New Democratic Party (NDP). At the July elections for the 20-seat constitutional commission, the SPPF won 58.4% of the votes, while the NDP received 33.7%. The PS, which took 4.4% of the votes, was the only other political party to obtain representation on the commission.

The commission, which comprised 11 representatives from the SPPF, eight from the NDP (now renamed the Democratic Party—DP) and one from the PS, completed its work in October 1992. In the previous month, however, the DP withdrew its delegation, on the grounds that the SPPF had allegedly refused to permit a full debate of reform proposals. The DP also expressed objections that the commission's meetings had been closed to the public and news media. Following publication of the draft Constitution, the DP challenged the proposed voting arrangements for a new National Assembly, whose members were to be elected on a basis of one-half by direct vote and one-half by proportional representation. The latter formula was to reflect the percentage of votes obtained by the successful candidate in presidential election, and was intended to ensure a legislative majority for the President's party. Other sections of the proposed Constitution, relating to social issues, were strongly opposed by the Roman Catholic Church, to which more than 90% of the islanders belong.

The draft Constitution, which required the approval of at least 60% of voters, was endorsed by only 53.7% at a referendum held in November 1992. A second constitutional commission, whose meetings were opened to the public, began work in January 1993 on proposals for submission to a further referendum, and in May the second commission unanimously agreed on a new draft Constitution, in which a compromise plan was reached on the electoral formula for a new National Assembly. With the joint endorsement of René and Mancham, the draft document was submitted to a national referendum in June, at which 73.9% of voters approved the constitutional plan. Opponents of the new constitutional arrangements comprised the PS, the Seychelles National Movement (SNM) and the National Alliance Party (NAP). At the presidential and legislative elections that followed in July, René received 59.5% of the vote, against 36.7% for Mancham and 3.8% for Philippe Boullé, the candidate representing an electoral alliance of the PS, the Seychelles Christian Democrat Party (SCDP), the SNM and the NAP. In the legislative elections, the SPPF secured 21 of the 22 seats elected by direct vote, and the DP one seat. Of the 11 additional seats allocated on a proportional basis, the SPPF received a further seven seats, the DP three seats and the PS one seat. Immediately following the elections, René, whose decisive victory was widely attributed to his promise of increased expenditure on social programmes, extensively reshuffled the Council of Ministers.

Following the 1993 elections, however, the Government began to promote a gradual transition from socialism to free-market policies, aimed at maximizing the country's potential as an 'offshore' financial and business centre. State-owned port facilities were transferred to private ownership in 1994, when plans were also announced for the creation of a duty-free International Trade Zone to provide transhipment facilities. Measures were introduced to implement the privatization of government activities in tourism, agriculture and tuna-processing.

In early 1995 tensions developed within the opposition DP, whose only directly elected MP, Christopher Gill, sought to remove Mancham from the party leadership on the grounds that the former President was insufficiently vigorous in opposing the policies of the René Government. Gill was suspended from the DP in June, and subsequently formed a breakaway 'New Democratic Party' with the aim of restructuring the DP under a new leader. The official registration of active political organizations, affording them corporate status, led to the formal amalgamation of the PS, the SNM, the SCDP and the NAP as a single party, the United Opposition (UO), under the leadership of Ramkalawan.

In the furtherance of its efforts to promote Seychelles as an international 'offshore' financial centre, the Government introduced, in November 1995, an Economic Development Act (EDA), under whose provisions investors of a minimum US $10m. would receive immunity in Seychelles from extradition or seizure of assets. It was feared in international financial circles, however, that the operation of the EDA would make Seychelles a refuge for the proceeds of drugs-trafficking and other crimes. Protest was led by the United Kingdom, France and the USA, and in February 1996 the EDA was described by the Financial Action Task Force on Money Laundering (see p. 389) as a 'serious threat to world financial systems.' The Government, while refusing to rescind the EDA, established an Economic Development Board under the chairmanship of René, to vet potential EDA investors. In April 1996 the Government introduced legislation aimed at preventing the use of the EDA for 'laundering' illicit funds. Following reports critical of Seychelles' financial sector from two international organizations, the EDA was finally repealed in July 2000.

In July 1996 the SPPF introduced a series of constitutional amendments, creating the post of Vice-President, to which James Michel, the Minister of Finance, Communications and Defence and a long-standing political associate of René, was appointed in the following month. The constitutional changes also provided for revisions in constituency boundaries, which were generally interpreted as favouring SPPF candidates in future parliamentary elections. Measures were also implemented whereby the number of seats in the National Assembly was to be increased (see Government).

Following the 1993 elections, effective opposition to the Government came increasingly to be led by Ramkalawan's UO, as the DP opted to pursue a policy of 'reconciliation' and 'non-confrontation' with the SPPF.

In January 1998 René announced that the elections would be held in March, and that he was to seek the second of a maximum of three consecutive five-year terms as president permitted under the 1993 Constitution. The outcome of the elections provided the SPPF with a decisive victory. René obtained 66.7% of the presidential ballot, while his party secured 30 of the 34 seats in the enlarged National Assembly. Ramkalawan, with 19.5% of the presidential vote, substantially exceeded support for Mancham, who received 13.8%. In the National Assembly the UO increased its representation from one to three seats, with the DP losing three of the four seats previously held. Mancham, who lost his parliamentary seat, subsequently announced his temporary withdrawal from active politics. The UO, which consequently emerged as the principal parliamentary opponent of the SPPF, boycotted a number of debates during 1998 in protest at allegedly partisan coverage of legislative proceedings by the Seychelles Broadcasting Corporation, and accused the Speaker of the National Assembly of authoritarian conduct. In mid-1998 the UO changed its name to the Seychelles National Party (SNP).

In July 2001 René declared a presidential election almost two years early, claiming that this was in order to reassure investors about the long-term stability of the country. The election was postponed from its scheduled date of 12 August until 31 August–2 September, in order to allow the opposition sufficient time to prepare. René was re-elected as President, but with the smallest mandate of his career, securing 54.2% of the valid votes cast. Ramkalawan, the SNP candidate, won 45.0% of the votes, but refused to accept the result, claiming serious irregularities in the electoral process, and subsequently filed a formal complaint with the Constitutional Court. Philippe Boullé, the first independent candidate in the country's history (who had contested the presidential election in July 1993 for an opposition alliance), secured only 0.9% of the votes. Legislative elections, which were due in 2003, took place early, on 4–6 December 2002. The SPPF retained its majority in the National Assembly, but with a reduced margin, securing 23 of the 34 seats, while the SNP won the remaining 11 seats. In March 2003 René indicated during the congress of the SPPF that he would progressively relinquish control of certain presidential duties to Vice-President Michel, who was also designated as the party's candidate for the next presidential election.

Following an announcement of his impending resignation in February 2004, on 14 April President René formally retired, having spent almost 27 years in office. He was succeeded by Vice-President Michel, who was inaugurated as President on the same day. René retained his position as President of the SPPF. Joseph Belmont was subsequently appointed Vice-President, retaining responsibility for tourism and transport. In July the portfolio for international trade and industry was subsumed into that of the Ministry of Economic Planning, which was to be headed by Jacquelin Dugasse.

Seychelles escaped relatively unscathed, in human terms, from the tsunamis that occurred in the Indian Ocean region in December, with only two deaths and some 100 families displaced; there was, however, significant economic and infrastructural damage.

In February 2005 President Michel reduced the number of government ministries from nine to seven. The Minister of Foreign Affairs, Jérémie Bonnelame, was appointed Permanent Representative to the United Nations and the USA and replaced by Patrick Pillay, hitherto Minister of Health. The health portfolio was merged with that of social affairs. The Minister of Manpower and Administration, Noellie Alexander, was also appointed elsewhere, but was not replaced; the areas of responsibility of the portfolio were reassigned to the Ministry of Education and Youth. Also in February Mancham resigned from the chairmanship of the DP and was succeeded on an interim basis by Nichol Gabriel. Michel was expected to conduct a more open government, especially with regard to economic measures, although it was anticipated that his policy agenda would necessarily be informed by the presidential elections to be held in 2006. In 2005, for the first time in his political career, Ramkalawan took a sabbatical leave from his role in the Anglican clergy, with the aim of focusing more exclusively on his political career and the presidential election to be held in 2006. In March Paul Chow became the leader of the DP; Nichol Gabriel retained his post as party secretary, however. Chow was believed to favour an electoral alliance with the SNP.

In early 2006 Seychelles was one of several Indian Ocean islands afflicted with an outbreak of both dengue fever and the chikungunya virus.

Seychelles has traditionally pursued a policy of non-alignment in international affairs, and supports movements for the creation of a 'zone of peace' in the Indian Ocean area. Until 1983 all naval warships wishing to dock at Seychelles had to provide a guarantee that they were not carrying nuclear weapons. The British and US Governments refused to agree to this condition, and their respective naval fleets were therefore effectively banned from using Seychelles port facilities. This requirement was withdrawn in September 1983, although Seychelles continued, in theory, to refuse entry to ships carrying nuclear weapons. In 1986 Seychelles and the USA renegotiated an agreement, signed in 1976 and renewed in 1981, which allowed the USA to maintain a satellite-tracking station on Mahé. This installation, however, was closed, simultaneously with the US diplomatic mission, in 1996, as part of cost-reduction measures by the US Government in its defence expenditure; the USA finally agreed to dismantle the structure in July 2000. Since the late 1980s Seychelles has expanded the scope of its formal diplomatic contacts. Relations have been established with the Comoros and with Mauritius, and agreements have been made with the latter for co-operation in health and economic development matters. In 1989 diplomatic relations were established with Morocco, Madagascar and Côte d'Ivoire, and in 1990 with Kenya. During 1992 formal relations were established with Israel and South Africa, and in 1998 Seychelles proposed to establish a diplomatic mission in Malaysia to expand its relations in Asia and Oceania. Libya opened a diplomatic mission in Seychelles in January 2000, and diplomatic ties were established with Sudan in October. Following years of minimal interaction between France and Seychelles, owing to Seychelles' accumulated debt to the Agence Française de Développement, the French Minister for Co-operation was the first minister in over four years to visit Seychelles in February 2001. It was hoped that a resolution to the situation could be found and a new schedule for repayments negotiated. In 2001 relations were restored with Japan, which granted a subsidy for fishery development to Seychelles; this was said to be a consequence of the reversal of Seychelles' whaling policy. President Michel paid a state visit to Mauritius in March 2005, as guest of honour at that country's annual celebration of independence;

various economic and co-operative agreements between the two countries were also signed. In December 2005, as a result of the seventh session of the Seychelles-Mauritius Commission on Bilateral Co-operation, a further agreement was signed on the sharing of expertise in a wide range of fields.

Government

Under the 1993 Constitution, executive power is vested in the President, who is Head of State and Commander-in-Chief of the Armed Forces. The President, who is elected by direct popular vote, appoints and leads the Council of Ministers, which acts in an advisory capacity to him. The President also appoints the holders of certain public offices and the judiciary. The President may hold office for a maximum period of three five-year terms. The legislature is the unicameral National Assembly, presently comprising 34 members, of whom 25 are directly elected for five years and nine allocated on a proportional basis. Constitutional changes, introduced in July 1996, provide for an enlargement to 35 members: 25 directly elected and a maximum of 10 allocated on a proportional basis.

Defence

At August 2005 the army numbered 450 men, including a coastguard of 200. Paramilitary forces comprised a 250-strong national guard. The defence budget for 2005 allocated an estimated SR 70m. to defence. Seychelles was to contribute servicemen to the East African Stand-by Brigade, part of the African Union (see p. 153) stand-by peace-keeping force; the unit was intended to be ready for rapid response by mid-2006.

Economic Affairs

In 2004, according to estimates by the World Bank, Seychelles' gross national income (GNI), measured at average 2002–04 prices, was US $685m., equivalent to $8,090 per head (or $15,590 per head on an international purchasing-power parity basis). During 1995–2004, it was estimated, the population increased at an average annual rate of 1.3%, while gross domestic product (GDP) per head increased, in real terms, by an average of 1.0% per year. Overall GDP increased, in real terms, at an average annual rate of 2.3% in 1995–2004. However, real GDP declined by 6.3% in 2003 and by 2.0% in 2004.

Agriculture (including hunting, forestry and fishing) contributed 2.7% of GDP in 2004 and accounted for 3.2% of total employment in that year. Much of Seychelles' production of coconuts has traditionally been exported in the form of copra, but there were no exports of copra in 1996–99. Other cash crops include cinnamon bark, tea, patchouli, vanilla and limes. Tea, sweet potatoes, cassava, yams, sugar cane, bananas, eggs and poultry meat are produced for local consumption. However, imports of food and live animals constituted 17.2% of the value of total imports in 2002. Fishing has become increasingly important since the 1980s, and exports of canned tuna alone contributed 91.4% of the value of total domestic exports in 2004. Licence fees from foreign fishing vessels, allowed to operate in Seychelles' waters, contribute significantly to foreign exchange. A three-year fishing protocol, worth €3.48m., was signed with the European Union in 2001; a further six-year protocol was agreed in October 2004, and in December 2005 an agreement, valid until 2011, increased the payment for fishing rights to €4.12m. a year as well as raising the value of some licences, meaning that the Government could expect payments of some €6.0m. a year. Agricultural GDP increased at an average annual rate of 2.0% during 1995–2004, according to the World Bank; it grew by 0.6% in 2003, but declined by 1.8% in 2004.

Industry (including mining, manufacturing, construction and power) contributed 29.1% of GDP in 2004 and accounted for 22.6% of total employment. Industrial GDP increased at an average annual rate of 5.9% during 1995–2004, according to the World Bank; however, the sector declined by 2.6% in 2003 and by 2.0% in 2004.

The mining sector is small; the sole mineral export is guano (of which 6,000 metric tons was exported in 1990, although consistent output was discontinued in the mid-1980s). Mineral production consists mainly of quantities of construction materials, such as clay, coral, stone and sand. There are deposits of natural gas, and during the 1980s concessions were sold to several foreign companies, allowing exploration for petroleum. Exploratory drilling has so far proved unsuccessful; however, an agreement to renew exploration was made in 2005. A survey of offshore areas, initiated in 1980, revealed the presence of nodules, containing deposits of various metals, on the sea-bed. The possibility of renewed commercial exploitation of Seychelles' granite reserves is under investigation and the future development of offshore petroleum reserves is a possibility.

Manufacturing contributed 17.3% of GDP in 2004 and accounted for 12.9% of total employment in that year. Apart from a tuna-canning plant (opened in 1987), the manufacturing sector consists mainly of small-scale activities, including boat-building, printing and furniture-making. According to the World Bank, manufacturing GDP increased at an average annual rate of 6.5% during 1995–2004. Manufacturing GDP declined by 3.8% in 2003 and by 2.0% in 2004.

Energy is derived principally from oil-fired power stations. In 2002 mineral fuels accounted for 1.1% of the value of total imports. The vast majority of fuel imports are re-exported, mainly as bunker sales to visiting ships and aircraft—exports of refined petroleum products contributed 30.0% of total export earnings in 1999 (in 2004 re-exports accounted for 36.9% of the value of total exports). In 2000 Seychelles generated SR 357m. from petroleum re-exports, and it was anticipated that in the early 2000s the proceeds from re-exports would fully fund fuel imports.

Services provided 68.2% of GDP in 2004 and accounted for 74.2% of total employment. In 1997 tourism generated 33.6% of total earnings from exports of goods and services. Tourist arrivals totalled some 122,038 in 2003; income from that source amounted to US $242m. in 2002. The majority of visitors were from western Europe, notably from France, Germany, Italy and the United Kingdom. The GDP of the services sector increased at an average annual rate of 0.9% during 1995–2004, according to the World Bank. However, services GDP declined by 8.3% in 2003 and by 2.0% in 2004.

In 2004 Seychelles recorded a visible trade deficit of US $116.5m. In the same year there was a deficit of $28.2m. on the current account of the balance of payments. The principal source of imports (16.2%) in 2002 was Saudi Arabia; other important suppliers were Germany, Italy, France, South Africa and the United Kingdom. The principal market for exports in that year was the United Kingdom (32.4% for exports incl. re-exports; 42.3% for domestic exports); other significant purchasers were France, Italy and Germany. The principal export in 2002 was canned tuna, following the expansion of the Indian Ocean Tuna Company in 1995 and increasing production thereafter; in 2004 canned tuna represented 91.5% of domestic exports. The main imports were machinery and transport equipment, food and live animals, and basic manufactures.

In 2004 Seychelles recorded a budgetary surplus of SR 409.6m. (equivalent to 10.6% of GDP). Seychelles' total external debt was US $547.9m. at the end of 2003, of which $439.0m. was long-term public debt. In that year the cost of debt-servicing was equivalent to 14.0% of the value of exports of goods and services. The annual rate of inflation averaged 3.0% in 1995–2003; consumer prices increased by an average of 3.8% in 2004. Some 8.3% of the labour force were registered as unemployed in 1993.

Seychelles is a member of the African Development Bank (see p. 151), of the Common Market for Eastern and Southern Africa (see p. 191) and of the Indian Ocean Commission (see p. 386), which aims to promote co-operation in the region. It was announced in December 1996 that Seychelles was to provide the headquarters of the Indian Ocean Tuna Commission.

Since the early 1970s tourism has been the mainstay of the Seychelles economy. Development of agriculture is impeded by the lack of cultivable land. Income from fisheries expanded greatly after the commissioning of a tuna-canning plant in 1987 and the establishment of a prawn farm in the early 1990s. Manufacturing growth is inhibited, however, by the lack of natural resources, although since 1988 the Government has offered incentives for new manufacturing enterprises. Measures were introduced in 1995 to develop Seychelles as an 'offshore' financial services centre (see Recent History), and to establish the islands as a centre for transhipment and air freight in the Indian Ocean area. An export-processing zone has been established, and most state-owned enterprises, with the exception of public utilities and transport, have been transferred to private-sector ownership. However, the continuing dependence of the economy on tourism leaves the country highly vulnerable to outside economic influences, while the cost of servicing the external debt remains a major impediment to balanced growth. In July 2003 a new macroeconomic reform programme took effect; intended to reduce costs and raise revenue, it included the introduction of a general sales and services tax of 12% on all imported items (except essential foodstuffs), most locally manufactured goods and all services. In September, as part of the programme, the Government announced several measures aimed at encouraging long-term settlement by investors in the country. The new regime of President James Michel (who was also the Minister of Finance) from 2004, and his avowed commitment to the programme of economic reform gave rise to a degree of economic optimism, particularly with regard to privatization (the Seychelles Marketing Board monopoly being the main target). However, a primary obstacle to relations with international monetary organizations such as the IMF was the country's refusal to devalue the national currency, owing to its fears of incurring inflation (related to the country's dependence on imported items). It was argued, though, that the over-valuation of the rupee was a contributing factor to the ongoing shortage of foreign-exchange. The tsunamis that affected many Indian-Ocean countries at the end of 2004 caused considerable damage to Seychelles' artisanal fishing sector and infrastructure. Recovery in the tourism sector, which had been slow during 2004, was further discouraged, in spite of the fact that the majority of facilities were unharmed. Damage from the event was estimated to amount to some 4%–5% of GDP. The World Bank pledged a US $2m. grant to aid recovery measures and the 'Paris Club' of creditors offered a temporary suspension of debt repayments. In 2005 it was claimed that high operating costs were rendering the country's fishing sector less competitive than those of rival countries such as Kenya and Tanzania. As of December 2005 trades taxes on raw materials, selected capital equipment and machinery for the manufacturing sector, as well as on domestic household appliances, were eliminated; it was intended that such taxes would only remain on fuel, motor vehicles, tobacco and alcohol. In March 2006 the National Assembly approved a new investment code, drawn up with the advice of the World Bank and the UN, which aligned policy more closely with international regulations; the code allows investors to repatriate rupee earnings in the form of foreign exchange, provides an incentive structure and a dispute-settlement facility and protects against expropriation, but also protects certain local activities and services.

Education

In 1979 free and compulsory primary education was introduced for children between six and 16 years of age. A programme of educational reform, based on the British comprehensive schools system, was introduced in 1980. The language of instruction in primary schools is English. The duration of primary education is six years, while that of general secondary education is five years (of which the first four years are compulsory), beginning at 12 years of age. Pre-primary and special education facilities are also available. There were 1,837 students in post-secondary (non-tertiary) education in 2005. A number of students study abroad, principally in the United Kingdom. Government expenditure on education in 2004 was SR 165.8m., or about 11.2% of total expenditure.

Public Holidays

2006: 1–2 January (New Year), 14–15 April (Easter), 1 May (Labour Day), 5 June (Liberation Day, anniversary of 1977 coup), 15 June (Corpus Christi), 18 June (National Day), 29 June (Independence Day), 15 August (Assumption), 1 November (All Saints' Day), 8 December (Immaculate Conception), 25 December (Christmas Day).

2007: 1–2 January (New Year), 6–7 April (Easter), 1 May (Labour Day), 7 June (Corpus Christi), 5 June (Liberation Day, anniversary of 1977 coup), 18 June (National Day), 29 June (Independence Day), 15 August (Assumption), 1 November (All Saints' Day), 8 December (Immaculate Conception), 25 December (Christmas Day).

Weights and Measures

The imperial system is being replaced by the metric system.

Statistical Survey

Source (unless otherwise stated): Statistics and Database Administration Section, Management and Information Systems Division, POB 206, Victoria; e-mail misdstat@seychelles.net; internet www.nsb.gov.sc.

AREA AND POPULATION

Area: 455.3 sq km (175.8 sq miles), incl. Aldabra lagoon (145 sq km).

Population: 74,331 at census of 26 August 1994; 75,876 (males 37,589, females 38,287) at census of 29 August 1997; 82,474 (official estimate) at mid-2004.

Density (mid-2004): 181.1 per sq km.

Principal Town: Victoria (capital), estimated population 60,000 (incl. suburbs) in 1994. *Mid-2003* (UN estimate, incl. suburbs): Victoria 20,050. (Source: UN, *World Urbanization Prospects: The 2003 Revision*.)

Births, Marriages and Deaths (registered at mid-2004): Live births 1,435 (birth rate 17.4 per 1,000); Marriages (of residents) 408 (marriage rate 4.9 per 1,000); Deaths 611 (death rate 7.2 per 1,000).

Expectation of Life (WHO estimates, years at birth): 72 (males 67; females 77) in 2003. Source: WHO, *World Health Report*.

Economically Active Population: 1987 census (persons aged 12 years and over): Employed 24,293; Unemployed 4,442; *Total labour force* 28,735 (Source: UN, *Demographic Yearbook*). June 1989 (persons aged 15 years and over): Total labour force 29,494 (males 16,964, females 12,530).

Employment (2004, averages): Agriculture, hunting, forestry and fishing 1,044; Manufacturing 4,213; Electricity and water 1,052; Quarrying and construction 2,141; Trade, restaurants and hotels 7,025; Transport, storage and communications 3,094; Other services 14,210; *Total* 32,782. (Figures exclude self-employed persons, unpaid family workers and employees in private domestic services; total may not be equal to the sum of components, owing to rounding.)

HEALTH AND WELFARE
Key Indicators

Total Fertility Rate (children per woman, 2003): 1.8.

Under-5 Mortality Rate (per 1,000 live births, 2004): 14.

Physicians (per 1,000 head, 1998): 1.32.

Hospital Beds (per 1,000 head, 1995): 6.28.

Health Expenditure (2002): US $ per head (PPP): 557.

Health Expenditure (2002): % of GDP: 5.2.

Health Expenditure (2002): public (% of total): 74.3.

Access to Water (% of persons, 2002): 87.

Human Development Index (2003): ranking: 51.

Human Development Index (2003): value: 0.821.

For sources and definitions, see explanatory note on p. vi.

AGRICULTURE, ETC.

Principal Crops (FAO estimates, metric tons, 2004): Coconuts 3,200; Vegetables 1,940; Bananas 1,970; Other fruit 505; Tea (green leaf) 213; Cinnamon 200.

Livestock (FAO estimates, '000 head, 2004): Cattle 1; Pigs 19; Goats 5.

Livestock Products (FAO estimates, '000 metric tons, 2004): Pig meat 1; Poultry meat 1; Hen eggs 2.

Fishing ('000 metric tons, live weight, 2003): Capture 85.8 (Skipjack tuna 36.8; Yellowfin tuna 34.7; Bigeye tuna 7.1); Aquaculture 1.1 (Giant tiger prawn 1.1); *Total catch* 86.9.

Source: FAO.

MINING AND INDUSTRY

Industrial Production (provisional figures, 1999): Canned tuna 33,234 metric tons; Beer 6,768,000 litres; Soft drinks 10,561,000 litres; Cigarettes 60 million. Source: IMF, *Seychelles: Recent Economic Developments* (December 2000). *2004:* Electric energy 226.0 million kWh.

FINANCE

Currency and Exchange Rates: 100 cents = 1 Seychelles rupee (SR). *Sterling, Dollar and Euro Equivalents* (30 December 2005): £1

SEYCHELLES

sterling = 9.470 rupees; US $1 = 5.500 rupees; €1 = 6.488 rupees; 1,000 Seychelles rupees = £105.59 = $181.82 = €154.12. *Average Exchange Rate* (Seychelles rupees per US $): 5.4007 in 2003; 5.5000 in 2004; 5.5000 in 2005. Note: In November 1979 the value of the Seychelles rupee was linked to the IMF's special drawing right (SDR). In March 1981 the mid-point exchange rate was set at SDR 1 = 7.2345 rupees. This remained in effect until February 1997, when the fixed link with the SDR was ended.

Budget (SR million, 2004): *Revenue:* Taxation 1,272.0 (Taxes on income, etc. 298.4; Domestic taxes on goods and services 622.4; Import duties 351.2); Other current revenue 614.0; Total 1,886.0, excl. grants received (5.1). *Expenditure:* General government services 294.7; Community and social services 314.1 (Education 165.8; Health 176.2); Economic services 68.8 (Agriculture, forestry, fishing and hunting 67.1; Transport and communications 44.9); Other purposes 423.4; Interest payments 262.9; Capital 118.0; Total 1,481.9, excl. lending minus repayments (-0.4). Note: Figures represent the consolidated accounts of the central Government, covering the operations of the Recurrent and Capital Budgets and of the Social Security Fund.

International Reserves (US $ million at 30 December 2005): IMF special drawing rights 0.0; Foreign exchange 57.50; Total 57.50. Source: IMF, *International Financial Statistics*.

Money Supply (SR million at 30 December 2005): Currency outside banks 325.7; Demand deposits at commercial banks 1,073.9; Total money (incl. others) 1,400.5. Source: IMF, *International Financial Statistics*.

Cost of Living (Consumer Price Index; base: 2000 = 100): All items 106.2 in 2002; 109.7 in 2003; 113.9 in 2004. Source: IMF, *International Financial Statistics*.

Expenditure on the Gross Domestic Product (SR million at current prices, 1998): Government final consumption expenditure 847.0; Private final consumption expenditure 1,603.9; Increase in stocks 56.0; Gross fixed capital formation 1,100.0; *Total domestic expenditure* 3,607.0; Exports of goods and services 2,045.5; *Less* Imports of goods and services 2,525.8; *GDP in purchasers' values* 3,126.7. Source: IMF, *International Financial Statistics*.

Gross Domestic Product by Economic Activity (SR million at current prices, 2004): Agriculture, hunting, forestry and fishing 100.7; Manufacturing 645.0; Electricity and water 61.1; Building and construction 379.8; Trade, restaurants and hotels 878.5; Transport, distribution and communications 683.6; Finance, insurance, real estate and business services 486.7; Government services 492.5; *Sub-total* 3,727.9; Import duties 397.4; *Less* Imputed bank service charge 258.3; *GDP in purchasers' values* 3,867.0.

Balance of Payments (US $ million, 2004): Exports of goods f.o.b. 300.46; Imports of goods f.o.b. −416.94; *Trade balance* −116.47; Exports of services 324.66; Imports of services −212.31; *Balance on goods and services* −4.12; Other income received 10.30; Other income paid −43.62; *Balance on goods, services and income* −37.43; Current transfers received 11.17; Current transfers paid −1.89; *Current balance* −28.15; Capital account (net) 0.99; Direct investment abroad −7.6; Direct investment from abroad 37.45; Portfolio investment assets −0.04; Portfolio investment liabilities 1.11; Other investment assets −12.27; Other investment liabilities −209.30; Net errors and omissions 32.54; *Overall balance* −185.27. Source: IMF, *International Financial Statistics*.

EXTERNAL TRADE

Principal Commodities (distribution by SITC, US $ million, 2002): *Imports c.i.f.:* Food and live animals 42.3 (Frozen fish, excl. fillets 22.1); Animal and vegetable oils, fats and waxes 8.6 (Olive oil 5.2); Chemicals and related products 10.6; Basic manufactures 41.8 (Iron and steel 7.8; Other metal manufactures 17.5); Machinery and transport equipment 62.8 (Road vehicles 7.7; Tankers 30.0); Miscellaneous manufactured articles 15.4; Total (incl. others) 245.7. *Exports f.o.b.:* Food and live animals 19.0 (Fish, crustaceans and molluscs, and preparations thereof 14.3); Kerosene 14.4; Machinery and transport equipment 1.6; Total (incl. others) 38.0 (Source: UN, *International Trade Statistics Yearbook*). 2004 (US $ million, exports f.o.b.): Canned tuna 923.2; Fish (fresh/frozen) 13.1; Frozen prawns 42.5; Other processed fish 8.3; Cinnamon bark 0.5; Other 21.4; Total 1,009.0.

Principal Trading Partners (US $ million, 2002): *Imports c.i.f.:* Australia 4.0; France (incl. Monaco) 26.2; Germany 32.5; India 6.0; Italy 28.7; Malaysia 5.5; Mauritius 8.0; Netherlands 3.3; Saudi Arabia 39.8; Singapore 13.3; South Africa 22.2; Spain 8.3; Thailand 2.7; United Kingdom 19.5; USA 3.9; Total (incl. others) 245.7. *Exports f.o.b.:* France (incl. Monaco) 12.8; Saudi Arabia 14.4; Total (incl. others) 38.0 (Source: UN, *International Trade Statistics Yearbook*). 2004 (US $ million): Total imports c.i.f. 2,739.0; Total exports f.o.b. 1,009.0 (United Kingdom 454.9; France 310.4; Italy 97.9; Germany 82.9); Re-exports 591.2.

TRANSPORT

Road Traffic (estimates, motor vehicles in use, 1996): Passenger cars 7,120; Lorries and vans 1,980. Source: International Road Federation, *World Road Statistics*. 2004 (registered motor vehicles): Private 6,252; Commercial 2,486; Taxis 270; Self-drive 851; Motor cycles 50; Omnibuses 200; Total 10,109.

Shipping: *Merchant Fleet* (registered at 31 December 2004): Vessels 33; Total displacement 66,851 grt (Source: Lloyd's Register-Fairplay, *World Fleet Statistics*); *International Sea-borne Freight Traffic* (2004): Freight ('000 metric tons): Imports 481; Exports 4,327; Transhipment 78.

Civil Aviation (traffic on scheduled services, 2001): Kilometres flown 9 million; Passengers carried 420,000; Passenger-km 925 million; Total ton-km 101 million (Source: UN, *Statistical Yearbook*). 2004: Aircraft movements 3,327; Passengers embarked 169,000; Passengers disembarked 163,000; Freight embarked 1,210 metric tons; Freight disembarked 3,305 metric tons.

TOURISM

Foreign Tourist Arrivals: 129,762 in 2001; 132,246 in 2002; 122,038 in 2003.

Arrivals by Country of Residence (2002): France 25,990; Germany 15,903; Italy 17,778; South Africa 5,003; Switzerland 4,737; United Kingdom 18,765. 2004: Total visitor arrivals 120,800.

Tourism Receipts (US $ million, incl. passenger transport): 221 in 2000; 210 in 2001; 242 in 2002.

Source: World Tourism Organization.

COMMUNICATIONS MEDIA

Radio Receivers (1997): 42,000 in use. Source: UNESCO, *Statistical Yearbook*.

Television Receivers (2000): 16,500 in use. Source: International Telecommunication Union.

Telephones (2004): 21,200 main lines in use. Source: International Telecommunication Union.

Facsimile Machines (2002): 590 in use.

Mobile Cellular Telephones (2004): 49,200 subscribers. Source: International Telecommunication Union.

Personal Computers (2004): 15,000 in use. Source: International Telecommunication Union.

Internet Users (2004): 20,000. Source: International Telecommunication Union.

Book Production (1980): 33 titles (2 books, 31 pamphlets).

Daily Newspapers (2004): 1 (average circulation in 1996 3,000 copies). Source: partly UNESCO, *Statistical Yearbook*.

Non-daily Newspapers (2004): 3 (average circulation in 1996 7,000 copies). Source: partly UNESCO, *Statistical Yearbook*.

EDUCATION

Pre-primary (2005): 32 schools; 189 teachers; 2,838 pupils.

Primary (2005): 25 schools; 670 teachers; 9,204 pupils.

Secondary (2005): 13 schools; 590 teachers; 7,895 pupils.

Post-secondary (2005): 8 schools; 183 teachers; 1,837 pupils.

Vocational (2004): 7 institutions; 82 teachers; 1,099 pupils.

Adult Literacy Rate (official estimate): 96% (males 96%; females 96%) in 2005.

Directory

The Constitution

The independence Constitution of 1976 was suspended after the coup in June 1977 but reintroduced in July with substantial modifications. A successor Constitution, which entered into force in March 1979, was superseded by a new Constitution, approved by national referendum on 18 June 1993.

The President is elected by popular vote simultaneously with elections for the National Assembly. The President fulfils the functions of Head of State and Commander-in-Chief of the armed forces and may hold office for a maximum period of three consecutive five-year terms. The Assembly, elected for a term of five years, consists of 34 seats, of which 25 are filled by direct election and nine are allocated on a proportional basis. Constitutional amendments, introduced in July 1996, provided for an Assembly of 25 directly elected seats and a maximum of 10 proportionally allocated seats. There is provision for an appointed Vice-President. The Council of Ministers is appointed by the President and acts in an advisory capacity to him. The President also appoints the holders of certain public offices and the judiciary.

The Government

HEAD OF STATE

President: JAMES MICHEL (took office 14 April 2004).
Vice-President: JOSEPH BELMONT.

COUNCIL OF MINISTERS
(April 2006)

President and Minister of Finance: JAMES MICHEL.
Vice-President and Minister of Tourism and Transport: JOSEPH BELMONT.
Minister of Foreign Affairs: PATRICK PILLAY.
Minister of Economic Planning and Employment: JACQUELIN DUGASSE.
Minister of Local Government, Sport and Culture: SYLVETTE POOL.
Minister of Land Use and Habitat: JOEL MORGAN.
Minister of Health and Social Services: VINCENT MERITON.
Minister of the Environment and Natural Resources: RONNIE JUMEAU.
Minister of Education and Youth: DANNY FAURE.

MINISTRIES

Office of the President: State House, POB 55, Victoria; tel. 224155; fax 224985; e-mail jmichel@statehouse.gov.sc.
Office of the Vice-President: State House, POB 1303, Victoria; tel. 225509; fax 225152; e-mail jbelmont@statehouse.gov.sc.
Ministry of Economic Planning and Employment: International Conference Centre, POB 648, Victoria; tel. 611200; fax 225374; e-mail mmep@seychelles.sc.
Ministry of Education and Youth: POB 48, Mont Fleuri; tel. 283283; fax 224859; e-mail pamedu@seychelles.net; internet www.education.gov.sc.
Ministry of the Environment and Natural Resources: Independence House, POB 166, Victoria; tel. 611120; fax 225438; e-mail minister@env.gov.sc; internet www.env.gov.sc.
Ministry of Foreign Affairs: Maison Queau de Quincy, POB 656, Mont Fleuri; tel. 283500; fax 225398; e-mail dazemia@mfa.gov.sc; internet seychelles.diplomacy.edu.
Ministry of Health and Social Services: POB 52, Mont Fleuri; tel. 388000; fax 226042; e-mail minister@moh.gov.sc.
Ministry of Land Use and Habitat: Independence House, POB 199, Victoria; tel. 284444; fax 225187; e-mail mluh@mluh.gov.sc.
Ministry of Local Government, Sport and Culture: Oceangate House, POB 731, Victoria; tel. 225477; fax 225254; e-mail frevet@seychelles.net.

President and Legislature

PRESIDENT*
Election, 31 August–2 September 2001

Candidate	Votes	% of votes
France Albert René (SPPF)	27,223	54.19
Wavel Ramkalawan (SNP)	22,581	44.95
Philippe Boullé (Independent)	434	0.86
Total	**50,238**	**100.00**

* On 14 April 2004 France Albert René resigned from the presidency and was succeeded by James Michel, hitherto Vice-President.

NATIONAL ASSEMBLY

Speaker: FRANCIS MACGREGOR.
Election, 4–6 December 2002

Party	Votes	% of votes	Seats*
Seychelles People's Progressive Front	28,075	54.3	23
Seychelles National Party	22,030	42.6	11
Democratic Party	1,605	3.1	0
Total	**51,710**	**100.0**	**34**

* Of the Assembly's 34 seats, 25 were filled by direct election and nine by allocation on a proportional basis.

Election Commission

Electoral Commission: POB 741, Victoria; Suite 306, Aarti Bldg, Mont Fleuri; tel. 225147; fax 225474; e-mail hendrick@seychelles.net; Electoral Commissioner HENDRICK PAUL GAPPY.

Political Organizations

Democratic Party (DP): POB 169, Mont Fleuri; tel. 224916; fax 224302; internet www.dpseychelles.org; f. 1992; successor to the Seychelles Democratic Party (governing party 1970–77); Leader PAUL CHOW; Sec.-Gen. NICHOL GABRIEL.

Mouvement Seychellois pour la Démocratie: Mont Fleuri; tel. 224322; fax 224460; f. 1992; Leader JACQUES HODOUL.

Seychelles National Party (SNP): Arpent Vert, Mont Fleuri, POB 81, Victoria; tel. 224124; fax 225151; e-mail snp2003@hotmail.com; internet www.seychelles.net/snp; f. 1995; as the United Opposition, comprising the fmr mem. parties of a coalition formed to contest the 1993 elections; adopted present name in 1998; Leader Rev. WAVEL RAMKALAWAN; Sec. ROGER MANCIENNE.

Seychelles People's Progressive Front (SPPF): POB 1242, Victoria; tel. 324622; fax 225351; e-mail admin@sppf.sc; internet www.sppf.sc; fmrly the Seychelles People's United Party (f. 1964), which assumed power in 1977; renamed in 1978; sole legal party 1978–91; Pres. FRANCE ALBERT RENÉ; Sec.-Gen. JAMES MICHEL.

Diplomatic Representation

EMBASSIES AND HIGH COMMISSIONS IN SEYCHELLES

China, People's Republic: POB 680, St Louis; tel. 266808; fax 266866; e-mail china@seychelles.net; Ambassador GENG WENBING.

Cuba: Belle Eau, POB 730, Victoria; tel. 224094; fax 224376; e-mail cubasey@seychelles.net; Ambassador DOMINGO ANGEL GARCÍA RODRÍGUEZ (designate).

France: La Ciotat Bldg, Mont Fleuri, POB 478, Victoria; tel. 382500; fax 382510; e-mail ambafran@seychelles.net; internet www.ambafrance-sc.org; Ambassador MICHEL TRÉTOUT.

India: Le Chantier, POB 488, Victoria; tel. 610301; fax 610308; e-mail hicomind@seychelles.net; internet www.seychelles.net/hicomind; High Commissioner ARUN KUMAR GOEL.

Russia: Le Niol, POB 632, Victoria; tel. 266590; fax 266653; e-mail rfembsey@seychelles.net; Ambassador ALEXANDER VLADIMIROV.

SEYCHELLES

United Kingdom: 3rd floor, Oliaji Trade Centre, POB 161, Victoria; tel. 283666; fax 283657; e-mail bhcvictoria@fco.gov.uk; High Commissioner DIANA SKINGLE.

Judicial System

The legal system is derived from English Common Law and the French Code Napoléon. There are three Courts, the Court of Appeal, the Supreme Court and the Magistrates' Courts. The Court of Appeal hears appeals from the Supreme Court in both civil and criminal cases. The Supreme Court is also a Court of Appeal from the Magistrates' Courts as well as having jurisdiction at first instance. The Constitutional Court, a division of the Supreme Court, determines matters of a constitutional nature, and considers cases bearing on civil liberties. There is also an industrial court and a rent tribunal.

Supreme Court: POB 157, Victoria; tel. 224071; fax 224197; Chief Justice VIVEKANAND ALLEEAR.

President of the Court of Appeal: (vacant).

Justices of Appeal: ANNEL SILUNGWE, A. PILLAY, G. P. S. DE SILVA, K. P. MATADEEN.

Puisne Judges: RANJAN PERERA, D. KARUNAKARAN, N. JUDDOO.

Attorney-General: ANTHONY F. FERNANDO.

Religion

The majority of the inhabitants are Christians, of whom more than 90% are Roman Catholics and about 8% Anglicans. Hinduism, Islam, and the Bahá'í Faith are also practised, however.

CHRISTIANITY

The Anglican Communion

The Church of the Province of the Indian Ocean comprises six dioceses: four in Madagascar, one in Mauritius and one in Seychelles. The Archbishop of the Province is the Bishop of Antananarivo, Madagascar.

Bishop of Seychelles: Rt Rev. SANTOSH MARRAY, POB 44, Victoria; tel. 224242; fax 224296; e-mail angdio@seychelles.net.

The Roman Catholic Church

Seychelles comprises a single diocese, directly responsible to the Holy See. At 31 December 2003 there were an estimated 70,103 adherents in the country, representing 85% of the total population.

Bishop of Port Victoria: Rt Rev. DENIS WIEHE, Bishop's House-Evêché, Olivier Maradan St, POB 43, Victoria; tel. 322152; fax 324045; e-mail rcchurch@seychelles.net.

The Press

L'Echo des Iles: POB 138, Victoria; tel. 322620; monthly; French, Creole and English; Roman Catholic; Editor P. SYMPHORIEN; circ. 2,800.

Le Nouveau Seychelles Weekly: Victoria; supports the Democratic Party.

The People: Maison du Peuple, Revolution Ave, Victoria; tel. 224455; owned by the SPPF; monthly; Creole, French and English; circ. 1,000.

Popsport: Premier Bldgs, POB 485, Victoria; tel. 323158.

Regar: Arpent Vert, Mont Fleuri, Victoria; tel. 224507; fax 224987; e-mail regar@seychelles.net; internet www.regar.sc; political weekly of the opposition SNP; Creole, English and French; Editor ROGER MANCIENNE.

Seychelles Nation: Information Technology and Communication Division, POB 800, Victoria; tel. 225775; fax 321006; e-mail seynat@seychelles.net; internet www.seychelles-online.com.sc; f. 1976; govt-owned; Mon.–Sat.; English, French and Creole; the country's only daily newspaper; Dir DENIS ROSE; circ. 3,500.

Seychelles Review: POB 29, Mahé, Victoria; tel. 241717; fax 241545; e-mail surmer@seychelles.net; monthly; business, politics, real estate and tourism; Editor ROLAND HOARAU.

Seychellois: POB 32, Victoria; f. 1928; publ. by Seychelles Farmers Asscn; quarterly; circ. 1,800.

NEWS AGENCY

Seychelles Agence de Presse (SAP): Victoria Rd, POB 321, Victoria; tel. 224161; fax 226006.

Broadcasting and Communications

TELECOMMUNICATIONS

Atlas (Seychelles) Ltd: POB 903, Victoria; tel. 304060; fax 324565; e-mail atlas@seychelles.net; internet www.seychelles.net; f. 1996; formed by a consortium of Space95, VCS and MBM; internet service provider.

Cable and Wireless (Seychelles) Ltd: Mercury House, Francis Rachel St, POB 4, Victoria; tel. 284000; fax 322777; e-mail cws@seychelles.net; internet www.cwseychelles.com; f. 1990; CEOs OSMAN SAADAT, CYRIL BONNELAME.

Telecom Seychelles Ltd (AirTel): POB 1358, Providence; tel. 345505; fax 345499; e-mail custcare@airtel.sc; internet www.airtel.sc; f. 1998; 80% owned by private investors, 10% by Govt of Seychelles; provides fixed-line, mobile and satellite telephone and internet services; Chief Exec. RAJAN SWAROOP.

BROADCASTING

Radio

Seychelles Broadcasting Corpn (SBC): Hermitage, POB 321, Victoria; tel. 224161; fax 225641; e-mail sbcradtv@seychelles.sc; internet www.sbc.sc; f. 1983; reorg. as independent corpn in 1992; programmes in Creole, English and French; Man. Dir IBRAHIM AFIF.

SBC Radio: Union Vale, POB 321, Victoria; tel. 289600; fax 289720; e-mail sbcradtv@seychelles.sc; internet www.sbc.sc; f. 1941; programmes in Creole, English and French; Man. Dir IBRAHIM AFIF.

Television

Seychelles Broadcasting Corpn (SBC): see Radio.

SBC TV: Hermitage, POB 321, Mahé; tel. 224161; fax 225641; e-mail sbcradtv@seychelles.sc; f. 1983; programmes in Creole, English and French; Head of Production PATRICK MATHIOT.

Finance

(cap. = capital; res = reserves; dep. = deposits; m. = million; brs = branches; amounts in Seychelles rupees)

BANKING

Central Bank

Central Bank of Seychelles (CBS): Independence Ave, POB 701, Victoria; tel. 225200; fax 224958; e-mail cbs@seychelles.net; internet www.cbs.sc; f. 1984; bank of issue; cap. 1.0m., res 105.6m., dep. 429.5m. (Dec. 2002); Gov. FRANCIS CHANG-LENG; Gen. Man. Dr PETER LAROSE.

National Banks

Development Bank of Seychelles: Independence Ave, POB 217, Victoria; tel. 224471; fax 224274; e-mail devbank@dbs.sc; internet www.dbs.sc; f. 1978; 55.5% state-owned; cap. 39.2m., res 43.7m., dep. 11.5m. (Dec. 2000); Chair. ANTONIO LUCAS; Man. Dir R. TOUSSAINT.

Seychelles International Mercantile Banking Corporation Ltd (Nouvobanq) (SIMBC): Victoria House, State House Ave, POB 241, Victoria; tel. 293000; fax 224670; e-mail nvb@nouvobanq.sc; f. 1991; 78% state-owned, 22% by Standard Chartered Bank (UK); cap. 50.0m., res 50.0m., dep. 1,509.7m. (Dec. 2003); Chair. CONRAD BENOÎTON; Pres. AHMED SAEED; 2 brs.

Seychelles Savings Bank Ltd (SSB): Kingsgate House, POB 531, Victoria; tel. 294000; fax 224713; e-mail ssb@savingsbank.sc; f. 1902; state-owned; term deposits, savings and current accounts; cap. and res 7.8m. (Dec. 1992), dep. 356.4m. (1999); Chair. JOSEPH NOURRICE; 4 brs.

Foreign Banks

Bank of Baroda (India): Trinity House, Albert St, POB 124, Victoria; tel. 323038; fax 324057; e-mail ce.seychelles@bankofbaroda.com; f. 1978; Man. M. M. PRASAD.

Mauritius Commercial Bank (Seychelles) Ltd (MCB Seychelles): POB 122, Manglier St, Victoria; tel. 284555; fax 322676; e-mail contact@mcbseychelles.com; internet www.mcbseychelles.com; f. 1978 as Banque Française Commerciale (BFCOI); changed name in 2003; cap. 14.0m., res 14.0m., dep. 958.4m. (Dec. 2003); Man. Dir JOCELYN AH-YU; 5 brs.

Barclays Bank (Seychelles) Ltd (United Kingdom): Independence Ave, POB 167, Victoria; tel. 383838; fax 224678; e-mail barclays.seychelles@barclays.com; f. 1959; Seychelles Dir M. P. LANDON; 3 brs and 4 agencies.

SEYCHELLES

Habib Bank Ltd (Pakistan): Frances Rachel St, POB 702, Victoria; tel. 224371; fax 225614; e-mail habibsez@seychelles.net; f. 1976; Vice-Pres. and Chief Man. SOHAIL ANWAR.

INSURANCE

H. Savy Insurance Co Ltd (HSI): Maison de la Rosière, 2nd Floor, POB 887; Victoria; tel. 322272; fax 321666; e-mail insurance@mail.seychelles.net; f. 1995; all classes; majority-owned by Corvina Investments; Gen. Dir JEAN WEELING-LEE.

Seychelles Assurance Company Ltd (SACL): Pirate's Arms Bldg, POB 636, Victoria; tel. 225000; fax 224495; e-mail sacos@sacos.sc; internet www.sacos.sc; f. 1980; state-owned; scheduled for privatization; all classes of insurance (excluding the Life Insurance Fund); subsidiaries include SUN Investments (Seychelles) Ltd, property-development company; fmrly State Assurance Corporation of Seychelles—SACOS; current name adopted 2006; Exec. Chair. ANTONIO A. LUCAS.

Trade and Industry

GOVERNMENT AGENCIES

Seychelles Fishing Authority (SFA): POB 449, Fishing Port, Victoria; tel. 670300; fax 224508; e-mail management@sfa.sc; internet www.sfa.sc; f. 1984; assessment and management of fisheries resources; Man. Dir RONDOLPH PAYET; Chair. FINLAY RACOMBO.

Seychelles Marketing Board (SMB): Latanier Rd, POB 634, Victoria; tel. 285000; fax 224735; e-mail mail@smb.sc; internet www.smb.sc; f. 1984; manufacturing and marketing of products, retailing, trade; CEO MUKESH VALABHJI.

DEVELOPMENT ORGANIZATIONS

Indian Ocean Tuna Commission (IOTC) (Commission de Thons de l'Océan Indien): POB 1011, Victoria; tel. 225494; fax 224364; e-mail iotc.secretary@iotc.org; internet www.iotc.org; f. 1997; an inter-governmental organization mandated to manage tuna and tuna-like species in the Indian Ocean and adjacent seas; to promote co-operation among its members with a view to ensuring, through appropriate management, the conservation and optimum utilisation of stocks and encouraging sustainable development of fisheries based on such stocks; Gen. Sec. ALEJANDRO ANGANUZZI.

Seychelles Agricultural Development Co Ltd (SADECO): POB 172, Victoria; tel. 375888; f. 1980; Gen. Man. LESLIE PRÉA (acting).

Seychelles Industrial Development Corporation (SIDEC): POB 537, Victoria; tel. 323151; fax 324121; e-mail sidec@sidec.sc; internet www.sidec.sc; f. 1988; promotes industrial development and manages leased industrial sites; CEO MAXWELL JULIE.

Seychelles International Business Authority (SIBA): POB 991, Victoria; tel. 380800; fax 380888; e-mail siba@seychelles.net; internet www.siba.net; f. 1995; to supervise registration of companies, transhipment and 'offshore' financial services in an international free-trade zone covering an area of 23 ha near Mahé International Airport; Man. Dir CONRAD BENOÎTON.

Seychelles Investment Bureau (SIB): POB 1167, Caravelle House, 2nd floor, Manglier St, Victoria; tel. 295500; fax 225125; e-mail sib@seychelles.sc; internet www.sib.sc; f. 2004; Chief Exec. JOSEPH NOURRICE.

CHAMBER OF COMMERCE

Seychelles Chamber of Commerce and Industry: Ebrahim Bldg, 2nd Floor, POB 1399, Victoria; tel. 323812; fax 321422; e-mail scci@seychelles.net; Chair. BERNARD POOL; Sec.-Gen. NICHOLE TIRANT-GHÉRARDI.

EMPLOYERS' ORGANIZATION

Federation of Employers' Associations of Seychelles (FEAS): POB 214, Victoria; tel. 324969; fax 324996; Chair. BASIL SOUNDY.

UTILITIES

Electricity

Public Utilities Corporation (Electricity Division): Electricity House, POB 174, Roche Caiman; tel. 678000; fax 321020; e-mail pmorin@puc.sc; Man. Dir PHILIPPE MORIN.

Water

Public Utilities Corporation (Water and Sewerage Division): Unity House, POB 34, Victoria; tel. 322444; fax 325612; e-mail pucwater@seychelles.net; Man. Dir STEPHEN ROUSSEAU.

TRADE UNION

Seychelles Federation of Workers' Unions (SFWU): Maison du Peuple, Latanier Rd, POB 154, Victoria; tel. 224455; fax 225351; e-mail sfwu@seychelles.net; f. 1978 to amalgamate all existing trade unions; affiliated to the Seychelles People's Progressive Front; 25,200 mems; Pres. OLIVIER CHARLES; Gen. Sec. ANTOINE ROBINSON.

Transport

RAILWAYS

There are no railways in Seychelles.

ROADS

In 2004 there were 498 km of roads, of which 478 km were surfaced. Most surfaced roads are on Mahé and Praslin.

SHIPPING

Privately owned ferry services connect Victoria, on Mahé, with the islands of Praslin and La Digue. At 31 December 2004 Seychelles' merchant fleet numbered 33 vessels, totalling 66,851 grt.

Port and Marine Services Division, Ministry of Tourism and Transport: POB 47, Mahé Quay, Victoria; tel. 224701; fax 224004; e-mail marineservices@seychellesports.sc; Dir-Gen. (Port of Victoria) Capt. W. ERNESTA.

Aquarius Shipping Agency Ltd: POB 865, Victoria; tel. 225050; fax 225043; e-mail aqua@seychelles.net; Gen. Man. ANTHONY SAVY.

Hunt, Deltel and Co Ltd: Victoria House, POB 14, Victoria; tel. 380300; fax 225367; e-mail hundel@seychelles.net; internet www.hundel.sc; f. 1937; Man. Dir E. HOUAREAU.

Mahé Shipping Co Ltd: Maritime House, POB 336, Victoria; tel. 380500; fax 380538; e-mail maheship@seychelles.net; shipping agents; Chair. Capt. G. C. C. ADAM.

Harry Savy & Co Ltd: POB 20, Victoria; tel. 322120; fax 321421; e-mail hsavyco@seychelles.net; shipping agents; Man. Dir GUY SAVY.

Seychelles Shipping Line Ltd: POB 977, Providence, Victoria; tel. 373737; fax 373647; e-mail ssl@gondwana.net; f. 1994; operates freight services between Seychelles and Durban, South Africa; Chair. SELWYN GENDRON; Man. Dir HASSAN OMAR.

CIVIL AVIATION

Seychelles International Airport is located at Pointe Larue, 10 km from Victoria. A new international passenger terminal and aircraft parking apron were to be constructed by 2007 on land reclaimed in 1990; the existing terminal (which underwent SR 3m. in renovations in 2002) was to be converted into a cargo terminal. The airport also serves as a refuelling point for aircraft traversing the Indian Ocean. There are airstrips on several outlying islands.

Seychelles Civil Aviation Authority (SCAA): POB 181, Victoria; tel. 384000; fax 384009; e-mail dcaadmin@seychelles.net; formerly Directorate of Civil Aviation; offers ground and cargo handling and refuelling services, as well as holding responsibility for the Flight Information Region of 2.6m. sq km of Indian Ocean airspace; Chair. GERARD LAFORTUNE; Chief Exec. CONRAD BENOÎTON.

Air Seychelles: The Creole Spirit Bldg, Quincy St, POB 386, Victoria; tel. 224305; fax 225933; e-mail airseymd@seychelles.net; internet www.airseychelles.net; f. 1979; operates scheduled internal flights from Mahé to Praslin; also charter services to Bird, Desroches and Denis Islands and to outlying islands of the Amirantes group; international services to Europe, Far East, East and South Africa; Chief Exec. Capt. DAVID SAVY.

Emirates Airlines: 5th June Ave and Manglier St, Victoria; tel. 292700; f. 2005; Dir ABDULRAHMAN AL BALOOSHI.

Tourism

Seychelles enjoys an equable climate, and is renowned for its fine beaches and attractive scenery. There are more than 500 varieties of flora and many rare species of birds. Most tourist activity is concentrated on the islands of Mahé, Praslin and La Digue, although the potential for ecological tourism of the outlying islands received increased attention in the late 1990s. It is government policy that the development of tourism should not blight the environment, and strict laws govern the location and construction of hotels. In 1998 the Government indicated that up to 200,000 visitors (although not more than 4,000 at any one time) could be accommodated annually without detriment to environmental quality. However, several new luxury resorts were constructed in the early 2000s, and the yachting sector was also under development. Receipts from tourism totalled an estimated US $242m. in 2002. In 2003 there were 122,038 tourist and business arrivals; most visitors (81.5% in 2004) are from Europe; in 2004 there were an average of 5,030 hotel beds available.

Compagnie Seychelloise de Promotion Hotelière Ltd: POB 683, Victoria; tel. 224694; fax 225291; e-mail cosproh@seychelles.net; promotes govt-owned hotels.

Seychelles Tourism Board (STB): POB 1262, Victoria; tel. 620000; fax 620620; e-mail seychelles@aspureasitgets.com; internet www.aspureasitgets.com; f. 1998 as Seychelles Tourism Marketing Board; merged with Seychelles Tourism Office in 2005; Chair. MAURICE LOUSTEAU-LALANNE.

SIERRA LEONE
Introductory Survey

Location, Climate, Language, Religion, Flag, Capital

The Republic of Sierra Leone lies on the west coast of Africa, with Guinea to the north and east, and Liberia to the south. The climate is hot and humid, with an average annual temperature of 27°C (80°F). The rainy season lasts from May to October. The average annual rainfall is about 3,436 mm (13.5 ins). English is the official language, while Krio (Creole), Mende, Limba and Temne are also widely spoken. The majority of the population follow animist beliefs, but there are significant numbers of Islamic and Christian adherents. The national flag (proportions 2 by 3) has three equal horizontal stripes, of green, white and blue. The capital is Freetown.

Recent History

Sierra Leone was formerly a British colony and protectorate. A new Constitution, which provided for universal adult suffrage, was introduced in 1951. In that year the Sierra Leone People's Party (SLPP) won the majority of votes in elections. The leader of the SLPP, Dr (later Sir) Milton Margai, became Chief Minister in 1953 and Prime Minister in 1958. On 27 April 1961 Sierra Leone achieved independence as a constitutional monarchy within the Commonwealth. The SLPP retained its majority at elections in May 1962. Margai died in April 1964 and was succeeded as Prime Minister by his half-brother, Dr (later Sir) Albert Margai, previously the Minister of Finance.

Following disputed elections in March 1967, the army assumed control and established a ruling body, the National Reformation Council. The Governor-General was subsequently forced to leave the country. In December a commission of inquiry announced that the All-People's Congress (APC) had won the elections in March. In April 1968 a further coup was staged by army officers, and power was subsequently transferred to a civilian Government; Dr Siaka Stevens, the leader of the APC, was elected as Prime Minister. In April 1971 a republican Constitution was introduced and Stevens became executive President.

The general election in May 1973 was not contested by the SLPP, and in 1976 Stevens, the sole candidate, was unanimously re-elected to the presidency for a second five-year term of office. In May 1977 the APC won the majority of votes in legislative elections, which were contested by the SLPP. In July the House of Representatives ruled that the SLPP was no longer the official opposition party, on the grounds that it was incapable of undertaking government administration. A new Constitution, which provided for a one-party system, was promulgated in May 1978, approved in a national referendum and adopted by the House of Representatives in June. The APC thus became the sole legitimate political organization. Stevens was inaugurated as President for a seven-year term on 14 June 1978. He subsequently released political detainees and allocated ministerial posts to several former SLPP members (who had joined the APC).

The Government faced increasing opposition in 1981, following a scandal involving government officials and several cabinet ministers in the misappropriation of public funds. Legislative elections took place in May 1982, amid serious incidents of violence. Civil unrest, prompted by economic hardship, subsequently increased. In April 1985 Stevens announced that (contrary to earlier indications) he would not seek re-election to the presidency upon the expiry, in June, of his existing mandate. Stevens' term of office was subsequently extended for six months, to allow time for registration of voters and the nomination of a presidential candidate. At a conference of the APC in August, Maj.-Gen. Joseph Momoh, a cabinet minister and the Commander of the Army, was the sole candidate for the leadership of the party and for the presidential nomination. Momoh was elected to the national presidency in October, with 99% of the votes cast, and was inaugurated on 28 November. Although retaining his military status, Momoh appointed a civilian Cabinet, which included several members of the previous administration. Elections to the House of Representatives took place in May 1986.

Despite a campaign against financial malpractice in the public sector, Momoh's administration failed to improve the serious economic situation, and popular discontent increased. In March 1987 the Government announced that it had suppressed an attempted coup; more than 60 people were subsequently arrested, including the First Vice-President, Francis Minah. In October Minah and 15 other defendants were sentenced to death for plotting to assassinate Momoh and to overthrow the Government, and two defendants received custodial sentences on charges of treason. In October 1989 Minah and five others were executed, despite international appeals for clemency.

Following the outbreak of civil conflict in Liberia in December 1989, an estimated 125,000 Liberians took refuge in Sierra Leone. The Sierra Leonean Government contributed troops to the cease-fire monitoring group (ECOMOG) of the Economic Community of West African States (ECOWAS, see p. 217), which was dispatched to Liberia in August 1990. In November of that year Charles Taylor, the leader of the principal Liberian rebel faction, the National Patriotic Front of Liberia (NPFL), threatened to attack Freetown International Airport (alleged to be a base for ECOMOG offensives against rebel strongholds). In early April 1991, following repeated border incursions by members of the NPFL, government forces entered Liberian territory and launched a retaliatory attack against NPFL bases. By the end of that month, however, NPFL forces had advanced 150 km within Sierra Leone. The Momoh Government alleged that the rebel offensive had been instigated by Taylor, in an attempt to force Sierra Leone's withdrawal from ECOMOG, and also accused the Government of Burkina Faso of actively assisting the rebels. It was reported, however, that members of a Sierra Leonean resistance movement, known as the Revolutionary United Front (RUF), had joined the NPFL in attacks against government forces. In mid-1991 government troops, with the assistance of military units from Nigeria and Guinea, initiated a counter-offensive against the rebels, and succeeded in recapturing several towns in the east and south of the country.

In August 1990, at a session of the Central Committee of the APC, Momoh (who had hitherto made clear his opposition to the establishment of a multi-party political system) conceded the necessity of electoral reforms, and announced an extensive revision of the Constitution, subsequently appointing a 30-member National Constitutional Review Commission. In March 1991 the Commission submitted a draft Constitution, which provided for the adoption of a multi-party system, for consideration by the Government. The new Constitution stipulated that the President, who was to appoint the Cabinet, was to be elected by a majority of votes cast nationally and by at least 25% of the votes cast in more than one-half of the electoral districts. Members of the legislature were to be elected by universal adult suffrage for a term of five years. The Government subsequently accepted the majority of the Commission's recommendations. In June the Government presented the draft Constitution to the House of Representatives, and announced that the parliamentary term, which was due to end that month, was to be extended until May 1992 to allow time for the transition to a multi-party system.

In early August 1991 the House of Representatives formally approved the new Constitution, and at a national referendum, which was conducted later in August, it was endorsed by 60% of voters, with 75% of the electorate participating. In the same month six newly created political associations formed an alliance, known as the United Front of Political Movements, which subsequently demanded that the forthcoming elections be monitored by international observers, and that the incumbent Government be dissolved and an interim administration established. On 23 September, following the resignation of the First Vice-President and Second Vice-President from both the APC and the Government, Momoh announced the formation of a new 18-member Cabinet, which retained only seven members of the previous Government. Later that month legislation that formally permitted the formation of political associations was introduced; several organizations were subsequently granted legal recognition.

On 29 April 1992 members of the armed forces, led by a five-member military junta, seized a radio station in Freetown and broadcast demands for improvements in conditions in the armed forces. The rebel troops later occupied the presidential offices, and the leader of the military junta, Capt. Valentine E. M. Strasser, announced that the Government had been overthrown. On the following day Momoh fled to Guinea, and Strasser announced the establishment of a governing council, to be known as the National Provisional Ruling Council (NPRC). Strasser affirmed the NPRC's commitment to the introduction of a multi-party system, and pledged to end the conflict in the country. On the same day the Constitution was suspended, the House of Representatives was dissolved and a state of emergency, which included a curfew, was imposed. On 1 May the NPRC (which principally comprised military officers), chaired by Strasser, was formed. Shortly afterwards a new 19-member Cabinet, which included a number of members of the NPRC, was appointed, and the Commander of the Armed Forces and the head of the security forces were replaced. On 6 May Strasser was inaugurated as Head of State.

In July 1992 Strasser replaced the three members of the NPRC in the Cabinet with civilians, and removed all civilian cabinet ministers from the NPRC. Later that month he announced extensive structural changes, which were designed to reduce the direct involvement of the NPRC in government administration: the NPRC was officially designated the Supreme Council of State, while the Cabinet was reconstituted as the Council of Secretaries (headed by the Chief Secretary of State), which was to be responsible for government administration, subject to the authority of the NPRC. In the same month the Government introduced legislation that imposed severe restrictions on the media.

In September 1992 the Deputy Chairman of the NPRC, Capt. Solomon A. J. Musa, temporarily assumed the office of Head of State during a visit by Strasser to the USA. In that month Musa suspended a number of senior army officers and members of the security forces. In November some 30 people, who were alleged to be supporters of Momoh, were arrested by the security forces and charged with involvement in subversive activities. In early December Strasser announced a reorganization of the Council of Secretaries, in which the two remaining members of the Momoh administration were replaced. In the same month Musa became Chief Secretary of State. Later in December, in an apparent attempt to regain public support, the Government established a 19-member National Advisory Council, comprising representatives of various non-governmental organizations, which was to draft a programme for transition to civilian rule.

At the end of December 1992 the Government announced that the security forces had suppressed a coup attempt by a group known as the Anti-Corruption Revolutionary Movement (which included former members of the army and security forces). Shortly afterwards nine of those accused of involvement in the attempted coup were convicted by a special military tribunal, and, together with 17 prisoners who had been convicted in November on charges of treason, were summarily executed. Human rights organizations subsequently contested the Government's statement that a coup attempt had been staged, and condemned the trial by special military tribunal. In January 1993 the United Kingdom announced the suspension of economic aid to Sierra Leone in protest at the executions.

In April 1993 Strasser announced that a programme providing for a transition to civilian rule within a period of three years was to be adopted; in addition, all political prisoners were to be released, press restrictions would be relaxed, and the function of special military tribunals was to be reviewed. In July Musa was replaced as Deputy Chairman of the NPRC and Chief Secretary of State by Capt. Julius Maada Bio, ostensibly on the grounds that false allegations against him had proved detrimental to the stability of the administration. Musa (who was widely believed to be responsible for the repressive measures undertaken by the Government) took refuge in the Nigerian high commission in Freetown, amid widespread speculation regarding his dismissal, and subsequently emigrated to the United Kingdom.

At the end of November 1993 Strasser announced the details of a two-year transitional programme, which provided for the installation of a civilian government by January 1996. The registration of political parties was to take place in June 1995, prior to a presidential election in November and legislative elections in December of that year. In December a five-member Interim National Electoral Commission was established to organize the registration of voters and the demarcation of constituency boundaries, in preparation for forthcoming local government elections. In the same month the National Advisory Council submitted constitutional proposals (which included a number of similar provisions to the 1991 Constitution), stipulating that: executive power was to be vested in the President, who was to be required to consult with the Cabinet, and was to be restricted to a tenure of two four-year terms of office; only Sierra Leonean nationals of more than 40 years of age were to qualify to contest a presidential election (thereby precluding Strasser and the majority of NPRC members, on grounds of age); the legislature was to comprise a House of Representatives, which was to be elected by universal adult suffrage for a term of five years, and a 30-member upper chamber, the Senate.

At the end of December 1993 the Government ended the state of emergency that had been imposed in April 1992 (although additional security measures remained in force). In April 1994 13 senior members of the armed forces were dismissed, following widespread criticism of the Government's failure to end continued conflict in the south-east of the country with the RUF, led by Foday Sankoh, which, in 1991, had joined Liberian rebels in attacks against government forces. In July a National Security Council, chaired by Strasser, was established to co-ordinate the operations of the armed forces. Later that month it was reported that the RUF (which had been joined by disaffected members of the armed forces) had besieged the principal town of Kenema, near the border with Liberia, and was exploiting diamond reserves in the region.

In October 1994 a draft Constitution was submitted to the NPRC. However, an increase in rebel activity in many parts of the country, with widespread looting and killing by armed groups, prevented the organization of district council elections, which had been scheduled to take place later that month. In January 1995 the RUF gained control of the mining installations owned by the Sierra Leone Ore and Metal Company (SIEROMCO) and Sierra Rutile Ltd, and seized a number of employees of the two enterprises, including eight foreign nationals. Later in January seven Roman Catholic nuns, together with a number of Sierra Leonean citizens, were abducted, following an attack by the RUF against the north-western town of Kambia. In the same month the RUF threatened to kill the British hostages if the Sierra Leonean authorities executed an officer, who had been convicted by military tribunal of collaborating with the rebels. In February the RUF rejected appeals by the UN and the Organization of African Unity (OAU, now the African Union, see p. 153) that peace negotiations be initiated, and demanded that all troops that had been dispatched by foreign Governments to assist the Strasser administration be withdrawn as a precondition to discussions. In mid-February government forces (which had succeeded in recapturing the mining installations owned by Sierra Rutile) launched an offensive against a principal rebel base in the Kangari region, east of Freetown. Meanwhile, continued atrocities perpetrated against civilians were increasingly attributed to disaffected members of the armed forces.

In February 1995 the military administration engaged 58 Gurkha mercenaries, who had previously served in the British army, prompting further concern regarding the safety of the British hostages in Sierra Leone. In March government forces regained control of the mining installations owned by SIEROMCO and the principal town of Moyamba, 100 km south-east of Freetown (which had been captured by the RUF earlier that month). Later that month the rebels released the seven nuns who had been abducted in January. Despite the successful counter-offensives by government forces, by April the RUF had advanced towards Freetown and had initiated a series of attacks against towns in the vicinity (including Songo, which was situated only 35 km east of Freetown), apparently prior to besieging the capital. Later in April the remaining foreign nationals who had been seized by the RUF were released.

In March 1995 the Council of Secretaries was reorganized to allow principal military officials in the Government to assume active functions within the armed forces (following the advance of RUF forces towards Freetown); Lt-Col Akim Gibril became Chief Secretary of State, replacing Bio, who was appointed Chief of Defence Staff. At the end of April, on the anniversary of the NPRC's assumption of power, Strasser formally announced that the ban on political activity was to be rescinded, and that a National Consultative Conference was to be convened to discuss the transitional process; he further indicated that elections were to take place by the end of that year, prior to the installation of a civilian government in January 1996, in accordance with the transitional programme. The ban on political activity was formally ended on 21 June; some 15 parties were subsequently granted registration (although the RUF failed to respond to government efforts to include the movement in the electoral process). Later in June 56 former government officials, including Momoh, were prohibited from assuming public office for a period of 10 years (and thereby precluded from contesting the elections), after the government commissions of inquiry concluded that they had misused public funds.

In May 1995 government forces initiated a number of counter-attacks against the RUF, and succeeded in recapturing Songo. The Governments of Guinea and Nigeria dispatched additional troops to Sierra Leone, while it was reported that mercenaries recruited via a private South African concern were assisting the authorities with military training and logistics. By the end of June government forces had regained control of significant diamond-mining regions in the eastern Kono District, and part of Bo District, in a successful counter-offensive, which was generally attributed to the assistance of the mercenaries. In September, however, the RUF launched further offensives in Bo District, while increasing reports of massacres and other violations of human rights perpetrated by the rebels against the civilian population emerged.

In October 1995, while Strasser was abroad, a coup attempt was suppressed by government forces; seven military officers were subsequently arrested on suspicion of attempting to overthrow the Government. In December it was announced that the presidential and legislative elections were to take place concurrently on 26 February 1996. In January 1996, however, Strasser was deposed by military officers, led by Bio, in a bloodless coup. Bio, who assumed the office of Head of State, announced that the coup had been instigated in response to efforts by Strasser to remain in power. (It was reported that Strasser had intended to amend restrictions on the age of prospective candidates to enable himself to contest the elections.) Strasser (who had been expelled to Guinea) claimed, however, that the new military administration planned to delay the transition to civilian government. A reconstituted Supreme Council of State and Council of Secretaries were formed, and, following a meeting of the new military leadership, the political parties and INEC, it was announced that the elections were to take place as scheduled. The RUF indicated that it was prepared to enter into negotiations with the new Government, and declared a temporary cease-fire to allow voter registration to proceed throughout the country, but urged a postponement of the elections, pending a peace settlement that would allow the movement to participate in the democratic process. However, delegates at the National Consultative Conference, which was convened by INEC in early February, voted in favour of adherence to the scheduled date. The RUF subsequently abandoned the cease-fire and launched a series of attacks in various parts of the country, in an apparent attempt to undermine the electoral process.

On 26 February 1996 presidential and legislative elections took place as scheduled. However, some 27 people were killed in attacks by armed groups, particularly in Bo and parts of Freetown, which were generally attributed to the RUF; voting was consequently extended for a further day. The reconstituted SLPP secured 36.1% of votes cast in the legislative elections, while its presidential candidate, Ahmed Tejan Kabbah, also received most support, with 35.8% of votes. Seven of the political parties demanded that the results be annulled, owing to the disruption of the elections in several regions caused by the civil violence. A second round of the presidential election, which took place on 15 March, was contested by Kabbah and the candidate of the United National People's Party (UNPP), John Karefa-Smart (who had obtained 22.6% of votes cast in the first round): Kabbah was elected President by 59.5% of the votes. Later in March seats in the new 80-member Parliament were allocated on a basis of proportional representation, with the SLPP securing 27, the UNPP 17, the People's Democratic Party 12 and the reconstituted APC only five seats; the 12 provincial districts were represented in the legislature by Paramount Chiefs. Kabbah was inaugurated on 29 March, when the military Government officially relinquished power to the new civilian administration. In April Kabbah appointed a new Cabinet, which was subsequently approved by the new Parliament.

Following the elections, the Government announced in March 1996 that the RUF had agreed to a cease-fire; at a meeting between Sankoh and Bio in Yamoussoukro, Côte d'Ivoire, later that month, the RUF undertook to observe the cease-fire for a period of two months and to continue negotiations with the newly elected civilian Government. Following discussions between Sankoh and Kabbah in April, the Government and RUF reaffirmed their commitment to a permanent cessation of hostilities, and announced the establishment of three joint committees, which would consider issues regarding the demobilization of rebel forces. However, Sankoh continued to refuse to recognize the legitimacy of the new Government, and demanded that a transitional administration be installed pending further elections. At continuing negotiations in May, agreement was reached on a number of issues, although the RUF demanded that the mercenaries be withdrawn from the country as a precondition to the demobilization of its forces. Despite the official cease-fire, sporadic attacks by the RUF were subsequently reported. Additional clashes occurred later that year between government forces and the Kamajors (traditional fighters reconstituted as an auxiliary defence force).

In July 1996 the Parliament adopted legislation that formally reinstated the Constitution of 1991. In September 1996 Kabbah ordered the compulsory retirement of some 20 officers, including Strasser and Bio, from the armed forces. Shortly afterwards it was reported that a conspiracy to overthrow the Government had been thwarted by senior military officers. About 17 members of the armed forces were arrested, of whom nine were subsequently charged with involvement in the conspiracy. Following reports of a further conspiracy to overthrow the Government in January 1997, Kabbah announced that an investigative mission from Nigeria had concluded that former members of the NPRC administration had instigated the coup attempt of September 1996.

In November 1996 Kabbah demanded that the RUF relinquish armaments within a period of two weeks, threatening that government forces would resume military operations. At the end of that month Kabbah and Sankoh signed a peace agreement in Abidjan, Côte d'Ivoire, whereby RUF forces were to be demobilized and the movement was to be reconstituted as a political organization, while all foreign troops were to be withdrawn from the country and replaced with foreign observers. A National Commission for the Consolidation of Peace was subsequently established to monitor the peace settlement. By February 1997 all foreign mercenaries had left Sierra Leone in accordance with the agreement, while the repatriation of Sierra Leonean refugees from Liberia had commenced. However, at the end of that month (when the implementation of the peace agreement was scheduled for completion) it was reported that members of the RUF had repeatedly violated the peace agreement and had failed to report to designated centres for disarmament. In March numbers of the political wing of the RUF issued a declaration that Sankoh had been removed as leader of the organization, owing to his failure to implement the peace accord. Later that month, however, RUF forces loyal to Sankoh kidnapped members of the movement who had supported his replacement, together with the Sierra Leonean ambassador to Guinea; the faction issued demands for the release of Sankoh, who had been detained in Nigeria earlier that month (being reportedly in possession of armaments).

On 25 May 1997 dissident members of the armed forces, led by Maj. Johnny Paul Koroma, seized power, deposing Kabbah, who fled to Guinea. Koroma claimed that the coup, which was condemned internationally, was in response to the Government's failure to implement the peace agreement with the RUF. (The coup leaders were believed to have connections with members of the NPRC administration, many of whom, it was reported, planned to return to Sierra Leone.) The Nigerian Government demanded that the junta relinquish power, and increased its military strength in Freetown to about 3,000 troops. The new authorities imposed a curfew in Freetown, following widespread violent looting by armed factions; most foreign nationals were evacuated. In early June Nigerian forces initiated a naval bombardment of Freetown in an effort to force the new military leaders to resign. However, forces loyal to the coup leaders, assisted by RUF members, succeeded in repelling Nigerian attacks. Koroma announced the establishment of a 20-member Armed Forces Revolutionary Council (AFRC), with himself as Chairman and Sankoh (who remained in detention in Nigeria) as Vice-Chairman; the AFRC (which was not internationally recognized as the legitimate Government) included a further three members of the RUF and several civilians. All political activity, the existing Constitution and government bodies were suspended, although Koroma pledged that democratic rule would be restored. Nigeria reiterated that it intended to reinstate the ousted Government with the support of ECO-WAS, and a further two Nigerian warships were dispatched to the region; further clashes between Nigerian troops, who had been serving under the mandate of ECOMOG in neighbouring Liberia (q.v.), and supporters of the new military leaders occurred at the international airport at Lungi. In mid-June the AFRC announced that it had suppressed a coup attempt, following the arrest of 15 people, including several senior military officers. In the same month it was reported that troops supporting the junta had repulsed an attack by Kamajors (who remained loyal to Kabbah) at the town of Zimmi, 250 km south-east of Freetown. On 17 June Koroma was formally inaugurated as the self-proclaimed Head of State. However, despite appeals from Koroma, a campaign of civil disobedience, organized by the labour congress in protest at the coup, continued.

By early July 1997 the new military Government had been completely isolated by the international community. The Commonwealth Ministerial Action Group on the Harare Declaration (CMAG—which had been established to ensure adherence to the principles of democracy by member states) suspended Sierra Leone from meetings of the Commonwealth, pending the restoration of constitutional order and the reinstatement of a democratically elected government. The UN Security Council also condemned the coup, and expressed support for ECOWAS efforts to resolve the situation. Meanwhile, a four-member ministerial committee, comprising representatives of Nigeria, Côte d'Ivoire, Guinea and Ghana, which had been established by ECOWAS, urged the Government to relinquish power during a series of negotiations with an AFRC delegation.

In mid-July 1997 Koroma formed a cabinet, known as the Council of Secretaries, comprising representatives of the RUF and the army, together with a number of civilians. Later that month, following further reports of clashes between Kamajors and forces loyal to the junta in the south of the country, AFRC representatives and the ECOWAS committee, meeting in Abidjan, agreed to an immediate cease-fire; negotiations were to continue, with the aim of restoring constitutional order. However, Nigeria subsequently accused the AFRC of violating the cease-fire, while further clashes between the Kamajors and the AFRC forces were reported at Zimmi. Renewed skirmishes between Nigerian and AFRC troops also occurred at Lungi airport. At the end of July continuing discussions between the ECOWAS committee and AFRC representatives in Abidjan were abandoned, after Koroma insisted that he retain power for a tenure of four years, and refused to restore the Constitution and to end the ban on political activity. Consequently, in late August an ECOWAS conference, which was convened at Abuja, Nigeria, officially endorsed the imposition of sanctions against Sierra Leone, with the aim of obliging the AFRC to relinquish power; however, the conference rejected demands by Kabbah, which were supported by the Nigerian Government, for military intervention to reinstate his administration. ECOMOG was granted a mandate to monitor the cease-fire and to enforce the economic embargo; it was also agreed that the ECOWAS monitoring committee would henceforth include Liberia (following the election of a democratic Government in that country).

In September 1997 ECOMOG troops stationed at the airport at Lungi bombarded container vessels that were suspected of attempting to violate the sanctions, and staged aerial attacks against commercial and military targets in Freetown, killing about 50 civilians. In the same month CMAG voted in support of the decision of the ECOWAS committee to effect the reinstatement of the Kabbah administration. In early October the UN Security Council imposed sanctions on the import of armaments and petroleum products to Sierra Leone. Following further aerial bombardments of Freetown by ECOMOG troops (in which large numbers of civilians were killed), a mass demonstration was held in the capital to demand that the Nigerian Government withdraw its troops from Sierra Leone. Negotiations between the AFRC and the five-member committee continued, however, and later in October an agreement, which was signed in Conakry, Guinea, provided for an immediate cease-fire, and the reinstatement of Kabbah's Government by April 1998, together with immunity from prosecution for AFRC members; all troops loyal to the incumbent military administration and RUF members were to be demobilized, under the supervision of a disarmament committee, comprising representatives of the AFRC, ECOMOG and local forces loyal to Kabbah. In November 10 people, including a senior RUF official, were arrested in connection with an alleged conspiracy to overthrow the military junta. In January 1998 ECOMOG forces again bombarded the port at Freetown (for the first time since the peace agreement in October), apparently with the aim of preventing merchant vessels from contravening the sanctions. Meanwhile, later that month Kamajors gained control of the town of Tongofield (where principal reserves of diamonds were located), 240 km east of Freetown, and in early February were reported to have captured the town of Bo.

In early February 1998 further clashes erupted near Freetown between ECOMOG troops and supporters of the military junta. Nigerian troops belonging to ECOMOG subsequently launched an intensive bombardment against Freetown and succeeded in gaining control of the capital, after senior members of the AFRC, including Koroma, fled into hiding, or surrendered to the ECOMOG forces; some 100 civilians were killed in the fighting, while more than 3,000 took refuge in Guinea. About 50 members of the military junta were arrested at James Spriggs Payne Airport at Monrovia, Liberia, prompting protests from the Liberian Government regarding the Nigerian military intervention. It was announced that the Government that had been ousted on 25 May 1997 was to be reinstated, and that all subsequent appointments were to be considered invalid. ECOMOG forces were to remain in the country to assist in the restructuring of the armed forces. Meanwhile, following reports that troops loyal to the former military junta, with the assistance of the RUF, had recaptured Bo, ECOMOG forces were deployed in the region to support the Kamajors, and rapidly succeeded in regaining control of most of the region (prompting speculation that the Nigerian military initiative had been undertaken with the aim of gaining access to Sierra Leone's mineral resources).

On 10 March 1998 Kabbah returned from exile and was officially reinstated as President; he subsequently appointed a Cabinet (which included a number of members of his previous administration). The new Government declared a state of emergency under which members of the former military junta could be detained for a maximum of 30 days without being formally charged. It was announced that some 1,500 civilians and members of the armed forces (including Momoh) had been placed in detention and were to be charged for their alleged connections with the former military junta. Also in March the UN Security Council voted to end its embargo on imports of petroleum products to Sierra Leone (which had resulted in severe fuel shortages), although an embargo on the supply of armaments was maintained. It was reported that ECOMOG forces had launched an offensive in the east of the country, in an effort to eradicate the remaining forces loyal to the former military junta and members of the RUF. In July the UN Security Council adopted a resolution establishing a UN Observer Mission in Sierra Leone (UNOMSIL), comprising 70 military observers, with an initial six-month mandate to monitor the security situation, supervise the disarmament of former combatants, and advise the authorities on the restructuring of the security forces. In the same month it was announced that the national army had been dissolved.

In late July 1998 the Nigerian Government returned Foday Sankoh (who had been in detention in Nigeria since early 1997) to Sierra Leone, where he was charged with treason following his support for the military coup of May 1997. In August 16 civilians, including five journalists, were sentenced to death, after being convicted of supporting the former military junta. In October 24 army officers were publicly executed, following their conviction for involvement with the military junta, provoking condemnation from many foreign Governments and human rights organizations, which had appealed for clemency. Death penalties imposed against a further 10 officers were commuted to terms of life imprisonment. In November a further 15 civilians, including several ministers who had served in the AFRC Government, were sentenced to death for their part in the May 1997 coup; Momoh received a custodial term of 10 years for colluding with the military junta.

Meanwhile, ECOMOG continued efforts to suppress rebel activity, particularly in the north and east of the country, and in October 1998 transferred its operational headquarters from the Liberian capital, Monrovia, to Freetown. In that month the RUF intensified hostilities, after it was announced that Sankoh had been sentenced to death by the High Court on charges of treason. In November ECOMOG forces commenced aerial bombardments of rebel bases. By late December, however, RUF forces, together with supporters of the former military junta, had advanced towards Freetown, and had seized control of the principal town of Makeni, 140 km north-east of Freetown. The Governments of Nigeria and Ghana dispatched additional troops to reinforce the ECOMOG contingent (which henceforth numbered about 15,000). At the end of December the acting Commander of the RUF, Sam Bockarie, rejected a government invitation to enter into peace negotiations, and ECOMOG forces, supported by Kamajors, attempted to repulse rebel attacks in the outskirts of Freetown.

On 6 January 1999 rebel forces attacked Freetown (where thousands of civilians from the surrounding area had taken refuge), releasing a number of supporters of the former junta from the capital's prison and seizing the Nigerian High Commission and government offices; Kabbah and a number of cabinet ministers were obliged to flee to ECOMOG headquarters. (It was subsequently discovered that two ministers had been killed by the rebels.) Bockarie announced that Freetown was under the control of the RUF, and demanded that Sankoh be released from detention. However, he rejected a subsequent offer by Kabbah to release Sankoh on condition that the rebels comply with the November 1996 peace agreement. ECOMOG troops initiated a counter-offensive, with an aerial bombardment of Freetown, forcing the rebels to retreat to the outskirts of the capital. It was estimated that about 3,000 people had been killed during the RUF occupation of the capital, and further large numbers of civilians were maimed by the rebels. The rebel forces had taken hostage the Roman Catholic Archbishop, Joseph Ganda, and about 11 European priests and nuns; Ganda and five priests were rescued by ECOMOG troops, but it was subsequently reported that some of the nuns had been killed. By late January ECOMOG forces claimed to have regained control of Freetown, and a cease-fire was agreed, pending peace negotiations, which were convened in Conakry, with mediation by the Governments of Guinea, Côte d'Ivoire and Togo. It was reported that Sankoh (who had been allowed by the Sierra Leonean authorities to attend the peace discussions) demanded his release and the official recognition of the RUF as a political movement as preconditions to the cessation of hostilities. Some 100 members of ECOMOG were arrested, following claims by a UN report (which were denied by ECOMOG) that suspected rebels had been summarily executed; the Kamajors were also implicated in summary killings. In late January the Government of Mali dispatched some 500 troops to join the ECOMOG contingent.

Following the rebel offensive in January 1999, a number of West African Governments, particularly those of Nigeria and Ghana, reiterated claims that the Liberian Government was supporting the RUF with mercenaries and illicit exports of armaments in exchange for diamonds. ECOMOG also accused Burkina Faso and Libya of assisting rebel operations. Charles Taylor (now the Liberian President) denied any connections with the RUF, dismissing the allegations as an attempt to destabilize his administration. In April the Nigerian President-elect, Olusegun Obasanjo, agreed that the Nigerian contingent (then numbering nearly 15,000) would remain in Sierra Leone until peace was restored, apparently in response to the influence of the international community; however, a gradual withdrawal of ECOMOG troops, to be completed by early 2000, was envisaged. Meanwhile, Kabbah authorized discussions between Sankoh and active RUF leaders to clarify RUF demands, and, following pressure from the Nigerian, US and British Governments, agreed to conduct formal peace negotiations with the rebels. In late April, following discussions between RUF leaders, formal negotiations between the RUF and a government delegation commenced in the Togolese capital, Lomé, with mediation by President Gnassingbé Eyadéma of Togo. In early May the Government and the RUF signed a cease-fire agreement, which came into effect later that month. Continuing negotiations on the proposed participation of the RUF in a coalition transitional administration, as part of a wider peace settlement, followed. In early July the Government and the RUF reached a power-sharing agreement, after government negotiators acceded to rebel demands that Sankoh be granted vice-presidential powers, with responsibility for the mineral resources industry, and the RUF be allocated a number of cabinet posts. The accord provided for the release of civilians who had been abducted by the rebels, and the disarmament and reintegration into the armed forces of former combatants; the RUF was to be reconstituted as a political organization. Following the completion of disarmament, legislative and presidential elections were to take place by February 2001. The office of the UN High Commissioner for Human Rights and human rights organizations objected to a general amnesty, under the provisions of the peace agreement, for perpetrators of atrocities against the civilian population.

In early August 1999 former supporters of the AFRC junta kidnapped some 32 members of ECOMOG and UNOMSIL who had been abducted by the rebels, after attempting to negotiate the release of about 200 civilians, held by the rebels. The dissidents issued demands for the extension of the amnesty to supporters of the former junta, and the release of Koroma, who, they believed, had been detained by the RUF. Koroma was transported by the UN to Monrovia, where he urged his supporters to free the hostages. Following negotiations between the Sierra Leonean authorities and the rebels, with the assistance of British mediators, the ECOMOG and UNOMSIL hostages were subsequently released.

In early October 1999 Sankoh (who had been conducting discussions with Taylor) and Koroma returned to Freetown from Monrovia, and pledged to co-operate with Kabbah in the implementation of the Lomé peace accord. Later that month the UN Security Council adopted Resolution 1270, establishing a 6,000-member force, the UN Mission in Sierra Leone (UNAMSIL), which was granted a six-month mandate to supervise the implementation of the peace agreement, and to assist in a programme for the disarmament and reintegration of the former rebel factions; at the same time the mandate of UNOMSIL was terminated. The withdrawal of the ECOMOG contingent was to be completed following the deployment of UNAMSIL, although, in effect, the new peace-keeping force (which was to comprise 4,000 Nigerian troops and 2,000 principally Kenyan and Indian troops) would incorporate a number of the Nigerian forces belonging to ECOMOG. On 2 November a new coalition Cabinet was officially installed; four former members of the RUF and the AFRC junta were allocated ministerial posts (but failed to secure any principal portfolios). Sankoh became Chairman of a commission supervising the reconstruction of the mineral resources industry, with vice-presidential status, while Koroma was nominated Chairman of the Commission for the Consolidation of Peace. In the same month the Government announced the establishment of a Truth and Reconciliation Commission, which was to make recommendations regarding compensation for victims of human rights violations. However, reports of atrocities perpetrated against the civilian population by rebels continued, and in November division between the AFRC and RUF leadership emerged, apparently as a result of the former junta's dissatisfaction with its cabinet posts. Fighting between the former allied factions was reported in northern Sierra Leone, with RUF forces ousting Koroma's supporters from the town of Makeni. The arrival of UNAMSIL troops in Sierra Leone commenced at the end of November.

In early 2000 reports emerged of RUF forces in the Kailahun District of eastern Sierra Leone (where illegal diamond-mining continued) resisting disarmament and the deployment of UNAMSIL troops. In February the UN Security Council adopted a resolution in favour of expanding UNAMSIL to number 11,100, and extended its mandate for six months; further African states, including Zambia, Ghana and Guinea, were to contribute troops. In March Kabbah established a commission to supervise the elections, which, under the terms of the peace agreement, were to take place following the disarmament of the former rebel factions. By the end of that month, however, only about 17,000 of the 45,000 former combatants had been disarmed.

In April 2000 UNAMSIL troops stationed in the eastern town of Kenema repulsed attacks from rebel forces. In early May, following a further dispute over disarmament, RUF forces attacked UNAMSIL troops in Makeni and the neighbouring town of Magburaka, killing at least four Kenyan members of the contingent, and seizing a number of UN personnel as hostages. Six civilian UN observers were subsequently released, following intervention by Taylor. However, rebel forces continued to hold about 300 members of UNAMSIL (principally Zambians) hostage at the towns of Makeni and Kailahun, while a further Zambian contingent of the peace-keeping force, numbering about 200, was reported missing (and was subsequently believed to have also been captured). The UN Secretary-General urged West African Heads of State to increase pressure on Sankoh to order the release of the hostages. Following a reported advance on Freetown by RUF forces, foreign nationals were advised to leave the country. The British Government dispatched a military task force to the region (stationing troops at the airport at Lungi, and in Senegal), which evacuated most European nationals. RUF supporters guarding Sankoh's residence in Freetown fired on civilian demonstrators, who were demanding that Sankoh comply with the peace agreement; some 20 protesters were killed. (UN officials were subsequently unable to contact Sankoh, who had fled from Freetown.) Sierra Leonean government forces, led by Koroma (who continued to support the Kabbah administration), were deployed to halt rebel advances, and claimed to have recaptured territory from the RUF. At an ECOWAS summit meeting in Abuja, Taylor was authorized to negotiate with the

RUF regarding their release of the hostages; the redeployment of Nigerian troops under an ECOMOG mandate was considered. In late May Sankoh was arrested in Freetown by troops loyal to Kabbah. By the end of that month, following mediation by Taylor, the hostages held by the RUF were released. In early June, however, 21 Indian members of UNAMSIL were seized by the RUF at the eastern town of Pendembu, while a further 233 peace-keeping troops were surrounded by rebels at nearby Kailahun. By mid-June most of the British forces had withdrawn (with about 250 troops remaining in the country to train new members of the Sierra Leone armed forces, and to assist in establishing the operations of a British military advisory team).

In early July 2000 the UN Security Council adopted a resolution, proposed by the British Government, imposing an international embargo on the purchase of unauthenticated diamonds (in an effort to prevent illicit trade from RUF-held regions, thereby ending the rebels' principal source of funding for armaments); the Sierra Leonean Government was to implement a system whereby officially mined diamonds would be granted certification. In the same month government forces clashed with one of the most notorious militia groups, the West Side Boys (WSB), which had hitherto supported the former AFRC junta. In mid-July the battalion of (principally Indian) peace-keeping personnel, who had been besieged by the RUF at Kailahun, were rescued in a military operation by UNAMSIL; one member of the contingent was killed during the offensive. In early August the UN Security Council approved the establishment of an international tribunal, where Sankoh and others responsible for atrocities committed during the civil conflict would be placed on trial. The RUF leadership announced the nomination of Gen. Issa Sesay (who was reported to be a more moderate commander) to replace Sankoh. Later in August the WSB abducted 11 British military personnel and one member of the Sierra Leonean armed forces, subsequently issuing a number of demands as a precondition to releasing the hostages. Five of the British personnel were freed after negotiations, but additional British troops were dispatched to Sierra Leone, following the failure of government officials to secure an agreement on the remaining hostages. In early September about 150 British troops attacked the main WSB base, 48 km east of Freetown, and succeeded in rescuing the other seven hostages. One member of the British armed forces died during the military operation, while 25 members of the WSB were killed, and a further 18 (including the movement's leader, Foday Kallay) were captured.

In September 2000 the Indian Commander of UNAMSIL, Maj.-Gen. Vijay Jetley, accused Nigeria of perpetuating the conflict in order to continue the illicit trade in diamonds in collusion with the RUF. The Nigerian authorities denied the allegations, and demanded Jetley's resignation. Later that month the Indian Government announced that it was to withdraw its contingent (then numbering 3,073 troops) from UNAMSIL, despite a proposal by the UN Secretary-General that the maximum strength of the peace-keeping force be increased. In October several nations, notably Bangladesh, Ghana and Kenya, pledged to dispatch additional troops to replace those of India. In early November the Kenyan Deputy Chief of Staff, Lieut-Gen. Daniel Opande, replaced Jetley as Commander of UNAMSIL. The number of British troops in the country had been increased to 400, while a 500-member naval task force was deployed off Freetown to provide additional support to the UN peace-keeping operations. On 10 November, following further negotiations mediated by ECOWAS, the Government and the RUF signed a cease-fire agreement in Abuja, providing for the demobilization and disarmament of all militia forces, and the deployment of UNAMSIL throughout the country.

Meanwhile, civilians continued to flee from the country, and by August 2000 some 331,000 Sierra Leonean refugees were registered in Guinea. In September the Guinean President, Gen. Lansana Conté, claimed that Liberian and Sierra Leonean refugees were supporting the activity of rebels attempting to overthrow his Government (see the chapter on Guinea), and ordered them to leave the country. Following clashes on Guinea's border with Liberia, tripartite discussions between Guinea, Liberia and Sierra Leone commenced in October. In March 2001, however, Taylor expelled the ambassadors of Guinea and Sierra Leone from Liberia, on the stated grounds that they had been engaged in activity incompatible with their office. Kabbah retaliated by ordering the Liberian chargé d'affaires to leave the country, and announced the closure of the joint border with Liberia. As a result of the continued violence and the hostility of the Guinean authorities, large numbers of the refugees in Guinea began to return to Sierra Leone. (Diplomatic links between Liberia and Sierra Leone and Guinea were normalized in August, following a request to Taylor by ECOWAS Heads of State.)

In February 2001 the National Assembly unanimously approved a proposal by Kabbah that presidential and legislative elections, scheduled to take place in February and March, respectively, be postponed for six months, owing to the continued civil unrest in the country. Following the extension of the mandate of the Government, Kabbah reorganized the Cabinet in early March. At the end of that month the UN Security Council adopted a resolution increasing the strength of UNAMSIL (which then numbered 9,500) to 17,500 troops. Some 650 British troops were to remain in the country until the end of the year. In April UNAMSIL began to deploy troops in northern regions of the country, including the towns of Lunsar and Makeni, formerly held by the RUF. In early May, however, it was reported that the pro-Government Kamajor militia, now known as the Civil Defence Forces (CDF), had attacked RUF positions in eastern towns. UNAMSIL accused the CDF, which had advanced within RUF-held territory, of instigating the hostilities. In mid-May the RUF and CDF signed an agreement, providing for the immediate cessation of hostilities and resumption of disarmament for both forces. In June UNAMSIL and (British-trained) government forces regained control of part of the significant diamond-mining regions and the eastern border with Guinea and Sierra Leone (thereby forestalling renewed rebel activity originating from the neighbouring countries). Further clashes between the RUF and CDF continued to impede the disarmament process, and in mid-July discussions regarding the implementation of the peace agreement were conducted at Bo; the Government, the RUF and UNAMSIL agreed to a ban on diamond-mining in eastern regions still controlled by the rebels, in order to facilitate the demobilization of combatants.

In early September 2001 the Government announced that presidential and legislative elections would take place, under the aegis of the UN, on 14 May 2002 (after a further postponement, owing to the continued uncertainty of the security situation). A number of political prisoners, including senior RUF members, were released from detention. The RUF, however, protested at the delay and threatened to withdraw from the peace process unless an interim coalition administration replaced the incumbent Government. In response to the progress made in the peace process, the United Kingdom reduced its military presence in Sierra Leone, although some 335 British troops remained in the country to support UNAMSIL and to continue with the reorganization of the armed forces. In November representatives of the Government, the RUF and civil society agreed that parliamentary deputies in the forthcoming elections were to be elected by district (rather than under the previous system of proportional representation). In December the UN Security Council extended its ban on trade in uncertified diamonds for a further 11 months (effective from 5 January 2002).

In preparation for the forthcoming elections, a three-week process of voter registration commenced in mid-January 2002. The disarmament of an estimated 45,000 former combatants was officially completed on 18 January. Later that month the UN and the Government reached agreement on the establishment of a war crimes tribunal, to be known as the Special Court, which was to be based in Sierra Leone; the Special Court had a three-year mandate to prosecute crimes perpetrated from the end of November 1996. Meanwhile, the continuing rebel insurgency in northern Liberia, which had advanced rapidly towards Monrovia by early 2002, prompted concern that the resumption of civil conflict there would cause further instability in Sierra Leone. Despite UN pressure on the Liberian Government to end assistance for the RUF, it was reported that Bockarie, supported by 4,000 rebel forces, continued to be based in Liberia.

Following the completion of disarmament, the RUF announced its reconstitution as a political organization, the Revolutionary United Front Party (RUFP), with the aim of contesting the elections. In early March 2002, however, Sankoh (who remained titular leader of the RUFP) was formally charged with murder, in connection with the killing of some 20 civilian protesters by his supporters in May 2000. (The trial of Sankoh, together with a further 49 former RUF members, commenced later in March.) In mid-March Kabbah was elected unopposed as the presidential candidate of the SLPP. A total of 24 political parties had officially registered by this time, notably the Peace and Liberation Party (PLP), led by Koroma. However, after the collapse of an opposition alliance, which had been established in late 2001, no serious challenge to the SLPP had emerged. In early April, after the authorities announced that Sankoh would not be permitted to contest the elections on behalf of the RUFP, the party's Secretary-General, Pallo Bangura, was nominated as its presidential candidate. By the end of that month an estimated 60,000 of the 150,000 Sierra Leonean refugees in Guinea and Liberia had returned voluntarily in order to participate in the elections.

Presidential and legislative elections took place peacefully on 14 May 2002. Kabbah was elected to a second term in office by 70.1% of the votes cast, while Ernest Bai Koroma of the APC received 22.4% of the votes. The SLPP also secured an outright majority in the expanded 124-member Parliament, with 83 seats, while the APC won 27 seats and the PLP two. Later that month Solomon Berewa (hitherto Minister of Justice) became the new Vice-President, and a reorganized Cabinet was installed.

In July 2002 the authorities announced that a seven-member Truth and Reconciliation Commission had been established. At the end of that month the British military presence in Sierra Leone was reduced to number some 100 officers, who were to continue the reorganization and training of the armed forces. In August Pallo Bangura resigned his RUFP office, having secured less than 2% of votes cast in the presidential election. In September the UN Security Council adopted a resolution extending the mandate of UNAMSIL for a further six months, but also advocating that the contingent be reduced in size. In December the UN embargo on illicit trade in diamonds was renewed for a further six months. In February 2003 a further 300 British troops were deployed in Sierra Leone, owing to concern that the intensification of hostilities between government and rebel Liberians United for Reconciliation and Democracy (LURD) forces in Liberia might destabilize the situation in Sierra Leone.

After the appointment of a British lawyer, Geoffrey Robertson, as President of the Special Court and a US lawyer, David Crane, as Chief Prosecutor, trial activities commenced at the end of 2002. In March 2003 the Special Court approved indictments for war crimes against seven former faction leaders, notably Sankoh, Koroma, the former RUF Commanders, Bockarie and Sesay, and the incumbent Minister of the Interior (and Kamajor leader), Sam Hinga Norman. Five of those indicted, including Hinga Norman, were taken into custody. Koroma went into hiding, following an attempt by the authorities to arrest him, while it was reported that Bockarie was supporting Liberian government forces against the LURD. In April Hinga Norman pleaded not guilty at the Special Court to charges relating to atrocities perpetrated during the civil war. Public hearings before the Truth and Reconciliation Commission commenced in mid-April. In early May the Liberian authorities announced that Bockarie had been killed near the border with Côte d'Ivoire, after clashing with Liberian troops attempting to arrest him, and ordered an investigation. Officials at the Special Court claimed that Bockarie and his immediate family had been captured and murdered by Liberian security forces, in an effort to prevent him from testifying against prominent regional figures. In June it was reported that Koroma had also been killed while at large in Liberia.

On 4 June 2003 the Special Court officially indicted Taylor for crimes against humanity, owing to his alleged long-standing support for the RUF, and an international warrant was issued for his arrest. The indictment against Taylor immediately precipitated a major offensive against the Liberian capital by rebels demanding his resignation (see the chapter on Liberia). The renewed humanitarian crisis in Liberia during June resulted in further large numbers of Liberian refugees fleeing to southern Sierra Leone. Having accepted an offer of asylum from the Nigerian Head of State, Olusegun Obasanjo, Taylor formally resigned his office and left for exile in Nigeria on 11 August, thereby evading arrest for the charges brought against him by the Special Court. Meanwhile, progress in the case against Sankoh was hindered by the deterioration of his state of health, and, after receiving medical treatment in hospital under UN custody from March, he finally died at the end of July. Also in July the UN Security Council adopted a resolution recommending the gradual withdrawal of UNAMSIL by the end of 2004, in view of improved security conditions.

In early February 2004 the five-year programme for 'disarmament, demobilization and reintegration' (in which 72,490 former combatants, including 6,845 children, had been disarmed) officially ended. In March Robertson was removed from the office of President of the Special Court, after being accused of demonstrating bias against the RUF in a book he had written concerning the atrocities committed during the civil conflict. At the end of that month, owing to renewed concern that the Sierra Leone authorities would be unable to maintain stability, particularly in view of the security situations in Guinea and Côte d'Ivoire, the UN Security Council approved a resolution in favour of maintaining a reduced UNAMSIL contingent in the country until the end of September, with further extensions possible. UNAMSIL also assisted in subsequent preparations for local government elections (regarded as significant in decentralization and in enabling the provision of public services), which had been postponed from late 2003 until May 2004. The APC won majorities in the municipal councils of both Freetown and Makeni in the local elections, reflecting widespread disaffection with the continuing poor state of the economy and the SLPP Government's failure to address corruption.

In June 2004 trials of prominent former combatants officially commenced at the Special Court. In August Kabbah replaced the Minister of Justice in a government reorganization believed to be related to the SLPP's poor performance in the local government elections. On 23 September UNAMSIL officially transferred primary responsibility for security in the remaining parts of the country where it was deployed, including Freetown, to government forces. The UN Security Council approved a further resolution in the same month, authorizing the contingent's continued presence in the country until the end of June 2005 to assist in the maintenance of security. In December 2004 10 former army officers and rebel combatants were sentenced to death on charges of treason for involvement in an attempt to overthrow the Government in an attack on a barracks in January 2003; six of those convicted were former members of the AFRC and the remaining four were former RUF combatants.

In early September 2005 Kabbah reorganized the Cabinet. Most notably, John Oponjo Benjamin replaced Joseph Dauda as Minster of Finance, while Pascal Egbenda assumed the internal affairs portfolio and Lloyd During was appointed Minister of Energy and Power.

At the end of June 2005 the UN Security Council extended the mandate of UNAMSIL for a final six months, until the end of that year. In August a further resolution provided for the creation of United Nations Integrated Office in Sierra Leone (UNIOSIL). Following the complete withdrawal of UNAMSIL as scheduled, UNIOSIL was established on 1 January 2006, for an initial period of one year; the mission was authorized to support the consolidation of peace and assist the Government in strengthening state institutions, the rule of law, human rights, and the security sector, and the organization of elections in the following year. Later in January a former prominent member of the RUF was arrested and detained on suspicion of subversive activities. In February the trial of Hinga Norman officially commenced at the Special Court; proceedings against him were expected to be highly controversial, owing to the popular support retained by the Kamajors.

In March 2006 Nigeria announced that it had received a formal request from the new Liberian Government (see chapter on Liberia) to extradite Taylor to the Special Court. Later that month Taylor fled from his residence in Nigeria in an attempt to evade custody, but was apprehended two days later, near the border with Cameroon, and dispatched to Liberia, from where he was immediately extradited by peace-keeping forces to the Special Court. In early April Taylor (who initially refused to accept the authority of the Court) pleaded not guilty to 11 charges relating to his involvement in the civil conflict in Sierra Leone. Tribunal officials subsequently requested that his trial be transferred to the International Criminal Court (see p. 291) at the Hague (while remaining under the jurisdiction of the Special Court), in the interests of regional stability.

Government

Under the terms of the Constitution of 1991, executive power is vested in the President, who is directly elected by universal adult suffrage. The President appoints the Cabinet (subject to approval by the legislature). The maximum duration of the President's tenure of office is limited to two five-year terms. Legislative power is vested in a unicameral Parliament, which is elected for a five-year term and comprises 112 members elected by a system of proportional representation, in 14 constituencies, and 12 Paramount Chiefs, who represent the provincial districts.

The country is divided into four regions: the Northern, Eastern and Southern Provinces, and the Western Area, which comprise 12 districts. There are 147 chiefdoms, each controlled by a Paramount Chief and a Council of Elders, known as the Tribal Authority.

Defence

In August 2005 active members of the armed forces of the Republic of Sierra Leone numbered about 12,000–13,000, with a navy of 200. In October 1999 the UN Security Council adopted a resolution establishing the UN Mission in Sierra Leone (UNAMSIL), which was to supervise the implementation of a peace agreement between the Government and rebel forces, signed in July of that year. Following the completion of disarmament in January 2002, a new army, restructured with British military assistance, was established. Some 100 British troops remained in the country to support peace-keeping operations and to continue reorganization of the Sierra Leone armed forces. Following the completion of UNAMSIL's mandate, the United Nations Integrated Office in Sierra Leone (UNIOSIL) was established on 1 January 2006 for an initial period of one year (in accordance with a Security Council resolution of 31 August 2005). Expenditure on defence in 2004 was budgeted at Le 37,793m. (equivalent to 4.6% of total expenditure).

Economic Affairs

In 2004, according to the World Bank, Sierra Leone's gross national income (GNI), measured at average 2002–04 prices, was US $1,113m., equivalent to $200 per head (or $790 per head on an international purchasing-power parity basis). During 1995–2004, it was estimated, the population increased at an average annual rate of 2.1%, while gross domestic product (GDP) per head rose, in real terms, by an average of 2.0% per year. Overall GDP increased, in real terms, at an average annual rate of 4.2% in 1995–2004; growth was 7.4% in 2004.

Agriculture (including forestry and fishing) contributed 53.2% of GDP in 2004. About 60.6% of the labour force were employed in the sector in 2003. The principal cash crops are cocoa beans and coffee. Staple food crops include cassava, rice and bananas. Cattle, sheep and poultry are the principal livestock. During 1990–2003 the GDP of the agricultural sector declined at an average annual rate of 4.4%; however, growth in agricultural GDP was 6.7% in 2003.

Industry (including mining, manufacturing, construction and power) contributed 29.6% of GDP in 2004, and employed an estimated 17.1% of the labour force in 1996/97. The GDP of the industrial sector declined by an average of 2.9% per year in 1990–2003; however, industrial GDP increased by 8.5% in 2003.

Mining and quarrying contributed 17.5% of GDP in 1994/95. The principal mineral exports are diamonds (which, according to official figures, accounted for 90.4% of total export earnings in 2004), rutile (titanium dioxide), bauxite and gold. The production of iron ore, previously an important mineral export, was suspended in 1985. In 1995 increased rebel activity effectively suspended official mining operations (although illicit exports of diamonds by rebel forces continued). In October 2000 official exports of diamonds were resumed under a certification scheme. Following reinvestment in a major kimberlite diamond field at Koidu, production commenced at the end of 2003. The Sierra Rutile mines (the largest source of private-sector employment and foreign-exchange earnings prior to 1995) resumed full mining operations in early 2006, while rehabilitation of the country's bauxite mine was completed in 2005, also allowing production to recommence in early 2006.

Manufacturing contributed 5.3% of GDP in 2004. The manufacturing sector consists mainly of the production of palm oil and other agro-based industries, textiles and furniture-making. During 1990–96 the GDP of the manufacturing sector increased at an average annual rate of 2.5%. Manufacturing GDP declined by 9.9% in 1995, but increased by 1.7% in 1996.

Energy is derived principally from oil-fired thermal power stations. With the electricity sector continuing to deteriorate, the Government planned to bring a delayed hydroelectric project at Bumbuna, in the north of the country, into operation by 2006. Imports of mineral fuels comprised 33.1% of the value of total imports in 2004.

The services sector contributed 17.2% of GDP in 2004, and employed 22.1% of the labour force in 1996/97. The GDP of the services sector declined by an average of 0.3% per year in 1990–2003, rising by 6.8% in 2003.

In 2004 Sierra Leone recorded an estimated trade deficit of US $98.4m., and there was a deficit of $74.3m. on the current account of the balance of payments. In 2003, according to official estimates, the principal source of imports (42.8%) was Germany; other major suppliers were the United Kingdom and France. Belgium was the principal market for exports (taking 57.0% of the total); the other significant purchaser was Germany. The principal export in 2004 was diamonds. The principal imports in that year were mineral fuels, food and live animals, machinery and transport equipment, and basic manufactures.

The overall budget deficit for 2004 was Le 70,273m. (equivalent to 2.4% of GDP). Sierra Leone's external debt totalled US $1,612m. at the end of 2003, of which $1,419m. was long-term public debt. In that year the cost of debt-servicing was equivalent to 12.4% of the value of exports of goods and services. The annual rate of inflation averaged 16.1% in 1992–2003. Consumer prices declined by 3.3% in 2002, but increased by 7.6% in 2003, by 14.2% in 2004 and by an estimated 12.1% in 2005. An estimated 50% of the labour force were unemployed in early 1990.

Sierra Leone is a member of the Economic Community of West African States (see p. 217) and of the Mano River Union (see p. 387), which aims to promote economic co-operation with Guinea and Liberia.

The civil conflict, which commenced in 1991, resulted in the progressive destruction of Sierra Leone's infrastructure, and severe disruption, or complete suspension, of traditional economic activities. Following a peace agreement between the Government and the rebels, which was signed in July 1999, a new coalition administration was installed, and a recovery and rehabilitation programme was adopted. Subsequent improvements in fiscal control and considerable post-conflict support from the international financial institutions resulted in some progress in reconstruction. Under a further cease-fire agreement, signed in November 2000 (see Recent History), presidential and legislative elections were conducted in May 2002. The reorganized Government's priorities were to alleviate widespread poverty, resettle displaced civilians (amounting to nearly one-half of the population at the end of 2001), reintegrate disarmed former combatants, reconstruct the country's infrastructure, and reduce dramatically high debt levels. In March 2002 the IMF, which had approved a further three-year credit arrangement in September 2001, commended the Government's progress in advancing the peace process and the country's improved economic and financial performance. In response to the implementation of structural reforms, the IMF and World Bank pledged debt relief to Sierra Leone under the concessionary terms of the enhanced heavily indebted poor countries (HIPC) initiative (conditional on the Government complying with the stipulated measures of fiscal control). The IMF approved further disbursements to Sierra Leone in September 2002 and April 2003, under the existing Poverty Reduction and Growth Facility (PRGF). The Fund advocated an accelerated implementation of structural reforms, including the privatization of state-owned enterprises, and measures to improve governance, and the legal and judicial systems (with the aim of encouraging private investment). A major peace agreement reached between the combatant factions in Liberia in August 2003 improved conditions for sustained peace in Sierra Leone; nevertheless, continuing instability in neighbouring countries posed a continued threat to the security situation. Following a further performance review in early 2004, the IMF concluded that the country had made continued progress in economic stabilization and achieving growth under the PRGF-supported programme. Although the Government had failed to meet some fiscal and structural criteria, the Fund approved the disbursement of further credit and extended the arrangement to March 2005. Strong rates of growth were recorded from 2003 (albeit with a concomitant rise in inflation), while levels of state revenue from exports of officially registered diamonds increased sharply, following the reduction in illicit trade and improvement in the security situation. In mid-2005 the IMF completed a further review under the extended PRGF arrangement, enabling the Government to draw further credit; the country was also approved additional interim assistance for the period to the end of that year, under the HIPC Initiative. The IMF welcomed progress made in post-conflict transition and the decision by the UN Security Council for the UN Mission in Sierra Leone (UNAMSIL) to remain in the country and support the Government in security maintenance until the end of 2005. The country remained heavily dependent on international aid, with, despite improved business confidence, private sector investment projects remaining problematic. In June, however, a critical donor conference in Paris, France, at which Sierra Leone was expected to receive pledges of substantial assistance for the following three years, was cancelled, owing to increasing concern at the Government's failure to address corruption. The country's economic prospects improved significantly with the resumption of rutile and bauxite production in

SIERRA LEONE

early 2006, together with the continuing increase in revenue from diamonds. Nevertheless, an expected decline in foreign assistance and the maintenance of the security situation, following the withdrawal of UNAMSIL at the end of the year, prior to elections scheduled for May 2007, remained a cause of concern.

Education

Primary education in Sierra Leone begins at six years of age and lasts for six years. Secondary education, beginning at the age of 12, lasts for a further six years, comprising two three-year cycles. In 2000/01 primary enrolment was equivalent to 92.8% of children in the relevant age-group (males 106.0%; females 79.8%), while about 26.5% of children in the relevant age-group were enrolled at secondary schools (males 29.0%; females 24.0%). There is one university, which comprises six colleges. A total of 8,795 students were enrolled in tertiary education in 2000/01. Following the onset of the civil conflict in 1991, large numbers of children were forced to join rebel militia, and to participate in atrocities. After peace was largely restored in July 1999, the reintegration of young former combatants into the community was a priority for the new administration. Education was allocated Le 30,700m. in the 2001 budget, increasing to a projected Le 36,400m. (equivalent to 5.2% of total expenditure) in 2002.

Public Holidays

2006: 1 January (New Year's Day), 10 January*† (Id al-Adha, Feast of the Sacrifice), 10 April (Mouloud, Birth of the Prophet)*, 14–17 April (Easter), 27 April (Independence Day), 23 October (Id al-Fitr, end of Ramadan)*, 25–26 December (Christmas and Boxing Day), 31 December*† (Id al-Adha, Feast of the Sacrifice).

2007: 1 January (New Year's Day), 31 March (Mouloud, Birth of the Prophet)*, 6–9 April (Easter), 27 April (Independence Day), 13 October (Id al-Fitr, end of Ramadan)*, 20 December (Id al-Adha, Feast of the Sacrifice)*, 25–26 December (Christmas and Boxing Day).

* These holidays are dependent on the Islamic lunar calendar and may vary by one or two days from the dates given.

† This festival occurs twice (in the Islamic years AH 1426 and 1427) within the same Gregorian year.

Weights and Measures

The metric system is in force.

Statistical Survey

Source (unless otherwise stated): Central Statistics Office, PMB 595, Tower Hill, Freetown; tel. (22) 223287; fax (22) 223897; internet www.sierra-leone.org/cso.html and www.statistics-sierra-leone.org.

Area and Population

AREA, POPULATION AND DENSITY

Area (sq km)	71,740*
Population (census results)†	
8 December 1974	2,735,159
14 December 1985	
Males	1,746,055
Females	1,769,757
Total	3,515,812
Population (UN estimates at mid-year)‡	
2002	4,892,000
2003	5,119,000
2004	5,336,000
Density (per sq km) at mid-2004	74.4

* 27,699 sq miles.

† Excluding adjustment for underenumeration, estimated to have been 10% in 1974 and 9% in 1985. The adjusted total for 1974 (based on a provisional total of 2,729,479 enumerated) is 3,002,426.

‡ Source: UN, *World Population Prospects: The 2004 Revision*.

PRINCIPAL TOWNS
(population at 1985 census)

Freetown (capital)	384,499		Kenema	52,473
Koindu	82,474		Makeni	49,474
Bo	59,768			

Mid-2003 (UN estimate, including suburbs): Freetown 920,717 (Source: UN, *World Urbanization Prospects: The 2003 Revision*).

BIRTHS AND DEATHS
(UN estimates, annual averages)

	1990–95	1995–2000	2000–05
Birth rate (per 1,000)	47.5	46.9	46.7
Death rate (per 1,000)	26.1	24.6	23.7

Source: UN, *World Population Prospects: The 2004 Revision*.

Expectation of life (WHO estimates, years at birth): 38 (males 37; females 39) in 2003 (Source: WHO, *World Health Report*).

ECONOMICALLY ACTIVE POPULATION
(% of labour force)

	1994/95	1995/96	1996/97
Agriculture, etc.	61.08	60.96	60.83
Industry	16.99	17.04	17.10
Services	21.93	22.00	22.07

Mid-2003 (estimates in '000): Agriculture, etc. 1,119; Total 1,847 (Source: FAO).

Health and Welfare

KEY INDICATORS

Total fertility rate (children per woman, 2003)	6.5
Under-5 mortality rate (per 1,000 live births, 2004)	283
HIV/AIDS (% of persons aged 15–49, 2001)	7.00
Physicians (per 1,000 head, 1996)	0.07
Health expenditure (2002): US $ per head (PPP)	27
Health expenditure (2002): % of GDP	2.9
Health expenditure (2002): public (% of total)	60.3
Access to water (% of persons, 2002)	57
Access to sanitation (% of persons, 2002)	39
Human Development Index (2003): ranking	176
Human Development Index (2003): value	0.298

For sources and definitions, see explanatory note on p. vi.

SIERRA LEONE

Agriculture

PRINCIPAL CROPS
('000 metric tons)

	2002	2003	2004
Rice (paddy)*	260	265	265
Maize	12.0	10.0†	10.0†
Millet	10.5	10.0†	10.0†
Sorghum	18.5	21.0*	21.0*
Sweet potatoes	25.4	25.5*	25.5*
Cassava (Manioc)	340.0*	377.2	390.0*
Sugar cane*	80	60	70
Pulses*	56.4	60.7	58.7
Groundnuts (in shell)*	16.0	18.2	16.0
Oil palm fruit*	180	195	195
Tomatoes*	13.5	15.0	15.0
Other vegetables*	205	220	220
Plantains*	30	33	33
Citrus fruit*	80	85	85
Other fruit*	64.0	68.0	66.5
Coffee (green)*	17	18	18
Cocoa beans*	11	12	11
Spices*	3.5	3.5	3.5

* FAO estimate(s).
† Unofficial figure.
Source: FAO.

LIVESTOCK
(FAO estimates, unless otherwise indicated, '000 head, year ending September)

	2002	2003	2004
Cattle	400	400	400
Pigs	52*	52	52
Sheep	370	375	375
Goats	220	220	220
Chickens	7,000	7,500	7,500
Ducks	70	70	70

* Official figure.
Source: FAO.

LIVESTOCK PRODUCTS
(FAO estimates, '000 metric tons)

	2001	2002	2003
Beef and veal	5.4	5.4	5.4
Poultry meat	10.6	10.5	11.3
Other meat	6.4	6.5	6.5
Cows' milk	21.3	21.3	21.3
Hen eggs	8.3	8.3	8.3

2004: Production as in 2003 (FAO estimates).
Source: FAO.

Forestry

ROUNDWOOD REMOVALS
(FAO estimates, '000 cubic metres, excl. bark)

	2002	2003	2004
Sawlogs, veneer logs and logs for sleepers*	3.6	3.6	3.6
Other industrial wood†	120.0	120.0	120.0
Fuel wood	5,373.6	5,386.7	5,403.1
Total	5,497.2	5,510.3	5,526.7

* Annual output assumed to be unchanged since 1993.
† Annual output assumed to be unchanged since 1980.
Source: FAO.

SAWNWOOD PRODUCTION
('000 cubic metres, incl. railway sleepers)

	1991	1992	1993
Total (all broadleaved)	9.0	9.0*	5.3

* FAO estimate.
1994–2004: Annual production as in 1993 (FAO estimates).
Source: FAO.

Fishing

('000 metric tons, live weight of capture)

	2001	2002	2003
West African ilisha	0.0	1.4	1.5
Tonguefishes	0.5	0.7	1.2
Bobo croaker	0.7	3.2	5.8
Sardinellas	9.8	13.3	15.4
Bonga shad	24.8	31.5	28.5
Tuna-like fishes	7.1	0.5	1.0
Marine molluscs	0.1	2.4	3.1
Total catch (incl. others)	75.2	83.0	96.9

Source: FAO.

Mining

(metric tons, unless otherwise indicated)

	2001	2002	2003
Gypsum*	4,000	4,000	4,000
Diamonds ('000 carats)	223	352	507
Salt	2,900	1,800	1,800*

* Estimate(s).
Source: US Geological Survey.

Industry

PETROLEUM PRODUCTS
('000 metric tons)

	1999*	2000*	2001
Jet fuels	17	17	18
Motor spirit (petrol)	29	30	30
Kerosene	9	9	9*
Distillate fuel oils	72	72	74*
Residual fuel oils	55	55	55*

* Provisional.
Source: UN, *Industrial Commodity Statistics Yearbook*.

SELECTED OTHER PRODUCTS
('000 metric tons, unless otherwise indicated)

	2003	2004
Beer and stout ('000 cartons)	771	809
Malt drink ('000 cartons)	172	133
Soft drinks ('000 crates)	1,171	1,582
Confectionery ('000 lbs)	3,319	2,734
Soap (metric tons)	491	268
Paint ('000 gallons)	181	165
Cement	170	180
Plastic footwear ('000 pairs)	731	86
Flour	n.a.	19.1
Electric energy (million kWh)	109.4	84.8

Source: Bank of Sierra Leone, *Annual Report*.

SIERRA LEONE

Finance

CURRENCY AND EXCHANGE RATES

Monetary Units
100 cents = 1 leone (Le).

Sterling, Dollar and Euro Equivalents (30 December 2005)
£1 sterling = 5,049.5 leones;
US $1 = 2,932.5 leones;
€1 = 3,459.5 leones;
10,000 leones = £1.98 = $3.41 = €2.89.

Average Exchange Rate (leones per US $)
2003   2,347.94
2004   2,701.30
2005   2,889.59

BUDGET
(Le million)

Revenue*	2002	2003	2004†
Income tax department	62,881	75,581	94,775
Customs and excise department	160,589	192,379	220,150
Mines department	2,034	3,040	6,662
Other departments	6,262	6,811	11,413
Road user charges	6,925	9,847	15,083
Total	**238,691**	**287,657**	**348,083**

Expenditure‡	2002	2003	2004†
Recurrent expenditure	474,811	509,760	567,802
Wages and salaries	142,769	160,092	173,825
Goods and services	154,606	192,389	187,929
Security-related expenditures	51,446	63,091	60,089
Defence	33,371	40,774	37,793
Democratization and DDR§	33,736	9,512	9,065
Grants to educational institutions	14,041	19,000	21,093
Transfers to road fund	6,925	9,847	15,083
Socially oriented outlays	—	3,007	844
Elections	17,937	750	6,586
Interest payments	104,797	115,163	153,377
Development expenditure	85,768	112,315	254,333
Subsidies	450	500	—
Total	**561,029**	**622,575**	**822,135**

* Excluding grants received (Le million): 161,336 in 2002; 179,344 in 2003; 260,440 in 2004 (forecast).
† Forecasts.
‡ Excluding lending minus repayments (Le million): 1,223 in 2002; –183 in 2003; –58 in 2004 (forecast).
§ Disarmament, demobilization and reintegration.

Source: IMF, *Sierra Leone: 2004 Article IV Consultation, the Fifth Review Under the Poverty Reduction and Growth Facility, and Requests for Waiver of Performance Criteria and Extension of Arrangement—Staff Report; Staff Statement; Public Information Notice and Press Release on the Executive Board Discussion; and Statement by the Executive Director for Sierra Leone* (January 2005).

INTERNATIONAL RESERVES
(US $ million at 31 December)

	2003	2004	2005
IMF special drawing rights	34.5	51.0	32.8
Foreign exchange	32.1	74.1	137.7
Total	**66.6**	**125.1**	**170.5**

Source: IMF, *International Financial Statistics*.

MONEY SUPPLY
(Le million at 31 December)

	2003	2004	2005
Currency outside banks	188,448	204,733	231,274
Demand deposits at commercial banks	94,415	127,416	176,649
Total money (incl. others)	**292,950**	**344,524**	**424,215**

Source: IMF, *International Financial Statistics*.

COST OF LIVING
(Consumer Price Index for Freetown; base: 2000 = 100)

	2001	2002	2003
Food	105.2	104.4	112.2
All items (incl. others)	**102.2**	**98.8**	**106.3**

All items: 121.3 in 2004; 135.9 in 2005.

Source: IMF, *International Financial Statistics*.

NATIONAL ACCOUNTS
(Le million at current prices)

National Income and Product
(year ending 30 June)

	1992/93	1993/94	1994/95*
Compensation of employees	86,503.1	107,650.3	138,658.6
Operating surplus	313,873.8	352,605.6	467,380.1
Domestic factor incomes	**400,376.9**	**460,255.8**	**606,038.7**
Consumption of fixed capital	30,097.2	35,104.2	41,907.3
Gross domestic product (GDP) at factor cost	**430,474.1**	**495,360.0**	**647,946.1**
Indirect taxes, *less* subsidies	36,713.4	48,351.0	62,443.2
GDP in purchasers' values	**467,187.5**	**543,711.0**	**710,389.3**
Factor income received from abroad / *Less* Factor income paid abroad	–66,914.8	–70,237.5	–84,216.0
Gross national product (GNP)	**400,272.7**	**473,473.5**	**626,173.3**
Less Consumption of fixed capital	30,097.2	35,104.2	41,907.3
National income in market prices	**370,175.5**	**438,369.3**	**584,265.9**
Other current transfers received from abroad / *Less* Other current transfers paid abroad	11,483.0	12,438.6	15,067.8
National disposable income	**381,658.5**	**450,807.9**	**599,333.7**

* Provisional figures.

Expenditure on the Gross Domestic Product

	2001	2002	2003
Government final consumption expenditure	255,265	325,223	353,541
Private final consumption expenditure	1,398,461	1,528,299	1,713,929
Gross fixed capital formation	90,091	114,690	322,945
Total domestic expenditure	**1,743,817**	**1,968,212**	**2,390,415**
Exports of goods and services	228,694	293,879	323,534
Less Imports of goods and services	484,986	618,709	850,982
Statistical discrepancy	112,644	321,245	460,701
GDP in purchasers' values	**1,600,169**	**1,964,627**	**2,323,668**
GDP at constant 1989/90 prices	**72,874**	**92,886**	**101,513**

GDP in purchasers' values: 2,894,326 in 2004; 3,356,686 in 2005.
GDP at constant 1989/90 prices: 108,986 in 2004; 117,193 in 2005.

Source: IMF, *International Financial Statistics*.

SIERRA LEONE

Gross Domestic Product by Economic Activity
(year ending 30 June)

	1992/93	1993/94	1994/95*
Agriculture, hunting, forestry and fishing	162,194.6	188,884.1	275,327.5
Mining and quarrying	98,615.8	96,748.8	119,229.2
Manufacturing	39,567.0	47,816.7	61,475.3
Electricity, gas and water	469.8	757.3	2,816.8
Construction	4,655.4	12,544.4	15,788.2
Trade, restaurants and hotels	69,139.9	77,251.0	98,270.1
Transport, storage and communications	37,056.5	50,047.1	61,267.5
Finance, insurance, real estate and business services	15,947.0	17,988.0	14,732.2
Government services	14,500.0	17,884.0	19,844.9
Other community, social and personal services	8,998.3	9,769.0	12,308.9
Sub-total	451,143.3	519,690.4	681,060.6
Import duties	18,994.0	27,410.0	32,942.0
Less Imputed bank service charge	2,950.8	3,389.8	3,612.3
GDP in purchasers' values	467,187.5	543,711.0	710,389.3

* Provisional figures.

BALANCE OF PAYMENTS
(US $ million)

	2002	2003	2004
Exports of goods f.o.b.	59.8	110.8	154.1
Imports of goods f.o.b.	−254.9	−310.7	−252.5
Trade balance	−195.1	−199.9	−98.4
Exports of services	38.3	66.1	61.4
Imports of services	−80.8	−93.8	−89.4
Balance on goods and services	−237.5	−227.6	−126.5
Other income received	18.3	1.7	4.1
Other income paid	−21.1	−16.7	−71.1
Balance on goods, services and income	−240.4	−242.6	−193.5
Current transfers received	170.8	167.6	122.0
Current transfers paid	−3.6	−5.0	−2.8
Current balance	−73.2	−80.0	−74.3
Capital account (net)	50.6	71.0	81.3
Direct investment from abroad	1.6	3.1	26.1
Other investment assets	8.1	0.5	10.1
Other investment liabilities	0.2	24.4	21.2
Net errors and omissions	−7.4	−47.6	−59.5
Overall balance	−20.1	−28.6	4.9

Source: IMF, *International Financial Statistics*.

External Trade

PRINCIPAL COMMODITIES
(US $ '000)

Imports c.i.f.	2002	2003	2004
Food and live animals	70,783.2	74,510.8	57,058.5
Beverages and tobacco	11,320.0	11,049.4	11,122.5
Crude materials (inedible) except fuels	9,212.1	6,880.4	7,578.3
Mineral fuels, lubricants, etc.	51,728.9	78,211.2	94,865.4
Animal and vegetable oils and fats	2,826.6	2,221.4	1,966.8
Chemicals	18,302.7	19,266.3	17,534.0
Basic manufactures	35,900.5	42,185.7	31,843.9
Machinery and transport equipment	50,216.8	56,396.2	50,861.2
Miscellaneous manufactured articles	13,986.2	12,964.3	13,633.4
Total	264,277.0	303,685.7	286,464.0

Exports f.o.b.	2002	2003	2004
Coffee	272.1	40.1	52.8
Cocoa beans	1,218.7	2,572.8	5,259.4
Diamonds	41,732.2	76,665.9	126,330.0
Total (incl. others)	46,361.6	92,395.4	139,694.9

Source: Bank of Sierra Leone.

PRINCIPAL TRADING PARTNERS

Imports c.i.f. (US $ million)	2002
Canada	23.0
China, People's Repub.	11.8
Côte d'Ivoire	129.1
Germany	9.1
India	13.2
Japan	14.9
Netherlands	19.4
United Kingdom	11.9
USA	17.4
Total (incl. others)	352.0

Source: UN, *International Trade Statistics Yearbook*.

Exports (Le million)	1992	1993	1994
Belgium	25,770	54	11,412
Germany	1,060	2,486	1,328
Guinea	1,315	817	1,331
Netherlands	5,307	1,201	2,815
Switzerland	7,546	486	215
United Kingdom	5,567	5,988	11,767
USA	13,832	17,564	30,431
Total (incl. others)	75,034	67,077	67,930

Source: Central Statistics Office, Freetown.

Transport

ROAD TRAFFIC
(motor vehicles in use at 31 December)

	2000	2001	2002
Passenger cars	2,045	2,263	11,353
Buses and coaches	2,597	3,516	4,050
Goods vehicles	2,309	2,898	3,565
Motorcycles	1,398	1,532	1,657

Source: IRF, *World Road Statistics*.

SHIPPING

Merchant Fleet
(registered at 31 December)

	2002	2003	2004
Number of vessels	43	45	46
Displacement (gross registered tons)	22,733	23,157	26,999

Source: Lloyd's Register-Fairplay, *World Fleet Statistics*.

International Sea-borne Freight Traffic
(estimates, '000 metric tons)

	1991	1992	1993
Goods loaded	1,930	2,190	2,310
Goods unloaded	562	579	589

Source: UN Economic Commission for Africa, *African Statistical Yearbook*.

SIERRA LEONE

CIVIL AVIATION
(traffic on scheduled services)

	1999	2000	2001
Passengers carried ('000)	19	19	14
Passenger-km (million)	30	93	73
Total ton-km (million)	3	18	13

Source: UN, *Statistical Yearbook*.

Tourism

	2001	2002	2003
Tourist arrivals	24,067	28,463	37,201
Tourism receipts (US $ million, excl. passenger transport)	14	38	60

Source: World Tourism Organization.

Communications Media

	2000	2001	2002
Television receivers ('000 in use)	64	65	n.a.
Telephones ('000 main lines in use)	19.0	22.7	24.0
Mobile cellular telephones ('000 subscribers)	11.9	26.9	67.0
Internet users ('000)	5	7	8

2004 ('000): Internet users 10.
Radio receivers ('000 in use): 1,120 in 1997.
Facsimile machines (number in use, year beginning 1 April): 2,500 in 1998.
Daily newspapers: 1 (average circulation 20,000) in 1996.
Sources: UNESCO, *Statistical Yearbook*; UN, *Statistical Yearbook*; and International Telecommunication Union.

Education

(2001/02)

	Schools	Teachers	Males	Females	Total
Primary	2,704	14,932	323,924	230,384	554,308
Secondary	246	5,264	66,745	41,031	107,776
University*	n.a.	n.a.	1,163	300	1,463

*Full-time undergraduate students in 1995.

Adult literacy rate (UNESCO estimates): 29.6% (males 39.8%; females 20.5%) in 2003 (Source: UN Development Programme, *Human Development Report*).

Directory

The Constitution

Following the transfer of power to a democratically elected civilian administration on 29 March 1996, the Constitution of 1991 (which had been suspended since April 1992) was reinstated. The Constitution provided for the establishment of a multi-party system, and vested executive power in the President, who was to be elected by the majority of votes cast nationally and by at least 25% of the votes cast in each of the four provinces. The maximum duration of the President's tenure of office was limited to two five-year terms. The President was to appoint the Cabinet, subject to approval by the Parliament. The Parliament was elected for a five-year term and comprised 124 members, 112 of whom were elected by a system of proportional representation, in 14 constituencies, while 12 Paramount Chiefs also represented the provincial districts in the legislature. Members of the Parliament were not permitted concurrently to hold office in the Cabinet.

The Government

HEAD OF STATE

President and Commander-in-Chief of the Armed Forces: Alhaji AHMED TEJAN KABBAH (took office 29 March 1996; reinstated 10 March 1998; re-elected 14 May 2002).
Vice-President: SOLOMON BEREWA.

CABINET
(April 2006)

Minister of Foreign Affairs and International Co-operation: MOMODU KOROMA.
Minister of Finance: JOHN OPONJO BENJAMIN.
Minister of Development and Economic Planning: MOHAMED B. DARAMY.
Minister of Trade and Industry: Dr KADI SESAY.
Minister of Transport and Communications: Dr PRINCE A. HARDING.
Minister of Marine Resources: Dr CHERNOR JALLOH.
Minister of Health and Sanitation: ABBATOR THOMAS.
Minister of Education, Science and Technology: Dr ALPHA T. WURIE.
Minister of Mineral Resources: Alhaji MOHAMED SWARRAY DEEN.
Minister of Local Government and Community Development: SIDIKIE BRIMA.
Minister of Tourism and Culture: OKERE ADAMS.
Minister of Lands, Housing, Country Planning, Forestry and the Environment: Dr ALFRED BOBSON SESAY.
Minister of Information and Broadcasting: Prof. SEPTIMUS KAIKAI.
Minister of Works, Housing and Technical Maintenance: Dr CAISER J. BOIMA.
Minister of Labour and Industrial Relations, and Social Security: ALPHA O. TIMBO.
Minister of Social Welfare, Gender and Children's Affairs: SHIRLEY GBUJAMA.
Minister of Justice and Attorney-General: FRANCIS M. CAREW.
Minister of Internal Affairs: PASCAL EGBENDA.
Minister of Youth and Sports: Dr DENNIS BRIGHT.
Minister of Energy and Power: LLOYD DURING.
Minister of Agriculture and Food Security: Dr SAMA S. MONDEH.
Minister of Political and Parliamentary Affairs: EYA MBAYO.
Minister of State of Presidential Affairs: Dr SHEKOU SESAY.
Minister of the Northern Region: ALEX ALIE KARGBO.
Minister of the Southern Region: Dr S. U. M. JAH.
Minister of the Eastern Region: SAHR RANDOLPH FILLIE-FABOE.

SIERRA LEONE

MINISTRIES

Office of the President: Freetown; tel. (22) 232101; fax (22) 231404; e-mail info@statehouse-sl.org; internet www.statehouse-sl.org/president.html.

Ministry of Agriculture and Food Security: Youyi Bldg, 3rd Floor, Brookfields, Freetown; tel. (22) 222242; fax (22) 241613.

Ministry of Lands, Housing, Country Planning, Forestry and the Environment: Youyi Bldg, 4th Floor, Brookfields, Freetown; tel. (22) 242013.

Ministry of Defence: State Ave, Freetown; tel. (22) 227369; fax (22) 229380.

Ministry of Development and Economic Planning: Youyi Bldg, 6th Floor, Brookfields, Freetown; tel. (22) 225236; fax (22) 241599.

Ministry of Education, Science and Technology: New England, Freetown; tel. (22) 240881; fax (22) 240137.

Ministry of Energy and Power: Electricity House, Siaka Stevens St, Freetown; tel. (22) 226566; fax (22) 228199.

Ministry of Finance: Secretariat Bldg, George St, Freetown; tel. (22) 225612; fax (2) 228472.

Ministry of Foreign Affairs and International Co-operation: Gloucester St, Freetown; tel. (22) 223260; fax (22) 225615; e-mail mfaicsl@yahoo.com.

Ministry of Health and Sanitation: Youyi Bldg, 6th Floor, Brookfields, Freetown; tel. (22) 240427; fax (22) 241613.

Ministry of Information and Broadcasting: Youyi Bldg, 8th Floor, Brookfields, Freetown; tel. (22) 240339; fax (22) 241757.

Ministry of Internal Affairs: Liverpool St, Freetown; tel. (22) 226979; fax (22) 227727.

Ministry of Justice: Guma Bldg, Lamina Sankoh St, Freetown; tel. (22) 227444; fax (22) 229366.

Ministry of Labour and Industrial Relations, and Social Security: New England, Freetown; tel. (22) 241947.

Ministry of Local Government and Community Development: New England, Freetown; tel. (22) 226589; fax (22) 222409.

Ministry of Marine Resources: Marine House, 11 Old Railway Line, Brookfields, Freetown; tel. (22) 242117.

Ministry of Mineral Resources: Youyi Bldg, 5th Floor, Brookfields, Freetown; tel. (22) 240142; fax (22) 241757.

Ministry of Political and Parliamentary Affairs: State House, State Ave, Freetown; tel. (22) 228698; fax (22) 222781.

Ministry of Presidential Affairs: State House, State Ave, Freetown; tel. (22) 229728; fax (22) 229799.

Ministry of Social Welfare, Gender and Children's Affairs: New England, Freetown; tel. (22) 241256; fax (22) 242076.

Ministry of Trade and Industry: Ministerial Bldg, George St, Freetown; tel. (22) 225211.

Ministry of Transport and Communications: Ministerial Bldg, George St, Freetown; tel. (22) 221245; fax (22) 227337.

Ministry of Tourism and Culture: Ministerial Bldg, George St, Freetown; tel. (22) 222588.

Ministry of Works, Housing and Technical Maintenance: New England, Freetown; tel. (22) 240937; fax (22) 240018.

Ministry of Youth and Sports: New England, Freetown; tel. (22) 240881; fax (22) 240137.

President and Legislature

PRESIDENT

Presidential Election, 14 May 2002

Candidate	% of votes
Ahmed Tejan Kabbah (SLPP)	70.06
Ernest Bai Koroma (APC)	22.35
Johnny Paul Koroma (PLP)	3.00
Pallo Bangura (RUFP)	1.73
Dr John Karefa-Smart (APC)	1.04
Dr Raymond Kamara (GAP)	0.59
Zainab Hawa Bangura (MOP)	0.55
Bamidele Thompson (CUPP)	0.47
Andrew Turay (YPP)	0.20
Total	**100.00**

PARLIAMENT

Speaker: Justice E. K. Cowan.

General Election, 14 May 2002

Party	Seats
Sierra Leone People's Party (SLPP)	83
All-People's Congress (APC)	27
Peace and Liberation Party (PLP)	2
Total	**112***

*A further 12 seats were allocated to Paramount Chiefs, who represented the 12 provincial districts.

Election Commission

National Electoral Commission (NEC): Freetown; f. 2000; Chair. Christiana Ayoka Mary Thorpe.

Political Organizations

A ban on political activity was rescinded in June 1995. Numerous political parties were officially granted registration, prior to elections in May 2002.

All-People's Congress (APC): 39 Siaka Stevens St, Freetown; e-mail info@new-apc.org; internet www.new-apc.org; f. 1960; sole authorized political party 1978–91; merged with the Democratic People's Party in 1992; reconstituted in 1995; Leader Ernest Bai Koroma.

Citizens United for Peace and Progress (CUPP): e-mail info@cupp.org; internet www.cupp.org; f. 2002; Chair. Abubakarr Yanssaneh.

Grand Alliance Party (GAP): Freetown; f. 2002; Pres. Dr Raymond Kamara.

Movement for Progress (MOP): Freetown; f. 2002; Pres. Zainab Hawa Bangura.

National Alliance Democratic Party (NADP): Leader Mohamed Yahya Sillah.

National Democratic Alliance (NDA): Leader Amadu M. B. Jalloh.

National Unity Movement (NUM): Leader Desmond Luke.

National Unity Party (NUP): e-mail johnben@nupsl.org; internet www.nupsl.org; Leader John Oponjo Benjamin (acting).

Peace and Liberation Party (PLP): Freetown; f. 2002; Leader Johnny Paul Koroma.

People's Democratic Party (PDP): Freetown; supported Sierra Leone People's Party in May 2002 elections; Leader Osman Kamara.

People's Movement for Democratic Change (PMDC): Freetown; f. April 2006 by fmr mems of Sierra Leone People's Party; Leader Charles Margai; Sec.-Gen. Ansu Lansana.

People's National Convention (PNC): Leader Edward John Kargbo.

People's Progressive Party (PPP): Leader Abass Chernor Bundu.

Revolutionary United Front Party (RUFP): 15 Charlotte St, Freetown; tel. (22) 231624; fax (22) 232329; e-mail info@rufp.org; internet www.rufp.org; f. 1991 as rebel movement in conflict with govt forces; after disarmament in Jan. 2002, reconstituted as political party; Leader Gen. Issa Hassan Sesay (acting); Sec.-Gen. Pallo Bangura.

Sierra Leone People's Party (SLPP): 29 Rawdon St, Freetown; tel. and fax (22) 228222; e-mail sq-slpp@hotmail.com; internet www.slpp.ws; Chair. Dr A. K. Turay.

Social Democratic Party (SDP): Leader Andrew Victor Lungay.

United National People's Party (UNPP): Leader Dr John Karefa-Smart.

Young People's Party (YPP): 19 Lewis St, Freetown; tel. (22) 232907; e-mail info@yppsl.org; internet www.yppsl.org; f. 2002; Leader Sylvia Blyden; Sec.-Gen. Abdul Rahman Yilla.

Diplomatic Representation

EMBASSIES AND HIGH COMMISSIONS IN SIERRA LEONE

China, People's Republic: 29 Wilberforce Loop, Freetown; tel. (22) 231797; fax (22) 231797; Ambassador Fan Guijin.

Egypt: 174c Wilkinson Rd, POB 652, Freetown; tel. (22) 231245; fax (22) 272231; Ambassador Tarek Abdel Monem Ghoneim.

SIERRA LEONE

Directory

France: 1 College Rd, Cline Town, Freetown; tel. (22) 224584; Ambassador JEAN MICHEL BERRIT.
Gambia: 6 Wilberforce St, Freetown; tel. (22) 225191; fax (22) 226846; High Commissioner Lt-Col (retd) ANOUMAN SAHO.
Ghana: 13 Walpole St, Freetown; tel. (22) 223461; fax (22) 227043; High Commissioner KABRAL BLAY-AMIHERE.
Guinea: 6 Wilkinson Rd, Freetown; tel. (22) 232584; fax (22) 232496; Ambassador MOHAMED LAMIN SOMPARE.
Lebanon: 22A Spur Rd, Wilberforce, Freetown; tel. (22) 222513; fax (22) 234665; Ambassador GHASSAN ABDEL SATER.
Liberia: 10 Motor Rd, Brookfields, POB 276, Freetown; tel. (22) 230991; Chargé d'affaires a.i. SAMUEL PETERS.
Libya: 1A and 1B P. Z. Compound, Wilberforce, Freetown; tel. (22) 235231; fax (22) 234514; Chargé d'affaires a.i. ALI TELLISI.
Nigeria: 37 Siaka Stevens St, Freetown; tel. (22) 224224; fax (22) 2242474; High Commissioner ADAMU A. ABBAS.
United Kingdom: 6 Spur Rd, Wilberforce, Freetown; tel. (22) 232565; fax (22) 231070; e-mail bhc@sierratel.sl; High Commissioner Dr JOHN MITCHINER.
USA: Walpole and Siaka Stevens Sts, Freetown; tel. (22) 226481; fax (22) 225471; e-mail TaylorJB2@state.gov; internet freetown.usembassy.gov; Ambassador THOMAS N. HULL.

Judicial System

The Supreme Court
The ultimate court of appeal in both civil and criminal cases. In addition to its appellate jurisdiction, the Court has supervisory jurisdiction over all other courts and over any adjudicating authority in Sierra Leone, and also original jurisdiction in constitutional issues.
Chief Justice: DESMOND LUKE.
Supreme Court Justices: C. A. HARDING, AGNES AWUNOR-RENNER.

The Court of Appeal
The Court of Appeal has jurisdiction to hear and determine appeals from decisions of the High Court in both criminal and civil matters, and also from certain statutory tribunals. Appeals against its decisions may be made to the Supreme Court.
Justices of Appeal: S. C. E. WARNE, C. S. DAVIES, S. T. NAVO, M. S. TURAY, E. C. THOMPSON-DAVIS, M. O. TAJU-DEEN, M. O. ADOPHY, GEORGE GELAGA KING, Dr A. B. Y. TIMBO, VIRGINIA A. WRIGHT.

High Court
The High Court has unlimited original jurisdiction in all criminal and civil matters. It also has appellate jurisdiction against decisions of Magistrates' Courts.
Judges: FRANCIS C. GBOW, EBUN THOMAS, D. E. M. WILLIAMS, LAURA MARCUS-JONES, L. B. O. NYLANDER, A. M. B. TARAWALLIE, O. H. ALGHALLI, W. A. O. JOHNSON, N. D. ALHADI, R. J. BANKOLE THOMPSON, M. E. T. THOMPSON, C. J. W. ATERE-ROBERTS (acting).
Magistrates' Courts: In criminal cases the jurisdiction of the Magistrates' Courts is limited to summary cases and to preliminary investigations to determine whether a person charged with an offence should be committed for trial.
Local Courts have jurisdiction, according to native law and custom, in matters that are outside the jurisdiction of other courts.

Religion

A large proportion of the population holds animist beliefs, although there are significant numbers of Islamic and Christian adherents.

ISLAM
In 1990 Islamic adherents represented an estimated 30% of the total population.
Ahmadiyya Muslim Mission: 15 Bath St, Brookfields, POB 353, Freetown; Emir and Chief Missionary KHALIL A. MOBASHIR.
Kankaylay (Sierra Leone Muslim Men and Women's Association): 15 Blackhall Rd, Kissy, POB 1168, Freetown; tel. (22) 250931; e-mail kankaylay@yahoo.com; f. 1972; 500,000 mems; Pres. Alhaji IBRAHIM ALPHA TURAY; Lady Pres. Haja MARIAM TURAY.
Sierra Leone Muslim Congress: POB 875, Freetown; Pres. Alhaji MUHAMMAD SANUSI MUSTAPHA.

CHRISTIANITY
Council of Churches in Sierra Leone: 4A King Harman Rd, Brookfields, POB 404, Freetown; tel. (22) 240568; fax (22) 241109; e-mail ccsl@sierratel.sl; f. 1924; 17 mem. churches; Pres. Rev. MOSES B. KHANU; Gen. Sec. ALIMAMY P. KOROMA.

The Anglican Communion
Anglicans in Sierra Leone are adherents of the Church of the Province of West Africa, comprising 12 dioceses, of which two are in Sierra Leone. The Archbishop of the Province is the Bishop of Koforidua, Ghana.
Bishop of Bo: Rt Rev. SAMUEL SAO GBONDA, MacRobert St, POB 21, Bo, Southern Province.
Bishop of Freetown: Rt Rev. JULIUS O. PRINCE LYNCH, Bishopscourt, Fourah Bay Rd, POB 537, Freetown.

Baptist Churches
Sierra Leone Baptist Convention: POB 64, Lunsar; Pres. Rev. JOSEPH S. MANS; Sec. Rev. N. T. DIXON.
The Nigerian Baptist Convention is also active.

Methodist Churches
Methodist Church Sierra Leone: Wesley House, George St, POB 64, Freetown; tel. (22) 222216; autonomous since 1967; Pres. of Conf. Rev. GERSHON F. H. ANDERSON; Sec. Rev. CHRISTIAN V. A. PEACOCK; 26,421 mems.
United Methodist Church: Freetown; Presiding Bishop T. S. BANGURA; 36,857 mems.
Other active Methodist bodies include the African Methodist Episcopal Church, the Wesleyan Church of Sierra Leone, the Countess of Huntingdon's Connexion and the West African Methodist Church.

The Roman Catholic Church
Sierra Leone comprises one archdiocese and two dioceses. At 31 December 2003 there were an estimated 187,226 adherents in the country, representing about 3.1% of the total population.

Inter-territorial Catholic Bishops' Conference of The Gambia and Sierra Leone
Santanno House, POB 893, Freetown; tel. (22) 228240; fax (22) 228252.
f. 1971; Pres. Rt Rev. GEORGE BIGUZZI (Bishop of Makeni).
Archbishop of Freetown and Bo: Most Rev. JOSEPH HENRY GANDA, Santanno House, POB 893, Freetown; tel. (22) 224590; fax (22) 224075; e-mail archbis@hotmail.com.

Other Christian Churches
The following are represented: the Christ Apostolic Church, the Church of the Lord (Aladura), the Evangelical Church, the Missionary Church of Africa, the Sierra Leone Church and the United Brethren in Christ.

AFRICAN RELIGIONS
There is a diverse range of beliefs, rites and practices, varying between ethnic and kinship groups.

The Press

DAILIES
Daily Mail: 29–31 Rawdon St, POB 53, Freetown; tel. (22) 223191; f. 1931; state-owned; Editor AIAH MARTIN MONDEH; circ. 10,000.
For di People: Freetown; independent; Editor PAUL KAMARA.

PERIODICALS
African Crescent: 15 Bath St, POB 353, Brookfields, Freetown; Editor MAULANA-KHALIL A. MOBASHIR.
The Catalyst: Christian Literature Crusade Bookshop, 92 Circular Rd, POB 1465, Freetown; tel. (22) 224382; Editor ELIAS BANGURA.
Concord Times: 139 Pademba Rd, Freetown; 3 a week; Editor DOROTHY GORDON.
Leonean Sun: 49 Main Rd, Wellington, Freetown; tel. (22) 223363; f. 1974; monthly; Editor ROWLAND MARTYN.
Liberty Voice: 139 Pademba Rd, Freetown; tel. (22) 242100; Editor A. MAHDIEU SAVAGE.
New Breed: Freetown; weekly; independent; Man. Editor (vacant).
New Citizen: 5 Hanna Benka-Coker St, Freetown; tel. (22) 241795; Editor I. BEN KARGBO.
The New Globe: 49 Bathurst St, Freetown; tel. (22) 228245; weekly; Man. Editor SAM TUMOE; circ. 4,000.

SIERRA LEONE

The New Shaft: 60 Old Railway Line, Brookfields, Freetown; tel. (22) 241093; 2 a week; independent; Editor Franklin Bunting-Davies; circ. 10,000.

The Pool Newspaper: 1 Short St, 5th Floor, Freetown; tel. and fax (22) 220102; e-mail pool@justice.com; internet www.poolnewspaper.tripod.com; f. 1992; 3 a week; independent; Man. Dir Chernor Ojuku Sesay; circ. 3,000.

Progress: 1 Short St, Freetown; tel. (22) 223588; weekly; independent; Editor Fode Kandeh; circ. 7,000.

Sierra Leone Chamber of Commerce Journal: Sierra Leone Chamber of Commerce, Industry and Agriculture, Guma Bldg, 5th Floor, Lamina Sankoh St, POB 502, Freetown; tel. (22) 226305; fax (22) 228005; monthly.

Unity Now: 82 Pademba Rd, Freetown; tel. (22) 227466; Editor Frank Kposowa.

The Vision: 60 Old Railway Line, Brookfields; tel. (22) 241273; Editor Siaka Massaquoi.

Weekend Spark: 7 Lamina Sankoh St, Freetown; tel. (22) 223397; f. 1983; weekly; independent; Editor Rowland Martyn; circ. 20,000.

Weekly Democrat: Freetown; Editor Jon Foray.

NEWS AGENCY

Sierra Leone News Agency (SLENA): 15 Wallace Johnson St, PMB 445, Freetown; tel. (22) 224921; fax (22) 224439; f. 1980; Man. Dir Abdul Karim Jalloh (acting).

Publishers

Njala University Publishing Centre: Njala University College, PMB, Freetown; science and technology, university textbooks.

Sierra Leone University Press: Fourah Bay College, POB 87, Freetown; tel. (22) 22491; fax (22) 224439; f. 1965; biography, history, Africana, religion, social science, university textbooks; Chair. Prof. Ernest H. Wright.

United Christian Council Literature Bureau: Bunumbu Press, POB 28, Bo; tel. (32) 462; books in Mende, Temne, Susu; Man. Dir Robert Sam-Kpakra.

Broadcasting and Communications

TELECOMMUNICATIONS

Sierra Leone Telecommunications Co (SIERRATEL): 7 Wallace Johnson St, POB 80, Freetown; tel. (22) 222804; fax (22) 224439.

BROADCASTING

Sierra Leone Broadcasting Service: New England, Freetown; tel. (22) 240403; f. 1934; state-controlled; programmes mainly in English and the four main Sierra Leonean vernaculars, Mende, Limba, Temne and Krio; weekly broadcast in French; television service established 1963; Dir-Gen. Jeana Bandatomo.

Finance

(cap. = capital; res = reserves; dep. = deposits; m. = million; brs = branches; amounts in leones)

BANKING

Central Bank

Bank of Sierra Leone: Siaka Stevens St, POB 30, Freetown; tel. (22) 226501; fax (22) 224764; e-mail info@bankofsierraleone-centralbank.org; internet www.bankofsierraleone-centralbank.org; f. 1964; cap. 24,001.5m., res 6,069.0m., dep. 482,567.1m. (Dec. 2002); Gov. James D. Rogers; Dep. Gov. Mohamed S. Fofana; 1 br.

Other Banks

Guaranty Trust Bank: Sparta Bldg, 12 Wilberforce St, Freetown; tel. (22) 228493; fax (22) 228318; e-mail gtbsl@sierratel.sl; f. Feb. 2002 through the acquisition of 90% of shareholding of First Merchant Bank of Sierra Leone by Guaranty Trust Bank of Nigeria; cap. 2,261.0m., total assets 17,769.0m. (Dec. 2003); Chair. Tayo Aderinokun.

National Development Bank Ltd: Leone House, 6th Floor, 21–23 Siaka Stevens St, Freetown; tel. (22) 226792; fax (22) 224468; e-mail ndbrisk@sierratel.sl; f. 1968; 99% state-owned; provides medium- and long-term finance and tech. assistance to devt-orientated enterprises; cap. 1,604.3m., total assets 2,200m. (Dec. 2003); Chair. Murray E. S. Lamin; Man. Dir Mohamed M. Turay; 3 brs.

Rokel Commercial Bank of Sierra Leone Ltd: 25–27 Siaka Stevens St, POB 12, Freetown; tel. (22) 222501; fax (22) 222563; e-mail rokelsl@sierratel.sl; internet www.rokelsl.com; f. 1971; cap. 1,119.7m., res 1,776.7m., dep. 83,685.5m. (Dec. 2003); 51% govt-owned; Chair. A. D. A. M'Cormack; Man. Dir Henry Akin Macauley; 7 brs.

Sierra Leone Commercial Bank Ltd: 29–31 Siaka Stevens St, Freetown; tel. (22) 225264; fax (22) 225292; e-mail slcb@sierratel.sl; internet www.slcb.biz; f. 1973; state-owned; cap. 1,000.0m., res 5,759.9m., dep. 88,911.6m. (Dec. 2003); Chair. I. I. May-Parker; Man. Dir A. Kakay; 5 brs.

Standard Chartered Bank Sierra Leone Ltd: 9 and 11 Lightfoot-Boston St, POB 1155, Freetown; tel. (22) 225022; fax (22) 225760; e-mail scbsl@sierratel.sl; f. 1971; cap. and res 13,073.0m., total assets 102,179.9m. (Dec. 2003); Chair. Lloyd A. During; Man. Dir Lamin Kemba Manjang; 14 brs.

Union Trust Bank Ltd: Howe St, PMB 1237, Freetown; tel. (22) 226954; fax (22) 226214; e-mail utb@sierratel.sl; fmrly Meridien BIAO Bank Sierra Leone Ltd; adopted present name in 1995; cap. and res 8,221.1m., total assets 29,025.0m. (Dec. 2003); Chair. S. B. Nicol-Cole; Man. Dir John D. Okrafo-Smart.

INSURANCE

Aureol Insurance Co Ltd: Kissy House, 54 Siaka Stevens St, POB 647, Freetown; tel. (22) 223435; fax (22) 229336; f. 1987; Man. Dir S. G. Benjamin.

National Insurance Co Ltd: 18–20 Walpole St, PMB 84, Freetown; tel. (22) 224328; fax (22) 226097; e-mail nic@sierratel.sl; f. 1972; state-owned; Chair. S. Macauley; CEO A. N. Yaskey.

New India Assurance Co Ltd: 18 Wilberforce St, POB 340, Freetown; tel. (22) 226453; fax (22) 222494; Man. Dir A. Chopra.

Reliance Insurance Trust Corpn Ltd: 24 Siaka Stevens St, Freetown; tel. (22) 225115; fax (22) 228051; f. 1985; Chair. Mohamed B. Cole; Man. Dir Alice M. Onomake.

Sierra Leone Insurance Co Ltd: 31 Lightfoot Boston St, POB 836, Freetown; tel. (22) 224920; fax (22) 222115; Man. Dir Idrisse Yille.

Trade and Industry

GOVERNMENT AGENCY

Government Gold and Diamond Office (GGDO): c/o Bank of Sierra Leone, Siaka Stevens St, Freetown; tel. (22) 222600; fax (22) 229064; f. 1985; govt regulatory agency for diamonds and gold; combats illicit trade; Chair. Alhaji M. S. Deen.

CHAMBER OF COMMERCE

Sierra Leone Chamber of Commerce, Industry and Agriculture: Guma Bldg, 5th Floor, Lamina Sankoh St, POB 502, Freetown; tel. (22) 226305; fax (22) 228005; e-mail cocsl@sierratel.sl; internet www.cocsl.com; f. 1961; 215 mems; Pres. Alhaji Mohamed Musa King.

TRADE AND INDUSTRIAL ASSOCIATIONS

Sierra Leone Export Development and Investment Corpn (SLEDIC): 18–20 Walpole St, PMB 6, Freetown; tel. (22) 227604; fax (22) 229097; e-mail sledic@sierratel.sl; f. 1993; Man. Dir Chris Jasabe.

Small-Medium Scale Businesses Association (Sierra Leone): O.A.U. Drive, Tower Hill, PMB 575, Freetown; tel. (22) 222617; fax (22) 224439; Dir Abu Conteh.

EMPLOYERS' ORGANIZATIONS

Sierra Leone Employers' Federation: POB 562, Freetown; Chair. Amadu B. Ndoeka; Exec. Officer L. E. Johnson.

Sierra Leone Chamber of Mines: POB 456, Freetown; tel. (22) 226082; f. 1965; mems comprise the principal mining concerns; Pres. D. J. S. Fraser; Exec. Officer N. H. T. Boston.

UTILITIES

Electricity

National Power Authority: Electricity House, Siaka Stevens St, Freetown; tel. (30) 700000; fax (22) 227584; e-mail Sierra_Leone@iaeste.org; supplies all electricity in Sierra Leone.

Water

Guma Valley Water Co: Guma Bldg, 13/14 Lamina Sankoh St, POB 700, Freetown; tel. (22) 25887; e-mail gumasl@sierratel.com; f. 1961; responsible for all existing water supplies in Freetown and surrounding villages, including the Guma dam and associated works.

TRADE UNIONS

Artisans', Ministry of Works Employees' and General Workers' Union: 4 Pultney St, Freetown; f. 1946; 14,500 mems; Pres. IBRAHIM LANGLEY; Gen. Sec. TEJAN A. KASSIM.

Sierra Leone Labour Congress: 35 Wallace Johnson St, POB 1333, Freetown; tel. (22) 226869; f. 1966; 51,000 mems in 19 affiliated unions; Pres. H. M. BARRIE; Sec.-Gen. KANDEH YILLA.

Principal affiliated unions:

Clerical, Mercantile and General Workers' Union: 35 Wallace Johnson St, Freetown; f. 1945; 3,600 mems; Pres. M. D. BENJAMIN; Gen. Sec. M. B. WILLIAMS.

Sierra Leone Association of Journalists: Freetown; Pres. SIAKA MASSAQUOI.

Sierra Leone Dockworkers' Union: 165 Fourah Bay Rd, Freetown; f. 1962; 2,650 mems; Pres. D. F. KANU; Gen. Sec. A. C. CONTEH.

Sierra Leone Motor Drivers' Union: 10 Charlotte St, Freetown; f. 1960; 1,900 mems; Pres. A. W. HASSAN; Gen. Sec. ALPHA KAMARA.

Sierra Leone Teachers' Union: Regaland House, Lowcost Step—Kissy, POB 477, Freetown; f. 1951; 18,500 mems; Pres. FESTUS E. MINAH; Sec.-Gen. A. O. TIMBO.

Sierra Leone Transport, Agricultural and General Workers' Union: 4 Pultney St, Freetown; f. 1946; 1,600 mems; Pres. S. O. SAWYERR-MANLEY; Gen. Sec. S. D. KARGBO.

United Mineworkers' Union: 35 Wallace Johnson St, Freetown; f. 1944; 6,500 mems; Pres. H. M. BARRIE; Gen. Sec. S. D. GBENDA.

Also affiliated to the Sierra Leone Labour Congress: **General Construction Workers' Union**, **Municipal and Local Government Employees' Union**, **Sierra Leone National Seamen's Union**.

Transport

RAILWAYS

There are no passenger railways in Sierra Leone.

Marampa Mineral Railway: Delco House, POB 735, Freetown; tel. (22) 222556; 84 km of track linking iron ore mines at Marampa (inactive since 1985) with Pepel port; Gen. Man. SYL KHANU.

ROADS

In 2002 there were an estimated 11,300 km of classified roads, including 2,138 km of main roads and 1,950 km of secondary roads; about 904 km of the total network was paved.

Sierra Leone Road Transport Corpn: Blackhall Rd, POB 1008, Freetown; tel. (22) 250442; fax (22) 250000; f. 1965; state-owned; operates transport services throughout the country; Gen. Man. DANIEL R. W. FAUX.

INLAND WATERWAYS

Established routes for launches, which include the coastal routes from Freetown northward to the Great and Little Scarcies rivers and southward to Bonthe, total almost 800 km. Although some of the upper reaches of the rivers are navigable only between July and September, there is a considerable volume of river traffic.

SHIPPING

Freetown, the principal port, has full facilities for ocean-going vessels.

Sierra Leone National Shipping Co Ltd: 45 Cline St, POB 935, Freetown; tel. (22) 229883; fax (22) 229513; e-mail nsc@sierratel.sl; f. 1972; state-owned; shipping, clearing and forwarding agency; representatives for foreign lines; Chair. Alhaji B. M. KOROMA; Man. Dir SYLVESTER B. FOMBA.

Sierra Leone Ports Authority: Queen Elizabeth II Quay, PMB 386, Cline Town, Freetown; tel. (22) 226480; fax (22) 226443; f. 1965; parastatal body, supervised by the Ministry of Transport and Communications; operates the port of Freetown; Gen. Man. Capt. P. E. M. KEMOKAI.

Sierra Leone Shipping Agencies Ltd: Deep Water Quay, Clinetown, POB 74, Freetown; tel. (22) 223453; fax (22) 220021; e-mail slsa@sl.dti.bollore.com; f. 1949; Man. Dir MICHEL MEYNARD.

Silver Star Shipping Agency Ltd: PMB 1023, Freetown; tel. (22) 221035; fax (22) 226653; e-mail silver2_star@hotmail.com; Dir Capt. H. A. BLOOMER.

CIVIL AVIATION

There is an international airport at Lungi.

Directorate of Civil Aviation: Ministry of Transport and Communications, Ministerial Bldg, George St, Freetown; tel. (22) 221245; Dir T. T. A. VANDY.

Sierra National Airlines: Leone House, 25 Pultney St, POB 285, Freetown; tel. (22) 222075; fax (22) 222026; e-mail alpha@kanu; f. 1982; state-owned; operates domestic and regional services, and a weekly flight to Paris, France; operations resumed, following civil conflict, in Nov. 2000; Chair. TAMBA MATTURI; Man. Dir ADAM CORMACK.

Tourism

The main attractions for tourists are the coastline, the mountains and the game reserves. Civil conflict throughout most of the 1990s effectively suspended tourist activity. By 2003, however, according to the World Tourism Organization, tourist arrivals had increased to 37,201, compared with 10,615 in 1999. Receipts from tourism totalled an estimated US $60m. in 2003.

National Tourist Board of Sierra Leone: Cape Sierra Hotel, Room 100, Aberdeen, POB 1435, Freetown; tel. (22) 236620; fax (22) 236621; e-mail ntbslinfo@yahoo.com; internet www.welcometosierraleone.org/visitsierraleone.org; f. 1990; Gen. Man. CECIL J. WILLIAMS.

SINGAPORE

Introductory Survey

Location, Climate, Language, Religion, Flag, Capital

The Republic of Singapore lies in South-East Asia. The country comprises one main island and some 64 offshore islands, situated approximately 137 km (85 miles) north of the Equator, off the southernmost tip of the Malay Peninsula, to which it is linked by a causeway. The climate is equatorial, with a uniformly high daily and annual temperature varying between 24°C and 27°C (75°F–80°F). Relative humidity is high (often exceeding 90%), and the average annual rainfall is 235 cm (93 ins). There are four official languages—Malay (the national language), Chinese (Mandarin), Tamil and English. The language of administration is English. Chinese dialects were spoken as a first language by 24% of the population in 2000. The principal religions are Daoism, Buddhism, Islam, Christianity and Hinduism. The national flag (proportions 2 by 3) has two equal horizontal stripes of red and white, with a white crescent moon and five white stars, arranged in a pentagram, in the upper hoist. The capital is Singapore City.

Recent History

In 1826 the East India Company formed the Straits Settlements by the union of Singapore and the dependencies of Penang and Malacca on the Malay Peninsula. They came under British rule in 1867 as a crown colony. Singapore was occupied by Japan for three years during the Second World War. At the end of the war, following Japan's defeat, Singapore was governed by a British military administration. When civil rule was restored in 1946, Singapore was detached from the other Straits Settlements and became a separate crown colony. A new Constitution, adopted in February 1955, introduced some measure of self-government, and in June 1959 the state achieved complete internal self-government, with Lee Kuan Yew as Prime Minister. The Federation of Malaysia came into being in September 1963, with Singapore as a constituent state. On 9 August 1965, following irreconcilable differences with the central Government in Malaysia, Singapore seceded from the federation and became an independent country. Singapore joined the UN in September and became a member of the Commonwealth in October. In December Singapore was proclaimed a republic, with a President as constitutional Head of State. In May 1973 the last major ties with Malaysia, concerning currency and finance, were renounced. In September 1972 Lee Kuan Yew's ruling People's Action Party (PAP) won all 65 parliamentary seats in a general election.

After independence the Government supported a strong US military presence in South-East Asia. However, with the collapse of US influence in the area during 1974–75, Singapore adopted a conciliatory attitude towards the People's Republic of China and its communist neighbours. The Government called for the removal of foreign bases from member states of the Association of South East Asian Nations (ASEAN, see p. 172), and advocated a policy of neutrality. Singapore sought to consolidate its trade links with China, although diplomatic relations were not established until 1982.

At general elections in December 1976 and again in December 1980, the PAP won all 69 seats in the enlarged Parliament. The PAP's monopoly ended in October 1981, however, when the Secretary-General of the opposition Workers' Party, J. B. Jeyaretnam, won a by-election. This posed no direct threat, but, in order to reassert its authority, the Government increased its control over trade unions and restructured the ownership of major newspapers. The PAP was again returned to power in December 1984 with a large majority in Parliament (now enlarged to 79 seats), but the party lost two seats to opposition parties, and its share of the total votes was reduced to 62.9% from 75% in 1980. A constitutional amendment approved in July 1984 provided for up to three 'non-constituency' parliamentary seats for the opposition (with restricted voting rights) if none was won in the election. One extra seat was subsequently offered to the losing opposition candidate with the highest percentage of votes. However, this seat was refused by the Workers' Party in January 1985. In March the state President, Devan Nair, resigned. A new President, Wee Kim Wee (hitherto the Chairman of the Singapore Broadcasting Corporation), was elected by Parliament in August.

During 1986 the Government exhibited signs of increasing intolerance towards its critics. In August amendments to the Parliament (Privileges, Immunities and Powers) Act were hurriedly adopted, enabling Parliament to fine, expel or imprison members who were deemed to have abused their parliamentary privileges. In the same month Parliament also approved a Newspaper and Printing Presses (Amendment) Act, which empowered the Government to restrict the distribution of foreign publications deemed to be interfering in domestic political affairs; the circulation of several foreign periodicals was subsequently restricted.

In November 1986 Jeyaretnam (one of the two opposition members of Parliament) was sentenced to one month's imprisonment and fined S $5,000 (enough, according to the Constitution, to deprive him of his parliamentary seat and prevent him from standing for election for five years), when the Supreme Court upheld a conviction for perjury in connection with bankruptcy proceedings brought against the Workers' Party four years previously. In February 1987 Jeyaretnam was also fined by a parliamentary committee for abuse of privilege, having made allegations of government interference in the judiciary; further fines were imposed on him for publishing 'distorted' accounts of an earlier hearing of the committee, and (in May) for alleged contempt of Parliament and abuse of parliamentary privilege. In October Jeyaretnam's removal from the Law Society register was ordered by a three-judge court. An appeal to the Judicial Committee of the Privy Council in the United Kingdom (then the highest court of appeal for Singapore) resulted, in October 1988, in his reinstatement as a practising lawyer. During the course of the appeal, investigations into Jeyaretnam's previous convictions found that they had been 'fatally flawed'. However, since the criminal case had been considered in the District Court, where there was no right of appeal to the Privy Council, the original convictions prevented Jeyaretnam from re-entering Parliament without a presidential pardon. This was refused by Wee Kim Wee in May 1989.

In May and June 1987 the Government detained 22 people (including 10 Roman Catholic church workers and four members of the Workers' Party) without trial, under the Internal Security Act, for alleged involvement in a 'Marxist conspiracy' to subvert state organizations. The arrests were denounced by Jeyaretnam, who claimed that the Government wished to intimidate Singaporeans so that they would not support opposition parties. In November the Government was also criticized by international human rights groups, including Amnesty International, for its refusal to present evidence of such a conspiracy in court. By December most of the alleged conspirators had been released, but eight of them were rearrested in April 1988, after complaining that they had been tortured while in detention. Four prisoners were released by June, and in December a further four detainees were released in accordance with a ruling by the Court of Appeal, based on a fault in their detention orders. They were immediately rearrested. The trial had, however, established a precedent for the judicial review of cases brought under the Internal Security Act, including the acceptability to the courts of evidence used in warrants for the arrest of suspects. In January 1989 Parliament approved legislation ensuring that the judiciary could examine such detentions only on technical grounds, and abolishing the right of appeal to the Privy Council in cases brought under the Internal Security Act. In March three detainees were released. The two remaining prisoners (of the original 22) remained in detention until June 1990.

A general election was held in September 1988. The electoral system was altered so that 39 of the existing 79 constituencies were replaced by 13 'group representation constituencies', to be contested by teams of three representatives for each party, at least one of whom was to be a member of an ethnic minority (i.e. non-Chinese). The declared aim was to ensure the presence of racial minorities in Parliament; in practice, however, opposition parties with few resources were handicapped by the difficulty of presenting three candidates. The PAP won 80 of the elective seats (which now totalled 81); one was taken by the leader of the Singapore Democratic Party (SDP), Chiam See Tong. Two 'non-constituency' seats were offered to Francis Seow (Workers' Party) and Lee Siew Choh (Socialist Front). In December, however, while Seow (who had already been detained in May under the Internal Security Act for organizing a meeting between a US diplomat and lawyers critical of the Government) was undergoing medical treatment in the USA, he was convicted *in absentia* for tax evasion and fined S $19,000: he was thus debarred from taking his seat in Parliament.

In January 1989 Lee began his eighth term as Prime Minister, and announced that he would retire from the premiership before the expiry of the term. This announcement was followed by a statement from the First Deputy Prime Minister, Goh Chok Tong (Lee's chosen successor), that Lee was adopting a second- ary and more advisory role in the government of the country. In August Parliament unanimously re-elected Wee Kim Wee for a further four-year term as President. In early 1990 Parliament approved legislation enabling the Government to nominate as many as six unelected MPs. The politically-neutral nominated MPs would be appointed for two years, and would be able to vote on all legislative proposals except those concerning financial and constitutional affairs.

On 28 November 1990 Lee was duly replaced as Prime Minister by Goh Chok Tong. Lee remained in the Cabinet as Senior Minister in the Prime Minister's Office, and retained the position of Secretary-General of the PAP, while Lee's son, Brig.-Gen. Lee Hsien Loong, was appointed as a Deputy Prime Minister.

In January 1991 the Constitution was amended to provide for a popularly elected presidency with extensive powers of veto on proposed financial legislation, a role as final arbiter in cases of detention for reasons of national security, and influence in civil and military appointments. The changes to the (hitherto highly ceremonial) functions of the President were initially proposed by Lee in 1984, and were criticized by members of opposition parties as being intended to accommodate the former Prime Minister. Under the amendment, Wee Kim Wee was to continue in office until October 1993. Legislation empowering him with the authority of an elected president took effect from 30 November 1991. Candidates for the presidency were limited to those who had held the post of a minister, chief justice or senior civil servant or were at the head of a large company. The candidates were to be scrutinized by a new presidential election committee, which was to comprise the head of the Society of Accountants, the Chairman of the Public Service Commission and a member of the Presidential Council of Human Rights. The last two officials were appointed by the Government, prompting fears that the selected candidates would be those favoured by the PAP. The constitutional amendment also included a clause increasing the number of candidates required to contest a 'group representation constituency' in a general election to a minimum of three and a maximum of four, one of whom was to be a member of an ethnic minority.

In early 1991 the Government promoted the acceptance of five 'shared values', based on Confucian philosophy, as the basis of a national ideology. Critics alleged that the ideology would be used to reinforce support for the PAP and to obviate opposition challenges. Goh attempted, in principle, to introduce a more 'open', consultative form of government. He instituted an extensive programme of community visits to assess popular opinion, showing solicitude for the views of the minority Malay and Indian communities. Although film censorship was relaxed, the Internal Security Act and restrictions on the foreign press remained in force. In early August, seeking a popular mandate for his style of government, Goh announced that there would be a general election at the end of the month. Under a plan conceived by Chiam, the opposition parties contested only 40 of the 81 seats, thus guaranteeing an absolute majority for the incumbent PAP. Chiam issued an appeal to the electorate to take the opportunity to elect a strong opposition. Goh indicated that a failure to receive a popular endorsement would result in a return to a more authoritarian and paternalistic form of government. At the election, held on 31 August, the PAP's share of the vote was 61.0% (compared with 63.2% in 1988), and the party won 77 seats (compared with 80 in 1988). Chiam's SDP secured three seats, and the Workers' Party one seat. Jeyaretnam was unable to contest the election, as his disqualification remained in force until the beginning of November 1991. In response to Jeyaretnam's accusations that he had been deliberately excluded from the election, and also because the election schedule had prevented the PAP from presenting enough new candidates, Goh had announced, prior to the polls, that he would organize by-elections within 12–18 months of the general election.

In October 1991 Seow, who had remained in exile in the USA since 1988, was convicted *in absentia* of a further 60 offences involving tax evasion, rendering him ineligible to contest any potential by-election. Later that month Jeyaretnam paid S $392,838 in legal costs to Lee, thus avoiding bankruptcy, which would have prevented his candidacy. Lee had instituted a successful defamation suit against Jeyaretnam in 1990, over remarks made by Jeyaretnam at a 1988 election rally.

Following the general election, Lee, who had temporarily withdrawn from public attention after Goh's accession to the premiership, resumed a prominent role in domestic politics. He attributed the decline in PAP support to neglect of the Mandarin-educated ethnic Chinese majority, and advocated a greater emphasis on Chinese culture and language. In April 1991 Goh announced that the level of electoral support among residents would be one of the criteria used to determine the order in which refurbishments would be undertaken in public housing estates. Since about 86% of Singaporeans lived in public housing, this was widely interpreted as a warning against voting for the opposition in the forthcoming by-elections.

Prior to the convening of Parliament in September 1992 the Government appointed the maximum of six nominated MPs. This too was generally regarded as an attempt to discourage support for opposition candidates in the impending by-elections. In October the implementation of legislation prohibiting MPs from using the ground floors of public housing blocks as office space adversely affected all four opposition MPs, who, because of a shortage of party funds, were unable to afford commercial rents.

In November 1992 Goh announced to the Central Executive Committee of the PAP that the renewal of national leadership was the party's most urgent consideration. This statement was followed two days later by the public disclosure that both Deputy Prime Ministers, Lee Hsien Loong and Ong Teng Cheong, had been diagnosed as suffering from cancer. The revelation strengthened Goh's position as Prime Minister, since many had previously regarded his incumbency as an interim arrangement prior to Lee Hsien Loong's assumption of the premiership. In December Goh was unanimously elected to replace Lee Kuan Yew (who proposed his candidacy) as Secretary-General of the PAP.

In December 1992 Goh relinquished his parliamentary seat (which formed part of a four-member 'group representation constituency') in order to contest a by-election. Jeyaretnam was unable to contest the by-election as only three candidates from the Workers' Party registered with the authorities. The results of the by-election were regarded as an endorsement of Goh's leadership, as the four PAP candidates received 72.9% of the votes cast, while the opposition SDP secured 24.5%.

In March 1993 Chee Soon Juan, who contested the December by-election as a candidate for the SDP, was dismissed from his post as a lecturer at the National University of Singapore for 'dishonest conduct'. The Government denied that the dismissal was politically motivated, and defamation proceedings were initiated by university officials against Chee. In June, following a rejection by the SDP Central Committee of a motion of censure proposed by Chiam against Chee for bringing the party into disrepute, Chiam resigned as Secretary-General of the party. Chee replaced him as acting Secretary-General, pending party elections in early 1995. In August 1993 the SDP expelled Chiam for alleged indiscipline; however, a High Court ruling in December declared the expulsion 'illegal and invalid'. (This enabled Chiam to retain his seat in Parliament: under the Constitution a member of the legislature is obliged to relinquish his seat if he resigns or is expelled from the party he has been elected to represent.) The following month, under a judicial ruling, a 'breakaway' central executive committee, formed in 1993 by a faction of the SDP that remained loyal to Chiam, was declared void. Chee subsequently published a book entitled *Dare to Change*, which demanded greater democracy and was adopted as official party policy by the SDP in June 1994. Chee was formally elected Secretary-General of the SDP in January 1995.

Meanwhile, in August 1993 Ong Teng Cheong was elected President with 58.7% of the votes cast. Contrary to expectation, however, the only other candidate, Chua Kim Yeow, a former government official, who adopted an apolitical position, secured a substantial proportion (41.3%) of the vote. The candidacies of both Jeyaretnam and Tan Soo Phuan, another member of the

Workers' Party, were rejected by the Presidential Election Committee on the grounds that they were unsuitable 'in regard to integrity, good character and reputation'.

In July 1995 Lee Kuan Yew, Lee Hsien Loong and Goh were awarded record damages by the Supreme Court in Singapore following a successful defamation suit, in January, against the US-owned *International Herald Tribune*. The newspaper had published an article in the previous year implying that Lee Hsien Loong's position had been attained through nepotism and that the Singapore Government suppressed democratic activity by using a compliant judiciary to bankrupt political opponents through defamation suits. Lee revived the libel suit in March 1996, and in April was awarded further damages for which the author of the article in question was to be liable. In November 1995 Lee Kuan Yew received further damages from the newspaper following its publication of an article referring to intolerant regimes in the region.

In late October 1996 Parliament approved amendments to the Constitution that redefined the role of the President and partially reformed the voting system. The President's powers were restricted by new provisions empowering the Government to call a referendum if the President vetoed certain constitutional amendments, and also enabling Parliament to overturn (by a two-thirds' majority) a presidential veto on key civil service appointments. A further amendment expanded the number of 'group representation constituencies' and increased the maximum number of group candidates from four to six. The electoral reforms were opposed by the opposition parties on the grounds that the amendments favoured large, well-established parties such as the PAP, while smaller parties would have difficulty both in finding and funding large numbers of candidates.

Prior to the general election, which took place on 2 January 1997, the success of the PAP was predetermined by the opposition parties' decision to contest only 36 of the 83 seats. Nevertheless, the PAP conducted a rigorous campaign in an effort to ensure that the party received two-thirds of the total votes cast, a margin regarded as sufficient endorsement of Goh and his administration. During the campaign, it was again announced that public housing improvements would be prioritized according to levels of electoral support for the PAP. The party secured a resounding victory, winning 65% of the votes and 81 seats (including all nine single-member constituencies). The remaining two elective seats were won by Chiam See Tong of the Singapore People's Party (for the fourth time, although previously he had been elected as a representative of the SDP) and Low Thia Khiang of the Workers' Party (for a second time). The Workers' Party, as the opposition party with the most votes but less than three seats, was also allocated a non-constituency seat; this was accepted by Jeyaretnam. The SDP lost the three seats it had previously held.

Seemingly a particular focus for attack by the PAP during the election campaign was Tang Liang Hong, a candidate of the Workers' Party. The PAP accused Tang of being anti-Christian, of promoting Chinese interests over those of Singapore's ethnic minorities and of attempting to foment discontent amongst the ethnic Chinese community. Tang, standing in the same 'group representation constituency' as Jeyaretnam, failed to secure election. (Goh, unopposed in a single-member constituency, personally campaigned against Tang in the group constituency.) Tang's public rebuttal of the accusations of the PAP leaders prompted them to issue writs against him for defamation. Tang fled to Malaysia in January 1997, claiming to have received anonymous death threats. Tang was found guilty of defamation by the High Court in March, as he failed to attend the trial and provide a defence, and was ordered in May to pay a record sum of S $8m. in libel damages to Goh and 10 senior PAP leaders. Tang appealed against the judgment in September on the grounds that it contained legal errors and that the cases had been brought for political motives. The Court of Appeal ruled in November that the damages awarded against Tang were disproportionate to the injury caused, and reduced the sum to S $4.53m. In February 1998, despite this concession, Tang, against whom a warrant for arrest had been issued on 33 counts of tax evasion, was declared bankrupt.

Goh and 10 senior PAP members also sued Jeyaretnam for alleged defamation following remarks made at an election rally concerning two police reports submitted by Tang accusing the PAP leadership of criminal conspiracy and lying. In September 1997 Jeyaretnam was ordered to pay damages of S $20,000; the award was, however, only one-tenth of the amount sought by the PAP leadership, and the judge, who criticized Goh's lawyers for their handling of the case, ordered that Jeyaretnam pay only 60% of the legal costs. During the trial Goh admitted under cross-examination that he had authorized the unofficial disclosure of the police reports to the press, and it was put to him that the legal suits were an attempt to bankrupt Jeyaretnam and thus disqualify him from Parliament. However, the Court of Appeal dismissed an appeal by Jeyaretnam in July 1998, increasing the damages to S $100,000, and awarding full costs against him. It was subsequently agreed, however, that Jeyaretnam would be permitted to pay the damages in five instalments, thereby enabling him to avoid bankruptcy proceedings and to continue as a legislator.

On 26 November 1998 the Government revoked the remaining restrictions on the activities of the political activist Chia Thye Poh. Chia had been arrested in 1966, imprisoned for more than 22 years without trial under the Internal Security Act, confined to a fortress on an island off the coast of Singapore for a further three years, then permitted to reside in Singapore from 1992, although prohibited from taking part in any political activity. Despite this concession to Chia, government suppression of expressions of opposition continued. In January 1999 Chee was charged twice under the Public Entertainment Act for making unlicensed public speeches in December 1998 and January 1999. Chee had deliberately refused to apply for licences to make the two public speeches, in which he criticized government policy, on the grounds that freedom of expression was guaranteed under the Constitution. During the first trial Chee was represented by Jeyaretnam, who attempted to expose the alleged use of the above Act to restrict political opposition. However, Chee was found guilty at the beginning of February, and was sentenced to seven days' imprisonment, owing to his refusal to pay a fine of S $1,400. Following his release, Chee appeared in court for a second time in February, and was sentenced, with the Assistant Secretary-General of the SDP, Wong Hong Toy, who had reportedly assisted Chee at the speech, to 12 days' imprisonment after Chee and Wong refused to pay respective fines of S $2,500 and S $2,400. The level of the fines automatically disqualified both men from seeking political office for five years; however, following an appeal, the two had their fines reduced to S $1,900 each, below the level that would have rendered them ineligible to stand for election. For its part, the Government maintained that opposition politicians had adequate opportunity to expound their views in Parliament or in the media (although in February 1998 the Government had banned political parties from producing videos and from promoting their opinions on television). In April 1999 it was reported that, subsequent to his release from prison after serving his second term of imprisonment, Chee had been fined S $600 for illegal sales of a book he had produced on Asian opposition leaders. In March members of the PAP filed a petition to close the Workers' Party, owing to its inability to pay more than S $280,000 in damages and costs awarded against it in a defamation case. The party's closure would force the resignation of its two parliamentary representatives. In May it was reported that the party had lost a judicial appeal against the award.

On 5 May 2000 Jeyaretnam was declared bankrupt by the High Court after he failed to make payments of S $30,000 in libel damages arising from a lawsuit concerning an article that appeared in the Workers' Party newspaper, *The Hammer*, in 1995. The bankruptcy ruling would have disqualified Jeyaretnam from serving in Parliament, but on 11 May the orders were set aside after the outstanding debt was paid, and he was authorized to retain his non-constituency seat. In January 2001, however, Jeyaretnam was once again declared bankrupt by the High Court, with a S $235,000 debt as a result of a defamation claim against a Workers' Party newsletter. The appeal against the bankruptcy ruling was dismissed in February. In May Jeyaretnam was replaced as Secretary-General of the Workers' Party by Low Thia Khiang. In July he finally lost his seat in Parliament when the Court of Appeals confirmed that it would not overturn the bankruptcy ruling against him.

Meanwhile, legislation introduced in May 1997 increased the number of nominated MPs from six to nine; the Constitution was amended accordingly in September. During the year nine Community Development Councils (CDCs) were formed. The CDCs encompassed all constituencies, including the two opposition wards, which, despite election campaign threats, were to receive the same services as other constituencies, although opposition representatives would not be permitted to stand as council chairmen and would have no power to disburse funds.

SINGAPORE

During 1999 Lee Hsien Loong, who had been appointed Chairman of the Monetary Authority of Singapore (MAS) in December 1997, began to assume a more prominent political role. Goh acknowledged that Lee's succession to the premiership was likely to take place after the next election. George Yeo, hitherto the Minister for Information and the Arts, also gained prominence following his promotion to the trade and industry portfolio in a minor cabinet reorganization in June 1999. Singapore's second presidential election was scheduled to take place in August 1999. President Ong, despite his PAP affiliation, had proved an independent President, whose determination to exercise the full powers of the elected presidency had resulted in strained relations with his former government colleagues. His allegations of government obstruction of his efforts to establish the details of the Republic's financial reserves (in order to fulfil his role of guardian of those reserves as specified in the constitutional amendments of 1991) had led to a rare display of disunity amongst senior PAP officials, involving public disputes with both Goh and Lee. Despite a medical report confirming that Ong was in complete remission from a cancer diagnosed in 1992, the PAP announced that, on the grounds of health, they would not support his candidacy should he choose to seek a second term of office. Ong, who was widely believed to command sufficient popular support to secure the presidency without a government endorsement, informed Goh that his candidacy remained a personal decision. He finally announced his decision not to contest the election in July, but unexpectedly proceeded to enumerate his political difficulties while in office. Despite Goh's expressed support for a more consultative style of governance, in mid-August a government-appointed committee declared that only one of three potential presidential candidates, S. R. Nathan (a former Singaporean ambassador to the USA whose presidential candidature was supported by the Cabinet), had fulfilled the criteria set by the committee; Nathan was subsequently nominated as the new President of Singapore on 18 August, and was formally appointed to the position on 1 September, prompting criticism of the Government's autocratic approach.

In September 2000 the Government appeared to have relaxed its tight control over public speaking, with the opening of a 'Speakers' Corner', theoretically allowing a forum for any citizen to air issues of concern. In practice, however, speakers were obliged to register with the police beforehand, and to refrain from speaking on certain racial issues. The opportunity to speak was taken up by members of two Singaporean policy centres, after they were refused a permit to organize a marathon run to protest against the Internal Security Act in December. The gathering of around 50 people was not dispersed, but a report on the event broadcast by the Radio Corporation of Singapore was later edited at the request of the management, and the presenter who publicized the re-editing was dismissed. In April 2001 the Government permitted a rare opposition political rally. It was the first authorized protest to be openly critical of the Government since independence. The rally, intended as a pro-democracy fund-raising event for Jeyaretnam, was attended by over 1,000 people, the permit having been issued after organizers assured police that security guards would be hired to prevent disturbances. It was suspected that there was substantial government surveillance of the rally.

In July 2001 four opposition parties—the Singapore People's Party, the Singapore Malay National Organization, the National Solidarity Party and the Singapore Justice Party—formed the Singapore Democratic Alliance (SDA). The new coalition was chaired by Chiam See Tong, and it was hoped that its formation would strengthen the fragmented political opposition to the PAP in the forthcoming general election. In October President Nathan unexpectedly dissolved Parliament and announced that a general election was to be held on 3 November 2001, significantly in advance of the August 2002 deadline. During the campaign the Government declared that the allocation of priority to public housing improvements would again be affected by levels of electoral support. Electoral boundaries were also redrawn, leading to the enlargement of 14 multi-member constituencies and to an increase in the number of parliamentary seats to 84, in order to accommodate a rise in the number of registered voters. The opposition protested that it had been disadvantaged by the rearrangements. When nominations closed in late October PAP candidates were unopposed in 55 of the 84 seats available. The Government thus secured victory by default before the polls opened. The Prime Minister, however, urged voters to turn out on election day to decide the outcome of the contests for the remaining 29 seats, warning that Singapore faced its 'gravest challenge since independence'. He also officially announced that he would leave office upon the conclusion of his next term.

The elections were held on 3 November 2001. The level of voter participation was low, owing to the large number of uncontested seats. Despite speculation that the PAP would lose some ground in the election because of the deterioration in the economy (see Economic Affairs), it succeeded in winning 82 seats and increasing its share of the votes cast to 75.3%. The remaining two seats went to Chiam See Tong, Chairman of the SDA, and Low Thia Khiang of the Workers' Party. Steve Chia of the SDA was awarded a non-constituency seat.

Shortly after the election it was reported that Lee and Goh were suing Chee Soon Juan of the SDP for defamation. Chee had alleged that the Government had lent more than S $17,000m. of public money to the Suharto administration in Indonesia during the 1997–98 financial crisis. He had issued a public apology for the comments soon afterwards and admitted fabricating the accusation, but had later retracted his statement, claiming that it had been made under duress. Goh claimed that, while the loan had been offered to the Suharto administration, it had never been disbursed. In February 2002 Chee faced further legal action after contravening the rule banning the discussion of racial and religious issues in 'Speakers' Corner'. He had criticized the Government's policy of banning Muslim girls from wearing headscarves in public schools and called for the promotion of cultural diversity. His comments came after three Muslim girls were suspended from school for wearing headscarves.

In April 2002 Jeyaretnam made a public apology in the High Court in an attempt to bring to an end the series of defamation suits that had been brought against him by the Government; seven outstanding lawsuits were subsequently abandoned. In the same month Chee stated that he intended to defend the lawsuits against him. In May Chee and the Vice-Chairman of the SDP, Ghandi Ambalam, led an unauthorized rally outside the presidential palace demanding workers' rights. Following the rally, Chee and Ambalan were both sentenced to brief prison terms, having elected not to pay the fines imposed upon them. However, Ambalan's family subsequently paid his fine, in order to enable his release from prison on the grounds of ill health. In August the High Court ordered Chee to pay damages of S $500,000 to Lee and Goh, after his request for a trial was rejected; Chee appealed against the verdict. Meanwhile, a constitutional amendment was passed stipulating that any member of Parliament declared bankrupt or found guilty of a crime would be banned from speaking or voting in Parliament for the duration of any appeal. In February 2003 Ambalam's appeal against his fine (which was sufficient to prohibit him from standing for political office for five years) was rejected by the Chief Justice. In October 2004 the Jeyaretnam affair resumed when he again appealed for early discharge from bankruptcy in order to secure re-entry into the political arena. However, the Court of Appeal deemed him to have been dishonest about his assets, ruling that he had failed to declare property in Johor Baru worth more than $350,000. Consequently, the Court's original decision was upheld and Jeyaretnam's application for clemency was denied. In February 2006 Chee was declared bankrupt by the High Court, having failed to pay the stipulated damages. In the following month Chee was convicted of contempt of court for his criticism of Singapore's judiciary during the February court hearing, and was ordered to pay a fine of $6,000; upon Chee's refusal to pay the fine, he was imprisoned for seven days, after which duration he again refused to pay and his imprisonment was subsequently extended for another seven days.

In April 2003, meanwhile, Prime Minister Goh announced a cabinet reshuffle. The acting Minister for Information, Communications and the Arts, David Lim Tik En, resigned and was replaced by Dr Lee Boon Yang, the former Minister for Manpower, who was succeeded by Dr Ng Eng Hen. Khaw Boon Wan was appointed to be acting Minister for Health, replacing Lim Hng Kiang, who became a Minister in the Prime Minister's Office. Meanwhile, Deputy Prime Minister and former Minister for Defence Dr Tony Tan Keng Yam was appointed to the newly created position of Co-ordinating Minister for Security and Defence in the Prime Minister's Office (effective from August 2003). The defence portfolio was allocated to the former Minister for Education, Teo Chee Hean, who was to be succeeded in an acting capacity by Tharman Shanmugaratnam.

In August 2003 Prime Minister Goh announced that he intended to resign from his post at least two years prior to the country's next general election, scheduled to be held in 2007. He designated his deputy, Lee Hsien Loong, as his successor. In a speech in early 2004 Lee indicated that, following his accession to power, he would implement measures to reduce the control of the Government over Singaporean citizens and to promote a culture of political 'openness' in the country.

On 12 August 2004 Lee was formally sworn in as Prime Minister, amidst claims that a dynastic succession had been contrived. Both former Prime Ministers were included within the new Cabinet: Goh was retained as Senior Minister, while Lee Kuan Yew was redesignated as Minister Mentor. Shanmugam Jayakumar became Singapore's first Deputy Minister of Indian origin, and Dr Tony Tan Keng Yam was also reappointed to this position. Lee retained the finance portfolio but, in an unexpected development, relinquished the chairmanship of the MAS to Goh. Wong Kan Seng remained the Minister for Home Affairs but was also designated as successor to Dr Tan as Deputy Prime Minister upon the latter's retirement, scheduled for June 2005. Brig.-Gen. George Yeo was named the new Minister for Foreign Affairs and Rear-Adm. Teo Chee Hean retained the defence portfolio, while Tharman Shanmugaratnam was confirmed in the permanent position of Minister for Education. Two women were appointed as Ministers of State: Lim Hwee Hua was named Minister of State for Finance and Transport, and Yu-Foo Yee Shoon became Minister for State for Community Development and Sports.

The reversal of the decline in Singapore's birth rate was immediately rendered a major government priority following Lee's inauguration. In late August 2004 Lee added responsibility for the revival of the country's population growth to the brief of Wong Kan Seng and implemented an array of measures aimed at increasing the birth rate, which since the 1960s had decreased sharply. Government bonuses were offered to parents producing a third or fourth child, maternity leave was lengthened and tax rebates were introduced for working mothers.

In April 2005 Prime Minister Lee announced that the Government was no longer opposed to the construction of two major casino resorts in Singapore, to be built at an estimated cost of US $3,000m. In the same month the Government approved a draft bill to legalize gambling on the island, thereby proposing to remove a ban that had been in place for 40 years. It was hoped that the resorts, which were expected to become operational by 2009, would significantly boost the country's tourism industry and contribute to the Government's campaign to double the number of tourist arrivals by 2015. Moreover, it was envisaged that the existence of these resorts would allow Singapore to retain the money of its nationals who had hitherto been obliged to travel abroad in order to engage in gambling activities. The decision encountered widespread disapproval, however, particularly from religious groups, which accused the Government of prioritizing profit over the country's moral standing. Following a series of bomb attacks targeting commuters on London's public transport network in July 2005, Minister for Transport Yeo Cheow Tong announced the creation of the Singaporean Police Mass Rapid Transport (MRT) Unit, intended to protect the island's transport system from terrorist attack; the unit commenced random patrols in the following month. Also in July, a scandal concerning the National Kidney Foundation (NKF) emerged; amidst allegations of misuse of funds, the entire executive board of the charitable organization tendered its resignation and the wife of Senior Minister Gok Chok Tong, hitherto the patron of NKF, also relinquished her position.

Presidential elections were scheduled to be held in August 2005. However, of the four candidates who had applied for inclusion in the contest only the incumbent, S. R. Nathan, was granted a Certificate of Eligibility, the other three candidates being deemed to be lacking in political experience. Consequently, Nathan was returned unopposed for a second term in office; he was formally sworn in on 1 September. In October the Deputy Prime Minister and Co-ordinating Minister for Security and Defence, Shanmugam Jayakumar, announced the development of the Risk Assessment and Horizon Scanning programme, an early warning system intended to identify and monitor the activities of newly emerging threats to national and regional security. In April 2006, following months of speculation that Prime Minister Lee Hsien Loong was to call an early legislative election in order to take advantage of Singapore's strong economic position, it was announced that the poll (which had not been due until June 2007) would be held on 6 May. At the election, opposition parties contested 47 of the 84 parliamentary seats. The PAP won 82 seats, as it had done at the 2001 election, while the SDA and the Workers' Party secured one seat each. However, the PAP's share of the votes cast decreased to 66.6%, compared with 75.4% at the 2001 election.

Singapore's foreign policy has been dominated by its membership of the regional grouping, ASEAN (which comprised all 10 South-East Asian nations by mid-1999), although it has also maintained strong political and military links with more distant allies, including the USA.

In November 2000 the fourth informal summit meeting of the ASEAN + 3 group of leaders was convened in Singapore. The summit comprised the leaders of all 10 ASEAN members, as well as those of the People's Republic of China, Japan and the Republic of Korea. An outcome of the meeting was the commissioning of an East Asia Study Group to report on the feasibility of a larger East Asia political and economic grouping and free trade area.

Singapore's relations with Indonesia improved in the late 1980s: the process of establishing joint military training facilities with Indonesia, which had begun in 1986, was accomplished in February and March 1989 by the signing of two agreements. In January 1995 the two countries launched a bilateral Defence Forum and signed a Defence Co-operation Pact. In June 1996 Singapore and Indonesia jointly opened the Bintan tourist resort in the Riau Islands. Following the resignation of President Suharto in May 1998, relations deteriorated, in part owing to Lee's criticism of the new President, Prof. Dr Ir B. J. Habibie. In February 1999 Habibie accused Singapore of racism for allegedly discriminating against its Malay minority. The principal problem was, however, Singapore's refusal to meet Indonesia's high expectations of aid from Singapore in response to the regional economic crisis. In March the Singaporean Minister for Foreign Affairs, Shanmugam Jayakumar, defused tensions in relations between Singapore and Indonesia by declaring in Parliament that Singapore had a vested interest in the economic and political stability of the Indonesian archipelago and pledging the Singaporean Government's intention to co-operate with the Indonesian administration. Relations improved temporarily following Habibie's replacement as President by Abdurrahman Wahid in October 1999. In November 2000, however, Wahid jeopardized the relationship by accusing Singapore of discriminating against Malays, after Singapore rejected certain motions proposed by its neighbour at the ASEAN summit. Nevertheless, Singapore subsequently concluded an agreement with Indonesia to supply the city-state with natural gas for the next 22 years. In February 2002 bilateral relations deteriorated again following the publication of an article in *The Straits Times* in which Lee Kwan Yew remarked that Singapore's national security was being compromised by the fact that terrorists remained at large in Indonesia. In response, the Indonesian Government summoned the Singaporean envoy to Jakarta and lodged an objection to the accusations, claiming that they were provocative and unsubstantiated. Meanwhile, Indonesian Islamic groups held protests outside Singapore's embassy in Jakarta. The situation was further exacerbated by the suspension of three Muslim schoolgirls in Singapore for wearing headscarves while at school. In March 2002 Abu Bakar Bashir, an Indonesian cleric accused of being linked to the international terrorist al-Qa'ida (Base) network, issued a writ of defamation against Lee in relation to his comments. In February 2006 the Indonesian authorities agreed to the deportation to Singapore of Mas Selamat Kastari, the alleged leader of the Singaporean branch of Jemaah Islamiah, following his rearrest in Indonesia on suspicion of immigration offences. Kastari, first arrested in Indonesia in 2003, also on charges of suspected illegal immigration, had been the subject of several previous extradition requests from Singapore, which accused Kastari of a central role in an alleged plot, thwarted in late 2001, to crash a hijacked aeroplane into Changi International Airport. The Indonesian Government had rejected those requests, on the grounds that Indonesia and Singapore had no formal extradition treaty; it was unclear why Indonesia subsequently chose to reverse its decision.

In September 1994 Singapore and Malaysia agreed to settle their long-standing dispute over the ownership of Pedra Branca Island (Batu Putih) by referring the case to the International Court of Justice in The Hague, the Netherlands. An agreement on the referral was finally signed in early 2003. In August 1995 Singapore and Malaysia agreed on the permanent boundary of their territorial waters following 15 years of negotiations. In March 1997 Lee Kuan Yew provoked tension between the two countries by making disparaging comments about security in the Malaysian State of Johor. Lee subsequently made an apology to Malaysia, which was accepted. In April 1999 Singapore and

Malaysia undertook joint defence exercises within the context of the regional Five-Power Defence Arrangements; Malaysia had withdrawn from similar exercises in 1998, citing tensions between the two countries as well as economic difficulties.

In February 1998 Goh made an official visit to Malaysia. In the latter half of 1998, however, relations between the two countries deteriorated as a result of conflict over a number of issues. In early August the Malaysian Prime Minister condemned Singapore for requesting that Malaysia move its customs, immigration and quarantine facilities from Tanjung Pagar, a railway station in central Singapore situated on land owned by the Malaysian Government; Malaysia subsequently decided to continue using its facilities at Tanjung Pagar, while Singapore moved its customs office to a new location. In September Malaysia announced its decision to insist on prior clearance for Singaporean military aircraft wishing to enter its airspace; combined operations and exercises between the two countries' air forces were also terminated. In the same month the publication of the memoirs of Lee Kuan Yew, which referred to the events surrounding the secession of Singapore from the Federation of Malaysia, exacerbated tensions in bilateral relations. However, an improvement in relations between the two countries was perceived in November, when Goh visited Malaysia at the invitation of Malaysian Prime Minister Mahathir. Lee Kuan Yew further angered Malaysian politicians in August 2000, however, when he publicly criticized Mahathir over his handling of the dismissal and detention of Malaysia's former Deputy Prime Minister, Anwar Ibrahim.

In September 2001 Lee Kuan Yew visited Malaysia and held talks with Mahathir to address the outstanding issues affecting the relationship between the two countries. A framework agreement was subsequently signed under which Malaysia agreed to relocate its facilities at Tanjung Pagar in return for Singapore's agreement to construct a railway tunnel under the strait. Lee also reported that the two countries would work together to construct a suspension bridge, which would enable the demolition of the causeway linking the two countries. However, in January 2002 the Malaysian Government denied the existence of such an agreement and proposed that Malaysia should build a suspension bridge and a railway swing bridge to replace its half of the road link, enabling the Malaysian half of the causeway to be demolished without Singapore's co-operation. Tension was also promoted by the ongoing renegotiation of the terms upon which Malaysia would continue to supply water to Singapore (based upon an agreement originally concluded in 1961 and due to expire in 2061). While an agreement had provisionally been reached in September 2001, the Malaysian Government was dissatisfied with its terms and continued to increase its demands. In March 2002 relations were further strained when Malaysia claimed that reclamation work being carried out by Singapore in the Tebrau Straits was too close to its border and was obstructing ships sailing into ports in Johor. Malaysia later applied to the International Tribunal for the Law of the Sea (see p. 300) for a suspension of the reclamation work. The issue was among those discussed when Deputy Prime Minister Lee Hsien Loong visited Malaysia in the same month. In July the two countries held talks in an attempt to find a solution to the ongoing water supply problem; further negotiations over the issue also took place in September and October of that year. Whilst the Government wished to link resolution of the matter to other issues it considered to be a cause of tension in the bilateral relationship, Malaysia threatened to take Singapore to an international court of arbitration to seek a solution. In February 2003 Mahathir pledged that his country would continue to supply water to Singapore indefinitely. However, he stated that Malaysia would cease its provision of untreated water to the city-state upon the termination of an existing agreement in 2011 and provide filtered water instead, at what it considered to be a reasonable price. Singapore continued to insist that any proposed price was too high and that it received too little for the treated water that it supplied to Malaysia in return.

In October 2003 the International Tribunal for the Law of the Sea ruled that the land reclamation work being carried out by Singapore in the Tebrau Straits was in accordance with international law and could, therefore, proceed. The long-running dispute was ostensibly resolved in January 2005 when the respective Governments of Singapore and Malaysia issued a joint statement declaring their agreement that the Tebrau Straits constituted a shared body of water and that the two countries had 'a common interest in co-operating to protect the environment, including the monitoring of water quality'.

Meanwhile, following Mahathir's retirement at the end of October 2003 and the accession of Abdullah Ahmad Badawi to the Malaysian premiership, it was hoped that Singapore's relations with Malaysia would improve. In January 2004 Abdullah Badawi visited Singapore and held talks with Prime Minister Goh in an attempt to ease the tensions between the two countries. Moreover, the transfer of the premiership to Lee augured well for bilateral relations; in his first National Day Rally speech, in August 2004, the incoming Prime Minister stressed his deep commitment to working in close unison with Abdullah Badawi, whom he had known for many years, in order to consolidate Singapore's links with Malaysia. Discussions aimed at strengthening relations between the two countries were resumed in March 2005. In mid-2005 Badawi announced the abandonment of his predecessor's plans for the construction of a replacement causeway linking Singapore and Malaysia. It was hoped that this decision would dissipate bilateral tensions. Further negotiations were held in September. However, in January 2006 Malaysia unexpectedly announced that it was to commence construction of its section of the new bridge, also referred to as the 'scenic bridge', in the hope that Singapore would agree in due course to the construction of its part. Construction of the Malaysian section of the bridge began in March, but was halted by Badawi in the following month; the Malaysian Prime Minister announced that all negotiations with Singapore pertaining to the bridge were also to be abandoned.

In November 1990 representatives of the Governments of the USA and Singapore signed an agreement providing the US navy and air force with increased access to existing bases in Singapore following the planned US withdrawal from military installations in the Philippines. In January 1992 the two countries reached an agreement, in principle, on the relocation of a naval logistic command headquarters from Subic Bay, in the Philippines. However, relations with the USA were occasionally strained by attacks on the authoritarian style of government in Singapore by the liberal US media. Following the terrorist attacks on the USA in September 2001 (see the chapter on the USA), Singapore affirmed its support for the US-led alliance against terrorism. In January 2002 it was reported that 15 people had been arrested in December 2001 under the Internal Security Act for allegedly participating in terrorist activities. The suspects were believed to be linked to terrorist organizations in Malaysia and Indonesia, as well as to al-Qa'ida. Several of those detained were junior national servicemen, prompting concerns about security in the country, particularly in the aftermath of the September attacks. Shortly afterwards the Government declared that the arrests had dismantled a network of militants plotting to blow up the US embassy and US businesses in Singapore. In order to address the ensuing national security concerns, the Government announced the establishment of a national security secretariat within the Ministry of Defence intended to strengthen co-ordination between the security services.

In September 2002 it was announced that 21 people had been detained in August on suspicion of engaging in terrorist activities. Of those arrested, 19 were believed to be members of Jemaah Islamiah. In March 2003 the Government announced its support for the US-led military campaign to oust the regime of Saddam Hussain in Iraq. Security measures within Singapore were strengthened subsequently, as the conflict was perceived to have raised the level of the terrorist threat to the country. In December the Government announced that it had arrested two Singaporean nationals under the Internal Security Act in late October, believing them to be members of Jemaah Islamiah. In an apparent display of approval for Singapore's firm stance on terrorism, the US Government dispatched Secretary of Homeland Security Tom Ridge to Singapore's National Day reception held in Washington, DC, in August 2004. It was the first time that a US official of cabinet rank had attended this annual event during the nine-year tenure of Singapore's ambassador to the USA, Chan Heng Chee. In November 2005 the Government announced that it had detained for a two-year period under the Internal Security Act Mohammad Sharif Rahmat, an alleged member of Jemaah Islamiah.

In October 2004 officials from Bahrain, Bangladesh, Egypt, Jordan, Kuwait, Malaysia, Singapore and Thailand convened in Singapore and agreed to hold the inaugural Asia-Middle East Dialogue (AMED) in mid-2005. This diplomatic initiative had been instigated by former Prime Minister Goh owing to concern that terrorism was being equated with Islam and also out of respect for Middle Eastern states' general suspicion of dialogues initiated by the USA or Europe. It was to focus on improving political, economic and business links between the two regions, as well as on promoting a greater level of mutual cultural understanding. The meeting was held in Singapore in June and was attended by representatives of approximately 50 Asian and Middle Eastern states. It was agreed that AMED would convene on a biennial basis, at venues alternating between Asia and the Middle East; Egypt and Thailand indicated their intention to host the 2007 and 2009 sessions, respectively.

Despite the establishment of important economic links during the 1980s, Singapore's relations with the People's Republic of China were adversely affected by the perceived threat of Chinese domination, owing to the preponderance of ethnic Chinese in Singapore (76.8% in 2000). Relations were also strained by Singapore's close military and economic ties with Taiwan. In October 1990, however, Singapore and the People's Republic of China established diplomatic relations at ambassadorial level. This development was prompted mainly by the resumption of diplomatic relations between the People's Republic of China and Indonesia, and followed a visit by the Chinese Premier, Li Peng, to Singapore in August. Singapore's relations with Taiwan were apparently unaffected by these events, and Goh made his first official visit to that country in October 1993. In October 1996 Singapore and Australia issued a joint communiqué urging the integration of the People's Republic of China into the Asian regional security structure, and reaffirming their commitment to a co-operative dialogue with the People's Republic. However, a private visit to Singapore in January 1998 by the Taiwanese Vice-President, Lien Chan, during which he met with Goh and with Singaporean cabinet ministers, provoked the disapproval of the People's Republic. Relations improved in November 1998 when Goh made an official visit to the People's Republic, and in November 1999 the Chinese Premier, Zhu Rongji, made a reciprocal visit to Singapore. However, further visits to Taiwan, by Lee Kuan Yew in September 2000 and September 2002, and by Lee Hsien Loong in July 2004 shortly before he assumed the premiership, caused further damage to bilateral relations. The diplomatic furore caused by Lee's visit in 2004 served to delay the start of negotiations concerning a free-trade pact between the People's Republic and Singapore, which had been due to commence in November 2004, despite Lee's insistence that his visit in no way weakened his country's commitment to the 'One China' policy that denied recognition of Taiwan. The Chinese Prime Minister, Wen Jiabao, and Lee consequently agreed to commence free-trade talks as planned, but they withheld from offering any indication as to when negotiations might begin. In October 2005, at a meeting in Beijing of Singaporean and Chinese delegates, led by Lee Hsien Loong and Wen Jiabao, both countries affirmed their commitment to accelerating the holding of free-trade negotiations. The two countries also agreed to work together to address the regional threats of terrorism and piracy in the Straits of Melaka (Malacca).

Government

Legislative power is vested in the unicameral Parliament, with 84 members who are elected by universal adult suffrage for five years (subject to dissolution—within three months of which a general election must be held) in single-member and multi-member constituencies. As many as three additional 'non-constituency' seats may be offered to opposition parties, and up to nine non-elected, neutral MPs may be nominated: all have restricted voting rights. The President is directly elected by universal adult suffrage for a six-year term as a constitutional Head of State, vested with limited powers of veto in financial matters, public appointments and detentions for reasons of national security. Effective executive authority rests with the Cabinet, led by the Prime Minister, which is appointed by the President and responsible to Parliament.

Defence

In August 2005 the Singapore armed forces had an estimated total active strength of 72,500 troops (including 35,000 conscripts): 50,000 in the army, an estimated 9,000 in the navy and 13,500 in the air force. The length of compulsory military service was 24 months. Paramilitary forces comprised a civil defence force (numbering an estimated 81,800) and a police force (numbering an estimated 8,500). Singapore is a participant in the Five-Power Defence Arrangements (with Australia, Malaysia, New Zealand and the United Kingdom). In 2005 the Government budgeted S $9,250m. for defence.

Economic Affairs

In 2004, according to estimates by the World Bank, Singapore's gross national income (GNI), measured at average 2002–04 prices, was US $104,994m., equivalent to US $24,220 per head (or US $26,590 per head on an international purchasing-power parity basis). During 1995–2004, it was estimated, the population increased at an average annual rate of 2.3%, while gross domestic product (GDP) per head increased, in real terms, at an average rate of 2.4% per year. Overall GDP increased, in real terms, at an average annual rate of 4.7% in 1995–2004. According to official figures, GDP expanded by 8.7% in 2004 and by 6.4% in 2005.

Agriculture (including fishing and quarrying) contributed an estimated 0.1% of GDP in 2005, and engaged only 0.2% of the employed labour force in 2003. Vegetables, plants and orchid flowers are the principal crops. According to the Asian Development Bank (ADB), agricultural GDP (again including fishing and quarrying) declined at an average annual rate of 1.3% during 1995–2004. According to official figures, agricultural GDP increased by 12.3% in 2004, but declined by 2.5% in 2005.

Industry (including manufacturing, construction and utilities) contributed an estimated 32.5% of GDP in 2005, and engaged 24.1% of the employed labour force in 2003. During 1995–2004, according to the ADB, industrial GDP increased at an average annual rate of 4.0%. According to official figures, the GDP of the sector expanded by 10.5% in 2004 and by 7.8% in 2005.

Mining (chiefly the quarrying of granite) accounted for only an estimated 0.01% of GDP in 1998 and 0.05% of employment in 2003. According to the ADB, the GDP of the mining sector declined at an average annual rate of 17.4% in 1990–98; it declined by 22.4% in 1998.

Manufacturing contributed an estimated 27.3% of GDP in 2005 and engaged 21.4% of the employed labour force in that year. The principal branches of manufacturing in 2004 (measured in terms of the value of output) were electronic products and components (which accounted for 38.8% of total manufacturing production), refined petroleum products, chemicals and chemical products, non-electrical machinery and equipment, biomedical and pharmaceutical products, and transport equipment (especially shipbuilding). According to the ADB, manufacturing GDP increased at an average annual rate of 4.9% in 1995–2004. According to official figures, manufacturing GDP increased by 13.9% in 2004 and by 9.3% in 2005.

Singapore relies on imports of hydrocarbons to fuel its three thermal power stations. In 2002 natural gas accounted for 58.3% of the total amount of electrical energy produced; petroleum accounted for 39.6%. In 2005 imports of crude petroleum accounted for 9.2% of merchandise imports.

The services sector contributed an estimated 67.4% of GDP in 2005, and engaged 69.6% of the employed labour force in that year. Finance and business services provided an estimated 23.8% of GDP in 2005, and engaged 15.8% of the employed labour force in 2005. The GDP of the financial services sector increased by 5.4% in 2004 and by 6.5% in 2005. Singapore is an important foreign-exchange dealing centre in Asia and the Pacific. Banking is also a significant sector, with a total of 111 commercial banks in operation in April 2005. Tourism is a significant source of foreign exchange, and receipts from tourism amounted to approximately S $10,800m. in 2005. In the same year the number of tourist arrivals exceeded 8.9m., an increase of 7.4% compared with 2004. In 2005 transport and communications contributed an estimated 12.1% of GDP. The GDP of the transport and communications sector increased by 8.5% in 2004 and by 4.5% in 2005. Singapore is the world's busiest port in tonnage terms and has one of the largest merchant shipping registers in the world. According to the ADB, the GDP of the services sector increased at an average annual rate of 5.1% in 1995–2004. According to official figures, the sector expanded by 7.3% in 2004 and by 5.8% in 2005.

In 2005 Singapore recorded a visible trade surplus of US $37,953m., and there was a surplus of US $33,265m. on the current account of the balance of payments. In 2005 the principal sources of imports were Malaysia (13.7%) and the USA (11.6%); other major suppliers were the People's Republic of China and Japan. Malaysia (13.2%) and the USA (10.2%) were also the principal markets for exports in that year; other major purchasers were Indonesia, Hong Kong and China. Principal imports in 2005 included machinery and equipment (notably electronic components and parts), mineral fuels, miscellaneous manufactured articles, basic manufactures and chemicals. Principal exports included machinery and equipment (notably electronic components and parts), mineral fuels, chemicals and miscellaneous manufactured articles. Singapore is an important entrepôt, and re-exports accounted for 45.8% of total exports in 2005.

According to the ADB, the 2006/07 budget projected an operating deficit of S \$2,900m., equivalent to 1.4% of GDP, compared with a deficit of approximately S \$700m. (0.3% of GDP) in the previous year. According to the ADB, at the end of 2005 Singapore's external debt totalled US \$245,983m. The annual rate of inflation averaged 0.8% in 1995–2004; consumer prices increased by 1.7% in 2004 and by 0.4% in the following year. According to the provisional results of the General Household Survey in 2005, the rate of unemployment stood at 4.3% of the labour force in mid-2005, having declined from 4.4% in the previous year. By December 2005 the official rate of unemployment had declined to just 2.5%. According to the ADB, approximately 113,300 new jobs were created during 2005.

Singapore is a member of the UN Economic and Social Commission for Asia and the Pacific (ESCAP, see p. 33), of the Asian Development Bank (ADB, see p. 169), of the Association of South East Asian Nations (ASEAN, see p. 172), of Asia-Pacific Economic Co-operation (APEC, see p. 164) and of the Colombo Plan (see p. 385). As a member of ASEAN, Singapore signed an accord in January 1992 pledging the creation of a free-trade zone to be known as the ASEAN Free Trade Area (AFTA). A reduction of tariffs to between 0% and 5% was originally envisaged to be completed by 2008 but this was subsequently advanced to 2002, when AFTA was formally implemented. However, Malaysia applied for an extension of this date for its automotive industry, fearing direct competition. Target dates for the removal of all tariffs were brought forward from 2015 to 2010 in November 1999.

Singapore's economic success has been based largely on its central location in the region, efficient planning, advanced infrastructure and highly skilled work-force. Singapore was less affected than its neighbours by the regional financial crisis of the late 1990s, owing partly to its high savings and investment rates, and to its substantial foreign-exchange reserves. The country was thus able to consolidate its position as a financial and trading centre through various reforms. As the programme to transfer many state-owned corporations to the private sector continued, the comprehensive deregulation of the telecommunications industry was effected in April 2000, and plans were announced for the deregulation of the power and insurance sectors. In 2001, however, GDP contracted by 2.3%, as Singapore experienced its worst recession since independence in 1965. This was due to the global economic downturn, particularly in the electronics sector, which was exacerbated by the effects of the September 2001 terrorist attacks on the USA (a major export market). Largely as a result of high levels of government spending, the economy avoided a further recession in 2002. In the first half of 2003 economic growth was severely constrained, owing both to the epidemic of Severe Acute Respiratory Syndrome (SARS) in the region early in that year, and to the disruption to international trade caused by the US-led military campaign in Iraq. In the last quarter of the year a recovery in the electronics sector, stimulated by increasing global demand for electronics, underpinned an upturn in economic performance, resulting in a GDP growth rate of 2.9% for the year. At almost 9%, GDP growth in 2004 reached its highest level since 2000, as the economy recovered from the adverse impact of the SARS outbreak in 2003. Of all manufacturing and services sub-sectors, only that of construction failed to register growth in 2004, signifying a broad foundation to the country's economic recovery. The Government's substantial ongoing investment in the development of the biomedical and pharmaceuticals was reflected in this sector's growth of 25.7% in that year, although in the first six months of 2005 the Singaporean pharmaceutical industry's output was reported to have declined, before resuming its strong expansion in the third quarter of the year. The global electronics industry, furthermore, also weakened in the first half of 2005, but demand had reportedly recovered by the end of the year. At 4.7%, in 2003 the rate of unemployment had reached its highest level in 17 years. The steady creation of new jobs within the services sector during the latter half of 2004 ameliorated the situation and, although many companies continued to shift their operations away from the island in favour of low-cost countries such as the People's Republic of China, by the end of 2005 the unemployment rate had declined substantially. Meanwhile, the Government had embarked upon a series of free-trade agreement (FTA) initiatives. By the end of 2003 FTAs had been concluded with New Zealand, Japan, the European Free Trade Association (EFTA, see p. 386), Australia and the USA, and with Jordan in mid-2004. By early 2006 negotiations had also been concluded with India, the Republic of Korea and Panama, and discussions were in progress with ASEAN, the Pacific Three (which comprised Chile and New Zealand, together with Singapore), and 11 other countries, including Canada, the People's Republic of China and Pakistan. The implementation of the FTA with the USA in January 2004 led to an increase of 11.7% in bilateral trade during the year compared with the level of 2003 and a further increase of 8.0% in 2005 compared with the previous year. In order further to diversify Singapore's economy, however, additional resources were to be allocated to the enhancement of the financial and tourism sectors. In 2004 three Singaporean budget airlines were launched, and in January 2006 construction of an airport terminal at Changi International Airport for the exclusive use of these and other low-cost airlines was completed, at an estimated cost of S \$45m.; the terminal commenced operations in late March, although at that time Tiger Airways was the only airline to make use of it. It was hoped that the cheaper operational fees offered by the new terminal would encourage more airlines to make the transition thereto. It was also hoped that the increased availability of inexpensive air fares would attract additional visitors to the city-state. In September 2004 Singapore signed an 'open skies' agreement with Australia, allowing the airlines of both countries to use the airport(s) of the other to service international destinations. This important accord initially excluded US destinations, pending the successful completion of a pact relating to routes between Australia and Los Angeles, USA, which was ultimately expected to secure significant additional revenue for the government-controlled Singapore Airlines Ltd. However, in February 2006 Australia formally rejected Singapore's application for an extension of the 'open skies' agreement to cover US destinations. It was hoped that the legalization of gambling in April 2005 and the proposed construction of two casinos on the island (see Recent History) would result in a significant increase in the number of tourists visiting Singapore. In an attempt to stimulate foreign investment, the Government announced in January 2003 that it intended to offer preferential tax rates over a three-year period to companies establishing regional headquarters in Singapore. National security concerns, owing to an increasing number of incidents of terrorism in the region from 2002, threatened to deter overseas investors. By 2005 the annual amount being allocated to defence had increased to reach the equivalent of approximately 6% of GDP, as a result of the growing likelihood of Singapore itself becoming a direct target of a terrorist attack, in view of the Government's public support for the US Administration as well as the high number of Western companies operating on the island. The Straits of Melaka (Malacca), through which the vast majority of mainland China's and Japan's petroleum imports and about 25% of the world's maritime trade was carried, had been identified as a particularly vulnerable target for terrorists seeking to disrupt the global economy. In late 2004 the Monetary Authority of Singapore (MAS) announced further incentives for potential foreign investors, including the offer of immediate residency on the island for those investing S \$5m. in local financial companies and of full Singaporean citizenship after five years of consecutive investment above this threshold; it was hoped that the proposed schemes would be sufficient to counterbalance the ongoing threat of militancy in the region. Foreign direct investment was reported to have increased from US \$6,307m. in 2004 to US \$14,562m. in 2005. The budget for the fiscal year ending 31 March 2006 included a proposed reduction of the highest rate of income tax from the existing level of 22% to 20%, over a two-year period. In the same fiscal year the Government was expected to record its first budgetary surplus for three years. In 2006 the Government projected overall GDP growth of 4.6% for that year.

Education

Primary and secondary education is available in the four official languages of Malay, Chinese, Tamil and English. In 1978, as part of a policy of bilingualism, examinations in English and Mandarin Chinese became compulsory for pupils seeking to enter secondary education. In 1987 English became the medium of instruction in all schools. Primary education begins at six years of age and lasts for six years. Secondary education lasts for four or five years from the age of 12. Post-secondary education lasts for two or three years and provides pre-university instruction. Outside the school system there are several higher education

SINGAPORE

centres and vocational institutes, providing craft and industrial training, and technical institutes providing advanced craft training. According to UNESCO, in 1996 total enrolment in tertiary-level education was equivalent to 38.5% of those in the relevant age-group (males 41.5%; females 35.3%). Adult education courses are conducted by a statutory board. In 2003 the Government introduced a six-year period of compulsory education; despite schooling previously having been optional, in 1996 the number of children attending primary schools was equivalent to 94% of children in the relevant age-group (males 95%; females 93%) and secondary school enrolment was equivalent to 74% of children in the relevant age-group. In 2004 57.8% of resident non-students aged 15 years and over held secondary or higher qualifications. In the same year the total number of students enrolled at Singapore's four universities was 41,628, with a further 56,266 students enrolled at the country's five polytechnics. Operating expenditure on education by the central Government in the financial year 2005/06 was estimated at S $4,980.7m. (24.1% of total spending).

Public Holidays

2006: 1 January (New Year's Day), 10 January* (Hari Raya Haji, Feast of the Sacrifice), 29–30 January (Chinese New Year), 14 April (Good Friday), 1 May (Labour Day), 12 May (Vesak Day), 9 August (National Day), 21 October (Deepavali), 24 October* (Hari Raya Puasa, end of Ramadan), 25 December (Christmas Day), 31 December* (Hari Raya Haji, Feast of the Sacrifice).

2007: 1 January (New Year's Day), 18–19 February (Chinese New Year), 6 April (Good Friday), 1 May (Labour Day), 31 May (Vesak Day), 9 August (National Day), 9 October (Deepavali), 13 October* (Hari Raya Puasa, end of Ramadan), 20 December* (Hari Raya Haji, Feast of the Sacrifice), 25 December (Christmas Day).

* These holidays are dependent on the Islamic lunar calendar and may vary by one or two days from the dates given.

Weights and Measures

The metric system is in force, but the following local units are also used:

Weight

1 tahil = 1 1/3 oz (37.8 grams).
16 tahils = 1 kati = 1 1/3 lb (604.8 grams).
100 katis = 1 picul = 133 1/3 lb (60.48 kg).
40 piculs = 1 koyan = 5,333 1/3 lb (2,419.2 kg).

Capacity

1 chupak = 1 quart (1.1365 litres).
1 gantang = 1 gallon (4.5461 litres).

Statistical Survey

Source (unless otherwise stated): Department of Statistics, 100 High St, 05-01 The Treasury, Singapore 179434; tel. 63327686; fax 63327689; e-mail info@singstat.gov.sg; internet www.singstat.gov.sg.

Area and Population

AREA, POPULATION AND DENSITY

Area (sq km)	699.4*
Population (census results)†	
30 June 1990	3,047,132‡
30 June 2000	
Males	2,061,800§
Females	1,955,900§
Total	4,017,733
Population (official estimates at mid-year)§	
2003	4,185,200
2004	4,240,300
2005	4,351,400
Density (per sq km) at mid-2005	6,225.2

* 270.0 sq miles.
† Includes non-residents, totalling 311,264 in 1990 and 754,524 in 2000.
‡ Includes resident population temporarily residing overseas.
§ Rounded figure(s).

ETHNIC GROUPS
(at census of 30 June 2000)*

	Males	Females	Total
Chinese	1,245,782	1,259,597	2,505,379
Malays	228,174	225,459	453,633
Indians	134,544	123,247	257,791
Others	21,793	24,613	46,406
Total	1,630,293	1,632,916	3,263,209

* Figures refer to the resident population of Singapore.

BIRTHS, MARRIAGES AND DEATHS*

	Registered live births		Registered Marriages		Registered deaths	
	Number	Rate (per 1,000)	Number	Rate (per 1,000)†	Number	Rate (per 1,000)
1993	50,225	15.4	25,298	7.8	14,461	4.4
1994	49,554	14.7	24,662	7.3	14,946	4.4
1995	48,635	14.0	24,974	7.2	15,569	4.5
1996	48,577	13.2	24,111	6.6	15,590	4.2
1997	47,333	12.5	25,667	8.2	15,307	4.0
1998	43,838	11.2	23,106	7.3	15,657	4.0
1999	43,336	11.0	25,648	8.0	15,516	3.9
2000†	46,631	11.3	22,561	6.9	15,692	3.8

* Data are tabulated by year of registration, rather than by year of occurrence.
† Provisional figures.

Source: mainly UN, *Demographic Yearbook*.

2003: Registered live births 37,633 (birth rate 9.0 per 1,000); Registered marriages 21,962 (marriage rate 6.4 per 1,000); Deaths 16,033 (death rate 3.8 per 1,000) (Source: partly UN, *Population and Vital Statistics Report*).

2004: Registered live births 37,174 (birth rate 10.1 per 1,000); Registered deaths 15,860 (death rate 4.3 per 1,000).

2005 (preliminary figures): Registered live births 37,593 (birth rate 10.0 per 1,000); Registered deaths 16,217 (death rate 4.3 per 1,000).

Expectation of life (WHO estimates, years at birth): 80 (males 78; females 82) in 2003 (Source: WHO, *World Health Report*).

SINGAPORE

ECONOMICALLY ACTIVE POPULATION
('000 persons aged 15 years and over, at June of each year)

	2001	2002	2003
Agriculture, hunting, forestry and fishing	6.3	6.1	5.0
Mining and quarrying	0.6	1.0	1.0
Manufacturing	384.0	367.6	364.8
Electricity, gas and water supply	10.4	9.0	10.0
Construction	124.9	119.1	114.5
Wholesale and retail trade; repair of motor vehicles, motorcycles and personal and household goods	303.6	304.4	296.5
Hotels and restaurants	128.3	125.3	128.4
Transport, storage and communications	228.2	218.8	216.0
Financial intermediation	108.7	107.9	104.7
Real estate, renting and business activities	243.1	237.4	243.0
Public administration and defence; compulsory social security	133.9	135.4	148.0
Education, health and social work	159.9	166.2	174.0
Other community, social and personal service activities; private households with employed persons	212.4	217.2	226.0
Extra-territorial organizations and bodies	2.4	2.3	2.0
Total employed	2,046.7	2,017.4	2,033.7
Unemployed	72.9	111.2	116.4
Total labour force	2,119.7	2,128.6	2,150.1
Males	1,190.4	1,202.1	1,188.2
Females	929.2	926.5	961.9

Source: ILO.

2005 ('000 persons aged 15 years and over, at June): Manufacturing 485.1; Construction 184.4; Wholesale and retail trade 350.6; Hotels and restaurants 124.2; Transport and storage 185.8; Information and communications 74.3; Financial intermediation 111.2; Real estate, renting and business services 246.4; Community, social and personal services 485.1; Others (Agriculture, Fishing, Mining and quarrying, Utilities and Activities not defined) 19.8; *Total* 2,266.7.

Health and Welfare

KEY INDICATORS

Total fertility rate (children per woman, 2003)	1.3
Under-5 mortality rate (per 1,000 live births, 2004)	3
HIV/AIDS (% of persons aged 15–49, 2003)	0.2
Physicians (per 1,000 head, 2001)	1.40
Hospital beds (per 1,000 head, 1994)	3.57
Health expenditure (2002): US $ per head (PPP)	1105
Health expenditure (2002): % of GDP	4.3
Health expenditure (2002): public (% of total)	30.9
Access to water (% of persons, 2000)	100
Access to sanitation (% of persons, 2000)	100
Human Development Index (2003): ranking	25
Human Development Index (2003): value	0.907

For sources and definitions, see explanatory note on p. vi.

Agriculture

PRINCIPAL CROPS
(FAO estimates, '000 metric tons)

	2002	2003	2004
Vegetables	5.0	5.0	5.0

Note: Annual output assumed to be unchanged since 1997 (FAO estimates).
Source: FAO.

Statistical Survey

LIVESTOCK
(FAO estimates, '000 head, year ending September)

	2002	2003	2004
Pigs	250	250	250
Chickens	2,000	2,000	2,000
Ducks	600	600	600

Source: FAO.

LIVESTOCK PRODUCTS
('000 metric tons)

	2002	2003	2004
Pig meat	21.3	19.0	19.5*
Poultry meat*	95.8	91.5	95.9
Hen eggs	21.7	23.5	22.7

*FAO estimate(s).
Source: FAO.

Forestry

SAWNWOOD PRODUCTION
(FAO estimates, '000 cubic metres, incl. railway sleepers)

	1990	1991	1992
Coniferous (softwood)	5	10	5
Broadleaved (hardwood)	50	20	20
Total	55	30	25

1993–2004: Annual production assumed to be unchanged since 1992 (FAO estimates).
Source: FAO.

Fishing

(metric tons, live weight)

	2001	2002	2003
Capture	3,342	2,769	2,085
Shrimps and prawns	250	222	220
Common squids	186	185	135
Aquaculture	4,443	5,027	5,024
Indonesian snakehead	613	455	535
Milkfish	656	956	1,492
Green mussel	2,454	2,903	2,362
Total catch	7,785	7,796	7,109

Note: Figures exclude crocodiles, recorded by number rather than by weight. The number of estuarine crocodiles caught was: 1,041 in 2001; 1,058 in 2002; 1,074 in 2003.

Source: FAO.

Industry

PETROLEUM PRODUCTS
('000 metric tons)

	1999	2000	2001
Liquefied petroleum gas	972	883	857
Naphtha	3,710	3,933	3,446
Motor spirit (petrol)	3,959	3,973	3,838
Kerosene	859	798	428
Jet fuel	6,336	5,844	5,558
Gas-diesel (distillate fuel) oils	13,818	11,618	11,397
Residual fuel oil	6,918	4,497	4,542
Lubricating oils	1,326	1,347	1,339
Petroleum bitumen (asphalt)	1,370	1,246	941

Source: UN, *Industrial Commodity Statistics Yearbook*.

SINGAPORE

SELECTED OTHER PRODUCTS

	1988	1989	1990
Paints ('000 litres)	48,103.6	52,746.9	58,245.9
Broken granite ('000 metric tons)	6,914.0	7,007.5	6,371.7
Bricks ('000 units)	103,136	116,906	128,386
Soft drinks ('000 litres)	269,689.4	252,977.6	243,175.1
Plywood, plain and printed ('000 sq m)	31,307.0	28,871.3	26,106.9
Vegetable cooking oil (metric tons)	75,022	103,003	102,854
Animal fodder (metric tons)	110,106	115,341	104,541
Electricity (million kWh)	13,017.5	14,039.0	15,617.6
Gas (million kWh)	681.1	722.4	807.1
Cassette tape recorders ('000 sets)	15,450	14,006	18,059

Source: UN, *Industrial Commodity Statistics Yearbook*.

Plywood ('000 cu m, estimates): 280 per year in 1991–2003 (Source: FAO).

Electricity (million kWh): 34,665 in 2002; 35,331 in 2003; 36,810 in 2004 (Source: Asian Development Bank, *Key Indicators of Developing Asian and Pacific Countries*).

Finance

CURRENCY AND EXCHANGE RATES

Monetary Units
100 cents = 1 Singapore dollar (S $).

Sterling, US Dollar and Euro Equivalents (30 December 2005)
£1 sterling = S $2.8656;
US $1 = S $1.6642;
€1 = S $1.9633;
S $100 = £34.90 = US $60.09 = €50.94.

Average Exchange Rate (Singapore dollars per US $)
2003   1.7422
2004   1.6902
2005   1.6644

BUDGET
(S $ million)

Revenue*	2003	2004	2005†
Tax revenue	20,736	22,699	28,117
Income tax	10,414	10,218	25,201
Corporate and personal income tax	10,028	10,100	11,209
Contributions by statutory board	386	119	1,446
Assets taxes	1,243	2,139	1,819
Taxes on motor vehicles	1,290	1,547	1,438
Customs and excise duties	1,802	1,883	1,995
Betting taxes	1,566	1,522	1,531
Stamp duty	648	898	813
Goods and services tax	2,724	3,297	3,815
Others	1,048	1,195	1,136
Fees and charges	3,587	3,509	2,567
Total (incl. others)	24,643	26,346	28,116

* Figures refer to operating revenue only. The data exclude investment income and capital revenue.
† Preliminary figures.

Expenditure	2003	2004	2005*
Operating expenditure	19,236	19,936	20,675
Security and external relations	9,249	9,348	10,443
Social development	8,202	8,982	8,548
Education	4,876	5,162	4,981
Health	1,655	1,890	1,671
Community development and sports	581	808	818
Environment	452	460	443
Economic development	994	867	924
Trade and industry	515	382	444
Transport†	304	287	285
Government administration	792	737	759
Development expenditure	7,953	8,482	8,107
Total	27,189	28,418	28,781

* Preliminary figures.
† The Ministry of Communications and Information Technology was renamed the Ministry of Transport in November 2001. Its portfolio of information technology and telecommunications was transferred to the Ministry of Information, Communications and the Arts.

INTERNATIONAL RESERVES
(US $ million at 31 December)

	2002	2003	2004
Gold and foreign exchange	81,367	94,975	111,498
IMF special drawing rights	177	207	293
Reserve position in the IMF	478	564	440
Total	82,021	95,746	112,232

Source: IMF, *International Financial Statistics*.

MONEY SUPPLY
(S $ million at 31 December)

	2002	2003	2004
Currency outside banks	12,360	12,838	13,694
Demand deposits at commercial banks	23,468	25,884	30,468
Total money	35,828	38,722	44,162

Source: IMF, *International Financial Statistics*.

COST OF LIVING
(National Consumer Price Index; base: 2004 = 100)

	2002	2003	2005
Food	97.4	97.9	101.3
Transport and communication	98.7	98.8	97.8
Clothing	99.4	99.8	99.9
Housing	100.6	100.1	100.8
Education	93.8	95.9	102.0
Health	92.5	94.4	100.4
All items (incl. others)	97.8	98.3	100.4

NATIONAL ACCOUNTS
(S $ million at current prices)
National Income and Product

	2002	2003	2004*
Compensation of employees	72,710.5	72,974.4	75,829.4
Gross operating surplus	72,446.1	74,462.0	87,563.8
Gross domestic product (GDP) at factor cost	145,156.6	147,436.4	163,393.2
Taxes, less subsidies, on production and imports	12,111.3	12,848.2	14,613.2
Statistical discrepancy	1,119.8	639.0	2,548.0
GDP in market prices	158,387.7	160,923.6	180,554.4
Net primary incomes received from abroad	−3,777.9	−2,500.4	−4,528.2
Gross national income (GNI)	154,609.8	158,423.2	176,026.2

* Preliminary figures.

SINGAPORE

Expenditure on the Gross Domestic Product

	2003	2004	2005*
Government final consumption expenditure	19,108.0	19,363.9	20,686.6
Private final consumption expenditure	74,311.6	79,165.5	81,525.8
Change in inventories	−13,704.8	−7,909.4	−6,276.0
Gross fixed capital formation	38,901.1	43,202.5	42,384.2
Statistical discrepancy	−2,535.9	−2,272.9	−2,222.9
Total domestic expenditure	116,080.0	131,549.6	137,097.7
Trade in goods and services (net)	45,466.6	50,154.0	58,262.1
GDP in market prices	161,546.6	181,703.6	194,359.8
GDP at constant 2000 prices	167,270.6	181,850.7	193,453.0

* Preliminary figures.

Gross Domestic Product by Economic Activity

	2003	2004	2005*
Agriculture, fishing and quarrying	164.1	195.1	191.1
Manufacturing	38,689.3	47,812.6	52,127.5
Electricity, gas and water	2,782.3	2,938.4	2,844.2
Construction	6,930.7	6,819.0	7,044.3
Wholesale and retail trade	22,856.3	26,242.2	28,838.1
Hotels and restaurants	2,982.9	3,386.9	3,637.9
Transport and communications	19,221.5	21,488.8	23,142.6
Financial services	18,025.0	19,219.7	20,906.9
Business services	21,627.3	22,515.6	24,584.2
Owner-occupied dwellings	6,788.5	6,739.5	6,890.4
Other services	19,446.0	20,542.2	20,791.4
Sub-total	159,513.9	177,900.0	190,998.6
Less Financial intermediation services indirectly measured	8,057.3	7,272.6	7,673.5
Gross value added at basic prices	151,456.6	170,627.4	183,325.1
Taxes on products	10,090.0	11,076.2	11,034.7
GDP in market prices	161,546.6	181,703.6	194,359.8

* Preliminary figures.

BALANCE OF PAYMENTS
(US $ million)

	2002	2003	2004
Exports of goods f.o.b.	137,747	158,440	197,343
Imports of goods f.o.b.	−120,166	−130,310	−166,104
Trade balance	17,581	28,130	31,239
Exports of services	30,833	34,573	41,179
Imports of services	−29,424	−33,174	−40,691
Balance on goods and services	18,990	29,529	31,726
Other income received	13,285	14,566	15,408
Other income paid	−15,408	−16,007	−18,094
Balance on goods, services and income	16,867	28,088	29,041
Current transfers received	126	130	134
Current transfers paid	−1,266	−1,267	−1,278
Current balance	15,727	26,951	27,897
Capital account (net)	−160	−168	−182
Direct investment abroad	−4,118	−3,710	−10,601
Direct investment from abroad	5,725	9,348	16,032
Portfolio investment assets	−13,114	−13,473	−13,683
Portfolio investment liabilities	−346	3,004	2,338
Other investment assets	−6,973	−19,396	−36,626
Other investment liabilities	8,530	4,594	29,667
Net errors and omissions	−3,943	−475	−2,753
Overall balance	1,327	6,675	12,087

Source: IMF, *International Financial Statistics*.

External Trade

PRINCIPAL COMMODITIES
(distribution by SITC, S $ million)

Imports c.i.f.	2003	2004	2005
Mineral fuels, lubricants, etc.	31,867.5	43,632.7	59,145.2
Crude petroleum	14,496.2	21,108.3	30,819.8
Chemicals and related products	15,380.6	18,404.0	20,743.8
Basic manufactures	16,279.4	20,284.4	25,040.0
Machinery and equipment	139,508.5	171,301.9	185,980.5
Electric generators	9,801.8	10,927.9	12,028.0
Electronic components and parts	51,228.9	64,900.3	71,392.5
Aircraft and vessels	7,525.6	7,207.7	7,240.5
Miscellaneous manufactured articles	20,898.6	25,269.8	26,525.7
Total (incl. others)	237,316.5	293,337.5	333,190.8

Exports f.o.b.	2003	2004	2005
Mineral fuels, lubricants, etc.	30,430.7	41,421.9	57,414.5
Petroleum products	22,975.3	32,845.1	45,880.9
Chemicals and related products	32,196.4	38,947.1	43,610.8
Basic manufactures	11,608.1	13,985.3	17,497.7
Machinery and equipment	170,667.3	203,519.6	224,980.2
Electronic components and parts	66,419.5	83,763.8	91,654.0
Miscellaneous manufactured articles	23,414.2	26,308.2	26,048.6
Total (incl. others)	278,577.7	335,615.0	382,532.0

Source: International Enterprise Singapore.

PRINCIPAL TRADING PARTNERS
(S $ million)

Imports c.i.f.	2003	2004	2005
Australia	3,805.1	3,884.3	4,850.5
China, People's Republic	19,276.3	27,356.7	34,169.8
France	4,326.9	7,027.3	6,345.5
Germany	8,455.8	9,597.9	9,915.0
Hong Kong	5,380.0	6,171.5	7,008.7
India	2,510.2	4,700.9	6,788.2
Italy	2,775.6	3,529.8	3,593.5
Japan	26,808.3	32,266.6	32,033.7
Korea, Republic	8,637.4	11,851.1	14,322.9
Kuwait	3,682.9	5,338.1	6,138.3
Malaysia	37,527.7	42,201.4	45,526.6
Netherlands	1,898.0	2,777.0	3,007.1
Philippines	4,920.6	7,137.9	7,741.6
Saudi Arabia	6,823.4	9,373.4	14,894.3
Switzerland	3,508.0	3,905.8	3,834.8
Taiwan	11,263.0	15,826.9	19,719.6
Thailand	9,587.1	11,330.2	12,515.6
United Arab Emirates	3,285.7	3,339.9	4,242.0
United Kingdom	4,428.5	5,307.3	6,553.6
USA	31,060.2	34,573.6	38,792.7
Total (incl. others)	237,316.5	293,337.5	333,190.8

SINGAPORE

Exports f.o.b.	2003	2004	2005
Australia	8,148.1	11,167.9	14,045.4
China, People's Republic	17,638.2	25,972.1	32,909.3
France	3,508.3	4,006.6	5,460.1
Germany	7,624.8	10,535.8	10,504.1
Hong Kong	25,116.2	29,807.2	35,849.2
India	5,382.7	7,050.8	9,816.6
Japan	16,875.4	19,533.1	20,874.1
Korea, Republic	10,550.2	12,481.7	13,412.2
Malaysia	39,672.4	46,072.9	50,612.3
Netherlands	8,042.7	9,191.4	9,128.7
Philippines	5,636.1	6,618.2	6,969.5
Taiwan	12,011.8	14,075.2	14,938.0
Thailand	10,710.7	13,077.8	15,661.6
United Arab Emirates	2,527.7	3,211.0	6,115.1
United Kingdom	7,969.8	10,646.9	10,524.6
USA	33,460.1	37,500.7	39,024.3
Viet Nam	4,194.5	5,366.9	7,364.0
Total (incl. others)	278,577.7	335,615.0	382,532.0

Source: International Enterprise Singapore.

Transport

ROAD TRAFFIC
(registered vehicles)

	2002	2003	2004
Cars*	404,274	405,328	417,103
Motorcycles and scooters	131,437	134,767	136,122
Motor buses	12,707	12,653	12,892
Taxis	19,106	19,384	20,407
Goods vehicles (incl. private)	125,931	125,023	126,709
Others	13,501	13,888	14,162
Total	706,956	711,043	727,395

* Including private, company, tuition and private hire cars.

SHIPPING

Merchant Fleet
(at 31 December)

	2002	2003	2004
Number of vessels	1,768	1,761	1,842
Displacement (grt)	21,148,090	23,240,945	26,282,777

Source: Lloyd's Register-Fairplay, *World Fleet Statistics*.

International Sea-borne Shipping
(vessels of over 75 net registered tons)

	2002	2003	2004
Vessels entered	142,745	135,386	133,185
Vessels cleared	142,765	n.a.	n.a.

Cargo ('000 freight tons, 1997): Loaded 159,272; Unloaded 188,234.

Note: One freight ton equals 40 cubic feet (1.133 cubic metres) of cargo.

Source: mainly UN, *Statistical Yearbook*.

CIVIL AVIATION

	1995	1996	1997
Passengers:			
arrived	10,919,739	11,587,394	11,915,969
departed	10,823,457	11,542,408	11,883,259
in transit	1,453,046	1,384,446	1,375,116
Mail (metric tons):			
landed	9,521	10,572	10,813
dispatched	9,543	10,380	10,978
Freight (metric tons):			
landed	577,749	622,019	696,710
dispatched	528,024	568,438	639,544

Source: Civil Aviation Authority of Singapore.

1998: Kilometres flown (million) 293; Passengers carried ('000) 13,316; Passenger-km (million) 58,174; Total ton-km (million) 10,381.

1999: Kilometres flown (million) 326; Passengers carried ('000) 15,283; Passenger-km (million) 65,471; Total ton-km (million) 11,824.

Source: UN, *Statistical Yearbook*.

Passengers carried ('000): 23,163 in 2002; 28,637 in 2003; 30,762 in 2004.

Freight handled ('000 metric tons): 804.7 landed and 810.8 dispatched in 2003; 873.0 landed and 907.3 dispatched in 2004; 894.4 landed and 943.9 dispatched in 2005.

Tourism

FOREIGN VISITOR ARRIVALS
('000, incl. excursionists)

Country of nationality	2003	2004	2005
Australia	392,864	561,181	620,237
China, People's Republic	568,449	880,188	857,792
Germany	121,365	142,358	154,775
Hong Kong	226,246	271,683	313,814
India	309,423	471,181	583,532
Indonesia	1,341,568	1,765,321	1,813,444
Japan	434,036	598,807	588,500
Korea, Republic	261,381	360,979	364,192
Malaysia*	439,411	537,254	577,882
Philippines	176,553	245,883	319,923
Taiwan	144,923	182,434	213,950
Thailand	235,787	341,935	379,013
United Kingdom	387,943	457,238	467,144
USA	250,642	333,117	371,422
Total (incl. others)*	6,126,569	8,328,118	8,942,408

* Figures exclude arrivals of Malaysians by land.

Tourism receipts (US $ million, excl. passenger transport): 4,617 in 2001; 4,463 in 2002; 3,998 in 2003.

Source: World Tourism Organization.

Communications Media

(at 31 December)

	2002	2003	2004
Telephones ('000 main lines in use)	1,927.2	1,889.5	1,864.0
Mobile cellular telephones ('000 subscribers)	3,312.6	3,577.5	3,860.6
Personal computers ('000 in use)	2,590	n.a.	3,194
Internet users ('000)	2,100	2,135	2,421.8

Radio receivers ('000 in use): 2,550 in 1997.

Television receivers ('000 in use): 1,200 in 2000.

Facsimile machines ('000 in use, estimate): 100 in 1998.

Daily newspapers: 9 (with average circulation of 1,096,000 copies) in 2000.

Non-daily newspapers: 3 (with average circulation of 115,000 copies) in 2000.

Sources: mainly International Telecommunication Union; UNESCO, *Statistical Yearbook*; UN, *Statistical Yearbook*.

Education

(June 2003)

	Institutions	Students	Teachers
Primary	175	299,939	12,356
Secondary	165	206,426	11,146
Centralized Institutes	2	851	106
Junior Colleges	16	23,708	1,991
Institute of Technical Education	1	17,941	1,257*
Polytechnics	5	55,376	3,931*
National Institute of Education	1	2,953	561*
Universities	4	40,095	2,826*

* June 2000 figure.

Adult literacy rate (UNESCO estimates): 92.5% (males 96.6%; females 88.6%) in 2003 (Source: UN Development Programme, *Human Development Report*).

Directory

The Constitution

A new Constitution came into force on 3 June 1959, with the establishment of the self-governing State of Singapore. This was subsequently amended as a consequence of Singapore's affiliation to Malaysia (September 1963 to August 1965) and as a result of its adoption of republican status on 22 December 1965. The Constitution was also amended in January 1991 to provide for the election of a President by universal adult suffrage, and to extend the responsibilities of the presidency, which had previously been a largely ceremonial office. A constitutional amendment in October 1996 placed restrictions on the presidential right of veto. The main provisions of the Constitution are summarized below:

HEAD OF STATE

The Head of State is the President, elected by universal adult suffrage for a six-year term. He normally acts on the advice of the Cabinet, but is vested with certain functions and powers for the purpose of safeguarding the financial reserves of Singapore and the integrity of the Public Services.

THE CABINET

The Cabinet, headed by the Prime Minister, is appointed by the President and is responsible to Parliament.

THE LEGISLATURE

The Legislature consists of a Parliament of 84 elected members, presided over by a Speaker who may be elected from the members of Parliament themselves or appointed by Parliament although he may not be a member of Parliament. Members of Parliament are elected by universal adult suffrage for five years (subject to dissolution) in single-member and multi-member constituencies.* Additionally, up to three 'non-constituency' seats may be offered to opposition parties, in accordance with a constitutional amendment approved in 1984, while legislation approved in 1990, and amended in 1997, enables the Government to nominate up to nine additional, politically-neutral members for a term of two years; these members have restricted voting rights.

A 21-member Presidential Council, chaired by the Chief Justice, examines material of racial or religious significance, including legislation, to see whether it differentiates between racial or religious communities or contains provisions inconsistent with the fundamental liberties of Singapore citizens.

CITIZENSHIP

Under the Constitution, Singapore citizenship may be acquired either by birth, descent or registration. Persons born when Singapore was a constituent State of Malaysia could also acquire Singapore citizenship by enrolment or naturalization under the Constitution of Malaysia.

* A constitutional amendment was introduced in May 1988, whereby 39 constituencies were merged to form 13 'group representation constituencies', which would return 'teams' of three Members of Parliament. At least one member of each team was to be of minority (non-Chinese) racial origin. In January 1991 the Constitution was further amended, stipulating that the number of candidates contesting 'group representation constituencies' should be a minimum of three and a maximum of four. The maximum was increased to six by constitutional amendment in October 1996.

The Government

HEAD OF STATE

President: SELLAPAN RAMANATHAN (S. R.) NATHAN (took office 1 September 1999).

CABINET
(April 2006)

Prime Minister and Minister for Finance: Brig.-Gen. (retd) LEE HSIEN LOONG.

Senior Minister in the Prime Minister's Office: GOH CHOK TONG.

Minister Mentor: LEE KUAN YEW.

Deputy Prime Minister, Co-ordinating Minister for National Security and Minister for Law: Prof. SHANMUGAM JAYAKUMAR.

Minister for Foreign Affairs: Brig.-Gen. (retd) GEORGE YONG-BOON YEO.

Deputy Prime Minister and Minister for Home Affairs: WONG KAN SENG.

Minister for Trade and Industry: LIM HNG KIANG.

Minister for Information, Communications and the Arts: Dr LEE BOON YANG.

Minister for Manpower: Dr NG ENG HEN.

Minister for Health: KHAW BOON WAN.

Minister for Education: THARMAN SHANMUGARATNAM.

Minister for Transport: YEO CHEOW TONG.

Ministers in the Prime Minister's Office: LIM SWEE SAY, LIM BOON HENG, RAYMOND LIM SIANG KEAT.

Minister for National Development: MAH BOW TAN.

Minister for Community Development, Youth and Sports: Dr VIVIAN BALAKRISHNAN.

Minister for Defence: Rear-Adm. (retd) TEO CHEE HEAN.

Minister for the Environment and Water Resources and Minister-in-charge of Muslim Affairs: Dr YAACOB IBRAHIM.

Minister of State for Community Development and Sports: YU-FOO YEE SHOON.

Minister of State for Finance and Transport: LIM HWEE HUA.

Minister of State for the Environment and Manpower: GAN KIM YONG.

SINGAPORE

MINISTRIES

Office of the President: The Istana, Orchard Rd, Singapore 238823; e-mail istana_general_office@istana.gov.sg; internet www.istana.gov.sg.

Office of the Prime Minister: The Istana, Orchard Rd, Singapore 238823; tel. 62358577; fax 63328983; e-mail lee_hsien_loong@pmo.gov.sg; internet www.pmo.gov.sg.

Ministry of Community Development, Youth and Sports: 512 Thomson Rd, MCYS Bldg, Singapore 298136; tel. 62589595; fax 63536695; e-mail mcys_email@mcys.gov.sg; internet www.mcys.gov.sg.

Ministry of Defence: Gombak Drive, off Upper Bukit Timah Rd, Mindef Bldg, Singapore 669645; tel. 67608844; fax 67646119; e-mail esc@miw.com.sg; internet www.mindef.gov.sg.

Ministry of Education: 1 North Buona Vista Drive, MOE Bldg, Singapore 138675; tel. 68722220; fax 67755826; e-mail contact@moe.edu.sg; internet www.moe.gov.sg.

Ministry of the Environment and Water Resources: 40 Scotts Rd, Environment Bldg, 22nd Floor, Singapore 228231; tel. 67327733; fax 67319456; e-mail mewr_feedback@mewr.gov.sg; internet www.mewr.gov.sg.

Ministry of Finance: 100 High St, 10-01 The Treasury, Singapore 179434; tel. 62259911; fax 63327435; e-mail mof_qsm@mof.gov.sg; internet www.mof.gov.sg.

Ministry of Foreign Affairs: Tanglin, Singapore 248163; tel. 63798000; fax 64747885; e-mail mfa@mfa.gov.sg; internet www.mfa.gov.sg.

Ministry of Health: 16 College Rd, College of Medicine Bldg, Singapore 169854; tel. 63259220; fax 62241677; e-mail moh_info@moh.gov.sg; internet www.moh.gov.sg.

Ministry of Home Affairs: New Phoenix Park, 28 Irrawaddy Rd, Singapore 329560; tel. 64787010; fax 62546250; e-mail mha_feedback@mha.gov.sg; internet www.mha.gov.sg.

Ministry of Information, Communications and the Arts: 140 Hill St, 02-02 MITA Bldg, Singapore 179369; tel. 62707988; fax 68379837; e-mail mica@mica.gov.sg; internet www.mica.gov.sg.

Ministry of Law: 100 High St, 08-02 The Treasury, Singapore 179434; tel. 63328840; fax 63328842; e-mail contact@mlaw.gov.sg; internet www.minlaw.gov.sg.

Ministry of Manpower: 18 Havelock Rd, 07-01, Singapore 059764; tel. 64385122; fax 65344840; e-mail mom_hq@mom.gov.sg; internet www.mom.gov.sg.

Ministry of National Development: 5 Maxwell Rd, 21/22-00, Tower Block, MND Complex, Singapore 069110; tel. 62221211; fax 63257254; e-mail mnd_hq@mnd.gov.sg; internet www.mnd.gov.sg.

Ministry of Trade and Industry: 100 High St, 09-01 The Treasury, Singapore 179434; tel. 62259911; fax 63327260; e-mail mti_email@mti.gov.sg; internet www.mti.gov.sg.

Ministry of Transport: 460 Alexandra Rd, 39-00 PSA Bldg, Singapore 119963; tel. 62707988; fax 63757734; e-mail mot@mot.gov.sg; internet www.mot.gov.sg.

President and Legislature

PRESIDENT

On 13 August 2005, at the end of his six-year term, the incumbent SELLAPAN RAMANATHAN (S. R.) NATHAN was again nominated as President by a state-appointed committee. S. R. Nathan was the sole candidate for the Presidency, following the rejection by the committee of three other potential candidates on the grounds of their insufficient experience. He was officially reappointed to the post on 1 September.

PARLIAMENT

Parliament House
1 Parliament Place, Singapore 178880; tel. 63326666; fax 63325526; e-mail parl@parl.gov.sg; internet www.parliament.gov.sg.
Speaker: ABDULLAH TARMUGI.
General Election, 6 May 2006

	Seats
People's Action Party	82*
Workers' Party	1
Singapore Democratic Alliance	1
Total	**84**

* 37 seats were unopposed.

Election Commission

Elections Department of Singapore (ELD): Prime Minister's Office, 11 Prinsep Link, Singapore 187949; fax 63323428; internet www.elections.gov.sg; govt body; Chair. ROBIN CHAN.

Political Organizations

Angkatan Islam (Singapore Muslim Movement): Singapore; f. 1958; Pres. MOHAMED BIN OMAR; Sec.-Gen. IBRAHIM BIN ABDUL GHANI.

National Solidarity Party: Blk 531, Upper Cross St, Hong Lim Complex, 03-30, Singapore 050531; tel. and fax 65366388; e-mail nsp-cec@yahoogroups.com; internet www.nsp-singapore.org; f. 1987; joined Singapore Democratic Alliance (SDA) in July 2001; Pres. YIP YEW WENG; Sec.-Gen. STEVE CHIA.

People's Action Party (PAP): Blk 57B, PCF Bldg, 01-1402 New Upper Changi Rd, Singapore 463057; tel. 62444600; fax 62430114; e-mail paphq@pap.org.sg; internet www.pap.org.sg; f. 1954; governing party since 1959; 12-member Cen. Exec. Cttee; Chair. LIM BOON HENG; Sec.-Gen. LEE HSIEN LOONG.

Pertubuhan Kebangsaan Melayu Singapura (PKMS) (Singapore Malay National Organization): 218F Changi Rd, 4th Floor, PKM Bldg, Singapore 1441; tel. 64470468; fax 63458724; f. 1950 as the United Malay National Organization (UMNO) of Malaysia; renamed as UMNO Singapore in 1954 and as PKMS in 1967; seeks to advance the implementation of the special rights of Malays in Singapore, as stated in the Constitution, to safeguard and promote the advancement of Islam and to encourage racial harmony and goodwill in Singapore; joined Singapore Democratic Alliance (SDA) in July 2001; Pres. Haji BORHAN ARIFFIN; Sec.-Gen. MOHD RAHIZAN YAACOB.

Singapore Democratic Alliance (SDA): Singapore; f. 2001; est. to contest 2001 general election; coalition of Pertubuhan Kebangsaan Melayu Singapura (PKMS), Singapore People's Party (SPP), National Solidarity Party and the Singapore Justice Party; Chair. CHIAM SEE TONG.

Singapore Democratic Party (SDP): 1357A Serangoon Rd, Singapore 328240; tel. and fax 63981675; e-mail speakup@singaporedemocrats.org; internet www.singaporedemocrats.org; f. 1980; 12-mem. Cen. Cttee; Chair. LING HOW DOONG; Sec.-Gen. CHEE SOON JUAN.

Singapore Justice Party: Singapore; f. 1972; joined Singapore Democratic Alliance (SDA) in July 2001; Pres. A. R. SUIB; Sec.-Gen. MUTHUSAMY RAMASAMY.

Singapore People's Party (SPP): Singapore; f. 1993; a breakaway faction of the SDP, espousing more moderate policies; joined Singapore Democratic Alliance (SDA) in July 2001; 12-mem. Cen. Exec. Cttee; Chair. SIN KEK TONG; Sec.-Gen. CHIAM SEE TONG.

Workers' Party: 216G Syed Alwi Rd 02-03, Singapore 207799; tel. 62984765; fax 64544404; e-mail wp@wp.org.sg; internet www.wp.org.sg; f. 1961; active as opposition party in Singapore since 1957, merged with Barisan Sosialis (Socialist Front) in 1988; seeks to establish a democratic socialist govt with a constitution guaranteeing fundamental citizens' rights; Chair. SYLVIA LIM SWEE LIAN; Sec.-Gen. LOW THIA KHIANG.

Other parties are the Alliance Party Singapura, Barisan Sosialis (Socialist Front), the Democratic People's Party, the Democratic Progressive Party, the National Party of Singapore, the Partai Rakyat, the People's Front, the Parti Kesatuan Ra'ayat (United Democratic Party), the People's Republican Party, the Persatuan Melayu Singapura, the Singapore Chinese Party, the Singapore Indian Congress, the Singapore National Front, the United National Front, the United People's Front and the United People's Party.

Diplomatic Representation

EMBASSIES AND HIGH COMMISSIONS IN SINGAPORE

Angola: 9 Temasek Blvd, 44-03 Suntec Tower Two, Singapore 038989; tel. 63419360; fax 63419367; e-mail embangola@pacific.net.sg; Ambassador ELISIO AVILA DE JESUS FIGUEIREDO.

Australia: 25 Napier Rd, Singapore 258507; tel. 68364100; fax 67375481; e-mail public-affairs-sing@dfat.gov.au; internet www.australia.org.sg; High Commissioner MILES KUPA.

Austria: 600 North Bridge Rd, 24-04/05 Parkview Sq., Singapore 188778; tel. 63966350; fax 63966340; e-mail embassy.singapore@austriantrade.org; internet www.austria.org.sg; Chargé d'affaires a.i. GERHARD MESCHKE.

SINGAPORE

Bangladesh: 101 Thomson Rd, 05-04 United Sq., Singapore 307591; tel. 62550075; fax 62551824; e-mail bdoot@singnet.com.sg; internet www.bangladesh.org.sg; High Commissioner MUNSHI FAIZ AHMAD.

Belgium: 8 Shenton Way, 14-01 Temasek Tower, Singapore 068811; tel. 62207677; fax 62226976; e-mail singapore@diplobel.org; internet www.diplomatie.be/singapore; Ambassador MARC A. M. CALCOEN.

Brazil: 101 Thomson Rd, 10-05 United Sq., Singapore 307591; tel. 62566001; fax 62564565; e-mail consular1@brazil.org.sg; internet web.singnet.com.sg/~cinbrem; Ambassador JOÃO GUALBERTO MARQUES-PORTO.

Brunei: 325 Tanglin Rd, Singapore 247955; tel. 67339055; fax 67375275; High Commissioner Pengiran Dato' YUSOF Pengiran KULA.

Cambodia: 152 Beach Rd, 11-05 Gateway East, Singapore 189721; tel. 62993028; fax 62993622; e-mail cambodiaembassy@pacific.net.sg; internet www.geocities.com/cambodiabusiness/Embassy.html; Ambassador KEM MONGKOL.

Canada: 1 George St 11-01, Singapore 049145; tel. 68545900; fax 68545930; e-mail echiesg@pacific.net.sg; internet www.dfait-maeci.gc.ca/singapore; High Commissioner ALAN VIRTUE.

Chile: 105 Cecil St, 25-00 The Octagon, Singapore 069534; tel. 62238577; fax 62250677; e-mail echilesg@pacific.net.sg; Ambassador ANGEL FLISFISCH FERNÁNDEZ.

China, People's Republic: 150 Tanglin Rd, Singapore 247969; tel. 64712117; fax 64795345; e-mail chinaemb_sg@fmprc.gov.cn; internet www.chinaembassy.org.sg; Ambassador ZHANG YUN.

Czech Republic: 7 Temasek Blvd, 18-02 Suntec Tower 1, Singapore 038987; tel. 63322378; fax 63322372; e-mail singapore@embassy.mzv.cz; internet www.mfa.cz/singapore; Chargé d'affaires a.i. LUDĚK ZAHRADNÍČEK.

Denmark: 101 Thomson Rd, 13-01/02 United Sq., Singapore 307591; tel. 63555010; fax 62533764; e-mail sinamb@um.dk; internet www.denmark.com.sg; Ambassador KLAVS A. HOLM.

Egypt: 75 Grange Rd, Singapore 249579; tel. 67371811; fax 67323422; Ambassador MOHAMED ELZORKANY.

Finland: 101 Thomson Rd, 21-03 United Sq., Singapore 307591; tel. 62544042; fax 62534101; e-mail sanomat.sin@formin.fi; internet www.finland.org.sg; Ambassador RISTO R. REKOLA.

France: 101–103 Cluny Park Rd, Singapore 259595; tel. 68807800; fax 68807801; e-mail ambassadeur@france.org.sg; internet www.france.org.sg; Ambassador JEAN-PAUL REAU.

Germany: 12-00 Singapore Land Tower, 50 Raffles Place, Singapore 048623; tel. 65336002; fax 65331132; e-mail germany@singnet.com.sg; internet www.sing.diplo.de; Ambassador ANDREAS MICHAELIS.

Hungary: 250 North Bridge Rd, 29-01 Raffles City Tower, Singapore 179101; tel. 68830882; fax 68830177; e-mail hunemsin@singnet.com.sg; Ambassador TAMAS MAGDA.

India: 31 Grange Rd, India House, Singapore 239702; tel. 67376777; fax 67326909; e-mail indiahc@pacific.net.sg; internet www.embassyofindia.org; High Commissioner ALOK PRASAD.

Indonesia: 7 Chatsworth Rd, Singapore 249761; tel. 67377422; fax 67375037; e-mail info@kbrisingapura.com; internet www.kbrisingapura.com; Chargé d'affaires a.i. ANDRADJATI.

Ireland: Ireland House, 541 Orchard Rd, 8th Floor, Liat Towers, Singapore 238881; tel. 62387616; fax 62387615; e-mail ireland@starhub.net.sg; internet www.ireland.org.sg; Ambassador DICK O'BRIEN.

Israel: 24 Stevens Close, Singapore 257964; tel. 68349200; fax 67337008; e-mail press@singapore.mfa.gov.il; internet singapore.mfa.gov.il; Ambassador ILAN BEN-DOV.

Italy: 101 Thomson Rd, 27-02/03 United Sq., Singapore 307591; tel. 62506022; fax 62533301; e-mail ambitaly@italyemb.org.sg; internet www.italyemb.org.sg; Ambassador FOLCO DE LUCA GABRIELLI.

Japan: 16 Nassim Rd, Singapore 258390; tel. 62358855; fax 67331039; e-mail eojsingfv@vsystem.com.sg; internet www.sg.emb-japan.go.jp; Ambassador TAKAAKI KOJIMA.

Korea, Democratic People's Republic: 7500A Beach Rd, 09-320 The Plaza, Singapore 199591; tel. 64403498; fax 63482026; Ambassador JI JAE-SUK.

Korea, Republic: 47 Scotts Rd, 08-00 Goldbell Towers, Singapore 228233; tel. 68362263; fax 62352581; e-mail info@koreaembassy.org.sg; internet www.koreaembassy.org.sg; Ambassador JOON-WOO PARK (designate).

Laos: 101 Thomson Rd, 03-05A United Sq., Singapore 307591; tel. 62506044; fax 62506014; e-mail laoembsg@singnet.com.sg; Ambassador DONE SOMVORACHIT.

Malaysia: 30 Hill St, 02-01, Singapore 179360; tel. 62350111; fax 67336135; e-mail mwspore@singnet.com.sg; High Commissioner Dato' NAGALINGAM PARAMESWARAN.

Mexico: 152 Beach Rd, 06-07/08, 6th Floor, Gateway East Tower, Singapore 189721; tel. 62982678; fax 62933484; e-mail embamexsing@embamexsing.org.sg; internet www.embamexsing.org.sg; Ambassador JUAN JOSÉ GOMEZ CAMACHO.

Myanmar: 15 St Martin's Drive, Singapore 257996; tel. 67350209; fax 67356236; e-mail ambassador@mesingapore.org.sg; Ambassador WIN MYINT.

Netherlands: 541 Orchard Rd, 13-01 Liat Towers, Singapore 238881; tel. 67371155; fax 67371940; e-mail nlgovsin@singnet.com.sg; internet www.nethemb.org.sg; Ambassador CHRISTIAAN CORNELIS SANDERS.

New Zealand: 391A Orchard Rd, Tower A, 15-06/10 Ngee Ann City, Singapore 238873; tel. 62359966; fax 67339924; e-mail enquiries@nz-high-com.org.sg; internet www.nzembassy.com/singapore; High Commissioner Dr RICHARD STURGE GRANT.

Nigeria: 390 Havelock Rd, 06-06 King's Centre, Singapore 169662; tel. 67321743; fax 67321742; e-mail highcommission@nigerian-singapore.org.sg; High Commissioner Dr OZICHI J. ALIMOLE (acting).

Norway: 16 Raffles Quay, 44-01 Hong Leong Bldg, Singapore 048581; tel. 62207122; fax 62202191; e-mail emb.singapore@mfa.no; internet www.norway.org.sg; Ambassador ENOK NYGAARD.

Pakistan: 1 Scotts Rd, 24-02/04 Shaw Centre, Singapore 228208; tel. 67376988; fax 67374096; e-mail parep@singnet.com.sg; internet www.parep.org.sg; High Commissioner SAJJAD ASHRAF.

Panama: 16 Raffles Quay, 41-06 Hong Leong Bldg, Singapore 048581; tel. 62218677; fax 62240892; e-mail pacosin@pacific.net.sg; Ambassador ARLEEN SUCRE GARCIA.

Peru: 390 Orchard Rd, 12-03 Palais Renaissance, Singapore 238871; tel. 67388595; fax 67388601; e-mail embperu@pacific.net.sg; Ambassador J. ARTURO MONTOYA.

Philippines: 20 Nassim Rd, Singapore 258395; tel. 67373977; fax 67339544; e-mail php@pacific.net.sg; internet www.philippine-embassy.org.sg; Ambassador BELEN FULE-ANOTA.

Poland: 435 Orchard Rd, 10-01/02 Wisma Atria, Singapore 238877; tel. 67340466; fax 67346129; e-mail polish_embassy@pacific.net.sg; internet www.singapore.polemb.net; Ambassador BOGUSLAW MAJEWSKI.

Romania: 48 Jalan Harom Setangkai, Singapore 258827; tel. 64683424; fax 64683425; e-mail comofrom@starhub.net.sg; Chargé d'affaires a.i. SEVER COTU.

Russia: 51 Nassim Rd, Singapore 258439; tel. 62351834; fax 67334780; e-mail rosposol@pacific.net.sg; internet www.singapore.mid.ru; Ambassador SERGEY B. KISELEV.

Saudi Arabia: 40 Nassim Rd, Singapore 258449; tel. 67345878; fax 67385291; Ambassador Dr MOHAMAD AMIN KURDI.

South Africa: 331 North Bridge Rd, 15/01-06 Odeon Towers, Singapore 188720; tel. 63393319; fax 63396658; e-mail sahcp@singnet.com.sg; internet www.southafricahc.org.sg; High Commissioner ZANELE MAKINA.

Spain: 7 Temasek Blvd, 39-00 Suntec Tower 1, Singapore 038987; tel. 67259220; fax 63333025; e-mail embassy@embspain.org.sg; internet www.embspain.org.sg; Ambassador FRANCISCO JOSÉ RABENA BARRACHINA.

Sri Lanka: 13-07/12 Goldhill Plaza, 51 Newton Rd, Singapore 308900; tel. 62544595; fax 62507201; e-mail slhcs@lanka.com.sg; internet www.lanka.com.sg; High Commissioner WINITHKUMAR SHEHAN RATNAVALE.

Sweden: 111 Somerset Rd, 05-01 Singapore Power Bldg, Singapore 238164; tel. 64159720; fax 64159747; e-mail ambassaden.singapore@foreign.ministry.se; internet www.swedenabroad.com/singapore; Ambassador TEPPO TAURIAINEN.

Switzerland: 1 Swiss Club Link, Singapore 288162; tel. 64685788; fax 64668245; e-mail sin.vertretung@eda.admin.ch; internet www.eda.admin.ch/singapore; Ambassador Dr DANIEL WOKER.

Thailand: 370 Orchard Rd, Singapore 238870; tel. 67372158; fax 67320778; e-mail thaisgp@singnet.com.sg; internet www.thaiembsingapore.org; Ambassador CHALERMPOL THANCHITT.

Turkey: 2 Shenton Way 10-03, SGX Centre 1, Singapore 068804; tel. 65333390; fax 65333360; e-mail turksin@singnet.com.sg; Ambassador HAYRI EROL.

Ukraine: 50 Raffles Place, 16-05 Singapore Land Tower, Singapore 048623; tel. 65356550; fax 65352116; e-mail emb_sg@mfa.gov.ua; internet www.embassy-ukraine.com; Ambassador Dr OLEKSANDR O. HORIN.

United Arab Emirates: 600 North Bridge Road, 09-01/05 Parkview Sq., Singapore 188778; tel. 62388206; fax 62380081; e-mail emarat@singnet.com.sg; internet www.uaeembassy-sg.com; Chargé d'affaires a.i. ASIM MIRZA ALRAHMAH.

SINGAPORE

United Kingdom: 100 Tanglin Rd, Singapore 247919; tel. 64244200; fax 64244218; e-mail commercial.singapore@fco.gov.uk; internet www.britain.org.sg; High Commissioner ALAN COLLINS.

USA: 27 Napier Rd, Singapore 258508; tel. 64769100; fax 64769340; e-mail singaporeusembassy@state.gov; internet singapore.usembassy.gov; Ambassador PATRICIA LOUISE HERBOLD.

Viet Nam: 10 Leedon Park, Singapore 267887; tel. 64625938; fax 64625936; e-mail vnemb@singnet.com.sg; Ambassador Dr DUONG VAN QUANG.

Judicial System

Supreme Court: 1 Supreme Court Lane, Singapore 178879; tel. 63360644; fax 63379450; e-mail supcourt_qsm@supcourt.gov.sg; internet www.supcourt.gov.sg.

The judicial power of Singapore is vested in the Supreme Court and in the Subordinate Courts. The Judiciary administers the law with complete independence from the executive and legislative branches of the Government; this independence is safeguarded by the Constitution. The Supreme Court consists of the High Court and the Court of Appeal. The Chief Justice is appointed by the President if the latter, acting at his discretion, concurs with the advice of the Prime Minister. The other judges of the Supreme Court are appointed in the same way, in consultation with the Chief Justice. At 1 June 2004 there were two judges of appeal, including the Chief Justice, and 10 judges in the Supreme Court. Under a 1979 constitutional amendment, the position of judicial commissioner of the Supreme Court was created 'to facilitate the disposal of business in the Supreme Court'. A judicial commissioner has the powers and functions of a judge, and is appointed for such period as the President thinks fit. At 1 June 2004 there were two judicial commissioners in the Supreme Court.

The Subordinate Courts consist of District Courts and Magistrates' Courts. In addition, there are also specialized courts such as the Coroner's Court, Family Court, Juvenile Court, Mentions Court, Night Court, Sentencing Courts and Filter Courts. The Primary Dispute Resolution Centre and the Small Claims Tribunals are also managed by the Subordinate Courts. The Subordinate Courts have also established the Multi-Door Courthouse, which serves as a one-stop centre for the screening and channelling of any cases to the most appropriate forum for dispute resolution.

District Courts and Magistrates' Courts have original criminal and civil jurisdiction. District Courts try offences for which the maximum penalty does not exceed 10 years of imprisonment and in civil cases where the amount claimed does not exceed S $250,000. Magistrates' Courts try offences for which the maximum term of imprisonment does not exceed three years. The jurisdiction of Magistrates' Courts in civil cases is limited to claims not exceeding S $60,000. The Coroners' Court conducts inquests. The Small Claims Tribunal has jurisdiction over claims relating to a dispute arising from any contract for the sale of goods or the provision of services and any claim in tort in respect of damage caused to any property involving an amount that does not exceed S $10,000. The Juvenile Court deals with offences committed by young persons aged under 16 years.

The High Court has unlimited original jurisdiction in criminal and civil cases. In its appellate jurisdiction it hears criminal and civil appeals from the District Courts and Magistrates' Courts. The Court of Appeal hears appeals against the decisions of the High Court in both criminal and civil matters. In criminal matters, the Court of Appeal hears appeals against decisions made by the High Court in the exercise of its original criminal jurisdiction. In civil matters, the Court of Appeal hears appeals against decisions made by the High Court in the exercise of both its original and appellate jurisdiction.

With the enactment of the Judicial Committee (Repeal) Act 1994 in April of that year, the right of appeal from the Court of Appeal to the Judicial Committee of the Privy Council in the United Kingdom was abolished. The Court of Appeal is now the final appellate court in the Singapore legal system.

Attorney-General: CHAN SEK KEONG.

Chief Justice: YONG PUNG HOW.

Judges of Appeal: CHAO HICK TIN, ANDREW PHANG BOON LEONG.

Judges of the High Court: KAN TING CHIU, LAI SIU CHIU, JUDITH PRAKASH, TAN LEE MENG, CHOO HAN TECK, BELINDA ANG, WOO BIH LI, TAY YONG KWANG.

Judicial Commissioners: V. K. RAJAH, ANDREW ANG.

Religion

According to the 2000 census, 64.4% of ethnic Chinese, who constituted 76.8% of the population, professed either Buddhism or Daoism (including followers of Confucius, Mencius and Lao Zi) and 16.5% of Chinese adhered to Christianity. Malays, who made up 13.9% of the population, were 99.6% Muslim. Among Indians, who constituted 7.9% of the population, 55.4% were Hindus, 25.6% Muslims, 12.1% Christians and 6.3% Sikhs, Jains or adherents of other faiths. There are small communities of Zoroastrians and Jews. Freedom of worship is guaranteed by the Constitution.

BAHÁ'Í FAITH

National Spiritual Assembly: 110D Wishart Rd, Singapore 098733; tel. 62733023; fax 62732497; e-mail secretariat@bahai.org.sg; internet www.bahai.org.sg.

BUDDHISM

Buddhist Union: 28 Jalan Senyum, Singapore 418152; tel. 64435959; fax 64443280.

Singapore Buddhist Federation: 12 Ubi Ave 1, Singapore 408932; tel. 67444635; fax 67473618; e-mail buddhist@singnet.com.sg; internet www.buddhist.org.sg; f. 1948.

Singapore Buddhist Sangha Organization: 88 Bright Hill Drive, Singapore 579644.

CHRISTIANITY

National Council of Churches: 6 Mt Sophia, Singapore 228457; tel. 63372150; fax 63360368; e-mail nccs@cyberway.com.sg; f. 1948; six mem. churches, six assoc. mems; Pres. Bishop JOHN TAN; Gen. Sec. Rev. Canon Dr JAMES WONG.

Singapore Council of Christian Churches (SCCC): Singapore; f. 1956.

The Anglican Communion

The Anglican diocese of Singapore (also including Indonesia, Laos, Thailand, Viet Nam and Cambodia) is part of the Province of the Anglican Church in South-East Asia.

Bishop of Singapore: The Rt Rev. Dr JOHN HIANG CHEA CHEW, 4 Bishopsgate, Singapore 249970; tel. 64741661; fax 64791054; e-mail bpoffice@anglican.org.sg.

Orthodox Churches

The Orthodox Syrian Church and the Mar Thoma Syrian Church are both active in Singapore.

The Roman Catholic Church

Singapore comprises a single archdiocese, directly responsible to the Holy See. In December 2003 there were an estimated 162,711 adherents in the country, representing 3.9% of the total population.

Archbishop of Singapore: Most Rev. NICHOLAS CHIA, Archbishop's House, 31 Victoria St, Singapore 187997; tel. 63378818; fax 63334725; e-mail nc@veritas.org.sg.

Other Christian Churches

Brethren Assemblies: Bethesda Hall (Ang Mo Kio), 601 Ang Mo Kio Ave 4, Singapore 569898; tel. 64587474; fax 64566771; e-mail bethesda@pacific.net.sg; internet www.bethesdahall.com; f. 1864; Hon. Sec. WONG TUCK KEONG.

Evangelical Fellowship of Singapore (EFOS): Singapore; f. 1980.

Methodist Church in Singapore: 70 Barker Rd, Singapore 309936; tel. 64784786; fax 64784794; e-mail episcopacy@methodist.org.sg; internet www.methodist.org.sg; f. 1885; 32,663 mems (Dec. 2004); Bishop Dr ROBERT SOLOMON.

Presbyterian Church: 3 Orchard Rd, cnr Penang Rd, Singapore 238825; tel. 63376681; fax 63391979; e-mail orpcenglish@orpc.org.sg; f. 1856; services in English, Chinese (Mandarin), Indonesian and German; 2,000 mems; Chair. Rev. DAVID BURKE.

Singapore Baptist Convention: 01 Goldhill Plaza, 03-19 Podium Blk, Singapore 308899; tel. 62538004; fax 62538214; e-mail sbcnet@gala.com.sg; internet www.baptistconvention.org.sg; f. 1974; Chair. Rev. SEBASTIAN CHUA; Asst Exec. Dir ALAN PHUA.

Other denominations active in Singapore include the Lutheran Church and the Evangelical Lutheran Church.

HINDUISM

Hindu Advisory Board: c/o 397 Serangoon Rd, Singapore 218123; tel. 62963469; fax 62929766; e-mail heb@pacific.net.sg; f. 1985; Chair. AJAIB HARI DASS; Sec. E. SANMUGAM.

Hindu Endowments Board: 397 Serangoon Rd, Singapore 218123; tel. 62963469; fax 62929766; e-mail heb@pacific.net.sg; internet www.heb.gov.sg; f. 1968; Chair. V. R. NATHAN; Sec. SATISH APPOO.

SINGAPORE   Directory

ISLAM

Majlis Ugama Islam Singapura (MUIS) (Islamic Religious Council of Singapore): Islamic Centre of Singapore, 273 Braddell Rd, Singapore 579702; tel. 62568188; fax 62537572; e-mail info@muis.gov.sg; internet www.muis.gov.sg; f. 1968; Pres. Haji MOHD ALAMI MUSA; Sec. SYED HAROON ALJUNIED.

Muslim Missionary Society Singapore (JAMIYAH): 31 Lorong, 12 Geylang Rd, Singapore 399006; tel. 67431211; fax 67450610; e-mail info@jamiyah.org.sg; internet www.jamiyah.org.sg; Pres. Haji ABU BAKAR MAIDIN; Sec.-Gen. ISMAIL ROZIZ.

SIKHISM

Sikh Ad: c/o 2 Towner Rd, 03-01, Singapore 327804; tel. and fax 62996440; Chair. BHAJAN SINGH.

The Press

Compulsory government scrutiny of newspaper management has been in operation since 1974. All newspaper enterprises must be public companies. In August 1986 there were more than 3,700 foreign publications circulating in Singapore. The Newspaper and Printing Presses (Amendment) Act 1986 empowers the Government to restrict the circulation of foreign periodicals that are deemed to exert influence over readers on domestic political issues. An amendment to the Newspaper and Printing Presses Act was promulgated in October 1990. Under this amendment, all publications of which the 'contents and editorial policy were determined outside Singapore' and which dealt with politics and current events in South-East Asia would be required to obtain a ministerial licence, renewable annually. The permit would limit the number of copies sold and require a deposit in case of legal proceedings involving the publication. Permits could be refused or revoked without any reason being given. In November, however, a statement was issued exempting 14 of the 17 foreign publications affected by the amendment, which came into effect in December.

DAILIES

English Language

Business Times: 1000 Toa Payoh North, Podium Blk, Level 3, Singapore 318994; tel. 63196319; fax 63198277; e-mail btnews@sph.com.sg; internet business-times.asia1.com.sg; f. 1976; morning; Editor ALVIN TAY; circ. 28,000 (Singapore only).

The New Paper: 1000 Toa Payoh North, Annexe Blk, Level 6, Singapore 318994; tel. 63196319; fax 63198266; e-mail tnp@asia1.com.sg; internet newpaper.asia1.com.sg; f. 1988; afternoon tabloid; Editor IVAN FERNANDEZ; circ. 120,394 in Aug. 2003 (Singapore only).

Streats: 1000 Toa Payoh North, Podium Blk, Level 1, Singapore 318994; tel. 63192421; fax 63198191; e-mail streats@sph.com.sg; f. 2000; Mon.-Fri.; morning tabloid; Editor PAUL JANSEN; circ. 280,000 in Aug. 2003 (Singapore only).

The Straits Times: 1000 Toa Payoh North, Singapore 318994; tel. 63196319; fax 67320131; e-mail stlocal@sph.com.sg; internet straitstimes.asia1.com.sg; f. 1845; morning; Editor HAN FOK KWANG; circ. 389,248 in Aug. 2003 (Singapore only).

Today: 24 Raffles Place, 28–01/06 Clifford Centre, Singapore 048621; tel. 62364889; fax 64812098; e-mail news@newstoday.com.sg; internet www.todayonline.com; f. 2000; free morning tabloid; Editor P. N. BALJI; circ. 550,000.

Chinese Language

Lianhe Wanbao: 1000 Toa Payoh North, Podium Blk, Level 4, Singapore 318994; tel. 63196319; fax 63198133; e-mail wanbao@sph.com.sg; f. 1983; evening; Editor KOH LIN HOE; circ. 127,021 (week), 120,879 (weekend) in Aug. 2003.

Lianhe Zaobao: 1000 Toa Payoh North, Podium Blk, Level 4, Singapore 318994; tel. 63196319; fax 63198119; e-mail cnzbmgt@sph.com.sg; internet www.zaobao.com; f. 1923; Editor LIM JIM KOON; circ. 200,761.

Shin Min Daily News (S) Ltd: 1000 Toa Payoh North, Podium Blk, Level 4, Singapore 318994; tel. 63196319; fax 63198166; e-mail shinmin@sph.com.sg; f. 1967; evening; Editor TOH LAM HHAT; circ. 126,541 (week), 122,029 (weekend) in Aug. 2003.

Malay Language

Berita Harian: 1000 Toa Payoh North, Singapore 318994; tel. 63195137; fax 63198255; e-mail aadeska@sph.com.sg; internet cyberita.asia1.com.sg; f. 1957; morning; Editor MOHD GUNTOR SADALI; circ. 61,177 in Aug. 2003 (Singapore only).

Tamil Language

Tamil Murasu: 82 Genting Lane 06-07, Singapore 349567; tel. 63196319; fax 63194001; e-mail murasu4@cyberway.co.sg; internet tamilmurasu.asia1.com.sg; f. 1935; Editor CHITRA RAJARAM; circ. 7,928 (week), 15,119 (Sunday) in Aug. 2003.

WEEKLIES

English Language

The New Paper on Sunday: 1000 Toa Payoh North, Annexe Blk, Level 6, Singapore 318994; tel. 63196319; fax 63198266; e-mail tnp@asia1.com.sg; internet newpaper.asia1.com.sg; f. 1999; tabloid; Editor IVAN FERNANDEZ; circ. 152,080 in Aug. 2003.

The Sunday Times: 1000 Toa Payoh North, Singapore 318994; tel. 63195397; fax 67320131; e-mail stlocal@sph.com.sg; internet straitstimes.asia1.com.sg; f. 1931; Editor-in-Chief CHEONG YIP SENG; circ. 387,205 in Aug. 2003 (Singapore only).

Weekend Today: 24 Raffles Place, 28–01/06 Clifford Centre, Singapore 048621; tel. 62364889; fax 64812098; e-mail sales_enquiry@newstoday.com.sg; internet www.todayonline.com; f. 2002; Editor P. N. BALJI; circ. 300,000.

Malay Language

Berita Minggu: 1000 Toa Payoh North, Singapore 318994; tel. 63196319; fax 63198255; e-mail aadeska@sph.com.sg; internet cyberita.asia1.com.sg; f. 1960; Sunday; Editor MOHD GUNTOR SADALI; circ. 68,209 in Aug. 2003 (Singapore only).

SELECTED PERIODICALS

English Language

Accent: Accent Communications, 215 Intrepid Warehouse Complex, 4 Ubi Ave, Singapore 1440; tel. 67478088; fax 67472811; f. 1983; monthly; lifestyle; Senior Editor DORA TAY; circ. 65,000.

Cherie Magazine: 12 Everton Rd, Singapore 0208; tel. 62229733; fax 62843859; f. 1983; bimonthly; women's; Editor JOSEPHINE NG; circ. 20,000.

8 Days: 10 Ang Mo Kio St 65, 01–06/08 Techpoint, Singapore 569059; tel. 62789822; fax 62724800; e-mail feedback@8daysonline.com; internet www.8days.sg; f. 1990; weekly; Editor-in-Chief TAN LEE SUN; circ. 113,258.

Her World: SPH Magazines Pte Ltd, 82 Genting Lane, Singapore 349567; tel. 63196319; fax 63196345; e-mail nguislc@sph.com.sg; internet www.herworld.com; f. 1960; monthly; women's; Editor CAROLINE NGUI; circ. 60,883.

Her World Brides: SPH Magazines Pte Ltd, 82 Genting Lane, Singapore 349567; tel. 63196319; fax 63196345; e-mail sphmag@sph.com.sg; f. 1998; quarterly; circ. 13,193.

Home and Decor: SPH Magazines Pte Ltd, 82 Genting Lane, Singapore 349567; tel. 63196319; fax 63196345; e-mail hdecor@cyberway.com.sg; f. 1981; 6 a year; home-owners; Editor SOPHIE KHO; circ. 19,814.

LIME: 10 Ang Mo Kio St 65, 01-06/08 Techpoint, Singapore 569059; tel. 64837118; fax 64837286; internet lime.mediacorppublishing.com; f. 1996; Editor PAMELA QUEK; circ. 34,947.

Mondial Collections: Singapore; f. 1990; bimonthly; arts; Chair. CHRIS CHENEY; circ. 100,000.

NSman: SAFRA National Service Association, 5200 Jalan Bukit Merah, Singapore 159468; tel. 62786011; fax 63779898; e-mail hq@safra.org.sg; internet www.safra.sg; f. 1972; bimonthly; publication of the SAF National Service; Gen. Man. TAN KEE BOO; circ. 130,000.

Republic of Singapore Government Gazette: SNP Corpn Ltd, 1 Kim Seng Promenade, 18-01 Great World City East Tower, Singapore 237994; tel. 68269600; fax 68203341; e-mail egazinfo@snpcorp.com; internet www.egazette.com; weekly; Friday.

Reservist: 5200 Jalan Bukit Merah, Singapore 0315; tel. 62786011; fax 6273441; f. 1973; bimonthly; men's; Editor SAMUEL EE; circ. 130,000.

Singapore Medical Journal: Singapore Medical Association, Level 2, Alumni Medical Centre, 2 College Rd, Singapore 169850; tel. 62231264; fax 62247827; e-mail smj@sma.org.sg; internet www.sma.org.sg/smj; monthly; Editor Prof. W. C. G. PEH; circ. 4,700.

Times Guide to Computers: 1 New Industrial Rd, Times Centre, Singapore 536196; tel. 62848844; fax 62850161; e-mail ttd@corp.tpl.com.sg; internet www.tpl.com.sg; f. 1986; annually; computing and communications; Vice-Pres. LESLIE LIM; circ. 30,000.

Visage: Ubi Ave 1, 02-169 Blk 305, Singapore 1440; tel. 67478088; fax 67472811; f. 1984; monthly; Editor-in-Chief TENG JUAT LENG; circ. 63,000.

WEEKENDeast: 82 Genting Lane, News Centre, Singapore 349567; tel. 67401200; fax 67451022; e-mail focuspub@cyberway.com.sg; f. 1986; Editor VICTOR SOH; circ. 75,000.

SINGAPORE

Woman's Affair: 140 Paya Lebar Rd, 04-10 A-Z Bldg, Singapore 1440; tel. 67478088; fax 67479119; f. 1988; 2 a month; Editor Dora Tay; circ. 38,000.

Young Parents: SPH Magazines Pte Ltd, 82 Genting Lane, Singapore 349567; tel. 63196319; fax 63196345; e-mail yparents@cyberway.com.sg; internet www.youngparents.com.sg; f. 1986; monthly; family; Editor Crispina Robert; circ. 13,187.

Chinese Language

Characters: 1 Kallang Sector, 04-04/04-05 Kolam Ayer Industrial Park, Singapore 349276; tel. 67458733; fax 67458213; f. 1987; monthly; television and entertainment; Editor Sam Ng; circ. 45,000.

The Citizen: People's Association, 9 Stadium Link, Singapore 397750; tel. 63405138; fax 63468657; monthly; English, Chinese, Tamil and Malay; Man. Editor Ooi Hui Mei.

i-weekly: 10 Ang Mo Kio St 65, 01–06/08 Techpoint, Singapore 569059; tel. 62789822; fax 62724811; e-mail feedback@i-weeklyonline.com; internet i-weekly.mediacorppublishing.com; f. 1981; weekly; radio and television; Editor-in-Chief Loke Tai Tay; circ. 113,000.

Punters' Way: 4 Ubi View (off Ubi Rd 3), Pioneers and Leaders Centre, Singapore 408557; tel. 67458733; fax 67458213; e-mail pnlhldg@pcl.com.sg; f. 1977; biweekly; English and Chinese; sport; Editor T. S. Phan; circ. 90,000.

Racing Guide: 1 New Industrial Rd, Times Centre, Singapore 1953; tel. 62848844; fax 62881186; f. 1987; 2 a week; English and Chinese; sport; Editorial Consultant Benny Ortega; Chinese Editor Kuek Chiew Teong; circ. 20,000.

Singapore Literature: Singapore Literature Society, 122B Sims Ave, Singapore 1438; quarterly; Pres. Yap Koon Chan; Editor Luo-Ming.

Tune Monthly Magazine: Henderson Rd 06-04, Blk 203A, Henderson Industrial Park, Singapore 0315; tel. 62733000; fax 62749538; f. 1988; monthly; women's and fashion; Editor Chan Eng; circ. 25,000.

You Weekly: SPH Magazines Pte Ltd, 82 Genting Lane, Singapore 349567; tel. 63196319; fax 63196345; e-mail sphmag@sph.com.sg; f. 2001; weekly; entertainment; circ. 80,000.

Young Generation: SNP Panpac Pte Ltd, 97 Ubi Avenue 4, Singapore 408754; tel. 67412500; fax 67454129; e-mail yg@snpcorp.com; internet www.snpcorp.com; monthly; children's; Editor Evelyn Tang; circ. 80,000.

Malay Language

Manja: 10 Ang Mo Kio St 65, 01-06/08 Techpoint, Singapore 569059; tel. 64837118; fax 64812098; e-mail hello@manjaonline.com.sg; internet www.manja.sg; monthly; entertainment and lifestyle; Editor Tuminah Sapawi.

NEWS AGENCIES

Foreign Bureaux

Agence France-Presse (AFP): 10 Hoe Chiang Rd, 07-03 Keppel Towers, Singapore 089315; tel. 62228581; fax 62247465; e-mail afpsin@afp.com; Bureau Chief Roberto Z. Coloma.

Agenzia Nazionale Stampa Associata (ANSA) (Italy): Blk 628, 8 Hougang Ave, 04-94, Singapore 530628; tel. 63855514; fax 63855279; e-mail kuttynng@pacific.net.sg; Correspondent N. G. Kutty.

Associated Press (AP) (USA): 10 Anson Rd, 32-11 International Plaza, Singapore 079903; tel. 62201849; fax 62212753; e-mail sgutkin@ap.org; Chief of South-East Asian Services Steven Gutkin.

Central News Agency Inc (CNA) (Taiwan): 78A Lorong N, Telok Kurau, Ocean Apartments, Singapore 425223; tel. 63445746; fax 63467645; e-mail cnanews@singnet.com.sg; South-East Asia Correspondent Sherman Shean-Shen Wu.

Inter Press Service (IPS) (Italy): Marine Parade Rd, 10-42 Lagoon View, Singapore 1544; tel. 64490432; Correspondent Surya Gangadharan.

Jiji Tsushin (Jiji Press) (Japan): 10 Anson Rd, 24-16A International Plaza, Singapore 079903; tel. 62244212; fax 62240711; e-mail jijisp@jiji.com.sg; internet www.jiji.com; Bureau Chief Makio Shimatani.

Kyodo News (Japan): 138 Cecil St, Cecil Court, Singapore; tel. 62233371; fax 62249208; e-mail goinrk@kyodonews.or.jp; Chief Noriko Goi.

Reuters Asia Pte Ltd: 18 Science Park Drive, Singapore 118229; tel. 68703080; fax 67768112; e-mail singapore.newsroom@reuters.com; Bureau Chief Richard Hubbard.

Rossiiskoye Informatsionnoye Agentstvo—Vesti (RIA—Vesti) (Russia): 8 Namly Grove, Singapore 1026; tel. 64667998; fax 64690784; Correspondent Mikhail I. Idamkin.

United Press International (UPI) (USA): Singapore; tel. 63373715; fax 63389867; Man. Dean Visser.

Bernama (Malaysia), United News (India) and Xinhua (People's Republic of China) are also represented.

Publishers

ENGLISH LANGUAGE

Butterworths Asia: 1 Temasek Ave, 17-01 Millenia Tower, Singapore 039192; tel. 63369661; fax 63369662; e-mail sales@butterworths.com.sg; internet www.lexisnexis.com.sg/butterworths-online; f. 1932; law texts and journals; Man. Dir Graham J. Marshall.

Caldecott Publishing Pte Ltd: 10 Ang Mo Kio St 65, 01-06/08 Techpoint, Singapore 569059; tel. 64837118; fax 64837286; f. 1990; Editorial Dir Michael Chiang; Group Editor Tan Lee Sun.

EPB Publishers Pte Ltd: Blk 162, 04-3545 Bukit Merah Central, Singapore 150162; tel. 62780881; fax 62782456; e-mail epb@sbg.com.sg; fmrly Educational Publications Bureau Pte Ltd; textbooks and supplementary materials, general, reference and magazines; English and Chinese; Gen. Man. Roger Phua.

FEP International Pte Ltd: 11 Arnsal Chetty Rd, 03-02, Singapore 239949; tel. 67331178; fax 67375561; f. 1960; textbooks, reference, children's and dictionaries; Gen. Man. Richard Toh.

Flame of the Forest Publishing Pte Ltd: Blk 5, Ang Mo Kio Industrial Park 2A, 07-22/23, AMK Tech II, Singapore 567760; tel. 64848887; fax 64842208; e-mail editor@flameoftheforest.com; internet www.flameoftheforest.com; Man. Dir Alex Chacko.

Graham Brash Pte Ltd: 45 Kian Teck Drive, Blk 1, Level 2, Singapore 628859; tel. 62624843; fax 62621519; e-mail graham_brash@giro.com.sg; internet www.grahambrash.com.sg; f. 1947; general, academic, educational; English, Chinese and Malay; CEO Chuan I. Campbell; Dir Helene Campbell.

HarperCollins, Asia Pte Ltd: 970 Toa Payoh North, 04-24/26, Singapore 1231; tel. 62501985; fax 62501360; f. 1983; educational, trade, reference and general; Man. Dir Frank Foley.

Institute of Southeast Asian Studies: 30 Heng Mui Keng Terrace, Pasir Panjang Rd, Singapore 119614; tel. 67780955; fax 67781735; e-mail admin@iseas.edu.sg; internet www.iseas.edu.sg; f. 1968; scholarly works on contemporary South-East Asia and the Asia-Pacific; Chair. Prof. Wang Gungwu; Dir K. Kesavapany.

Intellectual Publishing Co: 113 Eunos Ave 3, 04-08 Gordon Industrial Bldg, Singapore 1440; tel. 67466025; fax 67489108; f. 1971; Man. Poh Be Leck.

Marshall Cavendish International (Singapore) Pte Ltd: Times Centre, 1 New Industrial Rd, Singapore 536196; tel. 62139300; fax 62854871; e-mail mca@sg.marshallcavendish.com; internet www.marshallcavendish.com/academic; f. 1957; fmrly Times Media Pte Ltd; academic texts; Group Publr Elsa Tan; Man. Editor Anthony Thomas.

Pearson Education South Asia Pte Ltd: 23/25 First Lok Yang Rd, Jurong Town, Singapore 629733; tel. 63199388; fax 63199171; e-mail asia@pearsoned.com.sg; educational; Reg. Dir Low Chwee Leong.

Simon & Schuster Asia Pte Ltd: 317 Alexandra Rd, 04-01 Ikea Bldg, Singapore 159965; tel. 64764688; fax 63780370; e-mail prenhall@signet.com.sg; f. 1975; educational; Man. Dir Gunawan Hadi.

Singapore University Press (Pte) Ltd: National University of Singapore, 3 Arts Link, AS3–01–02, Singapore 117569; tel. 67761148; fax 67740652; e-mail nusbooks@nus.edu.sg; internet www.nus.edu.sg/npu; f. 1971; scholarly; Man. Dir Paul Kratoska.

Stamford College Publishers: Colombo Court 05-11A, Singapore 0617; tel. 63343378; fax 63343080; f. 1970; general, educational and journals; Man. Lawrence Thomas.

Times Editions Pte Ltd: Times Centre, 1 New Industrial Rd, Singapore 536196; tel. 62139288; fax 62844733; e-mail tpl@tpl.com.sg; internet www.tpl.com.sg; f. 1978; political, social and cultural books, general works on Asia; Chair. Lim Kim San; Pres. and CEO Lai Seck Khui.

World Scientific Publishing Co Pte Ltd: 5 Toh Tuck Link, Singapore 596224; tel. 64665775; fax 64677667; e-mail wspc@wspc.com.sg; internet www.worldscientific.com; f. 1981; academic texts and science journals; Chair. and Man. Editor Prof. K. K. Phua; Man. Dir Doreen Liu.

MALAY LANGUAGE

Malaysia Press Sdn Bhd (Pustaka Melayu): Singapore; tel. 62933454; fax 62911858; f. 1962; textbooks and educational; Man. Dir Abu Talib bin Ally.

Pustaka Nasional Pte Ltd: 2 Joo Chiat Rd, 05-1125 Joo Chiat Complex, Singapore 420002; tel. 67454321; fax 67452417; e-mail info@pustaka.com.sg; internet www.pustaka.com.sg; f. 1965; Malay and Islamic religious books and CD-Roms; Man. Dir SYED AHMAD BIN MUHAMMED.

CHINESE LANGUAGE

Shanghai Book Co (Pte) Ltd: 231 Bain St, 02-73 Bras Basah Complex, Singapore 180231; tel. 63360144; fax 63360490; e-mail shanghaibook@pacific.net.sg; f. 1925; educational and general; Man. Dir MA JI LIN.

Shing Lee Publishers Pte Ltd: 120 Hillview Ave, 05-06/07 Kewalram Hillview, Singapore 2366; tel. 67601388; fax 67625684; e-mail shingleebook@sbg.com.sg; f. 1935; educational and general; Man. PEH CHIN HUA.

Union Book Co (Pte) Ltd: 231 Bain St 03-01, Bras Basah Complex, Singapore 0718; tel. 63380696; fax 63386306; general and reference; Gen. Man. CHOW LI-LIANG.

TAMIL LANGUAGE

EVS Enterprises: Singapore; tel. 62830002; f. 1967; children's books, religion and general; Man. E. V. SINGHAN.

Government Publishing House

SNP Corpn Ltd: 1 Kim Seng Promenade, 18-01 Great World City East Tower, Singapore 237994; tel. 68269600; fax 68203341; e-mail enquiries@snpcorp.com; internet www.snpcorp.com; f. 1973; printers and publishers; Pres. and CEO YEO CHEE TONG.

PUBLISHERS' ORGANIZATIONS

National Book Development Council of Singapore (NBDCS): 50 Geylang East Ave 1, Singapore 389777; tel. 68488290; fax 67429466; e-mail info@bookcouncil.sg; internet www.bookcouncil.sg; f. 1969; independent non-profit org.; promotes reading, writing and publishing and organizes the annual Asian Congress of Storytellers and Asian Children's Writers and Illustrators' Conference; offers professional training programmes through Centre for Literary Arts and Publishing; Chair. LIM LI KOK.

Singapore Book Publishers' Association: 86 Marine Parade Central 03–213, Singapore 440086; tel. 63447801; fax 64470897; e-mail twcsbpa@singnet.com.sg; internet www.publishers-sbpa.org.sg; Pres. TAN WU CHENG.

Broadcasting and Communications

TELECOMMUNICATIONS

Infocomm Development Authority of Singapore: 8 Temasek Blvd, 14-00 Suntec Tower Three, Singapore 038988; tel. 62110888; fax 62112222; e-mail info@ida.gov.sg; internet www.ida.gov.sg; f. 1999; formed as result of merger of National Computer Board and Telecommunication Authority of Singapore; the national policy maker, regulator and promoter of telecommunications in Singapore; Chair. LAM CHUAN LEONG; CEO CHAN YENG KIT.

Netrust Pte Ltd: 10 Collyer Quay, 09-05/06 Ocean Bldg, Singapore 049315; tel. 62121388; fax 62121366; e-mail infoline@netrust.net; internet www.netrust.net; f. 1997; the only licensed Certification Authority (CA) in Singapore, jtly formed by the National Computer Board and the Network for Electronic Transfers; the authority verifies the identity of parties doing business or communicating in cyberspace through the issuing of electronic identification certificates, in order to enable government organizations and private enterprises to conduct electronic transactions in a secure manner; CEO FOO JONG AI.

Singapore Technologies Telemedia: 51 Cuppage Rd, 10-11/17, Starhub Centre, Singapore 229469; tel. 67238777; fax 67207277; e-mail contactus@stt.st.com.sg; internet www.sttelemedia.com; Pres. and CEO LEE THENG KIAT.

Singapore Telecommunications Ltd (SingTel): 19-00 Comcentre, 31 Exeter Rd, Singapore 239732; tel. 68383388; fax 67328428; e-mail contact@singtel.com; internet www.singtel.com; f. 1992; a postal and telecommunications service operator and a holding company for a number of subsidiaries, serving both the corporate and consumer markets; 61.79%-owned by Temasek Holdings (Private) Ltd (a government holding company), 38.21% transferred to the private sector; Chair. CHUMPOL NALAMLIENG; Group CEO LEE HSIEN YANG.

StarHub Pte Ltd: Head Office, 51 Cuppage Rd, 07-00 StarHub Centre, Singapore 229469; tel. 68255000; fax 67215000; e-mail corpcomms@starhub.com; internet www.starhub.com.sg; f. 2000; telecommunications service provider; consortium includes Singapore Technologies Telemedia Pte Ltd, Singapore Power Ltd, Nippon Telegraph and Telephone Corpn (NTT) and British Telecom (BT); Pres. and CEO TERRY CLONTZ.

BROADCASTING

Regulatory Authority

Media Development Authority (MDA): MITA Bldg 04-01, 140 Hill St, Singapore 179369; tel. 68379973; fax 63368023; internet www.mda.gov.sg; f. 1994; fmrly Singapore Broadcasting Authority, name changed as above in Jan. 2003; licenses and regulates the media industry in Singapore; encourages, promotes and facilitates the development of media industries in Singapore, ensures the provision of an adequate range of media services to serve the interests of the general public, maintains fair and efficient market conduct and effective competition in the media industry, ensures the maintenance of a high standard of media services, regulates public service broadcasting; Chair. TAN CHIN NAM; CEO LIM HOCK CHUAN.

Radio

Far East Broadcasting Associates: 30 Lorong Ampas, 07-01 Skywaves Industrial Bldg, Singapore 328783; tel. 62508577; fax 62508422; e-mail febadmin@febasgp.com; f. 1960; Chair. GOH EWE KHENG; Exec. Dir Rev. JOHN CHANG.

Media Corporation of Singapore: Caldecott Broadcast Centre, Andrew Rd, Singapore 299939; tel. 63333888; fax 62515628; e-mail cherfern@mediacorpradio.com; internet www.mediacorp.com.sg; f. 1994; est. as Singapore International Media (SIM), following the corporatization of the Singapore Broadcasting Corpn; holding co for seven operating cos—Television Corpn of Singapore (TCS), Singapore Television Twelve (STV12), Radio Corpn of Singapore (RCS), MediaCorp Studios, MediaCorp News, MediaCorp Interactive and MediaCorp Publishing; Chair. CHENG WAI KEUNG.

Radio Corpn of Singapore Pte Ltd (RCS): Caldecott Broadcast Centre, Radio Bldg, Andrew Rd, Singapore 299939; tel. 62518622; fax 62569533; e-mail feedback@rcs.com.sg; internet www.mediacorpradio.com; f. 1936; operates 12 domestic services—in English (five), Chinese (Mandarin) (three), Malay (two), Tamil (one) and foreign language (one)—and three international radio stations (manages Radio Singapore International (RSI)—services in English, Mandarin and Malay for three hours daily and service in Bahasa Indonesia for one hour daily); COO CHUA FOO YONG.

Union Works Pte Ltd: Singapore; internet www.wrkz913.com; f. 1991; fmrly Radio Heart; name changed as above in 2000; first private radio station; broadcasts in English; 2 channels broadcasting a total of 336 hours weekly.

Rediffusion (Singapore) Pte Ltd: 6 Harper Rd, 04-01/08 Leong Huat Bldg, Singapore 369674; tel. 63832633; fax 63832622; e-mail md@rediffusion.com.sg; internet www.rediffusion.com.sg; f. 1949; commercial audio wired broadcasting service and wireless digital audio broadcasting service; broadcasts two programmes in Mandarin (18 hours daily) and English (24 hours daily); Man. Dir WONG BAN KUAN.

SAFRA Radio: Bukit Merah Central, POB 1315, Singapore 911599; tel. 63731924; fax 62783039; e-mail power98@pacific.net.sg; internet www.power98.com.sg/; f. 1994; broadcasts in Chinese (Mandarin) and English.

Television

CNBC Asia Business News (S) Pte Ltd: 10 Anson Rd, 06-01 International Plaza, Singapore 079903; tel. 63230488; fax 63230788; e-mail talk2us@cnbcasia.com; internet www.cnbcasia.com.sg; f. 1998; cable and satellite broadcaster of global business and financial news; US controlled; broadcasts in English (24 hours daily) and Mandarin; Pres. PAUL FRANCE.

Media Corporation of Singapore: see Radio.

Starhub CableVision Ltd: 51 Cuppage Rd 07-00, Singapore 229469; tel. 68255000; fax 67215000; internet www.starhub.com; f. 1992; fmrly Singapore CableVision Ltd; name changed as above in 2002 following acquisition by Starhub Ltd; broadcasting and communications co, subscription television service; launched cable service in June 1995; offers 83 digital channels (March 2005); offers broadband access services.

Singapore Television Twelve Pte Ltd (STV12): 12 Prince Edward Rd, 05-00 Bestway Bldg, Singapore 079212; tel. 62258133; fax 62203881; internet www.stv12.com.sg; f. 1994; terrestrial television station; 2 channels—Suria (Malay, 58 hours weekly) and Central (110.5 hours weekly); COO WOON TAI HO.

SPH MediaWorks Ltd: 82 Genting Lane, Singapore 349567; tel. 63197988; fax 67443318; e-mail mwcc@sphmediaworks.com; internet www.sphmediaworks.com; f. 2000; subsidiary of Singapore Press Holdings Ltd (SPH); two channels—Channel U (Mandarin) and Channel i (English); also owns two radio stations; Exec. Dir WEE LEONG HOW.

SINGAPORE

Television Corpn of Singapore (TCS): Caldecott Broadcast Centre, Andrew Rd, Singapore 299939; tel. 62560401; fax 62538119; e-mail webmaster@mediacorptv.com; internet www.mediacorptv.com; f. 1994; est. following the corporatization of Singapore Broadcasting Corpn; four channels—TCS 5 (English), TCS 8 (Mandarin), Suria (Malay) and Central; teletext service on two channels; also owns TVMobile, Singapore's first digital television channel, and Digital TV; Chair. Cheng Wai Keung; CEO Lim Hup Seng.

Finance

(cap. = capital; res = reserves; dep. = deposits; m. = million; brs = branches; amounts in Singapore dollars)

BANKING

The Singapore monetary system is regulated by the Monetary Authority of Singapore (MAS) and the Ministry of Finance. The MAS performs all the functions of a central bank and also assumed responsibility for the issuing of currency following its merger with the Board of Commissioners of Currency in October 2002. In September 2004 there were 113 commercial banks (five local, 108 foreign) and 48 representative offices in Singapore. Of the foreign banks, 23 had full licences, 37 had wholesale licences and 48 had offshore banking licences.

Government Financial Institution

Monetary Authority of Singapore (MAS): 10 Shenton Way, MAS Bldg, Singapore 079117; tel. 62255577; fax 62299491; e-mail webmaster@mas.gov.sg; internet www.mas.gov.sg; merged with Board of Commissioners of Currency Oct. 2002; cap. 100m., res 16,993m., dep. 96,146m. (March 2004); Chair. Goh Chok Tong; Man. Dir Heng Swee Keat.

Domestic Full Commercial Banks

Bank of Singapore Ltd: 18 Church St, 01-00 OCBC Centre South, Singapore 049479; tel. 65863200; fax 64383718; e-mail clientservice@finatiq.com; internet www.bankofsingapore.com; f. 1954; subsidiary of Oversea-Chinese Banking Corpn Ltd; cap. 50m., res 207m., dep. 2,984.5m. (Dec. 1997); Chair. David Philbrick Conner; CEO Tan Ngiap Joo.

DBS Bank (Development Bank of Singapore Ltd): 6 Shenton Way, DBS Bldg, Tower One, Singapore 068809; tel. 68788888; fax 64451267; e-mail dbs@dbs.com; internet www.dbs.com/sg; f. 1968; 29% govt-owned; merged with Post Office Savings Bank in 1998; cap. 1,962m., res 14,288m., dep. 87,250m. (Dec. 2003); Chair. S. Dhanabalan; Vice-Chair. and CEO Jackson Tai; 107 local brs, 9 overseas brs.

Far Eastern Bank Ltd: 156 Cecil St, 01-00 FEB Bldg, Singapore 069544; tel. 62219055; fax 62242263; internet www.uobgroup.com; f. 1959; subsidiary of United Overseas Bank Ltd; cap. 100m., res 48.5m., dep. 644.7m. (Dec. 2003); Chair. and CEO Wee Cho Yaw; Pres. Wee Ee Cheong; 3 brs.

Oversea-Chinese Banking Corpn (OCBC) Ltd: 65 Chulia St, 08-00 OCBC Centre, Singapore 049513; tel. 65357222; fax 65337955; e-mail info@ocbc.com.sg; internet www.ocbc.com; f. 1932; merged with Keppel TatLee Bank Ltd in Aug. 2001; cap. 1,284.1m., res 8,774.8m., dep. 67,398.2m. (Dec. 2003); Chair. Dr Cheong Choong Kong; CEO David Phillbrick Conner; 63 local brs, 52 overseas brs.

United Overseas Bank Ltd: 80 Raffles Place, UOB Plaza, Singapore 048624; tel. 65394439; fax 65342334; internet www.uobgroup.com; f. 1935; merged with Overseas Union Bank Ltd in Jan. 2002 and Industrial and Commercial Bank Ltd in Aug. 2002; cap. 1,571.7m., res 7,463.6m., dep. 79,367.2m. (Dec. 2003); Chair. and CEO Wee Cho Yaw; Pres. Wee Ee Cheong; 61 local brs, 21 overseas brs.

Foreign Banks

Full Commercial Banks

ABN AMRO Asia Merchant Bank (Singapore) Ltd (Netherlands): 63 Chulia St, Singapore 049514; tel. 62318888; fax 65323108; Chair. Rajan Ray; Man. Dir Geoffrey W. S. McDonald.

American Express Bank Ltd (USA): 16 Collyer Quay, Hitachi Tower, Singapore 049318; tel. 65384833; fax 65343022; Sr Country Exec. S. Lachlan Hough.

Bangkok Bank Public Co Ltd (Thailand): 180 Cecil St, Bangkok Bank Bldg, Singapore 069546; tel. 62219400; fax 62255852; e-mail torpong.cha@bbl.co.th; Sr Vice-Pres. and Gen. Man. Torphong Charungchareonveji.

Bank of America NA (USA): 9 Raffles Place, 18-00 Republic Plaza Tower 1, Singapore 048619; tel. 62393888; fax 62393068; CEO Alan Koh; Man. Dir Goetz Eggelhoefer.

Bank of China (People's Republic of China): 4 Battery Rd, Bank of China Bldg, Singapore 049908; tel. 65352411; fax 65343401; Gen. Man. Zhu Hua.

Bank of East Asia Ltd (Hong Kong): 137 Market St, Bank of East Asia Bldg, Singapore 048943; tel. 62241334; fax 62251805; e-mail info@hkbea.com.sg; Gen. Man. Khoo Kee Cheok.

Bank of India (India): 01-01 to 03-01, Hong Leong Centre, 138 Robinson Rd, Singapore 068906; tel. 62220011; fax 62254407; Chief Exec. Vijay Mehta; Gen. Man. B. Ramasubramaniam.

PT Bank Negara Indonesia (Persero) Tbk (Indonesia): 158 Cecil St, 01-00 to 04-00 Dapenso Bldg, Singapore 069545; tel. 62257755; fax 62254757; e-mail ptbni@starhub.net.sg; Gen. Man. Muhammad Yazeed.

Bank of Tokyo-Mitsubishi UFJ Ltd (Japan): 9 Raffles Place, 01-01 Republic Plaza, Singapore 048619; tel. 65383388; fax 65388083; Gen. Man. Hakoto Nakagawa; Dep. Gen. Man. Hidemitsu Otsuka.

BNP Paribas (France): 20 Collyer Quay, 18-01 Tung Centre, Singapore 049319; tel. 62101288; fax 62243459; internet www.bnpparibas.com.sg; Regional Man. Jean-Pierre Bernard.

Citibank NA (USA): Capital Square, 23 Church St, 01-01, Singapore 049481; tel. 62255225; fax 6325880; internet www.citibank.com.sg; Country Corporate Officer Sanjiv Misra.

Crédit Agricole Indosuez (France): 6 Raffles Quay, 17-00 John Hancock Tower, Singapore 048580; tel. 65354988; fax 65322422; e-mail cai.singapore@sg.ca-indosuez.com; internet www.ca-indosuez.com; f. 1905; Sr Country Man. Jean-Francois Cahet.

HL Bank (Malaysia): 20 Collyer Quay, 01-02 and 02-02 Tung Centre, Singapore 049319; tel. 65352466; fax 65339340; Country Head Gan Hui Tin.

Hongkong and Shanghai Banking Corpn Ltd (Hong Kong): 01-00 HSBC Bldg, 21 Collyer Quay, Singapore 049320; tel. 65305000; fax 62214676; e-mail direct@hsbc.com.sg; internet www.hsbc.com.sg; CEO (Singapore) Paul Lawrence.

Indian Bank (India): 3 Raffles Place, Bharat Bldg, Singapore 048617; tel. 65343511; fax 65331651; e-mail ceibsing@mbox3.singnet.com.sg; Chief Exec. V. Srinivasan.

Indian Overseas Bank (India): 94 Serangoon Rd, Singapore 217999; tel. 62941385; fax 62970701; e-mail iobrem@iob.com.sg; Chief Exec. Konidala Perumal Munirathnam.

JP Morgan Chase Bank (USA): 168 Robinson Rd, 15th Floor, 14-01 Capital Tower, Singapore 068912; tel. 68822888; fax 68821756; Sr Country Officer Raymond Chang.

Maybank (Malaysia): Maybank Chambers, 2 Battery Rd 01-00, Singapore 049907; tel. 65507122; fax 65327909; e-mail maybank@maybank.com.sg; internet www.maybank2u.com.sg; Sr Gen. Man. Spencer Lee Tien Chye; 22 brs.

RHB Bank Bhd (Malaysia): 5th Floor, 90 Cecil St 05-00, Singapore 069531; tel. 62202736; fax 62216646; internet www.rhbbank.com.my/cbob/singapore.shtm; Country Head Anthony Yeo.

Southern Bank Bhd (Malaysia): 39 Robinson Rd, 01-02 Robinson Point, Singapore 068911; tel. 65321318; fax 65355366; Dir Yeap Lam Yang.

Standard Chartered Bank (UK): 6 Battery Rd, Singapore 049909; tel. 62258888; fax 67893756; internet www.standardchartered.com.sg; Group Exec. Dirs Mike DeNoma, Kai Nargolwala; Chief Exec. (Singapore) Euleen Goh.

Sumitomo Mitsui Banking Corpn (Japan): 3 Temasek Ave, 06-01 Centennial Tower, Singapore 039190; tel. 68820001; fax 68870330; Gen. Man. Masami Tashiro.

UCO Bank (India): 3 Raffles Place, 01-01 Bharat Bldg, Singapore 048617; tel. 65325944; fax 65325044; e-mail general@ucobank.com.sg; Chief Exec. R. K. Mukherjee.

Wholesale Banks

Australia and New Zealand Banking Group Ltd (Australia): 10 Collyer Quay, 17-01/07 Ocean Bldg, Singapore 049315; tel. 65358355; fax 65396111; Regional Gen. Man. John Winders.

Bank of Nova Scotia (Canada): 10 Collyer Quay, 15-01/09 Ocean Bldg, Singapore 049315; tel. 65358688; fax 65363325; Country Head, Vice-Pres. and Man. Seong Koon Wah Sun.

Barclays Bank PLC (UK): 23 Church St, 13-08 Capital Sq., Singapore 049481; tel. 63953000; fax 63953139; Regional Head James Loh; Country Man. Quek Suan Kiat.

Bayerische Hypo- und Vereinsbank AG (Germany): 30 Cecil St, 26-01 Prudential Tower, Singapore 049712; tel. 64133688; fax 65368591; Gen. Man. Peter Ng Poh Lian.

Bayerische Landesbank Girozentrale (Germany): 300 Beach Rd, 37-01 The Concourse, Singapore 199555; tel. 62933822; fax 62932151; e-mail sgblb@blb.de; Gen. Man. and Sr Vice-Pres. Manfred Wolf; Exec. Vice-Pres. Heinz Hoffmann.

SINGAPORE

Directory

BNP Paribas Private Bank (France): 20 Collyer Quay, 18-01 Tung Centre, Singapore 049319; tel. 62101037; fax 62103671; internet www.bnpparibas.com.sg; CEO Serge Forti.

Chiao Tung Bank Co Ltd (Taiwan): 80 Raffles Place, 23-20 UOB Plaza II, Singapore 048624; tel. 65366311; fax 65360680; Sr Vice-Pres. and Gen. Man. Chiang Sheng-Li.

Commerzbank AG (Germany): 8 Shenton Way, 41-01 Temasek Tower, Singapore 068811; tel. 63110000; fax 62253943; Gen. Man. Michael Oliver.

Crédit Lyonnais (France): 3 Temasek Ave, 11-01 Centennial Tower, Singapore 039190; tel. 63336331; fax 63336332; Gen. Man. Pierre Eymery.

Crédit Suisse (Switzerland): 1 Raffles Link, 05-02, Singapore 039393; tel. 62126000; fax 62126200; e-mail ask.us@credit-suisse.com; internet www.cspb.com.sg; Br. Man. Didier von Daeniken.

Crédit Suisse First Boston (Switzerland): 1 Raffles Link, 03/04-01 South Lobby, Singapore 039393; tel. 62122000; fax 62123100; Br. Man. Eric M. Varvel.

Deutsche Bank AG (Germany): 6 Shenton Way, 15-08 DBS Bldg, Tower Two, Singapore 068809; tel. 64238001; fax 62259442; Gen. Man. Ronny Tan Chong Tee.

Dresdner Bank AG (Germany): 20 Collyer Quay, 22-00 Tung Centre, Singapore 049319; tel. 62228080; fax 62244008; Man. Dirs Andreas Ruschkowski, Raymond B. T. Koh, Piers Willis; CEO Baudouin Groonenberghs.

First Commercial Bank (Taiwan): 76 Shenton Way, 01-02 ONG Bldg, Singapore 079119; tel. 62215755; fax 62251905; e-mail fcbsin@singnet.com.sg; Gen. Man. Wu Ho-Li.

Fortis Bank SA/NV (Belgium/Netherlands): 63 Market St, 21-01, Singapore 048942; tel. 65394988; fax 65394933; Dep. Gen. Man. Ng Chuey Peng.

Habib Bank Ltd (Pakistan): 3 Phillip St, 01-03 Commerce Pt, Singapore 048693; tel. 64380055; fax 64380644; e-mail gmhbl@singnet.com.sg; Regional Gen. Man. Ashraf Mahmood Wathra.

HSBC Republic Bank (Suisse) SA (Switzerland): 21 Collyer Quay, 21-01 HSBC Bldg, Singapore 049320; tel. 62248080; fax 62237146; CEO Kenneth Sit Yiu Sun.

Industrial and Commercial Bank of China (People's Republic of China): 6 Raffles Quay, 12-01 John Hancock Tower, Singapore 048581; tel. 65381066; fax 65381370; e-mail icbcsg@icbc.com.sg; Gen. Man. Shi Qilu.

ING Bank NV (Netherlands): 9 Raffles Place, 19-02 Republic Plaza, Singapore 048619; tel. 65353688; fax 65338329; Country Head J. Kestemont.

KBC Bank NV (Belgium): 30 Cecil St, 12-01/08 Prudential Tower, Singapore 049712; tel. 63952828; fax 65342929; Gen. Man. Thierry Mezeret.

Korea Exchange Bank (Republic of Korea): 30 Cecil St, 24-03/08 Prudential Tower, Singapore 049712; tel. 65361633; fax 65382522; e-mail kebspore@singnet.com.sg; Gen. Man. Kim Seong Jung.

Landesbank Baden-Württemberg (Germany): 25 International Business Park, 01-72 German Centre, Singapore 609916; tel. 65627722; fax 65627729; Man. Dr Wolfhart Auer van Herrenkirchen.

Mizuho Corporate Bank Ltd (Japan): 168 Robinson Rd, 13-00 Capital Tower, Singapore 068912; tel. 64230330; fax 64230012; Gen. Man. Tadao Ogoshi.

Moscow Narodny Bank Ltd (UK): 50 Robinson Rd, MNB Bldg, Singapore 068882; tel. 62209422; fax 62250140; Man. Dir Evgeny Mikhailovich Grevtsev.

National Australia Bank Ltd (Australia): 5 Temasek Blvd, 15-01 Suntec City Tower Five, Singapore 038985; tel. 63380038; fax 63380039; Gen. Man. Cheo Chai Hong.

National Bank of Kuwait SAK (Kuwait): 9 Raffles Place, 51-01/02 Republic Plaza, Singapore 048619; tel. 62225348; fax 62245438; Gen. Man. R. J. McKegney.

Norddeutsche Landesbank Girozentrale (Germany): 6 Shenton Way, 16-08 DBS Bldg Tower Two, Singapore 068809; tel. 63231223; fax 63230223; e-mail nordlb.singapore@nordlb.com; Gen. Man. and Regional Head Asia/Pacific Heinz Werner Frings.

Northern Trust Company (USA): 1 George St, 12-06, Singapore 049145; tel. 64376666; fax 64376609; e-mail LA16@ntrs.com; Sr Vice-Pres. Lawrence Au.

Rabobank International (Netherlands): 77 Robinson Rd, 09-00 SIA Bldg, Singapore 068896; tel. 65363363; fax 65363236; Exec. Vice-Pres. Christian H. A. M. Mol.

Royal Bank of Scotland PLC (UK): 50 Raffles Place, 08-00 Singapore Land Tower, Singapore 048623; tel. 64168600; fax 62209827; Gen. Man. Alan Roy Goodyear.

San Paolo IMI SpA (Italy): 6 Temasek Blvd, 42/04-05 Suntec Tower Four, Singapore 038986; tel. 63338270; fax 63338252; e-mail singapore.sg@sanpaoloimi.com; Gen. Man. Lim Khai Seng.

Société Générale (France): 80 Robinson Rd, 25-00, Singapore 068898; tel. 62227122; fax 62252609; Chief Country Officer Eric Wormser.

State Street Bank and Trust Co (USA): 8 Shenton Way, 33-03 Temasek Tower, Singapore 068811; tel. 63299600; fax 62259377; Br. Man. Lee Yow Fee.

UBS AG (Switzerland): 5 Temasek Blvd, 18-00 Suntec City Tower, Singapore 038985; tel. 64318000; fax 64318188; e-mail rolf-w.gerber@wdr.com; Man. Dir and Head of Br. (Singapore) Brad Orgill.

UFJ Bank Ltd (Japan): 6 Raffles Quay, 24-01 John Hancock Tower, Singapore 048580; tel. 65384838; fax 65384636; Gen. Man. Toru Kojima.

UniCredito Italiano SpA (Italy): 80 Raffles Place, 51-01 UOB Plaza 1, Singapore 048624; tel. 62325728; fax 65344300; e-mail singaporebranch@gruppocredit.it; Gen. Man. Maurizio Brentegani.

WestLB AG (Germany): 3 Temasek Ave, 33-00 Centennial Tower, Singapore 039190; tel. 63332388; fax 63332399; Gen. Man. Teo Ee-Ngoh.

Offshore Banks

ABSA Bank Ltd (South Africa): 9 Temasek Blvd, 40-01 Suntec Tower Two, Singapore 038989; tel. 63331033; fax 63331066; Gen. Man. David Meadows.

Agricultural Bank of China (People's Republic of China): 80 Raffles Place, 27-20 UOB Plaza 2, Singapore 048624; tel. 65355255; fax 65387960; e-mail aboc@abchina.com.sg; Gen. Man. Sun Meiyu.

Arab Bank PLC (Jordan): 80 Raffles Place, 32-20 UOB Plaza 2, Singapore 048624; tel. 65330055; fax 65322150; e-mail abplc@pacific.net.com.sg; Exec. Vice-Pres. and Area Exec. Asia Pacific Kim Eun-Young.

Banca Monte dei Paschi di Siena SpA (Italy): 10 Collyer Quay, 13-01 Ocean Bldg, Singapore 0104; tel. 65352533; fax 65327996; Gen. Man. Giuseppe De Giosa.

Banca di Roma (Italy): 9 Raffles Place, 20-20 Republic Plaza II, Singapore 048619; tel. 64387509; fax 65352267; e-mail bdrsi@singnet.com.sg; Gen. Man. Mario Fattorusso.

Bank of Communications (People's Republic of China): 50 Raffles Place, 26-04 Singapore Land Tower, Singapore 048623; tel. 65320335; fax 65320339; Gen. Man. Niu Ke Rong.

PT Bank Mandiri (Persero) (Indonesia): 16 Collyer Quay, 28-00 Hitachi Tower, Singapore 049318; tel. 65320200; fax 65320206; Gen. Man. Muhadjir Sangidu.

Bank of New York (USA): 1 Temasek Ave, 02-01 Millenia Tower, Singapore 039192; tel. 64320222; fax 63374302; Sr Vice-Pres. and Man. Dir Jai Arya.

Bank of New Zealand (New Zealand): 5 Temasek Blvd, 15-01 Suntec City Tower, Singapore 038985; tel. 63322990; fax 63322991; Gen. Man. Cheo Chai Hong.

Bank of Taiwan (Taiwan): 80 Raffles Place, 28-20 UOB Plaza 2, Singapore 048624; tel. 65365536; fax 65368203; Gen. Man. Chiou Ye-Chin.

Bumiputra Commerce Bank Bhd (Malaysia): 7 Temasek Blvd, 37-01/02/03 Suntec Tower One, Singapore 038987; tel. 63375115; fax 63371335; e-mail bpsp3700@pacific.net.sg; Gen. Man. Raja Sulong Ahmad bin Raja Abdul Razak.

Canadian Imperial Bank of Commerce (Canada): 16 Collyer Quay, 04-02 Hitachi Tower, Singapore 049318; tel. 65352323; fax 65357565; Br. Man. Norman Sim Chee Beng.

Chang Hwa Commercial Bank Ltd (China): 1 Finlayson Green, 08-00, Singapore 049246; tel. 65320820; fax 65320374; Gen. Man. Yang Jih-Cheng.

China Construction Bank (People's Republic of China): 9 Raffles Place, 33-01/02 Republic Plaza, Singapore 048619; tel. 65358133; fax 65356533; e-mail enquiry@ccb.com.sg; internet www.ccb.com.sg; Gen. Man. Kong Yong Xin.

Chohung Bank (Republic of Korea): 50 Raffles Place, 04-02/03 Singapore Land Tower, Singapore 048623; tel. 65361144; fax 65331244; Gen. Man. Choi Heung Min.

Commonwealth Bank of Australia (Australia): 3 Temasek Ave, 20-01 Centennial Tower, Singapore 039190; tel. 63497000; fax 62245812; Gen. Man. Robert Lewis Buchan.

Crédit Industriel et Commercial (France): 63 Market St, 15-01, Singapore 048942; tel. 65366008; fax 65367008; internet www.cic.com.sg; Gen. Man. Jean-Luc Anglada.

SINGAPORE

Crédit Lyonnais (Suisse) SA (Switzerland): 3 Temasek Ave 11-01, Centennial Tower, Singapore 039190; tel. 68320900; fax 63338590; e-mail singaporebranch@creditlyonnais.ch; Man. Dir ANTOINE CANDIOTTI.

Dexia Banque Internationale à Luxembourg (Luxembourg): 9 Raffles Place, 42-01 Republic Plaza, Singapore 048619; tel. 62227622; fax 65360201; Gen. Man. ALEXANDRE JOSSET.

Deutsche Zentral Genossenschaftsbank (DZ Bank AG); Germany: 50 Raffles Place, 40-01 Singapore Land Tower, Singapore 048623; tel. 64380082; fax 62230082; Gen. Man. KLAUS GERHARD BORIG.

Hana Bank (Republic of Korea): 8 Cross St, 23-06 PWC Bldg, Singapore 048424; tel. 64384100; fax 64384200; Gen. Man. CHOI CHEONG-IL.

Hang Seng Bank Ltd (Hong Kong): 21 Collyer Quay, 14-01 HSBC Bldg, Singapore 049320; tel. 65363118; fax 65363148; e-mail sgp@hangseng.com; Country Man. ANTHONY KAM PING LEUNG.

HSH Nordbank AG (Germany): 3 Temasek Ave, 32-03 Centennial Tower, Singapore 039190; tel. 65509000; fax 65509003; e-mail info@hsh-nordbank.com.sg; Gen. Man. and Regional Head KLAUS HEINER BORITZKA.

Hua Nan Commercial Bank Ltd (Taiwan): 80 Robinson Rd, 14-03, Singapore 068898; tel. 63242566; fax 63242155; Gen. Man. OLIVER HSU.

ICICI Bank Ltd (India): 9 Raffles Place, 50-01 Republic Plaza, Singapore 048619; tel. 67239288; fax 67239268; internet www.icicibank.com.sg; Chief. Exec. SUVEK NAMBIAR.

International Commercial Bank of China (Taiwan): 6 Battery Rd, 39-03, Singapore 049909; tel. 62277667; fax 62271858; Vice-Pres. and Gen. Man. YEN-PING HSIANG.

Korea Development Bank (Republic of Korea): 8 Shenton Way, 07-01 Temasek Tower, Singapore 068811; tel. 62248188; fax 62256540; Gen. Man. KIM BYOUNG SOO.

Krung Thai Bank Public Co Ltd (Thailand): 65 Chulia St, 32-05/08 OCBC Centre, Singapore 049513; tel. 65336691; fax 65330930; e-mail ktbs@pacific.net.sg; Gen. Man. PUMIN LEELAYOOVA.

Land Bank of Taiwan: UOB Plaza 1, 34-01 Raffles Place, Singapore 048624; tel. 63494555; fax 63494545; Gen. Man. WILSON W. B. LIN.

Lloyds TSB Bank PLC (UK): 1 Temasek Ave 18-01, Millenia Tower, Singapore 039192; tel. 65341191; fax 65322493; e-mail mktg@lloydstsb.com.sg; internet www.lloydstsb.com.sg; Country Head BARRY LEA.

Mitsubishi Trust and Banking Corpn (Japan): 50 Raffles Place, 42-01/06 Singapore Land Tower, Singapore 048623; tel. 62259155; fax 62241857; Gen. Man. MIKIO KOBAYASHI.

Natexis Banques Populaires (France): 50 Raffles Place, 41-01, Singapore Land Tower, Singapore 048623; tel. 62241455; fax 62248651; Gen. Man. PHILIPPE PETITGAS.

Nedcor Bank Ltd (South Africa): 30 Cecil St, 10-05 Prudential Tower, Singapore 049712; tel. 64169438; fax 64388350; e-mail nedsing@nedcor.com; Gen. Man. BRIAN SHEGAR.

Nordea Bank Finland Plc (Finland): 3 Anson Rd, 22–01 Springleaf Tower, Singapore 079909; tel. 63176500; fax 63275616; e-mail singapore@nordea.com; Gen. Man. THOR ERLING KYLSTAD.

Norinchukin Bank (Japan): 80 Raffles Place, 53-01 UOB Plaza 1, Singapore 048624; tel. 65351011; fax 65352883; Gen. Man. YUJI SHIMAUCHI.

Den norske Bank ASA (Norway): 8 Shenton Way, 48-02 Temasek Tower, Singapore 068811; tel. 62206144; fax 62249743; e-mail dnb.singapore@dnb.no; Gen. Man. PÅL SKOE.

Philippine National Bank (Philippines): 96 Somerset Rd, 04-01/04 UOL Bldg, Singapore 238183; tel. 67374646; fax 67374224; e-mail singapore@pnb.com.ph; Vice-Pres. and Gen. Man. RODELO G. FRANCO.

Raiffeisen Zentralbank Oesterreich Aktiengesellschaft (Austria): 50 Raffles Place, 45-01 Singapore Land Tower, Singapore 048623; tel. 62259578; fax 62253973; Gen. Man. RAINER SILHAVY.

Royal Bank of Canada (Canada): 20 Raffles Place, 27-03/08 Ocean Towers, Singapore 048620; tel. 65369206; fax 65322804; Gen. Man. TREVOR DAVID WYNN.

Siam Commercial Bank Public Company Ltd (Thailand): 16 Collyer Quay, 25-01 Hitachi Tower, Singapore 049318; tel. 65364338; fax 65364728; Vice-Pres. and Gen. Man. NATTAPONG SAMIT AMPAIPISARN.

Skandinaviska Enskilda Banken AB Publ (Sweden): 50 Raffles Place, 36-01 Singapore Land Tower, Singapore 048623; tel. 62235644; fax 62253047; Gen. Man. SVEN BJÖRKMAN.

State Bank of India (India): 6 Shenton Way, 22-08 DBS Bldg Tower Two, Singapore 068809; tel. 62222033; fax 62253348; e-mail sbinsgsg@pacific.net.sg; CEO PADMA RAMASUBBAN.

Sumitomo Trust & Banking Co Ltd (Japan): 8 Shenton Way, 45-01 Temasek Tower, Singapore 068811; tel. 62249055; fax 62242873; Gen. Man. MASAYUKI IMANAKA.

Svenska Handelsbanken AB (publ) (Sweden): 65 Chulia St, 21-01/04 OCBC Centre, Singapore 049513; tel. 65323800; fax 65344909; Gen. Man. JAN BIRGER DJERF.

Toronto-Dominion (South East Asia) Ltd (Canada): 15-02 Millenia Tower, 1 Temasek Ave, Singapore 039192; tel. 64346000; fax 63369500; Br. Dir AKHILESHWAR LAMBA.

Union de Banques Arabes et Françaises (UBAF) (France): 6 Temasek Blvd, 25-04-05 Suntec Tower Four, Singapore 038986; tel. 63336188; fax 63336789; e-mail ubafsg@singnet.com.sg; Gen. Man. BENOIT GUEROULT.

Westpac Banking Corpn (Australia): 77 Robinson Rd, 19-00 SIA Bldg, Singapore 068896; tel. 65309898; fax 65326781; e-mail yhlee@westpac.wm.au; Gen. Man. CHRISTOPHER DAVID RAND.

Woori Bank (Republic of Korea): 5 Shenton Way, 17-03 UIC Bldg, Singapore 068808; tel. 62235855; fax 62259530; e-mail combksp@singnet.com.sg; Gen. Man. PARK DONG YOUNG.

Bankers' Association

Association of Banks in Singapore: 10 Shenton Way, 12-08 MAS Bldg, Singapore 079117; tel. 62244300; fax 62241785; e-mail banks@abs.org.sg; internet www.abs.org.sg; Chairs. WEE EE CHEONG, TERENCE ONG SEA ENG.

STOCK EXCHANGE

Singapore Exchange Limited (SGX): 2 Shenton Way, 19-00 SGX Centre One, Singapore 068804; tel. 62368888; fax 65356994; e-mail webmaster@sgx.com; internet www.sgx.com; f. 1999; est. as a result of the merger of the Stock Exchange of Singapore (SES, f. 1930) and the Singapore International Monetary Exchange Ltd (SIMEX, f. 1984); Chair. J. Y. PILLAY; CEO HSIEH FU HUA; Pres. ANG SWEE TIAN.

INSURANCE

The insurance industry is supervised by the Monetary Authority of Singapore (see Banking). In September 2004 there were 136 insurance companies, comprising 52 direct insurers (six life insurance, 39 general insurance, seven composite insurers), 29 professional reinsurers (three life reinsurers, 19 general reinsurers, seven composite reinsurers) and 55 captive insurers.

Domestic Companies

Life Insurance

The Asia Life Assurance Society Ltd: 2 Finlayson Green, 05-00 Asia Insurance Bldg, Singapore 049247; tel. 62243181; fax 62239120; e-mail asialife@asialife.com.sg; internet www.asialife.com.sg; f. 1948; Chair. TAN ENG HENG.

Axa Life Insurance Singapore Pte Ltd: 143 Cecil St, 03-01/10 GB Bldg, Singapore 069542; tel. 68805500; fax 68805501; e-mail comsvc@axa-life.com.sg; internet www.axa-life.com.sg; Prin. Officer GARY HARVEY.

China Life Insurance Co Ltd: 105 Cecil St, 18-00 and 19-00 The Octagon, Singapore 069534; tel. 62222366; fax 62221033; Prin. Officer SHEN NAN NING.

Manulife (Singapore) Pte Ltd: 491B River Valley Rd, 07-00 Valley Pt, Singapore 248373; tel. 67371221; fax 62359158; e-mail service@manulife.com; internet www.manulife.com.sg; acquired John Hancock Life Assurance Co Ltd in Dec. 2004; Pres. and CEO PHILLIP HAMPDEN-SMITH.

UOB Life Assurance Ltd: 156 Cecil St, 10-01 Far Eastern Bank Bldg, Singapore 069544; tel. 62278477; fax 62243012; e-mail uoblife@uobgroup.com; internet www.uoblife.com.sg; Man. Dir RAYMOND KWOK CHONG SEE.

General Insurance

Allianz Insurance Company of Singapore Pte Ltd: 3 Temasek Ave, 09-01 Centennial Tower, Singapore 039190; tel. 62972529; fax 62971956; e-mail askme@allianz.com.sg; internet www.allianz.com.sg; formed by merger between Allianz Insurance (Singapore) Pte Ltd and AGF Insurance (Singapore) Pte Ltd; Man. Dir ROWAN D'ARCY.

Asia Insurance Co Ltd: 2 Finlayson Green, 03-00 Asia Insurance Bldg, Singapore 049247; tel. 62243181; fax 62214355; e-mail asiains@asiainsurance.com.sg; internet www.asiainsurance.com.sg; f. 1923; cap. p.u. S $75m.; Prin. Officer and Exec. Dir LARRY CHAN; Gen. Man. TAN KAH HO.

Asian Securitization and Infrastructure Assurance (Pte) Ltd: 9 Temasek Blvd, 38-01 Suntec Tower 2, Singapore 038989; tel. 63342555; fax 63342777; e-mail general@asialtd.com; Dir ELEANOR L. LIPSEY.

SINGAPORE

Directory

Axa Insurance Singapore Pte Ltd: 143 Cecil St, 01-01 GB Bldg, Singapore 069542; tel. 68804741; fax 68804740; e-mail customer.service@axa.com.sg; internet www.axa.com.sg; CEO BERNARD MARSEILLE.

Cosmic Insurance Corpn Ltd: 410 North Bridge Rd, 04-01 Cosmic Insurance Bldg, Singapore 188726; tel. 63387633; fax 63397805; e-mail query@cosmic.com.sg; internet www.cosmic.com.sg; f. 1971; Gen. Man. SWEE LEE CHUN.

ECICS-COFACE Guarantee Co (Singapore) Ltd: 7 Temasek Blvd, 11-01 Suntec City Tower 1, Singapore 038987; tel. 63374779; fax 63389267; e-mail ecics@ecics.com.sg; internet www.ecics.com.sg; Chair. KWAH THIAM HOCK; Asst Vice-Pres. JONATHAN TANG.

First Capital Insurance Ltd: 6 Raffles Quay 21-00, Singapore 048580; tel. 62222311; fax 62223547; e-mail enquiry@first-insurance.com.sg; internet www.first-insurance.com.sg; Gen. Man. RAMASWAMY ATHAPPAN.

India International Insurance Pte Ltd: 64 Cecil St, 04-00/05-00 IOB Bldg, Singapore 049711; tel. 62238122; fax 62244174; e-mail insure@iii.com.sg; internet www.iii.com.sg; f. 1987; all non-life insurance; Chair. HWANG SOO JIN; CEO R. ATHAPPAN.

Kemper International Insurance Co (Pte) Ltd: 3 Shenton Way, 22-09 Shenton House, Singapore 068805; tel. 68369120; fax 68369121; e-mail vchia@kemper.com.sg; internet www.kemper.com.sg; Gen. Man. VIOLET CHIA.

Liberty Citystate Insurance Pte Ltd: 51 Club St, 03-00 Singapore 069428; tel. 62218611; fax 62263360; e-mail koh.peter@libertycitystate.com.sg; internet www.libertycitystate.com.sg; fmrly Citystate Insurance Pte Ltd; Man. Dir PETER KOH TIEN HOE.

Mitsui Sumitomo Insurance (Singapore) Pte Ltd: 16 Raffles Quay, 24-01 Hong Leong Bldg, Singapore 048581; tel. 62209644; fax 62256371; internet www.ms-ins.com.sg; fmrly Mitsui Marine and Fire Insurance (Asia) Private Ltd; merged with The Sumitomo Marine and Fire Insurance Co Ltd and name changed as above in 2001; Man. Dir YOSHIO IIJIMA; Dep. Gen. Man. NOBORI OMORI.

SHC Capital Ltd: 302 Orchard Rd, 09-01 Tong Bldg, Singapore 238862; tel. 68299199; fax 68299249; e-mail tnicl@nanyanginsurance.com.sg; internet www.nanyanginsurance.com.sg; f. 1956; fmrly The Nanyang Insurance Co Ltd; name changed as above following takeover in June 2004; Dir and Prin. Officer FREDDIE YEO.

Overseas Union Insurance Ltd: 50 Collyer Quay, 02-02 Overseas Union House, Singapore 049321; tel. 62251133; fax 62246307; internet www.oub.com.sg; f. 1956; in early 2006 was in the process of winding down all operations; Gen. Man. PETER YAP KIM KEE; Asst Gen. Man. YEO TIAN CHU.

Royal & Sun Alliance Insurance (Singapore) Ltd: 77 Robinson Rd, 17-00 SIA Bldg, Singapore 068896; tel. 64230888; fax 64230798; e-mail customer.service@sg.royalsun.com; internet www.royalsunalliance.com.sg; Man. Dir and CEO EDMUND LIM.

Singapore Aviation and General Insurance Co (Pte) Ltd: 25 Airline Rd, 06-A Airline House, Singapore 819829; tel. 65423333; fax 65450221; f. 1976; Man. Dir AMARJIT KAUR SIDHU.

Standard Steamship Owners' Protection and Indemnity Association (Asia) Ltd: 140 Cecil St, 10-02 PIL Bldg, Singapore 069540; tel. 62211060; fax 62211082; e-mail central@ctg-ap.com; internet www.standard-club.com; Prin. Officer DAVID ALWYN.

Tenet Insurance Co Ltd: 10 Collyer Quay, 04-01 Ocean Bldg, Singapore 049315; tel. 65326022; fax 65333871; Chair. ONG CHOO ENG.

The Tokio Marine & Fire Insurance Co (Singapore) Pte Ltd: 6 Shenton Way, 23-08 DBS Bldg Tower Two, Singapore 068809; tel. 62216111; fax 62240895; Man. Dir KYOZO HANAJIMA.

United Overseas Insurance Ltd: 156 Cecil St, 09-01 Far Eastern Bank Bldg, Singapore 069544; tel. 62227733; fax 63273870; e-mail contactus@uoi.com.sg; internet www.uoi.com.sg; f. 1971; Man. Dir DAVID CHAN MUN WAI.

Yasuda Fire and Marine Insurance Co (Asia) Pte Ltd: 50 Raffles Place, 03-03 Singapore Land Tower, Singapore 048623; tel. 62235293; fax 62257947; e-mail yasudaqa@yasudaasia.com; internet www.yasudaasia.com; f. 1989; Man. Dir and Gen. Man. KOJI OTSUKA.

Zürich Insurance (Singapore) Pte Ltd: 78 Shenton Way, 06-01, Singapore 079120; tel. 62202466; fax 62255749; Prin. Officer and Man. Dir RONALD CHENG JUE SENG.

Composite Insurance

American International Assurance Co Ltd: 1 Robinson Rd, AIA Tower, Singapore 048542; tel. 62918000; fax 65385802; internet www.aia.com.sg; Prin. Officer MARK O'DELL.

Aviva Ltd: 4 Shenton Way, 01-01 SGX Centre 2, Singapore 068807; tel. 68277988; fax 68277900; internet www.aviva-singapore.com.sg; Prin. Officer KEITH PERKINS.

Great Eastern Life Assurance Co Ltd: 1 Pickering St, 13-01 Great Eastern Centre, Singapore 048659; tel. 62482000; fax 65322214; e-mail wecare@lifeisgreat.com.sg; internet www.lifeisgreat.com.sg; f. 1908; Dir and CEO TAN BENG LEE.

HSBC Insurance (Singapore) Pte Ltd: 3 Killiney Rd, 10-01/09, Winsland House 1, Singapore 239519; tel. 62256111; fax 62212188; internet www.insurance.hsbc.com.sg; Prin. Officer JASON DOMINIC SADLER.

NTUC Income Insurance Co-operative Ltd: 75 Bras Basah Rd, NTUC Income Centre, Singapore 189557; tel. 63363322; fax 63381500; e-mail inbox@income.wm.sg; internet www.income.com.sg; CEO TAN KIN LIAN; Gen. Man. ALOYSIUS TEO SENG LEE.

Overseas Assurance Corpn Ltd: 1 Pickering St, 13-01 Great Eastern Centre, Singapore 048659; tel. 62482000; fax 65322214; e-mail general@oac.com.sg; internet www.oac.com.sg; f. 1920; fully-owned subsidiary of Great Eastern Holdings; Chair. MICHAEL WONG PAKSHONG.

Prudential Assurance Co Singapore (Pte) Ltd: 30 Cecil St, 30-01 Prudential Tower, Singapore 049712; tel. 65358988; fax 65354043; e-mail customer.service@prudential.com.sg; internet www.prudential.com.sg; CEO TAN SUEE CHIEH.

Associations

General Insurance Association of Singapore: 112 Robinson Rd, 05-03 HB Robinson, Singapore 068902; tel. 62218788; fax 62272051; internet www.gia.org.sg; f. 1965; Pres. TERENCE TAN; Vice-Pres. STELLA TAN.

Life Insurance Association, Singapore: 20 Cross St, 02-07/08 China Court, China Sq. Central, Singapore 048422; tel. 64388900; fax 64386989; e-mail lia@lia.org.sg; internet www.lia.org.sg; f. 1967; Pres. JASON SADLER.

Reinsurance Brokers' Association: 69 Amoy St, Singapore 069888; tel. 63723189; fax 62241091; e-mail secretariat@rbas.org.sg; internet www.rbas.org.sg; f. 1995; Chair. RICHARD AUSTEN.

Singapore Insurance Brokers' Association: 138 Cecil St, 15-00 Cecil Court, Singapore 069538; tel. 62227777; fax 62220022; e-mail siba@stcsamasmgt.com.sg; Pres. ANTHONY LIM; Vice-Pres. DAVID LUM.

Singapore Reinsurers' Association: 85 Amoy St, Singapore 069904; tel. 63247388; fax 62248910; e-mail secretariat@sraweb.org.sg; internet www.sraweb.org.sg; f. 1979; Chair. CHRISTOPHER HO.

Trade and Industry

GOVERNMENT AGENCIES

Housing and Development Board: 480 Lorong 6, Toa Payoh, Singapore 310480; tel. 64901111; fax 63972070; e-mail hdbmailbox@hdb.gov.sg; internet www.hdb.gov.sg; f. 1960; public housing authority; Chair. Dr ALINE WONG.

Singapore Land Authority (SLA): 8 Shenton Way, 26-01 Temasek Tower, Singapore 068811; tel. 63239829; fax 63239937; e-mail SLA_enquiry@sla.gov.sg; internet www.sla.gov.sg; responsible for management and development of state land resources; Chair. LIEW HENG SAN.

Urban Redevelopment Authority (URA): 45 Maxwell Rd, URA Centre, Singapore 069118; tel. 62216666; fax 62275069; e-mail ura_email@ura.gov.sg; internet www.ura.gov.sg; statutory board; responsible for national planning; Chair. BOBBY CHIN; CEO CHEONG-CHUA KOON HEAN.

DEVELOPMENT ORGANIZATIONS

Agency for Science, Technology and Research (A*STAR): 20 Biopolis Way 01-03, Singapore 138668; tel. 68266111; fax 67771711; e-mail astar_contact@a-star.gov.sg; internet www.a-star.gov.sg; f. 1990; fmrly National Science and Technology Board; statutory board; responsible for the development of science and technology; Chair. PHILIP YEO; Man. Dir BOON SWAN FOO.

Applied Research Corpn (ARC): independent non-profit-making research and consultancy org. aiming to facilitate and enhance the use of technology and expertise from the tertiary institutions to benefit industry, businesses and joint institutions.

Asian Infrastructure Fund (AIF): Singapore; f. 1994; promotes and directs investment into regional projects; Chair. MOEEN QURESHI.

Economic Development Board (EDB): 250 North Bridge Rd, 24-00 Raffles City Tower, Singapore 179101; tel. 68326832; fax 68326565; e-mail webmaster@edb.gov.sg; internet www.edb.gov.sg; f. 1961; statutory body for industrial planning, development

SINGAPORE

and promotion of investments in manufacturing, services and local business; Chair. TEO MING KIAN; Man. Dir KO KHENG HWA.

Government of Singapore Investment Corp Pte Ltd (GSIC): 168 Robinson Rd, 37-01 Capital Tower, Singapore 068912; tel. 68898888; fax 68898722; e-mail contactus@gic.com.sg; internet www.gic.com.sg; f. 1981; Man. Dir LEE EK TIENG.

Infocomm Development Authority of Singapore (IDA): see under Telecommunications.

International Enterprise Singapore: 230 Victoria St, 07-00 Bugis Junction Office Tower, Singapore 188024; tel. 63376628; fax 63376898; e-mail enquiry@iesingapore.gov.sg; internet www.iesingapore.gov.sg; f. 1983; formed to develop and expand international trade; fmrly Trade Development Board; statutory body; Chair. STEPHEN LEE; CEO LEE YI SHYAN.

Jurong Town Corpn (JTC): The JTC Summit, 8 Jurong Town Hall Rd, Singapore 609434; tel. 65600056; fax 65655301; e-mail askjtc@jtc.gov.sg; internet www.jtc.gov.sg; f. 1968; statutory body responsible for planning, promoting and developing industrial space; Chair. SOO KOK LENG; CEO CHONG LIT CHEONG.

Singapore Productivity and Standards Board (PSB): PSB Bldg, 2 Bukit Merah Central, Singapore 159835; tel. 62786666; fax 62786667; e-mail queries@psb.gov.sg; internet www.psb.gov.sg; f. 1996; est. following merger of Singapore Institute of Standards and Industrial Research and the National Productivity Board; carries out activities in areas including workforce development, training, productivity and innovation promotion, standards development, ISO certification, quality programmes and consultancy, technology application, product and process development, system and process automation services, testing services, patent information, development assistance for small and medium-sized enterprises; Chief Exec. LEE SUAN HIANG.

CHAMBERS OF COMMERCE

Singapore Business Federation (SBF): 10 Hoe Chiang Rd, 22-01 Keppel Towers, 089315 Singapore; tel. 68276828; fax 68276807; e-mail webmaster@sbf.org.sg; internet www.sbf.org.sg; f. 2002 as result of restructuring of Singapore Federation of Chambers of Commerce and Industry; Chair. STEPHEN LEE; mems include the following:

Singapore Chinese Chamber of Commerce and Industry: 47 Hill St, 09-00 Singapore 179365; tel. 63378381; fax 63390605; e-mail corporate@sccci.org.sg; internet www.sccci.org.sg; f. 1906; promotes trade and industry and economic development of Singapore.

Singapore Indian Chamber of Commerce and Industry: 101 Cecil St, 23-01/04 Tong Eng Bldg, Singapore 069533; tel. 62222855; fax 62231707; e-mail sicci@sicci.com; internet www.sicci.com; Exec. Dir PREDEEP KUMAR MENON.

Singapore International Chamber of Commerce: 6 Raffles Quay, 10-01 John Hancock Tower, Singapore 048580; tel. 62241255; fax 62242785; e-mail general@sicc.com; internet www.sicc.com.sg; f. 1837; Chair. RENATO S. SIRTORI.

Singapore Malay Chamber of Commerce: 72A Bussorah St, Singapore 199485; tel. 62979296; fax 63924527; e-mail smcci@smcci.org.sg; internet www.smcci.org.sg; Pres. Dato' MOHAMAD ZAIN ABDULLAH.

Singapore Manufacturers' Federation (SMa): The Enterprise 02-02, 1 Science Centre Rd, Singapore 609077; tel. 68263000; fax 68228828; e-mail hq@smafederation.org.sg; internet www.smafederation.org.sg; f. 1932 as Singapore Manufacturers' Association; renamed Singapore Confederation of Industries in 1996; name changed as above in 2002; Pres. LEW SYN PAU; Sec.-Gen. Dr ROGER LOW.

INDUSTRIAL AND TRADE ASSOCIATIONS

Association of Singapore Marine Industries (ASMI): 1 Maritime Sq., 09-54 Harbour Front Centre, Singapore 099253; tel. 62704730; fax 62731867; e-mail asmi@pacific.net.sg; internet www.asmi.com; f. 1968; 12 hon. mems, 70 assoc. mems, 51 ord. mems (Oct. 2003); Pres. MICHAEL CHEA; Exec. Dir WINNIE LOW.

Singapore Commodity Exchange (SICOM): 111 North Bridge Rd, 23-04/05 Peninsula Plaza, Singapore 179098; tel. 63385600; fax 63389116; e-mail marketing@sicom.com.sg; internet www.sicom.com.sg; f. 1968 as Rubber Association of Singapore; adopted present name 1994; to regulate, promote, develop and supervise commodity futures trading in Singapore, including the establishment and dissemination of official prices for various grades and types of rubber; provides clearing facilities; endorses certificates of origin and licences for packers, shippers and mfrs; Chair. LIM HOW TECK; Gen. Man. LIM TOH ENG.

EMPLOYERS' ORGANIZATION

Singapore National Employers' Federation: Keppel Towers 22-00, 10 Hoe Chiang Rd, Singapore; tel. 68276827; fax 68276800; e-mail webmaster@snef.org.sg; internet www.sgemployers.com; f. 1948; Pres. STEPHEN LEE CHING YEN; Vice-Pres ALEX CHAN, BOB TAN BENG HAI, LANDIS W. HICKS.

UTILITIES

Electricity and Gas

Singapore Power Ltd: 111 Somerset Rd 10-01, Singapore Power Bldg, Singapore 238164; tel. 68238888; fax 68238188; e-mail corpcomms@singaporepower.com.sg; internet www.spower.com.sg; incorporated in 1995 to take over the piped gas and electricity utility operations of the Public Utilities Board (see Water), which now acts as a regulatory authority for the privately owned cos; 100% owned by government holding company, Temasek Holdings Pte Ltd; subsidiaries include PowerGrid, PowerGas, Power Supply, Singapore Power International, Development Resources, Power Automation, SP E-Services, SP Systems, Singapore District Cooling and SP Telecommunications; Chair. NG KEE CHOE; CEO QUEK POH HUAT.

Water

Public Utilities Board: 111 Somerset Rd 15-01, Singapore 238164; tel. 62358888; fax 67313020; e-mail pub_pr@pub.gov.sg; internet www.pub.gov.sg; statutory board responsible for water supply; manages Singapore's water system to optimize use of water resources, develops additional water sources; Chair. TAN GEE PAW.

TRADE UNIONS

At the end of 2003 there were 68 employees' trade unions and associations, with 417,166 members, and three employer unions, with 2,052 members.

In December 1998 the largest private-sector union, the United Workers of Electronics and Electrical Industries, had 40,433 members, while the largest public-sector union, the Amalgamated Union of Public Employees, had 20,872 members.

National Trades Union Congress (NTUC): NTUC Centre, 1 Marina Blvd B1-01, Singapore 018989; tel. 62138008; fax 63273740; e-mail bizcentre@ntuc.org.sg; internet www.ntuc.org.sg; f. 1961; 63 affiliated unions, 6 affiliated associates and 458,379 mems (Dec. 2005); Pres. JOHN DE PAYVA; Sec.-Gen. LIM BOON HENG.

Transport

RAILWAYS

In 1993 there was 26 km of 1-m gauge railway, linked with the Malaysian railway system and owned by the Malayan Railway Pentadbiran Keretapi Tanah Melayu—KTM. The main line crosses the Johor causeway (1.2 km) and terminates near Keppel Harbour. Branch lines link it with the industrial estate at Jurong.

Construction began in 1983 on the Mass Rapid Transit (MRT) system. The first section was completed in 1987, and the remaining sections by 1990. The system extends for 83 km and consists of two lines with 48 stations (32 elevated, 15 under ground and one at ground level). The construction of a further 20-km line, the North–East Line, began in 1997; the line has 16 stations and one depot, and was completed in 2003. In 2002 the extension of the East–West line to Changi Airport was completed; the Changi Airport Line (CAL) has one underground and one elevated station. In the early 2000s construction was under way on the Circle Line, a 34-km orbital line running entirely under ground which was to link all the radial lines into the city. The line was to start at Dhoby Ghaut and terminate at Harbour Front and was to be implemented in five stages, the last of which was scheduled for completion in 2010.

Singapore's first Light Rapid Transit (LRT) system, the Bukit Panjang LRT (a 7.8-km line with 14 stations), was completed in April 1998. In January 2003 an LRT line in Sengkang also became operational, and work on a further LRT line, in Punggol, was completed in 2004.

Land Transport Authority: 1 Hampshire Rd, Singapore 219428; tel. 63757100; fax 63757200; internet www.lta.gov.sg; Chair. FOCK SIEW WAH; Chief Exec. Maj.-Gen. HAN ENG JUAN.

ROADS

In 1999 Singapore had a total of 3,066 km of roads, of which 150 km were motorway; in that year 100% of the road network was paved. In 1990 the Government introduced a quota system to control the number of vehicles using the roads. A manual road-pricing system was introduced on one expressway in June 1996 and extended to two further expressways in May 1997. It was replaced by a system of Electronic Road Pricing (ERP) in 1998, whereby each vehicle was charged according to road use in congested areas. The ERP was first introduced on one expressway in April 1998, and was subsequently extended to include two other expressways and the Area Licensing Scheme gantry areas by early September of that year. In 2001 construction of the 12-km Kallang–Paya Lebar expressway began; an estimated 9 km of the expressway was to be under ground, which would render it the longest underground expressway in South-East Asia. It was scheduled for completion in 2007, and was expected to cost approximately S $1,800m.

SHIPPING

The Port of Singapore is the world's busiest in tonnage terms; Singapore handled an estimated 135,386 vessels with a total displacement of 986.4m. grt in 2003.

The Port of Singapore Authority operates six cargo terminals: Tanjong Pagar Terminal, Keppel Terminal, Brani Terminal, Pasir Panjang Terminal, Sembawang Terminal and Jurong Port.

Tanjong Pagar Terminal and Keppel Terminal have the capacity to handle 10.7m. 20-foot equivalent units (TEUs).

The third container terminal, Brani, built on an offshore island connected to the mainland by a causeway, has a capacity of 5.5m. TEUs.

Pasir Panjang Terminal, Singapore's main gateway for conventional cargo (particularly timber and rubber), has five deep-water berths and eight coastal berths and 17 lighter berths.

Sembawang Terminal has three deep-water berths and one coastal berth. This terminal is the main gateway for car carriers as well as handling steel and timber products.

Jurong Port (which handles general and dry-bulk cargo, is situated in south-western Singapore, and serves the Jurong Industrial Estate) has 20 deep-water berths and one coastal berth.

A new container terminal, at Pasir Panjang, was officially opened in 2000, following the completion of the second of four planned phases of building work. Upon completion, scheduled for 2009, the terminal was to have 49 berths and a handling capacity of 35m. TEUs.

Maritime and Port Authority of Singapore: 460 Alexandra Rd, 18-00 PSA Bldg, Singapore 119963; tel. 63751600; fax 62759247; e-mail mpa@mpa.gov.sg; internet www.mpa.gov.sg; f. 1996; regulatory body responsible for promotion and development of the port, overseeing all port and maritime matters in Singapore; Chair. PETER ONG BOON KWEE; Chief Exec. TAY LIM HENG.

Port of Singapore Authority: 460 Alexandra Rd, 36-00 PSA Bldg, Singapore 119963; tel. 62747111; fax 62795713; e-mail ccd1@psa.com.sg; internet www.singaporepsa.com; f. 1964 as a statutory board under the Ministry of Communications; made a corporate entity in 1997 in preparation for privatization; responsible for the provision and maintenance of port facilities and services; Chair. Dr YEO NING HONG; Pres. KHOO TENG CHYE.

Major Shipping Companies

American President Lines Ltd (APL): 456 Alexandra Rd, 08-00 NOL Bldg, Singapore 119962; tel. 62789000; fax 62742113; e-mail hung-song-goh@apl.com; internet www.apl.com; container services to North and South Asia, the USA and the Middle East; COO ED ALDRIDGE.

Glory Ship Management Private Ltd: 24 Raffles Place 17-01/02, Clifford Centre, Singapore 048621; tel. 65361986; fax 65361987; e-mail gene@gloryship.com.sg.

Guan Guan Shipping Pte Ltd: 2 Finlayson Green, 13-05 Asia Insurance Bldg, Singapore 049247; tel. 65343988; fax 62276776; e-mail golden@golden.com.sg; f. 1955; shipowners and agents; cargo services to East and West Malaysia, Indonesia, Pakistan, Sri Lanka, Bengal Bay ports, Persian (Arabian) Gulf ports, Hong Kong and China; Man. Dir RICHARD THIO.

IMC Shipping Co Pte Ltd: 5 Temasek Blvd, 12-01 Suntec City Tower, Singapore 038985; tel. 63362233; fax 63379715; e-mail biz@imcpaa.com; internet www.imcshipping.com; Man. Dir PETER CHEW.

Nedlloyd Lines Singapore Pte Ltd: 138 Robinson Rd, 01-00 Hong Leong Centre, Singapore 068906; tel. 62218989; fax 62255267; f. 1963; Gen. Man. F. C. SCHUCHARD.

Neptune Orient Lines Ltd: 456 Alexandra Rd, 05-00 NOL Bldg, Singapore 119962; tel. 62789000; fax 62784900; e-mail nol_group_corp_comms@nol.com.sg; internet www.nol.com.sg; f. 1968; liner containerized services on the Far East/Europe, Far East/North America, Straits/Australia, South Asia/Europe and South-East Asia, Far East/Mediterranean routes; tankers, bulk carriers and dry cargo vessels on charter; 36% govt-owned; Chair. CHENG WAI KEUNG; Group Pres. and CEO DAVID LIM.

New Straits Shipping Co Pte Ltd: 51 Anson Rd, 09-53 Anson Centre, Singapore 0207; tel. 62201007; fax 62240785.

Ocean Tankers (Pte) Ltd: 41 Tuas Rd, Singapore 638497; tel. 68632202; fax 68639480; e-mail admin@oceantankers.com.sg; Marine Supt V. LIM.

Osprey Maritime Ltd: 8 Cross St, 24-02/03 PWC Bldg, Singapore 048424; tel. 62129722; fax 65570450; CEO PETER GEORGE COSTALAS.

Pacific International Lines (Pte) Ltd: 140 Cecil St, 03-00 PIL Bldg, POB 3206, Singapore 069540; tel. 62218133; fax 62273933; e-mail sherry.chua@sgp.pilship.com; shipowners, agents and managers; liner services to South-East Asia, the Far East, India, the Red Sea, the Persian (Arabian) Gulf, West and East Africa; container services to South-East Asia; world-wide chartering, freight forwarding, container manufacturing, depot operators, container freight station operator; Exec. Chair. Y. C. CHANG; Man. Dir S. S. TEO.

Petroships Private Ltd: 460 Alexandra Rd, 25-04 PSA Bldg, Singapore 119963; tel. 62731122; fax 62732200; e-mail gen@petroships.com.sg; Man. Dir KENNETH KEE.

Singa Ship Management Private Ltd: 78 Shenton Way 16-02, Singapore 079120; tel. 62244308; fax 62235848; e-mail agency@singaship.com.sg; Chair. OLE HEGLAND; Man. Dir EILEEN LEONG.

Syabas Tankers Pte Ltd: 10 Anson Rd, 34-10 International Plaza, Singapore 0207; tel. 62259522.

Tanker Pacific Management (Singapore) Private Ltd: 1 Temasek Ave, 38-01 Millenia Tower, Singapore; tel. 63365211; fax 63375570; Man. Dir HUGH HUNG.

CIVIL AVIATION

Singapore's international airport at Changi was opened in 1981. Construction on a third terminal at Changi, solely for the use of budget carriers, was completed in January 2006, and became operational in March of that year, thereby increasing the airport's total capacity to 64m. passengers a year. A second airport at Seletar operates as a base for charter and training flights.

Civil Aviation Authority of Singapore: Singapore Changi Airport, POB 1, Singapore 918141; tel. 65421122; fax 65421231; e-mail thennarasee_R@caas.gov.sg; internet www.caas.gov.sg; responsible for regulatory and advisory services, air services development, airport management and development and airspace management and organization; Chair. TJONG YIK MIN; Dir-Gen. WONG WOON LIONG.

SilkAir: 77 Robinson Rd, 25-01 SIA Bldg, Singapore 068896; tel. 65428111; fax 65426286; internet www.silkair.com; f. 1975; fmrly Tradewinds Private; wholly owned subsidiary of Singapore Airlines Ltd; began scheduled services in 1989; Chair. CHEW CHOON SENG; Gen. Man. PAUL TAN.

Singapore Airlines Ltd (SIA): 7D Airline House, 25 Airline Rd, Singapore 819829; tel. 65415880; fax 65423002; e-mail investor_relations@singaporeair.com.sg; internet www.singaporeair.com; f. 1972; passenger services to 88 destinations in 42 countries; Chair. STEPHEN LEE CHING YEN; CEO CHEW CHOON SENG.

Tiger Airways: Singapore Changi Airport, POB 82, Singapore 918143; tel. 65384437; fax 65807564; internet www.tigerairways.com; f. 2003; 49%-owned by Singapore Airlines, 24%-owned by US co Indigo Partners, 11%-owned by Temasek Holdings Pte Ltd; services to 10 regional destinations; Chair. WILLIAM FRANKE; CEO TONY DAVIS.

ValuAir: POB 323, Singapore 918144; tel. 68222288; e-mail feedback@valuair.com.sg; internet www.valuair.com.sg; f. 2003; regional destinations; Chair. LIM CHIN BENG.

Tourism

Singapore's tourist attractions include its blend of cultures and excellent shopping facilities. In April 2005 the Government approved draft legislation to permit gambling on the island for the first time in 40 years. The new law opened the way for the construction of two major casino resorts, at Marina Bay and on Sentosa Island. The resorts were scheduled to become operational by 2009 and were expected significantly to boost the number of visitors to Singapore. Tourist arrivals totalled 8,942,408 in 2005. Receipts from tourism (excluding passenger transport) totalled S $3,998m. in 2003.

Singapore Tourism Board: Tourism Court, 1 Orchard Spring Lane, Singapore 247729; tel. 67366622; fax 67369423; e-mail feedback@stb.com.sg; internet www.stb.com.sg; f. 1964; Chair. SIMON ISRAEL; Dep. Chair. and Chief Exec. LIM NEO CHIAN.

SLOVAKIA

Introductory Survey

Location, Climate, Language, Religion, Flag, Capital

The Slovak Republic (formerly a constituent republic of the Czech and Slovak Federative Republic, or Czechoslovakia) is a land-locked state located in central Europe, bordered to the north by Poland, to the east by Ukraine, to the south by Hungary, to the west by Austria and to the north-west by the Czech Republic. The climate is typically continental, with cold, dry winters and hot, humid summers. Average temperatures in Bratislava range from −0.7°C (30.7°F) in January to 21.1°C (70.0°F) in July. Average annual rainfall in the capital is 649 mm (26 ins). The official language is Slovak, although Hungarian, Czech and other languages are also spoken. The major religion is Christianity, the Roman Catholic Church being the largest denomination, followed by the Evangelical Church of the Augsburg (Lutheran) Confession. The national flag (proportions 2 by 3) consists of three equal horizontal stripes, of white, blue and red; in the centre hoist there is a white-rimmed red shield containing a silver archiepiscopal (double-barred) cross surmounted on the central (and highest) of three blue hillocks. The capital is Bratislava.

Recent History

Slovaks and Czechs (who are closely related members of the western Slavic peoples) were first united in the ninth century AD, in the Great Moravian Empire, but were divided following the Empire's dissolution in 907. While the Slovaks came under Hungarian rule (which was to last, in different forms, until the early 20th century), the Czechs established a kingdom that remained an important political force until the incorporation of the Czech Lands into the Habsburg Empire in the 16th and 17th centuries.

A movement of nationalist revival, closely linked with a similar movement in the Czech Lands, evolved in Slovakia in the late 18th and 19th centuries. During the First World War (1914–18) Slovaks joined with Czechs in campaigning for an independent state, which would be composed of the Czech Lands and Slovakia. The Republic of Czechoslovakia was established on 28 October 1918, as one of the successor states to the Austro-Hungarian Empire. The country's boundaries were defined by the Treaty of Trianon of 1920, under which a large Hungarian minority was incorporated into Slovakia. Czechoslovakia's first Constitution, promulgated in 1920, made no provision for a proper federal system, and Slovak proposals for self-government were rejected by the central authorities in the capital, Prague. A further cause of Slovak disaffection was the fact that the Czech Lands were the focus of the country's economic development, while Slovakia remained comparatively undeveloped. There was also an ideological divide between the two parts of the country: while the majority of Slovaks were strict Roman Catholics, the central Government in Prague was professedly anticlerical.

In October 1938, following the Munich Agreement of 29 September (whereby the predominantly German-populated areas of Czechoslovakia were ceded to Germany), nationalists declared Slovak autonomy. On 14 March 1939, one day before Nazi armed forces occupied the Czech Lands, Adolf Hitler agreed to the establishment of a separate Slovak state, under the pro-Nazi 'puppet' regime of Fr Jozef Tiso. Under the wartime Slovak state any opposition to the Tiso regime was ruthlessly suppressed, and the treatment of Jews was particularly severe. In August 1944 an armed resistance (the Slovak National Uprising) against Tiso's regime was begun, but it was suppressed within two months by German troops.

Following the restoration of the Czechoslovak state in 1945, at the end of the Second World War, certain concessions were made to Slovak demands for autonomy, including the establishment of a regional legislature with restricted powers (the Slovenská národná rada—Slovak National Council) and an executive, both in Bratislava, the Slovak capital. However, communists (led by Gustav Husák) seized power in Slovakia in late 1947, and in the whole of the country in 1948. In May 1948 a new Constitution was approved, which declared Czechoslovakia to be a 'people's democracy'. The communists' consolidation of power was completed in the following month with the election to the post of President of Klement Gottwald, a Czech and the leader of the Communist Party of Czechoslovakia (CPCz), who had been Prime Minister since 1946.

In the first years of communist rule there was widespread repression. Expressions of Slovak nationalism were harshly suppressed, and in 1954 Husák and other Slovaks were imprisoned on charges of separatism. The new Constitution of 1960 restricted Slovak autonomy: the executive in Bratislava was dissolved and legislative authority was removed from the Slovenská národná rada. In January 1968 Alexander Dubček (a Slovak and hitherto the leader of the Communist Party of Slovakia—CPS) was appointed First Secretary of the CPCz. The wide-ranging political and economic reforms introduced by Dubček and the new Government included plans for the creation of a federal system of two equal republics. This period of political tolerance and freedom of expression (subsequently known as the 'Prague Spring') was abruptly ended in August 1968 by the armed intervention of some 600,000 troops of the USSR and its allies. Dubček was replaced by Husák as First (subsequently General) Secretary of the CPCz, and there was a severe purge of party members, in particular reformists and associates of Dubček. Nevertheless, the federal system was realized in January 1969: separate Czech and Slovak Socialist Republics were established, each with its own government and legislature (Národná rada—National Council). Supreme legislative and executive power, meanwhile, were vested, respectively, in the Federal Assembly and the Federal Government. However, the reimposition of centralized communist rule, under the leadership of Husák, left the new regional institutions largely powerless.

In 1975 Husák was appointed President of Czechoslovakia. In December 1987 he was replaced as General Secretary of the CPCz by Miloš Jakeš, a Czech member of the CPCz Presidium. Although the administration publicly avowed its commitment to introduce political and economic reforms similar to those taking place in the USSR under Mikhail Gorbachev, political liberalization was not forthcoming. The Government continued its repressive treatment of both the Roman Catholic Church and the several dissident groups that had been established since the late 1970s (the most important being Charter 77). Nevertheless, the dissident movement was instrumental in organizing a series of anti-Government demonstrations, beginning in 1988, which were to culminate in the anti-communist revolution of late 1989 (see the chapter on the Czech Republic).

Elections to the Federal Assembly and to the Czech and Slovak National Councils on 8–9 June 1990 were the first to be held freely since 1946. Of the Slovak parties and movements, Public Against Violence (PAV), which, with its Czech counterpart, Civic Forum, had been the principal force in effecting the end of communist rule, emerged with the largest representation at both federal and republican level. A coalition Slovak Government, dominated by PAV, was subsequently formed, with Vladimír Mečiar as Prime Minister.

The future of Czech-Slovak relations emerged in the latter half of 1990 as the dominant topic of political debate. Although most Czech and Slovak citizens appeared to favour the preservation of a common state, there was increasing support in Slovakia for a more decentralized form of the existing federation. Among the Slovak political parties, the Christian Democratic Movement (CDM), which formed part of the Slovak coalition Government, advocated greater Slovak autonomy within a common state; however, more radical parties—most notably the Slovak National Party (SNP), which held seats in both the federal and republican legislatures—advocated the complete secession of Slovakia from the federation. The debate over the future of the country (which since April 1990 had been officially known as the Czech and Slovak Federative Republic) led to increasing political turmoil in Slovakia during 1991. In March Mečiar was forced to resign as Slovak Prime Minister, accused of harming Czech-Slovak relations by his increasingly strident advocacy of full autonomy for Slovakia. Mečiar left PAV and formed a new party, the Movement for a Democratic Slovakia (MDS). He was replaced as Prime Minister by Ján Carnogurský, the leader of the CDM. Proposals by the Czechoslovak President, Václav Havel, for a referendum to determine the country's future were repeatedly rejected by the Federal Assembly.

Following elections to the federal and republican legislatures on 5–6 June 1992, the MDS emerged as the dominant Slovak party both in the Federal Assembly and the Slovenská národná rada. In the latter body the MDS won 74 of the 150 seats available, compared with only 18 won by the CDM and 15 by the SNP. The Party of the Democratic Left (PDL—the successor to the CPS) won the second largest representation (29 seats). In late June Mečiar was reinstated as Prime Minister, at the head of a new, MDS-dominated Slovak Government.

On 17 July 1992 the Slovenská národná rada overwhelmingly approved a declaration of Slovak sovereignty, as a result of which the dismantling of the Czechoslovak federation appeared inevitable. In late July Mečiar and his Czech counterpart, Václav Klaus, reached agreement on the necessary measures to permit the separation of the two republics. On 1 September the new Slovak Constitution was adopted by the Slovenská národná rada. In November the Federal Assembly finally approved (albeit at the third attempt and by a margin of only three votes) legislation to permit the constitutional dissolution (to be effected on 1 January 1993) of Czechoslovakia.

During the remainder of 1992 there was an acceleration of the process of dividing federal assets and liabilities, as well as the armed forces, between the Czech and Slovak Republics. In late December the two republics signed a co-operation agreement, and subsequently established formal diplomatic relations. With the dissolution of all federal structures at midnight on 31 December, the Czech Republic and the Slovak Republic came into existence. Recognition was rapidly accorded to the new countries by all those states that had maintained relations with Czechoslovakia, as well as by various international bodies.

Slovakia's MDS-dominated Government and legislature remained in place. In February 1993 the Národná rada Slovenskej republiky (National Council of the Slovak Republic, as the legislature was redesignated—Národná rada) elected Michal Kováč, the Deputy Chairman of the MDS and the former Chairman of Czechoslovakia's Federal Assembly, as President. Meanwhile, there were increasing internal divisions in the MDS, which culminated in March 1993 with the dismissal of Milan Kňažko, the strongest critic of Mečiar within the party, from his post of Deputy Prime Minister and Minister of Foreign Affairs. Kňažko subsequently formed a liberal party, the Alliance of Democrats of the Slovak Republic (ADSR), in opposition to Mečiar's Government. Also in March the SNP leader, Ludovít Černák, resigned as Minister of the Economy, leaving the Government (with the exception of two independent ministers) composed exclusively of members of the MDS. However, as a result of several defections, the party (plus affiliates) lost its majority in the legislature. A new coalition Government, in which the SNP held several principal portfolios, was formed in November. One of Mečiar's ministerial nominees was rejected by Kováč, who had become severely critical of the Prime Minister. In December Mečiar ignored a demand by the President for his resignation.

Mečiar's position was further undermined in early 1994 by resignations and defections. In February six SNP deputies left the party to form what became the National Democratic Party—New Alternative (NDP—NA), led by Černák. In the same month the Minister of Foreign Affairs, Jozef Moravčík, and the Deputy Prime Minister, Roman Kováč, resigned from the Government, subsequently establishing another new opposition party, the Democratic Union of Slovakia (DUS). In March the Národná rada approved a motion expressing 'no confidence' in Mečiar's Government (the MDS and SNP both abstained from voting). Following the resignation of Mečiar's administration, a new, five-party, interim coalition was installed in mid-March. The new Government, with Moravčík as Prime Minister, comprised members of the CDM and the PDL, as well as the three new formations: the NDP—NA, the DUS and the ADSR (the last was subsequently absorbed into the DUS). Early legislative elections were scheduled for September.

The MDS emerged as the leading party at elections to the Národná rada, held on 30 September and 1 October 1994 (with the participation of some 76% of the electorate). The renewed success of the MDS (which, in alliance with the Farmers' Party of Slovakia, secured 35.0% of the total votes cast and 61 seats) was attributed to Mečiar's populist election campaign. The Common Choice bloc (an alliance of left-wing parties, led by the PDL) won 10.4% of the votes cast and 18 seats, followed by a coalition of Hungarian parties (17) and the CDM (also 17). The remaining seats were taken by the DUS (15), the Association of Workers of Slovakia (AWS—formed earlier in the year, following a split in the PDL—13 seats) and the SNP (nine seats).

Subsequent inter-party negotiations proved inconclusive, and in late October 1994 Kováč requested that Mečiar form a Government. Finally, in mid-December a coalition of the MDS, the SNP and the AWS was announced. In January 1995 the new Government attempted to annul all decisions on privatization made by the previous administration and overturn a presidential veto. However, opposition deputies submitted the controversial legislation to the Constitutional Court, which in May declared the suspension of the privatization programme to have been illegal. The personal enmity between Mečiar and Kováč culminated in an unsuccessful motion of 'no confidence' in the President, following allegations that the Slovak Intelligence Service (SIS), which had been under presidential control until April) had provided Kováč with confidential information concerning the activities of political parties, in particular the MDS, and of state officials.

In February 1996 President Kováč claimed that there was evidence to suggest that the SIS had been responsible for the abduction of one of his sons (also called Michal) from Bratislava. Michal Kováč had subsequently been detained by police on an international arrest warrant in Austria, in connection with allegations of embezzlement, but later permitted to return to Slovakia. Mečiar alleged that the President, too, had been involved in the embezzlement affair, and that his son had organized his own abduction in order to divert attention from the financial scandal; President Kováč subsequently filed libel charges against Mečiar. However, investigations into both the abduction of Kováč's son and the libel suit were adjourned owing to lack of evidence.

The Ministers of the Economy, of Foreign Affairs and of the Interior were replaced in August 1996, in what was interpreted by some observers as an attempt to address the international concern at Slovakia's apparent lack of commitment to democratic reform. Opposition deputies, meanwhile, campaigned for a referendum to be held on their proposals that the Head of State be elected by direct popular vote, rather than chosen by the legislature. President Kováč scheduled a referendum for 23–24 May 1997. Although the Constitutional Court ruled that the Government had no authority to participate in constitutional disputes concerning the organization of a referendum, when the poll took place the question on presidential elections was omitted from the ballot papers, on the orders of Gustáv Krajči, the Minister of the Interior. The majority of voters consequently boycotted the referendum, and the rate of electoral participation (less than 10%) was too low to render the vote valid. The Minister of Foreign Affairs, Pavol Hamžík, resigned in protest at what he regarded as the Government's manipulation of the democratic process. In early June several thousand people attended a rally organized by the opposition to protest against the Government's intervention in the referendum. Later that month Krajči survived a vote of 'no confidence' in the Národná rada. In mid-February 1998, following a ruling by the Constitutional Court that Krajči had violated citizens' rights to vote in the referendum, and in response to appeals from the opposition, Kováč announced that a new referendum would be held in April.

Meanwhile, the Slovak Democratic Coalition (SDC), a new grouping of five opposition parties (including the CDM and the DUS), demanded Mečiar's resignation, accusing his administration of endangering Slovakia's political and economic future, following the failure of Slovakia to be invited to join the North Atlantic Treaty Organization (NATO, see p. 314) or to be recommended by the European Commission for negotiations on membership of the European Union (EU, see p. 228) in mid-1997. In mid-October, despite ongoing tension between the President and the Prime Minister, Kováč and Mečiar issued a joint statement affirming Slovakia's commitment to future membership of the EU and other international organizations, amid increasing concern about the country's image abroad. In December the Constitutional Court settled a protracted dispute between Mečiar and Kováč, when it ruled that the President's term of office would end five years after his inauguration (on 2 March 1998), rather than five years after his election, as Mečiar had claimed.

During January–March 1998 several attempts to elect a new President failed in the Národná rada, when candidates were unable to secure the required three-fifths' majority. The MDS had not contested the first rounds of voting, apparently confirming opposition fears that Mečiar was attempting to ensure that the presidency would remain vacant when Kováč left office, enabling him to assume a number of presidential powers. On 2 March Kováč's term expired and a number of presidential powers were transferred to the Government, in accordance with the Constitution. Mečiar immediately cancelled the referendum scheduled for April and announced the dismissal of some 28 of Slovakia's ambassadors abroad. He also granted an amnesty to various prisoners, including those suspected of abducting Kováč's son in 1995, and halted criminal proceedings relating to the May 1997 referendum. The Prime Minister's actions prompted a series of widely supported protest rallies organized by opposition parties, and were strongly criticized by the EU and the USA. In mid-April 1998 a further round of voting in the presidential election was contested for the first time by an MDS candidate; however, the Národná rada again failed to elect a new Head of State. Subsequent attempts were also unsuccessful.

At the end of May 1998, in preparation for legislative elections scheduled for September, the Národná rada approved amendments to the electoral law, including a stipulation that political parties obtain at least 5% of the votes cast in order to secure parliamentary representation. Legislation was also approved that restricted pre-election campaigning to the state-run media. In June three ethnic Hungarian parties formally merged to create the Party of the Hungarian Coalition (PHC) and the SDC registered officially as a single party. In July a constitutional amendment providing for the transfer of a number of presidential powers to the Chairman of the Národná rada, in the event of the presidency becoming vacant, was supported by deputies from all parties. The election campaign was marked by disagreements over access to the media, with the SDC accusing Slovak Television of bias towards the MDS. A dispute over the ownership of Slovakia's principal independent television channel, TV Markiza, culminated in the dismissal of its Director-General, Pavel Rusko, and thousands of opposition supporters reportedly participated in demonstrations (however, Rusko was reappointed in October).

The elections to the Národná rada were held, as scheduled, on 25–26 September 1998, with the participation of 84.2% of the electorate. The MDS narrowly retained its position as the strongest party in the legislature, winning 43 seats (with 27.0% of the votes cast), but was unable to form a government, with its only possible ally, the SNP, holding 14 seats. The SDC obtained 42 seats (26.3% of the votes), the PDL won 23 seats (14.7%), the PHC took 15 seats and the Party of Civic Understanding (PCU—formed earlier that year) won 13 seats. With a combined total of 93 seats, the SDC, the PDL, the PHC and the PCU agreed to attempt to form a new administration. Negotiations took place throughout October, and a new coalition Government, headed by Mikuláš Dzurinda, the leader of the SDC, was appointed at the end of the month. Jozef Migaš, of the PDL, was elected Chairman of the Národná rada. The opposition's victory was welcomed both by Western institutions and by neighbouring countries, which anticipated improved relations with Slovakia. Dzurinda emphasized the new Government's intention to pursue early membership of the EU and NATO, pledged to combat organized crime, and outlined measures to improve Slovakia's economic situation. In December the European Parliament adopted a resolution on Slovakia's application for membership of the EU, recommending that the European Commission consider initiating entry talks in 1999.

In January 1999 the Národná rada approved a government-sponsored constitutional amendment providing for the introduction of direct presidential elections. The ruling coalition nominated Rudolf Schuster, the Chairman of the PCU, as its presidential candidate. Nine candidates contested the first round of the presidential election, which was held on 15 May. Schuster won 47.4% of the votes cast, and Mečiar obtained 37.2%. (Despite announcing his intention to stand for re-election, Kováč had withdrawn his candidature prior to the first round, in favour of Schuster.) Schuster defeated Mečiar in a second round of voting on 29 May, with 57.2% of the votes cast, and was duly inaugurated as President on 15 June, having resigned the chairmanship of the PCU.

Investigations into the circumstances surrounding the abduction of Kováč's son in August 1995 and the failed referendum of May 1997 resumed in early 1999, following Dzurinda's cancellation of the amnesties granted by Mečiar in March 1998. In February 1999 the Národná rada revoked Krajči's parliamentary immunity, and in June he was charged with sabotaging the referendum and abusing public office. In April Ivan Lexa, the former head of the SIS, was also deprived of his immunity from prosecution and arrested in connection with Michal Kováč's abduction and other offences alleged to have been committed by the SIS under his leadership. The prosecution of Krajči and Lexa was effectively halted in July, however, when the Constitutional Court ruled that Dzurinda had not been entitled to revoke the amnesties. (In December 2002 Lexa was arrested and charged with having organized the murder of a former police-officer in 1996, in an attempt to obstruct the investigation into the kidnapping of Michal Kováč. Lexa was acquitted in September 2004.)

In September 1999 a large demonstration was staged in Bratislava to protest against rising unemployment and declining living standards, resulting from a series of austerity measures implemented by the Government. In October Černák resigned as Minister of the Economy; his ministerial post was assumed by Ľubomír Harach, the Chairman of the DUS. In January 2000, following several weeks of disputes over the future structure of the SDC, during which he had failed to consolidate the unity of the party, Dzurinda announced plans to form a new party, the Slovak Democratic and Christian Union (SDCU). The SDCU was officially registered in February 2000, and was joined by several government ministers. Further SDC deputies subsequently resigned from the CDM and the DUS to join the SDCU, while retaining membership of the SDC. In April the MDS announced its intention to propose legislation, aimed at SDC members that had joined the SDCU, to prohibit membership of more than one political party. Following Dzurinda's election as SDCU Chairman at the party's opening congress in November, the SDC became effectively defunct. Meanwhile, in June Schuster underwent emergency surgery, and later that month was transferred to Austria for further medical treatment. The President resumed office in mid-August.

In early 2001 discussions commenced in the Národná rada regarding proposed revisions to the Constitution, which, although opposed by the MDS and SNP, were adopted by a narrow majority in the legislature in late February. The revisions (which officially entered into effect on 1 July) redefined the relationship between national and international law, thereby facilitating the process of joining foreign alliances; strengthened the powers of the Constitutional Court; granted greater independence to the judiciary; and provided for public-administration reform. In early May Schuster replaced Pavol Hamzik, the Deputy Prime Minister for European Integration, held responsible for the misuse of EU funds, which had led to the suspension of payments in the previous month. Also in May the Minister of the Interior tendered his resignation, following increasing criticism of an investigation into mismanagement under the Mečiar administration. Later in May opposition parties strongly criticized the Deputy Prime Minister for the Economy, Ivan Mikloš, for lack of progress in economic and public-administration reform. However, a motion expressing 'no confidence' in him was defeated in the legislature, after Dzurinda indicated that he would resign if Mikloš was removed. The Government subsequently announced the adoption of a programme of extensive economic reforms.

In July 2001 the Government pledged to introduce measures to restore public confidence in the security forces, after the death of a Roma in police custody. In the same month dissension increased between the government coalition parties over new legislation providing for the establishment of a higher level of regional self-administration. Following the adoption of the reforms, which provided for the creation of eight 'higher territorial units' (VÚCs), local government elections took place in two rounds, on 1 and 15 December. In a reflection of increasing popular support for the party, MDS representatives secured 146 of the 401 seats in the regional councils and six of the eight gubernatorial posts. (However, voter participation in the second round was estimated at only 22% of the registered electorate.)

In January 2002 the PDL demanded the resignation of the reformist Minister of Finance, Brigita Schmögnerová (a PDL member), after she allegedly withheld information regarding the privatization programme. Although Dzurinda initially refused to dismiss her, threats by the PDL to withdraw from the coalition finally resulted in her replacement. Schmögnerová subsequently left the PDL and formed a new political party, the Social Democratic Alternative (SDA). In mid-February Mikloš (who was principally responsible for the programme of structural reforms) survived a further motion of 'no confidence' in the Národná rada.

In July 2002 members of the MDS who had not been selected by the party to contest the forthcoming legislative elections established a new party, known as the Movement for Democracy. At the elections to the Národná rada on 20–21 September, the MDS received the highest proportion of the votes cast (19.5%), obtaining 36 mandates. The SDCU received 15.1% of the votes cast and 28 seats; a centre-right party, known as Direction (Směr), 13.5% and 25 seats; the PHC 11.2% and 20 seats; and the CDM 8.3% and 15 seats. The New Citizen's Alliance (NCA), established in 2001, won 8.0% of the votes and 15 seats, while the Slovak Communist Party (SCP) significantly increased its share, securing 6.3% and 11 seats. However, Mečiar subsequently proved unable to negotiate alliances with other parties, in order to form a coalition government, and in late September Schuster invited Dzurinda to establish a new administration. A coalition agreement was signed in early October by four reformist, centre-right parties (the SDCU, the PHC, the CDM and the NCA), which together commanded a narrow majority, holding a total of 78 of the 150 seats in the Národná rada. On 16 October Schuster formally appointed a new coalition Government, comprising representatives of the four parties. The leader of the Democratic Party (DP), which had supported the SDCU in the elections, was also allocated a portfolio, although the party was not a coalition member. Mikloš was retained in the administration as the new Minister of Finance. The adoption of an austerity budget in November prompted popular protests, and the MDS urged deputies in the Národná rada to reverse the legislation. Local government elections took place on 6–7 December; mayoral offices were equally divided between the government coalition parties and the MDS.

In May 2003 a new party, the People's Union, was formed by disaffected members of the MDS. Former MDS Deputy Chairman Vojtech Tkáč was elected Chairman of the party. In the following month Mečiar was re-elected as Chairman of the MDS for a further two-year term. At the same time, MDS members approved changing the party's name to the People's Party—Movement for a Democratic Slovakia (PP—MDS). In early July tensions emerged within the ruling coalition, after the Národná rada approved legislative amendments proposed by the NCA, easing restrictions on abortion, which were strongly opposed by the CDM. In late July Schuster vetoed the legislation, fearing the collapse of the Government. In early September the Deputy Prime Minister and Minister of the Economy, Robert Nemcsics, officially resigned his post, after losing the support of the NCA, following his criticism of Pavel Rusko, the Chairman of the party. In late September Rusko was appointed as Deputy Prime Minister and Minister of the Economy. In October Juraj Liska was appointed as Minister of Defence, replacing Ivan Simko, who had been dismissed in September. In December Simko defected from the SDCU, in favour of his new Free Forum Party. A number of deputies subsequently left the SDCU to join the party, rendering the ruling coalition a minority Government, with just 68 parliamentary seats. In mid-March 2004 Mikloš survived a further motion of 'no confidence', proposed by the PP—MDS.

In the first round of voting in the presidential election of 3 April 2004, former Prime Minister Vladimír Mečiar won 32.7% of the votes cast, followed by Movement for Democracy leader (and former ally of Mečiar) Ivan Gašparovič, who won 22.3% of the votes. Eduard Kukan of the SDCU, the Minister of Foreign Affairs and the preferred candidate of Dzurinda's Government, took third place, with 22.1% of the votes, and was thus disqualified from the second round of voting. Schuster, the incumbent, obtained just 7.4% of the votes. The failure of Kukan's presidential bid prompted demands in the Národná rada for the resignation of Dzurinda, whereas Mečiar's success, which was unexpected by many observers, was seen as a potential threat to the success of Slovakia's accession to the EU (due at the beginning of May). In the second round of voting, held on 17 April, Gašparovič was elected as President, receiving 59.9% of the votes cast; the rate of participation by the electorate in the second round was 43.5%. Gašparovič, who subsequently announced his resignation from the leadership of the Movement for Democracy, was inaugurated on 15 June, and pledged to co-operate with other EU states while representing Slovakia's interests. Meanwhile, at Slovakia's first elections to the European Parliament in mid-June a rate of participation by the electorate of just 17.0% was recorded—the lowest rate recorded in any EU member state. The SDCU received 17.1% of the votes, the MDS 17.0%, Direction 16.9% and the CDM 16.2%; the four parties were each allocated three seats in the European Parliament. The PHC, which won 13.2% of votes, obtained two seats.

In October 2004 Ivan Šimko left the Free Forum Party. In January 2005 a new party, Direction-Social Democracy, was founded by the merger of Direction, the Social Democratic Party of Slovakia, the SDA and the PDL. In November 2004, meanwhile, the National Memory Institute had announced that it was to publish thousands of hitherto secret official files from Slovakia's communist era, detailing names of collaborators with the former regime; a deputy minister resigned in January 2005, after he was revealed to be a former agent of the communist security services.

In early July 2005 Dzurinda survived a motion of 'no confidence' in the Národná rada, which had been proposed by the Chairman of Direction-Social Democracy, Robert Fico, and supported by PP—MDS Chairman Vladimír Mečiar. Fico had criticized Dzurinda for his failure to combat corruption, and argued that his reforms had increased poverty. In late August President Gašparovič dismissed Rusko from his post as Deputy Prime Minister and Minister of the Economy, after he was implicated in a loan scandal, which revealed an apparent conflict of interest between his private business activities and his ministerial duties. (Rusko had refused to comply with an earlier request that he tender his resignation, after the CDM threatened to withdraw its 15 deputies from the Národná rada if he remained in the Government.) Deputy Prime Minister and Minister of Finance Ivan Mikloš assumed the economy portfolio, in an acting capacity. Rusko, who remained leader of the NCA, subsequently urged Dzurinda to dismiss the Minister of Health, Rudolf Zajac (who had been nominated by the NCA, but was not a party member), and the Minister of Culture, František Tóth (an NCA member), both of whom had supported Rusko's removal. According to the coalition agreement, the NCA was authorized to nominate the Ministers of the Economy, of Culture and of Health: Rusko threatened to withdraw the NCA from the Government should Dzurinda refuse to replace the ministers, which he considered a breach of the coalition agreement. Members of the NCA opposed to Rusko's leadership, including two party Vice-Chairmen, Lubomír Lintner and Jirko Malchárek, and Tóth, formed a splinter faction, led by Lintner. At the beginning of September the SDCU, the CDM and the PHC agreed to expel the NCA from the ruling coalition; Zajac and Tóth were permitted to retain their posts. Lintner's group of deputies pledged its co-operation with the governing parties, and proposed Malchárek for the post of Minister of the Economy. On 11 September the NCA expelled nine members from the party, including Tóth and five Vice-Chairmen (among them Lintner and Malchárek). The following day the Government signed a co-operation agreement with Lintner's group of deputies. Opposition parties boycotted the Národná rada, but after nine days the Government narrowly managed to secure sufficient support to open a legislative session. In early October Gašparovič appointed Malchárek as Deputy Prime Minister and Minister of the Economy.

In early October 2005 DP leader Ľudovít Kaník resigned his post as Minister of Labour, Social Affairs and the Family. Kaník, who was replaced by Iveta Radičová in mid-October, subsequently proposed a merger of the DP and the SDCU. In early December a congress of the DP approved a draft agreement on the merger, which was confirmed in late January 2006 at an extraordinary congress of the SDCU. The new political union was known as the SDCU-DP. Also in late January Malchárek, Tóth and a former Deputy Minister of Health founded a new political party, Hope, which was officially registered in early March.

Meanwhile, on 26 November and 10 December 2005 an estimated 18% of the electorate took part in local government elections. Just 11% of the electorate participated in the second round, the lowest rate of participation in Slovakia's history. Of the parties represented in the Národná rada, the CDM secured 87 of the 412 seats in the VUCs, Direction-Social Democracy took 70 and the SDCU won 64.

In late January 2006 the Minister of Defence, Juraj Liška, tendered his resignation, after a military aircraft crashed on the Hungarian–Slovak border, killing some 42 people. Although the cause of the accident was unknown, the Government had been criticized for its decision to modernize Soviet-manufactured aircraft, rather than buying new equipment. Liška was replaced by Martin Fedor. On 6 February the CDM announced the withdrawal of its three ministers from the Government, following Dzurinda's refusal to submit for discussion a proposal to approve a treaty with the Vatican that would enable workers to refuse to perform duties on the basis of religious objections.

Dzurinda argued that any such treaty would permit the Roman Catholic Church to interfere in civil affairs. The leader of the CDM subsequently resigned as Chairman of the Národná rada, and was replaced, in an acting capacity, by the PHC leader and Deputy Chairman of the legislature, Béla Bugár. As a result of the CDM's withdrawal, the ruling coalition controlled just 53 seats in the legislature, and three days later the Národná rada approved a proposal by Dzurinda for legislative elections, originally due to take place in September, to be held on 17 June. Gašparovič subsequently appointed Martin Pado of the SDCU-DP as Minister of the Interior, László Szigeti (of the PHC) as Minister of Education, and Lucia Žitňanská, an independent, as Minister of Justice. In early April Tóth was dismissed from his position as Minister of Culture, after being accused of misusing state funds; Rudolf Chmel, who held the position until May 2005, was subsequently re-appointed to the culture portfolio.

At the end of October 1997 Mečiar appealed to the Gypsy (Roma) population not to seek asylum abroad, after a number of Roma were repatriated from the United Kingdom. However, Slovakia's Roma continued to seek political asylum abroad (largely unsuccessfully), prompting several countries to introduce mandatory visa requirements, on a temporary basis, for Slovak citizens. Although, according to the 2001 census, there were some 89,900 Roma in Slovakia, the community was unofficially estimated to number around 200,000. In January 2004 a report by the Council of Europe (see p. 211) concluded that Slovakia's Roma were frequently victims of racial prejudice and were disadvantaged socially. In the following month proposed reductions in social welfare prompted violent protests by the Roma minority, and some 1,000 troops were deployed to control rioting. In July new legislation was introduced prohibiting discrimination on the grounds of ethnicity. However, in October Minister of Justice Daniel Lipšic challenged a clause proposed by the Deputy Prime Minister for European Integration, Human Rights and Minorities, Pál Csáky, which temporarily provided for 'positive discrimination'. According to this aspect of the law, the most disadvantaged groups in society were to be given special help until social divisions had been reduced. Lipšic argued that, according to the Constitution, any form of discrimination was illegal, and submitted his case to the Constitutional Court, which annulled the clause in October 2005.

Slovakia's relations with Hungary have been strained by the issue of the large Hungarian minority (numbering some 520,500 at the 2001 census) resident in Slovakia, who are campaigning for cultural and educational autonomy. The two countries are also involved in a dispute over the Gabčíkovo-Nagymaros hydroelectric project, a scheme initiated by the Governments of Czechoslovakia and Hungary in 1977, which involved the construction of two dams and the diversion of the River Danube. Despite Hungary's decision in 1989 to abandon the project (following pressure by environmentalist groups), the Czechoslovak Government announced that it would proceed unilaterally with its part of the construction. In early 1993 Slovakia and Hungary agreed to forward the dispute to the International Court of Justice (ICJ) in The Hague, Netherlands and to operate a temporary water-management scheme in the mean time. In March 1995, none the less, an historic bilateral Treaty of Friendship and Co-operation was signed by the Prime Ministers of Hungary and Slovakia. The Treaty, notably, guaranteed the rights of ethnic minorities in each republic, while confirming the existing state border. However, the language law approved by the Slovak legislature in November, declaring Slovak the only official language and thereby potentially restricting the use of minority languages, was criticized both by Hungarian residents of Slovakia, and also by the Hungarian Government, as a violation of the Treaty. In August 1997 the Hungarian Prime Minister, Gyula Horn, and Mečiar agreed on the establishment of a joint commission to assess the implementation of the 1995 Treaty, although there was subsequently disagreement over its composition.

In September 1997 relations became tense, after it emerged that Mečiar had proposed the initiation of a voluntary repatriation programme for the ethnic minorities of both countries. Later in September the ICJ pronounced its judgment on the Gabčíkovo-Nagymaros hydroelectric project, ruling that both countries had breached international law: Hungary was not justified in suspending work on the project, while the former Czechoslovakia should not have proceeded unilaterally. Both countries were to pay compensation for damages, and to negotiate regarding the realization of the original agreement. The participation of the PHC in the new Slovak Government appointed in October 1998 improved prospects for the protection of minority rights. In February 1999 the first meeting of the joint minorities commission to monitor the implementation of the 1995 Treaty was held in Budapest, Hungary. In July 1999 the Národná rada approved legislation that provided for the use of an ethnic minority language in towns where the minority accounted for at least 20% of the population.

In December 1999 Hungary renounced any claim to a share of the hydroelectric energy produced by the Gabčíkovo-Nagymaros dam project, but requested an increase in the common flow of water along the Danube, for ecological reasons. In February 2001 Slovakia accepted that it had no legal means to compel Hungary to complete the project, but stated that it was to seek compensation. In December 2003 an intergovernmental commission was established to co-ordinate negotiations on the issue. Meanwhile, in January 2002 relations between Slovakia and Hungary had again became acrimonious, following Hungary's adoption of legislation that granted ethnic Hungarians resident in six neighbouring states, including Slovakia, education, employment and medical benefits. The Slovak Government protested that the new legislation violated Slovakia's sovereignty, and demanded that it be cancelled or amended. In early March 2003 Hungary agreed to suspend the application of the law in Slovakia, and in December the Ministers of Foreign Affairs of Hungary and Slovakia signed an agreement on the issue. The provisions of the status law were effectively superseded by the accession of Hungary and Slovakia to the EU in May 2004 (see below). In December 2005, at a meeting in Bratislava with President Gašparovič, the President of Hungary, László Sólyom, described the two countries' relations as very good. In February 2006 it was announced that Slovakia and Hungary had agreed to implement the 1997 ICJ ruling on the Gabčíkovo-Nagymaros hydroelectric project. The two Governments were to draft an agreement on the implementation of the ruling and amend the 1977 agreement on the construction and operation of the system.

Relations with neighbouring Austria were strained by the issue of the partially constructed, Soviet-designed nuclear power station at Mochovce (north-east of Bratislava), operated by Slovenské elektrárne (Slovak Electricity), the completion of which was opposed by the Austrian Government, owing to safety concerns. An agreement on completion of the project was signed in April 1996, with western European, Russian and Czech companies, according to which the first reactor would be commissioned by July 1998 and the second by March 1999. Tension increased in June 1998, when the first reactor was activated, despite a request from the Austrian Government that Slovakia delay the opening of the plant until an international team of inspectors, who had visited Mochovce in May, had submitted a final report on the plant's safety. In late 1999 the Slovak Government announced its decision to close two existing reactors at Jaslovské-Bohunice between 2006 and 2008, further antagonizing Austria, which had favoured closure by 2000. In May 2004, shortly after Slovakia's accession to the EU, tensions between the two countries heightened, following the Slovak Government's announcement that it intended to complete work on the Mochovce plant. In August 2005 the Italian electricity group Enel, which had bought a majority stake in Slovenské elektrárne in February, agreed to invest some €1,600m. in Mochovce; Enel intended to complete the construction of the two unfinished reactors by 2010.

In December 1999 Slovakia was among six countries formally invited to commence talks on accession with the EU; entry negotiations opened in February 2000. Following the return to power of a reformist coalition Government in October 2002 (see above), at an EU summit meeting held in Copenhagen, Denmark, in December, Slovakia was one of 10 nations invited to become a member in 2004. At a national referendum, which was conducted on 16–17 May 2003, 92.5% of votes were cast in favour of membership of the EU; some 52% of the electorate participated in the ballot. Slovakia's Treaty of Accession was formally ratified by the Národná rada on 1 July, and the country became a full member of the EU on 1 May 2004. On 11 May Slovakia became the seventh country to ratify the proposed constitutional treaty of the EU (which was subsequently rejected by referendums in, notably, France and the Netherlands).

Meanwhile, in February 1994 Slovakia joined NATO's 'Partnership for Peace' programme. At a NATO summit meeting in Prague at the end of November 2002, Slovakia (together with six other countries) was formally invited to join the Alliance, and it became a full member on 29 March 2004. In May Slovakia hosted a plenary session of the NATO Parliamentary Assembly, and in

SLOVAKIA

February 2005 it hosted a summit meeting between US President George W. Bush and Russian President Vladimir Putin. President Bush praised the deployment of 100 Slovak troops to Iraq to participate in the US-led military operations there.

Government

Supreme legislative power is vested in the Národná rada Slovenskej republiky (National Council of the Slovak Republic), the 150 members of which are elected for a term of four years by universal adult suffrage. The President of the Republic (Head of State) is directly elected by universal adult suffrage for a five-year term. The President, who is restricted to two consecutive terms of office, appoints the Prime Minister and, on the latter's recommendation, the other members of the Government (the supreme body of executive power). For administrative purposes, Slovakia is divided into eight 'higher territorial units' (VUCs), each with a regional council (together totalling 401 seats), and 79 electoral districts.

Defence

In August 2005 the total active strength of Slovakia's armed forces was 20,195: army 12,860, air force 5,160, and some 2,175 centrally controlled personnel, logistical and support staff. The duration of military service was reduced from nine to six months in January 2004. In July 2005 it was announced that compulsory military service was to be abandoned from 1 August, and in December the army became fully professional. Slovakia became a full member of the North Atlantic Treaty Organization (NATO, see p. 314) in 29 March 2004. The 2005 budget allocated 25,600m. koruny to defence, compared with 23,100m. koruny in 2004.

Economic Affairs

In 2004, according to the World Bank, Slovakia's gross national income (GNI), measured at average 2002–04 prices, was US $34,907m., equivalent to $6,480 per head (or $14,370 per head on an international purchasing-power parity basis). During 1995–2004, it was estimated, the population increased at an annual average rate of 0.1%, while gross domestic product (GDP) per head increased, in real terms, by an average of 4.0% per year. Overall GDP increased, in real terms, at an annual average rate of 4.1% in 1995–2004; according to official figures, real GDP increased by 4.5% in 2003 and by 5.5% in 2004.

In 2004 the agricultural sector (including hunting, forestry and fishing) contributed 3.6% of GDP and employed 5.1% of the labour force. The principal crops are wheat and other grains, sugar beet, potatoes and other vegetables. Livestock breeding is also important. During 1995–2004, according to the World Bank, the GDP of the agricultural sector decreased, in real terms, by an annual average of 0.7%. Agricultural GDP increased by 4.4% in 2003, but decreased by 24.4% in 2004.

Industry (including mining, manufacturing, construction and power) contributed 29.7% of GDP in 2004, when it engaged 39.0% of the employed labour force. According to the World Bank, the GDP of the industrial sector increased, in real terms, by an annual average of 2.6% during 1995–2004. Industrial GDP increased by 9.2% in 2003 and by 7.0% in 2004.

Mining and quarrying contributed 0.5% of GDP in 2004, and engaged 0.7% of the employed labour force. The principal minerals extracted include brown coal and lignite, copper, zinc, lead, iron ore and magnesite. There are also deposits of crude petroleum, natural gas and mercury, as well as materials used in construction (including limestone, gravel and brick loam). According to IMF estimates, the GDP of the mining and quarrying sector increased by an annual average of 2.5% in 1995–2001. Mining GDP declined by 9.2% in 2001.

The manufacturing sector contributed 19.4% of GDP in 2004, when it engaged 26.8% of the employed labour force. The GDP of the manufacturing sector increased by an annual average of 3.4% in 1995–2004. Manufacturing GDP increased by 6.6% in 2003 and by 6.1% in 2004.

Energy is derived principally from nuclear power. According to the US-based Nuclear Energy Institute, nuclear energy provided some 57.4% of electricity generated in 2003. In 2002 coal accounted for 17.3% of electricity production, and hydroelectric power for 16.4%. A nuclear power station at Jaslovské-Bohunice has been in operation since the early 1980s, although in 1999 the Government pledged to close two reactors there by 2008. In mid-1998 the first block of a new nuclear power installation, at Mochovce, commenced operations; construction work on two unfinished reactors there was due to be completed by 2010. Slovakia has been heavily dependent on imported fuel and energy products. According to preliminary data, mineral products accounted for 15.4% of the value of total merchandise imports in 2005.

The services sector contributed 66.7% of GDP in 2004, when the sector engaged 55.7% of the employed labour force. During 1995–2003, according to the World Bank, the GDP of the services sector increased, in real terms, by an annual average of 5.0%. Services GDP increased by 6.9% in 2002 and by 2.4% in 2003.

In 2003 Slovakia recorded a trade deficit of US $641m., and there was a deficit of $280m. on the current account of the balance of payments. In 2005 the principal source of imports was Germany, which accounted for 21.0% of the total, according to preliminary figures; other major suppliers were the Czech Republic and Russia. Germany was also the principal market for exports in that year (accounting for an estimated 26.1%); other important purchasers were the Czech Republic, Austria, Italy, Poland and Hungary. The main exports in 2005 were machinery and electrical equipment, vehicles and transport equipment, base metals, mineral products, and rubber and plastics. The principal imports were machinery and electrical equipment, mineral products, vehicles and transport equipment, base metals, chemical products, and rubber and plastics.

Slovakia's overall budgetary deficit was 41,822m. koruny in 2004, equivalent to 3.2% of GDP. At the end of 2003 Slovakia's total external debt was US $18,379m., of which $4,508m. was long-term public debt. In that year the cost of debt-servicing was equivalent to 13.4% of the value of exports of goods and services. The annual rate of inflation averaged 7.5% in 1995–2004; consumer prices increased by 7.5% in 2004 and by 2.8% in 2005. In 2005 the average rate of unemployment was 16.2%.

Slovakia is a member of the IMF, the World Bank and the European Bank for Reconstruction and Development (EBRD, see p. 224). In 2000 Slovakia was admitted to the Organisation for Economic Co-operation and Development (OECD, see p. 320). Slovakia signed an association agreement with the European Community (now European Union—EU, see p. 228) in October 1993, and became a full member of the EU on 1 May 2004.

Following independence in 1993, Slovakia achieved sustained economic growth. The economy successfully shifted from its traditional reliance on industry to services, and from state to private ownership. The privatization programme was extended in 2000, and in November 2003 the Národná rada approved an amendment to legislation on privatization, to permit the sale of majority stakes in large state-owned utilities and natural monopolies (hitherto, the Government had retained a minimum 51% stake, although management control had been divested to investors). In January 2004 a 19% uniform rate of income tax, corporate tax and value-added tax was introduced, and in that year total foreign direct investment was the second highest in the region, apparently because investors were attracted by the relatively low rate of corporate taxation. The economy continued to record strong growth in 2005, with official preliminary data indicating that GDP increased by 6.0%, in real terms. Export trade also expanded rapidly, but high global energy prices contributed to an increased deficit on the current account of the balance of payments. The budgetary deficit for 2005, at an estimated 3.1% of GDP, was smaller than had been anticipated. Slovakia was admitted to the EU's exchange rate mechanism (ERM 2) in November 2005, when the koruna was linked to the common European currency, the euro. Slovakia aimed to adopt the euro in 2007, before becoming a member of the euro zone in 2009. In March 2006 the IMF warned that Slovakia needed to reduce both the high rate of unemployment (which was subject to significant regional disparities) and the rate of consumer-price inflation, in accordance with EU criteria (which stipulated that the rate of inflation should not exceed that of the three euro-zone countries with the lowest rates). The Government hoped to raise up to 90,000m. koruny from privatization in 2006, which, it was proposed, would be used to reduce the state debt. Growth in GDP was expected to remain buoyant, at some 5.8% in 2006 and 6.8% in 2007, stimulated by production at two new car factories and a concomitant increase in export trade.

Education

Education in Slovakia is provided free of charge at all levels in state-controlled and church-affiliated schools. Children between the ages of three and six may attend kindergarten (materská škola). Compulsory education begins at six years of age, when children enter basic school (základná škola), which takes nine years to complete (although the ninth year is optional). In 2004 555,335 pupils were enrolled at primary schools. There are three types of secondary school: the grammar school (gymnázium), which prepares students for higher education, and of which there

SLOVAKIA

were 234 in 2004, secondary specialized school (stredná odborná škola, 262) and secondary vocational school (stredné odborné učilište, 233), with a total enrolment of 260,796 students. In the 2002/03 academic year secondary enrolment was equivalent to 88% of children in the relevant age-group (males 88%; females 88%). In 2004 there were 24 institutions of higher education, with a total enrolment of 108,608 students. Children who, owing to disabilities, cannot attend regular schools may receive instruction at special schools. There are also private schools (basic and secondary). Of total estimated government expenditure (excluding wages) in 2001, 1,800m. koruny (0.5%) was allocated to education.

Public Holidays

2006: 1 January (Anniversary of the Slovak Republic), 6 January (Epiphany, Orthodox Christmas Day), 14 April (Good Friday), 17 April (Easter Monday), 1 May (Labour Day), 8 May (Anniversary of Liberation), 5 July (Day of the Slav Apostles, Cyril and Methodius), 29 August (National Day, Anniversary of the Slovak National Uprising), 1 September (Constitution Day), 15 September (Our Lady of Seven Sorrows), 1 November (All Saints' Day), 17 November (Day of Freedom and Democracy), 24–26 December (Christmas).

2007: 1 January (Anniversary of the Slovak Republic), 6 January (Epiphany, Orthodox Christmas Day), 6 April (Good Friday), 9 April (Easter Monday), 1 May (Labour Day), 8 May (Anniversary of Liberation), 5 July (Day of the Slav Apostles, Cyril and Methodius), 29 August (National Day, Anniversary of the Slovak National Uprising), 1 September (Constitution Day), 15 September (Our Lady of Seven Sorrows), 1 November (All Saints' Day), 17 November (Day of Freedom and Democracy), 24–26 December (Christmas).

Weights and Measures

The metric system is in force.

Statistical Survey

Source: Statistical Office of the Slovak Republic, Miletičova 3, 824 67 Bratislava; tel. (2) 5023-6340; fax (2) 5556-1361; e-mail agnesa.kralikova@statistics.sk; internet www.statistics.sk.

Area and Population

AREA, POPULATION AND DENSITY

Area (sq km)	49,033*
Population (census results)	
3 March 1991	5,274,335
26 May 2001	
Males	2,612,515
Females	2,766,940
Total	5,379,455
Population (official estimates at 31 December)	
2002	5,379,161
2003	5,380,053
2004	5,384,822
Density (per sq km) at 31 December 2004	109.8

* 18,932 sq miles.

POPULATION BY NATIONALITY
(at 2001 census)

	Number	%
Slovak	4,614,854	85.79
Hungarian	520,528	9.68
Gypsy (Roma)	89,920	1.67
Czech, Moravian, Silesian	46,968	0.87
Ruthenian and Ukrainian	35,015	0.65
German	5,405	0.10
Polish	2,602	0.05
Russian	1,590	0.03
Others (incl. undeclared)	62,573	1.16
Total	**5,379,455**	**100.00**

REGIONS
(at 2001 census)

	Area (sq km)	Population	Density (per sq km)
Banská Bystrica	9,455	662,121	70
Bratislava	2,053	599,015	292
Košice	6,753	766,012	113
Nitra	6,343	713,422	112
Prešov	8,993	789,968	88
Trenčín	4,501	605,582	135
Trnava	4,148	551,003	133
Žilina	6,788	692,332	102
Total	**49,034**	**5,379,455**	**110**

PRINCIPAL TOWNS
(estimated population at 31 December 2002)

Bratislava (capital)	427,049	Trnava	69,868
Košice	235,509	Martin	60,017
Prešov	92,486	Trenčín	57,413
Nitra	86,958	Poprad	55,982
Žilina	85,347	Prievidza	52,658
Banská Bystrica	82,493	Zvolen	43,674

BIRTHS, MARRIAGES AND DEATHS

	Registered live births		Registered marriages		Registered deaths	
	Number	Rate (per 1,000)	Number	Rate (per 1,000)	Number	Rate (per 1,000)
1997	59,111	11.0	27,955	5.2	52,124	9.7
1998	57,582	10.7	27,494	5.1	53,156	9.9
1999	56,223	10.4	27,340	5.1	54,402	9.8
2000	55,151	10.2	25,903	4.8	52,724	9.8
2001	51,136	9.5	23,795	4.4	51,980	9.7
2002	50,841	9.5	25,062	4.7	51,532	9.6
2003	51,713	9.6	26,002	4.8	52,230	9.7
2004	53,747	10.0	27,885	5.2	51,852	9.6

Expectation of life (WHO estimates, years at birth): 74 (males 70; females 78) in 2003 (Source: WHO, *World Health Report*).

SLOVAKIA

EMPLOYMENT
(labour force surveys, '000 persons)

	2002	2003	2004
Agriculture, hunting, forestry and fishing	131.4	125.3	109.8
Mining and quarrying	21.4	18.7	14.5
Manufacturing	573.5	570.0	582.5
Electricity, gas and water	46.1	45.4	44.3
Construction	176.0	194.9	205.3
Wholesale and retail trade; repair of motor vehicles, motorcycles and personal and household goods	271.5	270.0	260.2
Hotels and restaurants	68.5	79.5	84.3
Transport, storage and communications	154.4	149.4	140.7
Financial intermediation	39.8	43.6	45.8
Real estate, renting and business services	103.3	108.7	120.4
Public administration and defence; compulsory social security	149.7	159.7	151.6
Education	162.8	158.9	161.0
Health and social work	141.5	152.9	154.4
Other community, social and personal service activities	79.1	77.0	83.9
Private households with employed persons	7.9	8.0	7.3
Extraterritorial organizations	0.4	0.9	0.4
Activities not adequately defined	0.2	1.9	4.1
Total	**2,127.0**	**2,164.6**	**2,170.4**

Registered unemployed (annual averages, '000 persons): 486.9 in 2002, 459.2 in 2003; 480.7 in 2004.

Health and Welfare

KEY INDICATORS

Total fertility rate (children per woman, 2003)	1.3
Under-5 mortality rate (per 1,000 live births, 2004)	9
HIV/AIDS (% of persons aged 15–49, 2003)	<0.1
Physicians (per 1,000 head, 2002)	3.6
Hospital beds (per 1,000 head, 2000)	7.8
Health expenditure (2002): US $ per head (PPP)	723
Health expenditure (2002): % of GDP	5.9
Health expenditure (2002): public (% of total)	89.4
Access to water (% of persons, 2002)	100
Access to sanitation (% of persons, 2002)	100
Human Development Index (2003): ranking	42
Human Development Index (2003): value	0.849

For sources and definitions, see explanatory note on p. vi.

Agriculture

PRINCIPAL CROPS
('000 metric tons)

	2002	2003	2004
Wheat	1,554.4	930.4	1,764.8
Barley	695.0	804.2	915.9
Maize	753.8	601.4	862.4
Rye	96.5	62.3	124.3
Oats	43.4	57.9	55.6
Triticale	48.7	31.1	65.8
Potatoes	484.3	392.4	381.9
Sugar beet	1,346.2	1,171.7	1,598.8
Dry peas	25.1	19.1	31.4
Sunflower seed	116.9	252.7	196.4
Rapeseed	257.3	53.0	262.7
Cabbages (white)	84.1	86.5	85.2

—continued

	2002	2003	2004
Tomatoes	38.7	54.1	61.5
Chillies and green peppers*	36.0	36.0	36.0
Cucumbers and gherkins	27.1	26.4	23.6
Onions	29.7	26.3	36.9
Carrots	43.3	42.8	41.6
Apples	51.2	60.7	51.5
Grapes	45.1	66.0	56.5
Watermelons	7.6	14.0	11.4
Other fruits (incl. canteloupes and other melons)*	133.2	90.4	86.1
Tobacco (leaves)	2.0	1.9	1.3

* FAO estimates.
Source: FAO.

LIVESTOCK
('000 head, year ending 30 September)

	2002	2003	2004
Cattle	608	593	540
Pigs	1,517	1,443	1,149
Sheep	316	326	321
Goats	40	39	39
Horses	8	8	9*
Chickens	6,462†	6,372†	6,300*

* FAO estimate.
† Unofficial estimate.
Source: FAO.

LIVESTOCK PRODUCTS
('000 metric tons, unless otherwise indicated)

	2002	2003	2004
Beef and veal	41.6	40.0	41.2
Pig meat	154.3	158.1	136.5
Poultry meat*	127.5	127.3	127.3
Cows' milk	1,197.8	1,142.2	1,078.6
Goats' milk	9.1	9.0	8.9
Butter	17.8	14.8	10.8
Cheese	57.1	56.3	51.4
Hen eggs	66.2	67.7	63.3
Other poultry eggs*	1.9	3.1	4.3
Cattle hides (fresh)*	3.9	3.7	—

* FAO estimates.
Source: FAO.

Forestry

ROUNDWOOD REMOVALS
('000 cubic metres, excl. bark)

	2002	2003	2004
Sawlogs, veneer logs and logs for sleepers	2,365	2,533	3,119
Pulpwood	2,956	3,217	3,397
Other industrial wood	202	301	420
Fuel wood	259	304	304
Total	**5,782**	**6,355**	**7,240**

Source: FAO.

SAWNWOOD PRODUCTION
('000 cubic metres, incl. railway sleepers)

	2002*	2003	2004
Coniferous (softwood)	845	1,150	1,251
Broadleaved (hardwood)	420	501	586
Total	**1,265**	**1,651**	**1,837**

* FAO estimates.
Source: FAO.

SLOVAKIA

Fishing

(metric tons, live weight)

	2001	2002	2003
Capture	1,531	1,746	1,646
Common carp	967	1,166	1,046
Northern pike	73	64	56
Pike-perch	62	79	78
Breams	95	103	98
Aquaculture	999	829	881
Common carp	256	154	139
Rainbow trout	690	634	682
Total catch (incl. others)	2,530	2,575	2,527

Source: FAO, *Yearbook of Fishery Statistics*.

Mining

('000 metric tons, unless otherwise indicated)

	2001	2002	2003
Coal (brown and lignite)	3,424	3,401	3,077
Iron ore:			
gross weight	888	1,300	1,324
metal content	238	175	200
Crude petroleum	54	53	48
Natural gas (million cu metres)	212	212	212
Limestone and other calcareous stones for cement	3,596	3,694	3,453
Sands and gravel ('000 cubic metres)	1,272	1,399	1,300

Source: US Geological Survey.

Industry

SELECTED PRODUCTS
('000 metric tons, unless otherwise indicated)

	2000	2001	2002
Wheat flour	327	312	333
Bread	151	145	138
Refined sugar	25	38	35
Beer ('000 hectolitres)	4,491	4,520	4,800
Wine ('000 hectolitres)	480	450	374
Distilled alcoholic beverages ('000 hectolitres)	130	123	111
Cotton yarn	3.5	3.6	n.a.
Footwear ('000 pairs)*	8,503	8,994	9,555
Paper and paperboard	925	988	994
Paints and enamels	32.3	32.9	34.6
Black-coal coke	1,706	1,697	n.a.
Residual fuel oils	543	718	n.a.
Gas-diesel (distillate fuel) oil	2,125	2,406	n.a.
Cement	3,045	3,123	3,141
Pig-iron†	3,166	3,255	3,533
Crude steel†	3,733	3,989	4,275
Aluminium	250.1	250.4	275.1
Household refrigerators and freezers ('000 units)	177	27	2
Passenger motor cars ('000 units)	181	277	226
Lorries (number)	37	70	n.a.
Colour television receivers ('000 units)	431	594	712
Electric energy (million kWh)	31,993	32,046	n.a.

* Excluding rubber footwear.
† Source: US Geological Survey.

Source: UN, *Industrial Commodity Statistics Yearbook*.

Cement ('000 metric tons): 3,147 in 2003 (Source: US Geological Survey).

Pig-iron ('000 metric tons, estimate): 3,500 in 2003 (Source: US Geological Survey).

Crude steel ('000 metric tons): 4,549 in 2003 (Source: US Geological Survey).

Aluminium ingot, primary (metric tons): 133.7 in 2001; 147.0 in 2002; 165.3 in 2003 (Source: US Geological Survey).

Finance

CURRENCY AND EXCHANGE RATES

Monetary Units
100 halierov (singular: halier) = 1 Slovenská koruna (Slovak crown or Sk; plural: koruny).

Sterling, Dollar and Euro Equivalents (30 December 2005)
£1 sterling = 55.01 koruny;
US $1 = 31.95 koruny;
€1 = 37.69 koruny;
1,000 koruny = £18.18 = $31.30 = €26.53.

Average Exchange Rate (koruny per US $)
2003   36.773
2004   32.257
2005   31.018

Note: In February 1993 Slovakia introduced its own currency, the Slovak koruna, to replace (at par) the Czechoslovak koruna.

STATE BUDGET
(million koruny)

Revenue*	2001	2002	2003
Current revenue	347,090	385,656	408,674
Tax revenue	304,962	365,243	363,840
Non-tax revenue	42,128	40,143	44,834
Capital revenue	6,004	4,208	3,835
Total	353,094	389,864	412,509

Expenditure†	2001	2002	2003
Current expenditure	354,402	401,361	419,537
Wages	58,908	64,743	73,609
Goods and services	98,221	106,365	116,753
Transfers to households and non-profit institutions	144,906	173,051	175,933
Transfers abroad	707	745	852
Subsidies	20,033	17,200	20,354
Interest payments	31,627	39,257	32,036
Capital expenditure	54,326	57,372	41,740
Total	408,728	458,733	461,277

* Excluding grants received (million koruny): 263 in 2001; 376 in 2002; and 66 in 2003.
† Excluding net lending and repayments (million koruny): –24,885 in 2001; –177,709 in 2002; –16,578 in 2003.

2004 (million koruny): Total revenue 508,237; Total expenditure 550,059.

Source: Ministry of Finance.

INTERNATIONAL RESERVES
(US $ million at 31 December)

	2002	2003	2004
Gold (national valuation)	55	67	77
IMF special drawing rights	1	1	1
Foreign exchange	8,808	11,677	14,416
Total	8,864	11,745	14,494

Source: IMF, *International Financial Statistics*.

MONEY SUPPLY
(million koruny at 31 December)

	2002	2003*	2004
Currency outside banks	84,211	91,826	100,450
Demand deposits at commercial banks	160,560	261,072	303,057
Total money (incl. others)	244,771	353,971	404,722

* From August 2003 data compiled in accordance with European Central Bank's national residency approach.

Source: IMF, *International Financial Statistics*.

SLOVAKIA

COST OF LIVING
(Consumer Price Index; base December 2000 = 100)

	2003	2004	2005
Foodstuffs and non-alcoholic beverages	108.3	113.5	111.9
Alcoholic beverages and tobacco	126.5	137.2	136.3
Clothing and footwear	107.0	107.5	106.5
Housing, water, electricity, gas and other fuels	135.8	153.8	165.9
All items (incl. others)	118.1	127.0	130.5

NATIONAL ACCOUNTS

Expenditure on the Gross Domestic Product
(million koruny at current prices)

	2002	2003	2004
Final consumption expenditure	854,351	917,663	1,008,332
Households	624,532	667,453	738,671
Non-profit institutions serving households	9,031	10,622	11,935
General government	220,788	239,588	257,726
Gross capital formation	322,363	305,525	349,095
Gross fixed capital formation	303,481	308,404	327,226
Changes in inventories	18,882	−2,879	21,869
Total domestic expenditure	1,176,714	1,223,188	1,357,427
Exports of goods and services	788,245	933,235	1,018,011
Less Imports of goods and services	866,301	951,121	1,053,626
Statistical discrepancy	—	−4,106	3,674
GDP in purchasers' values	1,098,658	1,201,196	1,325,486

Gross Domestic Product by Economic Activity
(million koruny, current prices)

	2002	2003	2004
Agriculture, hunting, forestry and fishing	44,452	43,677	48,151
Mining and quarrying	6,754	6,074	6,226
Manufacturing	218,108	230,004	256,974
Electricity, gas and water supply	32,811	56,095	61,753
Construction	52,722	58,791	68,518
Wholesale and retail trade; repair of motor vehicles	141,941	154,841	173,821
Hotels and restaurants	12,797	11,216	11,464
Transport and storage	114,607	119,346	131,227
Financial intermediation	52,676	61,107	83,598
Real estate, renting, business activities	141,567	160,660	177,689
Public administration, defence and compulsory social security	77,105	84,999	86,824
Education	34,730	40,002	43,009
Health and social work	37,696	44,074	45,201
Other community, social, personal services activities	34,087	32,767	31,765
Private households with employed persons	0	0	0
Other	96,605	97,543	99,266
Total	1,098,658	1,201,196	1,325,486

BALANCE OF PAYMENTS
(US $ million)

	2001	2002	2003
Exports of goods f.o.b.	12,631	14,365	21,838
Imports of goods f.o.b.	−14,766	−16,497	−22,479
Trade balance	−2,135	−2,131	−641
Exports of services	2,490	2,786	3,286
Imports of services	−2,010	−2,330	−3,050
Balance on goods and services	−1,655	−1,675	−404
Income (net)	−313	−456	−120
Balance on goods, services and income	−1,968	−2,131	−524
Current transfers	212	193	245
Current balance	−1,756	−1,939	−280
Capital transfers	78	107	101
Medium and long-term credits	−114	27	−347
Short-term capital (net)	835	524	2,009
Foreign investment (net)	920	4,517	−25
Net errors and omissions	180	409	35
Overall balance	143	3,645	1,493

Source: IMF, *Slovak Republic: Statistical Appendix* (March 2005).

External Trade

COMMODITY GROUPS
(million koruny)

Imports f.o.b.	2001	2002	2003
Prepared foodstuffs, beverages and tobacco	22,779	24,973	23,306
Mineral products	117,890	109,190	108,522
Products of the chemical or allied industries	61,769	65,648	63,989
Rubber and plastics, and articles thereof	37,035	45,547	57,007
Wood pulp, cellulose and paper, and articles thereof	20,882	22,488	22,662
Textiles and textile articles	40,625	41,989	42,545
Base metals and articles of base metal	59,533	66,893	74,163
Machinery and electrical equipment	180,458	191,509	217,842
Vehicles, aircraft, vessels and transport equipment	89,858	95,434	123,652
Optical, photographic, measuring and medical apparatus; clocks and watches; musical instruments	16,715	17,091	20,648
Total (incl. others)	713,898	747,975	826,673

Exports f.o.b.	2001	2002	2003
Mineral products	47,519	46,644	48,405
Products of the chemical or allied industries	30,126	31,046	27,353
Rubber and plastics, and articles thereof	32,499	37,807	41,618
Wood pulp, cellulose and paper, and articles thereof	31,376	31,710	30,409
Textiles and textile articles	41,578	43,305	40,964
Base metals and articles of base metal	92,402	93,469	108,206
Machinery and electrical equipment	114,424	122,860	151,033
Vehicles, aircraft, vessels and transport equipment	126,077	137,943	233,225
Total (incl. others)	611,325	652,018	803,238

SLOVAKIA

PRINCIPAL TRADING PARTNERS
(million koruny)

Imports f.o.b.	2002	2003	2004
Austria	31,480	36,206	40,258
Belgium	13,498	13,947	15,697
China, People's Republic	n.a.	20,437	24,927
Czech Republic	113,332	118,317	124,620
France	32,984	35,068	34,485
Germany	169,195	210,632	224,397
Hungary	20,425	28,379	31,849
Italy	51,540	50,995	52,645
Japan	13,863	15,636	18,681
Korea, Republic	2,467	7,076	17,042
Netherlands	13,134	13,627	14,064
Poland	24,088	29,150	36,674
Russia	93,858	88,665	88,509
Spain	23,511	22,420	19,151
Switzerland	10,198	9,593	8,919
Ukraine	8,478	8,586	13,348
United Kingdom	18,952	17,627	17,132
USA	15,959	16,106	15,399
Total (incl. others)	747,975	826,673	942,160

Exports f.o.b.	2002	2003	2004
Austria	50,084	59,726	70,230
Belgium	13,535	15,971	18,946
Czech Republic	99,052	103,649	119,266
France	27,206	28,196	32,340
Germany	169,529	247,680	256,791
Hungary	35,539	39,124	70,230
Italy	69,934	60,132	57,051
Netherlands	19,842	21,683	27,330
Poland	34,768	38,383	49,144
Russia	6,495	9,817	10,824
Spain	10,572	13,123	16,026
Switzerland	8,156	8,860	7,379
Ukraine	7,064	8,152	9,556
United Kingdom	15,528	16,960	25,759
USA	9,425	42,216	42,630
Total (incl. others)	652,018	803,238	895,205

Transport

	2002	2003	2004
Railway transport:			
freight ('000 tons)	—	—	50,445
passengers ('000)	59,430	51,274	50,325
Public road transport:			
freight ('000 tons)	49,863	50,521	49,769
passengers ('000)	536,613	493,706	461,772
Waterway transport: freight ('000 tons)	1,699	1,451	1,636

ROAD TRAFFIC
(motor vehicles in use at 31 December)

	2002	2003	2004
Passenger cars ('000)	1,327	1,356	1,197
Buses and coaches ('000)	11	11	9
Goods vehicles ('000)	130	142	140

Civil Aviation
(traffic on scheduled services)

	2002	2003	2004
Passengers carried ('000)	272	428	974
Freight carried ('000 metric tons)	1	1	0

Tourism

FOREIGN TOURIST ARRIVALS
(visitors at accommodation facilities)

Country of origin	1999	2000	2001
Austria	32,643	36,779	44,046
Czech Republic	275,031	277,401	327,607
France	14,833	16,015	19,523
Germany	137,964	155,129	172,446
Hungary	53,057	59,322	73,937
Italy	27,076	28,097	32,737
Netherlands	16,540	18,772	22,068
Poland	173,135	201,082	264,631
Russia	22,361	30,861	19,876
Ukraine	31,732	24,212	18,863
USA	23,310	28,851	28,183
Total (incl. others)	975,105	1,045,614	1,219,099

Total foreign visitors at accommodation facilities: 1,219,000 in 2001; 1,399,000 in 2002; 1,387,000 in 2003.

Tourism receipts (US $ million, incl. passenger transport): 649 in 2001; 742 in 2002; 876 in 2003 (Source: World Tourism Organization).

Communications Media

	2002	2003	2004
Telephones ('000 main lines in use)	1,442.6	1,294.7	1,250.4
Mobile cellular telephones ('000 subscribers)	2,923.4	3,678.8	4,275.2
Personal computers ('000 in use)	1,010	1,270	1,593
Internet users ('000)	862.8	1,375.8	2,276.0
Newspapers: titles	478	463	95
Newspapers: circulation ('000 copies)	287,022	270,498	218,722
Periodicals: titles	1,108	1,076	791
Periodicals: circulation ('000 copies)	188,878	153,799	166,228

Radio receivers (licensed): 1,255,624 in 1998; 1,368,863 in 1999; 1,347,477 in 2000.

Television receivers (licensed): 1,392,883 in 1998; 1,241,663 in 1999; 1,211,773 in 2000.

Newspapers: 939,000 (daily), 3,752,000 (non-daily) in 1998; 851,000 (daily), 4,201,000 (non-daily) in 1999; 705,000 (daily), 2,651,000 (non-daily) in 2000.

Book production (number of titles): 2,064 in 1997; 4,386 in 1998; 3,153 in 1999.

Telefax stations (number registered): 54,037 in 1998.

Sources: partly International Telecommunication Union and UNESCO Institute for Statistics.

Education
(2004)

	Institutions	Teachers	Students
Kindergarten	3,046	13,931	149,232
Primary (basic)	2,342	35,984	555,335
Secondary: grammar	234	7,543	99,738
Secondary: specialized	262	8,274	87,533
Secondary: vocational	233	3,767	73,525
Higher	24	10,069	108,608

Directory

The Constitution*

On 1 September 1992 the Slovenská národná rada (Slovak National Council) adopted the Constitution of the Slovak Republic (which entered into force on 1 January 1993), the main provisions of which, as amended in January 1999, are summarized below:

FUNDAMENTAL PROVISIONS

The Slovak Republic is a democratic and sovereign state, ruled by law. It is bound neither to an ideology, nor to a religion. State power belongs to the people, who exercise it either through their representatives or directly. The state authorities shall act only on the basis of the Constitution and to the extent and in the manner stipulated by law.

The territory of the Slovak Republic is integral and indivisible. The conditions for naturalization or deprival of state citizenship of the Slovak Republic are regulated by law. No person may be deprived of citizenship against his or her will. The Slovak language is the state language in the republic. The use of languages other than the state language in administrative relations is regulated by law. The capital of the republic is Bratislava.

BASIC RIGHTS AND FREEDOMS

The people are free and equal, and the rights and freedoms of every citizen are guaranteed, irrespective of sex, race, colour, language, faith, political or other conviction, national or social origin, nationality or ethnic origin. No person may be tortured, nor be subjected to cruel, inhuman or humiliating treatment or punishment. Capital punishment is not practised.

Every person has the right to own property. The place of abode is inviolable. The freedom of migration and the freedom of domicile are guaranteed.

The freedom of expression and the right to information are guaranteed. Censorship is prohibited. The right to assemble peacefully is guaranteed. Every person has the right to be a member of a union, community, society or any other association. Citizens have the right to found political parties and movements. Such parties and movements, as well as other associations, are separate from the state.

The citizens have the right to participate in the administration of public affairs, either directly or through the free election of their representatives. The right to vote is universal, direct and equal and is exercised by secret ballot.

The universal advancement of citizens who are members of national minorities and ethnic groups is guaranteed, above all the right to develop their own culture, to broadcast and receive information in their mother tongue, to join national associations and to found and maintain educational and cultural institutions. The languages of national minorities may also be used in administrative relations.

Every person has the right to the free choice of profession and vocational training as well as to do business and to perform other commercial activities. Employees are entitled to fair and satisfactory working conditions. Citizens may form free associations to protect their economic and social interests. Trade unions are independent of the state. The right to strike is guaranteed.

Every citizen is entitled to adequate old-age and disability benefits; widow's allowances; free health care; family support; and education.

NÁRODNÁ RADA SLOVENSKEJ REPUBLIKY

Supreme legislative power is vested in the Národná rada Slovenskej republiky (National Council of the Slovak Republic—Národná rada), which has 150 deputies, elected for a four-year term. The deputies represent the citizens and are elected by them in general, equal and direct elections, by secret ballot.

The Národná rada has the power to: adopt the Constitution, constitutional and other laws and supervise their execution; decide on proposals to call a referendum; prior to their ratification, give consent to international political, economic or other agreements; establish ministries and other bodies of state administration; supervise the activities of the Government and pass a vote of confidence or censure on the Government or its members; approve the state budget and supervise its execution; elect judges, including the Chairman and Vice-Chairmen of the Supreme Court and of the Constitutional Court; adopt a resolution to declare war if the Slovak Republic is attacked, or if such a declaration ensues from the obligations of international treaties.

THE PRESIDENT OF THE REPUBLIC

The President is the Head of State of the Slovak Republic. He or she is directly elected by universal adult suffrage for a five-year term. The President is responsible to the Národná rada. He/she may not be elected for more than two consecutive terms.

The President represents the Slovak Republic internationally; negotiates and ratifies international agreements; receives and gives credentials to envoys; convenes constituent sessions of the Národná rada; may dissolve the Národná rada; signs laws; appoints and recalls the Prime Minister and other members of the Government and receives their resignation; grants amnesty, pardons and commutes sentences imposed by courts; may declare a state of emergency on the basis of constitutional law; may declare a referendum.

THE GOVERNMENT

The Government of the Slovak Republic is the highest organ of executive power. It is composed of the Prime Minister and Ministers. The Prime Minister is appointed by the President of the Republic. On the Prime Minister's recommendation, the President appoints and recalls the members of the Government and puts them in charge of their ministries. For the execution of office, the Government is responsible to the Národná rada.

The Government has the power to prepare bills; issue decrees; adopt fundamental provisions for economic and social policy; authorize drafts for the state budget and closing account of the year; decide international agreements; decide principal questions of internal and international policy; submit bills to the Národná rada; request the legislature for a vote of confidence.

* Further revisions to the Constitution were approved in February 2001 and officially entered into effect on 1 July. The amendments redefined the relationship between national and international law, incorporated Slovakia's aim of joining foreign alliances, strengthened the powers of the Constitutional Court, granted greater independence to the judiciary (by the establishment of a new judicial council), and provided for public administration reform, with the creation of a higher level of regional self-government.

The Government

HEAD OF STATE

President of the Republic: Ivan Gašparovič (elected 17 April 2004; inaugurated 15 June 2004).

GOVERNMENT
(April 2006)

The Government comprises members of the Slovak Democratic and Christian Union-Democratic Party (SDCU-DP), the Party of the Hungarian Coalition (PHC) and independents (Ind.).

Prime Minister: Mikuláš Dzurinda (SDCU-DP).

Deputy Prime Minister for European Integration, Human Rights and Minorities: Pál Csáky (PHC).

Deputy Prime Minister and Minister of Finance: Ivan Mikloš (SDCU-DP).

Deputy Prime Minister and Minister of the Economy: Jirko Malchárek (Ind.).

Minister of Foreign Affairs: Eduard Kukan (SDCU-DP).

Minister of Defence: Martin Fedor (SDCU-DP).

Minister of the Environment: László Miklós (PHC).

Minister of the Interior: Martin Pado (SDCU-DP).

Minister of Justice: Lucia Žitňanská (Ind.).

Minister of Labour, Social Affairs and the Family: Iveta Radičová (Ind.).

Minister of Culture: Rudolf Chmel (Ind.).

Minister of Education: László Szigeti (PHC).

Minister of Health: Rudolf Zajac (Ind.).

Minister of Agriculture: Zsolt Simon (PHC).

Minister of Transport, Posts and Telecommunications: Pavol Prokopovič (SDCU-DP).

Minister of Construction and Regional Development: László Gyurovszky (PHC).

MINISTRIES

Office of the President: Hodžovo nám. 1, 810 00 Bratislava, POB 128; tel. (2) 5720-1121; fax (2) 5441-7010; e-mail informacie@prezident.sk; internet www.prezident.sk.

Office of the Government: nám. Slobody 1, 813 70 Bratislava; tel. (2) 5729-5111; fax (2) 5249-7595; e-mail urad@vlada.gov.sk; internet www.government.gov.sk.

SLOVAKIA

Ministry of Agriculture: Dobrovičova 12, 812 66 Bratislava; tel. (2) 5296-6111; fax (2) 5296-6311; e-mail tlacove@land.gov.sk; internet www.mpsr.sk.

Ministry of Construction and Regional Development: Špitálska 8, 816 44 Bratislava; tel. (2) 5975-1111; fax (2) 5293-1203; e-mail informacie@build.gov.sk; internet www.build.gov.sk.

Ministry of Culture: nám. SNP, 81101 Bratislava; tel. (2) 5939-1111; fax (2) 5926-6457; e-mail mksr@culture.gov.sk; internet www.culture.gov.sk.

Ministry of Defence: Kutuzovova 7, 832 28 Bratislava; tel. (2) 4425-0320; fax (2) 4425-3242; e-mail linka.dovery@mod.gov.sk; internet www.mod.gov.sk.

Ministry of the Economy: Mierová 19, 827 15 Bratislava; tel. (2) 4854-1111; fax (2) 4333-7827; e-mail icom@economy.gov.sk; internet www.economy.gov.sk.

Ministry of Education: Stromová 1, 813 30 Bratislava; tel. (2) 5937-4111; fax (2) 5937-4335; e-mail inform@education.gov.sk; internet www.education.gov.sk.

Ministry of the Environment: nám. L'. Štúra 1, 812 35 Bratislava; tel. (2) 5956-1111; fax (2) 5956-2222; e-mail info@enviro.gov.sk; internet www.enviro.gov.sk.

Ministry of Finance: Štefanovičova 5, POB 82, 817 82 Bratislava; tel. (2) 5958-1111; fax (2) 5249-3048; e-mail podatelna@mfsr.sk; internet www.finance.gov.sk.

Ministry of Foreign Affairs: Hlboká cesta 2, 833 36 Bratislava; tel. (2) 5978-1111; fax (2) 5978-2213; e-mail informacie@foreign.gov.sk; internet www.mzv.sk.

Ministry of Health: Limbová 2, POB 52, 837 52 Bratislava; tel. (2) 5937-3111; fax (2) 5477-7983; e-mail office@health.gov.sk; internet www.health.gov.sk.

Ministry of the Interior: Pribinova 2, 812 72 Bratislava; tel. (2) 5094-1111; fax (2) 5094-4397; e-mail tokmv@minv.sk; internet www.minv.sk.

Ministry of Justice: Župné nám. 13, 813 11 Bratislava; tel. (2) 5935-3111; fax (2) 5935-3600; e-mail tlacove@justice.sk; internet www.justice.gov.sk.

Ministry of Labour, Social Affairs and the Family: Špitálska 4–6, 816 43 Bratislava; tel. (2) 5975-1617; fax (2) 5292-1258; e-mail tothova@employment.gov.sk; internet www.employment.gov.sk.

Ministry of Transport, Post and Telecommunications: nám. Slobody 6, 810 05 Bratislava; tel. (2) 5949-4111; fax (2) 5249-4794; e-mail info@telecom.gov.sk; internet www.telecom.gov.sk.

President

Presidential Election, First Ballot, 3 April 2004

Candidates	Number of votes	%
Vladimír Mečiar	650,242	32.74
Ivan Gašparovič	442,564	22.28
Eduard Kukan	438,920	22.10
Rudolf Schuster	147,549	7.43
František Mikloško	129,414	6.52
Martin Bútora	129,387	6.51
Others	48,138	2.42
Total	1,986,214	100.00

Second Ballot, 17 April 2004

Candidates	Number of votes	%
Ivan Gašparovič	1,079,592	59.91
Vladimír Mečiar	722,368	40.09
Total	1,801,960	100.00

Legislature

Národná rada Slovenskej republiky
(National Council of the Slovak Republic)

Mudronova 1, 812 80 Bratislava; tel. (2) 5934-1111; fax (2) 5441-5324; e-mail valdpete@nrsr.sk; internet www.nrsr.sk.

Chairman: BÉLA BUGÁR (acting).

General Election, 20–21 September 2002

Party	Votes	% of votes	Seats
Movement for a Democratic Slovakia	560,691	19.50	36
Slovak Democratic and Christian Union	433,953	15.09	28
Direction (Smer)	387,100	13.46	25
Party of the Hungarian Coalition	321,069	11.16	20
Christian Democratic Movement	237,202	8.25	15
New Citizens' Alliance	230,309	8.01	15
Communist Party of Slovakia	181,872	6.32	11
Others	522,885	18.19	—
Total*	2,875,081	100.00	150

* Excluding 34,917 invalid votes.

Election Commission

Odbora volieb a referenda, Ministerstva vnútra (Department of Elections and Referendums, Ministry of the Interior): Drieňova 22, 812 72 Bratislava; tel. (2) 4859-2706; fax (2) 4333-5857; e-mail petkova.linda@mvsr.vs.sk; internet www.civil.gov.sk; organ of the Ministry of the Interior; Chair. LÍVIA ŠKULTÉTYOVÁ.

Political Organizations

Christian Democratic Movement (CDM) (Krest'ansko-demokratické hnutie—KDH): Miletičova 21, 821 09 Bratislava; tel. (2) 5057-4006; fax (2) 5057-4049; e-mail tlacove@kdh.sk; internet www.kdh.sk; f. 1990; conservative; supports Christian and family values; Chair. PAVOL HRUŠOVSKY.

Civic Conservative Party (Občianska konzervatívna strana—OKS): Panenská 26, Bratislava 811 03; internet www.oks.sk; e-mail oks@oks.sk; tel. 908437009; f. and regd 2001; Chair. PETER TATÁR.

Communist Party of Slovakia (CPS) (Komunistická strana Slovenska—KSS): Ústredný výbor, Hattalova 12A, 831 03 Bratislava; tel. and fax (2) 4437-2540; e-mail sekr@kss.sk; internet www.kss.sk; f. 1992 following merger of two Marxist parties, the Union of Communists of Slovakia (Zväz komunistov Slovenska) and the Communist Party of Slovakia—91 (Komunistická strana Slovenska—91), which were established by Orthodox communists opposed to the transformation of the Communist Party of Slovakia into the non-Marxist Party of the Democratic Left (Strana demokratickej l'avice); Pres. JOZEF ŠEVC; Gen.-Sec. Dr LADISLAV JAČA; 10,000 mems.

Democratic Party of Slovakia (Demokratická strana Slovenska): Bratislava; f. 2006 by former mems of the Democratic Party who opposed its merger with the Slovak Democratic and Christian Union; in March reached agreement on co-operation with the Free Forum Party, the Green Party and the Democratic Union of Slovakia ahead of the June legislative elections; Leader DUŠAN BOBRÍK.

Democratic Union of Slovakia (DUS) (Demokratická únia Slovenska): Medená 10, 811 04 Bratislava; f. 1994 by former mems of the Movement for a Democratic Slovakia; in 1995 absorbed the National Democratic Party—New Alternative; splinter group, Liberal Democratic Union, f. in 2000; in March 2006 reached agreement on co-operation with the Free Forum Party, the Green Party and the Democratic Party of Slovakia, ahead of legislative elections in June; Chair. L'UBOMÍR HARACH; First Deputy Chair. MILAN KŇAŽKO.

Direction-Social Democracy (Smer-Sociálna demokracia): Súmračná 27, 821 02 Bratislava; tel. and fax (2) 4342-6297; e-mail tajomnik@strana-smer.sk; internet www.strana-smer.sk; f. and regd in 1999 as Direction (Smer); absorbed the Party of Civic Understanding in 2003; merged with the Social Democratic Alternative, the Social Democratic Party of Slovakia and the Party of the Democratic Left in Jan. 2005, and name changed as above; Chair. ROBERT FICO.

Free Forum Party (Slobodné fórum) (SF): Bazová 9, 821 08 Bratislava; tel. (2) 5564-2494; fax (2) 5564-2496; e-mail sf@slobodneforum.sk; internet www.slobodneforum.sk; f. 2003; regd 2004; centre-right; in March 2006 reached agreement on co-operation with the Democratic Party of Slovakia, the Democratic Union of Slovakia and the Green Party, ahead of legislative elections in June; Chair. ZUZANA MARTINÁKOVÁ.

Green Party (Strana zelených): Sienkiewiczova 4, 811 09 Bratislava; tel. and fax (2) 5292-3231; e-mail sekretariat@stranazelenych.sk; internet www.stranazelenych.sk; f. 1989, regd 1991; in March 2006 reached agreement on co-operation with the Democratic Party

SLOVAKIA   Directory

of Slovakia, the Democratic Union of Slovakia and the Free Forum, ahead of legislative elections in June; Chair. PAVEL PETRÍK.

Movement for Democracy (Hnutie za demokraciu—HZD): Nevädzová 5, 821 01, Bratislava; tel. (2) 4828-7638; fax (2) 4828-7417; e-mail hzd@hzd.sk; internet www.hzd.sk; f. and regd 2002; by former mems of the Movement for a Democratic Slovakia; Chair. JOZEF GRAPA.

Hope (Nádej): Palisády 51, 811 06 Bratislava; tel. 910425188; f. 2006 by former members of New Citizens' Alliance; registered in 2006; supports free-market economy, protection of human rights and representative government.

New Citizens' Alliance (NCA) (Aliancia nového občana—ANO): Drobného 27, 841 01 Bratislava; tel. (2) 6920-2918; fax (2) 6920-2920; e-mail ano@ano-aliancia.sk; internet www.ano-aliancia.sk; f. 2001; registered; centre-right, pro-reform; Dir PAVEL RUSKO.

Party of the Hungarian Coalition (PHC) (Strana maďarskej koalície/Magyar Koalíció Pártja): Čajakova 8, 811 05 Bratislava; tel. (2) 5249-5164; fax (2) 5249-5264; e-mail smk@smk.sk; internet www.mkp.sk; f. 1998 by merger of Coexistence (Spolužitie/Együttélés), the Hungarian Christian Democratic Movement and the Hungarian Civic Party; Chair. BÉLA BUGÁR.

Party of the Romany Coalition in the Slovak Republic (Strana rómskej koalície v Slovenskej republike—SRK): Pribinova 172, 960 01 Zvolen; regd in 2000 as Romany Intelligentsia for Co-existence in the Slovak Republic (Rómska inteligencia za spolunažívanie v Slovenskej republike); name changed as above in 2001; represents interests of the Romany population; Chair. LADISLAV FÍZIK.

People's Party—Movement for a Democratic Slovakia (PP—MDS) (Ľudová strana—Hnutie za Demokratické Slovensko—LS—HZDS): POB 49, Tomášikova 32A, 830 00 Bratislava; tel. (2) 4822-0203; fax (2) 4822-0223; e-mail krampl@hzds.sk; internet www.hzds.sk; f. 1991 as Movement for a Democratic Slovakia; present name adopted 2003; Chair. VLADIMÍR MEČIAR.

People's Union (Ľudová únia—LU): Hanulova 5B, 841 01 Bratislava; tel. (2) 6428-8312; fax (2) 6428-7567; e-mail ludovaunia@ludovaunia.sk; internet www.ludovaunia.sk; f. 2003 by fmr mems of Movement for a Democratic Slovakia; regd 2003; Chair. GUSTÁV KRAJČI.

Slovak Democratic and Christian Union-Democratic Party (SDCU-DP) (Slovenská demokratická a kresťanská únia-Demokratická strana—SDKÚ-DS): Ružinovská 28, 827 35 Bratislava; tel. (2) 4341-4102; fax (2) 4341-4106; e-mail sdku@sdkuonline.sk; internet www.sdkuonline.sk; f. and regd 2000 as the Slovak Democratic and Christian Union; name changed as above following merger with the Democratic Party in Jan. 2006; Leader MIKULÁŠ DZURINDA.

Slovak National Party (SNP) (Slovenská národná strana—SNS): Šafárikovo nám. 3, 814 99 Bratislava; tel. (2) 5292-4260; fax (2) 5296-6188; e-mail sns@sns.sk; internet www.sns.sk; f. and regd 1990; Chair. JÁN SLOTA.

Diplomatic Representation

EMBASSIES IN SLOVAKIA

Angola: Mudroňova 47, 811 03 Bratislava 1; tel. (2) 5441-2164; fax (2) 5441-2182; e-mail embangola1@embangola.sk; Ambassador DOMINGOS CULOLO.

Austria: Ventúrska 10, 811 01 Bratislava; tel. (2) 5930-1500; fax (2) 5443-2486; e-mail pressburg-ob@bmaa.gv.at; internet www.embassyaustria.sk; Ambassador Dr MARTIN BOLLDORF.

Belarus: Kuzmányho 3A, 811 06 Bratislava; tel. (2) 5441-6325; fax (2) 5441-6328; e-mail slovakia@belembassy.org; internet www.belembassy.org/slovakia; Ambassador Dr VALERY I. VORONETSKY.

Belgium: Fraňa kráľa 5, 811 05 Bratislava; tel. (2) 5710-1211; fax (2) 5249-4296; e-mail ambabelbratis@stonline.sk; internet www.diplomatie.be/bratislava; Ambassador OLIVIER BELLE.

Bulgaria: Kuzmányho 1, 811 06 Bratislava; tel. (2) 5441-5308; fax (2) 5441-2404; e-mail bulharskoet@stonline.sk; internet www.bulgarianembassy.sk; Ambassador YAROSLAV GOLEV.

China, People's Republic: Jančova 8, 811 02 Bratislava; tel. (2) 6280-3348; fax (2) 6280-4285; e-mail chinask@gtinet.sk; Ambassador HUANG ZHONGPO.

Croatia: Mišikova 21, 811 06 Bratislava; tel. (2) 5443-3647; fax (2) 5443-5365; e-mail croemb.bratislava@mvp.hr; Ambassador ANDREA GUSTOVIĆ-ERGEGOVAC.

Cuba: Somolického 1A, 811 05 Bratislava; tel. (2) 5249-2777; fax (2) 5249-4200; e-mail embacuba@zutom.sk; Ambassador CARIDAD YAMIRA CUETO MILIAN.

Czech Republic: POB 208, Hviezdoslavovo nám. 8, 810 00 Bratislava; tel. (2) 5920-3303; fax (2) 5920-3330; e-mail bratislava@embassy.mzv.cz; internet www.mzv.cz/bratislava; Ambassador VLADIMÍR GALUŠKA.

Denmark: Panská 27, 816 06 Bratislava; tel. 5930-0200; fax 5443-3653; e-mail btsamb@um.dk; internet www.denmark.sk; Ambassador JORGEN MUNK RASMUSSEN.

Finland: Palisády 29, 811 06 Bratislava; tel. 5980-5111; fax 5980-5120; e-mail sanomat.brt@formin.fi; Ambassador RAUNO VIEMERÖ.

France: Hlavné nám. 7, 811 01 Bratislava; tel. (2) 5934-7111; fax (2) 5934-7199; e-mail diplo@france.sk; internet www.france.sk; Ambassador JACQUES FAURE.

Germany: Hviezdoslavovo nám. 10, 813 03 Bratislava; tel. (2) 5920-4400; fax (2) 5441-9634; e-mail info@germanembassy.sk; internet www.germanembassy.sk; Ambassador Dr JOCHEN TREBESCH.

Greece: Hlavné nám. 4, 811 01 Bratislava; tel. (2) 5443-4143; fax (2) 5443-4064; e-mail embassy@greece.sk; internet www.greece.sk; Ambassador (vacant).

Holy See: Nekrasovova 17, 811 04 Bratislava (Apostolic Nunciature); tel. (2) 5479-3528; fax (2) 5479-3529; Apostolic Nuncio Most Rev. HENRYK JÓZEF NOWACKI (Titular Archbishop of Blera).

Hungary: Sedlárska 3, 814 25 Bratislava; tel. (2) 5920-5200; fax (2) 5443-5484; e-mail pozsony@embhung.sk; internet www.hungemb.sk; Ambassador CSABA GYŐRFFY.

India: Dunajská 4, 811 08 Bratislava; tel. (2) 5296-2915; fax (2) 5296-2921; e-mail india@slovanet.sk; internet www.indianembassy.sk; Ambassador MYSORE KAPANAIAH LOKESH.

Indonesia: Mudroňova 51, 811 02 Bratislava; tel. (2) 5441-9886; fax (2) 5441-9890; e-mail indonesia@indonesia.sk; internet www.indonesia.sk; Ambassador BINTANG PARLINDUNGAN SIMORANGKIR.

Ireland: Carlton Savoy Bldg, Mostavá 2, 811 02 Bratislava 1; tel. (2) 5930-9611; fax (2) 5443-0690; e-mail bratislava@iveagh.irlgov.ie; Ambassador DECLAN CONNOLLY.

Italy: Palisády 49, 811 06 Bratislava; tel. (2) 5980-0011; fax (2) 5441-3202; e-mail amb@ambitaba.sk; internet www.ambbratislava.esteri.it; Ambassador ANTONINO PROVENZANO.

Japan: Hlavné nám. 2, 813 27 Bratislava; tel. (2) 5980-0100; fax (2) 5443-2771; e-mail info@jpembassy.sk; internet www.sk.emb-japan.go.jp; Ambassador MAKOTO WASHIZU.

Libya: Révova ul. 45, 811 02 Bratislava 1; tel. (2) 5441-0324; fax (2) 5441-0730; e-mail lpb@stonline.sk; Sec. of People's Bureau AHMED KHALIFA.

Netherlands: Fraňa Kraľa 5, 811 05 Bratislava; tel. (2) 5262–5081; fax (2) 5249-1075; e-mail info@holandskoweb.com; internet www.holandskoweb.com; Ambassador LAURWENT L. STOKVIS.

Norway: Palisády 29, 811 06 Bratislava; tel. (2) 5910-0100; fax (2) 5910-0115; e-mail emb.bratislava@mfa.no; internet www.norway.sk; Ambassador BRIT LØVSETH.

Poland: Hummelova 4, 814 91 Bratislava; tel. (2) 5441-3174; fax (2) 5441-3184; e-mail bratampl@nextra.sk; internet www.polskevelvyslanectvo.sk; Ambassador ZENON KOSINIAK-KAMYSZ.

Romania: Fraňa Kráľa 11, 811 05 Bratislava; tel. (2) 5249-1665; fax (2) 5244-4056; e-mail ro-embassy@ba.sknet.sk; Ambassador VALERICA EPURE.

Russia: Godrova 4, 811 06 Bratislava; tel. (2) 5441-4436; fax (2) 5443-4910; e-mail embrus@chello.sk; internet www.slovakia.mid.ru; Ambassador ALEKSANDR I. UDALTSOV.

Serbia and Montenegro: Búdková 38, 811 04 Bratislava; tel. (2) 5443-1927; fax (2) 5443-1933; e-mail info@embassyscg.sk; Ambassador VOJISLAV MILENKOVIĆ.

Slovenia: Moyzesova 4, 813 15 Bratislava; tel. (2) 5245-0005; fax (2) 5245-0009; e-mail vbs@mzz-dkp.gov.si; Ambassador MAJA MARIJA LOVRENČIČ SVETEK.

Spain: Prepoštská 10, 811 01 Bratislava; tel. (2) 5441-5724; fax (2) 5441-7565; e-mail embespsk@mail.mae.es; Ambassador MIGUEL AGUIRRE DE CÁRCER GARCÍA DEL ARENAL.

Sweden: Palisády 29, 811 06 Bratislava; tel. (2) 5910-2200; fax (2) 5910-2233; e-mail ambassaden.bratislava@foreign.ministry.se; Ambassador CECILIA JULIN.

Switzerland: Tolstého 9, 811 06 Bratislava; tel. (2) 5930-1111; fax (2) 5930-1100; e-mail vertretung@bts.rep.admin.ch; Ambassador JOSEF AREGGER.

Turkey: Holubyho 11, 811 03 Bratislava; tel. (2) 5441-5504; fax (2) 5441-3145; e-mail testta@nextra.sk; Ambassador SUNA COKGÜR ILICAK.

Ukraine: Radvaňská 35, 811 01 Bratislava; tel. (2) 5920-2810; fax (2) 5441-2651; e-mail ukremb@ukrembassy.sk; internet ; Ambassador INNA OHNYIVETS.

United Kingdom: Panská 16, 811 01 Bratislava; tel. (2) 5998-2000; fax (2) 5998-2237; e-mail bebra@internet.sk; internet www.britishembassy.sk; Ambassador JUDITH ANNE MACGREGOR.

SLOVAKIA

USA: Hviezdoslavovo nám. 5, 811 02 Bratislava; tel. (2) 5443-3338; fax (2) 5443-0096; e-mail cons@usembassy-bratislava.sk; internet www.usembassy.sk; Ambassador RODOLPHE M. (SKIP) VALLEE.

Judicial System

The judicial system of Slovakia has three levels: District Courts (55), Regional Courts (eight) and the Supreme Court. Regional Courts serve as courts of appeal to the District Courts, as well as serving as Courts of First Instance in some cases: the Supreme Court is the highest judicial authority in the country, operating as a Court of Cassation and appeal for Regional Courts. There is also a Constitutional Court to ensure compliance with the Constitution. In April 2002 an 18-member Judicial Council was elected, all of whom were lawyers, and nine of whom were judges. Three members are nominated by the President, three by the legislature, three by the Government, and eight elected by the judges themselves. The final member is the Chairman of the Supreme Court. The Council proposes candidates for judgeships, decides on the assignment of judges, comments on the budget, and elects the Chief Justice of the Supreme Court.

Supreme Court of the Slovak Republic
(Najvyšší súd Slovenskej republiky)

Župné nám. 13, Bratislava 81 490; tel. (2) 5935-3111; fax (2) 5441-1535; internet www.nssr.gov.sk; f. 1993.

Chairman: MILAN KARABÍN.

Office of the Prosecutor-General: Štúrova ul. 2, 812 85 Bratislava; tel. (2) 5953-2505; fax (2) 5953-2653; internet www.genpro.gov.sk; Prosecutor-General DOBROSLAV TRNKA.

Constitutional Court of the Slovak Republic
(Ústavný súd Slovenskej republiky)

Hlavná 72, 042 65 Košice; tel. (55) 720-7211; fax (55) 622-7639; e-mail ochodni@concourt.sk; internet www.concourt.sk.

Chairman: JÁN MAZÁK.

Religion

The principal religion in Slovakia is Christianity, of which the largest denomination (representing some 69% of the total population according to the census of May 2001) is the Roman Catholic Church. About 10% of the population profess no religious belief.

CHRISTIANITY
The Roman Catholic Church

Slovakia consists of two archdioceses and five dioceses, including one (directly responsible to the Holy See) for Catholics of the Slovak (Byzantine) rite. At 31 December 2003 there were an estimated 3,808,276 adherents.

Bishops' Conference: Kapitulská 11, 81499 Bratislava; tel. (2) 5443-5234; fax (2) 5443-5913; e-mail kbs@kbs.sk; internet www.rcc.sk; f. 1993; Pres. Rt Rev. FRANTIŠEK TONDRA (Bishop of Spiš).

Latin Rite

Archbishop of Bratislava-Trnava: Most Rev. JÁN SOKOL, Hollého 10, 917 66 Trnava; tel. (33) 591-2111; fax (33) 551-1224; e-mail abu@abu.sk.

Archbishop of Košice: Most Rev. ALOJZ TKÁČ, Hlavná 28, 041 83 Košice; tel. (55) 682-8111; fax (55) 622-1034; e-mail abukosice@kbs.sk.

Slovak Rite

Bishop of Prešov: Rt Rev. JÁN HIRKA, Hlavná ul. 1, 081 35 Prešov; tel. (51) 772-2814; fax (51) 772-2723; e-mail grkbupo@nextra.sk; internet www.home.nextra.sk/greckoka; 175,000 adherents, 199 parishes (Dec. 1999).

The Orthodox Church

Orthodox Church in the Czech Lands Slovakia
(Pravoslávna cirkev v českých krajinách a na Slovensku)
Theological Faculty of Prešov University, Masarykova 15, 080 80 Prešov; tel. (51) 772-4736; fax (51) 773-4045; e-mail dzugan@orthodox.sk; internet www.orthodox.sk.

Divided into four eparchies in the former Czechoslovakia: Prague and Olomouc (Czech Republic), Prešov and Michalovce (Slovakia); Archbishop of Prešov and Metropolitan of the Czech Lands and Slovakia (vacant); 53,613 mems (March 1991); 127 parishes; Theological Faculty in Charles University, Prague, Czech Republic.

Archbishop of Prešov: (vacant), Budovateľská 1, 080 01 Prešov; e-mail metropolita@orthodox.sk; tel. (51) 773-2174; fax (51) 773-3612.

Bishop of Michalovce and Chair. of the Eparchial Assembly: His Holiness JÁN, Duklianska 16, 071 01 Michalovce; tel. (56) 642-4156; fax (56) 643-1500; e-mail uerpc.mi@stonline.sk.

Protestant Churches

Apostolic Church in Slovakia (Apoštolská cirkev na Slovensku): Sreznevského 2, 831 03 Bratislava; tel. and fax (2) 4425-0913; e-mail rada@acs-net.sk; internet www.acs-net.sk; f. 1956; affiliated to international Assemblies of God; 4,000 mems; Pres. JÁN LACHO.

Baptist Union of Slovakia: Súľovská 2, 821 05 Bratislava; tel. and fax (2) 4342-1145; e-mail jozef-kulacik@computel.sk; f. 1994; 2,038 mems (April 2000); Pres. Rev. TOMÁŠ KRIŠKA; Gen. Sec. Rev. Dr JOZEF KULAČÍK.

Evangelical Church of the Augsburg (Lutheran) Confession in Slovakia (Evanjelická cirkev augsburského vyznania na Slovensku): Palisády 46, POB 289, 811 00 Bratislava; tel. (2) 5443-2842; fax (2) 5443-2940; e-mail tlac@ecav.sk; internet www.ecav.sk; 327 parishes in 14 seniorates and two districts; 374,000 mems (Nov. 2001); Bishop-Gen. JÚLIUS FILO; Inspector-Gen. JÁN HOLČÍK.

Reformed Christian Church of Slovakia: Synodal Office, Hlavné nám. 23, 979 01 Rimavská Sobota; tel. (47) 562-1936; fax (47) 563-3090; e-mail reformata@reformata.sk; 109,735 mems and 325 parishes (2001); Bishop Dr GÉZA ERDÉLYI.

JUDAISM

Central Union of the Jewish Religious Communities in the Slovak Republic (Ústredný zväz židovských náboženských obcí v Slovenskej republike): Kozia ul. 21, 814 47 Bratislava; tel. (2) 5441-2167; fax (2) 5441-1106; e-mail uzzno@netax.sk; 3,300 mems; Exec. Chair. FERO ALEXANDER; Rabbi BARUCH MYERS.

The Press

In 2004 95 newspapers and 791 periodicals were published in Slovakia.

The publications listed below are in Slovak, unless otherwise indicated.

PRINCIPAL DAILIES
Banská Bystrica

Smer dnes (Direction Today): Čs. armády 26, 974 01 Banská Bystrica; tel. (48) 433-43; fax (48) 433-41; f. 1948; independent; Editor-in-Chief JURAJ KUČERA; circ. 20,000.

Večerník (Evening Paper): nám. SNP 3, 974 00 Banská Bystrica; tel. (48) 539-01; fax (48) 526-03; Editor-in-Chief EVA BENČÍKOVÁ; circ. 5,000.

Bratislava

Hospodárske noviny (Economic News): Pribinova 25, 810 11 Bratislava; tel. (2) 5063-3627; fax (2) 5063-4724; e-mail hn@hnx.sk; internet www.hnonline.sk; morning; Editor-in-Chief SLAVOMÍR MALIČKAY; circ. 40,000.

Nový čas (New Time): Gorkého 5, 812 78 Bratislava; tel. (2) 363-070; fax (2) 363-104; f. 1991; morning; Editor-in-Chief ZUZANA RAČKOVÁ; circ. 230,000.

Pravda (Truth): Trnavská cesta 39A, 831 04 Bratislava; tel. (2) 4959-6111; internet www.pravda.sk; f. 1920; independent; left-wing; Editor-in-Chief PAVOL MINARIK; circ. 165,000.

Roľnícke noviny (Agricultural News): Dobrovičova 12, 813 78 Bratislava; tel. (2) 368-449; fax (2) 321-282; f. 1946; Editor-in-Chief JURAJ ŠESTÁK; circ. 20,000.

Slovenská republika (Slovak Republic): Ružová dolina 6, 824 70 Bratislava; tel. (2) 5022-1505; fax (2) 5022-1500; e-mail redakcia@republika.sk; Editor-in-Chief EDUARD FAŠUNG; circ 78,000.

Sme (We Are): Mytná 33, 810 05 Bratislava; tel. (2) 498-726; fax (2) 498-306; internet www.sme.sk; f. 1993; merged with Práca (Labour) in Oct. 2002; Editor-in-Chief MARTIN SIMECKA; circ. 95,613.

Šport (Sport): Svätoplukova 2, 819 23 Bratislava; tel. (2) 600-53; fax (2) 211-380; Editor-in-Chief ZDENO SIMONIDES; circ. 85,000.

Új szó (New Word): nám. SNP 30, 814 64 Bratislava; tel. (2) 5923-3421; fax (2) 523-8321; e-mail redakcia@ujszo.com; internet www.ujszo.com; f. 1948; midday; in Hungarian; Editor-in-Chief ATTILA LOVÁSZ; circ. 42,000.

Večerník (Evening Paper): Dunajská 4, 811 08 Bratislava; tel. 5710-4021; fax 5292-0741; e-mail vecernik@vecernikba.sk; internet www

SLOVAKIA

.vecernikba.sk; f. 1956; evening; Editor-in-Chief Mgr Míchaela Conzarová; circ. 30,000.

Košice

Košický večer (Košice Evening): tr. SNP 24, 042 97 Košice; tel. (55) 429-820; fax (55) 421-214; f. 1990; Editor-in-Chief Mikuláš Jesenský; circ. 25,000.

Lúč (Ray): B. Němcovej 32, 042 62 Košice; tel. (55) 633-2117; fax (55) 359-090; f. 1992; Editor-in-Chief Edita Pačajová-Kardošová; circ. 15,000.

Slovenský východ (Slovak East): Letná 45, 042 66 Košice; tel. (55) 539-79; fax (55) 539-50; Editor-in-Chief Dušan Klinger; circ. 30,000.

Prešov

Prešovský večerník (Prešov Evening Paper): Jarkova 4, 080 01 Prešov; tel. (51) 724-563; fax (51) 723-398; f. 1990; Editor-in-Chief Peter Ličák; circ. 13,000.

PRINCIPAL PERIODICALS

A Het (The Week): Bratislava; weekly; Hungarian-language magazine; Editor-in-Chief Attila Lovász.

Deák–Avízo: Seberíniho 1, 821 03 Bratislava; tel. (2) 4823-2123; e-mail obchod@avizo.sk; internet www.avizo.sk; 3 a week; advertising and information; Dir Ernest Deak; circ. 70,000.

Domino Efekt: Hlavná 68, 040 01 Košice; tel. and fax (55) 622-7692; f. 1992; weekly; Editor-in-Chief Andrej Hrico; circ. 20,000.

Elektrón + Zenit: Pražská 11, 812 84 Bratislava; tel. (2) 417-225; fax (2) 493-385; monthly; science and technology for young people; Editor-in-Chief Ladislav Gyorffy; circ. 22,000.

Eurotelevízia (Eurotelevision): Pribinova 25, 819 14 Bratislava; tel. (2) 5063-4194; fax (2) 5063-4152; e-mail etv@euroskopringier.sk; weekly; Editor-in-Chief Taňa Lucká; circ. 290,000.

Eva: Pribinova 25, 819 39 Bratislava; tel. (2) 5063-3340; fax (2) 5063-4128; e-mail eva@euroskop.sk; internet www.euroskop.ringier.sk; monthly; magazine for women; Editor-in-Chief Katarina Patvarošová; circ. 120,000.

International: Štúrova 4, 815 80 Bratislava; tel. (2) 367-808; fax (2) 326-685; weekly; current affairs; Editor-in-Chief Tatiana Jaglová; circ. 60,000.

Kamarát (Friend): POB 73, 820 14 Bratislava; tel. and fax (2) 240-8777; f. 1950; fortnightly; magazine for teenagers; Editor-in-Chief Vladimír Topercer; circ. 30,000.

Katolícke noviny (Catholic News): Kapitulská 20, 815 21 Bratislava; tel. (2) 533-1790; fax (2) 533-3178; f. 1849; weekly; Editor-in-Chief Mária Kotesová; circ. 116,000.

Krásy Slovenska (Beauty of Slovakia): Vajnorská 100A, 832 58 Bratislava; tel. (2) 279-0641; fax (2) 279-0587; illustrated bi-monthly; Editor-in-Chief Milan Kubiš; circ. 10,000.

Línia: Pribišova 19A, 841 05 Bratislava; tel. (2) 6025-1123; fax (2) 6025-1130; monthly; life-style; Editor-in-Chief Ján Hanuška; circ. 25,000.

Móda (Fashion): Štefánikova 4, 812 64 Bratislava; tel. (2) 765-704; fax (2) 491-191; quarterly; Editor-in-Chief Dana Lapšanská; circ. 20,000.

Ohník (Little Flame): Pražská 11, 812 84 Bratislava; tel. (2) 417-233; monthly; youth; Editor-in-Chief Stanislav Bebjak; circ. 35,000.

Plus 7 dní: Ružová dolina 27, 825 06 Bratislava; tel. (2) 656-83; fax (2) 201-6309; weekly; social magazine; Editor-in-Chief Miloš Luknár; circ. 60,000.

Poradca podnikateľa (Entrepreneurs' Adviser): Národná 18, POB 29, 010 01 Žilina; tel. (41) 705-3610; fax (41) 705-3613; e-mail zidekova@epi.sk; internet www.epi.sk; f. 1993; monthly; Gen. Dir Zoja Žideková; circ. 30,000.

Rodina (Family): Pribinova 25, POB 122, 810 11 Bratislava; tel. (2) 210-4027; monthly; family magazine; Editor-in-Chief M. Város; circ. 145,000.

Romano nevo Ïil (Rómsky nový list) (The New Romany Journal): Jarková 4, 080 01 Prešov; tel. (51) 7725283; fax (51) 7733439; e-mail redakcia@rnl.sk; internet www.rnl.sk; f. 1991; in Romany, Slovak and English; publ. by the Association Jekhetane-Spolu (Together); Chief Editors Jozef Ferenc, Denisa Havrľová, Daniela Hivešová-Šilanová, Roman Čonka; circ. 8,500.

Slovenka (Slovak Woman): Jaskový rad 5, 833 80 Bratislava; tel. (2) 5478-9652; fax (2) 5477-6118; e-mail slovenka@slovenka.sk; f. 1948; weekly; illustrated magazine; Editor-in-Chief Zuzana Krútka; circ. 220,000.

Slovenské národné noviny (Slovak National News): Matica slovenská, Mudroňova 1, 036 52 Martin; tel. and fax (43) 345-35; f. 1845; weekly; organ of Matica slovenská cultural organization; Editor-in-Chief Peter Mišák; circ. 7,000.

Slovenský profit: Pribinova 25, 810 11 Bratislava; tel. (2) 563-3817; fax (2) 563-4581; economic weekly; Editor-in-Chief Iveta Seifertová; circ. 25,000.

Stop: Exnárova 57, 820 12 Bratislava; tel. (2) 4342-5052; fax (2) 4342-0554; e-mail stop@ba.telecom.sk; fortnightly; motoring; Editor-in-Chief Ľuboš Kríž; circ. 47,000.

Szabad újság (Free Journal): Michalská 9, 814 99 Bratislava; tel. (2) 333-012; fax (2) 330-519; f. 1991; Hungarian-language economic weekly; Editor-in-Chief Géza Szabó; circ. 40,000.

Trend: Rezedova 5, POB 31, 820 07 Bratislava; tel. (2) 4341-1652; fax (2) 4333-1336; e-mail redakcia@trend.sk; internet www.trend.sk; f. 1991; weekly; for entrepreneurs; publ. by Trend Holding; Editor-in-Chief Jaroslav Matyas; circ. 25,000.

Vasárnap (Sunday): SNP 30, 814 64 Bratislava 1; tel. (2) 5923-3235; fax (2) 5923-3295; e-mail reklama@ujszo.com; f. 1948; weekly; independent Hungarian-language magazine; Editor-in-Chief József Szilvássy; circ. 97,000.

Výber (Digest): Kominárska 2, 832 03 Bratislava; tel. (2) 203-4486; fax (2) 203-4521; f. 1968; weekly; digest of home and foreign press; Editor-in-Chief Miroslava Avramovová; circ. 15,000.

Život (Life): Pribinova 25, 819 37 Bratislava; tel. (2) 210-4135; fax (2) 210-4145; f. 1951; illustrated family weekly; Editor-in-Chief Milan Város; circ. 255,000.

Zmena (Change): Sabinovská 14, 821 02 Bratislava; tel. (2) 237-758; fax (2) 522-6420; f. 1989; weekly; independent; Editor-in-Chief Vladimír Mohorita; circ. 20,000.

NEWS AGENCIES

Rómska tlačová agentúra (Roma Press Agency): Slovenskej jednoty 44, 040 01 Košice; tel. (55) 6321372; e-mail rpa@rpa.sk; internet www.rpa.sk; reports on matters relating to the Romany minority, and aims to bring attention to issues affecting the community; Dir Ivan Hriczko.

SITA: Mýtna 15, 811 07 Bratislava; tel. (2) 5249-6106; fax (2) 5249-3466; e-mail slovakam@sita.sk; internet www.sita.sk; f. 1997; independent; Dir-Gen. Pavol Mudry.

Tlačová agentúra Slovenskej republiky (TASR) (News Agency of the Slovak Republic): Pribinova 23, 819 28 Bratislava; tel. (2) 5921-0152; fax (2) 5296-2468; e-mail market@tasr.sk; internet www.tasr.sk; f. 1992; has overseas bureaux in Belgium, Czech Republic, Germany and Russia; Dir Peter Nedavska.

Foreign Bureaux

Česká tisková kancelář (ČTK) (Czech Republic): Župné nám. 7, Bratislava 815 68; tel. (2) 210-4633; fax (2) 210-4605.

ITAR—TASS (Information Telegraph Agency of Russia—Telegraphic Agency of the Sovereign Countries) (Russia): Jancova 8A, 811 01 Bratislava; tel. (2) 315-797; Correspondent Valerii I. Rzhevskii.

The following news agencies are also represented in Slovakia: Reuters (United Kingdom), Deutsche Presse-Agentur (Germany), Austria Presse-Agentur (Austria), Agence France-Presse (France), Magyar Távirati Iroda (Hungary), RIA—Novosti (Russia), Polska Agencja Prasowa (Poland), Agenzia Nazionale Stampa Associata (Italy), Novinska Agencija Tanjug (Serbia and Montenegro) and Viet Nam News Agency (Viet Nam).

PRESS ASSOCIATIONS

Slovenský syndikát novinárov (Slovak Syndicate of Journalists): Župné nám. 7, 815 68 Bratislava; tel. (2) 5443-5071; fax (2) 5443-2438; e-mail krutka.zuzana@ssn.sk; internet www.ssn.sk; f. 1968; reorganized 1990; 2,600 mems; Chair. Zuzana Krútka.

Združenie slovenských novinárov (Association of Slovak Journalists): Šafárikovo nám. 4, 811 02 Bratislava; tel. and fax (2) 363-184; f. 1992; 700 mems; Chair. Ján Smolec.

Publishers

Academic Electronic Press: Bajzova 7, 821 08 Bratislava; tel. (2) 5556-4495; fax (2) 5556-4495; non-fiction.

Dajama: Ľublanská 2, 831 02 Bratislava; tel. (2) 4463-1702; fax (2) 4463-1702; e-mail info@dajama.sk; internet www.dajama.sk; guidebooks for Slovakia in Slovak, Hungarian, German, Polish, Russian and English.

Enigma: POB 12A, 949 01 Nitra 1; tel. (87) 6555-551; e-mail enigma@nr.psg.sk; internet www.enigma.sk; textbooks; study guides; translations of fiction for children and adults.

Epos, Ing. Miroslav Mračko: Pečnianska 27, 851 01 Bratislava 5; tel. and fax (2) 6241-2357; e-mail epos@epos.sk; internet www.epos.sk; f. 1990; economics; law; non-fiction.

SLOVAKIA

Koloman Kertész Bagala (L.C.A. Publishers Group): POB 99, 810 00 Bratislava 1; tel. (2) 5441 5366; fax (2) 5464 7393; e-mail lca@lca.sk; internet www.lca.sk; f. 1991; fiction; Dir. KOLOMAN KERTÉSZ BAGALA.

Matica slovenská: J. C. Hronského, 036 52 Martin; tel. (43) 413-2454; fax (43) 413-3188; e-mail msba@matica.sk; internet www.matica.sk; f. 1863; literary science, bibliography, biography and librarianship; literary archives and museums; Chair. Ing. JOZEF MARKUŠ.

Príroda a.s. (Nature): Križkova 9, 811 04 Bratislava; tel. (2) 396-335; fax (2) 397-564; e-mail priroda@priroda.bts.sk; f. 1949; school textbooks, encyclopaedias, reference books, etc. for children and youth; Chair. Ing. EMILIA JANKOVITSOVÁ.

Slovenské pedagogické nakladetel'stvo—Mladé léta, s.r.o. (Slovakian Pedagogical Publishers—Young Years): Sasinkova 5, 815 19 Bratislava; tel. (2) 5557-2454; fax (2) 5557-1894; e-mail spn@spn.sk; internet www.spn.sk; f. 1920; pedagogical literature, educational, school texts, dictionaries; Dir MÁRIA SEDLÁKOVÁ.

Slovenský spisovatel a.s. (Slovak Writer): A. Plávku 12, 813 67 Bratislava; tel. (2) 499-736; fax (2) 499-736; e-mail slovspis@slovspis.sk; fiction, poetry; Dir MARTIN CHOVANEC.

Smena (Change): Pražská 11, 812 84 Bratislava; tel. (2) 498-018; fax (2) 493-305; f. 1949; fiction, literature for young people, newspapers and magazines; Dir Ing. JAROSLAV SIŠOLÁK.

Šport: Vajnorská 100/A, 832 58 Bratislava; tel. (2) 691-95; sport, physical culture, guide books, periodicals; Dir Dr BOHUMIL GOLIAN.

Tatran: Michalská 9, 815 82 Bratislava; tel. (2) 5443-5849; fax (2) 5443-5777; f. 1949; fiction, art books, children's books, literary theory; Dir Dr EVA MLÁDEKOVÁ.

Veda (Science): Bradáčova 7, 852 86 Bratislava; tel. (2) 832-254; fax (2) 832-254; f. 1953; publishing house of the Slovak Academy of Sciences; scientific and popular scientific books and periodicals; Man. EVA MAJESKÁ.

PUBLISHERS' ASSOCIATION

Publishers' and Booksellers' Asscn of the Slovak Republic (Združenie vydavateľov a kníhkupcov Slovenskej republiky): Gregorovej 8, 821 03 Bratislava; tel. and fax (2) 4333-6700; e-mail alex.aust@post.sk; Pres. Dr ALEX AUST.

Broadcasting and Communications

TELECOMMUNICATIONS

Regulatory Authority

Telecommunications Office of the Slovak Republic: Továrenská 7, POB 18, 810 06 Bratislava 16; tel. (2) 5788-1111; fax (2) 5293-2096; e-mail eduard.mracka@teleoff.gov.sk; internet www.teleoff.gov.sk; Chair. MILAN LUKNÁR.

Service Providers

Orange Slovensko (Orange Slovakia): Prievozská 6, 821 09 Bratislava; e-mail info@orange.sk; internet www.orange.sk; f. 1997 as Globtel; present name adopted 2002; 64% owned by Orange (France); provides mobile cellular telecommunications services; Dir-Gen. PAVOL LANČARIČ.

T-Com, a.s.: nám. Slobody 6, 817 62 Bratislava 15; tel. (2) 5249-2324; fax (2) 5249-2492; e-mail sekr.gr@st.sk; internet www.t-com.sk; 51% owned by Deutsche Telekom (Germany), 34% owned by Ministry of Transport, Posts and Telecommunications, 15% owned by the National Property Fund of the Slovak Republic; formerly Slovenské Telekomunikácie; name changed to Slovak Telecom in Jan. 2004; name changed as above in March 2006; Pres. and Chief Exec. MIROSLAV MAJOROŠ.

T-Mobil Slovensko, a.s.: Vajnorská 100A, 831 03 Bratislava; tel. (2) 4955-1111; internet www.t-mobile.sk; f. 1997; 100% owned by T-Com; provides mobile cellular telecommunications services; Gen. Dir ROBERT CHVÁTEL.

BROADCASTING

Radio

Slovenský rozhlas (Slovak Radio): Mýtna 1, POB 55, 817 55 Bratislava; tel. (2) 5727-3560; fax (2) 5249-8923; e-mail interrel@slovakradio.sk; internet www.slovakradio.sk; f. 1926; Dir-Gen. MIROSLAVA ZEMKOVÁ.

Television

Slovenská televízia (STV) (Slovak Television): Mlynská dolina 28, 845 45 Bratislava; tel. (2) 6542-3001; fax (2) 6542-2341; internet www.stv.sk; f. 1956; public broadcasting co; Chair. of Council JAROSLAV FRANEK; Dir RICHARD RYBNIČEK.

Slovenská Televizná Spoločnosť: tel. (2) 6827-4111; fax (2) 6595-6824; internet tv.markiza.sk; e-mail markiza@markiza.sk; f. 1996; broadcasts as Markiza TV; first privately owned television channel; owned by Central European Media Enterprises Ltd; Dir-Gen. VLADIMÍR REPČÍK.

TA3: Gagarinova 12, POB 31, 820 15 Bratislava; e-mail web@ta3.com; internet www.ta3.com; f. 2001; privately owned; Dir-Gen. MARTIN LENGYEL; Editor-in-Chief ZDENEK SAMAL.

TV Joj: Grešákova 10, 040 01 Kosiče; tel. (55) 622-2664; fax (55) 6221-027; e-mail joj@joj.sk; internet www.joj.sk; f. 2002; privately owned subsidiary of Nova TV (Czech Republic); Dir-Gen. VLADIMÍR ŽELEZNÝ; Dir MILAN KNAŽKO.

TV Markíza: Bratislavská 1A, POB 7, 843 56 Bratislava 48; tel. (2) 6827-4111; fax (2) 6595-6824; e-mail markiza@markiza.sk; internet tv.markiza.sk; 80% owned by Central European Media Enterprises Ltd (USA); Dir-Gen. VÁCLAV MIKA.

Finance

(cap. = capital; res = reserves; dep. = deposits; m. = million; brs = branches; amounts in Slovak koruny)

BANKING

Central Bank

National Bank of Slovakia (Národná banka Slovenska): Imricha Karvaša 1, 813 25 Bratislava; tel. (2) 5787-1111; fax (2) 5787-1100; e-mail info@nbs.sk; internet www.nbs.sk; f. 1993; res. 14,595.8m., dep. 345,980.2m. (Dec. 2003); determines monetary policy, issues banknotes and coins, controls circulation of money, co-ordinates payments and settlements between banks, supervises the performance of banking activities; Gov. IVAN ŠRAMKO.

Commercial Banks

Banka Slovakia, a.s.: Janka Krála, POB 76, 974 01 Banská Bystrica; tel. (48) 431-7111; fax (48) 413-2222; e-mail sekretar@basl.sk; internet www.basl.sk; f. 1996; cap. 756.9m., res 43.7m., dep. 3,484.5m. (Dec. 2002); Chair. VILIAM OSTROŽLÍK.

Calyon Bank Slovakia, a.s.: Klemensova 2A, POB 70, 811 09 Bratislava; tel. (2) 5926-2111; fax (2) 5926-2112; internet www.calyon.sk; f. 2004; fmrly Crédit Lyonnais Bank Slovakia; cap. 500.0m., res 80.8m., dep. 6,740.3m. (Dec. 2003); Gen. Man. JEAN-MICHEL GIOVANNETTI.

Citibank (Slovakia), a.s.: Viedenská cesta 5, 851 01 Bratislava; tel. (2) 6827-8111; fax (2) 6827-8200; e-mail citibank.slovakia@citibank.com; internet www.citibank.sk; f. 1995; cap. 1,650m., res 668.2m., dep. 21,682.7m. (Dec. 2003); Gen. Dir IGOR THAM.

Dexia banka slovensko, a.s.: Hodžova 11, 010 11 Žilina; tel. (41) 511-1111; fax (41) 562-4129; e-mail webinfo@dexia.sk; internet www.dexia.sk; f. 1993; fmrly Prvá komunálna banka, name changed as above Oct. 2003; cap. 1,202.4m., res 143.3m., dep. 24,070.0m. (Dec. 2003); Pres. MARC LAUWERS; 46 brs.

HVB Bank Slovakia, a.s.: Mostovà 6, 811 02 Bratislava; tel. (2) 5969-1111; fax (2) 5969-9406; e-mail info@sk.hvb-cee.com; internet www.hvb-bank.sk; f. Sept. 2001 by merger of Bank Austria Creditanstalt Slovakia and Hypo-Vereinsbank Slovakia; cap. 62.6m., res 91.9m., dep. 1,023.8m. (Dec. 2003); Chair. CHRISTIAN SUPPANZ.

Istrobanka, a.s.: Laurinská 1, POB 109, 810 00 Bratislava; tel. (2) 5939-7111; fax (2) 5443-1744; e-mail info@istrobanka.sk; internet www.istrobanka.sk; f. 1992; cap. 1,750.0m., res 323.0m., dep. 23,084.4m. (Dec. 2003); Chair. and Gen. Man. VOLKER PICHLER; 11 brs.

Komerční Banka Bratislava, a.s.: Medená 6, POB 137, 810 00 Bratislava; tel. (2) 5927-7405; fax (2) 5296-4801; e-mail koba@koba.sk; internet www.koba.sk; f. 1995; cap. 500.0m., res 73.4m., dep. 2,894.0m. (Dec. 2003); Chair. and CEO JAROMÍR CHABR.

Ľudová banka, a.s. (People's Bank): Vysoká 9, POB 81, 810 00 Bratislava; tel. (2) 5965-1111; fax (2) 5441-2453; e-mail market@luba.sk; internet www.luba.sk; f. 1992; cap. 1,000.0m., res 2,390.2m., dep. 23,237.3m. (Dec. 2003); Chair. JOZEF KOLLÁR; 12 brs.

OTP Banka Slovensko, a.s. (Investment and Development Bank): Stúrova 5, 813 54 Bratislava; tel. (2) 5979-1111; fax (2) 5296-3484; e-mail info@otpbank.sk; internet www.otpbank.sk; f. 1992 as Investičná a rozvojová banka; 95.7% of shares divested to NSB Ltd (Hungary) in April 2002; Aug. 2002 name changed as above; cap. 2,064.4m., res 208.8m., dep. 23,243.7m. (Dec. 2003); Pres. KÁROLY HODOSSY; 53 brs.

Poštová banka, a.s. (Postal Bank): Prievozska 2B, 824 64 Bratislava 26; tel. (2) 5960-3109; fax (2) 5960-3133; e-mail luboslava

.olejarova@pabk.sk; internet www.pabk.sk; f. 1993; scheduled for privatization; cap. 2,947m., dep. 20,049m. (Dec. 2005); res 11.3m. (Dec. 2003); Gen. Dir and Chair. TOMÁŠ SALOMON; 24 brs.

Tatra banka, a.s.: POB 42, Hodzovo nam. 3, 850 05 Bratislava 55; tel. (2) 5919-1111; fax (2) 5919-1110; e-mail info@tatrabanka.sk; internet www.tatrabanka.sk; f. 1990; cap. 1,044.3m., res 10,554.4m., dep. 123,896.3m. (Dec. 2003); Chair. and Gen. Man. RAINER FRANZ; 30 brs.

UniBanka, a.s.: Vajnorská 21, 832 65 Bratislava; tel. (2) 4950-2111; fax (2) 4437-3975; internet www.unibanka.sk; f. 1990; April 2002 name changed as above from Polnobanka; cap. 2,377.1m., res 35.6m., dep. 35,096.9m. (Dec. 2002); Chair. of Bd JIŘI KUNERT; 10 brs.

Všeobecná úverová banka, a.s. (General Credit Bank): Mlynské Nivy 1, POB 90, 829 90 Bratislava 25; tel. (2) 5055-1111; fax (2) 5556-6650; e-mail webmaster@vub.sk; internet www.vub.sk; f. 1990; sold to Banka Intesa (Italy) in 2001; cap. 12,978.0m., res 2,182.0m., dep. 167,364.0m. (Dec. 2003); Chair. and CEO TOMAS SPURNY; 226 brs.

Savings Banks

Prvá stavebná sporiteľňa, a.s.: Bajkalská 30, POB 48, 829 48 Bratislava; tel. (2) 5823-1111; fax (2) 5341-1131; internet www.pss.sk; f. 1992; cap. 1,000m.; Chair. of Bd JÁN ROLAND BURGER.

Slovenská sporiteľňa, a.s. (Slovak Savings Bank): Suché mýto 4, 816 07 Bratislava; tel. (2) 5957-4500; fax (2) 5957-4503; e-mail postmaster@slsp.sk; internet www.slsp.sk; f. 1969; fmrly state-owned; absorbed operations of Priemyselná banka (Industrial Bank) in 1999; privatized in 2000, majority stake bought by Erste Bank (Austria); total assets 205,037.0m. (Dec. 2002); Chair. REGINA OVENSKY-STRAKA; 638 brs and agencies.

COMMODITY AND STOCK EXCHANGES

Bratislava Commodity Exchange (Komoditná burza Bratislava): 29 Augusta 2, 811 07 Bratislava; tel. (2) 5293-1010; fax (2) 5293-1007; e-mail burza@kbb.sk; internet www.kbb.sk; Gen. Sec. IGOR KREJČÍ.

Bratislava Stock Exchange (Burza cenných papierov v Bratislave a.s.): Vysoká 17, POB 151, 814 99 Bratislava; tel. (2) 4923-6111; fax (2) 4923-6102; e-mail info@bsse.sk; internet www.bsse.sk; Dir-Gen. MÁRIA HURAJOVÁ; Chair. MARIÁN SEDO.

INSURANCE

Slovak Insurance Co (Slovenská poisťovňa, a.s.): Strakova 1, 815 74 Bratislava; tel. (2) 533-2949; fax (2) 533-1272; majority stake divested to Allianz (Germany) in Dec. 2001; Chair. and Pres. RUDOLF JANAC.

Trade and Industry

GOVERNMENT AGENCIES

National Property Fund of the Slovak Republic (Fond Národného Majetku Slovenskej Republiky): Drieňová 27, 821 01 Bratislava; tel. (7) 4827-1111; fax (7) 4827-1289; e-mail fnm@natfund.gov.sk; internet www.natfund.gov.sk; f. 1993; supervises the privatization process; Pres. JOZEF KOJDA.

SARIO—Slovak Investment and Trade Development Agency (SARIO—Slovenská agentúra pre rozvoj investícií a obchodu): Martinčekova 17, 821 01 Bratislava; tel. (2) 5826-0100; fax (2) 5826-0109; e-mail sario@sario.sk; internet www.sario.sk; f. 1991; Gen. Dir MILAN JURÁŠKA.

CHAMBERS OF COMMERCE

Slovak Chamber of Commerce and Industry (Slovenská obchodná a priemyselná komora): Gorkého 9, 816 03 Bratislava; tel. (2) 5443-3291; fax (2) 5413-1159; e-mail sopkurad@scci.sk; internet www.scci.sk; Pres. Dr PETER MIHÓK.

Banská Bystrica Chamber of Commerce and Industry: Svermeva 43, 974 01 Banská Bystrica; tel. (48) 345-057; fax (48) 363-88; e-mail sopkrbb@sopk.sk; internet www.bb.scci.sk.

Košice Chamber of Commerce and Industry: Juźna Trieda 2A, 040 01 Košice; tel. (45) 641-9477; fax (45) 641-9470; e-mail sopkrkke@scci.sk; internet www.sopk.sk/ko/sk; Dir STEFAN KARAŠ.

Trenčín Chamber of Commerce and Industry: Jilemnickeho St 2, 911 01 Trenčín; tel. (32) 652-3834; fax (32) 652-1023; e-mail sopkrktn@scci.sk; internet www.commerce-and-industry.com.

Žilina Chamber of Commerce and Industry: ul. Halková 31, 010 01 Žilina; tel. (41) 7235655; fax (41) 7235653; e-mail sekrza@za.scci.sk; internet www.sopk.sk/za/sk; Dir JÁN MIŠURA.

UTILITIES
Electricity

Slovenské elektrárne, a.s. (SE) (Slovak Electricity): Hraničná 12, 827 36 Bratislava 212; tel. (2) 5866-1111; fax (2) 5341-7525; e-mail info@hq.seas.sk; internet www.seas.sk; fmr state-owned utility, 66% share acquired by Enel (Italy) in April 2006; 34% owned by the Slovak National Property Fund; Dir-Gen. and Chair. PAOLO RUZZINI; Deputy Chair. MARCO ARCELLI.

Gas

Slovenský Plynárenský Priemysel (SPP) (Slovak Gas Co): Mlynské nivy 44A, 825 11 Bratislava; tel. (2) 5869-2111; fax (2) 5341-5590; e-mail spp@spp.sk; internet www.spp.sk; partially privatized in July 2002; Gen. Dir MIROSLAV LAPUNÍK.

TRADE UNIONS

Confederation of Trade Unions of the Slovak Republic (Konfederácia odborových zväzov Slovenskej republiky): Odborárské nám. 3, 815 70 Bratislava; tel. (2) 622-65; fax (2) 213-303; e-mail press@kozsr.sk; internet www.kozsr.sk; Pres. IVAN SAKTOR; 1.1m. mems; affiliated unions listed below.

Metalworkers' Federation: Miletičova 24, 815 70 Bratislava; tel. (2) 5556-5383; fax (2) 5556-5387; e-mail oskovo@kovo.sk; Pres. EMIL MACHYNA.

Trade Union of Workers in Agriculture: Vajnorská 1, 815 70 Bratislava; tel. (2) 542-4186; fax (2) 542-1673; Pres. SVETOZÁR KORBEĽ.

Trade Union of Workers in the Chemical Industry: Osadná 6, 831 03 Bratislava; tel. (2) 273-527; fax (2) 273-538; Pres. JURAJ BLAHÁK.

Trade Union of Workers in Construction and Construction Materials: Vajnorská 1, 815 70 Bratislava; tel. (2) 5542-4180; fax (2) 5542-2764; e-mail stavba@nextra.sk; Pres. DUŠAN BARČIK.

Trade Union of Workers in Cultural and Social Organizations: Vajnorská 1, 815 70 Bratislava 1; tel. and fax (2) 5542-3760; e-mail sozkaso@nextra.sk; Pres. MÁRIA KRIŠTOFIČOVÁ.

Trade Union of Workers in Energy: Vajnorská 1, 815 70 Bratislava; tel. and fax (2) 542-1622; f. 1992; Pres. VLADIMIR MOJŠ.

Trade Union of Workers in the Food-processing Industry: Vajnorská 1, 815 70 Bratislava; tel. (2) 5542-1575; fax (2) 566-2506; e-mail ozp@isnet.sk; Pres. MAGDALENA MELLENOVA.

Trade Union of Workers in the Glass Industry: ul. Matice Slovenskej 19, 911 05 Trenčín; tel. (32) 743-7200; Pres. MIROSLAV BUČEK.

Trade Union of Workers in the Health and Social Services: Vajnorská 1, 815 70 Bratislava 3; tel. (2) 5024-0257; fax (2) 5542-5330; e-mail sekretariat@sozpzass.sk; Pres. ANDREJ KUČINSKÝ.

Trade Union of Workers in Radio, Television and Newspapers: Vajnorská 1, 815 70 Bratislava; tel. (2) 211-844; Pres. PETER JÁCHIN.

Trade Union of Workers in the Textile, Clothing and Leather Industry: Vajnorská 1, 815 70 Bratislava; tel. (2) 213-389; fax (2) 526-2570; Pres. Ing. KONŠTANTÍN BALÁŽ.

Trade Union of Workers in the Wood-working, Furniture and Paper Industries: Vajnorská 1, 815 70 Bratislava; tel. (2) 213-660; fax (2) 213-163; Pres. BORISLAV MAJTÁN.

Transport
RAILWAYS

In 2004 the total length of railways in Slovakia was estimated at 3,660 km, of which 1,556 km were electrified. In June 2005 Slovakia agreed to modernize its railway network in order to meet European Union rail transport standards. The cost of the process, expected to be completed in 2020, was estimated at €2,000m.

Železničná spoločnosť Cargo Slovakia, a.s. (ZSSK Cargo): Drieňová 24, 820 09 Bratislava; e-mail infoservis@zscargo.sk; internet www.zscargo.sk; f. 2005, following division into two of the state railway company, Železničná spoločnosť, a.s. (ZSSK); operation of rail freight transport and freight-related commercial activities; state-owned; due for privatization.

Železničná spoločnosť Slovensko, a.s.: Žabotova 14, 813 13 Bratislava; tel. (2) 5058-7015; fax (2) 5341 0128; e-mail info@slovakrail.sk; internet www.slovakrail.sk; f. 2005, following division into two of the state railway comapny, Železničná spoločnosť, a.s. (ZSSK); passenger transport; state-owned; Dir-Gen. ONDREJ MATEJ.

Železnice Slovenskej republiky (Slovak State Railways): Klemensova 8, 813 61 Bratislava; tel. (2) 2029-1111; fax (2) 5296-2296; e-mail gr@zsr.sk; internet www.zsr.sk; f. 1993; became a joint-stock co with responsibility for management of rail infrastructure in 2001, when responsibility for operations was transferred to the newly established state-owned concern, Železničná spoločnosť; Dir-Gen. ANDREJ EGYED.

Dopravný podnik Bratislava, a.s. (Bratislava Transport): Olejkárska 1, 814 52 Bratislava; tel. (2) 5950-1111; fax (2) 5950-1400; e-mail zad@dpb.sk; internet www.dpb.sk; tramway being upgraded to light-rail system; 11 routes with 154 stops; Dir-Gen. J. ZACHAR.

ROADS

In 2004 the total length of the road system (including motorways) was estimated at 17,780 km.

Slovak Road Administration (Slovenská správa ciest): Miletičova 19, 826 19 Bratislava; tel. (2) 5025-5111; fax (2) 5556-7976; e-mail info@ssc.sk; internet www.ssc.sk; f. 1996; Gen. Man. PETER HAVRILA.

INLAND WATERWAYS

The total length of navigable waterways in Slovakia (on the River Danube) is 172 km. The Danube provides a link with Germany, Austria, Hungary, Serbia and Montenegro, Bulgaria, Romania and the Black Sea. The main river ports are Bratislava and Komárno.

State Shipping Authority (Štátna plavebná správa): ul. Prístavná 10, 821 09 Bratislava; tel. (2) 5541-0851; fax (2) 5556-6335; internet www.sps.sk; Dir Ing. JÁN JURIA.

Slovak Shipping and Ports Co a.s. (Slovenská plavba a prístavy a.s.): Pribinova 24, 815 24 Bratislava; tel. (2) 5827-1111; fax (2) 5827-1114; e-mail spap@spap.sk; internet www.spap.sk; Chair. of Advisory Committee PETER PLANÝ; Chair. of Bd JOZEF BLAŠKO; Gen. Man. ANTON PRNO.

CIVIL AVIATION

There are five international airports in Slovakia: Bratislava (M. R. Štefánik Airport), Košice, Piešťany, Poprad and Sliač. Until Slovak Airlines, the national carrier, began operations in March 1998, ČSA (Czech Airlines) provided air transport services for both Slovakia and the Czech Republic. In February 2006 the TwoOne consortium, led by Flughafen Wien (Austria), won a bid to purchase the Government's 66% stake in Bratislava and Košice airports. The consortium was to secure approval from the anti-monopoly office by 15 August. (The privatization process was temporarily suspended later in February, after the Government decided to postpone decisions on privatizations, pending legislative elections in June.)

Air Slovakia: Pestovateľská ul. 2, 821 04 Bratislava; tel. and fax (2) 4342-2744; e-mail airslovakia@airslovakia.sk; internet www.airslovakia.sk; f. 1993; scheduled passenger flights between Slovakia and Cyprus, India, Israel, Italy, Kuwait and United Kingdom; charter and cargo services; Gen. Dir AUGUSTIN BERNAT.

SkyEurope Airlines, a.s.: Ivanská 26, POB 24, 821 04 Bratislava 21; tel. (2) 4850-1111; fax (2) 4850-1000; e-mail info@skyeurope.com; internet www.skyeurope.com; f. 2001; first budget airline in Central Europe; joint venture with Spanish and Belgian interests; scheduled and charter passenger and cargo services; domestic and international services; Chief Exec. CHRISTIAN MANDL; Chair. ALAIN SKOWRONEK.

Slovenské aerolínie, a.s. (Slovak Airlines): Letisko M. R. Štefánika, 820 01 Bratislava 21; tel. (2) 4445-0096; fax (2) 4445-0097; e-mail sll@sll.sk; internet www.sll.sk; f. 1995; 62% stake acquired by Austrian Airlines in Jan. 2005; scheduled and charter passenger and cargo services; scheduled international services between Bratislava and Brussels (Belgium) and Moscow (Russia); international charter services to Russia, Spain, Italy, Bulgaria, Cyprus, Turkey, Greece and Tunisia; Chair. CHRISTIANE BÖHM-MAYER.

Tatra Air: Banská Bystrica; tel. (48) 412-4509; e-mail tatraair@tatraair.sk; internet www.tatraair.sk; f. 1990; scheduled passenger flights between Silac and Prague (Czech Republic), charter flights, air taxi service; Chair. ANDREJ KVASNA.

Tourism

Slovakia's tourist attractions include ski resorts in the High and Low Tatras and other mountain ranges, more than 20 spa resorts (with thermal and mineral springs), numerous castles and mansions, and historic towns, including Bratislava, Košice, Nitra, Bardejov, Kežmarok and Levoča. In 2003 1,387,000 foreign tourists visited Slovakia; in that year revenue from tourism totalled US $876m.

Slovak Tourist Board: nám. L. Stura 1, POB 35, 974 05 Banska Bystrica; tel. (48) 413-6146; fax (48) 413-6149; e-mail sacr@sacr.sk; internet www.slovakiatourism.sk.

SLOVENIA

Introductory Survey

Location, Climate, Language, Religion, Flag, Capital

The Republic of Slovenia (formerly the Socialist Republic of Slovenia, a constituent republic of the Socialist Federal Republic of Yugoslavia) is situated in south-central Europe. It is bounded by Austria to the north, Hungary to the north-east, Croatia to the south and east and by Italy to the west, and it has a short (40-km—25-mile) western coastline on the Adriatic Sea. The climate is Alpine in the mountainous areas, Mediterranean along the coast and continental in the interior. Average temperatures range from between 0°C (32°F) and 22°C (71.6°F) inland, and between 2°C (35.6°F) and 24°C (75.2°F) on the coast. Average annual rainfall ranges from 800 mm (31.5 ins) in the east to 3,000 mm (118.1 ins) in the north-west. The official language is Slovene, and in ethnically-mixed regions also Hungarian and Italian. The majority religion in Slovenia is Roman Catholicism, although there are small communities of other Christian denominations and of Muslims and Jews. The national flag (proportions 2 by 3) consists of three horizontal stripes of white, blue and red, with a shield in the upper hoist depicting a white three-peaked mountain (Triglav), below which are two horizontal wavy blue lines and above which are three six-pointed yellow stars. The capital is Ljubljana.

Recent History

Following the collapse of the Austro-Hungarian empire, the Kingdom of Serbs, Croats and Slovenes was proclaimed on 4 December 1918. (The territory of Slovenia was formally ceded by Austria by the Treaty of Saint-Germain in 1919.) In 1929 the name of the country was changed to Yugoslavia. Yugoslavia collapsed under German attack in 1941 and, during the Second World War, Germany annexed lower Styria and Yugoslav Carinthia, while Italy annexed Istria and the territory around Ljubljana. (There was a continuing dispute with Italy over Istria; in 1954 Italy was awarded the city of Trieste, and Yugoslavia the remainder of the territory, giving Slovenia access to the sea.) Hungary occupied the plains along the Mura in north-eastern Slovenia.

The Slovene Liberation Front, formed in 1941, joined with the communist-led all-Yugoslav Partisan Army of Josip Broz (Tito), which was eventually recognized as an ally by the British and US Governments. Following the post-war proclamation of the Federal People's Republic of Yugoslavia (from 1963 the Socialist Federal Republic of Yugoslavia—SFRY), Slovenia became the most prosperous of the Yugoslav republics, but was increasingly suspicious of Serb domination. On 27 September 1989 the Slovene Assembly voted in favour of radical amendments to the Constitution of Slovenia, confirming Slovenia's sovereignty and its right to secede from the SFRY. The organization of multi-party elections was envisaged, and the establishment of opposition parties (the local League of Communists of Slovenia—LCS—having hitherto been the only legal party) was formally authorized. Slovenia was warned that the amendments contravened the Federal Constitution, and the Serbian leader, Slobodan Milošević, attempted to arrange protests in Slovenia against the Slovene leadership; the planned demonstrations were, however, banned in November. Milošević subsequently instructed all Serbian enterprises to sever links with Slovenia, which retaliated by imposing reciprocal economic sanctions. Relations between Slovenia and the other republics deteriorated sharply.

In January 1990 the Slovenian delegation withdrew from the 14th (Extraordinary) Congress of the League of Communists of Yugoslavia (LCY), following the overwhelming rejection of their proposals to reform the federal party and to give greater autonomy to the respective Leagues of Communists of the republics. The LCY suffered a further reverse in February, when its Central Committee was unable to secure the quorum necessary to set a date for the reconvening of the Congress. A boycott by the entire Slovene contingent was supported by members of the Leagues of Communists of Croatia and Macedonia. The LCS suspended its links with the LCY, and changed its name to the Party of Democratic Reform (PDR). In that month Stefan Korosec of Slovenia was removed from the position of Secretary of the Presidium of the LCY Central Committee, in advance of the expiry of his mandate, and was replaced by a Serb. In March Slovenia was redesignated the Republic of Slovenia. Meanwhile, opposition parties had been formed, and in December 1989 six of the main parties formed a coalition, the Democratic Opposition of Slovenia (DEMOS). In multi-party elections, held in April 1990, DEMOS won a majority in the republican parliament, and subsequently formed a Government under Lojze Peterle, the leader of the Slovenian Christian Democrats (SCD). However, the leader of the PDR, Milan Kučan (an opponent of Milošević), was elected President of the State Presidency and the PDR remained the largest single party in the legislature.

On 2 July 1990 the Slovenian legislature declared the sovereignty of the Republic and resolved that republican laws should take precedence over federal laws. This was confirmed by an amendment to the republican Constitution, approved by the legislature on 27 September. The Republic also assumed control over the local territorial defence force, thereby bringing Slovenia into direct confrontation with the Serb-dominated federal army, which attempted to reassert its authority by confiscating weapons and seizing the headquarters of the republican force. Slovenian and Croatian proposals to reform the Yugoslav Federation were rejected, and Serbia imposed economic sanctions on imports from the secessionist states. None the less, in a referendum held in Slovenia on 23 December 1990, some 89% of those who voted (about 94% of the electorate) endorsed Slovenian independence.

Relations between Slovenia and the SFRY deteriorated further in January 1991, when the Slovenian authorities refused to implement an order by the SFRY Presidency to disarm all paramilitary groups. In the same month Slovenia and Croatia signed friendship and military co-operation agreements. Although the Slovenian Government approved a programme for Slovenian dissociation from the SFRY in February, both Slovenia and Croatia remained willing to consider a federation of sovereign states. However, following the Serbian-led crisis in the Federal State Presidency in March (see the chapter on Serbia and Montenegro), the Slovenian Government became more resolved to withdraw from the federation. In May Slovenia declared its intention to secede before the end of June, and legislation was adopted that would enable eventual independence, including the establishment of a Slovenian army. Tensions with the federal authorities were exacerbated when Slovenia attempted to take control of the collection of customs duties.

Slovenia and Croatia declared their independence from the SFRY on 25 June 1991. In response, Serb-dominated federal troops were mobilized on 27 June, and tanks were dispatched from Belgrade. Sporadic fighting ensued and, despite attempts by the European Community (EC—now European Union—EU, see p. 228) to arrange a cease-fire, there was an aerial bombardment of Brnik (Ljubljana) airport. On 7–8 July an EC-mediated cease-fire agreement between Slovenia and the SFRY ended all hostilities in Slovenia (which, in contrast to Croatia, had only a small Serb population). According to official figures, 79 people were killed in the fighting in Slovenia. On 8 October (following the expiry of a three-month moratorium on dissociation, agreed as part of the EC cease-fire accord) Slovenia proclaimed its full independence, introduced its own currency, the tolar, and recalled all its citizens serving in federal institutions. All federal army units had withdrawn from Slovenia by 26 October. A new Slovenian Constitution, providing for a bicameral legislature, was promulgated on 23 December. Slovenia was recognized by the EC in January 1992. The USA recognized the country in April, and withdrew sanctions against Slovenia (imposed on all states in the territory of the former SFRY in the previous year) in August. Slovenia was admitted to the UN in May.

Peterle's administration experienced increasing difficulties, as the struggle for independence became less of a unifying factor. In October 1991 the Slovenian Democratic Union, one of the larger and most influential of the DEMOS parties, split into two factions, both of which remained in the coalition. A minority liberal wing formed the Democratic Party (DP) under the

Minister of Foreign Affairs, Dr Dmitrij Rupel, while the majority of the party's parliamentary delegates supported a more right-wing programme and formed the National Democratic Party, led by the Minister of Justice and Administration, Dr Rajko Pirnat. DEMOS, undermined by such factionalism, was dissolved in December, although it was envisaged that the Peterle administration would remain in power pending the organization of elections (to take place under the terms of the new Constitution). However, the Government lost a parliamentary motion of 'no confidence' in April 1992, and Peterle resigned. He was replaced by Dr Janez Drnovšek, the leader of the Liberal Democratic Party (LDP) and a former President of the SFRY Presidency.

Parliamentary and presidential elections took place on 6 December 1992. About 85% of the registered electorate participated in elections to the Državni zbor (National Assembly). Although the LDP returned the greatest number of deputies (22) to the 90-member body, it failed to secure a majority of seats in the legislature. Among the groupings that obtained representation were the SCD, with a total of 15 seats, the United List (a four-party electoral alliance), with 14 seats, and the extreme right-wing Slovenian National Party (SNP), which won 12 seats. In the presidential election Kučan (standing as an independent candidate) was re-elected to what had become, under the terms of the 1991 Constitution, a largely ceremonial post, obtaining 63.9% of the votes cast. His nearest rival, Ivan Bizjak of the SCD, secured 21.1% of the votes. Voting was held concurrently for the 22 directly elected members of the advisory Državni svet (National Council); its remaining 18 members were chosen by an electoral college shortly afterwards.

In January 1993 Drnovšek formed a coalition Government, comprising members of the LDP, the SCD, the United List (later renamed the United List of Social Democrats—ULSD), the Greens of Slovenia and the Social Democratic Party of Slovenia (SDPS). Peterle was appointed Minister of Foreign Affairs, and Bizjak Minister of Internal Affairs. In July the Minister of Defence, Janez Janša, was among senior politicians implicated in a scandal involving the sale of armaments to Bosnian Muslims, in contravention of the UN embargo on the transfer of military equipment between the former Yugoslav republics. Earlier in the year Janša (the President of the SDPS) had accused Kučan of protecting former officials of the communist regime. Janša was dismissed from the Government in March 1994, after a ministerial commission found that security forces under the command of the Ministry of Defence had ill-treated a former ministry employee. The SDPS withdrew from the Government, protesting that the coalition agreement had been breached. In addition, the party cited as its reasons for leaving the Government continuing high-level corruption and the change in the coalition's structure, following the merger in March of the LDP with three other organizations to form a new party, Liberal Democracy of Slovenia (LDS). The LDS, led by Drnovšek, also included the DP and the Greens of Slovenia—Eco-Social Party (comprising the parliamentary members of the Greens of Slovenia, which had divided into two factions), and numbered 30 deputies in the Državni zbor. Drnovšek subsequently formed a new coalition Government with the SCD and the ULSD. However, Bizjak resigned as Minister of Internal Affairs in May, following allegations that security forces controlled by his ministry had been involved in criminal activities in Austria. In September the appointment of an LDS member, Jožef Školjč, to the presidency of the Državni zbor prompted Peterle's resignation from the Government, in protest at what he regarded as the excessive concentration of authority among members of the LDS. Although the SCD remained within the government coalition, Drnovšek refused to accede to the party's demand that Peterle's successor should also be a member of the SCD. In January 1995 an agreement was finally reached whereby Zoran Thaler of the LDS was appointed Minister of Foreign Affairs, and Janko Deželak of the SCD assumed the post of Minister of Economic Relations and Development (a portfolio hitherto held by the LDS).

In January 1996 the ULSD withdrew from the governing coalition, following the Prime Minister's proposal to replace the ULSD Minister of Economic Affairs, Dr Maks Tajnikar, which, it claimed, violated the coalition agreement. Tajnikar was subsequently replaced by an independent deputy, Metod Dragonja, and the three other positions left vacant by the ULSD withdrawal were allocated to one member of the LDS and two of the SCD. The coalition, which had lost its overall majority in the Državni zbor (it controlled 45 of the 90 seats), subsequently came under pressure to relax its economic austerity measures by a series of public-sector strikes for wage increases. The forthcoming general election apparently prompted the Government to agree to the demands of certain groups. In May Thaler was defeated in a motion of 'no confidence', prompted by his acceptance of a compromise solution to a dispute with Italy (which had prevented Slovenia's accession to associate membership of the EU—see below) opposed by the SCD.

At the elections to the Državni zbor, which took place on 10 November 1996, the LDS returned 25 deputies to the 90-member assembly, and subsequently increased its overall strength to 45 seats, having gained the support of the ULSD, the Democratic Party of Pensioners of Slovenia (DeSUS), the SNP and the representatives of the Hungarian and Italian minorities (see Government, below). A newly formed opposition alliance, Slovenian Spring, comprising the Slovenian People's Party (SPP), the SCD and the SDPS, also held 45 seats in the Državni zbor. Consequently, Kučan's nomination that Drnovšek be returned to the office of Prime Minister failed to obtain the requisite majority of more than one-half of the deputies. Following a protracted delay, an SCD deputy announced his withdrawal from the party to become an independent deputy, and agreed to support Drnovšek's candidacy, and in January 1997 Drnovšek was re-elected to the office of Prime Minister. However, the continued absence of a majority in the Državni zbor impeded the formation of a new government, with the parties belonging to Slovenian Spring refusing to accept an administration headed by Drnovšek. Drnovšek consequently failed to secure sufficient support for his proposed new coalition government, which was to include representatives of all the political parties in the legislature. In late February the SPP (which held 19 seats in the Državni zbor) finally agreed to join a coalition government with the LDS and DeSUS, which was subsequently approved by 52 votes in the Državni zbor.

Following an agreement in July 1997 by parliamentary party leaders to co-operate over the country's bid to join the EU, a two-thirds' majority of the Državni zbor voted to amend the Constitution, to allow foreigners to purchase land in Slovenia, thereby meeting the requirements for ratification of the EU association agreement. The agreement was ratified by the legislature on the following day. The European Commission subsequently recommended that the EU begin membership negotiations with Slovenia in 1998. Despite this positive development, in late July 1997 Thaler resigned as Minister of Foreign Affairs, reportedly as the result of disunity on the issue of Slovenia's accession. Boris Frlec was appointed to the post in September.

A presidential election took place on 23 November 1997. Kučan won a second term of office, with 55.6% of the votes cast. His nearest rival, the President of the Državni zbor, Janez Podobnik, secured 18.4% of the votes. Indirect elections to the Državni svet followed on 26 November.

In February 1998 the Minister of Defence, Tit Turnšek, tendered his resignation, after the arrest in early January of two Slovenian military intelligence agents, who had entered Croatian territory with electronic surveillance equipment. (They were later released.) In October the Minister of Defence, Alojz Krapež, resigned, following allegations of corruption. Franci Demšar, a member of the SPP, was approved as Krapež's successor by the Državni zbor in February 1999. In the same month the Minister of Internal Affairs, Mirko Bandelj, lost a vote of confidence in the Državni zbor and was dismissed; Borut Šuklje was subsequently appointed as his successor.

In January 2000 Frlec tendered his resignation as Minister of Foreign Affairs, following criticism of his failure to resolve long-standing disputes between the Governments of Slovenia and Croatia (particularly regarding the joint sea border between the two countries and over the Krško nuclear power station—see below). He was replaced in early February by Dr Dmitrij Rupel. In March it was announced that, following lengthy negotiations between the SPP and the SCD, the two parties were to merge in the following month, and that the nine ministers belonging to the SPP would resign from the Government. In early April Drnovšek attempted to form a new government. However, the proposed Government was rejected by the Državni zbor, and Drnovšek (who no longer commanded a parliamentary majority, following the departure of the SPP from the government coalition) was obliged to resign. The SPP and SCD merged as planned in mid-April, and subsequently formed a new alliance, Coalition Slovenia, with the SDPS. Coalition Slovenia nominated Andrej Bajuk as a candidate for the premiership, and in early May, after having twice been narrowly rejected by the Državni zbor, Bajuk was endorsed as Prime Minister. The Government, which was approved by the Državni zbor in early June, notably included Lojze Peterle as Minister of Foreign Affairs and Janez Janša as Minister of Defence.

In late July 2000 the approval by 70 of the 90 deputies in the Državni zbor of constitutional amendments, providing for the introduction of a system of proportional representation in the forthcoming elections, resulted in division within the SPP. Bajuk (who had opposed the new legislation and favoured a majority electoral system) announced his resignation from the reconstituted SPP and his intention of establishing a new breakaway party. Kučan subsequently declared that the legislative elections would take place on 15 October; Bajuk's administration was to remain in office until then, despite the collapse of the government coalition. In early August Bajuk was elected Chairman of the newly formed New Slovenia—Christian People's Party (NSi), which was also joined by Peterle. The elections to the Državni zbor on 15 October were conducted under the new system, whereby 40 deputies were directly elected, and the remaining 50 were elected on a proportional basis by the parties represented in the chamber (which held the requisite minimum of 3% of votes cast). The LDS secured 34 seats (an increase of nine seats compared with 1996), while the SDPS won 14 seats, the ULSD 11 seats, the SPP nine seats, and the NSi eight seats. Consequently, Drnovšek was re-elected to the premiership by the Državni zbor in early November. Following inter-party negotiations, a coalition agreement was reached by the LDS, the ULSD, the SPP and DeSUS. A new Government, which included several prominent members of Drnovšek's previous administrations, was endorsed by the legislature at the end of November; the Cabinet comprised eight representatives of the LDS, three of the ULSD and three of the SPP. Drnovšek undertook to expedite administrative reforms essential to EU requirements. In March 2001 a member of the LDS, Mitja Gaspari, was appointed Governor of the National Bank.

The presidential election on 10 November 2002 was contested by Drnovšek and Barbara Brezigar, a state prosecutor, who was supported by the SDPS and the NSi, together with a further seven candidates. (Kučan was prohibited, under the terms of the Constitution, from seeking election for a third term.) Drnovšek won the highest proportion of votes, with 44.4%, but failed to secure an outright majority; a second round between him and Brezigar (who had received 30.8% of the votes) was scheduled for 1 December. At this second ballot Drnovšek was elected to the presidency, with 56.5% of the votes cast. Anton Rop, also a member of the LDS and hitherto Minister of Finance, was nominated to replace Drnovšek as Prime Minister, and on 19 December a new Government was approved by the Državni zbor. Drnovšek was inaugurated as President on 22 December. In September 2003 the SDPS was reconstituted as the Slovenian Democratic Party (SDP).

In early 2004 the Državni zbor approved legislation providing for the restoration of citizenship to 18,000 nationals of former Yugoslav republics, who (resident in Slovenia at the time of its independence) had been removed from population records and lost their residency rights. However, at a referendum, which was conducted in early April, following pressure from the SNP and three right-wing parties, some 94% of the votes cast by 31% of the electorate rejected adoption of the new legislation. Following the referendum, the SPP, the only party in the governing coalition to have supported the referendum, withdrew from the Government (which was subsequently reorganized). Following the accession of Slovenia to full membership of the EU on 1 May (see below), the first elections to the European Parliament took place on 13 June, although only about 28% of the electorate participated. In the elections, the NSi, the SDP and the LDS each obtained two mandates, while the ULSD received one seat. In July Rop dismissed Dimitrij Rupel as Minister of Foreign Affairs; Rupel had announced that he was transferring his support to a newly established opposition group prior to forthcoming legislative elections. Ivo Vajgl, hitherto ambassador to Germany, was subsequently appointed to the post.

At the legislative elections on 3 October 2004 the centre-right SDP secured 29.1% of votes cast and 29 seats in the 90-member Državni zbor, defeating the ruling LDS (with 22.8% of the votes and 23 seats). The leader of the SDP, Janez Janša, was appointed Prime Minister on 9 November. Following lengthy inter-party negotiations, the SDP reached a coalition agreement with the SPP, the NSi and DeSUS, and a new Government was approved by 51 votes in the Državni zbor on 3 December.

In late November 2005 trade unions organized a mass demonstration in Ljubljana (the largest to be staged since 1991), in protest at government plans for extensive reforms, and to demand dialogue on the main issues, such as the proposed introduction of a uniform rate of value-added tax. The programme was also strongly criticized by the LDS. In December the Državni zbor approved the appointment of an economist as Minister without Portfolio; Jože Damijan was to head a newly established government development office and be responsible for the implementation of the reform strategy. Later that month, despite a lack of public support and continued trade union opposition, the Državni zbor approved the economic reform strategy, which was designed to facilitate Slovenia's planned adoption of the common European currency, the euro, at the beginning of 2007 (see Economic Affairs). In late March 2006 Damijan announced his resignation, but Janša announced that the reform programme would continue as planned.

Areas of disputed border territory with Croatia, most notably the Bay of Piran in Istria, undermined otherwise harmonious relations between the two countries following independence. In July 1993 tensions between the two countries prevented the signing of agreements on friendship and co-operation and on the regulation of bilateral payments (although protocols governing other issues, including trade and economic relations, were concluded). In November Slovenian proposals to decommission the country's nuclear power plant, at Krško (constructed by the former federal authorities to supply energy to both Slovenia and Croatia), prompted protests by Croatia, which was reliant on the installation for one-quarter of its energy requirements. Little progress was achieved during 1994 in efforts to delineate the joint border, and the resumption of construction by Croatia of border facilities on Slovenian territory provoked renewed protests by the Slovenian Government. In October the Croatian Government submitted a formal protest to Slovenia, following the approval of legislation providing for a reorganization of local government boundaries in Slovenia, as part of which four villages in the disputed area were to be included within the Slovenian municipality of Piran. A subsequent proposal by the Slovenian Government to revise the law to exclude the villages was rejected by the Državni zbor, although deputies agreed to delay implementation of the law (and thus the holding of elections) in three villages, pending a resolution of the border issue. In February 1995 a meeting of the Slovenian-Croatian joint border commission agreed that, since the process of delineating the border would be lengthy, this should be pursued separately from other bilateral concerns. In March Slovenia and Croatia agreed to divide ownership of the Krško nuclear station equally between the two countries.

In December 1997 Drnovšek strongly criticized the removal from the Croatian Constitution of Slovenes as a recognized minority. Tension between the two countries escalated in early 1998, with the arrest in January of two Slovenian intelligence agents (see above). Negotiations on border issues and other areas of contention continued, none the less, and in March the Slovenian Minister of Foreign Affairs met with his Austrian and Croatian counterparts in Split, Croatia, with the aim of developing trilateral links within the framework of the Central European Initiative (see p. 395).

In July 1998 Slovenia ceased distributing electricity generated at the Krško nuclear power plant to Croatia, claiming that it had failed to pay for power, valued at some US $14m., already supplied. In the same month Slovenia privatized the Krško power plant. Croatia was reported to have resumed payments to Slovenia in August, and subsequently the transfer of electricity was restored. In November it was announced that the dispute over the Krško nuclear power plant would be resolved on the basis of co-ownership. Following the election of a new Government in Croatia in early 2000, bilateral relations improved significantly. After lengthy negotiations between Drnovšek and the Croatian Prime Minister, Ivica Račan, an agreement resolving the outstanding issues of contention between Slovenia and Croatia was signed in July 2001. The accord (which required endorsement by the legislatures of the two countries) granted Slovenia access to the Adriatic Sea through the Bay of Piran, and provided for continued joint management of the Krško nuclear installation; the four disputed border villages were to remain under Croatian sovereignty. In 2003 a further dispute erupted between Slovenia and Croatia, after the Croatian Government announced plans to establish an economic zone in the Adriatic Sea, which would remove Slovenia's direct access to international waters. The Slovenian Government threatened to obstruct Croatia's envisaged accession to the EU in 2007 (which was, in any case, subsequently postponed—see the chapter on Croatia), and at the end of August 2003 withdrew its ambassador to Croatia. In early September the ambassador was returned to Croatia, as a gesture of reconciliation, and trilateral discussions on the issue were initiated between Slovenia, Croatia and Italy. In September 2004, however, the Slovenian Government temporarily withdrew its ambassador, after a number of Slovenian citizens, including an opposition leader, were arrested by Croatian security forces in the disputed border region.

In August 2005 it was announced that Croatia had withdrawn its ambassador to Slovenia, following the Slovenian Government's decision to declare a fishing zone in the border region. The ambassador was returned by early September. After the Državni zbor approved the Government's decision, Croatia declared the fishing zone to be illegitimate and demanded that the issue be referred to international arbitration. The Slovenian Government demonstrated reluctance to enter into international arbitration and, following the official opening of Croatia's accession negotiations with the EU earlier that month, again threatened to withdraw support for Croatian membership. The Slovenian Government also continued to reject claims by Croatia that it was liable for outstanding debts owed to Croatian citizens by the former Ljubljanska Banka of Slovenia. At the end of 2005 the Croatian national power utility submitted to an international centre for investment disputes a demand for compensation for undelivered electricity from the Krško installation.

Slovenia and Croatia are united in their opposition to movements for Istrian autonomy and to any revision to their detriment of the 1975 Treaty of Osimo, which had defined the borders between the SFRY and Italy, and had provided for the payment by the SFRY of compensation for Italian property transferred to Yugoslav sovereignty after 1947. Although Slovenia asserted that its debt in this matter (in accordance with the Treaty of Osimo and the 1983 Treaty of Rome) had been discharged in full, in 1993 some 35,000 Italians were reported to be demanding compensation for, or the restitution of, property in Slovenia. In July 1994 the Italian Government of Silvio Berlusconi stated that until the Slovenian authorities agreed to compensate Italian nationals who had fled after 1947 from territory now held by Slovenia, and whose property had been confiscated under communist rule, Italy would block efforts by Slovenia to achieve further integration with western Europe. Italy thus prevented scheduled negotiations on an association agreement between Slovenia and the EU until March 1995, when the new Italian Government of Lamberto Dini withdrew the veto. Preliminary agreement on trade and political co-operation was reached in June. However, it was not until May 1996 that Slovenia and Italy agreed to a compromise solution proposed by Spain, whereby Slovenia was to allow EU nationals to purchase property in Slovenia, on a reciprocal basis, within four years of the association agreement's ratification, and EU citizens who had previously permanently resided in Slovenia for a period of three years (thus including Italian nationals who had fled after the Second World War) would be permitted to buy immediately. In June Slovenia finally signed an association agreement with the EU, and simultaneously applied for full membership of the organization. In July 1997 the Državni zbor voted in favour of amending the Constitution in accordance with the agreement.

In April 1993 Slovenia was the first former Yugoslav republic to sign a trade and economic co-operation accord with the EC, and it achieved associate membership of the EU in June 1996 (see above). Slovenia joined the Council of Europe (see p. 211) in May 1993, and in December was granted observer status at the Western European Union (see p. 365) conference in Paris, France. In March 1994 it was announced that Slovenia was to join NATO's 'Partnership for Peace' (see p. 316) programme. In January 1996 Slovenia was admitted to the Central European Free Trade Agreement (now Association). Formal accession negotiations with the EU commenced in November 1998. In December 2002, at a summit meeting in Copenhagen, Denmark, Slovenia was one of 10 nations officially invited to become members of the EU in May 2004. Meanwhile, at a summit meeting in Prague, Czech Republic, in November 2002, Slovenia was formally invited to join NATO in 2004. A national referendum on the issue of joining both organizations was conducted on 23 March 2003; some 89.6% of voters endorsed membership of the EU, and 66.1% membership of NATO. On 29 March 2004 Slovenia was officially admitted to NATO, together with Bulgaria, Estonia, Latvia, Lithuania, Romania and Slovakia, at a ceremony in Washington, DC (the USA being the depository nation for the North Atlantic Treaty). Slovenia's accession to the EU followed on 1 May. In early February 2005 the Državni zbor voted in favour of ratifying the EU draft constitutional treaty.

Government

Under the terms of the 1991 Constitution, legislative power is vested in the 90-member Državni zbor (National Assembly). Of the 90 deputies, who serve a term of four years, 40 are directly elected, while 50 are elected on a proportional basis by the parties represented in the chamber; two members are representatives of the Hungarian and Italian minorities. The Državni svet (National Council), which is elected for five years, comprises 22 directly elected members, and 18 members chosen by an electoral college to represent various social, economic, trading, political and local interest groups; the Council's role is mainly advisory, but it is empowered to veto decisions of the Državni zbor. The Prime Minister, who is elected by the Državni zbor, nominates the Government (subject to the approval of the legislature). The President of the Republic has largely ceremonial powers, and is directly elected for a maximum of two five-year terms. For administrative purposes, Slovenia is divided into 193 municipalities, 11 of which are designated as city municipalities.

Defence

In August 2005 the active Slovenian armed forces numbered 6,550; reserve forces totalled 20,000. There was a paramilitary police force of 4,500 (with 5,000 reserves). In September 2003 the Government announced the abolition of compulsory military service, prior to the country's official accession to the North Atlantic Treaty Organization (NATO, see p. 314) on 29 March 2004. The estimated defence budget for 2005 was SIT 110,000m.

Economic Affairs

In 2004, according to the World Bank, Slovenia's gross national income (GNI), measured at average 2002–04 prices, was US $29,555m., equivalent to $14,810 per head (or $20,730 per head on an international purchasing-power parity basis). During 1995–2004, it was estimated, the population neither increased nor declined, while gross domestic product (GDP) per head increased, in real terms, by an average of 3.8% per year. Overall GDP increased, in real terms, at an average annual rate of 3.8% in 1995–2004. Real GDP increased by 2.5% in 2003 and by 4.6% in 2004.

Agriculture (including hunting, forestry and fishing) contributed 2.5% of GDP in 2004. In that year the sector engaged 9.6% of the employed labour force. The principal crops are cereals (particularly maize and wheat), potatoes, sugar beet and fruits (especially grapes and apples). Slovenia's forests, which cover about one-half of the country, are an important natural resource. Agricultural GDP declined at an average rate of 0.5% per year during 1995–2004. The GDP of the sector declined by 15.4% in 2003, but increased by 11.2% in 2004.

Industry (including mining, manufacturing, construction and power) contributed 35.1% of GDP in 2004. In that year the industrial sector engaged 35.9% of the employed labour force. Industrial GDP increased at an average rate of 4.6% per year in 1995–2004. Sectoral GDP increased by 3.3% in 2003 and by 4.6% in 2004.

Mining and quarrying contributed 0.5% of GDP and engaged 0.6% of the employed labour force in 2004. The principal activity is coal-mining; lead and zinc are also extracted, together with relatively small amounts of natural gas, petroleum and salt. Slovenia also has small deposits of uranium. The GDP of the mining sector increased at an average rate of 0.9% per year in 1995–2000. Mining GDP declined by 7.3% in 2000.

Manufacturing contributed 25.9% of GDP in 2004, when it engaged 28.5% of the employed labour force. Manufacturing GDP increased at an average rate of 4.9% per year in 1995–2004. GDP in the manufacturing sector increased by 3.9% in 2003 and by 5.4% in 2004.

A nuclear power station was constructed in Slovenia by the former Yugoslav authorities to provide energy for both Slovenia and Croatia (see Recent History). In 2002 nuclear power stations provided 37.6% of energy requirements, coal-fired electricity generating stations provided 36.1%, and hydroelectric power stations provided 23.2%. Imports of fuel products comprised 8.2% of the value of merchandise imports in 2004.

The services sector contributed 62.3% of GDP and engaged 54.5% of the employed labour force in 2004. Tourism is a significant source of revenue; tourist activity was adversely affected by the political instability of 1991, but the number of arrivals recovered, reaching 1,498,900 in 2004. The GDP of the services sector increased at an average rate of 3.4% per year in 1995–2004. Growth in the services sector was 2.9% in 2003 and 4.3% in 2004.

In 2004 Slovenia recorded a visible trade deficit of US $1,257.5m., and there was a deficit of $669.7m. on the current account of the balance of payments. In that year Slovenia's principal source of imports was Germany (accounting for 20.3% of the total); other major suppliers were Italy (18.9%), Austria (13.2%) and France (8.2%). Germany was also the principal market for exports (taking 21.6% of the total in that year); Italy (13.0%), Croatia (9.1%), Austria (7.5%) and France (6.4%) were also significant purchasers. The major imports in 2004 were machinery and transport equipment (particularly road vehicles and parts), basic manufactures, chemical products, miscellaneous manufactured articles, mineral fuels, crude materials and food and live animals. The principal exports in that year were machinery and transport equipment (particularly road vehicles and parts and electrical machinery), basic manufactures, miscellaneous manufactured articles and chemicals.

Slovenia's overall budgetary deficit for 2004 was 77,000m. SIT, equivalent to 1.2% of GDP. In 2002 (according to the IMF) total external debt amounted to US $11,350m., and the cost of debt-servicing was equivalent to 13.6% of the value of exports of goods and services. The annual rate of inflation averaged 10.9% in 1992–2004. Consumer prices increased by 3.6% in 2004 and by 2.5% in 2005. An estimated 10.2% of the total labour force were unemployed in 2005.

Slovenia has joined several international organizations, including the IMF, the World Bank and (as a 'Country of Operations') the European Bank for Reconstruction and Development (see p. 224). The country became a full member of the World Trade Organization (see p. 370) in July 1995. Slovenia became a full member of the European Union (EU, see p. 228) on 1 May 2004.

Slovenia's economy was severely disrupted by secession from the Yugoslav Federation, and by the international economic blockade of Serbia and Montenegro, together with the conflicts in Croatia and in Bosnia and Herzegovina. By the mid-1990s, however, important advances in the transformation of the economy (such as the full convertibility of the tolar) had allowed Slovenia to gain a favourable position among the countries chosen to participate in negotiations to join the EU. All remaining restrictions to foreign investment in Slovenia were removed in 2002, and Slovenia's scheduled accession to the EU was officially announced in December of that year. At April 2003 Slovenia had achieved sustained convergence in per-head income to about 70% of the EU average. Slovenia formally acceded to the EU on 1 May 2004 and, following the successful adoption of measures to reduce inflation, achieved entry into the exchange-rate mechanism (ERM-2) in June. The continued reduction of inflation in order to meet EU levels, with the aim of adopting the euro in January 2007, was central to government policy. The coalition Government installed in December 2004 expressed commitment to the removal of administrative restraints, further liberalization of the financial sector and progress in privatization (notably of the state telecommunications sector). In November 2005 the Government announced extensive economic reforms, which were designed to facilitate entry into the euro zone, including measures to increase competitiveness, reform the labour market and the pension and health systems, and resume the privatization of state-owned enterprises. Trade unions responded by organizing mass protests, in particular against plans to introduce a uniform rate of value-added tax, which they claimed would adversely affect the standard of living. Nevertheless, the economic reform strategy was officially approved by the legislature in December, to be implemented from the beginning of 2006 (although continued trade union opposition was expected to prove an impediment). In early 2006 Slovenia's sustained ability to meet euro-zone membership criteria appeared extremely favourable, the IMF having concluded that at the end of 2005 long-term interest rates, the fiscal deficit, the public-debt ratio and the rate of inflation were within the requisite limits. In May 2006 the European Commission formally accepted, subject to ratification by the European Parliament and EU member states, Slovenia's application to join the euro zone on 1 January 2007.

Education

Primary education is free and compulsory for all children between the ages of six and 15 years. In ethnically mixed regions, two methods of schooling have been developed: bilingual or with instruction in the minority languages. Various types of secondary education, beginning at 15 and lasting between two and five years, are also available. In 2002/03 93% of children in the relevant age-group (males 94%; females 93%) were enrolled at primary schools, while the equivalent rate for secondary education was also 93% of children of the appropriate age-group (males 93%; females 94%). Slovenia's two universities are situated in Ljubljana and Maribor, with 58,265 and 25,621 students, respectively, in 2004/05. Expenditure on education by all levels of government in 2003 was estimated at SIT 350,062m., representing 6.1% of total government spending.

Public Holidays

2006: 1–2 January (New Year), 8 February (Prešeren Day, National Day of Culture), 14–17 April (Easter), 27 April (Resistance Day), 1–2 May (Labour Days), 25 June (National Statehood Day), 15 August (Assumption), 31 October (Reformation Day), 1 November (All Saints' Day), 25 December (Christmas Day), 26 December (Independence Day).

2007: 1–2 January (New Year), 8 February (Prešeren Day, National Day of Culture), 6–9 April (Easter), 27 April (Resistance Day), 1–2 May (Labour Days), 25 June (National Statehood Day), 15 August (Assumption), 31 October (Reformation Day), 1 November (All Saints' Day), 25 December (Christmas Day), 26 December (Independence Day).

Weights and Measures

The metric system is in force.

SLOVENIA

Statistical Survey

Source (unless otherwise indicated): Statistical Office of the Republic of Slovenia, 1000 Ljubljana, Vožarski pot 12; tel. (1) 2415104; fax (1) 2415344; e-mail info.stat@gov.si; internet www.stat.si.

Area and Population

AREA, POPULATION AND DENSITY

Area (sq km)	20,273*
Population (census results)	
31 March 1991	1,913,355
31 March 2002	
Males	958,576
Females	1,005,460
Total	1,964,036
Population (official estimates at 31 December)†	
2002	1,995,033
2003	1,996,433
2004	1,997,590
Density (per sq km) at 31 December 2004	98.5

* 7,827 sq miles.
† Estimates are calculated on a *de jure* basis.

POPULATION BY ETHNIC GROUP
(2002 census)

Ethnic group	Number	%
Slovenes	1,631,363	83.1
Serbs	38,964	2.0
Croats	35,642	1.8
Bosniaks	21,542	1.1
Muslims*	10,467	0.5
Hungarians	6,243	0.3
Albanians	6,186	0.3
Macedonians	3,972	0.2
Montenegrins	2,667	0.1
Italians	2,258	0.1
Total (incl. others)	1,964,036	100.0

* Including persons claiming Muslim ethnicity rather than religious adherence.

PRINCIPAL TOWNS
(population at 2002 census)

Ljubljana (capital)	265,881	Koper (Capodistria)	47,539
Maribor	110,668	Novo mesto	40,925
Kranj	51,225	Nova Gorica	35,640
Celje	48,081		

BIRTHS, MARRIAGES AND DEATHS

	Registered live births		Registered marriages		Registered deaths	
	Number	Rate (per 1,000)	Number	Rate (per 1,000)	Number	Rate (per 1,000)
1996	18,788	9.5	7,555	3.8	18,620	9.4
1997	18,165	9.1	7,500	3.8	18,928	9.5
1998	17,856	9.0	7,528	3.8	19,039	9.6
1999	17,533	8.8	7,716	3.9	18,885	9.5
2000	18,180	9.1	7,201	3.6	18,588	9.3
2001	17,477	8.8	6,935	3.5	18,508	9.3
2002	17,501	8.8	7,064	3.5	18,701	9.4
2003	17,321	8.7	6,756	3.4	17,321	9.7

2004: Live births 17,961 (birth rate 9.0 per 1,000).

Expectation of life (years at birth): 77 (males 73; females 81) in 2003 (Source: WHO, *World Health Report*).

IMMIGRATION AND EMIGRATION

	2001	2002	2003
Long-term immigrants	7,803	9,134	9,279
Long-term emigrants	4,811	7,269	5,867

ECONOMICALLY ACTIVE POPULATION
('000 persons aged 15 years and over, April-June)

	2002	2003	2004
Agriculture, hunting, forestry and fishing	89	75	91
Mining and quarrying	4	6	6
Manufacturing	287	264	270
Electricity, gas and water supply	11	9	10
Construction	54	52	54
Wholesale and retail trade; repair of motor vehicles, motorcycles and personal and household goods	120	118	120
Hotels and restaurants	36	36	38
Transport, storage and communications	55	59	56
Financial intermediation	22	22	22
Real estate, renting and business activities	45	53	58
Public administration and defence; compulsory social security	50	50	56
Education	61	62	65
Health and social work	51	47	48
Other social and personal services	33	37	40
Total employed (incl. others)	922	896	946
Unemployed	58	63	61
Total labour force	981	959	1,007
Males	530	519	543
Females	451	440	464

Health and Welfare

KEY INDICATORS

Total fertility rate (children per woman, 2003)	1.1
Under-5 mortality rate (per 1,000 live births, 2004)	4
HIV/AIDS (% of persons aged 15–49, 2003)	<0.1
Physicians (per 1,000 head, 2001)	2.19
Hospital beds (per 1,000 head, 2001)	5.16
Health expenditure (2002): US $ per head (PPP)	1,547
Health expenditure (2002): % of GDP	8.3
Health expenditure (2002): public (% of total)	74.9
Access to water (% of persons, 2000)	100
Human Development Index (2003): ranking	26
Human Development Index (2003): value	0.904

For sources and definitions, see explanatory note on p. vi.

SLOVENIA

Agriculture

PRINCIPAL CROPS
('000 metric tons)

	2002	2003	2004
Wheat	174.9	122.9	146.8
Barley	48.1	39.7	59.7
Maize	371.4	224.2	357.6
Oats	5.9	3.6	5.3
Triticale (wheat-rye hybrid)	6.6	5.5	8.9
Mixed grain	3.6	3.6*	3.6*
Potatoes	166.0	107.6	171.5
Sugar beet	232.2	202.1	213.1
Cabbages	22.0	17.8	24.4
Lettuce	6.6	5.4	7.4
Tomatoes	4.4	4.2	5.4
Chillies and green peppers	6.8	4.9	6.1
Dry onions	5.7	5.6	7.4
Other vegetables	13.7	11.5	13.0
Apples	141.7	167.2	230.0†
Pears	13.0	11.3	14.2
Peaches and nectarines	10.0	6.0	14.4
Plums	5.4	7.7	10.0
Grapes	123.0	104.4	134.8
Other fresh fruit	6.8	5.4	7.2

* FAO estimate.
† Unofficial figure.
Source: FAO.

LIVESTOCK
('000 head)

	2002	2003	2004
Cattle	477	473	450
Pigs	600	656	621
Sheep	94	107	106
Goats	20	22	23
Horses	17	17	18†
Chickens	5,217	4,981	4,534
Ducks*	200	200	200
Geese*	270	270	270
Turkeys	417	209	130

* FAO estimates.
† Unofficial figure.
Source: FAO.

LIVESTOCK PRODUCTS
('000 metric tons)

	2002	2003	2004
Beef and veal	42.7	51.8	46.9
Pig meat	62.0	63.6	71.3
Mutton and lamb	1.2	1.2	1.1*
Chicken meat	53.1	54.3	47.0†
Duck meat	1.2	1.2*	1.2*
Goose meat	3.4	3.4*	3.4*
Turkey meat*	8.4	8.4	8.4
Cows' milk	706.4	642.4	651.0
Cheese	22.8	24.6	22.0*
Butter	4.5	3.5*	3.5*
Hen eggs	22.7	18.2	20.0*

* FAO estimate(s).
† Unofficial figure.
Source: FAO.

Forestry

ROUNDWOOD REMOVALS
('000 cubic metres, excl. bark)

	2002	2003	2004
Sawlogs, veneer logs and logs for sleepers	1,164	1,291	1,372
Pulpwood	414	572	283
Other industrial wood	425	369	171
Fuel wood	280	359	725
Total	2,283	2,591	2,551

Source: FAO.

SAWNWOOD PRODUCTION
('000 cubic metres, incl. railway sleepers)

	2002	2003	2004
Coniferous (softwood)	337	340	304
Broadleaved (hardwood)	169	171	157
Total	506	511	461

Source: FAO.

Fishing

(metric tons, live weight)

	2001	2002	2003
Capture	1,827	1,686	1,281
Common carp	75	83	82
European pilchard (sardine)	1,219	1,223	771
European anchovy	97	72	58
Aquaculture	1,262	1,289	1,353
Common carp	216	208	201
Rainbow trout	832	891	861
Mediterranean mussel	88	83	135
Total catch	3,089	2,976	2,634

Source: FAO.

Mining

(metric tons, unless otherwise indicated)

	2001	2002	2003
Brown coal ('000 metric tons)	685	639	608
Lignite ('000 metric tons)	3,448	4,048	4,222
Natural gas ('000 cubic metres)	6,100	6,000	4,900
Crude petroleum	700*	763	482
Bentonite	3,738	4,122	4,000*
Quartz and quartzite (incl. glass sand)*	200,000	200,000	200,000
Sand and gravel (excl. glass sand)	11,510	10,897	11,000*
Pumice*	40,000	40,000	40,000
Salt	107,755	128,212	125,000*

* Estimate(s).
Source: US Geological Survey.

SLOVENIA

Industry

SELECTED PRODUCTS
('000 metric tons, unless otherwise indicated)

	2000	2001	2002
Wine ('000 hectolitres)	413	545	322
Beer ('000 hectolitres)	2,571	2,546	n.a.
Cigarettes (million)	7,855	n.a.	n.a.
Footwear (excl. rubber) ('000 pairs)	4,691	4,690	4,256
Veneer sheets ('000 cubic metres)	23	28	38
Plywood ('000 cubic metres)	35	37	26
Mechanical wood pulp	32	32	32
Chemical wood pulp	121	121	121
Newsprint	61	30	n.a.
Other printing and writing paper	200	147	186
Household and sanitary paper	61	229	131
Wrapping and packaging paper and paperboard	78	229	131
Rubber tyres ('000)	5,629	n.a.	n.a.
Cement	1,252	1,520	1,495
Crude steel ingots (incl. crude steel for casting)*	n.a.	462	481
Refined lead†	15.3	15.4	13.0
Passenger motor cars ('000)	123	119	127
Bicycles ('000)	142	n.a.	n.a.
Electric energy (million kWh)	13,527	14,466	n.a.

* Source: International Iron and Steel Institute (Brussels).
† Source: US Geological Survey.
Source (unless otherwise indicated): UN, *Industrial Commodity Statistics Yearbook*.

Finance

CURRENCY AND EXCHANGE RATES

Monetary Units
100 stotins = 1 tolar (SIT).

Sterling, Dollar and Euro Equivalents (30 December 2005)
£1 sterling = 348.564 tolars;
US $1 = 202.430 tolars;
€1 = 238.807 tolars;
1,000 tolars = £2.87 = $4.94 = €4.19.

Average Exchange Rate (tolars per US $)
2003   207.10
2004   192.38
2004   192.71

Note: The tolar was introduced in October 1991, replacing (initially at par) the Yugoslav dinar.

BUDGET
('000 million tolars)*

Revenue	2002	2003	2004
Tax revenue	2,002	2,291	2,447
Taxes on income and profits	395	461	507
Taxes on payroll, property etc.	128	142	157
Social security contributions	774	839	899
Domestic taxes on goods and services	673	815	857
Value-added tax	423	524	539
Excises	171	198	218
Others	78	91	100
Taxes on international trade and transactions	31	35	19
Other current revenue	134	149	162
Capital revenue and grants	29	29	23
Transferred revenues	11	8	8
Receipts from EU budget	—	—	44
Total	2,176	2,477	2,683

Expenditure†	2002	2003	2004
Current expenditure (excl. transfers)	1,119	1,226	1,234
Wages and salaries	515	561	589
Expenditure on goods and services	418	451	430
Interest payments	84	93	92
Current transfers	1,007	1,097	1,250
Subsidies	60	69	78
Transfers to individuals and households	910	986	1,053
Capital expenditure (excl. transfers)	129	142	151
Capital transfers	78	91	92
Payments to EU budget	—	—	41
Total	2,332	2,556	2,768

* Figures represent a consolidation of the accounts of the central Government (State Budget, Pension Fund and Health Insurance Fund) and local administrative authorities.
† Excluding net lending ('000 million tolars): 104 in 2002; −1 in 2003; −8 in 2004.

INTERNATIONAL RESERVES
(US $ million at 31 December)

	2003	2004	2005
Gold (market prices)	101.09	105.80	83.35
IMF special drawing rights	9.18	11.15	11.63
Reserve position in IMF	144.65	119.98	51.62
Foreign exchange	8,343.09	8,662.27	8,013.12
Total	8,598.00	8,899.20	8,159.72

Source: IMF, *International Financial Statistics*.

MONEY SUPPLY
(million tolars at 31 December)

	2002	2003	2004
Currency outside banks	143,050	156,040	167,920
Demand deposits at commercial banks	533,300	608,480	808,110
Total money (incl. others)	680,490	767,700	982,240

Note: Figures are rounded to the nearest 10,000 tolars.
Source: IMF, *International Financial Statistics*.

COST OF LIVING
(Consumer Price Index for urban areas; base: 2000 = 100)

	2002	2003	2004
Food (incl. beverages)	117.5	123.1	124.2
Fuel and light	112.2	116.7	123.8
Clothing (incl. footwear)	105.9	112.4	114.4
Rent	124.5	152.9	177.8
All items (incl. others)	116.5	123.0	127.4

Source: ILO.

SLOVENIA

NATIONAL ACCOUNTS

National Income and Product
(million tolars at current prices)

	2002	2003	2004
Compensation of employees	2,824,112	3,044,680	3,295,800
Net operating surplus	503,340	660,599	698,917
Net mixed income	335,991	336,009	365,345
Domestic primary incomes	3,663,443	4,041,288	4,360,062
Consumption of fixed capital	884,756	907,943	971,217
Gross domestic product (GDP) at factor cost	4,548,199	4,949,231	5,331,279
Taxes on production and imports	878,945	963,120	1,029,868
Less Subsidies	71,703	98,810	109,903
GDP in market prices	5,355,440	5,813,540	6,251,244
Net primary income from abroad	−27,640	−36,137	−57,705
Gross national income	5,327,800	5,777,403	6,193,539
Less Consumption of fixed capital	884,756	907,943	971,217
Net national income	4,443,044	4,869,460	5,222,322

Expenditure on the Gross Domestic Product
(million tolars at current prices)

	2002	2003	2004
Final consumption expenditure	4,030,681	4,381,303	4,680,583
Households	2,903,381	3,167,384	3,386,182
Non-profit institutions serving households	69,814	74,791	75,309
General government	1,057,486	1,139,128	1,219,092
Gross capital formation	1,250,957	1,436,604	1,646,171
Gross fixed capital formation	1,211,519	1,353,058	1,506,015
Changes in inventories / Acquisitions, less disposals, of valuables	39,438	83,547	140,156
Total domestic expenditure	5,281,638	5,817,907	6,326,754
Exports of goods and services	3,059,976	3,246,747	3,761,522
Less Imports of goods and services	2,986,173	3,251,114	3,837,032
GDP in purchasers' values	5,355,440	5,813,540	6,251,244
GDP at constant 2000 prices	4,511,414	4,625,302	n.a.

Gross Domestic Product by Economic Activity
(million tolars at current prices)

	2002	2003	2004
Agriculture, hunting and forestry	146,949	127,794	136,096
Fishing	854	1,060	903
Mining and quarrying	22,229	26,378	28,489
Manufacturing	1,210,946	1,332,453	1,406,406
Electricity, gas and water supply	141,645	147,844	166,900
Construction	264,710	290,297	308,827
Wholesale and retail trade; repair of motor vehicles, motorcycles and personal and household goods	538,756	592,019	631,270
Hotels and restaurants	107,183	117,075	123,092
Transport, storage and communications	321,742	360,735	389,902
Financial intermediation	212,234	222,434	241,702
Real estate, renting and business activities	721,283	788,799	863,880
Public administration and defence; compulsory social security	298,445	333,583	366,389
Education	263,963	288,351	315,597
Health and social work	235,140	252,472	270,670
Other community, social and personal services	152,897	165,966	184,470
Private households with employed persons	1,728	1,336	1,349
Gross value added at basic prices	4,640,703	5,048,599	5,435,944
Taxes on products	737,786	794,799	846,737
Less Subsidies	23,048	29,857	31,436
GDP in market prices	5,355,440	5,813,540	6,251,244

BALANCE OF PAYMENTS
(US $ million)

	2002	2003	2004
Exports of goods f.o.b.	10,471.1	12,916.3	16,064.6
Imports of goods f.o.b.	−10,718.9	−13,538.5	−17,322.1
Trade balance	−247.7	−622.1	−1,257.5
Exports of services	2,315.8	2,791.2	3,454.5
Imports of services	−1,732.0	−2,181.7	−2,604.4
Balance on goods and services	336.1	−12.5	−407.4
Other income received	469.6	625.7	734.1
Other income paid	−605.0	−805.6	−1,034.2
Balance on goods, services and income	200.8	−192.4	−707.5
Current transfers received	452.1	508.0	677.7
Current transfers paid	−317.9	−400.8	−640.0
Current balance	334.9	−85.3	−669.7
Capital account (net)	−158.3	−190.9	−134.2
Direct investment abroad	−147.7	−471.9	−550.5
Direct investment from abroad	1,636.4	333.2	827.2
Portfolio investment assets	−93.9	−220.0	−753.3
Portfolio investment liabilities	26.7	−37.0	60.5
Financial derivatives assets	—	—	−2.7
Other investment assets	−623.7	−904.3	−1,731.6
Other investment liabilities	1,049.6	1,800.0	2,793.8
Net errors and omissions	−207.4	86.5	−135.9
Overall balance	1,816.7	310.2	−296.5

Source: IMF, *International Financial Statistics*.

External Trade

PRINCIPAL COMMODITIES
(distribution by SITC, € million)

Imports c.i.f.	2002	2003	2004
Food and live animals	604.1	621.4	713.6
Crude materials (inedible) except fuels	574.7	601.4	720.1
Mineral fuels, lubricants, etc.	814.7	946.5	1,162.6
Petroleum, petroleum products, etc.	584.6	629.3	803.7
Chemicals and related products	1,547.9	1,631.1	1,849.6
Basic manufactures	2,661.3	2,799.3	3,293.2
Textile yarn, fabrics, etc.	387.3	343.6	412.6
Iron and steel	526.7	585.1	825.0
Non-ferrous metals	347.6	352.3	427.5
Other metal manufactures	468.6	494.7	526.5
Machinery and transport equipment	3,937.3	4,212.1	4,831.5
Machinery specialized for particular industries	336.5	402.5	379.8
General industrial machinery equipment and parts	531.1	621.6	655.0
Electrical machinery, apparatus etc.	759.6	756.0	867.6
Road vehicles (incl. air-cushion vehicles) and parts (excl. tyres engines and electrical parts)	1,237.4	1,356.0	1,688.2
Miscellaneous manufactured articles	1,318.5	1,319.6	1,437.8
Clothing and accessories (excl. footwear)	371.1	351.4	290.2
Total (incl. others)	11,574.1	12,238.9	14,143.0

SLOVENIA

Exports f.o.b.	2002	2003	2004
Chemicals and related products	1,354.3	1,551.3	1,711.0
Medicinal and pharmaceutical products	633.6	788.4	855.4
Basic manufactures	2,860.1	2,890.2	3,279.2
Paper, paperboard and articles thereof	438.4	408.4	444.7
Textile yarn, fabrics, etc.	377.4	346.1	379.6
Iron and steel	309.3	343.5	473.0
Non-ferrous metals	365.0	370.9	442.6
Other metal manufactures	502.5	526.1	578.9
Machinery and transport equipment	4,064.4	4,126.1	4,839.6
General industrial machinery equipment and parts	513.0	540.6	677.9
Electrical machinery, apparatus etc.	1,259.1	1,312.7	1,471.2
Road vehicles (incl. air-cushion vehicles) and parts (excl. tyres engines and electrical parts)	1,353.3	1,292.0	1,595.7
Miscellaneous manufactured articles	1,968.1	1,974.7	2,161.4
Furniture and parts; bedding mattresses, etc.	762.1	776.9	885.8
Clothing and accessories (excl. footwear)	346.3	304.4	271.8
Total (incl. others)	10,962.0	11,285.0	12,783.1

PRINCIPAL TRADING PARTNERS
(€ million)

Imports c.i.f.	2002	2003	2004
Austria	1,490.9	1,665.1	1,863.9
Belgium	193.4	208.6	267.9
China, People's Republic	70.1	89.1	150.0
Croatia	427.9	455.7	514.2
Czech Republic	282.8	303.6	345.1
France	1,145.3	1,069.4	1,166.2
Germany	2,477.9	2,586.6	2,871.7
Hungary	411.2	432.1	540.4
Italy	2,135.6	2,322.19	2,672.7
Japan	36.6	37.8	62.9
Netherlands	358.5	392.9	508.0
Poland	148.2	162.0	188.8
Russia	234.8	280.3	299.6
Slovakia	152.3	154.4	173.0
Spain	291.6	300.1	385.3
Sweden	98.8	115.9	145.9
Switzerland	282.1	295.8	229.4
Turkey	77.6	101.7	109.9
United Kingdom	223.1	226.2	242.8
USA	146.5	132.9	165.6
Total (incl. others)	11,574.1	12,238.9	14,143.0

Exports f.o.b.	2002	2003	2004
Austria	774.1	827.1	955.4
Belgium	96.9	93.2	140.7
Bosnia and Herzegovina	492.1	471.3	490.7
Croatia	954.4	1,006.9	1,166.7
Czech Republic	200.8	204.8	244.5
France	734.5	638.3	822.2
Germany	2,714.2	2,610.6	2,759.6
Hungary	195.8	222.8	248.9
Italy	1,322.7	1,477.8	1,663.9
Macedonia, former Yugoslav republic	158.8	142.8	139.2
Netherlands	182.6	197.0	190.5
Poland	304.6	310.9	343.7
Russia	319.7	347.5	420.2
Serbia and Montenegro	346.6	345.8	454.5
Slovakia	131.9	161.8	173.7
Spain	116.0	164.2	194.7
Switzerland	180.2	150.5	138.6
United Kingdom	268.1	252.3	288.5
USA	297.3	410.1	399.7
Total (incl. others)	10,962.0	11,285.0	12,783.1

Transport

RAILWAYS
(traffic)

	2002	2003	2004
Passenger journeys ('000)	14,519	15,066	14,835
Passenger-kilometres (million)	749	777	764
Freight carried ('000 metric tons)	16,339	17,266	17,876
Freight ton-kilometres (million)	3,078	3,279	3,466

ROAD TRAFFIC
(registered motor vehicles at 31 December)

	2002	2003	2004
Motorcycles	12,047	12,156	11,669
Mopeds	38,732	30,393	28,716
Passenger cars	873,962	889,580	910,723
Buses and coaches	2,189	2,188	2,257
Lorries	53,362	55,100	57,700
Agricultural tractors	67,485	68,410	70,690
Total (incl. others)	1,082,233	1,094,020	1,120,336

* Registration not compulsory for mopeds until 2002.

SHIPPING

Merchant Fleet
(at 31 December)

	2002	2003	2004
Number of vessels	11	8	6
Displacement (grt)	2,251	1,737	1,499

Source: Lloyd's Register-Fairplay, *World Fleet Statistics*.

International Sea-borne Freight Traffic
('000 metric tons)

	2002	2003	2004
Goods loaded	153	87	154
Goods unloaded	2,916	2,848	2,976

CIVIL AVIATION
(traffic)

	2002	2003	2004
Kilometres flown ('000)	13,589	14,644	15,783
Passengers carried ('000)	814	864	885
Passenger-kilometres (million)	794	837	896
Freight carried (metric tons)	4,620	3,854	3,530
Freight ton-kilometres ('000)	4,521	3,538	3,201

Tourism

FOREIGN TOURIST ARRIVALS
('000)*

Country of origin	2002	2003	2004
Austria	193.4	201.4	205.7
Bosnia and Herzegovina	27.8	27.6	23.5
Croatia	94.2	93.6	92.0
Czech Republic	30.0	31.3	32.1
France	27.9	34.7	50.4
Germany	229.2	229.4	237.9
Hungary	32.8	37.1	38.0
Israel	32.0	39.9	35.4
Italy	274.8	288.5	313.4
Netherlands	38.7	46.8	56.2
Serbia and Montenegro	19.6	25.1	30.0
United Kingdom	46.1	50.2	76.3
USA	30.1	29.6	38.5
Total (incl. others)	1,302.0	1,373.2	1,498.9

* Figures refer to arrivals at accommodation establishments.

Tourism receipts (US $ million, incl. passenger transport): 1,059 in 2001; 1,152 in 2002; 1,427 in 2003 (Source: World Tourism Organization).

Communications Media

	2000	2001	2002
Telephone subscribers (main lines)	808,012	945,295	998,414
Facsimile machines (subscribers)	19,739	11,072	8,850
Mobile cellular telephones (subscribers)	468,351	662,619	847,759
Television and radio subscriptions	547,885	564,977	n.a.
Personal computers ('000 in use)	548	550	600
Internet users ('000)	300	600	750
Book production (titles published)*	3,917	3,598	3,735
Daily newspapers	5	6	6
Non-daily newspapers	200	227	208
Other periodicals	1,296	1,515	1,451

* Including pamphlets.

2003: Telephone subscribers (main lines in use) 812,300; Mobile cellular telephones (subscribers) 1,739,100; Television and radio subscriptions ('000) 619; Internet users ('000) 800; Personal computers in use ('000) 650.

2004: Internet users ('000) 950; Personal computers in use ('000) 704.

Source: partly International Telecommunication Union.

Education

(2004/05, unless otherwise indicated)

	Institutions	Teachers	Males	Females	Total
Pre-primary	752	6,762	28,782	26,033	54,815
Elementary*†	477	17,613	92,378	86,868	179,246
Upper secondary*†	281	12,898	61,098	60,766	121,864
Higher education	49*	5,673*	37,066‡	54,163‡	91,229‡

* 2003/04.
† Including education of adults.
‡ Excluding post-graduate students.

Adult literacy rate (UNESCO estimates): 99.7% (males 99.7%; females 99.6%) in 2003 (Source: UN Development Programme, *Human Development Report*).

Directory

The Constitution

The Constitution of the Republic of Slovenia was enacted on 23 December 1991. Its provisions for the independence and sovereignty of Slovenia had been endorsed by a plebiscite held on 23 December 1990. The following is a summary of the Constitution's main articles:

INTRODUCTION

Slovenia is a democratic republic, governed by the rule of law. Slovenia is a territorially indivisible state. Human rights and fundamental freedom—including the rights of the autochthonous Italian and Hungarian ethnic communities—are protected. Slovenia attends to the welfare of the autochthonous Slovenian minorities in neighbouring countries and of Slovenian emigrants and migrant workers abroad.

The separation of church and state is guaranteed. Religious groups enjoy equal rights under the law and are guaranteed freedom of activity.

The autonomy of local government in Slovenia is guaranteed. The capital of the republic is Ljubljana. The official language of Slovenia is Slovene. In those areas where Italian or Hungarian ethnic communities reside, the official language is also Italian or Hungarian.

HUMAN RIGHTS AND FUNDAMENTAL FREEDOMS

All persons are guaranteed equal human rights and fundamental freedoms, irrespective of national origin, race, sex, language, religion, political or other beliefs, financial status, birth, education or social status, and all persons are equal before the law. Human life is inviolable, and there is no capital punishment. No person may be subjected to torture, inhuman or humiliating punishment or treatment. The right of each individual to personal liberty is guaranteed.

Respect for the humanity and dignity of the individual is guaranteed in all criminal or other proceedings. The use of violence of any sort on any person whose liberty has been restricted in any way is forbidden. Except for certain situations (as determined by statute), all court proceedings are conducted in public and all judgments are delivered in open court. Each person is guaranteed the right of appeal. Any person charged with a criminal offence is presumed innocent until proven guilty by due process of the law.

Each person has the right to freedom of movement, to choose his place of residence, to leave the country and to return at any time he wishes. The right to own and to inherit property is guaranteed. The dwellings of all persons are inviolable, and the protection of personal data relating to the individual is guaranteed. Freedom of expression of thought, freedom of speech and freedom to associate in public, together with freedom of the press and of other forms of public communication and expression, are guaranteed. The right to vote is universal and equal. Each citizen who has attained the age of 18 years is eligible both to vote and to stand for election.

The freedom of work is guaranteed. Each person may freely choose his employment. Forced labour is forbidden. All citizens who fulfil such conditions as are laid down by statute, have the right to social security. The State regulates compulsory health, pension, disability and other social insurance, and ensures the proper administration thereof. Education is free, and the State provides the opportunity for all citizens to obtain a proper education.

Each person is entitled freely to identify with his national grouping or ethnic community, to foster and give expression to his culture and to use his own language and script. All incitement to ethnic, racial, religious or other discrimination, as well as the inflaming of ethnic, racial, religious or other hatred or intolerance, is unconstitutional, as is incitement to violence or to war. The autochthonous Italian and Hungarian ethnic communities are guaranteed the right freely to use their national symbols and to establish organizations, to foster economic, cultural, scientific and research activities, as well as activities associated with the mass media and publishing. These two communities have the right to education and schooling in their own languages. They are also entitled to establish autonomous organizations in order to exercise their rights. The Italian and Hungarian communities are directly represented both at the local level and in the Državni zbor (National Assembly). The status and special rights of Gypsy (Roma) communities living in Slovenia are determined by statute.

ECONOMIC AND SOCIAL RELATIONS

The State is responsible for the creation of opportunities for employment. Each person has the right to a healthy environment, and the State is responsible for such an environment. The protection of animals from cruelty is regulated by statute. State and local government bodies are responsible for the preservation of the natural and cultural heritage.

Free enterprise is guaranteed. The establishment of trade unions, and the operation and membership thereof, is free. Workers enjoy the right to strike. The State creates the conditions necessary to enable each citizen to obtain proper housing.

ADMINISTRATION OF THE STATE

The Državni zbor (National Assembly)

The Državni zbor consists of 90 deputies, who serve a four-year term; 40 deputies are directly elected, while 50 are elected on a proportional basis by the parties represented in the chamber (which are required to hold a minimum of 3% of the votes). The Italian and Hungarian ethnic communities are entitled to elect one deputy each to the Državni zbor. The President of the Državni zbor (Speaker) is elected by a majority vote of all elected deputies.

The Državni zbor enacts laws; makes other decisions; authorizes adherence to international agreements; may call a referendum; may proclaim a state of war or a state of emergency, at the initiative of the Government; may establish parliamentary inquiries with respect to matters of public importance.

The Državni svet (National Council)

The Državni svet represents social, economic, trade and professional and local interests. It is composed of 40 councillors: four representing employers; four representing employees; four representing farmers, small business persons and independent professional persons; six representing non-profit-making organizations; and 22 representing local interests. Councillors are elected for a five-year term.

The Državni svet may: propose the enactment of statutes by the Državni zbor; demand that the Državni zbor reconsider statutes prior to their proclamation; demand the holding of a referendum; and demand the establishment of a parliamentary inquiry. The Državni zbor may require the Državni svet to provide its opinions on specific matters. A councillor of the Državni svet may not be simultaneously a deputy of the Državni zbor.

The President of the Republic

The President of the Republic of Slovenia is Head of State and Commander-in-Chief of the Defence Forces. The President is elected on the basis of universal, equal and direct suffrage by secret ballot. The President's term of office is five years (with a maximum of two consecutive terms). Only a citizen of Slovenia may be elected President of the Republic. Presidential elections are called by the President of the Državni zbor. The office of President of the Republic is incompatible with other public offices or other employment. In the event that the President of the Republic is permanently incapacitated, dies, resigns or is otherwise permanently unable to perform his functions, the President of the Državni zbor temporarily occupies the office of the President of the Republic until such time as a replacement is elected.

The President of the Republic is empowered to: call elections to the Državni zbor; proclaim statutes; appoint state officers and functionaries; accredit, and revoke the accreditation of, Slovenian ambassadors to foreign states, and to accept the credentials of foreign diplomatic representatives; grant amnesties; and confer state honours, decorations and honorary titles.

If, in the course of carrying out his office, the President of the Republic acts in a manner contrary to the Constitution or commits a serious breach of the law, he may be brought before the Constitutional Court upon the request of the Državni zbor. The President may be dismissed from office upon the vote of no less than two-thirds of all of the judges of the Constitutional Court.

The Government

The Government is composed of the Prime Minister and ministers. The Government is independent, and individual ministers are independent within their own particular portfolios. Ministers are accountable to the Državni zbor. After consultations with the leaders of the various political groups within the Državni zbor, the President of the Republic proposes to the Državni zbor a candidate for the office of Prime Minister. The Prime Minister is elected by the Državni zbor by a majority vote. Ministers in the Government are appointed or dismissed by the Državni zbor, upon the proposal of the Prime Minister. The Prime Minister is responsible for the political unity, direction and administrative programme of the Government and for the co-ordination of the work of the various ministers. The Državni zbor may, upon the motion of no fewer than 10 deputies and by a majority vote, elect a new Prime Minister (such a vote is deemed a vote of 'no confidence' in the Government). Furthermore, the Državni zbor may bring the Prime Minister or any minister before the Constitutional Court to answer charges relating to breaches of the Constitution.

The Judiciary

Judges independently exercise their duties and functions in accordance with the Constitution and with the law. The Supreme Court is the highest court for civil and criminal cases in the republic. The Državni zbor elects judges upon the recommendation of the Judicial Council, which is composed of 11 members. The office of a judge is incompatible with office in any other state body, local government body or organ of any political party.

The Office of the Public Prosecutor

The Public Prosecutor is responsible for the preferment of criminal charges, for prosecuting criminal matters in court and for the performance of such other duties as are prescribed by statute.

LOCAL SELF-GOVERNMENT

Slovenians exercise local government powers and functions through self-governing municipalities and other local government organizations. A municipality may comprise a single community or a number of communities, whose inhabitants are bound together by common needs and interests. The State supervises the proper and efficient performance of municipalities and wider self-governing local administrative bodies. Municipalities raise their own revenue. Municipalities are at liberty to join other municipalities in establishing wider self-governing local administrative bodies or regional local government bodies to exercise administrative powers and to deal with matters of wider common interest. Citizens may join together and form self-governing local bodies to further their common interests.

PUBLIC FINANCE

The State and local government bodies fund the performance of their respective duties and functions from taxes and other mandatory charges levied by them and from such other income as they may derive from their assets. All revenues raised, and all monies expended, for public purposes by the State and by local government bodies must be accounted for in their respective budgets.

The Auditor General's office is the body with ultimate responsibility for auditing state finances, the state budget and monies expended for public purposes. The Auditor General's office is independent in the performance of its functions. Officers of the Auditor General's office are appointed by the Državni zbor.

The Bank of Slovenia is the central bank. It is independent in its operations and accountable to the Državni zbor. The Governor of the Bank of Slovenia is appointed by the Državni zbor.

THE CONSTITUTIONAL COURT

The Constitutional Court is composed of nine judges, elected by the Državni zbor, upon the nomination of the President of the Republic, for a term (non-extendable) of nine years. The President of the Constitutional Court is elected by the judges from amongst their own number to hold office for a period of three years.

The Constitutional Court is empowered to decide upon matters relating to: the conformity of statutes with the Constitution and with international agreements; complaints of breaches of the Constitution involving individual acts infringing human rights and fundamental freedoms; juridical disputes between the state and local government bodies or among such local government bodies; juridical disputes between the Državni zbor, the President of the Republic and the Government; and unconstitutional acts or activities of political parties.

The Government

HEAD OF STATE

President: Dr JANEZ DRNOVŠEK (elected 1 December 2002; inaugurated 22 December 2002).

GOVERNMENT
(April 2006)

A coalition comprising representatives of the Slovenian Democratic Party (SDP), New Slovenia—Christian People's Party (NSi), Slovenian People's Party (SPP) and the Democratic Party of Pensioners of Slovenia (DeSUS).

Prime Minister: JANEZ JANŠA (SDP).
Minister of Finance: Dr ANDREJ BAJUK (NSi).
Minister of Internal Affairs: DRAGUTIN MATE (SDP).
Minister of Foreign Affairs: Dr DIMITRIJ RUPEL (SDP).
Minister of Justice: Dr LOVRO ŠTURM (NSi).
Minister of Defence: KARL ERJAVEC (DeSUS).
Minister of Labour, Family and Social Affairs: JANEZ DROBNIČ (NSi).
Minister of the Economy: ANDREJ VIZJAK (SDP).
Minister of Agriculture, Forestry and Food: MARIJA LUKAČIČ (SDP).
Minister of Culture: Dr VASKO SIMONITI (SDP).
Minister of the Environment and Physical Planning: JANEZ PODOBNIK (SPP).
Minister of Transport: JANEZ BOŽIČ (SPP).
Minister of Education and Sport: Dr MILAN ZVER (SDP).
Minister of Health: ANDREJ BRUČAN (SDP).
Minister of Public Administration: Dr GREGOR VIRANT (SDP).
Minister of Higher Education, Science and Technology: Dr JURE ZUPAN (NSi).
Minister without Portfolio, responsible for Local Self-Government and Regional Policy: Dr IVAN ŽAGAR (SPP).

MINISTRIES

Office of the President: 1000 Ljubljana, Erjavčeva 17; tel. (1) 4781222; fax (1) 4781357; e-mail gp.uprs@up-rs.si; internet www.up-rs.si.

Office of the Prime Minister: 1000 Ljubljana, Gregorčičeva 20; tel. (1) 4781000; fax (1) 4781721; e-mail gp.kpv@gov.si; internet www.kpv.gov.si/index.php?id=225&L=1.

Ministry of Agriculture, Forestry and Food: 1000 Ljubljana, Dunajska 56–58; tel. (1) 4789000; fax (1) 4789021; e-mail gp.mkgp@gov.si; internet www.gov.si/mkgp.

Ministry of Culture: 1000 Ljubljana, ul. Maistrova 10; tel. (1) 3695900; fax (1) 3695901; e-mail mkinfo@gov.si; internet www.kultura.gov.si.

Ministry of Defence: 1000 Ljubljana, Kardeljeva ploščad 25; tel. (1) 4712211; fax (1) 4318164; e-mail info@mors.si; internet www.mors.si.

Ministry of the Economy: 1000 Ljubljana, Kotnikova 5; tel. (1) 4783600; fax (1) 4331031; e-mail info.mg@gov.si; internet www.mg-rs.si.

Ministry of Education and Sport: 1000 Ljubljana, trg OF 13; tel. (1) 4784600; fax (1) 4784719; e-mail milan.zver@gov.si; internet www.mss.edus.si.

Ministry of the Environment and Physical Planning: 1000 Ljubljana, Dunajska cesta 48; tel. (1) 4787400; fax (1) 4787422; e-mail info.mop@gov.si; internet www.gov.si/mop.

Ministry of Finance: 1502 Ljubljana, Županičeva 3; tel. (1) 4785211; fax (1) 4785655; e-mail gp.mf@gov.si; internet www.gov.si/mf.

Ministry of Foreign Affairs: 1000 Ljubljana, Prešernova 25; tel. (1) 4782000; fax (1) 4782340; e-mail info.mzz@gov.si; internet www.mzz.gov.si/.

Ministry of Health: 1000 Ljubljana, Štefanova 5; tel. (1) 4786001; fax (1) 4786058; e-mail ministrstvo.zdravje@gov.si; internet www.gov.si/mz.

Ministry of Higher Education, Science and Technology: 1000 Ljubljana, trg Of 13; tel. (1) 4784000; fax (1) 4784719; e-mail gp.mvzt@gov.si.

Ministry of Internal Affairs: 1501 Ljubljana, Štefanova 2; tel. (1) 4325125; fax (1) 2514330; e-mail ssj@mnz.si; internet www.mnz.si.

Ministry of Justice: 1000 Ljubljana, Županičeva 3; tel. (1) 3695200; fax (1) 3695519; e-mail lovro.sturm@gov.si; internet www.gov.si/mp.

Ministry of Labour, Family and Social Affairs: 1000 Ljubljana, Kotnikova 5; tel. (1) 4783330; fax (1) 4783344; e-mail janez.drobnic@gov.si; internet www.gov.si/mddsz.

Ministry of Public Administration: 1508 Ljubljana, Tržaška cesta 21; tel. (1) 4788003; fax (1) 4788375; internet www.mju.gov.si.

Ministry of Transport: 1535 Ljubljana, Langusova ul. 4; tel. (1) 4788000; fax (1) 4788139; e-mail mpz.info@gov.si; internet www.gov.si/mpz.

President and Legislature

PRESIDENT

Presidential Election, First Ballot, 10 November 2002

Candidate	Votes	% of votes
Janez Drnovšek (Liberal Democracy of Slovenia)	506,800	44.40
Barbara Brezigar (Independent)	351,049	30.76
Zmago Jelinčič (Slovenian National Party)	97,103	8.51
France Arhar (Independent)	86,678	7.60
Others	99,700	8.74
Total*	1,141,330	100.00

* Excluding 15,019 invalid votes.

Second Ballot, 1 December 2002

Candidate	Votes	% of votes
Janez Drnovšek (Liberal Democracy of Slovenia)	583,570	56.54
Barbara Brezigar (Independent)	448,482	43.46
Total*	1,032,052	100.00

* Excluding 13,803 invalid votes.

LEGISLATURE

**Državni zbor
(National Assembly)**

1000 Ljubljana, Šubičeva 4; tel. (1) 4789400; fax (1) 4789845; e-mail france.cukjati@dz-rs.si; internet www.dz-rs.si.

President: Dr France Cukjati.

General Election, 3 October 2004

	Votes	% of votes	Seats
Slovenian Democratic Party	281,710	29.08	29
Liberal Democracy of Slovenia	220,848	22.80	23
United List of Social Democrats	98,527	10.17	10
New Slovenia—Christian People's Party	88,073	9.09	9
Slovenian People's Party	66,032	6.82	7
Slovenian National Party	60,750	6.27	6
Democratic Party of Pensioners of Slovenia	39,150	4.04	4
Others*	113,682	11.73	2
Total	968,772	100.00	90

* Two of the 90 seats in the Državni zbor are reserved for representatives of the Italian and Hungarian minorities.

**Državni svet
(National Council)**

1000 Ljubljana, Šubičeva 4; tel. (1) 4789798; fax (1) 4789851; e-mail janez.susnik@ds-rs.si; internet www.ds-rs.si..

There are 40 councillors in the Državni svet, who are indirectly elected for a five-year term by an electoral college.

President: Janez Sušnik.

Election Commission

Republic Electoral Commission: 1000 Ljubljana, Slovenska 54; tel. (1) 4322002; fax (1) 4331269; e-mail rvk@gov.si; internet www.sigov.si/elections/rvk.html; Chair. Marko Golubić.

Political Organizations

Christian Social Union (KSU) (Krščansko-Socialna unija): 1000 Ljubljana, Mariborska 26; f. 1995; Pres. Franc Miklavič; Sec.-Gen. Ivan Kepič.

Democratic Party of Pensioners of Slovenia (DeSUS) (Demokratična stranka upokojencev Slovenije): 1000 Ljubljana, Kersnikova 6; tel. (1) 324171; fax (1) 1314113; internet www.desus.si; Pres. Janko Kusar.

Democratic Party of Slovenia (Demokratska stranka Slovenije): 1000 Ljubljana, Linhartova 13; tel. (1) 1261073; fax (1) 1255077; f. 1994; by mems of Democratic Party who opted not to join the LDS (see below); Pres. Anton Peršak; 2,200 mems.

Greens of Slovenia (Zeleni Slovenije): 1000 Ljubljana, Komenskega 11; tel. (2) 7710035; fax (2) 7781071; internet www.zeleni.si; f. 1989; in 1993 the party split into two factions, one retaining the original name, the other, more radical wing adopting the title, Greens of Slovenia—Eco-Social Party; Chair. Prof. Vlado Čuš.

Liberal Democracy of Slovenia (Liberalna demokracija Slovenije—LDS): 1000 Ljubljana, Republike trg 3; tel. (1) 2000310; fax (1) 1256150; e-mail lds@lds.si; internet www.lds.si; f. 1994 by a merger of the Liberal Democratic Party, the Greens of Slovenia—Eco-Social Party, the Democratic Party and the Socialist Party of Slovenia; Chair. Jelko Kacin; 18,000 mems.

National Democratic Party (NDP) (Narodna demokratska stranka): 1000 Ljubljana; Pres. Marjan Vidmar.

New Party (Nova Stranka): 1000 Ljubljana, Linhartova cesta 13; tel. (1) 3063995; fax (1) 2310567; Pres. Dr Gorazd Drevenšek.

New Slovenia—Christian People's Party (NSi) (Nova Slovenija—Krščanska ljudska stranka): 1000 Ljubljana, Cankarjeva 11; tel. (1) 5004180; fax (1) 5004190; e-mail tajnistvo@nsi.si; internet www.nsi.si; f. 2000 by mems of the Slovenian People's Party; Pres. Dr Andrej Bajuk.

Party of Albanian Democratic Union: Ljubljana; f. 2000; Chair. Besnik Tallaj.

Slovenian Democratic Party (SDP) (Slovenska Demokratska Stranka—SDS): 1000 Ljubljana, Komenskega 11; tel. (1) 4345450; fax (1) 4345452; e-mail tajnistvo@sds.si; internet www.sds.si; f. 1989 as Social Democratic Party of Slovenia; name changed in Sept. 2003; centre-right; Pres. Janez Janša; Sec.-Gen. Dušan Strnad; 20,000 mems.

Slovenian National Party (SNP) (Slovenska nacionalna stranka—SNS): 1000 Ljubljana, Tivolska 13; tel. (1) 2529020; fax (1) 2529022; e-mail info@sns.si; internet www.sns.si; f. 1991; right-wing nationalist party; Pres. Zmago Jelinčič; Vice-Pres. Sašo Peče; Sec.-Gen. Miša Glažar; 6,500 mems.

SLOVENIA

Slovenian National Right (SNR) (Slovenska nacionalna desnica—SND): f. 1993; by a 'breakaway' faction of the SNP; Pres. SAŠO LAP.

Slovenian People's Party (SPP) (Slovenska ljudska stranka) (SLS): 1000 Ljubljana, Zarnikova 3; tel. (1) 301891; fax (1) 301871; internet www.sls.si; f. 1989 as the Slovenian Farmers' Association; conservative; merged with the Slovenian Christian Democrats in April 2000; Pres. FRANC ZAGOZEN; Chair. JOŽE ZUPANČIČ.

Social Democrats (SD) (Social Democrats) (Socialni demokrati): 1000 Ljubljana, Levstikova 15; tel. (1) 2444100; fax (1) 2444111; e-mail info@socialnidemokrati.si; internet www.socialnidemokrati.si; f. 1993; Pres. BORUT PAHOR; Gen. Sec. UROS JAUSEVEC; 23,000 mems.

Youth Party of Slovenia (Stranka mladih Slovenije—SMS): 1000 Ljubljana, Rimska cesta 8; tel. (1) 4211400; e-mail info@sms.si; internet www.sms.si; Pres. DARKO KRAJNC.

Diplomatic Representation

EMBASSIES IN SLOVENIA

Albania: 1000 Ljubljana, Ob Ljubljanici 12; tel. (1) 4322324; fax (1) 4322053; e-mail albania@siol.net; Ambassador DAUT GUMENI.

Austria: 1000 Ljubljana, Prešernova cesta 23; tel. (1) 4790700; fax (1) 2521717; e-mail laibach-ob@bmaa.gv.at; internet www.aussenministerium.at/laibach; Ambassador Dr VALENTIN INZKOV.

Belgium: 1000 Ljubljana, trg Republike 3/IX; tel. (1) 2006010; fax (1) 4266395; e-mail ljubljana@diplobel.org; Ambassador JEAN-LOUIS MIGNOT.

Bosnia and Herzegovina: 1000 Ljubljana, Korlajeva 26; tel. (1) 4324042; fax (1) 4322230; Ambassador IZMIR TALIĆ.

Bulgaria: 1000 Ljubljana, Rozna dolina XV/18; tel. (1) 4265744; fax (1) 4258845; e-mail bgembassysl@siol.net; Ambassador SVETLOZAR VLADISLAVOV PANOV.

China, People's Republic: 1111 Ljubljana, Koblarjeva ul. 3; tel. (1) 4202855; fax (1) 2822199; e-mail kitajsko.veleposlanistvo@siol.net; Ambassador WANG FUYUAN.

Croatia: 1000 Ljubljana, Gruberjevo nabrežje 6; tel. (1) 4256220; fax (1) 4258106; e-mail croemb.slovenia@siol.net; Ambassador Dr MARIO NOBILO.

Czech Republic: 1000 Ljubljana, Riharjeva 1; tel. (1) 4202450; fax (1) 2839259; e-mail ljubljana@embassy.mzv.cz; internet www.mzv.cz/ljubljana; Ambassador TOMÁŠ SZUNYOG.

Denmark: 1000 Ljubljana, Tivolska 48, EuroCenter; tel. (1) 4380800; fax (1) 4317417; e-mail ljuamb@um.dk; internet www.ambljubljana.um.dk; Ambassador LARS MØLLER.

Finland: 1000 Ljubljana, Ajdovščina 4/8; tel. (1) 3002120; fax (1) 3002139; e-mail sanomat.lju@formin.fi; Ambassador BIRGITTA STENIUS-MLADENOV.

France: 1000 Ljubljana, Barjanska cesta 1; tel. (1) 4790400; fax (1) 4790410; e-mail info@ambafrance.si; internet www.ambafrance.si; Ambassador DOMINIQUE GAZUY.

Germany: 1000 Ljubljana, Prešernova cesta 27; tel. (1) 4790300; fax (1) 4250899; e-mail germanembassy-slovenia@siol.net; internet www.ljubljana.diplo.de; Ambassador HANS JOCHEN PETERS.

Greece: 1000 Ljubljana, Trnovski Pristan 14; tel. (1) 4201400; fax (1) 2811114; e-mail emb.gr.slo@siol.net; Ambassador JOHN N. BOUCAOURIS.

Holy See: 1000 Ljubljana, Krekov trg 1; tel. (1) 4339204; fax (1) 4315130; e-mail apostolska.nunciatura@rkc.si; Apostolic Nuncio Most Rev. ABRIL Y CASTELLÓ SANTOS (Titular Archbishop of Tamada).

Hungary: 1210 Ljubljana, ul. Konrada Babnika 5; tel. (1) 5121882; fax (1) 5121878; e-mail huemblju@siol.net; internet www.hu-embassy.si; Ambassador GÁBOR BAGI.

Italy: 1000 Ljubljana, Snežniška 8; tel. (1) 4262194; fax (1) 4253302; e-mail amblubiana@siol.net; Ambassador Dr DANIELE VERGA.

Japan: 1000 Ljubljana, trg Republike 3/11; tel. (1) 4700884; fax (1) 4700886; Ambassador TSUNESHIGE IIYAMA.

Macedonia, former Yugoslav republic: 1000 Ljubljana, Prešernova Cesta 2; tel. (1) 4210021; fax (1) 4210023; e-mail makamb@siol.net; Ambassador ILJAZ SABRIU.

Netherlands: 1000 Ljubljana, Palača Kapitelj, Polijanski nasip 6; tel. (1) 4201460; fax (1) 4201470; e-mail lju@minbuza.nl; internet www.netherlands-embassy.si; Ambassador Dr JAN C. HENNEMAN.

Norway: 1000 Ljubljana, Miklošičeva 20; tel. (1) 4302611; fax (1) 4302613; Ambassador MAY BRITT BROFOSS.

Poland: 1000 Ljubljana, Rožna dolina XV, št. 18; tel. (1) 4232882; fax (1) 4232881; e-mail ambpol.si@siol.net; internet www.poland-embassy.si; Ambassador JANUSZ JESIONEK.

Romania: 1000 Ljubljana, Podlimbarskega 43; tel. (1) 5058294; fax (1) 5055432; e-mail embassy.of.romania@siol.net; Ambassador VICTOR CHIUJDEA.

Russia: 1000 Ljubljana, Tomšičeva 9; tel. (1) 4256875; fax (1) 4256878; e-mail ambrus.slo@siol.net; internet www.rus-slo.mid.ru; Ambassador MIKHAIL VANIN.

Serbia and Montenegro: 1000 Ljubljana, Slomskova 1; tel. (1) 4380111; fax (1) 4342688; e-mail ambasada.scg.ljubljana@siol.net; Ambassador RANKO MILOVIĆ.

Slovakia: 1000 Ljubljana, Tivolska cesta 4, POB 395; tel. (1) 4255425; fax (1) 4210524; e-mail embass@lublana.mfa.sk; internet lublana.mfa.sk; Ambassador Dr ROMAN PALDAN.

Spain: 1000 Ljubljana, Trnovski pristan 24; tel. (1) 4202330; fax (1) 4202333; Ambassador PABLO ZALDIVAR MIQUELARENA.

Sweden: 1000 Ljubljana, Ajdovščina 4/8, POB 1680; tel. (1) 3000270; fax (1) 3000271; e-mail ambassaden.ljubljana@foreign.ministry.se; Ambassador JOHN HAGARD.

Switzerland: 1000 Ljubljana, trg Republike 3/VI; tel. (1) 2008640; fax (1) 2008669; e-mail vertretung@lju.rep.admin.ch; Ambassador PAUL KOLLER.

Turkey: 1000 Ljubljana, Livarska 4; tel. (1) 4368149; fax (1) 4368148; e-mail vrtucije@siol.net; Ambassador BALKAN KIZILDELI.

United Kingdom: 1000 Ljubljana, trg Republike 3/IV; tel. (1) 2003910; fax (1) 4250174; e-mail info@british-embassy.si; internet www.british-embassy.si; Ambassador TIMOTHY SIMMONS.

USA: 1000 Ljubljana, Prešernova cesta 31; tel. (1) 2005500; fax (1) 2005555; e-mail email@usembassy.si; internet slovenia.usembassy.gov; Ambassador THOMAS B. ROBERTSON.

Judicial System

The Slovenian Constitution guarantees the independence of the judiciary.

The 44 district courts decide minor cases (criminal acts incurring a maximum sentence of three years' imprisonment, property disputes where the value of the disputed property is not more than SlT 2m., and certain other civil cases). The 11 regional courts act as courts of the first instance in all cases other than those for which the district courts have jurisdiction. Four regional courts act as courts of the second instance. There are, in addition, labour courts, which have jurisdiction in labour disputes, and social courts, which adjudicate in disputes over pensions, welfare allocations and other social benefits. A higher labour and social court has jurisdiction in the second instance. The Supreme Court is the highest authority for civil and criminal law. There is also a Constitutional Court, composed of nine judges, each elected for a single term of nine years, which determines, *inter alia*, the conformity of national legislation and all other regulations with the Constitution.

Constitutional Court of the Republic of Slovenia (Ustavno sodišča Republike Slovenije): 1000 Ljubljana, Beethovnova 10; tel. (1) 4776400; fax (1) 2510451; e-mail info@us-rs.si; internet www.us-rs.si; Pres. Dr JANEZ ČEBULJ.

Supreme Court of the Republic of Slovenia (Vrhovno Sodišče Republike Slovenije): 1000 Ljubljana, Tavčarjeva 9; tel. (1) 3664200; fax (1) 3664301; e-mail franc.testen@sodisce.si; internet www.sodisce.si; Pres. FRANC TESTEN.

Office of the Public Prosecutor: 1511 Ljubljana, Dunajska 22; tel. (1) 2320396; fax (1) 4310381; e-mail dtrs@dt-rs.si; Public Prosecutor BARBARA BREZIGAR.

Religion

Most of the population are Christian, predominantly adherents of the Roman Catholic Church. The Archbishop of Ljubljana is the most senior Roman Catholic prelate in Slovenia. There is also a Slovene Old Catholic Church. There are few Protestant Christians, despite the importance of a Calvinist sect (the Church of Carniola) to the development of Slovene literature in the 16th century. There are some members of the Eastern Orthodox Church, some Muslims and a small Jewish community.

CHRISTIANITY

The Roman Catholic Church

The Roman Catholic Church in Slovenia comprises two archdioceses and six dioceses. At 31 December 2003 there were an estimated 1,623,986 adherents (equivalent to about 81.3% of the total population).

SLOVENIA

Bishops' Conference
1000 Ljubljana, p.p. 121/III, Ciril Metodov trg 4; tel. (1) 2342600; fax (1) 2342612; e-mail ssk@rkc.si.
f. 1993; Pres. Rt Rev. Franc Kramberger (Archbishop of Maribor).

Archbishop of Ljubljana: Most Rev. Alojzij Uran, 1001 Ljubljana, p.p. 1990, Ciril Metodov trg 4; tel. (1) 2342600; fax (1) 2314169; e-mail nadskofija.lubljana@rkc.si.

Archbishop of Maribor: Most Rev. Franc Kramberger, 2000 Maribor, Slomskov trg 19; tel. (2) 2290401; fax (2) 2523092.

Old Catholic Church
Slovene Old Catholic Church: 1000 Ljubljana; Maribor, Vita Kraigherja 2; f. 1948; Bishop Rev. Josip Kvočić.

Protestant Church
Evangelical Lutheran Church of Slovenia: 9226 Moravske Toplice, 11 Levstikova; tel. (2) 5381323; fax (2) 5381324; e-mail evang.cerkev.si@siol.net; f. 1561; 20,000 mems; Chair. Geza Erniša.

JUDAISM
Jewish Community of Slovenia: 1000 Ljubljana, Trzaska 2, POB 37; tel. and fax (1) 2521836; e-mail jss@siol.net; Pres. Andrej Kožar Beck.

The Press

The publications listed below are in Slovene, unless otherwise indicated.

PRINCIPAL DAILIES

Delo (Event): 1509 Ljubljana, Dunajska 5; tel. (1) 4727402; fax (1) 4737406; e-mail webmaster@delo.si; internet www.delo.si; f. 1959; morning; Editor-in-Chief Peter Jancic; circ. 93,781.

Dnevnik (Daily): 1510 Ljubljana, Kopitarjeva 2; tel. (1) 3082100; fax (1) 3082189; e-mail info@dnevnik.si; internet www.dnevnik.si; f. 1951; evening; independent; Man. Dir Branko Bergant; Editor-in-Chief Zlatko Šetinc; circ. 63,000.

Slovenske novice (Slovene News): 1509 Ljubljana, Dunajska 5; tel. (1) 1737700; fax (1) 1737352; f. 1991; Editor-in-Chief Marjan Bauer; Man. Editor Tit Dobersek; circ. 80,000.

Večer (Evening): 2000 Maribor, Svetozarevska 14; tel. (2) 2353500; fax (2) 2353368; e-mail desk@vecer.com; internet www.vecer.si; f. 1945; Dir Boris Cekov; Editor-in-Chief Milan Predan; circ. 70,000.

PERIODICALS

7D: 2000 Maribor, Svetozarevska 14; tel. (2) 224221; fax (2) 211264; f. 1972; weekly; general, travel; Man. Dir Božo Zorka; Editor-in-Chief Milan Predan; circ. 20,000.

Antena: 1000 Ljubljana, Slovenska 15; tel. (1) 1253418; fax (1) 1253367; f. 1965; weekly; youth magazine concerned with popular culture; Editor-in-Chief Jasmin Petan Malachovsky; circ. 20,000.

Ars Vivendi: 1000 Ljubljana, Poljanska 6; tel. and fax (1) 317058; f. 1987; quarterly; visual arts and design; publ. in Slovene and English; Editor-in-Chief Sonja Tomažič; circ. 10,000.

Avto magazin: 1000 Ljubljana, Dunajska 5; tel. (1) 1738251; fax (1) 1738220; f. 1967; fortnightly; cars, motorcycles and sports; Editor Boštjan Jevšek; circ. 16,000.

Delavska enotnost: 1000 Ljubljana, Dalmatinova 4; tel. (1) 1310033; fax (1) 1313942; f. 1942; weekly; trade union issues; Dir and Editor-in-Chief Marjan Horvat; circ. 16,000.

Dolenjski list: 8000 Novo mesto, Glavni trg 24; tel. (7) 3323606; fax (7) 3322898; f. 1950; weekly; general and local information; Editor-in-Chief Marjan Legan; circ. 24,000.

Družina: 1000 Ljubljana, Krekov trg 1; tel. (1) 1316202; fax (1) 1316152; e-mail druzina@siol.net; f. 1952; Christian; Editor-in-Chief Janez Gril; circ. 70,000.

Finance: 1509 Ljubljana, Dunajska 5; tel. (1) 1330137; fax (1) 1312223; internet www.finance-on.net; f. 1992; 2 a week; Editor-in-Chief Jože Petrovčič; circ. 8,500.

Flaneur: 1000 Ljubljana, Šaranovičeva 12; f. 1992; bi-monthly; English; politics, economy, culture and leisure; Editor-in-Chief Tadej Čater; circ. 2,500.

Gea: 1536 Ljubljana, Slovenska 29; tel. (1) 2413230; fax (1) 1252836; e-mail gea@mkz-lj.si; internet www.mkz-lj.si; f. 1990; monthly; popular science; Editor-in-Chief Jana Leskovec; circ. 23,000.

Gorenjski glas: 4000 Kranj, Zoisova ul. 1; tel. (4) 2014200; fax (4) 2014213; f. 1947; 2 a week; general and regional information; Editor-in-Chief Marija Volejak; circ. 23,300.

Gospodarski vestnik: 1509 Ljubljana, Dunajska 5; tel. (1) 3091700; fax (1) 3091705; e-mail gvrevija@gvestnik.si; internet www.gvestnik.si; f. 1952; weekly; business; Editor-in-Chief Jože Petrovčič; circ. 9,500.

Jana: 1509 Ljubljana, Dunajska 5; tel. (1) 319260; fax (1) 1334320; f. 1972; weekly; women's interest; Editor-in-Chief Bernarda Jeklin; circ. 62,000.

Kaj: 62000 Maribor, Svetozarevska 14; tel. (2) 26951; fax (2) 227736; f. 1984; weekly; popular; Editor-in-Chief Milan Predan; circ. 16,500.

Kmečki glas: 1000 Ljubljana, p.p. 47, Železna 14; tel. (1) 1735350; fax (1) 1735376; weekly; general and agricultural news; Dir Boris Dolničar; circ. 38,000.

Lipov list: 1000 Ljubljana, Miklosičeva 38/6; tel. (1) 312087; fax (1) 1332338; e-mail tzs@siol.net; monthly; Editor-in-Chief Marjetica Novak.

Mag: 1000 Ljubljana, Njegoševa 14; tel. (1) 319480; fax (1) 1329158; f. 1995; weekly; news and politics; Editor-in-Chief Janez Markes.

Manager: 1000 Ljubljana, Dunajska 5; tel. (1) 3091990; fax (1) 3091705; internet www.gvrevija.com/manager; f. 1990; monthly; business management; Editor-in-Chief Jože Petrovčič; circ. 3,000.

Mladina: 1000 Ljubljana, Resljeva 16; tel. (1) 1328175; fax (1) 1331239; f. 1942; weekly; news magazine; Editor-in-Chief Jani Sever; circ. 30,000.

Moj mikro: 1509 Ljubljana, Dunajska 5; tel. (1) 4738261; fax (1) 4738109; e-mail marjan.kodelja@delo-revije.si; internet www.mojmikro.si; monthly; personal computers; Editor-in-Chief Marjan Kodelja.

Muska: 1000 Ljubljana, Kersnikova 4; tel. (1) 1317039; fax (1) 322570; e-mail kaja.sivic@kiss.uni_lj.si; monthly; music; Editor-in-Chief Kaja Sivič.

Naš Čas (Our Time): 63320 Velenje, Foltova 10; tel. (3) 855450; fax (3) 851990; f. 1956; weekly; general and regional information; Editor-in-Chief Stane Vovk; circ. 6,250.

Nedeljski dnevnik (Weekly Record): 1000 Ljubljana, Kopitarieva 2; tel. (1) 1325261; fax (1) 1321020; f. 1961; weekly; popular; Editor-in-Chief Zlatko Šetinc; circ. 171,000.

Novi tednik (New Weekly): 3000 Celje, Prešernova 19; tel. (3) 442500; fax (3) 441032; f. 1945; weekly; general and local information; Editor-in-Chief Brane Stamejčič; circ. 16,980.

Obrtnik: 1000 Ljubljana, Celovška 71; tel. (1) 5830507; fax (1) 5193496; e-mail revija.obrtnik@ozs.si; internet www.ozs.si; f. 1971; monthly; small businesses; Editor-in-Chief Miran Jarec; circ. 60,000.

Pavliha: 1000 Ljubljana, Slovenska 15; tel. (1) 221661; monthly; satire; Editor-in-Chief Jože Petelin.

PIL: 1000 Ljubljana, Nazorjeva 1; tel. (1) 2413220; fax (1) 4252836; e-mail pil@mkz-lj.si; internet www.mkz-lj.si; teenagers' interest; Editor-in-Chief Yana Zizkelbach; circ. 30,000.

Podjetnik: 1000 Ljubljana, Dunajska 51; tel. (1) 1330102; fax (1) 1330450; f. 1992; monthly; business and management; Editor-in-Chief Jože Vilfan; circ. 8,500.

Primorske novice (News from the Primorska region): 6000 Koper, OF ul. 12; tel. (5) 6648100; fax (5) 6648110; e-mail editors@prim-nov.si; internet www.prim-nov.si; f. 1947; daily; general and regional information; Editor-in-Chief Bojan Gluhak; circ. 23,000.

Profit: 1000 Ljubljana, Dunajska 7; tel. (1) 4304310; fax (1) 2318940; e-mail profit.uredmistvo@sid.net; 2 a month; business; Editor-in-Chief Jože Simčič.

Rodna gruda (Native Bosom): 1000 Ljubljana, Cankarjeva 1/II, Združenje Slovenska izseljenska matica; tel. (1) 2410288; fax (1) 4251673; e-mail rodna.gruda@zdruzenje-sim.si; internet www.zdruzenje-sim.si; f. 1951; monthly; ethnic issues and news; Editor-in-Chief Vida Posinković; circ. 2,100.

Slovenia Weekly: 1000 Ljubljana, Hradeckega 38; tel. (1) 4261412; fax (1) 5402027; e-mail marketing@vitrum.si; internet weekly.vitrum.si; f. 1994; weekly; politics and business; Editor-in-Chief Tomaž Gerdina; circ. 3,000.

Slovenian Business Report: 1000 Ljubljana, Dunajska 5; tel. (1) 3091924; fax (1) 3091705; f. 1991; monthly; in English; economic affairs; Editor-in-Chief Jože Petrovčič; circ. 4,000.

Slovenija: 1000 Ljubljana, Cankarjeva 1/II; tel. (1) 2410284; fax (1) 4251673; e-mail sim@siol.net; internet sim.kivi-com.si/default3.asp?type=3&MenuID=1512; f. 1987; quarterly; in English; ethnic issues and news; Man. Editor Jože Prešeren; circ. 3,500.

Slovenske brazde (Slovenian Tracks): 1000 Ljubljana, Zarnikova 3; tel. (1) 4301891; fax (1) 4301871; f. 1990; weekly; Man. Editor Nace Potocnik.

Stop: 1000 Ljubljana, Dunajska 5; tel. (1) 319190; fax (1) 1330403; f. 1967; weekly; leisure, film, theatre, pop music, radio and television programmes; Editor Igor Savič; circ. 44,600.

SLOVENIA

Tednik: 2250 Ptuj, Raičeva 6; tel. (2) 7493410; fax (2) 7493435; e-mail tednik@radio-tednik.si; internet www.radio-tednik.si; f. 1948; weekly; politics, local information; Editor-in-Chief JOŽE ŠMIGOC; circ. 12,000.

Tretji dan (Third Day): 1000 Ljubljana, Jurčičev trg 2; tel. (1) 1263071; fax (1) 223864; weekly; Editor-in-Chief Dr TONE JAMNIK.

Tribuna: 1000 Ljubljana, Kersnikova 4; tel. (1) 319496; fax (1) 319448; 3 a week; student newspaper; Editor-in-Chief BOJAN KORENINI.

Vestnik Murska Sobota (Murska Sobota Herald): 9000 Murska Sobota, ul. Arhitekta Novaka 13; tel. (2) 5311960; fax (2) 5321175; e-mail vestnik@eunet.si; internet www.p-inf.si; f. 1949; weekly; popular; Editor-in-Chief JANEZ VOTEK; circ. 20,000.

Zdravje (Health): 1000 Ljubljana, Smartinska 10; tel. (1) 2319360; e-mail mica.kotnik@zalozba.ara.si; monthly; Editor-in-Chief MARIJA MICA KOTNIK.

PRESS AGENCIES

Morel: 1000 Ljubljana, Reboljeva 13, statti Parmova 41–45; tel. (1) 4361222; fax (1) 4361223; e-mail morel@si21.com; internet www.morel.si; f. 1993; Dir and Chief Editor EMIL LUKANČIČ-MORI.

Slovenska Tiskovna Agencija (STA): 1000 Ljubljana, Cankarjeva 5, p.p. 145; tel. (1) 2410100; fax (1) 4266050; e-mail desk@sta.si; internet www.sta.si; f. 1991; Dir-Gen. IGOR VEZOVNIK; Editor-in-Chief TADEJA ŠERGAN.

Publishers

Cankarjeva Založba: 1000 Ljubljana, Kopitarjeva 2; tel. (1) 3603720; fax (1) 3603787; e-mail import.books@cankarjeva-z.si; internet www.cankarjeva-z.si; f. 1945; philosophy, science and popular science; dictionaries and reference books; Slovenian and translated literature; import and export; international co-productions; Dir-Gen. JOŽE KORINŠEK.

DZS d.d.: 1538 Ljubljana, Dalmatinova 2; tel. (1)3069700; fax (1) 3069877; e-mail info@dzs.si; internet www.dzs.si; f. 1945; textbooks, manuals, world classics, natural sciences, art books, encyclopedias, dictionaries, educational CD-ROMs; import and export; Exec. Dir ANDREJ ZALOŽNIK.

Mladinska Knjiga Založba d.d.: 1000 Ljubljana, Slovenska 29; tel. (1) 2413098; fax (1) 4252294; e-mail intsales@mkz-lj.si; f. 1945; books for youth and children, including general, fiction, science, travel and school books, language courses, magazines and videos; international co-operation; Dir MILAN MATOS.

Slovenské Matica: 1000 Ljubljana, Kongresni trg 8; tel. and fax (1) 2514200; e-mail drago.jancar@siol.net; f. 1864; poetry, science, philosophy; Pres. Prof. Dr JOŽA MAHNIČ.

Založba Lipa Koper: 66000 Koper, Muzejski trg 7; tel. (5) 6274883; fiction; Dir Prof. JOŽE A. HOČEVAR.

Založba Obzorja d.d. Maribor: 2000 Maribor, Partizanska 3–5; tel. (2) 2348100; fax (2) 22348135; e-mail info@zalozba-obzorja.si; internet www.zalozba-obzorja.si; f. 1950; popular science, general literature, periodicals, etc.; Man. Dir GORAZD ZEMLJARIČ.

Broadcasting and Communications

TELECOMMUNICATIONS

Telecommunications Agency (Agencija za telekomunikacije, radiodifuzijo in pošto Republike Slovenije—ATRP): 1000 Ljubljana, Kotnikcva 19a; tel. (1) 4734900; fax (1) 4328036; e-mail urst.box@gov.si; internet www.atrp.si; Dir JOŽE KLEŠNIK (acting).

Mobitel: 1537 Ljubljana, Vilharjeva 23; tel. (1) 4722200; fax (1) 4722990; e-mail info@mobitel.si; internet www.mobitel.si; f. 1991; mobile cellular telecommunications services; Dir ANTON MAJZELJ.

Si.mobil—Vodafone: 1000 Ljubljana, Šmartinska cesta 134B; tel. (1) 5440000; fax (1) 5440099; e-mail info@simobil.si; internet www.simobil.com; f. 1999; subsidiary of Mobilkom Austria; Chair. of Bd BOJAN DREMELJ.

Telekom Slovenije: 1000 Ljubljana, Cigaletova 15; tel. (1) 2341200; fax (1) 2302014; internet www.telekom.si; f. 1949; 65% state-owned, further transfer to private-sector ownership proposed; Pres. LIBOR VONČINA; 2,184 employees.

Vega—Western Wireless International: 1231 Ljubljana, Brnčičeva 49; e-mail info@vega070.com; internet www.vega070.com; f. 2001; subsidiary of Western Wireless International (USA).

BROADCASTING
Regulatory Authority

Slovenian Broadcasting Council (Svet za Radiodifuzijo—SRDF): 1000 Ljubljana, Parmova 53; tel. (1) 1363596; fax (1) 1363595; e-mail info.srdf@srd.gov.si; internet www.sigov.si/srd; f. 1994; nine mems; protects independence of radio and television programmes; supervises the activities of broadcasting and cable operators.

Radio

Radiotelevizija Slovenija (RTV Slo): 1550 Ljubljana, Kolodvorska 2; tel. (1) 4752154; fax (1) 4752150; e-mail webmaster@rtvslo.si; internet www.rtvslo.si/html/radio-slo; f. 1928; 3 radio programmes nationally; broadcasts in Slovene, Hungarian and Italian; Gen. Man. ALEKS ŠTAKUL.

Radio Koper Capodistria: 6000 Koper, OF ul. 15; tel. (5) 6485483; fax (5) 6485488; e-mail radio.koper@rtvslo.si; internet www.rtvslo.si; Dir DRAGOMIR MIKELIĆ.

Radio Maribor: 2000 Maribor, Ilichova 33; tel. (2) 4299132; fax (2) 4299215; e-mail srecko.trglec@rtvslo.si; internet www.rtvslo.si; Editor SREČKO TRGLEC.

Radio Murski val: 9000 Murska Sobota, Arhitekta Novaka ul. 13; tel. (2) 5311960; fax (2) 5321175; e-mail radio-murski.val@siol.net; internet www.p-inf.si; f. 1958; Editor-in-Chief MARJAN DORA.

Radio Ptuj: 2250 Ptuj, Raiceva 6; tel. (2) 7493410; fax (2) 7493435; e-mail nabiralnik@radio-tednik.si; internet www.radio-teknik.si.

Television

Radiotelevizija Slovenija (RTV Slo): 1550 Ljubljana, Kolodvorska 2; tel. (1) 4752154; fax (1) 4752150; e-mail webmaster@rtvslo.si; internet www.rtvslo.si/html/radio-slo; f. 1928; 2 television programmes (TV1 and TV2) nationally; broadcasts in Slovene, Hungarian and Italian; Gen. Man. ALEKS ŠTAKUL.

Kanal A: 1000 Ljubljana, Tivolska 50; tel. (1) 1334133; fax (1) 1334222; Pres. DOUGLAS FULTON.

Pop TV: 1000 Ljubljana, Kranjčeva 26; tel. (1) 1893200; fax (1) 1612222; Editor TOMAŽ PEROVIČ.

TV 3: 1210 Ljubljana, Štula 23; tel. (1) 1831200; fax (1) 1521512; Editor-in-Chief MLADEN SICHROVSKY.

Finance
BANKS
(cap. = capital; res = reserves; dep. = deposits; m. = million; amounts in Slovene tolars unless otherwise stated; brs = branches)

The Slovenian banking sector has undergone a rationalization process, involving a conversion to commercial banking (new regulations took effect in January 1995) and the merging of smaller banks. In January 1999 new banking legislation allowed foreign banks to establish branches in Slovenia for the first time.

National Bank

Banka Slovenije (Bank of Slovenia): 1505 Ljubljana, Slovenska 35; tel. (1) 4719000; fax (1) 2515516; e-mail bsl@bsi.si; internet www.bsi.si; formerly National Bank of Slovenia, as part of the Yugoslav banking system; assumed central bank functions in 1991; bank of issue since Oct. 1991; res 179,873.0m., dep. 1,223,881.12m., total assets 1,617,314.9m. (Dec. 2004); Gov. MITJA GASPARI.

Selected Banks

Abanka Vipa d.d.: 1517 Ljubljana, Slovenska 58, POB 368; tel. (1) 4718100; fax (1) 4325165; e-mail info@abanka.si; internet www.abanka.si; f. 1955 as Ljubljana Branch of Yugoslav Bank for Foreign Trade; present name adopted 1989; cap. 7,155.5m., res 27,653.5m., dep. 336,277.3m. (Dec. 2003); Pres. and Chief Exec. ALJOŠA TOMAŽ; 32 brs.

Bank Austria Creditanstalt d.d. Ljubljana: 1000 Ljubljana, Smartinska 140; tel. (1) 5876600; fax (1) 5411860; e-mail info@si.bacai.com; internet www.ba-ca.si; f. 1991; cap. 3,101.4m., res 12,445.1m., dep. 206,633.6m. (Dec. 2003); Chair. FRANCE ARHAR.

Banka Celje d.d.: 3000 Celje, Vodnikova 2, POB 431; tel. (3) 4221000; fax (3) 4221100; e-mail info@banka-celje.si; internet www.banka-celje.si; cap. 3,377.0m., res 21,241.6m., dep. 235,770.4m. (Dec. 2003); Pres. NIKO KAČ; 16 brs.

Banka Koper d.d.: 6502 Koper, Pristaniška 14; tel. (5) 6661000; fax (5) 6662006; e-mail info@banka-koper.si; internet www.banka-koper.si; f. 1955; cap. 5,064.9m., res 25,983.7m., dep. 235,081.4m. (Dec. 2003); Pres. of the Management Bd VOJKO ČOK; 13 brs.

Deželna banka Slovenije dd: 1000 Ljubljana, Kolodvorska 9; tel. (1) 4727100; fax (1) 4727411; e-mail info@dbs.si; internet www.dbs

SLOVENIA

.si; f. 1990 as Slovenska Zadružna Kmetijska Banka d.d. Ljubljana; changed name to above in 2004 following merger with Zveza HKS Slovenije; cap. 1,759.2m., res 4,802.1m., dep. 59,434.3m. (Dec. 2003); Pres. MILAN KNEŽEVIČ; 6 brs.

Factor Banka d.d.: 1001 Ljubljana, Tivolska cesta 48; tel. (1) 2306600; fax (1) 2307760; e-mail info@factorb.si; internet www.factorb.si; f. 1993; cap. 1,749.2m., res 1,565.3m., dep. 39,770.5m. (Dec. 2003); Chair. BORIS PESJAK.

Gorenjska Banka d.d. Kranj: 4000 Kranj, Bleiweisova cesta 1, POB 147; tel. (4) 2084000; fax (4) 2021718; e-mail info@gbkr.si; internet www.gbkr.si; f. 1955; cap. 4,043.8m., res 52,034.0m., dep. 157,560.0m. (Dec. 2003); Pres. and Chief Exec. ZLATKO KAVČIČ; 5 brs.

Hypo Alpe-Adria-Bank dd: 1000 Ljubljana, Dunajska cesta 117; tel. (1) 5804000; fax (1) 5804001; e-mail hypo-bank@hypo.si; internet www.hypo-alpe-adria.si; f. 1999; cap. 10,535m., res 1,004.2m., dep. 73,699.8m.; Pres. BOŽIDAR ŠPAN.

Nova Kreditna Banka Maribor d.d. (NKBM): 2505 Maribor, Vita Kraigherja 4; tel. (2) 2292290; fax (2) 2524333; e-mail info@nkbm.si; internet www.nkbm.si; f. 1955; adopted present name 1994; 90% state-owned; cap. 5,600m., res 40,419m., dep. 427,170m. (Dec. 2002); Pres. and Chief Exec. CRTOMIR MESARIĆ; 81 brs and sub-brs.

Nova Ljubljanska Banka d.d. (NLB): 1520 Ljubljana, Republike trg 2; tel. (1) 4250155; fax (1) 4250331; e-mail info@nlb.si; internet www.nlb.si; f. 1994; commercial, investment and savings bank; 34% of shares divested to KBC Bank NV (Belgium) in May 2002; cap. 15,295m., res 40,777m., dep. 1,451,578m. (Dec. 2002); Pres. MARJAN KRAMAR; 16 brs.

Probanka d.d.: 2000 Maribor, Gosposka Ulica 23; tel. (2) 2520500; fax (2) 2526029; e-mail info@probanka.si; internet www.probanka.si; f. 1991; cap. 1,740m., res 11,913.9m., dep. 74,346.8m. (Dec. 2003); Pres. and Chair. ROMANA PAJENK.

Raiffeisen Krekova Banka d.d. Maribor: 2000 Maribor, Slomškov trg 18; tel. (2) 2293100; fax (2) 2223502; e-mail info@r-kb.si; internet www.r-kb.si; f. 1992; cap. 2,058.0m., res 4,832.2m., dep. 65,558.1m. (Dec. 2001); Chair. ALEŠ ŽAJDELA; 14 brs.

SKB Banka d.d.: 1000 Ljubljana, Ajdovščina 4; tel. (1) 4715918; fax (1) 4715513; e-mail info@skb.si; internet www.skb.si; f. 1978; shares acquired by Société Générale in May 2001; cap. 30,795.1m., res 4,840.5m., dep. 276,392.6m. (Dec. 2003); Pres. and Chief Exec. CVETKA SELŠEK; 56 brs.

STOCK EXCHANGE

Ljubljana Stock Exchange (Ljubljanska Borza d.d.): 1000 Ljubljana, Slovenska 56; tel. (1) 4710211; fax (1) 4710213; e-mail info@ljse.si; internet www.ljse.si; f. 1989; operative 1990; Pres. and Chief Exec. Dr MARKO SIMONETI.

INSURANCE

Adriatic Insurance Co: 6503 Koper, Ljubljanska cesta 3A; tel. (5) 6643100; fax (5) 6643303; e-mail info@adriatic.si; internet www.adriatic.si; f. 1990.

Grawe Insurance Co d.d.: 2000 Maribor, Gregorčičeva 39; tel. (2) 2285500; fax (2) 2285526; e-mail prima@prima.si.

Maribor Insurance Co: 2507 Maribor, Cankarjeva 3; tel. (2) 224111.

Merkur Insurance Co: 1000 Ljubljana, Dunajska 58; tel. (1) 3005450; fax (1) 4361092; e-mail info@merkur-zav.si; internet www.merkur-zav.si; f. 1992; Gen. Man. DENIS STROLIGO.

Triglav Insurance Co (Zavarovalnica Triglav d.d.): 1000 Ljubljana, Miklošičeva 19; tel. (1) 4747200; fax (1) 4326302; e-mail info-triglav@triglav.si; internet www.zav-triglav.si; Pres. ANDREJ KOCIČ; Chair. DAMJAN MIHEVC.

Trade and Industry

GOVERNMENT AGENCY

Agency of the Republic of Slovenia for Restructuring and Privatization (Agencija Republike Slovenije za Prestrukturiranje in Privatizacijo—ARSPIP): 1000 Ljubljana, Kotnikova 28; tel. (1) 1316030; fax (1) 1316011; e-mail webmaster@arspip.si; Dir MIRA PUC.

DEVELOPMENT ORGANIZATION

Development Corporation of Slovenia (Slovenska Razvojna Druzba): 1000 Ljubljana, Dunajska 160; tel. (1) 1894800; fax (1) 1894819; e-mail jana.bogdanovski@srd.si; Pres. BOGDAN TOPIČ; Chair. MARJAN REKAR.

Directory

CHAMBERS OF COMMERCE

Chamber of Commerce and Industry of Slovenia (Gospodarska Zbornica Slovenije): 1504 Ljubljana, Dimičeva 13; tel. (1) 5898313; fax (1) 5898317; e-mail infolink@gzs.si; internet www.gzs.si; Pres. JOSKO CUK.

Chamber of Small Businesses of Slovenia: 1000 Ljubljana, Celovška 71; tel. (1) 4593241; fax (1) 4559270; Pres. MIHA GRAH; Sec. ANTON FILIPIČ; 50,000 mems.

UTILITIES

Electricity

Elektro-Slovenija d.o.o. (ELES): 1000 Ljubljana, Hajdrihova 2; tel. (1) 1301440; fax (1) 1250333; e-mail info@eles.si; internet www.eles.si; national electricity distributor; Chief Exec. VEKOSLAV KOROŠEC.

Nuklearna Elektrarna p.o. (NEK): 8270 Krško, Vrbina 12; tel. (7) 4802000; fax (7) 4921528; internet www.nek.si; f. 1974; jointly owned by Slovenia and Croatia, pending privatization; production and distribution of electricity; Man. Dir STANE ROŽMAN.

Gas

Geoplin d.o.o.: 1000 Ljubljana, Ljubljanska brigade 11; tel. (1) 5820600; fax (1) 5820601; e-mail info@geoplin.si; internet www.geoplin.si; f. 1975; national gas co; Gen. Man. JANEZ MOŽINA.

TRADE UNIONS

The Association of Independent Trade Unions of Slovenia: 1000 Ljubljana, Dalmatinova 4; tel. (1) 4317983; fax (1) 4318294; Pres. DUŠAN SEMOLIČ.

Independence—Confederation of New Trade Unions of Slovenia: 1000 Ljubljana, Linhartova 13; tel. (1) 4329141; fax (1) 4302868; Pres. FRANCE TOMŠIČ.

Transport

RAILWAYS

The rail link between Western Europe and Greece, Turkey and the Near and Middle East runs through Slovenia. In 1999 there were 1,201 km of railway lines in Slovenia, of which 499 km were electrified.

Slovenske Železnice (SŽ) (Slovenian Railways): 1506 Ljubljana, Kolodvorska 11; tel. (1) 2914001; fax (1) 2914800; e-mail boris.zivec@slo-zeleznice.si; internet www.slo-zeleznice.si; Dir-Gen. BORIS ŽIVEC.

ROADS

In 2001 the country had 20,236 km of roads, of which 435 km were motorways, 1,101 km were highways, main or national roads and 4,796 km were secondary or regional roads. An 84-km motorway links Ljubljana, Postojna and Sežana with the coastal region in the south-west, and a 25-km motorway connects the capital with Kranj and the Gorenjska region in the north-east.

Directorate of the Republic of Slovenia for Roads: Ministry of Transport, 1535 Ljubljana, Langusova ul. 4; tel. (1) 1788000; fax (1) 1788139; e-mail drsc-info@gov.si.

SHIPPING

Slovenia's principal international trading port, at Koper, handles some 6m. tons of freight annually, and has terminals for general, bulk and liquid cargo, containers and 'roll on, roll off' traffic, as well as warehousing facilities. The port is a duty-free zone. There are also major ports at Portorož and Izola.

Luka Koper d.d.: 6501 Koper, Vojkovo nabrežje 38; tel. (5) 6656100; fax (5) 6395020; e-mail portkoper@luka-kp.si; internet www.luka-kp.si; f. 1957; Chief Exec. BRUNO KORELIČ.

Principal Shipping Company

Splošna Plovba: 6320 Portorož, Obala 55, POB 60; tel. (5) 6766000; fax (5) 6766130; e-mail plovba@5-plovba.si; transport of all types of cargo; regular liner service; Man. Dir ALDO KREJAČIČ.

CIVIL AVIATION

There are three international airports in Slovenia, at Brnik (Ljubljana), Maribor and Portorož.

Adria Airways: 1000 Ljubljana, Kuzmičeva 7; tel. (1) 3691000; fax (1) 4369233; e-mail info@adria.si; internet www.adria.si; f. 1961; operates international scheduled services to destinations in Europe and the Middle East; Pres. BRANKO LUCOVNIK.

Tourism

Slovenia offers a variety of tourist attractions, including Mediterranean resorts to the west, the Julian Alps and the lakes of Bled and Bohinj to the north and, in the south, the 'karst' limestone regions, with more than 6,000 caves. The number of foreign tourist arrivals increased steadily from the mid-1990s, reaching 1,498,900 in 2004. Tourism receipts totalled US $1,427m. in 2003.

Slovenian Tourist Board: 1000 Ljubljana, Dunajska 156; tel. (1) 5891840; fax (1) 5891841; e-mail info@slovenia-tourism.si; internet www.slovenia-tourism.si; Exec. Man. BOJAN MEDEN.

SOLOMON ISLANDS

Introductory Survey

Location, Climate, Language, Religion, Flag, Capital

Solomon Islands is a scattered Melanesian archipelago in the south-western Pacific Ocean, east of Papua New Guinea. The country includes most of the Solomon Islands (those to the north-west being part of Papua New Guinea), Ontong Java Islands (Lord Howe Atoll), Rennell Island and the Santa Cruz Islands, about 500 km (300 miles) to the east. The climate is equatorial, with small seasonal variations, governed by the trade winds. In Honiara the average temperature is about 27°C (81°F) and the average annual rainfall about 2,160 mm (85 ins). The official language is standard English, although pidgin English is more widely used and understood. More than 80 different local languages exist, and no vernacular is common to the whole country. More than 95% of the inhabitants profess Christianity, and most of the remainder follow traditional beliefs. The national flag (proportions 1 by 2) comprises two triangles, one of blue (with its base at the hoist and its apex in the upper fly) and one of dark green (with its base in the fly and its apex in the lower hoist), separated by a narrow yellow diagonal stripe (from lower hoist to upper fly), with five white five-pointed stars (arranged to form a diagonal cross) in the upper hoist. The capital is Honiara, on the island of Guadalcanal.

Recent History

The northern Solomon Islands became a German protectorate in 1885 and the southern Solomons a British protectorate in 1893. Rennell Island and the Santa Cruz Islands were added to the British protectorate in 1898 and 1899. Germany ceded most of the northern Solomons and Ontong Java Islands to the United Kingdom between 1898 and 1900. The whole territory, known as the British Solomon Islands Protectorate, was placed under the jurisdiction of the Western Pacific High Commission (WPHC), with its headquarters in Fiji.

The Solomon Islands were invaded by Japan in 1942, but, after a fierce battle on Guadalcanal, most of the islands were recaptured by US forces in 1943. After the Second World War the protectorate's capital was moved from Tulagi Island to Honiara. In January 1953 the headquarters of the WPHC also moved to Honiara. Meanwhile, elected local councils were established on most of the islands, and by 1966 almost the whole territory was covered by such councils.

Under a new Constitution, introduced in October 1960, a Legislative Council and an Executive Council were established for the protectorate's central administration. Initially, all members of both bodies were appointed, but from 1964 the Legislative Council included elected members, and the elective element was gradually increased. Another Constitution, introduced in March 1970, established a single Governing Council of 17 elected members, three *ex-officio* members and (until the end of 1971) up to six public service members. A new Governing Council of 24 directly elected members was formed in 1973, when a ministerial system was introduced.

A further new Constitution, adopted in April 1974, instituted a single Legislative Assembly, containing 24 members who chose a Chief Minister with the right to appoint his own Council of Ministers. A new office of Governor of the Protectorate was also created, to assume almost all of the functions previously exercised in the territory by the High Commissioner for the Western Pacific. Solomon Mamaloni, leader of the newly founded People's Progressive Party (PPP), was appointed the first Chief Minister in August 1974. The territory was officially renamed the Solomon Islands in June 1975, although it retained protectorate status.

In January 1976 the Solomon Islands received internal self-government, with the Chief Minister presiding over the Council of Ministers in place of the Governor. In June elections were held for an enlarged Legislative Assembly, and in July the Assembly elected one of its new members, Peter Kenilorea, to the position of Chief Minister. Solomon Islands (as it was restyled) became an independent state, within the Commonwealth, on 7 July 1978. The Legislative Assembly became the National Parliament and designated Kenilorea the first Prime Minister. The main political issue confronting the new nation was the proposed decentralization of authority to the regions, support for which was particularly strong in the Western District, the most commercially developed part of the country. The first general election since independence took place in August 1980. Independent candidates won more seats than any of the three parties. Parliament again elected Kenilorea Prime Minister by an overwhelming majority. In August 1981, however, Parliament approved a motion expressing 'no confidence' in Kenilorea, and chose Mamaloni, who now led the People's Alliance Party (PAP) following the merger of the PPP with the Rural Alliance Party in 1979, to succeed him as Prime Minister.

After legislative elections in October 1984, Sir Peter Kenilorea (as he had become) was again elected as Prime Minister. The new Government consisted of a coalition of nine members of Kenilorea's Solomon Islands United Party (SIUPA), three members of the newly formed Solomone Ano Sagufenua (SAS) party and three independents. The five provincial ministries, established by Mamaloni, were abolished, in accordance with Kenilorea's declared policy of restoring to central government control some of the powers held by the provincial governments.

In October 1985 a new political party, which sought a resolution of ongoing land disputes, the Nationalist Front for Progress (NFP), was formed, under the leadership of Andrew Nori. The SAS subsequently withdrew from the coalition, and Kenilorea formed a new Cabinet, comprising nine members of the SIUPA, three of the NFP and three independents. Kenilorea resigned following the approval of a motion of 'no confidence' (two others having previously been defeated); in December Ezekiel Alebua, the former Deputy Prime Minister assumed the premiership.

A report by a specially commissioned constitutional review committee, chaired by Mamaloni, was published in March 1988, and proposed that Solomon Islands become a federal republic within the Commonwealth, and that the President of the Republic be a native of the territory. In January 1989 the PAP announced that Solomon Islands would be declared a republic if the party won the next general election, scheduled to take place in February. At the election the PAP won 11 of the 38 seats, the largest representation obtained by any party, while Alebua's party, the United Party, won only four seats. In March Mamaloni was elected Prime Minister. His Cabinet included the former Governor-General of Solomon Islands, Sir Baddeley Devesi, and was described as the first since independence to comprise the members of a single party.

In October 1990 Mamaloni resigned as leader of the PAP, one week before Parliament was due to vote on another motion of 'no confidence' in his premiership, declaring that he would remain as an independent Prime Minister. He dismissed five members of the Cabinet, replacing them with four members of the opposition and a PAP back-bencher. The Prime Minister defied persistent demands for his resignation by a majority of the members of Parliament. The remaining 10 ministers of the PAP were expelled from the party in February 1991, following their refusal to resign from their posts in the interests of party unity. Later that year, as a result of continuing economic decline, the Solomon Islands Council of Trade Unions issued an ultimatum demanding Mamaloni's resignation.

At elections to the recently enlarged National Parliament in May 1993 the Group for National Unity and Reconciliation (GNUR), led by Mamaloni, won 21 of the 47 seats. However, a newly formed coalition of opposition parties and independents, the National Coalition Partners (NCP), was successful in electing an independent member, Francis Billy Hilly, to the premiership in June. Hilly defeated Mamaloni by a single vote.

In October 1994 a constitutional crisis arose, following attempts by the Governor-General, Moses (later Sir Moses) Pitakaka, to dismiss Hilly on the grounds that he no longer held a parliamentary majority. Hilly remained in office, however, with the support of a High Court ruling, and confusion intensified when Pitakaka appointed the opposition leader, Mamaloni, to the position of Prime Minister. Hilly finally resigned on 31 October, and the post was declared vacant. In a parliamentary election to the premiership on 8 November, Mamaloni defeated the former Governor-General, Devesi, by 29 votes to 18.

In late 1995 and early 1996 Mamaloni's Government suffered a series of allegations of corruption and misconduct, particularly in relation to allegations that seven ministers had received payments from foreign logging companies between 1993 and 1995, although in February 1996 all seven were acquitted.

Controversy arose in July 1996 when it was reported that members of the National Parliament had begun to present gifts to their constituencies in preparation for the general election scheduled for 1997. This followed the reinstatement of the controversial Constituency Development Fund, which entitled each member to US $66,000, and which had been widely used by members at the previous general election to secure re-election by purchasing gifts for voters. In September the regional trades union organization, SPOCTU, cited the prevalence of corruption as the greatest obstacle to the islands' development, and stated that, in consequence, investors and aid donors would remain reluctant to make financial commitments to Solomon Islands.

In early August 1996 the National Parliament approved legislation to reform the provincial government system, which the Government claimed was inefficient and costly to maintain. Under the new system, the legislative and administrative powers of the nine provincial governments were to be transferred to 75 area assemblies and councils, with financial control vested wholly in the central Government. In February 1997, however, the legislation, which had been vehemently opposed by the larger provinces, was declared invalid by the High Court.

In May 1997 Mamaloni announced his intention to hold an early general election, following which he would resign as leader of the GNUR. Meanwhile, Alebua resigned from the leadership of the NCP, following accusations of misconduct, and was replaced by Edward Hunuehu. A general election took place on 6 August to a legislature that had recently been enlarged to 50 seats. The GNUR won 24 seats and a new grouping, the Solomon Islands Alliance for Change Coalition (SIACC), secured the remainder. A period of intense political manoeuvring followed the election, in attempts to form a parliamentary majority. On 27 August Bartholomew Ulufa'alu was elected Prime Minister, defeating the newly elected leader of the GNUR, Danny Philip, by 26 votes to 22. The new Government announced a programme of extensive structural reforms, including a rationalization of the public sector, a reduction in the number of ministerial portfolios (from 16 to 10), and measures to expand the private sector and to encourage greater participation of non-governmental organizations in the country's socio-economic development. The measures aimed to restore a degree of economic stability to Solomon Islands and to attract increased foreign investment. Legislation proposing that a politician seeking to change party allegiance would automatically lose his or her seat and be subject to a by-election was similarly intended to increase political stability.

In early 1998 a shipment of weapons (including a helicopter gunship, two military aircraft and smaller armaments) ordered by the previous administration for use in defending the maritime border with Papua New Guinea, arrived in the country from the USA. Ulufa'alu requested assistance from Australia in impounding the weapons, following widespread concern that unofficial organizations (particularly the Bougainville secessionist rebels within Papua New Guinea) might intercept the shipment. A dispute subsequently arose between Ulufa'alu and the former Prime Minister, Solomon Mamaloni, who had ordered the weapons. Mamaloni accused Ulufa'alu of treason for surrendering sovereign property to a foreign government, while the Prime Minister claimed that serious irregularities had occurred in procuring the arms, citing missing files and apparent overpayment.

In April 1998 Job Dudley Tausinga, whose Coalition for National Advancement (CNA) constituted the largest group outside the Government, was appointed Leader of the Opposition. Following the defection of six government members in July–August 1998, the opposition claimed to hold a parliamentary majority (with 25 of the 49 sitting members), and consequently sought to introduce a motion of 'no confidence' in the Prime Minister. A vote eventually took place on 18 September, after the failure of an attempt by the Government to declare the vote unlawful in the High Court, but was deemed to have been defeated as an equal number of votes were cast for and against the motion. Three opposition members subsequently defected to the Government, thus increasing its representation to 27 members. The climate of ongoing political instability prompted the Government to reiterate its proposal for legislation to restrict the rights of elected members of the National Parliament to change party allegiance. In late September Solomon Mamaloni was elected Leader of the Opposition. Mamaloni died in January 2000 and was succeeded by Manasseh Sogavare, under whose leadership the CNA subsequently reverted to its original name of the PPP.

From April 1998 violent unrest in Honiara was attributed to ethnic tensions, mainly between the inhabitants of Guadalcanal and Malaita provinces. One underlying cause of the disturbances was the alienation of land by the Government since independence. Title to some land thus expropriated had been returned to Guadalcanal in late November, but this had not allayed a widespread feeling of resentment in the province at the financial burden imposed by hosting the capital. It was reported that a group styling itself the 'Guadalcanal Revolutionary Army' (GRA) had begun a campaign of militancy to force the Government to relocate the capital. The unrest intensified in early 1999, prompting the Government to establish a peace committee for the province. In mid-1999 talks between the Premier of Guadalcanal Province, Ezekiel Alebua, and the Solomon Islands Prime Minister failed to alleviate inter-ethnic tensions in the province. Riots broke out in Honiara, and some 80 Malaitan immigrants were evacuated following threats by armed GRA militants. Following Ulufa'alu's demands that peace be restored to the province before the implementation of any further measures, the GRA ordered an immediate halt to its activities. The Guadalcanal Provincial Assembly subsequently declared that it had accepted an initial payment of SI $500,000 in compensation for accommodating the national capital. A reconciliation ceremony was held between the two parties, during which Alebua appealed to the GRA to lay down its arms. However, the Malaitans subsequently demanded that they too be compensated, to the sum of US $600,000, for damage to their property by the GRA militants.

Following an increase in violence during which three Malaitan immigrants were reported to have been killed, and an estimated 10,000 forced to flee their villages, in mid-June 1999 a state of emergency was declared in Guadalcanal. A leader of the Isatabu Freedom Movement (IFM, formerly the GRA, and also known in 1999 as the Isatabu Freedom Fighters—IFF), Andrew Te'e, announced that the movement was willing to surrender in return for a full amnesty for the militants; however, this was rejected by Ulufa'alu. The former Prime Minister of Fiji, Sitiveni Rabuka, was appointed Commonwealth Special Envoy, following a request for assistance by Ulufa'alu. After meeting with the parties concerned, Rabuka announced on 28 June that a peace agreement had been reached, and a UN delegation and police officers from Fiji and Vanuatu were dispatched to help implement the peace plan. As part of the Honiara Peace Accord, the Solomon Islands Government agreed to pay SI $2.5m. into a Reconciliation Trust Fund, which was to be jointly administered by Guadalcanal Province and the national Government, to compensate the victims of the unrest. In return, the IFM agreed to disarm and to abandon their demands for a full amnesty for their supporters. In early August, however, Rabuka and the UN monitoring team returned to the province, after four members of the IFM were reported to have been shot by police near Honiara. On 12 August, however, a new peace agreement was signed by Rabuka, Alebua and others. The agreement, known as the Panatina Agreement, allowed for a reduction in police activity in the province followed by the eventual revocation of the state of emergency, in return for the surrender of weapons by the IFM. Despite the extension of the disarmament deadline into September, the state of emergency was ended in mid-October and, following negotiations in Honiara and the signing of an agreement in Fiji, a multinational peace-monitoring group from Fiji and Vanuatu, jointly funded by Australia and New Zealand, arrived in Guadalcanal late in October. In early December the peace-keeping force's mandate was extended into January 2000, and subsequently further extended by three months, following renewed outbreaks of violence and the emergence of a new guerrilla group, the Malaita Eagle Force (MEF), demanding US $40m. in compensation payments for loss of property incurred by Malaitans as a result of the conflict. Among their spokesmen was the former Minister of Finance, Andrew Nori.

Following further outbreaks of violence in the province that led to the death of four people, including two policemen, in February 2000, the Governor-General issued a decree outlawing membership of both the IFM and the MEF. Further clashes between the two rebel groups were reported in early March, and later that month riots took place in Honiara during which Malaitan immigrants stoned the headquarters of the Guadalcanal provincial government. Peace talks took place in May without members of the IFM and the MEF, both of which refused to attend in protest at the decision to outlaw them. However, a document, known as the Buala Peace Communiqué, was issued as the outcome of these talks on 5 May. Later that month the order that outlawed the groups was suspended. On 5 June members of the MEF, armed with weapons obtained in raids on police armouries, seized control of Honiara, placing Ulufa'alu under house arrest. The rebels demanded the immediate resignation of the Prime Minister, claiming that he, himself an ethnic Malaitan, had failed to compensate displaced Malaitans within the established deadline (allegedly set for that day) and also demanded the appointment of a new Commissioner of Police, the *de facto* head of national security. In renewed outbreaks of violence, up to 100 people were reportedly killed. The MEF, meanwhile, claimed to have gained control of the Police Force, 98% of the military-style weapons in the territory, broadcasting services and the telecommunications infrastructure. Ulufa'alu was released after four days, following an agreement between the MEF and government negotiators that a special parliamentary sitting would be convened during which Ulufa'alu would be subject to a motion of 'no confidence'. A 14-day cease-fire was called to guarantee the safe passage of a Commonwealth monitoring team. On 14 June Ulufa'alu resigned, one day before the scheduled 'no confidence' vote; he would, however, remain as 'caretaker' Prime Minister for a 14-day transitional period during which negotiations between the MEF, the IFM and a Commonwealth Special Envoy, Prof. Ade Adefuye of Nigeria, were to take place. However, negotiations collapsed following the MEF's refusal to hand over its weapons, pending the appointment of a new Prime Minister, which was to occur in an extraordinary parliamentary session on 28 June. As this session failed to raise the necessary quorum, the election of a new Prime Minister was delayed until 30 June, when Sogavare, the leader of the opposition, defeated Rev. Leslie Boseto, incumbent Minister for Lands and Housing, by 23 votes to 21. (The third candidate, Hilly, withdrew in support of Boseto.) Sogavare declared that he would seek to establish peace without making significant changes to the policy of the previous Government. None the less, Sogavare announced a comprehensive reallocation of ministerial posts and restructuring of ministries. A new Ministry for National Unity, Reconciliation and Peace was established, and plans to create a Solomon Islands Defence Force and Ministry of Defence were announced. (Previously defence issues had fallen within the remit of the police service, which had become compromised because of alleged MEF infiltration, and by allegations that about 75% of officers were ethnic Malaitans.)

New cease-fire negotiations in August 2000 resulted in the declaration of a 90-day cease-fire between the IFM and the MEF, although intermittent violent disorder continued in Guadalcanal. In late August IFM dissidents kidnapped the brother of Deputy Prime Minister Allan Kemakeza, demanding that SI $6.5m. in compensation be paid to the displaced persons of Guadalcanal. Kemakeza was released unharmed after 10 days without the payment of a ransom. Logistical problems delayed the onset of further peace talks until early September, when a further communiqué concerning potential methods of advancing the peace process was issued. In mid-September a breakaway group from the IFM, which had reverted to the former name of the GRA under the leadership of Harold Keke, held an airline pilot hostage with a demand for SI $2m.; he was released unharmed without the demands being acceded to, although Keke later claimed that the Government had paid him US $200,000.

A further round of peace talks in Queensland, Australia, led to the signing on 15 October 2000 of a peace treaty known as the Townsville Agreement, by the MEF, the IFM, the Solomon Islands Government and the Provincial Governments of Malaita and Guadalcanal. An amnesty for all those involved in crimes associated with the ethnic conflict would be granted, subject to the surrender of all weaponry within 30 days. The agreement also envisaged the creation of an international peace-monitoring team, and the repatriation to their home villages of all MEF and IFM soldiers at the expense of the Solomon Islands Government. Infrastructure and service in the two provinces would be restored and developed. The two provinces would also be granted a greater degree of administrative autonomy. Malaita Province was to receive additional funding to reflect the demands placed on the region by the influx of 20,000 displaced persons from Guadalcanal. Public displays of forgiveness, reconciliation and confession were organized, and a Peace and Reconciliation Committee was to be established.

The implementation of the peace process, overseen by monitors from Australia and New Zealand, was threatened in mid-November 2000, when four people were killed in a shooting in Gizo, Western Province. Among the dead were two members of Papua New Guinea's Bougainville Revolutionary Army (BRA). Moreover, delays in the disarmament process involving the MEF and the IFM caused the deadline for the surrender of arms to be extended from 15 November until the end of that month, and then further until 15 December. In mid-November, following an announcement that the Guadalcanal Provincial Government headquarters, which had been occupied by members of the MEF since June, was to be rehabilitated as a symbol of national unity, arsonists, believed to be linked with the MEF, attacked the building. Despite a series of ceremonies in late November and early December, in which members of the IFM and MEF surrendered weapons, it was believed that at least 400 illegally held weapons remained in circulation at the end of December. The legislation granting immunity to those who had committed crimes during the conflict was passed by Parliament in mid-December, and was criticized by the prominent human rights organization, Amnesty International. In late December one man was wounded in an attack on a motel, in Honiara, in which disarmed former IFM rebels recruited into the police were resident. Responsibility for the attack was attributed to a group calling itself the Marau Eagle Force, from the eastern Marau region of Guadalcanal, which was subject to separate peace negotiations. The Guadalcanal Liberation Force (GLF) as it was restyled, led by Harold Keke, also announced that it had not accepted the cease-fire. In early January 2001 concerns were expressed that, as a result of the ongoing economic crisis and a larger number of rebels having opted to join the police than had been anticipated, the Government might be unable to pay the former rebels, thus precipitating further concerns about security.

In early December 2000 new legislation had permitted the appointment of two further ministers, a Minister of Rehabilitation, Reconstruction and Redirection, and a Minister of Economic Reform and Structural Adjustment. In early January 2001 it was reported that the Government was contemplating an extension of the amnesty. Further violence broke out between Guadalcanal militants and members of the Marau Eagle Force. A peace agreement between the group and the IFM was signed in early February, although the Peace Monitoring Council observed that the infrastructure of the Marau region had been almost entirely destroyed since 1998 and that there was little immediate prospect of recovery. In early March 2001 peace in the Marau region appeared to be threatened following an incident in which police officers, in connection with a drink-driving charge, opened fire on a vehicle owned by a former commander of the Marau Eagle Force. It was also reported that two other former Marau commanders had demanded SI $100,000 from the Government, and that other Marau militants would refuse to surrender their arms, in conformity with the agreement signed in February, unless the GLF were also disarmed. In mid-March tensions heightened following a security operation against the GLF leader, Keke, in which a government patrol boat fired at villages on the western coast of Guadalcanal. In the same month police disarmed and arrested a group of villagers from Munda, Western Province. Further incidents in early April, in which a boat fired at coastal targets in southern Guadalcanal, led the international peace monitoring force from Australia to state that the cease-fire arrangement reached under the Townsville Agreement might have been breached. The Assistant Commissioner of Police Operations protested that the Townsville Agreement did not require the police to surrender their guns, although a report published in April claimed that some of the weapons used in the security operation should have been surrendered the previous year. In June the Premier of Guadalcanal, Ezekiel Alebua, was shot and seriously injured in an assassination attempt, apparently carried out on the orders of former leaders of the IFM. Harold Keke met the Deputy Prime Minister and the secretary of the Peace Monitoring Council in June and, in October, he voiced his support for the imminent general elections. However, the failure of former militia groups to surrender their guns was the main obstacle to a lasting peace throughout 2001, and officials estimated that there remained some 500 high-powered weapons in the community, in addition to hand-made weapons. The Government declared an 'arms amnesty' in April 2002. Militants surrendered some 2,000 guns with impunity. Weapons disposal began in June, coinciding with the International Peace Monitoring Team's departure from the country.

SOLOMON ISLANDS

Introductory Survey

In the second half of 2000 Western, Choiseul, and Temutu provinces all declared themselves to be semi-autonomous states within Solomon Islands; on 1 September the legislature of the latter, representing 20,000 inhabitants, approved a bill allowing for a referendum on the province's proposed independence; the worsening economic situation caused by the conflict in Guadalcanal was believed to be a determining factor; additionally, movements in Guadalcanal and Makira provinces demanding greater autonomy were reported to have gained strength at this time. In late November the Minister of Provincial Government and Rural Development Nathaniel Waena announced that legislation to amend the Constitution would be submitted in 2001, in order to institute a federal system of government. Controversy arose following an announcement by the Government, in mid-March 2001, that it intended to introduce legislation to extend the life of Parliament for a further year, to expire in August 2002, stating that the social and economic position of the islands would not facilitate the holding of elections as scheduled in August 2001. This proposal attracted widespread opposition, including that of churches, trade unions, all provincial premiers, and the principal overseas aid donors to Solomon Islands. When it became apparent that he would not possess a parliamentary majority to support the legislation, Sogavare withdrew the bill from Parliament in early May; later that month it was announced that the elections would be held, as scheduled, funded wholly from overseas. In September the National Parliament approved a bill to increase national general election registration fees by 150%; Walter Folotalu, former member of the National Parliament for Baegu, successfully challenged the proposed legislation in the High Court in October. In the same month the High Court also began hearing the case brought by former Prime Minister Bartholomew Ulufa'alu; he had challenged the legality of the Government, seeking a ruling that the coup and subsequent election that ousted him were unconstitutional (he lost the case in November 2001).

In October 2001 public services deteriorated as nation-wide power cuts resulted from the Solomon Islands Electricity Authority's inability to pay for its supplies of diesel fuel. The Government announced the introduction of health charges in order to maintain medical services, and was forced to appeal to Australia and New Zealand for assistance in policing, as violent crime was becoming endemic. A storage container holding weapons relinquished under the Townsville peace agreement was broken into and, in November, the revelation that compensation totalling SI $17.4m. had been paid to former members of the MEF for alleged property damage precipitated a violent demonstration by protesters demanding similar recompense. The Prime Minister was prevented from leaving his office (to attend a session of the UN General Assembly in New York), while the house of the Deputy Prime Minister was vandalized.

Accusations and rumours of bribery and intimidation were rife during the campaigning that preceded the general election, held on 5 December 2001. The electoral grouping of the SIACC won 12 seats, the PAP secured nine and the PPP six, while 22 seats were won by independent candidates. In the absence of a clear SIACC leader, 11 elected members of the coalition convened with 11 elected independents to decide upon a satisfactory premier. Following various shifts in allegiances, Sir Allan Kemakeza (as he had become), leader of the PAP and former Deputy Prime Minister, was declared Prime Minister. Despite having been previously accused of misappropriating state funds, the former Minister of Finance, Snyder Rini, was appointed Deputy Prime Minister and Minister for National Planning.

The new Government, however, was unable to improve the increasingly desperate political and economic situation on the islands. A peace summit, organized by the Peace Monitoring Council, scheduled to be held in March 2002 was postponed until June, and, as the security situation in the country deteriorated further, numerous international peace monitors began withdrawing from the islands. Later in March the New Zealand Deputy High Commissioner to Solomon Islands, Bridget Nichols, was discovered at her home suffering from severe knife wounds, and died shortly afterwards in hospital, in what was initially believed to have been an incident linked to the recent escalation in violence. However, subsequent investigations by both the New Zealand and Solomon Islands authorities concluded that the diplomat's death had been an accident. Also in March Kemakeza dismissed Michael Maina, the Minister of Finance, after Maina failed to consult the Cabinet prior to announcing a number of drastic budgetary measures, the most significant of which was his decision to devalue the national currency by 25%. Maina was replaced by Laurie Chan, who in early April revalued the currency.

There were reports of further disturbances on the western coast of Guadalcanal in early June 2002 during which it was claimed that 11 Malaitans, who were part of a force attempting to capture the GLF leader, Harold Keke, had been killed. In mid-July water and electricity supplies to the capital were interrupted after the Solomon Islands Electricity Authority (SIEA) was once again unable to purchase fuel to power its generators, and the Solomon Islands Water Authority (SIWA) had failed to pay rental arrears to the landowners of the Kongulai water source. The country was further adversely affected by a series of strikes in mid-August by public-sector workers in protest at the non-payment of their salaries. Later that month the Minister for Youth and Sports and Women's Affairs, Rev. Augustin Greve, was assassinated. It was subsequently reported that Harold Keke had claimed responsibility for the murder. In September a church deacon was found beheaded on a beach on Guadalcanal's southern coast, an area considered to be a stronghold of the GLF. In a separate incident in the same month a woman and three children were shot dead and 11 others wounded in an assault which local chiefs attributed to Keke's organization. In late September Kemakeza made a formal request to the UN for a peace-keeping force to address the increasing state of lawlessness in the country and in the following month a delegation of four UN officials visited the islands to assess the situation.

In mid-October 2002 the Cabinet approved the establishment of the National Peace Council, an interim body, to replace the Peace Monitoring Council, the mandate of which expired on 15 October under the terms of the Townsville Peace Agreement. A permanent body was to be established after 16 January 2003. It was confirmed, however, in the same month that more weapons were in circulation in the country than when the peace agreement was signed in October 2000. The National Peace Council expressed a belief that many of the weapons surrendered under the arms amnesty of April 2002 had been removed for use by police officers in their campaign to capture Keke.

In mid-December 2002 the Minister of Finance, Laurie Chan, resigned. The Government claimed that this action was in response to criticism of his budget, which had recently been approved by the Cabinet. However, Radio New Zealand reported that his resignation was in protest at the Government's decision to pay unscheduled allowances to the 'special constables' (former militants from the ethnic conflict who were allowed to join the police force as part of the peace agreement) who had demanded the payments with threats and violence. The latter had included an incident in which gunshots were fired at the Prime Minister's residence by a group of 'special constables'. The Government faced a serious challenge in mid-December when six independent members of Parliament resigned because of what they described as a 'leadership problem' within the coalition. However, the Government defeated an opposition motion of 'no confidence' by 28 votes to 17. Meanwhile, several financial advisers fled the country, reportedly as a result of threats they had received.

In late December 2002 the remote islands of Tikopia and Anuta in the province of Temotu were struck by Cyclone Zoe and lost contact with the rest of the country. The islands suffered widespread devastation with the loss of all crops, buildings and water supplies, and heavy casualties were feared. The dispatch of a boat containing relief supplies was delayed by several days because of the Government's inability to pay for a crew or fuel for the vessel. When aid finally reached the islands, it was found that, contrary to all expectations, there had been no fatalities among the combined population of some 4,000, despite the severity of the storms. Islanders were believed to have used their knowledge of tunnels and caves on the islands to shelter from the cyclone.

The country's precarious peace process suffered a major reversal in February 2003 when a leading member of the National Peace Council, Sir Frederick Soaki, was assassinated. The motive for the killing was not immediately apparent, although there was speculation that it might have been connected to his involvement in a 'demobilization' programme for 'special constables'. A report by the human rights organization, Amnesty International, in March 2003 claimed that the country's 'special constables' had tortured and killed numerous people in the operation against Harold Keke along the southern coast of Guadalcanal. In April three of Keke's close associates deserted him and reported that they had witnessed him carry out nine murders in recent weeks. The killings were mostly thought to have involved his own supporters whom he had suspected of

SOLOMON ISLANDS

Introductory Survey

collaborating with the police. In May it was reported that Keke had taken six missionaries hostage in southern Guadalcanal. In a separate incident on Malaita, in the same month, an Australian missionary was beheaded.

In early June 2003 Kemakeza travelled to Canberra for a meeting with the Australian Prime Minister, John Howard, at which he requested direct foreign intervention in order to halt the islands' worsening law and order crisis. (Former Prime Minister Manasseh Sogavare had made a similar appeal for Australia to send troops to the country at the time of the signing of the Townsville Peace Agreement in October 2000, but the request had been rejected.) In mid-June senior officials from Australia and New Zealand arrived in Solomon Islands to assess the possibility of mounting a regional intervention in the country. At a meeting of the Pacific Islands Forum in Sydney, Australia, later that month, delegates from the 16 nations agreed unanimously to send a multinational intervention force to Solomon Islands; eight island members stated their intention to commit personnel to the force. The proposed action was to constitute the largest armed intervention in the South Pacific since the Second World War.

Meanwhile, reports of violence and intimidation by Harold Keke and his rebel forces continued during June 2003. At least 23 people (including 11 members of a religious order) were taken hostage and several more were killed. An estimated 1,000 villagers fled their homes after Keke took control of a police post, thereby expanding the area under his control. The rebel leader also burned two villages where he believed that local people had informed the authorities of his activities. Furthermore, in the same month his militia forced some 1,200 people at gun-point to stand along several stretches of beach in order to serve as a human shield and thereby prevent a planned police landing in the area. Atrocities continued in the following month when another settlement (of some 500 people) was burned on Keke's orders and a number of people (including several children) were beaten to death or beheaded.

Discussions continued throughout July 2003 regarding the nature of the proposed regional intervention force and its role in the country. The Australian Government presented a document to Kemakeza stating its requirements for the intervention to proceed, which included unhindered access to the country's financial records and the appointment of up to 100 foreign nationals to senior positions in the islands' public service and government sectors. The economic component of the proposed intervention would also provide for the payment of Solomon Islands' domestic and foreign debts through increased aid from Australia and New Zealand. Displaced villagers (estimated to total 20,000 since ethnic violence intensified in 2000) were to receive a specific allocation of $A100,000 in aid from Australia. On 10 July the Solomon Islands Government unanimously approved legislation to allow the Australian-led force into the country. The Australian Cabinet approved the deployment on 22 July, and two days later the warship HMAS *Manoora* arrived in Honiara with 400 personnel. Howard had said, in relation to the intervention, that it was 'not in Australia's interests to have a number of failed states in the Pacific', which led some commentators to speculate that Australia was acting out of fears for its own security rather than through concern for the people of Solomon Islands. In the following days a total of 2,225 troops and police arrived in the islands from various other countries including New Zealand, Papua New Guinea, Fiji, Tonga, Vanuatu and Samoa. In November 2004 Tuvalu sent two police officers to join the regional forces, bringing the number of countries involved in the operation to 11. The murder of an Australian soldier in the same month prompted Australia to increase the number of its defence personnel in Solomon Islands by 100.

In early August 2003 the UN Secretary-General, Kofi Annan, commended the Pacific island countries for their efforts to support Solomon Islands and stated that the UN was prepared to contribute actively to any future peace process in the country. On 13 August Harold Keke surrendered and was arrested, along with 10 of his close associates. Thousands of villagers gathered to watch as Keke handed over a large number of firearms and was taken away on HMAS *Manoora* for his own safety. Two days later the MEF surrendered around 100 weapons in a decommissioning ceremony presided over by Nick Warner, the senior diplomat in charge of the multinational force. Later that month a 17-member 'economic assistance team' arrived in Solomon Islands, some of whom were to assume key roles in government and the public service in order to implement major reforms. The Australian Prime Minister also made a one-day visit to the islands. By early September the regional forces announced that they had collected a total of 3,850 weapons since the start of a firearms amnesty a month earlier. Australia began to withdraw its troops in late October and by early December more than one-half of its personnel had left the islands.

The capture and arrest of members of various militia groups, including two individuals who had been signatories to the Townsville Peace Agreement, continued during late 2003. Two senior members of the MEF, including Police Superintendent Mannaseh Maelanga, who had served as its Supreme Commander were arrested in November. Maelanga was sentenced to one year's imprisonment in March 2004. Meanwhile, Andrew Te'e, former Supreme Commander of the Isatabu Freedom Movement, was arrested and charged with the murder of three people. Moreover, the trial of Keke and three of his closest associates on multiple charges of murder and abduction began in February 2004. Keke and two of his associates were found guilty of the murder in 2002 of Augustine Geve, a cabinet minister and Catholic priest. He was expected to stand trial for other alleged offences, including the murder of seven missionaries, in the following months.

The Government was subject to considerable embarrassment in December 2003 when the Minister for Communications, Aviation and Meteorology, Daniel Fa'afunua, was arrested and charged with the assault of his wife and of a female police officer, with being drunk and disorderly and of demanding money with menaces. The former minister was found guilty in February 2004 and received a lengthy prison sentence. In September of that year the Minister for Agriculture and Livestock, Alex Bartlett, was arrested on charges relating to violent offences that had occurred during 2000, when he was involved in the leadership of the MEF. In June 2004 Nathaniel Waena, the former Minister for National Unity, Reconciliation and Peace, was elected Governor-General, with 27 parliamentary votes, and in the following month was duly sworn in.

Further controversy within the Cabinet arose in early 2005 when the Minister for Provincial Government, Clement Rojumana, was arrested on 25 corruption charges and the Minister for Police, Michael Maina, was charged with theft. Both ministers were replaced in March. In April the former Minister for Finance, Francis Zama, was charged with official corruption over the alleged granting to himself of an exemption from the payment of goods tax during his period in office. Moreover, a police investigation in mid-2005 claimed that the Minister for Health, Benjamin Una, had been involved in two shooting incidents in 2004 that had targeted personnel from the regional intervention force, including the killing of an Australian officer. Una denied the allegations and accused the Australian-led intervention force of demonstrating a lack of respect towards Solomon Islands leaders, chiefs, customs and culture. In October 2005 the Minister for Fisheries and Marine Resources, Paul Maenu'u, was obliged to resign, following intense criticism of his decision to vote, at a meeting of the International Whaling Commission, in favour of a reintroduction of commercial whaling, in defiance of the Government's stated position. Mathias Taro was appointed to replace Maenu'u. In November Benjamin Una submitted his resignation as Minister for Health, having been arrested and charged with stealing aid funds that had been donated for a development project in his parliamentary constituency. Johnson Koli was named as the new Minister for Health. Alfred Sasako was appointed as Minister for Infrastructure and Development in the same month, but was dismissed in March 2006 following allegations of misconduct. In January 2006, meanwhile, Simeon Bouro was named as Minister for Mines and Energy.

In November 2005 the Prime Minister became involved in controversy with regard to the allocation of loans from a Taiwanese bank. It was claimed that during his tenure of the post of Minister for National Unity and Reconciliation in 2001, Sir Allan Kemakeza had received compensation of US $121,000 for personal losses incurred during ethnic unrest. Following an audit, it was revealed that millions of dollars could not be accounted for and that no apparent effort to locate the missing funds had been made, with the Cabinet having remained unaware of the situation.

In the legislative election held on 5 April 2006 around one-half of the incumbent members of the National Parliament were reported to have lost their seats. It was believed that only 16 of the 50 incoming members had formally declared their party affiliation prior to the election, a situation that drew attention to the weaknesses of the political system prevailing in the country, whereby electors tended to vote for individuals rather than for representatives of specific political parties. It was subsequently reported that independents occupied 30 seats and that the recently formed Solomon Islands Party for Rural Advancement (SIPRA), led by Job Dudley Tausinga, held four seats, the National Party four seats, the PAP three seats and the Solomon Islands Democratic Party three seats, with the remainder being distributed among various other parties. Lobbying then began, in advance of a secret parliamentary ballot to elect the Prime Minister, with a view to the formation of a coalition Government. On 18 April three candidates participated in the contest for the post of Prime Minister, but none secured the requisite majority in the first session of voting in Parliament. Manasseh Sogavare was thus eliminated and a second ballot took place, at which Snyder Rini, leader of the Association of Independent Members of Parliament and former Deputy Prime Minister, received 27 parliamentary votes, while Job Dudley Tausinga won 23.

Rini's appointment as Prime Minister led to widespread protests. A group calling itself People's Power delivered a petition to the Governor-General demanding Rini's immediate resignation, claiming that he had been involved in corruption and bribery. It was variously alleged that Rini had accepted funding from the local Chinese business community and from both mainland Chinese and Taiwanese supporters who hoped to influence the electoral process. Snyder Rini was nevertheless sworn in on 20 April. Public dissatisfaction mounted, however, culminating in two days of the most serious rioting witnessed in the country for many years. Much of the capital was left in ruins, and in particular many local Chinese businesses and homes were destroyed in arson attacks. It was reported that more than 300 citizens of the People's Republic of China had been evacuated from Honiara to their homeland. A curfew was imposed, and in an attempt to restore law and order in the capital Australia dispatched reinforcements of 110 soldiers and 70 police officers. Several opposition politicians were among those arrested in connection with the rioting. Shortly before a parliamentary vote of 'no confidence' was scheduled to take place, however, and after just eight days in the post of Prime Minister, Snyder Rini announced his decision to resign. The announcement led to scenes of jubilation in Honiara, although Rini remained in office in an acting capacity, pending a fresh parliamentary ballot to choose the next Prime Minister. On 4 May Manasseh Sogavare was elected, securing 28 votes; Fred Fono, who had briefly served as Deputy Prime Minister in the interim Government, received 22 votes. The majority of Solomon Islanders appeared to welcome the appointment of Manasseh Sogavare, who on the following day announced the composition of his Cabinet. Job Dudley Tausinga was appointed as Deputy Prime Minister, also assuming responsibility for the portfolio of forestry, environment and conservation. Bartholomew Ululfa'alu was named Minister for Finance and Treasury; Patteson Oti became Minister for Foreign Affairs; and Bernard Ghiro was appointed Minister for Home Affairs. Australia and New Zealand were highly critical of the appointments of Charles Dausabea, the Minister for Police and National Security, and of Nelson Ne'e, Minister for Culture and Tourism, who had been charged in connection with their alleged incitement of the recent riots. Both Ministers remained in custody and were unable to attend the swearing-in ceremony of the new Cabinet. Following his assumption of office, the new Prime Minister announced that the country's economic strategies were to be reorientated (see Economic Affairs) and that a new policy regarding the management of Taiwanese financial aid to Solomon Islands was to be formulated, to permit greater transparency in the use of such funds. In mid-May it was announced that Taiwan's first quarterly payment in relation to the Rural Constituency Development Fund (RCDF) had been released. Total Taiwanese aid was projected at US $2.9m. annually.

From 2004 the huge increase in the production of round logs in Solomon Islands led to considerable disquiet among community representatives, landowners and environmentalists. The total harvest of round logs in that year was estimated at more than 900,000 cu m, which was equivalent to five times the sustainable limit for timber production in the country. In November a petition of more than 1,000 signatures was delivered to the Government, demanding a reduction in the current rate of logging, increased regulation of logging activity by foreign companies and a greater role for local communities in decisions made about their forestry resources. The petition, which contained endorsements from every province in Solomon Islands, urged the Government to approve legislation known as the Forests Bill 2004, providing for the sustainable management of the forestry industry in the country. However, the Government postponed consideration of the proposed legislation, and it was reported that logging rates had increased yet further in anticipation of its introduction. Concerns were again aroused in late 2005, and in December the people of Maniwiriwiri village on Makira island staged a peaceful protest, successfully preventing bulldozers from passing through the village and gaining access to a logging project located near the site of the residents' water supply and dam. This was one of many peaceful protests in an area where the local community was taking an increasingly strong stance against logging operations.

In 1990 relations between Papua New Guinea and Solomon Islands deteriorated, following allegations by the Solomon Islands' Government that patrol boats from Papua New Guinea were interfering with the traditional crossing between Bougainville Island (Papua New Guinea) and the Shortland Islands, while the Papua New Guinea Government accused Solomon Islands of harbouring members of the rebel BRA and of providing them with supplies. Despite the signing that year of an agreement on joint border surveillance and arrangements to host peace negotiations between the BRA and the Papua New Guinea Government, relations worsened considerably in 1992 when Papua New Guinea forces carried out several unauthorized incursions into the Shortland Islands, in which a fuel depot was destroyed and two Solomon Islanders were killed. Alleging Australian involvement in the incursions, Mamaloni suspended surveillance flights by the Australian air force over its territory, and relations between the two countries deteriorated significantly. Despite the initiation of discussions between Solomon Islands and Papua New Guinea in January 1993, further incursions were reported in April. Following the election of a new Government in May in Solomon Islands, however, relations appeared to improve, and subsequent negotiations between the two countries resulted in an agreement to close the BRA office in Honiara. Tensions with Papua New Guinea, however, increased in 1996 as violence on Bougainville intensified. Numerous incursions by Papua New Guinea defence forces into Solomon Islands' waters were reported, while the Papua New Guinea Government repeated accusations that Solomon Islands was harbouring BRA activists. However, in June 1997 Papua New Guinea and Solomon Islands concluded a maritime border agreement, following several years of negotiations. The purpose of the agreement was not only to delineate the sea boundary between the two countries but also to provide a framework for co-operation in matters of security, natural disaster, customs, quarantine, immigration and conservation. In December 1997 the Prime Ministers of the two countries paid an extended visit to Bougainville to express support for the recently established truce agreement. Furthermore, the Governor of Bougainville was sympathetic to the problem of increasing numbers of Solomon Islanders from the Western Province crossing to Bougainville in late 2001. Many were trading goods in Bougainville in exchange for food and services. Discussions regarding the border of Papua New Guinea were held in April 2002; both Governments were concerned about the increase of weapons trafficking from Bougainville to the Western Province. Renewed border discussions took place between the two countries in June 2003. A development agreement that included joint infrastructural development, technical assistance and information sharing was signed by the two Governments in March 2005.

In March 1988 Solomon Islands signed an agreement with Vanuatu and Papua New Guinea to form the Melanesian Spearhead Group. The new group regarded as its principal aims the preservation of Melanesian cultural traditions and the attainment of independence by the French Overseas Territory of New Caledonia. In March 1990 the Melanesian Spearhead Group admitted the FLNKS (the main Kanak, or Melanesian, political group in New Caledonia). In mid-1994 the group concluded an agreement regarded as the first step towards the establishment of a free-trade area by the three countries. Fiji was admitted to the group in mid-1996. Solomon Islands announced its commitment to further economic integration between the countries of the Melanesian Spearhead Group in late 1997. In October 1995 Solomon Islands became a signatory of the Federated States of Micronesia Agreement on Regional Fisheries Access. In early 1997 Solomon Islands and Vanuatu agreed to undertake negotiations on the maritime boundaries between the two countries in an attempt to clarify uncertainty regarding fishing rights.

Solomon Islands attracted international criticism in mid-2003 for its practice of capturing and exporting large numbers of live dolphins. Police mounted a large-scale security operation around

Honiara airport to prevent journalists from filming some 200 dolphins being loaded into a cargo aeroplane bound for Mexico. Several reports of harassment and violence against foreign journalists were received. It was believed that, owing to the high price commanded by the sale of the animals, senior Solomon Islands officials were likely to be involved. The trade in wild dolphins has been prohibited by most developed countries under a Convention on International Trade in Endangered Species of Wild Flora and Fauna. The trade was not only a cause for concern among foreigners, however, and in late 2003 one of the country's important traditional houses of chiefs, the Gela, expressed disquiet over the treatment that the animals had received. In December 2004 a consignment of dolphins was prevented from being exported after representatives from the fishing industry complained that the trade was harming the reputation of the islands' important tuna industry (widely perceived by Western countries to be 'dolphin-friendly'). The export of dolphins was subsequently banned upon the entry into force in November 2005 of a new law; those found to have contravened the regulations would face a minimum fine and the possibility of a prison sentence of six months.

A seven-member parliamentary delegation, including five cabinet ministers, travelled to Taiwan in September 2004 to discuss mutual co-operation. One of the most important issues to be debated was the review of Taiwan's annual aid programe to Solomon Islands.

Solomon Islands' relations with Japan attracted international attention in mid-2005, when, following receipt of US $6.7m. from the Japanese Government for a major project to improve Honiara Airport, Solomon Islands voted with Japan (see above) to remove a 20-year moratorium on commercial whaling at a meeting of the International Whaling Commission (thereby reneging on a recent commitment to abstain from the vote). Its decision to support Japan's pro-whaling position resulted in the removal of Solomon Islands from a list of destinations promoted by several international diving organizations, which was likely to have a negative impact on the country's tourism industry.

Government

Under the 1978 Constitution, executive authority is vested in the British monarch, as Head of State, and is exercisable by the monarch's representative, the Governor-General, who is appointed on the advice of Parliament and acts on the advice of the Cabinet. Legislative power is vested in the unicameral National Parliament, with 47 members elected by universal adult suffrage for four years (subject to dissolution) in single-member constituencies. The Cabinet is composed of the Prime Minister, elected by Parliament, and other ministers appointed by the Governor-General on the Prime Minister's recommendation. The Cabinet is responsible to Parliament. The country comprises four Districts, within which there are nine local government councils, elected by universal adult suffrage. The Constitution provides for further devolution of power to provincial authorities.

Defence

Prior to the coup of June 2000, a unit within the Police Force, the Police Field Force, received technical training and logistical support from Australia and New Zealand. The Force latterly had two patrol boats and undertook surveillance activities in Solomon Islands' maritime economic zone. The Solomon Islands Peace Plan, signed in July 2000, provided for the establishment of a Ministry of Defence, which was to be independent of the Ministry of Police, Justice and Legal Affairs. The Ministry of Defence would, as one of its first tasks, introduce legislation to permit the establishment of a Solomon Islands Defence Force. A national reconnaissance and surveillance force was founded in 1995, and was also to become answerable to the new ministry.

Economic Affairs

In 2004, according to estimates by the World Bank, Solomon Islands' gross national income (GNI), measured at average 2002–04 prices, was US $260.3m., equivalent to US $550 per head (or $1,760 on an international purchasing-power parity basis). During 1995–2004, it was estimated, the population increased at an average annual rate of 2.8%, while gross domestic product (GDP) per head decreased, in real terms, at an average annual rate of 4.3%. Overall GDP decreased, in real terms, at an average annual rate of 1.6% in 1995–2004. According to the Asian Development Bank (ADB), GDP increased by 3.6% in 2003 and by 4.5% in 2004. It was estimated that GDP expanded by 4.4% in 2005.

Agriculture (including hunting, forestry and fishing) contributed 47.7% of GDP (measured at constant 1985 prices) in 2002. In 2003 an estimated 72% of the working population were involved in agriculture. The principal cash crops have traditionally included coconuts, cocoa, rice and oil palm. Earnings from copra (which was for many years the country's main export) rose from SI $7.8m. in 2003 to SI $25.5m. in 2004. High prices on the world market for cocoa in the early 2000s increased the value of exports of that commodity, which reached SI $53.2m. in 2003, before declining to SI $40.4m. in 2004. In April 2003 the Government announced plans to reopen a major palm oil plant that had remained closed since 1999 owing to civil unrest. By November 2005 the rehabilitation of the palm oil mill in Guadalcanal had created many new jobs, with more than 1,000 people being employed in reconstruction work. The new operating company, Guadalcanal Plains Palm Oil Ltd, intended to replant thousands of ha of the former plantations; it was hoped that in due course as many as 3,000 new jobs would be created, with an area of 12,000 ha being cleared for new plantations. Spices are cultivated for export on a small scale, while in the 1990s the production of honey became increasingly important. The main subsistence crops are root crops, garden vegetables and fruit. Pigs and cattle are also reared. Seaweed farming has been introduced, and sea-shells are exported. The country's first shipment of seaweed was exported to France in early 2004. However, adverse weather conditions during late 2005 destroyed much of the crop in Solomon Islands. Income from this source decreased further when a reduction in seaweed prices was announced in March 2006. The Solomon Seaweed Company's buyer in France was forced to lower the price of seaweed as a result of an oversupply of stock and higher fuel costs. Giant-clam farming became an important activity in the mid-1990s. Fish accounted for 18.1% of export earnings in 2004. In March 2006 an agreement between Soltai Fishing and Processing Ltd, the Solomon Islands' fish exporter, and Tri Marine International Ltd was concluded, allowing for an expansion of the islands' tuna production and progression towards supplying tuna in catering-sized cans for the previously impenetrable European market. The deal brought the prospect of some 350 jobs, and the arrangements were to be extended to encompass the production of fish meal. The forestry sector is an extremely important source of revenue, timber exports accounting for 64.3% of total export receipts in 2004. A dramatic increase in the production of timber in the early 1990s prompted several international organizations, including the World Bank, to express alarm at the rate of logging in the country. None the less, by the late 1990s Solomon Islands was one of the few remaining countries in the world to allow the export of round logs. It was estimated in the early 2000s that, if logging continued at current levels, all remaining virgin forest in Solomon Islands would be removed by 2015. The rate of logging continued to increase during 2004 and 2005 (see Recent History). The ADB estimated that agricultural GDP grew by 5.6% in 2002, before expanding by 33.1% in 2003 and by 14.0% in 2004.

Industry (including mining, manufacturing, construction and power) contributed 8.2% of GDP in 2002 (at 1985 prices), and employed 13.7% of wage-earners in 1993. The ADB estimated that industrial GDP increased by 4.0% in 2002, 4.5% in 2003 and 6.0% in 2004. Mining employed 0.5% of the working population in 1988. The mining sector's contribution to GDP, which was an estimated 3.1% in 2000, had declined to a negligible percentage by 2002. Compared with the previous year, the mining sector's GDP decreased by 93.6% in 2001, and contracted by a further 83.3% in 2002. Gold is the sole mineral export, but revenue from this source declined from SI $1.3m. (from exports of 50 kg) in 1991 to only SI $57,000 (from 2 kg) in 1997. Other (mainly undeveloped) mineral resources include deposits of copper, lead, zinc, silver, cobalt, asbestos, phosphates, nickel and high-grade bauxite. In early 2005 there was a surge of interest in mineral prospecting by potential overseas investors and the Government received a large number of applications for the prospecting of gold, nickel and diamonds. An application for the renewal of nickel-prospecting licences submitted by Pacrim Resources, however, was rejected in August 2005 after the company failed to pay the fees required and to provide reports on its activities. The company had also invested less in the area than originally anticipated.

Manufacturing contributed 4.1% of GDP (at 1985 prices) in 2002, and employed 15.6% of wage-earners in 1995. The most important branches are food-processing (notably fish-canning), coconut-based products, brewing, saw-milling, logging and handicrafts. Compared with the previous year, The manufacturing sector's GDP contracted by 19.4% in 2001 and by 5.4% in 2002.

Energy is derived principally from hydroelectric power, with solar energy being increasingly utilized. Mineral fuels accounted for 27.4% of the total value of imports in 2004. In 1992 exploratory projects revealed several potential petroleum-producing areas in the islands. Electricity output totalled 58m. kWh in 2003.

Service industries contributed 44.1% of GDP (at 1985 prices) in 2002 and engaged 58.8% of wage-earners in 1993. Tourist arrivals totalled only 1,718 in 2003. The riots of April 2006 (see Recent History) were expected to have a detrimental effect on the tourism sector. Earnings from the sector had declined from some US $13m. in 1998 to an estimated $6m. in 1999. The ADB estimated that the GDP of the services sector contracted by 5.8% in 2002 and by 3.9% in 2003, before expanding by 2.6% in 2004.

In 2005, according to the ADB, there was a visible trade deficit of US $40m. and a deficit of US $31m. on the current account of the balance of payments. In 2004 the principal sources of imports were Australia (25.3%) and Singapore (23.8%), while the principal markets for exports were the People's Republic of China (28.2%), Thailand (15.7%) and the Republic of Korea (15.7%). The principal exports in that year were timber, copra, fish and other marine products, and cocoa. The principal imports were foodstuffs, mineral fuels, machinery and transport equipment and basic manufactures.

In 2004 there was an estimated budgetary surplus of SI $102.1m. According to the ADB, there was a fiscal deficit equivalent to 0.2% of GDP in 2003 and a surplus of 8.3% of GDP in 2004. Budgetary expenditure in 2004 was estimated at SI $608.8m., part of which was to be financed by grants from Australia and New Zealand. Official development assistance declined from US $68.4m. in 2000 to $26.3m. in 2002; of the latter figure $21.3m. was bilateral aid. Aid from Australia totalled $A201.6m. in 2004/05 and a $A246.8m. was projected for 2005/06. Financial assistance from New Zealand rose from $NZ14m. in 2004/05 to a projected $NZ18m. in 2005/06. In 2004, according to the ADB, the country's external debt totalled US $160m. and the cost of debt-servicing was equivalent to 6.4% of the value of exports of goods and services. The average annual rate of inflation in Honiara in 1995–2004 was 9.6%. Compared with the previous year, the rate of inflation was estimated by the ADB at 7.1% in 2004 and at 6.9% in 2005.

Solomon Islands is a member of the Pacific Community (see p. 350), the Pacific Islands Forum (see p. 352), the Asian Development Bank (see p. 169) and the UN Economic and Social Commission for Asia and the Pacific (ESCAP, see p. 33), and is a signatory to the Lomé Conventions and the successor Cotonou Agreement (see p. 277) with the European Union (EU). The country is also a member of the Melanesian Spearhead Group, which provides for free trade among member countries.

The economy of Solomon Islands remains one of the least developed in the Pacific region. Progress has been impeded by inadequate infrastructure, inclement weather, a very high rate of population growth and fluctuations in prices on the international market for the country's major agricultural exports. Increasing environmental concerns over the exploitation of the country's natural resources and its vulnerability to unscrupulous foreign operators have continued to threaten the islands' economic stability. Furthermore, the country's dependence upon forestry—logging being the prime constituent of both taxation and export revenues—rendered the economy vulnerable to the low international prices for round logs prevailing in the early 2000s. The country's logging industry attracted renewed international attention in early 2004 when a chain of islands in the Western Solomons (one of which was the site of a World Bank-funded conservation project) was devastated by intensive logging carried out by a number of foreign companies. Reports indicated that some islands had been completely deforested within a matter of weeks and that coral reefs had been destroyed by the heavy machinery used in the area. The dramatic rise in crime, which in part had occurred as a result of the alleged infiltration of the police force by rebel groups (see Recent History), appeared to be a further deterrent to growth and investment. Youth unemployment remained a particular problem. The expansion of education facilities, plans for which were announced in March 2006 (see Education, below), was expected to provide work experience placements for local youths, who would assist with the construction of buildings and assembly of school furniture. It was hoped that the benefits of broadband internet access introduced by this scheme would also have an impact on other areas of rural development. In July 2003 an Australian-led regional intervention force arrived in the country to restore law and order (see Recent History). The intervention, which had been requested by the Government of Solomon Islands, included an economic recovery programme involving increased assistance from Australia (totalling some $A1,000m. over 10 years) and the appointment of numerous Australian officials to key posts within the Government and public service and finance sectors. The country's development budget for 2005 was to be financed mainly through external grants, most of the funding being allocated to strategic areas of the National Economic Recovery, Reform and Development Plan for 2003–06. Although the resumption of economic growth from 2003 had created inflationary pressures, by 2005 the rate of inflation appeared to have stabilized somewhat, despite the substantial increases in international petroleum prices in the latter year. The ADB originally envisaged a GDP growth rate of 5.0% for 2006; however, the violence that in April accompanied the election to office and brief tenure of Prime Minister Snyder Rini was expected to have a negative impact on the economy. Numerous businesses, owned predominantly by Chinese entrepreneurs, were destroyed in the rioting. Foreign investment, which had remained subdued for several years, was expected to be further depressed. Upon taking office as Prime Minister in May 2006, Manasseh Sogavare announced his intention to reorganize budgetary strategy in order to address the issue of rural development, envisaging the implementation of a programme of land reform. He aimed to accelerate the process of decentralizing major development activities from Honiara to the country's provinces, with greater emphasis to be placed on the role of the private sector. The particular problems faced by indigenous businesses were also to be addressed.

Education

Education is not compulsory in Solomon Islands. Primary education generally begins at six years of age and lasts for six years. Secondary education, normally beginning at the age of 12, lasts for up to five years. In 1994 an estimated 97% of children (104% of boys; 90% of girls) in the relevant age-group were enrolled in primary education, while 17% of children (21% of boys; 14% of girls) in the relevant age-group attended secondary schools. In 1993 there were 523 primary schools, with a total of 55,093 pupils in 2002, while in 1993 there were 23 secondary schools, with a total of 46,082 pupils in 2002. In 1993 10 of the country's secondary schools were national secondary schools, which are run either by the Government or by one of the churches, and the remaining 13 were provincial secondary schools, which are run by provincial assemblies and provide courses of a practical nature, mainly in agriculture and development studies. There are two teacher-training schools and a technical institute. Scholarships are available for higher education at various universities overseas, which in 1987 were attended by 413 students from Solomon Islands. In 1977 the Solomon Islands Centre of the University of the Pacific opened in Honiara. Government expenditure on education was SI $51m. (9.7% of total spending) in 1998. In late 2003 New Zealand announced that it was to provide some US $8.3m. for education projects in Solomon Islands. In the following year US $1.2m. was received from the Japanese Government to upgrade school buildings. In 2005 plans to construct several new educational centres were announced. In an attempt to reduce the number pupils abandoning their studies each year, many new community high schools were to be built over a period of 15 years. The islands were also granted funding for nine new distance learning centres, one to be built in each of the provinces. In November 2005 it was also announced that the University of the South Pacific was to establish a fourth campus in Solomon Islands, thereby reducing the amount of government funding needed to send students overseas. In March 2006 eight schools, four in Western Province and four in South Malaita, were selected for funding to construct new class rooms and to provide, equipment, desks and other facilities.

Public Holidays

2006: 1 January (New Year's Day), 14–17 April (Easter), 5 June (Whit Monday), 6 June (Queen's Official Birthday), 7 July (Independence Day), 25 December (Christmas Day), 26 December (Boxing Day).

2007 (provisional): 1 January (New Year's Day), 6–9 April (Easter), 4 June (Whit Monday), 5 June (Queen's Official Birthday), 7 July (Independence Day), 25 December (Christmas Day), 26 December (Boxing Day).

Statistical Survey

Source (unless otherwise stated): Statistics Office, POB G6, Honiara; tel. 23700; fax 20392.

AREA AND POPULATION

Area: 27,556 sq km (10,639 sq miles).

Population: 285,176 at census of 23–24 November 1986; 409,042 (males 211,381, females 197,661) at census of 21–22 November 1999. *Mid-2004* (UN estimate): 466,000 (Source: UN, *World Population Prospects: The 2004 Revision*).

Density (mid-2004): 16.9 per sq km.

Ethnic Groups (census of November 1986): Melanesians 268,536; Polynesians 10,661; Micronesians 3,929; Europeans 1,107; Chinese 379; Others 564.

Principal Towns (population in '000, 2000): Honiara (capital) 50.1; Gizo 7.0; Auki 5.0. Source: Stefan Helders, *World Gazetteer* (internet www.world-gazetteer.com). *Mid-2003* (UN estimate, incl. suburbs) Honiara 56,339 (Source: UN, *World Urbanization Prospects: The 2003 Revision*).

Births and Deaths (mid-2004): Birth rate 34 per 1,000; Death rate 8 per 1,000.

Expectation of Life (WHO estimates, years at birth): 70 (males 69; females 73) in 2003. Source: WHO, *World Health Report*.

Employment (employees only, June 1993): Agriculture, hunting, forestry and fishing 8,106; Manufacturing (incl. mining and quarrying) 2,844; Electricity and water 245; Construction 977; Trade, restaurants and hotels 3,390; Transport, storage and communications 1,723; Finance, insurance, real estate and business services 1,144; Community, social and personal services 11,148; *Total* 29,577. *1996*: Total employed 34,200 (Source: UN, *Statistical Yearbook for Asia and the Pacific*). *Mid-2003* (estimates, '000): Agriculture, etc. 177; Total labour force 245 (Source: FAO).

HEALTH AND WELFARE
Key Indicators

Total Fertility Rate (children per woman, 2003): 4.4.

Under-5 Mortality Rate (per 1,000 live births, 2004): 56.

Physicians (per 1,000 head, 1999): 0.13.

Hospital Beds (per 1,000 head, 1992): 2.75.

Health Expenditure (2002): US $ per head (PPP): 83.

Health Expenditure (2002): % of GDP: 4.8.

Health Expenditure (2002): public (% of total): 93.2.

Access to Water (% of persons, 2002): 70.

Access to Sanitation (% of persons, 2002): 31.

Human Development Index (2003): ranking: 128.

Human Development Index (2003): value: 0.594.

For sources and definitions, see explanatory note on p. vi.

AGRICULTURE, ETC.

Principal Crops (FAO estimates, '000 metric tons, 2004): Coconuts 240; Oil palm fruit 155; Rice 5.5; Cocoa beans 5; Sweet potatoes 86; Yams 29; Taro 40; Vegetables and melons 7.9; Fruit 19.

Livestock (FAO estimates, '000 head, year ending September 2004): Cattle 13.5; Pigs 652; Chickens 230.

Livestock Products (FAO estimates, '000 metric tons, 2004): Beef and veal 0.7; Pig meat 2.3; Hen eggs 0.5.

Forestry (FAO estimates, '000 cu m, 2004): *Roundwood Removals* (excl. bark): Industrial wood 554; Fuel wood 138; Total 692; *Sawnwood Production*: 12 (all broadleaved, incl. railway sleepers).

Fishing (FAO estimates, metric tons, live weight, 2003): Skipjack tuna 19,014; Yellowfin tuna 6,762; Bigeye tuna 1,526; Total catch (all capture, incl. others): 39,849.

Source: FAO.

MINING

Production (kilograms, 2000): Gold 338; Silver 200 (estimate). Source: US Geological Survey.

INDUSTRY

Production (metric tons, 2004, unless otherwise stated): Copra 22,000; Coconut oil 9,000 (unofficial figure from FAO, 2004); Palm oil 34,000 (unofficial figure from FAO, 2004); Fish 27,000; Electric energy 58 million kWh (2003). Source: Asian Development Bank, *Key Indicators of Developing Asian and Pacific Countries*, unless otherwise indicated.

FINANCE

Currency and Exchange Rates: 100 cents = 1 Solomon Islands dollar (SI $). *Sterling, US Dollar and Euro Equivalents* (30 December 2005): £1 sterling = SI $13.0447; US $1 = SI $7.5758; €1 = SI $8.9371; SI $100 = £7.67 = US $13.20 = €11.19. *Average Exchange Rate* (SI $ per US $): 7.5059 in 2003; 7.4847 in 2004; 7.5299 in 2005.

Budget (SI $ million, 2004): *Revenue*: Taxes 472.1; Other current revenue 37.8; Total 509.9; *Expenditure*: Total 608.8 (Current 506.2; Capital 102.6). Source: Asian Development Bank, *Key Indicators of Developing Asian and Pacific Countries*.

Official Development Assistance (US $ million, 2000): Bilateral 22.1; Multilateral 46.3; Total 68.4 (Grants 69.7, Loans –1.3). Source: UN, *Statistical Yearbook for Asia and the Pacific*.

International Reserves (US $ million at 31 December 2004): IMF special drawing rights 0.00; Reserve position in IMF 0.85; Foreign exchange 79.72; Total 80.58. Source: IMF, *International Financial Statistics*.

Money Supply (SI $ million at 31 December 2004): Currency outside banks 123.24; Demand deposits at deposit money banks 251.11; Total money 374.35. Source: IMF, *International Financial Statistics*.

Cost of Living (Consumer Price Index for Honiara; base: 2000 = 100): 117.7 in 2002; 129.5 in 2003; 138.7 in 2004. Source: IMF, *International Financial Statistics*.

Gross Domestic Product (SI $ million at current prices): 1,721 in 2000; 1,766 in 2001; 1,848 in 2002. Source: IMF, *International Financial Statistics*.

Gross Domestic Product by Economic Activity (official estimates, SI $ million at constant 1984/85 prices, 2002): Agriculture 124.2; Mining 0.1; Manufacturing 10.6; Electricity, gas and water 4.6; Construction 6.1; Trade 27.2; Transport and communications 11.2; Finance 15.2; Other services (including public administration) 61.2; *GDP at factor cost* 260.4. Source: Asian Development Bank, *Key Indicators of Developing Asian and Pacific Countries*.

Balance of Payments (US $ million, 2004): Exports of goods f.o.b. 97.29; Imports of goods f.o.b. –72.19; *Trade balance* 25.09; Exports of services and income 41.34; Imports of services and income –49.65; *Balance on goods, services and income* 16.77; Current transfers (net, obtained as residual) 50.41; *Current balance* 67.18; Capital account (net) 1.50; Direct investment 1.56; Other investments –23.56; Net errors and omissions –3.98; *Overall balance* 43.01. Source: Asian Development Bank, *Key Indicators of Developing Asian and Pacific Countries*.

EXTERNAL TRADE

Principal Commodities (SI $ '000, 2004): *Imports c.i.f.*: Food and live animals 101,492; Beverages and tobacco 7,775; Mineral fuels, etc. 174,766; Chemicals 12,605; Basic manufactures 48,402; Total (incl. others) 637,694. *Exports f.o.b.*: Fish 132,052; Copra 25,549; Timber 468,175; Cocoa 40,419; Total (incl. others) 727,701.

Principal Trading Partners (US $ million, 2004): *Imports*: Australia 35.59; Fiji 5.40; Hong Kong 1.46; India 6.70; Japan 5.48; Malaysia 2.12; New Zealand 7.39; Papua New Guinea 5.25; Singapore 33.42; USA 2.70; Total (incl. others) 140.70. *Exports*: Australia 3.77; China, People's Republic 48.23; India 2.25; Japan 16.60; Korea, Republic 26.84; Philippines 8.73; Singapore 4.97; Thailand 26.89; Viet Nam 5.31; Total (incl. others) 170.76.

Source: Asian Development Bank, *Key Indicators of Developing Asian and Pacific Countries*.

TRANSPORT

Road Traffic (motor vehicles in use at 30 June 1986): Passenger cars 1,350; Commercial vehicles 2,026.

Shipping (international traffic, '000 metric tons, 1990): Goods loaded 278; Goods unloaded 349 (Source: UN, *Monthly Bulletin of Statistics*). *Merchant Fleet* (registered at 31 December 2004): Vessels 28; Total displacement ('000 grt) 8.4 (Source: Lloyd's Register-Fairplay, *World Fleet Statistics*).

Civil Aviation (traffic on scheduled services, 2001): Passengers carried 81,000; Passenger-km 52 million; Total ton-km 6. Source: UN, *Statistical Yearbook*.

SOLOMON ISLANDS

TOURISM

Foreign Tourist Arrivals: 1,245 in 2001; 1,658 in 2002; 1,718 in 2003. Source: Solomon Islands Visitors' Bureau.

Visitor Arrivals by Country (2000, excl. cruise-ship passengers): Australia 1,949; Fiji 231; Japan 182; New Zealand 414; Papua New Guinea 542; United Kingdom 166; USA 433; Vanuatu 280; Total (incl. others) 5,198. Source: Solomon Islands Visitors' Bureau.

Tourism Receipts (US $ million): 16 in 1997; 13 in 1998; 6 in 1999. Source: World Tourism Organization.

COMMUNICATIONS MEDIA

Non-daily Newspapers (1996): 3; estimated circulation 9,000.

Radio Receivers (1997): 57,000 in use.

Television Receivers (2001): 12,000 in use.

Telephones (2004): 6,200 main lines in use.

Mobile Cellular Telephones (2004): 1,500 subscribers.

Personal Computers (2002): 18,000 in use.

Internet Users (2004): 3,000.

Facsimile Machines (1999): 764 in use.

Sources: UNESCO, *Statistical Yearbook*; International Telecommunication Union.

EDUCATION

Pre-primary (1994): 12,627 pupils.

Primary: 523 schools (1993); 2,514 teachers (1994); 55,093 pupils (2002).

Secondary: 23 schools (1993); 618 teachers (1994); 46,082 pupils (2002).

Overseas Centres (1988): 405 students.

Source: mainly UNESCO, *Statistical Yearbook*.

Adult Literacy Rate (estimate based on census data): 76.6% in 2003. Source: UN Development Programme, *Human Development Report*.

Directory

The Constitution

A new Constitution came into effect at independence on 7 July 1978.

The main provisions are that Solomon Islands is a constitutional monarchy with the British sovereign (represented locally by a Governor-General, who must be a Solomon Islands citizen) as Head of State, while legislative power is vested in the unicameral National Parliament composed of 50 members (increased from 47 in 1997), elected by universal adult suffrage for four years (subject to dissolution), and executive authority is exercised by the Cabinet, led by the Prime Minister. The Governor-General is appointed for up to five years, on the advice of Parliament, and acts in almost all matters on the advice of the Cabinet. The Prime Minister is elected by and from members of Parliament. Other ministers are appointed by the Governor-General, on the Prime Minister's recommendation, from members of Parliament. The Cabinet is responsible to Parliament. Emphasis is laid on the devolution of power, and traditional chiefs and leaders have a special role within these arrangements. Legislation approved in August 1996 provided for the abolition of the provincial government system and the transfer of legislative and administrative powers from the nine provincial governments to 75 area assemblies and councils controlled by central Government.

The Constitution contains comprehensive guarantees of fundamental human rights and freedoms, and provides for the introduction of a 'leadership code' and the appointment of an Ombudsman and a Public Solicitor. It also provides for 'the establishment of the underlying law, based on the customary law and concepts of the Solomon Islands people'. Solomon Islands citizenship was automatically conferred on the indigenous people of the islands and on other residents with close ties with the islands upon independence. The acquisition of land is reserved for indigenous inhabitants or their descendants.

In mid-1999 it was announced that two review committees had been established to amend the Constitution. They were expected to examine ways in which the traditions of the various ethnic groups could be better accommodated.

The Government

HEAD OF STATE

Monarch: HM Queen ELIZABETH II.

Governor-General: Sir NATHANIEL WAENA (sworn in 7 July 2004).

THE CABINET
(May 2006)

Prime Minister: MANASSEH SOGAVARE.

Deputy Prime Minister and Minister for Forestry, Environment and Conservation: JOB DUDLEY TAUSINGA.

Minister for Public Service, assisting the Prime Minister: JOSES WAWARI SANGA.

Minister for National Reform and Aid Co-ordination: GORDON DARCY LILO.

Minister for Finance and Treasury: BARTHOLOMEW ULUFA'ALU.

Minister for Police and National Security: CHARLES DAUSABEA.

Minister for Justice and Legal Affairs: SAMUEL MANETOALI.

Minister for Education and Human Resources Development: Dr DEREK SIKUA.

Minister for Health and Medical Services: CLAY FORAU SOALAOI.

Minister for Foreign Affairs: PATTESON OTI.

Minister for Commerce, Industries and Employment: FRANCIS BILLY HILLY.

Minister for Culture and Tourism: NELSON NE'E.

Minister for Agriculture and Livestock: TREVOR OLAVAE.

Minister for Lands and Surveys: LESLIE BOSETO.

Minister for Infrastructure and Development: STANLEY FESTUS SOFU.

Minister for Communications, Aviation and Meteorology: PATRICK VAHOE.

Minister for Fisheries and Marine Resources: NOLLEN LENI.

Minister for Mines and Energy: TOSWELL KAUA.

Minister for Provincial Government and Constituency Development: JAPHET WAIPORA.

Minister for Home Affairs: BERNARD GHIRO.

Minister for National Reconciliation and Peace: SAM S. IDURI.

MINISTRIES

There are 21 departments, each headed by a minister, within the 10 Ministries listed below.

Office of the Prime Minister: POB G1, Honiara; tel. 21867; fax 26088; internet www.pmc.gov.sb.

Ministry of Agriculture and Lands: POB G13, Honiara; tel. 21327; fax 21955; e-mail drsteve@solomon.com.sb.

Ministry of Education and Human Resources Development: POB G28, Honiara; tel. 23900; fax 20485.

Ministry of Finance, National Reform and Planning: POB 26, Honiara; tel. 22535; fax 20392; e-mail finance@welkam.solomon.com.sb.

Ministry of Foreign Affairs, Commerce and Tourism: POB G10, Honiara; tel. 2476; fax 20351; e-mail commerce@commerce.gov.sb; internet www.commerce.gov.sb.

Ministry of Health and Medical Services: POB 349, Honiara; tel. 20830; fax 20085.

Ministry of Infrastructure and Development: POB G30, Honiara; tel. 38255; fax 38259; e-mail kudu@mnpd.gov.sb.

Ministry of Natural Resources: POB G24, Honiara; tel. 25848; fax 21245; e-mail kdfmp@welkam.solomon.com.sb.

Ministry of Police, National Security and Justice: POB 1723/404, Honiara; tel. 22208; fax 25949.

Ministry of Provincial Government, National Reconciliation and Peace: POB G35, Honiara; tel. 21140; fax 21289.

SOLOMON ISLANDS

Legislature

National Parliament
POB G19, Honiara; tel. 21751; fax 23866.
Speaker: Sir PETER KENILOREA.
General Election, 5 April 2006 (provisional results)

Party	Seats
Solomon Islands Party for Rural Advancement	4
National Party	4
People's Alliance Party	3
Solomon Islands Democratic Party	3
Social Credit Party	2
Solomon Islands Liberal Party	2
LAFARI Party	2
Independents and others	30
Total	**50**

Election Commission

Electoral Commission: Parliament House, POB G19, Honiara; tel. 20683; e-mail kenilorea@welkam.solomon.com.sb; Chair. Sir PETER KENILOREA.

Political Organizations

Parties in the National Parliament can have a fluctuating membership and an influence disproportionate to their representation. There is a significant number of independents who are loosely associated in the amorphous, but often decisive, 'Independent Group'. The following parties represent the main groupings:

LAFARI Party: c/o National Parliament, POB G19, Honiara; supports an increased role for tribal chiefs in society.

National Party: Honiara; f. 1996; Leader FRANCIS BILLY HILLY.

People's Alliance Party (PAP): Honiara; f. 1979 by a merger of the People's Progressive Party (f. 1973) and the Rural Alliance Party (f. 1977); advocates the establishment of a federal republic; Leader Sir ALLAN KEMAKEZA; Sec. EDWARD KINGMELE.

Social Credit Party: c/o National Parliament, POB G19, Honiara; f. 2006; focuses on the underlying issues of communal tension and economic underdevelopment; Leader MANASSEH SOGAVARE.

Solomon Islands Democratic Party: c/o National Parliament, POB G19, Honiara; campaigns for self-reliance and for ending of country's dependence on external aid.

Solomon Islands Liberal Party (SILP): Honiara; f. 1976 as the National Democratic Party (NADEPA); present name adopted in 1986; Leader BARTHOLOMEW ULUFA'ALU.

Solomon Islands Party for Rural Advancement (SIPRA): Honiara; f. 2006; advocates the decentralization of powers and the recognition of community governance structures and traditional values; Pres. and Leader JOB DUDLEY TAUSINGA; Sec.-Gen. SAM ALASIA.

Other parties that contested the 2006 election included the Christian Alliance Party, the Solomon Islands Labour Party, the Solomons First Party, the One Nation Party and the United Party.

Diplomatic Representation

EMBASSIES AND HIGH COMMISSIONS IN SOLOMON ISLANDS

Australia: Hibiscus Ave, POB 589, Honiara; tel. 21561; fax 23691; internet www.embassy.gov.au/sb.html; High Commissioner PATRICK COLE.

China (Taiwan): Pantina Plaza, POB 586, Honiara; tel. 38050; fax 38060; Ambassador ANTONIO CHEN.

Japan: National Provident Fund Bldg, Mendana Ave, POB 560, Honiara; tel. 22953; fax 21006; Chargé d'affaires (vacant).

New Zealand: Mendana Ave, POB 697, Honiara; tel. 21502; fax 22377; e-mail nzhicom@solomon.com.sb; High Commissioner BRIAN SANDERS.

Papua New Guinea: POB 1109, Honiara; tel. 20561; fax 20562; High Commissioner PARAI TAMEI.

United Kingdom: Telekom House, Mendana Ave, POB 676, Honiara; tel. 21705; fax 21549; e-mail bhc@solomon.com.sb; High Commissioner RICHARD JOHN LYNE.

Judicial System

The High Court is a Superior Court of Record with unlimited original jurisdiction and powers (except over customary land) as prescribed by the Solomon Islands Constitution or by any law for the time being in force in Solomon Islands. The Judges of the High Court are the Chief Justice, resident in Solomon Islands and employed by its Government, and the Puisne Judges (of whom there are usually three). Appeals from this Court go to the Court of Appeal, the members of which are senior judges from Australia, New Zealand and Papua New Guinea. The Chief Justice and judges of the High Court are ex officio members of the Court of Appeal.

In addition there are Magistrates' Courts staffed by qualified and lay magistrates exercising limited jurisdiction in both civil and criminal matters. There are also Local Courts staffed by elders of the local communities, which have jurisdiction in the areas of established native custom, petty crime and local government by-laws. In 1975 Customary Land Appeal Courts were established to hear land appeal cases from Local Courts, which have exclusive original jurisdiction over customary land cases.

Office of the Registrar

High Court and Court of Appeal, POB G21, Honiara; tel. 21632; fax 22702; e-mail chetwynd@welkam.solomon.com.sb.

President of the Court of Appeal: Lord GORDON SLYNN.

Chief Justice of the High Court: ALBERT ROCKY PALMER.

Puisne Judges: ALBERT ROCKY PALMER, JOHN RODNEY BROWN, FRANK KABUI.

Registrar and Commissioner of the High Court: DAVID CHETWYND.

Chief Magistrate: SEKOVE NAQIOLEVU.

Attorney-General: PRIMO AFEAU.

Director of Public Prosecutions: FRANCIS MWANESALUA.

Solicitor-General: RANJIT HEWEGAMA.

Auditor-General: AUGUSTINE FATAI.

Public Solicitor: KENNETH HALL AVERRE.

Chair of Law Reform Commission: (vacant).

Religion

More than 95% of the population profess Christianity, and the remainder follow traditional beliefs. According to the census of 1976, about 34% of the population adhered to the Church of Melanesia (Anglican), 19% were Roman Catholics, 17% belonged to the South Seas Evangelical Church, 11% to the United Church (Methodist) and 10% were Seventh-day Adventists. Most denominations are affiliated to the Solomon Islands Christian Association. In many areas Christianity is practised alongside traditional beliefs, especially ancestor worship.

CHRISTIANITY

Solomon Islands Christian Association: POB 1335, Honiara; tel. 23350; fax 26150; e-mail essica@solomon.com.sb; f. 1967; five full mems, seven assoc. mem. orgs; Chair. Most Rev. ADRIAN SMITH; Gen. Sec. EMMANUEL IYABORA.

The Anglican Communion

Anglicans in Solomon Islands are adherents of the Church of the Province of Melanesia, comprising eight dioceses: six in Solomon Islands (Central Melanesia, Malaita, Temotu, Ysabel, Hanuato'o and Central Solomons, which was established in May 1997) and two in Vanuatu (one of which also includes New Caledonia). The Archbishop is also Bishop of Central Melanesia and is based in Honiara. The Church had an estimated 180,000 members in 1988.

Archbishop of the Province of Melanesia: Most Rev. Sir ELLISON POGO, Archbishop's House, POB 19, Honiara; tel. 21892; fax 21098; e-mail epogo@comphq.org.sb.

General Secretary: GEORGE KIRIAU, Provincial Headquarters, POB 19, Honiara; tel. 21892; fax 21098; e-mail gkiriau@comphq.oeg.sb.

The Roman Catholic Church

For ecclesiastical purposes, Solomon Islands comprises one archdiocese and two dioceses. At 31 December 2003 there were an estimated 92,286 adherents in the country. The Bishops participate in the Bishops' Conference of Papua New Guinea and Solomon Islands (based in Papua New Guinea).

SOLOMON ISLANDS

Archbishop of Honiara: Most Rev. ADRIAN THOMAS SMITH, Holy Cross, POB 237, Honiara; tel. 21943; fax 26426; e-mail ahonccsi@solomon.com.sb.

Other Christian Churches

Assembly of God: POB 928, Honiara; tel. and fax 25512; f. 1971; Gen. Supt Rev. JERIEL OTASUI.

Christian Fellowship Church: Church, Paradise, Munda, Western Province; f. 1960; over 5,000 mems in 24 villages; runs 12 primary schools in Western Province.

Seventh-day Adventist Mission: POB 63, Honiara; tel. 21191; over 9,000 mems on Guadalcanal and over 6,800 on Malaita (Oct. 2000); Pres. of Western Pacific Region NEIL WATTS; Sec. Pastor J. PIUKI TASA.

South Seas Evangelical Church: POB 16, Honiara; tel. 22388; fax 20302; Pres. ERIC TAKILA; Gen. Sec. CHARLES J. RAFEASI.

United Church in Solomon Islands: POB 82, Munda, Western Province; tel. 61125; fax 61143; e-mail ucsihq@solomon.com.sb; a Methodist church; Bishop of Solomon Islands Region Rev. PHILEMON RITI; Gen. Sec. GINA TEBULU.

BAHÁ'Í FAITH

National Spiritual Assembly: POB 245, Honiara; tel. 22475; fax 25368; e-mail bahainsa@welkam.solomon.com.sb.

ISLAM

Solomon Islands Muslim League: POB 219, Honiara; tel. 21773; fax 24243; Gen. Sec. Dr MUSTAPHA RAMO; 66 mems.

The Press

Agrikalsa Nius (Agriculture News): POB G13, Honiara; tel. 21211; fax 21955; f. 1986; monthly; Editor ALFRED MAESULIA; circ. 1,000.

Citizens' Press: Honiara; monthly.

Link: Solomon Islands Development Trust, POB 147, Honiara; tel. 21130; fax 21131; pidgin and English; 3 or 4 a year.

Solomon Nius: POB 718, Honiara; tel. 22031; fax 26401; monthly; Dept of Information publication; Editor-in-Chief THOMAS KIVO; monthly; circ. 2,000.

Solomon Star: POB 255, Honiara; tel. 22913; fax 21572; f. 1982; daily; English; Dir JOHN W. LAMANI; Editor OFANI EREMAI (acting); circ. 4,000.

Solomon Times: POB 212, Honiara; tel. 39197; fax 39197; weekly; Chief Editor and Man. Dir EDWARD KINGMELE.

Solomon Voice: POB 1235, Honiara; tel. 20116; fax 20090; f. 1992; daily; circ. 3,000; Editor CAROL COLVILLE.

Broadcasting and Communications

TELECOMMUNICATIONS

Telekom (Solomon Telekom Company Ltd): POB 148, Honiara; tel. 21576; fax 23110; e-mail sales@telekom.com.sb; internet www.solomon.com.sb; 59.14% owned by Solomon Islands National Provident Fund, 37.75% by Cable and Wireless plc., 3.11% by Investment Corpn of Solomon Islands; operates national and international telecommunications links; Chair. JOHN BEVERLEY; Gen. Man. MARTYN ROBINSON.

BROADCASTING

Radio

Solomon Islands Broadcasting Corporation: POB 654, Honiara; tel. 20051; fax 23159; e-mail sibcnews@solomon.com.sb; internet www.sibconline.com.sb; f. 1976; daily transmissions in English and Pidgin; broadcasts total 112 hours per week; Chair. FRANK PULE; Broadcast Operations Man. DAVID PALAPU; Gen. Man. JOHNSON HONIMAE; Editor WALTER NALANGU.

Finance

The financial system is regulated and monitored by the Central Bank of Solomon Islands. There are three commercial banks and a development bank. Financial statutory corporations include the Home Finance Corpn (which took over from the Housing Authority in 1990), the Investment Corporation of Solomon Islands (the state holding company) and the National Provident Fund. At the end of 1996 there were 142 credit unions, with some 17,000 members and total assets estimated at SI $18m.

BANKING

(cap. = capital; res = reserves; dep. = deposits; brs = branches; amounts in Solomon Islands dollars)

Central Bank

Central Bank of Solomon Islands: POB 634, Honiara; tel. 21791; fax 23513; e-mail cbsi-it@welkam.solomon.com.sb; internet www.cbsi.com.sb; f. 1983; sole bank of issue; cap. 2.6m., res 31.0m., dep. 179.0m. (Dec. 2003); Gov. RICK HOUWENIPWELA; Deputy Gov. JOHN KAITU.

Development Bank

Development Bank of Solomon Islands: POB 911, Honiara; tel. 21595; fax 23715; e-mail dbsi@welkam.solomon.com.sb; f. 1978; cap. 8.6m., res 4.6m. (Dec. 1998); declared insolvent in Sept. 2004; remained under the administration of the Central Bank of Solomon Islands in 2006; Chair. JOHN MICHAEL ASIPARA; Man. Dir LUKE LAYMAN ETA; 4 brs; 5 sub-brs.

Commercial Banks

Australia and New Zealand Banking Group Ltd (Australia): Mendana Ave, POB 10, Honiara; tel. 21835; fax 22957; Gen. Man. TAIT JENKIN (acting).

National Bank of Solomon Islands Ltd: Mendana Ave, POB 37, Honiara; tel. 21874; fax 24358; e-mail nbsi@welkam.solomon.com.sb; f. 1982; 51% owned by the Bank of Hawaii; 49% owned by Solomon Islands National Provident Fund; cap. 2.0m., res 17.4m., dep. 183.8m. (Dec. 2001); Chair. M. BAUER; Gen. Man. R. CANNOLES; 11 brs and 6 agencies.

Westpac Banking Corporation (Australia): 721 Mendana Ave, POB 466, Honiara; tel. 21222; fax 23419; e-mail gtaviani@westpac.com.au; Man. GIAN TAVIANI.

INSURANCE

About 10 major British insurance companies maintain agencies in Solomon Islands. In mid-1995 the Government announced a joint venture with an Australian insurance company to establish the Solomon Islands Insurance Company.

Trade and Industry

GOVERNMENT AGENCY

Investment Corporation of Solomon Islands: POB 570, Honiara; tel. 22511; fax 21263; holding company through which the Government retains equity stakes in a number of corporations; Chair. THOMAS KO CHAN.

DEVELOPMENT ORGANIZATION

Solomon Islands Development Trust (SIDT): POB 147, Honiara; tel. 21130; fax 21331; e-mail sidt@welkam.solomon.com.sb; f. 1982; development org.; Chief Officer ABRAHAM BALANISIA.

CHAMBER OF COMMERCE

Solomon Islands Chamber of Commerce and Industry: POB 650, Honiara; tel. 39542; fax 39544; e-mail chamberc@solomon.com.sb; 69 member cos (July 2004); Chair. IVAN DYER; Gen. Sec. SALLY ZIKU.

INDUSTRIAL AND TRADE ASSOCIATIONS

Association of Mining and Exploration Companies: c/o POB G24, Honiara; f. 1988; Pres. NELSON GREG YOUNG.

Commodities Export Marketing Authority: POB 54, Honiara; tel. 22528; fax 21262; e-mail cema@solomon.com.sb; sole exporter of copra; agencies at Honiara and Yandina; Chair. HUGO RAGOSO; Gen. Man. MOSES PELOMO.

Livestock Development Authority: Honiara; tel. 29649; fax 29214; f. 1977; privatized 1996; Man. Dir WARREN TUCKER.

Solomon Islands Business Enterprise Centre: POB 972, Honiara; tel. 26651; fax 26650; e-mail simbec@solomon.com.sb.

Solomon Islands Forest Industries Association: POB 1617, Honiara; tel. 26026; fax 20267; Chair. and Sec. KAIPUA TOHI.

EMPLOYERS' ORGANIZATIONS

Chinese Association: POB 1209, Honiara; tel. 22351; fax 23480; asscn of businessmen from the ethnic Chinese community.

SOLOMON ISLANDS

Federation of Solomon Islands Business: POB 320, Honiara; tel. 22902; fax 21477.

UTILITIES

Electricity

Solomon Islands Electricity Authority (SIEA): POB 6, Honiara; tel. 39442; fax 39472; e-mail mike@siea.com.sb; f. 1961; autonomous, govt-owned entity responsible for generation, transmission, distribution and sale of electrical energy; Chair. DONN TOLIA; CEO M. L. NATION.

Water

Solomon Islands Water Authority (SIWA): POB 1407, Honiara; tel. 23985; fax 20723; f. 1994; Gen. Man. DONALD MAKINI.

CO-OPERATIVE SOCIETIES

In 1986 there were 156 primary co-operative societies, working mostly outside the capital. There are two associations running and aiding co-operative societies in Solomon Islands:

Central Co-operative Association (CCA): Honiara.

Salu Fishing Cooperative Association: POB 1041, Honiara; tel. 26550.

Solomon Islands Consumers Co-operative Society Ltd: Honiara; tel. 21798; fax 23640.

Solomon Islands Farmers and Producers Cooperative Association Ltd: Honiara; tel. 30908.

Western General Co-operative Association (WGCA): Gizo, Western Province.

TRADE UNIONS

There are 14 registered trade unions in Solomon Islands.

Solomon Islands Council of Trade Unions (SICTU): National Centre for Trade Unions, POB 271, Honiara; tel. 22566; fax 23171; f. 1986; Pres. DAVID P. TUHANUKU; Sec. BENEDICT ESIBAEA; the principal affiliated unions are:

Media Association of Solomon Islands (MASI): POB 654, Honiara; tel. 20051; fax 23300; e-mail sibcnews@welkam.solomon.com.sb; Pres. ROBERT IROGA.

Solomon Islands Medical Association: Honiara.

Solomon Islands National Teachers' Association (SINTA): POB 967, Honiara; f. 1985; Pres. K. SANGA; Gen. Sec. BENEDICT ESIBAEA.

Solomon Islands National Union of Workers (SINUW): POB 14, Honiara; tel. 22629; Pres. DAVID P. TUHANUKU; Gen. Sec. TONY KAGOVAI.

Solomon Islands Post and Telecommunications Union: Honiara; tel. 21821; fax 20440; Gen. Man. SAMUEL SIVE.

Solomon Islands Public Employees' Union (SIPEU): POB 360, Honiara; tel. 21967; fax 23110; Pres. MARTIN KARANI; Sec.-Gen. CLEMENT WAIWORI.

Solomon Islands Seamen's Association: POB G32, Honiara; tel. 24942; fax 23798.

Transport

ROADS

There are about 1,300 km of roads maintained by the central and provincial governments; in 1976 main roads covered 455 km. In addition, there are 800 km of privately maintained roads mainly for plantation use. Road construction and maintenance is difficult because of the nature of the country, and what roads there are serve as feeder roads to the main town of an island.

Honiara has a main road running about 65 km each side of it along the north coast of Guadalcanal, and Malaita has a road 157 km long running north of Auki and around the northern end of the island to the Lau Lagoon, where canoe transport takes over; and one running south for 35 km to Masa. On Makira a road links Kira Kira and Kakoranga, a distance of 35 km. Before it abandoned mining investigations in 1977, the Mitsui Mining and Smelting Co built 40 km of road on Rennell Island.

SHIPPING

Regular shipping services (mainly cargo) exist between Solomon Islands and Australia, New Zealand, Hong Kong, Japan, Singapore, Taiwan and European ports. In 1994 internal shipping was provided by 93 passenger/cargo ships, 13 passenger-only ships, 61 fishing vessels and 17 tugs. The four main ports are at Honiara, Yandina, Noro and Gizo. The international seaports of Honiara and Noro are controlled by the Solomon Islands Ports Authority. A new wharf, constructed with EU funding, was opened in Gizo in mid-2004. Six further wharves were to be constructed in other parts of the country with similar funding.

Solomon Islands Ports Authority: POB 307, Honiara; tel. 22646; fax 23994; e-mail ports@solomon.com.sb; f. 1956; responsible for the ports of Honiara and Noro; Chair. NELSON BOSO; Gen. Man. N. B. KABUI.

Sullivans (SI) Ltd: POB 3, Honiara; tel. 21643; fax 23889; e-mail shipping@sullivans.com.sb; shipping agents, importers, wholesalers; CEO MARK WILLIAM CARROLL.

Tradco Shipping Ltd: POB 114, Honiara; tel. 22588; fax 23887; e-mail tradco@solomon.com.sb; f. 1984; shipping agents; Man. Dir GERALD STENZEL.

CIVIL AVIATION

Two airports are open to international traffic and a further 25 serve internal flights. Air Niugini (Papua New Guinea), Air Nauru and Qantas (Australia) fly to the principal airport of Honiara International Airport (located 13 km from the capital), at which a major renovation project financed by Japan was completed in December 2005. In late 2004 Air Pacific (Fiji) resumed a weekly service to Honiara some 20 years after it last operated a regular flight to the country.

Director of Civil Aviation: DEMETRIUS T. PIZIKI.

Solomon Airlines Limited: POB 23, Honiara; tel. 20031; fax 20232; e-mail gzoleveke@solair.com.sb; internet solomonairlines.com.au; f. 1968; govt-owned; international and domestic operator; scheduled services between Honiara and Port Moresby (Papua New Guinea), Nadi (Fiji), Brisbane (Australia) and Port Vila (Vanuatu); Chair. STEPHEN TONAFALEA; Gen. Man. GIDEON ZOLEVEKE, Jr.

Tourism

Tourism is hindered by the relative inaccessibility of the islands and the inadequacy of tourist facilities. Tourist arrivals declined from 25,127 in 2000 to just 1,718 in 2003. The industry earned US $6m. in 1999, compared with $13m. in the previous year.

Solomon Islands Visitors Bureau: POB 321, Honiara; tel. 22442; fax 23986; e-mail visitors@solomon.com.sb; internet www.commerce.gov.sb/tourism/index.htm; f. 1980; Gen. Man. MICHAEL TOKURU; Marketing Man. ANDREW NIHOPARA.

SOMALIA

Introductory Survey

Location, Climate, Language, Religion, Flag, Capital

The Somali Democratic Republic lies on the east coast of Africa, with Ethiopia to the north-west and Kenya to the west. There is a short frontier with Djibouti to the north-west. Somalia has a long coastline on the Indian Ocean and the Gulf of Aden, forming the 'Horn of Africa'. The climate is generally hot and dry, with an average annual temperature of 27°C (80°F). It is hotter in the interior and on the Gulf of Aden, but cooler on the Indian Ocean coast. Average annual rainfall is less than 430 mm (17 ins). The national language is Somali, but Arabic is also in official use. English and Italian are widely spoken. The state religion is Islam, and the majority of Somalis are Sunni Muslims. There is a small Christian community, mostly Roman Catholics. The national flag (proportions 2 by 3) is pale blue, with a large five-pointed white star in the centre. The capital is Mogadishu.

Recent History

Somalia was formed by a merger of two former colonial territories: British Somaliland, in the north, and its larger and more populous neighbour, Italian Somaliland. The United Kingdom established a protectorate in British Somaliland in 1886. Italian Somaliland originated in 1889, when Italy concluded agreements with two local rulers, who placed their territories under Italian protection. Italy's occupation of the region was subsequently extended along the coast and inland, and Italian control was completed in 1927. Italian forces in Somaliland and Eritrea invaded and occupied neighbouring Abyssinia (Ethiopia) in 1935–36. During the Second World War British Somaliland was conquered temporarily by Italian troops, but in 1941 it was recaptured by a British counter-offensive, which also forced the Italians to withdraw from Eritrea, Italian Somaliland and Ethiopia. A British military administration was then established in British and Italian Somaliland.

Under the provisions of the post-war peace treaty of February 1947, Italy renounced all rights to Italian Somaliland. In December 1950, however, the pre-war colony became the UN Trust Territory of Somalia, with Italy returning as the administering power for a 10-year transitional period, prior to independence. The territory's first general election on the basis of universal adult suffrage was held in March 1959, when 83 of the 90 seats in the Legislative Assembly were won by the Somali Youth League (SYL), a pro-Western party led by the Prime Minister, Seyyid Abdullah Issa.

British Somaliland reverted to civilian rule in 1948. The British colonial authorities prepared the territory for self-government, and the first general election took place in March 1959. Fresh elections, for a new legislative council, were held in February 1960, with all parties in favour of early independence and the unification of all Somali territories. Representatives of British Somaliland and the Trust Territory of Somalia met in April and agreed on a merger of the two territories in an independent republic. British Somaliland was granted independence on 26 June 1960, and the merger received unanimous approval by the legislature on the following day.

Accordingly, the union of former British and Italian Somaliland took effect on 1 July 1960, when the independent Somali Republic was proclaimed. Dr Aden Abdullah Osman, hitherto President of the legislature of the southern territory, was elected to be the first President of the new Republic, and the legislatures of the two Somali regions merged to create a single National Assembly. The two dominant parties in former British Somaliland joined with the SYL to form a tripartite coalition government. Dr Abd ar-Rashid Ali Shermarke of the SYL became Prime Minister. In June 1964 Shermarke resigned as Prime Minister and was replaced by Abd ar-Razak Hussein, who formed a cabinet exclusively from members of the SYL. In June 1967, however, Shermarke was elected by the National Assembly to replace President Osman. He appointed a new Cabinet, led by Mohamed Ibrahim Egal, the former Prime Minister of British Somaliland.

On 15 October 1969 President Shermarke was assassinated. Six days later the army seized control in a coup on the eve of a planned presidential election. Power was assumed by the armed forces Commander-in-Chief, Maj.-Gen. Mohamed Siad Barre. The 1960 Constitution was suspended, political parties were abolished and the National Assembly was dissolved. A new Government was formed by the Supreme Revolutionary Council (SRC), chaired by Siad Barre, which proclaimed the Somali Democratic Republic. In October 1970 Siad Barre declared Somalia a socialist state and began a revolutionary programme of national unification and social and economic reform. In July 1976 the SRC dissolved itself, and power was transferred to the newly formed Somali Revolutionary Socialist Party (SRSP), with Siad Barre as Secretary-General.

A new Constitution came into force in September 1979. Elections were held in December for a new legislature, the People's Assembly, which, in January 1980, elected Siad Barre as President of the Republic. Constitutional amendments, approved by the Assembly in November 1984, effectively transferred all powers of government to the President. Despite continuing internal unrest, at elections to the Assembly, in December, a single list of SRSP candidates was reportedly endorsed by 99.9% of voters.

A presidential election, at which Siad Barre was the sole candidate, took place in December 1986, confirming his presidency for a further seven-year term by 99.9% of a reported 4.9m. votes cast. Although Lt-Gen. Mohamed Ali Samater was appointed to the newly created post of Prime Minister in February 1987, the President continued to dominate Somalia's political life.

In October 1981 the Somali Salvation Front formed the Democratic Front for the Salvation of Somalia (DFSS, later renamed the Somali Salvation Democratic Front—SSDF) with two other opposition groups. Together with another group founded in 1981, the Somali National Movement (SNM), and with substantial Ethiopian military support, DFSS guerrillas invaded the central border area of Somalia in July 1982. The invasion was contained by the Somali national forces but, despite US and Italian military aid, they failed to expel the rebel troops from the country. Following a meeting between Siad Barre and Lt-Col Mengistu, the Ethiopian leader, in January 1986, Ethiopian military support for the insurgent groups was reduced, particularly in respect of the DFSS.

Anti-Government demonstrations in Mogadishu in July 1989, in protest at the arrest of several leading Muslim clerics, were violently suppressed by the armed forces, resulting in the deaths of more than 400 demonstrators. Two recently created opposition groups, the United Somali Congress (USC—composed of Hawiye clan intellectuals) and the National United Front of Somalia (allegedly dominated by disaffected army officers), were thought to have orchestrated the demonstrations. In August, amid reports that the ruling Marehan clan had lost the crucial support of the Ogadeni clan, the President offered to relinquish power and announced that the next elections would take place in the context of a multi-party system. At the same time there were reports of fighting between government troops and members of the Ogadeni clan in southern Somalia, and Western sources claimed that the only areas of the country that remained under government control were Mogadishu, parts of Hargeysa and Berbera.

Meanwhile, the USC gained support in the south, where its forces were fighting alongside those of the Somali Patriotic Movement (SPM). In the north the emergence of the Somali Democratic Alliance (SDA), led by Mohamed Farah Abdullah, intensified the challenge to Siad Barre's authority. The President responded to these pressures by dismissing the Government in January 1990 and offering posts (which were refused) in a successor administration to prominent opposition leaders. A new Government, headed by Samater, took office in February.

In July 1990 the Council of Ministers endorsed the proposals of August 1989 for the democratization of Somalia's political system. It was decided that, following a review by the People's Assembly, a new constitution would be submitted to a national referendum in October, and that multi-party legislative and local government elections would be held in February 1991. In August 1990 the USC, the SNM and the SPM agreed to co-ordinate their separate military campaigns to overthrow Siad Barre. In October the Government announced the immediate introduction of the new Constitution and a new electoral code. Siad Barre relinquished the post of Secretary-General of the SRSP, in accordance with the Constitution, which stipulated that the President should hold no responsibilities other than those of the presidency. Despite the apparent readiness of the new Government to hasten the process of political reform, the principal insurgent groups showed no signs of relaxing their military campaigns, and in November SPM forces seized control of Kismayu, in southern Somalia. On 25 December legislation was introduced to permit the establishment of political parties opposed to the Government.

On 1 January 1991 the USC announced that it had captured most areas of Mogadishu and that it had besieged the home of Siad Barre. On 27 January Siad Barre was reported to have fled the capital with those forces remaining loyal to him, and the USC took power. It immediately invited all former opposition groups to participate in a national conference to discuss the democratization of Somalia. On 29 January the USC appointed Ali Mahdi Mohamed (a government minister in the 1960s) as President, in a temporary capacity, and he, in turn, invited Umar Arteh Ghalib (a former foreign affairs minister) to form a government that would prepare the country for democracy. The provisional Government was approved by the President on 2 February. However, both the SNM and the SPM opposed the appointment of Ali Mahdi as interim President.

The USC emphasized that it did not intend to form a permanent government independently of the other insurgent movements that had collaborated in the overthrow of Siad Barre; however, by mid-March 1991 Somalia was close to anarchy. Siad Barre was reported to have relocated to his native region of Gedo, near the border with Kenya, accompanied by loyal armed forces. Opposition movements rejected the USC's invitation to take part in a national conference, and the SNM was reported to have formed an 11-member administration and a legislature to govern the former territory of British Somaliland.

In May 1991 the SNM announced its official support for the secession of the former territory of British Somaliland, and later that month the SNM Central Committee elected Abd ar-Rahman Ahmed Ali 'Tur' as President of the self-proclaimed 'Republic of Somaliland'. In June the Committee approved a 17-member government to administer the territory for a period of two years, after which free elections were to be held.

The SNM declined an invitation issued by the USC to participate in a conference of national reconciliation in June 1991, stating that it did not concern 'Somaliland'. The conference, convened in Djibouti, was attended by representatives of the USC, the Somali Democratic Movement (SDM), the SPM and the DFSS, and was chaired by former President Osman. The conference mandated delegates from the four organizations to travel to 'Somaliland' to persuade the SNM to abandon its declaration of independence. The SNM insisted, however, that the secession of 'Somaliland' from Somalia was irreversible. At a second reconciliation conference in July the four groups that had met in June were joined by the United Somali Front (USF) and the SDA. The leaders of the six groups signed a manifesto, which, *inter alia*, committed them to defeat the forces of Siad Barre (which had regrouped as the Somali National Front—SNF), to readopt the 1960 Constitution, which Barre had suspended in 1969, and to implement a general cease-fire. The manifesto also confirmed Ali Mahdi in his position as Somalia's President for a period of two years pending free elections. The participants in the conference agreed that a transitional government was to be formed, with an equitable distribution of major posts and portfolios among each of the groups. Ali Mahdi was sworn in as President on 18 August 1991, and in September he reappointed Umar Arteh Ghalib as Prime Minister; in October the latter announced the formation of a newly expanded Government, comprising 72 ministers and deputy ministers, in order to ensure equal representation for the six participating groups.

In June 1991 a major rift developed within the USC, and supporters of President Ali Mahdi clashed with those of the USC's military commander, Gen. Mohamed Farah Aidid, in Mogadishu. Aidid objected to Ali Mahdi's assumption of the presidency, since he had commanded the military campaign to overthrow Siad Barre. In July Aidid was elected Chairman of the USC. The internal conflict appeared to have abated following Ali Mahdi's inauguration as President in August: Aidid pledged to support the new President, and the two signed a co-operation agreement. However, in October Aidid rejected the legitimacy of the Government appointed earlier that month, and in November his faction launched a major offensive on the President's positions in the capital. The fighting intensified, and in December Ali Mahdi appealed to the UN to send a peace-keeping force to intervene in the conflict. The UN responded by sending a special envoy to Mogadishu in January 1992. However, the envoy's attempts to negotiate a cease-fire were thwarted by Aidid's refusal to agree to UN involvement in Somalia's internal affairs, and the mission was followed by an escalation in violence. In mid-January Aidid appointed his own, 21-member administration. By the end of March it was estimated that 14,000 people (mostly civilians) had been killed and 27,000 wounded in the hostilities in Mogadishu.

In January 1992 the UN imposed an embargo on the sale of armaments to Somalia. In the following month the UN, the Organization of African Unity, now the African Union—AU (see p. 153), the League of Arab States (the Arab League, see p. 306) and the Organization of the Islamic Conference (OIC, see p. 340) issued a joint appeal for a cease-fire, stating that it was a prerequisite for the granting of humanitarian aid to Somalia. Representatives from the rival factions in Mogadishu subsequently joined the conference and agreed to the terms of a cease-fire accord devised by the international organizations. In March, in discussions with a joint mission of the UN, the OAU, the OIC and the Arab League in Mogadishu, Aidid agreed to some form of monitoring of the cease-fire by a foreign observer mission. In April the UN Security Council approved the establishment of a 'UN Operation in Somalia' (UNOSOM), to comprise a 50-strong observer mission to monitor the cease-fire, while it also agreed, in principle, to the dispatch of a peace-keeping force to protect UN personnel and supplies at Mogadishu's port, and to escort food supplies to distribution points. However, the Security Council needed to obtain consent for the peace-keeping force from both parties involved in the conflict, and Aidid was opposed to the deployment of foreign military personnel in Somalia.

In April 1992 the SNF advanced on Mogadishu, with Siad Barre apparently intent on recapturing the capital. Forces of the SNF came to within 40 km of the capital, but Gen. Aidid's militias decisively repelled them, pursuing them to the south of the country. At the end of April the USC captured the town of Garba Harre, in the south-west, which had served as Siad Barre's base since his overthrow. Siad Barre fled, with some 200 supporters, to Kenya. (Siad Barre was refused political asylum in Kenya, and in May he moved to Nigeria, where he died in exile in January 1995.) In May Aidid's forces and those of the SPM, the SDM and the Southern Somali National Movement (SSNM), with which he had formed a military alliance known as the Somali Liberation Army (SLA), captured Kismayu, which had been held by the SNF. By June the SLA was in control of the majority of central and southern Somalia, making Aidid the most powerful of the country's warlords. In late June the UN secured agreement from the principal factions in Mogadishu for the deployment of the 50-strong observer mission envisaged in the March cease-fire accord. In August Aidid agreed to the deployment of 500 UN troops entrusted with escorting food aid from Mogadishu's port and airport to distribution points.

Also in August 1992 the coalition of Gen. Aidid's faction of the USC with the SPM, the SDM and the SSNM was consolidated with the formation of the Somali National Alliance (SNA), of which Aidid was the leader. Meanwhile, Ali Mahdi strengthened ties with other armed groups hostile to Aidid, notably the SSDF and a faction of the SPM, and forged links with Gen. Mohamed Siad Hersi 'Morgan' (who had led the SNF since the departure of his father-in-law, Siad Barre).

In September 1992 'Somaliland' stated its categorical opposition to the deployment of UN troops within its borders. By early November UNOSOM's 500 armed troops still had not been deployed. However, later in the month UNOSOM secured Mogadishu's airport with the agreement of the clan controlling it. The USA subsequently offered to lead a military operation in the country, with a US contingent of up to 30,000 men. The proposed US operation was sanctioned by the Security Council in early December. Shortly afterwards an advance contingent of 1,800 US marines landed on the beaches of Mogadishu and took control of the port and airport. Aidid and Ali Mahdi had instructed their supporters that the US forces were amicable, and consequently they encountered little resistance. The arrival of the foreign force, however, provoked fierce fighting in Kismayu, Baidoa and the north-east, with rival factions attempting to gain territory before the expected imposition of a cease-fire.

The US members of the Unified Task Force (UNITAF) were reinforced subsequently by troops from 21 other countries.

Shortly after the arrival of UNITAF, Gen. Aidid and Ali Mahdi signed a peace agreement, providing for an end to hostilities between the two USC factions. Aidid and Ali Mahdi subsequently met again and agreed to implement fully their initial peace accord, which had been flouted by both sides. However, shortly afterwards heavy fighting was reported between the SNA and militants of the Murusade clan in north-west Mogadishu.

In January 1993 14 of Somalia's political organizations attended peace negotiations in Addis Ababa, Ethiopia, held under the auspices of the UN. The talks resulted in agreements on an immediate cease-fire, disarmament under UN supervision and the holding of a conference of national reconciliation in March. Despite the cease-fire agreement, hostilities were resumed in various parts of the country almost immediately. In mid-March the national reconciliation conference opened in Addis Ababa, but proceedings were adjourned almost immediately, when Aidid withdrew in protest at an SNF attack on Kismayu. Discussions subsequently resumed, and in late March the leaders agreed to an accord providing for the establishment of a Transitional National Council as the supreme authority in Somalia, with a mandate to hold elections within two years. The Council was to comprise 74 members: one from each of the 15 organizations represented at the conference, three from each of the 18 proposed administrative regions (inclusive of 'Somaliland') and five from Mogadishu.

Agreement on the future government of Somalia was reached hours after the UN Security Council approved the establishment of UNOSOM II, which was to take over responsibility for maintaining security from UNITAF by 1 May 1993. UNOSOM II was to be the UN's largest ever peace-keeping operation, comprising 28,000 military personnel and 2,800 civilian staff, and its first where peace-enforcement without consent from parties within the country was authorized. UNOSOM II was, in addition, to be responsible for overseeing the rehabilitation of the country and the repatriation of Somali refugees. By April Gen. 'Morgan' appeared to be in control of Kismayu, with the SNA accusing UNITAF of supporting the SNF by failing to oppose its advances (a claim that was not wholly refuted by the Belgian forces responsible for the city). In May the USA transferred responsibility for international efforts in Somalia to UNOSOM II whose forces embarked on a series of armed initiatives, including air strikes, against suspected strategic positions of the SNA. Despite the increased scale of UNOSOM operations, Aidid avoided injury or capture during June, prompting the Security Council to issue a formal warrant for his arrest. The violent deaths of three Italian UNOSOM soldiers in July provoked Italian media claims that the military emphasis of the mission, promoted by the USA in pursuit of Aidid, was threatening the security of UN personnel and jeopardizing diplomatic initiatives undertaken by the Italian Government. The situation was exacerbated by a US helicopter attack on a suspected pro-Aidid command centre, which resulted in the deaths of 50–100 Somalis, and the murder, in retaliation, of four foreign journalists by enraged Somali crowds.

Uncompromising media coverage of the aftermath of the deaths of three US soldiers in September 1993, and a violent exchange in the capital in October (which resulted in the deaths of some 300 Somalis, 18 US servicemen and the capture, by local militiamen, of a US helicopter pilot and a Nigerian soldier), prompted widespread public outrage in the USA and encouraged US congressional demands for a reassessment of the US role in Somalia. The US President, Bill Clinton, subsequently announced that all US troops were to be withdrawn by the end of March 1994, regardless of the outcome of attempts to negotiate a political settlement to the conflict by that date. (In the mean time the US military presence was to be increased significantly.) Clinton's decision, announced in October, to withdraw the US Ranger élite forces (which had actively sought to apprehend Aidid) prompted speculation that the release of the US pilot and the Nigerian soldier, secured in mid-October following lengthy discussions between representatives of the US Government and Aidid, had been achieved as part of an undisclosed bilateral agreement. Despite Aidid's declaration of a unilateral cease-fire prior to the talks, and subsequent indications of his willingness to enter into negotiations with the USA (in preference to the UN), fighting between pro-Aidid and pro-Mahdi factions escalated. In December Aidid and Ali Mahdi (who in November reportedly assumed the leadership of the Somali Salvation Alliance—SSA, a coalition of 12 factions opposed to Aidid) attended negotiations in Addis Ababa, but discussions disintegrated with little progress.

In February 1994, in the context of the imminent withdrawal of UNOSOM contingents from the USA and several other Western nations, the UN Security Council revised UNOSOM's mandate, reducing the troop strength of the mission to a maximum of 22,000. In March, following protracted negotiations, initiated by the UN, an agreement on the restoration of peace was signed by Aidid and Ali Mahdi (on behalf of the SSA) in Nairobi, Kenya, committing both sides to a cease-fire, disarmament and the organization of a conference of national reconciliation in May to elect a president, vice-presidents and a prime minister. (A similar agreement, concluded in Nairobi days later between community leaders from the lower Juba region, sought to restore order to the port of Kismayu, where fighting between factions had intensified in February.) Electoral procedures and a future legislative structure were to be decided at a meeting of all signatories to the 1993 Addis Ababa agreement and the SNM, to be convened in April. By mid-1994, however, no such meeting had taken place, with accusations of failure to adhere to the terms of the Nairobi agreement proceeding from both Aidid and the SSA.

In June 1994 the UN Security Council agreed to renew UNOSOM's mandate by four months; in November it extended the mandate to a final date of 31 March 1995. In October 1994 fierce fighting erupted in Mogadishu between Ali Mahdi's Abgal clan and the Murusade clan. Hostilities continued sporadically into January 1995 (resulting in as many as 200 fatalities), in which month the two clans brokered a peace agreement. As the deadline for UNOSOM's departure approached, the competition for control of installations currently held by the UN, in particular the port and airport, became the focus of factional hostility.

In November 1994 UN forces began to withdraw from positions outside Mogadishu in the first stages of UNOSOM's departure. In December Harti and Marehan clansmen fought for control of Kismayu port in the wake of the UN's withdrawal from that town. 'Operation United Shield', to ensure the safe evacuation of the UN troops and civilian personnel, as well as most of the equipment brought in under UNOSOM, was organized and led by the USA. The USA stationed several thousand marines in warships off the Somali coast in December, and in early 1995 they were joined by a multinational force of naval and air force units (comprising some 10,000 armed personnel) in order to protect departing UN employees (by early 1995 some 136 members of UNOSOM had been killed since the beginning of the operation).

In late February 1995 1,800 US and 400 Italian marines landed on Mogadishu's beaches, and command of the remaining 2,400 UN troops and of the whole operation was passed from the UN to the US commander. The marines secured the port and airport, and evacuated the remaining UN soldiers. The departure of the last UN personnel on 2 March (almost one month ahead of schedule) was closely followed by that of the US and Italian marines themselves. Somali looters overran the airport, but armoured cars from Aidid's faction, reportedly accompanied by UN-trained police-officers, took control of the area. Ali Mahdi's Abgal clansmen gained control of the eastern section of the airport, and skirmishes were reported between the two sides. Aidid and Ali Mahdi subsequently agreed on the reopening of the port and set out detailed terms for the 'technical peace committee' that was to administer the port and airport; however, the terms of the agreement were promptly violated by both sides, and fighting for control of the crucial sites resumed.

Significant divisions within the SNA became more apparent in June 1995, following an attempt by disaffected members to replace Aidid with his former aide, Osman Hassan Ali 'Ato', as Chairman of the party. SNA members loyal to Aidid immediately rejected the legitimacy of the actions of the Ali 'Ato' faction and announced the expulsion of the faction from the SNA. In mid-June a conference of reconciliation, convened in southern Mogadishu by representatives of 15 pro-Aidid factions, elected Aidid President of the Republic of Somalia for a three-year term. Five Vice-Presidents, representing the interests of distinct clans, were also elected, and the composition of a comprehensive cabinet was subsequently announced. However, Aidid's presidency and mandate to govern were immediately rejected in a joint statement issued by Ali Mahdi and Ali 'Ato'. In September Aidid's forces seized Baidoa.

Fighting between Gen. Aidid's supporters and those loyal to Ali 'Ato' intensified in early 1996. In July pro-Aidid factions clashed with supporters of Ali Mahdi in Mogadishu, resulting in some 90 fatalities. Aidid was wounded during the skirmishes, and on 1 August he died as a result of his injuries. Despite initial hopes that Aidid's death might result in a cessation of hostilities and the resumption of peace negotiations, on 4 August one of his sons, Hussein Mohamed Aidid (a former US marine and hitherto Aidid's chief of security), was appointed interim President by the SNA leadership council. Hussein Aidid (who was subsequently elected Chairman of the SNA) vowed to continue his father's struggle, and factional fighting quickly resumed.

In October 1996, during negotiations in Nairobi, Ali 'Ato', Hussein Aidid and Ali Mahdi agreed to a series of measures, including the cessation of hostilities; however, fighting resumed in late October and intensified in the following months. In December representatives of some 26 Somali factions (notably excluding the SNA) held protracted talks in Sodere, Ethiopia, under the auspices of the Ethiopian Government and the Inter-governmental Authority on Development (IGAD). The conference culminated in January 1997 in the formation of a 41-member National Salvation Council (NSC), with an 11-member executive committee and a five-member joint chairmanship committee, to act as an interim government charged with drafting a transitional charter and holding a national reconciliation conference. Aidid condemned the establishment of the NSC and accused the Ethiopian authorities of interfering in Somali affairs.

International mediation efforts continued, and in March 1997 representatives of Somali factions participated in talks in Cairo, Egypt, under the auspices of the Egyptian Government and the Arab League. In May Ali 'Ato' and Hussein Aidid were reported to have reaffirmed their commitment to the Nairobi agreement, during a meeting held in San'a, Yemen. Later in the month Aidid and Ali Mahdi signed a reconciliation agreement in Cairo. In December, moreover, at the culmination of negotiations that began in November, 26 Somali faction leaders (including Aidid and Ali Mahdi) signed an accord in Cairo, establishing an end to all hostilities and providing for the eventual formation of a transitional government, charged with holding a general election within three years. A condition of the accord was that a national reconciliation conference be held in Baidoa in February 1998 in order to elect a 13-member presidential council (three representatives from each of Somalia's four principal clans and one from a minority group), a prime minister and a 189-seat legislature. The conference was later postponed on two occasions, not least because troops loyal to Aidid remained stationed in Baidoa.

In September 1999 the UN Secretary-General, Kofi Annan, announced that the UN Security Council was to consider a solution to the Somalia problem, following a proposal made by the Somali Peace Alliance (under the chairmanship of 'Puntland' Leader Abdullahi Yussuf) that central authority in Somalia be gradually rebuilt, beginning with regionally based administrations. This proposal was, however, immediately rejected by the Mogadishu faction leaders and President Egal of 'Somaliland'. In October IGAD delegates met in Addis Ababa to discuss President Gelleh of Djibouti's proposed peace plan for Somalia. They agreed to refer the proposal, which included the involvement of clan elders, religious leaders, non-governmental organizations and the business community in the peace discussions, to an IGAD summit conference to be held in Nairobi in November. In February 2000 IGAD member states finally endorsed Gelleh's peace plan for Somalia, which envisaged the staging of a Somali national reconciliation conference in Djibouti in late April and early May, to be attended by up to 1,500 delegates from various cross-sections of Somali society. Under the plan they would elect members to a new national legislature to be based in Mogadishu, which would, in turn, elect a President. The President would be responsible for choosing a Prime Minister, subject to the approval of the legislature, who would lead a transitional government for a period of no longer than two years, during which time a national constitution would be drafted and a date for elections would be selected. However, although the peace plan was unanimously approved by OAU foreign ministers in March, and also won the approval of the UN and the USA, Egal announced that 'Somaliland' would refuse any attempts to unite it with Somalia. A preliminary peace conference meeting scheduled for mid-March was postponed, owing to the absence of the majority of the participants, although in mid-April 'Puntland' delegates agreed to participate in the conference in Djibouti, provided the conference acknowledge the legitimacy of the 'Puntland' administration.

The Somali national reconciliation conference opened in Arta, Djibouti, on 2 May 2000, with some 400 delegates, representing various Somali clans and political and armed groups, in attendance. By mid-June the number of delegates had risen to around 900, although notably only one of the principal Somali faction leaders, Ali Mahdi Mohamed, was present. Later that month it was reported that the 'Puntland' administration had announced its rejection of the peace conference initiatives and stated that it would not recognize the outcome of the conference. In early July the conference produced a draft national charter, which envisaged the Somali Republic adopting a federal system of government, after a three-year interim period, comprising 18 regional administrations. Furthermore, it provided for the creation of the Somali Transitional National Assembly (TNA), which would consist of 225 members, of whom 25 would be women. In mid-July the Charter was approved by 638 votes to four and the process of electing members to the TNA began. The Charter, which was to serve as the Somali constitution for the three-year interim period, guaranteed freedom of expression and association for all Somali citizens, as well as free access to health and education services. The Charter also distinctly separated the executive, legislative and judiciary and guaranteed the independence of the latter. By late July the commission appointed by the peace conference participants to apportion the parliamentary seats among the various Somali clans had submitted its report. Each of the four major Somali clans (Dir, Hawiye, Darod and Oigil and Mirifleh) was allocated 44 seats, and an alliance of small clans was to receive 24 seats; the remaining 25 seats were reserved for women from the four major clans and the alliance of small clans, each of which would receive five seats. However, disagreements between clans and sub-clans over the distribution of seats ensued, and in early August President Gelleh intervened, suggesting the appointment of a further 20 members to the assembly, thus increasing the total number to 245. Gelleh's proposal was accepted, and on 13 August the TNA held its inaugural session in Arta. On 26 August it was announced that Abdulkasim Salad Hasan, a member of the Hawiye clan, who had held several ministerial positions in the Siad Barre administration, had been elected President of Somalia by the members of the TNA. Hasan obtained 145 of the 245 votes, defeating his nearest rival, Abdallah Ahmed Addow, who gained 92. Hasan was sworn in as President on the following day at a ceremony in Arta, attended by numerous regional leaders, including the Ethiopian Prime Minister, Meles Zenawi, and the Sudanese President, Omar Hassan Ahmad al-Bashir.

On 30 August 2000 President Hasan returned to Mogadishu, where he was greeted by tens of thousands of Somalis. At the same time several Mogadishu faction leaders opposed to the outcome of the Djibouti conference, including Hussein Aidid, Ali 'Ato' and Hussein Haji Bod, met in San'a for talks with Yemeni President Ali Abdullah Saleh, who attempted to persuade them to lend their support to Hasan's administration. However, on his return to Somalia, Aidid implored the international community not to recognise the legitimacy of Hasan's appointment. Furthermore, the authorities of both 'Somaliland' and 'Puntland' subsequently issued directives ordering the immediate arrest of those elected to the TNA should they enter either territory.

On 8 October 2000 President Hasan appointed Ali Khalif Galaydh, a former Minister of Industry in the Siad Barre regime, to the post of Prime Minister; later that month Galaydh announced a 32-member Cabinet.

Throughout late 2000 and early 2001 Hasan and Galaydh made numerous visits abroad, as they attempted to consolidate foreign support for the new Somali administration. However, most notably, relations between Somalia and Ethiopia deteriorated in January 2001, after Galaydh accused Ethiopia of providing arms to factions opposed to the Transitional National Government (TNG). Relations between the two countries were further strained in March, when the Ethiopian authorities allowed several Somali faction leaders to convene in Addis Ababa for a series of meetings, which resulted in the creation of the Somali Reconciliation and Restoration Council (SRRC), headed by Aidid. The following month the SRRC announced its intention to form a national government in direct opposition to the TNG within six months.

In early May 2001 Galaydh appointed 25 members to a Peace and Reconciliation Committee (PRC), chaired by former Prime Minister Abd ar-Razak Hussein, which was charged with obtaining recommendations from a cross-section of Somali factions for ways of accelerating the reconciliation process, defining the most suitable means of establishing a federal system in the country and addressing property and land issues. In mid-July violent clashes were again reported to have taken place in Mogadishu between followers of Aidid and Ali 'Ato' and troops loyal to the TNG, resulting in numerous fatalities. In late July the new administration suffered a further major set-back after Abd ar-Razak Hussein resigned as Chairman of the PRC, claiming that Galaydh had demonstrated a lack of co-operation with the committee and had failed actively to support its work. Abdiqadir Muhammad Adan Zope was subsequently appointed acting Chairman of the PRC.

In mid-October 2001 a group of dissatisfied TNA members proposed a motion of 'no confidence' in the TNG, citing the administration's failure to promote the reconciliation process and its lack of progress regarding the constitution of regional administrations. Later that month 141 of the 174 TNA members participating in the vote approved the motion to dismiss the Galaydh administration, with just 29 deputies indicating their support for the TNG; four members abstained. Galaydh's deputy, Uthman Jama' Ali, became acting Prime Minister. In early November talks, sponsored by President Moi of Kenya, took place in Nairobi between a delegation of TNA members, headed by President Hasan, and moderate members of the SRRC. Aidid declined to attend. Nevertheless, following the conclusion of discussions, both sides reported that some progress had been made and agreed to meet again to continue the *rapprochement* process.

On 12 November 2001 President Hasan appointed Col Hassan Abshir Farah, hitherto Minister of Water and Mineral Resources, as Prime Minister. Farah announced that his first priority was to implement a programme of national reconciliation, and thus the appointment of a new cabinet was delayed until after the conclusion of further peace talks between the SRRC and members of the TNA, which were scheduled to take place in Nairobi later that month. Although the talks were subsequently delayed until mid-December, they were attended by senior members of the SNA (again with the notable exception of Aidid) and representatives of several other Mogadishu faction leaders. On 24 December, in the Kenyan town of Nakura, Farah, on behalf of the TNA, and Mowlid Ma'aneh Mohamed, the Secretary-General of the SRRC, signed a peace agreement, which provided for the formation of an 'all-inclusive government' to ensure equitable power-sharing among all Somali clans and the establishment of a Nairobi-based secretariat to oversee the implementation of the Somali peace process and to solicit funds for it. The parties also agreed to propose an increase in the number of members appointed to both the TNA and the Cabinet. Furthermore, the signatories appealed to those groups currently outside the peace process to join it. However, it was subsequently reported that Aidid had announced his rejection of the agreement.

In mid-February 2002 Farah formed a new 31-member Cabinet, which notably included Dr Hussein Mohamed Usman Jimbir, a former senior member of the SRRC, as Minister of Education. However, several members of factions that had signed the Nakura peace agreement in December 2001, who were expected to be represented in the new administration, were reported to have requested to be excluded from the new Government until a parliamentary committee established to investigate the proposed increase in the number of parliamentary seats had released its recommendations. The reconciliation process in Somalia was further endangered in early April 2002, when the Rahanwin Resistance Army (RRA) announced that it had established a new autonomous region in south-western Somalia, based in Baidoa, to be known as the 'State of South-western Somalia'. The Chairman of the RRA, Mohamed Hasan Nur, was elected as 'President' of the new region for a four-year period.

In late June 2002 the TNG confirmed that it would attend an IGAD-sponsored reconciliation conference scheduled to be held in Kenya in July. The conference was subsequently postponed until September, and early that month the authorities in 'Somaliland' announced that they would not attend the talks. Following a further postponement, the conference opened in the Kenyan town of Eldoret in mid-October in the presence of representatives of the Governments of Ethiopia, Kenya, Uganda, Sudan, Djibouti and Eritrea. Some 350 delegates from various Somali factions attended the opening sessions, including a delegation from the TNG led by Prime Minister Farah. The conference was to be conducted in three phases and in late October, following the conclusion of the first phase, the TNG and a number of Somali factions signed a temporary cease-fire and agreed to abide by the final outcome of the conference; to establish an all-inclusive federal system of government; to combat terrorism; and to enhance the safety of aid workers in the country. Further progress was slowed by continuing deadlock over the allocation of seats to the plenary session of the conference. However, by early December it appeared that the impasse had been overcome, and the TNG and Mogadishu-based faction leaders Aidid, Mohammed Qanyare Afrah, Yalahow and Ali 'Ato' signed a declaration committing themselves to ending violence in the Somali capital. In January 2003, however, Yalahow announced that he would no longer participate in the conference. Yalahow's departure followed the earlier withdrawal of Qanyare Afrah from the proceedings. In February the conference was moved to Nairobi, and, despite a number of cease-fire violations, in the following month the TNG and the remaining faction leaders provisionally agreed on the formation of an administration for Mogadishu and further measures to bring peace to the capital.

In March 2003 faction leaders Qanyare Afrah and Ali 'Ato', along with representatives of the TNG, the RRA and the Juba Valley Alliance (JVA), led by Bare Adan Shire, agreed to establish a new administration for the Banaadir region, which encompasses Mogadishu and its environs. They also expressed their lack of confidence in the IGAD-sponsored peace talks in Kenya and pledged to convene a new national reconciliation conference.

In early July 2003 delegates at the Nairobi conference reached a provisional agreement on the formation of an interim government. The arrangement provided for a transitional unicameral parliament, whose 351 members would be selected by political leaders, and which would remain in operation for four years. The nomination of members of parliament was to be made by the signatories of the December 2002 cease-fire declaration and politicians who were originally, and officially, invited to the conference. However, President Hasan rejected the agreement, which had been signed by Farah, stating that it would divide the country, and in August 2003 divisions between Hasan and Farah intensified. Later that month, just days before the expiry of the three-year mandate of the TNG, Hasan reportedly dismissed Farah and the Speaker of the TNA. Hasan insisted that the current governing institutions would remain in place, despite the expiry of their mandate, until a new President, government and parliament had been installed. Dr Abdi Guled Mohamed, the Minister of Air and Land Transport, was appointed premier, in an acting capacity.

In November 2003 the Somali National Salvation Council, a recently formed alliance of 12 factions, chaired by Yalahow, pledged to boycott any further talks in Nairobi. Despite the expiry of his mandate in August 2003, President Hasan appointed Mohamed Abdi Yusuf, hitherto Deputy Speaker of the TNA, as Prime Minister in early December. In the following month the TNA approved the appointment of a new 37-member TNG, which included three Deputy Prime Ministers. Also in January 2004 talks reconvened in Nairobi with the aim of restoring the faltering peace process. Following a period of intense negotiations, during which Yalahow and the leaders of the JVA, the RRA and the SNF rejoined the discussions, later that month representatives from more than 20 factions in attendance agreed to establish a new transitional parliament, comprising 275 members (rather than the 351 previously agreed), who would serve a five-year term. Once formed, the parliament would appoint a President, who, in turn, would nominate a Prime Minister to form a government. It was envisaged that each of the four major Somali clans would select 61 members of the new legislature, while a coalition of smaller clans would be responsible for choosing the remaining 31 members. Initial optimism that a new government could be swiftly formed proved false, however, as several faction leaders expressed concern at perceived favouritism towards certain groups on the part of the Kenyan and Djiboutian authorities overseeing the talks. Furthermore, there were continuing disagreements over the procedure for selecting the members of the new parliament. Notably, in mid-March more than 150 delegates threatened to withdraw from the Nairobi talks if IGAD failed to address their concerns, and continued attempts to initiate the third phase of talks were delayed. The third phase eventually commenced in mid-May, with the stated aim of selecting and inaugurating a new government by early July.

In mid-June 2004 an arbitration committee was formed in Nairobi to oversee the nomination of members to the new parliament. The deadline for nominations of 21 July was not observed by the Darod and Dir clans; however, by mid-August the majority of the new members of the Transitional Parliament (TP) had been nominated and inauguration ceremonies commenced in Nairobi. On 15 September Shariff Hassan Sheikh Adan, a Mogadishu-based business executive, was elected Speaker of the TP and later that month nominations were invited for the position of President. Following two rounds of voting by the 275 members of the TP on 10 October two presidential candidates remained: Col Abdullahi Yussuf Ahmed, the President of the autonomous region of 'Puntland' (see below), and Abdallah Ahmed Addow, a former Somali ambassador to the USA. At a third round of voting held later that day, Yussuf secured 189 of the 268 votes cast and was sworn in as President of Somalia at a ceremony in Nairobi on 14 October. In early November Yussuf appointed Ali Mohammed Ghedi, a member of the Hawiye clan and a former AU official, as Prime Minister.

On 7 December 2004 Ghedi unveiled a new 31-member Cabinet. Hussein Aidid was appointed Deputy Prime Minister and Minister of the Interior and Security, while Qanyare Afrah became Minister of National Security. Other notable appointees included Ali 'Ato' as Minister of Public Works and Housing and Bare Adan Shire as Minister of Reconstruction and Resettlement. However, the following day a number of ministers resigned from the Government, maintaining that the new administration was too large and did not represent a fair distribution of power among the major clans, and on 12 December the TP, which remained based in Nairobi, overwhelmingly approved a motion of 'no confidence' in Ghedi, effectively dissolving the new Government. Two days later President Yussuf reappointed Ghedi as Prime Minister and in late December that decision was endorsed by 229 members of the TP. Ghedi was tasked with forming a government that more accurately represented the major clans and in early January 2005 Ghedi announced an amended Cabinet, which comprised some 90 ministers, assistant ministers and state ministers. Aidid, Qanyare Afrah, Ali 'Ato' and Adan Shire retained the posts previously awarded to them, while Salim Aliow Ibrow was appointed Deputy Prime Minister and Minister of Finance and Mahmud Abdullahi Jama Deputy Prime Minister and Minister of Information. Later in January 2005 the new Cabinet was approved by the TP.

Shortly after he had taken office, President Yussuf had appealed to the AU and the UN to approve the deployment of a peace-keeping force of up to 20,000 troops to assist with the relocation of the TP and the Government to Mogadishu and to disarm militias in the Somali capital. However, ongoing violence in the city caused plans to be stalled. In early January 2005 the AU stated its readiness 'in principle' to deploy a contingent of peace-keepers to Somalia, although no indication was given of the size of the force or the likely date of its arrival in the country. In mid-January Ghedi announced that the Government would begin the relocation to Mogadishu by the end of that month and envisaged that with the support of international peace-keepers the entire Government and Parliament would be settled in the capital by early May. In late January the head of the Somali police force, Gen. Yusuf Ahmed Sarinle, was killed by gunmen in Mogadishu, reportedly as a result of his support for the Government's plans to deploy foreign peace-keepers in Somalia. Despite further concerns over the security situation in the capital, plans for the relocation of the Government and the Parliament proceeded, and in early February a delegation of 30 members of the TP, led by the Minister of Trade, Muse Sudi Yalahow, arrived in Mogadishu followed by a further 50 parliamentarians, led by Sheikh Adan, a few days later. It was subsequently announced, however, that members of the Cabinet would travel to various parts of Somalia to establish possible locations for the Government's new base and that ministers remained deeply divided on the most suitable course of action. As an AU mission arrived in Mogadishu in mid-February to assess the security situation, thousands of people staged protests against the proposed peace-keeping force and a bomb exploded in the capital killing two people and seriously injuring six others. In late February Yussuf and Ghedi arrived in Somalia to head a delegation, which would investigate potential bases for the new Government; notably, the President and the Prime Minister did not visit Mogadishu as part of their tour. The delegation returned to Kenya in early March and Ghedi's special adviser announced that other towns were being considered as a temporary base for the new Government until violence in the capital subsided.

In mid-March 2005 IGAD defence ministers agreed to deploy a 10,000-strong peace-keeping force, the IGAD Peace Support Mission to Somalia (IGASOM) in the country from 30 April, to be replaced at an unspecified later date by an AU force. Demonstrations were held days later in Mogadishu opposing the deployment of peace-keeping troops from neighbouring countries, and members of the TP were involved in a violent confrontation following a vote to reject the planned deployment. In an attempt to allay fears in Somalia, the IGAD Council of Ministers proposed a compromise solution, in which a reduced IGASOM force of 6,800 would initially be deployed, comprised solely of Sudanese and Ugandan troops. In late March the Somali Government announced that it would temporarily relocate to Baidoa and Jowhar, 90 km north of Mogadishu. However, heavy fighting in Baidoa later in March between supporters of Yussuf and militia opposed to the relocation of the Government outside of Mogadishu resulted in at least 14 fatalities, and in late April the 80 parliamentarians situated in Mogadishu rejected calls from the President and the UN-led Joint Co-ordination and Monitoring Committee to return to Nairobi, stating that a return to exile would jeopardize ongoing efforts to 'pacify' the capital.

At the end of April 2005 a bomb exploded in Mogadishu, killing 15 people and injuring at least 50 others, at a rally attended by Ghedi, who was visiting the city for the first time since December 2004. In early May 2005 100 members of the TP opposed to Yussuf's relocation plans, including Sheikh Adan, boycotted a parliamentary vote in Nairobi, where supporters of the President approved the planned relocation to Baidoa and Jowhar and the deployment of the proposed peace-keeping force. Days later Qanyare Afrah, Yalahow and Ali 'Ato' undertook to combine their militias and to withdraw militiamen and armoured vehicles from Mogadishu, and a partial disarmament of their forces took place at a ceremony in the capital. Also in April, the AU approved plans to send 1,700 peace-keeping troops to Somalia but stated that the force would only arrive when its security could be guaranteed. In mid-May 30 members of the TP accompanied Sheikh Adan upon his return to Mogadishu, while a spokesman for the President announced that Jama had been removed from office. In late May up to 19 people were reportedly killed during heavy fighting in Baidoa between militia affiliated to two opposing members of the TP. In mid-June Ghedi and the remaining ministers and members of parliament left Nairobi and arrived in Jowhar, despite the opposition of local militia. Talks were held concurrently between Yussuf and Sheikh Adan in San'a but failed to resolve the disagreement. Fears of renewed conflict between the opposing factions were raised in early July as Yussuf announced plans to gather a group of militiamen in Jowhar and in August tensions escalated when the Mogadishu-based members of the TP accused Yussuf of planning a civil war with military assistance from Ethiopia. In September, speaking before the UN General Assembly, Yussuf urged the UN Security Council to lift the arms embargo, which he claimed had hindered the establishment of a national security force and had prevented the deployment of peace-keepers in Somalia. A convoy carrying Ghedi on a visit to Mogadishu was attacked with grenades and a land mine in early November. Three people were killed in the apparent assassination attempt, although Ghedi was uninjured in the attack. Later that month 11 people were killed during fighting in Mogadishu after the Union of Islamic Courts of Mogadishu, which had established a court system in the capital based on Shari'a (Islamic) law, attempted to seize control of cinemas it had accused of encouraging immoral and criminal behaviour.

In early January 2006 Yussuf and Sheikh Adan signed an agreement for the TP to meet in Somalia within 30 days, following further talks held in San'a, and in late January members of the group led by Sheikh Adan signalled their willingness to support a process of reconciliation. It was subsequently confirmed that the first meeting of the TP on Somali soil would take place in Baidoa on 26 February. In late February a number of formerly opposed faction leaders, including Qanyare Afrah and Yalahow, formed a new political alliance—the Alliance for the Restoration of Peace and Counter-Terrorism (ARPCT)—which aimed to combat Islamist extremism in Somalia. Militia supported by the ARPCT were in conflict with forces loyal to the Union of Islamic Courts in the south of Mogadishu and at least 33 people were killed before a cease-fire was negotiated by Somali elders. However, some 140 people were killed and thousands fled the capital in late March as fighting resumed, and attempts by elders to renegotiate a cease-fire between the two factions continued. Unrest continued in the capital during early May with more than 80 people reported to have been killed in clashes between the two sides. Meanwhile, despite the absence of Ali 'Ato', Yalahow and several other prominent ministers opposed to Yussuf, 205 parliamentarians assembled in Baidoa on 26 February as the TP met for the first time since returning from Kenya.

Meanwhile, the tsunamis generated by a massive earthquake in the Indian Ocean on 26 December 2004 resulted in the deaths of at least 120 Somalis and caused widespread damage along the coast. The Somali authorities subsequently reported that a further 35 people remained missing, primarily on the Hafun peninsula in the north-east of the country, where it was estimated that up to 80% of homes had been destroyed. Prime Minister Ghedi also estimated that some 50,000 people had been displaced by the tsunamis and called upon the international community for aid in the form of clean water, food, medicine and shelter. The UN deployed German and US troops to distribute aid; however, their efforts were severely hampered by damage to roads in the area. In early March 2005 it was reported that the tsunamis had spread hazardous waste along the coastline, adversely affecting the health of residents in coastal areas. (Owing to the absence of a central government, Somalia had been identified by European firms throughout the 1990s as a prime location for dumping radioactive and chemical waste.) By March 2005 aid agencies estimated the total number of deaths as a result of the tsunamis to be around 150, although the Somali authorities maintained that the actual figure was almost double that number. The relief effort was further hampered by an increase in piracy along the coast of Somalia. In June 2005 a ship chartered by the World Food Program (WFP) to transport aid to victims of the tsunami, the MV Semlow, was seized by pirates as it sailed to the north-eastern port of Bossaso from Mombasa, Kenya. Despite subsequent threats from the WFP to suspend aid shipments, the ship and its 10 crew members were held until October. In mid-October, a WFP-chartered ship was hijacked as its cargo of food aid was being unloaded in Merka, in the south of the country. However, the ship was released three days later.

In May 1993 Egal, who had been Somalia's Prime Minister in 1967–69, was elected as the new President of 'Somaliland'. In June Egal announced the composition of a 14-member council of ministers for 'Somaliland'. By late September a two-year transitional programme for reconstruction had been approved by a 47-member bicameral parliament (comprising a council of elders and a council of representatives). The administration's hopes that the prevailing atmosphere of peace in the north-western region would inspire the international community's prompt recognition of 'Somaliland' were largely frustrated, in October, by the OAU Secretary-General's rejection of the territory's independent status. Relations between the Egal administration and UNOSOM officials improved in late 1993, following the assurances of the UN Secretary-General that the mission would not interfere in the region's affairs but would provide funding for reconstruction and the rehabilitation of the police force. Nevertheless, in August 1994 Egal expelled UN representatives from 'Somaliland', accusing them of interfering in internal affairs. This was apparently precipitated by talks between the new UN Special Representative to Somalia, James Victor Gbeho (appointed in July), and Ahmed Ali 'Tur', who was courted by both the UN and Gen. Aidid following his disavowal of secession for 'Somaliland'. In October the rift between Egal and Ahmed Ali 'Tur' culminated in violent confrontations in Hargeysa between military units remaining loyal to Egal and those defecting to support Ahmed Ali 'Tur'. By mid-December it was estimated that three-quarters of the population of Hargeysa had fled, many thousands of them seeking refuge in Ethiopia (see below). Fighting spread to other parts of 'Somaliland', and in April government forces were in conflict with fighters from the Garhadji clan who had recently formed an alliance with Issa militiamen belonging to the anti-secessionist USF. Despite Egal's weakened position, he persevered with the introduction of a new currency for the territory, the 'Somaliland shilling'.

In August 1995 four sub-committees were established to draft a new constitution for 'Somaliland'. A provisional document was published in March 1996. Peace talks between the territory's warring factions were conducted in December 1995, and in May 1996 it was reported that rebel armed forces had surrendered their weapons at an official disarmament ceremony in Hargeysa. In February 1997, shortly after it was announced that the constitution had become effective for a three-year interim period, Egal was re-elected (by an electoral college) President of 'Somaliland' for a five-year term. In October 1999 Egal visited the USA in an attempt to persuade the UN to confer observer status on 'Somaliland' and to gain US support for a peace conference.

At a referendum held in late May 2001, according to official results, 91.7% of the voters in 'Somaliland' approved a new constitution for the territory, which contained a clause confirming the self-declared state's independence. However, the outcome appeared unlikely to persuade the international community to grant recognition to 'Somaliland'. In mid-January 2002 Egal's term of office, which had been due to expire at the end of February, prior to scheduled presidential and parliamentary elections, was extended for one year by the council of elders. In early May, however, Egal died from complications following surgery at a military hospital in South Africa; a seven-day period of national mourning was declared, and the Vice-President, Dahir Riyale Kahin, was inaugurated as President of 'Somaliland'. Kahin appointed Ahmed Yusuf Yassin as Vice-President later that month, and in July Kahin announced that a presidential election would be held in January 2003. The election was delayed on a number of occasions, but finally proceeded on 14 April. According to results published by the 'Somaliland' Election Commission, Kahin defeated his nearest rival, Ahmad Muhammad Silanyo, by just 80 votes, securing 205,595 (42.1%) of the total 498,639 votes cast. A third candidate, Faysal Ali Warabe, received 77,433 votes (15.5%). An estimated 800,000 of the population of 'Somaliland' were eligible to vote. Silanyo immediately contested the result of the election and announced his intention to appeal against the outcome. However, in the following month the 'Somaliland' constitutional court confirmed the legitimacy of Kahin's victory, and he was sworn in as President on 16 May.

In October 2003 Kahin announced that all foreigners not in possession of a legal resident's permit would be expelled from 'Somaliland'. The decision followed the recent murders of four international aid workers, who the President maintained had been killed by 'outsiders' with the aim of discrediting 'Somaliland'. Security forces later arrested ten men in connection with three of the murders. During 2004–05 'Somaliland' continued its attempts to secure international recognition and reiterated that it would not participate in ongoing peace negotiations taking place in Kenya (see above). Indeed, following the election of Yussuf to the Somali presidency in mid-October 2004, Kahin again stated the readiness of 'Somaliland' to defend its territorial integrity and that it would seek to retain its independent status. In March 2005 the trial of the ten men arrested for murder in October 2003 commenced in Hargeysa, and in November eight of the defendants were found guilty and sentenced to death. Meanwhile, elections to the lower chamber of the legislature, the House of Representatives, scheduled to be held in late March 2005, were postponed by Kahin. Members of parliament had objected to the allocation of seats in the new legislature by clan, rather than on a one-person, one-vote basis, and demanded a national census to determine voter eligibility. Nevertheless, an amended elections bill was approved by the House of Representatives in early April. On 29 September candidates from three political parties contested the 82 seats in the House of Representatives. Kahin's Unity, Democracy and Independence Party (UDUB) emerged as the largest of the three parties with 33 seats, the Peace, Unity and Development Party (KULMIYE) won 28 seats and the Justice and Development Party (UCID) 21. At the official opening of parliament in November a disagreement over the election of a speaker developed into a physical confrontation between members of the Council. The role was eventually allocated to Abdirahman Mohamed Abdullahi of the UCID, and in mid-December the 'Somaliland' parliament held its first full session.

In July 1998 Col Abdullahi Yussuf Ahmed, a former leader of the SSDF, announced the formation of 'Puntland', a new autonomous administration in north-eastern Somalia. In August Abdullahi Yussuf, as President of the new administration, appointed a cabinet, which was subsequently approved by the recently inaugurated 69-member parliament (empowered to act as the legislature for a three-year transitional period, prior to the holding of regional elections). A charter for 'Puntland', released shortly afterwards, precluded 'Puntland' from seceding from Somalia, while it envisaged the adoption of a federal system of national government, with similar regional governments emerging around the country. Hussein Aidid declared his opposition to the administration, accusing the Ethiopian authorities of encouraging 'Puntland' to secede. In late June 2001 Yussuf's mandate was controversially extended for a further three years by the 'Puntland' parliament, at the behest of clan elders. The constitutionality of the decision was challenged by several opposition figures, and the 'Puntland' High Court issued a decree, effective from 1 July, placing all security services and other government institutions under its supervision. The Chief Justice of 'Puntland', Yussuf Haji Nur, subsequently proclaimed himself President of the territory; senior clan elders confirmed Haji Nur as acting President until 31 August. However, Yussuf rejected this decision, and heavy fighting ensued between followers of Yussuf and Haji Nur. In late August a general congress, attended by representatives of all major 'Puntland' clans, opened in Garowe, the region's capital, to elect a new President and Vice-President, as well as members to a new 'Puntland' assembly, and in mid-November Jama Ali Jama and Ahmad Mahmud Gunle were sworn in as President and Vice-President, respectively. Just days later violent clashes were reported to have taken place in Garowe between troops loyal to Yussuf and Ali Jama. In April 2002 Yussuf and Ali Jama met for talks in Ethiopia, but no agreement was reached. Fighting continued in 'Puntland' during 2002 and early 2003, with numerous casualties reported on both sides. In May 2003 Yussuf sought to stabilize 'Puntland' by concluding a power-sharing agreement with opposition forces, under the terms of which opposition members were granted a number of ministerial portfolios. In July 2004, following a presidential decree which reduced the Government's term in office from two years to six months, Yussuf formed a new 15-member Government. In October Yussuf was elected President of Somalia (see above) and Mohamed Abdi Hashi succeeded him as President of 'Puntland' in an acting capacity. In early January 2005 Gen. Mohamud Muse Hersi 'Adde', a former Somali diplomat, secured the support of 35 members of the 'Puntland' parliament, thus defeating Hashi, who won 30 votes, and was elected President of 'Puntland'. Hassan Dahir Afqurac was elected Vice-President. In late February 2006 an armed confrontation near the parliament building between security forces and a group loyal to the Minister for Planning, Abdirahman Farole, resulted in at least three deaths. Security forces had surrounded the building, which the group had occupied the previous day. In early March members of parliament approved a new Cabinet, in which incumbent ministers retained their portfolios, with the exception of Farole, whom Hersi had dismissed following the siege. Meanwhile, in October 2005 it emerged that 'Puntland' had issued mineral and oil exploration rights to Range Resources of Australia in an agreement that included the regions of Sanaag and Sool, disputed by 'Puntland' and the neighbouring region of 'Somaliland', prompting vociferous criticism from the 'Somaliland' administration. From September 2004 troops from both regions had reportedly been engaged in heavy fighting near the border between the two self-declared states.

In 1992 severe drought, combined with the disruption to agriculture and relief efforts caused by conflict in many parts of the country, resulted in the deaths from starvation and famine-related diseases of some 500,000 people. UNITAF's operations greatly increased the amount of food reaching people in need, and by February 1993 deaths from starvation had been virtually eliminated. As a result of good rains, harvests were much better in 1993–94 than in previous years, and the country was expected to become self-sufficient in food once again. During 1994 the incidence of attacks on foreign aid workers increased, and, in anticipation of the departure of UNOSOM, which had provided a measure of protection, aid organizations withdrew many of their personnel from Somalia, thus impeding many relief and rehabilitation projects. In July 1999 the US Agency for International Development announced that, effective from October, it would no longer be disbursing aid to Somalia. In September the UN Children's Fund (UNICEF) suspended its operations in southern Somalia, following the murder of its highest-ranking health officer and the wounding of five UNICEF workers during a robbery attempt in Dibi Arab in central Somalia. Despite good seasonal rains in 2004–05 some 2.1m. people were estimated to be in need of food aid as a result of severe drought that affected the south of the country in 2005. It was reported in February 2006 that at least seven people had died of dehydration as a result of the ongoing drought, and in March the UN appealed for US $327m. in emergency aid to relieve an estimated 11.5m. people in Somalia and six other East African countries affected. International aid agencies warned that renewed conflict was obstructing the supply of aid to those in need and that famine was a likely prospect should rains fail later in the year as predicted.

The escalation of hostilities between the Siad Barre Government and the rebel forces increased the flow of refugees from Somalia to Ethiopia and Kenya. Following the SNM's assumption of control in northern Somalia in early 1991, thousands of refugees returned from Ethiopia. Many more returned to their home territory in 'Somaliland' in late 1991 and early 1992, as a result of the ethnic conflict in south-western Ethiopia. The intensification of hostilities in the south of Somalia from April 1992 precipitated a huge movement of refugees: by the end of 1992 there were approximately 400,000 Somali refugees in Kenya, more than 300,000 in Ethiopia, up to 100,000 in Yemen, and hundreds of thousands in the Persian (Arabian) Gulf region, in Europe and North America. In early 1993 the International Committee of the Red Cross estimated that three-quarters of Somalia's population had been internally displaced by the civil conflict, although by late 1994 many thousands had returned to their villages. However, in November some 30,000 civilians fled to Ethiopia to escape fighting in Hargeysa, 'Somaliland'. According to the office of the UN High Commissioner for Refugees, at the end of 2004 there were an estimated 389,272 Somali refugees world-wide, including 153,627 in Kenya, 63,511 in Yemen, 36,106 in the United Kingdom, 31,110 in the USA, 17,331 in Djibouti and 16,470 in Ethiopia. During 2004 some 18,069 Somali refugees, primarily from Ethiopia, were repatriated voluntarily.

In April 1988 a decade of hostile relations between Somalia and Ethiopia, following the war in 1977–78 over the Ogaden area of Ethiopia (which is inhabited by ethnic Somalis), ended with a peace accord. It was agreed to re-establish diplomatic relations, to withdraw troops from border areas and to exchange prisoners of war. Following the overthrow of the Mengistu regime in May 1991, the new Government in Ethiopia declared itself neutral with regard to the factions fighting for control of Somalia. Ethiopia hosted peace conferences for the warring Somali factions in 1993, 1996 and 1997. The Egyptian, Kenyan and Libyan authorities also fostered peace initiatives for Somalia from the late 1990s.

In March 1998 Ethiopian troops reportedly occupied several towns in Somalia's Gedo region, following the capture of the SNF-controlled town of Elwak (in Kenya) by the Islamist, Somali-based group al-Ittihad al-Islam. In April 1999 the Ethiopian Government denied reports that its forces were occupying two districts in western Somalia, while Hussein Aidid and Ali Mahdi reiterated their claims that Ethiopia was encouraging the division of Somalia by providing armaments and ammunition to autonomous administrations in the country.

Following the outbreak of the Eritrean–Ethiopian border conflict in mid-1998, rival Somali factions were the recipients of increasingly large consignments of weapons from the two warring countries, which sought to secure Somali allegiance to their causes. Growing concern about the activities of Eritrean-supported Somali militias prompted Ethiopia to launch cross-border raids into Somalia against warlords, and in June 1999 the RRA, assisted by some 3,000 Ethiopian troops, captured the town of Baidoa from Aidid's SNA. Aidid's continuing support of the Eritrean Government and Ethiopian insurgent groups led neutral observers to believe that the conflict was in danger of spreading elsewhere in the Horn of Africa. The Ethiopian Government claimed, however, that its actions were merely attempts to protect the border from attacks initiated by Somali-based rebel opposition groups. In September Ali 'Ato' and Aidid attended a meeting with the Ethiopian Minister of Foreign Affairs, Seyoum Mesfin, in Libya where an agreement was reached whereby Aidid would withdraw support for Ethiopian Oromo rebels in return for Ethiopian disengagement from Somalia. In November the SNA announced that it had disarmed several hundred Oromo Liberation Front (OLF) rebels living in Somalia, had closed down their offices and had asked the OLF leaders to leave the country. It was, however, reported that Ethiopian incursions into Somalia continued in early 2000. During late 2000 and early 2001 relations between the two countries deteriorated after the Hasan administration accused Ethiopia of offering support to faction leaders hostile to the TNA (see above). Relations between the two countries improved following the visit of a Somali government delegation to Ethiopia in June 2001. However, in September it was reported that Ethiopia had ordered the closure of the common border, fearing an increase in terrorist activity in Somalia after the events of 11 September. In November the Prime Ministers of the two countries met for talks in Addis Ababa, at which Ethiopia reiterated its concern over the suspected presence of Islamist terrorist elements in Somalia. Nevertheless, both sides pledged to improve bilateral relations, and Ethiopia affirmed its support for a comprehensive reconciliation process in Somalia. In February 2003 relations between the two countries were again strained after the Ethiopian Prime Minister admitted sending Ethiopian troops into Somali territory in pursuit of members of al-Ittihad al-Islam.

Following the suicide attacks on New York and Washington, DC, on 11 September 2001, for which the USA held the al-Qa'ida (Base) organization of Osama bin Laden responsible, the USA 'froze' the foreign assets of Somalia's al-Barakat bank, as it suspected that much of the estimated US $500m. remitted from Somalis abroad to the bank was being funnelled to terrorist organizations. Furthermore, al-Ittihad al-Islam was among 27 groups designated as foreign terrorist organizations in September by the US Government, which believed that al-Ittihad al-Islam had links to al-Qa'ida. In November the new Somali Prime Minister, Hassan Abshir Farah, denied that his Government had any links to al-Ittihad al-Islam or to al-Qa'ida and stated that he would not object to the deployment of US troops inside Somalia to monitor and detect alleged terrorist activities. In the following month US officials were reported to have held talks with several Somali faction leaders regarding the possible existence of al-Qa'ida camps in areas under their control. US special forces raided a Mogadishu hospital in March 2003 and seized a suspected al-Qa'ida operative, who was believed to have been involved in the bombing of an Israeli-owned hotel in Mombasa, Kenya, in November 2002, which resulted in the deaths of 18 people. A report published by the UN in November 2003 stated that the al-Qa'ida cell that had launched the attack on the hotel had used Somalia as a base, and warned of the possibility of further acts of terrorism being plotted, after it discovered evidence of attempts by extremist groups to procure weapons in Mogadishu. US naval forces stationed in Djibouti and Bahrain conducted patrols along the coast of Somalia throughout 2005 following a reported increase in piracy, and in late January 2006 13 suspected pirates were captured following an armed pursuit near the coast involving a US guided-missile destroyer.

Government

In July 2000 a Somali national reconciliation conference, sponsored by President Gelleh of Djibouti, approved a national Charter, which envisaged the Somali Republic adopting a federal system of government, comprising 18 regional administrations, after a three-year interim period. The Charter provided for the creation of a Transitional National Assembly (TNA), which was to exercise legislative power in Somalia during the interim period. The 245-member TNA, comprising members of the four major clans and of an alliance of smaller clans, as well as 20 influential Somalis, was inaugurated in August and elected a President of Somalia. In October the President nominated a Prime Minister, who formed a Cabinet. Despite the expiry of its mandate in August 2003, the TNA remained in place, pending the election of a new legislative body. In late January 2004, following protracted negotiations in Kenya, an agreement was signed that provided for the establishment of a new 275-member national parliament, to comprise 61 representatives from each of the four major clans and 31 from an alliance of smaller clans. Once established, the parliament elected a national President, who, in turn, nominated a Prime Minister to form a government.

Defence

Of total armed forces of 64,500 in June 1990, the army numbered 60,000, the navy 2,000 and the air force 2,500. In addition, there were 29,500 members of paramilitary forces, including 20,000 members of the People's Militia. Following the overthrow of the Siad Barre regime in January 1991, there were no national armed forces. Somalia was divided into areas controlled by different armed groups, which were based on clan, or sub-clan, membership. In March 1994 the UN announced that 8,000 former Somali police-officers had been rehabilitated throughout the country, receiving vehicles and uniforms from the UN. Following the UN withdrawal from Somalia in early 1995, these police-officers ceased receiving payment and their future and their hitherto neutral stance appeared uncertain. In December 1998 a 3,000-strong police force was established for the Banaadir region (Mogadishu and its environs). An additional 3,000 members (comprising former militiamen and police-officers) were recruited to the force in early 1999; however, the force was disbanded within months. Following his election to the presidency in August 2000, Abdulkasim Salad Hasan announced his intention to recruit former militiamen into a new national force: by December some 5,000 Somalis had begun training under the supervision of Mogadishu's Islamic courts. However, efforts to establish a new national armed force have made little progress since the Government's return to Somalia from exile in 2005. In August 2004 the total armed forces of the self-proclaimed 'Republic of Somaliland' were estimated to number 7,000.

Economic Affairs

In 1990, according to estimates by the World Bank, Somalia's gross national income (GNI), measured at average 1988–90 prices, was US $946m., equivalent to $150 per head. According to UN figures, in 2001 gross domestic product (GDP) was $1,000m., equivalent to $110 per head. During 1995–2004, it was estimated, the population increased at an average annual rate of 3.4%. GDP declined, in real terms, at an average annual rate of 3.3% in 1990–99; however, growth of 2.1% was recorded in 1999.

Agriculture (including forestry and fishing) contributed 66% of GDP in 1990. An estimated 66.9% of the working population were employed in agriculture in 2002. Agriculture is based on the breeding of livestock, which accounted for 49% of GDP in 1989 and 38.4% of the total value of exports in 1988. Bananas are the principal cash crop, accounting for 40.3% of export earnings in 1988. The GDP of the agricultural sector declined by an average of 4.1% per year in 1990–99; agricultural GDP increased by 12.0% in 1999. Although crop production in 1996 was reported to have increased by 50% compared with the previous year, output was still some 37% lower than it had been prior to the civil war. Severe flooding in southern Somalia during 1997 led to widespread crop failure and resulted in the loss of as many as 30,000 cattle. Total cereals production was 207,800 metric tons in 1999, the lowest annual yield since 1993, but recovered to an estimated 304,900 in 2002. Southern Somalia experienced severe drought in 2005, causing harvests to fail for the third consecutive year and provoking acute shortages of food among the population.

Industry (including mining, manufacturing, construction and power) contributed 8.6% of GDP in 1988, and employed an estimated 12.0% of the working population in 2002. The combined GDP of the mining, manufacturing and power sectors increased by an average of 2.3% per year in 1990–99; growth in 1999 was 13.8%. The GDP of the construction sector increased at an average annual rate of 0.8% in 1990–99; growth of 16.8% was recorded in 1999.

Mining contributed 0.3% of GDP in 1988. Somalia's mineral resources include salt, limestone, gypsum, gold, silver, nickel, copper, zinc, lead, manganese, uranium and iron ore. Deposits of petroleum and natural gas have been discovered, but remain unexploited: US petroleum companies were granted exploration rights covering two-thirds of the country by Siad Barre, and were expected to start investigations once there was a durable peace. In February 2001 it was reported that the French petroleum company TotalFinaElf had signed an agreement with the transitional Somali Government to carry out oil exploration in the south of the country. Discussions commenced in January 2003 between the 'Somaliland' administration and a British-based company regarding the possible granting of contracts for petroleum exploration. An Australian mining company, Range Resources, began mineral and petroleum exploration in 'Puntland' and in October 2005 it signed a contract with the 'Puntland' Government, granting it 50.1% of exploration rights for the entire region, including territory disputed by neighbouring 'Somaliland'.

Manufacturing contributed almost 5% of GDP in 1988. The most important sectors are food-processing, especially sugar-refining, the processing of hides and skins, and the refining of petroleum. Manufacturing GDP increased by an average of 2.0% per year in 1990–99; growth in 1999 was 18.0%.

Energy is derived principally from oil-fired generators. Imports of fuel products comprised 14% of the value of merchandise imports in 1990.

The services sector contributed 24.6% of GDP in 1988, and engaged an estimated 21.1% of the employed labour force in 2002. Tourism accounted for some 9.3% of GDP in 1988.

In 1989 Somalia recorded a visible trade deficit of US $278.6m., and there was a deficit of $156.7m. on the current account of the balance of payments. In 1982 the principal source of imports (34.4%) was Italy, while Saudi Arabia was the principal market for exports (86.5%). Other major trading partners in that year were the United Kingdom, the Federal Republic of Germany and Kenya. The principal exports in 1988 were livestock and bananas. The principal imports were petroleum, fertilizers, foodstuffs and machinery. Livestock and bananas remained the principal exports in the late 1990s, while the United Arab Emirates emerged as Somalia's main trading partner.

SOMALIA

In 1988 Somalia recorded a budget deficit of 10,009.4m. Somali shillings. A provisional budget for 1991 was projected to balance at 268,283.2m. Somali shillings. Somalia's total external debt was US $2,838m. at the end of 2003, of which $1,936m. was long-term public debt. In 1990–2001 the average annual rate of inflation was 20.6%. Consumer prices increased by 11.5% in 2001. The rate of unemployment was estimated at 47.4% in 2002.

Somalia is a member of the African Development Bank (see p. 151) and the Islamic Development Bank (see p. 303).

Somalia's long history of civil unrest, together with unreliable climatic conditions, have undermined the traditional agricultural base of the economy. By the mid-1990s a significant recovery had been recorded in livestock numbers, sorghum output and exports of bananas, although the production and export of the last exacerbated factional fighting, with rival clansmen competing for control of the industry in order to fund their war efforts. Following the establishment of the Transitional National Assembly in August 2000, it was hoped that Somalia's economic situation would improve. On his appointment, President Hasan appealed for foreign donors to provide assistance with the rehabilitation of basic infrastructures and to finance development projects. However, the Government's attempts to establish control over the economy by issuing large quantities of currency notes resulted in a rapid rise in the rate of inflation and a further depreciation in the value of the shilling. Although the economy subsequently began to show signs of a recovery, in December 2001 the UN announced that Somalia was on the verge of an economic collapse unparalleled in modern history. This was attributed largely to the US Administration's decision to enforce the closure of the al-Barakat banking and telecommunications organization (see Recent History), owing to its suspected links to terrorist organizations, thus severing the remittance process on which so much of the country is heavily dependent. The formation of a new Government in late 2004 again raised hopes that central authority would be restored to the country, thus enabling the possible creation of financial institutions and providing a degree of stability, which would, in turn, encourage the development of the economy. Indeed, in July 2004 Coca-Cola opened a soft drinks plant in Mogadishu representing the largest single investment in the country and in February 2005 Somalia signed a trade agreement with Kenya providing for co-operation in various sectors, including livestock farming, fisheries, telecommunications and industry. However, despite pledges of significant humanitarian aid by the international community, divisions within the Government and ongoing conflict continued to prevent the development of an economic infrastructure and analysts do not expect any real economic growth in the coming years. Meanwhile in mid-2003 the World Bank resumed operations in Somalia (which had been suspended in 1991) under its initiative for low-income countries under stress.

Education

All private schools were nationalized in 1972, and education is now provided free of charge. Primary education, lasting for eight years, is officially compulsory for children aged six to 14 years. However, in 2002 enrolment at primary schools was equivalent to only 16.9% of the school-age population (boys 20.8%; girls 12.7%). Secondary education, beginning at the age of 14, lasts for four years, but is not compulsory. In 1985 the enrolment at secondary schools included 3% of children (boys 4%; girls 2%) in the relevant age-group. Current expenditure on education in the Government's 1988 budget was 478.1m. Somali shillings (equivalent to 1.9% of total current spending). Following the overthrow of Siad Barre's Government in January 1991 and the descent of the country into anarchy, Somalia's education system collapsed. In January 1993 a primary school was opened in the building of Somalia's sole university, the Somali National University in Mogadishu (which had been closed in early 1991). The only other schools operating in the country were a number run by Islamist groups and some that had been reopened in 'Somaliland' in mid-1991.

Public Holidays

2006: 1 January (New Year's Day), 10 January*† (Id al-Adha, Feast of the Sacrifice), 9 February* (Ashoura), 10 April* (Mouloud, Birth of the Prophet), 1 May (Labour Day), 26 June (Independence Day), 1 July (Foundation of the Republic), 23 October* (Id al-Fitr, end of Ramadan), 31 December*† (Id al-Adha, Feast of the Sacrifice).

2007: 1 January (New Year's Day), 29 January* (Ashoura), 31 March* (Mouloud, Birth of the Prophet), 1 May (Labour Day), 26 June (Independence Day), 1 July (Foundation of the Republic), 13 October* (Id al-Fitr, end of Ramadan), 20 December* (Id al-Adha, Feast of the Sacrifice).

* These holidays are dependent on the Islamic lunar calendar and may vary by one or two days from the dates given.

† This festival occurs twice (in the Islamic years AH 1426 and 1427) within the same Gregorian year.

Weights and Measures

The metric and imperial systems are both used.

Statistical Survey

Sources (unless otherwise stated): Economic Research and Statistics Dept, Central Bank of Somalia, Mogadishu, and Central Statistical Dept, State Planning Commission, POB 1742, Mogadishu; tel. (1) 80385.

Area and Population

AREA, POPULATION AND DENSITY

Area (sq km)	637,657*
Population (census results)†	
7 February 1975	3,253,024
February 1986 (provisional)	
Males	3,741,664
Females	3,372,767
Total	7,114,431
Population (UN estimates at mid-year)‡	
2002	7,461,000
2003	7,708,000
2004	7,964,000
Density (per sq km) at mid-2004	12.5

* 246,201 sq miles.
† Excluding adjustment for underenumeration.
‡ Source: UN, *World Population Prospects: The 2004 Revision*.

2002: Total population 6,799,079 (males 3,499,523, females 3,299,556) (Source: The World Bank and United Nations Development Programme, *Socio-Economic Survey 2002 Somalia*).

PRINCIPAL TOWNS
(estimated population in 1981)

Mogadishu (capital)	500,000	Berbera	. . .	65,000
Hargeysa	70,000	Merca	. . .	60,000
Kismayu	70,000			

Mid-2003 (UN projection, including suburbs): Mogadishu 1,174,881 (Source: UN, *World Urbanization Prospects: The 2003 Revision*).

BIRTHS AND DEATHS
(UN estimates, annual averages)

	1990–95	1995–2000	2000–05
Birth rate (per 1,000)	45.7	47.7	45.8
Death rate (per 1,000)	23.5	20.3	18.4

Source: UN, *World Population Prospects: The 2004 Revision*.

Expectation of life (WHO estimates, years at birth): 44 (males 43; females 45) in 2003 (Source: WHO, *World Health Report*).

SOMALIA

ECONOMICALLY ACTIVE POPULATION
(estimates, '000 persons, 1991)

	Males	Females	Total
Agriculture, etc.	1,157	1,118	2,275
Industry	290	46	336
Services	466	138	604
Total labour force	1,913	1,302	3,215

Source: UN Economic Commission for Africa, *African Statistical Yearbook*.

2002 (percentage distribution): Agriculture 66.9; Industry 12.0; Services 21.1 (Source: The World Bank and United Nations Development Programme, *Socio-Economic Survey 2002 Somalia*).

Health and Welfare

KEY INDICATORS

Total fertility rate (children per woman, 2003)	7.2
Under-5 mortality rate (per 1,000 live births, 2004)	225
HIV/AIDS (% of persons aged 15–49, 2001)	1.00
Physicians (per 1,000 head, 1997)	0.04
Hospital beds (per 1,000 head, 1997)	0.75
Health expenditure (2001): US $ per head (PPP)	13
Health expenditure (2001): % of GDP	2.6
Health expenditure (2001): public (% of total)	44.6
Access to water (% of persons, 2002)	29
Access to sanitation (% of persons, 2002)	25

For sources and definitions, see explanatory note on p. vi.

Agriculture

PRINCIPAL CROPS
('000 metric tons)

	2001	2002	2003
Rice (paddy)	4*	4†	4†
Maize*	288	269	164
Sorghum*	137	141	121
Sweet potatoes†	6	6	6
Cassava (Manioc)†	85	85	85
Sugar cane†	200	200	200
Pulses†	16	16	16
Groundnuts (in shell)	3*	4*	4†
Sesame seed†	25	25	25
Vegetables*	61	58	58
Watermelons	15*	6*	6†
Sugar cane†	200	200	200
Grapefruit and pomelos	6†	6*	6†
Bananas	36*	37*	35†
Oranges†	8	8	8
Lemons and limes	8*	8*	8†
Dates†	11	11	11

* Unofficial figure(s).
† FAO estimate(s).
Source: FAO.

LIVESTOCK
('000 head, year ending September)

	2001	2002	2003
Cattle	5,256	5,300*	5,350*
Sheep	14,084	13,100*	13,100*
Goats*	12,700	12,700	12,700
Pigs*	4	4	4
Asses*	21	21	21
Mules*	19	19	19
Camels	7,079	7,100*	7,000*
Chickens*	3,000	3,000	3,000

* FAO estimate(s).
Source: FAO.

LIVESTOCK PRODUCTS
(FAO estimates, '000 metric tons)

	2000	2001	2002
Cows' milk	530	557	557
Goats' milk	390	392	392
Sheep's milk	430	445	445
Beef and veal	59	63	62
Mutton and lamb	35	43	43
Goat meat	37	32	38
Hen eggs	3	3	3
Cattle hides	11	11	11
Sheepskins	7	7	8
Goatskins	6	5	6

2003: Figures for 2003 assumed to be unchanged from 2002 (FAO estimates).
Source: FAO.

Forestry

ROUNDWOOD REMOVALS
(FAO estimates, '000 cubic metres, excl. bark)

	2002	2003	2004
Sawlogs, veneer logs and logs for sleepers*	28	28	28
Other industrial wood	82	82	82
Fuel wood	9,827	10,141	10,466
Total	9,937	10,251	10,576

* Annual output assumed to be unchanged since 1975.
Source: FAO.

SAWNWOOD PRODUCTION
('000 cubic metres, incl. railway sleepers)

	1973	1974	1975
Total (all broadleaved)	15*	10	14

* FAO estimate.
1976–2004: Annual production as in 1975 (FAO estimates).
Source: FAO.

Fishing

(FAO estimates, '000 metric tons, live weight)

	2001	2002	2003
Marine fishes	18.9	17.2	17.2
Total catch (incl. others)	20.0	18.0	18.0

Source: FAO.

Mining

(estimates, '000 metric tons)

	2002	2003	2004
Salt	1	1	1
Gypsum	2	2	2

Source: US Geological Survey.

SOMALIA

Industry

SELECTED PRODUCTS
('000 metric tons, unless otherwise indicated)

	1986	1987	1988
Sugar*	30.0	43.3	41.2
Canned meat (million tins)	1.0	—	—
Canned fish	0.1	—	—
Pasta and flour	15.6	4.3	—
Textiles (million yards)	5.5	3.0	6.3
Boxes and bags	15.0	12.0	5.0
Cigarettes and matches	0.3	0.2	0.1
Petroleum products	128	44	30
Electric energy (million kWh)†	253	255‡	257‡

Sugar (unofficial estimates, '000 metric tons)*: 21 in 1996; 18 in 1997; 19 in 1998.

Electric energy (million kWh)†: 271 in 1994‡; 272 in 1995‡; 275 in 1996.

* Data from FAO.
† Source: UN, *Industrial Commodity Statistics Yearbook*.
‡ Provisional figure.

Finance

CURRENCY AND EXCHANGE RATES

Monetary Units
100 cents = 1 Somali shilling (So. sh.).

Sterling, Dollar and Euro Equivalents (30 November 2005)
£1 sterling = 26,572 Somali shillings;
US $1 = 15, 386 Somali shillings;
€1 = 18,108 Somali shillings;
100,000 Somali shillings = £3.76 = $6.50 = €5.52.

Average Exchange Rate (Somali shillings per US $)
1987   105.18
1988   170.45
1989   490.68

Note: A separate currency, the 'Somaliland shilling', was introduced in the 'Republic of Somaliland' in January 1995. The exchange rate was reported to be US $1 = 2,750 'Somaliland shillings' in March 2000.

CURRENT BUDGET
(million Somali shillings)

Revenue	1986	1987	1988
Total tax revenue	8,516.4	8,622.4	12,528.1
Taxes on income and profits	1,014.8	889.7	1,431.0
Income tax	380.5	538.8	914.8
Profit tax	634.3	350.9	516.2
Taxes on production, consumption and domestic transactions	1,410.4	1,274.2	2,336.4
Taxes on international transactions	6,091.2	6,458.5	8,760.6
Import duties	4,633.2	4,835.2	6,712.1
Total non-tax revenue	6,375.2	8,220.4	7,623.4
Fees and service charges	274.1	576.1	828.8
Income from government property	633.4	656.4	2,418.9
Other revenue	5,467.2	6,987.9	4,375.7
Total	14,891.6	16,842.8	20,151.5

Expenditure	1986	1987	1988
Total general services	11,997.7	19,636.7	24,213.6
Defence	2,615.9	3,145.0	8,093.9
Interior and police	605.0	560.7	715.4
Finance and central services	7,588.3	14,017.8	12,515.6
Foreign affairs	633.0	1,413.9	2,153.1
Justice and religious affairs	248.5	290.2	447.0
Presidency and general administration	93.0	148.0	217.4
Planning	189.0	24.9	24.3
National Assembly	25.0	36.2	46.9
Total economic services	1,927.6	554.1	600.3

Expenditure—continued	1986	1987	1988
Transportation	122.2	95.2	94.5
Posts and telecommunications	94.3	76.7	75.6
Public works	153.9	57.5	69.8
Agriculture	547.2	59.4	55.3
Livestock and forestry	459.0	89.5	109.9
Mineral and water resources	318.8	85.2	93.1
Industry and commerce	131.0	45.1	43.9
Fisheries	101.2	45.5	58.2
Total social services	1,050.5	900.1	930.8
Education	501.6	403.0	478.1
Health	213.8	203.5	255.2
Information	111.5	135.0	145.8
Labour, sports and tourism	139.6	49.3	51.7
Other	84.0	109.3	—
Total	14,975.8	21,091.0	25,744.7

1989 (estimates): Budget to balance at 32,429.0m. Somali shillings.
1990 (estimates): Budget to balance at 86,012.0m. Somali shillings.
1991 (estimates): Budget to balance at 268,283.2m. Somali shillings.

CENTRAL BANK RESERVES
(US $ million at 31 December)

	1987	1988	1989
Gold*	8.3	7.0	6.9
Foreign exchange	7.3	15.3	15.4
Total	15.6	22.3	22.3

* Valued at market-related prices.
Source: IMF, *International Financial Statistics*.

MONEY SUPPLY
(million Somali shillings at 31 December)

	1987	1988	1989
Currency outside banks	12,327	21,033	70,789
Private-sector deposits at central bank	1,771	1,555	5,067
Demand deposits at commercial banks	15,948	22,848	63,971
Total money	30,046	45,436	139,827

Source: IMF, *International Financial Statistics*.

COST OF LIVING
(Consumer Price Index; base: 1995 = 100)

	1999	2000	2001
All items	173.3	193.2	215.4

Source: African Development Bank.

NATIONAL ACCOUNTS

Expenditure on the Gross Domestic Product*
(estimates, million Somali shillings at current prices)

	1988	1989	1990
Government final consumption expenditure	33,220	58,530	104,760
Private final consumption expenditure	240,950	481,680	894,790
Increase in stocks	14,770	n.a.	n.a.
Gross fixed capital formation	44,780	134,150	240,030
Total domestic expenditure	333,720	674,360	1,239,580
Exports of goods and services	7,630	8,890	8,660
Less Imports of goods and services	49,430	57,660	58,460
GDP in purchasers' values	291,920	625,580	1,189,780

* Figures are rounded to the nearest 10m. Somali shillings.
Source: UN Economic Commission for Africa, *African Statistical Yearbook*.

SOMALIA

Gross Domestic Product by Economic Activity
(million Somali shillings at constant 1985 prices)

	1986	1987	1988
Agriculture, hunting, forestry and fishing	54,868	59,378	61,613
Mining and quarrying	291	291	291
Manufacturing	4,596	4,821	4,580
Electricity, gas and water	77	62	57
Construction	3,289	3,486	2,963
Trade, restaurants and hotels	8,587	9,929	8,599
Transport, storage and communications	6,020	6,153	5,873
Finance, insurance, real estate and business services	3,743	4,095	3,890
Government services	1,631	1,530	1,404
Other community, social and personal services	2,698	2,779	2,863
Sub-total	85,800	92,524	92,133
Less Imputed bank service charges	737	748	748
GDP at factor cost	85,064	91,776	91,385
Indirect taxes, *less* subsidies	5,301	4,250	3,262
GDP in purchasers' values	90,365	96,026	94,647

GDP at factor cost (estimates, million Somali shillings at current prices): 249,380 in 1988; 500,130 in 1989; 923,970 in 1990 (Source: UN Economic Commission for Africa, *African Statistical Yearbook*).

BALANCE OF PAYMENTS
(US $ million)

	1987	1988	1989
Exports of goods f.o.b.	94.0	58.4	67.7
Imports of goods f.o.b.	−358.5	−216.0	−346.3
Trade balance	−264.5	−157.6	−278.6
Imports of services	−127.7	−104.0	−122.0
Balance on goods and services	−392.2	−261.6	−400.6
Other income paid	−52.0	−60.6	−84.4
Balance on goods, services and income	−444.2	−322.2	−485.0
Current transfers received	343.3	223.7	331.2
Current transfers paid	−13.1	—	−2.9
Current balance	−114.0	−98.5	−156.7
Investment liabilities	−22.8	−105.5	−32.6
Net errors and omissions	39.0	22.4	−0.8
Overall balance	−97.9	−181.7	−190.0

Source: IMF, *International Financial Statistics*.

External Trade

PRINCIPAL COMMODITIES
(million Somali shillings)

Imports*	1986	1987	1988
Foodstuffs	1,783.3	3,703.6	1,216.1
Beverages and tobacco	298.1	183.6	6.2
Manufacturing raw materials	230.0	626.9	661.4
Fertilizers	1.8	238.0	2,411.4
Petroleum	2,051.0	3,604.2	3,815.9
Construction materials	981.4	2,001.9	307.8
Machinery and parts	1,098.3	1,203.6	957.1
Transport equipment	1,133.8	1,027.6	195.2
Total (incl. others)	8,443.4	13,913.7	11,545.5

* Figures cover only imports made against payments of foreign currencies. The total value of imports in 1986 was 20,474 million Somali shillings.

Exports	1986	1987	1988
Livestock	4,420.3	7,300.0	3,806.5
Bananas	1,207.2	2,468.8	3,992.3
Hides and skins	294.0	705.2	492.0
Total (incl. others)	6,372.5	10,899.9	9,914.1

1992 (estimates, US $ million): Imports 150; Exports 80.

PRINCIPAL TRADING PARTNERS
('000 Somali shillings)

Imports	1980	1981	1982
China, People's Repub.	46,959	40,962	89,772
Ethiopia	43,743	146,853	155,775
Germany, Fed. Repub.	104,117	430,548	214,873
Hong Kong	5,351	13,862	3,972
India	41,467	19,638	4,801
Iraq	2,812	67,746	402
Italy	756,800	662,839	1,221,146
Japan	28,900	54,789	48,371
Kenya	86,515	105,627	198,064
Saudi Arabia	120,208	160,583	82,879
Singapore	18,569	15,592	73,652
Thailand	19,296	40,527	106,474
United Kingdom	172,613	935,900	238,371
USA	201,662	141,823	154,082
Total (incl. others)	2,190,627	3,221,715	3,548,805

Exports	1980	1981	1982
Djibouti	6,640	3,209	2,458
Germany, Fed. Repub.	11,376	1,956	20,086
Italy	107,661	58,975	77,870
Kenya	2,425	6,929	4,211
Saudi Arabia	583,768	803,631	1,852,936
United Kingdom	1,233	—	3,169
USA	1,301	—	6,970
Yemen, People's Dem. Repub.	3,182	—	—
Total (incl. others)	844,012	960,050	2,142,585

Source: the former Ministry of Planning, Mogadishu.

1986: *Imports* (estimates, million Somali shillings) USA 1,816; Japan 836; China, People's Repub. 553; United Kingdom 773; France 341; Germany, Fed. Repub. 1,481; Total (incl. others) 8,443; *Exports* (estimates, million Somali shillings) USA 5; China, People's Repub. 4; United Kingdom 31; France 27; Germany, Fed. Repub. 11; Total (incl. others) 6,373 (Source: UN Economic Commission for Africa, *African Statistical Yearbook*).

Transport

ROAD TRAFFIC
(estimates, '000 motor vehicles in use)

	1994	1995	1996
Passenger cars	2.8	2.0	1.0
Commercial vehicles	7.4	7.3	6.4

Source: International Road Federation, *World Road Statistics*.

SHIPPING

Merchant Fleet
(registered at 31 December)

	2002	2003	2004
Number of vessels	17	17	18
Total displacement ('000 grt)	6.3	6.3	7.3

Source: Lloyd's Register-Fairplay, *World Fleet Statistics*.

International Sea-borne Freight Traffic
('000 metric tons)

	1989	1990	1991
Goods loaded	325	324	n.a.
Goods unloaded	1,252*	1,118	1,007*

* Estimate.

Source: UN Economic Commission for Africa, *African Statistical Yearbook*.

SOMALIA

CIVIL AVIATION
(traffic on scheduled services)

	1989	1990	1991
Kilometres flown (million)	3	3	1
Passengers carried ('000)	89	88	46
Passenger-km (million)	248	255	131
Freight ton-km (million)	8	9	5

Source: UN, *Statistical Yearbook*.

Tourism

	1996	1997	1998
Tourist arrivals ('000)	10	10	10

Source: World Bank.

Communications Media

	1995	1996	1997
Radio receivers ('000 in use)	400	450	470
Television receivers ('000 in use)	124	129	135
Telephones ('000 main lines in use)*	15	15	15
Daily newspapers	1	2	n.a.

* Estimates.

2002: Mobile cellular telephones (subscribers) 35,000; Telephones (main lines in use, estimate) 100,000; Internet users 89,000.

Sources: UNESCO, *Statistical Yearbook*; International Telecommunication Union.

Education

(1985)

	Institutions	Teachers	Pupils
Pre-primary	16	133	1,558
Primary	1,224	10,338	196,496
Secondary:			
general	n.a.	2,149	39,753
teacher training	n.a.	30*	613*
vocational	n.a.	637	5,933
Higher	n.a.	817†	15,672†

* Figure refers to 1984.
† Figure refers to 1986.

Source: UNESCO, *Statistical Yearbook*.

1990 (UN estimates): 377,000 primary-level pupils; 44,000 secondary-level pupils; 10,400 higher-level pupils.

1991: University teachers 549; University students 4,640.

Adult literacy rate (UNESCO estimates): 24.0% in 2002 (Source: UN Development Programme, *Human Development Report*).

Directory

The Constitution

The Constitution promulgated in 1979 and amended in 1990 was revoked following the overthrow of President Siad Barre in January 1991. In July 2000 delegates at the Somali national reconciliation conference in Arta, Djibouti, overwhelmingly approved a national Charter, which was to serve as Somalia's constitution for an interim period of three years. The Charter, which is divided into six main parts, guarantees Somali citizens the freedoms of expression, association and human rights, and distinctly separates the executive, the legislature and the judiciary, as well as guaranteeing the independence of the latter.

The Government

HEAD OF STATE

President: Col ABDULLAHI YUSSUF AHMED (took office 14 October 2004).

CABINET
(March 2006)

Prime Minister: ALI MOHAMMED GHEDI.
Deputy Prime Minister and Minister of Interior and Security: HUSSEIN MOHAMED AIDID.
Deputy Prime Minister and Minister of Finance: SALIM ALIOW IBROW.
Deputy Prime Minister and Minister of Information: MUHAMMAD ABDI HAYR.
Minister of Justice: ADAN MUHAMMAD NUR.
Minister of Religious Affairs and Endowment: UMAR MUMAHHAD MAHMUD.
Minister of Foreign Affairs: ABDULLAHI SHAYKH ISMA'IL.
Minister of Defence: ABDIRAHMAN MAHMUD ALI.
Minister of National Security: MOHAMED QANYARE AFRAH.
Minister of Agriculture: HASAN MOHAMED NUR.
Minister of Fishery and Marine Resources: HASSAN ABSHIR FARAH.
Minister of Animal Husbandry and Forestry: IBRAHIM MUHAMMAD ISAQ.
Minister of Petroleum: YUSUF MUHAMMAD AHMAD HARARE.
Minister of Trade: MUSE SUDI YALAHOW.
Minister of Health: ABDIAZIZ SHAYKH YUSUF.
Minister of Minerals and Water Resources: MAHMUD SALAD NUR.
Minister of Aviation and Land Transport: IBRAHIM ADAN HASAN.
Minister of Monetary Affairs: ABDIKARIM AHMAD ALI.
Minister of Co-operative Development: MUHAMMAD ABDULLAHI KAMIL.
Minister of Ports and Sea Transport: ALI ISMA'IL ABDI GIIR.
Minister of Posts and Telecommunications: ALI AHMAD JAMA JANGALI.
Minister of Energy: MUHAMMAD NURANI BAKAR.
Minister of Public Works and Housing: OSMAN HASSAN ALI 'ATO'.
Minister of Industry: ABDI MUHAMMAD TARAH.
Minister of Reconstruction and Resettlement: BARE ADAN SHIRE.
Minister of Lands and Settlement: MOWLID MA'ANE MAHMUD.
Minister of Rural Development: MUHAMMAD MAHMUD GULED.
Minister of Higher Education: HUSAYN MAHMUD SHAYKH HUSAYN.
Minister of Education: ALI ABDULLAHI OSOBLE.
Minister of Culture and Social Services: ABDI HASHI ABDULLAHI.

SOMALIA

Minister of Settlement and Disaster Management: Muhammad Usman Maye.
Minister of Regional Co-operation: Isma'il Mahmud Hure.
Minister for National Assets and Equipment: Mahmud Siyad Adan.
Minister of Tourism and Wildlife: Muhammad Mahmud Hayd.
Minister of Labour Development: Salah Ali Farah.
Minister of Sports and Youth Affairs: Ahmad Abdullahi Dakir.
Minister of Science and Technology: Isma'il Hasan Jama.
Minister of Reconciliation and Somali Communities Abroad: Shaykh Adan Shaykh Muhammad.
Minister of National Planning and International Co-operation: Abdirizaq Usman Hasan.
Minister of Constitutional and Federal Affairs: Abdallah Derow Isaq.
Minister of Women's Development and Family Affairs: Fowziya Muhammad Shaykh Hasan.
Minister for the Welfare of the Disabled and Orphans: Husayn Elabe Fahiye.
Minister for Rehabilitation and Training of Militia: Botan Ise Alin.
State Minister of Foreign Affairs: Ibrahim Shaykh Ali Hafun.
State Minister in the Office of the President: Khalid Umar Hashi.
State Minister in the Office of the Prime Minister: Abdulqadir H. Mahmud Dakane.
State Minister of Defence: Ali Muhammad Hared.
State Minister of Parliament and Government Relations: Abdrahman Adan Ibbi.
There are, in addition, 42 Assistant Ministers.

MINISTRIES

Until mid-2005 the Somali Government was based in Nairobi, Kenya, for security reasons. The President, the Prime Minister and several ministers relocated to Jowhar, Somalia, in June; however, a significant number of ministers returned to Mogadishu in defiance of the President and in April 2006 the Government remained divided.

Legislature

TRANSITIONAL PARLIAMENT

Speaker: Shariff Hassan Sheikh Adan.

In August 2000, following the successful completion of the Somali national reconciliation conference, which commenced in Arta, Djibouti, in May, a Transitional National Assembly (TNA), comprising 245 members, was established. Despite the expiry of its mandate in August 2003, the TNA remained in place, pending the election of a new legislative body. In late January 2004, following protracted negotiations in Kenya, an agreement was signed that provided for the establishment of a new 275-member transitional national parliament, to comprise 61 representatives from each of the four major clans (Dir, Hawiye, Darod and Oigil and Mirifleh) and 31 from an alliance of smaller clans. Members were sworn in to the Transitional Parliament in late August.

Political Organizations

Alliance Party: Hargeysa; f. 2001; Chair. Sulayman Mahmud Adan.
Islamic Party (Hizb al-Islam): radical Islamist party; Chair. Sheikh Ahmad Qasim.
Islamic Union Party (al-Ittihad al-Islam): aims to unite ethnic Somalis from Somalia, Ethiopia, Kenya and Djibouti in an Islamic state.
Juba Valley Alliance (JVA): f. 1999; alliance of militia and businessmen from the Haber Gedir and Marehan clans; Pres. Bare Adan Shire.
National Democratic League: Beled Weyne; f. 2003; Chair. Dr Abdirahman Abdulle Ali; Sec.-Gen. Abdikarim Husayn Idow.
Northern Somali Alliance (NSA): f. 1997 as alliance between the United Somali Front and the United Somali Party.
  United Somali Front (USF): f. 1989; represents Issas in the north-west of the country; Chair. Abd ar-Rahman Dualeh Ali; Sec.-Gen. Mohamed Osman Ali.
  United Somali Party (USP): opposes the SNM's declaration of the independent 'Republic of Somaliland'; Leader Mohamed Abdi Hashi.
Peace and Development Party: Mogadishu; f. 2002; Chair. Abdullahi Hasan Afrah.
Rahanwin Resistance Army (RRA): guerrilla force active around Baidoa; Chair. Mohamed Hasan Nur.
Somali Democratic Alliance (SDA): f. 1989; represents the Gadaburi ethnic grouping in the north-west; opposes the Isaaq-dominated SNM and its declaration of an independent 'Republic of Somaliland'; Leader Mohamed Farah Abdullah.
Somali Democratic Movement (SDM): represents the Rahanwin clan; movement split in early 1992, with this faction in alliance with Ali Mahdi Mohamed; Leader Abdulkadir Mohamed Adan.
Somali Eastern and Central Front (SECF): f. 1991; opposes the SNM's declaration of the independent 'Republic of Somaliland'; Chair. Hirsi Ismail Mohamed.
Somali National Alliance (SNA): f. 1992 as alliance between the Southern Somali National Movement (which withdrew in 1993) and the factions of the United Somali Congress, Somali Democratic Movement and Somali Patriotic Movement given below; Chair. Hussein Mohamed Aidid.
  Somali Democratic Movement (SDM): represents the Rahanwin clan; Chair. Adam Uthman Abdi; Sec.-Gen. Dr Yasin Ma'alim Abdullahi.
  Somali Patriotic Movement (SPM): f. 1989; represents Ogadenis (of the southern Darod clan); Chair. Gedi Ugas Madhar.
  United Somali Congress (USC): f. 1989; overthrew Siad Barre in 1991; party split in mid-1991, and again in mid-1995; Chair. Osman Hassan Ali 'Ato'.
Somali National Front (SNF): f. 1991; guerrilla force active in southern Somalia, promoting Darod clan interests and seeking restoration of SRSP Govt; a rival faction (led by Omar Haji Masaleh) is active in southern Somalia; Leader Gen. Mohamed Siad Hersi 'Morgan'.
Somali National Salvation Council: f. 2003; Chair. Muse Sudi Yalahow.
Somali Patriotic Movement (SPM): f. 1989 in southern Somalia; represents Ogadenis (of the Darod clan) in southern Somalia; this faction of the SPM has allied with the SNF in opposing the SNA; Chair. Gen. Aden Abdullahi Noor ('Gabio').
Somali Peace Loving Party: Mogadishu; f. 2002; Dr Khalid Umar Ali.
Somali People's Democratic Union (SPDU): f. 1997; breakaway group from the SSDF; Chair. Gen. Mohamed Jibril Museh.
Somali Reconciliation and Restoration Council (SRRC): f. 2001 by faction leaders opposed to the establishment of the Hasan administration; aims to establish a rival national government; Co-Chair. Hussein Mohamed Aidid, Hilowle Iman Umar, Aden Abdullahi Noor, Hasan Mohamed Nur, Abdullahi Shaykh Isma'il; Sec.-Gen. Mowlid Ma'aneh Mohamed.
Somali Revolutionary Socialist Party (SRSP): f. 1976 as the sole legal party; overthrown in Jan. 1991; conducts guerrilla operations in Gedo region, near border with Kenya; Sec.-Gen. (vacant); Asst Sec.-Gen. Ahmed Suleiman Abdullah.
Somali Salvation Democratic Front (SSDF): f. 1981 as the Democratic Front for the Salvation of Somalia (DFSS), as a coalition of the Somali Salvation Front, the Somali Workers' Party and the Democratic Front for the Liberation of Somalia; operates in cen. Somalia, although a smaller group has opposed the SNA around Kismayu in alliance with the SNF; Chair. Mohamed Abshir Monsa.
Somali Solidarity Party: Mogadishu; f. 1999; Chair. Abd ar-Rahman Musa Mohamed; Sec.-Gen. Sa'id Isa Mohamed.
Southern Somali National Movement (SSNM): based on coast in southern Somalia; Chair. Abdi Warsemeh Isar.
United Somali Congress (USC): f. 1989 in cen. Somalia; overthrew Siad Barre in Jan. 1991; party split in 1991, with this faction dominated by the Abgal sub-clan of the Hawiye clan, Somalia's largest ethnic group; Leader Abdullahi Ma'alin; Sec.-Gen. Musa Nur Amin.
  United Somali Congress—Somali National Alliance (USC—SNA): f. 1995 by dissident mems of the SNA's USC faction; represents the Habr Gidir sub-clan of the Hawiye; Leader Osman Hassan Ali 'Ato'.
  United Somali Congress—Somali Salvation Alliance (USC—SSA): Leader Muse Sudi Yalahow.
Unity for the Somali Republic Party (USRP): f. 1999; the first independent party to be established in Somalia since 1969; Leader Abdi Nur Darman.

In November 1993 interim President Ali Mahdi Mohamed was reported to have assumed the leadership of the **Somali Salvation**

SOMALIA

Alliance (SSA), a coalition of 12 factions opposed to Gen. Aidid, including the Somali African Muki Organization (SAMO), the Somali National Union (SNU), the USF, the SDA, the SDM, the SPM, the USC (pro-Mahdi faction), the SSDF, the Somali National Democratic Union (SNDU), the SNF and the SSNM. In May 1994 the SNU announced its intention to leave the alliance and join the SNA.

Diplomatic Representation

EMBASSIES IN SOMALIA

Note: Following the overthrow of Siad Barre in January 1991, all foreign embassies in Somalia were closed and all diplomatic personnel left the country. Some embassies were reopened, including those of France, Sudan and the USA, following the arrival of the US-led Unified Task Force (UNITAF) in December 1992; however, nearly all foreign diplomats left Somalia in anticipation of the withdrawal of the UN peace-keeping force, UNOSOM, in early 1995.

Algeria: POB 2850, Mogadishu; tel. (1) 81696.
Bulgaria: Hodan District, Km 5, off Via Afgoi, POB 1736, Mogadishu; tel. (1) 81820.
China, People's Republic: POB 548, Mogadishu; tel. (1) 20805.
Cuba: Mogadishu.
Djibouti: Mogadishu.
Egypt: Via al-Mukarah Km 4, POB 76, Mogadishu; tel. (1) 80781; Ambassador Dr SALIH HALIM.
Ethiopia: POB 368, Mogadishu.
France: Corso Primo Luglio, POB 13, Mogadishu; tel. (1) 21715.
Germany: Via Mahamoud Harbi, POB 17, Mogadishu; tel. (1) 20547.
India: Via Jigjiga, Shingani, POB 955, Mogadishu; tel. (1) 21262.
Iran: Via al-Mukarah, POB 1166, Mogadishu; tel. (1) 80881.
Italy: Via Alto Giuba, POB 6, Mogadishu; tel. (1) 20544; Ambassador FRANCESCO LANATA.
Kenya: Via Mecca, POB 618, Mogadishu; tel. (1) 80857; Ambassador MOHAMMED AFFEY.
Korea, Democratic People's Republic: Via Km 5, Mogadishu; Ambassador KIM RYONG SU.
Kuwait: First Medina Rd, Km 5, POB 1348, Mogadishu.
Libya: Via Medina, POB 125, Mogadishu; Ambassador MOHAMED ZUBEYD.
Nigeria: Via Km 5, Mogadishu; tel. (1) 81362.
Oman: Via Afgoi, POB 2992, Mogadishu; tel. (1) 81658.
Pakistan: Via Afgoi, Km 5, POB 339, Mogadishu; tel. (1) 80856.
Qatar: Via Km 4, POB 1744, Mogadishu; tel. (1) 80746.
Romania: Via Lido, POB 651, Mogadishu.
Saudi Arabia: Via Benadir, POB 603, Mogadishu; tel. (1) 22087.
Serbia and Montenegro: Via Mecca, POB 952, Mogadishu; tel. (1) 81729.
Sudan: Via al-Mukarah, POB 552, Mogadishu; Chargé d'affaires a.i. ALI HASSAN ALI.
Syria: Via Medina, POB 986, Mogadishu.
Turkey: Via Km 6, POB 2833, Mogadishu; tel. (1) 81975.
United Arab Emirates: Via Afgoi, Km 5, Mogadishu; tel. (1) 23178.
United Kingdom: Waddada Xasan Geedd Abtoow 7/8, POB 1036, Mogadishu; tel. (1) 20288.
USA: Via Afgoi, Km 5, POB 574, Mogadishu; tel. (1) 39971.
Yemen: Via Km 5, POB 493, Mogadishu; Ambassador AHMED HAMID ALI UMAR.
Zimbabwe: Mogadishu.

Judicial System

Constitutional arrangements in operation until 1991 provided for the Judiciary to be independent of the executive and legislative powers. Laws and acts having the force of law were required to conform to the provisions of the Constitution and to the general principles of Islam.

Attorney-General: ABDULLAH DAHIR BARRE.
Supreme Court: Mogadishu; the court of final instance in civil, criminal, administrative and auditing matters; Chair. Sheikh AHMAD HASAN.
Military Supreme Court: Mogadishu; f. 1970; tried mems of the armed forces.
National Security Court: Mogadishu; heard cases of treason.
Courts of Appeal: Mogadishu; sat at Mogadishu and Hargeysa, with two sections, General and Assize.
Regional Courts: There were eight Regional Courts, with two sections, General and Assize.
District Courts: There were 84 District Courts, with Civil and Criminal Divisions. The Civil Division had jurisdiction over all controversies where the cause of action had arisen under *Shari'a* (Islamic) Law or Customary Law and any other Civil controversies where the matter in dispute did not involve more than 3,000 shillings. The Criminal Division had jurisdiction with respect to offences punishable with imprisonment not exceeding three years, or fines not exceeding 3,000 shillings, or both.
Qadis: Districts Courts of civil jurisdiction under Islamic Law.

In September 1993, in accordance with Resolution 865 of the UN Security Council, a judiciary re-establishment council, composed of Somalis, was created in Mogadishu to rehabilitate the judicial and penal systems.

Judiciary Re-establishment Council (JRC): Mogadishu; Chair. Dr ABD AL-RAHMAN HAJI GA'AL.

Following the withdrawal of the UN peace-keeping force, UNOSOM, in early 1995, most regions outside of Mogadishu reverted to clan-based fiefdoms where Islamic (*Shari'a*) law (comprising an Islamic Supreme Council and local Islamic high courts) prevailed. In October 1996 Ali Mahdi Mohamed endorsed a new Islamic judicial system under which appeals could be lodged on all sentences passed by Islamic courts, and no sentence imposed by the courts could be implemented prior to an appeal court ruling. In August 1998 the Governor of the Banaadir administration announced the application of *Shari'a* law in Mogadishu and its environs thenceforth.

Religion

ISLAM

Islam is the state religion. Most Somalis are Sunni Muslims.
Imam: Gen. MOHAMED ABSHIR.

CHRISTIANITY

The Roman Catholic Church

Somalia comprises a single diocese, directly responsible to the Holy See. At 31 December 2003 there were an estimated 100 adherents.
Bishop of Mogadishu: (vacant), POB 273, Ahmed bin Idris, Mogadishu; tel. (1) 20184.

The Anglican Communion

Within the Episcopal Church in Jerusalem and the Middle East, the Bishop in Egypt has jurisdiction over Somalia.

The Press

The Country: POB 1178, Mogadishu; tel. (1) 21206; f. 1991; daily.
Dalka: POB 388, Mogadishu; tel. (1) 500533; e-mail dalka@somalinternet.com; internet www.dalka-online.com; f. 1967; current affairs; weekly.
Heegan (Vigilance): POB 1178, Mogadishu; tel. (1) 21206; f. 1978; weekly; English; Editor MOHAMOUD M. AFRAH.
Horseed: POB 1178, Mogadishu; tel. (1) 21206; e-mail horseednet@gmail.com; internet www.horseednet.com; weekly; in Somali and English.
Huuriya (Liberty): Hargeysa; daily.
Jamhuuriya (The Republic): Hargeysa; e-mail jamhuria@emirates.net.ae; internet members.tripod.com/~jamhuria; independent; daily; Editor-in-Chief HASSAN SAID FAISAL ALI; circ. 2,500.
Al Mujeehid: Hargeysa; weekly.
New Era: POB 1178, Mogadishu; tel. (1) 21206; quarterly; in English, Somali and Arabic.
Qaran (Nation): Mogadishu; e-mail qaranpress@hotmail.com; internet www.qaranpress.com; financial information; daily; in Somali; Editor ABDULAHI AHMED ALI; circ. 2,000.
Riyaaq (Happiness): Boosaaso.
Sahan (Pioneer): Boosaaso; Editor MUHAMMAD DEEQ.
Somalia in Figures: Ministry of National Planning, POB 1742, Mogadishu; tel. (1) 80384; govt statistical publ; 3 a year; in English.
Somalia Times: POB 555, Mogadishu BN 03040; e-mail info@somalpost.com; internet www.somaliatimes.com; Somali; weekly; circ. 50,000.

NEWS AGENCIES

Horn of Africa News Agency: Mogadishu; e-mail info@hananews.org; internet www.hananews.org; f. 1990.

SOMALIA

Somali National News Agency (SONNA): POB 1748, Mogadishu; tel. (1) 24058; Dir MUHAMMAD HASAN KAHIN.

Foreign Bureaux

Agence France-Presse (AFP) (France): POB 1178, Mogadishu; Rep. MOHAMED ROBLE NOOR.

Agenzia Nazionale Stampa Associata (ANSA) (Italy): POB 1399, Mogadishu; tel. (1) 20626; Rep. ABDULKADIR MOHAMOUD WALAYO.

Publishers

Government Printer: POB 1743, Mogadishu.

Somalia d'Oggi: Piazzale della Garesa, POB 315, Mogadishu; law, economics and reference.

Broadcasting and Communications

TELECOMMUNICATIONS

Ministry of Information: POB 1748, Mogadishu; tel. (1) 999621; Dir-Gen. A. ALI ASKAR.

Somali Telecom (Olympic Telecommunications): Mogadishu.

Somaliland Telecommunications Corpn: Hargeysa; Dir MOHAMED ARWO.

BROADCASTING

Radio

Holy Koran Radio: Mogadishu; f. 1996; religious broadcasts in Somali.

Radio Awdal: Boorama, 'Somaliland'; operated by the Gadabursi clan.

Radio Banaadir: Tahlil Warsame Bldg, 4 Maka al-Mukarama Rd, Mogadishu; tel. (5) 944176; e-mail rbb@radiobanadir.com; internet www.radiobanadir.com; f. 2000; serves Mogadishu and its environs.

Radio Free Somalia: f. 1993; operates from Galacaio in northeastern Somalia; relays humanitarian and educational programmes.

Radio Gaalkayco: operates from 'Puntland'.

Radio Hargeysa, the Voice of the 'Republic of Somaliland': POB 14, Hargeysa; tel. 155; e-mail radiohargeysa@yahoo.com; internet www.radiosomaliland.com/radiohargeisa.html; serves the northern region ('Somaliland'); broadcasts in Somali, and relays Somali and Amharic transmission from Radio Mogadishu; Dir of Radio IDRIS EGAL NUR.

Radio HornAfrique: Mogadishu; f. 1999; commercial independent station broadcasting music and programmes on social issues; Dir AHMAD ABDI SALAN HAJI ADAN.

Radio Mogadishu, Voice of the Masses of the Somali Republic: southern Mogadishu; f. 1993 by supporters of Gen. Aidid after the facilities of the fmr state-controlled radio station, Radio Mogadishu (of which Gen. Aidid's faction took control in 1991), were destroyed by UNOSOM; broadcasts in Somali, Amharic, Arabic, English and Swahili; Chair. FARAH HASAN AYOBOQORE.

Radio Mogadishu, Voice of Somali Pacification: Mogadishu; f. 1995 by supporters of Osman Hassan Ali 'Ato'; broadcasts in Somali, English and Arabic; Dir-Gen. MUHAMMAD DIRIYEH ILMI.

Radio Mogadishu, Voice of the Somali Republic: northern Mogadishu; f. 1992 by supporters of Ali Mahdi Mohamed; Chair. FARAH HASSAN AYOBOQORE.

Radio Somaliland: e-mail radio@radiosomaliland.com; internet www.radiosomaliland.com.

Voice of Peace: POB 1631, Addis Ababa, Ethiopia; f. 1993; aims to promote peace and reconstruction in Somalia; receives support from UNICEF and the AU.

Some radio receivers are used for public address purposes in small towns and villages.

Television

A television service, financed by Kuwait and the United Arab Emirates, was inaugurated in 1983. Programmes in Somali and Arabic are broadcast for three hours daily, extended to four hours on Fridays and public holidays. Reception is limited to a 30-km radius of Mogadishu.

Somali Television Network (STN): Mogadishu; f. 1999; broadcasts 22 channels in Somali, English, French, Hindi, Gujarati, Bengali, Punjabi, Italian and Arabic; Man. Dir ABURAHMAN ROBLEY ULAYEREH.

Television HornAfrique: Mogadishu; f. 1999; broadcasts 6 channels in Somali and Arabic; CEO ALI IMAN SHARMARKEH.

Finance

(cap. = capital; res = reserves; m. = million; brs = branches; amounts in Somali shillings unless otherwise stated)

BANKING

Central Bank

Central Bank of Somalia (Bankiga Dhexe ee Soomaaliya): Corso Somalia 55, POB 11, Mogadishu; tel. (1) 657733; f. 1960; bank of issue; cap. and res 132.5m. (Sept. 1985); Gov. BASHIR ISSE ALI; Gen. Man MOHAMED MOHAMED NUR.

A central bank (with 10 branches) is also in operation in Hargeysa (in the self-proclaimed 'Republic of Somaliland').

Commercial Banks

Commercial Bank of Somalia: Via Primo Luglio, POB 203, Mogadishu; tel. (1) 22861; f. 1990 to succeed the Commercial and Savings Bank of Somalia; state-owned; cap. 1,000m. (May 1990); 33 brs.

Universal Bank of Somalia: Mogadishu; f. 2002; cap. US $10m.; Gen. Man. MAHAD ADAN BARKHADLE (acting).

Private Bank

Somali-Malaysian Commercial Bank: Mogadishu; f. 1997; cap. US $4m.

Development Bank

Somali Development Bank: Via Primo Luglio, POB 1079, Mogadishu; tel. (1) 21800; f. 1968; state-owned; cap. and res 2,612.7m. (Dec. 1988); Pres. MOHAMED MOHAMED NUR; 4 brs.

INSURANCE

Cassa per le Assicurazioni Sociali della Somalia: POB 123, Mogadishu; f. 1950; workers' compensation; Dir-Gen. HASSAN MOHAMED JAMA; 9 brs.

State Insurance Co of Somalia: POB 992, Mogadishu; f. 1974; Gen. Man. ABDULLAHI GA'AL; brs throughout Somalia.

Trade and Industry

DEVELOPMENT ORGANIZATIONS

Agricultural Development Corpn: POB 930, Mogadishu; f. 1971 by merger of fmr agricultural and machinery agencies and grain marketing board; supplies farmers with equipment and materials and purchases growers' cereal and oil seed crops; Dir-Gen. MOHAMED FARAH ANSHUR.

Livestock Development Agency: POB 1759, Mogadishu; Dir-Gen. HASSAN WELI SCEK HUSSEN; brs throughout Somalia.

Somali Co-operative Movement: Mogadishu; Chair. HASSAN HAWADLE MADAR.

Somali Oil Refinery: POB 1241, Mogadishu; Chair. NUR AHMED DARAWISH.

Water Development Agency: POB 525, Mogadishu; Dir-Gen. KHALIF HAJI FARAH.

CHAMBER OF COMMERCE

Chamber of Commerce, Industry and Agriculture: Via Asha, POB 27, Mogadishu; tel. (1) 3209; Chair. MOHAMED IBRAHIM HAJI EGAL.

TRADE ASSOCIATION

National Agency of Foreign Trade: POB 602, Mogadishu; major foreign trade agency; state-owned; brs in Berbera and over 150 centres throughout Somalia; Dir-Gen. JAMA AW MUSE.

UTILITIES

Water Development Agency: POB 525, Mogadishu; Dir-Gen. KHALIF HAJI FARAH.

TRADE UNIONS

General Federation of Somali Trade Unions: POB 1179, Mogadishu; Chair. MOHAMED FARAH ISSA GASHAN.

National Union of Somali Journalists (NUSOJ): Tree Biano Bldg, Via al-Mukarah Km4, Mogadishu; fax (1) 859944; e-mail nusoj@nusoj.org; internet www.nusoj.org; f. 2002 as Somali Journal-

SOMALIA

ists' Network (SOJON); name changed as above in 2005; Sec.-Gen. OMAR FARUK OSMAN; 6 brs across Somalia.

Transport

RAILWAYS

There are no railways in Somalia.

ROADS

In 1999 there were an estimated 22,100 km of roads, of which some 11.8% were paved.

SHIPPING

Merca, Berbera, Mogadishu and Kismayu are the chief ports. An EU-sponsored development project for the port of Berbera (in 'Somaliland') was announced in February 1996. It was reported that the port of Mogadishu, which had been largely closed since 1995, was reopened in early 2000. In 2005 the International Maritime Bureau warned ship operators to avoid the coast of Somalia following an increase in piracy.

Somali Ports Authority: POB 935, Mogadishu; tel. (1) 30081; Port Dir MOHAMED JUMA FURAH.

Juba Enterprises Beder & Sons Ltd: POB 549, Mogadishu; privately owned.

National Shipping Line: POB 588, Mogadishu; tel. (1) 23021; state-owned; Gen. Man. Dr ABDULLAHI MOHAMED SALAD.

Puntland Shipping Service: Boosaaso.

Shosman Commercial Co Ltd: North-Eastern Pasaso; privately owned.

Somali Shipping Corpn: POB 2775, Mogadishu; state-owned.

CIVIL AVIATION

Mogadishu has an international airport. There are airports at Hargeysa and Baidoa and six other airfields. It was reported that a daily service had been inaugurated in April 1994 between Hargeysa (in the self-declared 'Republic of Somaliland') and Nairobi, Kenya. Mogadishu international airport (closed since 1995) was officially reopened in mid-1998, but continuing civil unrest limited services significantly.

Air Somalia: Mogadishu; f. 2001; operates internal passenger services and international services to destinations in Africa and the Middle East; Chair. ALI FARAH ABDULLEH.

SOUTH AFRICA

Introductory Survey

Location, Climate, Language, Religion, Flag, Capital

The Republic of South Africa occupies the southern extremity of the African mainland. It is bordered by Namibia to the north-west, by Botswana and Zimbabwe to the north, by Mozambique to the north-east, and by Swaziland to the east. Lesotho is completely surrounded by South African territory. The climate is generally sub-tropical, but with considerable regional variations. Temperatures in Cape Town, on the south-west coast, vary from 7°C (45°F) to 26°C (79°F), with an annual average of about 17°C (63°F). Annual rainfall averages 510 mm (20 ins) at Cape Town, and 1,101 mm (43 ins) at Durban, on the east coast. The official languages are Sepedi, Sesotho, Setswana, siSwati, Tshivenda, Xitsonga, Afrikaans, English, isiNdebele, isiXhosa and isiZulu. About 77.8% of the population are black, 10.2% are white, 8.7% are Coloured (of mixed race), and 2.5% are Asian (mainly of Indian origin). Most of the inhabitants profess Christianity, although traditional African religions are still adhered to. There are also small minorities of Hindus (nearly all Asians) and Muslims (mainly Coloureds and Asians). The national flag (proportions 2 by 3) has a green 'Y' shape extending from the upper and lower hoist corners to the centre of the fly end, bordered in white on its outer edges, and in light orange on its inner edges near the hoist; the areas above and below the horizontal band of the 'Y' are red and blue respectively, with a black triangle at the hoist. The administrative capital is Pretoria, the legislative capital is Cape Town, and the judicial capital is Bloemfontein.

Recent History

On 31 May 1910 four British dependencies were merged to form the Union of South Africa, a dominion under the British Crown. In 1931 the British Parliament recognized the Union as an independent country within the Commonwealth. From the establishment of South Africa until 1984, national administration was the exclusive preserve of the white population.

The National Party (NP), which acceded to power in 1948, introduced the doctrine of apartheid (in theory the separate, but equal, development of all racial groups, in practice leading to white, particularly Afrikaner, supremacy). The principal opposition to government policy during the 1950s took the form of a campaign of civil disobedience, led by the multiracial African National Congress of South Africa (ANC). In 1959 some members of the ANC formed the exclusively black Pan-Africanist Congress (PAC). In 1960 the ANC and the PAC conducted opposition to the 'pass laws' (which required blacks to be in possession of special documentation in designated white urban areas); at one demonstration, in Sharpeville, 67 blacks were killed by security forces, prompting international outrage, and further demonstrations within South Africa, as a result of which the ANC and the PAC were declared illegal. Both movements subsequently formed military wings, based outside South Africa, to conduct campaigns of sabotage. An influential leader of the ANC, Nelson Mandela, was detained in 1962 and sentenced to life imprisonment on a charge of sabotage in 1964, but remained a focus for opposition to apartheid.

On 31 May 1961, following a referendum among white voters in October 1960, South Africa became a republic, and left the Commonwealth. Dr Hendrik Verwoerd was Prime Minister from 1958 until his assassination in September 1966. He was succeeded by the former Minister of Justice, Balthazar Johannes (B. J.) Vorster.

As an integral part of the policy of apartheid, the territorial segregation of African ethnic groups was enforced, on the grounds that the Native Reserves (comprising only 13% of national territory) constituted the historic 'homelands' (Bantustans) of different African nations. In 1963 Transkei was accorded 'self-governing' status, with an Executive Council, headed by a Chief Minister, to be elected by a Legislative Assembly. Bophuthatswana (June 1972), Ciskei (August 1972), Lebowa (October 1972), Gazankulu (February 1973), KwaZulu (April 1973), Qwaqwa (November 1974), KwaNdebele (October 1977), and KaNgwane (August 1984) were subsequently granted 'self-government'. Transkei was declared 'independent' in October 1976, Bophuthatswana in December 1977, Venda in September 1979 and Ciskei in December 1981. The population of the 'independent homelands' was not entitled to South African citizenship. The 'independent homelands' were not recognized by any government other than that of South Africa.

The numerous discriminatory laws regulating the lives of the country's black, 'Coloured' (a term used to denote people of mixed race) and 'Indian' (Asian) populations, combined with stringent security legislation, led to the detention without trial of many of the Government's opponents, the banning of black political organizations outside the 'homelands', and the forced removal of hundreds of thousands of blacks in accordance with the provisions of the Group Areas Act of 1966 (which imposed residential segregation of the races) and the 'homelands' policy. In June 1976 violent riots occurred in Soweto (South-Western Townships), near Johannesburg, and rapidly spread to other black urban areas. Vorster used the executive's virtually limitless powers, conferred by the newly adopted Internal Security Act, to suppress riots and strikes. Several hundred people died in confrontations with the security forces, and many more were detained without trial. Allegations of human rights violations by security forces culminated in international indignation at the death in detention of a black community leader, Steve Biko, in September 1977. In 1978 black, Coloured and Indian activists founded the Azanian People's Organization (AZAPO).

In September 1978 Vorster resigned as Prime Minister, and was succeeded by Pieter Willem (P. W.) Botha, hitherto the Minister of Defence. In February 1981 a new, 60-member advisory body, the President's Council, comprising representatives of the white, Coloured and Indian population, was formed to consider constitutional reform. Its recommendations to include Coloureds and Indians (but not blacks) in a three-chamber Parliament, with a multiracial government (led by an executive President), exacerbated inter-party differences: the 'verligte' (liberal) wing of the NP, led by Botha, advocated the establishment of a confederation of South Africa and the 'homelands', with separate citizenships but a common South African nationality, and was strongly opposed by the 'verkrampte' (uncompromising) wing of the party. In March 1982 16 extreme right-wing parliamentary deputies who had opposed the constitutional recommendations were expelled from the NP; they subsequently formed the Conservative Party of South Africa (CP), in conjunction with other right-wing elements.

Throughout 1983 and 1984, despite opposition from both the CP and the Progressive Federal Party (PFP), Botha pursued his policy of constitutional reform. The majority vote of the Coloured Labour Party (LP) in 1983 to participate in the reform programme caused divisions within the party. The constitutional body representing the Indian population, the South African Indian Council (SAIC), provisionally agreed to the proposals, subject to approval by an Indian community referendum. This decision was, however, opposed by the Transvaal Anti-SAIC Committee, an organization that had been formed in 1981 in protest at participation in elections to the SAIC. In August 1983 the Committee established the United Democratic Front (UDF), to organize resistance on a national scale to Indian and Coloured participation in the constitutional reforms. The UDF rapidly became the principal legal opposition movement.

The constitutional reforms were approved by the House of Assembly in September 1983, and by about 66% of voters in an all-white referendum in November. In the same month the PFP decided to take part in the reformed system. However, six 'homeland' leaders, including Chief Mangosuthu Gatsha Buthelezi, the Chief Minister of KwaZulu (who had consistently opposed the 'homelands' policy), rejected the constitutional reforms on the grounds that blacks remained excluded from participation in the central Government. Despite a previous pledge by the Prime Minister to assess Coloured and Indian opinion on the reforms, elections to the Coloured and Indian chambers of the new Parliament, known as the House of Representatives and the House of Delegates respectively, took place in August 1984, without prior referendums. As a result, the boycott that had been organized by the UDF was widely observed: about 18% of the eligible Coloured population voted in the elections to the House of Representatives, with the LP winning 76 of the 80 directly elected seats, while only 16.6% of eligible Indian voters participated in the elections to the House of Delegates, with the National People's Party (NPP) winning 18 and the Solidarity Party 17 of the 40 directly elected seats. (The House of Assembly, as elected in 1981, remained in office.)

The new Constitution came into effect in September 1984. Under the terms of the Constitution, legislative power was vested in the State President and the tricameral Parliament, comprising the 178-member House of Assembly (for the representation of whites), the 85-member House of Representatives (for Coloureds) and the 45-member House of Delegates (for Indians). Following the adoption of the Constitution in September, the post of Prime Minister was abolished, and Botha was unanimously elected to the new office of State President (which combined the powers of Head of State and Prime Minister) by an electoral college, comprising members of all three parliamentary chambers. A President's Council, a new Cabinet and three Ministers' Councils (one for each population group) were subsequently established. The Cabinet comprised only two non-white members, the Chairmen of the Indian and Coloured Ministers' Councils, neither of whom was given a portfolio.

During 1985–86 a number of the laws on which apartheid was based were modified or repealed, prompting strong right-wing opposition. The Immorality Act (1927) and the Prohibition of Mixed Marriages Act (1949), which banned sexual relations and marriage between members of different races, were repealed in April 1985, and in the following month it was announced that the Prohibition of Political Interference Act (1967), prohibiting members of different racial groups from belonging to the same political party, was to be abrogated. In April 1986 the Government promulgated legislation that provided for the removal of a number of restrictions on the movement, residence and employment of blacks in white urban areas. On 1 July the 'pass laws' were officially repealed, with the introduction of uniform identity documents for all South African citizens. On the same day reforms concerning the structure of local and provincial government were implemented, and legislation granting blacks limited rights to own property in black urban areas entered into force. In the same month it was announced that citizens of the four 'independent homelands' who were residing and working permanently in South Africa were to regain South African citizenship; in effect, however, only a small proportion of the population of the 'homelands' was eligible. Following discussions, initiated by Buthelezi in April 1986, regarding the establishment of a joint authority for his 'homeland', KwaZulu, and the province of Natal, the Government agreed to the formation of an administrative body, the Joint Executive Authority (which was installed in November 1987).

The introduction of the new Constitution in September 1984 prompted severe rioting in the black townships, which was violently repressed by the security forces. Factional clashes within the black community also occurred, notably between supporters of the ANC and of the Inkatha Movement, a Zulu organization led by Buthelezi. In July 1985 the Government declared a state of emergency in 36 districts; by March 1986 it was estimated that 757 people had been killed, and almost 8,000 arrested. In June of that year Botha declared a nation-wide state of emergency, on the grounds that national security was endangered by subversive elements. Press censorship subsequently became progressively stricter, and the powers of the security forces were extended. Opposition to the Government emerged from the influential Congress of South African Trade Unions (COSATU).

At a general election to the House of Assembly in May 1987, the NP secured 123 of the 166 directly-elective seats. The CP increased its representation from 17 to 22 elective seats, thereby replacing the PFP as the official opposition. In June the Government renewed the state of emergency, and further stringent press restrictions were imposed.

In January 1989 Botha withdrew from his official duties, owing to ill health; in February he resigned as leader of the NP, and was succeeded by Frederik Willem (F. W.) de Klerk, hitherto Minister of National Education. Despite almost unanimous demands from the party that he should share power with de Klerk before retiring at the next general election, Botha refused to allow his power as State President to be eroded, and in March he resumed his official duties. In April the PFP, the Independent Party (which had been formed by one of a number of 'verligte' defectors from the NP in 1988) and the National Democratic Movement (established by dissident PFP members in late 1987) merged to form the Democratic Party (DP).

The state of emergency was extended for a further 12 months in June 1989. In August Botha claimed that members of his Cabinet had omitted to inform him of a prospective visit by de Klerk to Zambia to meet with President Kenneth Kaunda (which he opposed, owing to Kaunda's support for the ANC). Following a confrontation with the Cabinet, Botha resigned as State President. Shortly afterwards de Klerk was appointed acting President.

Elections to the three Houses of Parliament took place in September 1989. The NP won 93 of the 166 elective seats in the House of Assembly, while the CP secured 39 seats, and the DP 33 seats. Less than 12% of the Coloured electorate voted in the general election to the House of Representatives, at which the LP won 69 of the 80 directly-elective seats. Some 20% of the Indian electorate voted in the general election to the House of Delegates: the Solidarity Party secured 16 of the 40 directly-elective seats, while the NPP won nine. In mid-September, following his inauguration as State President, de Klerk stated that the implementation of constitutional reforms was his highest priority.

On 2 February 1990 de Klerk announced several radical reforms, including the legalization of the ANC, the PAC, the South African Communist Party (SACP), the UDF and more than 30 other banned political organizations. Nelson Mandela and a further 120 political prisoners were to be released unconditionally. In addition, most emergency regulations restricting the media were to be removed, as were repressive measures imposed on former political detainees; detention without trial was to be limited to a maximum of six months. De Klerk confirmed that the Government intended to initiate negotiations with the black opposition, with the aim of drafting a new democratic constitution. Leaders of the extreme right-wing parties reacted to de Klerk's reforms with threats of violence.

Mandela's release from prison, on 11 February 1990, received much international attention. In March he was elected Deputy President of the ANC. In spite of appeals by Mandela for reconciliation between rival factions within the black community, the continuing violence in Natal between supporters of the Inkatha Movement and mainly Xhosa-speaking supporters of the ANC intensified in March and April, and unrest erupted in several black townships. The first formal discussions between the ANC and the de Klerk Government took place in early May. In mid-May legislation was introduced that granted temporary immunity from prosecution to political exiles who had committed crimes, including leaders of the ANC. In June de Klerk repealed the state of emergency in all provinces except Natal. In July Buthelezi reconstituted the Inkatha Movement as the Inkatha Freedom Party (IFP), in order to participate in future constitutional negotiations. At a second series of discussions in August, the ANC and the Government reached an agreement whereby, in preparation for constitutional negotiations, the ANC was to suspend its guerrilla activities, and the Government was to release more than 3,000 political prisoners and to facilitate the return to South Africa of an estimated 40,000 exiles. However, the ANC subsequently continued to train recruits for its military wing (known as Umkhonto we Sizwe—MK) and to stockpile ammunition, thereby contravening the terms of its cease-fire and causing the Government to delay the release of political prisoners and the repatriation of exiles.

During August 1990 factional fighting between supporters of the IFP and of the ANC, which was no longer confined to Natal, escalated in the black townships surrounding Johannesburg; more than 500 people were reported to have been killed by the end of that month. Nevertheless, in October the state of emergency was revoked in Natal. Also that month the Separate Amenities Act of 1953 (which had imposed racial segregation with regard to public amenities) was repealed, prompting right-wing protests, particularly from the Afrikaanse Weerstandsbeweging (AWB), a paramilitary organization that had been formed in 1973 under the leadership of Eugene Terre'Blanche. During October the NP opened its membership to all races. In December Oliver Tambo, the President of the ANC, returned after more than 30 years in exile.

In February 1991 de Klerk announced that he was to introduce draft legislation to repeal the principal remaining apartheid laws: the Land Acts of 1913 and 1936 (which stipulated that the black population was entitled to own only 13.6% of the land), the Group Areas Act, the Black Communities Act of 1984 (which enforced the separate status of black townships) and the Population Registration Act of 1950 (which decreed that all South Africans should be registered at birth according to race) were subsequently abolished. In the same month the Government agreed to assume joint administrative powers in Ciskei, following increasing pressure within the 'independent homeland' for its reincorporation into South Africa and for the resignation of its military ruler. In mid-February the Government and the ANC reached agreement on a wide range of issues, including the release of political prisoners, the return of exiles and the curtailment of activities by the MK. However, increasing township violence continued to impede constitutional negotiations. In May Winnie Mandela, the wife of Nelson Mandela, was found guilty of assaulting and kidnapping a young ANC activist, Stompie Moeketsi Seipei, in 1988, and was sentenced to six years' imprisonment, causing considerable embarrassment for the ANC. (Winnie Mandela, who became separated from Nelson Mandela in 1992, remained at liberty, pending an appeal against the verdict; in June 1993 the conviction for assault was overturned, and her sentence was commuted to a fine and a suspended term of imprisonment.) In July 1991, at a national congress of the ANC, Nelson Mandela was elected as its President and Cyril Ramaphosa, hitherto leader of the National Union of Mineworkers, was elected Secretary-General of the organization.

In August 1991 the Government declared an amnesty for all political exiles. During that month the UDF was dissolved. In September the Government, the ANC, the IFP and 23 other political organizations signed a national peace accord, in an attempt to end township violence; however, unrest continued to escalate. In October a judicial commission of inquiry was established to assess the causes of civil violence.

A multi-party conference on South Africa's future, known as the Convention for a Democratic South Africa (CODESA), was convened in December 1991. CODESA was attended by the Government and 18 political organizations, including the ANC, the NP, the DP, the LP, the NPP, New Solidarity (formerly the Solidarity Party) and representatives of the 'homelands' (including the IFP, which represented KwaZulu); the conference was boycotted by the PAC, AZAPO and the CP. The negotiating body's stated aim to create an undivided South Africa was rejected by the IFP, which favoured the concept of a South African federation of independent states, and by the Bophuthatswana administration, which demanded total independence from South Africa.

In March 1992 a referendum of the white population, aimed at determining the level of support for the negotiation of a democratic constitution, resulted in an overwhelming mandate for the continuation of the process of reform. In May, however, constitutional negotiations were suspended, owing to the Government's insistence on having a majority vote in CODESA. The ANC subsequently organized a campaign of mass protests. In June several residents of Boipatong, a black township, were massacred, apparently by Inkatha supporters and allegedly with the complicity of the security forces. Following a visit to the township by de Klerk, 30 demonstrators were killed as the security forces suppressed an anti-Government protest. The ANC subsequently withdrew from all bilateral discussions with the Government, pending the latter's agreement to a number of demands, including the immediate release of all remaining political prisoners and effective action to curtail township violence. In August the ANC, SACP and COSATU intensified their campaign of anti-Government protests. In the same month several parliamentary deputies belonging to the CP defected to form a new extreme right-wing party, the Afrikaner Volksunie (AVU).

In mid-1992 the ANC announced that it was to organize a series of demonstrations in protest against 'homeland' leaders who wished their territories (Bophuthatswana, Ciskei, KwaZulu and Qwaqwa) to retain a strong measure of autonomy in the future South Africa. In September Ciskei security forces killed 28 ANC demonstrators, and injured about 200, prompting international outrage. The ANC accused the South African security forces (some of whose members had been seconded to Ciskei) of complicity in the incident. In mid-September de Klerk announced that measures to reduce the 'independence' of the 'homelands' would be implemented. In late 1992 the leaders of Bophuthatswana, Ciskei and KwaZulu, in conjunction with the IFP, the AVU and the CP, formed a pressure group (the Concerned South Africans Group—COSAG) to campaign for a maximum degree of regional autonomy.

In late September 1992, following intense negotiations, a peace summit was held, at which the Government accepted the ANC's preconditions for the resumption of constitutional negotiations. A 'record of understanding' was signed, which stated that the new Constitution would be drafted by an elected constitutional assembly and that there would be a non-racial elected interim government. In October the Constitution was amended to permit blacks to serve in the Cabinet. Later in that month legislation was approved that granted immunity from prosecution to perpetrators of politically motivated offences committed prior to 8 October 1990. In December Buthelezi published a draft constitution for a planned state comprising the KwaZulu 'homeland' and the province of Natal, which would retain a strong measure of autonomy within a future South African federation.

In February 1993 the ANC and the Government agreed to the immediate resumption of multi-party discussions. In March, at a meeting between the Government and 25 delegations from national political parties (including the formerly unco-operative PAC, IFP and CP) and the 'homeland' Governments, it was decided that CODESA was to be reconstituted, with the PAC, the IFP and the CP granted equal status with the other representatives. In May an informal alliance was established of 21 right-wing organizations (including the AVU, the CP and the AWB), known as the Afrikaner Volksfront (AVF), to co-ordinate opposition to the negotiating process.

In June 1993 legislation providing for the abolition of the President's Council was approved by Parliament. In July the negotiating forum confirmed that the elections would take place on 27 April 1994, despite continuing opposition from COSAG. The IFP, CP and KwaZulu delegations subsequently withdrew from the negotiations, while the remaining representatives in the forum continued discussions on the precepts of a multiracial interim constitution, which was to remain in force pending the preparation and adoption of a permanent constitution. The confirmation of the election date prompted increased clashes between supporters of the IFP and those of the ANC. At the end of July a draft interim Constitution was promulgated. The interim Constitution entrenched equal rights for citizens regardless of race, and vested executive power in a President and a Cabinet, which was to comprise representatives of the political parties that held a stipulated number of seats in the legislature. Legislative authority was vested in a bicameral Parliament, comprising a 400-member National Assembly (to be elected by proportional representation) and a Senate (with 10 members elected by each regional legislature). The National Assembly and Senate were together to form a 'constitution-making body' (later designated the Constitutional Assembly), which was to draft a new constitution, with adherence to the principles stipulated by the negotiating forum. Failure to adopt the draft by a majority of two-thirds within a period of two years would require the new document to be submitted for approval at a national referendum. Although the interim Constitution included provisions for the establishment of regional legislatures, it was rejected by COSAG (while the IFP, KwaZulu and CP delegations continued to boycott negotiations).

In early September 1993 the negotiating forum approved legislation providing for the establishment of a multiracial Transitional Executive Council (TEC), which was to rule in conjunction with the existing Government pending the elections, thereby allowing blacks to participate in central government for the first time. The TEC was to comprise representatives of the groups involved in the negotiating process; however, the IFP, the CP, the governments of Bophuthatswana, Ciskei and KwaZulu, and the PAC refused to participate. Later in September Parliament adopted legislation providing for the installation of the TEC, and the establishment of an Independent Electoral Commission (IEC), and an independent media commission and broadcasting authority.

In October 1993 the constituent members of COSAG, together with the AVF, formed the Freedom Alliance (FA), with the stated objective of negotiating concessions regarding regional autonomy. The Bophuthatswana and Ciskei delegations subsequently withdrew from the negotiating forum. In November the negotiating forum repealed legislation providing for detention without trial. Later that month agreement was reached regarding the establishment of a new security force, which was to be under the control of both central and provincial government, and a reconstituted national defence force, which was to comprise members of the existing armed forces of South Africa and the 'independent homelands', and the military wings of political organizations.

On 18 November 1993, following intensive discussions, 19 of the 21 delegations remaining in the negotiating forum approved the interim Constitution, which incorporated several amendments to the draft promulgated in July. A number of significant compromises between the Government and the ANC had been achieved: the Government abandoned its demand that cabinet decisions require a two-thirds' majority (thereby accepting that power-sharing would not be constitutionally entrenched), while the ANC agreed to a fixed five-year period for transition to majority rule. The President was to be elected by the National Assembly, and was to exercise executive power in consultation with at least two Deputy Presidents, who were to be nominated by parties with a minimum of 80 seats in the National Assembly (equivalent to 20% of the national vote). A Constitutional Court was to be appointed by the President from a list of candidates nominated by an independent judicial commission. As a concession to the FA, the interim Constitution included a provision that entitled the legislatures of the nine redesignated provinces to draft their own constitutions, subject to the principles governing the national Constitution. Nevertheless, the FA, together with the PAC, rejected the interim Constitution.

In early December 1993 the negotiating forum reached agreement on the reincorporation of the four 'independent homelands' into South Africa on 27 April 1994, when the interim Constitution was to enter into force. On 1 January South African citizenship was to be restored to the population of the 'homelands', who would be entitled to vote in the elections. However, the governments of Bophuthatswana and Ciskei refused to recognize the decision. On 7 December 1993 the TEC commenced sessions, but was, as expected, boycotted by a number of delegations. In mid-December the IEC was established. On 22 December Parliament ratified the interim Constitution, thereby effecting its own dissolution as an organ of the apartheid regime.

In December 1993 the judicial commission of inquiry into political violence that had been established in October 1991 announced that several members of the KwaZulu security forces, who had been trained by the South African armed forces, had killed ANC members in Natal. In January 1994 the military wing of the PAC, the Azanian People's Liberation Army (APLA), was implicated in further indiscriminate killings of civilians; the PAC, however, denied responsibility for the violence and announced that it had suspended the activities of the APLA. In January the Ciskei government decided to join the TEC and subsequently withdrew from the FA.

In February 1994, in accordance with a decision by the TEC, de Klerk announced that the elections, which were to be monitored by international observers, would take place between 26 and 28 April. The ANC's list of candidates incorporated members of the SACP, COSATU, the 'homeland' governments and parties representing the Indian and Coloured communities; the inclusion of Winnie Mandela (who had been elected President of the ANC's Women's League in December 1993) attracted widespread criticism. The IFP confirmed that it intended to boycott the elections, after the Zulu tribal monarch, King Goodwill Zwelithini (who was Buthelezi's nephew), rejected the interim Constitution and declared sovereignty over the territory traditionally owned by the Zulus, prompting increased fears of civil conflict. In mid-February Nelson Mandela announced a number of proposed amendments to the interim Constitution, in an effort to comply with the demands of the IFP and the AVF. The proposed constitutional amendments recognized the right to regional self-determination, including the concept of a separate Afrikaner state, provided for a 'double-ballot system', whereby the electorate was to vote separately for national and provincial candidates, allowed each province to determine its legislative and executive structure, and redesignated Natal as KwaZulu/Natal. The FA, however, rejected the concessions, on the grounds that the powers of regional government remained inadequate, and refused to attend discussions on the proposed amendments, which were, nevertheless, adopted by the negotiating forum. During that month a series of bomb attacks, which were attributed to right-wing extremists, took place in Orange Free State and Transvaal. In early March, after the ANC and IFP agreed to accept international mediation regarding the issue of regional autonomy, Buthelezi announced that he was to register the IFP provisionally to contest the elections. The leader of the AVU, Gen. (retd) Constand Viljoen (who had increasingly dissociated himself from extreme right-wing elements in the AVF) also provisionally registered a new party, the Freedom Front (FF). Despite the insistence of the AVF that its constituent groups were to boycott the elections, the FF subsequently submitted a list of candidates, which included several prominent members of the CP. The IFP failed to present a list of candidates by the stipulated date, while Zwelithini continued to urge his followers to boycott the elections.

In March 1994 the President of Bophuthatswana, Lucas Mangope (a member of the FA), announced that the population of the 'homeland' would not participate in the elections. Following widespread protests in Bophuthatswana, Mangope fled from the capital, Mmabatho, after disaffected members of the security forces demanded that he allow participation in the elections and refused to take action against the demonstrators. At the apparent instigation of the AVF, some 5,000 armed right-wing extremists, principally members of the AWB, entered Bophuthatswana and occupied Mmabatho, with the aim of reinstating Mangope. Shortly afterwards the Government dispatched some 2,000 members of the armed forces to Bophuthatswana, which, together with disaffected local troops, regained control of the 'homeland'. The Government and the TEC formally deposed Mangope, whose removal signified the effective dissolution of the FA. Later in March members of the armed forces were deployed in Ciskei to maintain civil order, following the resignation of the 'homeland's' military ruler in response to a strike by reformist members of the security forces. (The TEC and the Government assumed joint responsibility for administration in Bophuthatswana and Ciskei pending the elections.) In the same month de Klerk announced the conclusions of a report by the judicial commission of inquiry into political violence, which implicated three senior officials in the security forces and prominent members of the IFP in a conspiracy to organize political assassinations, with the aim of undermining national stability prior to the elections. The security forces and the IFP denied the accusations. De Klerk subsequently stated that the allegations would be investigated by an international task force and suspended a number of members of the security forces, including the three officials.

Following renewed clashes between members of the IFP and the ANC in KwaZulu/Natal in March 1994, the ANC urged the Government to dispatch troops to the region. Later that month de Klerk, with the approval of the ANC, imposed a state of emergency in KwaZulu/Natal; some 3,000 troops were subsequently deployed in the province to maintain civil order during the election period, but political violence continued. In April, following protracted negotiations between the Government, the ANC and the IFP, with international mediation, an agreement was reached whereby the IFP was to participate in the elections, in exchange for guarantees that the institutions of the Zulu monarch and kingdom were to be recognized in the interim Constitution. Under the terms of a proposed draft constitution for KwaZulu/Natal, the Zulu monarch was to be granted additional territorial powers and sovereignty with regard to traditional law and custom. However, the AVF announced that it would continue to boycott the elections. At the end of April about 32 members of the AWB, including prominent party officials, were arrested in connection with a bombing offensive conducted during that month, in which a total of 21 people were killed. Terre'Blanche subsequently threatened that the campaign would continue unless the Government acceded to demands for Afrikaner self-determination. Under the terms of an accord between the Government, the ANC and the FF earlier in April, the level of support for the FF in the elections was to be used to determine whether a separate Afrikaner state might be established in any region with the approval of the majority of the resident population. Prior to the elections, the Government also reached an agreement with the PAC, which provided for the inclusion of members of the APLA in the new national defence force, in exchange for a guaranteed cessation of hostilities.

On 27 April 1994 the interim Constitution came into force, with voting commencing on the previous day, as scheduled. However, a number of logistical difficulties led to widespread delays. On 28 April voting was extended by one day in KwaZulu/Natal and other regions affected by administrative confusion. Although a number of reports of electoral malpractice emerged, the IEC declared that the elections had been free and fair. The promulgation of the official results was delayed, owing, in part, to disputed ballots in KwaZulu/Natal; following negotiations between the IFP and the ANC, it was agreed that the IFP would be allocated 50.3% of the vote in the province, thereby allowing it a majority of one seat in the regional legislature. On 2 May, after partial results indicated a substantial majority in favour of the ANC, de Klerk conceded defeat, prompting widespread jubilation. Shortly afterwards it was announced that the ANC had secured 62.7% of votes cast, while the NP had won 20.4%, the IFP 10.5% and the FF 2.2%. Consequently, the ANC narrowly failed to obtain a parliamentary majority of two-thirds, which, under the terms of the interim Constitution, would have allowed its members to draft and adopt the new constitution without consulting other parties. The NP, which secured a majority in the province of Northern Cape, received the stipulated percentage of the national vote entitling it to nominate a Deputy President. Mandela subsequently appointed a senior official of the ANC, Thabo Mbeki, as First Deputy President, while de Klerk was nominated as Second Deputy President.

Mandela was officially elected as President by the National Assembly on 9 May 1994, and was inaugurated on the following day at a ceremony that was attended by a large number of international heads of state. A Cabinet of National Unity, comprising 18 representatives of the ANC, six of the NP and three of the IFP, was subsequently formed, with Buthelezi allocated the portfolio of home affairs. The appointment of Winnie Mandela as a deputy minister was widely interpreted as an attempt to prevent her from criticizing the new administration. Later in May the provincial legislatures elected a 90-member Senate, comprising 60 representatives of the ANC, 17 of the NP, five of the IFP and FF, respectively, and three of the DP. The ANC consequently held a slightly higher majority in the Constitutional Assembly than in the National Assembly, but failed, nevertheless, to obtain a two-thirds' majority. The Secretary-General of the ANC, Cyril Ramaphosa, was subsequently elected Chairman of the Constitutional Assembly.

The new Government adopted a Reconstruction and Development Programme (RDP), which comprised extensive measures for social and economic development, including the reform of the education and health services. The Government also announced plans to establish a 'Truth and Reconciliation Commission' (TRC), composed of eminent citizens, which would investigate violations of human rights perpetrated under the apartheid regime; the TRC was to be empowered to grant indemnity to individuals who confessed to politically motivated crimes committed before 5 December 1993 (when the TEC was effectively installed). Although the FF had failed to obtain the level of support in the elections stipulated as a precondition to the consideration of its demands, the Government subsequently agreed to the establishment of a 'volkstaat council', in which Viljoen and other right-wing Afrikaners were to debate the issue of self-determination. Meanwhile, it was disclosed that de Klerk had authorized the transfer of state-owned land (comprising one-third of the territory of KwaZulu/Natal) to Zwelithini shortly before the elections. The ANC denied knowledge of the agreement, which, it was speculated, had been designed to prevent attempts to include the territory in the ANC's land reform programme (whereby communities or individuals were entitled to claim restitution for land dispossessed under regional legislation from 1913).

In June 1994 it was announced that the new South African National Defence Force (SANDF) was to be constituted over a period of three years (to allow the integration of former members of the MK and APLA). In mid-June a cabinet committee decided that Zwelithini was to remain the statutory trustee of the territory in KwaZulu/Natal that had been transferred to his control prior to the elections. At the end of June nine former MK officials were allocated prominent positions within the SANDF. (The commander of the former defence forces, Gen. George Meiring, had been reappointed Chief of the SANDF in May.) In September the Government officially ended the state of emergency in KwaZulu/Natal that had been imposed in March. In October the IFP majority in the provincial legislature of KwaZulu/Natal adopted legislation that provided for the establishment of an advisory council of Zulu chiefs, the House of Traditional Leaders, in which Zwelithini would be equal in status to other chiefs (including Buthelezi).

In November 1994 the Government adopted legislation that formally restored the rights of land ownership to members of the black population who had been dispossessed following the introduction of discriminatory legislation beginning in 1913; the Restitution of Land Rights Act provided for the establishment of a special commission and court to investigate and arbitrate claims.

In January 1995 the National Intelligence Service (NIS) was replaced with two new bodies, incorporating elements of the ANC's security department and agencies of the former 'homelands': the South African Secret Service, under the command of the former head of the NIS, was to control international intelligence, while the National Intelligence Agency (NIA), headed by a former ANC security official, was to be responsible for internal intelligence. In the same month, amid reports of increasing political violence between ANC and IFP supporters in KwaZulu/Natal, Buthelezi was elected Chairman of the House of Traditional Leaders.

An 11-member Constitutional Court was installed in February 1995; the Court was to ensure that the executive, legislative and judicial organs of government adhered to the principles entrenched in the interim Constitution, and was to endorse a final constitutional text with respect to these principles. In the same month Mandela confirmed that he would not contest the elections in 1999.

In February 1995 Buthelezi claimed that the ANC and NP had reneged on a pledge (which had been made shortly before the elections in April 1994) to invite international mediators to arbitrate on IFP demands for the devolution of power to KwaZulu/Natal, and IFP deputies consequently suspended participation in Parliament and the Constitutional Assembly. At a special party congress, which took place in March, the IFP agreed to resume participation in Parliament and in the Constitutional Assembly, but issued a resolution to the effect that IFP deputies would resume the boycott if Mandela failed to invite international mediators for negotiations on the issue of regional autonomy. Meanwhile, Winnie Mandela's position in the Cabinet appeared to be increasingly untenable, as a result of her continued autocratic behaviour. In late March Mandela finally removed her from the Cabinet, after she publicly criticized government expenditure on the visit to South Africa of the British monarch.

At a party conference on constitutional policy in April 1995, the ANC rejected NP proposals that the principle of power-sharing be entrenched in the final constitution, thereby extending the tenure of the coalition Government. The conference also failed to accept IFP demands for international mediation on regional autonomy, and adopted constitutional proposals that provided for a Senate comprising members of provincial legislatures, which would be empowered to veto provincial legislation. Buthelezi implemented his threat to suspend IFP participation in the Constitutional Assembly, and indicated that the IFP would not accept a constitution that had been drafted by the remaining parties in the Assembly.

In May 1995, following reports that factional hostilities in KwaZulu/Natal had increased, Mandela accused Buthelezi of inciting political violence and threatened to suspend government funds to the province. None the less, it was announced shortly afterwards that Mandela and Buthelezi had agreed to resolve their differences and to negotiate regarding the issue of international mediation. Later in May Mandela consented to foreign mediation on constitutional discussions. In the same month the National Assembly approved draft legislation providing for the establishment of the TRC; only the FF deputies opposed the enactment of the legislation.

In September 1995 the Constitutional Court ruled that Mandela had exceeded his presidential powers in overruling electoral boundaries that had been determined by the Western Cape Provincial Government prior to the local elections in November. The Court declared an amendment to the Local Government Transition Act (which had granted the President authority to issue decrees regarding the local elections) to be unconstitutional; the legislation was amended accordingly at an emergency session of Parliament in October. Elections in KwaZulu/Natal were postponed until March 1996, owing to continuing violence in the region. Voting took place in some parts of Western Cape, but not in the metropolitan area of Cape Town, nor in some rural areas of the province, as a result of delays in the demarcation of electoral boundaries. At the local elections, which took part in most parts of the country on 1 November 1995, the ANC secured 66.4% of the votes cast and the majority of the seats on the local councils, while the NP won 16.2% and the FF 4.0%.

In November 1995 Gen. Magnus Malan, the Minister of Defence in 1980–91, and a further 10 prominent officials in the former armed forces were arrested on charges relating to the killing of 13 people in KwaMakutha (south of Durban) in 1987; they were accused of involvement in the establishment in 1985 of a military camp in Namibia where IFP commandos were trained to perpetrate attacks on prominent ANC supporters. The arrest and subsequent indictment of Gen. Malan and the other former officers provoked great controversy; Mandela was accused by members of the NP and FF of political bias in his refusal to grant temporary indemnity to the accused until their cases could be heard by the TRC, which was to commence sessions in April 1996. (In late November 1995 Archbishop Desmond Tutu was appointed as Chairman of the Commission.) Buthelezi was cited in the indictment as having in 1985 requested the assistance of the security forces in creating paramilitary units to combat the ANC.

Renewed violence in KwaZulu/Natal in December 1995 culminated in an attack by some 600 IFP supporters against the village of Shobashobane, an ANC enclave in the south of the province, in which some 19 people were killed. In early February 1996 the NP Minister of Provincial Affairs and Constitutional Development, Roelf Meyer, announced that he was to resign from the Government and would assume the new post of Secretary-General of the NP. Later in the month Abraham Williams, also of the NP, resigned from the post of Minister of Welfare and Population Development, following allegations that he had defrauded social security funds. In March Mandela was granted a divorce from Winnie Mandela (who subsequently became known as Winnie Madikizela-Mandela). Later that month, in a cabinet reorganization, Mandela appointed Trevor Manuel, hitherto the Minister of Trade and Industry, to the finance portfolio. The NP protested at the appointment of an ANC member to the ministry, claiming that it breached an agreement reserving the position for a nominee without political affiliations.

The trial of Gen. Malan and his 19 co-defendants began in Durban in early March 1996. (In May charges were abandoned against three of the former security force commanders, owing to insufficient evidence.) In mid-March the Government withdrew indemnity from prosecution that had been granted by de Klerk's Government to 73 ANC members, including Mbeki and Modise. In April the TRC, comprising Archbishop Tutu (who retired from the archbishopric in June) and 16 other members drawn from all racial groups and a variety of professions, commenced hearings, which were to continue for up to two years. The Commission was empowered to grant judicial amnesties to perpetrators of human rights violations committed during the apartheid era, if it were satisfied that a full disclosure had been made and that the crime in question had been politically motivated, also depending on the gravity of the crime. The TRC was also to advise on appropriate reparations to the victims (or to their families) of crimes committed.

On 8 May 1996 Parliament approved the final version of the Constitution, with the NP voting in favour, in spite of its reservations over some provisions. The IFP maintained its boycott of the Constitutional Assembly, while the 10 FF deputies abstained; only the two deputies of the African Christian Democratic Party (ACDP) voted against the adoption of the Constitution. The new Constitution incorporated an extensive Bill of Rights, and provided for the establishment of a commission to guarantee the rights of the white minority. A National Council of Provinces was to replace the existing Senate, and was designed to increase the influence of the provinces on the policy of the central Government (although falling short of the provincial powers demanded by the IFP). De Klerk subsequently announced that the NP was to withdraw from the Government of National Unity, attributing the decision to the diminishing influence of his party on government policy, the refusal of the ANC to include power-sharing arrangements in the new Constitution, and the necessity, in the interests of democracy, for an effective opposition. The NP later withdrew from all the Provincial Governments except for that of Western Cape (where it was in the majority). Mandela appointed members of his own party to the ministerial portfolios vacated by NP members and abolished the position of Second Deputy President.

Local elections in KwaZulu/Natal had been postponed from March 1996 until 29 May; however, renewed violence in the province, which was regarded as threatening the democratic process, prompted the Government to postpone the elections still further. However, elections took place on 29 May in Cape Town and the remaining areas of Western Cape province where elections had not been held in November 1995: the NP increased its share of the votes cast compared with the general election in 1994, and secured control of the majority of the local councils in the areas in which polling took place. Following negotiations between the province's political leaders, the local elections in KwaZulu/Natal took place on 26 June, amid relative calm. The IFP won the largest share (44.5%) of the votes cast.

In late August 1996 Mbeki made a statement to the TRC regarding violations of human rights perpetrated during the apartheid era, including the execution of 34 people at the ANC's camps in Angola, asserting that these were justified in the context of the struggle against apartheid. De Klerk apologized before the TRC for the suffering that the apartheid policies of the NP had caused, but denied that any violations of human rights had been authorized during his time in government. Also in late August Eugene de Kock, a former commander of the notorious counter-insurgency 'hit squad', the Vlakplaas, was convicted of 89 charges relating to the activities of the unit, including six charges of murder. In September de Kock detailed to the Supreme Court his involvement in the apartheid regime's campaign against its opponents, claiming that de Klerk and Botha had both had full knowledge of these operations, which included assassinations.

In early September 1996 the Constitutional Court ruled that the new Constitution failed to adhere to the principles enshrined in the interim Constitution in a number of respects, notably with regard to the powers of the provinces, which the Court deemed insufficient. The Constitutional Assembly was to amend the document accordingly within a period of 90 days. In a separate ruling the Court rejected an alternative constitution that had been drafted by Buthelezi, stating that the proposed constitution attempted to encroach on the powers of national government. The IFP (which had boycotted the Constitutional Assembly in the negotiations resulting in the adoption of the national Constitution) rejoined the negotiations in early October, but withdrew shortly afterwards. (The IFP had argued for a greater role for traditional leaders in regional and local government than the other parties would accept.) The amended Constitution was approved by both chambers of Parliament on 11 October, with the ANC and the NP having negotiated a slight increase in the powers of the provinces. The new Constitution was returned to the Constitutional Court for final endorsement, and was promulgated by the President at a ceremony in Sharpeville on 10 December.

In mid-October 1996 Gen. Malan and his co-defendants were acquitted of all charges in connection with the massacre in Kwa-Makutha. Although it was accepted that the killings had been committed by IFP supporters who had been trained by the former armed forces, the prosecution failed to prove that the attack had been authorized by military or political leaders. The judgment was regarded as a set-back for the TRC, with Gen. Malan urging former members of the armed forces not to seek amnesties from the TRC, but to submit to trial in the courts if charged (thus discouraging potential confessions to the Commission). Later in October the TRC proposed that the final date for indemnity be extended from 6 December 1993 to 10 May 1994 (the date of Mandela's inauguration as President). Shortly afterwards a former police commissioner submitted evidence to the TRC implicating Botha in an attack against the headquarters of the South African Council of Churches in 1988. Botha declared that he would not submit evidence to the Commission and denied involvement in any crimes for which he needed to apply for amnesty. Following discussions with Tutu, however, he agreed to co-operate with the TRC by means of correspondence. In late October Tutu criticized the ANC for failing to submit amnesty applications from its members, and subsequently threatened to resign from the TRC if such applications were not made. The ANC responded by assuring the TRC that applications by its members would be made where necessary.

On 13 December 1996 (the eve of the deadline for applications for amnesty from the TRC) Mandela announced that the final date for the period in which crimes had been committed and the deadline for the receipt of amnesty applications were to be extended, to 10 May 1994 and 10 May 1997, respectively. The ANC confirmed that some 360 of its members, including three cabinet ministers, had applied for amnesty.

From January 1997 South Africa's main political parties conducted discussions regarding possible inter-party co-operation. Mandela issued invitations to both the DP and the PAC to participate in the Government of National Unity (which, however, both parties subsequently declined). In late January the IFP appeared to be in crisis, following the resignations of the KwaZulu/Natal Premier, Frank Mdlalose, the IFP Secretary-General and the Chairman of the IFP in Gauteng. Although ill health was the stated reason for Mdlalose's departure, it was reported that he had become disaffected following continual interference from Buthelezi in the affairs of the provincial administration. The new Constitution entered into force on 4 February 1997. On 6 February the inaugural session of the new National Council of Provinces, which replaced the Senate as the second chamber of Parliament, was held.

By the 10 May 1997 deadline nearly 8,000 amnesty applications had been received. In mid-May Meyer resigned from the NP and from the National Assembly, following opposition from within the NP to his proposal that the party be reconstituted in order to attract black support. Meyer, in alliance with Bantu Holomisa, the former ruler of Transkei (who, in 1996, had been dismissed from the Government and expelled from the ANC for indiscipline, in connection with allegations he had made at a hearing of the TRC), subsequently established a new political movement, the United Democratic Movement (UDM). Also in May 1997 de Klerk made a second appearance before the TRC; his continued insistence that he had been unaware of the violations of human rights perpetrated during the period of apartheid prompted an angry response from Tutu, who accused de Klerk of being responsible for abuses. The NP subsequently suspended co-operation with the TRC, and initiated legal action against the TRC on the grounds of political bias.

In June 1997 the leader of the AWB, Eugene Terre'Blanche, received a custodial term of six years for the attempted murder of a black employee, and a further one-year sentence for assault; he was released on bail pending an appeal against his conviction. In the same month Buthelezi invited the ANC to enter into negotiations with the aim of reaching an agreement to end political violence in KwaZulu/Natal. However, in July the killing of five ANC members, including two newly elected municipal councillors, in KwaZulu/Natal reflected the continuing political tensions in the province. In early August the IFP withdrew from the peace discussions, after it was alleged during hearings of the TRC that Buthelezi had been aware of political killings perpetrated by supporters of the IFP during apartheid. At the end of August de Klerk resigned from the leadership of the NP and retired from active politics; he was subsequently replaced by Marthinus van Schalkwyk.

In September 1997 five members of the former security forces appeared before the TRC to apply for amnesty for the killing of Steve Biko in 1977 (see below); it was admitted during the hearing that some of the evidence presented at the inquest into Biko's death had been fabricated. In the same month the publication of a book, based on statements by a former bodyguard of Winnie Madikizela-Mandela, Katiza Cebekhulu, attracted considerable publicity; Cebekhulu alleged that Winnie Madikizela-Mandela had been actively involved in the killing of Stompie Moeketsi Seipei in 1988, and that she had subsequently ordered that a physician who had examined the victim prior to his death be killed. Nevertheless, Madikizela-Mandela continued to receive widespread public support, and was nominated for the post of Deputy President of the ANC by the party's Women's League prior to the ANC's December 1997 congress. Later in September Madikizela-Mandela appeared before the TRC, having been implicated by previous applicants for amnesty in 18 incidences of human rights violations, including eight killings. The TRC subsequently acceded to Madikizela-Mandela's request that hearings of her testimony be conducted in public. In November representatives of the business community (principally state corporations and banks) applied for amnesty for their involvement with the apartheid system; however, Tutu criticized the failure of much of the private business sector, including three multinational petroleum companies, to participate in the TRC. During hearings of the TRC regarding the allegations against Madikizela-Mandela later that month, a number of witnesses testified that she had assaulted and killed several people. Cebekhulu appeared before the TRC to reiterate the claims that had been published in September 1997. Madikizela-Mandela subsequently denied involvement in any violations of human rights, and initiated legal action against Cebekhulu for libel.

At the ANC congress in December 1997 Mandela resigned from the presidency of the party, as anticipated, and was succeeded by Mbeki, who was elected unopposed. (Mandela's refusal to be re-elected to the party's National Executive Committee (NEC) further confirmed his stated intention to retire from active politics in May 1999.) Jacob Zuma was elected Deputy President of the party. Madikizela-Mandela, who had refused her nomination to contest the post of Deputy President, was, however, elected to the NEC.

In August 1998, following considerable delays, Botha, who had failed to comply with three subpoenas ordering him to testify at the TRC regarding his enforcement of apartheid through emergency rule in the 1980s, was convicted of being in contempt of the TRC, receiving a fine of R 10,000 and a one-year suspended sentence (which could be brought into effect if he failed to comply with a further TRC subpoena). In September Parliament adopted legislation guaranteeing employment equity, whereby corporations were required to employ a certain proportion of blacks, women and disabled people.

In October 1998 the TRC commenced reparation payments to victims of human rights violations under the apartheid system. Shortly before the TRC was due to release the report of its findings, de Klerk appealed to the Cape Town High Court to prevent the publication of sections alleging that he had prior knowledge of the bomb attacks against anti-apartheid bodies in the 1980s. The TRC agreed to remove provisionally the sections concerned, which were, however, to be contested at the High Court in early 1999. However, the Cape Town High Court dismissed a legal challenge by the ANC to the publication of findings that it had perpetrated human rights violations in armed opposition to apartheid, on the grounds that it had failed to appeal against previous drafts of the report. Tutu condemned the ANC's efforts to prevent the release of part of the report, which had been opposed by Mandela and had resulted in division within the party. At the end of October 1998 Tutu presented to Mandela the TRC's interim report detailing human rights violations committed in 1960–64, based on statements from some 21,000 victims of abuses and about 7,000 amnesty applicants. The report concluded that the apartheid system constituted a crime against humanity; it was alleged that, while the State was primarily accountable for violations of human rights, the ANC had also committed abuses in its legitimate struggle against apartheid (notably in the MK's torture and execution of suspected dissidents in detention camps outside South Africa). Botha, as President of the State Security Council in 1978–89, was considered to be responsible for an increase in killings of government opponents and to have ordered the bomb attacks by state agents in the 1980s. Buthelezi was deemed accountable for human rights violations perpetrated by the IFP (which was responsible for the highest proportion of killings in 1990–94). The report also cited Viljoen, Terre'Blanche, and Winnie Madikizela-Mandela as being responsible for serious violations of human rights. It was stated that the South African business community had benefited from the apartheid system, and the introduction of a 'wealth tax' to assist in social reconstruction was proposed. The prosecution of those responsible for human rights violations who had not applied for amnesty, or who had been denied amnesty, was recommended. Buthelezi and Viljoen dismissed the findings of the report as reflecting pro-ANC bias in the TRC, and Buthelezi subsequently threatened to prosecute the Commission, particularly with regard to the report's allegation that the IFP had colluded with the apartheid regime. In November 1998 one of the members of the security forces implicated in the 1977 killing of Steve Biko was refused amnesty, on the grounds that the killing was not politically motivated. Amnesty applications of the remaining four members of the security forces involved in the incident were rejected in early 1999. In December 1998 Mandela confirmed that perpetrators of crimes committed under the apartheid regime would not be granted a general amnesty, which had been urged by the NP, IFP and some members of the ANC. Under TRC regulations, applicants would only be granted amnesty after submitting a full confession and evidence that the crime was politically motivated. However, in October 2003 the Ministry of Justice and Constitutional Development announced that none of the men implicated in the killing of Steve Biko would be prosecuted, largely owing to insufficient evidence.

In January 1999 the Secretary-General of the UDM, Sifiso Nkabinde, was assassinated (apparently by ANC supporters) in KwaZulu/Natal. Some 11 ANC members were killed in a retaliatory attack by armed assailants. Further clashes between UDM and ANC supporters around Richmond were reported. Also in January a bomb attack at a Cape Town police station was widely attributed to an Islamist group, People Against Gangsterism and Drugs (PAGAD). Meanwhile, an increasing number of attacks against farmers by organized armed groups were reported. The South African Agricultural Union claimed that the attacks (in which more than 550 members of the farming community had been killed in 1994–98) were part of a campaign to force farmers to abandon their land.

In March 1999 the TRC rejected the amnesty applications of the 37 senior members of the ANC, including Mbeki, whose amnesties had been revoked in May 1998. In April 1999 a further 79 ANC supporters were refused amnesty by the TRC. In May the ANC and IFP signed an agreement to end hostilities between their supporters in KwaZulu/Natal during the forthcoming electoral period.

More than 16m. voters participated in legislative elections, which took place peacefully, at national and provincial level, on 2 June 1999. Some 32 political parties had registered to contest the elections. The ANC secured 266 of the 400 seats in the National Assembly, with 66.4% of votes cast; the DP increased its representation in the Assembly from seven to 38 seats, while the IFP won 34, and the New National Party (NNP, as the NP had been reconstituted), which had lost much support to the DP, only 28 seats. The ANC subsequently formed a coalition with an Indian party, the Minority Front, thereby securing a two-thirds' majority in the National Assembly. The IFP reached a coalition agreement with the ANC in KwaZulu/Natal, where the IFP Premier retained his post. In Western Cape no party won a majority of seats in the provincial legislature, and, after intensive negotiations, the NPP and DP established a coalition Government to prevent the ANC, which had obtained the highest number of votes, from gaining power. On 16 June Mbeki was inaugurated as President, in a ceremony that also marked the formal retirement of Mandela. The IFP joined the ANC in a further coalition Government, in which Buthelezi remained Minister of Home Affairs. Zuma became Deputy President.

In June 1999 Botha's appeal against his conviction was upheld, on the technical grounds that the TRC's subpoena was invalid since its mandate had temporarily expired. In July the TRC released a report containing evidence from former members of the security forces that implicated Botha in the killing of eight anti-apartheid activists in 1988. In August the TRC granted amnesty to Vlok, the former Commissioner of Police, Gen. Johan van der Merwe, de Kock, and a further 14 members of the former security forces, in respect of ordering the bombing of the offices of the South African Council of Churches in 1988. In September the Minister of Justice announced the closure of the commission investigating incidences of public-sector corruption, following disagreements between the head of the commission and the Government over financing; further cases were to be submitted to judges specially nominated by Mbeki. In the same month a PAC deputy submitted a motion urging a judicial inquiry into allegations that senior ANC officials had accepted bribes from armaments traders. In October the trial of Wouter Basson, the head of the apartheid regime's chemical and biological armaments programme in 1982–92, on 64 charges (including responsibility for the killing of 200 members of the South West Africa People's Organisation of Namibia—SWAPO), commenced at the High Court in Pretoria. He was acquitted of 15 charges in June 2001, and the remaining charges in April 2002. Later in October 1999 the TRC granted amnesty to nine former members of the security forces, including de Kock, who had provided evidence regarding the bombing of the ANC offices in London in 1982. In December 1999 10 members of the AWB were granted amnesty for the bombing campaign in 1994. At the end of December four members of PAGAD were arrested in connection with more than 80 bombing incidents in the region of Cape Town (including one bomb explosion in a restaurant in November, in which some 46 people were killed).

In January 2000 the National Assembly adopted extensive legislation prohibiting discrimination on any grounds and the use of racist terms in language. Meanwhile, the principal opposition parties (the DP, NNP, UDM and the FA) announced their intention to form an alliance prior to local government elections due in November; the DP also signed an electoral agreement with the smaller ACDP. In February, however, seven senior UDM officials left the party to join the ANC (increasing the total number of defections from the UDM since late 1999 to 34). In March, following the rejection of an appeal in October 1999, Terre'Blanche was ordered by the Pretoria High Court to surrender to the authorities to serve the one-year sentence he had received for assault, pending a further appeal against his six-year sentence. He was subsequently released on parole from the shorter sentence, but the longer sentence was confirmed on appeal in March 2001. (Terre'Blanche was released on parole in June 2004 after serving three years of the sentence. In November 2003 he was also convicted of involvement in terrorist activities prior to the 1994 elections and received a further, suspended, six-year sentence.) In June 2000 it was announced that the NNP and DP were to form a new coalition, known as the Democratic Alliance (DA), to contest the local government elections.

President Mbeki was criticized by many observers, including religious leaders, trade-union officials and prominent ANC members, as a result of statements he made throughout 2000, questioning the causal link between HIV and AIDS, and asserting that poverty could also cause the disease. Responsibility for policy on HIV/AIDS was subsequently transferred to a newly created cabinet committee. In April 2001 a court began hearing a petition, made by a group of 39 pharmaceutical manufacturers, to invalidate legislation, passed in 1997 (but suspended following an interim court ruling in the companies' favour in 1998), that enabled South Africa to purchase less expensive generic versions of patented anti-AIDS drugs from third parties. However, following international criticism, the companies abandoned the action unconditionally before the conclusion of the hearing. In September 2001 the South African Medical Research Council reported that HIV/AIDS was the largest single cause of death in South Africa, responsible for approximately 40% of adult deaths, and estimated that, without effective treatment, up to 7m. people could die from the disease by 2010. Mbeki had attracted further criticism in August 2001 after urging the Minister of Health to reduce the budget for HIV/AIDS treatment, citing mortality figures from 1995 (when the disease accounted for only 2.2% of deaths). In December the Ministry of Health lost a case brought by the Treatment Action Campaign (TAC), a group of AIDS activists, when the High Court in Pretoria ordered it to provide antiretroviral drugs to all pregnant women infected with HIV to reduce the chance of transmission to their children; the Government had argued that the drugs were toxic and excessively expensive to administer. (The Government lost its appeal against the ruling in April 2002.) In February 2002 Buthelezi, as Minister of Home Affairs, ordered the distribution of anti-retroviral drugs in Kwazulu/Natal, in contravention of official government policy, and in March the High Court upheld the ruling that ordered state provision of antiretroviral drugs. The Government sought leave to appeal the ruling, but it was overturned by the Constitutional Court in July; in October the Government announced that it would investigate means of providing antiretroviral drugs through the public health system. In September 2002 the TAC commenced legal action against two large European pharmaceutical companies, claiming that they had taken advantage of patent protection on their AIDS drugs and charged excessive prices for them. Following ruling against the companies by the South African Competition Commission, in December 2003 they agreed to license patents for antiretroviral drugs to generic manufacturers in South Africa. In the previous month the Government also announced that it would spend R 12,100m. on combating HIV/AIDS over the next four years; R 1,900m. was to be allocated for the provision of antiretroviral drugs. At that time the Government committed to providing free antiretroviral treatment to some 53,000 people by March 2004; however, by November of that year the number of people receiving treatment was estimated at only 18,500. In September 2004 the National Assembly approved legislation to regulate the country's 200,000 practitioners of traditional medicine, thereby granting them formal recognition; some 70% of the population were believed to consult traditional healers.

Municipal elections were held throughout the country in December 2000, including in the newly created urban regions around South Africa's six largest cities (the so-called 'megacities'), which generally merged the city proper and the surrounding townships into one administrative unit. Nationally, the ANC won approximately 60% of the votes cast, and gained control of five of the six conurbations, the DA winning control of Cape Town.

In January 2001 allegations of corruption were made against senior politicians, including ministers, regarding the award of weapons contracts, with an estimated combined value of R 43,000m. The Minister of Justice, Penuell Maduana, and President Mbeki were criticized for rejecting a demand from the National Assembly that a judge specializing in the investigation of corruption allegations join the inquiry into the issue. The Government was cleared of all charges when the inquiry report was published in November, although opposition parties accused the ANC of manipulating the investigations and suppressing parts of the report. The ANC chief whip, Tony Yengeni, resigned in October after being charged with corruption, forgery and perjury, following allegations that he had received favours from a weapons manufacturer while chairman of the parliamentary defence committee. He pleaded guilty to charges of defrauding the Government in February 2003, and was sentenced to four years' imprisonment in March.

In July 2001 the PAC drew attention to what it considered the Government's inadequate housing and land redistribution policies, by seizing land belonging to farmers and the Provincial

Government in east Johannesburg and inviting thousands of homeless people to settle there; many constructed shacks, believing that they were part of a resettlement scheme. Within two weeks the Government had removed the estimated 7,000 squatters from the land, using armed police-officers. COSATU and affiliated unions organized a two-day general strike in August in protest at the proposed privatization of public assets, which, it claimed, would result in large-scale redundancies. COSATU estimated that 4m. workers had participated in the strike, a figure that the Government described as exaggerated. Violence erupted in a squatter camp in Johannesburg in October, directed principally at Zimbabweans (with dual South African nationality) and women who lived with Zimbabwean men; it was reported that the attacks were economically motivated, despite the fact that most of the Zimbabweans in the camp were unemployed. More than 70 shacks were burned down, and a further 100 were looted, while hundreds of people were forced to seek refuge at a local police station.

In August 2001 Agri South Africa, an organization representing commercial farmers (mainly white) and 'emerging' black farmers, reported that there had been more than 6,000 attacks on South African farms since 1991, resulting in the deaths of more than 1,000 people; it was widely feared that the motivation for the attacks was land redistribution, as had been the case in Zimbabwe since the late 1990s. The South African Government declared land seizures illegal in August, and the Department of Safety and Security established a committee of inquiry to determine the reasons for the attacks.

The leader of the NNP, van Schalkwyk, announced in October 2001 that the party was suspending its participation in the DA, following differences with the DP; the DP had dismissed the mayor of Cape Town, a prominent figure in the NNP, while the DP suspected the NNP of attempting to increase membership in an attempt to take overall control of the DA. Van Schalkwyk announced that the NNP would seek an accommodation with the ANC, as the IFP had done, retaining its independence, but holding positions in the Cabinet. In late November the ANC and NNP announced a power-sharing agreement in Western Cape (the only province not previously under ANC control), and the NNP also took seats in seven of the eight other Provincial Governments (all except Kwazulu/Natal, where the ANC had an agreement with the IFP). Discord within the NNP emerged when Gerald Morkel resigned as Premier of Western Cape in November, after publicly refusing to support closer co-operation with the ANC; he was replaced by Peter Marais. Meanwhile, in October COSATU accused the ANC of attempting to discredit it and suppress criticism of the Government, after a leaked report from the ANC national executive suggested that COSATU intended to establish a rival, extreme left-wing party. Marais resigned in May over allegations of sexual harassment and was replaced by van Schalkwyk.

A ruling by the Constitutional Court in late 2002, allowing national and provincial deputies to change parties without losing their seats, led to significant changes in the political landscape: in April 2003 the ANC secured a two-thirds' parliamentary majority when members of the UDM and the NNP defected to the ruling party, while the FA and the Afrikaner Eenheidsbeweging lost all their seats. At provincial level, members of the IFP defected to the ANC in KwaZulu/Natal and assumed further positions in the Cabinet, although the premiership of the province remained under IFP control. In April Madikizela-Mandela, who had been re-elected to the NEC of the ANC in December, was convicted of fraud and theft for obtaining bank loans using the fabricated names of employees of the ANC Women's League, and sentenced to five years' imprisonment.

The TRC's final report was presented to Mbeki in March 2003. The Commission had granted amnesty to 1,200 people, but had rejected more than 5,000 applications. Tutu recommended that some US $240m. ($12,000 each) be paid to the 20,000 people identified as victims of apartheid, and urged companies that had benefited through their involvement with the apartheid regime to contribute to the reparations process. Publication of the final report had been delayed by a legal challenge brought by the IFP, which was heavily implicated in the perpetration of human rights violations. In April, having rejected the suggestion that a special tax be imposed on companies that had gained from apartheid, Mbeki announced that those designated victims by the TRC would receive single payments of just over $3,800 each.

During its campaign for the 2004 general election the ANC pledged to halve levels of poverty and unemployment by increasing public expenditure in relevant areas, such as social services, public works and health care, and to accelerate both the empowerment programme, which aimed to transfer control of the economy to black citizens, and the stalled land reform programme. An empowerment charter for the financial sector, released in October 2003, envisaged that within four years 25% of all company executives would be non-white; and that 50% of goods bought by financial companies would be sourced from black-owned suppliers, rising to 70% by 2014. The mining sector had released a similar charter in March 2003: this pledged that 26% of mines would be black-owned within 10 years; the first conversions of mineral rights were expected by the end of 2004. In 1994 the Government had promised to transfer 30% of white-owned farms to non-whites over the next five years, but by 2004 only 2% had been transferred. In October of that year the Minister of Agriculture and Land Affairs, Angela Thoko Didiza, announced that some R 30,000m. would be required to settle outstanding land claims by the Government's 2005 deadline.

Elections to the National Assembly and the provincial legislatures took place concurrently on 14 April 2004. A total of 21 parties presented candidates in the national ballot, while 37 parties contested the provincial polls; 76.7% of the registered electorate participated. Final results, announced by the IEC on 17 April, confirmed the overwhelming victory of the ANC, which won 279 of the National Assembly's 400 seats, with 69.7% of the valid votes cast. The DA took 50 seats, with 12.4% of votes cast, and the IFP 28, with 7.0%. The ANC secured overall control of seven of the nine provincial assemblies; although it failed to win outright majorities in Kwazulu/Natal and Western Cape, the ANC subsequently nominated premiers to head all nine provincial governments. The IEC declared the elections to have been free and fair, although the IFP lodged complaints concerning the conduct of polling in KwaZulu/Natal. However, the IFP later announced that it had withdrawn these complaints in the interests of national unity. On 23 April members of the National Assembly voted unanimously to re-elect Mbeki to the presidency. President Mbeki was sworn in to serve a second term of office on 27 April, amid celebrations to mark 10 years of multi-racial democracy. Mbeki announced the composition of a new Cabinet, which included most senior members of the previous administration: Zuma was reappointed Deputy President, while Mantombanza (Manto) Tshabalala-Msimang retained the health portfolio despite the slow progress regarding the provision of antiretroviral drugs to combat HIV/AIDS (see above). Kader Asmal was replaced as Minister of Education by G. Naledi Pandor and Buthelezi who had held the post of Minister of Home Affairs since 1994, was dismissed. Van Schalkwyk, was appointed Minister of Environment and Tourism and Mosibudi Mangena, the leader of AZAPO, became Minister of Science and Technology. The two IFP representatives who had been allocated ministerial portfolios did not take up their posts when the new Government was sworn in on 29 April. Of the 49 posts in the new Government 22 ministerial portfolios were held by women.

In August 2004 van Schalkwyk announced that the NNP was to merge with ANC and that the NNP would be disbanded in September 2005. The NNP leader also stated his intention to join the ANC and urged all NNP members to do the same. Former President de Klerk subsequently announced his resignation from the NNP in protest at the decision. (The NNP officially ceased to exist at the end of February 2006.)

Meanwhile, in August 2003, the National Director of Public Prosecutions, Bulelani Ngcuka, had announced that Deputy President Zuma would not be prosecuted for alleged corruption in connection with an arms-procurement deal, despite an apparent recommendation from investigators that he be charged. This prompted accusations of government interference in the legal process and opposition demands for Zuma's resignation. Zuma repeatedly rejected the allegations against him; however, in early June 2005 his financial adviser, Schabir Shaik, was found guilty of corruption and fraud and sentenced to fifteen years' imprisonment by the Durban High Court. The Court found evidence of a corrupt relationship between Shaik and Zuma, and that a series of payments made by Shaik on behalf of Zuma were intended to influence Zuma to benefit Shaik's business. Although Zuma did not give evidence, the trial revealed that Zuma had been party to a bid to solicit a bribe from a French defence company involved in the arms-procurement deal.

President Mbeki came under increasing pressure to dismiss Zuma and on 14 June 2005 he announced that the Deputy President would be 'released' from his duties. Zuma was replaced by Phumzile Mlambo-Ngcuka, hitherto the Minister of Energy and Mineral Affairs; Lindiwe Hendricks assumed Mlambo-

Mgucka's vacated portfolio. In early August it was reported that the new Deputy President advocated the forced expropriation of white farms to accelerate the process of land distribution. At an education conference later that month Mlambo-Ngcuka was also reported to have called for South Africa to model its land redistribution programme on that of Zimbabwe. Following a preliminary hearing in October, in mid-November Zuma was provisionally indicted at Durban Magistrates' Court; his trial was set to commence in the High Court on 31 July 2006. Later in November 2005 it was also reported that Zuma was under investigation for the alleged rape of a female family friend; he was charged with the offence in early December but strenuously denied the allegation and was acquitted in early May 2006. Also in early December 2005 the Constitutional Court ruled that same-sex marriages deserved the same legal status as those between men and women and called on the legislature to amend the existing marriage law within 12 months.

South Africa became increasingly isolated politically in southern Africa after Zimbabwe (formerly Rhodesia) underwent the transition to independence in April 1980. During the 1980s South Africa's continued occupation of Namibia resulted in frequent clashes between SWAPO guerrillas and South African troops (see the chapter on Namibia). In 1971 the International Court of Justice had declared South Africa's presence in Namibia to be illegal and the UN had, in 1973, recognized SWAPO as the 'authentic representative of the Namibian people'. Following the collapse of the semi-autonomous internal administration, South Africa resumed direct rule of Namibia in January 1983. In February 1984 South Africa and Angola agreed on a cease-fire along the Angola–Namibia border, and established a joint commission to monitor the withdrawal of South African troops from Angola. In May 1988 negotiations began between Angola, Cuba and South Africa, with the USA acting as mediator. On 22 December Angola, Cuba and South Africa signed a formal treaty designating 1 April 1989 as the commencement date for the process leading to Namibian independence, as well as a treaty requiring all 50,000 Cuban troops to be withdrawn from Angola by July 1991. Elections were held in Namibia in November 1989, and independence for the former South African territory was achieved on 21 March 1990, under a SWAPO-controlled Government. The strategic port of Walvis Bay and 12 offshore islands, to which Namibia laid claim, remained under South African jurisdiction until September 1991, when the two countries agreed to administer the disputed territories jointly. In August 1993 South Africa relinquished sovereignty over Walvis Bay and the 12 islands, which were officially transferred to Namibia in March 1994. In August 2001 the South African and Namibian foreign ministers met to discuss the issue of their joint border on the Orange river; Namibia claimed the border extended to the middle of the river, while South Africa claimed it lay on the northern bank, provoking differences over mineral and fishing rights.

In 1984 South Africa signed a mutual non-aggression pact with Mozambique (the Nkomati accord), which implied that South Africa would withdraw its covert support for the Resistência Nacional Moçambicana (Renamo), while Mozambique would prevent the ANC from using its territory as a base for attacks on South Africa. In September 1985 the South African Government conceded that there had been 'technical' violations of the accord. In May 1988 Mozambican and South African officials agreed to reactivate the Nkomati accord, and in September President Botha visited President Joaquim Chissano of Mozambique, his first state visit to a black African nation. Following his election as President, Mandela made an official visit to Mozambique in July 1994. In August of that year South Africa, Mozambique and Swaziland signed a security co-operation accord, in an effort to combat the continuing illicit transport of armaments. In February 1997 South Africa appealed to the Government of Swaziland to release Swazi trade union leaders from detention. The Swazi Government protested at action mounted by COSATU in support of its Swazi counterparts, stating that it represented interference in the internal affairs of Swaziland.

In 1979 the Southern African Development Co-ordination Conference (SADCC) was established by southern African countries, to work towards a reduction of their economic dependence on South Africa. SADCC reformed in August 1992 as the Southern African Development Community (SADC, see p. 358), which aimed to achieve closer economic integration between its member states. South Africa was admitted to SADC in August 1994. In April 1997 members of the South African armed forces participated in military training exercises in Zimbabwe, as part of a nascent SADC regional peace-keeping force. In September 1998 about 600 South African and 200 Botswanan troops were dispatched to restore order in the Lesotho capital, Maseru, under the aegis of SADC, following a coup attempt by junior military officers. The rebels subsequently withdrew from the capital, after fighting in which about 66 people were killed. About 750 South African troops, together with some 350 Botswanan troops, remained in Lesotho to maintain civil order, before their withdrawal in May 2000.

In April 2000 Mbeki, together with the Presidents of Namibia and Mozambique, visited Zimbabwe to increase pressure on President Robert Mugabe to prevent the illegal occupation of white-owned farmland (see the chapter on Zimbabwe). Despite international condemnation of Mugabe and requests by a number of countries, most notably the United Kingdom, for more unequivocal criticism of President Mugabe's actions from South Africa, President Mbeki attempted to maintain 'constructive engagement' towards Zimbabwe. Relations with the United Kingdom were strained in January 2001, when a British government minister openly criticized South African policy on the issue. Following Mugabe's re-election as President in March 2002, the ANC issued a statement endorsing the ballot, despite allegations that Mugabe's party, the Zimbabwe African National Union—Patriotic Front, had intimidated voters and engaged in electoral fraud. The South African Government's position strained relations with the United Kingdom and the USA, and the latter threatened to withdraw support for the New Partnership for Africa's Development (NEPAD, see below) if the Government did not condemn Mugabe. However, later in March Mbeki was part of a Commonwealth troika (also comprising the President of Nigeria and the Prime Minister of Australia) that decided to suspend Zimbabwe from meetings of that organization for a period of one year. Mbeki had previously ignored pleas from Morgan Tsvangirai, the leader of the main opposition party in Zimbabwe, the Movement for Democratic Change, to impose sanctions on Zimbabwe prior to the election. In March 2003 Donald (Don) McKinnon, the Secretary-General of the Commonwealth, stated that the troika had concluded that Zimbabwe's suspension from the organization's meetings should remain in force for a further nine months. However, South Africa subsequently denied that it had agreed to the extension of the suspension. Zimbabwe withdrew from the Commonwealth in December 2003, shortly before the conclusion of the organization's Heads of Government meeting, at which the country's suspension had been extended indefinitely. Mbeki had criticized the decision to maintain the suspension, claiming that some Commonwealth members had failed to understand the question of land ownership in Zimbabwe. The Commonwealth appointed South Africa to a six-member advisory panel charged with monitoring the situation in Zimbabwe. Mbeki met separately with Mugabe and Tsvangirai in that month in an unsuccessful attempt to persuade them to form a coalition government. In early 2005 it was estimated that some 2.5m. Zimbabweans were living in South Africa, the majority illegally. In November 2004 it was reported that South Africa was deporting some 45,000 Zimbabweans annually at a cost of R 720m. In February 2005 the expulsion from Zimbabwe of 18 senior members of COSATU, who were taking part in a 'fact-finding' mission prior to the legislative elections in that country in March, prompted a succession of large protests by civil society movements in South Africa against the Mugabe regime.

In November 1996 South Africa was criticized for its approval of a substantial sale of weapons to Rwanda, which was believed to be providing military support to rebels in eastern Zaire who were engaged in conflict with the Zairean army. In response to international pressure, the South African Government subsequently decided to suspend the sale of armaments to Rwanda. During 1996 South Africa supported efforts to achieve reconciliation in Angola and in early 1997 was involved in intensive diplomatic activity, along with other African countries, with the aim of negotiating an end to the civil war in Zaire. Following the assumption of power by Alliance des forces démocratiques pour la libération du Congo-Zaïre, led by Laurent-Désiré Kabila, in May, South Africa became the first foreign government to recognize the new regime and pledged to assist in reconstruction efforts and in the holding of elections in the renamed Democratic Republic of the Congo (DRC). In October 2001 South African soldiers were dispatched to Burundi (q.v.) as part of a proposed 700-member peace-keeping mission, in an effort to enforce national security and to support the formation of a multi-ethnic transitional government. Mandela had been instrumental in negotiating a peace accord (signed in August 2000), whereby the Hutu and Tutsi ethnic groups, which had been engaged in civil conflict since 1993, were each to hold the presidency for 18 months during a three-year transitional period. South African mediation was ongoing in March 2005, represented by Deputy President Zuma. In May 2003 1,400 South African troops were deployed in the DRC as part of a UN peace-keeping mission, rising to 1,750 at January 2004. In November 2004 President Mbeki was mandated by the African Union (AU, see p. 153) to lead peace negotiations in Côte d'Ivoire (q.v), following the breakdown of a cease-fire between the Government of that country and rebels. In March 2005 South Africa dispatched some 300 troops to Darfur, Sudan (q.v.), as part of an AU mission to investigate and monitor events in the region.

During the 1980s, despite appeals by anti-apartheid groups within and outside the country for the imposition of economic sanctions, South Africa retained vital trading links with many Western countries, and its economy was supported by considerable foreign investment. Nevertheless, following the violent events of 1984–85, the UN Security Council imposed a number of economic sanctions and restrictions on sport and cultural relations. The US Government (which had hitherto maintained a policy of 'constructive engagement' with South Africa) imposed a series of limited economic sanctions, as did members of the European Community (EC, now the European Union—EU, see p. 228) and Nordic countries. In 1986 the Heads of Government of seven Commonwealth countries agreed (with the exception of the United Kingdom) to adopt wide-ranging sanctions.

Following the implementation of political reforms in South Africa from February 1990, international sanctions were reviewed. During 1991 South Africa was readmitted to international sporting competition, after many years of exclusion. In July the USA officially withdrew sanctions (which were, however, retained by a number of US states and cities). In October Commonwealth Heads of Government endorsed the withdrawal of cultural sanctions against South Africa; however, sanctions on finance, arms and trade and investment remained. Japan ended all its sanctions during that month. In 1992 the EC withdrew a number of sanctions against South Africa. In September 1993, following the adoption of legislation providing for the installation of a multiracial transitional administration (see above), the international community ended the remaining economic sanctions against South Africa. The UN Security Council ended its mandatory embargo on armaments, following the establishment of an interim Government of National Unity in May 1994; South Africa subsequently established diplomatic relations with more than 165 countries. South Africa became a member of the Commonwealth on 1 June, and joined the Organization of African Unity (OAU—now the AU) later that month. The People's Republic of China refused to establish formal diplomatic links while South Africa maintained relations with Taiwan. In November 1996 President Mandela announced that South Africa's diplomatic relations with Taiwan were to be severed in favour of the People's Republic of China, with effect from the end of 1997. In response, Taiwan withdrew its ambassador indefinitely and announced that the majority of its aid projects in South Africa would be suspended.

Despite the ANC Government's commitment to an independent foreign policy and consequent good relations with regimes that are unpopular with Western nations, including Cuba, Iran and Libya, South Africa's relations with the USA were considerably strengthened following the transition to multiracial, democratic rule. In December 1995 a joint US-South African commission was established, chaired by Mbeki and the US Vice-President, Al Gore. In February 1998 it was announced that South Africa and the USA were to normalize their defence trade agreement, thereby allowing South African armaments companies to trade with their US counterparts for the first time. In August 1998 two people were killed, and about 27 injured, in a bomb attack on a US restaurant in Cape Town. A supporter of an organization styled Muslims Against Global Oppression (MAGO) claimed to have perpetrated the bombing, apparently in retaliation for US air attacks on Sudan and Afghanistan (although MAGO officially denied responsibility for the incident). Several members of PAGAD were subsequently arrested in connection with the bombing. A series of further bombings in the Cape Town area, and the killing of a local magistrate in July 2000, were also attributed by the authorities to PAGAD.

In March 1998, following four years of negotiations, the EU approved the terms for a comprehensive free-trade agreement with South Africa. The agreement provisionally came into force on 1 January 2000; a continuing dispute with the Governments of Italy, Spain, Portugal and Greece, which had refused to sign the accord on wines and spirits, was resolved after South Africa agreed to discontinue the use of traditional European names for alcoholic drinks within five years. In December 2000 a framework agreement was reached on a free-trade accord with the Southern Common Market (known as Mercosur—Mercado Común del Sur, comprising Argentina, Brazil, Paraguay and Uruguay); trade negotiations were ongoing in early 2004.

In mid-September 2004 the announcement by the South African Government that it had established diplomatic links with the Sahrawi Arab Democratic Republic precipitated a deterioration in relations between Morocco and South Africa. Morocco subsequently recalled its ambassador to South Africa 'for consultations'.

In October 2001 the New Partnership for Africa's Development (NEPAD) was launched, as part of a long-term strategy for socio-economic recovery in Africa, in accordance with a decision taken at the OAU summit held in Lusaka, Zambia, in July. Mbeki formulated NEPAD's founding documents, in conjunction with the heads of state of Algeria, Egypt, Nigeria and Senegal, and South Africa was to host the Secretariat. In mid-2004 the AU agreed that the Pan-African Parliament (PAP) would be based in South Africa; the Government then announced that the PAP would be housed in Midrand (between Johannesburg and Pretoria). The second session of the PAP—its first in South Africa—took place at temporary headquarters in Midrand in mid-September that year.

Government

Under the terms of the Constitution, which was adopted on 8 May 1996 and entered into force on 4 February 1997, legislative power is vested in a bicameral Parliament, comprising a National Assembly and a National Council of Provinces (formerly the Senate). The National Assembly is elected by universal adult suffrage under a system of proportional representation and has between 350 and 400 members. The 90-member National Council of Provinces comprises six permanent delegates and four special delegates from each of the provincial legislatures (see below). The President, who is elected by the National Assembly from among its members, exercises executive power in consultation with the other members of the Cabinet. Any party that holds a minimum of 80 seats in the National Assembly (equivalent to 20% of the national vote) is entitled to nominate an Executive Deputy President. A Constitutional Court ensures that the executive, legislative and judicial organs of government adhere to the provisions of the Constitution.

Each of the nine provinces has a legislature, which is elected under a system of proportional representation. Each legislature is entitled to draft a constitution for the province, subject to the principles governing the national Constitution, and to elect a Premier, who heads an Executive Council. Parties that hold a minimum of 10% of seats in the provincial legislature are entitled to a proportional number of portfolios in the Executive Council.

Defence

In August 2005 the South African National Defence Force (SANDF) totalled about 55,750: army 36,000, navy 4,500, air force 9,250 and a medical corps numbering 6,000. The SANDF comprised members of the former South African armed forces, together with personnel from the former military wings of the ANC and the Pan-Africanist Congress, and the former 'homelands'. Budgetary expenditure on defence was estimated at R22,400.0m. in 2005.

Economic Affairs

In 2004, according to estimates by the World Bank, South Africa's gross national income (GNI), measured at average 2002–04 prices, was US $165,326m., equivalent to $3,630 per head (or $10,960 per head on an international purchasing-power parity basis). During 1995–2004, it was estimated, the population increased at an average annual rate of 1.7%, while gross domestic product (GDP) per head, in real terms, increased by 1.2%. Overall GDP increased, in real terms, at an average annual rate of 3.0% in 1995–2004, according to the World Bank; growth was 3.7% in 2004.

Agriculture (including forestry and fishing) contributed 2.5% of GDP in 2005. Some 7.8% of the employed labour force were engaged in the sector at March 2004. Maize (also the principal subsistence crop), fruit and sugar are exported, and livestock-rearing is also important; wool is another significant export. The

GDP of the agricultural sector increased by an average of 2.9% per year in 1995–2004, according to the World Bank. Agricultural GDP increased by 1.2% in 2004.

Industry (including mining, manufacturing, construction and power) contributed 30.3% of GDP in 2005, and engaged 21.7% of the employed labour force at March 2004. Industrial GDP increased at an average annual rate of 1.8% in 1995–2004, according to the World Bank. Industrial GDP increased by 3.2% in 2004.

Mining contributed 7.0% of GDP in 2005, and engaged 4.9% of the employed labour force at March 2004. South Africa is the world's leading producer of gold, which is the major mineral export, accounting for about 15% of total world production in 2002. Coal, platinum, iron ore, diamonds, chromium, manganese, vanadium, vermiculite, antimony, limestone, asbestos, fluorspar, uranium, copper, lead and zinc are also important mineral exports. There are reserves of petroleum, natural gas, sillimanite, titanium and zirconium. The GDP of the mining sector increased by an average of 1.0% per year in 1998–2005. Mining GDP increased by 3.1% in 2005.

Manufacturing contributed 18.6% of GDP in 2005, and engaged 12.4% of the employed labour force at March 2004. The GDP of the manufacturing sector increased at an average annual rate of 2.2% in 1995–2004, according to the World Bank. Manufacturing GDP increased by 2.6% in 2004.

Energy is derived principally from coal-based electricity (93.1% in 2002); this is supplemented by nuclear power and by hydroelectric power (5.5% and 1.3%, respectively). The construction of a plant to convert natural gas into liquid fuel was completed in 1992. Exploitation of petroleum reserves in oilfields located 140 km south-west of the Southern Cape commenced in 1997. In 2001 substantial reserves of natural gas were discovered off the Western Cape. Imports of mineral fuels and lubricants comprised 12.5% of the value of total imports in 2002.

The services sector contributed 67.1% of GDP in 2004, and engaged 70.5% of the employed labour force at March 2004. The real GDP of the services sector increased by an average of 3.7% per year in 1995–2004, according to the World Bank. Services GDP increased by 4.1% in 2004.

In 2004 South Africa recorded a visible trade deficit of US $281m., while there was a deficit of $7,442m. on the current account of the balance of payments. In 2002 the principal source of imports for the Southern African Customs Union (SACU, see below) was Germany (an estimated 15.6%); other major suppliers of imports were the USA, the United Kingdom, Japan and the People's Republic of China. The principal market for exports in that year was the United Kingdom (10.9%); other important purchasers were the USA, Germany, Japan and the Netherlands. The principal exports in 2003 were basic manufactures (particularly iron and steel and diamonds), machinery and transport equipment, mineral fuels, crude materials, food and live animals and chemical products. The principal imports were machinery and transport equipment, basic manufactures, mineral fuels (particularly petroleum), and chemical products.

In the financial year 2005/06 South Africa's estimated budget deficit was R 6,734.1m. At the end of 2003 South Africa's total foreign debt was US $27,807m., of which $20,448 was long-term public debt. The cost of debt-servicing in that year was equivalent to 9.0% of the value of exports of goods and services. The annual rate of inflation averaged 8.7% in 1990–2002; consumer prices increased by 5.8% in 2003 and by 1.4% in 2004. According to official figures, 27.8% of the labour force were unemployed at March 2004.

South Africa is a member of SACU (with Botswana, Lesotho, Namibia and Swaziland), of the Southern African Development Community (SADC, see p. 358) and of the African Development Bank (see p. 151). The Secretariat of the New Partnership for Africa's Development (see p. 157) is located in South Africa.

Despite South Africa's mineral wealth and highly developed manufacturing sector, economic progress was hindered during the 1980s following the imposition of economic sanctions by the international community in protest at apartheid (see Recent History). In late 1993, in response to the Government's adoption of political reforms, the remaining economic sanctions were ended, relations with international financial institutions were normalized, and an agreement with foreign creditor banks regarding the country's outstanding debt was reached. Following democratic elections in April 1994, foreign Governments pledged considerable financial assistance to South Africa. The new Government initiated a Reconstruction and Development Programme; however, subsequent progress in social and economic development was impeded by the necessity for fiscal restraint. In mid-1996 the Government announced its long-term strategy for 'growth, employment and redistribution' (GEAR), which placed emphasis on continued fiscal discipline, reductions in the budgetary deficit and the removal of exchange controls. By 1999 financial market conditions had improved considerably, resulting in lower inflation, increased real GDP and an increase in investor confidence. Meanwhile, the IMF urged the Government to accelerate the implementation of the structural reforms of the GEAR strategy, particularly the reduction of unemployment (which remained critically high), trade liberalization and privatization. The mining sector, one of the most significant in the South African economy, underwent significant rationalization and consolidation in the late 1990s, and in June 2002 the National Assembly approved legislation transferring the control of mineral rights from private companies to the Government, which would then lease them. In 2003 gold contributed an estimated US $5,400m. to total foreign currency earnings, second only to tourism, which earned US $8,240m. in that year. In late 2003 the Government announced its intention to increase public expenditure on infrastructure, social services and health care in an attempt to reduce levels of poverty and unemployment. Despite several positive developments in 2004, including an increase in business and consumer confidence, the lowering of the rate of inflation, the appreciation of the rand against the US dollar and the first recorded reduction in the rate of unemployment since 1994, the South African economy was confronted with a number of difficulties. The distribution of income in the country remained one of the most unequal in the world with poverty still widespread among vast sections of the population, while the HIV/AIDS epidemic continued to have a devastating social and economic impact. The 2005/06 budget envisaged GDP growth of 3.9% for that year (revised to 5.0% in the 2006/07 budget). Under the 2006/07 budget an additional R 3,090m. was to be allocated to education, public health and social welfare services over the next three years.

Education

School attendance is compulsory for children of all population groups between the ages of seven and 16 years. From 1991 state schools were permitted to admit pupils of all races, and in 1995 the right to free state education for all was introduced. In 1998/99 the total enrolment at primary schools included 95.2% of pupils in the relevant age-group (males 94.9%; females 95.5%), while in 1999/2000 secondary enrolment was equivalent to 90.2% of pupils in the relevant age-group (males 85.8%; females 94.7%). During the 1980s universities, which were formerly racially segregated, began to admit students of all races. In 1999 there were 21 universities and 15 'technikons' (tertiary education institutions offering technological and commercial vocational training); in 2002 it was announced that the number of universities was to be reduced to 11, the number of technikons reduced to six, and that four comprehensive institutions and two national higher education institutes would be created. Budget estimates for 2005/06 indicated the allocation of R 12,397.1m. (3.0% of total expenditure) to education.

Public Holidays

2006: 1 January (New Year's Day), 21 March (Human Rights Day), 14 April (Good Friday), 17 April (Family Day), 27 April (Freedom Day), 1 May (Workers' Day), 16 June (Youth Day), 9 August (National Women's Day), 24 September (Heritage Day), 16 December (Day of Reconciliation), 25 December (Christmas Day), 26 December (Day of Goodwill).

2007: 1 January (New Year's Day), 21 March (Human Rights Day), 6 April (Good Friday), 9 April (Family Day), 27 April (Freedom Day), 1 May (Workers' Day), 16 June (Youth Day), 9 August (National Women's Day), 24 September (Heritage Day), 17 December (for Day of Reconciliation), 25 December (Christmas Day), 26 December (Day of Goodwill).

Weights and Measures

The metric system is in use.

SOUTH AFRICA

Statistical Survey

Source (unless otherwise indicated): Statistics South Africa, Private Bag X44, Pretoria 0001; tel. (12) 3108911; fax (12) 3108500; e-mail info@statssa.pwv.gov.za; internet www.statssa.gov.za.

Area and Population

AREA, POPULATION AND DENSITY*

Area (sq km)	1,219,090†
Population (census results)	
9 October 1996	40,583,573
9 October 2001	
Males	21,434,033
Females	23,385,737
Total	44,819,770
Population (official estimates at mid-year)‡	
2003	46,429,823
2004	46,586,607
2005	46,888,200§
Density (per sq km) at mid-2005	38.5

* Excluding data for Walvis Bay (area 1,124 sq km or 434 sq miles, population 22,999 in 1991), sovereignty over which was transferred from South Africa to Namibia on 1 March 1994.
† 470,693 sq miles.
‡ Figures exclude the effect of additional deaths caused by HIV/AIDS and have not been revised to take account of the 2001 census.
§ Rounded estimate.

ETHNIC GROUPS
(at census of October 2001)*

	Number	% of total
Africans (Blacks)	35,416,164	79.02
Europeans (Whites)	4,293,638	9.58
Coloureds	3,994,507	8.91
Asians	1,115,461	2.49
Total	44,819,770	100.00

* Figures exclude the effect of additional deaths caused by HIV/AIDS.

PROVINCES
(at census of October 2001)

	Area (sq km)	Population	Density (per sq km)	Capital
KwaZulu/Natal	92,100	9,426,019	102.3	Pietermaritzburg
Gauteng*	17,010	8,837,172	519.5	Johannesburg
Eastern Cape	169,580	6,436,761	38.0	Bisho
Limpopo†	123,910	5,273,637	42.6	Pietersburg
Western Cape	129,370	4,524,335	35.0	Cape Town
North-West	116,320	3,669,350	31.5	Mmabatho
Mpumalanga‡	79,490	3,122,994	39.3	Nelspruit
Free State§	129,480	2,706,776	20.9	Bloemfontein
Northern Cape	361,830	822,726	2.3	Kimberley
Total	1,219,090	44,819,770	36.8	

* Formerly Pretoria-Witwatersrand-Vereeniging.
† Known as Northern Province (formerly Northern Transvaal) until February 2002.
‡ Formerly Eastern Transvaal.
§ Formerly the Orange Free State.

PRINCIPAL TOWNS
(metropolitan areas, population at 2001 census)

Johannesburg	3,225,812	Springs	80,776
Durban	3,090,122	Vanderbijlpark	80,201
Cape Town*	2,893,247	Vereeniging	73,288
Pretoria*	1,985,983	Uitenhage	71,668
Port Elizabeth	1,005,779	Rustenburg	67,201
Soweto	858,649	Kimberley	62,526
Tembisa	348,687	Brakpan	62,115
Pietermaritzburg	223,518	Witbank	61,092
Botshabelo	175,820	Somerset West	60,609
Mdantsane	175,783	Klerksdorp	59,511
Boksburg	158,650	Midrand	44,566
East London	135,560	Newcastle	44,119
Bloemfontein*	111,698	Welkom	34,158
Benoni	94,341	Potchefstroom	26,725
Alberton	89,394	Carletonville	18,362
Krugersdorp	86,618	Westonaria	8,440

* Pretoria is the administrative capital, Cape Town the legislative capital and Bloemfontein the judicial capital.

Mid-2003 (UN estimates, incl. suburbs): Cape Town 2,967,088; Durban 2,551,257; East Rand (Ekurhuleni) 2,808,417; Johannesburg 3,084,207; Pretoria 1,208,537 (Source: UN, *World Urbanization Prospects: The 2003 Revision*).

BIRTHS AND DEATHS
(UN estimates, annual averages)

	1990–95	1995–2000	2000–05
Birth rate (per 1,000)	27.8	25.4	23.8
Death rate (per 1,000)	8.1	10.1	16.2

Source: UN, *World Population Prospects: The 2004 Revision*.

Expectation of life (WHO estimates, years at birth): 49 (males 48; females 50) in 2003 (Source: WHO, *World Health Report*).

IMMIGRATION AND EMIGRATION

	2001	2002	2003
Immigrants:			
Africa	1,450	2,472	4,961
Europe	1,714	1,847	2,567
Asia	1,398	1,738	2,328
Americas	213	244	354
Oceania	51	65	99
Total (incl. others and unspecified)	4,832	6,545	10,578
Emigrants:			
Africa	1,710	1,461	2,611
Europe	5,316	4,637	6,827
Asia	506	218	445
Americas	1,713	1,473	2,090
Oceania	2,912	2,523	3,248
Total (incl. others and unspecified)	12,260	10,890	16,165

SOUTH AFRICA

ECONOMICALLY ACTIVE POPULATION
(household survey, '000 persons aged 15 to 65 years, September 2001)*

	Males	Females	Total
Agriculture, hunting, forestry and fishing	727	324	1,051
Mining and quarrying	470	17	487
Manufacturing	1,004	602	1,605
Electricity, gas and water	80	15	95
Construction	534	60	594
Trade, restaurants and hotels	1,186	1,212	2,397
Transport, storage and communications	448	94	543
Financing, insurance, real estate and business services	547	428	975
Community, social and personal services	878	1,110	1,988
Private households	150	905	1,055
Total employed (incl. others)	6,049	4,783	10,833
Unemployed†	2,139	2,386	4,525
Total labour force	8,188	7,169	15,358

* Figures have been assessed independently, so that totals are not always the sum of the component parts.
† Based on the official definition. According to the expanded definition, the number of unemployed (in '000) was 7,698 (males 3,280, females 4,418).

March 2004 ('000): Agriculture, hunting, forestry and fishing 930; Mining and quarrying 584; Manufacturing 1,484; Electricity, gas and water 107; Construction 427; Wholesale and retail 1,590; Transport, storage and communications 467; Financing, insurance, real estate and business services 1,023; Community, social and personal services 2,114; Total employed (incl. others) 11,984; Unemployed 4,611; Total labour force 16,595.

Health and Welfare

KEY INDICATORS

Total fertility rate (children per woman, 2003)	2.6
Under-5 mortality rate (per 1,000 live births, 2004)	67
HIV/AIDS (% of persons aged 15–49, 2003)	21.5
Physicians (per 1,000 head, 2001)	0.69
Health expenditure (2002): US $ per head (PPP)	689
Health expenditure (2002): % of GDP	8.7
Health expenditure (2002): public (% of total)	40.6
Access to water (% of persons, 2002)	87
Access to sanitation (% of persons, 2002)	67
Human Development Index (2003): ranking	120
Human Development Index (2003): value	0.658

For sources and definitions, see explanatory note on p. vi.

Agriculture

PRINCIPAL CROPS
('000 metric tons)

	2002	2003	2004
Wheat	2,437.7	1,546.8	1,680.0
Barley	180	240	185
Maize	10,076	9,705	9,965
Oats	58.2	32.9	36.9
Sorghum	264.9	264.3	449.1
Potatoes	1,555.9	1,619.8	1,818.6
Sweet potatoes	52.4	50.1	54.8
Sugar cane	23,012.6	20,418.9	19,094.8
Dry beans	62.3	68.3	85.1
Soybeans	223.0	136.5	220.0
Groundnuts (in shell)	133.7	66.9	128.0
Sunflower seed	966.5	682.2	677.4
Cottonseed	47.0	41.1	71.7
Cabbages	177.9	171.4	174.0
Tomatoes	450.4	413.6	436.5
Pumpkins, squash and gourds	340.0*	357.1	367.8
Onions (dry)	344.1	360.4	403.3
Carrots	111.7	124.2	132.9
Green corn (maize)	296	322*	320*
Watermelons	52.3	61.2	64.9

—continued	2002	2003	2004
Other fresh vegetables (incl. melons)*	430.2	469.4	466.4
Bananas	280.0	209.7	220.0*
Oranges	1,267.1	1,342.1	1,154.3
Tangerines, mandarins, clementines and satsumas	109.8	112.2	112.6
Lemons and limes	190.2	197.6	215.0
Grapefruit and pomelos	268.3	256.2	233.3
Apples	580.3	714.3	707.8
Pears	304.3	306.3	308.9
Apricots	56.5	67.7	82.3
Peaches and nectarines	217.8	291.9	226.4
Plums	40.2	57.5	70.2
Grapes	1,521.7	1,663.5	1,683.0
Mangoes	86.1	81.8	77.2
Avocados	84.7	63.3	56.2
Pineapples	177.3	163.8	162.4
Other fresh fruit (excl. melons)*	91.7	90.2	93.7
Tobacco (leaves)	28.5	35.8	31.9

* FAO estimate(s).
Source: FAO.

LIVESTOCK
('000 head, year ending September)

	2002	2003	2004
Cattle	13,635	13,538	13,512
Pigs	1,663	1,662	1,651
Sheep	26,000*	25,820	25,360*
Goats	6,452	6,358	6,372
Horses*	270	270	270
Mules*	14	14	14
Asses*	150	150	150
Chickens*	148,000	144,000	145,000
Ducks*	360	360	360
Geese*	128	128	130
Turkeys*	380	410	500

* FAO estimate(s).
Source: FAO.

LIVESTOCK PRODUCTS
('000 metric tons)

	2002	2003	2004
Beef and veal	580	635	655
Mutton and lamb	105	120	120
Goat meat*	36.0	36.0	36.4
Pig meat	111	134	145
Poultry meat	930.1	905.0	912.4
Cows' milk	2,685	2,642	2,552
Butter	10.0	11.8	12.0
Cheese	38.0*	38.0	41.7*
Hen eggs	340	328	340
Wool: greasy	47.5	44.2	44.2*
Wool: scoured*	32	32	32
Cattle hides (fresh)*	76.1	75.5	76.8
Sheepskins (fresh)*	18.0	18.4	18.4

* FAO estimate(s).
Source: FAO.

Forestry
(including Namibia)

ROUNDWOOD REMOVALS
('000 cubic metres, excl. bark)

	2002*	2003	2004*
Sawlogs, veneer logs and logs for sleepers	6,002	5,235.9†	5,235.9
Pulpwood	9,223	14,833.3†	14,833.3
Other industrial wood	3,391	1,090.2†	1,090.2
Fuel wood*	12,000	12,000	12,000
Total	30,616	33,159.4*	33,159.4

* FAO estimate(s).
† Unofficial figure.

Source: FAO.

SAWNWOOD PRODUCTION
('000 cubic metres, incl. railway sleepers)

	2002*	2003†	2004*
Coniferous (softwood)	1,396	2,076.6	2,076.6
Broadleaved (hardwood)	102	94.7	94.7
Total	1,498	2,171.3	2,171.3

* FAO estimates.
† Unofficial figures.

Source: FAO.

Fishing
('000 metric tons, live weight)

	2001	2002	2003
Capture*	750.1	766.3	822.9
Cape hakes (Stokvisse)	146.4	149.5	139.2
Southern African pilchard	192.2	260.7	290.0
Whitehead's round herring	55.3	54.8	42.5
Southern African anchovy	287.2	213.4	258.9
Cape horse mackerel	9.7	21.9	28.3
Aquaculture	4.2	4.5*	4.9
Total catch*†	754.3	770.8	827.8

* FAO estimate(s).
† Excluding aquatic plants ('000 metric tons): 32.3 in 2001; 32.2 in 2002 (FAO estimate); 32.2 in 2003 (FAO estimate).

Note: Figures exclude aquatic mammals, recorded by number rather than weight. The number of Nile crocodiles captured was: 33,174 in 2001; 45,787 in 2002; 31,113 in 2003. The number of toothed whales caught was 37 in 2001; 78 in 2002; 70 in 2003.

Source: FAO.

Mining
('000 metric tons, unless otherwise indicated)

	2001	2002	2003*
Hard coal	223,500	220,200	239,311
Crude petroleum ('000 barrels)	13,870	10,950	4,068
Natural gas†	1,800	2,000	2,500
Iron ore‡	22,240	23,200	24,200
Copper ore (metric tons)‡	141,865	129,589	89,501
Nickel ore (metric tons)‡	36,443†	38,546	40,842†
Lead concentrates (metric tons)‡	50,771	49,444	39,941
Zinc ore (metric tons)‡	61,221	64,173	41,239
Manganese ore and concentrates (metallurgical and chemical)§	3,266	3,322	3,501
Chromium ore§	5,502	6,436	7,406
Vanadium ore (metric tons)‡	18,184	25,227	15,000
Zirconium concentrates (metric tons)†§	245,000	274,000	300,000

—continued	2001	2002	2003*
Antimony concentrates (metric tons)‡	4,927	5,746	5,310
Cobalt ore (metric tons)†‡	550	540	404
Silver (kg)	109,570	113,266	81,000
Uranium oxide (metric tons)	1,065	998	901
Gold (kg)	394,800	398,300	372,767
Platinum-group metals (kg)	229,913	243,033	266,150
Kaolin	85.6	91.4	85.3
Magnesite—crude	33.9†	40.0	40.0
Phosphate rock§	2,550	2,803	2,643
Fluorspar	286.4	267.0	235.0
Salt	354.0	430.6	438.3
Diamonds ('000 carats)	11,163	10,876	12,684
Gypsum—crude	382.8	415.4	394.1
Asbestos	13.4	—	6.2
Mica (metric tons)	937	821	1,003
Talc (metric tons)	3,030	2,511	6,719
Pyrophyllite (metric tons)	14,047	15,587	14,350

* Preliminary figures.
† Estimate(s).
‡ Figures refer to metal content of ores and concentrates.
§ Gross weight.

Source: US Geological Survey.

Industry

SELECTED PRODUCTS
('000 metric tons, unless otherwise indicated)

	2000	2001	2002
Wheat flour	1,836	1,926	2,070
Sugar—refined	1,148	1,096	1,141
Wine*	695	647	719
Cotton yarn—incl. mixed	67.4	74.5	78.8
Woven cotton fabrics (million sq metres)	219	216	215
Footwear ('000 pairs)	20,195	17,552	19,699
Mechanical wood pulp	270	275	275
Chemical wood pulp	1,372	1,354	1,354
Newsprint paper	328	328	328
Other printing and writing paper	506	533	533
Other paper and paperboard	1,062	1,245	1,245
Rubber tyres ('000)	11,862	10,923	12,038
Nitrogenous fertilizers	694	467	657
Phosphate fertilizers	370	309	369
Motor spirit (petrol)	7,979	7,948	n.a.
Kerosene	1,493	1,437	n.a.
Jet fuel	1,746	1,690	n.a.
Distillate fuel oils	6,935	7,150	n.a.
Lubricating oils	387	402	n.a.
Petroleum bitumen—asphalt	222	231	n.a.
Cement	8,715	8,036†	8,525†
Pig-iron†	6,292	5,820	5,823
Crude steel†	8,481	8,821	9,095
Refined copper—unwrought†	126.1‡	132.1‡	n.a.
Colour television receivers ('000)	290	260	271
Passenger motor cars—assembled ('000)	261	294	300
Lorries—assembled ('000)	131	126	129
Electric energy (million kWh)	210,670	213,137	n.a.

* Source: FAO.
† Source: US Geological Survey.
‡ Estimate.

Source: UN, *Industrial Commodity Statistics Yearbook*.

SOUTH AFRICA

Finance

CURRENCY AND EXCHANGE RATES

Monetary Units
100 cents = 1 rand (R).

Sterling, Dollar and Euro Equivalents (30 December 2005)
£1 sterling = 10.891 rand;
US $1 = 6.325 rand;
€1 = 7.462 rand;
1,000 rand = £91.82 = $158.10 = €134.02.

Average Exchange Rate (rand per US $)
2003   7.5648
2004   6.4597
2005   6.3593

BUDGET
(million rand, year ending 31 March)

Revenue	2003/04	2004/05	2005/06*
Tax revenue (gross)	302,507.5	354,980.3	417,050.0
Taxes on incomes and profits	171,962.8	195,219.1	228,730.0
Individuals	98,495.1	110,981.9	125,760.0
Companies (including secondary tax)	67,013.7	78,269.0	96,750.0
Retirement funds	4,897.7	4,406.1	4,500.0
Taxes on payroll and workforce.	3,896.4	4,443.3	5,000.0
Taxes on property	6,707.5	9,012.6	11,120.0
Domestic taxes on goods and services	110,173.5	131,982.8	152,370.0
Value-added tax	80,681.8	98,157.9	115,000.0
Excise duties	11,364.6	13,066.7	14,599.0
Levies on fuel	16,652.4	19,190.4	20,700.0
Stamp duties and fees	1,360.1	1,167.7	870.0
State Miscellaneous Revenue	−7.1	−130.9	—
Taxes on international trade and transactions	8,414.3	13,285.7	18,960.0
Other current revenue	5,931.4	5,520.4	7,454.1
Capital revenue	714.9	681.6	725.9
Sub-total	309,153.9	361,182.2	425,230.0
Less SACU payments†	9,722.7	13,327.8	14,144.9
Total	299,431.2	347,854.4	411,085.1

Expenditure	2003/04	2004/05‡	2005/06*
Central government administration	16,257.8	20,593.6	27,593.5
The Presidency	142.7	167.7	213.5
Parliament	448.5	580.8	677.3
Foreign affairs	2,163.8	2,393.1	2,595.1
Home affairs	2,022.0	2,069.4	2,972.7
Provincial and local government	9,456.3	13,138.2	15,580.8
Public works	2,024.5	2,244.4	5,554.1
Financial and administrative services	12,944.3	15,011.1	15,329.9
Government communication and information system	186.0	211.3	249.1
National treasury	12,111.9	13,510.0	13,990.7
Public enterprises	84.0	678.7	92.0
Public services and administration	155.9	128.5	167.7
Public service commission	69.3	77.0	82.1
SA management development institute	36.9	34.4	57.0
Statistics South Africa	300.3	371.2	691.3
Social services	59,869.9	70,121.4	81,371.7
Arts and culture	924.1	1,113.8	1,082.7
Education	10,557.0	11,340.4	12,397.1
Health	7,735.6	8,454.9	9,825.2
Labour	1,071.8	1,163.5	1,314.0
Social development	39,357.3	47,766.3	56,549.1
Sport and Recreation South Africa	224.1	282.5	203.6
Justice and protection services	55,325.0	59,161.6	65,272.1
Correctional services	7,849.7	8,828.8	9,234.1
Defence	20,504.7	20,201.3	22,459.4
Independent complaints directorate	41.3	47.0	49.5
Justice and constitutional development	4,236.4	4,670.0	5,072.1
Safety and security	22,692.9	25,414.5	28,457.0

Expenditure—continued	2003/04	2004/05‡	2005/06*
Economic services and infrastructure	25,733.1	28,131.8	31,838.6
Agriculture	1,194.8	1,408.2	1,684.7
Communications	849.5	1,663.9	1,017.5
Environmental affairs and tourism	1,455.6	1,660.5	1,723.1
Housing	4,560.0	4,808.4	5,191.7
Land affairs	1,635.9	2,022.0	3,881.5
Minerals and energy	1,812.5	1,876.4	2,117.6
Science and technology	1,391.6	1,632.9	1,986.6
Trade and industry	2,349.2	2,521.9	3,076.3
Transport	6,232.5	6,679.9	7,602.2
Water affairs and forestry	4,251.5	3,857.7	3,557.4
Contingency reserve	—	—	2,500.0
Sub-total	170,129.9	193,019.4	223,905.8
State debt costs	46,312.9	48,851.2	53,125.0
Provincial equitable share	107,538.4	120,884.5	134,706.2
Skills levy and seats	3,777.0	4,725.4	5,000.0
Members' remuneration	191.3	203.9	208.3
Judges' salaries	729.7	829.4	850.0
President and deputy-president salary	1.7	2.0	2.0
Standing appropriations	28.2	25.4	22.0
Total§	328,709.2	368,541.2	417,819.2

* Estimates.
† Payments to Botswana, Lesotho, Namibia and Swaziland, in accordance with Southern African Customs Union agreements.
‡ Provisional figures.
§ Based on unrounded data.
Source: National Treasury, Pretoria.

INTERNATIONAL RESERVES
(US $ million at 31 December)

	2003	2004	2005
Gold (national valuation)	1,476	1,578	2,051
IMF special drawing rights	331	346	319
Reserve position in IMF	1	1	1
Foreign exchange	6,164	12,794	18,260
Total	7,972	14,719	20,630

Source: IMF, *International Financial Statistics*.

MONEY SUPPLY
(million rand at 31 December)

	2002	2003	2004
Currency outside banks	29,219	33,718	39,084
Demand deposits at deposit money banks	328,047	352,627	379,842
Total (incl. others)	357,470	386,681	424,288

Source: IMF, *International Financial Statistics*.

COST OF LIVING
(Consumer Price Index; base: 2000 = 100)

	2001	2002	2003
Food	105.4	122.0	131.9
Housing	103.7	114.0	120.9
All items (incl. others)	105.7	115.4	122.1

SOUTH AFRICA

Statistical Survey

NATIONAL ACCOUNTS
(provisional figures, million rand at current prices)

National Income and Product

	2003	2004	2005
Compensation of employees	570,697	624,529	680,056
Net operating surplus	385,546	420,005	454,281
Consumption of fixed capital	161,653	172,496	189,952
Gross domestic product (GDP) at factor cost	1,117,896	1,217,030	1,324,289
Taxes on production	148,183	176,655	208,015
Less Subsidies	9,053	7,027	9,049
GDP at market prices	1,257,026	1,386,658	1,523,255
Primary incomes received from abroad	21,373	20,975	29,304
Less Primary incomes paid abroad	56,244	49,083	60,338
Gross national income at market prices	1,222,155	1,358,550	1,492,221
Current transfers received from abroad	1,841	1,622	1,536
Less Current transfers paid abroad	8,190	11,108	12,571
Gross national disposable income at market prices	1,215,806	1,349,064	1,481,186

Expenditure on the Gross Domestic Product

	2003	2004	2005
Government final consumption expenditure	242,913	273,361	307,395
Private final consumption expenditure	785,632	870,411	967,940
Increase in stocks	14,091	19,289	16,489
Gross fixed capital formation	198,904	223,478	256,590
Residual item	−8,973	9,990	−2,854
Total domestic expenditure	1,232,567	1,396,529	1,545,560
Exports of goods and services	350,793	368,412	412,727
Less Imports of goods and services	326,334	378,283	435,032
GDP at market prices	1,257,026	1,386,658	1,523,255
GDP at constant 2000 prices	1,011,556	1,056,771	1,108,774

Gross Domestic Product by Economic Activity

	2003	2004	2005
Agriculture, forestry and fishing	40,889	37,946	34,441
Mining and quarrying	84,258	87,493	94,322
Manufacturing	221,652	236,822	251,596
Electricity, gas and water	28,316	29,426	31,029
Construction (contractors)	26,947	29,182	33,400
Wholesale and retail trade, catering and accommodation	157,728	175,570	197,252
Transport, storage and communication	110,439	122,298	135,713
Finance, insurance, real estate and business services	229,013	260,940	285,757
Government services	171,995	186,802	204,560
Other community, social and personal services	69,895	76,385	84,882
Gross value added at basic prices	1,141,132	1,242,864	1,352,952
Taxes on products	119,940	146,240	174,167
Less Subsidies	4,046	2,446	3,864
GDP at market prices	1,257,026	1,386,658	1,523,255

Source: South African Reserve Bank.

BALANCE OF PAYMENTS
(US $ million)

	2002	2003	2004
Exports of goods f.o.b.	31,772	38,700	48,237
Imports of goods f.o.b.	−27,016	−35,270	−48,518
Trade balance	4,756	3,431	−281
Exports of services	4,673	7,910	9,010
Imports of services	−5,393	−8,230	−10,340
Balance on goods and services	4,037	3,110	−1,611
Other income received	2,179	2,857	3,259
Other income paid	−4,975	−7,447	−7,617
Balance on goods, services and income	1,240	−1,481	−5,970
Current transfers received	139	252	257
Current transfers paid	−695	−1,094	−1,730
Current balance	684	−2,323	−7,442
Capital account (net)	−15	44	52
Direct investment abroad	402	−553	−1,305
Direct investment from abroad	735	783	701
Portfolio investment assets	−875	−138	−950
Portfolio investment liabilities	457	862	7,100
Other investment assets	−288	−5,212	−216
Other investment liabilities	−1,884	2,297	2,065
Net errors and omissions	461	3,887	6,320
Overall balance	−322	−354	6,324

Source: IMF, *International Financial Statistics*.

External Trade

PRINCIPAL COMMODITIES
(distribution by SITC, US $ million)

Imports c.i.f.	2001	2002	2003
Food and live animals	775.1	924.8	1,184.3
Crude materials (inedible) except fuels	712.4	841.8	1,098.3
Mineral fuels, lubricants, etc.	3,752.7	3,286.2	4,126.0
Petroleum, petroleum products, etc.	3,553.2	3,151.7	3,955.2
Crude petroleum oils, etc.	3,112.9	2,796.4	3,597.9
Chemicals and related products	2,878.9	3,080.2	3,713.0
Basic manufactures	2,624.5	3,221.4	4,206.5
Non-metallic mineral manufactures	451.2	829.3	1,085.6
Machinery and transport equipment	8,783.5	9,826.0	13,579.4
Power generating machinery and equipment	489.3	581.6	809.3
Machinery specialized for particular industries	1,134.9	1,275.4	1,643.2
General industrial machinery, equipment and parts	1,400.7	1,493.2	2,051.0
Office machines and automatic data-processing equipment	1,150.7	1,080.4	1,616.0
Telecommunications and sound equipment	1,556.9	1,613.5	1,722.7
Other electrical machinery, apparatus, etc.	1,224.4	1,189.5	1,548.8
Road vehicles	1,301.0	1,662.5	2,441.5
Passenger motor vehicles (excl. buses)	644.3	959.7	1,455.2
Other transport equipment	351.0	737.7	1,486.6
Miscellaneous manufactured articles	2,187.8	2,307.3	2,887.9
Total (incl. others)	24,188.3	26,212.1	34,543.1

SOUTH AFRICA

Statistical Survey

Exports f.o.b.	2001	2002	2003
Food and live animals	1,801.9	1,898.9	2,381.5
Vegetables and fruit	767.2	846.4	1,238.0
Beverages and tobacco	475.7	482.1	670.1
Crude materials (inedible) except fuels	2,373.7	2,377.3	2,672.6
Metalliferous ores and metal scrap	1,349.8	1,305.4	1,348.6
Mineral fuels, lubricants, etc.	2,328.8	2,857.3	3,111.9
Coal, lignite and peat	1,440.6	1,839.0	1,804.8
Petroleum, petroleum products, etc.	871.3	1,009.6	1,296.9
Chemicals and related products	2,007.1	2,134.0	2,369.1
Basic manufactures	10,180.7	6,790.8	12,131.7
Non-metallic mineral manufactures	5,415.6	1,753.6	2,011.5
Pearl, precious and semi-precious stones, unworked or worked	5,204.9	1,550.9	1,764.0
Diamonds (non-industrial), not mounted or set	5,196.2	1,543.8	1,754.6
Iron and steel	2,185.9	2,416.1	3,874.9
Pig-iron, etc.	922.7	1,109.8	1,722.4
Ferro-alloys	808.1	1,029.2	1,626.2
Non-ferrous metals	1,041.8	1,098.7	4,418.3
Silver, platinum and other platinum group metals	12.8	20.3	3,206.7
Platinum group metals, unwrought, unworked or semi-manufactured	0.5	0.1	3,196.1
Aluminium	821.0	887.8	956.5
Aluminium and aluminium alloys, unwrought	654.7	704.2	679.0
Machinery and transport equipment	4,255.8	5,255.5	6,541.0
General industrial machinery, equipment and parts	1,110.5	1,318.1	1,671.6
Road vehicles	1,551.5	2,396.7	3,114.5
Passenger motor vehicles (excl. buses)	871.9	1,614.5	2,099.3
Miscellaneous manufactured articles	1,060.3	1,193.5	1,487.0
Total (incl. others)	27,927.7	23,064.4	31,635.9

Source: UN, *International Trade Statistics Yearbook*.

PRINCIPAL TRADING PARTNERS
(US $ million)*

Imports f.o.b.	2000	2001	2002
Australia	661.6	709.1	741.1
Austria	218.6	265.9	279.1
Belgium-Luxembourg	409.7	370.6	371.2
Brazil	294.4	324.1	467.2
China, People's Repub.	995.9	1,067.1	1,359.0
Finland	368.1	307.7	157.9
France (incl. Monaco)	1,138.0	959.9	1,075.8
Germany	3,523.8	2,541.6	4,076.3
Hong Kong	278.6	241.6	223.1
India	253.4	248.1	280.5
Iran	1,163.8	5.3	920.8
Ireland	339.2	349.4	290.4
Italy	894.0	945.8	943.9
Japan	2,131.2	1,318.9	1,818.6
Korea, Repub.	506.5	451.7	427.7
Malaysia	297.3	287.0	345.8
Netherlands	513.2	479.5	478.5
Nigeria	183.0	236.7	344.0
Saudi Arabia	2,020.5	169.0	1,299.6
Spain	297.8	280.9	337.4
Sweden	417.2	304.7	316.8
Switzerland-Liechtenstein	652.3	477.3	453.9
Thailand	264.6	258.8	283.1
United Kingdom	2,251.0	1,785.6	2,372.1
USA	3,187.0	2,658.9	3,084.0
Total (incl. others)	26,606.7	24,188.3	26,212.1

Exports f.o.b.	2000	2001	2002
Angola	197.3	308.3	322.7
Australia	480.2	445.2	486.7
Belgium-Luxembourg	965.3	809.5	865.6
China, People's Repub.	335.2	461.3	450.3
France (incl. Monaco)	564.2	565.9	664.5
Germany	1,900.0	1,308.8	1,883.7
Hong Kong	326.4	307.4	316.1
India	371.7	376.4	351.5
Israel	511.8	515.6	521.2
Italy	838.3	780.9	743.0
Japan	1,354.6	1,284.2	1,490.2
Korea, Repub.	594.4	446.0	478.1
Mauritius	294.9	247.1	255.1
Mozambique	708.6	662.8	600.9
Netherlands	1,010.4	804.2	1,188.9
Nigeria	102.3	200.6	258.9
Spain	494.3	559.8	641.7
Switzerland-Liechtenstein	316.7	207.1	240.5
United Kingdom	2,288.0	1,806.6	2,519.2
USA	2,409.2	2,090.2	2,439.2
Zambia	645.5	574.5	525.6
Zimbabwe	683.9	631.5	692.4
Total (incl. others)	26,075.3	27,927.7	23,064.4

* Imports by country of origin; exports by country of destination.

Note: Data for trade between South Africa and other members of the Southern African Customs Union (SACU—comprising South Africa, Namibia, Botswana, Lesotho and Swaziland) are included in totals; however, data for transactions with individual SACU members (although known to be significant) were not available.

Source: UN, *International Trade Statistics Yearbook*.

Transport

RAILWAYS
(traffic, year ending 31 March)*

	1997/98	1998/99	1999/2000
Passenger-km (million)	1,775	1,794	3,930
Net ton-km (million)	103,866	102,777	106,786

* Including Namibia.

Source: UN, *Statistical Yearbook*.

ROAD TRAFFIC
(registered motor vehicles)

	2002
Heavy load vehicles	326,798
Heavy passenger motor vehicles	164,369
Light load vehicles	1,875,234
Light passenger motor vehicles	4,135,037
Motorcycles	159,266
Special vehicles	296,518
Other vehicles	17,955
Total (incl. others)	6,975,177

SHIPPING

Merchant Fleet
(vessels registered at 31 December)

	2002	2003	2004
Number of vessels	196	251	246
Displacement ('000 grt)	144.5	170.9	170.0

Source: Lloyd's Register-Fairplay, *World Fleet Statistics*.

SOUTH AFRICA

International Sea-borne Freight Traffic

	2003	2004	2005
Goods loaded (metric tons)	128,477,183	124,370,762	127,408,557
Goods unloaded (metric tons)	42,845,843	43,820,161	43,847,748
Containers loaded (20-foot equivalent units—TEUs)	1,194,400	1,290,883	1,484,009
Containers unloaded (20-foot equivalent units—TEUs)	1,220,167	1,341,888	1,530,227

Source: National Ports Authority of South Africa.

CIVIL AVIATION
(traffic on scheduled services)

	1999	2000	2001
Kilometres flown (million)	144	151	167
Passengers carried ('000)	7,374	8,001	7,948
Passenger-km (million)	19,021	21,015	22,061
Total ton-km (million)	2,381	2,579	2,746

Source: UN, *Statistical Yearbook*.

Tourism

FOREIGN VISITOR ARRIVALS*

Country of origin	2001	2002	2003
Botswana	644,253	782,189	797,315
France	85,663	114,797	130,365
Germany	207,511	253,411	261,194
Lesotho	1,288,160	1,162,786	1,291,242
Mozambique	506,077	579,768	474,790
Namibia	203,667	217,077	216,978
Swaziland	751,538	788,842	809,049
United Kingdom	363,825	449,166	463,021
USA	176,412	187,681	192,561
Zambia	96,666	123,081	115,650
Zimbabwe	501,698	612,543	568,626
Total (incl. others and unspecified)	5,908,024	6,549,916	6,640,095

* Figures include same-day visitors (excursionists), but exclude arrivals of South African nationals resident abroad. Border crossings by contract workers are also excluded.

Tourism receipts (US $ million, incl. passenger transport): 3,257 in 2001; 3,695 in 2002; 5,232 in 2003.

Source: World Tourism Organization.

Communications Media

	2002	2003	2004
Telephones ('000 main lines in use)	4,844.0	n.a.	4,821.0*
Mobile cellular telephones ('000 subscribers)	13,702	16,860.0	19,500.0
Internet users ('000)	3,100	n.a.	3,566.0
Personal computers in use ('000)	3,300	n.a.	3,740

* Estimate.

Facsimile machines (number in use): 150,000 in 1997.

Radio receivers ('000 in use): 11,696 in 2001.

Television receivers ('000 in use): 7,708 in 2001.

Book production: 5,418 titles in 1995.

Daily newspapers (average circulation, '000): 1,233.4 in 2001.

Daily newspapers: 21 titles in 2001.

Sources: partly UNESCO, *Statistical Yearbook*; UN, *Statistical Yearbook*; International Telecommunication Union.

Education

(2002)*

	Institutions	Teachers	Students
Primary	17,197	179,222	6,37,8178
Secondary	5,752	113,171	3,514,162
Combined	3,921	52,343	1,659,227
Intermediate and middle	755	10,994	365,450
ABET centres†	1,895	13,099	249,578
ELSEN centres‡	370	12,482	79,589
Further education and training§	50	7,088	406,145
Higher education§	36	14,810	677,913

* Figures for public and independent institutions, unless otherwise indicated.
† Adult basic education and training.
‡ Education for learners with special needs.
§ Figures refer to public institutions only.

Source: Department of Education.

Adult literacy rate (UNESCO estimates): 82.4% (males 84.1%; females 80.9%) in 1995–99 (Source: UN Development Programme, *Human Development Report*).

Directory

The Constitution

The Constitution was adopted by the Constitutional Assembly (comprising the National Assembly and the Senate) on 8 May 1996, and entered into force on 4 February 1997. Its main provisions are summarized below:

FOUNDING PROVISIONS

The Republic of South Africa is one sovereign democratic state founded on the following values: human dignity, the achievement of equality and advancement of human rights and freedoms; non-racialism and non-sexism; supremacy of the Constitution and the rule of law; universal adult suffrage, a national common voters' roll, regular elections, and a multi-party system of democratic government, to ensure accountability, responsiveness and openness. There is common South African citizenship, all citizens being equally entitled to the rights, privileges and benefits, and equally subject to the duties and responsibilities of citizenship.

BILL OF RIGHTS

Everyone is equal before the law and has the right to equal protection and benefit of the law. The state may not unfairly discriminate directly or indirectly against anyone on one or more grounds, including race, gender, sex, pregnancy, marital status, ethnic or social origin, colour, sexual orientation, age, disability, religion, conscience, belief, culture, language and birth. The rights that are enshrined include: protection against detention without trial, torture or any inhuman form of treatment or punishment; the right to privacy; freedom of conscience; freedom of expression; freedom of assembly; political freedom; freedom of movement and residence; the right to join or form a trade union or employers' organization; the right to a healthy and sustainable environment; the right to property, except in the case of the Government's programme of land reform and redistribution, and taking into account the claims of people who were dispossessed of property after 19 June 1913; the right to adequate housing; the right to health care, food and water and social security assistance, if needed; the rights of children; the right to education in the official language of one's choice, where this is reasonably practicable; the right to use the language and to participate in the cultural life of one's choice, but not in a manner inconsistent with any provision of this Bill of Rights; access to state information; access to the courts; the rights of people who have been arrested or detained; and the right to a fair trial.

CO-OPERATIVE GOVERNMENT

Government is constituted as national, provincial and local spheres of government, which are distinctive, interdependent and interrelated. All spheres of government and all organs of state within each sphere must preserve the peace, national unity and indivisibility of the Republic; secure the well-being of the people of the

Republic; implement effective, transparent, accountable and coherent government for the Republic as a whole; respect the constitutional status, institutions, powers and functions of government in the other spheres; not assume any power or function except those conferred on them in terms of the Constitution.

PARLIAMENT

Legislative power is vested in a bicameral Parliament, comprising a National Assembly and a National Council of Provinces. The National Assembly has between 350 and 400 members and is elected, in general, by proportional representation. National and provincial legislatures are elected separately, under a 'double-ballot' electoral system. Each provincial legislature appoints six permanent delegates and nominates four special delegates to the 90-member National Council of Provinces, which is headed by a Chairperson, who is elected by the Council and has a five-year term of office. Parliamentary decisions are generally reached by a simple majority, although constitutional amendments require a majority of two-thirds.

THE NATIONAL EXECUTIVE

The Head of State is the President, who is elected by the National Assembly from among its members, and exercises executive power in consultation with the other members of the Cabinet. No person may hold office as President for more than two terms. Any party that holds a minimum of 80 seats in the National Assembly (equivalent to 20% of the national vote) is entitled to nominate an Executive Deputy President. If no party, or only one party, secures 80 or more seats, the party holding the largest number of seats and the party holding the second largest number of seats in the National Assembly are each entitled to designate one Executive Deputy President from among the members of the Assembly. The President may be removed by a motion of no-confidence or by impeachment. The Cabinet comprises a maximum of 27 ministers. Each party with a minimum of 20 seats in the National Assembly (equivalent to 5% of the national vote) is entitled to a proportional number of ministerial portfolios. The President allocates cabinet portfolios in consultation with party leaders, who are entitled to request the replacement of ministers. Cabinet decisions are reached by consensus.

JUDICIAL AUTHORITY

The judicial authority of the Republic is vested in the courts, which comprise the Constitutional Court; the Supreme Court of Appeal; the High Courts; the Magistrates' Courts; and any other court established or recognized by an Act of Parliament. (See Judicial System.)

PROVINCIAL GOVERNMENT

There are nine provinces: Eastern Cape, Free State (formerly Orange Free State), Gauteng (formerly Pretoria-Witwatersrand-Vereeniging), KwaZulu/Natal, Limpopo (formerly Northern Transvaal, subsequently Northern Province), Mpumalanga (formerly Eastern Transvaal), Northern Cape, North-West and Western Cape. Each province is entitled to determine its legislative and executive structure. Each province has a legislature, comprising between 30 and 80 members (depending on the size of the local electorate), who are elected by proportional representation. Each legislature is entitled to draft a constitution for the province, subject to the principles governing the national Constitution, and elects a Premier, who heads a Cabinet. Parties that hold a minimum of 10% of seats in the legislature are entitled to a proportional number of portfolios in the Cabinet. Provincial legislatures are allowed primary responsibility for a number of areas of government, and joint powers with central government in the principal administrative areas.

LOCAL GOVERNMENT

The local sphere of government consists of municipalities, with executive and legislative authority vested in the Municipal Council. The objectives of local government are to provide democratic and accountable government for local communities; to ensure the provision of services to communities; to promote social and economic development, and a safe and healthy environment; and to encourage the involvement of communities and community organizations in the matters of local government. The National Assembly is to determine the different categories of municipality that may be established, and appropriate fiscal powers and functions for each category. Provincial Governments have the task of establishing municipalities, and of providing for the monitoring and support of local government in each province.

STATE INSTITUTIONS SUPPORTING CONSTITUTIONAL DEMOCRACY

The following state institutions are designed to strengthen constitutional democracy: the Public Protector (whose task is to investigate any conduct in state affairs, or in the public administration in any sphere of government, that is alleged or suspected to be improper); the Human Rights Commission; the Commission for the Protection and Promotion of the Rights of Cultural, Religious and Linguistic Communities; the Commission for Gender Equality; the Auditor-General; and the Electoral Commission.

TRADITIONAL LEADERS

The institution, status and role of traditional leadership, according to customary law, are recognized, subject to the Constitution. A traditional authority that observes a system of customary law may function subject to any applicable legislation and customs. National and provincial legislation may provide for the establishment of local or provincial houses of traditional leaders; the National Assembly may establish a national council of traditional leaders.

The Government

HEAD OF STATE

President: THABO MBEKI (inaugurated 16 June 1999; re-elected by vote of the National Assembly 23 April 2004).
Deputy President: PHUMZILE MLAMBO-NGCUKA (ANC).

THE CABINET
(May 2006)

The African National Congress of South Africa (ANC), the Azanian People's Organization (AZAPO), and the South African Communist Party (SACP) are represented in the Cabinet.

Minister of Agriculture and Land Affairs: LULAMA XINGWANA (ANC).
Minister of Arts and Culture: Dr Z. PALLO JORDAN (ANC).
Minister of Communications: IVY MATSEPE-CASABURRI (ANC).
Minister of Correctional Services: NGCONDE BALFOUR (ANC).
Minister of Defence: MOSIUOA LEKOTA (ANC).
Minister of Education: G. NALEDI PANDOR (ANC).
Minister of Environmental Affairs and Tourism: MARTHINUS VAN SCHALKWYK (ANC).
Minister of Finance: TREVOR A. MANUEL (ANC).
Minister of Foreign Affairs: NKOSAZANA C. DLAMINI-ZUMA (ANC).
Minister of Health: MANTOMBAZANA (MANTO) TSHABALALA-MSIMANG (ANC).
Minister of Home Affairs: NOSIVIWE MAPISA-NQAKULA (ANC).
Minister of Housing: LINDIWE NONCEBA SISULU (ANC).
Minister of Intelligence: RONNIE KASRILS (ANC).
Minister of Justice and Constitutional Development: BRIGITTE S. MABANDLA (ANC).
Minister of Labour: MEMBATHISI M. S. MDLADLANA (ANC).
Minister of Minerals and Energy: BUYELWA P. SONJICA (ANC).
Minister of Provincial and Local Government: F. SYDNEY MUFAMADI (ANC).
Minister of Public Enterprises: ALEC ERWIN (ANC).
Minister of Public Service and Administration: GERALDINE J. FRASER-MOLEKETI (ANC).
Minister of Public Works: ANGELA THOKO DIDIZA (ANC).
Minister of Safety and Security: CHARLES NQAKULA (SACP).
Minister of Science and Technology: MOSIBUDI MANGENA (AZAPO).
Minister of Social Development: ZOLA S. T. SKWEYIYA (ANC).
Minister of Sport and Recreation: Rev. MAKHENKESI STOFILE (ANC).
Minister of Trade and Industry: MANDISI B. M. MPAHLWA (ANC).
Minister of Transport: JEFFREY T. RADEBE (ANC).
Minister of Water Affairs and Forestry: LINDIWE HENDRICKS (ANC).
Minister in the Presidency: Dr ESSOP G. PAHAD (ANC).

MINISTRIES

The Presidency: Union Bldgs, West Wing, Government Ave, Pretoria 0001; Private Bag X1000, Pretoria 0001; tel. (12) 3005200; fax (12) 3238246; e-mail president@po.gov.za; internet www.gov.za/president/index.html.

Ministry of Agriculture and Land Affairs: Agriculture Bldg, 20 Beatrix St, Arcadia, Pretoria 0002; Private Bag X250, Pretoria 0001; tel. (12) 3197298; fax (12) 3218558; e-mail nanaz@nda.agric.za; internet www.nda.agric.za.

Ministry of Arts and Culture: Dept of Arts and Culture, Nassau Bldg, Rm 7060, 188 Schoeman St, Pretoria 0002; Private Bag X727,

SOUTH AFRICA

Pretoria 0001; tel. (12) 32440968; fax (12) 3242687; e-mail andile.xaba@dac.gov.za; internet www.dac.gov.za.

Ministry of Communications: Nkululeko House, iParioli Office Park, 399 Duncan St, cnr Park St, Hatfield, Pretoria 0083; Private Bag X860, Pretoria 0001; tel. (12) 4278000; fax (12) 4278026; e-mail elna@doc.gov.za; internet www.doc.gov.za.

Ministry of Correctional Services: Poyntons Bldg, West Block, cnr Church and Schubart Sts, Pretoria 0002; Private Bag X853, Pretoria 0001; tel. (12) 3072000; fax (12) 3286149; e-mail communications@dcs.gov.za; internet www.dcs.gov.za.

Ministry of Defence: Armscor Bldg, Block 5, Nossob St, Erasmusrand 0181; Private Bag X161, Pretoria 0001; tel. (12) 3556321; fax (12) 3556398; e-mail info@mil.za; internet www.mil.za.

Ministry of Education: Sol Plaatje House, 123 Schoeman St, Pretoria 0002; Private Bag X603, Pretoria 0001; tel. (12) 3125911; fax (12) 3256260; e-mail webmaster@doe.gov.za; internet www.education.gov.za.

Ministry of Environmental Affairs and Tourism: Fedsure Forum Bldg, North Tower, cnr Van der Walt and Pretorius Sts, Pretoria; Private Bag X447, Pretoria 0001; tel. (12) 3103911; fax (12) 3222682; internet www.environment.gov.za.

Ministry of Foreign Affairs: Union Bldgs, East Wing, 1 Government Ave, Arcadia, Pretoria 0002; Private Bag X152, Pretoria 0001; tel. (12) 3511000; fax (12) 3510253; e-mail minister@foreign.gov.za; internet www.dfa.gov.za.

Ministry of Health: DTI Bldg, Rm 1105, Prinsloo St, Pretoria 0001; Private Bag X828, Pretoria 0001; tel. (12) 3120000; fax (12) 3264395; e-mail masint@health.gov.za; internet www.health.gov.za.

Ministry of Home Affairs: 270 Maggs St, Watloo; Private Bag X114, Pretoria 0001; tel. (12) 3148911; fax (12) 3216491; internet www.home-affairs.gov.za.

Ministry of Housing: Govan Mbeki House, 240 Walker St, Sunnyside, Pretoria 0002; Private Bag X644, Pretoria 0001; tel. (12) 4211311; fax (12) 3418510; internet www.housing.gov.za.

Ministry of Intelligence: Bogare Bldg, 2 Atterbury Rd, Menlyn, Pretoria 0063; POB 37, Menlyn 0063; tel. (12) 3670700; fax (12) 3670749.

Ministry of Justice and Constitutional Development: Momentum Centre, 329 Pretorius St, cnr Pretorius and Prinsloo Sts, Pretoria 0001; Private Bag X81, Pretoria 0001; tel. (12) 3151111; fax (12) 3571112; e-mail haugustyn@justice.gov.za; internet www.doj.gov.za.

Ministry of Labour: Laboria House, Schoeman St, Pretoria 0002; Private Bag X117, Pretoria 0001; tel. (12) 3094000; fax (12) 3094030; e-mail page.boikanyo@labour.gov.za; internet www.labour.gov.za.

Ministry of Minerals and Energy: Mineralia Centre, 391 Andries St, Pretoria 0002; Private Bag X59, Pretoria 0001; tel. (12) 3179000; fax (12) 3204327; internet www.dme.gov.za.

Ministry of Provincial and Local Government: 87 Hamilton St, Arcadia, Pretoria 0001; Private Bag X804, Pretoria 0001; tel. (12) 3340600; fax (12) 3340603; e-mail enquiry@dplg.gov.za; internet www.dplg.gov.za.

Ministry of Public Enterprises: Infotech Bldg, Suite 401, 1090 Arcadia St, Hatfield, Pretoria 0083; Private Bag X15, Hatfield 0028; tel. (12) 4311000; fax (12) 4302853; e-mail info@dpe.gov.za; internet www.dpe.gov.za.

Ministry of Public Service and Administration: Batho Pele House, 22nd Floor, Vermeulen and van der Walts Sts, Pretoria 0002; Private Bag X916, Pretoria 0001; tel. (12) 3147911; fax (12) 3232386; internet www.dpsa.gov.za.

Ministry of Public Works: Central Government Bldg, cnr Bosman and Vermeulen Sts, Pretoria 0002; Private Bag X65, Pretoria 0001; tel. (12) 3372000; fax (12) 3252856; internet www.publicworks.gov.za.

Ministry of Safety and Security: Van Erkom Bldg, 8th Floor, Van Erkom Arcade, 217 Pretorius St, Pretoria 0002; Private Bag X922, Pretoria 0001; tel. (12) 3392500; fax (12) 3392536; e-mail stratfordm@saps.org.za; internet www.gov.za/sss.

Ministry of Science and Technology: Oranje Nassau Bldg, 7th Floor, 188 Schoeman St, Pretoria 0001; Private Bag X727, Pretoria 0001; tel. (12) 3174302; fax (12) 3242687; e-mail nelvis.qekema@dst.gov.za; internet www.dst.gov.za.

Ministry of Social Development: HSRC Bldg, North Wing, 134 Pretorius St, Pretoria 0002; Private Bag X901, Pretoria 0001; tel. (12) 3127654; fax (12) 3127943; internet www.welfare.gov.za.

Ministry of Sport and Recreation: Oranje Nassau Bldg, 3rd Floor, 188 Schoeman St, Pretoria; Private Bag X896, Pretoria 0001; tel. (12) 3343220; fax (12) 3264026; e-mail denver@sport1.pwv.gov.za; internet www.srsa.gov.za.

Ministry of Trade and Industry: 77 Meintjies St, Sunnyside, Pretoria 0002, Pretoria 0002; Private Bag X84, Pretoria 0001; tel. (12) 2549405; fax (12) 2549406; e-mail contactus@thedti.gov.za; internet www.thedti.gov.za.

Ministry of Transport: 159 Forum Bldg, cnr Bosman and Struben Sts, Pretoria 0002; Private Bag X193, Pretoria 0001; tel. (12) 3093657; fax (12) 3093462; e-mail khozac@dot.gov.za; internet www.transport.gov.za.

Ministry of Water Affairs and Forestry: Sedibeng Bldg, 10th Floor, 185 Schoeman St, Pretoria 0002; Private Bag X313, Pretoria 0001; tel. (12) 3368733; fax (12) 3284254; e-mail zay@dwaf.gov.za; internet www-dwaf.pwv.gov.za.

National Treasury: 40 Church Sq., Private Bag X115, Pretoria 0001; tel. (12) 3155645; fax (12) 3155126; e-mail thoraya.pandy@treasury.gov.za; internet www.treasury.gov.za.

Legislature

PARLIAMENT

National Council of Provinces

Chairman: MOSIUOA LEKOTA.

The National Council of Provinces (NCOP), which replaced the Senate under the new Constitution, was inaugurated on 6 February 1997. The NCOP comprises 90 members, with six permanent delegates and four special delegates from each of the nine provinces.

National Assembly

Speaker: BALEKA MBETE.

General Election, 14 April 2004

Party	Votes	% of votes	Seats
African National Congress	10,878,251	69.68	279
Democratic Alliance	1,931,201	12.37	50
Inkatha Freedom Party	1,088,664	6.97	28
United Democratic Movement	355,717	2.28	9
Independent Democrats	269,765	1.73	7
New National Party	257,824	1.65	7
African Christian Democratic Party	250,272	1.60	6
Freedom Front Plus	139,465	0.89	4
United Christian Democratic Party	117,792	0.75	3
Pan-Africanist Congress of Azania	113,512	0.73	3
Minority Front	55,267	0.35	2
Azanian People's Organisation	41,776	0.27	2
Others	113,161	0.72	—
Total	**15,612,667**	**100.00**	**400**

Provincial Governments
(March 2006)

EASTERN CAPE

Premier: NOSIMO BALINDELA (ANC).
Speaker of the Legislature: NOXOLO KIVIET (ANC).

FREE STATE

Premier: BEATRICE MARSHOFF (ANC).
Speaker of the Legislature: MXOLISI DUKWANA (ANC).

GAUTENG

Premier: MBHAZIMA SHILOWA (ANC).
Speaker of the Legislature: RICHARD MDAKANE (ANC).

KWAZULU/NATAL

Premier: SIBUSISO NDEBELE (ANC).
Speaker of the Legislature: WILLIES MCHUNU (ANC).

LIMPOPO

Premier: SELLO MOLOTO (ANC).
Speaker of the Legislature: Dr TSHENUWANI FARISANI (ANC).

MPUMALANGA

Premier: SAMPSON PHATHAGE (THABANG) MAKWETLA (ANC).
Speaker of the Legislature: YVONE (PINKY) PHOSA (ANC).

SOUTH AFRICA   *Directory*

NORTHERN CAPE
Premier: DIPUO PETERS (ANC).
Speaker of the Legislature: CONNIE SEOPOSENGWE (ANC).

NORTH-WEST
Premier: EDNA MOLEWA (ANC).
Speaker of the Legislature: THANDI MODISE (ANC).

WESTERN CAPE
Premier: EBRAHIM RASOOL (ANC).
Speaker of the Legislature: SHAUN BYNEVELDT (ANC).

Election Commission

Independent Electoral Commission: Election House, 260 Walker St, Sunnyside, Pretoria; tel. 428-5700; fax 428-5863; e-mail iec@elections.org.za; internet www.elections.org.za; f. 1996; Chair. Dr BRIGALIA BAM.

Political Organizations

A total of 21 parties contested the elections to the National Assembly in April 2004, while 37 parties presented candidates in the concurrent provincial elections.

African Christian Democratic Party (ACDP): Alberton; tel. (11) 8693941; fax (11) 8693942; internet www.acdp.org.za; f. 1993; Leader Rev. KENNETH MESHOE.

African National Congress of South Africa (ANC): 54 Sauer St, Johannesburg 2001; POB 61884, Marshalltown 2107; tel. (11) 3761000; fax (11) 3761134; internet www.anc.org.za; f. 1912; in alliance with the South African Communist Party (SACP) and the Congress of South African Trade Unions (COSATU); governing party since April 1994; incl. fmr mems of the New National Party (disbanded Feb. 2006); Pres. THABO MBEKI; Deputy Pres. JACOB ZUMA; Sec.-Gen. KGALEMA MOTLANTHE.

Afrikaner Eenheidsbeweging (AEB) (Unity Movement): Pretoria; right-wing movement; Leader CASPERUS AUCAMP.

Afrikaner Weerstandsbeweging (AWB) (Afrikaner Resistance Movement): POB 4712, Kempton Park 1620, Johannesburg; tel. and fax (18) 2642516; e-mail awb@awb.co.za; internet www.awb.co.za; f. 1973; extreme right-wing paramilitary group; Leader EUGENE TERRE' BLANCHE.

Azanian People's Organization (AZAPO): 100 President St, 7th Floor, Balmoral House, Johannesburg 2001; POB 4230, Johannesburg 2000; tel. (11) 3363551; e-mail azapo@sn.apc.org; internet www.azapo.org.za; f. 1978; to seek the establishment of a unitary, democratic, socialist republic; excludes white mems; Pres. MOSIBLIDI MANGENA; Nat. Chair. ZITHULELE N. A. CINDI.

Blanke Bevrydingsbeweging (BBB) (White Protection Movement): f. 1987; extreme right-wing activist group; Leader Prof. JOHAN SCHABORT.

Boerestaat Party (Boer State Party): POB 3456, Randburg 2125; tel. and fax (11) 7081988; f. 1988; seeks the reinstatement of the Boer Republics in a consolidated Boerestaat; Leader COEN VERMAAK.

Cape Democrats: f. 1988; white support; liberal.

Democratic Alliance (DA): POB 15, Cape Town 8000; e-mail headoffice@da.org.za; internet www.da.org.za; f. 2000 by opposition parties, including the Democratic Party, the Federal Alliance and the New National Party (NNP), to contest that year's municipal elections; NNP withdrew in late 2001; Leader ANTHONY (TONY) LEON; Chair. JOE SEREMANE.

Democratic Reform Party (DRP): f. 1988; Coloured support; Leader CARTER EBRAHIM.

Democratic Workers' Party (DWP): Cape Town; f. 1984 by breakaway faction of the People's Congress Party; mainly Coloured support; Leader DENNIS DE LA CRUZ.

Freedom Front Plus (Vryheidsfront Plus—FF Plus/VF Plus): 203 Soutpansberg Ave, Rietondale, Pretoria; POB 74693, Lynnwood Ridge 0040; tel. (12) 3291220; fax (12) 3294466; e-mail info@vf.co.za; internet www.vf.co.za; f. 1994 as Freedom Front; name changed after incorporating the Conservative Party and Afrikaner Eenheidsbeweging in Sept. 2003; right-wing electoral alliance, including some mems of the CPSA; Leader Dr PIETER W. A. MULDER; Sec.-Gen. Col (retd) PIET UYS.

Freedom Party: Coloured support; Leader ARTHUR BOOYSEN.

Herstigte Nasionale Party (HNP) (Reconstituted National Party): 1043 Pretorius St, Hatfield, POB 1888, Pretoria 0001; tel. (12) 3423410; fax (12) 3423417; e-mail info@hnp.org.za; internet www.hnp.org.za; f. 1969 by fmr mems of the National Party; advocates 'Christian Nationalism'; Leader WILLEM MARAIS; Gen. Sec. L. J. VAN DER SCHYFF.

Independent Democrats (ID): Rm 28, Marks Bldg, Parliament Plein St, POB 751, Cape Town 8000; tel. (21) 4038696; fax (21) 4032350; e-mail id@id.org.za; internet www.id.org.za; f. 2003; Leader PATRICIA DE LILLE.

Inkatha Freedom Party (IFP): Albany House North, 4th Floor, Albany Grove, POB 4432, Durban 4000; tel. (31) 3651300; fax (31) 3010252; internet www.ifp.org.za; f. as Inkatha Movement, liberation movement with mainly Zulu support; reorg. in 1990 as a multiracial political party; Leader Chief MANGOSUTHU GATSHA BUTHELEZI; Nat. Chair. L. P. H. M. MTSHALI; Sec.-Gen. M. ZAKHELE KHUMALO.

Justice and Freedom Alliance (JAFA): ME Store Bldg, 4th Floor, 155 Smit St, Johannesburg; Private Bag X49, Johannesburg; tel. (11) 3397129; fax (11) 3396982; f. 1997; CEO BARRY NILSSON; Sec.-Gen. A. DLOMO.

Minority Front: Law Society Bldg, Suite 17, Chancery Lane, Pietermaritzburg; tel. (33) 3557667; internet www.mf.org.za; f. 1993; Indian support; formed political alliance with the ANC in June 1999; Leader AMICHAND RAJBANSI.

New Freedom Party of Southern Africa: 15 Eendrag St, Bellville 7530; Coloured support.

New Solidarity: POB 48687, Qualbert 4078; tel. (11) 3055692; fax 3011077; f. 1989; Indian support; Leader Dr J. N. REDDY.

Die Oranjewerkers: POB 74550, Lynwoodrif 0040; tel. and fax (12) 3485607; seeks to establish several small, self-governing white states; Leader HENDRIK FRENSCH VERWOERD.

Pan-Africanist Congress of Azania (PAC): Umoya House, 5th Floor, 2–6 cnr Rissik and New South Sts, Ghandi Sq., Johannesburg; POB 6010, Johannesburg 2000; tel. (11) 3372193; fax (11) 3376400; internet www.paca.org.za; f. 1959; Pres. Dr MOTSOKO PHEKO; Sec.-Gen. THAMI PLAATJIE.

Progressive Independent Party (PIP): Indian support; Leader FAIZ KHAN.

South African Communist Party (SACP): Cosatu House, 3rd Floor, 1 Leyds St, Braamfontein; POB 1027, Johannesburg 2000; tel. (11) 3393633; fax (11) 3396880; e-mail info@sacp.org.za; internet www.sacp.org.za; f. 1921; reorg. 1953; supports the ANC; Chair. CHARLES NQAKULA; Gen. Sec. BLADE NZIMANDE.

Transvaal Indian Congress: f. 1902; reactivated 1983; Pres. Dr ESSOP JASSAT.

United Christian Democratic Party (UCDP): POB 3010, Mmabatho; tel. (18) 3815691; fax (18) 3817346; e-mail ucdpheadoff@ucdp.org.za; internet www.ucdp.org.za; f. 1986; multiracial; Leader KGOSI L. M. MANGOPE; Sec.-Gen. M. N. MATLADI; Nat. Chair. I. S. MFUNDISI.

United Democratic Movement: Tomkor Bldg, 2nd Floor, cnr Vermeulen and Du Toit Sts, Pretoria; POB 26290, Arcadia 0007; tel. (12) 3210010; fax (12) 3210014; internet www.udm.org.za; f. 1997; multiracial support; demands effective measures for enforcement of law and order; Pres. BANTU HOLOMISA.

United Democratic Reform Party: POB 14048, Reigerpark 1466; f. 1987 by merger; mainly Coloured and Indian support; Leader JAKOBUS (JAC) ALBERT RABIE; Nat. Chair. NASH PARMANAND.

Workers' Organization for Socialist Action (WOSA): c/o Univ. of Cape Town, Private Bag, Rondebosch 7701; e-mail nalexand@humanities.uct.ac.za; f. 1990; Trotskyist; Chair. Dr NEVILLE ALEXANDER; Gen. Sec. C. BRECHER.

Diplomatic Representation

EMBASSIES AND HIGH COMMISSIONS IN SOUTH AFRICA

Algeria: 950 Arcadia St, Hatfield, Pretoria 0083; POB 57480, Arcadia 0007; tel. (12) 3425074; fax (12) 3426479; e-mail embalgpta@intekom.co.za; Ambassador MOURAD BENCHEIKH.

Angola: 1030 Schoeman St, Hatfield, Pretoria 0083; POB 8685, Pretoria 0001; tel. (12) 3420049; fax (12) 320284; Ambassador MIGUEL GASPAR FERNANDES NETO.

Argentina: 200 Standard Plaza, 440 Hilda St, Hatfield, Pretoria 0083; POB 11125, Pretoria 0028; tel. (12) 4303524; fax (12) 4303521; e-mail argembas@global.co.za; Ambassador CARLOS SERSALE DI CERISANO.

Australia: 292 Orient St, Pretoria; Private Bag X150, Pretoria 0001; tel. (12) 3423740; fax (12) 3428442; e-mail philip.green@dfat.gov.au; internet www.australia.co.za; High Commissioner PHILIP GREEN.

Austria: Momentum Office Park, 1109 Duncan St, Brooklyn, Pretoria 0181; POB 95572, Waterkloof 0145; tel. (12) 4529155; fax (12)

SOUTH AFRICA

4601151; e-mail pretoria-ob@bmaa.gv.at; Ambassador Dr HELMUT FREUDENSCHUSS.

Bangladesh: 410 Farenden St, Sunnyside, Pretoria 0002; tel. (12) 3432105; fax (12) 3435222; e-mail bdoot@global.co.za; High Commissioner NASIMA HAIDER.

Belarus: 327 Hill St, Arcadia, Pretoria 0083; POB 4107, Pretoria 0001; tel. (12) 4307664; fax (12) 3426280; e-mail sa@belembassy.org; Ambassador Dr ANATOLY AKHRAMCHUK.

Belgium: 625 Leyds St, Muckleneuk, Pretoria 0002; tel. (12) 4403201; fax (12) 4403216; e-mail pretoria@diplobel.org; internet www.diplomatie.be/pretoria; Ambassador PIERRE LABOUVERIE.

Benin: 900 Park St, cnr Orient and Park Sts, Arcadia, Pretoria 0083; POB 26484, Arcadia 0007; tel. (12) 3426978; fax (12) 3421823; e-mail embbenin@yebo.co.za; Ambassador JEAN-PIERRE ADÉLUI EDON.

Bosnia and Herzegovina: 25 Stella St, Brooklyn, Pretoria 0181; POB 11464, Hatfield 0028; tel. (12) 3465547; fax (12) 3462295; e-mail bih@mweb.co.za; Ambassador DRAGAN BOŽANIĆ.

Botswana: 24 Amos St, Colbyn, Pretoria 0083; POB 57035, Arcadia 0007; tel. (12) 4309640; fax (12) 3421845; High Commissioner MOTLHWARE KGORI JAMES MASISI.

Brazil: Hadefields, Block C, 1st Floor, 1267 Pretorius St, Hatfield, Pretoria 0083; POB 3269, Pretoria 0001; tel. (12) 4269400; fax (12) 4269494; internet www.brazil.co.za; Ambassador LUCIO AMORIM.

Bulgaria: 1071 Church St, Hatfield, Pretoria 0083; POB 26296, Arcadia 0007; tel. (12) 3423720; fax (12) 3423721; Ambassador KOSYO P. KITIPOV.

Burundi: Infotech Bldg, Suite 405, 1090 Arcadia St, Hatfield, Pretoria 0083; POB 12914, Hatfield 0028; tel. (12) 3424881; fax (12) 3424885; Ambassador PATRICE RWIMO.

Cameroon: 924 Pretorius St, Arcadia, Pretoria 0083; POB 13790, Hatfield 0028; tel. (12) 3422477; fax (12) 3422478; e-mail hicocam@cameroon.co.za; High Commissioner WILLIAM EYAMBE EYAMBE (acting).

Canada: 1103 Arcadia St, cnr Hilda St, Hatfield, Pretoria 0083; Private Bag X13, Hatfield 0028; tel. (12) 4223000; fax (12) 4223052; internet www.dfait-maeci.gc.ca/southafrica/menu-en.asp; High Commissioner SANDELLE SCRIMSHAW.

Chile: Brooklyn Gardens, cnr Veale St and Middle St, Block B, 1st Floor, New Muckleneuk, Pretoria; POB 2449, Brooklyn Sq. 0075; tel. (12) 4608090; fax (12) 4608093; e-mail chile@iafrica.com; internet www.embchile.co.za; Ambassador CLAUDIO E. HERRERA ALAMOS.

China, People's Republic: 972 Pretorius St, Arcadia, Pretoria 0083; POB 95764, Waterkloof 0145; tel. (12) 3424194; fax (12) 3424244; internet www.chinese-embassy.org.za; Ambassador GUIJIN LIU.

Colombia: 1105 Park St, 3rd Floor, Hatfield, Pretoria 0083; POB 12791, Hatfield 0028; tel. (12) 3420211; fax (12) 3420216; e-mail emcolsf@mweb.co.za; Ambassador VICTOR G. RICARDO PIÑEROS.

Congo, Democratic Republic: 791 Schoeman St, Arcadia, Pretoria 0083; POB 28795, Sunnyside 0132; tel. (12) 3441478; fax (12) 3441510; e-mail rdcongo@lantic.net; Ambassador BENE M'POKO.

Congo, Republic: 960 Arcadia St, Arcadia, Pretoria 0083; POB 40427, Arcadia 0007; tel. (12) 3425508; fax (12) 3425510; e-mail congo@telkomsa.net; Ambassador ROGER ISSOMBO.

Côte d'Ivoire: 795 Government Ave, Arcadia, Pretoria 0083; POB 13510, Hatfield 0028; tel. (12) 3426913; fax (12) 3426713; Ambassador BOUBAKAR KONE.

Croatia: 1160 Church St, Colbyn, Pretoria 0083; POB 11335, Hatfield 0028; tel. (12) 3421206; fax (12) 3421819; e-mail vrhjar@iafrica.com; Ambassador IVAN PICUKARIĆ.

Cuba: 45 Mackenzie St, Brooklyn, Pretoria 0181; POB 11605, Hatfield 0028; tel. (12) 3462215; fax (12) 3462216; e-mail sudafri@iafrica.com; Ambassador ESTHER ARMENTEROS CÁRDENAS.

Cyprus: cnr Church St and Hill St, Arcadia, Pretoria 0083; POB 14554, Hatfield 0028; tel. (12) 3425258; fax (12) 3425596; e-mail cyprusjb@mweb.co.za; High Commissioner COSTA LEONTIOU.

Czech Republic: 936 Pretorius St, Arcadia, Pretoria 0083; POB 13671, Hatfield 0028; tel. (12) 4312380; fax (12) 4302033; e-mail pretoria@embassy.mzv.cz; Ambassador JAROSLAV SIRO.

Denmark: iParioli Office Park, Block B2, Ground Floor, 1166 Park St, Hatfield, Pretoria; POB 11439, Hatfield 0028; tel. (12) 4309340; fax (12) 3427620; e-mail pryamb@um.dk; internet www.ambpretoria.um.dk; Ambassador TORBEN BRYLLE.

Egypt: 270 Bourke St, Muckleneuk, Pretoria 0002; POB 30025, Sunnyside 0132; tel. (12) 3431590; fax (12) 3431082; Ambassador HAGER ABD ELHAMED AL-ISLAMBOULI.

Equatorial Guinea: 48 Florence St, Colbyn, Pretoria; POB 12720, Hatfield 0028; tel. (12) 3429945; fax (12) 3427250; Ambassador JUAN ANTONIO BIBANG NCHUCHUMA.

Eritrea: 1281 Cobham Rd, Queenswood, Pretoria 0186; POB 11371, Queenswood 0186; tel. (12) 3331302; fax (12) 3332330; Ambassador TESFAMICAEL GERAHTU OGBAGHIORGHIS.

Ethiopia: 47 Charles St, Bailey's Muckleneuk, Brooklyn 0181; POB 11469, Hatfield 0028; tel. (12) 3463542; fax (12) 3463867; e-mail ethiopia@sentechsa.com; Chargé d'affaires a.i. MEBRAT BEYENE.

Finland: 628 Leyds St, Muckleneuk, Pretoria 0002; POB 443, Pretoria 0001; tel. (12) 3430275; fax (12) 3433095; e-mail sanomat.pre@formin.fi; internet www.finland.org.za; Ambassador HEIKKI TUUNANEN.

France: 250 Melk St, cnr Melk and Middle Sts, New Muckleneuk, Pretoria 0181; tel. (12) 4251600; fax (12) 4251689; e-mail carolize.jansen@diplomatie.gouv.fr; internet www.ambafrance-rsa.org; Ambassador JEAN FÉLIX-PAGANON.

Gabon: 921 Schoeman St, Arcadia, Pretoria 0083; POB 9222, Pretoria 0001; tel. (12) 3424376; fax (12) 3424375; e-mail embagarsap@telkomsa.net; Ambassador MARCEL-JULES ODONGUI-BONNARD.

Germany: 180 Blackwood St, Arcadia, Pretoria 0083; POB 2023, Pretoria 0001; tel. (12) 4278900; fax (12) 4278982; internet www.pretoria.diplo.de; Ambassador HARRO ADT.

Ghana: 1038 Arcadia St, Hatfield, Pretoria 0083; POB 12537, Hatfield 0028; tel. (12) 3425847; fax (12) 3425863; e-mail ghcom27@icon.co.za; High Commissioner HANNAH NYARKO (acting).

Greece: 1003 Church St, Arcadia, Pretoria 0083; tel. (12) 3427136; fax (12) 4304313; e-mail embgrsaf@global.co.za; Ambassador ARISTIDIS SANDIS.

Guinea: 336 Orient St, Arcadia, Pretoria 0083; POB 13523, Hatfield 0028; tel. (12) 3424906; fax (12) 3427348; e-mail embaguinea@iafrica.com; Ambassador ALEXANDRE CÉCÉ LOUA.

Haiti: 808 George St, Arcadia, Pretoria 0007; POB 14362, Hatfield 0028; tel. (12) 4307560; fax (12) 3427042; Ambassador YOLETTE AZOR-CHARLES.

Holy See: 800 Pretorius St, Arcadia, Pretoria 0083; POB 26017, Arcadia 0007; tel. (12) 3443815; fax (12) 3443595; e-mail nunziosa@iafrica.com; Apostolic Nuncio Most Rev. BLASCO FRANCISCO COLLAÇO.

Hungary: 959 Arcadia St, Arcadia, Pretoria 0083; POB 13843, Hatfield 0028; tel. (12) 4303020; fax (12) 4303029; Ambassador ANDRÁS DALLOS.

Iceland: iParioli Office Park, Phase II, Block A2, 1166 Park St, Pretoria; POB 14325 Hatfield 0028; tel. (12) 3425885; fax (12) 3425885; e-mail emb.pretoria@mfa.is; Ambassador BENEDIKT ASGEIRSSON.

India: 852 Schoeman St, Arcadia, Pretoria 0083; POB 40216, Arcadia 0007; tel. (12) 3425392; fax (12) 3425310; e-mail polinf@hicomind.co.za; High Commissioner SATYABRATA PAL.

Indonesia: 949 Schoeman St, Arcadia, Pretoria 0083; POB 13155, Hatfield 0028; tel. (12) 3423350; fax (12) 3423369; e-mail indonemb@intekom.co.za; Ambassador SUGENG RAHARDJO.

Iran: 1002 Schoeman St, Hatfield, Pretoria 0083; POB 12546, Hatfield 0083; tel. (12) 3425880; fax (12) 3421878; e-mail office@iranembassy.org.za; internet www.iranembassy.org.za; Ambassador MOHAMMAD ALI GHANEZADEH.

Iraq: 803 Duncan St, Brooklyn, Pretoria; POB 11089, Hatfield 0028; tel. (12) 3622012; fax (12) 3622027; Ambassador QASIM ABDLBAQI SHAKIR AL-RAMMAH.

Ireland: Southern Life Plaza, 1st Floor, 1059 Schoeman St, cnr Festival and Schoeman Sts, Arcadia, Pretoria 0083; POB 4174, Arcadia 0001; tel. (12) 3425062; fax (12) 3424752; e-mail pretoria@iveagh.irlgov.ie; internet www.embassyireland.org.za; Ambassador GERARD CORR.

Israel: 428 King's Hwy, Elizabeth Grove St, Lynnwood, Pretoria; POB 3726, Pretoria 0001; tel. (12) 3480470; fax (12) 3488594; Ambassador ILAN BARUCH.

Italy: 796 George Ave, Arcadia, Pretoria 0083; tel. (12) 4230000; fax (12) 4305547; e-mail ambital@iafrica.com; internet www.ambital.org.za; Ambassador VALERIO AUGUSTO ASTRALDI.

Japan: 259 Baines St, cnr Frans Oerder St, Groenkloof, Pretoria 0181; Private Bag X999, Pretoria 0001; tel. (12) 4521500; fax (12) 46038001; e-mail info@embjapan.org.za; internet www.japan.org.za; Ambassador TOSHINORI SHIGEIE.

Jordan: 209 Festival St, Hatfield, Pretoria 0083; POB 55755, Arcadia 0007; tel. (12) 3428026; fax (12) 3427847; Ambassador Dr MAZIM IZZEDINE TAL.

Kenya: 302 Brooks St, Menlo Park, Pretoria 0081; POB 35954, Menlo Park 0012; tel. (12) 3622249; fax (12) 3622252; e-mail kenrep@mweb.co.za; High Commissioner TABITHA J. SEII.

Korea, Democratic People's Republic: 958 Waterpoort St, Faerie Glen, Pretoria; POB 1238, Garsfontein 0042; tel. (12) 9918661; fax (12) 9918662; e-mail dprkembassy@lantic.net; Ambassador KUN GWANG PAK.

SOUTH AFRICA

Korea, Republic: Greenpark Estates, Bldg 3, 27 George Storrar Dr., Groenkloof, Pretoria 0081; POB 939, Groenkloof 0027; tel. (12) 4602508; fax (12) 4601158; Ambassador EUN-SOO KIM.

Kuwait: 890 Arcadia St, Arcadia, Pretoria 0083; Private Bag X920, Pretoria 0001; tel. (12) 3420877; fax (12) 3420876; e-mail safarku@global.co.za; Ambassador SALEM AL-ZAMANAN.

Lebanon: 290 Lawley St, Waterkloof, Pretoria 0081; POB 941, Groenkloof 0027; tel. (12) 3467020; fax (12) 3467022; Chargé d'affaires a.i. MICHEL KATRA.

Lesotho: 391 Anderson St, Menlo Park, Pretoria 0081; POB 55817, Arcadia 0007; tel. (12) 4607648; fax (12) 4607469; High Commissioner MOSUOE CHARLES MOTEANE.

Liberia: Infotech Bldg, Suite 105/113, 1090 Arcadia St, Hatfield, Pretoria 0083; POB 25917, Monument Park 0105; tel. (12) 3460880; fax (12) 3468006; Chargé d'affaires A. N. NIMLEY.

Libya: 900 Church St, Arcadia, Pretoria 0083; POB 40388, Arcadia 0007; tel. (12) 3423902; fax (12) 3423904; e-mail libyansa@yebo.co.za; Ambassador Dr ABDULLAH ABDUSSALAM AL-ZUBEDI.

Madagascar: 90B Tait St, Colbyn, Pretoria; POB 11722, Queenswood 0121; tel. (12) 3420983; fax (12) 3420995; Ambassador YVAN RANDRIASANDRATRINIONY.

Malawi: 770 Government Ave, Arcadia, Pretoria 0083; POB 11172, Hatfield 0028; tel. and fax (12) 3421759; fax (12) 3420147; e-mail mhc@easun.co.za; High Commissioner MICHAEL KAMPHAMBE-NKHOMA.

Malaysia: 1007 Schoeman St, Arcadia, Pretoria 0083; POB 11673, Hatfield 0028; tel. (12) 3425990; fax (12) 4307773; High Commissioner YAHAYA BIN ABDUL JABAR.

Mali: 876 Pretorius St, Arcadia 0083; POB 12978, Hatfield, Pretoria 0028; tel. (12) 3427464; fax (12) 3420670; Ambassador SINALY COULIBALY.

Mauritius: 1163 Pretorius St, Hatfield, Pretoria 0083; tel. (12) 3421283; fax (12) 3421286; e-mail mhcpta@mweb.co.za; Chargé d'affaires a.i. MOHAMED ISMAEL DOSSA.

Mexico: 1 Hatfield Sq., 3rd Floor, 1101 Burnett St, Hatfield, Pretoria 0083; POB 9077, Pretoria 0001; tel. (12) 3622822; fax (12) 3621380; e-mail embamexza@mweb.co.za; Ambassador MAURICIO DE MARIA Y CAMPOS.

Morocco: 799 Schoeman St, cnr Farenden St, Arcadia, Pretoria 0083; POB 12382, Hatfield 0028; tel. (12) 3430230; fax (12) 3430613; Ambassador TALAL RHOUFRANI.

Mozambique: 529 Edmund St, Arcadia, Pretoria 0083; POB 40750, Arcadia 0007; tel. (12) 4010300; fax (12) 3266388; High Commissioner VICENTE MABUNIO VELOSO.

Myanmar: 201 Leyds St, Arcadia, Pretoria 0083; POB 12121, Queenswood 0121; tel. (12) 3415207; fax (12) 3413867; e-mail euompta@global.co.za; Ambassador U OHN THWIN.

Namibia: 197 Blackwood St, Arcadia, Pretoria 0083; POB 29806, Sunnyside 0132; tel. (12) 4819100; fax (12) 3445998; e-mail secretary@namibia.co.za; High Commissioner WILBARD MANIQUE SHIHEPO HELLAO.

Netherlands: 825 Arcadia St, Arcadia, Pretoria 0083; POB 117, Pretoria 0001; tel. (12) 3443910; fax (12) 3439950; internet www.dutchembassy.co.za; Ambassador FRANS A. ENGERING.

New Zealand: Block C, Hatfield Gardens, 1110 Arcadia St, Hatfield, Pretoria 0083; Private Bag X17, Hatfield 0028; tel. (12) 3428656; fax (12) 3428640; e-mail nzhc@global.co.za; High Commissioner MALCOLM MCGOUN.

Nigeria: 971 Schoeman St, Arcadia, Pretoria 0083; POB 27332, Sunnyside 0132; tel. (12) 3420805; fax (12) 3421668; High Commissioner Dr OLUGBENGA AYODEJI ASHIRU.

Norway: iParioli Bldg, A2, 1166 Park St, Hatfield, Pretoria 0083; POB 11612, Hatfield 0028; tel. (12) 3426100; fax (12) 3426099; e-mail emb.pretoria@mfa.no; internet www.norway.org.za; Ambassador OVE THORSHEIM.

Oman: 42 Nicholson St, Muckleneuk, Pretoria 0081; POB 2650, Brooklyn 0075; tel. (12) 3460808; fax (12) 3461660; Chargé d'affaires a.i. FAKHRI MOHAMMED SAID AL-SAID.

Pakistan: 312 Brooks St, Menlo Park, Pretoria 0181; POB 11803, Hatfield 0028; tel. (12) 3624072; fax (12) 3623967; e-mail parepretoria@worldonline.co.za; High Commissioner AKBAR ZEB.

Paraguay: 189 Strelitzia Rd, Waterkloof Heights, Pretoria 0181; POB 95774, Waterkloof 0145; tel. (12) 3471047; fax (12) 3470403; Chargé d'affaires a.i. ARNALDO R. SALAZAR.

Peru: Infotech Bldg, Suite 202, 1090 Arcadia St, Hatfield, Pretoria 0083; POB 907, Groenkloof 0027; tel. (12) 3422390; fax (12) 3424944; e-mail emperu@telkomsa.net; Ambassador FÉLIX CÉSAR CALDERÓN.

Philippines: 54 Nicholson St, Muckleneuk, 0181 Pretoria; POB 2562, Brooklyn Sq. 0075; tel. (12) 3460451; fax (12) 3460454; e-mail pretoriape@mweb.co.za; Ambassador VIRGILIO A. REYES.

Poland: 14 Amos St, Colbyn, Pretoria 0083; POB 12277, Queenswood 0121; tel. (12) 4302631; fax (12) 4302608; Ambassador ROMUALD SZUNIEWICZ.

Portugal: 599 Leyds St, Muckleneuk, Pretoria 0002; POB 27102, Sunnyside 0132; tel. (12) 3412340; fax (12) 3413975; e-mail portemb@satis.co.za; Ambassador PAULO COUTO BARBOSA.

Qatar: 355 Charles St, Waterkloof, Pretoria 0181; Private Bag X13, Brooklyn Sq. 0075; tel. (12) 4521700; fax (12) 3466732; e-mail qatar-emb@lantic.net; Ambassador ZAYED RASHED AL-NAEMI.

Romania: 117 Charles St, Brooklyn, Pretoria 0181; POB 11295, Hatfield 0028; tel. (12) 4606940; fax (12) 4606947; e-mail romembsa@telkomsa.co.za; Ambassador VALER GABRIEL PAUL POTRA.

Russia: 316 Brooks St, Menlo Park, Pretoria 0081; POB 6743, Pretoria 0001; tel. (12) 3621337; fax (12) 3620116; e-mail ruspospr@mweb.co.za; internet www.russianembassy.org.za; Ambassador ANDREI A. KUSHAKOV.

Rwanda: 983 Schoeman St, Arcadia, Pretoria; POB 55224, Arcadia 0007; tel. (12) 3426536; fax (12) 3427106; Ambassador JAMES KIMONYO.

Saudi Arabia: 711 Duncan St, cnr Lunnon St, Hatfield, Pretoria 0083; POB 13930, Hatfield 0028; tel. (12) 3624230; fax (12) 3624239; e-mail reosa4@lantic.net; Chargé d'affaires FAIFAL MOALLA.

Senegal: Charles Manor, 57 Charles St, Baileys Muckleneuk, Pretoria 0181; POB 2948, Brooklyn Sq. 0075; tel. (12) 4605263; fax (12) 3465550; e-mail ambassene@mweb.co.za; Ambassador SAMBA BURI MBOUP.

Serbia and Montenegro: 163 Marais St, Brooklyn, Pretoria; POB 13026, Hatfield 0028; tel. (12) 4605626; fax (12) 4606003; e-mail info@scgembassy.org.za; internet www.scgembassy.org.za; Ambassador SRDJAN HOFMAN.

Singapore: 980 Schoeman St, Arcadia, Pretoria 0083; POB 11809, Hatfield 0028; tel. (12) 4306035; fax (12) 3424425; e-mail sporehc@cis.co.za; High Commissioner MOHIDEEN P. H. RUBIN.

Slovakia: 930 Arcadia St, Pretoria 0083; POB 12736, Hatfield 0028; tel. (12) 3422051; fax (12) 3423688; e-mail slovakemb@telkomsa.net; Ambassador PAVOL IVAN.

Spain: 169 Pine St, Arcadia, Pretoria 0083; POB 1633, Pretoria 0001; tel. (12) 3443875; fax (12) 3434891; e-mail embspain@mweb.co.za; Ambassador SANTIAGO MARTÍNEZ-CARO.

Sri Lanka: 410 Alexander St, Brooklyn, Pretoria 0181; tel. (12) 4607690; fax (12) 4607702; e-mail srilanka@global.co.za; internet www.srilanka.co.za; High Commissioner TIKIRI B. MADUWEGEDARA.

Sudan: 1203 Pretorius St, Hatfield, Pretoria 0083; POB 25513, Monument Park 0105; tel. (12) 3424538; fax (12) 3424539; e-mail embassy@sudani.co.za; internet www.sudani.co.za; Ambassador KUOL ALOR KUOL.

Swaziland: 715 Government Ave, Arcadia, Pretoria 0007; POB 14294, Hatfield 0028; tel. (12) 3441910; fax (12) 3430455; High Commissioner PHILLIP NHLANHLA MUNTU MSWANE.

Sweden: iParioli Bldg, 1166 Park St, Hatfield, Pretoria 0083; POB 13477, Hatfield 0028; tel. (12) 4266400; fax (12) 4266464; e-mail sweden@iafrica.com; Ambassador ANDERS MÖLLANDER.

Switzerland: 225 Veale St, Parc Nouveau, New Muckleneuk, Pretoria 0181; POB 2508, Brooklyn Sq. 0075; tel. (12) 4520660; fax (12) 3466605; e-mail vertretung@pre.rep.admin.ch; internet www.swissembassy.co.za; Ambassador VIKTOR CHRISTEN.

Syria: 963 Schoeman St, Arcadia, Pretoria 0083; POB 12830, Hatfield 0028; tel. (12) 342 4701; fax (12) 342 4702; e-mail syriaemb@telkomsa.net; Chargé d'affaires a.i. Dr A. AL-SHAMMAT.

Tanzania: 822 George Ave, Arcadia, Pretoria 0007; POB 56572, Arcadia 0007; tel. (12) 3424393; fax (12) 4304383; e-mail tanzania@cis.co.za; High Commissioner EMMANUEL A. MWAMBULUKUTU.

Thailand: 428 cnr Hill and Pretorius Sts, Arcadia, Pretoria 0028; POB 12080, Hatfield 0028; tel. (12) 3424600; fax (12) 3424601; e-mail thailand@thaiembpta.co.za; Ambassador DOMEDEJ BUNNAG.

Tunisia: 850 Church St, Arcadia, Pretoria 0083; POB 56535, Arcadia 0007; tel. (12) 3426282; fax (12) 3426284; Ambassador ALI GOUTALI.

Turkey: 1067 Church St, Hatfield, Pretoria 0083; POB 56014, Arcadia 0007; tel. (12) 3426053; fax (12) 3426052; e-mail pretbe@global.co.za; internet www.turkishembassy.co.za; Ambassador FERHAT ATAMAN.

Uganda: 882 Church St, Pretoria 0083; POB 12442, Hatfield 0083; tel. (12) 3426031; fax (12) 3426206; High Commissioner JOSEPH TOMUSANGE.

Ukraine: 398 Marais St, Brooklyn, Pretoria 0181; POB 36463, Menlo Park 0102; tel. (12) 4601943; fax (12) 4601944; Ambassador MYKHAILO V. SKURATOVSKYI.

United Arab Emirates: 992 Arcadia St, Arcadia, Pretoria 0083; POB 57090, Arcadia 0007; tel. (12) 3427736; fax (12) 3427738; e-mail uae@mweb.co.za; Ambassador ISMAEL OBAID YUSUF AL-ALI.

United Kingdom: 255 Hill St, Arcadia, Pretoria 0002; tel. (12) 4217500; fax (12) 4217555; e-mail media.pretoria@fco.gov.uk; internet www.britain.org.za; High Commissioner PAUL BOATENG.

USA: 877 Pretorius St, Arcadia, Pretoria 0083; POB 9536, Pretoria 0001; tel. (12) 4314000; fax (12) 3422299; e-mail embassypretoria@state.gov; internet southafrica.usembassy.gov; Chargé d'affaires a.i. DONALD TEITELBAUM.

Uruguay: 301 MIB House, 3rd Floor, Hatfield Sq., 1119 Burnett St, Hatfield, Pretoria 0083; POB 3247, Pretoria 0001; tel. (12) 3626521; fax (12) 3626523; Ambassador GUILLERMO JOSÉ POMI BARIOLA.

Venezuela: Hatfield Gables South Bldg, 1st Floor, Suite 4, 474 Hilda St, Pretoria 0083; POB 11821, Hatfield 0028; tel. (12) 3626593; fax (12) 3626591; e-mail embasudaf@icon.co.za; Chargé d'affaires a.i. R. PACHECO.

Viet Nam: 87 Brooks St, Brooklyn, Pretoria 0181; POB 13692, Hatfield 0028; tel. (12) 3628119; fax (12) 3628115; e-mail embassy@vietnam.co.za; Ambassador Dr TRAN DUY THI.

Yemen: 329 Main St, Waterkloof 0181; POB 13343, Hatfield 0028; tel. (12) 4250760; fax (12) 4250762; e-mail info@yemenembassy.org.za; internet www.yemenembassy.org.za; Chargé d'affaires a.i. MOHAMED JAMIL MUHARRAM.

Zambia: 570 Ziervogel St, Arcadia, Pretoria 0083; POB 12234, Hatfield 0028; tel. (12) 3261854; fax (12) 3262140; e-mail zahpta@mweb.co.za; High Commissioner LESLIE SAINOT MBULA.

Zimbabwe: Zimbabwe House, 798 Merton St, Arcadia, Pretoria 0083; POB 55140, Arcadia 0007; tel. (12) 3425125; fax (12) 3425126; Ambassador SIMON KHAYA MOYO.

Judicial System

The common law of the Republic of South Africa is the Roman-Dutch law, the uncodified law of Holland as it was at the time of the secession of the Cape of Good Hope in 1806. The law of England is not recognized as authoritative, although the principles of English law have been introduced in relation to civil and criminal procedure, evidence and mercantile matters.

The Constitutional Court, situated in Johannesburg, consists of a Chief Justice, a Deputy Chief Justice and nine other justices. Its task is to ensure that the executive, legislative and judicial organs of government adhere to the provisions of the Constitution. It has the power to reverse legislation that has been adopted by Parliament. The Supreme Court of Appeal, situated in Bloemfontein, comprises a President, a Deputy President and a number of judges of appeal, and is the highest court in all but constitutional matters. There are also High Courts and Magistrates' Courts. A National Director of Public Prosecutions is the head of the prosecuting authority and is appointed by the President of the Republic. A Judicial Service Commission makes recommendations regarding the appointment of judges and advises central and provincial government on all matters relating to the judiciary.

THE SUPREME COURT OF APPEAL
President: CRAIG HOWIE.

THE CONSTITUTIONAL COURT
Chief Justice: ARTHUR CHASKALSON.

Religion

Some 80% of the population profess the Christian faith. Other religions that are represented are Hinduism, Islam, Judaism and traditional African religions.

CHRISTIANITY

At mid-2000 there were an estimated 12.4m. Protestants and 18.7m. adherents of other forms of Christianity.

South African Council of Churches: POB 62098, Marshalltown 2107; tel. (11) 2417817; fax (11) 8384818; e-mail tmm@sacc.org.za; internet www.sacc.org.za; f. 1936; 26 mem. churches; Pres. Prof. RUSSEL BOTMAN; Gen. Sec. Rev. Dr MOLEFE TSELE.

The Anglican Communion

Most Anglicans in South Africa are adherents of the Church of the Province of Southern Africa, comprising 23 dioceses (including Lesotho, Namibia, St Helena, Swaziland and two dioceses in Mozambique). The Church had an estimated 2.7m. members at mid-2000.

Archbishop of Cape Town and Metropolitan of the Province of Southern Africa: Most Rev. NJONGONKULU WINSTON HUGH NDUNGANE, 20 Bishopscourt Dr., Bishopscourt, Claremont, Cape Town 7700; tel. (21) 7612531; fax (21) 7614193; e-mail archbish@bishopscourt-cpsa.org.za; internet www.cpsa.org.za.

The Dutch Reformed Church (Nederduitse Gereformeerde Kerk–NGK)

In 1996 the Dutch Reformed Churches in South Africa consisted of the Dutch Reformed Church, with 1,288,837 (mainly white) mems, the Uniting Reformed Church, with 1,216,252 (mainly Coloured and black) mems, and the Reformed Church in Africa, with 2,386 Indian mems. All congregations were desegregated in 1986.

General Synod: POB 4445, Pretoria 0001; tel. (12) 3228900; fax (12) 3223803; e-mail ngkdrc@mweb.co.za; Moderator Dr C. BURGER; Scribe Rev. J. C. CARSTENS; CEO Dr W. J. BOTHA.

The Lutheran Churches

Lutheran Communion in Southern Africa (LUCSA): POB 7170, Bonaero Park 1622; tel. (11) 9731873; fax (11) 3951615; e-mail lucsa@iafrica.com; f. 1991; co-ordinating org. for the Lutheran churches in southern Africa, incl. Angola, Botswana, Malawi, Mozambique, Namibia, South Africa, Swaziland, Zambia and Zimbabwe; 1,618,720 mems (1999); Pres. Bishop P. J. ROBINSON; Exec. Dir Bishop Dr A. MOYO.

Evangelical Lutheran Church in Southern Africa (ELCSA): POB 7231, 1622 Bonaero Park; tel. (11) 9731853; fax (11) 3951888; e-mail elcsaadmin@mweb.co.za; f. 1975 by merger of four non-white churches; Pres. Bishop LOUIS SIBIYA; 624,567 mems.

Evangelical Lutheran Church in Southern Africa (Cape Church): 240 Long St, Cape Town 8001; tel. (21) 4244932; fax (21) 4249618; e-mail rohwernj@adept.co.za; Pres. Bishop NILS ROHWER; 4,099 mems.

Evangelical Lutheran Church in Southern Africa (N-T): Church Council, 24 Geldenhuis Rd, Bonaero Park, Johannesburg; POB 7095, Bonaero Park 1622; tel. (11) 9731851; fax (11) 3951862; e-mail elksant@elksant.co.za; internet www.elcsant.org.za; f. 1981; Pres. Bishop DIETER R. LILJE; 9,700 mems (2006).

Moravian Church in Southern Africa: POB 24111, Lansdowne 7779; tel. (21) 7614030; fax (21) 7614046; e-mail mcsa@iafrica.com; f. 1737; Pres. ANGELENE H. SWART; 100,000 mems (2002).

The Roman Catholic Church

South Africa comprises four archdioceses, 21 dioceses and one Apostolic Vicariate. At 31 December 2003 there were an estimated 3,110,665 adherents in the country, representing about 6.4% of the total population.

Southern African Catholic Bishops' Conference (SACBC) Khanya House, 399 Paul Kruger St, Pretoria 0002; POB 941, Pretoria 0001; tel. (12) 3236458; fax (12) 3266218; internet www.sacbc.org.za.

f. 1947mems representing South Africa, Botswana and Swaziland; Pres. Cardinal WILFRID NAPIER (Archbishop of Durban); Sec.-Gen. Fr RICHARD MENATSI.

Archbishop of Bloemfontein: (vacant), Archbishop's House, 7A Whites Rd, Bloemfontein 9300; POB 362, Bloemfontein 9300; tel. (51) 4481658; fax (51) 4472420; e-mail bfnarch@mweb.co.za.

Archbishop of Cape Town: Most Rev. LAWRENCE HENRY, Cathedral Place, 12 Bouquet St, Cape Town 8001; POB 2910, Cape Town 8001; tel. (21) 4622417; fax (21) 4619330; e-mail catholic@intekom.co.za; internet www.catholic-ct.co.za.

Archbishop of Durban: Cardinal WILFRID NAPIER, Archbishop's House, 154 Gordon Rd, Durban 4001; POB 47489, Greyville 4023; tel. (31) 3031417; fax (31) 3121848; e-mail chancery@catholic-dbn.org.za.

Archbishop of Pretoria: Most Rev. GEORGE FRANCIS DANIEL, Jolivet House, 140 Visagie St, Pretoria 0002; POB 8149, Pretoria 0001; tel. (12) 3265311; fax (12) 3253994; e-mail ptadiocese@absamail.co.za.

Other Christian Churches

In addition to the following Churches, there are a large number of Pentecostalist groups, and more than 4,000 independent African Churches.

African Gospel Church: POB 32312, 4060 Mobeni; tel. (31) 9074377; Moderator Rev. F. D. MKHIZE; Gen. Sec. O. MTOLO; 100,000 mems.

Afrikaanse Protestantse Kerk (Afrikaans Protestant Church): POB 11488, Hatfield 0028; tel. (12) 3621390; fax (12) 3622023; f. 1987 by fmr mems of the Dutch Reformed Church (Nederduitse Gereformeerde Kerk) in protest at the desegregation of church congregations; c. 46,400 mems.

SOUTH AFRICA   *Directory*

Apostolic Faith Mission of South Africa: POB 890197, 2106 Lyndhurst; tel. (11) 7868550; fax (11) 8871182; e-mail afmgens@mweb.co.za; f. 1908; Gen. Sec. Pastor M. G. MAHLABO; 136,000 mems.

Assemblies of God: POB 51065, Musgrave 4062; tel. (31) 231341; fax (31) 231342; f. 1915; Chair. Rev. ISAAC HLETA; Gen. Sec. Rev. C. P. WATT; 300,000 mems.

Baptist Union of Southern Africa: Private Bag X45, Wilropark 1731; tel. (11) 7685980; fax (11) 7685983; e-mail busa@icon.co.za; f. 1877; Pres. Rev. STEPHEN MANN; Gen. Sec. Rev. ANGELO SCHEEPERS; 51,769 mems (2004).

Black Dutch Reformed Church: POB 137, Bergvlei 2012; Leader Rev. SAM BUTI; *c.* 1m. mems.

Church of England in South Africa: POB 2180 Clareinch 7740; tel. (21) 6717070; fax (21) 6712553; e-mail cameronb@cesa.org.za; internet www.cesa.org.za; Bishop Rt Rev. F. RETIEF (presiding), Bishop Rt Rev. M. MORRISON, Bishop Rt Rev. Dr W. COLE-EDWARDES, Bishop Rt Rev. D. INGLESBY; 207 churches.

Evangelical Presbyterian Church in South Africa: POB 31961, Braamfontein 2017; tel. (11) 3391044; Gen. Sec. Rev. J. S. NGOBE; Treas. Rev. H. D. MASANGU; 60,000 mems.

The Methodist Church of Southern Africa: Methodist Connexional Office, POB 50216, Musgrave 4062; tel. (31) 2024214; fax (31) 2017674; internet www.users.club.co.za/mco; f. 1883; Pres. Bishop I. M. ABRAHAMS; Sec. Rev. ROSS A. J. OLIVER; 696,353 mems.

Nederduitsch Hervormde Kerk van Afrika: POB 2368, Pretoria 0001; tel. (12) 3228885; fax (12) 3227907; internet www.nhk.co.za; e-mail fanie@nhk.co.za; Gen. Sec. Prof. J. BUITENDAG; 193,561 mems.

Nederduitse Gereformeerde Kerk in Afrika: Portland Pl., 37 Jorissen St, 2017 Johannesburg; tel. (11) 4031027; 6 synods (incl. 1 in Swaziland); Moderator Rev. S. P. E. BUTI; Gen. Sec. W. RAATH; 350,370 mems.

Presbyterian Church of Africa: POB 54840, Umlazi 4031; tel. (31) 9072366; f. 1898; 8 presbyteries (incl. 1 in Malawi and 1 in Zimbabwe); Chief Clerk Rev. S. A. KHUMALO; 1,231,000 mems.

Reformed Church in South Africa (Die Gereformeerde Kerke): POB 20002, Noordbrug 2522, Potchefstroom; tel. (148) 2973986; fax (148) 2931042; f. 1859; Prin. Officer Dr C. J. SMIT; 158,973 mems.

Seventh-day Adventist Church: POB 468, Bloemfontein 9300; tel. (51) 4478271; fax (41) 4488059; Pres. Pastor V. S. WAKABA; Sec. Pastor B. H. PARKERSON; 150,000 mems.

United Congregational Church of Southern Africa: POB 96014, Brixton; tel. and fax (21) 6839665; e-mail dave@uccsa.co.za; internet www.uccsa.org.za; f. 1799; Pres. Rev. IAN BOOTH; Gen. Sec. Rev. DES VAN DER WATER; 400,000 mems in 350 churches.

Uniting Presbyterian Church in Southern Africa: POB 96188, Brixton 2019; tel. (11) 8371258; fax (11) 8371653; e-mail gensec@presbyterian.org.za; f. 1999; Moderator Rt Rev. Dr J. PILLAY; Gen. Sec. Rev. V. S. VELLEM; Clerk of the Assembly T. W. COULTER; 130,000 mems.

Zion Christian Church: Zion City, Moria; f. 1910; South Africa's largest black religious group; Leader Bishop BARNABAS LEKGANYANE; *c.* 4m. mems.

JUDAISM

There are about 100,000 Jews in South Africa, and about 200 organized Jewish communities.

South African Jewish Board of Deputies: POB 87557, Houghton 2041; tel. (11) 6452523; fax (11) 6452559; e-mail sajbod@iafrica.com; internet www.jewish.org.za; f. 1903; the representative institution of South African Jewry; Pres. RUSSELL GODDIN; Chair. MICHAEL BAGRAM; Nat. Dir YEHUDA KAY.

BAHÁ'Í FAITH

National Spiritual Assembly: 209 Bellairs Dr., North Riding 2169, POB 932, Banbury Cross 2164; tel. (11) 4620100; fax (11) 4620129; e-mail nsa.sec@bahai.org.za; internet www.bahai.org.za; f. 1956; Sec. SHOHREH RAWHANI; 11,000 mems resident in 320 localities.

The Press

In December 1993 legislation was adopted that provided for the establishment of an Independent Media Commission, which was to ensure the impartiality of the press.

Government Communication and Information System (GCIS): Midtown Bldg, cnr Vermeulen and Prinsloo Sts, Pretoria; Private Bag X745, Pretoria 0001; tel. (12) 3142911; fax (12) 3233831; e-mail govcom@gcis.pwv.gov.za; internet www.gcis.gov.za; govt agency; CEO JOEL NETSHITENZHE.

Press Ombudsman of South Africa: POB 47221, Parklands 2121; tel. (11) 7884837; fax (11) 7884990; e-mail pressombudsman@ombudsman.org.za; Ombudsman ED H. LININGTON.

DAILIES

Eastern Cape

Die Burger (Oos-Kaap): 52 Cawood St, POB 525, Port Elizabeth 6001; tel. (41) 5036111; fax (41) 5036138; f. 1937; morning; Afrikaans; Editor LEON VAN DER VYVER; circ. 23,849.

Cape Times: Newspaper House, 122 St George's Mall, Cape Town 8001; POB 11, Cape Town 8000; tel. (21) 4884911; fax (21) 4884744; internet www.iol.co.za; f. 1876; morning; English; Editor TYRONE AUGUST (acting); circ. 50,000.

Daily Dispatch: 35 Caxton St, POB 131, East London 5200; tel. (43) 7022000; fax (43) 7435155; e-mail phyliciao@dispatch.co.za; internet www.dispatch.co.za; f. 1872; morning; English; Editor PHYLICIA OPPELT; circ. 70,486.

Eastern Province Herald: Newspaper House, 19 Baakens St, POB 1117, Port Elizabeth 6000; tel. (41) 5047911; fax (41) 554966; f. 1845; morning; English; Editor RIC WILSON; circ. 30,000 (Mon.–Fri.), 25,000 (Sat.).

Evening Post: Newspaper House, 19 Baakens St, POB 1121, Port Elizabeth 6000; tel. (41) 5047911; fax (41) 554966; f. 1950; evening; English; Editor NEVILLE WOUDBERG; circ. 19,000.

Free State

Die Volksblad: 79 Voortrekker St, POB 267, Bloemfontein 9300; tel. (51) 4047600; fax (51) 4306949; e-mail nuus@volksblad.com; internet www.naspers.com; f. 1904; morning; Afrikaans; Editor JONATHAN CROWTHER; circ. 28,000 (Mon.–Fri.), 23,000 (Sat.).

Gauteng

Beeld: Media Park, Kingsway 69, Auckland Park, Johannesburg; POB 333, Auckland Park 2006; tel. (11) 7139000; fax (11) 7139960; e-mail rvanderm@beeld.com; f. 1974; morning; weekly: *Kampus-Beeld*, student news and information, and *JIP* youth supplement; Afrikaans; Editor PEET KRUGER; Gen. Man. LUCILLE VAN NIEKERK; circ. 105,618 (Mon.–Fri.), 88,402 (Sat.).

Business Day: POB 1745, Saxonwold 2132; tel. (11) 2803000; fax (11) 2805505; internet www.bday.co.za; f. 1985; morning; English; financial; incl. *Wanted* arts and leisure magazine; Editor JIM JONES; circ. 44,000.

The Citizen: POB 7712, Johannesburg 2000; tel. (11) 4022900; fax (11) 4026862; f. 1976; morning; English; Editor M. A. JOHNSON; circ. 14,000 (Mon.–Fri.), 108,000 (Sat.).

The Pretoria News: 216 Vermeulen St, Pretoria 0002; tel. (12) 3002000; fax (12) 3287166; e-mail ptanews@ptn.independent.co.za; f. 1898; morning; English; Editor PHILANI MGWABA; circ. 25,500 (Mon.–Fri.), 14,000 (Sat.).

Sowetan: 61 Commando Rd, Industria West, POB 6663, Johannesburg 2000; tel. (11) 4714000; fax (11) 4748834; e-mail swtnedit@sowetan.co.za; internet sowetan.co.za; f. 1981; Mon.–Fri.; English; Editor Z. AGGREY KLAASTE; circ. 225,000.

The Star: 47 Sauer St, POB 1014, Johannesburg 2000; tel. (11) 6332334; fax (11) 8366186; e-mail webmaster@star.co.za; internet www.star.co.za; f. 1887; English; two editions; Editor MOEGSIEN WILLIAMS; circ. 168,539 (Mon.–Fri.).

Transvaaler: 28 Height St, Doornfontein, POB 845, Johannesburg 2000; tel. (11) 7769111; fax (11) 4020037; afternoon; Afrikaans; Editor G. JOHNSON; circ. 40,000.

KwaZulu/Natal

The Daily News: 18 Osborne St, Greyville 4001; POB 47549, Greyville 4023; tel. (31) 3082107; fax (31) 3082185; internet www.iol.co.za; f. 1878; Mon.–Fri., afternoon; English; Editor D. PATHER; circ. 50,000.

Mercury: 18 Osborne St, Greyville 4001; POB 47549, Greyville 4023; tel. (31) 3082336; fax (31) 3082333; e-mail mercnews@nn.independent.co.za; internet themercury.co.za; f. 1852; morning; English; Editor DAVID CANNING; circ. 40,000.

The Witness: 45 Willowton Rd, POB 362, Pietermaritzburg 3200; tel. (33) 3551111; fax (33) 3551122; e-mail newsed@witness.co.za; internet www.witness.co.za; f. 1846; morning; English; Editor J. CONYNGHAM; circ. 30,000.

Northern Cape

Diamond Fields Advertiser: POB 610, cnr Bean and Villiers Sts, Kimberley 8300; tel. (53) 8326261; fax (53) 8321141; e-mail pbe@dfa.co.za; internet www.iol.co.za; morning; English; Editor KEVIN RITCHIE; circ. 8,149.

SOUTH AFRICA   *Directory*

North-West

Rustenburg Herald: 28 Steen St, POB 2043, Rustenburg 0300; tel. (14) 5928329; fax (14) 5921869; e-mail mailbag@rustenburgherald.co.za; f. 1924; English and Afrikaans; Man. Editor C. THERON; circ. 20,368.

Western Cape

Die Burger: 40 Heerengracht, POB 692, Cape Town 8000; tel. (21) 4062222; fax (21) 4062913; f. 1915; morning; Afrikaans; Editor E. DOMMISSE; circ. 105,841 (Mon.–Fri.), 97,881 (Sat.).

Cape Argus: 122 St George's St, POB 56, Cape Town 8000; tel. (21) 4884911; fax (21) 4884075; f. 1857; English; independent; Editor MOEGSIEN WILLIAMS; circ. 85,000.

WEEKLIES AND FORTNIGHTLIES

Eastern Cape

Imvo Zabantsundu (Black Opinion): 35 Edes St, POB 190, King William's Town 5600; tel. (433) 23550; fax (433) 33865; f. 1884; weekly; English and Xhosa; Editor W. MNYIKIZO; Gen. Man. WILL FERREIRA; circ. 31,000.

Weekend Post: POB 1141, Port Elizabeth 6000; tel. (41) 5047911; fax (41) 554966; English; Editor N. M. WOUDBERG; circ. 38,000.

Free State

Vista: POB 1027, Welkom 9460; tel. (57) 3571304; fax (57) 3532427; e-mail avaneck@volksblad.com; internet www.media24.com/eng/newspapers/vista.html; f. 1971; weekly; English and Afrikaans; Editor MARTI WILLN; circ. 38,000 (2005).

Gauteng

African Jewish Newspaper: Johannesburg 2000; tel. (11) 6468292; f. 1931; weekly; Yiddish; Editor LEVI SHALIT.

Die Afrikaner: POB 1888, Pretoria 0001; tel. (12) 3423410; fax (12) 3423417; e-mail afrikaner@hnp.org.za; internet www.hnp.org.za/afrikaner; f. 1970; Wednesday; organ of Herstigte Nasionale Party; Editor Dr J. L. BASSON; circ. 10,000.

Benoni City Times en Oosrandse Nuus: 28 Woburn Ave, POB 494, Benoni 1500; tel. (11) 8451680; fax (11) 4224796; English and Afrikaans; Editor HILARY GREEN; circ. 32,000.

City Press: POB 3413, Johannesburg 2000; tel. (11) 4021632; fax (11) 4026662; f. 1983; weekly; English; Editor-in-Chief KHULU SIBIYA; circ. 251,748.

Financial Mail: Johncom Bldg, 4 Biermann Ave, Rosebank 2196; POB 1744, Saxenwold 2132; tel. (11) 2803016; fax (11) 2805800; e-mail fmmail@fm.co.za; internet www.financialmail.co.za; weekly; English; Editor BARNEY MTHOMBOTHI; circ. 33,000.

The Herald Times: POB 31015, Braamfontein 2017; tel. (11) 8876500; weekly; Jewish interest; Man. Dir R. SHAPIRO; circ. 5,000.

Mail and Guardian: POB 32362, Braamfontein 2017; tel. (11) 4037111; fax (11) 4031025; CEO GOVIN REDDY; Editor PHILIP VAN NIEKERK; circ. 38,000.

Mining Week: Johannesburg; tel. (11) 7892144; f. 1979; fortnightly; Editor VAL PIENAAR; circ. 10,000.

Die Noord-Transvaler: POB 220, Ladanna, Pietersburg 0704; tel. (152) 931831; fax (152) 932586; weekly; Afrikaans; Editor A. BUYS; circ. 12,000.

Noordwes Gazette: POB 515, Potchefstroom 2520; tel. (18) 2930750; e-mail potchherald@media24.com; weekly; English and Afrikaans; Editor H. STANDER; circ. 35,000.

Northern Review: 16 Grobler St, POB 45, Pietersburg 0700; tel. (152) 2959167; fax (152) 2915148; weekly; English and Afrikaans; Editor R. S. DE JAGER; circ. 10,300.

Potchefstroom and Ventersdorp Herald: POB 515, Potchefstroom 2520; tel. (18) 2930750; fax (18) 2930759; e-mail potchherald@media24.com; f. 1908; Friday; English and Afrikaans; Editor H. STANDER; Man. Dir RASSIE VAN ZYL; circ. 8,000.

Rapport: POB 8422, Johannesburg 2000; tel. (11) 4022620; fax (11) 4026163; internet www.naspers.co.za/rapport; Sunday; Afrikaans; Sr Gen. Man. and Publr SAREL DU PLESSIS; Editor IZAK DE VILLIERS; circ. 353,000.

Springs and Brakpan Advertiser: POB 138, Springs 1560; tel. (11) 8121600; fax (11) 8121908; f. 1916; English and Afrikaans; Editor CATHY GROSVENOR; circ. 13,000.

Sunday Times: POB 1742, Saxonwold 2132; tel. (11) 2805104; fax (11) 2805111; e-mail makhanyam@sundaytimes.co.za; internet www.sundaytimes.co.za; English; Editor MONDLI MAKHANYA; circ. 508,000.

Vaalweekblad: 27 Ekspa Bldg, D. F. Malan St, POB 351, Vanderbijlpark 1900; tel. (16) 817010; fax (16) 810604; weekly; Afrikaans and English; Editor W. J. BUYS; circ. 16,000.

Vrye Weekblad: 153 Bree St, Newtown, Johannesburg 2001; tel. (11) 8362151; fax (11) 8385901; f. 1988; weekly; Afrikaans; Editor MAX DU PREEZ; circ. 13,000.

KwaZulu/Natal

Farmers' Weekly: POB 32083, Mobeni 4060; tel. (31) 422041; fax (31) 426068; f. 1911; weekly; agriculture and horticulture; Editor CORRIE VENTER; circ. 17,000.

Ilanga: 19 Timeball Blvd, The Point, Durban 4001; POB 2159 Durban, 4000; tel. (31) 3374000; fax (31) 3379785; e-mail peterc@ilanganews.co.za; f. 1903; 2 a week; Zulu; Editor S. NGOBESE; circ. 107,000.

Independent On Saturday: 18 Osborne St, Greyville 4001, POB 47549, Greyville 4023; tel. (31) 3082390; fax (31) 3082185; e-mail satmail@nn.independent.co.za; internet www.nn.independent.co.za; f. 1878; English; Editor RAFIQ ROHAN; circ. 77,500.

Keur: POB 32083, Mobeni 4060; tel. (31) 422041; fax (31) 426068; f. 1967; Afrikaans; Editor CARL STEYN; circ. 69,496.

Ladysmith Gazette: POB 10019, Ladysmith 3370; tel. (36) 6376801; fax (36) 6372283; f. 1902; weekly; English, Afrikaans and Zulu; Editor DIANA PROCTER; circ. 7,000.

Post: 18 Osborne St, Greyville 4000, POB 733, Durban 4000; tel. (31) 3082400; fax (31) 3082427; e-mail post@nn.independent.co.za; internet www.iol.co.za; f. 1950 as *Golden City Post*; weekly; English; focus on the Indian community; Editor BRIGLALL RAMGUTHEE; circ. 40,000.

Sunday Tribune: 18 Osborne St, POB 47549, Greyville 4023; tel. (31) 3082911; fax (31) 3082355; e-mail tribnews@nn.independent.co.za; internet www.iol.co.za; f. 1937; weekly; English; Editor ALAN DUNN; circ. 114,304.

Umafrika: 35A Intersite Ave, Umgeni Business Park, Durban; tel. (31) 2630263; fax (31) 2630270; e-mail editor@umafrika.co.za; f. 1911; Friday; Zulu and English; Editor CYRIL MADLALA; circ. 25,000.

Northern Cape

Die Gemsbok: POB 60, Upington 8800; tel. 27017; fax 24055; English and Afrikaans; Editor D. JONES; circ. 8,000.

Western Cape

Eikestadnuus: 44 Alexander St, POB 28, Stellenbosch 7600; tel. (2231) 72840; fax (2231) 99538; weekly; English and Afrikaans; Editor R. GERBER; circ. 7,000.

Fair Lady: POB 785266, Cape Town 2146; tel. (11) 3220858; fax (11) 8836611; e-mail adonald@fairlady.com; internet www.natmags.com; fortnightly; English; Editor ANN DONALD; circ. 103,642.

Huisgenoot: 40 Heerengracht, POB 1802, Cape Town 8000; tel. (21) 4062279; fax (21) 4063316; e-mail eweidema@media24.com; internet www.huisgenoot.com; f. 1916; weekly; Afrikaans; Editor ESMARÉ WEIDEMAN; circ. 355,487.

Sarie: POB 785266, Sandton 2146; tel. and fax (21) 4062366; e-mail mvanbre@sarie.com; internet www.natmags.com; fortnightly; Afrikaans; women's interest; Editor MICHELLE VAN BREDA; circ. 166,840.

South: 6 Russel St, Castle Mews, Woodstock 7925; POB 13094, Sir Lowry Rd 7900; tel. (21) 4622012; fax (21) 4615407; weekly; black interest; Editor Dr GUY BERGER; circ. 25,000.

The Southern Cross: POB 2372, Cape Town 8000; tel. (21) 4655007; fax (21) 4653850; e-mail scross@global.co.za; f. 1920; weekly; English; Roman Catholic; Editor GUNTHER SIMMERMACHER; circ. 10,500 (2004).

Tyger-Burger: 40 Heerengracht, POB 2271, Cape Town 8000; tel. (21) 4062121; fax (21) 4062913; weekly; Afrikaans and English; Editor ABIE VON ZYL.

Weekend Argus: 122 St George's Mall, POB 56, Cape Town 8000; tel. (21) 4884911; fax (21) 4884762; internet www.iol.co.za; f. 1857; Sat. and Sun.; English; Editor CHRIS WHITFIELD; circ. 108,294.

You Magazine: 40 Heerengracht, Cape Town 8000; tel. (21) 4062366; fax (21) 4063289; f. 1987; weekly; English; Editor-in-Chief ANDRIES VAN WYK; circ. 258,138.

MONTHLIES

Free State

Wamba: POB 1097, Bloemfontein; publ. in seven vernacular languages; educational; Editor C. P. SENYATSI.

Gauteng

Centre News: Johannesburg; tel. (11) 5591781; English; publ. by R. J. J. Publications; circ. 30,000.

SOUTH AFRICA

Directory

Nursing News: POB 1280, Pretoria 0001; tel. (12) 3432315; fax (12) 3440750; f. 1978; English and Afrikaans; magazine of the Democratic Nursing Org; circ. 76,000.

Pace: POB 48985, Roosevelt Park 2129; tel. (11) 8890600; fax (11) 8805942; Man. Editor FORCE KOSHANI; circ. 131,000.

Postal and Telkom Herald: POB 9186, Johannesburg 2000; tel. (11) 7255422; fax (11) 7256540; f. 1903; English and Afrikaans; Staff Asscn (Workers' Union); Editor F. A. GERBER; circ. 13,000.

Telescope: POB 925, Pretoria 0001; tel. (12) 3217121; fax (12) 3114031; f. 1970; English, Afrikaans and vernacular languages; telecom staff journal; Editor MOSES MUDZWITI; circ. 60,000.

KwaZulu/Natal

Bona: POB 32083, Mobeni 4060; tel. (31) 422041; fax (31) 426068; f. 1956; English, Sotho, Xhosa and Zulu; Editor DAIZER MQHABA; circ. 256,631.

Living and Loving: POB 218, Parklands, Johannesburg 2121; tel. (11) 8890621; fax (11) 8890668; e-mail livingandloving@caxton.co.za; internet www.livingandloving.co.za; English; Editor KERESE THOM; circ. 55,000.

Rooi Rose: POB 412982, Craighall 2024; tel. (11) 8890665; fax (11) 8890975; e-mail rooirose@caxton.co.za; internet www.rooirose.co.za; Afrikaans; women's interest; Editor MARTIE PANSEGROUW; circ. 145,690.

Tempo: POB 16, Pinetown 3600; tel. (31) 7013225; fax (31) 7012166; f. 1984; weekly; Afrikaans; Editor Dr HILDA GROBLER; circ. 7,000.

World Airnews: POB 35082, Northway 4065; tel. (31) 5641319; fax (31) 5637115; e-mail tom@airnews.co.za; internet www.airnews.co.za; f. 1973; aviation news; Editor TOM CHALMERS; circ. 12,842 (2005).

Your Family: POB 32083, Mobeni 4060; tel. (31) 422041; fax (31) 426068; f. 1973; English; cooking, crafts, DIY; Editor ANGELA WALLER-PATON; circ. 164,115.

Western Cape

Boxing World: 5A Dover St, Randburg, Gauteng; tel. (11) 8868558; e-mail info@boxingworld.co.za; f. 1976; Editor PETER LEOPENG; circ. 10,000.

Car: Ramsay, Son & Parker (Pty) Ltd, Digital Publishing, 3 Howard Dr., Pinelands, Cape Town; POB 180, Howard Place 7450; tel. (21) 5303100; fax (21) 5322698; e-mail car@rsp.co.za; internet www.cartoday.com; Editor J. WRIGHT; circ. 111,639 (2004).

Drum: Media 24 Bldg, 2nd Floor, 5 Protea Place, Sandown 2096; POB 653284, Benmore 2010; tel. (11) 3220888; fax (11) 3220891; e-mail jrelihan@media24.co.za; internet www.natmags.com; f. 1951; English and Zulu; Editor ESMARE WEIDEMAN; Publr JOHN RELIHAN; circ. 67,012 (2005).

Femina: 21 St. John's St, POB 3647, Cape Town 8000; tel. (21) 4646248; fax (21) 4612501; e-mail robynne@assocmags.co.za; Editor ROBYNNE KAHN; circ. 68,591.

Learning Roots: POB 1161, Cape Town 8000; tel. (21) 6968414; fax (21) 6968346; f. 1980; newsletter for black schools in the Western Cape; circ. 50,000.

Nursing RSA Verpleging: Private Bag XI, Pinelands 7430; tel. (21) 5312691; fax (21) 5314126; f. 1986; professional nursing journal; Editor LILLIAN MEDLIN; circ. 10,000.

Reader's Digest (South African Edition): Ilford House, Ground Floor, Hampton Park, 20 Georgian Crescent, Bryanston, Johannesburg 2196; POB 784483, Sandton 2146; tel. (11) 7071200; fax (11) 4630491; e-mail magazine.sa@readersdigest.com; internet www.readersdigest.co.za; f. 1948; English; Editor ANTHONY JOHNSON; circ. 112,000.

South African Medical Journal: MASA House, Central House, Private Bag X1, Pinelands 7430; tel. (21) 5306520; fax (21) 5314126; e-mail publishing@samedical.co.za; f. 1884; publ. by the South African Medical Asscn; Editor DANIEL J. NCAYIYANA; circ. 20,000.

Die Unie: POB 196, Cape Town 8000; tel. (21) 4616340; fax (21) 4619238; e-mail saoukaap@jaywalk.com; f. 1905; educational; publ. by the South African Teachers' Union; Editor H. M. NEL; circ. 7,200.

Die Voorligter: Private Bag, Tyger Valley 7536; tel. (21) 9177000; fax (21) 9141333; e-mail lig@cnw-inter.net; internet www.christene.co.za; f. 1937; journal of the Dutch Reformed Church of South Africa; Editor Dr F. M. GAUM; circ. 50,000.

Wineland Magazine: VinPro, POB 1411, Suider-Paarl 7624; tel. (21) 8073267; fax (21) 8631562; e-mail cas@wineland.co.za; internet www.wineland.co.za; f. 1931; publ. by VinPro wine producers' org.; viticulture and the wine and spirit industry; incorporates *Wynboer* technical guide for wine producers; Editor CASSIE DU PLESSIS; circ. 10,000.

The Wisden Cricketer: POB 16368, Vlaeberg 8018; tel. (21) 4083813; e-mail jkrohn@touchline.co.za; internet www.wisdencricketer.co.za; f. 2005; Publr NIC WIDES; Editor ROB HOUWING.

Woman's Value: POB 1802, Cape Town 8000; tel. (21) 4062629; fax (21) 4062929; e-mail wvdited@womansvalue.com; internet www.women24.com/women24/womanswalue/wv_template; English; Editor and Publr TERENA LE ROUX; circ. 134,749.

PERIODICALS

Eastern Cape

African Journal of AIDS Research: CADRE, Institute for Social and Economic Research, Rhodes Univ., POB 94, Grahamstown 6140; tel. (46) 6038553; fax (46) 6038770; e-mail ajar@ru.ac.za; internet www.cadre.org.za; f. 2002; quarterly; Man. Editor KEVIN KELLY.

Gauteng

Africa Insight: Africa Institute of South Africa, POB 630, Pretoria 0001; tel. (12) 3286970; fax (12) 3238153; e-mail beth@ai.org.za; internet www.ai.org.za; f. 1970; quarterly; journal of the Africa Institute of South Africa; Editor ELIZABETH LE ROUX; circ. 1,200.

African Journal of Political Science: 195 Beckett St, Arcadia, Pretoria; POB 13995, The Tramshed 0126; tel. (12) 3430409; fax (12) 3443622; e-mail program@aaps.org.za; 2 a year; articles in English and French; Editor ADEKUNLE AMUWO.

Africanus: Unisa Press, POB 392, UNISA, 0003 Pretoria; tel. (12) 4292953; fax (12) 4293449; e-mail delpoa@unisa.ac.za; 2 a year; journal of the Centre for Development Studies, Unisa; African and Third World developmental issues; Editor LINDA CORNWELL.

Codicillus: Unisa Press, POB 392, UNISA, 0003 Pretoria; tel. (12) 4292953; fax (12) 4293449; e-mail delpoa@unisa.ac.za; 2 a year; journal of the School of Law at the Univ. of South Africa; South African and int. law; Editor Prof. H. C. ROODT.

The Motorist: Highbury Monarch Pty, 8th Floor, Metlife Centre, 7 Coen Steytler Ave, Foreshore, 8001 Cape Town; tel. (21) 4160141; fax (21) 4187312; e-mail themotorist@monarchc.co.za; f. 1966; journal of the Automobile Asscn of SA; Editor FIONA ZERBST; circ. 131,584 (2000).

The ScienceScope: POB 395, Pretoria 0001; tel. (12) 8414625; fax (12) 8413789; e-mail edaconceicao@csir.co.za; internet www.csir.co.za; f. 1991 as *Technobrief*; quarterly; publ. by the South African Council for Scientific and Industrial Research; Editor EUNICE DA CONCEIÇÃO; circ. 6,000.

South African Journal of Chemistry: POB 806, Ruimsig 1732; e-mail wolfgang.meyer@sasol.com; f. 1921; digital; Editor WOLFGANG H. MEYER.

South African Journal of Economics: 4.45 EBW Bldg, Univ. of Pretoria, Pretoria 0002; POB 73354, Lynnwood Ridge 0040; tel. (12) 4203525; fax (12) 3625266; e-mail saje@up.ac.za; internet www.essa.org.za; f. 1933; quarterly; English and Afrikaans; journal of the Economic Soc. of South Africa; publ. by Blackwells; Man. Editor P. A. BLACK.

South African Journal of Wildlife Research: POB 217, Bloubergstrand 7436; tel. (21) 5541297; e-mail elma@mweb.co.za; internet www.sawma.co.za; f. 1970; journal of the Southern African Wildlife Management Asscn; 2 a year; Editor Prof. MICHAEL CHERRY.

Kwa/Zulu Natal

African Journal on Conflict Resolution: ACCORD, Private Bag X018, Umhlanga Rocks 4320; tel. (31) 5023908; fax (31) 5024160; e-mail info@accord.org.za; internet www.accord.org.za/ajcr/intro.htm; f. 1999; annually; conflict transformation in Africa; Chair. JAKES GERWEL; Editor Prof. JANNIE MALAN.

Indilinga: African Journal of Indigenous Knowledge Systems (IAJIKS): Private Bag X10, Isipingo 4110; tel. (31) 9077000; fax (31) 9073011; e-mail nmkabela@pan.uzulu.ac.za; internet www.indilinga.org.za; f. 2001; 1–2 a year; issues relating to the transmission of local or traditional knowledge; Editor-in-Chief QUEENETH MKABELA.

North-West

Historia: School of Basic Sciences, Potchefstroom Univ. for Christian Higher Education, Vaal Triangle Campus, POB 1174, 1900 Vanderbijlpark; e-mail gskjwnt@puknet.puk.ac.za; f. 1956; 2 a year; journal of the Historical Asscn of South Africa; South African and African history; Editor LIZA KRIEL.

Western Cape

African Finance Journal: African Finance Association, ACIA, Univ. of Stellenbosch Business School, POB 610, Bellville 7535; tel. (21) 9184347; fax (21) 9184262; e-mail afa@acia.sun.ac.za; f. 1999; 2 a year; finance, accounting and economics; Exec. Editor NICHOLAS BIEKPE.

SOUTH AFRICA

Economic Prospects: Bureau for Economic Research, Economics and Management Sciences Bldg, 7th Floor, Bosman St, Stellenbosch 7600; Private Bag 5050, Stellenbosch 7599; tel. (21) 8872810; fax (21) 8839225; e-mail hhman@sun.ac.za; quarterly; forecast of the South African economy for the coming 18–24 months; Man. Editor P. LAUBSCHER.

Ecquid Novi: c/o South African Journal for Journalism Research, POB 106, Stellenbosch 7599; tel. (21) 8082625; fax (21) 8083488; e-mail novi@sun.ac.za; internet www.sun.ac.za/ecquidnovi; f. 1980; 2 a year; focus on role of the media in southern Africa and Africa; Editor ARNOLD S. DE BEER.

Journal for the Study of Religion: Dept of Religious Studies, Room 5.40, Leslie Social Science Bldg, Upper Campus, Univ. of Cape Town, Private Bag, Rondebosch 7701; tel. (21) 6503452; fax (21) 6897575; Editor Prof. DAVID CHIDESTER; Man. Editor RAFFAELLE DELLE DONNE.

South African Journal for Research in Sport, Physical Education and Recreation: Dept of Sport Science, Univ. of Stellenbosch, Private Bag X1, Matieland, Stellenbosch 7602; tel. (21) 8084724; fax (21) 8084817; e-mail floris@sun.ac.za; 2 a year; Editor Prof. FLORIS J. G. VAN DER MERWE; circ. 75.

South African Law Journal: Faculty of Law, Univ. of Cape Town, Private Bag Rondebosch 7700; POB 24299, Lansdowne 7779; tel. (21) 7633600; fax (21) 7970121; e-mail salj@law.uct.ac.za; f. 1884; Editor C. H. LEWIS; circ. 1,000.

NEWS AGENCIES

East Cape News (ECN) Pty Ltd: POB 897, Grahamstown 6140; tel. (46) 6361013; e-mail editor@ecn.co.za; internet www.ecn.co.za; f. 1997; fmrly East Cape News Agencies; Dir MIKE LOEWE.

South African Press Association (SAPA): Cotswold House, Greenacres Office Park, cnr Victory and Rustenburg Rds, Victory Park; POB 7766, Johannesburg 2000; tel. (11) 7821600; fax (11) 7821587; e-mail comms@sapa.org.za; internet www.sapa.org.za; f. 1938; Man. WIM J. H. VAN GILS; Editor MARK A. VAN DER VELDEN; 40 mems.

Foreign Bureaux

Agence France-Presse (AFP): Nixdorf Centre, 6th Floor, 37 Stanley Ave, Milpark; POB 3462, Johannesburg 2000; tel. (11) 4822170; fax (11) 7268756; Bureau Chief MARC HUTTEN.

Agenzia Nazionale Stampa Associata (ANSA) (Italy): POB 32312, Camps Bay, Cape Town 8040; tel. (21) 7903991; fax (21) 7904444; Correspondent LICINIO GERMINI.

Associated Press (AP) (USA): 15 Napier St, Richmond, Johannesburg 2092; tel. (11) 7267022; fax (11) 7267834; Bureau Chief TERRY LEONARD.

Central News Agency (Taiwan): Kine Centre, 1st Floor, 141 Commissioner St, Johannesburg 2001; tel. (11) 3316654; fax (11) 3319463; Chief CHANG JER SHONG.

Deutsche Presse-Agentur (dpa) (Germany): 96 Jorrisen St, POB 32521, Braamfontein 2017; tel. (11) 4033926; fax (11) 4032849; Chief Dr ARNO MAYER.

Informatsionnoye Telegrafnoye Agentstvo Rossii—Telegrafnoye Agentstvo Suverennykh Stran (ITAR—TASS) (Russia): 1261 Park St, Atfield, Pretoria; tel. (12) 436677; fax (12) 3425017; Bureau Chief YURII K. PICHUGIN.

IPS—Inter Press Service (Italy): Media Mill, 7 Quince Rd, Milpark 2092, Johannesburg; POB 1062, Auckland Park 2006; tel. (11) 4034967; fax (11) 4032516; e-mail farai@ips.org; internet www.ipsnews.net/africa; Regional Dir (Africa) FARAI SAMHUNGU.

Kyodo News (Japan): Sandton Office Towers, 6th Floor, cnr Rivonia Rd and 5th St; POB 787522 Sandton 2146; tel. (11) 8834995; fax (11) 8834996; e-mail nako@kyodo.co.jp; Rep. DAI KANEKO.

Reuters Ltd (UK): Surrey House, 7th and 8th Floors, 35 Rissik St, Johannesburg; Man. CHRIS INWOOD.

United Press International (UPI) (USA): Nedbank Centre, 2nd Floor, POB 32661, Braamfontein 2017; tel. (11) 4033910; fax (11) 4033914; Bureau Chief PATRICK COLLINS.

Agencia EFE (Spain) is also represented.

PRESS ASSOCIATIONS

Newspaper Association of South Africa: Nedbank Gardens, 5th Floor, 33 Bath Ave, Rosebank 2196, Johannesburg; POB 47180, Parklands 2121; tel. (11) 7213200; fax (11) 7213254; e-mail na@printmedia.org.za; internet www.printmedia.org.za; f. 1882; represents 42 national daily and weekly newspapers, and 128 community newspapers; Pres. TREVOR NCUBE.

Print Media SA: North Wing, Nedbank Gardens, 5th Floor, 33 Bath Ave, Rosebank 2196, Johannesburg; POB 47180, Parklands 2121; tel. (11) 7213200; fax (11) 7213254; e-mail printmediasa@printmedia.org.za; internet www.printmedia.org.za; f. 1995 following the restructuring of the Newspaper Press Union of Southern Africa; represents all aspects of the print media (newspapers and magazines); 680 mems; Pres. T. NCUBE.

Publishers

Acorn Books: POB 4845, Randburg 2125; tel. (11) 8805768; fax (11) 8805768; e-mail acorbook@iafrica.com; f. 1985; Africana, general, natural history; Propr and Publr ELEANOR-MARY CADELL.

Albertyn Publishers (Pty) Ltd: Andmar Bldg, Van Ryneveld St, Stellenbosch 7600; tel. (21) 8871202; fax (21) 8871292; f. 1971; encyclopaedias; Editorial Man. S. CARSTENS.

BLAC Publishing House: POB 17, Athlone, Cape Town; f. 1974; general fiction, poetry; Man. Dir JAMES MATTHEWS.

Jonathan Ball Publishers: POB 33977, Jeppestown 2043; tel. (11) 6222900; fax (11) 6223553; fiction, reference, bibles, textbooks, general.

Ad. Donker (Pty) Ltd: POB 33977, Jeppestown 2043; tel. (11) 6222900; fax (11) 6223553; Africana, literature, South African history, general non-fiction.

Bible Society of South Africa: POB 5500, Tyger Valley 7536; tel. (21) 9108777; fax (21) 9108799; e-mail biblia@biblesociety.co.za; internet www.biblesociety.co.za; f. 1820; CEO Rev. G. S. KRITZINGER.

Book Promotions (Pty) Ltd: Prime Park, Unit 1 (Sec. B), Mocke Rd, Diep River 7800; POB 5, Plumstead 7800; tel. (21) 7060949; fax (21) 7060941; e-mail enquiries@bookpro.co.za; internet www.bookpro.co.za; CEO R. MANSELL.

Book Studio (Pty) Ltd: POB 121, Hout Bay 7872.

Books of Africa (Pty) Ltd: POB 10, Muizenberg 7950; tel. (21) 888316; f. 1947; biography, history, Africana, art; Man. Dir T. V. BULPIN.

Brenthurst Press (Pty) Ltd: POB 87184, Houghton 2041; tel. (11) 6466024; fax (11) 4861651; e-mail orders@brenthurst.co.za; internet www.brenthurst.org.za; f. 1974; Southern African history; Dir MARCELLE GRAHAM.

Clever Books: POB 13186, Hatfield 0028; tel. (12) 3423263; fax (12) 432376; e-mail elizabeth@cleverbooks.co.za; f. 1981; subsidiary of MacMillan Publishers.

College of Careers/Faircare Books: POB 10207, Caledon Sq., Cape Town 7905; tel. (21) 4614411; f. 1946; general, educational; Man. Dir MICHAEL IRVING.

CUM Books: POB 1599, Vereeniging 1930; tel. (16) 4214781; fax (16) 4211748; e-mail cabooks@cum.co.za; internet www.cum.co.za.

Da Gama Publishers (Pty) Ltd: MWU Bldg, 6th Floor, 19 Melle St, Braamfontein 2017; tel. (11) 4033763; fax (11) 4031263; travel; Publr DERMOT SWAINE.

Digma Publications: POB 95466, Waterkloof 0145; tel. (11) 3463840; fax (11) 3463845.

Dreyer Printers and Publishers: POB 286, Bloemfontein 9300; tel. (51) 4479001; fax (51) 4471281.

Educum Publishers: POB 3068, Halfway House 1685.

Eksamenhulp: POB 55555, Arcadia 0007.

Fisichem Publishers: Private Bag X3, Matieland 7602; tel. (21) 8870900; fax (21) 8839635; e-mail fisichem@iafrica.com; Man. RETHA JORDAAN.

Flesch Publications: 11 Peninsula Rd, Zeekoevlei, Cape Town 7941; POB 31353, Grassy Park 7888; tel. (21) 7054317; fax (21) 7060766; e-mail sflesch@iafrica.com; f. 1954; Prin. Officer STEPHEN FLESCH.

Fortress Books: POB 2475, Knysna 6570; tel. and fax (44) 3826805; fax (44) 3826848; e-mail fortress@iafrica.com; internet www.uys.com; f. 1973; military history, biographies, financial; Man. Dir I. UYS.

HAUM: Prima Park 4 and 6, cnr Klosser and King Edward Rds, Porow 7500; tel. (21) 926123; f. 1894; Man. C. J. HAGE.

Kagiso Publishers: POB 629, Pretoria 0001; tel. (12) 3284620; fax (12) 3284705; school textbooks and other materials for schools and tertiary institutions in all 11 official South African languages; Man. Dir L. M. MABANDLA.

University Publishers & Booksellers (Pty) Ltd: POB 29, Stellenbosch 7599; tel. (21) 8870337; fax (21) 8832975; f. 1947; educational; Man. Dir B. B. LIEBENBERG.

Heinemann Publishers (Pty) Ltd: POB 781940, Sandown, Sandton 2146; tel. (11) 3228600; fax (11) 3228715; internet www.heinemann.co.za; educational; incl. imprints Lexicon, Isando and Centaur; Man. Dir O. KRUT.

Home Economics Publishers (Huishoudkunde Uitgewers): POB 7091, Stellenbosch 7599; tel. (21) 8864722; fax (21) 8864722; e-mail mcv1@sun.ac.za; Man. M. C. VOSLOO.

Human and Rousseau (Pty) Ltd: Naspers Bldg, 40 Heerengracht, Cape Town 8000; POB 5050, Cape Town 8000; tel. (21) 4063033; fax (21) 4063812; e-mail humanhk@humanrousseau.com; internet www.humanrousseau.com; f. 1959; subsidiary of NB Publrs; English, Afrikaans, Xhosa and Zulu; children and adult trade books; Head of Publishing C. T. BREYTENBACH.

Incipit Publishers: POB 28754, Sunnyside, Pretoria 0132; tel. and fax (12) 6502626; e-mail feenstra@protem.uct.ac.za; f. 1987; music education; Man. MARIANNE FEENSTRA.

Juta and Co Ltd: POB 14373, Kenwyn 7790, Cape Town; tel. (11) (21) 7633600; fax (21) 7627424; e-mail books@juta.co.za; internet www.juta.co.za; f. 1853; academic, educational, law, electronic; CEO R. J. WILSON.

Klipbok Publishers: POB 170, Durbanville 7550; tel. and fax (21) 9762293; f. 1979; prose, poetry, drama.

Knowledge Unlimited (Pty) Ltd: POB 781337, Sandton 2146; tel. (11) 6521800; fax (11) 3142984; children's fiction, educational; Man. Dir MIKE JACKLIN.

Konsensus Publishers: 213 Orion St, Waterkloof 0180.

Lemur Books (Pty) Ltd (The Galago Publishing Co): POB 1645, Alberton 1450; tel. (11) 9072029; fax (11) 8690890; e-mail lemur@mweb.co.za; internet www.galago.co.za; military, political, history, hunting, general; Man. Dir F. STIFF.

LexisNexis Butterworths SA: 215 North Ridge Rd, Morningside, Durban 4001; POB 792, Durban 4000; tel. (31) 2683266; fax (31) 2683109; e-mail liane.mulholland@lexisnexis.co.za; internet www.lexisnexis.co.za; law, tax, accountancy; Man. Dir WILLIAM J. LAST.

LMA (Pty) Ltd: 341 West St, Durban 4001; tel. (31) 3048571; primary school educational.

Lovedale Press: Private Bag X1346, Alice; tel. (040) 6531135; fax (040) 6531871; f. 1841; Gen. Man. Rev. B. NTISANA.

Lux Verbi-BM: POB 1822, Cape Town 8000; tel. (21) 8648237; fax (21) 8648292; e-mail epi@luxverbi-bm.co.za; internet www.luxverbi-bm.com; f. 1818 as the Dutch Reformed Church Publishing Co; merged with Bible Media in 1999; subsidiary of the Naspers Group; imprints incl. Hugenote, NG Kerk Uitgewers, Protea, and Waterkant; Christian media; CEO H. S. SPIES; Editor-in-Chief D. FOURIE.

Macdonald Purnell (Pty) Ltd: POB 51401, Randburg 2125; tel. (11) 7875830; South African flora, fauna, geography and history; Man. Dir E. ANDERSON.

Marler Publications (Pty) Ltd: POB 27815, Sunnyside, Pretoria 0132; tel. (12) 573770; f. 1987; educational; Man. Dir C. J. MULLER.

Maskew Miller Longman (Pty) Ltd: cnr Forest Dr. and Logan Way, Pinelands 7405; POB 396, Cape Town 8000; tel. (21) 5326000; fax (21) 5310716; e-mail tembela@mml.co.za; internet www.mml.co.za; f. 1893 as Miller Maskew; merged with Longman in 1983; jtly owned by Pearson Education and Caxton Publrs and Printers Ltd; imprints incl. Kagiso Education; educational and general.

Methodist Publishing House: POB 13128, Woodstock, Cape Town 7915; tel. (21) 4483640; fax (21) 4483716; e-mail mark@methbooks.co.za; internet www.methodist.org.za; religion and theology; Gen. Man. Rev. TERRY MOULT (acting).

Nasionale Boekhandel: POB 122, Parow 7500; tel. (21) 5911131; English, Afrikaans and several African languages; fiction, general, educational, academic; Man. Dir P. J. BOTMA.

Nasou—Via Afrika: POB 5197, Cape Town 8000; tel. (21) 406331; fax (21) 4063086; internet www.nasou-viaafrika.com; f. 1963; educational; CEO LOUISE NAUDÉ.

New Holland Publishing (South Africa) (Pty) Ltd: POB 1144, Cape Town 8000; tel. (21) 4624360; fax (21) 4619378; Dir S. CONNOLLY, P. C. DESAI, F. M. LEE, A. C. B. MOLUSI, L. O'BRIEN, S. RYLANDS, R. P. WILKINSON, B. D. WOOTTON.

Oxford University Press: POB 12119, N1 City, Cape Town 7463; tel. (21) 5954400; fax (21) 5954430; e-mail oxford@oup.com; internet www.oup.com/za; f. 1914; Man. Dir KATE MCCALLUM.

David Philip Publishers (Pty) Ltd: POB 23408, Claremont 7735; tel. (21) 6744136; fax (21) 6743568; f. 1971; general, academic, literature, reference, fiction; Man. Dir BRIAN WAFOWAROWA.

Pretoria Boekhandel: POB 23334, Innesdale, Pretoria 0031; tel. (12) 761531; f. 1971; Prin. Officer L. S. VAN DER WALT.

Random House (Pty) Ltd South Africa: POB 2002, Houghton 2041; tel. (11) 4843538; fax (11) 4846180; e-mail mail@randomhouse.co.za; f. 1966; general fiction; Man. Dir S. E. JOHNSON.

Ravan Press (Pty) Ltd: POB 145, Randburg 2125; tel. (11) 7897636; fax (11) 7897653; f. 1972; political, sociological, fiction, business studies, gender, history, autobiography, biography, educational; Man. Dir DAVID LEA.

Saayman and Weber (Pty) Ltd: POB 673, Cape Town 8000; f. 1980.

Sasavona Publishers and Booksellers: Private Bag X8, Braamfontein 2017; tel. (11) 4032502; fax (11) 3397274; Northern Sotho, Tshwa, Tsonga, Tswana, Venda and Zulu; Man. A. E. KALTENRIEDER.

Shuter and Shooter Publishers (Pty) Ltd: 21C Cascades Crescent, Pietermaritzburg 3201; POB 13016, Cascades, Pietermaritzburg 3202; tel. (33) 3476100; fax (33) 3476130; internet www.shuter.co.za; f. 1921; educational, general and African languages; Man. Dir DAVE F. RYDER.

Study Aids Ltd: 13 Darrock Ave, Albemarle Park, Germiston 1401; study aids.

Hans Strydom Publishers: Private Bag 10, Mellville 2109.

Sunray Publishers: 96 Queen St, Durban 4001; tel. (31) 3052543.

Tafelberg Publishers Ltd: 12th Floor Naspers 40 Heerengracht Roggebaai 8012; POB 879, Cape Town 8000; tel. (21) 4063033; fax (21) 4063812; e-mail tafelbrg@tafelberg.com; internet www.tafelberg.com; f. 1950; subsidiary of NB Publrs; juvenile, fiction and non-fiction, arts and crafts, nature and tourism; Gen. Man. J. P. VAN ZYL.

Thomson Publications: Johannesburg 2123; tel. (11) 7892144; fax (11) 7893196; f. 1948; trade and technical; Man. Dir JOE M. BRADY.

UCCSA Publications Dept: POB 31083, Braamfontein 2017; tel. (11) 8360065; f. 1946; Gen. Man. W. WESTENBORG.

University of KwaZulu-Natal Press (UKZN Press): Private Bag X01, Scottsville 3209; tel. (33) 2605226; fax (33) 2605801; e-mail books@ukzn.ac.za; internet www.ukznpress.co.za; Publr GLENN COWLEY.

Van der Walt and Son, J. P. (Pty) Ltd: POB 123, Pretoria 0001; tel. (12) 3252100; fax (12) 3255498; f. 1947; general; Man. Dir C. J. STEENKAMP.

Chris van Rensburg Publications (Pty) Ltd: POB 29159, Mellville 2109; tel. (31) 7264350; yearbooks, general; Man. Dir. C. C. VAN RENSBURG.

Van Schaik Publishers: POB 12681, Hatfield 0028; tel. (12) 3422765; fax (12) 4303563; e-mail vanschaik@vanschaiknet.com; internet www.vanschaiknet.com; f. 1915; English and Afrikaans; academic; CEO. L. MARTINI.

Wits University Press: PO Wits, Johannesburg 2050; tel. (11) 4845910; fax (11) 4845971; e-mail klippv@wup.wits.ac.za; internet witspress.ac.za; f. 1922; academic; Publr VERONICA KLIPP.

PUBLISHERS' ASSOCIATION

Publishers' Association of South Africa: Centre for the Book, 62 Queen Victoria St, Cape Town; POB 15277, Vlaeberg 8018; tel. (21) 426278; fax (21) 4261733; internet www.publishsa.co.za; f. 1992; Exec. Dir. DUDLEY H. SCHROEDER.

Broadcasting and Communications

TELECOMMUNICATIONS

South African Telecommunications Regulatory Authority (SATRA): 164 Katherine St, Sandton 2146; Private Bag X1, Marlboro 2063; tel. (11) 3218200; fax (11) 3218551; internet www.satra.gov.za.

Mobile Telephone Network: PMB 9955, Sandton 2146; tel. (11) 3016000; fax (11) 3016111; internet www.mtn.co.za.

Telkom SA Ltd: Private Bag X74, Pretoria 0001; tel. (12) 3111028; fax (12) 3114031; internet www.telkom.co.za; f. 1991; privatized in 2003; Chair. E. D. MOSENEKE; CEO SIZWE NXASANA.

BROADCASTING

Regulatory Authority

Independent Broadcasting Authority: Pinmill Farm, 164 Katherine St, Sandton 2146; tel. (22) 7220000; fax (11) 4441919; internet www.iba.org.za; f. 1993; Chair. MANDLA LANGA.

Radio

South African Broadcasting Corpn (SABC)—Radio: Private Bag X1, Auckland Park 2006; tel. (11) 7143407; fax (11) 7142635; e-mail info@sabc.co.za; internet www.sabc.co.za; Chair. Prof. PAULUS ZULU; CEO CHARLOTTE MAMPANE.

Domestic Services

Radio South Africa; Afrikaans Stereo; Radio 5; Radio 2000; Highveld Stereo; Good Hope Stereo; Radio Kontrei; RPN Stereo; Jacaranda Stereo; Radio Algoa (regional services); Radio Lotus (Indian service in English); Radio Metro (African service in English); Radio Lebowa; Radio Ndebele; Radio Sesotho; Setswana Stereo; Radio Swazi; Radio Tsonga; Radio Xhosa; Radio Zulu.

SOUTH AFRICA

External Service

Channel Africa Radio: POB 91313, Auckland Park 2006; tel. (11) 7142255; fax (11) 7142072; e-mail ntentenit@sabc.co.za; internet www.channelafrica.org; f. 1966; SABC's external service; broadcasts 217 hours per week in English, French, Portuguese, Kiswahili, Chinyanja and Silozi; Exec. Editor THAMI NTENTENI.

Television

South African Broadcasting Corpn (SABC)—Television: Private Bag X41, Auckland Park 2006; tel. (11) 7149111; fax (11) 7145055; e-mail info@sabc.co.za; internet www.sabc.co.za; transmissions began in 1976; operates television services in seven languages over three channels; Channel One (TV1) broadcasts in English and Afrikaans; Channel Two (CCV-TV) broadcasts in English, Northern and Southern Sotho, Tswana, Xhosa and Zulu; Channel Three (NNTV) broadcasts documentaries, educational programmes and sport; Chair. Prof. PAULUS ZULU; CEO MOLEFE MOKGATLE.

Finance

(cap. = capital; auth. = authorized; res = reserves; dep. = deposits; m. = million; brs = branches; amounts in rand)

BANKING

Central Bank

South African Reserve Bank: 370 Church St, POB 427, Pretoria 0002; tel. (12) 3133911; fax (12) 3133197; e-mail hopub01@resbank.co.za; internet www.resbank.co.za; f. 1921; cap. 2.0m., res 3,429.1m., dep. 71,821.9m. (March 2002); Gov. TITO T. MBOWENI; Sen. Dep. Gov. X. P. GUMA; 7 brs.

Commercial Banks

ABSA Bank Ltd: ABSA Towers East, 3rd Floor, 170 Main St, Johannesburg 2001; tel. (11) 3504000; fax (11) 3503768; e-mail absa@absa.co.za; internet www.absa.co.za; total assets 306,848m. (Mar. 2004); Chair. Dr DANIE CRONJÉ; CEO STEVE F. BOOYSEN; 726 brs.

African Bank Investments Ltd: 59 16th Rd, Private Bag X170, Midrand 1685; tel. (11) 2569000; fax (11) 2569217; internet www.abil.co.za; f. 1975; cap. 1,876.4m., res 186.7m., dep. 706.2m. (Sept. 2002); CEO LEONIDAS KIRKINIS; 268 brs.

Albaraka Bank Ltd: 134 Commercial Rd, 1st Floor, Durban 4001; POB 4395, Durban 4000; tel. (31) 3662800; fax (31) 3052631; e-mail albaraka@icon.co.za; tel. www.albaraka.co.za; f. 1989; operates according to Islamic principles; cap. 41.0m., res 13.5m., dep. 551.7m. (Dec. 2002); Chair. A. A. SABBAHI; Deputy CEO M. G. MCLEAN.

AMB Holdings Ltd: The Forum, 9th Floor, cnr Maude and Fifth Sts, POB 786833, Sandton 2146; tel. (11) 3022000; fax (11) 7849211; e-mail asprague@amb.co.za; internet www.amb.co.za; Exec. Dir ZENZO LUSENGO; CEO ANDREW SPRAGUE.

Brait South Africa Ltd: 9 Fricker Rd, Illovo Blvd, Illovo, Sandton 2196; Private Bag X1, Northlands 2116; tel. (11) 5071000; fax (11) 5071001; internet www.brait.com; f. 1998; subsidiary of Brait S.A., Luxembourg; total assets 802.3m. (Mar. 2004); CEO JOHN COULTER.

FirstRand Bank Ltd: 4 Merchant Place, 4th Floor, cnr Fredman Dr. and Rivonia Rd, Sandton 2196; POB 786273, Sandton 2146; tel. (11) 2821808; fax (11) 2828065; e-mail information@firstrand.co.za; internet www.firstrand.co.za; f. 1971 as First National Bank of Southern Africa; merged with Rand Bank in 1998; total assets 323,500m. (June 2004); Chair. GERRIT T. FERREIRA; CEO LAURITZ L. DIPPENAAR; 650 brs.

GBS Mutual Bank: 18–20 Hill St, Grahamstown 6139; POB 114, Grahamstown 6140; tel. (46) 6227109; fax (46) 6228855; e-mail gbs@gbsbank.co.za; internet www.gbsbank.co.za; f. 1877; total assets 301.1m. (Dec. 2003); Chair. C. K. M. STONE; Man. Dir T. C. S. TAGG; 1 br.

HBZ Bank Ltd: 209 Grey St, POB 48449, Qualbert 4078; tel. (31) 3600400; fax (31) 3072731; e-mail sazone@hbzbank.co.za; internet www.habibbank.com; f. 1995; subsidiary of Habib Bank Ltd; total assets 650.4m. (Dec. 2003); Chair. MUHAMMAD HABIB; CEO N. A. CHODHARI; 4 brs.

Imperial Bank Ltd: 140 Boeing Rd, East Elma Park, Edenvale, Gauteng 1610; POB 3567, Edenvale 1610; tel. (11) 8792000; fax (11) 8792234; e-mail phassim@imperialbank.co.za; internet www.imperialbank.co.za; f. 1996; 51.1% owned by Nedbank, 49.9% Imperial Holdings; total assets 12,955.0m. (Dec. 2003); Chair. W. G. LYNCH; CEO R. VAN WYK.

Meeg Bank Ltd: Meeg Bank Bldg, 60 Sutherland St, Umtata; POB 332, Umtata 5100; tel. (47) 5026200; fax (47) 5311098; internet www.meegbank.co.za; f. 1977; fmrly Bank of Transkei; name changed Oct. 1998; total assets 782.4m. (March 2003); Chair. Prof. WISEMAN LUMKILE NKUHLU; Man. Dir. EMIL G. KALTENBRÜNN; 5 brs.

Mercantile Bank Ltd: Mercantile Lisbon House, 142 West St, Sandown 2196; POB 782699, Sandton 2146; tel. (11) 3020300; fax (11) 3020729; internet www.mercantile.co.za; f. 1965; subsidiary of Mercantile Lisbon Bank Holdings; total assets 2,224.8m. (Dec. 2003); Chair. Dr JOAQUIM A. S. DE ANDRADE CAMPOS; CEO D. J. BROWN; 14 brs.

Nedbank Ltd: 135 Rivonia Rd, Sandown 2196, Johannesburg 2001; POB 1144, Johannesburg 2000; tel. (11) 2940999; fax (11) 2950999; e-mail nedbankgroupir@nedbank.co.za; internet www.nedbankgroup.co.za; f. 1988; name changed from Nedcor Bank Ltd Nov. 2002; subsidiary of Nedbank Group Ltd; cap. 395m., res 9,657m., dep. 262,946m. (Jun. 2005); Chair. WARREN CLEWLOW; CEO THOMAS ANDREW BOARDMAN; 242 brs.

Rennies Bank Ltd: Rennie House, 11th Floor, 19 Ameshoff St, Braamfontein 2001, Johannesburg; POB 185, Johannesburg 2000; tel. (11) 4073000; fax (11) 4073322; e-mail agent2@bank.rennies.co.za; internet www.renniesbank.co.za; f. 1850; subsidiary of Bidvest Group Ltd; foreign exchange, trade finance and related activities; total assets 313,772m. (June 2003); Chair. J. J. PAMENSKY; CEO DAVID WALKER; over 60 brs.

South African Bank of Athens Ltd: Bank of Athens Bldg, 116 Marshall St, Johannesburg 2001; POB 7781, Johannesburg 2000; tel. (11) 8321211; fax (11) 8381001; e-mail karenc@bankofathens.co.za; internet www.bankofathens.co.za; f. 1947; 99.46% owned by National Bank of Greece; cap. 94.5m., dep. 531.7m. (Dec. 2004); Chair. TAKIS ARAPOGLOU; CEO HECTOR ZARCA; 10 brs.

Standard Bank Ltd: Standard Bank Centre, 5 Simmonds St, Johannesburg 2000; POB 7725, Johannesburg 2000; tel. (11) 6369111; fax (11) 6364207; e-mail information@standardbank.co.za; internet www.standardbank.co.za; f. 1862; cap. 5,703.0m., res 9,472.0m., dep. 204,812.0m. (Dec. 2003); Chair. DEREK E. COOPER; CEO JACKO H. MAREE; 997 brs.

Teba Bank Ltd: 238 Roan Cres., Corporate Park North, Midrand; Private Bag X174, Halfway House, 1685; tel. (11) 2031500; fax (11) 2031554; e-mail corpcomm@tebabank.com; internet www.tebabank.co.za; f. 2000; fmrly Teba Savings Fund; specializes in micro-finance and providing financial services to mining communities; total assets 1,715.1m. (Feb. 2004); Man. Dir JENNIFER HOFFMAN; 20 brs and over 50 agencies.

Merchant Bank

Marriott Merchant Bank Ltd: Kingsmead Office Park, Durban 4001; POB 3211, Durban 4000; tel. (31) 3661007; fax (31) 366 1250; e-mail mmb@marriott.co.za; internet www.marriott.co.za; f. 1994; CEO D. A. POLKINGHORNE.

Investment Banks

Cadiz Investment Bank Ltd: Fernwood House, 1st Floor, The Oval, 1 Oakdale Rd, Newlands 7700; POB 44547, Claremont 7735; tel. 6578300; fax 6578301; e-mail reception@cadiz.co.za; internet www.cadiz.co.za; f. 1993; 15% owned by Investec, 11% Makana Financial Services; total assets 298.1m. (Dec. 2003); Chair. COLIN HALL; CEO RAM BARKAI.

Investec Bank Ltd: 100 Grayston Dr., Sandown, Sandton 2196; POB 785700, Sandton 2146; tel. (11) 2867000; fax (11) 2867777; e-mail investorrelations@investec.co.za; internet www.investec.com; f. 1974; cap. 12.6m., res 6,200m., dep. 60,400m. (December 2004); CEO S. KOSEFF; 6 brs.

Sasfin Bank Ltd: Sasfin Pl., 13–15 Scott St, Waverley 2090; POB 95104, Grant Park 2051; tel. (11) 809 7500; fax (11) 8872489; e-mail info@sasfin.com; internet www.sasfin.com; f. 1951; subsidiary of Sasfin Holdings Co; total assets 1,382.7m.; Chair. MARTIN GLATT; CEO ROLAND SASSOON.

Development Bank

Development Bank of Southern Africa (DBSA): 1258 Lever Rd, Headway Hill; POB 1234, Halfway House, Midrand 1685; tel. (11) 3133911; fax (11) 3133086; e-mail info@dbsa.org; internet www.dbsa.org; total assets 23,684.5m. (March 2004); f. 1983; Chair. JAYASEELAN NAIDOO; CEO MANDLA S. V. GANTSHO.

Discount Houses

Discount House Merchant Bank Ltd: 66 Marshall St, Johannesburg 2001; POB 61574, Marshalltown 2107; tel. (11) 8367451; fax (11) 8369636; f. 1957; cap. 18.8m.; Exec. Chair. C. J. H. DUNN; Man. Dir M. R. THOMPSON.

Interbank Ltd: 108 Fox St, POB 6035, Johannesburg; tel. (11) 8344831; fax (11) 8345357; f. 1971; cap. 15.5m., dep. 564m. (1990); Chair. A. KELLY; Man. Dir M. SWART.

SOUTH AFRICA

The National Discount House of South Africa Ltd: Loveday House, 1st Floor, 15 Loveday St, Johannesburg; tel. (11) 8323151; f. 1961; auth. cap. 10m., dep. 357.1m. (1987); Chair. M. MACDONALD; Man. Dir G. G. LUND.

Bankers' Association

Banking Council of South Africa: 17 Harrison St, 10th Floor, POB 61674, Marshalltown 2107; tel. (11) 3703500; fax (11) 8365509; e-mail banking@banking.org.za; internet www.banking.org.za; f. 1993; 15,000 mems; Chair. E. R. BOSMAN; CEO ROBERT S. K. TUCKER.

STOCK EXCHANGE

JSE Securities Exchange: 17 Diagonal St, POB 1174, Johannesburg 2000; tel. (11) 3772200; fax (11) 8387106; internet www.jse.co.za; f. 1887 as Johannesburg Stock Exchange; name changed as above in 2001; in late 1995 legislation was enacted providing for the deregulation of the Stock Exchange; automated trading commenced in June 1996; CEO R. M. LOUBSER.

INSURANCE

Allianz Insurance Ltd: Allianz House, 13 Fraser St, Johannesburg 2001; POB 62228, Marshalltown 2107; tel. (11) 2804300; fax (11) 2804309; Chair. D. DU PREEZ; Man. Dir Dr U. F. DELIUS.

Clientèle Life Assurance Co: Clientèle House, Morning View Office Park, cnr Rivonia and Alon Rds, Morningside, Johannesburg; POB 1316, Rivonia 2128; tel. (11) 3203333; e-mail services@clientelelife.com; internet www.clientelelife.com; f. 1997; subsidiary of Hollard Insurance Group; Chair. G. Q. ROUTLEDGE; Man. Dir G. J. SOLL.

Credit Guarantee Insurance Corpn of Africa Ltd: 31 Dover St, POB 125, Randburg 2125; tel. (11) 8897000; fax (11) 8861027; e-mail info@cgic.co.za; internet www.creditguarantee.co.za; f. 1956; Chair. K. T. M. SAGGERS; Man. Dir CHRIS LEISEWITZ.

Discovery: Discovery Bldg, 155 West St cnr Alice Lane, Sandton 2146; POB 786722 Sandton 2146; tel. (11) 5292888; fax (11) 5293590; e-mail worldinfo@discovery.co.za; internet www.discoveryworld.co.za; f. 1992; 64% owned by FirstRand; health and life assurance; Chair. LAURITZ L. DIPPENAAR; CEO ADRIAN GORE.

Liberty Group Ltd (LGL): Liberty Life Centre, 1 Ameshoff St, Johannesburg 2001; POB 10499, Johannesburg 2000; tel. (11) 4083911; fax (11) 4082109; e-mail info@liberty.co.za; internet www.liberty.co.za; f. 1958; Chair. D. E. COOPER; CEO MYLES RUCK.

Metropolitan Life Ltd: 7 Coen Steytler Ave, Foreshore, Cape Town; POB 2212, Bellville 7535; tel. (21) 9405911; fax (21) 9405730; internet www.metropolitan.co.za; Chair. D. E. MOSENEKE; Man. Dir P. R. DOYLE.

Momentum Life Assurers Ltd: Momentum Park, 267B West Ave, Centurion 0157; POB 7400, Centurion 0046; tel. (12) 6718911; fax (12) 6636288; internet www.momentum.co.za; f. 1967; Chair. LAURIE DIPPENAAR; Man. Dir HILLIE P. MEYER.

Mutual & Federal Insurance Co Ltd: Mutual Federal Centre, 75 President St, POB 1120, Johannesburg 2000; tel. (11) 3749111; fax (11) 3742652; internet www.mf.co.uk; f. 1970; Chair. K. T. M. SAGGERS; Man. Dir B. CAMPBELL.

Old Mutual (South African Mutual Life Assurance Society): Mutualpark, Jan Smuts Dr., POB 66, Cape Town 8001; tel. (21) 5099111; fax (21) 5094444; internet www.oldmutual.com; f. 1845; Chair. MICHAEL J. LEVETT; CEO JAMES SUTCLIFFE.

Santam Ltd: Santam Head Office, 1 Sportica Cres., Bellville 7530; POB 3881, Tyger Valley 7536; tel. (21) 9157000; fax (21) 9140700; internet www.santam.co.za; f. 1918; Chair. M. H. DALING; Man. Dir L. VERMAAK.

South African Eagle Insurance Co Ltd: SA Eagle House, The Braes, 193 Bryanston Dr., Bryanston 2021; POB 61489, Marshalltown 2107; tel. (11) 5404000; fax (11) 5404444; internet www.saeagle.co.za; Chair. M. C. SOUTH; CEO N. V. BEYERS.

South African National Life Assurance Co Ltd (SANLAM): 2 Strand Rd, Bellville; POB 1, Sanlamhof 7532; tel. (21) 9165000; fax (21) 9479440; e-mail life@sanlam.co.za; internet www.sanlam.co.za; f. 1918; Chair. Dr J. VAN ZYL.

Association

South African Insurance Association: JCC House, 3rd Floor, 27 Owl St, Milpark; POB 30619, Braamfontein 2017; tel. (11) 7265381; fax (11) 7265351; e-mail info@sainsurance.co.za; e-mail info@saia.co.za; internet www.saia.co.za; f. 1973; represents short-term insurers; Chair. RONALD S. NAPIER; CEO BARRY SCOTT.

Trade and Industry

DEVELOPMENT ORGANIZATIONS

Business Partners Ltd: 5 Wellington Rd, Parktown, Johannesburg 2193; POB 7780, Johannesburg 2000; tel. (11) 4808700; fax (11) 6422791; internet www.businesspartners.co.za; f. 1981 as Small Business Devt Corpn; invests in, and provides services to, small and medium enterprises; Chair. J. P. RUPERT; Man. Dir JO' SCHWENKE.

Industrial Development Corpn of South Africa Ltd (IDC): 19 Fredman Dr., Sandown 2196; POB 784055, Sandton 2146; tel. (11) 2693000; fax (11) 2693116; e-mail callcentre@idc.co.za; internet www.idc.co.za; f. 1940; promotes entrepreneurship and competitiveness; total assets 36,593m.; Chair. Dr WENDY Y. N. LUHABE; CEO G. M. QHENA.

The Independent Development Trust: 129 Bree St, Cape Town 8001; POB 16114, Vlaeberg 8018; tel. (21) 238030; fax (21) 238401; f. 1990; finances health and rural devt, housing and urban devt, micro-enterprises, education, school and clinic-building projects; Chair. Dr MAMPHELA RAMPHELE.

National Productivity Institute: Private Bag 235, Midrand 1685; tel. (11) 8485300; fax (11) 8485555; e-mail info@npi.co.za; internet www.npi.co.za; f. 1968; Exec. Dir Dr YVONNE DLADLA.

CHAMBER OF COMMERCE

South African Chamber of Business (SACOB): 24 Sturdee Ave, Rosebank, Johannesburg; POB 213, Saxonwold 2132; tel. (11) 4463800; fax (11) 4463847; internet www.sacob.co.za; f. 1990 by merger of Asscn of Chambers of Commerce and Industry and South African Federated Chamber of Industries; Pres. D. PENFOLD; CEO JAMES LENNOX.

CHAMBERS OF INDUSTRIES

Bloemfontein Chamber of Trade and Industry: POB 87, Kellner Heights, Bloemfontein 9300; tel. (51) 473368; fax (51) 475064.

Cape Chamber of Commerce and Industry: Cape Chamber House, 19 Louis Gradner St, Foreshore, Cape Town 8001; tel. (21) 4184300; fax (21) 4181800; f. 1994; Pres. DENIS SKEATE; 3,800 mems.

Chamber of Commerce and Industry–Johannesburg: JCC House, 6th Floor, Empire Rd, Milpark; Private Bag 34, Auckland Park 2006; tel. (11) 7265300; fax (11) 4822000; e-mail info@jcci.co.za; internet www.jcci.co.za; f. 1890; CEO MARIUS DE JAGER; 3,800 mems.

Durban Chamber of Commerce and Industry: POB 1506, Durban 4000; tel. (31) 3351000; fax (31) 3321288; e-mail chambers@durbanchamber.co.za; internet www.durbanchamber.co.za; CEO Dr J. WILSON; 5,500 mems.

Gauteng North Chamber of Commerce and Industry (GNCCI): Tshwane Events Centre, Soutter St, Pretoria; POB 2164, Pretoria 0001; tel. (12) 3271487; fax (12) 3271490; e-mail gncci-info@gncci.co.za; internet www.gncci.co.za; f. 1929; fmrly Pretoria Business and Agricultural Centre; merged with Pretoria Sakekamer in 2004; Chair. BERT BADENHORST; CEO WIM DU PLESSIS; over 900 mems.

Pietermaritzburg Chamber of Industries: POB 637, Pietermaritzburg 3200; tel. (331) 452747; fax (331) 944151; f. 1910; Dir R. J. ALLEN; 300 mems.

Port Elizabeth Regional Chamber of Commerce and Industry (PERCCI): KPMG House, 1 Norvic Dr., Greenacres, Port Elizabeth; POB 63866, Greenacres 6057; tel. (41) 3731122; fax (41) 3731142; e-mail info@pechamber.org.za; internet www.percci.co.za; f. 1995; CEO A. DA COSTA; 1,100 mems.

Wesvaal Chamber of Business (WESCOB): POB 7167, Flamwood 2572; tel. (18) 4687111; fax (18) 4687419; e-mail chamber@gds.co.za; Pres. EMÉL BROWN; c. 320 mems.

INDUSTRIAL AND TRADE ORGANIZATIONS

Association of Cementitious Material Producers: POB 10181, Centurion 0046; tel. (12) 6635146; fax (12) 6636036; e-mail naudek.acmp@mweb.co.za; Chair. P. K. STRAUSS.

Building Industries Federation South Africa: POB 1619, Halfway House, Midrand 1685; tel. (11) 3151010; fax (11) 3151644; e-mail bifsa@bifsa.org.za; internet www.bifsa.org.za; f. 1904; 5,000 mems.

Chamber of Mines of South Africa: Chamber of Mines Bldg, 5 Hollard St, POB 61809, Marshalltown 2107; tel. (11) 4987100; fax (11) 8341884; e-mail webmaster@bullion.org.za; internet www.bullion.org.za; f. 1889; Pres. RICK MENELL.

Clothing Trade Council (CloTrade): 35 Siemers Rd, 6th Floor, Doornfontein; POB 2303, Johannesburg 2000; tel. (11) 4020664; fax (11) 4020667; f. 2002; successor to the Clothing Federation of South Africa; Pres. JACK KIPLING.

SOUTH AFRICA

Grain Milling Federation: POB 7262, Centurion 0046; tel. (12) 6631660; fax (12) 6633109; e-mail info@grainmilling.org.za; internet www.grainmilling.org.za; f. 1944; Exec. Sec. JANNIE DE VILLIERS.

Industrial Rubber Manufacturers' Association of South Africa: POB 91267, Auckland Park 2006; tel. (11) 4822524; fax (11) 7261344; f. 1978; Chair. Dr D. DUNCAN.

Master Diamond Cutters' Association of South Africa: S.A. Diamond Centre, Suite 310, 240 Commissioner St, Johannesburg 2001; tel. (11) 3341930; fax (11) 3341933; e-mail diam@pixie.co.za; f. 1928; 76 mems.

National Association of Automobile Manufacturers of South Africa: Nedbank Plaza, 1st Floor, cnr Church and Beatrix Sts, Pretoria 0002; POB 40611, Arcadia 0007; tel. (12) 3232980; fax (12) 3263232; e-mail naamsa@iafrica.com; f. 1935; Dir N. M. W. VERMEULEN; 17 full mems and 8 associate mems.

National Chamber of Milling, Inc: Braamfontein; tel. (11) 4033739; f. 1936; Dir Dr J. B. DE SWARDT.

National Textile Manufacturers' Association: POB 1506, Durban 4000; tel. (31) 3013692; fax (31) 3045255; f. 1947; Sec. PETER MCGREGOR; 9 mems.

Plastics Federation of South Africa: 18 Gazelle Rd, Corporate Park South, Old Pretoria Rd, Midrand; Private Bag X68, Halfway House, Midrand 1685; tel. (11) 3144021; fax (11) 3143764; internet www.plasticsinfo.co.za; f. 1979; Exec. Dir BILL NAUDE; 3 mems.

Printing Industries Federation of South Africa (PIFSA): Printech Ave, Laser Park, POB 1084, Honeydew 2040; tel. (11) 6993000; fax (11) 6993010; e-mail pifsa@pifsa.org; internet www.pifsa.org; f. 1916; CEO C.W.J. SYKES; c. 900 mems (representing 65% of printers in South Africa).

Retail Motor Industry Organization (RMI): POB 2940, Randburg 2125; tel. (11) 8866300; fax (11) 7894525; e-mail rmi@rmi.org.za; internet www.rmi.org.za; affiliates throughout southern Africa; Dir JEFF OSBORNE; 7,800 mems.

South African Dairy Foundation: POB 72300, Lynnwood Ridge, Pretoria 0040; tel. (2712) 3485345; fax (2712) 3486284; f. 1980; Sec. S. L. VAN COLLER; 59 mems.

South African Federation of Civil Engineering Contractors (SAFCEC): POB 644, Bedfordview 2008; tel. (11) 4551700; fax (11) 4501715; e-mail admin@safcec.org.za; internet www.safcec.org.za; f. 1939; Dir H. P. LANGENHOVEN; 300 mems.

South African Fruit and Vegetable Canners' Association (Pty) Ltd (SAFVCA): Hoofstraat 258 Main St, POB 6175, Paarl 7622; tel. (21) 8711308; fax (21) 8725930; e-mail safvpa@mweb.co.za; f. 1953; Gen. Man. TERRY R. M. MALONE; 9 mems.

South African Inshore Fishing Industry Association (Pty) Ltd: POB 2066, Cape Town 8000; tel. (21) 251500; f. 1953; Chair. W. A. LEWIS; Man. S. J. MALHERBE; 4 mems.

South African Lumber Millers' Association: Private Bag X686, Isando 1600; tel. (11) 9741061; fax (11) 9749779; e-mail jmort@salma.org.za; internet www.salma.org.za; f. 1941; Exec. Dir J. H. MORTIMER; 88 mems.

South African Oil Expressers' Association: Cereal Centre, 6th Floor, 11 Leyds St, Braamfontein 2017; tel. (11) 7251280; f. 1937; Sec. Dr R. DU TOIT; 14 mems.

South African Paint Manufacturers' Association: POB 751605, Gardenview, Johannesburg 2047; tel. (11) 4552503; fax (11) 4552502; e-mail sapma@sapma.org.za; internet www.sapma.org.za; Chair. DERYCK SPENCE; 80 mems.

South African Petroleum Industry Association (SAPIA): Cape Town; represents South Africa's six principal petroleum cos; Chair. FRED PHASWANA.

South African Sugar Association (SASA): 170 Flanders Dr., POB 700, Mount Edgecombe 4300; tel. (31) 5087000; fax (31) 5087199; e-mail sugarmail@sasa.org.za; internet www.sugar.org.za; Exec. Dir M. K. TRIKAM.

Includes:

South African Sugar Millers' Association Ltd (SASMAL): POB 1000, Mt Edgecombe 4300; tel. (31) 5087300; fax (31) 5087310; e-mail sasmal@sasa.org.za; represents interests of sugar millers and refiners within the operations of SASA; Exec. Dir D. W. HARDY; 6 mem cos.

Sugar Manufacturing and Refining Employers' Association (SMREA): POB 1000, Mount Edgecombe 4300; tel. (31) 5087300; fax (31) 5087310; e-mail sasmal@sasa.org.za; f. 1947; regulates relations between mems and their employees; participates in the Bargaining Council for the sugar manufacturing and refining industry; Chair. C. H. KYLE; 6 mem. cos.

South African Wool Board: POB 2191, Port Elizabeth 6056; tel. (41) 544301; fax (41) 546760; f. 1946; 12 mems: nine appointed by wool-growers and three by the Minister of Agriculture and Land Affairs; Chair. H. F. PRINSLOO; CEO Dr J. W. GIESELBACH.

South African Wool Textile Council: POB 2201, North End, Port Elizabeth 6056; tel. (41) 4845252; fax (41) 4845629; Sec. BEATTY-ANNE STARKEY.

Steel and Engineering Industries Federation of South Africa (SEIFSA): POB 1338, Johannesburg 2000; tel. (11) 8336033; fax (11) 8381522; e-mail angelique@seifsa.co.za; internet www.seifsa.co.za; f. 1943; Exec. Dir. B. ANGUS; 39 affiliated trade asscns representing 2,350 mems.

VinPro (SA): POB 1411, Suider-Parl 7624; tel. (21) 8073322; fax (21) 8632079; e-mail info@vinpro.co.za; internet www.vinpro.co.za; f. 1979; represents wine producers; Chair. ABRIE BOTHA; Exec. Dir JOS LE ROUX.

UTILITIES

Electricity

Electricity Supply Commission (ESKOM): POB 1091, Johannesburg 2000; tel. (11) 8008111; fax (11) 8004390; internet www.eskom.co.za; f. 1923; state-controlled; CEO A. J. MORGAN.

Gas

SASOL Gas: POB 4211, Randburg 2125; tel. (11) 8897600; fax (11) 8897955; internet www.sasol.com/gas; f. 1964; Man. Dir HANS NAUDÉ.

Water

Umgeni Water: 310 Burger St, Pietermaritzburg 3201; tel. (331) 3411111; fax (331) 3411167; internet www.umgeni.co.za/contact.html.

Water Research Commission: Private Bag X03, Gezina 0031; tel. (12) 3300340; fax (12) 3312565; e-mail orders@wrc.org.za; internet www.wrc.org.za; Chair. Prof. H. C. KASAN; CEO Dr RIVKA KFIR.

TRADE UNIONS

In 1994 the number of registered unions totalled 213, with a membership that represented about 24% of the economically active population. In addition there were an estimated 65 unregistered unions, with a membership of about 510,000. According to COSATU, some 40% of workers were unionized at March 2005.

Trade Union Federations

Congress of South African Trade Unions (COSATU): COSATU House, 4th Floor, 1–5 Leyds St, Braamfontein; POB 1019, Johannesburg 2000; tel. (11) 3394911; fax (11) 3396940; e-mail cosatu@wn.apc.org; internet www.cosatu.org.za; f. 1985; 19 trade union affiliates representing c. 1.8m. mems; Pres. WILLIE MADISHA; Gen. Sec. ZWELINZIMA VAVI.

Principal affiliates include:

Construction and Allied Workers' Union: POB 1962, Johannesburg 2000; tel. (11) 294321; fax (11) 3371578; Pres. D. NGCOBO; Gen. Sec. L. MADUMA.

Food and Allied Workers' Union: POB 234, Salt River 7925; tel. (21) 6379040; fax (21) 6383761; Pres. ERNEST THERON; Gen. Sec. MANDLA GXANYANA.

Health and Allied Workers' Union: POB 47011, Greyville 4023; tel. (11) 3063993; Gen. Sec. S. NGCOBO.

National Education, Health and Allied Workers' Union: 56 Marshall St, Marshalltown, POB 10812, Johannesburg 2000; tel. (11) 8332902; fax (11) 8343416; Pres. VUSI NHLAPO; Gen. Sec. FIKILE MAJOLE.

National Union of Metalworkers of South Africa (NUMSA): 153 Bree St, Newtown, POB 260483, Johannesburg 2001; tel. (11) 8322031; fax (11) 8384092; e-mail dumisan@numsa.org.za; internet www.numsa.org.za; Pres. M. TOM; Gen. Sec. SILUMKO NONDWANGU; 232,000 mems (2000).

National Union of Mineworkers: 7 Rissik St, POB 2424, Johannesburg 2000; tel. (11) 3772000; fax (11) 8366051; e-mail tmlabatheki@num.org.za; internet www.num.org.za; f. 1982; Pres. SENZENI ZOKWANA; Gen. Sec. GWEDE MANTASHE; 350,000 mems.

Paper, Printing, Wood and Allied Workers' Union: POB 3528, Johannesburg 2000; tel. (11) 3317721; fax (11) 3313750; Pres. P. DYANI; Gen. Sec. B. MTHOMBENI.

Post and Telecommunications Workers' Association: POB 260100, Excom 2023; tel. (11) 234351; Pres. K. MOSUNKULU; Gen. Sec. V. A. KHUMALO.

Southern African Clothing and Textile Workers' Union (SACTWU): POB 203, Woodstock 7915; tel. (21) 4474570; fax (21) 4472194; e-mail lynnt@sactwu.co.za; Pres. A. NTULI; Gen. Sec. EBRAHIM PATEL; 110,000 mems.

SOUTH AFRICA

Directory

South African Railways and Harbours Workers' Union: POB 8059, Johannesburg 2000; tel. (11) 8343251; fax (11) 8344664; Pres. J. LANGA; Gen. Sec. M. SEBEKOANE.

South African Transport and Allied Workers' Union: POB 9451, Johannesburg 2000; tel. (11) 3319321; fax (11) 3315418; Pres. EZROM MABYANA; Gen. Sec. RANDALL HOWARD.

Federation of Unions of South Africa (FEDUSA): Fedusa House, 10 Kingfisher St, Horizon Park, POB 7779, Westgate 1734; tel. (11) 2791800; fax (11) 2791821; e-mail fedusa@fedusa.org.za; internet www.fedusa.org.za; Gen. Sec. CHEZ MILANI.

National Council of Trade Unions (NACTU): Lekton House, 7th Floor, 5 Wanderers St, POB 10928, Johannesburg 2000; tel. (11) 3368031; fax (11) 3337625; f. 1986; fed. of 22 African trade unions; Pres. JAMES MDLALOSE; Gen. Sec. CUNNINGHAM MCGUKAMU.

Principal affiliates include:

Building, Construction and Allied Workers' Union: POB 96, Johannesburg 2000; tel. (11) 236311; Pres. J. SEISA; Gen. Sec. V. THUSI.

Hotel, Liquor and Catering Trade Employees' Union: POB 1409, Johannesburg 2000; tel. (11) 234039; Pres. E. NKOSI (acting); Gen. Sec. K. KEELE (acting).

Metal and Electrical Workers' Union of South Africa: POB 3669, Johannesburg 2000; tel. (11) 8369051; fax (11) 8369002; f. 1989; Pres. RUSSELL SABOR; Gen. Sec. ZITHULELE CINDI.

National Union of Farm Workers: POB 10928, Johannesburg 2000; tel. (11) 333054; fax (11) 337625; Pres. E. MUSEKWA; Gen. Sec. T. MOLETSANE.

National Union of Food, Beverage, Wine, Spirits and Allied Workers: POB 5718, Johannesburg 2000; tel. (11) 3335561; fax (1) 3333480; Pres. M. L. KWELEMTINI; Gen. Sec. L. SIKHAKHANE.

National Union of Public Service Workers: POB 10928, Johannesburg 2000; tel. (11) 232812; Pres. K. NTHUTE; Gen. Sec. S. RADEBE.

South African Chemical Workers' Union: POB 236, Johannesburg 2000; tel. (11) 8386581; fax (11) 8386622; Pres. W. THUTHANI; Gen. Sec. O. H. NDABA.

Steel, Engineering and Allied Workers' Union of South Africa: POB 4283, Johannesburg 2001; tel. (11) 3364865; fax (11) 294869; Pres. G. MABIDIKAMA; Gen. Sec. N. RAMAEMA.

South African Confederation of Labour: POB 19299, Pretoria West 0117; tel. (12) 793271; 7 mems; Pres. I. J. ELS; Sec. L. N. CELLIERS.

South African Independent Trade Unions Confederation (SAITUCO): f. 1995 by 14 independent trade unions that opposed the new draft legislation on labour relations; Pres. PIET SKHOSANA; Gen. Sec. THEMBA NCALO.

Transport

Most of South Africa's railway network and the harbours and airways are administered by the state-owned Transnet Ltd. There are no navigable rivers. Private bus services are regulated to complement the railways.

Transnet Ltd: 8 Hillside Rd, Parktown, Johannesburg; POB 72501, Parkview 2122; tel. (11) 4887055; fax (11) 4887511; e-mail sakim@transnet.co.za; internet www.transnet.co.za; Chair. BONGANI AUG KHUMALO; CEO MARIA RAMOS.

RAILWAYS

With the exception of commuter services, the South African railways system is operated by Spoornet Ltd (the rail division of Transnet). The network comprised 31,400 track-km in 1996, of which 16,946 km was electrified. Extensive rail links connect Spoornet with the rail networks of neighbouring countries.

Spoornet: Paul Kruger Bldg, 30 Wolmarans St, Private Bag X47, Johannesburg 2001; tel. (11) 7735090; fax (11) 7733033; internet www.spoornet.co.za; CEO ZANDILE JAKARULA.

ROADS

In 1999 there were an estimated 534,131 km of classified roads, including 2,032 km of motorways. In 2004 there were 7,200 km of main roads.

South African National Roads Agency Ltd (SANRAL): Ditsela Pl., 1204 Park St, cnr Duncan St, Hatfield, Pretoria; POB 415, Pretoria 0001; tel. (12) 4266000; fax (12) 3622116; e-mail info@nra.co.za; internet www.nra.co.za; f. 1998; responsible for design, construction, management and maintenance of 13,933 km of the nat. road network (2005); Chair. LOT NDLOVU; CEO NAZIR ALLI.

SHIPPING

The principal harbours are at Richards Bay, Durban, Saldanha, Cape Town, Port Elizabeth, East London and Mossel Bay. Construction of an eighth port, at Ngqura (Coega), was ongoing in early 2006. The deep-water port at Richards Bay has been extended and its facilities upgraded. Both Richards Bay and Saldanha Bay are major bulk-handling ports, while Saldanha Bay also has an important fishing fleet. More than 30 shipping lines serve South African ports.

National Ports Authority (NPA): POB 32696, Braamfontein 2017; tel. (11) 2424022; fax (11) 2424027; internet www.npa.co.za; f. 2000; fmrly part of Portnet; subsidiary of Transnet; controls and manages the country's seven major seaports; CEO KHOMOTSO PHIHLELA (acting).

South African Maritime Safety Authority: Block E, Hatfield Gardens, 333 Grosvenor St, Hatfield, Pretoria SAMSA; POB 13186, Hatfield 0028; tel. (12) 3423049; fax (12) 3423160; e-mail samsa@iafrica.com; advises the Govt on matters connected with sea transport to, from or between South Africa's ports, incl. safety at sea, and prevention of pollution by petroleum; CEO Capt. B. R. WATT.

South African Port Operations (SAPO): Marine Parade, POB 10124, Durban 4056; tel. (31) 3088333; fax (31) 3088352; e-mail webmaster@saportops.co.za; internet www.saponet.co.za; f. 2000; fmrly part of Portnet; subsidiary of Transnet; operates 13 container, bulk, breakbulk and car terminals at six of the country's major ports; CEO TAU MORWE.

CIVIL AVIATION

Civil aviation is controlled by the Minister of Transport. The Chief Directorate: Civil Aviation Authority at the Department of Transport is responsible for licensing and control of domestic and international air services.

Airports Company South Africa (ACSA): 24 Johnson Rd, Riverwoods, Bedfordview 2008; POB 75480, Gardenview 2047; tel. (11) 9216991; internet www.airports.co.za; f. 1993; owns and operates South Africa's nine principal airports, of which three (at Johannesburg, Cape Town and Durban) are classified as int. airports; Chair. TOMMY OLIPHANT; Man. Dir MONHLA HLAHLA.

Civil Aviation Authority (CAA): Ikhaya Lokundiza, Bldg 16, Treur Close, Waterfall Park, Bekker St, Midrand; Private Bag X73, Halfway House 1685; tel. (11) 5451000; fax (12) 5451465; e-mail mail@caa.co.za; internet www.caa.co.za; Chair. DUKE MOOROSI; CEO MONGEZI INDIA (acting).

Air Cape (Pty) Ltd: POB D. F. Malan Airport, Cape Town 7525; tel. (21) 9340344; fax (21) 9348379; scheduled internal passenger services and charters, engineering services and aerial surveys; Chair. Dr P. VAN ASWEGEN; Gen. Man. G. A. NORTJE.

Airlink Airline: POB 7529, Bonaero Park 1622; tel. (11) 3953579; fax (11) 3951319; internet www.saairlink.co.za; f. 1992; internal and external scheduled services and charters in Southern Africa; Man. Dirs RODGER FOSTER, BARRIE WEBB.

COMAIR Ltd: POB 7015, Bonaero Park 1622; tel. (11) 9210111; fax (11) 9733913; e-mail comair.co.za; internet www.comair.co.za; f. 1946; scheduled domestic, regional and international services; Chair. D. NOVICK; Man. Dir P. VAN HOVEN.

Safair (Pty) Ltd: POB 938, Kempton Park 1620; tel. 9280000; fax 3951314; e-mail marketing@safair.co.za; internet www.safair.co.za; f. 1965; subsidiary of Imperial Holdings Ltd; aircraft leasing, engineering and maintenance services; Chair. R. J. BOËTTGER; CEO C. KOK.

South African Airways (SAA): Airways Park, Jones Rd, Private Bag X13, Johannesburg 1627; tel. (11) 9781111; fax (11) 9781106; internet www.flysaa.com; f. 1934; state-owned; internal passenger services linking all the principal towns; international services to Africa, Europe, North and South America and Asia; Chair. JAKES GERWEL; CEO KHAYA NGQULA.

Tourism

Tourism is an important part of South Africa's economy. The chief attractions for visitors are the climate, scenery and wildlife reserves. In 2003 some 6.6m. tourists visited South Africa. In that year receipts from tourism amounted to US $5,232m.

South African Tourism (SATOUR): Bojanala House, 90 Protea Rd, Chislehurston, Johannesburg 2196; Private Bag X10012, Sandton 2146; tel. (11) 8953000; fax (11) 8953001; e-mail info@southafrica.net; internet www.southafrica.net; f. 1947; 11 overseas brs; CEO MOEKETSI MOSOLA.

SPAIN

Introductory Survey

Location, Climate, Language, Religion, Flag, Capital

The Kingdom of Spain, in south-western Europe, forms more than four-fifths of the Iberian peninsula. The country also includes the Balearic Islands in the Mediterranean Sea, the Canary Islands in the Atlantic Ocean and a few small enclaves in Morocco. Mainland Spain is bounded to the north by France and to the west by Portugal. To the east is the Mediterranean Sea, and Morocco lies 30 km to the south. The climate is less temperate than in most of western Europe, with hot summers and, in the hilly interior, cold winters. The principal language is Castilian Spanish. Catalan is widely spoken in the north-east, Basque in the north and Galician in the north-west. The overwhelming majority of the population are Roman Catholics, but the 1978 Constitution laid down that Spain had no official state religion. The national flag (proportions 2 by 3) carries three horizontal stripes, of red, yellow (half the depth) and red. The state flag carries, in addition, the national coat of arms. The capital is Madrid.

Recent History

After winning the civil war of 1936–39, the Nationalist forces, led by Gen. Francisco Franco y Bahamonde, established an authoritarian rule which provided peace and stability, while restricting individual liberties and severely repressing challenges to its power. In 1942 Gen. Franco revived the traditional legislative assembly, the Cortes ('Courts'), with limited powers. After keeping Spain neutral in the Second World War, Gen. Franco announced in 1947 that the monarchy (abolished in 1931) would be restored after his death or retirement. In 1967, in the first elections since the civil war, a portion of the Cortes was directly elected under a limited franchise. In July 1969 Gen. Franco nominated Prince Juan Carlos de Borbón (grandson of the last reigning monarch, King Alfonso XIII) as his successor, and in June 1973 relinquished the post of President of the Council of Ministers to Adm. Luis Carrero Blanco, who was killed in December. Responsibility for the assassination was claimed by Euskadi ta Askatasuna (ETA, Basque Homeland and Liberty), the Basque separatist organization. Carlos Arias Navarro became Prime Minister in January 1974.

Gen. Franco died in November 1975. He was succeeded as Head of State by King Juan Carlos, and in December a more liberal Council of Ministers was formed. In 1976 restrictions on political activity were lifted, but the slow progress of the reforms resulted in widespread demonstrations. In July Arias Navarro resigned at the King's request, and was replaced by Adolfo Suárez González. The introduction of democratic government then proceeded rapidly. Political reforms included the establishment of an elected bicameral legislature. Most of the numerous *de facto* political parties were able to take part in the general elections for the Cortes, held in June 1977. An overall majority was won by the Unión de Centro Democrático (UCD), a coalition party headed by the Prime Minister. In December 1978 a new Constitution was endorsed by referendum and ratified by the King. It confirmed Spain as a parliamentary monarchy, with freedom for political parties, and guaranteed the right of Spain's 'nationalities and regions' to autonomy.

A general election was held in March 1979, resulting in little change in the distribution of seats in the Cortes, although there was stronger support for the regionalist parties. The new Government was again headed by Suárez. Basque and Catalan autonomous parliaments were established in March 1980 and, in both elections, the UCD was heavily defeated by the moderate regionalist parties. Confidence in Suárez diminished and in January 1981, as a result of growing opposition from right-wing factions within the UCD, he unexpectedly resigned. Leopoldo Calvo Sotelo, hitherto the Deputy Prime Minister, succeeded him.

In February 1981 a group of armed civil guards, led by Lt-Col Antonio Tejero Molina, stormed into the Cortes, taking hostage 350 deputies. The military commander of Valencia, Lt-Gen. Jaime Milans del Bosch, declared a state of emergency in that region and sent tanks on to the streets of the city of Valencia. King Juan Carlos acted swiftly to secure the loyalty of other military commanders, and by the following morning had been able to persuade Lt-Gen. Milans himself to stand down. Lt-Col Tejero surrendered, and the deputies were released unharmed. More than 30 military officers were subsequently brought to trial, and both Lt-Col Tejero and Lt-Gen. Milans received lengthy prison sentences. Lt-Gen. Milans was released in 1990, and Lt-Col Tejero was released in 1996.

Immediately after the attempted coup, Calvo Sotelo formed a new Council of Ministers, resisting pressure to establish a coalition government. The Prime Minister addressed various contentious issues during his term of office, including his decision to take Spain into the North Atlantic Treaty Organization (NATO, see p. 314). At the election for the first Galician Parliament, held in October 1981, the Alianza Popular (AP) won two seats more than the UCD. The overwhelming Socialist victory at the election for the Parliament of Andalucía in May 1982 was a grave set-back for the central Government. Following Calvo Sotelo's replacement as party leader by Landelino Lavilla Alsina in July, Suárez defected to found a rival party, the Centro Democrático y Social (CDS). Desertion from the UCD continued and by August the party no longer commanded a workable majority, and an early general election was called. In October, however, shortly before the election, a right-wing plot to stage a pre-emptive military coup was uncovered. Four colonels were arrested (three of whom were subsequently sentenced to prison terms), and Lt-Gen. Milans was also implicated. The election resulted in a decisive victory for the Partido Socialista Obrero Español (PSOE—Socialist Workers' Party), led by Felipe González Márquez, who formed a new Council of Ministers in December 1982.

One of the most serious problems facing the new Government was the continuing tension in the Basque region (see below). The Government's proposals for the rationalization of Spain's industry and bureaucracy, instigated in 1983, met with strong opposition from the trade unions and the general public. In June 1985 hundreds of thousands of workers, motivated by the Unión General de Trabajadores (UGT—the socialist trade union) and supported by the Confederación Sindical de Comisiones Obreras (CCOO—the left-wing trade union), protested against proposed reforms in the social security system and consequent reductions in pension rights. Following large-scale demonstrations against Spain's continued membership of NATO, in March 1986 the long-awaited referendum on the question of Spain's membership of NATO was held. Contrary to expectations, the Spanish people voted to remain within the alliance, following Prime Minister González's reversal on the issue and an extensive pro-NATO campaign by the Government.

In an early general election held in June 1986 the PSOE was returned to power, winning 184 of the 350 seats in the Congreso de los Diputados (Congress of Deputies), 18 fewer than at the 1982 election, while the conservative Coalición Popular (CP), which incorporated the AP, the Partido Demócrata Popular (subsequently Democracia Cristiana) and the Partido Liberal, won 105 seats. The new Council of Ministers was appointed in late July, again led by González. Following its defeat, the CP fell into disarray, and in December Manuel Fraga, the leader of the AP, the principal component of the conservative grouping, resigned. Industrial unrest continued with frequent strikes against the Government's economic policies, notably its commitment to pay restraint; the public transport sector was particularly badly affected.

In June 1987 the results of the elections for the European Parliament, for 13 of the 17 regional parliaments and for the municipal governments confirmed the continuing decline in support for the PSOE. The AP also sustained losses, while the centre-left CDS was able to strengthen its position. The growing rift between the Prime Minister and the UGT became increasingly evident during 1987, and in October Nicolás Redondo, the UGT leader, and a union colleague resigned from their seats as PSOE deputies in the Cortes, in protest against the Government's economic policies. The UGT and the CCOO then combined forces to organize a new campaign of protests against the Government, which continued throughout 1988, culminating in

December in a one-day general strike (the first since 1934), which was supported by almost 8m. workers. In April 1989 Madrid was brought to a halt by strikers demanding pay increases of up to 8%. Similar strikes elsewhere in Spain followed.

In January 1989 Fraga returned to the leadership of the AP, which was relaunched as the Partido Popular (PP) and was subsequently joined by Democracia Cristiana and the Partido Liberal. The unity of the PSOE was undermined by the establishment of a dissident faction and by the defection to the Izquierda Unida (IU, an alliance comprising the Partido Comunista de España (PCE) and other left-wing parties) of 100 PSOE members. Nevertheless, at the general election, held eight months early, in late October 1989, the PSOE was returned to power on a provisional basis, pending investigations into allegations of polling irregularities. After several months of controversy, the PSOE's final representation in the Congreso de los Diputados was reduced to 175 of the 350 seats, the PP holding 107 seats. The PSOE, however, was able to retain a majority by subsequently entering into a tactical alliance with the CDS, the Catalan Convergència i Unió (CiU) and the Partido Nacionalista Vasco (PNV, also known as Euzko Alderdi Jeltzalea—Basque Nationalist Party).

In April 1990 a corruption scandal involving the financing of the opposition PP was revealed, and a number of party officials and business executives were arrested in connection with allegations of bribery. It was alleged that the PP had received funds from companies that were seeking planning permission or hoping to win municipal contracts. Furthermore, it was suggested that both José María Aznar, the new leader of the PP, and Fraga, his predecessor, had been aware of these illegal activities. The integrity of the PP, and indeed of other political parties, was therefore brought into question.

Following the revelation of a scandal involving his brother, in January 1991 the Deputy Prime Minister, Alfonso Guerra, resigned. He was replaced by Narcís Serra, hitherto Minister of Defence. An extensive government reorganization followed in March. Local elections were held in May, to coincide with elections to the regional parliaments. Although remaining the most widely supported party, the PSOE lost control of several major cities. The CDS suffered heavy losses, as a result of which Suárez, the party leader and former Prime Minister, resigned. In June Carlos Navarro, a senior PSOE treasurer, was obliged to resign, following the exposure of a scandal concerning alleged illicit donations to the ruling party. In January 1992, as labour unrest and protests against the Government's programme of industrial restructuring and attendant job losses continued, a fresh scandal arose, leading to the resignation of the Minister of Health and Consumer Affairs, Julián García Valverde. It was alleged that in 1990, while head of RENFE (the state railways organization), García Valverde had been responsible for fraudulent land purchases. Public concern at apparent widespread corruption increased further in February, when a new financial scandal was revealed, this time involving the Governor of the Central Bank, Mariano Rubio, who was accused of irregularities relating to his personal investments.

In early 1993 the PSOE's reputation was further damaged by new revelations concerning the party's financing. Having refused to permit inspection of its accounts, in late 1992 the PSOE headquarters had been forcibly searched on the orders of the judge investigating the allegations. The 'Filesa case', as the principal scandal became known, was named after a bogus Barcelona holding company which, it was claimed, had been administered by senior PSOE officials, including Navarro. It was alleged that during 1989–91 illicit contributions, totalling an estimated 1,000m. pesetas, had been made to Filesa by both private companies and public corporations, in return for fictitious consultancy work. Following a Supreme Court inquiry into the affair, PSOE officials, business executives and bankers were charged; the trial of 12 defendants, including Navarro, opened in July 1997. In September González, the previous Prime Minister, and Guerra, his former deputy, were obliged to give evidence in court. In late October Navarro was sentenced to a total of 11 years' imprisonment. Seven other defendants were sentenced to terms of imprisonment, including former Senator Josep Maria Sala, who received three years. In December 1997, however, Sala was released pending an appeal. (The sentences of Navarro and the remaining defendants had also been suspended by July 2001.) In May 1993 the ruling party's difficulties were compounded by fresh allegations of misconduct, this time concerning the funding in 1986 of the campaign for the referendum to remain in NATO and for the legislative elections of that year.

At the general election in June 1993 the PSOE failed to obtain an absolute majority in the Congreso de los Diputados, where its strength declined to 159 of the 350 seats. The PP increased its representation to 141 seats, while the IU won 18 seats, the CiU 17 and the PNV five. The CDS lost all of its seats. The PSOE's negotiations with the CiU (which insisted upon greater control over taxes in return for support) and with the PNV failed to result in the conclusion of a formal coalition agreement. In July, therefore, González commenced his fourth term as Prime Minister, at the head of a minority administration. With the Spanish economy in recession the Prime Minister appealed for support for drastic measures to address the economic crisis. In November, however, thousands of protesters demonstrated against the Government's economic policies. Controversial labour legislation, as amended to comply with CiU requests, was approved by the Congreso in March 1994.

In November 1993 the Government was embarrassed by the discovery of an illegal telephone 'tapping' network, centred on a respected Barcelona newspaper. The existence of a complex espionage and extortion operation was subsequently revealed, in which former agents of the country's military intelligence service, Centro Superior de Información de la Defensa (CESID), were implicated. In late June 1995 González accepted the resignations of Serra, the former Minister of Defence and current Deputy Prime Minister, and of Julián García Vargas, Serra's successor as Minister of Defence, following the exposure of the operation. In May 1999 Lt-Gen. Emilio Alonso Manglano, the former director of CESID, and Col Juan Alberto Perote, the intelligence service's former head of operations, both received a six-month prison sentence and were barred from public office for eight years for their part in the illegal recording of private telephone conversations during 1984–91, victims having included King Juan Carlos and senior politicians. Manglano and Perote were both pardoned in May 2001.

In April 1994 fresh accusations of tax evasion and 'insider' stock trading were made against Rubio, the former Governor of the Central Bank. In May he was arrested and imprisoned, along with Manuel de la Concha, a former chairman of the Madrid stock exchange. Meanwhile, in April another government appointee, Luis Roldán, the former head of the paramilitary Civil Guard, absconded while under investigation on charges of tax fraud and embezzlement of government funds. It was alleged that Roldán's substantial personal wealth was derived from the misappropriation of the Ministry of the Interior's covert-operations reserves (notably for the financing of the counter-terrorist grouping Grupos Antiterroristas de Liberación—GAL, see below). Antoni Asunción, who had been appointed Minister of the Interior in November 1993, was obliged to resign. Having been captured in Laos in 1995, Roldán was found guilty in February 1998 of fraud, embezzlement and tax evasion, and was sentenced to a total of 28 years' imprisonment; in December 1999 his sentence was increased to 31 years. (In May 1996 Roldán also became implicated in the murders of José Antonio Lasa and José Ignacio Zabala—see below.)

In May 1994 the Minister of Agriculture resigned, following an admission of his failure, 10 years previously, to fulfil tax obligations on personal investments also handled by Manuel de la Concha. Furthermore, a number of former government ministers, including Carlos Solchaga, Minister of Finance during Rubio's tenure of office and a close associate of González, announced their intention to relinquish their seats in the Cortes.

Following the failure in December 1993 of the Banco Español de Crédito (Banesto) and the revelation of its huge debts and of irregularities, in June 1994 Mario Conde, the bank's former head, was accused of having conducted fraudulent operations. He was formally charged in November 1994, along with several other former executives of the bank. In March 1997 Conde received a six-year prison sentence, was fined 18m. pesetas and was ordered to pay 600m. pesetas in compensation to Banesto. At the opening in December of a new trial on other charges of fraud and embezzlement, Conde reappeared in court along with 10 former associates. In February 1998 the Supreme Court confirmed a prison sentence of four-and-a-half years (instead of the original six years). Conde was released in August 1999, but in March 2000 he was sentenced to 10 years' imprisonment upon conviction on charges of fraud and misappropriation during his chairmanship of Banesto.

Confidence in the country's financial system was further undermined by the arrest in October 1994 of Javier de la Rosa, the prominent Barcelona financier, pending the investigation of charges of fraud and misappropriation of funds, brought in the United Kingdom by the Kuwait Investment Office. In July 1997, furthermore, it was reported that (during the campaign for elections to the Catalan Parliament in 1991) de la Rosa had made a substantial contribution to PP funds. Appearing in court in November 1997, de la Rosa confirmed the donation. In November 2002 de la Rosa was sentenced to 20 months' imprisonment.

Meanwhile, in mid-1988 the PSOE Government had been embarrassed by suggestions that it had been involved in the establishment of GAL, which had been formed in 1983 with the aim of combating ETA. It was alleged that members of the Ertzaintza (Basque police force) had given support to these death squads, which were suspected of responsibility for the murders of numerous ETA members exiled in France. The Ministry of the Interior in Madrid was also implicated in the scandal. In July 1988 a senior police-officer in Bilbao, José Amedo Fouce, and an accomplice, Michel Domínguez, were formally charged with organizing the groups of mercenaries. Their trial concluded in mid-1991, both defendants receiving long prison sentences. In December 1994, following further questioning of the pair and the reopening of the case, Julián Sancristóbal, a former director-general of state security in the Ministry of the Interior, was arrested on suspicion of financing and assisting GAL. The Prime Minister denied that the Government had been connected in any way with the so-called 'dirty war' against ETA. At the end of the month the Minister of Justice and the Interior was obliged to appear before a congressional commission of inquiry.

In January 1995 the investigating judge, Baltasar Garzón, ordered the arrest of the former personal assistant of Rafael Vera, ex-Secretary of State for Security, on suspicion of embezzlement. Vera himself was detained in the following month, accused of involvement in the kidnapping in 1983 of Segundo Marey, a French business executive mistaken for an ETA member, and of misappropriation of public funds. In early 1995 the Prime Minister came under increasing pressure over the GAL affair. In March the remains of José Antonio Lasa and José Ignacio Zabala, two ETA members apparently tortured before being murdered by GAL in 1983, were identified by forensic scientists. An inquiry into their fate had been closed in 1988, ostensibly owing to lack of evidence. A new inquiry into their deaths was instigated. In April 1995, concluding that GAL had been established and financed by the Ministry of the Interior, Judge Garzón indicted a total of 14 former officials, including Vera and Sancristóbal, both of whom were subsequently released on bail.

Despite the gravity of the latest scandals and the PSOE's heavy losses at the municipal and regional elections of May 1995, the Prime Minister continued to reject demands for his resignation. In July, however, he announced that a general election would be held in early 1996. At the end of July 1995 Judge Garzón submitted to the Supreme Court a report of his investigations into the origins and financing of GAL. His findings implicated González, the former Deputy Prime Minister and Minister of Defence, Serra, the Minister of the Interior during 1982–88, José Barrionuevo, the Basque socialist leader, Txiki Benegas and other PSOE officials. In a separate development, it was reported that, prior to their murders in 1983, Lasa and Zabala had been abducted by a group of civil guards and detained in San Sebastián in a building owned by the Ministry of the Interior. In August 1995, appearing before Judge Garzón, Lt-Gen. Manglano, who in June had resigned as director of CESID prior to being formally charged, denied the existence of secret service documents relating to GAL.

In September 1995, shortly after the Supreme Court's appointment of Judge Eduardo Móner to examine the allegations against the Prime Minister and the other senior politicians, the CiU formally withdrew its support for the ruling party. In the same month the Prime Minister's claim that there existed a plot to discredit his administration appeared to assume some credibility when it was reported that Conde, the disgraced banker, had attempted to blackmail the Government by threatening to release stolen CESID documents relating to GAL, if the legal action against him were not withdrawn and compensation paid. In June 1997 Conde admitted to having used the stolen documents in his blackmail attempts. (In July 1997 Col Perote, the former head of operations at CESID, was sentenced by a military court to seven years' imprisonment for the theft of the documents; he was released in April 1999.) In a magazine interview in February 1998, Luis María Anson, former director of the conservative newspaper *ABC*, disclosed that he had been a member of a media group that had indeed conspired to bring down the Government of González. The PP was also implicated in the affair.

Also in September 1995 Sancristóbal declared before Judge Móner that the abduction of Marey in 1983 had been approved by both Barrionuevo and Vera. In October 1995 José Luis Corcuera (who had succeeded Barrionuevo as Minister of the Interior), Sancristóbal and Vera were charged with misuse of public funds.

In January 1996, his parliamentary immunity having been removed, Barrionuevo was indicted by the Supreme Court. His alleged involvement in the 'dirty war' of the 1980s related to three charges: illegal detention (the abduction of Marey); misuse of public funds; and association with an armed group. In April Judge Móner reported that he had found no evidence linking González to the activities of the death squads, believed to be responsible for the murders of 27 ETA members. Serra and Benegas were also exonerated. In May several members of the Civil Guard, including Gen. Enrique Rodríguez Galindo and two other senior generals, were detained in connection with the GAL inquiry. Charges included involvement in the murders of Lasa and Zabala. In June 1996 Vera was charged with concealing these two murders, while the former Governor of Guipúzcoa, Julen Elgorriaga, was also imprisoned in connection with the case.

In August 1996 the Government approved draft legislation clarifying the regulations on official secrets. In late August, however, the investigating judge, Javier Gómez de Liaño, accused the Government of obstructing his inquiry by refusing to declassify CESID documents relating to the 'dirty war'. The matter was referred to the Supreme Court. In November 1996 the Supreme Court voted not to pursue the case against González, Serra and Benegas, as there was insufficient evidence to connect the former Prime Minister and his colleagues to the activities of GAL. (In November 1999 the Supreme Court refused a further request for an investigation into González's alleged involvement in the events of the 'dirty war'.)

In December 1996 the General Council of Judicial Power ordered an investigation into the release to the press of the CESID documents in question. In March 1997 the Supreme Court ordered the declassification of 13 of the 16 CESID documents, thereby permitting their use as evidence in court. In April Judge Móner concluded his inquiry into the abduction of Marey. In September the Supreme Court confirmed that 12 defendants were to stand trial: Barrionuevo, former Minister of the Interior; Vera, former Secretary of State for Security; Ricardo García Damborenea, a former PSOE official; Sancristóbal, Amedo and Domínguez, the former civil guards; and six others. In April 1998 the Supreme Court ruled that González, the former Prime Minister, and Francisco Alvarez-Cascos, the current Deputy Prime Minister, were to give evidence in court in relation to the abduction of Marey. The trial concluded in July 1998. Barrionuevo, Vera and Sancristóbal were found guilty of kidnapping and misappropriation of public funds, each receiving a prison sentence of 10 years. The sentences of the other nine defendants ranged from two to nine years. The 12 defendants were also ordered to pay 30m. pesetas in compensation to Marey. During September the immediate commencement of the prison terms of Barrionuevo and Vera (the pair having refused to request a pardon) and of the other defendants was ordered. By the end of December, however, 11 of the prisoners had been set free, their sentences having been suspended, while the 12th was released in June 2000. In March 2001 the Constitutional Court rejected Barrionuevo and Vera's appeal against the ruling, and in late May they returned to prison, together with seven others, to complete their terms. A further trial began in September, with González among some 100 witnesses called to testify. In January 2002 Barrionuevo and Corcuera were absolved of the charges of misappropriation of funds. However, Vera was sentenced to seven years' imprisonment and barred from holding public office for 18 years. The former Chief of the National Police, José Maria Rodriguez Colorado, received a six-year sentence, Sancristóbal one of four years and Alvarez-Cascos one of 11 months.

At the general election, held 15 months early, in March 1996, and in which 78% of the electorate participated, the PP took 156 of the 350 seats in the Congreso de los Diputados, thus falling short of an outright majority. The PSOE won 141 seats, the IU 21 and the CiU 16. In the Senado (Senate) the PP received 132 of the 256 seats (winning 111 by direct election), while the PSOE took 96 (81 by direct election). The King invited José María Aznar of the PP to form a government. After protracted negotiations, the PP and the CiU reached agreement on a pact enabling Aznar to take office. Having also secured the support of the five PNV deputies and of the four representatives of Coalición Canaria (CC), the new Prime Minister's investiture finally took place in early May. The incoming Government included three independent ministers.

One of the new administration's main priorities was the reduction of the budget deficit. Several aspects of the Government's policies, however, aroused intense opposition. In late 1996 thousands of public-sector workers attended demonstrations to protest against the Government's imposition of a pay 'freeze'. In December a 24-hour strike by civil servants took place, demonstrators being joined by students and teachers protesting against reductions in the education budget. A two-week strike by truck drivers, in support of improved working conditions, caused severe disruption and led to the closure of the country's road borders in February 1997. In early 1998 one miner died during violent protests in northern Spain, where the coal-miners of Asturias were demonstrating against proposed job losses (the Government having been obliged to plan decreases in coal output in order to comply with European Union (EU, see p. 228) directives regarding reductions in subsidies to state-owned industries). At the end of January, after a month-long strike that attracted much public sympathy, agreement was reached when the Government granted concessions on the terms of early retirement for miners.

Public concern regarding the functioning of the country's judicial system was aroused in October 1996 when Miguel Moreiras, a National Court judge, was removed from office as a result of having disclosed to a newspaper (in October 1995) confidential information relating to his handling of the cases against the disgraced Conde (see above). Furthermore, in December 1996 the General Prosecutor ordered the removal of José Aranda, chief prosecutor of the National Court, and the instigation of disciplinary proceedings against four of its judges. The General Council of Judicial Power warned the judges of the National Court that it would not tolerate 'excesses', a reference to the judges' perceived disregard for the law and for the Constitution; many observers were critical of the judges' wide-ranging powers. In May 1997, after only eight months in office, the General Prosecutor himself, Juan Ortiz Urculo, was abruptly dismissed by the Government. He was replaced by Jesús Cardenal. The crisis surrounding the National Court worsened in June when, despite the rejection of his nomination by prosecutors of the Supreme Court, the Government appointed Eduardo Fungairiño to replace Aranda.

In May 1997 the Prime Minister announced that CESID was to be reformed and that responsibility for the secret service was to be transferred from the Ministry of Defence to his own office, under the direct supervision of the Deputy Prime Minister. In April 1998, however, the Government was embarrassed by the revelation that surveillance devices, which lacked the requisite legal authorization, had been found in the headquarters of Herri Batasuna (HB, the political wing of ETA) in Vitoria and that, moreover, this operation by CESID had been approved, *inter alia*, by the Minister of Defence in March 1997. (Devices in numerous other HB offices had apparently been dismantled by the PSOE administration in late 1995, following the exposure of the scandal relating to stolen CESID documents.) In May 2001 the Government implemented the reforms and for the first time CESID was directed by a civilian. Additionally, new legislation was to be introduced to supervise intelligence operations more closely.

At the PSOE congress in June 1997, after leading the party for 23 years, González unexpectedly announced his resignation as Secretary-General. Joaquín Almunia, hitherto the party's parliamentary spokesman and a loyal associate of González, was chosen to succeed him. In April 1998, in a new procedure that required the holding of primary elections in the contest for the selection of the PSOE's next prime ministerial candidate, Almunia was defeated by Josep Borrell, a former member of the Council of Ministers. The former's offer of resignation from the party leadership was rejected. In November, in a bid to restore party unity, the PSOE designated Borrell as party leader and sole spokesman, while Almunia was to remain responsible for political affairs, at the head of the party's federal executive committee.

In September 1997, as a result of a regional financing dispute, the PNV declared that it considered the pact with the PP to have ended. Nevertheless, Xabier Arzallus, the PNV leader, expressed his willingness to co-operate with the Government on individual issues. In late 1997 PP-CiU relations were strained by a disagreement relating to the introduction of a new national curriculum for the teaching of history in schools (the Government being obliged to withdraw its proposals) and by the Catalan Parliament's approval in December of a CiU-proposed law to promote the Catalan language. In January 1998, however, the CiU formally renewed its collaboration agreement with the PP until the end of the incumbent legislature. The CC gave a similar undertaking in April.

In April 1998, meanwhile, after an inquiry lasting three years, Judge Gómez de Liaño concluded his investigation into the fate of Lasa and Zabala, the two ETA activists allegedly killed by GAL members during the 'dirty war'. Criminal proceedings were instigated against seven suspects, including Vera, Elgorriaga (former Governor of Guipúzcoa) and Gen. Rodríguez Galindo. In April 2000 Galindo and Elgorriaga were found guilty of involvement in the abduction and murder in 1983 of Lasa and Zabala. Both were sentenced to 71 years' imprisonment.

In December 1998 Francisco Frutos replaced Julio Anguita as Secretary-General of the PCE, Anguita retaining his leadership of the IU. At the PP congress in January 1999 Javier Arenas, hitherto Minister of Labour and Social Affairs, succeeded Álvarez-Cascos as the ruling party's Secretary-General. The opposition was thrown into disarray in May by the abrupt resignation of Borrell, the PSOE prime ministerial candidate, following the revelation of a financial scandal, involving allegations of malpractice by two former colleagues during the 1980s.

In July 1999 Almunia, the PSOE Secretary-General, was selected unopposed as the party's prime ministerial candidate. In early December, owing to the deteriorating situation in the Basque region (see below), the five PNV members of the Congreso de los Diputados finally withdrew their support for the minority Government.

In February 2000, only three weeks before the forthcoming general election, Manuel Pimentel, the Minister of Labour and Social Affairs, abruptly resigned, owing to allegations of departmental corruption in relation to the allocation of state contracts. In the same month the opposition PSOE and IU agreed to conduct a joint electoral campaign aimed at increasing their representation in the Senado.

The ruling party's strong performance at the legislative election held on 12 March 2000 was largely attributed to the Government's record of economic success (in particular its reduction of the unemployment rate). In the lower house the PP won 183 of the 350 seats, thus unexpectedly securing an absolute majority. The PSOE's representation was reduced to 125 seats, while the moderate regional parties, the CiU and the PNV, took 15 and seven seats respectively. The IU suffered a sharp decline in support, the communist-led coalition losing 13 of its 21 seats in the Congreso de los Diputados. In the Senado the PP increased its strength to 127 of the 208 directly-elective seats, whereas the PSOE's representation decreased to 61 seats. The level of voter participation was less than 70%. Almunia immediately conceded defeat and resigned as leader of the PSOE. At the party congress in July José Luis Rodríguez Zapatero, a lawyer, was unexpectedly elected to the leadership of the PSOE. Zapatero, who excluded left-wingers from the new national executive committee, declared his intention to modernize the party in order to form an effective opposition.

At the end of April 2000, with the support of the 15 CiU and four CC deputies, Aznar, who expressed a desire to govern largely by consensus, was sworn in for a second term of office. The Prime Minister announced the composition of the new Council of Ministers on the following day. Mariano Rajoy, hitherto Minister of Education, was appointed Deputy Prime Minister and Minister of the Presidency. Rodrigo Rato also remained a Deputy Prime Minister, retaining the economy portfolio, while that of finance was allocated to Cristóbal Montoro. Josep Piqué i Camps became Minister of Foreign Affairs. The incoming Government's programme included the reduction of taxes, reforms in the financing of the Autonomous Communities and improvements in the judicial system.

In February 2001 Jaime Mayor resigned as Minister of the Interior to run as the PP candidate for Lehendakari (President of the Basque Government) in the Basque regional election. He was replaced by Rajoy, who was in turn replaced by Juan José Lucas.

During 2001 the Government suffered from the alleged involvement of several PP members in corruption cases. In mid-June the Supreme Court decided to proceed with an investigation into the role of the Minister of Foreign Affairs, Josep Piqué, in the fraudulent sale of Ertoil, a subsidiary of the Spanish fuel company Ercros, of whose board Piqué was a member, to the French company Elf Aquitaine. Aznar announced that he would wait for the results of the investigation before reviewing Piqué's position in the Council of Ministers. The Government's reputation was further undermined by the collapse of the Antonio Camacho Gescartera stockbroking company in mid-2001, as a result of which several prominent charities and organizations lost significant sums of money. In September the President of the National Securities and Exchange Commission (Comisión Nacional del Mercado de Valores—CNMV), Pilar Valiente, was remanded in custody following the publication of her personal diaries, in which it was revealed that she had long been aware of discrepancies in the stockbroker's accounts. Since Valiente had been appointed by the Deputy Prime Minister and Minister of the Economy, Rodrigo Rato, his position also came under scrutiny and a full reorganization of the CNMV was ordered in early 2002, following the implication of several more of its members in the case. In November 2002 a €2.1m. fine was imposed on the Spanish arm of the HSBC Bank, for its role in laundering Gescartera funds worth some €100m. in 138 numbered accounts.

In January 2002 the PP re-elected Aznar as its President, but he made clear his intention not to seek a third term as Prime Minister in 2004. In May 2002, after the trial of Arnaldo Otegi of Batasuna (as HB had been renamed) was shelved by the Supreme Court, a request by Aznar for reconsideration was strongly criticized by the judiciary as misplaced government intervention. Also in May the first general strike since 1988 was called for 20 June by the CCOO and the UGT in protest at proposed government reforms to unemployment subsidies. The reforms were approved by the PP in the Senado on 13 June, with all other parties abstaining. The general strike proceeded one week later, with the UGT claiming a rate of participation of 80%. The largest demonstrations took place in Seville on the eve of the EU summit to conclude Spain's presidency of the Union. The Seville summit itself, at Spain's instigation, was dominated by the issue of illegal immigration (see below), including the proposition of more extensive visa restrictions.

In June 2002 disagreements between Aznar and Jordi Pujol i Soley, the President of the CiU, in which Aznar accused the latter of disloyalty to the Government and support for the general strike, led to a 'freezing' of relations between the PP and the CiU for a 'period of reflection'. Instability in the PP following the strike led to a major ministerial reshuffle by Aznar in mid-July; notably, the Minister of Foreign Affairs, Josep Piqué, was transferred to the Ministry of Science and Technology and was replaced by Ana Palacio, while Mariano Rajoy was promoted from the position of Minister of the Interior to that of Deputy Prime Minister and was replaced by Angel Acebes.

In mid-November 2002 the Aznar Government was faced with a serious crisis following the sinking of the Liberian-registered, Greek-owned oil tanker *Prestige* 240 km off the coast of Galicia. The vessel, which had reported to the authorities on 13 November that its hull had ruptured and that it was leaking oil, had been refused landfall and had been towed out to sea, where it split in two and sank on 19 November. An estimated 12,000 metric tons of the vessel's 77,000-ton capacity was believed to have been released into the sea in the first slick, around one-half of which soon reached the Galician Costa da Morte, requiring the imposition of a fishing ban between Finisterre and A Coruña. On 27 November Deputy Prime Minister Mariano Rajoy refuted claims by French and Portuguese investigators that the wreck was still issuing oil and that a second leak was possible. However, it was subsequently revealed that the oil remaining in the wreck was indeed still leaking (in early January 2003 the total amount of spillage was revised to 25,000 tons). The Spanish Minister of Foreign Affairs, Ana Palacio, accused Gibraltar of failing properly to report the vessel's condition, and named the British territory as the intended destination of the *Prestige*, thus precipitating a minor diplomatic fracas. The British Government immediately denied her claim, claiming that the ship had last docked near Gibraltar in June, but that an inspection had not been required as the vessel had not entered the port, and affirmed that the ship's actual destination in November had been Singapore. Massive clean-up operations were launched, mostly by environmental groups and by the local population; a significant lack of aid from the Spanish military aroused widespread public discontent. Demonstrations were attended by some 150,000 people in Santiago de Compostela in December and by around 100,000 people in Vigo in January 2003, at which participants protested at the perceived mishandling of the disaster by both the regional and national PP authorities and demanded the resignation of Aznar. A local commission launched by the Regional Government of Galicia met with obstruction from the central Government, which also delayed the setting up of a national investigation. Meanwhile, the oil slicks spread to the Basque region, incurring €6m. worth of damages, and also reached the coastlines of France and Portugal. The total cost of the cleaning-up process to the Spanish Government was projected at more than €1,000m. In November 2003 the World Wildlife Fund published a report that was highly critical of the role that the Spanish Government had played in the *Prestige* disaster, and maintained that the sea had not been adequately cleaned and that fishing grounds had been reopened too early.

Amid the increasing likelihood of US-led military action against the Iraqi regime of Saddam Hussain in early 2003, Aznar was one of eight European leaders to sign a declaration at the end of January in support of US moves towards an ultimatum. Public opinion, however, already swayed against the PP by the Government's handling of the *Prestige* disaster, was, in general, strongly against military action, with 3m. people participating in anti-war demonstrations in mid-February, and opinion polls suggesting that at least 80% of the population were against the launching of armed conflict in Iraq. None the less, in late February Aznar expressed his support for US-led military action with a UN mandate, although he remained guarded as to the line Spain would adopt should a UN resolution not be achieved. As the US intention to commence armed intervention with or without UN approval became clear, Aznar assured the Spanish people that Spain would not contribute to any military coalition. A summit meeting hosted in the Azores in March led to a joint declaration by Aznar, the British Prime Minister, Anthony (Tony) Blair, and the US President George W. Bush, condemning the regime of Saddam Hussain and expressing support for necessary military actions. Aznar publicly maintained the importance of continuing attempts to secure UN backing for military action; however, the subsequent announcement by the USA of its intention to act, if need be, without international ratification received the PP Government's concerted support, which provoked strong criticism from the national media. Although the PP Government strongly supported Aznar's policy on Iraq, by 1 April six parliamentary motions rejecting war had been proposed by opposition parties, and on 29 March a number of non-governmental organizations filed charges against Aznar before the Supreme Court, accusing him of exceeding his authorities. Public demonstrations continued in March and April, with a march in Madrid on 6 April supported by Spain's most respected judge, Baltasar Garzón, and another comprising up to 200,000 protesters in Barcelona on 12 April. In April seven diplomatic staff at the Iraqi embassy in Madrid were expelled at the request of the USA, ostensibly on the grounds of alleged espionage, while the dispatch of 900 Spanish non-combative troops to Iraq aroused specific anger among protesters. After the fall of Saddam Hussain's regime in mid-April, Spain pledged forces for peace-keeping duties and humanitarian activities in Iraq, while the Minister of Foreign Affairs, Ana Palacio, emphasized the importance of UN involvement in Iraq's reconstruction.

The scale of public protest against the Iraqi conflict prompted the drafting of legislation by the PP in April 2003 that would extend the jurisdiction of military courts to include trial (with a maximum sentence of six years) for acts of protest staged to discredit Spain's participation in international armed conflict; the proposed legislation, which was the first of its kind since the reintroduction of democracy in 1975, was accused of being reactionary and a threat to civil rights. In July, despite the level of popular feeling against the war and the dissent of all the opposition parties, the Government committed 1,300 troops to the peace-keeping force. In November seven Spanish intelligence officers were killed in Iraq, bringing the total number of Spaniards to have died as a direct result of the conflict to 10. Questions were subsequently raised over whether intelligence failures had led to the deaths of the officers. Opinion polls reported that an estimated 90% of the Spanish population believed that the instigation of armed conflict in Iraq by the US-led coalition had been a mistake, and Zapatero, the leader of the PSOE, stated that if his party won the general election in March 2004, the Spanish troops would be withdrawn from Iraq.

Following the holding of local elections in late May 2003, in which the PSOE won more votes than the PP, the former party became embroiled in scandal when two of its members in the Government of the Comunidad de Madrid defected to the PP, provoking PSOE allegations (later proved to be unfounded) of PP corruption in local politics. The PSOE-led coalition Government in Madrid was dissolved, and a further election, which was held in late October, was won (with a small majority) by the PP,

Esperanza Aguirre becoming the first woman to head a regional government. The episode damaged the PSOE's image in the run-up to the 2004 general election. In early September 2003 the Deputy Prime Minister, Mariano Rajoy, was appointed as the PP's prime ministerial candidate for the general election following his nomination by Aznar.

In opinion polls held before the general election of March 2004 it was widely predicted that the PP would win with a reduced majority. Aznar's popularity had suffered as a result of his policy towards Iraq and ongoing questions over the Government's handling of the *Prestige* disaster. The PSOE's chances of winning the general election, which had been damaged by the events surrounding Madrid's local elections in 2003, appeared to be further reduced by the revelation that Josep-Lluís Carod-Rovira, the Secretary-General of the Esquerra Republicana de Catalunya (ERC)—the PSOE's coalition partner in Cataluña—had held secret meetings with ETA leaders.

Four days before the general election, on 11 March 2004, Spain was thrown into turmoil when 10 bombs exploded in three commuter trains in Madrid. A total of 191 people were killed and more than 1,500 people injured. The Minister of the Interior, Angel Acebes, immediately indicated that ETA was the principal suspect; Batasuna, however, was swift to condemn the attacks. Campaigning for the election was suspended, and three days of national mourning were declared. On 12 March demonstrations against the atrocity were held throughout Spain, and more than 2m. people marched through the centre of Madrid. Despite the Government's initial supposition that the bombings had been carried out by ETA, suspicion increasingly came to rest on Islamist militants; in the days following the attacks three Moroccans suspected of having links to al-Qa'ida and to the May 2003 suicide bombings in Casablanca, Morocco, were arrested.

The bombings became the central issue in the general election, which took place as scheduled on 14 March 2004. It was predicted that in the few days prior to voting proof of ETA's involvement would help the cause of the PP, which had pursued an active anti-terrorism policy against the Basque separatists. Conversely, evidence that Islamist militants had been responsible would naturally provide a connection between the bombings and the Government's already deeply unpopular involvement in Iraq. As the likelihood of ETA being responsible for the attacks receded, the Government was criticized for its seemingly premature response in blaming the illegal Basque group and its perceived unwillingness to consider other possibilities. In the event, the PSOE secured an unexpected victory in the elections to the lower house, winning 42.7% of the votes (164 seats), while the PP obtained 37.7% of the votes (148 seats). The PP retained its majority in the Senado, however, winning 102 of the directly-elective seats, compared with the 93 directly-elective seats secured by the PSOE and its Catalan allies. The PP held 126 seats in the final composition of the Senado, and the PSOE 111. The election turn-out, at 77.2%, was 9% higher than in 2000. Immediately after his party's victory Zapatero reiterated his pledge to withdraw Spanish troops from Iraq if control in that country were not handed over by the US-led coalition authorities to the UN by 30 June; however, on assuming office he announced that the troops would be withdrawn as quickly as possible, since the successful transfer of power by 30 June in Iraq seemed increasingly unlikely. (In the event, the Spanish withdrawal was completed by the end of May.) Zapatero announced that he did not intend to form a coalition government; rather, the PSOE made pacts with smaller parties in the Congreso de los Diputados and Senado, effectively isolating the PP. Having won a congressional vote of confidence, Zapatero and his new Council of Ministers were inaugurated on 17 April. María Teresa Fernández de la Vega became the first female to hold the post of First Deputy Prime Minister (she was also appointed Minister of the Presidency), while Pedro Solbes, previously the EU Commissioner for Economic and Monetary Affairs, was appointed Second Deputy Prime Minister and Minister of the newly reunited departments of the economy and finance. Miguel Angel Moratinos assumed the position of Minister of Foreign Affairs and Co-operation, and José Antonio Alonso was appointed Minister of the Interior. The new Government's programme included constitutional reform, transforming the Senado into a more regionally representative body, fiscal reform, the implementation of a co-ordinated anti-terrorism policy, and a focus on improving gender equality and reducing domestic violence.

On 2 April 2004, meanwhile, a bomb of the same type discovered on the trains involved in the earlier Madrid attacks was defused on the railway line between Madrid and Seville. The following day seven men who were suspected of involvement in the bombings apparently blew themselves up, killing one police officer, during a police raid on an apartment in Leganes, a suburb of Madrid; Farkhet was among the dead. In May a parliamentary commission of inquiry into the train bombings, presided over by Paulino Rivero, was established. Specifically, the commission was to investigate information on the attacks provided by the PP Government, that Government's anti-terrorist policy, and the trafficking of illegal arms in Spain. In late November the former Prime Minister, Aznar, was questioned by the commission. Aznar maintained that ETA was linked to the Islamist militants suspected of carrying out the bomb attacks. Zapatero, who subsequently appeared before the commission, alleged that the PP administration had deleted all government computer records relating to the train bombings before leaving office. In March 2005 the preliminary findings of the commission, supported by all the parliamentary groups except the PP, were published. Recommendations included an increase in the implementation of security measures; however, the commission was criticized by some observers for being overly political in its handling of the inquiry.

During its first two years in office Zapatero's Government relied less on support from the opposition in major policy areas than the previous Government. In particular, the PP did not support the Government in its attempts to begin negotiations with ETA, or on the Catalan statute (see below), and the Government passed its legislative agenda mainly with the support of the ERC and the IU. In December 2004 the Government's budget was approved by the Congreso de los Diputados, despite having been vetoed in the PP-dominated Senado. This was the first time since the restoration of democracy that a budget had been vetoed in the Senado.

Despite opposition from leaders of the Roman Catholic church, legislation permitting marriage between couples of the same sex was adopted by the Senado in June 2005, following its approval by the Congreso de los Diputados in April. In November new defence legislation was passed that required any deployment of Spanish troops abroad to be approved by the Cortes, and limited the circumstances in which such a deployment might occur.

In February 2006 Spain's highest consultative body, the Council of State, voted to support the Government's proposed amendments to the Constitution. Among the changes anticipated were the alteration of the law of royal succession, removing the preference for a male heir, a restructuring of the Senado, and an increase in the power of the Autonomous Communities in the upper house; also to be addressed was the contentious issue of whether the Autonomous Communities should be regarded as 'nations'.

In April 2006 Zapatero announced an unexpected government reshuffle, prompted by the resignation of the Minister of Defence, José Bono, who was replaced by José Antonio Alonso, hitherto Minister of the Interior. Alfredo Pérez Rubalcaba took the interior portfolio.

In elections to the European Parliament, held on 13 June 2004, the PSOE won 25 seats, of a total of 54, equivalent to 43.3% of the votes cast, while the PP won 23 seats (41.3%). Voter turn-out was, however, only 45.9%. A national referendum on the EU Treaty establishing a Constitution for Europe took place in Spain on 20 February 2005, with 76.2% of the votes cast being in favour of ratifying the treaty. The turn-out, at 42.3% of the electorate, however, was the lowest since the introduction of democracy. Both the PSOE and the PP were in favour of the proposed constitution.

Autonomous regional parliaments were established in the Basque Country and in Cataluña in 1980. The parliaments of Galicia and Andalucía were established in October 1981 and May 1982 respectively, and the remaining 13 Legislative Assemblies of the Comunidades Autónomas (Autonomous Communities) were elected in May 1983. In 2001 proposals were announced to complete the development process of the Autonomous Communities with a policy of co-operation between the Communities, through meetings and conferences. The presidents of each Autonomous Community were to be incorporated into the Senado, thus making it more representative of Spain as a whole. (See Legislative Assemblies of the Autonomous Communities for details of the most recent elections to all regional parliaments.)

Prior to the regional elections in Cataluña in 2003, Jordi Pujol y Soley, who had been President of a CiU-led Government for 23 years, announced that he would step down. In the event, no party won an absolute majority in the Catalan regional elections held on 16 November, and the two leading parties both entered negotiations to form a coalition with the nationalist ERC, which, having almost doubled its representation to 23 seats, held the balance of power. A coalition was subsequently formed comprising the Partit dels Socialistes de Catalunya (PSC), the ERC and the Iniciativa per Catalunya-Verds (IC-V). The PSC candidate, Pasqual Maragall, was inaugurated as President of Cataluña on 15 December. In September 2005 the Catalan Parliament overwhelmingly approved a revised statute increasing the region's autonomy. The statute provoked considerable controversy elsewhere in the country over its definition of Cataluña as a nation and its provision for greater fiscal and judicial independence. In mid-January 2006 Lt-Gen. José Mena Aguado, the head of the army's ground forces, was dismissed and placed under house arrest after appearing to suggest that the military should intervene to preserve the unity of Spain, should the statute become law. Later that month Prime Minister Zapatero bypassed the left-wing parties traditionally allied to the national PSOE, and negotiated an agreement with the centre-right CiU to limit the extent of financial independence granted to Cataluña under the proposed statute. In late March the Congreso de los Diputados approved the statute, despite the opposition of the ERC, which favoured full independence, and the PP, which claimed that the statute violated the Constitution. It was then to be subject to votes in the Senado and the Catalan Parliament and to a referendum in Cataluña to be held on 18 June. In May Maragall dismissed the ERC members of the Catalan Parliament in response to the ERC's refusal to support the autonomy statute. Maragall also announced that early elections would take place following the referendum.

In March 2006 the Senado approved a new statute for Valencia, which, *inter alia*, defined Valencia as an 'historic nationality', made Valencian an official language and increased judicial and tax-raising independence. The statute was still to be considered by the Valencian Parliament.

In the Basque region, meanwhile, terrorist activity by the separatist organization, ETA, founded in 1959, continued. Having claimed its first victim in 1961, between 1978 and 1992 alone a total of 711 murders was attributed to the group. Despite bomb attacks in Bilbao in February 1983 and Madrid in July 1986, the central Government maintained its offer of social reintegration, instigated in mid-1984, to former ETA members. The explosion in June 1987 of a bomb beneath a crowded Barcelona supermarket, which killed 21 and injured 45, was the most devastating ETA attack ever, prompting HB's first condemnation of a terrorist attack. Co-operation with the authorities of France and Algeria (where numerous ETA members were discovered to be living) was strengthened, and in October the French police arrested 67 Basque suspects. In December five children were among the 12 killed in a bomb attack on the married quarters of a Civil Guard barracks in Zaragoza, which provoked a further public outcry. In January 1988, after protracted negotiations, six Basque parties (excluding HB) signed the Ajuria Enea Pact, rejecting terrorism as a means of determining the region's future. In January 1989 a unilateral truce was declared by ETA, in an effort to reopen negotiations with the Government, broken off in early 1988. Secret discussions between representatives of the Government and of ETA commenced in Algeria, but collapsed in April 1989, and violent action recommenced, resulting in reprisals by GAL in which a HB deputy-elect, Josu Muguruza, was murdered. In February 1990 a resolution declaring the right of the Basque people to self-determination was approved by the Basque Parliament.

The authorities continued to make arrests and to convict members of ETA, including José Javier Zabaleta Elósegui ('Waldo'), alleged to be ETA's second-in-command, who was sentenced to 57 years' imprisonment for three attempted murders. Nevertheless, ETA's campaign of violence continued during the 1990s. In December 1991, following an apparent rift within ETA over the organization's future policy, the central Government denied that it was planning to resume direct negotiations with the terrorists. The capture in March of Francisco Múgika Garmendia ('Pakito'), ETA's military leader, along with other senior commanders, represented a particular achievement in the Government's increasingly successful anti-terrorist campaign. Between mid-1992 and early 1993 more than 500 ETA suspects were arrested. In July 1992 ETA's offer of a truce (to coincide with the forthcoming Olympic Games in Barcelona), in return for the reopening of dialogue, was rebuffed by the Government, which continued to insist upon the group's permanent renunciation of violence. Hopes that ETA's campaign might be ended were raised in February 1993, upon the discovery of a major arsenal in France and the capture of Rafael Caride, thought to be ETA's operational head. In June, however, following the conclusion of the trial in Paris of six ETA members, two car bombs exploded in Madrid, one of which killed seven people.

The Basque people's growing revulsion at ETA's actions, demonstrated by HB's loss of two of its four seats in the Congreso de los Diputados at the general election, was intensified by the abduction in July 1993 of industrialist Julio Iglesias Zamora, leading to a resurgence of the peace movement within the region. He was released in October, reportedly upon the payment of a large ransom. In August there were violent clashes in San Sebastián and Bilbao between peace demonstrators and supporters of ETA. In September there was renewed unrest in the Basque region, following the deaths in custody of two ETA suspects and the disclosure of medical evidence suggesting violent treatment of a third detainee. Detentions in Spain of terrorist suspects totalled 127 in 1993, including eight suspects believed to be part of an extortion network responsible for the attempted blackmailing of numerous Basque enterprises.

In March 1994 Henri Parot, a French member of ETA, was sentenced to a total of 1,802 years' imprisonment for the bomb attack on the Zaragoza barracks in 1987. Both attacks by ETA and arrests by the authorities continued in 1994; Pedro Picabea Ugalde ('Kepa'), believed to be responsible for 24 murders and for the abduction of Iglesias Zamora, and Idoia López Riaño ('Margarita' or 'La Tigresa') were arrested in France in July and August. At the end of August the ETA leadership ordered its imprisoned members to embark upon a hunger strike, in an attempt to reassert its authority and to obstruct the process of 'reinsertion' into society. About 100 of the 600 ETA prisoners had expressed an interest in the Government's offer of reintegration, in return for the renunciation of violence.

The results of the election to the Basque Parliament in October 1994 demonstrated the continuing decline in support for HB. ETA suffered a major reverse in mid-November, when several activists were arrested, including José Luis Martín Carmona ('Koldo'), believed to be the head of the notorious Vizcaya unit, who was captured near Bilbao, and Félix Alberto López de la Calle Gauna ('Mobutu'), the terrorist group's alleged second-in-command, who was detained in the French city of Toulon.

In January 1995, as attacks on police-officers continued, Gregorio Ordóñez, a member of the Basque Parliament and the PP candidate for the mayoralty of San Sebastián at the forthcoming municipal elections, was shot dead, the first politician since 1992 to be murdered by ETA. Thousands of Basque citizens took to the streets of San Sebastián and Bilbao to protest against the assassination. In April Aznar, leader of the then opposition PP, narrowly survived a car-bomb attempt on his life in Madrid, which injured 19 others. ETA warned that its campaign of violence would continue if the Basque Country were not granted self-determination. Upon his renunciation of violence and subsequent extradition to the Dominican Republic in July, Juan Manuel Soares Gamboa confessed to his involvement in a total of 29 murders. In April 2000 he received a prison sentence of 1,401 years for the murder of the 12 civil guards in 1986.

In August 1995 it was revealed that, with assistance from the French authorities, a plot to assassinate King Juan Carlos had been foiled; 18 ETA suspects were arrested, and three were convicted in 1997, receiving sentences of 35–37 years. In February 1996 the shooting dead in San Sebastián of Fernando Múgica Herzog, a Basque socialist leader, followed by the murder of Francisco Tomás y Valiente, a former President of the Constitutional Court and a close associate of the then Prime Minister, González, provoked a public outcry. Some 1m. citizens, including González and many other political leaders, attended an anti-ETA march in Madrid. As the general election approached, Jon Idígoras, the veteran HB leader, was arrested, amid controversy arising from a campaign video that apparently supported the activities of ETA. The arrest of Valentín Lasarte, believed to be responsible for the murders of Ordóñez and of Múgica Herzog, led to the discovery of a large bomb-making factory near San Sebastián. (In May 1998 Lasarte, who had previously received three prison sentences of 30 years, including one in January 1995 for the murder of Ordóñez, was sentenced to a further 82 years' imprisonment for the murder of Múgica Herzog.)

In July 1996, following a brief truce and the PP Government's conditional offer of dialogue in the previous month, ETA renewed its bombing campaign, this time targeting the tourism industry. In January 1997 Jesús Arkautz Arana ('Josu de Mondragón'), a senior ETA member detained in 1991, was expelled from France and handed over to the Spanish authorities (In June 1998 he received a prison sentence of 83 years.) This expulsion was followed by the capture near Bordeaux of José Luis Urrusolo Sistiaga, sought by the authorities for 15 years and believed to be responsible for 16 murders.

A resurgence of violence in 1997 culminated in the abduction in July of Miguel Angel Blanco, a young PP councillor in the Basque town of Ermua. ETA issued an ultimatum that prisoners belonging to the separatist organization be transferred to gaols in the Basque region. Despite numerous appeals, including a message from the Pope, Blanco was duly shot upon the expiry of ETA's 48-hour deadline. His death provoked an unprecedented display of public outrage, which united most of the country against ETA. In the largest demonstration since the attempted military coup of 1981, millions of Spaniards took to the streets, including the Prime Minister, who led a protest march in Madrid. In response to public feeling, the Prime Minister vowed to intensify the Government's campaign against ETA, while urging (along with the moderate Basque parties) the isolation of HB.

ETA's suspected head of intelligence, Igor Urrestarazu Garijo, was arrested in southern France in early August 1997. Following the deportation of Eugenio Etxebeste Arizcuren ('Antxon') and two other ETA exiles from the Dominican Republic to Spain, the Dominican Government indicated that it would not extradite any further ETA members. Etxebeste Arizcuren was sentenced to 10 years' imprisonment in April 2001.

In September 1997 the Government confirmed that more than 100 businesses in Navarra had received letters of extortion from ETA, in which sums of between 5m. and 40m. pesetas had been demanded. In the same month, following the death of two alleged leaders of the Vizcaya unit in an exchange of gunfire with the Civil Guard in Bilbao, 12 suspected ETA collaborators were detained and a large arsenal was discovered. In October an attempt to plant remote-controlled grenades outside the new Guggenheim Museum in Bilbao, which was due to be inaugurated by the King, was thwarted by the police, but resulted in the death of one officer.

In December 1997 the 23 members of the collective leadership of HB were each sentenced to seven years' imprisonment for collaborating with an armed group. In a significant development, for the first time the direct relationship between ETA and HB, which continued to claim to be independent of the terrorist organization, was recognized by the judiciary. The members of the collective leadership were released in July 1999, when their imprisonment was ruled unconstitutional.

In January 1998, as ETA continued its attacks against local councillors belonging to the PP, Alberto Jiménez Becerril and his wife were shot in Seville, provoking renewed outrage. The murder of Jiménez Becerril was the first of a PP councillor outside the Basque region. In February a dispute arose between the President of the Basque regional Government, which administered its own police force, and the central Government, following the disclosure that national forces had been clandestinely deployed in the Basque region. At a meeting in early 1998 HB elected a new collective leadership, which pledged to continue the policies of its predecessor. In May 1998 Tomás Caballero, spokesman for the Unión del Pueblo Navarro (UPN), was murdered in Pamplona. The capture of several ETA activists in San Sebastián, as they prepared to launch mortar bombs at a police barracks, resulted in the discovery of another plot to assassinate King Juan Carlos.

Following a dispute relating to a proposal to oblige all members of the Basque Parliament to accord formal recognition to the Spanish Constitution in June 1998, after 12 years of co-operation, the Partido Socialista de Euskadi-Euskadiko Ezkerra (PSE-EE) withdrew from the Basque coalition Government. In July Judge Garzón, who was investigating ETA's fund-raising activities, ordered the closure of *Egin*, a radical Basque newspaper, and that of an associated radio station, on the grounds of their connections to ETA. A series of fire-bomb attacks on Basque media groups followed.

In early September 1998, apparently attempting to pre-empt any ban on its activities and while still declining to renounce the use of violence, HB announced that it was to contest the forthcoming elections to the Basque Parliament as the newly formed Euskal Herritarrok (EH). In mid-September both the PP and the opposition PSOE expressed reservations at the conclusion of an agreement (the 'Lizarra Pact') by the PNV, Eusko Alkartasuna (EA), HB and IU on proposals for unconditional discussions with ETA. Nevertheless, following several months of secret talks between representatives of the PNV and HB, on 16 September ETA declared an indefinite truce. In response, the central Government urged the separatist organization to disarm and to respect the results of the forthcoming elections to the Basque Legislative Assembly. In a conciliatory gesture, the Prime Minister indicated his willingness to transfer a number of ETA convicts to prisons in the Basque Country.

At the Basque elections, held in October 1998, the PNV again received the greatest support, while the PP supplanted the PSE-EE as the party with the second largest representation in the regional parliament. At the end of October it was announced that the State was to assume responsibility for compensation of the victims of ETA, the total sum in question now estimated at 60,000m. pesetas. However, the Government refused to compensate members of GAL. The Prime Minister also stated that, while being required to renounce the use of violence, ETA would not be obliged to relinquish all its weapons. In November the central Government announced the inauguration of direct contact with representatives of ETA, the separatist organization reaffirming its commitment to the cease-fire. In December, with the support of EH, an entirely nationalist Basque Government was established; the coalition was headed by Juan José Ibarretxe of the PNV. In the same month, as transfers of ETA convicts to prisons located in the Basque region continued, the Prime Minister invited EH to join discussions on the region's future. In January 1999, however, EH refused to attend the inauguration ceremony of the Basque region's new Lehendakari (President). As street disturbances and arson attacks began to escalate in early 1999, in January thousands of Basques participated in a march to demonstrate support for the transfer of ETA inmates to prisons nearer their homes.

In February 1999, in France, the first arrest since the cease-fire of an ETA suspect was made. The failure of EH categorically to condemn the continuing street violence further hindered the faltering peace process. In March the police arrested six ETA activists, including José Javier Arizkuren Ruiz ('Kantauri'), the alleged head of ETA's military wing, who was believed to have been involved in 20 murders and also the 1995 plot to kill King Juan Carlos; he was convicted in April 2002.

In May 1999 the Spanish Government announced that 304 (of an estimated 550) exiles, who had been obliged to leave Spain on account of their alleged connections to ETA, were to be permitted to return to their homeland. In early June the Prime Minister admitted that direct talks between government representatives and members of ETA had taken place in the previous month, the first such official acknowledgement since 1989. In late June a newly-elected deputy to the parliament of Navarra and member of ETA, José Luis Barrios, was sentenced to 60 years' imprisonment, along with an accomplice, upon conviction for the murder in 1998 of the PP councillor Jiménez Becerril and his wife.

In July 1999, for the first time, EH joined other Basque parties in signing a declaration rejecting the use of violence. In August ETA stated that dialogue with the Government was being suspended, owing to the latter's perceived attempt to gain political advantage from the peace process. The Government reiterated its willingness to resume contact. In early September, as the first anniversary of the truce approached, it was revealed that a total of 180 ETA prisoners had been released within the last year. At the end of September, following the theft of a substantial quantity of industrial dynamite from a depot in Brittany (and only a few days prior to an official visit to Spain by the French President, Jacques Chirac), the French authorities arrested three ETA suspects, including Jon Bienzobas Arreche ('Karaka'), alleged to be responsible for the murder in 1996 of Tomás y Valiente.

In October 1999 ETA's proposals for the resumption of direct peace talks were rejected by the central Government on the grounds that the release of hundreds of ETA prisoners, as urged by the terrorist organization, was not negotiable. At the end of October ETA members exiled overseas were reported to be returning to Europe and regrouping in France. On 28 November, on the eve of the opening in Paris of the trial of Arizkuren Ruiz and 12 other ETA defendants, the terrorist organization announced the end of the 14-month cease-fire. Thousands of dismayed citizens took to the streets to urge that the truce be maintained. Hours before the expiry of the truce on 3 December, the PNV, along with other members of the Lizarra Pact, invited HB to sign a document demanding full sovereignty for the Basque region and criticizing the policies of both the Spanish and French Governments.

Despite the authorities' recent interception of vehicles laden with explosives, and the detention of three ETA suspects belonging to the Vizcaya unit, in January 2000, nevertheless, ETA successfully exploded two car-bombs in Madrid, one of which killed an army officer. More than 1m. people, led by the Prime Minister, participated in a protest march in the capital. At the end of the month it was reported that ETA's international network, responsible for the co-ordination of financial and logistical support, had been dismantled. In February, in Vitoria, a Basque socialist politician, Fernando Bueso, and his bodyguard died in a bomb attack, prompting Ibarretxe to sever all links with EH. In April it was reported that, since July 1999, the PNV had been attempting unsuccessfully to hold direct discussions with ETA. EH subsequently announced that it was withdrawing from the Basque Parliament.

In early May 2000 the central Government discounted the possibility of renewed contact with ETA unless a cease-fire were reinstated. Also in May the Spanish and French Governments determined to intensify collaboration to combat terrorism. In June a PP politician, Jesús María Pedrosa Urquiza, was assassinated, resulting in the abolition of local government pacts between the PNV and EH. In July the interior ministries of Madrid and the Basque Country established a joint co-ordinating committee to share and assess intelligence regarding ETA. Attacks in July and August claimed the lives of six people, including a former socialist governor. In September 20 financial and political organizers of EKIN, ETA's fund-raising wing, were arrested. Seven of these were convicted in April 2001, on the same day that Judge Garzón pronounced EKIN illegal, owing to its associations with ETA. On 15 September 2000 the French authorities arrested the suspected former leader of ETA, Ignacio Gracia Arregui ('Iñaki de Rentería') on charges of terrorism and attempting to assassinate the King in 1995. In December he was sentenced to five years' imprisonment, added to a previous sentence of 11 years. In retaliation for Arregui's arrest, José Luis Ruiz Casado, a PP politician, was assassinated in Barcelona. On the following day some 100,000 Catalans, led by the Prime Minister, Aznar, demonstrated in Barcelona.

In September 2000 the EH abandoned the ruling coalition, leaving the PNV without a majority in the Basque Government. In October Ibon Muñoa, a former HB politician, was convicted of providing ETA with information to aid the assassination of Blanco. In the same month a public prosecutor in Andalucía, Luis Portero, and Lt-Col Antonio Muñoz Cariñanos were assassinated, and five people were killed by car-bombs. Demonstrations were held in Madrid and in the Basque Country. In November a former socialist health minister, Ernest Lluch, was assassinated in Barcelona, and in the following month a PP politician, Francisco Cano Consuegra, was killed in a car-bomb. During 2000 some 100 members or collaborators of ETA were detained following covert Civil Guard operations; six command units were dismantled; and 12 members of ETA were successfully extradited. However, street disturbances in Basque cities continued to escalate, many caused by the youth wing of ETA, and there were 23 fatalities resultant from ETA attacks.

In January 2001, in an attempted car-bomb attack on Princess Alexia of Greece, one man was killed. In February French police arrested a key ETA leader, Francisco Javier García Gaztelu ('Txapote'), and the Spanish Civil Guard arrested 10 members of the Donosti unit. On 20 February the Ibarretxe announced that Basque regional elections would be held early, on 13 May. The PP and PSOE had proposed an all-party anti-terrorist pact to follow the elections, and a co-ordinating committee was established to form anti-terrorist policy. In March 16 people, who were believed to be leaders of Haika (Rise Up), the youth wing of ETA, were arrested; in May Judge Garzón pronounced Haika illegal. Following retaliatory attacks throughout March, ETA warned that it was to target holiday resorts.

Elections to the Basque Parliament took place on 13 May 2001. The PNV/EA electoral coalition, led by Ibarretxe, retained power, taking 33 of the 75 seats. The PP retained its position as the party with the second largest representation, gaining 19 seats, while the PSE-EE won 13 seats, the EH seven seats and the IU-EB three. The PNV/EA now controlled more seats than the combined forces of the PP and the PSOE.

As the violence continued throughout April and May 2001, with a number of attempted bombings, Ibarretxe reiterated his refusal to allow EH to attend peace talks owing to its support for ETA. Attacks during May included the assassination of the financial director of the regional newspaper El Diario Vasco, and the fire-bombing of a Civil Guard barracks in Vizcaya; there were a number of arrests in June, and in July a court case against 33 members of EKIN opened. Garzón had announced earlier in the month that he would investigate members of ETA who had been interviewed by the newspapers Gara and Euskaldunon Egunkaria. In late June a parcel-bomb in Madrid injured 20 people, including Brig.-Gen. Justo Oreja Pedraza, who died a month later. Earlier bomb attacks in Logrono, San Sebastián and a conspiracy to bomb a ferry en route to Plymouth, United Kingdom, had failed. Following its losses in the elections of 13 May, HB elected new members to its leadership and declared that henceforth it wished to be known as Batasuna (Unity).

On 2 July 2001 Spain secured an agreement with Mexico for the extradition of 20 suspected ETA members and further co-operation against ETA. On 14 July the inauguration of Ibarretxe as Lehendakari was accompanied by ETA action in Tolosa, where a member of the Ertzaintza was assassinated, and in Leitxa, Navarra, where a local councillor was killed in a bomb attack. Two days later 50,000 people demonstrated on the streets of Pamplona in protest at the violence. In late July it became apparent that ETA had planned a series of bomb attacks on Spain's holiday resorts to coincide with the summer tourist season. A car-bomb at Málaga airport was defused on 26 July and a series of co-ordinated bomb attacks took place in towns across the Basque Country. The following day, a bomb injured three people in Barcelona. On 30 July the National High Court in Madrid sentenced two former leading ETA members, Francisco Mujika Garmendia ('Pakito') and José Maria Arregi Erostarbe ('Fiti'), to 1,128 years' imprisonment for various crimes, including 46 counts of murder. ETA's campaign of violence and bombing continued throughout August. At the end of the month it was estimated that, so far in 2001, some 51 arrests of alleged ETA members had been made.

There was a brief interlude in ETA violence during September 2001. Nevertheless, the Minister of the Interior reported that month that police had discovered a list, compiled by ETA, of potential targets, which included more than 2,000 politicians, police and military personnel. In late September police in France captured the alleged chief of ETA logistics, Asier Oiartzabal Txapartegi ('Baltza') and four other suspects. In early October Ibarretxe warned that he was determined to hold a referendum on self-determination for the Basque Country, should the Government in Madrid continue to reject dialogue and ETA continue its campaign of violence. However, the Prime Minister, Aznar, condemned the proposal as unconstitutional, and the violence resumed with the bombing of a courthouse in Vitoria. On 12 October a car-bomb exploded in Madrid, injuring 17 people. It was later reported that the bomb had been intended to be detonated at a military parade earlier in the day, at which members of the royal family were present, to commemorate National Day. On 26 October the French courts confirmed the expulsion of 17 Basques resident in France, who were suspected of links with ETA. In the same month police also carried out operations against the ETA prisoners' support group, Gestoras Pro Amnista, which the Minister of the Interior accused of inciting violence.

On 17 November 2001 some 35,000 people marched through Bilbao to demand the right for self-determination for the region. This followed two high-profile bomb attacks on Madrid earlier that month, of which one took place during the city's 'rush hour' and injured 95 people. On the same day, two ETA gunmen assassinated a judge, José Maria Lidon, who had presided over the regional court of Vizcaya. Members of Ertzainta again became the targets of ETA when two were shot dead in Guipuzcoa province on 23 November. On the same day it was reported that Pedro José Pikabea Ugalde had been convicted in France in connection with a plot to assassinate King Juan Carlos. In December seven people were arrested in the Urretxe and Zumarraga provinces in connection with the summer bombing campaign on tourist resorts.

Basque groups took advantage of the beginning of Spain's presidency of the EU in January 2002 to demand greater representation in the European Parliament. The central Government, however, welcomed the introduction of an EU-wide arrest warrant, which it hoped would help capture ETA suspects, due to come into effect in 2004. ETA claimed responsibility for several terrorist attacks in March 2002. In the following month a demand from independent, left-wing Basque parties for a cease-fire was denounced by Batasuna and ETA. A total of 122 arrests of ETA members were carried out during 2002 as part of a crackdown on the organization. In May the trial of Arnaldo Otegi of

Batasuna for vocal support of ETA was dismissed by the Supreme Court, to the consternation of the Government which attempted to intervene. After a number of ETA actions during the EU summit in Seville in June, however, the Senado approved measures to outlaw political parties deemed to support terrorist organizations. The legislation was widely seen as targeting Batasuna, and, indeed, in August a parliamentary vote outlawed the party, while a separate Supreme Court order enforced the closure of party offices and a three-year suspension of party activities. Subsequently, in March 2003, the Supreme Court officially outlawed Batasuna. (The party was banned for a further two years in early 2006.) Meanwhile, ETA declared its intention to attack the political offices of the PP and PSOE, and a number of violent actions were attempted in late 2002, including a thwarted attack on shopping centres in Madrid with five linked bombs in late December. In September ETA leaders Olarra Guridi and Ainhoa Mújika were arrested; this was followed in December by the arrest, in France, of their successors, one of whom, Ibon Fernandez de Iradi ('Susper'), subsequently escaped from custody. (He was recaptured a year later.) In November Judge Garzón accused 20 Batasuna leaders of membership of ETA, while in December an attempt to circumvent the illegalization of the party led Batasuna to establish another organization, the Sozialsta Abertzaleak (Patriotic Socialists), in the hope of contesting regional elections in May 2003. On 22 December 2002 a silent rally in Bilbao organized by Lehendakari Ibarretxe, who had put forward a set of proposals for the establishment of an independent Basque state in October, protested against ETA's political use of violence. As part of a global crackdown on terrorism, an anti-terrorist bill was passed by the national legislature in January 2003, raising the maximum sentence for terrorist activities from 30 to 40 years, and in February the Basque-language newspaper *Euskaldunon Egunkari* was shut down, on the grounds of its alleged links with ETA. Aznar's hope for external support in the eradication of ETA was widely believed to have been one of the reasons for his backing of US-led military action in Iraq during 2003 (see above). Prior to regional and municipal elections in May 2003, the central Government banned some 1,500 candidates from standing on the grounds of their alleged links with ETA. In response, ETA urged the lodging of protest votes in support of the banned politicians. In July two members of ETA were given terms of imprisonment of 790 years and six months for the 1987 bombing of a supermarket in Barcelona, in which 21 people had died. In September 2003 Ibarretxe presented to the regional parliament his plan for shared Spanish and Basque sovereignty over the Basque region, which proposed the 'free association' of the Basque Country with Spain, the creation of a separate judiciary and education system, and the right of the Basque Country to conduct international relations. The proposals—known as the Ibarretxe plan—were not widely supported in the region, and were strongly criticized by Madrid-based politicians and media, including Aznar, who accused Ibarretxe of treason. In early October 34 suspected ETA members were arrested as part of a joint Franco-Spanish operation, and in mid-November a further 12 suspected leaders of the illegal body were taken into custody. The following month four others, including Gorka Palacios Alday, the alleged military leader of ETA, were arrested in France. In December Spanish police foiled a planned attack by suspected ETA terrorists on a railway station in Madrid, and in February 2004, in the run-up to the general election in March, two men were captured driving towards Madrid with 500 kg of explosives. In the same month letters purporting to be from ETA were sent to businesses in the Spanish tourism sector warning that, as had been the case in 2003, tourists would be targeted during the summer season. At the same time ETA declared a cease-fire in Cataluña.

In January 2004 the Constitutional Court rejected Batasuna's appeal for legalization. Earlier that month a UN human rights specialist alleged that suspected ETA terrorists were being tortured while in custody. This was strenuously denied by the Government. Immediately following the PSOE's victory in the general election in March, ETA expressed a desire to begin a dialogue with the new Government; this was rejected, however, by José Luis Rodríguez Zapatero, the Prime Minister-elect. Responsibility for a series of bombs in seaside towns in mid-2004, the tourist season, was claimed by ETA. In late 2004, following the establishment of a Franco-Spanish anti-terrorism police force in September, a series of arrests of suspected members of ETA took place in France and Spain, including the capture in October of the alleged leader of the terrorist group, Mikel "Antza" Albizu Iriarte, in France. Subsequently Batasuna, the illegal political wing of ETA, announced that it was prepared to negotiate. However, in December and January 2005 a series of bombs were detonated around Spain, and in early February ETA exploded a car bomb, injuring over 40 people, at a conference centre in Madrid, which was due to be visited by the King and President Fox of Mexico. In 2004 a total of 135 suspected members of ETA were arrested, 74 in Spain and the others in France and Belgium. In December Baltasar Garzón, the leading anti-terrorism investigating judge, published a report stating that in the previous 10 years ETA had been responsible for the deaths of more than 800 people, and had caused some €8,000m. of damage; however, 2004 was notable for being the first year since the early 1970s in which ETA had not been responsible for any deaths. This was ascribed by many to the train bombings in March.

In December 2004 the Basque Parliament voted in favour of the Ibarretxe plan, with the last-minute support of Socialista Abertzaleak, the perceived successor to Batasuna, and thus the new political wing of ETA. In early February 2005 the plan was debated, and rejected by an overwhelming majority, by the Congreso de los Diputados, although Zapatero declared that he was prepared to enter into negotiations on the status of the Basque Country within Spain. Ibarretxe responded by bringing the date of the Basque regional elections forward to 17 April, and declaring that he would go ahead with plans for a referendum on the Ibarretxe plan, despite claims by the central Government that this was unconstitutional. The election was seen as a gauge of the popularity of the Ibarrexte plan. Prior to the poll, Aukera Guztiak, a nationalist party, was banned on the grounds of being close to ETA. In the event, Ibarretxe's PNV/EA coalition won a reduced majority of 29 seats, equivalent to 38.7% of votes cast.

In May 2005 the Congreso de los Diputados approved government plans to open negotiations with ETA, should the group consent to disarm. An estimated 300,000 demonstrators opposed to talks with ETA marched through north-east Madrid in early June. In October Harriet Aguirre, an alleged senior leader of ETA, was arrested in France, and in November, in the largest ever such prosecution, the trial commenced of 56 people suspected of belonging to, or aiding, ETA. ETA continued its bombing campaign around Spain during 2005 and early 2006, although no fatalities were caused. On 24 March 2006 a permanent cease-fire, which had been announced by ETA two days earlier, came into force. It was speculated that the cease-fire had been prompted by the arrest of many of ETA's leaders in recent years. Zapatero responded cautiously to ETA's unilateral declaration, stating in early April that talks on the political future of the Basque region could only begin once the cease-fire was confirmed.

Catalan and Galician nationalist groups, meanwhile, had continued their terrorist activities, the Catalan organization, Terra Lliure, claiming its first victim in September 1987 and the Galician Exército Guerrilheiro do Pobo Galego Ceibe (EGPGC) carrying out its first murder, of a civil guard, in February 1989. In mid-1989 the Catalan Government was reported to be negotiating with Terra Lliure. In July 1991 the dissolution of Terra Lliure was announced, following the group's renunciation of the use of violence. In mid-1992, however, a dissident faction planted several bombs. The trial of 24 alleged members of Terra Lliure concluded in July 1995, 18 being found guilty; 15 were pardoned in June 1996. The EGPGC's campaign continued intermittently. In September 1991 the alleged leader of the group was apprehended by the authorities and, upon the arrest in November of eight suspected EGPGC members, it was believed that the organization had been annihilated. In June 1994 six EGPGC activists received prison sentences, while two others were acquitted. In September 1998 proceedings for the extradition of an EGPGC suspect from Mexico were instigated.

In January 1985 the police arrested 17 members of Grupos de Resistencia Antifascista Primero de Octubre—GRAPO, an extreme left-wing organization. Detainees included the alleged leader of GRAPO, Mercedes Padrós Corominas. After a period of inactivity, GRAPO resumed its guerrilla campaign in 1988. In December 1989 GRAPO announced an intensification of its activities, shooting dead two civil guards shortly afterwards. In January 1990, as a hunger strike by more than 50 GRAPO prisoners progressed, the Minister of Justice confirmed that the Government would not negotiate with the terrorist organization. In September GRAPO claimed responsibility for various bomb attacks, targets including the stock exchange and the Ministry of Finance in Madrid and the PSC-PSOE headquarters in Barcelona. Two further bombs at government offices in Barcelona in

November again caused extensive damage. GRAPO remained active in 1992, the bombing of a gas pipeline in Zaragoza in February being attributed to the grouping. Between its foundation in 1975 and 1992, GRAPO was believed to have been responsible for a total of 70 murders. In December 1992 Laureano Ortega and two other leaders of the grouping were captured in Santander. In March 1993, however, three bombs planted by GRAPO exploded at offices in Madrid. Similar bomb attacks were carried out in May and in January 1994. At the end of the latter month four GRAPO suspects were arrested. Several members of GRAPO, including Ortega, received long prison sentences upon the conclusion of their trial in June 1995. Responsibility for the abduction later that month of Publio Cordón, a Zaragoza business executive, was claimed by GRAPO. In November more than 20 suspects were detained. Judicial proceedings against four GRAPO members, who claimed to have released Cordón in August 1995 upon receipt of a ransom, began in August 1996. Reports that the Government was negotiating with GRAPO prisoners, regarding the group's dissolution in return for certain concessions, were denied by José María Sánchez Casas, co-founder of GRAPO, upon his release from prison in July 1997. Having been imprisoned in October 1979 on various charges, including murder, Sánchez Casas vowed to resume the armed struggle. Also in July 1997 another GRAPO leader, Olegario Sánchez, was released after serving 20 years' imprisonment. Resuming its campaign, GRAPO detonated several devices in Madrid during 1998. In November three members of GRAPO were sentenced to 27 years' imprisonment for the abduction in 1995 of Cordón, the fate of the businessman remaining unknown. In April 1999 GRAPO claimed responsibility for an explosion at the tomb of Gen. Franco. In June GRAPO was linked to the bombing of a PP office in Carabanchel, and in May 2000 GRAPO claimed responsibility for an attack in Vigo on an armoured vehicle transporting 390m. pesetas, in which two security guards were killed. In June and September a number of bombs exploded, targeting locations in Seville, Valencia and Vigo. Later in the month bombs were found in Madrid and in the *El Mundo* office in Barcelona, both of which were attributed to GRAPO. In November an alleged leader, Manuel Perez, and a further six members of GRAPO were arrested in Paris, France. In retaliation for their arrest, Francisco Javier Sanz Morales, a civil guard, was assassinated in Madrid. In July 2002 14 GRAPO members were arrested in police operations in Paris, Madrid and Vitoria, including suspected leader Hierro Txomon; this was followed by a second series of arrests in November. In January 2006 a court in Paris sentenced nine senior members of GRAPO convicted of conspiring with a terrorist group to between 18 months' and seven years' imprisonment; Hierro Txomon received a seven-year sentence.

Following the terrorist attacks in the USA on 11 September 2001, it was reported that 16 Islamist activists had been arrested in Spain in late 2001. They were accused of belonging to the al-Qa'ida (Base) organization of Osama bin Laden, the Saudi-born militant Islamist held principally responsible for the attacks, and charged with terrorist activities. Further arrests were made during April and June 2002. In January 2003 16 North Africans, mostly from Algeria, were arrested near Barcelona and Girona following the discovery of a cache of chemicals and explosives, which were purportedly intended to be used in terrorist attacks around Europe. In September five men of Syrian origin were arrested in Spain on suspicion of having links with al-Qa'ida. Baltasar Garzón issued an arrest warrant for Osama bin Laden, and a further 34 individuals were charged with belonging to a terrorist organization. The trial of 24 alleged members of al-Qa'ida, some of whom were charged with organizing the 11 September attacks, commenced in Madrid in April 2005. In September 18 of the defendants were found guilty of being members of al-Qa'ida; Syrian-born Imad Yarkas was sentenced to 27 years' imprisonment for involvement in the 11 September attacks, while the others received prison sentences of between six and 11 years for a range of terrorism offences.

In late March 2004 international arrest warrants were issued for six suspected terrorists with Moroccan connections, including Abdelmajid Farkhet, a Tunisian, who was suspected of having masterminded the 11 March train bombings in Madrid (see above) and was known to have been preaching *jihad* (holy Islamic war) in the capital since mid-2003. Throughout the rest of 2004 and in early 2005 further arrests were made in Spain and in other European countries in connection with the Madrid train bombings; by early April 2005 a total of 24 people, mainly North Africans, had been charged on counts of terrorism and murder. In October and November 2004 33 suspected Islamist militants, reportedly with links to Moroccan fundamentalist groups, were arrested in connection with an alleged plot to detonate explosive devices in the high court and other public buildings in Madrid. In March 2006 32 people were charged in connection with the plot.

The first trial in connection with the Madrid train bombings was held in November 2004, and a 16-year-old Spaniard received a prison sentence of six years for trafficking explosives that were subsequently used in the attacks. In December Rabei Osman el Sayed, known as *The Egyptian*, one of the suspected leaders of the plot to blow up the trains in Madrid, was extradited from Italy, and in the same month Hassan al-Haski, who was alleged to be a leader of the Moroccan Islamist group, Groupe islamique combattant Marocain (GICM), was arrested and charged with 191 counts of murder. The GICM was reportedly connected to the May 2003 suicide bombings in Casablanca, Morocco. In November and December 2005 17 people were arrested on suspicion of providing logistical and financial assistance to a Algerian-based Islamist militant group, the Groupe salafiste pour la prédication et le combat (GSPC). It was reported that a total of around 90 suspected Islamist militants were arrested in Spain during 2005, some of whom were alleged to have been involved in recruiting other radicals to join the insurgency in Iraq. In April 2006 29 people, mostly Moroccan nationals, were charged with involvement in the Madrid train bombings; their trial was not expected to commence until early the following year.

In the late 1990s there was growing concern over the increasing number of illegal immigrants entering Spain, mostly from Latin America and North Africa. In 2000 some 14,893 people were apprehended, compared with 3,569 in the previous year. The influx of illegal immigrants had resulted in social unrest in some areas, with anti-immigration protests and violent attacks against the immigrant population. Despite intense opposition from the other parties in the Congreso de los Diputados, in July 2000 the Government announced proposals for the reform of the immigration law (adopted by the Congreso in December 1999), introducing severe penalties for illegal immigrants, and for traffickers and employers of illegal immigrants. Those entering the country illegally could be deported within 48 hours. Illegal workers would be deprived of the right to strike and to join a trade union, and their use of public services would be limited. They would gain the right to remain in the country only after five years of employment, rather than the two years previously specified. The reforms entered into force in January 2001, at which time there were an estimated 200,000 illegal immigrants in Spain. Demonstrations against the reforms were staged across the country, and in Barcelona 300 illegal immigrants locked themselves into the Santa Maria Pi Church and declared a hunger strike. In June the Government agreed to grant the protesters legal status. The authorities estimated in mid-2001 that there had been a 10% increase in illegal immigration compared with the previous year, and in August there were further protests in Barcelona when police arrested some 100 African illegal immigrants who had established a camp in one of the city's parks. Despite criticism from the opposition, amendments to the electoral legislation received parliamentary approval in late July: these specified modalities whereby immigrants who could prove that they had been working in Spain since January 2001 could obtain residency, but otherwise imposed a strict quota system linked to the needs of the labour market.

In January 2003 changes to immigration legislation, allowing South Americans of Spanish ancestry to apply for Spanish citizenship, were expected to lead to some 1m. applications. At the same time, greater strictures were placed on applications from other non-EU countries.

In February 2005 an amnesty was granted to the estimated 800,000 illegal immigrants in Spain, the terms of which required employers to register illegal immigrants, thereby allowing them to receive working permits. Immigration was becoming an increasingly important factor in the Spanish economy, with the number of registered immigrants living in Spain rising from 900,000 in 2000 to 3.7m. in 2005, equivalent to 8.4% of the resident population. In March 2006 the Spanish Government announced its intention to open the Spanish labour market from May to citizens of the eight central and eastern European countries that joined the EU in May 2004, removing restrictions that had been imposed at that time. Meanwhile, large numbers of Africans continued to attempt to enter Spain, often by highly dangerous routes. In October 2005 hundreds of would-be immigrants attempted to climb the barriers separating Morocco from the Spanish enclaves of Ceuta and Melilla, while in March 2006 it was estimated that some 1,200 Africans had died in the previous four months attempting to sail from Mauritania to the Canary Islands. Spain and Mauritania subsequently agreed to tighten their borders in an effort to deter African migrants from trying to enter Europe.

In foreign relations, in December 1988 Spain and the USA renewed their bilateral defence agreement, permitting the USA's use of bases in Spain for a further eight years from May 1989. In late 1996 the accord was extended until May 1998. In November 1999 the US Government requested permission to establish their principal base in southern Europe in Cádiz. Spain was admitted to Western European Union (WEU, see p. 365) in November 1988. In November 1992 Spain dispatched a substantial contingent of troops to Bosnia and Herzegovina, the first Spanish soldiers to serve in a UN peace-keeping operation. Continuing to assume a greater international role, Spain contributed troops to the multinational force deployed in Albania in April 1997, and again in April 1999 during the NATO offensive against Yugoslavia. The Spanish Government also offered temporary accommodation to as many as 10,000 refugees from the Yugoslav province of Kosovo. Spain committed 1,200 ground troops to the international peace-keeping force deployed in Kosovo in June 1999. In mid-2003, despite widespread public opposition, Spain sent 1,300 peace-keeping troops to Iraq to join the US-led coalition forces, and in October of that year pledged €250m. to the reconstruction process in Iraq. Following the devastating bomb attacks in Madrid in March 2004 and the consequent election of the PSOE Government, however, the withdrawal of the Spanish troops was completed by the end of May. In early 2006 Spain was contributing to a number of international peace-keeping missions, including the International Security Assistance Force Afghanistan, in which some 800 Spanish troops were serving.

From 1998, under Spanish law persons accused of crimes against humanity, no matter where they had taken place, could be tried in a Spanish court. In the late 1990s criminal proceedings continued in Spain against former Argentine and Chilean officials of the military dictatorships of Argentina (1976–83) and of Chile (1979–90), during which numerous Spanish citizens had been killed. In November 1999 the investigating judge, Garzón, issued international arrest warrants for 98 citizens of Argentina. In January 2000, however, the judge's request for the extradition of 48 Argentines, accused of various atrocities, was refused. In August 2003 Ricardo Cavallo, a naval officer during Argentina's 'dirty war', was extradited from Mexico on charges of human rights abuses. In November 1998, following the arrest in the United Kingdom of Gen. Augusto Pinochet and the instigation by Garzón of extradition proceedings against the former Chilean President, Chile's ambassador to Madrid was recalled for consultations. In October 1999 a British judge ruled that the former Chilean President could be extradited to Spain to answer 35 charges of torture and conspiracy. In March 2000, however, Pinochet was permitted to return to Chile from the United Kingdom, where he had remained under house arrest, extradition proceedings having been abandoned on medical grounds. In early 2005, following an indictment by Garzón, Adolfo Scilingo, an Argentine former army officer, was given a prison sentence of 640 years for crimes against humanity under the military rule in Argentina between 1976–1983.

The success of the PSOE in general elections in March 2004 led to a shift in foreign relations emphasis from the USA to Europe, and accords were signed on the creation of a joint anti-terrorism police force with France, and on increased military co-operation between EU member states, including the creation of a European rapid-reaction force. Relations with the Vatican were strained in 2005, however, due to the legalization of same-sex marriage. In late 2005 tensions arose with the USA over a Spanish agreement to sell military equipment to Venezuela. In April 2006 the foreign affairs committee of the Congreso de los Diputados requested that the Government compile a detailed report on alleged flights by the USA's Central Intelligence Agency (CIA) via Spain. This followed claims that the CIA had used European airports to transport suspected Islamist militants to third countries for interrogation.

Spanish ratification of the Maastricht Treaty on European Union was completed in November 1992. The dispute between Spain and the United Kingdom over the sovereignty of the neighbouring British dependent territory of Gibraltar remained unresolved. Relations deteriorated in 1995 upon Spain's announcement that, in protest at the apparent inadequacy of British efforts, it was to implement stricter border controls to combat the problem of drugs- and tobacco-smuggling from Gibraltar. In May 1996, upon the election of a new Government in the territory, border controls were further strengthened by the Spanish authorities, leading to even greater delays for travellers and to renewed protests from the British Government. In 1997 the United Kingdom rejected Spanish initiatives entailing joint sovereignty for up to 100 years prior to the eventual transfer of power to Spain. In December Spanish proposals that, following a period of joint sovereignty, Gibraltar became an Autonomous Community were similarly rebuffed by the British Government. In 1998 tension was renewed over the issue of access to fishing grounds. The seizure of a Spanish fishing vessel in early 1999 led to a serious escalation of the dispute and the imposition of new border controls and travel restrictions by Spain. In September 1996, meanwhile, it was announced that Gibmed, the NATO base in Gibraltar, was to be phased out, thus facilitating Spain's full integration into the alliance's military structure. In July 1998 Spain and the United Kingdom were reported to have reached agreement regarding the removal of restrictions on the use of Gibraltar as a communications centre during NATO exercises. In April 2000 Spain and the United Kingdom signed an agreement relating to the administrative status of Gibraltar. The territory's identity cards would henceforth be accepted by Spain as valid for travel within the EU. While emphasizing that the accord did not alter its claim to Gibraltar, Spain was expected to co-operate more fully with the territory's police force. Furthermore, the agreement permitted the implementation of numerous EU directives, long obstructed by Spain, which had refused to recognize the Government of Gibraltar as a 'competent authority' in EU affairs. It was also agreed that Spain and Gibraltar would communicate indirectly through a facility, based in London, provided by the British authorities. In March 2001 Spain condemned plans by the political parties of Gibraltar to request reforms to the 1969 Constitution, allowing self-determination, and to hold a referendum on decolonization. Following a meeting between Spanish and British officials in Brussels in mid-2001, the Minister of Foreign Affairs, Josep Piqué, and his British counterpart, Jack Straw, held discussions in October, at which they agreed to work towards solving the dispute by December 2002. The issue of the right of Gibraltarians to vote on any agreement reached by the two Governments continued to impede the progress of the discussions, Piqué warning the British Government that Spain would not accept the results of such a referendum. At further talks in November, however, Piqué announced plans to increase the number of telephone lines available to Gibraltar, from 35,000 to 100,000, and provide access to Spanish health care for the inhabitants of the territory. The deadline for achieving a solution was also brought forward to September 2002. In January 2002 it was reported that the Spanish Government had agreed to modify its demand for outright sovereignty over the territory and reconsider the option of sharing sovereignty over the territory with the United Kingdom for an indefinite period. In an open letter published in the Gibraltan press, Piqué attempted to persuade the citizens of Gibraltar of the advantages of Spanish sovereignty and urged its Chief Minister, Peter Caruana, to join the discussions; Caruana had hitherto boycotted the negotiations. At a meeting in March, the Spanish and British Governments agreed to seek EU funding for proposals for the development of Gibraltar's port, airport and other infrastructure. During May, however, Aznar announced that Spain would never withdraw its territorial claim to the British enclave. Negotiations progressed in mid-2002, although a stalemate emerged when Spain disagreed with the British conditions for joint sovereignty—that it be permanent, that the military base would remain under British control, and that all changes be approved by a referendum put to the people of Gibraltar. In a referendum organized by the local administration of Gibraltar in November, which was not, however, recognized by the Spanish or British Government, the electorate voted overwhelmingly (by 99%, of a turn-out of 87.9%) against joint sovereignty with Spain. Relations were further strained in November 2003 when the Spanish Government ordered that the frontier with Gibraltar be closed for the first time since 1985. The Spanish authorities maintained that this action was taken as a precautionary measure when a cruise-ship carrying passengers suffering from a virulent stomach virus was docked in Gibraltar. In August 2004 relations between Spain and the United Kingdom were strained following the attendance of the British Secretary of State for Defence at a celebration of the colony's 300th anniversary. Following informal talks between

Spanish and Gibraltarian officials in September, Spain lifted its ban on cruise ships from outside the EU visiting both Gibraltar and Spain and announced that it would be seeking to reopen negotiations with the United Kingdom. In December the first of what was to be an annual tripartite meeting between the United Kingdom, Spain and Gibraltar was held in the United Kingdom, and it was subsequently announced that henceforth decisions on the territory's future must be agreed by all three parties. In early 2006 Spain opposed the inclusion of references to the right to self-determination of Gibraltarians in a proposed new constitution for Gibraltar. However, in March Straw assured the Spanish Government that the draft constitution, which was to be subject to a referendum in Gibraltar, would not change the current international status or sovereignty of the territory, nor affect Spanish rights over Gibraltar under the Treaty of Utrecht, which would constrain the right to self-determination, in the view of the British Government, and that independence would therefore only be a future option for Gibraltar with Spain's consent.

Relations with Portugal, traditionally tense, improved throughout the 1980s, culminating in 1989 when King Juan Carlos became the first Spanish monarch to address the Portuguese parliament. In the mid-1990s the principal bilateral issue between the two countries was the division of water resources; an accord over the sharing over river resources was reached in 1998. During 1997 relations were strained by Portugal's refusal to extradite an ETA terrorist. In 2002 tensions rose again, firstly over a border incident in which two Portuguese MPs were refused entry into Spain in July, then, later in the year, over mutual accusations of responsibility for the *Prestige* disaster (see above). In January 2003 a clash between Portuguese maritime police and Spanish fishermen accused of using illegal fishing nets in Portuguese territorial waters led to the instigation of legal proceedings by Portugal, souring relations further between the two countries. However, in December a reciprocal 10-year agreement on access to fishing grounds was reached by the two countries.

Relations with Morocco have been dominated by the issues of sovereignty of the enclaves of Ceuta and Melilla, illegal immigration and drugs-trafficking, and by disputes over fishing rights. By early 2000 the problems of illegal immigration (not only via Spanish North Africa but increasingly via the Canary Islands) had become a major political issue. In May, during a visit to Morocco, the Spanish Prime Minister confirmed that the recently implemented immigration law, one of the most liberal within the EU, was to be reformed (see above). Since its entry into force earlier in the year, the new legislation had encouraged more than 82,000 immigrants to apply for Spanish residency permits. Protests against the reforms were staged in Spanish North Africa as well as in Spain. Negotiations on the renewal of the fishing agreement between Morocco and the EU, permitting Spanish vessels access to Moroccan waters, commenced in mid-September 1999. The agreement expired at the end of November and Morocco indicated that the accord would not be renewed. Spanish vessels were once again required to withdraw from Moroccan waters and more than 4,000 Spanish fishermen remained without work. Despite extensive negotiations, by early 2001 the EU had failed to reach an agreement with Morocco, and Prime Minister José María Aznar announced that the consequences would be felt in the relations between the two countries. In October the Moroccan Government recalled its ambassador to Spain at short notice after declaring that it was dissatisfied with the level of bilateral relations following the failure of the EU negotiations. In the following month a Spanish fishing vessel was apprehended by the Moroccan authorities and charged with fishing without a licence. In early April 2002, however, it was reported that the two Governments were preparing to reinstate their respective ambassadors. Relations were threatened again in mid-July, following the occupation of a small islet near Ceuta, the Isla de Perejil, by 12 Moroccan soldiers. Spain lodged a formal protest against this action on 12 July, but Morocco refused to withdraw its men, claiming that Perejil (known as Laila by the Moroccans) had been a part of Morocco since independence in 1956. Four Spanish gunboats were dispatched to patrol the locality and Spanish soldiers reoccupied the island on 17 July. A subsequent US-mediated agreement between Spain and Morocco left the island unoccupied. Issues over the sovereignty of Ceuta and Melilla continued to be problematic, however, especially in relation to negotiations on Gibraltar, and in September Morocco accused Spain of repeated violations of its airspace and territorial waters and reasserted its claims over the enclaves before the UN. Relations improved somewhat in November, however, when Morocco offered the temporary use of its territorial waters to 64 Spanish fishing boats after the *Prestige* oil disaster. Meetings in December 2002 and January 2003 contributed to the re-establishment of diplomatic relations between the two countries in February 2003. During an official visit by Aznar to Morocco in December 2003 Spain and Morocco agreed to instigate a feasibility survey for a tunnel linking the two countries. A decision on whether to construct the tunnel was expected to be made in 2008. Relations between Morocco and Spain improved following the election of the PSOE in March 2004, and co-operation with regard to suspected militant Islamist activity in Spain increased.

Government

Under the Constitution approved in 1978, Spain is an hereditary monarchy, with the King as Head of State. He appoints the President of the Government (Prime Minister) and, on the latter's recommendation, other members of the Council of Ministers. Legislation is initiated for discussion in the Cortes (national assembly) in Madrid, in the Parliaments of the Autonomous Communities, or by popular petition. The King's actions in state affairs must receive the prior approval of the Cortes, to which the Government is responsible. The Council of State is the supreme consultative organ and comprises 23 members.

Legislative power is vested in the Cortes Generales, comprising two Houses, elected by direct universal adult suffrage for four years (subject to dissolution). The Congreso de los Diputados (Congress of Deputies) has 350 members, elected by proportional representation, and the Senado (Senate) has 208 directly elected members, plus 51 regional representatives, elected by the autonomous parliaments. A party can gain representation only if it obtains at least 3% of the votes.

The process of regional self-government was initiated in 1967. In October 1979 the statutes of the first of 17 Autonomous Communities were approved by referendum. The first Legislative Assemblies (Basque and Catalan) were elected in March 1980. The Galician Legislative Assembly was elected in October 1981, and that of Andalucía in May 1982. The remaining 13 were constituted in May 1983, thus completing the process of devolution. The regions possess varying degrees of autonomy. Each Legislative Assembly is elected for four years.

Spain comprises 50 provinces, each with its own Council (Diputación Provincial). The system of Civil Governors was replaced (by royal decree) in April 1997: a government sub-delegate is appointed by each Autonomous Community's government delegate.

Defence

Plans for the gradual abolition of military service and for the establishment of professional armed forces were announced in early 1996; conscription was abolished in 2000, while the final stages of professionalization were completed in 2003. Legislation to permit the entry of women to all sections of the armed forces took effect in early 1989. In August 2005 the total strength of the armed forces was 147,255, comprising: army 95,600, navy 19,455 (including 5,300 marines), air force 22,750, and 9,450 in joint service. The paramilitary Guardia Civil (Civil Guard) numbered 73,360. Spain became a member of the North Atlantic Treaty Organization (NATO, see p. 314) in May 1982. In December 1997 Spain's full integration into the military structure of NATO (with effect from January 1999) was approved by the alliance. Spain joined Western European Union (WEU, see p. 365) in November 1988. The US military presence in Spain comprised a naval force of 282 in August 2005. In September 2004 an agreement on the establishment of a *gendarmerie* comprising 3,000 troops was signed by Spain, France, Italy, Portugal and the Netherlands. In the same year Spain pledged some 2,000 troops to a European rapid reaction force, which was intended to be fully established by 2007. The 2006 draft budget for defence was €7,123.4m., equivalent to 2.6% of total expenditure.

Economic Affairs

In 2004, according to estimates by the World Bank, Spain's gross national income (GNI), measured at average 2002–04 prices, was US $875,818m., equivalent to $21,210 per head (or $25,070 per head on an international purchasing-power parity basis). During 1995–2004, it was estimated, the population increased at an average annual rate of 0.6%, while gross domestic product (GDP) per head increased, in real terms, by an average of 2.7% per year. Overall GDP increased, in real terms, at an average annual rate of 3.6% in 1995–2004, according to official estimates; growth was 3.0% in 2003 and 3.1% in 2004.

Agriculture (including forestry and fishing) contributed an estimated 3.5% of GDP and engaged 5.4% of the employed labour force in 2004. The principal crops are barley, wheat, sugar beet, vegetables, citrus fruits, grapes and olives; wine and olive oil are important products. Farmers were seriously affected by the infection of cattle with both bovine spongiform encephalopathy (BSE) and foot and mouth disease during 2000–01. Agricultural GDP grew at an average annual rate of 3.7% in 1995–2004, according to official estimates; it decreased by 0.1% in 2003, and by 1.0% in 2004. The fishing industry is significant. The Spanish fishing fleet is one of the largest in the world, and has been involved in various international disputes. In November 2002 the oil-tanker *Prestige* sank off the Galician coast, polluting an estimated 3,000 km of coastline. It was predicted that the area would take 10 years to recover, at a cost of some €5,000m. to the fishing and tourism industries. Catches of shellfish and inshore fish were reported to have declined by 80% following the tanker's sinking.

Industry (including mining, manufacturing, power and construction) contributed an estimated 29.2% of GDP and engaged 30.1% of the employed labour force in 2004. According to the World Bank, industrial GDP increased at an average annual rate of 3.5% in 1995–2003; it increased by 1.8% in 2002 and by 2.0% in 2003.

The mining and quarrying industry provided less than 1.0% of GDP and engaged 0.3% of the employed labour force in 2004. Hard coal and brown coal are the principal minerals extracted, although production fell in the late 1990s owing to environmental standards imposed by the European Union (EU, see p. 228). In 2005, according to the Energy Information Administration (a section of the US Department of Energy), proven oil reserves amounted to 158m. barrels.

Manufacturing contributed an estimated 16.0% of GDP and engaged 17.2% of the employed labour force in 2004. In 2005 Spain was the world's fifth largest exporters of passenger cars. In that year exports of passenger vehicles numbered 2.25m. units. Other important industries are shipbuilding, chemicals, steel, textiles and footwear; some of these sectors underwent a process of rationalization in the 1980s. Investment is being made in new manufacturing industries, such as information technology and telecommunications equipment. Manufacturing GDP increased at an average annual rate of 3.3% in 1995–2004, according to official estimates; the rate of growth was 0.9% in 2003 and 0.4% in 2004.

Energy (comprising mining and power) contributed an estimated 2.5% of GDP and employed 0.9% of the labour force in 2004. Energy is derived principally from petroleum, most of which is imported. In 2003 imports of mineral fuels and petroleum products accounted for 10.3% of total import costs. Natural gas became an increasingly important fuel source in the late 1990s. Some natural gas requirements are obtained from the Bay of Biscay, the remainder being imported by pipeline from Algeria. Nuclear energy provided 55.0% of total electricity production in 2003, while coal provided 24.4%, and hydroelectric power 12.1%. In 2001 the electricity sector underwent major restructuring. By 2004 wind power provided €3,000m. of energy, the equivalent of 6% of total electricity demand. According to official estimates, energy GDP increased by 1.7% in 1995–2004; energy GDP grew by 1.3% in 2003, and by 2.0% in 2004.

In 2004 the services sector accounted for an estimated 67.3% of GDP and engaged 64.5% of the employed labour force. The tourism industry makes an important contribution to the Spanish economy. In 2005 the number of tourist arrivals was estimated at 55.6m., and receipts from tourism reached €46,060m. In April 2001 several areas, including the Balearic Islands, introduced an environmental tourist tax, included in the cost of tourist accommodation, to protect the environment and repair the damage caused by the annual influx of tourists. Remittances from emigrants are also significant. In 2004 remittances amounted to €4.2m., while immigrants living in Spain remitted €3.4m. According to official estimates, the GDP of the services sector increased at an average annual rate of 3.3% in 1995–2004; services GDP increased by 2.9% in 2003 and by 3.6% in 2004.

In 2004 Spain recorded a visible trade deficit of US $65,830m. and there was a deficit of $55,380m. on the current account of the balance of payments. In 2003 the principal sources of imports were Germany (16.4%) and France (16.2%), while the latter was the main export market, purchasing 19.2%, followed by Germany (12.0%). Italy, the United Kingdom and other EU countries, and the USA, are also important trading partners. The principal imports in 2003 were machinery and transport equipment, chemical products, mineral fuels and petroleum products, and food and live animals. The main exports were machinery and transport equipment, food and live animals (particularly fruit and vegetables), and chemical products.

In 2005 an overall budget surplus equivalent to 1.1% of GDP was estimated. The annual rate of inflation averaged 2.6% in 1995–2000 and 3.2% in 2001–04; consumer prices increased by an average of 3.0% in 2004 and 3.4% in 2005. The unemployment rate fell for the first time since 2001 in 2004, to 10.8%, and declined further, to 8.7%, in 2005.

Spain became a member of the EU in January 1986, and joined the exchange rate mechanism of the European Monetary System in June 1989. According to the draft budget for 2006, in that year Spain was due to receive €16,705m. from the EU, while contributing €10,946m. Spain is also a member of the Organisation for Economic Co-operation and Development (OECD, see p. 320).

Upon taking office in May 1996, the PP Government declared its commitment to European economic and monetary union (as agreed by EU members at Maastricht in December 1991). In order to meet the EU convergence criteria, Spain's budget deficit was duly reduced to the equivalent of below 3.0% of GDP by 1997. Spain was thus able to qualify for membership of the single European currency, introduced in January 1999. As a direct consequence of entering the single European currency, from early 1999 there was a sudden and sustained rise in inflation. In addition to high consumer demand, the introduction of the euro also encouraged stronger GDP growth. Following the enlargement of the EU in May 2004, only Andalucía and Extremadura, with an income per head of less than 75% of the EU average, remained eligible for EU funding in 2007–13. The PSOE Government that took office in April 2004 pledged to continue with the fiscal policies of the previous administration, which had predicted annual budgetary surpluses for 2004–07. In early 2005 a plan to generate economic growth by developing infrastructure and increasing competition was unveiled, and the IMF recommended reform of the pensions system, the phasing out of tax deductions for home owners, and the limiting of government spending. Negotiations between the Government and labour representatives were under way in 2005 with the aim of reforming labour regulations; measures proposed included an increase in the retirement age. The budget for 2006, approved by the Congreso de los Diputados in December 2005, provided for an increase of 11.3% in central government transfers to the regional governments, in line with the Government's policy of increasing regional autonomy. Notably, the Government had decentralized health-care provision, although funding this was proving to be problematic. Spain's economic performance in 2005 was generally favourable: real GDP increased by 3.4%, a budgetary surplus was recorded and the rate of unemployment declined. Nevertheless, strong domestic demand contributed to high inflation and a significant increase in imports, causing the current-account deficit to widen to an estimated 7.3% of GDP. GDP growth of 3.3% was forecast for 2006. In February 2006 the Government proposed a series of moderate tax reforms, which were to be introduced from 2007 with the aim of simplifying the system and lowering overall taxes. A reduction in the base rate of corporate tax, from 35% to 30%, was envisaged.

Education

In 2005/06 some 1.48m. children were attending pre-school institutions. In that year 2.48m. children were enrolled at primary schools and a total of 2.99m. were enrolled in secondary education. Under reforms implemented in 1991, basic education is compulsory, and available free of charge, from the ages of six to 16 years. It comprises primary education, which begins at six years of age and lasts for six years, and secondary education, composed of two two-year cycles, followed between the ages of 12 and 16. Thereafter, students may take either a vocational training course, lasting one or two years, or the two-year *Bachillerato* course, in preparation for university entrance. Private schools, many of which are administered by the Roman Catholic Church, are responsible for the education of more than 30% of Spanish children. In the Autonomous Communities the teaching of languages other than Spanish (such as Catalan) is regulated by decree. In 2002/03 enrolment at primary schools included 100% of children (males 100%; females 99%) in the relevant age-group, while enrolment at secondary schools in that year included 96% of children (males 94%; females 98%) in the appropriate age-group. In 2004 the Government announced a reform of the education system, part of which included the designation of religious education as an optional, rather than compulsory, subject.

SPAIN

Statistical Survey

Some 1.44m. students were attending university in 2005/06. In that year there were 72 universities, including the open university (UNED, established in 1972). There are three cycles within university education. The first cycle lasts for three years and leads to the degree of *Diplomatura*. The second cycle lasts for two or three years and leads to the degree of *Licenciatura*. The degree of Doctor is awarded upon completion of the two-year third cycle and the writing of a thesis. Higher technical studies in engineering and architecture are followed at Escuelas Técnicas de Grado Medio and Escuelas Técnicas de Grado Superior. The 2006 draft budget allocated €1,888.2m. (0.7% of total expenditure) to education.

Public Holidays

2006: 1 January (New Year's Day), 6 January (Epiphany), 13 April (Maundy Thursday), 14 April (Good Friday), 1 May (Labour Day), 15 August (Assumption), 12 October (National Day, anniversary of the discovery of America), 1 November (All Saints' Day), 6 December (Constitution Day), 8 December (Immaculate Conception), 25 December (Christmas Day).

2007: 1 January (New Year's Day), 6 January (Epiphany), 5 April (Maundy Thursday), 6 April (Good Friday), 1 May (Labour Day), 15 August (Assumption), 12 October (National Day, anniversary of the discovery of America), 1 November (All Saints' Day), 6 December (Constitution Day), 8 December (Immaculate Conception), 25 December (Christmas Day).

In addition, various regional holidays are observed.

Weights and Measures

The metric system is in force.

Statistical Survey

Source (unless otherwise stated): Instituto Nacional de Estadística, Paseo de la Castellana 183, 28071 Madrid; tel. (91) 5839100; fax (91) 5839158; internet www.ine.es.

Area and Population

AREA, POPULATION AND DENSITY*

Area (sq km)	505,988†
Population (census results)	
1 March 1991	38,872,268
1 November 2001	
Males	20,021,850
Females	20,825,521
Total	40,847,371
Population (official estimates at 1 January)	
2003	42,717,064
2004	43,197,684
2005	44,108,530
Density (per sq km) at 1 January 2005	87.2

* Including the Spanish External Territories (Spanish North Africa—area 33 sq km), an integral part of Spain. Ceuta had a population of 75,276 on 1 January 2005, while Melilla's population was 65,488.
† 195,363 sq miles.

PROVINCES
(population at 1 January 2005)*†

Alava	299,957		Lugo	357,625
Albacete	384,640		Madrid	5,964,143
Alicante	1,732,389		Málaga	1,453,409
Almería	612,315		Murcia	1,335,792
Avila	167,032		Navarra	593,472
Badajoz	671,299		Ourense	339,555
Illes Balears			Oviedo (Principado	
(Balearic Is)	983,131		de Asturias)	1,076,635
Barcelona	5,226,354		Palencia	173,471
Burgos	361,021		Las Palmas	1,011,928
Cáceres	412,580		Pontevedra	938,311
Cádiz	1,180,817		Salamanca	352,414
Castellón (Castelló)			Santa Cruz de	
de la Plana	543,432		Tenerife	956,352
			Santander	
Ciudad Real	500,060		(Cantabria)	562,309
Córdoba	784,376		Segovia	155,517
A Coruña	1,126,707		Sevilla	1,813,908
Cuenca	207,974		Soria	92,773
Girona (Gerona)	664,506		Tarragona	704,907
Granada	860,898		Teruel	141,091
Guadalajara	203,737		Toledo	598,256
Guipúzcoa	688,708		Valencia	2,416,628
Huelva	483,792		Valladolid	514,674
Huesca	215,864		Vizcaya	1,136,181
Jaén	660,284		Zamora	198,045
La Rioja	301,084		Zaragoza	912,072
León	495,902			
Lleida (Lérida)	399,439		**Total**	**43,967,766**

* Excluding the Spanish External Territories (Spanish North Africa).
† Including residents temporarily abroad.

PRINCIPAL TOWNS*
(population at 1 January 2005)

Madrid (capital)	3,155,359		Vitoria-Gasteiz	226,490
			Santa Cruz de	
Barcelona	1,593,075		Tenerife	221,567
Valencia	796,549		Badalona	218,553
Sevilla (Seville)	704,154		Elche	215,137
Zaragoza	647,373		Oviedo	212,174
Málaga	558,287		Móstoles	204,463
Murcia	409,810		Cartagena	203,945
Las Palmas de Gran				
Canaria	378,628		Alcalá de Henares	197,804
Palma de Mallorca	375,773		Sabadell	196,971
Bilbao	353,173		Jerez de la Frontera	196,275
Córdoba	321,164		Fuenlabrada	195,131
Valladolid	321,001		Terrassa	194,947
Alicante (Alacant)	319,380		Pamplona	193,328
Vigo	293,725		Santander	183,955
			Donostia-San	
Gijón	273,931		Sebastián	182,930
Hospitalet de				
Llobregat	252,884		Almería	181,702
(A) Coruña	243,349		Leganés	181,284
Granada	236,982		Burgos	172,421

* Population figures refer to *municipios*, each of which may contain some rural area as well as the urban centre.

BIRTHS, MARRIAGES AND DEATHS

	Registered live births		Registered marriages		Registered deaths	
	Number	Rate (per 1,000)	Number	Rate (per 1,000)	Number	Rate (per 1,000)
1997	369,035	9.3	196,499	5.0	349,521	8.8
1998	365,193	9.2	207,041	5.2	360,511	9.1
1999	380,130	9.5	208,129	5.2	371,102	9.3
2000	397,632	9.9	216,451	5.4	360,391	9.0
2001	406,380	10.1	208,057	5.1	360,131	8.9
2002	418,846	10.1	211,522	5.1	368,618	8.9
2003	441,881	10.5	212,300	5.0	384,828	9.2
2004	454,591	10.6	216,149	5.1	371,934	8.7

Expectation of life (WHO estimates, years at birth): 80 (males 76; females 83) in 2003 (Source: WHO, *World Health Report*).

SPAIN

ECONOMICALLY ACTIVE POPULATION
('000 persons aged 16 years and over)

	2002	2003	2004
Agriculture, hunting and forestry	905.6	892.7	868.1
Fishing	55.7	49.4	51.6
Mining and quarrying	63.2	63.3	57.7
Manufacturing	2,999.1	2,960.5	2,936.8
Electricity, gas and water supply	91.5	99.6	103.7
Construction	1,913.2	1,984.6	2,058.7
Wholesale and retail trade; repair of motor vehicles, motorcycles and personal and household goods	2,552.3	2,638.9	2,747.1
Hotels and restaurants	1,018.9	1,042.3	1,076.7
Transport, storage and communications	993.7	1,026.9	1,033.6
Financial intermediation	400.6	398.4	398.4
Real estate, renting and business activities	1,293.2	1,370.6	1,481.9
Public administration and defence; compulsory social security	1,046.2	1,096.8	1,137.4
Education	943.1	951.8	996.3
Health and social work	913.2	987.8	1,016.4
Other community, social and personal service activities	649.5	688.1	696.5
Private households with employed persons	416.8	441.7	454.6
Extra-territorial organizations and bodies	1.8	1.2	1.1
Total employed	16,257.6	16,694.6	17,116.6
Total unemployed	2,082.9	2,127.3	2,073.8
Total labour force	18,340.4	18,821.9	19,190.3
Males	11,034.5	11,199.1	11,300.6
Females	7,305.9	7,622.8	7,889.8

Health and Welfare

KEY INDICATORS

Total fertility rate (children per woman, 2003)	1.2
Under-5 mortality rate (per 1,000 live births, 2004)	5
HIV/AIDS (% of persons aged 15–49, 2003)	0.7
Physicians (per 1,000 head, 2002)	2.9
Hospital beds (per 1,000 head, 2000)	4.1
Health expenditure (2002): US $ per head (PPP)	1,640
Health expenditure (2002): % of GDP	7.6
Health expenditure (2002): public (% of total)	71.3
Human Development Index (2003): ranking	21
Human Development Index (2003): value	0.928

For sources and definitions, see explanatory note on p. vi.

Agriculture

PRINCIPAL CROPS
('000 metric tons)

	2002	2003	2004
Wheat	6,822	6,290	7,018
Rice (paddy)	819	855	900
Barley	8,362	8,698	10,609
Maize	4,425	4,339	4,748
Oats	916	873	1,019
Potatoes	3,078	2,665	2,745
Sugar cane	79	83	58
Sugar beet	8,197	6,365	7,015
Olives	4,415	7,554	4,966
Sunflower seed	771	769	785
Lettuce	1,037	1,045	967
Tomatoes	3,980	3,947	4,442
Chillies and green peppers	1,056	1,056	1,006
Dry onions	1,022	937	1,084

	2002	2003	2004
—*continued*			
Other vegetables*	500	500	500
Oranges	2,963	3,052	2,690
Tangerines, mandarins, clementines and satsumas	2,068	2,060	2,458
Lemons and limes	934	1,130	729
Apples	695	881	603
Pears	631	728	562
Peaches and nectarines	1,276	1,271	916
Grapes	5,935	7,266	7,286
Watermelons	623	733	765
Cantaloupes and other melons	1,012	1,071	1,102

* FAO estimates.
Source: FAO.

LIVESTOCK
('000 head, year ending September)

	2002	2003	2004
Horses*	238	238	238
Mules*	110	110	110
Asses*	140	140	140
Cattle	6,478	6,548	6,653
Pigs	23,518	24,056	24,895
Sheep	23,813	23,486	22,672
Goats	3,047	3,164	2,833
Chickens*	128,000	128,000	129,000

* FAO estimates.
Source: FAO.

LIVESTOCK PRODUCTS
('000 metric tons)

	2002	2003	2004
Beef and veal	679	706	702
Mutton and lamb	237	236	231
Goat meat	15	14	13
Pig meat	3,070	3,190	3,176
Horse meat	6	5	5
Rabbit meat	119	112	107
Poultry meat	1,210	1,209	1,289
Cows' milk	6,809	7,234	6,300*
Sheep's milk	420	440	380†
Goats' milk	529	517	455†
Butter	55	52	50
Cheese	163	179	128
Hen eggs	734	768	700*
Other poultry eggs	1	1	1†
Honey	36	35	37
Wool: (greasy)	42	30	22
Wool: (scoured)	19	18	18
Cattle hides†	70	75	80
Sheepskins†	23	23	23

* Unofficial estimate.
† FAO estimate(s).
Source: FAO.

Forestry

ROUNDWOOD REMOVALS
('000 cubic metres, excl. bark)

	2002	2003	2004
Sawlogs, veneer logs and logs for sleepers	7,603	7,700	7,795
Pulpwood	5,373	5,470	5,520
Other industrial wood	874	905	920
Fuel wood	1,989	2,030	2,055
Total	15,839	16,105	16,290

Source: FAO.

SPAIN

SAWNWOOD PRODUCTION
('000 cubic metres, incl. railway sleepers)

	2002	2003	2004
Coniferous (softwood)	2,681	2,710	2,730
Broadleaved (hardwood)	843	920	1,000
Total	3,524	3,630	3,730

Source: FAO.

Fishing

('000 metric tons, live weight)

	2001	2002	2003
Capture*	1,093.0	893.0	896.3
European pilchard (sardine)	71.1	54.4	55.8
Skipjack tuna	122.2	140.3	155.4
Yellowfin tuna	90.4	90.2	108.7
Jack and horse mackerels	47.0	38.3	37.0
Aquaculture	312.6	322.7	313.3
Blue mussel	246.0	260.0	248.8
Total catch*	1,405.7	1,215.8	1,209.6

* FAO estimates.

Note: Figures exclude aquatic plants ('000 metric tons, capture only): 14.0 in 2001; n.a. in 2002; n.a. in 2003. Also excluded are Sardinia coral (metric tons): 6.6 in 2001; 7.8 in 2002; 9.1 in 2003; and sponges (metric tons): 0.7 in 2001 (FAO estimate); 0.7 in 2002 (FAO estimate); 0.5 in 2003.

Source: FAO.

Mining

('000 metric tons, unless otherwise indicated)

	2001	2002	2003
Anthracite	4,694	4,3	3,863
Lignite	12,193	8,762	7,981
Crude petroleum ('000 barrels)	2,505	2,427	2,404
Natural gas (million cubic metres)	556.6	553.2	550.0
Copper*	9.7	1.2	0.6
Lead*	36.0	6.2	1.8
Zinc (metric tons)*	164.9	69.9	44.6
Kaolin	400.0†	419.5	450.0
Potash salts (crude)	569.1	481.3	594.4
Pyrites	152	100	0
Sepiolite	897.0	733.1	690.4
Dolomite	9,628	11,537	12,000
Fluorspar‡	134.0	141.4	139.7
Salt (unrefined)	3,700	3,894	3,963
Gypsum (crude)	10,901	11,218	12,000

* Figures refer to the metal content of ores.
† Estimated figure.
‡ Figures refer to total CaF_2 content (acid and metallurgical grades).

Source: US Geological Survey.

Industry

SELECTED PRODUCTS
('000 metric tons, unless otherwise indicated)

	2000	2001	2002
Fish (tinned)	342.9	347.9	368.9
Wheat flour	2,673	2,811	2,932
Vinegar	820	938	947
Distilled alcohol ('000 hectolitres)	1,605	1,863	2,907
Wine ('000 hectolitres)	n.a.	n.a.	27,891
Beer ('000 hectolitres)	26,388	26,802	28,631
Soft drinks ('000 hectolitres)	45,355	47,305	48,424
Cigarettes (million units)	74,799	n.a.	n.a.
Caustic soda	707	704	n.a.
Washing powders and detergents	2,073.9	2,122.9	2,306.8
Aluminium (primary)	365.7*	376.4*	380.0†
Refined copper (primary)†	315.8	290.7	309.0
Pig-iron‡	4,059	4,219	4,021
Cement (Portland)†	38,154	40,512	42,500
Motorcycles ('000)	89	117	74
Passenger cars ('000)	2,619	2,406	2,518
Merchant ships launched ('000 gross tons)	527	263	141
Electricity (million kWh)	224,737	237,579	n.a.

* Data from *World Metal Statistics* (London).
† Data from the US Geological Survey.
‡ Date from International Iron and Steel Institute.

Source: mainly UN, *Industrial Commodity Statistics Yearbook*.

2003 ('000 metric tons unless otherwise stated): Ham and other prepared meats 746.8; Tuna, bonito and other tinned fish 208.9; Olive oil 828.0; Wheat flour 2,950.1; Wine (hectolitres) 8,523.8; Beer (hectolitres) 31,028.4; Soft drinks ('000 litres) 4,243.6; Cement (Portland) 42,162.9; Concrete 182,768.5.

2004 ('000 metric tons unless otherwise stated): Ham and other prepared meats 880.6; Tuna, bonito and other tinned fish 224.1; Olive oil 1,109.0; Wheat flour 2,965.0; Wine (hectolitres) 8,909.8; Beer (hectolitres) 31,466.9; Soft drinks ('000 litres) 5,911.8; Cement (Portland) 42,256.7; Concrete 185,508.7.

Finance

CURRENCY AND EXCHANGE RATES

Monetary Units
100 cent = 1 euro (€).

Sterling and Dollar Equivalents (30 December 2005)
£1 sterling = 1.4596 euros;
US $1 = 0.8477 euros;
€100 = £68.51 = $117.97..

Average Exchange Rate (euros per US $)
2003   0.8860
2004   0.8054
2005   0.8041

Note: The national currency was formerly the peseta. From the introduction of the euro, with Spanish participation, on 1 January 1999, a fixed exchange rate of €1 = 166.386 pesetas was in operation. Euro notes and coins were introduced on 1 January 2002. The euro and local currency circulated alongside each other until 28 February, after which the euro became the sole legal tender.

SPAIN

BUDGET
(€ million)

Revenue	2004	2005	2006
Current operations	108,905	116,097	127,078
Direct taxation	58,087	63,689	72,036
Indirect taxation	39,836	43,051	45,032
Rates and other revenue	2,874	2,237	2,298
Current transfers	5,480	5,353	5,605
Estate taxes	2,627	1,767	1,837
Capital operations	1,591	1,494	1,513
Transfer of real investments	65	94	98
Capital transfers	1,527	1,400	1,415
Financial assets	568	706	955
Total	**111,064**	**118,297**	**129,546**

Expenditure*	2004	2005	2006
Current	100,131	106,209	113,605
Social security	4,620	4,822	5,243
Autonomous communities	26,679	29,620	32,668
State foundations	37	40	41
State enterprises	2,329	2,125	2,832
Autonomous organs	2,523	2,680	3,070
Local corporations	10,509	11,078	12,769
Private companies	246	181	421
Foreign contributions	9,622	10,435	11,300
Families	2,295	2,585	2,625
Personnel	19,486	20,447	22,124
Purchase of goods and services	2,740	2,905	3,069
Interest	19,047	19,293	17,443
Contingency fund	2,345	2,491	2,873
Capital	14,783	15,827	17,473
Investment	7,611	8,841	9,338
Capital transfers	7,172	6,986	8,134
Financial assets	6,532	7,782	9,677
Financial liabilities	33,369	30,070	31,348
Total	**157,161**	**162,379**	**174,976**

* Calculated according to recognized obligations rather than payments made.

Source: Ministerio de Economía y Hacienda, Madrid.

INTERNATIONAL RESERVES
(US $ million at 31 December)

	2003	2004	2005
Gold*	7,021	7,370	7,550
IMF special drawing rights	413	332	418
Reserve position in IMF	1,862	1,575	752
Foreign exchange*	17,513	10,481	8,594
Total	**26,809**	**19,758**	**17,314**

* Figures for gold and foreign exchange exclude deposits made with the European Monetary Institute (now the European Central Bank). Gold is valued at market-related prices.

Source: IMF, *International Financial Statistics*.

MONEY SUPPLY
(€ '000 million at 31 December)

	2003	2004	2005
Currency issued*	46.38	52.70	59.36
Demand deposits at banking institutions	191.06	214.72	433.87

* Currency put into circulation by the Banco de España was €65,730m. in 2003, €74,200m. in 2004 and €83,090m. in 2005.

Source: IMF, *International Financial Statistics*.

COST OF LIVING
(Consumer Price Index; base: 2001 = 100)

	2003	2004	2005
Food (excl. alcoholic beverages and tobacco)	108.9	113.2	116.7
Household expenses	104.0	105.6	107.9
Clothing (incl. footwear)	109.1	111.1	112.6
Rent	105.2	108.9	114.7
All items (incl. others)	106.7	109.9	113.6

NATIONAL ACCOUNTS
(€ million at current prices, provisional)

National Income and Product

	2002	2003	2004
Compensation of employees	355,653	378,653	401,878
Gross operating surplus and mixed income	302,724	323,327	348,276
Gross domestic product (GDP) at factor cost	658,377	701,980	750,154
Taxes, less subsidies on production and imports	70,644	78,570	87,162
GDP in market prices	729,021	780,550	837,316
Primary incomes received from abroad	28,690	28,245	31,389
Less Primary incomes paid abroad	41,288	40,412	46,240
Gross national income	716,423	768,383	822,465
Current transfers from abroad	8,458	8,293	9,265
Less Current transfers paid abroad	9,214	11,366	12,155
Gross national disposable income	715,667	765,310	819,575

Expenditure on the Gross Domestic Product

	2002	2003	2004
Final consumption expenditure	549,929	583,760	632,137
Households	418,063	441,133	475,916
Non-profit institutions serving households	6,469	6,708	7,323
General government	125,397	135,919	148,898
Gross capital formation	193,911	214,263	236,756
Gross fixed capital formation	191,004	211,334	233,647
Changes in inventories	2,907	2,929	3,109
Total domestic expenditure	743,840	798,023	868,893
Exports of goods and services	134,551	139,398	147,934
Less Imports of goods and services	213,857	223,270	248,433
GDP in market prices	729,021	780,550	837,316

Gross Domestic Product by Economic Activity

	2002	2003	2004
Agriculture, hunting, forestry and fishing	25,628	25,880	26,217
Mining and quarrying; electricity, gas and water supply*	17,219	17,914	18,472
Manufacturing	112,386	116,527	120,504
Construction	62,401	70,586	80,870
Private sector service industries	349,664	372,191	398,332
Public sector service industries	94,242	101,578	108,918
Gross value added in basic prices	661,540	704,676	753,313
Import duties	1,039	1,115	1,376
Value-added tax	42,407	46,773	51,080
Other taxes, less subsidies on products	24,035	27,986	31,547
GDP in market prices	729,021	780,550	837,316

* Including refinery products.

SPAIN

BALANCE OF PAYMENTS
(US $ million)

	2002	2003	2004
Exports of goods f.o.b.	127,162	159,049	184,153
Imports of goods f.o.b.	−161,794	−203,205	−249,983
Trade balance	−34,632	−45,155	−65,830
Exports of services	60,247	74,308	84,877
Imports of services	−38,712	−47,951	−57,382
Balance on goods and services	−13,097	−18,798	−38,335
Other income received	21,132	25,524	30,749
Other income paid	−32,768	−38,589	−47,735
Balance on goods, services and income	−24,734	−31,862	−55,320
Current transfers received	13,420	16,495	19,218
Current transfers paid	−11,278	−16,370	−19,278
Current balance	−22,592	−31,737	−55,380
Capital account (net)	7,236	9,274	10,601
Direct investment abroad	−33,653	−27,570	−50,211
Direct investment from abroad	39,983	25,716	16,594
Portfolio investment assets	−29,089	−90,833	−37,153
Portfolio investment liabilities	34,105	44,763	139,275
Financial derivatives liabilities	−4,720	−3,785	1,477
Other investment assets	−22,970	−13,304	−51,177
Other investment liabilities	35,000	70,916	20,823
Net errors and omissions	390	1,070	−1,259
Overall balance	3,690	−15,489	−6,412

Source: IMF, *International Financial Statistics*.

External Trade

PRINCIPAL COMMODITIES
(distribution by SITC, US $ million)

Imports c.i.f.	2001	2002	2003
Food and live animals	11,944.0	13,308.5	16,288.6
Fish, crustaceans and molluscs, and products thereof	3,866.4	3,986.1	5,031.6
Vegetables and fruit	1,897.8	1,964.0	2,560.2
Beverages	1,228.5	1,243.8	1,693.5
Tobacco	1,058.5	1,147.5	1,530.6
Mineral products	17,401.3	18,019.4	21,625.5
Products of the chemical industries and related industries	17,306.0	20,344.7	25,896.7
Medicinal and pharmaceutical products	4,407.0	5,724.4	7,293.6
Organic chemicals	3,958.2	4,675.3	6,029.3
Paper, paperboard and related products	2,954.9	3,313.4	3,987.2
Plastics and related manufactures	3,270.1	3,816.3	4,740.4
Textiles and their manufactures	3,384.4	3,556.6	4,224.2
Iron and steel	4,487.2	4,826.5	6,885.9
Machinery and transport equipment	60,899.1	63,001.6	81,789.9
Total (incl. others)	154,992.6	165,918.6	210,860.5

Exports f.o.b.	2001	2002	2003
Food and live animals	13,883.0	15,285.5	19,307.4
Vegetables and fruit	7,363.8	8,550.8	10,796.0
Beverages and tobacco	1,887.3	2,017.2	2,540.0
Mineral products	3,415.5	3,338.9	4,996.2
Products of the chemical industries and related industries	11,297.5	13,402.2	16,974.1
Plastic materials, etc.	2,799.2	2,817.9	3,523.7
Paper, paperboard and related products	2,091.7	2,345.9	2,885.1
Textiles and their manufactures	3,101.3	3,265.3	3,739.3
Ceramic products	1,696.9	1,875.2	2,131.9
Iron and steel	3,467.2	3,648.9	4,621.6
Machinery and transport equipment	47,573.9	50,579.0	65,208.8
Total (incl. others)	116,148.8	125,872.3	158,213.2

Source: UN, *International Trade Statistics Yearbook*.

PRINCIPAL TRADING PARTNERS*
(US $ million)

Imports c.i.f.	2001	2002	2003
Algeria	3,009.4	2,804.3	3,082.8
Belgium	5,177.3	5,292.5	6,423.4
China, People's Republic	5,545.0	5,463.1	7,518.5
France (incl. Monaco)	25,956.9	27,251.3	34,079.9
Germany	24,084.5	26,779.3	34,551.5
Italy	14,311.3	15,025.0	19,348.6
Japan	3,888.0	4,031.4	5,507.5
Netherlands	6,046.7	6,524.1	8,525.6
Portugal	4,346.3	5,158.1	6,778.4
Russia	1,845.8	2,565.5	3,335.6
Sweden	1,923.8	2,166.2	3,212.8
United Kingdom	10,895.8	10,823.9	13,719.8
USA	7,044.2	6,819.9	7,639.6
Total (incl. others)	154,992.6	165,916.6	210,860.5

Exports f.o.b.	2001	2002	2003
Belgium	3,332.7	3,334.0	4,756.3
France (incl. Monaco)	22,668.0	23,945.6	30,394.1
Germany	13,763.1	14,466.8	19,008.0
Greece	1,217.4	1,479.7	1,898.6
Italy	10,481.2	11,863.6	15,486.4
Mexico	1,775.5	2,211.1	2,508.1
Morocco	1,340.7	1,601.2	2,133.4
Netherlands	4,103.1	4,075.3	5,318.6
Turkey	995.2	1,373.3	1,989.8
United Kingdom	10,485.7	12,150.5	14,644.8
USA	5,060.7	5,468.0	6,478.9
Total (incl. others)	116,148.8	125,872.3	158,213.2

* Imports by country of production; exports by country of last consignment. For exports the distribution by country excludes stores and bunkers for ships and aircraft.

Source: UN, *International Trade Statistics Yearbook*.

Transport

RAILWAYS
(RENFE only)

	2002	2003	2004
Number of passengers ('000)	484,460	490,440	484,461
Passenger-kilometres (million)	19,480	19,309	19,017
Freight ('000 metric tons)	26,359	26,929	26,806
Freight ton-kilometres (million)	11,660	11,866	11,927

Source: Red Nacional de los Ferrocarriles Españoles (RENFE), Madrid.

SPAIN

ROAD TRAFFIC
('000 motor vehicles in use at 31 December)

	2002	2003	2004
Passenger cars	18,732.6	18,688.3	19,541.9
Buses	57.0	56.0	57.0
Lorries	4,091.9	4,188.9	4,418.0
Motorcycles	1,517.2	1,513.5	1,612.1
Tractors	167.0	174.5	185.4
Other vehicles	500.1	548.2	618.3

SHIPPING
Merchant Fleet
(registered at 31 December)

	2002	2003	2004
Number of vessels	1,568	1,613	1,611
Displacement (grt)	2,371,201	2,651,007	2,869,127

Source: Lloyd's Register-Fairplay, *World Fleet Statistics*.

International Sea-borne Freight Traffic

	2002	2003	2004
Goods loaded ('000 metric tons)	63,045	68,227	74,576
Goods unloaded ('000 metric tons)	213,995	221,455	236,199
Passengers embarked ('000)	1,952	2,227	2,094
Passengers disembarked ('000)	2,156	2,351	2,034

Source: partly Puertos del Estado, Ministerio de Fomento, Madrid.

CIVIL AVIATION
(domestic and international traffic on scheduled services)

	2003	2004	2005*
Passengers carried ('000)	151,739	163,889	179,435
Goods carried ('000 metric tons)	576,835	629,396	673,829

* Provisional figures.

Source: Dirección General de Aviación Civil, Ministerio de Fomento, Madrid.

Tourism

FOREIGN TOURIST ARRIVALS
('000 persons, incl. Spaniards resident abroad)

Country of residence	2003	2004	2005
Belgium	1,766	1,743	1,734
France	7,654	7,499	8,765
Germany	9,754	10,022	9,928
Ireland	1,361	1,489	1,367
Italy	2,367	2,610	3,004
Netherlands	2,362	2,294	2,495
Portugal	1,680	2,006	2,041
Switzerland	1,044	1,080	1,146
United Kingdom	15,925	16,383	16,109
USA	929	934	882
Total (incl. others)	51,830	53,599	55,576

Receipts from tourism (€ million): 36,871 in 2003; 44,166 in 2004; 46,060 in 2005.

Source: Instituto de Estudios Turísticos, Madrid.

Communications Media

	2002	2003	2004
Telephones ('000 main lines in use)	18,640.7	17,657.5	17,752.0
Mobile cellular telephones ('000 subscribers)	33,531.0	37,506.7	38,622.6
Personal computers ('000 in use)	7,972	n.a.	10,957
Internet users ('000)	7,856	9,789	14,333

Facsimile machines (1996): 700,000 in use (estimate).
Radio receivers ('000 in use, 1997): 13,100.
Book production (2003): titles ('000) 72.0; copies (million) 238.7.
Daily newspapers (2000): 87 (with combined average circulation of 4,003,000 copies per issue).
Non-daily newspapers (1999): 11 (with combined average circulation of 5,371,000).

Sources: partly UN, *Statistical Yearbook*; UNESCO Institute for Statistics; UNESCO, *Statistical Yearbook*; and International Telecommunication Union.

Education

(estimates, 2005/06 unless otherwise indicated)

	Institutions	Teachers	Students
Pre-primary	3,985	19,237*	1,480,810
Primary	9,805†	117,753*	2,481,667
Special education	486	6,396*	29,892
Secondary: general	4,569†	216,361*‡	1,843,313
Secondary: vocational and university entrance			1,142,713
Universities, etc.	72	89,305	1,442,081

* 2003/04 figures.
† Excluding institutions providing primary education and the first cycle of secondary education (2,475), or institutions providing both primary and secondary education (1,268).
‡ Excluding personnel teaching at institutions that provide both primary and secondary education (147,300).

Source: Ministerio de Educación, Cultura y Deporte, Madrid.

Adult literacy rate (UNESCO estimates): 97.7% (males 98.6%; females 96.9%) in 2001 (Source: UN Development Programme, *Human Development Report*).

Directory

The Constitution

The Constitution of the Kingdom of Spain was approved by popular referendum on 6 December 1978, and promulgated on 29 December 1978.

According to the final provisions, all the fundamental laws of the Franco regime are repealed, together with all measures incompatible with the Constitution.

The following is a summary of the main provisions:

PRELIMINARY PROVISIONS

Spain is established as a social and democratic State whose supreme values are freedom, justice, equality and political pluralism. National sovereignty and power reside with the Spanish people, the political form of the State being a parliamentary Monarchy.

The Constitution is based on the indissoluble unity of the Spanish nation, and recognizes and guarantees the right to autonomy of the nationalities and regions.

FUNDAMENTAL RIGHTS, DUTIES AND FREEDOMS

Standards concerning fundamental rights and freedoms recognized in the Constitution are to be interpreted in accordance with the Universal Declaration of Human Rights and other international treaties and agreements of a similar nature ratified by Spain.

All Spaniards are equal under the law and no Spaniard by birth may be deprived of his nationality. The age of majority is 18, suffrage is free and universal and every person has a right to public service.

The main freedoms listed are described below, bearing in mind that the Constitution contains the proviso that no person, group or action pose a threat to public order and safety. Free entry to and exit from Spain, freedom of thought, belief and expression are guaranteed, as is the right of access to state and public communications media by significant social and political groups and to administrative archives and registers by individuals, except in matters concerning state security and defence, and the private life and home of the individual, which are inviolable.

The Constitution states that there is no state religion but that it will maintain co-operation with the Roman Catholic Church and other religious groups.

Freedom of association is guaranteed, except for criminal, paramilitary and secret associations, all associations being bound to inscribe themselves in a public register; the right to form trade unions and to strike is also guaranteed, military personnel being subject to special laws in these cases.

Every person has a right to work for a just remuneration, including paid holiday, under conditions of safety, hygiene and a healthy environment. The State is to be run on the principles of a market economy. Taxation is determined according to means and consumer protection is encouraged by the State. Social-security payments are provided for and it is stipulated that special care be taken of the handicapped and the elderly.

In criminal matters, the death penalty is abolished except under military criminal law in time of war. Extradition functions on the principle of reciprocity but the terms do not apply to political crimes, acts of terrorism, however, not being considered as such. All persons are presumed innocent before trial, and a habeas corpus clause provides for a detainee to be freed within 72 hours of arrest or to be brought before a court.

THE CROWN

The King is the Head of State, the symbol of its unity and permanence, and the highest representative of the Spanish State in international relations. The person of the King is inviolable. His decisions and acts must be approved by the Government, without which they are deemed invalid, and responsibility for the King's actions is borne by those who approve them. The Crown is hereditary descending to the sons of the Sovereign in order of seniority or, if there are no sons, to the daughters. Persons marrying against the wishes of the King or Cortes (national assembly) are excluded from the succession. The Constitution lays down the procedure for establishing the Regency.

The King's duties are as follows:

to approve and promulgate laws;

to convene and dissolve the Cortes Generales and to call elections and referendums (according to the Constitution);

to propose a candidate for the presidency of the Cortes and dismiss him;

to appoint the members of the Cortes on the proposal of the President;

to issue decrees approved by the Council of Ministers, and to confer civil and military posts and grant honours and distinctions in accordance with the laws;

to be informed of the affairs of State, and to preside over the Council of Ministers when he deems it necessary on the request of the President of the Government;

to command the Armed Forces;

to grant mercy according to the law (which may not authorize general pardons);

to accredit ambassadors and other diplomatic representatives;

to express the State's assent to bind itself to international treaties;

to declare war and peace on the prior authorization of the Cortes.

THE CORTES GENERALES
(National Assembly)

The Cortes represent the Spanish people and comprise the Congreso de los Diputados (Congress of Deputies—lower house) and the Senado (Senate—upper house).

The Congreso has a minimum of 300 deputies and a maximum of 400, elected by universal, free, equal, direct and secret suffrage. Each province forms one constituency, the number of deputies in each one being determined according to population and elected by proportional representation for four years, Ceuta and Melilla having one deputy each. Elections must be held between 30 and 60 days after the end of each parliamentary mandate, and the Congreso convened within 25 days of the elections.

The Senado is based on territorial representation. Each province elects four senators for four years. Each island or group of islands forms one constituency. Gran Canaria, Mallorca and Tenerife return three senators each, the others one each. The Autonomous Communities return, in addition, one senator, plus one more for each million inhabitants, appointed by the legislative assembly of the community.

Each House lays down its own rules of procedure and elects its own president and governing body. Each year there are two ordinary sessions of the Cortes, of four and five months each, and a standing committee of 21 members in each House looks after affairs while the Cortes are in recess or during electoral periods. Plenary sessions are normally public. Measures are adopted by a majority in both Houses providing that a majority of the members is present. If agreement is not reached between the Congreso and the Senado, a joint committee must attempt to solve the differences by drawing up a text to be voted on again by both Houses. In the case of further non-agreement, the issue is decided by an absolute majority vote in the Congreso. Members may not vote by proxy.

LEGISLATION

Laws may not be retroactive.

Organic laws concern the development of fundamental rights and public freedoms, the approval of statutes of autonomy, the general electoral system, and other matters specified in the Constitution. Any approval, modification or repeal of these laws requires an absolute majority in the Congreso. The Cortes may delegate the power to issue measures called Legislative Decrees with the status of law to a governmental legislative body. In urgent cases the Government may issue provisional measures in the form of Decree-Laws not affecting the fundamental laws and rights of the nation, which must be voted upon by the Cortes within 30 days.

All laws must be sanctioned by the King within 15 days of their approval by the Cortes.

Provision is made for the popular presentation of bills if they are supported by 500,000 reputable signatures. Petitions to the Cortes by public demonstration are prohibited.

THE GOVERNMENT

The Government is the executive power and is composed of a President proposed by the King on the Cortes' approval and voted into office by the Congreso by absolute majority. If no President is elected within two months, the King will dissolve the Cortes and convene new elections with the approval of the President of the Congreso. The President of the Government designates the Ministers.

The Council of State is the supreme consultative organ of the Government. (An organic law will regulate its composition.)

Further articles provide for the procedure for declaring a state of alarm, emergency or siege.

THE JUDICIARY

Justice derives from the people and is administered in the name of the King by judges and magistrates subject only to the law. The principle of jurisdictional unity is the basis of the organization and functioning of the Courts, which are established in an organic law of judicial power. Emergency courts are prohibited.

The Judiciary is governed by the General Council of Judicial Power (Consejo General del Poder Judicial), presided over by the President of the Supreme Court and made up of 20 members appointed by the King for five years, of whom 12 are judges or magistrates, four are nominated by the Congreso and four by the Senado, these eight being elected by a three-fifths' majority from lawyers and jurists of more than 15 years' professional service.

The Attorney-General is appointed by the King on the Government's approval. Citizens may act on juries.

TERRITORIAL ORGANIZATION

The State is organized into municipalities, provinces and Autonomous Communities, all of which have local autonomy. The Constitution states that the differences between the Statutes of the Autonomous Communities shall not imply economic or social privileges.

THE AUTONOMOUS COMMUNITIES

The peripheral provinces, with their own historical, cultural and economic characteristics, are entitled to accede to self-government, but the Constitution states that in no case will the federation of the Autonomous Communities be permitted.

Article 148 lists the matters in which the Communities may assume competence, among which are: land use and building, public

SPAIN — Directory

works and transport, ports, agriculture, environment, minerals, economic development, culture, tourism, social aid, health and local policing, all within the framework of national laws and policy and as long as nothing outside the regional boundaries is involved. Areas solely under state control are listed in article 149. In the specific case of financial autonomy, revenue proceeds from the State and from each Autonomous Community's own taxes, and a State Compensation Fund acts to correct any imbalances between the Communities. State competence will always prevail over regional competence should conflict arise over matters not under the exclusive control of the Autonomous Communities.

Although the State will delegate state power wherever possible, legislative measures must always be guided by state law. The State, in the general public interest, may pass laws by absolute majority to establish the principles for the harmonization of measures taken by the Autonomous Communities, even concerning matters directly under their authority.

The institutional organization of the Communities is based on a Legislative Assembly elected by universal suffrage and proportional representation, a Governing Council with executive and administrative functions, and a President elected by the Assembly from its members and appointed by the King to be the supreme representative of the Community to the State, and the ordinary representative of the State in the Community, and finally a High Court of Justice, inferior only to the Supreme Court.

THE CONSTITUTIONAL COURT

This court monitors observance of the Constitution and comprises 12 members appointed by the King, of whom four are elected by the Congreso and four by the Senado by three-fifths' majority, two on the proposal of the Government and two on the proposal of the General Council of Judicial Power. The members must satisfy the conditions for membership of the aforesaid Council. They are appointed for nine years, with three members resigning every three years.

Three further articles establish the procedure for constitutional reform.

The Government

HEAD OF STATE

King of Spain, Head of State, Commander-in-Chief of the Armed Forces and Head of the Supreme Council of Defence: HRH King JUAN CARLOS (succeeded to the throne 22 November 1975).

COUNCIL OF MINISTERS
(April 2006)

Prime Minister and President of the Government: JOSÉ LUIS RODRÍGUEZ ZAPATERO.

First Deputy Prime Minister, Minister of the Presidency and Government Spokesperson: MARÍA TERESA FERNÁNDEZ DE LA VEGA SANZ.

Second Deputy Prime Minister and Minister of the Economy and Finance: PEDRO SOLBES MIRA.

Minister of Labour and Social Affairs: JESÚS CALDERA SÁNCHEZ-CAPITÁN.

Minister of the Interior: ALFREDO PÉREZ RUBALCABA.

Minister of Foreign Affairs and Co-operation: MIGUEL ÁNGEL MORATINOS CUYAUBÉ.

Minister of Defence: JOSÉ ANTONIO ALONSO SUÁREZ.

Minister of Justice: JUAN FERNANDO LÓPEZ AGUILAR.

Minister of Development: MAGDALENA ÁLVAREZ ARZA.

Minister of Trade, Industry and Tourism: JOSÉ MONTILLA AGUILERA.

Minister of Education and Science: MERCEDES CABRERA CALVO-SOTELO.

Minister of Housing: MARÍA ANTONIA TRUJILLO RINCÓN.

Minister of Agriculture, Fisheries and Food: ELENA ESPINOSA MANGANA.

Minister of Public Administration: JORDI SEVILLA SEGURA.

Minister of Health and Consumer Affairs: ELENA SALGADO MENDÉZ.

Minister of Environment: CRISTINA NARBONA RUÍZ.

Minister of Culture: CARMEN CALVO POYATO.

MINISTRIES

Prime Minister's Chancellery: Complejo de la Moncloa, Avda de Puerta de Hierro s/n, 28071 Madrid; internet www.la-moncloa.es.

Ministry of Agriculture, Fisheries and Food: Paseo Infanta Isabel 1, 28071 Madrid; tel. (91) 3475368; fax (91) 4675854; e-mail sministr@mapa.es; internet www.mapa.es.

Ministry of Culture: Plaza del Rey 1, 28071 Madrid; tel. (91) 7017000; fax (91) 7017352; e-mail contacte@mcu.es; internet www.mcu.es.

Ministry of Defence: Paseo de la Castellana 109, 28071 Madrid; tel. (91) 3955000; e-mail infodefensa@mde.es; internet www.mde.es.

Ministry of Development: Paseo de la Castellana 67, 28071 Madrid; tel. (91) 5978787; fax (91) 5978573; e-mail portal@administracion.es; internet www.mfom.es.

Ministry of the Economy and Finance: Alcalá 9, 28014 Madrid; tel. (91) 5958348; fax (91) 5958486; e-mail informacion.alcala@meh.es; internet www.meh.es.

Ministry of Education and Science: Alcalá 36, 28071 Madrid; tel. (91) 7018000; fax (91) 7018648; e-mail infociencia@mec.es; internet www.mec.es.

Ministry of Environment: Nuevos Ministerios, Plaza San Juan de la Cruz s/n, 28071 Madrid; tel. (91) 5976000; internet www.mma.es.

Ministry of Foreign Affairs and Co-operation: Plaza de la Provincia 1, 28012 Madrid; tel. (91) 3799700; e-mail informae@mae.es; internet www.mae.es.

Ministry of Health and Consumer Affairs: Paseo del Prado 18–20, 28014 Madrid; tel. 901 400100; fax (91) 5964480; e-mail atencionciudadano@msc.es; internet www.msc.es.

Ministry of Housing: Paseo de la Castellana 112, 28071 Madrid; tel. (91) 7284004; fax (91) 7284861; e-mail portal.vivienda@mviv.es; internet www.mviv.es.

Ministry of the Interior: Paseo de la Castellana 5, 28046 Madrid; tel. (91) 5371111; fax (91) 5371003; e-mail estafeta@mir.es; internet www.mir.es.

Ministry of Justice: San Bernardo 45, 28015 Madrid; tel. (91) 3904500; internet www.mju.es.

Ministry of Labour and Social Affairs: Nuevos Ministerios, Agustín de Bethencourt 4, 28071 Madrid; tel. (91) 3631135; e-mail gprensa@mtas.es; internet www.mtas.es.

Ministry of the Presidency: Complejo de la Moncloa, Avda de Puerta de Hierro s/n, 28071 Madrid; tel. (91) 3214000; e-mail sec@mpr.es; internet www.mpr.es.

Ministry of Public Administration: Paseo de la Castellana 3, 28071 Madrid; tel. (91) 2731029; fax (91) 2731012; e-mail portal@map.es; internet www.map.es.

Ministry of Trade, Industry and Tourism: Paseo de la Castellana 160, 28071 Madrid; tel. 902 446006; fax (91) 4578066; e-mail info@mityc.es; internet www.mityc.es.

COUNCIL OF STATE

Consejo de Estado: Mayor 79, 28013 Madrid; tel. (91) 5166262; fax (91) 5166244; e-mail tramitaciones@consejo-estado.es; internet www.consejo-estado.es.

The Council of State has nine permanent members, eight hereditary members and six elected members, as well as a President.

President: FRANCISCO RUBIO LLORENTE.

Legislature

LAS CORTES GENERALES

Congreso de los Diputados
(Congress of Deputies)

Carrera de San Jerónimo s/n, 28071 Madrid; tel. (91) 3906000; fax (91) 3906435; e-mail guias.congreso@sgral.congreso.es; internet www.congreso.es.

President: MANUEL MARÍN GONZÁLEZ (PSOE).

First Vice-President: CARME CHACÓN PIQUERAS (PSOE).

SPAIN

General Election, 14 March 2004

	Votes	% of votes	Seats
Partido Socialista Obrero Español (PSOE)	11,026,163	42.59	164
Partido Popular (PP)	9,763,144	37.71	148
Convergència i Unió (CiU)	835,471	3.23	10
Esquerra Republicana de Catalunya (ERC)	652,196	2.52	8
Euzko Alderdi Jeltzalea/ Partido Nacionalista Vasco (EAJ/PNV)	420,980	1.63	7
Izquierda Unida (IU)	1,284,081	4.96	5
Coalición Canaria (CC)	235,221	0.91	3
Bloque Nacionalista Galego (BNG)	208,688	0.81	2
Chunta Aragonesista (ChA)	94,252	0.36	1
Eusko Alkartasuna (EA)	80,905	0.31	1
Nafarroa Bai (Na-Bai)	61,045	0.24	1
Total (incl. others)	25,891,299	100.00	350

There were 8,416,395 abstentions, 407,795 blank votes and 264,137 spoiled votes

Senado (Senate)

Plaza de la Marina Española 8, 28071 Madrid; tel. (91) 5381000; fax (91) 5381003; e-mail webmaster@senado.es; internet www.senado.es.

The Senate comprises 259 members, 208 of whom are directly elected, the remaining 51 regional representatives being chosen by the assemblies of the autonomous regions.

President: JAVIER ROJO (PSOE).

First Vice-President: ISIDRE MOLAS I BATLLORI (PSC-PSOE).

General Election, 14 March 2004

	Directly elected seats	Total seats
Partido Popular (PP)	102	126
Partido Socialista Obrero Español (PSOE)	93	111
Euzko Alderdi Jeltzalea/Partido Nacionalista Vasco (EAJ/PNV)	6	7
Convergència i Unió (CiU)	4	6
Coalición Canaria (CC)	3	4
Izquierda Unida (IU)	0	2
Bloque Nacionalista Galego (BNG)	0	1
Eusko Alkartasuna (EA)	0	1
Partido Aragonés (PAR)	0	1
Total	208	259

Legislative Assemblies of the Autonomous Communities

(For full names of political parties, see Political Organizations)

ANDALUCÍA (ANDALUSIA)

President of the Government: MANUEL CHAVES GONZÁLEZ (PSOE).
President of the Parliament: MARÍA DEL MAR MORENO (PSOE).

Election, 14 March 2004

	Seats
PSOE	61
PP	37
IU-LV-CA*	6
PA	5
Total	109

* Convocatoria por Andalucía.

ARAGÓN

President of the Government: MARCELINO IGLESIAS RICOU (PSOE).
President of the Parliament: FRANCISCO PINA CUENCA (PSOE).

Election, 25 May 2003

	Seats
PSOE	27
PP	22
ChA	9
PAR	8
IU	1
Total	67

ASTURIAS

President of the Government: VICENTE ÁLVAREZ ARECES (PSOE).
President of the Parliament: MARÍA JESÚS ÁLVAREZ GONZÁLEZ (PSOE).

Election, 25 May 2003

	Seats
PSOE	22
PP	19
IU	4
Total	45

BALEARES (BALEARIC ISLANDS)

President of the Government: JAUME MATAS PALOU (PP).
President of the Parliament: PERE ROTGER I LLABRÉS (PP).

Election, 25 May 2003

	Seats
PP	29
PSOE	15
PACTE	5
PSM-EN	4
UM	3
EU	2
AIPF*	1
Total	59

* Agrupació Independent Popular de Formentera.

BASQUE COUNTRY (SEE EUSKADI)

CANARIAS (CANARY ISLANDS)

President of the Government: ADÁN MARTÍN MENIS (CC).
President of the Parliament: D. GABRIEL MATO ADROVER (PP).

Election, 25 May 2003

	Seats
CC	22
PSOE	18
PP	17
FNC*	3
Total	60

* Federación Nacionalista Canaria.

CANTABRIA

President of the Government: MIGUEL ÁNGEL REVILLA ROIZ (PRC).
President of the Parliament: MIGUEL ÁNGEL PALACIO GARCÍA (PSOE).

Election, 25 May 2003

	Seats
PP	18
PSOE	13
PRC	8
Total	39

CASTILLA Y LEÓN (CASTILE AND LEON)

President of the Government: JUAN VICENTE HERRERA CAMPO (PP).
President of the Parliament: JOSÉ MANUEL FERNÁNDEZ DE SANTIAGO (PP).

Election, 25 May 2003

	Seats
PP	48
PSOE	31
UPL	3
Total	82

CASTILLA-LA MANCHA

President of the Government: José María Barreda Fontes (PSOE).
President of the Parliament: Fernando López Carrasco (PSOE).
Election, 25 May 2003

	Seats
PSOE	29
PP	18
Total	47

CATALUÑA/CATALUNYA (CATALONIA)

President of the Government (Generalitat): Pasqual Maragall i Mira (PSC).
President of the Parliament: Ernest Benach i Pascual (ERC).
Election, 16 November 2003

	Seats
CiU	46
PSC-PSOE	42
ERC	23
PP	15
IC-V-EUiA*	9
Total	135

*Coalition of Iniciativa per Catalunya-Verds (IC-V) and Esquerra Unida i Alternativa (EUiA).

EUSKADI (BASQUE COUNTRY)

Lehendakari (President): Juan José Ibarretxe Markuartu (PNV).
President of the Parliament: Izaskun Bílbao Barandíka (PNV).
Election, 17 April 2005

	Seats
PNV*/EA	29
PSE-EE	18
PP	15
PCTV-EHAK	9
IU-EB†	3
ARALAR	1
Total	75

*Also known as Euzko Alderdi Jeltzalea (EAJ).
† Ezker Batua.

EXTREMADURA

President of the Government: Juan Carlos Rodríguez Ibarra (PSOE).
President of the Parliament: Federico Suárez Hurtado (PSOE).
Election, 25 May 2003

	Seats
PSOE-Progresista	36
PP	26
IU-SIEX*	3
Total	65

*Socialistas Independientes de Extremadura.

GALICIA/GALIZA

President of the Government (Xunta): Emilio Pérez Touriño (PS de G-PSOE).
President of the Parliament: Dolores Villarino Santiago (PS de G-PSOE).
Election, 19 June 2005

	Seats
PP	37
PS de G-PSOE	25
BNG	13
Total	75

MADRID

President of the Government: Esperanza Aguirre (PP).
President of the Parliament: Concepción Dancausa Teviño (PP).
Election, 26 October 2003

	Seats
PP	57
PSOE	45
IU	9
Total	111

MURCIA

President of the Government: Ramón Luis Valcárcel Siso (PP).
President of the Parliament: Francisco Celdrán Vidal (PP).
Election, 25 May 2003

	Seats
PP	28
PSOE	16
IU	1
Total	45

NAVARRA (NAVARRE)

President of the Government: Miguel Sanz Sesma (UPN).
President of the Parliament: Rafael Gurrea Induraín (UPN).
Election, 25 May 2003

	Seats
UPN	23
PSN-PSOE	11
IU/EBN*	4
ARALAR	4
CDN	4
EAJ-PNV/EA	4
Total	50

*Ezker Batua de Navarra.

LA RIOJA

President of the Government: Pedro María Sanz Alonso (PP).
President of the Parliament: José Ignacio Ceniceros González (PP).
Election, 25 May 2003

	Seats
PP	17
PSOE	14
PR	2
Total	33

VALENCIA

President of the Government (Generalitat): Francisco Enrique Camps Ortiz (PP).
President of the Parliament: Julio Francisco de España Moya (PP).
Election, 25 May 2003

	Seats
PP	48
PSPV-PSOE	36
L'Entesa*	5
Total	89

*Coalition of EU, LV and EV.

Political Organizations

In 2005 around 500 political parties were officially registered.

PRINCIPAL NATIONAL PARTIES

Izquierda Unida (IU): Olimpo 35, 28043 Madrid; tel. (91) 7227500; fax (91) 3880405; e-mail org.federal@izquierda-unida.es; internet www.izquierda-unida.es; Co-ordinator-Gen. GASPAR LLAMAZARES TRIGO; f. 1989; by left-wing parties to contest elections; includes:

Izquierda Republicana (IR): Meléndez Valdés 33, 1° dcha, 28015 Madrid; tel. (91) 5436930; fax (91) 5437649; e-mail info@izquierdarepublicana.org; internet www.izquierdarepublicana.com; f. 1934; ran independently in general election of 2004; Sec.-Gen. ISABELO HERREROS MARTÍN-MAESTRO.

Partido de Acción Socialista (PASOC): Félix Boix 7, 6E, 28036 Madrid; tel. and fax (91) 3507747; e-mail pasoc@pasoc.org; internet www.pasoc.org; f. 1879; took present name 1982; fmrly Partido Socialista Obrero Español—Histórico (PSOE(h), Partido Socialista); Pres. ANDRÉS CUEVAS GONZÁLEZ; Sec.-Gen. LUIS AURELIO SÁNCHEZ SUÁREZ.

Partido Comunista de España (PCE): Olimpo 35, 28043 Madrid; tel. (91) 3004969; fax (91) 3004744; e-mail webmasterpce@pce.es; internet www.pce.es; f. 1922; Euro-communist; absorbed Partido Comunista Obrero Español (PCOE) in 1986, and most of Partido Comunista de los Pueblos de España (PCPE) in Jan. 1989; Sec.-Gen. FRANCISCO FRUTOS.

Partido Popular (PP): Génova 13, 28004 Madrid; tel. (91) 5577300; fax (91) 3122322; e-mail atencion@pp.es; internet www.pp.es; f. 1976; fmrly Alianza Popular, name changed Jan. 1989; absorbed Democracia Cristiana (fmrly Partido Demócrata Popular) and Partido Liberal in early 1989; centre-right, Christian Democrat; 600,000 mems (Feb. 2000); Pres. MARIANO RAJOY BREY; Sec.-Gen. ÁNGEL ACEBES PANIGUA.

Partido Socialista Obrero Español (PSOE): Ferraz 68 y 70, 28008 Madrid; tel. (91) 5820444; fax (91) 5820422; e-mail administrador-web@psoe.es; internet www.psoe.es; f. 1879; socialist workers' party; affiliated to the Socialist International; merged with the Partido Socialista Popular in 1978; joined by Partido de los Trabajadores de España-Unidad Comunista (PTE-UC) in 1991 and Partido de Nueva Izquierda (PDNI) in 2001; 366,000 mems (1996); Pres. MANUEL CHAVEZ GONZÁLEZ; Sec.-Gen. JOSÉ LUIS RODRÍGUEZ ZAPATERO.

Los Verdes (LV): Navellos 9, 2°, 46003 Valencia; tel. (96) 2817581; fax (96) 3921314; e-mail verdes@verdes.es; internet www.verdes.es; f. 1984; green party; confederation of 12 national and regional parties, and 1 observer; Sec.-Gen. PEDRO J. COLLADO GÓMEZ.

REGIONAL PARTIES

There are branches of the main national parties in most Spanish regions, and numerous regional parties including the following:

Andalucía
(Andalusia)

Partido Andalucista (PA): Vidrio 32, 41003 Sevilla; tel. (95) 4502157; fax (95) 4210446; e-mail prensa@partidoandalucista.org; internet www.partidoandalucista.org; f. 1965; Sec.-Gen. JULIAN ALVAREZ ORTEGA.

Aragón

Chunta Aragonesista (ChA): Conde de Aranda 14–16, 1°, 50003 Zaragoza; tel. (976) 284242; fax (976) 281311; e-mail sedenacional@chunta.com; internet www.chunta.com; left-wing regional party of Aragón; Pres. BIZÉN FUSTER.

Partido Aragonés (PAR): Coso 87, 50001 Zaragoza; tel. (976) 200616; e-mail sugerencias@partidoaragones.es; internet www.partidoaragones.es; f. 1977; fmrly Partido Aragonés Regionalista; Pres. JOSÉ ANGEL BIEL; Sec.-Gen. JUAN CARLOS TRILLO.

Asturias

Unión Renovadora Asturiana (URAS): Palacio Valdés 2, 1°, 33201 Gijón; tel. (98) 5353245; internet www.uras.org; f. 1998; following split in PP of Asturias; in 2004 formed coalition, Unión Asturianista, with Partíu Asturianista (PAS); Pres. SERGIO MARQUÉS FERNÁNDEZ; Sec.-Gen. MARTA AURORA PRIETO BUSTO.

Baleares
(Balearic Islands)

Pacte Progressista d'Eivissa (PACTE): Eivissa (Ibiza), Illes Balears; e-mail webmaster@pacte.org; internet www.pacte.org; local alliance of the PSOE, EU, ERC and Entesa Nacionalista Ecologista.

Partit Socialista de Mallorca—Entesa Nacionalista de Mallorca (PSM—EN): Isidoro Antillón 9, baixos, 07006 Palma de Mallorca; tel. (971) 775252; fax (971) 774848; e-mail mallorca@psm-entesa.org; internet www.psm-entesa.org; f. 1994; Sec.-Gen. GABRIEL VINCENS Y MIR.

Unió Mallorquina (UM): Via Sindicat 21, 07002 Palma de Mallorca; tel. (971) 726336; fax (971) 728116; e-mail um@unio-mallorquina.com; internet www.unio-mallorquina.com; f. 1982; liberal party; Pres. MARÍA ANTÒNIA MUNAR; Sec.-Gen. DAMÍA NICOLAU.

Canarias
(Canary Islands)

Agrupación Herreña Independiente (AHI): La Constitución 4, 38900 Valverde, El Hierro, Santa Cruz de Tenerife; tel. (922) 551134; fax (922) 551224; Canary Islands group; Pres. TOMÁS PADRÓN HERNÁNDEZ.

Coalición Canaria (CC): Buenos Aires 24, 35001 Las Palmas, Gran Canaria; tel. (928) 363142; internet www.coalicioncanaria.es; Canary Islands coalition; Pres. PAULINO RIVERO BAUTE; coalition includes:

Agrupaciones Independientes de Canarias (AIC): Galcerán 7–9, 1°, Edif. El Drago, 38003 Santa Cruz de Tenerife; tel. (922) 279702; e-mail agrupacion-ati@jet.es; federation of Canary Islands groupings (incl. Agrupación Tinerfeña de Independientes—ATI; Pres. MANUEL HERMOSO ROJAS; Sec.-Gen. PAULINO RIVERO); Pres. VICTORIANO RÍOS.

Asamblea Majorera (AM): La Venta 11, 35600 Puerto del Rosario, Fuerteventura; tel. (928) 850798; fax (928) 531591; e-mail info@asambleamajorero.com; internet www.asambleamajorero.com; f. 1977; progressive, left-wing Canary Islands nationalist party; Gen. Co-ordinator VICTOR M. ALONSO FALCON; Organizing Sec. TOMAS QUESADA DE SAA.

Centro Canario Nacionalista (CCN): General Mas de Gaminde 15 y Villalba, Hervás, 38004 Santa Cruza de Tenerife; tel. and fax (922) 273223; e-mail prensa@centrocanario.org; internet www.centrocanario.org; f. 1992 as Centro Canario Independiente (CCI); Pres. LUIS HERNÁNDEZ PÉREZ; Sec.-Gen. IGNACIO GONZÁLEZ SANTIAGO.

Iniciativa Canaria (I.CAN): Buenos Aires 24, 35002 Las Palmas de Gran Canaria; tel. (928) 363142; fax (928) 380356; f. 1991; as Canary Islands grouping of Communists and left-wing nationalists; Co-ordinators JOSÉ CARLOS, MAURICIO RODRÍGUEZ.

Partido Nacionalista Canario (PNC): Sagasta 92, 35008 Las Palmas de Gran Canaria; tel. and fax (928) 221736; e-mail pnc@partidonacionalistacanario.com; internet www.narias.com/pnc; f. 1977; as Canary Islands nationalist group; National Pres. JUAN MANUEL GARCÍA RAMOS; National Sec.-Gen. GUSTAVO DAVILA DE LEÓN.

Cantabria

Partido Regionalista de Cantabria (PRC): Amos de Escalante 3, 2°D, 39002 Santander; tel. (942) 229177; fax (942) 362337; e-mail prc@prc.es; internet www.prc.es; centre-right; Sec.-Gen. MIGUEL ANGEL REVILLA.

Castilla y León
(Castile and Leon)

Unión del Pueblo Leonés (UPL): Avda República Argentina 13, 1°, 24004 León; tel. (987) 263309; fax (987) 204499; internet www.uniondelpuebloleones.com; León separatist party; Pres. MELCHOR MORENO DE LA TORRE; Sec.-Gen. JOAQUÍN OTERO PEREIRA.

Cataluña/Catalunya
(Catalonia)

Convergència i Unió (CiU): Còrsega 331, 08037 Barcelona; tel. (93) 2363100; e-mail ciu@ciu.info; internet www.ciu.info; f. 1979; as an electoral coalition; became confederation of parties in March 2001; Pres. ARTUR MAS I GAVARRÓ; Sec.-Gen. JOSEP ANTONI DURAN I LLEIDA; an alliance of the following two parties:

Convergència Democràtica de Catalunya (CDC): Còrsega 331–333, 08037 Barcelona; tel. (93) 2363100; fax (93) 2363115; e-mail cdc@convergencia.org; internet www.convergencia.org; f. 1977; Catalan nationalist; centre; 45,523 mems (2000); Pres. JORDI PUJOL I SOLEY; Sec.-Gen. ARTUR MAS I GAVARRÓ.

Unió Democràtica de Catalunya (UDC): Travessera de Gràcia 17–21, àtic, 08021 Barcelona; tel. (93) 2402200; fax (93) 2402201; e-mail info@unio.org; internet www.unio.org; f. 1931; 34,255 mems (1998); Pres. of National Council RAMON ESPADALER I PARCERISAS; Pres. of Exec. Cttee JOSEP ANTONI DURAN I LLEIDA; Sec.-Gen. JOSEP M. PELEGRÍ.

Esquerra Republicana de Catalunya (ERC) (Republican Left of Catalonia): Carrer Villarroel 45, 08011 Barcelona; tel. (93) 4536005; fax (93) 3237122; e-mail administracio@esquerra.org; internet www

.esquerra.org; f. 1931; advocates independence for Catalonia within European context, a just society and national solidarity of Catalan people; Pres. Josep Lluís Carod-Rovira; Sec.-Gen. Joan Puigcercós.

Esquerra Unida i Alternativa (EUiA): Doctor Aiguader 10, 08003 Barcelona; tel. (93) 317034; fax (93) 3179251; e-mail euia@euia.org; internet www.euia.org; anti-capitalist Catalan republican party; Co-ordinator-General Jordi Miralles i Conte.

Iniciativa per Catalunya-Verds (IC-V): Ciutat 7, 08002 Barcelona; tel. (93) 3010612; fax (93) 4124252; e-mail iniciativa@ic-v.org; internet www.ic-v.org; f. 1987; as Iniciativa per Catalunya, a left-wing alliance comprising the Partit Socialista Unificat de Catalunya (PSUC, see below) and Entesa des Nacionalistes d'Esquerra (ENE); in 1995 formed a coalition with the above name, incl. Els Verds, L'Espai roig-verd-violeta, and individual citizens; Pres. Joan Saura Laporta.

Partit Socialista Unificat de Catalunya (PSUC): Ciutat 7, 08002 Barcelona; tel. (93) 3010612; fax (93) 4124252; internet www.psuc.es; f. 1936; Communist.

Partit dels Socialistes de Catalunya (PSC-PSOE): Nicaragua 75, 08029 Barcelona; tel. (93) 4955400; fax (93) 4955435; e-mail info@socialistes.org; internet www.psc.es; f. 1978; by merger of various Catalan parties of socialist ideology; Pres. Pasqual Maragall.

Euskadi
(Basque Country)

ARALAR: Hurtado de Amezaga 10, 1 izqda, 48008 Bilbao; tel. (94) 4028647; fax (94) 4028646; e-mail bizkaia@aralar.net; internet www.aralar.net; Co-ordinator-Gen. Patxi Zabaleta.

Eusko Alkartasuna (EA) (Basque Solidarity): Camino de Portuetxe 23, 1°, 20018 San Sebastián; tel. (943) 020130; fax (943) 020131; e-mail gipuzkoa@euskoalkartasuna.org; internet www.euskoalkartasuna.org; f. 1985 (as Eusko Abertzaleak—Basque Nationalists) by dissident group of progressive PNV mems; 15,000 mems; Pres. Begoña Errazti Esnal; Sec.-Gen. Gorka Knörr Borras.

Euzko Alderdi Jeltzalea/Partido Nacionalista Vasco (EAJ/PNV): Ibáñez de Bilbao 16 (Sabin Etxea), 48001 Bilbao; tel. (94) 4039400; fax (94) 4039413; e-mail prensa@eaj-pnv.com; internet www.eaj-pnv.com; f. 1895; Basque nationalist; seeks to achieve autonomy through peaceful means; 31,000 mems (1998); Pres. Josu Jon Imaz; Sec. Josune Ariztondo.

Partido Socialista de Euskadi-Euskadiko Ezkerra (PSE-EE) (Basque Socialist Party-Basque Left): Alameda de Recalde 27, 4°, 48009 Bilbao; tel. (94) 4242142; fax (94) 4238904; internet www.pse-ee.psoe.es; f. 1993; by merger of PSE-PSOE and EE; Pres. Jesús Eguiguren; Sec.-Gen. Paxti López.

Unidad Alavesa (UA): Calle San Antonio 27, 1°, 01005 Vitoria-Gasteiz; e-mail uaforal@unidadalavesa.es; internet www.unidadalavesa.es; f. 1989; splinter group of PP; supports rights of province of Alava, within Basque Country; Pres. José Luis Añúa Ajuria; Sec.-Gen. Enriqueta Benito.

Other parties include the following: the Partido Comunista de las Tierras Vascas—Euskal Herrialdeetako Alderdi Komunista (PCTV—EHAK); Aukera Guztiak (AG), a Basque separatist party that was banned from standing in the 2004 Basque elections; and Socialista Abertzaleak. Batasuna (f. 1978 as Herri Batasuna), a separatist party, was banned by the Supreme Court in March 2003 due to its links to ETA (see below). It is led by Arnaldo Otegi Mondragón.

Galicia/Galiza

Bloque Nacionalista Galego (BNG): Avda Rodríguez de Viguri 16, baixo, 15703 Santiago de Compostela; tel. (981) 555850; fax (981) 555851; e-mail sedenacional@bng-galiza.org; internet www.bng-galiza.org; f. 1982; Galician nationalist organization; Leader Anxo Quintana.

Esquerda de Galicia (EdeG): San Lazaro, 95°C, 15700 Santiago de Compostela; e-mail edeg@ctv.es; internet www.ctv.es/USERS/edeg/; left-wing Galician party; fmrly Esquerda Galega Unida; National Sec. Anxo Guerrero Carreiras.

Partido dos Socialistas de Galicia (PS de G-PSOE) (Galician Socialist Party): Rua do Pino 1–9, 15704 Santiago de Compostela; tel. (981) 552030; fax (981) 588708; e-mail ceng@psdeg-psoe.org; internet www.psdeg-psoe.org; Sec.-Gen. Emilio Pérez Touriño.

Navarra
(Navarre)

Convergencia de Demócratas de Navarra (CDN): Avda Carlos III 7, 1°, Pamplona; tel. (948) 228185; fax (948) 227336; e-mail cdn@cdn.es; internet www.cdn.es; f. 1995; as progressive centre party; social-Christian ideology; Pres. Juan Cruz Alli; Sec. Carlos Pérez-Nievas.

Nafaroa Bai (Na-Bai): Plaza del Castillo 32, 1° izqda, Iruña 31001; tel. (948) 203033; fax (948) 203034; e-mail nafarroabai@nafaroabai.net; internet www.nafarroabai.org; coalition of Basque nationalist parties in Navarre (ARALAR, Batzarre, Eusko Alkartasuna, EAJ-PNV) won one seat in the general election of March 2004

Batzarre: Navarrería 15, 1°C, Iruñea 31001; tel. (948) 224757; fax (948) 211063; e-mail batzarre@batzarre.org; internet www.batzarre.org; f. 1987; left wing Basque nationalist party of Navarre.

Partido Socialista de Navarra (PSN): Paseo de Sarasate 15, 2°, 31002 Pamplona; tel. (948) 225003; fax (948) 221534; e-mail info@psn-psoe.org; internet www.psn-psoe.org; Sec.-Gen. Carlos Chivite.

Unión del Pueblo Navarro (UPN): Plaza Príncipe de Viana 1, 4° dcha, 31002 Pamplona; tel. (948) 223402; fax (948) 210810; e-mail info@upn.org; internet www.upn.org; f. 1979; social Christian; Pres. Miguel Sanz Sesma; Sec.-Gen. Alberto Catalán Higueras.

La Rioja

Partido Riojano (PR): Portales 17, 1°, 26001 Logroño; tel. (941) 238199; fax (941) 254396; e-mail partidoriojano@partidoriojano.es; internet www.partidoriojano.es; Pres. Miguel González de Legarra; Sec.-Gen. Javier Sáenz Torre Merino.

Valencia

Esquerra Unida (EU): Gran Via Ramón i Cajál 55, 2°, 46007 Valencia; e-mail eu.pvalencia@izquierda-unida.es; tel. (963) 841888; fax (963) 847678; internet www.eupv.org; left-wing; Pres. Glòria Marcos i Martí.

Esquerra Valenciana (EV): 13129-4621994 Valencia; e-mail esquerravalenciana@ono.com; internet www.esquerravalenciana.org; f. 1934; as part of Front Popular; Pres. Roberto Moro; Sec.-Gen. Víctor Baeta Subias.

Partido Socialista del País Valenciano (PSPV-PSOE) (Valencian Socialist Party): Las Cortes Valencianas, Palau de les Corts Valencianes, Plaza San Lorenzo 4, 46003 Valencia; internet www.pspv-psoe.org; Pres. Diego Macía Antón; Sec.-Gen. Joan Ignasi Pla i Durà.

ILLEGAL ORGANIZATIONS

Illegal terrorist organizations include the Basque separatist Euskadi ta Askatasuna (ETA, Basque Homeland and Liberty, f. 1959) and the extreme left-wing Grupos de Resistencia Antifascista Primero de Octubre (GRAPO, First of October Anti-Fascist Resistance Groups, f. 1975). The Grupos Antiterroristas de Liberación (GAL) were formed in 1983 to oppose ETA, and were subsequently revealed to have received government funding. Catalan nationalist movements have included the right-wing anti-separatist Milicia Catalana (f. 1986 to oppose Terra Lliure), Moviment de Defensa de la Terra (MDT) and Ejército Rojo Catalán de Liberación (ERCA); Terra Lliure (Free Land, f. 1975), which had links with ETA, was dissolved in July 1991, but a dissident faction subsequently became active. A Galician nationalist movement, Exército Guerrilheiro do Pobo Galego Ceibe (EGPGC), was active between 1987 and 1991. Following the Madrid train bombings in March 2004, it was revealed that fundamentalist Islamist groups, thought to be connected to the Moroccan Groupe islamique combattant Marocain (GICM), were operating in Spain.

Election Commission

Junta Electoral Central: Congreso de los Diputados, Floridablanca, 28071 Madrid; tel. (91) 3906367; fax (91) 3906991; independent; Pres. José María Ruiz-Jarabo Ferrán.

Diplomatic Representation

EMBASSIES IN SPAIN

Albania: María de Molina 64, 5°B, 28006 Madrid; tel. (91) 5626985; fax (91) 5613775; e-mail albania@albania.e.telefonica.net; Ambassador Anila Bitri Lani.

Algeria: General Oráa 12, 28006 Madrid; tel. (91) 5629705; fax (91) 5629877; e-mail embargel@tsai.es; Ambassador Mohammed Haneche.

Andorra: Alcalá 73, 28009 Madrid; tel. (91) 4317453; fax (91) 5776341; e-mail embajada@embajadaandorra.es; Ambassador Vicenç Mateu-Zamora.

Angola: Serrano 64, 3°, 28001 Madrid; tel. (91) 4356430; fax (91) 5779010; e-mail gabinete@embajadadeangola.com; internet www.embajadadeangola.com; Ambassador Armando da Cruz Neto.

SPAIN

Argentina: Pedro de Valdivia 21, 28006 Madrid; tel. (91) 7710500; fax (91) 7710526; e-mail embajada@portalargentino.net; internet www.portalargentino.net; Ambassador CARLOS ANTONIO BETTINI.

Australia: Plaza del Descubridor Diego de Ordás 3, Edif. Santa Engracia 120, 2°, 28003 Madrid; tel. (91) 3536600; fax (91) 3536692; e-mail pilar.sanchez@dfat.gov.au; internet www.spain.embassy.gov.au; Ambassador SUSAN ELIZABETH TANNER.

Austria: Paseo de la Castellana 91, 9°, 28046 Madrid; tel. (91) 5565315; fax (91) 5973579; e-mail madrid-ob@bmaa.gv.at; internet www.bmaa.gv.at/madrid; Ambassador ULRIKE TILLY.

Azerbaijan: Ronda de la Avutarda 38, 28043 Madrid; tel. (91) 7596010; fax (91) 7597056; Ambassador MAMMAD NOVRUZOGLU ALIYEV.

Bangladesh: Diego de León 69, 2°D, 28006 Madrid; tel. (91) 4019932; fax (91) 4029564; e-mail chancery@bdoot-mad.e.telefonica.net; Ambassador ANWAR UI ALAM.

Belgium: Paseo de la Castellana 18, 6°, 28046 Madrid; tel. (91) 5776300; fax (91) 4318166; e-mail madrid@diplobel.org; internet www.diplobel.org/spain; Ambassador CLAUDE RIJMENANS.

Bolivia: Velázquez 26, 3°, 28001 Madrid; tel. (91) 5780835; fax (91) 5773946; e-mail embajada@embajadadebolivia.es; internet www.embajadadebolivia.es; Chargé d'affaires a.i. ALVARO DEL POZO CARAFA.

Bosnia and Herzegovina: Lagasca 24, 2° izqda, 28001 Madrid; tel. (91) 5750870; fax (91) 4355056; e-mail ambasada@ctv.es; Ambassador JOSIP BRKIC.

Brazil: Fernando el Santo 6, 28010 Madrid; tel. (91) 7004650; fax (91) 7004660; e-mail ambe@embajadabrasil.es; internet www.brasil.es; Ambassador JOSÉ VIEGAS, Filho.

Bulgaria: Santa María Magdalena 15, 28016 Madrid; tel. (91) 3455761; fax (91) 3591201; e-mail embulmad@tyahoo.es; Ambassador VASSILIY HHRISTOV TAKEV.

Cameroon: Rosario Pino 3, 28020 Madrid; tel. (91) 5711160; fax (91) 5712504; e-mail ambcammadrid@telefonica.net; Ambassador (vacant).

Canada: Núñez de Balboa 35, Edif. Goya, 28001 Madrid; tel. (91) 4233250; fax (91) 4233253; e-mail madrid@dinternational.gc.ca; internet www.canada-es.org; Ambassador MARC LORTIE.

Chile: Lagasca 88, 6°, 28001 Madrid; tel. (91) 4319160; fax (91) 5775560; e-mail echilees12@pc-compatible.co; Ambassador ENRIQUE KRAUSS RUSQUE.

China, People's Republic: Arturo Soria 113, 28043 Madrid; tel. (91) 5194242; fax (91) 5192035; e-mail chinaemb-es@emfa.gov.cn; internet www.embajadachina.es; Ambassador QIU XIAOQI.

Colombia: General Martínez Campos 48, 28010 Madrid; tel. (91) 7004770; fax (91) 3102869; e-mail emadrid@minrelext.gov.co; Ambassador MARTHA NOEMÍ SANÍN POSADA.

Congo, Democratic Republic: Paseo de la Castellana 255, 1°, 28046 Madrid; tel. (91) 7332647; fax (91) 3231575; e-mail ambardcmadrid@yahoo.es; Ambassador (vacant).

Costa Rica: Paseo de la Castellana 164, 17°A, 28046 Madrid; tel. (91) 3459622; fax (91) 3533709; e-mail embajada@embcr.org; Ambassador MARÍA ELENA POZUELO PAGÉS.

Côte d'Ivoire: Serrano 154, 28006 Madrid; tel. (91) 5626916; fax (91) 5622193; e-mail costamarfil@ic1.inycom.es; Ambassador JEANNE GUEHE MOULOT.

Croatia: Claudio Coello 78, 2°, 28001 Madrid; tel. (91) 5776881; fax (91) 5776905; e-mail croemb.madrid@mvp.hr; Ambassador FILIP VUČAK.

Cuba: Paseo de la Habana 194, 28036 Madrid; tel. (91) 3592500; fax (91) 3596145; e-mail secrembajada@cubamad.com; internet www.ecubamad.com; Ambassador ALBERTO VELAZCO SAN JOSÉ.

Cyprus: Paseo de la Castellana 45, 4–5°, 28046 Madrid; tel. (91) 5783114; fax (91) 5782189; e-mail embajadachipre@telefonica.net; Ambassador REA YIORDAMLIS.

Czech Republic: Avda de Pío XII 22–24, 28016 Madrid; tel. (91) 3531880; fax (91) 3531885; e-mail madrid@embassy.mzv.cz; internet www.mfa.cz/madrid; Ambassador MARTIN KOŠATKA.

Denmark: Claudio Coello 91, 4°, 28006 Madrid; tel. (91) 4318445; fax (91) 4319168; e-mail madamb@um.dk; internet www.embajadadinamarca.es; Ambassador NIELS PULTZ.

Dominican Republic: Paseo de la Castellana 30, 1° dcha, 28046 Madrid; tel. (91) 4315395; fax (91) 4358139; e-mail oficrdes@infonegocio.com; Ambassador ALEJANDRO GONZÁLEZ PONS.

Ecuador: Velázquez 114, 2°, 28006 Madrid; tel. (91) 5627215; fax (91) 7450244; e-mail embajada@mecuador.es; Ambassador ANTONIO PARRA GIL.

Egypt: Velázquez 69, 28006 Madrid; tel. (91) 5776308; fax (91) 5781732; Ambassador MOHAMED EL-AMIR KHALIL.

El Salvador: General Oraá 9, 5° dcha, 28006 Madrid; tel. (91) 5628002; fax (91) 5630584; e-mail embasalvamadrid@yahoo.com; internet www.embasalva.com; Ambassador ENRIQUE BORGO BUSTAMANTE.

Equatorial Guinea: Claudio Coello 91, 5°, 28006 Madrid; tel. (91) 7810472; fax (91) 5782263; Ambassador (vacant).

Estonia: Claudio Coello 91, 1° dcha, 28006 Madrid; tel. (91) 4261671; fax (91) 4261672; e-mail embassy.madrid@mfa.ee; internet www.estemb.es; Ambassador ANDRES RUNDU.

Finland: Paseo de la Castellana 15, 4°, 28046 Madrid; tel. (91) 3196172; fax (91) 3083901; e-mail sanomat.mad@foemin.fi; internet www.finlandia.es; Ambassador MAIJA LAHTEENMAKI.

France: Salustiano Olózaga 9, 28001 Madrid; tel. (91) 4238900; fax (91) 4238908; e-mail chancellerie@ctv.es; internet www.ambafrance-es.org; Ambassador CLAUDE MARIE BLANCHEMAISON.

Gabon: Francisco Alcántara 3A, 28002 Madrid; tel. (91) 4138211; fax (91) 4131153; e-mail emb-gabon-es@nemo.es; Ambassador CARLOS VICTOR BOUNGOU.

Georgia: Carrera de San Jerónimo 15, Palacio de Miraflores, 2° despacho 28, 28014 Madrid; tel. (91) 4547261; fax (91) 4547001; Ambassador ZURAB POLOLIKASHVILI.

Germany: Fortuny 8, 28010 Madrid; tel. (91) 5579000; fax (91) 3102104; e-mail zreg@madri.auswaertiges-amt.de; internet www.embajada-alemania.es; Ambassador WOLF-RUTHART BORN.

Ghana: Capitán Haya 38, 10°A, 28020 Madrid; tel. (91) 5670390; fax (91) 5670393; Ambassador FRANCIS TSEGAH.

Greece: Avda del Dr Arce 24, 28002 Madrid; tel. (91) 5644653; fax (91) 5644668; e-mail embajadadegrecia@telefonica.net; Ambassador ARISTIDES AGATHOCLES.

Guatemala: Rafael Salgado 3, 10° dcha, 28036 Madrid; tel. (91) 3441417; fax (91) 4587894; e-mail embespana@minex.gob.gt; Ambassador ROBERTO EDUARDO GEREDA TARACENA.

Haiti: Marques del Duero 3, 1°, 28001 Madrid; tel. (91) 5752624; fax (91) 4314600; e-mail embhaiti@ctv.es; Ambassador YOLETTE AZOR CHARLES.

Holy See: Avda de Pío XII 46, 28016 Madrid; tel. (91) 7668311; fax (91) 7667085; e-mail nunap@planalfa.es; Apostolic Nuncio Most Rev. MANUEL MONTEIRO DE CASTRO (Titular Archbishop of Benevento).

Honduras: Paseo de la Castellana 164, 2° dcha, 28046 Madrid; tel. (91) 5790251; fax (91) 3450665; e-mail info@embahonduras.es; internet www.embahonduras.es; Ambassador JOSÉ EDUARDO MARTELL MEJÍA.

Hungary: Fortuny 6, 4°, 28010 Madrid; tel. (91) 4137011; fax (91) 4134138; e-mail info@embajada-hungria.org; internet www.embajada-hungria.org; Ambassador GÁBOR TÓTH.

India: Avda de Pío XII 30–32, 28016 Madrid; tel. (91) 1315100; fax (91) 3451112; Ambassador SURYAKANTHI TRIPATTHI.

Indonesia: Agastia 65, 28043 Madrid; tel. (91) 4130294; fax (91) 4138994; e-mail kbri@embajadadeindonesia.es; internet www.embajadadeindonesia.es; Ambassador SLAMET SANTOSO MUSTAFA.

Iran: Jerez 5, Villa El Altozano, Chamartín, 28016 Madrid; tel. (91) 3450112; fax (91) 3451190; e-mail embiran@hotmail.com; internet www.embajadairan.es/madrid; Ambassador MORTEZA ALVIRI.

Iraq: Ronda de Sobradiel 67, Parque Conde de Orgaz, 28043 Madrid; tel. (91) 7591282; fax (91) 7593180; internet www.embassyiraqmadrid@hotmail.com; Ambassador TALAL H. AL-KHUDAIRI.

Ireland: Paseo de la Castellana 46, 4°, 28046 Madrid; tel. (91) 4364093; fax (91) 4351677; e-mail embajada@irlanda.es; Ambassador PETER GUNNING.

Israel: Velázquez 150, 7°, 28002 Madrid; tel. (91) 7829500; fax (91) 7829555; e-mail embajada@embajada-israel.es; internet www.embajada-israel.es; Ambassador VICTOR HAREL.

Italy: Lagasca 98, 28006 Madrid; tel. (91) 4233300; fax (91) 5757776; e-mail ambitalsp@cempresarial.com; internet www.ambitaliamadrid.org; Ambassador AMEDEO DE FRANCIS.

Japan: Serrano 109, 28006 Madrid; tel. (91) 5907600; fax (91) 5901321; e-mail embjapon@embjapon.es; internet www.embjapon.es; Ambassador KEN SHIMANOUCHI.

Jordan: General Martínez Campos 41, 5°, 28010 Madrid; tel. (91) 3191100; fax (91) 3082536; e-mail jordania@telefonica.net; Ambassador ZAID M. AL-LOZI.

Kazakhstan: Cascanueces 25, Parque Conde de Orgaz, 28043 Madrid; tel. (91) 7216290; fax (91) 7219374; e-mail embajada@kazesp.org; internet www.kazesp.org; Ambassador NURLAN DANENOV.

Korea, Republic: González Amigó 15, 28033 Madrid; tel. (91) 3532000; fax (91) 3532001; e-mail embspain.adm@mofa.go.kr; internet www.mofat.go.kr/spain; Ambassador CHUN-SEUN LEE.

SPAIN

Kuwait: Paseo de la Castellana 141, 16°, 28046 Madrid; tel. (91) 5792467; fax (91) 5702109; Ambassador Dr SALEM AL-JABER AL-AHMAD AL-JABER AL-SABAH.

Latvia: Alfonso XII 52, 1°, 28014 Madrid; tel. (91) 3691362; fax (91) 3690020; e-mail lespan@telefonica.net; Ambassador MARTINS PERTS.

Lebanon: Paseo de la Castellana 178, 3° izqda, 28046 Madrid; tel. (91) 3451368; fax (91) 3455631; e-mail leem_e@teleline.es; Ambassador SAMIR MOUBARAK.

Libya: Pisuerga 12, 28002 Madrid; tel. (91) 5635753; fax (91) 5643986; e-mail oficinapopularlibia-madrid@hotmail.com; Secretary of People's Bureau ABDULWAHED R. GAMMUDI.

Lithuania: Pisuerga 5, 28002 Madrid; tel. (91) 7022116; fax (91) 3104018; e-mail amb.es@urm.lt; internet www.emblituania.es; Ambassador MEČYS LAURINKUS.

Luxembourg: Claudio Coello 78, 1°, 28001 Madrid; tel. (91) 4359164; fax (91) 5774826; e-mail madrid.amb@mae.etat.lu; internet www.mae.lu/espagne; Ambassador JEAN-PAUL SENNINGER.

Macedonia, former Yugoslav republic: Don Ramón de la Cruz 107, 2°B, 28006 Madrid; tel. (91) 5717298; fax (91) 5713481; e-mail rep.mac.madrid@terra.es; Chargé d'affaires a.i. DANICA RUZIN.

Malaysia: Paseo de la Castellana 91, Edif. Centro 23, 10°, 28046 Madrid; tel. (91) 5550684; fax (91) 5555208; e-mail mwmadrid@adv.es; Ambassador Dato' Dr MOHD YUSOF AHMAD.

Malta: Paseo de la Castellana 45, 6° dcha, 28046 Madrid; tel. (91) 3913061; fax (91) 3913066; e-mail maltaembassy.madrid@gov.mt; Ambassador GAETAN A. NAUDI.

Mauritania: Velázquez 90, 3°, 28006 Madrid; tel. (91) 5757006; fax (91) 4359531; Ambassador SALEM OULD MEMMOU.

Mexico: Carrera de San Jerónimo 46, 28014 Madrid; tel. (91) 3692814; fax (91) 4202292; e-mail embamex@embamex.es; internet www.embamex.es; Ambassador GABRIEL JIMÉNEZ REMUS.

Monaco: Villanueva 12, 28001 Madrid; tel. (91) 5782048; fax (91) 4357132; e-mail ambmonacomad@hotmail.com; Ambassador JOSÉ BADIA.

Morocco: Serrano 179, 28002 Madrid; tel. (91) 5631090; fax (91) 5617887; e-mail simafa1@infonegocio.com; internet www.maec.gov.ma/madrid; Ambassador OMAR AZZIMAN.

Mozambique: Goya 67, 1° izqda, 28001 Madrid; tel. (91) 5776382; fax (91) 5776705; e-mail embamocmadrid@worldonline.es; Ambassador ALVARO MANUEL T. DA SILVA.

Netherlands: Avda del Comandante Franco 32, 28016 Madrid; tel. (91) 3537500; fax (91) 3537565; e-mail nlgovmad@telefonica.net; internet www.embajadapaisesbajos.es; Ambassador J. G. S. M. VAN HELLENBERG HUBAR.

New Zealand: Plaza de la Lealtad 2, 3°, 28014 Madrid; tel. (91) 5230226; fax (91) 5230171; e-mail nuevaz@grupouni2.com; internet www.nzembassy.com/spain; Ambassador GEOFFREY KENYON WARD.

Nicaragua: Paseo de la Castellana 127, 1° B, 28046 Madrid; tel. (91) 5555510; fax (91) 4555737; e-mail embanic@tsai.es; Ambassador JORGE SALAVERRY ROMERO.

Nigeria: Segre 28, 28002 Madrid; tel. (91) 5630911; fax (91) 5636320; e-mail nigerian-emb-sp@jet.es; Ambassador Dr KINGSLEY SUNNY EBENGUI.

Norway: Paseo de la Castellana 31, 9°, 28046 Madrid; tel. (91) 3103116; fax (91) 3190969; e-mail emb.madrid@mfa.no; internet www.noruega.es; Ambassador PER LUDVIG MAGNUS.

Pakistan: Avda de Pio XII 11, 28016 Madrid; tel. (91) 3458995; fax (91) 3458158; e-mail cancilleria@embajada-pakistan.org; internet www.embajada-pakistan.org; Ambassador HASAN SARMAD.

Panama: Claudio Coello 86, 1° dcha, 28006 Madrid; tel. (91) 5765001; fax (91) 5767161; Ambassador HUMBERTO LÓPEZ TIRONE.

Paraguay: Eduardo Dato 21, 4° izqda, 28010 Madrid; tel. (91) 3082746; fax (91) 3084905; e-mail embapar@arrakis.es; Ambassador (vacant).

Peru: Príncipe de Vergara 36, 5° dcha, 28001 Madrid; tel. (91) 4314242; fax (91) 5776861; e-mail lepru@embajadaperu.es; Ambassador ARMANDO LECAROS DE COSSIO.

Philippines: Eresma 2, 28002 Madrid; tel. (91) 7823830; fax (91) 4116606; e-mail madridpe@terra.es; internet www.philmadrid.com; Ambassador JOSEPH DELANO BERNARDO Y MEDINA.

Poland: Guisando 23 bis, 28035 Madrid; tel. (91) 3736605; fax (91) 3736624; e-mail embajada@polonia.es; internet www.polonia.es; Ambassador GRAZYNA BERNATOWICZ.

Portugal: Pinar 1, 28006 Madrid; tel. (91) 7824960; fax (91) 7824972; e-mail embaportugal@mtelefonica.net; Ambassador JOSÉ FILIPE MORAES CABRAL.

Qatar: Paseo de la Castellana 92, Hotel Villamagna, 28046 Madrid; tel. (91) 3106926; fax (91) 3104851; Ambassador FAHAD BIN AWIDA ATH-THANI.

Romania: Alfonso XIII 157, 28016 Madrid; tel. (91) 3504436; fax (91) 3452917; e-mail secretariat@roembmad.tiscalibiz.com; internet www.embajadarumana.com; Ambassador MARIA LIGOR.

Russia: Velázquez 155, 28002 Madrid; tel. (91) 4110807; fax (91) 5629712; e-mail embrues@infonegocio.com; internet www.spain.mid.ru; Ambassador ALEXANDER I. KUZIVETSOV.

San Marino: Padre de Jesús Ordóñez 18, 3°, 28002 Madrid; tel. (91) 5639000; fax (91) 5631931; e-mail rsm_madrid@accessnet.es; Ambassador ENRICO MARIA PASQUINI.

Saudi Arabia: Dr Alvarez Sierra 3, 28033 Madrid; tel. (91) 3834300; fax (91) 3021212; e-mail info@arabiasaudi.org; internet www.arabiasaudi.org; Ambassador Prince SA'UD BIN NAIF BIN ABD AL-AZIZ AS-SA'UD.

Senegal: Príncipe de Vergara 90, 1° A y B, 28001 Madrid; tel. (91) 7451003; fax (91) 7451148; e-mail senegal@repsenmadrid.e.telefonica.net; Ambassador ABAS NDIOUR.

Serbia and Montenegro: Velázquez 162, 28002 Madrid; tel. (91) 5635045; fax (91) 5630440; e-mail madrid@embajada-yugoslavia.es; internet www.embajada-yugoslavia.es; Ambassador IVO ARMENKO.

Slovakia: Pinar 20, 28006 Madrid; tel. (91) 5903861; fax (91) 5903868; e-mail mail@embajadaeslovaquia.es; Ambassador JÁN VALKO.

Slovenia: Hermanos Bécquer 7, 2°, 28006 Madrid; tel. (91) 4116893; fax (91) 5646057; e-mail vma@mzz-dkp.gov.si; internet www.gov.si/mzz/vma; Ambassador TOMAŽ LOVRENČIČ.

South Africa: Claudio Coello 91, 6° y 7°, 28006 Madrid; tel. (91) 4363780; fax (91) 5777414; e-mail embassy@sudafrica.com; internet www.sudafrica.com; Ambassador (vacant).

Sudan: Paseo de la Castellana 115, 11 izqda, 28046 Madrid; tel. (91) 4174903; fax (91) 5972516; e-mail sudani49@hotmail.com; Chargé d'affaires SIDDIG MOHAMED ABDALLA MOHAMED.

Sweden: Caracas 25, 28010 Madrid; tel. (91) 7022000; fax (91) 7022040; e-mail ambassaden.madrid@foreign.ministry.se; internet www.swedenabroad.com/spain; Ambassador ANDERS RÖNQUIST.

Switzerland: Núñez de Balboa 35, 7°, 28001 Madrid; tel. (91) 4363960; fax (91) 4363980; e-mail vertretung@mad.rep.admin.ch; internet www.eda.admin.ch/madrid; Ambassador ARMIN RITZ.

Syria: Plaza de Platerías Martínez 1, 1°, 28014 Madrid; tel. (91) 4203946; fax (91) 4202681; Ambassador (vacant).

Thailand: Joaquín Costa 29, 28002 Madrid; tel. (91) 5632903; fax (91) 5640033; e-mail madthai@wanadoo.es; internet www.mfa.go.th; Ambassador BUSBA BUNNAG.

Tunisia: Avda Alfonso XIII 64–68, 28016 Madrid; tel. (91) 4473508; fax (91) 5938416; Ambassador HABIB M'BAREK.

Turkey: Rafael Calvo 18, 2°, 28010 Madrid; tel. (91) 3198111; fax (91) 3086602; e-mail info@tcmadridbe.org; internet www.tcmadridbe.org; Ambassador VOLKAN VURAL.

Ukraine: Ronda de Abubilla 52, 28043 Madrid; tel. (91) 7489360; fax (91) 3887178; e-mail ukremb@ukremb.e.telefonica.net; internet www.embucraina.org.es; Chargé d'affaires OLEH VLASENKO.

United Arab Emirates: Capitán Haya 40, 28020 Madrid; tel. (91) 5701003; fax (91) 5715176; Ambassador Sultan MOHAMED ALI KHALFAN.

United Kingdom: Fernando el Santo 16, 28010 Madrid; tel. (91) 7008200; fax (91) 7008210; e-mail enquiries.madrid@fco.gov.uk; internet www.ukinspain.com; Ambassador Sir STEPHEN WRIGHT.

USA: Serrano 75, 28006 Madrid; tel. (91) 5872200; fax (91) 5872303; internet www.embusa.es; Ambassador EDUARDO AGUIRRE.

Uruguay: Paseo del Pintor Rosales 32, 1° dcha, 28008 Madrid; tel. (91) 7580475; fax (91) 5428177; e-mail urumatri@urumatri.com; Ambassador JOSÉ MARÍA ARANEO GALLART.

Venezuela: Avda Capitán Haya 1, 13°, Edif. Eurocentro, 28020 Madrid; tel. (91) 5981200; fax (91) 5971583; e-mail embajada@venezuela.es; internet www.venezuela.es; Ambassador ARÉVAL ENRIQUE MÉNDEZ ROMERO.

Vietnam: Arturo Soria 201, 1°A, 28043 Madrid; tel. (91) 5102867; fax (91) 4157067; e-mail claudiomes@yahoo.com; internet www.embavietnam-madrid.org; Ambassador NGUYEN XUAN PHONG.

Yemen: Paseo de la Castellana 114, 3° esc. 1, 1°, 28046 Madrid; tel. (91) 4119950; fax (91) 5623865; internet www.embajadayemen.es; Chargé d'affaires ABDULRAHMAN KAMARAMI.

Judicial System

Consejo General del Poder Judicial (CGPJ)
(General Council of Judicial Power)

Marqués de la Ensenada 8, 28071 Madrid; tel. (91) 7006100; fax (91) 7006358; e-mail webmaster@cgpj.es; internet www.poderjudicial.es.

SPAIN

The highest governing body of the judiciary; comprises the President of the Supreme Court, 20 members elected by the Cortes and appointed by the King for a five-year term (10 by the Congress of Deputies and 10 by the Senate); supervises the judicial system; independent of the Ministry of Justice; Pres. FRANCISCO JOSÉ HERNANDO SANTIAGO

General Prosecutor: CANDIDO CONDE-PUMPIDO.

SUPREME COURT
Tribunal Supremo
Palacio de Justicia, Plaza de la Villa de París s/n, 28071 Madrid; tel. (91) 3971200; internet www.poderjudicial.es.

Composed of five courts, civil, criminal, litigation, company and military, each with its president and its respective judges.

President: FRANCISCO JOSÉ HERNANDO SANTIAGO.

HIGH COURTS

Audiencia Nacional (National Court): García Gutiérrez 1, 28004 Madrid; tel. (91) 3973339; fax (91) 3973306; established in 1977; consists of three divisions—Penal, Social and Contencioso-Administrativo—each with its president and respective judges; attached to Second Court of Supreme Court; deals primarily with crimes associated with a modern industrial society, such as corruption, forgery, drugs-trafficking and also terrorism; Pres. CARLOS DIVAR.

Tribunales Superiores de Justicia de las Comunidades Autónomas (Autonomous Communities' Superior Courts of Justice): consist of civil and criminal division, administrative division and labour division.

Audiencias Provinciales (Provincial Courts): hear oral public proceedings, in single instance, for prosecutions of offences punishable by major prison terms, and appeals against decisions, sentences and judgments of lower courts.

OTHER COURTS

Lower courts are the Criminal, Administrative, Labour, Juvenile and Prison Supervisory Courts of First Instance and Trial Courts. In municipalities where there are no Courts of First Instance and Trial, there is a Magistrates' Court.

Religion
CHRISTIANITY

About 90% of Spain's inhabitants profess adherence to Roman Catholicism, and the country contains some 61,000 churches, with about 500 persons in each parish. Opus Dei, which seeks to integrate religious faith and professional work, plays an important role in Spanish society. There are some 30,000 Protestants in Spain.

The Roman Catholic Church

For ecclesiastical purposes, Spain (including Spanish North Africa) comprises 14 metropolitan archdioceses and 55 dioceses. The archdiocese of Barcelona was directly responsible to the Holy See until mid-2004, when it became a metropolitan see. Each diocese is suffragan to a metropolitan see. At 31 December 2003 adherents were equivalent to some 89.2% of the population.

Bishops' Conference

Conferencia Episcopal Española, Añastro 1, 28033 Madrid; tel. (91) 3439615; fax (91) 3439616; e-mail conferenciaepiscopal@planalfa.es; internet www.conferenciaepiscopal.es.
f. 1977; Pres. Mons. RICARDO BLÁSQUEZ PÉREZ (Bishop of Bilbao); Sec.-Gen. JUAN ANTONIO MARTÍNEZ CAMINO.

Archbishop of Barcelona: LLUÍS MARTÍNEZ SISTACH.
Archbishop of Burgos: FRANCISCO GIL HELLÍN.
Archbishop of Granada: FRANCISCO JAVIER MARTÍNEZ FERNÁNDEZ.
Archbishop of Madrid: Cardinal ANTONIO MARÍA ROUCO VARELA.
Archbishop of Mérida-Badajoz: SANTIAGO GARCÍA ARACIL.
Archbishop of Oviedo: CARLOS OSORO SIERRA.
Archbishop of Pamplona y Tudela: FERNANDO SEBASTIÁN AGUILAR.
Archbishop of Santiago de Compostela: JULIÁN BARRIO BARRIO.
Archbishop of Sevilla: Cardinal CARLOS AMIGO VALLEJO.
Archbishop of Tarragona: JAUME PUJOL BALCELLS.
Archbishop of Toledo: Cardinal ANTONIO CAÑIZARES LLOVERA.
Archbishop of Valencia: AGUSTÍN GARCÍA-GASCO VICENTE.
Archbishop of Valladolid: BRAULIO RODRÍQUEZ PLAZA.
Archbishop of Zaragoza: MANUEL UREÑA PASTOR.

The Anglican Communion

Anglicans in Spain are adherents of the Spanish Reformed Episcopal Church (Iglesia Española Reformada Episcopal), founded in 1860. The Church had 17 congregations in 2004.

Bishop: Rt Rev. CARLOS LÓPEZ, Beneficencia 18, 28004 Madrid; tel. (91) 4452560; fax (91) 5944572; e-mail eclesiae@arrakis.es; internet www.iere.cjb.net.

Other Christian Churches

Iglesia Evangélica Española (Spanish Evangelical Church): Noviciado 5, 28015 Madrid; tel. (91) 5313947; fax (91) 5234137; f. 1869; by merger of Presbyterians, Methodists, Congregationalists and Lutherans; 3,000 mems (1994); Pres. JOEL CORTÉS; Sec. ALFREDO ABAD.

Iglesia Ortodoxa Griega (Greek Orthodox Church): Nicaragua 12, 28016 Madrid; tel. (91) 3454085; fax (91) 3509374; internet iglesiaortodoxa.net; Rector Arcipreste DIMITRI TSIAMPARLIS.

Unión Evangélica Bautista Española (UEBE) (Baptist Evangelical Union of Spain): Salvador Ferrandis Luna 45, 26°, 46018 Valencia; tel. (96) 3591633; fax (96) 3134581; e-mail secretaria@uebe.org; internet www.uebe.org; f. 1922; Gen. Sec. Rev. MANUEL SARRIAS; Pres. PABLO SIMARRO.

ISLAM

Centro Islámico: Alfonso Cano 3, 28010 Madrid; tel. (91) 4480554.

Comisión Islámica de España: Anastasio Herrero 5, 28020 Madrid; tel. (91) 5714040; fax (91) 5708889; e-mail cie@teleline.es; umbrella org.; negotiates with Govt on Islamic affairs; Sec.-Gen. RIAY TATARY BAKRY.

Federación Española de Entidades Religiosas Islámicas (FEERI): Madrid; e-mail feeri@feeri.org; internet www.feeri.org; f. 1989; 57 mem. groups; Pres. FÉLIX ANGEL HERRERO.

Unión de Comunidades Islámicas de España (UCIDE): Anastasio Herrero 5, Madrid 28020; tel. (91) 5714040; e-mail webmaster@islamhispania.org; internet www.islamhispania.org; Pres. RIAY TATARY BAKRY.

Comunidad Ahmadía del Islam en España: La Mezquita Basharat, 14630 Pedro Abad (Córdoba); tel. (957) 186203; fax (957) 186300; e-mail info@alislam.org; internet www.alislam.org; Pres. MUBARIK AHMAD KHAN.

JUDAISM

There are an estimated 15,000 Jews in Spain.

Comunidad Judia (Jewish Community): Balmes 3, 28010 Madrid; tel. (91) 5913131; fax (91) 5941517; e-mail secretaria@comjudiamadrid.org.

Federación de Comunidades Israelitas de España (Federation of Jewish Communities of Spain): Balmes 3, 28010 Madrid; tel. (91) 7001208; fax (91) 3915717; e-mail fcje@fcje.org; Pres. JACOBO ISRAEL GARZÓN.

OTHER RELIGIOUS GROUPS

There are minorities of Bahá'ís (2,000 adherents), Buddhists and Jehovah's Witnesses.

The Press

There are four national newspapers: *ABC*, *Marca*, *El Mundo* and *El País*. Others, such as *As*, *El Correo*, *El Periódico de Catalunya* and *La Vanguardia*, may readily be obtained outside the region in which they are published. In 2000 there were 87 daily newspapers in Spain, with a total daily circulation estimated at 4.0m.

PRINCIPAL NEWSPAPERS
(arranged alphabetically by province)

Alava

El Periódico de Alava—Arabako Egunkaria: General Alava 5, interior, 01005 Vitoria; tel. (945) 230032; fax (945) 133086; e-mail prensa@elperiodicodealava.com; f. 1996; daily; Dir IÑIGO MUÑOZ TRIGO; circ. 15,000.

Albacete

La Tribuna de Albacete: Paseo de la Cuba 14, 02005 Albacete; tel. (967) 191000; fax (967) 240386; e-mail redaccion@latribunadealbacete.es; internet www.latribunadealbacete.es; daily; Dir DIMAS CUEVAS CUERDA.

La Verdad de Albacete: Plaza Catedral 6, 02005 Albacete; tel. (967) 219311; fax (967) 210781; Dir EDUARDO SAN MARTÍN MONTILLA.

SPAIN

Alicante

Ciudad de Alcoy: Avda Puente San Jorge 8 y 10, 03803 Alcoy; tel. (96) 6521548; fax (96) 6521551; e-mail ciudaddealcoy@elperiodico.com; internet www.ciudaddealcoy.com; daily; Dir JOSÉ VICENTE BOTELLA.

Información: Avda Dr Rico 17, Apdo 214, 03005 Alicante; tel. (96) 5989100; fax (96) 5989165; e-mail redaccion@epi.es; internet www.diarioinformacion.com; f. 1941; morning; Dir-Gen. JESÚS PRADO SÁNCHEZ; circ. 21,269.

La Verdad de Alicante: Avda Oscar Esplá 4, Bajo 5, 03003 Alicante; tel. (96) 5921950; fax (96) 5922248; e-mail alicante@la-verdad.com; internet www.la-verdad.com; Dir EDUARDO SAN MARTÍN MONTILLA.

Almería

La Voz de Almería: Avda Mediterráneo 159, 1°, Edif. Cadena Ser, 04007 Almería; tel. (950) 280036; fax (950) 256458; e-mail lavoz@lavozdealmeria.com; internet www.lavozdealmeria.com; morning; Dir PEDRO MANUEL DE LA CRUZ ALONSO; circ. 7,737.

Asturias—see Oviedo

Avila

El Diario de Ávila: Pta del Ejército 8, Ávila; tel. (920) 351852; fax (920) 351853; e-mail redaccion@diariodeavila.com; f. 1888; morning; Dir JUAN CARLOS FERNÁNDEZ AGANZO; circ. 8,000.

Badajoz

Hoy—Diario de Extremadura: Carretera Madrid–Lisboa 22, 06008 Badajoz; tel. (924) 252511; fax (924) 205297; e-mail hoyredaccion@hoy.es; internet www.hoy.es; f. 1933; morning; Catholic; Badajoz and Cáceres editions; Dir TERESIANO RODRÍGUEZ NÚÑEZ; circ. 21,815.

Barcelona

Avui: Consell de Cent 425, 08009 Barcelona; tel. (93) 3163900; fax (93) 3163936; e-mail info@avui.es; internet www.avui.es; f. 1976; morning; in Catalan; Exec. Pres. ANTONI CAMBREDÓ; circ. 50,000.

Diari de Sabadell: Sant Quirze 37–41, 2°, 08201 Sabadell; tel. (93) 7261100; fax (93) 7270865; e-mail redaccio@diarisabadell.com; f. 1977; 5 a week; Dir RAMÓN RODRÍGUEZ ZORRILLA; circ. 7,164.

Diari de Terrassa: Vinyals 61, 08221 Terrassa; tel. (93) 7283700; fax (93) 7283719; e-mail opinion@diariterrasa.net; f. 1977; daily; Dir ANA MUÑOZ NÚÑEZ; circ. 5,590.

Metro Directo: General Almirante 2–6, 8°, 08014 Barcelona; tel. (93) 3903500; fax (93) 3903595; e-mail redaccion@metrospain.com; internet www.metrodirecto.com; free daily; partly in Catalan; editions in Alicante, Castilla-La Mancha, Elche, Galicia, Málaga, Sevilla, Valencia and Zaragoza; Dir-Gen. CARLOS OLIVA-VÉLEZ.

Mundo Deportivo: Tallers 62–64, 4°, 08001 Barcelona; tel. (93) 3444100; fax (93) 3444250; e-mail cd@elmundodeportivo.es; internet www.elmundodeportivo.es; f. 1906; morning; sport; Dir SANTI NOLLA ZAYAS; circ. 102,480.

El 9 Punt: Sardà 1, baixos, 08203 Sabadell; tel. (93) 7209990; fax (93) 7121025; Dir JAUME ESPUNY.

El País: Consell de Cent 341, 08007 Barcelona; tel. (93) 4010500; fax (93) 4010631; internet www.elpais.es; daily; f. 1982; Assistant Editor-in-Chief XAVIER VIDAL-FOLCH; circ. 80,000 (Sun. 143,000).

El Periódico de Catalunya: Consell de Cent 425–427, 08009 Barcelona; tel. (93) 2655353; fax (93) 4846512; e-mail redaccionp@elperiodico.com; internet www.elperiodico.com; daily; f. 1978; Dir ANTONIO FRANCO ESTADELLA; circ. 210,000, (Sun. 380,000).

Regió 7 Informatiu Intercomarcal: Sant Antoni M. Claret 32, 08240 Manresa; tel. (93) 8772233; fax (93) 8740352; e-mail regio7@regio7.com; internet www.regio7.com; f. 1978; daily; Dir GONÇAL MAZCUÑÁN BOIX; circ. 8,658 (Sat. 11,232).

Sport: Valencia 49–51, 08015 Barcelona; tel. (93) 2279400; fax (93) 2279410; e-mail redaccion@diariosport.com; internet www.diariosport.com; daily; Editor JOSÉ MARÍA CASANOVAS; Dir JOSÉ PRATS FIOL; circ. 130,000.

La Vanguardia: Pelayo 28, 08001 Barcelona; tel. (93) 4812200; fax (93) 3185587; e-mail lavanguardia@lavanguardia.es; internet www.lavanguardia.es; f. 1881; morning; Dir JOSÉ ANTICH; circ. 210,153 (Sun. 339,528).

20 Minutos: Plaça Universitat 3, 7°, 3A, 08007 Barcelona; tel. (93) 4706250; fax (93) 4706257; e-mail noesven@20minutos.es; internet www.20minutos.es; free daily; partly in Catalan; Dir ARSENIO ESCOLAR.

Burgos

Diario de Burgos: San Pedro de Cardeña 34, Apdo 46, 09002 Burgos; tel. (947) 267280; fax (947) 268003; e-mail redaccion@diariodeburgos.es; internet www.diariodeburgos.es; f. 1891; morning; Catholic; independent; Dir VICENTE RUIZ DE MENCÍA; circ. 15,028 (Sun. 21,600).

Cáceres

El Periodico de Extremadura: Doctor Marañón 2, Local 7, 10002 Cáceres; tel. (927) 620600; fax (927) 620626; e-mail epextremadura@elperiodico.es; internet www.elperiodico.es/extremadura; f. 1926; morning; Dir JULIÁN RODRÍGUEZ MOSCOSO; circ. 12,000.

Cádiz

Area: Gibraltar 13–15, 11300 La Línea de la Concepción (Cádiz); tel. (956) 690620; fax (956) 172060; e-mail direcdiarioarea@telefonica.net; f. 1956; morning; Dir JOSÉ ANTONIO GÓMEZ AMADO; circ. 2,601.

Diario de Cádiz: Ceballos 1, Apdo 57, 11003 Cádiz; tel. (956) 297900; fax (956) 224883; e-mail redaccion@diariodecadiz.es; internet www.diariodecadiz.es; f. 1867; morning; independent; Dir MANUEL DE LA PEÑA MUÑOZ; circ. 32,120.

Diario de Jerez: Patricio Garvey s/n, Apdo 316, 11402 Jerez de la Frontera; tel. (956) 321411; fax (956) 349904; e-mail redaccion@diariojerez.es; internet www.diariodejerez.com; f. 1984; Dir RAFAEL NAVAS RENEDO; circ. 10,265.

Europa Sur: Muro 3, 11201 Algeciras; tel. (956) 568250; fax (956) 631167; f. 1989; daily; Dir JORGE BEZARES BERMÚDEZ; circ. 6,485.

Información Jerez: Oso s/n, 11405 Jerez de la Frontera; tel. (956) 319833; fax (956) 307912; Dir JUAN MANUEL GARRO REMENTERÍA.

Cantabria (Santander)

Alerta de Cantabria: 1 de Mayo s/n, Barrio San Martín, 39011 Peñacastillo; tel. (942) 320033; fax (942) 322046; e-mail alerta@cantabria.org; f. 1937; morning; Dir CIRIACO DÍAZ PORRAS; circ. 30,619.

El Diario Montañés: La Prensa s/n, La Albericia, 39012 Santander; tel. (942) 354000; fax (942) 341806; internet www.eldiariomontanes.es; f. 1902; morning; independent; Dir MANUEL ANGEL CASTAÑEDA PÉREZ; circ. 40,610 (Sun. 56,409).

Castellón

Mediterráneo: Carretera de Almassora s/n, 12005 Castellón de la Plana; tel. (964) 349500; fax (964) 349505; e-mail mediterraneo@elperiodico.com; internet www.elperiodicomediterraneo.com; f. 1938; morning; Dir JESÚS MONTESINOS CERVERA; circ. 15,000.

Ciudad Real

Canfali: Plaza España 8, 1°, Edif. Mercado de Abastos, 13600 Alcazar de San Juan; tel. (926) 550940; fax (926) 550944; Dir MANUEL ESQUEMBRE BAÑULS.

El Día de Ciudad Real: Toledo 8, Edif. Miró, 3°, 3001 Ciudad Real; tel. (926) 223033; fax (926) 227185; e-mail redaccion@eldiadeciudadreal.com; f. 2002; Dir SANTIAGO MATEO SAHUQUILLO; circ. 4,500.

Lanza—Ciudad Real: Ronda del Carmen s/n (antiguo Hospital provincial), 13002 Ciudad Real; tel. (926) 274690; fax (926) 274746; e-mail redaccion@lanzadigital.com; internet www.lanzadigital.com; morning; Dir LAURA ESPINAR SÁNCHEZ; circ. 5,000.

La Tribuna de Ciudad Real: Juan II 7, 1°, 13001 Ciudad Real; tel. (926) 215301; fax (926) 215306; e-mail redaccion@diariolatribuna.com; Dir MARISA GARCÍA CARRETERO.

Córdoba

Córdoba: Ing. Juan de la Cierva 18 (Polígono Industrial de la Torrecilla), Apdo 2, 14013 Córdoba; tel. (957) 295531; fax (957) 420302; e-mail cordoba1@elperiodico.es; f. 1941; morning; Dir ALFONSO S. PALOMARES; circ. 18,660.

El Día de Córdoba: Avda Gran Capitán 23, 2°, 14008 Córdoba; tel. (957) 222050; fax (957) 222072; e-mail eldia@eldiadecordoba.com; internet www.eldiadecordoba.com; Dir ALFREDO MARTÍNEZ PÉREZ.

A Coruña

El Correo Gallego: Preguntoiro 29, 15704 Santiago de Compostela; tel. (981) 543700; fax (981) 543701; e-mail grupocorreogallego@elcorreogallego.es; internet www.elcorreogallego.es; morning; Dir JOSÉ MANUEL REY NÓVOA; circ. 18,238.

O Correo Galego: f. 1994; Galician edn of above; circ. 10,000.

Deporte Campeón: Polígono de Pocomaco, C12, 2°, 15190 Mesoiro; tel. (981) 138586; fax (981) 138575; e-mail dxt@deportecampeon.com; f. 1995; daily; sport; Dir JUAN CARLOS BOGA SÁNCHEZ.

SPAIN

El Ideal Gallego: Polígono de Pocomaco, C12, 15190 Mesoiro; tel. (981) 173040; fax (981) 299327; e-mail elidealgallego@elidealgallego.com; internet www.elidealgallego.com; f. 1917; morning; Dir JUAN RAMÓN DÍAZ GARCÍA; circ. 15,500 (Sun. 20,000).

La Voz de Galicia: Avda de la Prensa 84–85, Polígono de Sabón, 15142 Arteixo; tel. (981) 180180; fax (981) 180410; e-mail redac@lavoz.com; internet www.lavozdegalicia.com; f. 1882; daily; commercial; Dir BIEITO RUBIDO RAMONDE; circ. 130,728 (Sun. 160,974).

Cuenca

El Día de Cuenca: Polígono 'El Cantorral' 13, 16004 Cuenca; tel. (969) 212291; fax (969) 225351; internet www.eldia-digital.com; f. 1984; Dir SANTIAGO MATEO SAHUQUILLO; circ. 7,500.

Girona

Diari de Girona: Passeig General Mendoza 2, 17002 Girona; tel. (972) 202066; fax (972) 202005; e-mail diaridegirona@epi-es; internet www.diaridegirona.es; f. 1891; morning; Dir JORDI XARGAYO I TEIXIDOR; circ. 6,208.

El Punt: Santa Eugènia 42, 17005 Girona; tel. (972) 186400; fax (972) 186420; e-mail elpunt@elpunt.com; internet www.elpunt.com; f. 1979; Dir JOAN VALL I CLARA; circ. 27,642 (2004).

Granada

Ideal: Huelva 2, Polígono 'La Unidad' de Asegra, 18210 Peligros; tel. (958) 809809; fax (958) 402480; e-mail ideal@ideal.es; internet www.ideal.es; f. 1932; morning; Dir EDUARDO PERALTA DE ANA; circ. 40,000; edns in Granada, Jaén and Almería.

Guipúzcoa

El Diario Vasco: Camino de Portuetxe 2, Barrio de Ibaeta, Apdo 201, 20018 San Sebastián; tel. (943) 410700; fax (943) 410814; internet www.diariovasco.com; f. 1934; morning; liberal; Dir JOSE GAVRIEL MUGICA; circ. 103,000 (Sat./Sun. 125,000).

Euskaldunon Egunkaria: Gudarien Etorbidea Z/G, 20140 Andoain; tel. (943) 300222; fax (943) 300707; e-mail egunkaria@egunkaria.com; f. 1990; daily; entirely in Basque; shut down by Government in February 2002; Dir MARTXELO OTAMENDI; circ. 15,000.

Gara: Camino Portuetxe 23, 2°, 20018 San Sebastián; tel. (943) 316999; fax (943) 316998; internet www.gara.net; Dir MERTXE AIZPURUA.

Huelva

Huelva Información: Plaza San Pedro 7, Apdo 176, 21004 Huelva; tel. (959) 541150; fax (959) 260608; e-mail redaccion@huelvainformacion.es; internet www.huelvainformacion.es; Dir MANUEL CAPELO HERNÁNDEZ; circ. 7,047.

Huesca

Diario del Altoaragón: Ronda Estación 4, 22005 Huesca; tel. (974) 215656; fax (974) 215658; e-mail redaccion@diariodelaltoaragon.es; internet www.diariodelaltoaragon.es; fmrly Nueva España; morning; Dir ANTONIO ANGULO ARAGUÁS.

Heraldo de Huesca: Coso Bajo 28, 22001 Huesca; tel. (974) 239000; fax (974) 239005; e-mail huescaredaccion@heraldo.es; Dir GUILLERMO FATÁS CABEZA.

Jaén

Diario Jaén: Torredonjimeno 1, Polígono los Olivares, 23009 Jaén; tel. (953) 221810; fax (953) 280207; e-mail diariojaen@diariojaen.es; internet www.diariojaen.es; f. 1941; morning; Dir JUAN ESPEJO GONZÁLEZ; circ. 7,466.

León

La Crónica/El Mundo de León: Moisés de León, Bloque 49, bajo, 24006 León; tel. (987) 212512; fax (987) 213152; e-mail la-cronica@alehep.com; f. 1986; daily; Dir JOSÉ LUIS ESTRADA LIÉBANA; circ. 9,800.

Diario de León: Carretera de León–Astorga, Km 4–6, 24010 León; tel. (987) 840300; fax (987) 840340; e-mail diarioleon@diarioleon.com; internet www.diarioleon.com; morning; Dir FERNANDO ALLER GONZÁLEZ; circ. 18,366.

El Faro Astorgano: Manuel Gullón 5, 24700 Astorga; tel. (987) 617012; fax (987) 617025; e-mail elfaro@astorga.com; internet www.astorga.com; f. 1980; 5 a week; Dir ISIDRO MARTÍNEZ RODRÍGUEZ; circ. 2,250.

Lleida (Lérida)

La Mañana-Diari de Ponent: Polígono Industrial El Segre 118, Apdo 11, 25080 Lérida; tel. (973) 204600; fax (973) 201646; e-mail manyana@lamanyana.es; internet www.lamanyana.es; f. 1938; morning; Dir JORDI PÉREZ ANSÓTEGUI; circ. 7,510.

Segre: Riu 6, Apdo 543, 25007 Lérida; tel. (973) 248000; fax (973) 246031; e-mail redaccio@diariosegre.com; internet www.diarisegre.com; f. 1982; morning; Dir JUAN CAL SÁNCHEZ; circ. 19,416 (Sun. 25,084).

Lugo

El Progreso: Ribadeo 5, 27002 Lugo; tel. (982) 298100; fax (982) 298102; e-mail correo@elprogreso.es; f. 1908; morning; independent; Dir LUIS RODRÍGUEZ GARCÍA; Editor-in-Chief BLANCA GARCÍA MONTENEGRO; circ. 13,177.

Madrid

ABC: Juan Ignacio Luca de Tena 7, 28027 Madrid; tel. (91) 3399000; fax (91) 3203680; e-mail info@abc.es; internet www.abc.es; f. 1905; morning; monarchist, independent; Dir JOSÉ ANTONIO ZARZALEJOS; circ. 334,696 (Sun. 765,668).

As: Albasanz 14, 4°, 28037 Madrid; tel. (91) 3752500; fax (91) 3752558; e-mail diarioas@diarioas.es; internet www.as.com; f. 1967; morning, sporting paper; Dir ALFREDO RELAÑO ESTAPÉ; circ. 162,420.

El Boletín de la Tarde: Bárbara de Braganza 11, 1°, 28004 Madrid; tel. (91) 3197000; fax (91) 3195831; e-mail redaccion@elboletin.com; internet www.elboletin.com; Dir CARLOS HUMANES FERNÁNDEZ.

Cinco Días: Gran Vía 32, 2°, 28013 Madrid; tel. (91) 3537900; fax (91) 3537991; e-mail redaccion@5dias.com; internet www.cincodias.es; f. 1978; morning, incl. Sat. and Sun.; economic; Dir FÉLIX MONTEIRA; Gen. Man. JUAN JOSÉ MANCEBO ZAFORAS; circ. 21,011.

Diario de Alcalá: Plaza de Navarra 1°c y D, 28804 Alcalá de Henares; tel. (91) 8894162; fax (91) 8895115; e-mail diarioalcala@tsai.es; Dir ANTONIO NARANJO; Editor JULIO R. NARANJO.

El Economista: Condesa de Venadito 1, 3°, 28027 Madrid; tel. (91) 3246700; fax (91) 3246727; e-mail comunicacion@eleconomista.es; internet www.eleconomista.es; f. 2006; daily; Pres. ALFONSO DE SALAS; Dir CARLOS SALAS; circ. 250,000.

Expansión: Paseo de la Castellana 66, 28046 Madrid; tel. (91) 3373220; fax (91) 3373266; e-mail expansion@recoletos.es; internet www.expansion.com; daily; Dir IGNACIO GARAY; circ. 50,000.

La Gaceta de los Negocios: Pantoja 14, 28002 Madrid; tel. (91) 4327600; fax (91) 4327733; e-mail jpv@negocios.com; internet www.negocios.com; f. 1989; daily; business and finance; Dir JUAN PABLO DE VILLANUEVA; circ. 45,000.

Marca Deportivo: Paseo de la Castellana 66, 2°, 28046 Madrid; tel. (91) 3373220; fax (91) 3373276; e-mail marca@recoletos.es; internet www.marca.com; f. 1938; as weekly in San Sebastián, 1942 as daily in Madrid; morning; sports; Editor LUIS INFANTE BRAVO; Dir ELIAS ISRAEL; circ. 474,405.

Metro Directo: Serrano 90, 6°, 28006 Madrid; e-mail redaccion.mdr@metrospain.com; internet madrid.metrodirecto.com; free daily; Dir RAMÓN PEDRÓS.

El Mundo (del Siglo Veintiuno): Pradillo 42, 28002 Madrid; tel. (91) 5864800; fax (91) 5864848; internet www.elmundo.es; f. 1989; daily; Dir PEDRO J. RAMÍREZ CODINA; circ. 315,000 (2005).

El País: Miguel Yuste 40, 28037 Madrid; tel. (91) 3378200; fax (91) 3377758; e-mail suscripciones@elpais.es; internet www.elpais.es; f. 1976; morning; Dir JAVIER MORENO BARBER; Dir-Gen. VICENTE JIMÉNEZ; circ. 578,499 (Sun. 1,040,808); various regional and international edns.

La Razón: Josefa Valcárcel 42, 28027 Madrid; tel. (91) 3247000; fax (91) 7423604; internet www.larazon.es; f. 1998; Pres. LUIS MARÍA ANSÓN; Dir ALEJANDRO VARA.

20 Minutos: Palacio de la Prensa, Plaza del Callao 4, 2°, 28013 Madrid; tel. (91) 7015600; fax (91) 7015660; e-mail nosevende@20minutos; internet www.20minutos.es; f. 2000; free, daily; Dir ARSENIO ESCOLAR; circ. 850,000.

Málaga

Diario Málaga-Costa del Sol: Avda García Morato 50, 29004 Málaga; tel. (95) 2244353; fax (95) 2245540; e-mail redaccion@diariomalaga.com; internet www.diariomalaga.com; Dir JAVIER CHECA.

La Opinión de Málaga: Granada 42, 29015 Málaga; tel. (95) 2126200; fax (95) 2126255; e-mail secretaria@epi.es; internet www.laopiniondemalaga.es; Dir JOAQUÍN MARÍN ALARCÓN.

Sur: Avda Dr Marañón 48, 29009 Málaga; tel. (95) 2649600; fax (95) 2279508; e-mail redaccion.su@diariosur.es; internet www.diariosur

.es; f. 1937; morning; Dir José Antonio Frías Ruiz; circ. 60,000; also publishes free English weekly; circ. 42,975.

Murcia

La Opinión de Murcia: Plaza Condestable 3, 30009 Murcia; tel. (968) 281888; fax (968) 281417; f. 1988; Dir Paloma Reverte de Luis; circ. 8,415.

La Verdad de Murcia: Camino Viejo de Monteagudo s/n, 30160 Murcia; tel. (968) 369100; fax (968) 369147; internet www.laverdad.es; f. 1903; morning; independent; Dir Eduardo San Martín Montilla; circ. 42,724.

Navarra

Diario de Navarra: Zapatería 49, Apdo 5, 31001 Pamplona; tel. (948) 236050; fax (948) 237940; internet www.diariodenavarra.es; f. 1903; morning; independent; Dir Julio Martínez Torres; circ. 64,406.

Diario de Noticias: Polígono Areta Huarte s/n, 31620 Huarte; tel. (948) 332533; fax (948) 332518; e-mail redacción@noticiasdenavarra.com; internet www.noticiasdenavarra.com; f. 1994; daily; Dir Pablo Muñoz Peña; circ. 17,000.

Ourense

La Región (Ourense): Polígono Industrial de San Ciprián de Viñas C4, 32091 Orense; tel. (988) 383838; fax (988) 244449; e-mail laregion@laregion.net; internet www.lri.laregion.net; f. 1910; morning; Dir Alfonso Sánchez Izquierdo; circ. 12,273 (weekly international edn; f. 1966; circ. 44,259).

Oviedo (Asturias)

El Comercio: Diario El Comercio 1, 33207 Gijón; tel. (98) 5179800; fax (98) 5340955; e-mail elcomercio@elcomercio-sa.es; internet www.elcomerciodigital.com; f. 1878; morning; Dir Juan Carlos Martínez Gauna; circ. 27,483.

La Nueva España: Calvo Sotelo 7, Edif. Sedes, 33007 Oviedo; tel. (98) 5279700; fax (98) 5279711; internet www.lanuevaespaña.es; f. 1937; morning; Dir Isidoro Nicieza; circ. 57,561.

El Periódico-La Voz de Asturias: La Lila 6, bajo, 33002 Oviedo; tel. (98) 5101500; fax (98) 5101505; e-mail vozredaccion@elperiodico.com; internet www.lavozdeasturias.es; f. 1923; morning; independent; Dir Luis Muguetta San Martín; circ. 23,500.

La Voz de Avilés: La Camara 47, 33402 Avilés; tel. (98) 5522456; fax (98) 5569899; internet www.elcomerciodigital.com/lavozdeaviles; morning; Dir Juan Manuel Wes López; circ. 3,541.

Palencia

Diario Palentino-El Día de Palencia: Mayor Principal 67, Apdo 17, 34001 Palencia; tel. (979) 744822; fax (979) 743360; e-mail redaccion@diariopalentino.es; internet www.diariopalentino.es; f. 1882; morning; independent; Dir Carlos Martín Santoyo; circ. 10,000.

Pontevedra

Atlántico Diario: Camelias 104, 36211 Vigo; tel. (986) 208686; fax (986) 201269; e-mail atlantico@atlantico.net; f. 1987; daily; Dir Fernando R. Ojea; circ. 5,470.

Diario de Pontevedra: Lepanto 5, 36002 Pontevedra; tel. (986) 011100; fax (986) 011142; morning; Dir Antón Galocha López; circ. 3,903.

Faro de Vigo: Colón 30, Apdo 91, 36201 Vigo; tel. (986) 814600; fax (986) 814615; e-mail redaccion@farodevigo.es; internet www.farodevigo.es; f. 1853; morning; Dir Pedro Pablo Alonso García; circ. 36,862.

Terceiro Tempo: Rúa Barcelona 33, entresuelo, 36205 Vigo; tel. and fax (986) 410706; e-mail tempovision@mundo-r.com; internet www.tercertiempo.net; Dir Daniel Soto Rodrigo.

La Rioja (Logroño)

La Rioja: Vara del Rey 74, Apdo 28, 26002 Logroño; tel. (941) 279107; fax (941) 279106; e-mail director@larioja.com; internet www.diariolarioja.com; f. 1889; morning; Dir José María Esteban Ibáñez; circ. 15,043.

Salamanca

El Adelanto: Gran Vía 56, 37001 Salamanca; tel. (923) 280228; fax (923) 280260; e-mail eladelanto@elperiodico.com; internet www.eladelanto.com; f. 1883; morning; independent; Dir Nunchi Prieto García; circ. 6,100.

La Gaceta Regional de Salamanca: Avda de los Cipreses 81, 37004 Salamanca; tel. (923) 252020; fax (923) 256155; e-mail opinion@lagacetadesalamanca.com; f. 1920; morning; Dir Iñigo Domingúez de Calatayud; circ. 13,740 (Sun. 25,377).

Tribuna de Salamanca: Cañón de Riolobos 14 (Polígono Montalvo II), 37008 Salamanca; tel. (923) 191111; fax (923) 191152; e-mail info@tribuna.net; internet www.tribuna.net; Dir Javier Melero Suárez; Man. Daría Rodríguez Mateos.

Santander—see Cantabria

Segovia

El Adelantado de Segovia: Peñalara 3 (Polígono Industrial El Cerro), 40006 Segovia; tel. (921) 437261; fax (921) 442432; e-mail adelantado@eladelantado.com; internet www.eladelantado.com; f. 1901; evening; Dir Carlos Herranz Cano; circ. 5,000.

Sevilla

ABC: Albert Einstein s/n, Isla de la Cartuja, 41092 Sevilla; tel. (95) 4488600; fax (95) 4488601; f. 1929; morning; monarchist; independent; Dir Alvaro Ybarra Pacheco; circ. 59,874; see also under Madrid.

El Correo de Andalucía: Avda de la Prensa 1, Polígono Carretera Amarilla, 41007 Sevilla; tel. (95) 4999251; fax (95) 4517635; e-mail redaccion@correodeandalucia.es; internet www.correodeandalucia.es; f. 1899; morning; independent; Dir Fernando Orgambides; circ. 27,204.

Diario de Andalucía: Sevilla; e-mail diarioandalucia@arrakis.es; Dir Juan Emilio Ballesteros.

Diario de Sevilla: Rioja 13, pasaje, 41001 Sevilla; tel. (95) 4506200; fax (95) 4506222; e-mail secretaria@diariodesevilla.es; internet www.diariodesevilla.es; Dir Manuel Jesús Florencio.

Estadio Deportivo: Avda San Francisco Javier, Edif. Sevilla 2, 11°, 41018 Sevilla; tel. (95) 4933940; fax (95) 4637839; e-mail estadio@estadiodeportivo.com; internet www.estadiodeportivo.com; sport; Dir José Ángel Muñoz Ramírez; Man. Francisco J. García Moreno; circ. 10,235.

El País: Cardenal Bueno Monreal s/n, Edif. Columbus, 41013 Sevilla; tel. (95) 4246100; fax (95) 4246124; e-mail andalucia@elpais.es; f. 1986; regional edition of the Madrid daily; Dir Román Orozco; circ. 74,000.

Soria

Diario de Soria: Morales Contreras 2, bajo, 42003 Soria; tel. (975) 212063; fax (975) 221504; e-mail diariosoria@maptel.es; internet www.gumaro.com/diariosoria; daily; Dir Patxi Veramendi Moreno.

Heraldo Soria 7 Días: El Collado 17, 1°A–C, 42001 Soria; tel. (975) 233607; fax (975) 229211; e-mail soriaredaccion@heraldo.es; internet www.heraldo.es; Dir Esther Guerrero Gijón; circ. 5,000.

Tarragona

Diari de Tarragona: Domènech Guansé 2, 43005 Tarragona; tel. (977) 299700; fax (977) 223013; e-mail diari@diaridetarragona.com; internet www.diaridetarragona.com; f. 1808; morning; Dir Antonio Coll i Gilabert; circ. 12,302.

Teruel

Diario de Teruel: Avda de Sagunto 27, 44002 Teruel; tel. (978) 617086; fax (978) 600682; e-mail redaccion@diariodeteruel.net; internet www.diariodeteruel.net; daily, morning; Dir Julio Zapater García; circ. 23,800.

Toledo

El Día de Toledo: Cuesta de Carlos V 4, 3° izqda, 45001 Toledo; tel. (925) 221170; fax (925) 214065; e-mail diadetoledo@ticom.es; internet www.eldia-digital.com; f. 1987; daily; Dir Santiago Mateo Sahuquillo; circ. 6,500.

Valencia

Levante—El Mercantil Valenciano: Traginers 7, 46014 Valencia; tel. (96) 3992200; fax (96) 3992276; e-mail levante-emv@epi.es; internet www.levante-emv.es; f. 1872; morning; Dir Pedro Muelas Navarrete; circ. 54,860 (Sun. 86,779).

Mini Diario de la Comunidad Valenciana: Avda Campanar 33, 1°, 46009 Valencia; tel. (96) 3462624; fax (96) 3173140; e-mail valencia@minidiario.com; internet www.minidiario.com; f. 1992; free, daily; Dir Juan Pérez; circ. 55,000.

El País: Poeta Querol 11, 1°, 46002 Valencia; tel. (96) 3981150; fax (96) 3511731; e-mail valencia@elpais.es; internet www.elpais.es; Dir Josep Torrent; f. 1986; regional edn of national daily.

Las Provincias: Polígono Industrial Vara de Quart, Gremis 4, 46014 Valencia; tel. (96) 3502211; fax (96) 3590188; e-mail lasprovincias@lasprovincias.es; internet www.lasprovincias.es;

f. 1866; morning; rightist, independent; Dir Pedro Ortiz Simarro; circ. 59,370 (Sun. 85,084).

The Spanish World: Irlanda 1, 46901 Vedat de Torrent; tel. (96) 1553799; fax (96) 1561583; e-mail spia@spia.com; internet www.thespanishworld.com; Dir Patricia Murray.

Super Deporte: Avda de Aragón 2, Entresuelo, 46021 Valencia; tel. (96) 3371818; fax (96) 3372045; e-mail super@superdeporte.es; sport; Dir Vicente Bau Miquel.

Valladolid

El Norte de Castilla: Vázquez de Menchaca 10 (Polígono de Argales), 47008 Valladolid; tel. (983) 412100; fax (983) 412111; internet www.nortecastilla.es; f. 1854; morning; agricultural and economic interests; Dir Carlos Roldán San Juan; circ. 34,111 (Sun. 45,522).

El Día de Valladolid: Edif. Promecal, Los Astros s/n, 47009 Valladolid; tel. (983) 325045; fax (983) 325047; e-mail redaccion@diavalladolid.es; f. 2000; Dir David Frontela.

Vizcaya

El Correo Español-El Pueblo Vasco: Pintor Losada 7, Apdo 205, 48004 Bilbao; tel. (94) 4870100; fax (94) 4870111; e-mail info@diario-elcorreo.es; internet www.elcorreodigital.com; f. 1910; morning; independent; Dir Ángel Arnedo Gil; circ. 133,032.

Deia: Carretera Bilbao Galdácano 8 (Bolueta), 48004 Bilbao; tel. (94) 4599100; fax (94) 4599120; internet www.deia.com; f. 1997; morning; Basque; Dir Juan José Banõs Loinaz; circ. 50,690.

Diario El Boletín de Bolsa, Economía y Finanzas: Alameda de Mazarredo 31, 3° izqda, 48009 Bilbao; tel. (94) 4235504; fax (94) 4248394; f. 1987; daily; finance; Dir Fernando Mata Iriondo; circ. 10,500.

El País: Epalza 8, 7°, 48007 Bilbao; tel. (94) 4132300; regional edn of Madrid daily; Dir Ander Landáburu.

Zamora

La Opinión-El Correo de Zamora: Rua de los Francos 20, 49001 Zamora; tel. (988) 534759; fax (988) 513552; internet www.laopiniondezamora.es; f. 1896; morning; Dir Francisco García Alonso; circ. 6,404.

Zaragoza

Equipo: Plaza Mariano Arregui 15–16, 50005 Zaragoza; tel. (976) 700440; fax (976) 700449; internet www.diarioequipo.com; Dir Manuel de Miguel Guillén.

Heraldo de Aragón: Avda de la Independencia 29, Apdo 175, 50001 Zaragoza; tel. (976) 765000; fax (976) 765001; e-mail redaccion1@heraldo.es; internet www.heraldo.es; f. 1895; morning; independent; Dir Guillermo Fatás; circ. 55,696.

El Periódico de Aragón: Hernán Cortés 37, bajo, 50005 Zaragoza; tel. (976) 700400; fax (976) 700458; e-mail eparagon@elperiodico.es; internet www.elperiodicodearagon.com; f. 1990; Dir Miguel Angel Liso Tejada; circ. 14,446.

Balearic Islands

Diari de Balears: Paseo Mallorca, 9°A, 07011 Palma de Mallorca; tel. (971) 788322; fax (971) 455740; e-mail mc.dbalears@bitel.es; internet www.diaridebalears.com; f. 1939; fmrly Baleares; morning; in Catalan; Dir Miguel Serra Magraner; circ. 11,777.

Diario de Ibiza: Fray Vicente Nicolás 27, 07800 Ibiza; tel. (971) 190000; fax (971) 190322; e-mail diariodeibiza@epi.es; internet www.diariodeibiza.es; morning; Dir Joan Serra Tur; circ. 6,496.

Diario de Mallorca: Puerto Rico 15, Polígono de Levante, 07006 Palma de Mallorca; tel. (971) 170300; fax (971) 170301; e-mail nacional.diariodemallorca@epi.es; internet www.diariodemallorca.es; f. 1953; morning; daily; Dir José Eduardo Iglesias Barca; circ. 27,202.

Majorca Daily Bulletin: Paseo Mallorca 9A, Palau de la Premsa, Apdo 304, 07011 Palma de Mallorca; tel. (971) 788400; fax (971) 719706; e-mail editorial@majorcadailybulletin.es; internet www.majorcadailybulletin.es; f. 1962; 6 a week; English language; Dir Jason Moore; circ. 5,300.

Menorca, Diario Insular: Cap de Cavalleria 5, 07714 Mahón, Menorca; tel. (971) 351600; fax (971) 351983; e-mail redaccion@menorca.info; internet www.menorca.info; f. 1941; morning; Dir Joan Bosco Marqués Bosch; circ. 6,316.

El Mundo/El Día de Baleares: 16 de Julio 75, Polígono de Son Castelló, 07009 Palma de Mallorca; tel. (971) 767600; fax (971) 767656; e-mail eldia.redaccion@el-mundo.es; internet www.elmundo-eldia.com; f. 1981; daily; Dir Luis Fidalgo Hortelano; circ. 18,000.

Última Hora: Edif. Palacio de la Prensa, Paseo de Mallorca 9°A, 07011 Palma de Mallorca; tel. (971) 788333; fax (971) 454190; internet www.ultimahora.es; f. 1893; morning; Dir Pedro Comas Barceló; circ. 33,100.

Canary Islands—Lanzarote

La Voz Diario de Lanzarote: Canalejas 2, 2° izqda, 35500 Arrecife, Lanzarote; tel. (928) 803949; fax (928) 814225; Dir Francisca Trujillo Eugenio.

Canary Islands—Las Palmas

Canarias 7: Profesor Lozano 7, Urbanización El Sebadal, 35008 Las Palmas; tel. (928) 301300; fax (928) 301434; e-mail infocan@canarias7.es; internet www.canarias7.es; f. 1982; daily; Dir Francisco Suárez Alamo; circ. 36,229.

La Provincia—Diario de las Palmas: Alcalde Ramírez Bethencourt 8, 35003 Las Palmas; tel. (928) 479410; fax (928) 479401; e-mail laprovincia@editorialprensacanaria.es; internet www.la-provincia.com; La Provincia; f. 1911; Diario de las Palmas; f. 1895; morning; independent; Dir Julio Puente; circ. 40,316.

Canary Islands—Santa Cruz de Tenerife

El Día: Avda de Buenos Aires 71, Apdo 97, 38005 Santa Cruz; tel. (922) 238300; fax (922) 214247; e-mail redaccioneldia@eldia.es; internet www.eldia.es; f. 1910; morning; Dir José E. Rodríguez Ramírez; circ. 25,437.

Diario de Avisos: Salamanca 5, 38006 Santa Cruz; tel. (922) 272350; fax (922) 241039; e-mail redaccion@diariodeavisos.com; internet www.diariodeavisos.com; f. 1890; re-f. 1976; morning; Dir Leopoldo Fernández Cabeza de Vaca; circ. 12,293.

La Gaceta de Canarias: Polígono Industrial Los Majuelos, Fernando Díaz Cutillas s/n, 38108 La Laguna; tel. (922) 821555; fax (922) 821460; e-mail lagaceta@teide.net; f. 1989; Dir Andrés González de Chaves y Sotomayor; circ. 11,407.

Jornada Deportiva: Avda Buenos Aires 71, Apdo 714, 38005 Santa Cruz; tel. (922) 238300; fax (922) 213834; f. 1953; morning; general information; Gen. Man. José E. Rodríguez Ramírez; circ. 10,000 (Tue.–Sat.), 26,000 (Mon.).

La Opinión de Tenerife: Plaza Santa Cruz de la Sierra 2, 38003 Santa Cruz; tel. (922) 471800; fax (922) 471801; e-mail lectores@la-opinion.com; internet www.la-opinion.com; Dir Francisco Pomares.

GENERAL INTEREST PERIODICALS

A Nosa Terra: Rúa Príncipe 22, 36202 Vigo; tel. (986) 222405; fax (986) 223101; e-mail info@anosaterra.com; internet www.anosaterra.com; f. 1907; weekly; Galician; Dir Afonso Eiré López.

Aceprensa: Núñez de Balboa 125, 28006 Madrid; tel. (91) 5158975; fax (91) 5631243; e-mail redaccion@aceprensa.com; internet www.aceprensa.com; f. 1973; weekly; news and features; Dir Ignacio Aréchaga; circ. 4,000.

Cambio 16: Arroyo Fontarron 51, 28030 Madrid; tel. (91) 4201199; fax (91) 3601302; e-mail cambio16@cambio16.info; internet www.cambio16.info; f. 1972; weekly (Wed.); general; Pres. Manuel Domínguez Moreno; Dir Gorka Landaburu.

El Ciervo: Calvet 56, 08021 Barcelona; tel. (93) 2005145; fax (93) 2011015; e-mail redaccion@elciervo.es; internet www.elciervo.es; f. 1951; monthly; Dir Lorenzo Gomis Sanahuja; circ. 5,000.

Ciudad Nueva: José Picón 28, 28028 Madrid; tel. (91) 7259530; fax (91) 7130452; e-mail revista@ciudadnueva.com; internet www.ciudadnueva.com; f. 1958; monthly; Dir Javier Rubio; circ. 7,000.

La Clave: Avda de Argón 336, 28022 Madrid; tel. (91) 8373131; fax (91) 8373138; e-mail redaccion@laclave.com; internet www.laclave.com; f. 2001; weekly; news magazine; Dir José Luis Balbin; circ. 60,000.

Diez Minutos: Avda Cardenal Herrera Oria 3, 28034 Madrid; tel. (91) 7287000; fax (91) 7289132; e-mail diezminutos@hachette.es; internet www.diezminutos.es; f. 1951; weekly; Dir Cristina Acebal; circ. 209,208.

El Empresario: Diego de León 50, 3°, 28006 Madrid; tel. (91) 4116161; fax (91) 5645269; e-mail elempresario@cepyme.es; internet www.cepyme.es; monthly; Dir Carlota Domínguez Núñez; circ. 15,000.

Época: Paseo de la Castellana 36–38, 28046 Madrid; tel. (91) 5109100; fax (91) 5109149; e-mail epoca@epoca.es; internet www.epoca.es; weekly; Dir Alfonso Basallo Fuentes.

Gaceta Internacional: Alonso Cano 66, 1°6, 28003 Madrid; tel. (91) 5547354; fax (91) 5539395; e-mail info@aphis.org; monthly; international magazine produced by the Asociación de la Prensa Hispanamerica; Dir Armando Restrepo Bretón; Editor-in-Chief

SPAIN

Yolanda Arratia García; circ. 16,500 in Spain; 150,000 internationally.

Geo: Albasanz 15, Edif. A, 28037 Madrid; tel. (91) 4369800; fax (91) 4369781; e-mail geo@gyj.es; internet www.georevista.es; f. 1987; monthly; Dir David Corral; circ. 61,427.

Guía del Ocio—Barcelona y Área Metropolitana: Muntaner 492, bajos, 08022 Barcelona; tel. (93) 4185005; fax (93) 4179471; e-mail redaccion@guiadelociobcn.com; internet www.guiadelociobcn.com; f. 1977; weekly; Dir Xavier Muniesa Calderó; circ. 50,000.

Guía del Ocio—La Semana de Madrid: Alcalá 106, 2°, 28009 Madrid; tel. (91) 4316080; fax (91) 5769307; e-mail guiadelocio@guiadelocio.es; internet wwwguiadelocio.com; weekly; Dir-Gen. Juan Miguel Alonso Seco.

¡Hola!: Miguel Angel 1, 4°, 28010 Madrid; tel. (91) 7021300; fax (91) 3196444; f. 1944; weekly; general illustrated; Dir Eduardo Sánchez Junco; circ. 582,778.

Insula: Complejo Atica, Edif. 4, Vía de las Dos Castillas 33, 28224 Pozuelo de Alarcón, Madrid; tel. (91) 7848200; fax (91) 3589505; e-mail insula@espasa.es; internet www.insula.es; f. 1946; monthly; literature and social sciences; Editor Carlos Alvarez-Ude; circ. 6,000.

Interviú: O'Donnell 12, 5°, 28009 Madrid; tel. (91) 5863300; fax (91) 5863555; e-mail interviu@grupozeta.es; internet www.zetainterviu.com; f. 1976; weekly; Dir Teresa Viejo; circ. 494,347.

El Jueves: Avda Diagonal 468, 5°, 08006 Barcelona; tel. (93) 2922217; fax (93) 2375824; e-mail redaccion@eljueves.es; internet www.eljueves.es; f. 1977; weekly; satirical; Dir Manuel Fontdevila; circ. 130,000.

Muy Interesante: Marqués de Villamagna 4, 28001 Madrid; tel. (91) 4369800; fax (91) 5759128; e-mail publicidad@gyj.es; internet www.muyinteresante.es; f. 1981; monthly; Dir José Pardina Cancer; circ. 283,690.

Natura: Islas Marquesas 28B, 28035 Madrid; tel. (91) 3865152; fax (91) 3860265; e-mail redaccion@mundonatura.es; f. 1983; bimonthly; wildlife, archaeology, research, travel, food; Dir Jesús Iniesta; circ. 69,913.

El Nuevo Lunes de la Economía y la Sociedad: Plaza de España 18, 7°, Of. 3, 28008 Madrid; tel. (91) 5160803; fax (91) 5160819; e-mail nuevolunes@elnuevolunes.com; internet www.elnuevolunes.com; weekly; Dir Rosa del Río Cabrerizo.

Nuevo Vale: Gran Vía de Carlos III 124, 5°, 08034 Barcelona; tel. (93) 2061540; fax (93) 2805555; e-mail buzon@publicacionesheres.com; weekly; Dir Esther Giralt; circ. 200,000.

Pronto: Gran Vía de Carlos III 124, 5°, 08034 Barcelona; tel. (93) 2061540; fax (93) 2805555; e-mail pronto@publicacionesheres.com; f. 1972; weekly; general information; Dir Antonio Gómez Abad; circ. 960,000.

Semana: Cuesta de San Vicente 28, 28008 Madrid; tel. (91) 5472300; fax (91) 5414488; e-mail redaccion@semana.es; internet www.semana.es; f. 1942; weekly; general, illustrated; Pres. Vicente Montiel y Rodríguez de la Encina; Dir Rosario Montiel Armada; circ. 340,590.

El Semanal Digital: Ferraz 82, 2° izqda, 28008 Madrid; tel. and fax (91) 5482349; e-mail elsemanaldigital@elsemanaldigital.com; internet www.elsemanaldigital.com; f. 1999; weekly; online only; Dir Antonio Martín Beaumont; Editor-in-Chief Isabel García.

El Socialista: Gobelas 31, 28023 Madrid; tel. (91) 5820044; fax (91) 5820045; e-mail elsocialista@elsocialista.es; internet www.elsocialista.es; f. 1866; monthly; general information; Dir Joaquín Tagar; circ. 185,000.

Super Pop: Gran Vía Carlos III 124, 5°, 08034 Barcelona; tel. (93) 2061540; fax (93) 2805555; e-mail superpop@publicacionesheres.com; f. 1976; fortnightly; teenage magazine; Dir Carmen Grasa; circ. 125,000.

Supertele: Cardenal Herrera Oria 3, 28034 Madrid; tel. (91) 7287000; fax (91) 7289129; e-mail supertele@hachette.es; internet www.supertele.es; f. 1992; weekly; TV magazine; Dir Agustín de Tena.

Tele Digital: Vallehermoso 32, 28015 Madrid; tel. (91) 4451950; fax (91) 4450621; internet www.telesatellite.com; Dir José da Cunha.

Tele Indiscreta: Cardenal Herrera Oria 3, 28034 Madrid; tel. (91) 7287000; fax (91) 7289142; e-mail teleindiscreta@hachette.es; internet www.teleindiscreta.es; weekly; popular illustrated; TV programmes; Dir Agustín de Tema; circ. 80,000.

Telenovela: Cardenal Herrera Oria 3, 28034 Madrid; tel. (91) 7287051; fax (91) 7289142; e-mail telenovela@hachette.es; internet www.tele-novela.com; f. 1993; TV series; Dir Irene González; 200,000.

El Temps: Avinguda del Baró de Càrcer 40, 13°, 46001 Valencia; tel. (96) 3535100; fax (96) 3534569; e-mail eltemps@eltemps.com; internet www.eltemps.com; f. 1984; weekly; general information; Dir Jordi Fortuny i Batalla; circ. 25,000.

Tiempo de Hoy: O'Donnell 12, 3°, 28009 Madrid; tel. (91) 5863300; fax (91) 5863346; e-mail tiempo@grupozeta.es; internet www.tiempodehoy.es; weekly; Dir Jesús Maraña.

TP Teleprograma: Avda Cardenal Herrera Oria 3, 28034 Madrid; tel. (91) 7287000; fax (91) 7289141; e-mail tp@hachette.es; internet www.t-p.es; f. 1966; weekly; TV, cinema and video; Dir Agustín de Tena; circ. 300,000.

Viajar: O'Donnell 12, 3°, 28009 Madrid; tel. (91) 5863630; fax (91) 5869711; e-mail viajar@grupozeta.es; f. 1978; monthly; travel magazine; Dir Mariano López; circ. 75,000.

Vida Nueva: Impresores 15, Urbanización Prado del Espino, 28660 Boadilla del Monte, Madrid; tel. (91) 4226255; fax (91) 4226118; e-mail vidanueva@ppc-editorial.com; f. 1958; weekly; Dir Ninfa Watt; circ. 20,000.

SPECIALIZED PUBLICATIONS
Arts, Literature, etc.

Amadeus: RBA Revistas, SA, Pérez Galdós 36 bis, 08012 Barcelona; tel. (93) 4157374; fax (93) 2177378; e-mail amadeus@rba.es; internet www.rba.es; monthly; classical music; Editorial Dir José Luis Córdoba del Águila.

Arquitectura y Diseño: RBA Revistas, SA, Pérez Galdós 36 bis, 08012 Barcelona; internet www.rba.es; monthly; architecture and design.

Claves de Razón Práctica: Fuencarral 6, 2°, 28004 Madrid; tel. (91) 5386100; fax (91) 5222291; e-mail claves@progresa.es; monthly; books and culture; Dirs Javier Pradera, Fernando Savater.

Clio: Gran Vía de les Corts Catalanes 133, 2°, 08014 Barcelona; tel. (93) 2232136; fax (93) 4218048; e-mail clio@hachette.es; internet www.cliorevista.com; f. 2001; monthly; history; Dir Josep A. Borrell; circ. 36,401.

El Croquis: Avda de los Reyes Católicos 9, El Escorial, 28280 Madrid; tel. (91) 8969410; fax (91) 8969411; e-mail elcroquis@infornet.es; internet www.elcroquis.net; six a year; architecture, in Spanish and English.

Experimenta: Churruca 27, 4° dcha, 28004 Madrid; tel. (91) 5214049; fax (91) 5213212; e-mail publi@revistaexperimenta.com; internet www.revistaexperimenta.com; design; Dir Pierluigi Cattermole Fioravanti.

Historia 16: Rufino González 23 bis, 28037 Madrid; tel. (91) 3271171; fax (91) 3271220; e-mail h16redaccion@terra.es; f. 1976; monthly; history; Dir María Aldave; circ. 25,000.

Letra Internacional: Monte Esquinza 30, 2° dcha, 28010 Madrid; tel. (91) 3104313; fax (91) 3194585; e-mail redaccion@fpabloiglesias.es; internet www.fpabloiglesias.es; quarterly; culture; Dir Salvador Clotas i Cierco.

Matador: Alameda 9, 28014 Madrid; tel. (91) 3601320; fax (91) 3601322; e-mail matador@lafabrica.com; internet www.lafabrica.com; f. 1995; annual; art; Dir Alberto Arnaut; Editor-in-Chief Camino Brasa; circ. 7,000.

Ritmo: Isabel Colbrand 10, 4°, Oficina 95, 28050 Madrid; tel. (91) 3588774; fax (91) 3588944; e-mail correo@revistaritmo.com; internet www.revistaritmo.com; classical music; Dir Antonio Rodríguez Moreno.

Qué Leer: Gran Vía de les Corts Catalanes 133, 2°, 08014 Barcelona; tel. (93) 2232136; fax (93) 42180487; e-mail queleer@hachette.es; internet www.que-leer.com; f. 1996; monthly; book news, etc.; Dir Jorge de Cominges; circ. 26,608.

Finance

Actualidad Económica: Paseo de la Castellana 66, 3°, 28046 Madrid; tel. (91) 3373220; fax (91) 5628415; e-mail aeconomica@recoletos.es; internet www.recoletos.es/económica; f. 1958; Mon.; Gracia Cardador Moreno; circ. 46,000.

Dinero: Pantoja 14, 28002 Madrid; tel. (91) 4327600; fax (91) 4327765; e-mail srodriguez@negocios.com; internet www.negocios.com/dinero; weekly; business and finance; Dir Miguel Ormaetxea Arroyo; circ. 35,000.

Información Comercial Española—Revista de Economía: Paseo de la Castellana 162, 5°, 28046 Madrid; tel. (91) 3493627; fax (91) 3493634; 8 a year; published by Ministry of the Economy; Dir Antonio Hernández García.

Inversión y Capital: José Abascal 56, 7°, 28003 Madrid; tel. (91) 4563320; fax (91) 4563328; e-mail r.rubio@inverca.com; internet www.inverca.com; Dir Rafael Rubio Gómez-Caminero.

El Mundo Financiero: Peña Sacra 1, 28260 Madrid; tel. and fax (91) 8583547; e-mail mundofinanciero@nauta.es; internet www.elmundofinanciero.com; f. 1946; monthly; Dir José Luis Barceló Mezquita; circ. 15,000.

Politics, Sociology, Religion, etc.

Ecclesia: Alfonso XI 4, 28014 Madrid; tel. (91) 5315400; fax (91) 5225561; e-mail ecclesia@planalfa.es; f. 1941; weekly; religious information; Dir JESÚS DE LAS HERAS MUELA; Editor-in-Chief MIGUEL DE SANTIAGO; Propr Conferencia Episcopal Española; circ. 24,000.

Mundo Cristiano: Paseo de la Castellana 210, 2°B, 28046 Madrid; tel. (91) 3459855; fax (91) 3590230; e-mail mundoc@edicionespalabra.es; f. 1963; monthly; Dir DARIO CHIMENO CANO; circ. 46,852.

Nueva Revista: Javier Ferrero 2, 28002 Madrid; tel. (91) 5199756; fax (91) 4151254; e-mail nuevarevista@tst.es; internet www.nuevarevista.net; f. 1990; six a year; politics, culture, art; Pres. ANTONIO FONTÁN PÉREZ.

El Nuevo Lunes de la Economía y la Sociedad: Plaza de España 18 (Torre de Madrid), 3/11, 28008 Madrid; tel. (91) 5160803; fax (91) 5160819; e-mail nuevolunes@elnuevolunes.com; internet www.elnuevolunes.com; Editor JOSÉ GARCÍA ABAD.

Política—Revista Republicana: Meléndez Valdés 33, 1° dcha, 28015 Madrid; tel. (91) 5436930; fax (91) 5437649; e-mail ir@bitmailer.net; internet www.izquierdarepublicana.com; f. 1935; bimonthly; organ of the Izquierda Republicana; Dir ISABEL O. HERREROS.

Revista de Estudios Políticos: Plaza de la Marina Española 9, 28071 Madrid; tel. (91) 5401950; fax (91) 5419574; e-mail publicrev@cepc.es; f. 1941; quarterly; Dirs PEDRO DE VEGA, JUAN J. SOLOZÁBAL; publ. by Centro de Estudios Politicos y Constitucionales; circ. 1,000.

Treball: Ciutat 7, 08002 Barcelona; tel. (93) 3010612; fax (93) 4124252; e-mail treball@ic-v.org; f. 1991; fortnightly; organ of Iniciativa per Catalunya-Verds; Dir MARC RIUS; circ. 6,000.

Science and Medicine

Arbor: Vitruvio 8, 28006 Madrid; tel. (91) 5616651; fax (91) 5855326; e-mail arbor@csic.es; internet www.csic.es/arbor; f. 1944; monthly; science, thought and culture; publ. by Consejo Superior de Investigaciones Científicas (CSIC); Dir PEDRO GARCÍA BARRENO.

El Ecologista: Marqués de Laganés 12, 28004 Madrid; tel. (91) 5312389; fax (91) 5312611; e-mail comunicacion@ecologistasenaccion.org; internet www.ecologistasenaccion.org; quarterly; ecological issues; Dir JOSÉ LUIS GARCÍA CANO; circ. 13,000.

Gaceta Médica de Bilbao: Lersundi 9, Apdo 5073, 48080 Bilbao; tel. (94) 4233768; fax (94) 4230111; f. 1894; quarterly; official publication of the academy of medical sciences; Dir Prof. Dr JUAN B. ZARRANZ; circ. 5,000.

Investigación y Ciencia: Muntaner 339, Pral 1°, 08021 Barcelona; tel. (93) 4143344; fax (93) 4145413; e-mail precisa@investigacionyciencia.es; internet www.investigacionyciencia.es; f. 1976; quarterly; Dir JOSÉ MARÍA VADERAS GALLARDO; circ. 14,000.

Mundo Científico: Pérez Galdós 36, 08012 Barcelona; tel. (93) 4157374; fax (93) 2177378; monthly; Editorial Dir JOSÉ LUIS CÓRDOBA DE ÁGUILA.

Tiempos Médicos: Editores Médicos, SA, Gabriela Mistral 2, 28035 Madrid; tel. (91) 3768140; fax (91) 3739907; e-mail edimsa@edimsa.es; 10 issues per year; Dir Dr A. CHICHARRO PAPIRI; circ. 10,000.

Women's Magazines

Clara: Muntaner 40–42, 08011 Barcelona; tel. (93) 5087000; fax (93) 4545949; e-mail clara@hymsa.com; internet www.clara.es; f. 1992; monthly; Dir ASSUMPTA SORIA BADIA; circ. 292,990.

Cosmopolitan: Marqués de Villamagna 4, 28001 Madrid; tel. (91) 4369820; fax (91) 4358701; e-mail cosmopolitan@gyj.es; internet www.cosmopolitan.es; monthly; Dir SARAH GLATTSTEIN FRANCO; circ. 175,594.

Elle: Avda Cardenal Herrera Oria 3, 28034 Madrid; tel. (91) 7287000; fax (91) 7289135; e-mail elle@hachette.es; internet www.elle.navegalia.com; f. 1986; monthly; Dir SUSANA MARTÍNEZ VIDAL; circ. 180,000.

Elle Decoración: Avda Cardenal Herrera Oria 3, 28034 Madrid; tel. (91) 7287000; fax (91) 7289144; e-mail malvarez@hachette.es; 5 a year; Dir MILAGROS ALVAREZ GORTARI.

Labores del Hogar: Muntaner 40–42, 08011 Barcelona; tel. (93) 5087000; fax (93) 4540551; e-mail labores@hymsa.com; f. 1925; monthly; home textile crafts; Dir EULALIA UBACH; circ. 96,627.

Lecturas: Muntaner 40–42, 08011 Barcelona; tel. (93) 5087000; fax (93) 4541322; e-mail lecturas@hymsa.com; f. 1921; Fri.; Dir CATALINA VIDAL SERRA; Man. XAVIER ELIES; circ. 339,028.

Marie Claire: Marqués de Villamagna 4, 28001 Madrid; tel. (91) 4369800; fax (91) 5751392; e-mail cblanchuelo@gyj.es; f. 1987; monthly; Dir JOANA BONET CAMPRUBÍ; circ. 118,243.

Mía: Albasanz 15, Edif. A, 28037 Madrid; tel. (91) 4369889; fax (91) 5758880; e-mail mia@gyj.es; internet www.miarevista.es; f. 1986; weekly; Dir KETTY RICO OLIVER; circ. 257,222.

Telva: Paseo de la Castellana 66, 28046 Madrid; tel. (91) 3373220; fax (91) 3373143; e-mail telva@recoletos.es; internet www.estarguapa.com; f. 1963; beauty, fashion, weddings, interviews, cookery and fitness; monthly; Dir NIEVES FONTANA LÍBANO; circ. 175,000.

Vogue España: Paseo de la Castellana 9–11, 28046 Madrid; tel. (91) 7004170; fax (91) 3199325; e-mail vogue@condenast.es; internet www.vogue.es; f. 1988; monthly; Dir YOLANDA SACRISTÁN; circ. 117,515.

Woman: Bailén 84, 2°, 08009 Barcelona; tel. (93) 4846600; fax (93) 2324630; e-mail woman@grupozeta.es; f. 1992; monthly; Dir INMA SEBASTIA; circ. 125,000.

Miscellaneous

Automóvil: Ancora 40, 28045 Madrid; tel. (91) 3470100; fax (91) 3470204; e-mail pubautos@mpib.es; internet www.motorpress-iberica.es; monthly; motoring; Dir FERNANDO GÓMEZ BLANCO; circ. 88,000.

Autopista: Ancora 40, 28045 Madrid; tel. (91) 3470100; fax (91) 3470135; e-mail autopista@mpib.es; internet www.motorpress-iberica.es; weekly; motoring; Dir ARANCHA PATO; circ. 65,088.

Avión Revue: Ancora 40, 28045 Madrid; tel. (91) 3470100; fax (91) 3470152; e-mail pubavion@mpib.es; f. 1982; monthly; aeroplanes; Dir JOSÉ MARÍA PARÉS; circ. 30,000.

Boletín Oficial del Estado: Avda Manoteras 54, 28050 Madrid; tel. (91) 3841500; fax (91) 5382121; internet www.boe.es; f. 1936; successor of *Gaceta de Madrid*, f. 1661; daily except Sundays; laws, decrees, orders, etc.; Dir-Gen. JULIO SEAGE MARIÑO; circ. 60,000.

Cinemanía: Progresa (Grupo Prisa), Fuencarral, 6, 28004 Madrid; tel. (91) 5386104; fax (91) 5222291; e-mail cinemania@progresa.es; internet www.progresa.es; f. 1995; monthly; films; Dir INMA GARRIDO; circ. 125,000.

Coche Actual: Ancora 40, 28045 Madrid; tel. (91) 3470100; fax (91) 3470119; e-mail cocheactual@mpib.es; internet www.motorpress-iberica.es; weekly; cars; Dir ANTONIO RONCERO FERNÁNDEZ; circ. 65,394.

Computerworld: Fortuny 18, 4°, 28010 Madrid; tel. (91) 3496600; fax (91) 3196104; e-mail computerworld@idg.es; internet www.idg.es/computerworld; f. 1981; weekly; also available: PCWorld, Comunicaciones World, Digital World, MacWorld, Dealer World, iWorld; Editor-in-Chief MARÍA JOSÉ MARZAL; circ. 10,327.

Don Balón: Avda Diagonal 435, 1–2°, 08036 Barcelona; tel. (93) 2092000; fax (93) 2412358; e-mail info@donbalon.org; internet www.donbalon.com; f. 1975; weekly; sport; Editor-in-Chief JUAN CARLOS CASAS.

Fotogramas & Video: Gran Vía de les Corts Catalanes 133, 2°, 08014 Barcelona; tel. (93) 2232790; fax (93) 4322907; e-mail fotogramas@hachette.es; internet www.fotogramas.es; f. 1946; monthly; cinema and video; Dir ELISENDA NADAL GAÑÁN; circ. 107,598.

GQ: Paseo de la Castellana 9–11, 28046 Madrid; tel. (91) 7004170; fax (91) 3199325; e-mail gq@condenast.es; internet www.revistagq.com; monthly; men's magazine; Dir MIGUEL DE SANTOS.

El Magisterio Español: Javier Ferrero 2, 28002 Madrid; tel. (91) 5199131; fax (91) 4151124; e-mail jmoya@magisnet.com; internet www.magisnet.com; f. 1866; Wed.; education; Dir JOSÉ MARÍA DE MOYA ANEGÓN; circ. 24,200.

Man: Consejo de Ciento 425, 5°, 08009 Barcelona; tel. (93) 4846600; fax (93) 2324542; monthly; men's fashion, etc.; Dir JUAN CARLOS DE LA IGLESIA GONZÁLEZ; circ. 95,782.

Motociclismo: Ancora 40, 28045 Madrid; tel. (91) 3470100; fax (91) 3470119; e-mail pubmotos@mpib.es; f. 1951; weekly; motorcycling; Dir and Editor AUGUSTO MORENO DE CARLOS; circ. 110,000.

Nuevo Estilo: Avda Cardenal Herrera Oria 3, 28034 Madrid; tel. (91) 7287000; fax (91) 7289338; e-mail nuevoestilo@hachette.es; f. 1977; monthly; home decoration; Dir MARTA RIOPÉREZ; circ. 172,000.

PC Actual: San Sotero 8, 4°, 28037 Madrid; tel. (91) 3137900; fax (91) 3273704; e-mail fercla@bpe.es; internet www.pc-actual.com; Dir FERNANDO CLAVER.

PC World: Fortuny 18, 4°, 28010 Madrid; tel. (91) 3496600; fax (91) 3496796; e-mail pcworld@idg.es; internet www.idg.es/pcworld; f. 1988; monthly; for users of personal computers; Editor-in-Chief ARANXTA G. AGUILERA.

Ser Padres Hoy: Marqués de Villamagna 4, 28001 Madrid; tel. (91) 4369800; fax (91) 5767881; e-mail publicidad@gyj.es; f. 1974; monthly; for parents; Dir JAVIER J. GARCÍA GONZÁLEZ; circ. 60,577.

SPAIN

Sport Life: Ancora 40, 28045 Madrid; tel. (91) 3470100; fax (91) 3470204; e-mail pubsportlife@mpib.es; internet www.motorpress-iberica.es; monthly; Editor MONTSE SALA.

Tu Bebé: Muntaner 40–42, 08011 Barcelona; tel. (93) 5087000; fax (93) 4545949; e-mail tu_bebe@hymsa.com; f. 1993; monthly; for parents; Dir PEDRO RIAÑO MARTÍNEZ; circ. 60,000.

Vinos de España: Islas Marquesas 28B, 28035 Madrid; tel. (91) 3865152; fax (91) 3860265; e-mail vinos@mundonatura.es; f. 1996; wines and viniculture; bimonthly; also trimonthly in German; Dir ALBERTO HUERTA; circ. 30,000.

NEWS AGENCIES

Agencia EFE, SA: Espronceda 32, 28003 Madrid; tel. (91) 3467100; fax (91) 3467134; e-mail efe@efe.es; internet www.efe.es; f. 1939; national and international news; 140 bureaux and correspondents abroad; sports, features, radio and television, and photographic branches; Pres. and Dir-Gen. ÁLEX GRIJELMO.

Colpisa: José Abascal 56, 1°, 28003 Madrid; tel. (91) 4564600; fax (91) 4564701; f. 1972; Pres. JOSÉ MARÍA BERGARECHE; Dir ROGELIO RODRÍGUEZ.

Europa Press Noticias: Paseo de la Castellana 210, 3°, 28046 Madrid; tel. (91) 3592600; fax (91) 3503251; e-mail noticias@europapress.es; internet www.europapress.es; Dir ANGEL EXPÓSITO MORA.

Iberia Press: Velázquez 46, 1°, 28001 Madrid; tel. and fax (91) 8155319; e-mail press-bulletin@jet.es; f. 1977; Dir JOSÉ RAMÓN ALONSO.

Foreign Bureaux

Agence France-Presse (AFP): Paseo de Recoletos 18, 28001 Madrid; tel. (91) 4358740; fax (91) 5755380; e-mail afp.madrid@afp.com; Chief Correspondent XAVIER BARON.

Agenzia Nazionale Stampa Associata (ANSA) (Italy): Vergara 3, 1°D, 28013 Madrid; tel. (91) 5488867; fax (91) 5488989; e-mail ansa.madrid@infonegocio.com; Chief Correspondent JAVIER FERNÁNDEZ BONELLI.

AICA (Argentina): Toledo 109, 5°D, 28005 Madrid; tel. and fax (91) 3661827; e-mail arp41228@wanadoo.es; f. 1947; financial; Correspondent ARMANDO PUENTE.

Algerie Presse Service (APS): Alcalde Sáinz de Baranda 44, 5°A, 28009 Madrid; tel. (91) 5040076; Correspondent YACINE SEMCH-EDDINE BENTAHAR.

Anadolu Ajansı (AA) (Turkey): Monte Esquinza 41, 5°E, 28010 Madrid; tel. and fax (91) 3083933; e-mail madrid@anadoluajansi.com.tr; Correspondent SENHAN BOLELLI.

Associated Press (AP) (USA): Espronceda 32, 5°, 28003 Madrid; tel. (91) 3992433; fax (91) 4423612; internet www.ap.org; Chief of Iberian Services KERNAN TURNER.

Bulgarska Telegrafna Agentsia (BTA) (Bulgaria): Fernando Garrido 4, 2°B, 28015 Madrid; tel. and fax (91) 5940203; Correspondent IOSSIF DAVIDOV SOLOMONOV.

Ceibo Producciones (Chile): Cuchilleros 10, 4°B, 28005 Madrid; tel. (91) 3650210; e-mail andreapacheco@worldonline.es; Correspondent ANDREA PAOLA PACHECO GONZÁLEZ.

Deutsche Presse-Agentur (dpa) (Germany): Espronceda 32, 5°, 28003 Madrid; tel. (91) 3391002; fax (91) 4427706; Chief Correspondent HUBERT KAHL.

Informatsionnoye Telegrafnoye Agentstvo Rossii—Telegrafnoye Agentstvo Suverennykh Stran (ITAR—TASS) (Russia): General Díaz Porlier 18, 5°F, 28001 Madrid; tel. (91) 4314864; e-mail medved@arrakis.es; Correspondent SERGEY SEREDA.

IRNA (Iran): Padre Damián 40, 28036 Madrid; tel. (91) 4570434; fax (91) 4570414; e-mail aajavan321@hotmail.com; Correspondent ALI AKBAR JAVANFEKER.

Lusa (Agência de Notícias de Portugal, SA): Espronceda 32, 6°, 28003 Madrid; tel. (91) 4424308; fax (91) 4421938; e-mail asampaio@lusa.pt; Correspondent ANTÓNIO SAMPAIO.

Maghreb Arabe Presse (Morocco): Talavera de la Reina, Sebastián de los Reyes 28027, Madrid; tel. and fax (91 3467615; e-mail mapmad@wanadoo.es; Chief Correspondent MOHAMED BOUNDI.

Magyar Távirati Iroda (MTI) (Hungary): Taibilla 1, 4° izqda, 03130 Santa Pola, Alicante; tel. and fax (96) 6696959; e-mail xantus@ciberia.es; Correspondent JUDIT XANTUS SZARVAS.

Notimex (Mexico): San Bernardo 63, 3°B, 28015 Madrid; tel. (91) 5214022; fax (91) 5317699; e-mail notimexeuropa@notimex.e.telefónica.net; internet www.notimex.com.mx; Chief Correspondent LUIS CASTRO OBREGÓN.

Prensa Latina (Cuba): Perú 23, 4°, 28820 Coslada, Madrid; tel. (91) 6693859; fax (91) 6693645; e-mail plmadrid@mi.madritel.es; Correspondent RAFAEL JUSTO CALCINES ARMAS.

Reuters (United Kingdom): Paseo de la Castellana 36–38, 5°, 28046 Madrid; tel. (91) 5852160; fax (91) 4359666; e-mail madrid.newsroom@reuters.com; internet www.reuters.com; Chief Correspondent ADRIAN CROFT.

Septimus International (Egypt): Julio Palacios 2, portal 3, 9°, 28029 Madrid; tel. and fax (91) 5721179; Correspondent ELMEHDI KAJIJI.

Tanjug (Serbia and Montenegro): Madrid; Correspondent SVETLANA BOSCOVIĆ.

Xinhua (New China) News Agency (People's Republic of China): Arturo Soria 154, Bloque 3, 1°F, 28043 Madrid; tel. (91) 4131620; fax (91) 4168543; e-mail guojibu@jet.es; Correspondent RUICHANG LIU.

PRESS ASSOCIATIONS

National Organizations

Asociación de Editores de Diarios Españoles (AEDE): Orense 69, 2°, 28020 Madrid; tel. (91) 4251085; fax (91) 5796020; e-mail maribel@aede.es; internet www.aede.es; f. 1978; 32 mems. representing 88 daily newspapers; Pres. JUAN LUIS CEBRIAN; Dir-Gen. IGNACIO M. BENITO GARCÍA.

Asociación de Revistas Culturales en España (ARCE): Hortaleza 75, 28004 Madrid; tel. (91) 3086066; fax (91) 3199267; e-mail info@arce.es; internet www.arce.es; f. 1983.

Federación de Asociaciones de la Prensa de España (FAPE): Juan Bravo 6, 28006 Madrid; tel. (91) 5850038; fax (91) 5850038; e-mail fape@infonegocio.com; internet www.fape.es; f. 1922; Pres. FERNANDO GONZÁLEZ URBANEJA; Sec.-Gen. JOSÉ MARÍA LORENTE TORIBIO; 41 mem. asscns.

Unión de Escritores e Periodistas Españoles: Madrid; f. 1978; journalists' asscn; Pres. ANTONIO ARIAS PIQUERAS; Sec.-Gen. ELOY S. CASTAÑARES; 4,000 mems.

Asociación de Corresponsales de Prensa Extranjera (ACPE): Monte Esquinza 41, 1°, 28010 Madrid; tel. (91) 3101433; fax (91) 3080950; e-mail acpe.corresponsales@wanadoo.es; f. 1923; foreign correspondents' asscn; Pres. LUIS CASTRO OBREGÓN; Sec.-Gen. KARLA CASTILLAS; 150 mems.

Provincial Organizations

Barcelona

Centre Internacional de Premsa de Barcelona: Rambla de Catalunya 10, 1°, 08007 Barcelona; tel. (93) 4121111; fax (93) 3178386; e-mail cipb@periodistes.org; internet www.periodistes.org; f. 1988; facilities and services for journalists; Pres. CARLES SENTÍS I ANFRUNS; Dir MONICA VIÑAS.

Bilbao

Asociación de Periodistas de Bizkaia (Bizkaiko Kazetarien Elkartea): Dr Achucarro 10, 1°, 48011 Bilbao; tel. and fax (94) 4168748; e-mail asociacion@periodistasvascos.com; internet www.periodistasvascos.com; Pres. JOSÉ MANUEL ALONSO; Sec. BLANCA GARCÍA-EGOCHEAGA.

Madrid

Asociación de la Prensa de Madrid: Juan Bravo 6, 28006 Madrid; tel. (91) 5850010; fax (91) 5850050; e-mail apm@apmadrid.es; internet www.apmadrid.es; f. 1895; Pres. FERNANDO GONZÁLEZ URBANEJA; Sec.-Gen. JOSÉ MARÍA LORENTE TORIBIO; 5,518 mems.

Centro de Prensa de Madrid: Claudio Coello 98, 28006 Madrid; tel. (91) 5850010; fax (91) 5850050; Sec.-Gen. JOSÉ MARÍA LORENTE TORIBIO.

Sevilla

Asociación de la Prensa de Sevilla: Plaza de San Francisco 9, 1°, 41004 Sevilla; tel. (95) 4500468; fax (95) 4225299; e-mail aps@asociacionprensa.org; internet www.asociacionprensa.org; f. 1909; Pres. SANTIAGO SÁNCHEZ TRAVER; Sec.-Gen. JUAN TERUEL SALMERÓN.

Zaragoza

Centro de Prensa de Zaragoza: Cinco de Marzo 9, 50004 Zaragoza; tel. (976) 223210; fax (976) 222963; e-mail aparagon@aparagon.es; Pres. RAMÓN J. BUETAS CORONAS; Sec. ROBERTO GARCÍA BERMEJO.

Publishers

Actar: Roca i Batlle 2, 08023 Barcelona; tel. (93) 4187759; fax (93) 4186707; e-mail info@actar-mail.com; internet www.actar.es; architecture, photography, art, design.

SPAIN

Barcino Editorial: Montseny 9, 08012 Barcelona; tel. and fax (93) 2186888; e-mail info@editorialbarcino.com; internet www.editorialbarcino.com; f. 1924; Catalan classics, general; Dir CARLES DUARTE MONTSERRAT.

Carroggio, SA de Ediciones: Pelai 28–30, 08001 Barcelona; tel. (93) 4949922; fax (93) 4949923; e-mail carroggio@carroggio.com; internet www.carroggio.com; f. 1911; art, literature, reference books, multimedia; Man. Dir SANTIAGO CARROGGIO GUERIM.

Durvan, SA de ediciones: Colón de Larreátegui 13, 3°, 48001 Bilbao; tel. (94) 4230777; fax (94) 4243832; e-mail editorial@durvan.com; internet www.durvan.com; f. 1960; Administrator Gen. LORENZO PORTILLO SISNIEGA.

EDHASA (Editora y Distribuidora Hispano-Americana, SA): Avda Diagonal 519–521, 2°, 08029 Barcelona; tel. (93) 4949720; fax (93) 4194584; e-mail info@edhasa.es; internet www.edhasa.es; f. 1946; contemporary fiction, non-fiction, pocket books, historical fiction and non-fiction, crime, philosophy; Editorial Dir and Man. DANIEL FERNÁNDEZ.

Ediciones de Cultura Hispánica: General Pardiñas 55, 28006 Madrid; tel. (91) 37999494; fax (91) 5838311; internet www.aeci.es; f. 1943; arts, law, history, economics for circulation in Latin America; Literary and Artistic Dir ANTONIO PAPELL.

Ediciones Encuentro: Cedaceros 3, 2°, 28014 Madrid; tel. (91) 5322607; fax (91) 5322346; e-mail encuentro@ediciones-encuentro.es; internet www.ediciones-encuentro.es; f. 1978; theology, philosophy, art, history, literature.

Ediciones Morata, SL: Mejía Lequerica 12, 28004 Madrid; tel. (91) 4480926; fax (91) 4480925; e-mail morata@edmorata.es; internet www.edmorata.es; f. 1920; psychology, psychiatry, pedagogics, sociology; Dir FLORENTINA GÓMEZ MORATA.

Ediciones Mensajero, SAU: Sancho de Azpeitia 2, 48014 Bilbao; tel. (94) 4470358; fax (94) 4472630; e-mail mensajero@mensajero.com; internet www.mensajero.com; f. 1915; arts, biography, theology, psychology, pedagogy, social science and paperbacks; Dir ANGEL ANTONIO PÉREZ GÓMEZ.

Ediciones Obelisco: Pedro IV 78, 3 y 5°, 08005 Barcelona; tel. (93) 3098525; fax (93) 3098523; e-mail info@edicionesobelisco.com; internet www.edicionesobelisco.com; f. 1981; general fiction and non-fiction; Dir JULI PERADEJORDI.

Ediciones Omega, SA: Platón 26, 08006 Barcelona; tel. (93) 2010599; fax (93) 2097362; e-mail omega@ediciones-omega.es; internet www.ediciones-omega.es; f. 1948; biology, field guides, geography, geology, agriculture, photography; Chair. ANTONIO PARICIO; Mans ANTONIO, GABRIEL PARICIO.

Ediciones Polígrafa, SA: Balmes 52, 08009 Barcelona; tel. (93) 4882381; fax (93) 4877392; e-mail info@edicionespoligrafa.com; internet www.edicionespoligrafa.com; f. 1960; arts, leisure; Man. Dir JUAN DE MUGA DÒRIA; Editor-in-Chief FRANCISCO REI.

Ediciones Siruela, SA: Almagro 25, 28010 Madrid; tel. (91) 3555720; fax (91) 3552201; e-mail atencionlector@siruela.com; internet www.siruela.com; f. 1982; history, literature, art, children's books, translations; Dir JACOBO FITZ-JAMES STUART.

Ediciones Universidad de Navarra, SA (EUNSA): Plaza de los Sauces 1 y 2, 31010 Barañain (Navarra); tel. (948) 256850; fax (948) 256854; e-mail info@eunsa.es; internet www.eunsa.es; f. 1967; architecture, natural sciences, law, history, social sciences, theology, philosophy, medical, engineering, journalism, education, economics and business administration, biology, literature, library science, paperbacks, etc.; Chair. GUIDO STEIN.

Editorial Anagrama, SA: Pedró de la Creu 58, 08034 Barcelona; tel. (93) 2037652; fax (93) 2037738; e-mail anagrama@anagrama-ed.es; internet www.anagrama-ed.es; f. 1969; foreign literature in translation; Editor and Dir JORGE HERRALDE.

Editorial Aranzadi SA: Camino de Galar 15, 31190 Cizur Menor, Navarra; tel. (948) 297297; fax (948) 297200; e-mail clientes@aranzadi.es; internet www.aranzadi.es; f. 1929; law; Dir JUAN CARLOS FRANQUET.

Editorial Biblioteca Nueva, SL: Almagro 38, 28010 Madrid; tel. (91) 3100436; fax (91) 3198235; e-mail editorial@bibliotecanueva.com; internet www.bibliotecanueva.es; f. 1920; literature, essays, poetry, history, psychiatry, psychology, philosophy, economy, law; Dir ANTONIO ROCHE.

Editorial Bosch, SA: Comte d'Urgell 51 bis, Apdo 928, 08011 Barcelona; tel. (93) 4521050; fax (93) 4521057; e-mail bosch@bosch.es; internet www.bosch.es; f. 1934; law, social science, classics; Man. ALBERT FERRÉ.

Editorial Castalia: Zurbano 39, 28010 Madrid; tel. (91) 3195857; fax (91) 3102442; e-mail castalia@castalia.es; internet www.castalia.es; f. 1945; classics, literature; Pres. AMPARO SOLER GIMENO; Dir FEDERICO IBAÑEZ SOLER.

Editorial Desclée de Brouwer, SA: Henao 6, 3° dcha, 48009 Bilbao; tel. (94) 4246843; fax (94) 4237594; e-mail info@edesclee.com; internet www.edesclee.com; f. 1945; general non-fiction in Spanish and Basque; Pres. JAVIER GOGEASKOETXEA.

Editorial Edaf, SA: Jorge Juan 30, 1°, 28001 Madrid; tel. (91) 4358260; fax (91) 4315281; e-mail edaf@edaf.net; internet www.edaf.net; f. 1967; literature, dictionaries, occult, natural health, paperbacks; Dir-Gen. JOSÉ ANTONIO FOSSATI SEDDON.

Editorial Everest, SA: Carretera León–Coruña, Km 5, Apdo 339, 24080 León; tel. (987) 844200; fax (987) 844202; e-mail marketing@everest.es; internet www.everest.es; f. 1957; general; Dir-Gen. JOSÉ ANTONIO LÓPEZ MARTÍNEZ.

Editorial Galaxia: Reconquista 1, 36201 Vigo; tel. (986) 432100; fax (986) 223205; e-mail editorial@editorialgalaxia.es; internet www.editorialgalaxia.es; f. 1950; literary works, reviews, popular, children's, Galician literature; Dir VÍCTOR F. FREIXANES.

Editorial Gredos, SA: Sánchez Pacheco 85, 28002 Madrid; tel. (91) 7444920; fax (91) 5192033; e-mail comercial@editorialgredos.com; internet www.editorialgredos.com; f. 1944; linguistics, philology, humanities, art, literature, dictionaries; Dir MANUEL OLIVEIRA CALVET.

Editorial Gustavo Gili, SA: Roselló 87–89, 08029 Barcelona; tel. (93) 3228161; fax (93) 3229205; e-mail info@ggili.com; internet www.ggili.com; f. 1902; photography, art, architecture, design; Dirs GABRIEL GILI, MÓNICA GILI.

Editorial Hispano-Europea, SA: Bori y Fontestá 6, 08021 Barcelona; tel. (93) 2018500; fax (93) 4142635; e-mail hispanoeuropea@hispanoeuropea.com; internet www.hispanoeuropea.com; f. 1954; technical, scientific, sport, pet books and reference; Propr and Man. Dir JORGE J. PRAT ROSAL.

Editorial Juventud, SA: Provença 101, 08029 Barcelona; tel. (93) 4441800; fax (93) 4398383; e-mail info@editorialjuventud.es; internet www.editorialjuventud.es; f. 1923; general fiction, biography, history, art, music, reference, dictionaries, travel books, children's books, paperbacks; Dir LUIS ZENDRERA.

Editorial Marfil, SA: San Eloy 17, 03804 Alcoy; tel. (96) 5523311; fax (96) 5523496; e-mail editorialmarfil@editorial.marfil.com; internet www.editorialmarfil.com; f. 1947; textbooks, psychology, pedagogy, university texts, literature; Man. VERÓNICA CANTÓ DOMÉNECH.

Editorial Molino: Calabria 166, 08015 Barcelona; tel. (93) 2260625; fax (93) 2266998; e-mail molino@rba.es; internet www.editorialmolino.com; f. 1933; crime, children's books, reference books; Dir LUIS ANTONIO DEL MOLINO JOVER.

Editorial Nerea, SA: San Bartolomé 2, 5° dcha, 20007 Donostia/San Sebastián (Guipúzcoa); tel. (943) 432227; fax (943) 433379; e-mail nerea@nerea.net; internet www.nerea.net; f. 1987.

Editorial Paraninfo, SA: Magallanes 25, 28015 Madrid; tel. (91) 4463350; fax (91) 4456218; e-mail info@paraninfo.es; internet www.paraninfo.es; f. 1946; technical, reference and educational; Man. MIGUEL MANGADA FERBER.

Editorial Reus, SA: Preciados 23, 2°, 28013 Madrid; tel. (91) 5213619; fax (91) 5312408; e-mail reus@editorialreus.es; internet www.editorialreus.es; f. 1852; law, literature; Pres. JESÚS M. PINTO VARELA.

Editorial Reverté, SA: Loreto 13–15, Local B, 08029 Barcelona; tel. (93) 4193336; fax (93) 4195189; e-mail reverte@reverte.com; internet www.reverte.com; f. 1947; engineering, general science, university and scientific books; Dir JAVIER REVERTÉ MASCÓ.

Editorial Teide, SA: Viladomat 291, 08029 Barcelona; tel. 902 233030; fax (93) 3212646; e-mail info@editorialteide.com; internet www.editorialteide.es; f. 1942; educational, scientific, technical and art; Man. Dir FEDERICO RAHOLA.

La Esfera de los Libros, SL: Avda de Alfonso XIII 1, bajos, 28002 Madrid; tel. (91) 2960200; fax (91) 2960206; e-mail laesfera@esferalibros.com; internet www.esferalibros.com; history, journalism, biography; Dir JOSÉ MARÍA CALVÍN.

Fondo de Cultura Económica de España, SL (FCE España): Librería Juan Rulfo México, Fernando el Católico 86, 28015 Madrid; tel. (91) 7632800; e-mail fondodeculturae@terra.es; internet www.fcede.es; f. 1974; pocket collections, sciences, literature, children's books, history, academic; Dir JUAN GUILLERMO LÓPEZ.

Galaxia Gutenberg: Traverssera de Gràcia 47–49, 08021 Barcelona; tel. (93) 3660100; fax (93) 3660104; e-mail galaxiagutenberg@circulo.es; internet www.galaxiagutenberg.com; f. 1995.

Grup 62, SA: Peu de la Creu 4, 08001 Barcelona; tel. (93) 4437100; fax (93) 4437130; e-mail correu@grup62.com; internet www.grup62.com; f. 1962; imprints include Edicions 62, Editorial Empúries, Editorial Selecta, Ediciones Península, El Aleph Editores, Luciérnaga, Salsa Books; Pres. J. M. MARTOS; Man. ROSA COLLELL.

Grupo Anaya, SA: Juan Ignacio Luca de Tena 15, 28027 Madrid; tel. (91) 3554405; fax (91) 3933937; e-mail administrador@anaya.es; internet www.anaya.es; f. 1959; imprints include Algaida, Anaya, Barçanova, Clé Internacional, Del Prado, Eudema, Larousse and

Oberon, as well as companies listed below; reference, sciences, arts, literature, education; Pres. JOSÉ MANUEL GÓMEZ.

Alianza Editorial, SA: Juan Ignacio Luca de Tena 15, 28027 Madrid; tel. (91) 3938888; fax (91) 7414343; e-mail alianza@anaya.es; internet www.alianzaeditorial.es; f. 1959; advanced textbooks, fiction, general non-fiction, reference, paperbacks; Pres. JOSÉ MANUEL GÓMEZ; Gen. Man. VALERIA CIOMPI.

Ediciones Cátedra: Juan Ignacio Luca de Tena 15, 28027 Madrid; tel. (91) 3938787; fax (91) 7412118; e-mail catedra@catedra.com; internet www.catedra.com; f. 1973; literature, literary criticism, history, humanities, linguistics, arts, cinema, music, feminism; Pres. JOSÉ MANUEL GÓMEZ; Man. Dir EMILIO PASCUAL.

Ediciones Pirámide: Juan Ignacio Luca de Tena 15, 28027 Madrid; tel. (91) 3938989; fax (91) 7423661; e-mail piramide@anaya.es; internet www.edicionespiramide.es; f. 1973; scientific and technical books (business, economics and psychology); Pres. JOSÉ MANUEL GÓMEZ; Man. Dir MARIANO JOSÉ NORTE.

Edicións Xerais de Galicia, SA: Doutor Marañón 12, 36211 Vigo; tel. (986) 214888; fax (986) 201366; e-mail xerais@xerais.es; internet www.xerais.es; f. 1979; literature, education, history and reference books in Galician.

Editorial Tecnos, SA: Juan Ignacio Luca de Tena 15, 28027 Madrid; tel. (91) 3938550; fax (91) 7426631; e-mail foro_tecnos@anaya.es; internet www.tecnos.es; f. 1947; law, social and political science, philosophy and economics; Pres. JOSÉ MANUEL GÓMEZ; Man. MANUEL GONZÁLEZ MORENO.

Grupo EDEBE: Paseo San Juan Bosco 62, 08017 Barcelona; tel. (93) 2037408; fax (93) 2054670; e-mail informacion@edebe.net; internet www.edebe.com; f. 1968; imprints include Giltza, Rodeira, Marjal and Guadiel; children's and educational publications; Man. JOSÉ ALDUNATE JURÍO.

Grupo Editorial Bruño: Maestro Alonso 21, 28028 Madrid; tel. (91) 7244800; fax (91) 3613133; e-mail informacion@editorial-bruno.es; internet www.editorial-bruno.es; f. 1898; education, children's books; Dir-Gen. JOSÉ ANTONIO CAMACHO.

Grupo Editorial Luis Vives: Xaudaró 25, 28034 Madrid; tel. (91) 3344893; fax (91) 3344882; e-mail dediciones@edelvives.es; internet www.grupoeditorialluisvives.com; f. 1890; children's books, textbooks, reference under the imprints Edelvives, Baula (Catalan), Alhucema, Ibaizabal (Basque) and Tambre (Galician).

Grupo Editorial Santillana: Torrelaguna 60, 28043 Madrid; tel. (91) 7449060; fax (91) 7449019; e-mail grupo@santillana.es; internet www.gruposantillana.com; f. 1960; imprints include Aguilar, Alfarguara, Altea, Richmond Publishing and Taurus; Pres. EMILIANO MARTÍNEZ.

Grupo Océano: Milanesado 21–23, 08017 Barcelona; tel. (93) 2802020; fax (93) 2041073; e-mail info@oceano.com; internet www.oceano.com; f. 1950; imprints include Oceano, Circe and co listed below; general; Chair. JOSÉ LLUIS MONREAL.

Instituto Gallach de Librería y Ediciones, SL: Milanesado 21–23, 08017 Barcelona; tel. (93) 2802020; fax (93) 2045958; e-mail infopresid@oceano.com; f. 1924; illustrated and reference books, encyclopaedias; Chair. JOSÉ LLUIS MONREAL; Gen. Man. JOSÉ MARÍA MARTI COSTA.

Grupo Planeta, SA: Avda Diagonal 662–664, 08034 Barcelona; tel. (93) 4928900; fax (93) 4928565; internet www.planeta.es; f. 1949; owns companies listed below, and Ediciones Minotauro, Ediciones Temas de Hoy, Editorial Crítica, Editorial Planeta, Emcé Editores, GeoPlaneta, Timun Mas among others; popular, literature, children's; Pres. JOSÉ MANUEL LARA BOSCH.

Columna Edicions: Provença 260, 6A, 08008 Barcelona; tel. (93) 4967061; fax (93) 4967062; e-mail bbruna@grupocolumna.com; internet www.columnaedicions.com; f. 1985; fiction and non-fiction in Catalan.

Ediciones del Bronce: Avda Diagonal 662–664, 08034 Barcelona; tel. (93) 4928710; fax (93) 4967051; e-mail abalaguer@planeta.es; f. 1996; non-western literature.

Ediciones Destino, SA: Provenza 260, 5°, 08008 Barcelona; tel. (93) 4967001; fax (93) 4967002; e-mail edicionesdestino@stl.logicontrol.es; internet www.edestino.es; f. 1942; general fiction, history, art, children's books.

Ediciones Deusto, SA: Alameda Recalde 27, 7°, 48009 Bilbao; tel. (94) 4356161; fax (94) 4356166; e-mail deustomail@ediciones-deusto.es; internet www.ediciones-deusto.es; f. 1960; diaries, newsletters, management and law books; Man. Dir ENRIQUE IGLESIAS MONTEJO.

Editorial Ariel, SA: Avda Diagonal 662–664, 7°, 08034 Barcelona; tel. (93) 4967030; fax (93) 4967033; e-mail editorial@ariel.es; internet www.ariel.es; f. 1942; social and political science, economics, history, sciences and law; Editorial Dir JOSÉ LUIS CASTILLEJO.

Editorial CEAC, SA: Perú 164, 08020 Barcelona; tel. (93) 2660247; fax (93) 3084392; e-mail info@ceacedit.com; internet www.editorialceac.com; f. 1947; unit includes Deusto and Gestion 2000; textbooks, education, leisure; Man. JAIME PINTANEL.

Editorial Seix Barral: Avda Diagonal 662–664, 7°, 08034 Barcelona; tel. (93) 4967003; fax (93) 4967004; e-mail editorial@seix-barral.es; internet www.seix-barral.es; f. 1911; literature.

Espasa-Calpe, SA: Complejo Ática, Edif. 4B, Vía de las Dos Castillas 33, 28224 Pozuelo de Alárcon (Madrid); tel. (91) 7848200; fax (91) 3525020; e-mail surgerencias@espasa.es; internet www.espasa.com; f. 1860; encyclopaedias, history, dictionaries, literature, biographies, paperbacks, etc.; Editorial Dir PILAR CORTÉS GARCÍA-MORENO.

MR Ediciones, SA: Recoletos 4, 3°, 28001 Madrid; tel. (91) 4230314; fax (91) 4230306; e-mail info@ediciones-martinez-roca.es; internet www.edicionesmartinezroca.com; f. 1965; fmrly Ediciones Martínez Roca; fiction, New Age, spirituality, sport, 'how-to' books, psychology, psychiatry; Dir LAURA FALCÓ.

Herder Editorial, SA: Provença 388, 08025 Barcelona; tel. (93) 4762626; fax (93) 2073448; e-mail herder@herdereditorial.com; internet www.herdereditorial.com; f. 1944; literature, language, theology, sociology, psychology.

Iberoamericana de Libros y Ediciones, SL: Amor de Dios 1, 28014 Madrid; tel. (91) 4293522; fax (91) 4295397; e-mail info@iberoamericanalibros.com; internet www.ibero-americana.net; f. 1996; owned by Verveut Verlagsgesellschaft (Frankfurt); academic books.

Marcombo, SA de Boixareu Editores: Gran Vía de les Corts Catalanes 594, 08007 Barcelona; tel. (93) 3180079; fax (93) 3189339; e-mail info@marcombo.com; internet www.marcombo.com; f. 1945; reference, sciences, textbooks; Pres. and Man. Dir JOSEP M. BOIXAREU VILAPLANA.

Montagud Editores: Ausiàs Marc 25, 1°, 08010 Barcelona; tel. (93) 3182082; fax (93) 3025083; e-mail montagud@montagud.com; internet www.montagud.com; f. 1906; business; Chair. FRANCISCO ANTOJA GIRALT.

Narcea, SA de Ediciones: Avda Dr Federico Rubio y Galí 9, 28039 Madrid; tel. (91) 5546484; fax (91) 5546487; e-mail narcea@narceaediciones.es; internet www.narceaediciones.es; f. 1968; humanities, pedagogy, psychology, spiritualism and textbooks; Man. Dir ANA MARÍA DE MIGUEL CARRO.

Nivola Libros y Ediciones, SL: Sector Islas 12, Local 38, Tres Cantos, 28760 Madrid; tel. (91) 8045817; fax (91) 8041482; e-mail nivola@nivola.com; internet www.nivola.com; science.

Noguer y Caralt Editores, SA: Santa Amèlia 22, bajos, 08034 Barcelona; tel. (93) 2801399; fax (93) 2801993; e-mail contact@noguercaralt.com; internet www.noguercaralt.com; f. 1993; includes Editorial Noguer and Luis de Caralt Editores; dictionaries, children's, philosophy, art; Man. EMILIO ARDÉVOL.

Oikos-Tau, SL—Editorial—Gráficas: Barcelona; tel. (93) 7590759; fax (93) 7506825; f. 1963; economics, science, geography, history, marketing, management, agriculture, sociology, urban planning, education, school-books; Man. JORDI GARCÍA-JACAS.

Random House Mondadori, SA: Travessera de Gràcia 47–49, 08021 Barcelona; tel. (93) 3660300; fax (93) 3660449; internet www.randomhousemondadori.es; f. 2001; Spanish imprints include Areté, Beascoa, Debate, Electa, Lumen, Montena, Rosa dels Vents, and co listed below; Gen. Man. RICARDO CAVALLERO.

Plaza y Janés, Editores, SA: Travessera de Gràcia 47–49, 08021 Barcelona; tel. (93) 3660300; fax (93) 2002219; internet www.plaza.es; f. 1959; fiction and non-fiction, reference; owned by Mondadori, SA; Dir-Gen. JUAN PASCUAL.

Salvat Editores, SA: Mallorca 45, 08029 Barcelona; tel. (93) 4955700; fax (93) 4955779; e-mail infosalvat@salvat.com; internet www.salvat.com; f. 1869; art, history, dictionaries, encyclopaedias, English courses, music; Pres. JEAN-LOUIS LISIMACHIO.

Siglo XXI de España, Editores, SA: Príncipe de Vergara 78, 2°, 28006 Madrid; tel. (91) 5617748; fax (91) 5615819; e-mail sigloxxi@sigloxxieditores.com; internet www.sigloxxieditores.com; f. 1967; pocket collections, reference, history, social sciences; Pres. PABLO GARCÍA-ARENAL.

SM Grupo: Impresores 15, Urbanización Prado del Espino, 28660 Boadilla del Monte, Madrid; tel. (91) 4228800; fax (91) 5089927; e-mail comunicacion@grupo-sm.com; internet www.grupo-sm.com; f. 1939; textbooks, children's, reference, travel, literature; Pres. JUAN DE ISASA GONZÁLEZ UBIETA; Man. Dir JAVIER CORTÉS SORIANO.

SPES Editorial, SL: Aribau 197–199, 3°, 08021 Barcelona; tel. (93) 2413505; e-mail larousse@larousse.es; internet www.vox.es, www.larousse.es, www.diccionarios.com; encyclopaedias, dictionaries, atlases, linguistics; f. 2000; by merger of Larousse Editorial and Biblograf.

Susaeta Ediciones, SA: Campezo 13, 28022 Madrid; tel. (91) 3009100; fax (91) 3009118; e-mail general@susaeta.com; internet www.susaeta.com; f. 1963; non-fiction, children's books; Dir Javier Susaeta.

Tusquets Editores, SA: Cesare Cantú 8, 08023 Barcelona; tel. (93) 2530400; fax (93) 4176703; internet www.tusquets-editores.es; art, general fiction and non-fiction.

Vicens Vives, SA: Polígono Industrial Pratense, 111, parcela 16, 08820 El Prat de Llobregat (Barcelona); tel. (93) 4782755; fax (93) 4783659; e-mail e@vicensvives.es; internet www.vicensvives.es; f. 1961; school and university, educational; Dir Rosario Rahola de Espona.

Visor Libros, SL: Isaac Peral 18, 28015 Madrid; tel. (91) 5493409; fax (91) 5448695; e-mail visor-libros@visor-libros.com; internet www.visor-libros.com; poetry, linguistics, philology.

PUBLISHERS' ASSOCIATIONS

Federación de Gremios de Editores de España (Federation of Publishers' Associations of Spain): Cea Bermúdez 44, 2° dcha, 28003 Madrid; tel. (91) 5345195; fax (91) 5352625; e-mail fgee@fge.es; internet www.federacioneditores.org; f. 1978; Pres. Emiliano Martínez Rodríguez; Exec. Dir Antonio Avila; 719 mem. publishing houses.

Asociación de Editoriales Universitarias Españolas (AEUE): Plaza de las Cortes 2, 7°, 28014 Madrid; tel. (91) 3600698; fax (91) 3601201; e-mail secretaria.tecnica@aeue.es; internet www.aeue.es; university and research institutes; Pres. Antonio Pérez Lasheras.

Associació d'Editors en Llengua Catalana (Association of Publishers in Catalan Language): València 279, 1°, 08009 Barcelona; tel. (93) 2155091; fax (93) 2155273; e-mail associacio.editors@retemail.es; internet www.catalanpublishers.org; Pres. Manuel Sanglas Muchart; Sec.-Gen. Segimon Borràs.

Gremi d'Editors de Catalunya: València 279, 1°, 08009 Barcelona; tel. (93) 2155091; fax (93) 2155273; e-mail info@gremieditorscat.es; internet www.gremieditorscat.es; Pres. Josep M. Puig de la Bellacasa; Sec.-Gen. Segimon Borràs.

Gremio de Editores de Euskadi (Euskadiko Editoreen Elkartea): Lehendakari Aguirre 11, 3°, 48014 Bilbao; tel. (94) 4764313; fax (94) 4761980; internet www.editores-euskadi.com; Pres. Javier Gogeascoechea Arrien; Man. Dir Andrés Fernández Seco.

Gremio de Editores de Madrid: Santiago Rusiñol 8, 28040 Madrid; tel. (91) 5544745; fax (91) 5532553; e-mail editoresmadrid@editoresmadrid.org; internet www.editoresmadrid.org; f. 1977; Pres. Emiliano Martínez Rodríguez; Sec.-Gen. Amalia Martín Pereda.

Broadcasting and Communications

TELECOMMUNICATIONS

The telecommunications market was fully deregulated in December 1998.

ALÓ Comunicaciones, SA: Príncipe de Vergara 112, 28002 Madrid; tel. (91) 5634717; internet www.alo.es; f. 1997; Contact Alejandro Rivas-Micoud.

BT España: Edif. Herre, Salvador de Madariaga 1, 28027 Madrid; tel. (91) 270800; fax (91) 2708888; internet www.btglobalservices.com.

Grupo Auna: Avda Diagonal 579–585, 08014 Barcelona; tel. (93) 5020000; internet www.auna.es; telecommunications group; f. 2000; by merger of Endesa, Unión Fenosa, Telecom Italia and various financial companies; operates the cable telecommunications providers Aragón de Cable, Cabletelca, Cable i Televisió de Catalunya, Madritel, Supercable de Andalucía, Supercable Sevilla and Supercable Almería and the broadcasting and telecommunications providers Amena (mobile telecommunications) and Retevisión; Pres. Luis Alberto Salazar-Simpson Bos; Dir-Gen. Miguel Iraburu Elizondo.

Jazztel, SA: Avda de Europa 14, La Moraleja, 28108 Alcobendas, Madrid; tel. (91) 2917200; fax (91) 2917201; e-mail contact@jazztel.com; internet www.jazztel.com; Pres. Leopoldo Fernández Pujals.

ONO: Basauri 7 y 9, 28023 Madrid; tel. (91) 1809300; internet www.ono.es; broadband internet, telephone and television; Pres. Eugenio Galdón; Dirs-Gen. Philip Blanchette, Fernando Ojeda.

Telefónica, SA: Gran Vía 28, 28013 Madrid; tel. (91) 7406918; e-mail prensa@telefonica.es; internet www.telefonica.es; f. 1924; privatized in 1997; monopoly on telephone services removed in 1998, merged its digital services with the television company Sogecable (see below) in 2003; provides services in 41 countries; Pres. César Alierta; Sec.-Gen. Antonio Alonso Ureba.

Uni 2: Juan Esplandiú 11–13, Edif. Juan Esplandiú, 28007 Madrid; tel. (91) 2521200; e-mail informacion@uni2.es; internet www.uni2.es; f. 1998; owned by France Télécom; land-line telecommunications; Exec. Pres. Victoria Hernández Valcárcel.

Vodafone España: Avda Europa 1 (Central), Parque Empresarial La Moraleja, 28108 Alcobendas, Madrid; tel. 607 133333; internet www.vodafone.es; f. 1998; fmrly Airtel; mobile services; Pres. José Manuel Entrecanales; CEO Francisco Román.

In March 2000 the Spanish Government awarded 3G ('third generation') licences to the three existing mobile operators, the fourth being granted to the Xfera consortium. The 3G technology, also known as Universal Mobile Telephone Services (UMTS), permits users to receive and deliver internet data and video images on cellular handsets. In 2001 the Government issued provisional licences for the resale of mobile telecommunications services to the following companies: Affinalia, Aló Comunicaciones, Aviron, Globatel, Primus, Timón, Vallehermoso Telecom and British Telecom.

Regulatory Authorities

Comisión del Mercado de las Telecomunicaciones (CMT): Alcalá 37, 28014 Madrid; tel. (91) 3724300; fax (91) 3724205; e-mail cmt@cmt.es; internet www.cmt.es; f. 1996; Pres. Reinaldo Rodríguez Illera.

Secretaría de Estado de Telecommunicaciones y para la Sociedad de la Información: Ministerio de Industria, Turismo y Comercio, Paseo de la Castellana 160, 28071 Madrid; tel. 902 446006; internet www.setsi.mcyt.es.

BROADCASTING

Grupo Radio Televisión Española (RTVE): Edif. Prado del Rey, 28223 Pozuelo de Alarcón, Madrid; tel. (91) 5815461; fax (91) 5815454; e-mail direccion.comunicacion@rtve.es; internet www.rtve.es; state organization; controls and co-ordinates radio and television; incorporates: Televisión Española, Televisión Española Internacional, Televisión Española Temática, Radio Nacional de España, Instituto Oficial de Radio y Televisión and the Orquesta Sinfónica y Coro; undergoing structural reform in 2005 to become independent of government influence; Dir-Gen. Carmen Caffarel; Sec.-Gen. Jaime Gaiteiro.

Independent Companies

Compañía de Radio y Televisión de Galicia (CRTVG): San Marcos, Apdo 707, 15780 Santiago de Compostela; tel. (981) 540640; fax (981) 540619; f. 1985; Galician language station; Dir-Gen. Francisco Campos Freire.

Corporació Catalana de Ràdio i Televisió (CCRTV): Ganduxer 117, 08022 Barcelona; tel. (93) 4444800; fax (93) 4444824; e-mail comunicacio@ccrtv.es; internet www.ccrtv.es; f. 1983; Catalan language station; three television channels and four radio stations; Dir-Gen. Vicenç Villatorio i Lamolla; Sec.-Gen. Josep Badia i Sánchez.

Euskal Irrati Telebista (EITB)/Radiotelevisión Vasca: 48215 Iurreta (Vizcaya); tel. (94) 6031000; fax (94) 6031095; e-mail info@eitb.com; internet www.eitb.com; f. 1982; Basque station; two television channels, two international television channels and five radio stations; Dir-Gen. Andoni Ortuzar Arruabarrena.

Onda Regional de Murcia: Avda Libertad 6, bajo, 30009 Murcia; tel. (968) 200000; fax (968) 230850; e-mail ondaregional.or@carm.es; internet www.ondaregionalmurcia.es; Dir-Gen. Juan Manuel Máiquez Estévez.

Ràdiotelevisió Valenciana (RTVV): Polígono Accés Ademús s/n, 46100 Burjassot (Valencia); tel. (96) 3183000; fax (96) 3183001; e-mail dgen@rtvv.es; internet www.rtvv.es; f. 1984; Dir-Gen. Pedro García Gimeno.

Radio Televisión de Andalucía (RTVA): Sede Central RTVA, Pabellón de Canal Sur (Antigua Pabellón de Andalucía), José de Gálvez s/n, 41092 Isla de la Cartuja (Sevilla); tel. (95) 5054600; fax (95) 5054937; e-mail comunicacion@rtva.es; internet www.canal.sur.es; Dir-Gen. Rafael Camacho.

Radio Televisión Madrid (RTVM): Paseo del Príncipe 3, Ciudad de la Imagen, 28223 Pozuelo de Alarcón, Madrid; tel. (91) 5128200; fax (91) 5128300; Dir-Gen. Francisco Giménez-Alemán.

Radiotelevisión Canaria (RTVC): Avda Bravo Murillo 5, Edif. Mapfre, 1°, 38003 Santa Cruz de Tenerife; tel. (922) 470200; fax (922) 273173; internet www.tvcanaria.tv; f. 1997; broadcasts in the Canaries; Dir-Gen. Francisco Moreno García.

Radiotelevisión Castilla-La Mancha (RTVCM): Río Alberche s/n, Edif. RTVCM, Polígono Santa María de Benquerencia, 45007 Toledo; tel. (925) 288600; fax (925) 287883; e-mail comunicacion@rtvcm.es; internet www.rtvcm.es; Dir-Gen. Jordi García Candau.

Retevisión: Avda Diagonal 579–585, 08014 Barcelona; tel. (93) 5020000; fax (93) 5022850; internet www.retevision.es; privatized in 1997; in 1998 acquired internet providers Redes TB, Servicom and Xarxa Cirnet; services include: cable and digital terrestrial television, radio broadcasting, fixed-line and mobile telephones, satellite communications and the internet; operates digital terrestrial company Onda Digital.

Federation

Federación de Asociaciones de Radio y Televisión de España: Evaristo San Miguel 8, 28008 Madrid; tel. (91) 5481222; fax (91) 5593630; e-mail artv@jazzfree.com; Pres. FEDERICO SÁNCHEZ AGUILAR; Sec.-Gen. JOSÉ ESTEBAN VERDES.

RADIO

RNE: Casa de la Radio, Prado del Rey, 28223 Pozuelo de Alarcón (Madrid); tel. (91) 5817000; fax (91) 5183240; e-mail secretario_general.rne@rtve.es; internet www.rtve.es/rne; broadcasts Radio 1, Radio Clásica, Radio 3, Radio 4, Radio 5 Todo Noticias; 17 regional stations; Dir-Gen. PEDRO PIQUERAS; Sec.-Gen. EDUARDO HERNÁNDEZ.

Radio Exterior de España (REE): Apdo 156.202, 28080 Madrid; tel. (91) 3461081; fax (91) 3461815; e-mail dir_radioexterior.rne@rtve.es; overseas service of RNE; broadcasts in 10 languages; includes a world service in Spanish; Dir FRANCISCO JAVIER GARRIGÓS.

Independent Stations

Ambiente Musical, SA: Paseo de la Castellana 210, 10°, 28046 Madrid; tel. (91) 3454000; fax (91) 3591321; e-mail estudio@musicam.net; Dir-Gen. MANEL SALLÉS CARCELLER.

Antena Boreal Radio: Real 8, 28340 Valdemoro (Madrid); tel. (91) 8095321; fax (91) 8082434; e-mail antenaboreal@nsi.es; Dir CRISTINA FONTÁN OÑATE.

Cadena 100: Alfonso XI 4, 28014 Madrid; tel. (91) 5951200; fax (91) 5317517; e-mail casoliva@cadena100.es; internet www.cadena100.es; Dir JORDI CASOLIVA.

Cadena M80: Gran Vía 32, 8°, 28013 Madrid; tel. (91) 3470700; fax (91) 5228693; e-mail programas@m80radio.com; internet www.m80radio.com; Dir MANUEL DÁVILA MORENO.

Cadena Dial: Gran Vía 32, 8°, 28013 Madrid; tel. (91) 3470700; fax (91) 5211753; internet www.cadenadial.com; Dir FRANCISCO HERRERA.

Cadena Europa FM (Medipress, SA): Bueso Pineda 7, 28043 Madrid; tel. (91) 4134361; fax (91) 4137175; e-mail europafm@europafm.com; internet europafm.com; Pres. FRANCISCO GAYA GONZÁLEZ.

Cadena Flaix FM: Passeig de Gràcia 54, 08007 Barcelona; tel. (93) 5055555; fax (93) 4880775; Dirs-Gen. CARLES CUNÍ, MIQUEL CALÇADA.

Cadena Herri Irratia/Radio Popular: Garibai 19, 20004 San Sebastián; tel. (943) 423644; fax (943) 427821; e-mail info@herri-irratia.com; internet herri-irratia.com; Dir GORKA BARAÑANO.

Cadena NGRadio (NGR)/Cadena Nervión-Gorbea-Rabel Radio: Hurtado de Amézaga 27, 17°, 48008 Bilbao; tel. (94) 4433317; fax (94) 4448302; Dir-Gen. ENRIQUE CAMPOS LED.

Cadena Ona Catalana, SA: Aragón 390–394, 2°, 08013 Barcelona; tel. (93) 2449990; fax (93) 2459459; e-mail onacatalana@onacatalana.com; internet www.onacatalana.com; Dir-Gen. JOSEP PUIGBÓ.

Cadena Ondacero Radio Voz Galicia: Ronda de Outeiro 1, bajo, 15009 A Coruña; tel. (981) 180600; fax (981) 180477; e-mail mantilla@radiovoz.com; internet www.radiovoz.com; Man. Dir MANUEL MANTILLA FERNÁNDEZ.

Cadena de Ondas Populares Españolas/Radio Popular, SA (COPE): Alfonso XI 4, 3°, 28014 Madrid; tel. (91) 5951200; fax (91) 5322008; e-mail postmaster@cope.es; internet www.cope.es; f. 1959; numerous medium-wave and FM stations; Pres. ALFONSO CORONEL DA PALMA; Dir-Gen. JENARO GONZÁLEZ DEL YERRO VALDÉS; Council Delegate RAFAEL PÉREZ DEL PUERTO RODRÍGUEZ.

Cadena Radio Club 25: Gütemberg 3–16, 6°, 08224 Terrassa (Barcelona); tel. (93) 7806166; fax (93) 7803358; e-mail radioclub25@radioclub25.com; internet www.radioclub25.com; Dir FRANCISCO JAVIER SALILLAS PINILLOS; Man. Dir JOSÉ MANUEL SALILLAS GARCÍA.

Cadena Radio España/Radio España Madrid: Manuel Silvela 9, 28010 Madrid; tel. (91) 4475300; fax (91) 5938413; internet www.radioes.es; Pres. and Dir-Gen. JOSÉ ANTONIO SÁNCHEZ.

Cadena Radio Estudio: Pasaje de la Radio 1, 28100 Alcobendas (Madrid); tel. (91) 6531199; fax (91) 6533072; e-mail radioestudio@futurnet.es; internet www.radioestudio.com; Dir-Gen. ROMÁN BEITIA ALONSO.

Cadena Radiolé: Gran Vía 32, 8°, 28013 Madrid; tel. (91) 3470886; Dir MANUEL DÁVILA MORENO.

Cadena Sinfo Radio: Gran Vía 32, 8°, 28013 Madrid; tel. (91) 3470808; fax (91) 5228693.

Cadena Top FM Radio: Gordóniz 44, 12°, 6–8 dtos, 48002 Bilbao; tel. (94) 4101156; fax (94) 4444054; e-mail topbilbao@topbilbao.com; internet www.topbilbao.com; f. 1986; Dir RICARDO FONTANES MATO.

Cadena TOP Radio España: Manuel Silvela 9, 28010 Madrid; tel. (91) 4475300; fax (91) 4477026; internet www.topradio.es; Pres. JOSÉ ANTONIO SÁNCHEZ.

Canal 28 Producciones, SL: Sao Paulo 40, 2°, 35008 Las Palmas de Gran Canaria; tel. and fax (928) 475126; e-mail radioeconomia@telecan.es; Pres. JOSÉ MIGUEL GONZALO RODRÍGUEZ.

Catalunya Ràdio, SRG, SA: Avda Diagonal 614–616, 08021 Barcelona; tel. (93) 3069200; fax (93) 3069201; e-mail correo@catradio.com; internet www.catradio.com; f. 1983; run by Catalan autonomous govt; four channels: Catalunya Ràdio, Catalunya Música, Catalunya Informació, Catalunya Cultura; Dir MONTSERRAT MINOBIS I PUNTONET.

Compañía de Radiodifusión Intercontinental, SA (INTER): Modesto Lafuente 42, 28003 Madrid; tel. (91) 5544603; fax (91) 5331302; Dir-Gen. FERNANDO SERRANO-SUÑER POLO.

COMRàdio: Pavelló Cambó, Recinte de la Maternitat, Travessera de les Corts 131–159, 08028 Barcelona; tel. (93) 5080600; fax (93) 5080810; e-mail comradio@comradio.com; internet www.comradio.com; Dir-Gen. JORDI LLONCH MASSANÉS; Dir of Programmes JOSEP MARIA FRANCINO.

EITB Radio: Miramón Pasealekua 172, 20014 San Sebastián; tel. (943) 012300; fax (943) 012295; e-mail info@eitb.com; internet www.eitb.com; run by Basque autonomous govt; broadcasts on FM and MW as Euskadi Irratia, Radio Euskadi (Bilbao), Radio Vitoria (Vitoria-Gasteiz) and EITB Irratia; Dir JULIAN BELOKI GERRA.

Grupo Pavesa Comunicación, SL—Radio Ondas Riojanas: Sabto Domingo 5, 26580 Arnedo; tel. (941) 383350; fax (941) 383383; e-mail ondarioja@ondarioja.com; internet www.ondarioja.com; Pres. PEDRO VEGA HERNÁNDEZ.

Los 40 Principales: Gran Vía 32, 8°, 28013 Madrid; tel. (91) 3470705; fax (91) 5317370; internet www.los40.com; Dir JAUME BARÓ GARRIGA.

Muinmo, SL: Apolonio Morales 6–10, 28036 Madrid; tel. (91) 3536017; fax (91) 3536019; Dir-Gen. MIGUEL ANGEL MONTERO QUEVEDO.

Onda Cero Radio (OCR): José Ortega y Gasset 22–24, 28006 Madrid; tel. (91) 436400; fax (91) 436101; e-mail ondacero@ondacero.es; internet www.ondacero.es; owned by Telefónica, SA; Pres. JAVIER GONZÁLEZ FERRARI; Dir-Gen. JOSÉ LUIS OROSA ROLDAN.

Onda Rambla Catalunya: Avda Diagonal 441, 1°, 08036 Barcelona; tel. (93) 4448000; fax (93) 4106662; e-mail ondarrambla@ondarrambla.es; internet www.ondarrambla.es; Pres. LUIS DEL OLMO MAROTE; Dir-Gen. FRANCESC X. OLONA CABASSÉS.

Radio Autonomía Madrid, SA: Paseo del Príncipe 3, Ciudad de la Imagen, 28223 Pozuelo de Alarcón, Madrid; tel. (91) 5128679; fax (91) 5128670; e-mail telemadridradio@telemadrid.com; internet www.telemadrid.es; f. 1985; broadcasts on 101.3 and 106.0 MHz; Dir MIGUEL PÉREZ-PLA DE VIU.

Ràdio Autonomia Valenciana, SA/Ràdio Nou: Avda Blasco Ibáñez 136, 46022 Valencia; tel. (96) 3183600; fax (96) 3183602; internet www.radionou.com; Dir JESÚS WOLLSTEIN ALCARAZ.

Radio ECCA: Avda Mesa y López 38, Apdo 994, 35080 Las Palmas de Gran Canaria; tel. (928) 257400; fax (928) 207395; e-mail info@radioecca.es; internet www.radioecca.org; adult education; Dir-Gen. LUCAS LÓPEZ PÉREZ.

Radio Galega, SA (RG): San Marcos, 15780 Santiago de Compostela; tel. (981) 540940; fax (981) 540919; internet www.crtvg.es/rtg/hisradio.htm; f. 1985; run by Galician autonomous govt; Man. Dir LUIS PÉREZ FERNÁNDEZ.

Radio Surco-Castilla La Mancha: Concordia 14, Bajo C, 13700 Tomelloso (Ciudad Real); tel. (926) 505959; fax (926) 505961; e-mail r.surco@retemail.es; internet www.radiosurco.es; Dir FRANCISCO CASTELLANOS CUELLAR.

Punto Radio: e-mail info@puntoradio.com; internet www.puntoradio.com; f. 2005; Pres. JOSÉ MARÍA BERGARECHE.

Sociedad Española de Radiodifusión (SER): Gran Vía 32, 28013 Madrid; tel. (91) 3470700; fax (91) 3470709; internet www.cadenaser.es; f. 1924; 235 regional stations; Pres. JESÚS DE POLANCO; Dir-Gen. MANUEL SABIDO DURÁN.

Digital Radio

In March 1999 two digital radio licences were awarded for the frequencies MF-1 and MF-2. MF-1 was controlled by Cope, Intereconomía, Recoletos and El Mundo, while MF-2 was controlled by SER, Onda Rambla-Planeta, Onda Cero, Radio España, Onda Digital and Prensa Española. MF-1 began broadcasting in Madrid and Barcelona in July 2000.

SPAIN

Radio Association

Asociación Española de Radiodifusión Comercial (AERC): Plaza Independencia 2, 4° dcha, 28001 Madrid; tel. (91) 4357072; fax (91) 4356196; e-mail aerc@retemail.es; groups nearly all commercial radio stations; Pres. Rafael Pérez del Puerto; Sec.-Gen. Alfonso Ruíz de Assin.

TELEVISION

Legislation relating to the ending of TVE's monopoly and the regulation of private TV stations was approved in April 1988. In 2005 there were plans to increase the number of private terrestrial broadcasters from three (Antena 3, Telecinco and Canal+). It was also envisaged that analogue broadcasts would cease in 2010.

Televisión Española (TVE): Edif. Prado del Rey, 28223 Pozuelo de Alarcón, Madrid; tel. (91) 3464968; fax (91) 3463055; e-mail consultas@rtve.es; internet www.tve.es; broadcasts on TVE-1 and La 2; production centres in Barcelona and Las Palmas de Gran Canaria and 15 regional centres; broadcasts to Europe and the Americas on Canal Internacional; Dir Manuel Pérez Estremena; Sec.-Gen. Javier Martín Domínguez.

Independent Stations

Antena 3 Televisión: Avda de Isla Graciosa s/n, 28700 San Sebastián de los Reyes, Madrid; tel. (91) 6230500; fax (91) 6230994; e-mail antena3tv@antena3tv.com; internet www.antena3tv.com; f. 1989; private commercial national network; owned by Grupo Planeta; Pres. José Manuel Lara Bosch; Sec.-Gen. Adolfo Lefort.

Canal 9—Televisió Autonómica Valenciana (TVV): Polígon Accés Ademús, 46100 Burjassot (Valencia); tel. (96) 3183000; fax (96) 3183001; e-mail wmaster@rtvv.es; internet www.rtvv.es; commenced regular transmissions Oct. 1989; second channel commenced operations in Oct. 1997; Dir Genoveva Reig.

Canal Sur Televisión, SA: Carretera San Juan de Aznalfarache, Apdo 132, 41920 San Juan de Aznalfarache, Sevilla; tel. (95) 5607600; fax (95) 5054740; e-mail csalinas@cica.es; internet www.canalsur.es; commenced transmissions in 1989; regional station for Andalucía; controlled by RTVA; Dir-Gen. Rafael Camacho.

Euskal Telebista—ETB (TV Vasca): 48215 Iurreta (Vizcaya); tel. (94) 6031000; fax (94) 6031095; e-mail info@eitb.com; internet www.eitb.com; f. 1982; broadcasts in Basque Country in Basque language on ETB-1 and in Spanish on ETB-2; mem. of EITB; Dir Bingen Zupiria Gorostidi; Dir of Programmes Pello Sarasola.

Popular TV: Alfonso XI 4, 28014 Madrid; tel. (91) 3096669; e-mail populartv@populartv.net; internet www.populartv.net; broadcasts on a local and national level; Pres. Bernardo Herráez Rubio; Dir-Gen. Alejandro Samanes Prat.

Sogecable, SA: Avda de los Artesanos 6, 28760 Tres Cantos, Madrid; tel. (91) 7367000; internet www.sogecable.es; f. 1989; private commercial national network; services include satellite and digital television, film rights production and management, film distribution and exhibition, thematic channels, sports rights production and management, and internet services; operates Canal+, Canal Satélite Digital, CNN+, Compañía Independiente de Televisión, Gestsport, Sogecine, the Plus.es internet portal; partly owned by Telefónica (see above); Pres. Rodolfo Martín Villa; Sec.-Gen. Iñigo Dago.

Grupo Telecinco: Carretera de Irún, Km 11,700, 28049 Madrid; tel. (91) 155555; e-mail oinf@telecinco.es; internet www.telecinco.es; f. 1990; private commercial national network; joint owned by Grupo Mediaset (Italy), Grupo Correo de Comunicación, Ice Finance (The Netherlands); Pres. Alejandro Echevarría.

Televisió de Catalunya, SA: Carrer de la TV3, s/n, 08970 Sant Joan Despi, Barcelona; tel. (93) 4999333; fax (93) 4730671; internet www.tvcatalunya.com; f. 1983; broadcasts on TV-3, Canal 33 and K3 in Catalan over north-eastern Spain; controlled by CCRTV; Dir Francesc Escribano.

Televisión de Galicia (TVG): San Marcos, Apdo 707, 15820 Santiago de Compostela; tel. (981) 540640; fax (981) 540719; e-mail crtvg@crtvg.es; internet www.crtvg.es; f. 1985; broadcasts in Galician; controlled by CRTVG; Man. Dir Angel Quintanilla Louzao.

Televisión Autonomía Madrid, SA (Telemadrid): Paseo del Príncipe de España 1, 28223 Pozuelo de Alarcón (Madrid); tel. (91) 5128200; fax (91) 5128300; e-mail correo@telemadrid.com; internet www.telemadrid.es; commenced transmissions in 1989; controlled by RTVM; cultural channel, laOtra, commenced transmission in March 2001; Dir-Gen. Francisco Giménez Alemán; Man. Dir Fernando Jeréz.

Other Satellite, Cable and Digital Television

By early 1996 more than 1.1m. Spanish homes were receiving programmes by satellite. These companies used the Hispasat and Astra satellites. Legislation relating to the regulation of cable television received the Government's approval in late 1996. The first licences were awarded during 1997. The country is divided into 43 operating sectors. Each of these is served by Telefónica de España, and 36 sectors are also served by one of the other cable companies operating in Spain, offering television, telephone and internet access. By 2000 more than 2m. Spanish homes and businesses were served by cable telecommunications and some 900,000 received digital television. In 1999 the first licence for a terrestrial digital network was awarded. By 2000 there were more than 100 satellite, cable and digital television broadcasters in Spain. Many of these were operated by existing broadcasting companies. Others include:

Aragón de Cable, SA (Able): Avda Diagonal, 579–585, Barcelona 08014; internet www.auna.es; cable; part of Grupo Auna; Dir-Gen. José Antonio Royo Pueyo.

Grupo Auna: Avda Diagonal 579–585, 08014 Barcelona; internet www.auna.es; telecommunications, internet and cable TV.

Digital+: Gran Vía 32, 4°, 28013 Madrid; tel. (91) 201515; fax (91) 213121; e-mail contactnos@cplus.es; internet www.plus.es; f. 2002 by merger of Canal Satélite Digital (CSD) with Via Digital; Dir-Gen. Santiago Tapia.

Euskaltel: Vizcaya; internet www.euskaltel.es; cable; operator for Vizcaya; part of Grupo Auna.

Hispasat: Gobelas 41, 28023 Madrid; tel. (91) 7102540; fax (91) 3729000; e-mail comunicacion@hispasat.es; internet www.hispasat.com; satellite system; part of Grupo Auna, Telefónica, BBVA and Eutelsat; Pres. Petra Mateos.

Madritel: Obenque 4, Madrid; internet www.madritel.es; cable and digital; part of Grupo Auna.

Menta: Moll de Barcelona s/n, 08039 Barcelona; tel. 900 700900; e-mail info@menta.es; internet www.auna.es; f. 1997; cable; part of Grupo Auna.

Multicanal: Saturno 1, Pozuelo de Alarcón, 28224 Madrid; tel. (91) 7141080; fax (91) 3515884; e-mail multicanal@multicanaltps.com; internet www.multicanaltps.com; f. 1996; cable; operates five thematic channels.

Net TV: Madrid; f. 2001; digital.

ONO: Basauri 7–9, Urbanización La Florida, 28023 Madrid; tel. (91) 7089300; fax (91) 7089337; internet www.ono.es; Cable Pres. Eugenio Galdón.

Paquete Digital RTVE: Avda Radio Televisión Española 4, 29223 Pozuelo de Alarcón, Madrid; tel. (91) 5817000; fax (91) 5818824; e-mail direccion.comunicacion@rtve.es; internet www.rtve.es; digital; operates five thematic channels; part of RTVE; Dir Eladio Gutiérrez Montes.

R: Real 85, 15003 A Coruña; tel. (981) 911000; fax (981) 911002; e-mail fala-con-R@mundo-R.net; internet www.mundo-R.com; cable; operator for Galicia.

Retecal: Bajada al Molino 15, 09400 Aranda de Duero (Burgos); tel. (947) 500828; fax (947) 508885; e-mail info-aranda@retecal.es; internet www.retecal.com; cable; operator for Castilla y León.

Retena: Carretera Zaragoza Km 3, 31191 Cordovilla (Navarra); tel. (948) 070707; e-mail info@retena.es; internet www.retena.es; cable; operator for Navarra.

Reterioja: Piqueras 38–40, 26006 Logroño (La Rioja); tel. (941) 585858; internet www.reterioja.es; cable; operator for La Rioja.

Retevisión: Avda Diagonal 579–585, 08014 Barcelona; tel. (93) 5020000; fax (93) 5022850; internet www.retevision.es; cable, digital and satellite; operates digital terrestrial company Onda Digital; part of Grupo Auna.

Telecable de Asturias, SAU: Marqués de Pidal 11, bajo, 33004 Oviedo, Asturias; tel. (985) 081111; fax (985) 081112; e-mail info@telecable.es; internet www.telecable.es; cable; f. 1995; operator for Asturias.

Telecom Canarias: internet www.canariastelecom.com; f. 1998; as Cabletelca, SA; cable; part of Grupo Auna.

Telefónica Cable, SA: Calle Virgilio 2, Edif. 2, 2°, 28223 Pozuelo de Alarcón (Madrid); tel. (91) 5129510; e-mail cac@tcable.es; internet www.telefonica-cable.com; f. 1997; cable; operates in all sectors.

Veo TV: Madrid; f. 2001; 25.5% owned by Recoletos, 25.5% owned by Unedisa; digital; Dir Eduardo Sánchez Illana.

Associations

Agrupación de Operadores de Cable (AOC): Obenque 4, 28042 Madrid; f. 1998; by CYC Madrid, Retecal, Telecable and Grupo Cable; group of cable telecommunications operators; Dir Jesús Pelegrín.

Promoción e Identificación de Servicios Emergentes de Telecomunicaciones Avanzadas (PISTA): Secretaria de Estado de Telecomunicaciones y para la Sociedad de la Información, Capitán Haya 41, 28071 Madrid; tel. (91) 3462820; fax (91) 3461567; e-mail jmontalban@mityc.es; part of Ministry of Trade, Industry and

SPAIN   Directory

Tourism; initiative for the promotion and identification of emerging advanced telecommunications.

Unión de Televisiones Comerciales Asociadas (UTECA): Maldonado 4, bajo C, 28006 Madrid; tel. (91) 5759778; fax (91) 5776754; e-mail uteca@uteca.com; internet www.uteca.com; f. 1998; represents commercial television interests; Pres. José Manuel Lara Bosch; Sec.-Gen. Jorge del Corral y Díez del Corral.

Finance

(cap. = capital, res = reserves, dep. = deposits, br. = branch, m. = million)

BANKING

Central Bank

Banco de España: Alcalá 50, 28014 Madrid; tel. (91) 3385000; fax (91) 5310059; e-mail bde@bde.es; internet www.bde.es; f. 1829; granted exclusive right of issue in 1874; nationalized 1962; granted a degree of autonomy in 1994; cap. €1.4m., res €4,484.2m., dep. €31,763.2m. (Dec. 2003); Gov. Jaime Caruana (due to stand down July 2006); 42 brs.

Principal Commercial and Development Banks

Altae Banco Privado: Monteesquinza 48, 28010 Madrid; tel. (91) 3915380; fax (91) 3915414; internet www.altae.es; f. 1983; as Banco de Crédito y Ahorro, changed to current name 1995; private banking; part of Grupo Caja Madrid; cap. €18.0m., res €4.7m., dep. €91.4m. (Dec. 2002); Pres. Miguel Blesa de la Parra; Gen. Man. José Manuel Dabrio Achabal; 7 brs.

Banca March, SA: Avda Alejandro Rosselló 8, 07002 Palma de Mallorca; tel. (971) 779100; fax (971) 779187; e-mail divinter@bancamarch.es; internet www.bancamarch.es; f. 1926; cap. €29.2m., res €330.6m., dep. €3,342.3m. (Dec. 2003); Pres. José Carlos March Delgado; Man. Dir Francisco Verdú Pons; 210 brs.

Banco Arabe Español (Aresbank): Castellana Hall, Paseo de la Castellana 257, 28046 Madrid; tel. (91) 3149595; fax (91) 3149768; e-mail aresbank@aresbank.es; internet www.aresbank.es; f. 1975; cap. €71.4m., res –€25.2m., dep. €235.9m. (Dec. 2002); Chair. Luis Vaño; 3 brs.

Banco de Andalucía: Fernández y González 4, 41001 Sevilla; tel. (95) 4594700; fax (95) 4594802; internet www.bancoandalucia.es; f. 1844; cap. €16.3m., res €484.1m. (Dec. 2001), dep. €4,161.0m. (Dec. 2002); Pres. Miguel de Solís y Martínez Campos; Gen. Man. Francisco Fernández Dopico; 298 brs.

Banco Atlántico: Avda Diagonal 407 bis, Apdo 424, 08008 Barcelona; tel. (93) 4020100; fax (93) 2188317; internet www.batlantico.es; f. 1901; as Banca Nonell; changed name as above in 1946; 99.9% owned by Banco Sabadell, SA; cap. €125.6m., res €388.9m., dep. €8,675.9m. (Dec. 2003); Chair. Abdulmohsen Y al-Hunaif; First Gen. Man Manuel Montecelos; 269 brs.

Banco Bilbao Vizcaya Argentaria (BBVA): Paseo de la Castellana 81, 28046 Madrid; tel. (91) 3746000; fax (91) 3746202; internet www.bbva.es; f. 2000; through merger; absorbed Banca Catalana, Banco del Comercio and Banco de Negocios Argentaria in same year; cap. €1,566.0m., res €13,518.3m., dep. €237,001.3m. (Dec. 2003); Pres. Francisco González Rodríguez; Chief Exec. José Ignacio Goirigolzarri Tellaeche.

Banco de Castilla: Plaza de los Bandos 10, 37002 Salamanca; tel. (923) 290000; fax (923) 211902; internet www.bancocastilla.es; f. 1915; part of Grupo Banco Popular; cap. €26.0m., res €292.1m., dep. €2,142.2m. (Dec. 2002); Gen. Man. José Bravo Jiménez; 199 brs.

Banco Cooperativo Español, SA: Virgen de los Peligros 6, 28013 Madrid; tel. (91) 5956700; fax (91) 5956800; internet www.cajarural.com; f. 1990; cap. €72.9m., res €93.4m., dep. €6,203.9m. (Dec. 2003); Chair. José Luis Palacios; Gen. Man. Javier Petit Asumendi; 3,671 brs.

Banco de Crédito Balear, SA: Plaza de España 1, 07002 Palma de Mallorca; tel. (971) 170100; fax (971) 170152; internet www.escredit.es; f. 1872; 64.5% owned by Banco Popular Español; Gen. Man. Eladio Sebastián Gil; 101 brs.

Banco Español de Crédito (Banesto): Gran Vía de Hortaleza 3, 28043 Madrid; tel. (91) 3383100; fax (91) 3381883; e-mail uninternac@banesto.es; internet www.banesto.es; f. 1902; cap. €1,229.0m., res €1,325.9m., dep. €47,860.8m. (Dec. 2003); Chair. Ana Patricia Botín-Sanz de Sautuola y O'Shea; CEO Federico Outon del Moral; 1,906 brs.

Banco Espírito Santo, SA (BESSA): Velázquez 108, 28006 Madrid; tel. (91) 5667100; fax (91) 5625679; internet www.bes.es; f. 1972; as Banco Industrial de Mediterraneo, SA; name changed to above in 1993; 89.6% owned by Banco Espirito Santo, SA, Lisbon; cap. €86.5m., res €3.1m., dep. €1,915.9m. (Dec. 2002); Pres. José Manuel Pinheiro; CEO Manuel María de Olazábal y Albuquerque; 33 brs.

Banco de Finanzas e Inversiones, SA (FIBANC): Avda Diagonal 668–670, 08034 Barcelona; tel. (93) 2535400; fax (93) 2535492; e-mail info@fibanc.es; internet www.fibanc.es; f. 1988; 85.1% owned by Banco Mediolanum, SpA; cap. €6.9m., res €32.4m., dep. €520.4m. (Dec. 2003); Pres. Carlos Tusquets; Man. and Gen. Dir Gianluca Bosisio.

Banco de Galicia: Policarpo Sanz 23, 36202 Vigo (Pontevedra); tel. (986) 822100; fax (986) 822101; f. 1918; total assets €2,597.3m. (Dec. 2003); Gen. Man. José Fernando Martínez Isach; 141 brs.

Banco Gallego, SA: Avda Linares Rivas 30, 15005 A Coruña; tel. (981) 127950; fax (981) 126582; e-mail intervenciongeneral@bancgellego.com; internet www.bancogallego.es; f. 1847; cap. €83.4m., res €38.9m., dep. €1,574.3m. (Dec. 2003); Pres. Juan Manuel Urgoiti López-Ocaña; Gen. Man. José Luis Losada Rodríguez; 158 brs.

Banco Guipuzcoano: Avda de la Libertad 21, 20004 San Sebastián; tel. (943) 418100; fax (943) 418337; e-mail bgintnal@bancogui.com; internet www.bancogui.es; f. 1899; cap. €31.2m., res €220.8m., dep. €5,672.9m. (Dec. 2003); Pres. José María Aguirre González; Gen. Man. Juan Luis Arrieta; 208 brs.

Banco Inversión: Recoletos 3, 28004 Madrid; tel. (91) 5950200; fax (91) 5226821; e-mail info@bancoinversion.es; internet www.bancoinversion.es; f. 2001; Pres. and Chair. Harm Bishoff; CEO Armando Mayo; 13 brs.

Banco Pastor, SA: Cantón Pequeño 1, Edif. Pastor, 15003 La Coruña; tel. (981) 127600; fax (981) 210301; internet www.bancopastor.es; f. 1776; cap. €54.5m., res €557.6m., dep. €9,123.5m. (Dec. 2003); Chair. José María Arias Mosquera; Vice-Chair., CEO and Gen. Man. Fulgencio García Cuellar; 496 brs.

Banco de la Pequeña y Mediana Empresa, SA (Bankpyme): Travessera de Gràcia 11, 08021 Barcelona; tel. (93) 3163333; fax (93) 3163170; e-mail info@bankpyme.es; internet www.bankpyme.es; f. 1978; cap. €75.8m., res –€9.4m., dep. €796.8m. (Dec. 2003); Chair. Jordi Conejos; Gen. Man. Francesc Saldaña; 24 brs.

Banco Popular Español: Velázquez 34 (esquina a Goya), 28001 Madrid; tel. (91) 5207000; fax (91) 5783274; internet www.bancopopular.es; f. 1926; absorbed Banco Popular Industrial (Eurobanco), 1995; cap. €113.7m., res €2,868.2m., dep. €45,542.4m. (Dec. 2003); Pres. and CEO Ángel Carlos Ron Guimil; 1,227 brs.

Banco de Sabadell: Plaza de Catalunya 1, 08201 Sabadell; tel. (93) 7289289; fax (93) 7270606; e-mail infobs@bancsabadell.com; internet www.bancsabadell.com; f. 1881; cap. €102.0m., res €2,069.1m., dep. €26,144.5m. (Dec. 2003); Chair. and CEO Josep Oliu; Dir and Gen. Man. Joan M. Nin; 1,160 brs..

Banco Santander Central Hispano (BSCH): Plaza de Canalejas 1, 28014 Madrid; tel. (91) 5581111; internet www.bsch.com; f. 1999 through merger; cap. €2,384.2m., res €19,445.0m., dep. €279,357.1m. (Dec. 2003); Chair. Emilio Botín-Sanz de Sautuola y García de los Ríos; Man. Dir Juan Botín; 8,848 brs.

Banco Siméon, SA: María del Molina 39, 28006 Madrid; tel. (91) 3099100; fax (91) 4116381; internet www.grupocgde.com; f. 1969; as Banco Industrial Fierro; name changed to above in 2002; 99.6% owned by Caixa Geral de Depósitos, SA, Lisbon; cap. €167.8m., res €8.6m., dep. €2,228.5m. (Dec. 2003); Chair. and Pres. Carlos Prieto Traguelho; 171 brs.

Banco de Valencia: Pintor Sorolla 2–4, 46002 Valencia; tel. (96) 3984500; fax (96) 3984570; internet www.bancodevalencia.es; f. 1900; cap. €97.0m., res €365.5m., dep. €6,760.0m. (Dec. 2003); Pres. and Chair. Julio de Miguel Aynat; Gen. Man. Domingo Parra Soria; 352 brs.

Banco de Vasconia, SA: Plaza del Castillo 39, 31001 Pamplona; tel. (948) 179600; fax (948) 179665; e-mail servicioscentrales@bancovasconia.es; internet www.bancovasconia.es; f. 1901; 96.84% owned by Banco Popular Español; total assets €2,278.0m. (Dec. 2003); Pres. José R. Rodríguez García; Gen. Man. Miguel Mozolobato; 121 brs.

Banco de Vitoria, SA: Postas 22–24, 01001 Vitoria, Alava; tel. (945) 163300; fax (945) 163345; internet www.bancovitoria.es; f. 1900; 98% owned by Banco Español de Crédito, SA; Pres. José Ángel Merodio Zubiarrain; Chair. Carlos Sabanza Teruel; 121 brs.

Bancoval, SA: Fernando el Santo 20, 28010 Madrid; tel. (91) 3609900; fax (91) 3609997; e-mail info@bancoval.es; internet www.bancoval.es; f. 1881; as Banco de Valls; 1989 name changed to above; cap. €12.5m., res €42.9m., dep. €1,375.7m. (Dec. 2003); CEOs José María Alonso Gamo, José Luis Velasco.

Bankinter, SA: Paseo de la Castellana 29, 28046 Madrid; tel. (91) 3397500; fax (91) 3397556; e-mail international@bankinter.es; internet www.ebankinter.com; f. 1965; finances industrial and business dealings with medium- and long-term loans and investments; cap. €113.9m., res €258.7m., dep. €21,171.9m. (Dec. 2003); Chair. Juan Arena de la Mora; CEO Jaime Echegoyen ; 253 brs.

SPAIN   *Directory*

BANKOA, SA (Banco Industrial de Guipuzcoa): Avda de la Libertad 5, 20004 San Sebastián; tel. (943) 410145; fax (943) 410174; internet www.bankoa.es; f. 1975; cap. €23.1m., res €69.1m., dep. €826.8m. (Dec. 2003); Pres. RENEE TALAMONA; 44 brs.

Instituto de Crédito Oficial (ICO): Paseo del Prado 4, 28014 Madrid; tel. (91) 5921600; fax (91) 5921700; e-mail ico@ico.es; internet www.ico.es; f. 1971; state credit bank; Pres. AURELIO MARTÍNEZ ESTÉVEZ.

Foreign Banks

Barclays Bank SA: Plaza de Colón 1, 28046 Madrid; tel. (91) 3361000; fax (91) 3361134; internet www.barclays.es; f. 1979; as Banco de Valladolid, name changed in 1982; cap. €157.8m., res €450.7m., dep. €13,170.9m. (Dec. 2003); Chair. C. MARTÍNEZ DE CAMPOS; Man. Dir JACOBO GONZALEZ-ROBATTO; 163 brs.

Banco Urquijo: Príncipe de Vergara 131, 28002 Madrid; tel. (91) 3372000; fax (91) 3372096; internet www.bancourquijo.es; f. 1870; 99.66% owned by Kredietbank SA (Luxembourg); cap. €92.7m., res €36.2m., dep. €2,008.6m. (Dec. 2003); Pres. FERDINAND VERDONCK; CEO ALFONSO TOLCHEFF ALVAREZ; 59 brs.

Deutsche Bank SAE: Avda Diagonal 446, 08006 Barcelona; tel. (93) 5818181; fax (93) 5818544; internet www.deutsche-bank.es; f. 1950; cap. €67.4m., res €430.1m., dep. €11,124.3m. (Dec. 2003); Chair. HERMANN-JOSEF LAMBERTI; CEO JUAN CARLOS GARAY; 277 brs.

Other major foreign banks include Banca Nazionale del Lavoro, BNP Paribas, Citibank, Commerzbank, ING Bank, Societé Génerale, and JP Morgan Chase.

Savings Banks

Bilbao Bizkaia Kutxa: Gran Vía 30–32, 48009 Bilbao; tel. (94) 4017000; fax (94) 4017800; e-mail bbktelefono@bbk.es; internet www.bbk.es; f. 1907; res €1,790.7m., dep. €12,650.8m. (Dec. 2003); Chair. and CEO XABIER DE IRALA; 330 brs.

Caixa de Aforros de Vigo, Ourense e Pontevedra (CAIXANOVA): Avda García Barbon 1–3, 36201 Vigo; tel. (986) 828200; fax (986) 828238; e-mail internacionalcx@caixanova.com; internet www.caixanova.com; f. 1929 as Caixa de Vigo e Ourense; merged with Caixa de Pontevedra in 2000 and changed name as above; cap. €0.01m., res €687.1m., dep. €9,976.7m. (Dec. 2003); Pres. and Chair. RAMÓN CORNEJO MOLINS; Gen. Man. JULIO FERNÁNDEZ GAYOSO; 403 brs.

Caixa d'Estalvis de Catalunya: Plaza Antonio Maura 6, 08003 Barcelona; tel. (93) 4845000; fax (93) 4845141; e-mail international.services@caixacatalunya.es; internet www.caixacatalunya.es; f. 1926; res €1,026.0m., dep. €27,899.0m. (Dec. 2003); Pres. NARCÍS SERRA; Gen. Man. JOSEP MARÍA LOZA; 936 brs.

Caixa d'Estalvis de Sabadell: Gràcia 17, 08201 Sabadell (Barcelona); tel. (93) 7286700; fax (93) 7286555; e-mail info@caixasabadell.es; internet www.caixasabadell.com; f. 1859; res €303.0m., dep. €5,635.2m. (Dec. 2004); Pres. LLUÍS BRUNET BERCH; Gen. Man. PERE RIFÁ PUJOL; 284 brs.

Caixa d'Estalvis de Tarragona: Plaza Imperial Tàrraco 6, 43005 Tarragona; tel. (977) 299200; fax (977) 299250; e-mail liniapreferent@caixatarragona.es; internet www.caixatarragona.es; f. 1952; res €267m., dep. €4,154m. (Dec. 2004); Pres. GABRIEL FERRATÉ PASCUAL; Gen. Man. RAFAEL JENÉ VILLAGRASA; 289 brs.

Caixa d'Estalvis de Terrassa: Ramble d'Ègara 350, 08221 Terrasa; tel. (93) 7397700; fax (93) 7397777; internet www.caizaterrassa.es; f. 1877; res €218.6m., dep. €3,783.4m. (Dec. 2002); Pres. FRANCES ASTALS COMA; Gen. Man. ENRIC MATA TARRAGO; 164 brs.

Caja de Ahorros de Asturias (CAJASTUR): Plaza de la Escandalera 2, 33003 Oviedo; tel. (98) 5102222; fax (98) 5215649; e-mail extranjero@cajastur.es; internet www.cajastur.es; f. 1945; res €572.1m., dep. €6,180.2m. (Dec. 2003); Chair., Pres. and CEO MANUEL MENÉNDEZ MENÉNDEZ; 223 brs.

Caja de Ahorros de Galicia/Caixa Galicia: Rúa Nueva 30, 15003 A Coruña; tel. (981) 188000; fax (981) 188001; internet www.caixagalicia.es; f. 1978; res €1,135.1m., dep. €24,151.5m. (Dec. 2003); Pres. MAURO VARELA PÉREZ; Dir-Gen. JOSÉ LUIS MÉNDEZ LÓPEZ; 703 brs.

Caja de Ahorros de la Inmaculada de Aragón: Paseo Independencia 10, 50004 Zaragoza; tel. (976) 718100; fax (976) 718377; e-mail planif@cai.es; internet www.cai.es; f. 1905; cap. €632.5m., res €479.6m., dep. €5,191.6m. (Dec. 2003); Pres. FERNANDO GIL MARTÍNEZ; Gen. Man. LUIS CALVERA SERRANO; 212 brs.

Caja de Ahorros del Mediterráneo (CAM): San Fernando 40, 03007 Alicante; tel. (96) 5905000; fax (96) 5905044; e-mail cam@cam.es; internet www.cam.es; f. 1976; cap. €3.0m., res €1,295.3m., dep. €20,948.6m. (Dec. 2003); Chair. VICENTE SALA BELLÓ; Gen. Man. ROBERTO LÓPEZ ABAD; 870 brs.

Caja de Ahorros y Monte de Piedad de las Baleares 'Sa Nostra': Ramón Llull 2, 07001 Palma de Mallorca; tel. (971) 171717; fax (971) 171797; e-mail sanostra@sanostra.es; internet www.sanostra.es; res €308.5m., dep. €5,412.1m. (Dec. 2003); Chair. LORENÇ HUGUET ROTGER; Gen. Man. PEDRO BATLE MAYO; 244 brs.

Caja de Ahorros y Monte de Piedad del Círculo Católico de Obreros de Burgos: Avda de los Reyes Católicos 1, 09005 Burgos; tel. (947) 288200; fax (947) 288210; internet www.cajacirculo.es; f. 1909; res €424m., dep. €2,835m. (Dec. 2005); Chair. JOSÉ IGNACIO MIJANGOS LINAZA; 176 brs.

Caja de Ahorros y Monte de Piedad de Gipuzkoa y San Sebastián/Gipuzkoa eta Donstiako Aurrezki Kutxa: Garibai 15, Apdo 1389, 20004 San Sebastián; tel. (943) 001000; fax (943) 001045; e-mail admin@kutxa.es; internet www.kutxa.es; f. 1896; cap. €180.3m. (Dec. 2002), res €1,420.8m., dep. €8,817.5m. (Dec. 2003); Pres. and Chair. CARLOS ETXEPARE ZUGASTI; Gen. Mans JESÚS MARÍA ITURRIOZ, XABIER ALKORTA; 200 brs.

Caja de Ahorros y Monte de Piedad de Madrid—Caja Madrid: Paseo de la Castellana 189, 28046 Madrid; tel. (91) 3792000; fax (91) 5216980; internet www.cajamadrid.es; f. 1869; res €4,215.6m., dep. €64,813.7m. (Dec. 2003); Pres. MIGUEL BLESA DE LA PARRA; 1,914 brs.

Caja de Ahorros y Monte de Piedad de Navarra: Avda de Carlos III 8, 25, 31002 Pamplona; tel. (948) 222333; fax (948) 224179; e-mail can@can.es; internet www.can.es; f. 1921 as Caja de Ahorros de Navarra; merged with Caja de Ahorros Municipal de Pamplona in 2000 and changed name as above; cap. €0.003m., res €589.5m., dep. €7,419.1m. (Dec. 2003); Pres. MIGUEL SANZ SESMA; Gen. Man. ENRIQUE GOÑI BELTRÁN DE GARIZURIETA; 164 brs.

Caja de Ahorros y Monte de Piedad de Zaragoza, Aragón y Rioja 'IBERCAJA': Plaza del Paraíso 2, 50008 Zaragoza; tel. (976) 767676; fax (976) 214417; internet www.ibercaja.es; f. 1876; res €1,407.0m., dep. €15,726.2m. (Dec. 2003); Chair. AMADO FRANCO; Gen. Man. JOSÉ LUIS AGUIRRE; 943 brs.

Caja de Ahorros de Murcia: Gran Vía Escultor Salzillo 23, 30005 Murcia; tel. (968) 361600; fax (968) 306160; internet www.cajamurcia.es; f. 1965; res €457.1m., dep. €7,454.8m. (Dec. 2003); Pres. JUAN ROCA GUILLAMÓN; Gen. Man. CARLOS EGEA KRAUEL; 367 brs.

Caja de Ahorros y Pensiones de Barcelona 'La Caixa': Avda Diagonal 621–629, 08028 Barcelona; tel. (93) 4046000; fax (93) 3395703; e-mail estudis@lacaixa.es; internet www.lacaixa.es; f. 1990; res €6,004.9m., dep. €107,464.9m. (Dec. 2004); Chair. RICARD FORNESA; Pres. and CEO ISIDRO FAINÉ; 4,841 brs.

Caja de Ahorros de Valencia, Castellón y Alicante/Caixa d'Estalvis de València, Castelló i Alacant (BANCAJA): Pintor Sorolla, 8, 46002 Valencia; tel. (96) 3875500; fax (96) 3527550; internet www.bancaja.es; f. 1878; res €1,227.3m., dep. €30,860.2m. (Dec. 2003); Chair. JOSÉ LUIS OLIVAS MARTÍNEZ; Gen. Man. JOSÉ FERNANDO GARCÍA CHECA; 864 brs.

Caja Badajoz (Monte de Piedad y Caja General de Ahorros de Badajoz): Paseo de San Francisco 18, 06001 Badajoz; tel. (924) 214000; fax (924) 214073; e-mail buzon@cajabadajoz.es; internet www.cajabadajoz.es; f. 1889; Pres. JOSÉ MANUEL SÁNCHEZ ROJAS.

Caja Duero: Plaza de los Bandos 15–17, 37002 Salamanca; tel. (923) 279300; fax (923) 270680; internet www.cajaduero.es; f. 1881 as Caja de Ahorros y Monte Piedad de Salamanca; changed name as above in 1997; res €553.4m., dep. €9,817.0m. (Dec. 2002); Pres. and Chair. JULIO FERMOSO; Gen. Man. LUCAS HERNANDEZ; 559 brs.

Caja España: Ordoño II 17, 24001 León; tel. (987) 218683; fax (987) 218067; e-mail buzon@cajaespana.es; internet www.cajaespana.es; f. 1900; cap. 2m. (Dec. 2000), res €805.2m., dep. €11,210.6m. (Dec. 2003); Chair. VICTORINO GONZÁLEZ OCHOA; Gen. Man. JOSÉ IGNACIO LAGARTOS RODRÍGUEZ; 538 brs.

Caja Laboral Popular (S Coop. de Crédito Ltda): Paseo José María Arizmendiarrieta s/n, 20500 Mondragón, Guipúzcoa; tel. (943) 719500; fax (943) 719778; e-mail cajalaboral.net@cajalaboral.es; internet www.cajalaboral.es; f. 1959; cap. €302.6m., res €680.1m., dep. €8,467.7m. (Dec. 2003); Pres. JUAN M. OTAEGUI MURUA; Gen. Man. JUAN JOSÉ ARRIETA SUDUPE; 336 brs.

Confederación Española de Cajas de Ahorros (CECA): Alcalá 27, 28014 Madrid; tel. (91) 5965000; fax (91) 5965742; e-mail admin@ceca.es; internet www.ceca.es; f. 1928; national asscn of savings banks; cap. €30.0m., res €334.0m., dep. €7,360.6m. (Dec. 2003); Chair. JUAN RAMÓN QUINTÁS SEOANE; Gen. Man. J. A. OLAVARREITA; 47 affiliates, 19,297 brs.

Montes de Piedad y Caja de Ahorros de Ronda, Cádiz, Almería, Málaga y Antequera (Unicaja): Avda Andalucía 10–12, 29007 Málaga; tel. (952) 138000; fax (952) 611349; e-mail info@personal.unicaja.es; internet www.unicaja.es; f. 1991; res €175.1m., dep. €1,895.2m. (Dec. 2003); Pres. BRAULIO MEDEL CAMARA; Gen. Man. MIGUEL ANGEL CABELLO JURADO; 740 brs.

Banking Associations

Asociación Española de Banca Privada (AEB): Velázquez 64–66, 28001 Madrid; tel. (91) 5777015; fax (91) 5777022; f. 1977; Pres. José Luis Leal Maldonado; Sec. Manuel Torres Rojas.

Fondo de Garantía de Depósitos (FGD): José Ortega y Gasset 22, 28006 Madrid; tel. (91) 4316645; fax (91) 5755728; e-mail fogade@fgd.es; internet www.fgd.es; f. 1977; deposit guarantee fund; Pres. Gonzalo Gil García.

STOCK EXCHANGES

Bolsa de Barcelona: Paseo de Gracia 19, 08007 Barcelona; tel. (93) 4013555; fax (93) 4013625; e-mail estudios@borsabcn.es; internet www.borsabcn.es; f. 1915; Pres. Hortalà i Arau.

Bolsa de Bilbao: José M. Olabarri 1, 48001 Bilbao; tel. (94) 4034400; fax (94) 4034430; e-mail bolsabilbao@bolsabilbao.es; internet www.bolsabilbao.es; f. 1890; Chair. José Luis Marcaida; CEO José Luis Damborenea.

Bolsa de Madrid: Plaza de la Lealtad 1, 28014 Madrid; tel. (91) 5891161; fax (91) 5312290; e-mail internacional@bolsamadrid.es; internet www.bolsamadrid.es; f. 1831; 49 mems; Chair. and CEO Antonio Zoido.

Bolsa de Valores de Valencia: Libreros 2 y 4, 46002 Valencia; tel. (96) 3870100; fax (96) 3870133; e-mail mjose.medialdea@bolsavalencia.es; internet www.bolsavalencia.es; f. 1980; Vice-Pres. and CEO Manuel Escámez Sánchez.

Regulatory Authority

Comisión Nacional del Mercado de Valores (CNMV): Paseo de la Castellana 19, 28046 Madrid; tel. (91) 5851500; fax (91) 3193373; e-mail inversores@cnmv.es; internet www.cnmv.es; f. 1988; national securities and exchange commission; Pres. Manuel Conthe.

INSURANCE

Aegon Unión Aseguradora, SA: Príncipe de Vergara 156, 28002 Madrid; tel. (91) 5636222; fax (91) 5639715; internet www.aegon.es; f. 1944; merged with Unión Levantina in 1986, Unión Previsora in 1987 and Labor Médica, La Sanitaria and Caja de Previsión y Socorro in 1996; owned by Aegon NV (The Netherlands); life, property, health and personal insurance and reinsurance; total premiums €289.9m. (2000); also owns Aegon Salud, Aegon Inversión and Aegon Money Maxx; Chair. Alejandro Royo-Villanova Payá; CEO Jesús Quintanal San Emeterio.

Allianz, Compañía de Seguros y Reaseguros, SA: Paseo de la Castellana 39, 28046 Madrid; tel. (91) 5960400; fax (91) 5578702; internet www.allianz.es; f. 1999 after fusion of AGF Unión-Fénix, Allianza Ras and Athena.

Ascat Vida, SA: Provença 398–404, 08025 Barcelona; tel. (93) 484600; tel. (93) 4846002; e-mail info_ascat@caixacatalunya.es; internet www.ascat.es; f. 1986.

Asistencia Sanitaria Interprovincial de Seguros, SA (ASISA): Caracas 12, 28010 Madrid; tel. (91) 3190191; fax (91) 4103836; e-mail asisa.informacion@asisa.es; internet www.asisa.es; Pres. Francisco Carreño Castilla.

Axa Seguros: Paseo de la Castellana 79, 28046 Madrid; tel. (91) 5388200; fax (91) 5553197; e-mail webmaster@axa-seguros.es; internet www.axa-seguros.es; Pres. Eduardo de Aguirre Alonso-Allende.

Banco Vitalicio de España, Compañía Anónima de Seguros: Paseo de Gracia 11, 08007 Barcelona; tel. (93) 4840100; fax (93) 4840226; internet www.vitalicio.es; f. 1880; Pres. Alfonso Escámez López; Man. Dir José Luis Pérez Torres.

BBVA Seguros, SA: Alcalá 17, 28014 Madrid; tel. (91) 5379231; fax (91) 3747266; internet www.bbvaseguros.com.

Bilbao, Cía Anónima de Seguros y Reaseguros: Paseo del Puerto 20, 48990 Neguri-Getxo (Vizcaya); tel. (94) 4898100; fax (94) 4898263; internet www.segurosbilbao.com; f. 1918; gen. insurance, represented throughout Spain; Pres. Patrick de la Sota MacMahon; Man. Dir Iñaki Alvares.

Caja de Seguros Reunidos, Cía de Seguros y Reaseguros, SA (Caser): Plaza de la Lealtad 4, 28014 Madrid; tel. (91) 5955000; fax (91) 5955018; internet www.caser.es; f. 1942; represented throughout Spain; Dir-Gen. Ignacio Eyries García de Vinuesa.

Crédito y Caución, SA (Compañía Española de Seguros y Reaseguros): Paseo de la Castellana 4, 28046 Madrid; tel. (91) 4326300; fax (91) 4326506; e-mail comunicacion@creditoycaucion.es; internet www.creditoycaucion.com; Pres. Jesús Serra Farré.

La Estrella, SA: Paseo de la Castellana 130, 28046 Madrid; tel. (91) 5905656; fax (91) 3301400; e-mail clientes@laestrella.es; internet www.laestrella.es; f. 1901; all classes of insurance and reinsurance; Pres. Duque D. Carlos Zurita Delgado; Man. Dir Luis Espacio Casanovas; 124 brs.

Grupo Catalana Occidente, SA: Avda Alcalde Barnils 63, 08190 Sant Cugat del Vallés (Barcelona); tel. (93) 5820500; fax (93) 5820560; internet www.catalanaoccidente.com; insurance and reinsurance; total premiums €1,117m. (1999); Pres. José María Serra Farré.

Mapfre Mutualidad (Mapfre Mutualidad de Seguros y Reaseguros): Carretera de Pozuelo a Majadahonda, Km 3800, 28820 Majadahonda, Madrid; tel. (91) 6262100; fax (91) 6262308; internet www.mapfre.com; f. 1933; car insurance; total premiums €7,085.9m. (2002); Pres. José A. Rebuelta García.

Mapfre Seguros Generales, SA: Paseo de Recoletos 23, 28004 Madrid; tel. (91) 5816300; fax (91) 5815252; internet www.mapfre.com; Pres. Rafael Galarraga Solores.

Mapfre Vida, SA: Avda General Perón 40, 28020 Madrid; tel. (91) 5811400; fax (91) 5811592; internet www.mapfre.com; life and health insurance; Pres. José Manuel Martínez Martínez; Man. Dir Sebastián Homet Dupra.

Multinacional Aseguradora, SA: Doctor Ferrán 3 y 5, 08034 Barcelona; tel. (93) 4847000; fax (93) 4847070; internet www.ascat-mna.com.

Musini, Sociedad Anónima de Seguros y Reaseguros: Manuel Cortina 2, 6°, 28006 Madrid; tel. (91) 5509090; fax (91) 5509000; internet www.musini.com; f. 1968; CEO Alvaro Muñoz López.

Mutua General de Seguros: Avda Diagonal 543, 08029 Barcelona; tel. (93) 3221212; fax (93) 3220971; e-mail mutua@mgs.es; internet www.mgs.es; f. 1907; total premiums €206m. (2003); Pres. Jorge Luque Vico; Dirs-Gen. Fernando Jiménez Pérez, Juan José Candelas Fernández; brs throughout Spain.

Mutua Madrileña Automovilista: Almagro 9, 28010 Madrid; tel. (91) 5578200; internet www.mutua-mad.es; f. 1930; Pres. Gabriel Gancedo.

Ocaso, SA, Compañía de Seguros y Reaseguros: Princesa 23, 28008 Madrid; tel. (91) 5380100; fax (91) 5418509; e-mail ocaso@ocaso.es; internet www.ocaso.es; f. 1920; total premiums €513m., cap. €100m. (2002); 370 brs in Spain, 1 in London, 1 in Puerto Rico; Pres. Isabel Castelo d'Ortega; Dir-Gen. D. Antonio Domínguez Cuerdo.

Plus Ultra: Plaza de las Cortes 8, 28014 Madrid; tel. (91) 5899292; fax (91) 4298921; e-mail plus.ultra@plusultra.es; internet www.plusultra.es; life premiums 33,626m. pesetas, non-life premiums 59,748m. pesetas (2000); Pres. Gerardo Aróstegui Gómez.

Sanitas de Seguros, SA: Ribera del Loira 52, 28042 Madrid; tel. 902230220; fax (91) 5852516; e-mail iferrando@sanitas.es; internet www.sanitas.es; health insurance; Pres. Juan José López-Ibor.

Santa Lucía, SA: Plaza de España 15, 28008 Madrid; tel. (91) 5419387; fax (91) 5410133; e-mail atencion@santalucia.es; internet www.santalucia.es; f. 1922; cap., res, etc. €1.106,254m. (2000); Pres. Carlos J. Alvarez Navarro.

Vidacaixa, SA: General Almirante 6, 08014 Madrid; tel. (93) 2278700; fax (93) 3324441; internet www.vidacaixa.es; Pres. Tomás Muniesa Arantegui.

Winterthur Seguros: Avda Diagonal 575, 08029 Barcelona; tel. (93) 2909761; fax (93) 3637240; e-mail winterthur-seguros@winterthur.es; internet www.winterthur.es; f. 1996; by merger; Pres. and Dir-Gen. César Bardají.

Zurich: Vía Augusta 192–200, 08021 Barcelona; tel. (93) 2099111; fax (93) 2014849; internet www.zurichspain.com.

Insurance Associations

Dirección General de Seguros y Fondos de Pensiones: Paseo de la Castellana 44, 28046 Madrid; tel. (91) 3397000; fax (91) 3397113; e-mail dirseguros@mineco.es; internet www.dgseguros.mineco.es; supervisory body; part of Ministry of the Economy and Finance; Dir-Gen. Ricardo Lozano Aragües.

Comisión Liquidadora de Entidades Aseguradoras (CLEA): Marqués de la Ensenada 16, 2°, 28004 Madrid; tel. (91) 7005500; fax (91) 3195390; e-mail clea@clea.es; internet www.clea.es; f. 1984; empowered to liquidate companies dissolved by the Public Administration; part of Ministry of the Economy and Finance; Pres. Concepción Bermúdez Meneses.

Unión Española de Entidades Aseguradoras y Reaseguradoras (UNESPA): Núñez de Balboa 101, 28006 Madrid; tel. (91) 7451530; fax (91) 7451531; internet www.unespa.es; professional asscn; Pres. Alvaro Muñoz; Sec. Aranzazu del Valle.

Trade and Industry

GOVERNMENT AGENCIES

Secretaría General de Comercio Exterior: Secretaria de Estado de Comercio y Turismo, Paseo de la Castellana 162, 28046 Madrid;

e-mail buzon.oficial@secgcomex.sscc.mcx.es; internet www.mcx.es; Sec.-Gen. ALFREDO BONET BAIGET.

Instituto Español de Comercio Exterior (ICEX): Paseo de la Castellana 14, 28046 Madrid; tel. (91) 3496100; fax (91) 4316128; internet www.icex.es; f. 1982; institute for foreign trade; Pres. MARÍA ELENA PISONERO RUIZ.

DEVELOPMENT ORGANIZATIONS

Instituto Andaluz de la Reforma Agraria (IARA): Tabladilla s/n, 41013 Sevilla; tel. (95) 5032271; fax (95) 5032149; empowered to expropriate land under the agricultural reform programme; Pres. JUAN ÁNGEL FERNÁNDEZ BATANERO.

Instituto Galego de Promoción Económica (IGAPE): Complexo Administrativo Barrio de San Lázaro s/n, 15703 Santiago de Compostela; tel. (902) 300903; e-mail igape@igape.es; internet www.igape.es.

Instituto Madrileño de Desarrollo: José Abascal 57, 28003 Madrid; tel. (91) 5802600; fax (91) 5802589; e-mail informacion@imade.es; internet www.imad.es; f. 1984; public development institution for Madrid region; Man. RODOLFO DEL OLMO LÓPEZ.

Sociedad de Desarrollo de Navarra (SODENA): Avda Carlos III el Noble 36, 1° dcha, 31003 Pamplona; tel. (948) 421942; fax (948) 421943; e-mail info@sodena.com; internet www.sodena.com.

Sociedad para el Desarrollo de las Comarcas Mineras (SODECO): La Unión 21, La Felguera, 33930 Langreo, Asturias; tel. (98) 5678116; fax (98) 5678172; internet www.sodeco.es.

Sociedad para el Desarrollo Económico de Canarias, SA: Villalba Hervás 4, 6°, 38002 Santa Cruz de Tenerife; tel. (922) 298020; fax (922) 298131; e-mail sodecantf@sodecan.es; internet www.sodecan.es; Pres. EUSEBIO BAUTISTA VIZCAINO.

Sociedad para el Desarrollo Industrial de Andalucía (SODIAN): República Argentina 29, 41011 Sevilla; tel. (95) 4278705; fax (95) 4276806.

Sociedad para el Desarrollo Industrial de Castilla y León, SA (SODICAL): Doctrinos 6, 4°, 47001 Valladolid; tel. (983) 343811; e-mail sodical@sodical.es; internet www.sodical.es; f. 1982; Dir-Gen. MANUEL FERNÁNDEZ DÍEZ.

Sociedad para el Desarrollo Industrial de Extremadura (SODIEX): Avda Virgen de Guadalupe, 10001 Cáceres; tel. (927) 224878; fax (927) 243304; e-mail sodiex@sodiex.es; internet www.sodiex.es; f. 1977.

Sociedad para el Desarrollo Industrial de Galicia, SA (SODIGA): Orense 6, La Rosaleda, 15701 Santiago de Compostela; tel. (981) 566100; fax (981) 566183.

CHAMBERS OF COMMERCE

Cámara de Comercio Internacional (International Chamber of Commerce): Avda Diagonal 452–4, 08006 Barcelona; tel. (93) 4169300; fax (93) 4169301; e-mail iccspain@cambrabcn.es; internet www.iccspain.org; f. 1922; Pres. GUILLERMO DE LA DEHESA; Sec.-Gen. LUIS SOLÁ VILARDELL.

Consejo Superior de Cámaras Oficiales de Comercio, Industria y Navegación de España (High Council of Official Chambers of Commerce, Industry, and Navigation of Spain): Ribera del Loira 12, 28042 Madrid; tel. (91) 5906900; fax (91) 5906913; e-mail comunicacion@cscamaras.es; internet www.camaras.org; f. 1922; Pres. JAVIER GÓMEZ-NAVARRO; Dir-Gen. FERNANDO GÓMEZ AVILES-CASCO; Sec.-Gen. FERNANDO FERRERO; comprises 85 Chambers throughout Spain, incl. the following:

Cámara de Comercio de Bilbao (Bilboko Merkataritza Ganbera): Licenziado Poza 17, Bilbao; tel. (94) 4702485; e-mail info@camaranet.com; internet www.camarabilbao.com; Pres. IGNACIO MARÍA ECHEBERRIA MONTEBERRIA.

Cámara Oficial de Comercio e Industria de Madrid: Ribera del Loira 56–58, 28042 Madrid; tel. (91) 5383500; fax (91) 5383677; e-mail camara@camaramadrid.es; internet www.camaramadrid.es; f. 1887; Pres. FERNANDO FERNÁNDEZ-TAPIAS; Dir JOSÉ MARÍA ISARDO; 370,000 mems.

Cámara Oficial de Comercio, Industria y Navegación de Sevilla: Plaza de la Contratación 8, 41004 Sevilla; tel. (954) 211005; fax (954) 225619; e-mail ccinsevilla@camaradesvilla.com; internet www.camaradesevilla.com.

Cámara Oficial de Comercio, Industria y Navegación de Valencia: Poeta Querol 15, 46002 Valencia; tel. (96) 3103900; fax (96) 3516349; e-mail info@camaravalencia.com; internet www.camaravalencia.com; f. 1886; Pres. ARTURO VIROSQUE RUIZ; Dir FERNANDO ZÁRRAGA QUINTANA; Sec.-Gen. ANTONIO RICO GIL.

Cambra Oficial de Comerç, Indústria i Navegació de Barcelona: Avda Diagonal 452–454, 08006 Barcelona; tel. (90) 2448448; fax (93) 4169301; internet www.cambrabcn.es; f. 1886; Pres. MIQUEL VALLS MASEDA; Dir XAVIER CARBONELL ROURA.

Confederación Española de Comercio: Diego de León 50, 28006 Madrid; tel. (91) 4116161; fax (91) 5645269; Pres. PERE LLORENS LORENTE; Sec.-Gen. MIQUEL ÁNGEL FRAILE; 400,000 mems.

INDUSTRIAL AND TRADE ASSOCIATIONS

Agrupación de Exportadores del Centro de España (AGRECE): Ribera del Loira 56–58, 28042 Madrid; tel. (91) 5383613; fax (91) 5383676; e-mail cex2@camaramadrid.es; exporters.

Agrupación de Fabricantes de Cemento de España (OFICEMEN): José Abascal 53, 28003 Madrid; tel. (91) 4411688; fax (91) 4423817; internet www.oficemen.com; cement manufacturers; Pres. MANUEL DE MELGAR; Dir-Gen. RAFAEL FERNÁNDEZ.

Agrupación de Importadores y Exportadores de Productos Agrícolas: Londres 96, 08036 Barcelona; tel. (93) 2093478; agricultural products.

Associación Española de Centros Comerciales (AECC): Mauricio Legendre 19, 1°A, 28046 Madrid; tel. (91) 3084844; fax (91) 3105535; e-mail asociacion@aedecc.com; internet www.aedecc.es; f. 1980; Dir MARÍA VICTORIA GOZÁLVEZ.

Asociación de Comercio de Cereales y Oleaginosas de España (ACCOE) (Spanish Association of Oilseeds and Cereals Traders): Doctor Fleming 56, 3°D, 28036 Madrid; tel. (91) 3504305; fax (91) 3455009; e-mail info@accoe.org; internet www.accoe.org; f. 1977; cereal traders; Pres. PELAYO MORENO SÁNCHEZ; Sec.-Gen. JOSÉ M. ALVAREZ BLASCO.

Asociación de Criadores Exportadores de Sherry (ACES): Avda Alcalde Alvaro Domecq 6, 2° dcha, 11405 Jerez de la Frontera; tel. (956) 341046; fax (956) 346081; e-mail fedejerez@fedejerez.com; internet www.fedejerez.com; sherry exporters; Pres. FRANCISCO VALENCIA JAÉN.

Asociación Española de Comercio Exterior de Cereales y Productos Análogos (AECEC): Calle Orense 85, Edif. Lexington, 28020 Madrid; tel. (91) 678400; fax (91) 5714244; e-mail aecec@arrakis.es; cereal exporters; Pres. J. CORNEJO; Sec.-Gen. GUILLERMO LORENZO ZAMORANO.

Asociación Española de Exportadores de Electrónica e Informática (SECARTYS): Gran Vía de les Corts Catalanes 774, 4°, 08013 Barcelona; tel. (93) 2478560; fax (93) 2478561; e-mail secartys@secartys.org; internet www.secartys.org; f. 1968; electronics exporters; Pres. JOSÉ BELTRÁN; Dir-Gen. IGNACIO TORMO MARXUACH.

Asociación Española de Extractores de Aceite de Orujo de Aceitunas (ANEO): Paseo Reina Cristina 6, 28014 Madrid; tel. (91) 4376585; fax (91) 5515013; olive oil extractors; Pres. ALVARO ESPUNY RODRÍGUEZ; Sec. JUAN JOSÉ VÁZQUEZ CANSINO.

Asociación Española de Fabricantes de Automóviles y Camiones (ANFAC): Fray Bernardino Sahagún 24, 28036 Madrid; tel. (91) 3431343; fax (91) 3594488; e-mail prensa@anfac.com; internet www.anfac.com; car and lorry manufacturers; Pres. JUAN ANTONIO FERNÁNDEZ DE SEVILLA; Gen. Sec. LUIS VALERO.

Asociación Española de Fabricantes de Equipos y Componentes para Automoción (SERNAUTO): Castelló 120, 28006 Madrid; tel. (91) 5621041; fax (91) 5618437; e-mail sernauto@sernauto.es; internet www.sernauto.es; asscn of manufacturers of equipment and components for automobile industry; Pres. JOSÉ MARÍA PUJOL; Gen. Man. JOSÉ A. JIMÉNEZ SACEDA.

Asociación Española de la Industria y Comercio Exportador de Aceite de Oliva (ASOLIVA): José Abascal 40, 2°, 28003 Madrid; tel. (91) 4468812; fax (91) 5931918; e-mail asoliva@asoliva.es; internet www.asoliva.es; f. 1928; olive oil exporters; Pres. JOSÉ PONT AMENOS.

Asociación Española de Productoras de Fibras Químicas (PROFIBRA): Vía Layetana 46, 2°, 08003 Barcelona; tel. (93) 2682644; fax (93) 2682630; e-mail profibra@profibra.com; internet www.profibra.com; chemical fibre producers; Pres. RAFAEL ESPAÑOL NAVARRO; Sec.-Gen. GUILLERMO GRAELL DENIEL.

Asociación de Exportadores de Pescado y Cefalopodos Congelados (AEPYCC): Diego de León 44, 28006 Madrid; tel. (91) 4112407; fax (91) 5618178; fish exporters; Pres. RAMÓN MASO; Sec. IGNACIO MONTENEGRO GONZÁLEZ.

Asociación Industrial Textil de Proceso Algodonero (AITPA): Gran Vía de les Corts Catalanes 670, 08010 Barcelona; tel. (93) 3189200; fax (93) 3026235; e-mail aitpa@aitpa.es; internet www.aitpa.es; cotton textile industry; Pres. ADRIA SERRA; Exec. Vice-Pres. SALVADOR MALUQUER.

Asociación Nacional Española de Fabricantes de Hormigón Preparado (ANEFHOP): Bretón de los Herreros 43, bajo, 28003 Madrid; tel. (91) 4416834; fax (91) 4418341; e-mail anefhop@nauta.es; internet www.anefhop.com; concrete manufacturers; Pres. MANUEL A. SOBRAL CRUZ; Dir-Gen. FRANCISCO JAVIER MARTÍNEZ DE EULATE.

Asociación Nacional de Fabricantes de Pastas Papeleras, Papel y Cartón (ASPAPEL): Alcalá 85, 4°, 28009 Madrid; tel. (91) 5763002; fax (91) 5774710; e-mail c.reinoso@aspapel.es; paper and cardboard manufacturers; Pres. FERNANDO ARRIETA SAN MIGUEL; Dir-Gen. CARLOS REINOSO TORRES.

Asociación Nacional de Industrias Electrónicas y de Telecomunicaciones (ANIEL): Príncipe de Vergara 74, 28006 Madrid; tel. (91) 5902300; fax (91) 4114000; e-mail aniel@aniel.es; internet www.aniel.es; f. 1984; electronic, information and telecommunication industries; Man. Dir GONZALO CARO.

Comité de Gestión de la Exportación de Frutos Cítricos: Monjas de Santa Catalina 8, 4°, 46002 Valencia; tel. (96) 3521102; fax (96) 3510718; citrus fruit exporters; Pres VICENTE BORDILS RAMÓN, ANTONIO MUÑOZ ARMERO; Dir JOSÉ MARTÍNEZ SERRANO.

Confederación de Cooperativas Agrarias de España (CCAE): Agustín de Bethencourt 17, 4°, 28003 Madrid; tel. (91) 5351035; fax (91) 5540047; e-mail prensa@ccae.es; internet www.ccae.es; Pres. JOSÉ MARÍA LUQUI GARDE.

Confederación Española de Organizaciones Empresariales del Metal (CONFEMETAL): Príncipe de Vergara 74, 5°, 28006 Madrid; tel. (91) 5625590; fax (91) 5628477; internet www .confemetal.es; metal organizations; Pres. CARLOS PÉREZ DE BRICIO OLARIAGA; Sec.-Gen. ANDRÉS SÁNCHEZ DE APELLANIZ.

Confederación Nacional de la Construcción (CNC): Diego de León 50, 2°, 28006 Madrid; tel. (91) 2619715; fax (91) 2615269; construction industry; Pres. JOSÉ LUIS ALONSO; Sec. Pastor JOSÉ LUIS RODRÍGUEZ-PONGA.

Confederación Nacional de Empresarios de la Minería y de la Metalurgia (CONFEDEM): Jorge Juan 28, 2°, 28001 Madrid; tel. (91) 4319402; fax (91) 4317162; e-mail confedem@terra.es; mining and metallurgy; Pres. UBALDO USUNÁRIZ BALANZATEGUI; Sec. ANDRÉS VILLALOBOS BELTRÁN.

Consejo Intertextil Español (CIE): Gran Vía 670, E-08010 Barcelona; tel. (93) 3189200; fax (93) 3026235; e-mail cie@consejointertextil.com; internet www.consejointertextil.com; textile industry; Pres. ADRIA SERRA; Sec.-Gen. SALVADOR MALUQUER; 8 mem. asscns.

CONSTRUNAVES—CNE, SA: Orense 11, 1°, 28020 Madrid; tel. (91) 5560458; fax (91) 5555216; e-mail construnaves@construnaves .es; f. 1959; private shipbuilders' asscn; Man. Dir RAMÓN LÓPEZ-EADY.

Federación Empresarial de la Industria Química Española (FEIQUE): Hermosilla 31, 1°, 28001 Madrid; tel. (91) 4317964; fax (91) 5763381; e-mail info@feique.org; internet www.feique.org; chemical industry; Pres. FRANCISCO BELIL CREIXELL.

Federación Española de Asociaciones de Productores Exportadores de Frutas y Hortalizas (FEPEX): Miguel Angel 13, 4A, 28010 Madrid; tel. (91) 3191050; fax (91) 3103812; e-mail fepex@fepex.es; internet www.fepex.es; fruit and vegetable producers and exporters; Pres. ANDRÉS CUARTERO RUIZ; Dir JOSÉ MARÍA POZANCOS.

Federación Espanõla de Exportadores de Frutos Cítricos (FECIT): Hernan Cones 4E, 46004 Valencia; tel. (96) 3521284; fax (96) 3513187; citrus fruit exporters; Pres. ANTONIO PELUFO; Sec. LUIS RIBERA PERIS.

Federación Española de Industrias de la Alimentación y Bebidas (FIAB): Diego de León 44, 1° izqda, 28001 Madrid; tel. (91) 4117211; fax (91) 4117344; e-mail fiab@fiab.es; internet www .fiab.es; f. 1977; food and drink industries; Pres. ARTURO GIL PÉREZ ANDUJAR; Sec.-Gen. JORGE JORDANA BUTTICAZ DE POZAS.

Federación de la Industria Textil Lanera: San Quirico 30, 08201 Sabadell; tel. (93) 7450944; fax (93) 7261526; e-mail gremifab@textilespain.com; internet www.gremifab.es; wool industry; Pres. JOSEP ROCA VALLRRIBERA; Sec. BENET ARMENGOL OBRADORS.

Federación de Industrias del Calzado Español (FICE): Núñez de Balboa 116, 3°, Ofs 5 y 6, 28006 Madrid; tel. (91) 5627001; fax (91) 5620094; e-mail fice@inescop.es; internet www.paso-paso.com; footwear; Pres. RAFAEL CALVO RODRÍGUEZ.

Fundacíon Cotec: Marqués de Salamanca 11, 2 izqda, 28006 Madrid; tel. (91) 4364776; fax (91) 4311239; internet www.cotec.es; f. 1990; promotes technological innovation and understanding; Pres. JOSÉ ÁNGEL SÁNCHEZ ASIAÍN; Dir JUAN MULET.

Servicio Comercial de la Industria Textil Lanera (SCITL): Rosellón 216, 08008 Barcelona; tel. (93) 2150170; fax (93) 2158463; wool industry; Pres. PEDRO GUITART; Sec. ANTONIO AIZPÚN.

Sociedad Estatal de Participaciones Industriales (SEPI): Velasquez 134, 28006 Madrid; tel. (91) 3961000; fax (91) 5628789; e-mail informacion@sepi.es; internet www.sepi.es; f. 1996; asscn of state-owned companies; Pres. ENRIQUE MARTÍNEZ ROBLES; Sec.-Gen. ENRIQUE HERNÁNDEZ PÉREZ; 36 mems.

Unión de Empresas Siderúrgicas (UNESID): Castelló 128, 3°, 28006 Madrid; tel. (91) 5624010; fax (91) 5626584; e-mail unesid@unesid.org; internet www.unesid.org; f. 1967; asscn of Spanish producers of steel; Chair. GONZALO URQUIJO; Dir-Gen. JUAN I. BARTOLOMÉ.

EMPLOYERS' ORGANIZATIONS

Confederación Española de Organizaciones Empresariales (CEOE) (Spanish Confederation of Employers' Organizations): Diego de León 50, 28006 Madrid; tel. (91) 5663400; fax (91) 5628023; e-mail ceoe@ceoe.es; internet www.ceoe.es; f. 1977; covers industry, agriculture, commerce and service sectors; comprises 210 orgs; Pres. JOSÉ MARÍA CUEVAS SALVADOR; Sec.-Gen. JUAN JIMÉNEZ DE AGUILAR.

Círculo de Empresarios: Serrano 1, 4°, 28001 Madrid; tel. (91) 5781472; fax (91) 5774871; e-mail asociacion@circulodeempresarios .org; internet www.circulodeempresarios.org; f. 1977; comprises CEOs of more than 180 major companies; Pres. CLAUDIO BOADA PALLERÉS; Sec.-Gen. PEDRO MORENÉS EULATE.

Confederación Empresarial Valenciana (CEV): Plaza Conde de Carlet 3, 46003 Valencia; tel. (96) 3155720; fax (96) 3923199; e-mail cev@cev.es; internet www.cev.es; f. 1977; Pres. JOSÉ VICENTE GOUTÁLET; Sec.-Gen. ENRIQUE SOTO.

Confederación Empresarial Vasca (CONFEBASK) (Euskal Entrepresarien Konfederakuntza): Gran Vía 45, 2°, 48011 Bilbao; tel. (94) 4021331; fax (94) 4021333; e-mail webmaster@confebask.es; internet www.confebask.es; f. 1983; Pres. ROMÁN KNÖRR BORRAS; Sec.-Gen. JOSÉ GUILLERMO ZUBÍA GUINEA.

Confederación de Empresarios y Industrías de la Comunidad de Madrid (CEIM-CEOE): Diego de León 50, 1°, 28006 Madrid; tel. (91) 4115317; fax (91) 5627537; internet internacional@ceim.es; internet www.ceim.es; small, medium and large businesses; Pres. GERARDO DIAZ FERRÁN; Sec. ALEJANDRO COUCEIRO.

Confederación Española de la Pequeña y Mediana Empresa (CEPYME): Diego de León 50, 3°, 28006 Madrid; tel. (91) 4116161; fax (91) 5645269; e-mail cepyme@cepyme.es; internet www.cepyme .es; small and medium businesses; Pres. ANTONIO MASA GODOY; Sec.-Gen. ELÍAS APARICIO BRAVO.

Fomento del Trabajo Nacional/Foment del Treball Nacional—Confederación Empresarial de Catalunya: Vía Layetana 32, 08003 Barcelona; tel. (93) 4841200; fax (93) 4841230; internet www.foment.com; f. 1771 as Real Compañía de Hilados de Algodón del Principado de Catalunya; development of national labour; Pres. JOAN ROSELL LASTORTRAS; Sec.-Gen. JUAN PUJOL SEGARRA.

Tribunal de Defensa de la Competencia: Velázquez 147, 28002 Madrid; tel. (91) 5680510; fax (91) 5680590; e-mail secretaria .general@tdcompetencia.es; internet www.tdcompetencia.es; f. 1963; Pres. GONZALO SOLANA GONZÁLEZ; Sec. RAFAEL GARCÍA MONTEYS.

UTILITIES

Instituto para la Diversificación y Ahorro de la Energía (IDAE): Madera 8, 28004 Madrid; tel. (91) 4564900; fax (91) 5551389; e-mail comunicacion@idae.es; internet www.idae.es; f. 1974 as Centro de Estudios de la Energía; under control of Secretary of State for Energy, Industrial Devlopment and Small and Medium Enterprises, Ministry of the Economy and Finance; Dir-Gen. MARÍA ISABEL MONREAL PALOMINO.

Electricity

In 2001 Spain and Portugal signed an agreement on the establishment of an integrated electricity market, the Mercado Ibérico de Electricidade (MIBEL), to be introduced incrementally by 2006.

Asociación Española de la Industria Eléctrica (UNESA): Francisco Gervás 3, 28020 Madrid; tel. (91) 5674800; fax (91) 5674987; e-mail info@unesa.es; internet www.unesa.es; f. 1944; groups principal electricity cos; Pres. IÑIGO DE ORIOL; Dir-Gen. PEDRO RIVERO.

Comisión Nacional de Energía (CNE): Alcalá 47, 28014 Madrid; tel. (91) 4329600; fax (91) 5776218; e-mail dre@cne.es; internet www .cne.es; Pres. MARÍA TERESA COSTA.

Red Eléctrica de España (REE): Paseo del Conde de los Gaitanes 177, 28109 La Moraleja (Madrid); tel. (91) 6508500; fax (91) 6504542; internet www.ree.es; manages and operates the national grid; Chair. LUIS ATIENZA; Dir-Gen. VICTORIANO CASSIÚS DÍAZ.

Principal Electricity Companies

Endesa, SA: Príncipe de Vergara 187, 28002 Madrid; tel. (91) 5668625; fax (91) 5668655; internet www.endesa.es; f. 1983; generator, distributor and vendor of electricity; also provides gas; negotiating merger with Gas Natural in early 2006; Pres. MANUEL PIZARRO MORENO; CEO RAFAEL MIRANDA.

Hidroeléctrica del Cantábrico, SA (Hidrocantábrico): Plaza de la Gesta 2, 33007 Oviedo; tel. (98) 5230300; internet www.hcenergia .com; f. 1919; generator, distributor and vendor of electricity; also provides gas; owned by Electricidade de Portugal; Pres. MANUEL MENÉNDEZ MENÉNDEZ.

Iberdrola, SA: Hermosilla 3, 28001 Madrid; tel. (91) 5776565; fax (91) 5777101; internet www.iberdrola.es; generator, distributor and vendor of electricity; supplies mainly hydroelectric power; also provides gas; Pres. IÑIGO DE ORIOL Y IBARRA; CEO JAVIER HERRERO.

Unión Fenosa, SA: Avda San Luis 77, 28033 Madrid; tel. (91) 5676000; fax (91) 5676658; e-mail unionfenosa@unionfenosa.es; internet www.unionfenosa.es; generator, distributor and vendor of electricity; also provides gas; Chair. PEDRO LÓPEZ JIMÉNEZ; Sec.-Gen. RAMÓN NOVO.

Viesgo: Medio 12, 39003 Santander; tel. (942) 246000; fax (942) 246034; internet www.viesgo.es; f. 1906; 100% owned by Enel SpA (Italy); distributor; Pres. MIGUEL ANTOÑANZAS.

Gas

As a part of the restructuring of the sector, in 2000 the Government awarded 11 licences for the transportation of gas.

BilboGas, SA: Ledesma 10, bajos, 48001 Bilbao; tel. (94) 4354960; fax (94) 4239572; internet www.bilbogas.es; distributor of gas; Pres. IBÓN ARESO MENDUGUREN.

Compañía Española de Gas, SA: Grabador Esteve 14, 46004 Valencia; tel. (96) 3537700; distributor of gas; Dir-Gen. PEDRO SÁENZ DE SANTA MARÍA.

Donostigas, SA: Alto de Errondo 2, 20009 San Sebastián; tel. (94) 3445090; fax (94) 3455559; internet www.donostigas.es; 49% owned by Ente Vaso de la Energía; distributor of gas; Dir-Gen. GONZALO SUBIJANA.

Endesa Gas, SA: Aznar Molina 2, 50002 Zaragoza; tel. (976) 760000; fax (976) 760044; internet www.endesa.es; distributor of gas; comprises five subsidiaries; also provides electricity; Pres. AMADO FRANCO LAHOZ; Dir-Gen. FERNANDO CORTINA GONZÁLEZ.

Gas Natural SDG, SA: Avda Portal de l'Angel 22, 08002 Barcelona; tel. (93) 4025100; fax (93) 4029317; internet www.gasnatural.com; distributor of gas; also provides electricity and communications; comprises regional distribution companies; negotiating merger with Endesa in early 2006; Pres. SALVADOR GABARRÓ.

NaturGas—Sociedad de Gas de Euskadi, SA: Plaza Pío Baroja 3, 2°, 48001 Bilbao; tel. (94) 4355600; fax (94) 4249733; e-mail webnaturgas@naturgas.es; internet www.naturgas.es; f. 1982; 79.5% owned by Ente Vasco de la Energía; distributor of gas; Pres. JESÚS GOIRI BASTERRA.

Water

Aguas de Valencia, SA: Gran Vía Marqués del Turia 19, 46005 Valencia; tel. (96) 3860600; internet www.aguasdevalencia.es; water and sewerage services; Chair. V. BOLUDA FOS.

Sociedad General de Aguas de Barcelona, SA (Agbar): Torre Agbar, Avda Diagonal 211, 08009 Barcelona; tel. (93) 3422000; fax (93) 3422662; e-mail comunicacion@agbar.es; internet www.agbar.es; treatment of water and waste liquid; provision of sanitation and certification services; Chair. RICARDO FORNESA RIBÓ; Dir-Gen. ANGEL SIMÓN.

TRADE UNIONS

Central Sindical Independiente y de Funcionarios (CSI-CSIF): Fernando El Santo 17, 1° y 2°, 28010 Madrid; tel. (91) 2735900; fax (91) 2735991; e-mail presidente@csi-scif.es; internet www.csi-csif.es; Pres. DOMINGO FERNÁNDEZ VEIGUELA; Sec.-Gen. LOURDES BLANCO AMILLATEGUI.

Confederación General de Trabajo (CGT) (General Confederation of Labour): Sagunto 15, 28010 Madrid; tel. (91) 4475769; fax (91) 4453132; e-mail spcc.cgt@cgt.es; internet www.cgt.es; Sec.-Gen. ELADIO VILLANUEVA SARAVIA.

Confederación Intersindical Galega (CIG): Rua Miguel Ferro Caaveiro 10, 3°, 15073 Santiago de Compostela; tel. (981) 564300; fax (981) 571082; e-mail secretarioxeral@galizacig.net; internet www.galizacig.com; Galician confederation; Sec.-Gen. XÉSUS E. SEIXO FERNÁNDEZ.

Confederación Nacional del Trabajo (CNT) (National Confederation of Labour): Secretariado Permanente del Comité Nacional, Imagen 8, 5°B, 41003 Sevilla; tel. (945) 257660; fax (91) 4202749; e-mail sp_cn@cnt.es; internet www.cnt.es; Sec.-Gen. RAFAEL CORRALES.

Confederación Sindical de Comisiones Obreras (CCOO) (Workers' Commissions): Fernández de la Hoz 12, 28010 Madrid; tel. (91) 7028000; fax (91) 3104804; e-mail ccoo@ccoo.es; internet www.ccoo.es; f. 1956; independent left-wing; Sec.-Gen. JOSÉ MARÍA FIDALGO; 1,050,000 mems (2005).

Eusko Langilleen Alkartasuna/Solidaridad de Trabajadores Vascos (ELA/STV) (Basque Workers' Solidarity): Barrainkua 13, Apdo 1391, 48009 Bilbao; tel. (94) 4037700; fax (94) 4037777; e-mail fundm001@sarenet.es; internet www.ela-sindikatua.org; f. 1911; legally recognized 1977; independent; Sec.-Gen. JOSÉ ELORRIETA AURREKOETXEA; 110,000 mems.

Unión General de Trabajadores (UGT) (General Union of Workers): Hortaleza 88, 28004 Madrid; tel. (91) 5897601; fax (91) 5897603; e-mail info@cec.ugt.org; internet www.ugt.es; f. 1888; eight affiliated federations; Sec.-Gen. CÁNDIDO MÉNDEZ; 738,000 mems (2002).

Unión Sindical Obrera (USO) (Workers' Trade Union): Príncipe de Vergara 13, 7°, 28001 Madrid; tel. (91) 5774113; fax (91) 5772959; e-mail uso@uso.es; internet www.uso.es; f. 1960; independent; Sec.-Gen. BENITO LÓPEZ GONZÁLEZ; 105,000 mems.

Transport

RAILWAYS

In August 2000 it was announced that rail transport was to be liberalized by 2008, with private operators using the state rail infrastructure. In January 2001 Spain and Portugal agreed on the route of a high-speed train to be built, linking the two countries. The infrastructure was to be completed by 2008. A high-speed link from Madrid to the French border, via Barcelona, was scheduled to be completed in 2009. There were also plans for a high-speed link between Madrid and Valencia, and a new railway between Valencia and the Basque Country. From January 2005 the state railway company, RENFE, was divided into an operating and a management division, and the goods transport sector was open to competition. RENFE's monopoly on passenger transport was to end in 2010. In 2005 the total rail network was 12,624.5 km, 483.7 km of which was high-speed track.

Administrador de Infraestructuras Ferroviarias (Adif): Paseo del Rey 30, 28008 Madrid; tel. (91) 3008080; e-mail rrhh@adif.es; internet www.infraestructuras-ferroviarias.com; f. 2005; state-owned; fmrly part of state-owned railway company, Red Nacional de los Ferrocarriles Españoles (RENFE); manages railway infrastructure following liberalization of rail sector in 2005; Pres. ANTONIO GONZÁLEZ MARÍN; Sec.-Gen. MARÍA ROSA SANZ CEREZO.

RENFE Operadora: Avda Pío XII 110, 28036 Madrid; tel. (91) 3006600; e-mail comunicacion@renfe.es; internet www.renfe.es; f. 2005 following liberalization of railway sector; fmrly Red Nacional de los Ferrocarriles Españoles (RENFE); state owned; Pres. JOSÉ SALGUEIRO CARMONA; Sec.-Gen. JOSÉ L. MARROQUÍN MOCHALES.

Eusko Trenbideak—Ferrocarriles Vascos (ET/FV), SA (EuskoTren): Atxuri 6, 48006 Bilbao; tel. (94) 4019900; fax (94) 4019901; e-mail attcliente@euskotren.es; internet www.euskotren.es; f. 1982; controlled by the Basque Government; 188 km of 1,000 mm gauge; passengers carried 25.6m. (1995); Dir-Gen. JOSÉ MIGUEL MÚGICA PERAL.

Ferrocarriles de Vía Estrecha (Feve) (Narrow Gauge Railways): Plaza de los Ferroviarios, 33012 Oviedo; tel. (98) 5297656; fax (98) 5281708; e-mail info@feve.es; internet www.feve.es; f. 1965; by integration of private companies; operates mainly in suburban areas of northern cities; 1,194 km (2006) of narrow-gauge track (of which 317 km were electrified); Pres. EUGENIO DAMBORIENA Y OSA; Dir-Gen. JUAN DE LA CRUZ PACHECO.

Ferrocarrils de la Generalitat de Catalunya (FGC): Pau Casals 24, 8°, 08021 Barcelona; tel. (93) 3663000; fax (93) 3663350; e-mail rrpp@fgc.net; internet www.fgc.net; f. 1979; 290 km, of which 161 km are electrified; Pres. JOAN TORRES I CAROL.

Ferrocarrils de la Generalitat de Valencia (FGV): Partida de Xirivelleta, 46014 Valencia; tel. (96) 3976565; fax (96) 3976580; e-mail webmaster_fgv@gva.es; internet www.fgv.es; f. 1986; 228 km of track; also operates Metro Valencia, with four lines and 134 km of line, and Tram Alicante (43 km); Pres. JOSÉ RAMÓN GARCÍA ANTÓN; Dir-Gen. MARISA GRACIA GIMÉNEZ.

Metro de Bilbao: Navarra 2, 48001 Bilbao; tel. (94) 4254000; e-mail info@metrobilbao.net; internet www.metrobilbao.net; f. 1995; Dir-Gen. JOSU SAGASTAGOITIA.

Metro de Madrid: Cavanilles 58, 28007 Madrid; tel. 902 444403; fax (91) 7212957; e-mail prensa@metromadrid.es; internet www.metromadrid.es; 13 lines; Pres. MANUEL MELIS MAYNAR; Dir ILDEFONSO DE MATÍAS JÍMENEZ.

Transports Metropolitans de Barcelona (TMB): Carrer 60, 21–31, Sector A. Polígon industrial Zona Franca, 08040 Barcelona; tel. (93) 2987000; e-mail tmb@tmb.net; internet www.tmb.net; five lines.

Association

Fundación de los Ferrocarriles Espanoles: Santa Isabel 44, 28012 Madrid; tel. (91) 1511024; fax (91) 1511066; internet www.vialibre.org; foundation of Spanish railways; mems: RENFE Operadora, Eusko Tren, FEVE, FGC, FGV, GIF, Metro Bilbao, Metro de Madrid and TMB.

ROADS

The total road network at December 2002 was 676,598 km, including 11,406 km of motorway and 24,641 km of main roads. By the end of 2004 there were 12,440 km of motorway and 25,155 km of main roads.

Dirección General de Carreteras: Paseo de la Castellana 67, 28071 Madrid; tel. (91) 5977000; fax (91) 5978535; Dir-Gen. JUAN FRANCISCO LAZCANO ACEDO.

Empresa Nacional de Autopistas (ENA): Paseo de la Castellana 83–85, 4°, 28046 Madrid; tel. (91) 5455000; fax (91) 5455432; e-mail ena@gruposyv.com; internet www.ena.es; motorway authority; privatized in 2003; Pres. JOSÉ MIGUEL ORTÍ BORDÁS.

SHIPPING

Spain has many ports. Among the most important, measured by tonnage in 2002, are Algeciras, Barcelona, Valencia, Tarragona, Bilbao, Cartagena, Gijón, Huelva and Santa Cruz de Tenerife. The 1,611 ships of the merchant fleet totalled 2,869,127 grt in December 2004.

Asociación de Navieros Españoles (ANAVE): Dr Fleming 11, 1° dcha, 28036 Madrid; tel. (91) 4580040; fax (91) 4579780; e-mail anave@anave.es; internet www.anave.es; shipowners' asscn; Pres. JUAN RIVA FRANCOS; Dir MANUEL CARLIER DE LAVALLE.

Dirección General de la Marina Mercante: Ruíz de Alarcón 1, 28014 Madrid; tel. (91) 5979118; fax (91) 5979120; Dir-Gen. FELIPE MARTÍNEZ.

Ente Público Puertos del Estado: Campo de las Naciones, Avda del Partenón 10, 28042 Madrid; tel. (91) 5245500; fax (91) 5245501; internet www.puertos.es; Pres. MARIANO NAVAS GUTIÉRREZ.

Principal Shipping Companies

Agencia Marítima Española Evge, SA: Avda Francesc Cambó 17, 8°, 08003 Barcelona; tel. (93) 2689030; fax (93) 2681750; e-mail evge@evgebcn.com; internet www.evgebcn.com; f. 1959; international shipping agents; Man. Dir RAMÓN OLIETE COSSIO.

Auxiliar Marítima, SL: Miño 4, 28002 Madrid; tel. (91) 7454300; fax (91) 7454303; e-mail central@auximar.es; f. 1957; ship management, refrigerated cargo vessels, liquefied gas tankers; Dirs IÑIGO DE SENDAGORTA, JAVIER DE SENDAGORTA.

Compañía Remolcadores Ibaizabal, SA: Muelle de Tomás Olabarri 4, 5°, 48930 Las Arenas-Getxo; tel. (94) 4645133; fax (94) 4645565; e-mail ibaizabal@sarenet.es; f. 1906; ocean-going, coastal, harbour, salvage, fire-fighting; Pres. ALEJANDRO AZNAR SAINZ; Man. Dir FRANCISCO GARAYGORDOBIL AMORRORTU.

Compañía Trasatlántica Española, SA: José Abascal 58, 3°, 28003 Madrid; tel. (91) 4514244; fax (91) 3993736; internet www.trasatlantica.com; f. 1850; freight services to Europe, North Africa, Caribbean, South America; Man. Dir JAVIER VILLASANTE.

Compañía Trasmediterránea, SA: Alcalá 61, 28014 Madrid; tel. (91) 4238500; fax (91) 4238555; internet www.transmediterranea.es; f. 1917; Spanish ports, Balearic and Canary Is and Spanish North African ports; Pres. MIGUEL ANGEL FERNÁNDEZ VILLAMANDOS; Dir-Gen. JOSÉ MANUEL FERNÁNDEZ VILLAMANDOS.

Empresa Naviera Elcano, SA: José Abascal, 4°, 28003 Madrid; tel. (91) 5369800; fax (91) 4474275; e-mail elcano@elcano.sa.es; Pres. JOSÉ SILVERA.

Ership: Don Ramón de la Cruz 13, 28001 Madrid; tel. (91) 4355620; fax (91) 5750883; fmrly TAC; Pres. GUILLERMO ZATARAÍN GUTIÉRREZ DE LA CONCHA.

Ibarra y Cía, SA: Menéndez Pelayo 4, Apdo 15, 41004 Sevilla; tel. (95) 4421658; fax (95) 4410112; f. 1881; cargo vessels to South America from Italy, France, Spain and Portugal; Pres. LUIS DE YBARRA YBARRA.

Naviera Pinillos, SA: Capitán Haya 21, 28020 Madrid; tel. (91) 5556711; fax (91) 5569777; e-mail pinillos@pinillos.com; internet www.pinillos.com; f. 1840; part of Grupo Boluda; services between Canary Is and other Spanish ports; Pres. VICENTE BOLUDA; Dir ANGEL MATO.

Nenufar Shipping, SA: Manuel Ferreo 13, 28036 Madrid; tel. (91) 3158393; fax (91) 3158384; e-mail nenufar@nenufar.com; internet www.nenufar.com; f. 1983; part of Grupo Boluda; services to Spanish ports, Canary Is, Italy, Portugal, the United Kingdom, Morocco and Mauritania.

Repsol Naviera Vizcaina, SA: Juan de Aguriaguerra 35, 2°, 48009 Bilbao; tel. (94) 4251100; fax (94) 4251143; f. 1956; world-wide, but particularly Mediterranean, Near East and Persian Gulf to Spain and transatlantic trade; Man. Dir JAVIER GONZÁLEZ JULIÁ.

CIVIL AVIATION

In 2004 there were 45 airports, almost all of which were equipped to receive international flights. A new terminal at Barájas airport in Madrid opened in 2006.

Dirección General de Aviación Civil: Paseo de la Castellana 67, 28071 Madrid; tel. (91) 5975356; fax (91) 5975357; internet www.mfom.es/aviacioncivil/; Dir-Gen. ENRIQUE SANMARTÍ AULET.

Aeropuertos Españoles y Navegación Aérea (AENA): Arturo Soria 109, 28043 Madrid; tel. (91) 3211000; fax (91) 3212571; internet www.aena.es; f. 1990; network of airports in Spain; Pres. MANUEL AZUAGA MORENO; Dir-Gen. PEDRO ARGÜELLES SALAVERÍA.

Principal Airlines

Air Europa Líneas Aéreas, SA: Centro Empresarial Globalia, POB 132, Baleares; tel. (971) 178190; fax (971) 178353; internet www.air-europa.com; f. 1986; charter and scheduled services to Canary and Balearic Islands, North Africa, Western and Northern Europe; also Thailand, Egypt, Mexico, USA, Cuba and Dominican Republic; Pres. JUAN JOSÉ HIDALGO ACERA; Dir-Gen. MANUEL PANADERO.

Air Madrid: Avda de la Industría 6–8, 28108 Alcobendas, Madrid; tel. (91) 2016010; fax (91) 2016020; e-mail airmadrid@airmadrid.com; internet www.airmadrid.com; f. 2004; low-cost airline flying to destinations in Latin America; Pres. JOSÉ LUIS CARRILLO.

Cygnus Air, SA: Aguetol 7, Barajas, 28042 Madrid; tel. (91) 3293031; fax (91) 3966899; e-mail cygnus@gestair.es; f. 1998; part of Grupo Gestair; freight services; Pres. JESÚS MACARRÓN; Gen. Man. FRANCISCO BERNALTE.

Futura International Airways (Compañía Hispano-Irlandesa de Aviación): Gran Vía Asima 17, 07009 Palma de Mallorca; tel. (971) 432053; fax (971) 434401; e-mail comercial@futura-aer.com; internet www.futura-aer.com; charter services within Europe.

Gestair Executive Jet, SA: Aguetol 7, Barajas, 28042 Madrid; tel. (91) 3290500; fax (91) 3293323; e-mail infoair@gestair.es; internet www.gestair.es; f. 1977; air-taxi operator, domestic and international services; part of Grupo Gestair; Pres. JESÚS MACARRÓN; Man. Dir CESÁR PITA.

Grupo Iberia: Velazquez 130, 28006 Madrid; tel. (91) 5877462; fax (91) 5877949; e-mail prensaintl@iberia.es; internet www.iberia.com; f. 1927; domestic and international passenger and freight services to 101 destinations in 40 countries; partner in airline alliance OneWorld; Chair. and CEO FERNANDO CONTE; Chief Operating Officer ANGEL MULLOR PARRONDO.

Binter Canarias, SA: Aeropuerto de Gran Canaria, Parcela 9, del ZIMA Apdo 50, Gran Canaria; tel. (928) 579601; fax (928) 579603; e-mail info@bintercanarias.es; internet www.bintercanarias.com; f. 1988; scheduled services within Canary Islands and to Madeira; Pres. ANGEL MULLOR PARRONDO; Dir-Gen. LUIS GREGORIO GARCÍA RUIZ.

Iberia Regional/Air Nostrum: Avda Comarques del País Valencià 2, 46930 Quart de Poblet (Valencia); tel. (96) 1960200; fax (96) 1960218; e-mail direccion@airnostrum.es; internet www.airnostrum.es; f. 1996; domestic scheduled passenger and freight services; Chair. CARLOS BERTOMEU; Pres. EMILIO SERRATOSA.

Iberworld Airlines, SA: Gran Vía Asima 23, Polígono Son Castelló, 07009 Palma de Mallorca; tel. (91) 229144; fax (91) 713184; e-mail iberworld@iberworld.com; internet www.iberworld.com; charter flights from Spanish islands to rest of Europe.

LTE International Airways, SA (also known as Volar Airlines): Carrer del Ter 27, 07009 Palma de Mallorca; tel. (971) 475700; fax (971) 478886; e-mail dgeneral@lte.es; f. 1987; charter flights between Spanish islands and Europe; Pres. JOSÉ M. GOYA; Dir CASIMIRO BERMÚDEZ.

Oasis International Airlines: Madrid; f. 1986; fmrly Andalus Air; charter services to Europe, Canary Islands and Caribbean; Pres. and Gen. Man. ANTONIO MARA.

Pan Air Líneas Aéreas, SA: Edif. TNT, 2°, Centro de Cargo Aérea, Aeropuerto de Madrid-Barajas, 28022 Madrid; tel. (91) 3120422; fax (91) 3120440; f. 1987; international and domestic freight charter; Pres. (vacant).

Spanair: Aeropuerto de Palma, Apdo 50.086, Palma de Mallorca; tel. (971) 745020; fax (971) 492553; e-mail spanair@spanair.es; internet www.spanair.com; f. 1986; passenger scheduled and charter services within Spain, incl. Canary and Balearic Islands and within Europe; owned by Teinver and Scandinavian Airlines System; Pres. GONZALO PASCUAL; Dir-Gen. LARS NYGAARD.

Vueling Airlines, SA: Edif. Muntadas, Berguedà 1, Parque de Negocios Mas Blau, El Prat de Llobregat, 08820 Barcelona; tel. (93) 3787878; fax (93) 3787879; e-mail clients@vueling.com; internet www.vueling.com; f. 2004; low-cost airline; domestic and international flights; Pres. JOSEP MIQUEL ABAD; CEO CARLOS MUÑOZ.

Tourism

Spain's tourist attractions include its climate, beaches and historic cities. Tourism makes an important contribution to the country's economy. In 2005 55.6m. foreign tourists visited Spain. Receipts from tourism totalled an estimated €46,060m. in that year.

Instituto de Turismo de España (Turespaña): José Lázaro Galdiano 6, 28071 Madrid; tel. (91) 3433500; e-mail infosmile@tourspain.es; internet www.tourspain.es; promotes tourism; offices in Spain and abroad; Dir-Gen. AMPARO FERNÁNDEZ GONZÁLEZ.

Secretaria de Estado de Comercio y Turismo: Paseo de la Castellana 160, 28071 Madrid; fax (91) 4578066; internet www.mcx.es; Sec. PEDRO MEJÍA GÓMEZ.

SPANISH EXTERNAL TERRITORIES

The Spanish External Territories comprise mainly Ceuta and Melilla, two enclaves within Moroccan territory on the north African coast. Attached to Melilla, for administrative purposes, are Peñón de Vélez de la Gomera, a small fort on the Mediterranean coast, and two groups of islands, Peñón de Alhucemas and the Chafarinas. Ceuta and Melilla are seen as integral parts of Spain by the Spanish Government and have the status of autonomous cities, although Morocco has put forward a claim to both. Sovereignty over the uninhabited island of Perejil (known as Laila to the Moroccans) is disputed between Spain and Morocco.

CEUTA

Introductory Survey

Location, Climate, Language, Religion

Ceuta, one of the two main enclaves of Spanish North Africa, is situated on the north African coast opposite Gibraltar, the Strait here being about 25 km wide. The average temperature is 17°C. Spanish and Arabic are spoken. Most Europeans are Roman Catholic, most North Africans being Muslim. There are small Hindu and Jewish communities.

Recent History

The population of the enclave is mostly Spanish. The proportion of Arab residents, however, has increased, owing to the large number of illegal immigrants from Morocco. Those born in the territory are Spanish citizens and subjects. An ancient port and walled city, Ceuta was retained by Spain upon Moroccan independence from France in 1956. Having developed as a military and administrative centre for the former Spanish Protectorate in Morocco, Ceuta now functions as a bunkering and fishing port. In 1974 the town became the seat of the Capitanía General de Africa. Two-thirds of Ceuta's land area are used exclusively for military purposes.

In November 1978 King Hassan of Morocco stated his country's claim to Ceuta and the other main Spanish enclave in North Africa, Melilla, a claim that was reiterated following the opening of the Spanish frontier with Gibraltar in early 1985. In October 1981 Spain declared before the UN that Ceuta and Melilla were integral parts of Spanish territory. Spain rejects any comparison between the two enclaves and Gibraltar. From 1984 there was increasing unease over Spanish North Africa's future, following rioting in Morocco in January and the signing of the treaty of union between Libya and Morocco in August. In July 1985 the joint Libyan-Moroccan assembly passed a resolution calling for the 'liberation' of Ceuta and Melilla.

Details of Ceuta and Melilla's new draft statutes, envisaging the establishment of two local assemblies, with jurisdiction over such matters as public works, agriculture, tourism, culture and internal trade, were announced in August 1985 and approved by the central Government in December. Unlike Spain's other regional assemblies, however, those of Ceuta and Melilla were not to be vested with legislative powers. After negotiations with representatives of the Muslim community, in May 1986 the central Government in Madrid agreed to grant Spanish nationality to more than 2,400 Muslims resident in the enclaves. At the general election held in June the ruling Partido Socialista Obrero Español (PSOE) was successful in Ceuta.

In February 1988 it was announced that, in accordance with regulations of the European Community (EC, now European Union—EU, see p. 228), to which Spain had acceded in 1986, Moroccan citizens would in due course require visas to enter Spain. Entry to Spanish North Africa, however, was to be exempt from the new ruling.

In March 1988, after several months of negotiations, the central Government and principal opposition parties in Madrid reached a broad consensus on draft autonomy statutes for Spanish North Africa. Although it was envisaged that Spain would retain the territories, the possibility of a negotiated settlement with Morocco was not discounted. In July, seven years after the enclaves' first official request for autonomy, the central Government announced that the implementation of the territories' autonomy statutes was to be accelerated. Meanwhile, in October Morocco's Minister of Foreign Affairs formally presented his country's claim to Ceuta and Melilla to the UN General Assembly. In 1989 Spain and Morocco agreed to hold annual summit meetings in an effort to improve relations. At the general election held in October 1989 the ruling PSOE retained its Ceuta seats, despite allegations by the opposition Partido Popular (PP) that many names on the electoral register were duplicated.

In April 1990 the Spanish Government presented the autonomy statutes for discussion in the territories. It was confirmed that the enclaves were to remain an integral part of Spain, and that they were to be granted self-government at municipal, rather than regional, level. Moroccan political parties were united in their denunciation of what they considered an attempt to legalize Spanish possession of the territories. The draft autonomy statutes of Ceuta and Melilla were submitted to the Congreso de los Diputados (Congress of Deputies) in Madrid for discussion in October 1991. In November thousands of demonstrators, many of whom had travelled from the enclaves, attended a protest march in Madrid (organized by the Governments of Ceuta and Melilla), in support of demands for full autonomy for the territories. In early 1992, however, the central Government confirmed that the assemblies of Ceuta and Melilla were not to be granted full legislative powers. At the general election of June 1993 the PSOE of Ceuta lost its one seat in the Congreso and its two seats in the Senado (Senate) to the PP.

The final statutes of autonomy were approved by the Spanish Government in September 1994, in preparation for their presentation to the Cortes (parliament). The statutes provided for 25-member local assemblies with powers similar to those of the municipal councils of mainland Spain. Each assembly would elect from among its members a city president. The proposals for limited self-government were not well received in Ceuta where, in October, a general strike received widespread support, while demonstrations subsequently took place in both Ceuta and Madrid. Following their approval by the Congreso de los Diputados in December, the autonomy statutes were ratified by the Senado in February 1995. Approval of the statutes by the Spanish Cortes was denounced by Morocco, which declared that the recovery of Ceuta and Melilla was to be one of its major objectives.

Elections for the new local assemblies were held in May 1995. In Ceuta the PP won nine of the 25 seats, Progreso y Futuro de Ceuta (PFC) six, the nationalist Ceuta Unida (CEU) four and the PSOE three. Basilio Fernández López of the PFC was re-elected Mayor/President, heading a coalition with CEU and the PSOE. Mustafa Mizziam Ammar, leader of the Partido Democrático y Social de Ceuta (PDSC), became the first Muslim candidate ever to be elected in the territory. Fewer than 57% of those eligible voted in the polls.

In February 1996 the Spanish and Moroccan Prime Ministers met in Rabat, Morocco, for their first summit meeting since December 1993. At the general election held in March 1996 the three PP delegates to the Cortes in Madrid were re-elected. In July Mayor/President Fernández López resigned after seven months at the head of a minority administration, and was replaced by Jesús Fortes Ramos of the PP, who urged that the enclave be considered a fully autonomous region.

In mid-1996 attention focused once again on the issue of illegal immigration from Africa. Both Ceuta and Melilla appealed to the EU for financial assistance to counter the problems arising from the enclaves' attractive location as an entry point to Europe and from the recent implementation of the EU's Schengen Agreement permitting the free movement of persons among the accord's signatory countries. Negotiations in Madrid in October between the Spanish Minister of the Interior and his Moroccan counterpart resulted in an agreement on the establishment of two joint commissions to address the specific problems of illegal immigration and drugs-trafficking. At further discussions in December, for the first time since the signing of a joint accord in 1992, Morocco agreed to the readmission of illegal immigrants held in the Spanish enclaves. In September the Secretary-General of NATO confirmed that Ceuta and Melilla would remain outside the alliance's sphere of protection if Spain were to be fully integrated into NATO's military structure.

At the elections of June 1999 the most successful party was the Grupo Independiente Liberal (GIL), which secured 12 of the 25 seats in the Assembly. Antonio Sampietro Casarramona of the GIL replaced Jesús Fortes Ramos of the PP as Mayor/President in August, following the latter's removal from office by a motion of censure supported by a rebel PSOE deputy, Susana Bermúdez. The defection to the GIL of the socialist deputy was ostensibly due to the PSOE's apparent refusal to allocate her the education and culture portfolio, as desired. The authorities subsequently announced that a judicial inquiry into the defection of Bermúdez was to be conducted. Both the PSOE and the PP accused the GIL of having bribed the deputy to transfer her allegiance. In March 2000 Sampietro and Bermúdez were charged with bribery. At the general election held on 12 March Ceuta's three PP representatives in Madrid, one deputy and two senators, all secured re-election.

In early 1999 it was conceded that the security barrier along Ceuta's border with Morocco was proving inadequate. The EU-funded project had been initiated five years previously but remained unfinished. Between January and July alone a total of 21,411 illegal immigrants were apprehended on Ceuta's frontier and returned to Morocco. In November border security was reinforced by the army. Further improvements to the barrier were completed in February 2000. The implementation in that month of new legislation relating to immigrants' rights obliged the border post at Ceuta to provide legal assistance to those being denied entry to Spain by the police. In May the Government of Ceuta estimated that more than 25,000 potential immigrants, mainly Moroccans, were concentrated on the North African coast, awaiting an opportunity to travel to southern Spain. It was also revealed that during 1999 a total of 700,000 illegal immigrants had been refused admission to Spanish North Africa.

In Morocco, meanwhile, King Hassan died in July 1999. In January 2000, in the first visit by a Spanish premier in 19 years, Prime Minister José María Aznar López visited Ceuta and Melilla, describing the enclaves as constant parts of Spain's future. Morocco subsequently cancelled a scheduled official visit of the Spanish Minister of Foreign Affairs (although the official reason given by the Moroccan authorities for the cancellation was that King Muhammad was on holiday). In May Aznar declared that the controversial immigration law, which had taken effect in February, would need to be reviewed, as, since its entry into force, more than 82,000 immigrants had applied for Spanish residency permits. Large numbers of immigrants continued to enter the two enclaves illegally throughout 2000, and further clashes between migrants and the security forces were reported. The immigration law reforms, which entered into force on 23 January 2001, intended to assist those seeking asylum but offered severe penalties to illegal immigrants and to traffickers in and employers of illegal immigrants. Protests against the reforms were staged in Spanish North Africa, as in Spain.

In early September 2000, following a ruling in the Spanish courts that Ceuta and Melilla could not be considered to be autonomous communities, the ruling GIL proposed in the Ceuta Assembly that the Spanish Government grant Ceuta greater autonomy. Discussions on the proposal, which proved highly emotive, led to disturbances within the Assembly. However, the motion was subsequently carried by a majority vote.

In early January 2001 five Ceuta councillors resigned their posts and announced their departure from the GIL, thus depriving the party of its majority in the Assembly. Former PSOE deputy Bermúdez subsequently withdrew her support for the GIL which had previously enabled the party to assume office. A motion of censure was subsequently brought against Sampietro by the PP, the PSOE, the PDSC and one of the former GIL councillors, Aida Pietra. The motion was carried on 10 February, with the support of 17 of the 25 deputies, and Juan Jesús Vivas Lara of the PP was appointed Mayor/President of Ceuta. A new Council was subsequently announced, including the five 'rebel' councillors (now members of the Grupo Mixto). There was controversy in late July when the Vice-President of the Council, Jesús Simarro Marín resigned, ostensibly for personal and political reasons. Cristina Bernal Dúran was subsequently appointed to replace him.

The Government announced in September 2001 that the identification papers of Moroccans wishing to enter Ceuta and Melilla would be examined more closely and increased the police presence at the frontiers. In mid-August the human rights organization Amnesty International had accused the Spanish Government of the systematic abuse of the rights of homeless children from Morocco and Algeria, citing Melilla and Ceuta as regions where the worst offences occurred.

Relations with Morocco remained tense in late 2001, especially following that country's abrupt withdrawal of its ambassador from Madrid in October. A confrontation developed between Moroccan and Spanish police at the end of December when the Spanish authorities attempted to seize a vessel, allegedly laden with narcotics, which the Moroccans had already been pursuing through their own waters. In February 2002 the Spanish Ministry of Foreign Affairs rejected the Moroccan Government's comparison of the status of Ceuta and Melilla with that of Gibraltar, as talks between the Spanish and British governments regarding the British territory progressed. Relations were threatened again in July, after the occupation of Perejil, a small islet near Ceuta, by 12 Moroccan soldiers. Madrid made a formal protest to Rabat on 12 July, but Morocco refused to withdraw its men, claiming that Perejil (known as Laila to the Moroccans) had been a part of Morocco since independence in 1956. Four Spanish gunboats were dispatched to patrol the locality and Spanish soldiers reoccupied the island on 17 July. A subsequent US-mediated arrangement resulted in agreement by both countries to leave the islet unoccupied, although issues regarding the sovereignty of Ceuta and Melilla continued to be problematic.

Indeed, in September Morocco reasserted its claims to the enclaves at the UN. Later in the month Morocco additionally accused Spain of violating its airspace and territorial waters more than 90 times since July, and cancelled a scheduled meeting with Spain in protest against the alleged landing of a Spanish military helicopter on Perejil; Spain denied the claim. In response to several border incidents and in an attempt to halt illegal immigration, Spain ordered the permanent closure of the border with Morocco at Benzu in October; since this border was the principal commercial route from Morocco into Ceuta, there were some local fears that trade would be threatened and that the only official entrance, at Tarajal, would be placed under additional pressure.

A bilateral immigration accord signed by Spain and Morocco in February 2003 proposed the repatriation to Morocco of 200 illegal immigrant minors from Ceuta and Melilla in March. Early 2003 saw an increase in measures to strengthen border security. Moreover, a series of suicide bombings launched against Western targets in Casablanca in mid-May, killing up to 45 people, resulted in a further tightening of border security. It was believed that one of the leaders of the militant Islamist group thought to be responsible for the attacks was a resident of Ceuta, and that others involved in the bombings had subsequently fled to mainland Spain via Ceuta. In June the Spanish Government's delegate in Ceuta initiated a request to the Ministry of Foreign Affairs in Madrid to withdraw citizenship from any dual-nationals in the enclave who were proven criminals, members of fundamentalist groups or pro-Moroccan. At the regional elections held in May 2003 the PP achieved an absolute majority in Ceuta for the first time, winning 19 out of 25 seats, while the Unión Demócratica Ceutí, which represented the Muslim population, secured three. Juan José Vivas Lara remained as Mayor/President.

In September 2003 Aznar visited Morocco for bilateral discussions, although the issue of sovereignty over Spain's North African possessions was reportedly avoided. In 2003 it was estimated that around 3,000 immigrants passed through Ceuta, and the enclave received more than 1,400 asylum requests, compared with 372 in 2002 and 82 in 2001. Official figures stated that 18% of the requests processed in 2003 were successful. In December 2003 Morocco and Spain made progress towards reaching an accord on the repatriation of illegal immigrant minors; however, a final agreement was not signed. Human rights groups criticized the two centres provided by the Spanish Government for immigrants as inadequate.

At the general election held on 14 March 2004 the PP retained the deputy and senators elected by Ceuta. In September the Mayor/President, Juan Jesús Lara, met with the newly elected Spanish Prime Minister, José Luis Rodríguez Zapatero, to discuss the possible change in status of Ceuta from Ciudad Autónoma (Autonomous City) to Comunidad Autónoma (Autonomous Community), in line with other areas of Spain. In that year the height of the barrier separating Ceuta and Morocco reached 6 m. In November the central Government unveiled plans to build reception centres for immigrants on the mainland, to which illegal immigrants arrested in Ceuta and Melilla would be transported.

In 2005 potential immigrants continued to attempt to gain access to Europe through Ceuta and Melilla, with a succession of groups of would-be immigrants attempting to scale the walls separating the enclaves from Morocco. In September five would-be immigrants were killed by security forces during an attempt by some 600 people to climb the wall into Ceuta. It was announced at a Spanish-Moroccan summit held in late September in Seville, Spain, that security on both sides of the border would be increased following the attempts; however, the waves of immigration continued in early October, and more deaths resulted. Concern arose that immigrants captured by Moroccan security forces were being abandoned in Morocco's south-western desert. In October the Spanish Government authorized €3m. to improve facilities for immigrants in the enclaves. Heightened security reduced the number of attempts being made to climb the walls, but it appeared that immigrants were looking for new, and more dangerous, routes to Europe via the Canary Islands.

In October 2005 the Congreso de los Diputados in Madrid reaffirmed the integral Spanish nature of the enclaves. In early 2006 Zapatero made the first visit by a Prime Minister to the enclaves in over 25 years. His visit was condemned by the Moroccan authorities as a provocation, despite the fact that relations between Spain and Morocco had been favourable during the first two years of Zapatero's administration, with increasing co-operation on immigration issues.

Government

Following the adoption of statutes of autonomy and the establishment of local assemblies in 1995, Ceuta and Melilla remain integral parts of Spain, but have greater jurisdiction over matters such as public works, internal trade and tourism. Each enclave has its own Mayor/President. Ceuta, Melilla and the island dependencies are known as *plazas de soberanía*, fortified enclaves over which Spain has full sovereign rights. In both Ceuta and Melilla civil authority is vested in an official (Delegado del Gobierno) directly responsible to the Ministry of the Interior in Madrid. This official is usually assisted by a government sub-delegate. There is also one delegate from each of

SPANISH EXTERNAL TERRITORIES — Ceuta

the Ministries in Madrid. In 2005 the two enclaves were seeking to change their status from that of Ciudades Autónomas (Autonomous Cities) to Comunidades Autónomas (Autonomous Communities).

Defence
Military authority is vested in a commandant-general. The enclaves are attached to the military region of Sevilla. Spain had 8,100 troops deployed in its North African territories in August 2003.

Economic Affairs
In 2004 the gross domestic product (GDP) of Ceuta totalled an estimated €1,388.4m., equivalent to €17,548 per head. In that year GDP per head was equivalent to 89.4% of the average for Spain. In 2004 the city ranked 12th in terms of GDP per head in a list of the 17 Autonomous Communities, together with Ceuta and Melilla. The population of Ceuta increased by 0.04% in 2000–04, while GDP grew by 5.7% during that period, and by 7.0% in 2004.

Agricultural activity in Ceuta is negligible, and industry is on a limited scale. There is a local brewery. In 2004 the economically active population totalled 29,500, of whom 3,000 were unemployed. In that year, from a total labour force in Ceuta and Melilla of 58,600, 325 were employed in the agricultural sector, 5,300 in industry (including 3,675 in the construction sector), and 45,175 were employed in the services sector.

Most of the population's food is imported, with the exception of fish, which is obtained locally. Sardines and anchovies are the most important items. A large proportion of the tinned fish is sold outside Spain. More important to the economies of Ceuta and Melilla is the port activity; most of their exports take the form of fuel supplied—at very competitive rates—to ships. Most of the fuel comes from the Spanish refinery in Tenerife. Ceuta's port received a total of 8,785 ships in 2004. The main exports are frozen and preserved fish, foodstuffs and beer. Most trade is conducted with other parts of Spain. In 2003 Ceuta's trade deficit was €25,087m. Tourism makes a significant contribution to the territory's economy. In 2004 68,205 tourists visited Ceuta, attracted by duty-free goods. The average annual rate of inflation was 3.5% in 2004 and 2.5% in 2005.

Upon the accession in January 1986 of Spain to the European Community (EC, now European Union—EU, see p. 228), Ceuta was considered a Spanish city and therefore as European territory, and joined the organization as part of Spain. It retained its status as a free port. The statute of autonomy, adopted in early 1995, envisaged the continuation of the territory's fiscal benefits. Euro notes and coins became the sole legal tender on 28 February 2002.

The successive enlargements of the EU that took place in 2004 and were planned for 2007 were to limit Spain's access to EU aid, with Ceuta no longer to be eligible for support. An Action Plan for Ceuta was launched in late 2002, providing for €71m. in investment by mainland Spain to reduce the enclave's dependence upon Morocco.

Education
The education system is similar to that of mainland Spain; however, there are also teachers of the Islamic religion in the city.

Statistical Survey

Sources (unless otherwise stated): Administración General del Estado, Beatriz de Silva 4, 51001 Ceuta; tel. (956) 512616; fax (956) 511893; Instituto Nacional de Estadística, Paseo de la Castellana 183, 28071 Madrid; tel. (91) 5839100; fax (91) 5839158; internet www.ine.es; *Memoria Socioeconómico y Laboral de 2004*: Consejo Económico y Social, Edif. La Tahoma, Esquina Salud Tejero y Dueñas, Ceuta; tel. (956) 519131; fax (956) 519146; e-mail ces-ceuta@ceuta.es.

AREA AND POPULATION

Area: 19.7 sq km (7.6 sq miles).

Population (census results): 67,615 at 1 March 1991; 71,505 at 1 November 2001 (males 35,991, females 35,514). *2005* (official estimate at 1 January): 75,276 (males 38,315, females 36,961).

Density (1 January 2005): 3,821 per sq km.

Births, Marriages and Deaths (2004): Live births 1,061 (birth rate 14.9 per 1,000); Marriages 374 (marriage rate 5.2 per 1,000); Deaths 491 (death rate 6.9 per 1,000).

Expectation of Life (Ceuta and Melilla, years at birth, 2000): Males 74.7; Females 81.3.

Immigration and Emigration (2004): Immigrants 1,632; Emigrants 2,656.

Economically Active Population (2004): *Ceuta and Melilla:* Agriculture, hunting, forestry and fishing 325; Industry 5,300 (Construction 3,675); Services 45,175; Total employed 50,800; Unemployed 7,800; Total labour force 58,600. *Ceuta:* Total employed 26,500; Unemployed 3,000; Total labour force 29,500.

AGRICULTURE, ETC.

Livestock (animals slaughtered, 2004): Sheep 1,025; Goats 108.

Fishing (metric tons, live weight of catch): 304.1 in 2002; 310.8 in 2003; 236.8 in 2004.

FINANCE

Currency and Exchange Rates: 100 cent = 1 euro (€). *Sterling and Dollar Equivalents* (30 December 2005): £1 Sterling = 1.4596 euros; US $1 = 0.8477 euros; 100 euros = £68.51 = $117.97. *Average Exchange Rate* (euros per US $): 0.8860 in 2003; 0.8054 in 2004; 0.8041 in 2005. Note: The local currency was formerly the Spanish peseta. From the introduction of the euro, with Spanish participation, on 1 January 1999, a fixed exchange rate of €1 = 166.386 pesetas was in effect. Euro notes and coins were introduced on 1 January 2002. The euro and local currency circulated alongside each other until 28 February, after which the euro became the sole legal tender.

Budget (€ '000, 2004): *Revenue:* Current operations 170,621.8 (Direct taxation 6,397.6, Indirect taxation 90,247.4, Rates and other revenue 14,342.8, Current transfers 54,106.2, Estate taxes 5,527.7); Capital operations 49,002.7 (Capital transfers 31,715.2, Transfers of real investments 3,073.4, Assets 704.3, Liabilities 13,509.7); Total 219,624.5. *Expenditure:* Current operations 153,214.7 (Wages and salaries 74,948.9, Goods and services 55,016.6, Financial 3,561.4, Current transfers 19,687.8); Capital operations 65,659.8 (Real investments 53,365.5, Capital transfers 0.0, Assets 1,705.0, Liabilities 10,589.2); Total 218,874.5.

Cost of Living (Consumer Price Index; base: 2001 = 100): 107.2 in 2003; 110.9 in 2004; 113.7 in 2005.

Gross Domestic Product (€ million, provisional): 1,235.9 in 2002; 1,304.3 in 2003; 1,388.4 in 2004.

Gross Domestic Product by Economic Activity (€ million, 2004, provisional): Agriculture, hunting, forestry and fishing 3.6; Energy 46.8; Industry 30.9; Construction 88.8; Services 955.0; *Sub-total* 1,125.2; Net taxes on products 125.5; *GDP at market prices* 1,250.6.

EXTERNAL TRADE

Principal Commodities (€ '000, 2004): *Imports:* Fuel, lubricants, etc. 29,859; Milk and dairy products 29,797; Textile and clothing 34,706; Transport vehicles 10,023; Total (incl. others) 191,145. *Exports:* Machines 21; Transport vehicles 4; Total 166,058.

Principal Trading Partners: *Imports* (percentage of total imports, 2000): People's Republic of China 22.1; Germany 5.5; Indonesia 4.5; Italy 14.0; Netherlands 10.1; Russia 4.4; Republic of Korea 13.4; United Kingdom 3.7. *Exports:* In 2001 the most important export partners were the Republic of Korea, Morocco, Japan, China and Argentina.

TRANSPORT

Road Traffic (2004): Vehicles registered 49,811 (Passenger cars 38,227, Buses, etc. 66, Lorries 5,384, Motorcycles 5,527, Tractors 84, Other 523).

Shipping (2004): Goods loaded 933,162 metric tons; Goods unloaded 1,134,214 metric tons; Vessels entered 8,785; Passenger arrivals 1,049,310; Passenger departures 1,096,133.

Civil Aviation (2004, by helicopter): Journeys made 1,830; Passengers carried 15,649; Goods transported 5.7 metric tons.

TOURISM

Visitor Arrivals (by country of residence, 2002): France 2,653; Germany 700; Italy 1,076; Portugal 1,062; Spain 41,593; United Kingdom 1,430; USA 2,939; Total (incl. others) 61,356. *2004:* Foreign visitors 17,243; Spanish visitors 50,962; Total visitors 68,205.

COMMUNICATIONS MEDIA

Telephones (main lines in use, 2004): 24,849.

EDUCATION

(2004/05, preliminary)

Pre-primary: 2,897 students.

Primary: 22 schools (incl. 2 exclusively pre-primary, see above); 5,925 students; 602 teachers (incl. pre-primary, see above).

Secondary: First Cycle: 16 schools (of which 6 schools also provided second-cycle education and 5 provided vocational education, see below); 3,808 students; 568 teachers (all levels, see below).

Secondary: Second Cycle: 1,262 students.

Secondary: Vocational: 948 students.

Source: Ministry of Education and Science, Madrid.

Directory

Government

Government Delegate in Ceuta: JOSÉ JENARO GARCÍA-ARRECIADO.

Deputy elected to the Congress in Madrid: FRANCISCO ANTONIO GONZÁLEZ PÉREZ (PP).

Representatives to the Senate in Madrid: NICOLÁS FERNÁNDEZ CUCURULL (PP), PEDRO GORDILLO DURÁN (PP).

Commandant-General: LUIS GÓMEZ-HORTIGÜELA.

COUNCIL OF GOVERNMENT
(May 2006)

Mayor/President: JUAN JESÚS VIVAS LARA (PP).

Councillor of Development: JUAN ANTONIO RODRÍGUEZ FERRÓN (PP).

Councillor of the Economy and Finance: EMILIO CARRERIA RUIZ (Ind.).

Councillor of Education and Culture: MARÍA ISABEL DEU DEL OLMO (PP).

Councillor of the Environment: MARÍA CAROLINA PÉREZ GÓMEZ (PP).

Councillor of Health and Social Welfare: YOLANDA BEL BLANCA (PP).

Councillor of the Interior: MANUEL CORONADO MARTÍN (Ind.).

Councillor of the Presidency: JOSÉ LUIS MORALES MONTERO (PP).

GOVERNMENT OFFICES

Delegación del Gobierno: Beatriz de Silva 4, 51001 Ceuta; tel. (956) 984400; fax (956) 513671; e-mail roberto@ceuta.map.es.

Office of the Mayor/President: Plaza de Africa s/n, Asamblea, 1°, 51001 Ceuta; tel. and fax (956) 528309; e-mail presidencia@ceuta.es; internet www.ceuta.es.

Council of Development: Plaza de Africa s/n, Asamblea, 3°, 51001 Ceuta; tel. and fax (956) 528240; e-mail fomento@ceuta.es.

Council of the Economy and Finance: Edif. Ceuta Center, 1°, 51001 Ceuta; tel. and fax (956) 528262; e-mail economia@ceuta.es; e-mail hacienda@ceuta.info.

Council of Education and Culture: Plaza de Africa s/n, Asamblea, 2°, 51001 Ceuta; tel. (956) 528153; tel. and fax (956) 528166; e-mail cultura@ceuta.es; e-mail educacion@ceuta.es.

Council of the Environment: Plaza de Africa s/n, Asamblea, 3°, 51001 Ceuta; tel. and fax (956) 528164; e-mail medioambiente@ceuta.es.

Council of Health and Social Welfare: San Amaro s/n, Ceuta; tel. and fax (956) 200680; e-mail sanidad@ceuta.es; e-mail bsocial@ceuta.es.

Council of the Interior: Edif. Polifuncional, Avda España, 51001 Ceuta; tel. (956) 528076.

Council

Election, 25 May 2003

	Seats
Partido Popular (PP)	19
Unión Demócrata Ceutí (UDCE)	3
Partido Socialista Obrero Español (PSOE)	2
Partido Democrático y Social de Ceuta (PDSC)	1
Total	**25**

Election Commission

Junta Electoral de Zona y Provincial de Ceuta: Ceuta.

Political Organizations

Ceuta Unida (CEU): Teniente Arrabal 2, Ceuta; nationalist party; Sec.-Gen. JOSÉ ANTONIO QUEROL.

Izquierda Unida (IU): General Yaque, 4-1°, 11701 Ceuta; tel. (956) 513558; fax (956) 513558; e-mail org.federal@izquierda-unida.es; internet www.izquierda-unida.es; left-wing electoral alliance; Leader MOHAMMED HADDU MUSA.

Partido Democrático y Social de Ceuta (PDSC): Bolivia 35, 51001 Ceuta; Muslim party; Leader MUSTAFA MIZZIAM AMMAR.

Partido Popular (PP): Teniente Arrabal 4, Edif. Ainara, Bajo, 51001 Ceuta; tel. (956) 511636; fax (956) 513218; e-mail ceuta@pp.es; internet www.pp.es; fmrly Alianza Popular; national-level, centre-right party; Pres. PEDRO GORDILLO DURÁN; Sec.-Gen. MARÍA DOLORES PASTILLA.

Partido Socialista Obrero Español (PSOE): Daóiz 1, 51001 Ceuta; tel. (956) 515553; internet www.psoe.es/ambito/ceuta/index.do; national-level, left-wing party; Sec.-Gen. ANTONIA MARÍA PALOMO FERNÁNDEZ.

Partido Socialista del Pueblo de Ceuta (PSPC): Carretera del Embalse 10, 51001 Ceuta; tel. and fax (956) 518869; e-mail pspc@pspc.es; internet www.pspc.es; f. 1986; dissident group of PSOE; Sec.-Gen. JOSÉ ANTONIO ALARCÓN.

Unión Demócrata Ceutí (UDCE): Avda Teniente-Coronel Gautier 22, 2° dcha, Ceuta; Muslim party; Leader MUHAMMAD ALÍ.

There are branches of the major Spanish parties in Ceuta, and also various civic associations. The Organización 21 de Agosto para la Liberación de los Territorios Marroquíes Usurpados resumed its activities in 1995 (see Recent History).

Judicial System

Tribunal Superior de Justicia de Andalucía, Ceuta y Melilla: Plaza Nueva, 10, Palacio de la Real Chancillería, 18071 Granada, Spain; tel. (958) 002600; fax (958) 002720; e-mail webmaster.ius@juntadeandalucia.es; internet www.juntadeandalucia.es; Pres. AUGUSTO MÉNDEZ DE LUGO Y LÓPEZ DE AYALA.

Religion

CHRISTIANITY

The Roman Catholic Church

Bishop of Cádiz and Ceuta: ANTONIO CEBALLOS ATIENZA (resident in Cádiz), Vicar-General FRANCISCO CORRERO TOCÓN, Obispado de Ceuta, Plaza de Nuestra Señora de Africa, 51001 Ceuta; tel. (956) 517732; fax (956) 513208; e-mail obispadoceuta@planalfa.es; internet www.obispadodecadizyceuta.org.

OTHER RELIGIONS

There are also Muslim, Jewish and Hindu communities in Ceuta.

The Press

El Faro de Ceuta: Sargento Mena 8, 51001 Ceuta; tel. (956) 524148; fax (956) 524147; e-mail ceuta@elfaro.es; internet www.elfaroceutamelilla.com; f. 1934; morning; Dir CARMEN ETXARRI PIUDO; Editor-in-Chief ROCÍO ABAD DE LOS SANTOS; circ. 5,000.

El Pueblo de Ceuta: Independencia 11, 1°, 51001 Ceuta; tel. (956) 514367; fax (956) 517650; e-mail elpuebloredaccion@telefonica.net; internet www.elpueblodeceuta.com; daily; Dir and Editor-in-Chief SALVADOR VIVANCOS CANALES.

NEWS AGENCY

Agencia EFE: Milán Astray 1, 1°, Of. 8, 51001 Ceuta; tel. (956) 517550; Correspondent RAFAEL PEÑA SOLER.

PRESS ASSOCIATION

Asociación de la Prensa: Beatriz de Silva 14, 1° E, 51001 Ceuta; fax (95) 6528205; Pres. FRANCISCO RUIZ JIMÉNEZ CARMONA.

Broadcasting

RADIO

Onda Cero Radio Ceuta: Delgado Serrano, 1, 1° Dcha, 51001 Ceuta; tel. (956) 200068; fax (956) 200179; Dir RAFAEL ROMAGUERA MENA.

Radio Televisión Ceuta: Real 90, Portón 4, 1° Dcha, 51001 Ceuta; tel. (956) 511820; fax (956) 516820; f. 1934; commercial; owned by Sociedad Española de Radiodifusión; Dir ANTONIO ROSA GUERRERO.

Radio Nacional de España: Real 90, 51001 Ceuta; tel. (956) 524688; fax (956) 519067; Dir Eduardo Sánchez Dorado.

Radio Popular de Ceuta/COPE: Sargento Mena 8, 1°, 11701 Ceuta; tel. (956) 524200; fax (956) 524202; Dir Daniel Oliva.

TELEVISION

Televisión Ceuta: Ceuta; tel. (956) 514417; Dir Manuel González Bolorino.

Finance

BANKING

In 2004 there were 11 banks operating in Ceuta.

Banco Bilbao Vizcaya Argentaria (BBVA): Plaza de los Reyes s/n, 51001 Ceuta; tel. (956) 510415; internet www.bbva.es; 4 brs.

Banco de España: Plaza de España 2, 51001 Ceuta; tel. (956) 513253; fax (956) 513108; internet www.bde.es.

Banco Español de Crédito (Banesto): Camoens 5, 51001 Ceuta; tel. (956) 524028; internet www.banesto.es.

Banco Popular Español: Paseo del Revellín 1, 51001 Ceuta; tel. (956) 515340; fax (956) 512970; internet www.bancopopular.es.

Banco Santander Central Hispano (BSCH): Paseo del Revellin 17–19, 51001 Ceuta; tel. (956) 511371; internet www.gruposantander.es; 2 brs.

Caja Duero: Sargento Coriat 5, 51001 Ceuta; tel. (956) 518040; fax (956) 517019; tel. www.cajaduero.es; 1 br.

Caja Madrid: Plaza de los Reyes s/n, 51001 Ceuta; tel. (956) 524016; fax (956) 524017; internet www.cajamadrid.es; 6 brs.

Caja Rural Intermediterránea (Cajamar): Paseo Alcalde Sanchez Prado, 51001 Ceuta; tel. (956) 516952; e-mail cajamar@cajamar.es; internet www.cajamar.es; 2 brs.

INSURANCE

MAPFRE: Cervantes 14, 51001 Ceuta; tel. (956) 519638; fax (956) 513916; internet www.mapfre.com.

Trade and Industry

Cámara Oficial de Comercio, Industria y Navegación: Dueñas 2, 51001 Ceuta; tel. (956) 509590; fax (956) 509589; e-mail sgeneralceuta@camaras.org; internet www.camaraceuta.org; chamber of commerce; Pres. Luis Moreno Naranjo; Sec.-Gen. María del Rosario Espinosa Suárez.

Confederación de Empresarios de Ceuta: Teniente Arrabal 2, 51001 Ceuta; tel. (956) 516912; employers' confederation; Pres. Miguel Angel Azcoitia León; Sec.-Gen. Evaristo Rivera Gómez.

UTILITIES

Aguas de Ceuta Empresa Municipal, SA (ACEMSA): Solis 1, Edif. San Luis, Ceuta; tel. (956) 524619; e-mail aguasdeceuta@acemsa.es; internet www.acemsa.es; Pres. María Carolina Pérez Gómez; Dir-Gen. Manuel Gómez Hoyos.

Empresa de Alumbrado Eléctrico de Ceuta SA: Beatriz de Silva 2, Ceuta; generates and transmits electricity; Rep. Alberto Ramón Gaitán Rodríguez.

TRADE UNION

Confederación Sindical de Comisiones Obreras (CCOO): Alcalde Fructuoso Miaja 1, 51001 Ceuta; tel. (956) 516243; fax (956) 517991; e-mail ccoo.ce@ceuta.ccoo.es; internet www.ccoo.es; 3,214 mems (2004); Sec.-Gen. Juan Luis Arostegui Ruiz.

Transport

Much of the traffic between Spain and Morocco passes through Ceuta; there are ferry services to Algeciras, Melilla, Málaga and Almería. Plans for an airport are under consideration. Helicopter services to Málaga are provided by Helisureste. There were 28 km of paved roads in Ceuta in 2004; in 2005 the road to Morocco was being upgraded. The Port of Ceuta is one of the most important in the Mediterranean. In 2004 2.1m. tons of goods, 2.1m. passengers and 8,785 boats passed through the port.

Port of Ceuta: Autoridad Portuaria de Ceuta, Muelle de España s/n, 51001 Ceuta; tel. (956) 527000; fax (956) 527001; e-mail apceuta@puertodeceuta.com; internet www.puertodeceuta.com.

Compañía Trasmediterránea: Muelle Cañorero Dato 6, 51001 Ceuta; tel. (956) 505390; fax (956) 522239; internet www.trasmediterranea.es; f. 1917; services between Algeciras and Ceuta.

Euroferrys: Muelle Cañorero Dato, 51001 Ceuta; tel. (956) 507070; fax (956) 505588; e-mail clientes@euroferrys.com; internet www.euroferrys.com; f. 1998; passenger and cargo services between Algeciras and Ceuta; Pres. Joaquin González Sanjuán.

Tourism

Visitors are attracted by the historical monuments, the Parque Marítimo and the museums, as well as by the Shrine of Our Lady of Africa. There were 68,205 visitors to Ceuta in 2004, of whom 50,962 were from mainland Spain. In that year Ceuta had five hotels.

Viceconsejería de Turismo de Ceuta: Baluarte de los Mallorquines, 51001 Ceuta; tel. (956) 200560; e-mail turismo@ceuta.es; internet www.ceuta.es.

Patronato Municipal de Turismo: Estación Marítima s/n, 51001 Ceuta; tel. (956) 506275.

MELILLA

Introductory Survey

Location, Climate, Language, Religion

Melilla is situated on a small peninsula jutting into the Mediterranean Sea. The average temperature is 17°C. Spanish and Arabic are spoken. Most Europeans are Roman Catholic, most North Africans being Muslim.

Recent History

The population of Melilla is mostly Spanish. The proportion of Arab residents, however, has greatly increased, owing to the large number of illegal immigrants from Morocco. Those born in the territory are Spanish citizens and subjects. Melilla was the first Spanish town to rise against the Government of the Popular Front in July 1936, at the beginning of the Spanish Civil War. Like Ceuta, Melilla was retained by Spain when Morocco became independent in 1956. In addition to its function as a port, Melilla now serves as a military base, more than one-half of the enclave's land area being used solely for military purposes. In October 1978 King Hassan of Morocco attempted to link the question of the sovereignty of Melilla to that of the return of the British dependent territory of Gibraltar to Spain. (See the chapter on Ceuta for details on Morocco's relationship with Spain and the north African enclaves.)

After negotiations with representatives of the Muslim community, in May 1986 the central Government in Madrid agreed to grant Spanish nationality to more than 2,400 Muslims resident in Melilla and Ceuta, under the terms of legislation introduced in July 1985 requiring all foreigners resident in Spain to register with the authorities. At that time only some 7,000 of the estimated 27,000-strong Muslim community in Melilla held Spanish nationality. In response to protests, particularly in Melilla, the central Government had given assurances that it would assist the full integration into Spanish society of Muslims in the enclaves. By mid-1986, however, the number of Muslims applying for Spanish nationality in Melilla had reached several thousand. As a result of delays in the processing of the applications, Aomar Muhammadi Dudú, the leader of the newly founded Muslim Partido de los Demócratas de Melilla (PDM), accused the Government of failing to fulfil its pledge to the Muslim residents.

At the general election of June 1986 the ruling Partido Socialista Obrero Español (PSOE) was defeated by the centre-right Coalición Popular (CP) in Melilla, the result indicating the strong opposition of the Spanish community to the Government's plan to integrate the Muslim population. Tight security surrounded the elections, and 'parallel elections', resulting in a vote of confidence in the PDM leader, were held by the Muslim community. Polling was accompanied by several days of unrest. Talks in Madrid between representatives of the main political parties in Melilla and the Ministry of the Interior resulted in concessions to the enclave. In September Dudú agreed to accept a senior post in the Ministry, with responsibility for relations with the Muslim communities of Spain. In November, however, Muslim leaders in Melilla announced that they wished to establish their own administration in the enclave, in view of the Madrid Government's failure to fulfil its promise of Spanish citizenship for Muslim residents. The Spanish Minister of the Interior reiterated assurances of the Government's commitment to integrating the Muslim community. Later in the month thousands of Muslims took part in a peaceful demonstration in support of Dudú, who had resigned his Madrid post after only two months in office. (He subsequently went into exile in Morocco and lost the support of Melilla's Muslim community.)

In February 1987 police reinforcements were dispatched from Spain, in response to a serious escalation of inter-racial tensions in Melilla. Numerous demonstrators were detained, and several prominent Muslims were charged with sedition and briefly held in custody. King Hassan reaffirmed his support for the Muslims of the Spanish enclaves.

In March 1988, after several months of negotiations, the central Government and main opposition parties in Madrid reached a broad consensus on draft autonomy statutes for the Spanish External Territories. (See the chapter on Ceuta for details of the statutes.)

At the general election held in October 1989 the election results were declared invalid, following the discovery of serious irregularities. At the repeated ballot, in March 1990, both seats in the Senado (Senate) and the one seat in the Congreso de los Diputados (Congress of Deputies) were won by the Partido Popular (PP), the latter result depriving the PSOE of its overall majority in the Madrid lower chamber. By 1990 almost all residents were in possession of an identity card.

At elections to the municipal council held in May 1991, the PP secured 12 of the 25 seats and Ignacio Velázquez Rivera of the right-wing Partido Nacionalista de Melilla (PNM) was elected Mayor of the enclave, replacing the previous PSOE mayor. At the general election of June 1993 the PSOE candidate defeated the incumbent PP member in the Congreso de los Diputados; the PP also lost one of its two seats in the Senado.

The final statutes of autonomy for Ceuta and Melilla were approved by the Spanish Government in September 1994, in preparation for their presentation to the Cortes (parliament—see the chapter on Ceuta). At elections for the new local assembly, held in May 1995, the level of participation was less than 62%. The PP won 14 of the 25 seats, the PSOE five seats, Coalición por Melilla (CpM), a new Muslim grouping, four seats and the right-wing Unión del Pueblo Melillense (UPM) two seats. Ignacio Velázquez (PP/PNM) returned to the position of Mayor/President.

At the general election held in March 1996, the PSOE lost its seat in the lower house to the PP, which also took both seats in the Senado. In the same month thousands of Muslims took part in a demonstration, organized by CpM, to protest against their position on the margins of society.

In March 1997 a motion of censure against Ignacio Velázquez resulted in the Mayor/President's defeat, owing to the defection to the opposition of two PP councillors, Enrique Palacios and Abdelmalik Tahar. The opposition then declared Palacios to be Mayor/President, although the central Government continued to recognize Velázquez as the rightful incumbent. In May, for the first time, the Mayor/Presidents of both Ceuta and Melilla attended a conference of the autonomous regions' presidents, held in Madrid. Despite the attempted 'coup' in Melilla, the territory was represented by Ignacio Velázquez. In November, from Tenerife, Abdelmalik Tahar accused Velázquez and five associates of having subjected him to blackmail and threats, as a result of which he had relinquished his seat on the Council, thereby permitting the PP to replace him and to regain its majority. In December Tahar, who was now under police protection, declared to the investigating judge that he had been offered 50m. pesetas (of which he had received 3m.) and a monthly sum of 200,000 pesetas. Following a judicial ruling leading to the successful revival of the motion of censure against Velázquez in February 1998, Palacios took office as Mayor/President of Melilla, accusing his predecessor of serious financial mismanagement. A new motion of censure, presented by the PP urging that (despite the bribery charges against him) Velázquez be restored to office, was deemed to be illegal and therefore rejected in a decree issued by Palacios, who also ordered the temporary closure of the local assembly. In July Palacios accused the PP of having employed public funds, amounting to more than 200m. pesetas, to secure the votes of some 2,500 Muslims at the 1995 local elections. The allegations were denied by the PP.

During 1997 there was increased concern regarding the numbers of illegal immigrants. In June police reinforcements were drafted into Melilla, following renewed disturbances in which one immigrant died. More than 100 illegal immigrants were immediately returned to Morocco as part of a special security operation, and on the same day a total of 873 Moroccans were denied entry to Melilla. (More than 10,000 Moroccans continued to cross the border legally each day, in order to work in the enclave.) In August the Spanish General Prosecutor demanded emergency measures to address the immigration crisis, having urged the Ministry of the Interior in June to find an immediate solution. In the same month various non-governmental organizations condemned the rudimentary conditions in which more than 900 illegal immigrants, mainly from sub-Saharan Africa and Algeria, were being held in Melilla. In December the Spanish Government announced that 1,206 sub-Saharan Africans were to be transferred from Ceuta and Melilla to the mainland.

In January 1999, after 12 years' exile in Morocco, Aomar Muhammadi Dudú, the former Muslim leader, returned to Melilla, in preparation for the local elections to be held in June. At the elections the Grupo Independiente Liberal (GIL), recently founded by Jesús Gil, the controversial Mayor of Marbella, Spain, secured seven of the 25 seats in the assembly of Melilla. In July the two newly elected PSOE councillors defied a central directive to vote with the five PP delegates (in order to obstruct the accession of the GIL to the city presidency), and instead gave their support to Mustafa Aberchán Hamed of the CpM, which had won five seats. The Muslim Aberchán was thus elected to replace Enrique Palacios as Mayor/President of Melilla. In mid-July Aberchán and the GIL agreed to form a minority Government. The two rebel PSOE councillors subsequently relinquished their seats. In October, following a disagreement between the CpM and the GIL, Aberchán was able to reach a broad agreement with members of the PP and UPM, enabling him to remain in office. In November the Melilla branch of the GIL announced that henceforth it was to operate independently of the mainland party. In the same month, a new agreement between Aberchán and the GIL having been concluded, the latter grouping declared its intention to renew its participation in the Government of Melilla. As a result, the socialist councillors withdrew from the administration.

In early December 1999 the Mayor/President announced the composition of a new coalition Government, the post of First Vice-President being allocated to Crispin Lozano, the local leader of the GIL, while Enrique Palacios of the newly founded Partido Independiente de Melilla (PIM) became Second Vice-President. In the same month Ignacio Velázquez, the former PP Mayor/President, was barred from public office for six years, having been found guilty of neglecting his duty during his tenure of office. The conviction was in respect of an incident in 1992 when Velázquez had convened a session of the Council, which was due to vote on a motion of censure against him, in full knowledge of the fact that at least one member was due to be in Madrid that day, thus rendering any vote invalid. However, he was acquitted of charges of misappropriation of public funds. In May 2000, following the defection to the opposition of two GIL deputies and one UPM representative, Aberchán declared that, despite the Government's loss of its majority, he would not resign. The opposition subsequently announced that they would request a vote of 'no confidence' in Aberchán's Government at the earliest opportunity. Later in the month the national leadership of the PP and the PSOE met in Madrid in an attempt to negotiate a solution to the political crisis in Melilla. The two parties agreed that, if Aberchán's Government were removed from office, they would form a coalition government in partnership with the UPM, whose leader, Juan José Imbroda Ortiz, would be nominated Mayor/President. In early July the remaining five GIL members left the Government and joined the opposition. The opposition subsequently introduced a motion of censure against Aberchán, whom they accused of nepotism, a lack of transparency and of harassment of the opposition. Aberchán, who described the accusations as being racially motivated, announced that the CpM was to withdraw from the legislature. In mid-July some 2,000 Muslim citizens of Melilla demonstrated in support of Aberchán. At the same time Palacios suspended the motion of censure by decree, reportedly without having consulted Aberchán. (Palacios was subsequently barred from public office for seven years, having been found guilty of perversion of the course of justice.) The opposition later successfully overturned the decree in the courts, and the vote on the motion of censure against Aberchán was therefore able to proceed. The motion was adopted on 17 September, with the support of 16 of the 25 deputies, and Imbroda was elected as Mayor/President. In late 2000 four members of the GIL announced their departure from the party. In January 2002 Velázquez resigned as Councillor of the Presidency, after the Supreme Court upheld his 1999 conviction.

At the regional elections held in May 2003 a coalition of the PP and the UPM won 15 seats, with the CpM taking seven. The incumbent Mayor/President, Juan José Imbroda Ortiz, remained in power. The PP's success was, in part, the result of a concerted effort to prevent the perpetuation of unstable government that had characterized the previous four years under the GIL. A rising fear of immigration was another likely factor.

In May 2004 the Government of Melilla announced plans to improve security along the border with Morocco; however, in early August, in the first mass entry for three years, approximately 450 people attempted to enter Melilla illegally by climbing the security fence. It was believed that up to 40 people succeeded in entering the territory. At the general election held on 14 March 2004, meanwhile, the PP retained Melilla. On 1 September Juan José Imbroda met the recently elected Spanish Prime Minister, José Luis Zapatero, to discuss the possibility that Melilla would become a 'Comunidad Autónoma' (Autonomous Community), a move that would give legislative powers to the government of the territory.

During August–October 2005 increasing numbers of would-be immigrants attempted to scale the security barriers separating

SPANISH EXTERNAL TERRITORIES

Melilla from Morocco, leading to the deaths of a number of people. In early October six potential immigrants were reportedly shot in clashes with Moroccan security forces. It was announced that one barrier would be doubled in height, and that border security would be increased; in October plans to build a third barrier were unveiled. In the same month the Spanish Government announced funding of €17m. for security in Mellila.

Government
See the chapter on Ceuta.

Defence
See the chapter on Ceuta.

Economic Affairs

In 2004 the gross domestic product (GDP) of Melilla totalled an estimated €1,135.8m., equivalent to €16,950 per head. An unofficial report issued in October 1996 classified Melilla as by far the poorest city in Spain; in 2004 the city ranked 10th in terms of GDP per head in a list of the 17 Autonomous Communities, together with Ceuta and Melilla. In 2004 GDP per head was equivalent to 86.3% of the Spanish average in Melilla. The population increased by an estimated 0.5% in 2000–04, while GDP grew by some 5.6% during that period. GDP increased by 7.1% in 2004.

Agricultural activity in Melilla is negligible, and industry is on a limited scale. In 2003 the economically active population of the enclave totalled 25,100, of whom 2,300 were unemployed. In 2002 2,500 were employed in the construction sector, 3,000 in industry, 200 in agriculture, hunting, forestry and fishing, and 20,400 in the services sector.

Most of the population's food is imported, with the exception of fish which is obtained locally. Sardines and anchovies are the most important items. A large proportion of the tinned fish is sold outside Spain. More important to the economies of Melilla and Ceuta is the port activity; most of their exports take the form of fuel supplied—at very competitive rates—to ships. Most of the fuel comes from the Spanish refinery in Tenerife. Apart from the ferries from Málaga and Almería in mainland Spain, Melilla's port is not busy—a total of 1,032 vessels entered in 2004—and its exports are correspondingly low. Most trade is conducted with other parts of Spain. Tourism makes a significant contribution to the territory's economy. The average annual rate of inflation was 3.9% in 2004 and 3.1% in 2005.

Upon the accession in January 1986 of Spain to the European Community (EC, now European Union—EU, see p. 228), Melilla was considered a Spanish city and European territory, and joined the organization as part of Spain. It retained its status as a free port. The statute of autonomy, adopted in early 1995, envisaged the continuation of the territory's fiscal benefits. Euro notes and coins became the sole legal tender on 28 February 2002.

In June 1994 the EU announced substantial regional aid: between 1995 and 1999 Melilla was to receive a total of ECU 45m., of which ECU 18m. was to be in the form of direct aid. However, the enlargement of the EU which took place in 2004 and the enlargement scheduled for 2007 were to limit Spain's access to EU aid; Melilla would no longer be eligible for support. The Spanish budget for 2006 anticipated a 15% increase, to €50m., in central government expenditure in Melilla. In 2005 the city achieved a budget surplus of €7.1m.

Education

The education system is similar to that of mainland Spain. In addition to the conventional Spanish facilities, the Moroccan Government finances a school for 600 Muslim children, the languages of instruction being Arabic and Spanish. The curriculum includes Koranic studies. In 1982 only 12% of Muslim children were attending school, but by 1990 the authorities had succeeded in achieving an attendance level of virtually 100%. The open university (UNED) maintains a branch.

The Peñón de Vélez de la Gomera, Peñón de Alhucemas and Chafarinas Islands

These rocky islets, situated, respectively, just west and east of al-Hocima (Alhucemas) and east of Melilla off the north coast of Morocco, are administered with Melilla. The three Chafarinas Islands lie about 3.5 km off Ras el-Ma (Cabo de Agua). The Peñón de Alhucemas is situated about 300 m from the coast. The Peñón de Vélez de la Gomera is situated about 80 km further west, lying 85 m from the Moroccan shore, to which it is joined by a narrow strip of sand. A small military base is maintained on the Peñón de Vélez, while a military garrison of fewer than 100 men is stationed on the Peñón de Alhucemas, and a garrison of about 100 Spanish soldiers is maintained on the Isla del Congreso, the most westerly of the Chafarinas Islands. A supply ship calls at the various islands every two weeks. Prospective visitors must obtain the necessary military permit in Ceuta or Melilla.

Melilla

Statistical Survey

Source (unless otherwise stated): Instituto Nacional de Estadística, Paseo de la Castellana 183, 28071 Madrid; tel. (91) 5839100; fax (91) 5839158; internet www.ine.es.

AREA AND POPULATION

Area: 12.5 sq km (4.8 sq miles).

Population (census results): 56,600 at 1 March 1991; 66,411 at 1 November 2001 (males 33,224, females 33,187). *2005* (official estimate at 1 January): 65,488 (males 33,322, females 32,166).

Density (1 January 2005): 5,239 per sq km.

Births, Marriages and Deaths (provisional figures, 2004): Live births 995 (birth rate 14.8 per 1,000); Marriages 407 (marriage rate 6.1 per 1,000); Deaths 455 (death rate 6.8 per 1,000).

Expectation of Life (Ceuta and Melilla, years at birth, 2000): Males 74.7; Females 81.3.

Immigration and Emigration (2004): Immigrants 1,973; Emigrants 2,688.

Economically Active Population: *2002* ('000 persons) Agriculture, hunting, forestry and fishing 0.2; Industry 3.0 (Construction 2.5); Services 20.4; Total employed 23.6. *2003* ('000 persons): Total employed 22.8; Total unemployed 2.3; Total labour force 25.1. *2004* (Ceuta and Melilla): Agriculture, hunting, forestry and fishing 325; Industry 5,300 (Construction 3,675); Services 45,175; Total employed 50,800; Unemployed 7,800; Total labour force 58,600.

FINANCE

Currency and Exchange Rates: 100 cent = 1 euro (€). *Sterling and Dollar Equivalents* (30 December 2005): £1 Sterling = 1.4596 euros; US $1 = 0.8477 euros; 100 euros = £68.51 = $117.97. *Average Exchange Rate* (euros per US $): 0.8860 in 2003; 0.8054 in 2004; 0.8041 in 2005. Note: The local currency was formerly the Spanish peseta. From the introduction of the euro, with Spanish participation, on 1 January 1999, a fixed exchange rate of €1 = 166.386 pesetas was in effect. Euro notes and coins were introduced on 1 January 2002. The euro and local currency circulated alongside each other until 28 February, after which the euro became the sole legal tender.

Cost of Living (Consumer Price Index, annual averages; base: 2001 average = 100): 106.6 in 2003; 110.8 in 2004; 114.2 in 2005.

Gross Domestic Product (€ million, provisional): 1,006.7 in 2002; 1,051.6 in 2003; 1,135.8 in 2004.

Gross Domestic Product by Economic Activity (€ million, provisional, 2004): Agriculture, hunting, forestry and fishing 9.2; Energy 21.4; Industry 25.1; Construction 96.7; Services 869.4; *Sub-total* 1,021.8; Net taxes on products 113.9; *GDP at market prices* 1,135.8.

EXTERNAL TRADE

Melilla is a duty-free port. Most imports are from Spain but over 90% of exports go to non-Spanish territories. The chief export is fish.

TRANSPORT

Road Traffic (2004): Vehicles registered 42,805 (Passenger cars 30,759, Buses, etc. 48, Lorries 7,926, Motorcycles 3,250, Tractors 95, Other 727).

International Shipping (2004): Goods loaded 157,968 metric tons; Goods unloaded 584,447 metric tons; Vessels entered 1,032; Passenger arrivals 178,876; Passenger departures 184,644 (Source: partly Puertos del Estado, Ministerio de Fomento, Madrid).

Civil Aviation (2004): Journeys made 8,072; Passengers transported 229,338; Goods transported 386.4 metric tons.

TOURISM

Tourist Arrivals (by country of residence, 2002): France 476; Germany 432; Italy 331; Netherlands 425; Spain 23,648; Total (incl. others) 31,812.

EDUCATION

(2004/05, preliminary)

Pre-primary: 5 schools; 3,151 students.

Primary: 20 schools; 6,060 students; 603 teachers (incl. pre-primary).

Secondary: First Cycle: 9 schools (of which 8 schools also provided second-cycle education and 4 provided vocational education); 3,768 students; 562 teachers (all levels, see below).

Secondary: Second Cycle: 1,314 students.

Secondary: Vocational: 607 students.

Source: Ministry of Education and Science, Madrid.

Directory

Government

Government Delegate in Melilla: JOSÉ FERNÁNDEZ CHACÓN.
Deputy elected to the Congress in Madrid: ANTONIO GUTIÉRREZ MOLINA (PP-UPM).
Representatives to the Senate in Madrid: CARLOS A. BENET CAÑETE (PP-UPM), JUAN JOSÉ IMBRODA ORTIZ (PP-UPM).
Commandant-General: Gen. VICENTE DÍAZ DE VILLEGAS.

COUNCIL OF GOVERNMENT
(April 2006)

Mayor/President of Melilla: JUAN JOSÉ IMBRODA ORTIZ (PP-UPM).
First Vice-President and Councillor of Public Administration: MIGUEL MARÍN COBOS (PP-UPM).
Second Vice-President and Councillor of the Interior, Education, Youth and Women: ANTONIO MIRANDA MONTILLA (PP-UPM).
Councillor of Finance, Contracting and Heritage: GUILLERMO FRÍAS BARERRAS (PP-UPM).
Councillor of the Economy, Employment and Tourism: DANIEL CONESA MÍNGUEZ (PP-UPM).
Councillor of Development: RAFAEL MARÍN FERNÁNDEZ (PP-UPM).
Councillor of Social Welfare and Health: MARÍA ANTONIA GARBÍN ESPIGARES (PP-UPM).
Councillor of the Environment: RAMÓN GAVILÁN ARAGÓN (PP-UPM).
Councillor of Culture and Festivals: SIMI CHOCRÓN CHOCRÓN (PP-UPM).
Councillor of the President and Government: ABDELMALIK EL-BARKANI ABDELKADER (PP-UPM).
Councillor of Civic Security: RAMÓN ANTÓN MOTA (PP-UPM).

GOVERNMENT OFFICES

Delegación del Gobierno: Avda de la Marina Española 3, 52001 Melilla; tel. (95) 2675840; fax (95) 2672657; e-mail puri@melilla.map.es.
Office of the Mayor/President: Palacio de la Asamblea, Plaza de España, 52001 Melilla; tel. (95) 2699100; fax (95) 2679230; e-mail presidencia@melilla.es; internet www.melilla.es.
Council of Civic Security: Jefatura Policía Local, General Astilleros 25, Melilla; tel. (95) 2698110; fax (95) 2698121; e-mail policialocal@melilla.es.
Council of Culture and Festivals: Palacio de la Asamblea, Plaza de España, 52001 Melilla; tel. (95) 2699193; fax (95) 2699158; e-mail consejeriacultura@melilla.es.
Council of Development: Antiguo Edif. Mantelete, Duque de Ahumada s/n, Melilla 52071; tel. (95) 2699223; fax (95) 2699224; e-mail consejeriafomento@melilla.es.
Council of the Economy, Employment and Tourism: Justo Sancho Miñano 2, 52801 Melilla; tel. (95) 2690381; fax (95) 2690036; e-mail consejeriaeconomia@melilla.es.
Council of Education, Youth and Women: Querol 7, 52001 Melilla; tel. (95) 2699214; fax (95) 2699279; e-mail educacionmelilla@melilla.com.
Council of the Environment: Palacio de la Asamblea, Plaza de España, 52001 Melilla; tel. (95) 2699134; fax (95) 2699161; e-mail consejeriamedioambiente@melilla.es.
Council of Finance, Contracting and Heritage: Palacio de la Asamblea, Plaza de España, 52001 Melilla; tel. (95) 2699157; fax (95) 2699160.
Council of the Presidency and the Interior: Palacio de la Asamblea, Plaza de España, 52001 Melilla; tel. (95) 2699207; fax (95) 2699137; e-mail consejeriapresidencia@melilla.es.
Council of Public Administration: Palacio de la Asamblea, Plaza de España, 52001 Melilla; tel. (95) 2699102; fax (95) 2699103.

Council of Social Welfare and Health: Carlos Ramírez de Arellano 10, Melilla; tel. (95) 2699301; fax (95) 2699302; e-mail consejeriabienstarsocial@melilla.es.

Council

Election, 25 May 2003

	Seats
Partido Popular-Unión del Pueblo Melillense (PP-UPM)	15
Coalición por Melilla (CpM)	7
Partido Socialista Obrero Español (PSOE)	3
Total	**25**

Election Commission

Junta Electoral de Zona y Provincial de Melilla: Melilla; Sec. RUPERTO MANUEL GARCÍA HERNÁNDEZ.

Political Organizations

Coalición por Melilla (CpM): Querol 46, 52001 Melilla; e-mail cpm-grupo@sociored.net; f. 1995 by merger of Partido del Trabajo y Progreso de Melilla and Partido Hispano Bereber; Leader MUSTAFA HAMED MO ABERCHÁN; Sec.-Gen. JUAN MOLINA PEÑA FIEL.
Partido de los Demócratas de Melilla (PDM): Avda del General Aizpuru 29, Melilla; f. 1985; Muslim party; Leader ABDELKÁDER MOHAMED ALÍ.
Partido Independiente de Melilla (PIM): Avda Juan Carlos I Rey 23, 1° Izqda, Melilla; f. 1999; Leader ENRIQUE PALACIOS.
Partido Nacionalista del Rif de Melilla (PNRif): Chafarinas 12, Barrio del Zoco, 52001 Melilla; Muslim party formed by ex-PP militant to contest elections of 2003; Leader MIMÓN KADDUR.
Partido Popular (PP): Roberto Cano 2, 1° izqda, POB 384, 52001 Melilla; tel. (95) 2681095; fax (95) 2684477; e-mail melilla@pp.es; internet melilla.pp.es; centre-right; Pres. ARTURO ESTEBAN ALBERT.
Partido Social Demócrata de Melilla (PSDM): General O'Donnell, 8, 1° izqda, Melilla; f. 1998.
Partido Socialista de Melilla-Partido Socialista Obrero Español (PSME-PSOE): Cándido Lobera 7-1°, Melilla; tel. (95) 2681820; e-mail info@psoemelilla.com; internet www.psoemelilla.com; socialist workers' party; favours self-government but not full autonomy; Pres. ANDRÉS VISIEDO SEGURA; Sec.-Gen. DIONISIO MUÑOZ PÉREZ.
Unión del Pueblo Melillense (UPM): Ejército Español 7, 1° dcha, Apdo 775, 52001 Melilla; tel. (95) 2681987; fax (95) 2684677; f. 1985; right-wing; Pres. DANIEL CONESA MÍNGUEZ; Sec.-Gen. GUILLERMO MERINO BARRERA.

There are branches of the major Spanish parties in Melilla, and also various civic associations.

Religion

As in Ceuta, most Europeans are Roman Catholics. The registered Muslim community numbered 20,800 in 1990. The Jewish community numbered 1,300. There is also a Hindu community.

ISLAM

Comisión Islámica de Melilla (CIM): García Cabrelles 13, Melilla; Pres. ABDERRAMAN BENYAHYA.

CHRISTIANITY

The Roman Catholic Church

Melilla is part of the Spanish diocese of Malaga.

The Press

Diario Sur: Músico Granados 2, 52001 Melilla; tel. (95) 2691283; fax (95) 2673674; e-mail diariosurml@terra.es; internet www.diariosur.es; Perm. Rep. AVELINO GUTIÉRREZ PÉREZ.
El Faro de Melilla: General Marina 11, 1°, 52001 Melilla; tel. (95) 2690029; fax (95) 2680010; e-mail melilla@elfaro.es; internet melilla.elfaro.es; Dir JUAN ANTONIO CALLEJA FLÓREZ.
Melilla Hoy: Polígono Industrial SEPES, La Espiga, Naves A-1/A-2, 52006 Melilla; tel. (95) 2690000; fax (95) 2675725; e-mail redaccion@melillahoy.es; internet www.melillahoy.es; f. 1985; Dir IRENE FLORES SÁEZ; Editor-in-Chief MARÍA ANGELES JIMÉNEZ PADILLA; circ. 2,000.
El Telegrama de Melilla: Polígono La Espiga, Nave A-8, 52006 Melilla; tel. (95) 2691443; fax (95) 2691469; e-mail redaccion@

eltelegrama.com; internet www.eltelegrama.com; Dir JUAN CARLOS HEREDIA.

NEWS AGENCY

Agencia EFE: Candido Lobera 4, 1° Izqda, 52001 Melilla; tel. (95) 2685235; fax (95) 2680043; e-mail melilla@efe.es; Correspondent JUAN IGNACIO POVEDA.

PRESS ASSOCIATION

Asociación de la Prensa: Apartado de Correos 574, 52001 Melilla; tel. (95) 2681854; fax (95) 2675725; Pres. MIGUEL GÓMEZ BERNARDI.

Broadcasting

RADIO

40 Melilla: Muelle Ribera 1°, 29805 Melilla; tel. (95) 2681708; fax (95) 2681573; Dir ANTONIA RAMOS PELÁEZ.

Antena 3: Edif. Melilla, Urbanización Rusadir, 29805 Melilla; tel. (95) 2688840; Dir TOÑI RAMOS PELÁEZ.

Cadena Rato: Melilla; Dir ANGEL VALENCIA.

Dial Melilla: Urbanización Rusadir, Edif. Melilla, 52005 Melilla; tel. (95) 2673333; fax (95) 2678342; Rep. NURIA FERNÁNDEZ.

Ingar Radio: Abdelkader 3 bajo, 52000 Melilla; tel. (952) 682100.

Onda Cero Radio Melilla: Músico Granados 2, 52004 Melilla; tel. (95) 2691283; e-mail ondaceromelilla@ondaceromelilla.net; internet www.ondaceromelilla.net; Dir JOSÉ JESÚS NAVAJAS TROBAT.

Radio Melilla: Muelle Ribera 1, 52005 Melilla; tel. (95) 2681708; fax (95) 2681573; commercial; owned by Sociedad Española de Radiodifusión (SER); Dir ANTONIA RAMOS PELÁEZ.

Radio Nacional de España (RNE): Duque de Ahumada 5, 52001, Melilla; tel. (95) 2681907; fax (95) 2683108; internet www.rtve.es/me; state-controlled; Rep. MONTSERRAT COBOS RUANO.

TELEVISION

A fibre optic cable linking Melilla with Almería was laid in 1990. From March 1991 Melilla residents were able to receive three private TV channels from mainland Spain: Antena 3, Canal+ and Tele 5.

Finance

BANKING

Banco de España: Plaza de España 3, 52001 Melilla; tel. (95) 2683940; internet www.bde.es.

Banco Español de Crédito (Banesto): Avda Juan Carlos I 12, 52001 Melilla; tel. (95) 2684348; internet www.banesto.es.

Banco Popular Español: Avda Juan Carlos I 14, 52001 Melilla; tel. (95) 2684847; fax (95) 2676844.

Banco Santander Central Hispano (BSCH): Ejército Español 1, 52001 Melilla; tel. (95) 2681790; internet www.gruposantander.es; 3 brs.

Caja de Ahorros y Pensiones de Barcelona 'la Caixa': Avda Juan Carlos I 28, 52001 Melilla; tel. (95) 2685670; fax (95) 2960276; internet www.lacaixa.es; 2 brs.

Caja Rural Intermediterránea (Cajamar): Plaza de España, 52001 Melilla; tel. (95) 2685858; internet www.cajamar.es; 2 brs.

INSURANCE

MAPFRE: Avda Democracia 9, 52004 Melilla; tel. (95) 2673189; fax (95) 2674977; internet www.mapfre.com.

Trade and Industry

Cámara Oficial de Comercio, Industria y Navegación: Cervantes 7, 298901 Melilla; tel. (95) 2684840; fax (95) 2683119; f. 1906; chamber of commerce; Pres. MARGARITA LÓPEZ ALMENDÁRIZ; Sec.-Gen. MARÍA JESÚS FERNÁNDEZ DE CASTRO Y PEDRAJAS.

Confederación de Empresarios de Melilla (CEME): Plaza 1 de Mayo, Bajo Dcha, 52003 Melilla; tel. (95) 2673696; fax (95) 2676175; e-mail ceme@cemelilla.org; internet www.cemelilla.org; f. 1979; employers' confederation; Pres. MARGARITA LÓPEZ ALMENDÁRIZ; Sec.-Gen. JERÓNIMO PÉREZ HERNÁNDEZ.

UTILITIES

In early 2005, the Spanish electricity company Endesa, announced a plan to construct a new electricity generator in Melilla.

TRADE UNION

Confederación Sindical de Comisiones Obreras (CCOO): Plaza 1° de Mayo s/n, 3°, 29803 Melilla; tel. (95) 2676535; fax (95) 2672571; e-mail orga.melilla@melilla.ccoo.es; internet www.ccoo.es; Sec.-Gen. ANGEL GUTIERREZ GOMEZ.

Transport

There is a daily ferry service to Málaga and a service to Almería. Melilla airport, situated 4 km from the town, is served by daily flights to various destinations on the Spanish mainland, operated by Iberia and by Melilla Jet/Pauknair. There are also services to Madrid and Granada. There were 30 km of paved roads in Melilla in 2004.

Port of Melilla: Autoridad Portuaria de Melilla, Avda de la Marina Española 4, 52001 Melilla; tel. (95) 2673600; fax (95) 2674838; e-mail info@puertomelilla.com; internet www.puertomelilla.com; Dir LUIS A. FERNÁNDEZ MUÑOZ.

Compañía Trasmediterránea: Avda General Marina 1, 52001 Melilla; tel. (95) 2681635; fax (95) 2682685; e-mail correom@trasmediterranea.es; internet www.trasmediterranea.es; operates ferry service between Melilla and Almería and Málaga, in mainland Spain.

Tourism

There is much of historic interest to the visitor, while Melilla is also celebrated for its modernist architecture. Several new hotels, including a luxury development, were constructed in the 1990s. In 2002 tourist arrivals, including visitors from mainland Spain, numbered 31,812.

Oficina Provincial de Turismo: Pintor Fortuny 21, 52004 Melilla; tel. (95) 2675444; fax (95) 2679616; e-mail info@melillaturismo.com; internet www.melillaturismo.com.

Viceconsejería de Turismo: Calle Pintor Fortuny 20, Palacio de Congresos y Exposiciones, 52004 Melilla; tel. (95) 2675444; fax (95) 2691232; e-mail info@melillaturismo.com; internet www.melillaturismo.com; part of Council of Culture and Festivals; Vice-Councillor JAVIER MATEO FIGUEROA.

SRI LANKA

Introductory Survey

Location, Climate, Language, Religion, Flag, Capital

The Democratic Socialist Republic of Sri Lanka lies in southern Asia. It comprises one large island and several much smaller ones, situated in the Indian Ocean, about 80 km (50 miles) east of the southern tip of India. The climate is tropical, with an average annual temperature of about 27°C (81°F) in Colombo. There is very little seasonal variation in temperature: the monthly average in Colombo ranges from 25°C (77°F) to 28°C (82°F). The south-western part of the island receives rain from both the south-west and the north-east monsoons: average annual rainfall in Colombo is 2,365 mm (93 ins). Sinhala and Tamil are recognized national languages. One of the official languages, Sinhala, is spoken by more than 70% of the population. Tamil was made the country's second official language in 1988. According to the 2001 census, in 18 out of 25 districts 76.7% of the population are Buddhist, 8.5% are Muslim, 7.9% are Hindu and 6.1% are Roman Catholic. The census results did not cover the Tamil-dominated (and therefore mainly Hindu) northern and eastern districts. The national flag (proportions 1 by 2) consists mainly of a dark crimson rectangular panel, with a yellow border, in the fly. In the centre of the panel is a gold lion, carrying a sword, while in each corner (also in gold) there is a leaf of the bo (bodhi) tree, which is sacred to Buddhists. At the hoist are two vertical stripes, also edged in yellow, to represent Sri Lanka's minorities: one of green (for Muslims) and one of orange (for Tamils). The commercial capital is Colombo. In 1982 the ancient capital of Sri Jayawardenepura (Kotte) became the administrative capital.

Recent History

Sri Lanka, known as Ceylon until 1972, gained its independence from the United Kingdom in February 1948. From then until 1956, for a brief period in 1960 and from 1965 to 1970 the country was ruled, latterly in coalition, by the United National Party (UNP), which was concerned to protect the rights of the Tamils, Hindu members of an ethnic minority (closely linked with the inhabitants of the southern Indian state of Tamil Nadu), who are concentrated in the north (and, to a lesser extent, in the east) of the main island. The socialist Sri Lanka Freedom Party (SLFP), formed in 1951 by Solomon Bandaranaike, emphasized the national heritage, winning the support of groups that advocated the recognition of Sinhala as the official language and the establishment of Buddhism as the predominant religion. The SLFP won the 1956 elections decisively and remained in power, except for a three-month interruption in 1960, until 1965, having formed a coalition Government with the Lanka Sama Samaj Party (LSSP), a Trotskyist group, in 1964. Following the assassination of Solomon Bandaranaike in 1959, his widow, Sirimavo Bandaranaike, assumed the leadership of the SLFP. At the 1970 elections the SLFP became the leading partner of a United Front coalition Government with the LSSP and the Communist Party of Sri Lanka.

In 1971 the United Front Government suppressed an uprising led by the left-wing Janatha Vimukthi Peramuna (JVP—People's Liberation Front). A state of emergency was declared, and the party was banned. In 1976 the main Tamil party, the Federal Party, and other Tamil groups formed the Tamil United Liberation Front (TULF), demanding a separate Tamil state ('Eelam') in the northern and eastern parts of the country.

In December 1976 the communists supported strikes of transport unions, which were initiated by the UNP and the LSSP (the latter had been expelled from the coalition in 1975). The strikes ended in January 1977, and in February Sirimavo Bandaranaike prorogued the National State Assembly until May. Several members of the SLFP resigned, and seven members of the Communist Party left the coalition Government, forming an independent group within the opposition. In February the state of emergency, which had been imposed in 1971, was lifted and the JVP was legalized again. A general election was held in July 1977, accompanied by widespread violence. The UNP won the election, with an overwhelming majority, and the party's leader, Junius Richard Jayewardene, became Prime Minister. In August riots broke out between the Sinhalese majority and the Tamil minority. The TULF, which had become the main opposition party, increased its demands for an independent Tamil state. In October a constitutional amendment was passed to establish a presidential system of government, and in February 1978 Jayewardene became the country's first executive President.

Continued violence and pressure from the Tamils during 1978 led the Government to make some concessions, such as the recognition of the Tamil language, in the new Constitution of the Democratic Socialist Republic of Sri Lanka, which came into force in September. In view of this, the Ceylon Workers' Congress (CWC) joined the Government, but the TULF remained undecided, mainly for fear of reprisals by Tamil extremists. Continuing violence prompted the declaration of a state of emergency in July 1979 in the northern district of Jaffna, where the Tamils are in a majority. At the same time, stringent anti-terrorist legislation was passed in Parliament (as the National State Assembly had been renamed in 1978), and a presidential commission was established to study the Tamil problem.

In June 1980 a general strike, called by left-wing trade unions seeking higher wages, led to the declaration of a state of emergency between July and August, and more than 40,000 government workers lost their jobs. In August the TULF agreed to the establishment of District Development Councils, providing for a wide measure of regional autonomy. Elections to these, held in June 1981, were boycotted by the SLFP, the LSSP and the Communist Party, and the UNP won control of 18 of the 24 Councils. Subsequent communal disturbances between Sinhalese and Tamils led to the imposition of a state of emergency in the north for five days in June, and throughout the country from August 1981 to January 1982. Tamil MPs proposed a motion of 'no confidence' in the Government and subsequently boycotted Parliament until November 1981, when a peace initiative to ease racial tension was proposed by the Government.

Meanwhile, in October 1980 the former Prime Minister, Sirimavo Bandaranaike, was found guilty of having abused power by a special presidential commission, which deprived her of all civic rights and effectively prevented her from standing in the next elections.

In August 1982 Parliament approved an amendment to the 1978 Constitution which enabled President Jayewardene to call a presidential election before his term of office expired, i.e. after four years instead of six. Sri Lanka's first presidential election was held in October 1982, and Jayewardene was returned to office with 53% of the votes cast. The SLFP candidate, Hector Kobbekaduwa, polled 39%, despite his party's disarray and Sirimavo Bandaranaike's loss of civic rights.

Following this success, the President announced, with the approval of Parliament and the Supreme Court, that, instead of a general election, a referendum would be held to decide whether to prolong the life of Parliament for a further six years after the session ended in July 1983. A state of emergency was in force between October 1982 and January 1983, and all opposition newspapers were closed by the Government. Sirimavo Bandaranaike was allowed to campaign in the referendum, which took place in December 1982 and resulted in approval of the proposal to prolong Parliament until 1989. On a 71% turn-out, 55% (3.1m.) voted in favour, with the dissenting minority of 2.6m. being concentrated mainly in and around Jaffna.

In May 1983 by-elections were held for seats where the UNP had fared badly in both the presidential election and the referendum, and the UNP won 14 of the 18 seats. This was accompanied by success for the UNP in the local government elections, held concurrently, although the TULF was successful in Tamil-speaking areas.

A state of emergency was declared in May 1983 to combat mounting terrorism, and in June Tamil terrorist activity led to army reprisals and the worst outbreak of violence for many years, with more than 400 deaths and particularly severe rioting in Jaffna and Colombo. A curfew and press censorship were imposed, and three left-wing parties (including the JVP) were banned. In July the 16 TULF MPs resigned in protest at the extension of Parliament, as approved by the referendum. In

August Parliament passed a 'no-separation' amendment to the Constitution, depriving those espousing Tamil separatism of their civic rights. In October the TULF MPs were found to have forfeited their seats because of their parliamentary boycott. After much discussion and with the informal mediation of India, an All-Party Conference (APC) began in January 1984. The APC comprised representatives of the Buddhist, Christian and Muslim faiths as well as political leaders from the Sinhalese and Tamil communities. The Government proposed to establish provincial councils, with some regional autonomy, throughout the country. The TULF, however, demanded regional devolution that would enable the northern province, with its Tamil majority, to amalgamate with the eastern province where the Tamils were in a minority and thus create a Tamil state within the framework of a united Sri Lanka. The Sinhalese and the Muslims were implacably opposed to this proposal. The APC was finally abandoned in December, without agreement on the crucial question of the extent of regional autonomy.

Further violent outbursts in the northern part of the island in November and December 1984 led to the proclamation of another state of emergency. There were widespread accusations of gross military indiscipline, and there was condemnation of government-sponsored settlement of Sinhalese in Tamil areas in the eastern province. A restricted zone was established between Mannar and Mullaitivu, to prevent contact with the Indian state of Tamil Nadu, where many of the Tamil militants were based.

In February 1986 there was a resurgence of violence in the northern and eastern provinces. In May a series of explosions in Colombo was widely believed to have been carried out by Tamil terrorists. In the same month, the Government intensified its campaign against the insurgents by increasing defence expenditure and by launching an offensive against the militant Tamils in the Jaffna peninsula. This offensive made little headway, but the government cause was helped by internecine fighting between two of the principal Tamil militant groups, the Tamil Eelam Liberation Organization (TELO) and the Liberation Tigers of Tamil Eelam (LTTE—also known as the Tamil Tigers), which, over the year, emerged as the dominant Tamil separatist group under the leadership of Velupillai Prabhakaran. In May Tamil terrorists renewed their attacks on Sinhalese villagers who had been settled by the Government in Tamil-dominated areas in the eastern province. In June the Government presented fresh devolution proposals to a newly convened APC, in which the TULF was not invited to participate, while the SLFP boycotted the talks. The proposals again envisaged the formation of provincial councils, but did not satisfy the Tamils' demand for amalgamation of the northern and eastern provinces. The proposals were also rejected by the SLFP, on the grounds that they conceded too much to the Tamils.

In January 1987, in response to an announcement by the LTTE that they intended to seize control of the civil administration of Jaffna, the Government suspended, indefinitely, the distribution of all petroleum products to the peninsula. In the same month all the powers previously vested in the Prime Minister, Ranasinghe Premadasa, as Minister of Emergency Civil Administration were transferred to a new Ministry of National Security, directly supervised by the President. In February the Government launched an offensive against the terrorists in the Batticaloa district of the eastern province. The situation worsened in April, when the LTTE, having rejected an offer of a cease-fire by the Sri Lankan Government, carried out a series of outrages against the civilian population, including a bomb explosion in Colombo's main bus station, which killed more than 100 people. In response, the Government attempted to regain control of the Jaffna peninsula, the stronghold of the LTTE. During the resultant struggle between the LTTE and government forces, India demonstrated its support for the Tamils by violating Sri Lankan airspace to drop food and medical supplies in Jaffna. On 29 July, however, an important breakthrough was made when President Jayewardene and the Indian Prime Minister, Rajiv Gandhi, signed an accord regarding an attempted settlement of the country's ethnic crisis. The main points of this accord were: the provision of an Indian Peace-Keeping Force (IPKF) to oversee its proper implementation; a complete cessation of hostilities, and the surrender of all weapons held by the Tamil militants; the amalgamation of the northern and eastern provinces into one administrative unit, with an elected provincial council (together with the creation of provincial councils in the seven other provinces); the holding of a referendum in the eastern province at a date to be decided by the Sri Lankan President, to determine whether the mixed population of Tamils, Sinhalese and Muslims supported an official merger with the northern province into a single Tamil-dominated north-east province; a general amnesty for all Tamil militants; the repatriation of some 130,000 Tamil refugees from India to Sri Lanka (by early 1991 the number of Tamil refugees in India had risen to an estimated 210,000, and in early 1992 the Indian Government began to repatriate them, allegedly on a voluntary basis); the prevention of the use of Indian territory by Tamil militants for military or propaganda purposes; the prevention of the military use of Sri Lankan ports by any country in a manner prejudicial to Indian interests; and the provision that Tamil and English should have equal status with Sinhala as official languages. The accord encountered widespread disapproval among the Sinhalese population and from the SLFP, which claimed that it granted too much power to the Tamil minority.

In July and August 1987 more than 7,000 Indian troops were dispatched to Sri Lanka. After a promising start in August, the surrender of arms by the Tamil militant groups became more sporadic in September, and the implementation of the peace accord was impeded by further bitter internecine fighting among the Tamil militias (involving the LTTE in particular), which necessitated direct intervention by the IPKF. Under arrangements reported to have been negotiated in September with the Indian authorities, the LTTE were to be allocated a majority of seats on an interim council, which was to administer the northern and eastern provinces, pending the holding of elections. Despite this concession, the surrender of arms by the LTTE had virtually ceased by early October; the group had resumed its terrorist attacks on Sinhalese citizens, and had declared itself to be firmly opposed to the peace accord. In response to the resurgence in violence, the IPKF launched an offensive against the LTTE stronghold in the Jaffna peninsula in October. The Indian troops encountered fierce and prolonged resistance from the Tamil militants, which necessitated the deployment of thousands of reinforcements. By the end of the month, however, the IPKF had gained control of Jaffna city, while most of the LTTE militants had escaped to establish a new base for guerrilla operations, in the Batticaloa district of the eastern province. Both sides had suffered heavy casualties.

Because of the continuing violence, the Sri Lankan Government abandoned its plan to create an interim administrative council for the northern and eastern provinces. However, in November 1987, despite strong opposition from the SLFP (which vehemently opposed the proposed merger of the northern and eastern provinces), Parliament adopted the legislation establishing provincial councils.

Another major threat to the successful implementation of the peace accord was the re-emergence in 1987 of the outlawed Sinhalese group, the JVP, which had been officially banned in August 1983 and which was based mainly in the south of the island. This group claimed that the accord conceded too much power to the Tamils. As part of its anti-accord campaign, the JVP was widely believed to have been responsible for an assassination attempt on President Jayewardene in August, in which one MP was killed and several cabinet ministers were seriously wounded, and to have murdered more than 200 UNP supporters by February 1988, including the Chairman of the UNP, Harsha Abeywardene, and the leader of the left-wing Sri Lanka Mahajana (People's) Party (SLMP), Vijaya Kumaratunga, who supported the accord. In May 1988 the Government revoked the five-year ban on the JVP in return for an agreement by the party to end its campaign of violence, but JVP leaders disowned the agreement as a hoax.

In February 1988 a new opposition force emerged when an alliance, named the United Socialist Alliance (USA), was formed between the SLMP, the LSSP, the Communist Party of Sri Lanka, the Nava Sama Samaja Party, and (most notably) the Tamil rights group entitled the Eelam People's Revolutionary Liberation Front (EPRLF). Although the USA group, led by Chandrika Bandaranaike Kumaratunga (the widow of the SLMP leader and the daughter of Sirimavo Bandaranaike), comprised opposition parties, it expressed support for the peace accord.

Elections to seven of the new provincial councils were held in April and June 1988 (in defiance of the JVP's threats and violence); elections in the northern and eastern provinces were postponed indefinitely. The UNP won a majority and effective control in all seven (with 57% of the elective seats), while the USA emerged as the main opposition group (with 41% of the seats). The SLFP boycotted the elections, in protest at the continuing presence of the IPKF (which now numbered about 50,000) in Sri Lanka. In September President Jayewardene officially authorized the merger of the northern and eastern provinces into a single north-eastern province, prior to provincial council elections there. The JVP reacted violently, and was widely believed to have been responsible for the murder of the Minister of Rehabilitation and Reconstruction at the end of the month. In protest against the proposed elections in the new north-eastern province and the presidential election (due to be held in December), the JVP organized a series of disruptive strikes and violent demonstrations in the central, western and southern provinces in October. In an effort to curb the increasing violence, the Government applied extensive emergency regulations, imposed curfews in areas of unrest, and deployed armed riot police. Despite boycotts and threats by both the JVP and the LTTE, elections to the new north-eastern provincial council took place in November. The moderate and pro-accord Tamil groups, the EPRLF and the Eelam National Democratic Liberation Front (ENDLF), together with the Sri Lanka Muslim Congress (SLMC), were successful in the elections, while the UNP won only one seat. In early December Parliament unanimously approved a Constitution Amendment Bill to make Tamil one of the country's two official languages (with Sinhala), thus fulfilling one of the major commitments envisaged in the peace accord. On 19 December the presidential election took place, in circumstances of unprecedented disruption, and was boycotted by the LTTE and the JVP. None the less, about 55% of the total electorate was estimated to have voted. The Prime Minister, Ranasinghe Premadasa (the UNP's candidate), won by a narrow margin, with 50.4% of the total votes, while Sirimavo Bandaranaike, the President of the SLFP (whose civil rights had been restored in January 1986), received 44.9%. On the following day, as promised earlier in the month by the Government, Parliament was dissolved in preparation for a general election.

In early January 1989 Premadasa was sworn in as Sri Lanka's new President, and an interim Cabinet was appointed. In the same month, the Government repealed the state of emergency, which had been in force since May 1983, and abolished the Ministry of National Security. Concurrently, however, special security measures were invoked in an attempt to arrest the escalating violence. Shortly after his inauguration, Premadasa offered to confer with the extremists and invited all groups to take part in the electoral process. The JVP and the LTTE, however, intensified their campaigns of violence in protest at the forthcoming general election. In early February 1989 the moderate, pro-accord Tamil groups, the EPRLF, the ENDLF and the TELO, formed a loose alliance, under the leadership of the TULF, to contest the general election. In the election, which was held on 15 February and which was, again, marred by widespread violence, the UNP won 125 of the 225 contested seats. The new system of proportional representation, which was introduced at this election, was especially advantageous to the SLFP, which became the major opposition force in Parliament, with 67 seats. The comparatively low electoral participation of 64% confirmed, again, that intimidatory tactics, employed by the LTTE and the JVP, had had an effect on the voters. A few days later, President Premadasa installed a new Cabinet, and in March he appointed the Minister of Finance, Dingiri Banda Wijetunga, as the country's new Prime Minister. Although both the LTTE and the JVP rejected a conciliatory offer made by the President in April, in a surprising development, representatives of the LTTE began discussions with government officials in Colombo in the following month.

Between January and April 1989 five battalions of the IPKF left Sri Lanka, and in May the Sri Lankan Government announced that it wanted all Indian troops to have left Sri Lanka by the end of July. In response, Rajiv Gandhi stressed that the timetable for a complete withdrawal would have to be decided mutually, and that, before the Indian forces left, he wanted to ensure the security of the Tamils and the devolution of real power to the elected local government in the north-eastern province. In protest against the continued presence of the IPKF in Sri Lanka, the JVP organized a series of demonstrations and strikes. As a result of the escalating unrest, the Government reimposed a state of emergency on 20 June. In the same month, shortly after the murders of several prominent Tamil leaders, the peace negotiations between the Sri Lankan Government and the LTTE were temporarily discontinued. In September the Governments of Sri Lanka and India signed an agreement in Colombo, under which India promised to make 'all efforts' to withdraw its remaining 45,000 troops from Sri Lanka by the end of the year, and the IPKF was to declare an immediate unilateral cease-fire. In turn, the Sri Lankan Government pledged immediately to establish a peace committee for the north-eastern province in an attempt to reconcile the various Tamil groups and to incorporate members of the LTTE into the peaceful administration of the province.

The JVP suffered a very serious set-back when its leader, Rohana Wijeweera, and his principal deputy were shot dead by the security forces in November 1989. In the following month the leader of the military wing of the JVP, Saman Piyasiri Fernando, was killed in an exchange of gunfire in Colombo. Between September 1989 and the end of January 1990 the Sri Lankan security forces effectively destroyed the JVP as a political force, thus substantially transforming the country's political scene. All but one member of the JVP's political bureau and most leaders at district level had been killed. It was estimated, however, that the number of civilians killed in the lengthy struggle between the JVP and the Government might have been as high as 25,000–50,000.

As the Indian troops increased the speed of their withdrawal from Sri Lanka in the latter half of 1989, the LTTE initiated a campaign of violence against its arch-rivals, the more moderate Indian-supported EPRLF, which was mustering a so-called Tamil National Army, with Indian help, in the north-eastern province, to resist the LTTE. The LTTE accused the EPRLF and its allies of forcibly conscripting thousands of Tamil youths into the Tamil army. Following months of peace talks with the Government, however, the political wing of the LTTE was recognized as a political party by the commissioner of elections in December. The LTTE leaders then proclaimed that the newly recognized party would take part in the democratic process (it demanded immediate fresh elections in the north-eastern province) under the new name of the People's Front of the Liberation Tigers (PFLT). By the end of 1989 the inexperienced and undisciplined Tamil National Army had been virtually destroyed by the LTTE, who now appeared to have the tacit support of the central Government and had taken control of much of the territory in the north-eastern province.

Following further talks between the Governments of Sri Lanka and India, the completion date for the withdrawal of the IPKF was postponed until the end of March 1990. In early March the EPRLF-dominated north-eastern provincial council, under the leadership of Annamalai Varadharajah Perumal, renamed itself the 'National Assembly of the Free and Sovereign Democratic Republic of Eelam' and gave the central Government a one-year ultimatum to fulfil a charter of demands. Two weeks later, however, Perumal was reported to have fled to southern India. The last remaining IPKF troops left Sri Lanka on 24 March, a week ahead of schedule. In the next month the Government eased emergency regulations (including the ban on political rallies) in an effort to restore a degree of normality to the country after years of violence. At the same time, Sri Lanka's security forces, encouraged by the relative lull in violence, halted all military operations against the now much-weakened JVP and the Tamil militant groups. A fragile peace was maintained until June, when the LTTE abandoned their negotiations with the Government and renewed hostilities with surprise attacks on military and police installations in the north and north-east. Consequently, the Sri Lankan security forces were compelled to launch a counter-offensive. In mid-June the Government dissolved the north-eastern provincial council (despite protests by the EPRLF), and the holding of fresh elections in the province was postponed indefinitely pending the LTTE's agreement to participate in them (as earlier promised). In August the LTTE intensified their campaign of violence in the eastern province against the Muslim population, which retaliated with counterattacks. At the end of August the Government launched a major offensive against the Tamil strongholds in the Jaffna peninsula. In March 1991 it was widely suspected that the LTTE were responsible for the assassination of a senior Sri Lankan cabinet member, the Minister of Plantation Industries and Minister of State for Defence, Ranjan Wijeratne (who had been in charge of both the government forces' successful offensive against the JVP, several years earlier, and the ongoing offensive against the LTTE), and for the bomb attack on an armed-forces building in Colombo in June. More significantly, for its regional implications, the LTTE were believed to have been responsible for the assassination of the former Indian Prime Minister, Rajiv Gandhi, near Madras (now known as Chennai), the state capital of Tamil Nadu, in May. In early 1992 the Indian Government proscribed the LTTE in India and banned their activities on Indian territory.

In May 1991 President Premadasa consolidated his political position when the UNP won a decisive victory in the local government elections. In August, however, the opposition, with the support of a number of UNP parliamentary members, began proceedings for the impeachment of the President. The impeachment motion listed 24 instances of alleged abuse of power and constituted a serious challenge to the authority of Premadasa and to the stability of his Government. However, it was rejected in October by the Speaker of Parliament on the grounds that some of the signatures on the resolution were invalid. Eight erstwhile UNP parliamentary members, including two former cabinet members, Lalith Athulathmudali and Gamini Dissanayake, who were expelled from the party (thus losing their parliamentary seats as well) by Premadasa for supporting the impeachment motion, formed a new party in December, called the Democratic United National Front (DUNF), to which they hoped to attract dissident members of the UNP.

The security forces suffered a serious reversal in August 1992, when 10 senior officers, including the northern military commander and the Jaffna peninsula commander, were killed in a land-mine explosion near Jaffna. Tension between the Muslim and Tamil populations in the north-eastern district of Polonnaruwa drastically increased following the massacre of more than 170 Muslim villagers by suspected LTTE guerrillas in October. In the next month the LTTE were also widely believed to have been responsible for the murder of the naval commander, Vice-Admiral Clancy Fernando, in Colombo. The LTTE themselves lost one of their most senior leaders when Velupillai Prabhakaran's chief deputy was killed at sea in January 1993.

In late April 1993 the opposition DUNF accused Premadasa's Government of having been responsible for the assassination of the party's leader, Lalith Athulathmudali. In response, Premadasa alleged that the perpetrators of the murder had been LTTE terrorists; the LTTE, however, denied any responsibility for the killing. The country was thrown into greater political turmoil on 1 May, when President Premadasa was assassinated in a bomb explosion in Colombo. The LTTE were officially blamed for the murder, although, again, they strenuously denied any involvement. A few days later Parliament unanimously elected the incumbent Prime Minister, Dingiri Banda Wijetunga, to serve the remaining presidential term (expiring in December 1994), and the erstwhile Minister of Industries, Science and Technology, Ranil Wickremasinghe, was appointed to replace him in the premiership. In provincial elections held in mid-May 1993 the UNP won control of four of the seven councils; no polling was carried out in the area covered by the now defunct north-eastern province. Although the ruling party received 47% of the votes, it was the first time since 1977 that its percentage of total votes had fallen below 50%, an indication of an erosion of its support base that became more pronounced in the early part of 1994.

The Sri Lankan forces achieved considerable success in their fight against ethnic violence in the eastern province in 1993, but were forced to abandon a massive military offensive in the Jaffna peninsula in October owing to the ferocity of the LTTE resistance. In the following month both sides suffered heavy casualties in the course of the battle over the military base at Pooneryn on the Jaffna lagoon. As a result of this military débâcle, in which, according to official figures, more than 600 army and naval personnel were either killed or captured, the Government established a new combined security forces command for the Jaffna and Kilinochchi districts to counter the LTTE threat.

Despite the continuing violence, provincial elections were held in the eastern province and in the northern town of Vavuniya in early March 1994; the UNP secured the greatest number of seats, while independent Tamil groups also performed well. The LTTE and the TULF boycotted the poll. The ruling party suffered its first major electoral reverse for 17 years at the end of the month, however, when an opposition grouping known as the People's Alliance (PA, of which the main constituents were the SLFP and the traditional Marxist left and which was headed by the former leader of the USA group, Chandrika Kumaratunga) won a clear majority in elections to the southern provincial council. On 24 June, in an apparent attempt to catch the opposition by surprise, the President dissolved Parliament and announced that early legislative elections were to be held on 16 August, ahead of the presidential election. Wijetunga's ploy failed, however: the PA obtained 48.9% of the votes, thus securing a narrow victory over the UNP, which received 44% of the poll. Under the prevailing system of proportional representation, this translated to 105 seats for the PA and 94 for the UNP in the 225-seat Parliament. The 17-year rule of the UNP had thus come to an end. On 18 August President Wijetunga abandoned hope of forming a UNP minority Government and appointed Kumaratunga as Prime Minister, the PA having secured the support of the SLMC, the TULF, the Democratic People's Liberation Front and a small, regional independent group. A new Cabinet was appointed on the following day, almost all members of which belonged to the SLFP. In line with her electoral pledge to abolish the executive presidency and to establish a parliamentary system in its place, the Prime Minister removed the finance portfolio from the President and assumed responsibility for it herself. Although Wijetunga retained the title of Minister of Defence, actual control of the ministry was expected to be exercised by the Deputy Minister of Defence. The Prime Minister's mother, Sirimavo Bandaranaike, was appointed as Minister without Portfolio. With regard to the Tamil question, overtures were made between the new Government and the LTTE concerning unconditional peace talks (these commenced in mid-October) and at the end of August, as a gesture of goodwill, the Government partially lifted the economic blockade on LTTE-occupied territory. In addition, the Prime Minister created a new Ministry of Ethnic Affairs and National Integration and assumed the portfolio herself, thus revealing her determination to seek an early solution to the civil strife.

In September 1994 Kumaratunga was unanimously elected by the PA as its candidate for the forthcoming presidential poll, while Gamini Dissanayake, the leader of the opposition (who had left the DUNF and returned to the UNP in 1993), was chosen as the UNP's candidate. The election campaign was thrown into confusion, however, on 24 October 1994, when Dissanayake was assassinated by a suspected LTTE suicide bomber in a suburb of Colombo; more than 50 other people, including the General Secretary of the UNP, Gamini Wijesekara, and the leader of the SLMP, Ossie Abeyagoonasekera, were killed in the blast. The Government declared a state of emergency and suspended the ongoing peace talks with the LTTE. Dissanayake had been an outspoken critic of these talks and had been one of the architects of the 1987 Indo-Sri Lankan accord. His widow, Srima Dissanayake, was chosen by the UNP to replace him as the party's presidential candidate. The state of emergency was revoked on 7 November (with the exception of the troubled areas in the north and east) to facilitate the fair and proper conduct of the presidential election, which was held on 9 November. Kumaratunga won the election, with 62.3% of the votes, while Srima Dissanayake obtained 35.9%. The Government viewed the victory as a clear mandate for the peace process initiated earlier that year. Sirimavo Bandaranaike was subsequently appointed Prime Minister, for the third time. The new President pledged to abolish the executive presidency before mid-July 1995, on the grounds that she believed that the post vested too much power in one individual, and promised to initiate a programme of social, economic and constitutional change.

The Government and the LTTE resumed peace talks in early January 1995, which resulted in the drawing up of a preliminary agreement on the cessation of hostilities as a prelude to political negotiations. This important development constituted the first formal truce since fighting was renewed in the north-east in June 1990. In April 1995, however, following several rounds of deadlocked negotiations, with both sides accusing each other of making unreasonable demands and proposals, the LTTE unilaterally ended the truce, withdrew from the peace talks and resumed hostilities against the government forces. In response, the Government cancelled all the concessions made to the guerrillas during the peace negotiations and placed the security forces on alert. A disturbing escalation in the violence was demonstrated at the end of the month by the LTTE's deployment, for the first time, of surface-to-air missiles.

In July 1995 the Government launched another major offensive in the Jaffna peninsula. As the offensive was intensified in mid-October, tens of thousands of civilians were compelled by the LTTE to flee the area. In retaliation against the army's attack, rather than actively confronting the troops, the LTTE detonated explosives on the country's two largest oil storage facilities near Colombo, which received virtually all of Sri Lanka's imported petroleum. As a result, about 20% of the island's petroleum supply was destroyed. In November two LTTE suicide bombers caused 18 deaths and more than 50 injuries in Colombo. In early December, however, the Sri Lankan army achieved a major victory in capturing the city of Jaffna and subsequently much of the Jaffna peninsula. Although the LTTE's military strength and morale were undermined, the rebels, as expected, reverted to guerrilla warfare and further terrorist activity. The day after the armed forces had raised the national flag above Jaffna, the LTTE rejected the President's offer of an amnesty in exchange for disarmament and announced a new recruitment drive. The Government's short-term strategy with regard to the Jaffna peninsula was to attempt to persuade the tens of thousands of civilians now living in refugee camps to return there and to establish a fully functional civil administration in the region. As widely feared, there was an escalation in LTTE-organized terrorist activity following the recapture of Jaffna; at the end of January 1996 more than 100 people were killed and about 1,400 were injured as a result of a suicide bomb attack on the Central Bank in Colombo. This devastating attack appeared to be the LTTE's response to the Government's release of the legal draft of devolution proposals earlier that month. Against a background of continuing conflict between the Tamil militants and the government forces in the north and east of the country, the President extended the state of emergency to cover the whole country in April (since coming to power in November 1994, the PA administration had restricted the emergency provisions to the troubled northern and eastern regions and Colombo). In mid-May 1996 the army announced that it now controlled the whole of the Jaffna peninsula and claimed that, of the 300,000 Tamil civilians who had been displaced by the ethnic violence, about 250,000 had returned to the government-held areas. Despite the army's controlling presence in the Jaffna peninsula, the LTTE were, by no means, a spent force. In mid-July the Tamil militants attacked and overran the isolated military base at Mullaitivu on the north-eastern coast of Sri Lanka, inflicting very heavy casualties on the army (according to the LTTE, at least 1,200 government soldiers were killed; according to official figures, the army death toll was about 300). About one week later the LTTE were suspected of planting a bomb on a crowded suburban train near Colombo, which left more than 70 people dead. In September the army seized control of the northern town of Kilinochchi, which had served as the LTTE's new headquarters since April. In the following month Prabhakaran and nine other militants were charged with more than 700 criminal acts of terrorism, including the bombing of the Central Bank in January. This constituted the first occasion that the Government had taken legal action against the LTTE leader. Fierce fighting between the Tamil militants and government troops continued into 1997, both in the north and east of the country; in early March it was estimated that more than 50,000 people had died and about one million people had been displaced as a result of the 14-year civil war.

The Government was given a considerable boost in March 1997, following its overwhelming success in local elections, in which it won more than 80% of the contested bodies (voting did not take place in the troubled northern and eastern provinces). However, although the Government secured control over a majority of the local bodies, its share of the total vote decreased to 48%, compared with the 62% it achieved in the presidential election of November 1994. The UNP obtained nearly 42% of the poll. None the less, the Government viewed the election results as a mandate to continue preparing its devolution plans offering limited autonomy to the Tamil secessionists (plans that had, so far, been blocked by the UNP). In May the Government launched a fresh military offensive against the LTTE, with the aim of gaining control of the 75-km stretch of the A9 highway between Vavuniya and Elephant Pass, which is the point of entry to the Jaffna peninsula. In late August the Government announced that it would submit its devolution proposals for parliamentary debate in October. In mid-October, however, 18 people were killed and more than 100 injured (including about 35 foreigners) when a bomb exploded in the car park of a Colombo hotel. It was widely believed that the LTTE deliberately targeted foreigners in this attack following the US Government's decision a few days earlier to place the organization on its official proscribed list of international terrorist groups. At the end of the month, despite protests from the UNP, the draft of the proposed constitutional amendments was presented to Parliament. The prospect of peace, however, appeared increasingly remote in late January 1998, when 16 people were killed in a suspected LTTE suicide bombing in Kandy at Sri Lanka's most sacred Buddhist temple, the Dalada Maligawa ('Temple of the Tooth'). The following day the Government retaliated by formally outlawing the LTTE, thus apparently ruling out the prospect of further peace negotiations in the near future and focusing instead on a military solution. (In October 2003 two Tamils were sentenced to death for carrying out the bombing; a third defendant was sentenced *in absentia* to 20 years' imprisonment. Death sentences were normally commuted to life imprisonment in Sri Lanka.) The Government suffered another set-back in late January 1998 when the UNP effectively rejected the proposed devolution package. The UNP disagreed with the Government's proposal to devolve wide-ranging powers to regional councils—including a Tamil-administered area—and favoured the concept of power-sharing at the centre. Also at the end of January, polls were conducted in Jaffna for the first time in 15 years. The local authority elections, which were monitored by tens of thousands of troops, were contested by a number of moderate Tamil political parties but were, not surprisingly, boycotted by the LTTE. The largest number of seats was won by the Eelam People's Democratic Party, but the turn-out was a mere 28%, owing to LTTE threats to disrupt the voting.

In mid-May 1998 the recently elected mayor of Jaffna (the first person to hold that position in 14 years), Sarojini Yogeswaran, who was a member of the moderate TULF, was assassinated by two suspected LTTE gunmen after refusing demands by Tamil militants to resign. In September Yogeswaran's replacement, Ponnuthurai Sivapalan, who was also a leading member of the TULF, was killed, along with 19 others, in a suspected LTTE bomb explosion in Jaffna city hall.

In early June 1998 the Government imposed an indefinite 'total ban' on news coverage (both local and foreign) of the ongoing civil war. In late September hundreds of troops on both sides were killed when the LTTE recaptured Kilinochchi and the army seized Mankulam, the last major town held by the guerrillas on the vital northern highway. By the end of the year, despite fierce fighting and large numbers of casualties on both sides, the army had still failed to capture completely the northern highway, which, if opened, would provide the military with a vital land route to the Jaffna peninsula (hitherto during the civil war, all government troops and supplies had had to be transported by sea or air). In early December the Government announced its decision to cancel the operation to capture the highway, which, since it was launched in May 1997, had cost the lives of more than 3,000 government troops. There were also indications that the army had a serious manpower problem (it needed to recruit 20,000 fresh troops), caused partly by desertions and growing numbers of casualties.

In late January 1999 the ruling PA won the elections to the north-western provincial council by a significant margin, but amid allegations of widespread electoral fraud and violence against opposition activists. A few days later the Supreme Court in Colombo overruled an order made by President Kumaratunga in August 1998 postponing elections to five other provincial councils. The Court stated that the presidency had no constitutional right to postpone the elections through the declaration of a state of emergency, as it had done, and asked the election commission to hold the polls within the next three months and to hold all five of them on a single day. In the provincial elections, which were eventually held in early April, the PA won control in four provinces and retained power in the fifth—the polls were very keenly contested, however, with the PA achieving about 43% of the total votes and the UNP obtaining around 41%. Elections to the southern province, which were held in May, also resulted in a PA-led administration. One noteworthy feature of this series of provincial polls was the resurgence of the JVP as a credible political force (it won 8% of the vote in all of the contested provincial councils, and, specifically, as much as 20% in the Hambantota district of the southern province).

Meanwhile, in March 1999 the army launched another offensive against the LTTE in the northern province, the objective of which was to reduce the area under the effective control of the Tamil guerrillas. In mid-June, in an unprecedented order, the President temporarily dissolved the powerful National Security Council and divested the Chief of Defence Staff of sweeping powers. Prospects of achieving a peace settlement in Sri Lanka appeared even more distant in late July, following the assassination by a suspected LTTE suicide bomber in Colombo of the TULF Vice-President, Neelan Tiruchelvam, who was a leading peace campaigner and human rights activist. In the same month Kumaratunga promoted 15 PA members to the position of deputy minister, in a move that was widely interpreted as an attempt to ensure that politicians remained loyal to the Alliance prior to and during the forthcoming general election. The promotions were heavily criticized by the opposition as financially profligate.

In October 1999 President Kumaratunga announced the holding of an early presidential election in December (about

11 months ahead of schedule), prompting the opposition to claim that her decision was aimed at bolstering the foundering ruling coalition prior to the legislative elections, which were due to be held in October 2000. In November 1999, however, the Government suffered a debilitating set-back following a rapid series of LTTE victories in the north-eastern Wanni region, thus reversing more than two years of territorial gains by the military. Following these demoralizing defeats and amidst reports of large-scale desertions and mutiny in the army ranks, the Government announced a tightening of existing military censorship on domestic news coverage in an attempt to stem adverse publicity and reorganized the northern military command.

A few days before the presidential election, which was held on 21 December 1999, Kumaratunga survived an assassination attempt by a suspected LTTE suicide bomber in Colombo; the explosion killed more than 20 people and injured more than 100, while the President sustained wounds to her right eye. The election, which was contested by 13 candidates and attracted a 73% turn-out of the electorate, was marred by widespread allegations of vote-rigging, intimidation and violence. Kumaratunga was returned to power by a narrow majority (possibly having garnered a considerable sympathy vote), winning 51% of the total votes, while her main rival, Ranil Wickremasinghe of the UNP, secured 43%.

At the end of January 2000, in a dramatic reversal of policy, Wickremasinghe announced that, in spite of reservations, the UNP would henceforth offer legislative support to the Government's proposed constitutional amendments regarding devolution (first unveiled in 1995), which were designed to prepare the ground for peace talks with the LTTE; the opposition party, however, later appeared to vacillate with regard to their support, following indications that Kumaratunga intended to retain the executive presidency for a further six years. In early 2000 the Government confirmed that, at Kumaratunga's request, the Norwegian Government had agreed to play an intermediary role in any peace negotiations. The Norwegian Minister of Foreign Affairs, Knut Vollebæk, arrived in Colombo in February to discuss with Kumaratunga and Wickremasinghe the modalities for commencing direct peace talks between the Sri Lankan Government and the LTTE. Earlier that month Vollebæk had met a senior LTTE official in London, United Kingdom, to assess the separatists' opinions regarding peace negotiations. According to commentators, the preconditions of both sides (respectively, the withdrawal of all government troops from Tamil areas and the abandonment by the LTTE of their demand for an independent state) were the most serious obstacles to the commencement of talks.

Despite the steps being taken towards the instigation of peace talks, heavy fighting continued between the army and the LTTE in the north. In April 2000, having made several significant gains, the LTTE announced that they had captured the large military base at Elephant Pass at the strategic entrance point to the peninsula (the garrison had been under government control since the IPKF's withdrawal in 1990). In early May President Kumaratunga came under intense pressure from various quarters to seek Indian assistance in an attempt to halt the rapid LTTE march to recapture Jaffna; the Indian Government firmly ruled out military intervention, but offered to provide humanitarian aid (including mediation and the evacuation of troops). India also announced that it was extending its ban on the outlawed LTTE for a further two years. In response to the escalating military crisis, the Government imposed draconian security measures, banning all activities perceived as a threat to national security and giving extensive powers to the armed forces and police, and renewed press censorship on the foreign media. By mid-May the LTTE claimed to be only 1 km from the administrative centre of Jaffna, and thousands of terrified civilians were reported to be fleeing from the embattled city. In late May, as the army and the LTTE continued to struggle for control of the peninsula, the Government appealed for new army recruits, and Norway launched a fresh diplomatic initiative to find a peaceful solution to the ethnic crisis. In early June the Minister of Industrial Development, Clement V. Gunaratna, and more than 20 others were killed by a suspected LTTE suicide bomber in Colombo. At the end of the month President Kumaratunga and the leader of the opposition UNP, Ranil Wickremasinghe, began discussions on the draft of the new Constitution designed to resolve the conflict with the LTTE. The LTTE, however, immediately denounced the proposals. At the same time, the Supreme Court ruled that the recently renewed press censorship was illegal as the appointment of the official censor had not been approved by Parliament. Nevertheless, the President reimposed a series of restrictions on the local and foreign press and reappointed the official censor under the same emergency regulations employed in May. The Government and UNP then agreed on a draft constitution, which recommended converting the country into a *de facto* federal state through the establishment of eight semi-autonomous regional councils. However, the Tamil parliamentary parties, the TULF, PLOTE and Eelam People's Democratic Party (EPDP), rejected the proposals as providing inadequate autonomy to the Tamil regions of the country. Senior Buddhist monks rejected the reforms, owing to fears that devolution would threaten the Sinhalese-dominated population and prominence of Buddhism in Sri Lanka. In late July the UNP withdrew its support for the reforms. Street demonstrations were held in protest at the proposals. In August the President indefinitely postponed a parliamentary vote on the issue, and hence any further discussion of the reform programme, once it became clear that the Government would not obtain the two-thirds' majority required to secure the passage of the requisite legislation. The LTTE intensified attacks on security forces. On 10 August Sirimavo Bandaranaike announced her resignation as Prime Minister, owing to ill health. She was replaced by Ratnisiri Wickremanayake, the erstwhile Minister of Public Administration, Home Affairs and Plantation Industries. Parliament was dissolved in preparation for a general election.

Meanwhile, a report issued by the University Teachers for Human Rights in mid-July 2000 claimed that there had been a dramatic increase in the number of child soldiers forcibly recruited by the LTTE, in preparation for a major assault on Jaffna city. In September heavy fighting between the LTTE and Sri Lankan army continued; the army reclaimed a naval base and Jaffna's second largest town, Chavakachcheri. By the end of September, however, the LTTE had managed to regain some territory. In the same month the Minister of Shipping and Shipping Development, Mohammad H. M. Ashraff, and the President of the SLMC, along with 14 others, were killed in a helicopter crash in Kegalle District. A high-level investigation into the incident was ordered; there was widespread speculation that the aircraft had been shot down by LTTE guerrillas.

The parliamentary elections of 10 October 2000 were marred by allegations of electoral malpractice and by systematic violence and intimidation (particularly on the part of the incumbent PA). Nevertheless, the elections attracted a turn-out of 75% of the electorate. Despite the electoral irregularities, neither the PA nor the UNP won an absolute majority (taking 107 and 89 of the 225 parliamentary seats, respectively), but, having gained the support of the EPDP and National Unity Alliance (NUA—primarily a constituent of the SLMC), the PA was able to form a new, expanded coalition under the premiership of Wickremanayake. The former Prime Minister, Sirimavo Bandaranaike, died shortly after casting her vote. On 18 October Parliament elected Anura Bandaranaike, a member of the UNP and the President's estranged brother, as parliamentary Speaker; this was the first time in 40 years that the position had been held by a member of the opposition. This development was followed by an agreement between the PA and UNP to preserve the stability of the new Government for the next two years. On 19 October a new Cabinet was announced. In exchange for its support, the NUA established a 100-day deadline for the President to introduce a new constitution and to open negotiations with the LTTE. At the end of the month the JVP announced its willingness to support the Government in order to prevent the NUA from wielding excessive influence.

In late October 2000 negotiations between the leader of the LTTE, Velupillai Prabhakaran, and the Norwegian peace envoy, Erik Solheim, commenced. Discussions between Solheim and the President were also initiated. In early November Prabhakaran proposed direct peace negotiations with the Government, without any preconditions, but demanded a reduction in fighting and the lifting of an economic embargo on areas controlled by the LTTE to create a suitable atmosphere for talks. The Government did not immediately respond to the offer, although it had made it clear that it was willing to attempt to reach a peace accord. The Prime Minister ruled out an imminent cease-fire, declaring that the army would continue to fight LTTE guerrillas. In mid-December the Government announced that it was prepared to enter immediate peace negotiations, but would not scale down its offensive or lift the embargo until talks were under way. The LTTE rejected peace talks without the prior implementation of a cease-fire and later declared a unilateral one-month cease-fire, to begin from 24 December, as a 'goodwill gesture' to assist the peace process. Shortly afterwards, however, government troops launched an offensive in the Jaffna peninsula, and violence continued. The Government rejected the cease-fire, dismissing it as a strategic manoeuvre, and insisted that it would not discuss a cease-fire until the two parties entered peace negotiations.

On 23 January 2001, and at regular intervals thereafter, the LTTE extended the cease-fire by one month. The Government refused to reciprocate with a cease-fire. Nevertheless, dialogue between Solheim and representatives of the LTTE and Government, respectively, resumed in late January. In early March both sides appeared to react positively to Solheim's efforts to broker peace; however, in mid-March violence escalated and continued into April. Meanwhile, the United Kingdom banned the LTTE under its anti-terrorism legislation. At the end of April Solheim held negotiations with the President. Talks between Solheim and the Government and the LTTE, respectively, in mid-May ended inconclusively.

In early June 2001 a motion for the impeachment of Chief Justice Sarath Silva, accusing him of misconduct, was submitted to Parliament. Later that month the President dismissed the leader of the SLMC, Abdul Rauf Hakeem, from his position as Minister of Internal and International Trade, Commerce, Muslim Religious Affairs and Shipping Development, later accusing him of making anti-Government statements and refusing to support government policies. The President's strategy foundered, however, when Hakeem and six other members of the SLMC withdrew their support for the ruling PA, thereby reducing the coalition Government to a minority in Parliament. Immediately afterwards, opposition parties challenged the Government with a no-confidence motion. In order to prevent the motion from being debated in Parliament in mid-July, the President suspended the legislature on 10 July until 7 September, and announced that a referendum on a new constitution would take place on 21 August. The rulings, which were undemocratic and unconstitutional, respectively, caused a constitutional crisis. The UNP-led opposition organized a series of demonstrations against the President's decision to prorogue Parliament. The President also faced opposition within the Cabinet, particularly to the referendum. As a result, Kumaratunga announced in early August that the referendum would be postponed until mid-October.

In the mean time, in early June 2001 the Norwegian Minister of Foreign Affairs, Thorbjørn Jagland, arrived in Colombo, at the request of the President, in an attempt to bolster the peace initiative. The LTTE, however, protested against this development, claiming that it was an effort to reduce in importance Solheim's position. In early July President Kumaratunga circumvented Parliament and reimposed a state of emergency under anti-terrorist regulations. The President also extended a ban on the LTTE. On 24 July, the 18th anniversary of the start of the LTTE's separatist campaign, Tamil militants attacked the capital's international airport and an adjacent air base. Several hours of shooting between Tamil militants and the army ended with all 13 guerrillas and seven soldiers killed. The LTTE had destroyed eight military aircraft and three civilian aircraft, and damaged others. The attack on the country's only international airport, renowned for its impenetrable security, adversely affected the tourist industry and, thus, the economy and raised questions about the air force and airport's defence system. Following the incident, the army launched a retaliatory air attack on LTTE bases; violence between the army and guerrillas escalated. At the end of August the LTTE rejected the Government's offer of a cease-fire, dismissing it as a strategic manoeuvre.

In an attempt to resolve the political crisis, the Prime Minister and senior cabinet members conducted negotiations with the UNP on the possible establishment of a coalition government. The UNP, however, opted to form a UNP-led coalition with other opposition parties. Consequently, the President entered into negotiations with the left-wing, radical JVP. On 5 September 2001 the JVP formally agreed to support the minority Government for one year (but not to join the administration), in return for a set of conditions laid out in a 28-point memorandum of understanding. The JVP's 10 seats in Parliament raised the Government's share to a majority of 119 out of 225 seats. The President had already granted the JVP two of its demands by cancelling the referendum and announcing that Parliament would be reconvened one day earlier. In addition, the President agreed to suspend negotiations with the LTTE for one year and to postpone the privatization programme. According to the JVP's demands, in mid-September the size of the Cabinet was halved to 22 members. However, three senior cabinet members resigned, refusing to participate in an administration supported by the left-wing party. Several members of the PA criticized the pact and doubted its longevity. Later that month Parliament approved an item of legislation to establish a Constitutional Council, which would be responsible for removing political influence from major institutions and appointing independent commissions for public service, the judiciary, the police and elections. At the end of September a motion of 'no confidence' in the Government was resubmitted to Parliament. On 8 October the SLFP removed its General Secretary, S. B. Dissanayake. (In December 2004 Dissanayake was sentenced to a two-year prison term, having been convicted of making 'defamatory comments' about the judges of the Supreme Court during his tenure as General Secretary.) Two days later 13 members of the PA, including several ministers, defected to the opposition, reducing the coalition to a minority. In order to forestall defeat in the vote of 'no confidence' due to take place the next day, President Kumaratunga dissolved Parliament. The opposition condemned the decision, although the dissolution was constitutional (one year had passed since the previous legislative elections).

The general election on 5 December 2001, reportedly one of the most violent in Sri Lanka's history, was marred by incidents of vote-rigging and other electoral malpractices. Some tens of thousands of Tamil voters were barred from voting after the army prevented them from leaving LTTE-controlled areas to cast their vote. The outgoing Government claimed that the UNP had signed a secret pact with the LTTE, an allegation strongly denied by the opposition. Nevertheless, 72% of the electorate voted. The UNP won 109 of the 225 seats (45.6% of the vote) and the PA received 77 seats (37.2%). The JVP secured 16 seats (9.1%) and the Tamil Nationalist Alliance (TNA—a Tamil opposition alliance comprising the TULF, TELO, EPRLF and All Ceylon Tamil Congress formed prior to the election) won 15 seats (3.9%). The UNP leader, Ranil Wickremasinghe, formed the United National Front (UNF) with the SLMC to ensure a majority of 114 seats in Parliament. Two days after the election Wickremasinghe was invited to form a government and on 9 December he was sworn in as Prime Minister. For the first time since 1984, the Prime Minister and the President were from two opposing parties; consequently, the relationship between the PA President and the UNF Government proved to be uneasy at times. The President was at first reluctant to relinquish her defence and finance portfolios, which she eventually gave up in return for full control over the élite Presidential Security Division that was deployed for her personal protection, and refused initially to allow members of her former administration who had defected to the UNP to join the Government. After long negotiations, a new coalition Government, including the TNA and 12 members of the former PA administration, was sworn in on 12 December. In 2002 the right of the President to dissolve Parliament after one year from the date of the last election loomed over the new Government. In an attempt to curb the President's powers and to ensure stability for the peace process (see below), the Government recommended that parliamentary resolutions determine future elections; however, the President refused to support this suggestion. In September the Government introduced to Parliament a constitutional amendment which would restrict the right of the President to dissolve the legislature when the governing party has a majority in Parliament. In October, however, the Supreme Court ruled that the proposed statute required not only a two-thirds' majority in the legislature, but also endorsement by a national referendum.

The UNP's victory was largely attributed to the party's keenness to resume negotiations with the LTTE; on his accession, the Prime Minister reiterated this willingness. Significantly, the TNA was a member of the coalition Government. Although the LTTE launched major attacks against army troops and the police, during which 26 were killed, to mark the inauguration of the new Cabinet, on 19 December the Tamil extremists announced a unilateral one-month cease-fire from 25 December. On 21 December the Government responded with the declaration of a cease-fire as a 'gesture of goodwill'. The Prime Minister also announced that the free movement of food, medicine and other non-military supplies into the Tamil-controlled areas would be allowed; a concession refused, hitherto, by the President. In early January 2002 the Government announced the reduction of economic sanctions on the northern areas controlled by the LTTE. One week later a delegation of Norwegian diplomats, led by Norway's Deputy Minister of Foreign Affairs, Vidar

Helgesen, arrived in Colombo to conduct negotiations with the Prime Minister and President, and eventually to facilitate peace talks between the Government and the LTTE. At the end of January both sides extended the cease-fire by one month. At the same time, the LTTE released 10 army and civilian prisoners. As a further confidence-building measure, the Government restored the electricity supply to part of the northern Tamil-controlled Vavuniya district.

On 22 February 2002 the Government and LTTE signed an agreement on an internationally monitored indefinite cease-fire to take effect the following day. Norway was requested to monitor the cease-fire. It was hoped that this breakthrough would lead to peace negotiations and end years of fighting in which more than 60,000 people had been killed. However, in mid-February there were several reports that the LTTE was continuing forcibly to recruit Tamil children.

In mid-March 2002 Prime Minister Wickremasinghe visited Jaffna, the first premier to do so since 1982. In early April the Government lifted a six-year ban on domestic flights and allowed commercial airlines to resume flights to Jaffna. A week later an important road linking the Jaffna peninsula with the rest of the country was opened for the first time in 12 years. On 10 April Prabhakaran addressed an international press conference for the first time in more than 10 years. He demanded the lifting of the ban on the LTTE as a prerequisite to negotiations and declared his commitment to peace and full support of the cease-fire. A few days later he signed a pact with the SLMC, allowing the largest Muslim party in Sri Lanka to participate in proposed negotiations with the Government. It was also agreed that nearly 100,000 Muslims expelled from the north by the LTTE about 10 years ago would be allowed to return to their homes. At the end of April the Prime Minister rejected the LTTE's demand for an independent Tamil state, or eelam, raising doubts about resolving the ethnic conflict. Meanwhile, Kumaratunga, who had reportedly criticized the Government for making too many concessions to the Tamil militants, expressed her support in late April for a public demonstration against the proposal to grant legal status to the LTTE.

In May 2002 a Tamil-owned trawler, reported to have been illegally importing weapons, was destroyed by the Sri Lankan navy in an exchange of gunfire off the coast of the eastern Batticaloa district—the first major violation of the cease-fire to have occurred. The LTTE refuted allegations that they had been smuggling arms and accused the army of attacking a civilian fishing boat in an effort to undermine the cease-fire. Later in the month the Norwegian-led Sri Lanka Monitoring Mission issued a statement conveying concern over the increasing number of cases of civilians being harassed by the LTTE. In June incidents of violence between Hindu Tamils and Muslims in eastern Sri Lanka resulted in eight deaths and several injuries.

Meanwhile, also in May 2002 the first direct talks for seven years between the Government and the LTTE took place on the Jaffna peninsula. Although the August deadline for the commencement of formal peace negotiations was not achieved, the cease-fire was maintained. According to the office of the UN High Commissioner for Refugees (UNHCR, see p. 62), by mid-August 103,000 displaced families had returned to their homes since the beginning of the cease-fire in February. On 4 September the Government lifted the official ban on the LTTE, a prerequisite to negotiations set by the LTTE. (The President, however, firmly opposed the removal of the ban until the talks were under way.) The first round of negotiations took place on 16–18 September in Thailand. The minister G. L. Peiris was chief negotiator for the Government; Anton Balasingham led negotiations on behalf of the LTTE. The talks were successful: both sides agreed to establish a joint committee to deal with security issues, and a joint task force to concentrate on the reconstruction of areas destroyed by war, the clearing of land-mines and the resettling of 800,000 internally displaced people to high-security zones. On the last day of negotiations Balasingham unexpectedly renounced the LTTE's long-standing demand for independence, instead agreeing to consider regional autonomy and self-government.

In early October 2002 four people were killed and 15 injured in clashes between government and LTTE forces in Ampara district, in one of the most serious violations of the cease-fire to date. On 31 October a Sri Lankan court convicted *in absentia* Prabhakaran for his role in a 1996 truck bombing in Colombo and sentenced him to 200 years' imprisonment. The sentencing did not have an effect on the second round of negotiations, which began on 31 October in Thailand. The four-day talks concentrated mainly on humanitarian issues, but concluded in a breakthrough with both sides agreeing to create a subcommittee to examine a political solution to the conflict. Balasingham announced that the LTTE were willing to participate in democracy, would allow other political parties to operate in the areas under their control and would cease the recruitment of child soldiers. The LTTE also abandoned their demand for an interim government in the north-east. Both sides agreed to establish subcommittees to deal with rehabilitation and military de-escalation. However, while the talks progressed, a curfew was imposed in large parts of Colombo after three days of rioting between the majority Sinhalese and members of the Muslim community. Meanwhile, Sinhalese nationalists opposed to the peace process questioned the sincerity of the LTTE, dismissing the progress at the negotiations as an attempt to win publicity and international favour. Nevertheless, the peace process gained momentum in late November when Balasingham arrived in Norway to enter negotiations with the Prime Minister on the eve of a one-day international donor conference in support of the peace process. A few days later Prabhakaran confirmed in his annual address that the LTTE were prepared to accept regional autonomy rather than an independent state, but warned that violence would resume if negotiations collapsed.

In December 2002, at the third round of peace talks in Oslo, Norway, the two sides agreed on 'internal self-determination' based on a federal system of government within a united Sri Lanka. Peiris and Balasingham described the developments as unprecedented and historic. However, in order to achieve the two-thirds' majority required in Parliament to pass a constitutional amendment, the Government needed to secure the support of the President. Although Kumaratunga welcomed the peace agreement, she had repeatedly criticized the Government for making too many concessions during the peace process. In mid-December a close adviser of the President stated that the PA would not support a political solution unless the LTTE disarmed. However, at the fourth round of negotiations, held in early January 2003 in Thailand, Balasingham refused to yield to pressure to disarm the Tamil guerrillas prior to a political settlement and rejected Kumaratunga's demand that the LTTE's squad of suicide bombers disband. The talks concluded with an agreement to accelerate the rate of return and resettlement of up to 250,000 displaced people. Meanwhile, despite Tamil promises to halt the involuntary recruitment of children, the Sri Lanka Monitoring Mission reported that the LTTE had enlisted hundreds of child soldiers since the beginning of the cease-fire. In late January the President ordered police and military chiefs to curb the recruitment of child soldiers within one week. Representatives of UNICEF conducted training sessions with the Sri Lankan military and talks with the LTTE on the recruitment of child soldiers, as well as issues of child protection and rehabilitation. The fifth round of negotiations, held in Germany in early February, was overshadowed by a serious violation of the cease-fire. On 7 February three LTTE guerrillas committed suicide by setting fire to their trawler after the Sri Lankan navy intercepted the vessel and Norwegian peace monitors discovered arms on board. The two-day negotiations focused on human rights issues; it was agreed that UNICEF would monitor a joint programme to rehabilitate child soldiers.

Meanwhile, the SLMC split in early December 2002 after two members of the party mounted a challenge to Hakeem's leadership. In early February 2003 President Kumaratunga censured the Prime Minister for granting a licence to the LTTE radio station, Voice of Tigers, amid rising tension in the cohabitation Government. On 7 February the PA and JVP began negotiations to form a joint front against the UNF Government. The JVP strongly opposed the LTTE and attempted to persuade the President to dismiss the governing coalition. Prabhakaran failed to attend a meeting with Norwegian peace mediators in mid-March, reportedly owing to the sinking of a civilian Tamil ship by the Sri Lankan navy several days earlier. The LTTE declared that they were considering abandoning the peace talks as a result of the incident. Furthermore, the sixth round of negotiations on 18–21 March, held in Japan, ended without agreement, amid reports of renewed violence in Sri Lanka (some progress had been made, however, including an agreement by the LTTE to permit other Tamil parties to function in LTTE-controlled areas). Both sides reaffirmed their commitment to the cease-fire after a Chinese fishing trawler was attacked by suspected LTTE guerrillas off the coast of Sri Lanka. An international donor meeting in Washington, DC, USA, to consider aid for Sri Lanka's reconstruction in preparation for a major donor conference to be held in Japan in June, took place in mid-April. The LTTE, however, were not invited: the USA had not yet lifted its ban on the Tamil organization; neither had India, one of the attendees at the meeting. On 21 April the LTTE announced that they were temporarily withdrawing from the peace negotiations and that they would not attend the donor conference in Japan in June because they were excluded from the aid conference in the USA. They were also dissatisfied with the manner in which the cease-fire had been implemented (government troops remained stationed in many parts of the Tamil-controlled areas in a clear violation of the cease-fire) and the way in which the Government was carrying out rehabilitation and relief measures. Following the LTTE announcement, the President placed the security forces on high alert; however, the LTTE intended to uphold the cease-fire and there were no signs of renewed tension.

Efforts to revive the peace process suffered a set-back in May 2003. In a letter to the Prime Minister, Balasingham demanded that the Government establish an interim administration for the north-east of the country. The Government refused to agree, offering instead a 'development-orientated' structure for the area, with greater financial authority for the LTTE. The LTTE rejected this proposal as not extensive enough, and attempts to resume the peace negotiations failed. Informal talks, however, continued to take place. In mid-June a senior leader of the Varadharajah faction of the Eelam People's Revolutionary Front, Subathran, was shot dead. Subathran was the most senior of 30 politicians from rival Tamil parties and suspected army informants to have been assassinated since the beginning of the cease-fire; the LTTE were believed to have been responsible for the attack, creating serious doubts over the Tamil organization's commitment to multi-party politics. At the same time, an LTTE oil tanker exploded and sank during a confrontation with a Sri Lankan navy patrol. The LTTE and Government offered conflicting versions of the incident: military officials reported that the ship was smuggling weapons and that Tamil militants aboard the vessel refused to stop despite several warnings and caused the explosion to avoid being caught; the LTTE denied the charges, claiming that the Sri Lankan navy fired at the ship after capturing the crew. At the end of the month the LTTE organized a demonstration to demand the return of thousands of homes on the Jaffna peninsula occupied by the Sri Lankan army as high-security zones since the 1980s; some 150,000 people attended the rally. Although the Government was committed to vacating these zones, the army believed a sudden withdrawal would give the LTTE the opportunity to seize complete control of the Jaffna peninsula. Meanwhile, in early June an international donor Conference on the Reconstruction and Development of Sri Lanka took place in Tokyo, Japan, despite the refusal of the LTTE to attend. The international community agreed to give Sri Lanka US $4,500m. in aid over four years as long as the stalled peace process began again.

In July 2003 the Government requested Norwegian peace envoy Jon Westbørg to inform the LTTE of the Government's new proposals for an interim administration, which reportedly included greater financial and political powers for the LTTE. The JVP opposed government plans to share power with Tamil militants in the north-east of the country and announced that it would organize public demonstrations in protest against the proposal. The LTTE agreed to consider the offer. In the same month the Sri Lankan administration decided to grant Sri Lankan citizenship to more than 160,000 Tamils of Indian origin who had been unable to return home since the beginning of the civil war. In August the Sri Lankan Monitoring Mission reported that the Tamil militants had failed to comply with the terms of the cease-fire agreement by refusing to dismantle a camp in the north-eastern district of Trincomalee. Following talks with Norwegian monitors, and under pressure from the international community, the LTTE agreed to reconsider their position. However, at the end of August the Tamil rebels refused to dismantle the camp, insisting that it had existed before the cease-fire agreement was reached and should, therefore, be allowed to remain. This claim was rejected by the security forces and independent truce monitors. Controversy over the issue continued with allegations by the military and opposition that the LTTE had established 13 new camps since the beginning of the cease-fire; the Tamil militants denied the charges. The matter had also become a source of contention between the Prime Minister and President. Wickremasinghe censured the President for discussing security issues publicly, while President Kumaratunga continued to criticize the Government's conduct in the peace process. Meanwhile, the Kumaratunga-led PA and left-wing JVP failed to form an alliance owing to differences over their approach to the peace process and devolution of power.

Despite the political wrangling and the LTTE's increasingly rigid stance, the Prime Minister remained optimistic in late September 2003 that the stalled peace process would resume. However, on 9 October the Minister of Defence accused the LTTE of having increased their military strength two-fold and of having continued to conscript child soldiers since the beginning of the truce in February 2002. In late October the LTTE revealed a detailed plan for an Interim Self-Governing Authority (ISGA) to administer north-eastern Sri Lanka. The LTTE demanded an authority with a guaranteed Tamil majority and full control over regional administration for five years pending the achievement and implementation of a final settlement. The Government reacted cautiously to the plan; nevertheless, the Government announced that it would request Norwegian mediators to facilitate the resumption of talks. President Kumaratunga, however, condemned the offer, claiming that it was the first step towards a separate state.

On 4 November 2003 the country was plunged into a constitutional crisis when Kumaratunga took advantage of the Prime Minister's absence (he was attending trade negotiations in the USA) and suspended the legislature for a period of two weeks, dismissed the Minister of Interior and Christian Affairs, the Minister of Defence and of Transport, Highways and Aviation, and the Minister of Mass Communication, assuming the important portfolios herself, and deployed troops to key positions in the capital, Colombo, in the stated interest of preserving national security. It was reported that Kumaratunga had declared a state of emergency on 5 November, but withdrew the decree two days later on Wickremasinghe's return from the USA. The President claimed that the Prime Minister had made too many concessions to the LTTE during peace negotiations. Kumaratunga and Wickremasinghe held two meetings in an attempt to resolve the crisis, with little success: Wickremasinghe rejected the offer to form a government of national unity and suggested that, since the President had assumed the defence portfolio, Kumaratunga should lead the peace negotiations. However, the two leaders agreed to appoint a committee to establish by mid-December new power-sharing arrangements. In the mean time, in mid-November the Norwegian peace negotiators announced that they would withdraw from the peace process until it was made clear who held power and authority in Sri Lanka.

In mid-January 2004 the crisis worsened when Kumaratunga declared that she had held an undisclosed swearing-in ceremony in 2000 to give herself another year in office, thereby extending her term to December 2006. Analysts debated whether the action was constitutional. Later in January the Kumaratunga-led SLFP and the JVP formed the United People's Freedom Alliance (UPFA). The UPFA was joined by four more left-wing parties, which were members of the erstwhile PA, in early February. On 7 February Kumaratunga dissolved Parliament and called a general election for 2 April, almost four years ahead of schedule. Hours before the dissolution, the President created two new cabinet appointments for her supporters; the existing Cabinet was to operate in an acting capacity prior to the general election. Both the Cabinet and the LTTE condemned the decision, amid fears that the election would further undermine the peace process with the LTTE. The LTTE, however, pledged to maintain the cease-fire. Meanwhile, it was reported in late January that a Christian church at Mattegoda, near Colombo, had been attacked. The incident was the latest of at least 30 attacks on Christian churches since November 2003, which had allegedly been encouraged by hardline Buddhist clergy. Christians had been accused of sympathizing with the LTTE and carrying out unethical conversions. President Kumaratunga warned that anyone guilty of promoting religious tension would be severely punished.

In early March 2004 a rift within the LTTE appeared after a senior Tamil eastern regional commander declared his independence from the rest of the group. V. Muralitharan (commonly known as Col Karuna) withdrew his 6,000 fighters from the 15,000-strong LTTE in a dispute with the northern-based LTTE leader, Prabhakaran. Karuna, who accused northern Tamil groups of ignoring and discriminating against eastern groups, made it clear that he would not resume violence. However, he would not recognize the cease-fire agreement between the Government and Prabhakaran, and instead demanded a separate truce agreement with the Sri Lankan administration. Analysts feared that the schism might escalate into factional war; the split also raised questions about Prabhakaran's control over the LTTE and undermined the Tamil militants' claims that the main obstacle in the peace process was political divisions among Sinhalese political parties. The rift also adversely affected Norway's fresh attempt to revive the peace initiative. In late March the LTTE vowed to remove Karuna from Sri Lanka. The Tamil political candidate and supporter of Karuna, Rajan Sathyamoorthy, was shot dead by suspected Tamil militants in the eastern town of Batticaloa, raising fears of factional fighting. Although the LTTE denied any involvement in the killing, government troops were deployed to Batticaloa to maintain law and order. On 9 April fighting between the two factions broke out. The conflict ended on 13 April with Karuna reported to have fled from his base and gone into hiding, his forces having dispersed and the LTTE assuming full control of the eastern areas.

At the general election, which took place on 2 April 2004, the UPFA won 105 of the 225 seats, having taken 45.6% of the votes cast; Wickremasinghe's UNP retained 82 seats (with 37.8% of the votes), while the TNA won 22 seats (with 7%). In an unexpected development, the Buddhist Jathika Hela Urumaya (JHU—National Heritage Party) won nine seats. The LTTE had openly supported the TNA during the election campaign and described the large number of seats won by the alliance as an endorsement and recognition of the LTTE as 'the sole representative' of the Tamil population. Participation at the election was reported to have reached 75% of eligible voters. The poll concluded peacefully. However, there were claims of voter intimidation and electoral malpractice, particularly in the north and east of the country. The UPFA, which had not secured an outright majority of seats in Parliament, undertook negotiations with a view to forming a coalition administration. Meanwhile, Mahinda Rajapakse, a senior member of the UPFA and former fisheries minister, was sworn in as Prime Minister on 6 April. By 10 April the UPFA still needed the support of at least eight legislators to achieve an absolute majority in Parliament; nevertheless, a 31-member Cabinet was sworn in. While Kumaratunga retained the defence portfolio, Lakshman Kadirgamar was appointed Minister of Foreign Affairs. In late April, having resolved a dispute with the UPFA, four members of the JVP were also sworn in as ministers.

Meanwhile, the LTTE responded to the election result with a threat to return to violence if their demands for self-rule were not met. They later requested the Government to open negotiations on the basis of the proposed ISGA that they had submitted in late October. President Kumaratunga had already agreed to abide by the cease-fire and pledged to resume negotiations with the LTTE; however, it was widely acknowledged that she would not be willing to grant the degree of devolution that was desired by the Tamil organization. The JVP was also hostile towards the LTTE's campaign for regional autonomy.

From June 2004 onwards the cease-fire between the LTTE and the Government came under increasing pressure. During discussions with Hagrup Haukland, leader of the Norwegian team monitoring the ongoing peace process, the LTTE accused the Sri Lankan armed forces of sheltering Col Karuna and of assisting him in waging a campaign against them. The armed forces initially denied that they had helped Karuna to escape following the April conflict; however, later in that month the Minister of Ports and Aviation and of Information and Media, Mangala Saramaraweera, admitted that the army had helped Karuna to escape, while insisting that the plan had been carried out without government knowledge. Fears that the cease-fire was close to collapse were heightened when a suicide bomber blew herself up during questioning at a police station in Colombo in early July, having first attempted to meet the Tamil Secretary-General of the EPDP, Douglas Devananda, who was a long-standing opponent of the LTTE. Although the LTTE denied any involvement in the attack, they were widely believed to have been responsible both for the bombing, and for the assassination of an EPDP politician in Ampara district later in that month. Meanwhile, clashes continued to occur between the LTTE and members of the faction that had broken away under the leadership of Karuna. At the end of July Norway's Deputy Minister of Foreign Affairs, Vidar Helgesen, arrived in Sri Lanka to attempt to restart peace talks, accusing both the Government and the LTTE of complacency. The opposition UNP subsequently offered to support the Government in any parliamentary vote on the resumption of talks. However, in September it was reported that Norwegian envoy Erik Solheim had failed in his attempts to instigate new peace talks.

In September 2004 the UPFA Government achieved a legislative majority for the first time since its formation in April when the CWC, which had eight seats in Parliament, announced that it would join the ruling coalition. Muttu Sivalingam of the CWC was subsequently appointed Minister of Community Development and Estate Infrastructure. In the following month three members of the opposition SLMC defected to the UPFA, further strengthening the Government.

In December 2004 the LTTE formally rejected a new proposal by the Government that the two sides restart peace negotiations. The LTTE attributed their decision to the fact that the JVP, one of the members of the coalition Government, opposed their condition that any negotiations should be based upon their proposed ISGA. The LTTE had warned in November that they would return to their violent struggle for self-rule unless the Government agreed to discuss the ISGA. Concerns were raised by several prominent donor countries that the JVP's stance was undermining the peace process.

Sri Lanka was one of the countries most seriously affected by the devastating tsunami caused by a massive earthquake in the Indian Ocean on 26 December 2004. More than 31,000 Sri Lankans were killed in the disaster, which also left thousands homeless and without livelihoods. The tourism industry was badly affected by the catastrophe, with many hotels and resorts being damaged or destroyed. It was initially hoped that the scale of the disaster would serve to ease tensions between the Government and the LTTE, particularly as the Tamil areas of the island were amongst those worst hit. However, conflicts soon surfaced over the distribution of aid; the LTTE claimed that the Government was restricting the flow of international aid into Tamil-controlled areas and demanded that it be delivered directly to them. Talks intended to resolve the dispute held at the end of January ended without agreement. The situation deteriorated further in the following month, when it was revealed that around 70% of the survivors of the tsunami disaster had yet to receive any government relief, apparently owing to a combination of bureaucratic incompetence and corruption. The Tamil Relief Organization (TRO), controlled by the LTTE, alleged that only one-third of the aid was reaching the Tamil-controlled northern and eastern areas, despite government claims that two-thirds of the aid was destined for these areas.

Meanwhile, in February 2005 the Government announced that it was prepared to resume peace negotiations with the LTTE, based on the ISGA, prompting the JVP to threaten its withdrawal from the UPFA. Earlier in that month a senior LTTE leader, E. Kaushalyan, was murdered in his car near the town of Batticaloa. The police blamed the LTTE faction led by Col Karuna; however, the LTTE accused the armed forces of collaborating with Karuna's faction to fight against them. Karuna's faction continued to clash with the LTTE sporadically during the following months, and was suspected to be responsible for the assassination of a prominent Tamil journalist in April.

In June 2005 the Government finally signed an agreement—the Post-Tsunami Operational Management Structure (P-TOMS)—that would allow the LTTE to participate in the distribution of aid for the reconstruction effort. The agreement had been reached only following the withdrawal from the ruling coalition of the JVP, which had remained stringently opposed to any deal with the LTTE. The JVP's withdrawal left the Government with a minority in the legislature, although the opposition UNP had assured the Government of its support for the aid-sharing mechanism. In the following month, however, in response to a petition from the JVP and the JHU, the Supreme Court suspended the implementation of the P-TOMS, ruling that several of its clauses were illegal. Meanwhile, increasing tensions between the LTTE and government forces, complicated by the former's ongoing clashes with the rebel Karuna faction, led to an upsurge in violence that prompted international donors to warn the two sides that the ongoing cease-fire was under threat. At the end of May the chief of military intelligence in Colombo, Maj. Nizam Muthalif, had become the most senior official to have been assassinated by the LTTE since the agreement of the cease-fire in February 2002.

In August 2005 the peace process between the Government and the LTTE was seriously threatened when the Minister of Foreign Affairs, Lakshman Kadirgamar, was assassinated by unidentified gunmen at his home in Colombo. Although they denied responsibility, the LTTE were held responsible for the attack. In the aftermath of the murder, President Kumaratunga declared a state of emergency, granting the security forces broad powers of detention. Amidst widespread fears that the cease-fire would collapse, both sides announced their commitment to its maintenance, and the LTTE agreed to meet with the Government to review the truce agreement. Later in August Kumaratunga announced the appointment of her brother, Anura Bandaranaike, already Minister of Tourism in the Cabinet, as Kadirgamar's successor. Bandaranaike continued to hold the tourism portfolio. Meanwhile, there was uncertainty over the venue at which talks between the LTTE and the Government could take place. In September the LTTE declined a Norwegian proposal that the talks should be held at the international airport near Colombo, while the Government rejected the LTTE's suggestion that they be held in Kilinochchi, the political centre of LTTE-controlled northern Sri Lanka. Later in the same month the European Union (EU) issued a statement banning LTTE delegations from visiting any of its member states. Sporadic violence continued throughout the following months.

Meanwhile, there was controversy over when the country's next presidential election was scheduled to take place. While, under the terms of the Constitution, the next election was due to be held in December 2005, President Kumaratunga claimed that the holding of an undisclosed swearing-in ceremony in 2000 (see above) had actually extended her second term until December 2006. In July the SLFP announced that its presidential candidate would be Prime Minister Mahinda Rajapakse. In August the Supreme Court brought an end to the controversy, ruling that the election should be held by 22 November 2005. In September it was announced that the election would take place on 17 November. Former Prime Minister Ranil Wickremasinghe subsequently declared that he would stand as the candidate of the UNP. The JVP offered its support to Rajapakse, on the condition that were he to secure victory he would commit his government to the retention of a unitary state, renegotiate the ongoing cease-fire with the LTTE and end the privatization of state assets. Rajapakse concluded a similar agreement with the JHU.

On 17 November 2005 14 candidates contested the presidential election. Mahinda Rajapakse secured a narrow victory over his closest rival, Ranil Wickremasinghe, winning 50.29% of the vote, compared with 48.43% for Wickremasinghe. The election was notable for the low turn-out amongst the country's Tamil population, particularly in the LTTE-controlled northern and eastern areas; this was thought to have played a significant part in Wickremasinghe's defeat, as he had stressed his commitment to the ongoing cease-fire agreement during the electoral campaign. While the LTTE had stated that they would not prevent people from voting, there was widespread evidence that they had done so. Rajapakse subsequently nominated Minister of Agriculture, Public Security, Law and Order and of Buddha Sasana, Ratnasiri Wickremanayake, as Prime Minister. In the new Cabinet, announced shortly afterwards, Minister of Ports and Aviation Mangala Samaraweera was additionally allocated the foreign affairs portfolio, while Anura Bandaranaike continued as Minister of Tourism. Neither the JVP nor the JHU were awarded any cabinet portfolios.

In December 2005 violence in the country escalated. At least 60 people died over the course of the month as a result of various attacks believed to have been co-ordinated by the LTTE. At the end of that month President Rajapakse stated that he was ready to hold talks with the LTTE. Shortly before his announcement, Norwegian peace envoy Erik Solheim had urged both sides to enter into new peace talks, stressing that the cease-fire was in imminent danger of collapse. In early January 2006 a suicide bomb attack on a naval patrol vessel resulted in the deaths of 13 sailors, equalling the largest loss of military life since the cease-fire began. A further nine sailors were killed in a land-mine explosion later in that month, as the number of violent incidents continued to increase. In February negotiators representing the LTTE and the Government convened in Geneva, Switzerland, to hold talks on how to control the recent increase in violence. A joint statement issued following the conclusion of the talks committed both sides to uphold the cease-fire. The LTTE agreed to try and prevent further attacks on the security forces, while the Government pledged to try and disarm the Karuna faction of the LTTE, which was thought to have been acting on behalf of the armed forces against its erstwhile colleagues. However, prior to the second round of talks, scheduled to take place in Geneva in mid-April, the violence intensified once again. Several days before the talks were due to commence, the LTTE requested that they be postponed, in order that members of their delegation could first meet with LTTE commanders. Later that month the LTTE stated that they would not attend talks, alleging that government forces had perpetrated attacks on Tamil civilians. In late April a suicide bombing believed to have been perpetrated by the LTTE at the army headquarters in Colombo killed at least 11 people and seriously injured the Chief of Staff of the Army, Lt-Gen. Sarath Fonseka. The Government subsequently ordered a number of air strikes on the LTTE. Violence continued into May, placing the ongoing cease-fire in further jeopardy.

In foreign policy, Sri Lanka has adopted a non-aligned role. Sri Lanka is a founder member of the South Asian Association for Regional Co-operation (SAARC, see p. 356), formally established in 1985.

Government

A presidential form of government was adopted in October 1977 and confirmed in the Constitution of September 1978. The Constitution provides for a unicameral Parliament as the supreme legislative body, its members being elected by a system of modified proportional representation. Executive powers are vested in the President, who is Head of State. The President is directly elected for a term of six years and is not accountable to Parliament. The President has the power to appoint or dismiss the Prime Minister and members of the Cabinet; may assume any portfolio; and is empowered to dismiss Parliament. In 1982 the Constitution was amended, allowing the President to call a presidential election before his/her first term of office was completed. In 1983 the Constitution was further amended to include a 'no-separation' clause, making any division of Sri Lanka illegal, and any advocates of separatism liable to lose their civic rights.

Sri Lanka comprises nine provinces and 25 administrative districts, each with an appointed Governor and elected Development Council. In November 1987 a constitutional amendment was adopted, providing for the creation of eight provincial councils (the northern and eastern provinces were to be merged as one administrative unit). A network of 68 Pradeshiya Sabhas (district councils) was inaugurated throughout the country in January 1988.

Defence

In August 2005 the armed forces totalled 151,000 (including recalled reservists): army 118,000, navy 15,000, air force 18,000. There were also paramilitary forces of around 88,600 (including 13,000 Home Guard, an estimated 15,000 National Guard and a 3,000-strong anti-guerrilla unit). Defence expenditure for 2005 was budgeted at Rs 56,200m. Military service is voluntary.

Economic Affairs

In 2004, according to estimates by the World Bank, Sri Lanka's gross national income (GNI), measured at average 2002–04 prices, was US $19,618m., equivalent to $1,010 per head (or $4,000 per head on an international purchasing-power parity basis). During 1995–2004, it was estimated, the population increased at an average annual rate of 1.3%, while gross domestic product (GDP) per head increased, in real terms, by an average of 3.0% per year. Overall GDP increased, in real terms, at an average annual rate of 4.4% in 1995–2004. According to the Asian Development Bank (ADB), real GDP increased by 5.5% in 2004 and by 5.7% in 2005.

Agriculture (including hunting, forestry and fishing) contributed 17.8% of GDP in 2004, and in the first quarter of that year 32.1% of the employed labour force were engaged in the sector. The principal cash crops are tea (which accounted for 12.8% of total export earnings in 2004), rubber and coconuts. In 2004 Sri Lanka was the world's second largest tea exporter, having been overtaken by Kenya in that year. Rice production is also important. Cattle, buffaloes, goats and poultry are the principal livestock. During 1995–2004 agricultural GDP increased at an average annual rate of 0.8%. According to the ADB, agricultural GDP declined by 1.8% in 2004 but increased by 0.5% in 2005.

Industry (including mining and quarrying, manufacturing, construction and power) contributed 26.8% of GDP in 2004, and engaged 24.4% of the employed labour force (excluding inhabitants of the districts of Vavuniya, Mullaitivu and Kilinochchi) in the first quarter of that year. During 1995–2004 industrial GDP increased at an average annual rate of 4.5%. According to the ADB, industrial GDP increased by 5.4% in 2004 and by 6.1% in 2005.

Mining and quarrying contributed 2.0% of GDP in 2004, and, according to the ADB, engaged 1.8% of the employed labour force in 2001. Gemstones are the major mineral export (accounting for an estimated 1.9% of total export earnings in 2004). Another commercially important mineral in Sri Lanka is graphite, and there are also deposits of iron ore, monazite, uranium, ilmenite sands, limestone and clay. During 2000–04 sectoral GDP increased by an annual average of 3.2%, according to the ADB.

Manufacturing contributed 15.3% of GDP in 2004, and engaged 16.9% of the employed labour force in the first quarter of that year. The principal branches of manufacturing include wearing apparel (excluding footwear), textiles, food products, and also petroleum and coal products. The garment industry is Sri Lanka's largest earner of foreign exchange, with sales of garments and textiles providing an estimated 46.0% of total export earnings in 2004. During 1995–2004 manufacturing GDP increased by an average of 4.7% per year. The GDP of the manufacturing sector rose by 4.2% in 2003 and by 5.1% in 2004.

Energy is derived principally from petroleum, which accounted for 61.2% of electricity production in 2002. In the same year hydroelectric power accounted for 38.7% of electricity produced. Imports of mineral fuels and lubricants comprised 14.2% of the value of total imports in 2004.

The services sector, which is dominated by tourism, contributed 55.4% of GDP in 2004, and engaged 43.5% of the employed labour force (excluding inhabitants of the districts of Vavuniya, Mullaitivu and Kilinochchi) in the first quarter of that year. During 1995–2004 services GDP increased at an average annual rate of 5.5%. The sector's GDP grew by 8.1% in 2004 and by 7.1% in 2005.

In 2004 Sri Lanka recorded a visible trade deficit of US $1,442.6m., and there was a deficit of $677.2m. on the current account of the balance of payments. In 2004 the principal source of imports (14.0%) was India, while the USA was the principal market for exports (31.0%). Other major trading partners were the People's Republic of China, Singapore and the United Kingdom. The principal exports in 2004 were basic manufactures, including clothing, and tea. The principal imports were basic manufactures, machinery and transport equipment, and miscellaneous manufactured articles.

The projected budgetary deficit, before grants, for 2005 totalled Rs 171,146m. (7.5% of GDP). Sri Lanka's total external debt was US $10,238m. at the end of 2003, of which $9,106m. was long-term public debt. In that year the cost of debt-servicing was equivalent to 7.5% of earnings from the exports of goods and services. During 1995–2004 the average annual rate of inflation was 9.2%; the rate was 7.9% in 2004 and 11.6% in 2005. According to the ADB, an estimated 8.8% of the labour force were unemployed in 2005.

Sri Lanka is a member of the Asian Development Bank (ADB, see p. 169), a founder member of the South Asian Association for Regional Co-operation (SAARC, see p. 356), which seeks to improve regional co-operation, particularly in economic development, a founder member of the Colombo Plan (see p. 385), which seeks to promote economic and social development in Asia and the Pacific, and a member of the UN Economic and Social Commission for Asia and the Pacific (ESCAP, see p. 33).

Unemployment, a persistent fiscal deficit and inflation, together with the economic dislocation resulting from the ethnic conflict, are among the country's main economic problems. Following the declaration of a cease-fire between the Government and the Liberation Tigers of Tamil Eelam (LTTE) in February 2002, the economy showed clear signs of recovery. The export sector improved, and tourist arrivals increased. A privatization programme was also under way: the insurance, utilities, petroleum and telecommunications sectors were opened to private investment. In 2003 substantial progress was also made in public enterprise reform: several key public corporations were privatized and the electricity sector was opened to private investment. Donors at an international conference in June of that year pledged US $4,500m. in aid over the next five years to help rebuild the country's economy and infrastructure. The prerequisites to the assistance were a serious commitment from the Government to a restructuring programme and a permanent peace agreement between the LTTE and the Government. In 2004 the progress of economic reforms was constrained by the failure of the Government that was elected in April to achieve a majority in the legislature until September, and by the concomitant stalling of the peace process with the LTTE. However, growth was sustained in that year. Despite the continued economic expansion, drought and high global petroleum prices did have an adverse effect upon economic performance, reflected in a rise in the rate of inflation over the course of the year attributable to higher food and fuel prices and increased domestic demand. Furthermore, the fiscal deficit was estimated to have increased to some 8.2% of GDP in 2004, compared with 8.1% in the previous year, contributing to an increase in public debt to the equivalent of 108% of GDP (compared with 100.9% in 2003). The reconstruction effort necessitated by the devastating effect upon much of Sri Lanka's coastline of the massive tsunami in late December 2004 shaped the country's economic performance to an extent in 2005. However, although the fisheries and tourism sectors sustained extensive damage, resulting in the loss of many livelihoods, the more commercial areas in the west of the country were unaffected, limiting the economic impact of the disaster. In May 2005, at a forum on post-tsunami reconstruction, international donors pledged an estimated $3,000m. in financial assistance to Sri Lanka. The momentum generated by reconstruction efforts, together with the financial support offered by international donors, served to sustain economic expansion in 2005, with GDP increasing by 5.7% in that year. However, inflation increased further and the fiscal deficit once again exceeded budgetary targets. The 2006 budget, announced in December 2005, focused on reducing poverty through the introduction of decreases in taxation and new allowances for the poor and increasing investment in rural industries. In early 2006 an expansion in agricultural output contributed to a decline in the rate of inflation, although continued high global petroleum prices were expected to prevent any significant decrease in consumer prices over the course of the year. Meanwhile, political instability and security problems continued to deter potential investors. Escalating violence in late 2005 and early 2006 led to renewed fears of civil war, which, if realized, would have significant economic repercussions for Sri Lanka. In the long term, the achievement of a durable solution to the conflict with the LTTE and the Government's ability to implement structural reforms and to manage the country's considerable level of debt would be central to Sri Lanka's economic performance. The Government targeted GDP growth of 8.0% in 2006, while the ADB forecast that GDP would expand by 5.3% in that year.

Education

Education is officially compulsory for 11 years between five and 15 years of age, and it is available free of charge from lower kindergarten to university age. There are three types of school: state-controlled schools (mostly co-educational), denominational schools and Pirivenas (for Buddhist clergy and lay students). Primary education begins at the age of five and lasts for five years. Secondary education, beginning at 10 years of age, lasts for up to eight years, comprising a first cycle of six years and a second of two years. In 1998/99 the total enrolment at primary and secondary schools was equivalent to 84% of the school-age population (boys 84%; girls 85%). Primary enrolment in that year was equivalent to 106% of children in the relevant age-group (boys 107%; girls 104%); the comparable ratio for secondary enrolment was 72% (boys 70%; girls 74%) in 1995. There are 26 teacher-training colleges, 12 universities, 13 polytechnic institutes, eight junior technical colleges and an open university. Budgeted expenditure on education by the central Government in 2005 was Rs 63,360m. (11.2% of total government spending).

Public Holidays

2006: 11 January (Id al-Adha, Hadji Festival Day), 15 January (Tamil Thai Pongal Day), 4 February (Independence Commemoration Day), 26 February (Maha Shivaratri), 11 April (Milad un-Nabi, Birth of the Prophet), 13 April (Sinhala and Tamil New Year's Eve), 14 April (Good Friday and Sinhala and Tamil New Year's Day), 1 May (May Day), 21 October (Diwali—Festival of Lights), 24 October (Id al-Fitr, Ramazan Festival Day), 25 December (Christmas Day), 31 December (Id al-Adha, Hadji Festival Day).

2007: 14 January (Tamil Thai Pongal Day), 4 February (Independence Commemoration Day), 16 February (Maha Shivaratri), 31 March (Milad un-Nabi, Birth of the Prophet), 6 April (Good Friday), 13 April (Sinhala and Tamil New Year's Eve), 14 April (Sinhala and Tamil New Year's Day), 1 May (May Day), 13 October (Id al-Fitr, Ramazan Festival Day), 9 November (Diwali—Festival of Lights), 20 December (Id al-Adha, Hadji Festival Day), 25 December (Christmas Day).

Note: A number of Hindu, Muslim and Buddhist holidays depend on lunar sightings. There is a holiday every lunar month on the day of the full moon.

Weights and Measures

Legislation passed in 1974 provided for the introduction of the metric system, but imperial units are still used for some purposes.

SRI LANKA

Statistical Survey

Source (unless otherwise stated): Department of Census and Statistics, 15/12 Maitland Crescent, POB 563, Colombo 7; tel. (11) 2682176; fax (11) 2697594; e-mail dcensus@lanka.ccom.lk; internet www.statistics.gov.lk.

Area and Population

AREA, POPULATION AND DENSITY

Area (sq km)	65,525*
Population (census results)	
17 March 1981	14,846,750
17 July 2001 (provisional)†	
Males	8,343,964
Females	8,520,580
Total	16,864,544
Population (official estimates at mid-year)	
2001	18,700,000
2002	19,007,000
2003	19,253,000
Density (per sq km) at mid-2003	293.8

* 25,299 sq miles. This figure includes inland water (3,189 sq km).
† Figures refer to 18 out of 25 districts where enumeration was carried out completely. Enumeration was only partially conducted in Mannar, Vavuniya, Batticaloa and Trincomalee districts, owing to security concerns; data from these districts brought the total enumerated population to approximately 17,560,000. The census was not conducted in the districts of Jaffna, Mullaitivu and Kilinochchi, also owing to security concerns. The total estimated population for the entire country at July 2001 was 18,732,255.

ETHNIC GROUPS
(census results)

	1981	2001*†
Sinhalese	10,979,561	13,810,664
Sri Lankan Tamil	1,886,872	736,484
Indian Tamil	818,656	855,888
Sri Lankan Moors	1,046,926	1,349,845
Others	114,735	111,663
Total	14,846,750	16,864,544

* Provisional.
† Figures refer to 18 out of 25 districts.

DISTRICTS
(population estimates at mid-2003)

	Area (sq km, excl. inland water)*	Population ('000)	Density (persons per sq km)
Colombo	676	2,305	3,410
Gampaha	1,341	2,089	1,558
Kalutara	1,576	1,077	683
Kandy	1,917	1,307	682
Matale	1,952	453	232
Nuwara Eliya	1,706	714	419
Galle	1,617	1,011	625
Matara	1,270	780	614
Hambantota	2,496	533	214
Jaffna	929	589	634
Mannar	1,880	97	52
Vavuniya	1,861	139	75
Mullaitivu	2,415	141	58
Kilinochchi	1,205	140	116
Batticaloa	2,610	536	205
Ampara	4,222	605	143
Trincomalee	2,529	377	149
Kurunegala	4,624	1,475	319
Puttalam	2,882	722	251
Anuradhapura	6,664	764	115
Polonnaruwa	3,077	368	120
Badulla	2,827	801	283
Moneragala	5,508	405	74
Ratnapura	3,236	1,036	320
Kegalle	1,685	789	468
Total	62,705	19,253	307

* As at 1988; revised total land area is 62,336 sq km.

PRINCIPAL TOWNS
(provisional, population at 2001 census)

Colombo (Kolamba) (commercial capital)	642,020	Sri Jayawardenepura (Kotte) (administrative capital)	115,826
Dehiwala-Mount Lavinia	209,787	Kandy (Maha Nuwara)	110,049
Moratuwa	177,190	Kalmunai (Galmune)	94,457
Jaffna (Yapanaya)	145,600*	Galle (Galla)	90,934
Negombo (Migamuwa)	121,933		

* Estimated population at mid-1997 (Source: Provincial Councils, Department of Elections).

Source: Thomas Brinkhoff, *City Population* (internet www.citypopulation.de).

BIRTHS, MARRIAGES AND DEATHS*

	Registered live births		Registered marriages		Registered deaths	
	Number	Rate (per 1,000)	Number	Rate (per 1,000)	Number	Rate (per 1,000)
1996	340,649	18.6	172,306	9.3	122,161	7.0
1997†	333,219	18.8	164,407	n.a.	114,782	6.5
1998†	325,821	18.2	169,813	9.0	111,405	6.2
1999†	329,521	18.1	169,634	n.a.	114,472	6.3
2000†	340,144	18.4	186,548	n.a.	112,569	6.1
2001†	354,101	18.9	186,698	n.a.	111,100	5.9
2002†	363,549	19.1	190,832	n.a.	110,637	5.8
2003†	363,343	18.9	193,387	n.a.	114,310	5.9

* Data are tabulated by year of registration, rather than by year of occurrence.
† Provisional.

Expectation of life (WHO estimates, years at birth): 71 (males 68; females 75) in 2003 (Source: WHO, *World Health Report*).

ECONOMICALLY ACTIVE POPULATION
('000 persons aged 10 years and over, January–March of each year)

	2002*	2003†	2004§
Agriculture, hunting, forestry and fishing	2,341.8	2,380.9	2,354.9
Manufacturing	1,125.2	1,106.3	1,242.4
Mining and quarrying	164.0	120.0	165.6
Electricity, gas and water‡			
Construction	297.1	397.2	383.3
Trade, restaurants and hotels	973.1	987.7	1,140.6
Transport, storage and communications	282.2	375.7	400.5
Financing, insurance, real estate and business services	153.5	216.8	170.9
Community, social and personal services	1,326.1	1,358.1	1,478.5
Total employed	6,662.8	6,942.8	7,336.7
Unemployed	632.8	700.4	650.2
Total labour force	7,295.6	7,643.2	7,986.9

* Excluding northern and eastern provinces.
† Excluding northern but including eastern province.
‡ Including extraterritorial organizations and activities not adequately defined.
§ Excluding Vavuniya, Mullaitivu and Kilinochchi districts.

SRI LANKA

Health and Welfare

KEY INDICATORS

Total fertility rate (children per woman, 2003)	2.0
Under-5 mortality rate (per 1,000 live births, 2004)	14
HIV/AIDS (% of persons aged 15–49, 2003)	<0.1
Physicians (per 1,000 head, 2000)	0.43
Hospital beds (per 1,000 head, 1990)	2.74
Health expenditure (2002): US $ per head (PPP)	131
Health expenditure (2002): % of GDP	3.7
Health expenditure (2002): public (% of total)	48.7
Access to water (% of persons, 2002)	78
Access to sanitation (% of persons, 2002)	91
Human Development Index (2003): ranking	93
Human Development Index (2003): value	0.751

For sources and definitions, see explanatory note on p. vi.

Agriculture

PRINCIPAL CROPS
('000 metric tons)

	2002	2003	2004
Rice (paddy)	2,859	3,071	2,628
Maize	26	30	35
Potatoes	89	72	81
Sweet potatoes	47	44	40
Cassava (Manioc)	225	229	221
Sugar cane	963	1,015	990
Dry beans	10	11	11*
Dry cow-peas	10	13	13*
Coconuts	1,818	1,947	1,950*
Copra	59	49	80†
Cabbages	49	52	61
Tomatoes	41	45	54
Pumpkins, squash and gourds	100*	71	74
Cucumbers and gherkins	26*	23	23
Aubergines (Eggplants)	70*	74	80
Chillies and green peppers	46	46	40
Dry onions	67	68	77
Green beans	33	32	40
Carrots	28	27	34
Other vegetables*	70	70	65
Plantains*	590	590	600
Lemons and limes*	21	24	22
Mangoes	97	100	92
Pineapples	51	49	58
Other fresh fruit*	71	67	62
Coffee (green)	10	9	9
Tea (made)	310	303	308
Pepper	17	18	18*
Cinnamon	13	13	13*
Other spices*	15	13	13
Natural rubber	91	92	95

* FAO estimate(s).
† Unofficial figure.
Source: FAO.

LIVESTOCK
('000 head, year ending September)

	2002	2003	2004
Buffaloes	282	281	302
Cattle	1,113	1,139	1,161
Sheep	9*	9	11
Goats	351*	415	405
Pigs	82	67	79
Chickens	11,564	9,772	11,042

* Unofficial figure.
Source: FAO.

LIVESTOCK PRODUCTS
('000 metric tons)

	2002	2003	2004
Beef and veal	27.9	29.4	28.2
Buffalo meat*	3.4	3.3	3.5
Goat meat	1.6	1.4	1.4
Pig meat	1.9	2.2	2.1
Poultry meat	85.7	88.1	94.7
Cows' milk	129.1	132.2	134.9
Buffaloes' milk	25.6	25.6	25.8
Goats' milk*	4.8	5.0	4.9
Hen eggs	50.5	50.2	49.6
Cattle and buffalo hides*	5.1	5.3	5.2

* FAO estimates.
Source: FAO.

Forestry

ROUNDWOOD REMOVALS
(FAO estimates, '000 cubic metres, excl. bark)

	2002	2003	2004
Sawlogs, veneer logs and logs for sleepers	117	117	117
Other industrial wood	577	577	577
Fuel wood	5,774	5,710	5,646
Total	6,468	6,404	6,340

Source: FAO.

SAWNWOOD PRODUCTION
('000 cubic metres, incl. railway sleepers)

	1999*	2000	2001
Coniferous (softwood)	—	—	30
Broadleaved (hardwood)	5	29	31
Total	5	29	61

* FAO estimates.

2002–04: Production assumed to be unchanged from 2001 (FAO estimates).

Source: FAO.

Fishing

('000 metric tons, live weight)

	2001	2002	2003
Capture	279.6	293.6	279.1
Tilapias	27.2	16.1	17.9
Demersal percomorphs	14.5	16.3	20.0
Clupeoids	49.3	52.3	56.4
Skipjack tuna	47.2	43.0	42.8
Carangids	10.0	10.8	14.9
Mackerels	16.8	17.3	17.8
Sharks, rays, skates etc.	15.9	18.5	17.6
Aquaculture	8.3	8.3	10.2
Total catch	287.9	301.9	289.3

Source: FAO.

SRI LANKA

Mining

('000 metric tons, unless otherwise indicated)

	2002	2003	2004*
Natural graphite (metric tons)	3,619	3,387	3,400
Salt—unrefined	73	79	79
Kaolin	9	9	9
Natural phosphates	39	41	42

* Estimates.

Ilmenite concentrates ('000 metric tons): 34.1 in 1998.

Zirconium concentrates ('000 metric tons): 13 in 1999.

Sources: US Geological Survey; UN, *Industrial Commodity Statistics Yearbook*.

Industry

SELECTED PRODUCTS
('000 barrels, unless otherwise indicated)

	2002	2003	2004
Raw sugar ('000 metric tons)	38	57	60
Cigarettes (million units)	5,015	4,765	5,003
Jet fuel	600	650	650*
Motor gasoline—petrol	2,100	2,100	2,100*
Kerosene	1,500	1,500	1,500*
Distillate fuel oil	4,900	5,000	5,100*
Residual fuel oil	5,200	5,200	5,100*
Cement ('000 metric tons)	1,018	1,164	1,400*
Plywood ('000 cu m)†	14	14	14
Electric energy (million kWh)	6,951	7,612	8,044

* Estimate.
† FAO estimates.

Naptha: 116 in 2000.

Sources: US Geological Survey; Asian Development Bank, *Key Indicators of Developing Asian and Pacific Countries*; FAO; UN, *Industrial Commodity Statistics Yearbook*.

Finance

CURRENCY AND EXCHANGE RATES

Monetary Units
100 cents = 1 Sri Lanka rupee (R).

Sterling, Dollar and Euro Equivalents (30 December 2005)
£1 sterling = Rs 175.84;
US $1 = Rs 102.12;
€1 = Rs 120.47;
1,000 Sri Lanka rupees = £5.69 = $9.79 = €8.30.

Average Exchange Rate (rupees per US $)
2003 96.521
2004 101.194
2005 100.498

BUDGET
(Rs million)

Revenue	2003	2004	2005*
Taxation	231,648	281,552	351,119
Taxes on income	39,397	41,372	55,361
Taxes on goods and services	97,230	120,382	142,690
Excise levy	50,972	65,790	76,865
Taxes on property	3,662	4,489	5,253
Taxes on international trade	39,667	48,655	66,243
Non-tax revenue	44,868	29,921	38,373
Property income	24,750	15,493	19,985
Other	15,618	7,981	11,934
Total	276,516	311,473	389,492

Expenditure	2003	2004	2005*
General public services	91,564	102,634	121,870
National security and defence	61,983	73,452	84,980
Social services	124,002	166,845	183,643
Education	39,116	42,340	63,360
Health	27,476	34,419	39,636
Economic services	77,559	83,545	123,753
Agriculture-related	15,422	17,083	27,023
Energy and water supply	23,810	22,395	24,386
Transport and communication	24,852	30,758	46,204
Interest payments	125,126	119,782	128,000
Other purposes	8,254	14,504	6,162
Total expenditure and net lending	426,505	487,310	563,428

* Forecasts.

Source: IMF, *Sri Lanka: Selected Issues and Statistical Appendix* (September 2005).

INTERNATIONAL RESERVES
(US $ million at 31 December)

	2002	2003	2004
IMF special drawing rights	2	1	—
Reserve position in IMF	65	71	74
Foreign exchange	1,564	2,193	2,058
Total (excl. gold)	1,631	2,265	2,132

Source: IMF, *International Financial Statistics*.

MONEY SUPPLY
(Rs million at 31 December)

	2002	2003	2004
Currency outside banks	75,292	85,601	99,669
Demand deposits at commercial banks	64,052	76,014	88,777
Total money (incl. others)	139,361	161,635	188,454

Source: IMF, *International Financial Statistics*.

COST OF LIVING
(Consumer Price Index for Colombo; base: 2000 = 100)

	2002	2003	2004
Food (incl. beverages)	127.5	134.9	145.5
Fuel and light	124.3	143.2	157.0
Clothing (excl. footwear)	108.9	111.6	112.7
Rent	100.0	100.0	100.0
All items (incl. others)	125.1	133.0	143.0

Source: ILO.

NATIONAL ACCOUNTS
(Rs million at current prices)

Expenditure on the Gross Domestic Product

	2002	2003	2004
Government final consumption expenditure	139,311	139,268	164,716
Private final consumption expenditure	1,214,117	1,341,896	1,542,107
Increase in stocks	4,261	2,135	268
Gross fixed capital formation	330,543	386,621	506,922
Total domestic expenditure	1,688,232	1,869,920	2,214,013
Exports of goods and services	570,833	632,907	738,687
Less Imports of goods and services	677,180	741,667	923,258
GDP in purchasers' values	1,581,885	1,761,161	2,029,441
GDP at factor cost, at constant 1996 prices	877,248	930,057	979,925

Source: IMF, *International Financial Statistics*.

SRI LANKA

Gross Domestic Product by Economic Activity

	2002	2003	2004
Agriculture, hunting, forestry and fishing	287,840	297,342	320,201
Mining and quarrying	25,821	27,489	35,965
Manufacturing	221,970	243,596	275,630
Construction	100,590	113,284	142,430
Electricity, gas and water	20,314	28,405	27,668
Transport, storage and communications	173,890	214,036	255,654
Wholesale and retail trade, restaurants and hotels	288,257	313,949	369,727
Finance	122,507	155,339	177,893
Public administration	81,525	81,549	97,485
Other services	80,572	87,748	95,288
GDP at factor cost	**1,403,286**	**1,562,737**	**1,797,941**
Indirect taxes, *less* subsidies	178,599	198,424	231,500
GDP in purchasers' values	**1,581,885**	**1,761,161**	**2,029,441**

Source: Asian Development Bank, *Key Indicators of Developing Asian and Pacific Countries*.

BALANCE OF PAYMENTS
(US $ million)

	2002	2003	2004
Exports of goods f.o.b.	4,699.2	5,133.2	5,757.2
Imports of goods f.o.b.	−5,495.1	−6,004.8	−7,199.8
Trade balance	**−795.9**	**−871.6**	**−1,442.6**
Exports of services	1,268.3	1,410.7	1,526.6
Imports of services	−1,584.3	−1,679.1	−1,907.9
Balance on goods and services	**−1,111.9**	**−1,140.0**	**−1,823.9**
Other income received	75.3	169.8	156.7
Other income paid	−327.8	−341.5	−360.3
Balance on goods, services and income	**−1,364.4**	**−1,311.7**	**−2,027.4**
Current transfers received	1,287.1	1,413.9	1,563.9
Current transfers paid	−190.2	−208.6	−213.7
Current balance	**−267.5**	**−106.4**	**−677.2**
Capital account (net)	65.0	74.1	64.2
Direct investment abroad	−11.5	−27.3	−5.8
Direct investment from abroad	196.5	228.7	232.8
Portfolio investment assets	78.0	144.8	111.3
Portfolio investment liabilities	−52.6	−143.2	−100.4
Other investment assets	104.4	−93.8	−353.5
Other investment liabilities	−510.7	−328.0	−17.0
Net errors and omissions	136.2	−113.9	−189.3
Overall balance	**−262.2**	**−365.0**	**−934.8**

Source: IMF, *International Financial Statistics*.

OFFICIAL DEVELOPMENT ASSISTANCE
(US $ million)

	1998	1999	2000
Bilateral donors	296.7	219.9	251.1
Multilateral donors	210.3	43.7	25.2
Total	**507.0**	**263.6**	**276.3**
Grants	195.6	198.4	187.2
Loans	311.4	65.2	89.1
Per caput assistance (US $)	28.3	14.5	15.0

Source: UN, *Statistical Yearbook for Asia and the Pacific*.

External Trade

PRINCIPAL COMMODITIES
(distribution by SITC, Rs million)

Imports c.i.f.	2002	2003	2004
Food and live animals	62,286	62,474	74,257
Beverages and tobacco	9,367	10,740	10,542
Crude materials (inedible), excluding fuels	8,034	9,804	10,114
Mineral fuels, lubricants, etc.	80,037	71,101	115,036
Animal, vegetable oil and fats	6,783	8,281	8,025
Chemicals	28,518	31,925	38,306
Basic manufactures	197,092	210,410	250,292
Machinery and transport equipment	105,944	131,904	163,985
Miscellaneous manufactured articles	79,500	92,183	125,351
Total (incl. others)	**584,491**	**643,749**	**811,138**

Exports f.o.b.	2002	2003	2004
Food and live animals	16,979	20,239	23,101
Beverages and tobacco	75,400	76,490	87,710
Tea	63,105	65,937	74,897
Basic manufactures	273,267	295,432	341,589
Garments	214,895	231,652	268,573
Machinery and transport equipment	20,720	24,513	34,694
Miscellaneous manufactured articles	49,920	47,001	56,432
Total (incl. others)	**449,850**	**495,426**	**583,967**

Source: Asian Development Bank, *Key Indicators of Developing Asian and Pacific Countries*.

PRINCIPAL TRADING PARTNERS
(US $ million)

Imports c.i.f.	2002	2003	2004
China, People's Republic	257.7	329.0	623.9
Hong Kong	489.7	559.5	480.1
India	832.1	1,076.2	1,143.8
Iran	183.2	249.5	312.5
Japan	354.2	448.1	372.7
Korea, Republic	302.8	282.9	300.7
Malaysia	203.9	270.4	379.5
Singapore	432.0	522.2	651.6
United Kingdom	262.1	272.9	278.5
USA	217.8	198.3	180.8
Total (incl. others)	**6,022.8**	**6,671.9**	**8,172.0**

Exports f.o.b.	2002	2003	2004
Belgium	—	—	295.3
France	93.3	87.1	78.8
Germany	199.3	232.4	290.6
India	170.6	245.1	306.9
Japan	140.3	161.0	179.2
Russia	126.6	140.8	165.6
United Arab Emirates	130.0	163.5	187.8
United Kingdom	590.3	640.5	774.8
USA	1,764.2	1,776.4	1,856.9
Total (incl. others)	**4,679.9**	**5,133.3**	**5,989.0**

Source: Asian Development Bank, *Key Indicators of Developing Asian and Pacific Countries*.

SRI LANKA

Transport

RAILWAYS

	2001	2002	2003
Passengers (million)*	92.9	108.6	113.0
Freight carried ('000 metric tons)	1,258	1,452	1,665

* Tickets and season tickets, counted once only.

Source: Sri Lanka Railways.

ROAD TRAFFIC
(motor vehicles in use at 31 December)

	2000	2001	2002
Passenger cars	233,018	241,444	253,447
Buses and coaches	64,963	66,273	67,702
Lorries and vans	300,712	312,495	328,913
Road tractors	133,092	138,879	146,043
Motorcycles and mopeds	834,586	868,705	923,467
Total	1,566,371	1,627,796	1,719,572

Source: International Road Federation, *World Road Statistics*.

SHIPPING

Merchant Fleet
(registered at 31 December)

	2002	2003	2004
Number of vessels	66	70	77
Displacement ('000 grt)	80.9	140.7	156.6

Source: Lloyd's Register-Fairplay, *World Fleet Statistics*.

International Sea-borne Shipping
(freight traffic, '000 metric tons)

	1999	2000	2001
Goods loaded	9,292	9,192	9,358
Goods unloaded	17,703	18,343	17,704

Source: UN, *Statistical Yearbook for Asia and the Pacific*.

CIVIL AVIATION
(traffic on scheduled services)

	1999	2000	2001
Kilometres flown (million)	28	47	34
Passengers carried ('000)	1,422	1,756	1,719
Passenger-km (million)	5,156	6,840	6,641
Total ton-km (million)	669	1,125	822

Source: UN, *Statistical Yearbook*.

Tourism

FOREIGN TOURIST ARRIVALS*

Country of residence	2001	2002	2003
Australia	11,457	11,217	19,958
Belgium	5,250	4,767	4,304
Canada	7,609	8,304	11,164
France	20,949	19,989	28,585
Germany	60,405	55,170	58,908
India	33,924	69,960	90,603
Italy	12,074	12,177	15,654
Japan	9,237	13,602	17,115
Maldives	9,019	9,861	11,583
Netherlands	12,569	11,748	18,197
Pakistan	8,562	6,756	9,704
Switzerland	6,228	9,375	11,240
United Kingdom	67,830	67,533	93,278
USA	8,374	11,565	13,946
Total (incl. others)	336,794	393,171	500,642

* Excluding Sri Lanka nationals residing abroad.

Tourism receipts (US $ million, incl. passenger transport): 347 in 2001; 594 in 2002; 692 in 2003.

Sources: Ceylon Tourist Board; World Tourism Organization.

Communications Media

	1999	2000	2001
Television receivers ('000 in use)	1,900	2,100	2,200
Telephones ('000 main lines in use)	669.1	767.4	822.1
Mobile cellular telephones ('000 subscribers)	256.7	430.2	667.7
Personal computers ('000 in use)	105	135	175
Internet users ('000)	65.0	121.5	150.0
Newspapers	174	180	189
Books published: titles	4,655	1,818	n.a.
Books published: copies ('000)	n.a.	25,459.3	7,439.1

Facsimile machines (in use): 11,000* in 1994.

Radio receivers ('000 in use): 3,850 in 1997.

2002 ('000): Telephones (main lines in use) 881.4; Mobile cellular telephones (subscribers) 931.6; Personal computers ('000 in use) 250; Internet users 200.0.

2003 ('000): Telephones (main lines in use) 939.0; Mobile cellular telephones (subscribers) 1,393.4; Personal computers ('000 in use) 325; Internet users 250.0.

2004 ('000): Telephones (main lines in use) 991.2; Mobile cellular telephones (subscribers) 2,211.2; Personal computers ('000 in use) 530; Internet users 280.0.

* Estimate.

Sources: UN, *Statistical Yearbook*; UNESCO, *Statistical Yearbook*; Telecommunications Regulatory Commission of Sri Lanka and International Telecommunication Union.

Education

(1995)

	Institutions	Teachers	Students
Primary	9,657	70,537	1,962,498
Secondary	5,771*	103,572	2,314,054
Universities and equivalent	n.a.	2,344	40,035
Distance learning	n.a.	206	20,601

* 1992 figure.

1996: Primary: 9,554 institutions, 66,339 teachers, 1,843,848 students.

1997: Primary: 60,832 teachers, 1,807,751 students; Secondary: 2,313,511 students.

1998: Primary: 1,798,162 students.

2001: Universities: 12 institutions, 2,999 teachers, 48,899 students.

2002: Universities: 12 institutions, 3,225 teachers (excl. open university), 48,667 students (excl. open university).

2003 (provisional): Universities: 12 institutions, 3,386 teachers (excl. open university), 59,734 students (excl. open university).

Sources: UNESCO, *Statistical Yearbook*; Ministry of Education, Colombo.

Adult literacy rate (UNESCO estimates): 90.4% (males 92.2%; females 88.6%) in 2003 (Source: UN Development Programme, *Human Development Report*).

Directory

The Constitution

The Constitution of the Democratic Socialist Republic of Sri Lanka was approved by the National State Assembly (renamed Parliament) on 17 August 1978, and promulgated on 7 September 1978. The following is a summary of its main provisions:

FUNDAMENTAL RIGHTS

The Constitution guarantees the fundamental rights and freedoms of all citizens, including freedom of thought, conscience and worship and equal entitlement before the law.

THE PRESIDENT

The President is Head of State, and exercises all executive powers, including defence of the Republic. The President is directly elected by the people for a term of six years, and is eligible for re-election. The President's powers include the right to:
  (i) choose to hold any portfolio in the Cabinet;
  (ii) appoint or dismiss the Prime Minister or any other minister;
  (iii) preside at ceremonial sittings of Parliament;
  (iv) dismiss Parliament at will; and
  (v) submit to a national referendum any Bill or matter of national importance which has been rejected by Parliament.

LEGISLATURE

The Parliament is the legislative power of the people. It consists of such number of representatives of the people as a Delimitation Commission shall determine. The members of Parliament are directly elected by a system of modified proportional representation. By-elections are abolished, successors to members of Parliament being appointed by the head of the party which nominated the outgoing member at the previous election. Parliament exercises the judicial power of the people through courts, tribunals and institutions created and established or recognized by the Constitution or established by law. Parliament has control over public finance.

OTHER PROVISIONS

Religion

Buddhism has the foremost place among religions and it is the duty of the State to protect and foster Buddhism, while assuring every citizen the freedom to adopt the religion of their choice.

Language

The Constitution recognizes two official languages, Sinhala and Tamil. Either of the national languages may be used by all citizens in transactions with government institutions.

Amendments

Amendments to the Constitution require endorsement by a two-thirds' majority in Parliament. In February 1979 the Constitution was amended by allowing members of Parliament who resigned or were expelled from their party to retain their seats, in certain circumstances. In January 1981 Parliament amended the Constitution to increase its membership from 168 to 169. An amendment enabling the President to seek re-election after four years was approved in August 1982. In February 1983 an amendment providing for by-elections to fill vacant seats in Parliament was approved. An amendment banning parties that advocate separatism was approved by Parliament in August 1983. In November 1987 Parliament adopted an amendment providing for the creation of eight provincial councils (the northern and eastern provinces were to be merged as one administrative unit). In December 1988 Parliament adopted an amendment allowing Tamil the same status as Sinhala, as one of the country's two official languages.

The Government

HEAD OF STATE

President: MAHINDA RAJAPAKSE (sworn in 19 November 2005).

THE CABINET
(April 2006)

Prime Minister and Minister of Disaster Management: RATNASIRI WICKREMANAYAKE.
Minister of Foreign Affairs and of Ports and Aviation: MANGALA SARAMARAWEERA.
Minister of Defence and of Finance and Planning: MAHINDA RAJAPAKSE.
Minister of Tourism: ANURA BANDARANAIKE.
Minister of Post and Telecommunications and of Rural Economy Development: D. M. JAYARATNE.
Minister of Justice and Judicial Reforms: AMARASIRI DODANGODA.
Minister of Healthcare and Nutrition: NIMAL SIRIPALA DE SILVA.
Minister of Transport, Railways and Petroleum Resources Development: A. H. M. FOWZIE.
Minister of Trade, Commerce and Consumer Affairs and of Highways: JEYARAJ FERNANDOPULLE.
Minister of Agriculture, Environment, Irrigation and Mahaweli: MAITHRIPALA SIRISENA.
Minister of Power and Energy: JOHN SENEVIRATNA.
Minister of Youth Affairs and Women's Empowerment: SUMEDHA G. JAYASENA.
Minister of Information and Media: ANURA PRIYADARSHANA YAPA.
Minister of Urban Development and Water Supply: DINESH GUNAWARDENE.
Minister of Social Services and Social Welfare: DOUGLAS DEVANANDA.
Minister of Public Administration and Home Affairs: Dr SARATHA AMUNUGAMA.
Minister of Housing and Construction Industry: FERIAL ASHRAFF.
Minister of Education: SUSIL PREMAJAYANTHA.
Minister of Labour Relations and Foreign Employment: ATHAUDA SENEVIRATNE.
Minister of Rural Industries and Self Employment: S. B. NAVINNA.
Minister of Vocational and Technical Education: PIYASENA GAMAGE.
Minister of Provincial Councils and Local Government: JANAKA BANDARA THENAKOON.
Minister of Fisheries and Housing Development: A. L. M. ATHAULLA.
Minister of Science and Technology: TISSA VITARANA.
Minister of National Enterprise Development and Investment Promotion: ROHITHA BOGOLLAGAMA.
Minister of Constitutional Affairs and National Integration: D. E. W. GUNASEKERA.

MINISTRIES

President's Secretariat: Republic Sq., Colombo 1; tel. (11) 2324801; fax (11) 2331246; e-mail gosl@presidentsl.org; internet www.presidentsl.org.
Prime Minister's Office: Sir Ernest de Silva Mawatha, Colombo 7; tel. (11) 2575317; fax (11) 2575454.
Ministry of Advanced Technology and National Enterprise Development: Colombo.
Ministry of Agricultural Marketing Development, Hindu Affairs and Tamil Language Schools and Vocational Training (North): 64 Galle Rd, Colombo 3; tel. (11) 2385367; fax (11) 2385383; e-mail admncode@sltnet.lk; internet www.hinduministry.lk.
Ministry of Agriculture, Livestock, Land and Irrigation: 'Govijana Mandiraya', 82 Rajamalwatta Rd, Battaramulla, Colombo; tel. (11) 2869553; fax (11) 2868919; e-mail minagr@slt.lk.
Ministry of Buddha Sasana: 135 Srimath Anagarika Dharmapala Mawatha, Colombo 7; tel. (11) 2326126; fax (11) 2424726; e-mail buddhasec@eureka.lk.
Ministry of Christian Affairs: 49/1 Ward Place, Colombo 7; tel. (11) 2686006; fax (11) 2667895; e-mail mdpa@sltnet.lk; internet www.christian.gov.lk.
Ministry of Constitutional Reform: 44B Horton Place, Colombo 7; tel. (11) 2662251; fax (11) 2662252; e-mail consas@sltnet.lk; internet www.constitution.gov.lk.
Ministry of Cultural Affairs and National Heritage: 8th Floor, 'Sethsiripaya', Battaramulla, Colombo; tel. (11) 2872001; fax (11) 2872021; e-mail mcasec@sltnet.lk.
Ministry of Defence: 15/5 Baladaksha Mawatha, POB 572, Colombo 3; tel. (11) 2430860; fax (11) 2446300; e-mail modsec@sltnet.lk; internet www.gov.lk/defense.

SRI LANKA

Ministry of Education: 'Isurupaya', Pelawatte, Battaramulla, Colombo; tel. (11) 2785141; fax (11) 2785162; e-mail secedu@moe.gov.lk; internet www.moe.gov.lk.

Ministry of Environment and Natural Resources: 'Sampathpaya', 82 Rajamalwatte Rd, Battaramulla, Colombo; tel. (11) 2877290; fax (11) 2877292; e-mail forest@sri.lanka.net.

Ministry of Estate Housing, Infrastructure and Community Development: 45 St Michael's Rd, Colombo 3; tel. (11) 2541369; fax (11) 2541371; e-mail secomdev@sltnet.lk.

Ministry of Finance and Planning: Galle Face Secretariat, Colombo 1; tel. (11) 2484510; fax (11) 2433349; e-mail st@sltnet.lk; internet www.treasury.gov.lk.

Ministry of Fisheries and Aquatic Resources: Maligawatte, Colombo 10; tel. (11) 2446184; fax (11) 2541184; e-mail secmof@sltnet.lk.

Ministry of Foreign Affairs: Republic Bldg, Colombo 1; tel. (11) 2325371; fax (11) 2446091; e-mail cypher@formin.gov.lk; internet www.slmfa.gov.lk.

Ministry of Healthcare, Nutrition and Uva Wellassa Development: 'Suwasiripaya', 385 Wimalawansha Mawatha, Colombo 10; tel. (11) 2698471; fax (11) 2698475; e-mail minister@health.gov.lk; internet www.health.gov.lk.

Ministry of Highways: 9th Floor, 'C' Wing, Sethsiripaya Office Complex, POB 53, Battaramulla, Colombo; tel. (11) 2871821; fax (11) 2862705; e-mail hiwaysec@sltnet.lk; internet www.mohsl.gov.lk.

Ministry of Housing and Construction Industry, Eastern Province Education and Irrigation Development: 'Sethsiripaya', Sri Jayawardenepura Kotte, Battaramulla, Colombo; tel. (11) 2862721; fax (11) 2864788; e-mail ministry@urbanlanka.lk; internet www.urbanlanka.lk.

Ministry of Indigenous Medicine: 330 Union Place, Colombo 2; tel. (11) 2399611; fax (11) 2314923; e-mail inmed@dialogsl.net.

Ministry of Industry and Investment Promotion: 73/1 Galle Rd, Colombo 3; tel. (11) 2392149; fax (11) 2449402; e-mail misec@sltnet.lk; internet www.industry.gov.lk.

Ministry of Information and Media: Levels 7, 17 & 18, West Tower, World Trade Centre, Echelon Sq., Colombo 1; tel. (11) 2422591; fax (11) 2323465; e-mail masscom@sltnet.lk.

Ministry of Infrastructure Development in the Eastern Province: 189 Galle Rd, Colombo 3; tel. (11) 2441296; fax (11) 2441299; e-mail mail@medemra.gov.lk; internet www.midep.gov.lk.

Ministry of Justice and Judicial Reforms: Superior Courts Complex Bldg, Colombo 12; tel. (11) 2323022; fax (11) 2320785; e-mail justices@sri.lanka.net; internet www.justiceministry.gov.lk.

Ministry of Labour Relations and Foreign Employment: Labour Secretariat, Narahenpita, Colombo 5; tel. (11) 2581991; fax (11) 2368165; e-mail moeladmn@sltnet.lk; internet www.labour.gov.lk.

Ministry of Mahaweli, River Basin Development and Rajarata Development: 500 T. B. Jayah Mawatha, Colombo 10; tel. (11) 2687491; fax (11) 2687386; e-mail dev123@sltnet.lk.

Ministry of Muslim Religious and Cultural Affairs: Colombo.

Ministry of Parliamentary Affairs: Colombo.

Ministry of Petroleum Resources Development: Colombo.

Ministry of Plantation Industries: 55/75 Vauxhall Lane, Colombo 2; tel. (11) 2320902; fax (11) 2328154; e-mail mpiadas@sltnet.lk.

Ministry of Ports and Aviation: 45 Leyden Bastian Rd, Colombo 1; tel. (11) 2438344; fax (11) 2435142; e-mail secpd@slpa.lk.

Ministry of Post and Telecommunications and Upcountry Development: Levels 7, 17 & 18, West Tower, World Trade Centre, Colombo 1; tel. (11) 2422591; fax (11) 2323465; e-mail spostele@sltnet.lk.

Ministry of Power and Energy: 80 Sir Ernest de Silva Mawatha, Colombo 7; tel. (11) 2564363; fax (11) 2564474; e-mail secrepe@sltnet.lk.

Ministry of Provincial Councils and Local Government: 330 Union Place, Colombo 2.

Ministry of Public Administration and Home Affairs: Independence Sq., Colombo 7; tel. (11) 2696211; fax (11) 2695279; e-mail minister@pubad.gov.lk; internet www.pubad.gov.lk.

Ministry of Public Security, Law and Order: 15/5 Baladaksha Mawatha, Colombo 3; tel. (11) 2430860; fax (11) 2389021; e-mail interior_1@sltnet.lk.

Ministry of Regional Infrastructure Development: 29 Galle Face Terrace, Colombo 3; tel. (11) 2307192; fax (11) 2307827; e-mail srid@sltnet.lk.

Ministry of Relief, Rehabilitation and Reconciliation: 177 Galle Rd, Colombo 3; tel. (11) 2382067; fax (11) 2382066; e-mail secmdrnn@sltnet.lk.

Ministry of Samurdhi and Poverty Alleviation: 7A Ried Ave, Colombo 7; tel. (11) 2689589; fax (11) 2688945.

Ministry of Science and Technology: 561/3 Etvigala Mawatha, Colombo 5; tel. (11) 2554848; fax (11) 2554845; e-mail milindamora@sltnet.lk; internet www.most.gov.lk.

Ministry of Skills Development, Vocational and Technical Education: Colombo.

Ministry of Small and Rural Industries: 780 Maradana Rd, Colombo 10; tel. (11) 2669269; fax (11) 2669273; e-mail ruraleco@sltnet.lk; internet www.msri.gov.lk.

Ministry of Tourism: 64 Galle Rd, Colombo 3; tel. (11) 2385341; fax (11) 2441505; e-mail slmts@sltnet.lk; internet www.slmts.slt.lk.

Ministry of Trade, Commerce and Consumer Affairs: Rakshana Mandiraya, 21 Vauxhall St, Colombo 3; tel. (11) 2421310; fax (11) 2863138.

Ministry of Transport: 1 D. R. Wijewardene Mawatha, POB 588, Colombo 10; tel. (11) 2687212; fax (11) 2687284; e-mail transplan@eol.lk; internet www.transport.gov.lk.

Ministry of Urban Development and Water Supply: 3rd Floor, 'Sethsiripaya', Battaramulla, Colombo 3; tel. and fax (11) 2872338; e-mail secudws@sltnet.lk.

Ministry of Women's Empowerment and Social Welfare: 5th Floor, 'Sethsiripaya', Battaramulla, Colombo; tel. (11) 2887349; e-mail mssplan@sltnet.lk; internet www.socialwelfare.lk.

Ministry of Youth Affairs and Sports: 420 Bauddhaloka Mawatha, Colombo 7; tel. (11) 2669234; fax (11) 2669237; e-mail youthmin@sltnet.lk; internet www.sportsministry.gov.lk.

President and Legislature

PRESIDENT

Presidential Election, 17 November 2005

Candidate	Valid votes	% of votes
Mahinda Rajapakse (UPFA)	4,887,152	50.29
Ranil Wickremasinghe (UNP)	4,706,366	48.43
Total (incl. others)	9,717,039	100.00

PARLIAMENT

Speaker: W. J. M. LOKUBANDARA.
Deputy Speaker: GEETHANJANA GUNAWARDENA.

General Election, 2 April 2004

Party	Seats
United People's Freedom Alliance (UPFA)*	105
United National Party (UNP)	82
Tamil National Alliance (TNA)	22
Jathika Hela Urumaya (JHU)	9
Sri Lanka Muslim Congress (SLMC)	5
Others	2
Total	225

* Coalition comprising the Sri Lanka Freedom Party, Janatha Vimukthi Peramuna, Communist Party of Sri Lanka, Democratic United National Front, Lanka Sama Samaja Party and Sri Lanka Mahajana Party.

Notes: Direct elections were held for 196 of the 225 seats on the basis of a proportional representation system involving preferential voting; the remaining 29 were chosen from party lists according to each party's national share of the vote.

Election Commission

Department of Elections: Elections Secretariat, Sarana Mawatha, Rajagiriya, Jayawardenapura; tel. (11) 2868441; fax (11) 2868445; e-mail comelesl@sltnet.lk; internet www.slelections.gov.lk; f. 1947; govt dept; independent commission to be established in 2006; Commr of Elections DAYANANDA DISSANAYAKE.

Political Organizations

Akhila Illankai Tamil United Front (AITUK): f. 2006; Tamil; advocates federal solution to ethnic conflict; Gen. Sec. K. VIGNESWARAN.

Ceylon Workers' Congress (CWC): 'Savumia Bhavan', 72 Ananda Coomarasamy Mawatha, POB 1294, Colombo 7; tel. (11) 2565082; fax (11) 2301355; e-mail cwcctuc@slt.lk; f. 1939; represents the interests of workers in the mercantile and local government sectors and of workers on tea, rubber and coconut plantations; 300,000 mems; Pres. and Gen. Sec. S. R. ARUMUGAM THONDAMAN.

Democratic People's Liberation Front (DPLF): 16 Haig Rd, Bambalapitiya, Colombo 4; tel. (11) 2586289; has operated as a national political party since Sept. 1988; political wing of the People's Liberation Organization of Tamil Eelam (PLOTE); Leader DHARMALINGAM SITHADTHAN.

Democratic Workers' Congress (DWC) (Political Wing): 70 Bankshall St, POB 1009, Colombo 11; tel. (11) 2439199; fax (11) 2435961; f. 1939 as trade union, f. 1978 as political party; aims to eliminate discrimination against the Tamil-speaking Sri Lankans of recent Indian origin; 201,382 mems (1994); Pres. and Gen. Sec. MANO GANESHAN.

Desha Vimukthi Janatha Pakshaya (National Liberation People's Party): 63/24, Wewewatte, Weliweriya; tel. 338812; has operated as a national political party since Sept. 1988; Sec. P. M. PODIAPPUHAMY.

Deshapriya Janatha Viyaparaya (DJV) (Patriotic People's Movement): militant, Sinhalese group; associated with the JVP.

Eelam National Democratic Liberation Front (ENDLF): 315 Kandy Rd, Kilinochchi; Tamil; supports 1987 Indo-Sri Lankan peace accord; has operated as a national political party since Sept. 1988; Gen. Sec. G. GNANASEKARAN; Dep. Gen. Sec. P. RAJARATNAM.

Eelam People's Democratic Party (EPDP): 121 Park Rd, Colombo 5; tel. (11) 2551015; fax (11) 2585255; e-mail epdp@sltnet.lk; internet www.epdpnews.com; Tamil; Sec.-Gen. DOUGLAS DEVANANDA.

Eelavar Democratic Front: 39 Temple Rd, Jaffna; fmrly known as Eelam Revolutionary Organization of Students (EROS); Tamil separatist group; Leader VELUPILLAI BALAKUMAR.

Eksath Lanka Podujana Pakshaya: 43/5 Galle Rd, Colombo 4; tel. (77) 2313321; Sec. U. LALITH WIJETHUNGA.

Janatha Vimukthi Peramuna (JVP) (People's Liberation Front): 198/19 Panchikawattha Rd, Colombo 10; tel. (11) 2822379; fax (11) 2819775; e-mail jvplanka@sltnet.lk; internet www.jvpsrilanka.com; f. 1964; banned following a coup attempt in 1971, regained legal status in 1977, banned again in 1983, but regained legal status in 1994; Marxist; Sinhalese support; Leader SOMAWANSA AMARASINGHE.

Jathika Hela Urumaya (JHU) (National Heritage Party): 152/B, Stanley Thilakarathna Mawatha, Nugegoda; tel. (11) 2810185; fax (11) 2811504; e-mail helaurumaya@gmail.com; internet www.jathikahelaurumaya.lk; f. 2004; Buddhist; Sinhalese nationalist; Deputy Leader Dr OMALPE SOBITHA THERO.

Liberal Party: 88/1 Rosmead Place, Colombo 7; tel. (11) 2691589; fax (11) 2699772; e-mail libparty@sri.lanka.net; Pres. Dr RAJIVA WIJESINHA.

Mahajana Eksath Peramuna (MEP) (People's United Front): 31/27 Narahenpita Rd, Nawala, Rajagiriya; tel. 872318; f. 1956; Sinhalese and Buddhist support; left-wing; advocates economic self-reliance; Pres. DINESH C. R. GUNAWARDENA.

Muslim United Liberation Front: 134 Hulftsdorp St, Colombo 12; tel. (11) 2501198; has operated as a national political party since Sept. 1988.

National Unity Alliance (NUA): Sama Mandiraya, 53 Vauxhall Lane, Colombo 2; tel. (11) 2424187; affiliate party of the Sri Lanka Muslim Congress; has operated as a national political party since 1986; Leader FARIEL ASHRAFF.

Nava Sama Samaja Party (NSSP) (New Equal Society Party): 17 Barracks Lane, Colombo 2; tel. (11) 2324053; fax (11) 2305963; e-mail nssp@visual.lk; internet www.nssp.info; f. 1977; Trotskyist; operates under the New Left Front; Gen. Sec. LINUS JAYATILAKE; Presidium Member Dr VICKRAMABAHU KARUNARATHNE.

People's Front of the Liberation Tigers (PFLT): 61 Abdul Caffoor Mawatha, Colombo 3; tel. (11) 2696889; f. 1989; political wing of the LTTE (see below); Leader GOPALSWAMY MAHENDRARAJAH ('Mahathya'); Gen. Sec. YOGARATNAM YOGI.

Singhalaye Nithahas Peramuna (Sinhalese Freedom Front): Sri Panchananda Charity Bldg, Kelani Railway Station Rd, Colombo; f. 1994; nationalist, Buddhist; Pres. ARYA SENA TERA; Sec. Prof. NALIN DE SILVA.

Sri Lanka Muslim Congress: Sama Mandiraya, 53 Vauxhall Lane, Colombo 2; tel. (11) 2431711; internet www.slmc.org; Leader RAUF HAKEEM.

Sri Lanka Progressive Front: 7 7th Lane, Pagoda Rd, Nugegoda; tel. 826564; Sec. ROHAN JAYATUNGA.

Tamil National Alliance (TNA): c/o Parliament, Colombo; f. 2001; alliance of Tamil parties.

Eelam People's Revolutionary Liberation Front (EPRLF): 85/9 Pokuna Rd, Hendala, Wattala; tel. 685826; Tamil rights group; the party split into two factions, one led by ANNAMALAI VARADHARAJAH PERUMAL, known as the Varadharajah faction, and the other by SURESH K. PREMACHANDRAN, known as the Premachandran faction; c. 1,000 mems.

Tamil Eelam Liberation Organization (TELO): C.28, MPs Quarters, Madiwela, Sri Jayawardenepura (Kotte); tel. 585620; supports 1987 Indo-Sri Lankan peace accord; has operated as a national political party since Sept. 1988; Leader Sri SABARATNAM.

Tamil United Liberation Front (TULF): 30/1B Alwis Place, Colombo 3; tel. (11) 2347721; fax (11) 2347721; f. 1976 following merger of All Ceylon Tamil Congress (f. 1945) and Federal Party (f. 1949); Pres. VEERASINGHAM ANANDASANGAREE; Sec.-Gen. R. SAMPANTHAN.

United National Party (UNP): Sirikotha, 400 Kotte Rd, Sri Jayawaredenepura; tel. (11) 2865375; fax (11) 2865347; e-mail gsunp@sltnet.lk; internet www.unplanka.org; f. 1946; democratic socialist; aims at a non-aligned foreign policy, supports Sinhala and Tamil as the official languages and state aid to denominational schools; Leader RANIL WICKREMASINGHE; Chair. M. H. MOHAMMED; Gen. Sec. N. V. K. K. WERAGODA.

United People's Freedom Alliance (UPFA): 121 Wijerama Mawatha, Colombo 7; tel. (11) 2868917; f. 2004 as a left-wing alliance, incl. communists and Trotskyists; Pres. RATNASIRI WICKREMANAYAKE; Chair. NANDANA GUNATILAKA.

Communist Party of Sri Lanka (CPSL): 91 Dr N. M. Perera Mawatha, Colombo 800; tel. (11) 2695328; fax (11) 2691610; e-mail dew128@dialogsl.net; f. 1943; advocates establishment of socialist society; seeks broadening of democratic rights and processes, political solution to ethnic problem, defence of social welfare and presses for social justice; supports national sovereignty, territorial integrity and national unity of the country; Gen. Sec. DEW GUNASEKERA.

Democratic United National Front (DUNF): 60 1st Lane, Rawathawatte, Moratuwa; tel. (11) 2645566; f. 1991 by a dissident group of UNP politicians; 500,000 mems; Leader ARIYAWANS DISSANAYAKE; Pres. D. M. G. EKANAYAKE; Gen. Sec. ARIYAWANSA DISSANAYAKE.

Lanka Sama Samaja Party (LSSP) (Lanka Equal Society Party): 457 Dr Colvin R. de Silva Mawatha, Colombo 2; tel. (11) 2676770; f. 1935; Trotskyist; Gen. Sec. WIMALASIRI DE MEL.

Sri Lanka Freedom Party (SLFP): 301 T. B. Jayah Mawatha, Colombo 10; tel. (11) 2696289; internet www.slfp.lk; f. 1951; democratic socialist; advocates a non-aligned foreign policy, industrial development in both the state sector and the private sector, rapid modernization in education and in the economy, and safeguards for minorities; Pres. CHANDRIKA BANDARANAIKE KUMARATUNGA.

Sri Lanka Mahajana (People's) Party (SLMP): 196 Kolonnawa Rd, Wellampitiya; f. 1984 by fmr mems of the SLFP; social democrats; Leader SARATH KONGAHAGE; Gen. Sec. PREMASIRI PERERA.

Upcountry People's Front: 56, Rosita Housing Scheme, Kotagala; tel. (52) 28286; represents interests of workers (mainly of Indian Tamil origin) on tea plantations; Sec. MURUGAN SIVALINGAM.

Tamil separatist groups also include the Liberation Tigers of Tamil Eelam (LTTE; Leader VELUPILLAI PRABHAKARAN), the Tamil Eelam Liberation Front (TELF; Gen. Sec. M. K. EELAVENTHAN), the People's Liberation Organization of Tamil Eelam (PLOTE; Leader DHARMALINGAM SIDDHARTHAN; Vice-Pres. KARUVAI A. SRIKANTHASAMI), the People's Revolutionary Action Group, the Ellalan Force and the Tamil People's Protection Party.

Diplomatic Representation

EMBASSIES AND HIGH COMMISSIONS IN SRI LANKA

Australia: 3 Cambridge Place, Colombo 7; tel. (11) 2698767; fax (11) 2686453; e-mail ahc@sri.lanka.net; internet www.srilanka.embassy.gov.au; High Commissioner Dr GREG FRENCH.

Bangladesh: 85 Dharmapala Mawatha, Colombo 7; tel. (11) 2303943; fax (11) 2303942; e-mail bdootlanka@eureka.lk; High Commissioner SHAHADAT HOSSAIN.

Canada: 6 Gregory's Rd, Cinnamon Gdns, POB 1006, Colombo 7; tel. (11) 5326232; fax (11) 5226296; e-mail clmbo@international.gc.ca; internet www.dfait-maeci.gc.ca/world/embassies/SriLanka; High Commissioner VALERIE RAYMOND.

China, People's Republic: 381A Bauddhaloka Mawatha, Colombo 7; tel. (11) 2694494; fax (11) 2693799; e-mail chinaemb_lk@mfa.gov.cn; internet lk.chineseembassy.org; Ambassador SUN GUOXIANG.

Cuba: 15/9 Maitland Crescent, Colombo 7; tel. (11) 2677170; fax (11) 2669380; e-mail embacub@eureka.lk; Ambassador ENNA VIANT VALDÉS.

Egypt: 39 Dickman's Rd, Colombo 5; tel. (11) 2583621; fax (11) 2585292; Ambassador GIHAN AMIN MOHAMED ALI.

France: 89 Rosmead Place, POB 880, Colombo 7; tel. (11) 2698815; fax (11) 2699039; e-mail ambfrclb@sltnet.lk; internet www.ambafrance-lk.org; Ambassador JEAN-BERNARD DE VAIVRE.

Germany: 40 Alfred House Ave, POB 658, Colombo 3; tel. (11) 2580431; fax (11) 2504104; e-mail info@colo.diplo.de; internet www.colombo.diplo.de; Ambassador JÜRGEN WEERTH.

Holy See: 220 Bauddhaloka Mawatha, Colombo 7 (Apostolic Nunciature); tel. (11) 2582554; fax (11) 2580906; e-mail aponun@sri.lanka.net; Apostolic Nuncio Most Rev. Dr MARIO ZENARI (Titular Archbishop of Zuglio).

India: 36–38 Galle Rd, Colombo 3; tel. (11) 2421605; fax (11) 2446403; e-mail hcicmbpl@sri.lanka.net; internet www.hcicolombo.org; High Commissioner NIRUPAMA RAO.

Indonesia: 400/50 Sarana Rd, off Bauddhaloka Mawatha, Colombo 7; tel. (11) 2674337; e-mail indocola@sri.lanka.net; Ambassador SUDARGO MANGUNWIDJOJO.

Iran: 17 Bullers Lane, Colombo 7; tel. (11) 2501137; fax (11) 2502691; e-mail iranemb@dailogst.net; Ambassador BEHNAM BEHRUZ.

Italy: 55 Jawatta Rd, Colombo 5; tel. (11) 2588388; fax (11) 2596344; e-mail ambasciata.colombo@esteri.it; internet sedi.esteri.it/colombo; Ambassador PIO MARIANI.

Japan: 20 Gregory's Rd, POB 822, Colombo 7; tel. (11) 2393831; fax (11) 2674555; e-mail cultujpn@sltnet.lk; internet www.lk.emb-japan.go.jp; Ambassador AKIO SUDA.

Korea, Democratic People's Republic: Colombo; Ambassador HAN CHANG-WON.

Korea, Republic: 98 Dharmapala Mawatha, Colombo 7; tel. (11) 2699036; fax (11) 2672358; e-mail kesl@koreanembassy.net; Ambassador LIM JAE-HONG.

Kuwait: 292 Bauddhaloka Mawatha, Colombo 7; tel. (11) 2597958; fax (11) 2597954; e-mail cmb@kuwaitembassysl.org; Ambassador ABDULLAH AL-SANOUSI.

Libya: 120 Horton Place, POB 155, Colombo 7; tel. (11) 2693700; fax (11) 5338881; e-mail libya@eureka.lk; Secretary of the People's Bureau ABDUL KARIM ALI ABDUL KARIM.

Malaysia: 33 Bagatalle Rd, Colombo 3; tel. (11) 2554683; fax (11) 2554684; e-mail mwcolmbo@eureka.lk; High Commissioner NAZIRAH HUSSAIN.

Maldives: 25 Melbourne Ave, Colombo 4; tel. (11) 2586762; fax (11) 2581200; High Commissioner Dr MOHAMED ASIM.

Myanmar: 120 Park Rd, Colombo 5; tel. (11) 2672197; fax (11) 2681196; Ambassador U TIN OO LWIN.

Nepal: 153 Kynsey Rd, Colombo 8; tel. (11) 2590559; fax (11) 2689655; e-mail balakunwar@eureka.lk; Ambassador DURGA PRASAD BHATTARI.

Netherlands: 25 Torrington Ave, Colombo 7; tel. (11) 2596914; fax (11) 2502855; e-mail nethemb@sri.lanka.net; internet www.netherlands.lk; Ambassador REYNOUT S. VAN DIJK.

Norway: 34 Ward Place, Colombo 7; tel. (11) 2469611; fax (11) 2695009; e-mail emb.colombo@mfa.no; internet www.colombo.mfa.no; Ambassador HANS BRATTSKAR.

Pakistan: 211 De Saram Place, Colombo 10; tel. (11) 2696301; fax (11) 2695780; e-mail parepcolombo@sltnet.lk; High Commissioner BASHIR WALI MOHMAND.

Qatar: 7 Bethesda Place, off Dickmen's Rd, Colombo 4; tel. (11) 2665477; fax (11) 2665476; Ambassador ALI HAMAD MUBARAK AL-MARRI.

Romania: A/1/111 New Parliament Rd, Sri Jayawardenepura Kotte, Battaramulla, Colombo; tel. (11) 5551666; fax (11) 2863587; e-mail romania@sri.lanka.net; Chargé d'affaires a.i. NICOLAE ALDEA.

Russia: 62 Sir Ernest de Silva Mawatha, Colombo 7; tel. (11) 2573555; fax (11) 2574957; e-mail rusemb@itmin.com; Ambassador ALEXEY L. SHEBARSHIN.

Saudi Arabia: 39 Sir Ernest de Silva Mawatha, Colombo 7; tel. (11) 2682087; fax (11) 2682088; e-mail lkemb@mofa.gov.sa; Ambassador MOHAMMED BIN MAHMOUD AL-ALI.

Sweden: 49 Bullers Lane, Colombo 7; tel. (11) 4795400; fax (11) 4795450; e-mail ambassaden.colombo@sida.se; Chargé d'affaires JERKER THUNBERG.

Switzerland: 63 Gregory's Rd, POB 342, Colombo 7; tel. (11) 2695117; fax (11) 2695176; e-mail vertretung@col.rep.admin.ch; Ambassador BERNARDINO REGAZZONI.

Thailand: 9th Floor, Greenlanka Towers, 46/46 Nawam Mawatha, Colombo 2; tel. (11) 2302500; fax (11) 2304511; e-mail thaicmb@sltnet.lk; internet www.thaiembassy.org/colombo; Ambassador KARN CHIRANOND.

United Arab Emirates: 44 Sir Ernest de Silva Maratha, Colombo 7; tel. (11) 2565052; Ambassador M. M. MOHAMOUD AL-MAHMOUD.

United Kingdom: 190 Galle Rd, Kollupitiya, POB 1433, Colombo 3; tel. (11) 2437336; fax (11) 2430308; e-mail bhc@eureka.lk; internet www.britishhighcommission.gov.uk/srilanka; High Commissioner DOMINICK CHILCOTT.

USA: 210 Galle Rd, POB 106, Colombo 3; tel. (11) 2448007; fax (11) 2437345; internet usembassy.state.gov/srilanka; Ambassador JEFFERY J. LUNSTEAD.

Judicial System

The judicial system consists of the Supreme Court, the Court of Appeal, the High Court, District Courts, Magistrates' Courts and Primary Courts. The last four are Courts of the First Instance and appeals lie from them to the Court of Appeal and from there, on questions of law or by special leave, to the Supreme Court. The High Court deals with all criminal cases and the District Courts with civil cases. There are Labour Tribunals to decide labour disputes.

The Judicial Service Commission comprises the Chief Justice and two judges of the Supreme Court, nominated by the President. All judges of the Courts of First Instance (except High Court Judges) and the staff of all courts are appointed and controlled by the Judicial Service Commission. The Supreme Court consists of the Chief Justice and not fewer than six and not more than 10 other judges. The Court of Appeal consists of the President and not fewer than six and not more than 11 other judges.

Chief Justice of the Supreme Court: SARATH NANDA SILVA.
Attorney-General: K. C. KAMALASABEYSON.

Religion

According to the 2001 census, the distribution of the population by religion in 18 out of 25 districts was: Buddhist 76.7%, Muslim 8.5%, Hindu 7.9%, Roman Catholics 6.1% and other Christians 0.8%. The census results did not cover the Tamil-dominated northern and eastern districts, where a higher proportion of Hindus could be expected.

BUDDHISM

Theravada Buddhism is the predominant sect. There are an estimated 53,000 Buddhist *Bhikkhus* (monks), living in about 6,000 temples.

All Ceylon Buddhist Congress: 380 Bauddhaloka Mawatha, Colombo 7; tel. (11) 2691695; fax (11) 2688517; e-mail acbc@isplanka.lk; internet www.acbc.lk; f. 1919; Pres. MILINA SUMATHIPALA; Jt Secs RANJITH EKANAYAKE, SUNIL SARATH KURUGAMA.

Sri Lanka Regional Centre of the World Fellowship of Buddhists: 380 Bauddhaloka Mawatha, Colombo 7; tel. (11) 2681886; e-mail nationlanka@sltnet.lk; Pres. S. PALITHA KANNANGARA; Sec. Dr MALANI DIAS.

HINDUISM

The majority of the Tamil population are Hindus. According to the 2001 census the Hindu population in 18 out of 25 districts was 1,329,020.

CHRISTIANITY

National Christian Council of Sri Lanka: 368/6 Bauddhaloka Mawatha, Colombo 7; tel. (11) 2671723; fax (11) 2671721; e-mail nccslsec@sltnet.lk; f. 1945; 13 mem. bodies; Gen. Sec. Rev. W. P. EBENEZER JOSEPH.

The Anglican Communion

The Church of Ceylon (Sri Lanka) comprises two Anglican dioceses. In 1985 there were about 78,000 adherents.

Bishop of Colombo: Rt Rev. DULEEP KAMIL DE CHICKERA, Bishop's House, 358/2 Bauddhaloka Mawatha, Colombo 7; tel. (11) 2684810; fax (11) 2684811; e-mail bishop@eureka.lk; diocese f. 1845.

Bishop of Kurunegala: Rt Rev. KUMARA BANDARA SAMUEL ILLANGASINGHE, Bishop's House, Kandy Rd, Kurunegala; tel. (37) 22191; fax (37) 26806; e-mail bishopkg@sltnet.lk; diocese f. 1950.

The Roman Catholic Church

For ecclesiastical purposes, Sri Lanka comprises one archdiocese and 10 dioceses. At 31 December 2003 there were an estimated 1,369,927 adherents in the country.

SRI LANKA

Catholic Bishops' Conference in Sri Lanka
19 Balcombe Place, Cotta Rd, Borella, Colombo 8; tel. (11) 2697062; fax (11) 2699619; e-mail neildias@rocketmail.com; f. 1975; Pres. Most Rev. FERNANDO JOSEPH VIANNEY (Bishop of Kandy); Sec.-Gen. Rt Rev. MARIUS PEIRIS.

Archbishop of Colombo: Most Rev. Dr OSWALD THOMAS COLMAN GOMIS, Archbishop's House, 976 Gnanartha Pradeepaya Mawatha, Colombo 8; tel. (11) 2695471; fax (11) 2692009; e-mail cyrilsp@sltnet.lk; internet www.ceylon.net/catholicchurchcolombo.

The Church of South India
The Church comprises 21 dioceses, including one, Jaffna, in Sri Lanka. The diocese of Jaffna, with an estimated 18,500 adherents in 1997, was formerly part of the South India United Church (a union of churches of the Congregational and Presbyterian/Reformed traditions), which merged with the Methodist Church in South India and the four southern dioceses of the (Anglican) Church of India to form the Church of South India in 1947.

Bishop in Jaffna: Rt Rev. Dr S. JEBANESAN, 41 4th Cross St, Jaffna; tel. (21) 2029; fax (1) 584836; e-mail jdcsiacm@panlanka.net.

Other Christian Churches
Dutch Reformed Church: General Consistory Office, 363 Galle Rd, Colombo 6; tel. (11) 2360190; fax (11) 2582469; e-mail drc1642@sltnet.lk; f. 1642; Pres. of Gen. Consistory Rev. CHARLES N. JANSZ; Admin. Mgr GODFREY B. EBENEZER.

Methodist Church: Methodist Headquarters, 252 Galle Rd, Colombo 3; tel. (11) 2575630; fax (11) 2436090; e-mail methhq@sltnet.lk; internet www.gbgm-umc.org/methchsrilan; 30,139 mems (2000); Pres. of Conference Rev. W. P. EBENEZER JOSEPH; Sec. of Conference Rev. J. C. S. ROHITHA DE SILVA.

Other denominations active in the country include the Sri Lanka Baptist Sangamaya.

BAHÁ'Í FAITH
Spiritual Assembly: Bahá'í National Centre, 65 Havelock Rd, Colombo 5; tel. and fax (11) 2587360; e-mail nsasrilanka@sltnet.lk.

The Press

NEWSPAPERS
Newspapers are published in Sinhala, Tamil and English. There are five main newspaper publishing groups:

Associated Newspapers of Ceylon Ltd: Lake House, 35 D. R. Wijewardene Mawatha, POB 248, Colombo 10; tel. (11) 2435641; fax (11) 2449069; e-mail webmgr@sri.lanka.net; internet www.lanka.net/lakehouse; f. 1926; nationalized 1973; publr of Daily News, Evening Observer, Thinakaran, Lak Janatha and Dinamina (dailies); three Sunday papers: Sunday Observer, Silumina and Thinakaran Vaara Manjari; and 11 periodicals; Chair. JANADASA PEIRIS; CEO TIKIRI KOBBEKADUWA.

Express Newspapers (Ceylon) Ltd: 185 Grandpass Rd, POB 160, Colombo 14; tel. (11) 2320881; fax (11) 2439987; e-mail md@expressnewspapers.lk; internet www.virakesari.lk; publr of Virakesari Daily, Mithran Varamalar, Metro News and Virakesari Weekly (Sunday); Man. Dir KUMAR NADESAN.

Leader Publications (Pvt) Ltd: 1st Floor, Colombo Commercial Bldg, 121 Sir James Peiris Mawatha, Colombo 2; tel. (75) 2365892; fax (75) 2365891; e-mail leader@sri.lanka.net; internet www.thesundayleader.lk; publr of The Sunday Leader and Irida Peramuna.

Upali Newspapers Ltd: 223 Bloemendhal Rd, POB 133, Colombo 13; tel. (11) 2324001; fax (11) 2448103; f. 1981; publr of The Island, Divaina (dailies), two Sunday papers, Sunday Island and Sunday Divaina, four weeklies, Vidusara, Navaliya, Bindu and The Island International (for sale abroad only), and one bi-weekly, Vathmana–News Magazine; English and Sinhala; Editor-in-Chief (vacant); Man. Dir J. H. LANEROLLE.

Wijeya Newspapers Ltd: 8 Hunupitiya Cross Rd, Colombo 2; tel. (11) 2314714; fax (11) 2449504; e-mail wnlgen@wijeya.lk; internet www.wijeya.lk; f. 1979; publr of Daily Mirror, The Sunday Times, Lankadeepa, Irida Lankadeepa, Sirikatha; Sinhala and English; Chair. RANJIT SUJIVA WIJEWARDENE.

Dailies
Daily Mirror: 8 Hunupitiya Cross Rd, Colombo 2; tel. (11) 2314714; fax (11) 2449504; e-mail mirror@wijeya.lk; internet www.dailymirror.lk; f. 1996; English and Sinhala; Editor LALITH ALAHAKOON; circ. 45,500.

Daily News: Lake House, D. R. Wijewardene Mawatha, POB 248, Colombo 10; tel. (11) 2429429; fax (11) 2429210; e-mail editor@dailynews.lk; internet www.dailynews.lk; f. 1918; morning; English; Editor GEOFF WIJEYESINGHE; circ. 65,000.

Dinakara: 95 Maligakanda Rd, Colombo 10; tel. (11) 2595754; f. 1978; morning; Sinhala; publ. by Rekana Publrs; official organ of the Sri Lanka Freedom Party; Editor MULEN PERERA; circ. 12,000.

Dinamina: Lake House, D. R. Wijewardene Mawatha, POB 248, Colombo 10; tel. (11) 2221181; internet www.dinamina.lk; f. 1909; morning; Sinhala; Editor G. S. PERERA; circ. 140,000.

Divaina: 223 Bloemendhal Rd, POB 133, Colombo 13; tel. (11) 2224001; fax (11) 2448103; e-mail gamini@unl.upali.lk; internet www.divaina.com; f. 1982; morning and Sunday; Chief Editor UPALI TENNAKOON.

Eelanadu: Jaffna; tel. (21) 22389; f. 1959; morning; Tamil; Chair. S. RAVEENTHIRANATHAN; Editor M. SIVANANTHAM; circ. 15,000.

The Island: 223 Bloemendhal Rd, Colombo 13; tel. (11) 2448102; fax (11) 4609198; e-mail prabath@unl.upali.lk; internet www.island.lk; f. 1981; English; Editor GAMINI WEERAKOON; circ. 80,000.

Lak Janatha: Lake House, D. R. Wijewardene Mawatha, Colombo 10; tel. (11) 2421181; f. 2005; evening; Sinhala; Editor SUJEEWA DISSANAYAKE.

Lankadeepa: 8 Hunupitiya Cross Rd, Colombo 2; tel. (11) 2448321; fax (11) 2438039; e-mail siri@wijeya.lk; internet www.lankadeepa.lk; f. 1986; Sinhala and English; Editor SIRI RANASINGHE; circ. 160,000.

Namathu Eelanadu: Jaffna; f. 2002; Tamil; Editor SIVASUBRAMANIAM RAGURAM.

Peraliya: 2nd Floor, Borella Supermarket Complex, Colombo 8; Editor SUJEEWA GAMAGE.

Thinakaran: Lake House, D. R. Wijewardene Mawatha, POB 248, Colombo 10; tel. (11) 2221181; f. 1932; morning; Tamil; Editor R. SIVAGURUNATHAN; circ. daily 14,000.

Thinakkural: 68 Ellie House Rd, Colombo 15; internet www.thinakkural.com; Tamil; also publ. from Jaffna; Editor A. SIYANESACHELVAN.

Uthayan: Jaffna; e-mail editorial@uthayan.com; internet www.uthayan.com; Tamil; Chief Editor M. V. KAANAMYLNATHAN.

Valampuri: Jaffna; f. 1999; Tamil; Editor S. WIJESUNDARAM.

Virakesari Daily: 185 Grandpass Rd, POB 160, Colombo 14; tel. (11) 2320881; fax (11) 2439987; e-mail kesari10@virakesari.lk; internet www.virakesari.lk; f. 1931; morning; Tamil; Man. Dir KUMAR NADESAN; Editor R. PRABAGAN; circ. 60,000.

Sunday Newspapers
Irida Lankadeepa: 8 Hunupitiya Cross Rd, Colombo 2; tel. (11) 2448321; fax (11) 2438039; e-mail siri@wijeya.lk; internet www.lankadeepa.lk; Sinhala; Chief Editor SIRI RANSINGHE.

Janasathiya: 47 Jayantha Weerasekara Mawatha, Colombo 10; f. 1965; Sinhala; publ. by Suriya Publishers Ltd; Editor SARATH NAWANA; circ. 50,000.

Mithran Varamalar: 185 Grandpass Rd, Colombo 14; tel. (11) 2320881; fax (11) 2448205; e-mail kesari25@virasekari.lk; internet www.virakesari.lk; f. 1969; Tamil; Man. Dir KUMAR NADESAN; Editor V. THEVARAJ; circ. 29,000.

Silumina: Lake House, 35 D. R. Wijewardene Mawatha, Colombo 10; tel. (11) 2324772; fax (11) 2449069; e-mail editor@silumina.lk; internet www.silumina.lk; f. 1930; Sinhala; Editor NIWAL HORANA; circ. 264,000.

Sunday Island: 223 Bloemendhal Rd, POB 133, Colombo 13; tel. (11) 2421599; fax (74) 609198; e-mail manik@unl.upali.lk; f. 1981; English; Editor MANIK DE SILVA; circ. 40,000.

The Sunday Leader: Colombo Commercial Bldg, 1st Floor, 121 Sir James Peiris Mawatha, Colombo 2; tel. (75) 2365892; fax (75) 2365891; e-mail editor@thesundayleader.lk; internet www.thesundayleader.lk; English; Editor LASANTHA WICKRAMATUNGA.

Sunday Observer: D. R. Wijewardene Mawatha, POB 248, Colombo 10; tel. (11) 2429231; fax (11) 2429230; e-mail editor@sundayobserver.lk; internet www.sundayobserver.lk; f. 1923; English; Editor JAYATILLEKE DE SILVA; circ. 125,000.

Sunday Thinakkural: 68 Ellie House Rd, Colombo 15; internet www.thinakkural.com/sundaythinakkural; Tamil; also publ. from Jaffna; Editor A. SIYANESACHELVAN.

The Sunday Times: 8 Hunupitiya Cross Rd, Colombo 2; tel. (11) 2326247; fax (11) 2423922; e-mail editor@sundaytimes.wnl.lk; internet www.sundaytimes.lk; f. 1986; English and Sinhala; Editor SINGHA RATNATUNGA; circ. 116,000.

Thinakaran Vaara Manjari: Lake House, 35 D. R. Wijewardene Mawatha, Colombo 10; tel. (11) 2221181; f. 1948; Tamil; Editor R. SRIKANTHAN; circ. 35,000.

SRI LANKA

Virakesari Weekly: 185 Grandpass Rd, Colombo 14; tel. (11) 2320881; fax (11) 2448205; e-mail webmaster@virakesari.lk; internet www.virakesari.lk; f. 1931; Tamil and English; Man. Dir KUMAR NADESAN; Editor MURUGESAMPILLAI SUBRAMANIAM; circ. 110,000.

PERIODICALS
(weekly unless otherwise stated)

Athavan: Colombo; Tamil.

Aththa: 91 Dr N. M. Perera Mawatha, Colombo 8; tel. (11) 2691450; fax (11) 2691610; e-mail dew128@dialogsl.net; f. 1964; Sinhala; publ. by the Communist Party of Sri Lanka; Editor GUNASENA VITHANA; circ. 28,000.

Business Lanka: Trade Information Service, Sri Lanka Export Development Board, Level 7, 42 Navam Mawatha, POB 1872, Colombo 2; tel. (11) 2300677; fax (11) 2300715; e-mail tisinfo@tradenetsl.lk; f. 1981; quarterly; information for visiting businessmen, etc.; Editor S. D. ISAAC.

Ceylon Commerce: National Chamber of Commerce of Sri Lanka, NCCSL Bldg, 450 D. R. Wijewardene Mawatha, POB 1375, Colombo 10; tel. (11) 2689597; fax (11) 2689596; e-mail nccsl@slt.lk; internet www.nationalchamberlk.org; monthly.

Ceylon Medical Journal: 6 Wijerama Mawatha, Colombo 7; tel. (11) 2693324; fax (11) 2698802; e-mail slma@eureka.lk; internet www.medinet.lk/cmj; f. 1887; quarterly; Editors Prof. COLVIN GOONARATNA, Prof. H. JANAKA DE SILVA.

The Economic Times: 130/C/8, Jothikarama Mawatha, Pannipitiya; tel. (11) 2796134; fax (11) 4305787; f. 1970; Editor THIMSY FAHIM.

The Financial Times: 323 Union Place, POB 330, Colombo 2; tel. (11) 2226181; quarterly; commercial and economic affairs; Man. Editor CYRIL GARDINER.

Gnanarthapradeepaya: Colombo Catholic Press, 2 Gnanarthapradeepaya Mawatha, Borella, Colombo 8; tel. (11) 2695984; fax (11) 2692586; e-mail catholic@eureka.lk; f. 1866; Sinhala; Roman Catholic; Chief Editor Rev. Fr W. DON BENEDICT JOSEPH; Exec. Dir Rev. Fr BERTRAM DABRERA; circ. 26,000.

Irudina: Lithira Publications (Pvt) Ltd, 98 Ward Place, Colombo 7; tel. (11) 5344202; fax (11) 5344200; internet www.irudina.lk; f. 2004; Sinhala; Editor MOHAN LAL PIYADASA.

Janakavi: 47 Jayantha Weerasekera Mawatha, Colombo 10; fortnightly; Sinhala; Assoc. Editor KARUNARATNE AMERASINGHE.

Manasa: 150 Dutugemunu St, Dehiwala, Colombo; tel. (11) 2553994; f. 1978; Sinhala; monthly; science of the mind; Editor SUMANADASA SAMARASINGHE; circ. 6,000.

Mihira: Lake House, 35 D. R. Wijewardene Mawatha, Colombo 10; tel. (11) 2419583; f. 1964; Sinhala children's magazine; Editor M. NEWTON PINTO; circ. 145,000.

Morning Star: 39 Fussels Lane, Colombo 6; tel. (11) 2511233; fax (11) 2584836; e-mail jdcsiacm@panlanka.net; f. 1841; English and Tamil; publ. by the Jaffna diocese of the Church of South India.

Nava Yugaya: Lake House, 35 D. R. Wijewardene Mawatha, Colombo 10; tel. (11) 2419581; f. 1956; literary fortnightly; Sinhala; Editor S. N. SENANAYAKE; circ. 57,000.

Navaliya: 223 Bloemendhal Rd, Colombo 13; tel. (11) 2324001; fax (11) 2448103; internet www.navaliya.com; Sinhala; women's interest; Editor CHANDANI WIJETUNGE; circ. 148,260.

Pathukavalan: POB 2, Jaffna; tel. (21) 22300; f. 1876; Tamil; publ. by St Joseph's Catholic Press; Editor Rev. Fr RUBAN MARIAMPILLAI; circ. 7,000.

Puthiya Ulaham: 115 4th Cross St, Jaffna; tel. (21) 22627; f. 1976; Tamil; six a year; publ. by Centre for Better Society; Editor Rev. Dr S. J. EMMANUEL; circ. 1,500.

Ravaya: Colombo; Sinhala; Editor VICTOR IVAN.

Samajawadhaya: 91 Dr N. M. Perera Mawatha, Colombo 8; tel. (11) 2595328; monthly; theoretical; publ. by the Communist Party of Sri Lanka.

Sarasaviya: Lake House, 35 D. R. Wijewardene Mawatha, Colombo 10; tel. (11) 2429586; f. 1963; Sinhala; films; Editor GRANVILLE SILVA; circ. 56,000.

Sinhala Bauddhaya: Maha Bodhi Mandira, 130 Rev. Hikkaduwe Sri Sumangala Nahimi Mawatha, Colombo 10; tel. (11) 2698079; f. 1906; publ. by The Maha Bodi Society of Ceylon; Editor-in-Chief KIRTHI KALAHE; circ. 25,000.

Sirikatha: 8 Hunupitiya Cross Rd, Colombo 2; tel. (11) 2314714; fax (11) 2449504; Sinhala women's magazine; Editor SIRI RANASINGHE.

Sri Lanka Government Gazette: Government Press, POB 507, Colombo; tel. (11) 2293611; f. 1802; Sinhala and Tamil; official govt bulletin; circ. 54,000.

Sri Lanka News: Lake House, 35 D. R. Wijewardene Mawatha, Colombo 10; tel. (11) 2429429; fax (11) 2449069; f. 1938; digest of news and features; printing temporarily suspended from March 2002; Editor RUWAN GODAGE.

Sri Lanka Today: Government Dept of Information, 7 Sir Baron Jayatilaka Mawatha, Colombo 1; tel. (11) 2228376; English; quarterly; Editor MANEL ABHAYARATNE.

Subasetha: Lake House, 35 D. R. Wijewardene Mawatha, Colombo 10; tel. (11) 2221181; f. 1967; Sinhala; astrology, the occult and indigenous medicine; Editor Capt. K. CHANDRA SRI KULARATNE; circ. 100,000.

Tharunee: Lake House, 35 D. R. Wijewardene Mawatha, Colombo 10; tel. (11) 2429588; fax (11) 2449069; f. 1969; Sinhala; women's journal; Editor SUMANA SAPRAMADU; circ. 95,000.

Vidusara: 223 Bloemendhal Rd, Colombo 13; tel. (11) 2324001; fax (11) 2448103; internet www.vidusara.com; Sinhala; Editor ANURA SIRIWARDENA; circ. 103,992.

NEWS AGENCIES

Lankapuvath (National News Agency of Sri Lanka): Transworks House, Lower Chatham St, Colombo 1; tel. (11) 2673483; fax (11) 2673011; internet www.lankapuvath.com; f. 1978; Chair. D. E. W. GUNASEKARA; Editor G. L. W. WIJESINHA.

TamilNet: e-mail tamilnet@tamilnet.com; internet www.tamilnet.com; f. 1997; reports on Tamil affairs.

Foreign Bureaux

Agence France-Presse (AFP): 100 Barnes Place, Colombo 7; tel. (11) 2695097; fax (11) 2694385; Chief of Bureau AMAL JAYASINGHE.

Deutsche Presse-Agentur (dpa) (Germany): Independent Newspapers Ltd, 5 Gunasena Mawatha, Colombo 12; tel. (11) 2545327; Correspondent REX DE SILVA.

Press Trust of India (PTI): Colombo; Correspondent K. DHARMARAJAN.

Reuters (United Kingdom): Level 27, East Tower, World Trade Centre, Echelon Sq., Colombo 1; tel. (11) 2431187; fax (11) 2338302; Sr Country Rep. DION SCHOORMAN.

United Press International (UPI) (USA): 'Jasmin Court', 60/1 Wijerama Lane, Udahamulla, Nugegoda; tel. (11) 2853923; fax (11) 2856496; Correspondent IQBAL ATHAS.

Xinhua (New China) News Agency (People's Republic of China): 24 Pathiba Rd, Colombo 5; tel. (11) 2589092; e-mail xhco@eureka.lk; Chief Correspondent ZHANG YADONG.

The Associated Press (USA) and Prensa Latina (Cuba) are also represented.

PRESS ASSOCIATIONS

Foreign Correspondents' Association of Sri Lanka: 20 1/1 Regent Flats, Sir Chittampalan Gardiner Mawatha, Colombo; tel. (11) 2231224.

Sri Lanka Press Association: Colombo; Pres. B. H. S. JAYEWARDENE.

Publishers

W. E. Bastian and Co (Pvt) Ltd: 23 Canal Row, Fort, Colombo 1; tel. (11) 2432752; f. 1904; art, literature, technical; Dirs H. A. MUNIDEVA, K. HEWAGE, N. MUNIDEVA, G. C. BASTIAN.

Buddhist Publication Society: 54 Sangharaja Mawatha, POB 61, Kandy; tel. (81) 2237283; fax (81) 2223679; e-mail bps@sltnet.lk; internet www.bps.lk; f. 1958; philosophy, religion and theology; Pres. Bhikkhu BODHI.

Colombo Catholic Press: 2 Gnanarthapradeepaya Mawatha, Borella, Colombo 8; tel. (11) 2678106; fax (11) 2692586; e-mail catholic@eureka.lk; f. 1865; religious; publrs of The Messenger, Gnanarthapradeepaya, The Weekly; Exec. Dir Rev. Fr BERTRAM DABRERA.

M. D. Gunasena and Co Ltd: 217 Olcott Mawatha, POB 246, Colombo 11; tel. (11) 2323981; fax (11) 2323336; e-mail mdgunasena@mail.ewisl.net; internet www.mdgunasena.com; f. 1913; educational and general; Chair M. D. PERCY GUNASENA; Man. Dir M. D. ANANDA GUNASENA.

Lake House Printers and Publishers Ltd: 41 W. A. D. Ramanayake Mawatha, POB 1458, Colombo 2; tel. (11) 2433271; fax (11) 2449504; e-mail wnl@wijeya.lk; f. 1965; Chair. R. S. WIJEWARDENE; Sec. D. P. ANURA NISHANTHA KUMARA.

Pradeepa Publishers: 34/34 Lawyers' Office Complex, Colombo 12; tel. (11) 2435074; fax (11) 2863261; e-mail kjaytie@slt.lk; academic and fictional; Propr K. JAYATILAKE.

Saman Publishers Ltd: 49/16 Iceland Bldg, Colombo 3; tel. (11) 2223058; fax (11) 2447972.

SRI LANKA

Sarexpo International Ltd: Caves Bookshop, 81 Sir Baron Jayatilleke Mawatha, POB 25, Colombo 1; tel. (11) 2422676; fax (11) 2447854; e-mail sarexpo@eureka.lk; f. 1876; history, arts, law, medicine, technical, educational; Man. Dir C. J. S. FERNANDO.

K. V. G. de Silva and Sons (Colombo) Ltd: Shop No. 5, Liberty Plaza, Colombo 3; tel. (11) 7455646; fax (11) 7555543; e-mail photowave@sltnet.lk; f. 1898; art, philosophy, scientific, technical, academic, 'Ceyloniana', fiction; Man. FREDERICK JAYARATNAM.

PUBLISHERS' ASSOCIATION

Sri Lanka Association of Publishers: 112 S. Mahinda Mawatha, Maradana, Colombo 10; tel. (11) 2695773; fax (11) 2696653; e-mail dayawansajay@hotmail.com; Pres. DAYAWANSA JAYAKODY; Sec.-Gen. GAMINI WIJESURIYA.

Broadcasting and Communications

TELECOMMUNICATIONS

Lanka Communication Services (Pvt) Ltd: 65C Dharmapala Mawatha, Colombo 7; tel. (11) 2437545; fax (11) 2537547; internet www.lankacom.net; f. 1991; subsidiary of Singapore Telecom International; Man. Dir ROHITH UDALAGAMA.

Lanka Internet Services Ltd: 443 Galle Rd, Colombo 3; tel. (11) 2559600; fax (11) 2559599; e-mail info@sri.lanka.net; internet lisl.lanka.net; Chair. UPALI KEPPITIPOLA.

MTN Networks (Pvt) Ltd: 475 Union Place, Colombo 2; tel. (11) 2678678; fax (11) 2678692; e-mail dialog@dialog.lk; internet www.dialog.lk; fully owned subsidiary of Telekom Malaysia; operates Dialog GSM, Sri Lanka's largest mobile phone network; Chief Exec. Dr HANS WIJAYASURIYA.

Sri Lanka Telecom Ltd: Telecom Headquarters, 7th Floor, Lotus Rd, POB 503, Colombo 1; tel. (11) 2329711; fax (11) 2440000; e-mail pr@slt.lk; internet www.slt.lk; 35% owned by Nippon Telegraph and Telephone Corpn (Japan), 49.5% by Govt of Sri Lanka and 3.5% by employees; Chair. THILANGA SUMATHIPALA; CEO SHUHEI ANAN.

Regulatory Authority

Telecommunications Regulatory Commission of Sri Lanka: 276 Elvitigala Mawatha, Manning Town, Colombo 8; tel. (11) 2689345; fax (11) 2689311; e-mail dgtsl@slt.lk; internet www.trc.gov.lk; f. 1996; Chair. S. S. EDIRIWEERA; Dir-Gen. THEMIYA HURULLE.

RADIO

Sri Lanka Broadcasting Corpn: Independence Sq., POB 574, Colombo 7; tel. (11) 2696525; fax (11) 2698576; e-mail slbcweb@lanka.net; internet www.slbc.lk; f. 1967; under Ministry of Information and Media; controls all broadcasting in Sri Lanka; regional stations at Anuradhapura, Kandy and Matara; transmitting stations at Ambewela, Amparai, Anuradhapura, Diyagama, Ekala, Galle, Kanthalai, Mahiyangana, Maho, Matara, Puttalam, Ratnapura, Seeduwa, Senkadagala, Weeraketiya; home service in Sinhala, Tamil and English; foreign service also in Tamil, English, Sinhala, Hindi, Kannada, Malayalam, Nepali and Telugu; 893 broadcasting hours per week: 686 on domestic services, 182 on external services and 126 on education; Chair. JANADASA PEIRIS; Dir-Gen. NIMAL LAKSHAPATHIARACHCHI.

Asura FM: No. 52, 5th Lane, Colombo 3; tel. (11) 2575000; fax (11) 2301082; internet www.asurafm.com; broadcasts 24 hrs daily in Sinhala; Chair. NIRAJ WICKREMESINGHE.

Colombo Communications (Pvt) Ltd: 2/9 2nd Floor, Liberty Plaza, 250 R. A. de Mel Mawatha, Colombo 3; tel. (11) 2577924; fax (11) 2577929; commercial station; three channels broadcast 24 hrs daily in English, Sinhala and Tamil.

Lite FM: No. 52, 5th Lane, Colombo 3; tel. (11) 2575000; fax (11) 2301082; e-mail info@tnlradio.com; internet www.tnlradio.com; commercial station; broadcasts 24 hrs daily in English; Chair. NIRAJ WICKREMESINGHE.

MBC Networks (Pvt) Ltd: 7 Braybrooke Place, Colombo 2; tel. (11) 5340111; fax (11) 5340124; internet www.maharaja.lk; commercial station comprising four channels; broadcasts 24 hrs daily in English, Sinhala and Tamil.

TNL Radio: No. 52, 5th Lane, Colombo 3; tel. (11) 2575000; fax (11) 2301082; e-mail info@tnlradio.com; internet www.tnlradio.com; f. 1993; commercial station; broadcasts 24 hrs daily in English; Chair. NIRAJ WICKREMESINGHE.

Trans World Radio: 125/3 3rd Lane, Subadrarama Rd, POB 123, Nugegoda; tel. (5) 559321; fax (11) 2817749; e-mail rkoch@twr.org; f. 1978; religious station; broadcasts 3 hours every morning and 6 hours each evening to Indian subcontinent; Dir (Finance/Administration) ROGER KOCH; Eng. P. VELMURUGAN.

Voice of Tigers: Vanni; internet www.eelam.com/vot; f. 1990 by the LTTE; banned until 2003; broadcasts 8.5 hrs daily in Tamil and Sinhala.

TELEVISION

Sri Lanka Rupavahini Corpn (SLRC): Independence Sq., POB 2204, Colombo 7; tel. (11) 2599506; fax (11) 2580929; e-mail ict@rupavahini.lk; internet www.rupavahini.lk; f. 1982; studio at Colombo; transmitting stations at nine locations; broadcasts 18 hrs daily on Channel I, 15 hrs daily on Channel II; Dir-Gen. NISHANTHA RANATUNGA; Chair. M. M. ZUHAIR.

Independent Television Network (ITN—Sri Lanka): Wickremasinghepura, Battaramulla; tel. (11) 2775494; fax (11) 2774591; e-mail itnch@slt.lk; internet www.itnsl.lk; broadcasts about 6 hrs daily; Chair. NEWTON GUNARATNE; Gen. Man. W. M. C. S. JAYAWEERA.

EAP Network (Pvt) Ltd: 676 Galle Rd, Colombo 3; tel. (11) 2503819; fax (11) 2503788; e-mail eapnet@slt.lk; Chair. SOMA EDIRISINGHE; Man. Dir JEEVAKA EDIRISINGHE.

MTV Channel (Pvt) Ltd: Araliya Uyana, Depanama, Pannipitiya; tel. (11) 5340111; e-mail info@media.maharaja.lk; f. 1992; broadcasts on three channels in English, Sinhala and Tamil.

National Television of Tamil Eelam (NTT): e-mail ntt_news@yahoo.com; f. 2005; broadcasts for 2 hrs daily.

Telshan Network (Pvt) Ltd (TNL): 9D Tower Bldg, 25 Station Rd, Colombo 4; tel. (11) 2596241; fax (11) 2706125; e-mail tnltvr@slt.lk; Chair. and Man. Dir SHANTILAL NILKANT WICKREMESINGHE.

Finance

(cap. = capital; res = reserves; dep. = deposits; m. = million; brs = branches; amounts in Sri Lanka rupees, unless otherwise indicated)

BANKING

Central Bank

Central Bank of Sri Lanka: 30 Janadhipathi Mawatha, POB 590, Colombo 1; tel. (11) 2477000; fax (11) 2477677; e-mail cbslgen@sri.lanka.net; internet www.centralbanklanka.org; f. 1950; sole bank of issue; cap. and res 64,144m., dep. 83,320m. (Dec. 2003); Gov. and Chair. of the Monetary Board SUNIL A. S. MENDIS; Dep. Govs Dr RANEE JAYAMAHA, W. A. WIJEWARDENA; 3 regional offices.

Commercial Banks

Bank of Ceylon: 4 Bank of Ceylon Mawatha, POB 241, Colombo 1; tel. (11) 2446811; fax (11) 2447171; e-mail boc@sri.lanka.net; internet www.bankofceylon.net; f. 1939; 100% state-owned; cap. 2,600m., res 11,242.7m., dep. 205,164.3m. (Dec. 2004); Chair. SUMITRA MOONESINGHE; Gen. Man. S. N. P. PALIHENA; 293 brs in Sri Lanka, 3 brs abroad.

Commercial Bank of Ceylon Ltd: Commercial House, 21 Bristol St, POB 856, Colombo 1; tel. (11) 2430416; fax (11) 2449889; e-mail e-mail@combank.net; internet www.combank.net; f. 1969; 29.77% owned by DFCC Bank, 29.91% by govt corpns and 40.32% by public; cap. 2,603.1m., res 9,080.9m., dep. 85,764.7m. (Dec. 2003); Chair. M. J. C. AMARASURIYA; Man. Dir A. L. GOONERATNE; 110 brs.

Hatton National Bank Ltd: 479 T. B. Jayah Mawatha, Colombo 10; tel. (11) 2664664; fax (11) 2446523; e-mail moreinfo@hnb.net; internet www.hnb.net; f. 1970; 15.7% owned by Standard Finance Ltd, 29.9% by public and 54.5% by others; cap. 715.0m., res 5,520.1m., dep. 87,884.4m. (Dec. 2002); Chair. RIENZIE T. WIJETILLEKE; Gen. Man. and CEO R. THEAGARAJAH; 111 brs.

Nations Trust Bank Ltd: 242 Union Place, Colombo 2; tel. (11) 2447655; fax (11) 2447659; e-mail bank@nationstrust.lk; internet www.nationstrust.com; f. 1999; privately owned; cap. 850.0m., res 274.5m., dep. 7,077.8m. (Dec. 2003); Chair. VIVENDRA LINTOTAWELA; CEO MOKSEVI R. PRELIS.

Pan Asia Banking Corpn Ltd: 450 Galle Rd, Colombo 3; tel. (11) 2565556; fax (11) 2565558; e-mail pabc@pabcbank.com; internet www.pabcbank.com; f. 1995; 100% privately-owned; cap. 556m., res –180m., dep. 6,557m. (Dec. 2004); Chair. W. M. ABEYRATNE BANDARA; Man. Dir, Gen. Man. and CEO R. NADARAJAH; 18 brs.

People's Bank: 75 Sir Chittampalam A. Gardiner Mawatha, POB 728, Colombo 2; tel. (11) 2327841; fax (11) 2446407; e-mail info@people.is.lk; internet www.peoplesbank.lk; f. 1961; 92% owned by Govt, 8% by co-operatives; cap. 1,202.0m., res –2,446.8m., dep. 157,486.9m. (Dec. 2003); Chair. P. AMARASINGHE; CEO and Gen. Man. DERECK J. KELLY; 324 brs.

Sampath Bank Ltd: 110 Sir James Peiris Mawatha, POB 997, Colombo 2; tel. (11) 2300153; fax (11) 2300143; e-mail mgr@oper.sampath.lk; internet www.sampath.lk; f. 1987; cap. 442.8m., res 2,940.1m., dep. 42,031.4m. (Dec. 2003); Chair. EDGAR GUNATUNGA; Man. Dir/CEO ANIL AMARASURIYA; 64 brs.

SRI LANKA

Directory

Seylan Bank Ltd: Ceylinco Seylan Towers, 90 Galle Rd, POB 400, Colombo 3; tel. (11) 2456789; fax (11) 2456456; e-mail info@seylan.lk; internet www.eseylan.com; f. 1988; cap. 869.5m., res 3,603.8m., dep. 59,362.9m. (Dec. 2003); Chair. J. L. B. KOTELAWALA; Gen. Man., Dir and CEO AJITA PASQUAL; 113 brs.

Union Bank of Colombo Ltd: 15A Alfred Place, Colombo 3; tel. (11) 2370870; fax (11) 2370692; e-mail shan@unionb.com; internet www.unionb.com; f. 1995; cap. 885.0m., res 6.4m., dep. 4,595.2m. (Dec. 2003); Chair. AJITA DE ZOYSA; CEO and Dir MAHENDRA FERNANDO.

Development Banks

Agricultural and Industrial Credit Corpn of Ceylon: POB 20, Colombo 3; tel. (11) 2223783; f. 1943; loan cap. 30m.; Chair. V. P. VITTACHI; Gen. Man. H. S. F. GOONEWARDENA.

DFCC Bank: 73/5 Galle Rd, POB 1397, Colombo 3; tel. (11) 2442442; fax (11) 2440376; e-mail info@dfccbank.com; internet www.dfccbank.com; f. 1956 as Development Finance Corpn of Ceylon; name changed as above 1997; provides long- and medium-term credit, investment banking and consultancy services; cap. 574.1m., res 8,368.0m., dep. 3,779.4m. (March 2005); Chair. Dr T. N. JINASENA; Gen. Man., Dir and CEO N. FONSEKA; 3 brs.

National Development Bank of Sri Lanka: 40 Navam Mawatha, POB 1825, Colombo 2; tel. (11) 2437701; fax (11) 2440262; e-mail info@ndb.org; internet www.ndb.org; f. 1979; provides long-term finance for projects, equity financing and merchant banking services; cap. 537.5m., res 6,847.4m. (Dec. 2003); Chair. SARATH KUSUM WICKREMESINGHE; Gen. Man. and Dir NIHAL WELIKALA.

State Mortgage and Investment Bank: 269 Galle Road, POB 156, Colombo 3; tel. (11) 2573563; fax (11) 2573346; e-mail smibgm@itmin.com; internet www.lanka.net/smib; f. 1979; Chair. Dr GAMINI FERNANDO; Gen. Man. U. H. D. PATHMASIRI.

Merchant Banks

Merchant Bank of Sri Lanka Ltd: Bank of Ceylon Merchant Tower, 28 St Michael's Rd, POB 1987, Colombo 3; tel. (11) 4711711; fax (11) 2565666; e-mail mbslbank@mbslbank.com; internet www.mbslbank.com; f. 1982; 53.8% owned by Bank of Ceylon; public ltd liability co; cap. 2,500m., total assets 2,128m. (2003); Chair. S. N. P PALIHENA; Man. Dir and CEO SUNIL G. WIJESINHA; 3 brs.

People's Merchant Bank Ltd: Level 4, Hemas House, 75 Braybrooke Place, Colombo 2; tel. (11) 2300191; fax (11) 2300190; e-mail pmbank@sltnet.lk; f. 1983; total assets 610m. (1999); Chair. Dr G. FERNANDO.

Foreign Banks

American Express Bank Ltd (USA): 104 Dharmapala Mawatha, Colombo 7; tel. (11) 2682787; fax (11) 2682786; Dir of Operations K. BALACHANDRARAJAN.

Citibank NA (USA): 65C Dharmapala Mawatha, POB 888, Colombo 7; tel. (11) 2447316; fax (11) 2445487; e-mail kapila.jayawardena@citicorp.com; Vice-Pres. KAPILA JAYAWARDENA.

Deutsche Bank AG (Germany): 86 Galle Rd, POB 314, Colombo 3; tel. (11) 2447062; fax (11) 2447067; Chief Country Officer STEFAN MAHRDT; 3 brs.

Emirates Bank International Ltd (United Arab Emirates): 64 Lotus Rd, POB 358, Colombo 1; tel. (11) 223467; Gen. Man. N. C. VITARANA.

Habib Bank Ltd (Pakistan): 140–142 Second Cross St, POB 1088, Colombo 11; tel. (11) 2326565; fax (11) 2447827; e-mail habiblk@lanka.ccom.lk; f. 1941; Vice-Pres. and Country Man. M. YUSUF SAUDAGAR.

The Hongkong and Shanghai Banking Corpn Ltd (Hong Kong): 24 Sir Baron Jayatilaka Mawatha, POB 73, Colombo 1; tel. (11) 2325435; fax (11) 2448388; internet www.hsbc.lk; CEO DAVID GRIFFITHS.

ICICI Bank (India): 58 Dharmapala Mawatha, Colombo 7; tel. (11) 4242448; e-mail customercare.srilanka@icicibank.com; internet www.icicibank.lk; Country Head NAVEEN K. AGARWAL.

Indian Bank (India): 22–24 Mudalige Mawatha, POB 624, Colombo 1; tel. (11) 2323402; fax (11) 2447562; e-mail ibcol@slnet.lk; internet www.indian-bank.com; Chief Exec. K. RAGHAVAN.

Indian Overseas Bank (India): 139 Main St, POB 671, Colombo 11; tel. (11) 2324422; fax (11) 2447900; e-mail iobch@lgo.lk; Country Head A. RAMASWAMY; 1 br.

Overseas Trust Bank Ltd (Hong Kong): YMCA Bldg, 39 Bristol St, POB 835, Colombo 1; tel. (11) 2547655.

Public Bank Berhad (Malaysia): Ground and First Floors, Jewelarts Bldg, 324 Galle Rd, Colombo 3; tel. (11) 2576289; fax (11) 2573958.

Standard Chartered Grindlays Bank Ltd (United Kingdom): 37 York St, Colombo 1; tel. (11) 2480000; fax (11) 2422618; e-mail wasim.saifi-sri-lanka@lk.standardchartered.com; internet www.standardchartered.com; f. 1853; CEO WASIM SAIFI.

State Bank of India: 16 Sir Baron Jayatilaka Mawatha, POB 93, Colombo 1; tel. (11) 2326133; fax (11) 2439404; e-mail ceosbilk@slt.lk; internet www.statebankofindia.net; f. 1955; CEO VINAY JAIN.

Union Bank Ltd (United Arab Emirates): 245 Dharmapala Mawatha, Colombo 7; tel. (11) 2679000; fax (75) 5331849; e-mail gohar@eureka.lk; Country Man. GOHARULAYN AFZAL.

Financial Association

The Finance Houses' Association of Sri Lanka: 181/1A Dharmapala Mawatha, Colombo 7; tel. (11) 2665865; fax (11) 2665864; e-mail finass@sltnet.lk; internet www.fha.lk; f. 1958; represents the finance cos registered and licensed by the Central Bank of Sri Lanka; Chair. VAGDEVI FERNANDO; Sec.-Gen. DENNIS VISWASAM.

STOCK EXCHANGES

Securities and Exchange Commission of Sri Lanka: 11–01 East Tower, World Trade Centre, Echelon Sq., Colombo 1; tel. (11) 2439144; fax (11) 2439149; e-mail mail@sec.gov.lk; internet www.sec.gov.lk; f. 1987.

Colombo Stock Exchange: 04–01, West Block, World Trade Centre, Echelon Sq., Colombo 1; tel. (11) 2446581; fax (11) 2445279; e-mail cse@cse.lk; internet www.cse.lk; f. 1896; stock market; 18 mem firms and 241 listed cos; Chair. ERAJ WIJESINGHE; Dir-Gen. HIRAN MENDIS.

INSURANCE

Ceylinco Insurance Co Ltd: Ceylinco House, 4th Floor, 69 Janadhipathi Mawatha, Colombo 1; tel. (11) 2485706; fax (11) 2485769; e-mail jagath@lanka.ccom.lk; f. 1987; Chair. and Man. Dir J. L. B. KOTELAWALA.

Eagle Insurance Co Ltd: 'Eagle House', 75 Kumaran Ratnam Rd, Colombo 2; tel. (11) 2437090; fax (11) 2447620; e-mail info@eagle.com.lk; internet www.eagle.com.lk; f. 1988 as CTC Eagle Insurance Co Ltd; general and life insurance; mem. of the Zurich Group; CEO DEEPAL SOORIYAARACHCHI; Man. Dir CHANDRA JAYARATNE.

Hayleys Ltd: Hayley Bldg, 400 Deans Rd, Colombo 10; internet www.hayleys.com; f. 1952; Chair. SUNIL MENDIS; Dep. Chair. R. YATAWARA.

National Insurance Corpn Ltd: 47 Muttiah Rd, POB 2202, Colombo 2; tel. (11) 2445738; fax (11) 2445733; e-mail nicopl@slt.lk; general; Chair. T. M. S. NANAYAKKARA; Sec. A. C. J. DE ALWIS.

Sri Lanka Insurance Corporation Ltd: 'Rakshana Mandiraya', 21 Vauxhall St, POB 1337, Colombo 2; tel. (11) 2357537; fax (11) 2447742; e-mail slic@srilankainsurance.com; internet www.srilankainsurance.com; f. 1961; privatized in 2003; all classes of insurance; Chair. D. H. S. JAYAWARDENE; Dep. Chair. RAJ OBEYESEKERE.

Union Assurance Ltd: Union Assurance Centre, 20 St Michael's Rd, Colombo 3; tel. (11) 2344171; fax (11) 2343065; e-mail info@union-assurance.com; internet www.union-assurance.com; f. 1987; general and life insurance; Chair. KEN BALENDRA; Dep. Chair. R. SIVARATNAM.

Trade and Industry

GOVERNMENT AGENCIES

Board of Investment of Sri Lanka: World Trade Centre, West Tower, 24th–26th Floors, Echelon Sq., Colombo 1; tel. (11) 2434403; fax (11) 2447995; e-mail infoboi@boi.gov.lk; internet www.boi.lk; f. 1978 as the Greater Colombo Economic Commission; promotes foreign direct investment and administers the eight Export Processing Zones at Katunayake, Biyagama, Koggala, Mirigama, Malwatta, Horana, Mawathagama and Polgahawela; also administers industrial township at Watupitiwala and industrial parks at Seetawaka and Kandy; Chair. and Dir-Gen. Prof. LAKSHMAN R. WATAWALA.

Public Enterprises Reform Commission (PERC): 11–01 West Tower, World Trade Centre, Colombo 1; tel. (11) 2338756; fax (11) 2326116; e-mail dg@perc.gov.lk; internet www.perc.gov.lk; f. 1995 to advise Govt on privatization and restructuring of loss-making state-sector enterprises; Chair. NIHAL SRI AMERESEKERE; Dir-Gen. LEEL WICKREMARACHCHI.

Sri Lanka Gem and Jewellery Exchange: Levels 4 and 5, East Low Block, World Trade Centre, Echelon Sq., Colombo 1; e-mail slgje@sltnet.lk; internet www.srilankagemautho.lk; f. 1990; testing and certification of gems, trading booths; Dir-Gen. M. WIJESEKERA; Sen. Man. (Export Promotion) AJITH PERERA.

SRI LANKA

National Gem and Jewellery Authority: 25 Galle Face Terrace, Colombo 3; tel. and fax (11) 2329352; e-mail ngja@sltnet.lk; internet www.srilankagemautho.com; f. 1971 as State Gem Corpn; Chair. ASOKA JAYAWARDENA; Dir-Gen. T. PIYADASA.

Trade Information Service: Sri Lanka Export Development Board, Level 7, POB 1872, 42 Navam Mawatha, Colombo 2; tel. (11) 2300677; fax (11) 2300715; e-mail tisinfo@edb.tradenetsl.lk; internet www.srilankabusiness.com; f. 1981 to collect and disseminate commercial information and to provide advisory services to trade circles; Dir W. M. D. S. WEERAKOON.

DEVELOPMENT ORGANIZATIONS

Coconut Development Authority: 11 Duke St, POB 386, Colombo 1; tel. (11) 2421027; fax (11) 2447602; e-mail cocoauth@panlanka.net; internet www.cda.lk; f. 1972; state body; promotes the coconut industry through financial assistance for mfrs of coconut products, market information, consultancy services and quality assurance; Chair. H. A. TILLEKERATNE.

Industrial Development Board of Ceylon (IDB): 615 Galle Rd, Katubedda, POB 09, Moratuwa; tel. (11) 2605326; fax (11) 2607002; e-mail idb@sltnet.lk; internet www.nsf.ac.lk/idb; f. 1969; under Ministry of Industrial Development; promotes industrial development through provincial network; Chair. C. T. S. B. PERERA; Gen. Man. CHANDRASIRI KALUPAHNAGE.

Centre for Entrepreneurship Development and Consultancy Services: 615 Galle Rd, Katubedda, POB 09, Moratuwa; tel. (11) 2632156; f. 1989; Dir T. M. KULARATHNE (acting).

Centre for Industrial and Technology Information Services (CITIS): 615 Galle Rd, Katubedda, POB 09, Moratuwa 10400; tel. (11) 2605372; fax (11) 2607002; e-mail idb@sltnet.lk; internet www.idb.lk; f. 1989; disseminates information to small and medium-sized enterprises; Dir G. J. K. ARIYADASA.

Information and Communication Technology Association of Sri Lanka (ICTA): 160/24 Kirimandala Mawatha, Colombo 5; tel. (11) 2369100; fax (11) 2369091; e-mail info@icta.lk; internet www.icta.lk; f. 2003; responsible for development of information communication technology in Sri Lanka; Man. Dir and CEO MANJU HATHOTUWA.

Janatha Estates Development Board: 55/75 Vauxhall St, Colombo 2; tel. (11) 2320901; fax (11) 2446577; f. 1975; manages 18 tea and spice plantations; 10,164 employees; 1 regional office.

Sri Lanka Export Development Board: Level 7, Trade Information Service, 42 Navam Mawatha, Colombo 2; tel. (11) 2300705; fax (11) 2300715; e-mail tisinfo@edb.tradenetsl.lk; internet www.tradenetsl.lk/edb; f. 1979; Chair. ROHANTHA ATHUKORALA.

CHAMBERS OF COMMERCE

Federation of Chambers of Commerce and Industry of Sri Lanka: Colombo; internet www.fccisl.lk; f. 1973; a central org. of 45 chambers of commerce and industry and trade asscns representing 10,000 cos throughout Sri Lanka; Pres. LAL DE MEL; Sec.-Gen. SAMANTHA ABEYWICKRAMA.

All Ceylon Trade Chamber: 212/45 1/3, Bodhiraja Mawatha, Colombo 11; tel. (11) 2432428; Pres. MUDLIYAR N. W. J. MUDALIGE; Gen. Sec. Y. P. MUTHUKUMARANA.

Ceylon Chamber of Commerce: 50 Navam Mawatha, POB 274, Colombo 2; tel. (11) 2421745; fax (11) 2449352; e-mail info@chamber.lk; internet www.chamber.lk; f. 1839; 517 mems; Chair. DEVA RODRIGO; Sec.-Gen. PREMA COORAY.

Ceylon National Chamber of Industries: Galle Face Court 2, 1st Floor, POB 1775, Colombo 3; tel. (11) 2423734; fax (11) 2423734; e-mail info@cnci.lk; internet www.cnci.lk; f. 1960; 325 mems; Chair. RANJITH HETTIARACHCHY.

International Chamber of Commerce Sri Lanka: 141/7 Vauxhall St, POB 1733, Colombo 2; tel. (11) 2307825; fax (11) 2307841; e-mail iccsl@sltnet.lk; internet www.iccsl.lk; f. 1955; Chair. TISSA JAYAWEERA; CEO GAMINI PEIRIS.

National Chamber of Commerce of Sri Lanka: NCCSL Bldg, 450 D. R. Wijewardene Mawatha, POB 1375, Colombo 10; tel. (11) 2689600; fax (11) 2689596; e-mail nccsl@slt.lk; internet www.nationalchamberlk.org; f. 1948; Pres. NIRMALI SAMARATUNGA; Sec.-Gen. NEIL C. SENEVIRATNE.

INDUSTRIAL AND TRADE ASSOCIATIONS

Association of Computer Training Organizations: 5 Clifford Ave, Colombo 3; tel. (11) 2565193; fax (11) 2713821; e-mail infotel@sri.lanka.net; f. 1991; 29 mems; Pres. KITHSIRI MANCHANAYAKE.

Ceylon Coir Fibre Exporters' Association: c/o Volanka Ltd, 193 Minuwangoda Rd, Kotugoda; tel. (11) 2232938; fax (11) 2237365; e-mail com@volanka.com; internet www.slcfa.lk; Chair. INDRAJITH PIYASENA.

Ceylon Hardware Merchants' Association: 159 1/5 Mahavidyalaya Mawatha, Colombo 13; tel. (11) 2433085; fax (11) 2423342; 191 mems; Pres. S. THILLAINATHAN.

Ceylon Planters' Society: 40/1 Sri Dhammadara Mawatha, Ratmalana; tel. (11) 2715656; fax (11) 2716758; e-mail plansoty@yahoo.com; f. 1936; 1,133 mems (plantation mans); 25 brs and nine regional organizations; Pres. C. BASNAYAKE; Sec. D. N. R. WIJEWARDENA.

Coconut Products Traders' Association: c/o Ceylon Chamber of Commerce, 50 Navam Mawatha, POB 274, Colombo 2; tel. (11) 2421745; fax (11) 2449352; e-mail info@chamber.lk; internet www.chamber.lk; f. 1925; Chair. NALIN JAYASINGHE; Sec. E. P. A. COORAY.

Colombo Rubber Traders' Association: c/o Ceylon Chamber of Commerce, 50 Navam Mawatha, POB 274, Colombo 2; tel. (11) 2421745; fax (11) 2449352; e-mail info@chamber.lk; internet www.chamber.lk; f. 1918; Chair. A. L. WEERASINGHE; Sec. E. P. A. COORAY.

Colombo Tea Traders' Association: c/o Ceylon Chamber of Commerce, 50 Navam Mawatha, POB 274, Colombo 2; tel. (11) 2421745; fax (11) 2449352; e-mail info@chamber.lk; internet www.chamber.lk; f. 1894; 203 mems; Chair. TYEAB AKBARALLY; Sec. E. P. A COORAY.

Free Trade Zone Manufacturers' Association: Plaza Complex, Unit 6 (Upper Floor), IPZ, Katunayake; tel. (11) 2252813; Chair. AJITH DIAS.

Joint Apparel Association Forum (JAAF): 16 De Fonseka Rd, Colombo 5; tel. (11) 2580493; fax (11) 2580099; e-mail info@jaafsl.com; internet www.jaafsl.com; f. 2002; co-ordinates and develops apparel industry; Chair. ASHROFF OMAR; Sec.-Gen. M. P. T. COORAY.

Sea Food Exporters' Association: c/o Andriesz & Co Ltd, 39 Nuge Rd, Peliyagoda; tel. 530021.

Software Exporters' Association: c/o Ceylon Chamber of Commerce, 50 Navam Mawatha, Colombo 2; tel. (11) 2343702; fax (11) 2449352; e-mail rukshika@chamber.lk; internet www.softwaresrilanka.com; f. 1999; 52 mems; Chair. JAYANTHA DE SILVA.

Sri Lanka Apparel Exporters' Association: 45 Rosmead Place, Colombo 7; tel. (11) 2670778; fax (11) 2683118; e-mail srilanka-apparel@eureka.lk; internet www.srilanka-apparel.com; f. 1982; Chair. RANJAN CASIE CHETTY; Sec. HEMAMALI SIRISENA.

Sri Lanka Association of Manufacturers and Exporters of Rubber Products (SLAMERP): 425 Thimbirigasyaya Rd, Colombo 5; tel. (11) 2521200; fax (11) 2521222; e-mail slamerp@panlanka.net; f. 1984; Chair. ANANDA CALDERA; Sec.-Gen. C. DIAS BANDARANAYAKE.

Sri Lanka Association of Printers: 290 D. R. Wijewardena, Colombo 10; tel. (11) 2472315; fax (11) 2386716; e-mail slap@sltnet.lk; internet www.lankaprint.org; f. 1956; 300 mems; publishes quarterly magazine *Print Ceylon*; Pres. KEERTHI GUNAWARDANE; Sec. DHARANI KARUNARATNA.

Sri Lanka Chamber of the Pharmaceutical Industry: 15 Tichbourne Passage, Colombo 10; tel. (11) 2694823; fax (11) 2671877; e-mail nimjay@sltnet.lk; Pres. N. DIAS JAYASINHA; Sec. NAUSHAD ISMAIL.

Sri Lanka Fruit and Vegetables Producers, Processors and Exporters' Association: c/o Sri Lanka Export Development Board, 42 Navam Mawatha, Colombo 2; tel. (11) 2300705; fax (11) 2304879; e-mail harz47@edb.tradenetsl.lk; internet www.tradenetsl.lk; Sec. M. A. JUNAID.

Sri Lanka Importers, Exporters and Manufacturers' Association (SLIEMA): POB 12, Colombo; tel. (11) 2696321; fax (11) 2684480; e-mail tradelink@slt.lk; f. 1955; Pres. WILLIAM JOHN TERRENCE PERERA.

Sri Lanka Jewellery Manufacturing Exporters' Association: Colombo; tel. (11) 2445141; fax (11) 2445105; Pres. IFTHIKHAR AZIZ; Sec. CHANAKA ELLAWELA.

Sri Lanka Shippers' Council: c/o Ceylon Chamber of Commerce, 50 Nawam Mawatha, POB 274, Colombo 2; tel. (11) 2422156; internet www.slsc.ws.

Sri Lanka Tea Board: 574 Galle Rd, POB 1750, Colombo 3; tel. (11) 2508991; fax (11) 2589132; e-mail teaboard@pureceylontea.com; internet www.pureceylontea.com; f. 1976 for development of tea industry through quality control and promotion in Sri Lanka and in world markets; Chair. NIRAJ DE MEL; Dir-Gen. H. D. HEMARATNE.

Sri Lanka Wooden Furniture and Wood Products Manufacturers' and Exporters' Association: c/o E. H. Cooray & Sons Ltd, 411 Galle Rd, Colombo 3; tel. (11) 2509227; fax (11) 2575198; Pres. PATRICK AMARASINGHE; Sec. PINSIRI FERNANDO.

Sugar Importers' Association of Sri Lanka: c/o C. W. Mackie & Co Ltd, 36 D. R. Wijewardena Mawatha, POB 89, Colombo 10; tel. (11) 2423554; fax (11) 2438069; e-mail nalin@export.cwmackie.com; Pres. M. THAVAYOGARAJAH; Sec. C. KAPUWATTA.

SRI LANKA

EMPLOYERS' ORGANIZATION

Employers' Federation of Ceylon: 385 J3 Old Kotte Rd, Rajagiriya, Colombo; tel. (11) 2867966; fax (11) 2867942; e-mail gkbd@eureka.lk; internet www.empfed.lk; f. 1929; mem. International Organization of Employers and Confederation of Asia Pacific Employers; 456 mems; Dir-Gen. G. K. B. DASANAYAKA.

UTILITIES

Electricity

Ceylon Electricity Board: 50 Sir Chittampalam A. Gardiner Mawatha, POB 540, Colombo 2; tel. (11) 2324471; fax (11) 2323935; e-mail chairceb@sri.lanka.net; internet www.ceb.lk; f. 1969; Chair. ARJUN DERANIYAGALA.

Water

National Water Supply and Drainage Board (NWSDB): Galle Rd, Ratmalana, Colombo; tel. (11) 2638999; fax (11) 2636449; e-mail gmnwsdb@sltnet.lk; internet waterboard.lk; f. 1975; govt corpn; Chair. S. L. SENEVIRATNE.

CO-OPERATIVES

In 2000 there were an estimated 11,793 co-operative societies in Sri Lanka, with membership totalling 17,235,000.

TRADE UNIONS

At the end of 2000 there were 1,588 trade unions functioning in Sri Lanka.

All Ceylon Federation of Free Trade Unions (ACFFTU): 94-1/6 York Bldg, York St, Colombo 1; tel. (11) 2431847; fax (11) 2470874; e-mail nwc@itmin.com; nine affiliated unions; 84,000 mems; Pres. M. C. RAJAHMONEY; Sec.-Gen. K. D. LALKANTHA.

Ceylon Federation of Labour (CFL): 457 Union Place, Colombo 2; tel. (11) 2694273; f. 1957; 16 affiliated unions; 155,969 mems; Pres. Dr COLVIN R. DE SILVA; Gen. Sec. S. S. SIRIWARDANE.

Ceylon Mercantile, Industrial and General Workers' Union (CMU): 3 22nd Lane, Colombo 3; tel. (11) 2328157; fax (11) 2434025; e-mail cgscmu@sltnet.lk; Gen. Sec. BALA TAMPOE.

Ceylon Trade Union Federation (CTUF): Colombo; tel. (11) 2220365; f. 1941; 24 affiliated unions; 35,271 mems; Sec.-Gen. L. W. PANDITHA.

Ceylon Workers' Congress (CWC): 'Savumia Bhavan', 72 Ananda Coomarasamy Mawatha, POB 1294, Colombo 7; tel. (11) 2301359; fax (11) 2301355; e-mail cwcctuc@slt.lk; f. 1939; represents mainly plantation workers of Indian Tamil origin; 50 district offices and 7 regional offices; 250,000 mems; Pres. and Gen. Sec. S. ARUMUGAN THONDAMAN.

Democratic Workers' Congress (DWC): 70 Bankshall St, POB 1009, Colombo 11; tel. (11) 2423746; fax (11) 2435961; f. 1939; 201,382 mems (1994); Pres. MANO GANESHAN; Gen. Sec. R. KITNAN.

Government Workers' Trade Union Federation (GWTUF): 457 Union Place, Colombo 2; tel. (11) 2295066; 52 affiliated unions; 100,000 mems; Leader P. D. SARANAPALA.

Jathika Sevaka Sangamaya (JSS) (National Employees' Union): 416 Kotte Rd, Pitakotte, Colombo; tel. (11) 2565432; f. 1959; 357,000 mems; represents over 70% of unionized manual and clerical workers of Sri Lanka; Pres. W. A. NEVILLE PERERA; Sec. SIRINAL DE MEL.

Lanka Jathika Estate Workers' Union (LJEWU): 60 Bandaranayakepura, Sri Jayawardenepura Mawatha, Welikada, POB 1918, Rajagiriya; tel. (11) 2865138; fax (11) 2862262; e-mail ctucljeu@sri.lanka.net; f. 1958; 350,000 mems; Pres. RAJAH SENEVIRATNE; Gen. Sec. K. VELAYUDAM.

Public Service Workers' Trade Union Federation (PSWTUF): 35/5, 19–20 Main St, Colombo 11; tel. (11) 2231125; 100 affiliated unions; 100,000 mems.

Sri Lanka Nidahas Sewaka Sangamaya (Sri Lanka Free Workers' Union): 301 T. B. Jayah Mawatha, POB 1241, Colombo 10; tel. and fax (11) 2694074; f. 1960; 478 br. unions; 193,011 mems; Gen. Sec. LESLIE DEVENDRA.

Union of Post and Telecommunication Officers: 11/4 Lotus Rd, POB 15, Colombo 1; tel. (11) 2350687; fax (11) 2341626; f. 1945; Pres. H. M. NAWARATNE BANDARA; Sec. K. S. WEERASEKERA.

Transport

RAILWAYS

Sri Lanka Railways Authority (SLRA): Colombo; f. 2003; responsible for running of national railway network; Chair. P. H. MANATUNGA.

Sri Lanka Railways (SLR): Olcott Mawatha, POB 335, Colombo 10; tel. (11) 2431177; fax (11) 2446490; e-mail slrail@itmin.com; internet www.scienceland.lk/railway; f. 1864; under Ministry of Transport; operates 1,447 track-km; there are 9 railway lines across the country and 164 stations, with 134 sub-stations (1997); Gen. Man. W. K. B. WERAGAMA.

ROADS

In 1999 there were an estimated 96,695 km of roads in Sri Lanka, of which 11,462 km were main roads. In April 2002 a major highway linking the Jaffna peninsula with the rest of the country was opened for the first time in 12 years.

Ministry of Transport: 1 D. R. Wijewardene Mawatha, POB 588, Colombo 10; tel. (11) 2687212; fax (11) 2687284; e-mail transplan@eol.lk; internet www.transport.gov.lk; maintains 11,147 km of national highways and 4,441 bridges through the Road Development Authority.

Department of Motor Traffic: 581-341 Elvitigala Mawatha, POB 533, Colombo 5; tel. (11) 2694331; fax (11) 2694338; e-mail dmtsl@sltnet.lk.

Sri Lanka Central Transport Board: 200 Kirula Rd, POB 1435, Colombo 5; tel. (11) 2581121; f. 1958; nationalized organization responsible for road passenger transport services consisting of a central transport board, 11 Cluster Bus Cos and one regional transport board; fleet of 8,900 buses (2001); Chair. AMAL KUMARAGE (acting); Sec. R. ARIYAGAMA.

SHIPPING

Colombo is one of the most important ports in Asia and is situated at the junction of the main trade routes. The other main ports of Sri Lanka are Trincomalee, Galle and Jaffna. Trincomalee is the main port for handling tea exports.

Ceylon Association of Ships' Agents (CASA): 56 Ward Place, Colombo 7; tel. (11) 2696227; fax (11) 2698648; e-mail casa@sltnet.lk; internet www.casa.lk; f. 1944; primarily a consultative organization; represents mems in dealings with govt authorities; 116 mems; Chair. Capt. A. V. RAJENDRA; Sec.-Gen. N. K. WARUSAVITHARANA.

Sri Lanka Ports Authority: 19 Chaithya Rd, POB 595, Colombo 1; tel. (11) 2421201; fax (11) 2440651; e-mail slpainfo@slpa.lk; internet www.slpa.lk; f. 1979; responsible for all cargo handling operations and harbour development and maintenance in the ports of Colombo, Galle, Kankasanthurai, Trincomalee, Oluvil and Point Pedro; Chair. DILEEPA WIJESUNDERA; Man. Dir W. G. SAMARATUNGA.

Shipping Companies

Ceylon Ocean Lines Ltd: 'Sayuru Sevana', 46/12 Nawam Mawatha, Colombo 2; tel. (11) 2434928; fax (11) 2439245; e-mail oceanlines@col.lk; f. 1956; shipping agents, freight forwarders, charterers, container freight station operators and bunkers; Dirs Capt. L. P. WEINMAN, Capt. A. V. RAJENDRA.

Ceylon Shipping Corpn Ltd: 6 Sir Baron Jayatilaka Mawatha, POB 1718, Colombo 1; tel. (11) 2328772; fax (11) 2447547; e-mail cscemail@sri.lanka.net; f. 1971 as a govt corpn; became govt-owned limited liability co in 1992; operates fully-containerized service to Europe, the Far East, the Mediterranean, USA and Canada (East Coast); Chair. SUNDRA JAYAWARDHANA; Gen. Man. M. S. P. GUNAWARDENA.

Ceylon Shipping Lines Ltd: 450 D. R. Wijewardena Mawatha, POB 891, Colombo 10; tel. (11) 2689500; fax (11) 2689510; shipping agents, travel agents, off dock terminal operators; Chair. E. A. WIRASINHA; Man. Dir T. D. V. GUNARATNE.

Ceyoceanic Ltd: 80 Reclamation Rd, POB 795, Colombo 11; tel. (11) 2236071; Dir M. T. G. ANAAM.

Colombo Dockyard Ltd: Port of Colombo, Graving Docks, POB 906, Colombo 15; tel. (11) 2522461; fax (11) 2446441; e-mail coldock@cdl.lk; internet www.cdl.lk; f. 1974; 51% owned by Onomichi Dockyard Co Ltd, Japan, and 49% by Sri Lankan public and government institutions; four dry-docks, seven repair berths (1,200 m), repair of ships up to 125,000 dwt, and builders of steel/aluminium vessels of up to 3,000 dwt; Chair. K. YAMANAKA; Gen. Man. M. P. B. YAPA.

Mercantile Shipping Co Ltd: Bohen House, 108 Aluthmawatha Rd, Colombo 15; tel. (11) 2331792; fax (11) 2331799.

Sri Lanka Shipping Co Ltd: 46/5 Navam Mawatha, POB 1125, Colombo 2; tel. (11) 2336853; fax (11) 2437420; e-mail lankaship@slsl.lk; internet www.srilankashipping.com; f. 1956.

INLAND WATERWAYS

There are more than 160 km of canals open for traffic.

CIVIL AVIATION

Civil aviation is controlled by the Government's Department of Civil Aviation. There are airports at Batticaloa, Colombo (Bandaranaike for external flights and Ratmalana for internal), Gal Oya, Palali, Jaffna and Trincomalee. In April 2002 the Government lifted a six-year ban on domestic flights and permitted commercial airlines to resume services to Jaffna.

SriLankan Airlines Ltd: 22–01 East Tower, World Trade Centre, Echelon Sq., Colombo 1; tel. (11) 97335555; e-mail ulweb@srilankan.aero; internet www.srilankan.aero; f. 1979 as Air Lanka Ltd, name changed as above in 1999; 51% state-owned, 44% owned by Emirates Airline (UAE) and 5% by employees; international services to Europe, the Middle East, South Asia and the Far East; Chair. D. PELPOLA; CEO P. M. HILL.

Helitours: Air Headquarters, POB 594, Colombo 2; tel. (11) 2508927; fax (11) 220541; e-mail slafgops@slk.lk; commercial wing of Sri Lankan Air Force; charter services to major tourist destinations.

Lionair (Pvt) Ltd: Asian Aviation Centre, Colombo Airport, Ratmalana, Colombo; tel. (11) 2622622; fax (11) 2611540; e-mail citadeld@sierra.lk; f. 1994; scheduled and charter services to eight domestic destinations; Chair. CHANDRAN RUTNAM; Man. Dir ASOKA PERERA.

Sky Cabs: 294 1/1 Union Place, POB 683, Colombo 2; tel. (11) 2333105; fax (11) 2635575; e-mail skycabs@lanka.com.lk; internet www.skycab.com; f. 1991; commenced operations 1993; privately owned; scheduled passenger and cargo services to Bahrain, India, Oman, the Maldives and Pakistan; Chair. ALI AKBER S. JEEVUNJEE; Man. Dir SURENDRA DE SILVA.

Tourism

As a stopping place for luxury cruises and by virtue of the spectacle of its Buddhist festivals, ancient monuments and natural scenery, Sri Lanka is one of Asia's most important tourist centres. Good motor roads connect Colombo to the main places of interest.

Owing to the continuing intercommunal violence, tourist arrivals decreased from 403,101 in 1995 to 302,265 in 1996 and tourism receipts fell from US $224m. to $168m. The tourism sector, however, recovered well in the latter half of the 1990s, with tourist arrivals reaching 436,440 in 1999. At the end of 2000 the industry appeared to be improving, although arrivals decreased to 400,414 in that year. However, the LTTE attack on Colombo's international airport in July 2001 caused severe damage to the tourist industry. As a result, the number of tourist arrivals in 2001 decreased to 336,794 and tourist receipts fell from $250.8m. to $211.1m. In 2002 the industry recovered; total arrivals reached 393,171 and tourist receipts increased to stand at an estimated $253.0m. Tourist arrivals rose by 27.3% in 2003 to reach 500,642; in the same year tourist receipts totalled an estimated $340.0m.

Sri Lanka (Ceylon) Tourist Board: 80 Galle Rd, Colombo 3; tel. (11) 2437759; fax (11) 2437953; e-mail tourinfo@sri.lanka.net; internet www.srilankatourism.org; f. 1966; Chair. PADDY VITHARANA; Dir-Gen. S. KALAISELVAM.

SUDAN

Introductory Survey

Location, Climate, Language, Religion, Flag, Capital

The Republic of Sudan lies in north-eastern Africa. It is bordered by Egypt to the north, by the Red Sea, Eritrea and Ethiopia to the east, by the Central African Republic, Chad and Libya to the west, and by Kenya, Uganda and the Democratic Republic of the Congo (formerly Zaire) to the south. The climate shows a marked transition from the desert of the north to the rainy equatorial south. Temperatures vary with altitude and latitude. The annual average for the whole country is about 21°C (70°F). Arabic is the official language, although other languages are spoken and English is widely understood. Most northern Sudanese are Muslims, while in the south most of the inhabitants are animists or Christians. The national flag (proportions 1 by 2) has three equal horizontal stripes, of red, white and black, with a green triangle at the hoist. The capital is Khartoum.

Recent History

The Sudan (as the country was known before 1975) achieved independence as a parliamentary republic on 1 January 1956. After a military coup in November 1958, a Supreme Council of the Armed Forces was established and ruled until October 1964, when it was overthrown in a civilian revolution. In May 1969 power was seized by a group of officers, led by Col Gaafar Muhammad Nimeri. All existing political institutions and organizations were abolished, and the 'Democratic Republic of the Sudan' was proclaimed, with supreme authority in the hands of the Revolutionary Command Council (RCC). In October 1971 a referendum confirmed Nimeri's nomination as President. A new Government was formed, the RCC was dissolved, and the Sudanese Socialist Union (SSU) was recognized as the only political party.

An early problem facing the Nimeri Government concerned the disputed status of the three southern provinces (Bahr al-Ghazal, Equatoria and Upper Nile), whose inhabitants are racially and culturally distinct from most of the country's population. Rebellion against rule from the north had first broken out in 1955, and fighting continued until March 1972, when an agreement to give the three provinces a degree of autonomy was concluded between members of the Government and representatives of the South Sudan Liberation Movement. A High Executive Council (HEC) for the Southern Region was established in April 1972, and Sudan's permanent Constitution was endorsed in April 1973. Elections to the Regional People's Assembly for southern Sudan took place in November 1973, followed by elections to the National People's Assembly in April 1974.

The establishment of a National Assembly and a political party broadened the Government's base of power, although the army continued to play an important role in the country's affairs. Regional and national elections were held in February 1978, with the provision that opposition candidates had to be approved by the SSU. About one-half of the 274 elective seats in the National Assembly were won by SSU candidates. Elections were held in May 1980 for the National and Regional Assemblies, and in October legislative proposals to legalize a regional system of government were approved. The National People's Assembly was dissolved in October 1981. When new elections were held in December, its membership had been reduced from 366 to 151, as many powers had been devolved to the regions. At the same time, the southern HEC was dissolved. The entire Sudanese Government was dismissed in November, although many individuals were later reinstated. In April 1982 a new Southern Region People's Assembly was elected.

In April 1983 President Nimeri was re-elected for a third six-year term. During that year Sudan's north–south conflict escalated, and in June Nimeri finally decided to redivide the south into three smaller regions, each with its own assembly, in an effort to quell the unrest. In September Nimeri suddenly announced the imposition of strict Islamic law (the *Shari'a*), provoking anger in the largely non-Muslim south, and in April 1984 Nimeri proclaimed a state of emergency. The subsequent stringent application of *Shari'a* law aggravated tensions within the country and strained relations between Sudan and its allies, Egypt and the USA.

In May 1984 Nimeri replaced his Council of Ministers with a 64-member Presidential Council, in accordance with the '*Shoura*' (consultation) principle of *Shari'a* law. In July, however, the National People's Assembly rejected his proposed constitutional amendments to make Sudan a formal Islamic state. In October Nimeri ended the state of emergency and offered to revoke the redivision of the south, if a majority of southerners desired it. The situation in the south continued to deteriorate, with the emergence of the Sudan People's Liberation Movement (SPLM), whose armed forces, the Sudan People's Liberation Army (SPLA), rapidly gained military control over large areas of the provinces of Bahr al-Ghazal and Upper Nile.

On 6 April 1985, while Nimeri was visiting the USA, he was deposed in a bloodless military coup. The country's new leader, Gen. Abdel-Rahman Swar ad-Dahab (who had recently been made Minister of Defence and Commander-in-Chief of the army by Nimeri), appointed a Transitional Military Council (TMC) to govern the country, but he pledged a return to civilian rule after a one-year transitional period. The SSU and the National People's Assembly were dissolved, and hundreds of Nimeri's officials were arrested; Nimeri went into exile in Cairo, Egypt. A transitional Constitution was introduced in October 1985 that allowed new political groupings to emerge in preparation for a general election, and in December the name of the country was officially changed to 'the Republic of Sudan'.

In a general election in April 1986 the Umma Party (UP), led by Sadiq al-Mahdi, won 99 of the 264 seats in the new National Assembly, followed by the Democratic Unionist Party (DUP), with 63 seats. A coalition Government was formed by the UP and DUP, with four portfolios in the Council of Ministers allocated to southern parties. Al-Mahdi became Prime Minister and Minister of Defence, and a six-member Supreme Council assumed the functions of Head of State. With these appointments, the TMC was dissolved, signifying a return to civilian rule.

In response to the April 1985 coup, the SPLM initially declared a cease-fire, but presented the new regime with a series of demands concerning the southern region. Despite Swar ad-Dahab's offer of various concessions to the south, the SPLM refused to negotiate with the TMC, and fighting resumed. In May 1987, following increasing instability in the south, a temporary Council for the Southern Sudan (CSS) was established. Its influence on the army and the SPLM, the two contending *de facto* ruling powers that now existed in the south, was, however, negligible. In June al-Mahdi announced that the coalition parties had agreed on guide-lines for the conduct of government policy and that laws based on a 'Sudanese legal heritage' would replace those unacceptable to non-Muslims, who would be exempted from Islamic taxation and special penalties. However, the SPLM continued to demand a total abrogation of Islamic law as a precondition for peace negotiations, while the National Islamic Front (NIF) demanded that the Islamic code be imposed on the whole country. On 25 July the Government imposed a 12-month state of emergency, aimed at bringing under control the worsening economic situation.

In May 1988 a new Government of National Unity, comprising members of the UP, the DUP, the NIF and some southern Sudanese political parties, was formed. In November representatives of the SPLM met senior members of the DUP and reached agreement on proposals to end the civil war. A statement issued by the two sides stipulated that, prior to the convening of a national constitutional conference, the Islamic legal code should be suspended, that military agreements between Sudan and other countries should be abandoned, and that the state of emergency be lifted and a cease-fire implemented in the south. In December, however, a state of emergency was again declared, amid reports of an attempted military coup. The DUP withdrew from the Government. The political crisis was caused by al-Mahdi's requesting the National Assembly to convene the national constitutional conference, while refusing to incorporate the agreement between the SPLM and the DUP into his proposal.

In February 1989 Dr Hassan at-Turabi, the leader of the NIF, was appointed Deputy Prime Minister. Although the peace agreement concluded by the DUP and the SPLM in November had been widely endorsed, the NIF opposed its provision for the suspension of Islamic laws as a prelude to the negotiation of a peace settlement. The NIF was consequently excluded from a new Government formed in March. Peace negotiations between a government delegation and the SPLM commenced in Ethiopia in April, and at the beginning of May the SPLM leader, Col John Garang, proclaimed a one-month cease-fire (subsequently extended to 30 June), renewing hopes for peace and aiding the work of famine relief. The negotiations culminated in an agreement to suspend Islamic laws, pending the proposed convening, in September, of a constitutional conference.

On 30 June 1989 a bloodless coup, led by Brig. (later Lt-Gen.) Omar Hassan Ahmad al-Bashir, removed al-Mahdi's Government. Al-Bashir formed a 15-member Revolutionary Command Council for National Salvation (RCC), which declared its primary aim to be the resolution of the southern conflict. Al-Bashir, who became Head of State, Chairman of the RCC, Prime Minister and Minister of Defence, and Commander-in-Chief of the armed forces, abolished the Constitution, the National Assembly and all political parties and trade unions, and declared a state of emergency.

The SPLM's response to the coup was cautious. In July 1989 Lt-Gen. al-Bashir declared a one-month unilateral cease-fire and offered an amnesty to those opposing the Government 'for political reasons'. By August the SPLM's terms for a negotiated settlement to the conflict included the immediate resignation of the RCC, prior to the establishment of an interim government, in which the SPLM, the banned political parties and other groupings would be represented. However, the new regime's proximity to the NIF had become apparent, and the negotiations collapsed immediately over the issue of Islamic law. Hostilities, which had been in abeyance since the beginning of May, resumed at the end of October.

In February 1991 the RCC enacted a decree instituting a new, federal system of government. Sudan was divided into nine states, each of which had its own governor, deputy governor and cabinet of ministers, and assumed responsibility for local administration and the collection of some taxes. The central Government retained control over foreign policy, military affairs, the economy and the other principal areas of administration. At the beginning of February it had been announced that a new penal code, based on *Shari'a* law, would take effect in March, but would not apply in the three southern states, pending the establishment there of elected assemblies to resolve the issue. The SPLM nevertheless regarded the application of Islamic law in the northern states as unacceptable, citing the large numbers of non-Muslims resident there.

The overthrow, in May 1991, of the Ethiopian Government, led by Mengistu Haile Mariam, had implications for the SPLA forces, who had previously enjoyed Ethiopian support. In late May armed clashes were reported within Ethiopia between SPLA forces and those of the new Ethiopian Government, and the Sudanese Government declared its recognition of, and support for, the new Ethiopian regime. In October Sudan and Ethiopia signed a treaty of friendship and co-operation.

In February 1992 al-Bashir appointed all 300 members of a new transitional National Assembly, which included the entire RCC, all government ministers and the governors of Sudan's nine states. The Assembly was accorded legislative authority, with the power to examine all decrees issued by the RCC, and responsibility for preparing the country for parliamentary elections. In March government forces commenced an offensive in southern Sudan against the SPLA, which had split into two rival factions.

In early 1993 the NIF was reported to be opposed to the continued military character of the Government, and to favour the dissolution of the RCC. Regional councils were in the process of being elected, and the Government had reportedly undertaken, in 1992, to dissolve the RCC once the regional councils were in place. In January 1993 al-Bashir effected an extensive reorganization of the Cabinet, but stated that the RCC would not be dissolved. Rather, in 1994 the gradual transfer of power to the regional councils would begin. Talks between the Government and the SPLA ended inconclusively in January 1993. By this time the SPLA was reported to have split into three factions.

In July 1993 Garang's faction of the SPLA launched a major offensive after attacks by government troops, aided by rival SPLA factions. Renewed fighting between government troops and the SPLA in July 1993 caused the influx of some 100,000 starving people into the area around the southern provincial capital of Malakal. In August the Nuba people were reported to be threatened by government forces in central Sudan. Independent observers urged the UN to establish 'safe havens' for refugees and to extend its Operation Lifeline Sudan to the Nuba Mountains.

In mid-October 1993 al-Bashir announced political reforms in preparation for presidential and legislative elections in 1994 and 1995, respectively. The RCC was dissolved after it had appointed al-Bashir as President and as head of a new civilian Government. Cabinet ministers were requested to remain in office until elections took place. Later in October al-Bashir appointed a new Minister of Defence—a portfolio that he had formerly held himself—and a new Vice-President.

In January 1994 the two principal rival factions of the SPLA were reported to have agreed on a cease-fire. In February Sudan was redivided into 26 states instead of the nine that had formed the basis of administration since 1991. The executive and legislative powers of each state government were to be expanded, and southern states were to be exempted from *Shari'a* law. In March delegations representing the Government and two factions of the SPLA participated in peace talks held in Nairobi under the auspices of the Intergovernmental Authority on Drought and Development (IGADD—superseded in 1996 by the Intergovernmental Authority on Development—IGAD, see p. 286), which in September 1993 had formed a committee on the Sudanese conflict comprising the Heads of State of Kenya, Ethiopia, Uganda and Eritrea. All parties to the talks agreed to allow the free passage of relief supplies to southern Sudan. In April 1994 the Government adopted legislation providing for the appointment, by the President, of an independent commission to supervise legislative elections scheduled to take place in the second half of 1994, and for a constitutional referendum.

A further round of IGADD-sponsored peace negotiations was held in Nairobi on 18–28 July 1994. On 23 July the Government announced a unilateral cease-fire, to which Garang's faction of the SPLA reportedly responded on 28 July with a cease-fire of its own. However, when the negotiations resumed in early September, divergent positions on the issues of the governance of the south and the role of religion in government quickly led to deadlock. In late September President al-Bashir announced the creation of a peace council, which was formally inaugurated in November as the Supreme Council for Peace. The severing, in December, of diplomatic relations between Sudan and Eritrea led Sudan to inform the IGADD in early 1995 that it no longer considered Eritrea to be a suitable intermediary in the Sudanese conflict. A cabinet reshuffle in February suggested a reinforcement of the Islamic character of the Government.

In mid-March 1995 Garang announced that his faction of the SPLA was to mount a new northern offensive in collaboration with other northern rebels. This grouping, the New Sudan Brigade, aimed to unite other insurgent groups against the Government, but did not appear to gain the support of rival SPLA factions. In late March it was reported that former US President Jimmy Carter had persuaded the Government to declare a unilateral cease-fire for a period of two months, and to offer rebel groups an amnesty if they surrendered their weapons. The SPLA and the South Sudan Independence Movement (SSIM) responded by also declaring cease-fires. In late May the Government extended its cease-fire for two months. However, it soon became apparent that the army was continuing to conduct military operations. In June a conference of groups and parties opposed to the Sudanese Government commenced in Asmara, Eritrea. The conference, hosted by the Eritrean People's Front for Democracy and Justice and organized by the Asmara-based National Democratic Alliance (NDA), was attended, among others, by representatives of the DUP, the UP and the Sudanese Communist Party. It was agreed that, once the al-Bashir regime had been ousted, religion would be separated from politics and that a referendum would be held regarding the secession of the southern provinces. The conference was also reported to have achieved a *rapprochement* between the SPLA and other opposition groups.

In August 1995 a reshuffle of the Cabinet was announced. The DUP claimed that those ministers who had been dismissed had been involved in the attempted assassination of President Mubarak of Egypt in June (see below). Later in August President al-Bashir announced that legislative and presidential elections would be held in 1996. At the end of January 1996 the USA announced the withdrawal of its diplomatic personnel from

Sudan, owing to doubts about the Government's ability to guarantee their safety. Prior to their withdrawal, the UN Security Council had unanimously adopted Resolution 1044, which accused Sudan of supporting terrorism and condemned its role in the attempted assassination of Mubarak. The resolution also demanded that Sudan immediately extradite three individuals implicated in the attempted assassination.

The first legislative and presidential elections to be held in Sudan since 1989 took place in March 1996. Some 5.5m. of Sudan's 10m. eligible voters were reported to have participated in the election of 275 deputies to a new, 400-seat National Assembly. The remaining 125 deputies had been appointed at a national conference in January. Representatives of opposition groups and parties alleged that electoral malpractice had been widespread. In the presidential election al-Bashir (who was reportedly opposed only by token candidates) obtained 75.7% of the total votes cast, and formally commenced a five-year term of office on 1 April. On the same day Dr Hassan at-Turabi, the Secretary-General of the NIF, was unanimously elected President of the National Assembly.

Rumours of an attempted *coup d'état* in late March 1996 prejudiced the newly constituted regime's claim that the elections signified the beginning of a new period of stability and reconciliation, as did reports of serious unrest in Khartoum in early April and the decision not to appoint a new Cabinet until it became clear whether the UN would impose sanctions on Sudan for its failure to comply with the terms of UN Security Council Resolution 1044. On 10 April, however, a substantial breakthrough in the southern conflict appeared to be achieved through the signing of a 'political charter for peace', by the Government, the SSIM and the SPLA-United, which pledged to preserve Sudan's national unity and to take joint action to develop those areas of the country that had been affected by the civil war. The charter also provided for the holding of a referendum as 'a means of realizing the aspirations of southern citizens' and affirmed that Islamic law would be the basis of future legislation. On 17 April Sudan's First Vice-President was reported to have invited Garang to sign the charter on behalf of his faction of the SPLA, prompting speculation that this was part of an ongoing attempt to form a new government of national unity. However, the new Cabinet, announced on 21 April, retained the military, Islamist cast of its predecessor. On 28 April the UN Security Council adopted Resolution 1054, which imposed diplomatic sanctions on Sudan for its failure to comply with the terms of Resolution 1044. In mid-May a second faction of the SPLA was reported to have concluded a peace agreement with the Government. In October al-Bashir appointed eight deputies to the National Assembly to represent constituencies in the south where, owing to the civil war, it had not been possible to hold elections in March.

In January 1997 the Government was reported to be seeking assistance from Egypt, after its forces suffered a series of defeats by allied rebel forces. Sudan claimed that Ethiopia was lending active support to the rebels and appealed to the UN Security Council to intervene. In April a peace accord, covering major issues such as power-sharing and *Shari'a* law, and promising a referendum on southern secession after a four-year transition period, was signed by six of the rebel groups (two of which later merged). Both the NDA and the SPLA, however, rejected the agreement. In August, in accordance with the terms of the agreement, the Southern States Co-ordination Council (SSCC) was established; Dr Riek Mashar Teny-Dhurgon, the leader of the Southern Sudan Defence Force (SSDF), was sworn in as its Chairman. At the beginning of September the SPLA-United declared a cease-fire, and its commander, Dr Lam Akol, returned to Khartoum in the following month.

In March 1998 al-Bashir announced a government reorganization in which a number of former rebel leaders were appointed to the Cabinet, including Akol as Minister of Transport. In April a new Constitution was approved by the National Assembly, and was presented to al-Bashir. The new Constitution was endorsed by 96.7% of voters in a referendum held between 1 and 20 May. Under its terms, executive power would be vested in the Council of Ministers, which would be appointed by the President but responsible to the National Assembly. Legislative power was to be vested in the National Assembly. The Constitution also guaranteed freedoms of thought and religion, and the right to lawful political association.

New legislation approved in November 1998 provided for the establishment of an independent election commission and of a Constitutional Court, and for the legalization of political associations. Registration of political parties began in January 1999; all parties were required to have 100 founding members, none of whom was to have a criminal record.

Clashes were reported between government and rebel forces in early January 1999, in which the rebels claimed to have captured seven soldiers and to have killed a further 48. In April three government officials and a Sudanese aid worker were killed by rebel forces; the four had been kidnapped with two Red Cross workers who had subsequently been released. Following this incident, the Government suspended all contacts with the rebels through IGAD. The rebels, however, claimed that the four had been killed in cross-fire during a rescue attempt by government forces, despite ongoing negotiations for their release, and that the Government was, in fact, seeking an alternative mediator to IGAD.

In May 1999 former President Nimeri returned to Sudan after 14 years in exile in Egypt. His return was welcomed by the Government, and he held meetings with both al-Bashir and at-Turabi, although opposition parties demanded his prosecution for crimes he had allegedly committed while President. In the same month at-Turabi held talks in Switzerland with Sadiq al-Mahdi, with the aim of initiating a process of reconciliation. At the end of May a meeting took place in Kampala, Uganda, between al-Mahdi, Garang and Mubarak al-Mahdi (of the NDA), to discuss several issues regarding their conflict with the Sudanese Government.

In August 1999 the Government accepted a Libyan peace initiative, which envisaged a cease-fire, an end to media propaganda, direct talks through a conference of national dialogue and the establishment of a preparatory committee. The peace effort was to be co-ordinated jointly by Egypt and Libya. The Government did, however, express reservations over a number of conditions proposed by the NDA, which included the suspension of articles in the Constitution that restricted public liberty and the release of political prisoners. In September the SPLA stated that it supported the Egyptian-Libyan peace initiative 'in principle', although after a meeting with the US Secretary of State in October (see below) Garang discounted the Egyptian-Libyan initiative in favour of the IGAD-sponsored peace process.

In May 1999 a new pipeline, which was to transport oil some 1,600 km from oilfields in southern Sudan to Port Sudan on the Red Sea, had been inaugurated. Despite heavy security, a number of bomb attacks on the pipeline were carried out by rebel fighters during 1999, and in September Sudan formally requested the extradition from Egypt of the deputy commander of the NDA in connection with one of these attacks. The pipeline and the oilfields were operated by Greater Nile Oil, a joint venture that was led by a Canadian firm, Talisman Energy. In early 2000 a Canadian government investigation found that Talisman was contributing to human rights violations in Sudan through its operations, although no action was taken against the company. In February the USA imposed a ban on trade with Greater Nile Oil.

At a conference, held in Cairo in October 1999, the leaders of the NDA decided to examine ways of combining the peace initiative sponsored by IGAD and the Egyptian-Libyan initiative, in order to unite the parties of the NDA, a number of whom opposed the pursuit of two parallel initiatives. In November the NDA leader, al-Mirghani, held talks with the Egyptian Minister of Foreign Affairs to discuss the Egyptian-Libyan peace initiative. Al-Mirghani expressed his dissatisfaction at the lack of progress made towards establishing a conference of national dialogue and urged co-ordination with the IGAD peace initiative. Al-Bashir reiterated his offer of a general amnesty for rebel fighters at that time, and the Peace and National Accord Committee announced its decision to pardon all political prisoners, as well as to return confiscated property.

At the end of November 1999 Djibouti hosted a regional IGAD summit meeting, attended by Kenya, Ethiopia and Sudan, to discuss issues related to development and stability in the region. While in Djibouti, President al-Bashir met the UP leader, al-Mahdi, following which the Sudanese Government and the UP signed a declaration of principles, which envisaged a federal system of government and the holding of a referendum within four years to allow southerners to choose between the division of the country or unity with decentralized powers. The agreement was welcomed by many parties; however, the NDA responded by stating that it would escalate the war in the south, not end it. Garang later condemned and disavowed the Djibouti agreement.

During 1999 there were increasing reports of rivalry between al-Bashir and at-Turabi, particularly following the introduction of a bill in the National Assembly that sought to remove the President's power to appoint and dismiss state governors. Consideration of the draft legislation was repeatedly delayed, but a vote was scheduled to be held in mid-December in which the National Assembly was widely expected to approve it. However, on 12 December al-Bashir dissolved the National Assembly and imposed a three-month state of emergency, claiming that he had taken these measures in order to end the 'duality' in the administration. An emergency order suspended some articles of the Constitution, although provincial councils and governors were to continue working. At-Turabi accused al-Bashir of having carried out a *coup d'état*, although a legal challenge, mounted against the measures, was later rejected by the Constitutional Court.

In January 2000 the Libyan and Egyptian foreign ministers visited Sudan and discussed recent developments with al-Bashir; at the end of the meeting they stressed that the Egyptian-Libyan peace initiative would continue. IGAD peace efforts continued in that month with a visit by IGAD officials to southern Sudan, where they held talks with rebel leaders. IGAD-sponsored talks held in Nairobi in January made some progress on the issue of a referendum. At the end of January al-Bashir appointed a new Cabinet and state governors. An emergency development programme, formulated by the SSCC, for the southern states was approved by the Government in February. Teny-Dhurgon resigned as Chairman of the SSCC in February in protest at the Government's failure to implement the terms of the peace accords and at al-Bashir's disregard for the Constitution. In mid-February Teny-Dhurgon claimed a major victory over government forces and announced the establishment of the Sudan People's Defence Force (SPDF).

In March 2000 the Government extended the state of emergency until the end of the year, and approved a law allowing the formation of political parties (superseding the 1998 law), although this was rejected by the opposition, as it still incorporated provisions to suspend the activities of any party. In the same month the UP announced its decision to suspend its membership of the NDA during a meeting in Asmara. Relations between the UP and the NDA had deteriorated after December 1999, when al-Mahdi initiated independent talks with al-Bashir following the dissolution of the National Assembly. The NDA accused the UP of a lack of co-operation and of violating the NDA's principles, while the UP stated that it advocated co-operation with the Government. In April 2000 it was reported that a presidential election was planned for October; the ruling National Congress (NC) had nominated al-Bashir as its candidate in October 1999. However, most opposition parties, including the UP, indicated that they would not participate in any elections prior to the convening of a national conference to discuss the problems in Sudan.

A meeting between the leaders of Egypt, Sudan and Libya was held in Cairo in April 2000 to discuss the Egyptian-Libyan peace initiative. At that time al-Bashir revealed that discussions were under way for the return of al-Mahdi to Sudan. In May al-Bashir announced the suspension of the secretariat of the NC, including the activities of at-Turabi and his deputies, and affirmed his intention to restructure the party.

IGAD-sponsored peace talks, held in April 2000, ended inconclusively, and in May the SPLM suspended its participation in protest at the Government's alleged continued bombing of civilian targets. It reaffirmed its commitment to the unification of the IGAD process and the Egyptian-Libyan initiative, but did not indicate on what conditions it would resume talks. The next round of IGAD-sponsored talks had been scheduled to begin on 17 May. In June the SPLM announced it would rejoin the peace talks, and in that month al-Bashir declared a general amnesty for all opponents of the Government; however, it was rejected by a number of opposition groups, including the SPLM. Later that month at-Turabi announced the formation of a new political party, the Popular National Congress (PNC), whose registration was formally approved in August.

In September 2000 al-Mahdi confirmed the withdrawal of the UP from the NDA alliance. Later that month al-Bashir visited Asmara, where he met with an NDA delegation led by al-Mirghani. The two parties discussed possible political settlements to the situation in Sudan and agreed to meet for further direct talks, although no date for such discussions was set. In October it was reported that al-Bashir had dismissed Maj.-Gen. George Kongor Arop from the post of Second Vice-President. The following month al-Mahdi returned to Sudan from his four-year self-imposed exile in Eritrea and Egypt, but announced that he would not participate in the forthcoming elections.

Presidential and legislative elections were held concurrently over a 10-day period in mid-December 2000, although they were boycotted by the main opposition parties. As expected, al-Bashir was re-elected President, with 86.5% of the votes cast, comfortably defeating his nearest rival, former President Nimeri, who obtained 9.6% of the vote. Voting did not take place in the three southern states. The NC secured 355 seats in the new 360-member National Assembly; the remaining five seats were won by small opposition parties. On 3 January 2001 al-Bashir extended the state of emergency for a further year.

On 21 February 2001 at-Turabi was arrested at his home in Khartoum after it was announced that the PNC and the SPLM had signed a memorandum of understanding in Switzerland, which urged the Sudanese people to participate in 'peaceful popular resistance' against the al-Bashir regime. Over the following days some 30 associates of at-Turabi were also taken into police custody, and in early March at-Turabi and several other members of the PNC's leadership council were reported to have been charged with criminal conspiracy, undermining the constitutional order, waging war on the state and calling for violent opposition to public authority. (In late May at-Turabi was released from prison and placed under house arrest.) Meanwhile, the day after at-Turabi's arrest, al-Bashir implemented a major reorganization of the Cabinet and replaced many of the country's state governors. Several new ministries were created, and, although the new, 32-member Cabinet was dominated by NC members, al-Bashir incorporated four members of two minor opposition parties into the Government. Two members of the UDSF retained their positions in the Cabinet, but the UP, despite earlier indications to the contrary, refused to participate in the new administration and officially stated that it would not accept ministerial posts before the holding of free and fair elections in the south of the country and the resolution of the armed conflict in that region.

In late May 2001 the Government announced the suspension of air strikes against southern rebel groups, but stated that it reserved the right to protect individuals and lines of supply and to counter any rebel offensives. The cessation proved short-lived, as heavy fighting swiftly broke out, and in early June an SPLA offensive resulted in the capture of the strategically important town of Raga in the Bahr al-Ghazal province. Just days later the Government officially revoked the suspension of air strikes, although it stated that it would attempt to avoid the bombing of densely populated areas. Despite these clashes, in early June al-Bashir and Garang both attended an IGAD-sponsored meeting in Nairobi; notably, it was the first time that they had both been present at the same talks since 1997. However, there was no face-to-face meeting between the two, and the negotiations concluded without producing a cease-fire.

In early July 2001 it was reported that the Sudanese Government and the NDA had both provisionally accepted a renewed Libyan-Egyptian peace initiative, which provided for an immediate cease-fire, the establishment of a transitional government and a number of constitutional reforms. Later that month the leadership council of the NC approved the Libyan-Egyptian plan. However, al-Bashir maintained that he would not support any proposals that involved the separation of state and religion or the partition of the country, thus endangering the success of the initiative, as the NDA concurrently reiterated its demand for the right of the southern states to be granted self-determination. In August the SPLA claimed that it had attacked a petroleum-producing facility at Heglig, owned by Talisman, and inflicted heavy casualties. Representatives of the petroleum company denied that any damage to facilities had occurred, although they did confirm that production had been temporarily suspended. Fierce fighting between government forces and rebels continued during September–October; some 170 government fatalities were reported in late September. In the following month, however, government troops recaptured Raga from the SPLA.

Meanwhile, in late September 2001 the UN Security Council voted to remove the sanctions imposed on Sudan in 1996 (see above) and praised the country's recent efforts to combat terrorism. Notably, the USA, which had previously used its vote to veto the lifting of sanctions, abstained, enabling the motion to be carried. In mid-December the state of emergency was again extended for a further 12 months. In January 2002 Teny-Dhurgon and Garang announced the merger of the SPDF and the SPLA. Teny-Dhurgon had defected from the SPLM/SPLA in 1991 and had signed a peace accord with the Government in 1997 (as leader of the SSDF); however, this agreement had collapsed in early 2001.

In mid-January 2002 talks sponsored jointly by the USA and Switzerland commenced in Buergenstock, Switzerland. Following six days of intensive discussions, the Sudanese Government and the SPLA agreed to observe a six-month cease-fire, to be supervised by a joint military commission, in the central Nuba region in order to facilitate the delivery of vital aid supplies to the area. However, the following month the USA announced that it had suspended discussions with the Sudanese Government, after two separate incidents earlier that month in which Sudanese air force planes had bombed civilians collecting food supplies in the Bahr al-Ghazal province. In the second incident at least 24 civilians were killed when a UN World Food Programme (WFP) relief centre came under fire. Although the Government insisted that the earlier incident was accidental, the US Department of State insisted that discussions would not recommence until it had received a full explanation for the attacks from the Sudanese Government. The Sudanese Minister of External Relations subsequently issued an apology for the attack and in mid-March the USA brokered an agreement between the SPLA and the Sudanese Government, which aimed to guarantee the protection of civilians from military attacks; the agreement was to be monitored by two teams of international observers. In early July the cease-fire was extended for a further six months, and in late December it was agreed that it would continue until July 2003.

In May 2002 the Minister of Finance, Adb ar-Rahim Muhammad Hamdi, reportedly resigned owing to ill health. There was, however, speculation that he had been dismissed by al-Bashir following the implementation of several unpopular economic measures. Hamdi was subsequently replaced by Muhammad al-Hasan az-Zubayr. In June three members of the NC, including the Minister of Transport, Dr Lam Akol, resigned from the party in protest at the increasing dominance of al-Bashir. In mid-August al-Bashir renewed the detention order that had been placed on at-Turabi the previous year for a further 12 months, and in September at-Turabi was transferred to prison. In the previous month al-Bashir had effected a minor reorganization of the Council of Ministers, and in September Akol was dismissed; Akol was one of a number of former NC members who had, earlier that month, established a new political party, the Justice Party. In November al-Bashir carried out a further reshuffle of the Council of Ministers and created two new ministries. In December the state of emergency was once again extended for a further 12 months.

Meanwhile, in mid-June 2002 a new round of IGAD-sponsored peace talks between the Government and the SPLM opened in Machakos, Kenya. Despite the ongoing discussions, fighting between the two sides continued, and there were numerous reports of heavy civilian casualties following bombing raids on southern towns by government forces. Nevertheless, a major breakthrough in the conflict was achieved on 20 July, when delegations from the SPLM and the Government signed an accord, known as the Machakos Protocol, which provided for a six-year period of autonomy for the south, to be followed by an internationally monitored referendum on self-determination. The Protocol also stated that Sudan's Constitution would be rewritten to ensure that *Shari'a* law would not be applied to non-Muslim southerners. Government and SPLM delegations reconvened in Machakos in mid-August for talks. However, further outbreaks of fighting between the two sides were reported, and in early September, in response to the SPLA's capture of Torit, the Government announced that it had suspended talks with the SPLM and launched an offensive to try and reclaim the town. Despite agreeing to cease hostilities and resume peace talks, government forces recaptured Torit in early October. Later that month the two sides reconvened in Machakos and signed a cease-fire agreement for the duration of the ongoing discussions. Both sides subsequently accused each other of breaking the cease-fire, and it was reported that some 300 government troops had been killed by rebel forces just hours after the signing of the accord. Negotiations between the Government and the SPLM were halted in mid-November, after no agreement could be reached on the number of government and civil service posts to be allocated to southerners and the distribution of petroleum revenues. Disputes also remained over control of the Abeyi, Blue Nile and Nuba Mountains provinces in central Sudan and the religious status of Khartoum. The two sides did, however, agree to extend the cease-fire until the end of March 2003.

Talks resumed in Nairobi in mid-January 2003, and the following month a memorandum of understanding was signed under which the Government and the SPLM agreed to allow international observers to monitor the cease-fire. In April al-Bashir and Garang met for only the second time in 20 years and announced that they anticipated that the peace talks would be concluded by the end of June; they also reaffirmed their commitment to the Machakos Protocol and pledged to facilitate unrestricted delivery of humanitarian assistance to those in the south of the country. However, in May it became apparent that the talks would not be concluded as expected, after negotiations between the Government and the SPLM ended with a number of key issues, including wealth- and power-sharing, still unresolved. In July the government delegation rejected a document presented by the IGAD mediators, providing for a separate army and an independent central bank for the south, as it maintained that this was in conflict with the Machakos Protocol, which had enshrined the unity of Sudan. In mid-August talks between the Government and the SPLM recommenced in the Kenyan town of Nanyuki, and later that month the discussions were extended until mid-September in order to give both sides additional time to resolve their outstanding differences.

In mid-September 2003 the SPLA and the Sudanese Government agreed to extend their cease-fire for a further two months, and days later the two sides signed a landmark security agreement. Under the terms of the arrangement, two separate armed forces were to be created, as well as a number of integrated units, comprising both government and SPLA troops. Both sides agreed to contribute 12,000 soldiers to a joint force to be deployed in southern Sudan, and a further 6,000 soldiers from each side were to be dispatched to the disputed Nuba Mountains and Blue Nile provinces. Furthermore, 80% of the government forces in southern Sudan would be withdrawn to the north no later than two and a half years after the signing of a comprehensive peace agreement. It was also agreed that both sides' forces would be reduced at a later, unspecified date and that they would be placed under the command of a joint defence board composed of SPLM and government officials. In October the US Secretary of State, Colin Powell, secured assurances from the Sudanese Government and the SPLM that a comprehensive settlement would be reached by the end of the year. Nevertheless, later in October US sanctions on Sudan (see below) were extended for a further 12 months. Also in October at-Turabi was released from detention, and all restrictions on the NPC's activities were lifted. In late March 2004 the Sudanese security forces arrested some 27 people, among them at-Turabi, five other members of the PNC and 10 military officers, on suspicion of plotting to overthrow the Government. In January 2005 a number of those apprehended were released, however, at-Turabi remained in detention along with some 12 other PNC members. Meanwhile, in October 2004 al-Bashir dismissed the Assistant President, Mubarak al-Fadil al-Mahdi, who was reportedly not replaced.

In early December 2003 SPLM delegates visited Khartoum for the first time since the escalation of the north–south conflict in 1983, prior to convening for further talks with the Government in Naivasha, Kenya. The discussions were expected to focus on the division of oil and water resources, the application of *Shari'a* law in Khartoum, the distribution of ministerial and civil service posts, and the boundary between the north and the south of the country. Later in December the Government and the SPLM agreed 'in principle' to divide petroleum revenues equally between the north and the south, and it was reported that they had also reached preliminary agreement on the distribution of tax revenues and the role of the new central bank. Nevertheless, no final agreement was concluded by the end of the month, and talks recommenced in early January 2004. On 7 January the two sides signed an accord on wealth- and revenue-sharing, which also provided for the establishment of two separate banking systems for the north and the south, as well as a new national currency on the signing of a final peace settlement. Although talks resumed in Kenya in mid-February, progress on other matters remained stalled, and by mid-May, despite intense international pressure, the two sides had still not concluded a definitive peace agreement. Furthermore, in mid-April the UN announced it had been forced to suspend aid operations in southern Sudan, owing to renewed violence, and that some 50,000 people had fled their homes in the region during the previous month.

Following further talks in Nairobi, the Government and the SPLM signed three protocols on 26 May 2004, which removed the remaining obstacles to the conclusion of a comprehensive peace accord. Specifically, the protocols stated that the SPLM and other southern groups would hold 30% of government seats in the north, while holding 70% of seats in the south; that the contested regions of the Blue Nile and the Nuba Mountains would be governed by an administration in which 55% of the seats would be taken by government officials and 45% by the SPLM, while the petroleum-rich region of Abeyi would be granted special status and be governed by the presidential office; and that Khartoum would remain under Islamic law with certain protections for non-Muslims. The final round of the IGAD-sponsored talks began in Naivasha, Kenya, in late June with the stated aim of finalizing and implementing a comprehensive cease-fire and it was announced that the two sides hoped to conclude a definitive agreement by August. Progress was delayed, however, by the Sudanese authorities' attempts to involve other pro-government southern militias in the talks. On 31 August the cease-fire was extended for a further three months and in early October the Naivasha talks recommenced. In early November the UN Security Council met in Nairobi in an attempt to prompt a definitive conclusion to proceedings, and it was announced that the Government and the SPLM had agreed to finalize a peace agreement by the end of the year.

In early December 2004 Garang met with the Sudanese Vice-President, Ali Osman Muhammad Taha, in Nairobi and on 31 December, at a ceremony in Naivasha, a permanent cease-fire was agreed by the Sudanese Government and the SPLM in compliance with the deadline established with the UN in November. On 9 January 2005 Garang and Taha signed the Comprehensive Peace Agreement (CPA) in Nairobi in the presence of Powell and representatives from the UN, the EU, the African Union—AU (see p. 153) and IGAD, thus formally bringing an end to more than 20 years of civil conflict between the SPLA and successive governments. The agreement provided for the implementation of the protocols and accords already agreed upon (see above), while Garang was to assume the position of Sudanese Vice-President in late February and would act as President of southern Sudan during the six-year period of autonomy, after which a referendum on secession would be held. However, by mid-April Garang had yet to take up either position and it was announced that the commission charged with formulating a new constitution would not be appointed until later that month. Meanwhile, in mid-January, following several months of talks, the Government signed a peace accord with the NDA in Cairo, Egypt, which allowed for the return of NDA leaders to Sudan and granted them the right to conduct their political activities in the country.

In late January 2005 it was announced that the administrative capital of southern Sudan would be established at Rumbek, a town with limited electricity and running water, which had been extensively damaged by bombing during the civil conflict. The UN appealed for the international community to assist with the reconstruction of southern Sudan's infrastructure (several million people who had been displaced by the war were expected to return to Sudan). On 25 January the UN announced that it had restored diplomatic ties with Sudan and would contribute some €50m. in aid, to be divided equally between the north and the south, and in early February the UN Secretary-General, Kofi Annan, announced plans to deploy some 10,000 peace-keeping troops to Sudan to monitor the cease-fire and assist with the disarmament process. In mid-February it was announced that with the assistance of the International Committee of the Red Cross, the SPLM intended to release some 750 prisoners of war. In mid-March the Government launched its six-year recovery and development plan, the main priority of which was to rebuild the country's infrastructure, a project which the Government claimed would cost US $8,000m. over two years. In late March the UN Security Council unanimously approved Resolution 1590, which provided for the establishment of the new UN Mission in Sudan (UNMIS), comprised of up to 10,000 peace-keeping troops and 715 civilian personnel and to be deployed in southern Sudan for an initial period of six months. In early April it was reported that the UP had been banned from all political activities following the arrest of a number of party officials in the city of Omdurman. Security forces also prevented al-Mahdi from speaking at a rally held to commemorate his period as Prime Minister. The UN announced in late April that peace-keeping troops and observers would arrive in southern Sudan within a month, and a contingent of 12 Nepalese soldiers duly commenced duties at the end of the month. Talks began in early May between the Government, the SPLM and opposition parties regarding an interim constitution which was to incorporate the provisions of the CPA into law and to enable the formation of a government of national unity. However, the UP refused to enter the talks and demanded greater representation for opposition parties.

In early June 2005 the UP, the PNC and 14 smaller opposition parties signed an agreement to form a new coalition, styled the National Forces Coalition. At a meeting held in Cairo in mid-June Taha and al-Mirghani signed an agreement for the NDA to join a power-sharing administration and the NDA subsequently nominated 27 of its members to the commission charged with drafting the new interim Constitution. In late June al-Bashir announced the release of 'all political detainees', among them at-Turabi. Earlier that month the President had lifted the ban prohibiting all political activity by the PNC. On 6 July the National Assembly ratified the new interim Constitution (see below) and on 9 July Garang was appointed First Vice-President of the new presidential council, replacing Taha who took the role of Vice-President, and as President of southern Sudan. In mid-July Government troops withdrew from Juba and the surrounding area in accordance with the CPA, which stipulated that 17% of Government troops be redeployed within six months of signing the agreement, and Garang named the SPLM deputy leader, Commdr. Salva Kiir Mayardit, as Vice-President of the new southern administration. Interim governors were also appointed to each of the 10 states in southern Sudan. On 1 August it was announced that Garang had been killed in a helicopter crash as he travelled to Rumbek from Kampala, Uganda. During 1–4 August at least 130 people were killed in Khartoum during violent clashes between protesters angry at Garang's death and the security forces. Salva Kiir succeeded Garang as leader of the SPLA/SPLM, and in early August was appointed as First Vice-President of Sudan and President of southern Sudan. Also in early August al-Bashir announced the formation of a committee to investigate the circumstances surrounding Garang's death.

During August 2005 differences regarding wealth-sharing and the allocation of the energy portfolio continued to obstruct the formation of a government of national unity. However, in late September an agreement was reached and the list of government ministers was announced, in which 16 portfolios (including those of defence, interior, finance and energy and mining) were awarded to members of the NC, nine to the SPLM and four to members of smaller opposition parties. In late January 2006 at the sixth AU summit, which took place in Khartoum, the emergence of al-Bashir as the leading candidate for the chairmanship of the organization provoked widespread criticism from the international community and proved unacceptable to representatives from a number of AU member states. Following two days of negotiations, it was agreed that the President of the Republic of Congo, Gen. Denis Sassou-Nguesso, would assume the chairmanship in 2006, to be succeeded by al-Bashir in 2007.

In February 2003 a new area of conflict emerged in the Darfur region of western Sudan. The Sudan Liberation Movement (SLM) announced the commencement of an armed campaign to end Darfur's political and economic marginalization and to combat the Government's 'ethnic cleansing' activities in the region. The SLM, which was reported to have some 1,500 troops and received support from Eritrea, subsequently attacked the provincial capital, Al-Fasher, and claimed to have killed more than 70 government soldiers. The SLM also attacked government positions in Melit and other towns in the Jebel Marra area. In an attempt to suppress the revolt the Sudanese authorities armed pro-Government ethnic Arab militias, known as the *Janjaweed*, who systematically razed entire villages to the ground and carried out indiscriminate killings. In April the Sudanese authorities refused offers of talks with the rebels, dismissed senior security officials in the region, and deployed additional forces to Darfur to retake most of the territory that had been lost to the SLM. Fighting continued in the area until early September, when, following mediation from the Chadian Government, a cease-fire was agreed between the Sudanese Government and the SLM. Under the accord, the Government agreed to release more than 50 suspected SLM members from detention. However, there were reports of ongoing incidents in Darfur during late 2003, with large numbers of Sudanese, fleeing alleged human rights abuses, crossing the border into Chad to seek refuge. In December aid agencies maintained that the Sudanese Government was preventing food and medical supplies from reaching the Darfur region, and in January 2004 Sudanese planes reportedly bombed a number of villages in the border area, just weeks after the rebels claimed to have killed some 700 government troops. Talks, again with Chadian mediation, broke down without making any progress, and by March it was estimated that more than 130,000 Sudanese had entered Chad and as many as 900,000 people had been displaced as a result of the ongoing conflict and the rapidly deteriorating humanitarian situation. At the end of that month indirect peace talks between the Government, the SLM and the Sudan Justice and Equality Movement (SJEM), attended by international observers, commenced in Chad, and on 8 April a 45-day humanitarian cease-fire was signed by representatives of the three parties. In mid-April the UN requested that donors provide some US $115m. to alleviate the humanitarian crisis in the Darfur region. Further talks were held in Chad between the Government, the SLM and the SJEM later that month, although little progress was made. There were also reports of serious human rights violations by government troops in the Darfur region and in early May a series of clashes occurred between Sudanese militiamen pursuing Sudanese rebels across the border and Chadian troops. By early June it was estimated that as a result of the violence in Darfur more than 30,000 people had been killed and a further 1m. people had been displaced, with 350,000 of those at risk from starvation and disease. The UN and the international human rights organization Amnesty International, along with the US and British Governments, placed renewed pressure on the Government to address the situation.

Following visits from Annan and Powell to refugee camps in Darfur in late June 2004 and the threat of the imposition of UN sanctions on the *Janjaweed*, in early July the Sudanese authorities committed to a series of actions, including the more aggressive use of the security forces to deal with the militia, the easing of travel restrictions for aid workers and the deployment of AU troops in Darfur. Both the UN and the USA had stated in June that they believed that the Sudanese Government was providing support to the *Janjaweed* and that the militia forces had carried out summary executions of civilians in Darfur. There followed a marginal improvement in access granted to humanitarian aid agencies but the security situation remained precarious as militias continued to attack civilian populations. In mid-July AU-sponsored peace talks between the Sudanese Government and the rebels opened in Addis Ababa, Ethiopia. The talks swiftly collapsed after the Government rejected the preconditions set out by the SLM and the SJEM for further negotiations, which included the disarmament of the *Janjaweed* and the removal of those *Janjaweed* fighters absorbed by the police and army; the observation of the April cease-fire agreement; the prosecution of the perpetrators of crimes and an inquiry into allegations of genocide; unimpeded humanitarian access for aid agencies; the release of prisoners of war; and a 'neutral' venue for future talks. In late July the US House of Representatives approved a resolution declaring the human rights abuses in Darfur a 'genocide' and on 30 July the UN Security Council adopted a resolution (No. 1556), that called on the Sudanese Government to end the conflict in Darfur, to facilitate the delivery of humanitarian aid, and to grant AU peace monitors access to the region. The resolution was rejected by the Sudanese Government and the armed forces spokesman, Gen. Muhammad Bashir Suleiman, described it as a 'declaration of war'.

In early August 2004 the UN Special Envoy to Sudan, Jan Pronk, agreed a number of measures with the Sudanese Government, aimed at averting the imposition of sanctions if certain conditions were fulfilled. However, in mid-August aid workers continued to report government-imposed travel restrictions and incidences of government-assisted violence occurring across the Darfur region. On 20 August the Sudanese Government admitted to the UN that it had control over certain *Janjaweed* members and stated that it would divulge the names of those fighters it was aware of. On 25 August the Government agreed to allow further foreign troops into Darfur. However, as the UN Security Council resolution expired at the end of the month, observers of the cease-fire reported that the government forces had launched attacks on civilians in Darfur only one week previously and Annan announced that the Sudanese authorities had failed to meet the requirements set out by the UN.

In mid-September 2004 the UN Security Council approved a second resolution (No. 1564), stating that it would consider imposing sanctions affecting Sudan's petroleum industry should it fail to take steps to disarm the *Janjaweed* and protect civilians from further attacks. The UN was also to establish a commission to investigate claims that the human rights abuses in Darfur amounted to genocide, while the AU was to increase the size of its monitoring force in the region from 350 to some 3,500. Further peace talks held days earlier between the Government, the SLA and the SJEM in Abuja, Nigeria, ended without agreement. In early October 2004 the British Prime Minister, Anthony (Tony) Blair, arrived in Sudan for talks with President al-Bashir in an attempt to resolve the Darfur issue. A five-point peace plan, proposed by Blair, was accepted by the President. In agreeing to the plan, the Sudanese Government pledged to allow an increase in the number of AU troops in the country; to identify its forces in Darfur to enable the effective monitoring of the cease-fire; to commit to a cessation of hostilities in Darfur within three months and to negotiate a comprehensive agreement to the ongoing conflict in southern Sudan (see above) by the end of 2004; and to assist with the distribution of humanitarian aid.

A second round of AU-sponsored peace talks between the Government and the Darfur rebel groups commenced in Abuja in October 2004 and in mid-November an agreement was signed according to which the two sides pledged to end hostilities, with the Government also agreeing to establish a 'no-fly' zone over the Darfur region (the rebels had accused government forces of using aircraft to support *Janjaweed* attacks). During late 2004, however, aid workers reported attacks on refugee camps by Sudanese police and several aid agencies were forced to temporarily withdraw their staff from the region. In mid-December AU cease-fire monitors reported that they had witnessed large quantities of arms and ammunition being delivered to government forces in Darfur. Days later, following the expiry of a deadline imposed by the AU for both sides to cease all hostilities, the Sudanese authorities agreed to end military operations in Darfur on the condition that the rebels also refrained from acts of violence. By that time it was estimated that some 70,000 people had been killed and 2m. people had been displaced since the start of the conflict. Despite the agreement, the AU reported later in December that government forces had attacked the village of Labado in the south of the Darfur region.

International relief organizations continued to report attacks on villages carried out by both government and rebel forces throughout January 2005. In early February a UN commission of inquiry, established to investigate the atrocities in Darfur, revealed that although serious crimes against humanity had taken place, these did not amount to genocide. It did, however, identify 51 suspected war criminals and recommended that they be tried by the International Criminal Court—(ICC, see p. 291). In late March the UN Security Council adopted Resolution 1593, referring the situation prevailing in Darfur since 1 July 2002 to the Prosecutor of the ICC. The resolution demanded that the Sudanese Government and all other parties to the Darfur conflict co-operate fully with the ICC, which was to undertake preparatory analysis of the situation prior to deciding whether to commence a full investigation into allegations of war crimes committed in Darfur. The decision prompted the Government to organize a mass demonstration in Khartoum, which was reportedly attended by up to 1m. people. For his part, al-Bashir pledged not to send any Sudanese national abroad for trial, but the Minister of External Relations, Dr. Mustafa Osman Ismail, subsequently offered to hold any future ICC trial in Sudan. In late April the AU confirmed that a new round of talks between the Government and rebel groups would begin in Abuja in May, and it was also announced that 3,320 additional AU peace-keeping troops would arrive in Darfur by the end of September, increasing the number of troops in the AU contingent to 7,731.

In mid-May 2005 the SLM and the SJEM agreed to maintain a cease-fire and to engage in further talks with the Government. However, the UN reported an increase in the number of reported instances of rape and kidnapping in the region during the month of April and stated that attacks on civilians by *Janjaweed* fighters continued. In late May a conference for international donor countries was held in Addis Ababa and US $200m. was pledged by countries including Canada, the USA and the United Kingdom for the enlarged AU peace-keeping operation in Darfur. NATO had previously announced that it would provide training, logistics and technical support to the mission. In early June the ICC commenced an investigation into allegations that the Sudanese Government and the *Janjaweed* had committed crimes against humanity in the Darfur region. Talks between rebels and the Government resumed in Abuja in mid-June, and following four weeks of negotiations, the two sides signed a declaration of principles. Meanwhile, in mid-June the Government established a court at which 162 people accused of committing crimes against humanity in the Darfur region were to be tried, and referred to the institution as 'an alternative' to the ICC. The court was rejected by rebel groups in Darfur, who claimed that Sudanese officials would escape trial, and Pronk dismissed the notion that the court could replace the ICC. In mid-July the SLM and SJEM signed an agreement to end their dispute and to normalize relations following a meeting in Tripoli, Libya. However, talks between the Government and the two rebel groups, scheduled to be held in Abuja during late August, were postponed for one month. Despite the absence of an SLM faction, talks resumed in mid-September amid reports of increasing violence in Darfur. In early October a rebel faction captured 18 AU peace-keeping staff close to the border with Chad, although most were released after one day. Also in early October four AU peace-keepers were killed in southern Darfur during the same weekend and in mid-October concerns over escalating violence prompted the UN to withdraw all non-essential staff from Darfur. In late November Annan reported a further increase in violence against civilians in the region and the AU called for an end to the killing of civilians as peace talks resumed in Abuja. The human rights organization Human Rights Watch (HRW) released a report in mid-December, which accused al-Bashir, Taha and several other senior Government officials of involvement in crimes against humanity committed in Darfur. The report also called for them to be investigated by the ICC and added to a UN list of suspects eligible for sanctions. Later in December ICC investigators were refused permission by the Government to visit Darfur to gather evidence of alleged crimes against humanity.

In early January 2006 30 Senegalese peace-keeping troops were attacked by gunmen in the west of Darfur. One soldier died and 10 others were injured in the attack, which the Sudanese armed forces blamed on Chadian forces and Sudanese rebels supported by the Chadian Government. In mid-January Annan called upon the USA and European countries to contribute logistical support and troops for a planned UN peace-keeping mission in Darfur. The AU had earlier warned that a lack of funds would lead to the eventual withdrawal of African peace-keepers from the region. Sudan declared its vehement opposition to the proposal and al-Bashir reportedly stated that Darfur would become a 'graveyard' for any foreign troops deployed in the region. In late January the SLM and the SJEM announced the formation of the Alliance of Revolutionary Forces in West Sudan, in a move intended to strengthen the rebels' position in the Abuja negotiations. In early March the UNHCR reduced the budget intended for Darfur in 2006 to US $18.5m., from an original figure of $33m., as a result of increased violence in the region. Also in early March the AU voted to extend the mandate of its peace-keeping mission until September, when a UN force was expected to assume peace-keeping duties. However, Arab League heads of state, meeting in Khartoum in late March, agreed to provide funds for the AU force to remain and voted to support Sudanese opposition to the deployment of non-African peace-keeping troops. In late April the UN Security Council approved a resolution (No. 1672) imposing sanctions on four individuals it suspected of involvement in crimes committed in the Darfur region. Maj.-Gen. Gaafar Muhammad el-Hassan, Commander of the Western Military Region for the Sudanese Air Force; the Commander of the SLA, Adam Yacub Shant; the Field Commander of the rebel National Movement for Reform and Development, Gabril Abdulkareem Badri; and Sheikh Musa Hilal of the *Janjaweed* militia were banned from travelling outside of Sudan and any assets they held abroad were to be 'frozen'. Also in late April, following further talks in Abuja, AU mediators submitted a proposed peace agreement to representatives of the Sudanese Government and rebel groups. Days later the Government agreed to accept the proposals. However, the 30 April deadline was twice extended by two days, and officials from the USA and United Kingdom arrived in Abuja to aid the negotiations. On 4 May the SJEM and the SLM faction led by Abd al-Wahid Muhammad al-Nur rejected the agreement. Nevertheless, the faction led by Minni Minawi announced that it had accepted the proposals, despite reservations regarding certain conditions, and the Darfur Peace Agreement was signed on 5 May. The measures stipulated in the document included a Government undertaking to disarm completely the *Janjaweed* by mid-October 2006; the establishment of buffer zones around refugee camps and access routes for humanitarian aid organizations; the integration of rebel forces into the Sudanese armed forces and police; the allocation of eight seats in the National Assembly to Minawi's group; and the transfer of US $300m. to a reconstruction and development fund for Darfur, and further annual transfers of $200m. for two years thereafter. In mid-May the deadline for the two remaining rebel groups to accept the peace deal was extended until the end of May and negotiations continued.

Concerns were raised in late 2005 that the ongoing conflict in Darfur could spread into neighbouring Chad. In late November Sudan accused the Chadian air force of violating Sudanese airspace by flying over the Darfur region and claimed that Chadian armed forces had crossed the border into Darfur to steal cattle. Chad responded with accusations that Sudan had provided weapons to a group of soldiers who had deserted the Chadian army and were planning to overthrow the President of Chad, Gen. Idriss Deby. In mid-December Chadian rebels based in Darfur attacked the town of Adre, near the border between Chad and Sudan and the Chadian Government declared 'a state of belligerence' with Sudan, which it held ultimately responsible for the assault. In February 2006 HRW reported that the *Janjaweed* had regularly crossed the border into Chad from Darfur and had carried out similar crimes to those it was accused of committing in Darfur. Later that month the two countries held talks in Libya aimed at preventing further escalation in the dispute and agreement was reached to restore diplomatic relations and to prevent rebels from using territory to launch cross-border raids. However, in March Deby publicly questioned Sudan's commitment to the accord following a series of attacks on villages in Chad by the *Janjaweed*, allegedly with Sudanese 'material and financial' assistance. In mid-April Deby expelled the Sudanese ambassador to Chad and ordered the closure of the land border between the two countries following an attack on the Chadian capital, N'djamena, by rebel forces. However, a threat to forcibly return Sudanese refugees was subsequently withdrawn.

In addition to civil war and economic crisis, Sudan has experienced drought and famine, and the problem has been compounded by a very large number of refugees in the southern provinces, mainly from Ethiopia and Chad. International relief operations to provide food aid, in years of drought and failed harvests, have frequently been obstructed by the civil war and by the Government's refusal to recognize the need for them. Even when successful, they have done little to solve the problems of under investment in, and mismanagement of, Sudanese agriculture, and the economic impoverishment that has resulted from drought and famine.

At the end of 2004, according to estimates by the office of the UN High Commissioner for Refugees (UNHCR), there were some 730,612 Sudanese refugees abroad, of whom 224,924 were in Chad, 214,673 in Uganda, 90,451 in Ethiopia, 67,556 in Kenya, 45,226 in the Democratic Republic of the Congo (DRC, formerly Zaire), 19,470 in the Central African Republic, and 17,994 in the USA. Sudan was also host to more than 141,588 refugees at that time, of whom 110,927 were originally from Eritrea and 14,812 were from Ethiopia. During 1997 there had been large-scale refugee repatriation, particularly to Ethiopia and the DRC, and during 1998 a further 37,000 refugees arrived in Sudan, including 10,300 from Kenya and 9,500 from Uganda. During 2000 more than 94,000 Eritrean refugees fleeing the border war with Ethiopia entered Sudanese territory; by the end of that year, however, some 68,000 had been repatriated. In early 2003 the US Committee for Refugees stated that Sudan possessed the largest internally displaced population in the world, officially estimated at 4m. people. By late 2004, as a result of the Darfur conflict, it was estimated by the UNHCR that some 1.6m. people were displaced within Darfur and that some 200,000 people had fled to neighbouring Chad. In December 2002 the refugee status of Eritreans living in Sudan expired, and in the following month UNHCR convoys, which would return Eritreans to their country, recommenced. It was reported that since May 2001 more than 100,000 Eritreans had been repatriated. In 2002 some 18,000 Sudanese were repatriated from Kenya. In late December 2005 the UNHCR announced that some 500,000 refugees were to be repatriated to southern Sudan from neighbouring countries. The process commenced earlier that month when 90,000 Sudanese refugees left northern Kenya. However, in mid-March 2006 a UNHCR compound in the town of Yei was attacked by armed men, and UNHCR operations in southern Sudan were subsequently suspended for two weeks.

In June 1997 the Government banned relief flights to the south—an act that caused concern to aid agencies; the UN Children's Fund stated that thousands of children were at risk and announced that there had been a rise in the infant mortality rate in that area. By April 1998 many aid agencies were warning of widespread famine in the south if immediate action was not taken. The Government initially refused to act, as it claimed that aid would fall into rebel hands. However, in May, following UN requests, the Government agreed to reopen all relief corridors in the worst affected areas and to allow the aid agencies to operate a total of 22 food distribution sites. It also agreed to increase the frequency of relief flights and to provide some food aid from that year's surplus in the north. Relief operations continued throughout mid-1998. In October, however, the Government banned aid agency flights in the country. In November, following two days of negotiations in Rome, Italy, the Government and the rebels signed an agreement to guarantee the safety of aid workers and to facilitate access to the worst affected areas, despite the continuing fighting. In March 1999 further warnings were issued of impending famine. Hostilities again escalated in the south in August 2000, and the Sudanese Government was accused of deliberately bombing relief facilities in that region. In response, the UN announced the suspension of all aid flights under the Operation Lifeline Sudan programme. However, later that month, following personal assurances from al-Bashir that measures were being taken to ensure the safety of all humanitarian workers in the region, the UN agreed to resume relief flights. In February 2001 WFP launched an appeal for US $135m. of food aid, required to feed the estimated 2.9m. people in Sudan under threat of starvation as a result of the ongoing civil war and severe drought. Appeals for significant humanitarian assistance were repeated in May, as conditions in Sudan reached critical levels. However, in that month the International Committee of the Red Cross temporarily suspended all aid deliveries, after the co-pilot of one of its planes was killed while flying over southern Sudan. Aid flights were subsequently resumed later that month. In mid-April 2005 donors from the international community, including the USA, the European Commission, and the United Kingdom, pledged $4,500m. in aid which was to go directly to southern Sudan. By March 2006, however, the UN Special Envoy to Sudan, Jan Pronk, acknowledged that only a small portion of the money pledged had thus far been spent.

Following an unsuccessful coup attempt in 1976, Sudan severed diplomatic relations with Libya and established a mutual defence pact with Egypt. Diplomatic links between Sudan and Libya were restored in 1978, but relations became strained in 1981, during Libya's occupation of Chad, and President Nimeri frequently accused Libya of supporting plots against him. After the 1985 coup, Libya was the first country to recognize the new regime, and relations between the two countries improved significantly. Although Libya's military involvement in Chad declined, some Libyan forces remained in north-western Sudan, despite repeated Sudanese demands for their withdrawal. The regime that took power in Sudan in 1985 adopted a foreign policy of non-alignment, in contrast to Nimeri's strongly pro-Western attitude, and sought improved relations with Ethiopia and the USSR, to the concern of Sudan's former allies, Egypt and the USA. In 1990, after Lt-Gen. al-Bashir had visited Col Qaddafi, the Libyan leader, in Tripoli, Sudan and Libya signed a 'declaration of integration' that envisaged the complete union of the two countries within four years. In 1995 Sudan, Libya and Chad were reported to be discussing integration after eventual legislative elections in Chad. Tension subsequently arose between Libya and Sudan as a result of Libya's expulsion of Sudanese expatriate workers, but did not, apparently, detract from the two countries' commitment to integration, reiterated in 1996.

Relations with Ethiopia have fluctuated since 1987, but, until late 1995, were mostly characterized by harmony and co-operation. In September 1995, however, Ethiopia accused Sudan of harbouring terrorists implicated in the attempted assassination of President Mubarak in June and, in response, announced the closure of some Sudanese diplomatic facilities in the country and of non-governmental organizations connected with Sudan. In April 1996 Sudan claimed that Ethiopian government forces had collaborated with the SPLA in attacks on two towns in southeastern Sudan, while in June Ethiopia accused Sudan of attempting to destabilize the region. In January 1997 relations deteriorated further when, following alleged attacks on Sudan, President al-Bashir declared a *jihad* (holy war) against Ethiopian aggression and ordered a general mobilization. Ethiopia, however, denied any involvement in the attacks. An improvement in relations was reported during 1998, although in December the Ethiopian Minister of Foreign Affairs stated that relations between the two countries would not improve until Sudan handed over those responsible for the attempted assassination of the Egyptian President. One of the suspects was extradited in 1999 (see below), and in November, on his return from a visit to Ethiopia, al-Bashir stated that relations with that country were fully normalized. The common border was reopened in early 2000, and in March the Sudanese and Ethiopian Governments signed a number of agreements, which provided for increased co-operation in political, cultural, commercial and transport sectors. Further agreements regarding border security were signed in the following month. Relations between the two countries were temporarily strained in late April 2001 after an internal Ethiopian flight was hijacked and diverted to Khartoum. Although the incident was brought to a swift conclusion, and all passengers on board the aircraft were released unharmed, the Sudanese authorities refused Ethiopia's request for the hijackers to be extradited to Ethiopia for trial.

Sudan's relations with Eritrea deteriorated after 1991, and in December 1994 Eritrea severed diplomatic relations with Sudan. Eritrea has sponsored meetings of the principal groups opposed to the Sudanese regime, which it accuses of lending support to the insurgent Eritrean Islamic Jihad. In December 1994 Eritrea sponsored a meeting between various Sudanese opposition groups, which resulted in a 'Declaration of Political Agreement'. The signatories included the SPLA, the UP and the DUP. In January 1995 Sudan demanded that Eritrea withdraw from the IGADD peace committee (see above), which also included Ethiopia, Kenya, and Uganda. A further deterioration in relations occurred after a conference of the Sudanese opposition, organized by the NDA, was held in Asmara in June (see above). In July 1996 Sudanese government forces claimed that attacks had been launched against them from within Eritrea. In October the National Assembly endorsed a report by the Sudanese Security and National Defence Committee, which recommended—with reference to Eritrea—the strengthening of defence facilities and a firm response to military provocation. In April 1997 Sudan protested to the UN over Eritrean aggression on its territory. In June Sudan denied Eritrean accusations that the Sudanese Government had masterminded a plot to assassinate the Eritrean President. At the end of the month Sudan closed the border with Eritrea and mobilized its forces to maximum levels for fear of a military strike against Sudan. The border was again closed in February 1998 in order to prevent Eritrean troops entering the country following reported border clashes between the two countries. Further attacks were reported in the border area by both Eritrea and Sudan throughout 1998. Following talks held in November 1998, in Qatar, the two sides signed an agreement for the open discussion of bilateral issues. A further meeting, held in May 1999, resulted in an accord, signed by the Presidents of Sudan and Eritrea, in which they agreed to restore diplomatic relations, to refrain from hostile propaganda and to establish joint committees, both to implement the terms of the accord and to study any further issues that might arise between the two countries. However, tensions between the two countries remained, and in June Sudan accused Eritrea of violating the Doha agreement, following an NDA conference in Asmara. At that time the two countries established joint committees in accordance with the terms of the Doha agreement. In August it was reported that Eritrea had ordered the Sudanese opposition to cease political activity and to leave the Sudanese embassy, which it had occupied since December 1994. A further agreement was signed in Asmara in January 2000, providing for the immediate reopening of the two countries' borders and embassies and the resumption of flights between their airports. In February the Presidents of Eritrea and Sudan held talks in Khartoum, and it was agreed to issue passports to residents in the border area. Furthermore, they declared that they would not allow opposition groups located in their respective countries to launch cross-border raids. However, relations between the two countries deteriorated in July, when the Sudanese Government accused Eritrea of assisting the NDA with a planned offensive in eastern Sudan. In October President Afewerki visited Khartoum, where he held talks with al-Bashir, during which both sides expressed their desire for a fresh beginning to their bilateral relations and agreed to take measures to settle differences between the two countries in a peaceful manner. In July 2001 Eritrea and Sudan signed an agreement on border security, which aimed to eradicate smuggling and illegal infiltration, as well as ensure the safe passage of people and goods. Relations between the two countries deteriorated again in mid-2002, and in October the Sudanese authorities closed the common border, claiming that Eritrea had been involved in an NDA offensive in eastern Sudan. Following a meeting with the Yemeni President, Ali Abdullah Saleh, and the Ethiopian Prime Minister, Meles Zenawi, in December 2003, President al-Bashir accused Eritrea of arming and training rebels in the Darfur region of Sudan and maintained that Eritrea was a destabilizing force in the region. Eritrea refuted the allegations. In mid-January 2004 Eritrea claimed that the Sudanese authorities had arrested several Eritreans and closed community centres used by Eritreans in Khartoum. In late May the Eritrean authorities accused Sudan of carrying out a bomb attack which killed seven people in Barentu, Eritrea. Sudan vehemently denied any involvement in the incident and stated that the explosion had been the work of Eritrean opposition forces. In mid-October Eritrea accused Sudan of complicity in an attempt to assassinate President Afewerki, while Sudan maintained that Eritrea had provided rebels with arms in an attempt to destabilize the Sudanese Government. In mid-March 2005 it was announced that talks between the NDA and Sudanese authorities would take place in a further attempt to normalize relations. Relations between the two countries were again strained in late June when Sudan accused Eritrea of providing assistance to rebel forces who had attacked Sudanese government troops in eastern Sudan earlier that month. However, at a meeting in Khartoum in October Akol, who had earlier been appointed Minister of Foreign Affairs, signed an agreement with his Eritrean acting counterpart to work towards normalizing relations between Sudan and Eritrea.

Sudan and Uganda have accused each other of supporting groups opposed to their respective regimes, and in 1995 Uganda broke off diplomatic relations with Sudan. A further deterioration in relations in December brought the two countries to the brink of open war. In 1996, following mediation by President Rafsanjani of Iran, Sudan and Uganda agreed to restore diplomatic relations, provided that each side undertook to cease its support for rebel factions operating from the other's territory, and to participate in an international committee to monitor the agreement. In February 1997, in response to protests about its deployment of troops on the Sudan–Uganda border, Uganda denied accusations that it intended to invade Sudan. In late April Sudan denied allegations that its forces had invaded northern Uganda and, at the end of the month Dr Riek Mashar Teny-Dhurgon, the Chairman of the SSCC, visited Uganda to discuss relations between the two countries prior to the forthcoming IGAD summit meeting. Talks held in Kenya in May achieved little progress in easing tension, and the planned IGAD summit meeting was later cancelled, owing to a concurrent meeting of leaders of the Organization of African Unity (OAU, now the AU). In August President Mandela of South Africa hosted talks between the two countries. Mandela later said that the talks had been successful, although he did not reveal what progress had been made. At the end of the year there were reports of Ugandan attacks in the border area; Uganda, however, denied the reports and said that the attacks had been made by the SPLA and had been wrongly attributed to Uganda. Relations with Uganda improved during 1999, and in December, following a meeting in Nairobi, mediated by former US President Jimmy Carter, the two countries signed an accord in which they agreed to restore diplomatic relations and to end support to each other's rebel groups; shortly afterwards it was announced that eight leaders of the Lord's Resistance Army (LRA) were to be relocated from Sudan to a country of their choice in accordance with the agreement. In February 2000, however, Uganda expressed its dissatisfaction with Sudan's implementation of the accord and called for Sudan to disarm the LRA and to disband all LRA camps within Sudan. Sudan reaffirmed its commitment to the agreement. In October it was agreed that Egyptian and Libyan observers would be deployed on the Uganda–Sudan border to prevent any further violations by the SPLA and the LRA. In mid-May 2001 President al-Bashir attended the inauguration of the Ugandan President, Yoweri Museveni, in Kampala, and in the following month the two countries exchanged diplomats. In August the Ugandan embassy in Khartoum reopened, and a chargé d'affaires was appointed. In March 2002 the two countries signed an agreement whereby Sudan temporarily authorized Ugandan troops to pursue LRA rebels within Sudan, and later that month the Ugandan Government announced that its troops had captured all four main bases in Sudan belonging to the LRA. In late November 2002 the Sudanese authorities agreed to extend permission for Ugandan troops to remain on its territory for as long as Uganda deemed necessary. Meanwhile, the two countries upgraded relations to ambassadorial level.

President Nimeri was one of very few Arab leaders to support President Sadat of Egypt's initiative for peace with Israel in 1978. Sudan's close relations with Egypt were consolidated in 1982, when a 'charter of integration' was signed. The first session of the joint 'Nile Valley Parliament', created by the charter, was convened in 1983 with 60 Sudanese and 60 Egyptian members. After the 1985 coup, the leaders of the two countries reaffirmed links between Khartoum and Cairo, despite the change of government in Sudan. Relations with Egypt deteriorated in 1991, as a result of the Sudanese Government's support for Iraq during the Gulf crisis. Egypt also expressed concern at the perceived growth of Islamic 'fundamentalism' in Sudan. The two countries are involved in a dispute over the Halaib border area, and in early 1992 relations deteriorated sharply following the announcement that Sudan had awarded a Canadian company a concession to explore for petroleum there. Relations deteriorated further, as Egypt repeatedly accused Sudan of supporting illegal Islamic fundamentalist groups in Egypt, while Sudan alleged that Egypt was supporting the SPLA. In August the Sudanese Government sought international arbitration on the Halaib issue, claiming that Egypt had been settling families in the area in an effort to bring it under Egyptian control. A series of bilateral meetings held during the second half of 1992 failed to resolve the issue, and in January 1993 Sudan complained to the UN Security Council that Egyptian troops had infringed Sudan's territorial integrity. In March Egypt announced the construction of a new road link to Halaib. Sudan retaliated by appropriating the Khartoum campus of the University of Cairo. In June Sudan announced that it was closing two Egyptian consulates in Sudan and two of its own consulates in Egypt. A meeting between Lt-Gen. al-Bashir and President Mubarak of Egypt, during a summit session of the OAU at the end of June appeared, however, to ease tensions between the two countries, and was followed by a meeting of their respective Ministers of Foreign Affairs at the end of July. In May 1994 Sudan accused Egypt of establishing military posts on Sudanese territory, and at the end of the month the Sudanese Ministry of Foreign Affairs announced that Sudan wished to refer its dispute with Egypt to the International Court of Justice (ICJ) in The Hague, Netherlands, for arbitration. In January 1995 Egypt rejected a request by Sudan to refer the dispute over the Halaib border area to a meeting of the OAU's council of Ministers of Foreign Affairs in Addis Ababa. On 26 June relations suffered a further, serious setback after the attempted assassination of President Mubarak of Egypt on his arrival in Addis Ababa to attend the annual conference of the OAU. The Egyptian Government immediately accused Sudan of complicity in the attack, and the OAU made the same allegation in September. In January 1996 the UN Security Council condemned Sudan's role in the attempted assassination and adopted a resolution (No. 1044) seeking the extradition of three individuals implicated in the attack. Relations between Sudan and Egypt appeared to improve in 1997; in December talks were held between President al-Bashir and senior Egyptian officials, and in January 1998 it was agreed that a joint chamber of commerce would be established. In May a joint Sudanese-Egyptian technical committee met in Khartoum to finalize details for the return of several institutions in Sudan to Egyptian control. Both sides were agreed that the institutions, such as the appropriated University of Cairo in Khartoum, should be returned, although differences remained over the time period for this operation. The Sudanese Minister for Foreign Trade made a three-day visit to Egypt in April 1998, during which he praised the *rapprochement* between the two countries, although in August the Sudanese Government stated that it found the Egyptian decision to host an NDA conference regrettable. During the conference meetings were held with Egyptian officials including President Mubarak; Egypt had requested the meetings as it feared that the ongoing civil war in the Sudan could affect control of the Nile, its source of water. In October Sudan and Egypt agreed on a plan to hasten the normalization of relations, and a further meeting was held in Cairo in January 1999 to discuss bilateral relations. Following further meetings, in June it was announced that diplomatic relations between the two countries were to be upgraded. Relations improved further in July when it was announced that Sudan had extradited one of the three suspects implicated in the attempted assassination of Mubarak. In December the two countries agreed to normalize their relations and to resolve their dispute over the Halaib issue amicably. In March 2000 it was announced that the University of Cairo in Khartoum was to be reopened, and later that month Egypt appointed an ambassador to Sudan for the first time since the assassination attempt on Mubarak. The two countries also agreed to establish an Egyptian-Sudanese joint committee. In September the Sudanese and Egyptian ministers responsible for foreign affairs held the first session of the Egyptian-Sudanese Commission for 10 years, at which the two countries expressed their commitment to further bilateral economic development. In May 2003 Mubarak visited Khartoum for the first time since the attempted assassination and held talks with al-Bashir, during which the two leaders reaffirmed their commitment to improving relations between Egypt and Sudan.

The USA has been one of the severest critics of the present Sudanese Government, frequently expressing concern about Sudan's links with Iran. Allegations of Sudanese involvement in terrorism resulted in the detention in the USA, in 1993, of five Sudanese residents suspected of plotting to blow up buildings and road tunnels in New York, and to assassinate President Mubarak of Egypt on a visit to the USA; the USA subsequently added Sudan to its list of countries accused of sponsoring terrorism. In August 1997 the USA imposed economic sanctions against Sudan, owing to its alleged continued support for terrorism. The USA reiterated its accusations of Sudanese involvement in terrorism following bomb explosions in its embassies in Kenya and Tanzania in August 1998; the bombings were believed to have been orchestrated by Osama bin Laden, a Saudi-born Islamist activist exiled in Afghanistan. In late August the USA launched a missile attack on what it claimed was a chemical weapons factory in Khartoum in which bin Laden was believed to hold a financial interest. Immediately after the attack, however, the Sudanese Government denied these claims and stated that it was, in fact, a private pharmaceuticals plant. Sudan recalled its ambassador to the USA and refused permission for US aircraft to use its airspace; its requests for a UN inquiry into the attack were unanimously refused by the Security Council, despite backing from the League of Arab States (see p. 306) and the Organization of the Islamic Conference (see p. 340). By February 1999 it had become evident that the US intelligence on which the attack had been based was fundamentally flawed and that bin Laden had had links only with the previous owner. In May Sudan requested compensation for the damage caused by the bomb attack, and in July 2000 the proprietor of the factory announced his intention to sue the US Government for damages. Meanwhile, in April 1999 the USA had announced its decision to ease sanctions on the export of food and medicine to Sudan, and at the end of May Sudan fulfilled one of the conditions set by the USA for a review of the sanctions regime by signing a treaty banning chemical weapons. In September the USA appointed a special envoy to Sudan, whose role was to focus international attention on Sudan's human rights record, highlight the consequences of the civil war and strengthen the IGAD-sponsored peace process. Sudan described the appointment as an 'arrogant decision'. The US Secretary of State, Madeleine Albright, visited Sudan during a tour of Africa in October and held meetings with John Garang, during which she urged him to reinvigorate the IGAD-sponsored peace process and discouraged the rival Egyptian-Libyan initiative. In November, however, the USA enacted controversial legislation allowing food aid to be delivered directly to the Sudanese rebels. An improvement in relations was evident in March 2000 following a visit to Sudan by a US diplomat to discuss the possibility of reopening the US embassy in Khartoum. In mid-April the embassy was duly reopened and a chargé d'affaires appointed. However, relations once again deteriorated in December, when Sudan lodged an official complaint with the UN after the US Assistant Secretary of State, Susan Rice, visited rebel-held areas of southern Sudan in November, without the permission of the Sudanese Government. Following the election of a new US Administration, under the leadership of President George W. Bush, in January 2001, there was some uncertainty regarding the USA's policy towards Sudan. In early May Bush appointed Andrew Natsios, administrator of the US Agency for International Development (USAID), as special humanitarian co-ordinator for Sudan, charged with monitoring the delivery of aid supplies and ensuring they reached their intended destinations. In July the Bush administration outlined its three main policy objectives for Sudan: to deal with the humanitarian crisis, to end Sudan's role as a sanctuary for terrorism, and to promote a just peace by bringing the warring parties together. In September Bush appointed a former senator, John Danforth, as his special envoy to Sudan.

Following the September 2001 suicide attacks on New York and Washington, DC, Sudan agreed to assist the USA with its search for terrorist suspects, and by late September the Sudanese authorities had arrested some 30 individuals resident in Sudan who were suspected of having links to bin Laden and the al-Qa'ida (Base) organization, which the USA held responsible for the attacks. Nevertheless, US sanctions remained in place, and Sudan continued to be listed by the US Department of State as a sponsor of terrorism. Furthermore, two Sudanese banks (al-Shamal Islamic Bank and Tadamon Islamic bank) were among numerous institutions under US investigation as possible sources of financial support for bin Laden. Sudan expressed criticism of the US-led military strikes on Afghanistan, which commenced in November, and later that month the USA extended sanctions until November 2002. In February 2002 a suspected senior member of al-Qa'ida, who had been indicted for his alleged involvement in the bombing of the US embassies in Kenya and Tanzania in 1998 and was also believed to have played a significant role in the September 2001 attacks on the USA, was arrested in Sudan. In October 2002 Bush approved legislation that allowed the USA to impose further sanctions, including the suspension of multilateral loans, on the Sudanese Government, should it fail to negotiate in good faith with the southern rebels or interfere with humanitarian efforts in the south of the country. The USA also froze the financial assets of 12 Sudanese companies, including the National Broadcasting Corporation. Under the Sudan Peace Act, conditions in Sudan would be evaluated every six months, although the law also made provision for the expenditure of US $100m. a year by the USA until 2005 in areas of Sudan not under the Sudanese Government's control. In October 2003 USAID pledged a further $40m. to finance initiatives to assist Sudan to recover from the civil war. However, Natsios warned that the additional aid was conditional on the implementation of a comprehensive peace agreement. In mid-November the US embassy in Khartoum was temporarily closed in response to a 'specific threat' to US interests in Sudan. The conflict in Darfur (see above) resulted in the deterioration of relations between Sudan and the USA and in September 2004 the US Administration accused the Sudanese Government of committing genocide. The USA subsequently proposed a draft UN resolution, which threatened to impose sanctions on Sudan's petroleum industry if the Sudanese authorities did not act to end the violence in the region. In late July 2005 the US Secretary of State, Condoleezza Rice, met with al-Bashir in Khartoum and also visited the Abu Shouk refugee camp in the Darfur region, and called for 'actions, not words' from the Sudanese administration to resolve the conflict in Darfur. During the visit, Rice also indicated that the USA was to send an ambassador to Khartoum for the first time since 1997. In early August, two US envoys arrived in Sudan tasked with assisting the reinforcement of the Comprehensive Peace Agreement following the death of Garang.

Sudan's relations with the United Kingdom deteriorated in May 1998, following a statement made by the British Secretary of State for International Development in which she accused Sudan of using food aid as a weapon in Bahr al-Ghazal. The Sudanese Government vehemently denied this and accused the United Kingdom of having a negative attitude towards forthcoming peace negotiations. In August, following British support for the US bombing of Sudan (see above), Sudan announced that it would recall its ambassador to the United Kingdom and asked the British ambassador to leave. Negotiations were held in an attempt to avert this, but the British envoy was withdrawn in September. Relations improved during 1999, and in September the two countries agreed to appoint ambassadors; both appointments were made by the end of April 2000. The British Government played an active role in attempting to end the violence in Darfur—the British Secretary of State for Foreign and Commonwealth Affairs, Jack Straw, visited the region in August 2004, and Prime Minister Blair visited Khartoum in October to increase diplomatic pressure on the Sudanese Government.

Government

In October 1993 the Revolutionary Command Council for National Salvation, which had assumed power after the military coup of 30 June 1989, was dissolved after appointing Lt-Gen. al-Bashir as President and head of a new civilian Government. In April 1998 a new Constitution was endorsed by the National Assembly, and was presented to President al-Bashir. The document was endorsed by 96.7% of voters in a national referendum held in May. Under its terms, executive power is vested in the Council of Ministers, which is appointed by the President, but is responsible to the National Assembly. Legislative power is vested in the National Assembly. The 360-member National Assembly serves a term of four years. Of its 360 members, 270 are directly elected in single seat constituencies, 35 members represent women, 26 represent university graduates and 29 represent trade unions.

In February 1994 Sudan was redivided into 26 states (rather than the nine that had formed the basis of administration since 1991). A governor assumed responsibility for each state, assisted by five—in the case of the southern states six—state ministers.

In early July 2005 the National Assembly approved an interim Constitution as part of the Comprehensive Peace Agreement signed in January between the Sudanese Government and the Sudan People's Liberation Movement (SPLM). The interim Constitution provided for the establishment of a Government of National Unity, representation in which was to be divided between northerners and southerners, with the former holding 70% of the posts and the latter 30%. The interim Constitution also stipulated that, pending legislative elections, which were to be held no later than the end of the fourth year of the interim period, the National Assembly shall be composed of 450 members who shall be appointed by the President of the Republic in consultation with the First Vice-President, according to the 70%/30% north and south ratio.

Provision was also made in the interim Constitution for the election of the President of the Government of Southern Sudan and the establishment of a transitional Southern Sudan Assembly. The President of Government of Southern Sudan shall be elected directly by the people of southern Sudan for a five-year mandate, renewable only once. The transitional Southern Sudan Assembly shall be an inclusive, constituent legislature composed of 170 appointed members with 70% representing the SPLM; 15% representing the National Congress; and 15% representing the other southern Sudanese political forces.

Defence

In August 2005 the armed forces comprised: army an estimated 100,000, navy an estimated 1,800, air force 3,000. A paramilitary Popular Defence Force included 17,500 active members and 85,000 reserves. Budgeted defence expenditure in 2005 was an estimated US $483m. Sudan has a defence agreement with Egypt and has received military aid from the USA. The People's Republic of China and Iran all provide a number of military advisers. Military service is compulsory for males aged 18–30 years and lasts for up to two years.

Economic Affairs

In 2004, according to estimates by the World Bank, Sudan's gross national income (GNI), measured at average 2002–04 prices, was US $18,151.2m., equivalent to $530 per head (or $1,870 on an international purchasing-power parity basis). During 1995–2004, it was estimated, the population increased at an average annual rate of 2.3%, while gross domestic product (GDP) per head increased, in real terms, by an average of 3.8% per year. Overall GDP increased, in real terms, at an average annual rate of 6.2% in 1995–2004; growth in 2004 was 6.0%.

Agriculture (including forestry and fishing) contributed 39.2% of GDP in 2002 and employed about 58.3% of the labour force in 2003. The principal cash crop is sesame seed (including oilcake), which accounted for 4.3% of total export earnings in 2002. The principal subsistence crops are sorghum, millet and wheat. The GDP of the agricultural sector increased by an average of 10.9% per year in 1995–2002. Agricultural GDP increased by 7.5% in 2002.

Industry (including mining, manufacturing, construction and power) contributed 18.3% of GDP in 2002, and employed 7.9% of the labour force in 1983. In 1995–2002 industrial GDP increased at an average annual rate of 8.0%. Industrial GDP increased by 7.5% in 2002.

Mining accounted for only 0.1% of employment in 1983 and an estimated 0.9% of GDP in 1999. Sudan has reserves of petroleum (estimated at 563m. barrels in July 2005), chromite, gypsum, gold, iron ore and wollastonite. Sudan began to develop its petroleum reserves in the mid-1990s, and production reached about 500,000 barrels per day (b/d) in 2005, and this was expected to increase to 650,000 b/d by the end of 2006. In 2005 Sudan was the seventh largest producer of petroleum in Africa. In 2002 petroleum and petroleum products accounted for 69.2% of total export earnings. The GDP of the mining sector increased by 22.5% in 2001.

Manufacturing contributed 9.3% of GDP in 2002. The most important branch of the sector is food-processing, especially sugar-refining, while the textile industry, cement production and petroleum-refining are also significant. Some 4.6% of the labour force were employed in manufacturing in 1983. In 1995–2002 manufacturing GDP increased at an average annual rate of 0.2%. Manufacturing GDP increased by 2.1% in 2002.

Energy is derived from petroleum (which contributed 55.6% of total output in 2002) and hydroelectric power (44.4%). In May 2004 the Government announced plans to provide 90% of the country with electricity over the following five years by harnessing more of the hydro-electric potential of the Nile. Sudan is a net exporter of fuels, with imports of petroleum and petroleum products comprising an estimated 4.7% of the total value of imports in 2002.

Services contributed 42.5% of GDP in 2002, and employed 18.8% of the labour force in 1983. During 1995–2002 the GDP of the services sector increased at an average annual rate of 2.7%. In 2002 the GDP of the services sector rose by 4.0%.

In 2004 Sudan recorded a visible trade surplus of US $191.6m., and there was a deficit of $870.9m. on the current account of the balance of payments. In 2002 the principal sources of imports were Saudi Arabia (accounting for 12.7% of the total), the People's Republic of China, the United Arab Emirates, Japan and the United Kingdom. In that year the principal markets for Sudanese exports were the People's Republic of China (taking 58.2%) and Saudi Arabia. The principal exports in 2002 were petroleum and petroleum products, and live animals. The principal imports in that year were machinery and transport equipment, basic manufactures, food and live animals, and chemicals and related products.

In 2004 Sudan recorded an overall budget deficit of 45,100m. Sudanese dinars. At the end of 2003 Sudan's total external debt was US $17,496m., of which $9,569m. was long-term public debt. In that year the cost of debt-servicing was equivalent to 0.9% of the total value of exports of goods and services. In 1992–2000 the average annual rate of inflation was 64.8%. Consumer prices increased by an annual average of 8.5% in 2004.

Sudan is a member of the African Development Bank (see p. 151), the Arab Bank for Economic Development in Africa (see p. 307), the Council of Arab Economic Unity (see p. 208) and the Islamic Development Bank (see p. 303). In 1997 Sudan's membership of both the Arab Fund for Economic and Social Development (AFESD, see p. 161) and the Arab Monetary Fund (see p. 163) was suspended. Membership of the AFESD was restored in April 2000.

Sudan's formidable economic problems can be traced back to the 1970s, when the country's agricultural potential was neglected and the Government began to borrow heavily. The problems were compounded by civil conflict in the south, which, in addition to depressing economic activity in the areas where it was waged, caused a massive waste of state resources. Relations with the IMF, which had deteriorated over the preceding years, began to improve in 1997, and in August 2000 Sudan's voting rights and full membership of the Fund were restored. Sudan began exporting petroleum in late 1999 and, as a result, in 2000 recorded a trade surplus for the first time in modern history. Further discoveries of petroleum in 2001 led to a vast increase in export revenues; however, much of these earnings were used by the Government to fund the war against the rebels in the south, which was estimated to cost US $1m. per day, and the country's reliance on petroleum has caused some concern in recent years. In late 2002, in return for the rescheduling of its repayments to the IMF, the Sudanese Government pledged to display more transparency in the management of its petroleum revenues and to reduce its military expenditure drastically. The creation of an oil-revenue savings account and the introduction of a managed-float exchange-rate system reinforced economic stability, and the rate of inflation, which had been as high as 132.8% in 1996, was estimated to have declined to just 8.4% by 2004. Much of Sudan's proven reserves of oil are located in the south of the country and following the Comprehensive Peace Agreement signed by the Government and the SPLM in January 2005, levels of foreign investment were expected to increase as well as growth, thus providing capital for reconstruction programs in the regions affected by the civil war. Significantly, while many companies from Europe and North America have been reluctant to invest in Sudan, due in part to the ongoing conflict and humanitarian crisis in the Darfur region, companies from the People's Republic of China, India and Malaysia have acquired major stakes in a number of Sudanese oil concessions. In late 2005 negotiations regarding two new oil blocks in northern Sudan commenced. By early 2006, however, only seven of Sudan's 21 petroleum blocks were producing and large-scale investment was required to improve the country's basic infrastructure, most notably in the south. Despite a number of

SUDAN

positive macro-economic indications, widespread famine, drought and the significant number of refugees and internally displaced people in the country continue adversely to affect the Sudanese economy. In recent years international financial institutions have been reluctant to provide funding and the donor community remained deeply concerned regarding recent events in the Darfur region.

Education

The Government provides free primary education from the ages of six to 13 years. Secondary education begins at 14 years of age and lasts for up to three years. In 1996 the total enrolment at primary and secondary schools was equivalent to 44% of children in the appropriate age-groups (47% of boys; 40% of girls). In 2000/01 enrolment at primary schools included 49% of children in the relevant age-group (boys 54%; girls 45%), according to UNESCO estimates, while in 1998/99 enrolment at secondary schools was equivalent to 30% of children in the relevant age-group (boys 31%; girls 29%). About 15% of current government expenditure in 1985 was for primary and secondary education. Pupils from secondary schools are accepted at the University of Khartoum, subject to their reaching the necessary standards. There are three universities at Omdurman: Omdurman Islamic University; Omdurman Ahlia University; and Ahfad University for Women. New universities were opened at Juba and Wadi Medani (University of Gezira) in 1977. There is also a University of Science and Technology in Khartoum.

Public Holidays

2006: 1 January (Independence Day), 10 January*† (Id al-Adha, Feast of the Sacrifice), 31 January* (Islamic New Year), 6 April (Uprising Day, anniversary of 1985 coup), 11 April* (Mouloud, Birth of the Prophet), 12 April (Sham an-Nassim, Coptic Easter Monday), 30 June (Revolution Day), 23 October* (Id al-Fitr, end of Ramadan), 25 December (Christmas), 31 December*† (Id al-Adha, Feast of the Sacrifice).

2007: 1 January (Independence Day), 29 January* (Islamic New Year), 31 March* (Mouloud, Birth of the Prophet), 6 April (Uprising Day, anniversary of 1985 coup), 9 April (Sham an-Nassim, Coptic Easter Monday), 30 June (Revolution Day), 13 October* (Id al-Fitr, end of Ramadan), 20 December* (Id al-Adha, Feast of the Sacrifice), 25 December (Christmas).

* The dates of Islamic holidays are determined by sightings of the moon, and may be slightly different from those given above.

† This festival occurs twice (in the Islamic years AH 1426 and 1427) within the same Gregorian year.

Weights and Measures

The metric system is gradually replacing traditional weights and measures.

Statistical Survey

Source (unless otherwise stated): Department of Statistics, Ministry of Finance and National Economy, POB 735, Khartoum; tel. (183) 777563; fax (183) 775630; e-mail info@mof-sudan.net; internet www.mof-sudan.net.

Area and Population

AREA, POPULATION AND DENSITY

Area (sq km)	2,505,813*
Population (census results)†	
1 February 1983	20,594,197
15 April 1993‡	
Males	12,518,638
Females	12,422,045
Total	24,940,683
Population (UN estimates at mid-year)§	
2003	34,856,000
2004	35,523,000
2005	36,233,000
Density (per sq km) at mid-2005	14.5

* 967,500 sq miles.
† Excluding adjustments for underenumeration, estimated to have been 6.7% in 1993.
‡ Provisional result.
§ Source: UN, *World Population Prospects: The 2004 Revision*.

PROVINCES
(1983 census, provisional)*

	Area (sq miles)	Population	Density (per sq mile)
Northern	134,736	433,391	3.2
Nile	49,205	649,633	13.2
Kassala	44,109	1,512,335	34.3
Red Sea	84,977	695,874	8.2
Blue Nile	24,009	1,056,313	44.0
Gezira	13,546	2,023,094	149.3
White Nile	16,161	933,136	57.7
Northern Kordofan	85,744	1,805,769	21.1
Southern Kordofan	61,188	1,287,525	21.0
Northern Darfur	133,754	1,327,947	9.9
Southern Darfur	62,801	1,765,752	28.1
Khartoum	10,883	1,802,299	165.6
Eastern Equatoria	46,073	1,047,125	22.7
Western Equatoria	30,422	359,056	11.8
Bahr al-Ghazal	52,000	1,492,597	28.7
Al-Buhayrat	25,625	772,913	30.2
Sobat	45,266	802,354	17.7
Jonglei	47,003	797,251	17.0
Total	**967,500**	**20,564,364**	**21.3**

* In 1991 a federal system of government was inaugurated, whereby Sudan was divided into nine states, which were sub-divided into 66 provinces and 281 local government areas. A constitutional decree, issued in February 1994, redivided the country into 26 states.

PRINCIPAL TOWNS
(population at 1993 census)

Omdurman	1,271,403	Nyala	227,183
Khartoum (capital)	947,483	El-Gezira	211,362
Khartoum North	700,887	Gedaref	191,164
Port Sudan	308,195	Kosti	173,599
Kassala	234,622	El-Fasher	141,884
El-Obeid	229,425	Juba	114,980

Source: UN, *Demographic Yearbook*.

Mid-2003 (UN projection, including suburbs): Khartoum 4,285,542 (Source: UN, *World Urbanization Prospects: The 2003 Revision*).

SUDAN

BIRTHS AND DEATHS
(UN estimates, annual averages)

	1990–95	1995–2000	2000–05
Birth rate (per 1,000)	37.8	35.9	33.5
Death rate (per 1,000)	13.0	11.8	11.2

Source: UN, *World Population Prospects: The 2004 Revision*.

Expectation of life (WHO estimates, years at birth): 59 (males 57; females 62) in 2003 (Source: WHO, *World Health Report*).

ECONOMICALLY ACTIVE POPULATION*
(persons aged 10 years and over, 1983 census, provisional)

	Males	Females	Total
Agriculture, hunting, forestry and fishing	2,638,294	1,390,411	4,028,705
Mining and quarrying	5,861	673	6,534
Manufacturing	205,247	61,446	266,693
Electricity, gas and water	42,110	1,618	43,728
Construction	130,977	8,305	139,282
Trade, restaurants and hotels	268,382	25,720	294,102
Transport, storage and communications	209,776	5,698	215,474
Financing, insurance, real estate and business services	17,414	3,160	20,574
Community, social and personal services	451,193	99,216	550,409
Activities not adequately defined	142,691	42,030	184,721
Unemployed persons not previously employed	387,615	205,144	592,759
Total	**4,499,560**	**1,843,421**	**6,342,981**

* Excluding nomads, homeless persons and members of institutional households.

Mid-2003 (estimates in '000): Agriculture, etc. 7,836; Total 13,434 (Source: FAO).

Health and Welfare

KEY INDICATORS

Total fertility rate (children per woman, 2003)	4.3
Under-5 mortality rate (per 1,000 live births, 2004)	91
HIV/AIDS (% of persons aged 15–49, 2003)	2.3
Physicians (per 1,000 head, 2000)	0.16
Hospital beds (per 1,000 head, 1990)	1.09
Health expenditure (2002): US $ per head (PPP)	58
Health expenditure (2002): % of GDP	4.9
Health expenditure (2002): public (% of total)	20.7
Access to water (% of persons, 2002)	69
Access to sanitation (% of persons, 2002)	34
Human Development Index (2003): ranking	141
Human Development Index (2003): value	0.512

For sources and definitions, see explanatory note on p. vi.

Agriculture

PRINCIPAL CROPS
('000 metric tons)

	2002	2003	2004
Wheat	247	332	332*
Rice (paddy)	8	16	16*
Maize	60	60*	60*
Millet	581	784	784*
Sorghum (Durra)	2,825	5,188†	2,600†
Potatoes*	16	16	16
Cassava (Manioc)*	10	10	10
Yams*	137	137	137
Sugar cane*	5,500	5,500	5,500
Dry beans	25	30*	30*
Dry broad beans	146	140*	140*
Other pulses	102	102*	102*
Groundnuts (in shell)	1,267	1,200*	1,200*
Sunflower seed	19	18	18*
—*continued*	2002	2003	2004
Sesame seed	122	325†	325*
Melonseed	46	46*	46*
Cottonseed	111	162	175†
Tomatoes	707	700*	700*
Pumpkins, etc.*	68	68	68
Aubergines (Eggplants)	227	230*	230*
Dry onions*	59	59	59
Garlic*	18	18	18
Melons*	28	28	28
Watermelons*	144	145	145
Dates	330†	330*	330*
Oranges*	18	18	18
Lemons and limes*	62	63	63
Grapefruits and pomelos*	68	68	68
Mangoes*	194	195	195
Bananas*	74	74	74

* FAO estimate(s).
† Unofficial figure.

Source: FAO.

LIVESTOCK
('000 head, year ending September)

	2002	2003*	2004*
Horses*	26	26	26
Asses*	750	750	750
Cattle	38,183	38,325	38,325
Camels	3,342	3,300	3,300
Sheep	48,136	48,000	48,000
Goats	41,485	42,000	42,000
Poultry*	37,000	37,000	37,000

* FAO estimates.

Source: FAO.

LIVESTOCK PRODUCTS
('000 metric tons)

	2002	2003	2004
Beef and veal*	325	325	325
Mutton and lamb*	144	144	144
Goat meat*	126	126	126
Poultry meat*	27	30	30
Other meat*	80	80	80
Cows' milk*	3,216	3,264	3,264
Sheep's milk	464	465*	465*
Goats' milk	1,295	1,295*	1,295*
Butter and ghee*	16	16	16
Cheese*	152	152	152
Hen eggs*	47	47	47
Wool: greasy*	46	46	46
Wool: scoured*	24	24	24
Cattle hides*	56	56	56
Sheepskins*	23	23	23
Goatskins*	24	24	24

* FAO estimate(s).

Source: FAO.

Forestry

ROUNDWOOD REMOVALS
(FAO estimates, '000 cubic metres)

	2002	2003	2004
Sawlogs, veneer logs and logs for sleepers	123	123	123
Other industrial wood	2,050	2,050	2,050
Fuel wood	17,068	17,272	17,482
Total	**19,241**	**19,445**	**19,655**

Source: FAO.

Gum arabic ('000 metric tons, year ending 30 June): 24 in 1993/94; 27 in 1994/95; 25 in 1995/96 (Source: IMF, *Sudan—Recent Economic Developments*, March 1997).

SUDAN

Fishing

('000 metric tons, live weight)

	2001	2002	2003*
Capture	58.0	58.0	58.0
Nile tilapia	20.0	20.0	20.0
Other freshwater fishes	33.0	33.0	33.0
Marine fishes	4.9	4.9	4.9
Aquaculture	1.0	1.6	1.6
Total catch	59.0	59.6	59.6

* FAO estimates.
Source: FAO.

Mining

('000 metric tons, unless otherwise stated)

	2002	2003	2004*
Crude petroleum ('000 barrels)	87,759	103,400	118,000
Salt (unrefined)	83.3	61.1	62.0
Chromite	14.0	37.0	26.0
Gold ore (kilograms)†	5,239	5,106	5,000

* Estimated figures.
† Figures refer to the metal content of ores.
Source: US Geological Survey.

Industry

PETROLEUM PRODUCTS
('000 metric tons)

	1999	2000	2001
Motor spirit (petrol)	50	618	842
Aviation gasoline	6	6*	6
Naphtha*	25	25	n.a.
Jet fuels	95*	95*	115
Kerosene*	27	36	30
Gas-diesel (distillate fuel) oils*	331	835	965
Residual fuel oils	325	305	249
Liquefied petroleum gas	5*	162	215

* Estimate(s).
Source: UN, *Industrial Commodity Statistics Yearbook*.

SELECTED OTHER PRODUCTS

	2000	2001	2002
Flour ('000 metric tons)	600	n.a.	n.a.
Raw sugar ('000 metric tons)	664	693	732
Refined sugar ('000 metric tons)	610	637	n.a.
Vegetable oils ('000 metric tons)	27	32	63
Cement ('000 metric tons)	146*	190	190

* Estimate.
Source: UN, *Industrial Commodity Statistics Yearbook*.

Finance

CURRENCY AND EXCHANGE RATES

Monetary Units
100 piastres = 1 Sudanese dinar.

Sterling, Dollar and Euro Equivalents (30 December 2005)
£1 sterling = 396.97 dinars;
US $1 = 230.254 dinars;
€1 = 271.97 dinars;
1,000 Sudanese dinars = £2.52 = $4.34 = €3.68.

Average Exchange Rate (Sudanese dinars per US $)
2003   260.98
2004   257.91
2005   243.61

Note: On 1 March 1999 the Sudanese pound (£S) was replaced by the Sudanese dinar, equivalent to £S10. The pound was withdrawn from circulation on 31 July 1999.

CENTRAL GOVERNMENT BUDGET
('000 million Sudanese dinars)

Revenue	2002	2003	2004*
Tax revenue	213.4	260.9	259.8
Direct taxes	41.2	46.6	49.5
Indirect taxes	172.2	214.3	210.3
Taxes on international transactions	97.6	103.8	92.8
Taxes on domestic transactions	33.2	48.5	55.1
Value-added tax	41.4	62.0	62.4
Non-tax revenue	257.2	337.6	472.3
Departmental fees	13.0	18.4	13.0
National revenues	244.2	319.2	459.3
Non-petroleum revenues	33.5	50.6	48.4
Petroleum revenues	210.7	268.6	410.9
Total	470.7	598.5	732.0

Expenditure	2002	2003	2004*
Current expenditure	384.8	472.9	534.0
Wages, salaries and pensions	165.1	196.5	237.4
Other current spending	186.8	219.3	226.3
Debt service paid	51.1	65.2	37.5
Goods and services	50.5	53.0	54.6
General reserve	50.4	45.7	62.5
Other obligations	34.8	55.5	71.7
Transfers to states	32.9	57.1	70.3
Capital expenditure	118.6	161.4	243.1
Locally financed	108.9	123.0	204.0
Foreign financed	9.6	38.4	39.1
Total	503.4	634.3	777.1

* Projected figures.
Source: IMF, *Sudan: 2003 Article IV Consultation and First Review of the 2003 Staff-Monitored Program—Staff Report; and Public Information Notice on the Executive Board Discussion* (December 2003).

INTERNATIONAL RESERVES
(US $ million at 31 December)

	2002	2003	2004
IMF special drawing rights	0.2	0.3	—
Foreign exchange	440.7	847.2	1,626.1
Total	440.9	847.5	1,626.1

Source: IMF, *International Financial Statistics*.

MONEY SUPPLY
('000 million Sudanese dinars at 31 December)

	2002	2003	2004
Currency outside banks	193.58	240.21	304.90
Demand deposits at deposit money banks	147.46	194.63	279.46
Total money (incl. others)	352.26	458.48	604.37

Source: IMF, *International Financial Statistics*.

SUDAN

Statistical Survey

COST OF LIVING
(Consumer Price Index; base: 1992 = 100)

	1998	1999	2000
Food, beverages and tobacco	3,930.8	4,670.3	4,883.3
Clothing and footwear	3,615.7	4,010.5	3,985.6
Housing	3,826.8	5,257.2	6,192.9
Household operations	3,677.7	3,899.3	3,706.4
Health care	5,277.9	6,313.5	6,984.7
Transport and communications	7,107.7	8,661.7	9,082.8
Entertainment	2,261.2	3,046.0	4,149.7
Education	5,947.8	7,057.0	8,048.7
All items (incl. others)	4,299.8	5,077.0	5,451.9

Source: Bank of Sudan.

All items (Consumer Price Index; base: 2000 = 100): 107.2 in 2001; 116.2 in 2002; 125.2 in 2003; 135.8 in 2004 (Source: IMF, *International Financial Statistics*).

NATIONAL ACCOUNTS
(estimates, '000 million Sudanese dinars at current prices)

Expenditure on the Gross Domestic Product

	1997	1998	1999
Government final consumption expenditure	91.3	88.5	118.3
Private final consumption expenditure	1,465.9	1,882.2	2,172.6
Gross fixed capital formation	210.7	259.1	318.7
Total domestic expenditure	1,767.9	2,229.8	2,609.6
Exports of goods and services	98.4	122.4	205.7
Less Imports of goods and services	255.4	393.9	383.8
GDP in purchasers' values	1,676.9	2,062.1	2,536.3
GDP at constant 1981/82 prices*	1,201.9	1,262.1	1,338.2

*Million Sudanese dinars.

Source: IMF, *Sudan—Statistical Appendix* (July 2000).

Gross Domestic Product by Economic Activity

	1997	1998	1999
Agriculture and forestry	745.7	841.6	1,040.3
Mining and quarrying	4.2	5.5	20.9
Manufacturing and handicrafts	100.7	177.4	217.3
Electricity and water	14.3	16.1	19.0
Construction	73.1	132.5	156.8
Trade, restaurants and hotels	260.5	405.9	492.0
Transport and communications	150.5	116.3	142.3
Other services	266.0	290.8	354.1
GDP at factor cost	1,615.1	1,986.0	2,442.7
Indirect taxes, *less* subsidies	61.9	76.1	93.6
GDP in purchasers' values	1,677.0	2,062.1	2,536.3

Source: IMF, *Sudan—Statistical Appendix* (July 2000).

BALANCE OF PAYMENTS
(US $ million)

	2002	2003	2004
Exports of goods f.o.b.	1,949.1	2,542.2	3,777.8
Imports of goods f.o.b.	−2,293.8	−2,536.1	−3,586.2
Trade balance	−344.7	6.1	191.6
Exports of services	132.2	36.5	44.1
Imports of services	−818.2	−830.3	−1,064.5
Balance on goods and services	−1,030.7	−787.7	−828.8
Other income received	29.2	10.0	21.8
Other income paid	−638.0	−879.2	−1,134.5
Balance on goods, services and income	−1,639.5	−1,657.0	−1,941.5
Current transfers received	1,085.9	1,218.4	1,580.2
Current transfers paid	−454.5	−516.8	−509.6
Current balance	−1,008.1	−955.4	−870.9
Direct investment from abroad	713.2	1,349.2	1,511.1
Portfolio investment assets	14.8	35.3	19.9
Other investment assets	−148.0	381.4	598.8
Investment liabilities	181.2	−481.5	−702.0
Net errors and omissions	492.2	−2.4	225.5
Overall balance	245.3	326.6	782.4

Source: IMF, *International Financial Statistics*.

External Trade

PRINCIPAL COMMODITIES
(US $ million)

Imports c.i.f.	2000	2001	2002
Food and live animals	331.6	397.5	411.4
Cereals and cereal preparations	219.4	225.4	243.1
Unmilled durum wheat	174.2	156.2	203.3
Mineral fuels, lubricants, etc.	122.4	127.9	120.1
Refined petroleum products	115.9	123.7	117.5
Chemicals and related products	190.0	236.0	246.1
Medicinal and pharmaceutical products	55.6	63.9	73.2
Basic manufactures	296.5	425.8	504.6
Textiles and textile products (excl. clothing)	55.2	87.7	90.2
Cement	22.4	34.0	91.8
Iron and steel	58.9	102.6	113.5
Machinery and transport equipment	560.4	915.5	943.9
Power generating machinery and equipment	60.0	97.6	122.3
Machinery specialized for particular industries	84.7	141.3	151.8
Miscellaneous industrial machinery	74.4	125.3	122.7
Telecommunication and recording equipment	76.1	79.1	73.2
Road vehicles	166.5	324.2	285.0
Passenger vehicles (excl. buses)	35.6	88.0	91.1
Lorries and special purpose vehicles	58.8	127.0	96.9
Miscellaneous manufactured articles	102.1	152.9	171.7
Total (incl. others)	1,657.4	2,342.4	2,492.8

SUDAN

Exports f.o.b.	2000	2001	2002
Food and live animals	152.1	46.9	192.0
Live animals	60.5	—	122.8
Sheep and goats	60.5	—	122.2
Sheep	—	—	121.0
Crude materials (inedible) except fuels	238.7	187.2	172.9
Oil seeds and oleaginous fruit	149.0	117.9	82.4
Sesame seeds	132.1	94.8	68.8
Cotton	59.3	41.2	55.2
Mineral fuels, lubricants, etc.	1,402.7	1,342.1	1,118.0
Petroleum and petroleum products	1,398.4	1,322.1	1,100.0
Crude petroleum and bituminous oils	—	—	128.8
Refined petroleum products	1,398.4	1,322.1	971.2
Other commodities and transactions	61.4	68.6	75.1
Non-monetary gold, unwrought	57.3	67.2	72.7
Total (incl. others)	1,898.9	1,701.6	1,616.6

Source: UN, *International Trade Statistics Yearbook*.

PRINCIPAL TRADING PARTNERS
(US $ million)

Imports c.i.f.	2000	2001	2002
Australia	83.5	82.4	90.3
Canada	26.0	53.0	83.6
China, People's Repub.	117.5	246.1	254.2
Egypt	42.6	69.8	83.0
France (incl. Monaco)	74.6	70.0	48.0
Germany	100.6	—	—
India	81.3	127.0	114.1
Indonesia	28.7	53.0	46.6
Iran	11.9	25.4	20.1
Italy	43.2	51.4	75.8
Japan	99.5	155.2	135.2
Jordan	18.2	29.3	50.9
Kenya	30.4	44.8	32.8
Korea, Repub.	37.2	80.7	68.3
Malaysia	22.7	23.9	24.2
Netherlands	22.8	33.7	42.5
Saudi Arabia	196.5	220.9	316.7
Switzerland-Liechtenstein	20.4	24.7	48.5
Turkey	35.1	39.3	48.1
United Arab Emirates	97.9	158.2	189.5
United Kingdom	164.5	182.2	127.1
USA	33.0	31.5	21.6
Total (incl. others)	1,657.4	2,324.4	2,492.8

Exports f.o.b.	2000	2001	2002
China, People's Repub.	983.8	935.8	940.2
Egypt	61.3	32.8	38.9
Germany	28.5	—	—
Indonesia	55.7	14.6	0.5
Italy	32.1	17.7	17.4
Japan	130.8	77.2	24.7
Korea, Repub.	44.4	63.3	7.1
Lebanon	12.4	26.7	24.9
Malta	19.2	6.2	4.8
Saudi Arabia	102.5	35.2	167.7
Singapore	111.0	158.0	65.5
Syria	17.6	32.1	14.3
United Arab Emirates	38.6	39.3	70.9
United Kingdom	71.6	64.0	64.0
Yemen	16.0	34.0	16.3
Total (incl. others)	1,898.9	1,701.6	1,616.6

Source: UN, *International Trade Statistics Yearbook*.

Transport

RAILWAY TRAFFIC*

	1991	1992	1993
Freight ton-km (million)	2,030	2,120	2,240
Passenger-km (million)	1,020	1,130	1,183

* Estimates.

Source: UN Economic Commission for Africa, *African Statistical Yearbook*.

2000 (passengers carried): 258,000 (Source: Sudan Railways).

ROAD TRAFFIC
(motor vehicles in use)

	1999	2000	2001
Passenger cars	40,600	46,000	46,000
Commercial vehicles	53,900	60,500	60,500

Source: UN, *Statistical Yearbook*.

SHIPPING
Merchant Fleet
(registered at 31 December)

	2002	2003	2004
Number of vessels	17	16	17
Displacement (grt)	33,287	23,899	15,650

Source: Lloyd's Register-Fairplay, *World Fleet Statistics*.

International Sea-borne Freight Traffic
(estimates, '000 metric tons)

	1991	1992	1993
Goods loaded	1,290	1,387	1,543
Goods unloaded	3,800	4,200	4,300

Source: UN Economic Commission for Africa, *African Statistical Yearbook*.

CIVIL AVIATION
(traffic on scheduled services)

	1999	2000	2001
Kilometres flown (million)	7	6	6
Passengers carried ('000)	390	414	415
Passenger-km (million)	693	748	761
Total ton-km (million)	94	101	98

Source: UN, *Statistical Yearbook*.

Tourism

	2001	2002	2003
Tourist arrivals	50,000	52,000	51,000
Tourism receipts (US $ million, excl. passenger transport)	3	108	118

Source: World Tourism Organization.

Communications Media

	2002	2003	2004
Telephones ('000 main lines in use)	671.8	900.0	1,028.9
Mobile cellular telephones ('000 subscribers)	191	650	1,049
Personal computers ('000 in use)	300	300	606
Internet users ('000)	200	n.a.	1,140

Source: International Telecommunication Union.

1996: Daily newspapers 5 (average circulation 737,000 copies) (Source: UNESCO, *Statistical Yearbook*).

1997: Radio receivers ('000 in use) 7,550 (Source: UNESCO, *Statistical Yearbook*).

1998: Non-daily newspapers 11 (average circulation 5,644,000); Periodicals 54 (average circulation 68,000 copies) (Source: UN, *Statistical Yearbook*).

2000: Television receivers ('000 in use) 8,500 (Source: International Telecommunication Union).

Education

(1998)

	Institutions	Teachers*	Students
Pre-primary	5,984	8,897	365,723
Primary	11,982	102,987	2,478,309
Secondary	3,512	14,743	1,010,060
Universities, etc.	n.a.	2,043	200,538

* Figures refer to 1996/97.

Source: UNESCO Institute for Statistics.

1999/2000: Primary: 11,923 schools; 117,151 teachers; 3,137,494 pupils. Secondary: 1,694 schools; 21,114 teachers; 401,424 pupils (Source: Ministry of Education).

Adult literacy rate (UNESCO estimates): 59.0% (males 69.2%; females 49.9%) in 2003 (Source: UN Development Programme, *Human Development Report*).

Directory

The Constitution

Following the coup of 6 April 1985, the Constitution of April 1973 was abrogated. A transitional Constitution, which entered into force in October 1985, was suspended following the military coup of 30 June 1989. In April 1998 a new Constitution was approved by the National Assembly, and presented to President al-Bashir. At a referendum held in June, the new Constitution was endorsed by 96.7% of voters. This Constitution, which entered into force on 1 July 1998, vests executive power in the Council of Ministers, which is appointed by the President but responsible to the National Assembly. Legislative power is vested in the National Assembly. The Constitution guarantees freedom of thought and religion, and the right to political association, provided that such activity complies with the law.

In early July 2005 the National Assembly approved an interim Constitution as part of the Comprehensive Peace Agreement signed in January between the Sudanese Government and the Sudan People's Liberation Movement (SPLM). The interim Constitution provided for the establishment of a Government of National Unity (GONU), representation in which was to be divided between northerners and southerners, with the former holding 70% and the latter 30% of the posts. In the GONU, the National Congress shall be represented by 52% (49% northerners and 3% southerners); the SPLM shall be represented by 28% (21% southerners and 7% northerners); other northern political forces shall be represented by 14%; and other southern political forces shall be represented by 6%.

The interim Constitution also stipulated that, pending legislative elections, which were to be held by no later than the end of the fourth year of the interim period, the National Assembly shall be composed of 450 members who shall be appointed by the President of the Republic in consultation with the First Vice-President, according to the 70%/30% north and south ratio.

Provision was also made in the interim Constitution for the election of the President of the Government of Southern Sudan and for the establishment of a transitional Southern Sudan Assembly. The President of Government of Southern Sudan shall be elected directly by the people of Southern Sudan for a five-year mandate, renewable only once. The transitional Southern Sudan Assembly shall be an inclusive, constituent legislature composed of 170 appointed members with 70% representing the SPLM; 15% representing the National Congress; and 15% representing the other southern Sudanese political forces.

The Government

HEAD OF STATE

President: Lt-Gen. OMAR HASSAN AHMAD AL-BASHIR (took power as Chairman of the Revolutionary Command Council for National Salvation (RCC) on 30 June 1989; appointed President by the RCC on 16 October 1993; elected President in March 1996; re-elected in December 2000).

First Vice-President: Commdr SALVA KIIR MAYARDIT.

Second Vice-President: ALI OSMAN MUHAMMAD TAHA.

COUNCIL OF MINISTERS
(March 2006)

Prime Minister: Lt-Gen. OMAR HASSAN AHMAD AL-BASHIR (National Congress).

Minister of Foreign Affairs: Dr LAM AKOL (SPLM).

Minister of the Interior: Prof. ZUBEIR BESHIR TAHA (National Congress).

Minister of the Presidency: Maj. Gen. BAKRI HASSAN SALEH (National Congress).

Minister of Cabinet Affairs: DENG ALOR KOL (SPLM).

Minister of Defence: Maj.-Gen. Eng. ABD AR-RAHIM MUHAMMAD HUSSEIN (National Congress).

Minister of Justice: MUHAMMAD ALI AL-MARDI (National Congress).

Minister of Information and Communication: ZAHAWI IBRAHIM MALEK (UP).

Minister of Federal Government: ABD AL-BASIT SALEH SABDARAT (National Congress).

Minister of Finance and National Economy: AZ-ZOBEIR AHMED HASSAN (National Congress).

Minister of Foreign Trade: GEORGE BORENG NIYAMI (SPLM).

Minister of International Co-operation: AT-TIJANI SALEH FEDAIL (National Congress).

Minister of Industry: JALAL YUSUF MUHAMMAD AD-DUQAYR (DUP).

Minister of Investment: MALEK AGAR AYAR (SPLM).

Minister of Agriculture and Forestry: MUHAMMAD AL-AMIN ISSA ALAGHBASH (National Congress).

Minister of Animal Resources: GALWAK DENG (National Congress).

Minister of Irrigation and Water Resources: Eng. KAMAL ALI MUHAMMAD (National Congress).

Minister of Energy and Mining: Dr AWAD AHMAD AL-JAZ (National Congress).

Minister of Transport, Roads and Bridges: KUWAL MANIANG AJOK (SPLM).

Minister of Culture, Youth and Sport: MUHAMMAD YUSSUF ABDALLAH (National Congress).

Minister of Tourism and Wildlife: JOSEF MALWAL (UDSF).

Minister of Higher Education and Scientific Research: PETER NIYOT KOK (SPLM).

Minister of Education: PAUL MITHANQ (SPLM).

Minister of Labour, Public Services and Development of Human Resources: Maj.-Gen. (retd) ALISON MANANI MAGAYA (National Congress).

Minister of Health: Dr TABITA SOKAYA (SPLM).

Minister of Humanitarian Affairs: KOSTI MANYEBI (SPLM).

Minister of Religious Affairs and Waqf: AZHARI AT-TIGANI AWAD AS-SID (National Congress).

SUDAN

Minister of Welfare and Social Development: SAMIA AHMAD MUHAMMAD.
Minister of the Environment and Urban Development Construction: AHMED BABKIR NAHAR (National Congress).
Minister of Parliamentary Affairs: JOSEPH OKELLO (USAP).

In addition, there is one presidential adviser and 33 Ministers of State. The President also has 12 special advisers who are considered part of the Government.

GOVERNMENT OF SOUTHERN SUDAN
(March 2006)

President: Commdr SALVA KIIR MAYARDIT.
Vice-President and Minister for Housing, Lands and Public Service: Dr RIEK MACHAR.
Minister for Presidential Affairs: Dr JUSTIN YAAC AROP.
Minister for Police and Security: DANIEL AWET.
Minister of Finance and Economic Planning: ARTHA AKWIN CHUOL.
Minister of Regional Co-operation: NHIAL DENG NHIAL.
Minister for Legal Affairs and Constitutional Development: MICHAEL MAKUEI.
Minister for Education, Science and Technology: Dr MICHAEL MILA HUSSEIN.
Minister for Health: Dr THEOPHILUS OCHAN.
Minister for Industry and Mining: Maj.-Gen. (Retd) ALBINO AKOL.
Minister for Trade and Supplies: ANTHONY LINO MAKANA.
Minister for Information, Broadcasting and Television: Dr SAMSON KWAJE.
Minister for Communication and Postal Services: GEER CHAN.
Minister for Transport and Roads: REBECCA NYAN DENG DE MABIOR.
Minister for Environment and Protection of Wildlife: Lt-Gen. JAMES LORO.
Minister for Agriculture and Forestry: Dr MARTIN ALIA.
Minister for Public Services and Human Resource Development: DAVID DENG ATHORBI.
Minister for Animal Resources and Fisheries: Dr FESTO KUMBA.
Minister for Culture, Youth and Sports: Dr JOHN LUK.
Minister for Diversity and Social and Religious Affairs: MARY KIDEN.
Minister for Water and Irrigation: JOSEPH DWER.

In addition, there are seven presidential advisers.

MINISTRIES

All ministries are in Khartoum.

Ministry of Agriculture and Forestry: POB 285, al-Gamaa Ave, Khartoum; tel. (183) 780951; e-mail moafcc@sudanmail.net.
Ministry of Animal Resources: Khartoum.
Ministry of Cabinet Affairs: Khartoum.
Ministry of Culture, Youth and Sport: Khartoum.
Ministry of Defence: POB 371, Khartoum; tel. (183) 774910.
Ministry of Education: Khartoum; tel. (183) 772808; e-mail moe-sd@moe-sd.com; internet www.moe-sd.com.
Ministry of Energy and Mining: POB 2087, Khartoum; tel. (183) 775595; fax (183) 775428.
Ministry of the Environment and Urban Development Construction: POB 300, Khartoum; tel. (183) 462604.
Ministry of Federal Government: Khartoum.
Ministry of Finance and National Economy: POB 735, Khartoum; tel. (183) 777563; fax (183) 775630; e-mail info@mof-sudan.net; internet mof-sudan.com.
Ministry of Foreign Affairs: POB 873, Khartoum; tel. (183) 773101; e-mail aladinmofa@yahoo.com; internet www.sudanmfa.com.
Ministry of Foreign Trade: Khartoum; tel. (183) 772793; fax (183) 773950.
Ministry of Health: POB 303, Khartoum; tel. (183) 773000; e-mail inhsd@sudanet.net; internet www.fmoh.gov.sd.
Ministry of Higher Education and Scientific Research: POB 2081, Khartoum; tel. (183) 779312; e-mail mhesr@sudanmail.net.
Ministry of Humanitarian Affairs: POB 1976, Khartoum; tel. (183) 780675; e-mail human@mha.gov.sd; internet www.mha.gov.sd.
Ministry of Industry: POB 2184, Khartoum; tel. (183) 777830.
Ministry of Information and Communication: Khartoum.
Ministry of the Interior: POB 2793, Khartoum; tel. (183) 776554.
Ministry of International Co-operation: POB 2092, Khartoum; tel. (183) 772169; fax (183) 780115; e-mail info@micsudan.com; internet www.micsudan.com.
Ministry of Investment: POB 6286, Khartoum; tel. (183) 787193; fax (183) 787199; e-mail investment@sudanmail.net; internet www.sudaninvest.gov.sd.
Ministry of Irrigation and Water Resources: POB 878, Khartoum; tel. (183) 783221; fax (183) 773388; e-mail oehamad@hotmail.com.
Ministry of Justice: POB 302, an-Nil Ave, Khartoum; tel. (183) 774842; fax (183) 771479.
Ministry of Labour, Public Service and Development of Human Resources: Khartoum.
Ministry of Parliamentary Affairs: Khartoum.
Ministry of Religious Affairs and Waqf: Khartoum.
Ministry of Tourism and Wildlife: POB 2424, Khartoum; tel. (183) 471329; fax (183) 471437; e-mail admin@sudan-tourism.com.
Ministry of Transport, Roads and Bridges: POB 300, Khartoum; tel. (183) 781629; fax (183) 780507.
Ministry of Welfare and Social Development: Khartoum.

STATE GOVERNORS
(March 2006)

Al-Buhayrat: Brig. JOHN LAT ZAKARIA.
Bahr al-Jabal: Maj.-Gen. CLEMENT WANI KONGA.
Blue Nile: ABDALLAH UTHMAN AL-HAJ.
Eastern Equatoria: ALOYSIO AMOR.
Gadarif: ABD AR-RAHMAN AHMED AL-KHADR.
Gezira: Lt-Gen. (retd) ABD AR-RAHMAN SIR AL-KHATIM.
Jonglei: PHILLIP THON LEEK.
Kassala: Lt-Gen. FARUQ HASAN MUHAMMAD NUR.
Khartoum: Dr ABD-AL-HALIM ISMAIL AL-MUTA'AFI.
Northern: Maj.-Gen. (retd) AL-HADI BUSHRA HASSAN.
Northern Bahr al-Ghazal: MARYANG AKOI AGO.
Northern Darfur: OSMAN MUHAMMAD YUSUF KIBIR.
Northern Kordofan: GHULAM AD-DIN UTHMAN.
Red Sea: Maj.-Gen. (retd) HATIM AL-WASIL ASH-SHAYKH AS-SAMMANI.
River Nile: Dr BDELLA MASAR.
Sennar: AHMED ABBAS.
Southern Darfur: ADAM HAMID MUSA.
Southern Kordofan: SOMI ZAYDAN ATTIYAH.
Upper Nile: Dr DAK DOK BISHOK.
Wahdah: Brig. TABAN DENG GAI.
Warab: LOUIS ANI MADOT KONDIT.
Western Bahr al-Ghazal: MARK NABIBOSH OBONG.
Western Darfur: Staff Maj.-Gen. (retd) SULAYMAN ABDALLAH ADAM.
Western Equatoria: Col. PATRICK RAPHAEL ZAMOI.
Western Kordofan: Maj.-Gen. AT-TAYIB ABD AR-RAHMAN MUKHTAR.
White Nile: MAJDHUB YUSUF BABIKIR.

President

PRESIDENT

Election, 13–22 December 2000

Candidate	% of total votes cast
Omar Hassan Ahmad al-Bashir (National Congress)	86.5
Gaafar Muhammad Nimeri (Alliance of the People's Working Forces)	9.6
Malik Hussain	1.6
as-Samawi'it Husayn Osman Mansur (Independent Democrats)	1.0
Mahmoud Ahmad Juna	1.0

Legislature

MAJLIS WATANI
(National Assembly)

Speaker: AHMAD IBRAHIM AT-TAHIR.

SUDAN
Directory

Deputy Speakers: ANGELO BEDA, ABDALLAH AL-HARDELLO.
Election, 13–22 December 2000

	Seats
National Congress	355
Others	5
Total	**360***

*Of the 360 members, 270 are directly elected in single seat constituencies, 35 members represent women, 26 represent university graduates and 29 represent trade unions.

According to the interim Constitution approved by the National Assembly in July 2005, the National Assembly shall be composed of 450 members who shall be appointed by the President of the Republic in consultation with the First Vice-President. Legislative elections were to be held by no later than the end of the fourth year of the interim period.

Election Commission

General Election Commission (GEC): PO 14416, Omdurman; tel. (15) 558537; fax (15) 560950; e-mail info@sudan-parliament.org; comprises of a chairman and two mems appointed for the election period only; mems appointed by the President, subject to the approval of the National Assembly; responsible for the election of the President, provincial magistrates, and national, provincial and local assembly mems; Chairman ABD AL-MUN'IM AL-ZAYN AL-NAHHAS.

Political Organizations

National Congress: Khartoum; successor to National Islamic Front; Pres. Lt-Gen. OMAR HASSAN AHMAD AL-BASHIR; Sec.-Gen. Prof. IBRAHIM AHMAD UMAR.

The right to political association, subject to compliance with the law, was guaranteed in the Constitution approved by referendum in June 1998. (All political organizations had been banned following the military coup of 30 June 1989.) The registration of parties began on 6 January 1999, and by 14 February 32 parties had applied to register. The following parties are among the most active:

Alliance of the People's Working Forces: Khartoum; Head GAAFAR MUHAMMAD NIMERI; Acting Sec.-Gen. KAMAL AD-DIN MUHAMMAD ABDULLAH.

Democratic Unionist Party (DUP): Khartoum; Leader OSMAN AL-MIRGHANI; participates in National Democratic Alliance (see below).

Free Sudanese National Party (FSNP): Khartoum; Chair. Fr PHILIP ABBAS GHABBUSH.

Independent Democrats: Khartoum; Leader AS-SAMAWI'IT HUSAYN OSMAN MANSUR.

Islamic-Christian Solidarity: Khartoum; Founder HATIM ABDULLAH AZ-ZAKI HUSAYN.

Islamic Revival Movement: Khartoum; Founder SIDDIQ AL-HAJ AS-SIDDIQ.

Islamic Socialist Party: Khartoum; Leader SALAH AL-MUSBAH.

Islamic Ummah Party: Khartoum; Chair. WALI AD-DIN AL-HADI AL-MAHDI.

Justice Party: Khartoum; f. 2002 by fmr members of the National Congress.

Moderate Trend Party: Khartoum; Leader MAHMUD JIHA.

Muslim Brotherhood: Khartoum; Islamic fundamentalist; Leader Dr HABIR NUR AD-DIN.

National Democratic Party: Khartoum; f. 2002 following merger of the Union of Nationalistic Forces, the Communist Party and the National Solidarity Party.

Nile Valley Conference: Khartoum; Founder Lt-Gen. (retd) UMAR ZARUQ.

Popular Masses' Alliance: Khartoum; Founder FAYSAL MUHMAD HUSAYN.

Popular National Congress (PNC): Khartoum; f. 2000; Founder HASSAN AT-TURABI.

Socialist Popular Party: Khartoum; Founder SAYYID KHALIFAH IDRIS HABBANI.

Sudan Green Party: Khartoum; Founder Prof. ZAKARAIA BASHIR IMAM.

Sudan People's Liberation Movement (SPLM): e-mail webmaster@splmtoday.com; internet www.splmtoday.com; Leader Commdr SALVA KIIR MAYARDIT; Sec.-Gen. JAMES WANI IGGA.

Sudanese Central Movement: Khartoum; Founder Dr MUHAMMAD ABU AL-QASIM HAJ HAMAD.

Sudanese Initiative Party: Khartoum; Leader J'AFAR KARAR.

Sudanese National Party (SNP): Khartoum; Leader HASAN AL-MAHI; participates in the National Democratic Alliance (see below).

Umma Party (UP): e-mail hq@umma.org; internet www.umma.org; Mahdist party based on the Koran and Islamic traditions; Chair. Dr UMAR NUR AD-DA'IM; Leader SADIQ AL-MAHDI; withdrew from the National Democratic Alliance (see below) in March 2000.

Union of Sudan African Parties (USAP): f. 1987; Chair. JOSEPH OKELLO; Sec.-Gen. Prof. AJANG BIOR.

United Democratic Salvation Front (UDSF): Khartoum; political wing of the Sudan People's Defence Force; Chair. Dr RIEK MASHAR TENY-DHURGON.

A number of opposition movements are grouped together in the Asmara-based **National Democratic Alliance (NDA)** (Chair. OSMAN AL-MIRGHANI; Sec.-Gen. JOSEPH OKELU). These include the **Beja Congress** (Sec.-Gen. Amna Dirar), the **Legitimate Command (LC)**, the **Sudan Alliance Forces (SAF)** (f. 1994; Cmmdr-in-Chief Brig. ABD EL-AZIZ KHALID OSMAN), the **Sudan Federal Democratic Alliance (SFDA)** (f. 1994; advocates a decentralized, federal structure for Sudan; Chair. AHMAD DREIGE).

In 2003 two rebel groups, the **Sudan Liberation Movement (SLM)** (Leader MINNI ARKUA MINAWI) and the **Sudan Justice and Equality Movement (SJEM)**, began an armed rebellion in the Darfur region of western Sudan.

Diplomatic Representation

EMBASSIES IN SUDAN

Afghanistan: Madinatol Riyadh, Shareol Moshtal Sq. 10, House No. 81, Khartoum; tel. (183) 221852; fax (183) 222059; e-mail afembsudan@hotmail.com; Chargé d'affaires KHALILURRAHMAN HANANI.

Algeria: St 31, New Extension, POB 80, Khartoum; tel. (183) 741954; Ambassador SALIH BEN KOBBI.

Bulgaria: St 31, House No. 9, Block 10, al-Amarat, POB 1690, 11111 Khartoum; tel. (183) 560106; fax (183) 560107; e-mail bgembsdn@hotmail.com; Chargé d'affaires SVILEN BOZHANOV.

Chad: St 57, al-Amarat, Khartoum; tel. (183) 471612; Ambassador SAGOUR Y. MOHAMAD.

Congo, Democratic Republic: St 13, Block 12CE, New Extension, 23, POB 4195, Khartoum; tel. (183) 471125; Chargé d'affaires a.i. BAWAN MUZURI.

Egypt: University St, POB 1126, Khartoum; tel. (183) 777646; fax (183) 778741; e-mail sphinx-egysud@yahoo.com; Ambassador MUHAMMAD ASSEM IBRAHIM.

Eritrea: St 39, House No. 26, Khartoum 2; tel. (183) 483834; fax (183) 483835; e-mail erena@sudanet.net; Ambassador Gen. ISSA AHMED ISSA.

Ethiopia: Plot No. 4, Block 384BC, POB 844, Khartoum; tel. (183) 471379; fax (183) 471141; e-mail eekrt@hotmail.com; Ambassador Dr KADAFO MOHAMMED HANFARE.

France: al-Amarat, St 13, Plot No. 11, Block 12, POB 377, 11111 Khartoum; tel. (183) 471082; e-mail cad.khartoum-amba@diplomatie.fr; internet www.ambafrance-sd.org; Ambassador CHRISTINE ROBICHON.

Germany: Baladia St, Block No. 8DE, Plot No. 2, POB 970, Khartoum; tel. (183) 777990; fax (183) 777622; e-mail reg1@khar.auswaertiges-amt.de; Ambassador HANS-GÜNTER GNODTKE.

Greece: Sharia al-Gamhouria, Block 5, No. 30, POB 1182, Khartoum; tel. (183) 765900; fax (183) 765901; e-mail grembkrt@mfa.gr; Ambassador GEORGIOS VEIS.

Holy See: Kafouri Belgravia, POB 623, Khartoum (Apostolic Nunciature); tel. (183) 330037; fax (183) 330692; e-mail kanuap@yahoo.it; Apostolic Nuncio Most Rev. DOMINIQUE MAMBERTI (Titular Archbishop of Sagona).

India: 61 Africa Rd, POB 707, Khartoum; tel. (183) 471205; fax (183) 472266; e-mail indembsdn@yahoo.com; Ambassador SHRI DEEPAK VOHRA.

Indonesia: St 60, 84, Block 12, ar-Riyadh, POB 13374, Khartoum; tel. (183) 225106; fax (183) 225528; e-mail kbri_khartoum@sudanmail.com; Ambassador SYAMSUDIN YAHYA.

Iran: Sq. 15, House No. 4, Mogran, POB 10229, Khartoum; tel. (183) 781490; fax (183) 778668; e-mail alihasan@sudanmail.net; Ambassador HAMID BAYAT.

Iraq: Sharia ash-Shareef al-Hindi, POB 1969, Khartoum; tel. (183) 271867; fax (183) 271855; e-mail krtemb@iraqmofamail.net; Ambassador SAMIR KHAIREE ALNEEMA.

SUDAN

Italy: St 39, POB 793, Khartoum; tel. (183) 471615; fax (183) 471217; e-mail ambasciata.khartoum@esteri.it; internet www.ambkhartoum.esteri.it; Ambassador LORENZO ANGELONI.
Japan: St 43, House No. 67, POB 1649, Khartoum; tel. (183) 471601; fax (183) 471600; Ambassador YOSHINORI IMAGAWA.
Jordan: St 33, House No. 13, POB 1379, Khartoum; tel. (183) 483125; fax (183) 471038; e-mail joremb@sudanmail.net; Ambassador MOHAMMED JUMA ASANA.
Kenya: POB 8242, Khartoum; tel. (183) 460386; fax (183) 472265; Ambassador Col (Retd) ELIJAH M. MATIBO.
Korea, Republic: House No. 2, St 1, New Extension, POB 2414, Khartoum; tel. (183) 451136; fax (183) 452822; e-mail ssudan@mofat.go.kr; Ambassador DONG EOK KIM.
Kuwait: Africa Ave, near the Tennis Club, POB 1457, Khartoum; tel. (183) 781525; Ambassador MUNTHIR BADR SALMAN.
Lebanon: Khartoum; Ambassador NASR AJAJ BAZANA.
Libya: 50 Africa Rd, POB 2091, Khartoum; Secretary of People's Bureau GUMMA AL-FAZANI.
Malaysia: St 3, Block 2, al-Amarat, POB 11668, Khartoum; tel. (183) 482763; fax (183) 482762; e-mail mwktoum@sudanmail.net; Ambassador MOHD ZAMRI MOHD KASSIM.
Morocco: St 19, 32, New Extension, POB 2042, Khartoum; tel. (183) 473068; fax (183) 471053; e-mail sifmasoud@sudan.mail.net; Ambassador MUHAMMAD MAA EL-AININE.
Netherlands: St 47, House No. 6, POB 391, Khartoum; tel. (183) 471200; fax (183) 471204; e-mail nlgovkha@mail.com; Ambassador A. KOOIJMANS.
Nigeria: St 17, Sharia al-Mek Nimr, POB 1538, Khartoum; tel. (183) 779120; Ambassador IBRAHIM KARLI.
Norway: St 49, House No. 63, POB 13096, Khartoum; tel. (183) 578336; fax (183) 577180; e-mail emb.khartoum@mfa.no; internet www.norway-sudan.org; Chargé d'affaires STEIN UNDHEIM.
Oman: St 1, New Extension, POB 2839, Khartoum; tel. (183) 745791; Ambassador MOSLIM EBIN ZAIDAN AL-BARAMI.
Pakistan: Dr Mehmood Sharif St, House No. 13, Block 35, POB 1178, Khartoum; tel. (183) 265599; fax (183) 273777; e-mail parepkhartoum@yahoo.com; Ambassador KHALID HUSSAIN YOUSFANI.
Qatar: St 11, New Extension, POB 223, Khartoum; tel. (183) 261113; fax (183) 261116; e-mail qatarembkht@yahoo.com; Ambassador ALI HASSAN ABDULLAH AL-HAMADI.
Romania: Kassala Rd, Plot No. 172–173, Kafouri Area, POB 1494, Khartoum North; tel. (185) 338114; fax (185) 330113; e-mail ambromania@sudanmail.net; Chargé d'affaires a.i. LAURENTIU PINTE.
Russia: A10 St, B1, New Extension, POB 1161, Khartoum; tel. (183) 471042; fax (183) 471239; e-mail rfsudan@hotmail.com; Ambassador VALERII Y. SUKHIN.
Saudi Arabia: St 11, New Extension, POB 1161, Khartoum; tel. (183) 741938; Ambassador SAYED MOHAMMED SIBRI SULIMAN.
Somalia: St 23–25, New Extension, POB 1857, Khartoum; tel. (183) 744800; Ambassador Sheikh MUHAMMAD AHMED.
South Africa: St 11, House No. 16, Block B9, al-Amarat, Khartoum; tel. (183) 585301; fax (183) 585082; e-mail khartoum@foreign.gov.za; Ambassador REDDY MAMPANE.
Switzerland: St 15, POB 1707, al-Amarat, Khartoum; tel. (183) 471010; fax (183) 472804; e-mail vertretung@kha.rep.admin.ch; Chargé d'affaires a.i. GIANBATTISTA MONDADA.
Syria: St 3, New Extension, POB 1139, Khartoum; tel. (183) 744663; Ambassador MOHAMMED AL-MAHAMEED.
Tunisia: St 15, 35, al-Amarat, Khartoum; tel. (183) 487947; fax (183) 487950; e-mail at_khartoum@yahoo.fr; Ambassador ABDESSALEM BOUAÏCHA.
Turkey: St 29, 31, New Extension, POB 771, Khartoum; tel. (183) 451197; fax (183) 472542; e-mail trembkh@email.sudanet.net; Ambassador Dr ALI ENGIN OBA.
Uganda: POB 2676, Khartoum; tel. (183) 158571; fax (183) 797868; e-mail ugembkht@hotmail.com; Ambassador MULL KATENDE.
United Arab Emirates: St 3, New Extension, POB 1225, Khartoum; tel. (183) 744476; Ambassador ABDULLAH MATAR KHAMIS.
United Kingdom: St 10, off Baladia St, POB 801, Khartoum; tel. (183) 777105; fax (183) 776457; e-mail british@sudanmail.net; internet www.britishembassy.gov.uk/sudan; Ambassador IAN CLIFF.
USA: Sharia Ali Abdul Latif, POB 699, Khartoum; tel. (183) 774611; fax (183) 774137; internet khartoum.usembassy.gov; Chargé d'affaires CAMERON HUME.
Yemen: St 11, New Extension, POB 1010, Khartoum; tel. (183) 743918; Ambassador ABDOULJALIL AZZOUZ.

Judicial System

Until September 1983 the judicial system was divided into two sections, civil and Islamic, the latter dealing only with personal and family matters. In September 1983 President Nimeri replaced all existing laws with Islamic (*Shari'a*) law. Following the coup in April 1985, the *Shari'a* courts were abolished, and it was announced that the previous system of criminal courts was to be revived. In June 1986 the Prime Minister, Sadiq al-Mahdi, reaffirmed that the *Shari'a* law was to be abolished. It was announced in June 1987 that a new legal code, based on a 'Sudanese legal heritage', was to be introduced. In July 1989 the military Government established special courts to investigate violations of emergency laws concerning corruption. It was announced in June 1991 that these courts were to be incorporated in the general court administration. Islamic law was reintroduced in March 1991, but was not applied in the southern states of Equatoria, Bahr al-Ghazal and Upper Nile.

Chief Justice: GALAL ED-DIN MUHAMMAD OSMAN.

Religion

The majority of the northern Sudanese population are Muslims, while in the south the population are principally Christians or animists.

ISLAM

Islam is the state religion. Sudanese Islam has a strong Sufi element, and is estimated to have more than 15m. adherents.

CHRISTIANITY

Sudan Council of Churches: Inter-Church House, St 35, New Extension, POB 469, Khartoum; tel. (183) 742859; f. 1967; 12 mem. churches; Chair. Most Rev. PAOLINO LUKUDU LORO (Roman Catholic Archbishop of Juba); Gen. Sec. Rev. CLEMENT H. JANDA.

Roman Catholic Church

Latin Rite

Sudan comprises two archdioceses and seven dioceses. At 31 December 2003 there were an estimated 4,020,548 adherents, representing about 9.1% of the total population.

Sudan Catholic Bishops' Conference
General Secretariat, POB 5011, Khartoum; tel. (183) 724365; fax (183) 724866; f. 1971; Pres. Most Rev. PAOLINO LUKUDU LORO (Archbishop of Juba); Sec.-Gen. JOHN DINGI MARTIN.

Archbishop of Juba: Most Rev. PAOLINO LUKUDU LORO, Catholic Church, POB 32, Juba, Equatoria State; tel. 20388; fax 20755.

Archbishop of Khartoum: Cardinal GABRIEL ZUBEIR WAKO, Catholic Church, POB 49, Khartoum; tel. (183) 782174; fax (183) 783518; e-mail rielei@hotmail.com.

Maronite Rite

Maronite Church in Sudan: POB 244, Khartoum; Rev. Fr YOUSEPH NEAMA.

Melkite Rite

Patriarchal Vicariate of Egypt and Sudan: Greek Melkite Catholic Patriarchate, 16 Sharia Daher, 11271 Cairo, Egypt; tel. (2) 5905790; fax (2) 5935398; e-mail grecmelkitecath_egy@hotmail.com; General Patriarchal Vicar in Egypt and Sudan Mgr (JOSEPH) JULES ZEREY (Titular Archbishop of Damietta); Patriarchal Vicar in Sudan Mgr. Exarkhos GEORGE BANNA; POB 766, Khartoum; tel. (183) 777910.

Syrian Rite

Syrian Church in Sudan: Under the jurisdiction of the Patriarch of Antioch; Protosyncellus Rt Rev. JOSEPH HANNOUCHE (Bishop of Cairo).

Orthodox Churches

Coptic Orthodox Church

Metropolitan of Khartoum, Southern Sudan and Uganda: Rt Rev. ANBA DANIAL, POB 4, Khartoum; tel. (183) 770646; fax (183) 785646; e-mail metaous@email-sudan.net.

Bishop of Atbara, Omdurman and Northern Sudan: Rt Rev. ANBA SARABAMON, POB 628, Omdurman; tel. (183) 550423; fax (183) 556973.

SUDAN

Greek Orthodox Church

Metropolitan of Nubia: POB 47, Khartoum; tel. (183) 772973; Archbishop DIONYSSIOS HADZIVASSILIOU.

The Ethiopian Orthodox Church is also active.

The Anglican Communion

Anglicans are adherents of the (Episcopal) Church of the Province of the Sudan. The Province, with 24 dioceses and about 1m. adherents, was established in 1976.

Archbishop in Sudan: Most Rev. JOSEPH BIRINGI HASSAN MARONA, POB 110, Juba; tel. (183) 20065.

Other Christian Churches

Evangelical Church: POB 57, Khartoum; c. 1,500 mems; administers schools, literature centre and training centre; Chair Rev. RADI ELIAS.

Presbyterian Church: POB 40, Malakal; autonomous since 1956; 67,000 mems (1985); Gen. Sec. Rev. THOMAS MALUIT.

SIM Sudan: POB 220, Khartoum; tel. (183) 472790; fax (183) 467213; e-mail fwilson@simintl.sim.org; f. 1937; Dir L. DICK.

The Africa Inland Church, the Sudan Interior Church and the Sudanese Church of Christ are also active.

The Press

DAILIES

Press censorship was imposed following the 1989 coup.

Abbar al-Youm: Khartoum; tel. (183) 779396; daily; Editor AHMED AL-BALAL AT-TAYEB.

Al-Anbaa: Khartoum; tel. (183) 466523; f. 1998; Editor-in-Chief NAJIB ADAM QAMAR AD-DIN.

An-Nasr: Khartoum; tel. (183) 772494; Editor Col YOUNIS MAHMOUD.

Ar-Rai al-Akhar: Khartoum; tel. (183) 777934; daily; Editor MOHI AD-DIN TITTAWI.

Ar-Rai al-Amm: Khartoum; tel. (183) 778182; fax (183) 772176; e-mail info@rayaam.net; internet www.rayaam.net; daily; Editor SALAH MUHAMMAD IBRAHIM.

Khartoum Monitor: St 61, New Extension, Khartoum; e-mail Khartoummonitor@hotmail.com; Chair. and Editor ALFRED TABAN; Man. Editor WILLIAM EZEKIEL.

Sudan Mirror: POB 59163, 00200 Nairobi, Kenya; tel. and fax (20) 570458; e-mail info@sudanmedia.org; internet www.sudanmirror.com; f. 2003.

Sudan Standard: Ministry of Information and Communication, Khartoum; daily; English.

Al-Wan: Khartoum; tel. (183) 775036; e-mail alwaan@cybergates.net; daily; independent; pro-Govt; Editor HOUSSEN KHOGALI.

PERIODICALS

Al-Guwwat al-Musallaha (The Armed Forces): Khartoum; f. 1969; publs a weekly newspaper and monthly magazine for the armed forces; Editor-in-Chief Maj. MAHMOUD GALANDER; circ. 7,500.

New Horizon: POB 2651, Khartoum; tel. (183) 777913; f. 1976; publ. by the Sudan House for Printing and Publishing; weekly; English; political and economic affairs, development, home and international news; Editor AS-SIR HASSAN FADL; circ. 7,000.

Sudanow: POB 2651, Khartoum; tel. (183) 777913; f. 1976; publ. by the Sudan House for Printing and Publishing; monthly; English; political and economic affairs, arts, social affairs and diversions; Editor-in-Chief AHMED KAMAL ED-DIN; circ. 10,000.

NEWS AGENCIES

Sudan News Agency (SUNA): Sharia al-Gamhouria, POB 1506, Khartoum; tel. (183) 775770; e-mail suna@sudanet.net; internet www.sudanet.net/suna.htm; Dir-Gen. ALI ABD AR-RAHMAN AN-NUMAYRI.

Sudanese Press Agency: Khartoum; f. 1985; owned by journalists.

Foreign Bureaux

Middle East News Agency (MENA) (Egypt): Dalala Bldg, POB 740, Khartoum.

Xinhua (New China) News Agency (People's Republic of China): No. 100, 12 The Sq., Riad Town, POB 2229, Khartoum; tel. (183) 224174; Correspondent SUN XIAOKE.

The Agence Arabe Syrienne d'Information – SANA (Syria) also has a bureau in Khartoum.

Publishers

Ahmad Abd ar-Rahman at-Tikeine: POB 299, Port Sudan.

Al-Ayyam Press Co Ltd: Aboulela Bldg, POB 363, United Nations Sq., Khartoum; f. 1953; general fiction and non-fiction, arts, poetry, reference, newspapers, magazines; Man. Dir BESHIR MUHAMMAD SAID.

As-Sahafa Publishing and Printing House: POB 1228, Khartoum; f. 1961; newspapers, pamphlets, fiction and govt publs.

As-Salam Co Ltd: POB 944, Khartoum.

Claudios S. Fellas: POB 641, Khartoum.

Khartoum University Press: POB 321, Khartoum; tel. (183) 776653; f. 1964; academic, general and educational in Arabic and English; Man. Dir ALI EL-MAK.

GOVERNMENT PUBLISHING HOUSE

El-Asma Printing Press: POB 38, Khartoum.

Broadcasting and Communications

TELECOMMUNICATIONS

A mobile cellular telephone network for Khartoum State was inaugurated in 1997.

Ministry of Information and Communication: Khartoum; regulatory body; Sec.-Gen. Eng. AWAD E. WIDAA.

Posts and Telegraphs Public Corpn: Khartoum; tel. (183) 770000; fax (183) 772888; e-mail sudanpost@maktoob.com; regulatory body; Dir-Gen. AHMAD AT-TIJANI ALALLIM.

Sudan Telecom Co (SUDATEL): Sudatel Tower, POB 11155, Khartoum; tel. (183) 797400; fax (183) 782322; e-mail info@sudatel.net; internet www.sudatel.net; f. 1993; service provider for Sudan; Chair. Dr AHMAD MAGZOUB; Gen. Man. EMAD ALDIN HUSSAIN AHMAD.

BROADCASTING

Radio

Sudan National Broadcasting Corpn: POB 572, Omdurman; tel. (15) 552100; state-controlled service broadcasting daily in Arabic, English, French and Swahili; Dir-Gen. SALAH AD-DIN AL-FADHIL USUD.

Voice of Sudan: e-mail sudanvoice@umma.org; active since 1995; run by the National Democratic Alliance; Arabic and English.

Television

An earth satellite station operated on 36 channels at Umm Haraz has much improved Sudan's telecommunications links. A nation-wide satellite network is being established with 14 earth stations in the provinces. There are regional stations at Gezira (Central Region) and Atbara (Northern Region).

Sudan Television: POB 1094, Omdurman; tel. (15) 550022; internet www.sudantv.net; f. 1962; state-controlled; 60 hours of programmes per week; Head of Directorate HADID AS-SIRA.

Finance

(cap. = capital; res = reserves; dep. = deposits; m. = million; brs = branches; amounts in Sudanese dinars, unless otherwise indicated)

BANKING

All domestic banks are controlled by the Bank of Sudan. Foreign banks were permitted to resume operations in 1976. In December 1985 the Government banned the establishment of any further banks. It was announced in December 1990 that Sudan's banking system was to be reorganized to accord with Islamic principles. In 2000 there were a total of 25 banks in Sudan. In May 2000 the Bank of Sudan issued new policy guide-lines under which Sudan's banks were to merge into six banking groups to improve their financial strength and international competitiveness; however, the mergers had not been implemented by early 2006.

Central Bank

Bank of Sudan: Gamaa Ave, POB 313, Khartoum; tel. (183) 774419; fax (183) 780273; e-mail cbank@sudanet.net; internet www.bankofsudan.org; f. 1960; bank of issue; cap. 300.2m., res 1,688.0m., dep. 530,580.1m. (Dec. 2001); Gov. Dr SABIR MUHAMMAD HASSAN; 9 brs.

Commercial Banks

Al-Baraka Bank: Al-Baraka Tower, Al-Qasr Ave, POB 3583, Khartoum; tel. (183) 780688; fax (183) 778948; e-mail info@albarakasudan.com; internet www.albarakasudan.com; f. 1984; investment and export promotion; cap. and res 1,639.0m., total assets 2,180.1m. (Dec. 2003); Chair. OSMAN AHMED SULIMAN; Gen. Man. ABDALLAH KHAIRY HAMID; 24 brs.

Al-Shamal Islamic Bank: Al-Shamal Islamic Tower, Es-Sayed Abd ar-Rahman St, POB 10036, 11111 Khartoum; tel. (183) 779078; fax (183) 772661; e-mail info@alshamalbank.com; internet www.alshamalbank.com; f. 1990; total assets 18,258.0m. (Dec. 2003); Pres. GAFAAR OSMAN FAGIR; Gen. Man. ABDELMONEIM HASSAN SAYED (acting); 15 brs.

Bank of Khartoum Group: Intersection Gamhouria St and El-Gaser St, POB 1008, Khartoum; tel. (183) 772800; fax (183) 781120; e-mail admin@bankofkhartoum.net; internet www.bankofkhartoum.net; f. 1913; 55% owned by Dubai Islamic Bank PLC; absorbed National Export/Import Bank and Unity Bank in 1993; cap. 11,800m., res 450.1m., dep. 48,600m. (Dec. 2003); Chair. OSMAN ALHADI IBRAHIM; Gen. Man. MUHAMMAD SALAH ELDIN; 118 brs.

Blue Nile Mashreg Bank: Parliament St, Khartoum; tel. (183) 784690; fax (183) 782562; e-mail bnbsudan@yahoo.com; internet www.bluemashreg.com; cap. and res 1,751.9m., total assets 16,757.9m. (Dec. 2003); Chair. MUHAMMAD ISMAIL MUHAMMAD; Gen. Man. ABDEL KHALIG ALSAMANI ABDEL RAZIG.

Farmers Commercial Bank: POB 1116, Al-Qasr St, Khartoum; tel. (183) 774960; fax (183) 779907; f. 1960 as Sudan Commercial Bank; name changed as above in 1999 following merger with Farmers Bank for Investment and Rural Development; cap. 1,517.7m., res 1,031.3m., dep. 12,545.1m. (Dec. 2002); Chair. ET-TAYB ELOBEID BADR; Gen. Man. BADER ELDIEN MAHMOUD ABBAS; 28 brs.

National Bank of Sudan: Kronfli Bldg, Al-Qasr Ave, POB 1183, Khartoum; tel. (183) 778151; fax (183) 779497; f. 1982; cap. 593.0m., res 313.6m., dep. 8,384.0m. (Dec. 2001); Chair. HASSAN IBRAHIM MALIK; Gen. Man. MUHAMMAD KHEIR ISMAIL; 13 brs in Sudan, 2 abroad.

Omdurman National Bank: POB 11522, Al-Qasr Ave, Khartoum; tel. (183) 770400; fax (183) 777219; e-mail omb@sudanmail.net; internet www.omd-bank.com; f. 1993; cap. 3,293.1m., res 2,762.8m., dep. 135,723.0m. (Dec. 2003); Gen. Man. AHMED MOHAMMED MUSA; 19 brs.

Sudanese French Bank: POB 2775, Plot No 6, Block A, Al-Qasr Ave, Khartoum; tel. (183) 771730; fax (183) 771740; e-mail sfbankb@sudanet.net; f. 1978 as Sudanese Investment Bank; cap. 1,013m. S. pounds, res 21,414m., dep. 148,624m. (Dec. 1998); Chair. Dr EZZELDEIN EBRAHIM; Gen. Man. MASSAD MOHAMMED AHMED; 11 brs.

Tadamon Islamic Bank: Baladia St, POB 3154, Khartoum; tel. (183) 771505; fax (183) 773840; e-mail tadamon@sudanmail.net; f. 1981; cap. 3,011m., res 1,295m., total assets 44,852m. (Dec. 2004); Chair. Dr HASSAN OSMAN ABDALLAH; Gen. Man. ABDALLAH NOGD ALLAH AHMAIDI; 18 brs.

Foreign Banks

Byblos Bank Africa Ltd: POB 8121, Al-Amarat St 21, Khartoum; tel. (183) 566444; fax (183) 566454; internet www.byblosbank.com.lb; f. 2003; Chair. Dr FRANÇOIS S. BASSIL; Gen. Man. NADIM GHANTOUS.

Faisal Islamic Bank (Sudan) (Saudi Arabia): POB 2415, Khartoum; tel. (183) 774027; fax (183) 780193; e-mail gaafarom@sudanmail.net; internet www.fibsudan.com; f. 1977; cap. 1,000.0m., res 241.9m., dep. 12,382.1m. (Dec. 2001); Chair. Prince MUHAMMAD AL-FAISAL AS-SAUD; Gen. Man. AHMED ABDALLAH DAWLA (acting); 33 brs.

Habib Bank (Pakistan): Al-Qasr St, POB 8246, Khartoum; tel. (183) 782820; fax (183) 781497; e-mail hblsudan@sudanmail.net.sd; internet www.habibbankltd.com; f. 1982; cap. and res 13.8m. S. pounds, total assets 27.3m. (Dec. 1987); Gen. Man. BAZ MUHAMMAD KHAN.

National Bank of Abu Dhabi (United Arab Emirates): Taka Bldg, Atbara St, POB 2465, Khartoum; tel. (183) 787203; fax (183) 774892; e-mail nbadkh@sudanmail.net; internet www.nbad.com; f. 1976; cap. and res 16.9m. S. pounds, total assets 12.5m. (Dec. 1987); Man. GAAFER OSMAN MUHAMMAD.

Saudi Sudanese Bank: Baladia St, POB 1773, Khartoum; tel. (183) 776700; fax (183) 781836; e-mail saudi-sud@saudisb.com; internet www.saudisb.com; f. 1986; Saudi Arabian shareholders have a 57.3% interest, Sudanese shareholders 42.7%; res 27,797.7m., dep. 16,800.9m. (Dec. 2003); Chair. ABDEL GALIL EL-WASIA; 13 brs.

Development Banks

Agricultural Bank of Sudan: Ghoumhoria Ave, POB 1363, Khartoum; tel. (183) 777432; fax (183) 777437; e-mail agribank@yahoo.com; f. 1957; cap. and res 1,679.4m., total assets 32,362.8m. (Dec. 2003); provides finance for agricultural projects; Man. Dir AWAD OSMAN MUHAMMAD AHMED; 40 brs.

Islamic Co-operative Development Bank (ICDB): Et-Tanmha Tower, Kolyat Eltib St, POB 62, Khartoum; tel. (183) 780223; fax (183) 777715; f. 1983; cap. and res 3,821.0m., total assets 28,250.4m. (Dec. 2003); Chair. EL-HAJ ATTA EL-MANAN IDRIS; 6 brs.

El-Nilein Industrial Development Bank: United Nations Sq., POB 1722, Khartoum; tel. (183) 781507; fax (183) 780776; e-mail nidbg@nidbg.com; f. 1993 by merger; provides tech. and financial assistance for private-sector industrial projects and acquires shares in industrial enterprises; cap. and res 4.1m., total assets 39.8m. (Dec. 2003); Chair. Dr SABIR MUHAMMAD EL-HASSAN; Man. Dir WUGIDALLA A. ALLAH; 40 brs.

NIMA Development and Investment Bank: Hashim Hago Bldg, As-Suk al-Arabi, POB 665, Khartoum; tel. (183) 779496; fax (183) 781854; f. 1982 as National Devt Bank; name changed as above 1998; 90%-owned by NIMA Groupe, 10% private shareholders; finances or co-finances economic and social development projects; cap. 4,000m. S. pounds, res 106m. (Dec. 1998); Dir-Gen. SALIM EL-SAFI HUGIR; 6 brs.

Sudanese Estates Bank: Baladia St, POB 309, Khartoum; tel. (183) 777917; fax (183) 779465; f. 1967; mortgage bank financing private-sector urban housing development; cap. and res 1,700m. S. pounds, total assets 9,500m. (Dec. 1994); Chair. Eng. MUHAMMAD ALI EL-AMIN; 6 brs.

STOCK EXCHANGE

Sudanese Stock Exchange: Al-Baraka Tower, 5th Floor, POB 10835, Khartoum; tel. (183) 776235; fax (183) 776134; f. 1995; Chair. HAMZA MUHAMMAD JENAWI; 27 mems.

INSURANCE

African Insurance Co (Sudan) Ltd: New Abu Ella Bldg, Parliament Ave, Khartoum; tel. (183) 173402; fax (183) 177988; f. 1977; fire, accident, marine and motor; Gen. Man. AN-NOMAN AS-SANUSI.

Blue Nile Insurance Co (Sudan) Ltd: Al-Qasr Ave, POB 2215, Khartoum; tel. (183) 170580; fax (183) 172405; Gen. Man. MUHAMMAD AL-AMIN MIRGHANI.

Foja International Insurance Co Ltd: POB 879, Khartoum; tel. (183) 784470; fax (183) 783248; fire, accident, marine, motor and animal; Gen. Man. MAMOON IBRAHIM ABD ALLA.

General Insurance Co (Sudan) Ltd: El-Mek Nimr St, POB 1555, Khartoum; tel. (183) 780616; fax (183) 772122; f. 1961; Gen. Man. ELSAMAWL ELSAYED HAFIZ.

Islamic Insurance Co Ltd: Al-Faiha Commercial Bldg, Ali Abdullatif St, POB 2776, Khartoum; tel. (183) 772656; e-mail islamicins@sudanmail.net; f. 1979; all classes; CEO Dr OTHMAN ABDUL WAHAB.

Khartoum Insurance Co Ltd: Al-Taminat Bldg, Al-Jamhouriya St, POB 737, Khartoum; tel. (183) 778647; f. 1953; Chair. MUDAWI M. AHMAD; Gen. Dir YOUSIF KHAIRY.

Juba Insurance Co Ltd: Al-Baladiya St, Sayen Osnam Al-Amin Bldg, 2nd Floor, POB 10043, Khartoum; tel. (183) 783245; fax (183) 781617; Gen. Man. ABDUL AAL ELDAWI ABDUL AAL.

Middle East Insurance Co Ltd: Al-Qasr St, Kuronfuli Bldg, 1st Floor, POB 3070, Khartoum; tel. (183) 772202; fax (183) 779266; f. 1981; fire, marine, motor and general liability; Chair. AHMAD I. MALIK; Gen. Dir ALI MUHAMMAD AHMED EL-FADL.

Sudanese Insurance and Reinsurance Co Ltd: Al-Gamhouria St, Nasr Sq., Middle Station Makati Bldg, 3rd Floor, POB 2332, Khartoum; tel. (183) 770812; f. 1967; CEO HASSAN ES-SAYED MUHAMMAD ALI.

United Insurance Co (Sudan) Ltd: Makkawi Bldg, Al-Gamhouria St, POB 318, Khartoum; tel. (183) 776655; fax (183) 770783; e-mail abdin@unitedinsurance.ws; internet www.unitedinsurance.ws; f. 1968; Chair. HASHIM EL-BERIER; Dir-Gen. MUHAMMAD ABDEEN BABIKER.

Trade and Industry

GOVERNMENT AGENCIES

Agricultural Research Corpn: POB 126, Wadi Medani; tel. (5118) 42226; fax (5118) 43213; e-mail arcsudan@sudanet.net; f. 1967; Dir-Gen. Prof. SALIH HUSSEIN SALIH.

Animal Production Public Corpn: POB 624, Khartoum; tel. (183) 778555; Gen. Man. Dr FOUAD RAMADAN HAMID.

General Petroleum Corpn: POB 2986, Khartoum; tel. (183) 771554; f. 1976; Chair. Dr OSMAN ABDULWAHAB; Dir-Gen. Dr ABD ER-RAHMAN OSMAN ABD ER-RAHMAN.

SUDAN
Directory

Gum Arabic Co Ltd: POB 857, Khartoum; tel. (183) 461061; fax (183) 471336; e-mail info@gum-arab.com; internet www.gum-arab.com; f. 1969; Chair. ABD EL-HAMID MUSA KASHA; Gen. Man. HASSAN SAAD AHMED.

Industrial Production Corpn: POB 1034, Khartoum; tel. (183) 771278; f. 1976; Dir-Gen. OSMAN TAMMAM.

    Cement and Building Materials Sector Co-ordination Office: POB 2241, Khartoum; tel. (183) 774269; Dir T. M. KHOGALI.

    Food Industries Corpn: POB 2341, Khartoum; tel. (183) 775463; Dir MUHAMMAD AL-GHALI SULIMAN.

    Leather Industries Corpn: POB 1639, Khartoum; tel. (183) 778187; f. 1986; Man. Dir IBRAHIM SALIH ALI.

    Oil Corpn: POB 64, Khartoum North; tel. (183) 332044; Gen. Man. BUKHARI MAHMOUD BUKHARI.

    Spinning and Weaving General Co Ltd: POB 765, Khartoum; tel. (183) 774306; f. 1975; Dir MUHAMMAD SALIH MUHAMMAD ABDALLAH.

    Sudan Tea Co Ltd: POB 1219, Khartoum; tel. (183) 781261.

    Sudanese Mining Corpn: POB 1034, Khartoum; tel. (183) 770840; f. 1975; Dir IBRAHIM MUDAWI BABIKER.

    Sugar and Distilling Industry Corpn: POB 511, Khartoum; tel. (183) 778417; Man. MIRGHANI AHMAD BABIKER.

Mechanized Farming Corpn: POB 2482, Khartoum; Man. Dir AWAD AL-KARIM AL-YASS.

National Cotton and Trade Co Ltd: POB 1552, Khartoum; tel. (183) 80040; f. 1970; Chair. ABD EL-ATI A. MEKKI; Man. Dir ABD AR-RAHMAN A. MONIEM; Gen. Man. ZUBAIR MUHAMMAD AL-BASHIR.

Port Sudan Cotton Trade Co Ltd: POB 590, Port Sudan; POB 590, Khartoum; Gen. Man. SAÏD MUHAMMAD ADAM.

Public Agricultural Production Corpn: POB 538, Khartoum; Chair. and Man. Dir ABDALLAH BAYOUMO; Sec. SAAD AD-DIN MUHAMMAD ALI.

Public Corpn for Building and Construction: POB 2110, Khartoum; tel. (183) 774544; Dir NAIM AD-DIN.

Public Corpn for Irrigation and Excavation: POB 619, Khartoum; tel. (183) 780167; Gen. Sec. OSMAN AN-NUR.

Public Corpn for Oil Products and Pipelines: POB 1704, Khartoum; tel. (183) 778290; Gen. Man. ABD AR-RAHMAN SULIMAN.

Rahad Corpn: POB 2523, Khartoum; tel. (183) 775175; financed by the World Bank, Kuwait and the USA; Man. Dir HASSAN SAAD ABDALLA.

The State Trading Corpn: POB 211, Khartoum; tel. (183) 778555; Chair. E. R. M. TOM.

    Automobile Corpn: POB 221, Khartoum; tel. (183) 778555; importer of vehicles and spare parts; Gen. Man. DAFALLA AHMAD SIDDIQ.

    Captrade Engineering and Automobile Services Co Ltd: POB 97, Khartoum; tel. (183) 789265; fax (183) 775544; e-mail cap1@sudanmail.net; f. 1925; importers and distributors of engineering and automobile equipment; Gen. Man. ESSAM MOHD EL-HASSAN KAMBAL.

    Gezira Trade and Services Co: POB 215, Khartoum; tel. (183) 772687; fax (183) 779060; e-mail gtco@sudanmail.net; f. 1980; importer of agricultural machinery, spare parts, electrical and office equipment, foodstuffs, clothes and footwear; exporter of oilseeds, grains, hides and skins and livestock; provides shipping insurance and warehousing services; agents for Lloyds and P and I Club; Chair. NASR ED-DIN M. OMER.

    Khartoum Commercial and Shipping Co: POB 221, Khartoum; tel. (183) 778555; f. 1982; import, export and shipping services, insurance and manufacturing; Gen. Man. IDRIS M. SALIH.

    Silos and Storage Corpn: POB 1183, Khartoum; stores and handles agricultural products; Gen. Man. AHMAD AT-TAIEB HARHOOF.

The Sudan Cotton Co Ltd: POB 1672, Khartoum; tel. (183) 771567; fax (183) 770703; e-mail sccl@sudanmail.net.sd; internet www.sudancottonco.com; f. 1970; exports and markets cotton; Chair. ABBAS ABD AL-BAGI HAMMAD; Dir-Gen. Dr ABDIN MUHAMMAD ALI.

Sudan Gezira Board: POB 884, HQ Barakat Wadi Medani, Gezira Province; tel. 2412; Sales Office, POB 884, Khartoum; tel. (183) 740145; responsible for Sudan's main cotton-producing area; the Gezira scheme is a partnership between the Govt, the tenants and the board. The Govt provides the land and is responsible for irrigation. Tenants pay a land and water charge and receive the work proceeds. The Board provides agricultural services at cost, technical supervision and execution of govt agricultural policies relating to the scheme. Tenants pay a percentage of their proceeds to the Social Development Fund. The total potential cultivable area of the Gezira scheme is c. 850,000 ha and the total area under systematic irrigation is c. 730,000 ha. In addition to cotton, groundnuts, sorghum, wheat, rice, pulses and vegetables are grown for the benefit of tenant farmers; Man. Dir Prof. FATHI MUHAMMAD KHALIFA.

Sudan Oilseeds Co Ltd: Parliament Ave, POB 167, Khartoum; tel. (183) 780120; f. 1974; 58% state-owned; exporter of oilseeds (groundnuts, sesame seeds and castor beans); importer of foodstuffs and other goods; Chair. SADIQ KARAR AT-TAYEB; Gen. Man. KAMAL ABD AL-HALIM.

DEVELOPMENT CORPORATIONS

Sudan Development Corpn (SDC): 21 al-Amarat, POB 710, Khartoum; tel. (183) 472151; fax (183) 472148; e-mail sdc@sudanmail.net; f. 1974 to promote and co-finance development projects with special emphasis on projects in the agricultural, agri-business, and industrial sectors; cap. p.u. US $200m.; Man. Dir ABDEL WAHAB AHMED HAMZA.

    Sudan Rural Development Co Ltd (SRDC): POB 2190, Khartoum; tel. (183) 773855; fax (183) 773235; e-mail srdfc@hotmail.com; f. 1980; SDC has 27% shareholding; cap. p.u. US $20m.; Gen. Man. EL-AWAD ABDALLA H. HIJAZI (designate).

    Sudan Rural Development Finance Co (SRDFC): POB 2190, Khartoum; tel. (183) 773855; fax (183) 773235; f. 1980; Gen. Man. OMRAN MUHAMMAD ALI.

CHAMBER OF COMMERCE

Union of Sudanese Chambers of Commerce: POB 81, Khartoum; tel. (183) 772346; fax (183) 780748; e-mail chamber@sudanchamber.org; internet www.sudanchamber.org; f. 1908; Pres. ELTAYEB AHMED OSMAN; Sec.-Gen. IBRAHIM MUHAMMAD OSMAN.

INDUSTRIAL ASSOCIATION

Sudanese Industries Association: Africa St, POB 2565, Khartoum; tel. (183) 773151; f. 1974; Chair. FATH AR-RAHMAN AL-BASHIR; Exec. Dir A. IZZ AL-ARAB YOUSUF.

UTILITIES

Public Electricity and Water Corpn: POB 1380, Khartoum; tel. (183) 81021; Dir Dr YASIN AL-HAJ ABDIN.

CO-OPERATIVE SOCIETIES

There are about 600 co-operative societies, of which 570 are officially registered.

Central Co-operative Union: POB 2492, Khartoum; tel. (183) 780624; largest co-operative union operating in 15 provinces.

TRADE UNIONS

All trade union activity was banned following the 1989 coup. The following organizations were active prior to that date.

Federations

Sudan Workers Trade Unions Federation (SWTUF): POB 2258, Khartoum; tel. (183) 777463; includes 42 trade unions representing c. 1.75m. public-service and private-sector workers; affiliated to the Int. Confed. of Arab Trade Unions and the Org. of African Trade Union Unity; Pres. MUHAMMAD OSMAN GAMA; Gen. Sec. YOUSUF ABU SHAMA HAMED.

Sudanese Federation of Employees and Professionals Trade Unions: POB 2398, Khartoum; tel. (183) 773818; f. 1975; includes 54 trade unions representing 250,000 mems; Pres. IBRAHIM AWADALLAH; Sec.-Gen. KAMAL AD-DIN MUHAMMAD ABDALLAH.

Transport

RAILWAYS

The total length of railway in operation in 2002 was 5,978 route-km. The main line runs from Wadi Halfa, on the Egyptian border, to al-Obeid, via Khartoum. Lines from Atbara and Sinnar connect with Port Sudan. There are lines from Sinnar to Damazin on the Blue Nile (227 km) and from Aradeiba to Nyala in the south-western province of Darfur (689 km), with a 445-km branch line from Babanousa to Wau in Bahr al-Ghazal province. In 2001 plans were announced for the construction of a rail link between Port Sudan and Moyale, Ethiopia.

Sudan Railways Corpn: POB 65, Atbara; tel. 2000; f. 1875; Gen. Man. OMAR MUHAMMAD NUR.

ROADS

Roads in northern Sudan, other than town roads, are only cleared tracks and often impassable immediately after rain. Motor traffic on roads in the former Upper Nile province is limited to the drier months of January–May. There are several good gravelled roads in Equa-

SUDAN

toria and Bahr al-Ghazal provinces which are passable all the year, but in these districts some of the minor roads become impassable after rain.

Over 48,000 km of tracks are classed as 'motorable'; there were 3,160 km of main roads and 739 km of secondary roads in 1985. A 1,190-km tarmac road linking the capital with Port Sudan was completed during 1980. In 1996, according to World Bank estimates, some 36.3% of Sudan's roads were paved. By 1997 a 270-km road linking Jaili with Atbara had been completed, as part of a scheme to provide an alternative route from Khartoum to the coast. A 484-km highway linking Khartoum, Haiya and Port Sudan was scheduled for completion in 2006.

National Transport Corpn: POB 723, Khartoum; Gen. Man. MOHI AD-DIN HASSAN MUHAMMAD NUR.

Public Corpn for Roads and Bridges: POB 756, Khartoum; tel. (183) 770794; f. 1976; Chair. ABD AR-RAHMAN HABOUD; Dir-Gen. ABDOU MUHAMMAD ABDOU.

INLAND WATERWAYS

The total length of navigable waterways served by passenger and freight services is 4,068 km, of which approximately 1,723 km is open all year. From the Egyptian border to Wadi Halfa and Khartoum navigation is limited by cataracts to short stretches, but the White Nile from Khartoum to Juba is almost always navigable.

River Transport Corpn (RTC): POB 284, Khartoum North; operates 2,500 route-km of steamers on the Nile; Chair. ALI AMIR TAHA.

River Navigation Corpn: Khartoum; f. 1970; jtly owned by Govts of Egypt and Sudan; operates services between Aswan and Wadi Halfa.

SHIPPING

Port Sudan, on the Red Sea, 784 km from Khartoum, and Suakin are the only commercial seaports.

Axis Trading Co Ltd: POB 1574, Khartoum; tel. (183) 775875; f. 1967; Chair. HASSAN A. M. SULIMAN.

Red Sea Shipping Corpn: POB 116, Khartoum; tel. (183) 777688; fax (183) 774220; e-mail redseaco@sudan.net; Gen. Man. OSMAN AMIN.

Sea Ports Corpn: Port Sudan; f. 1906; Gen. Man. MUHAMMAD TAHIR AILA.

Sudan Shipping Line Ltd: POB 426, Port Sudan; tel. 2655; and POB 1731, Khartoum; tel. (183) 780017; f. 1960; 10 vessels totalling 54,277 dwt operating between the Red Sea and western Mediterranean, northern Europe and United Kingdom; Chair. ISMAIL BAKHEIT; Gen. Man. SALAH AD-DIN OMER AL-AZIZ.

United African Shipping Co: POB 339, Khartoum; tel. (183) 780967; Gen. Man. MUHAMMAD TAHA AL-GINDI.

CIVIL AVIATION

Civil Aviation Authority: Sharia Sayed Abd ar-Rahman, Khartoum; tel. (183) 772264; Dir-Gen. ABOU BAKR GAAFAR AHMAD.

Air West Express: POB 10217, Khartoum; tel. (183) 452503; fax (183) 451703; f. 1992; passenger and freight services to destinations in Africa; Chair. SAIF M. S. OMER.

Azza Transport: POB 11586, Mak Nimir St, Khartoum; tel. (183) 783761; fax (183) 770408; e-mail sawasawa@sudanet.net; f. 1993; charter and dedicated freight to Africa and the Middle East; Man. Dir Dr GIBRIL I. MOHAMED.

Sudan Airways Co Ltd: POB 253, Sudan Airways Complex, Obeid Khatim St 19, Khartoum; tel. (183) 243708; fax (183) 243722; internet www.sudanair.com; f. 1947; internal flights and international services to Africa, the Middle East and Europe; Man. Dir AHMED ISMAEL ZUMRAWI.

Sudanese Aeronautical Services (SASCO): POB 8260, al-Amarat, Khartoum; tel. (183) 7463362; fax (183) 4433362; fmrly Sasco Air Charter; chartered services; Chair. M. M. NUR.

Trans Arabian Air Transport (TAAT): POB 1461, Africa St, Khartoum; tel. (183) 451568; fax (183) 451544; e-mail ftaats@sudanmail.net; f. 1983; dedicated freight; services to Africa, Europe and Middle East; Man. Dir Capt. EL-FATI ABDIN.

United Arabian Airlines: POB 3687, Office No. 3, Elekhwa Bldg, Atbara St, Khartoum; tel. (183) 773025; fax (183) 784402; e-mail krthq@uaa.com; internet www.uaa.com; f. 1995; charter and dedicated freight services to Africa and the Middle East; Man. Dir M. KORDOFANI.

Tourism

Public Corpn of Tourism and Hotels: POB 7104, Khartoum; tel. (183) 781764; f. 1977; Dir-Gen. Maj.-Gen. EL-KHATIM MUHAMMAD FADL.

SURINAME

Introductory Survey

Location, Climate, Language, Religion, Flag, Capital

The Republic of Suriname lies on the north-east coast of South America. It is bordered by Guyana to the west, by French Guiana to the east, and by Brazil to the south. The climate is sub-tropical, with fairly heavy rainfall and average temperatures of between 21°C (70°F) and 30°C (86°F). Average annual rainfall varies from 3,720 mm (146 ins) in the north to 804 mm (32 ins) in the south. The official language is Dutch. The other main languages are Hindustani and Javanese. The majority of the people can speak the native language Sranang Tongo, a Creole language known as Negro English or taki-taki, while Chinese, English, French and Spanish are also used. The principal religions are Christianity (professed by about 40% of the population), Hinduism (27%) and Islam (22%). The national flag (proportions 2 by 3) has five horizontal stripes: a broad central band of red (with a five-pointed yellow star in the centre), edged with white, between bands of green. The capital is Paramaribo.

Recent History

Settlers from England landed in Suriname in the 1630s, and the territory was alternately a British and a Dutch colony until it was eventually awarded to the Netherlands by the Treaty of Vienna in 1815. The colony's economy depended on large sugar plantations, for which labour was provided by slaves of African origin. Following the abolition of slavery in 1863, immigration of labourers from India and the then Dutch East Indies was encouraged, and many of them settled permanently in Suriname. This history explains the country's current ethnic diversity: there are small communities of the original Amerindian population (mainly in the interior) and of ethnic Chinese and Europeans; a Creole population, largely of African descent, constitutes about one-third of the population, as do the Asian-descended 'East' Indians (known locally as Hindustanis); the Indonesian-descended 'Javanese' form about 15% of the population, and another Creole group, the 'boschnegers' or Bush Negroes, forms a further 10% (the Bush Negroes are the Dutch-speaking descendants of escaped slaves, long-established in the rainforest as a tribalized society of four clans). Under a Charter signed in December 1954, Suriname (also known as Dutch Guiana) became an equal partner in the Kingdom of the Netherlands, with the Netherlands Antilles and the Netherlands itself, and gained full autonomy in domestic affairs.

The Hindustani-dominated Government, in power since 1969 and led by Dr Jules Sedney, resigned in February 1973. General elections in November were won by an alliance of parties, the Nationale Partij Kambinatie (NPK), which favoured complete independence from the Netherlands, and in December Henck Arron, leader of the Nationale Partij Suriname (NPS—a predominantly Creole party), became Prime Minister. Suriname became independent on 25 November 1975. Dr Johan Ferrier, hitherto the Governor of Suriname, became the new republic's first President. Some 40,000 Surinamese emigrated to the Netherlands after independence, leaving Suriname with a severely underskilled work-force. Border disputes with French Guiana and Guyana also ensued. The general election of October 1977 resulted in a clear majority for the NPK, and Henck Arron continued as Prime Minister.

The Arron administration was overthrown in February 1980 by a group of soldiers, who formed a military council, the Nationale Militaire Raad (NMR). President Ferrier refused to agree to the retention of supreme power by the NMR, and in March he appointed a civilian administration led by Dr Henk Chin-A-Sen, a former leader of the Partij Nationalistische Republiek. In August the Army Chief of Staff, NMR member Sgt-Maj. (later Lt-Col) Désiré (Desi) Bouterse (subsequently Commander-in-Chief of the armed forces), led a coup. Ferrier was replaced by Chin-A-Sen; the legislature was dissolved, and a state of emergency declared. A Hindustani-inspired counter-coup, led by Sgt-Maj. Wilfred Hawker, failed in March 1981. In September the President announced details of a draft Constitution, which sought to limit the army to a supervisory role in government. The army responded with the formation of the Revolutionary People's Front, a comprehensive political alliance headed by Bouterse and two other members of the NMR, Maj. Roy Horb and Lt (later Commdr) Iwan Graanoogst, together with three leaders of workers' and students' organizations. In February 1982 the NMR, led by Bouterse, seized power from Chin-A-Sen and his civilian Government. The Vice-President of the Supreme Court, L. Fred Ramdat Misier, was appointed interim President. Hawker was executed after attempting a further coup in March. (Chin-A-Sen left for the Netherlands, where, in January 1983, he formed the Movement for the Liberation of Suriname, which aimed to remove Bouterse from power by peaceful means.)

A state of siege was declared, and martial law was imposed in December 1982. In order to prevent the Netherlands from suspending its aid, a 12-member Cabinet of Ministers with a civilian majority was appointed, and a moderate economist, Henry Neyhorst, became Prime Minister, although Bouterse remained effectively in control. Failure to effect promised social and economic changes lost Bouterse the support of left-wing groups and trade unions, which supported the business community in demanding a return to constitutional rule. In October the arrest of Cyriel Daal, the leader of Suriname's principal trade union (De Moederbond), prompted strikes and demonstrations. In order to avert a general strike, Bouterse agreed to arrange for the election of a constituent assembly to draft a new constitution by March 1983 (to be followed by the establishment of an elected government), but he later reneged on this commitment. In December 1982 members of the armed forces burned down several buildings used by the opposition. During the ensuing disturbances, 15 prominent citizens, including Daal, were killed, in what became known as the 'December Murders'. The Government resigned, the Netherlands and the USA halted all aid, and the country was placed under rule by decree; an interim, military-dominated Government was appointed. An attempted coup in January 1983, the sixth since February 1980, resulted in the dismissal of two-thirds of the officers of the armed forces and the death of Maj. Horb. In February 1983 Dr Errol Alibux, a former Minister of Social Affairs, was appointed Prime Minister. He formed a new Cabinet of Ministers, composed of members of two left-wing parties, the Progressieve Arbeiders en Landbouwers Unie (PALU) and the Revolutionaire Volkspartij. The new Government immediately ended the restrictions imposed in December 1982.

In January 1984, after a series of widely observed strikes in support of demands for the restoration of civilian rule and the organization of free elections, Bouterse dismissed the Cabinet of Ministers. Agreement was reached with the strike organizers, following the withdrawal of proposals to increase taxation rates. An interim Government, with Wim Udenhout, a former adviser to Bouterse, as Prime Minister, was created in February to formulate a timetable for the gradual restoration of constitutional rule. Nominees of the trade unions and business sector were also included in the new Government. Bouterse hoped to consolidate his position by securing a political base through Standvaste (the 25 February Movement), which he had founded in November 1983. In December 1984 plans for a nominated National Assembly (comprising representatives of Standvaste, the trade unions and the business community) were announced. The Netherlands Government, however, refused to consider the changes as a significant move towards democratic rule, deeming them insufficient to merit the resumption of aid. None the less, the National Assembly was inaugurated in January 1985. A new Cabinet of Ministers, based on the previous administration, was formed by Udenhout.

The tripartite administration collapsed in April 1985, after the withdrawal from the Cabinet of Ministers of three of the four trade union nominees. A reconstituted Cabinet, formed in June, contained new members with links to traditional political parties. In November the ban on political parties was revoked, and in the same month, former NPS Prime Minister Arron, together with Jaggernath Lachmon of the Hindustani-based Vooruitstrevende Hervormings Partij (VHP) and Willy Soemita of the Kaum-Tani Persuatan Indonesia (KTPI), accepted an invitation to join the NMR, renamed the Topberaad (Supreme Council). By

July 1986 only two military officers remained on the Topberaad. In that month Bouterse appointed a new Cabinet of Ministers, including representatives from industry, business, political parties, trade unions and Standvaste. Pretaap Radhakishun, a business executive and member of the VHP, was appointed Prime Minister. The Cabinet drafted a new Constitution, which was approved by a national referendum in September 1987.

From July 1986 anti-Government guerrillas began a series of attacks on military posts on the eastern border of the country. The guerrillas were led by Ronnie Brunswijk (a former presidential bodyguard). Mainly Bush Negroes, they claimed that government resettlement policies threatened the autonomy of their tribal society, as guaranteed by treaties, signed in 1760, with the former Dutch authorities. It was reported that financial support for the guerrillas (known as the Jungle Commando, or Surinamese Liberation Army—SLA) was being provided by Surinamese exiles in the Netherlands, in particular by members of the Movement for the Liberation of Suriname. By November most of the eastern district of Marowijne was under guerrilla control, and the rebels had also occupied the area near Zanderij (later renamed Johan Adolf Pengel) International Airport, south of Paramaribo. Rebel attacks on the mining town of Moengo forced the closure of the country's principal bauxite mines. The town was recaptured by the armed forces in December, but the mines remained closed. At the beginning of December a state of emergency was declared in eastern and southern Suriname, and a curfew was imposed. Reports that some 200 civilians had been massacred by government troops in the search for guerrillas led to protests by the Netherlands and US Governments.

In February 1987 five members of the Cabinet of Ministers, including Radhakishun, resigned. Jules Wijdenbosch, hitherto the Minister of Internal Affairs and a member of Standvaste, was appointed Prime Minister. The entire Cabinet resigned at the end of March 1987, and a new Cabinet, led by Wijdenbosch, was appointed by Bouterse in April.

In 1987, in preparation for the general election that was to be held in November, several political parties resumed their activities. Standvaste was reconstituted, under Wijdenbosch, as the Nationale Democratische Partij (NDP—National Democratic Party). Three major opposition parties, the NPS, the VHP and the KTPI (whose name was changed to the Kerukanan Tulodo Pranatan Ingil in October 1987), announced an electoral alliance, the Front voor Demokratie en Ontwikkeling (FDO—Front for Democracy and Development). Brunswijk's SLA observed a cease-fire for the duration of the voting.

The FDO won a decisive victory in elections to the 51-seat National Assembly held on 25 November 1987. In January 1988 the National Assembly unanimously elected Ramsewak Shankar (a former Minister of Agriculture) as President of the Republic, and Henck Arron was elected Vice-President and thus (in accordance with the new Constitution) Prime Minister. In December 1987 Bouterse was appointed leader of a five-member Military Council, established under the new Constitution to 'guarantee a peaceful transition' to democracy. In July 1988 the Netherlands Government agreed to resume aid to Suriname, but under more restrictive conditions than hitherto. Aid was to be provided only on a project-by-project basis until the Suriname Government implemented the IMF's structural-adjustment programme, considered necessary to correct the economic crisis. However, relations remained tense, largely owing to the Dutch administration's mistrust of the intentions of the Surinamese army.

In July 1989 representatives of the Government and the SLA, meeting in French Guiana, signed an agreement at Kourou, which was ratified by the National Assembly in August. The main provisions of the Kourou Accord were: a general amnesty for those involved in the recent conflicts; the ending of the state of emergency; the incorporation of many members of the SLA into a special police unit for the interior of the country; and significant investment in the interior. The armed forces declared their opposition to the Accord, but took no direct action against continuing negotiations. However, at the end of August there was a further outbreak of guerrilla activity, in the west of the country, by an Amerindian group critical of some of the provisions of the Accord. The group, known as the Tucayana Amazonica, principally opposed the involvement of the SLA in the proposed police force for the interior; it also requested the restoration of the Bureau for Amerindian Affairs. Several of the group's demands were similar to those of the army command, and there were allegations that Tucayana were being armed and encouraged by the military, exploiting the traditional antipathy between the Amerindians and many of the Bush Negroes. In October, however, the Tucayana spokesmen were augmented by elected representatives of the Amerindian communities (the Commission of Eight) and the two groups met representatives of the National Assembly, who stated that the Government was prepared to supplement, but not rescind, the Kourou Accord.

Also in October 1989 Tucayana received the support of another new insurgent group, the Mandela Bush Negro Liberation Movement (BBM), which declared itself to be dissatisfied with the Kourou Accord. The BBM was formed by members of the most westerly (and, hitherto, least involved in the civil war) of the Bush Negro clans, the Matauriërs. In the same month, however, Brunswijk's SLA secured the support of another new insurgent group, the Union for Liberation and Democracy (UBD), which occupied the mining town of Moengo. Apparently composed of radical former members of the SLA, the UBD declared its support for the Accord.

On 22 December 1990 Bouterse resigned as Commander-in-Chief of the armed forces, after President Shankar failed to issue an official protest at the Netherlands' treatment of Bouterse, who was denied access to the country while in transit at Amsterdam's airport. Suspicions that Bouterse's resignation might portend a military coup were realized two days later, when the acting Commander-in-Chief of the armed forces, Graanoogst, seized power from the Government. The coup was immediately condemned by the Dutch Government, which suspended development aid to Suriname. Johan Kraag (honorary chairman of the NPS and a former Minister of Labour) was appointed provisional President on 29 December, and promptly invited Bouterse to resume command of the armed forces, thus substantiating speculation that Kraag was merely acting on behalf of Bouterse. A transitional Government (led by Jules Wijdenbosch) was sworn in on 7 January 1991, and it was announced that a general election would take place within 100 days, later extended to 150 days. In March Brunswijk and Bouterse (who had continued negotiations intermittently since 1989) signed a peace accord in the rebel stronghold of Drietabbetje. In April four rebel groups, the SLA, Tucayana, the BBM and Angula (or 'Defiance', led by Carlos Maassi), signed a further agreement with the Government, promising to respect the law and not to obstruct the conduct of free elections.

The elections, which were monitored by a delegation from the Organization of American States (OAS, see p. 333), were held on 25 May 1991. The Nieuw Front (NF), an electoral alliance comprising the members of the former FDO and the Surinaamse Partij van de Arbeid, secured 30 seats in the National Assembly, while the NDP won 12. The remaining nine seats were won by a new coalition, Democratisch Alternatief 1991 (DA '91), mainly comprising former members of the FDO critical of the Government's failure to curb the political influence of the military. Despite the fact that it had not secured the two-thirds' majority in the Assembly necessary to elect automatically its presidential candidate, Runaldo R. Venetiaan, the NF refused to consider the possibility of any agreement involving the formation of a coalition government or the cession of ministerial posts or policy commitments to either the NDP or DA '91. When a series of meetings of the National Assembly in July failed to result in any one presidential candidate securing a majority, the Chairman of the Assembly, Jaggernath Lachman, in accordance with provisions incorporated in the Constitution, convened the Vereinigde Volksvergadering (United People's Assembly), a body comprising the members of the National Assembly and representatives of the municipal and district councils, in order to elect a President. On 7 September Venetiaan was elected with an overwhelming 79% of the votes. One of Venetiaan's first acts as President was to announce, in October, the reduction of the armed forces by two-thirds and a reduction in the defence budget of 50%. These measures were introduced as part of a government programme of 'socialization' of the armed forces. In addition, amendments to the Constitution, approved in March 1992, included measures to curb the political influence of the military, removing all its constitutional duties except those of national defence and the combating of organized subversion, and banning serving members of the security forces from holding representative public office. In April the Military Council, established under the 1987 Constitution, was abolished.

In August 1992 a peace agreement was signed by the Government and the SLA and the Tucayana; the BBM also committed itself to the agreement. Under the terms of the agreement, the amnesty law envisaged under the Kourou Accord of 1989, covering all civil conflicts since 1985 and amended to include insurgent groups formed since the ratification of the Kourou Accord, was to be implemented. All weapons were to be surrendered to the Government, under OAS supervision. Following disarmament, members of all the groups would be eligible for recruitment into a special police force for the interior of the country. In addition, the Government gave assurances that the interior would receive priority in its programmes for economic development and social welfare. However, in March 2005 former guerrillas claimed that the Government had not fulfilled its pledge to provide them with jobs and medical care.

In November 1992 Bouterse resigned as Commander-in-Chief of the armed forces, prompting public concern that the move might once again signal a coup. Venetiaan's appointment of Col (retd) Arthy Gorré as Bouterse's successor resulted in a confrontation between the Government and senior military officers in April 1993. (Gorré had supported the 1980 coup staged by Bouterse, but had resigned from the armed forces in 1987, following a disagreement with the latter.) Graanoogst, who had occupied the position of Commander-in-Chief on an interim basis since Bouterse's resignation, refused to concede the post to Gorré. He was supported by his fellow members of the military high command and by Bouterse, who, despite his resignation, remained effectively in control of the armed forces. Venetiaan subsequently deferred Gorré's appointment until mid-May, when it was endorsed by a majority in the National Assembly, despite veiled threats of a military coup and an attack on the national television station, which had allegedly been instigated by Bouterse. All four members of the military high command subsequently acceded to a request by the National Assembly for their resignations. Three of them, including Graanoogst, later accepted posts as advisers to the Government, thus assuaging fears of an escalation of the conflict. Indications that the Netherlands might intervene to assist the Government were also considered influential in averting further military defiance of civilian rule.

At a general election conducted on 23 May 1996 no single party secured a legislative majority, much less the two-thirds' majority necessary to elect its presidential candidate. The NF secured 24 seats, the NDP 16, DA '91 four, Pendawa Lima four and Alliantie the remaining three seats. Venetiaan, having rejected an offer from Bouterse to form a coalition government, began negotiations with the three other parties with representation in the legislature. However, the negotiations failed to produce agreement on a coalition. Neither Venetiaan nor the candidate of the NDP, former Prime Minister Jules Wijdenbosch, were able to command the two-thirds' majority in the National Assembly necessary to secure the presidency, and responsibility for electing the president consequently passed to the Vereinigde Volksvergadering. With only a simple majority required to win, Wijdenbosch obtained 438 votes, against 407 for Venetiaan, and was inaugurated as President on 14 September. The KTPI and a dissident faction of the VHP, the Beweging voor Vernieuwing en Democratie (BVD), subsequently left the NF alliance, joining an NDP-led coalition. However, the support of the KTPI and the BVD was conditional upon Bouterse's exclusion from the new Government. The parties also stipulated that the portfolios of Foreign Affairs, Finance, Defence and Internal Affairs should not be allocated to the NDP. The new coalition Government, appointed in September, comprised members of the NDP, KTPI, BVD and the Hernieuwde Progressieve Partij (HPP).

In August 1997 the Government recalled its ambassador to the Netherlands for consultations, following the decision by the Netherlands Government to seek an international arrest warrant for Bouterse on charges of illegal drugs-trafficking. Bouterse was reportedly in hiding following the issue of the warrant. Talks aimed at improving relations between the Governments of Suriname and the Netherlands were conducted, at ministerial level, in New York, USA, in April 1998. However, the fact that Bouterse was continuing to serve on the Council of State, as part of the Suriname Government, remained a serious source of dissatisfaction for the Netherlands' delegation, which refused a request from Suriname's chief of police that the warrant for Bouterse's arrest be withdrawn. In March 1999 the Dutch authorities began legal proceedings against Bouterse *in absentia*, on charges of corruption and drugs-trafficking. Similar *in absentia* court proceedings were initiated in the Netherlands against the guerrilla leader Ronnie Brunswijk (who was found guilty on charges of drugs-trafficking in April, and sentenced to eight years' imprisonment) and the President of the Central Bank of Suriname, Henk Goedschalk, who was accused of deliberate financial mismanagement. Despite the Suriname Government's refusal to accede to the demands of the Netherlands Government for the apprehension and extradition of Bouterse, in April President Wijdenbosch dismissed Bouterse from the Council of State, claiming that he represented a divisive force in Surinamese politics. In mid-July Bouterse was convicted and sentenced, *in absentia*, to 16 years in prison (later reduced to 11 years) and fined US $2.3m. The Attorney-General of the Netherlands filed further charges (this time for torture resulting in death) against Bouterse in January 2000. The new charges concerned the 1982 December Murders and arose because of a complaint filed by relatives of the victims.

Dissatisfaction with the Government's management of the economy increased in 1998 and 1999. In June 1998 widespread industrial action brought chaos to the country for several days. There was further labour unrest in the agriculture and mining sectors later in the year. Following another national strike, which brought the country to a virtual standstill, the entire Cabinet resigned in late May 1999. On 1 June the National Assembly passed a vote of 'no confidence' in the President. However, the result fell short of the two-thirds' majority needed to force him from office and Wijdenbosch refused to tender his own resignation. Instead he called for early elections to be held by 25 May 2000 and asked the cabinet members to remain in office. However, in early December the Government resubmitted its resignation after several of its members were implicated in financial and sexual scandals. President Wijdenbosch accepted several ministers' resignations, distributing their portfolios among the remaining ministers. Prior to the election, in an apparent attempt to distance himself from Bouterse, Wijdenbosch left the NDP and formed a new electoral coalition, Democratisch Nationaal Platform 2000 (DNP 2000).

Voting proceeded on 25 May 2000, when Venetiaan's NF (an electoral alliance comprising the NPS, the Pertajah Luhur, the Surinaamse Partij van de Arbeid, and the VHP) secured 33 of the 51 seats; the Millenium Combinatie (an alliance including the NDP) took 10, and DNP 2000 three. Having narrowly failed to secure the two-thirds' majority to appoint a new President directly, the NF entered into coalition negotiations with the smaller parties. On 4 August Venetiaan was elected to the presidency for the second time, winning 37 of the 51 votes cast in the National Assembly. On assuming office on 12 August, the new President pledged to fight corruption, accelerate economic development and reduce debt. In October the Dutch Government agreed to resume aid to Suriname, which had been suspended since 1998.

On 1 November 2000 the Suriname Court of Justice ruled that Bouterse must stand trial in Suriname in connection with the December Murders. In May 2001 a key witness in the case against Bouterse, the former activist and founder of the Labour Party, Fred Derby, died. In September, the Dutch High Court ruled that Bouterse could not be prosecuted in the Netherlands under the UN's Convention on Torture, as the legislation had not been ratified in that country until 1989, seven years after the atrocities took place. However, in the following month it upheld Bouterse's 1999 conviction for drugs-trafficking and demanded he be extradited to serve his 11-year prison sentence. However, the Surinamese Constitution prohibited extradition of its citizens.

The arrival of a detachment of Dutch marines in June 2002 prompted speculation that the Dutch Government would attempt to arrest Bouterse; the Netherlands claimed that the troops were merely engaged in a joint military exercise. However, in the same month, the Dutch Government dispatched forensic specialists to assist Surinamese police-officers investigating the December Murders. In December a judge presiding over the case ordered the exhumation of the remains of the 15 murder victims. A series of burglaries at the homes of the Minister of Justice and a leading judge in April 2003 were thought to be connected to the investigation; a former police-officer was subsequently arrested for questioning. In December 2004, following a four-year investigation, a military court indicted Bouterse and 25 other suspects for the 1982 December Murders. The trials were expected to begin in 2006. In August 2005 the OAS's Inter-American Court of Human Rights instructed the Government to investigate a massacre that occurred in the Maroon village of Moiwana in 1986, during Bouterse's presidency, and to pay US $13,000 compensation to the 130 survivors.

Legislative elections were scheduled to be held on 25 May 2005. In March the NDP formally nominated Bouterse as its candidate in the indirect presidential election that was to follow the legislative ballot, in June. The USA reacted to the NDP's nomination by threatening to sever diplomatic links with Suriname in the event of Bouterse being re-elected President. The NDP accused the USA of political interference and lodged a formal complaint with the Caribbean Community and Common Market (CARICOM, see p. 183) and the OAS. The other main contenders for the presidency were the incumbent Venetiaan, who was seeking a third term in office, and former President Jules Wijdenbosch, representing the Volksalliantie Voor Vooruitgang (VVV—People's Alliance for Progress), an alliance comprising the DNP 2000, the BVD and the Democratisch Alternatief.

The ruling NF's popularity waned in the months preceding the election. Mounting political pressure regarding allegations of corruption led, on 11 May 2005, to the resignation of the Minister of Public Works, Dewanand Balesar, pending an investigation into his alleged participation in a scheme that awarded contracts to fictitious contractors. (In September the National Assembly voted to remove Balesar's immunity from prosecution.) Nevertheless, at the election the NF retained its position as the largest party in the National Assembly, attracting 39.4% of the votes cast and securing 23 of the 51 seats. The NDP also performed well, obtaining 22.2% of the ballot and 15 seats, while the VVV secured just five seats (and 13.8% of the votes). Bouterse and former guerrilla leader Ronnie Brunswijk were both elected to the legislature.

Following the election the NF entered into negotiations with smaller parties in order to garner the two-thirds' parliamentary majority needed to re-elect Venetiaan to the presidency. As a result, on 13 July 2005 Venetiaan was nominated by a coalition of the NF, the DA '91 and the A-Combinatie (a coalition that included the Algemene Bevrijdings- en Ontwikkeling Partij—General Liberation and Development Party—led by Brunswijk). In a surprise move, two days later the NDP presidential candidate Bouterse withdrew from the contest, nominating his former running mate Rabin Parmessar in his stead. The NDP and the VVV formed a coalition, nominating Wilfried Roseval, formerly Wijenbosch's running mate, for the vice-presidency. However, neither Venetiaan or Parmessar secured the requisite two-thirds' majority during the two rounds of voting held on 19 and 26 July. Responsibility for electing the new head of state subsequently passed to the 891-member Vereinigde Volksvergadering. With only a simple majority required, on 3 August Venetiaan secured the presidency with 560 votes, compared with 315 for Parmessar. At his inauguration on 12 August President Venetiaan pledged to combat criminal activity and to continue to pursue established financial policies and budgetary discipline to secure economic stability.

In an attempt to reduce the cost of imported petroleum, in July 2005 the Government signed the PetroCaribe energy accord with Venezuela, thereby gaining access to favourable energy concessions and the option of preferential terms should the price of petroleum exceed US $40 per barrel. However, the steep increases in the retail cost of petroleum products, and consequently of transportation, led to civil unrest in the latter half of 2005 and early 2006. Public transport was disrupted across the country on 12–13 September as a result of industrial action by bus drivers; furthermore, on 30 January 2006 teachers, angry at the Government's failure to increase transport subsidies, began three days of demonstrations outside government buildings. Power shortages in the west of the country in February prompted further protests.

On 19 January 2006 the Minister of Trade and Industry, Siegfried Gilds, resigned following accusations of money-laundering and membership of a criminal organization. He was succeeded by Clifford Marica, hitherto Minister of Labour, Technological Development and Environment. Responsibility for this portfolio was assumed by Joyce Amarello-Williams.

On 13 March 2006 the Surinamese ambassador to the Netherlands, Edgar Amanh, tendered his resignation following an incident at Schiphol Airport, Amsterdam, during which the Surinamese Minister of Transport, Communications and Tourism, Alice H. Amafo, was requested to undergo an unexpected security inspection. Amanh was reportedly held responsible for failing to inform the Government about the new Dutch security measures.

The illegal trafficking of drugs continued to be a problem in Suriname. The UN's Drug Control Programme estimated that some 22 metric tons of cocaine were transported annually to Europe via Suriname. In March 2002 three Surinamese, three Brazilians and one Colombian were sentenced to up to 14 years' imprisonment for attempting to bring 1,198 kgs of cocaine into the country. The men had been arrested in March 2001 in what had been the largest ever seizure of illegal drugs by the Surinamese police. In October 2002 the Netherlands announced the provision of training and equipment to assist the Surinamese security forces' campaign against drugs-trafficking and funds for the construction of a new police headquarters in Paramaribo. Following negotiations held in January 2004 the two Governments agreed to co-operate on intelligence-gathering and sea patrols; it was also agreed that security would be increased on both passenger and cargo flights from Suriname.

Suriname has a territorial dispute with Guyana over an estimated 15,000 sq km (6,000 sq miles) of land in the Corentije region, and another with French Guiana over land to the east of the Litani river. In April 1990, with the mediation of the UN High Commissioner for Refugees, France and Suriname agreed terms providing for the repatriation of an estimated 10,000 Surinamese refugees from French Guiana. In October French Guiana was reported to have begun forcible repatriation of Surinamese refugees. In April 1992, under a plan agreed between France, Suriname and the UN, some 6,000 Surinamese refugees were offered voluntary repatriation. In late July the Suriname Government delivered an official protest to the French authorities concerning the alleged compulsory repatriation of refugees. By that time some 2,500 Surinamese refugees had returned to Suriname.

In 1995 Guyana and Suriname reached agreement on the establishment of a joint commission in order to seek a resolution of the countries' territorial dispute. In June 1998 Guyana granted the Canadian-based company, CGX Energy Inc, a concession to explore for petroleum and gas along the continental margin off Guyana, part of which lay within the disputed maritime area. In May 2000 Suriname formally claimed that Guyana had violated its territorial integrity, and invited Guyana to begin negotiations regarding the maritime boundary. In early June the Surinamese Navy forced CGX to remove the drilling platform. In June 2001 the Ministers of Foreign Affairs of the two countries issued a declaration of their Governments' commitment to peace and co-operation. The Guyana–Suriname Bilateral Co-operation Council was revived in January 2002 and members agreed to investigate the possibility of a joint exploration for petroleum in the disputed territory. The two Governments also agreed to improve co-operation in trade, investments and joint ventures. However, relations again became strained in March 2003 when the Surinamese Government decreed that maps of the country circulated by all diplomatic missions in Paramaribo must include the disputed territory. Guyana lodged a formal protest and sent a naval detachment to patrol the Corentijn River. Both countries subsequently strengthened their military presence in the area and in February 2004 two Surinamese gunboats expelled a Canadian company, exploring for oil with Guyana's permission, from the area. At the end of that month Guyana referred the maritime boundary dispute to arbitration under the provisions of the UN Convention on the Law of the Sea. Representatives of the two countries participated in talks in Hamburg, Germany, in May. Guyana also requested a number of interim measures that would allow gas and oil exploration to continue. It was anticipated that a provisional ruling would be followed by a substantive hearing within three years. In December, at Suriname's behest, the Netherlands denied Guyana access to its archived documents on the border issue. The British Government made its archives available to both Guyana and Suriname. Guyana subsequently filed a protest with the International Tribunal for the Law of the Sea and the case was submitted to court in March 2005.

In March 2002 the Surinamese and Dutch Ministers of Foreign Affairs approved the establishment of a Returned Emigration Committee to oversee the voluntary repatriation of Surinamese with Dutch nationality without the loss of social benefits. In October 2004 customs officials in Suriname and the Netherlands reached an agreement to share information in an attempt to reduce tax evasion on imports from the Netherlands.

Government

Under the provisions of the 1987 Constitution, legislative power is held by the National Assembly, with 51 members, elected by universal adult suffrage for a five-year term. The Assembly elects the President and the Vice-President of the Republic. Executive power is vested in the President, who appoints the Cabinet of Ministers, led by the Vice-President, who is also the Prime Minister. The Cabinet is responsible to the National

Assembly. A Council of State, comprising civilians and members of the armed forces, advises the President and the Cabinet of Ministers on policy, and has power of veto over legislation approved by the Assembly. Suriname comprises 10 administrative districts.

Defence

Suriname's armed forces numbered 1,840 men and women in August 2005. There is an army of 1,400, a navy of 240, and an air force of about 200. Defence expenditure in 2004 was estimated at US $7.7m.

Economic Affairs

In 2004, according to estimates by the World Bank, Suriname's gross national income (GNI), measured at average 2002–04 prices, was US $996.7m., equivalent to $2,250 per head. During 1995–2004, it was estimated, the population increased at an average annual rate of 0.9%, while gross domestic product (GDP) per head increased, in real terms, by an average of 1.9% per year. Overall GDP increased, in real terms, at an average annual rate of 2.8% in 1995–2004; growth was 4.6% in 2004.

Agriculture (including hunting, forestry and fishing) contributed an estimated 6.9% of GDP (excluding the informal sector) and employed 8.0% of the employed population in 2004. The principal crop is rice, which supplies domestic demand and provided 1.4% of export earnings in 2003. Bananas are cultivated for export, together with plantains, sugar cane and citrus fruits, while Suriname also produces coconuts, maize and vegetables. In April 2002 the Government closed the state-run banana company Surland after it accumulated debt of some US $8m. However, the company was subsequently restructured with the aid of a US $6m. loan from the Inter-American Development Bank (IDB, see p. 284), and production and exports resumed in March 2004. In January 2005 some US $23m. was granted by the Dutch Government to assist the diversification of the agricultural sector and to improve rural roads and irrigation systems. Livestock is being developed, as are the extensive timber reserves (more than 80% of Suriname's total land area is covered by forest). Commercial fishing is important (providing an estimated 5.8% of total export revenue in 2003). According to government estimates, agricultural GDP increased by 2.5% per year in 2000–04; the sector grew by an estimated 6.1% in 2003 and by 6.2% in 2004.

Industry (including mining, manufacturing, public utilities and construction) contributed 38.3% of GDP (excluding the informal sector) and engaged some 22.9% of the employed labour force in 2004. The principal activity is the bauxite industry, which dominates both the mining and manufacturing sectors. In early 2005 Alcoa World Alumina and Chemicals (AWAC) completed a project to increase production at the refinery in Paranam by 250,000 metric tons, to 2.2m. tons per year. In the early 2000s there were plans to build an industrial development zone near to Johan Adolf Pengel International Airport at Zanderij. According to government estimates, industrial GDP increased by an annual average of 7.1% in 2000–04; the sector increased by 4.9% in 2003 and by a dramatic 13.7% in 2004.

Mining and quarrying contributed an estimated 11.3% of GDP (excluding the informal sector) and engaged 5.9% of the employed labour force in 2004. The principal product is bauxite (used in the manufacture of aluminium), of which Suriname is one of the world's leading producers (producing an estimated 4.2m. metric tons in 2003). In early 2003 the US-based aluminium company Alcoa reached an accord with the Government to allow Alcoa to increase the capacity of its existing bauxite operations in the country. Alcoa was also granted permission for a joint venture with the Australian company BHP for an aluminium melting plant and hydroelectric dam in the Backhuis Mountains. In November 2004 Alcoa and BHP Billiton announced joint plans to invest in two new bauxite mines, which were scheduled to begin operations in 2006. The large-scale exploitation of gold in central-eastern Suriname was postponed in the late 1990s, owing to falling gold prices; gold reserves at the Gross Rosebel mine, situated some 80 km south of Paramaribo, were estimated at 2.4m. ounces (oz). In late 2002 the Canadian gold-mining corporation Cambior began construction on new facilities at Gross Rosebel. Extraction began in January 2004 and in that year as a whole gold production reportedly reached a record 694,100 oz. In 2003 gold contributed some 22.0% of total export revenue. Reserves of petroleum in Suriname are exploited at a rate of around 12,500 b/d. Some 40% of production is for export, but much is used domestically in the bauxite industry. Unproven reserves are also thought to exist in the Saramacca district. Suriname also has extensive deposits of iron ore and reserves of manganese, copper, nickel, platinum and kaolin. According to government estimates, the GDP of the mining sector increased by an average of 10.6% per year in 2000–04; sectoral GDP remained steady in 2003 before increasing by 31.3% in 2004.

Manufacturing contributed an estimated 17.2% of GDP (excluding the informal sector) and engaged an estimated 7.0% of the employed labour force in 2004. Bauxite refining and smelting is the principal industry (alumina accounted for an estimated 52.6% of export revenue in 2003), but there are also important food-processing industries and manufacturers of cigarettes, beverages and chemical products. According to government figures, manufacturing GDP increased by an estimated average of 6.0% per year in 2000–04; the sector expanded by an estimated 5.6% in 2003 and by a robust 9.4% in 2004.

Energy is currently derived principally from hydrocarbon fuels, which are mainly imported; in 2003 fuels and lubricants accounted for 13.8% of total merchandise imports. The country has considerable potential for the development of hydroelectric power; there is a hydroelectric station for the aluminium industry. In April 2004 the Government announced plans to install a major power line from the Afobakka hydroelectric dam to Paramaribo. The three-year project would be undertaken by two companies based in India and financed by a loan from the Indian Government. In 2001 Suriname produced 1,870m. kWh of electricity, derived mostly from hydroelectric power.

The services sector contributed some 54.8% of GDP (excluding the informal sector) and engaged an estimated 64.3% of the employed labour force in 2004. The GDP of the services sector increased by an estimated average of 5.3% per year in 2000–04; sectoral growth was 7.7% in 2003 and 5.1% in 2004.

In 2004 Suriname recorded a visible trade surplus of US $67.8m., and there was a deficit of $145.7m. on the current account of the balance of payments. The principal source of imports was the USA (providing 31.2% of total imports in 2003); other significant suppliers were the Netherlands (17.8%), Trinidad and Tobago (11.9%) and the People's Republic of China (6.9%). The principal markets for exports in 2003 were the USA (an estimated 21.0% of the total), Norway (16.5%) and France (9.1%). The principal imports in 2003 were machinery and transport equipment, mineral fuels and lubricants, manufactured goods, and food and live animals. The principal exports the same year were alumina, gold, and shrimp and fish.

In 2003 there was an estimated budgetary deficit of 3.2m. Surinamese dollars (equivalent to 0.1% of GDP). At the end of 2002 the total external public debt stood at an estimated US $319.8m., of which $161.9m. was long-term public debt. By the end of December 2004 total external public debt had declined to US $235.6m. The annual rate of inflation averaged 30.0% in 1995–2002. Consumer prices increased by an average of 15.5% in 2002 and by an average of 23.0% in 2003. According to official sources, the rate of unemployment was 9.5% in 2004. It was estimated that the informal sector contributed an estimated 15.7% of GDP in 2004.

In February 1995 Suriname was granted full membership of the Caribbean Community and Common Market (CARICOM, see p. 183). It was also one of the six founder members of CARICOM's Caribbean Single Market and Economy (CSME), established on 1 January 2006. The CSME was intended to enshrine the free movement of goods, services and labour throughout the CARICOM region.

Economic activity is relatively diversified in range, but the dominant sector is the bauxite industry. On assuming office in September 2000, the Government of Runaldo Venetiaan discovered that most of the country's gold reserves had been converted into US dollars. With the country nearing bankruptcy, in October the new President announced a series of measures intended to stabilize the exchange rate and the domestic inflation rate. The official exchange rate was devalued by 89% and tariffs on utilities were raised. As a result, the annual inflation rate fell to 38.6% in 2001 and to 15.5% in 2002. Following relatively slow growth of 3.0% in 2002, public-sector salaries were 'frozen' and sales tax was increased by 3%. In its annual report in 2003 the IMF commended the Venetiaan Government's economic policy and recommended further fiscal consolidation, through economic diversification, continued privatization and further tax reform. The improved macroeconomic stability was reflected by the increased confidence of international investors and a recommencement of international aid negotiations. However, owing to rising international oil prices, government fuel

SURINAME

subsidies contributed to a widening of the fiscal deficit, which reached an estimated 4.0% of GDP in 2005. The raising of the fixed fuel retail price in late 2005 prompted protests from fuel retailers. The annual rate of increase in consumer prices increased in 2003, to 23.0%, but fell to an estimated 8.8% in 2005 and, despite the steep increase in the price of fuel, was expected to decline further, to 8.0%, in 2006. In his third term in office (2005–), President Venetiaan proposed to establish a new tax collection agency and to proceed with the privatization of Surland, the rice producer Stichting Machinale Landbouw and the timber company Bruynzeel Houtmaatschappij. The economy benefited from strong international bauxite prices in 2005, which contributed to estimated GDP growth of 4.1%. The economy was forecast to increase by a more modest 2.8% in 2006. The stricter fiscal regime implemented by Venetiaan's administration contributed to a stable economic outlook, but in 2005 the IMF nevertheless highlighted Suriname's dependence on a non-renewable resource and recommended that the Government establish a revenue stabilization fund in preparation for the eventual depletion of bauxite deposits.

Education

Primary education is compulsory for children between seven and 12 years of age. Primary education begins at six years of age and lasts for six years. Secondary education comprises a first cycle of four years and a second cycle of three years. All education in government and denominational schools is provided free of charge. In 2002/03 the total enrolment in primary education was equivalent to 97.0% of children in the relevant age-group (males 95.8%; females 98.2%), while the total enrolment in secondary education was equivalent to 63.7% of children in the relevant age-group (males 53.6%; females 74.1%). The traditional educational system, inherited from the Dutch, was amended after the 1980 revolution to place greater emphasis on serving the needs of Suriname's population. This included a literacy campaign and programmes of adult education. Higher education is provided by technical and vocational schools and by the University of Suriname at Paramaribo, which has faculties of law, economics, medicine, social sciences and technology. Of total expenditure by the Central Government in 1996, an estimated Sf 3,480.5m (3.2%) was for education. In March 2003 the Inter-American Development Bank (IDB, see p. 284) approved a US $12.5m. loan to fund the reform of the basic education system into a single 10-year cycle. It was also intended to provide for a modernized curriculum with redesigned text books and a reform of the examination system. It was hoped that the funds would result in a 10% increase in the number of pupils who finished sixth grade and a 20% reduction in drop-out and repetition rates. A further $13m. grant for the sector was approved by the Dutch Government in January 2005.

Public Holidays

2006: 1 January (New Year's Day), March* (Phagwa), 14–17 April (Easter), 1 May (Labour Day), 1 July (National Union Day), 23 October (Id al-Fitr, end of Ramadan), 25 November (Independence Day), 25–26 December (Christmas).

2007: 1 January (New Year's Day), March* (Phagwa), 6–9 April (Easter), 1 May (Labour Day), 1 July (National Union Day), 13 October (Id al-Fitr, end of Ramadan), 25 November (Independence Day), 25–26 December (Christmas).

* Exact date dependent upon sightings of the moon.

Weights and Measures

The metric system is in force.

Statistical Survey

Sources (unless otherwise stated): Algemeen Bureau voor de Statistiek, Kromme Elleboogstraat 10, POB 244, Paramaribo; tel. 473927; fax 425004; e-mail info@statistics-suriname.org; internet www.statistics-suriname.org; Ministry of Trade and Industry, Havenlaan 3, POB 9354, Paramaribo; tel. 475080; fax 477602.

AREA AND POPULATION

Area: 163,820 sq km (63,251 sq miles).

Population: 355,240 (males 175,814, females 179,426) at census of 1 July 1980; 492,829 (males 247,846, females 244,618, not known 365) at census of 2 August 2004.

Density (census of 2004): 3.0 per sq km.

Ethnic Groups (1980 census, percentage): Creole 34.70; Hindustani 33.49; Javanese 16.33; Bush Negro 9.55; Amerindian 3.10; Chinese 1.55; European 0.44; Others 0.84.

Religious Affiliation (census of 2 August 2004): Christianity 200,744; Hinduism 98,240; Islam 66,307; Other (incl. none) 50,334; Not reported 77,204; *Total* 492,829.

Administrative Districts (population at census of 2 August 2004): Paramaribo 242,946; Wanica 85,986; Nickerie 36,639; Coronie 2,887; Saramacca 15,980; Commewijne 24,649; Marowijne 16,642; Para 18,749; Brokopondo 14,215; Sipaliwini 34,136; *Total* 492,829.

Principal Towns (estimated population at 1 July 1996): Paramaribo (capital) 205,000; Lelydorp 15,600; Nieuw Nickerie 11,100. Source: Thomas Brinkoff, *City Population* (internet www.citypopulation.de).

Births and Deaths (2000): Registered live births 9,804 (birth rate 22.5 per 1,000); Registered deaths 3,090 (death rate 7.1 per 1,000).

Expectation of Life (WHO estimates, years at birth): 66 (males 63; females 69) in 2003. Source: WHO, *World Health Report*.

Economically Active Population ('000 persons aged 15–64 years, census of 2004): Agriculture, hunting, forestry and fishing 12,593; Mining and quarrying 9,308; Manufacturing 10,971; Utilities 1,659; Construction 14,031; Trade 25,012; Hotels, restaurants and bars 4,833; Transport, storage and communication 8,711; Financial intermediation 2,723; Real estate, renting and business activities 6,350; Public administration and defence 27,995; Education 8,355; Health and social work 6,797; Other community, social and personal service activities 9,911; Unknown 7,456; *Total employed* 156,705 (males 101,919, females 54,768, unknown 18); Unemployed 16,425; *Total labour force* 173,130.

HEALTH AND WELFARE
Key Indicators

Total Fertility Rate (children per woman, 2003): 2.4.
Under-5 Mortality Rate (per 1,000 live births, 2004): 39.
HIV/AIDS (% of persons aged 15–49, 2003): 1.7.
Physicians (per 1,000 head, 2000): 0.45.
Hospital Beds (per 1,000 head, 1996): 3.74.
Health Expenditure (2002): US $ per head (PPP): 385.
Health Expenditure (2002): % of GDP: 8.6.
Health Expenditure (2002): public (% of total): 41.8.
Access to Water (% of persons, 2002): 92.
Access to Sanitation (% of persons, 2002): 93.
Human Development Index (2003): ranking: 86.
Human Development Index (2003): value: 0.755.

For sources and definitions, see explanatory note on p. vi.

AGRICULTURE, ETC.

Principal Crops (FAO estimates, '000 metric tons, 2004): Rice (paddy) 195.0; Roots and tubers 5; Sugar cane 120; Coconuts 9; Vegetables 22; Bananas 43; Plantains 12; Oranges 13; Other citrus fruit 4.

Livestock (FAO estimates, '000 head, 2004): Cattle 137; Sheep and Goats 15; Pigs 25; Chickens 3,800.

Livestock Products (FAO estimates, '000 metric tons, 2004): Beef and veal 2; Pig meat 1; Poultry meat 6; Cows' milk 9; Hen eggs 3.

Forestry (FAO estimates, '000 cu metres, 2004): *Roundwood Removals:* Sawlogs, veneer logs and logs for sleepers 156; Other industrial wood 7; Fuel wood 44; Total 207. *Sawnwood Production:* Total (incl. railway sleepers) 46.

Fishing (FAO estimates, '000 metric tons, 2002): Capture 28.2 (Marine fishes 11.6; Penaeus shrimps 2.4; Atlantic seabob 13.9); Aquaculture 0.2; *Total catch* 28.4.

Source: FAO.

SURINAME

MINING

Production (2003, unless otherwise indicated): Crude petroleum ('000 barrels) 4,300; Bauxite ('000 metric tons) 4,215. Source: US Geological Survey.

INDUSTRY

Production ('000 metric tons, unless otherwise indicated, 2001): Gold-bearing ores (kg) 300; Gravel and crushed stone 85; Distillate fuel oil 26; Residual fuel oils 258; Cement 60; Alumina 1,900; Beer of barley 16; Coconut oil 0.82; Palm oil 0.22; Cigarettes 483 million (1996); Plywood ('000 cubic metres) 3; Electricity (million kWh) 1,870. Sources: mainly UN, *Industrial Commodity Statistics Yearbook* and FAO. *2003:* Alumina 2,005. Source: IMF, *Suriname: Selected Issues and Statistical Appendix* (November 2003 and March 2005).

FINANCE

Currency and Exchange Rates: 100 cents = 1 Surinamese dollar. *Sterling, Dollar and Euro Equivalents* (30 December 2005): £1 sterling = 4.718 Surinamese dollars; US $1 = 2.740 Surinamese dollars; €1 = 3.232 Surinamese dollars; 1,000 Surinamese dollars = £211.95 = $364.96 = €309.37. *Average Exchange Rate* (Surinamese dollars per US $): 2.625 in 2003; 2.734 in 2004; 2.732 in 2005. *Note:* Between 1971 and 1993 the official market rate was US $1 = 1.785 guilders. A new free market rate was introduced in June 1993, and a unified, market-determined rate took effect in July 1994. A mid-point rate of US $1 = 401.0 guilders was in effect between September 1996 and January 1999. A new currency, the Surinamese dollar, was introduced on 1 January 2004, and was equivalent to 1,000 old guilders. Some data in this survey are still presented in terms of the former currency.

Budget (million Surinamese dollars, 2003): *Revenue:* Direct taxation 308.7; Indirect taxation 429.5 (Domestic taxes on goods and services 175.2, Taxes on international trade 251.2, Other taxes (incl. bauxite levy) 3.0); Non-tax revenue 119.1; Total 857.3 (excl. grants 62.3). *Expenditure:* Wages and salaries 406.0; Current transfers 139.1; Goods and services 203.6; Interest payments 65.2; Capital 98.7; Total 912.6 (excl. net lending 10.2). Source: IMF, *Suriname: Selected Issues and Statistical Appendix* (March 2005).

International Reserves (US $ million at 31 December 2004): Gold (national valuation) 7.52; IMF special drawing rights 1.89; Reserve position in IMF 9.51; Foreign exchange 118.00; Total 136.92. Source: IMF, *International Financial Statistics*.

Money Supply (million Surinamese dollars at 31 December 2004): Currency outside banks 246,826; Demand deposits at deposit money banks 414,364; Total money (incl. others) 701,316. Source: IMF, *International Financial Statistics*.

Cost of Living (Consumer Price Index for Paramaribo area; base: October–December 2000 = 100): 138.6 in 2001; 160.1 in 2002; 196.9 in 2003. Source: IMF, *International Financial Statistics*.

National Income and Product (Sf million at current prices, 1998): Compensation of employees 213,371; Operating surplus 109,143; *Domestic factor incomes* 322,514; Consumption of fixed capital 38,697; *GDP at factor cost* 361,210; Indirect taxes 53,644; *Less* subsidies 7,726; *GDP in purchasers' values* 407,128; Net factor income from abroad −244; *Gross national product* 406,884; *Less* consumption of fixed capital 38,697; *National income in market prices* 368,187. Source: UN Economic Commission for Latin America and the Caribbean, *Statistical Yearbook*.

Expenditure on the Gross Domestic Product ('000 Surinamese dollars at current prices, preliminary figures, 2003): Public consumption 814,013; Private consumption 1,971,593; Public investment 47,667; Private investment 674,337; Exports of goods and non-factor services 654,589; *Less* Imports of goods and non-factor services 1,508,804; *GDP in purchasers' values* 2,653,396. Source: IMF, *Suriname: Selected Issues* (March 2005).

Gross Domestic Product by Economic Activity ('000 Surinamese dollars at current prices, preliminary figures, 2004): Agriculture, hunting and forestry 180,247; Fishing 37,970; Mining and quarrying 359,090; Manufacturing 546,829; Electricity, gas and water 194,127; Construction 119,063; Wholesale and retail trade 397,342; Restaurants and hotels 61,634; Transport, storage and communications 307,544; Financial intermediation 234,490; Real estate, renting and business activities 233,552; Public administration 268,064; Education 163,528; Health and social work 22,576; Other community, social and personal services 54,067; Informal sector 593,753; *Sub-total* 3,773,876; *Less* Imputed bank service charge 96,411; *GDP at factor cost* 3,677,465; Taxes on products, less subsidies 429,852; *GDP in purchasers' values* 4,107,318.

Balance of Payments (US $ million, preliminary figures, 2004): Exports of goods f.o.b. 880.6; Imports of goods f.o.b. −812.8; *Trade balance* 67.8; Exports of services 64.5; Imports of services −208.4; *Balance on goods and services* −76.1; Other income (net) −138.9; *Balance on goods, services and income* −215.0; Current transfers received (net) 69.3; *Current balance* −145.7; Capital account (net) 23.0; Financial account (net) 146.0; Net errors and omissions 7.6; *Overall balance* 30.9. Source: IMF, *Staff Report for the 2004 Article IV Consultation* (March 2005).

EXTERNAL TRADE

Principal Commodities (US $ million, 2003): *Imports c.i.f.:* Food and live animals 84.2; Mineral fuels, lubricants, etc. 96.9; Chemicals 61.8; Manufactured goods 116.3; Machinery and transport equipment 239.2; Total (incl. others, excl. re-exports) 703.9. *Exports:* Alumina 335.8; Gold 140.3; Shrimp and fish 36.9; Crude oil 34.7; Rice 9.1; Total (incl. others) 638.5. Source: IMF, *Suriname: Selected Issues* (March 2005).

Principal Trading Partners (US $ million, 2003): *Imports:* Belgium 14.6; Brazil 18.6; China, People's Republic 48.4; Germany 20.7; Italy 9.3; Japan 43.1; Netherlands 125.5; Trinidad and Tobago 83.8; United Kingdom 18.2; USA 219.9; Total (incl. others) 703.9. *Exports:* Barbados 9.8; France 58.2; Iceland 26.5; Japan 12.1; Netherlands 23.9; Norway 105.6; Trinidad and Tobago 11.1; USA 134.3; Total (incl. others) 638.5. Source: IMF, *Suriname: Selected Issues* (March 2005).

TRANSPORT

Road Traffic (registered motor vehicles, 2000 estimates): Passenger cars 61,365; Buses and coaches 2,393; Lorries and vans 20,827; Motorcycles and mopeds 30,598.

Shipping: *International Sea-borne Freight Traffic* (estimates, '000 metric tons, 2001): Goods loaded 2,306; Goods unloaded 1,212. *Merchant Fleet* (registered at 31 December 2004): Number of vessels 13; Total displacement 5,229 grt Source: Lloyd's Register-Fairplay, *World Fleet Statistics*.

Civil Aviation (traffic on scheduled services, 2001): Kilometres flown (million) 5; Passengers carried ('000) 203; Passenger-km (million) 898; Total ton-km (million) 103. Source: UN, *Statistical Yearbook*.

TOURISM

Tourist Arrivals (number of non-resident arrivals at airports, '000): 72 in 1999; 72 in 2000; 68 in 2001 (preliminary figure).

Tourism Receipts (US $ million, excl. passenger transport): 26 in 2001; 17 in 2002; 18 in 2003.

Source: World Tourism Organization.

COMMUNICATIONS MEDIA

Radio Receivers (1997): 300,000 in use.

Television Receivers (2000): 110,000 in use.

Telephones (2004): 81,300 main lines in use.

Facsimile Machines (1996): 800 in use.

Mobile Cellular Telephones (2004): 212,800 subscribers.

Personal Computers (2001): 20,000 in use.

Internet Users (2004): 30,000.

Daily Newspapers (2001): 3.

Non-daily Newspapers (2000): 10.

Sources: mainly UNESCO, *Statistical Yearbook*; UN, *Statistical Yearbook*; International Telecommunication Union.

EDUCATION

Pre-primary (2002/03): 704 teachers; 17,049 pupils.

Primary (2002/03 unless otherwise stated, incl. special education): 308 schools (2001/02); 3,324 teachers; 64,659 pupils.

Secondary (2002/03 unless otherwise stated, incl. teacher-training): 141 schools (2001/02); 2,714 teachers; 41,000 pupils.

University (2001/02): 1 institution; 350 teachers; 3,250 students.

Other Higher (2001/02): 3 institutions; 200 teachers; 1,936 students.

Adult Literacy Rate (UNESCO estimates): 88.0% (males 92.3%; females 84.1%) in 2003 (Source: UN Development Programme, *Human Development Report*).

Source: mainly UNESCO Institute for Statistics.

Directory

The Constitution

The 1987 Constitution was approved by the National Assembly on 31 March and by 93% of voters in a national referendum in September.

THE LEGISLATURE

Legislative power is exercised jointly by the National Assembly and the Government. The National Assembly comprises 51 members, elected for a five-year term by universal adult suffrage. The Assembly elects a President and a Vice-President and has the right of amendment in any proposal of law by the Government. The approval of a majority of at least two-thirds of the number of members of the National Assembly is required for the amendment of the Constitution, the election of the President or the Vice-President, the decision to organize a plebiscite and a People's Congress and for the amendment of electoral law. If it is unable to obtain a two-thirds' majority following two rounds of voting, the Assembly may convene a People's Congress and supplement its numbers with members of local councils. The approval by a simple majority is sufficient in the People's Congress.

THE EXECUTIVE

Executive authority is vested in the President, who is elected for a term of five years as Head of State, Head of Government, Head of the Armed Forces, Chairman of the Council of State, the Cabinet of Ministers and the Security Council.

The Government comprises the President, the Vice-President and the Cabinet of Ministers. The Cabinet of Ministers is appointed by the President from among the members of the National Assembly. The Vice-President is the Prime Minister and leader of the Cabinet, and is responsible to the President.

In the event of war, a state of siege, or exceptional circumstances to be determined by law, a Security Council assumes all government functions.

THE COUNCIL OF STATE

The Council of State comprises the President (its Chairman) and 14 additional members, composed of two representatives of the combined trade unions, one representative of the associations of employers, one representative of the National Army and 10 representatives of the political parties in the National Assembly. Its duties are to advise the President and the legislature and to supervise the correct execution by the Government of the decisions of the National Assembly. The Council may present proposals of law or of general administrative measures to the Government. The Council has the authority to suspend any legislation approved by the National Assembly which, in the opinion of the Council, is in violation of the Constitution. In this event, the President must decide within one month whether or not to ratify the Council's decision.

The Government

HEAD OF STATE

President: Runaldo Ronald Venetiaan (assumed office 12 August 2000; re-elected by vote of the United People's Assembly 3 August 2005).

Council of State: Chair. Runaldo Ronald Venetiaan (President of the Republic); 14 mems; 10 to represent the political parties in the National Assembly, one for the Armed Forces, two for the trade unions and one for employers.

CABINET OF MINISTERS
(April 2006)

Vice-President: Ramdien Sardjoe (VHP).
Minister of Finance: Humphrey Hildenberg (NPS).
Minister of Foreign Affairs: Lygia L. Kraag-Keteldijk (NPS).
Minster of Defence: Ivan C. Fernald (NPS).
Minister of the Interior: Maurits S. H. Hassankhan (VHP).
Minister of Justice and the Police: Chandrikapersad Santokhie (VHP).
Minister of Planning and Community Development: Ricardo O. van Ravenswaay (DA'91).
Minister of Agriculture, Livestock and Fisheries: Kermechend Stanley Raghoebarsing (VHP).
Minister of Transport, Communications and Tourism: Alice H. Amafo (AC).
Minister of Public Works: Ganeshkoemar Khandai (VHP).
Minister of Social Affairs and Housing: Hendrik S. Setrowidjojo (PL).
Minister of Trade and Industry: Clifford Marica (SPA).
Minister of Regional Development: Michel Felisi (AC).
Minister of Education and Community Development: Edwin T. Wolf (PL).
Minister of Health: Celcius W. Waterberg (AC).
Minister of Labour, Technological Development and the Environment: Joyce Amarello-Williams (SPA).
Minister of Natural Resources and Energy: Gregory A. Rusland (NPS).
Minister of Physical Planning and Land and Forestry Management: Michael Jong Tjien Fa (PL).

MINISTRIES

Ministry of Agriculture, Livestock and Fisheries: Letitia Vriesdelaan, Paramaribo; tel. 477698; fax 470301.

Ministry of Defence: Kwattaweg 29, Paramaribo; tel. 474244; fax 420055.

Ministry of Education and Community Development: Dr Samuel Kafiluddistraat 117–123, Paramaribo; tel. 498383; fax 495083; e-mail minond@sr.net.

Ministry of Finance: Onafhankelijkheidsplein 3, Paramaribo; tel. 472610; fax 476314.

Ministry of Foreign Affairs: 25 Lim A Po St, POB 25, Paramaribo; tel. 471209; fax 410411.

Ministry of Health: Henck Arronstraat 64 boven, POB 201, Paramaribo; tel. 474841; fax 410702; e-mail narsur@sr.net.

Ministry of the Interior: Wilhelminastraat 3, Paramaribo; tel. and fax 476461; fax 421170; e-mail gensur@sr.net.

Ministry of Justice and the Police: Henck Arronstraat 1, Paramaribo; tel. 473033; fax 410465.

Ministry of Labour, Technological Development and the Environment: Verlengde Gemenelandsweg 132B, POB 911, Paramaribo; tel. 432921; fax 433167; e-mail nvb@sr.net.

Ministry of Natural Resources and Energy: Dr J. C. de Mirandastraat 11–13, Paramaribo; tel. 410160; fax 472911.

Ministry of Physical Planning and Land and Forestry Management: Paramaribo.

Ministry of Planning and Community Development: Dr S. Redmondstraat 118, Paramaribo; tel. 473628; fax 421056.

Ministry of Public Works: Verlengde Coppenamestraat 167, Paramaribo; tel. 462500; fax 464901.

Ministry of Regional Development: Van Rooseveltkade 2, Paramaribo; tel. 471574; fax 424517.

Ministry of Social Affairs and Housing: Waterkant 30–32, Paramaribo; tel. 472340; fax 470516.

Ministry of Trade and Industry: Havenlaan 3, POB 9354, Paramaribo; tel. 402886; fax 402602; e-mail dhisur@yahoo.com.

Ministry of Transport, Communications and Tourism: Prins Hendrikstraat 24–26, Paramaribo; tel. 411951; fax 420425; e-mail mintct@sr.net; internet www.mintct.sr.

Legislature

NATIONAL ASSEMBLY

Chairman: Paul Salam Somohardjo.

SURINAME

General Election, 25 May 2005

Party	Seats	% of votes cast
Nieuwe Front*	23	39.37
Nationale Democratische Partij	15	22.20
Volksalliantie Voor Vooruitgang†	5	13.79
A-Combinatie‡	5	7.21
A1§	3	5.86
Unie van Progressieve Surinamers/Partij voor Democratie en Ontwikkeling in Eenheid	—	4.67
Nieuw Suriname	—	1.57
Progressieve Arbeiders en Landbouwers Unie	—	0.89
Progressieve Politieke Partij	—	0.17
Total	**51**	**100.00‖**

* An alliance of the Nationale Partij Suriname (NPS), the Pertajah Luhur (PL), the Surinaamse Partij van de Arbeid (SPA) and the Vooruitstrevende Hervormingspartij (VHP).
† An alliance of the Democratisch Nationaal Platform 2000 (DNP 2000), the Basispartij voor Vernieuwing en Democratie (BVD), the Kerukanan Tulodo Pranatan Ingigil (KTPI) and the Democratisch Alternatief.
‡ Including candidates of the Algemene Bevrijdings- en Ontwikkelingspartij (ABOP) and the Broederschap en Eenheid in Politiek (BEP).
§ Including candidates from the Democratisch Alternatief 1991 (DA '91), the Democraten van de 21 (D21) and the Politieke Vleugel van de FAL (PVF).
‖ Including invalid votes.

Election Commission

Centraal Hoofdstembureau (CHS) (Central Polling Authority): Wilhelminastraat 3, Paramaribo; tel. 410362; internet www.cq-link.sr/verkiezingen2005; independent; Chair. LOTHAR BOKSTEEN.

Political Organizations

Algemene Bevrijdings- en Ontwikkeling Partij (ABOP) (General Liberation and Development Party): Jaguarstraat 15, Paramaribo; f. 1986; contested the 2005 election as part of the A-Combinatie (AC) electoral list; Pres. RONNIE BRUNSWIJK.

Alternatief Forum (AF) (Alternative Forum): Gladiolenstraat 26–28, Paramaribo; tel. 432342; Chair. GERARD BRUNINGS.

Amazone Partij Suriname (APS) (Suriname Amazon Party): Wilhelminastraat 91, Paramaribo; tel. 452081; Pres. KENNETH VAN GENDEREN.

Broederschap en Eenheid in Politiek (BEP): Ariestraat BR 34, S. O. B. Projekt, Paramaribo; tel. 494466; f. 1986; contested the 2005 election as part of the A-Combinatie (AC) electoral list; Chair. CAPRINO ALLENDY.

Democraten Van de 21 (D21) (Democrats of the 21st Century): Goudstraat 22, Paramaribo; f. 1986; contested the 2005 election as part of the A1 electoral list; Chair. SOEWARTO MUSTADJA.

Democratisch Alternatief 1991 (DA '91) (Democratic Alternative 1991): POB 91, Paramaribo; tel. 470276; fax 493121; e-mail info@da91.sr; internet www.da91.sr; f. 1991; contested the 2005 election as part of the A1 electoral list; social-democratic; Chair. DJAGENDRE RAMKHELAWAN.

Hernieuwde Progressieve Partij (HPP) (Renewed Progressive Party): Tourtonnelaan 51, Paramaribo; tel. 426965; e-mail hpp@cq-link.sr; f. 1986; Chair. HARRY KISOENSINGH.

Nationale Democratische Partij (NDP) (National Democratic Party): Dr. H. D. Benjaminstraat 38, Paramaribo; tel. 499183; fax 432174; e-mail ndpsur@sr.net; internet www.ndp.sr; f. 1987 by Standvaste (the 25 February Movt); army-supported; Chair. DESIRÉ (Desi) BOUTERSE.

Nationale Partij Voor Leiderschap en Ontwikkeling (NPLO) (National Party for Leaderhip and Development): Tropicaweg 1, Paramaribo; tel. 551252; f. 1986; Chair. OESMAN WANGSABESARIE.

Naya Kadam (New Choice): Naarstraat 5, Paramaribo; tel. 482014; fax 481012; e-mail itsvof@sr.net; Chair. INDRA DJWALAPERSAD; Sec. WALDO RAMDIHAL.

Nieuw Front (NF) (New Front): Paramaribo; f. 1987 as Front voor Demokratie en Ontwikkeling (FDO—Front for Democracy and Devt); name changed as above in 1991; Pres. RONALD R. VENETIAAN; an alliance comprising:

Nationale Partij Suriname (NPS) (Suriname National Party): Wanicastraat 77, Paramaribo; tel. 477302; fax 475796; e-mail nps@sr.net; internet www.nps-suriname.com; f. 1946; predominantly Creole; Sec. OTMAR ROEL RODGERS.

Pertajah Luhur (PL) (Full Confidence Party): Hoek Gemenlandsweg-Daniel Coutinhostraat, Paramaribo; tel. 401087; fax 420394; Pres. PAUL SOMOHARDJO.

Surinaamse Partij van de Arbeid (SPA) (Suriname Labour Party): Rust en Vredestraat 64, Paramaribo; tel. 425912; fax 420394; f. 1987; affiliated with C-47 trade union; social democratic party; joined NF in 1991; Leader SIEGFRIED F. GILDS.

Vooruitstrevende Hervormings Partij (VHP) (Progressive Reformation Party): Coppenamestraat 130, Paramaribo; tel. 425912; fax 420394; internet www.parbo.com/vhp; f. 1949 as Verenigde Hindostaanse Partij (United Indian Party); name changed as above in 1973; leading left-wing party; predominantly Indian; Leader R. SARDJOE.

Nieuw Suriname (NS) (New Suriname): Paramaribo; contested the 2005 election.

Partij voor Demokratie en Ontwikkeling in Eenheid (DOE) (Party for Democracy through Unity and Development): Kamperfoeliestraat 23, Paramaribo; internet www.angelfire.com/nv/DOE; f. 1999.

Pendawa Lima: Bonistraat 115, Geyersvlij, Paramaribo; tel. 551802; f. 1975; predominantly Indonesian; Chair. RAYMOND SAPOEN.

Politieke Vleugel van de FAL (PVF): Keizerstraat 150, Paramaribo; political wing of farmers' org. Federatie van Agrariërs en Landarbeiders; contested the 2005 election as part of the A1 electoral list; Chair. JIWAN SITAL.

Progressieve Arbeiders en Landbouwers Unie (PALU) (Progressive Workers' and Farm Labourers' Union): Dr S. Kafiluddistraat 27, Paramaribo; tel. 400115; e-mail palu@sr.net; socialist party; Chair. JIM K. HOK; Vice-Chair. HENK RAMNANDANLAL.

Progressieve Bosneger Partij (PBP): f. 1968; resumed political activities 1987; represents members of the Bush Negro (Boschneger) ethnic group; associated with the Pendawa Lima (see above).

Progressieve Politieke Partij (PPP) (Progressive Political Party): Paramaribo; contested the 2005 election; Chair. SURINDER MUNGRA.

Progressieve Surinaamse Volkspartij (PSV) (Suriname Progressive People's Party): Keizerstraat 122, Paramaribo; tel. 472979; f. 1946; resumed political activities 1987; Christian democratic party.

Unie van Progressieve Surinamers/Partij voor Democratie en Ontwikkeling in Eenheid (UPS/DOE): Paramaribo; contested the 2005 election.

Volksalliantie Voor Vooruitgang (People's Alliance for Progress): Paramaribo; contested the 2005 election; Leader JULES WIJDENBOSCH; alliance comprising:

Basispartij voor Vernieuwing en Democratie (BVD) (Base Party for Renewal and Democracy): Hoogestraat 28–30, Paramaribo; tel. 422231; e-mail info@bvdsuriname.org; internet www.bvdsuriname.org; Chair. TJAN GOBARDHAN.

Democratisch Alternatief (Democratic Alternative): Jadnanansinghlaan 5, Paramaribo.

Democratisch Nationaal Platform 2000 (DNP 2000) (National Democratic Platform 2000): Gemenlandsweg 83, Paramaribo; f. 2000; Pres. JULES WIJDENBOSCH; alliance including:

Democratische Partij (DP) (Democratic Party): Paramaribo; f. 1992; Leader FRANK PLAYFAIR.

Democraten Van de 21 (D21) (Democrats of the 21st Century): Goudstraat 22, Paramaribo; f. 1986; contested the 2005 election as part of the A1 electoral list; Chair. SOEWARTO MUSTADJA.

Kerukanan Tulodo Pranatan Ingigil (KTPI) (Party for National Unity and Solidarity): Bonistraat 64, Geyersvlijt, Paramaribo; tel. 456116; f. 1947 as the Kaum-Tani Persuatan Indonesia; largely Indonesian; Leader WILLY SOEMITA.

Diplomatic Representation

EMBASSIES IN SURINAME

Brazil: Maratakkastraat 2, POB 925, Paramaribo; tel. 400200; fax 400205; e-mail brasemb@sr.net; Ambassador CARVALHO DO NASCIMENTO BORGES.

China, People's Republic: Anton Dragtenweg 154, POB 3042 Paramaribo; tel. 451570; fax 452540; e-mail chinaemb_sr@mfa.gov.cn; Ambassador CHEN JINGHUA.

France: Henck Arronstraat 5–7 boven, POB 2648, Paramaribo; tel. 476455; fax 471208; e-mail ambafrance.paramaribo@diplomatie

SURINAME

.gouv.fr; internet www.amfrance@sr.net; Ambassador JEAN-MARIE BRUNO.
Guyana: Henck Arronstraat 82, POB 785, Paramaribo; tel. 475209; fax 472679; e-mail guyembassy@sr.net; Ambassador KARSHANJEE ARJUN.
India: Rode Kruislaan 10, POB 1329, Paramaribo; tel. 498344; fax 491106; e-mail india@sr.net; Ambassador ASHOK KUMAR SHARMA.
Indonesia: Van Brusselaan 3, POB 157, Paramaribo; tel. 431230; fax 498234; e-mail indoemb@sr.net; internet www.indonesia.nl; Ambassador SUPARMIN SUNJOYO.
Japan: Henck Arronstraat 23–25, POB 2921, Paramaribo; tel. 474860; fax 412208; e-mail eojparbo@sr.net; Ambassador YASUO MATSUI (resident in Venezuela).
Netherlands: Van Roseveltkade 5, POB 1877, Paramaribo; tel. 477211; fax 477792; e-mail prm@minbuza.nl; internet www.mfa.nl/prm; Ambassador HENDRIK J. W. SOETERS.
Russia: Anton Dragtenweg 7, POB 8127, Paramaribo; tel. 472387; fax 472387; Ambassador VLADIMIR LVOVITCH TYURDENEV.
USA: Dr Sophie Redmondstraat 129, POB 1821, Paramaribo; tel. 472900; fax 425-690; e-mail embuscen@sr.net; internet paramaribo.usembassy.gov; Ambassador MARSHA BARNES.
Venezuela: Henck Arronstraat 23–25, POB 3001, Paramaribo; tel. 475401; fax 475602; e-mail vzla@sr.net; internet www.embajadavzla.org.sr; Ambassador FRANCISCO DE JESÚS SIMANCAS.

Judicial System

The administration of justice is entrusted to a Court of Justice, the six members of which are nominated for life, and three Cantonal Courts. Suriname recognized the Caribbean Court of Justice (CCJ) on matters of original jurisdiction pertaining to international trade. The CCJ was inaugurated in Port of Spain, Trinidad and Tobago on 16 April 2005.

President of the Court of Justice: (vacant).
Attorney-General: SUBHAAS PUNWASI.

Religion

Many religions are represented in Suriname. According to official sources, Christians represent approximately 40% of the population, Hindus 27% and Muslims 22%.

CHRISTIANITY

Committee of Christian Churches: Paramaribo; Chair. Rev. JOHN KENT (Praeses of the Moravian Church).

The Roman Catholic Church

For ecclesiastical purposes, Suriname comprises the single diocese of Paramaribo, suffragan to the archdiocese of Port of Spain (Trinidad and Tobago). The Bishop participates in the Antilles Episcopal Conference (currently based in Port of Spain, Trinidad and Tobago). At 31 December 2003 there were an estimated 110,664 adherents in the diocese, representing about 23% of the population.
Bishop of Paramaribo: WILHELMUS ADRIANUS JOSEPHUS MARIA DE BEKKER, Bisschopshuis, Henck Arronstraat 12, POB 1230, Paramaribo; tel. 425918; fax 471602; e-mail azichem@sr.net.

The Anglican Communion

Within the Church in the Province of the West Indies, Suriname forms part of the diocese of Guyana. The Episcopal Church is also represented.
Anglican Church: St Bridget's, Hoogestraat 44, Paramaribo.

Protestant Churches

Evangelisch-Lutherse Kerk in Suriname: Waterkant 102, POB 585, Paramaribo; tel. 425503; fax 481856; e-mail elks@sr.net; Pres. WIM LOOR; 4,000 mems.
Moravian Church in Suriname (Evangelische Broeder Gemeente): Maagdenstraat 50, POB 1811, Paramaribo; tel. 473073; fax 475797; e-mail ebgs@sr.net; f. 1735; Praeses MAARLEN MINGUERN; 40,000 mems (2004).
Adherents to the Moravian Church consitute some 15% of the population. Also represented are the Christian Reformed Church, the Dutch Reformed Church, the Baptist Church, the Evangelical Methodist Church, Pentecostal Missions, the Seventh-day Adventists and the Wesleyan Methodist Congregation.

HINDUISM

Sanatan Dharm: Koningstraat 31–33, POB 760, Paramaribo; tel. 404190; f. 1930; Pres. Dr R. M. NANNAN PANDAY; over 150,000 mems.

ISLAM

Surinaamse Moeslim Associatie: Kankantriestraat 55–57, Paramaribo; Javanese Islamic org.; Chair. A. ABDOELBASHIRE.
Surinaamse Islamitische Organisatie (SIO): Watermolenstraat 10, POB 278, Paramaribo; tel. 475220; f. 1978; Pres. Dr I. JAMALUDIN; Sec. C. HASRAT; 6 brs.
Stichting Islamitische Gemeenten Suriname: Verlengde Mahonielaan 39, Paramaribo; Indonesian Islamic org.; Chair. Dr T. SOWIRONO.
Federatie Islamitische Gemeenten in Suriname: Paramaribo; Indonesian Islamic org.; Chair. K. KAAIMAN.

JUDAISM

The Dutch Jewish Congregation and the Dutch Portuguese-Jewish Congregation are represented in Suriname.
Jewish Community: The Synagogue Neve Shalom, Keizerstraat, POB 1834, Paramaribo; tel. 400236; fax 402380; e-mail rene-fernandes@cq-link.sr; internet www.ujcl.org; f. 1854; mem. of Union of Jewish Congregations of Latin America and the Caribbean (UJCL); Officiant JACQUES VAN NIEL; 300 mems (2005).

OTHER RELIGIONS

Arya Dewaker: Dr S. Kafilludistraat 1, Paramaribo; tel. 400706; members preach the Vedic Dharma; disciples of Maha Rishi Swami Dayanand Sarswati, the founder of the Arya Samaj in India; f. 1929; Chair. INDERDATH TILAKDHARIE.
The Bahá'í faith is also represented.

The Press

DAILIES

Dagblad Suriname: Zwartenhovenbrugstraat 154, POB 975, Paramaribo; tel. 426336; fax 471718; e-mail general@dbsuriname.com; internet www.dbsuriname.com; f. 2002; Dir FARIED PIERKHAN; Editor SERENA HOLLAND.
De Ware Tijd: Malebatrumstraat 9, POB 1200, Paramaribo; tel. 472823; fax 411169; e-mail webmanager@dwt.net; internet www.dwtonline.com; f. 1957; morning; Dutch; independent/liberal; Dir STEVE JONG TJIEN FA; Editor-in-Chief DESI TRUIDMAN.
De West: Dr J. C. de Mirandastraat 2–6, POB 176, Paramaribo; tel. 6923338; fax 470322; e-mail dewest@cq-link.sr; internet www.dewestonline.cq-link.sr; f. 1909; midday; Dutch; liberal; Editors G. D. C. FINDLAY, L. KETTIE; circ. 15,000–18,000.

PERIODICALS

Advertentieblad van de Republiek Suriname: Henck Arronstraat 120, POB 56, Paramaribo; tel. 473501; fax 454782; f. 1871; 2 a week; Dutch; government and official information bulletin; Editor E. D. FINDLAY; circ. 1,000.
CLO Bulletin: Gemenelandsweg 95, Paramaribo; f. 1973; irregular; Dutch; labour information published by civil servants' union.
Kerkbode: Burenstraat 17–19, POB 219, Paramaribo; tel. 473079; fax 475635; e-mail stadje@sr.net; f. 1906; weekly; religious; circ. 2,000.
Omhoog: Henck Arronstraat 21, POB 1802, Paramaribo; tel. 425992; fax 426782; e-mail rkomhoog@sr.net; weekly; f. 1952; Dutch; Catholic bulletin; Editor S. MULDER; circ. 5,000.
Xtreme Magazine: Uranusstraat 49, Paramaribo; tel. 456969.

NEWS AGENCIES

Foreign Bureau

Inter Press Service (IPS) (Italy): Malebatrumstraat 1–5, POB 5065, Paramaribo; tel. 471818; Correspondent ERIC KARWOFODI.

Publishers

Afaka International NV: Residastraat 23, Paramaribo; tel. and fax 530640; internet www.afaka.com; f. 1996; Dir GERRIT BARRON.
Educatieve Uitgeverij Sorava NV: Latourweg 10, POB 8382, Paramaribo; tel. and fax 480808.

SURINAME

IMWO, Universiteit van Suriname: Universiteitscomplex, Leysweg 1, POB 9212, Paramaribo; tel. 465558; fax 462291; e-mail bmhango@yahoo.com.

Ministerie van Onderwijs en Volksontwikkeling (Ministry of Education and Community Development): Dr Samuel Kafilludistraat 117–123, Paramaribo; tel. 498850; fax 495083.

Okopipi Publ. (Publishing Services Suriname): Van Idsingastraat 133, Paramaribo; tel. 472746; e-mail pssmoniz@sr.net; fmrly I. Krishnadath.

Papaya Media: Plutostraat 30, POB 8304, Paramaribo; tel. and fax 454530; e-mail roy_bhikharie@sr.net; f. 2002; Man. Dir ROY BHIKHARIE.

Stichting Wetenschappelijke Informatie (Foundation for Information and Development): Prins Hendrikstraat 38, Paramaribo; tel. 475232; fax 422195; e-mail swin@sr.net; f. 1977.

Tabiki Productions: Weidestraat 34, Paramaribo; tel. 478525; fax 478526; e-mail insightsuriname@yahoo.com.

VACO, NV: Domineestraat 26, POB 1841, Paramaribo; tel. 472545; fax 410563; f. 1952; Dir EDUARD HOGENBOOM.

PUBLISHERS' ASSOCIATION

Publishers' Association Suriname: Domineestraat 32, POB 1841, Paramaribo; tel. 472545; fax 410563.

Broadcasting and Communications

TELECOMMUNICATIONS

Telecommunication Corporation Suriname (Telesur): Heiligenweg 1, POB 1839, Paramaribo; tel. 473944; fax 404800; internet www.telesur.sr; supervisory body; Man. Dir DIRK M. R. CURRIE (acting).

BROADCASTING

Radio

ABC Radio (Ampie's Broadcasting Corporation): Maystraat 57, Paramaribo; tel. 464609; fax 464680; e-mail info@abcsuriname.com; internet www.abcsuriname.com; f. 1975; re-opened in 1993; commercial; Dutch and some local languages.

Radio Apintie: Verlengde Gemenelandsweg 37, POB 595, Paramaribo; tel. 498855; fax 400684; e-mail apintie@sr.net; internet www.apintie.sr; f. 1958; commercial; Dutch and some local languages; Gen. Man. CHARLES VERVUURT.

Radio Bersama: Bonniestraat 115, Paramaribo; tel. 551804; fax 551803; f. 1997; Dir AJOEB MOENTARI.

Radio Boskopou: Roseveltkade 1, Paramaribo; tel. 410300; govt-owned; Sranang Tongo and Dutch; Head Mr VAN VARSEVELD.

Radio Garuda: Goudstraat 14–16, Paramaribo; tel. 422422; Dir TOMMY RADJI.

Radio Nickerie (RANI): Waterloostraat 3, Nieuw Nickerie; tel. 231462; commercial; Hindi and Dutch.

Radio Paramaribo (Rapar): Verlengde Coppenamestraat 34, POB 975, Paramaribo; tel. 499995; fax 493121; e-mail rapar@sr.net; f. 1957; commercial; Dutch and some local languages; Dir RASHIED PIERKHAN.

Radio Radika: Indira Gandhiweg 165, Paramaribo; tel. 482800; fax 482910; e-mail radika@sr.net; re-opened in 1989; Dutch, Hindi; Dir ROSHNI RADHAKISHUN.

Radio Sangeet Mala: Indira Gandhiweg 73, Paramaribo; tel. 485893; Dutch, Hindi; Dirs RADJEN SOEKHRADJ, SOEDESH RAMSARAN.

Radio SRS (Stichting Radio Omroep Suriname): Jacques van Eerstraat 20, POB 211, Paramaribo; tel. 498115; fax 498116; e-mail radiosrs@sr.net; f. 1965; commercial; govt-owned; Dutch and some local languages; Dir LEOPOLD DARTHUIZEN.

Radio Ten: Letitia Vriesdelaan 5, Paramaribo; tel. 410881; fax 410885; e-mail radio10@cq-link.sr; internet www.radio10.cq-link.sr. Other stations include: Radio KBC, Radio Koyeba, Radio Pertjaya, Radio Shalom, Radio Zon, Ramasha Radio, Rasonic Radio and Trishul Radio.

Television

ABC Televisie (Ampie's Broadcasting Corporation): Maystraat 57, Paramaribo; tel. 464555; fax 464680; e-mail info@abcsuriname.com; internet www.abcsuriname.com; Channel 4.

Algemene Televisie Verzorging (ATV): Adrianusstraat 55, POB 2995, Paramaribo; tel. 404611; fax 402660; e-mail info@atv.sr; internet www.atv.sr; f. 1985; govt-owned; commercial; Dutch, English, Portuguese, Spanish and some local languages; Channel 12; Man. GUNO COOMAN.

STVS (Surinaamse Televisie Stichting): Letitia Vriesdelaan 5, POB 535, Paramaribo; tel. 473031; fax 477216; e-mail adm@stvs.info.sr; internet www.parbo.com/stvs; f. 1965; govt-owned; commercial; local languages, Dutch and English; Channel 8; Dir KENNETH OOSTBURG.

Finance

(cap. = capital; res = reserves; dep. = deposits; m. = million; amounts in Suriname guilders unless otherwise stated)

BANKING

Central Bank

Centrale Bank van Suriname: 18–20 Waterkant, POB 1801, Paramaribo; tel. 473741; fax 476444; e-mail info@cbvs.sr; internet www.cbvs.sr; f. 1957; Pres. ANDRE E. TELTING.

Commercial Banks

Finabank NV: Dr Sophie Redmondstraat 59–61, Paramaribo; tel. 476111; fax 410471; e-mail finabank@sr.net.

Handels-Krediet- en Industriebank (Hakrinbank NV): Dr Sophie Redmondstraat 11–13, POB 1813, Paramaribo; tel. 477722; fax 472066; e-mail hakrindp@sr.net; internet www.hakrinbank.com; f. 1936; cap. 69,854m., res 11,901m., dep. 86,874m. (Dec. 2003); Pres. and Chair. A. K. R. SHYAMNARAIN; Man. Dirs M. TJON-A-TEN, J. D. BOUSAID; 6 brs.

Landbouwbank NV: FHR Lim A Postraat 34, POB 929, Paramaribo; tel. 475945; fax 411965; e-mail lbbank@sr.net; f. 1972; govt-owned; agricultural bank; Chair. D. FERRIER; Pres. R. MERHAI; 5 brs.

RBTT Bank NV: Kerkplein 1, Paramaribo; tel. 471555; fax 411325.

De Surinaamsche Bank NV: Henck Arronstraat 26–30, POB 1806, Paramaribo; tel. 471100; fax 411750; internet www.dsbbank.sr; f. 1865; cap. 17.5m., res 26,558.1m., dep. 572,666.4m. (Dec. 2003); Chair. S. SMIT; Pres. Dr SIGMUND L. J. PROEVE; 7 brs.

Surinaamse Postspaarbank: Knuffelsgracht 10–14, POB 1879, Paramaribo; tel. 472256; fax 472952; e-mail spsbdir@sr.net; f. 1904; savings and commercial bank; cap. and res 1,044m., dep. 66,533m. (Dec. 2004); Man. ALWIN R. BAARH (acting); 2 brs.

Surinaamse Volkscredietbank: Waterkant 104, POB 1804, Paramaribo; tel. 472616; fax 473257; e-mail btlsvcb@sr.net; f. 1949; cap. and res 170.3m. (Dec. 1997); Man. Dir THAKOERDIEN RAMLAKHAN; 3 brs.

Development Bank

Nationale Ontwikkelingsbank van Suriname NV: Jagernath Lachmonstraat 160–162, POB 677, Paramaribo; tel. 465000; fax 497192; f. 1963; govt-supported devt bank; cap. and res 34m. (Dec. 1992).

INSURANCE

Assuria NV: Grote Combeweg 37, POB 1501, Paramaribo; tel. 477955; fax 472390; e-mail assuria@sr.net; internet www.assuria.sr; f. 1961; life and indemnity insurance; Man. Dir Dr S. SMIT.

Assuria Schadeverzekering NV: Henck Arronstraat 5–7, POB 1030, Paramaribo; tel. 473400; fax 476669; e-mail assuria@sr.net; internet www.assuria.net; Dir M. R. CABENDA.

CLICO Life Insurance Company (SA) Ltd: Klipstenenstraat 29, POB 3026, Paramaribo; tel. 472525; fax 476777; e-mail clicosur@sr.net; internet www.clico.com/suriname; COO GEETA SINGH.

Fatum Levensverzekering NV: Noorderkerkstraat 5–7, Paramaribo; tel. 471541; fax 410067; e-mail fatum@sr.net; internet www.fatum-suriname.com.

Hennep Verzorgende Verzekering NV: Dr Sophie Redmondstraat 246, Paramaribo; tel. 425205; e-mail hennep@sr.net; internet www.uitvaarthennep.com; Dir H. J. HENNEP.

Parsasco NV: Henck Arronstraat 117 boven, Paramaribo; tel. 421212; e-mail parsasco@sr.net; internet www.parsasco.com; Dir L. KHEDOE.

Self Reliance: Herenstraat 22, Paramaribo; tel. 472582; fax 472475; e-mail self-reliance@sr.net; internet www.self-reliance.sr; life insurance; Dir N. J. VEIRA.

Trade and Industry

DEVELOPMENT ORGANIZATIONS

Centre for Industry and Export Development: Rust en Vredestraat 79–81, POB 1275, Paramaribo; tel. 474830; fax 476311; f. 1981; Man. R. A. LETER.

SURINAME

Stichting Planbureau Suriname (National Planning Bureau of Suriname): Dr Sophie Redmondstraat 118, POB 172, Paramaribo; tel. 447408; fax 475001; e-mail dirsps@sr.net; internet www.planbureau.net; responsible for regional and socio-economic long- and short-term planning; Man. Dir LILIAN J. M. MONSELS-THOMPSON.

CHAMBER OF COMMERCE

Kamer van Koophandel en Fabrieken (Chamber of Commerce and Industry): Dr J. C. de Mirandastraat 10, POB 149, Paramaribo; tel. 474536; fax 474779; e-mail chamber@sr.net; internet www.surinamedirectory.com; f. 1910; Pres. R. L. A. AMEERALI; Sec. R. RAMDAT; 16,109 mems.

Surinaams–Nederlandse Kamer voor Handel en Industrie (Suriname–Netherlands Chamber of Commerce and Industry): Jagernath Lachmonstraat 158, Paramaribo; tel. 463201; fax 463241.

INDUSTRIAL AND TRADE ASSOCIATIONS

Associatie van Surinaamse Fabrikanten (ASFA) (Suriname Manufacturers' Asscn): Jaggernath Lachmonstraat 187, POB 3046, Paramaribo; tel. 439797; fax 439798; e-mail asfa@sr.net; Chair. KATHLEEN LIEUW KIE SONG; 317 mems.

Vereniging Surinaams Bedrijfsleven (Suriname Trade and Industry Association): Prins Hendrikstraat 18, POB 111, Paramaribo; tel. 475286; fax 475287; e-mail vsbtia@sr.net; internet www.vsbstia.org; Pres. MARCEL A. MEYER; 290 mems.

UTILITIES

Electricity

Energy Company Suriname (EBS): Nieuw Nickerie; state-owned electricity supplier.

TRADE UNIONS

Council of the Surinamese Federation of Trade Unions (RAVAKSUR): f. 1987; Sec. FREDDY WATERBERG; comprises:

Algemeen Verbond van Vakverenigingen in Suriname 'De Moederbond' (AVVS) (General Confederation of Trade Unions): Verlengde Coppenamestraat 134, POB 2951, Paramaribo; tel. 463501; fax 465116; e-mail avvsmoederbonds51@hotmail.com; right-wing; Pres. IMRO GREP; Gen. Sec. ALESSANDRO SPRONG; 15,000 mems.

Centrale Landsdienaren Organisatie (CLO) (Central Organization for Civil Service Employees): Gemenelandsweg 743, Paramaribo; tel. 499839; Pres. HENDRIK SYLVESTER; 13,000 mems.

Organisatie van Samenwerkende Autonome Vakbonden (OSAV): Noorderkerkstraat 2–10, Paramaribo; Pres. SONNY CHOTKAN; Gen. Sec. RONNY HEK.

Progressieve Werknemers Organisatie (PWO) (Progressive Workers' Organization): Limesgracht 80, POB 406, Paramaribo; tel. 475840; f. 1948; covers the commercial, hotel and banking sectors; Pres. ANDRE KOORNAAR; Sec. EDWARD MENT; 4,000 mems.

Progressive Trade Union Federation (C-47): Wanicastraat 230, Paramaribo; tel. 494365; fax 401149; Gen. Sec. R. NAARENDORP.

Federation of Civil Servants Organization (CLO): Verlengde Gemenelandsweg 74, Paramaribo; tel. 464200; fax 493918; Pres. RONALD HOOGHART; Gen. Sec. DOROTHY TELTING.

Federation of Farmers and Agrarians (FAL): Keizerstraat 150, Paramaribo; tel. 464200; fax 499839; Pres. JIWAN SITAL; Gen. Sec. ANAND DWARKA.

Transport

RAILWAYS

There are no public railways operating in Suriname.

ROADS

In 2000 Suriname had an estimated 4,492 km (2,750 miles) of roads, of which 1,220 km (758 miles) were main roads. The principal east–west road, 390 km (242 miles) in length, links Albina, on the eastern border, with Nieuw Nickerie, in the west.

SHIPPING

Suriname is served by many shipping companies and has about 1,500 km (930 miles) of navigable rivers and canals. A number of shipping companies conduct regular international services (principally for freight) to and from Paramaribo including EWL, Fyffesgroup, the Alcoa Steamship Co, Marli Marine Lines, Bic Line, Nedlloyd Line, Maersk Lines and Tecmarine Lines (in addition to those listed below). There are also two ferry services linking Suriname with Guyana, across the Corentijn river, and with French Guiana, across the Marowijne river.

Dienst voor de Scheepvaart (Suriname Maritime Authority): Cornelis Jongbawstraat 2, POB 888, Paramaribo; tel. 476769; fax 472940; e-mail dvsmas@sr.net; govt authority supervising and controlling shipping in Surinamese waters; Man. of Nautical Affairs NAOMI EERSEL.

Scheepvaart Maatschappij Suriname NV (SMS) (Suriname Shipping Line Ltd): Waterkant 44, POB 1824, Paramaribo; tel. 472447; fax 474814; e-mail surinam_line@sr.net; f. 1936; regular cargo and passenger services in the interior; Chair. F. VAN DER JAGT; Dir J. AMARELLO-WILLIAMS.

NV VSH Scheepvaartmij United Suriname Shipping Company: Van het Hogerhuysstraat 9–11, POB 1860, Paramaribo; tel. 402558; fax 403515; e-mail united@sr.net; internet www.vshunited.com/shipping.html; shipping agents and freight carriers; Man. PATRICK HEALY.

Staatsolie Maatschappij Suriname NV: Dr Ir Adhinstraat, POB 4069, Paramaribo; tel. 499649; fax 491105; e-mail mailstaatsolie@staatsolie.com; internet www.staatsolie.com; Chair. H. G. COLERIDGE; Man. Dir Dr S. E. JHARAP.

Suriname Coast Traders NV: Flocislaan 4, Industrieterrein Flora, POB 9216, Paramaribo; tel. 463040; fax 463831; internet www.pasonsgroup.com; f. 1981; subsidiary of Pasons Group.

CIVIL AVIATION

The main airport is Johan Adolf Pengel International Airport (formerly Zanderij International Airport), 45 km from Paramaribo. Domestic flights operate from Zorg-en-Hoop Airport, located in a suburb of Paramaribo. There are 35 airstrips throughout the country.

Surinaamse Luchtvaart Maatschappij NV (SLM) (Suriname Airways): Mr. Jagernath Lachmonstraat 136, POB 2029, Paramaribo; tel. 465700; fax 491213; e-mail publicrelations@slm.firm.sr; internet www.surinamairways.net; f. 1962; services to Amsterdam (the Netherlands) and to destinations in North America, South America and the Caribbean; Vice-Pres. CLYDE CAIRO.

Gonini Air Service Ltd: Doekhiweg 1, Zorg-en-Hoop Airport, POB 1614, Paramaribo; tel. 499098; fax 498363; f. 1976; privately owned; licensed for scheduled and unscheduled national and international services (charters, lease, etc.); Man. Dir GERARD BRUNINGS.

Gum Air NV: Rijweg naar Kwatta 254, Paramaribo; tel. 498888; fax 497670; privately owned; unscheduled domestic flights; Man. HENK GUMMELS.

Tourism

Efforts were made to promote the previously undeveloped tourism sector in the 1990s. Attractions include the varied cultural activities, a number of historical sites and an unspoiled interior with many varieties of plants, birds and animals. There are 13 nature reserves and one nature park. There were an estimated 68,000 foreign tourist arrivals at the international airport in 2001. In 2003 tourism receipts totalled US $18m.

Suriname Tourism Foundation: Dr J. F. Nassylaan 2, Paramaribo; tel. 410357; fax 477786; e-mail stsur@sr.net; internet www.parbo.com/tourism; f. 1996; Exec. Dir ARMAND LI-A-YOUNG.

SWAZILAND

Introductory Survey

Location, Climate, Language, Religion, Flag, Capital

The Kingdom of Swaziland is a land-locked country in southern Africa, bordered by South Africa to the north, west, south and south-east, and by Mozambique to the east. The average annual temperature is about 16°C (61°F) on the Highveld, and about 22°C (72°F) in the sub-humid Lowveld, while annual rainfall ranges from 1,000 mm (40 ins) to 2,280 mm (90 ins) on the Highveld, and from 500 mm (20 ins) to 890 mm (35 ins) in the Lowveld. English and siSwati are the official languages. About 60% of the population profess Christianity, while most of the remainder adhere to traditional beliefs. The national flag (proportions 2 by 3) is blue, with a yellow-edged horizontal crimson stripe (one-half of the depth) in the centre. On this stripe is a black and white Swazi shield, superimposed on two spears and a staff, all lying horizontally. The capital is Mbabane.

Recent History

Swaziland, which was previously under the joint rule of the United Kingdom and the South African (Transvaal) Republic, became a British protectorate in 1903, and one of the High Commission Territories in 1907, the others being the colony of Basutoland (now the Kingdom of Lesotho) and the protectorate of Bechuanaland (now the Republic of Botswana). The British Act of Parliament that established the Union of South Africa in 1910 also provided for the inclusion in South Africa of the three High Commission Territories, subject to consultation with the local inhabitants.

Swaziland's first Constitution, which was introduced by the British Government, entered into force in January 1964. The Paramount Chief (Ngwenyama—the Lion), King Sobhuza II, subsequently established a traditionalist political party, the Imbokodvo National Movement (INM), which secured all of the seats in the new Legislative Council at elections in June of that year. In 1965, in response to continued pressure from the INM, the British Government established a committee to draft proposed constitutional amendments. A new Constitution, which was promulgated in 1966 and came into effect in April 1967, provided for the introduction of internal self-government pending the attainment of full independence by the end of 1969. Executive power was vested in King Sobhuza as the hereditary monarch and constitutional Head of State. The Legislative Council was dissolved in March 1967, and elections to the new bicameral Parliament took place in April. The INM secured all 24 elective seats in the House of Assembly, although the Ngwane National Liberatory Congress (NNLC) received 20% of the votes cast. In May King Sobhuza formed Swaziland's first Cabinet, appointing the leader of the INM, Prince Makhosini Dlamini, as Prime Minister. On 6 September 1968 Swaziland was granted full independence within the Commonwealth, and a new Constitution (based on the existing Constitution) was adopted.

At elections to the House of Assembly in May 1972, the INM secured 21 seats, while the NNLC won the remaining three elective seats. In April 1973, in accordance with a parliamentary resolution, King Sobhuza repealed the Constitution, imposed a state of emergency under which all political activity was suspended, introduced legislation providing for detention without trial for a period of 60 days, and announced the formation of a national army. A new Constitution, promulgated on 13 October 1978, confirmed the King's control of executive and legislative decisions. The functions of the bicameral parliament, comprising a House of Assembly and a Senate, were confined to debating government proposals and advising the King. The existing 40 traditional local councils (Tinkhundla—singular: Inkhundla) were each to nominate two members to an 80-member electoral college, which was, in turn, to elect 40 deputies to the House of Assembly. Members of the House of Assembly were to select 10 members of the Senate, while the King was to nominate a further 10 members to each chamber. All political parties (including the INM) were prohibited. Legislative elections took place later that year, and the parliament was inaugurated in January 1979. In June 1982 the Swaziland National Council, an advisory body on matters of Swazi tradition, comprising members of the royal family, was redesignated as the Supreme Council of State (Liqoqo).

King Sobhuza died in August 1982. In accordance with Swazi tradition, the powers of Head of State devolved upon the Queen Mother (Indlovukazi—Great She Elephant) Dzeliwe, who was authorized to act as Regent until King Sobhuza's designated successor, Prince Makhosetive (born in 1968), attained the age of 21. Shortly afterwards Queen Regent Dzeliwe appointed the Liqoqo, which was to advise her in all affairs of State. Competition to secure supreme executive power subsequently emerged between the Prime Minister, Prince Mabandla N. F. Dlamini, and several prominent members, led by Prince Mfanasibili Dlamini, of the Liqoqo. In March 1983 Prince Mabandla was replaced as Prime Minister by a traditionalist, Prince Bhekimpi Dlamini. In August, under the powers of the 'Authorized Person' (an important hereditary post, held by Prince Sozisa Dlamini, the Chairman of the Liqoqo), Queen Regent Dzeliwe was deposed, apparently as a result of her reluctance to dismiss Prince Mabandla. Following an attempt by Queen Regent Dzeliwe to appeal against her deposition, Prince Mfanasibili and his followers obtained an official declaration that the High Court had no jurisdiction in matters concerning Swazi custom and tradition. Widespread opposition to the deposition of Queen Regent Dzeliwe was suppressed, and in September Queen Ntombi, the mother of Prince Makhosetive, was officially invested as Regent. In November elections to the Libandla took place, and a new Cabinet was appointed, in which only Prince Bhekimpi and the Minister of Foreign Affairs, Richard Dlamini, were retained.

In October 1985, following protests by prominent members of the royal family at the Liqoqo's monopoly of power, Queen Regent Ntombi dismissed Prince Mfanasibili. It was subsequently announced that the Liqoqo was to be reconstituted in its former capacity as an advisory body on matters pertaining to traditional law and custom. In December all those convicted of conspiracy in late 1984 were pardoned and released. In January 1986 it was announced that Prince Makhosetive was to be crowned in April, three years earlier than expected, in order to end the competition for power among vying royal factions. In February Prince Mfanasibili and an associate, Majiji Simelane, were arrested on charges of attempting to subvert justice.

Prince Makhosetive was crowned on 25 April 1986, and assumed the title of King Mswati III. In May King Mswati dissolved the Liqoqo, thereby consolidating his power. In July King Mswati reorganized the Cabinet, and in October he appointed a former senior member of the security forces, Sotsha Dlamini, as Prime Minister. In May 1987 12 prominent officials, including Prince Bhekimpi and Prince Mfanasibili, were charged with sedition and treason, in connection with the removal from power of Queen Regent Dzeliwe in 1983. In November King Mswati established a special tribunal to preside over all cases involving alleged offences against the King or the Queen Regent; defendants appearing before the tribunal were not to be granted the right to legal representation or appeal. In March 1988 10 of those accused of involvement in the deposition of Queen Regent Dzeliwe were convicted of treason by the special tribunal, and received custodial sentences; two defendants were acquitted. In July, however, it was reported that the 10 convicted in March had been released.

In November 1987 elections to the legislature took place, one year earlier than scheduled. Later that month King Mswati reappointed Sotsha Dlamini as Prime Minister. In July King Mswati dismissed Sotsha Dlamini for alleged disobedience, replacing him with Obed Dlamini, a former leader of the Swaziland Federation of Trade Unions (SFTU). This appointment was widely regarded as a measure to appease increasing discontent within some sectors of the labour force; nevertheless, unrest continued throughout 1989.

In early 1990 the People's United Democratic Movement (PUDEMO), which had been established in 1983, distributed tracts questioning the legitimacy of the monarchy in its existing form and demanding constitutional reform. Security forces subsequently arrested a number of suspected members of

PUDEMO, who were variously charged with treason, sedition or conspiring to form a political party. All the defendants were acquitted of the principal charges, although five were convicted of illegally attending a political gathering (the sentences of two of the five were annulled on appeal in October 1991). In November King Mswati dismissed the reformist Minister of Justice, Reginald Dhladhla, reportedly on the advice of the Swaziland National Council (which had been reconstituted from the former Liqoqo), prompting public concern that it continued to exert undue influence on government policies. Later in November five members of PUDEMO (who had previously been acquitted of all charges) were arrested under legislation enabling the detention of suspects without trial. In March 1991 the prisoners were released, as a result of international pressure. In an attempt to advance its objectives through legal bodies, PUDEMO subsequently established a number of affiliated organizations, including the Human Rights Association of Swaziland (HUMARAS) and the Swaziland Youth Congress (SWAYOCO), but these were not accorded official recognition.

In September and October 1991 a committee, termed Vusela (Greetings), conducted a series of public forums throughout the country to elicit popular opinion on political reforms. Widespread demands for the abolition of the existing electoral system were reported, while there was substantial criticism of the composition of the Vusela committee itself. In subsequent months several peaceful demonstrations, organized by SWAYOCO to demand the establishment of a democratic system of government, were suppressed by security forces. In October King Mswati announced an extensive reorganization of the Cabinet. In February 1992 PUDEMO declared itself a legal opposition party (in contravention of the prohibition on political association), rejected King Mswati's efforts to institute political reform, and demanded a constitutional referendum. Two further opposition movements, the Swaziland United Front (SUF) and the Swaziland National Front (SWANAFRO), subsequently re-emerged. In February King Mswati appointed a second committee (Vusela 2), which was to present recommendations for consideration by the King, based on the conclusions of the first committee.

In October 1992 King Mswati approved several proposals submitted by Vusela 2. The House of Assembly (redesignated the National Assembly) was to be expanded to 65 deputies (of whom 55 were to be directly elected by secret ballot from candidates nominated by the Tinkhundla, and 10 appointed by the King), and the Senate to 30 members (10 selected by the National Assembly and 20 appointed by the King); in addition, the legislation providing for detention without trial was to be abrogated, and a new constitution, incorporating the amendments, enshrining an hereditary monarchy and confirming the fundamental rights of the individual and the independence of the judiciary, was to be drafted. However, opposition groups protested at the committee's failure to recommend the immediate restoration of a multi-party political system: the issue was to be postponed until the forthcoming elections, in order to determine the extent of public support. PUDEMO announced its opposition to the electoral reforms, and demanded that the Government organize a national convention to determine the country's constitutional future. King Mswati subsequently dissolved parliament, and announced that he was to rule by decree, with the assistance of the Council of Ministers (as the Cabinet had been restyled), pending the adoption of a new constitution and the holding of parliamentary elections. Later in October King Mswati announced that elections to the National Assembly would take place in the first half of 1993. At a series of public meetings doubts were expressed as to the viability of the reformed electoral system; in early 1993, in response to public concern, it was announced that legislation preventing the heads of the Tinkhundla from exerting undue influence in the nomination of candidates had been introduced.

In early 1993 additional security measures were imposed in order to prevent political meetings from taking place. In March more than 50 opposition activists were arrested and charged in connection with the organization of illegal political gatherings. Although those arrested were subsequently released on bail, legal restrictions prevented them from participating in opposition activity, thereby effectively undermining efforts to prevent the elections. None the less, the subsequent low level of voter registration appeared to reflect widespread objections to the reforms.

The first round of elections to the expanded National Assembly, which was contested by 2,094 candidates nominated by the Tinkhundla, took place on 25 September 1993. At the end of September King Mswati repealed the legislation providing for detention without trial. The second round of parliamentary elections, on 11 October, was contested by the three candidates in each Inkhundla who had obtained the highest number of votes in the first poll; the majority of members of the former Council of Ministers (which had been dissolved in late September), including Obed Dlamini, failed to secure seats in the Assembly. Later in October King Mswati nominated a further 10 deputies to the National Assembly, which elected 10 of its members to the Senate; King Mswati subsequently appointed the remaining 20 senators, among them Obed Dlamini and Prince Bhekimpi. In November the former Minister of Works and Construction, Prince Jameson Mbilini Dlamini, considered a traditionalist, was appointed Prime Minister, and a new Council of Ministers (with Nxumalo as Deputy Prime Minister) was formed.

In February 1994, following a report by the US Department of State that stated that the parliamentary elections had been 'undemocratic', the Government claimed that the majority of the Swazi people were opposed to the establishment of a multi-party political system. It was announced, however, that King Mswati was to appoint a 15-member commission, comprising representatives of organs of State and non-governmental organizations, to draft a new constitution, and a national policy council, which was to prepare a manifesto of the Swazi people. Elections to the Tinkhundla (which had been postponed from March) finally took place, although a high rate of abstention by voters was reported. (The heads of the Tinkhundla had previously been appointed by the King.)

In March 1995 the SFTU undertook a two-day general strike (which was widely observed) in support of a set of 27 demands (first presented in January 1994) that included the repeal of the 1973 decree banning all political activity. The unions subsequently suspended further strike action after the Government established an independent committee to consider the SFTU's demands. Further planned strike action was abandoned in July, after the National Assembly approved legislation enabling the Government to impose custodial and financial penalties on organizers of industrial action. In August the Senate approved a motion supporting a statement made by King Mswati (during a visit to South Africa) to the effect that the Swazi population was not in favour of a multi-party system.

In January 1996 PUDEMO announced a campaign of protests and civil disobedience, owing to the Government's failure to respond to demands for the installation of a multi-party system and for the adoption of a constitution restricting the monarch to a largely ceremonial role. Strike action took place later in the month, following a failed attempt by the authorities to have the strike declared illegal. Security forces intervened to suppress demonstrations by SFTU members, and violent clashes ensued, in which three people were reported to have been killed. The SFTU refused to enter into negotiations with the Government, stipulating that the 1973 decree and restrictions on trade unions be revoked prior to discussions. Meanwhile, it was reported that some members of the Government, including Obed Dlamini, also favoured political reform. King Mswati accused the trade unions of attempting to overthrow the monarchy, and threatened to order his traditional warriors to suppress the strike. The SFTU subsequently suspended strike action to allow negotiations to proceed with the Government (which continued to reject the unions' preconditions for discussions). In February 1996 King Mswati announced that the process of drafting a new constitution would be initiated later that year, and that the ban on political activity would also be reviewed. In May King Mswati indicated that a 'People's Parliament', comprising a series of consultative meetings between citizens and government leaders, had been initiated to solicit public opinion regarding constitutional reform. At the same time King Mswati dismissed Prince Mbilini as Prime Minister, and announced that he would appoint his successor in consultation with the Swaziland National Council. The country was effectively paralysed in mid-1996 by strike action in the public sector, in support of pay demands. The Government declared the strike illegal. Although the industrial action was abandoned, the Government deducted approximately one-half from teachers' and civil servants' salaries for July and August.

In late July 1996, following an emergency meeting (attended by the Heads of State of Mozambique, Botswana, Zimbabwe and South Africa) to discuss Swaziland's political situation, King Mswati appointed a Constitutional Review Commission, comprising chiefs, political activists and trade unionists, to collate submissions from the Swazi people and subsequently draft proposals for a new constitution. (The Commission received substantial funds from international donors.) At the same time, Dr Barnabas Sibusiso Dlamini, an IMF Executive Director and former Minister of Finance, was appointed Prime Minister. In August PUDEMO expressed its dissatisfaction with the composition of the Constitutional Review Commission under the chairmanship of the King's brother, Prince Mangaliso, and appealed for regional and international assistance in the review process. In response to accusations by the SFTU of police brutality at a PUDEMO rally in September, the Minister of Commerce and Industry defended police action and blamed political parties for ignoring the 1973 decree prohibiting political activity.

In December 1996 the Prime Minister announced that a 'task force', composed of workers, employers and government representatives, had discussed the SFTU's demands made in March 1995, and that the implementation of the recommendations outlined in the resulting report was to be overseen by the Labour Advisory Board. In January 1997, however, the SFTU claimed that there had been no response to its demands for democratic reform, and resolved to begin indefinite strike action from February. Meanwhile, the PUDEMO President, Mario Masuku, declared that Swaziland's leaders were not committed to change, and withdrew from the Constitutional Review Commission. At the end of January the four main leaders of the SFTU were arrested and subsequently charged with intimidating bus owners into joining the forthcoming strike. The strike, pronounced illegal by the Government, proceeded, and was apparently observed by approximately one-half of the labour force. On the ninth day of industrial action six strikers were seriously injured in violent clashes with the security forces. The SFTU leaders declined the Government's offer to release them on condition that they end the strike; their trial was dismissed in February, owing to lack of evidence. At the beginning of March the Congress of South African Trade Unions (COSATU), which had asserted its support for the SFTU throughout the strike, initiated a one-day blockade of the Swazi border. The SFTU decided to suspend the strike shortly afterwards, as the Government had agreed to commence negotiations, but resolved to continue industrial action on the first two days of each month until its 27 demands had been met. It was subsequently announced that King Mswati was reviewing the 1973 decree. In April 1997 the SFTU postponed a further blockade indefinitely, in order to allow the Government adequate time to review the situation.

In October 1997 the SFTU called a nation-wide strike in support of its ongoing demands for democratic reform, after talks with the Government failed to produce any agreement, although support for the strike was low. Teachers none the less resolved to continue with separate industrial action in support of pay demands. Meanwhile, SFTU and other protesters demanded the recall from Swaziland of the British High Commissioner, whom they accused of colluding with the King and interfering in domestic affairs.

In August 1998 King Mswati dissolved the National Assembly, in preparation for elections scheduled for October. Opposition groups urged voters to boycott the polls, in the absence of the immediate legalization of political parties. Some 350 candidates were nominated by the Tinkhundla to contest the 55 elective seats in the Assembly. Voting took place on 16 and 24 October; turn-out was reportedly low. A new Cabinet, with Sibusiso Dlamini as Prime Minister, was appointed in mid-November, and a new Senate and Swaziland National Council were formed.

In April 1999 the NNLC, PUDEMO and the SFTU united to form the Swaziland Democratic Alliance (SDA). The NNLC leader, Obed Dlamini, was elected Chairman. The formal launch of the SDA was scheduled for 11 April, to coincide with the end of the Southern African Development Community (SADC, see p. 358) labour conference in Mbabane. However, following warnings from the police that the proposed inauguration, which had been rescheduled for 19 April, was illegal and would not be permitted to take place, the executive of the SDA met and cancelled the event.

In September 1999, as a result of an article criticizing the King's choice of a new wife, the Sunday editor of *The Times of Swaziland* was arrested and charged with criminal libel. He was released on bail, but had his passport confiscated. New anti-defamation legislation passed in October required the licensing of all journalists and threatened reporters with criminal penalties for publishing inaccurate stories. The *Swazi Observer*, owned by a national trust controlled by the King, was abruptly closed in February 2000, reportedly as a result of government intervention following the newspaper's recent exposés of power struggles between ministers and of politicians' alleged criminal involvement; the newspaper resumed publication in March 2001, although in October its editor was shot dead, apparently in an indiscriminate attack.

In October 2000 there was unrest in several areas following an operation by the armed forces to evict some 200 people from their home villages, allegedly in response to the residents' refusal to abandon support for their local chieftains, in favour of Prince Maguga, the King's brother. Pro-democracy campaigners and trade unions met in South Africa in November to support the displaced residents and to initiate a plan of action in support of democratic reforms. A two-day strike was partially observed, and activists subsequently blockaded the country's border with South Africa for two days in late November. Meanwhile, Masuku was arrested and charged with sedition after allegedly demanding the overthrow of King Mswati at a public meeting. He was subsequently released on bail. A judicial crisis developed in late 2002 when, with reference to decrees issued by the King in connection with the evictions, the six South African judges of the Swaziland Court of Appeal resigned in protest at the Government's refusal to accept two rulings that the King had no power to overrule the National Assembly. The judges of the High Court subsequently announced that they would refuse to sit or set dates for hearings, and a strike by members of the legal profession ensued. In April 2003 a report by the International Bar Association attributed the judicial crisis to the lack of clearly defined roles for the executive, legislature and judiciary. In May the Government withdrew a statement in which it had accused the judges of being under external influence. In mid-September 2004 the Government reversed its position on the rulings which had provoked the crisis. Hearings were scheduled to resume at the Court of Appeal in November on condition that the people evicted in October 2000 were allowed to return to their villages.

Meanwhile, in June 2001 King Mswati provoked international criticism by promulgating a decree that, it was claimed, effectively amounted to the declaration of a state of emergency; the legislation ensured that no person or body, including the courts, had the authority to challenge the King, prevented newspapers from challenging publishing bans, allowed the King to appoint judges and traditional chiefs personally, and made ridiculing or impersonating the King a criminal offence. Opposition groups in Swaziland condemned the decree as reinforcing tyrannical rule, and criticized the international community's lack of interest in the country's political situation. The King revoked the decree in July, in response to international diplomatic pressure, notably a threat by the USA to impose economic sanctions. However, at the same time the King issued a new decree that retained certain sections of the original decree, including a provision allowing the detention of Swazi citizens without the option of bail for some offences.

In August 2001 the Constitutional Review Commission submitted its report, which recommended that the King's powers be extended and political parties remain outlawed, but stated that the introduction of a bill of rights that was not in conflict with Swazi laws and customs was a possibility. The SFTU and PUDEMO rejected the Commission's proposals. In February 2002 a 15-member committee, appointed by the King, began drafting a new constitution; PUDEMO criticized the Government for allegedly manipulating the Commission's report and selecting members of the drafting committee who were sympathetic to government policy. In April King Mswati stated again his opinion that multi-party democracy was not a suitable system for Swaziland. In May Prince David, the King's brother, and Chairman of the constitution-drafting committee, announced a new draft constitution, which, *inter alia*, envisaged the retention of the Tinkhundla system for forthcoming elections to the National Assembly. Meanwhile, in October 2001 Masuku was rearrested for defying his bail conditions; his trial on charges of sedition, which he denied, began in February 2002, and in August he was acquitted and released after the High Court ruled that the State had failed to prove its case.

King Mswati introduced the Internal Security Bill in June 2002, intended to suppress political dissent. It provided variously for fines and prison sentences for those found guilty of carrying or wearing banners or flags of banned political formations, or of participating in mass strikes or boycotts. Training abroad to commit acts of insurgency in Swaziland would be punishable by up to 20 years' imprisonment. The bill was severely criticized by the SFTU, PUDEMO and various foreign governments, which considered it to be inconsistent with the bill of rights and the proposed constitutional reform.

In October 2002 the King was the subject of a legal challenge from the mother of a girl chosen to be his 10th wife; the woman alleged that her daughter had been abducted by two of the King's emissaries. However, she withdrew the case in early November, when her daughter stated that she had no objection to becoming a queen. Chief Justice Stanley Sapire was dismissed following the incident, after ignoring a decree issued by the King to abandon the case against him. Further controversy arose over the King's order for a private aircraft costing around US \$45m. The National Assembly voted against the purchase of the aircraft in November, after it was revealed that development funds from international donors had been diverted to pay for it, but the vote was overruled by the Council of Ministers. The European Union (EU) had previously suspended financial aid to the country over the issue in September 2002. In August 2003 the Prime Minister denied newspaper reports that claimed that the aircraft had been purchased. In January 2004 the King's request for funds to construct a new palace for each of his 11 wives provoked further controversy.

In April 2003 a cabinet reshuffle was effected; nine portfolios were redistributed, and the Minister of Public Works and Transport, Titus Mlangeni, was dismissed on suspicion of fraud. On 31 May King Mswati announced the dissolution of the National Assembly. Pending elections to a new Assembly, scheduled for October, a council, styled the King's Order-in-Council, was charged with debating and enacting legislation in collaboration with the King. The elections to the National Assembly, duly held in October, were reportedly marked by a very low turn-out, many voters having apparently heeded an appeal by pro-democracy groups for a boycott of the polls. Although several members of proscribed political organizations stood as independent candidates, a Commonwealth monitoring team subsequently declared that the elections had been largely meaningless, in view of the lack of basic democratic freedoms that prevailed in Swaziland. In November the King appointed Themba Dlamini, a former incumbent on various parastatal bodies and a close associate of the royal family, as the new Prime Minister. At the same time, the King accepted a new draft constitution that, observers noted, safeguarded many of the monarchy's existing prerogatives. Among the provisions of the proposed new basic law was that the King should remain the head of the executive and retain responsibility for appointing the Prime Minister. He would, furthermore, retain a power of veto over any bill that received parliamentary approval. However, the draft Constitution did propose the removal of the King's power to rule by decree and provided for the replacement of the Court of Appeal by a new Supreme Court as Swaziland's highest judicial body.

Meanwhile, in March 2004 Marwick Khumalo resigned as Speaker of the National Assembly and was replaced, in May, by Charles S'gayoyo Magongo. Khumalo claimed that he had been forced to resign, owing to his opposition to government attempts to purchase a private aircraft for the King. In May the National Assembly voted to suspend itself in protest at the Government's stated intention to review (or reject) the Industrial Court's ruling that the Clerk of Parliament had been illegally dismissed by the previous Prime Minister and should be reinstated. Also in May the National Constituent Assembly (NCA—a pressure group composed of churches, political parties, labour and human rights organizations) announced a legal challenge to what it claimed was the King's intention of promulgating the proposed new Constitution by decree. In mid-June the NCA petitioned the High Court, demanding that the constitution-drafting committee should be required to hold public hearings and receive submissions from interested parties. The High Court agreed that it would hear the petition in August, although no date was fixed.

In January 2005 the SFTU commenced a two-day general strike in protest at the proposed constitutional reform, which it maintained entrenched the power of the monarchy. The new Constitution was finally approved by a joint sitting of the Senate and the National Assembly in early June. It was ratified by King Mswati on 26 July and came into effect on 7 February 2006. The Constitution was viewed as being socially progressive, according greater rights to women—legally recognized as adults for the first time—and guaranteeing the right to primary education, but politically conservative: executive power was concentrated in the King and the Tinkhundla remained as the basis of the parliamentary system; the King would also continue to appoint the Prime Minister and the Council of Ministers, Chiefs and High Court judges and could dissolve the legislature. A bill of rights guaranteed freedom of assembly and speech; however, these rights could be suspended by the King if he considered it to be in the public interest. Furthermore, while there existed provision for the judiciary to interpret the Constitution, ultimate authority was vested with the King. There also remained considerable ambiguity regarding the legality of political parties, although the NNLC announced its intention to submit an application to the registrar of companies. In February 2006, the President of the Swaziland Law Society instigated legal proceedings at the High Court to clarify the issue.

Meanwhile, in late December 2005 nine members of SWAYOCO were arrested and charged with treason following a series of arson attacks on government buildings and private residences during that year. Subsequent arrests brought the total number detained to 16, among whom was the PUDEMO Secretary-General, Bong'nkosi Dlamini. It was claimed that the defendants and several witnesses were tortured in police custody. In mid-March 2006 the acting Chief Justice, Jacobus Annandale, released 15 of the suspects on bail and demanded that the Prime Minister commence a public investigation into the allegations of torture.

In late February 2006 the King effected a reshuffle of the Council of Ministers. Moses Mathendele Dlamini was appointed Minister of Foreign Affairs and Trade, replacing Mabili Dlamini, who assumed the housing and urban development portfolio vacated by Dumsile Sukati. Sukati was appointed Minister of Natural Resources and Energy replacing Mfofmfo Nkambule, who took over the health and social welfare portfolio from Chief Sipho Shongwe.

Swaziland has been severely affected by the HIV/AIDS pandemic. The Government has been criticized for its reluctance to confront the problem directly; proposed measures have included sterilizing or branding those infected with HIV. In an attempt to prevent the spread of the disease, in September 2001 the Government ordered women aged 18 years or younger to remain celibate and avoid shaking hands with men for a period of five years. In February 2004 the Prime Minister declared a national disaster, brought about by Swaziland's high incidence of HIV infection in combination with drought, land degradation and rising poverty. Following a visit to the country, in mid-March 2006 the UN Secretary-General's special envoy reported that 42.6% of the adult population (aged between 15 and 49 years) was infected with HIV; a recent survey of pregnant women between the ages of 25 and 29 had indicated a prevalence rate of 56.3%. It was anticipated that by 2010 orphaned children would represent between 10% and 15% of the population.

During the apartheid era Swaziland pursued a policy of dialogue and co-operation with South Africa. In 1982 the two countries signed a secret non-aggression pact; several members of the African National Congress of South Africa (ANC), which had increasingly used Swaziland as a base for guerrilla attacks into South Africa, were subsequently arrested and expelled from Swaziland. The signing, in March 1984, of the Nkomati accord between South Africa and Mozambique (which banned both countries from harbouring dissidents) led many ANC members to flee from Mozambique to neighbouring Swaziland. Following the murder, in 1984, of the deputy chief of the Swazi security police, the Government initiated a campaign to arrest all ANC fugitives remaining in the country (the ANC denied involvement in the killing). In 1986 leading Swazi politicians expressed opposition to the imposition of economic sanctions against South Africa, owing to the dependence of Swaziland's own economy on that country. Detentions and deportations of ANC members by the Swazi Government continued, while several suspected ANC members were abducted by South African security forces or killed in Swaziland by gunmen who were widely assumed to be South African. Following the legalization of the ANC in 1990, the Swazi Prime Minister, Obed Dlamini, pledged to conduct an inquiry (which, however, he failed to initiate) into state operations against ANC members. Formal diplomatic relations were established in 1993. From the late 1990s prominent South African organizations, including the ANC and COSATU, expressed support for the SFTU's demands for political reform, prompting the Swazi Government to protest of interference in its domestic affairs. In April 1995 the South African Government announced that it had rejected a long-standing claim by Swaziland to a region in the Mpumalanga province (formerly Eastern Transvaal). However, King Mswati declared in a letter to South African President, Thabo Mbeki, in early 2001 that he had not abandoned his intention to reincorporate parts of Mpumalanga and KwaZulu/Natal provinces into Swaziland. In 2003 the Chairperson of the Swaziland Border Adjustment Committee, Prince Khuzulwandle, criticized Mbeki for declining to discuss realignments of the border.

Following the ratification of the October 1992 peace accord in Mozambique (q.v.), an agreement signed by the Governments of Swaziland and Mozambique and the office of the UN High Commissioner for Refugees in August 1993 provided for the repatriation of some 24,000 Mozambican nationals from Swaziland. In December the number of Swazi troops deployed at the border with Mozambique was increased, following clashes between Swazi and Mozambican forces in the region. Mozambique subsequently protested at alleged border incursions by members of the Swazi armed forces. In early 1994 discussions took place between Swazi and Mozambican officials to seek mutually satisfactory arrangements for the joint patrol of the border, and in 1995 it was announced that the Mhlumeni border post, closed since the 1970s, would reopen as the second official transit point between the two countries. In September 1997, during the first visit to Swaziland made by a Mozambican Prime Minister, a bilateral extradition agreement was signed, with the aim of reducing cross-border crime. In December 1999 the Swazi authorities expelled some 500 Mozambican citizens who had been declared illegal immigrants. In the following month a campaign began to encourage Mozambicans living in Swaziland to register for military service there.

Government

The Constitution of 13 October 1978 vests supreme executive and legislative power in the hereditary King, who is the Head of State, and provides for a bicameral legislature, comprising a House of Assembly and a Senate. The functions of the legislature are confined to debating government proposals and advising the King. Executive power is exercised through the Cabinet (later redesignated the Council of Ministers), which is appointed by the King. The Swaziland National Council (Libandla), which comprises members of the royal family and is headed by the King and the constitutional dual monarch, the Queen Mother, provides advice on matters regulated by traditional law and custom.

Following a number of amendments to the electoral system, which were approved by King Mswati in October 1992, the House of Assembly was redesignated as the National Assembly and expanded to 65 deputies (of whom 55 are directly elected from candidates nominated by traditional local councils, known as Tinkhundla, and 10 appointed by the King), and the Senate to 30 members (of whom 20 are appointed by the King and 10 elected by the National Assembly). Elections to the National Assembly are conducted by secret ballot, in two rounds of voting; the second round of the elections is contested by the three candidates from each of the Tinkhundla who secure the highest number of votes in the first poll. Swaziland is divided into 273 regional tribal areas, comprising 55 elected Tinkhundla.

A new constitution came into effect on 7 February 2006. Executive power remained concentrated in the King, who appoints the Prime Minister and the Council of Ministers, and who has the power to dissolve the bicameral legislature.

Defence

The Umbutfo Swaziland Defence Force, created in 1973, totalled 2,657 regular troops in November 1983. Swaziland also has a paramilitary police force. Military service is compulsory and lasts for two years. Of total current expenditure by the central Government in 2001/02, E 168m. (6.6%) was allocated to defence.

Economic Affairs

In 2004, according to estimates by the World Bank, Swaziland's gross national income (GNI), measured at average 2002–04 prices, was US $1,859m., equivalent to $1,660 per head (or $4,970 per head on an international purchasing-power parity basis). During 1995–2004, it was estimated, the population increased at an average annual rate of 2.5%, while gross domestic product (GDP) per head increased, in real terms, by an average of 0.4% per year. Overall GDP increased, in real terms, at an average annual rate of 2.9% in 1995–2004; growth in 2004 was 2.1%.

Agriculture (including forestry) contributed an estimated 11.2% of GDP in 2004. About 32.3% of the labour force were employed in the agricultural sector in mid-2003. The principal cash crops are sugar cane (sugar accounted for 5.9% of domestic export earnings in 2002, compared with 9.3% in 2001), cotton, citrus fruits, pineapples and maize. Tobacco and rice are also cultivated. Livestock-rearing is traditionally important. Poor harvests in 2001 and 2002 necessitated the imports of basic foods in those years and substantial food imports were required in 2004, owing to low cereal production caused by drought. An estimated 70% of the maize crop was destroyed by drought in February 2005. At that time the UN World Food Programme was supplying food aid to some 260,000 people. Commercial forestry (which employs a significant proportion of the population) provides wood for the manufacture of pulp. During 1995–2004, according to the World Bank, agricultural GDP increased by an average of 2.3% per year. Agricultural GDP increased by 1.8% in 2004.

Industry (including mining, manufacturing, construction and power) contributed an estimated 46.4% of GDP in 2004. During 1995–2003, according to the World Bank, industrial GDP increased at an average annual rate of 2.6%. Industrial GDP increased by 1.8% in 2004.

Mining contributed an estimated 0.6% of GDP in 2004. Swaziland has extensive reserves of coal, much of which is exported. Asbestos is also an important mineral export. In addition, Swaziland has reserves of tin, kaolin, talc, iron ore, pyrophyllite and silica. During 2000–04, according to the IMF, mining GDP declined by an average of 5.0% per year; mining GDP declined by 20.2% in 2003 but increased by 9.0% in 2003.

Manufacturing contributed an estimated 35.9% of GDP in 2004, and is mainly based on the processing of agricultural, livestock and forestry products. Some 26% of the labour force were employed in the manufacturing sector in 1996/97. During 1995–2004, according to the World Bank, manufacturing GDP increased at an average annual rate of 2.1%. Manufacturing GDP increased by 2.0% in 2003 and by 1.8% in 2004.

Swaziland imports most of its energy requirements from South Africa. The Swazi Government aimed to increase domestic energy output to cover approximately 50% of the country's needs, following the construction of a hydroelectric power station on the Maguga Dam, which began operations in 2002. However, in 2004 89.9% of total electrical energy generated and imported was imported from South Africa, compared with 77.1% in 2002. Mineral fuels and lubricants accounted for an estimated 2.4% of imports in 2002. In November 2004 plans were being discussed for the construction of a 100-MW thermal power station in the Lowveld using bagasse, the waste left from processing sugar cane.

The services sector contributed an estimated 42.4% of GDP in 2004. According to the World Bank, the GDP of the services sector increased by an average of 3.4% per year in 1995–2004. Services GDP increased by 2.7% in 2004.

In 2004, according to estimates, Swaziland recorded a visible trade surplus of US $24.3m., while there was a surplus of $114.2m. on the current account of the balance of payments. In 2002 the principal source of imports was South Africa (84.6%) which was also the principal market for exports (67.5%); the USA and Mozambique were also important markets. The principal imports in 2002 year were machinery and transport equipment, basic manufactures, food and live animals, and chemicals and chemical products. The principal exports in that year were chemicals and chemical products, clothing and textiles, food and live animals and wood pulp.

In the financial year ending 31 March 2005 there was an overall budgetary deficit of E 715.1m.. Swaziland's external debt totalled US $399.8m. at the end of 2003, of which $346.3m. was long-term public debt. In that year the cost of debt-servicing was equivalent to 1.6% of the value of exports of goods and services. In 2000–04 annual inflation averaged 7.5%; consumer prices increased by an average of 3.5% in 2004. It was estimated that 40% of the labour force were unemployed in 1995.

Swaziland is a member of the Common Market for Eastern and Southern Africa (see p. 191), of the Southern African Development Community (SADC, see p. 358) and of the Southern African Customs Union (SACU), which also includes Botswana, Lesotho, Namibia and South Africa.

Swaziland's economy is vulnerable to fluctuations in international prices for some major exports, including sugar, as well as to the effects of unfavourable weather conditions. In addition, prevailing economic conditions in neighbouring South Africa have a pronounced impact on the Swazi economy: although Swaziland may determine the exchange rate of its currency, the lilangeni, this has remained at par with the South African rand. The decline in value of the rand and, consequently, the lilangeni from the late 1990s had a detrimental effect on Swaziland's economic performance, although there was some recovery

SWAZILAND

in the value of both currencies from 2003. In 1997 the Government presented the Economic and Social Reform Agenda, prepared in consultation with the IMF and the World Bank, which aimed to accelerate economic growth, reduce the level of unemployment and encourage investment in the private sector. In 1999 the IMF urged further fiscal and other reforms to strengthen Swaziland's public finances, in order to offset the effects of the new revenue-sharing agreement within SACU (the IMF projected that Swaziland's receipts from SACU would decline from 16% of GDP in 2000 to about 14% in 2004), and of free-trade agreements within SADC and between South Africa and the EU. In January 2003, and again in October of that year, the IMF urged fiscal discipline and increased social and humanitarian spending, and attributed low GDP growth to the country's lack of competitiveness in the region. At the beginning of 2004 the new Prime Minister, Themba Dlamini, made a number of proposals for the improvement of Swaziland's economic prospects, including a review of government spending, the encouragement of foreign investment and the promotion of small businesses; however, any progress was expected to be slow. In response to industrial action in the increasingly significant textiles industry, which employed an estimated 30,000 people, in early 2004 the Government announced its intention to establish a wages council for the sector. The removal in January 2005 of WTO quotas for textile exports to the USA brought Swaziland into direct competition with exporters based in Asia; the situation was compounded by the strengthening of the South African rand—and thus the lilangeni—and some 15,000 jobs in the textile industry were reportedly endangered, although Swaziland was still eligible for certain tariff preferences on exports to the USA under the African Growth and Opportunity Act until the end of September 2007. In 2004 the EU announced plans to reduce the price at which it purchased sugar from Swaziland by some 36% by 2007; it was anticipated that the price reduction would cost the industry some E 370m. during 2007–10. The EU did, however, allocate €100m. to assist Swazi farmers in diversifying into alternative crops, such as cotton, while domestically the Government continued to encourage farmers to grow geraniums for their essential oils. The medium-term prospects of the Swazi economy were also seriously threatened by the extremely high rate of HIV/AIDS infection among the labour force, while the securing of significant amounts of much-needed foreign investment in Swaziland remained dependent on a satisfactory political settlement.

Education

Education is neither free nor compulsory in Swaziland. Primary education begins at six years of age and lasts for seven years; the Government announced in the 2001 budget that it hoped to provide free primary education in the future. Secondary education begins at 13 years of age and lasts for up to five years, comprising a first cycle of three years and a second of two years. In 2000/01 93% of children in the relevant age-group (males 92%; females 94%) were enrolled at primary schools, while in 1999/2000 secondary enrolment included 44% of children in the appropriate age-group (males 40%; females 47%). In 2003/04 4,198 students were enrolled at the University of Swaziland, which has campuses at Luyengo and Kwaluseni; there are also a number of other institutions of higher education. According to the IMF, of total expenditure by the central Government in the financial year 2004/05, E 27.9m. (5.0%) was for education.

Public Holidays

2006: 1 January (New Year's Day), 14–17 April (Easter), 19 April (Birthday of King Mswati), 25 April (National Flag Day), 1 May (Workers' Day), 25 May (Ascension Day), 22 July (Birthday of the late King Sobhuza), 6 September (Somhlolo—Independence—Day), 24 October (UN Day), 25–26 December (Christmas and Boxing Day).

2007: 1 January (New Year's Day), 6–9 April (Easter), 19 April (Birthday of King Mswati), 25 April (National Flag Day), 1 May (Workers' Day), 5 May (Ascension Day), 22 July (Birthday of the late King Sobhuza), 6 September (Somhlolo—Independence—Day), 24 October (UN Day), 25–26 December (Christmas and Boxing Day).

The Incwala and Umhlanga Ceremonies are held in December or January, and August or September (respectively), but the exact dates are variable each year.

Statistical Survey

Source (unless otherwise stated): Central Statistical Office, POB 456, Mbabane; internet www.gov.sz/home.asp?pid=75.

Area and Population

AREA, POPULATION AND DENSITY

Area (sq km)	17,363*
Population (census results)†	
25 August 1986	681,059
11–12 May 1997	929,718
Population (UN estimates at mid-year)‡	
2002	1,033,000
2003	1,035,000
2004	1,034,000
Density (per sq km) at mid-2004	59.6

* 6,704 sq miles.
† Excluding absentee workers.
‡ Source: UN, *World Population Prospects: The 2004 Revision*.

ETHNIC GROUPS
(census of August 1986)

Swazi	661,646
Other Africans	14,468
European	1,825
Asiatic	228
Other non-Africans	412
Mixed	2,403
Unknown	77
Total	**681,059**

REGIONS
(population at census of May 1997; provisional figures, excluding absentee workers)

	Area (sq km)	Population	Density (per sq km)
Hhohho	3,569	247,539	69.4
Manzini	5,945	276,636	46.5
Shiselweni	4,070	198,084	48.7
Lebombo	3,779	190,617	50.4
Total	**17,363**	**912,876**	**52.6**

PRINCIPAL TOWNS
(population at census of May 1997)

Mbabane (capital)	57,992	Manzini	25,571

Mid-2003 (UN estimate, incl. suburbs): Manzini 100,833 (Source: UN, *World Urbanization Prospects: The 2003 Revision*).

BIRTHS AND DEATHS

	1990–1995	1995–2000	2000–05
Birth rate (per 1,000)	38.6	33.1	29.6
Death rate (per 1,000)	10.9	16.5	26.7

Source: UN, *World Population Prospects: The 2004 Revision*.

Expectation of life (UN estimates, years at birth): 35 (males 33; females 36) in 2003 (Source: WHO, *World Health Report*).

SWAZILAND

EMPLOYMENT
(labour force sample survey, '000 persons in paid employment, June 1996)

	Males	Females	Total
Agriculture, hunting, forestry and fishing	18.34	4.10	22.44
Mining and quarrying	1.10	0.04	1.14
Manufacturing	12.53	3.64	16.17
Electricity, gas and water	1.05	0.14	1.19
Construction	4.81	0.19	5.00
Trade, restaurants and hotels	6.79	5.10	11.89
Transport, storage and communications	2.44	0.27	2.70
Financing, insurance, real estate and business services	4.17	2.00	6.17
Community, social and personal services	12.31	10.86	23.17
Total employed	63.54	26.32	89.86

Source: ILO.

Mid-2003 (FAO estimates, '000 persons): Agriculture, etc. 120; Total labour force 372 (Source: FAO).

Health and Welfare

KEY INDICATORS

Total fertility rate (children per woman, 2003)	4.5
Under-5 mortality rate (per 1,000 live births, 2004)	156
HIV/AIDS (% of persons aged 15–49, 2003)	38.8
Physicians (per 1,000 head, 1996)	0.15
Health expenditure (2002): US$ per head (PPP)	309
Health expenditure (2002): % of GDP	6.0
Health expenditure (2002): public (% of total)	59.5
Access to water (% of persons, 2002)	52
Access to sanitation (% of persons, 2002)	52
Human Development Index (2003): ranking	147
Human Development Index (2003): value	0.498

For sources and definitions, see explanatory note on p. vi.

Agriculture

PRINCIPAL CROPS
('000 metric tons)

	2002	2003	2004*
Maize	76.2	69.3†	70.0
Potatoes*	6	6	6
Sweet potatoes*	2.3	2.3	2.3
Sugar cane*	4,300	4,500	4,500
Groundnuts (in shell)*	4.1	4.1	4.1
Cottonseed	4	4*	6.5
Cotton (lint)*	2	2	2
Tomatoes	3.1	3.4*	3.4
Other fresh vegetables*	7.3	7.3	7.3
Oranges*	36	36	36
Grapefruit and pomelo*	37	37	37
Pineapples*	32	32	32
Other fresh fruit*	5	5	5

* FAO estimate(s).
† Unofficial figure.
Source: FAO.

LIVESTOCK
('000 head, year ending September)

	2002	2003	2004*
Horses*	1.4	1.4	1.4
Asses*	14.8	14.8	14.8
Cattle	522.3†	520*	580
Pigs*	30	30	30
Sheep*	27	35	27
Goats	350*	273.6†	274.0
Chickens*	3,200	3,200	3,200

* FAO estimate(s).
† Unofficial figure.
Source: FAO.

LIVESTOCK PRODUCTS
('000 metric tons)

	2001	2002	2003
Beef and veal	8.0	12.5	12.5*
Goat meat*	2.9	2.4	1.9
Pig meat*	1.1	1.1	1.1
Poultry meat*	6.0	5.0	5.0
Cows' milk*	37.5	37.5	37.5

* FAO estimate(s).
2004: Figures assumed to be unchanged from 2003 (FAO estimates).
Source: FAO.

Forestry

ROUNDWOOD REMOVALS
(FAO estimates, '000 cubic metres, excl. bark)

	1996	1997	1998
Sawlogs, veneer logs and logs for sleepers	260	260	260
Pulpwood	604	604	—
Other industrial wood	70	70	70
Fuel wood	560	560	560
Total	1,494	1,494	890

1999–2004: Production as in 1998 (FAO estimates).
Source: FAO.

SAWNWOOD PRODUCTION
(FAO estimates, '000 cubic metres, incl. railway sleepers)

	1995	1996	1997
Total (all coniferous)	90	100	102

1998–2004: Production as in 1997.
Source: FAO.

Fishing

(metric tons, live weight)

	1999	2000*	2001*
Capture	70*	70	70
Aquaculture	61	69	72
Common carp	18	20	20
Mozambique tilapia	20	25	25
Redbreast tilapia	12	13	15
North African catfish	5	6	6
Red claw crayfish	6	5	6
Total catch	131*	139	142

* FAO estimate(s).
2002–03 (FAO estimate, metric tons, live weight): Capture 70.

SWAZILAND

Mining

(metric tons, unless otherwise indicated)

	2002	2003	2004*
Coal	313,272	553,422	550,000
Ferrovanadium	—	1,011	1,150
Quarrystone ('000 cu m)	300*	283	300

* Estimate(s).

Source: US Geological Survey.

Industry

SELECTED PRODUCTS
('000 metric tons, unless otherwise indicated)

	1999	2000	2001
Raw sugar	534	545	528
Wood pulp	191	191	191
Electrical energy (million kWh)*	435	435	n.a.

* Estimates.

Source: UN, *Industrial Commodity Statistics Yearbook*.

Electrical energy (million kWh, excl. self-generated power of some industrial units): 203.7 in 2002; 123.0 in 2003; 103.5 in 2004.

Sources: Swaziland Electricity Board and IMF, *Kingdom of Swaziland: Statistical Appendix* (March 2006).

Finance

CURRENCY AND EXCHANGE RATES

Monetary Units
100 cents = 1 lilangeni (plural: emalangeni).

Sterling, Dollar and Euro Equivalents (30 December 2005)
£1 sterling = 10.8910 emalangeni;
US $1 = 6.3250 emalangeni;
€1 = 7.4616 emalangeni;
1,000 emalangeni = £91.82 = $158.10 = €134.02.

Average Exchange Rate (emalangeni per US $)
2003   7.5648
2004   6.4597
2005   6.3593

Note: The lilangeni is at par with the South African rand

BUDGET
(million emalangeni, year ending 31 March)

Revenue*	2002/03	2003/04	2004/05
Tax revenue	3,107.4	3,660.5	4,627.8
Taxes on net income and profits	827.5	1,105.4	1,164.0
Companies	259.6	322.4	324.0
Individuals	494.1	698.7	742.0
Non-resident dividends and interest	73.8	84.3	98.0
Taxes on property	6.0	9.0	12.0
Taxes on goods, services, and international trade	2,269.2	2,540.8	3,445.8
Receipts from Southern African Customs Union	1,618.6	1,878.1	2,772.8
Levies on sugar exports	21.8	12.1	22.0
Hotel and gaming taxes	3.7	4.4	5.0
Sales tax	528.6	547.7	549.0
Licenses and other taxes	96.6	98.5	97.0
Other taxes	4.7	5.3	6.0
Other current revenue	157.1	104.9	98.0
Property income	108.6	52.0	46.0
Fees, fines, and non-industrial sales	48.5	52.9	52.0
Total	3,264.5	3,765.4	4,725.8

Expenditure†	2002/03	2003/04	2004/05
Current expenditure	3,045.0	3,437.2	4,294.9
Wages and salaries	1,417.1	1,668.9	1,964.0
Other purchases of goods and services	905.6	1,003.0	1,421.0
Interest payments	167.3	173.8	168.0
Domestic	0.0	37.0	49.0
Foreign	163.7	136.8	119.0
Subsidies and other current transfers	555.0	591.5	742.0
Capital expenditure	935.5	817.8	1,259.0
Education	48.0	13.0	27.9
Agriculture	31.0	48.0	104.5
Transport and communications	427.0	125.0	347.6
Other	407.5	571.8	696.4
Total	3,980.5	4,255.0	5,553.9

* Excluding grants received (million emalangeni): 163.0 in 2002/03; 137.7 in 2003/04; 116.0 in 2004/05.

† Excluding net lending (million emalangeni): 37.7 in 2002/03; 59.0 in 2003/04; 3.0 in 2004/05.

Source: IMF, *Kingdom of Swaziland: Statistical Appendix* (March 2006).

INTERNATIONAL RESERVES
(excl. gold, US $ million at 31 December)

	2002	2003	2004
IMF special drawing rights	3.35	3.67	3.84
Reserve position in IMF	8.91	9.74	10.19
Foreign exchange	263.59	264.11	309.53
Total	275.84	277.51	323.56

Source: IMF, *International Financial Statistics*.

MONEY SUPPLY
(million emalangeni at 31 December)

	2002	2003	2004
Currency outside banks	155.44	213.45	235.85
Demand deposits at deposit money banks	670.09	834.39	843.08
Total	825.53	1,047.84	1,078.93

COST OF LIVING
(Consumer Price Index; base: 2000 = 100)

	2002	2003	2004
Food	129.8	145.7	155.7
All items (incl. others)	120.2	129.0	133.5

Source: ILO.

NATIONAL ACCOUNTS
(million emalangeni at current prices)

Expenditure on the Gross Domestic Product

	2002	2003	2004*
Government final consumption expenditure	2,334.7	2,681.0	3,422.6
Private final consumption expenditure	7,772.3	9,199.8	10,552.4
Gross fixed capital formation	2,486.4	2,590.4	2,831.6
Total domestic expenditure	12,593.4	14,471.2	16,806.6
Exports of goods and services	11,923.0	12,416.1	15,223.1
Less Imports of goods and services	11,956.4	12,464.9	15,767.4
GDP in purchasers' values	12,560.0	14,422.4	16,262.3

SWAZILAND

Gross Domestic Product by Economic Activity

	2002	2003	2004*
Agriculture and forestry	1,075.0	1,050.5	1,063.6
Mining	47.3	50.4	57.0
Manufacturing	2,983.3	3,269.7	3,403.0
Electricity and water	127.5	130.6	134.0
Construction	504.2	539.0	797.3
Wholesale and retail trade	642.5	715.7	797.3
Hotels and restaurants	143.2	146.8	147.8
Transport and communications	434.8	481.7	479.7
Banking, finance and insurance	285.1	314.2	382.4
Real estate	86.3	89.4	93.2
Government services	1,496.1	1,687.3	1,856.0
Other services	85.0	86.7	89.2
Owner-occupied dwellings	158.0	161.0	165.7
Sub total	8,068.3	8,723.0	9,466.2
Less Imputed bank service charge	192.6	212.3	240.9
GDP at factor cost	7,875.7	8,510.7	9,225.3
Indirect taxes / *Less* Subsidies	4,684.3	5,911.7	7,037.0
GDP at purchasers' values	12,560.0	14,422.4	16,262.3

* Estimates.

Source: IMF, *Kingdom of Swaziland: Statistical Appendix* (March 2006).

BALANCE OF PAYMENTS
(US $ million)

	2002	2003	2004
Exports of goods f.o.b.	1,029.2	1,625.6	1,938.3
Imports of goods f.o.b.	−938.7	−1,508.1	−1,913.3
Trade balance	−90.5	117.5	24.3
Exports of services	102.0	255.4	499.5
Imports of services	−195.6	−299.5	−533.8
Balance on goods and services	−3.1	73.4	−10.0
Other income received	143.9	143.5	160.6
Other income paid	−145.8	−147.1	−128.7
Balance on goods, services and income	−5.0	69.8	21.9
Current transfers received	198.5	333.3	424.4
Current transfers paid	−135.9	−287.0	−332.2
Current balance	57.5	116.2	114.2
Capital account (net)	0.5	—	−0.6
Direct investment abroad	−0.2	−10.5	−3.6
Direct investment from abroad	88.8	−60.9	68.4
Portfolio investment assets	3.9	−0.3	−10.7
Portfolio investment liabilities	−2.0	−0.1	−0.3
Other investment assets	−99.0	64.4	−117.5
Other investment liabilities	−45.9	−20.0	−46.6
Net errors and omissions	−29.3	−133.0	−21.9
Overall balance	−25.8	−44.1	−18.5

Source: IMF, *International Financial Statistics*.

External Trade

PRINCIPAL COMMODITIES
(distribution by SITC, US $ million)

Imports c.i.f.	2000	2001	2002
Food and live animals	164.9	129.4	131.9
Beverages and tobacco	27.3	19.7	18.1
Crude materials (inedible) except fuels	34.2	31.9	27.2
Mineral fuels and lubricants	138.5	95.7	19.9
Petroleum and petroleum products	121.3	84.9	3.9
Chemicals and related products	115.0	101.8	95.1
Manufactures classified chiefly by materials	179.7	145.1	182.6
Machinery and transport equipment	299.0	192.7	201.1
Specialized machinery	34.4	33.0	35.7
General industrial machinery	89.2	29.2	29.2
Electric machinery, apparatus appliances and parts	44.6	21.0	20.6
Road vehicles	96.6	79.2	73.6
Miscellaneous manufactures	114.4	99.9	98.8
Total (incl. others)	1,098.6	832.0	797.8

Exports f.o.b.	2000	2001	2002
Food and live animals	283.9	257.5	125.6
Sugar, sugar preparations and honey	120.1	96.5	74.6
Crude materials (inedible) except fuels	102.7	87.4	79.9
Wood pulp	60.5	60.7	56.3
Chemicals and related products	178.6	143.9	465.5
Manufactures classified chiefly by materials	44.9	28.3	31.9
Textile yarn, fabrics and related products	21.4	12.7	16.2
Machinery and transport equipment	86.4	31.2	35.3
General industrial machinery	26.8	6.5	9.3
Electric machinery, apparatus appliances and parts	30.2	3.1	4.9
Miscellaneous manufactures	174.1	114.1	211.8
Clothing and accessories	124.0	79.5	173.5
Total (incl. others)	890.8	677.8	974.1

Source: UN, *International Trade Statistics Yearbook*.

PRINCIPAL TRADING PARTNERS
(US $ million)

Imports c.i.f.	2000	2001	2002
China, People's Repub.	4.2	3.9	12.9
Hong Kong	11.9	8.2	19.6
Japan	8.1	7.5	8.1
South Africa	1,023.4	786.5	675.3
Total (incl. others)	1,098.6	832.0	797.8

Exports f.o.b.	2000	2001	2002
Angola	5.8	10.0	7.5
Mozambique	55.5	31.4	52.2
South Africa	531.5	528.6	657.5
Tanzania	27.1	9.4	13.3
United Kingdom	33.0	7.2	12.3
USA	78.8	26.8	78.3
Zimbabwe	33.4	7.3	28.2
Total (incl. others)	890.8	677.8	974.1

Source: UN, *International Trade Statistics Yearbook*.

SWAZILAND

Transport

RAILWAYS
(traffic)

	1999	2000	2001
Net total ton-km (million)	677	753	746

Source: UN, *Statistical Yearbook*.

ROAD TRAFFIC
(motor vehicles in use at 31 December)

	1997	1998
Passenger cars	31,882	34,064
Buses and coaches	3,495	4,089
Lorries and vans	29,277	30,941
Motorcycles and mopeds	n.a.	2,588

Source: International Road Federation, *World Road Statistics*.

CIVIL AVIATION
(traffic on scheduled services)

	1998	1999	2000
Kilometres flown (million)	1	1	2
Passengers carried ('000)	41	12	90
Passenger-km (million)	43	13	68
Total ton-km (million)	4	1	6

Source: UN, *Statistical Yearbook*.

Tourism

TOURIST ARRIVALS
(at hotels)

Country of residence	2001	2002	2003
Australia	3,784	1,496	701
Mozambique	19,455	17,304	11,642
Portugal	2,014	2,006	8,666
South Africa	112,157	146,286	85,899
United Kingdom	13,684	5,818	13,702
Total (incl. others)	283,177	255,927	218,813

Tourism receipts (US $ million): 31 in 2001; 31 in 2002; 16 in 2003.

Source: World Tourism Organization.

Communications Media

	2002	2003	2004
Television receivers ('000 in use)*	32	n.a.	n.a.
Telephones ('000 main lines in use)	35.1	46.2	46.2†
Mobile cellular telephones ('000 subscribers)	68.0	88.0	113.0
Personal computers ('000 in use)	25	30	36
Internet users ('000)	20.0	27.0	36.0

* Year ending 31 March.
† Estimate.

Source: International Telecommunication Union.

Radio receivers (year ending 31 March 1998): 155,000 in use (Source: UN, *Statistical Yearbook*).

Daily newspapers (1996): 3 (estimated circulation 24,000) (Source: UN, *Statistical Yearbook*).

Education

(2001, unless otherwise indicated)

	Institutions	Teachers	Students
Primary	541	6,594	212,064
Secondary	182	3,647	61,335
University*	1†	257‡	3,692†

* Figures exclude vocational, technical and teacher-training colleges. In 2000, there were 1,822 students enrolled at these institutions, which numbered 10 in 2003.
† Figure for 2000.
‡ Figure for 1996/97.

Source: partly UNESCO Institute for Statistics; SADC Education Policy Support Initiative.

Adult literacy rate (UNESCO estimates): 79.2% (males 80.4%; females 78.1%) in 2003 (Source: UN Development Programme, *Human Development Report*).

Directory

The Constitution

The Constitution of 13 October 1978 vests supreme executive and legislative power in the hereditary King (Ngwenyama—the Lion). Succession is governed by traditional law and custom. In the event of the death of the King, the powers of Head of State are transferred to the constitutional dual monarch, the Queen Mother (Indlovukazi—Great She Elephant), who is authorized to act as Regent until the designated successor attains the age of 21. The Constitution provides for a bicameral legislature, comprising a House of Assembly and a Senate. The functions of the Swaziland National Council (Libandla) are confined to debating government proposals and advising the King. Executive power is exercised through the Cabinet (later redesignated the Council of Ministers), which is appointed by the King. The Libandla, which comprises members of the royal family, and is headed by the King and Queen Mother, advises on matters regulated by traditional law and custom. The Constitution affirms the fundamental rights of the individual.

Following a number of amendments to the electoral system, which were approved by the King in October 1992, the House of Assembly (which was redesignated as the National Assembly) was expanded to 65 deputies (of whom 55 are directly elected from candidates nominated by traditional local councils, known as Tinkhundla, and 10 appointed by the King), and the Senate to 30 members (of whom 20 are appointed by the King and 10 elected by the National Assembly). Elections to the National Assembly are conducted by secret ballot, in two rounds of voting; the second round of the elections is contested by the three candidates from each of the Tinkhundla who secure the highest number of votes in the first poll. In July 1996 the King appointed a commission to prepare proposals for a draft constitution, which would subsequently be submitted for approval by the Swazi people. The commission submitted its report in August 2001, and in February 2002 a committee began drafting a new constitution, based on the commission's recommendations. In May 2003 the completion of the draft document was announced.

The draft Constitution was approved by a joint sitting of the National Assembly and the Senate in mid-June 2005, but was initially rejected by King Mswati. The King approved and signed an amended version on 26 July. The new Constitution came into effect on 7 February 2006 (see Recent History). Executive power remained concentrated in the King, who appoints the Prime Minister and the Council of Ministers, and who has the power to dissolve the bicameral legislature. Further details of the new Constitution were not immediately made available.

The Government

HEAD OF STATE

King: HM King Mswati III (succeeded to the throne 25 April 1986).

COUNCIL OF MINISTERS
(March 2006)

Prime Minister: Absalom Themba Dlamini.
Deputy Prime Minister: Albert Shabangu.
Minister of Justice and Constitutional Affairs: Prince David.
Minister of Finance: Majozi Sithole.
Minister of Home Affairs: Prince Gabheni.
Minister of Foreign Affairs and Trade: Moses Mathendele Dlamini.
Minister of Education: Constance Simelane.
Minister of Regional Development and Youth Affairs: Chief Sipho Shongwe.
Minister of Agriculture and Co-operatives: Mtiti Fakudze.
Minister of Enterprise and Employment: Lutfo Dlamini.
Minister of Economic Planning and Development: Rev. Absalom Dlamini.
Minister of Health and Social Welfare: Mfomfo Nkambule.
Minister of Public Service and Information: Themba Msibi.
Minister of Public Works and Transport: Elijah Shongwe.
Minister of Natural Resources and Energy: Dumsile Sukati.
Minister of Tourism, the Environment and Communication: Thandi Shongwe.
Minister of Housing and Urban Development: Mabili Dlamini.

MINISTRIES

Office of the Prime Minister: POB 433, Swazi Plaza, Mbabane; tel. 4042251; fax 4043943; internet www.gov.sz.
Office of the Deputy Prime Minister: POB 433, Swazi Plaza, Mbabane; tel. 4042723; fax 4044085.
Ministry of Agriculture and Co-operatives: POB 162, Mbabane; tel. 4042731; fax 4044700.
Ministry of Economic Planning and Development: POB 602, Mbabane; tel. 4043765; fax 4042157.
Ministry of Education: POB 39, Mbabane; tel. 4042491; fax 4043880.
Ministry of Enterprise and Employment: POB 451, Mbabane; tel. 4043201; fax 4044711; e-mail sglabour@realnet.co.sz.
Ministry of Finance: POB 443, Mbabane; tel. 4048148; fax 4043187; e-mail minfin@realnet.co.sz.
Ministry of Foreign Affairs and Trade: POB 518, Mbabane; tel. 4042661; fax 4042669.
Ministry of Health and Social Welfare: POB 5, Mbabane; tel. 4042431; fax 4042092; e-mail minhealth@realnet.co.sz.
Ministry of Home Affairs: POB 432, Mbabane; tel. 4042941; fax 4044303.
Ministry of Housing and Urban Development: POB 1832, Mbabane; tel. 4041739; fax 4045290.
Ministry of Justice and Constitutional Affairs: POB 924, Mbabane; tel. 4046010; fax 4043533; e-mail ps@justice.gov.sz.
Ministry of Natural Resources and Energy: POB 57, Mbabane; tel. 4046244; fax 4042436; e-mail nergyswa@realnet.co.sz.
Ministry of Public Service and Information: POB 338, Mbabane; tel. 4042761; fax 4042774.
Ministry of Public Works and Transport: POB 58, Mbabane; tel. 4042321; fax 4042364; e-mail minister-moptw@realnet.co.sz.
Ministry of Regional Development and Youth Affairs: Phutfumani Bldg, Warner St, Mbabane; POB 125, Mbabane H100.
Ministry of Tourism, the Environment and Communication: POB 2652, Mbabane; tel. 4046556; fax 4045415; internet www.mintour.gov.sz.

Legislature

SENATE

There are 30 senators, of whom 20 are appointed by the King and 10 elected by the National Assembly.
President: Muntu Msawane.

NATIONAL ASSEMBLY

There are 65 deputies, of whom 55 are directly elected from candidates nominated by the Tinkhundla and 10 appointed by the King. The latest elections to the National Assembly took place on 18 October 2003.
Speaker: Charles S'gayoyo Magongo.

Political Organizations

Party political activity was banned by royal proclamation in April 1973, and formally prohibited under the 1978 Constitution. Since 1991, following indications that the Constitution was to be revised, a number of political associations have re-emerged.

Imbokodvo National Movement (INM): f. 1964 by King Sobhuza II; traditionalist movement, which also advocates policies of development and the elimination of illiteracy; Leader (vacant).
Ngwane National Liberatory Congress (NNLC): Ilanga Centre, Martin St, Manzini; tel. 5053935; f. 1962 by fmr mems of the SPP; advocates democratic freedoms and universal suffrage, and seeks abolition of the Tinkhundla electoral system; Pres. Obed Dlamini; Sec.-Gen. Dumisa Dlamini.
People's United Democratic Movement (PUDEMO): POB 4588, Manzini; tel. and fax 5054181; internet www.members.nbci.com/pudemo; f. 1983; seeks constitutional limitation of the powers of the monarchy; affiliated orgs include the Human Rights Asscn of Swaziland and the Swaziland Youth Congress (SWAYOCO—Pres. Bongani Masuku; Sec.-Gen. Kenneth Kunene); Pres. Mario Masuku; Sec.-Gen. Bong'nkosi Dlamini.
Swaziland National Front (SWANAFRO): Mbabane; Pres. Elmond Shongwe; Sec.-Gen. Glenrose Dlamini.
Swaziland Progressive Party (SPP): POB 6, Mbabane; tel. 2022648; f. 1929; Pres. J. J. Nquku.
Swaziland United Front (SUF): POB 14, Kwaluseni; f. 1962 by fmr mems of the SPP; Leader Matsapa Shongwe.

Diplomatic Representation

EMBASSIES IN SWAZILAND

China (Taiwan): Embassy House, Warner St, POB 56, Mbabane; tel. 4042379; fax 4046688; e-mail chineseembassy@africaonline.co.sz; Ambassador George Jin-gou Chang.
Mozambique: Princess Dr., POB 1212, Mbabane; tel. 4043700; fax 4048402; Ambassador Amour Zacarias Kapela.
South Africa: The New Mall, 2nd Floor, Plasmall St, POB 2597, Mbabane; tel. 4044651; fax 4044335; e-mail sahc@africaonline.co.sz; High Commissioner Dr Mzolisi Mabude.
USA: Central Bank Bldg, Warner St, POB 199, Mbabane; tel. 4046442; fax 4045959; e-mail usembswd@realnet.co.sz; internet usembassy.state.gov/posts/wz1/wwwhhome.html; Ambassador Lewis W. Lucke.

Judicial System

Swaziland's legal system operates on a dual basis, comprising both traditional Swazi National Courts as well as Constitutional Courts. The latter are based on Roman-Dutch law and comprise a High Court (which is a Superior Court of Record) with subordinate courts in all the administrative districts. The Court of Appeal sits at Mbabane. The Constitutional Courts are headed by a Chief Justice, subordinate to whom are judges and magistrates. There is also an Industrial Court.

There are 17 Swazi National Courts, including two Courts of Appeal and a Higher Court of Appeal, which have limited jurisdiction in civil and criminal cases. Their jurisdiction excludes non-Swazi nationals. The Constitutional Courts have the final ruling in the event of any conflict between the two legal systems.

Chief Justice: Jacobus Annandale (acting).
Judge President of the Court of Appeal: Ray Leon.

Religion

About 60% of the adult Swazi population profess Christianity. Under the new Constitution, which came into effect on 7 February 2006, Christianity ceased to be recognized as the country's official religion. At mid-2005 there was a growing Muslim population, reported to number some 10,000 adherents. Most of the remainder of the population hold traditional beliefs.

SWAZILAND

CHRISTIANITY

At mid-2000 there were an estimated 153,000 Protestants and 466,000 adherents professing other forms of Christianity.

Council of Swaziland Churches: Mandlenkosi Ecumenical House, 142 Esser St, Manzini; POB 1095, Manzini; tel. 5053697; fax 5055841; e-mail c.o.c@africaonline.co.sz; f. 1976; Chair. Rev. M. B. MABUZA; Gen. Sec. MARIA MBELU; 12 mem. churches incl. Roman Catholic, Anglican, Kukhanya Okusha Church in Zion and Lutheran.

League of African Churches: POB 230, Lobamba; asscn of 48 independent churches; Chair. SAMSON HLATJWAKO.

Swaziland Conference of Churches: 175 Ngwane St, POB 1157, Manzini; tel. 5055259; fax 5054430; f. 1929; Pres. Rev. NICHOLAS NYAWO; Gen. Sec. JOHANNES V. MAZIBUKO.

The Anglican Communion

Swaziland comprises a single diocese within the Church of the Province of Southern Africa. The Metropolitan of the Province is the Archbishop of Cape Town, South Africa. The Church had some 40,000 members at mid-2000.

Bishop of Swaziland: Rt Rev. MESHACK BOY MABUZA, Bishop's House, Muir St, POB 118 Mbabane; tel. 4043624; fax 4046759; e-mail anglicanchurch@africaonline.co.sz.

The Roman Catholic Church

The Roman Catholic Church was established in Swaziland in 1913. For ecclesiastical purposes, Swaziland comprises the single diocese of Manzini, suffragan to the archdiocese of Pretoria, South Africa. At 31 December 2003 there were an estimated 55,130 adherents in Swaziland (some 5.6% of the total population). The Bishop participates in the Southern African Catholic Bishops' Conference (based in Pretoria, South Africa).

Bishop of Manzini: Rt Rev. LOUIS NCAMISO NDLOVU, Bishop's House, Sandlane St, POB 19, Manzini; tel. 5056900; fax 5056762; e-mail bishop@africaonline.co.sz.

Other Christian Churches

Church of the Nazarene: POB 1460, Manzini; tel. 5054732; f. 1910; 7,649 adherents (1994).

The Evangelical Lutheran Church in Southern Africa: POB 117, Mbabane; tel. 4046453; f. 1902; Bishop R. SCHIELE; 2,800 adherents in Swaziland (1994).

Lutheran Development Service: POB 388, Mbabane; tel. 4042562; fax 4043870; e-mail lds@realnet.co.sz; Dir BJORN BRANDBERG.

Mennonite Central Committee: POB 329, Mbabane; tel. 4042805; fax 4044732; f. 1971; Co-ordinators JON RUDY, CAROLYN RUDY.

The Methodist Church in Southern Africa: POB 218, Mbabane; tel. 4042658; f. 1880; 2,578 adherents (1992).

United Christian Church of Africa: POB 253, Nhlangano; tel. 2022648; f. 1944; Pres. Rt Rev. JEREMIAH NDZINISA; Founder and Gen. Sec. Dr J. J. NQUKU.

The National Baptist Church, the Christian Apostolic Holy Spirit Church in Zion and the Religious Society of Friends (Quakers) are also active.

BAHÁ'Í FAITH

National Spiritual Assembly: POB 298, Mbabane; tel. 5052689; f. 1960; mems resident in 153 localities.

ISLAM

Ezulwini Islamic Institute: Al Islam Dawah Movement of Swaziland, POB 133, Ezulwini; c. 3,000 adherents (1994).

The Press

PRINCIPAL PERIODICALS

Farming in Swaziland: POB 592, Mbabane; tel. 4043400; e-mail cft@realnet.co.sz; quarterly; Editor CHRISTINA FORSYTH THOMPSON; circ. 3,000.

The Nation: Mbabane House, 3rd Floor, Warner St, POB 4547, Mbabane; tel. 4046611; e-mail thenation@realnet.co.sz; f. 1997; monthly; independent news magazine; publ. suspended briefly May 2001; Editor BHEKI MAKHUBU.

Swaziview: Mbabane; tel. 4042716; monthly magazine; general interest; circ. 3,500.

UNISWA Journal of Agriculture: Faculty of Agriculture, University of Swaziland, Luyengo Campus, PO Luyengo M205; tel. and fax 5283021; fax 5283441; e-mail mwendera@agric.uniswa.sz; annually; Editor-in-Chief Prof. EMMANUEL J. MWENDERA.

UNISWA Research Journal of Agriculture, Science and Technology: Private Bag 4, Kwaluseni; tel. 5186126; fax 5185276; 2 a year; publ. of the Faculties of Agriculture, Health Sciences and Science of the Univ. of Swaziland; Chair. Prof. H. M. MUSHALA.

Publishers

Apollo Services (Pty) Ltd: POB 35, Mbabane; tel. 4042711.

GBS Printing and Publishing (Pty) Ltd: POB 1384, Mbabane; tel. 5052779.

Jubilee Printers: POB 1619, Matsaka; tel. 5184557; fax 5184558.

Longman Swaziland (Pty) Ltd: POB 2207, Manzini; tel. 5053891.

Macmillan Boleswa Publishers (Pty) Ltd: POB 1235, Manzini; tel. 5184533; fax 5185247; Man. Dir T. BALL.

Swaziland Printing & Publishing Co Ltd: POB 28, Mbabane; tel. 4042716; fax 4042710.

Whydah Media Publishers Ltd: Mbabane; tel. 4042716; f. 1978.

Broadcasting and Communications

TELECOMMUNICATIONS

MTN Swaziland: Smuts St, POB 5050, H100 Mbabane; tel. 4060000; fax 4046217; e-mail yellohelp@mtn.co.sz; internet www.mtn.co.sz; f. 1998; operates mobile cellular telephone network; CEO THEMBA KHUMALO.

Swaziland Posts and Telecommunications Corpn (SPTC): Phutfumani Bldg, Warner St, POB 125, H100 Mbabane; tel. 4052000; fax 4052020; e-mail info@sptc.co.sz; internet www.sptc.co.sz; f. 1986; Chair. WINNIE NXUMALO-MAGAGULA; Man. Dir VUSUMUZI N. MKHUMANE.

BROADCASTING

Radio

Swaziland Broadcasting and Information Service: POB 338, Mbabane; tel. 4042763; fax 4042774; e-mail sbisnews@africaonline.co.sz; f. 1966; broadcasts in English and siSwati; Dir STAN MOTSA.

Swaziland Commercial Radio (Pty) Ltd: POB 1586, Alberton 1450, South Africa; tel. (11) 4344333; fax (11) 4344777; privately-owned commercial service; broadcasts to southern Africa in English and Portuguese; music and religious programmes; Man. Dir A. DE ANDRADE.

Trans World Radio: POB 64, Manzini; tel. 5052781; fax 5055333; f. 1974; religious broadcasts from five transmitters in 30 languages to southern, central and eastern Africa and to the Far East; Pres. DAVID TUCKER.

Television

Swaziland Television Authority: POB A146, Swazi Plaza, Mbabane; tel. 4043036; fax 4042093; e-mail swazitv.eng@africaonline.co.sz; f. 1978; state-owned; broadcasts seven hours daily in English; colour transmissions; CEO CELANI NDZIMANDZE (acting).

Finance

(cap. = capital; res = reserves; dep. = deposits; m. = million; brs = branches; amounts in emalangeni)

BANKING

Central Bank

Central Bank of Swaziland: POB 546, Warner St, Mbabane; tel. 4082000; fax 4042636; e-mail info@centralbank.org.sz; internet www.centralbank.org.sz; f. 1974; bank of issue; cap. 21.8m., res 188.3m., dep. 322.2m. (March 2002); Gov. MARTIN G. DLAMINI; Dep. Gov. S. G. MDLULI.

Commercial Banks

First National Bank of Swaziland Ltd: Sales House Bldg, 2nd Floor, POB 261, Mbabane; tel. 4045401; fax 4044735; f. 1988; fmrly Meridien Bank Swaziland Ltd; cap. and res 61.5m., dep. 484.5m. (June 2002); Chair. Dr D. M. J. VON WISSEL; Man. Dir R. A. PAWSON; 7 brs and 1 agency.

Nedbank (Swaziland) Ltd: Nebank House, Dr Sishayi and Sozisa Rds, Swazi Plaza, POB 68, Mbabane; tel. 4081000; fax 4044060; e-mail bmvubu@nedcor.com; internet www.nedbank.co.sz; f. 1974;

fmrly Standard Chartered Bank Swaziland Ltd; 23.1% state-owned; cap. and res 77.8m., dep. 649.0m., total assets 752.1m. (Dec. 2004); Chair. Z. M. NKOSI; Man. Dir AMBROSE DLAMINI; 6 brs and 1 agency.

Development Banks

Standard Bank Swaziland Ltd: Standard House, 1st Floor, Swazi Plaza, POB A294, Mbabane; tel. 4046930; fax 4045899; internet www.standardbank.co.sz; f. 1988; fmrly Stanbic Bank Swaziland, present name adopted 1997; merged with Barclays Bank of Swaziland in Jan. 1998; 10% state-owned; cap. and res 88.0m., total assets 1,156.1m. (Dec. 2001); Chair. R. J. ROSSOUW (acting); Man. Dir MERVYN LUBBE; 10 brs; 1 agency.

Swaziland Development and Savings Bank (SwaziBank—Libhange LeSive): Engungwini Bldg, Gwamile St, POB 336, Mbabane; tel. 4042551; fax 4042550; e-mail swazibank@swazibank.sz; internet www.swazibank.sz; f. 1965; state-owned; taken over by central bank in 1995; under independent management since 2000; cap. and res 143.0m., total assets 557.9m. (Mar. 2002); Chair NOKUKHANYA GAMEDZE; Man. Dir STANLEY M. N. MATSEBULA; 8 brs.

Financial Institution

Swaziland National Provident Fund: POB 1857, Manzini; tel. 5053731; fax 5054377; total assets 290m. (June 1996).

STOCK EXCHANGE

Swaziland Stock Exchange: Capital Markets Development Unit, Infumbe Bldg, 1st Floor, Warner St, POB 546, Mbabane; tel. 4082164; fax 4049493; e-mail info@ssx.org.sz; internet www.ssx.org.sz; f. 1990; state-owned; Chair. MARTIN G. DLAMINI.

INSURANCE

Between 1974 and 1999 the state-controlled Swaziland Royal Insurance Corpn (SRIC) operated as the country's sole authorized insurance company, although cover in a number of areas not served by SRIC was available from several specialized insurers. In 1999 it was proposed that legislation would be enacted to end SRIC's monopoly and provide for the company's transfer to private-sector ownership. Parliamentary debate over the legislation was ongoing in 2006.

Insurance Companies

Swaziland Employee Benefit Consultants (Pty) Ltd: Sales House Bldg, 2nd Floor, Swazi Plaza, POB 3159, Mbabane; tel. 4044776; fax 4046413; e-mail hollands@aforbes.co.sz; 50% owned by Alexander Forbes Ltd; specialized medical cover; Man. SIMON HOLLAND.

Swaziland Royal Insurance Corpn (SRIC): Liluga House, Gilfillan St, POB 917, H100 Mbabane; tel. 4043231; fax 4046415; e-mail zrmagagula@sric.sz; internet www.sric.sz; 51% state-owned; 49% owned by Munich-Reinsurance Co of Africa Ltd., Commercial Union Insurance Co of South Africa Ltd, Swiss Re Southern Africa Ltd and S.A. Eagle Insurance Co Ltd; sole auth. insurance co 1974–99; Chair. Dr E. T. GINA; Gen. Man. ZOMBODZE R. MAGAGULA.

Insurance Association

Insurance Brokers' Association of Swaziland (IBAS): Swazi Plaza H101, POB A32, Mbabane; tel. 4046411; fax 4046412; f. 1983; 4 mems.

Trade and Industry

GOVERNMENT AGENCY

Swaziland Investment Promotion Authority (SIPA): POB 4194, Mbabane; tel. 4040470; fax 4043374; e-mail info@sipa.org.uk; internet www.sipa.org.sz; f. 1998; Gen. Man. BHEKI R. DLAMINI.

DEVELOPMENT ORGANIZATIONS

National Industrial Development Corpn of Swaziland (NIDCS): POB 866, Mbabane; tel. 4043391; fax 4045619; f. 1971; state-owned; administered by Swaziland Industrial Development Co; Admin. Dir P. K. THAMM.

Small Enterprise Development Co (SEDCO): POB A186, Swazi Plaza, Mbabane; tel. 4042811; fax 4040723; e-mail business@sedco.co.sz; internet www.sedco.co.sz; f. 1970; government devt agency; supplies workshop space, training and expertise for 120 local entrepreneurs at seven sites throughout the country; CEO BERTRAM B. STEWART.

Swaziland Coalition of Concerned Civic Organisations (SCCCO): Smithco Industrial Centre, Mswati III Ave, 11th St, MatsaphaPOB 4173, Mbabane; tel. and fax 5187688; e-mail webmaster@swazicoalition.org.sz; internet www.swazicoalition.org.sz; f. 2003; promotes constitutional democracy, poverty alleviation, fiscal discipline, economic stability, competitive regional and international trade, social justice, and the rule of law; Sec.-Gen. MUSA HLOPE; 9 mems:

Coordinating Assembly of Non-Governmental Organisations (CANGO): POB A67, Swazi Plaza, Mbabane; tel. 4044721; fax 4045532; e-mail cango@africaonline.co.sz; internet www.cango.org.sz; f. 1983; Dir EMMANUEL NDLANGAMANDLA; over 70 mem. orgs.

Swaziland Industrial Development Co (SIDC): Dhlan'Ubeka House, 5th Floor, cnr Tin and Walker Sts, POB 866, Mbabane; tel. 4044010; fax 4045619; e-mail info@sidc.co.sz; internet www.sidc.co.sz; f. 1986; 34.9% state-owned; finances private-sector projects and promotes local and foreign investment; cap. E24.1m., total assets E178.4m. (June 1999); Chair. TIM ZWANE; Man. Dir TAMBO GINA.

Swaki (Pty) Ltd: Liqhaga Bldg, 4th Floor, Nkoseluhlaza St, POB 1839, Manzini; tel. 5052693; fax 5052001; jtly owned by SIDC and Kirsh Holdings; comprises a number of cos involved in manufacturing, services and the production and distribution of food (especially maize).

Tibiyo Taka Ngwane (Bowels of the Swazi Nation): POB 181, Kwaluseni; tel. 5184306; fax 5184399; e-mail info@tibiyo.com; internet www.tibiyo.com; f. 1968; national devt agency, with investment interests in all sectors of the economy; participates in domestic and foreign jt investment ventures; total assets: E604m. (1999); Chair. Prince MANGALISO; Man. Dir NDUMISO MAMBA.

Swaziland Solidarity Network (SSN): c/o COSATU House, 3rd Floor, 1–5 Leyds St, Braamfontein, South AfricaPOB 1019, Johannesburg 2000; tel. (11) 3393621; fax (11) 3394244; e-mail swaziland@union.org.za; internet www.swazisolidarity.org; f. 1997; umbrella org. promoting democracy; incorporates mems from Swaziland and abroad incl. PUDEMO, SWAYOCO, and the Swaziland Democratic Alliance (f. 1999); also incl., from South Africa, the ANC, SACP and COSATU; Sec.-Gen. BONGANI MASUKU.

CHAMBERS OF COMMERCE

Sibakho Chamber of Commerce: POB 2016, Manzini; tel. 5057347.

Swaziland Chamber of Commerce and Industry: see Federation of Swaziland Employers and Chamber of Commerce.

INDUSTRIAL AND TRADE ASSOCIATIONS

National Agricultural Marketing Board: POB 4261, Manzini; tel. 5055314; fax 5054072; internet www.swazibusiness.com/namboard; Chair Prince MABANDLA; CEO OBED HLONGWANE.

National Maize Corpn: POB 158, Manzini; tel. 5187432; fax 5184461; e-mail nmc@swazi.net; f. 1985.

Swaziland Citrus Board: Sokhamila Bldg, cnr Dzeliwe and Mdada Sts, POB 343, Mbabane H100; tel. 4044266; fax 4043548; e-mail citrus@realnet.co.sz; f. 1969.

Swaziland Commercial Board: POB 509, Mbabane; tel. 4042930; Man. Dir J. M. D. FAKUDZE.

Swaziland Cotton Board: POB 230, Manzini; tel. 5052775; Gen. Man. TOM JELE.

Swaziland Dairy Board: Liqhaga Bldg, 3rd Floor, POB 2975, Manzini; tel. 5058262; fax 5058260; e-mail ceo-swazidairy@africaonline.co.sz; Gen. Man. N. T. GUMEDE.

Swaziland Sugar Association: 4th Floor, cnr Dzeliwe and Msakato Sts, POB 445, Mbabane; tel. 4042646; fax 4045005; e-mail info@ssa.co.sz; internet www.ssa.co.sz; CEO Dr MICHAEL MATSEBULA.

EMPLOYERS' ORGANIZATIONS

Building Contractors' Association of Swaziland: POB 518, Mbabane; tel. 4040071; fax 4044258.

Swaziland Association of Architects, Engineers and Surveyors: Swazi Plaza, POB A387, Mbabane; tel. 4042309; e-mail ribar@africaonline.co.sz.

Swaziland Institute of Personnel and Training Managers: c/o UNISWA, Private Bag, Kwaluseni; tel. 5184011; fax 5185276.

Employers' Federation

Federation of Swaziland Employers and Chamber of Commerce (FSECC): POB 72, Mbabane; tel. 4040768; fax 4090051; e-mail fsecc@business-swaziland.com; internet www.business-swaziland.com; f. 2005 by merger of Federation of Swaziland Employers and Swaziland Chamber of Commerce; CEO TREASURE MAPHANGA.

UTILITIES

Electricity

Swaziland Electricity Board: Mhlambanyatsi Rd, Eluvatsini House, POB 258, Mbabane; tel. 4042521; fax 4042335; e-mail fikeld@seb.co.sz; internet www.seb.co.sz; statutory body; f. 1963; Man. Dir (vacant).

Water

Swaziland Water Services Corpn: Dhlan'Ubeka House, 6th and 7th Floor, POB 20, Mbabane; tel. 4043161; fax 4045585; internet www.swsc.co.sz; state authority; Chair. ESAU N. ZWANE; CEO PETER N. BHEMBE.

CO-OPERATIVE ASSOCIATIONS

Swaziland Central Co-operatives Union: POB 551, Manzini; tel. 5052787; fax 5052964.

There are more than 123 co-operative associations, of which the most important is:

Swaziland Co-operative Rice Co Ltd: handles rice grown in Mbabane and Manzini areas.

TRADE UNIONS

At mid-2005 there were 55 organizations recognized by the Department of Labour. These included: the Association of Lecturers and Academic Personnel of the University of Swaziland, the Building and Construction Workers Union of Swaziland, Swaziland Commercial and Allied Workers' Union, Swaziland Conservation Workers' Union, Swaziland Electricity Supply, Maintenance and Allied Workers' Union, Swaziland Engineering, Metal and Allied Workers' Union, Swaziland Hotel, Catering and Allied Workers' Union, Swaziland Manufacturing and Allied Workers' Union, Swaziland Mining, Quarrying and Allied Workers' Union, Swaziland National Association of Civil Servants, Swaziland National Association of Teachers, Swaziland Post and Telecommunications Workers' Union, Swaziland Transport Workers' Union, Swaziland Union of Financial Institutions and Allied Workers, University of Swaziland Workers' Union, Workers' Union of Swaziland Security Guards, Workers' Union of Town Councils.

Trade Union Federations

Swaziland Federation of Labour: mems include workers from the banking sector and mems of the Swaziland Manufacturing and Allied Workers' Union.

Swaziland Federation of Trade Unions (SFTU): POB 1158; Manzini; tel. 5056575; internet www.cosatu.org.za/sftu/index.html; f. 1973; prin. trade union org. since mid-1980s; mems from public and private sectors, incl. agricultural workers; Pres. ELLIOT MKATSHWA (acting); Sec.-Gen. JAN SITHOLE; 83,000 mems.

Staff Associations

Three staff associations exist for employees whose status lies between that of worker and that of management: the Nyoni Yami Irrigation Scheme Staff Association, the Swazican Staff Association and the Swaziland Electricity Board Staff Association.

Transport

Buses are the principal means of transport for many Swazis. Bus services are provided by private operators who are required to obtain annual permits for each route from the Road Transportation Board, which also regulates fares.

RAILWAYS

The rail network, which totalled 297 km in 1998–99, provides a major transport link for imports and exports. Railway lines connect with the dry port at Matsapha, the South African ports of Richards Bay and Durban in the south, the South African town of Komatipoort in the north and the Mozambican port of Maputo in the east. Goods traffic is mainly in wood pulp, sugar, molasses, coal, citrus fruit and canned fruit. In June 1998 the Trans Lebombo rail service was launched to carry passengers from Durban to Maputo via Swaziland. The service was terminated in May 2000, owing to insufficient demand. In August 2004 the Government announced plans to privatize Swaziland Railways.

Swaziland Railways: Swaziland Railway Bldg, cnr Johnston and Walker Sts, POB 475, Mbabane; tel. 4047211; fax 4047210; f. 1962; Chair. B. A. G. FITZPATRICK; CEO GIDEON J. MAHLALELA.

ROADS

In 1998 there were an estimated 3,247 km of roads, including 1,660 km of main roads and 1,587 km of secondary roads. About 28.2% of the road network was paved in 1994. The rehabilitation of about 700 km of main and 600 km of district gravel-surfaced roads began in 1985, financed by World Bank and US loans totalling some E18m. In 1991 work commenced on the reconstruction of Swaziland's main road artery, connecting Mbabane to Manzini, via Matsapha, and in 2001 the Government announced the construction of two main roads in the north of the country, financed by Japanese loans.

Roads Department: Ministry of Public Works and Transport, POB 58, Mbabane; tel. 4042321; fax 4042364; e-mail mopwt_rd@realnet.co.sz; Sr Roads Engineer A. MANANA.

SHIPPING

Royal Swazi National Shipping Corpn Ltd: POB 1915, Manzini; tel. 5053788; fax 5053820; f. 1980 to succeed Royal Swaziland Maritime Co; 76% owned by Tibiyo Taka Ngwane; owns no ships, acting only as a freight agent; Gen. Man. M. S. DLAMINI.

CIVIL AVIATION

Swaziland's only airport is at Matsapha, near Manzini, about 40 km from Mbabane. In mid-1997 the Government initiated a three-year programme to upgrade the airport. In early 2003 construction began of an international airport at Sikhupe, in eastern Swaziland. In March 2006 Swaziland Airlink was one of 92 airlines banned from landing at European Union airports owing to safety concerns.

African International Airways (AIA): Suite 108, Development House, Swazi Plaza, POB 569, Mbabane; tel. 4043875; fax 4043876; e-mail ams@global.co.za; f. 1985; operates cargo services; Chair. PATRICK CORBIN; Man. Dir MARTIN LONGMORE.

Air Swazi Cargo: Dhlan'Ubeka House, Walker St, POB 2869, Mbabane; tel. 4045575; fax 4045003; charter services for freight to destinations in Africa and Europe; Man. BRIAN PARMENTER.

Swaziland Airlink: POB 939, Matsapha Airport, Manzini; tel. 5186155; fax 5186148; f. 1999; fmrly Royal Swazi National Airways Corpn; joint venture between SA Airlink of South Africa (40%) and the Govmt of Swaziland; scheduled passenger services from Manzini to Johannesburg, South Africa; Chair. LINDIWE KHUMALO-MATSE.

Tourism

Swaziland's attractions for tourists include game reserves (at Malolotja, Hawane, Mlawula and Mantenga) and magnificent mountain scenery. In 2001 tourist arrivals numbered 283,177, declining to 255,927 the following year; receipts from tourism totalled US $31m. during both years. In 2003 the number of visitors fell again, to 218,813; receipts amounted to $16m.

Hotel and Tourism Association of Swaziland: Oribi Court, 1st Floor, Gwamile St, 462, Mbabane; tel. 4042218; fax 4044516; e-mail aliand@realnet.co.sz; f. 1979.

Swaziland National Trust Commission (SNTC): POB 100, Lobamba, Swaziland; tel. 4161481; fax 4161875; e-mail staff@swazimus.org.sz; internet www.sntc.org.sz; f. 1972; parastatal org. responsible for conservation of nature and cultural heritage, incl. the Nat. Museum; Dir SKUMBUZO DLAMINI (acting).

Swaziland Tourism Authority: Swazi Plaza, POB A1030, Mbabane; tel. 4049693; fax 4049683; e-mail secretary@tourismauthority.org.sz; internet www.welcometoswaziland.com; CEO M. N. 'POPPY' KHOZA.

SWEDEN

Introductory Survey

Location, Climate, Language, Religion, Flag, Capital

The Kingdom of Sweden lies in north-western Europe, occupying about two-thirds of the Scandinavian peninsula. It is bordered by Finland to the north-east, and by Norway to the north-west and west. About 15% of Sweden's area lies north of the Arctic Circle. The Baltic Sea and the Gulf of Bothnia are to the east, the Skagerrak and Kattegat channels to the south-west. The country is relatively flat and is characterized by thousands of inland lakes and small coastal islands. There is a mountain range, the Kjolen mountains, in the north-west. Winters are cold and summers mild. In Stockholm the mean summer temperature is 18°C (64°F) and the mean winter temperature −3°C (27°F). The national language is Swedish, but there are Finnish and Lapp (Sámi) minorities (the latter numbering between 17,000 and 20,000), retaining their own languages. A majority of the inhabitants profess Christianity, and about 78% are adherents of the Evangelical Lutheran Church of Sweden. The national flag (proportions 5 by 8) is light blue with a yellow cross, the upright of the cross being to the left of centre. The capital is Stockholm.

Recent History

Sweden has been a constitutional monarchy, traditionally neutral, since the early 19th century. During this time the country has not participated in any war or entered any military alliance. Norway, formerly united with Sweden, became independent in 1905. Sweden adopted parliamentary government in 1917, and universal adult suffrage was introduced in 1921. From 1932 until 1976, except for a short break in 1936, Sweden was governed by the Socialdemokratiska Arbetareparti (SAP—Social Democratic Labour Party), either alone or as the senior partner in coalitions (1936–45 and 1951–57). During those 44 years the country had only three Prime Ministers, all Social Democrats. Since the Second World War Sweden has become an active member of many international organizations, including the UN (to which it has given military support), the Council of Europe (see p. 211) and, from 1995, the European Community (EC—now European Union—EU, see p. 228).

Olof Palme succeeded Dr Tage Erlander as Prime Minister and leader of the SAP in October 1969. After a general election in September 1970, Palme formed a minority Government. Under a constitutional reform, the Riksdag (Parliament) was reconstituted from January 1971, its two chambers being replaced by a unicameral assembly. King Gustaf VI Adolf, who had reigned since 1950, died in September 1973 and was succeeded by his grandson, Carl XVI Gustaf. A revised Constitution, effective from January 1975, ended the monarch's prerogative to appoint the Prime Minister: the Speaker of the Riksdag was to have this responsibility in future.

At the September 1976 election, dissatisfaction with high rates of taxation, necessary to maintain the advanced social welfare system that Sweden had developed, brought about the defeat of the SAP. Thorbjörn Fälldin, leader of the Centerpartiet (CP—Centre Party), formed a centre-right coalition in October. The wish of the CP to abandon Sweden's nuclear power programme caused serious controversy in June 1978, when an independent commission recommended its continued use as an energy source. This view was endorsed by the Folkpartiet (FP—Liberals) and Moderata Samlingspartiet (Moderates), whose rejection of a proposal by Fälldin to submit the nuclear issue to a national referendum led to the resignation of the Government in October 1978. The FP formed a minority Government, led by Ola Ullsten. Following a general election in September 1979, Fälldin returned as Prime Minister of a coalition comprising members of the CP, the Moderates and the FP, with an overall parliamentary majority of only one seat. A referendum on the future of nuclear power was held in March 1980, at which a narrow majority of the electorate approved a limited programme of nuclear reactor development, to be progressively eliminated by 2010 and replaced by alternative energy resources.

During 1980 the Government's economic policies came under attack, mainly because of the rising rate of inflation, and there was severe industrial unrest. The Moderates, who disagreed with proposed tax reforms, left the coalition in May 1981. At the next general election, held in September 1982, the SAP was returned to power, winning 45.6% of the votes cast (and 166 of the 349 seats in the Riksdag), but gaining an overall majority over the three non-socialist parties. In October Palme formed a minority Government, following an undertaking by the Vänsterpartiet—Kommunisterna (VpK—Left Party—Communists), which held 20 parliamentary seats, that they would support the SAP. Palme's Government was returned to power in September 1985, with the support of the VpK. The SAP and the VpK together won 50.0% of the votes cast (securing 178 seats in the Riksdag), while the three main non-socialist parties won 48.0% (and the remaining 171 seats). The FP increased its share of seats in the Riksdag from 21 to 51, attracting voters from all of the other main parties. Palme undertook to continue to follow his 'third way' economic policy, seeking to combat inflation and recession while avoiding both excessively high levels of public spending and reductions in social welfare benefits.

In February 1986 Olof Palme was murdered by an unknown assailant in Stockholm. In March the Deputy Prime Minister, Ingvar Carlsson, took office as Prime Minister and was also appointed acting Chairman of the SAP, pending ratification by the National Congress in 1987. Carlsson retained Palme's Cabinet and declared that he would continue the policies of his predecessor. During 1986–87 little progress was made towards discovering Palme's assassin, and considerable controversy surrounded the case, as disputes increased between the police and successive public prosecutors. In December 1988 Christer Pettersson, a man with a history of mental illness and violent crime, was arrested, and in mid-1989 he was tried for the murder of Palme. He was convicted amid some controversy, only to be acquitted on appeal in October. In December 1997 the public prosecutor's office petitioned the Supreme Court to re-examine the case against Pettersson in the light of the discovery of new, allegedly incriminating, evidence. In May 1998, however, the Supreme Court ruled that there was insufficient new evidence to conduct a retrial.

Meanwhile, ecological concerns were heightened in 1988 by two disasters, both of which were attributed to the effects of pollutants: an increase in the concentration of algae devastated the marine environment along the west coast, and this was followed by an outbreak of a virus that reduced the seal population of the North and Baltic Seas by up to two-thirds. At the general election in September the environmentalist Miljöpartiet de Gröna (MP—Green Party) gained parliamentary representation for the first time, but the SAP remained in power with the continued support of the VpK. The conservative Moderates remained the second largest party in the Riksdag. In February 1990 the VpK (subsequently restyled the Vänsterpartiet—VP—Left Party) and the MP refused to support the Government's proposed austerity measures. Carlsson resigned, but, having secured support for a more moderate set of proposals, he formed another minority Government.

During 1990 the Swedish economy entered into recession, and in December the Riksdag approved a new programme of austerity measures, intended to reduce inflation and to restore confidence in the economy. The Government was forced to abandon the long-held belief that the commitment to full employment and the defence of the welfare state (supported by high levels of taxation and of public expenditure) should be overriding priorities.

However, the popularity of the SAP continued to decline, and in the general election of September 1991 the party did not win enough seats to form a government, although it remained the largest party in the Riksdag, with 138 seats. The Moderates increased their representation to 80 seats, while the Kristdemokratiska Samhällspartiet (KdS—Christian Democrats) and a recently formed right-wing party, Ny demokrati (ND—New Democracy), won 26 and 25 seats respectively, at the expense of the FP and the CP; the MP failed to secure 4% of the total votes cast, and thereby lost all its seats. Ingvar Carlsson resigned as Prime Minister, and in early October Carl Bildt, the leader of the Moderates (the largest non-socialist party in the legislature), was invited to form a government. He formed a coalition comprising members of four non-socialist parties—the Moderates, the CP, the FP and the KdS. Since these four parties, even in combination, still formed a minority in the Riksdag, they were obliged to rely on the ND for support in securing approval for legislation. Without delay, the new Government began to accelerate the deregulation of the economy already undertaken by its predecessor.

During 1992 the recession continued in Sweden. Although the Government's austerity measures succeeded in reducing inflation, the high level of the budgetary deficit was a cause of concern. In September speculation on the international currency markets caused a rapid outflow of capital, and in November a fresh outflow of capital, following the SAP's refusal to approve reductions in public expenditure, forced the Government to allow the krona to 'float' in relation to other currencies, thereby effectively devaluing it by some 10%. In March 1993 the Government was defeated in the Riksdag when the ND refused to support budgetary proposals, but later in the same month the Government won a parliamentary vote of confidence (the ND abstained from voting).

At the general election in September 1994 the SAP secured 45.3% of the votes cast, increasing its representation to 161 seats. The VP won 22 seats (compared with 16 in 1991) and the MP won 18 seats. Although the Moderates maintained the level of support they gained at the previous election, the other parties in the incumbent coalition Government fared badly. Bildt resigned as Prime Minister, and in October 1994 Ingvar Carlsson formed a minority SAP Government. The results appeared to indicate a trend of increased support for parties opposed to Sweden's joining the EU (as the EC had become). Despite opposition to EU membership within the SAP, Carlsson declared that a major objective of his Government would be to secure a mandate for Sweden to join the EU in the forthcoming national referendum (see below). He also emphasized the need for stringent economic measures (introduced from late 1994) to reduce unemployment, stabilize the budgetary deficit and safeguard welfare provisions.

In March 1996 Carlsson relinquished his dual posts as Prime Minister and leader of the SAP, in order to retire from political life. Göran Persson, hitherto Minister of Finance, was elected unopposed as Prime Minister and leader of the SAP. Persson immediately initiated a broad cabinet reorganization.

In October 1996 Persson urged that the process to enlarge the EU be accelerated in order to strengthen European security. In November an independent study group, which had been commissioned by the Government to consider Sweden's proposed participation in Economic and Monetary Union (EMU, see p. 265), recommended that Sweden should not join EMU until the unemployment rate had been significantly reduced. In February 1997, however, the central bank advocated membership of EMU from its inception in 1999. Nevertheless, in June 1997 the Government announced that Sweden would not be participating in the first wave of EMU, citing a lack of public support for the project. The Government reiterated this stance in October, when it was also announced that Sweden had no intention of participating in the European Exchange Rate Mechanism (ERM).

In August 1997 details of a national programme of enforced sterilization conducted during 1935–75 against some 60,000 individuals assessed to be of inferior intellectual or physical capabilities, reported in the Swedish daily newspaper *Dagens Nyheter*, provoked national outrage and prompted the Government to announce the creation of a comprehensive public inquiry into the country's post-First World War eugenics programme. It was subsequently revealed that minimal compensation had been paid to just 16 victims of the programme during the previous 10 years. In March 1999 the Ministry of Health and Social Affairs announced that compensation amounting to a maximum of 175,000 kronor would be paid to each surviving victim of the programme. In August 2001 the State Sterilization Compensation Board stated that some 2,000 people had sought financial reparation, and that, of these, about 1,500 had received compensation, the total amount paid out being approximately 256m. kronor.

In March 1991 the Swedish and Danish Governments agreed to construct a 16-km combined bridge and tunnel for road and rail traffic, across the Öresund strait, between Malmö and Copenhagen (to be known as the Öresund Link). The plan aroused opposition in Sweden, on the grounds that the link might hinder the flow of water into the Baltic Sea, as well as increasing pollution by emissions from vehicles. In May 1994 a Swedish marine commission concluded that plans for the link did not provide sufficient guarantees to protect the flow of water into the Baltic. In the following month, however, the Swedish Government approved construction plans, prompting the resignation from the Government of the Minister of the Environment and leader of the CP, Olof Johansson. The link was opened in July 2000.

Prior to Sweden's membership of the EU (see below), trade with EU countries was conducted by means of a free-trade area, the European Economic Area (EEA), created in 1994 under the aegis of the European Free Trade Association (EFTA, see p. 386). Negotiations on admission to the EU began in February 1993, when the Bildt Government declared that the country's tradition of neutrality would not prevent Sweden from participating fully in the common foreign and security policy of the EU. The negotiations were concluded in March 1994. Sweden obtained safeguards for its traditional policy of freedom of official information, and for its strict environmental standards, and won concessions on the maintenance of subsidies for agriculture in remote areas. A national referendum on membership was held on 13 November, producing a 52.2% majority in favour of joining the EU. The Riksdag formally ratified membership in December, and Sweden's accession to the EU took effect from 1 January 1995 (whereupon Sweden withdrew from EFTA). It was widely held that concern about the possible effects on the domestic economy of remaining outside the EU, together with fears regarding Sweden's ability to influence international affairs, such as the maintenance of effective environmental controls, had been major factors in the outcome of the referendum. Following the vote, the Carlsson Government reiterated that Sweden would retain its non-aligned policy within the EU and therefore remain outside the North Atlantic Treaty Organization (NATO, see p. 314), although it would apply for observer status within Western European Union (WEU, see p. 365).

At the general election held in September 1998 the SAP maintained its position as the largest party in the Riksdag, but suffered a substantial reduction in the number of parliamentary seats that it held—131, compared with 161 in the outgoing Riksdag. This was the SAP's worst electoral performance for some 70 years, and the party was only able to remain in government by subsequently securing the support of the VP and the MP. The Moderates retained the position of second largest party in the Riksdag, obtaining 82 parliamentary seats. Like the CP and the the Kristdemokraterna (Kd, as the KdS had been renamed), the Moderates indicated their unwillingness to support the SAP in government. At about 81%, the participation rate at the election was the lowest for some 50 years. Post-electoral analysis identified the SAP's pursuit of financial regularity at the perceived expense of socialist policies as the probable cause of its poor performance: many voters had transferred their allegiance from the SAP to the VP. It was reported that, in return for its support, the VP would seek to persuade the Government to increase expenditure on social welfare and employment, and would encourage the slower repayment of Sweden's national debt, higher taxes, the complete decommissioning of Sweden's nuclear power stations, and a less stringent programme of privatization. Both the VP and the MP remained strongly opposed to any future participation by Sweden in EMU. In early October a new Cabinet was announced. At the same time the Government presented its statement of policy, which envisaged a more active role in Europe for Sweden. The Government would also seek to achieve sustainable economic growth in order to increase labour-force participation to a targeted 80% by 2004. This aim was reflected in the reconstitution of the Ministry of Industry as a so-called 'superministry', with additional responsibility for labour, energy, information technology and infrastructure. In April 1999 the Minister of Finance, Erik Asbrink, resigned following a reported disagreement with the Prime Minister over the content of the forthcoming spring budget; he was replaced by Bosse Ringholme. Following the announcement of former Prime Minister Carl Bildt's retirement from party politics, in August Bo Lundgren was elected to succeed him as leader of the Moderates.

In late 1999 it was reported that public spending on defence equipment was to be reduced drastically. Additionally, proposed reform of the national defence system was likely to result in the loss of some 10,000 military and civilian jobs. Earlier in the year the military high command had indicated that the Government's programme of defence rationalization would lead to an eventual halving of the strength of the armed forces, in terms of both personnel and hardware, prompting speculation that Sweden might be about to reconsider its non-aligned status with regard to regional security. In November 2000 Persson announced proposals to that effect. He asserted that neutrality was no longer relevant after the end of the Cold War, and that it did not cover all aspects of Sweden's security policy, such as disarmament, the non-proliferation of nuclear weapons and stability in Europe. However, Persson ruled out any move to join NATO, asserting that it was essential for the stability of northern Europe that Sweden remain non-aligned.

At the general election held on 15 September 2002 the SAP maintained its position as the largest party in the Riksdag, winning 39.8% of the votes cast and securing 144 of the 349 seats. Persson formed a minority SAP Government with the parliamentary support of the MP and the VP. In return for their support, the MP and the VP required the Government to espouse some of their policies, including, among others, a reduction of 6,000m. kronor in defence expenditure over five years and a moratorium on cod-fishing in the Baltic Sea from 1 January 2003, with compensation for the fishing industry.

In March 2000 a national congress of the SAP endorsed the adoption of future EMU entry as official party policy, despite a significant degree of opposition. Following the 2002 general election, Persson announced that a referendum would be held on the adoption of the euro in September 2003. In December 2002 opinion polls reported equal proportions in favour of and against adopting the euro, but by May 2003 the proportion of those opposing the euro had increased to 47%, while the proportion of those in favour had fallen to 40% and the number of undecided voters had increased to 13%. Meanwhile, the SAP remained sharply divided on the issue. Five of the party's 22 cabinet ministers were opposed to joining EMU, among them the Deputy Prime Minister, Margareta Winberg. The Moderates and other parties of the centre-right supported Sweden's entry into EMU. The campaign for the adoption of the euro was supported by the national media and the business community, whereas opposition to the new currency was focused in the trade unions, the MP and the VP. Most Swedes, and especially those in rural and northern areas or in public-sector employment, wanted to keep their generous social welfare provisions, which were funded through high taxation, and opponents of EMU feared that membership would force Sweden to reduce public spending so as not to breach the 3% budget deficit limit imposed by the EU's Stability and Growth Pact.

Anna Lindh, the Minister for Foreign Affairs, was one of the Government's most effective campaigners for entry into EMU, and was widely seen as a potential future SAP leader. In September 2003, four days prior to the referendum, she was stabbed in central Stockholm; she died of her injuries the following day. The referendum was held as planned on 14 September, and speculation that support for the euro would be enhanced as a result of sympathy in the immediate aftermath of Lindh's death, thereby undermining the legitimacy of the decision, proved unfounded, as voters decisively rejected transition from the krona to the euro. The result of the referendum, for which turn-out was 82.6%, was 42.0% in favour, 55.9% against and 2.1% blank. Only in Stockholm did the propoposal to adopt the euro receive a majority of votes cast.

Mijail Mijailović, a Swede of Serbian origin, was arrested in September 2003 on suspicion of the murder of Anna Lindh. He initially denied any involvement in the killing but later confessed to police during his interrogation. Mijailović, who had a history of mental illness and claimed there was no political motive for the attack, was tried in January 2004, and was convicted of murder and sentenced to life imprisonment. Mijailović appealed against his conviction, and in July the Court of Appeal in Stockholm ruled that he should be sent to a psychiatric institution rather than serving a prison sentence. The Lindh family challenged the decision in the Supreme Court, which in December confirmed Mijailović's sentence of life imprisonment.

With the prospect of the enlargement of the EU from 15 to 25 countries on 1 May 2004, concerns arose that the Swedish welfare system would be unduly burdened by an influx of workers from the new member states. In March of that year, following similar action by other EU member states, the Government introduced legislation in the Riksdag proposing welfare and labour restrictions for migrant workers from the 10 accession countries for at least two years. However, the Riksdag rejected the bill at the end of April by 187 votes to 137. This defeat was seen as a major reverse for the Government, and meant that Sweden was one of the few EU countries without any restrictions limiting access to jobs or social security to citizens of the new member states.

The perceived failure of the main political parties adequately to address the strong current of EU scepticism expressed in Sweden's rejection of the euro led to the formation, in February 2004, of a new political grouping, the Junilistan (June List), which opposed further integration with the EU but did not advocate withdrawal. The grouping stressed that it was not itself a political party, and went as far as appending its candidates' usual party affiliation to their names on the ballots for the forthcoming elections to the European Parliament. Thus voters would be able to support the June List on the issue of the EU while not altogether abandoning their usual party. This strategy proved successful, allowing the June List to draw support from across the political spectrum. At the elections, held on 13 June, the June List won 14.4% of the votes cast and three of Sweden's 19 seats in the European Parliament. The SAP, in contrast, suffered its worst electoral result since 1912, obtaining just 24.7% and five seats, while the Moderates won 18.2% and four seats. The VP and FP each won two seats, and the CP, MP and Kd each won one. It was widely believed that the June List's success in the European elections might increase pressure on the Government to consider holding a national referendum on the ratification of the EU constitutional treaty, which had finally been approved by the Council of the EU in June 2004. However, the Government chose to present the treaty for approval (or otherwise) in the Riksdag: legislation was to be presented by September 2005, with a view to adoption in December of that year. However, following the rejection of the treaty at national referendums in France and the Netherlands in mid-2005, Sweden was one of several member states to decide to delay the ratification process indefinitely.

Meanwhile, in mid-September 2004 Lars Engqvist was replaced at the Ministry of Health and Social Affairs by Ylva Johansson, and in late October Persson implemented a wider reorganization of the Cabinet. Pär Nuder, previously Minister for Policy Co-ordination, was appointed Minister for Finance, in place of Bosse Ringholm (who became Deputy Prime Minister). Thomas Östros, hitherto Minister for Education and Science, replaced Leif Pagrotsky as Minister for Industry and Trade, while Pagrotsky became head of a reorganized Ministry of Education, Research and Culture (which also included Ibrahim Baylan as Minister for Schools). Mona Sahlin, formerly Minister for Democracy, Integration and Gender Equality, took responsibility for the new Ministry of Sustainable Development. The reorganization was widely viewed as an attempt by the Prime Minister, following the SAP's poor performance in the European parliamentary elections in June, to renew, and revive support for, his administration in advance of the general election scheduled for 2006.

In May 2005 the UN Committee against Torture ruled that Sweden had violated the 1984 UN Convention against Torture and Other Cruel, Inhuman or Degrading Treatment or Punishment in December 2001 by returning an asylum seeker to Egypt, where he had been convicted *in absentia* of membership of a terrorist group; the Committee stated that the Swedish authorities should have known at the time of the expulsion that Egypt used torture against detainees. Human rights groups had earlier expressed concern at the treatment of the asylum seeker and another Egyptian national deported at the same time; the two men had controversially been flown to Egypt in a US-leased aircraft, having been handed over to US security officials by the Swedish authorities. In November 2005 the Swedish Government ordered the Civil Aviation Authority to investigate media reports that aircraft used by the US Central Intelligence Agency (CIA) had landed at Swedish airports while transporting suspected terrorists to third countries for interrogation. In the following month the Authority, which examined the period from January 2002, reported that it could not substantiate the claims.

In September 2005 the Riksdag rejected a proposed amnesty for illegal immigrants living in Sweden, despite considerable public support for such a measure. Following the vote, a number of protests took place and 150,000 signatures were collected in favour of an amnesty. In November the Riksdag approved legislation allowing failed asylum seekers to reapply for a residence permit before the end of March 2006. It was estimated that 20,000 asylum seekers whose deportation orders had not been carried out due to conditions in their home countries or who had gone into hiding after having their original applications refused would be eligible to submit new applications under the law.

In February 2006 the Government announced its intention for Sweden to overcome its dependency on petroleum within 15 years, without constructing any further nuclear power stations. A committee of industrialists, academics, farmers, vehicle manufacturers, civil servants and others was charged with devising a plan to achieve this, and was to report to the Riksdag later that year. The Government hoped to protect Sweden from the adverse economic effects of climate change and from fluctuations in the price of petroleum, which had increased substantially in recent years.

In March 2006 Laila Freivalds resigned as Minister for Foreign Affairs, following criticism of her ministry's involvement in forcing the temporary closure, in February, of the website of *SD-Kuriren*—the newspaper of the far-right Sverigedemokraterna (SD—Swedish Democrats)—which had asked readers to submit cartoons of the Prophet Muhammad. (The publication of caricatures depicting the Prophet in a Danish newspaper in late 2005, and in a number of other European newspapers in early 2006, had led to world-wide protests by Muslims—see the chapter on Denmark.) Freivalds had initially denied responsibility for the decision to intervene, which Persson had denounced as being contrary to the freedom of the press. She had already come under pressure to resign in December 2005 after an independent commission held her partly responsible for the Government's slow response to the tsunamis in South-East Asia on 26 December 2004 (which killed more than 500 Swedes). Jan Eliasson, the President of the UN General Assembly, was appointed as the new Minister for Foreign Affairs; he was to hold both positions until the expiry of his UN term in September.

The Swedish Government expressed its opposition to the US-led military operation against the regime of Saddam Hussain in Iraq from early 2003. In October of that year, however, Sweden pledged 250m. kronor towards the reconstruction of Iraq (in addition to a substantial amount of humanitarian aid).

Government

Sweden is a constitutional monarchy. The hereditary monarch is Head of State but has very limited formal prerogatives. Executive power rests with the Cabinet (Regeringen), which is responsible to the legislature (Riksdag). The unicameral Riksdag was introduced in January 1971. It has 349 members, elected by universal adult suffrage for four years, on the basis of proportional representation. The Prime Minister is nominated by the Speaker of the Riksdag and later confirmed in office by the whole House. The country is divided into 21 counties (Län) and 288 municipal districts (Kommun): both counties and municipalities have popularly elected councils.

Defence

Proposals for a significant reduction in defence spending and resources were announced during 1999 (see Recent History). In August 2005 Sweden maintained total armed forces of 27,600, compared with 53,100 in 1999. The army consisted of 13,800 men, of whom 8,600 were conscripts; the navy 7,900 men, including 2,000 conscripts, and the air force 5,900 men, including 1,500 conscripts. In addition, there were voluntary defence reservists totalling 262,000, compared with 570,000 in 1999. Military service for males (aged between 19 and 47) lasts between seven and 15 months in the army and navy, and between eight and 12 months in the air force. Basic training for women is voluntary. In 2005 defence was allocated 44,174m. kronor in the budget. In October 2004 Prime Minister Göran Persson and the Finnish Prime Minister, Matti Vanhanen, announced that Sweden and Finland were to establish a joint Nordic battle group as their contribution to the rapid reaction force of the European Union (EU). Sweden was to contribute 900 troops and Finland 300; Norway later agreed to contribute a further 300 troops. The group, one of 13 such battle groups envisaged by the EU, was to be ready for international deployment to carry out peace-keeping activities at crisis points around the world from 2008.

Economic Affairs

In 2004, according to estimates by the World Bank, Sweden's gross national income (GNI), measured at average 2002–04 prices, was US $321,401m., equivalent to $35,770 per head (or $29,770 on an international purchasing-power parity basis). During 1995–2004, it was estimated, the population grew at an average annual rate of 0.2%, while gross domestic product (GDP) per head increased, in real terms, by an average of 2.5% per year. Sweden's overall GDP increased, in real terms, by an average of 2.7% per year in 1995–2004. GDP rose by 1.5% in 2003 and by 3.6% in 2004.

Agriculture (including hunting, forestry and fishing) contributed 1.8% of GDP in 2004, and employed 2.1% of the working population in that year. The main agricultural products are dairy produce, meat, cereals and potatoes, primarily for domestic consumption. In 2004 forestry products (wood, pulp and paper) accounted for 12.2% of total merchandise exports. Agricultural GDP increased by an average of 0.9% per year during 1995–2003; it increased by 1.7% in 2002 and by 1.1% in 2003.

Industry (including mining, manufacturing, construction and power) provided 28.1% of GDP in 2004, and employed 22.7% of the working population in that year. Industrial GDP increased by an average of 3.7% per year in 1995–2003. Industrial GDP grew by 3.2% in 2002 and by 1.1% in 2003.

Mining contributed 0.3% of GDP in 2004, and employed 0.1% of the working population in that year. The principal product is iron ore, but there are also large reserves of uranium (some 15% of the world's total known reserves), copper, lead and zinc. The GDP of the mining and quarrying sector declined, in real terms, by an average of 2.0% per year in 1999–2004, according to Statistics Sweden; it decreased by 2.5% in 2003, but increased by 7.9% in 2004.

Manufacturing contributed 20.5% of GDP in 2004, and employed 16.1% of the working population in that year. In 1995 the most important manufactures (measured by total value of output) were paper and paper products (10.5% of the total), motor vehicles (9.3%), chemicals (7.2%), basic iron and steel (6.8%), television and radio transmitters and other communications apparatus (6.4%), and general purpose machinery (5.4%). Manufacturing GDP increased, in real terms, by an average of 4.9% per year in 1999–2004, according to Statistics Sweden; it rose by 2.6% in 2003 and by 9.4% in 2004.

Energy is derived principally from nuclear power, which provided some 46.3% of electricity generated in 2002, and hydroelectric power, which provided 45.6% of electricity generated in the same year. Sweden has 10 nuclear reactors. (The last reactor at Barsebäck was closed in May 2005.) Alternative sources of energy are being developed, because of strict environmental legislation, the lack of potential for further hydroelectric projects and, primarily, the Riksdag's resolution to phase out nuclear power. In February 2006 the Government announced its intention for Sweden to overcome its dependency on petroleum within 15 years, without constructing any further nuclear power stations. Imports of petroleum and petroleum products accounted for 8.1% of total imports in 2004.

The services sector contributed 70.1% of GDP in 2004, and engaged 75.2% of the employed population in that year. The GDP of the services sector increased, in real terms, at an average annual rate of 2.3% during 1995–2003; it grew by 1.5% in both 2002 and 2003.

In 2004 Sweden recorded a visible trade surplus of US $23,415m., and there was a surplus of $27,485m. on the current account of the balance of payments. The European Union (EU, see p. 228) dominates Swedish trade: in 2004 it provided 72.8% of imports and took 58.6% of exports. The European Free Trade Association (EFTA, see p. 386) is also an important trading partner. In 2004 the principal single source of imports was Germany (contributing 18.7% of total imports); other major suppliers were Denmark (9.2%), Norway (7.6%), the United Kingdom (7.5%), the Netherlands (6.8%) and Finland (6.4%). The USA was the principal market for exports in that year (accounting for 10.7% of total exports); other major purchasers were Germany (10.2%), Norway (8.6%), the United Kingdom (7.8%), Denmark (6.7%) and Finland (5.7%). The principal exports in 2004 were machinery and transport equipment (principally road vehicles and telecommunications equipment), basic manufactured goods (notably paper) and chemicals. The principal imports in 2004 were machinery and transport equipment, and basic and other manufactures.

In 2004 there was a budget deficit of 53,343m. kronor, equivalent to 2.1% of GDP; the deficit was projected to decrease to 32,716m. kronor in 2005. At the end of 1999 the central Government's total external debt was 409,440m. kronor. The annual rate of inflation averaged 1.0% in 1995–2004. Consumer prices increased by an average of 1.9% in 2003 and 0.4% in 2004. An estimated 5.6% of the labour force were unemployed in February 2006.

Sweden is a member of the Nordic Council (see p. 397) and the Nordic Council of Ministers (see p. 397). In January 1995 Sweden

SWEDEN

became a full member of the EU. Sweden joined the EU's Schengen Agreement (see p. 257) in March 2001.

Sweden's economy is more diversified than is usual for a country of its size. Alongside traditional industries based on iron ore and wood (Sweden's most significant raw materials), the engineering industry and high-technology sectors have become increasingly important. Unlike many relatively small countries, Sweden has significant domestic aviation and nuclear power industries, as well as automotive manufacturers, an advanced arms industry, a world-leading telecommunications industry and major pharmaceutical and medical research capabilities. In the late 1990s, following the country's most serious economic recession in some 60 years (triggered by unwieldy inflation and public-sector salary bills), Sweden experienced a considerable economic recovery. Expansion in the high-technology sector fuelled exports and helped to achieve robust GDP growth. In 2002–03 Sweden's economy compared favourably with the members of the euro area—apparently one reason influencing its rejection of participation in European Economic and Monetary Union (EMU, see p. 265) in a national referendum held in September 2003. Sweden continued to outperform the euro area during 2004, with a strong export performance, GDP growth of 3.6% and low inflation. While growth in 2004 was largely export-driven, domestic demand and investment became the main impetus for growth in 2005, when GDP increased by an estimated 2.7%, a situation that was expected to continue in 2006–07. In its budget for 2006, the Government forecast GDP growth of 3.1% for that year, and announced reductions in income tax and an increase in expenditure on government work programmes aimed at reducing unemployment. Job creation measures introduced at the beginning of 2006 were targeted particularly at young people and the long-term unemployed. The Government aimed to reduce the unemployment rate to around 4.0% by mid-2006 (from 5.6% in February of that year). The central bank raised interest rates in early 2006, citing strong GDP growth, improving labour-market conditions and an anticipated increase in household consumption.

Education

Basic education, which is compulsory, extends for nine years, starting at the age of six or seven years, and is received at the comprehensive school (grundskolan). At the end of this period a pupil may enter the integrated upper secondary school (gymnasieskolan). In accordance with legislation implemented in 1992–95, courses at upper secondary schools last three years, and are organized into 16 nationally defined study programmes, comprising two university entrance programmes and 14 vocational programmes. Enrolment at pre-primary level included 81% of children (81% of both boys and girls) in the relevant age-group in 2002/03. Enrolment at primary schools in that year included 100% of children (100% of boys; 99% of girls) in the relevant age-group, while the comparable ratio for secondary enrolment was 99% (99% of boys; 100% of girls). There are some 64 universities, university colleges, specialized institutions and university colleges of health science in Sweden. Slightly more than 30% of young people in Sweden proceed to higher education within five years of completing their upper secondary schooling. In 2002/03 enrolment in higher education was equivalent to 83% of people in the relevant age-group (males 66%; females 102%). The budget for 2005 allocated 43,331m. kronor (5.8% of total expenditure) to education and university research.

Public Holidays*

2006: 1 January (New Year's Day), 6 January (Epiphany), 14 April (Good Friday), 16 April (Easter), 17 April (Easter Monday), 1 May (May Day), 25 May (Ascension Day), 4 June (Whit Sunday), 6 June (National Day), 24 June (Midsummer Holiday), 4 November (All Saints' Day), 25 December (Christmas), 26 December (St Stephen's Day).

2007: 1 January (New Year's Day), 6 January (Epiphany), 6 April (Good Friday), 8 April (Easter), 9 April (Easter Monday), 1 May (May Day), 17 May (Ascension Day), 27 May (Whit Sunday), 6 June (National Day), 23 June (Midsummer Holiday), 4 November (All Saints' Day), 25 December (Christmas), 26 December (St Stephen's Day).

* The eve of a holiday is as important or more so than the holiday itself. Most Swedes have the day off, including those working in the civil service, banks, public transport, hospitals, shops and the media. Others have at least a half-day. This applies especially to Midsummer's Eve, All Saints' Day Eve and Christmas Eve. The eve of May Day is sometimes called Valborg Eve or St Walpurgis. When a holiday falls on a Thursday many Swedes have the following Friday off in addition. When a holiday falls on a Saturday or Sunday it is not taken on the following Monday.

Weights and Measures

The metric system is in force.

Statistical Survey

Sources (unless otherwise stated): Statistics Sweden, Klostergatan 23, 701 89 Örebro; tel. (19) 17-60-00; fax (19) 17-70-80; e-mail information@scb.se; internet www.scb.se; Nordic Statistical Secretariat (Copenhagen), *Yearbook of Nordic Statistics*.

Area and Population

AREA, POPULATION AND DENSITY

Area (sq km)	
Land	410,335
Inland waters	39,960
Total	450,295*
Population (census results)†	
1 November 1985	8,360,178
1 November 1990	
Males	4,242,351
Females	4,345,002
Total	8,587,353
Population (official estimates at 31 December)†	
2002	8,940,788
2003	8,975,670
2004	9,011,392
Density (per sq km) at 31 December 2004	22.0‡

* 173,859 sq miles.
† Population is *de jure*.
‡ Land area only.

COUNTIES
(31 December 2004)

	Land area (sq km)*	Population	Density (per sq km)
Stockholms län	6,519.3	1,872,900	287.3
Uppsala län	7,036.7	302,564	43.0
Södermanlands län	6,103.1	261,070	42.8
Östergötlands län	10,604.6	415,990	39.2
Jönköpings län	10,495.4	329,297	31.4
Kronobergs län	8,467.3	178,285	21.1
Kalmar län	11,219.1	234,496	20.9
Gotlands län	3,151.4	57,661	18.3
Blekinge län	2,946.7	150,335	51.0
Skåne län	11,035.4	1,160,919	105.2
Hallands län	5,461.6	283,788	52.0
Västra Götalands län	23,956.1	1,521,895	63.5

SWEDEN

—continued	Land area (sq km)*	Population	Density (per sq km)
Värmlands län	17,591.3	273,547	15.6
Örebro län	8,546.3	273,920	32.1
Västmanlands län	6,317.9	261,005	41.3
Dalarnus län	28,195.6	276,042	9.8
Gävleborgs län	18,200.1	276,599	15.2
Västernorrlands län	21,684.5	244,195	11.1
Jämtlands län	49,343.1	127,424	2.6
Västerbottens län	55,189.7	256,875	4.7
Norrbottens län	98,249.0	252,585	2.6
Total†	410,335.4	9,011,392	22.0

* According to new estimates for land area.
† Including area of 21.2 sq km outside of existing county boundaries.

PRINCIPAL TOWNS
(estimated population of municipalities at 31 December 2004)*

Stockholm (capital)	765,044	Örebro	126,982
Göteborg (Gothenburg)	481,410	Norrköping	124,410
Malmö	269,142	Helsingborg	121,179
Uppsala	182,076	Jönköping	119,927
Linköping	136,912	Umeå	109,390
Västerås	131,014	Lund	101,423

* According to the administrative subdivisions of 1 January 2005.

BIRTHS, MARRIAGES AND DEATHS

	Registered live births		Registered marriages		Registered deaths	
	Number	Rate (per 1,000)	Number	Rate (per 1,000)	Number	Rate (per 1,000)
1997	90,502	10.2	32,313	3.7	93,326	10.6
1998	89,028	10.1	31,598	3.6	93,271	10.5
1999	88,173	9.9	35,628	4.0	94,726	10.7
2000	90,441	10.2	39,895	4.5	93,461	10.5
2001	91,446	10.3	35,778	4.0	93,752	10.5
2002	95,815	10.7	38,012	4.3	95,009	10.6
2003	99,157	11.0	39,041	4.3	92,961	10.4
2004	100,928	11.2	43,088	4.8	90,532	10.0

Expectation of life (WHO estimates, years at birth): 81 (males 78; females 83) in 2003 (Source: WHO, *World Health Report*).

IMMIGRATION AND EMIGRATION

	2002	2003	2004
Immigrants	64,087	63,795	62,028
Emigrants	33,009	35,023	36,586

ECONOMICALLY ACTIVE POPULATION
(sample surveys, '000 persons aged 16 to 64 years)

	2002	2003	2004
Agriculture, hunting and forestry	88	87	89
Fishing	3	2	1
Mining and quarrying	7	7	6
Manufacturing	714	689	679
Electricity, gas and water supply	25	27	27
Construction	235	239	242
Wholesale and retail trade, repair of motor vehicles, motorcycles and personal and household goods	515	527	529
Hotels and restaurants	113	119	124
Transport, storage and communications	284	275	265
Financial intermediation	90	90	87
Real estate, renting and business activities	564	548	545

—continued	2002	2003	2004
Public administration and defence, compulsory social security, extra-territorial organizations and bodies	241	243	246
Education	348	471	472
Health and social work	792	687	683
Other community, social and personal service activities, private households with employed persons	217	219	214
Activities not adequately defined	6	4	3
Total employed	4,244	4,234	4,213
Unemployed	176	217	246
Total labour force	4,421	4,450	4,459
Males	2,298	2,314	2,323
Females	2,123	2,136	2,136

Source: ILO.

Health and Welfare

KEY INDICATORS

Total fertility rate (children per woman, 2003)	1.6
Under-5 mortality rate (per 1,000 live births, 2004)	4
HIV/AIDS (% of persons aged 15–49, 2003)	0.1
Physicians (per 1,000 head, 2000)	3.05
Hospital beds (per 1,000 head, 2000)	3.60
Health expenditure (2002): US $ per head (PPP)	2,512
Health expenditure (2002): % of GDP	9.2
Health expenditure (2002): public (% of total)	85.3
Access to water (% of persons, 2002)	100
Access to sanitation (% of persons, 2002)	100
Human Development Index (2003): ranking	6
Human Development Index (2003): value	0.949

For sources and definitions, see explanatory note on p. vi.

Agriculture

PRINCIPAL CROPS
('000 metric tons; holdings of more than 2 ha of arable land)

	2002	2003	2004
Wheat	2,112.6	2,282.7	2,412.3
Rye	128.2	118.1	133.4
Barley	1,777.9	1,546.3	1,691.9
Oats	1,180.7	1,102.3	925.3
Triticale (wheat-rye hybrid)	169.4	205.1	270.2
Potatoes	913.6	857.1	979.1
Rapeseed	159.2	129.5	227.5
Sugar beets	2,664.3	2,484.4	2,287.1

Source: FAO.

LIVESTOCK
('000 head, year ending September; holdings of more than 2 ha of arable land, or with large numbers of livestock)

	2002	2003	2004
Cattle	1,637.5	1,606.7	1,628.5
Sheep	426.8	448.3	465.6
Pigs	1,881.7	1,903.1	1,818.0
Horses	85.0*	95.5	95.7
Chickens	6,269	6,006	6,620
Turkeys*	200.0	200.0	200.0

* FAO estimate(s).

Source: FAO.

SWEDEN

LIVESTOCK PRODUCTS
('000 metric tons)

	2002	2003	2004
Beef and veal	146.5	140.4	142.4
Horse meat	1.5	1.4	1.4
Mutton and lamb	3.9	3.7	3.8
Pig meat	283.8	287.5	294.5
Poultry meat	103.4	99.9	93.2
Game meat	18.5	18.5	18.5*
Cows' milk	3,226.0	3,206.0	3,229.2
Butter	48.0	49.0	47.3†
Cheese	132.0	129.0	121.8
Hen eggs	93.4	92.3	92.3*

* FAO estimate.
† Unofficial figure.
Source: FAO.

Forestry

ROUNDWOOD REMOVALS
('000 cubic metres)

	2002	2003	2004
Sawlogs, veneer logs and logs for sleepers	33,800	35,500	35,400
Pulpwood	26,400	25,200	25,500
Fuel wood*	5,900	5,900	5,900
Other industrial wood*	500	500	500
Total	66,600	67,100	67,300

* FAO estimates.
Source: FAO.

SAWNWOOD PRODUCTION
('000 cubic metres, incl. railway sleepers)

	2002	2003	2004
Coniferous (softwood)	16,012	16,640	16,740
Broadleaved (hardwood)	160	160*	160*
Total	16,172	16,800	16,900

* FAO estimate.
Source: FAO.

Fishing

('000 metric tons, live weight)

	2001	2002	2003
Capture	311.8	295.0	286.9
Atlantic cod	24.1	17.4	16.3
Blue whiting (Poutassou)	2.1	18.5	65.5
Sandeels (Sandlances)	50.6	56.0	22.0
Atlantic herring	125.7	97.6	86.6
European sprat	88.6	78.4	76.7
Aquaculture	6.8	5.6	6.3
Total catch	318.6	300.6	293.2

Note: Figures exclude aquatic mammals, recorded by number rather than by weight. The number of harbour porpoises caught was: 3 in 2001; 3 in 2002; 5 in 2003.
Source: FAO.

Mining

('000 metric tons, unless otherwise indicated)

	2002	2003	2004
Iron ore*	13,400	14,100	14,700
Copper ore	72.1	83.1	85.5
Gold (kilograms)	4,500	4,300	5,300
Silver (metric tons)	293.9	306.8	292.6
Zinc ore	148.6	185.9	160.6
Lead ore	43.0	51.0	33.9

* Estimates.
Note: Figures relate to the metal content of ores.
Source: US Geological Survey.

Industry

SELECTED PRODUCTS
('000 metric tons, unless otherwise indicated)

	2002	2003	2004
Pig-iron and sponge-iron*	3,703	3,700†	3,600†
Crude steel*	5,754	5,707	5,949
Aluminium*‡	128.6	131.2	130.4
Copper (refined)*†‡	224	214	235
Lead (refined)*†‡	69.7	76.2	82.2
Mechanical wood pulp§	3,021.0	3,222.6	3,397.0
Chemical wood pulp§	8,052.0	8,236.0	8,417.0
Newsprint§	2,423.0	2,548.0	2,649.0
Printing and writing paper†§	2,807.0	2,817.0	3,033.0
Other paper and paperboard†§	5,494.0	5,696.6	5,907.0
Cement (hydraulic)*†	2,700	2,650	2,700
Dwellings completed (number)	19,941	19,986	25,283
Electricity (million kWh)	143,234	132,535	148,373

* Source: US Geological Survey.
† Estimate(s).
‡ Primary and secondary metals.
§ Source: FAO.

Finance

CURRENCY AND EXCHANGE RATES

Monetary Units
  100 öre = 1 Swedish krona (plural: kronor).

Sterling, Dollar and Euro Equivalents (30 December 2005)
  £1 sterling = 13.704 kronor;
  US $1 = 7.958 kronor;
  €1 = 9.389 kronor;
  1,000 Swedish kronor = £72.97 = $125.65 = €106.51.

Average Exchange Rate (kronor per US $)
  2003 8.0863
  2004 7.3489
  2005 7.4731

SWEDEN

STATE BUDGET
(million kronor)

Revenue	2003	2004	2005*
Tax revenue	608,462	637,001	650,657
Taxes on income, profits and capital gains	29,726	45,706	68,181
Statutory social security fees	259,037	266,040	272,349
Taxes on property	36,133	37,126	37,105
Taxes on goods and services	298,365	308,876	327,459
Reallocation fee†	−1,815	−5,776	−31,943
Adjustment for non-collection	−4,425	−5,458	−5,741
Tax reductions	−8,560	−9,513	−16,753
Other current revenue	29,242	35,082	38,692
Capital revenue	3	136	6,369
Loan repayment	2,524	2,391	2,235
Computed revenue	9,484	8,252	8,667
EU contributions	12,016	11,555	11,630
Total	**661,731**	**694,418**	**718,249**

Expenditure	2003	2004	2005*
Justice	25,513	26,318	27,576
Defence	45,129	42,846	44,174
Health	34,068	36,809	38,450
Social insurance for the sick and disabled	121,464	122,916	129,193
Social insurance for the elderly	51,954	51,229	46,331
Social insurance for families and children	52,223	53,925	55,381
Social insurance for the unemployed / Employment	65,356	68,572	69,253
Education and university research	42,046	43,981	43,331
Community planning and housing	8,805	8,723	8,895
Communications	25,281	29,139	31,347
Agriculture, forestry and fisheries	9,615	12,219	15,149
General grants to municipalities	72,400	69,834	57,466
Interest on central government debt	42,173	52,718	35,165
Contributions to the European Union	18,322	25,563	26,222
Total (incl. others)	**708,081**	**747,761**	**750,965**

* Forecasts.
† Includes refund for overcharging.

INTERNATIONAL RESERVES
(US $ million at 31 December)

	2003	2004	2005
Gold*	310	324	271
IMF special drawing rights	198	209	176
Reserve position in IMF	1,468	1,308	532
Foreign exchange	18,015	20,611	21,355
Total	**19,991**	**22,452**	**22,334**

* Valued at SDR 35 per troy ounce.

Source: IMF, *International Financial Statistics*.

MONEY SUPPLY
(million kronor at 31 December)*

	2003	2004	2005
Currency outside banks	97,130	98,190	100,370
Demand deposits	677,450	839,320	973,110
Total money	**774,580**	**937,510**	**1,073,480**

* Figures are rounded to the nearest 10m. kronor.

Source: IMF, *International Financial Statistics*.

COST OF LIVING
(Consumer Price Index; base: 1980 = 100)

	2002	2003	2004
Food and non-alcoholic beverages	240.0	240.8	239.7
Alcoholic beverages and tobacco	342.2	347.3	349.4
Clothing and footwear	164.5	164.5	161.4
Housing, water, electricity and fuels	312.1	325.6	326.2
Furniture and household goods	229.0	231.6	228.9
Health	686.0	705.3	732.0
Transport	328.7	334.7	347.3
Communication	227.8	224.5	214.6
Recreation and culture	197.8	197.4	194.5
Restaurants and hotels	370.7	381.0	388.6
Miscellaneous goods and services	227.4	286.6	295.4
All items	**272.9**	**278.1**	**279.1**

NATIONAL ACCOUNTS
(million kronor at current prices)

National Income and Product

	2002	2003	2004
Compensation of employees	1,349,763	1,390,128	1,427,888
Net operating surplus / Net mixed income	339,051	360,436	412,741
Domestic factor incomes	**1,688,814**	**1,750,564**	**1,840,629**
Consumption of fixed capital	302,276	304,100	311,159
Gross domestic product (GDP) at factor cost	**1,991,090**	**2,054,664**	**2,151,788**
Taxes on production and imports	407,723	426,874	438,982
Less Subsidies	45,875	43,091	45,020
GDP in market prices	**2,352,938**	**2,438,447**	**2,545,750**
Primary incomes received from abroad (net)	−6,713	−381	29,340
Gross national income	**2,346,225**	**2,438,066**	**2,575,090**
Less Consumption of fixed capital	302,276	304,100	311,159
Net national income	**2,043,949**	**2,133,966**	**2,263,931**
Other current transfers from abroad (net)	−24,176	−21,324	−35,571
Net national disposable income	**2,019,773**	**2,112,642**	**2,228,360**

Expenditure on the Gross Domestic Product

	2002	2003	2004
Final consumption expenditure	1,801,702	1,878,828	1,930,657
Households / Non-profit institutions serving households	1,144,415	1,188,154	1,224,478
General government	657,287	690,674	706,179
Gross capital formation	393,725	395,193	410,770
Gross fixed capital formation	392,067	384,568	407,209
Changes in inventories	1,272	10,292	3,166
Acquisitions, less disposals, of valuables	386	333	395
Total domestic expenditure	**2,195,427**	**2,274,021**	**2,341,427**
Exports of goods and services	1,038,338	1,068,037	1,178,067
Less Imports of goods and services	880,827	903,611	973,744
GDP in market prices	**2,352,938**	**2,438,447**	**2,545,750**
GDP at constant 2000 prices	**2,261,773**	**2,294,943**	**2,377,495**

Gross Domestic Product by Economic Activity

	2002	2003	2004
Agriculture, forestry and fishing	38,606	39,350	40,579
Mining and quarrying	5,056	5,262	6,559
Manufacturing	425,984	434,180	467,001
Electricity, gas and water	54,811	61,574	63,927
Construction	92,981	96,786	102,375
Wholesale and retail trade	219,267	224,743	233,792
Hotels and restaurants	32,734	33,142	33,853
Transport, storage and communications	156,039	159,948	165,803
Financial intermediation	75,580	78,896	80,603
Real estate and business services*	433,940	448,100	461,447

SWEDEN

Statistical Survey

—continued	2002	2003	2004
Government services	437,133	463,860	481,481
Education, health and social services	52,246	56,180	56,387
Other community, social and personal services	46,576	49,716	50,810
Other services†	31,262	32,423	33,606
Sub-total	2,102,215	2,184,160	2,278,223
Less Financial intermediation services indirectly measured	46,162	53,782	51,478
Gross value added in basic prices	2,056,053	2,130,378	2,226,745
Taxes on products	310,980	322,337	332,603
Less Subsidies on products	14,095	14,268	13,598
GDP in market prices	2,352,938	2,438,447	2,545,750

* Including imputed rents of owner-occupied dwellings.
† Domestic services and non-profit institutions serving households.

BALANCE OF PAYMENTS
(US $ million)

	2002	2003	2004
Exports of goods f.o.b.	84,172	102,080	125,214
Imports of goods f.o.b.	−67,541	−83,147	−101,799
Trade balance	16,631	18,933	23,415
Exports of services	24,009	30,654	38,719
Imports of services	−23,958	−28,771	−33,056
Balance on goods and services	16,682	20,816	29,079
Other income received	18,018	22,934	28,816
Other income paid	−19,044	−22,637	−25,592
Balance on goods, services and income	15,657	21,113	32,303
Current transfers received	3,345	3,577	3,680
Current transfers paid	−6,218	−1,845	−8,498
Current balance	12,784	22,844	27,485
Capital account (net)	−79	−46	94
Direct investment abroad	−10,673	−17,341	−15,369
Direct investment from abroad	11,709	3,268	−588
Portfolio investment assets	−4,038	−13,701	−24,796
Portfolio investment liabilities	−6,691	4,134	−265
Financial derivatives assets	37,720	40,045	27,730
Financial derivatives liabilities	−37,888	−38,964	−27,969
Other investment assets	−998	−8,349	−16,930
Other investment liabilities	155	10,744	23,417
Net errors and omissions	−1,336	−558	6,091
Overall balance	665	2,076	−1,100

Source: IMF, *International Financial Statistics*.

OFFICIAL ASSISTANCE TO DEVELOPING COUNTRIES
(million kronor)

	2002	2003	2004
Bilateral assistance	12,581	14,374	15,249
Multilateral assistance	7,212	5,014	4,747
Total	19,793	19,388	19,996

External Trade

PRINCIPAL COMMODITIES
(distribution by SITC, million kronor, provisional figures)

Imports c.i.f.	2002	2003	2004
Food and live animals	42,058	43,569	46,614
Crude materials (inedible) except fuels	23,061	21,927	25,890
Mineral fuels, lubricants, etc.	56,571	65,257	71,719
Petroleum, petroleum products, etc.	47,537	52,219	59,947
Chemicals and related products	70,402	74,128	79,114
Basic manufactures	95,448	99,161	111,565
Iron and steel	23,450	25,982	33,457
Machinery and transport equipment	267,768	274,378	297,308
Power-generating machinery and equipment	21,965	21,084	21,325
General industrial machinery, equipment and parts	36,445	35,944	37,749
Office machines and automatic data-processing equipment	29,491	28,758	30,672
Telecommunications and sound equipment	36,174	35,898	44,692
Other electrical machinery, apparatus, etc.	47,463	47,253	50,675
Road vehicles and parts*	64,337	72,908	80,800
Miscellaneous manufactured articles	91,851	90,971	94,245
Clothing and accessories (excl. footwear)	21,340	21,327	21,238
Other miscellaneous manufactured articles	28,963	29,151	30,084
Total (incl. others)	656,664	679,329	736,510

Exports f.o.b.	2002	2003	2004
Crude materials (inedible) except fuels	46,615	45,537	48,355
Mineral fuels, lubricants, etc.	23,619	28,149	37,629
Petroleum, petroleum products, etc.	21,118	24,032	32,083
Chemicals and related products	90,279	98,966	103,526
Medical and pharmaceutical preparations	44,835	53,299	52,948
Basic manufactures	171,069	171,197	185,490
Paper, paperboard and manufactures	66,894	66,624	66,663
Iron and steel	40,518	41,645	51,624
Manufactures of metals	24,242	24,303	26,298
Machinery and transport equipment	368,895	375,383	415,284
Power-generating machinery and equipment	31,655	31,887	34,561
Machinery specialized for particular industries	34,823	36,679	37,310
General industrial machinery, equipment and parts	52,990	54,102	58,831
Telecommunications and sound equipment	76,158	69,559	84,480
Other electrical machinery, apparatus, etc.	43,780	42,795	42,864
Road vehicles and parts*	100,139	113,775	128,989
Miscellaneous manufactured articles	77,085	76,870	80,803
Total (incl. others)	805,696	825,850	903,866

* Data on parts exclude tyres, engines and electrical parts.

SWEDEN

PRINCIPAL TRADING PARTNERS
(million kronor, provisional figures)

Imports c.i.f.	2002	2003	2004
Austria	7,865	9,077	8,050
Belgium	25,524	28,304	29,653
China, People's Repub.	11,280	14,494	17,570
Denmark	59,047	62,877	67,621
Finland	34,464	40,017	47,249
France	36,333	37,577	40,186
Germany	120,218	126,176	138,064
Hong Kong	7,620	7,120	6,928
Ireland	11,421	11,065	10,344
Italy	23,037	23,320	25,242
Japan	14,628	14,914	15,557
Netherlands	45,585	45,484	49,720
Norway	52,089	52,016	56,123
Poland	12,575	15,621	18,573
Russia	9,801	10,518	16,112
Spain	10,660	11,189	11,780
Switzerland	10,510	8,861	8,589
United Kingdom	57,402	54,255	54,884
USA	31,886	27,159	25,674
Total (incl. others)	656,664	679,329	736,510

Exports f.o.b.	2002	2003	2004
Australia	8,577	9,444	9,706
Austria	8,103	8,590	9,337
Belgium	36,953	37,061	40,781
Canada	9,574	10,365	10,239
China, People's Repub.	15,494	18,133	19,019
Denmark	49,096	52,766	60,258
Finland	45,682	47,102	51,587
France	40,596	39,959	43,255
Germany	80,775	82,210	91,859
Italy	29,751	29,356	33,370
Japan	19,116	16,109	16,682
Netherlands	42,038	40,472	43,166
Norway	69,781	71,167	78,062
Poland	12,698	13,650	15,914
Russia	11,065	11,359	13,607
Saudi Arabia	8,596	6,330	5,076
Spain	21,192	26,144	26,569
Switzerland	10,689	9,163	9,950
United Kingdom	65,985	64,036	70,584
USA	91,829	94,850	96,595
Total (incl. others)	805,696	825,850	903,866

Transport

RAILWAYS
(traffic)

	2001	2002	2003
Passenger-kilometres (million)	8,732	8,984	9,051
Freight ton-kilometres (million)	18,954	19,197	20,170

Freight ton-kilometres (million): 20,856 in 2004.

ROAD TRAFFIC
('000 motor vehicles in use at 31 December)

	2002	2003	2004
Passenger cars	4,043	4,075	4,113
Buses and coaches	14	14	13
Lorries and vans	409	422	440
Motorcycles	221	247	235

SHIPPING

Merchant Fleet
(registered at 31 December)

	2002	2003	2004
Number of vessels	571	581	579
Total displacement ('000 grt)	3,177.5	3,579.3	3,666.9

Source: Lloyd's Register-Fairplay, *World Fleet Statistics*.

International Sea-borne Freight Traffic

	2002	2003	2004
Vessels entered ('000 grt)	106,918	102,539	106,690
Vessels cleared ('000 grt)	103,012	98,180	102,311
Goods loaded ('000 metric tons)	58,911	60,990	65,547
Goods unloaded ('000 metric tons)	72,382	76,777	79,088

CIVIL AVIATION
(traffic on scheduled services)*

	1999	2000	2001
Kilometres flown (million)	150	167	167
Passengers carried ('000)	12,933	13,354	13,123
Passenger-kilometres (million)	10,607	11,192	11,277
Total ton-kilometres (million)	1,309	1,387	1,384

* Including an apportionment (3/7) of the international services of Scandinavian Airlines System (SAS), operated jointly with Denmark and Norway.

Source: UN, *Statistical Yearbook*.

Tourism*

VISITORS BY ORIGIN
('000 nights in all types of tourist accommodation)†

	2002	2003	2004
Denmark	669.6	686.5	680.4
Finland	328.9	323.0	308.8
France	171.5	162.0	175.1
Germany	818.4	844.7	844.6
Italy	171.5	156.3	215.4
Japan	137.6	109.6	118.2
Netherlands	208.9	202.2	237.6
Norway	1,062.9	1,076.5	968.6
Russia	163.8	113.1	132.0
United Kingdom	547.5	533.7	565.8
USA	391.8	364.8	383.2
Total (incl. others)	6,066.8	6,038.3	6,233.5

* Since the introduction of the Scandinavian Passport Control Area, there are no figures available for total arrivals in Sweden.
† Excluding nights at campsites (million, all nationalities, incl. Swedish): 15.8 in 2002; 17.1 in 2003; 15.6 in 2004.

Tourism receipts (US $ million, incl. passenger transport): 5,200 in 2001; 5,671 in 2002; 6,548 in 2003.

Source: World Tourism Organization, mainly *Yearbook of Tourism Statistics*.

Communications Media

	2002	2003	2004
Telephones ('000 main lines in use)	6,579	n.a.	6,873
Mobile cellular telephones ('000 subscribers)	7,949	8,801	9,302
Personal computers ('000 in use)	5,556	n.a.	6,861
Internet users ('000)	5,125	n.a.	6,800
Daily newspapers:			
titles	168	166	165
average net circulation ('000 copies)	4,064	4,055	4,000
Weekly newspapers and periodicals:			
titles	410	415	417
average net circulation ('000 copies)	22,256	22,785	22,668
Book production (titles)	9,002	9,981	16,031

Television receivers ('000 in use, 2001): 8,600.

Radio receivers ('000 in use, 1997): 8,250.

Facsimile machines (estimated '000 in use, 1996): 450.

Source: mainly International Telecommunication Union, UN, *Statistical Yearbook*, and UNESCO, *Statistical Yearbook*.

Education

(2004/05, unless otherwise indicated)

	Institutions	Teachers[1]	Students
Primary: grades 1–6	4,963	108,233	650,342
Secondary: grades 7–9			373,292
Integrated upper secondary schools	641[2]	37,640	347,713[3]
Higher education	64	20,000[4]	397,679[5]
People's colleges	147[2]	n.a.	108,742[6]
Municipal adult education	400[7]	6,593	226,851[5]

[1] Full-time and part-time teachers and teachers on leave.
[2] 1996/97.
[3] At 15 October 2004.
[4] 1994/95.
[5] 2003/04.
[6] Autumn term.
[7] 1993/94.

Directory

The Constitution

The Swedish Constitution is based on four fundamental laws: the Instrument of Government (originally dating from 6 June 1809), the Act of Succession (1810), the Freedom of the Press Act (1949) and the Riksdag Act. Following partial reforms in 1968 and 1969, a new Instrument of Government and a new Riksdag Act were adopted in 1973 and 1974, and the revised Constitution, summarized below, came into force on 1 January 1975.

GOVERNMENT

The Cabinet governs Sweden and is responsible to the Riksdag (Parliament). The Constitution of 1975 formalized the position of the Monarch relative to the Cabinet and the Riksdag, and laid down rules on the selection and resignation of the Cabinet. In 1978 the Riksdag amended the constitutional law of succession to allow the first-born royal child, whether male or female, to be heir to the throne, with effect from 1980.

As Head of State, the Monarch has representative and ceremonial duties only. The Monarch does not participate in the government of the country, which is conducted rather by the Cabinet at meetings not attended by the Monarch. Decisions of government do not require the Monarch's signature, and it is the Speaker of the Riksdag, and not the Monarch, who leads the procedure resulting in the formation of a new Government. Following consultations within the Riksdag, the Speaker nominates a candidate for Prime Minister. If not more than one-half of the total number of members of the Riksdag vote against the proposed candidate, he or she is approved. Failing this approval, the procedure has to be repeated. After four unsuccessful attempts to secure Riksdag approval of a candidate for the premiership, a new election to the Riksdag must be held within three months. A candidate for the premiership approved by the Riksdag nominates the other members of the Government.

The Prime Minister can be dismissed at his or her own request, by the Speaker of the Riksdag, or in the event of a vote of 'no confidence' in the Riksdag. Other ministers can be dismissed at their own request, by the Prime Minister or by a vote of 'no confidence'. If the Prime Minister should resign or die, all of the ministers in the Cabinet must resign. A Cabinet that is due to resign shall, however, remain in power until a new Prime Minister has been appointed.

A demand for a vote of 'no confidence' will be considered only if it is supported by 10% of the members of the Riksdag. A vote of 'no confidence' requires the support of more than one-half of the Riksdag members. If the Riksdag decides upon a vote of 'no confidence', the Cabinet can avoid resigning if it calls for an extra general election within one week. The Riksdag may continue its business, or be summoned to convene, even after a decision has been made to hold new elections. A Riksdag session may, however, be terminated by a special decision of the Cabinet. Existing terms of office do not expire until the new terms of office have begun.

LEGISLATURE

The Riksdag is the prime representative of the Swedish people. It enacts laws, decides the amount and use of taxation and examines the Government's actions. The Riksdag at present contains 349 members, elected for four years.

In accordance with tradition, the work of the Swedish Riksdag is, to a great extent, carried on in a non-partisan atmosphere. This is largely the result of the thorough attention given to all questions by numerous standing committees elected by the Riksdag on a basis of proportional representation. Besides the Utrikesnämnden (Advisory Council on Foreign Affairs) and Special Committees, every Riksdag appoints from within the assembly a Constitution Committee, a Finance Committee, a Taxation Committee and at least 12 other committees.

The Constitution Committee has to examine the minutes of the Cabinet and deal with or initiate proposals concerning alterations of the fundamental laws and of laws regulating local government.

ELECTORAL SYSTEM

In order that local and national government terms of office should coincide, the Constitution calls for local and general elections to be held on the same day. In both cases the term of office for the elected candidate is four years. Proportional representation was introduced in Sweden between the years 1906 and 1909, universal and equal suffrage by 1921. Under the provisions of legislation passed in 1976, all aliens resident in the country for three years are permitted to vote in local elections. The minimum voting age is 18 years. In allocating the 349 seats in the Riksdag, the seats are divided into two groups. The first group of 310 'constituency seats' is distributed among the constituencies according to the number of eligible voters, and within each constituency among the parties. The remaining 39 seats are distributed as 'adjustment seats'. First, it is calculated how many seats each party would have obtained if the whole country had been treated as a single constituency and if the distribution of seats had taken place according to a modified Lague method. From this figure is subtracted the number of 'constituency seats' received, the result being the number of 'compensatory seats' to be allocated to each party. These seats are filled by candidates nominated in the constituencies. There is a check to the emergence of small parties in that only parties that have received at least 4% of the total votes cast are entitled to a seat. However, any party that receives 12% or more of the votes in any constituency will be allowed to compete for a permanent seat in that constituency.

SWEDEN

The Government

HEAD OF STATE

Monarch: King CARL GUSTAF XVI (succeeded to the throne 15 September 1973).

THE CABINET
(April 2006)

Prime Minister: GÖRAN PERSSON.
Deputy Prime Minister: BOSSE RINGHOLM.
Minister for Agriculture, Food and Consumer Affairs: ANN-CHRISTIN NYKVIST.
Minister for Migration and Asylum Policy: BARBRO HOLMBERG.
Minister for Social Affairs: BERIT ANDNOR.
Minister for International Development Co-operation: CARIN JÄMTIN.
Minister for Employment: HANS KARLSSON.
Minister for Schools: IBRAHIM BAYLAN.
Minister for Foreign Affairs: JAN ELIASSON.
Minister for Integration, Metropolitan and Gender Equality Issues: JENS ORBACK.
Minister for Education and Culture: LEIF PAGROTSKY.
Minister for Pre-School Education, Youth Affairs and Adult Learning: LENA HALLENGREN.
Minister for the Environment: LENA SOMMESTAD.
Minister for Defence: LENI BJÖRKLUND.
Minister for Sustainable Development: MONA SAHLIN.
Minister for Public Health and Social Services: MORGAN JOHANSSON.
Minister for Finance: PÄR NUDER.
Minister for Local Government Finances and Financial Market Issues: SVEN-ERIK ÖSTERBERG.
Minister for Justice: THOMAS BODSTRÖM.
Minister for Industry and Trade: THOMAS ÖSTROS.
Minister for Communications and Regional Policy: ULRICA MESSING.
Minister for Health and Elderly Care: YLVA JOHANSSON.

MINISTRIES

Prime Minister's Office: Rosenbad 4, 103 33 Stockholm; tel. (8) 405-10-00; fax (8) 723-11-71; e-mail registrator@primeminister.ministry.se.
Ministry of Agriculture, Food and Consumer Affairs: Fredsgt. 8, 103 33 Stockholm; tel. (8) 405-10-00; fax (8) 20-64-96; e-mail registrator@agriculture.ministry.se; internet jordbruk.regeringen.se.
Ministry of Defence: Jakobsgt. 9, 103 33 Stockholm; tel. (8) 405-10-00; fax (8) 723-11-89; e-mail registrator@defence.ministry.se; internet forsvar.regeringen.se.
Ministry of Education, Research and Culture: Drottninggt. 16, 103 33 Stockholm; tel. (8) 405-10-00; fax (8) 723-11-92; e-mail registrator@educcult.ministry.se; internet utbildning.regeringen.se.
Ministry of Finance: Drottninggt. 21, 103 33 Stockholm; tel. (8) 405-10-00; fax (8) 21-73-86; e-mail registrator@finance.ministry.se; internet finans.regeringen.se.
Ministry for Foreign Affairs: Gustav Adolfs torg 1, 103 39 Stockholm; tel. (8) 405-10-00; fax (8) 723-11-76; e-mail registrator@foreign.ministry.se; internet utrikes.regeringen.se.
Ministry of Health and Social Affairs: Fredsgt. 8, 103 33 Stockholm; tel. (8) 405-10-00; fax (8) 723-11-91; e-mail registrator@social.ministry.se; internet social.regeringen.se.
Ministry of Industry, Employment and Communications: Jakobsgt. 26, 103 33 Stockholm; tel. (8) 405-10-00; fax (8) 411-36-16; e-mail registrator@industry.ministry.se; internet naring.regeringen.se.
Ministry of Justice: Rosenbad 4, 103 33 Stockholm; tel. (8) 405-10-00; fax (8) 20-27-34; e-mail registrator@justice.ministry.se; internet justitie.regeringen.se.
Ministry of Sustainable Development: Tegelbacken 2, 103 33 Stockholm; tel. (8) 405-10-00; fax (8) 24-16-29; e-mail registrator@sustainable.ministry.se; internet miljo.regeringen.se.
Office of Administrative Affairs: Fredsgt. 8, 103 33 Stockholm; tel. (8) 405-10-00; fax (8) 24-46-31.

Legislature

RIKSDAG

Sveriges Riksdag
100 12 Stockholm; tel. (8) 786-40-00; e-mail riksdagsinformation@riksdagen.se; internet www.riksdagen.se.
Speaker (Talman): BJÖRN VON SYDOW.
General Election, 15 September 2002

Party	Votes	% of votes	Seats
Sveriges Socialdemokratiska Arbetareparti (SAP)	2,113,560	39.85	144
Moderata Samlingspartiet (MS)	809,041	15.26	55
Folkpartiet liberalerna (FP)	710,312	13.39	48
Kristdemokraterna (Kd)	485,235	9.15	33
Vänsterpartiet (VP)	444,854	8.39	30
Centerpartiet (Centern) (CP)	328,428	6.19	22
Miljöpartiet de Gröna (MP)	246,392	4.65	17
Others	165,390	3.12	—
Total	5,303,212	100.00	349

Election Commission

Valmyndigheten: Solna Strandväg 78, POB 4210, 171 04 Solna; tel. (8) 50-52-91-00; fax (8) 50-52-91-30; e-mail valet@val.se; internet www.val.se; independent; Dir PETER LARSEN.

Political Organizations

Centerpartiet (CP) (Centre Party): Stora Nygt. 4, POB 2200, 103 15 Stockholm; tel. (8) 617-38-00; fax (8) 652-64-40; e-mail centerpartiet@centerpartiet.se; internet www.centerpartiet.se; f. 1910; as an agrarian party; aims at social, environmental and progressive development and decentralization; Leader MAUD OLOFSSON; Sec. JÖRAN HÄGGLUND; 140,000 mems.
Feministiskt initiativ (Feminist Initiative): POB 498, 101 29 Stockholm; tel. (0) 706-100-190; e-mail info@feministisktinitiativ.se; internet www.feministisktinitiativ.se; f. 2005; Leaders SOFIA KAROLINA KARLSSON, DEVRIM MAVI, GERD GUDRUN MARIA SCHYMAN.
Folkpartiet liberalerna (FP) (Liberal Party): POB 6508, Drottninggt. 97, 1st Floor, 113 83 Stockholm; tel. (8) 509-11-600; fax (8) 509-11-660; e-mail info@liberal.se; internet www.folkpartiet.se; f. 1902; advocates market-orientated economy and social welfare system; Chair. LARS LEIJONBORG; Sec.-Gen. JOHAN JAKOBSSON.
Junilistan: Vasagt. 40, 111 20 Stockholm; tel. (8) 23-01-11; e-mail info@junilistan.se; internet www.junilistan.se; f. 2004 to contest elections to the European Parliament; opposes further powers for EU; Leaders NILS LUNDGREN, LARS WOHLIN.
Kristdemokraterna (Kd) (Christian Democratic Party): POB 2373, 103 18 Stockholm; Munkbron 1, Stockholm; tel. (8) 723-25-00; fax (8) 723-25-10; e-mail info@kristdemokraterna.se; internet www.kristdemokraterna.se; f. 1964 as Kristdemokratiska Samhällspartiet (KdS); promotes emphasis on Christian values in political life; Chair. GÖRAN HÄGGLUND; Sec.-Gen. URBAN SVENSSON; 25,800 mems.
Miljöpartiet de Gröna (MP) (Green Party): International Secretary, Swedish Parliament, 100 12 Stockholm; tel. (8) 786-57-44; fax (8) 786-53-75; e-mail info@mp.se; internet www.mp.se; f. 1981; Co-Leaders MARIA WETTERSTRAND, PETER ERIKSSON; c. 8,000 mems.
Moderata Samlingspartiet (MS) (Moderate Party): Stord Nygatan 30, POB 2080, 113 12 Stockholm; tel. (8) 676-80-00; fax (8) 21-61-23; e-mail info@moderat.se; internet www.moderat.se; f. 1904; advocates liberal-conservative market-orientated economy; Chair. FREDRIK REINFELDT; Sec. SVEN OTTO LITTORIN; 100,000 mems.
Piratpartiet (Pirate Party): POB 307, 101 26 Stockholm; tel. (8) 720-04-00; e-mail info@piratpartiet.se; internet www.piratpartiet.se; f. 2006; advocates the citizen's right to complete and exclusive control of information pertaining to his or her private life and the abolition of copyright on all material for non-commercial use; Chair. RICKARD FALKVINGE.
Sverigedemokraterna (SD) (Swedish Democrats): POB 200 85, 104 60 Stockholm; tel. (8) 641-20-11; fax (8) 643-92-60; e-mail info@sverigedemokraterna.se; internet www.sverigedemokraterna.se; f. 1988; nationalist, anti-immigration; currently unrepresented in the Riksdag, but has won representation at local level; Leader JIMMIE ÅKESSON.

Sveriges Socialdemokratiska Arbetareparti (SAP) (Swedish Social Democratic Party): Sveavägen 68, 105 60 Stockholm; tel. (8) 700-26-00; fax (8) 21-93-31; e-mail info@sap.se; internet www.socialdemokraterna.se; f. 1889; egalitarian; Chair. GÖRAN PERSSON; Sec.-Gen. MARITA ULVSKOG; 143,000.

Vänsterpartiet (VP) (Left Party): Kungsgt. 84, POB 12660, 112 93 Stockholm; tel. (8) 654-08-20; fax (8) 653-23-85; e-mail vansterpartiet@riksdagen.se; internet www.vansterpartiet.se; f. 1917 as Left Social Democratic Party of Sweden; affiliated to the Communists International 1919; renamed the Communist Party in 1921; renamed Left Party—Communists in 1967; renamed Left Party in 1990; policies based on the principles of Marxism, feminism and other theories; Chair. LARS OHLY; Sec. ANKI AHLSTEN.

Diplomatic Representation

EMBASSIES IN SWEDEN

Albania: Capellavägen 7, 181 32 Lidingö; tel. (8) 731-09-20; fax (8) 767-65-57; Ambassador SHABAN MURATI.

Algeria: Danderydsgt. 3–5, POB 26027, 100 41 Stockholm; tel. (8) 679-91-30; fax (8) 611-49-57; e-mail embassy.algeria@telia.com; Ambassador MERZAK BEDJAOUI.

Angola: POB 3199, 103 64 Stockholm; Skeppsbron 8, 111 33 Stockholm; tel. (8) 24-28-90; fax (8) 34-31-27; e-mail info@angolaemb.se; internet www.angolaemb.se; Ambassador LEOVIGILDO DA COSTA E SILVA.

Argentina: Narvavägen 32, 3rd Floor, Apartment 3, POB 14039, 115 22 Stockholm; tel. (8) 663-19-65; fax (8) 661-00-09; e-mail cancilleria@argemb.se; Ambassador ELDA BEATRIZ SAMPIETRO.

Australia: Sergels Torg 12, POB 7003, 103 86 Stockholm; tel. (8) 613-29-00; fax (8) 613-29-82; e-mail reception@austemb.se; internet www.sweden.embassy.gov.au; Ambassador RICHARD ANTHONY ROWE.

Austria: Kommendörsgt. 35, 114 58 Stockholm; tel. (8) 665-17-70; fax (8) 662-69-28; e-mail stockholm-ob@bmaa.gv.at; internet www.aussenministerium.at/stockholm; Ambassador STEPHAN TOTH.

Bangladesh: Anderstorpsvägen 12, 1st Floor, 171 54 Solna; tel. (8) 730-58-50; fax (8) 730-58-70; e-mail banijya@bangladeshembassy.se; Ambassador SABIHUDDIN AHMED.

Belarus: Herserudsvägen 5, 4th Floor, 181 34 Lidingö; tel. (8) 731-57-45; fax (8) 731-57-46; e-mail belarusembassy@telia.com; internet www.belembassy.org/sweden; Ambassador ANDREI M. GRINKEVICH.

Belgium: Villagt. 13A, POB 26114, 100 41 Stockholm; tel. (8) 534-802-00; fax (8) 534-802-07; e-mail stockholm@diplobel.org; internet www.diplobel.be/stockholm; Ambassador RAOUL DELCORDE.

Bolivia: Södra Kungsvägen 60, 181 32 Lidingö; tel. (8) 731-58-30; fax (8) 767-63-11; e-mail embolivia-estocolmo@telia.com; Chargé d'affaires a.i. MARÍA ELENA GARCÍA DE BACCINO.

Bosnia and Herzegovina: POB 7102, 103 87 Stockholm; Birger Jarlsgt. 55, 111 45 Stockholm; tel. (8) 24-83-60; fax (8) 24-98-30; e-mail info@bosniaemb.se; internet www.bosniaemb.se; Ambassador JAKOV SKOČIBUŠIĆ.

Botswana: Tyrgt. 11, POB 26024, 100 41 Stockholm; tel. (8) 545-258-00; fax (8) 723-00-87; Ambassador BERNADETTE SEBAGE RATHEDI.

Brazil: Odengt. 3, 114 24 Stockholm; tel. (8) 545-163-00; fax (8) 545-163-14; Ambassador OTO AGRIPINO MAIA.

Bulgaria: Karlavägen 29, 114 31 Stockholm; tel. (8) 723-09-38; fax (8) 21-45-03; e-mail bg.embassy@telia.com; Ambassador GORAN YONOV.

Canada: Tegelbacken 4, 7th Floor, POB 16129, 103 23 Stockholm; tel. (8) 453-30-00; fax (8) 453-30-16; e-mail stkhm@international.gc.ca; internet www.canadaemb.se; Ambassador LORENZ I. FRIEDLAENDER.

Chile: 3rd Floor, Sturegt. 8, 114 35 Stockholm; tel. (8) 679-82-80; fax (8) 679-85-40; e-mail echilese@chileemb.se; Ambassador ALVARO GARCÍA.

China, People's Republic: Lidovägen 8, 115 25 Stockholm; tel. (8) 579-364-37; fax (8) 579-364-54; e-mail protocal@chinaembassy.se; internet www.chinaembassy.se; Ambassador LU FENGDING.

Colombia: 3rd Floor, Östermalmsgt. 46, POB 5627, 114 86 Stockholm; tel. (8) 21-43-20; fax (8) 21-84-90; e-mail embcol@telia.com; internet www.welcome.to/theembassyofcolombia; Ambassador CARLOS HOLMES TRUJILLO GARCÍA.

Congo, Democratic Republic: POB 1171, 181 23 Lidingö; tel. (8) 765-83-80; fax (8) 765-85-91; e-mail rdcongo6@hotmail.com; Chargé d'affaires a.i. MAYOLA MA LULENDO.

Croatia: 1st Floor, Birger Jarlsgt. 13, 111 45 Stockholm; tel. (8) 678-42-20; fax (8) 678-83-20; e-mail croemb.stockholm@mvp.hr; Ambassador Dr SVJETLAN BERKOVIĆ.

Cuba: Sturevägen 9, 182 73 Stocksund; tel. (8) 545-83-277; fax (8) 545-83-270; e-mail primero.enero59@swipnet.se; internet home.swipnet.se/embacubasuecia; Ambassador JORGE DESIDERIO PAYRET ZUBIAUR.

Cyprus: 4th Floor, Birger Jarlsgt. 37, POB 7649, 103 94 Stockholm; tel. (8) 24-50-08; fax (8) 24-45-18; e-mail info@cyprusemb.se; internet www.cyprusemb.se; Ambassador PAVLOS ANASTASIADES.

Czech Republic: Villagt. 21, POB 26156, 100 41 Stockholm; tel. (8) 440-42-10; fax (8) 440-42-11; e-mail stockholm@embassy.mzv.cz; internet www.mzv.cz/stockholm; Ambassador MARIE CHATARDOVÁ.

Denmark: Jakobs Torg 1, POB 16119, 103 23 Stockholm; tel. (8) 406-75-00; fax (8) 791-72-20; e-mail stoamb@um.dk; internet www.ambstockholm.um.dk; Ambassador OLE LØNSMANN POULSEN.

Dominican Republic: 4th Floor, Sibyllegt. 13, POB 5584, 114 85 Stockholm; tel. (8) 667-46-11; fax (8) 667-51-05; e-mail stockholm@domemb.se; Ambassador ABIGAÍL MEJÍA-RICART.

Ecuador: Engelbrektsgt. 13, 114 32 Stockholm; tel. (8) 679-60-43; fax (8) 611-55-93; e-mail suecia@embajada-ecuador.se; internet www.embajada-ecuador.se; Ambassador ROBERTO BETANCOURT RUALES.

Egypt: Strandvägen 35, POB 14230, 104 40 Stockholm; tel. (8) 662-96-03; fax (8) 661-26-64; e-mail egypt.embassy@chello.se; Ambassador SAMAH MOHAMED SOTOUHI.

El Salvador: 5th Floor, Herserudsvägen 5A, 181 34 Lidingö; tel. (8) 765-86-21; fax (8) 731-72-72; e-mail embassy@elsalvador.se; Ambassador MARTIN RIVERA GÓMEZ.

Eritrea: 4th Floor, Stjärnvägen 2B, POB 1164, 181 23 Lidingö; tel. (8) 441-71-70; fax (8) 446-73-40; e-mail info@eritrean-embassy.se; internet www.eritrean-embassy.se; Chargé d'affaires a.i. YONAS MANNA BAIRU.

Estonia: Tyrgt. 3, 114 27 Stockholm; POB 26076, 100 41, Stockholm; tel. (8) 545-122-80; fax (8) 545-122-99; e-mail info@estemb.se; internet www.estemb.se; Ambassador JÜRI KAHN.

Ethiopia: Löjtnantsgt. 17, POB 10148, 100 55 Stockholm; tel. (8) 665-60-30; fax (8) 660-81-77; e-mail ethio.embassy@telia.com; internet www.ethemb.se; Ambassador DINA MUFTI.

Finland: Gärdesgt. 11, POB 24285, 104 51 Stockholm; tel. (8) 676-67-00; fax (8) 20-74-97; e-mail info@finland.se; internet www.finland.se; Ambassador PERTTI TORSTILA.

France: Kommendörsgt. 13, POB 5135, 102 43 Stockholm; tel. (8) 459-53-00; fax (8) 459-53-41; e-mail info@ambafrance-se.org; internet www.ambafrance-se.org; Ambassador DENIS DELBOURG.

Germany: Skarpögt. 9, POB 27832, 115 93 Stockholm; tel. (8) 670-15-00; fax (8) 670-15-72; e-mail zreg@stoc.diplo.de; internet www.stockholm.diplo.de; Ambassador BUSSO VON ALVENSLEBEN.

Greece: POB 55565, 102 04 Stockholm; Kommendörsgt. 16, 114 48 Stockholm; tel. (8) 545-660-10; fax (8) 660-54-70; e-mail gremb.stockholm@beta.telenordia.se; internet www.greekembassy.se; Ambassador EVANGELOS CAROKIS.

Guatemala: Wittstocksgt. 30, 115 27 Stockholm; tel. (8) 660-52-29; fax (8) 660-42-29; e-mail embassy@guatemala.se; internet www.guatemala.se; Ambassador SUSANA BARRIOS BELTRANENA.

Holy See: Svalnäsvägen 10, 182 63 Djursholm; tel. (8) 446-51-10; fax (8) 622-51-10; e-mail nunciature@telia.com; Apostolic Nuncio Most Rev. GIOVANNI TONUCCI (Titular Archbishop of Torcello).

Honduras: 7th Floor, Stjärnvägen 2, 181 34 Lidingö; tel. (8) 731-50-84; fax (8) 636-99-83; e-mail embahon@telia.com; internet www.hondurasembassy.se; Ambassador IVÁN ROMERO-MARTÍNEZ.

Hungary: Dag Hammarskjölds Väg 10, POB 24125, 104 51 Stockholm; tel. (8) 661-67-62; fax (8) 660-29-59; e-mail secretariat@huembsto.se; internet www.huembsto.se; Ambassador GÁBOR IKLÓDY.

Iceland: Kommendörsgt. 35, 114 58 Stockholm; tel. (8) 442-83-00; fax (8) 660-74-23; e-mail icemb.stock@utn.strj.is; internet www.island.se; Ambassador SVAVAR GESTSSON.

India: Adolf Fredriks Kyrkogt. 12, POB 1340, 111 83 Stockholm; tel. (8) 10-70-08; fax (8) 24-85-05; e-mail information@indianembassy.se; internet www.indianembassy.se; Ambassador DEEPA GOPALAN WADHWA.

Indonesia: POB 12520, 102 29 Stockholm; Sysslomansgt. 18/I, 112 41 Stockholm; tel. (8) 545-55-880; fax (8) 650-87-50; e-mail subidpen@indonesiskaambassaden.se; internet www.indonesiskaambassaden.se; Chargé d'affaires a.i. ELISABETH HERI BUDIASTUTI.

Iran: Västra Yttringe Gård, Elfviksvägen, POB 6031, 181 06 Lidingö; tel. (8) 765-08-19; fax (8) 765-31-19; internet www.iran.se; Ambassador HASSAN GHASHGHAVI.

Iraq: Baldersgt. 6A, POB 26031, 100 41 Stockholm; tel. (8) 411-44-43; fax (8) 796-83-66; Ambassador AHMAD A. BAMARNI.

Ireland: Östermalmsgt. 97, POB 10326, 100 55 Stockholm; tel. (8) 661-80-05; fax (8) 660-13-53; e-mail irish.embassy@swipnet.se; Ambassador BARRIE ROBINSON.

Israel: Torstenssonsgt. 4, POB 14006, 104 40 Stockholm; tel. (8) 663-04-35; fax (8) 662-53-01; e-mail israel-info@stockholm.mfa.gov.il; internet stockholm.mfa.gov.il; Ambassador EVIATAR MANOR.

Italy: Oakhill, Djurgården, 115 21 Stockholm; tel. (8) 545-67-100; fax (8) 660-05-05; e-mail itemb@itemb.se; internet www.itemb.se; Ambassador FRANCESCO CARUSO.

Japan: Gärdesgt. 10, 115 27 Stockholm; tel. (8) 576-353-00; fax (8) 661-88-20; e-mail protocol@japansamb.se; internet www.japansamb.se; Ambassador SELICHIRO OTSUKA.

Kenya: 2nd Floor, Birger Jarlsgt. 37, POB 7694, 103 95 Stockholm; tel. (8) 21-83-00; fax (8) 20-92-61; e-mail kenya.embassy@telia.com; Ambassador MICHAEL KINYANJUI.

Korea, Democratic People's Republic: Norra Kungsvägen 39, 181 31 Lidingö; tel. (8) 767-38-36; fax (8) 767-38-35; e-mail koryo@telia.com; Ambassador JON IN CHAN.

Korea, Republic: Laboratoriegt. 10, POB 27237, 102 53 Stockholm; tel. (8) 545-894-00; fax (8) 660-28-18; e-mail koremb.sweden@mofat.go.kr; Ambassador JUNG YONG-JO.

Kuwait: Banérgt. 37, POB 10030, 100 55 Stockholm; tel. (8) 450-99-80; fax (8) 450-99-55; e-mail kuwaitambassad@telia.com; Ambassador SAMI MOHAMED AL-SULAIMAN.

Laos: Badstrandsvägen 11, POB 34050, 112 65 Stockholm; tel. (8) 618-20-10; fax (8) 618-20-01; e-mail laoembassy@telia.com; Ambassador PHOU RASPHONE.

Latvia: Odengt. 5, POB 19167, 104 32 Stockholm; tel. (8) 700-63-00; fax (8) 14-01-51; e-mail embassy.sweden@mfa.gov.lv; internet www.stockholm.mfa.gov.lv; Ambassador ELITA KUZMA.

Lebanon: Kommendörsgt. 35, POB 5360, 102 49 Stockholm; tel. (8) 665-19-65; fax (8) 662-68-24; Ambassador MOUNIR TALHOUK.

Libya (People's Bureau): Valhallavägen 74, POB 10133, 100 55 Stockholm; tel. (8) 14-34-35; fax (8) 10-43-80; e-mail libya69bstock@yahoo.com; Chargé d'affaires a.i. RADWAN ALSHAREF SWEEY.

Lithuania: Grevgt. 5, 114 53 Stockholm; tel. (8) 667-54-55; fax (8) 667-54-56; e-mail info@litemb.se; internet www.litemb.se; Ambassador PETRAS ZAPOLSKAS.

Macedonia, former Yugoslav republic: Riddargt. 35, POB 10128, 100 55 Stockholm; tel. (8) 661-18-30; fax (8) 661-03-25; e-mail macedonian.embassy@telia.com; Chargé d'affaires a.i. SLAVICA CANEVSKA.

Malaysia: Karlavägen 37, POB 26053, 100 41 Stockholm; tel. (8) 791-76-90; fax (8) 791-87-60; e-mail mwstholm@algohotellet.se; Ambassador JASMI MD YUSOFF.

Mexico: Grevgt. 3, 114 53 Stockholm; tel. (8) 663-51-70; fax (8) 663-24-20; e-mail suecia.embamex@telia.com; internet www.sre.gob.mx/suecia; Ambassador FERNANDO ESTRADA SÁMANO.

Morocco: Kungsholmstorg 16, 112 21 Stockholm; tel. (8) 545-511-30; fax (8) 545-511-39; e-mail sifamastock@stockholm.mail.telia.com; Ambassador FARIDA JAÏDI.

Mozambique: Sturegt. 46, POB 5801, 102 48 Stockholm; tel. (8) 666-03-50; fax (8) 663-67-29; e-mail info@embassymozambique.se; internet www.mozambique.mz/governo/minec/msuecia; Chargé d'affaires a.i. ALEXANDRE ANTÓNIO CHEMANE.

Namibia: POB 19151, 104 32 Stockholm; Luntmakargt. 86–88, 113 51 Stockholm; tel. (8) 442-98-00; fax (8) 612-66-55; e-mail info@embassyofnamibia.se; internet www.embassyofnamibia.se; Ambassador PANDULENI K. SHINGENGE.

Netherlands: Götgt. 16A, POB 15048, 104 65 Stockholm; tel. (8) 556-993-00; fax (8) 556-933-11; e-mail info@nlemb.se; internet www.nlemb.se; Ambassador ANTOINE FRANÇOIS VAN DONGEN.

Nicaragua: 6th Floor, Sandhamnsgt. 40, 115 28 Stockholm; tel. (8) 667-18-57; fax (8) 662-41-60; e-mail embajada.nicaragua@telia.com; Ambassador ALVARO MONTENEGRO MALLONA.

Nigeria: Tyrgt. 8, POB 628, 101 32 Stockholm; tel. (8) 26-39-0; fax (8) 24-63-98; e-mail nigerian.embassy@swipnet.se; Ambassador F. ADEBO-KIENCEE.

Norway: Skarpögt. 4, POB 27829, 115 27 Stockholm; tel. (8) 665-63-40; fax (8) 782-98-99; e-mail emb.stockholm@mfa.no; internet www.norge.se; Ambassador ODD L. FOSSEIDBRÅTEN.

Pakistan: 1st Floor, Karlavägen 65, 114 49 Stockholm; tel. (8) 20-33-00; fax (8) 24-92-33; e-mail info@pakistanembassy.se; internet www.pakistanembassy.se; Chargé d'affaires a.i. MUHAMMED AEJAZ.

Panama: Östermalmsgt. 59, 114 50 Stockholm; POB 55547, 102 04 Stockholm; tel. (8) 662-65-35; fax (8) 662-89-91; Chargé d'affaires a.i. LUZ LESCURE FRÜHLING.

Peru: 2nd Floor, Brunnsgt. 21B, 111 38 Stockholm; tel. (8) 440-87-40; fax (8) 20-55-92; e-mail info@peruembassy.se; internet www.peruvian-embassy.se; Ambassador MAX DE LA FUENTE PREM.

Philippines: 1st Floor, Skeppsbron 20, 111 30 Stockholm; POB 2219, 103 15 Stockholm; tel. (8) 23-56-65; fax (8) 14-07-14; e-mail stockholm@philembassy.se; internet www.philembassy.se; Ambassador VICTORIA S. BATACLAN.

Poland: Karlavägen 35, 114 31 Stockholm; tel. (8) 505-750-00; fax (8) 505-750-86; e-mail info.polen@tele2.se; internet www.polemb.se; Ambassador MICHAŁ CZYŻ.

Portugal: POB 10194, 100 55 Stockholm; 2nd Floor, Narvavägen 32, 115 22 Stockholm; tel. (8) 662-60-28; fax (8) 662-53-29; e-mail portugal@chello.se; internet www.embassyportugal.se; Ambassador JOÃO PEDRO ZANATTI.

Romania: Östermalmsgt. 36, POB 26043, 100 41 Stockholm; tel. (8) 10-86-03; fax (8) 10-28-52; e-mail info@romanianembassy.se; internet www.romanianembassy.se; Ambassador VICTORIA POPESCU.

Russia: Gjörwellsgt. 31, 112 60 Stockholm; tel. (8) 13-04-41; fax (8) 618-27-03; e-mail rusembassy@telia.com; internet www.ryssland.se; Ambassador ALEXANDER MIHAJLOVITCH KADAKIN.

Saudi Arabia: Sköldungagt. 5, POB 26073, 100 41 Stockholm; tel. (8) 23-88-00; fax (8) 796-99-56; Ambassador BADR O. BAKHSH.

Senegal: Blanchegt. 16, 115 33 Stockholm; tel. and fax (8) 660-02-40; Ambassador HENRI-ANTOINE TURPIN.

Serbia and Montenegro: Valhallavägen 70, POB 26209, 100 41 Stockholm; tel. (8) 21-84-36; fax (8) 21-84-95; e-mail scgemb.office@telia.com; Ambassador Prof. Dr NINOSLAV D. STOJADINOVIĆ.

Slovakia: POB 7183, 103 88 Stockholm; 3rd Floor, Arsenalsgt. 2, 111 47 Stockholm; tel. (8) 611-90-05; fax (8) 611-90-02; e-mail info@slovakemb.se; internet www.stockholm.mfa.sk; Chargé d'affaires a.i. JURAJ TOMÁŠ.

Slovenia: 1st Floor, Styrmansgt. 4, 114 54 Stockholm; tel. (8) 545-65-885; fax (8) 662-92-74; e-mail vst@mzz-dkp.gov.si; Ambassador DARJA BAVDAŽ KURET.

South Africa: Linnégt. 76, 115 23 Stockholm; tel. (8) 24-39-50; fax (8) 660-71-36; e-mail saemb.swe@telia.com; internet www.southafricanemb.se; Ambassador GLADYS SONTO KUDJOE.

Spain: POB 10295, 100 55 Stockholm; Djurgårdsvägen 21, Djurgården, 115 21 Stockholm; tel. (8) 667-94-30; fax (8) 663-79-65; e-mail spain.amb.stock@telia.com; Ambassador JAVIER GARRIGUES FLÓREZ.

Sri Lanka: Strandvägen 39, POB 24055, 104 50 Stockholm; tel. (8) 663-65-23; fax (8) 660-00-89; e-mail slembassy@chello.se; internet www.srilanka-travel.com; Ambassador NAGOORPITCHAI SIKKANDER.

Sudan: POB 26142, 100 41 Stockholm; Stockholmsvägen 43, Lidingö; tel. (8) 611-77-80; fax (8) 611-77-82; e-mail sudanembassy@telia.com; Ambassador ZEINAB MOHAMED MAHMOUD.

Switzerland: Valhallavägen 64, POB 26143, 100 41 Stockholm; tel. (8) 676-79-00; fax (8) 21-15-04; e-mail vertretung@sto.rep.admin.ch; internet www.eda.admin.ch/stockholm; Ambassador ROBERT REICH.

Syria: Narvavägen 32, 115 22 Stockholm; POB 24262, 104 51 Stockholm; tel. (8) 660-88-10; fax (8) 660-88-05; internet www.syrianembassy.se; Ambassador MOHAMMAD BASSAM HATEM IMADI.

Tanzania: Wallingatan 11, POB 7255, 111 60 Stockholm; tel. (8) 503-206-00; fax (8) 503-206-02; e-mail balozi@tanemb.se; internet www.tanemb.se; Ambassador JAMES LUTA KATEKA.

Thailand: Floragt. 3, POB 26220, 100 40 Stockholm; tel. (8) 791-73-40; fax (8) 791-73-51; e-mail info@thaiembassy.se; internet www.thaiembassy.se; Ambassador APICHART CHINWANNO.

Tunisia: 1st Floor, Narvavägen 32, 115 22 Stockholm; tel. (8) 545-855-20; fax (8) 662-19-75; e-mail tunamb@swipnet.se; Chargé d'affaires a.i. AMEL BEN YOUNES.

Turkey: POB 24105, 104 51 Stockholm; Dag Hammarskjölds Väg 20, 115 27 Stockholm; tel. (8) 23-08-40; fax (8) 663-55-14; e-mail turkbe@turkemb.se; internet www.turkemb.se; Ambassador NECIP EGÜZ.

Ukraine: Stjärnvägen 2A, 181 34 Lidingö; tel. (8) 731-76-90; fax (8) 731-56-90; e-mail ukraina.embassy@ukrainaemb.se; internet www.ukrainaemb.se; Chargé d'affaires a.i. EDUARD TERPYTSKY.

United Arab Emirates: Norrlandsgt. 20, POB 7485, 103 92 Stockholm; tel. (8) 411-12-44; fax (8) 411-12-45; Ambassador (vacant).

United Kingdom: Skarpögt. 6–8, POB 27819, 115 93 Stockholm; tel. (8) 671-30-00; fax (8) 671-310-49; e-mail info@britishembassy.se; internet www.britishembassy.se; Ambassador ANTHONY CARY.

USA: Dag Hammarskjölds Väg 31, 115 89 Stockholm; tel. (8) 783-53-00; fax (8) 661-19-64; e-mail stockholmweb@state.gov; internet www.usemb.se; Ambassador M. TEEL BIVINS.

Uruguay: Kommendörsgt. 35, POB 10114, 100 55 Stockholm; tel. (8) 660-31-96; fax (8) 665-31-66; e-mail urustoc@uruemb.se; Ambassador JULIO MOREIRA MORÁN.

Venezuela: Engelbrektsgt. 35B, POB 26012, 100 41 Stockholm; tel. (8) 411-09-96; fax (8) 21-31-00; e-mail venezuela.embassy@chello.se; internet www.members.chello.se/embavene-sweden; Ambassador HORACIO ARTEAGA ACOSTA.

Viet Nam: Örby Slottsvägen 26, 125 71 Älvsjö; tel. (8) 556-210-70; fax (8) 556-210-80; e-mail jdh642o@tninet.se; internet www.vietnamemb.se; Ambassador NGUYEN NGOC TRUONG.

SWEDEN

Zambia: Engelbrektsgt. 7, POB 26013, 100 41 Stockholm; tel. (8) 679-90-40; fax (8) 679-68-50; e-mail info@zambiaembassy.se; internet www.zambiaembassy.se; Ambassador JOYCE MUSENGE.

Zimbabwe: 7th Floor, Herserudsvägen 5A, 181 34 Lidingö; POB 3253, 103 65 Stockholm; tel. (8) 765-53-80; fax (8) 21-91-32; e-mail mbuya@stockholm.mail.telia.com; Ambassador MARY SIBUSISIWE MUBI.

Judicial System

The judiciary and the executive are separate. Judges are appointed by the Government. A judge can be removed by an authority other than a court, but may, in such an event, request a judicial trial of the decision.

To supervise the courts in administrative matters, there is a central authority, the Domstolsverket, in Jönköping. This authority has no control over the judicial process, in which the court is independent even of the legislature and Government.

There are state officers who exercise control over the judiciary as well as the administrative authorities. The Justitiekansler (Chancellor of Justice or Attorney-General) and the four Justitieombudsmän supervise the courts and the general administration including the armed forces. The Justitiekansler performs his functions on behalf of the Government. The Justitieombudsmän are appointed by and act on behalf of the legislature.

Justitiekansler: GÖRAN LAMBERTZ.

SUPREME COURT

The Supreme Court in Stockholm (Högsta domstolen), consisting of 16 members, is the Court of Highest Instance. The Court works in three chambers, each of which is duly constituted of five members. Certain cases are decided by full session of the Court. There are also special divisions with three members (or, in simple cases, one member) which decide whether the Court is to consider a case.

Chairman of the Supreme Court: ANDERS KNUTSSON.

APPELLATE COURTS

The Court of Appeal, the Court of Second Instance, consists of a president, judges of appeal and associate judges of appeal. The work is apportioned between various divisions, each of which has five or six members. In criminal cases the bench consists of three professional judges and two lay assessors; in petty and civil cases there are three professional judges only. There are six Courts of Appeal (hovrätt).

President of the Court of Appeal (Stockholm): JOHAN HIRSCHFELDT.
President of the Court of Appeal (Jönköping): LARS ÅHLÉN.
President of the Court of Appeal (Malmö): B. BROOMÉ.
President of the Court of Appeal (Göteborg): O. LINDH.
President of the Court of Appeal (Sundsvall): H. WINBERG.
President of the Court of Appeal (Umeå): ANNA-KARIN LUNDIN.

DISTRICT COURTS

The District Court acts as a Court of First Instance in both civil and criminal cases. In January 1998 there were 96 District Courts (tingsrätt). In criminal cases the court is composed of a presiding professional judge and three or, in serious cases, five lay assessors; in petty cases the court consists of the professional judge only. In civil cases the court is ordinarily composed of three professional judges; however, preparatory sessions are conducted by one professional judge. In family law cases, the court is composed of a professional judge and three lay assessors. The lay assessors are elected for a period of four years (during which they are on duty for about 10 days a year). They act as members of the bench and should consequently be distinguished from the jurors of other countries. In certain types of case technical experts may sit alongside the judges.

ADMINISTRATIVE COURTS

In each of the 23 administrative districts of the country there is a County Administrative Court (länsrätten). This Court handles appeal cases concerning the assessment of social security and welfare. The bench ordinarily consists of a professional judge and three lay assessors, although in simple cases a professional judge may preside alone.

Appeals against decisions by the County Administrative Courts may be made to Administrative Courts of Appeal (kammarrätter) consisting of a president, judges of appeal and associate judges of appeal. The courts work in divisions, each of which normally has six members. The bench consists of at least three and not more than four judges. In certain cases there are, however, three professional judges and two lay assessors. There are four Administrative Courts of Appeal.

The Supreme Administrative Court of Sweden (Regeringsrätten) in Stockholm, consisting of 14 members, is the Court of Highest Instance in Administrative cases. The composition of the Court is governed by rules very similar to those that apply to the Supreme Court.

Chairman of the Supreme Administrative Court: GUNNAR BJÖRNE.
President of the Administrative Court of Appeal (Stockholm): R. LAURÉN.
President of the Administrative Court of Appeal (Göteborg): ELISABETH PALM.
President of the Administrative Court of Appeal (Sundsvall): B. ORRHEDE.
President of the Administrative Court of Appeal (Jönköping): J. FRANCKE.

SPECIAL COURTS

Special courts exist for certain categories of cases, e.g. fastighetsdomstolar (real estate courts) for cases concerning real estate.

OMBUDSMEN

The post of Justitieombudsman was created in 1800 to supervise the manner in which judges, government officials and other civil servants observe the laws, and to prosecute those who act illegally, misuse their position or neglect their duties. The Ombudsman is allowed access to all documents and information and has the right to be present at the considerations of the courts and other authorities. Government ministers in Sweden are not subject to supervision by the Ombudsman. The term of office is four years.

Ombudsmen: CLAES EKLUNDH, SUSANNE KNÖÖS, JAN PENNLÖV, RUNE LAVIN.

Religion

CHRISTIANITY

About 78% of the population are members of the Svenska Kyrkan (Church of Sweden). Since the constitutional link between the Church and the State was severed in 2000 a significant number of people have left the Church each year (68,145 in 2004).

Sveriges Kristna Råd (Christian Council of Sweden): 172 99 Sundbyberg; tel. (8) 453-68-00; fax (8) 453-68-29; e-mail info@skr.org; internet www.skr.org; f. 1993; 26 mem. churches; Gen. Sec. SVEN-BERNHARD FAST.

Church of Sweden

Svenska kyrkan

Kyrkans Hus, Sysslomansgt. 4, 751 70 Uppsala; tel. (18) 16-95-00; fax (18) 16-96-07; e-mail info@svenskakyrkan.se; internet www.svenskakyrkan.se.

Evangelical Lutheran; 13 dioceses, 2,200 parishes, 3,300 active clergy (including missionaries in the mission fields); the Archbishop of Uppsala is head of the Church.

Archbishop of Uppsala: Most Rev. K. G. HAMMAR, 751 70 Uppsala; tel. (18) 16-95-00; fax (18) 16-96-25.

Evangeliska Fosterlands-Stiftelsen (Swedish Evangelical Mission): Sysslomansgt. 4, 751 70 Uppsala; tel. (18) 16-98-00; fax (18) 16-98-01; e-mail efs@efs.svenskakyrkan.se; internet www.efs.nu; f. 1856; an independent mission organization within the Church of Sweden; 17,994 mems; Chair. RAY RAWALL; Mission Dir ANDERS SJÖBERG.

Other Protestant Churches

Eesti Evangeeliumi Luteri Usu Kirik (Estonian Evangelical Lutheran Church): POB 450 74, 104 30 Stockholm 45; tel. (8) 20-69-78; e-mail ingo.jaagu@bredband.net; 12,000 mems; Dean INGO TIIT JAAGU; Gen. Sec. IVAR NIPPAK.

Metodistkyrkan i Sverige (United Methodist Church): Danska vägen 20, 412 66 Göteborg; tel. (31) 733-78-40; fax (31) 733-87-49; e-mail info@metodistkyrkan.se; internet www.metodistkyrkan.se; f. 1868; 3,565 mems; Bishop ØYSTEIN OLSEN; Pres. of Conference Board ANDERS SVENSSON.

Sjundedags Adventistsamfundet (Seventh-day Adventists): POB 536, 101 30 Stockholm; tel. (8) 545-297-70; fax (8) 20-48-68; e-mail info@adventist.se; internet www.adventist.se; f. 1880; 2,800 mems; Pres. BJORN OTTESEN; Sec. AUDREY ANDERSSON.

Svenska Baptistsamfundet (Baptist Union of Sweden): 3rd Floor, Ekensbergsvägen 128, 172 69 Sundbyberg; tel. (8) 564-827-00; fax (8) 564-827-27; e-mail baptist@baptist.se; f. 1848; 270 churches, 18,631 mems (1997); Pres. Rev. SÖREN CARLSVÄRD; Gen. Sec. Rev. SVEN LINDSTRÖM.

Svenska Missionskyrkan (Mission Covenant Church of Sweden): Tegnérgt. 8, POB 6302, 113 81 Stockholm; tel. (8) 674-07-00; fax (8) 674-07-93; e-mail info@missionskyrkan.se; internet www.missionskyrkan.se; f. 1878; 67,041 mems; Gen. Sec. and Pres. GÖRAN ZETLERGREN; Chair. of Board ULF HÅLLMARKER.

The Roman Catholic Church

For ecclesiastical purposes, Sweden comprises the single diocese of Stockholm, directly responsible to the Holy See. At 31 December 2003 there were 144,000 adherents in the country, representing 1.6% of the total population.

Scandinavian Bishops' Conference

POB 135, 421 22 Västra Frölunda; tel. (31) 709-57-15; fax (31) 49-21-70; e-mail nbk@bishopsoffice.org; internet www.katolskakyrkan.se/nbk; f. 1960; new statutes approved 2000; covers Sweden, Norway, Denmark, Finland and Iceland; Pres. Mgr GERHARD SCHWENZER (Bishop of Oslo); Sec.-Gen. Rt Rev. WILLIAM KENNEY.

Bishop of Stockholm: Most Rev. ANDERS ARBORELIUS, Götgt. 68, POB 4114, 102 62 Stockholm; tel. (8) 462-66-00; fax (8) 702-05-55; e-mail biskop@katolskakyrkan.se.

Other Denominations

Other Christian Churches include the Pentecostal Movement (with an estimated 90,000 mems in 2004), the Orthodox Churches of the Greeks, Romanians, Russians, Serbians and Finnish (together numbering about 100,000 mems in 2004), the Church of Jesus Christ of Latter-day Saints (Mormons—9,000 mems in 2004) the Swedish Alliance Missionary Society (12,895 mems in 1997), the Jehovah's Witnesses (23,000 mems in 2004), and the Salvation Army (25,531 mems in 1997).

ISLAM

In 2004 there were approximately 300,000 to 350,000 Muslims in Sweden, of whom around 100,000 were believed to be religiously active. Muslim affiliations represented among immigrant groups are predominantly with the Shi'a and Sunni branches of Islam.

Islamiska Radet i Sverige (The Islamic Council of Sweden—IRIS): POB 3053, 14503 Norsborg; tel. (8) 531-707-95; fax (8) 531-706-65; f. 1986.

Islamiska Kulturcenterunionen i Sverige (Union of the Islamic Cultural Centres in Sweden—IKUS): POB 3053, 145 03 Norsborg; tel. (8) 531-707-95; fax (8) 531-706-65; f. 1984.

Sveriges Muslimska Förbund (SMUF): Stockholms Moske, Kapellgränd 10, 116 25 Stockholm; tel. and fax (8) 643-10-04; e-mail aldebe@arabia.com.

JUDAISM

In 2004 the total number of Jews living in Sweden was estimated to be approximately 18,500–20,000; however, the Jewish community estimated 10,000 active, or practising, members. There are Orthodox, Conservative and Reform Jewish synagogues. The largest Jewish community is in Stockholm.

Jewish Community in Stockholm: Wahrendorffsgt. 3B, POB 7427, 103 91 Stockholm; tel. (8) 587-858-00; fax (8) 587-858-58; e-mail info@jf-stockholm.org; internet www.jf-stockholm.org; c. 5,000 mems; Exec. Dir THOMAS BAB.

BAHÁ'Í FAITH

The Swedish Bahá'í Community: Solhagavägen 11, 163 52 Spånga; tel. (8) 21-51-90; fax (8) 21-51-91; e-mail secretariat@bahai.se; internet www.bahai.se.

OTHER RELIGIONS

In 2004 there were approximately 3,000–4,000 Buddhists and a similar number of Hindus in Sweden.

The Press

Press freedom in Sweden dates from a law of 1766. The 1949 Freedom of the Press Act, a fundamental law embodying the whole of the press legislation in the Constitution, guarantees the Press's right to print and disseminate ideas; protects those supplying information by forbidding editors to disclose sources under any circumstances; authorizes all public documents to be publicly available, official secrets being the only exception; and contains provision for defamation. Press offences are to be referred to common law, and all cases against the Press must be heard by jury.

In 1916 the Press Council was founded by press organizations to monitor ethical matters within the Press. Lacking judicial status, it has powers to rehabilitate persons wronged by the Press who refuse to apply to courts of law. Its judgments are widely published and highly respected.

In 1969 the office of Press Ombudsman was established to supervise adherence to ethical standards. Public complaints shall be directed to the Press Ombudsman, who is also entitled to act on his own initiative. He may dismiss a complaint if unfounded, or if the newspaper agrees to publish a retraction or rectification acceptable to the complainant. When he finds that the grievance is of a more serious nature, he will file a complaint with the Press Council, which will then publish a statement acquitting or criticizing the newspaper. The findings of the Council are published in the newspaper concerned.

The dominating influence of the few major dailies is largely confined to Stockholm, the provinces having a strong Press of their own. The major dailies are: *Expressen, Dagens Nyheter, Aftonbladet, Svenska Dagbladet* (all Stockholm), *Göteborgs-Posten* (Göteborg), *Sydsvenska Dagbladet, Arbetet Nyheterna* (Malmö). In 2004 there were an estimated 165 daily newspapers with a combined circulation of 4.0m.

The two principal magazine publishers in Sweden are the Bonnier group (also a large book publisher and the majority shareholder in the newspapers *Dagens Nyheter, Expressen* and *Sydsvenska Dagbladet*) and the Aller company. Four other companies produce most of the remainder of Sweden's magazine circulation. The most popular weekly periodicals include the family magazines *Aret Runt, Hemmets Veckotidning, Allers* and *Hemmets Journal*, and the home and household magazine *ICAKuriren*. *Vi* caters for serious cultural and political discussion and *Bonniers Litterära Magasin* specializes in literary topics.

PRINCIPAL NEWSPAPERS

Newspapers with a circulation exceeding 15,000 are listed below.

Ängelholm

Nordvästra Skånes Tidningar: 262 83 Ängelholm; tel. (431) 84-000; fax (431) 26-177; f. 1847; daily; Conservative; Editor-in-Chief BENNIE OHLSSON; circ. 42,400 (1996).

Borås

Borås Tidning: 501 85 Borås; tel. (33) 700-07-00; fax (33) 10-14-36; f. 1826; morning; Conservative; Editor JAN ÖJMERTZ; circ. 53,000 (2001).

Eksjö

Smålands-Tidningen: POB 261, 575 23 Eksjö; tel. (381) 13-200; fax (381) 17-145; f. 1899; morning; independent; Editor BENGT WENDLE; circ. 18,700 (1996).

Eskilstuna

Eskilstuna-Kuriren Strengnäs Tidning: POB 120, 631 02 Eskilstuna; tel. (16) 15-60-00; fax (16) 51-63-04; e-mail ek@ekuriren.se; internet www.ekuriren.se; f. 1890; morning; Liberal; Editors PEO WÄRRING, JERKER NORIN; circ. 33,000 (2002).

Falkenberg

Hallands Nyheter: 311 81 Falkenberg; tel. (346) 29-000; fax (346) 29-115; e-mail administration@hn.se; internet www.hn.se; f. 1905; morning; Centre; Editor KRISTIAN ALM; circ. 31,000 (2001).

Falun

Dala-Demokraten: POB 825, 791 29 Falun; tel. (23) 47-500; fax (23) 20-668; f. 1917; morning; Social Democrat; Editor WILLY BERGSTRÖM; circ. 24,400 (1996).

Falu-Kuriren: POB 265, 791 26 Falun; tel. (23) 93-500; fax (23) 12-073; e-mail red@falukuriren.se; internet www.falukuriren.se; f. 1894; morning; Liberal; Editor CHRISTER GRUHS; circ. 29,400 (1996).

Gävle

Arbetarbladet: POB 287, 801 04 Gävle; tel. (26) 15-93-00; fax (26) 12-14-06; f. 1902; morning; Social Democrat; Editor KENNET LUTTI; circ. 29,100 (1996).

Gefle Dagblad: POB 367, 801 05 Gävle; tel. (26) 15-95-00; fax (26) 15-97-00; f. 1895; morning; Liberal; Editor ROBERT ROSÉN; circ. 30,800 (1996).

Göteborg
(Gothenburg)

Göteborgs-Posten: Polhemsplatsen 5, 405 02 Göteborg; tel. (31) 62-40-00; fax (31) 62-45-85; e-mail redaktion@gp.se; internet www.gp.se; f. 1858; morning; Liberal; Editor-in-Chief JONATHAN FALCK; circ. 264,600 (2000).

SWEDEN

Halmstad

Hallandsposten: 301 81 Halmstad; tel. (35) 14-75-00; fax (35) 14-76-88; f. 1850; morning; Liberal; Editor Sverker Emanuelsson; circ. 32,200 (1996).

Härnösand

Nya Norrland: POB 120, 871 23 Härnösand; tel. (611) 88-800; fax (611) 17-247; f. 1907; morning; Social Democrat; Editor-in-Chief Per Åhlström; circ. 19,400 (1996).

Hässleholm

Norra Skåne: 281 81 Hässleholm; tel. (451) 74-50-00; fax (451) 74-50-32; e-mail chefred@nsk.se; internet www.nsk.se; f. 1899; morning; Centre; Editor Billy Bengtsson; circ. 21,800 (2001).

Helsingborg

Helsingborgs Dagblad: POB 822, 251 08 Helsingborg; tel. (42) 17-50-00; fax (42) 17-50-02; f. 1867; morning; independent; Editor-in-Chief Sven-Åke Olofsson; circ. 49,500 (1996).

SD-Kuriren: POB 130 45, 250 13 Helsingborg; tel. (73) 62-60-661; fax (455) 151-33; e-mail redaktion@sdkuriren.se; internet www.sdkuriren.se; f. 1988; organ of the Sverigedemokraterna; Editor-in-Chief Richard Jomshof; circ. 30,000.

Hudiksvall

Hudiksvalls Tidning: POB 1201, 824 15 Hudiksvall; tel. (650) 355-00; fax (650) 355-60; e-mail redaktion@ht.se; internet www.ht.se; f. 1909; includes Hälsinglands Tidning; morning; Centre; Man. Dir Ruben Jacobsson; Editor Jörgen Bengtson; circ. 17,600 (1998).

Jönköping

Jönköpings-Posten/Smålands Allehanda: 551 80 Jönköping; tel. (36) 30-40-50; fax (36) 12-61-11; f. 1865; morning; independent; Editor Stig Fredriksson; circ. 42,900 (1996).

Kalmar

Barometern med Oskarshamns-Tidningen: 391 88 Kalmar; tel. (480) 59-100; fax (480) 59-131; f. 1841; morning; Conservative; Editor Gunilla Andreasson; circ. 47,400 (1999).

Karlskrona

Blekinge Läns Tidning: 371 89 Karlskrona; tel. (455) 77-000; fax (455) 82-170; internet www.blt.se; f. 1869; morning; Liberal; Editor-in-Chief Kerstin Johansson; circ. 36,800 (2003).

Sydöstra Sveriges Dagblad: Landbrogt. 17, 371 88 Karlskrona; tel. (455) 19-000; fax (455) 82-237; f. 1903; morning; Social Democrat; Editor Anders Hagquist; circ. 18,000 (1998).

Karlstad

Nya Wermlands-Tidningen: POB 28, 651 02 Karlstad; tel. (54) 19-90-00; fax (54) 19-92-67; f. 1836; morning; Conservative; Editor Staffan Ander; circ. 59,500 (1996).

Värmlands Folkblad: POB 67, 651 03 Karlstad; tel. (54) 17-55-06; fax (54) 15-16-59; f. 1918; morning; Social Democrat; Editor Rolf H. Jansson; circ. 25,300 (1996).

Kristianstad

Kristianstadsbladet: 291 84 Kristianstad; tel. (44) 18-55-00; fax (44) 21-17-01; e-mail kb@kristianstadsbladet.se; internet www.kristianstadsbladet.se; f. 1856; morning; Liberal; Man. Dir Bo Wigernäs; Editor Hakan Bengtsson; circ. 31,900 (2004).

Lidköping

Nya Läns-Tidningen: 531 81 Lidköping; tel. (510) 89-700; fax (510) 89-796; e-mail post@nlt.se; f. 1903; morning; 3 a week; Liberal; Editor Lennart Hörling; circ. 26,300.

Linköping

Östgöta Correspondenten: 581 89 Linköping; tel. (13) 28-00-00; fax (13) 28-03-24; e-mail nyhet@corren.se; internet www.corren.se; f. 1838; morning; Liberal; Editor Ola Sigvardsson; circ. 63,300 (2003).

Luleå

Norrbottens-Kuriren: 971 81 Luleå; tel. (920) 37-500; fax (920) 67-107; f. 1861; morning; Conservative; Editor (vacant); circ. 30,700 (1996).

Directory

Norrländska Socialdemokraten: 971 83 Luleå; tel. (920) 36-000; fax (920) 36-279; f. 1919; morning; Social Democrat; Editor Lennart Håkansson; circ. 39,600 (1996).

Malmö

Kvällsposten: 205 26 Malmö; tel. (40) 28-16-00; fax (40) 93-92-24; f. 1990; evening; Liberal; Editor Lars Klint; circ. 62,900.

Skånska Dagbladet: Östergt. 11, POB 165, 201 21 Malmö; tel. (40) 660-55-00; fax (40) 97-47-70; f. 1888; morning; Centre; Editor Jan A. Johansson; circ. 29,400 (1996).

Sydsvenska Dagbladet: 205 05 Malmö; tel. (40) 28-12-00; fax (40) 93-54-75; e-mail sydsvenskan@sydsvenskan.se; internet sydsvenskan.se; f. 1848; morning; Liberal independent; Editors Peter Melin, Per T. Ohlsson; circ. 136,400 (2003).

Norrköping

Norrköpings Tidningar: 601 83 Norrköping; tel. (11) 20-00-00; fax (11) 20-02-40; e-mail chefred@nt.se; internet www.nt.se; f. 1758; morning; Conservative; Editor Karl-Åke Bredenberg; circ. 49,900 (2000).

Nyköping

Södermanlands Nyheter: 611 79 Nyköping; tel. (155) 76-700; fax (155) 21-83-50; e-mail redaktionen@sn.se; internet www.sn.se; f. 1893; morning; Centre; Editor Lars J. Eriksson; circ. 23,900 (1998).

Örebro

Nerikes Allehanda: 701 92 Örebro; tel. (19) 15-50-00; fax (19) 12-03-83; e-mail vd@nerikes.se; internet www.nerikes.se; f. 1843; morning; Liberal; Editor Krister Linner; circ. 68,000 (1999).

Örnsköldsvik

Örnsköldsviks Allehanda: POB 110, 891 23 Örnsköldsvik; tel. (660) 29-50-00; fax (660) 15-064; e-mail lars.nordstrom@allehanda.se; f. 1843; morning; Liberal; Editor Lars Nordström; circ. 20,800 (2001).

Östersund

Länstidningen: 831 89 Östersund; tel. (63) 15-55-00; fax (63) 15-55-95; f. 1924; morning; Social Democrat; Editors Peter Swedenmark, Christer Sjöström; circ. 17,000 (2003).

Östersunds-Posten: POB 720, 831 28 Östersund; tel. (63) 16-16-00; fax (63) 10-58-02; f. 1877; morning; Centre; Editors Bosse Svensson, Håkan Larsson; circ. 27,100 (1996).

Piteå

Piteå-Tidningen: POB 193, 941 24 Piteå; tel. (911) 64-500; fax (911) 64-650; f. 1915; morning; Social Democrat; Editor Olov Carlsson; circ. 17,600 (1996).

Skara

Skaraborgs Läns Tidning: POB 214, 532 23 Skara; tel. (511) 13-010; fax (511) 18-815; f. 1884; morning; Liberal; Editor Hans Olofsson; circ. 17,100 (1995).

Skellefteå

Norra Västerbotten: POB 58, 931 21 Skellefteå; tel. (910) 57-700; fax (910) 57-875; e-mail redaktionsavderlning@norran.se; internet www.norran.se; f. 1910; morning; 6 days a week; Liberal; Editor Ola Theander; circ. 30,500 (2000).

Skövde

Skaraborgs Allehanda: POB 407, 541 28 Skövde; tel. (500) 46-75-75; fax (500) 48-05-82; f. 1884; morning; Conservative; Editor Måns Johnson; circ. 23,700 (1997).

Södertälje

Länstidningen: 151 82 Södertälje; tel. (8) 550-921-00; fax (8) 550-877-72; e-mail redaktion@lt.se; f. 1861; morning; 6 a week; Centre; Editor Torsten Carlsson; circ. 17,600 (2002).

Stockholm

Aftonbladet: 105 18 Stockholm; tel. (8) 725-20-00; fax (8) 600-01-70; f. 1830; evening; Social Democrat independent; Editor-in-Chief Anders Gerdin; Political Editor Helle Klein; circ. 381,200 (1996).

Dagen: 105 36 Stockholm; tel. (8) 619-24-00; fax (8) 619-60-51; e-mail info@dagen.se; f. 1945; morning; 4 a week; Christian independent; Editor Daniel Grahn; circ. 20,200 (2003).

SWEDEN

Dagens Industri: 113 90 Stockholm; tel. (8) 736-50-00; fax (8) 31-19-06; f. 1976; 6 a week; business news; Editor HASSE OLSSON; circ. 110,200 (1998).

Dagens Nyheter: 105 15 Stockholm; tel. (8) 738-10-00; fax (8) 738-21-80; e-mail info@dn.se; internet www.dn.se; f. 1864; morning; independent; Editor-in-Chief JAN WIFSTRAND; CEO LENA HERRMANN; circ. 368,000 (2003).

Expressen: Gjörwellsgt. 30, 105 16 Stockholm; tel. (8) 738-30-00; fax (8) 738-33-40; e-mail redaktionen@expressen.se; internet www.expressen.se; f. 1945; evening; Liberal; Editor OTTO SJÖBERG; circ. 353,000 (2003).

Svenska Dagbladet: 105 17 Stockholm; tel. (8) 13-50-00; fax (8) 13-56-80; e-mail svd@svd.se; internet www.svd.se; f. 1884; morning; Conservative; Editor-in-Chief HANNU OLKINVORA; circ. 170,000 (2000).

Sundsvall

Sundsvalls Tidning: 851 72 Sundsvall; tel. (60) 19-70-00; fax (60) 15-44-33; e-mail kjell.carnbro@st.nu; f. 1841; morning; Liberal; Editor KJELL CARNBRO; circ. 35,700 (2005).

Trollhättan

Trollhättans Tidning: POB 54, 461 22 Trollhättan; tel. (520) 49-42-00; fax (520) 49-43-19; f. 1906; morning; 5 a week; independent; Editor TORBJÖRN HÅKANSSON; circ. 17,300 (1996).

Uddevalla

Bohusläningen med Dals Dagblad: 451 83 Uddevalla; tel. (522) 99-000; fax (522) 51-18-88; f. 1878; morning; Liberal; Editor ULF JOHANSSON; circ. 32,400 (1996).

Umeå

Västerbottens-Kuriren: 901 70 Umeå; tel. (90) 15-10-00; fax (90) 77-00-53; e-mail info@vk.se; internet www.vk.se; f. 1900; morning; Liberal; circ. 41,500 (1998).

Uppsala

Upsala Nya Tidning: POB 36, Danmarksgt. 28, 751 03 Uppsala; tel. (18) 478-00-00; fax (18) 12-95-07; e-mail hakan.holmberg@unt.se; internet www.unt.se; f. 1890; morning; Liberal; Editor-in-Chief LARS NILSSON; circ. 62,800 (2002).

Värnamo

Värnamo Nyheter: 331 84 Värnamo; tel. (370) 30-19-56; fax (370) 493-95; e-mail sten.ake.hjerpe@varnamonyheter.se; internet www.varnamonyheter.se; f. 1917; morning; independent; Editor STEN-ÅKE HJERPE; circ. 23,000 (2000).

Västerås

Vestmanlands Läns Tidning: POB 3, 721 03 Västerås; tel. (21) 19-90-00; fax (21) 19-90-60; e-mail nyheter@vlt.se; internet www.vlt.se; f. 1831; morning; Liberal; Editor ELISABETH BÄCK; circ. 48,000 (2003).

Växjö

Smålandsposten: 351 70 Växjö; tel. (470) 77-05-00; fax (470) 209-49; f. 1866; morning; Conservative; Editor CLAES-GÖRAN HEGNELL; circ. 41,500 (1996).

Ystad

Ystads Allehanda: 271 81 Ystad; tel. (411) 55-78-00; fax (411) 13-955; e-mail nyheter@ystadsallehanda.se; internet www.ystadsallehanda.se; f. 1873; morning; Liberal; Man. Dir BO WIGERNÄS; Editor MARGARETHA ENGSTRÖM; circ. 26,100 (2004).

POPULAR PERIODICALS

Allas Veckotidning: Allers Förlag, 205 35 Malmö; tel. (40) 38-59-00; fax (40) 38-59-64; e-mail allas@aller.se; f. 1931; weekly; family; Editor-in-Chief TINA JANSSON; circ. 138,400.

Allers: 251 85 Helsingborg; tel. (42) 17-35-00; fax (42) 17-35-68; e-mail redaktionen@allers.aller.se; f. 1877; weekly; family; Editor-in-Chief ÅSA TENGVALL; circ. 247,400.

Allt om Mat: Sveavägen 53, 105 44 Stockholm; tel. (8) 736-53-00; fax (8) 34-00-88; e-mail red@aom.bonnier.se; internet www.alltommat.se; f. 1970; 18 a year; food specialities; Editor-in-Chief JAN HOLMSTRÖM; circ. 125,800.

Antik och Auktion: Svenska Media Resia AB, POB 63, 827 22 Ljusdal; tel. (651) 15-050; fax (651) 13-333; e-mail ca@svenskamdeiaresia.se; internet www.antik-auktion.nu; f. 1978; monthly; antiques; Editor CHRISTIAN WOLLIN; circ. 57,900.

Året Runt: 105 44 Stockholm; tel. (8) 736-52-00; fax (8) 30-49-00; f. 1946; weekly; family; Editor LILLIAN EHRENHOLM-DAUN; circ. 243,500.

Bilsport: POB 529, 371 23 Karlskrona; tel. (455) 33-53-25; fax (455) 291-75; e-mail bilsport@fabas.se; internet www.bilsport.se; f. 1962; fortnightly; motor-sport, cars; Editor-in-Chief FREDRIK SJÖQVIST; circ. 67,300.

Damernas Värld: 105 44 Stockholm; tel. (8) 736-53-00; fax (8) 24-46-46; e-mail red@dv.bonnier.se; f. 1940; monthly; women's interest; Editor MONA JOHANSSON; circ. 118,800.

Elle: St Eriksplan 2, 113 93 Stockholm; tel. (8) 457-80-00; fax (8) 457-80-80; e-mail ellered@hachette.se; internet www.elle.se; f. 1988; monthly; women's interest; Editor KRISTINA ADOLFSSON; circ. 81,900.

Femina Månadens Magasin: 251 85 Helsingborg; tel. (42) 17-35-00; fax (42) 17-36-82; e-mail femina@aller.se; f. 1981; monthly; women's interest; Editor LISBETH LUNDAHL; circ. 118,000.

Frida: Hammarby Kajväg 14, 120 30 Stockholm; tel. (8) 587-481-00; fax (8) 587-481-07; e-mail frida@frida.forlag.se; internet www.frida.se; fortnightly; for teenage girls; Editor-in-Chief CAROLINE ENGVALL; circ. 67,000.

Hänt Extra: POB 27704, 115 91 Stockholm; tel. (8) 679-46-00; fax (8) 679-46-77; f. 1986; weekly; family; Editors-in-Chief JAN BARD, THORD SKÖLDEKRANS; circ. 113,300.

Hänt i Veckan: POB 27704, 115 91 Stockholm; tel. (8) 679-46-00; fax (8) 679-46-33; f. 1964; weekly; family; Editor-in-Chief STEN HEDMAN; circ. 132,300.

Hemmets Journal: Hemmets Journal AB, 212 05 Malmö; tel. (40) 38-52-00; fax (40) 29-42-82; f. 1920; weekly; family; Editor-in-Chief JANNE WALLES; circ. 272,900.

Hemmets Veckotidning: Allers Förlag AB, 205 35 Malmö; tel. (40) 38-59-00; fax (40) 38-59-14; f. 1929; weekly; family; Editor ULLA COCKE; circ. 215,300.

Hus & Hem: ICA Förlaget AB, POB 6630, 113 84 Stockholm; tel. (8) 728-23-00; fax (8) 34-56-37; e-mail led.husohem@publ.ica.se; internet www.husohem.com; 12 a year; for house-owners; circ. 153,000.

ICA Kuriren: POB 6630, 113 84 Stockholm; tel. (8) 728-23-00; fax (8) 728-23-50; e-mail red.kuriren@forlaget.ica.se; internet www.icakuriren.se; f. 1942; weekly; home and household; Editor (vacant); circ. 364,300.

Kalle Anka & Co: 205 08 Malmö; tel. (40) 693-94-00; fax (40) 693-94-95; e-mail kalle.anka@egmont.se; internet www.ankeborg.egmont.se; f. 1948; weekly; comics; Editor TORD JÖNSSON; circ. 138,000.

Kvällsstunden: Tidningshuset Kvällsstunden AB, POB 1080, 721 27 Västerås; tel. (21) 19-04-00; fax (21) 13-62-62; e-mail info@tidningshuset.com; internet www.tidningshuset.com; weekly; family magazine; Editor ÅKE LINDBERG; circ. 54,300.

Må Bra: POB 27780, 115 93 Stockholm; tel. (8) 679-46-00; fax (8) 667-34-39; f. 1978; monthly; health and nutrition; Editor-in-Chief INGER RIDSTRÖM; circ. 97,900.

OKEJ: Egmont Kärnan AB, Ö Förstadsgt. 34, 205 08 Malmö; tel. (40) 693-94-00; fax (40) 693-94-94; e-mail okej@egmont.se; internet www.okej.se; f. 1980; monthly; pop-music magazine; Editor ANDERS TENGNER; circ. 44,400.

Premium Motor: POB 6019, 175 06 Järfälla; tel. (8) 761-09-50; fax (8) 761-09-49; motoring; Editor STAFFAN SWEDENBORG; circ. 44,615.

Privata Affärer: Sveavägen 53, 105 44 Stockholm; tel. (8) 736-56-00; fax (8) 31-25-60; e-mail red@privataaffarer.se; internet www.privataaffarer.se; f. 1978; monthly; personal money management; Editor-in-Chief HANS BOLANDER; circ. 111,200.

Röster i Radio/TV: POB 27704, 115 91 Stockholm; tel. (8) 679-46-00; fax (8) 679-46-33; f. 1934; weekly; family magazine and programme guide to radio and television; Editor-in-Chief EDGAR ANTONSSON; circ. 140,000.

Sköna Hem: 105 44 Stockholm; tel. (8) 736-53-00; fax (8) 33-74-11; e-mail skonahem@skh.bonnier.se; internet www.skonahem.com; f. 1979 (Sköna Hem), 1956 (Allt i Hemmet), merged 1992; monthly; interior decoration; Editor-in-Chief LOTTI ANDER; circ. 102,500.

Svensk Damtidning: POB 27710, 115 91 Stockholm; tel. (8) 679-46-00; fax (8) 679-47-50; f. 1980; weekly; women's interest; Editor-in-Chief KARIN LENMOR; circ. 132,400.

Teknikens Värld: 105 44 Stockholm; tel. (8) 736-53-00; fax (8) 736-00-11; internet www.teknikensvarld.com; f. 1947; fortnightly; motoring; Editor-in-Chief DANIEL FRODIN; circ. 58,500.

Vår bostad: POB 12651, 112 93 Stockholm; tel. (8) 692-02-00; fax (8) 650-06-41; e-mail info@varbostad.se; internet www.varbostad.se; f. 1924; 11 a year; house and home; Editor ULRICA AMBJÖRN; circ. 928,700.

Vecko-Revyn: Kungsgt. 34, 105 44 Stockholm; tel. (8) 736-52-00; fax (8) 24-16-02; f. 1935; weekly; young women's interest; Editor ÅSA RYDGREN; circ. 91,100.

SWEDEN

Vi Bilägare: POB 23800, 104 35 Stockholm; tel. (8) 736-12-00; fax (8) 736-12-49; e-mail redaktionen@vibilagare.se; internet www.vibilagare.se; f. 1930; fortnightly; auto and travel; Editor NILS-ERIC FRENDIN; circ. 170,000.

Vi Föräldrar: 105 44 Stockholm; tel. (8) 736-53-00; fax (8) 34-00-43; e-mail red@vf.bonnier.se; f. 1968; monthly; parents' magazine; Editor-in-Chief HELENA RÖNNBERG; circ. 59,500.

SPECIALIST PERIODICALS

Aktuellt i Politiken: Sveavägen 68, 105 60 Stockholm; tel. (8) 700-26-00; fax (8) 11-65-42; weekly; social, political and cultural affairs; organ of Social Democratic Labour Party; circ. 55,000.

Allt om Jakt & Vapen: POB 3263, 103 65 Stockholm; tel. (8) 30-16-30; fax (8) 28-59-74; e-mail jaktochvapen@pressdata.se; internet www.jaktovapen.com; 11 a year; hunting; circ. 41,500.

Arbetsledaren: POB 12069, 102 22 Stockholm; tel. (8) 652-01-20; fax (8) 653-99-68; f. 1908; 10 a year; journal for foremen and supervisors; Editor INGRID ASKEBERG; circ. 87,400.

Barn: 107 88 Stockholm; tel. (8) 698-90-00; fax (8) 698-90-14; e-mail barn@rb.se; 6 a year; children's rights; circ. 125,700.

Båtliv: POB 8097, 371 08 Lyckeby; tel. (445) 297-80; fax (455) 36-97-99; e-mail info@batliv.se; internet www.batliv.se; 5 a year; for boat-owners and boat-club members; circ. 126,300.

Byggnadsarbetaren: 106 32 Stockholm; tel. (8) 728-49-00; fax (8) 728-49-80; e-mail kenneth.petterson@byggnadsarbetaren.se; internet www.byggnadsarbetaren.se; f. 1949; 18 a year; building; Editor KENNETH PETTERSON; circ. 132,900 (2004).

Dina Pengar: Konsument Göteborg, POB 11364, 404 28 Göteborg; tel. (31) 61-15-15; fax (31) 13-10-43; 9 a year; finance; circ. 83,000.

Du&jobbet: Maria Skolgt. 83, POB 17550, 118 91 Stockholm; tel. (8) 442-46-00; fax (8) 442-46-07; e-mail redaktionen@duochjobbet.com; internet www.duochjobbet.com; monthly; working environment; circ. 105,000.

Handelsnytt: POB 1146, 111 81 Stockholm; tel. (8) 412-68-00; fax (8) 21-43-33; e-mail handelsnytt@handels.se; internet www.handelsnytt.se; f. 1906; 11 a year; organ of the Union of Commercial Employees; circ. 71,300.

Hundsport: POB 11141, 100 61 Stockholm; tel. (8) 642-37-20; fax (8) 641-00-62; monthly; for dog-owners; Editor TORSTEN WIDHOLM; circ. 101,300.

Jaktmarker och Fiskevatten: Västra Torggt. 18, 652 24 Karlstad; tel. (54) 10-03-70; fax (54) 10-09-83; 11 a year; hunting and fishing; circ. 48,100.

Kommunalarbetaren: POB 19034, 104 32 Stockholm; tel. (8) 728-28-00; fax (8) 30-61-42; e-mail kommunalarbetaren@kommunal.se; internet www.kommunalarbetaren.se; 22 a year; organ of the Union of Municipal Workers; circ. 640,000.

Kyrkans Tidning: POB 15412, 104 65 Stockholm; tel. (8) 462-28-00; fax (8) 644-76-71; e-mail redaktionen@kyrkanstidning.com; internet www.kyrkanstidning.com; f. 1982; weekly; organ of the Church of Sweden; Man. Dir THOMAS GRAHL; Editor DAG TUVELIUS; circ. 46,700.

LAND-Familjetidningen: Gävlegt. 22, 113 92 Stockholm; tel. (8) 588-365-10; fax (8) 588-369-59; e-mail land@lrfmedia.lrf.se; internet www.tidningenland.com; f. 1971; weekly; organ of the farmers' asscn; circ. 231,200.

LAND Lantbruk: Gävlegt. 22, 113 92 Stockholm; tel. (8) 787-51-00; fax (8) 787-55-02; e-mail internetredaktionen@lantbruk.com; internet www.lantbruk.com; f. 1971; weekly; organ of the farmers' asscn; agriculture, forestry; circ. 121,800.

Lärarförbundet: Segelbåtsvägen 15, POB 12239, 102 26 Stockholm; tel. (8) 737-65-00; e-mail sten.svensson@lararforbundet.se; internet www.lararforbundet.se; 22 a year; for teachers; Editor-in-Chief STEN SVENSSON; circ. 213,700.

Lön & Jobb: POB 30102, 104 25 Stockholm; tel. (8) 737-80-00; fax (8) 618-67-22; e-mail lonjobb@htf.se; internet www.lon-jobb.nu; 18 a year; organ of the Union of Commercial Salaried Employees; Editor-in-Chief CARL VON SCHÉELE; circ. 147,300.

Metallarbetaren: Olof Palmesgt. 11, 105 52 Stockholm; tel. (8) 10-68-30; fax (8) 11-13-02; f. 1888; weekly; organ of Swedish Metal Workers' Union; Editor PER AHLSTRÖM; circ. 415,400.

Motor: POB 23142, 104 35 Stockholm; tel. (8) 690-38-00; fax (8) 690-38-22; monthly; cars and motoring; circ. 141,500.

Motorföraren: Heliosvägen 11, 120 30 Stockholm; tel. (8) 555-765-55; fax (8) 555-765-95; e-mail motorforaren@mhf.se; internet www.mhf.se; f. 1927; 7 a year; motoring and tourism; Editor SÖREN SEHLBERG; circ. 40,600.

Musiktidningen Musikomanen: POB 6903, 102 39 Stockholm; tel. (8) 31-00-07; e-mail alexander.scarlat@chello.se; f. 1964; 4 a year; classical and modern music; circ. 90,000.

Ny Teknik: Mäster Samuelsgt. 56, 106 12 Stockholm; tel. (8) 796-66-00; fax (8) 613-30-28; internet www.nyteknik.se; f. 1967; weekly; technical publication owned by the two largest engineering societies of Sweden; Editor-in-Chief DAN MAGNEROT; circ. 150,500.

PRO-Pensionären: POB 3274, 103 65 Stockholm; tel. (8) 701-67-00; fax (8) 20-33-58; e-mail info@pro.se; internet www.pro.se; f. 1942; 10 a year; magazine for pensioners; Editor AGNETA BERG-WAHLSTEDT; circ. 293,900.

SEKO-magasinet: Barnhusgt. 10, POB 1102, 111 81 Stockholm; tel. (8) 791-41-00; fax (8) 21-16-94; f. 1955; 11 a year; organ of the National Union of Services and Communications Employees; Editor-in-Chief JESPER BENGTSSON; circ. 154,700.

SIA-Skogsindustriarbetaren: Olof Palmesgt. 31, POB 1138, 111 81 Stockholm; tel. (8) 701-77-90; fax (8) 411-27-42; e-mail sia@skogstrafacket.org; monthly; forestry; circ. 69,100.

SIF-Tidningen: SIF-huset, Olof Palmesgt. 17, 105 32 Stockholm; tel. (8) 508-970-00; fax (8) 508-970-12; e-mail bjorn.oijer@sif.se; internet www.siftidn.sif.se; 19 a year; organ of the Union of Clerical and Technical Employees; Editor-in-Chief BJORN OIJER; circ. 331,800.

Skog & Såg: Sag i Syd, POB 37, 551 12 Jönköping; tel. (36) 19-86-20; fax (36) 12-86-10; f. 1966; 4 a year; sawmills and forestry; Editor HENRIK ASPLUND; circ. 72,500.

SKTF-Tidningen: POB 7825, 103 97 Stockholm; tel. (8) 789-63-00; fax (8) 789-64-79; e-mail sktftidningen@sktf.se; internet www.sktftidningen.nu; 20 a year; organ of the Union of Municipal Employees; circ. 182,800.

Sunt Förnuft: 114 95 Stockholm; tel. (8) 613-17-00; fax (8) 21-38-58; 8 a year; tax-payers' magazine; circ. 175,100.

Svensk Bokhandel (Journal of the Swedish Book Trade): Birkagt. 16C, POB 6888, 113 86 Stockholm; tel. (8) 545-417-70; fax (8) 545-417-75; e-mail redaktion@svb.se; internet www.svb.se; co-publ. by Swedish Publrs' Asscn and Swedish Booksellers' Asscn, for booksellers, publishers, antiquarians and librarians; Editor LARS WINKLER; circ. 4,400.

Svensk Golf: POB 84, 182 11 Danderyd; tel. (8) 622-15-00; fax (8) 622-69-30; e-mail info@golf.se; internet www.golf.se; monthly; golf; circ. 353,000.

Svensk Jakt: Skedhults Säteri, 575 96 Eksjö; tel. (381) 371-80; fax (381) 371-85; e-mail svenskjakt@telia.com; internet www.jagareforbundet.se/svenskjakt; f. 1862; 11 a year; for hunters and dog-breeders; circ. 157,800 (2004).

Sveriges Natur: POB 4625, 116 91 Stockholm; tel. (8) 702-65-00; fax (8) 702-27-02; e-mail sveriges.natur@snf.se; internet www.sveriges.natur.snf.se; f. 1909; 5 a year; organ of Swedish Society for Nature Conservation; circ. 120,000.

Tidningen C: POB 2200, 103 15 Stockholm; tel. (8) 617-38-30; fax (8) 617-38-10; e-mail c.redaktionen@centrepartiet.se; f. 1929; 10 a year; organ of the Centre Party; Editor EVA-KANN LIND; circ. 68,000.

Transportarbetaren: POB 714, 101 33 Stockholm; tel. (8) 723-77-00; fax (8) 723-00-76; 11 a year; organ of the Swedish Transport Workers' Union; Editor JAN LINDKVIST; circ. 72,000.

Turist: 101 20 Stockholm; tel. (8) 463-21-00; 6 a year; tourism and travel; Editor MONIKA TROZELL; circ. 215,000.

NEWS AGENCIES

Svenska Nyhetsbyrån (Swedish Conservative Press Agency): POB 16051, 103 21 Stockholm; tel. (8) 14-07-50; fax (8) 10-10-48; e-mail red@snb.se; internet www.snb.se; Pres. KJELL SVENSSON; Editor-in-Chief and Dir PATRIK STRÖMER.

Svensk-Internationella Pressbyrån AB (SIP) (Swedish-International Press Bureau): Skeppargt. 27, 114 52 Stockholm; tel. (8) 528-088-10; fax (8) 528-088-30; e-mail kjell@ins.se; internet www.publicitet.se; f. 1927; Editor-in-Chief KJELL ERIKSSON.

Tidningarnas Telegrambyrå (Swedish News Agency): Kungsholmsvarg 5, 105 12 Stockholm; tel. (8) 692-26-00; fax (8) 651-53-77; e-mail redaktionen@tt.se; internet www.tt.se; f. 1921; co-operative news agency, working in conjunction with Reuters, AFP, the 'Groupe 39' agencies, dpa and other telegraph agencies; Chair. GUNNAR STRÖMBLAD; Gen. Man. and Editor-in-Chief EBBA LINDSÖ.

Foreign Bureaux

Agence France-Presse (AFP): Kungsgt. 37, 111 56 Stockholm; tel. (8) 651-01-60; fax (8) 650-82-28; e-mail stockholm@afp.com; internet www.afp.com; Bureau Chief JÜRGEN HECKER.

Agenzia Autonoma Stampa Internationale Libera (AASIL) (Italy): Ynglingagt. 23, 113 47 Stockholm; tel. (8) 33-93-10; Man. GIACOMO OREGLIA.

Associated Press (AP) (USA): Klarabergsgt. 37, POB 1726, 111 87 Stockholm; tel. (8) 5451-30-80; fax (8) 21-24-71; internet www.ap.org; Man. PIERRE-YVES GLASS.

Informatsionnoye Telegrafnoye Agentstvo Rossii—Telegrafnoye Agentstvo Suverennykh Stran (ITAR—TASS) (Russia):

SWEDEN

Karlavägen 12, 2nd Floor, 114 31 Stockholm; tel. (8) 411-32-40; fax (8) 21-06-45; e-mail boris.zaytsev@telia.com; internet www.itar-tass.com; Man. BORIS ZAYTSEV.

Kyodo Tsushin (Kyodo News); Japan: POB 2130, 145 56 Norsborg; tel. (0753) 83-215.

Xinhua (New China) News Agency (People's Republic of China): Krokvägen 5, 181 33 Lidingö; tel. (8) 765-60-83; fax (8) 731-91-54; Man. LINFENG XIE.

PRESS ASSOCIATIONS

Pre Cent (Centre Party's Press Agency): POB 2033, 103 11 Stockholm; tel. (8) 786-48-84; fax (8) 24-30-04; e-mail red@precent.se; f. 1987; Editor-in-Chief JIMMY DOMINIUS; 33 mems.

Svenska Journalistförbundet (Swedish Union of Journalists): POB 1116, 111 81 Stockholm; tel. (8) 613-75-00; fax (8) 21-26-80; e-mail kansliet@sjf.se; internet www.sjf.se; f. 1901; Pres. AGNETA LINDBLOM HULTÉN; 19,000 mems.

Svenska Tidningsutgivareföreningen (Swedish Newspaper Publishers' Asscn): Kungsholmstorg 5, POB 22500, 104 22 Stockholm; tel. (8) 692-46-00; fax (8) 692-46-38; e-mail tidningsutgivarna@tu.se; internet www.tu.se; f. 1898; Man. Dir BARBRO FISCHERSTRÖM; 200 mems.

Sveriges Tidskrifter (Swedish Magazine Publishers' Asscn): Vasagt. 50, 111 20 Stockholm; tel. (8) 545-298-90; fax (8) 14-98-65; e-mail info@sverigestidskrifter.se; internet www.sverigestidskrifter.se; f. 1943; Man. Dir ÖSTEN JOHANSSON.

Sveriges Vänsterpressförening (The Liberal Press Asscn): 901 70 Umeå; tel. (90) 15-10-00; fax (90) 77-46-47; f. 1905; Pres. OLOF KLEBERG; Sec. MATS OLOFSSON; c. 130 mems.

Publishers

Alfabeta Bokförlag AB: POB 4284, 102 66 Stockholm; tel. (8) 714-36-30; fax (8) 643-24-31; e-mail info@alfamedia.se; internet www.alfamedia.se; fiction, psychology, biography, cinema, art, music, travel guides, children's books; Man. Dir DAG HERNRIED.

Bokförlaget Atlantis AB: Sturegt. 24, 114 36 Stockholm; tel. (8) 545-660-70; fax (8) 545-660-71; e-mail mail@atlantisbok.se; internet www.atlantisbok.se; f. 1977; fiction, non-fiction, art; Man. Dir PETER LUTHERSSON.

Berghs Förlag AB: Observatoriegt. 10, POB 45084, 104 30 Stockholm; tel. (8) 31-65-59; fax (8) 32-77-45; f. 1954; non-fiction for adults and children, picture books and fiction for children, craft books, popular science, 'New Age' literature; Man. Dir CARL HAFSTRÖM.

Bonnier Carlsen Bokförlag AB: POB 3159, 103 63 Stockholm; tel. (8) 696-89-30; fax (8) 696-89-31; e-mail info@carlsen.bonnier.se; internet www.bonniercarlsen.se; picture books, juvenile books, non-fiction, board books, comics; Man. Dir BODIL SJÖÖ.

Bonnierförlagen AB: Sveavägen 56, POB 3159, 103 63 Stockholm; tel. (8) 696-80-00; fax (8) 696-80-46; internet www.bok.bonnier.se; f. 1837; fiction, non-fiction, encyclopaedias, reference books, quality paperbacks; includes Albert Bonniers Förlag AB, Bonnier Utbildning AB, Bokförlaget Forum AB, AB Wahlström & Widstrand, Autumn Publishing, Bonnier Audio, Bonnier Carlsen, Bokförlaget Rebus, Bokförlaget Max Ström; Chair. MARIA CURMAN; Man. Dir KARIN LEIDOW.

Bokförlaget Bra Böcker: POB 892, 201 80 Malmö; tel. (40) 665-46-00; f. 1965; Man. Dir JOHAN MÖLLER.

Brombergs Bokförlag AB: Hantverkargt. 26, POB 12886, 112 98 Stockholm; tel. (8) 562-620-80; fax (8) 562-620-85; e-mail info@brombergs.se; internet www.brombergs.se; quality fiction, non-fiction; Man. Dir DOROTEA BROMBERG.

Brutus Östlings Bokförlag Symposion: POB 148, 241 22 Eslöv; tel. (413) 609-90; e-mail order.symposion@swipnet.se.

Carlsson Bokförlag AB: Stora Nygt. 31, 111 27 Stockholm; tel. (8) 411-23-49; fax (8) 796-84-57; art, photography, ethnology, history, politics; Man. Dir TRYGVE CARLSSON.

Bokförlaget DN: POB 703 21, 107 23 Stockholm; e-mail evafallenius@bokforlagetdn.se; internet www.bokforlagetdn.com; publishing division of Dagens Nyheter newspaper; Publr and Pres. ALBERT BONNDER.

Eriksson & Lindgren Bokförlag AB: St Eriksgt. 14, POB 12085, 102 23 Stockholm; tel. (8) 652-32-26; fax (8) 652-32-23; e-mail info@eriksson-lindgren.se; internet www.eriksson-lindgren.se; f. 1990; Man. Dir CLAES ERIKSSON.

Bokförlaget T. Fischer & Co: Näs Gård, 762 93 Rimbo; tel. (175) 620-52; fax (175) 620-54; e-mail bokforlaget@fischer-co.se; internet www.fischer-co.se; non-fiction; Man. Dir KIM MODIN.

Forum Publishers: POB 70321, 107 23 Stockholm; tel. (8) 696-84-40; fax (8) 696-83-67; internet www.forum.se; f. 1943; general fiction, non-fiction; Man. Dir MAGNUS NYTELL.

Gedins Förlag: Tystagt. 10, 115 20 Stockholm; tel. (8) 662-15-51; fax (8) 663-70-73; fiction, non-fiction, poetry, food, psychology, politics; Man. Dir PER I. GEDIN.

Gehrmans Musikförlag AB: POB 42026, 126 12 Stockholm; tel. (8) 610-06-00; fax (8) 610-06-27; e-mail info@gehrmans.se; internet www.gehrmans.se; f. 1893; orchestral and choral music; general music publishing; Pres. JOE LINDSTRÖM; Man. Dir MAGNUS FILIPSSON.

ICA-förlaget AB: 721 85 Västerås; tel. (21) 19-40-00; fax (21) 19-42-83; e-mail bok@publ.ica.se; internet www.publ.ica.se; f. 1945; non-fiction, cookery, handicrafts, gardening, natural history, popular psychology, health, domestic animals, sports; Publr GÖRAN SUNEHAG; Man. Dir HANS RINKEBORN.

Informationsförlaget: Sveavägen 61, POB 6884, 113 86 Stockholm; tel. (8) 545-560-50; fax (8) 31-39-03; f. 1979; publishers of books for companies and organizations on demand; reference, encyclopaedias, gastronomy, illustrated books; Man. Dir ULF HEIMDAHL.

Liber AB: 113 98 Stockholm; tel. (8) 690-90-00; fax (8) 690-94-70; e-mail export@liber.se; internet www.liber.se; general and educational publishing; Man. Dir BIRGITTA JOHANSSON-HEDBERG.

Liber Hermods AB: Råsundavägen 18, 113 98 Stockholm; tel. (8) 690-94-00; e-mail helena.holmstrom@liber.se; f. 1993; Man. Dir HELENA HOLMSTRÖM.

Abraham Lundquist AB Musikförlag: POB 93, 182 11 Danderyd; tel. (8) 732-92-35; fax (8) 732-92-38; e-mail info@abrahamlundquist.se; internet www.abrahamlundquist.se; f. 1838; music; Man. Dir (vacant).

Bokförlaget Natur och Kultur: Karlavägen 31, POB 27323, 102 54 Stockholm; tel. (8) 453-86-00; fax (8) 453-87-90; e-mail info@nok.se; internet www.nok.se; f. 1922; textbooks, general literature, fiction; Man. Dir LARS GRAHN.

Norstedts Förlag AB: Tryckerigt. 4, POB 2052, 103 12 Stockholm; tel. (8) 769-87-50; fax (8) 769-87-64; e-mail info@norstedts.se; internet www.norstedts.se; f. 1823; fiction, non-fiction; Man. Dir SVANTE WEYLER.

Norstedts Juridik AB: 106 47 Stockholm; tel. (8) 690-90-90; fax (8) 690-91-91; e-mail info.fritzes@nj.se; internet www.fritzes.com; f. 1837; fmrly C. E. Fritzes AB; Man. Dir DOMINIC RICHARDSON.

Bokförlaget Opal AB: Tegelbergsvägen 31, POB 20113, 161 02 Bromma; tel. (8) 28-21-79; fax (8) 29-66-23; e-mail opal@opal.se; internet www.opal.se; f. 1973; Man. Dir BENGT CHRISTELL.

Ordfront Förlag AB: Bellmansgt. 30, POB 17506, 118 91 Stockholm; tel. (8) 462-44-20; fax (8) 462-44-90; e-mail forlaget@ordfront.se; internet www.ordfront.se; fiction, history, politics; Man. Dir JAN-ERIK PETTERSSON.

Prisma Bokförlaget: Tryckerigt. 4, POB 2052, 103 12 Stockholm; tel. (8) 769-89-00; fax (8) 769-89-13; e-mail prisma@prismabok.se; internet www.prismabok.se; f. 1963; Dir VIVECA EKELUND.

Rabén & Sjögren Bokförlag: Tryckerigt. 4, POB 2052, 103 12 Stockholm; tel. (8) 789-30-00; fax (8) 789-30-52; e-mail raben-sjogren@raben.se; internet www.raben.se; f. 1942; general, juvenile; Dir SUZANNE ÖHMAN-SUNDEN.

Bokförlaget Semic: Landsvägen 57, POB 1243, 172 25 Sundbyberg; tel. (8) 799-30-50; fax (8) 799-30-64; e-mail bokforlaget@semic.se; internet www.semic.se; handbooks, calendars, comic magazines, juvenile; Pres. RICKARD EKSTRÖM.

Stenströms Bokförlag AB: Linnégt. 98, POB 24086, 104 50 Stockholm; tel. (8) 663-76-01; fax (8) 663-22-01; f. 1983; Man. Dir BENGT STENSTRÖM.

Streiffert Förlag AB: Skeppargt. 27, POB 5334, 102 47 Stockholm; tel. (8) 661-58-80; fax (8) 783-04-43; e-mail bo@streiffert.se; internet www.streiffert.se; f. 1990; Man. Dir BO STREIFFERT.

Svenska Förlaget liv & ledarskap AB: POB 3313, 103 66 Stockholm; e-mail kundservice@svenskaforlaget.com; internet www.svenskaforlaget.com; non-fiction.

Timbro/SFN: POB 5234, 102 45 Stockholm; tel. (8) 587-898-00; fax (8) 587-898-55; e-mail info@timbro.se; internet www.timbro.se; economics, political science; Pres. CECILIA STEGÖ CHILÒ.

Verbum Förlag AB: St Paulsgt. 2, POB 15169, 104 65 Stockholm; tel. (8) 743-65-00; fax (8) 641-45-85; e-mail gunnar.goranzon@verbum.se; internet www.verbum.se; f. 1911; theology, fiction, juvenile, music; Man. Dir GUNNAR GÖRANZON.

AB Wahlström & Widstrand: Sturegt. 32, POB 5587, 114 85 Stockholm; tel. (8) 696-84-80; fax (8) 696-83-80; f. 1884; fiction, non-fiction, biography, history, science, paperbacks; Man. Dir UNN PALM.

B. Wahlströms Bokförlag AB: Warfvingesvägen 30, POB 30022, 104 25 Stockholm; tel. (8) 619-86-00; fax (8) 618-97-61; e-mail bertil

.wahlstrom@wahlstroms.se; internet www.wahlstroms.se; fiction, non-fiction, juvenile, paperbacks; Man. Dir BERTIL WAHLSTRÖM.

PUBLISHERS' ASSOCIATIONS

Föreningen Svenska Läromedelsproducenter (Swedish Asscn of Educational Publishers): Drottninggt. 97, 113 60 Stockholm; tel. (8) 736-19-40; fax (8) 736-19-44; e-mail fsl@forlagskansli.se; f. 1973; Dir JERKER FRANKSSON; 25 mems.

Svenska Förläggareföreningen (Swedish Publishers' Asscn): Drottninggt. 97, 113 60 Stockholm; tel. (8) 736-19-40; fax (8) 736-19-44; e-mail svf@forlagskansli.se; internet www.forlagskansli.se; f. 1843; Chair. LARS GRAHN; Dir KRISTINA AHLINDER; 74 mems.

Broadcasting and Communications

TELECOMMUNICATIONS

Regulatory Authority

Post-och Telestyrelsen (PTS): POB 5398, Birger Jarlsgt. 16, 102 49 Stockholm; tel. (8) 678-50-50; fax (8) 678-55-05; e-mail pts@pts.se; internet www.pts.se; Dir-Gen. CURT ANDERSSON (acting).

Major Service Providers

Global One Services AB: POB 1, 171 18 Solna; tel. (8) 519-131-00; fax (8) 519-132-00; Dir PETER JERRY SØRENSEN.

Tele 2 AB: Borgarfjordsgt. 16, POB 62, 164 94 Kista; tel. (85) 626-40-00; fax (85) 626-42-00; Man. ULF JOHANSSON.

Telefonaktiebolaget LM Ericsson: Torshamngt. 23, 164 83 Stockholm; tel. (8) 719-00-00; fax (8) 18-40-85; e-mail investor.relations.se@ericsson.com; internet www.ericsson.com; parent company of the Ericsson group; mobile and fixed network provider; represented in 140 countries; Chair. MICHAEL TRESCHOW; CEO CARL-HENRIC SVANBERG.

TeliaSonera AB: Sutregt. 1, 106 63 Stockholm; tel. (8) 504-550-00; e-mail teliasonera@teliasonera.se; internet www.teliasonera.se; f. by merger of Telia AB (Sweden) with Sonera Ltd (Finland); Pres. and CEO ANDERS IGEL.

TERACOM AB: Medborgarplatsen 3, POB 17666, 118 92 Stockholm; tel. (8) 671-20-00; fax (8) 671-20-82; e-mail info@teracom.se; internet www.teracom.se; Dir VALDEMAR PERSSON.

Vodafone Sverige AB: 371 80 Karlskrona; tel. (4) 553-310-00; e-mail info@vodafone.se; internet www.vodafone.se; part of Vodafone Group PLC (United Kingdom); CEO JON RISFELT.

BROADCASTING

Until the end of 1992 public-service radio and television were organized within the state broadcasting corporation, Sveriges Radio AB, a public-service organization financed by licence fees; this operated two national television channels and three national radio channels, together with 24 local radio stations. On 1 January 1993 the state corporation was replaced by three companies, Sveriges Radio AB, Sveriges Television AB, and Sveriges Utbildningsradio AB, responsible for radio, television, and educational radio and television, respectively. The operations of these companies are regulated by law and by agreements with the Government. From 1 January 1994 the three companies came into the ownership of three foundations.

Radio

There are four public-service radio channels, as well as neighbourhood radio stations and private local radio stations (financed by advertising).

Sveriges Radio AB: Oxenstiernsgt. 20, 105 10 Stockholm; tel. (8) 784-50-00; fax (8) 667-83-36; e-mail anders.held@sr.se; internet www.sr.se; f. 1993; independent co responsible for national radio broadcasting; Man. Dir PETER ÖRN.

Sveriges Utbildningsradio AB: 113 95 Stockholm; tel. (8) 784-40-00; fax (8) 784-43-91; internet www.ur.se; f. 1978; public service co responsible for educational broadcasting on radio and television; CEO CHRISTINA BJÖRK.

IBRA Radio AB: POB 4033, 141 04 Huddinge; tel. (8) 608-96-80; fax (8) 608-96-89; e-mail ibra@ibra.se; internet www.ibra.org; non-commercial private Christian co broadcasting to all continents; Pres. PER-OVE MORBERG; Dir SUNE ELOFSON.

Television

There are two public-service television channels (SVT 1 and SVT 2). The broadcasts are financed by licence fees. In 1991 the Government awarded the licence for a third terrestrial nation-wide television channel to TV 4 (which is financed by advertising). Television channels transmitted by satellite and cable, and directed at the Swedish audience, include: TV 3, Kanal 5, TV 6, Z-TV, and the film channels TV 1000, FilmMax, Filmnet Plus and Filmnet Movie.

Kanal 5: 114 99 Stockholm; tel. (8) 674-15-00; fax (8) 612-05-95; commercial satellite channel.

Sveriges Television AB: TH T2, 105 10 Stockholm; tel. (8) 784-00-00; fax (8) 784-15-00; e-mail information@sut.se; f. 1956; independent; 2 public-service channels; Man. Dir SAM NILSSON.

Sveriges Utbildningsradio AB: see Radio.

TV 3: Stockholm; tel. (8) 562-023-00; fax (8) 562-023-30; e-mail info@tv3.se; internet www.tv3.se; commercial satellite channel.

TV 4: Tegeluddsvägen 3, 115 79 Stockholm; tel. (8) 459-40-00; fax (8) 459-44-44; internet www.tv4.se; commercial terrestrial channel; Man. Dir JAN SCHERMAN.

Finance

(cap. = capital; res = reserves; dep. = deposits; m. = million; brs = branches; amounts in kronor unless otherwise stated)

BANKING

In 2004 there were 50 commercial banks, with total assets of 3,879,110m. kronor, and 76 savings banks.

Central Bank

Sveriges Riksbank (Swedish Central Bank): Brunkebergstorg 11, 103 37 Stockholm; tel. (8) 787-00-00; fax (8) 21-05-31; e-mail registratorn@riksbank.se; internet www.riksbank.se; f. 1668; bank of issue; controlled by a board of eight delegates, seven of whom are appointed by the Riksdag and one, the Governor, by other board members; cap. 1,000m., res 80,697m., dep. 1,663m. (Dec. 2003); Chair. JAN BERGQVIST; Gov. STEFAN INGVES; 10 brs.

Commercial Banks

Danske Bank i Sverige: Norrmalmstorg 1, POB 7523, 103 92 Stockholm; tel. (8) 561-60-00; internet www.danskebank.se; f. 1837 as Östgöta Enskilda Bank; wholly owned subsidiary of Den Danske Bank; cap. 563.3m., res 236.5m., dep. 12,778.5m. (Dec. 1996); Chair. PETER STRAARUP; Pres. and CEO ULF LUNDAHL; 30 brs.

FöreningsSparbanken AB (Swedbank): Brunkebergstorg 8, 105 34 Stockholm; tel. (8) 585-900-00; fax (8) 796-80-92; e-mail info@foreningssparbanken.se; internet www.foreningssparbanken.se; f. 1997 as a result of merger between Föreningsbanken and Sparbanken Sverige; cap. 10,556m., res 18,603m., dep. 393,725m. (Dec. 2003); Chair. CARL ERIC STÅLBERG; Pres. and CEO JAN LIDÉN; 650 brs.

Nordea Bank AB: Hamngt. 10, 105 71 Stockholm; tel. (8) 614-70-00; fax (8) 20-08-46; internet www.nordea.com; f. 1974 as Post- och Kreditbanken, present name adopted Dec. 2001; part of Nordea Group; cap. €1,160m., res €9,527m., dep. €188,689m. (Dec. 2003); Chair. HANS DALBORG; CEO LARS G. NORDSTRÖM; 256 brs.

Skandinaviska Enskilda Banken AB: Kungsträdgårdsgt. 8, 106 40 Stockholm; tel. (8) 763-80-00; fax (8) 763-83-89; internet www.seb.se; f. 1972; cap. 7,046m., res 35,714m., dep. 959,395m. (Dec. 2003); Chair. MARCUS WALLENBERG; Pres. and Group CEO ANNIKA FALKENGREN; 260 brs.

Svenska Handelsbanken AB: Kungsträdgårdsgt. 2, 106 70 Stockholm; tel. (8) 701-10-00; fax (8) 701-24-37; e-mail info@handelsbanken.se; internet www.handelsbanken.se; f. 1871; cap. 2,859m., res 45,860m., dep. 964,716m. (Dec. 2003); Chair. ARNE MÅRTENSSON; Pres. and CEO LARS O. GRÖNSTEDT; 573 brs in Nordic countries and the United Kingdom.

Banking Organization

Svenska Bankföreningen (Swedish Bankers' Asscn): Regeringsgt. 38, POB 7603, 103 94 Stockholm; tel. (8) 453-44-00; fax (8) 79693-95; e-mail registrator@bankforeningen.se; internet www.bankforeningen.se; f. 1880; Pres. JAN. LIDÉN; Man. Dir ULLA LUNDQUIST; 31 mems.

STOCK EXCHANGE

Stockholmsbörsen (Stockholm Stock Exchange): Tullvaktsvägen 15, 105 78 Stockholm; tel. (8) 405-60-00; fax (8) 405-60-01; e-mail info.stockholmsborsen@omxgroup.com; internet www.se.omxgroup.com; f. 1863 under government charter; automated trading system introduced by 1990; owned by OMX AB; forms group with stock exchanges in Helsinki, Rīga, Tallinn and Vilnius; also part of an alliance (Nordic Exchanges, Norex) with the Copenhagen, Reykjavík and Oslo Stock Exchanges, launched June 1999; Pres. and CEO MAGNUS BÖCKER.

SWEDEN — Directory

INSURANCE

The total assets of Swedish insurance companies in 2004 was 446,284m. kronor.

Principal Insurance Companies

Folksam: Bohusgt. 14, 106 60 Stockholm; tel. (8) 772-60-00; fax (8) 643-40-26; e-mail info@floksam.se; internet www.folksam.se; f. 1908; all branches of life and non-life insurance; Pres. and CEO TORE ANDERSSON.

Försäkringsaktiebolaget Skandia (publ): Sveavägen 44, 103 50 Stockholm; tel. (8) 788-10-00; fax (8) 10-31-74; internet www.skandia.com; f. 1855; all branches of life insurance; Chair. LENNART JEANSSON; Pres. and CEO JULIAN ROBERTS.

Trygg-Hansa: Flemminggt. 18, 106 26 Stockholm; tel. (8) 693-10-00; fax (8) 650-93-67; internet www.trygghansa.se; f. 1828; all branches of non-life insurance; Pres. and CEO JENS ERIK CHRISTENSEN.

Insurance Associations

Konsumernternas försäkringsbyrå (Swedish Consumers' Insurance Bureau): Klara Norra Kyrkogt. 33, 111 22 Stockholm; tel. (8) 22-58-00; fax (8) 24-88-91; e-mail gunnar@konsumenternasforsakringsbyra.se; internet www.konsumenternasforsakringsbyra.se; f. 1979; provides free advice to consumers on various insurance matters; principles are the Konsumentverket (Swedish Consumer Agency), the Finansinpektionen (Financial Supervisory Authority) and the Sveriges Försäkringsförbund (Swedish Insurance Fed.); Chair. GUNNAR OLSSON.

Svenska Försäkringsföreningen (Swedish Insurance Society): Klara Norra Kyrkogt. 33, 111 22 Stockholm; tel. (8) 783-98-90; fax (8) 783-98-95; e-mail anders.kleverman@sff.a.se; internet www.sff.a.se; f. 1875; to promote sound development of the Swedish insurance business; Chair. LARS ROSÉN; Sec. ANDERS KLEVERMAN.

Sveriges Försäkringsförbund (Swedish Insurance Federation): POB 24043, 104 50 Stockholm; tel. (8) 522-785-00; fax (8) 522-785-15; e-mail kansli@forsakringsforbundet.com; internet www.forsakringsforbundet.com; Chair. TOMMY PERSSON; Man. Dir ANNIKA LUNDIUS.

SUPERVISORY BODY

Finansinspektionen (Financial Supervisory Authority): POB 6750, 113 85 Stockholm; tel. (8) 787-80-00; fax (8) 24-13-35; e-mail finansinspektionen@fi.se; internet www.fi.se; f. 1991 by merger of Bankinspektionen (Bank Inspection Board, f. 1907) and Försäkringsinspektionen (Private Insurance Supervisory Service, f. 1904), for the supervision of commercial and savings banks, financial companies, insurance companies, insurance brokers, friendly societies, mortgage institutions, securities firms and unit trusts, the stock exchange and clearing functions, the securities registry centre and the information registry centre; Dir-Gen. INGRID BONDE.

Trade and Industry

GOVERNMENT AGENCIES

Arbetsmarknadsstyrelsen (AMS) (Labour Market Board): 171 99 Solna, Stockholm; tel. (8) 730-60-00; fax (8) 27-83-68; e-mail ams-infocenter@ams.amv.se; internet www.ams.se; f. 1948; central authority within the National Labour Market Administration (Arbetsmarknadsverket—AMV); autonomous public agency, responsible for administration of Sweden's labour market; main aims: to provide social means for easing structural change in the economy, to organize labour market by balancing requirements of workers and employers, and to uphold commitment to concept of full employment; board mems appointed by Govt, employers and trades unions; Dir-Gen. ANDERS L. JOHANSSON.

Exportrådet (Swedish Trade Council): POB 240, 101 24 Stockholm; tel. (8) 588-660-00; fax (8) 588-661-90; e-mail infocenter@swedishtrade.se; internet www.swedishtrade.se; f. 1972; Chair. ANDERS NARVINGER; Man. Dir ULF BERG.

CHAMBERS OF COMMERCE

Handelskammaren i Jönköpings Län: Elmiavägen 11, 554 54 Jönköping; tel. (36) 30-14-30; fax (36) 12-95-79; e-mail info@jonkoping.cci.se; f. 1975; Pres. PER RISBERG; Man. Dir GÖRAN KINNANDER; 600 mems.

Handelskammaren Mälardalen: POB 8044, 700 08 Örebro; tel. (19) 611-22-23; fax (19) 11-77-50; e-mail info@malardalen.cci.se; internet www.malardalen.cci.se; f. 1907; Pres. EGON LINDEROTH; Sec. SVEN SVENSSON.

Handelskammaren Mittsverige (Mid-Sweden Chamber of Commerce): Kyrkogt. 26, 852 32 Sundsvall; tel. (60) 17-18-80; fax (60) 61-86-40; e-mail sdl@mid.chamber.cci.se; internet www.mid.chamber.cci.se; f. 1913; Chair. ROLF JOHANNESSON; Man. Dir STURE LARSSON; 400 mems.

Handelskammaren Värmland: Södra Kyrkogt. 6, 652 24 Karlstad; tel. (54) 22-14-80; fax (54) 22-14-90; e-mail info@wermland.cci.se; internet www.wermland.cci.se; f. 1912; Pres. TORBJÖRN JOGHED; Sec. ULF LJUNGDAHL; c. 600 mems.

Mellansvenska Handelskammaren: POB 296, 801 04 Gävle; tel. (26) 66-20-80; fax (26) 66-20-99; e-mail chamber@mhk.cci.se; internet www.mhk.cci.se; f. 1907; Pres. OVE ANONSEN; Man. Dir ANDERS FRANCK; 465 mems.

Norrbottens Handelskammare: Storgt. 9, 972 38 Luleå; tel. (920) 122-10; fax (920) 94-857; e-mail lundgren@north.cci.se; internet www.north.cci.se; f. 1904; Chair. INGA-LILL HOLMGREN; Dir STURE LUNDGREN.

Östsvenska Handelskammaren: Nya Rådstugugt. 3, 60224 Norrköping; tel. (11) 28-50-30; fax (11) 13-77-19; e-mail info@east.cci.se; internet www.east.cci.se; f. 1913.

Stockholms Handelskammare: V. Trädgårdsgt. 9, POB 16050, 103 21 Stockholm; tel. (8) 555-100-00; fax (8) 566-316-30; e-mail tradeofficer@chamber.se; internet www.chamber.se; f. 1902; Pres. MARGARETA BOSVED; Dir PETER EGARDT.

Sydsvenska Handelskammaren (Chamber of Commerce and Industry of Southern Sweden): Skeppsbron 2, 211 20 Malmö; tel. (40) 73-550; fax (40) 611-86-09; e-mail info@handelskammaren.com; f. 1905; Pres. HANS CAVALLI-BJÖRKMAN; Man. Dir STEPHAN MÜCHLER; 3,050 mems.

Västsvenska Industri- och Handelskammaren: POB 5253, 402 25 Göteborg; tel. (31) 83-59-00; fax (31) 83-59-36; e-mail info@handelskammaren.net; internet www.handelskammaren.net; f. 1661; Man. Dir ANDERS KÄLLSTRÖM; c. 2,500 mems.

INDUSTRIAL AND TRADE ASSOCIATIONS

Svenskt Näringsliv (Confederation of Swedish Enterprise): Storgt. 19, 114 82 Stockholm; tel. (8) 553-430-00; fax (8) 553-430-99; e-mail info@svensktnaringsliv.se; internet www.svensktnaringsliv.se; f. 2001 by merger of Sveriges Industriförbund (f. 1910) and Svenska Arbetsgivareföreningen (f. 1902); central organization representing Swedish business and industry; Pres. SÖREN GYLL; Vice-Pres BJÖRN ANDERSSON, SIGRUN HJELMQUIST, MICHAEL TRESCHOW; Dir-Gen. GÖRAN TUNHAMMAR; consists of 52 mem. asscns, representing c. 46,000 cos.

Företagarnas Riksorganisation (Federation of Private Enterprises): 106 67 Stockholm; tel. (8) 406-17-00; fax (8) 24-55-26; e-mail info@fr.se; internet www.fr.se; f. 1990; Chair. ARNE JOHANSSON; Man. Dir CARL-JOHAN WESTHOLM; 60,000 mems.

Grafiska Företagens Förbund (Graphic Companies' Federation): Karlavägen 108, POB 24184, 104 51 Stockholm; tel. (8) 762-68-00; fax (8) 611-08-28; e-mail info@grafiska.se; internet www.grafiska.se; Chair. LARS FREDRIKSON; Man. Dir LARS JOSEFSSON.

Järnverksföreningen (Swedish Steel Producers' and Distributors' Association): Kungsträdgårdsgt. 10, POB 1721, 111 87 Stockholm; f. 1889; Pres. BENGT LINDAHL; Sec. MATHIAS TERNELL; 35 mems.

Jernkontoret (Steel Producers' Asscn): Kungsträdgårdsgt. 10, POB 1721, 111 87 Stockholm; tel. (8) 679-17-00; fax (8) 611-20-89; e-mail office@jernkontoret.se; internet www.jernkontoret.se; f. 1747; Man. Dir ELISABETH NILSSON.

Lantbrukarnas Riksförbund (LRF) (Federation of Swedish Farmers): Klara Östra Kyrkogt. 12, 105 33 Stockholm; tel. (0) 771-573-573; e-mail info@lrf.se; internet www.lrf.se; 163,000 mems.

Plast- & Kemiföretagen (Swedish Plastics and Chemicals Asscn): Storgt. 19, POB 5501, 114 85 Stockholm; tel. (8) 783-86-00; fax (8) 663-63-23; e-mail info@plastkemiforetagen.se; internet www.plastkemiforetagen.se; f. 1917; Pres. MÅNS COLLIN; Man. Dir OWE FREDHOLM; 265 mems.

Skogsindustrierna (Swedish Forest Industries' Federation): POB 16006, 103 21 Stockholm; tel. (8) 762-72-60; fax (8) 762-72-14; internet www.forestindustries.se; Chair. KENNETH ERIKSSON; Dir-Gen. MARIE S. ARWIDSON.

SveMin (Föreningen för gruvor, mineral- och metallproducenter i Sverige) (Swedish Asscn of Mines, Mineral and Metal Producers): POB 1721, 111 87 Stockholm; tel. (8) 762-67-35; fax 8) 611-62-64; e-mail info@svemin.se; internet www.svemin.se; f. 2004; Pres. MARTIN IVERT; Man. Dir BENGT HULDL; 20 mem cos.

Svensk Handel (Swedish Federation of Trade): 103 29 Stockholm; tel. (8) 762-77-00; fax (8) 762-77-77; e-mail info@svenskhandel.se; internet www.svenskhandel.se; Chair. KENNETH BENGTSSON; Man. Dir DAG KLACKENBERG; 14,000 mems.

Svensk Industriförening (Swedish Industry Asscn): Flemingt. 14, POB 22307, 104 22 Stockholm; tel. (8) 440-11-70; fax (8) 440-11-

71; e-mail info@sinf.se; internet www.sinf.se; f. 1941; Man. Dir Sven Langenius; 1,500 mems.

Svenska Garveriidkareföreningen (Swedish Tanners' Asscn): c/o Elmo Leather AB, 512 81 Svenljunga; tel. (325) 66-14-00; fax (325) 61-10-04; f. 1901; Chair. Björn Johansson; Man. Dir C. Lennartson; 5 mems.

Svenska Glasbruksföreningen (Swedish Crystal Manufacturers' Asscn): POB 5501, 114 85 Stockholm; tel. (8) 783-86-00; fax (8) 663-63-23; e-mail jan.eriksson@plastkemiforetagen.se; internet www.plastkemiforetagen.se; Chair. Georg Wergeman.

Svenska Skofabrikantföreningen (Swedish Shoe Manufacturers' Asscn): c/o Arbesko-Gruppen AB, POB 1642, 701 16 Örebro; tel. (19) 30-66-00; fax (19) 30-66-50; f. 1910.

TEKOindustrierna (Textile and Clothing Industries' Asscn): Storgt. 5, POB 5510, 114 85 Stockholm; tel. (8) 762-68-80; fax (8) 762-68-87; f. 1907; Chair. Ivan L. Ludvigson; Man. Dirs Anders Sandgren, Sven Cele; 263 mems.

EMPLOYERS' ORGANIZATIONS

ALMEGA: POB 16105, 103 22 Stockholm; tel. (8) 762-69-00; fax (8) 762-69-48; e-mail almega.epost@almega.se; internet www.almega.se; f. 1921; Chair. Håkan Bryngelson; Dir-Gen. Jonas Milton; 8,500 mems.

ARBIO (Swedish Federation of Wood and Furniture Industry): Södra Blasieholmshamnen 4A, POB 16006, 103 21 Stockholm; tel. (8) 762-72-00; fax (8) 762-72-14; internet www.traindustrierna.org; Chair. Björn Hägglund; Man. Dir Karl-Ewert Lidman; 5,000 mems.

Biltrafikens Arbetsgivareförbund (Road Transport Employers): Blasieholmsgt. 4A, 111 48 Stockholm; tel. (8) 762-60-00; fax (8) 611-46-99; Chair. Reinhold Öhman; Man. Dir Göran Ljungström; 5,330 mem. cos.

Byggnadsämnesförbundet (Building Material Manufacturers Employers): POB 16347, 103 26 Stockholm; tel. (8) 762-65-07; fax (8) 762-65-12; Chair. Gull-Britt Jonasson; Man. Dir Gunnar Göthberg; 278 mem. cos.

Elektriska Installatörsorganisationen EIO (The Swedish Electrical Contractors' Association): POB 17537, 118 91 Stockholm; tel. (8) 762-75-00; fax (8) 668-86-17; e-mail info@eio.se; internet www.eio.se; Chair. Gösta Allthin; Man. Dir Hans Enström; 2,500 mem. cos.

Försäkringsbranschens Arbetsgivareorganisation (Insurance Employers): Klara Norra Kyrkogt. 33, 111 22 Stockholm; tel. (8) 783-98-60; fax (8) 783-98-95; e-mail info@fao.se; internet www.fao.se; Chair. Tommy Persson; Man. Dir Annika Lundius; 110 mem. cos.

Livsmedelsbranschens Arbetsgivareförbund (Food Producers): POB 16105, 103 22 Stockholm; tel. (8) 762-69-00; fax (8) 762-69-48; Chair. Sune Sigvardsson; Man. Dir Gunnar Göthberg; 385 mem. cos.

Maskinentreprenörerna (Earth-Moving Contractors): POB 1609, 111 86 Stockholm; tel. (8) 762-70-65; fax (8) 611-85-41; Chair. Rolf Gunnarsson; Man. Dir Sven-Ola Nilsson; 3,703 mem. cos.

Medie- och Informationsarbetsgivarna (Media and Information Employers' Association): POB 16383, 103 27 Stockholm; tel. (8) 762-70-30; fax (8) 611-41-47; e-mail info@mediearbetsgivarna.org; internet www.mediearbetsgivarna.org; Chair. Lennart Wiklund; Man. Dir Charlott Richardson; 400 mem. cos.

Motorbranschens Arbetsgivareförbund (Motor Trade Employers): Blasieholmsgt. 4A, POB 1621, 111 86 Stockholm; tel. (8) 762-71-00; fax (8) 611-46-99; e-mail info@transportgruppen.se; internet www.transportgruppen.se; Chair. Per Olav Persson; Dir Peter Jeppsson; 2,138 mem. cos.

Petroleumbranschens Arbetsgivareförbund (Petroleum Industry Employers): Blasieholmsgt. 4A, POB 1621, 111 86 Stockholm; tel. (8) 762-60-00; fax (8) 611-46-99; f. 1936; Chair. Hans von Uthmann; Man. Dir Göran Ljungström; 53 mem. cos.

Plåtslageriernas Riksförbund (Platers): Rosenlundsgt. 40, POB 17536, 118 91 Stockholm; tel. (8) 762-75-85; fax (8) 616-00-72; internet www.plr.se; Chair. Lars Sjöblom; Man. Dir Robert Kiejstut; 808 mem. cos.

Samhallförbundet (Samhall Employers' Association): POB 16105, 103 22 Stockholm; tel. (8) 762-69-00; fax (8) 762-69-48; Chair. Håkan Andersson; Man. Dir Johan Rimmerfeldt; 3 mem. cos.

Stål- och Metallförbundet (Steel and Metal Industry Employers): POB 1721, 111 87 Stockholm; tel. (8) 762-67-35; fax (8) 611-62-64; e-mail info@metallgruppen.se; internet www.metallgruppen.se; Pres. Peter Gossas; Man. Dir Bengt Huldt; 202 mems with 43,953 employees.

SveMek (Welding Engineering): POB 1721, 111 87 Stockholm; tel. (8) 762-67-35; fax (8) 611-62-64; e-mail info@metallgruppen.se; internet www.metallgruppen.se; fmrly Svets Mekaniska Arbetsgivareförbundet; Pres. Gunnar Sköld; Man. Dir Bengt Huldt; 414 mems with 4,629 employees.

Sveriges Bageriförbund (Bakery and Confectionery Employers): POB 16141, 103 23 Stockholm; tel. (8) 762-60-00; fax (8) 678-66-64; e-mail kansli@bageri.se; internet www.bageri.se; f. 1900; Chair. Mats Roséu; Man. Dir Björn Hellwau; 570 mems.

Sveriges Byggindustrier (Swedish Construction Federation): Norrlandsgt. 15, POB 7835, 103 98 Stockholm; tel. (8) 698-58-00; fax (8) 698-59-00; e-mail info@bygg.org; internet www.bygg.org; Pres. Bo Antoni; 2,400 mem. cos.

Sveriges Hamnar (Ports): POB 1621, 111 86 Stockholm; tel. (8) 762-71-00; fax (8) 611-46-99; e-mail ports@transportgruppen.se; internet www.transportgruppen.se/sweports; f. 1906; Vice-Pres. Mariav Nygren; 53 mem. cos.

Teknikföretagen (Asscn of Swedish Engineering Industries): Storgt. 5, POB 5510, 114 85 Stockholm; tel. (8) 782-08-00; fax (8) 782-09-00; e-mail info@teknikforetagen.se; internet www.teknikforetagen.se; f. 1896 as VI Sveriges Verkstadsindustrier; Pres. Lennart Nilsson; Man. Dir Anders Narvinger; 3,000 mem. cos.

Trä- och Möbelindustriförbundet (Swedish Wood Products Industry Employers' Asscn): POB 16006, 103 21 Stockholm; tel. (8) 762-72-00; fax (8) 611-60-25; e-mail info@traindustrin.org; Chair. Lars-Erik Sandström; Man. Dir Karl-Ewert Lidman; 700 mem. cos.

VVS-Installatörerna (Heating, Plumbing, Refrigeration and Insulation Employers): Rosenluundsgt. 40, 118 91 Stockholm; tel. (8) 762-75-00; fax (8) 669-41-19; e-mail roine.kristianson@vvsi.se; internet www.vvsi.se; f. 1918; Chair. Osten Lindgren; Man. Dir Roine Kristianson; 1,360 mems.

UTILITIES

Major Service Providers

Ängelholms Energi AB: Energigt. 1, 262 73 Ängelholm; tel. (431) 878-00.

Billeberga Kraft & Energi AB: Industrivägen 5, POB 53, 260 21 Billeberga; tel. (418) 45-08-50.

Gullspång: Forsövägen 4, POB 33, 820 10 Arbrå; tel. (278) 277-00.

Helsingborg Energi: V. Sandgt. 4, POB 642, 251 06 Helsingborg; tel. (42) 490-32-70; fax (42) 490-32-56.

Höganäs Energi AB: Stadshuset, 253 82 Höganäs; tel. (42) 33-71-00.

KREAB Energi AB: Ljungbygt. 22, 260 70 Lyungbyhed; tel. (20) 41-00-10.

Norrlands Energi Försäljning AB: Kyrkogt. 12, POB 736, 851 21 Sundsvall; tel. (60) 19-59-00.

NVSH Energi AB: Verkstadsgt. 1, POB 505, 267 25 Bjuv; tel. (42) 856-00.

Skövde Elnät: Badhusgt. 22, 541 83 Skövde; tel. (500) 46-82-14.

Sollefteå Energi: Sollefteå; tel. (620) 68-20-00; internet www.solleftea.se.

Sydkraft AB: 205 09 Malmö; tel. (42) 255-000; e-mail info@sydkraft.se; internet www.sydkraft.se.

Vattenfall AB: 162 87 Stockholm; tel. (8) 739-50-00; fax (8) 739-51-29; e-mail info@vattenfall.se; internet www.vattenfall.se; f. 1909; became limited liability company in 1992; 100% state-owned; power generation and distribution; some 90 directly or indirectly owned operational subsidiaries; interests in Germany, Poland, South-East Asia and Latin America; Pres. and CEO Carl-Erik Nyquist.

Vinninga Elektriska Förening Ek. för.: Vallmovägen, POB 3052, 531 03 Vinninga; tel. (510) 500-60.

TRADE UNIONS

The three principal trade union bodies are the Swedish Trade Union Confederation (LO), the Confederation of Professional Employees (TCO) and the Confederation of Professional Associations (SACO).

Landsorganisationen i Sverige (LO) (Swedish Trade Union Confederation): Barnhusgt. 18, 105 53 Stockholm; tel. (8) 796-25-00; fax (8) 796-28-00; e-mail info@lo.se; internet www.lo.se; f. 1898; affiliated to ICFTU; Pres. Wanja Lundby-Wedin; 15 affiliated unions with a total membership of c. 1,831,000 (Dec. 2005), including.

Byggnads (Building Workers): 106 32 Stockholm; tel. (8) 728-48-00; fax (8) 34-50-51; Chair. Ove Bengtsberg; 133,102 mems (Dec. 2000).

Fastighetsanställdas Förbund (Building Maintenance Workers): POB 70446, 107 25 Stockholm; tel. (8) 696-11-50; fax (8) 24-46-90; f. 1936; Chair. Barbro Palmerlund; 41,943 mems (Dec. 2000).

Grafiska Fackförbundet (Graphic and Media Workers): POB 1101, 111 81 Stockholm; tel. (8) 791-16-00; fax (8) 411-41-01; e-mail gf@gf.se; internet www.gf.se; Pres. Jan Österlind; Vice-Pres. Tommy Andersson; 39,140 mems (Dec. 2000).

Handelsanställdas Förbund (Commercial Employees): Upplandsgt. 5, POB 1146, 111 81 Stockholm; tel. (8) 412-68-00;

fax (8) 10-00-62; e-mail handels@handels.se; internet www.handels.se; f. 1916; Pres. NINEL JANSSON; 167,703 mems (Dec. 2000).

Hotell- och Restaurang Facket (Hotel and Restaurant Workers): POB 1143, 111 81 Stockholm; tel. (8) 781-02-00; fax (8) 411-71-18; internet www.hrf.net; Chair. JOHN HERRSTRÖM; 61,069 mems (Dec. 2004).

IF Metall: Olof Palmesgt. 11, 105 52 Stockholm; tel. (8) 786-80-00; fax (8) 240-86-74; e-mail postbox.fk@industrifacket.se; internet www.industrifacket.se; f. 2006 by merger of Industrifacket and Svenska Metallindustriarbetareförbundet; Chair. STEFAN LÖFVEN; c. 440,000 mems (2006).

SEKO—Facket för Service och Kommunikation (Services and Communications Employees): Barnhusgt. 6–10, POB 1105, 111 81 Stockholm; tel. (8) 791-41-00; fax (8) 21-89-53; e-mail seko@seko.se; internet www.seko.se; f. 1970; present name since 1995; Chair. SVEN-OLAF ARBESTÅL; 172,616 mems (Dec. 2000).

Skogs- och Träfacket (Swedish Forest and Wood Trade Union): POB 1152, 111 81 Stockholm; tel. (8) 701-77-00; fax (8) 20-79-04; e-mail postbox.fk@skogstrafacket.org; internet www.skogstrafacket.org; f. 1998; by merger of Svenska Skogsarbetareförbundet and Svenska Träindustriarbetareförbundet; Chair. and Pres. KJELL DAHLSTRÖM; 57,000 mems.

Svenska Elektrikerförbundet (Electricians): POB 1123, 111 81 Stockholm; tel. (8) 402-14-00; fax (8) 412-82-01; Pres. ALF NORBERG; 26,883 mems (Dec. 2000).

Svenska Kommunalarbetareförbundet (Swedish Municipal Workers' Union): POB 19039, 104 32 Stockholm; tel. (8) 728-28-00; fax (8) 31-87-45; e-mail kommunal.forbundet@kommunal.se; internet www.kommunal.se; Pres. YLVA THÖRN; 573,600 mems.

Svenska Livsmedelsarbetareförbundet (Food Workers): POB 1156, 111 81 Stockholm; tel. (8) 769-29-00; fax (8) 796-29-03; Chair. ÅKE SÖDERGREN; Sec. (vacant); 53,095 mems (Dec. 2003).

Svenska Målareförbundet (Painters): POB 1113, 111 81 Stockholm; tel. (8) 587-274-00; fax (8) 587-274-99; e-mail post@malareforbundet.a.se; internet www.malareforbundet.a.se; f. 1887; Chair. LARS-ÅKE LUNDIN; 18,062 mems.

Svenska Musikerförbundet (Musicians): POB 49144, 101 29 Stockholm; tel. (8) 5870-60-00; fax (8) 16-80-20; e-mail info@musikerforbundet.se; f. 1994; Pres. JAN GRANVIK; 3,700 mems (Dec. 2001).

Svenska Pappersindustriarbetareförbundet (Swedish Paperworkers' Union): POB 1127, 111 81 Stockholm; tel. (8) 796-61-00; fax (8) 411-41-79; e-mail info@pappers.se; internet www.pappers.se; Chair. SUNE EKBÅGE; Sec. BENGT HALLBERG; 25,760 mems.

Svenska Transportarbetareförbundet (Transport Workers): POB 714, 101 33 Stockholm; tel. (8) 723-77-00; fax (8) 24-03-91; e-mail transport.fk@transport.se; internet www.transport.se; Chair. PER WINBERG; 72,000 mems (Dec. 2002).

SACO (Confederation of Professional Asscns): POB 2206, Lilla Nygt. 14, 103 15 Stockholm; tel. (8) 613-48-00; fax (8) 24-77-01; e-mail kansli@saco.se; internet www.saco.se; f. 1947; Chair. ANNA EKSTRÖM; 569,000 mems (Dec. 2004); 26 affiliated unions and professional organizations, of which the following are the largest:

Civilingenjörsförbundet (Swedish Asscn of Graduate Engineers): Malmskillnadsgt. 13, POB 1419, 111 84 Stockholm; tel. (8) 613-80-00; fax (8) 796-71-02; e-mail info@cf.se; internet www.cf.se; Sec. JAN MARTIN; 98,000 mems.

Jusek: Drottninggt. 89, POB 5167, 102 44 Stockholm; tel. (8) 665-29-00; fax (8) 662-79-23; e-mail vaxel@jusek.se; internet www.jusek.se; asscn of graduates in law, business administration and economics, computer and systems science, personnel management and social science; 65,000 mems.

Lärarnas riksförbund (National Union of Teachers in Sweden): Sveavägen 50, POB 3529, 103 69 Stockholm; tel. (8) 613-27-00; fax (8) 21-91-36; e-mail lr@lr.se; internet www.lr.se; f. 1884; Pres. METTA FJELKNER; 80,000 mems.

Tjänstemännens Centralorganisation (TCO) (Confederation of Professional Employees): Linnégt. 14, 114 94 Stockholm; tel. (8) 782-91-00; fax (8) 663-75-20; e-mail tco@tco.se; f. 1944; affiliated to ICFTU, European Trade Union Confed. and Council of Nordic Trade Unions; Pres. STURE NORDH; 17 affiliated unions with total membership of 1.3m. (2006), of which the following are the largest:

Fackförbundet ST (Civil Servants): Sturegt. 15, POB 5308, 102 47 Stockholm; tel. (8) 790-51-00; fax (8) 24-29-24; e-mail st@st.org; internet www.st.org; fmrly Statstjänstemannaförbundet; Chair. ANNETTE CARNHEDE; 97,000 mems.

Finansförbundet (Bank Employees): Roselundsgt. 29B, POB 38151, 100 64 Stockholm; tel. (8) 614-03-00; fax (8) 611-38-98; e-mail info@finansforbundet.se; internet www.finansforbundet.se; Chair. LILLEMOR SMEDENVALL; 34,920 mems.

Lärarförbundet (Teachers): Segelbåtsvägen 15, POB 12229, 102 26 Stockholm; tel. (8) 737-65-00; fax (8) 656-94-15; e-mail kansli@lararforbundet.se; internet www.lararforbundet.se; Chair. EVA-LIS PREISZ; 228,000 mems.

Ledarna (Professional and Managerial Staff): St Eriksgt. 26, POB 12069, 102 22 Stockholm; tel. (8) 598-990-00; fax (8) 598-990-10; e-mail ledarna@ledarna.se; Chair. BJÖRN BERGMAN; 77,192 mems.

Sif (Clerical and Technical Employees in Industry): Olof Palmesgt. 17, 105 32 Stockholm; tel. (8) 508-970-00; fax (8) 508-970-19; e-mail postservice@sif.se; internet www.sif.se; f. as Svenska Industritjänstemannaförbundet, present name adopted 2001; Chair. MARI-ANN KRANTZ; 367,101 mems.

Sveriges Kommunaltjänstemannaförbund (Local Government Officers): Kungsgt. 28A, POB 7825, 103 97 Stockholm; tel. (8) 789-63-00; fax (8) 21-52-44; e-mail sktf@sktf.se; internet www.sktf.se; Chair. INGER EFRAIMSSON; 176,300 mems.

Tjänstemannaförbundet HTF (Commercial Salaried Employees): Franzengt. 5, POB 30102, 104 25 Stockholm; tel. (8) 737-80-00; fax (8) 618-22-45; fmrly Handelstjänstemannaförbundet; Chair. HOLGER ERIKSSON; 145,286 mems.

Vårdförbundet (Swedish Asscn of Health Professionals): Adolf Fredrik Kyrkogt. 11, POB 3260, 103 65 Stockholm; tel. (8) 14-77-00; fax (8) 411-42-29; e-mail mailbox@vardforbundet.se; internet www.vardforbundet.se; fmrly Svenska Hälso- och Sjukvårdens Tjänstemannaförbund; Chair. EVA FERNVALL MARKSTEDT; 112,186 mems.

Transport

RAILWAYS

At 31 December 2004 there were 11,050 km of standard- and narrow-gauge railways, of which 7,745 km of track was electrified. A railway line linking Stockholm and Arlanda international airport opened in September 1999.

SJ AB (Statens Järnvägar): 105 50 Stockholm; tel. (8) 762-20-00; fax (8) 762-24-24; e-mail sjinfo@sj.se; internet www.sj.se; f. 1856; state-owned; runs passenger and freight traffic on all state-owned railway track; the company also controls ferry-boats; 70,000 passengers per day; 3,500 employees; Man. Dir JAN FORSBERG.

BK Tåg AB: POB 91, 571 21 Nässjö; tel. (380) 55-44-00; e-mail info@bktag.se; internet www.bktag.se; passenger services on six routes; Gen. Man. T. HULT; 667 km.

Malmö-Limhamns Järnvägs AB: POB 30022, 200 61 Limhamn; tel. (40) 36-15-04; fax (40) 15-86-24; 5 km of 1,435-mm gauge; Dir UWE JÖHNSON; Traffic Man. K. HOLMBERG.

TGOJ Trafik och Rental AB: Gredbyvägen 3–5, 632 21 Eskilstuna; tel. (16) 17-26-61; fax (16) 17-26-45; e-mail info@tgojtrafik.se; internet www.tgojtrafik.se; f. 1877; 300 km of 1,435-mm gauge electrified railways; Chair. R. HELLSTADIUS; Pres. CURT BYLUND.

ROADS

At 31 December 2002 there were an estimated 213,237 km of roads, of which 1,542 km were motorways, 15,388 km were main or national roads and 82,870 km of secondary or regional roads. In 2001 a road-rail link between Malmö and Copenhagen (Denmark), across the 16-km Öresund strait, was opened. A bridge linking Sweden and Norway, at Svinesund, was opened in 2005.

SHIPPING

The principal ports in terms of cargo handled are Göteborg (Gothenberg), Brofjorden, Trelleborg, Luleå and Malmö. Stockholm is also an important port.

Principal Shipping Companies

B & N & Nordsjöfrakt AB: POB 32, 471 21 Skärhamn; tel. (304) 67-47-00; fax (304) 67-47-70; e-mail bn@bn.se; Man. Dir FOLKE PATRIKSSON.

Broström Ship Management AB: POB 39, 471 21 Skärhamn; tel. (304) 67-67-00; fax (304) 67-11-10; e-mail shipman@brostrom.se; internet www.brostrom.se; management company, operating specialized tanker services; Man. Dir OLLE NOORD.

Broström Tankers AB: 403 30 Göteborg; tel. (31) 61-60-00; fax (31) 61-60-12; e-mail brotank@brostrom.se; internet www.brostrom.se; f. 1990; specializes in transporting petroleum products, in north-west Europe and world-wide; Man. Dir TORE ANGERVALL.

EffJohn International: Stockholm; tel. (8) 666-34-00; f. 1990 following merger of Effoa Finland Steamship Co and Johnson Line (Sweden); passenger ferry operations; EffJohn Group covers operations in the Baltic: Silja Line, SeaWind Line, Wasa Ferries, Sally Line, JBT, Svea Management; elsewhere in Europe: Sally Line UK;

in USA: Commodore Cruise Line, Crown Cruise Line; Pres. Hans H. Christner.

N&T Argonaut AB: Skeppsbron 34, POB 1215, 111 82 Stockholm; tel. (8) 613-19-00; fax (8) 21-31-37; e-mail nt@ntargonaut.com; internet nt.argonaut.se; f. 1983; Pres. Bjorn Ersman.

Nordström & Thulin AB: Skeppsbron 34–36, POB 1215, 111 82 Stockholm; tel. (8) 613-19-00; fax (8) 21-22-28; f. 1850; Man. Dir Anders Berg.

Stena AB: 405 19 Göteborg; tel. (31) 85-80-00; fax (31) 12-06-51; f. 1939; Stena Line ferry service since 1962; in 1990 acquired Sealink (United Kingdom); Man. Dir Dan Sten Olsson.

Wallenius Lines AB/Wallenius Rederierna AB: Swedenborgsgt. 19, POB 17086, 104 62 Stockholm; tel. (8) 772-05-00; fax (8) 640-68-54; e-mail postmaster@wallenius.se; f. 1934; car and truck carriers; Pres. Christer Olsson.

Associations

Föreningen Sveriges Sjöfart och Sjöförsvar (Swedish Maritime League): Kastellet, Kastellholmen, 111 49 Stockholm; tel. (8) 611-74-81; fax (8) 611-74-76; e-mail fsss@algonet.se; f. 1983 by merger of Swedish General Shipping Asscn and Swedish Navy League; Pres. Claes Tornberg; Gen. Sec. Sten Göthberg; 2,000 mems.

Sveriges Redareförening (Swedish Shipowners' Asscn): POB 330, 401 25 Göteborg; tel. (31) 62-95-25; fax (31) 15-23-13; e-mail srf@sweship.se; internet www.sweship.se; f. 1906; Pres. Christer Olsson; Man. Dir Håkan Gezelius; mems 156 shipping companies with 259 ships (1996).

CIVIL AVIATION

The main international airport is at Arlanda, connected by bus service to Stockholm, 42 km away. There are other international airports at Landvetter, 25 km from Göteborg, and at Sturup, 28 km from Malmö. There are regular flights between the main cities in Sweden. Many domestic flights operate from Bromma (Stockholm's city airport). Measures on the deregulation of civil aviation took effect in 1992 and ended the virtual monopoly of domestic services previously held by the Scandinavian Airlines System.

Luftfartsstyrelsen (Swedish Civil Aviation Authority): Vikboplan 7, 601 73 Norrköping; tel. (11) 415-20-00; e-mail luftfartsstyrelsen@luftfartsstyrelsen.se; internet www.luftfartsstyrelsen.se; f. 1923 as Luftfartsverket, adopted present name 2005; state body; central govt authority for matters concerning civil aviation; Dir-Gen. Nils Gunnar Billinger.

Scandinavian Airlines System (SAS): Head Office: Frösundavik Allé 1, Solna, 195 87 Stockholm; tel. (8) 797-00-00; fax (8) 797-15-15; internet www.sas.se; f. 1946; the national carrier of Denmark, Norway and Sweden. It is a consortium owned two-sevenths by SAS Danmark A/S, two-sevenths by SAS Norge ASA and three-sevenths by SAS Sverige AB. Each parent organization is a limited company owned 50% by Govt and 50% by private shareholders. The SAS group includes the consortium and the subsidiaries in which the consortium has a majority or otherwise controlling interest; the Board consists of two members from each of the parent companies and the chairmanship rotates among the three national chairmen on an annual basis. SAS absorbed Linjeflyg AB (domestic passenger, newspaper and postal services in Sweden) in 1993; strategic alliance with Lufthansa (Germany) formed in 1995; Chair. Bo Berggren; Pres. and CEO Jan Stenberg.

Nordic East Airways: POB 79, 190 45 Stockholm; tel. (8) 594-906-00; fax (8) 593-614-44; f. 1991; charter services; Chair. and CEO Gunnar Ohlsson.

Swedair AB: 195 87 Stockholm; tel. (8) 797-00-00; fax (8) 85-96-38; f. 1975 as result of merger of Svensk Flygtjanst and Crownair; passenger services to destinations within Scandinavia; Pres. Benny Zakrisson.

Transwede Airways AB: POB 2011, 438 11 Landvetter; tel. (31) 94-79-89; fax (31) 94-79-90; e-mail jimmie.bergqvist@transwede.com; internet www.transwede.se; f. 1985 as Aerocenter Trafikflyg AB; current name adopted 1986; relaunched 2005; operates charter passenger services within Scandinavia; Pres. Jimmie Bergqvist.

West Air Sweden: POB 5433, 402 29 Göteborg; tel. (31) 703-04-50; fax (31) 703-04-55; e-mail info@westair.se; internet www.westair.se; f. 1963; present name since 1993; Pres. Oskar Nilsson.

Tourism

Sweden offers a variety of landscape, from the mountains of the 'Midnight Sun', north of the Arctic Circle, to the white sandy beaches of the south. There are many lakes, waterfalls and forests, and Stockholm is famed for its beautiful situation and modern architecture. Most tourists come from the other Scandinavian countries and from Germany. In 2003 tourism receipts totalled an estimated US $6,548m.

Svenska Turistföreningen (Swedish Touring Club): Ameralitetsbacken 1, POB 25, 101 20 Stockholm; tel. (8) 463-21-00; fax (8) 678-19-58; e-mail info@stfturist.se; internet www.stfturist.se; f. 1885; 300,000 mems; owns and operates mountain hotels and youth hostels; co-ordinates nature and cultural activities in local clubs; Pres. Torgny Håstad; Sec.-Gen. Torbjörn Widén.

Turistdelegationen (Swedish Tourist Authority): POB 860, 101 37 Stockholm; tel. (8) 5451-54-60; fax (8) 5451-54-69; e-mail kansli@tourist.se; internet www.tourist.se; f. 1995; state-owned; co-ordinates government-sponsored promotion of the tourist industry in Sweden, and monitors trends in the sector; Dir Dennis Bederoff (acting).

SWITZERLAND

Introductory Survey

Location, Climate, Language, Religion, Flag, Capital

The Swiss Confederation lies in central Europe, bounded to the north by Germany, to the east by Austria, to the south by Italy and to the west by France. The climate is generally temperate, but varies considerably with altitude and aspect. In Zürich the average temperature ranges from −1°C (30°F) in winter to 16°C (61°F) in summer. There are four national languages—German, French, Italian and Raeto-Romansch, spoken by 72.5%, 21.0%, 4.3% and 0.6% of resident Swiss nationals respectively in 2000. Other languages are spoken by the remaining 1.6% of the population. Including resident aliens, the linguistic proportions in 2000 were: German 63.7%, French 20.4%, Italian 6.5%, Romansch 0.5% and other languages 9.0%. Most Swiss citizens profess Christianity: in 2000 42.7% were Protestants and 41.2% Roman Catholics. Of the total resident population in 2000, 35.3% were Protestants and 41.8% Roman Catholics. The Federal flag, which is square, consists of a white upright cross in the centre of a red ground. The capital is Bern (Berne).

Recent History

Switzerland, whose origins date back to 1291, has occupied its present area since its borders were fixed by treaty in 1815. At the same time, it was internationally recognized as a neutral country. Despite the strategic importance of Switzerland, its 'permanent neutrality' has never since been violated. The country has not entered any military alliances, and it avoided participation in both World Wars. Executive authority is exercised on a collegial basis by the Federal Council (cabinet), with a President who serves, for only one year at a time, as 'the first among equals'. Owing to the restricted powers of the Federal Council, initiatives and referendums form the core of the political process. Switzerland is a confederation of 20 cantons and six half-cantons. In 1979 the mainly French-speaking region of Jura seceded from the predominantly German-speaking canton of Bern, becoming the first new canton to be established since 1815.

Despite the fact that Switzerland has long been the headquarters of many international organizations, the country did not join the UN until 2002, owing to concerns that it would conflict with the country's traditional neutrality. Switzerland was a founder member of the European Free Trade Association (EFTA, see p. 386) in 1960 and joined the Council of Europe (see p. 211) in 1963.

Switzerland began to emerge from its traditional isolation in the early 1990s. This was largely due to economic pressures resulting from the world recession and the further integration of the European Community (EC, now European Union—EU, see p. 228). In May 1992 the Government's proposal for Switzerland to join the IMF and the World Bank was approved in a referendum. On the following day, the Federal Council announced that it was to present an application for membership of the EC. During September and October 1992 the Swiss Parliament approved the necessary legislation to comply with an agreement, signed in May 1992, to create a free-trade zone, the European Economic Area (EEA), encompassing both EC and EFTA member states. In a referendum on 6 December, however, the Swiss electorate voted against ratification of the agreement, by 16 cantons to seven. (The EEA was established, without Switzerland, in January 1994.) Despite this set-back, the Government declared its intention to continue to pursue its application for membership of the EC. During 1993 Switzerland confined itself to seeking bilateral negotiations with the EC on issues of particular national interest, including transport and involvement in EC research programmes. In February 1994, however, in defiance of a government campaign, 52% of voters in a referendum approved a proposal to ban transit freight by road through Switzerland within 10 years (requiring its transportation by rail), in order to protect the Swiss Alps. In April 1996 the Federal Council approved the Neue Eisenbahn-Alpen-Transversale (NEAT) project to construct two new Alpine tunnels in order to expedite international freight transport by rail; it was announced that this was to be financed mainly by levying a weight and distance toll on heavy goods vehicles crossing Swiss territory. (Construction work on the tunnels was completed in April 2005.) Agreement was reached in December 1996 to phase out Swiss work permits for citizens of EU member states over a period of six years. At the beginning of December 1998 Switzerland and the EU concluded a bilateral trade agreement, having settled a lengthy dispute concerning the level of the tolls to be imposed on road freight traffic through Switzerland. By February 2000 the Government had negotiated seven bilateral free-trade agreements with the EU. The accords included the gradual elimination of immigration controls between Switzerland and the EU over a 12-year period in order to allay popular anxiety regarding the possibility of EU workers depriving the Swiss of employment. While the Government had taken care to ensure that Swiss sovereignty was not affected by the trade agreements, popular resentment at the EU's imposition of sanctions against Austria during 1999 in protest at the presence of the far-right in the Austrian Government prompted Swiss opponents of the EU to submit a petition to the Swiss Government, thereby forcing a referendum on the trade agreements. At the referendum, which was held in May 2000, 67.2% of those who voted approved the agreements. Following the submission of a petition by pro-EU lobbyists, a referendum was held in March 2001 on whether to begin 'fast-track' accession negotiations with the EU; the ballot attracted an unusually high participation rate and the motion was rejected by an unexpectedly large majority, 77% of the voters. The result was believed to have been influenced in part by a letter from the European Commission in February, widely perceived as coercive, which urged the acceleration of negotiations with the EU regarding co-operation against customs fraud and tax evasion. The Government announced that the vote did not represent a rejection of the EU, but rather reflected the desire to move towards membership at a slower pace, and that its plans for eventual membership of the EU remained unchanged.

Since 1959 government posts have been divided between the members of the Social Democratic Party, the Radical Democratic Party, the Christian Democratic People's Party and the Swiss People's Party. This coalition holds more than 80% of the seats in the National Council (the lower house of the Federal Assembly), and all of the seats in the Council of States (the upper house). The ruling coalition dominated the National Council at elections held between 1975 and 1995, although it lost some support to the Green Party of Switzerland, which grew to become the fifth largest party as public concern regarding ecological issues increased. The results of elections to the National Council and the Council of States, held in October 1999, challenged, initially at least, some of the assumptions generally made about the Swiss political process. They were characterized, above all, by the strong performance of the Swiss People's Party, which, in terms of votes gained, became the country's largest party. In the National Council the Swiss People's Party overtook both the Radical Democrats and the Christian Democratic People's Party to become the second largest party after the Social Democrats. Seats in the National Council are allotted in proportion to votes gained. However, the complex, 'cantonal' nature of the electoral system ensured ultimate victory for the Social Democratic Party. In the Council of States, the success of the Swiss People's Party was similarly diluted by the 'cantonal' nature of majority voting procedures; even so, the People's Party obtained a total of seven seats, thereby overtaking the Social Democrats as the third largest party (after the Radical Democrats and the Christian Democrats).

Analysis of the election results revealed that many of the Swiss People's Party's gains had been made at the expense of extreme right-wing groups. Spurred by one of its factions, the 'Association for an Independent and Neutral Switzerland', led by Christian Blocher, nationalist, isolationist policies had been at the fore of the Party's electoral campaign, together with populist proposals to adopt a more hard-line stance towards asylum-seekers and drug offenders, and to reduce taxation. There was speculation that if the party's representation in the Federal Council were not increased to two seats in December 1999, then Blocher would seek to detach the party from the governing coalition. In the event, Blocher's attempt to gain a seat on the Federal Council was defeated without provoking such a defection.

The enfranchisement of women in federal elections was approved at a referendum in February 1971. However, the half-cantons of Appenzell Ausserrhoden and Appenzell Innerrhoden introduced female suffrage only in 1989 and 1990, respectively. In October 1984 the Federal Assembly elected Switzerland's first female cabinet minister, Dr Elisabeth Kopp, a leading member of the Radical Democratic Party, who became Head of the Federal Department of Justice and Police. In December 1988 the Assembly elected Dr Kopp, by a large majority, to be Vice-President of the Swiss Confederation for 1989, concurrently with her other duties in the Federal Council. In the same month, however, she announced her resignation from her post as Head of the Federal Department of Justice and Police, following allegations that she had violated regulations concerning official secrecy. In February 1989, following an official investigation of the case, Dr Kopp was replaced as Vice-President; in February 1990, however, she was finally acquitted by the Federal Supreme Court.

In January 1993 the Head of the Federal Department of Foreign Affairs, René Felber, resigned from the Federal Council. Under the terms of the coalition, Felber was to be replaced by another francophone member of the Social Democratic Party. In March the official Social Democratic candidate, Christiane Brunner, a trade union leader, was rejected by other members of the coalition in favour of a male candidate, Francis Matthey, who, however, following pressure from within the party, refused to accept his election. The Social Democratic Party subsequently reconfirmed Brunner's candidacy but presented another female candidate as well, Ruth Dreifuss, also a trade union activist (and a former journalist and government aid worker). Following three rounds of voting, Dreifuss became the second woman to be elected to a ministerial position in Switzerland. In December 1998 the Federal Assembly elected Dreifuss (by then Head of the Federal Department of Home Affairs) as President of the Confederation for 1999. A female Christian Democratic People's Party candidate, Ruth Metzler, was elected Head of the Federal Department of Justice and Police in March 1999. In the following month 59.2% of voters in a national referendum approved a revised draft Constitution that included new provision for the right to undertake strike action by the labour force.

The commission that had investigated the allegations against Dr Kopp during 1989 subsequently revealed that the office of the Federal Public Prosecutor held about 900,000 secret files on some 200,000 Swiss citizens and foreigners. In March 1990 about 30,000 people demonstrated in Bern in protest at the existence of such files; the demonstration ended in rioting. The Government subsequently announced that it would commission a report on the activities of the security services and introduce new laws regulating state security; it also opened most of the files to public scrutiny. The completed report, which was published in June 1993, found that security service observation had been largely restricted to left-wing groups since 1945 and that security service personnel had at times behaved in an unprofessional manner.

In September 1995 the Swiss Bankers' Association (SBA) announced the introduction of measures that would enable relatives to trace and recover the assets deposited in Swiss bank accounts by victims of the Nazi massacre of Jews in the Second World War. To assist in this process an accord was signed in May 1996 by the SBA and the World Jewish Congress establishing an Independent Committee of Eminent Persons (ICEP), chaired by Paul Volcker, a former Chairman of the Board of Governors of the US Federal Reserve, which was to be responsible for auditing all dormant Swiss bank accounts. In September 1996 controversial documents were released from British and US archives, claiming that gold valued at several thousand million dollars, at current prices, had been deposited in Swiss banks during the Second World War. Much of it was suspected to have belonged to Jews killed in the Holocaust. The Swiss Federal Assembly subsequently approved legislation establishing an independent panel to investigate the ownership of these assets, and legislation ordering banks to release all records that might pertain to dealings with the Nazi regime in Germany or its victims. In December 1996 the Federal Government appointed an international commission to conduct a broad historical investigation of Switzerland's role as a financial centre during the Second World War.

Meanwhile, the issue of 'Nazi gold' had received much coverage in the international press. Jewish organizations threatened to boycott Swiss financial institutions, claiming that insufficient efforts were being made to recover their assets and expressing outrage at what they regarded as antagonistic comments made by Jean-Pascal Delamuraz (President of the Confederation in 1996) and by Carlo Jagmetti (who subsequently resigned as Switzerland's ambassador to the USA). In March 1997 three of Switzerland's most prominent banks, Crédit Suisse, Swiss Bank Corporation and UBS-Union Bank of Switzerland, established a special humanitarian fund for impoverished survivors of the Holocaust, under the administration of the Federal Government; the first payments from the fund were made in November. In December Swiss banks issued the first payments to claimants of funds from dormant accounts that had been opened prior to and during the Second World War. In March of that year the Swiss administration had announced a plan, subject to ratification by the Federal Assembly and the electorate, to establish a 'Swiss Foundation for Solidarity', a larger-scale fund with a general humanitarian brief, to be financed by a revaluation of a part of the Swiss National Bank's gold reserves. However, the proposals were rejected by the electorate at a referendum held in September 2002.

In March 1998 senior US public finance officials, threatening an imminent boycott of Swiss banks and industrial interests, placed the former under increasing pressure to agree to a swift 'global settlement' of the issue of Holocaust victims' accounts, involving the establishment of a victims' fund and a timetable for payment; soon afterwards (against the wishes of the Swiss Government, which believed the ICEP to be making adequate progress in assessing claims) Swiss Bank Corporation and UBS-Union Bank of Switzerland, which subsequently merged to form UBS AG, and Crédit Suisse announced their intention to negotiate such a 'global settlement'. In August UBS and Crédit Suisse agreed to pay US $1,250m. to the World Jewish Congress as compensation for the role of Swiss financial institutions in retaining dormant Jewish assets, handling gold deposited by the Nazis and lending money during the Second World War to German companies that had utilized Jewish slave labour. In return, all threats of boycotts and legal action against Swiss concerns were withdrawn. The settlement was not endorsed by the Swiss Government.

In December 1999 the ICEP reported that its audit of all dormant Swiss bank accounts had shown that some 54,000 of these might have belonged to Jews murdered in the Holocaust (although the figure was subsequently reduced to 36,000). The Committee recommended that details of 25,000 of the 54,000 accounts should be publicized in order to alert survivors of the Holocaust or their heirs to their existence, and it criticized some Swiss banks for their insensitivity and for their obstruction of legitimate claims. The Committee did not attempt to value the funds held in the accounts, but stated that the total would probably not exceed the US $1,250m. already committed by UBS and Crédit Suisse to the World Jewish Congress. The publication of the report of the ICEP was followed, almost immediately, by the release of that of the international historical commission appointed in December 1996. The commission concluded that, by closing its border to an estimated 24,500 fugitive Jews from 1942, Switzerland bore partial responsibility for their deaths at the hands of the Nazis. Following the release of the historical commission's report, the Government formally apologized for Switzerland's role in the Second World War. Further details emerged in August 2001, which indicated that several of Switzerland's largest companies, including Nestlé, had ignored reports of Nazi atrocities and pursued business as usual with Germany during the Second World War, thereby contributing to the German war effort. Moreover, it was revealed that, despite Switzerland's neutrality, the Government had issued Germany and Italy with credits to buy Swiss-made machinery and weapons. In December a further report indicated that Switzerland had harboured substantial amounts of Nazi funds and assets, and even dissimilated entire German companies, during the Second World War. The report also stated that Switzerland had provided a refuge for several prominent Nazi war criminals following the end of hostilities.

In May 2000 UBS and Crédit Suisse agreed to allow researchers to examine records of more than 2m. bank accounts in order to verify or reject claims by Holocaust survivors. The proposed settlement of US $1,250m. to end the threat of litigation by Holocaust survivors against Swiss banks was approved by a judge in the USA in July 2000. The two banks formally agreed the settlement in August; four Swiss insurers added a further $50m. in response to claims that the insurance policies of Holocaust survivors had not been honoured. Swiss companies that had used forced labour during the Second World War were also required to contribute. In February 2001, in preparation for the beginning of payments, Swiss banks published lists of dormant bank accounts, thought to be linked to the Holocaust, to be claimed by the account-holders or their heirs.

On 1 January 2004 legislation entered force pardoning many Swiss citizens who were condemned and punished for illegally helping refugees during the Second World War. Although almost 30,000 Jews took refuge in Switzerland during the war, more than 20,000 were turned away, many of whom later died in Nazi concentration camps. Many Swiss citizens who helped refugees across the border or hid them after their arrival were prosecuted and imprisoned and, in most cases, their criminal records were allowed to stand. The new legislation allowed those prosecuted, or their relatives and other organizations, to apply for a pardon via a parliamentary commission. There was, however, no provision for compensation.

During 1986 the Government introduced legislation that aimed to restrict the number of refugees who were to be granted political asylum in Switzerland. However, the new legislation was criticized by socialist, religious and humanitarian groups, and in April 1987 a national referendum on the issue was held. Of the 41.8% of the electorate who voted at the referendum, a substantial majority was in favour of the new restrictions. In a further national referendum, held in December 1988, 67% of voters rejected a proposal by a small extreme right-wing party to reduce by 300,000 the number of foreigners to be allowed to settle in Switzerland by 2003. In March 1994, in an attempt to control increasing drugs-related crime (following allegations that immigrants trading in illicit drugs were exploiting the asylum laws to avoid extradition), the Government approved legislation restricting the rights of asylum-seekers and immigrants, which included provisions for their arrest and detention without trial for failure to possess the requisite identification documents; further stringent measures against foreigners suspected of trafficking in illegal drugs were approved by national referendum in December. Civil rights groups accused the Government of yielding to popular xenophobic sentiment in an effort to divert attention from its failure to overcome the drugs problem. In December 1996 a proposal sponsored by the Swiss People's Party to confiscate the earnings of asylum-seekers in Switzerland and to expel automatically all those without sufficient documentation was narrowly rejected in a national referendum. In a referendum held in September 2000 63.7% of voters rejected a motion to reduce the number of foreigners allowed to settle in Switzerland from 20% of the total population to 18%. In November 2002 a national referendum was held on proposals, drawn up by the Swiss People's Party, under which would-be refugees arriving in Switzerland via any country free of political persecution (in practice, all neighbouring countries) would automatically be denied refugee status and sent back across the border: the proposal was only narrowly rejected (by 51.1% of votes cast). In January 2004 the town of Ostermundigen became the first in Switzerland to introduce written language tests for those applying for Swiss citizenship.

In the early years of the 21st century the stability of the 'grand coalition' that had governed Switzerland since 1959 was increasingly threatened by the growing influence of the Swiss People's Party. Under the so-called 'magic formula', government seats were shared among the coalition partners, with the Social Democratic Party, the Radical Democratic Party, the Christian Democratic People's Party each receiving two seats and the Swiss People's Party receiving only one. At the general election held on 19 October 2003 the Swiss People's Party received the largest share of the votes cast and thus for the first time became the largest party in the National Council, with 55 seats. The party demanded a second seat on the Federal Council to reflect this (to be taken by Christian Blocher), and threatened to withdraw from the coalition, effectively ending the era of consensus politics, if its demand was not met. (Traditionally, Swiss ministers are reappointed at each election, and keep their seats until such time as they resign.) When the Federal Assembly elected the Federal Council on 10 December, however, Blocher contested the seat held by Ruth Metzler (of the Christian Democratic People's Party) and, after three ballots, won with a majority of just five votes. This was the first ministerial deselection for 130 years, and the first time the composition of the governing coalition had been changed in 44 years. Joseph Deiss, now the Christian Democratic People's Party's only representative in Government, was elected as President for 2004. When the new Federal Council took office on 1 January 2004, Blocher, who had expressed his wish to become Head of the Federal Department of Finance, was instead made Head of the Federal Department of Justice and Police, which carried with it responsibility not only for policy on immigration and asylum but also for negotiating with the EU on Swiss membership of the Schengen Agreement (which binds signatories to the abolition of border controls) and the Dublin Convention on Asylum (relating to common formal arrangements on asylum) and on judicial co-operation.

In December 2004 the Federal Assembly approved a second set of bilateral agreements with the EU, which had been signed in October. Under the agreements Switzerland was to introduce (incrementally between 1 July 2005 and 2011) a withholding tax of 35% on the income of EU citizens' savings held in Switzerland, with banking secrecy to be retained. The agreements also provided for co-operation against customs fraud and for Switzerland's associate membership of the Schengen Agreement and Dublin Convention, as well as for the extension of the first set of bilateral agreements (see above) to the 10 new EU member states. The National Council voted against submitting the agreement on the Schengen/Dublin accords to an obligatory referendum. However, the Swiss People's Party gathered sufficient signatures to force a referendum on the issue. At the referendum, held on 5 June 2005, 54.6% of participating voters (56.6% of the electorate) supported Switzerland's adherence to the Schengen/Dublin accords. The extension of existing bilateral agreements to the new EU member states was approved by 56.0% of voters at a referendum held on 25 September 2005; a participation rate of 54.5% was recorded.

In June 2004 the National Council approved, by 64 votes to 48, a two-tier immigration policy whereby priority was to be given to EU and EFTA nationals, with immigration otherwise restricted to only highly skilled labour in the agricultural, construction, health and tourism sectors. A national referendum held in September 2004 rejected proposals to relax the country's laws on citizenship: a government plan to ease citizenship procedures for Swiss-born second-generation immigrants was opposed by 56.8% of those who participated, while a plan to grant automatic citizenship to third-generation immigrants was rejected by 51.6%. (Foreigners comprise approximately 20% of Switzerland's population.) In November 66.4% of voters in a referendum approved legislation allowing scientists to experiment on cells taken from human embryos (known as stem cell research), which was henceforth to be regulated by Federal law. Voters also approved a programme of fiscal reform for the redistribution of funds between the Federal Government and the cantons, and a Federal resolution that extended the Government's power to levy direct Federal and value-added taxes to 2020 (this mandate had been due to expire in 2006). In December 2004 Samuel Schmid of the Swiss People's Party was appointed as President of the Swiss Confederation for 2005.

A referendum on the registration of same-sex partnerships was held on 5 June 2005 (concurrently with the referendum on the Schengen/Dublin accords—see above), at which 58.0% of voters supported proposals to grant registered same-sex couples similar legal rights to married couples in areas such as taxation and pensions (although they would not be allowed to adopt children, nor would they be eligible for fertility treatment). The participation rate was 56.5%. In December Moritz Leuenberger of the Social Democratic Party was appointed as President of the Swiss Confederation for 2006.

In November 1989 64.4% of voters in a referendum rejected a proposal to abolish the armed forces by 2000. The referendum, which had been instigated by the Group for Switzerland Without an Army (an alliance of socialist, pacifist, youth and ecological organizations), attracted an unusually high level of participation, almost 70% of the electorate. Following the referendum, the Federal Military (Defence) Department established a working party to examine proposals for reforms in the armed forces; consequently, the strength of the armed forces was considerably reduced during the early 1990s. In June 1993 the Federal Assembly approved legislation that sought permission for Swiss forces to be included in future UN peace-keeping operations. However, at a referendum on the issue, which took place in June 1994, 57.3% of voters rejected the proposal. Switzerland did subsequently join the Partnership for Peace (see p. 316) programme of the North Atlantic Treaty Organization (NATO) in 1996. Swiss peace-keepers have participated in operations in Bosnia and Herzegovina, while Swiss truce-verifiers have worked in Kosovo under the Organization for Security and Co-operation in Europe (OSCE, see p. 327). In November 2000 plans were announced to reduce the size of the army. In the same month a referendum was held on proposals to reduce the military budget by one-third; the motion was rejected by 62% of voters. A further proposal to abolish the armed forces, instigated by the Group for Switzerland Without an Army, was rejected by 79% of voters in a referendum held in December 2001; 78% of voters also rejected a replacement civilian force.

Following the accident in April 1986 at the Chornobyl (Chernobyl) nuclear power station, in the former USSR (Ukraine), public concern about nuclear safety became a national issue in Switzerland. In June a large-scale anti-nuclear demonstration took place at Gösgen, the site of the largest of Switzerland's five nuclear power stations, and in the same month the Social Democratic Party initiated a campaign to collect signatures for a referendum on the nuclear issue, advocating the progressive elimination of the country's existing reactors and the cancellation of any future nuclear projects. In March 1989 the Federal Assembly, after protracted debate, approved legislation to cancel the projected construction of a sixth nuclear power station, at Kaiseraugst (near Basel), and to provide compensation for the construction consortium. The decision followed increasing public disapproval of the project. In a referendum held in September 1990, a majority of voters rejected proposals to abandon the use of nuclear power, but approved a proposal for a 10-year moratorium on the construction of further nuclear power stations in Switzerland. The Federal Council announced in October 1998 that the five existing nuclear plants would eventually be closed on environmental grounds; it did not, however, propose a timescale for the withdrawal from nuclear energy.

In September 2000 the Federal Prosecutor-General, Valentin Roschacher, investigated allegations that two Swiss companies had paid bribes to the former Kremlin property manager, Pavel Borodin, to secure contracts to refurbish the Kremlin in Moscow, Russia. Borodin, his daughter and his son-in-law were believed to have transferred the funds into Swiss bank accounts. As the Russian State Prosecutor was reluctant to investigate the case, Roschacher issued an international arrest warrant; Borodin was subsequently arrested in New York, and in April 2001 he agreed to be voluntarily extradited to Switzerland to face trial. This was just the latest in a series of high-profile money-laundering cases in Switzerland which included the 'freezing' of assets and accounts linked to Sani Abacha and Slobodan Milošević, the former leaders of Nigeria and Yugoslavia respectively, and the former head of the Peruvian secret service. Suspect funds found in Swiss banks accounts were linked to missing IMF aid paid to Russia and to the former leader of the Philippines, Ferdinand Marcos. The total value of suspect funds under investigation in Switzerland increased from 333m. Swiss francs in 1999 (representing 160 cases) to 1,543m. Swiss francs (representing 370 cases) in 2000. These cases, which involved some of Switzerland's most prestigious banks and financial institutions, seriously damaged the country's international reputation as a stable and reliable financial centre. Swiss laws denying foreign investigators access to information about bank accounts unless local laws are broken attracted criticism, as did Switzerland's continued (although diminished) use of anonymous bank accounts.

In August 2003 Switzerland declared itself willing to co-operate with Nigeria's efforts to recover funds stolen by its former President, Sani Abacha. The Nigerian Government estimated that Abacha had embezzled some US $2,000m., of which about $700m. was believed to have been deposited in Switzerland. The Swiss Government announced in April 2006 that it had returned all of the funds to the Nigerian Government. Appeals from the Abacha family for ownership of the money had been rejected. According to an agreement reached between Switzerland and Nigeria, the World Bank was to ensure the returned funds were used for development projects in health, education and basic infrastructure. In April 2005 Switzerland secured the extradition from Germany of Abacha's son, Abba Abacha; he was subsequently charged with money-laundering, fraud, forgery and participation in a criminal organization. In early 2006 Switzerland and Nigeria held discussions aimed at concluding a bilateral accord on the repatriation of Nigerians who had failed to obtain asylum in Switzerland. Large numbers of Nigerians had sought asylum in Switzerland in recent years, peaking at 1,100 in 2002.

Until 2002, although Switzerland maintained a permanent observer at the UN and had joined the organization's non-political specialized agencies, it was not a full member of the UN. At a referendum in 1986, although the Government campaigned in its favour, some 75.7% of voters rejected full membership of the UN. The proportion of the electorate voting in the referendum, at 50.2%, represented a higher than average level of participation in the Swiss system of direct democracy. In March 2000 a petition favouring membership of the UN forced a further future referendum on the issue and in December of that year it was announced that at the referendum, which was not to take place until 2002, the Government would support membership of the UN. In September 2001 the Federal Assembly approved proposals for Switzerland to join the organization. At the referendum, which was held on 3 March 2002, the proposals required not only the support of the majority of voters, but also the approval of at least one-half of the cantons in order to be adopted. In the event, 54.6% of voters and 12 (of 23) cantons supported the proposals; the participation rate at the referendum was 57.8%. Switzerland was formally admitted as a member of the UN in September of that year.

At a national referendum held in February 2003 70.3% of voters cast their ballots in favour of two proposed reforms whereby voters would be given the automatic right to challenge treaties signed between Switzerland and other countries (although in practice all important agreements are already subject to a referendum), and petitions with the requisite number of signatures could be used to introduce legislation, rather than solely constitutional amendments as was already the case. The rate of participation in the referendum, however, was markedly low, at only some 28%.

Government

The Swiss Confederation, composed of 20 cantons and six half-cantons, has a republican federal Constitution. Legislative power is held by the bicameral Federal Assembly: the Council of States, with 46 members representing the cantons (two for each canton and one for each half-canton), elected for three to four years; and the National Council, with 200 members directly elected by universal adult suffrage for four years, on the basis of proportional representation. Executive power is held by the Federal Council, which has seven members elected for four years by a joint session of the Federal Assembly. The Assembly also elects one of the Federal Councillors to be President of the Confederation (Head of State) for one year at a time.

National policy is the prerogative of the Federal Government, but considerable power is vested in the cantons. Under the Constitution, the autonomous cantons hold all powers not specifically delegated to the federal authorities. The Swiss citizen shares three distinct allegiances—communal, cantonal and national. Direct participation is very important in communal government, and all adult Swiss residents may take part in the communal assemblies or referendums, which decide upon local affairs. Each canton has its own written constitution, government and legislative assembly. The referendum, which can be on a communal, cantonal or national scale, further ensures the possibility of direct public participation in decision-making.

Defence

National defence is based on compulsory military service. Switzerland maintains no standing army except for a small permanent personnel of commissioned and non-commissioned officers primarily concerned with training. Military service consists of 18–21 weeks' compulsory recruit training at the age of 19–20 years, followed by six or seven three-week 'refresher' training courses between the ages of 20 and 30 years. Approximately 113,200 soldiers of all ranks were trained in 2004. Each soldier keeps his equipment in his own home, and receives compulsory marksmanship training between periods of service. In August 2005 the total strength of the armed forces, when mobilized, was 214,400, comprising an active force of 4,300 and reserves of 210,100 (army 153,200; air force 32,900; command support organization 14,000; and logistics organization 10,000). In addition, there is a paramilitary force numbering 105,000 reservists. The Confederation belongs to no international defence organizations, and the strategy of the army and air force is defensive. In December 1996 Switzerland signed the Partnership for Peace (see p. 316) framework document of the North Atlantic Treaty Organization (NATO). Defence expenditure for 2005 was budgeted at 4,700m. Swiss francs.

Economic Affairs

In 2004, according to estimates by the World Bank, Switzerland's gross national income (GNI), measured at average 2002–04 prices, was US $356,052m., equivalent to $48,230 per head (or $35,370 per head on an international purchasing-power parity basis). During 1995–2004, it was estimated, the population grew by an average of 0.5% per year, while gross domestic product (GDP) per head increased, in real terms, at an average annual rate of 0.9%. Overall GDP increased, in real terms, by an average of 1.4% per year in 1995–2004; real GDP declined by 0.4% in 2003, but increased by 1.7% in 2004.

Agriculture (including forestry and fishing) contributed an estimated 1.2% of GDP in 2003, and engaged 3.8% of the employed labour force in 2004. The principal cash crops are sugar beet, potatoes and wheat. Dairy products, notably cheese, are also important. At a national referendum held in November 2005, 55.7% of voters approved a five-year ban on the use of genetically modified crops. According to FAO, agricultural production declined at an average annual rate of 0.2% in 1995–2004; it decreased by 1.5% in 2003, but there was no discernible change in 2004.

Industry (including mining and quarrying, manufacturing, power and construction) contributed an estimated 26.5% of GDP in 2003, and engaged 23.6% of the employed labour force in 2004. Industrial GDP increased by 5.3% in 1998.

Switzerland is not richly endowed with mineral deposits, and only rock salt and building materials are mined or quarried in significant quantities. In 2004 only 0.1% of the working population were employed in mining and quarrying. The sector contributed just 0.2% of GDP in 2003.

The manufacturing sector, which contributed an estimated 18.5% of GDP in 2003, engaged 16.0% of the employed labour force in 2004. The most important branches are precision engineering (in particular clocks and watches, which provided 7.5% of export revenue in 2003), heavy engineering, machine-building, textiles, chocolate, chemicals and pharmaceuticals.

Of total electricity output in 2002, 54.2% was provided by hydroelectric power and 41.9% by nuclear power (from five reactors with a total generating capacity of 3,077 MW). In 1998 Switzerland imported 82% of the energy that it consumed, mainly in the form of petroleum and related products (which accounted for 61.2% of final energy consumption in that year). Imports of mineral fuels comprised 4.3% of the value of total imports in 2003. Switzerland is, however, a net exporter of electricity.

The services sector contributed 72.3% of GDP in 2003, and engaged 72.6% of the employed labour force in 2004. Switzerland plays an important role as a centre of international finance, and Swiss markets account for a significant share of international financial transactions. The insurance sector is also highly developed, and Swiss companies are represented throughout the world. The reputation of the banking sector abroad was adversely affected in the 1990s by revelations concerning the ignoble role played by Swiss banks in respect of funds deposited by Jewish victims of the Nazi Holocaust (see Recent History). The resolution of this issue in 2001 was overshadowed by a series of high-profile money-laundering scandals, which caused yet more damage to the reputation of Swiss banking. Switzerland draws considerable revenue from tourism; receipts from tourism totalled US $11,344m. in 2003.

In 2004 Switzerland recorded a visible trade surplus of US $15,737m., and there was a surplus of $58,294m. on the current account of the balance of payments. The European Union (EU, see p. 228) accounted for the majority of Switzerland's trade, providing 78.0% of the country's imports and taking 59.0% of exports in 2002. In 2003 the principal source of imports was Germany (providing 32.3% of total imports), followed by France (10.8%), Italy (10.7%) and the USA (5.1%). Germany was also the principal market for exports (taking 20.8% of total exports), followed by the USA (11.0%), France (8.7%) and Italy (8.3%). The principal exports in 2003 were chemicals, pharmaceutical products, machinery and clocks and watches. The main imports in that year were chemicals, machinery, pharmaceutical products and agricultural and forestry products.

Switzerland recorded a consolidated budgetary deficit of 6,577m. Swiss francs (equivalent to 1.5% of GDP) in 2004. General government external debt was equivalent to 0.2% of GDP in 1999. The annual rate of inflation averaged 0.7% in 1995–2004; consumer prices increased by 0.8% in 2004 and by 1.1% in 2005. The rate of unemployment averaged 4.3% in 2004. Of all the major European countries, Switzerland has the highest percentage of foreign workers (25.4% of the working population in 2004).

Switzerland is a founder member of the European Free Trade Association (EFTA, see p. 386).

Although Switzerland is not a member of the EU, it is nevertheless largely dependent on the euro area for economic growth. The poor performance of Germany, Switzerland's main trading partner, was particularly damaging for Switzerland as it went into recession in 2002–03. This was compounded by weakness in the world's financial markets, since financial services account for some 12% of Switzerland's GDP. GDP was estimated to have increased by 1.9% in 2005, with growth of 2.1% projected for 2006. Private consumption was likely to benefit from a gradual improvement in the labour market (with the unemployment rate forecast to decline from 3.8% in 2005 to 3.4% in 2006), which was expected to release considerable accumulated demand, following years of weak private consumption growth, and from low inflation, which was expected to decline from 1.1% in 2005 to 0.8% in 2006, despite high petroleum prices. An improvement in investment activity, particularly in the business sector, was also anticipated in 2006, with only investment in housing construction forecast to decline slightly, owing to its recent high level. Exports grew substantially in 2004, and remained strong in 2005, with significant increases in exports of precision instruments, jewellery and watches, and chemical products. Exports were forecast to rise again in 2006, although at a slower rate than 2004–05. In 2004–05 the emphasis of Switzerland's economic policy shifted to improving the country's business environment through structural measures. However, progress was expected to be slow. Legislation to liberalize the agricultural sector and the electricity market, measures to increase competition, the full privatization of the telecommunications company Swisscom (in which the Government still held a 62.45% stake) and market-orientated reforms of public healthcare and pensions insurance were all likely to be subject to referendums. However, the rejection in 2002 of a bill on the liberalization of the electricity market suggested that these proposals would prove difficult to carry, and that any reforms would have to be substantially amended before being approved.

Education

Primary and secondary education are controlled by the cantons, with the result that there are 26 different systems in operation. Responsibility for higher education is shared between the cantons and the Federal Government. Education is compulsory for children between the ages of seven and 16 years. The duration of primary education, which commences at the age of six or seven, is nine years. The duration and system of secondary education depends on individual cantonal policy. Some 20% of 17-year-olds continue their studies at a higher secondary school (Gymnasium/Collège), and a leaving certificate (Matura/Maturité) from one of these is a prerequisite for entry to academic higher education. About 70% proceed to vocational training (trade and technical) for a period of three to four years. There are 10 cantonal universities, two Federal Institutes of Technology (of university standing) and one Academic Institute (a teacher-training college of university standing), as well as seven universities of applied sciences. Numerous private schools exist, as well as one private university of applied sciences, and many foreign children receive part of their education in Switzerland. In 2002/03 enrolment at pre-primary level included 77% of children in the relevant age-group; the comparable ratios for primary and secondary education were 99% (for both boys and girls) and 87% (males 89%; females 84%), respectively. Enrolment at tertiary level in that year was equivalent to 49% of those in the relevant age-group (males 53%; females 44%). In 2003 federal, cantonal and communal expenditure on education amounted to 26,560m. Swiss francs (19.6% of total public expenditure).

Public Holidays

2006: 1–2 January (New Year), 14 April (Good Friday), 17 April (Easter Monday), 1 May (Labour Day), 25 May (Ascension Day), 5 June (Whit Monday), 1 August (National Day), 24 December (Christmas Eve)*, 25 December (Christmas), 26 December (St Stephen's Day), 31 December (New Year's Eve)*.
2007: 1–2 January (New Year), 6 April (Good Friday), 9 April (Easter Monday), 1 May (Labour Day), 17 May (Ascension Day), 28 May (Whit Monday), 1 August (National Day), 24 December (Christmas Eve)*, 25 December (Christmas), 26 December (St Stephen's Day), 31 December (New Year's Eve)*.

In addition, various cantonal and local holidays are observed.
* Half day only.

Weights and Measures

The metric system is in force.

SWITZERLAND

Statistical Survey

Source (unless otherwise stated): Federal Statistical Office, Information Service, Espace de l'Europe 10, 2010 Neuchâtel; tel. 327136011; fax 327136012; e-mail information@bfs.admin.ch; internet www.statistics.admin.ch.

Area and Population

AREA, POPULATION AND DENSITY

Area (sq km)	41,284*
Population (census results)	
4 December 1990	6,873,687
5 December 2000	
Males	3,567,567
Females	3,720,443
Total	7,288,010
Population (official estimates at 31 December)†	
2003	7,364,148
2004	7,415,102
2005‡	7,461,100
Density (per sq km) at 31 December 2005	180.7

* 15,940 sq miles.
† Figures refer to permanent resident population, and have not been adjusted to take the results of the 2000 census into account.
‡ Provisional.

LANGUAGES
(Swiss nationals, %)

	1980	1990	2000
German	73.5	73.4	72.5
French	20.1	20.5	21.0
Italian	4.5	4.1	4.3
Raeto-Romansch	0.9	0.7	0.6
Others	1.0	1.3	1.6

REGIONS AND CANTONS

Region/Canton	Area (sq km)*	Population (2004†) Total	Per sq km	Capital (with population, 2000‡)
Région lémanique	8,718.7	1,362,754	156.3	—
Genève	282.4	427,396	1,513.4	Genève (177,964)
Valais	5,224.4	287,976	55.1	Sion (27,171)
Vaud	3,211.9	647,382	201.6	Lausanne (124,914)
Espace Mittelland	10,062.0	1,690,135	168.0	—
Bern	5,959.3	955,378	160.3	Bern (128,634)
Fribourg	1,670.6	250,377	149.9	Fribourg (35,547)
Jura	838.5	69,091	82.4	Delémont (11,353)
Neuchâtel	802.9	167,910	209.1	Neuchâtel (32,914)
Solothurn	790.7	247,379	312.9	Solothurn (15,489)
Nordwestschweiz	1,958.2	1,017,180	519.4	—
Aargau	1,403.6	565,122	402.6	Aarau (15,470)
Basel-Stadt	37.0	186,753	5,047.4	Basel (166,558)
Basel-Landschaft	517.6	265,305	512.6	Liestal (12,930)
Zürich	1,728.9	1,261,810	729.8	Zürich (363,273)
Ostschweiz	11,521.1	1,059,586	92.0	—
Appenzell Ausserrhoden	242.8	52,841	217.3	Herisau (15,882)
Appenzell Innerrhoden	172.5	15,029	87.1	Appenzell (5,447)
Glarus	685.1	38,317	55.9	Glarus (5,556)
Graubünden	7,105.5	187,812	26.4	Chur (32,989)
St Gallen	2,025.7	458,821	226.5	St Gallen (72,626)
Schaffhausen	298.5	73,788	247.2	Schaffhausen (33,628)
Thurgau	991.0	232,978	235.1	Frauenfeld (21,954)
Zentralschweiz	4,483.6	703,706	157.0	—
Luzern	1,493.5	354,731	237.5	Luzern (59,496)
Nidwalden	275.9	39,497	143.2	Stans (6,983)
Obwalden	490.6	33,162	67.6	Sarnen (9,145)
Schwyz	908.2	135,989	149.7	Schwyz (13,802)
Uri	1,076.7	35,083	32.6	Altdorf (8,541)
Zug	238.7	105,244	440.9	Zug (22,973)
Ticino	2,812.2	319,931	113.8	Bellinzona (16,463)
Total	41,284.2	7,415,102	179.6	—

* Figures exclude lakes larger than 5 sq km (total area 1,289.5 sq km). Also excluded are special territories (total area 7.2 sq km).
† Estimated permanent resident population at 31 December.
‡ Census figures.

PRINCIPAL TOWNS
(estimated population at 31 December 2003)

Zürich (Zurich)	342,853	Biel (Bienne)	48,524
Genève (Genf or Geneva)	178,500	Thun (Thoune)	40,850
Basel (Bâle)	164,802	Köniz	37,134
Bern (Berne, the capital)	122,299	La Chaux-de-Fonds	36,882
Lausanne	116,811	Schaffhausen (Schaffhouse)	33,818
Winterthur (Winterthour)	91,159	Fribourg (Freiburg)	32,849
St Gallen (Saint-Gall)	70,628	Chur (Coire)	32,227
Luzern (Lucerne)	57,271	Neuchâtel (Neuenburg)	31,465

BIRTHS, MARRIAGES AND DEATHS

	Registered live births Number	Rate (per 1,000)	Registered marriages Number	Rate (per 1,000)	Registered deaths Number	Rate (per 1,000)
1997	80,584	11.4	39,102	5.5	62,839	8.9
1998	78,377	11.0	38,683	5.4	62,569	8.8
1999	78,408	11.0	40,646	5.7	62,503	8.7
2000	78,458	10.9	39,758	5.5	62,528	8.7
2001	73,509	10.2	35,987	5.0	61,287	8.5
2002	72,372	9.9	40,213	5.5	61,768	8.5
2003	71,848	9.8	40,056	5.4	63,070	8.6
2004	73,082	9.9	39,460	5.3	60,180	8.1

Expectation of life (WHO estimates, years at birth): 81 (males 78; females 83) in 2003 (Source: WHO, *World Health Report*).

SWITZERLAND

EMPLOYMENT*
(April-June, '000 persons aged 15 years and over)

	2002	2003	2004
Agriculture, hunting, forestry and fishing	177	173	159
Mining and quarrying	6	5	5
Manufacturing	713	678	668
Electricity, gas and water supply	22	25	26
Construction	307	292	289
Wholesale and retail trade; repair of motor vehicles, motorcycles and personal and household goods	679	651	655
Hotels and restaurants	246	241	244
Transport, storage and communications	258	273	276
Financial intermediation	221	221	219
Real estate, renting and business activities	440	487	490
Public administration and defence; compulsory social security	158	166	171
Education	272	274	274
Health and social work	437	460	470
Other community, social and personal service activities	182	178	180
Private households with employed persons	63	54	58
Total employed	**4,180**	**4,177**	**4,185**
Males	2,329	2,322	2,327
Females	1,851	1,855	1,857

* Refers to workers who are employed for at least one hour per week, and includes foreign workers ('000): 1,058 in 2002; 1,052 in 2003; 1,061 in 2004.

Health and Welfare

KEY INDICATORS

Total fertility rate (children per woman, 2003)	1.4
Under-5 mortality rate (per 1,000 live births, 2004)	5
HIV/AIDS (% of persons aged 15–49, 2003)	0.4
Physicians (per 1,000 head, 2002)	3.60
Hospital beds (per 1,000 head, 2000)	17.90
Health expenditure (2002): US $ per head (PPP)	3,446
Health expenditure (2002): % of GDP	11.2
Health expenditure (2002): public (% of total)	57.9
Access to water (% of persons, 2002)	100
Access to sanitation (% of persons, 2002)	100
Human Development Index (2003): ranking	7
Human Development Index (2003): value	0.947

For sources and definitions, see explanatory note on p. vi.

Agriculture

PRINCIPAL CROPS
('000 metric tons)

	2002	2003	2004
Wheat	517.6	453.7	563.0
Barley	247.2	224.9	265.4
Maize	194.8	94.0	186.5
Rye	24.1	10.9	11.4
Oats	22.2	22.0	16.2
Triticale (wheat-rye hybrid)	92.6	70.1	85.4
Potatoes	526.2	468.0	526.7
Sugar beet	1,407.9	1,257.3	1,449.0
Rapeseed	48.7	44.4	56.5*
Cabbages	21.2	21.0	25.9*
Lettuces	32.7	31.0	37.5*
Tomatoes	26.7	24.5*	29.6*
Green onions and shallots	26.8	24.5*	29.8*
Carrots	67.9	62.4*	75.4*
Other fresh vegetables*	136.5	114.7	147.8
Apples	275.0	207.5	284.3
Pears	52.2	89.7	73.8
Grapes	145.5	126.6	151.9

* Unofficial figure(s).
Source: FAO.

LIVESTOCK
('000 head, year ending September)

	2002	2003	2004
Cattle	1,593.7	1,564.8	1,570.2
Horses	51.2	52.7	53.7
Pigs	1,556.7	1,528.5	1,537.5
Sheep	429.5	449.4	440.5
Goats	66.0	67.6	70.6
Chickens	7,206	7,440	7,913

Source: FAO.

LIVESTOCK PRODUCTS
('000 metric tons)

	2002	2003	2004
Beef and veal	139.6	136.7	133.9
Mutton and lamb	5.9	6.1	6.6
Pig meat	235.8	229.6	227.1
Poultry meat	54.2	56.3	59.7
Cows' milk	3,944.0	3,886.7	3,916.9
Goats' milk	17.0	17.5	19.0
Butter	42.3	41.0	41.5
Cheese	177.8	173.2	172.4
Poultry eggs	39.1	37.5	36.2

Source: FAO.

Forestry

ROUNDWOOD REMOVALS
('000 cubic metres, excluding bark)

	2002	2003	2004
Sawlogs, veneer logs and logs for sleepers	3,046	3,500	3,200
Pulpwood	520	513	500
Fuel wood	991	1,107	1,000
Total	**4,557**	**5,120**	**4,700**

Source: FAO.

SAWNWOOD PRODUCTION
('000 cubic metres, including railway sleepers)

	2002	2003	2004
Coniferous (softwood)	1,276	1,240	1,410
Broadleaved (hardwood)	116	105	95
Total	**1,392**	**1,345**	**1,505**

Source: FAO.

Fishing

(metric tons, live weight)

	2001	2002	2003
Capture	1,715	1,544	1,815
Roach	137	159	162
European perch	262	288	485
Whitefishes	1,205	977	1,021
Aquaculture	1,135	1,135	1,135
Rainbow trout	1,100	1,100	1,100
Total catch	**2,850**	**2,679**	**2,950**

Source: FAO.

SWITZERLAND

Industry

SELECTED PRODUCTS
('000 metric tons, unless otherwise indicated)

	2000	2001	2002
Cement*	3,720	3,920	3,771
Cigars (million)	163	186	167
Cigarettes (million)	34,299	33,565	37,160
Aluminium (unwrought, primary)*†	35.5	36.2	40.0
Flour (wheat)	395	395	n.a.
Chocolate and chocolate products	138.4	141.2	142.2
Motor spirit (petrol, '000 barrels)*	9,000	8,690	9,000
Distillate fuel oils ('000 barrels)*	9,500	3,036	3,000
Residual fuel oil ('000 barrels)*	5,500	3,397	3,500
Electric energy (million kWh)‡	68,722	71,915	n.a.

* Source: US Geological Survey.
† Source: World Metal Statistics, London.
‡ Including Liechtenstein.

Source (unless otherwise indicated): UN, *Industrial Commodity Statistics Yearbook*.

Watches ('000 exported): 17,840 in 1984; 25,137 in 1985; 28,075 in 1986.

New dwellings (units completed): 35,961 in 1997; 33,734 in 1998; 33,108 in 1999.

2003 ('000 barrels, unless otherwise indicated): Cement 3,700 ('000 metric tons); Aluminium (primary, unwrought) 43,538 (metric tons); Motor spirit (petrol) 9,000; Distillate fuel oils 3,000; Residual fuel oil 3,500 (Source: US Geological Survey).

2004 ('000 barrels, unless otherwise indicated): Cement 3,800 ('000 metric tons); Aluminium (primary, unwrought) 44,538 (metric tons); Motor spirit (petrol) 9,000; Distillate fuel oils 3,000; Residual fuel oil 3,500 (Source: US Geological Survey).

Finance

CURRENCY AND EXCHANGE RATES

Monetary Units
100 Rappen (centimes) = 1 Schweizer Franken (franc suisse) or Swiss franc.

Sterling, Dollar and Euro Equivalents (30 December 2005)
£1 sterling = 2.2631 francs;
US $1 = 1.3143 francs;
€1 = 1.5505 francs;
100 Swiss francs = £44.19 = $76.09 = €64.50.

Average Exchange Rates (Swiss francs per US $)
2003 1.3467
2004 1.2435
2005 1.2452

BUDGET
(million Swiss francs)*

Revenue†	2001	2002	2003
Taxes	93,764	95,697	94,568
Taxes on income and wealth	62,163	64,935	63,418
Income and wealth tax	43,440	45,591	45,986
Corporation and capital gains tax	14,075	12,615	12,118
Pre-paid tax	896	2,628	1,641
Other taxes on income and wealth	3,752	4,101	3,673
Stamp duty	3,453	2,819	2,624
Taxes on property and goods	1,843	1,895	1,937
Taxes on motor vehicles	1,725	1,774	1,820
Taxes on consumption	24,168	23,735	24,204
Value-added tax	17,033	16,857	17,156
Taxes on traffic	978	1,067	999
Customs duty	1,067	1,091	1,090
Agricultural duty	0	3	3
Duty from drivers	92	86	105
Duty from casinos	—	65	189
Other revenue	37,118	38,913	35,246
Total	130,882	134,610	129,814

Expenditure	2001	2002	2003
General administration	8,848	8,818	9,204
Public order and safety	7,185	7,514	7,872
Defence	5,338	5,162	5,066
Foreign relations	2,691	2,373	2,365
Education	24,074	25,786	26,560
Culture and leisure activities	4,170	4,187	4,212
Health	16,856	18,047	18,839
Social welfare	24,187	25,411	26,481
Transport and administration	14,097	14,671	14,024
Environment	4,938	4,909	4,897
National economy	7,134	7,058	6,466
Finances and taxes	10,448	10,317	9,825
Total	129,966	134,253	135,811

* Incorporates federal, cantonal and communal budgets, but excludes social security obligations. The consolidated accounts (including social security obligations) were (million Swiss francs): *Revenue:* 157,669 in 2001, 162,213 in 2002, 161,932 in 2003; *Expenditure:* 157,494 in 2001, 163,687 in 2002, 167,981 in 2003.
† Not including parish taxes.

2004 (million Swiss francs): Revenue 134,421; Expenditure 139,511.

2005 (million Swiss francs, budget proposals): Revenue 135,536; Expenditure 141,977.

Consolidated accounts (million Swiss francs, incl. social security obligations): *Revenue:* 165,763 in 2004; 165,935 in 2005*. *Expenditure:* 172,340 in 2004; 175,545 in 2005*.

* Budget proposals.

INTERNATIONAL RESERVES
(US $ million at 31 December)

	2003	2004	2005
Gold (national valuation)	21,932	19,123	21,342
IMF special drawing rights	37	71	60
Reserve position in IMF	2,056	1,792	816
Foreign exchange	45,560	53,634	35,421
Total	69,584	74,620	57,639

Source: IMF, *International Financial Statistics*.

MONEY SUPPLY
(million Swiss francs at 31 December)

	2003	2004	2005
Currency outside banks	42,927	42,139	43,835
Demand deposits at deposit money banks	194,487	181,917	194,729
Total money	237,414	224,056	238,564

Source: IMF, *International Financial Statistics*.

COST OF LIVING
(Consumer Price Index; annual averages; base: December 2005 = 100)

	2003	2004	2005
Foodstuffs	101.5	102.0	101.3
Alcoholic beverages and tobacco	91.4	94.6	99.0
Clothing and footwear	95.0	92.4	92.3
Housing and energy	94.3	95.8	98.7
Household equipment, etc.	100.2	100.4	100.4
Health	98.6	99.5	100.1
Transport	94.2	95.5	98.8
Communication	112.8	112.0	105.6
Education	96.4	97.9	99.0
Recreation and culture	100.7	100.3	99.7
Restaurants and hotels	97.9	98.9	100.0
Other goods and services	97.9	99.0	99.9
All items	97.5	98.3	99.4

SWITZERLAND

NATIONAL ACCOUNTS
(million Swiss francs at current prices)

National Income and Product

	2002	2003*	2004*
Compensation of employees	273,864	274,480	276,082
Operating surplus	67,734	70,740	77,114
Domestic factor incomes	341,598	345,220	353,196
Consumption of fixed capital	77,217	77,695	79,468
Gross domestic product (GDP) at factor cost	418,815	422,915	432,664
Indirect taxes	30,452	30,882	32,373
Less Subsidies	18,741	19,235	19,106
GDP in purchasers' values	430,527	434,562	445,931
Factor income received from abroad	63,679	83,367	87,582
Less Factor income paid abroad	39,239	39,429	40,770
Gross national product	454,967	478,500	492,743
Less Consumption of fixed capital	77,217	77,695	79,468
National income in market prices	377,750	400,805	413,275
Other current transfers from abroad	1,904	2,068	1,945
Less other current transfers to abroad	11,149	11,660	11,536
National disposable income in market prices	368,505	391,273	403,684

* Provisional figures.

Expenditure on the Gross Domestic Product

	2002	2003*	2004*
Final consumption expenditure	309,739	314,959	322,449
Households and non-profit institutions serving households	259,342	263,080	269,516
General government	50,398	51,879	52,932
Gross capital formation	93,310	91,148	90,792
Gross fixed capital formation	92,812	89,946	93,410
Changes in inventories	−427	−20	−3,320
Acquisitions, less disposals, of valuables	926	1,222	702
Total domestic expenditure	403,049	406,107	413,214
Exports of goods and services	187,974	188,594	206,052
Less Imports of goods and services	160,497	160,138	173,362
GDP in market prices	430,527	434,562	445,931

* Provisional figures.

Gross Domestic Product by Economic Activity

	2002	2003*
Agriculture, hunting, forestry and fishing	5,693	5,426
Mining and quarrying	769	730
Manufacturing	81,979	81,093
Chemicals and products of petroleum refining	14,504	14,649
Medical and optical instruments, and watches	10,685	10,967
Electricity and water	10,340	10,253
Construction	23,599	23,914
Wholesale and retail trade; repair of motor vehicles, motorcycles and personal and household goods	55,830	56,422
Hotels and restaurants	11,321	10,588
Transport, storage and communications	27,065	27,504
Financial intermediation	40,189	40,210
Insurance, real estate and business activities	65,425	66,117
Renting	30,416	31,366

—*continued*	2002	2003*
Public administration	45,778	46,934
Education	2,705	2,593
Health and social work	24,395	24,956
Other community, social and personal service activities	10,228	10,403
Sub-total	435,734	438,507
Less Financial intermediation services indirectly measured	29,618	28,913
Gross value added in basic prices	406,116	409,594
Taxes on products	28,372	28,770
Less Subsidies on products	−3,962	−3,801
GDP in market prices	430,527	434,562

* Provisional figures.

BALANCE OF PAYMENTS
(US $ million)

	2002	2003	2004
Exports of goods f.o.b.	100,786	115,443	138,225
Imports of goods f.o.b.	−94,139	−108,484	−122,487
Trade balance	6,647	6,958	15,737
Exports of services	30,305	35,236	43,019
Imports of services	−17,218	−19,039	−23,804
Balance on goods and services	19,734	23,156	34,953
Other income received	42,150	63,757	72,854
Other income paid	−31,167	−36,598	−43,508
Balance on goods, services and income	30,717	50,316	64,299
Current transfers received	10,599	13,162	14,170
Current transfers paid	−16,385	−18,552	−20,175
Current balance	24,930	44,925	58,294
Capital account (net)	−1,159	−667	−1,409
Direct investment abroad	−8,585	−15,673	−26,639
Direct investment from abroad	6,783	17,487	1,627
Portfolio investment assets	−29,159	−32,902	−42,412
Portfolio investment liabilities	7,483	−1,662	2,858
Other investment assets	−38,290	−4,631	−29,349
Other investment liabilities	38,591	12,383	29,344
Net errors and omissions	1,955	−15,855	9,303
Overall balance	2,549	3,405	1,618

Source: IMF, *International Financial Statistics*.

External Trade

Note: Swiss customs territory includes the Principality of Liechtenstein, the German enclave of Büssingen and the Italian commune of Campione, but excludes the free zone of the Samnaun Valley.

PRINCIPAL COMMODITIES
(million Swiss francs)

Imports c.i.f.	2001	2002	2003
Agricultural and forestry products	9,935.9	9,863.8	10,287.4
Mineral fuels	6,420.4	5,368.7	5,548.5
Textiles and items of clothing	8,993.4	8,624.6	8,538.3
Clothing (excl. footwear)	5,496.6	5,385.5	5,372.3
Paper, paperboard and graphics	4,867.9	4,739.8	4,735.7
Leather, rubber and plastic products	4,394.3	4,264.0	4,435.6
Chemical products	26,256.3	27,255.5	27,298.6
Chemical elements and unmoulded plastics	7,760.0	6,995.8	6,573.0
Pharmaceutical products	13,743.3	15,449.5	15,984.1
Metal products	6,161.8	5,766.2	6,022.6
Machinery (incl. electrical)	29,583.4	25,925.1	25,600.8
Industrial machinery	9,651.7	8,868.6	8,798.3
Office machines	7,773.1	6,445.4	5,916.9
Electronics	8,669.8	7,195.1	7,378.2
Passenger cars	8,407.0	7,767.7	7,626.3
Precision instruments	4,547.6	4,476.4	4,374.1
Precious metals and gemstones	10,243.1	5,961.8	4,814.6
Total (incl. others)	141,889.3	130,193.3	129,742.8

SWITZERLAND

Statistical Survey

Exports f.o.b.	2001	2002	2003
Agricultural and forestry products	4,387.6	4,218.7	4,341.0
Chemical products	41,832.5	44,845.7	45,029.5
Chemical elements and unmoulded plastics	5,539.3	5,933.8	5,783.0
Pharmaceutical products	27,737.8	30,754.9	30,873.0
Metals and metal products	10,453.5	9,743.5	9,918.6
Machinery (incl. electrical)	36,022.0	31,692.5	30,832.2
Industrial machinery	22,474.4	20,572.2	19,907.8
Electronics	9,904.8	8,500.7	8,432.1
Precision instruments	8,396.1	8,901.5	9,696.8
Clocks and watches	10,653.5	10,639.8	10,176.9
Precious metals and gemstones	5,647.0	4,805.9	3,737.2
Total (incl. others)	138,491.7	136,522.9	135,405.0

PRINCIPAL TRADING PARTNERS
(million Swiss francs)*

Imports c.i.f.	2001	2002	2003
Austria	5,080.4	5,273.7	5,487.4
Belgium	4,237.9	3,852.5	3,943.0
China, People's Republic	2,257.7	2,206.9	2,413.9
France	14,555.0	13,014.9	13,983.3
Germany	42,743.7	40,868.7	41,895.5
Ireland	5,328.3	5,131.7	4,794.1
Italy	13,315.5	13,414.8	13,854.0
Japan	3,390.8	2,619.1	2,728.5
Netherlands	7,650.3	6,651.6	6,475.1
Russia	4,768.9	1,527.1	1,175.6
Spain	2,493.4	2,635.3	3,040.5
Sweden	1,486.7	1,494.6	1,660.8
United Kingdom	8,180.5	6,315.1	5,260.2
USA	8,381.7	7,987.1	6,634.8
Total (incl. others)	141,889.3	130,193.3	129,742.8

Exports f.o.b.	2001	2002	2003
Austria	4,472.7	4,543.1	4,469.4
Belgium	2,713.2	2,851.2	2,649.4
Canada	1,377.0	1,547.1	1,428.9
China, People's Republic	1,668.2	2,046.5	2,460.0
France	12,386.0	12,450.1	11,815.1
Germany	30,013.9	27,876.3	28,217.3
Hong Kong	4,039.3	4,479.7	4,002.2
Israel	1,276.6	644.1	626.6
Italy	11,038.7	11,215.6	11,186.0
Japan	5,383.1	5,179.4	5,405.7
Netherlands	4,222.8	4,092.2	4,402.1
Singapore	1,580.3	1,518.1	1,358.7
Spain	4,353.1	4,528.1	4,744.0
Sweden	1,611.9	1,475.4	1,620.2
Turkey	1,203.3	1,586.8	1,650.2
United Kingdom	7,677.3	7,011.2	6,582.1
USA	15,660.2	15,880.0	14,943.4
Total (incl. others)	138,491.7	136,522.9	135,405.0

* Imports by country of production; exports by country of consumption.

Transport

RAILWAY TRAFFIC

	2001	2002	2003
Passengers carried (million)*	301	319	327
Passenger-kilometres (million)	13,301	14,147	14,509
Freight carried (million metric tons)	62.9	60.9	62.4
Freight ton-kilometres (million)†	11,172	10,746	10,565

* Excluding multiple journeys.
† Net ton-kilometres (excl. weight of containers, etc.): 10,091 in 2001; 9,639 in 2002; 9,534 in 2003.

ROAD TRAFFIC
(motor vehicles in use at 30 September)

	2003	2004	2005
Passenger cars	3,753,890	3,811,351	3,863,807
Buses and coaches	43,629	44,784	45,785
Lorries and vans	292,329	298,193	307,264
Agricultural vehicles	180,295	180,898	182,093
Other industrial vehicles	50,795	50,957	51,860
Motorcycles	567,358	583,010	592,194

INLAND WATERWAYS
(freight traffic at port of Basel, '000 metric tons)

	1996	1997	1998
Goods loaded	876.9	837.5	688.4
Goods unloaded	6,283.4	7,002.4	7,420.3

Source: Federal Department of Transport.

SHIPPING

Merchant Fleet
(at 31 December)

	2002	2003	2004
Number of vessels	24	25	23
Displacement ('000 grt)	559.1	588.7	487.5

Source: Lloyds Register-Fairplay, *World Fleet Statistics*.

CIVIL AVIATION
(traffic on scheduled services)

	1999	2000	2001
Kilometres flown (million)	295	317	304
Passengers carried ('000)	16,209	17,268	16,915
Passenger-kilometres (million)	33,309	36,625	33,470
Total ton-kilometres (million)	5,195	5,616	4,970

Source: UN, *Statistical Yearbook*.

Tourism

FOREIGN TOURIST ARRIVALS
(at hotels, and similar establishments)

Country of residence	2001	2002	2003
Belgium	208,505	197,957	191,463
France	502,797	488,817	488,468
Germany	2,179,224	1,952,214	1,881,932
Italy	438,736	429,436	434,515
Japan	522,674	416,306	320,593
Netherlands	312,080	289,118	284,982
Spain	156,045	146,149	137,904
United Kingdom	661,497	619,313	612,435
USA	827,155	688,820	598,046
Total (incl. others)	7,454,855	6,867,696	6,530,112

Tourism receipts (US $ million, incl. passenger transport): 10,013 in 2001; 9,745 in 2002; 11,344 in 2003 (Source: World Tourism Organization).

Communications Media

	2002	2003	2004
Telephones ('000 main lines in use)	5,419.0	5,323.5	5,250.0
Mobile cellular telephones ('000 subscribers)	5,736.3	6,172.0	6,275.0
Personal computers ('000 in use)	5,160	n.a.	6,105
Internet users ('000)	2,556	2,916	3,500
Books published (titles)	10,817	11,226	10,376
Newspapers:			
number	224	224	216
circulation ('000)	2,513.8	2,490.3	2,415.3

Source: mainly International Telecommunication Union.

Television receivers ('000 in use): 4,000 in 2001.

Facsimile machines ('000 in use, 1996): 207.

Radio licences ('000, 1996): 2,805.

Education

(2004)

	Institutions	Teachers	Students
Pre-primary	4,825	11,900	156,157
Compulsory education*		72,900	
Primary	5,760	41,300	810,315
Compulsory secondary		31,600	
Upper secondary	1,196	10,600	
General	405	10,600	312,851
Vocational	791	n.a.	
Higher	351	69,050	
Vocational	331	n.a.	
Universities of applied sciences†	8	25,479‡	200,777
Universities	13	43,571‡	

* Excluding schools with special curricula.
† Excluding teacher-training colleges and other institutions offering courses of study at a similar level that are not integrated within the seven technical colleges.
‡ Including teaching assistants and administrative and technical personnel.

Directory

The Constitution

The Constitution (summarized below) was adopted on 29 May 1874. A revised version of the Constitution, which included new provision for the right to undertake strike action by the labour force, was approved by 59.2% of voters at a federal referendum on 18 April 1999 and entered into force in January 2000.

Switzerland is divided into federated cantons, which have sovereign authority except where the Constitution defines limits to their powers or accords responsibility to the Federal authority. After a referendum in September 1978, the Constitution was amended to allow for the formation of the canton of Jura, increasing the number of cantons to 23 (three of these are sub-divided and they are sometimes collectively referred to as the 26 states).

Principally, the Federal authority is responsible for civil, penal and commercial law, legislation concerning marriage, residence and settlement, export and import duties, defence, postal and telecommunications services, the mint, forestry, hunting and fishing, hydro-electric power, the economy, railways, important roads and bridges, social insurance, and international affairs. Administration is largely in the hands of the cantons, and in the combined management of Federal authorities and cantons. The cantons derive their revenue from direct taxation. The Federal authority draws its revenue from direct and indirect taxation. The profits from Federal enterprises and customs duties are received by the Federal authorities.

COMMUNES

Each of the more than 3,000 communes of Switzerland has local autonomy over such matters as public utilities and roads, and grants primary citizenship. Decisions are made by communal assemblies. The smallest communes have fewer than 20 inhabitants, the largest, Zürich, around 370,000.

CANTONS

The 26 cantons and half-cantons of the Swiss Confederation each have their own constitution and their own method of choosing the members of the cantonal assembly and cantonal government and the States Councillors who represent them at the federal level. Five cantons, Glarus, Appenzell Ausserrhoden and Innerrhoden, Obwalden and Nidwalden, retain the Landsgemeinde, an assembly of all citizens of the canton held annually, as their decision-making authority. Elsewhere, democracy is less direct, the secret ballot and the referendum having replaced the mass assembly.

FEDERAL ASSEMBLY

The Federal Assembly (Bundesversammlung/Assemblée Fédérale) is the supreme governing body of the Confederation. It is composed of two bodies, the National Council (Nationalrat/Conseil National) and the Council of States (Ständerat/Conseil des Etats), which deliberate separately. The 200 members of the National Council are elected directly, by proportional representation, every four years. The minimum age for voting and eligibility for election in the Confederation is 18 years. In 1971 women gained full political rights at federal level and in almost all the cantons (female suffrage had been introduced in all cantons by late 1990). The Council of States represents the cantons, each of which sends two councillors, elected by the people in various ways according to the cantonal constitutions. Legislative and fiscal measures must be accepted by both houses in order to be adopted, and the Federal Assembly supervises the army, the civil service and the application of the law, exercises the right of pardon and elects the Federal Supreme Court, the Federal Insurance Court, the General who commands the army in times of crisis, and the Federal Council.

FEDERAL COUNCIL

Executive authority is vested in the Federal Council, whose members are each in charge of a Federal Department. Each year the Federal Assembly appoints the President and Vice-President of the Confederation from among the Federal Councillors. Generally, the Councillors are chosen from the members of the Federal Assembly for four years after every general election.

REFERENDUMS AND INITIATIVES

Referendums are held on both cantonal and federal levels. In many cantons all legislation has to be accepted by a majority of the voters, and in some cantons major financial matters have to be submitted to the popular vote. In federal affairs the consent of a majority of the voters and of the cantons must be obtained for amendments to the Federal Constitution, for extraconstitutional emergency legislation and for the decision to join collective security organizations or international bodies, but referendums are optional for other legislation. A petition from 50,000 voters is needed to bring about a national referendum, which can accept or reject any legislation that has been passed by Parliament. The initiative gives voters in many cantons the right to propose a constitutional or legislative amendment and to demand a popular vote on it. A petition by 100,000 voters is needed to initiate a vote on an amendment to the Federal Constitution, but as federal laws cannot be proposed by means of an initiative, some constitutional amendments introduced in this manner concern relatively unimportant matters and participation of the voters is, on average, 30% to 45%. The initiative is also used by the political opposition to effect changes in government policy.

The Government

FEDERAL COUNCIL
(April 2006)

President of the Swiss Confederation for 2006 and Head of the Federal Department of Environment, Transport, Energy and Communications: MORITZ LEUENBERGER (Social Democratic Party).

Vice-President and Head of the Federal Department of Foreign Affairs: MICHELINE CALMY-REY (Social Democratic Party).

SWITZERLAND

Head of the Federal Department of Defence, Civil Protection and Sports: SAMUEL SCHMID (Swiss People's Party).
Head of the Federal Department of Economic Affairs: JOSEPH DEISS (Christian Democratic People's Party).
Head of the Federal Department of Home Affairs: PASCAL COUCHEPIN (Radical Democratic Party).
Head of the Federal Department of Justice and Police: CHRISTOPH BLOCHER (Swiss People's Party).
Head of the Federal Department of Finance: HANS-RUDOLF MERZ (Radical Democratic Party).
Chancellor of the Swiss Confederation: ANNEMARIE HUBER-HOTZ (Radical Democratic Party).

FEDERAL DEPARTMENTS

Federal Chancellery: Bundeshaus West, 3003 Bern; tel. 313222111; fax 313223706; e-mail webmaster@admin.ch; internet www.admin.ch.

Federal Department of Defence, Civil Protection and Sports: Bundeshaus Ost, 3003 Bern; tel. 313241211; fax 313235782; e-mail postmaster@gs-vbs.admin.ch; internet www.vbs-ddps.admin.ch.

Federal Department of Economic Affairs: Bundeshaus Ost, 3003 Bern; tel. 313222007; fax 313222194; e-mail info@gs-evd.admin.ch; internet www.evd.admin.ch.

Federal Department of Environment, Transport, Energy and Communications: Bundeshaus Nord, 3003 Bern; tel. 313225511; fax 313119576; e-mail webmaster@gs-uvek.admin.ch; internet www.uvek.admin.ch.

Federal Department of Finance: Bernerhof, Bundesgasse 3, 3003 Bern; tel. 313226033; fax 313233852; e-mail info@gs-efd.admin.ch; internet www.efd.admin.ch.

Federal Department of Foreign Affairs: Bundeshaus West, 3003 Bern; tel. 313222111; fax 31334041; e-mail info@eda.admin.ch; internet www.eda.admin.ch.

Federal Department of Home Affairs: Bundeshaus, Inselgasse, 3003 Bern; tel. 313229111; fax 313227901; e-mail info@gs-edi.admin.ch; internet www.edi.admin.ch.

Federal Department of Justice and Police: Bundeshaus West, Bundesgasse, 3003 Bern; tel. 313222111; fax 313224082; e-mail info@gs-ejpd.admin.ch; internet www.ejpd.admin.ch.

Legislature

BUNDESVERSAMMLUNG/ASSEMBLÉE FÉDÉRALE
(Federal Assembly)

Nationalrat/Conseil National
(National Council)

President: CLAUDE JANIAK (2005/06).
General Election, 19 October 2003

	Seats
Swiss People's Party	55
Social Democratic Party	52
Radical Democratic Party	36
Christian Democratic People's Party	28
Green Party	13
Liberal Party	4
Evangelical People's Party	3
Workers' Party	2
Union of Federal Democrats	2
Union of Ticino	1
Swiss Democrats	1
Christian Socialist Party	1
Links-Alternative	1
Socialist Solidarity Group	1
Total	**200**

Ständerat/Conseil des Etats
(Council of States)

President: ROLF BÜTTIKER (2005/06).

Elections, 2003

	Seats
Christian Democratic People's Party	15
Radical Democratic Party	14
Social Democratic Party	9
Swiss People's Party	8
Total	**46**

Note: Members are elected by canton; method and period of election differs from canton to canton

Political Organizations

Christlichdemokratische Volkspartei der Schweiz—Parti démocrate-chrétien suisse (Christian Democratic People's Party): Klaraweg 6, Postfach 5835, 3001 Bern; tel. 313573333; fax 313522430; e-mail info@cvp.ch; internet www.cvp.ch; f. 1912; advocates a Christian outlook on world affairs, federalism and Christian social reform by means of professional asscns; non-sectarian; Pres. DORIS LEUTHARD; Gen. Sec. RETO NAUSE; Leader of Parliamentary Group URS SCHWALLER.

Christlichsoziale Partei—Parti chrétien-social (Christian Socialist Party): Widenstr. 26, 6317 Oberwil-Zug; tel. 417116957; fax 417116947; e-mail monikamathers@gmx.ch; Sec. MONIKA MATHERS-SCHREGENBERGER.

Eidgenössisch-Demokratische Union—Union Démocratique Fédérale (Union of Federal Democrats): Postfach 2144, 3601 Thun; tel. 332223637; fax 332223744; e-mail info@edu-udf.ch; internet www.edu-udf.ch; Pres. HANS MOSER.

Evangelische Volkspartei der Schweiz—Parti évangélique suisse (Protestant People's Party): Josefstr. 32, Postfach 7334, 8023 Zürich; tel. 442727100; fax 442721437; e-mail info@evppev.ch; internet www.evppev.ch; f. 1919; Pres. RUEDI AESCHBACHER; Sec. JOEL BLUNIER.

Freiheits-Partei der Schweiz—Die Auto-Partei (Automobile Party): Postfach, 4622 Egerkingen; tel. 913890040; fax 913890045; e-mail fps@bluewin.ch; internet www.freiheits-partei.ch; f. 1985 to support motorists' rights; has subsequently campaigned for restricted immigration; Pres. JÜRG SCHERRER.

Freisinnig-Demokratische Partei der Schweiz—Parti radical-démocratique suisse (Radical Democratic Party): Postfach 6136, 3001 Bern; tel. 313203535; fax 313203500; e-mail gs@fdp.ch; internet www.fdp.ch; led the movement that gave rise to the Federative State and the Constitution of 1848; promotes a strong Fed. Govt, while respecting the legitimate rights of the cantons and all the minorities; liberal democratic principles; Pres. Dr FULVIO PELLI; Sec. GUIDO SCHOMMER; Leader of Parliamentary Group FELIX GUTZWILLER.

Grüne Partei der Schweiz—Parti écologiste suisse (Green Party of Switzerland): Waisenhauspl. 21, 3011 Bern; tel. 313126660; fax 313126662; e-mail gruene@gruene.ch; internet www.gruene.ch; f. 1983; Pres RUTH GENNER; Gen. Sec. HUBERT ZURKINDEN; Leader of Parliamentary Group CÉCILE BÜHLMANN.

Grünes Bündnis—Alliance verte et sociale (Green Alliance): Postfach 6411, 3001 Bern; tel. 313018209; fax 313028878; Sec. REGULA RYTZ.

Lega dei Ticinesi (Union of Ticino): via Monte Boglia 7, CP 2311, 6901 Lugano; tel. 919713033; fax 919727492; Pres. GIULIANO BIGNASCA; Sec. MAURO MALANDRA.

Liberale Partei der Schweiz—Parti libéral suisse (Liberal Party): Postfach 7107, Spitalgasse 32, 3001 Bern; tel. 313116404; fax 313125474; e-mail info@liberal.ch; internet www.liberal.ch; opposes centralizing tendencies; Pres. CLAUDE RUEY; Sec. CHRISTOPHE BERDAT; Leader of Parliamentary Group RÉMY SCHEURER.

Partei der Arbeit der Schweiz—Parti suisse du travail (Workers' Party): 25 rue du Vieux-Billard, CP 232, 1211 Geneva 8; tel. 223222290; fax 223222295; e-mail secret-pst-pda@gouvernement.ch; internet www.pst.ch; f. 1944; by Communist Party mems and left-wing Socialists; Pres. ALAIN BRINGOLF.

Progressive Organisationen der Schweiz—Organisations progressistes suisses (Progressive Swiss Orgs): Postfach 1461, Aarauerstr. 7, 4600 Olten; tel. 62266707; f. 1973; left-wing; Secs GEORGES DEGEN, EDUARD HAFNER.

Schweizer Demokraten—Démocrates suisses (Swiss Democrats): Postfach 8116, 3001 Bern; tel. 319742010; fax 319742011; fmrly Nationale Aktion für Volk und Heimat—Action nationale; 6,000 mems; main objectives are preservation of the country's political independence and of individual freedom, protection of the environment, and a population policy restricting the number of immigrants; Pres. BERNARD HESS; Gen. Sec. ROLAND SCHÖNI.

Schweizerische Volkspartei—Union démocratique du centre (Swiss People's Party): Brückfeldstr. 18, 3000 Bern 26; tel. 313005858; fax 313005859; e-mail gs@svp.ch; internet www.svp.ch; f. 1971; Pres. UELI MAURER; Gen. Sec. GREGOR A. RUTZ; Leader of Parliamentary Group CASPAR BAADER.

Sozialdemokratische Partei der Schweiz—Parti socialiste suisse (Social Democratic Party): Spitalgasse 34, 3001 Bern; tel. 313296969; fax 313296970; e-mail info@spschweiz.ch; internet www.spschweiz.ch; f. 1888; bases its policy on democratic socialism; mem. of Socialist International and assoc. mem. of Party of European Socialists; 43,000 mems; Pres. HANS-JÜRG FEHR; Sec.-Gen. THOMAS CHRISTEN; Leader of Parliamentary Group HILDEGARD FÄSSLER; International Sec. PETER HUG.

Partito Socialista, sezione ticinese PSS (Socialist Party): Piazza Governo 4, 6500 Bellinzona; tel. 918259462; fax 918259601; e-mail segreteria@ps-ticino.ch; f. 1992; fmrly the Partito Socialista Unitario; Pres. MANUELE BERTOLI.

Diplomatic Representation

EMBASSIES IN SWITZERLAND

Albania: Pourtalèsstr. 45A, 3074 Muri bei Bern; tel. 319526010; fax 319526012; e-mail emalb.ch@bluewin.ch; Ambassador MEHMET ELEZI.

Algeria: Willadingweg 74, 3000 Bern 15; tel. 313501050; fax 313501059; e-mail mbcybs@bluewin.ch; Ambassador ABDELMALEK GUENAIZIA.

Argentina: Jungfraustr. 1, 3005 Bern; tel. 313564343; fax 313564340; e-mail resembar@freesurf.ch; Ambassador GUILLERMO GONZALEZ.

Austria: Kirchenfeldstr. 77–79, 3005 Bern; tel. 313565252; fax 313515664; e-mail bern-ob@bmaa.gv.at; internet www.aussenministerium.at/bern; Ambassador Dr AUREL SAUPE.

Belarus: Quartierweg 6, CP 438, 3074 Muri bei Bern; tel. 319527914; fax 319527616; e-mail swiss@belembassy.org; Ambassador VLADIMIR KOROLEV.

Belgium: Jubiläumstr. 41, 3005 Bern; tel. 313500150; fax 313500165; e-mail bern@diplobel.org; Ambassador MARC BAPTIST.

Bosnia and Herzegovina: Thorackerstr. 3, 3074 Muri bei Bern; tel. 313511052; fax 313511079; e-mail emb-ch-brn@tiscalinet.ch; Ambassador JASMINA PAŠALIĆ.

Brazil: Monbijoustr. 68, 3007 Bern; POB 30, 3000 Bern 23; tel. 313718515; fax 313710525; e-mail brasbern@iprolink.ch; Ambassador CELINA MARIA ASSUMPÇÃO DO VALLE PEREIRA.

Bulgaria: Bernastr. 2–4, 3005 Bern; tel. 313511455; fax 313510064; e-mail bulembassy@bluewin.ch; internet www.bulembassy.ch; Ambassador ATANAS PAVLOV.

Cameroon: Brunnadernrain 29, 3006 Bern; tel. 313524734; fax 313524737; e-mail ambassade-cameroun@tiscalinet.ch; Ambassador FRANÇOIS-XAVIER NGOUBEYOU.

Canada: Kirchenfeldstr. 88, 3005 Bern; tel. 313573200; fax 313573210; e-mail bern@international.gc.ca; internet www.international.gc.ca/switzerland; Ambassador ROBERT COLLETTE.

Chile: 12th Floor, Eigerpl. 5, 3007 Bern; tel. 313700058; fax 313720025; e-mail embajada@embachile.ch; Ambassador CECILIA MACKENNA.

China, People's Republic: Kalcheggweg 10, 3006 Bern; tel. 313527333; fax 313514573; internet www.china-embassy.ch; Ambassador ZHU BANGZAO.

Colombia: Dufourstr. 47, 3005 Bern; tel. 313511700; fax 313527072; e-mail colombie@iprolink.ch; internet www.emcol.ch; Ambassador ELENA ECHAVARRIA OLANO.

Congo, Democratic Republic: Sulgenheimweg 21, 3007 Bern; tel. 313713538; fax 313727466; e-mail rdcambassy@bluewin.ch; Ambassador NDEZE MATABARO.

Costa Rica: Schwarztorstr. 11, 3007 Bern; tel. 313727887; fax 313727834; e-mail embajada.costa.rica@thenet.ch; Ambassador ISABEL MONTERO DE LA CÁMARA DE MEISSNER.

Côte d'Ivoire: POB 170, 3000 Bern 6; Thormannstr. 51, 3005 Bern; tel. 313508080; fax 313508081; e-mail acibe-1@acibe.org; internet www.acibe.org; Ambassador N'GORAN KOUAME.

Croatia: Thunstr. 45, 3005 Bern; tel. 313520275; fax 313520373; e-mail croemb.bern@mvp.hr; Ambassador Dr MLADEN ANDRLIC.

Cuba: Gesellschaftsstr. 8, CP 5275, 3012 Bern; tel. 313022111; fax 313029830; e-mail embacuba.berna@bluewin.ch; Ambassador TERESITA VICENTE SOTOLONGO.

Czech Republic: Muristr. 53, Postfach 537, 3000 Bern 31; tel. 313504070; fax 313504098; e-mail bern@embassy.mzv.cz; internet www.mfa.cz/bern; Ambassador JOSEF KREUTER.

Denmark: Thunstr. 95, 3006 Bern; tel. 313505454; fax 313505464; e-mail brnamb@um.dk; internet www.denmark.ch; Ambassador BJARNE BLADBJERG.

Dominican Republic: Wettposstr. 4, Postfach 22, 3000 Bern 15; tel. 313511585; fax 313511589; e-mail embaj.rep-dom@freesurf.ch.

Ecuador: Kramgasse 54, 3011 Bern; tel. 313511755; fax 313512771; e-mail embecusuiza@bluewin.ch; Ambassador Dr JAIME MARCHAN.

Egypt: Elfenauweg 61, 3006 Bern; tel. 313528012; fax 3135280625; Ambassador NIHAD ZIKRY.

Finland: Weltpoststr. 4, Postfach 11, 3015 Bern; tel. 313504100; fax 313504107; e-mail sanomat.brn@formin.fi; Ambassador PEKKA OJANEN.

France: Schosshaldenstr. 46, 3006 Bern; tel. 313592111; fax 313592191; e-mail scac@ambafrance-ch.org; internet www.ambafrance-ch.org; Ambassador JEAN-DIDIER ROISIN.

Germany: Willadingweg 83, Postfach 250, 3000 Bern 15; tel. 313594111; fax 313594444; e-mail poststelle@deutsche-botschaft.ch; internet www.bern.diplo.de; Ambassador ANDREAS VON STECHOW.

Ghana: Belpstr. 11, Postfach, 3001 Bern; tel. 313817852; fax 313814941; e-mail ghanaemb@tcnet.ch; Ambassador (vacant).

Greece: Bern; tel. 313561414; fax 313681272; e-mail gremb.brn@mfa.gr; Ambassador JOHN THOMOGLOU.

Holy See: Thunstr. 60, 3006 Bern (Apostolic Nunciature); tel. 313526040; fax 313525064; e-mail nunziatura-ch@datacomm.ch; Apostolic Nuncio Most Rev. FRANCESCO CANALINI (Titular Archbishop of Valeria).

Hungary: Muristr. 31, Postfach 216, 3000 Bern 15; tel. 313528572; fax 313512001; e-mail huembbrn@bluemail.ch; internet www.hungemb.ch; Ambassador JENŐ BOROS.

India: Kirchenfeldstr. 28, 3006 Bern; tel. 313511110; fax 313511557; e-mail india@spectraweb.ch; internet www.indembassybern.ch; Ambassador SHRI ARMITAVA TRIPATHI.

Indonesia: Elfenauweg 51, 3006 Bern; tel. 313520983; fax 313516765; e-mail kbribern@bgb.ch; internet www.indonesia-bern.org; Ambassador TATI SUMIYATI DARSOYO.

Iran: Thunstr. 68, 3006 Bern; tel. 313510801; fax 313515652; e-mail ambassador@iranembassy.ch; internet www.iranembassy.ch; Ambassador MAJID TAKHT RAVANCHI.

Ireland: Kirchenfeldstr. 68, 3005 Bern; tel. 313521442; fax 313521455; e-mail irlemb@bluewin.ch; Ambassador JOSEPH LYNCH.

Israel: Alpenstr. 32, 3006 Bern; tel. 313563588; fax 313563556; e-mail info@bern.mfa.gov.il; internet bern.mfa.gov.il; Ambassador AVIV SHIR-ON.

Italy: Elfenstr. 14, 3000 Bern 16; tel. 313500777; fax 313500711; e-mail ambasciata.berna@esteri.it; internet sedi.esteri.it/berna; Ambassador PIER BENEDETTO FRANCESE.

Japan: Engestr. 53, Postfach, 3000 Bern 9; tel. 313002222; fax 313002255; e-mail eojs@bluewin.ch; internet www.ch.emb-japan.go.jp; Ambassador YUJI NAKAMURA.

Jordan: Belpstr. 11, 3007 Bern; tel. 313810404; fax 313810405; e-mail jordanie@bluewin.ch; internet www.jordanie.ch; Ambassador MUHAMMAD AMIN SHAHANKARI.

Kazakhstan: Alleeweg 15, 3006 Bern; tel. 313517972; fax 313517975; e-mail mission.kazakstan@ties.itu.int; internet missions.itu.int/~kazaks; Ambassador ABUSEITOV KAIRAT HUATOVICH.

Korea, Democratic People's Republic: Pourtalèsstr. 43, 3074 Muri bei Bern; tel. 319516621; fax 319515704; e-mail dprk.embassy@bluewin.ch; Ambassador RI CHOL.

Korea, Republic: Kalcheggweg 38, 3006 Bern; tel. 313562444; fax 313562450; e-mail swiss@mofat.go.kr; internet www.mofat.go.kr/switzerland; Ambassador PARK WON-HWA.

Lebanon: Thunstr. 10, 3074 Muri bei Bern; tel. 319506565; fax 319506566; e-mail ambalibch@hotmail.com; Ambassador INAAM OSSEIRAN.

Libya: 25 rue Richemond, 1202 Geneva; tel. 229598900; fax 229598910; Ambassador NAJAT AL-HAJJAJI.

Liechtenstein: Willadingweg 65, Postfach, 3000 Bern 15; tel. 313576411; fax 313576415; e-mail info@bbrn.liv.li; internet www.bern.liechtenstein.li; Ambassador Prince STEFAN of Liechtenstein.

Luxembourg: Kramgasse 45, 3000 Bern 8; tel. 313114732; fax 313110019; e-mail berne.am@mae.etat.lu; Ambassador YVES SPAUTZ.

Macedonia, former Yugoslav republic: Kirchenfeldstr. 30, 3005 Bern; tel. 313520002; fax 313520057; e-mail makedamb@bluewin.ch.

SWITZERLAND

Malaysia: Jungfraustr. 1, 3005 Bern; tel. 313504700; fax 313504702; e-mail malberne@greenmail.ch; Ambassador Dato' ISMAIL MUSTAPHA.

Mali: 20 route du Pré-Bois, CP 1814, 1215 Geneva 15 Aéroport; tel. 227100960; fax 227100969; Ambassador LOUIS MARIE JOSEPH BASTIDE.

Mexico: Bernastr. 57, 3005 Bern; tel. 313574747; fax 313574748; e-mail embamex1@swissonline.ch; internet www.sre.gob.mx/suiza; Ambassador JOSÉ LUIS BERNAL RODRIGUEZ.

Monaco: Hallwylstr. 34, 3005 Bern; tel. 313562858; fax 313562855; e-mail ambassademonaco@bluewin.ch; Ambassador PHILIPPE BLANCHI.

Morocco: Helvetiastr. 42, 3005 Bern; tel. 313510362; fax 313510364; e-mail sifamaberne2@bluewin.ch; internet www.amb-maroc.ch; Ambassador MOHAMMED GUEDIRA.

Netherlands: Kollerweg 11, Postfach 261, 3000 Bern 6; tel. 313508700; fax 313508710; e-mail nlgovben@nlembassy.ch; internet www.nlembassy.ch; Ambassador EDO HOFLAND.

Nigeria: Zieglerstr. 45, Postfach 574, 3007 Bern; tel. 313842600; fax 313842619; e-mail juayalogu@nigeriabern.org; internet www.nigeriabern.org; Ambassador JOSEPH U. AYALOGU.

Norway: Bubenbergpl. 10, Postfach 5264, 3011 Bern; tel. 313105555; fax 313105550; e-mail emb.bern@mfa.no; internet www.amb-norwegen.ch; Ambassador LARS PETER FORBERG.

Pakistan: Bernastr. 47, 3005 Bern; tel. 313501790; fax 313501799; e-mail parepberne@bluewin.ch; Ambassador TAYYAB SIDDIQUI.

Paraguay: Kramgasse 58, Postfach 523, 3000 Bern 8; tel. 313123222; fax 313123234; e-mail embapar@embapar.ch.

Peru: Thunstr. 36, 3005 Bern; tel. 313518555; fax 313518570; e-mail lepruberna02@bluewin.ch; Ambassador CARLOS PAREJA.

Philippines: Kirchenfeldstr. 73–75, 3005 Bern; tel. 313501717; fax 313522602; e-mail berne_pe@bluewin.ch; internet www.mypage.bluewin.ch/berne_pe; Ambassador RORA NAVARRO-TOLENTINO.

Poland: Elfenstr. 20A, 3000 Bern 16; tel. 313580202; fax 313580216; e-mail polishemb@dial.eunet.ch; internet www.pol-amb.ch; Ambassador JANUSZ NIESYTO.

Portugal: Weltpoststr. 20, 3015 Bern; tel. 313528329; fax 313514432; e-mail embpt.berna@scber.dgaccp.pt; Ambassador MANUEL CORTE-REAL.

Romania: Kirchenfeldstr. 78, 3005 Bern; tel. 313523522; fax 313526455; e-mail amb@befree.ch; internet roembassy-berne.ew.ro; Ambassador IOAN MAXIM.

Russia: Brunnadernrain 37, 3006 Bern; tel. 313520566; fax 313525595; e-mail rusbotschaft@bluewin.ch; internet www.switzerland.mid.ru; Ambassador DMITRI CHERKASHIN.

Saudi Arabia: Kramburgstr. 12, 3006 Bern; tel. 313521555; fax 313521556; e-mail saudia.be@bluewin.ch; Chargé d'affaires a.i. IBRAHIM AMMAR.

Serbia and Montenegro: Seminarstr. 5, 3006 Bern; tel. 313526353; fax 313514474; e-mail info@yuamb.ch; internet www.yuamb.ch; Ambassador DRAGAN MARŠIĆANIN.

Slovakia: Thunstr. 99, 3006 Bern 1; tel. 313563930; fax 313563933; e-mail slovak@spectraweb.ch; Ambassador STEFAN SCHILL.

Slovenia: Schwanengasse 9, 3011 Bern; tel. 313109000; fax 313124414; e-mail vbe@mzz-dkp.gov.si; Ambassador MIHA VRHUNEC.

South Africa: Alpenstr. 29, Postfach, 3000 Bern 6; tel. 313501313; fax 313501310; e-mail political@southafrica.ch; internet www.southafrica.ch; Chargé d'affaires a.i. JOHANNES VAN NIEKERK.

Spain: Kalcheggweg 24, Postfach 99, 3016 Bern; tel. 313505252; fax 313505255; e-mail ambespch@mail.mae.es; Ambassador GONZALO DE BENITO SECADES.

Sweden: Bundesgasse 26, Postfach, 3001 Bern; tel. 313287000; fax 313287001; e-mail ambassaden.bern@foreign.ministry.se; Ambassador LARS MAGNUSON.

Thailand: Kirchstr. 56, 3097 Liebefeld-Bern; tel. 319703030; fax 319703035; e-mail thai.bern@bluewin.ch; Ambassador PRADAP PIBULSONGGRAM.

Tunisia: Kirchenfeldstr. 63, 3005 Bern; tel. 313528226; fax 313510445; e-mail at.berne@bluewin.ch; Ambassador AFIF HENDAOUI.

Turkey: Lombachweg 33, 3006 Bern; tel. 313597070; fax 313528819; e-mail tcbern@tr-botschaft.ch; internet www.tr-botschaft.ch; Ambassador ALEV KILIÇ.

Ukraine: Feldeggweg 5, 3005 Bern; tel. 313522316; fax 313516416; e-mail emb_ch@mfa.gov.ua; internet www.ukremb.ch; Ambassador (vacant).

United Kingdom: Thunstr. 50, 3000 Bern 15; tel. 313597700; fax 313597701; e-mail info@britain-in-switzerland.ch; internet www.britain-in-switzerland.ch; Ambassador SIMON FEATHERSTONE.

USA: Jubiläumsstr. 93, 3005 Bern; tel. 313577011; fax 313577344; internet bern.usembassy.gov; Ambassador PAMELA PITZER WILLEFORD.

Uruguay: Kramgasse 63, 3011 Bern; tel. 313122226; fax 313112747; e-mail uruguay@dial.eunet.ch; Ambassador LUIS A. CARROSSO.

Venezuela: Schocchaldenstr. 1, Postfach 1005, 3000 Bern 23; tel. 313505757; fax 313505758; e-mail embavenez@span.ch; Chargé d'affaires a.i. MAGDA RUIZ-PINEDA.

Viet Nam: Schlösslistr. 26, 3008 Bern; tel. 313887878; fax 313887879; e-mail vietsuisse@bluewin.ch; internet www.vietnamconsulate.ch; Ambassador NGUYEN NGOC SON.

Judicial System

Switzerland has possessed a common Civil Code since 1912, but the Penal Code was only unified in 1942. Under the Code capital punishment was abolished by the few cantons that still retained it. The individual cantons continue to elect and maintain their own magistracy, and retain certain variations in procedure. The canton of Zürich, for example, has justices of the peace (Friedensrichter—normally one for each commune), District Courts (Bezirksgerichte), Labour Courts (Arbeitsgerichte), Courts for Tenancy Matters, an Appeal Court (Obergericht) with various specialized benches, a Cassation Court (Kassationsgericht), and, for the more important cases under penal law, a Jury Court (Geschworenengericht). in 2007.

At the federal level, the Federal Supreme Court has, in principle, jurisdiction over judicial matters. However, federal appeals commissions adjudicate appeals against rulings by the federal authority. From 1997 a revision of the federal judicial system was undertaken that saw the establishment of two new judicial bodies of first instance, in order to alleviate the burden on the Federal Supreme Court. These were the Federal Criminal Court in Bellinzona (from April 2004) and the Federal Administrative Court in St-Gallen (to be established in 2007). There are also military courts at the federal level.

Most disputes relating to the application of federal administrative law are first judged by federal arbitration and appeals commissions. For instance, the federal appeals commissions adjudicate disputes in the fields of federal taxes or between the Confederation and its employees. In 2007 the Federal Administrative Court in St-Gallen was to replace some 30 federal appeals commissions as well as the current departmental appeals services.

FEDERAL SUPREME COURT

Schweizerisches Bundesgericht—Tribunal fédéral
Mon Repos, 1000 Lausanne 14; tel. 213189111; fax 213233700; internet www.bger.ch.

composed of 30 judges elected for a six-year term by the Federal Assembly. According to the Constitution any citizen eligible for election to the National Council can theoretically be elected Justice to the Court, but in practice only lawyers are considered for this office. All three official Swiss languages must be represented in the Court. The President of the Federal Supreme Court is elected by the Federal Assembly for a two-year term, with no possibility of re-election, from among the senior judges of the Court. The Court is divided into six permanent branches or chambers, each of which has jurisdiction over cases pertaining to a specific subject, namely: (a) two 'Public', i.e. Constitutional and Administrative Law Divisions, being composed of seven and six judges respectively; (b) two Civil or Private Law Divisions of six judges each, which serve mainly as Courts of Appeal in civil matters; (c) the Debt Execution and Bankruptcy Law Chamber of three judges (members of the Second Civil Law Division); (d) the Criminal Law Division, the so-called Court of Cassation, which is composed of five judges and which hears mainly appeals in criminal law matters. There are also four non-permanent divisions hearing exclusively cases that involve certain crimes against the Confederation, certain forms of terrorism, and other offences related to treason.

President: Dr GIUSEP NAY.
Vice-President: Dr BERNARD CORBOZ.

FEDERAL INSURANCE COURT

Eidgenössisches Versicherungsgericht—Tribunal fédéral des assurances
Schweizerhofquai 6, 6004 Luzern; tel. 414193555; fax 414193669; internet www.bger.ch; f. 1918; consists of 11 members; since 1969 it has been considered as the Court of Social Insurance (Sozialversicherungsabteilung, Cour des assurances sociales, Corte delle assicurazioni sociali) of the Federal Supreme Court.

President: Dr SUSANNE LENZINGER-NAEF.
Vice-President: PIERRE FERRARI.

SWITZERLAND   *Directory*

FEDERAL CRIMINAL COURT

Bundesstrafgericht—Tribunal pénal fédéral
CP 2720, 6501 Bellinzone; Viale Stefano Franscini 3, 6500 Bellinzone; tel. 918226262; fax 918226242; e-mail info@bstger.admin.ch; internet www.bstger.ch.
f. 2004; composed of 11 judges elected by the Federal Assembly; court of first instance for criminal cases assigned to federal jurisdiction; in particular, may adjudicate offences such as crimes and misdemeanours against the Confederation's interests, offences committed using explosives, economic crime, organized crime or money laundering beyond the internal or external borders of Switzerland.
President: ALEX STAUB.
Vice-President: ANDREAS J. KELLER.

Religion

According to the 2000 census, the religious adherence of the population was as follows: Roman Catholic 41.8%, Protestant 35.3%, Orthodox Church 1.8%, Old Catholic 0.2%, Muslim 4.3%, Jewish 0.2%, other religions (including Buddhist and Hindu) 0.8% and those without religion 11.1%.

CHRISTIANITY

The Roman Catholic Church

For ecclesiastical purposes, Switzerland comprises six dioceses and two territorial abbacies. All of the dioceses and abbacies are directly responsible to the Holy See. At 31 December 2003 there were an estimated 3,187,778 adherents (some 46.1% of the total population).

Bishops' Conference

Secrétariat de la Conférence des Evêques Suisses, ave du Moléson 21, CP 122, 1706 Fribourg; tel. 263224794; fax 263224993; e-mail sbk-ces@gmx.ch; internet www.kath.ch/sbk-ces-cvs; f. 1863; Pres. Mgr AMÉDÉE GRAB OSB (Bishop of Chur); Sec.-Gen. Abbé Dr AGNELL RICKENMANN.

Bishop of Basel: Rt Rev. Dr KURT KOCH, Bischöfliches Ordinariat, Baselstr. 58, Postfach 216, 4501 Solothurn; tel. 326255825; fax 326255845; e-mail generalvikariat@bistum-basel.ch; internet www.bistum-basel.ch.

Bishop of Chur: Rt Rev. AMÉDÉE GRAB OSB, Bischöfliches Ordinariat, Hof 19, Postfach 133, 7002 Chur; tel. 812586000; fax 812586001; e-mail kanzlei@bistum-chur.ch; internet www.bistum-chur.ch.

Bishop of Lausanne, Geneva and Fribourg: Rt Rev. BERNARD GENOUD, 86 rue de Lausanne, CP, 1701 Fribourg; tel. 263474850; fax 263474851; e-mail chancellerie@diocese-lgf.ch; internet www.catholink.ch/fr/lgf.

Bishop of Lugano: Rt Rev. PIER GIACOMO GRAMPA, CP 5382, Borghetto 6, 6901 Lugano; tel. 919138989; fax 919138990; e-mail curialugano@catt.ch; internet www.catt.ch.

Bishop of St Gallen: Rt Rev. Dr IVO FÜRER, Bischöfliches Ordinariat, Klosterhof 6B, Postfach 263, 9001 St Gallen; tel. 712273340; fax 712273341; e-mail kanzlei@bistum-stgallen.ch; internet www.bistum-stgallen.ch.

Bishop of Sion: Rt Rev. NORBERT BRUNNER, ave de la Tour 12, CP 2124, 1950 Sion 2; tel. 273291818; fax 273291836; e-mail diocese.sion@vtx.ch; internet www.cath-org.ch.

Old Catholic Church

Christkatholische Kirche der Schweiz (Old Catholic Church of Switzerland): Willadingweg 39, 3006 Bern; tel. 313513530; fax 313529560; e-mail bischof@christkath.ch; f. 1874; 14,000 mems (1996); Pres. URS STOLZ; Bishop Rt Rev. FRITZ RENÉ MÜLLER.

The Orthodox Church

Communauté Orthodoxe-Helvétique: POB 2082, 1950 Sion 2; e-mail admin@orthodox.ch; internet www.orthodox.ch; attached to the Celtic Orthodox Church; Archpriest Most Rev. DIMITRI MOTTIER (Provost of the Eparchy of Switzerland).

Protestant Churches

Federation of Swiss Protestant Churches (Schweizerischer Evangelischer Kirchenbund, Fédération des Eglises protestantes de Suisse): Sulgenauweg 26, Postfach, 3000 Bern 23; tel. 313702525; fax 313702580; e-mail info@sek-feps.ch; internet www.sek-feps.ch; f. 1920; comprises the 26 reformed cantonal churches of Aargau, Appenzell AI + AR, Basel-Stadt, Basel-Landschaft, Bern-Jura-Solothurn, Fribourg, Geneva, Glarus, Graubünden, Luzern, Neuchâtel, Nidwalden, St Gallen, Schaffhausen, Schwyz, Solothurn, Tessin, Thurgau, Unterwalden, Uri, Valais, Vaud, Zug, Zürich, the Eglise évangélique libre de Genève and the United Methodist Church; the exec. organ is the Council of the Federation (Rat des Schweizerischen Evangelischen Kirchenbundes, Conseil de la Fédération); Pres. Rev. THOMAS WIPF.

ISLAM

According to the 2000 census there were 310,807 Muslims recorded in Switzerland, making Islam the second largest religion in the country. There are two major mosques, one in Zürich and one in Geneva, and approximately 120 Muslim centres located throughout the country.

Föderation Islamischer Gemeinschaften in der Schweiz: Leutschenbachstr. 71, 8050 Zürich; tel. 443013151.

League of Muslims in Switzerland: rue Temple 23, 2400 Le Locle; tel. 329314595.

Musulmans, Musulmanes de Suisse (MMS): Postfach 7303, 3001 Bern; tel. 313229780; fax 313222235; e-mail mms@muslims.net.

JUDAISM

Approximately three-quarters of Jewish households in Switzerland are located in the urban areas of four major cities: Zürich, Geneva, Basel and Bern. There are four distinguishable Jewish subgroups: Orthodox, conservative, liberal and reformists. About 15% of Jews in Switzerland belong to the Orthodox branch.

Schweizerischer Israelitischer Gemeindebund—Fédération suisse des communautés israélites: Gotthardstr. 65, Postfach 2105, 8027 Zürich; tel. 433050777; fax 433050766; e-mail info@swissjews.org; internet www.swissjews.org; Pres. Prof. Dr ALFRED DONATH; Gen. Sec. DENNIS L. RHEIN.

BAHÁ'Í FAITH

Nationaler Geistiger Rat der Bahá'í der Schweiz—Assemblée spirituelle nationale des bahá'ís de Suisse: Dufourstr. 13, 3005 Bern; tel. 313521020; fax 313524716; e-mail bahai@bluewin.ch; internet www.bahai.ch; Chair. DIANE ALA'I; Sec. Dr JOHN-PAUL VADER.

The Press

Freedom of the Press in Switzerland is guaranteed by Article 55 of the amended 1874 Constitution, and the only formal restrictions on the press are the legal restraints concerned with abuses of this freedom. A federal law, enacted in 1968, protects the right of journalists to refuse, in administrative procedures, to reveal their sources of information, except in cases where state security is involved.

Switzerland's federal constitutional structure and the coexistence of diverse languages and religions have tended to produce a decentralized press, fragmented into numerous local papers, often with very low circulations. In 2001 there were 72 daily newspapers with a combined circulation of 2,871,100. The majority of newspapers are regional, even such high circulation ones as *Tages Anzeiger Zürich* and *Basler Zeitung* and national dailies such as *Neue Zürcher Zeitung*. About 67% of newspapers are printed in German, 27% in French, 4% in Italian and less than 1% in Raeto-Romansch. Some 100,000 copies of French, German, Italian and Spanish newspapers are imported daily.

PRINCIPAL DAILIES

Arbon

Bodensee Tagblatt: Romanshornerstr. 36, 9320 Arbon; tel. 714476060; fax 714476070; f. 1849; circ. 14,780.

Baden

Aargauer Zeitung: Stadtturmstr. 19, 5400 Baden; tel. 562042424; fax 562042425; f. 1996 by merger of *Aargauer Tagblatt* and *Badener Tagblatt*; non-party; Editor-in-Chief FRANZ STRAUB; Publr PETER WANNER; circ. 120,000.

Basel
(Bâle)

Basellandschaftliche Zeitung: Schützengasse 6, 4410 Liestal; tel. 619272600; fax 619212268; Publrs Verlag Lüdin AG; circ. 27,654.

Basler Zeitung: Aeschenpl. 7, 4002 Basel; tel. 616391111; fax 616311582; e-mail redaktion@baz.ch; internet www.baz.ch; f. 1976; liberal; Editor-in-Chief IVO BACHMANN; circ. 100,763.

Bellinzona

La Regione Ticino: Via Ghiringhelli 9, 6500 Bellinzona; tel. 918211121; fax 918211122; e-mail info@laregione.ch; internet www.laregione.ch; f. 1992; circ. 32,556.

SWITZERLAND

Bern
(Berne)

Berner Zeitung: Nordring/Dammweg 9, 3001 Bern; tel. 313303730; fax 313316087; internet www.bzonline.ch; f. 1844; independent; Chief Editor Andreas Z'graggen; circ. 131,515.

Der Bund: Bubenbergpl. 8, 3001 Bern; tel. 313851111; fax 313851112; e-mail redaktion@derbund.ch; internet www.ebund.ch; f. 1850; liberal; Chief Editor Hanspeter Spoerri; circ. 60,500.

Berneck

Der Rheintaler: Hafnerwisenstr. 1, 9442 Berneck; tel. 717472244; fax 717472240; e-mail rheintaler@rdv.ch; internet www.rheintaler.ch; independent; Editor-in-Chief Andreas Rüdisüli; circ. 11,023.

Bienne
(Biel)

Bieler Tagblatt/Seeländer Bote: Längfeldweg 135, 1501 Bienne; tel. 32428333; fax 32428335; independent; Publr W. Gassman; circ. 33,281.

Le Journal du Jura: 15 rue M.-Chipot, CP 624, 2501 Bienne; tel. 323219000; fax 323219009; e-mail redactionjj@journaldujura.ch; internet www.journaldujura.ch; f. 1863; independent; Publr W. Gassmann; circ. 13,131.

Brig

Walliser Bote: Furkastr. 21, 3900 Brig; tel. 279229988; fax 279229989; Catholic; Editor-in-Chief Pius Rieder; circ. 27,493.

Buchs

Werdenberger und Obertoggenburger: Bahnhofstr. 14, 9470 Buchs; tel. 817500202; f. 1869; liberal; circ. 10,450.

La Chaux-de-Fonds

L'impartial: 14 rue Neuve, 2300 La Chaux-de-Fonds; tel. 39210210; fax 39210360; f. 1880; independent; circ. 26,951.

Chur
(Coire)

Bündner Tagblatt: Commercialstr. 22, 7007 Chur; tel. 812555000; fax 812555123; e-mail redaktion-bt@suedostschweiz.ch; f. 1852; independent; circ. 13,000.

Bündner Zeitung: Kasernenstr. 1, 7007 Chur; tel. 812555050; fax 812555100; independent; Publr Gasser AG; circ. 56,144.

La Quotidiana: Via Centrala 4, 7130 Ilanz; tel. 819200710; fax 819200715; e-mail redaktion-lq@suedostschweiz.ch; f. 1997; Romansch-language; Publr Südostschweiz Presse AG; Editor-in-Chief Martin Cabalzar; circ. 10,154.

Die Südostschweiz: Comercialstr. 22, 7007 Chur; tel. 812255050; fax 812255102; e-mail zentralredaktion@suedostschweiz.ch; internet www.suedostschweiz.ch; independent; Publr Südostschweiz Presse AG; circ. 140,000.

Delémont

Le Quotidien Jurassien: 6 route de Courroux, 2800 Delémont; tel. 324211818; fax 324211890; e-mail lqj@lqj.ch; internet www.lqj.ch; f. 1993; independent; Editor M. Voisard; circ. 25,120.

Dielsdorf

Zürcher Unterländer: Schulstr. 12, 8157 Dielsdorf; tel. 18548282; fax 18530690; e-mail redaktion@zuonline.ch; internet www.zuonline.ch; circ. 19,696 (Thur. 74,417).

Flawil

Volksfreund/Wiler Zeitung/Gossauer Zeitung: Burgauerstr. 50, 9230 Flawil; independent; circ. 10,473.

Frauenfeld

Thurgauer Zeitung: Promenadenstr. 16, 8501 Frauenfeld; tel. 527235511; fax 527210002; f. 1798; independent; Publrs Huber & Co AG; circ. 31,866.

Fribourg
(Freiburg)

Freiburger Nachrichten: Bahnhofpl. 5, 1701 Fribourg; tel. 263473000; fax 263473019; e-mail fn.verlag@freiburger-nachrichten.ch; internet www.freiburger-nachrichten.ch; Catholic; circ. 16,393.

Geneva

Le Temps: pl. de Cornavin 3, CP 2570, 1211 Geneva 2; tel. 227995858; fax 227995859; e-mail info@letemps.ch; internet www.letemps.ch; f. 1998 by merger of *Journal de Genève* and *Le Nouveau Quotidien*.

Tribune de Genève: CP 5115, 1211 Geneva 11; tel. 22322400; fax 227810107; f. 1879; independent; morning; Editor Antoine Exchaquet; circ. 71,029.

Glarus

Glarner Nachrichten: Zwinglistr. 6, Postfach 366, 8750 Glarus; tel. 556401921; fax 556406440; f. 1875; liberal; Publrs Tschudi & Co AG; circ. 10,976.

Herisau

Appenzeller Zeitung: Kasernenstr. 64, 9100 Herisau; tel. 713546464; fax 713546465; radical democratic; f. 1828; Publrs Appenzeller Medienhaus Schläpfer AG; circ. 15,293.

Lausanne

Le Matin: 33 ave de la Gare, 1001 Lausanne; tel. 213494949; fax 21494929; e-mail matin-redaction@edicom.ch; internet www.lematin.ch; f. 1862; independent; Editor Daniel Pittard; circ. 66,000, Sunday 220,000.

Nouvelle Revue et Journal politique: 15 ave Ruchonnet, 1001 Lausanne; tel. 213400011; fax 213400030; f. 1868; radical democratic; circ. 6,790.

24 heures: 33 ave de la Gare, 1001 Lausanne; tel. 213494444; fax 213494419; f. 1762; independent; circ. 91,096.

Lucerne
(Luzern)

Neue Luzerner Zeitung: Maihofstr. 76, 6002 Lucerne; tel. 414295151; fax 414295181; e-mail redaktion@neue0lz.ch; f. 1996; Editor Thomas Bornhauser; circ. 133,820.

Lugano

Corriere del Ticino: Ai Mulini, 6933 Muzzano; tel. 919603131; fax 919682779; e-mail cdt@cdt.ch; internet www.cdt.ch; f. 1891; independent; circ. 37,000.

Giornale del Popolo: Via San Gottardo 50, 6900 Lugano; tel. 919232271; fax 919232805; f. 1926; independent; circ. 26,485.

Mels

Der Sarganserländer: Sarganserstr., 8887 Mels; tel. 817233761; fax 817237018; Catholic; circ. 10,272.

Montreux

La Presse: 22 ave des Planches, 1820 Montreux; tel. 219636131; fax 219635734; e-mail redac@lapresse.ch; internet www.lapresse.ch; f. 1867; independent; circ. 24,655.

Neuchâtel
(Neuenburg)

L'Express: CP 2216, 2001 Neuchâtel; tel. 327235300; fax 327235209; e-mail fwolfrath@lexpress.ch; internet www.lexpress.ch; f. 1738; independent; circ. 29,028.

St Gallen
(St-Gall)

Die Ostschweiz: Oberer Graben 8, 9001 St Gallen; tel. 71308580; f. 1873; Catholic; circ. 21,642.

St Galler Tagblatt: Fürstenlandstr. 122, 9001 St Gallen; tel. 712727711; fax 712727476; e-mail zentralredaktion@tagblatt.ch; internet www.tagblatt.ch; f. 1839; liberal; Editor-in-Chief Gottlieb F. Höpli; circ. 110,000.

Schaffhausen
(Schaffhouse)

Schaffhauser Nachrichten: Vordergasse 58, 8201 Schaffhausen; tel. 526333111; fax 526333401; e-mail redaktion@shn.ch; internet www.shn.ch; f. 1861; liberal; Editor-in-Chief Norbert Neiminger; circ. 26,000.

Sion

Le Nouvelliste et Feuille d'Avis du Valais: 13 rue de l'Industrie, 1950 Sion; tel. 273297511; fax 273297565; e-mail redaction@nouvelliste.ch; internet www.lenouvelliste.ch; Catholic; Publrs

SWITZERLAND

Imprimerie Moderne SA; Editorial Dir HERMAN PELLEGRINI; circ. 42,066.

Stäfa

Zürichsee-Zeitung: Seestr. 86, 8712 Stäfa; tel. 19285555; fax 19285550; e-mail redstaefa@zsz.ch; internet www.zsz.ch; f. 1845; radical democratic; Publr and Editor-in-Chief LUZI BERNET; circ. 53,000.

Thun
(Thoune)

Berner Oberländer: Rampenstr. 1, 3602 Thun; tel. 332251515; fax 332251505; e-mail redaktion-bo@bom.ch; internet www.berneroberlaender.ch; f. 1898; independent; Publrs Berner Oberland Medien AG; Dir KONRAD MAURER; Editor-in-Chief RENÉ E. GYGAX; circ. 23,500.

Thuner Tagblatt: Rampenstr. 1, 3602 Thun; tel. 332251515; fax 332251505; e-mail redaktion-tt@bom.ch; internet www.thunertagblatt.ch; independent; publ. by Berner Oberland Medien AG; Dir KONRAD MAURER; Editor-in-Chief RENÉ E. GYGAX; circ. 24,000.

Uster

Anzeiger von Uster: Oberlandstr. 100, 8610 Uster; tel. 19057979; fax 19057980; e-mail inserat@avu.ch; f. 1846; independent; Publr G. MÜLLER; circ. 11,524.

Wetzikon

Zürcher Oberländer: 8620 Wetzikon; tel. 19333333; fax 19323232; e-mail redaktion@zol.ch; internet www.zo-medien.ch; f. 1852; liberal; circ. 46,000.

Winterthur
(Winterthour)

Der Landbote: Postfach 778, 8401 Winterthur; tel. 522669901; fax 522669911; e-mail redaktion@landbote.ch; internet www.winti-guide.ch; f. 1836; independent; morning; Editor-in-Chief Dr RUDOLF GERBER; circ. 48,000.

Yverdon-les-Bains

La Presse Nord Vaudoise: 6 ave Haldimand, 1401 Yverdon-les-Bains; tel. 244248424; fax 244248425; e-mail redac@lapresse-nv.ch; f. 1773; independent; circ. 11,000.

Zofingen

Zofinger Tagblatt: Vordere Hauptgasse 33, 4800 Zofingen; tel. 627459350; fax 627459419; e-mail ztredaktion@ztonline.ch; f. 1873; liberal; Editor BEAT KIRCHHOFER; circ. 17,200.

Zürich

Blick: Dufourstr. 23, 8008 Zürich; tel. 442596262; fax 442622953; independent; Editor WERNER DE SCHEPPER; circ. 292,292.

Neue Zürcher Zeitung: Falkenstr. 11, Postfach, 8021 Zürich; tel. 442581111; fax 442521329; e-mail redaktion@nzz.ch; internet www.nzz.ch; f. 1780; independent-liberal; Chief Editor Dr HUGO BÜTLER; circ. 166,291.

Tages Anzeiger Zürich: Werdstr. 21, 8021 Zürich; tel. 442484411; fax 442484471; e-mail redaktion@tages-anzeiger.ch; internet www.tagesanzeiger.ch; f. 1893; independent; Chief Editor PETER HARTMEIER; circ. 250,000.

PERIODICALS AND JOURNALS

Allgemeine Schweizerische Militärzeitschrift: Verlag Huber & Co AG, Postfach, 8501 Frauenfeld; tel. 527235622; fax 527235632; e-mail redaktion@asmz.ch; f. 1834; 11 a year; Editor LOUIS GEIGER; circ. 23,200.

Die Alpen: Monbijoustr. 61, Postfach, 3000 Bern 23; tel. 313701818; fax 313701890; e-mail alpen@sac-cas.ch; internet www.sac-cas.ch; monthly; publ. by Schweizer Alpen-Club; circ. 90,000.

Annabelle création: Baslerstr. 30, 8048 Zürich; tel. 444046333; fax 444046218; e-mail redaktion@an-creation.ch; creative lifestyle and living magazine; f. 1998; monthly; circ. 102,866.

Auto & Lifestyle (ACS Clubmagazin): Wasserwerkgasse 39, 3000 Bern 13; tel. 313283111; fax 313110310; e-mail acszv@acs.ch; internet www.acs.ch; publ. by the Automobile Club of Switzerland; 10 a year; circ. 63,200.

Automobil Revue: Dammweg 9, 3001 Bern; tel. 313303034; fax 313303032; e-mail office@automobilrevue.ch; f. 1906; weekly publ. in German and French (*Revue automobile*); Editor MAX NÖTZLI; circ. 67,412.

Baukader Aktuelles Bauen: Schück Söhne, Bahnhofstr. 24, 8803 Rüschlikon; tel. 17247777; fax 17247877; f. 1944; 10 a year; magazine for the construction industry; publ. by Imprimerie Vogt-Schild AG; circ. 10,500.

Beobachter: Förrlibuckstr. 70, 8021 Zürich; tel. 434445111; fax 434445353; e-mail redaktion@beobachter.ch; internet www.beobachter.ch; f. 1927; 2 a month; circ. 335,226.

Bilanz: Förrlibuckstr. 70, 8021 Zürich; tel. 434445520; fax 434445521; internet www.bilanz.ch; f. 1977; review of business in Switzerland; circ. 57,548.

Courrier neuchâtelois: 2013 Colombier; tel. 328417250; fax 328411521; e-mail administration@editionsduchateau.ch; weekly; Editor RENÉ GESSLER; circ. 88,087.

Du (Zeitschrift für Kultur): Du Verlags AG, Schöntalstr. 27, Postfach 9530, 8036 Zürich; tel. 432434600; fax 432434611; e-mail redaktion@dumag.ch; internet www.dumag.ch; f. 1941; monthly art review; Editor Dr CHRISTOPH J. BÜCKKLE; circ. 31,915.

Echo Magazine: rue de Meyrin 12, CP 80, 1211 Geneva 7; tel. and fax 225930303; e-mail abo.echo.magazine@saripress.ch; f. 1929; weekly; circ. 22,000.

L'Eco dello Sport: Via Industria, 6933 Muzzano; tel. 919603131; fax 91575750; circ. 44,000.

Finanz und Wirtschaft: Hallwylstr. 71, Postfach, 8021 Zürich; tel. 442983535; fax 442983500; e-mail verlag@fuw.ch; internet www.finanzinfo.ch; f. 1928; 2 a week; finance and economics; circ. 44,308.

Freisinn: Postfach 6136, 3001 Bern; tel. 313203535; fax 313203500; e-mail zila@fdp.ch; internet www.fdp.ch; f. 1979; monthly; politics; Editor-in-Chief NICO ZILA; circ. 71,160.

Gauchebdo: 18 rue Dancet, CP 366, 1211 Geneva 4; tel. 223206335; fax 223200587; e-mail gauchebdo@worldcom.ch; f. 1944; weekly; left-wing; Publr A. BRINGOLF; Editor-in-Chief R. ABADI; circ. 5,000.

Glücks-Post: Dufourstr. 49, 8008 Zürich; tel. 442596912; fax 442596930; e-mail gluesckspost@ringier.ch; women's interest; f. 1977; weekly; Editor-in-Chief HELMUT-MARIA GLOGGER; circ. 148,737.

Graphis: Dufourstr. 107, 8008 Zürich; tel. 443838211; fax 443831643; f. 1944; bi-monthly; graphic art and applied arts; publ. by Graphis Press Corpn; Editor B. MARTIN PEDERSEN; circ. 29,000.

Handels Zeitung: Seestr. 37, 8027 Zürich; tel. 442883555; fax 442883575; e-mail redaktion@handelszeitung.ch; internet www.handelszeitung.ch; f. 1862; financial, commercial and industrial weekly; Publr RALPH BÜCHI; Chief Editor MARTIN SPIELER; circ. 33,044.

L'Hebdo: 3 Pont Bessières, 1005 Lausanne; tel. 213317600; fax 213317601; f. 1981; weekly; news magazine; Editor-in-Chief ALAIN JEANNET; circ. 48,376.

L'Illustré: Pont Bessières 3, 1005 Lausanne; tel. 213317500; fax 213317501; e-mail illustre@ringier.ch; internet www.ringier.ch; f. 1921; weekly; Chief Editor FREDERICO CAMPOMODO; circ. 97,974.

M: 33 ave de la Gare, 1001 Lausanne; tel. 23494545; fax 23494110; f. 1998; men's leisure; Dir PHILIPPE SIMON.

Museum Helveticum: Steinentorstr. 13, 4010 Basel; tel. 612789565; fax 612789566; e-mail verlag@schwabe.ch; internet www.schwabe.ch; f. 1944; quarterly; Swiss journal for classical philology, ancient history and classical archaeology; Editors Prof. M. BILLERBECK, Prof. A. GIOVANNINI, Prof. TH. GELZER, Prof. H. HARICH-SCHWARZBAUER; publ. by Schwabe AG.

Music Scene: 5401 Baden; tel. 562032200; fax 562032299; e-mail info@music-scene.ch; internet www.music-scene.ch; f. 1924; young people's fortnightly; circ. 50,000.

Nebelspalter: Bahnhofstr. 17, 9326 Horn; tel. 718468876; fax 718468876; e-mail redaktion@nebelspalter.ch; internet www.nebelspalter.ch; f. 1875; 10 a year; satirical; Editor-in-Chief MARCO RATSCHILLER; publ. By Engeli & Partner Verlag; circ. 12,600.

PRO: Im Morgental 35, 8126 Zumikou; tel. 19182728; f. 1951; monthly; Editor ANNEMARIE FREY.

Revue économique et sociale: BFSH 1, 1015 Lausanne/Dorigny; tel. 216915347; fax 216923385; e-mail infosees@hec.unil.ch; internet www.hec.unil.ch/sees; f. 1943; quarterly; Editors A. M. GUÉNETTE, W. RAHM; circ. 1,400.

Revue médicale de la suisse romande: Editions Médecine et Hygiene, 2 ave Bellefontaine, 1003 Lausanne; tel. 213417170; fax 213417179; f. 1880; monthly; Editors Dr J. P. BERGER, Prof. A. PECOUD; circ. 5,600.

Revue militaire suisse: 3 ave de Florimont, 1006 Lausanne; tel. 213114817; fax 213919709; e-mail jcrc@vtxnet.ch; f. 1856; 11 a year; Editor-in-Chief Col HERVÉ DE WECK.

Revue suisse de zoologie: Muséum d'Histoire Naturelle, CP 6434, 1211 Geneva 6; tel. 224186300; fax 224186301; e-mail danielle.decrouez@mhn.ville-ge.ch; internet www.ville-ge.ch/musinfo/mhng/page.rsz.htm; f. 1893; quarterly; Dir DANIELLE DECROUEZ.

SWITZERLAND

Schweizer Archiv für Neurologie und Psychiatrie (Archives Suisses de Neurologie et de Psychiatrie): Schwabe AG Verlag, Steinentorstr. 13, 4010 Basel; tel. 612789565; fax 612789566; internet www.schwabe.ch; f. 1917; 8 a year.

Schweizer Familie: Baslerstr. 30, Postfach, 8021 Zürich; tel. 444046106; fax 444046096; f. 1893; weekly; Editor ANDREAS DURISCH; Man. Dir JOSEF BURCH; circ. 205,529.

Schweizer Illustrierte: Dufourstr. 23, 8008 Zürich; tel. 442596111; fax 442620442; f. 1911; illustrated weekly; circ. 213,433.

Schweizer Monatshefte: Vogelsangstr. 52, 8006 Zürich; tel. 443612606; fax 443637005; e-mail info@schweizermonatshefte.ch; internet www.schweizermonatshefte.ch; f. 1921; political, economic and cultural monthly; Editors ROBERT NEF, SUZANN RENNINGER; circ. 2,500.

Schweizerisches Handelsamtsblatt (Feuille officielle suisse du commerce): Effingerstr. 1, Postfach 8164, 3001 Bern; tel. 313240992; fax 313240961; e-mail shab@seco.admin.ch; internet www.shab.ch; f. 1883; commercial daily; publ. by Federal Dept of Foreign Trade; circ. 16,200.

Ski: Vogt—Schild/Habesses Medien AG, Buchwilerstr. 21, 4501 Solothurn; tel. 326247685; fax 326247251; e-mail j.weibel@vsonline.ch; f. 1968; 7 a year; German and French/Italian editions; Editor JOSEPH WEIBEL; circ. 82,000.

Sport: Förrlibuckstr. 10, 8021 Zürich; tel. 444487373; fax 444487673; f. 1920; weekly; Chief Editor PETER ZWICKY; circ. 55,477.

Swiss Engineering (STZ): Chellenstr. 18E, 6318 Walchwil; tel. 417590202; fax 417590200; e-mail mediakom@bluewin.ch; internet www.swissengineering-stz.ch; 11 a year; technical journal in German; Editor-in-Chief HANNES GYSLING; circ. 18,000.

Swiss Journal of Psychology (Schweizerische Zeitschrift für Psychologie/Revue suisse de psychologie): Unitobler, Muesmattstr. 45, 3000 Bern 9; e-mail margit.oswald@psy.unibe.ch; f. 1942; quarterly; Editors Prof. Dr MARGIT E. OSWALD, Prof. Dr FRIEDRICH WILKENING.

Swiss Medical Weekly: EMH Swiss Medical Publrs Ltd, Steinentorstr. 13, 4010 Basel; tel. 614678555; fax 614678556; e-mail red@smw.ch; internet www.smw.ch; f. 1870; fortnightly; Man. Editor Dr N. MARTY; circ. 3,000.

TCS-Revue: Alfred-Escher-Str. 38, 8027 Zürich; tel. 442868613; fax 442868637; official organ of the Zürich Touring Club; monthly; Chief Editor RETO CAVEGN; circ. 200,000.

Tele: Dufourstr. 23, 8008 Zürich; tel. 442596111; fax 442598697; e-mail telesekr@ringier.ch; internet www.tele.ch; f. 1967; television, cinema and multimedia; weekly; Editor KLAUS KRIESEL; circ. 214,214.

Touring: Maulbeerstr. 10, 3001 Bern; tel. 313805000; fax 313805006; f. 1935; fortnightly; German, French and Italian editions; Chief Editor STEFAN SENN; circ. 1,306,000.

TV 8: 3 Pont Bessières, 1005 Lausanne; tel. 213317700; fax 213317701; e-mail tv8@ringier.ch; weekly; circ. 52,720.

Vox Romanica: Centre de dialectologie, Université de Neuchâtel, ave DuPeyiou 6, 2000 Neuchâtel; e-mail centre.dialectologie@unine.ch; internet www.unine.ch/dialectologie/vox/vox.html; f. 1936; annual review of Romance linguistics and medieval literature.

Weltwoche: Förrlibuckstr. 70, 8021 Zürich; tel. 434445111; fax 434445669; e-mail redaktion@weltwoche.ch; internet www.weltwoche.ch; f. 1933; weekly; independent; Editor-in-Chief ROGER KÖPPEL; circ. 92,337.

Werk, Bauen + Wohnen: Talstr. 39, 8001 Zürich; tel. 442181430; fax 442181434; e-mail wbw.zh@bluewin.ch; internet www.werkbauenundwohnen.ch; f. 1913; monthly; architecture; circ. 8,000.

Yakari: Yakari Verlag GmbH, Faselimatt 9A, 6252 Dagmersellen; tel. 627481010; fax 627481019; internet www.yakari-verlag.ch; children's monthly; Editor PATRICK WICKI; circ. 10,500.

Zeitschrift für Psychiatrie, Psychologie und Psychotherapie: Verlag Hans Huber, Länggass-Str. 76, 3000 Bern 9; e-mail zeitschriften@hanshuber.com; internet www.verlag-hanshuber.com/zppp; f. 1952; quarterly; Editor Prof. Dr F. PETERMANN; circ. 500.

NEWS AGENCIES

Schweizerische Depeschenagentur AG (SDA) (Agence Télégraphique Suisse SA (ATS), Swiss News Agency): Länggassstr. 7, 3001 Bern; tel. 313093333; fax 313018538; f. 1894; agency for political and general news; Chief Editor BERNARD REIST.

Foreign Bureaux

Agence France-Presse (AFP): Bureau C14, Palais des Nations, 1211 Geneva 10; tel. 229197979; fax 229197961; e-mail afpgva@afp.com; Bureau Chief ANDRÉ VIOLLAZ.

Agencia EFE (Spain): Bureau 49, Palais des Nations, 1211 Geneva 10; tel. 227336273; fax 227332041; e-mail efe-ginebra@bluewin.ch; Bureau Chief ELENA MORENO.

Agenzia Nazionale Stampa Associata (ANSA) (Italy): Salle de Presse 1, Palais des Nations, 1211 Geneva 10; tel. 227334872; fax 227345900; e-mail ansa@itu.ch; Bureau Chief FRANCESCO INDRACEOLO.

Allgemeiner Deutscher Nachrichtendienst (ADN) (Germany): Bureau 53, Palais des Nations, 1211 Geneva 10; Correspondent HELMUT SCHULZ.

Associated Press (AP) (USA): Palais des Nations, 1211 Geneva 10; tel. 229194222; fax 227331337; Bureau Chief ALEXANDER HIGGINS.

Deutsche Presse-Agentur (dpa) (Germany): Bureau 84, Palais des Nations, 1211 Geneva 10; tel. 227315117; fax 227332706; e-mail office.geneva@dpa.com; Bureau Chief HEINZ-PETER DIETRICH.

Informatsionnoye Telegrafnoye Agentstvo Rossii—Telegrafnoye Agentstvo Suverennykh Stran (ITAR—TASS) (Russia): Bureau 72, Palais des Nations, 1211 Geneva 10; tel. 227343321; fax 227401147; Correspondent KONSTANTIN F. PRIBYTKOV.

Inter Press Service (IPS) (Italy): Bureau C504, Palais des Nations, 1211 Geneva 10; tel. 227346011; fax 227342430; Correspondent CHAKRAVARTHI RAGHAVAN.

Jiji Tsushin (Jiji Press Ltd); Japan: 54 chemin du Grand Puits, 1217 Meyrin/Geneva; tel. 227341216; fax 227335115; Man. TOKIHIKO KITAHARA.

Kyodo Tsushin (Kyodo News); Japan: Bureau C521, Palais des Nations, 1211 Geneva 10; tel. 227343856; fax 227349669; e-mail kyodonews@bluewin.ch; internet home.kyodo.co.jp; f. 1945; Bureau Chief HAJIME OZAKI.

Reuters (UK): Bureau 70, Palais des Nations, 1211 Geneva 10; tel. 227333831; fax 227348760; Man. Dir ROBERT EVANS.

United Press International (UPI) (USA): Bureau 76, Palais des Nations, 1211 Geneva 10; tel. 227341740; fax 227341042; Bureau Chief MICHAEL HUGGINS.

Xinhua (New China) News Agency (People's Republic of China): Bureau 57, Palais des Nations, 1211 Geneva 10; tel. 229173710; fax 227343505; Correspondent DASHENG LU.

PRESS ASSOCIATIONS

Association Presse Suisse/Verband Schweizer Presse: Baumackerstr. 42, Postfach, 8050 Zürich; tel. 3186464; fax 3186462; e-mail contact@schweizerpresse.ch; internet www.schweizerpresse.ch; f. 1899; Pres. HANSPETER LEBRUMENT; 180 mems.

Schweizer Verband der Journalistinnen und Journalisten/Fédération suisse des journalistes/Federazione svizzera dei giornalisti: Postfach 518, Grand'Places 14A, 1701 Fribourg; tel. 263471500; fax 263471509; e-mail info@journalisten.ch; internet www.journalisten.ch; Pres ANTOINE GESSLER, STEFAN ROHRBACH.

Publishers

FRENCH-LANGUAGE PUBLISHING HOUSES

Editions l'Age d'Homme SA: 10 rue de Genève, BP B2, 1003 Lausanne 9; tel. 213120095; fax 213208440; e-mail info@agedhomme.com; internet www.agedhomme.com; f. 1966; fiction, biography, music, art, social science, science fiction, literary criticism; Man. Dir VLADIMIR DIMITRIJEVIC.

Editions de l'Aire SA: 15 rue de l'Union, BP 57, 1800 Vevey; tel. 219236836; fax 219236823; e-mail editionaire@bluewin.ch; internet www.editions-aire.ch; f. 1978; literature, history, philosophy, religion; Man. MICHEL MORET.

La Bibliothèque des Arts: 55 ave de Rumine, 1005 Lausanne; tel. 213123667; fax 213123615; e-mail webmaster@bibliotheque-des-arts.com; internet www.bibliotheque-des-arts.com; f. 1952; art, culture; Dir OLIVIER DAULTE.

Librairie Droz SA: 11 rue Firmin-Massot, 1211 Geneva 12; tel. 223466666; fax 223472391; e-mail droz@droz.org; internet www.droz.org; f. 1924; history, medieval literature, French literature, linguistics, social sciences, economics, archaeology; Dir MAX ENGAMMARE.

Edipresse Publications SA: 33 ave de la Gare, 1001 Lausanne; tel. 213494545; fax 213494110; e-mail epsa.info@edipresse.ch; internet www.edipresse.com; f. 1988; newspapers, magazines; Pres. PIERRE LAMUNIÈRE.

Editions Eiselé SA: Confrérie 42, CP 128, 1008 Prilly; tel. 21623650; fax 216236359; e-mail jleisele@worldcom.ch; internet www.eisele.ch; arts, education, popular science, textbooks.

Editions d'En Bas: 12 rue du Tunnel, 1005 Lausanne; tel. 213233918; fax 213123240; e-mail enbas@bluewin.ch; internet

SWITZERLAND

www.enbas.ch; literature, politics, memoirs, travel, poetry; Dir JEAN RICHARD.

Françoise Gonin Editions d'Art: 1 chemin du Grand-Praz, 1012 Lausanne; tel. 217285948; fax 217285948; internet www.lemeilleur.ch/editionsgonin; f. 1926; art books.

Editions du Grand-Pont: 2 place Bel-Air, 1003 Lausanne; tel. 213124466; fax 213113222; f. 1971; general, art books and literature; Dir JEAN-PIERRE LAUBSCHER.

Editions du Griffon: 17 Faubourg du Lac, 2000 Neuchâtel; tel. 327252204; f. 1944; science, arts.

Editions Ides et Calendes: Évole 19, 2001 Neuchâtel; tel. 327253861; fax 327255880; e-mail info@idesetcalendes.com; internet www.idesetcalendes.com; f. 1941; art, photography, literature; Dir ALAIN BOURET.

La Joie de Lire SA: 2 bis rue Saint-Léger, 1205 Geneva; tel. 228073399; fax 228073392; e-mail info@lajoiedelire.ch; internet www.lajoiedelire.ch; f. 1987; juvenile; Dir FRANCINE BOUCHET.

Editions Labor & Fides SA: 1 rue Beauregard, 1204 Geneva; tel. 223113290; fax 227813051; e-mail contact@laboretfides.com; internet www.laboretfides.com; f. 1924; theological and religious publs; Dir GABRIEL DE MONTMOLLIN.

Loisirs et Pédagogie SA (LEP): en Budron B4A, 1052 Le Mont-sur-Lausanne; tel. 216512570; fax 216535751; e-mail contact@editionslep.ch; internet www.editionslep.ch; Dir PHILIPPE BURDEL.

Médecine et Hygiène: 78 ave de la Roseraie, CP 456, 1211 Geneva 4; tel. 227029311; fax 227029355; e-mail librairie@medecinehygiene.ch; internet www.medhyg.ch; f. 1943; medicine, psychology, general science, university textbooks; Man. Dirs BERTRAND KIEFER, JACQUELINE MONNIER.

Editions Mondo SA: 7 passage St-Antoine, 1800 Vevey; tel. 219241450; fax 219244662; e-mail info@mondo.ch; internet www.mondo.ch; Dir ARSLAN ALAMIR.

Noir sur Blanc SA: Le Mottâ, 1147 Montricher; tel. 218645931; fax 218644026; e-mail noirsurblanc@bluewin.ch; f. 1986; literature.

Olizane: 11 rue des Vieux-Grenadiers, 1205 Geneva; tel. 223285252; fax 223285796; e-mail guides@olizane.ch; internet www.olizane.ch; f. 1981; travel, tourism, orientalism, photography; Dir MATTHIAS HUBER.

Editions Payot Lausanne: Nadir SA, 18 ave de la Gare, CP 529, 1001 Lausanne; tel. 213290264; fax 213290266; f. 1875; technical, textbooks, medicine, law, popular science, art books, tourism, history, music, general non-fiction, academic publs; Dir JACQUES SCHERRER.

Presses Polytechniques et Universitaires Romandes: EPFL, Centre-Midi, CP 119, 1015 Lausanne-Ecublens; tel. 216934131; fax 216934027; e-mail ppur@epfl.ch; internet www.ppur.org; f. 1980; technical and scientific; also publishes in English as EPFL Press; Man. Dir OLIVIER BABEL.

Editions Pro Schola: 3 pl. Chauderon, 1003 Lausanne; tel. 213236655; fax 213236777; f. 1928; education, language textbooks, audio-visual material; Dir JEAN BENEDICT.

Editions Scriptar SA: 25 chemin du Creux-de-Corsy, 1093 Geneva; tel. 217960096; fax 217914084; e-mail info@jsh.ch; internet www.jsh.ch; f. 1946; watches and jewellery, gemmology; Dir. F. MUGNIER.

Slatkine Reprints: 5 rue des Chaudronniers, CP 3625, 1211 Geneva 3; tel. 227762551; fax 227763527; e-mail slatkine@slatkine.com; internet www.slatkine.com; Dir M.-E. SLATKINE.

Editions du Tricorne: 14 rue Lissignol, 1201 Geneva; tel. 227388366; fax 227319749; e-mail tricorne@tricorne.org; internet www.tricorne.org; f. 1976; philosophy, human sciences, art, religion, psychology, mathematics; Dir SERGE KAPLUN.

Editions Universitaires SA: 42 blvd de Pérolles, 1705 Fribourg; tel. 264264311; fax 264264300; e-mail eduni@st-paul.ch; internet www.st-paul.ch/uni-press-fr; Man. Dir ANTON SCHERER.

Institut Universitaire d'Etudes du Développement: 20 rue Rothschild, CP 136, 1211 Geneva 21; tel. 229065940; fax 229065947; e-mail iued@unige.ch; internet www.iued.unige.ch; f. 1961; educational, health and development; Dir MICHEL CARTON.

Editions 24 heures: 33 ave de la Gare, 1001 Lausanne; tel. 213495013; fax 213495029; Dir J.-P. MÉROT.

Editions Zoé: 11 rue des Moraines, 1227 Carouge-Geneva; tel. 223093606; fax 223093603; e-mail info@editionszoe.ch; internet www.editionszoe.ch; literature, criticism, fiction, essays, theatre, art, music, cookery; Dir MARLYSE PIETRI-BACHMANN.

GERMAN-LANGUAGE PUBLISHING HOUSES

Arche Literatur Verlag AG: Niederdorfstr. 90, 8001 Zürich; tel. 442522410; fax 442611115; internet www.arche-verlag.com; f. 1944; literature; Dirs ELISABETH RAABE, REGINA VITALI.

Benteli Verlags AG: Seftigenstr. 310, 3084 Wabern-Bern; tel. 319608484; fax 319617414; e-mail info@benteliverlag.ch; internet www.benteliverlag.ch; f. 1898; fine arts, photography, non-fiction, philology; Dir TILL SCHAAP.

Birkhäuser Verlag AG: Viaduktstr. 42, Postfach 133, 4010 Basel; tel. 612050707; fax 612050799; e-mail info@birkhauser.ch; internet www.birkhauser.ch; scientific and technical books, architecture, periodicals; Man. Dir SVEN FUND.

Cosmos Verlag AG: Kräyigenweg 2, 3074 Muri bei Bern; tel. 319506464; fax 319506460; e-mail info@cosmosverlag.ch; internet www.cosmosverlag.ch; f. 1923; literature, local history, reference, children's, tax management; Dir RETO M. AEBERLI.

Diogenes Verlag AG: Sprecherstr. 8, 8032 Zürich; tel. 442548511; fax 442528407; e-mail info@diogenes.ch; internet www.diogenes.ch; f. 1952; belles-lettres, fiction, graphic arts, children's; Publrs DANIEL KEEL, RUDOLF C. BETTSCHART.

Europa Verlag AG: Rämistr. 5, 8024 Zürich; tel. 442611629; fax 442516081; e-mail info@europa-verlag.ch; internet www.europa-verlag.ch; f. 1933; politics, philosophy, history, biography, sociology, fiction; Dir MARLYS MOSER.

Hallwag Kümmerly+Frey AG: Grubenstr. 109, 3322 Schönbühl; tel. 318503131; fax 318503100; e-mail info@swisstravelcenter.ch; internet www.swisstravelcenter.ch; f. 1912; maps and guides, road maps, atlases, travel guides; CEO PETER NIEDERHAUSER.

H.E.P. Verlag AG: Brunngasse 36, Postfach, 3000 Bern 7; tel. 313183133; fax 313183135; e-mail info@hep-verlag.ch; internet www.hep-verlag.ch; imprints Baufachverlag and Ott Verlag; educational and training material; Dir PETER EGGER.

Huber & Co AG: Promenadenstr. 16, Postfach 382, 8501 Frauenfeld; tel. 527235511; fax 527235530; e-mail info@huber.ch; internet www.huber.ch; f. 1809; art, history, politics, marketing/communications, philology, military, textbooks; Gen. Man. HANSRUDOLF FREY.

S. Karger AG: Allschwilerstr. 10, Postfach, 4009 Basel; tel. 613061111; fax 613061234; e-mail karger@karger.ch; internet www.karger.com; f. 1890; in Berlin, 1937 in Basel; international medical journals, books on medicine, chemistry, psychology; Pres. Dr THOMAS KARGER; CEO STEVEN KARGER.

Peter Lang AG: Moosstr. 1, Postfach 350, 2542 Pieterlen; tel. 323761717; fax 323761727; e-mail info@peterlang.com; internet www.peterlang.com; f. 1977; humanities, social sciences, German language and literature, Romance literatures and languages, linguistics, music, art, theatre, ethnology; CEO TONY ALBALÁ.

Müller Rüschlikon Verlags AG: Gewerbestr. 10, 6330 Cham; tel. 417403040; fax 417417115; e-mail info@bucheli-verlag.ch; f. 1936; non-fiction; Dir HEINZ JANSEN.

Nagel & Kimche AG, Verlag: Nordstr. 9, Postfach, 8035 Zürich; tel. 523666680; fax 523666688; e-mail info@nagel-kimche.ch; internet www.nagel-kimche.ch; f. 1983; belles-lettres, juvenile; Dir Dr DIRK VAIHINGER.

Neptun Verlag AG: Erlenstr. 2, 8280 Kreuzlingen; tel. 716779655; fax 716779650; e-mail neptun@bluewin.ch; internet www.neptunart.ch; f. 1946; travel books, children's, contemporary history; Dir H. BERCHTOLD-MÜHLEMANN.

Neue Zürcher Zeitung, Buchverlag: Postfach, 8021 Zürich; tel. 442581505; fax 442581399; e-mail buch.verlag@nzz.ch; internet www.nzz-buchverlag.ch; Man. HANS-PETER THÜR.

Verlag Niggli AG: Steinackerstr. 8, Postfach 135, 8583 Sulgen; tel. 716449111; fax 716449190; e-mail info@niggli.ch; internet www.niggli.ch; f. 1950; art, architecture, typography; Gen. Man. Dr J. CHRISTOPH BÜRKLE.

Novalis Verlag AG: Stokarbergstr. 76, Postfach 1021, 8200 Schaffhausen; tel. 526258764; fax 526258766; e-mail redaktion@novalis.ch; internet www.novalis.ch; f. 1974; the arts, cultural and social sciences, education; Dirs Dr M. FRENSCH, Dr MAX RAPOLD.

Orell Füssli Verlag: Dietzingerstr. 3, Postfach, 8036 Zürich; tel. 444667711; fax 444667412; e-mail info@ofv.ch; internet www.ofv.ch; f. 1519; management, history, law, schoolbooks, trade directories; Gen. Man. MANFRED HIEFNER-HUG.

Verlag Pro Juventute/Atlantis Kinderbücher: Seehofstr. 15, 8032 Zürich; tel. 442567717; fax 442567778; e-mail info@projuventute.ch; internet www.projuventute.ch; social science, children's, families; Man. URS GYSLING.

Friedrich Reinhardt Verlag: Missionsstr. 36, Postfach 393, 4012 Basel; tel. 612646464; e-mail verlag@reinhardt.ch; internet www.reinhardt.ch; f. 1900; belles-lettres, theology, periodicals; Dir ALFRED RÜDISÜHLI.

Rex-Verlag: Arsenalstr. 24, 6011 Kreins; tel. 414194719; fax 414194711; e-mail info@rex-verlag.ch; internet www.rex-verlag.ch; f. 1931; theology, pedagogics, fiction, juvenile; Dir MARKUS KAPPELER.

Ringier AG: Dufourstr. 23, 8008 Zürich; tel. 442596111; fax 442598635; e-mail info@ringier.ch; internet www.ringier.ch; f. 1831; newspapers, magazines, online services, television, print; CEO MARTIN WERFELI.

Sauerländer Verlage AG: Ausserfeldstr. 9, 5036 Oberentfelden; tel. 628368626; fax 628268620; e-mail verlag@sauerlaender.ch; internet www.sauerlaender.ch; f. 1807; juvenile, school books, textbooks, history, chemistry, periodicals (professional, trade, science); Dir KLAUS WILLBERG.

Schulthess Juristische Medien AG: Zwinglipl. 2, 8022 Zürich; tel. 442002999; fax 442002998; e-mail werbung@schulthess.com; internet www.schulthess.com; f. 1791; legal, social science, university textbooks; Man. Dir WERNER STOCKER.

Schwabe AG: Steinentorstr. 13, 4010 Basel; tel. 612789565; fax 612789566; e-mail verlag@schwabe.ch; internet www.schwabe.ch; f. 1488; medicine, art, history, philosophy; Dirs R. BIENZ, Dr U. BREITENSTEIN.

Schweizer Spiegel Verlag: Zürich; tel. 444221666; f. 1925; art, philosophy, psychology, poetry, education, general; Dir Dr P. HUGGLER.

Stämpfli Verlag AG: Wölflistr. 1, Postfach 8326, 3001 Bern; tel. 313006311; fax 313006688; e-mail verlag@staempfli.com; internet www.staempfliverlag.com; f. 1799; law, economics, history, art; Man. Dir Dr RUDOLF STÄMPFLI.

Theologischer Verlag Zürich AG (TVZ): Badenerstr. 73, Postfach, 3026 Zürich; tel. 442993355; fax 442993358; e-mail tvz@ref.ch; internet www.tvz-verlag.ch; f. 1934; religion, theology; Dir MARIANNE STAUFFACKER.

Tobler Verlag AG: Trogenerstr. 80, Postfach 642, 9450 Altstätten; tel. 717556060; fax 717551254; e-mail books@tobler-verlag.ch; internet www.tobler-verlag.ch; f. 1995.

Ch. Walter Verlag AG: Dorfstr. 81, Postfach 121, 8706 Meilen; e-mail info@walter-verlag.ch; internet www.walter-verlag.ch; f. 1916; psychology, religion, history of civilization, literature; Pres. Dr T. AURELIO; Man. RAUL NIEMANN.

Wepf & Co AG Verlag: Eisengasse 5, 4001 Basel; tel. 612698515; fax 612630244; e-mail wepf@dial.eunet.ch; internet www.wepf.ch; f. 1755; architecture, engineering, ethnology, geography, geology, mineralogy; Dir H. HERRMANN.

PUBLISHERS' ASSOCIATIONS

Association Suisse des Editeurs de Langue Française: 2 ave Agassiz, CP 1215, 1001 Lausanne; tel. 213197111; fax 213197910; e-mail aself@centrepatronal.ch; f. 1975; asscn of French-speaking publrs; Pres. FRANCINE BOUCHET; Vice-Pres. OLIVIER BABEL; Sec.-Gen. FRANÇOIS PERRET; 75 mems.

Schweizer Buchhändler- und Verleger-Verband (SBVV): Alderstr. 40, Postfach, 8034 Zürich; tel. 444212800; fax 444212818; e-mail sbvv@swissbooks.ch; internet www.swissbooks.ch; f. 1849; asscn of German-speaking Swiss booksellers and publrs; Central Pres. MEN HAUPT; Dir Dr MARTIN JANN; 550 mem. and affiliated firms.

Broadcasting and Communications

TELECOMMUNICATIONS

Swisscom AG: Alte Tiefenaustr. 6, 3050 Bern; tel. 313421111; fax 313422549; e-mail swisscom@swisscom.com; internet www.swisscom.com; fmrly Swiss Telecom PTT; 62.45% owned by Government; full privatization proposed Nov. 2005; Pres. MARKUS RAUH; CEO JENS ALDER.

BROADCASTING

The Swiss Broadcasting Corporation (SBC) is a private non-profit-making company, which fulfils a public duty on the basis of a licence granted to it by the Federal Government. The SBC uses the electrical and radio-electrical installations of Swisscom AG for public broadcasting of radio and television programmes. Swisscom is responsible for all technical aspects of transmission. Some 75.1% of the receiver licence fee is allocated to the SBC, while Swisscom takes 24.2% and the remainder is distributed among local radio and television stations.

SRG SSR idée suisse (Swiss Broadcasting Co—SBC): Giacomettistr. 3, Postfach 26, 3000 Bern 15; tel. 313509111; fax 313509256; e-mail info@srgssrideesuisse.ch; internet www.srgssrideesuisse.ch; f. 1931; Pres. JEAN-BERNARD MÜNCH; Dir-Gen. ARMIN WALPEN; Deputy Dir-Gen. DANIEL ECKMANN; SRG SSR idée suisse is composed of the following regional companies:

Cuminanza Rumantscha Radio e Televisiun (CRR): Via dal teater 1, 7002 Chur; tel. 812557575; fax 812557500.

Radio-Télévision suisse romande (RTSR): 40 ave du Temple, 1010 Lausanne; tel. 213181111; fax 213181976; e-mail secretariat.general@rtsr.ch; internet www.rtsr.ch; Pres. JEAN CAVADINI; Sec.-Gen. ESTHER JOUHET.

Società cooperativa per la radiotelevisione nella Svizzera italiana (CORSI): Segreteria CORSI, Via Canevascini 5, 6903 Lugano; tel. 918039325; fax 918039300.

SRG Idée suisse DEUTSCHSCHWEIZ (Radio- und Fernsehgesellschaft DRS): Fernsehstr. 1–4, Postfach, 8052 Zürich; tel. 443056703; fax 443056710; e-mail info@srgdeutschschweiz.ch; internet www.srgdeutschschweiz.ch; formerly Radio- und Fernsehgesellschaft der Deutschen und der Rätoromanischen Schweiz (RDRS).

Radio

Digital audio broadcasting (DAB) began in 1999 in Bern, Biel, Interlaken and Solothurn, and was soon expanded to include Basel, Geneva, Lausanne and Zürich. Approximately 4m. people (60% of the population) can receive DAB programmes. SRG-SSR idée suisse is the main DAB operator, providing 11 channels in the German-speaking cantons and 10 channels in the French-speaking cantons.

Radio Rumantsch (RR): Via dal teater 1, 7002 Chur; tel. 812557575; fax 812557500; e-mail contact@rtr.ch; internet www.rtr.ch; operated by Radio e Televisiun Rumantscha (RTR); daily programming in Romansch from 6am to 9pm Monday to Friday and from 8am to 9pm at weekends; Dir BERNARD CATHOMAS.

Radio suisse romande (RSR): 40 ave du Temple, 1010 Lausanne; tel. 213181111; fax 216523719; e-mail webmaster@rsr.ch; internet www.rsr.ch; offers four stations: **La Première** news and background reports, stories, entertainment and music; **Espace 2** classical and contemporary music, jazz and folk, with features on the arts, history and society, radio plays and concert broadcasts; **Couleur 3** youth station playing rock and pop, with current affairs features; **Option Musique** music station with news bulletins, traffic reports and weather forecasts; Dir GÉRARD TSCHOPP; Dir of Programmes ISABELLE BINGGELI; Dir of Information PATRICK NUSSBAUM.

Radio svizzera di lingua italiana (RSI): CP, 6903 Lugano; tel. 918035111; fax 918035355; e-mail info@rtsi.ch; internet www.rtsi.ch; operated by Radiotelevisione svizzera di lingua italiana (RTSI); operates three Italian-language stations: **Rete Uno** current affairs and reportage, also general entertainment programmes and public service broadcasts, **Rete Due** educational and general interest programmes, music and news, **Rete Tre** rock and pop music; Dir of Radio JACKY MARTI.

Schweizer Radio DRS (SR DRS): Novarastr. 2, Postfach, 4024 Basel; tel. 613653411; fax 613653250; e-mail programminfo@srdrs.ch; internet www.drs.ch; has three main studios in Zürich, Basel and Bern from which it operates five radio stations; **DRS 1** current affairs, traffic and weather reports and entertainment, six regional news magazines report regularly from around Switzerland; **DRS 2** classical music, jazz, culture, science, economics, politics and philosophy; **DRS 3** pop music and information, specializes in live concert broadcasts; **Musigwälle 531** traditional music of all genres, with news and **DRS1** programmes; **Virus** youth and multimedia; Dir WALTER RÜEGG.

Swiss Satellite Radio (SsatR): Giacomettistr. 1, 3000 Bern 15; tel. 313509333; fax 313509663; three Swiss Satellite Radio music channels, broadcast via the internet, cable and satellite; **Radio Swiss Pop** music-only service; **Radio Swiss Classic** classical music service with minimal presentation; **Radio Swiss Jazz** music service playing jazz, blues and soul.

Swissinfo/Schweizer Radio International (SRI): Giacomettistr. 1, 3000 Bern 15; tel. 313509222; fax 313500544; e-mail contact_swissinfo@swissinfo.ch; internet www.swissinfo.org; f. 1935; news and information programmes in English, French, German, Italian, Spanish, Portuguese, Japanese, Chinese and Arabic, short-wave and via satellites, Eutelsat HB3 and Worldspace; short-wave transmitters are situated at Sottens; relay stations in Germany and French Guiana; Dir BEAT WITSCHI.

There are also 48 local and regional radio stations active in Switzerland.

Television

A complete TV programme service for each linguistic region and regular broadcasts in Romansch are provided on the 1st (VHF) channel. The 2nd and 3rd (UHF) channels are used in each linguistic region for transmitting programmes of the other two linguistic regions. Limited direct advertising is allowed.

Digital Video Broadcasting (DVB) began in 2005, with analogue broadcasting to be discontinued in 2015.

Schweizer Fernsehen DRS (SF DRS): Fernsehstr. 1–4, Postfach, 8052 Zürich; tel. 443056611; fax 443055660; e-mail sfdrs@sfdrs.ch; internet www.sfdrs.ch; operates **SF1**, **SF2** and a third channel, **SF info** which repeats current affairs programmes from **SF1**, **SF2** and **Presse TV** in hourly and half-hourly blocks; Dir INGRID DELTENRE.

Télévision suisse romande (TSR): 20 quai Ernest-Ansermet, CP 234, 1211 Geneva 8; tel. 227082020; fax 223204813; e-mail tsr@tsr

SWITZERLAND

.ch; internet www.tsr.ch; operates **TSR1** and **TSR2**; Dir GILLES MARCHAND.

Televisione svizzera di lingua italiana (TSI): CP, 6903 Lugano; tel. 918035111; fax 918035355; e-mail info@rtsi.ch; internet www.rtsi.ch; operated by Radiotelevisione svizzera di lingua italiana (RTSI); two Italian-language channels: **TSI1** full-service channel aimed at a broad audience, **TSI2** complementary channel with sport, children's programmes and repeats of news programmes from **TSI1**; Dir of TV RENIGIO RATTI.

Televisiun Rumantscha (TvR): Via dal teater 1, 7002 Chur; tel. 812557575; fax 812557500; e-mail contact@rtr.ch; internet www.rtr.ch; operated by Radio e Televisiun Rumantscha (RTR); provides programming in Romansch (*Telesguard* and *Cuntrasts*) which is broadcast on SF1; Dir BERNARD CATHOMAS.

There are also 83 local and regional television stations, 18 of which have high transmission activity.

Finance

(cap. = capital; dep. = deposits; res = reserves; m. = million; brs = branches; all values are in Swiss francs)

BANKING

Switzerland's banks have a long-standing reputation as a secure repository for foreign capital. The Swiss Banking Law of 1934 declared it a penal offence for a bank to provide information about its clients without their explicit authorization, unless a court had ordered otherwise. When foreign authorities wish to investigate Swiss accounts, criminal charges must have been made in a foreign court and accepted as valid by Switzerland. The system of numbered accounts has also shielded depositors' shares from investigation. However, the abuse of bank secrecy by organized crime led Switzerland and the USA to sign a treaty in May 1973, whereby banking secrecy rules may be waived in the case of common-law crime (although not for non-criminal tax evasion and anti-trust law infringements). Further amendments to banking secrecy legislation were introduced in 1990 and 1998.

In June 1977 the Swiss banks agreed a code of practice which required the introduction of stricter controls over the handling of foreign funds. The opening of numbered accounts was subjected to closer scrutiny and the practice of actively encouraging the flow of foreign money into the country was checked. The agreement was modified in 1982. In 1987, following the withdrawal from the agreement of the Swiss National Bank, the code was adapted by the Swiss Bankers' Association into rules of professional conduct; further modifications to the code were introduced in 1992. In 1978, in view of the steady increase in Swiss banks' international business, the Federal Banking Commission was given greater supervisory powers. Banks were required for the first time to submit consolidated balance sheets to the Commission and new consolidation requirements forced banks to raise capital to between 6% and 8% of total liabilities. The capital requirement is now one of the highest in the world.

During the 1990s significant restructuring of the retail banking sector was envisaged as a response to a long-term profitability problem which was blamed on overcrowding in the sector. By 1997 approximately one-third of all banks in operation in 1990 had disappeared, mostly through merger or acquisition. The most important amalgamations during the 1990s were the take-over of Swiss Volksbank by Crédit Suisse in 1993 and the creation in 1998 of UBS AG by the merger of UBS-Union Bank of Switzerland and Swiss Bank Corporation.

At the end of 2002 there were 2,712 bank branches (including 722 loan offices) in Switzerland, owned by 342 banks. The total assets of all banks operating in Switzerland at the end of 2002 was 2,251,874m. francs.

The 24 canton banks are mostly financed and controlled by the cantons, and their activities are co-ordinated by the Association of Swiss Cantonal Banks. In 2002 they had 748 branches and controlled more than one-third of Switzerland's savings deposits.

Central Bank

Schweizerische Nationalbank/Banque nationale suisse (Swiss National Bank): Börsenstr. 15, Postfach 2800, 8022 Zürich; tel. 446313111; fax 446313911; e-mail snb@snb.ch; internet www.snb.ch; f. 1907; the object of the bank is to regulate the circulation of money, to facilitate payments transactions and to pursue a credit and monetary policy serving the general interest; Dept I (Zürich) is responsible for economic studies, international affairs, statistics, legal matters, personnel and internal auditing; Dept II (Bern) issues notes, manages metal reserves, runs the main accounting section and banking transactions for the Fed. Govt; Dept III (Zürich) handles foreign-exchange business and credits to the commercial banks in addition to giro and clearing functions; cap. 50m., res 68m., dep. 10,810m. (Dec. 2003); Chair. of Governing Bd Dr JEAN-PIERRE ROTH.

Canton Banks

There are 24 cantonal banks, of which the following are the largest:

Aargauische Kantonalbank: Bahnhofstr. 58, 5001 Aarau; tel. 628357777; fax 628357925; e-mail akb@akb.ch; internet www.akb.ch; f. 1913; cap. 200m., res 193m., dep. and bonds 12,538m. (Dec. 2003); Pres. ARTHUR ZELLER; CEO U. GRÄTZER; 28 brs.

Banca dello Stato del Cantone Ticino: Viale H. Guisan 5, 6501 Bellinzona; tel. 918037111; fax 918261364; e-mail contatto@bsct.ch; internet www.bancastato.ch; f. 1915; cap. 100m., res 123m., dep. and bonds 5,834m. (Dec. 2003); Chair. FULUIO PELLI; 3 brs.

Banque Cantonale de Fribourg: Blvd de Pérolles 1, 1701 Fribourg; tel. 848223223; fax 263507709; internet www.bcf.ch; f. 1892; cap. 70m., res 633m., dep. and bonds 8,468m. (Dec. 2004); Chair. GILBERT MENNERON; CEO ALBERT MICHEL; 25 brs.

Banque Cantonale de Genève: quai de l'Ile 17, CP 2251, 1211 Geneva; tel. 223172727; fax 227935960; e-mail info@bcge.ch; internet www.bcge.ch; f. 1994; cap. 360m., res 292m., dep. and bonds 14,589m. (Dec. 2003); Chair. MICHEL MATTACCHINI; CEO BLAISE GOETSCHIN; 28 brs.

Banque Cantonale du Jura: 10 rue de la Chaumont, CP 278, 2900 Porrentruy; tel. 324651301; fax 324651495; e-mail bcj@bcju.ch; internet www.bcju.ch; cap. 45m., res 90m., dep. and bonds 1,494m. (Dec. 2004); Chair. Dr PAUL-ANDRÉ SANGLARD.

Banque Cantonale du Valais: CP 133, Pl. des Cèdres, 1951 Sion; tel. 273246111; fax 273246666; e-mail info@bcvs.ch; internet www.bcvs.ch; cap. 150m., res 213m., dep. and bonds 6,308m. (Dec. 2003); Pres., Chair and Gen. Man. JEAN-DANIEL PAPILLOUD.

Banque Cantonale Neuchâteloise: 4 pl. Pury, 2001 Neuchâtel; tel. 327236111; fax 327236236; e-mail info@bcn.ch; internet www.bcn.ch; f. 1883; cap. 125m., res 119m., dep. 3,941m. (Dec. 2003); Pres. JEAN-PIERRE GHELFI.

Banque Cantonale Vaudoise: 14 pl. St François, CP 300, 1003 Lausanne; tel. 212121212; fax 212121222; e-mail info@bcv.ch; internet www.bcv.ch; f. 1845; cap. 1,380m., res 1,026m., dep. and bonds 27,406m. (Dec. 2003); Chair. OLIVIER STEINER; 69 brs.

Basellandschaftliche Kantonalbank: Rheinstr. 7, 4410 Liestal; tel. and fax 619259494; e-mail info@blkb.ch; internet www.blkb.ch; f. 1864; cap. 240m., res 449m., dep. and bonds 12,375m. (Dec. 2003); Pres. WERNER DEGEN; CEO PAUL NYFFELER; 10 brs.

Basler Kantonalbank: Spiegelgasse 2, 4002 Basel; tel. 612662121; fax 612618434; e-mail bkb@bkb.ch; internet www.bkb.ch; f. 1899; cap. 299m., res 332m., dep. and bonds 10,760m. (Dec. 2003); Chair. Dr WILLI GERSTER; CEO HANS-RUDOLF MATTER; 22 brs.

BEKB/BCBE (Berner Kantonalbank/Banque Cantonale Bernoise): Bundesplatz 8, 3001 Bern; tel. 316661111; fax 316666040; e-mail bekb@bekb.ch; internet www.bekb.ch; f. 1834; cap. 401m., res 577m., dep. and bonds 17,570m. (Dec. 2003); Pres. PETER W. KAPPELER; CEO JEAN-CLAUDE NOBILI; 84 brs.

Graubündner Kantonalbank: Postfach, 7002 Chur; tel. 812569111; fax 812526729; e-mail info@gkb.ch; internet www.gkb.ch; f. 1870; cap. 270m., res 285m., dep. and bonds 10,620m. (Dec. 2004); Pres. Dr HANS HATZ.

Luzerner Kantonalbank: Pilatusstr. 12, 6002 Lucerne; tel. 412062222; fax 412062200; e-mail info@lukb.ch; internet www.lukb.ch; f. 1850; cap. 425m., res 417m., dep. and bonds 15,362m. (Dec. 2003); Chair. PETER GALLIKER; 28 brs.

Schwyzer Kantonalbank: Bahnhofstr. 3, 6431 Schwyz; tel. 418194111; fax 418117355; e-mail info@szkb.ch; internet www.szkb.ch; f. 1889; as Kantonalbank Schwyz, current name adopted 1997; cap. 160m., res 702m., dep. and bonds 7,955m. (June 2005); Pres. ALOIS CAMENZIND; Man. GOTTFRIED WEBER; 28 brs.

St Galler Kantonalbank: St Leonhardstr. 25, Postfach 2063, 9001 St Gallen; tel. 712313131; fax 712313232; e-mail info@sgkb.ch; internet www.sgkb.ch; f. 1868; cap. 500m., res 577m., dep. and bonds 17,160m. (Dec. 2003); Pres. Dr U. RÜEGSEGGER; 37 brs.

Thurgauer Kantonalbank: Bankpl. 1, 8570 Weinfelden; tel. 71848111444; fax 71848111445; e-mail info@tkb.ch; internet www.tkb.ch; f. 1871; cap. 400m., res 148m., dep. and bonds 12,635m. (Dec. 2003); Chair. Dr PETER LINDT; CEO THEODOR PRINZ; 15 brs.

Urner Kantonalbank: Bahnhofstr. 1, 6460 Altdorf; tel. 418756000; fax 418756313; e-mail info@urkb.ch; internet www.urkb.ch; f. 1915; cap. 30m., res 40m., dep. and bonds 1,523m. (Dec. 2003); Pres. Dr HANSRUEDI STADLER.

Zuger Kantonalbank: Baarerstr. 37, 6301 Zug; tel. 417091111; fax 417091555; e-mail service@zugerkb.ch; internet www.zugerkb.ch; f. 1892; cap. 144m., res 234m., dep. and bonds 5,282m. (Dec. 2003); Chair. and Pres. WALTER WEBER; Gen. Man. T. LUGINBÜHL; 12 brs.

Zürcher Kantonalbank: Bahnhofstr. 9, Postfach, 8010 Zürich; tel. 442201111; fax 442111525; e-mail info@zkb.ch; internet www.zkb

SWITZERLAND

.ch; f. 1870; cap. 1,925m., res 2,470m., total assets 64,506m. (Dec. 2003); Chair Dr URS OBERHOLZER; 86 brs.

Commercial Banks (Selected List)

Baloise Bank SoBa: Amthauspl. 4, 4502 Solothurn; tel. 326260202; fax 326233692; e-mail info@baloise.ch; internet www.baloise.ch; f. 1994; cap. 50m., res 252m., dep. 4,842m. (Dec. 2003); Chair. Dr ROLF SCHÄUBLE; CEO ALOIS MÜLLER.

Banca del Gottardo: viale S. Franscini 8, CP 2811, 6901 Lugano; tel. 918081111; fax 919239487; e-mail info@gottardo.ch; internet www.gottardo.ch; f. 1957; cap. 170m., res 593m., dep. and bonds 8,045m. (Dec. 2003); Chair. C. GENERALI; 6 brs.

Bank Julius Baer & Co AG: Bahnhofstr. 36, 8010 Zürich; tel. 442285111; fax 442112560; f. 1890; cap. 6m., res 1,357m., dep. 10,369m. (Dec. 2002); Chair. RAYMOND J. BAER.

Bank Leu AG: Bahnhofstr. 32, 8001 Zürich; tel. 442191111; fax 442193797; e-mail info@leu.com; internet www.leu.com; f. 1755; cap. 200m., res 169m., dep. and bonds 7,287m. (Dec. 2003); Chair. WALTER BERCHTOLD; Pres. and CEO HANS NÜTZI; 2 brs.

Banque Thaler SA: 3 rue Pierre-Fatio, 1211 Geneva 3; tel. 227070909; fax 227070910; e-mail info@banquethaler.ch; internet www.banquethaler.ch; f. 1982; as KBC Bank (Suisse) SA, current name adopted 2000; cap. 20m., res 4m., dep. 21m. (Dec. 2003); Pres. ROBERT CUYPERS; Gen. Man. DIRK EELBODE.

BDL (Banco di Lugano): Piazzetta San Carlo 1, 6901 Lugano; tel. 919108111; fax 919232631; e-mail info@banco-di-lugano.ch; internet www.banco-di-lugano.ch; f. 1947; current name adopted 1990; cap. 50m., res 168m., dep. 3,406m. (Dec. 2003); Chair. KARL JANJÖRI.

BNP Paribas (Suisse) SA: 2 pl. de Hollande, 1204 Geneva; tel. 227877111; fax 227878000; internet www.bnpparibas.com; f. 1961; as United Overseas Bank SA, current name adopted 2001; cap. 320m., res 1,109m., dep 23,925m. (Dec. 2003); Chair. MICHEL FRANÇOIS-PONCET; Pres. and CEO ROBERT RICCI; 4 brs.

BSI AG: via Magatti 2, 6900 Lugano; tel. 918093111; fax 918093678; e-mail info@bsi.ch; internet www.bsibank.com; f. 1873; cap. 290m., res 325m., dep. and bonds 7,611m. (Dec. 2004); Chair. Dr GIORGIO GHIRINGHELLI; 7 brs.

Coutts Bank von Ernst Ltd: Stauffacherstr. 1, Postfach, 8022 Zürich; tel. 432455111; fax 432455396; internet www.cvbe.com; f. 1930; current name adopted 1994; cap. 110m., res 748m., dep. 13,041m. (Dec. 2005); Chair. The Earl of HOME; 5 brs.

Crédit Suisse Group: Crédit Suisse: Paradepl. 8, 8001 Zürich, Postfach 100, 8070 Zürich; tel. 443331111; fax 443325555; internet www.credit-suisse.ch; f. 1869; cap. 1,190m., res 28,896m., dep. 702,701m. (Dec. 2002); Group Chair. WALTER B. KIELHOLZ; 290 brs.

Crédit Suisse First Boston: Uetlibergstr. 231, 8045 Zürich, Postfach 1, 8070 Zürich; tel. 443335555; fax 443335599; internet www.csfb.com; f. 1856; corporate and investment banking; cap. 4,400m., res 13,646m., dep. and bonds 449,632m. (Dec. 2003); CEO JOHN J. MACK; 70 brs.

Ehinger & Armand von Ernst AG: Morgartenstr. 1, 8004 Zürich; tel. 442952111; fax 442952010; e-mail info@eave.com; internet www.eave.com; f. 2003 by merger of Cantrade Privatbank AG, Bank Ehinger & Cie AG and Armand von Ernst & Co Inc Banquiers; cap. 21m., res 185m., dep. and bonds 2,126m. (Dec. 2003); Chair. HANS DE GIER; CEO JEAN-PIERRE KLUMPP.

Hyposwiss Privatbank AG: Schützengasse 4, 8023 Zürich; tel. 442143111; fax 442115223; e-mail info@hyposwiss.ch; internet www.hyposwiss.ch; f. 1889; cap. 26m., res 49m., dep. 476m. (Dec. 2003); Chair. Dr URS RUERGIEGGER; Exec. Pres. URS BOLZERN.

Luzerner Regiobank AG: Piulatusstr. 22, Postfach 4970, 6002 Lucerne; tel. 412486655; fax 412486792; e-mail lrb.direktion@valiant.ch; internet www.lrb.ch; f. 1882; Pres. ERWIN GRÜTER; Man. HANS BRUNNER; 18 brs.

Migrosbank AG: Seidengasse 12, 8023 Zürich; tel. 442298111; fax 442298715; e-mail migrosbank@migros.ch; internet www.migrosbank.ch; f. 1957; cap. 364m., res 1,510m., dep. 24,216m. (Dec. 2003); Chair. Dr ANTON SCHERRER; Pres. Dr HARALD NEDWED; 39 brs.

Neue Aargauer Bank: Bahnhofstr. 49, 5001 Aarau; tel. and fax 628388080; f. 1989; 98.6% owned by Crédit Suisse Group AG; cap. 137m., res 348m., dep. 14,749m. (Dec. 2003); Pres. JOSEF BÜRGE; CEO HANS-MATHIAS KÄPPELI; 42 brs.

Schweizer Verband der Raiffeisenbanken/Union Suisse des Banques Raiffeisen: Wassergasse 24, 9001 St Gallen; tel. 712258888; fax 712258887; internet www.raiffeisen.ch; f. 1902; cap. 320m., res 4,032m., dep. 95,264m. (Dec. 2003); Chair. FRANZ MARTY.

Swissfirst Bank AG: Bellariastr. 23, 8002 Zürich; tel. 442048000; fax 442048080; e-mail info@swissfirst.ch; internet www.swissfirst.ch; f. 1923; cap. 22m., res 86m., dep. 486m. (Dec. 2003); Pres. HANS E. BUCK.

Swissquote Bank: 16 route des Avouillons, 1196 Gland; tel. 229999411; internet www.swissquote.ch; f. 2000; cap. 25m., dep. 180m. (Dec. 2002); Chair. MARIO FONTANA; CEO and Gen. Man. MARC BÜRKI.

UBS AG: Bahnhofstr. 45, 8021 Zürich; tel. 442341111; fax 442365111; e-mail info@ubs.com; internet www.ubs.com; f. 1998 by merger of UBS-Union Bank of Switzerland (f. 1912) and Swiss Bank Corpn (f. 1872); cap. 946m., res 35,427m., dep. 808,465m. (Dec. 2003); Chair. MARCEL OSPEL; 357 brs.

Union Bancaire Privée: 96–98 rue du Rhône, CP 1320, 1211 Geneva 1; tel. 228192111; fax 228192100; e-mail ubp@ubp.ch; internet www.ubp.ch; f. 1990 by merger of TDB American Express Bank (f. 1956) and Compagnie de Banque et d'Investissements (f. 1969); in 2002 merged with Discount Bank and Trust Co (f. 1952); cap. 300m., res 1,060m., dep. 12,035m. (Dec. 2004); Chair. EDGAR DE PICCIOTTO; Pres. and CEO GUY DE PICCIOTTO.

Valiant Bank: Bundespl. 4, Postfach 5333, 3001 Bern; tel. 313209111; fax 313209112; internet www.valiant.ch; f. 1857 as Spar- und Leihkasse in Bern/Caisse d'Epargne et de Prêts à Berne, present name adopted 2001; cap. 70m., res 533m., dep. 6,983m. (Dec. 2003); Chair. Prof. Dr ROLAND VON BÜREN.

Private Banks

Switzerland's private banking sector is the largest, in terms of assets, in the world. In 2005 there were 14 privately owned banks in Switzerland, of which the following are among the most important:

Banque Privée Edmond de Rothschild SA: 18 rue de Hesse, 1204 Geneva; tel. 228189111; fax 228189121; internet www.lcf-rothschild.ch; f. 1924; cap. 45m., res 366m., dep. 969m. (Dec. 2003); Chair. Baron BENJAMIN DE ROTHSCHILD; Gen. Man. CLAUDE MESSULAM; 2 brs.

EFG Private Bank SA: Postfach 2255, Bahnhofstr. 16, 8022 Zürich; tel. 442261717; fax 442261726; internet www.efgprivatebank.com; f. 1983; as Royal Bank of Scotland AG, current name adopted 1997; incorporated Banque Edouard Constant SA (f. 1964) in 2003; cap. 56m., res 111m., dep. 329m. (Dec. 2003); Chair. JEAN-PIERRE CUONI; CEO LAWRENCE D. HOWELL.

HSBC Private Bank (Suisse) SA: 2 quai Général Guisan, CP 3580, 1211 Geneva 3; tel. 587055555; fax 587055151; internet www.hsbcprivatebank.com; f. 1988 as Republic National Bank New York (Suisse) SA, present name adopted 2004; cap. 683m., res 1,143m., dep. 533,054m. (Dec. 2004); Chair. PETER WIDMER; 6 brs.

Lombard Odier Darier Hentsch & Cie: 11 rue de la Corraterie, 1211 Geneva 11; tel. 227092111; fax 227092911; e-mail contact@lodh.com; internet www.lodh.com; f. 2002 by merger of Lombard Odier & Cie (f. 1798) and Daroeer Hentsch & Cie (f. 1991); Snr Partners PIERRE DARIER, THIERRY LOMBARD; Partners JEAN A. BONNA, ERIC DEMOLE, PATRICK ODIER, RICHARD DE TSCHARNER, JACQUES ROSSIER, JEAN PASTRÉ, BARTHÉLEMY HELG, BERNARD DROUX, ANNE MARIE DE WECK, CHRISTOPHE HENTSCH.

Pictet & Cie Banquiers: 29 blvd Georges-Favon, CP 5130, 1211 Geneva 11; tel. 583232323; fax 583232324; e-mail info@pictet.com; internet www.pictet.com; f. 1805; Snr Partner IVAN PICTET; Partners CLAUDE DEMOLE, JACQUES DE SAUSSURE, NICOLAS PICTET, PHILIPPE BERTHERAT, JEAN-FRANÇOIS DEMOLE, RENAUD DE PLANTA, RÉMY BEST.

Central Co-operative Credit Institution

Bank Coop AG: Aeschenpl. 3, 4002 Basel; tel. 612862121; fax 612714595; e-mail netteam@bankcoop.ch; internet www.bankcoop.ch; f. 1927; fmrly Coop Bank/Banque Coop, present name adopted 2001; cap. 338m., res 312m., dep. 8,855m. (Dec. 2003); Chair. WILLI GERSTER; Exec. Pres. DAVID BECHER; 33 brs.

Regulatory Authorities

Eidgenössische Bankenkommission (Federal Banking Commission): Sekretariat, Schwanengasse 12, Postfach, 3001 Bern; tel. 313226911; fax 313226926; e-mail info@ebk.admin.ch; internet www.ebk.admin.ch; Dir DANIEL ZUBERBÜHLER.

Swiss Banking Ombudsman: Bahnhofpl. 9, Postfach 1818, 8021 Zürich; tel. 432661414; fax 432661415; internet www.bankingombudsman.ch; Ombudsman HANSPETER HÄNI.

Bankers' Organizations

Association of Foreign Banks in Switzerland: Postfach 6229, 8023 Zurich; Löwenstr. 51, 8001 Zurich; tel. 442244070; fax 442210029; e-mail info@foreignbanks.ch; internet www.foreignbanks.ch; f. 1972; Chair. Dr ALFREDO GYSI; Sec. Gen. Dr MARTIN MAURER.

Association Suisse des Banquiers/Schweizerische Bankiervereinigung (Swiss Bankers' Asscn): Aeschenpl. 7, Postfach 4182, 4002 Basel; tel. 612959393; fax 612725382; e-mail office@sba.ch; internet www.swissbanking.org; f. 1912; 934 mems; Chair. PIERRE MIRABAUD; CEO Dr URS P. ROTH.

SWITZERLAND

Verband Schweizerischer Kantonalbanken/Union des Banques Cantonales Suisses (Asscn of Swiss Cantonal Banks): Wallstr. 8, Postfach, 4002 Basel; tel. 612066666; fax 612066667; e-mail vskb@vskb.ch; internet www.kantonalbank.ch; f. 1907; perm. office est. 1971; Chair. PAUL NYFFELER; Man. CARLO MATI.

STOCK EXCHANGES

BX Berne Exchange (Berner Börsenverein): Aarbergergasse 36, 3011 Bern; tel. 313114042; fax 313115309; e-mail office@berne-x.com; internet www.bernerboerse.ch; f. 1884; 9 mems, 2 assoc. mems; Dir JÜRG NIEDERHÄUSER.

SWX Swiss Exchange: Selnaustr. 30, 8021 Zürich; tel. 442292111; fax 442292233; e-mail swx@swx.com; internet www.swx.com; f. 1873; 51 mems; Pres. PETER GOMEZ; CEO Dr HEINRICH HENCKEL; Man. A. HUNZIKER-EBNETER.

INSURANCE

In 2003 there were 158 insurance companies in Switzerland.

Allianz Continentale Allgemeine Versicherungs AG: Seestr. 356, 8038 Zürich; tel. 444889191; fax 444823580; f. 1974; general; Pres. Dr PETER ALTHER.

Allianz Continentale Lebensversicherungs AG: Seestr. 356, 8038 Zürich; tel. 444889191; fax 444823580; f. 1964; life; Pres. Dr PETER ALTHER.

Basler Lebens-Versicherungs-Gesellschaft: Aeschengraben 21, Postfach, 4002 Basel; tel. 612858585; fax 612857070; e-mail group.konzern@basler.ch; f. 1864; life, annuity; Chair. Dr ROLF SCHÄUBLE; Vice-Chair. WALTER FREHNER.

Basler Versicherungs-Gesellschaft: Aeschengraben 21, Postfach, 4002 Basel; tel. 612858585; fax 612857070; e-mail group.konzern@basler.ch; f. 1864; all classes except life; Chair. Dr ROLF SCHÄUBLE; Vice-Chair. WALTER FREHNER.

ELVIA-Life Swiss Life Insurance Co: 2 ave du Bouchet, 1211 Geneva 28; tel. 227344000; f. 1924; life; Pres. Dr HEINZ R. WUFFLI; Gen. Man. P. JUNGO.

GAN Incendie Accidents, Compagnie Française d'Assurances et de Réassurances: 70 ave C.-F. Ramuz, 1009 Pully-Lausanne; Head Office, Paris; tel. 217297121; fax 217288076; f. 1830.

La Genevoise, Compagnie d'Assurances sur la Vie: 16 ave Eugène-Pittard, 1211 Geneva 25; tel. 227042424; fax 227042704; f. 1872; life; Gen. Man. M. C. MEYER.

La Genevoise, Compagnie générale d'Assurances: 16 ave Eugène-Pittard, 1211 Geneva 25; tel. 227042424; fax 227042704; f. 1950; Gen. Man. M. C. MEYER.

Lebensversicherungs-Gesellschaft: Gen. Guisan-Str. 10, 8401 Winterthur; tel. 522611111; fax 522136620; f. 1923; life; Chair. Dr P. SPÄLTI.

Helvetia Patria Holding: Dufourstr. 40, 9001 St Gallen; tel. 714935111; fax 714935100; e-mail investor@helvetiapatria.com; internet www.helvetiapatria.com; f. 1861; life, fire, burglary, accident liability, motor; Chair. Dr HANS-RUDOLF MERZ; CEO ERICH WALSER.

Pax, Schweizerische Lebensversicherungs-Gesellschaft: Aeschenpl. 13, 4002 Basel; tel. 612776666; fax 612776565; e-mail info@pax.ch; internet www.pax.ch; f. 1876; life; Pres. GIANFRANCO BALESTRA.

Schweizerische Mobiliar: Bundesgasse 35, 3001 Bern; tel. 313896111; fax 313896852; e-mail mobi@mobi.ch; internet www.mobi.ch; f. 1826; accident, sickness, fire and damage by the elements, theft, valuables, damage by water, glass breakage, machines, construction work, interruption of business, epidemics, warranty, guarantee, third-party liability, motor vehicles, travel, transport; Pres. of Exec. Bd URS BERGER.

Swiss Life/Rentenanstalt: General Guisan-Quai 40, 8002 Zürich; tel. 442834311; fax 442842080; e-mail info.com@swisslife.ch; internet www.swisslife.ch; f. 1857; specializes in international employee benefit and pension plans; brs in Belgium, France, Germany and Netherlands; CEO ROLF DOERIG.

Swiss Re (Schweizerische Rückversicherungs-Gesellschaft) (Swiss Reinsurance Co): Mythenquai 50/60, 8022 Zürich; tel. 442852121; fax 442852999; internet www.swissre.com; f. 1863; world-wide reinsurance; Chair. Prof. Dr PETER FORSTMOSER; CEO JOHN COOMBER.

Winterthur Schweizerische Versicherungs-Gesellschaft: Gen. Guisan-Str. 40, Postfach 357, 8401 Winterthur; tel. 522611111; fax 522136620; e-mail info@winterthur.com; internet www.winterthur.com; f. 1875; merged with Crédit Suisse Group in 1997; Chair. OSWALD J. GRÜBEL.

Zenith Vie, Compagnie d'assurances sur la vie: 6 ave de la Tour Haldimand, 1009 Pully-Lausanne; tel. 217217000; fax 217217120; f. 1987; life; Gen. Man. GILBERT SMADJA.

Zürich Financial Services: Mythenquai 2, 8022 Zürich; tel. 446252525; internet www.zurich.com; f. 1998 by merger of Zürich Versicherungsgesellschaft (f. 1872) and BAT Industries PLC (UK); non-life, life, reinsurance, asset management; Chair. MANFRED GENTZ; CEO JAMES J. SCHIRO.

Zürich Lebensversicherungs-Gesellschaft: Austr. 46, 8036 Zürich; tel. 442052890; fax 442052029; f. 1922; life; CEO Dr GÜNTHER GOSE.

Insurance Organization

Schweizerischer Versicherungsverband (Swiss Insurance Asscn): C. F. Meyer-Str. 14, 8022 Zürich; tel. 442082828; fax 442082801; e-mail info@svv.ch; f. 1901; Pres. Dr H J. FREI; 80 mems.

Trade and Industry

GOVERNMENT AGENCIES

Osec Business Network Switzerland: Stampfenbachstr. 85, Postfach 492, 8035 Zürich; tel. 443655151; fax 443655221; e-mail info.zurich@osec.ch; internet www.osec.ch; promotes trade; CEO BALZ HÖSLY.

Staatssekretariat für Wirtschaft—SECO/Secrétariat d'Etat à l'économie—SECO/State Secretariat for Economic Affairs: Effingerstr. 31, 3003 Bern; tel. 313230710; fax 313248600; e-mail invest@seco.admin.ch; internet www.standortschweiz.ch; promotes investment in Switzerland.

PRINCIPAL CHAMBERS OF COMMERCE

Aargauische Industrie- und Handelskammer: Entfelderstr. 11, 5001 Aarau; tel. 628371818; fax 628371819; Pres. H. P. ZEHNDER.

Berner Handelskammer: Gutenbergstr. 1, 3001 Bern; tel. 313821711; fax 313821715; Pres. WALTER LEUENBERGER.

Bündner Handels- und Industrieverein: Poststr. 43, 7002 Chur; tel. 812526306; fax 812520449; Pres. OTTO BECK.

Camera di commercio dell'industria e dell'artigianato del Cantone Ticino: Corso Elvezia 16, 6901 Lugano; tel. 919115111; fax 919115112; e-mail cciati@cci.ch; internet www.cciati.ch; f. 1917; Pres. FRANCO AMBROSETTI; Dir CLAUDIO CAMPONOVO; 900 mems.

Chambre fribourgeoise du commerce, de l'industrie et des services: 37 route du Jura, 1706 Fribourg; tel. 263471220; fax 263471239; e-mail info@cfcis.ch; internet www.cfcis.ch; f. 1917; Pres. BERNARD SOTTAS; Dir ANDRÉ UEBERSAX.

Chambre de commerce et d'industrie de Genève: 4 blvd du Théâtre, 1211 Geneva 11; tel. 228199111; fax 228199100; e-mail ccig@cci.ch; internet www.ccig.ch; f. 1865; Pres. MICHEL BALESTRA; Dir JACQUES JEANNERAT; 1,500 mems.

Chambre de commerce et d'industrie du Jura: 23 rue de l'Avenir, CP 274, 2800 Delémont 1; tel. 324214545; fax 324214540; e-mail ccjura@cci.ch; internet www.ccij.ch; Pres. JEAN-PAUL RENGGLI; Dir JEAN-FRÉDÉRIC GERBER.

Chambre neuchâteloise du commerce et de l'industrie: 4 rue de la Serre, 2001 Neuchâtel; tel. 327257541; fax 327247092; Pres. YANN RICHTER; Dir CLAUDE BERNOULLI.

Chambre valaisanne de commerce et d'industrie: 6 rue Pré-Fleuri, CP 288, 1951 Sion; tel. 273273535; fax 273273536; Pres. JACQUES-ROLAND COUDRAY; Dir THOMAS GSPONER; 492 mems.

Chambre vaudoise du commerce et de l'industrie: 47 ave d'Ouchy, CP 315, 1001 Lausanne; tel. 216133535; fax 216133505; e-mail cvci@cvci.ch; internet www.cvci.ch; Pres. HUBERT BARDE; Dir JEAN-LUC STROHM; 2,100 mems.

Glarner Handelskammer: Spielhof 14A, 8750 Glarus; tel. 556401173; fax 556403639; e-mail glhk@landolt-partner.ch; Pres. ANDERS HOLTE; Sec. Dr KARLJÖRG LANDOLT.

Handelskammer beider Basel: Aeschenvorstadt 67, Postfach, 4010 Basel; tel. 612706060; fax 612706065; e-mail hkbb@hkbb.ch; internet www.hkbb.ch; Pres. THOMAS STAEHELIN; 800 mems.

Handelskammer und Arbeitgebervereinigung Winterthur (HAW): Neumarkt 15, 8401 Winterthur; tel. 522137352; Pres. Dr VIKTOR BEGLINGER.

Industrie- und Handelskammer St Gallen-Appenzell: Gallusstr. 16, Postfach, 9001 St Gallen; tel. 712241010; fax 712241060; e-mail sekretariat@ihk.ch; internet www.ihk.ch; f. 1466; Pres. Dr KONRAD HUMMLER.

Industrie- und Handelskammer Thurgau: Schmidstr. 9, Postfach, 8570 Weinfelden; tel. 716221919; fax 716226257; e-mail info@ihk-thurgau.ch; internet www.ihk-thurgau.ch; Pres. P. A. SCHIFFERLE.

Junior Chamber Switzerland: c/o Unirevisa AG, Spielhof 14A, 8750 Glarus; tel. 556407252; fax 556407435; e-mail zs@

SWITZERLAND

Directory

juniorchamber.ch; internet www.juniorchamber.ch; Sec. F. Dällenbach.

Schweizerische Zentrale für Handelsförderung/Office suisse d'expansion commerciale (OSEC): Stampfenbachstr. 85, 8035 Zürich; and ave de l'Avant-Poste 4, 1001 Lausanne; tel. 443655151; fax 443655221; e-mail info.zurich@osec.ch; tel. 213203231; fax 213207337; f. 1927; Pres. Philippe Lévy; Dir Martin Monsch; 2,000 mems.

Solothurner Handelskammer: Grabackerstr. 6, Postfach 1554, 4502 Solothurn; tel. 326262424; fax 326226426; e-mail info@sohk.ch; internet www.sohk.ch; f. 1874; Pres. Kurt Hoosli; Dir Dr Hans-Rudolf Meyer.

Zentralschweizerische Handelskammer: Kapellpl. 2, 6002 Lucerne; tel. 414106865; fax 414105288; e-mail info@hkz.ch; internet www.hkz.ch; f. 1889; Pres. Dr Werner Steinegger; Dir Alex Bruckert; 500 mems.

Zürcher Handelskammer: Bleicherweg 5, Postfach 3058, 8022 Zürich; tel. 442174050; fax 442174051; e-mail direktion@zurichcci.ch; internet www.zurichcci.ch; Pres. Andreas W. Keller; CEO Dr Lukas Briner; 1,300 mems.

INDUSTRIAL AND TRADE ASSOCIATIONS

Associazione Industrie Ticinesi: Corso Elvezia 16, 6901 Lugano; tel. 919235041; fax 919234636; Pres. Giancarlo Bordoni.

Basler Volkswirtschaftsbund: Aeschenvorstadt 71, Postfach 4010 Basel; tel. 612059600; fax 612059609; e-mail bvb@bvb.ch; internet www.bvb.ch; Pres. Marc R. Jaquet; Dir Barbara Gutzwiller-Holliger; 9,000 mems.

Chocosuisse—Verband Schweizerischer Schokoladefabrikanten: Münzgraben 6, 3000 Bern 7; tel. 313100990; fax 313100999; e-mail info@chocosuisse.ch; internet www.chocosuisse.ch; f. 1901; asscn of chocolate mfrs; Dir Dr F. U. Schmid; 22 mems.

Economiesuisse (Swiss Business Federation): Hegibachstr. 47, Postfach 1072, 8032 Zürich; tel. 444213535; fax 444213434; e-mail info@economiesuisse.ch; internet www.economiesuisse.ch; f. 1870; as Schweizerischer Handels- und Industrie-Verein, present name adopted 2000; Pres. Ueli Forster; Exec. Dir Dr Rudolf Ramsauer; 171 mems.

Fédération de l'Industrie Horlogère Suisse (FH): 6 rue d'Argent, 2501 Bienne; tel. 323280828; fax 323280880; e-mail info@fhs.ch; internet www.fhs.ch; f. 1876; watch industry fed; Pres. J. D. Pasche; 542 mems.

Föderation der Schweizerischen Nahrungsmittel-Industrien: Thunstr. 82, 3000 Bern 16; Münzgraben 6, 3000 Bern 7; and Elfenstrasse 19, 3000 Bern 16; tel. 313562121; fax 313510065; e-mail info@advo-emmenegger.ch; foodstuffs; Secs B. Hodler, G. Emmenegger, Dir F. U. Schmid; 216 mems.

Schweizerischer Baumeisterverband (SBV): Weinbergstr. 49, Postfach, 8035 Zürich; tel. 442588111; fax 442588335; e-mail verband@baumeister.ch; internet www.baumeister.ch; f. 1897; building contractors; Pres. W. Messmer; 3,000 mems.

Schweizerischer Elektrotechnischer Verein (SEV): Luppmenstr. 1, 8320 Fehraltorf; tel. 19561111; fax 19561122; electronics; Pres. Andreas Bellwald.

Schweizerischer Gewerbeverband (SGV) (Swiss Union of Small and Medium Enterprises): Schwarztorstr. 26, 3007 Bern; tel. 313801414; fax 313801415; e-mail info@sgv-usam.ch; internet www.sgv-usam.ch; f. 1879; Pres. Edi Engelberger; 284 sections.

Schweizerischer Verband für visuelle Kommunikation (Viscom): Alderstr. 40, Postfach, 8034 Zürich; tel. 444212828; fax 444212829; e-mail visc.schweiz@viscom.ch; internet www.viscom.ch; f. 1869; printing industry; Pres. Peter Edelmann; Dir Hans-Ulrich Bigler; 900 mems.

Schweizerischer Versicherungsverband: (see under Insurance).

SGCI Chemie Pharma Schweiz (Swiss Society of Chemical Industries): Nordstr. 15, Postfach 8035 Zürich; tel. 443681711; fax 443681770; e-mail mailbox@sgci.ch; internet www.sgci.ch; f. 1882; chemical and pharmaceutical industry; Pres. Dr R. Wehrli; Dir Dr B. Moser; 180 mems.

Swiss Cigarette: rue de l'Hôpital 15, CP 1376, 1701 Fribourg; tel. 264255050; fax 264255055; e-mail office@cisc.ch; internet www.swiss-cigarette.ch; f. 1933; formerly Communauté de l'industrie suisse de la cigarette; cigarette mfrs; Pres. (vacant); Sec.-Gen. Chantal Aeby Purro.

Swiss Retail Federation: Marktgasse 50, 3000 Bern 7; tel. 313124040; fax 313124041; e-mail info@swiss-retail.ch; internet www.swiss-retail.ch; formerly Verband der Schweizerischen Waren- und Kaufhäuser; Pres. Dr Klaus Hug.

Textilverband Schweiz: Beethovenstr. 20, Postfach 2900, 8022 Zürich; tel. 442897979; fax 442897980; e-mail contact@tvs.ch; internet www.swisstextiles.ch; f. 1874; textiles and fashion; Pres. Thomas Isler; Dir Dr Th. Schweizer; 230 mems.

Verband der Schweizerischen Gasindustrie: Grütlistr. 44, Postfach, 8027 Zürich; tel. 412883131; fax 412021834; f. 1920; Pres. J. Cavadini.

Verband Schweizerischer Kreditbanken und Finanzierungsinstitute (VSKF): Toblerstr. 97/Neuhausstr. 4, 8044 Zürich; tel. 442504340; fax 442504349; e-mail office@gigersimmen.ch; internet www.vskf.org; asscn of credit banks and finance institutes; Sec. Dr Robert Simmen.

Verband Schweizerische Ziegelindustrie: c/o Herrn RA Dr Peter R. Burkhalter, Advokatbüro Hodler & Emmenegger, Elfenstr. 19, Postfach, 3000 Bern 16; tel. 313521188; fax 313521185; e-mail info@chziegel.ch; internet www.chziegel.ch; f. 1874; heavy clay; Sec.-Gen. Dr Peter R. Burkhalter.

EMPLOYERS' ORGANIZATIONS

Central Organizations

Schweizerischer Arbeitgeberverband (Confed. of Swiss Employers): Hegibachstr. 47, Postfach, 8032 Zürich; tel. 444211717; fax 444211718; e-mail verband@arbeitgeber.ch; internet www.arbeitgeber.ch; f. 1908; Pres. Dr Rudolf Staempfli; Vice-Pres. Hubert Barde; Dir Dr Peter Hasler; 74 mems.

Schweizerischer Bauernverband (Union Suisse des Paysans, Lega svizzera dei contadini, Swiss Farmers' Union): Laurstr. 10, 5201 Brugg; tel. 564625111; fax 564415348; e-mail info@sbv-usp.ch; internet www.bauernverband.ch; f. 1897; Pres. H. J. Walter; Dir Jacques Bourgeois.

Principal Regional Organizations

Fédération des entreprises romandes: 98 rue de Saint-Jean, CP 5278, 1211 Geneva 11; tel. 227153111; fax 227153213; e-mail info@fer-ge.ch; internet www.fer-ge.ch; Pres. Daniel Delay; Sec.-Gen. Michel Barde.

Luzerner Industrie-Vereinigung: Kapellpl. 2, Postfach 3142, 6002 Lucerne; tel. 4106889; e-mail info@hkz.ch; internet www.hkz.ch; Pres. Werner Hug.

Union des associations patronales genevoises: 98 rue de Saint-Jean, 1211 Geneva 11; tel. 227153241; fax 227380434; e-mail uapg@uapg.ch; union of employers' asscns in Geneva; Pres. Nicolas Brunschwig.

Union des industriels valaisans: CP 2106, 1905 Sion; tel. 273232992; fax 273232288; Pres. Jurg Herold.

Verband der Arbeitgeber Region Bern (VAB): Kapellenstr. 14, Postfach 6916, 3001 Bern; tel. 313902581; fax 313902582; f. 1919; employers' asscn for the Bern region; Pres. Dr Rudolf Stämpfli.

Vereinigung Zürcherischer Arbeitgeberorganisationen: Selnaustr. 30, 8021 Zürich; tel. 588542827; fax 588542833; e-mail dieter.sigrist@swx.com; asscn of Zürich employers' orgs; Pres. Thomas Isler; Sec. Dieter Sigrist.

Sectional Organizations

Arbeitgeberverband Schweizerischer Papier-Industrieller: Bergstr. 110, 8032 Zürich; tel. 442669921; fax 442669949; e-mail zpk@zpk.ch; internet www.zpk.ch; paper mfrs; Pres. Heinz Hohl; Dir M. Fritz; 11 mems.

Convention Patronale de l'Industrie Horlogère Suisse: 65 ave Léopold-Robert, 2301 La Chaux-de-Fonds; tel. 329100383; fax 329100384; e-mail info@cpih.ch; internet www.cpih.ch; f. 1937; watch mfrs; Pres. J. Cavadini; Gen. Sec. F. Matile; 9 mems.

Swissmem (ASM and VSM) (Swiss Mechanical and Electrical Engineering Industries): Kirchenweg 4, Postfach, 8032 Zürich; tel. 443844111; fax 443844242; e-mail info@swissmem.ch; internet www.swissmem.ch; f. 1905; Pres. J. N. Schneider-Ammann; Dir Thomas Daum; c. 930 mems.

UTILITIES

Electricity

Verband Schweizerischer Elektrizitätsunternehmen: Hintere Bahnhofstr. 10, Postfach, 5001 Aarau; tel. 628252525; fax 628252526; e-mail info@strom.ch; internet www.strom.ch; electricity producers' asscn; f. 1895; Pres. Dr R. Steiner; Dir A. Bucher.

Gas

Verband der Schweizerischer Gasindustrie: Grütlistr. 44, 8002 Zürich; tel. 442883131; fax 442021834; e-mail vsg@erdgas.ch; internet www.erdgas.ch; gas industry asscn.

Water

The cantons are responsible for the supply of water, but delegate to the municipalities and communes. As a result Switzerland has some 3,000 water companies. Water is usually supplied by a public company or co-operative, such as the municipal water suppliers for Winterthur, Basel and Zürich (Städische Werke Winterthur, Industrielle Werke Basel, Wasserversorgung Zürich).

TRADE UNIONS

Schweizerischer Gewerkschaftsbund (Swiss Fed. of Trade Unions): Monbijoustr. 61, 3007 Bern; tel. 313770101; fax 313770102; e-mail info@sgb.ch; internet www.sgb.ch; f. 1880; main trade union org.; affiliated to ICFTU; Pres. PAUL RECHSTEINER; total affiliated membership 393,128.

The principal affiliated unions are:

Comedia (Media): Postfach 6336, 3001 Bern; tel. 313906611; fax 313906691; e-mail sekretariat@comedia.ch; internet www.comedia.ch; f. 1858; Pres. C. TIREFORT; 17,000 mems.

Gewerkschaft Kommunikation (Communications Union): Looslistr. 15, Postfach 370, 3027 Bern; tel. 319395211; fax 319395262; e-mail zentralsekretariat@gewerkschaftkom.ch; internet www.gewerkschaftkom.ch; f. 1999; Pres. CHRISTIAN LEVRAT; 37,000 mems.

Schweizerischer Eisenbahn- und Verkehrspersonal-Verband (SEV) (Railway Workers): Steinerstr. 35, Postfach, 3000 Bern 6; tel. 313575757; fax 313575858; e-mail info@sev-online.ch; internet www.sev-online.ch; f. 1919; Pres. PIERRE-ALAIN GENTIL; 54,000 mems.

Schweizerischer Verband des Personals öffentlicher Dienste (Public Services): Sonnenbergstr. 83, Postfach, 8030 Zürich; tel. 442665252; fax 442665253; e-mail vpod@vpod-ssp.ch; internet www.vpod-ssp.ch; f. 1905; Pres. CHRISTINE GOLL; Gen. Sec. DORIS SCHUEPP; 38,000 mems.

Unia: Monbijoustr. 61, Postfach 3000, Bern 23; tel. 313760900; fax 313760904; e-mail info@unia.ch; internet www.unia.ch; f. 2004 by merger of Gewerkschaften Bau und Industrie (GBI), Gewerkschaft Industrie, Gewerbe, Dienstleistungen (SMUV), Gewerkschaft Verkauf, Handel, Transport, Lebensmittel (VHTL) and Gewerkschaft Unia; represents construction and engineering industries as well as employees in the retail and catering sectors; 200,000 mems; Pres VASCO PEDRINA, RENZO AMBROSETTI.

Syna, die Gewerkschaft (Syndicat Interprofessionnel, Sindicato Interprofessionale): Josefstr. 59, 8031 Zürich; tel. 442797171; fax 442797172; e-mail zuer@syna.ch; internet www.syna.ch; f. 1998 to replace Landesverband freier Schweizer Arbeitnehmer (f. 1919); Pres. MAX HAAS; Sec. Dr ANDREAS HUBLI; 68,000 mems.

Travail Suisse (CNG) (Confed. of Christian Trade Unions): Hopfenweg 21, Postfach 5775, 3001 Bern; tel. 313702111; fax 313702109; e-mail info@travailsuisse.ch; internet www.travailsuisse.ch; f. 1907; as Christlichnationaler Gewerkschaftsbund der Schweiz; Pres. H. FASEL; Sec THERESE SCHMID; 102,274 mems.

Transport

RAILWAYS

The boring of the 35-km Lötschberg tunnel was completed in May 2005; it was the longest overland tunnel in the world at that time and the third longest tunnel. The tunnel was to carry both transalpine freight and passenger traffic by rail, thereby easing congestion on the roads above. Construction of the railway within the new tunnel was expected to be completed by 2007, and was expected to shorten travel time between Germany and the Italian city of Milan by about one hour. Excavation of a further 57-km rail tunnel, the Gotthard Base Tunnel, was underway in 2006 and was scheduled for completion in 2015. The St Gotthard rail tunnel was opened in 1982.

Schweizerische Bundesbahnen (SBB) (Chemins de fer fédéraux suisses): Hochschulstr. 6, 3000 Bern 65; tel. 512201111; fax 512204265; e-mail railinfo@sbb.ch; internet www.sbb.ch; f. 1901; 2,910 km in 1998 (of which 2,902 km were electrified); Pres. THIERRY LALIVE D'EPINAY; Gen. Man. Dr BENEDIKT WEIBEL.

Small private companies control private railways in Switzerland, chiefly along short mountain routes, with a total length of around 2,032 km. The following are among the principal private railways:

BLS Loetschbergbahn Ltd: Genfergasse 11, Postfach, 3001 Bern; tel. 313272727; fax 313272910; e-mail info@bls.ch; internet www.bls.ch; f. 1906; 245 km; 11 passenger routes; cargo services on Lötschberg–Simplon route; direct car-train connection from Bern to the Valais and Italy; boat services on Lakes Thun and Brienz; 5 commuter rail services in Bern; Man. Dr M. TROMP.

Centovalli Railway: Via Franzoni 1, CP 146, 6601 Locarno; tel. 917560400; fax 917560499; e-mail fart@centovalli.ch; internet www.centovalli.ch; f. 1909; 19 km; Locarno–Camedo; Dir DIRK MEYER.

Matterhorn Gotthard Bahn AG: Nordstr. 20, 3900 Brig; tel. 279277777; fax 279277779; e-mail info@mgbahn.ch; internet www.mgbahn.ch; f. 2003; merger between BVZ Zermatt-Bahn AG and Furka Oberalp Bahn AG; 25% state-owned, 75% owned by BVZ Holding AG; Zermatt–Brig–Disentis and Andermatt–Göschenen; 144 km; Chair. DANIEL LAUBER; Dir HANS MOOSER.

Matterhorn Gotthard Bahn Verkehrs AG: 75% owned by BVZ Holding AG, 25% state-owned; controls all railway operation, incl. rolling atock, depots and related maintenance; Pres. DANIEL LAUBER.

Matterhorn Gotthard Bahn Infrastruktur AG: 100% state-owned; responsible for track, overhead catenary equipment, operating control centres, station bldgs and workshops; Pres. ROLF ESCHER.

Montreux-Oberland Bernois: CP 1426, 1820 Montreux; tel. 219898181; fax 219898100; e-mail mob@mob.ch; internet www.mob.ch; f. 1899; 75 km; Montreux–Château d'Oex–Gstaad–Zweisimmen–Lenk i/S; operates tour services incl. GoldenPass Panoramic, Belle Epoque, Rochers-de-Naye, Les Pléiades and the Chocolate Train; operates funicular railways on Vevey–Chardonne–Mont-Pèlerin and Les Avants–Sonloup routes; Dir R. KUMMROW.

Rhaetian Railway: Bahnhofstr. 25, 7002 Chur; tel. 812549100; fax 812549118; e-mail info@rhaetische-bahn.ch; internet www.rhaetische-bahn.ch; f. 1889; 375 km; the most extensive of the privately run railways; Dir S. FASCIATI.

Südostbahn AG: Bahnhofplatz 1A, 9001 St Gallen; tel. 712282323; fax 712282333; e-mail info@sob.ch; internet www.sob.ch; f. 1889; founded by a merger between Schweizerische Südostbahn and Bodensee–Toggenburg-Bahn in 2001; 119km; Pres. GEORG HESS.

ROADS

In 2002 Switzerland had 71,212 km of roads: 1,706 km of motorways and expressways, 18,109 km of other main roads and 51,397 km of secondary roads. The construction of a national network of approximately 1,857 km of motorways is scheduled for completion by 2010. The 17-km road tunnel through the Saint Gotthard Pass, a European road link of paramount importance, was opened in 1980. Vehicles of more than 39 metric tons are prohibited from traversing Switzerland.

Swiss Federal Roads Authority (Bundesamt für Strassen/Office fédéral des routes): Worblentalstr. 68, Ittigen, 3003 Bern; tel. 313229411; fax 313232303; e-mail webmaster@astra.admin.ch; internet www.astra.admin.ch; Dir RUDOLF DIETERLE.

INLAND WATERWAYS

In 2000 there were some 190 passenger vessels, 15 of which were steamships, on the Swiss rivers and lakes, representing a tourist attraction of major importance. The vessels had a seating capacity of around 67,000 passengers and carried some 12m. passengers over 2m. km.

Inland navigation legislation is the responsibility of the Confederation, but sovereignty over the waterways rests with the Cantons. This means, in practice, that the Confederation limits its activities to the supervision of the licensed shipping companies (passenger ships and the related infrastructure, such as landing stages) and pilots; the Cantons supervise pleasure-boat navigation (sports boats, i.e. sail and motor boats, etc.) and the non-licensed passenger vessels and goods shipping on the lakes and rivers. In 2000 24 shipping companies held a federal licence.

SHIPPING

In 2004 Switzerland's registered merchant fleet comprised 23 vessels, with an aggregate displacement of 487,500 grt. The principal shipping companies in Switzerland are:

Keller Shipping Ltd: Holbeinstr. 68, Postfach 3479, 4002 Basel; tel. 612818686; fax 612818679; Pres. A. R. KELLER.

Mediterranean Shipping Co SA: 40 ave Eugène-Pittard, 1206 Geneva; tel. 227038888; fax 227038787; Dir G. APONTE.

Natural van Dam AG: Westquaistr. 62, 4019 Basel; tel. 616399233; fax 616399250; e-mail naturalvandam@nvd.ch; internet www.nvd.ch; shipping management; Dir HEINZ AMACKER.

Navirom AG: St Alban-Anlage 64, 4052 Basel; tel. 613135816; fax 613135805.

Schweizerische Reederei & Neptun AG: Wiesendamm 4, 4019 Basel; tel. 616393333; fax 616393466; e-mail info@srn.ch; internet www.srn.ch; Dir H. SCHMITT.

Stolt-Nielsen AG: Uferstr. 90, Postfach, 4057 Basel; tel. 616388200; fax 616388211.

SWITZERLAND

Suisse-Atlantique, Société de Navigation Maritime SA: 7 ave des Baumettes, CP 48, 1020 Renens 1; tel. 216372201; fax 216372202; e-mail activity@suisse-atlantique.ch; world-wide tramping services; Pres. E. ANDRE; Dir C. DIDAY; mans of:

Navemar SA: 1 Grand' Places, 1700 Fribourg.

Van Ommeren (Schweiz) AG: Hafenstr. 87–89, Postfach, 4127 Birsfelden.

Vinalmar SA: 7 rue du Mont-Blanc, 1211 Geneve 1; tel. 229060431; fax 227386467.

CIVIL AVIATION

Switzerland's principal airports are situated at Zürich, Geneva and Basel-Mulhouse.

Swiss (Swiss International Airlines Ltd): Postfach, 4002 Basel; tel. 615820000; fax 615823333; e-mail communications@swiss.com; internet www.swiss.com; f. 1979 as Crossair, took over operations from Swissair and adopted current name in 2002; national carrier operating routes to 44 countries; 20.4% owned by Federal Govt, 12.2% by cantons; Chair. and CEO PIETER BOUW.

Tourism

Switzerland's principal attractions are the lakes and lake resorts and the mountains. Walking, mountaineering and winter sports are the chief pastimes. Foreign tourist arrivals at hotels and similar establishments totalled 6.5m. in 2003. Receipts from tourism were US $11,344m. in 2003.

Switzerland Tourism: Head Office: Tödistr. 7, 8027 Zürich; tel. 442881111; fax 442881205; e-mail info@switzerland.com; internet www.myswitzerland.com; f. 1917; Dir JÜRG SCHMID; offices in most major cities of the world.

SYRIA

Introductory Survey

Location, Climate, Language, Religion, Flag, Capital

The Syrian Arab Republic lies in western Asia, with Turkey to the north, Iraq to the east and Jordan to the south. Lebanon and Israel are to the south-west. Syria has a coastline on the eastern shore of the Mediterranean Sea. Much of the country is mountainous and semi-desert. The coastal climate is one of hot summers and mild winters. The inland plateau and plains are dry but cold in winter. Average temperatures in Dimashq (Damascus) range from 2°C to 12°C (36°F to 54°F) in January and from 18°C to 37°C (64°F to 99°F) in August. The national language is Arabic, with Kurdish a minority language. At December 2005 there were 432,048 Palestinian refugees registered in Syria. More than 80% of the population are Muslims (mostly Sunnis), but there is a substantial Christian minority of various sects. The national flag (proportions 2 by 3) has three equal horizontal stripes, of red, white and black, with two five-pointed green stars in the centre of the white stripe. The capital is Damascus.

Recent History

Syria was formerly part of Turkey's Ottoman Empire. Turkish forces were defeated in the First World War (1914–18) and Syria was occupied in 1920 by France, in accordance with a League of Nations mandate. Syrian nationalists proclaimed an independent republic in September 1941. French powers were transferred in January 1944, and full independence was achieved on 17 April 1946. In December 1949 Syria came under a military dictatorship, led by Brig. Adib Shishekly. He was elected President in July 1953, but was overthrown by another army coup in February 1954.

In February 1958 Syria merged with Egypt to form the United Arab Republic (UAR). In September 1961, following a military coup in Damascus, Syria seceded and formed the independent Syrian Arab Republic. In 1963 Maj.-Gen. Amin al-Hafiz formed a Government in which members of the Arab Socialist Renaissance (Baath) Party were predominant. In February 1966 the army deposed the Government of President al-Hafiz, replacing him with Dr Nur ed-Din al-Atasi. However, in November 1970, after a bloodless coup, the military (moderate) wing of the Baath Party seized power, led by Lt-Gen. Hafiz al-Assad, who was elected President in March 1971. In March 1972 the National Progressive Front (NPF), a grouping of the five main political parties (including the Baath Party), was formed under the leadership of President Assad.

Increasing border tension between Syria and Israel was a major influence leading to the Six-Day War of June 1967, when Israel attacked its Arab neighbours in reprisal for the closure of the Strait of Tiran by the UAR (Egypt). Israeli forces made swift territorial gains, including the Golan Heights region of Syria, which remains under Israeli occupation. An uneasy truce lasted until October 1973, when Egyptian and Syrian forces launched simultaneous attacks on Israeli-held territory. On the Syrian front, there was fierce fighting in the Golan Heights until a cease-fire was agreed after 18 days. In May 1974 the US Secretary of State, Henry Kissinger, secured an agreement for the disengagement of forces. Israel's formal annexation of the Golan Heights in December 1981 effectively impeded the prospect of a negotiated Middle East settlement at this time.

Syria disapproved of the second interim Egyptian-Israeli Disengagement Agreement, signed in September 1975, but agreed to acknowledge it as a *fait accompli* in return for Egypt's acceptance of Syria's role in Lebanon. Syria had progressively intervened in the Lebanese civil war during 1976, finally providing the bulk of the 30,000-strong Arab Deterrent Force (ADF). Syria condemned the Egyptian President, Anwar Sadat, for Egypt's peace initiative with Israel in November and December 1977, the Camp David agreements signed by Egypt and Israel in September 1978, and the subsequent peace treaty concluded between them.

From 1977 frequent assassinations of Alawites (the minority Islamic sect to which Assad belonged) indicated sectarian tension within Syrian society. Assad attributed much of the opposition to the Muslim Brotherhood, a conservative Islamist group, and he ordered the brutal suppression of an uprising in Hamah (Hama), led by the outlawed Brotherhood, in February 1982. From November 1983, after Assad suffered a heart attack, rivals to the succession—including Col Rifaat al-Assad, the President's brother—vied for pre-eminence. In March 1984, following Assad's recovery, the appointment of three Vice-Presidents had the effect of equally distributing power among the President's potential successors and giving none the ascendancy. Assad was also able to rely on a cadre of loyal officers who ensured the army's continued support for the President.

The ADF, based in northern Lebanon, was unable to act when Israel invaded southern Lebanon in June 1982 and surrounded Beirut, trapping Syrian troops and fighters of the Palestine Liberation Organization (PLO). The Syrian and Palestinian forces in Beirut were evacuated in August, under the supervision of a multinational peace-keeping force, and some 50,000 Syrian troops, deployed in the Beka'a valley and northern Lebanon, faced 25,000 Israelis in the south of the country, even though the ADF's mandate had expired. Syria rejected the May 1983 Israel-Lebanon peace agreement, formulated by US Secretary of State George Shultz, refusing to withdraw its forces from Lebanon and continuing to supply the militias of the Lebanese Druze and Shi'ite factions in their fight against the Lebanese Government and the Christian Phalangists. From May 1983 Syria supported a revolt against Yasser Arafat and the leadership of Fatah (the Palestine National Liberation Movement) and by November Syrian and rebel PLO forces had cornered Arafat, the PLO Chairman, in the Lebanese port of Tarabulus (Tripoli). Arafat and some 4,000 of his supporters were eventually evacuated, under UN protection, in December.

In March 1984 President Amin Gemayel of Lebanon capitulated to Syria's influence over Lebanese affairs, and abrogated the May 1983 agreement with Israel. In April President Assad approved Gemayel's plans for a Lebanese government of national unity, giving equal representation to Muslims and Christians. In September Syria arranged a truce to end fighting in Tripoli between the pro-Syrian Arab Democratic Party and the Sunni Tawheed Islami (Islamic Unification Movement). The Lebanese army entered the city in late 1984, under the terms of a Syrian-backed extended security plan, to assert the authority of the Lebanese Government. Syria also authorized Lebanon's participation in talks with Israel to co-ordinate the departure of the Israeli Defence Force (IDF) from southern Lebanon (with that of other security forces), in order to prevent an outbreak of civil violence. After the final stage of the Israeli withdrawal in early June 1985, several hundred Israeli troops and advisers remained in Lebanon to assist the Israeli-backed 'South Lebanon Army' (SLA) in policing a narrow buffer zone along the Lebanese side of the international border. Syria removed 10,000–12,000 troops from the Beka'a valley in July, leaving some 25,000 in position.

President Assad was re-elected for a third seven-year term of office in February 1985, and in early 1985 Syria involved itself in seeking to resolve Lebanon's sectarian unrest. Through its proxy, Amal, Syria sought to prevent Yasser Arafat from re-establishing a power-base in Beirut, and around 650 people died in the fighting before a cease-fire was agreed in Damascus in June. In Damascus in December the three main Lebanese militias—the Druze, Amal and Lebanese Forces (LF) Christian militia—signed a Syrian-brokered accord outlining a politico-military settlement of the civil war. However, the Shi'ite Hezbollah and Sunni Murabitoun militias were not party to the accord and President Gemayel, who had not been consulted during the drafting of the agreement, refused to endorse it. Opposition to the accord was further manifested following Samir Gaegea's promotion to the leadership of the LF in January 1986. Syria brokered another cease-fire in June, this time in the Palestinian refugee camps around Beirut (where fighting between Palestinian guerrillas and Shi'ite Amal militiamen had recently escalated); this proved to be the first stage in a Syrian-sponsored peace plan for Muslim west Beirut. The co-operation of the Amal, Druze and Sunni militias was dependent upon the deployment of uniformed Syrian troops in Beirut for the first time since 1982. Though the activities of the militias in west Beirut were temporarily curbed, the plan was strongly opposed in Christian east Beirut and was not extended to the predominantly Shi'ite southern suburbs, where most of the city's Palestinian refugees lived. By early 1987 heavy fighting had resumed in west Beirut, between Amal forces and an alliance of Druze, Murabitoun and Communist Party militias. Syrian troops (soon numbering some 7,500) succeeded in enforcing a cease-fire in the central and northern areas of west Beirut, but were not deployed in the southern suburbs.

At a general election held in February 1986 the Baath Party and other members of the NPF (excluding the Communist Party, which contested the poll independently) obtained 151 of the 195 seats in the People's Assembly. The communists won nine seats, and independents 35. In November 1987, following the resignation of Abd ar-Rauf al-Kassem as Prime Minister, Mahmoud az-Zoubi, the Speaker of the Assembly, was appointed premier. In May 1988 Syria's interest in the Lebanese presidential election, scheduled to be held in August of that year, prompted an intense period of fighting between Amal and Hezbollah in Beirut's southern suburbs. Overt Syrian support for the candidacy of Sulayman Franjiya (President of Lebanon during 1970–76), and later for Mikhail ad-Daher (after the first postponement of the election), aroused the opposition of Lebanese Christian leaders, who objected to candidates imposed by foreign powers. Consequently, Syria refused to recognize the interim military administration appointed by President Gemayel shortly before his term of office expired. From March 1989 Christian forces, commanded by Gen. Michel Awn (the head of the interim Lebanese Government), attempted to expel Syrian forces from Lebanon, thereby provoking one of the most violent confrontations of the entire civil war.

In October 1989, under the auspices of the League of Arab States (the Arab League, see p. 306), the Lebanese National Assembly endorsed a charter of national reconciliation (the Ta'if agreement). The Lebanese authorities envisaged a continuing role for the Syrian army in Lebanon by stipulating that it should assist in the implementation of two security plans incorporated in the accord, which also included the constitutional amendments that Syria had long sought to effect in Lebanon. (For further details concerning the Ta'if agreement, see the chapter on Lebanon.) In May 1991 Syria and Lebanon signed a treaty of 'fraternity, co-operation and co-ordination', which was immediately denounced by Israel as a further step towards the formal transformation of Lebanon into a Syrian protectorate. Israel responded by deploying armed forces inside the buffer zone in southern Lebanon, and any likelihood of Israel's compliance with UN Security Council Resolution 425 (adopted in March 1978), which demanded the withdrawal of Israeli armed forces from southern Lebanon, diminished. Syria was the only Arab state which refused to recognize the independent Palestinian state (proclaimed by the Palestine National Council in November 1988), in accordance with its long-standing policy of preventing any other force in Lebanon from acquiring sufficient power to challenge Syrian interests. Meanwhile, Syria persistently denied claims, principally by the USA, that it was sponsoring international terrorism, and refused to restrict the activities of Palestinian groups on its territory. Following a series of bomb attacks in Europe in 1985–86, in November 1986 members of the European Community (EC, now European Union—EU, see p. 228), excluding Greece, imposed limited diplomatic and economic sanctions against Syria, as did the USA and Canada. However, the EC (with the exception of the United Kingdom) ended its ban on ministerial contacts with Syria in July 1987; financial aid was resumed in September, although a ban on the sale of weapons to Syria remained in force.

At elections to the People's Assembly (now expanded to 250 seats) in May 1990, the Baath Party won 134 seats and other parties 32, while 84 seats were reserved for independent candidates. In December 1991 it was announced that 2,864 political prisoners were to be released; this was regarded as the first indication of President Assad's intention to liberalize Syria's political system. In March 1992 Assad indicated that new political parties might in future be established, but he rejected the implementation of foreign democratic frameworks as unsuited to the country's level of economic development. In January 1994 Basel al-Assad, President Assad's eldest son and presumed successor, was killed in a road accident; the President's second son, Bashar, was reportedly instructed to assume the role of his late brother in order to avoid a power struggle. In August senior government officials, including the Commander of the Special Forces, were removed from office in an apparent attempt by Assad to consolidate his position and improve Syria's international standing.

At elections to the People's Assembly held in August 1994, the ruling Baath Party and its NPF allies reinforced their dominance of Syrian affairs, winning 167 of the Assembly's 250 seats. In November 1995—the 25th anniversary of President Assad's seizure of power—some 1,200 political prisoners, including members of the banned Muslim Brotherhood, were released under an amnesty, while a number of the Brotherhood's leaders were allowed to return from exile. During 1996 there were reports of several explosions in Damascus, in addition to a number of attacks on Syrian targets in Lebanon. In January 1997 the Syrian-based Islamic Movement for Change claimed responsibility for a bomb attack in central Damascus in December 1996, in which 11 people died.

In February 1998 President Assad unexpectedly dismissed his brother, Col Rifaat al-Assad, as Vice-President (a post he had held since 1984, although he had spent much of the intervening period overseas). In July President Assad appointed new chiefs of both the Syrian army and the intelligence service, prompting speculation that he was seeking to extend the political influence of his second son, Bashar.

Elections to the People's Assembly were held on 30 November and 1 December 1998, at which the NPF, led by the ruling Baath Party, again won 167 of the 250 seats. On 11 February 1999 a national referendum ratified the incoming Assembly's decision to nominate President Assad for a fifth term of office. It was widely speculated that Bashar would be promoted to the vice-presidency in a new administration, having already been promoted to the rank of army colonel in January, and reportedly granted new powers over important domestic matters. In June the Syrian authorities were said to be undertaking an 'unprecedented' campaign, led by Bashar al-Assad, to counter corruption in public office. Several leading officials and businessmen were subsequently incarcerated, and in October, following a nine-month trial, a former director of Syria's intelligence service received a lengthy prison sentence for alleged corruption and embezzlement of public funds. Details emerged in September of large-scale arrests (involving 1,000 people, according to some reports) by security forces in Damascus and Al-Ladhiqiyah (Latakia) against supporters and relatives of Rifaat al-Assad. Subsequent closures of Rifaat's interests (including port facilities in Latakia) provoked several days of violent clashes between his supporters and the security forces, in which, according to reports rejected by the Government, hundreds of people were killed or injured.

In July 1999 President Assad ordered a general amnesty for prisoners convicted of certain economic crimes, and for army deserters and those who had evaded military service. The amnesty was to affect hundreds (some reports claimed thousands) of prisoners, including a number of Muslim Brotherhood activists. In February 2000, however, a report by the British-based Amnesty International alleged that in recent months several hundred Syrians (including many Islamists) opposed to a future peace accord with Israel had been arrested. Meanwhile, it was reported that Syria's military intelligence chief, Gen. Ali Duba, had been removed from his post, owing to alleged 'administrative offences', and replaced by his deputy, Maj.-Gen. Hassan Khalil.

Having accepted the resignation of Mahmoud az-Zoubi and his administration in March 2000, President Assad named Muhammad Mustafa Mero, formerly governor of Halab (Aleppo), as Prime Minister. A new Cabinet was subsequently inaugurated, with a programme to accelerate social and economic reforms, to strengthen anti-corruption measures, and to resume peace negotiations with Israel. In all, 22 new ministers were appointed (including a number of younger technocrats and supporters of Bashar al-Assad), although the foreign affairs, defence and interior portfolios remained unchanged. In mid-May az-Zoubi was expelled from the Baath Party for alleged 'irregularities and abuses' during his period in office. His assets were subsequently seized, and he was expected to stand trial on corruption charges. However, in late May official sources reported that az-Zoubi had committed suicide. (In early June 2002 Mufid Abd al-Karim, a former Minister of Transport in the az-Zoubi Government, was convicted on corruption charges and given a 10-year gaol term.)

President Assad died on 10 June 2000. Shortly after his death the People's Assembly amended the Constitution, lowering the minimum age required of a president from 40 to 34 years, thus enabling Bashar al-Assad to assume the presidency. Bashar al-

Assad was also nominated as Commander-in-Chief of the Armed Forces, and his military rank was upgraded to that of Lieutenant-General. Following approval of Bashar's nomination for the presidency by the People's Assembly in late June (the Baath Party having already endorsed his candidacy), a nation-wide referendum on the succession was scheduled to be held in July. Meanwhile, the First Vice-President, Abd al-Halim Khaddam, assumed the role of acting President. In mid-June Bashar al-Assad was elected Secretary-General of the Baath Party. Rifaat al-Assad claimed that the assumed succession by Bashar was unconstitutional, and declared that he would challenge his nephew for the presidency. (The Syrian authorities reportedly issued a warrant for Rifaat's arrest should he attempt to enter the country from exile.) At the national referendum, which proceeded on 10 July, Bashar al-Assad (the sole presidential candidate) received the endorsement of a reported 97.29% of voters. In his inaugural address to the People's Assembly on 17 July, President al-Assad emphasized as priorities for his administration economic reform, elimination of official corruption and the conclusion of a peace treaty with Israel.

In late July 2000 the new President released a significant number of political prisoners, the majority of whom were communists and members of the Muslim Brotherhood. Nevertheless, in September a statement by 99 Syrian intellectuals, published in the Lebanese press, demanded increased democracy and freedom of expression, an end to the state of emergency (in force since 1963) and the release of political detainees. In November the army deployed tanks and armoured vehicles in the southern region of As-Suweida, in order to quell three days of violent clashes between members of the Sunni bedouin and Druze communities; 20 people died in the fighting, and some 200 were injured. On the 30th anniversary of his father's seizure of power, commemorated in mid-November, President Bashar al-Assad declared an amnesty for about 600 political detainees, as well as a general amnesty for several non-political offences. The decision to free as many as 100 Lebanese prisoners was widely viewed as a gesture of 'goodwill' at a time when influential elements within Lebanon were demanding a lessening of Syrian influence in Lebanese political life.

In January 2001 a group of at least 1,000 intellectuals, among them a prominent businessman and deputy, Riad Seif, urged the Syrian regime to approve political reforms. They demanded the suspension of martial law, the holding of free elections, a free press, the release of political prisoners and an end to discrimination against women. Later that month a new 'liberal' political organization, the Movement for Social Peace, was reportedly established under Seif's leadership. The formation of a new nationalist party, the Grouping for Democracy and Unity, was also reported. Meanwhile, following a decision by the Baath Party in November 2000 to permit the other political parties in the NPF to issue their own newspapers, it was announced in early 2001 that the first non-state-controlled newspaper for several decades was to be published by the Communist Party. Syria's first privately owned newspaper for almost 40 years was also issued from February, while the launch was announced of the official newspaper of the Syrian Arab Socialist Unionist Party.

Reports emerged in February 2001 that the Baath Party was to restrict the activities of civic discussion forums being held by Syrian intellectuals by requiring that groups should henceforth apply for permission several days in advance of convening meetings. In early April the Deputy Prime Minister and Minister of Defence, Maj.-Gen. Mustafa Tlass, accused Syrian intellectuals of being agents of the US Central Intelligence Agency. Later in the month another civil rights document was issued, defining for President al-Assad a list of the principles on which reforms should be based. Also in April a report published by the UN Human Rights Committee expressed concerns regarding violations of human rights in Syria, including unfair trials and the torture of prisoners, the practice of extra-judicial executions and the continued imposition of martial law.

During August and September 2001 a series of actions by the authorities against influential opposition activists revived speculation that, contrary to early impressions, the President was less than willing to tolerate dissent. In early August an independent deputy, Mamoun al-Homsi, was detained after starting a hunger strike in protest at official corruption and the Government's failure to end martial law. In early September the leader of the Communist Party, Riad at-Turk, was taken into custody on charges of defaming the presidency (he had reportedly criticized the system of 'hereditary succession'). A few days later Riad Seif, who had held an 'illegal' discussion forum on political reform, was arrested. The crack-down continued, with about 10 'pro-reform' campaigners being detained by the authorities during the first part of September. Trial proceedings began at the end of October against al-Homsi and Seif, and in late March 2002 al-Homsi was convicted of 'attempting to change the Constitution by illegal means' and sentenced to a five-year custodial term. Seif also received a five-year gaol sentence in early April, having been convicted on similar charges. In late June at-Turk was sentenced to two-and-a-half years' imprisonment, although he was freed by President al-Assad in November, reportedly on 'humanitarian grounds'. The convictions against both al-Homsi and Seif had been upheld by an appeals court in July of that year. Meanwhile, in late November 2001 some 120 political prisoners (mostly Islamists or communists) were released under a general amnesty. In January 2002 legislation relating to private broadcasting was relaxed.

President al-Assad effected an extensive reorganization of the Government on 13 December 2001. Prime Minister Mero retained his post, as did the Ministers of Defence and Foreign Affairs (the long-serving Minister of Foreign Affairs, Farouk ash-Shara', additionally became the fourth Deputy Prime Minister), although a new Minister of the Interior, Maj.-Gen. Ali Hammoud (former head of the intelligence service), was named. However, several 'pro-reform' ministers were appointed to strategic portfolios relating to the economy, among them Muhammad al-Atrash as Minister of Finance, Ghassan ar-Rifai as Minister of Economy and Foreign Trade and Ibrahim Haddad as Minister of Petroleum and Mineral Resources. In late January 2002 Maj.-Gen. Hasan at-Turkmani replaced Maj.-Gen. Ali Aslan as the new Chief of Staff of the Armed Forces. In mid-February al-Assad reportedly accepted the resignation of the Deputy Prime Minister and Minister of Defence, Maj.-Gen. Mustafa Tlass, effective from July; however, there were further reports in May that Tlass had been ordered by the President to remain in office for a further two years.

Elections to the People's Assembly were held on 2 and 3 March 2003, at which the NPF, led by the ruling Baath Party, again won 167 of the 250 seats, with the remaining 83 going to independents. Electoral turn-out was estimated to be 63.5%. Opposition parties, under an umbrella grouping called the National Democratic Rally, boycotted the election on the grounds that it was undemocratic. On 9 March the newly reconvened legislature elected the Deputy Prime Minister in charge of Public Services, Muhammad Naji al-Otari, as the new Speaker of the People's Assembly. Al-Otari was replaced as Deputy Prime Minister by Muhammad Safi Abu Wdan in late March.

The Government reacted to the outbreak of conflict in Iraq in March 2003 (see below) by authorizing large anti-war demonstrations in Damascus and other major cities. However, this new-found tolerance of public demonstrations had not been extended to protests by Syrian Kurds earlier in February, when hundreds of members of one of Syria's outlawed Kurdish parties had protested outside the People's Assembly, leading to the arrest of the party's leadership.

In early July 2003 it was reported that President Bashar al-Assad had passed a decree effectively ending the Baath Party's monopoly on government, military and public-sector positions. In early September Prime Minister Mero resigned, along with his Cabinet, apparently as a result of his failure to accelerate the process of political reform. Muhammad Naji al-Otari, the Speaker of the People's Assembly, was appointed as the new Prime Minister, and his first Cabinet was announced at the end of the month. Ministers who retained their portfolios from the previous administration included Maj.-Gen. Mustafa Tlass as Minister of Defence and Farouk ash-Shara' as Minister of Foreign Affairs; notable new appointments included Dr Muhammad al-Hussain, a former Deputy Prime Minister, as Minister of Finance, and Ahmad al-Hassan as Minister of Information. Soon after the appointment of the new Government at least 16 government officials were dismissed as part of a new anti-corruption campaign. At the end of September assets belonging to the former Minister of Industry in the Government of Prime Minister Mero, Dr Issam az-Zaim, were seized in connection with alleged corruption at a state-owned textile plant in Latakia. In May 2004 Tlass retired from the posts of Minister of Defence and Deputy Commander-in-Chief of the Armed Forces; he was succeeded in both posts by armed forces Chief of Staff Hasan at-Turkmani, who was in turn replaced by Gen. Ali Habib (hitherto Special Forces Commander).

Issues of civil rights came to the fore in early 2004. In February a prominent lawyer and human rights activist, Haitham Malih, was prevented from travelling to the United Arab Emirates; the Syrian Human Rights Association claimed that Malih was being punished for having criticized the ongoing state of emergency (in force since 1963) in a speech he made to the German Bundestag (Federal Assembly) two months earlier. At the same time the Lebanese newspaper *An-Nahar* published a petition signed by 1,500 Syrian intellectuals, democratic activists and lawyers urging the Government to instigate radical reforms, including the lifting of the state of emergency and the release of political prisoners. At the end of the month foreigners were banned from studying at the 20 Islamic schools licensed by the Ministry of Labour and Social Affairs; they would henceforth only be allowed to study Islamic law at Damascus University. Although the official reason given was that the degrees awarded by the schools were not yet officially recognized, the decision was widely regarded as a crack-down by the secular regime on foreign Islamists using their studies as a cover for militant, fund-raising or recruitment activities.

There was a widespread outbreak of violent, predominantly Kurdish, protest in mid-March 2004. The unrest started on 14 March in the north-eastern town of Al-Qamishli, close to the border with Turkey, when fighting at a football match escalated into large-scale anti-Government protests and fighting between the Arab majority and Kurdish minority; a number of deaths were reported. The Minister of the Interior, Maj.-Gen. Ali Hammoud, travelled to the region to oversee the quelling of the violence, and the Government accused Kurdish political groups of deliberately inciting the riots. However, the unrest quickly spread to the town of Al-Hasakah, and Kurdish émigrés in many European countries staged demonstrations of solidarity with the Kurds outside Syrian embassies. There were also outbreaks of violence at commemorations of the anniversary of a chemical attack by the former Iraqi regime of Saddam Hussain on the Kurdish town of Halabja, in northern Iraq, in 1988, and at least seven Kurds were reported to have been killed in Aleppo and Afrin. By early April 2004 it appeared that hundreds of Kurds were still being detained by the authorities in connection with the previous month's clashes, and Amnesty International called for an independent inquiry into the unrest and for any remaining detainees to be either charged or released. In connection with the violence, in early June it was alleged that Syrian military intelligence had announced to three senior Kurdish leaders the end of state tolerance of the acitivities of unlicensed Kurdish parties; hundreds of Kurds allegedly remained in custody, having been arrested on suspicion of involvement in the March incident. Meanwhile, in late April 2004 a car bomb exploded outside the former offices of the UN Disengagement Observer Force (UNDOF) in Damascus; an exchange of fire between police and four people fleeing the scene resulted in the deaths of two assailants, a police-officer and a bystander; the other two attackers were arrested by the authorities.

In July and August 2004, as part of an amnesty declared by President al-Assad, 251 political prisoners were freed, including members of the Muslim Brotherhood and Imad Shiash, who had been serving a prison sentence since 1975 for his membership of the proscribed Arab Communist Organization. In early October al-Assad announced a significant reorganization of the Council of Ministers, dismissing eight ministers from their posts. Prominent appointees included Maj.-Gen. Ghazi Kanaan, a former head of Syrian military intelligence in Lebanon, who assumed the interior portfolio from Maj.-Gen. Ali Hammoud; Mahdi Dakhlallah, a well-known journalist, who was appointed Minister of Information; and Muhammad al-Gafri, who became Minister of Justice. In mid-February 2005 it was reported that Syria's military intelligence chief, Maj.-Gen. Hassan Khalil, had reached retirement age, and had been replaced by Brig.-Gen. Asef Shawkat. (For further details regarding internal political developments, see below.)

In July 1991, following a meeting with the US Secretary of State, James Baker, President Assad agreed for the first time to participate in direct negotiations with Israel at a regional peace conference, for which the terms of reference would be a comprehensive settlement based on UN Security Council Resolutions 242 (of 1967) and 338 (1973). In August 1991 the Israeli Cabinet formally agreed to attend a peace conference on terms proposed by the USA and the USSR. An initial, 'symbolic' session of the conference was held in Madrid, Spain, in October, and attended by Israeli, Syrian, Egyptian, Lebanese and Palestinian-Jordanian delegations. Syria's principal aim was to recover the Golan Heights, occupied by Israel since 1967. However, it emphasized that it was not prepared to achieve national goals at the expense of a comprehensive Middle East peace settlement. Syria regarded the Declaration of Principles on Palestinian Self-Rule in the Occupied Territories—the basis of a peace settlement signed by Israel and the PLO in September 1993—as deeply flawed. Furthermore, President Assad viewed the secret negotiations between Israel and the PLO prior to the Declaration of Principles as having undermined the united Arab position in the peace process, and Syria gave no indication that it would cease to support those Palestinian factions, such as the Damascus-based Popular Front for the Liberation of Palestine—General Command (PFLP—GC), which actively opposed the accord.

President Assad met US President Bill Clinton in Geneva, Switzerland, in January 1994—his first such meeting with a US leader since 1977—in an attempt to give fresh impetus to the Syrian track of the peace process. In June Syria reacted warily to the signing by Jordan and Israel of 'sub-agendas' for future bilateral discussions, and continued to adhere to the principle of a united Arab approach to negotiation with Israel. In September Israel published details of a plan for the partial withdrawal of its armed forces from the Golan Heights; Syria rejected the proposals, although President Assad continued to affirm his willingness to achieve peace with Israel. Clinton visited Damascus in October for talks with Assad (the first visit by a US President to Syria for some 20 years), in a further attempt to facilitate the resumption of dialogue between Syria and Israel. However, it was not until March 1995 that bilateral negotiations finally resumed.

In May 1995 Israel and Syria concluded a 'framework understanding on security arrangements', in order to facilitate the participation in the discussions of the two countries' military Chiefs of Staff. Israel stated publicly that it had proposed a four-year timetable for the withdrawal of its armed forces from the Golan Heights, but that Syria had insisted on one of 18 months. In June the Israeli and Syrian Chiefs of Staff held talks in Washington, DC. Negotiations became deadlocked once again, however, and the situation was aggravated by political turmoil in Israel following the assassination of the Prime Minister, Itzhak Rabin, in November. The acting Israeli Prime Minister, Shimon Peres, indicated that no further discussions would take place until after the Israeli general election in May, owing to Syria's refusal to condemn the violence in Israel and to take firmer action against terrorism generally. Following the election to the Israeli premiership of Likud leader Binyamin Netanyahu, an emergency Arab League summit meeting, held in Cairo in June, urged the new right-wing Government in Israel not to abandon the principle of negotiating 'land-for-peace', and demanded the removal of all Israeli settlements in the Golan Heights and their return to Syria. Netanyahu rejected the 'land-for-peace' policies of his Labour predecessor and also insisted that continued Israeli sovereignty over the Golan Heights must be the basis of any peace settlement with Syria. The redeployment, in September, of Syrian armed forces in Lebanon to positions in the Beka'a valley gave rise to speculation in Israel that Syria, frustrated at the lack of progress in the peace process, might be preparing an attack on Israeli forces.

The Israeli-Syrian peace initiative was further interrupted by the construction of a controversial new Jewish settlement at Jabal Abu Ghunaim (Har Homa) in Arab East Jerusalem in March 1997. Prospects of a resumption in negotiations were further frustrated after the Israeli Knesset approved a preliminary reading of proposed legislation stipulating that the return of land to Syria would require the approval of at least two-thirds of deputies. In March 1998 Syria accused Israel of attempting to sabotage its relationship with Lebanon after the Israeli Prime Minister offered to withdraw from southern Lebanon in exchange for a security arrangement before reaching a formal agreement with Syria regarding the Golan Heights. Both Syria and Lebanon reiterated that any withdrawal must be unconditional, in compliance with UN Security Council Resolution 425. Syria was sceptical regarding the likely success of the US-brokered Wye Memorandum, signed in October by Israel and the Palestinian (National) Authority (PA), towards achieving a lasting peace in the Middle East, and President Assad again demanded a resumption of 'land-for-peace' negotiations.

Syria welcomed the success of Ehud Barak and his Labour-led One Israel coalition in the Israeli elections of May 1999. Barak reportedly proposed a five-phase plan to negotiate peace with Syria and to effect an Israeli withdrawal from southern Lebanon. Syria responded with the demand that Barak uphold his pre-election pledge to withdraw from Lebanon within one year of his election and to resume peace talks from their point of deadlock in 1996. At the inauguration of the new Israeli Cabinet in early July 1999, Barak promised to negotiate a bilateral peace with Syria, based on UN Security Council Resolutions 242 and 338, thus apparently signalling to the Assad regime his intention to return most of the occupied Golan Heights to Syria in exchange for peace and normalized relations. In mid-July, prior to a meeting in Washington, DC, between Barak and President Clinton, Syria was reported to have warned dissidents of Damascus-based Palestinian organizations to cease their military operations against Israel, and also to have interrupted the supply of Iranian weapons to Hezbollah guerrillas in southern Lebanon. Moreover, in late July Syria reported a 'cease-fire' with Israel, although mutual disagreements remained, most notably over the point at which previous negotiations had been suspended. At the beginning of September, as Israel and the PA signed the Sharm esh-Sheikh Memorandum (or Wye Two—see the chapter on Israel) in Egypt, US Secretary of State Albright held talks with President Assad in Damascus.

In early December 1999 Israel and Syria agreed to resume negotiations from the point at which they had stalled in 1996 (this was following mediation by Clinton). The first round of discussions between the Syrian Minister of Foreign Affairs, Farouk ash-Shara', and the Israeli premier, Ehud Barak, was opened by the US President in mid-December 1999 in Washington, DC. Both sides agreed to resume discussions in the following month, and in late December Syria and Israel were reported to have agreed an informal 'cease-fire' in order to limit the conflict in Lebanon. A second round of talks between ash-Shara' and Barak proceeded on 3–10 January 2000 (with the involvement of Clinton) in Shepherdstown, West Virginia. Syria and Israel had agreed meanwhile on the establishment of committees to discuss simultaneously the issues of borders, security, normalization of relations, and water sharing. However, in mid-January the peace talks were postponed indefinitely. Syria declared that it required a 'written' commitment from Israel to withdraw from the Golan Heights prior to a resumption of talks, while Israel demanded the personal involvement of President Assad in the negotiating process and that Syria take action to restrain Hezbollah in southern Lebanon. In March the Israeli Cabinet voted unanimously to withdraw its forces from Lebanon by July, even in the absence of peace settlement with Syria, while the Knesset voted to change the majority required in the event of an Israeli withdrawal from the Golan from 50% of participating voters to 50% of the registered electorate.

In May 2000 ash-Shara' hosted discussions in Palmyra with his Egyptian and Saudi Arabian counterparts in an effort to co-ordinate a united Arab position towards the USA and Israel prior to the planned Israeli withdrawal from southern Lebanon. Reports following the talks suggested that Saudi Arabia and Egypt had pledged military support to Syria in the event of Israeli aggression. The accelerated withdrawal of Israeli armed forces from southern Lebanon was completed on 24 May 2000, several weeks ahead of the original Israeli deadline. (See the chapters on Israel and Lebanon for further details of the Israeli withdrawal.) Following the death, in June, of President Assad, and the succession of his second son, Bashar al-Assad, in mid-July, the Israeli-Syrian track of the Middle East peace process remained stalled. Nevertheless, Bashar indicated a desire to resume negotiations in the near future, although he emphasized that Syrian policy on the Golan Heights remained unchanged. The escalation of the Palestinian al-Aqsa *intifada* from late September strained Syria's relations with Israel and, as tensions increased throughout the Middle East, Israel accused Syria of involvement in the abduction of Israeli military personnel by Hezbollah in the disputed Shebaa Farms area of southern Lebanon. (Shebaa Farms has been designated by the UN as being part of Syria, and thus subject to the Syrian track of the peace process.) During an emergency summit meeting of the Arab League held in Cairo in late October Farouk ash-Shara' urged all Arab countries to sever diplomatic ties with Israel.

Following the election of Likud leader Ariel Sharon to the Israeli premiership in early February 2001, President al-Assad again reiterated Syria's position: namely that negotiations would only be resumed upon a full Israeli withdrawal from the Golan Heights. Tensions between the two sides increased in mid-April following an attack by Israeli forces on a Syrian radar station in eastern Lebanon, in which at least one Syrian soldier died. In early December, following talks in Damascus between Egypt's President Mubarak and President al-Assad, Egypt and Syria issued a joint statement condemning Israeli military actions in the West Bank and Gaza, and called on the international community to put pressure on Israel to halt its 'aggression'. In early January 2003 a Syrian soldier was killed during a rare exchange of gunfire between Israeli and Syrian forces in the Golan Heights. In late November 2004 al-Assad announced that he was willing to resume peace talks with Israel unconditionally (although it was unclear whether the Syrian President intended for negotiations to resume from where they had collapsed in 2000—see above); however, Israel refused to conduct talks with Syria until it closed the headquarters of Hamas and Islamic Jihad, and al-Assad rejected Israel's setting of conditions as unacceptable.

In early December 2004 PLO leader Mahmud Abbas made the first official Palestinian visit to Damascus since 1996. Abbas, the Palestinian Prime Minister, Ahmad Quray, the Minister of Foreign Affairs, Dr Nasser al-Kidwa, and President al-Assad discussed the current situation in the Palestinian territories and preparations for the presidential election scheduled to be held there in January 2005. Al-Assad emphasized Syria's support for the Palestinian people and their struggle for national unity, while Abbas stressed the importance of co-operation between Syria and the PA.

At the end of April 2003 US President George W. Bush handed to the Israeli and Palestinian leaderships the so-called 'roadmap' peace plan, which had been drawn up by the Quartet group (comprising the USA, the UN, Russia and the EU). The plan envisaged an end to the Arab–Israeli conflict and the creation of a sovereign Palestinian state by 2005–06 (for full details of the roadmap, see the chapter on Israel). A fully negotiated peace settlement between Israel and Syria was one of the objectives of the roadmap, but Syria was keen to emphasize that the new plan must run in tandem with the Syrian track of negotiations on the Golan Heights issue; however, in mid-May 2003 President al-Assad reportedly assured Javier Solana, the EU's High Representative for Common Foreign and Security Policy, that Syria would unconditionally accept the roadmap. An offer from Syria to resume peace talks with Israel in late July was firmly rejected by Israeli Prime Minister Ariel Sharon as 'insincere'. In early August Israel accused Syria of masterminding an attack by Hezbollah in Shebaa Farms. At the beginning of October Israel launched an air attack against an alleged Palestinian militant training camp inside Syria. Israel claimed that the camp at Ain Saheb near Damascus was being used by Hamas and Islamic Jihad, which the latter group denied, while another Palestinian militant group, the Popular Front for the Liberation of Palestine (PFLP), stated that the facility at Ain Saheb was in fact not in use. Israel insisted that the attack was not directed against Syria, but was in retaliation for a suicide bomb attack in Haifa, Israel, in which 19 Israelis were killed. In mid-January 2004 President al-Assad rejected Israeli offers to resume peace negotiations, describing them as a 'media manoeuvre'. In late September, following an Israeli warning of military action against Syria for its presumed involvement in suicide attacks in Israel in late August that killed 16 people, a senior Hamas official was assassinated in Damascus in late September, provoking an angry response from Syrian officials.

There was increasing agitation in Lebanon for a cessation of Syrian influence on Lebanese political affairs after the inauguration of a new Syrian President and the Israeli withdrawal from southern Lebanon. In July 2000 Maronite Christian leaders in Lebanon requested that President al-Assad release all Lebanese political prisoners held in Syria, and in the following month a coalition of Christian political parties in Lebanon urged voters there to boycott the forthcoming parliamentary elections, on the grounds that Syria would predetermine the outcome of the poll. The results of the elections, at which former premier Rafik Hariri resoundingly defeated the Syrian-sponsored Government of Selim al-Hoss, served to intensify speculation about Syria's future role in Lebanese affairs. Syrian officials reacted angrily when the Lebanese Druze leader and traditional ally of Syria, Walid Joumblatt, demanded a 're-evaluation' of Syria's role in Lebanon. In December 46 Lebanese prisoners (many of whom were Christians detained by Syrian troops during the civil war) were released from Syrian detention; hitherto Syria had never confirmed that it was holding Lebanese political prisoners. In mid-June 2001 Syria withdrew some 6,000–10,000 of its armed forces from predominantly Christian districts of east and south Beirut, and from Mount Lebanon; some of the troops were redeployed in the Beka'a valley. However, Syria retained a number of military bases in strategic areas of the Lebanese capital. President al-Assad's discussions with President Lahoud in March 2002 reportedly centred on the forthcoming Arab League conference in Beirut, at which Saudi Arabia's Crown Prince Abdullah was formally to submit his proposals for a Middle East peace settlement (for further details, see the chapter on Lebanon). The two leaders reportedly demanded that any peace deal should include the right of return for Palestinian refugees. Redeployments of Syrian troops from central Lebanon took place in early April 2002, and from northern Lebanon in mid-February 2003. The new Lebanese Government formed under Hariri in mid-April was widely considered to be the most pro-Syrian administration in Lebanon for more than a decade. In June unidentified assailants fired rockets at the studios of Hariri's Future Television in central Beirut. Syria was blamed for having organized the attack, chiefly as a warning to the Lebanese Prime Minister following remarks he made on a state visit to Brazil in which Hariri appeared to call for an improvement in Arab–Israeli relations. Moreover, the attack coincided with a further redeployment of Syrian troops from Lebanon, emphasizing that while Syria was reducing its military presence in Lebanon, many believed that it was still keen to maintain its influence on Lebanese political affairs.

This influence appeared to be continuing in 2004: following meetings with Syrian officials, Lebanon decided not to effect any government changes in response to a strike in the southern suburbs of Beirut in late May, and Prime Minister Hariri, also following meetings with Syrian officials, withdrew his objection to the extension, in late August, of President Lahoud's mandate by three years. However, international pressure on Syria's presence in and influence on Lebanon increased following the adoption in early September of UN Security Council Resolution 1559, which, without referring to Syria explicitly, demanded that Lebanon's sovereignty be respected and that all foreign forces leave the country. (See the chapter on Lebanon for further details of Lebanese domestic affairs and of the UN resolution.) The Syrian army subsequently redeployed about 3,000 special forces from positions south of Beirut, and further troops were withdrawn in December from the northern town of Batrun and from Beirut's southern suburbs and airport to the Beka'a valley. However, the new Lebanese Government approved by the legislature in early November (in which Rafik Hariri had been replaced as Prime Minister by Omar Karami) was regarded as being more favourable than its predecessor to continued Syrian influence in Lebanese affairs. In mid-December a number of Lebanese political parties issued a joint statement demanding the cessation of foreign interference in the country.

Former Lebanese Prime Minister Rafik Hariri was killed in a car bombing in Beirut on 14 February 2005. Although President al-Assad condemned the attack, the USA, without accusing Syria of involvement in the incident, withdrew its ambassador to Syria for consultations, and later demanded the complete withdrawal of Syrian troops from Lebanon and a thorough and transparent investigation into the attack. Meanwhile, Syria and Iran agreed to form a 'united front' against foreign threats to their states. Syria declared later in the month that it would redeploy all of its troops in Lebanon to the Beka'a valley. Mass protests against Syria's influence on Lebanese affairs, and against the Syrian military presence in Lebanon, followed, and in late February President Bush demanded that Syria: withdraw all troops and security service personnel from Lebanon; stop using its territory to support militant groups; support free and fair elections in Lebanon; and adhere to UN Security Council Resolution 1559 (see above). The UN Secretary-General, Kofi Annan, called on Syria to withdraw its troops from Lebanon by April.

Meanwhile, in late February 2005 Karami announced the resignation of his administration, but, under Lahoud's request, he and his ministers remained in office in an interim capacity pending the appointment of a new government. Opposition groups continued to demand that Syrian army and intelligence personnel withdraw from Lebanon, and that senior Lebanese security officials resign. In early March the US Secretary of State, Condoleezza Rice, reiterated Bush's demands and warned Syria that it was threatening peace and preventing change in the Middle East. She also stated that there was evidence of the involvement of Islamic Jihad in a bombing in Tel-Aviv, Israel, in late February. Also in early March al-Assad and Lahoud agreed at a summit meeting to the withdrawal of Syrian troops to the Beka'a valley by the end of the month; Syria later promised to withdraw all troops before Lebanon's general election in May, and to provide the UN with a timetable for the withdrawal. Rice praised the decision, but urged the two countries to accelerate the process. Meanwhile, protests were held in Beirut in support of the Syrian military presence and the country's influence on affairs in Lebanon. Syria reportedly withdrew 4,000–6,000 of its troops from Lebanon to Syria in mid-March, removing Syrian troops and intelligence agents from their barracks and offices around Tripoli and Beirut; 8,000–10,000 troops reportedly remained in the Beka'a valley. A UN report released in late March blamed Syria for allowing political tension in Lebanon to mount before the murder of Hariri; it also criticized Lebanon's initial attempts to investigate the incident. In early April the UN Security Council approved Resolution 1595 establishing an International Independent Investigation Commission (UNIIIC) to investigate Hariri's murder. The German prosecutor Detlev Mehlis was appointed to head the commission. A UN envoy announced that Syria had declared its intention to completely withdraw all troops, military assets and the intelligence apparatus by the end of the month. The formation of a new Lebanese administration, headed by newly appointed Prime Minister Najib Mikati, was announced in mid-April. Later in the month Syria declared that it had withdrawn all of its troops and security forces from Lebanon, and in early May a UN team dispatched to Lebanon to confirm the withdrawal announced that thus far it had not found a single Syrian soldier in areas that it had inspected.

Legislative elections were held in Lebanon in four rounds between 29 May and 19 June 2005 (see the chapter on Lebanon). A broad anti-Syrian alliance, led by Rafik Hariri's son, Saad ed-Din al-Hariri, secured the highest number of seats in the National Assembly (72 of 128 seats). A pro-Syrian bloc that included Hezbollah and Amal secured 35 seats, and a bloc led by a former Commander-in-Chief of the Lebanese army, Gen. Michel Awn, who had allied himself with pro-Syrian factions immediately prior to the elections, won 21 seats. Pro-Syrian Nabih Berri was re-elected as President of the National Assembly in late June, and Fouad Siniora, a close ally of Rafik Hariri, was appointed as Prime Minister. A new Cabinet was installed in mid-July. Syrian President al-Assad and Prime Minister Otari met Fouad Siniora in Syria in early August. The two states reportedly agreed to improve relations based on mutual respect, and Siniora emphasized Lebanon's support of Syria and its commitment to bilateral agreements. Various prominent Lebanese figures opposed to Syrian influence in Lebanon were killed or injured in bomb attacks during mid- to late 2005, including the former Secretary-General of the Parti communiste libanais (Lebanese Communist Party), who was killed in a car bombing in Beirut in June.

At the 10th national congress of the Baath Party in early June 2005, President al-Assad was re-elected as Secretary-General. Vice-President and member of the party leadership Abd al-Halim Khaddam reportedly asked to be relieved of all of his duties, citing a wish to allow more young people to be represented in the party and state leadership. Although there was no confirmation that Khaddam's resignation as Vice-President had been accepted, it was announced that he had not been re-elected to the party leadership. The political committee of the Baath Party endorsed proposals to relax laws relating to the state of emergency, and to produce legislation allowing the formation of independent parties and increased freedom of the press; however, by early 2006 the proposed reforms had not received the required parliamentary approval. In late December 2005 Khaddam, who had been living in exile in Paris since his resignation, held an interview with the Dubai-based satellite television station Al-Arabia in which he accused al-Assad of having personally threatened Rafik Hariri a few months prior to his assassination. Khaddam subsequently declared that, in his view, al-Assad had ordered Hariri's killing, although he awaited the final decision of the investigating commission. He declared that the current Syrian regime could not be reformed, and called on opposition groups in Syria to co-operate to defeat it. In early January 2006 the Baath Party announced that it had formally expelled Khaddam from the party, accusing him of treachery against the party, his country and the Arab nation for his accusations against the Syrian President. Meanwhile, the People's Assembly unanimously approved a motion calling for Khaddam to be brought to trial on charges of treason and corruption.

In response to reports that Syrian intelligence agents might not have completely withdrawn from Lebanon, the UN announced in early June 2005 that it was considering sending a commission to the country to investigate the claims. (Syria continued to assert that it had removed all of its security personnel.) UNIIIC began its inquiry into Rafik Hariri's assassination in mid-June, with a three-month mandate. In late August UNIIIC arrested three former Lebanese security officials with close ties to Syria, who had tendered their resignations in April, for questioning regarding the assassination. A fourth security chief, who had retained his post after Hariri's murder, subsequently handed himself in to the organization. A former, pro-Syrian parliamentary deputy was also detained. In mid-October, shortly before the UNIIIC issued its report on the investigation, the official Syrian Arab News Agency announced the death, by suicide, of the Minister of the Interior, Maj.-Gen. Ghazi Kanaan; a formal investigation subsequently confirmed the cause of death. Shortly before his apparent suicide, Kanaan had issued a statement to a Lebanese radio station defending Syria's role in Lebanon and announcing that he had been questioned by UNIIIC, but had not given any evidence against Syria. Some analysts noted that Kanaan, a potential alternative to the Syrian President who had opposed the decision to extend Lebanese President Lahoud's tenure by three years in 2004 (see above), had been seen as a threat to al-Assad.

According to its first report, issued in late October 2005, UNIIIC had found evidence that Lebanese and Syrian intelligence and security services were directly involved in the assassination of Rafik Hariri. Moreover, the report reasoned, the act was too complex and too well planned to have taken place without the approval of senior Syrian security officials and their Lebanese counterparts. UNIIIC expressed its extreme concern at the lack of co-operation of the Syrian authorities. Lebanon and Syria both rejected the report, criticizing the investigation's findings as politically motivated, and Syria announced that it had established a special judicial commission to deal with all matters relating to the UNIIIC's mission. The commission was granted an extension to its mandate to mid-December. The UN Security Council reacted to the report by adopting Resolution 1636 at the end of October 2005, establishing measures against suspects in the assassination, including prohibitions on travel and the freezing of assets, and urging Syria to co-operate fully with the investigation commission and to detain suspects identified by the inquiry as suspects in Hariri's assassination, threatening unspecified 'further action' should Syria not fulfil the resolution's demands. The Security Council gave Syria until 15 December to comply with the resolution, which was sponsored by the USA, France and the United Kingdom. Syria reported in early November that it had arrested six government officials for questioning. Meanwhile, in late October 2005, the UN Special Envoy, Terje Roed-Larsen, published his report on compliance with UN Security Council Resolution 1559, in which he lauded Syria's withdrawal of its troops from Lebanon, but criticized Lebanon for not complying with the resolution's demands.

In his second report to the UN Security Council, issued in mid-December 2005, Mehlis noted that Syria had presented five officials suspected of involvement in the murder of Hariri to the UNIIIC for interrogation in Vienna, Austria. However, the report again accused Syria of reluctance to co-operate with the investigating body and of hindering the investigation. The UNIIIC had found further evidence of the involvement of the Lebanese and Syrian intelligence and security services in the assassination, and Mehlis identified 19 suspects, six of whom were Syrian (of which five were those currently under interrogation in Vienna). Mehlis resigned as head of the UNIIIC shortly after he presented the report, citing personal and professional reasons; he was replaced by Serge Brammertz. The UNIIIC's mandate was extended to 15 June 2006.

In early January 2006, after Abd al-Halim Khaddam accused President al-Assad of having personally threatened Hariri (see above), UNIIIC investigators declared that they wished to question the Syrian President and Minister of Foreign Affairs ash-Shara'. However, the following day the Minister of Information, Mahdi Dakhlallah, declared that Syria would not permit UNIIIC to interview al-Assad. Brammetz met ash-Shara' and other unspecified Syrian officials in late February. Ash-Shara' announced in early March that he had reached an agreement with UNIIIC providing for full Syrian co-operation with the investigation, while maintaining the country's 'sovereignty and dignity'.

In mid-February 2006 President al-Assad effected a comprehensive reorganization of the Council of Ministers. Ash-Shara' was appointed as Vice-President to replace Khaddam, and given additional responsibility for Foreign Affairs and Information; he was replaced as Minister of Foreign Affairs by Walid Mouallem. Brig.-Gen. Bassam Abd al-Majid assumed the interior portfolio, Mohsen Bilal was appointed as Minister of Information, and Sufian Allaw as Minister of Petroleum and Mineral Resources. In late March Dr Najah al-Attar was also named as a Vice-President.

The distribution and reprinting in both Western and Muslim-majority countries of caricatures of the Prophet Muhammad originally published in a Danish newspaper in September 2005 provoked considerable anger among Muslim communities worldwide (see the chapter on Denmark). Depiction of the Prophet is forbidden by Islamic tradition, and the cartoons in question were considered to be particularly offensive. Violent protests against the publication of the caricatures took place in a number of Muslim countries, and the Danish and Norwegian embassies in Damascus (as well as in the capitals of other majority-Muslim countries) were attacked and forced to close temporarily due to a perceived threat to their security.

The Syrian Government condemned the massive suicide attacks carried out against US citizens in New York and Washington, DC, on 11 September 2001. However, Syria was openly critical of the decision of the US Administration of George W. Bush—as part of its world-wide 'war on terror'—to launch a military campaign against targets in Afghanistan linked to the Taliban regime and to the militant Islamist organization held principally responsible for the attacks, the al-Qa'ida (Base) network of Osama bin Laden. At the end of October the British Prime Minister, Tony Blair, undertook an official visit to Syria, to garner Arab support for the US-led campaign in Afghanistan, and asked the Syrian leadership to end its support for militant groups such as Hezbollah and the PFLP. However, President al-Assad condemned the West's bombing of Afghan civilians and stated that organizations engaged in fighting the Israeli occupation were 'legitimate'. In mid-December 2002 President Bashar al-Assad became the first Syrian leader to visit the United Kingdom, where he expressed his opposition to a US-led military campaign to bring about 'regime change' in Iraq, and rejected Blair's demand to curb militant Palestinian groups operating in Syria.

President al-Assad visited Italy in late February 2002 for discussions with Italian political leaders concerning the US-led 'war on terror', the growing Israeli–Palestinian violence and bilateral trade issues. The Syrian leader was reported to have called for greater EU involvement in resolving the conflict in the Palestinian areas, and to have emphasized Syria's opposition to a possible US military offensive against the regime of Saddam Hussain in Iraq. In early April US Secretary of Defense Donald Rumsfeld accused Syria, Iran and Iraq of involvement in terrorism against Israeli civilians. Relations between Syria and the USA deteriorated further during late 2002 and early 2003. Several members of the US Administration proposed the imposition of economic sanctions against Syria as punishment for its continued support for militant Palestinian organizations such as Islamic Jihad, Hamas and the PFLP. US officials also accused Syria of involvement in the illegal purchase of oil from Iraq. In late November 2002 the Syrian leadership refused US demands that it close the Damascus office of Islamic Jihad, following a renewed campaign by that organization against targets in Israel.

As the US-led coalition forces launched a military campaign to oust the regime of Saddam Hussain in Iraq in mid-March 2003, the USA also increasingly hinted that Syria might be the next target for a US-imposed 'regime change'. Damascus referred to the campaign in Iraq as an 'illegal invasion'. Moreover, Syrians were angered in late March when a bus close to the border with Iraq was hit by a stray US missile, killing five Syrian civilians. Damascus strongly denied claims by the Bush Administration that it was providing military equipment to Iraq during the conflict. The USA alleged that Syria had assisted leading members of the Iraqi Baath Party to flee the country after the collapse of Saddam Hussain's regime and that Iraqi weapons of mass destruction might have been transported to cross the border into Syria. However, in late April President Bush declared that Syria was co-operating with the US-led coalition, having recently sealed its border with Iraq. Nevertheless, US officials from the Department of the Treasury estimated that US $3,000m. of Iraqi money was being held by Syrian-controlled banks in Damascus and Lebanon, in contravention of a UN resolution calling on all Iraqi funds held abroad to be handed over to the US-controlled Iraqi Fund for Development. In mid-December US President Bush signed the Syria Accountability Act, which allowed him to impose a range of sanctions on Syria unless the country met a series of conditions (including ending its support for terrorist groups). The sanctions were eventually put in place on 11 May 2004; they included a ban on all US exports to Syria other than food or medicine, and a halt to flights between the two countries. Syria rejected the sanctions, asserting that they would not affect the country or its economy, and in October Syria signed a bilateral agreement with the EU for greater economic co-operation, with Syria agreeing to renounce proliferation of nuclear weapons. In early December it was reported that evidence had been found that Syria was permitting the training on its territory of militants to be used as insurgent fighters in Iraq, as well as allowing insurgents across the border between the two countries; Syria denied the claims. In May 2005, following reports that Iraqi militants had planned recent bombings at a meeting in Syria, the USA and Iraq urged Syria to prevent foreign fighters from crossing the border into Iraq. Syria denied accusations that its authorities had allowed insurgents to enter Iraq from its territory, asserting that it was working hard to prevent such cross-border activity.

In August 1999 a diplomatic crisis developed between Syria and the Palestinian authorities after the Syrian Deputy Prime Minister and Minister of Defence, Maj.-Gen. Mustafa Tlass, publicly accused Yasser Arafat of having 'sold Jerusalem and the Arab nation' in peace agreements concluded with Israel since 1993, and made other personal insults against the Palestinian leader. The PA demanded that Tlass resign (and Fatah reportedly issued a death warrant against Tlass), while President Assad was apparently angered by the minister's remarks. Arafat attended the funeral of President Hafiz al-Assad, and in mid-2000 the PA renewed its demand that Syria free all remaining Palestinian prisoners from its gaols; seven Palestinians were released into Lebanese custody in December. Amid Syrian efforts to support the Palestinians in their escalating conflict with the Israelis, and after talks between al-Assad and Arafat during the summit meeting of Arab League states in Jordan in late March 2001, the two leaders declared that they had achieved a reconciliation.

In October 1998 the Jordanian Government demanded 'immediate answers' from Syria concerning a list of 239 Jordanians allegedly missing in Syria, and a further 190 who it claimed were being held in Syrian prisons. The Syrian authorities agreed to investigate the matter, but stated that most of those listed were in fact members of Palestinian organizations linked with Jordan and had violated Syrian laws. In February 1999 President Assad unexpectedly attended the funeral of King Hussein of Jordan, and reportedly held a private meeting with the new monarch. Syria had welcomed the succession of King Abdullah, and the new Jordanian King made his first official visit to Syria in April. The two leaders urged a resumption of the peace process and increased bilateral co-operation; Syria agreed to supply Jordan with water during 1999, as the latter was undergoing a drought, and both sides agreed to hold future discussions regarding the Jordanian prisoners in Syria. King Abdullah made an unscheduled visit to Syria in July, at a time when Jordan was concerned that any separate peace settlement between Syria and Israel might undermine the Palestinian position in future negotiations. The joint Syrian-Jordanian Higher Committee met in August in Amman, under the chairmanship of both countries' premiers—the first time in almost a decade that a senior Syrian delegation had visited Jordan's capital. Meanwhile, the Syrian Government stated that many of the Jordanian prisoners held in Syria had been released under a general amnesty granted in July (see above) and that the 'very few' who remained in Syrian gaols were non-political detainees. Later in August Syria ended a 10-year ban on the free circulation of Jordanian newspapers and publications in the country. A further 17 Jordanian prisoners were reportedly released from Syrian gaols in March 2000. Following the death of President Assad in June, King Abdullah visited Damascus in mid-July for talks with Syria's new President, Bashar al-Assad; Syria again agreed to supply Jordan with water during that summer. It was reported in November that Syria had upgraded its diplomatic representation in Jordan to ambassadorial level. In mid-January 2001 Syrian officials reportedly gave assurances to Jordan that all Jordanian political prisoners would soon be released. In early February 2004 Syria and Jordan launched the Wahdah Dam project on Jordan's River Yarmuk. The project, due to be completed at the end of 2005, aimed to provide Jordan with water and Syria with electricity; its launch effectively ended the diplomatic impasse of the previous couple of months which had been caused by Jordanian accusations that Syria was easing the passage of Islamist militants into Iraq to fight the US-led coalition.

Relations between Syria and Iraq had been strained since the early 1970s due to a rivalry between the respective factions of the Baath Party in Damascus and Baghdad. Notably, Syria supported Iran in its war with Iraq in 1980–88. Although an extraordinary summit meeting of the Arab League in November 1987 produced a unanimous statement expressing solidarity with Iraq and condemning Iran for prolonging the war and for its occupation of Arab territory, Syria announced subsequently that a reconciliation with Iraq had not taken place, and that Syrian relations with Iran remained fundamentally unchanged. Syria also used its veto to prevent the adoption of an Iraqi proposal to readmit Egypt to the Arab League, but it could not prevent the inclusion in the final communiqué of a clause permitting individual member nations to re-establish diplomatic relations with Egypt. However, Egypt's recognition of the newly proclaimed Palestinian state in November 1988 gave fresh impetus to attempts to achieve a reconciliation between Egypt and Syria. These culminated in the restoration of bilateral relations in December 1989, and in the visit of Egypt's President Hosni Mubarak to Damascus (the first such visit by an Egyptian head of state for more than 12 years).

Syria appeared keen to take advantage of the diplomatic opportunities arising from Iraq's invasion of Kuwait in August 1990, and in particular to improve its relations with the USA. Syria endorsed Egypt's efforts to co-ordinate an Arab response to the invasion, and agreed to send troops to Saudi Arabia as part of a pan-Arab deterrent force, supporting the US-led effort to deter an Iraqi invasion of Saudi Arabia; Syria also committed itself to the demand for an unconditional Iraqi withdrawal from Kuwait. Indications that Syria's participation in the multinational force was transforming its relations with the West were confirmed in November when diplomatic ties were restored with the United Kingdom. Iraq's overwhelming military defeat by the US-led multinational force in February 1991 strengthened Syria's position with regard to virtually all its major regional concerns. In March the Ministers of Foreign Affairs of the members of the Co-operation Council for the Arab States of the Gulf (Gulf Co-operation Council, see p. 205) met their Egyptian and Syrian counterparts in Damascus to discuss regional security. The formation of an Arab peace-keeping force, comprising mainly Egyptian and Syrian troops, was subsequently announced. (In early May, however, Egypt declared its intention to withdraw its forces from the Gulf region within three months, thus casting doubt on the future of joint Syrian-Egyptian security arrangements.) Moreover, Syria's decision to ally itself, in opposition to Iraq, with the Western powers and the 'moderate' Arab states led the USA to realize that it could no longer seek to exclude Syria from any role in the resolution of the Arab–Israeli conflict. A shift in Syria's relations with the USSR, a major source of military assistance but whose programmes of political liberalization President Assad had recently criticized, provided another reason for its realignment with the West.

After Iraq's defeat by the multinational force in February 1991, Syria became a centre for elements of the Iraqi opposition. However, it remains committed to the territorial integrity of Iraq, fearing that disintegration might encourage minorities within Syria (particularly the Kurds) to pursue their own autonomy. Three crossing points on the Syria–Iraq border were reopened in June 1997 to facilitate bilateral trade (Syria closed its border with Iraq in 1980), and in September 1998 Iraq, Iran and Syria agreed to establish a joint forum for foreign policy co-ordination (particularly with regard to the USA). In the same month Syria and Iraq reopened commercial centres in one another's capitals, and in April 1999 a series of mutual agreements were signed, as part of the process of normalizing relations. Throughout 1998–2002 the Syrian Government criticized US and British air-strikes against Iraqi air defence targets, as well as the maintenance of UN sanctions against Iraq. In August 2000 a rail link between Aleppo and the Iraqi capital was reopened after an interval of some 20 years, and in December the Syrian authorities reportedly removed all restrictions on Iraqi citizens travelling to Syria. In November, furthermore, Iraq was reported to have begun transporting crude petroleum to Syria via a pipeline not used since the early 1980s. When the US Secretary of State, Colin Powell, visited Damascus at the end of February 2001, his discussions with the Syrian President apparently centred on Syria's alleged violation of UN sanctions regarding the supply of petroleum from Iraq; in January 2002 British officials publicly accused Syria of sanctions violations. In mid-August 2001 the Syrian Prime Minister, leading a ministerial and commercial delegation, became the most senior Syrian official to visit Iraq for two decades. Syria was particularly concerned (as was Turkey) at the potential ascendance of Iraqi Kurdish groups should the incumbent regime in Baghdad be overthrown, although, visiting these countries in March 2002, the PUK leader, Jalal Talabani, gave assurances that Iraq's Kurdish groups had no intention of establishing their own state. There were reports in mid-2002 that Syria was involved in mediation efforts between Iraq and Kuwait. (In early October 2001 Syria had been elected as a non-permanent member of the UN Security Council for 2002–03.) Despite its unexpected support for UN Security Council Resolution 1441, approved in early November, which imposed strict terms according to which Iraq must disarm or else face probable military action, Syria expressed its firm opposition to the US-led military campaign against the Iraqi regime which began in mid-March 2003 (see the chapter on Iraq). Syria had been expected to abstain from the UN vote, but Syrian officials asserted that the resolution did not give the USA the right to use force against the Iraqi regime. In early February 2006 Syria and Iraq announced that they were to restore full diplomatic relations and exchange ambassadors as soon as a new government was installed in Iraq.

Meanwhile, in the context of a long-standing commitment to establish a regional common market under the auspices of the Council of Arab Economic Unity (see p. 208), plans for a quadripartite free-trade zone encompassing Iraq, Egypt, Libya and Syria were advanced following a meeting of the Council held in the Iraqi capital in early June 2001.

Relations between Syria and Turkey became increasingly strained in the 1990s, owing to disagreements over the sharing of water from the Euphrates river. No permanent agreement on this resource has been concluded, and both Syria and Iraq are concerned that new dams in Turkey will reduce their share of water from the Euphrates. Syria's relations with Turkey deteriorated sharply in April 1996 after it was revealed that Turkey and Israel had concluded a military co-operation agreement earlier in the year. In August 1997 Syria condemned the decision by the USA, Israel and Turkey to conduct joint naval manoeuvres, although the three countries claimed that the exercises (carried out in January 1998) were solely for humanitarian purposes. Tension between Syria and Turkey increased considerably in October 1998, when Turkey threatened to invade Syria if its demands for an end to alleged Syrian support for the separatist Kurdistan Workers' Party (Partiya Karkeren Kurdistan—PKK) were not met. The Turkish authorities also demanded the extradition of the PKK leader, Abdullah Öcalan (who, they claimed, was directing PKK operations from Damascus), and insisted that Syria renounce its historic claim on the Turkish province of Hatay. Turkey's aggressive stance was viewed by Syria as evidence of a Turkish-Israeli military and political alliance, and as a result both Syria and Turkey ordered troops to be deployed along their joint border. Diplomatic efforts to defuse the crisis by Egypt, Iran and the UN, and Syrian assurances that Öcalan was not residing in Syria, allowed a degree of normalization in bilateral relations. In late October, following two days of negotiations in southern Turkey, representatives of the two countries signed an agreement whereby the PKK was to be banned from entering Syrian territory, while the organization's active bases in Syria and Lebanon's Beka'a valley were to be closed. Turkey and Syria also agreed mutual security guarantees, and resolved to invite Lebanon to participate in further discussions regarding the issue of PKK activity. Despite persistent Syrian concerns regarding the close nature of Turkish-Israeli relations, it was reported in March 2000 that Syrian and Turkish officials were holding discussions in Damascus on a memorandum of principles, intended to establish a new framework for future bilateral relations. In September Syria and Turkey signed a co-operation agreement relating to countering terrorism and organized crime. It was reported in May 2001 that the two countries had agreed to conduct joint military training exercises, and in June 2002 they signed two military co-operation accords. Moreover, reports in February that the Turkish army was to begin the clearance of landmines along its border with Syria were seen as evidence of a steady improvement in bilateral relations. In December 2003 relations between the two countries were strengthened by Syria's decision to hand over 22 suspects sought by the Turkish authorities in connection with four suicide bomb attacks in Istanbul in mid-November, in which at least 60 people were killed. In early January 2004 President al-Assad made the first ever visit by a Syrian Head of State to Turkey. Turkey's membership of NATO, and hence its relatively close relationship with the USA, as well as shared concerns about a possible 'ripple-effect' of increased Kurdish autonomy in northern Iraq following the removal of the regime of Saddam Hussain, were believed to be among the principal reasons for Syria's initiative to improve its relations with Turkey, and in December Syria and Turkey agreed to create a bilateral free-trade zone.

In November 1998 Syria and Russia signed a military agreement, whereby Russia would assist in the modernization of Syria's defence systems and provide training to military personnel. However, in January 1999 Syria denied Western reports that it was receiving assistance from Russia in the development of chemical weapons. President Assad visited Moscow in July for talks with President Boris Yeltsin and the then Russian premier, Sergei Stepashin. During the discussions Russia reiterated its support for Syria's demand for a complete Israeli withdrawal from the Golan Heights and southern Lebanon, and that Israeli-Syrian peace negotiations be resumed from their point of suspension in 1996. In May 2000 it was reported that a major arms deal had been concluded whereby Russia would supply Syria with defensive weaponry worth some US $2,000m. In mid-January 2005 reports that Russia was to sell missiles to Syria that could be used against targets in Israel provoked anger in that country. In late January al-Assad held official talks in Russia with the Russian President, Vladimir Putin, and other senior officials; the two Presidents reportedly signed an agreement relating to greater co-operation. Russia confirmed its intention to sell missiles to Syria in mid-February, asserting that the weapons could only be used for defence purposes.

Government

Under the 1973 Constitution (as subsequently amended), legislative power is vested in the unicameral People's Assembly, with 250 members elected by universal adult suffrage to serve a four-year term. Executive power is vested in the President, elected by direct popular vote for a seven-year term. (Following the death of President Hafiz al-Assad on 10 June 2003, the Constitution was amended to allow his son, Lt-Gen. Bashar al-Assad, to accede to the presidency). He governs with the assistance of an appointed Council of Ministers, led by the Prime Minister. Syria has 14 administrative districts (*mohafazat*).

Defence

National service, which normally lasts 30 months, is compulsory for men. In August 2005 the regular armed forces totalled an estimated 307,600 men: an army of an estimated 200,000 (including conscripts), an air defence command of some 60,000, a navy of 7,600 and an air force of 40,000. In addition, Syria had 354,000-strong reserve forces (army 280,000; air force 70,000; navy 4,000). Paramilitary forces included a gendarmerie (connected to the Ministry of the Interior) of 8,000 and a Baath Party Workers' Militia of some 100,000. An estimated 8,000–10,000 Syrian troops were deployed in Lebanon in March 2005; however, in late April Syria claimed to have withdrawn all of its forces from that country (see the chapter on Lebanon). Budgeted defence expenditure for 2005 was estimated at £S90,000m.

Economic Affairs

In 2004, according to estimates by the World Bank, Syria's gross national income (GNI), measured at average 2002–04 prices, was US $21,125m., equivalent to $1,190 per head (or $3,550 per head on an international purchasing-power parity basis). During 1995–2004, it was estimated, the population increased at an average annual rate of 2.5%, while gross domestic product (GDP) per head increased, in real terms, by an average of 0.2% per year. Overall GDP increased, in real terms, at an average annual rate of 2.7% in 1995–2004; growth was 2.6% in 2003 and 3.6% in 2004.

Agriculture (including forestry and fishing) contributed an estimated 24.4% of GDP in 2004, and engaged 26.2% of the employed labour force (excluding foreign workers) in 2003. The principal cash crops are cotton (which accounted for about 2.4% of export earnings in 2003) and fruit and vegetables. Agricultural GDP increased at an average annual rate of 3.4% in 1995–2004; the sector's GDP increased by 0.4% in 2003 and by 7.8% in 2004.

Industry (comprising mining, manufacturing, construction and utilities) provided some 28.2% of GDP in 2004, and engaged 24.8% of the employed labour force (excluding foreign workers) in 2003. The GDP of the industrial sector increased by an average of 5.6% per year during 1995–2004; industrial GDP increased by 0.9% in 2003 and by 2.5% in 2004.

Mining contributed an estimated 6.6% of GDP in 1994, and employed 0.3% of the working population (excluding foreign workers) in 1999. Crude petroleum is the major mineral export, accounting for 69.3% of total export earnings in 2001, and phosphates are also exported. Syria also has reserves of natural gas and iron ore. At the end of 2004 Syria had proven oil reserves of 3,200m. barrels, and estimated average oil production was 536,000 barrels per day (b/d) (having declined from 596,000 b/d in 1995). Syria was estimated to have 370,000m. cu m of proven natural gas reserves at the end of 2004, and in that year production of natural gas reached an estimated daily average of 5,200m. cu m. In 2001 Syria and Lebanon signed an agreement under which Syria was to supply gas to northern Lebanon. However, although the pipeline intended to supply the natural gas was completed in 2005, the two countries did not implement the agreement owing to political differences (see Recent History, above).

Manufacturing contributed an estimated 3.6% of GDP in 2003, and employed 12.7% of the working population in 1999. The principal branches of manufacturing, measured by gross value of output, are: food products, beverages and tobacco; chemicals, petroleum, coal, rubber and plastic products; textiles, clothing, leather products and footwear; metal products, machinery, transport equipment and appliances; and non-metallic mineral products. The GDP of the manufacturing sector increased by an average of 6.5% per year during 1995–2004; manufacturing GDP increased by 0.9% in 2003 and by 2.5% in 2004.

Energy is derived principally from hydroelectric power (providing 39.7% of total electricity production in 2002), and also natural gas (35.2%) and petroleum (25.2%). Imports of mineral fuels and lubricants comprised an estimated 3.3% of the value of total imports in 2003.

Services engaged 49.0% of the employed labour force (excluding foreign workers) in 2003, and accounted for 47.4% of GDP in 2004. The GDP of the services sector increased at an average rate of 1.2% per year in 1995–2004; growth of the sector was 4.7% in 2003 and 1.6% in 2004.

In 2004 Syria recorded a visible trade deficit of US $374m., while there was a surplus of $205m. on the current account of the balance of payments. In 2003 the principal source of imports (7.2%) was Germany; other important suppliers were Italy, the People's Republic of China, France and Turkey. Germany was also the principal market for exports in that year (22.7%); other major purchasers were Italy, the United Arab Emirates, Lebanon and Turkey. The principal exports in 2003 were mineral fuels and lubricants, food and beverages, basic manufactures, and basic manufactures, while the principal imports were basic manufactures, machinery and transport equipment, and food and beverages.

A balanced budget was projected for 2003. At the end of 2003 Syria's total external debt was US $21,566m., of which $15,848m. was long-term public debt. The cost of debt-servicing in that year was equivalent to 4.2% of the total value of exports of goods and services. Annual inflation averaged 5.7% in 1990–2001. Consumer prices increased by 1.0% in 2002, by 7.8% in 2003 and by 4.4% in 2004. According to a study published by the Central Bureau of Statistics and the UN Development Programme in mid-2005, 8.2% of the labour force were unemployed; however, other sources estimated the unemployment rate to be more than double this rate.

Syria is a member of the UN Economic and Social Commission for Western Asia (ESCWA, see p. 41), the Arab Fund for Economic and Social Development (AFESD, see p. 161), the Arab Monetary Fund (see p. 163), the Council of Arab Economic Unity (see p. 208), the Islamic Development Bank (see p. 303) and the Organization of Arab Petroleum Exporting Countries (OAPEC, see p. 338).

The regime under President Bashar al-Assad, who assumed the presidency in July 2000, has implemented a bolder programme of economic reforms than his predecessor, Hafiz al-Assad, although progress has remained slow. The Syrian economy recently suffered from the temporary loss of Syria's trade with Iraq, as a result of the US-led military campaign to oust the regime of Saddam Hussain in March–April 2003. Moreover, the USA levied trade sanctions on Syria in May 2004 (see above). Although the economy reportedly recovered to a limited extent in 2004 and 2005, largely as a result of an increase in exports (especially tourism) and private investment, some sources predicted average growth of less than 1.5% per year during 2006–07. A decline in petroleum production limited economic growth, and it was considered likely that Syria would become a net importer of petroleum by 2010–15, and that its supplies would be exhausted by 2030, making a reduction of the economy's dependence on revenue from petroleum essential to ensuring long-term growth. According to an IMF survey published in November 2005, further structural and fiscal reforms were necessary to increase non-oil revenue and encourage domestic and external investment. A report published by the UN Development Programme (UNDP) in late 2005 concluded that non-petroleum exports would have to increase by at least 15% annually in order to compensate for the decrease in revenue from petroleum exports, which constituted around two-thirds of exports each year, according to the IMF. However, the UNDP report asserted that Syria would be unlikely to achieve such high growth rates, largely because of its restrictive macroeconomic policies, the protectionist trading policies of the EU and strong competition from other developing countries. In the short term, however, the high international petroleum prices were expected to offset reduced production. In reaction principally to the decreasing supplies of petroleum, in late 2005 Syria announced that it intended to secure US $6,000m. of annual investment in all sectors of the economy, and to increase the number of tourists to 15m. per year by 2015. The Government was also considering a law that would allow foreign investors to own 100% of shares in private banks. (According to a law introduced in 2001, foreign investors were permitted to own a maximum of 49% of share in private banks; domestic investors had to own at least 51% of the shares. By early 2006 there were at least six private banks operating in Syria.) Other planned reforms included the floating of the Syrian pound on the stock market in June 2006 and the introduction of a value-added tax by 2008, with IMF assistance. Meanwhile, unemployment remained high, at over 20%, according to some sources. Moreover, the population was growing rapidly and was expected to increase by 50% by 2020: the Government reportedly needed to invest some $100,000m. to create sufficient employment opportunities for the future greatly expanded labour force. According to a study by the Central Bureau of Statistics and UNDP published in mid-2005, some 10.4% of Syrians lived on less than $2 per day. In February 2006 it was reported that Prime Minister al-Otari had issued a decree ordering that all of the government and private-sector foreign-currency transactions be carried out in euros rather than dollars, reportedly in order to make foreign assets more secure and to strengthen Syria's ability to counter political pressure from the USA. After the USA prohibited transactions between US banks and the Central Bank of Syria, Syria announced that it was to use euros instead of dollars in its 2006 budget. The budget was valued at an estimated £S495,000m., compared with £S460,000m. in 2005, and provided for the creation of 57,000 new jobs in the manufacturing and service sectors. For the immediate future, further improvements to Syria's economic situation are expected to be dependent upon both domestic restructuring and reform, as well as the conclusion of a comprehensive peace agreement with Israel.

Education

Primary education, which begins at six years of age and lasts for six years, is officially compulsory. In 2002/03 primary enrolment included 98% of children in the relevant age-group (males 100%; females 96%). Secondary education, beginning at 12 years of age, lasts for a further six years, comprising two cycles of three years each. In 2002/03 enrolment at secondary schools included 43% of children in the appropriate age-group (males 44%; females 41%). There are agricultural and technical schools for vocational training, and higher education is provided by the universities of Damascus, Aleppo, Tishrin (the October University, in Latakia) and Hims (Homs—the Baath University, formerly the Homs Institute of Petroleum). There were 201,689 students enrolled in higher education in 2002/03. Expenditure on education by all levels of government in 1999 was estimated at £S26,324m. (10.3% of total government expenditure).

The United Nations Relief and Works Agency (UNRWA) provides education for Palestinian refugees in Syria. During the academic year 2005/06 UNWRA operated 118 elementary and preparatory schools in Syria, with a total enrolment of 64,169 pupils.

Public Holidays

2006: 1 January (New Year's Day), 10 January*† (Id al-Adha, Feast of the Sacrifice), 31 January* (Muharram, Islamic New Year), 8 March (Revolution Day), 21 March (Mother's Day), 10 April* (Mouloud/Yum an-Nabi, Birth of Muhammad), 17 April (Independence Day), 21–24 April (Greek Orthodox Easter), 1 May (Labour Day), 6 May (Martyrs' Day), 21 August* (Leilat al-Meiraj, Ascension of Muhammad), 6 October (Anniversary of October War), 23 October* (Id al-Fitr, end of Ramadan),

SYRIA

25 December (Christmas Day), 31 December*† (Id al-Adha, Feast of the Sacrifice).

2007: 1 January (New Year's Day), 20 January* (Muharram, Islamic New Year), 8 March (Revolution Day), 21 March (Mother's Day), 31 March* (Mouloud/Yum an-Nabi, Birth of Muhammad), 6–9 April (Greek Orthodox Easter), 17 April (Independence Day), 1 May (Labour Day), 6 May (Martyrs' Day), 10 August* (Leilat al-Meiraj, Ascension of Muhammad), 6 October (Anniversary of October War), 13 October* (Id al-Fitr, end of Ramadan), 20 December* (Id al-Adha, Feast of the Sacrifice), 25 December (Christmas Day).

* These holidays are dependent on the Islamic lunar calendar and may vary by one or two days from the dates given.

† This festival ocurs twice (in the Islamic years AH 1426 and 1427) within the same Gregorian year.

Weights and Measures

The metric system is in force.

Statistical Survey

Source (unless otherwise stated): Central Bureau of Statistics, rue Abd al-Malek bin Marwah, Malki Quarter, Damascus; tel. (11) 3335830; fax (11) 3322292; e-mail cbs@mail.sy; internet www.cbssyr.org.

Area and Population

AREA, POPULATION AND DENSITY

Area (sq km)	
Land	184,050
Inland water	1,130
Total	185,180*
Population (census results)†	
8 September 1981	9,052,628
3 September 1994	
Males	7,048,906
Females	6,733,409
Total	13,782,315
Population (UN estimates at mid-year)‡	
2002	17,683,000
2003	18,129,000
2004	18,582,000
Density (per sq km) at mid-2004	101.0

* 71,498 sq miles.

† Official estimates at mid-year, including Palestinian refugees. According to the United Nations Relief and Works Agency for Palestine Refugees in the Near East (UNRWA), there were 432,048 Palestinian refugees in Syria at 31 December 2005.

‡ Source: UN, *World Population Prospects: The 2004 Revision*.

PRINCIPAL TOWNS
(population at census of 3 September 1994)

Halab (Aleppo)	1,582,930		Ar-Raqqah (Rakka)	165,195
Dimashq (Damascus, capital)	1,394,322		Al-Qamishli	144,286
Hims (Homs)	540,133		Deir ez-Zor	140,459
Al-Ladhiqiyah (Latakia)	311,784		Al-Hasakah	119,798
Hamah (Hama)	264,348			

Source: UN, *Demographic Yearbook*.

Mid-2000 (UN estimates, incl. suburbs): Aleppo 2,188,000; Damascus 2,105,000; Homs 797,000 (Source: UN, *World Urbanization Prospects: The 2003 Revision*).

Mid-2003 (UN estimate, incl. suburbs): Damascus 2,228,000 (Source: UN, *World Urbanization Prospects: The 2003 Revision*).

BIRTHS, MARRIAGES AND DEATHS
(estimates, excl. nomad population and Palestinian refugees)

	Registered live births — Number	Rate (per 1,000)	Registered marriages	Registered deaths
1994	447,987	n.a.	115,994	51,003
1995	478,308	n.a.	n.a.	52,214
1996	500,953	n.a.	127,963	53,786
1997	496,140	32.9	128,146	53,366
1998	505,008	32.4	130,835	57,893
1999	503,473	31.3	136,157	56,564
2000	505,484	31.0	139,843	57,759
2001	524,212	31.4	153,842	60,814

Source: UN, *Demographic Yearbook*.

Expectation of life (WHO estimates, years at birth): 72 (males 69; females 74) in 2003 (Source: WHO, *World Health Report*).

ECONOMICALLY ACTIVE POPULATION
(labour force sample survey, persons aged 15 years and over, 2003)*

	Males	Females	Total
Agriculture, hunting, forestry and fishing	816,598	352,145	1,168,743
Mining and quarrying; manufacturing; and electricity, gas and water	558,324	50,381	608,705
Construction	492,657	7,727	500,384
Trade, restaurants and hotels	650,835	26,394	677,229
Transport, storage and communications	258,541	6,946	265,487
Financing, insurance, real estate and business services	78,585	11,162	89,747
Community, social and personal services	851,357	306,922	1,158,279
Total employed	3,706,897	761,677	4,468,574
Unemployed	334,066	214,372	548,438
Total labour force	4,040,963	976,049	5,017,012

* Figures refer to Syrians only, excluding armed forces.

SYRIA

Health and Welfare

KEY INDICATORS

Total fertility rate (children per woman, 2003)	3.3
Under-5 mortality rate (per 1,000 live births, 2004)	16
HIV/AIDS (% of persons aged 15–49, 2003)	<0.1
Physicians (per 1,000 head, 2001)	1.4
Hospital beds (per 1,000 head, 1999)	1.4
Health expenditure (2002): US $ per head (PPP)	109
Health expenditure (2002): % of GDP	5.1
Health expenditure (2002): public (% of total)	45.8
Access to water (% of persons, 2002)	79
Access to sanitation (% of persons, 2002)	77
Human Development Index (2003): ranking	106
Human Development Index (2003): value	0.721

For sources and definitions, see explanatory note on p. vi.

Agriculture

PRINCIPAL CROPS
('000 metric tons)

	2002	2003	2004
Wheat	4,775.4	4,913.0	4,537.5
Barley	919.5	1,079.1	527.2
Maize	231.9	226.7	180.0*
Potatoes	515.2	486.6	500.0
Sugar beet	1,480.5	1,205.2	1,100.0*
Chick-peas	88.8	87.0	45.3
Lentils	132.8	168.4	125.3
Almonds	139.0	130.0*	130.0
Olives	999.0	552.3	950.0*
Cabbages	49.7	29.6	32.2
Lettuce	28.3	54.2	52.4
Tomatoes	900.6	900.0*	920.0*
Cauliflowers	35.4	25.7†	28.0*
Pumpkins, squash and gourds	110.2	111.0*	110.0*
Cucumbers and gherkins	141.0	141.0*	140.0*
Aubergines (Eggplants)	133.4	133.0*	132.0*
Chillies and green peppers	40.5	40.5*	40.0*
Green onions and shallots	76.8	75.0*	75.0*
Dry onions	96.9	94.7	95.0*
Oranges	427.1	410.0*	427.0*
Lemons and limes	84.9	80.0*	84.0*
Apples	215.8	306.7	215.0*
Apricots	100.9	100.9*	100.0*
Cherries	39.7	39.7*	39.7*
Peaches and nectarines	35.3	36.0*	36.0
Grapes	341.9	307.3	300.0*
Watermelons	480.1	674.2	620.0*
Cantaloupes and other melons	100.1	116.2	100.0*
Figs	43.4	43.4*	43.4*

* FAO estimate.
† Unofficial figure.
Source: FAO.

LIVESTOCK
('000 head, year ending September)

	2002	2003	2004*
Horses	16.8	17.0*	17.0
Mules	7.0	7.0*	7.0
Asses	130.0	130.0*	130.0
Cattle	866.7	937.0	940.0
Camels	12.5	15.2	15.0
Sheep	13,497.5	15,292.7	15,300.0
Goats	931.9	1,017.3	1,018.0
Chickens	28,634	29,000*	30,000

* FAO estimate(s).
Source: FAO.

LIVESTOCK PRODUCTS
('000 metric tons)

	2002	2003	2004
Beef and veal	47.0	47.3	47.4
Mutton and lamb*	183.6	207.0	207.0
Chicken meat	123.2	123.2*	123.3*
Cows' milk	1,173.5	1,200.0*	1,250.0*
Sheep's milk	535.9	604.2*	604.2*
Goats' milk	56.0	62.1*	62.1*
Cheese	91.2	95.4	95.4
Butter and ghee	15.3	16.3	16.3
Hen eggs	166.0	172.5	167.0*
Wool: greasy	29.7†	33.6*	33.6*
Cattle hides*	7.3	7.3	7.3
Sheepskins*	30.6	34.5	34.5

* FAO estimate(s).
† Unofficial figure.
Source: FAO.

Forestry

ROUNDWOOD REMOVALS
('000 cubic metres, excl. bark)

	2002	2003	2004
Sawlogs, veneer logs and logs for sleepers	16	16	16
Other industrial wood	19*	24	24*
Fuel wood	16*	18	18*
Total	51*	58	58*

* FAO estimate.

Sawnwood production ('000 cubic metres): *1980*: Coniferous (softwood) 6.6; Broadleaved (hardwood) 2.4; Total 9.0. *1981–2004*: Production as in 1980 (FAO estimates).

Source: FAO.

Fishing

(metric tons, live weight)

	2001	2002	2003
Capture	8,291	9,178	8,911
Freshwater fishes	5,969	6,335	5,851
Demersal percomorphs	449	n.a.	n.a.
Aquaculture	5,880	5,988	7,217
Common carp	2,248	2,722	2,937
Tilapias	3,195	2,571	3,439
Total catch	14,171	15,166	16,128

Source: FAO.

Mining

('000 metric tons, unless otherwise indicated)

	2002	2003	2004*
Phosphate rock	2,483	2,414	2,883
Salt (unrefined)	146	146*	146
Gypsum	351	375*	375

* Estimate(s).
Source: US Geological Survey.

Crude petroleum ('000 cu m, estimates): 33,568 in 2001; 36,222 in 2002; 33,568 in 2003.

Crude petroleum ('000 metric tons): 26,700 in 2004 (Source: BP, *Statistical Review of World Energy*).

SYRIA

Statistical Survey

Industry

SELECTED PRODUCTS
(metric tons, unless otherwise indicated)

	2000	2001	2002
Cotton yarn (pure)	82,975	78,019	61,680
Silk textiles	25	10	20
Cotton textiles	25,067	21,559	23,477
Woollen fabrics	7,244	6,481	6,887
Plywood (cu m)	37,237	38,622	43,076
Cement ('000 metric tons)	5,428	4,631	5,134
Glass and pottery products	72,715	69,062	69,639
Soap	17,653	17,649	18,863
Refined sugar ('000 metric tons)	121	109	158
Olive oil	95,384	165,354	80,000
Vegetable oil	106,506	88,786	78,235
Cottonseed cake ('000 metric tons)	328	312	288
Manufactured tobacco	12,007	11,097	10,991
Refrigerators	109,812	96,322	119,687
Washing machines	62,105	66,168	64,661
Television receivers	139,485	169,291	149,711
Electricity (million kWh)	26,896	25,544	23,946

Finance

CURRENCY AND EXCHANGE RATES

Monetary Units
100 piastres = 1 Syrian pound (£S).

Sterling, Dollar and Euro Equivalents (30 December 2005)
£1 sterling = £S19.328;
US $1 = £S11.225;
€1 = £S13.242;
£S1,000 = £51.74 sterling = $89.09 = €75.52.

Exchange Rate: Between April 1976 and December 1987 the official mid-point rate was fixed at US $1 = £S3.925. On 1 January 1988 a new rate of $1 = £S11.225 was introduced. In addition to the official exchange rate, there is a promotion rate (applicable to most travel and tourism transactions) and a flexible rate. For calculating the value of transactions in the balance of payments, the Central Bank of Syria used the following average exchange rates: $1 = £S44.88 in 1997; $1 = £S49.27 in 1998; $1 = £S48.83 in 1999.

BUDGET
(estimates, £S million)

Revenue	2001	2002	2003
Taxes and duties	115,932	135,844	151,558
Services, commutations and revenues from state properties and their public investments	29,885	29,547	30,652
Various revenues	68,625	68,595	15,058
Supply surplus	69,317	70,029	97,428
Exceptional revenues	38,241	52,375	125,304
Total	322,000	356,390	420,000

Expenditure	2001	2002	2003
Community, social and personal services	171,325	186,757	237,123
Agriculture, forestry and fishing	27,486	29,375	32,074
Mining and quarrying	11,449	14,606	16,490
Manufacturing	17,936	22,839	25,515
Electricity, gas and water	30,667	32,421	32,645
Building and construction	1,095	1,240	1,228
Trade	2,752	2,943	4,102
Transport, communications and storage	35,549	39,697	39,064
Finance, insurance and companies	2,888	3,385	2,658
Non-distributed funds	20,850	23,127	29,101
Total	322,000	356,390	420,000

CENTRAL BANK RESERVES
(US $ million at 31 December)

	1986	1987	1988
Gold*	29	29	29
Foreign exchange	144	223	193
Total	173	252	222

*Valued at $35 per troy ounce.

1989–2003 (US $ million, national valuation): Gold 29.

Source: IMF, *International Financial Statistics*.

MONEY SUPPLY
(£S million at 31 December)

	2001	2002	2003
Currency outside banks	229,266	258,359	285,015
Demand deposits at commercial banks	176,845	222,391	329,809
Total money (incl. others)	419,911	494,681	628,279

Source: IMF, *International Financial Statistics*.

COST OF LIVING
(Consumer Price Index; base: 2000 = 100)

	2001	2002	2003
Food and beverages	100.2	99.6	107.3
Electricity, gas and other fuels (incl. water)	100.0	111.2	119.5
Clothing and footwear	100.5	96.5	102.9
Rent	100.7	102.9	124.0
All items (incl. others)	100.4	101.4	109.3

2004: Food and beverages 112.8; All items (incl. others) 114.1.

Source: ILO.

NATIONAL ACCOUNTS
(£S million at current prices)

Expenditure on the Gross Domestic Product

	2001	2002	2003
Government final consumption expenditure	121,723	124,785	143,528
Private final consumption expenditure	571,863	603,243	634,928
Gross capital formation	198,166	206,587	243,652
Total domestic expenditure	891,752	934,615	1,022,108
Exports of goods and services	359,278	404,102	345,964
Less Imports of goods and services	296,893	324,176	315,151
GDP in market prices	954,137	1,014,541	1,052,921
GDP at constant 2000 prices	938,678	978,482	1,004,348

Gross Domestic Product by Economic Activity

	2001	2002	2003
Agriculture, hunting, forestry and fishing	242,610	249,520	258,391
Mining and quarrying	190,511	189,360	200,351
Manufacturing	57,305	54,613	36,741
Electricity, gas and water	8,689	13,374	13,237
Construction	28,257	30,401	36,063
Wholesale and retail trade	148,914	172,959	174,685
Transport and communications	118,349	125,721	131,072
Finance and insurance	31,147	32,968	34,957
Government services	85,002	92,903	105,865
Other community, social and personal services	22,577	24,751	27,304
Non-profit private services	541	558	614
Sub-total	933,902	987,128	1,019,280
Import duties	20,445	25,310	33,175
Less imputed bank service charges	211	−2,104	−467
GDP in market prices	954,136	1,014,542	1,052,922

SYRIA

BALANCE OF PAYMENTS
(US $ million)

	2002	2003	2004
Exports of goods f.o.b.	6,668	5,762	5,561
Imports of goods f.o.b.	−4,458	−4,430	−5,935
Trade balance	2,210	1,332	−374
Exports of services	1,559	1,331	2,614
Imports of services	−1,883	−1,806	−1,980
Balance on goods and services	1,886	857	260
Other income received	250	282	385
Other income paid	−1,175	−1,139	−1,114
Balance on goods, services and income	961	0	−469
Current transfers received	499	743	690
Current transfers paid	−20	−15	−16
Current balance	1,440	728	205
Capital account (net)	20	20	18
Direct investment from abroad	115	160	275
Other investment assets	1,180	—	—
Other investment liabilities	−1,545	−298	−335
Net errors and omissions	−160	85	254
Overall balance	1,050	695	417

Source: IMF, *International Financial Statistics*.

External Trade

PRINCIPAL COMMODITIES
(US $ million)

Imports c.i.f.	2001	2002	2003
Food and beverages	675.1	763.2	767.0
Cereals and cereal preparations	198.4	207.5	208.4
Crude materials, inedible	256.0	291.9	293.0
Mineral fuels and lubricants	264.0	155.5	156.2
Chemicals and related products	669.1	727.8	731.0
Basic manufactures	1,548.1	1,508.5	1,515.4
Machinery and transport equipment	1,158.4	1,333.0	1,338.9
Total (incl. others)	4,587.4	4,780.8	4,803.1

Exports f.o.b.	2001	2002	2003
Food and beverages	501.5	674.1	739.9
Cereals and cereal preparations	13.2	17.7	13.5
Crude materials, inedible, except fuels	316.8	425.8	251.8
Mineral fuels and lubricants	4,373.4	4,763.2	4,195.0
Crude petroleum and oils obtained from bituminous materials	4,098.1	4,179.4	3,367.9
Chemicals and related products	51.9	69.8	62.6
Basic manufactures	428.1	575.3	477.8
Machinery and transport equipment	35.5	47.7	34.8
Total	5,707.1	6,556.0	5,761.9

Source: Arab Monetary Fund, *Foreign Trade Statistics*.

PRINCIPAL TRADING PARTNERS
(US $ million)

Imports c.i.f.	2001	2002	2003
Argentina	80.5	84.5	84.4
Brazil	72.0	65.7	42.4
China, People's Republic	205.5	268.0	305.8
Cyprus	73.9	19.5	10.7
Egypt	61.5	45.6	46.8
France	389.2	214.2	284.0
Germany	341.3	358.9	346.0
Greece	46.3	24.6	54.9
India	71.4	64.3	115.0
Indonesia	71.6	44.5	25.3
Iran	48.6	35.3	37.8
Italy	535.5	390.2	341.2
Japan	170.6	136.1	117.1
Jordan	28.2	52.4	61.8
Korea, Repub.	301.8	224.1	174.3
Lebanon	31.2	23.1	23.7
Malaysia	55.7	49.9	98.2
Netherlands	98.4	82.1	82.6
Romania	75.4	72.2	79.2
Russia	97.4	103.5	132.7
Saudi Arabia	134.0	97.3	104.3
Spain	105.7	72.6	88.9
Sri Lanka	61.2	48.8	39.8
Sweden	49.1	52.9	46.1
Switzerland	72.2	75.0	51.6
Thailand	48.9	62.6	59.9
Turkey	309.3	200.3	261.4
United Arab Emirates	46.5	33.8	36.2
United Kingdom	105.7	95.0	85.5
USA	249.0	205.8	136.3
Total (incl. others)	4,587.4	4,780.8	4,803.1

Exports f.o.b.	2001	2002	2003
Algeria	22.3	114.8	127.6
Austria	168.9	161.1	119.4
Canada	39.6	31.8	68.4
Cyprus	137.6	132.5	107.6
Czech Republic	14.1	103.7	141.5
Egypt	44.1	47.9	60.6
France	535.5	440.4	335.5
Germany	1,163.7	1,133.7	1,308.5
Iran	1.6	31.6	35.1
Italy	1,004.8	1,028.1	785.6
Japan	14.9	19.9	43.8
Jordan	60.4	88.1	139.3
Kuwait	64.5	66.7	74.1
Lebanon	284.3	308.5	390.5
Libya	31.2	32.3	35.9
Netherlands	58.1	207.7	60.2
Portugal	37.5	50.2	29.0
Qatar	19.7	30.0	23.2
Romania	32.3	68.1	4.3
Saudi Arabia	183.2	189.5	210.7
Singapore	68.4	99.0	129.8
Spain	226.1	227.4	110.0
Turkey	421.3	460.2	375.8
United Arab Emirates	515.5	426.0	473.5
United Kingdom	115.1	160.5	85.4
USA	151.1	145.2	256.0
Total (incl. others)	5,707.1	6,556.0	5,761.9

Source: Arab Monetary Fund, *Foreign Trade Statistics*.

Transport

RAILWAYS
(traffic)

	2001	2002	2003
Passenger-km ('000)	306,929	384,321	525,357
Freight ('000 metric tons)	5,297	5,927	6,416

ROAD TRAFFIC
(motor vehicles in use)

	2001	2002	2003
Passenger cars	148,884	181,017	206,130
Buses and coaches	44,579	46,560	473,014
Lorries, trucks, etc.	348,688	367,048	382,179
Motorcycles	105,150	99,009	104,732

SHIPPING

Merchant Fleet
(registered at 31 December)

	2002	2003	2004
Number of vessels	190	178	173
Total displacement ('000 grt)	472.1	477.2	446.7

Source: Lloyd's Register-Fairplay, *World Fleet Statistics*.

International Sea-borne Traffic

	1996	1997	1998
Vessels entered ('000 net reg. tons)	2,901*	2,640	2,622
Cargo unloaded ('000 metric tons)	4,560	4,788	5,112
Cargo loaded ('000 metric tons)	1,788	2,412	2,136

* Excluding Banias.

Vessels entered ('000 net registered tons): 2,928 in 1999; 2,798 in 2000; 2,827 in 2001.

Source: mainly UN, *Monthly Bulletin of Statistics* and *Statistical Yearbook*.

CIVIL AVIATION
(traffic on scheduled services)

	1999	2000	2001
Kilometres flown (million)	12	15	15
Passengers carried ('000)	668	750	761
Passenger-km (million)	1,287	1,422	1,465
Total ton-km (million)	134	149	153

Source: UN, *Statistical Yearbook*.

Tourism

FOREIGN VISITOR ARRIVALS
(incl. excursionists)*

Country of nationality	2001	2002	2003
Iran	216,542	310,839	213,931
Iraq	187,954	278,934	253,120
Jordan	609,225	692,211	752,935
Kuwait	80,344	99,906	72,693
Lebanon	1,025,101	1,410,511	1,654,001
Saudi Arabia	330,639	371,601	361,758
Turkey	281,459	467,648	470,900
Total (incl. others)	3,389,091	4,272,911	4,388,119

* Figures exclude Syrian nationals resident abroad.

Tourism receipts (US $ million, excl. passenger transport): 1,150 in 2001; 970 in 2002; 1,147 in 2003.

Source: World Tourism Organization.

Communications Media

	2001	2002	2003
Telephones ('000 main lines in use)	1,817	2,099	n.a.
Mobile cellular telephones ('000 in use)	200	400	1,185
Personal computers ('000 in use)	270	330	500
Internet users ('000)	60	365	610

1992: Book production 598 titles.
1996: Daily newspapers 8 (average circulation 287,000 copies).
1997 ('000 in use): Radio receivers 4,150.
1998 ('000 in use): Facsimile machines 22.
2000 ('000 in use): Television receivers 1,080.

Sources: UNESCO, *Statistical Yearbook*; UN, *Statistical Yearbook*; International Telecommunication Union.

Education

(2002/03)

	Institutions	Teachers	Males	Females	Total
Pre-primary	1,431	6,365	73,198	65,339	138,537
Primary		204,264	2,016,372	1,804,674	3,821,046
Secondary: general	1,140	26,273	134,088	132,108	266,196
Secondary: vocational	595	14,597	62,824	66,034	128,858
Higher	4	8,702	106,975	94,714	201,689

Adult literacy rate (UNESCO estimates): 82.9% (males 91.0%; females 74.2%) in 2003 (Source: UN Development Programme, *Human Development Report*).

Directory

The Constitution

A new and permanent Constitution was endorsed by 97.6% of voters in a national referendum held on 12 March 1973. The 157-article Constitution defines Syria as a 'Socialist popular democracy' with a 'pre-planned Socialist economy'. Under the new Constitution, Lt-Gen. Hafiz al-Assad remained President, with the power to appoint and dismiss his Vice-President, Premier and government ministers, and also became Commander-in-Chief of the Armed Forces, Secretary-General of the Baath Socialist Party and President of the National Progressive Front. According to the Constitution, the President is elected by direct popular vote for a seven-year term. Legislative power is vested in the People's Assembly, with 250 members elected for a four-year term by universal adult suffrage (83 seats are reserved for independent candidates).

Following the death of President Hafiz al-Assad on 10 June 2000, the Constitution was amended to allow his son, Lt-Gen. Bashar al-Assad, to accede to the presidency. Bashar al-Assad also became Commander-in-Chief of the armed forces, Secretary-General of the Baath Socialist Party and President of the National Progressive Front.

SYRIA

The Government

HEAD OF STATE

President: Lt-Gen. BASHAR AL-ASSAD (assumed office 17 July 2000).
Vice-President, responsible for Foreign Affairs and Information: FAROUK ASH-SHARA'.
Vice-President: Dr NAJAH AL-ATTAR.

COUNCIL OF MINISTERS
(April 2006)

Prime Minister: MUHAMMAD NAJI AL-OTARI.
Deputy Prime Minister, responsible for Economic Affairs: ABDULLAH AD-DARDARI.
Minister of Defence: Lt-Gen. HASAN AT-TURKMANI.
Minister of Foreign Affairs: WALID MOUALLEM.
Minister of Information: MOHSEN BILAL.
Minister of the Interior: Brig.-Gen. BASSAM ABD AL-MAJID.
Minister of Local Administration and Environment: HILAL AL-ATRASH.
Minister of Education: ALI SA'D.
Minister of Higher Education: GHIATH BARAKAT.
Minister of Electricity: AHMAD KHALED AL-ALI.
Minister of Culture: RIYAD NA'ASAN AGHA.
Minister of Transport: YAAROB SULEIMAN BADR.
Minister of Petroleum and Mineral Resources: SUFIAN ALLAW.
Minister of Industry: FOUAD ISSA JONI.
Minister of Finance: Dr MUHAMMAD AL-HUSSEIN.
Minister of Housing and Construction: HAMOUD AL-HUSSEIN.
Minister of Justice: MUHAMMAD AL-GAFRI.
Minister of Agriculture: ADEL SAFAR.
Minister of Irrigation: NADER AL-BUNI.
Minister of Communications and Technology: AMR NAZIR SALEM.
Minister of Health: Dr MAHER HUSSAMI.
Minister of Awqaf (Islamic Endowments): MUHAMMAD ZIAD AYOUBI.
Minister of Labour and Social Affairs: DIALA HAJ-AREF.
Minister of Tourism: Dr SAADALLAH AGHA AL-QALLA.
Minister of Presidential Affairs: GHASSAN AL-LAHHAM.
Minister of Expatriates: BOUTAINA SHA'BAN.
Ministers of State: YOUSUF SULEIMAN AL-AHMAD, BASHAR ASH-SH'AR, HUSSEIN MAHMOUD FARZAT, JOSEPH SWEID, HASSAN AS-SARRI, GHIATH JARAATLY.

MINISTRIES

Office of the President: Damascus; internet www.basharassad.org.
Office of the Prime Minister: rue Chahbandar, Damascus; tel. (11) 2226000.
Ministry of Agriculture: rue Jabri, place Hedjaz, Damascus; tel. (11) 2213613; fax (11) 2216627; e-mail agre-min@syriatel.net; internet www.syriangriculture.org.
Ministry of Awqaf (Islamic Endowments): Rukeneddin, Damascus; tel. (11) 4419079; fax (11) 419969.
Ministry of Communications and Technology: rue Abed, Damascus; tel. (11) 3320807; fax (11) 2246403; e-mail admin@moct.gov.sy; internet www.moct.gov.sy.
Ministry of Construction: rue Sa'dallah al-Jaberi, Damascus; tel. (11) 2223595.
Ministry of Culture: rue George Haddad, ar-Rawda, Damascus; tel. (11) 3331556; fax (11) 3320804.
Ministry of Defence: place Omayad, Damascus; tel. (11) 7770700.
Ministry of Economy and Trade: rue Maysaloun, Damascus; tel. (11) 2213514; fax (11) 2225695; e-mail econ-min@net.sy; internet www.syrecon.org.
Ministry of Education: rue Shahbander, al-Masraa, Damascus; tel. (11) 4444703; fax (11) 4420435.
Ministry of Electricity: BP 4900, rue al-Kouatly, Damascus; tel. (11) 2223086; fax (11) 2223686.
Ministry of Finance: BP 13136, rue Jule Jammal, Damascus; tel. (11) 2239624; fax (11) 2224701; e-mail mof@net.sy; internet www.syriafinance.org.
Ministry of Foreign Affairs: ave Shora, Muhajireen, Damascus; tel. (11) 3331200; fax (11) 3320686.
Ministry of Health: rue Majlis ash-Sha'ab, Damascus; tel. (11) 3311020; fax (11) 3311114; e-mail health-min@net.sy; internet www.moh.gov.sy.
Ministry of Higher Education: ave Kasem Amin, ar-Rawda, Damascus; tel. (11) 3330700; fax (11) 3337719.
Ministry of Housing and Construction: place Yousuf al-Azmeh, as-Salheyeh, Damascus; tel. (11) 2217571; fax (11) 2217570; e-mail mhu@net.sy.
Ministry of Industry: BP 12835, rue Maysaloun, Damascus; tel. (11) 2231834; fax (11) 2231096; e-mail min-industry@syriatel.net; internet www.syrianindustry.org.
Ministry of Information: Immeuble Dar al-Baath, Autostrade Mezzeh, Damascus; tel. (11) 6622141; fax (11) 6617665; e-mail moi@net.sy; internet www.moi-syria.com.
Ministry of the Interior: rue al-Bahsah, al-Marjeh, Damascus; tel. (11) 2238682; fax (11) 2246921.
Ministry of Irrigation: rue Fardoss; tel. (11) 2212741; fax (11) 3320691.
Ministry of Justice: rue an-Nasr, Damascus; tel. (11) 2214105; fax (11) 2246250.
Ministry of Labour and Social Affairs: place Yousuf al-Azmeh, as-Salheyeh, Damascus; tel. (11) 2210355; fax (11) 2247499.
Ministry of Local Administration and Environment: Damascus; e-mail webmaster@mlae-sy.org.
Ministry of Petroleum and Mineral Resources: BP 40, al-Adawi, Insha'at, Damascus; tel. (11) 4451624; fax (11) 4463942; e-mail mopmr@net.sy; internet www.mopmr-sy.org.
Ministry of Tourism: Barada St, Damascus; tel. (11) 2233183; fax (11) 2456143; e-mail min-tourism@mail.sy; internet www.syriatourism.org.
Ministry of Transport: BP 134, rue al-Jalaa, Damascus; tel. (11) 3336801; fax (11) 3323317; internet www.mot.gov.sy.

Legislature

MAJLIS ASH-SHA'AB
(People's Assembly)

Speaker: MAHMOUD AREF AL-ABRASH.
Election, 2 and 3 March 2003

Party	Seats
National Progressive Front*	167
Independents	83
Total	250

*The National Progressive Front reportedly comprised seven political parties, including the Baath Party, Syrian Communist Party, Arab Socialist Unionist Party, Syrian Arab Socialist Union Party, Arab Socialist Party and Democratic Socialist Unionist Party.

Political Organizations

The **National Progressive Front (NPF—Al-Jabha al-Wataniyah at-Taqadumiyah)**, headed by the late President Hafiz al-Assad, was formed in March 1972 as a coalition of five political parties. The Syrian Constitution defines the Baath Arab Socialist Party as 'the leading party in the society and the state'. At mid-2005 the NPF consisted of 10 parties, including the following:

Arab Socialist Party: Damascus; a breakaway socialist party; contested the 1994 election to the People's Assembly as two factions; Leader ABD AL-GHANI KANNOUT.

Arab Socialist Unionist Party: Damascus; f. 1964, following merger of four parties; Nasserite; supportive of the policies of the Baath Arab Socialist Party; Leader SAFWAN QUDSI.

Baath Arab Socialist Party: National Command, BP 9389, Autostrade Mezzeh, Damascus; tel. (11) 6622142; fax (11) 6622099; e-mail baath@baath-party.org; internet www.baath-party.org; Arab nationalist socialist party; f. 1947; result of merger of the Arab Revival (Baath) Movement (f. 1940) and the Arab Socialist Party (f. 1940); brs in most Arab countries; in power since 1963; supports creation of a unified Arab socialist society; Sec.-Gen. Lt-Gen. BASHAR AL-ASSAD; more than 800,000 mems in Syria.

Democratic Arab Union Party (Ittihad ad-Dimuqrati al-'Arabi): f. 1992; considers the concerns of the Arab world in general as secondary to those of Syria itself in the pursuit of pan-Arab goals; Chair. GHASSAN AHMAD OTHMAN.

SYRIA

Democratic Socialist Unionist Party (Hizb al-Wahdawi al-Ishtiraki al-Dimuqrati): f. 1974, following split from the Party of Socialist Unionists; Chair. FADLLAH NASIR ADEEN.

Party of Socialist Unionists (Hizb al-Wahiduin al-Ishtirakin): e-mail f.ismail@alwahdawi.org; f. 1961, through split from the Baath Arab Socialist Party, following that organization's acceptance of Syria's decision to secede from the United Arab Republic; Nasserite; aims for Arab unity; produces weekly periodical *Al-Wehdawi*; Chair. FAYEZ ISSMA'EL.

Syrian Arab Socialist Union Party: Damascus; tel. (11) 239305; Nasserite; Sec.-Gen. SAFWAN KOUDSI.

Syrian Communist Party (Bakdash): Damascus; f. 1924 by Fouad Shamal in Lebanon and Khalid Bakdash (died 1995); until 1943 part of joint Communist Party of Syria and Lebanon; party split into two factions, Bakdash and Faisal (q.v.), in 1986; Marxist-Leninist; publishes fortnightly periodical *Sawt ash-Shaab*; Sec.-Gen. WESAL FARHT BAKDASH.

Syrian Communist Party (Faisal): f. 1986, following split of Syrian Communist Party into two factions, known as Faisal and Bakash (q.v.); aims to end domination of Baath Arab Socialist Party and the advantages given to members of that party at all levels; advocates the lifting of the state of emergency and the release of all political prisoners; publishes weekly periodical *An-Nour*; Sec.-Gen. YOUSUF FAISAL.

Syrian Social Nationalist Party (Centralist Wing) (Al-Hizb as-Suri al-Qawmi al-Ijtima'i): internet www.ssnp.net; f. 1932 in Beirut, Lebanon; also known as Parti populaire syrien; seeks creation of a 'Greater Syrian' state, incl. Syria, Lebanon, Jordan, Palestine, Iraq, Kuwait and Cyprus; advocates separation of church and state, the redistribution of wealth, and a strong military; supports Syrian involvement in Lebanese affairs; has brs world-wide; joined the NPF in 2005; Chair. ISSAM MAHAYIRI.

The **Syrian Democratic People's Party** (leader RIAD AT-TURK) was founded in 1973 as the Syrian Communist Party (Political Bureau), following at-Turk's decision to split from that party after its leader, Khalid Bakdash, decided to allow the organization to join the NPF. At-Turk's party adopted its current name in 2005.

There is also a **Marxist-Leninist Communist Action Party**, which regards itself as independent of all Arab regimes.

An illegal Syrian-based organization, the **Islamic Movement for Change (IMC)**, claimed responsibility for a bomb attack in Damascus in December 1996.

Two new political organizations were formed in early 2001: the **Grouping for Democracy and Unity** (nationalist; Sec.-Gen. MUHAMMAD SAWWAN) and the **Movement for Social Peace** (pro-democratic; Leader RIAD SEIF); however, the latter was reportedly disbanded later that year.

Diplomatic Representation

EMBASSIES IN SYRIA

Afghanistan: BP 12217, ave Secretariat, West Villas, Mezzeh, Damascus; tel. (11) 6112910; fax (11) 6133595; Ambassador MUHAMMADULLAH HAIDARI.

Algeria: Immeuble Noss, Raouda, Damascus; tel. (11) 3331446; fax (11) 3334698; Ambassador SALEM BOUJOUMAA.

Argentina: BP 116, Damascus; tel. (11) 3334167; fax (11) 3327326; e-mail easir@net.sy; Ambassador HERNÁN ROBERTO PLORUTTI.

Armenia: POB 33241, Ibrahim Hanono St, Malki, Damascus; tel. (11) 6133560; fax (11) 6130952; e-mail am309@net.sy; Chargé d'affaires YOURI BABAKHANIAN.

Austria: BP 5634, Immeuble Mohamed Naim ad-Deker, 1 rue Farabi, East Villas, Mezzeh, Damascus; tel. (11) 6116730; fax (11) 6116734; e-mail damaskus-ob@bmaa.gv.at; Ambassador Dr iur. KARL SHRAMEK.

Belgium: 3 rue Salaam, Bâtiment 101, 2e and 3e étage, Mezzeh East, Damascus; tel. (11) 6124682; fax (11) 6124684; e-mail damascus@diplobel.org; internet www.diplomatie.be/damascus; Ambassador JORIS COUVREUR.

Brazil: BP 2219, 39 rue Al-Farabi, Mezzeh Charkieh, Damascus; tel. (11) 6124551; fax (11) 6124553; e-mail braemsyr@net.sy; Ambassador EDUARDO MONTEIRO DE BARROS ROXO.

Bulgaria: POB 2732, 8 rue Pakistan, place Arnous, Damascus; tel. (11) 3318445; fax (11) 4419854; e-mail bul-emb@scs-net.org; Ambassador GEORGI YANKOV.

Canada: BP 3394, Damascus; tel. (11) 6116692; fax (11) 6114000; e-mail dmcus@dfait-maeci.gc.ca; internet www.dfait-maeci.gc.ca/syria; Ambassador BRIAN J. DAVIS.

Chile: BP 3561, Immeuble du Patriarcat Catholique, rue Chakib Areslan, Abou Roumane, Damascus; tel. (11) 3338443; fax (11) 3331563; e-mail echilesy@scs-net.org; Ambassador RICARDO FIEGELIST.

China, People's Republic: 83 rue Ata Ayoubi, Damascus; tel. (11) 3339594; fax (11) 3338067; e-mail chinaemb_sy@mfa.gov.cn; Ambassador ZHOU XIUHUA.

Cuba: Immeuble Istouani and Charbati, 40 rue ar-Rachid, Damascus; tel. (11) 3339624; fax (11) 3333802; e-mail embacubasy@net.sy; Ambassador ORLANDO LANCÍS SUÁREZ.

Cyprus: BP 9269, 106 Akram al-Ojjeh, Eastern Mezzeh-Fursan, Damascus; tel. (11) 6130812; fax (11) 6130814; e-mail cyembdam@scs-net.org; Ambassador EFSTATHIOS ORPHANIDES.

Czech Republic: BP 2249, place Abou al-Ala'a al-Maari, Damascus; tel. (11) 3331383; fax (11) 3338268; e-mail damascus@embassy.mzv.cz; Ambassador Dr JOSEF KOUTSKY.

Denmark: BP 2244, rue Chekib Arslan, Abou Roumaneh, Damascus; tel. (11) 3331008; fax (11) 3337928; e-mail damamb@um.dk; internet www.ambdamaskus.um.dk; Ambassador OLE EGBERG MIKKELSEN.

Egypt: POB 12443, rue al-Gala'a, Abu Rumana, Damascus; tel. (11) 3330756; fax (11) 3337961; fax egyemb@syria.net; Ambassador HAZEM AHDI KHAIRAT.

Eritrea: BP 12846, Autostrade Al-Mazen West, 82 rue Akram Mosque, Damascus; tel. (11) 6112356; fax (11) 6112358; Chargé d'affaires a.i. HUMMED MOHAMED SAEED KULU.

Finland: BP 3893, Immeuble Yacoubian, Hawakir, West Malki, Damascus; tel. (11) 3338809; fax (11) 3734740; Ambassador PERTIE HARFOLA.

France: BP 769, rue Ata Ayoubi, Damascus; tel. (11) 3327992; fax (11) 3338632; e-mail ambafr@net.sy; internet www.ambafrance-sy.org; Ambassador JEAN-FRANÇOIS GIRAULT.

Germany: BP 2237, 16 rue Abd al-Mun'im Riyad, al-Malki, Damascus; tel. (11) 37900000; fax (11) 3323812; e-mail germemb@scs-net.org; Ambassador VOLKMAR KARL WENZEL.

Greece: BP 30319, Immeuble Pharaon, 11 rue Farabi, Mezzeh, Damascus; tel. (11) 6113035; fax (11) 6114920; e-mail grembdam@mail.sy; Ambassador VASSILIS PAPAIOANNOU.

Holy See: BP 2271, 1 place Ma'raket Ajnadin, Malki, Damascus (Apostolic Nunciature); tel. (11) 3332601; fax (11) 3327550; e-mail noncesy@mail.sy; Apostolic Nuncio Most Rev. MORANDINI GIOVANNI BATTISTA (Titular Archbishop of Grado).

Hungary: BP 2607, 12 rue as-Salam, East Villas, Mezzeh, Damascus; tel. (11) 6117966; fax (11) 6117917; e-mail hungemb@scs-net.org; internet www.hungemb.com/damascus; Ambassador Prof. PÉTER MEDGYES.

India: POB 685, BP 685, Immeuble Yassin Noueilati, 40/46 ave Adnan al-Malki, Damascus; tel. (11) 3739082; fax (11) 3336231; e-mail indemcom@scs-net.org; Ambassador GOTAM MOKOBAD HAYA.

Indonesia: BP 3530, Immeble 26, Bloc 270A, rue Al-Madina al-Munawar, Mezzeh Eastern Villa, Damascus; tel. (11) 6119630; fax (11) 6119632; e-mail kbridams@cyberia.net.lb; Ambassador SUKARNI SIKAR.

Iran: POB 2691, Autostrade Mezzeh, nr ar-Razi Hospital, Damascus; tel. (11) 6117675; fax (11) 6110997; e-mail iran-dam@net.sy; Ambassador MUHAMMAD REZA BAQIRI.

Italy: BP 2216, rue al-Ayoubi, Damascus; tel. (11) 3338338; fax (11) 3320325; e-mail ambasciata.damasco@esteri.it; internet www.ambdamasco.esteri.it; Ambassador FRANCESCO CERULLI.

Japan: BP 3366, 18 rue al-Mihdi bin Baraka, Damascus; tel. (11) 3338273; fax (11) 3339920; Ambassador AZUSA HAYASHI.

Jordan: rue Abou Roumaneh, Damascus; tel. (11) 3334642; fax (11) 3336741; Ambassador Dr HASHEM MUHAMMAD TALEB ASH-SHABBOUL.

Korea, Democratic People's Republic: rue Fares al-Khouri-Jisr Tora, Damascus; Ambassador KIM PYONG-NAM.

Kuwait: rue Ibrahim Hanano, Damascus; Ambassador FAHED AHMAD AL-AWADI.

Libya: Abou Roumaneh, Damascus; Head of People's Bureau AHMAD ABD AS-SALAM BIN KHAYAL.

Malaysia: Bldng 15, Abd al-Kader al-Jazairy St, Abu Roumanneh, Damascus; tel. (11) 3343388; fax (11) 3341002; e-mail mwsyria@scs-net.org; Ambassador ZEIN EDDIN YEHYA.

Mauritania: ave al-Jala'a, rue Karameh, Damascus; Ambassador Dr ABDALLAH OUL BENHMEIDA.

Morocco: rue Farabi Villas, Est-Mezzeh, Damascus; tel. (11) 6110451; fax (11) 61178845; e-mail sifmar@scs-net.org; Ambassador ABDELOUAHAB BELLOUKI.

Netherlands: BP 702, Immeuble Tello, rue al-Jalaa, Abou Roumaneh, Damascus; tel. (11) 3336871; fax (11) 3339369; e-mail dmc@minbuza.nl; Ambassador R. VAN SCHREVEN.

Norway: BP 7703, Immeuble 271A, rue Munawara, Mezze-Madina, Damascus; tel. (11) 6115053; fax (11) 6131159; e-mail emb

.damascus@mfa.no; internet www.norway.org.sy; Ambassador SVEIN SEVJE.

Oman: BP 9635, rue Ghazzawi, West Villas, Mezzeh, Damascus; tel. (11) 6110408; fax (11) 6110944; Ambassador MUHAMMAD BIN SALEM BIN SAID ASH-SHANFARI.

Pakistan: BP 9284, rue al-Farabi, East Villas, Mezzeh, Damascus; tel. (11) 6132694; fax (11) 6132662; e-mail parepdam@scs-net.org; Ambassador ABD AL-MOIZ BOKHARI.

Panama: BP 2548, Apt 7, Immeuble az-Zein, rue al-Bizm, Malki, Damascus; tel. (11) 224743; Chargé d'affaires CARLOS A. DE GRACIA.

Poland: BP 501, rue George Haddad, Abou Roumaneh, Damascus; tel. (11) 3333010; fax (11) 3315318; e-mail dampol@cyberia.net.lb; Ambassador JACEK CHODOROWICZ.

Qatar: BP 4188, rue Ahmed Shouki, Abou Roumaneh, Damascus; e-mail damascus@mofa.gov.qa; tel. (11) 336717; fax (11) 3320531; Ambassador MAJED GHANEM AL-ALI AL-MAADEED.

Romania: BP 4454, 8 rue Ibrahim Hanano, Damascus; tel. (11) 3327570; fax (11) 3327574; e-mail ro.dam@net.sy; Ambassador ION DOBRECI.

Russia: rue Umar bin al-Khattab, ad-Dawi, Damascus; tel. (11) 4423155; fax (11) 4423182; e-mail rusemb@scs-net.org; Ambassador ROBERT V. MARKARYAN.

Saudi Arabia: ave al-Jala'a, Abou Roumaneh, Damascus; tel. (11) 3334914; fax (11) 3337383; e-mail syemb@mofa.gov.sa; Ambassador ABDULLAH BIN SALEH AL-FADL.

Serbia and Montenegro: BP 739, 18 ave al-Jala'a, Damascus; tel. (11) 3336222; fax (11) 3333690; e-mail yudamsy@scs-net.org; Chargé d'affaires JOVAN VUJASINOVIĆ.

Slovakia: BP 33115, place Mezzeh, rue ash-Shafei, East Villas, Damascus; tel. (11) 6132114; fax (11) 6132598; e-mail slovemb@scs-net.org; internet www.damascus.mfa.sk; Ambassador OLDRICH HLAVACEK.

Somalia: ave Ata Ayoubi, Damascus; Ambassador (vacant).

South Africa: POB 9141, al-Ghazaoui St, 7 Jadet Kouraish, West Mezzeh, Damascus; tel. (11) 6135 1520; fax (11) 6111714; e-mail saembdam@ses-net.org; Ambassador MUHAMMAD DANGOR.

Spain: BP 392, rue ash-Shafi, Mezzeh East, Damascus; tel. (11) 6132900; fax (11) 6132941; e-mail spainemda@net.sy; Ambassador JUAN RAMÓN SERRAT CUENCA-ROMERO.

Sudan: Damascus; tel. (11) 6111036; fax (11) 6112904; e-mail sud-emb@net.sy; Ambassador ABD AR-RAHMAN DERAR.

Sweden: BP 4266, Immeuble du Patriarcat Catholique, rue Chakib Arslan, Abou Roumaneh, Damascus; tel. (11) 33400700; fax (11) 3327749; e-mail ambassaden.damaskus@foreign.ministry.se; Ambassador KATRINA KIBB.

Switzerland: BP 234, 2 rue ash-Shafi, East Villas, Mezzeh, Damascus; tel. (11) 6111972; fax (11) 6111976; e-mail vertretung@dam.rep.admin.ch; Ambassador ROBERT MAYOR.

Tunisia: BP 4114, 6 rue ash-Shafi, blvd Fahim, Mezzeh, Damascus; tel. (11) 6132700; fax (11) 6132704; e-mail at.damas@net.sy; Ambassador HEDI BEN NASR.

Turkmenistan: Miset, 4097 Ruki ed-Din, 2e étage, Damascus; tel. (11) 2241834; fax (11) 3320905.

Turkey: BP 3738, 56–58 ave Ziad bin Abou Soufian, Damascus; tel. (11) 33501930; fax (11) 3339243; e-mail sambe@mfa.gov.tr; Ambassador KHALED CEVIK.

Ukraine: Mezzeh, East Villas, 14 rue as-Salam, Damascus; tel. (11) 6113016; fax (11) 6121355; e-mail ukrembassy@mail.sy; Ambassador VOLODYMYR KOVAL.

United Arab Emirates: Immeuble Housami, 62 rue Raouda, Damascus; Ambassador YOUSUF MUHAMMAD HUSSEIN AL-MADFA'AI.

United Kingdom: BP 37, Immeuble Kotob, 11 rue Muhammad Kurd Ali, Malki, Damascus; tel. (11) 3739241; fax (11) 3731600; e-mail british.embassy.damascus@fco.gov.uk; Ambassador PETER FORD.

USA: BP 29, 2 rue al-Mansour, Abou Roumaneh, Damascus; tel. (11) 3331342; fax (11) 2247938; e-mail damasweb-query@state.gov; internet syria.usembassy.gov; Ambassador MARGARET SCOBEY (recalled in Feb. 2005).

Venezuela: BP 2403, Immeuble at-Tabbah, 5 rue Lisaneddin bin al-Khateb, place Rauda, Damascus; tel. (11) 3335356; fax (11) 3333203; e-mail embavenez@net.sy; internet www.embavensiria.com; Ambassador IVAN URBINA ORTIZ.

Yemen: Abou Roumaneh, Charkassieh, Damascus; Ambassador SALAH ALI AHEMD AL-ANSI.

Note: Syria and Lebanon have very close relations but do not exchange formal ambassadors.

Judicial System

The Courts of Law in Syria are principally divided into two juridical court systems: Courts of General Jurisdiction and Administrative Courts. Since 1973 the Supreme Constitutional Court has been established as the paramount body of the Syrian judicial structure.

THE SUPREME CONSTITUTIONAL COURT

This is the highest court in Syria. It has specific jurisdiction over: (i) judicial review of the constitutionality of laws and legislative decrees; (ii) investigation of charges relating to the legality of the election of members of the Majlis ash-Sha'ab (People's Assembly); (iii) trial of infractions committed by the President of the Republic in the exercise of his functions; (iv) resolution of positive and negative jurisdictional conflicts and determination of the competent court between the different juridical court systems, as well as other bodies exercising judicial competence. The Supreme Constitutional Court is composed of a Chief Justice and four Justices. They are appointed by decree of the President of the Republic for a renewable period of four years.

Chief Justice of the Supreme Court: NASRAT MOUNLA-HAYDAR, Damascus; tel. (11) 3331902.

COURTS OF GENERAL JURISDICTION

The Courts of General Jurisdiction in Syria are divided into six categories: (i) The Court of Cassation; (ii) The Courts of Appeal; (iii) The Tribunals of First Instance; (iv) The Tribunals of Peace; (v) The Personal Status Courts; (vi) The Courts for Minors. Each of the above categories (except the Personal Status Courts) is divided into Civil, Penal and Criminal Chambers.

(i) The Court of Cassation: This is the highest court of general jurisdiction. Final judgments rendered by Courts of Appeal in penal and civil litigations may be petitioned to the Court of Cassation by the Defendant or the Public Prosecutor in penal and criminal litigations, and by any of the parties in interest in civil litigations, on grounds of defective application or interpretation of the law as stated in the challenged judgment, on grounds of irregularity of form or procedure, or violation of due process, and on grounds of defective reasoning of judgment rendered. The Court of Cassation is composed of a President, seven Vice-Presidents and 31 other Justices (Councillors).

(ii) The Courts of Appeal: Each court has geographical jurisdiction over one governorate (Mouhafazat). Each court is divided into Penal and Civil Chambers. There are Criminal Chambers which try felonies only. The Civil Chambers hear appeals filed against judgments rendered by the Tribunals of First Instance and the Tribunals of Peace. Each Court of Appeal is composed of a President and sufficient numbers of Vice-Presidents (Presidents of Chambers) and Superior Judges (Councillors). There are 54 Courts of Appeal.

(iii) The Tribunals of First Instance: In each governorate there are one or more Tribunals of First Instance, each of which is divided into several Chambers for penal and civil litigations. Each Chamber is composed of one judge. There are 72 Tribunals of First Instance.

(iv) The Tribunals of Peace: In the administrative centre of each governorate, and in each district, there are one or more Tribunals of Peace, which have jurisdiction over minor civil and penal litigations. There are 227 Tribunals of Peace.

(v) Personal Status Courts: These courts deal with marriage, divorce, etc. For Muslims each court consists of one judge, the 'Qadi Shari'i'. For Druzes there is one court consisting of one judge, the 'Qadi Mazhabi'. For non-Muslim communities there are courts for Roman Catholics, Orthodox believers, Protestants and Jews.

(vi) Courts for Minors: The constitution, officers, sessions, jurisdiction and competence of these courts are determined by a special law.

PUBLIC PROSECUTION

Public prosecution is headed by the Attorney-General, assisted by a number of Senior Deputy and Deputy Attorneys-General, and a sufficient number of chief prosecutors, prosecutors and assistant prosecutors. Public prosecution is represented at all levels of the Courts of General Jurisdiction in all criminal and penal litigations and also in certain civil litigations as required by the law. Public prosecution controls and supervises enforcement of penal judgments.

ADMINISTRATIVE COURTS SYSTEM

The Administrative Courts have jurisdiction over litigations involving the state or any of its governmental agencies. The Administrative Courts system is divided into two courts: the Administrative Courts and the Judicial Administrative Courts, of which the paramount body is the High Administrative Court.

MILITARY COURTS

The Military Courts deal with criminal litigations against military personnel of all ranks and penal litigations against officers only. There are two military courts: one in Damascus, the other in Aleppo.

SYRIA

Each court is composed of three military judges. There are other military courts, consisting of one judge, in every governorate, which deal with penal litigations against military personnel below the rank of officer. The different military judgments can be petitioned to the Court of Cassation.

Religion

In religion the majority of Syrians follow a form of Islamic Sunni orthodoxy. There are also a considerable number of religious minorities: Shi'a Muslims; Isma'ili Muslims; the Isma'ili of the Salamiya district, whose spiritual head is the Aga Khan; a large number of Druzes, the Nusairis or Alawites of the Jebel Ansariyeh (a schism of the Shi'ite branch of Islam, to which President Assad belongs, who comprise about 11% of the population) and the Yezidis of the Jebel Sinjar; and a minority of Christians.

The Constitution states only that 'Islam shall be the religion of the head of the state'. The original draft of the 1973 Constitution made no reference to Islam at all, and this clause was inserted only as a compromise after public protest. The Syrian Constitution is thus unique among the constitutions of Arab states (excluding Lebanon) with a clear Muslim majority in not enshrining Islam as the religion of the state itself.

ISLAM

Grand Mufti: Sheikh AHMAD HASSOUN, POB 7410, Damascus; tel. (11) 2777158; fax (11) 2764989; e-mail admin@kuftaro.org; internet www.drhassoun.com.

CHRISTIANITY

Orthodox Churches

Greek Orthodox Patriarchate of Antioch and all the East: BP 9, Damascus; tel. (11) 5424400; fax (11) 5424404; e-mail info@antiochpat.org; internet www.antiochpat.org; Patriarch of Antioch and all the East His Beatitude IGNATIUS HAZIM; has jurisdiction over Syria, Lebanon, Iran and Iraq.

Syrian Orthodox Patriarchate of Antioch and all the East: BP 22260, Bab Touma, Damascus; tel. (11) 54498989; e-mail patriarch-z-iwas@scs-net.org; Patriarch of Antioch and all the East His Holiness IGNATIUS ZAKKA I IWAS; the Syrian Orthodox Church includes one Catholicose (of India), 37 Metropolitans and one Bishop, and has an estimated 4m. adherents throughout the world.

The Armenian Apostolic Church is also represented in Syria.

The Roman Catholic Church

Armenian Rite

Patriarchal Exarchate of Syria: Exarchat Patriarcal Arménien Catholique, BP 22281, Bab Touma, Damascus; tel. (11) 5413820; fax (11) 5419431; f. 1985; represents the Patriarch of Cilicia (resident in Beirut, Lebanon); 4,500 adherents (31 December 2004); Exarch Patriarchal Bishop JOSEPH ARNAOUTIAN.

Archdiocese of Aleppo: Archevêché Arménien Catholique, BP 97, 33 33 at-Tilal, Aleppo; tel. (21) 2213946; fax (21) 2235303; e-mail armen.cath@mail.sy; 17,000 adherents (31 December 2003); Archbishop BOUTROS MARAYATI.

Diocese of Kamichlié: Evêché Arménien Catholique, BP 17, Al-Qamishli; tel. (53) 424211; fax (53) 426211; 4,000 adherents (31 December 2002); Bishop (vacant).

Chaldean Rite

Diocese of Aleppo: Evêché Chaldéen Catholique, BP 4643, 1 rue Patriarche Elias IV Mouawwad, Soulémaniyé, Aleppo; tel. (21) 4441660; fax (21) 4600800; e-mail chalalep@mail.sy; 15,000 adherents (31 December 2003); Bishop ANTOINE AUDO.

Latin Rite

Apostolic Vicariate of Aleppo: BP 327, 19 rue Antaki, Aleppo; tel. (21) 2210204; fax (21) 2219031; e-mail vicariatlatin@mail.sy; f. 1762; 17,000 adherents (31 December 2003); Vicar Apostolic GIUSEPPE NAZZARO (Titular Bishop of Forma).

Maronite Rite

Archdiocese of Aleppo: Archevêché Maronite, BP 203, 57 rue Fares-El-Khoury, Aleppo; tel. and fax (21) 2248048; fax (21) 2243048; e-mail maronite-aleppo@net.sy; 4,105 adherents (31 December 2003); Archbishop YOUSSEF ANIS ABI-AAD.

Archdiocese of Damascus: Archevêché Maronite, BP 2179, 6 rue ad-Deir, Bab Touma, Damascus; tel. (11) 5412888; 12,000 adherents (31 December 2003); Archbishop RAYMOND EID.

Diocese of Latakia: Evêché Maronite, BP 161, rue Hamrat, Tartous; tel. (43) 223433; fax (43) 322939; 31,000 adherents (31 December 2003); Bishop YOUSSEF-MASSOUD MASSOUD.

Melkite Rite

Melkite-Greek-Catholic Patriarchate of Antioch: Patriarcat Grec-Melkite Catholique, BP 22249, 12 ave az-Zeitoon, Bab Charki, Damascus; tel. (11) 5433129; fax (11) 5431266; e-mail gcp@pcg-lb.org; or BP 70071, Antélias, Lebanon; tel. (4) 413111; fax (4) 418113; jurisdiction over 1.5m. Melkites throughout the world (including 290,000 in Syria); Patriarch of Antioch, Alexandria and Jerusalem H. B. GREGORIOS III (Laham); The Melkite Church includes the patriarchal sees of Damascus, Cairo and Jerusalem and four other archdioceses in Syria; seven archdioceses in Lebanon; one in Jordan; one in Israel; and six Eparchies in the USA, Brazil, Canada, Australia, Venezuela, Argentina and Mexico).

Archdiocese of Aleppo: Archevêché Grec-Catholique, BP 146, place Farhat, Aleppo; tel. (21) 2213218; fax (21) 2223106; e-mail gr.melkcath@mail.sy; 17,000 adherents (31 December 2002); Archbishop JEAN-CLÉMENT JEANBART.

Archdiocese of Busra and Hauran: Archevêché Grec-Catholique, Khabab, Hauran; tel. (15) 855012; e-mail derbosra@hotmail.com; 27,000 adherents (31 December 2003); Archbishop BOULOS NASSIF BORKHOCHE.

Archdiocese of Homs: Archevêché Grec-Catholique, BP 1525, rue El-Mo'tazila, Boustan ad-Diwan, Homs; tel. and fax (31) 482587; e-mail a_nehme@postmaster.co.uk; 27,000 adherents (31 December 2003); Archbishop ABRAHAM NEHMÉ.

Archdiocese of Latakia: Archevêché Grec-Catholique, BP 151, rue al-Moutannabi, Latakia; tel. (41) 460777; fax (41) 467002; 10,000 adherents (31 December 2003); Archbishop NICOLAS SAWAF.

Syrian Rite

Archdiocese of Aleppo: Archevêché Syrien Catholique, place Mère Teresa de Calcutta, Azizié, Aleppo; tel. (21) 2241200; fax (21) 2286347; 8,000 adherents (31 December 2003); Archbishop ANTOINE CHAHDA.

Archdiocese of Damascus: Archevêché Syrien Catholique, BP 2129, 157 rue Al-Mustaqeem, Bab Charki, Damascus; tel. (11) 5445343; fax (11) 5445343; 6,500 adherents (31 December 2003); Archbishop GREGORIOS ELIAS TABÉ.

Archdiocese of Hassaké-Nisibi: Archevêché Syrien Catholique, BP 6, Hassaké; tel. (52) 320812; 5,630 adherents (31 December 2003); Archbishop JACQUES BEHNAN HINDO.

Archdiocese of Homs: Archevêché Syrien Catholique, BP 368, rue Hamidieh, Homs; tel. (31) 221575; fax (21) 224350; 10,000 adherents (31 December 2003); Archbishop THÉOPHILE GEORGES KASSAB.

The Anglican Communion

Within the Episcopal Church in Jerusalem and the Middle East, Syria forms part of the diocese of Jerusalem (see the chapter on Israel).

Other Christian Groups

Protestants in Syria are largely adherents of either the National Evangelical Synod of Syria and Lebanon or the Union of Armenian Evangelical Churches in the Near East (for details of both organizations, see the chapter on Lebanon).

The Press

Since the Baath Arab Socialist Party came to power, the structure of the press has been modified according to socialist patterns. Most publications are issued by political, religious or professional associations (such as trade unions), and several are published by government ministries. Anyone wishing to establish a new paper or periodical must apply for a licence.

The major dailies are *Al-Baath* (the organ of the party), *Tishrin* and *Ath-Thawra* in Damascus, *Al-Jamahir al-Arabia* in Aleppo and *Al-Fida'* in Hama.

PRINCIPAL DAILIES

Al-Baath (Renaissance): BP 9389, Autostrade Mezzeh, Damascus; tel. (11) 6622142; fax (11) 6622099; e-mail baath@baath-party.org; internet www.baath-party.org; f. 1946; morning; Arabic; organ of the Baath Arab Socialist Party; Editor ILYAS MURAD; circ. 45,000.

Barq ash-Shimal (The Syrian Telegraph): rue Aziziyah, Aleppo; morning; Arabic; Editor MAURICE DJANDJI; circ. 6,400.

Champress: internet www.champress.com; privately owned; political; internet only; Arabic; Dir ALI JAMALO.

Al-Fida' (Redemption): Hama; Al-Wihdat Press, Printing and Publishing Organization, BP 2448, Dawar Kafr Soussat, Damascus; tel. (11) 225219; e-mail fedaa@thawra.com; internet fedaa.alwehda.gov.sy; morning; Arabic; political; Editor A. AULWANI; circ. 4,000.

Al-Horubat: Homs; Al-Wihdat Press, Printing and Publishing Organization, BP 2448, Dawar Kafr Soussat, Damascus; tel. (11) 225219; morning; Arabic; circ. 5,000.

Al-Jamahir (The People): Aleppo; Al-Wihdat Press, Printing and Publishing Organization, BP 2448, Dawar Kafr Soussat, Damascus; tel. (21) 214309; fax (21) 214308; Arabic; political; Chief Editor MORTADA BAKACH; circ. 10,000.

Ash-Shabab (Youth): rue at-Tawil, Aleppo; morning; Arabic; Editor MUHAMMAD TALAS; circ. 9,000.

Syria Times: BP 5452, Medan, Damascus; tel. (11) 2247359; fax (11) 2231374; e-mail syriatimes@teshreen.com; internet syriatimes.tishreen.info; English; publ. by Tishreen Foundation for Press and Publishing; Editor FOUAD MARDOUD; circ. 15,000.

Ath-Thawra (Revolution): Al-Wihdat Press, Printing and Publishing Organization, BP 2448, Dawar Kafr Soussat, Damascus; tel. (11) 2210850; fax (11) 2216851; e-mail admin@thawra.com; internet thawra.alwehda.gov.sy/thakafi.asp; morning; Arabic; political; Editor-in-Chief FAYEZ AS-SAYEGH; circ. 40,000.

Tishreen (October): BP 5452, Medan, Damascus; tel. (11) 2131100; fax (11) 2231374; e-mail daily@teshreen.com; internet www.teshreen.com/daily; Arabic; publ. by the Tishreen Foundation for Press and Publishing; Chief Editor KHALAF AL-JARAAD; circ. 50,000.

Al-Wihdat (Unity): Latakia; Al-Wihdat Press, Printing and Publishing Organization, BP 2448, Dawar Kafr Soussat, Damascus; Arabic.

WEEKLIES AND FORTNIGHTLIES

Abyad wa Aswad (White and Black): f. 2002; weekly; Arabic; political; privately owned; Editor AYMAN AD-DAQUQ.

Al-Ajoua' (The Air): Compagnie de l'Aviation Arabe Syrienne, BP 417, Damascus; fortnightly; Arabic; aviation; Editor AHMAD ALLOUCHE.

Ad-Doumari (Lamplighter): Damascus; f. 2001; weekly; Arabic; political satire; privately owned; Publr ALI FARZAT.

Al-Esbou ar-Riadi (The Sports Week): Immeuble Tibi, ave Fardoss, Damascus; weekly; Arabic; sports; Asst Dir and Editor HASRAN AL-BOUNNI; circ. 14,000.

Al-Fursan (The Cavalry): Damascus; Arabic; political magazine; Editor RIFAAT AL-ASSAD.

Homs: Homs; weekly; Arabic; literary; Publisher and Dir ADIB KABA; Editor PHILIPPE KABA.

Al-Iqtisadiya: f. 2001; weekly; Arabic; economic; privately owned; Editor WADDAH ABD AR-RABBO.

Kifah al-Oummal al-Ishtiraki (The Socialist Workers' Struggle): Fédération Générale des Syndicats des Ouvriers, rue Qanawat, Damascus; weekly; Arabic; labour; published by General Federation of Labour Unions; Editor SAID AL-HAMAMI.

Al-Masirah (Progress): Damascus; weekly; Arabic; political; published by Federation of Youth Organizations.

Al-Maukef ar-Riadi (Sport Stance): Al-Wihdat Press, Printing and Publishing Organization, BP 2448, Dawar Kafr Soussat, Damascus; tel. (11) 225219; e-mail riadi@thawra.com; internet riadi.alwehda.gov.sy; weekly; Arabic; sports; circ. 50,000.

An-Nas (The People): BP 926, Aleppo; f. 1953; weekly; Arabic; Publisher VICTOR KALOUS.

Nidal al-Fellahin (Peasants' Struggle): Fédération Générale des Laboureurs, BP 9389, Autostrade Mezzeh, Damascus; weekly; Arabic; peasant workers; Editor MANSOUR ABU AL-HOSN; circ. 8,100.

Ar-Riada (Sport): BP 292, near Electricity Institute, Damascus; weekly; Arabic; sports; Dir NOUREDDINE RIAL; Publisher and Editor OURFANE UBARI.

As-Sakafat al-Usbouiya (Weekly Culture): BP 2570, Soukak as-Sakr, Damascus; weekly; Arabic; cultural; Publisher, Dir and Editor MADHAT AKKACHE.

Sawt ash-Shaab (Voice of the People): Damascus; f. 1937; but publication suspended in 1939, 1941, 1947 and 1958; relaunched in 2001; fortnightly; Arabic; organ of the Syrian Communist Party (Bakdash).

Al-Wehdawi (Unionist): Damascus; f. 2001; weekly; Arabic; organ of the Party of Socialist Unionists.

Al-Yanbu al-Jadid (New Spring): Immeuble Al-Awkaf, Homs; weekly; Arabic; literary; Publisher, Dir and Editor MAMDOU AL-KOUSSEIR.

OTHER PERIODICALS

Al-Arabieh (The Arab Lady): Syrian Women's Association, BP 3207, Damascus; tel. (11) 3316560; monthly; Editor S. BAKOUR.

Ad-Dad: rue Tital, Wakf al-Moiriné Bldg, Aleppo; monthly; Arabic; literary; Dir RIAD HALLAK; Publisher and Editor ABDULLAH YARKI HALLAK.

Al-Fikr al-Askari (The Military Idea): BP 4259, blvd Palestine, Damascus; fax (11) 2125280; f. 1950; 6 a year; Arabic; official military review published by the Political Administration Press.

Al-Ghad (Tomorrow): Association of Red Cross and Crescent, BP 6095, rue Maysat, Damascus; tel. (11) 2242552; fax (11) 7777040; monthly; environmental health; Editor K. ABED-RABOU.

Al-Irshad az-Zirai (Agricultural Information): Ministry of Agriculture, rue Jabri, Damascus; tel. (11) 2213613; fax (11) 2216627; 6 a year; Arabic; agriculture.

Jaysh ash-Sha'ab (The People's Army): Ministry of Defence, BP 3320, blvd Palestine, Damascus; fax (11) 2125280; f. 1946; monthly; Arabic; army magazine; published by the Political Department of the Syrian Army.

Al-Kalima (The Word): Al-Kalima Association, Aleppo; monthly; Arabic; religious; Publisher and Editor FATHALLA SAKAL.

Al-Kanoun (The Law): Ministry of Justice, rue an-Nasreh, Damascus; tel. (11) 2214105; fax (11) 2246250; monthly; Arabic; juridical.

Al-Maaloumatieh (Information): National Information Centre, BP 11323, Damascus; tel. (11) 2127551; fax (11) 2127648; e-mail nice@net.sy; f. 1994; quarterly; computer magazine; Editor ABD AL-MAJID AR-RIFAI; circ. 10,000.

Al-Ma'arifa (Knowledge): Ministry of Culture, rue ar-Rouda, Damascus; tel. (11) 3336963; f. 1962; monthly; Arabic; literary; Editor ABD AL-KARIM NASIF; circ. 7,500.

Al-Majalla al-Batriarquia (The Magazine of the Patriarchate): Syrian Orthodox Patriarchate, BP 914, Damascus; tel. (11) 4447036; f. 1962; monthly; Arabic; religious; Editor SAMIR ABDOH; circ. 15,000.

Al-Majalla at-Tibbiya al-Arabiyya (Arab Medical Magazine): rue al-Jala'a, Damascus; monthly; Arabic; published by Arab Medical Commission; Dir Dr Y. SAKA; Editor Prof. ADNAN TAKRITI.

Majallat Majma' al-Lughat al-Arabiyya bi-Dimashq (Magazine of the Arab Language Academy of Damascus): Arab Academy of Damascus, BP 327, Damascus; tel. (11) 3713145; fax (11) 3733363; e-mail mla@net.sy; f. 1921; quarterly; Arabic; Islamic culture and Arabic literature, Arabic scientific and cultural terminology; Chief Editor Dr SHAKER FAHAM; circ. 1,600.

Al-Mawkif al-Arabi (The Arab Situation): Ittihab al-Kuttab al-Arab, rue Murshid Khatir, Damascus; monthly; Arabic; literary.

Monthly Survey of Arab Economics: BP 2306, Damascus; BP 6068, Beirut; f. 1958; monthly; English and French editions; published by Centre d'Etudes et de Documentation Economiques, Financières et Sociales; Dir Dr CHAFIC AKHRAS.

Al-Mouallem al-Arabi (The Arab Teacher): National Union of Teachers, BP 2842-3034, Damascus; tel. (11) 225219; f. 1948; monthly; Arabic; educational and cultural.

Al-Mouhandis al-Arabi (The Arab Engineer): Order of Syrian Engineers and Architects, BP 2336, Immeuble Dar al-Mouhandisen, place Azme, Damascus; tel. (11) 2214919; fax (11) 2216948; e-mail lbosea@net.sy; f. 1961; 4 a year; Arabic; scientific and cultural; Dir Eng. M. FAYEZ MAHFOUZ; Chief Editor Dr Eng. AHMAD AL-GHAFARI; circ. 50,000.

Al-Munadel (The Militant): c/o BP 11512, Damascus; fax (11) 2126935; f. 1965; monthly; Arabic; magazine of Baath Arab Socialist Party; Dir Dr FAWWAZ SAYYAGH; circ. 100,000.

An-Nashra al-Iktissad (Economic Bulletin): Damascus Chamber of Commerce; tel. (11) 2218339; fax (11) 2225874; e-mail dcc@net.sy; f. 1922; quarterly; finance and investment; Editor GHASSAN KALLA; circ. 3,000.

Risalat al-Kimia (Chemistry Report): BP 669, Immeuble al-Abid, Damascus; monthly; Arabic; scientific; Publisher, Dir and Editor HASSAN AS-SAKA.

Saut al-Forat: Deir ez-Zor; monthly; Arabic; literary; Publisher, Dir and Editor ABD AL-KADER AYACHE.

Ash-Shourta (The Police): Directorate of Public Affairs and Moral Guidance, Damascus; monthly; Arabic; juridical.

As-Sinaa (Industry): Damascus Chamber of Commerce, BP 1305, rue Mou'awiah, Harika, Damacus; tel. (11) 2222205; fax (11) 2245981; monthly; commerce, industry and management; Editor Y. HINDI.

Souriya al-Arabiyya (Arab Syria): Ministry of Information, Immeuble Dar al-Baath, Autostrade Mezzeh, Damascus; tel. (11) 6622141; fax (11) 6617665; monthly; publicity; in four languages.

Syria Today: Baramkeh, Free Zone, Damascus; tel. (11) 8827031; fax (11) 2137343; e-mail info@idassociates.net; internet www.syria-today.com/index.htm; monthly; English; economic and social development; Man. Dir KINDA KANBAR.

SYRIA

At-Tamaddon al-Islami (Islamic Civilization Society): Darwichiyah, Damascus; tel. (11) 2240563; fax (11) 2233815; e-mail isltmddn@hotmail.com; f. 1932; monthly; Arabic; religious; published by At-Tamaddon al-Islami Association; Pres. of Asscn AHMAD MOUAZ AL-KHATIB.

At-Taqa Wattanmiya (Energy and Expansion): BP 7748, rue al-Moutanabbi, Damascus; tel. (11) 233529; monthly; Arabic; published by the Syrian Petroleum Co.

Al-Yakza (The Awakening): Al-Yakza Association, BP 6677, rue Sisi, Aleppo; f. 1935; monthly; Arabic; literary social review of charitable institution; Dir HUSNI ABD AL-MASSIH; circ. 12,000.

Az-Zira'a (Agriculture): Ministry of Agriculture, rue Jabri, Damascus; tel. (11) 2213613; fax (11) 2244023; f. 1985; monthly; Arabic; agriculture; circ. 12,000.

PRESS AGENCIES

Syrian Arab News Agency (SANA): BP 2661, Baramka, Damascus; tel. (11) 2228239; fax (11) 2220365; e-mail sanagm@sana.org; internet www.sana.org; f. 1966; supplies bulletins on Syrian news to foreign news agencies; 16 offices abroad; 16 foreign correspondents; Dir-Gen. GHAZI AD-DIB.

Foreign Bureaux

Agencia EFE (Spain): Damascus; Correspondent ZACHARIAS SARME.

Agence France-Presse (AFP): BP 2400, Immeuble Adel Charaj, place Saaba Bahrat, Damascus; tel. (11) 2318200; fax (11) 2312691; Correspondent JOSEPH GHASI.

Agenzia Nazionale Stampa Associata (ANSA) (Italy): Hotel Méridien, BP 2712, Damascus; tel. (11) 233116; f. 1962; Correspondent ABDULLAH SAADEL.

Associated Press (AP) (USA): c/o Hotel Méridien, BP 2712, Damascus; tel. (11) 233116; e-mail opc@scs-net.com; internet www.ap.org.

Deutsche Presse-Agentur (dpa) (Germany): c/o Hotel Méridien, BP 2712, Damascus; tel. (11) 332924.

Kuwait News Agency (KUNA) and Reuters (UK) are also represented in Syria.

Publishers

Arab Advertising Organization: BP 2842-3034, 28 rue Moutanabbi, Damascus; tel. (11) 2225219; fax (11) 2220754; e-mail sy-adv@net.sy; f. 1963; exclusive government establishment responsible for advertising; publishes *Directory of Commerce and Industry*, *Damascus International Fair Guide*, *Daily Bulletin of Official Tenders*; Dir-Gen. MONA F. FABAH.

Damascus University Press: Damascus; tel. (11) 2215100; fax (11) 2236010; f. 1946; 12 journals; medicine, engineering, social sciences, agriculture, arts; Dir HUSSEIN OMRAN.

Institut Français du Proche-Orient: BP 344, Damascus; tel. (11) 3330214; fax (11) 3327887; e-mail ifead@net.sy; internet www.univ-aix.fr/ifead; f. 1922; sociology, anthropology, Islamic archaeology, history, language, arts, philosophy, poetry, geography, religion; Dir CHRISTIAN DÉCOBERT.

OFA-Business Consulting Center—Documents Service: BP 3550, 3 place Chahbandar, Damascus; tel. (11) 3318237; fax (11) 4426021; e-mail ofa1@net.sy; f. 1964; numerous periodicals, monographs and surveys on political and economic affairs; Dir-Gen. SAMIR A. DARWICH; has one affiliated branch, OFA-Business Consulting Centre (foreign company representation and services).

The Political Administration Press: BP 3320, blvd Palestine, Damascus; fax (11) 2125280; publishes *Al-Fikr al-Askari* (6 a year) and *Jaysh ash-Sha'ab* (monthly).

Syrian Documentation Papers: BP 2712, Damascus; f. 1968; publishers of *Bibliography of the Middle East* (annual), *General Directory of the Press and Periodicals in the Arab World* (annual), and numerous publications on political, economic, literary and social affairs, as well as legislative texts concerning Syria and the Arab world; Dir-Gen. LOUIS FARÈS.

Tishreen Foundation for Press and Publishing: BP 5452, Medan, Damascus; tel. (11) 2131100; fax (11) 2246860; publishes *Syria Times* and *Tishreen* (dailies).

Al-Wihdat Press, Printing and Publishing Organization (Institut al-Ouedha pour l'impression, édition et distribution): BP 2448, Dawar Kafr Soussat, Damascus; tel. (11) 225219; publishes *Al-Fida'*, *Al-Horubat*, *Al-Jamahir*, *Ath-Thawra* and *Al-Wihdat* (dailies), *al-Maukef ar-Riadi* (weekly) and other commercial publications; Dir-Gen. FAHD DIYAB.

Broadcasting and Communications

TELECOMMUNICATIONS

Syrian Telecommunications Establishment (STE): BP 11774, Autostrade Mezzeh, Damascus; tel. (11) 6122226; fax (11) 6120000; e-mail ste-gm@net.sy; f. 1975; Gen. Dir. Dr IMAD SABOUNI.

Syriatel: Immeuble STE, 6e étage, rue Thawra, Damascus; fax (11) 3341900; e-mail cs@syriatel.com.sy; internet www.syriatel.com; f. 2000; provider of mobile telephone services; Chair. RAMI MAKHLOUF; CEO NADER KALAI.

BROADCASTING

Radio and Television

Directorate-General of Radio and Television: place Omayyad, Damascus; tel. (11) 720700.

Organisme de la Radio–Télévision Arabe Syrienne (ORTAS): place Omayyad, Damascus; tel. (11) 720700; fax (11) 2234930; radio broadcasts started in 1945, television broadcasts in 1960; Dir-Gen. RIAD ISMAT; Dirs NAIF HAMMOUD (Radio), Dr FOUAD SHERBAJI (Television).

Finance

(cap. = capital; res = reserves; dep. = deposits; m.= million; brs = branches; amounts in £S unless otherwise indicated)

BANKING

Central Bank

Central Bank of Syria: BP 2254, place At-Tajrida al-Mughrabia, Damascus; tel. (11) 2212642; fax (11) 2213076; e-mail mrksyba-bn@mail.sy; internet www.syrecon.org/establishments1a.html; f. 1956; cap. 63,315.0m., dep. 466,942.0m., total assets US$ 16,647.8m. (Dec. 2002); Gov. Dr MUHAMMAD BASHAR KABBARA; 11 brs.

Other Banks

Agricultural Co-operative Bank: BP 4325, rue at-Tajehiz, Damascus; tel. (11) 2213461; fax (11) 2241261; f. 1888; cap. 10,000m., res 671m., dep. 12,000m., (Dec. 2001); Chair. and Dir-Gen. YASSER AS-SAMOR; 106 brs.

Bank of Syria and Overseas: BP 3103, Lawyers' Syndicate Bldg, nr Chamber of Commerce, Damascus; tel. (11) 2460560; fax (11) 2460555; e-mail bsomail@bso.com.sy; f. 2004; Pres. Dr RATEB SHALLAH; Gen. Man. GEORGES SAYEGH.

Banque BEMO (Banque Européene pour le Moyen-Orient) Saudi Fransi SA: 39 rue Ayyar, Salhiah, Damascus; tel. (11) 2317778; fax (11) 2318778; e-mail bbsf@mail.sy; f. 2004; Pres., Chair. and Gen. Man. RIAD OBEGI.

Commercial Bank of Syria: BP 933, place Yousuf al-Azmeh, Damascus; tel. (11) 2218890; fax (11) 2216975; e-mail tec.cbs@mail.sy; internet www.cbs-bank.com; f. 1967; govt-owned bank; cap. 4,000m., res 3,796m., dep. 510,941m., total assets 768,229m. (Dec. 2001); Chair. and Gen. Man. Dr DOURAID DERGHAM; 50 brs.

Industrial Bank: BP 7578, Immeuble Dar al-Mohandessin, rue Maysaloon, Damascus; tel. (11) 2228200; fax (11) 2228412; e-mail ind-bank@mail.sy; f. 1959; nationalized bank providing finance for industry; cap. 257m., total assets 8,131m. (Dec. 2001); Chair. and Gen. Man. MUHAMMAD ABU AN-NASSER; 13 brs.

Popular Credit Bank: BP 2841, 6e étage, Immeuble Dar al-Mohandessin, rue Maysaloon, Damascus; tel. (11) 2227604; fax (11) 2211291; f. 1967; government bank; provides loans to the services sector and is sole authorized issuer of savings certificates; cap. 25m., res 42,765m., dep. 2,313m. (Dec. 1984); Pres. and Gen. Man. MUHAMMAD HASSAN AL-HOUJJEIRI; 50 brs.

Real Estate Bank: BP 2337, place Yousuf al-Azmeh, Damascus; tel. (11) 2218602; fax (11) 2237938; e-mail realestate@realestate-sy.com; internet www.realestatebank-sy.com; f. 1966; govt-owned bank; provides loans and grants for housing, schools, hospitals and hotel construction; cap. 1,000m. (Dec. 2001); Chair. and Gen. Man. MUHAMMAD AHMAD MAKHLOUF; 15 brs.

Syrian Lebanese Commercial Bank SAL: BP 933, Damascus; fax (11) 2243224; f. 1974; Pres., Chair. and Gen. Man. TAREK AS-SARRAJ.

INSURANCE

Syrian General Organization for Insurance (Syrian Insurance Co): BP 2279, 29 rue Ayyar, Damascus; tel. (11) 2218430; fax (11) 2220494; f. 1953; auth. cap. 1,000m.; a nationalized company; operates throughout Syria; Chair. and Gen. Man. GHASSAN BAROUDIT; Assistant Gen. Man. and Admin. Dir SULAYMAN AL-HASSAN.

SYRIA

Trade and Industry

STATE ENTERPRISES

Syrian industry is almost entirely controlled and run by the State. There are national organizations responsible to the appropriate ministry for the operation of all sectors of industry, of which the following are examples:

Cotton Marketing Organization: BP 729, rue Bab al-Faraj, Aleppo; tel. (21) 2238486; fax (21) 2218617; f. 1965; governmental authority for purchase of seed cotton, ginning and sales of cotton lint; Pres. and Dir-Gen. Dr AHMAD SOUHAD GEBBARA.

General Company for Phosphate and Mines (GECOPHAM): BP 288, Homs; tel. (31) 420405; fax (31) 412961; e-mail gecopham@net.sy; f. 1970; production and export of phosphate rock; Gen. Dir Eng. FARHAN AL-HUHSSIN.

General Organization for Engineering Industries: POB 3120, Damascus; tel. (11) 2122650; fax (11) 2123375; e-mail g.o.eng.ind@net.sy; 13 subsidiary cos.

General Organization for the Exploitation and Development of the Euphrates Basin (GOEDEB): Rakka; Dir-Gen. Dr Eng. Dr AHMAD SOUHAD GEBBARA.

General Organization for Food Industries (GOFI): BP 105, rue al-Fardous, Damascus; tel. (11) 2457008; fax (11) 2457021; e-mail foodindustry@mail.sy; internet www.syriafoods.net; f. 1975; food-processing and marketing; Chair. and Gen. Dir KHALIL JAWAD.

General Organization for the Textile Industries: BP 620, rue al-Fardoss, Bawabet As-Salhieh, Damascus; tel. (11) 2216200; fax (11) 2216201; e-mail syr-textile@mail.syr; internet www.syr-textile.org; f. 1975; control and planning of the textile industry and supervision of textile manufacture; 27 subsidiary cos.; Dir-Gen. YAHYA HAMDOUNI.

Syrian Petroleum Company (SPC): BP 2849, rue al-Moutanabbi, Damascus; tel. (11) 2228298; fax (11) 2225648; e-mail spcgenman@net.sy; f. 1958; state agency; holds the oil and gas concession for all Syria; exploits the Suweidiya, Karatchouk, Rumelan and Jbeisseh oilfields; also organizes exploring, production and marketing of oil and gas nationally; Gen. Man. Dr Eng. MUHAMMAD KHADDOUR.

Al-Furat Petroleum Company: BP 7660, Damascus; tel. (11) 6183333; fax (11) 6184444; e-mail afpc@afpc.net.sy; internet www.afpc-sy.com; f. 1985; owned 50% by SPC and 50% by a foreign consortium of Syria Shell Petroleum Development B.V. and Deminex Syria GmbH; exploits oilfields in the Euphrates river area; Chair. HAITHAM GHANEM; Gen. Man. JOHN MALCOLM.

DEVELOPMENT ORGANIZATIONS

State Planning Commission: Parliament Square, Damascus.

Syrian Consulting Bureau for Development and Investment: 17 Zuheir Ben Abi St, Rawda, Damascus; tel. (11) 3340710; fax (11) 33407; e-mail scb@scbdi.com; internet www.scbdi.com; f. 1981; independent; Chair. NABIL SUKKAR.

CHAMBERS OF COMMERCE AND INDUSTRY

Federation of Syrian Chambers of Commerce: BP 5909, rue Mousa Ben Nousair, Damascus; tel. (11) 3337344; fax (11) 3331127; e-mail syr-trade@mail.sy; internet www.fedcommsyr.org; f. 1975; Pres. Dr RATEB ASH-SHALLAH; Gen. Sec. Dr ABD AR-RAHMAN AL-ATTAR.

Aleppo Chamber of Commerce: BP 1261, Aleppo; tel. (21) 2238236; fax (21) 2213493; e-mail alepchmb@mail.sy; internet www.aleppochamber.com; f. 1885; Pres. MUHAMMAD SALEH AL-MALLAH; Sec. MUHAMMAD MANSOUR.

Aleppo Chamber of Industry: BP 1859, rue al-Moutanabbi, Aleppo; tel. (21) 3620601; fax (21) 3620049; e-mail alpindus@net.sy; internet www.aleppo-coi.org; f. 1935; Pres. GHASSAN KRAYYEM; 7,705 mems.

Alkalamoun Chamber of Commerce: BP 2507, rue Bucher A. Mawla, Damascus; fax (11) 778394; Pres. M. SOUFAN.

Damascus Chamber of Commerce: BP 1040, rue Mou'awiah, Damascus; tel. (11) 2211339; fax (11) 2225874; e-mail dcc@net.sy; internet www.dcc-sy.com; f. 1890; Pres. Dr RATEB ASH-SHALLAH; Gen. Dir HISHAM AL-HAMWY; 11,500 mems.

Damascus Chamber of Industry: BP 1305, rue Harika Mou'awiah, Damascus; tel. (11) 2215042; fax (11) 2245981; e-mail dci@mail.sy; internet www.dci-syria.org; Pres. SAMIR DIBS; Sec. AHMAD BACHAR HATAHET.

Hama Chamber of Commerce and Industry: BP 147, rue al-Kouatly, Hama; tel. (33) 233304; fax (33) 517701; e-mail ham-coci@net.sy; internet www.hama-chamber.com; f. 1934; Pres. HAMZEH KASSAB BASHI; Dir ABD AR-RAZZAK AL-HAIT.

Homs Chamber of Commerce and Industry: BP 440, rue Abou al-Of, Homs; tel. (31) 471000; fax (31) 464521; e-mail homschamber@homschamber.org; internet www.homschamber.org; f. 1928; Pres. Dr Eng. ADEL TAYYARA; Dir M. FARES AL-HUSSAMY.

Latakia Chamber of Commerce and Industry: 8 rue Attar, Latakia; tel. (41) 479531; fax (41) 478526; e-mail lattakia@chamberlattakia.com; internet www.chamberlattakia.com; Pres. JULE NASRI.

Tartous Chamber of Commerce and Industry: POB 403, Tartous; tel. (43) 329852; fax (43) 329728; e-mail contact@souria.com; Pres. WAHIB KAMEL MERI; Vice-Pres. ABD AL-KADR SABRA.

EMPLOYERS' ORGANIZATIONS

Fédération Générale à Damas: Damascus; f. 1951; Dir TALAT TAGLUBI.

Fédération de Damas: Damascus; f. 1949.

Fédération des Patrons et Industriels à Lattaquié: Latakia; f. 1953.

Order of Syrian Engineers and Architects: BP 2336, Immeuble Al Mohandessin, place Azmeh, Damascus; tel. (11) 2214916; fax (11) 2216948; e-mail lbosea@net.sy; Pres. M. FAYEZ MAHFOUZ.

UTILITIES

Electricity

Public Establishment for Electricity Generation and Transmission (PEEGT): BP 3386, rue Nessan 17, Damascus; tel. (11) 2119940; fax (11) 2229062; e-mail peegt@net.sy; internet www.peegt-syria.org; f. 1965; renamed 1994; state-owned; operates eleven power stations through subsidiary companies; Dir-Gen. Dr A. AL-ALI.

TRADE UNIONS

General Federation of Labour Unions (Ittihad Naqabat al-'Ummal al-'Am fi Suriya): BP 2351, rue Qanawat, Damascus; f. 1948; Chair. 'IZZ AD-DIN NASIR; Sec. MAHMOUD FAHURI.

Transport

RAILWAYS

In 2004 the railway system totalled 2,460 km of track.

Syrian Railways: BP 182, Aleppo; tel. (21) 2213900; fax (21) 2228480; e-mail cfs-syria@net.sy; f. 1897; Pres. and Dir-Gen. Eng. MUHAMMAD IYAD GHAZAL.

General Organization of the Hedjaz-Syrian Railway: BP 2978, rue Hedjaz, Damascus; tel. (11) 3331625; f. 1908; the Hedjaz Railway has 347 km of track (gauge 1,050 mm) in Syria; services operate between Damascus and Amman, on a branch line of about 24 km from Damascus to Katana, and there is a further line of 64 km from Damascus to Serghaya; Dir-Gen. S. AHMED.

ROADS

Arterial roads run across the country linking the north to the south and the Mediterranean to the eastern frontier. At 31 December 1999 Syria's total road network was 43,381 km, including 31,189 km of highways, main or national roads and 9,191 km of secondary or regional roads. In the late 1990s work was scheduled to commence on the first stage of a project costing £S1,800m. to improve the road linking Rakka with Deir ez-Zor. In 2001 the Syrian Government awarded a contract for the construction of a 100-km, four-lane highway, connecting the eastern port town of Latakia with Ariba in the northern governorate of Aleppo, at an estimated cost of US $207m. The project was to be financed by loans from the Kuwaiti-based Arab Fund for Economic and Social Development and the Kuwait Fund for Arab Economic Development.

General Co for Roads: BP 3143, Aleppo; tel. (21) 555406; f. 1975; Gen. Man. Eng. M. WALID EL-AJLANI.

PIPELINES

The oil pipelines that cross Syrian territory are of great importance to the national economy, representing a considerable source of foreign exchange. In the early 2000s a number of gas pipelines, linking gas fields in the Palmyra area to Aleppo and Lebanon, were under construction.

Syrian Co for Oil Transport (SCOT): BP 13, Banias; tel. (43) 711300; fax (43) 710418; f. 1972; Gen. Man. JIHAD HAMZEH.

SHIPPING

Latakia is the principal port; the other major ports are at Banias and Tartous. A project to expand the capacities of Latakia and Tartous, and to construct new port facilities near Tartous, commenced in 1997.

SYRIA

General Directorate of Syrian Ports: BP 505, Latakia; tel. (41) 473333; fax (41) 475805; e-mail danco@net.sy; Dir-Gen. Rear-Adm. MOHSEN HASSAN.

Syrian General Authorities for Maritime Transport (SYRIAMAR): BP 730, 2 rue Argentina, Damascus; tel. (11) 3316418.

Abdulkader, Abu Bakr: Arwad, Latakia; operates a fleet of 5 general cargo vessels.

Delta Marine Transport: POB 1908, rue de Baghdad, Latakia; tel. (41) 222426; fax (41) 226047.

Ismail, A. M., Shipping Agency Ltd: BP 74, rue al-Mina, Tartous; tel. (43) 221987; fax (43) 318949; operates 8 general cargo vessels; Man. Dir MAHMOUD ISMAIL.

Muhieddine Shipping Co: BP 779, rue al-Mina, Tartous; tel. (43) 323090; fax (43) 317139; operates 7 general cargo ships.

Riamar Shipping Co Ltd: Al Kornish ash-Sharki, BP 284, Immeuble Tarwin, rue du Port, Tartous; tel. (43) 314999; fax (43) 212616; e-mail tarekg@scs-net.org; operates 6 general cargo vessels; Chair. and Man. Dir ABD AL-KADER SABRA.

Samin Shipping Co Ltd: BP 62, rue al-Mina, Tartous; tel. (43) 318835; fax (43) 318834; operates 10 general cargo ships.

Syro-Jordanian Shipping Co: BP 148, rue Port Said, Latakia; tel. (41) 471635; fax (41) 470250; e-mail syjomar@net.sy; f. 1976; operates 2 general cargo ships; transported 70,551 metric tons of goods in 1992; Chair. OSMAN LEBBADY; Tech. Man. M. CHOUMAN.

CIVIL AVIATION

There is an international airport at Damascus, and the upgrading of Aleppo airport, to enable it to handle international traffic, is planned.

Directorate-General of Civil Aviation: BP 6257, place Nejmeh, Damascus; tel. (11) 3331306; fax (11) 2232201.

Syrian Arab Airlines (Syrianair): BP 417, 5th Floor, Social Insurance Bldg, Youssef al-Azmeh Sq., Damascus; tel. (11) 2220700; fax (11) 224923; e-mail syr-air@syriatel.net; internet www.syriaair.com; f. 1946; refounded 1961 to succeed Syrian Airways, after revocation of merger with Misrair (Egypt); domestic passenger and cargo services (from Damascus, Aleppo, Latakia and Deir ez-Zor) and routes to Europe, the Middle East, North Africa and the Far East; Chair. SHAFIK DAOUD.

Tourism

Syria's tourist attractions include a pleasant Mediterranean coastline, the mountains, town bazaars and antiquities of Damascus and Palmyra, as well as hundreds of deserted ancient villages in the north-west of the country. In 2003 some 4.4m. tourists visited Syria, and tourism receipts totalled US $1,147m.

Ministry of Tourism: Barada St, Damascus; tel. (11) 2233183; e-mail min-tourism@mail.sy; internet www.syriatourism.org; f. 1972; Counsellor to the Minister Mrs SAWSAN JOUZY; Dir of Tourism Promotion and Marketing NIDAL MACHFEJ.

Middle East Tourism: BP 201, rue Fardoss, Damascus; tel. (11) 2211876; fax (11) 2246545; f. 1954; Pres. MUHAMMAD DADOUCHE; 7 brs.

Syrian Arab Co for Hotels and Tourism (SACHA): BP 5549, Mezzeh, Damascus; tel. (11) 2223286; fax (11) 2219415; f. 1977; Chair. DIRAR JUMA'A; Gen. Man. ELIAS ABOUTARA.

TAJIKISTAN
Introductory Survey

Location, Climate, Language, Religion, Flag, Capital

The Republic of Tajikistan (formerly the Tajik Soviet Socialist Republic) is situated in the south-east of Central Asia. To the north and west it borders Uzbekistan, to the north-east Kyrgyzstan, to the east the People's Republic of China and to the south Afghanistan. The climate varies considerably according to altitude. The average temperature in January in Khujand (lowland) is −0.9°C (30.4°F); in July the average is 27.4°C (81.3°F). In the southern lowlands the temperature variation is somewhat more extreme. Rainfall is low in the valleys, in the range of 150–250 mm (6–10 ins) per year. In mountain areas winter temperatures can fall below −45°C (−51°F); the average January temperature in Murgab, in the mountains of south-east Kuhistoni Badakhshon, is −19.6°C (−3.3°F). Levels of rainfall are very low in mountain regions, seldom exceeding 60–80 mm (2–3 ins) per year. The official language is Tajik, an Iranian language; the Constitution grants Russian the status of a language of inter-ethnic communication, and all ethnic groups are guaranteed the right to use their native languages freely. The major religion is Islam. Most Tajiks and ethnic Uzbek residents follow the Sunni tradition, but the Pamiris are mostly Isma'ilis, a Shi'ite sect. The national flag (proportions 1 by 2) consists of three horizontal stripes from top to bottom of red, white and green, with a stylized gold crown surmounted by seven gold stars arranged in a semicircle in the centre of the white stripe. The capital is Dushanbe.

Recent History

In 1918 northern Tajikistan (which had been under the Russian Empire since the 19th century) was conquered by the Bolsheviks, and the territory was incorporated into the Turkestan Autonomous Soviet Socialist Republic (ASSR). However, Dushanbe and the other southern regions of Tajikistan (which were subject to the Emirate of Bukhara) did not come under the control of the Bolsheviks until 1921. Opposition to Soviet rule was led by the *basmachis* (local guerrilla fighters) and foreign interventionists. In 1924 the Tajik ASSR was established as a part of the Uzbek Soviet Socialist Republic (SSR), and in January 1925 the south-east of Tajikistan was designated a Special Pamir Region (later renamed the Kuhistoni Badakhshon—Gornyi Badakhshan Autonomous Viloyat) within the Tajik ASSR. On 16 October 1929 the Tajik ASSR became a full Union Republic of the USSR and was slightly enlarged by the addition of the Khujand district from the Uzbek SSR. Soviet rule brought economic and social benefits to Tajikistan, but living standards remained low, and cattle-breeding, the main occupation in the uplands, was severely disrupted by collectivization. During the repressions of the 1930s almost all ethnic Tajiks in the republican Government were replaced by Russians.

During the 1970s increased Islamic influence was reported, as was violence towards non-indigenous nationalities. In 1978 there were reports of an anti-Russian riot, involving some 13,000 people, and after 1979 there were arrests of some activists opposed to Soviet intervention in Afghanistan. As in other Central Asian republics of the USSR, the first manifestation of the policies of Mikhail Gorbachev, who came to power as Soviet leader in 1985, was a campaign against corruption. Rakhmon Nabiyev, who had been First Secretary of the Communist Party of Tajikistan (CPT) since 1982, was replaced in late 1985 by Kakhar Makhkamov, who accused his predecessor of tolerating nepotism and corruption. Makhkamov was also openly critical of the economic situation in the republic. Censorship was relaxed, and there was increased debate in the media of perceived injustices—such as alleged discrimination against Tajiks in Uzbekistan, and the legitimacy of the Uzbekistani–Tajikistani boundary. Greater freedom of expression allowed discussion of Tajik culture and language, and an increased interest in other Iranian cultures. Tajik was declared the state language in 1989, and the teaching of the Arabic script (used by Tajiks prior to sovietization) was begun in schools.

In February 1990, following reports that Armenian refugees were to be settled in the capital, Dushanbe, violence broke out at a protest rally, when about 3,000 demonstrators demanding democratic and economic reforms clashed with police. A state of emergency was declared, and some 5,000 troops of the USSR's Ministry of Internal Affairs, in conjunction with 'civilian militia' units, suppressed the demonstrations; 22 people were reported dead and 565 injured. The unrest prompted a more inflexible attitude towards political pluralism by the republic's leadership. Two nascent opposition parties, Rebirth (Rastokhez), which had been involved in the February demonstrations, and the Democratic Party of Tajikistan (DPT), were refused official registration, and the Islamic Rebirth Party (IRP) was denied permission to hold a founding congress. Opposition politicians were barred from contesting the elections to the republic's Supreme Soviet (Supreme Council—legislature), held in March; 94% of the deputies elected were members of the CPT. None the less, in an apparent concession to growing Tajik nationalism the Supreme Soviet adopted a declaration of sovereignty on 25 August. In November Makhkamov was elected to the new post of executive President of the Republic by the Supreme Soviet; his only opponent was Nabiyev.

The Tajikistani Government, possibly anxious about increased Turkic dominance in Central Asia, displayed enthusiasm for a new Union Treaty (effectively preserving the USSR), and 90.2% of eligible voters in the republic were reported to have voted for the preservation of the USSR in the all-Union referendum in March 1991. In August, however, before the Treaty could be signed, conservative communists staged a *coup d'état* in the Soviet and Russian capital, Moscow. Makhkamov did not oppose the coup, and on 31 August, after it had collapsed, he resigned as President, following demonstrations, which continued throughout much of September. On 9 September, following the declarations of independence by neighbouring Uzbekistan and Kyrgyzstan, the Tajikistani Supreme Soviet voted to proclaim an independent state, the Republic of Tajikistan. However, demonstrators demanded the dissolution of the CPT and new, multi-party elections. Kadriddin Aslonov, the Chairman of the Supreme Council and acting President, issued a decree that banned the CPT and nationalized its assets. In response, the communist majority in the Supreme Council demanded Aslonov's resignation, declared a state of emergency in the republic and rescinded the prohibition of the CPT. Aslonov resigned, and was replaced by Nabiyev. Nabiyev was, however, rapidly obliged to make substantial concessions to the opposition, and in early October the Supreme Council rescinded the state of emergency, suspended the CPT and legalized the IRP. Shortly afterwards he resigned as acting President, in advance of the presidential election.

Seven candidates contested the direct presidential election, which took place on 24 November 1991. Attracting strong support in rural areas, Nabiyev won 57% of the votes cast, compared with 30% for the candidate favoured by the main opposition parties, Davlat Khudonazarov. Nabiyev took office in December. In late December Tajikistan signed the declaration establishing the Commonwealth of Independent States (CIS, see p. 201), the successor body to the USSR. In January 1992 a new Prime Minister, Akbar Mirzoyev, was appointed.

Anti-Government demonstrations began in Dushanbe in March 1992, initially prompted by Nabiyev's dismissal of Mamadayez Navzhuvanov, a prominent Badakhshani, from the post of Minister of Internal Affairs. Protests against his dismissal were led by the group Lale Badakhshon, which advocated greater autonomy for the Pamiri peoples of the southern Kuhistoni Badakhshon Autonomous Viloyat. It was joined by Rebirth, the IRP and the DPT. Protesters demanding the resignation of Nabiyev and the Government remained encamped in the centre of Dushanbe for nearly two months; in response, the Government organized rival demonstrations, bringing supporters to the capital from the southern region of Kulob (Kulyab) and Leninabad (later Khujand, and now known as Soghd), in the north—the traditional areas of support for the CPT. In late April members of the newly formed national guard loyal to Nabiyev opened fire on the demonstrators, killing at least eight people. In early May the National Security Committee (NSC—the successor to the Soviet Committee for State Security—KGB) allegedly distributed weapons to pro-communist supporters, and the ensuing violent clashes escalated into civil war. Fighting in Dushanbe ended after Nabiyev negotiated a truce with opposition leaders and formed a new 'Government of National Reconciliation' led by Mirzoyev, in which eight of the 24 ministers were members of opposition parties. However, violent clashes erupted in Kulob Viloyat between pro-communist Kulyabi forces, who opposed the President's compromise with the opposition, and members of Islamist and democratic groups. In late May the conflict spread into Qurgonteppa (Kurgan-Tyube or Kurgan Teppe) Viloyat (the main base of support for the Islamist and democratic groups), where a Kulyabi militia, the Tajik People's Front (TPF), led by Sangak Safarov, attempted to suppress the local forces of the informal Islamist-democratic coalition. The Kulyabis alleged that their opponents were receiving weapons and assistance from Islamist groups in Afghanistan, and there were reports that Gulbuddin Hekmatyar, the leader of the Afghan *mujahidin* group, Hizb-i Islami, had established training camps in Afghanistan for Tajikistani fighters. The Islamic-democratic alliance, for its part, claimed that the ex-Soviet (Russian) garrisons were arming the pro-Government militias.

In late August 1992 several members of the DPT and Lale Badakhshon were killed by Kulyabi militia forces in Qurgonteppa. A violent conflict ensued between local members of the opposition and Kulyabis, in which several hundred people were reportedly killed. Meanwhile, in Dushanbe anti-Government demonstrations resumed, and at the end of August demonstrators entered the presidential palace and took 30 officials hostage. On 7 September Nabiyev was seized by opposition forces at Dushanbe airport, and was forced to announce his resignation. Akbarsho Iskandarov, the Chairman of the Supreme Council, temporarily assumed the responsibilities of Head of State. Mirzoyev also resigned, and Abdumalik Abdullojonov, a communist from Leninabad Viloyat, was appointed acting Prime Minister. Iskandarov's administration, which had the support of all the main Islamist and democratic groups, had little influence, however, outside Dushanbe; much of the south of the country was under the control of the TPF militia, and some leaders of Leninabad Viloyat (which had a large Uzbek community) threatened to secede from Tajikistan if there was any attempt to introduce an Islamic state. In October the Islamist-democratic alliance's control of Dushanbe was threatened when forces led by Safarali Kenjayev, a former Chairman of the Supreme Soviet and a supporter of Nabiyev, entered the capital and attempted to seize power. Kenjayev briefly proclaimed himself Head of State, but his troops were forced to retreat by forces loyal to the regime. During the ensuing two months, however, Kenjayev's militias effectively enforced an economic blockade of the capital.

In November 1992, having failed to end the civil war, Iskandarov and the Government resigned. The legislature abolished the office of President, and Imamali Rakhmonov, a collective-farm chairman from Kulob Viloyat, was appointed Chairman of the Supreme Council (equivalent to Head of State). The legislature appointed a new Government, in which Abdullojonov retained the post of Prime Minister. However, all members of the opposition parties lost their portfolios, and the majority of the new ministers were Kulyabis or supporters of Nabiyev. The Supreme Council also voted to combine Qurgonteppa and Kulob Viloyats into one unit, based in Qurgonteppa, and to be known as Khatlon Viloyat, in an apparent attempt to ensure control of the south of the country by pro-communist forces from Kulob.

In December 1992 forces loyal to the new Government, the TPF and Kulyabi-Hissarite militias, captured Dushanbe, hitherto under the control of the Popular Democratic Army (PDA), a recently formed military coalition of Islamist and democratic groups. Hundreds of PDA fighters were reportedly killed during the attack, and there were reports of atrocities committed by the militias both in the capital and in the south, particularly against people from Garm (a stronghold of the Islamist and democratic groups) and Kuhistoni Badakhshon. In February 1993 insurgents in Garm attempted to declare an 'autonomous Islamic republic', but the Government had secured control of most of the country by March. The Government estimated that 30,000 people had been killed and some 800,000 people displaced during the civil war; other sources claimed that as many as 100,000 people had died.

In December 1992 and January 1993 some 60,000 Tajikistanis fled to Afghanistan, after alleged reprisals against supporters of the democratic and Islamist forces. Among those who fled was the influential *kazi* of Tajikistan, Akbar Turajonzoda, a senior member of the IRP, who was accused by the new Government of attempting to establish an Islamist state. In February he was replaced as spiritual leader of Tajikistan's Muslims by Fatkhullo Sharifzoda, who was given the title of *mufti*.

Although the civil war effectively ended in early 1993, the continued insurgency of Islamist-democratic forces, notably from across the Afghan border, continued to destabilize the country. Rebel resistance near Garm was ended in March. In June the Supreme Court formally proscribed the IRP, Lale Badakhshon, Rebirth and the DPT, leaving the CPT as the only legal party. Two new parties established later in the year—the Party of Economic Freedom and the People's Democratic Party of Tajikistan (PDPT)—were founded or sponsored by members of the Government or its associates.

In December 1993 Abdullojonov resigned as premier; he was replaced by Abdujalil Samadov. From the end of 1993 Rakhmonov, who secured for his own office responsibility for the powerful Ministries of Defence and Internal Affairs, as well as for the NSC (and, in February 1994, operational supervision of the broadcast media), began to show signs of compromise. In March he announced his willingness to negotiate with the Islamist-democratic opposition, and talks began in April in Moscow, under the auspices of the UN and in the presence of representatives from Iran, Pakistan, Russia and the USA. The negotiations resulted in a protocol on the establishment of a joint commission on refugees. However, reconciliation was far from having been achieved: from March border incursions by Tajik guerrillas intensified, resulting in clashes with the CIS troops stationed on the frontier (see below), and there was renewed insurgency in Kuhistoni Badakhshon. In June 1994 a further round of negotiations took place in the Iranian capital, Tehran, at which both sides announced their support, in principle, for a cease-fire. However, attacks by opposition forces on CIS and Tajikistani government troops patrolling the border with Afghanistan intensified in July and August. The continuing conflict along the Tajikistani–Afghan border was interpreted by some observers as being partly a battle for control of drugs-smuggling routes: since securing independence Tajikistan had become a major conduit for illicit drugs (chiefly opium) from Pakistan, Iran and Afghanistan to Russia and western Europe.

In August 1994 the Government did not renew the state of emergency in effect since October 1992, claiming that greater political freedom would be permitted for the presidential election, scheduled to take place in September. In late August, however, the election was postponed, to allow time for opposition candidates to be included in the poll. In mid-September a temporary cease-fire was agreed. Nevertheless, in late September rebel forces launched a large-scale offensive in Tavil Dara, which was repelled by government troops. The cease-fire eventually came into effect in late October. In December the UN Security Council authorized the deployment of a Mission of Observers in Tajikistan (UNMOT).

When the presidential election eventually took place on 6 November 1994, the only two candidates were Rakhmonov and Abdullojonov. Some 85% of eligible voters were reported to have participated in the election, which was won by Rakhmonov, with some 58% of the votes cast; Abdullojonov received about 35% of the votes. The result reflected regional loyalties; Rakhmonov (a Kulyabi) secured most of his support in the south, and Abdullojonov received a large proportion of the votes in Khujand and in Kuhistoni Badakhshon. In a concurrent referendum, some 90% of voters approved a new constitution. Despite allegations of widespread electoral malpractice, Rakhmonov was inaugurated as President in mid-November. In December Jamshed Karimov was appointed as Chairman of the Council of Ministers.

In February 1995 renewed peace talks opened in Almaty, Kazakhstan, but little progress was achieved. In late February the newly formed Party of Popular Unity and Accord (PPUA—led by Abdullojonov) announced that it would not contest the legislative elections scheduled to take place later that month, after Abdullojonov's candidature had been disallowed by the electoral authorities. The Organization for Security and Co-operation in Europe (OSCE, see p. 327) refused to send observers to the elections, claiming that the electoral law was severely flawed. Despite the opposition boycott, elections to the new Majlisi Oli (Supreme Assembly) took place on 26 February, with the participation of an estimated 84% of the electorate. In some 40% of constituencies there was only one candidate, and most of those elected were reported to be state officials loyal to the President, largely without party affiliation. The CPT was reported to have won some 60 seats, and its ally, the People's

Party of Tajikistan, five seats. Despite the PPUA's boycott, two representatives of the party were said to have been elected to the legislature. A second round of voting was held on 12 March to decide 19 seats that had not been filled.

In March 1995 the opposition announced a unilateral, 50-day extension of the cease-fire, but later that month there were further attacks on border posts on the Tajikistani–Afghan frontier. In early April there was a serious escalation of the conflict in the region, and 34 border guards and 170 rebel troops were reportedly killed during one week of fighting. In response, Russian aircraft were alleged to have bombed the Afghan town of Taloqan (reported to be the rebels' base in Afghanistan), killing some 125 civilians. (Russian official sources denied the attack.) The opposition forces (comprising the IRP and Lale Badakhshon) claimed that they were responding to a large deployment of Tajikistani government troops and Russian border guards in Kuhistoni Badakhshon, in violation of the cease-fire agreement. The cease-fire was extended in late April, and subsequently extended for three months in May. An exchange of prisoners was agreed at further talks in May. In July Rakhmonov met the leader of the IRP, Sayed Abdullo Nuri, and other opposition leaders for talks in Tehran, and in mid-August the cease-fire was extended for six months. During the second half of 1995 conflict continued in the south of the country and on the border with Afghanistan. In mid-September fighting was reported in Qurgonteppa between two military units, both formerly loyal to the Government. By late September, when government forces regained control of the town, some 300 people had reportedly died. Further peace negotiations were convened, under UN auspices, in Aşgabat, Turkmenistan, in November. However, the opposition withdrew, in response to the Government's refusal to accede to its demand for the formation of a national reconciliation council to govern the country alongside Rakhmonov during a two-year transition period.

In January 1996 Sharifzoda was killed by gunmen. Although the Government accused the IRP of responsibility for his death, the opposition denied any involvement. At the end of January opposition forces began a major offensive in the Tavil Dara region, and military commanders of government troops initiated rebellions in two towns. The western town of Tursan-Zade was taken by forces under Ibodullo Boitmatov, and Makhmoud Khudoberdiyev took control of Qurgonteppa. The commanders (both ethnic Uzbeks) demanded changes to the Government, notably the removal of several Kulyabi ministers. In early February Khudoberdiyev's troops approached Dushanbe, but retreated when they encountered government forces. Following negotiations, Rakhmonov agreed to the commanders' demands; Karimov was replaced as premier by Yakhyo Azimov.

Despite the announcement of an indefinite extension of the cease-fire, fighting intensified in March and April 1996 near Tavil Dara, where it was reported that Russian border guards and aircraft were supporting Tajikistani government troops in attacks on rebel forces; in May opposition forces captured the town of Tavil Dara. Talks resumed in Aşgabat in early July. A cease-fire was brokered in Tavil Dara, and agreement was reached on the conduct of further peace negotiations and on a gradual exchange of prisoners of war. In late July the formation of a National Revival bloc, a new opposition movement chaired by three former premiers (Abdullojonov, Karimov and Samadov), was announced. Large-scale hostilities resumed around Tavil Dara in late July. Opposition forces regained control of the town in mid-August, and government and rebel troops fought for command of the strategic central region of Tajikistan, notably Garm. Negotiations between representatives of the two sides took place in Tehran in October, and in December a UN-sponsored meeting was held between Rakhmonov and Nuri in Khosdeh, northern Afghanistan. A further cease-fire agreement was reached, but was almost immediately violated as fierce fighting continued around Garm. However, later that month, in Moscow, Rakhmonov and Nuri agreed to form a National Reconciliation Council (NRC), to be headed by a representative of what had come to be known as the United Tajik Opposition (UTO), comprising both Islamists and supporters of democracy. The NRC was to have extensive executive powers to revise legislation on elections, political parties and the media, to debate constitutional amendments and to monitor the implementation of the peace agreement. A general amnesty was agreed, as were terms for an exchange of prisoners and the repatriation of refugees.

Negotiations were held in Tehran in January 1997 to determine the structure and composition of the NRC. Meanwhile, supporters of the National Revival bloc organized rallies in Khujand, protesting against the exclusion of the secular opposition movement from the peace talks. At further UN-mediated peace talks held in Mashhad, Iran, in February, it was agreed that the NRC was to comprise 26 seats divided equally between the Government and the UTO. Negotiations on the reintegration of opposition forces into Tajikistan's military structures, the exchange of prisoners and the legalization of opposition parties were held in Moscow and Tehran throughout March and April. In April Rakhmonov was wounded in an assassination attempt in Khujand. The UTO denied any involvement and condemned the attack. In May an agreement was signed on the legalization of the opposition parties and media, to be implemented after the disarmament of the rebel forces. Following talks held in Tehran later that month, a protocol was signed by government and UTO representatives, which guaranteed the provisions of the December 1996 peace agreement. These were confirmed in the General Agreement on Peace and National Accord in Tajikistan, signed by Rakhmonov and Nuri in Moscow on 27 June 1997, which formally ended the five-year civil conflict. In early July Nuri was elected Chairman of the NRC, at its inaugural session; a policy of 'mutual forgiveness' was concluded, as well as an amnesty to allow UTO fighters to return to Tajikistan. Constitutional amendments were to be made by the NRC, prior to early parliamentary elections. The return of refugees from Afghanistan commenced shortly afterwards.

In September 1997, for the first time in five years, Nuri arrived in Dushanbe, to participate in the NRC. Some 200 UTO fighters were deployed in the capital to guard members of the NRC, sessions of which formally commenced in mid-September. Meanwhile, opposition to the agreement led to a series of minor bomb explosions in Dushanbe in early September. In October an attack on the barracks of the presidential guard, attributed to Makhmoud Khudoberdiyev, resulted in the deaths of at least 14 servicemen.

By mid-November 1997 some 10,000 Tajikistani refugees had been repatriated from Afghanistan. Meanwhile, negotiations were held between Nuri and Rakhmonov to determine the allocation of portfolios in the new government (under the terms of the peace agreement, the UTO was to receive one-third of posts in both the central and regional administrations). In January 1998 the UTO delegation to the NRC temporarily suspended its participation in the Council, claiming that the Government had failed to implement the terms of the peace agreement. In mid-February, however, three portfolios, including those of Labour and Employment and of the Economy and Foreign Economic Relations, were formally allocated to UTO members. Turajonzoda, the deputy leader of the UTO, who had been living in exile in Iran, made his return to Tajikistan conditional on his appointment to the Government as a Deputy Chairman; he arrived in Tajikistan in late February, and was appointed First Deputy Chairman, with responsibility for relations with CIS countries.

In March 1998 several people, including the brother of the former Prime Minister, Abdullojonov, were sentenced to death for their part in the attempted assassination of Rakhmonov in April 1997. An upsurge in fighting between government and opposition forces, in the vicinity of Dushanbe, resulted in many civilian deaths. In April 1998 Rakhmonov, who had joined the PDPT in March, was elected Chairman of the party. In May a cease-fire was agreed, following the outbreak of fighting between government and opposition forces close to Dushanbe. In early August 1998 Rakhmonov confirmed the appointment of several UTO members to government posts. However, other opposition appointments were rejected by the President, bringing the number of UTO members in the Government to 11, rather than the 14 agreed under the terms of the peace accord. At the end of August five local officials in western Tajikistan were killed; the Government reportedly blamed supporters of Khudoberdiyev. In late September the trial of four men, said to be associates of Khudoberdiyev, accused of attempting to overthrow the Government in August 1997, began in Dushanbe. At the end of September 1998 a senior opposition member, Otakhon Latifi, was assassinated in the capital. Meanwhile, accusations by the Government of opposition involvement in the deaths of the four UNMOT workers in July prompted the UTO to announce its withdrawal from the Government and the NRC at the end of September. The crisis was defused after intensive talks between Rakhmonov and UTO representatives resulted in agreement on a 10-point programme (which included measures to ensure the safety of opposition groups and the formation of a joint commission to investigate Latifi's death) to accelerate the peace process.

(In early June 2000 a militant was imprisoned, having been found guilty of Latifi's murder.)

In mid-October 1998 an operation by government forces against two rebel factions in eastern Dushanbe resulted in some 13 deaths and the detention of six rebels. Heavy fighting was reported around Khujand in early November, in what was regarded as the most violent uprising since the 1997 peace agreement, following the seizure by Khudoberdiyev's forces of police and security headquarters and a nearby airport. An estimated 100–300 people were killed; some 500 were injured and a number of police-officers were taken hostage. Khudoberdiyev's forces were reportedly defeated after five days of fighting. President Rakhmonov accused Abdumalik Abdullojonov of having instigated the rebellion. Criminal proceedings were initiated against the former premier shortly afterwards, as well as against Khudoberdiyev and two other prominent figures.

In mid-November 1998 the Majlisi Oli endorsed the appointment of several UTO members to the Council of Ministers, including Zokir Vazirov as a Deputy Chairman and Davlat Usmon as Minister of the Economy and Foreign Economic Relations. Additional junior government posts were allocated to the UTO in December and in March 1999. In December 1998 Nuri announced that the UTO would disband its armed forces in early 1999. In March 1999 the re-registration of political parties was effected by the Ministry of Justice: of the eight parties previously registered, only five received new licences. Criminal charges against leading members of opposition parties, including Nuri and Turajonzoda, were abandoned, in accordance with the 1997 amnesty document; 360 UTO members were thus granted immunity from prosecution. At the end of the month the Supreme Court sentenced seven supporters of Khudoberdiyev to 10–14 years' imprisonment, following their conviction on charges of involvement in the attack on government forces in October 1997. In mid-April 1998 the activity of the Civil and Patriotic Party was suspended for six months (the third party to be suspended since March).

The Majlisi Oli adopted a resolution in mid-May 1999 whereby the estimated 5,500 opposition fighters registered were to receive a general amnesty. In late May the UTO leadership withdrew from the NRC: among its demands were the holding of elections to the Majlisi Oli in 1999, in advance of the presidential election scheduled for November, and further UTO appointments to government posts (so that it held one-third of all government positions, as specified by the 1997 peace agreement). In particular, the UTO demanded the appointment of its commander, Mirzo Ziyoyev, to the post of Minister of Defence. In mid-June 1999 President Rakhmonov and Nuri signed an agreement outlining a timetable for the implementation of the provisions of the peace agreement. A further four UTO members were appointed to government posts. In early July Rakhmonov appointed another five UTO representatives to government positions; Ziyoyev became Minister of Emergency Situations and Civil Defence. In the same month the President reportedly announced that 21 of the 69 local government posts would be offered to opposition members. In early August the UTO leadership announced that the integration of its fighters into the regular armed forces had been completed. Rakhmonov responded in mid-August by lifting a ban on opposition parties and their media that had been imposed in 1993.

At a referendum held on 26 September 1999, some 72% of the votes cast by an estimated 92% of the electorate gave their endorsement to amendments to the Constitution, proposed by President Rakhmonov, which included: the formation of a bilateral legislature; the extension of the presidential mandate from five to seven years; and the legalization of religious-based political parties. The IRP was subsequently permitted to register as a political party. In mid-October the UTO again temporarily withdrew from the NRC, alleging that pledges made by the Government had not been met. In particular, the UTO sought a postponement of the forthcoming presidential election, owing to the fact that three of its candidates had been prevented from contesting the presidency. Later in the month, however, a ruling by the Supreme Court enabled Usmon, an IRP member, to stand as a candidate. Meanwhile, it was reported in mid-October that the First Deputy Prime Minister and deputy leader of the UTO, Akbar Turajonzada, had been expelled from the organization and its largest constituent party, the IRP, after dissenting from party policy.

In the presidential election, held on 6 November 1999, Rakhmonov received some 97.0% of the total votes cast, according to official sources, defeating his only opponent, Usmon. The rate of participation by the electorate was reported to be almost 99%. However, the opposition demanded that the election be declared invalid, owing to alleged electoral malpractice; the OSCE had again refused to send any monitors to the election. Following the inauguration of President Rakhmonov on 16 November, the Government tendered its resignation, although ministers remained in office until the formation of a new Government in late December. Akil Akilov was appointed Chairman of the Council of Ministers.

In early December 1999 the legislature approved the reorganization of the Majlisi Oli as a bicameral parliament. It was announced that elections to the upper and lower chambers would take place, respectively, on 27 February and 23 March 2000. Although six political parties were registered to participate in the elections, it was reported that a number of opposition parties had been barred from contesting the poll. (The further re-registration of parties was carried out during the month.) In late December 1999 two death sentences were imposed on participants in the 1998 uprising in Khujand, bringing the total number to five. Many other supporters of Khudoberdiyev were given lengthy prison sentences.

In the elections to the new Majlisi Namoyandagon (Assembly of Representatives), the lower chamber of the Majlisi Oli, held on 27 February 2000, Rakhmonov's PDPT (with its allies) was reported to have won 64.5% of the total votes cast and secured 45 of the 63 seats. The CPT won around 20.6% of the votes (13 seats), while the IRP secured about 7.5% (two seats). According to official sources, some 93% of eligible voters participated in the election. There were claims by the OSCE and opposition parties that electoral malpractice had been widespread. Following the elections, Nuri made a formal complaint to Rakhmonov, the UN and the OSCE, alleging that the President had reneged on pledges made to him in November 1999 regarding electoral procedures. A second round of voting took place on 12 March 2000 for 11 constituencies in which the requisite quorum of 50% had not been achieved. Results in a further three constituencies had been declared invalid at the first round of voting; re-elections for two seats took place in April and December, respectively. Meanwhile, on 23 March indirect elections to the Majlisi Milliy (National Assembly), the legislative upper chamber, were held for the first time (25 members of the chamber were elected by regional deputies, with eight further members appointed by the President of the Republic). At the end of the month the NRC was dissolved. However, Nuri stated that unresolved issues included the repatriation of Tajikistani refugees and the achievement of the 30% quota for UTO representatives in government. In May UNMOT announced the cessation of its peace-keeping activities. In June a new opposition alliance, For the Promotion of Democracy, was formed by organizations that had been prohibited from participating in the legislative elections. In late October a new currency, the somoni, was introduced, replacing the Tajik rouble, which had been in use since May 1995.

In December 2000 the Supreme Court suspended the activities of the Justice (Adolatkhoh) Party for six months; the party claimed that the ruling was a consequence of its opposition to the President during the legislative elections. In August 2001 the party was banned, after it failed to re-register its members during its period of suspension. Meanwhile, in April several bomb attacks took place, which killed at least four people. In June state security forces launched an attack against a group of militants, led by a former UTO field commander, Rakhmon Sanginov, near Dushanbe; it was reported that some 36 rebels were killed. In August Sanginov was killed by security forces, and at the end of the month officials claimed that only about 10 of his supporters remained at large.

In early September 2001 the Minister of Culture, Press and Information, Abdurakhim Rakhimov, was assassinated; Karomatullo Olimov was appointed as his successor in October. It was reported in December that 10 men had been sentenced to between eight and 25 years' imprisonment on charges of treason, terrorism and sedition, relating to the November 1998 insurrection in Khujand. In January 2002 a new Ministry of Industry was created; Zaid Saidov, hitherto Chairman of the State Committee for Industry, was appointed Minister of Industry. At the same time Ghulomjon Boboyev was appointed to head a new Ministry of State Revenues and Tax Collection. In March a public accord agreement, signed in 1996 by pro-Government political parties and non-governmental organizations to express support for the peace process, and renewed in 1999, was extended indefinitely; the accord was signed by a representative of the IRP for the first time.

Drugs-smuggling remained a significant problem in Tajikistan, at times apparently involving government officials as well as Islamist militants. In August 2002 the former Deputy Minister of Defence, Col Nikolai Kim, was sentenced to 13 years' imprisonment for taking part in drugs-trafficking and embezzlement while in office in 1998. Organized crime also remained a problem: in October 2002 a senior police official was sentenced to 25 years' imprisonment on charges of murder, fraud and extortion. Meanwhile, in mid-October two men were sentenced to death, and a further six were reported to have received terms of imprisonment of between two and 25 years, after being found guilty of belonging to an armed grouping loyal to Khudoberdiyev. It was reported that almost 75 supporters of Khudoberdiyev had been convicted since 1999.

In late January 2003 President Rakhmonov carried out a major reorganization of the Council of Ministers and other government structures. On 22 June an estimated 96% of the electorate participated in a referendum on proposed amendments to the Constitution, which were approved by 93% of the votes cast. The amendments approved included: an extension of judges' terms of office from five to 10 years; the removal from the Constitution of references to religious parties; and the abolition of the right to both free health care and higher education. Significantly, Rakhmonov would also be permitted to stand for two further seven-year terms of office upon the expiry of his existing mandate in 2006.

A Deputy Chairman of the IRP, Shamsiddin Shamsiddinov, was arrested in late May 2003, and in early October he became the first person to be tried on charges relating to the period of civil conflict. Shamsiddinov's detention and trial was widely interpreted as a new initiative by the Government to suppress Islamist groups by accusing them of war crimes. Following a closed trial, in January 2004 Shamsiddinov was sentenced to 16 years' imprisonment. Meanwhile, in October 2003 the former commander of the interior ministry rapid-reaction forces, Maj. Shodi Alimadov, was sentenced to eight years in prison, after being convicted on charges of corruption, extortion and abuse of office. In December and in January 2004 Rakhmonov effected a number of high-level government changes. Notably, Jurabek Nurmakhmadov was appointed as Minister of Energy, in place of Abdullo Yorov.

In April 2004 the DPT, the IRP, the Social Democratic Party of Tajikistan (SDPT) and the Socialist Party of Tajikistan announced the formation of an electoral alliance, the Coalition for Just and Transparent Elections. Less than one month later, however, Rakhmonov apparently persuaded the DPT to leave the bloc. In mid-July President Rakhmonov signed into law amendments to the election code, reportedly in an attempt to make the election process more transparent.

In mid-September 2004 20 members of the banned transnational militant Islamist group Hizb-ut-Tahrir al-Islami (Party of Islamic Liberation—Hizb-ut-Tahrir) were sentenced to prison terms ranging from six months to 15 years. (According to the Office of the Prosecutor-General, between 2000 and July 2005 209 people were convicted of membership of Hizb-ut-Tahrir; no person arrested on suspicion of belonging to the organization had been acquitted. In January 2006 it was reported that 99 suspected members of the movement had been detained in 2005, of whom 40 had been tried and sentenced.)

In early January 2005 Rakhmonov removed Kozidavlat Koimdodov from the post of Deputy Prime Minister, appointing him ambassador to Turkmenistan. Zokir Vazirov was dismissed as Deputy Prime Minister in early February, and appointed Minister of Labour, Employment and Social Welfare. Meanwhile, in mid-January the Chairman of the DPT, Makhmadruzi Iskandarov, was denied permission to register as a candidate in the parliamentary elections scheduled for 27 February, owing to criminal charges; Iskandarov had been arrested in Moscow in December 2004, accused of corruption and involvement in an attack on the Tajikabad region Ministry of Internal Affairs and prosecutor's offices in August; the DPT asserted that the arrest was politically motivated. Sulton Kuvvatov, the leader of the Union and Development Party (which had been denied registration in March 2004), was also detained and refused permission to register as a candidate in the elections, having been accused of insulting Rakhmonov and inciting ethnic hatred. In late January 2005 a car bomb explosion outside the Ministry of Emergency Situations and Civil Defence in Dushanbe killed the driver of the vehicle and injured several others. A further bomb outside the same ministry in mid-June injured four people. In January 2006 the Minister of Internal Affairs, Khomiddin Sharipov, announced the completion of an investigation into the two bomb attacks of 2005. At least two people suspected of organizing the attacks were still to be apprehended, but a number of others, believed to be members of the militant Islamist Islamic Movement of Uzbekistan (IMU), had been imprisoned; one of the suspected IMU members was reported to have committed suicide while in detention.

Six political parties participated in the elections to the Majlisi Namoyandagon held on 27 February and 13 March 2005. Rakhmonov's PDPT reportedly won 74% of the votes cast nation-wide to decide the allocation of seats on the basis of party lists, securing a total of 52 of the 63 seats in the chamber. The CPT won 13% of the national vote on the basis of party lists (four seats in total), while the IRP secured 8% (two seats). Five independent candidates were also elected. A reported 92.6% of the electorate participated in the poll. The OSCE and opposition parties claimed that electoral malpractice was widespread; the OSCE stated that amendments to the constitutional law on elections adopted in July 2004 had not been fully implemented. Several members of the IRP and other opposition parties received gaol sentences, widely believed to be politically motivated, after being found guilty of charges of hooliganism, defamation and embezzlement. The first session of the newly elected Majlisi Namoyandagon was held on 17 March 2005. Indirect elections to the Majlisi Milliy took place on 24 March, and the eight presidential nominees were announced the following day. The first session of the new upper chamber convened on 15 April.

In late April 2005 it was reported that a former Minister of the Interior, Yakub Salimov, who had been extradited from Russia in February 2004, had been sentenced to 15 years' imprisonment for treason after a five-month closed trial; Salimov was subsequently reported to have lodged an appeal with the Supreme Court. Meanwhile, in early April 2005 the Russian authorities released Iskandarov, owing to a lack of evidence, after refusing a request by Tajikistan for his extradition. However, later in April Iskandarov was arrested in Dushanbe; he claimed that he had been kidnapped in Russia and brought to Tajikistan by unknown individuals. After the Russian and Tajikistani authorities failed to clarify the details of Iskandarov's transfer to Tajikistan, in early May the DPT announced its temporary withdrawal from the Public Council (a body established in 1994 by Rakhmonov, and usually comprising social and cultural organizations and five of Tajikistan's six officially registered parties); in addition, the DPT criticized alleged malpractice during the legislative elections. The IRP and CPT subsequently also announced their withdrawal from the Public Council, in protest at the conduct of the elections.

In late June 2005 the deputy leader of the Union and Development Party was found guilty of provoking ethnic discord and insulting President Rakhmonov, whom he had accused of genocide: he was sentenced to almost six years' imprisonment. In mid-October the Supreme Court sentenced Iskandarov to 23 years' imprisonment, after he was found guilty of charges of terrorism, embezzlement and the possession of illegal weapons. Iskandarov vehemently denied the charges, but in January 2006 the verdict was upheld by the court of appeal. In late March the Chairman of the SDPT, Rakhmatullo Zoirov, declared that there were some 1,000 political prisoners in Tajikistan. Also in late March the European Union (EU, see p. 228) released a statement in which it expressed concern at the unclear circumstances surrounding Iskandarov's transfer from Russia to Tajikistan, and at allegations that he was mistreated prior to his trial.

Concern was expressed regarding the freedom of the media in 2005. Media representatives accused state officials of withholding information from and threatening journalists, and no independent newspapers or magazines were registered. The authorities reportedly prevented several independent newspapers and printing houses from publishing, and in April a privately owned television station was closed, ostensibly for failing to submit the requisite documentation. Meanwhile, in November two new political parties were registered: the Party of Economic Reforms and the Agrarian Party of Tajikistan. Nevertheless, the Chairman of the SDPT, Rakhmatullo Zoirov, asserted that the organizations were instruments of the Government.

After the dissolution of the USSR, Russian troops remained in Tajikistan, officially adopting a neutral stance during the civil war. However, following the communist victory in Dushanbe in December 1992, they openly assisted pro-communist troops in quelling the opposition forces, and the Tajikistani Government became increasingly dependent on Russia, both militarily and economically. In January 1993 Russia, Kazakhstan, Kyrgyzstan and Uzbekistan committed themselves to the defence of Tajikistan's southern frontiers, thus supporting the Government in the continuing conflict on the Tajik–Afghan border. In practice, mainly Russian troops were responsible for repelling rebel fighters entering Tajikistan, with Russia defending the southern CIS border as if it were its own. In August Russia and the Central Asian states (excluding Turkmenistan) signed an agreement establishing a CIS peace-keeping force to police Tajikistan's border with Afghanistan.

Despite Russia's involvement in the civil conflict in Tajikistan, it also sought to mediate between the Government and the opposition leadership in exile. During 1994–95 relations between the Russian authorities and the Rakhmonov regime deteriorated. However, in 1996 and 1997 Russia hosted several rounds of the UN-sponsored negotiations for a political settlement in Tajikistan, which culminated in the signature of the peace agreement in Moscow, in June 1997. In April 1999 Russia and Tajikistan signed an agreement on the establishment of a Russian military base in Tajikistan; in the same month nine major bilateral agreements were signed, including a Treaty of Alliance and Co-operation. In October 2004 Russia officially opened a military base in Tajikistan and took formal control of the Nurek space monitoring centre, after a meeting between the Russian President, Vladimir Putin, and President Rakhmonov; in return, Russia agreed to cancel US $242m. of Tajikistan's $300m. debt to Russia.

During the civil conflict in Tajikistan, the leadership of Uzbekistan provided military and political support to the Rakhmonov administration. In October 1994 Tajikistan and Uzbekistan signed a Co-operation Agreement envisaging greater bilateral co-ordination, especially in foreign policy and security. However, the Uzbekistani Government reportedly criticized the treatment of the Uzbek ethnic minority in Tajikistan, alleging that many ethnic Uzbeks had been replaced in their posts by Kulyabis. None the less, Uzbekistan continued to provide considerable technical and military support for the Tajikistani administration. Following the signature of the peace agreement in June 1997, the Uzbekistani leadership expressed renewed concern at the possible Islamicization of Tajikistan. Further tensions arose in August 1999, when northern Tajikistan came under attack by unidentified aircraft, which, according to the Tajikistani leadership, belonged to Uzbekistani forces, which were assisting Kyrgyzstan to repel a group of Islamist militants in that country's nearby Osh region, in the Farg'ona valley. (The Uzbekistani Government subsequently admitted that its forces might accidentally have bombed the territory.) In April 2000 Tajikistan was strongly criticized by the Uzbekistani and Kyrgyzstani Governments for failing to expel the leader of a group of Uzbek anti-Government Islamist rebels, who had allegedly established a permanent base in Tajikistan. Armed incursions into those two countries by insurgents commenced in August. By the end of 2000 hostilities had subsided, although occasional violent incidents continued to be reported. In March 2001, in response to a claim by the Kyrgyzstani Government that Tajikistan harboured some 2,500 international terrorists, the Tajikistani Government declared there to be no members of any rebel organization on its territory, and invited the Kyrgyzstani Government to examine its borders. Uzbekistan, which had begun laying landmines along its border with Tajikistan from mid-2000, in an effort to prevent cross-border incursions by Islamist insurgents, officially informed Tajikistan of its actions only in May 2001. At the end of the month a Tajikistani border official accused Uzbekistan of violating international law by planting mines along the Tajikistani–Uzbekistani border, which had not been delineated in mountainous areas; it was further observed that, thus far, all of the casualties had been Tajikistani and Uzbekistani citizens. However, bilateral relations subsequently improved. President Rakhmonov visited President Karimov of Uzbekistan in December; it was announced that a crossing between the Penjakent region of Tajikistan and Uzbekistan's Samarqand region was to re-open, and the two leaders also agreed to collaborate to combat terrorism, crime and drugs-trafficking. In February 2002, at a meeting of the Tajikistani and Uzbekistani premiers, an agreement on border-crossing procedures was reached. In October a border agreement was signed by Presidents Rakhmonov and Karimov, although four areas in the northern Soghd Viloyat remained in dispute. None the less, landmines on the border with Uzbekistan continued to kill civilians and border guards in the mid-2000s, and the Government was co-operating with international organizations to remove the devices; 80 such deaths were reported in 2005.

Tajikistan had begun to develop relations outside the USSR before its dissolution in 1991, notably with Iran, with which the Tajiks have strong ethnic and linguistic ties. However, the effective collapse of central authority in Tajikistan in 1992 severely hindered further development of foreign relations, although several states attempted to influence the progress of the country's civil war. Anti-Islamist groups in Tajikistan asserted that Iran was supplying armaments and other goods to Islamist elements in Tajikistan, but the Iranian authorities insisted that they were providing only cultural and humanitarian assistance. In July 1995 President Rakhmonov visited Tehran, where a number of agreements on cultural and economic co-operation were signed. Further agreements were signed in late 1996, providing for Iranian investment in Tajikistan's industrial and agricultural sectors, followed by economic, cultural and defence accords in late 1998. UN-sponsored peace negotiations between Tajikistani government and opposition representatives were held in Tehran in 1996 and 1997. In April 2002 Tajikistan and Iran signed nine protocols on co-operation in economic, political and social affairs. In April 2005 the two countries signed a memorandum of understanding on enhanced co-operation in defence matters, and for the provision, *inter alia*, of equipment and training for Tajikistani military personnel. Iran explained the agreement as an attempt to prevent 'external powers' from increasing their military presence in the region and threatening Iranian national security, widely interpreted as an intention to prevent the USA from securing control of additional military bases in Central Asia.

Relations with Afghanistan were strained by the apparent inability of the Afghan Government to prevent *mujahidin* fighters and consignments of weapons from crossing the frontier into Tajikistan. The election of the largely pro-communist Tajikistani Government in late 1992 further strained bilateral relations, and in April 1993 the Tajikistani Government protested to the Afghan authorities about alleged incursions across the border by Afghans, apparently to assist rebel troops. In December the Afghan President, Burhanuddin Rabbani, made an official visit to Tajikistan, which resulted in the signature of a bilateral friendship and co-operation treaty, as well as agreements on economic co-operation and border security. A tripartite agreement was signed, together with the office of the UN High Commissioner for Refugees, on the safety of refugees returning to Tajikistan. In April 1995 Afghanistan protested strongly against alleged Russian attacks on rebel bases within Afghanistan, and continued to deny any official support of rebel Tajik factions within the country. The widespread victory of Taliban forces in Afghanistan in that year threatened to destabilize the fragile situation in Tajikistan and, as the Taliban increased their territorial gains in northern Afghanistan, there was increasing concern in Tajikistan and neighbouring countries, which feared an influx of large numbers of refugees. In July 1998, while heavy fighting occurred close to Tajikistan's border with Afghanistan, the frontier was reinforced by Russian troops. As fighting escalated in Afghanistan in September 2000, the Tajikistani Government closed its border with that country.

Following the suicide attacks on the mainland USA of 11 September 2001, attributed to the al-Qa'ida (Base) organization of the Saudi Arabian-born Islamist militant Osama bin Laden, Russian troops along the Tajikistani–Afghan border were placed on a state of alert, in anticipation of military strikes against Afghanistan by the USA and allied countries. Although Rakhmonov announced his willingness to co-operate with the USA, both Tajikistan and Russia initially dismissed the possibility of Tajikistani territory being used as a base for any US-led military action; however, US specialists were granted entry to the country to oversee the distribution of humanitarian aid to Afghanistan. The Tajikistani Government declared its support for the aerial bombardment of Taliban and al-Qa'ida targets in Afghanistan, which commenced on 7 October, and in early November it was confirmed that Tajikistan had permitted US troops and forces of the North Atlantic Treaty Organization (NATO, see p. 314) to utilize three of its airbases. In January 2002 it was announced that US restrictions on the transfer of defence equipment to Tajikistan, imposed in 1993, had been lifted. In February 2002 Tajikistan joined NATO's 'Partnership for Peace' programme of military co-operation. In October 2004 the Secretary-General of NATO, Jaap de Hoop Scheffer, signed a bilateral transit agreement with Rakhmonov in support of NATO's International Security Assistance Force in Afghanistan.

In December Russia began to transfer military control of the Pamir stretch of the Tajikistani–Afghan border to the Tajikistani authorities. The transfer was completed in September 2005; however, a Russian task force was to remain in Tajikistan, and Russia was to continue to train Tajikistan's border guards. Throughout the transfer, concern had been expressed at a possible increase in the cross-border smuggling of drugs from Afghanistan, and later in September international donors signed an agreement with Tajikistan on the security of the Tajikistani–Afghan border, according to which Tajikistan was to be provided with installations, equipment and training to help manage its borders. In early October the Majlisi Namoyandagon ratified a bilateral security agreement with Afghanistan on co-operation in countering terrorism, extremism and transnational organized crime.

In the mid-1990s Tajikistan sought to develop relations with other Asian states, in particular the People's Republic of China. In April 1996 Tajikistan signed (together with Russia, Kazakhstan and Kyrgyzstan) a wide-ranging border agreement with China. This was supplemented by a further border accord, signed in August 1999. In January 2002 Tajikistan signed a further treaty with China, resolving contentious issues regarding the two countries' joint border on the edge of Kuhistoni Badakhshon, and in mid-May Tajikistan signed a border agreement, conceding 1,000 sq km of disputed territory to China. Meanwhile, in April 1997 an agreement on confidence-building measures in the military sphere was concluded. Members of the Shanghai Co-operation Organization (SCO, see p. 398), comprising China, Kazakhstan, Kyrgyzstan, Russia, Tajikistan and Uzbekistan, signed the Shanghai Convention on Combating Terrorism, Separatism and Extremism in mid-2001. At an emergency meeting in October of that year, the members agreed to establish an anti-terrorism centre. In September 2004 members of the SCO, meeting in Bishkek, Kyrgyzstan, agreed to increase co-operation in trade, science, technology, and humanitarian projects, as well as to improve anti-terrorism measures.

In March 2000 joint military exercises were conducted in southern Tajikistan by Kazakhstan, Kyrgyzstan, Tajikistan, Uzbekistan and Russia, as part of a joint commitment to combat international terrorism in the region. In May 2001 the signatory countries of the Collective Security Treaty—Armenia, Belarus, Kazakhstan, Kyrgyzstan, Russia and Tajikistan—formed a Rapid Reaction Force to combat Islamist militancy in Central Asia; in January 2002 it was announced that the force was ready to undertake combat missions. In March the Central Asian Economic Community, which Tajikistan joined in March 1998, was superseded by the Central Asian Co-operation Organization (CACO). In April 2003 the signatories of the Collective Security Treaty inaugurated a successor organization, known as the Collective Security Treaty Organization (CSTO). In October 2005 it was announced that the CACO was to merge with the Eurasian Economic Community (EurAsEc).

Government

Under the Constitution of November 1994 (to which a number of amendments were passed in September 1999 and June 2003), Tajikistan has a presidential system of government. The President is Head of State and also heads the executive branch of power. The President appoints a Prime Minister (or Chairman) to head the Government (Council of Ministers). Legislative power is vested in the 63-member lower chamber, the Majlisi Namoyandagon (Assembly of Representatives), and the upper chamber, the Majlisi Milliy (National Assembly), which has a minimum of 33 members. For administrative purposes, the country is divided into three viloyats (regions or oblasts): Soghd (known as Leninabad in 1936–92, and subsequently Khujand, until 2000), in the north; Khatlon (formerly the two viloyats of Kulob and Kurgan-Tyube), in the south; and the nominally autonomous viloyat of Kuhistoni Badakhshon. These regions are further subdivided into districts and towns. The city of Dushanbe has a separate status. Three cities and 10 districts of central Tajikistan are not incorporated into any of the viloyats, and are known as the Regions of Republican Subordination.

Defence

Following the dissolution of the USSR in December 1991, Tajikistan became a member of the Commonwealth of Independent States (CIS, see p. 201) and its Collective Security Treaty. In April 2003 the Collective Security Treaty Organization (CSTO) was inaugurated as the successor to the CIS collective security system, with the participation of Armenia, Belarus, Kazakhstan, Kyrgyzstan, Russia and Tajikistan. A Ministry of Defence was established in September 1992; in December it was announced that Tajikistan's national armed forces were to be formed on the basis of the Tajik People's Front and other paramilitary units supporting the Government. Integration of United Tajik Opposition (UTO) force members into the Tajikistani armed forces took place from 1998. Military service lasts for 24 months (12 months for those with higher-education degrees). At August 2005 there was an army of 7,600, and 5,300 paramilitary border guards were attached to the Ministry of Internal Affairs. There were plans to form an Air Force squadron. State expenditure on defence in 2004 totalled 160m. somoni. The budget for 2005 allocated an estimated 139m. somoni to defence. Tajikistan became a member of the North Atlantic Treaty Organization's 'Partnership for Peace' (see p. 316) programme of military co-operation in February 2002.

Economic Affairs

In 2004, according to estimates by the World Bank, Tajikistan's gross national income (GNI), measured at average 2002–04 prices, was US $1,779m., equivalent to $280 per head (or $1,150 per head on an international purchasing-power parity basis). During 1995–2004, it was estimated, the population increased by an annual average of 1.1%, while gross domestic product (GDP) per head increased by an annual average of 3.2%, in real terms. Overall GDP increased, in real terms, by an average of 4.4% per year. According to the Asian Development Bank (ADB, see p. 169), GDP increased by 10.6% in 2004 and by 6.7% in 2005.

Despite the fact that only 7% of Tajikistan's land is arable (the remainder being largely mountainous), the Tajikistani economy has traditionally been predominantly agricultural: agriculture contributed 24.2% of GDP in 2004, and provided 67.6% of employment in 2003. According to IMF estimates, the rural population accounted for some 72.4% of the total in 2000–03. The principal crop is grain, followed in importance by cotton, vegetables and fruit. Approximately 95% of the country's arable land is irrigated. Agricultural production was severely disrupted by the civil war. In 1996 proposals were announced to transfer collective and state farms to private ownership. However, although in mid-1998 legislation was passed on the establishment of a centre to aid farm privatization, agricultural reform has proceeded slowly. The IMF estimated that 51% of Tajikistan's arable land was privately owned at the end of 2001. During 1995–2003 agricultural GDP increased, in real terms, by an average of 5.0% annually. Real agricultural GDP increased by 15.1% in 2002 and by 9.6% in 2003.

Industry (comprising manufacturing, mining, utilities and construction) contributed 28.1% of GDP in 2004, and provided 7.7% of employment in 2003. There is little heavy industry, except for mineral extraction, aluminium production and power generation. Light industry concentrates on food-processing, textiles and carpet-making. Industrial GDP increased, in real terms, by an annual average of 3.2% in 1995–2003. Sectoral GDP increased by 8.4% in 2002, but decreased by 10.2% in 2003.

Tajikistan has considerable mineral deposits, including gold, antimony, silver, aluminium, iron, lead, mercury and tin. There are deposits of coal as well as reserves of petroleum and natural gas. Mineral extraction is hampered by the mountainous terrain.

The GDP of the manufacturing sector increased, in real terms, by an annual average of 3.0% in 1995–2003. Real manufacturing GDP increased by 8.3% in 2002 and by 10.2% in 2003.

Although imports of fuel and energy comprised 29.5% of the value of merchandise imports in 2001 (mainly supplied by Turkmenistan, Uzbekistan, Kazakhstan and Russia), Tajikistan is believed to have sufficient unexploited reserves of petroleum and natural gas to meet its requirements. The mountain river system is widely used for hydroelectric power generation, and Tajikistan is one of the largest producers of hydroelectric power world-wide. In 2002 hydroelectricity accounted for 97.7% of energy production. In January 2005 Tajikistan signed a protocol with Russia and Iran on the construction of two hydroelectric power plants, Sangtuda-1 (originally conceived in the 1980s, but work on which had been suspended owing to lack of funding) and Sangtuda-2. At the end of March Tajikistan also signed an agreement with Pakistan on the construction of a 700-km transmission line to transport electricity from Tajikistan's Roghun plant to Pakistan, from 2009. Construction work on Sangtuda-2 commenced in February 2006; both power stations were scheduled for completion in 2009. The completion of Sangtuda-1 was to be fully funded by Russia, and Iran was to provide significant funding for the construction of the Sangtuda-2 plant, ownership of which was to be secured by Tajikistan in

2018. Meanwhile, also in February 2006 Uzbekistan announced that it was to reduce natural gas exports to Tajikistan by some 25%, because of the accumulation of arrears by Tojikgaz, the state-owned natural gas company. Tajikistan imports some 90% of its gas requirements, principally from Uzbekistan.

The services sector contributed 47.7% of GDP in 2004, and provided 24.6% of employment in 2003. The GDP of the services sector increased, in real terms, by an annual average of 7.8% in 1995–2003; real services GDP increased by 2.5% in 2002 and by 11.0% in 2003.

In 2004, according to IMF figures, Tajikistan recorded a visible trade deficit of US $151m., and there was a deficit of $83m. on the current account of the balance of payments. In 2004 the principal source of imports was Russia (accounting for 17.8% of the total); other important suppliers were Uzbekistan (13.4%), Kazakhstan (9.6%), Ukraine (6.3%) and Azerbaijan (6.3%). The major market for exports in that year was Latvia (accounting for 13.1% of the total). Switzerland (11.5%), Uzbekistan (11.3%), Norway (9.9%), Russia (8.2%), Iran (7.9%), Turkey (7.7%) and Italy (6.6%) were also significant purchasers. The principal exports in 2002 were non-precious metals and mineral products. The principal imports were mineral products and chemical.

According to the IMF, there was an overall budgetary deficit of 146m. somoni in 2004 (equivalent to some 2.4% of GDP). Tajikistan's total external debt was US $1,166m. at the end of 2003, of which $926m. was long-term public debt. The cost of debt-servicing in that year was equivalent to 9.1% of the value of exports of goods and services. The average annual rate of inflation was 303.4% in 1990–2000. The rate of inflation was 12.5% in 2001 and 14.5% in 2002. According to the ADB, the rate of inflation was 17.1% in 2003, and 7.1% in both 2004 and 2005. Figures from the ADB indicated that the rate of unemployment was 1.8% in 2004; however, other sources estimated the rate to be much higher.

In 1992 Tajikistan joined the Economic Co-operation Organization (ECO, see p. 223) and the European Bank for Reconstruction and Development (EBRD, see p. 224), as a 'Country of Operations'; it became a member of the IMF and the World Bank in 1993. In November 1996 Tajikistan joined the Islamic Development Bank (see p. 303) and it became a member of the ADB in 1998. In 2001 Tajikistan was granted observer status at the World Trade Organization (WTO, see p. 370).

Already the poorest of the republics of the former USSR, the Tajikistani economy was severely affected by the disruption to the former Soviet trading system caused by the collapse of the USSR, and by the civil war that broke out in 1992. Following the conclusion of a peace agreement in June 1997, international financial organizations allocated credit to facilitate the structural reform process and to assist in rebuilding the country's infrastructure. However, the Russian financial crisis of 1998 had an adverse effect on the economy, as did a decline in world cotton prices. A new currency, the somoni, was introduced in late 2000, and the country's economic performance improved significantly from that year. However, poverty remained widespread. According to a World Bank report published in October 2005, 74% of the population were living on less than US $2.15 per day in 2003, and it was estimated that some 900,000 Tajikistani citizens travelled to Russia each year to seek employment; remittances from abroad were estimated to account for some 20% of annual GDP. Although by 2005 some progress had been made in implementing structural reform, particularly in the banking sector and, to a lesser extent, in the energy sector, further reform remained essential in order to ensure continued economic growth. Tajikistan had managed significantly to reduce its public and publicly guaranteed external debt, from the equivalent of 96% of GDP at the end of 2000 to an estimated 36% of GDP at the end of 2005. Moreover, the initiation of a number of projects involving foreign investment was likely to be of enormous benefit to the economy, and Russian companies reportedly intended to invest some $2,000m. in Tajikistan's economy over a five-year period. In mid-June 2005 President Rakhmonov announced the removal of restrictions on the operations of foreign banks, in an attempt to attract increased foreign investment. The pace of growth slowed in 2005, mainly owing to a decline in cotton production, but the Government anticipated growth of some 8% in 2006, and the rate of consumer-price inflation was expected to be less than 7%.

Education

Education is controlled by the Ministry of Education. Education is officially compulsory for nine years, to be undertaken between seven and 17 years of age. Primary education begins at seven years of age and lasts for four years. Secondary education, beginning at the age of 11, lasts for up to seven years, comprising a first cycle of five years and a second of two years. In 1998/99 total enrolment at primary schools was equivalent to 94% of the relevant age-group (males 97%; females 91%). In the 2002/03 academic year, according to UN estimates, total enrolment at secondary schools was equivalent to 83% of the relevant age-group (males 90%; females 76%). Since independence, greater emphasis has been placed in the curriculum on Tajik language and literature, including classical Persian literature. In 2003 President Imamali Rakhmonov announced that the compulsory teaching of Russian was to be reintroduced. Constitutional amendments approved in June 2003 provided for the withdrawal of free higher education. In 2002/03 some 96,583 students were enrolled at 33 institutes of higher education. In 2005 expenditure on education by all levels of government was 250m. somoni (equivalent to 15.9% of government expenditure), according to preliminary figures. Spending was expected to be increased to 336 somoni in 2006 (17.3% of anticipated expenditure).

Public Holidays

2006: 1 January (New Year's Day), 11 January*† (Id-al-Adha, Feast of the Sacrifice), 8 March (International Women's Day), 20–22 March (Navrus), 1 May (International Labour Day), 9 May (Victory Day), 9 September (Independence Day), 24 October* (Id-al-Fitr, end of Ramadan), 6 November (Constitution Day), 31 December*† (Id-al-Adha, Feast of the Sacrifice).

2007: 1 January (New Year's Day), 8 March (International Women's Day), 20–22 March (Navrus), 1 May (International Labour Day), 9 May (Victory Day), 9 September (Independence Day), 13 October* (Id-al-Fitr, end of Ramadan), 6 November (Constitution Day), 20 December* (Id-al-Adha, Feast of the Sacrifice).

* These holidays are dependent on the Islamic lunar calendar and may vary by one or two days from the dates given.

† This festival occurs twice (in the Islamic years AH 1426 and 1427) within the same Gregorian year.

Weights and Measures

The metric system is in force.

TAJIKISTAN

Statistical Survey

Source (unless otherwise indicated): State Committee for Statistics, 734001 Dushanbe, Bokhtar 17; tel. (372) 23-25-53; fax (372) 21-43-75; e-mail stat@tojikiston.com; internet www.tajstat.org.

Area and Population

AREA, POPULATION AND DENSITY

Area (sq km)	143,100*
Population (census results)†	
12 January 1989	5,092,603
20 January 2000	
Males	3,069,100
Females	3,058,393
Total	6,127,493
Population (UN estimates at mid-year)‡	
2002	6,293,000
2003	6,360,000
2004	6,430,000
Density (per sq km) at mid-2004	44.9

* 55,251 sq miles.
† Figures refer to *de jure* population. The *de facto* total at the 1989 census was 5,108,576.
‡ Source: UN, *World Population Prospects: The 2004 Revision*.

POPULATION BY ETHNIC GROUP
(2000 census)

	Number ('000 persons)	%
Tajik	4,898.4	79.9
Uzbek	936.7	15.3
Russian	68.2	1.1
Kyrgyz	65.5	1.1
Lakaits	51.0	0.8
Turkmen	20.3	0.3
Tatar	18.9	0.3
Kongrat	15.1	0.2
Arab	14.5	0.2
Total (incl. others)	6,127.5	100.0

ADMINISTRATIVE DIVISIONS
(2000 census, rounded figures)

	Area (sq km)	Population	Density (per sq km)*	Capital city
Viloyats				
Khatlon	24,600	2,151,000	87.4	Qurgonteppa
Soghd	26,100	1,870,000	71.6	Khujand
Autonomous Viloyat				
Kuhistoni Badakhshon	63,700	206,000	3.2	Khorog
Capital City				
Dushanbe	300	562,000	1,873.3	—
Regions of Republican Subordination †	28,400	1,338,000	47.1	—
Total	143,100	6,127,000	42.8	

* Densities are calculated using rounded population and area data and are therefore subject to discrepancies.
† The Regions of Republican Subordination comprise 3 cities (Gissar; Kofarnikhon; Rogun) and 10 raions or districts (Faizabad; Garm; Gissar; Darban; Jirgital; Lenin; Shakhrinav; Tajikabad; Tavildara; and Varzov) in central Tajikistan where there is no higher tier of local government.

PRINCIPAL TOWNS
(population at 1 January 2002)

Dushanbe (capital)	575,900	Kanibadam		45,100
Khujand*	147,400	Kofarnihon‡		45,100
Kulob	79,500	Tursunzade		38,100
Qurgonteppa	61,200	Isfara		37,300
		Panjakent		
Istravshan†	51,700	(Pendzhikent)		33,200

* Known as Leninabad between 1936 and 1992.
† Also known as Urateppa (Ura-Tyube).
‡ Formerly Ordzhonikidzeabad.

Mid-2003 (UN estimate, incl. suburbs): Dushanbe 554,355 (Source: UN, *World Urbanization Prospects: The 2003 Revision*).

BIRTHS, MARRIAGES AND DEATHS

	Registered live births		Registered marriages		Registered deaths	
	Number	Rate (per 1,000)	Number	Rate (per 1,000)	Number	Rate (per 1,000)
1994	191,596	34.2	38,820	6.8	39,943	7.1
1995	193,182	34.1	32,078	5.7	34,274	6.0
1996	172,341	30.0	28,019	4.8	31,610	5.5
1997	178,127	30.6	27,250	4.7	27,888	4.8
1998	185,733	31.3	22,276	3.8	29,261	4.9
1999	180,888	29.8	22,536	3.9	25,384	4.2
2000	167,246	27.0	26,257	4.2	29,387	4.7
2001	171,623	27.2	28,827	4.6	32,015	5.1

Expectation of life (WHO estimates, years at birth): 61 (males 59; females 63) in 2003 (Source: WHO, *World Health Report*).

ECONOMICALLY ACTIVE POPULATION
(annual averages, '000 persons)

	1999	2000	2001
Activities of the material sphere	1,420	1,416	1,452
Agriculture*	1,118	1,135	1,167
Industry†	133	121	131
Construction	44	36	31
Trade and catering‡	70	72	72
Transport and communications	44	42	43
Activities of the non-material sphere	313	326	316
Housing and municipal services	24	27	29
Health care, social security, physical culture and sports	75	82	72
Education, culture and arts	179	179	178
Science, research and development	5	5	5
Government and finance	31	34	23
Total employed	1,737	1,745	1,769
Unemployed	54	49	43
Total labour force	1,791	1,794	1,812

* Including forestry.
† Comprising manufacturing (except printing and publishing), mining and quarrying, electricity, gas, water, logging and fishing.
‡ Including material and technical supply.

2002 (annual averages, '000 persons): Agriculture 1,255; Industry (incl. construction) 153; Others 449; Total employed 1,857; Unemployed (registered) 47; Total labour force 1,904.

2003 (annual averages, '000 persons): Agriculture 1,275; Industry (incl. construction) 146; Others 464; Total employed 1,885; Unemployed (registered) 47; Total labour force 1,932.

Source: Asian Development Bank, *Key Indicators of Developing Asian and Pacific Countries*.

TAJIKISTAN

Health and Welfare

KEY INDICATORS

Total fertility rate (children per woman, 2003)	3.0
Under-5 mortality rate (per 1,000 live births, 2004)	118
HIV/AIDS (% of persons aged 15–49, 2003)	<0.1
Physicians (per 1,000 head, 2001)	2.18
Hospital beds (per 1,000 head, 2001)	6.40
Health expenditure (2002): US $ per head (PPP)	47
Health expenditure (2002): % of GDP	3.3
Health expenditure (2002): public (% of total)	27.7
Human Development Index (2003): ranking	122
Human Development Index (2003): value	0.652

For sources and definitions, see explanatory note on p. vi.

Agriculture

PRINCIPAL CROPS
('000 metric tons)

	2002	2003	2004
Wheat	545	660	631
Rice (paddy)	50	59	51
Barley	36	51	63
Maize	55	95	113
Potatoes	357	473	527
Cottonseed*	296	325	330
Cabbages	29	38	65*
Tomatoes	155	170	226
Dry onions	140	153	191*
Carrots	87	95*	81*
Other vegetables*	51	111	101
Watermelons	111	139	150
Apples	87	45*	85*
Apricots*	25	22	25
Peaches and nectarines*	20	12	20
Plums*	2	1	2
Grapes	81	28	93
Other fruits and berries*	14	8	14
Cotton (lint)	113	172*	172*
Tobacco (leaves)	4	7	3

* Unofficial figure(s).
Source: FAO.

LIVESTOCK
('000 head at 1 January)

	2002	2003	2004
Horses	71	73	74
Asses	123	138	147
Cattle	1,091	1,136	1,219
Camels*	42	42	40
Sheep	1,490	1,591	1,672
Goats	779	842	920
Poultry	1,320	1,541	1,888

* FAO estimates.
Source: FAO.

LIVESTOCK PRODUCTS
('000 metric tons)

	2002	2003	2004
Beef and veal*	19.3	22.5	23.0
Mutton, lamb and goat meat*	14.4	19.0	18.0
Poultry meat*	2.1	2.8	2.5
Cows' milk*	381.1	424.7	450.0
Goats' milk*	31.0	34.4	40.0
Cheese†	8.5	9.5	11.2
Wool: greasy	2.9	3.6	2.9†
Wool: scoured	1.8	2.2	1.7†
Cattle hides (fresh)†	2.1	2.4	2.5
Sheepskins (fresh)†	1.9	2.5	2.3

* Unofficial figures.
† FAO estimate(s).
Source: FAO.

Fishing

(metric tons, live weight)

	2001	2002	2003
Capture	137	181	158
Freshwater bream	37	25	24
Common carp	24	51	52
Sichel	8	4	2
Asp	6	5	3
Other cyprinids	31	27	23
Wels catfish	10	12	9
Pike-perch	21	24	22
Aquaculture	99	143	167
Silver carp	73	95	88
Common carp	8	17	47
Grass carp	18	29	30
Total catch	236	324	325

Source: FAO.

Mining

(metric tons, unless otherwise indicated)

	2000	2001	2002
Coal	20,700	20,000	40,000
Crude petroleum	20,000*	20,000	20,000
Natural gas (million cu m)	40	50	30
Lead concentrate*†	800	800	800
Antimony ore*†	2,000	2,500	3,000
Mercury*†	40	40	20
Silver (kilograms)†	5,000	5,000*	5,000
Gold (kilograms)†	5,000	5,000*	5,000*
Gypsum (crude)*	35,000	35,000	35,000

* Estimated production.
† Figures refer to the metal content of ores and concentrates.
Source: US Geological Survey.

2003: Hard coal 47,000 metric tons; Crude petroleum 16,000 metric tons; Natural gas 33 million cu m (Source: Asian Development Bank, *Key Indicators of Developing Asian and Pacific Countries*).

2004: Hard coal 68,000 metric tons; Crude petroleum 19,000 metric tons; Natural gas 36 million cu m (Source: Asian Development Bank, *Key Indicators of Developing Asian and Pacific Countries*).

TAJIKISTAN

Industry

SELECTED PRODUCTS
('000 metric tons, unless otherwise indicated)

	2000	2001	2002
Cottonseed oil (refined)*	23	26	31
Wheat flour	307	315	304
Ethyl alcohol ('000 hectolitres)	23	25	18
Wine ('000 hectolitres)	39	56	63
Beer ('000 hectolitres)	4	8	9
Soft drinks ('000 hectolitres)	58	127	134
Cigarettes (million)	667	1,155	585
Wool yarn (pure and mixed)	0.5	0.6	0.7
Cotton yarn (pure and mixed)	15.0	14.9	8.5
Woven cotton fabrics (million sq metres)	11	14	20
Woven silk fabrics ('000 sq metres)	253	248	136
Footwear, excl. rubber ('000 pairs)	110	100	84
Caustic soda (Sodium hydroxide)	4	3	3
Clay building bricks (million)	30	24	29
Cement	55	69	89
Aluminium (unwrought): primary	269.0†	289.0†	308.0‡
Electric energy (million kWh)	14,197	14,397	n.a.

2003 ('000 metric tons, unless otherwise indicated): Cottonseed oil (refined) 34*; Wheat flour 399†; Cement 166†; Electric energy (million kWh) 16,509†.

2004 ('000 metric tons, unless otherwise indicated): Wheat flour 458†; Cement 194†; Electric energy (million kWh) 16,491†.

* Unofficial figure(s) from FAO.
† Source: Asian Development Bank, *Key Indicators of Developing Asian and Pacific Countries*.
‡ Source: US Geological Survey.

Source (unless otherwise indicated): UN, *Industrial Commodity Statistics Yearbook*.

Finance

CURRENCY AND EXCHANGE RATES

Monetary Units
100 diram = 1 somoni.

Sterling, Dollar and Euro Equivalents (30 December 2005)
£1 sterling = 5.509 somoni;
US $1 = 3.199 somoni;
€1 = 3.774 somoni;
100 somoni = £18.15 = $31.26 = €26.50.

Average Exchange Rate (somoni per US $)
2003 3.0614
2004 2.9705
2005 3.1166

Note: The Tajik rouble was introduced in May 1995, replacing the Russian (formerly Soviet) rouble at the rate of 1 Tajik rouble = 100 Russian roubles. A new currency, the somoni (equivalent to 1,000 Tajik roubles), was introduced in October 2000.

BUDGET
(million somoni)*

Revenue†	2004	2005‡	2006§
Tax revenue	934	1,169	1,374
Income and profit tax	105	142	156
Payroll taxes	120	146	172
Property taxes	34	51	66
Internal taxes on goods and services	482	625	728
International trade and operations tax	185	205	252
Non-tax revenue	129	143	154
Total	**1,063**	**1,312**	**1,528**

Expenditure‖	2004	2005‡	2006§
General administrative services	117	157	185
Protection services	134	194	239
Social services	438	664	805
Education	161	250	336
Health	62	91	106
Social security and welfare	153	228	238
Other	61	95	125
Economic services	119	148	167
Interest payments	43	56	57
Other purposes	211	144	156
External financing of public investment programme (PIP)	189	284	336
Total	**1,250**	**1,648**	**1,944**

* Figures refer to the consolidated operations of the State Budget, comprising the budgets of the central (republican) Government and local authorities, and the Social Security Fund.
† Excluding grants received (million somoni): 41 in 2004; 38 in 2005 (preliminary); 38 in 2006 (budget proposal).
‡ Preliminary figures.
§ Budget proposals.
‖ Including lending minus repayments (million somoni): 3 in 2004; 2 in 2005 (preliminary); 2 in 2006 (budget proposal).

Sources: IMF, *Republic of Tajikistan: Sixth Review Under the Poverty Reduction and Growth Facility—Staff Report; Staff Statement; Press Release on the Executive Board Discussion; and Statement by the Executive Director for the Republic of Tajikistan* (January 2006).

INTERNATIONAL RESERVES
(US $ million at 31 December)

	2003	2004	2005
Gold (national valuation)	5.7	14.6	20.7
IMF special drawing rights	0.9	1.3	5.4
Foreign exchange	111.0	156.2	162.8
Total	**117.6**	**172.1**	**188.9**

Source: IMF, *International Financial Statistics*.

MONEY SUPPLY
(million somoni at 31 December)

	2002	2003	2004
Currency outside banks	135.8	158.1	175.4
Demand deposits	36.3	61.8	64.4
Total money (incl. others)	**173.2**	**222.2**	**241.1**

Source: IMF, *International Financial Statistics*.

COST OF LIVING
(Consumer price index for December; base: previous December = 100)

	2000	2001	2002
Food	166.3	113.7	117.0
Other goods	144.2	110.5	106.3
Services	134.0	103.2	109.9
All items	**160.6**	**112.5**	**114.5**

NATIONAL ACCOUNTS
(million somoni at current prices)

Expenditure on the Gross Domestic Product

	2001	2002	2003
Government final consumption expenditure	222.0	290.2	393.5
Private final consumption expenditure	2,185.4	2,907.6	4,157.8
Increase in stocks	186.4	240.8	342.7
Gross fixed capital formation	233.5	362.1	515.4
Total domestic expenditure	**2,827.3**	**3,800.7**	**5,409.4**
Exports of goods and services	1,658.0	2,093.8	2,533.5
Less Imports of goods and services	1,956.4	2,529.0	3,185.1
GDP in purchasers' values	**2,528.8**	**3,365.5**	**4,757.8**

TAJIKISTAN

Gross Domestic Product by Economic Activity

	2002	2003	2004
Agriculture	886.8	1,199.0	1,330.0
Mining, manufacturing and electricity, gas and water	744.2	994.8	1,206.9
Construction	127.8	199.8	338.7
Transport and communications	123.5	180.8	338.7
Trade	671.4	904.0	1,213.0
Others, including public administration and finance	479.0	775.1	1,072.5
GDP at factor cost	3,032.8	4,253.5	5,499.8
Indirect taxes, less subsidies	332.8	504.3	657.7
GDP in purchasers' values	3,365.5	4,757.8	6,157.5

Source: Asian Development Bank, *Key Indicators of Developing Asian and Pacific Countries*.

BALANCE OF PAYMENTS
(US $ million)

	2004	2005*	2006*
Exports of goods f.o.b.	1,088	1,124	1,188
Imports of goods c.i.f.	−1,239	−1,403	−1,539
Trade balance	−151	−279	−351
Services (net)	−89	−76	−92
Balance on goods and services	−241	−355	−443
Other income (net)	−78	−89	−82
Balance on goods, services and income	−319	−444	−525
Current transfers (net)	236	357	406
Current balance	−83	−86	−118
Capital transfers (net)	13	21	24
Public sector (net)	−194	56	64
Other investment	360	42	76
Electricity credit	7	7	—
Other capital and errors and omissions	−81	−27	−37
Overall balance	23	14	8

* Projected figures.

Source: IMF, *Republic of Tajikistan: Sixth Review Under the Poverty Reduction and Growth Facility—Staff Report; Staff Statement; Press Release on the Executive Board Discussion; and Statement by the Executive Director for the Republic of Tajikistan* (February 2006).

External Trade

PRINCIPAL COMMODITIES
(US $ million)

Imports c.i.f.	1999	2000	2001
Alumina	81	198	184
Natural gas	36	35	27
Petroleum products	54	48	78
Electricity	179	119	98
Grain and flour	46	45	38
Total (incl. others)	663	675	688

Exports f.o.b.	1999	2000	2001
Aluminium	309	433	397
Cotton fibre	82	84	62
Electricity	175	92	79
Total (incl. others)	689	784	652

2002 (US $ million): *Imports c.i.f.*: Mineral products 225; Products of the chemical or allied industries 220; Articles of stone, cement, asbestos, mica, glass and glassware 10; Non-precious metals and articles of non-precious metal 13; Others 253; Total 721. *Exports c.i.f.*: Mineral products 72; Products of the chemical or allied industries 2; Articles of stone, cement, asbestos, mica, glass and glassware 2; Non-precious metals and articles of non-precious metal 401; Others 260; Total 737.

PRINCIPAL TRADING PARTNERS
(US $ million)

Imports	2002	2003	2004
Azerbaijan	41.1	62.3	66.2
Iran	15.6	23.7	29.7
Italy	25.8	22.8	13.7
Kazakhstan	72.3	95.8	101.8
Romania	—	38.9	41.3
Russia	163.5	178.1	187.3
Turkey	10.5	29.5	45.8
Turkmenistan	47.1	31.6	33.6
Ukraine	80.5	62.4	66.3
Uzbekistan	132.4	132.7	141.0
Total (incl. others)	710.3	880.8	1,055.1

Exports	2002	2003	2004
Hungary	39.9	12.0	32.8
Iran	28.4	51.4	59.0
Italy	6.9	8.4	48.8
Latvia	30.9	78.0	97.7
Netherlands	216.9	200.8	24.7
Norway	0.0	—	74.0
Russia	87.5	52.2	60.8
Switzerland	68.7	77.0	85.5
Turkey	118.5	193.2	57.1
Uzbekistan	72.9	67.1	84.0
Total (incl. others)	737.0	790.8	744.3

Source: Asian Development Bank, *Key Indicators of Developing Asian and Pacific Countries*.

Transport

RAILWAYS
(traffic)

	1999	2000	2001
Passenger-km (million)	61	73	32
Freight ton-km (million)	1,282	1,326	1,248

CIVIL AVIATION
(estimated traffic on scheduled services)

	1997	1998	1999
Kilometres flown (million)	7	5	4
Passengers carried ('000)	594	217	156
Passenger-km (million)	1,825	322	229
Freight ton-km (million)	166	32	23

Source: UN, *Statistical Yearbook*.

Communications Media

	2001	2002	2003
Telephones ('000 main lines in use)	226.9	237.6	245.2
Mobile cellular telephones ('000 subscribers)	1.6	13.2	47.6
Internet users ('000)	3.2	3.5	4.1

Television receivers ('000 in use): 2,000 in 2000.

Facsimile machines (number in use): 2,100 in 1999.

Books published (titles): 150 in 1997.

Books published (copies): 997,000 in 1996.

Daily newspapers (estimates): 2 titles and 120,000 copies (average circulation) in 1996.

Non-daily newspapers: 73 titles and 153,000 copies (average circulation) in 1996.

Other periodicals: 11 titles and 130,000 copies (average circulation) in 1996.

Radio receivers ('000 in use): 850 in 1997.

2004: Internet users ('000) 5.0.

Sources: UNESCO, *Statistical Yearbook*; International Telecommunication Union.

Education

(2001/02, unless otherwise indicated)

	Institutions	Teachers	Students
Pre-primary	501	6,615*	57,812
Primary	660		33,000
Secondary:		100,200	
general	2,861		1,487,600
specialist	128		39,400
vocational	55	n.a.	29,842†
Higher (incl. universities)	31	6,100	84,400

* 1996/97.
† 1994/95.

Source: partly UNESCO, *Statistical Yearbook*.

Primary and secondary schools (excl. vocational schools): 3,684 in 2002/03.

Students in primary and secondary schools ('000 persons, excl. vocational schools): 1,619.4 in 2002/03.

Higher institutions (incl. universities): 33 in 2002/03.

Students in higher institutions (incl. universities): 96,583 in 2002/03.

Adult literacy rate (UNESCO estimates): 99.5% (males 99.7%; females 99.3%) in 2003 (Source: UN Development Programme, *Human Development Report*).

Directory

The Constitution

Tajikistan's Constitution entered into force on 6 November 1994, when it was approved by a majority of voters in a nation-wide plebiscite. It replaced the previous Soviet republican Constitution, adopted in 1978. The following is a summary of its main provisions (including amendments approved by referendum on 26 September 1999 and 22 June 2003):

PRINCIPLES OF THE CONSTITUTIONAL SYSTEM

The Republic of Tajikistan is a sovereign, democratic, law-governed, secular and unitary state. The state language is Tajik, but Russian is accorded the status of a language of communication between nationalities.

Recognition, observance and protection of human and civil rights and freedoms is the obligation of the State. The people of Tajikistan are the expression of sovereignty and the sole source of power of the State, which they express through their elected representatives.

Tajikistan consists of Kuhistoni Badakhshon Autonomous Viloyat (Region), Viloyats, towns, districts, settlements and villages. The territory of the State is indivisible and inviolable. Agitation and actions aimed at disunity of the State are prohibited.

No ideology, including religious ideology, may be granted the status of a state ideology.

The Constitution of Tajikistan has supreme legal authority and its norms have direct application. Laws and other legal acts which run counter to the Constitution have no legal validity. The State, its bodies and officials are bound to observe the provisions of the Constitution.

Tajikistan will implement a peaceful policy, respecting the sovereignty and independence of other states of the world and will determine foreign relations on the basis of international norms. Agitation for war is prohibited.

The economy of Tajikistan is based on various forms of ownership. The State guarantees freedom of economic activity, entrepreneurship, equality of rights and the protection of all forms of ownership, including private ownership. Land and natural resources are under state ownership.

FUNDAMENTAL DUTIES OF INDIVIDUALS AND CITIZENS

The freedoms and rights of individuals are protected by the Constitution, the laws of the republic and international documents to which Tajikistan is a signatory. The State guarantees the rights and freedoms of every person, regardless of nationality, race, sex, language, religious beliefs, political persuasion, social status, knowledge and property. Men and women have the same rights. Every person has the right to life. No one may be subjected to torture, punishment or inhuman treatment. No one may be arrested, kept in custody or exiled without a legal basis, and no one is adjudged guilty of a crime except by the sentence of a court in accordance with the law. Every person has the right freely to choose their place of residence, to leave the republic and return to it. Every person has the right to profess any religion individually or with others, or not to profess any, and to take part in religious ceremonies. Every citizen has the right to take part in political life and state administration; to elect and be elected from the age of 18; to join and leave political parties, trade unions and other associations; to take part in meetings, rallies or demonstrations. Every person is guaranteed freedom of speech. State censorship is prohibited.

Every person has the right: to ownership and inheritance; to work; to housing; to social security in old age, or in the event of sickness or disability. Basic general education is compulsory.

A state of emergency is declared as a temporary measure to ensure the security of citizens and of the State in the instance of a direct threat to the freedom of citizens, the State's independence, its territorial integrity, or natural disasters. The period of a state of emergency is up to three months; it can be prolonged by the President of the Republic.

MAJLISI OLI (SUPREME ASSEMBLY)

The Majlisi Oli (Supreme Assembly) is the highest representative and legislative body of the republic. It is a bicameral legislative body, comprising a 63-member lower chamber, the Majlisi Namoyandagon (Assembly of Representatives), and an upper chamber, the Majlisi Milliy (National Assembly). The members of the Majlisi Namoyandagon are elected for a five-year term, 22 by proportional representation and 41 in single-mandate constituencies. Twenty-five members of the Majlisi Milliy are indirectly elected for a term of five years by regional deputies. Eight members of the chamber are appointed by the President of the Republic. Additionally, former Heads of State of the Republic of Tajikistan are entitled to a seat in the chamber.

The powers of the Majlisi Oli include: enactment and amendment of laws, and their annulment; interpretation of the Constitution and laws; determination of the basic direction of domestic and foreign policy; ratification of presidential decrees on the appointment and dismissal of the Chairman of the National Bank, the Chairman and members of the Constitutional Court, the Supreme Court and the Supreme Economic Court; ratification of the state budget; determining and altering the structure of administrative territorial units; ratification and annulment of international treaties; ratification of presidential decrees on a state of war and a state of emergency.

Laws are adopted by a majority of the legislative deputies. If the President does not agree with the law, he may return it to the Majlisi Oli. If the legislature once again approves the law, with at least a two-thirds' majority, the President must sign it.

TAJIKISTAN

THE PRESIDENT OF THE REPUBLIC

The President of the Republic is the Head of State and the head of the executive. The President is elected by the citizens of Tajikistan on the basis of universal, direct and equal suffrage for a seven-year term. Any citizen who knows the state language and has lived on the territory of Tajikistan for the preceding 10 years may be nominated to the post of President of the Republic.

The President has the authority: to represent Tajikistan inside the country and in international relations; to establish or abolish ministries with the approval of the Majlisi Oli; to appoint or dismiss the Chairman (Prime Minister) and other members of the Council of Ministers and to propose them for approval to the Majlisi Oli; to appoint and dismiss chairmen of regions, towns and districts, and propose new appointments for approval to the relevant assemblies of people's deputies; to appoint and dismiss members of the Constitutional Court, the Supreme Court and the Supreme Economic Court (with the approval of the Majlisi Oli); to appoint and dismiss judges of lower courts; to sign laws; to lead the implementation of foreign policy and sign international treaties; to appoint diplomatic representatives abroad; to be Commander-in-Chief of the armed forces of Tajikistan; to declare a state of war or a state of emergency (with the approval of the Majlisi Oli).

In the event of the President's death, resignation, removal from office or inability to perform his duties, the duties of the President will be carried out by the Chairman of the Majlisi Oli until further presidential elections can be held. New elections must be held within three months of these circumstances. The President may be removed from office in the case of his committing a crime, by the decision of at least two-thirds of deputies of the Majlisi Oli, taking into account the decisions of the Constitutional Court.

THE COUNCIL OF MINISTERS

The Council of Ministers consists of the Chairman (Prime Minister), the First Deputy Chairman, Deputy Chairmen, Ministers and Chairmen of State Committees. The Council of Ministers is responsible for implementation of laws and decrees of the Majlisi Oli and decrees and orders of the President. The Council of Ministers leaves office when a new President is elected.

LOCAL GOVERNMENT

The local representative authority in regions, towns and districts is the assembly of people's deputies. Assemblies are elected for a five-year term. Local executive government is the responsibility of the President's representative: the chairman of the assembly of people's deputies, who is proposed by the President and approved by the relevant assembly. The Majlisi Oli may dissolve local representative bodies, if their actions do not conform to the Constitution and the law.

KUHISTONI BADAKHSHON AUTONOMOUS VILOYAT

Kuhistoni Badakhshon Autonomous Viloyat is an integral and indivisible part of Tajikistan, the territory of which cannot be changed without the consent of the regional assembly.

JUDICIARY

The judiciary is independent and protects the rights and freedoms of the individual, the interests of the State, organizations and institutions, and legality and justice. Judicial power is implemented by the Constitutional Court, the Supreme Court, the Supreme Economic Court, the Military Court, the Court of Kuhistoni Badakhshon Autonomous Viloyat, and courts of viloyats, the city of Dushanbe, towns and districts. The term of judges is 10 years. The creation of emergency courts is not permitted.

Judges are independent and are subordinate only to the Constitution and the law. Interference in their activity is not permitted.

THE OFFICE OF THE PROCURATOR-GENERAL

The Procurator-General and procurators subordinate to him ensure the control and observance of laws within the framework of their authority in the territory of Tajikistan. The Procurator-General is responsible to the Majlisi Oli and the President, and is elected for a five-year term.

PROCEDURES FOR INTRODUCING AMENDMENTS TO THE CONSTITUTION

Amendments and addenda to the Constitution are made by means of a referendum. A referendum takes place with the support of at least two-thirds of the people's deputies. The President, or at least one-third of the people's deputies, may submit amendments and addenda to the Constitution. The form of public administration, the territorial integrity and the democratic, law-governed and secular nature of the State are irrevocable.

The Government

HEAD OF STATE

President: IMAMALI SH. RAKHMONOV (elected by popular vote 6 November 1994; re-elected 6 November 1999).

COUNCIL OF MINISTERS
(April 2006)

Chairman (Prime Minister) and Minister of Construction: AKIL AKILOV.
First Deputy Chairman: Haji AKBAR TURAJONZODA.
Deputy Chairman: KHAIRINISSO MAVLONOVA.
Minister of Agriculture: TURSUN RAKHMATOV.
Minister of Culture: RAJABMAD AMIROV.
Minister of Defence: Maj.-Gen. SHERALI KHAYRULLOYEV.
Minister of the Economy and Trade: KHAKIM SOLIYEV.
Minister of Education: ABDUJABBOR RAHMONOV.
Minister of Emergency Situations and Civil Defence: Maj.-Gen. MIRZO ZIYOYEV.
Minister of Energy: ABDULLO YEROV.
Minister of Finance: SAFARALI NAJMIDDINOV.
Minister of Foreign Affairs: TALBAK NAZAROV.
Minister of Grain Products: BEKMUROD UROKOV.
Minister of Health: NUSRATULLO FAIZULLOYEV.
Minister of Industry: ZAID SAIDOV.
Minister of Internal Affairs: KHOMIDDIN SHARIPOV.
Minister of Justice: KHALIFABOBO KHAMIDOV.
Minister of Labour, Employment and Social Welfare: ZOKIR VAZIROV.
Minister of Land Improvement and Water Economy: ABDUKAKHIR NAZIROV.
Minister of Security: KHAYRIDDIN ABDURAKHIMOV.
Minister of State Revenues and Tax Collection: GHULOMJON BOBOYEV.
Minister of Transport: ABDURAHIM ASHUROV.

Note: The Chairmen of State Committees are also members of the Council of Ministers.

MINISTRIES

Office of the President: 734023 Dushanbe, pr. Rudaki 80; tel. (372) 21-04-18; fax (372) 21-18-37.
Secretariat of the Prime Minister: 734023 Dushanbe, pr. Rudaki 80; tel. (372) 21-18-71; fax (372) 21-51-10.
Ministry of Agriculture: 734025 Dushanbe, pr. Rudaki 14; tel. (372) 21-15-96; fax (372) 21-57-94.
Ministry of Construction: 734025 Dushanbe, ul. Valamatzde 19/11; tel. (372) 23-18-82; fax (372) 27-86-17.
Ministry of Culture: 734025 Dushanbe, pr. Rudaki 34; tel. (372) 21-03-05; fax (372) 21-47-01.
Ministry of Defence: 734025 Dushanbe, ul. Bokhtar 59; tel. (372) 23-18-97; fax (372) 23-19-37.
Ministry of the Economy and Trade: 734002 Dushanbe, ul. Bokhtar 37; tel. (372) 27-34-34; fax (372) 21-04-04; e-mail sharipov_jamshed@hotmail.com; internet www.met.tj.
Ministry of Education: 734025 Dushanbe, ul. Chekhova 13 A; tel. (372) 21-46-05; fax (372) 21-70-41.
Ministry of Emergency Situations and Civil Defence: 734025 Dushanbe, ul. Bokhtar 59; tel. (372) 23-17-78; fax (372) 21-13-31.
Ministry of Energy: 734025 Dushanbe, pr. I. Somoni 64; tel. (372) 35-86-30.
Ministry of Finance: 734025 Dushanbe, ul. Ak. Rajabovykh 3; tel. (372) 21-62-37; fax (372) 21-33-29.
Ministry of Foreign Affairs: 734051 Dushanbe, pr. Rudaki 42; tel. (372) 21-18-08; fax (372) 21-02-59; e-mail dushanbe@mfaumo.td.silk.org; internet www.mid.tj.
Ministry of Grain Products: 734025 Dushanbe, pr. Rudaki 42; tel. (372) 27-61-31; fax (372) 27-95-71.
Ministry of Health: 734025 Dushanbe, ul. Shevchenko 69; tel. (372) 21-30-64; fax (372) 21-48-71.
Ministry of Industry: 734012 Dushanbe, pr. Rudaki 22; tel. (372) 21-69-97; fax (372) 21-82-81; e-mail minprom@netrt.org.
Ministry of Internal Affairs: 734025 Dushanbe, ul. Tekhron 29; tel. (372) 21-17-40; fax (372) 21-26-05.
Ministry of Justice: 734025 Dushanbe, pr. Rudaki 25; tel. (372) 21-44-05; fax (372) 21-80-66.

TAJIKISTAN

Ministry of Labour, Employment and Social Welfare: 734028 Dushanbe, ul. A. Navoi 52; tel. (372) 36-18-37; fax (372) 36-24-15.

Ministry of Land Improvement and Water Economy: 734001 Dushanbe, pr. Rudaki 78; tel. (372) 35-35-66.

Ministry of Security: 734025 Dushanbe, ul. Tekhron 8; tel. (372) 21-23-12; fax (372) 21-15-65.

Ministry of State Revenues and Tax Collection: 734025 Dushanbe, pr. Rudaki 80; tel. (372) 21-46-17.

Ministry of Transport: 734042 Dushanbe, ul. Aini 14; tel. (372) 21-17-13; fax (372) 21-20-03; e-mail mintrans@tajnet.com; internet www.mintrans.tajnet.com.

President and Legislature

PRESIDENT

Presidential Election, 6 November 1999

Candidates	Votes	%
Imamali Sh. Rakhmonov	2,749,908	96.97
Davlat Usmon	59,587	2.11
Total*	**2,835,590**	**100.00**

* Including invalid votes, numbering 18,774.

LEGISLATURE

Constitutional amendments approved by a referendum in September 1999 provided for the establishment of a bicameral legislative body, the Majlisi Oli (Supreme Assembly), comprising a 63-member lower chamber, the Majlisi Namoyandagon (Assembly of Representatives), and an upper chamber, the Majlisi Milliy (National Assembly), which has a minimum of 33 members.

Majlisi Milliy
(National Assembly)

734051 Dushanbe, pr. Rudaki 42; tel. (372) 23-19-33; fax (372) 21-51-10; e-mail mejparl@parliament.tojikiston.com.

President: MAKHMADSAID UBAYDULLOYEV.

The Majlisi Milliy has a minimum of 33 members, of whom 25 (five from each of the five administrative regions of Tajikistan) are indirectly elected for a term of five years by regional deputies. Eight members of the chamber, who also serve for a term of five years, are appointed by the President of the Republic. All former Presidents of Tajikistan are also entitled to a seat in the Majlisi Milliy. Elections to the Majlisi Milliy were held on 24 March 2005, and the eight presidential nominees were announced on 25 March. The new chamber convened on 15 April.

Majlisi Namoyandagon
(Assembly of Representatives)

734051 Dushanbe, pr. Rudaki 42; tel. (372) 21-23-66; fax (372) 21-92-81; e-mail mejparl@parliament.tojikiston.com.

President: SAIDULLO KHAIRULLAYEV.

Elections, 27 February and 13 March 2005*

	Party lists†		Seats	
	% of votes	Resulting seats	Constituency‡	Total
People's Democratic Party of Tajikistan (PDPT)	74	17	35	52
Communist Party of Tajikistan (CPT)	13	3	1	4
Islamic Rebirth Party of Tajikistan (IRP)	8	2	—	2
Independents	—	—	5	5
Total (incl. others)	**100**	**22**	**41**	**63**

* Final provisional results.
† Each party was required to obtain at least 5% of the total votes cast in order to win seats on the basis of party lists.
‡ Elected on basis of single mandate.

Election Commission

Central Commission for Elections and Referenda: 734051 Dushanbe, pr. Rudaki 42; tel. (372) 21-13-75; comprises Chair., Sec. and 13 mems, elected by the Majlisi Namoyandagon at the proposal of the President of the Republic; Chair. MIRZOALI BOLTUYEV; Sec. VERA NAIMOVA.

Political Organizations

At the end of November 2005 there were eight registered parties in Tajikistan.

Agrarian Party of Tajikistan (Agrarnaya partiya Tadzhikistana): Dushanbe; f. and regd 2005; supports creation of a civil society, and aims to protect the interests of the agricultural sector and its workers; Chair. AMIR KARAKULOV; c. 1,300 mems.

Communist Party of Tajikistan (CPT) (Kommunisticheskaya partiya Tadzhikistana): 734002 Dushanbe, ul. Fatekha Niyazi 37; tel. (372) 23-29-53; internet www.kpt.freenet.tj; f. 1924; sole registered party until 1991; Chair. SHODI D. SHABDOLOV; c. 60,000 mems (Jan. 2005).

Democratic Party of Tajikistan (DPT): 731000 Dushanbe, ul. Pushkina 64; tel. (372) 21-77-87; f. 1990; banned in 1993; permitted to re-register 1996 and 1999; secular nationalist and pro-Western; Chair. MAKHMADRUZI ISKANDAROV (sentenced to 23-year gaol term in Oct. 2005); c. 4,500 mems (Jan. 2005).

Islamic Rebirth Party of Tajikistan (IRP): Dushanbe, pos. Kalinina, ul. Tukhagul 55; tel. (372) 27-25-30; fax (372) 27-53-93; f. 1990 as a result of split from the All-Union Islamic Renaissance Party of the USSR; leadership formerly based in Tehran, Iran; registered in 1991; banned 1993–99; Chair. SAYED ABDULLO NURI; c. 20,000 mems (Jan. 2005).

Justice (Adolatkoh): ul. Sayeed Nosirov 41, Dushanbe; tel. (372) 24-90-55; f. and regd 1996; campaigns for the establishment of social justice and construction of a legal state; registration revoked 2001; Leader ABDURAKHMON KARIMOV; c. 10,000 mems.

Party of Economic Reforms (Partiya ekonomicheskikh reform): Dushanbe; f. and regd 2005; supports establishment of a market economy on the basis of democratic principles; aims to reduce poverty, undertake privatization and increase foreign investment; Chair. OLIM BOBOYEV; c. 1,000 mems.

Party of Popular Unity and Accord (PPUA): Dushanbe; f. 1994; represents interests of northern Tajikistan; banned 1998; Leader ABDUMALIK ABDULLOJONOV.

People's Democratic Party of Tajikistan (PDPT) (Hizbi Demokrati-Khalkii Tojikston): Dushanbe, pr. Rudaki 107; tel. (372) 21-63-21; e-mail ndpt1994@yahoo.com; f. 1994; campaigns for a united, democratic, secular and law-based state; Chair. IMAMALI SH. RAKHMONOV; First Dep. Chair. DAVLATALI DAVLATOV; 70,000 mems (Jan. 2005).

Rebirth (Rastokhez): f. 1990; nationalist-religious party favoured by intellectuals; unregistered; Chair. TAKHIR ABDUZHABBOROV.

Social Democratic Party of Tajikistan (SDPT): 731000 Dushanbe, pr. Rudaki 81/49; tel. (372) 23-47-40; f. 1998; regd 2002; fmrly Justice and Progress of Tajikistan; Chair. RAKHMATULLO KH. ZOIROV; 5,000 mems.

Socialist Party of Tajikistan (Sotsialisticheskaya partiya Tadzhikistana): 731000 Dushanbe, pr. Rudaki 137; tel. (372) 34-77-11; f. 1996; split into two factions in advance of 2005 legislative elections, only one of which was registered by the Ministry of Justice; Chairmen ABDUKHALIM GAFFOROV (Chair. of faction registered by the Ministry of Justice), MIRKHUSEYN NARZIYEV (Chair. of unregistered faction).

Union and Development Party (Hizb-i Ittihod va Taraqqiyot—Taraqqiyot): Dushanbe; f. 2000; unregistered; formerly a faction of the Democratic Party of Tajikistan; Chair. SULTON KUVVATOV; 3,000 mems (2001).

Unity Party (Hizb-i-Vahdat): Dushanbe; f. 2001; unregistered.

The transnational militant Islamist Hizb-ut-Tahrir al-Islami (Party of Islamic Liberation—Hizb-ut-Tahrir) was believed to be operative in Tajikistan. As in neighbouring states, the organization was banned in Tajikistan, and a number of people have received gaol sentences for their alleged membership of the group, despite its stated intention of using only peaceful means of pursuing its goals, notably the restoration of a caliphate.

Diplomatic Representation

EMBASSIES IN TAJIKISTAN

Afghanistan: 734000 Dushanbe, ul. Pushkina 34; tel. (372) 27-60-51; fax (372) 51-00-96; e-mail afghanemintj@yahoo.com; Ambassador SAID MUHAMMAD KHAIRKHOKH.

TAJIKISTAN

China, People's Republic: 734002 Dushanbe, ul. Parvin 8; tel. (372) 21-01-94; fax (372) 51-00-24; e-mail chinaembassy@tajnet.com; Ambassador Li Huilai.

France: 734017 Dushanbe, Varzovskaya 17; tel. (372) 21-78-55; fax (372) 51-00-82; Ambassador Pierre Andrieu.

Germany: 734017 Dushanbe, ul. Varzobskaya 16; tel. (372) 21-21-89; fax (372) 24-03-90; e-mail info@dusc.diplo.de; internet www.duschanbe.diplo.de; Ambassador Rainer Müller.

Holy See: 734006 Dushanbe, pr. Titova 21/10; tel. (372) 21-21-90; fax (372) 23-42-69; e-mail nuntius_kazakhstan@lycos.com; internet www.church.tj; Apostolic Nuncio Most Rev. József Wesołowski (Titular Archbishop of Slebte).

India: 734000 Dushanbe, ul. Bukhoro 45; tel. (372) 21-23-50; fax (372) 21-24-61; e-mail eoi@netrt.org; Ambassador Bondal Jaishankar.

Iran: 734000 Dushanbe, ul. Tekhron 18, POB 734025; tel. (372) 21-00-74; fax (372) 51-00-89; e-mail iran-embassy@tagnet.com; Ambassador Naser Sarmadi-Parsa.

Japan: Dushanbe, ul. Khlopkozavodskaya 80A; tel. (372) 21-39-70; fax (919) 01-50-30; Chargé d'affaires a.i. Hiroshi Takahashi.

Kazakhstan: 734000 Dushanbe, ul. Prof. Husseynzade 33/1; tel. (372) 21-11-08; fax (372) 21-89-40; e-mail dipmiskz7@tajik.net; Ambassador Erlan Abildayev.

Korea, Democratic People's Republic: Dushanbe; Ri Tong Phal.

Kyrgyzstan: 734000 Dushanbe, ul. Chekhova 41/3; tel. and fax (372) 27-20-08; e-mail kyremb@tajnet.com; Ambassador Turatbek Dzhunushaliyev.

Pakistan: 734000 Dushanbe, pr. Rudaki 37A; tel. (372) 21-19-65; fax (372) 21-17-29; e-mail pareptaj@netrt.org; Ambassador Ikramul-Lakh Mekhsud.

Russia: 734000 Dushanbe, ul. A. Sino 29/31; tel. (372) 21-10-05; fax (372) 21-10-85; e-mail rambtadjik@rambler.ru; internet www.rusembassy.tajnet.com; Ambassador Ramazan Abdulatipov.

Sweden: 734013 Dushanbe, pr. Druzhby Narodov 106; tel. (372) 24-62-65; e-mail sida@sida.tojikiston.com; Ambassador Hans Olsson.

Turkey: 734019 Dushanbe, pr. Rudaki 17/2; tel. (372) 21-00-36; e-mail turkdusa@tajnet.com; Ambassador Altay Jengizer.

Turkmenistan: 734000 Dushanbe, ul. S. Gani 21; tel. (372) 21-68-84; fax (372) 21-57-49; Ambassador Ata Gundogdyyev.

United Kingdom: Dushanbe, Lutfi 43; tel. (372) 24-22-21; e-mail reception@britishembassy-tj.com; internet www.britishembassy.gov.uk/tajikistan; Ambassador Graeme Loten.

USA: 734003 Dushanbe, ul. Pavlova 10; tel. (372) 21-03-48; fax (372) 21-03-62; e-mail reception@amemb.tajik.net; e-mail dushanbeconsular@state.gov; internet usembassy.state.gov/dushanbe; Ambassador Richard E. Hoagland.

Uzbekistan: 734003 Dushanbe, ul. L. Sherali 15; tel. (372) 21-21-84; fax (372) 24-90-77; Ambassador Shoqosim I. Shoislomov.

Judicial System

Chairman of the Constitutional Court: Zarif Aliyev, 734025 Dushanbe, ul. Bokhtar 48; tel. (372) 21-61-96.

Chairman of the Supreme Court: Izbillo Khojayev, 734000 Dushanbe, pr. N. Karabayeva 1; tel. (372) 33-93-69.

Procurator-General: Bobojon Bobokhonov, 734000 Dushanbe, ul. A. Sino 126; tel. (372) 35-19-72.

Higher Economic Court: 734000 Dushanbe, ul. F. Niyazi 37; tel. (372) 21-15-58; Chair. Amirkhoja Goibnazarov.

Religion

ISLAM

The majority of Tajiks are adherents of Islam and are mainly Sunnis (Hanafi school). Many of the Pamiri peoples, however, are Isma'ilis (followers of the Aga Khan), a Shi'ite sect. Under the Soviet regime the Muslims of Tajikistan were subject to the Muslim Board of Central Asia and a muftiate, both of which were based in Tashkent, Uzbekistan. The senior Muslim cleric in Tajikistan was the *kazi* (supreme judge). In 1992 the incumbent *kazi* fled to Afghanistan, and in 1993 the Government appointed an independent *mufti* (expert in Islamic law). The Tajikistani Government, however, abolished the post of *mufti* in 1996, following the murder of the incumbent, and established a Council of Islamic Scholars (or *ulema*), as the highest Islamic religious authority in the country.

Council of Islamic Scholars (Ulema): Dushanbe; Chair. Qari Amanulloh Nematzade.

CHRISTIANITY

Most of the minority Christian population is Slav, the main denomination being the Russian Orthodox Church. There are some Protestant and other groups, notably a Baptist Church in Dushanbe.

Roman Catholic Church

The Church is represented in Tajikistan by a Mission, established in September 1997. There were an estimated 245 adherents at 31 December 2003.

Superior: Rev. Carlos Avila, 734006 Dushanbe, pr. Titova 21/10; tel. (372) 27-68-21; e-mail carlosavila@tajnet.com.

The Russian Orthodox Church (Moscow Patriarchate)

The Church in Tajikistan comes under the jurisdiction of the Eparchy of Tashkent and Central Asia, based in Uzbekistan and headed by the Metropolitan of Tashkent and Central Asia, Vladimir (Ikim).

JUDAISM

Leader: Amnon Iyaev, Dushanbe 7340001, ul. Nazima Khikmata 26; tel. (372) 21-76-58.

The Press

In 2000 there were four national newspapers. In 1996 two daily newspapers and 73 non-daily newspapers were published in Tajikistan. There were also 11 periodicals published in that year.

PRINCIPAL NEWSPAPERS

Adabiyet va sanat (Literature and Art): 734001 Dushanbe, Ismail Somoni 8; tel. (372) 24-57-39; f. 1959; weekly; organ of Union of Writers of Tajikistan and Ministry of Culture; in Tajik; Editor Gulnazar Keldi; circ. 4,000.

Adolat (Justice): in Tajik; organ of the Democratic Party of Tajikistan; Editor-in-Chief Mukhiddinu Idizoda.

Biznes i Politika (Business and Politics): 734025 Dushanbe, ul. M. Tursun-Zade 30; tel. (372) 23-52-50; e-mail b_p@rambler.ru; f. 1992; weekly; in Russian; Editor-in-Chief U. Rahmon; circ. 10,000.

Charkhi gardun (Wheel of Fortune): 734018 Dushanbe, pr. S. Sherozi 16; tel. (372) 33-56-72; e-mail gazeta@tojikiston.com; f. 1996; weekly; in Tajik; Editor-in-Chief Khabibullo Yerov.

Daijest press (Press Digest): 734018 Dushanbe, pr. S. Sherozi 16; tel. (372) 33-25-03; e-mail gazeta@tojikiston.com; f. 1994; weekly; in Russian; overview of world press; economics; popular culture; Editor-in-Chief Markhabo Zununova.

Djavononi Tochikiston (Youth of Tajikistan): 734000 Dushanbe, ul F. Niyazi 32; tel. (372) 23-38-01; f. 1930; weekly; organ of the Union of Youth of Tajikistan; in Tajik; Editor Davlat Nazriyev; circ. 3,000.

Ittikhod (Unity): organ of the Socialist Party of Tajikistan.

Jumhuriyat (Republic): 734018 Dushanbe, pr. S. Sherozi 16; tel. (372) 33-08-11; e-mail jumhuriyat@tojikiston.com; f. 1925; organ of the Government and presidential administration; 3 a week; in Tajik; Editor-in-Chief Kamol Abdurahimov; circ. 8,000.

Khalk ovozi (Voice of the People): 734018 Dushanbe, pr. S. Sherozi 16; tel. (372) 33-05-04; f. 1929; organ of the President; 3 a week; in Uzbek; Editor I. Mukhsinov; circ. 8,600.

Kurer Tadzhikistana (Tajikistan Courier): 734018 Dushanbe, pr. S. Sherozi 16; tel. (372) 33-08-15; e-mail ttemirov@td.silk.org; weekly; independent; in Russian; Editor Kh. Yusipov; circ. 40,000.

Millat (Nation): Dushanbe; f. 2005; in Tajik; independent; Editor Adolat Umarovoi.

Minbari Khalk (National Tribune): 734018 Dushanbe, pr. S. Sherozi 16; tel. (372) 33-72-10; organ of the People's Democratic Party of Tajikistan; Editor Mansur Saifiddinov.

Najot (Salvation): 734000 Dushanbe, ul. Toktogulya 55; tel. (372) 31-47-38; organ of the Islamic Rebirth Party of Tajikistan; weekly; Editor-in-Chief Sidumar Khusaini.

Narodnaya Gazeta (People's Newspaper): 734018 Dushanbe, pr. S. Sherozi 16; tel. (372) 33-08-30; e-mail narodnaja2004@mail.ru; f. 1929; fmrly Kommunist Tadzhikistana (Tajik Communist); organ of the Govt; 1 a week; in Russian; Editor Vladimir Vorobiyev; circ. 3,000.

Nerui Sukhan (Power of the Word): 734018 Dushanbe, pr. S. Sherozi 16; weekly; f. 2003; Editor-in-Chief Mukhtor Bokizoda.

Nidoi ranchbar (Call of the Workers): 734018 Dushanbe, pr. S. Sherozi 16; tel. (372) 33-38-50; f. 1992; weekly; organ of the Communist Party of Tajikistan; in Tajik; Editor-in-Chief Khabibullo Yorov; circ. 6,000.

Odamu olam (Person and World): weekly; in Tajik; independent; socio-political; Editor-in-Chief MIRAHMAD AMIRSHO.

Oila: 734018 Dushanbe, S. Sherozi 16; tel. (372) 33-32-51; weekly; independent; Editor-in-Chief FIRUZA SATTORI.

Omuzgor (Teacher): 734000 Dushanbe, ul. Aini 45; tel. (372) 21-63-36; f. 1932; weekly; organ of the Ministry of Education; in Tajik; Editor-in-Chief SAMIULLO SAIFULLOYEV; circ. 3,000.

Ruzi Nav (New Day): 734018 Dushanbe, pr. S. Sherozi 16; tel. (372) 33-14-40; f. 2003; weekly; independent; politics and government; Chief Editor RAJABI MIRZO.

Sadoi mardum (The Voice of the People): 734018 Dushanbe, pr. S. Sherozi 16; tel. (372) 22-42-47; f. 1991; 3 a week; organ of the legislature; in Tajik; Editor MURADULLO SHERALIYEV; circ. 8,000.

Tojikiston (Tajikistan): 734018 Dushanbe, pr. S. Sherozi 16; tel. (372) 34-94-11; e-mail nt@tajnet.com; f. 1938; weekly; social and political; in Tajik; Editor-in-Chief SHARIF KHAMDAMPUR; circ. (annual) 9,000.

Tojikiston ovozi/Golos Tadzhikistana (Voice of Tajikistan): 734018 Dushanbe, pr. S. Sherozi 16; tel. (372) 33-06-08; f. 1992; organ of the Central Committee of the Communist Party of Tajikistan; weekly; in Tajik and Russian; Editors SULAYMAN ERMATOV, INOM MUSOYEV; circ. 24,700.

Vechernii Dushanbe (Dunshanbe Evening News): 734018 Dushanbe, pr. S. Sherozi 16; tel. (372) 33-08-15; fax (372) 33-30-25; e-mail anush@tajnet.com; f. 1968; weekly; social and political; in Russian; Editor-in-Chief SAIDALI SIDDIKOV.

Zindagi (Life): f. 2004; weekly; in Tajik; independent; politics; Editor-in-Chief KHURSHED ATOVULLO.

PRINCIPAL PERIODICALS

Monthly, unless otherwise indicated.

Adab: 734025 Dushanbe, ul. Chekhova 13; tel. (372) 23-49-36; organ of the Ministry of Education; in Tajik; Editor SH. SHOKIRZODA; circ. (annual) 24,000.

Avitsenna: 734018 Dushanbe, pr. S. Sherozi 16; tel. (372) 34-34-44; in Russian; weekly; medicine, health, sport; Editor-in-Chief RUSTAM TURSUNOV.

Bunyod-i Adab (Culture Fund): f. 1996 to foster cultural links among the country's Persian-speaking peoples; weekly; Editor ASKAR KHAKIM.

Djashma (Spring): 734018 Dushanbe, pr. S. Sherozi 16; tel. (372) 33-08-48; f. 1986; journal of the Ministry of Culture; for children; Editor KAMOL NASRULLO; circ. (annual) 10,000.

Farkhang (Culture): 734003 Dushanbe, pr. Rudaki 124; tel. (372) 24-02-39; f. 1991; journal of the Culture Fund and Ministry of Culture; in Tajik; Editor-in-Chief J. AKOBIR; circ. 15,000.

Firuza: 734018 Dushanbe, pr. S. Sherozi 16; tel. (372) 33-89-10; f. 1932; organ of the Ministry of Culture; social and literary journal for women; Editor ZULFIYA ATOI; circ. (annual) 29,400.

Ilm va khayot (Science and Life): 734025 Dushanbe, pr. Rudaki 34; tel. (372) 27-48-61; f. 1989; organ of the Academy of Sciences; popular science; Editor T. BOIBOBO; circ. (annual) 12,000.

Istikbol: 734018 Dushanbe, pr. S. Sherozi 16; tel. (372) 33-14-52; f. 1952; organ of the Ministry of Culture; in Tajik; Chief Editor L. KENJAYEVA; circ. (annual) 10,000.

Marifat: 734024 Dushanbe, kuchai Aini 45; tel. (372) 23-42-84; organ of the Ministry of Education; in Tajik; Editor O. BOZOROV; circ. (annual) 40,000.

Pamir: 734001 Dushanbe, Ismail Somoni 8; tel. (372) 24-56-56; f. 1949; journal of the Union of Writers of Tajikistan; fiction; in Russian; Editor-in-Chief BORIS PSHENICHNYI.

Sadoi shark (Voice of the East): 734001 Dushanbe, Ismail Somoni 8; tel. (372) 24-56-79; f. 1927; journal of the Union of Writers of Tajikistan; fiction; in Tajik; Editor URUN KUKHZOD; circ. 1,600.

NEWS AGENCIES

Asia-Plus TV-Radio Company: 734002 Dushanbe, Bokhtar 35/1, 8th Floor; tel. (372) 23-59-95; fax (372) 23-01-07; e-mail manager@asiaplus.tj; internet www.asiaplus.tj; f. 2002; independent; reports in Tajik and Russian; Gen. Dir UMED BABAKHANOV.

Khovar (East): 737025 Dushanbe, pr. Rudaki 40; tel. (372) 23-23-83; fax (372) 21-21-37; e-mail khovar@tojikiston.com; internet www.khovar.tj; f. 1925; govt information agency; Dir ZAFAR SAIDOV.

Mizon: Dushanbe; independent information agency; Dir ASATULLO VALIYOV.

Varorud: Khujand, Ferdovsi 123; tel. and fax (342) 24-09-33; e-mail varorud@varorud.org; internet www.varorud.org; f. 2000; independent; Dir ILKHOM JAMOLOV.

Foreign Bureau

RIA—Novosti (Russian Information Agency—News) (Russia): 734025 Dushanbe, Putovskogo 73/2; tel. (372) 23-49-06.

PRESS ASSOCIATIONS

Internews Tajikistan: 734025 Dushanbe, ul. Akademikov Rajabovikh 7; tel. (372) 21-99-33; fax (372) 21-99-34; e-mail troy@internews.tj; internet www.internews.tj; f. 1995; non-governmental org.; provides support and funding to media organizations, and in the training of journalists; Head TROY ETULAIN.

National Association of Independent Mass Media: 734025 Dushanbe, ul. Khuseynzode 34; tel. (372) 21-37-11; e-mail nansmit@tojikiston.com; internet www.nansmit.org; f. 1999; Chair. NURIDDIN KARSHIBOYEV.

Publishers

Adib (Writer): Dushanbe, pr. Rudaki 37; tel. (372) 23-08-92; fax (372) 23-37-94; state-owned; Tajik and Russian; fiction, incl. poetry, and non-fiction, incl. books on Tajikistani and Central Asian culture.

Donish (Knowledge): Dushanbe, pr. Akademiya Nauk pr. 33; state-owned; Russian and Tajik; non-fiction, incl. geography, literature, history, and art; associated with the Academy of Sciences.

Irfon (Light of Knowledge) Publishing House: 734018 Dushanbe, N. Karabayeva 17; tel. (372) 33-39-06; f. 1925; politics, social sciences, economics, agriculture, medicine and technology; Dir J. SHARIFOV; Editor-in-Chief A. OLIMOV.

Maorif va Farkhang (Education and Culture) Publishing House: 734018 Dushanbe, Nemat Karabayev 17; tel. and fax (372) 33-93-97; e-mail najmidin@netrt.org; f. 1958 as Maorif (Education) Publishing House; present name adopted 2003; educational, academic; Gen. Dir NAJMIDDIN ZAYNIDDINOV.

Sarredaksiyai Ilmii Entsiklopediyai Millii Tajik (Tajik National Scientific Encyclopaedia) Publishing House: 731000 Dushanbe, kuchai Ami 126; tel. (372) 25-81-55; e-mail encyclopedia@yahoo.com; f. 1969; Editor-in-Chief A. QURBONOV.

Sharki Ozod Publishing House: 734018 Dushanbe, pr. Saadi Sherozi 16; tel. (372) 34-94-11; e-mail tadjikis@tajnet.com; state-owned; Dir MANZURHON DODOHONOV.

Surushan Publishing House: 734025 Dushanbe, pr. Rudaki 37; tel. and fax (372) 21-54-62; e-mail surushan@net.org; f. 1997; literary fiction, educational; Dir NURIDDIN ZAYNIDDINOV.

Broadcasting and Communications

TELECOMMUNICATIONS

Babilon-Mobil (Babilon-M): 734001 Dushanbe, ul. I. Somoni 5; tel. (372) 24-20-21; e-mail babilon-m@tojikiston.com; internet www.babilon-m.com; f. 2002; mobile cellular telecommunications.

Indigo Tajikistan: 734000 Dushanbe, ul. M. Tursunzade 23; tel. (372) 23-21-21; fax (372) 23-21-23; e-mail sales@indigo.tajnet.com; internet www.indigo.tj; f. 2001; mobile cellular telecommunications.

Tajiktelecom: 734025 Dushanbe, pr. Rudaki 57 A; tel. (372) 21-31-78; fax (372) 23-21-19; e-mail ttelecom@rs.tj; internet www.tajiktelecom.tj; f. 1996; national telecommunications operator; Dir-Gen. GULMAHMAD KAYUMOV.

BROADCASTING

In December 2001 there were some 20 independent television stations.

Regulatory Authority

State Committee for Broadcasting: Dushanbe; Chair. A. K. RAKHMONOV.

Radio

State TV-Radio Broadcasting Co of Tajikistan: 734025 Dushanbe, kuchai Chapayev 31; tel. (372) 27-75-27; fax (372) 21-34-95; e-mail soro@ctvrtj.td.silk.org; Chair. ABDODZHABBOR RAKHMONOV.

Asia-Plus Radio: Dushanbe, Bokhtar 35/1, 8th Floor; tel. (372) 23-59-95; fax (371) 23-01-07; e-mail radio@asiaplus.tajik.net; f. 2002; country's first independent radio station; broadcasts 19 hours per day in Russian and Tajik; Dir UMED BABAKHANOV.

Tajik Radio: 734025 Dushanbe, kuchai Chapayev 31; tel. (372) 27-65-69; broadcasts in Russian, Tajik and Uzbek.

TAJIKISTAN

Directory

Tiroz: 735700 Khujand, Mikroraion 27; tel. (342) 25-66-89; e-mail trrktiroz@sugdien.com; internet www.tiroz.sugdien.com; Dir KHURSHED ULMASOV.

Television

State TV-Radio Broadcasting Co of Tajikistan: 734025 Dushanbe, kuchai Chapayev 31; tel. (372) 27-75-27; fax (372) 21-34-95; e-mail soro@ctvrtj.td.silk.org; Chair. ABDODZHABBOR RAKHMONOV.

Tajik Television (TTV): 734013 Dushanbe, kuchai Behzod 7; tel. (372) 22-43-57.

Poitakht: 734013 Dushanbe, Azizbekova 20; tel. (372) 23-26-29; independent; Dir RAKHMON OSTONOV.

Finance

(cap. = capital; res = reserves; dep. = deposits; brs = branches; m. = million; amounts in somoni, unless otherwise stated)

BANKING

Central Bank

National Bank of the Republic of Tajikistan: 734025 Dushanbe, pr. Rudaki 23/2; tel. (372) 21-26-28; fax (372) 51-00-68; e-mail info@natbank.tajnet.com; internet www.nbt.tj; f. 1991; cap. 0.8m., res 25.4m., dep. 604.8m. (Oct. 2003); Chair. MURODALI ALIMARDONOV.

State Savings Bank

Amonatbank State Savings Bank: 734025 Dushanbe, pr. Rudaki 67; tel. (372) 22-70-81; fax (372) 23-14-53; f. 1991; fmrly br. of USSR Sberbank; licensed by presidential decree and not subject to the same controls as the commercial and trading banks; Chair. of Bd M. B. MAKHMADAMUNOV ; 58 brs, 480 sub-brs.

Other Banks

In June 2005 President Rakhmonov announced the removal of all restrictions on the activities of foreign banks in Tajikistan. There were reported to be 16 commercial banks in operation in Tajikistan in early 2005, including the following:

Agroinvestbank: 734018 Dushanbe, pr. Saadi Sherazl 21; tel. (372) 36-50-05; fax (372) 36-51-66; e-mail info@aib-tj.com; internet www.agroinvestbank.tj; f. 1992; fmrly Agroprombank; cap. 15.0m., res 11.0m., dep. 73.2m. (Jan. 2005); Chair. NIYOZMUROD M. SAIDMURODOV; 60 brs (Jan. 2005).

Orienbank: 734001 Dushanbe, pr. Rudaki 95/1; tel. (372) 21-06-57; fax (372) 21-18-77; e-mail ved@orien.tojikiston.com; internet www.orienbank.com; f. 1922 as republican office of Industrial Bank; cap. 8.0m., res 3.3m., dep. 61.9m. (Dec. 2003); commercial bank; Chair. of Bd HASAN SADULLOEV; Chair. of Bank Council SHERMALIK MALIKOV; 30 brs.

Tajbank: 734064 Dushanbe, Ismail Somoni 59/1; tel. (372) 27-46-54.

Tajprombank (Tajik Joint-Stock Bank for Reconstruction and Development): 734025 Dushanbe, Kh. Dekhlavi 12/3; tel. (372) 21-27-20; e-mail tpb@tjinter.com; cap. US $1m., res $3m., dep. $4m.; Chair. DZHAMSHED ZIYAYEV; 8 brs.

Tojiksodirotbonk (Bank for Foreign Economic Affairs of the Republic of Tajikistan): 734017 Dushanbe, Dekhlavi 4; tel. (372) 21-59-52; fax (372) 21-47-38; e-mail sham@sodirotbonk.com; fmrly br. of USSR Vneshekonombank; underwent restructuring in 1999; Chair. I. L. LALBEKOV; 6 brs.

COMMODITY EXCHANGES

Tajik Republican Commodity Exchange (NAVRUZ): 374001 Dushanbe, Orjonikidze 37; tel. (372) 23-48-74; fax (372) 27-03-91; f. 1991; Chair. SULEYMAN CHULEBAYEV.

Vostok-Mercury Torgovyi Dom: Dushanbe; tel. and fax (372) 24-60-61; f. 1991; trades in a wide range of goods.

INSURANCE

Tajikgosstrakh (Tajik State Insurance Co): 731000 Dushanbe, Ak. Rajabovykh 3; tel. (372) 27-58-49; state-owned; Dir-Gen. MANSUR OCHILDEV.

Trade and Industry

GOVERNMENT AGENCY

Drug Control Agency: Dushanbe, Karabaeva 52; tel. (372) 34-81-30; fax (372) 34-81-29; e-mail dca@tojikiston.com; f. 1999; documents and curbs regional drugs-trafficking; receives financial and technical assistance from the UN Office on Drugs and Crime; Dir Col-Gen. RUSTAM NAZAROV.

CHAMBER OF COMMERCE

Chamber of Commerce and Industry of the Republic of Tajikistan: 734012 Dushanbe, Valamatzade 21; tel. (372) 21-52-84; fax (372) 21-14-80; e-mail chamber@tjinter.com; internet www.tpp.tj; brs in Khujant, Qurgonteppa, Khorog, and Chamber of Services in Dushanbe; Chair. SHARIF S. SAIDOV.

INDUSTRIAL ASSOCIATION

Tajikvneshtorg (Tajik External Trade) Industrial Asscn: 734035 Dushanbe, pr. Rudaki 25, POB 48; tel. (372) 23-29-03; fax (372) 22-81-20; f. 1988; co-ordinates trade with foreign countries in a wide range of goods; Pres. ABDURAKHMON MUKHTASHOV.

EMPLOYERS' ORGANIZATION

National Asscn of Small and Medium-Sized Businesses of Tajikistan: Dushanbe, Bofanda 9; tel. (372) 27-79-78; fax (372) 21-17-26; f. 1993 with govt support; independent org.; Chair. MATLJUBA ULJABAEVA.

UTILITIES

Electricity

Barqi Tojik (Tajik Electricity): Dushanbe, kuchai I. Somoni 64; tel. (372) 35-87-66; Chair. BAHROM SIROJEV.

Pamir Energy Co (PamirEnergy): Kuhistoni Badakhshon, Khorog; f. 2002; jt venture between Governments of Tajikistan and Switzerland, the Aga Khan Fund for Economic Development, the International Finance Corpn and the International Development Association to provide electricity to Kuhistoni Badakhshon.

Gas

Dushanbegaz: supplies gas to Dushanbe region.

Tojikgaz: state-owned; natural gas.

TRADE UNIONS

Federation of Trade Unions: 734012 Dushanbe, pr. Rudaki 20; tel. (372) 23-17-79; fax (372) 23-25-06; f. 1926; above name adopted in 1992; Chair. MURODALI S. SALIKHOV; 1.3m. mems.

Transport

RAILWAYS

There are few railways in Tajikistan. In 1999 the total length of the rail network was 482 km. Lines link the major centres of the country with the railway network of Uzbekistan, connecting Khujand to the Farg'ona (Fergana) valley lines, and the cotton-growing centre of Qurgonteppa to Termiz. A new line, between the town of Isfara, in Soghd Viloyat, and Xavast, in Uzbekistan, was opened in 1995 and in 1997 a passenger route between Dushanbe and Volgograd, Russia, was inaugurated. The first section of a new line between Qurgonteppa and Kulob, in the south-west of Tajikistan, was inaugurated in 1998. In October 2002 a route from Kulob to Astrakhan, Russia, was opened. The predominantly mountainous terrain makes the construction of a more extensive network unlikely.

Tajik Railways: 734012 Dushanbe, Nazarshoyeva 35; tel. (372) 21-88-54; fax (372) 21-83-34; e-mail belugin@railway.td.silk.glas.apc.org; Pres. AMONULLO KH. KHUKUMOV.

ROADS

In mid-2002 Tajikistan's road network totalled an estimated 30,000 km, including 13,747 km of highways. The principal highway links the northern city of Khujand, across the Anzob Pass (3,372 m), with the capital, Dushanbe, continuing to Khorog (Kuhistoni Badakhshon), before wending through the Pamir Mountains, to the east and north, to Osh, Kyrgyzstan, across the Akbaytal Pass (4,655 m). This arterial route exhibits problems common to much of the country's land transport: winter weather is likely to cause the road to be closed by snow for up to eight months of the year. In 2000 Tajikistan and the Asian Development Bank signed a memorandum of understanding for the rehabilitation of the road linking Dushanbe to the south-western cities of Qurgonteppa and Kulob. In the same year a road linking eastern Tajikistan with the People's Republic of China was completed, giving Tajikistan access to the Karakorum highway, which connects China and Pakistan.

CIVIL AVIATION

The main international airport is at Dushanbe, and there is also a major airport at Khujand. The country is linked to cities in Russia and other former Soviet republics, and to a growing number of destinations in Europe and Asia.

Tajikistan Airlines: 734006 Dushanbe, Dushanbe Airport, Titova 32/1; tel. (372) 21-21-45; fax (372) 21-86-85; e-mail tt_gart@tajnet.com; internet www.tajikistan-airlines.com; f. 1990; fmrly Tajik Air; state-owned; operates flights to destinations in Afghanistan, the People's Republic of China (Xinjiang Uygur autonomous region), Germany, India, Iran, Kazakhstan, Kyrgyzstan, Pakistan, Russia, Turkey and the United Arab Emirates; Gen. Dir HOKIMSHO TILLOYEV.

Tourism

There was little tourism in Tajikistan even before the 1992–97 civil war. There is some spectacular mountain scenery, hitherto mainly visited by climbers, and, particularly in the Farg'ona (Fergana) valley, in the north of the country, there are sites of historical interest, notably the city of Khujand.

Tajikistan Republican Council of Tourism and Excursions: 734008 Dushanbe, ul. Rudaki 20; tel. (372) 27-27-51; fax (372) 51-01-40; f. 1960; Chair. MADZHID SOBIROV.

Sayoh National Tourism Company: 734025 Dushanbe, Pushkinskaya 14; tel. (372) 23-14-01; fax (372) 23-42-33; e-mail gafarov@cada.tajik.net; internet www.tajiktour.tajnet.com; Chair. GAFAROV KASIM.

TANZANIA

Introductory Survey

Location, Climate, Language, Religion, Flag, Capital

The United Republic of Tanzania consists of Tanganyika, on the African mainland, and the nearby islands of Zanzibar and Pemba. Tanganyika lies on the east coast of Africa, bordered by Uganda and Kenya to the north, by Rwanda, Burundi and the Democratic Republic of the Congo (formerly Zaire) to the west, and by Zambia, Malawi and Mozambique to the south. Zanzibar and Pemba are in the Indian Ocean, about 40 km (25 miles) off the coast of Tanganyika, north of Dar es Salaam. The climate varies with altitude, ranging from tropical in Zanzibar and on the coast and plains to semi-temperate in the highlands. The official languages are Swahili and English, and there are numerous tribal languages. There are Muslim, Christian and Hindu communities. Many Africans follow traditional beliefs. The national flag (proportions 2 by 3) comprises two triangles, one of green (with its base at the hoist and its apex in the upper fly) and the other of blue (with its base in the fly and its apex at the lower hoist), separated by a broad, yellow-edged black diagonal stripe, from the lower hoist to the upper fly.

Recent History

Tanzania was formed in 1964 by a merger of the two independent states of Tanganyika and Zanzibar (see below).

Tanganyika became a German colony in 1884, and was later incorporated into German East Africa, which also included present-day Rwanda and Burundi. In 1918, at the end of the First World War, the German forces in the area surrendered, and Tanganyika was placed under a League of Nations mandate, with the United Kingdom as the administering power. In 1946 Tanganyika became a UN Trust Territory, still under British rule. Tanganyika's first general election was held in September 1958 and February 1959. A new Council of Ministers, including African members, was formed in July 1959. At the next election, in September 1960, the Tanganyika African National Union (TANU) won 70 of the 71 seats in the National Assembly. The party's leader, Dr Julius Nyerere, became Chief Minister. Internal self-government was achieved in May 1961, when Nyerere became Prime Minister. Tanganyika became independent, within the Commonwealth, on 9 December 1961, but Nyerere resigned as Prime Minister in January 1962, in order to devote himself to the direction of TANU. He was succeeded as premier by Rashidi Kawawa. On 9 December 1962, following elections in November, Tanganyika became a republic, with Nyerere as the country's first President. Kawawa became Vice-President. Zanzibar (including the island of Pemba), a British protectorate since 1890, became an independent sultanate in December 1963. Following an armed uprising by the Afro-Shirazi Party in January 1964, the Sultan was deposed and a republic proclaimed. The new Government signed an Act of Union with Tanganyika in April 1964, thus creating the United Republic. The union was named Tanzania in October 1964, and a new Constitution was introduced in July 1965, which provided for a one-party state (although, until 1977, TANU and the Afro-Shirazi Party remained the respective official parties of mainland Tanzania and Zanzibar, and co-operated in affairs of state). Nyerere was elected President of the United Republic in September 1965, and was subsequently re-elected in 1970, 1975 and 1980.

Despite its incorporation in Tanzania, Zanzibar retained a separate administration, which ruthlessly suppressed all opposition. In April 1972 Sheikh Abeid Karume, Chairman of the ruling Revolutionary Council of Zanzibar and First Vice-President of the United Republic, was assassinated. His successor, Aboud Jumbe, extended the powers of the Afro-Shirazi Party. A separate Constitution for Zanzibar was adopted in October 1979, providing for a popularly elected President and a House of Representatives elected by delegates of the ruling party. The first elections to the 40-member Zanzibar House of Representatives were held in January 1980. In June of that year a coup plot against Jumbe was thwarted; Jumbe won an overwhelming majority at Zanzibar's first presidential election, held in October. However, mounting dissatisfaction among Zanzibaris concerning the union with Tanganyika culminated in the resignation, in January 1984, of Jumbe and three of his ministers. In April Ali Hassan Mwinyi, a former Zanzibari Minister of Natural Resources and Tourism, was elected unopposed as President of Zanzibar, winning 87.5% of the votes cast. A new Constitution for Zanzibar came into force in January 1985, providing for the House of Representatives to be directly elected by universal adult suffrage.

In February 1977 TANU and the Afro-Shirazi Party were amalgamated to form Chama Cha Mapinduzi (CCM), the Revolutionary Party of Tanzania. In April the National Assembly approved a permanent Constitution for Tanzania; this provided for the election to the National Assembly of representatives from Zanzibar, in addition to those from the Tanzanian mainland. At a general election in October 1980 about one-half of the elected members of the Assembly, including several ministers, failed to retain their seats; this was interpreted as a protest by voters against commodity shortages and inefficient bureaucracy. Major changes to the Constitution were approved by the National Assembly in October 1984, limiting the President's powers and increasing those of the National Assembly.

President Nyerere retired in November 1985, and was succeeded by Ali Hassan Mwinyi (President of Zanzibar and Vice-President of Tanzania since April 1984), who, as the sole candidate, had won 96% of the votes cast at a presidential election in October. Elections to the National Assembly were held on the same day. Mwinyi appointed Joseph Warioba (previously Minister of Justice) as Prime Minister and First Vice-President. At presidential and legislative elections in Zanzibar, also held in October, Idris Abdul Wakil (formerly Speaker of the Zanzibar House of Representatives) was elected President of Zanzibar to replace Mwinyi; although the sole candidate, he received only 61% of the votes. Nyerere remained Chairman of the CCM.

In July 1986 Mwinyi declared an offensive against corruption and mismanagement within the CCM: in the following months several regional party officials and directors of parastatal bodies were dismissed or demoted, and in some cases expelled from the party. By late 1987 a division was apparent between 'conservative' socialists, who supported the CCM's traditional socialist ideology (as favoured by Nyerere), and 'pragmatists', who advocated a more liberal approach to government (as favoured by Mwinyi). It was thought that Nyerere's decision to accept renomination as Chairman of the CCM at this time reflected his desire to counter reformist influence in government: in October he was re-elected Chairman of the CCM. Nyerere resigned in August 1990, and Mwinyi was appointed Chairman of the CCM.

In early 1988 tension began to increase in Zanzibar, reflecting underlying rivalries between the inhabitants of the main island and those of the smaller island of Pemba, between Zanzibar's African and Arab populations, and between supporters and opponents of unity with Tanganyika. In January Wakil suspended the islands' Government, the Supreme Revolutionary Council, and assumed control of the armed forces from the office of his main rival, Chief Minister Seif Sharrif Hamad, following earlier claims by Wakil that a group of dissidents, including members of the Council, had been plotting the overthrow of his administration. When Wakil appointed a new Council later in that month, Hamad was among the five ministers dismissed. Dr Omar Ali Juma was appointed as the new Chief Minister. In May Hamad and six other officials were expelled from the CCM for allegedly opposing the party's aims and endangering Tanzanian unity.

In October 1990 concurrent parliamentary and presidential elections were held in Zanzibar. Wakil did not stand for re-election; the sole presidential candidate, Dr Salmin Amour, was elected as Wakil's successor by 97.7% of the votes cast. Amour subsequently reappointed Juma as Chief Minister of Zanzibar. At the end of October national parliamentary and presidential elections took place. Mwinyi, the sole candidate in the presidential election, was re-elected for a second term, taking 95.5% of the votes cast. In November Mwinyi replaced Warioba as Prime Minister with John Malecela, previously the Tanzanian High Commissioner to the United Kingdom. In December 1994 Mwinyi reorganized the Cabinet. Malecela was replaced as Prime Minister and First Vice-President by Cleopa Msuya, hitherto the

Minister of Industry and Trade and previously Prime Minister in 1980–83.

Meanwhile, in December 1991 a presidential commission published recommendations for the establishment of a multi-party political system. In February 1992 proposed constitutional amendments to this effect were ratified by a special congress of the CCM, which stipulated that, in order to protect national unity, all new political organizations should command support in both Zanzibar and mainland Tanzania, and should be free of tribal, religious and racial bias. In May the Constitutions of both the United Republic and Zanzibar were amended to enshrine a multi-party system. Several political organizations were officially registered from mid-1992. In December Zanzibar unilaterally joined the Organization of the Islamic Conference (OIC, see p. 340), thereby precipitating controversy regarding the future of the Tanzanian union. An ad hoc parliamentary commission concluded in February 1993 that Zanzibar's membership of the OIC contravened the Constitution of the United Republic. Zanzibar withdrew from the organization in August.

In October 1995 multi-party legislative elections were held for the first time, concurrently with presidential elections, both in Zanzibar and throughout the Tanzanian union. At elections on 22 October the CCM secured 26 of the 50 elective seats in the Zanzibari House of Representatives, while the Civic United Front (CUF, campaigning for increased Zanzibari autonomy) took 24 seats. Amour was re-elected President of the islands by 50.2% of the votes cast, only narrowly defeating Seif Sharrif Hamad (the former Zanzibari Chief Minister), who represented the CUF. Amour appointed a new ruling council, with Dr Mohamed Gharib Bilali, formerly a government official, as Chief Minister. The CUF contested the election results, accusing the Zanzibari authorities of electoral malpractice and refusing to recognize the legitimacy of the new Amour administration, while party delegates initially declined to take up their seats in the House of Representatives. The Tanzanian national elections, on 29 October, were disrupted by a combination of apparent organizational chaos and further allegations by opposition parties of electoral fraud. Administrative inefficiency led to the cancellation of the election results in seven constituencies in Dar es Salaam; these polls were repeated in mid-November. The opposition parties, alleging that the CCM was manipulating the voting process, refused to rerun, withdrew their candidates from the presidential election, and unsuccessfully petitioned the High Court to declare all results null and void. The Government proceeded to publish the results, whereby the CCM won 186 of the 232 elective seats in the National Assembly, the CUF 24, the National Convention for Reconstruction and Reform (NCCR—Mageuzi) 16, and Chama Cha Democrasia na Maendeleo (Chademas) and the United Democratic Party (UDP) three seats each. Benjamin Mkapa, hitherto Minister of Science, Technology and Higher Education, was deemed to have been elected President, winning 61.8% of the votes cast. Mrema, his closest rival, took 27.8% of the votes. President Mkapa was inaugurated in late November; Omar Ali Juma (hitherto Chief Minister of Zanzibar) was appointed Vice-President. Shortly afterwards Mkapa announced a new Cabinet, with Frederick Sumaye (formerly Minister of Agriculture) as Prime Minister.

In his election campaign Mkapa had promised a crusade against corruption in high public office, and in January 1996 he appointed a special presidential commission; in December the commission issued a report asserting that corruption was widespread in the public sector. At a special congress of the CCM in June, Mkapa was elected party Chairman. In September a parliamentary select committee investigating bribery allegations against the Minister of Finance, Simon Mbilinyi, published a report recommending that he be made accountable for having illegally granted tax exemptions. Mbilinyi subsequently resigned. Meanwhile, in October the former Minister of Home Affairs, Augustine Mrema, unexpectedly won a parliamentary by-election in a Dar es Salaam constituency for NCCR—Mageuzi, of which he had become Chairman following his dismissal from Government in 1995; although his campaign had focused on financial impropriety in government, Mrema had recently been accused of having presented false evidence to the parliamentary select committee on corruption in order to undermine the Government's credibility.

In May 1997 a faction of NCCR—Mageuzi attempted to remove Mrema from the party chairmanship, reportedly after he ordered an investigation into the disappearance of substantial party funds. In June the High Court banned a NCCR—Mageuzi special congress from taking place, apparently in order to prevent violent confrontation between the opposing factions. Following allegations that opposition members were frequently being harassed by the security forces, reports emerged in August that some opposition groupings had formed their own militias.

In February 1996 the Zanzibari Government banned demonstrations by the CUF in southern Pemba; allegations persisted that numerous human rights abuses were being perpetrated by the authorities against supporters of the CUF. During 1996 external donors began to suspend aid disbursements to Zanzibar in view of the continuing political deadlock between the CUF and the islands' administration. There were signs of a rapprochement in January 1997, when representatives of the mainland branch of the CUF reportedly agreed to accept the legitimacy of the Amour Government. During December 1997 and early January 1998, however, 17 members of the CUF, including some delegates to the House of Representatives, were arrested on suspicion of conspiring to overthrow the Amour Government. From January CUF members refused to attend sessions of the House of Representatives in protest; consequently, in February all CUF deputies were officially suspended from the House for 10 days as a punitive measure. During January the Secretary-General of the Commonwealth, Chief Emeka Anyaoku, visited Zanzibar and presented proposals for a peaceful solution to the dispute, including a cessation of confrontational statements, the removal of restrictions on party political activity and a return to the House of Representatives by CUF delegates. Both the CUF and the Zanzibari section of the CCM contained elements that were strongly opposed to negotiating a compromise. Chief Anyaoku subsequently appointed a special envoy, Dr Moses Anafu, to continue mediation efforts, and in early May the UN Secretary-General, Kofi Annan, declared the full support of his organization for the Commonwealth's initiative. During that month a member of a CUF delegation that had been negotiating with Dr Anafu was arrested on suspicion of treason. Treason charges against the 18 CUF members who had been detained in 1997 and 1998 were finally presented in February 1999. The Zanzibari CCM came under considerable pressure from senior mainland CCM officials to reach an agreement with the CUF, while that party's leadership eventually resigned itself to accepting Amour's tenure of the presidency until the end of his term of office in 2000; a mutual accord was finally concluded in June 1999. In January 2000 45 deputies of the mainland CCM were reported to have petitioned the Zanzibari President to withdraw the charges against the 18 CUF members being tried for treason. By that time the court proceedings had already been adjourned several times, and two days prior to the deputies' appeal the Zanzibari Attorney-General had been dismissed after he had ordered the arrest of two more leading members of the CUF. Nevertheless, in February President Amour declared that the trial would not be abandoned. (The charges were dropped in November by Amani Abeid Karume following his election as President of Zanzibar—see below.) Later in February the National Executive Committee of the CCM rejected a proposal to amend the Zanzibari Constitution in order to allow President Amour to serve a third term of office.

In August 1998 a car bomb exploded outside the US embassy in Dar es Salaam (concurrently with a similar attack at the US mission in Nairobi, Kenya); 11 people were killed in Dar es Salaam and some 75 were injured. The attacks were believed to have been co-ordinated by international Islamist terrorists led by a Saudi-born dissident, Osama bin Laden, and the USA retaliated by launching air-strikes against targets in Afghanistan and Sudan. In the aftermath of the bomb attacks, Tanzanian investigators and US federal agents made extensive nationwide inquiries. Four men were convicted of involvement in the bombings by a court in New York, USA, in May 2001 and were later sentenced to life imprisonment.

A committee was appointed by the Government in July 1998 to assess public opinion on constitutional reform. In September Mkapa reorganized the Cabinet, following the nullification of the election to the National Assembly, in 1995, of two ministers and the resignation in August of the Minister of State in the President's Office, Hassy Kitine, who was alleged to have used state funds to finance medical treatment abroad for his wife. In April 1999 Mrema and his faction of NCCR—Mageuzi defected to the Tanzania Labour Party (TLP). Mrema initially assumed the chairmanship of the TLP, but in May he was banned by the High Court from holding any official post in that party. There was speculation that the death in October of former President Nyerere might give rise to increased pressure for a restructuring of the United Republic of Tanzania. This was, to some extent,

TANZANIA

reinforced by the release in December of the report of the committee charged with assessing public opinion on constitutional reform. While it found that some 96.25% of Zanzibaris and 84.97% of mainland Tanzanians favoured a 'two-tier' government for the United Republic, the committee itself recommended the establishment of a 'three-tier' system. In so doing it was adjudged by President Mkapa to have exceeded its mandate. In February 2000 the National Assembly approved draft legislation to amend the Constitution in accordance with citizens' recommendations as reported by the committee. Among these recommendations was one that the President should henceforth be elected by a majority vote.

At a presidential election held on 29 October 2000 Benjamin Mkapa was re-elected as President, securing 71.7% of votes cast; Prof. Ibrahim Lipumba, the Chairman of the CUF, won 16.3% of the votes cast, Augustine Mrema 7.8% and John Cheyo 4.2%. The participation rate was 84%. The CUF, Chadema and the UDP had initially planned to field joint candidates, but in July a judge ruled that the Constitution forbade the presidential running-mate from being drawn from a different party to the presidential candidate. In the following month the CUF and Chadema agreed to form a five-year alliance and field joint candidates for the presidential elections in both the United Republic of Tanzania and in Zanzibar. It was agreed that if either candidate (both from the CUF) won, the respective prime minister would be drawn from Chadema. Candidates from the TLP and NCCR—Mageuzi failed to secure the minimum 200 referees and thus were not allowed to stand for election. At legislative elections, held concurrently, the CCM secured 244 seats in the National Assembly. The largest opposition group to obtain representation was the CUF, with 15 seats; the three other opposition parties (Chadema, the TLP and the UDP) won four, three and two seats, respectively. The polls were declared by international observers to have been freely and fairly conducted. In November Mkapa appointed a new Cabinet, reappointing Frederick Sumaye as Prime Minister.

In marked contrast, presidential and legislative elections were also held in Zanzibar and Pemba on 29 October 2000, amid widespread accusations of electoral fraud. Voting in 16 of the islands' 50 constituencies was annulled owing to a lack of ballot papers and voter registration lists. The Zanzibar Electoral Commission (ZEC) announced that new polls would be held in the 16 constituencies (all areas where the CUF enjoyed strong support), and that counting for the presidential elections for both Zanzibar and the United Republic would be delayed until the new results were received. Opposition parties and Commonwealth electoral observers called for a full rerun of the elections, but this was rejected by the ZEC. Following a week of confusion and violent clashes between the police and opposition supporters, the repeated polls were held on 5 November. Accusations of electoral fraud persisted, and the participation rate was reported to be low. Following the poll, the CCM claimed that it had won 67% of the votes cast (thereby winning 34 seats in the House of Representatives). The CUF refused to recognize the results of the ballot. Despite the concerns of the opposition parties and international observers, the ZEC proclaimed Amani Abeid Karume of the CCM as President of Zanzibar. The CUF refused to recognize Karume as President and demanded that a repeat election be held within four months. During Karume's subsequent appointment of a new Government, popular unrest and a series of bomb attacks occurred throughout the islands. In January 2001 police in Zanzibar and Pemba recovered 112 explosive devices and arrested 59 people in connection with the bomb attacks. In September John Tendwa, the Registrar of Political Parties, announced that he would investigate the results of the elections to ascertain whether electoral rules had been adhered to properly, and that he would consider whether a change of electoral legislation was necessary.

Meanwhile, throughout late 2000 and January 2001 there were, often violent, opposition demonstrations calling for new elections. In late January clashes between the police and opposition supporters left an estimated 37 people dead (including one police-officer and five other members of the security forces) and 100 people injured; more than 400 protesters were arrested and imprisoned.

In February 2001 two prominent CUF leaders, including the Deputy Secretary-General, were arrested and charged with the murder of a police-officer during the January demonstrations; the human rights organization Amnesty International criticized the charges as politically motivated. One of Karume's first acts as President had been to withdraw treason charges that the two, along with 16 other CUF members, had been facing since 1997

(see above). The Tanzania Court of Appeal had subsequently ruled that treason was not possible in Zanzibar because the isles were not a sovereign state. In November 2001 the 18 CUF members brought legal actions against the National Chief of Police, the Zanzibari Police Commissioner and the Zanzibari Attorney-General. The 18 were seeking damages for income lost and fees incurred during their three-year imprisonment, as well as for losing the chance to contend the 2000 elections.

In April 2001 an estimated 60,000 supporters of 12 opposition parties gathered peacefully in Dar es Salaam to demand that the Government hold fresh elections in Zanzibar, draft a new Constitution for the United Republic and establish independent electoral commissions. A similar, peaceful demonstration in Zanzibar later that month was attended by an estimated 60,000–85,000 protesters. President Karume, however, continued to reject the opposition's demands. In May 11 members of the Zanzibar House of Representatives and five members of the National Assembly were dismissed from their respective legislatures for having boycotted three successive sittings—their actions were part of the CUF's ongoing refusal to recognize the 2000 election results. The Attorney-General rejected subsequent demands from the CUF for their reinstatement. By-elections were held on 15 May 2003, at which the CUF won every seat it contested (amounting to 15 in the National Assembly and 11 in the Zanzibar House of Representatives). CUF candidates were disqualified from contesting six seats in the House of Representatives; these were won by CCM candidates.

At the beginning of July 2001 a week of official mourning was announced to mark the death of Vice-President Omar Ali Juma; his successor, Dr Ali Mohamed Sheni, was sworn in later that month.

In June 2001 it emerged that, following the violence of the 2000 elections, the CCM and the CUF had been holding a series of secret negotiations intended to resolve the political impasse in Zanzibar. The negotiations concluded with the signing of a *muafaka* (peace accord) between the two parties in Zanzibar in October 2001. Shortly afterwards the State withdrew all 109 legal cases related to the January demonstrations, including the murder charges against the two CUF leaders.

In accordance with the CCM-CUF accord signed in October 2001, amendments to the Zanzibari Constitution were approved by the House of Representatives in April 2002. The amendments provided for the restructuring of the electoral commission to include opposition representatives (duly appointed in October 2002), the creation of a permanent voters' register and the removal of legislation requiring a person to live in a particular area for five consecutive years in order to qualify as a voter. Also included were the introduction of the right to appeal against High Court decisions and the appointment of a separate director of public prosecutions for Zanzibar.

President Mkapa was re-elected Chairman of the CCM at the party's general convention, which was held in October 2002. Later that year 11 Tanzanian opposition parties (including Chadema, NCCR—Mageuzi and the CUF) agreed in principle to field a joint candidate to contest the 2005 presidential election; the proposal remained subject to approval by the parties' members. However, in July 2003 the CUF declared that it would not join the coalition, following its strong performance at May by-elections (see above).

In late 2003 and early 2004 political tension in Zanzibar intensified ahead of the elections due in late 2005. Supporters of the CUF were keen to avoid a repetition of the irregularities that had marred the elections of 1995 and 2000. Zanzibaris were reportedly particularly anxious as, according to the prevailing custom of the United Republic, they were to elect the next President. However, following remarks from President Mkapa that this custom was not guaranteed by law, many Zanzibaris feared that they were becoming marginalized. In November 2003 the CUF Chairman, Lipumba, threatened to obtain a court injunction blocking the 2005 elections unless the register of voters was completed in time, and in April 2004 the leader of the Democratic Party made a similar threat, stating his intention to sue the National Electoral Commission (NEC) and the ZEC unless both bodies were reformed to include members of parties other than the CCM and the CUF. Opposition supporters were also concerned that the Government's efforts to encourage mainlanders who had been living in Zanzibar for more than 10 years to register for Zanzibari citizenship (thus making them eligible to vote in Zanzibar) constituted an attempt to manipulate voter registration in favour of the CCM. The Government, in contrast, deplored the circulation of leaflets throughout

TANZANIA

Zanzibar urging mainlanders to leave and alleged intimidation of mainlanders.

In early 2004 Islamism appeared to be exerting an increasing influence on politics in Zanzibar. Members of religious groups from Pakistan and Afghanistan were reported to have entered Zanzibar in March 2003 and begun spreading 'seditious teachings'. Moderate Zanzibari Muslim leaders expressed concern about rising extremism, and in March 2004 the island's Mufti, Sheikh Harith bin Kalef, denounced a radical Islamic group, the Zanzibar Union for Awakening and Islamic Forums Community (also known as Uamsho), as a political organization that used religion to disguise its efforts to destabilize Zanzibar. Police banned a demonstration by Uamsho, which insisted that the Mufti should be elected by Muslims rather than appointed by the Government and, it was claimed, advocated killing secular leaders who refused to impose Islamic law in Zanzibar. The demonstration proceeded, none the less, becoming violent when protesters threw stones at the police, who retaliated by using tear gas to disperse the demonstrators. A series of bomb attacks followed, targeting Zanzibari power-stations, schools, and other government and private property. On one occasion, in late March, two bombs exploded in Stone Town, outside the residences of the Mufti and the Minister of Communications and Transport, Zubeir Ali Maulid, while a third bomb was defused in a bar; there were no casualties. A number of Uamsho leaders were subsequently arrested in connection with the bombings. In April legislation was passed outlawing homosexuality. Uamsho welcomed the legislation, which enjoyed rare, cross-party support in the House of Representatives. Meanwhile, there were reports of attacks on women deemed to be dressed inappropriately.

In early 2004 the Supreme Revolutionary Council stated that from 2005 Zanzibar was to fly its own, separate flag at its interests abroad rather than that of the United Republic of Tanzania. All of Zanzibar's national symbols had been abolished on 26 April 1964 when it entered into its union with Tanganyika. However, a separate Zanzibari flag was enshrined in the island's Constitution of 1985, and had been used within Zanzibar for some time.

It was reported in February 2004 that the Government was to prepare, for the first time in 10 years, a supplementary budget, in order to cover additional costs associated with the 2005 elections (including the introduction of identity cards and the establishment of a permanent register of voters), as well as to counteract the effects of drought. In August, amid growing tension in Zanzibar, the CUF petitioned the UN to dispatch observers to the 2005 elections. The CUF noted that a permanent voters' register had yet to be established, and that the reformed ZEC still lacked a director. Moreover, the Joint Presidential Supervisory Commission (JPSC), established to implement the 2001 *muafaka*, was being investigated following allegations of embezzlement. The JPSC was partly funded by international donors, who suspended their contributions following the allegations.

In February 2005 Lipumba declared his candidacy for the presidential election, at which he would represent the CUF. The CCM elected Jakaya Mrisho Kikwete as its presidential candidate at its national party congress in May. (Under the terms of the Constitution, Mkapa was prohibited from standing for re-election to the presidency.) There were sporadic outbreaks of civil unrest on Zanzibar during the voter registration period, where new legislation requiring voters to have lived in their constituencies for at least three years resulted in some 32,000 potential voters being disqualified. Hamad, the CUF's presidential candidate in Zanzibar, had initially been barred from registering (which would have disqualified him from standing in election) but appealed successfully against the decision. Campaigning was calm on the mainland. In August 12 of the 18 parties contesting the legislative election signed a code of conduct with the NEC that encouraged candidates to speak only in Swahili while campaigning, in order to avoid escalating ethnic tensions by using other languages. Campaigning in Zanzibar was marred by violence as opposition supporters clashed with the police on numerous occasions.

Following the death of a candidate, it was announced in October 2005 that the elections on the mainland would be delayed until December. The elections in Zanzibar proceeded as scheduled on 30 October 2005 at which Karume was elected President securing 53.2% of the valid votes cast; Hamad received 46.1% and the four other candidates who contested the presidential election received negligible support. In the legislative elections the CCM won 31 seats in the House of Representatives, and the CUF 18. The ballot in the one remaining constituency was rerun on 14 December, although the result was not made available. The ZEC declared the poll to have been free and fair, while Commonwealth observers generally agreed but recommended investigations into violence and irregularities in voting in Stone Town. There were reports of sporadic violence and numerous unsubstantiated claims of fraud. However, the extreme violence of previous elections was avoided; 30,000 security personnel had been deployed to keep the peace. Karume was sworn in as President of Zanzibar on 2 November.

On mainland Tanzania the delayed presidential and legislative elections were held concurrently on 14 December 2005. Turn-out was officially recorded at 72% and voting proceeded without notable incident. Kikwete was elected President with 80.3% of the votes cast, while Lipumba received 11.7%. The CCM won 207 seats in the National Assembly, the CUF 18, Chadema five and the TLP and UDP one seat each. The CCM received a further 59 of the 75 seats reserved for women (of the remainder the CUF received 10 and Chadema six) and six of the 10 seats reserved for presidential nominees (four remained vacant). Of the five representatives sent from the Zanzibari legislature, three were from the CCM and two from the CUF. The Attorney-General was also a CCM member. Thus, the CCM's final strength in the National Assembly came to 276 seats and the CUF's 30; Chadema secured 11 seats and the TLP and UDP one each. At his inauguration, on 21 December, Kikwete stated that his main priority as President would be to resolve the tensions on Zanzibar, while he also pledged to continue Mkapa's free-market economic policies. On 4 January 2006 Kikwete unveiled his new Cabinet; Sheni was retained as Vice-President, while Edward Lowassa, hitherto the Minister of Water Livestock and Development, was appointed Prime Minister.

Tanzania's relations with Uganda and Kenya were strained throughout the 1970s, particularly after the dissolution of the East African Community (EAC, see p. 385) in 1977. Uganda briefly annexed the Kagera salient from Tanzania in November 1978. In early 1979 Tanzanian troops supported the Uganda National Liberation Front in the overthrow of President Idi Amin Dada. In June 2000 Tanzania called on Uganda to pay 98,500m. shillings to cover the cost of the operation. President Mkapa later stated that the amount was to be regarded as a military debt and not, as some claimed, as compensation for those killed during the war. The Tanzania–Kenya border, closed since 1977, was reopened in November 1983, following an agreement on the distribution of the EAC's assets and liabilities. In the following month Tanzania and Kenya agreed to establish full diplomatic relations. The two countries reached agreement on a trade treaty and on the establishment of a joint co-operation commission in 1986. Tanzania pledged its support for the Government of Yoweri Museveni, which took power in Uganda in January of that year, and in November Tanzania began to send military instructors to Uganda to organize the training of Ugandan government troops. In November 1991 the Presidents of Tanzania, Kenya and Uganda met in Nairobi, Kenya, and declared their commitment to developing mutual co-operation. In November 1994, meeting in Arusha, the three leaders established a commission for co-operation; in March 1996 they met again in Nairobi to inaugurate formally the Secretariat of the Permanent Tripartite Commission for East African Co-operation, which aimed to revive the EAC. A treaty for the re-establishment of the EAC, providing for the creation of a free trade area (with the eventual introduction of a single currency), for the development of infrastructure, tourism and agriculture within the Community, and for the establishment of a regional legislative assembly and court, was formally ratified by the Tanzanian, Kenyan and Ugandan Heads of State in November 1999. The new East African Council of Ministers held its first meeting in Tanzania in January 2001. Talks on integrating the economies of the three EAC members followed, and in March 2004 Mkapa, Museveni, and President Mwai Kibaki of Kenya signed a protocol on the creation of a customs union, eliminating most duties on good within the EAC, which came into force on 1 January 2005.

In August 1993, following a protracted mediation effort by the Mwinyi Government, a peace agreement was signed in Arusha by the Rwandan authorities and the rebel Front patriotique rwandais. In April 1994, however, following the assassination of the Rwandan President, Juvénal Habyarimana, hundreds of thousands of Rwandans fled to Tanzania to escape the atrocities being perpetrated in their homeland: in one 24-hour period in late April some 250,000 refugees were reported to have crossed the Rwanda–Tanzania border. In May the Tanzanian authorities appealed for international emergency aid to assist in the care of the refugees, many of whom were sheltering in makeshift camps in the border region. In March 1995 Tanzania banned the admission of further refugees from both Rwanda and Burundi (where violent unrest had erupted in late 1994); some 800,000 Rwandan and Burundian refugees were reportedly sheltering in Tanzania in September 1995. The International Criminal Tribunal for Rwanda, authorized by the UN to charge and try Rwandan nationals accused of direct involvement in the genocide perpetrated in that country during 1994, was inaugurated in June 1995 in Arusha. After the Tutsi-led military coup, which took place in Burundi in July 1996 (following the failure of peace talks mediated by former President Nyerere), the Mkapa administration imposed economic sanctions against the new regime of President Pierre Buyoya, in co-operation with other regional governments. Relations between Tanzania and Burundi remained strained, owing both to the presence of Burundian rebels in northern Tanzania, which the Buyoya regime accused the Mkapa administration of supporting, and to the increasing numbers of Burundians seeking refuge in Tanzania throughout 1996 and 1997. Talks between the Buyoya Government and opposition politicians, once again mediated by Nyerere, were convened in Arusha, Tanzania, in 1998 and early 1999. The regional economic sanctions that were imposed against Burundi in 1996 were suspended in January 1999. In July 2002, following a meeting between President Mkapa and the Burundian Vice-President, Domitien Ndayizeye, the two countries stated that they were to normalize their relations. Peace negotiations between the Burundian transitional Government and rebel groups took place in Dar es Salaam in August and October of that year.

In December 1996 some of the Rwandan refugees remaining in Tanzania were repatriated, following the threat of forcible repatriation by the Tanzanian Government; however, 200,000 refugees, unwilling to return to Rwanda, reportedly fled their camps. In March 1997 the Tanzanian Government appealed for further international assistance in coping with the remaining refugees (an estimated 200,000 Burundians and 250,000 Zaireans). In June 1997 it was agreed to repatriate some 100,000 refugees to the Democratic Republic of the Congo (DRC—formerly Zaire). At the end of December the office of the UN High Commissioner for Refugees (UNHCR) estimated that some 74,300 refugees from the DRC remained in Tanzania, while the number of Burundian refugees was believed to have increased to 459,400.

In February 2000 the Government announced that nine refugee camps in the Kigoma region of west Tanzania had become saturated. Instability in Burundi and the DRC had recently led to further heavy influxes of refugees from those countries. At that time the number of officially registered refugees in west Tanzania reportedly totalled 468,000, but it was claimed that an additional 200,000 unregistered refugees were also present in the region. Burundians accounted for 70% of all refugees, and refugees from the DRC for 29%. In August 2000 a peace accord was signed in Arusha between the Burundian Government and various rebel groups; however, the main rebel groups refused to sign the agreement. Although the agreement neither stopped the fighting in Burundi, nor allowed the refugees to return home, it nevertheless resulted in a serious decline in the level of aid donations (for example, the UNHCR allocation for refugee camps in Tanzania was reduced by 55%). In May 2001 UNHCR and the Governments of Tanzania and Burundi signed an agreement to establish a tripartite commission for the voluntary repatriation of Burundian refugees in Tanzania, of whom there were an estimated 800,000 at that time. In August 2003 Burundi and Tanzania agreed to open additional border crossings to facilitate the return of refugees. An estimated 494,200 Burundian refugees remained in Tanzania in December of that year; by April 2004 a further 34,000 had returned to Burundi, and UNHCR aimed to repatriate a further 122,000 by the end of the year, in view of progress in the peace process and the improved security situation. In February 2004 the remaining Rwandan refugees in Tanzanian camps were repatriated. However, it was reported that an estimated 20,000 Rwandans were illegally resident in Tanzania at this time. At the end of 2003 there were some 150,160 refugees from the DRC in Tanzania.

Government

Under the provisions of the 1977 Constitution, with subsequent amendments, legislative power is held by the unicameral National Assembly, whose members serve for a term of five years. There is constitutional provision for both directly elected members (chosen by universal suffrage) and nominated members (including five members elected by and from the Zanzibar House of Representatives). The number of directly elected members exceeds the number of nominated members. The Electoral Commission may review and, if necessary, increase the number of constituencies before every general election. Executive power lies with the President, elected by popular vote for five years. The President must be at least 40 years of age and his mandate is limited to a maximum of two five-year terms. The President appoints a Vice-President, to assist him in carrying out his functions, and presides over the Cabinet, which is composed of a Prime Minister and other ministers who are appointed from among the members of the National Assembly.

Zanzibar has its own administration for internal affairs, and the amended Zanzibar Constitution, which came into force in January 1985, provides for the President, elected by universal adult suffrage, to hold office for a maximum of two five-year terms, and for the House of Representatives, of 45–55 members, to be directly elected by universal adult suffrage. The President of Zanzibar appoints the Chief Minister, and the two co-operate in choosing the other members of the Supreme Revolutionary Council, which has a maximum of 20 members.

In May 1992 the United Republic's Constitution was amended to legalize a multi-party political system.

Defence

In August 2005 the total active armed forces numbered an estimated 27,000, of whom about 23,000 were in the army, 1,000 in the navy and 3,000 in the air force. There are also paramilitary forces including a 1,400-strong Police Field Force and an 80,000-strong reservist Citizens' Militia. The estimated defence budget was 401,000m. shillings in 2004.

Economic Affairs

In 2004, according to estimates by the World Bank, mainland Tanzania's gross national income (GNI), measured at average 2002–04 prices, was US $11,561m., equivalent to $330 per head (or $660 per head on an international purchasing-power parity basis). During 1995–2004, it was estimated, the population of the country as a whole increased at an average annual rate of 2.4%, while gross domestic product (GDP) per head increased, in real terms, by an average of 2.8% per year. Overall GDP increased, in real terms, at an average annual rate of 5.2% in 1995–2004; growth was 6.3% in 2004.

Agriculture (including hunting, forestry and fishing) contributed an estimated 35.1% of GDP in 2003, and, according to FAO estimates, employed some 79.1% of the labour force in that year. The principal cash crops are cashew nuts (which provided an estimated 4.1% of export revenues in 2003/04), coffee (3.8%), cotton (3.4%) and cloves (Zanzibar's most important export, cultivated on the island of Pemba—they provided 0.9% of export revenues in 2003/04). Other cash crops include tobacco, tea, sisal, pyrethrum, coconuts, sugar and cardamom. Exports of cut flowers (grown in the vicinity of Kilimanjaro Airport and freighted to Europe) commenced in the mid-1990s. Seaweed production is an important activity in Zanzibar. Farmers have been encouraged to produce essential food crops, most importantly cassava and maize. Cattle-rearing is also significant. A large proportion of agricultural output is produced by subsistence farmers. Tanzania's agricultural GDP increased at an average annual rate of 4.0% during 1995–2004, according to the World Bank; agricultural GDP increased by 5.5% in 2004.

Industry (including mining, manufacturing, construction and power) contributed an estimated 21.2% of GDP in 2003; the sector employed 2.6% of the working population in 2001. During 1995–2004 industrial GDP increased by an average of 7.9% per year, according to the World Bank; growth in 2004 was 8.0%.

Mining provided an estimated 2.7% of GDP in 2003. The sector employed 0.2 of the working population on mainland Tanganyika in 2001. Gold, diamonds, other gemstones (including rubies and sapphires), salt, phosphates, coal, gypsum, tin, kaolin, limestone and graphite are mined, and it is planned to exploit reserves of natural gas. Other mineral deposits include nickel, silver, cobalt, copper, soda ash, iron ore and uranium. In late 2003 three companies were bidding for licences to explore for petroleum in the Rufiji delta, Zanzibar, Mafia and the Mkuranga district on the mainland coast. Petroleum was discovered on Tanzania's coastal belt in the 1960s, but was only recently being considered seriously by companies searching for sources of petroleum outside the Middle East. In January 2004 it was announced that a Canadian company, the Barrick Gold Corporation, was to construct a new 526,000-oz gold mine in Tulawaka.

According to the IMF, the GDP of the mining sector increased by an average of 12.9% per year in 1990–99; it grew by 9.1% in 1999.

Manufacturing contributed an estimated 9.9% of GDP in 2003. The sector employed 1.5% of the working population on mainland Tanganyika in 2001. The most important manufacturing activities are food-processing, textile production, cigarette production and brewing. Pulp and paper, fertilizers, cement, clothing, footwear, tyres, batteries, pharmaceuticals, paint, bricks and tiles and electrical goods are also produced, while other activities include oil-refining, metal-working, vehicle assembly and engineering. Tanzania's manufacturing GDP increased at an average annual rate of 6.2% in 1995–2004, according to the World Bank; it grew by 8.0% in 2004.

Energy is derived principally from hydroelectric power, which supplied 91.4% of Tanzania's electricity in 2002; the remainder was supplied by petroleum (5.1%) and coal (3.5%). Imports of petroleum and petroleum products accounted for an estimated 18.6% of the total value of imports in 2003.

The services sector contributed 43.7% of GDP in 2003; the sector employed 15.3% of the working population on mainland Tanganyika in 2001. Tourism is an important potential growth sector: tourism receipts were approximately US $450m. in 2003 (excluding passenger transport). According to the World Bank, the GDP of the services sector increased by an average of 5.1% per year in 1995–2004. Growth in the sector was 6.4% in 2004.

In 2004 Tanzania recorded a visible trade deficit of US $906.0m., and there was a deficit of $437.1m. on the current account of the balance of payments. In 2003 the principal sources of imports were South Africa (providing 14.1% of total imports), Japan (7.8%), India (7.7%) and the People's Republic of China (5.8%—including Hong Kong). The main markets for exports were the United Kingdom (taking 33.9% of total exports), Japan (7.8%), Kenya (7.0%) and India (6.2%). The European Union (EU, see p. 228) was an important trading partner, taking 56.7% of total exports in 2003 and supplying 19.7% of imports. The principal exports in 2003 were gold, fish and fish products, manufactured goods and tobacco. The principal imports were machinery, petroleum, transport equipment and raw materials for industry.

In the financial year ending 30 June 2004 there was a budgetary deficit of 1,084,200m. shillings. At the end of 2003 Tanzania's external debt totalled US $7,516m., of which $6,248m. was long-term public debt. In that year the cost of debt-servicing was equivalent to 5.1% of the value of exports of goods and services. On 14 January 2005 the British Chancellor of the Exchequer, Gordon Brown, signed a memorandum of understanding with the Government under which the United Kingdom would service 10% of the debt (both interest and capital repayments) owed by Tanzania to the World Bank, IMF and African Bank for Reconstruction. It was part of a wider move to ease the debt burden of heavily indebted poor countries, and it was hoped his move would persuade other rich nations to act similarly. However, the United Kingdom would cease to service Tanzanian debt if the Tanzanian Government breached undertakings on good governance and democracy. The annual rate of inflation for Tanganyika averaged 7.6% in 1995–2004; consumer prices there increased by 4.7% in 2004. The annual rate on inflation for Zanzibar averaged 6.0% in 1995–2003; consumer prices on the islands increased by 9.5% in 2003.

Tanzania is a member of the African Development Bank (see p. 151) and of the Southern African Development Community (see p. 358). Tanzania is a founder member (with Kenya and Uganda) of the restored East African Community (EAC, see p. 385).

In the past Tanzania faced falling incomes and the collapse of its agricultural exports and much of its manufacturing sector. Yet by the mid-2000s Tanzania had transformed into one of Africa's better-performing economies. Since 1996 real GDP growth has averaged 4.75% a year, of which agriculture and services (mostly trade, tourism and hotels) each accounted for about one-third. Tourism has been particularly successful: between 1990 and 2003 the number of tourist arrivals almost quadrupled, from 150,000 to 576,000, and receipts rose sevenfold, reaching US $450m. This was accompanied by strong productivity growth. Total factor productivity was negative in the early 1990s yet rose to replace increased employment as the main motor of GDP growth since 1997, largely as a result of economic reforms implemented by the Government during the 1990s and the impact of increased foreign investment on technology and efficiency. Increased government spending, partly funded by increased foreign aid, also contributed to more rapid growth. However, this economic improvement was accompanied by only a modest reduction in poverty. In terms of GNI per head, Tanzania is one of the world's poorest countries. One of the country's greatest economic problems is the very high level of its external debt. In September 1999 Tanzania was admitted to the World Bank's initiative for heavily indebted poor countries, thereby qualifying for concessionary debt relief. The IMF approved two three-year loans in 2000 and 2003 equivalent to some $208.5m. for Tanzania, under its Poverty Reduction and Growth Facility (PRGF), and in November 2001 the country was granted enhanced debt relief, effectively halving its external debt. However, there was concern about Tanzania's continued dependence on foreign aid. The new President, Jakaya Kikwete, stated that he would continue the free-market policies of his predecessor, Mkapa. Thus, it seemed likely that Tanzania's strong economic performance and good relations with donors would continue. However, there was a risk that drought or adverse commodity prices could depress growth. Daytime power cuts were introduced in February 2006 following a decline in hydroelectric production owing to drought. The power rationing was to last until a 60-MW gas turbine was installed at Ubungo power station in mid-March. It was also possible that increased government spending on education and training to counteract a lack of skills in the labour force could prove insufficient, and it was feared that HIV/AIDS could constrain productivity improvements.

Education

In 2004/05 enrolment at pre-pimary level was 23% (23% of both boys and girls). Education at primary level is officially compulsory and is provided free of charge. In secondary schools a government-stipulated fee is paid: from January 1995 this was 8,000 shillings per year for day pupils at state-owned schools and 50,000–60,000 shillings per year for day pupils at private schools. Villages and districts are encouraged to construct their own schools with government assistance. Almost all primary schools are government-owned. Primary education begins at seven years of age and lasts for seven years. In 2004/05 enrolment at primary level was 82% (83% of boys; 81% of girls). Secondary education, beginning at the age of 14, lasts for a further six years, comprising a first cycle of four years and a second of two years. Secondary enrolment in 1999/2000 included only 6% of children in the appropriate age-group (males 6%; females 5%), according to UNESCO estimates. In November 2001 it was announced that approximately 7m. children were to be enrolled in primary schools, under the Government's five-year plan to reintroduce universal primary education by 2005. Enrolment at tertiary level was included just 1% of those in the relevant age-group in 2004/05 (males 2%; females 1%). There is a university at Dar es Salaam. Tanzania also has an agricultural university at Morogoro, and a number of vocational training centres and technical colleges. Education was allocated 23% of total recurrent budgetary expenditure by the central Government in 1994.

Public Holidays

2006: 1 January (New Year's Day), 10 January*† (Id El Haji, Feast of the Sacrifice), 12 January (Zanzibar Revolution Day), 31 January* (Muharram, New Year), 5 February (Chama Cha Mapinduzi Day), 10 April* (Maulid, Birth of the Prophet), 14–17 April (Easter), 26 April (Union Day), 1 May (International Labour Day), 7 July (Saba Saba, Industry's Day), 8 August (Peasants' Day), 26 August (Sultan's Birthday)‡, 23 October* (Id El Fitr, end of Ramadan), 29 October (Naming Day), 9 December (Independence Day), 25–26 December (Christmas), 31 December*† (Id El Haji, Feast of the Sacrifice).

2007: 1 January (New Year's Day), 12 January (Zanzibar Revolution Day), 20 January* (Muharram, New Year), 5 February (Chama Cha Mapinduzi Day), 31 March* (Maulid, Birth of the Prophet), 6–9 April (Easter), 26 April (Union Day), 1 May (International Labour Day), 7 July (Saba Saba, Industry's Day), 8 August (Peasants' Day), 26 August (Sultan's Birthday)‡, 13 October* (Id El Fitr, end of Ramadan), 29 October (Naming Day), 9 December (Independence Day), 20 December* (Id El Haji, Feast of the Sacrifice), 25–26 December (Christmas).

* These holidays are dependent on the Islamic lunar calendar and may vary by one or two days from the dates given.

† This festival occurs twice (in the Islamic years AH 1426 and 1427) within the same Gregorian year.

‡ Zanzibar only.

Weights and Measures

The metric system is in force.

TANZANIA

Statistical Survey

Source (unless otherwise stated): Economic and Research Policy Dept, Bank of Tanzania, POB 2939, Dar es Salaam; tel. (22) 2110946; fax (22) 2113325; e-mail info@hq.bot-tz.org; internet www.bot-tz.org.

Area and Population

AREA, POPULATION AND DENSITY

Area (sq km)	945,087*
Population (census results)	
28 August 1988	23,126,310
25 August 2002	
Males	16,910,321
Females	17,658,911
Total	34,569,232
Population (UN estimates at mid-year)†	
2003	36,919,000
2004	37,627,000
Density (per sq km) at mid-2004	39.8

* 364,900 sq miles. Of this total, Tanzania mainland is 942,626 sq km (363,950 sq miles), and Zanzibar 2,461 sq km (950 sq miles).
† Source: UN, *World Population Prospects: The 2004 Revision*.

ETHNIC GROUPS
(private households, census of 26 August 1967)

African	11,481,595	Others	839
Asian	75,015	Not stated	159,042
Arabs	29,775	**Total**	11,763,150
European	16,884		

REGIONS
(at census of 25 August 2002)

Arusha	1,292,973	Mwanza	2,942,148
Dar es Salaam	2,497,940	Pwani	889,154
Dodoma	1,698,996	North Pemba†	186,013
Iringa	1,495,333	North Unguja†	136,953
Kagera	2,033,888	Rukwa	1,141,743
Kigoma	1,679,109	Ruvuma	1,117,166
Kilimanjaro	1,381,149	Shinyanga	2,805,580
Lindi	791,306	Singida	1,090,758
Manyara*	603,691	South Pemba†	176,153
Mara	1,368,602	South Unguja†	94,504
Mbeya	2,070,046	Urban West†	391,002
Morogoro	1,759,809	Tabora	1,717,908
Mtwara	1,128,523	Tanga	1,642,015

* Before the 2002 census Manyara was included in the region of Arusha.
† Part of the autonomous territory of Zanzibar.

PRINCIPAL TOWNS
(estimated population at mid-1988)

Dar es Salaam	1,360,850	Mbeya	152,844
Mwanza	223,013	Arusha	134,708
Dodoma	203,833	Morogoro	117,760
Tanga	187,455	Shinyanga	100,724
Zanzibar	157,634		

Source: UN, *Demographic Yearbook*.

BIRTHS AND DEATHS
(UN estimates, annual averages)

	1990–1995	1995–2000	2000–05
Birth rate (per 1,000)	42.4	40.2	38.1
Death rate (per 1,000)	13.7	15.6	16.7

Source: UN, *World Population Prospects: The 2004 Revision*.

Expectation of life (WHO estimates, years at birth): 45 (males 44; females 46) in 2003 (Source: WHO, *World Health Report*).

ECONOMICALLY ACTIVE POPULATION
(Mainland Tanganyika only, persons aged 10 years and over, at March 2001)

	Males	Females	Total
Agriculture, forestry, hunting and fishing	6,698.6	7,191.2	13,890.1
Mining and quarrying	15.5	13.8	29.2
Manufacturing	161.7	83.8	245.4
Electricity, gas and water supply	13.5	1.2	14.7
Construction	147.5	4.2	151.7
Wholesale and retail trade and restaurants and hotels	565.5	697.5	1,263.0
Transport, storage and communications	103.9	7.6	111.6
Financing, insurance, real estate and business services	22.2	4.3	26.5
Community, social and personal services	622.8	559.9	1,182.7
Total employed	8,351.3	8,563.5	16,914.8
Unemployed	388.4	524.4	912.8
Total labour force	8,739.7	9,087.9	17,827.6

Source: ILO.

Mid-2003 (estimates in '000): Agriculture, etc. 14,982; Total labour force 18,932 (Source: FAO).

Health and Welfare

KEY INDICATORS

Total fertility rate (children per woman, 2003)	5.1
Under-5 mortality rate (per 1,000 live births, 2004)	126
HIV/AIDS (% of persons aged 15–49, 2003)	8.8
Physicians (per 1,000 head, 2002)	0.02
Hospital beds (per 1,000 head, 1992)	0.89
Health expenditure (2002): US $ per head (PPP)	31
Health expenditure (2002): % of GDP	4.9
Health expenditure (2002): public (% of total)	54.8
Access to water (% of persons, 2002)	73
Access to sanitation (% of persons, 2002)	46
Human Development Index (2003): ranking	164
Human Development Index (2003): value	0.418

For sources and definitions, see explanatory note on p. vi.

Agriculture

PRINCIPAL CROPS
('000 metric tons)

	2002	2003	2004
Wheat	76.5	71.0*	75.0*
Rice (paddy)	640.2	650.0*	680.0*
Maize	2,704.8	2,550.0*	3,230.0*
Millet*	300.0	270.0	215.0
Sorghum	833.7	700.0*	800.0*
Potatoes†	240.0	260.0	260.0
Sweet potatoes†	950.0	970.0	970.0
Cassava (Manioc)	6,888.0	6,890.0†	6,890.0†
Sugar cane	1,750.0	2,000.0†	2,000.0†
Dry beans†	270.0	280.0	280.0
Cashew nuts†	100.0	100.0	100.0
Groundnuts (in shell)	75.0*	80.0†	83.0†
Coconuts†	370.0	370.0	370.0
Oil palm fruit†	65.0	65.0	65.0
Seed cotton*	190.0	155.0	330.0
Tomatoes†	145.0	145.0	145.0
Onions (dry)†	55.0	55.0	55.0
Other vegetables†	986.9	987.1	993.1

TANZANIA

—continued

	2002	2003	2004
Bananas	150.4	150.4†	150.4†
Plantains	601.6	601.6†	601.6†
Mangoes†	195.0	195.0	195.0
Pineapples†	77.5	77.5	77.5
Other fruit†	310.1	310.3	310.3
Coffee (green)*	49.5	54.0	57.0
Tea (made)†	25.5	25.5	25.5
Cloves (whole and stems)†	12.5	12.5	12.5
Tobacco (leaves)*	24.3	24.3	24.3
Cotton (lint)*	61.0	51.0	109.0

* Unofficial figure(s).
† FAO estimate(s).

Source: FAO.

LIVESTOCK
('000 head, year ending September)

	2002	2003	2004*
Asses*	182.0	182.0	182.0
Cattle	17,367.0	17,704.0	17,800.0
Pigs	458.0	455.0	455.0
Sheep	3,514.4	3,521.2	3,521.0
Goats	12,324.2	12,556.2	12,550.0
Chickens*	29,000	30,000	30,000

* FAO estimates.

Source: FAO.

LIVESTOCK PRODUCTS
(FAO estimates, '000 metric tons)

	2002	2003	2004
Beef and veal	246.3	246.3	246.3
Mutton and lamb	10.3	10.3	10.3
Goat meat	30.6	30.6	30.6
Pig meat	12.9	13.0	13.0
Poultry meat	45.4	47.0	47.0
Cows' milk	835.0	840.0	840.0
Goats' milk	100.0	104.0	104.0
Cheese	8.5	9.5	11.2
Hen eggs	33.8	35.1	35.1
Other poultry eggs	1.6	1.6	1.6
Honey	26.5	27.0	27.0
Cattle hides	48.3	48.3	48.3
Sheepskins	2.6	2.6	2.6
Goatskins	6.4	6.5	6.4

Source: FAO.

Forestry

ROUNDWOOD REMOVALS
(FAO estimates, '000 cubic metres, excluding bark)

	2002	2003	2004
Sawlogs, veneer logs and logs for sleepers	317	317	317
Pulpwood	153	153	153
Other industrial wood	1,844	1,844	1,844
Fuel wood	21,125	21,310	21,505
Total	**23,439**	**23,624**	**23,819**

Source: FAO.

SAWNWOOD PRODUCTION
(FAO estimates, '000 cubic metres, including railway sleepers)

	1992	1993	1994
Coniferous (softwood)	26	21	13
Broadleaved (hardwood)	22	18	11
Total	**48**	**39**	**24**

1995–2004: Production assumed to be unchanged from 1994 (FAO estimates).

Source: FAO.

Fishing
('000 metric tons, live weight)

	2001	2002	2003
Capture	335.9	323.5	351.1
Tilapias	45.0	43.0	50.0
Nile perch	96.0	92.0	98.5
Other freshwater fishes	86.0	84.4	98.8
Dagaas	43.0	43.0	43.5
Sardinellas	15.5	14.0	14.2
Aquaculture*	0.3	0.6	0.0
Total catch	**336.2**	**324.2**	**351.1**

* FAO estimates.

Note: Figures exclude aquatic plants ('000 metric tons): 12.0 (capture 5.0, aquaculture 7.0) in 2001; 11.5 (capture 4.5, aquaculture 7.0) in 2002; 11.5 (capture 4.5; aquaculture 7.0) in 2003. Also excluded are aquatic mammals, recorded by number rather than by weight. The number of Risso's dolphins caught was: 11 in 2001; 0 in 2002; 1 in 2003. The number of Indo-Pacific hump-backed dolphins caught was: 5 in 2001; 1 in 2002; 4 in 2003. The number of Bottlenose dolphins caught was: 12 in 2001; 12 in 2002; 16 in 2003. The number of Spinner dolphins caught was: 18 in 2001; 0 in 2002; 10 in 2003. The number of other spotted dolphins caught was: 4 in 2001; 0 in 2002; 2 in 2003. The number of Nile crocodiles caught was: 1,589 in 2001; 1,369 in 2002; 1,469 in 2003. One humpback whale was caught in 2002.

Source: FAO.

Mining
('000 metric tons, unless otherwise indicated)

	2001	2002	2003
Coal (bituminous)	78	79	55
Diamonds ('000 carats)*	254	240	237
Gold (refined, kilograms)	30,088	43,320	48,018
Salt	65	71	59
Gypsum and anhydrite	72	73	23
Limestone, crushed	2,269	2,857	1,100
Pozzolanic materials	41	52	24
Sand	n.a.	503	2,036

* Estimated at 85% gem-quality and 15% industrial-quality stones. Excluding smuggled artisanal production.

Source: US Geological Survey.

Industry

SELECTED PRODUCTS
('000 metric tons, unless otherwise indicated)

	2001	2002	2003*
Sugar	184.0	189.6	212.9
Cigarettes (million)	3.5	3.8	3.9
Beer (million litres)	175.7	175.9	194.1
Non-alcoholic beverages (million litres)	198.7	208.7	208.4
Textiles (million sq metres)	84.3	106.3	125.8
Cement	900.0	1,026.0	1,186.0
Rolled steel	16.1	25.4	39.6
Iron sheets	25.9	35.1	33.6
Aluminium	0.1	0.1	0.2
Sisal ropes	4.5	5.9	6.9
Paints (million litres)	9.0	13.6	16.8

* Provisional.

Source: IMF, *Tanzania—Selected Issues and Statistical Appendix* (September 2004).

TANZANIA

Finance

CURRENCY AND EXCHANGE RATES

Monetary Units
100 cents = 1 Tanzanian shilling.

Sterling, Dollar and Euro Equivalents (30 December 2005)
£1 sterling = 2,006.89 Tanzanian shillings;
US $1 = 1,165.51 Tanzanian shillings;
€1 = 1,374.95 Tanzanian shillings;
10,000 Tanzanian shillings = £4.98 = $8.58 = €7.27.

Average Exchange Rate (Tanzanian shillings per US $)
2003 1,038.42
2004 1,089.33
2005 1,128.93

BUDGET
('000 million shillings, year ending 30 June)*

Revenue†	2001/02	2002/03	2003/04‡
Tax revenue	938.5	1,105.7	1,325.1
Import duties	88.9	106.4	130.1
Value-added tax	352.3	424.3	494.8
Excises	177.6	187.3	216.6
Income tax	228.4	276.1	360.4
Other taxes	91.3	111.7	123.2
Non-tax revenue	104.5	111.8	122.3
Ministries and regions	68.0	78.0	85.4
Total	**1,042.9**	**1,217.5**	**1,447.3**

Expenditure	2001/02	2002/03	2003/04‡
Recurrent expenditure	1,171.4	1,488.6	1,887.1
Wages	342.0	397.8	464.1
Interest	121.1	99.8	121.7
Goods, services and transfers	708.3	991.1	1,301.4
Clearance of domestic payment arrears	59.1	—	—
Development expenditure and net lending	291.3	500.9	644.4
Local	50.2	95.7	136.1
Foreign	241.1	405.2	508.3
Total	**1,521.9**	**1,989.5**	**2,531.5**

* Figures refer to the Tanzania Government, excluding the revenue and expenditure of the separate Zanzibar Government.
† Excluding grants received.
‡ Provisional.

Source: IMF, *Tanzania—Selected Issues and Statistical Appendix* (September 2004).

INTERNATIONAL RESERVES
(excl. gold, US $ million at 31 December)

	2002	2003	2004
IMF special drawing rights	0.1	0.5	0.1
Reserve position in IMF	13.6	14.9	15.5
Foreign exchange	1,512.2	2,023.0	2,280.1
Total	**1,525.9**	**2,038.4**	**2,295.7**

Source: IMF, *International Financial Statistics*.

MONEY SUPPLY
('000 million shillings at 31 December)

	2002	2003	2004
Currency outside banks	495.45	553.05	664.15
Demand deposits at commercial banks	463.34	560.33	651.45
Total money	**958.79**	**1,113.38**	**1,315.61**

Source: IMF, *International Financial Statistics*.

COST OF LIVING
(Consumer Price Index)
Tanganyika
(Base: 2000 = 100)

	2002	2003	2004
Food (incl. beverages)	107.1	112.0	118.6
Fuel, light and water	105.1	107.7	112.9
Clothing (incl. footwear)	104.5	106.6	109.0
Rent	105.0	111.2	113.8
All items (incl. others)	106.2	109.8	114.5

Zanzibar
(Base: 2001 = 100)

	2002	2003
Food (incl. beverages)	106.9	116.7
Fuel, light and water	100.0	106.0
Clothing (incl. footwear)	106.7	128.3
Rent	104.9	118.0
All items (incl. others)	105.2	114.7

Source: ILO.

NATIONAL ACCOUNTS
(Tanzania mainland, current prices)
National Income and Product
(million shillings, provisional)

	1992	1993	1994
Compensation of employees	88,230	119,119	148,194
Operating surplus	906,923	1,132,774	1,462,193
Domestic factor incomes	995,153	1,251,894	1,610,387
Consumption of fixed capital	35,802	36,697	49,542
Gross domestic product (GDP) at factor cost	1,030,955	1,288,591	1,659,929
Indirect taxes	109,442	183,389	260,039
Less Subsidies	9,801	67,611	97,398
GDP in purchasers' values	1,130,596	1,404,369	1,822,570
Factor income received from abroad	2,563	7,934	8,648
Less Factor income paid abroad	72,969	67,842	78,173
Gross national product (GNP)	1,060,190	1,344,460	1,753,045
Less Consumption of fixed capital	35,802	36,697	49,542
National income in market prices	1,024,387	1,307,763	1,703,504
Other current transfers from abroad (net)	282,813	291,673	308,518
National disposable income	1,307,200	1,599,436	2,084,022

Expenditure on the Gross Domestic Product
('000 million shillings)

	2001	2002	2003*
Government final consumption expenditure	516.3	598.9	697.8
Private final consumption expenditure	6,917.6	7,499.6	8,765.5
Increase in stocks	15.7	17.9	17.5
Gross fixed capital formation	1,390.6	1,789.9	1,974.1
Total domestic expenditure*	8,840.2	9,906.3	11,454.9
Exports of goods and services	1,284.7	1,520.5	1,900.0
Less Imports of goods and services	1,962.8	2,106.9	2,857.4
Sub-total	8,162.1	9,319.9	10,497.5
Discrepancy	112.5	125.5	195.0
GDP in purchasers' values	8,274.6	9,445.5	10,692.4
GDP at constant 1992 prices	1,892.4	2,029.4	2,173.4

* Provisional figures.

Source: IMF, *Tanzania—Selected Issues and Statistical Appendix* (September 2004).

TANZANIA

Gross Domestic Product by Economic Activity
('000 million shillings)

	2001	2002	2003*
Agriculture, forestry, fishing and hunting	1,919.7	2,205.2	2,508.9
Mining and quarrying	120.5	153.0	191.2
Manufacturing	564.7	638.7	711.0
Electricity and water	124.8	145.8	157.0
Construction	335.9	389.7	454.2
Trade, restaurants and hotels	926.9	1,038.1	1,153.3
Transport and communications	361.6	404.9	454.0
Public administration	723.1	810.3	869.3
Financial and business services	421.5	494.8	564.3
Other services	73.9	82.7	86.9
Sub-total	5,572.4	6,363.1	7,150.0
Less Imputed bank service charge	157.8	168.8	182.3
Total monetary GDP	5,414.6	6,194.3	6,967.7
Non-monetary GDP	2,210.0	2,505.6	2,843.8
Agriculture, forestry, fishing and hunting	1,486.4	1,679.4	1,909.0
Construction	69.2	80.3	92.0
Owner-occupied dwellings	654.3	745.9	842.9
Total GDP at factor cost	7,624.6	8,699.9	9,811.6
Net taxes	650.0	745.6	880.9
Total GDP at market prices	8,274.6	9,445.5	10,692.4

* Provisional figures.

Source: IMF, *Tanzania—Selected Issues and Statistical Appendix* (September 2004).

BALANCE OF PAYMENTS
(US $ million)

	2002	2003	2004
Exports of goods f.o.b.	911.6	1,156.6	1,278.1
Imports of goods f.o.b.	−1,526.5	−1,980.4	−2,184.1
Trade balance	−614.9	−823.7	−906.0
Exports of services	675.3	707.6	901.4
Imports of services	−675.3	−792.6	−1,012.3
Balance on goods and services	−614.9	−908.8	−1,016.9
Other income received	68.6	89.2	78.2
Other income paid	−91.5	−134.0	−116.9
Balance on goods, services and income	−637.8	−953.6	−1,055.6
Current transfers received	482.8	624.7	680.8
Current transfers paid	−61.9	−64.5	−62.3
Current balance	−217.0	−393.4	−437.1
Capital account (net)	793.6	709.5	385.4
Direct investment from abroad	242.8	253.8	249.1
Other investment assets	2.9	−60.5	−10.5
Other investment liabilities	−1,163.4	−218.5	−20.1
Net errors and omissions	668.1	103.7	33.4
Overall balance	327.0	394.7	200.2

Source: IMF, *International Financial Statistics*.

External Trade

PRINCIPAL COMMODITIES
(US $ million)

Imports c.i.f.	2001	2002	2003*
Capital goods	739.7	721.2	852.4
Transport equipment	189.8	218.3	263.2
Building and construction	144.0	134.7	168.3
Machinery	406.0	368.3	420.9
Intermediate goods	440.8	423.0	679.7
Petroleum and petroleum products	220.7	194.8	403.4
Fertilizers	15.5	20.1	28.5
Industrial raw materials	204.6	208.0	247.7
Consumer goods	531.8	514.2	633.7
Food and foodstuffs	169.4	147.3	183.1
Total (incl. others)	1,714.8	1,660.8	2,168.2

Exports f.o.b.	2001/02	2002/03	2003/04*
Coffee	36.9	48.9	44.8
Cotton	31.9	42.3	39.7
Sisal	6.9	6.5	7.2
Tea	26.4	29.6	21.4
Tobacco	43.0	42.5	48.6
Cashew nuts	37.4	44.1	48.5
Cloves	11.9	9.8	11.1
Minerals and metals	349.5	432.3	623.2
Gold	311.2	383.1	581.6
Diamonds	18.7	29.3	20.5
Manufactured goods	64.2	75.8	95.5
Fish and fish products	108.3	125.8	123.7
Horticulture	11.4	13.3	12.9
Total (incl. others)	816.1	1,010.0	1,173.1

* Provisional.

Source: IMF, *Tanzania—Selected Issues and Statistical Appendix* (September 2004).

PRINCIPAL TRADING PARTNERS
(million shillings)

Imports c.i.f.	1997	1998	1999
Argentina	1,798.4	4,338.4	14,256.2
Australia	1,177.2	18,966.6	60,646.6
Belgium	15,632.2	16,236.8	17,166.0
Brazil	5,258.3	9,685.7	12,936.4
Canada	7,651.9	11,080.2	19,853.0
China, People's Repub.	37,671.0	32,401.2	43,213.3
Denmark	5,281.6	17,828.7	17,865.7
France	12,449.2	10,513.2	15,993.3
Germany	30,368.5	51,601.1	46,524.0
India	47,443.7	59,659.7	70,444.1
Iran	38,938.0	43,556.5	59,734.3
Italy	23,730.2	45,348.5	36,418.0
Japan	45,322.9	87,044.5	132,711.7
Kenya	58,558.4	70,319.2	70,799.0
Malaysia	10,510.4	23,346.9	17,865.9
Netherlands	17,246.4	62,065.2	27,425.0
Pakistan	6,387.6	11,827.3	11,660.7
Singapore	23,716.2	8,546.5	7,266.9
South Africa	58,757.8	86,885.6	127,231.3
Sweden	11,183.6	19,466.5	13,299.4
Switzerland	18,209.9	11,917.0	10,918.3
Thailand	11,821.9	16,016.1	13,345.6
United Arab Emirates	57,200.3	39,704.7	38,006.4
United Kingdom	75,342.0	81,558.9	95,553.6
USA	32,215.4	54,046.5	73,963.0
Zambia	15,303.8	11,324.2	5,408.4
Total (incl. others)	808,167.9	1,403,096.9	1,219,957.4

Exports	1997	1998	1999
Belgium	5,019.1	17,353.5	12,527.6
China, People's Repub.	10,595.9	1,320.1	90.6
France	8,769.1	1,885.7	1,672.9
Germany	41,518.3	32,560.0	26,178.0
Hong Kong	11,153.6	3,321.4	5,828.0
India	40,710.6	76,272.7	84,022.3
Indonesia	11,711.3	3,922.9	6,737.9
Ireland	1,115.4	13,304.2	10,716.9
Italy	7,499.9	4,374.3	4,797.2
Japan	36,729.9	30,276.2	32,702.9
Kenya	7,807.5	17,306.9	15,630.9
Netherlands	24,537.9	30,035.6	23,234.5
Pakistan	7,067.9	6,147.6	5,662.3
Portugal	9,207.8	7,988.8	4,678.3
St Helena	0.6	3,556.7	6,546.0
Singapore	8,922.9	7,267.6	18,399.4
South Africa	4,852.0	4,190.1	4,771.0

TANZANIA

Exports—continued	1997	1998	1999
Spain	7,807.5	3,703.6	2,548.8
Switzerland	3,596.1	7,463.0	1,802.0
Taiwan	12,672.8	4,617.5	2,210.7
Thailand	8,624.1	5,086.1	2,870.0
Uganda	7,096.0	4,336.8	3,467.2
United Arab Emirates	3,031.0	4,546.4	4,969.7
United Kingdom	22,864.8	39,679.4	69,113.2
USA	13,076.7	8,519.9	13,372.8
Zambia	6,134.5	2,442.0	2,119.5
Total (incl. others)	459,549.0	391,804.4	407,118.1

Source: Bank of Tanzania.

Transport

RAILWAYS

	2002	2003	2004
Passengers ('000)	1,897	927	854
Freight ('000 metric tons)	2,123	1,590	1,300

Source: National Bureau of Statistics, *Tanzania in Figures 2004*.

ROAD TRAFFIC
(estimates, '000 motor vehicles in use)

	1994	1995	1996
Passenger cars	28.0	26.0	23.8
Buses and coaches	78.0	81.0	86.0
Lorries and vans	27.2	27.7	29.7
Road tractors	6.7	6.7	6.6

Source: IRF, *World Road Statistics*.

SHIPPING
Merchant fleet
(registered at 31 December)

	2002	2003	2004
Number of vessels	58	52	51
Displacement ('000 grt)	47.1	38.9	38.9

Source: Lloyd's Register-Fairplay, *World Fleet Statistics*.

International sea-borne traffic

	2002	2003	2004
Vessels docked	3,500	2,722	3,168
Cargo ('000 metric tons)	5,107	5,746	4,410
Passengers ('000)	579	684	539

Source: National Bureau of Statistics, *Tanzania in Figures 2004*.

CIVIL AVIATION
(traffic on scheduled services)

	1999	2000	2001
Kilometres flown (million)	2	3	3
Passengers carried ('000)	75	90	77
Passenger-km (million)	115	146	134
Total ton-km (million)	12	15	15

Source: UN, *Statistical Yearbook*.

Tourism

FOREIGN VISITOR ARRIVALS
(by country of origin)

	2001	2002	2003
Burundi	5,869	6,951	11,907
Canada	6,782	12,042	10,354
Congo, Democratic Repub.	7,837	12,784	6,850
France	16,990	22,059	22,103
Germany	21,190	17,855	19,222
India	24,068	21,973	22,215
Italy	8,035	23,459	24,675
Kenya	102,235	112,036	119,406
Malawi	16,573	17,531	14,267
Netherlands	10,514	15,891	15,272
Rwanda	6,016	4,090	12,061
South Africa	17,568	22,916	35,071
Spain	8,295	16,054	9,565
Uganda	25,330	28,618	34,664
United Kingdom	34,125	43,269	43,656
USA	30,806	38,159	36,419
Zambia	9,577	13,096	10,670
Total (incl. others)	525,122	575,296	576,198

Tourism receipts (US $ million, incl. passenger transport unless otherwise indicated): 424 in 2001; 441 in 2002; 450 in 2003 (excl. passenger transport).

Source: World Tourism Organization.

Communications Media

	2002	2003	2004
Telephones ('000 main lines in use)	161.6	149.1	149.1
Mobile cellular telephones ('000 subscribers)	760.0	891.2	1,640.0
Personal computers ('000 in use)	144	200	278
Internet users ('000)	80	250	333

Source: International Telecommunication Union.

Television receivers ('000 in use, 2000): 700.

Radio receivers ('000 in use, estimate, 1997): 8,800 (Source: UNESCO, *Statistical Yearbook*).

Daily newspapers (1996): 3; average circulation ('000 copies, estimate) 120 (Source: UNESCO, *Statistical Yearbook*).

Education

(2004)

	Institutions	Teachers	Students
Primary (state)	13,533	119,773	1,893,000
Primary (private)	156	1,775	10,734
Secondary (state)	828	18,754	151,048
Secondary (private)	463	7,434	88,304
Higher (state)*	64	n.a.	14,527
Higher (private)†	13	n.a.	1,820

*Comprising 34 teacher training colleges, 4 technical colleges, 5 full universities, 3 constituent universities and 18 other higher institutions.
† Comprising 11 teacher training colleges and 13 universities.

Source: National Bureau for Statistics, *Tanzania in Figures 2004*.

Adult literacy rate (UNESCO estimates): 69.4% (males 77.5%; females 62.2%) in 2003 (Source: UN Development Programme, *Human Development Report*).

Directory

The Constitution

The United Republic of Tanzania was established on 26 April 1964, when Tanganyika and Zanzibar, hitherto separate independent countries, merged. An interim Constitution of 1965 was replaced, on 25 April 1977, by a permanent Constitution for the United Republic. In October 1979 the Revolutionary Council of Zanzibar adopted a separate Constitution, governing Zanzibar's internal administration, with provisions for a popularly elected President and a legislative House of Representatives elected by delegates of the then ruling party. A new Constitution for Zanzibar, which came into force in January 1985, provided for direct elections to the Zanzibar House of Representatives. The provisions below relate to the 1977 Constitution of the United Republic, as subsequently amended.

GOVERNMENT

Legislative power is exercised by the Parliament of the United Republic, which is vested by the Constitution with complete sovereign power, and of which the present National Assembly is the legislative house. The Assembly also enacts all legislation concerning the mainland. Internal matters in Zanzibar are the exclusive jurisdiction of the Zanzibar executive, the Supreme Revolutionary Council of Zanzibar, and the Zanzibar legislature, the House of Representatives.

National Assembly

The National Assembly comprises both directly elected members (chosen by universal adult suffrage) and nominated members (including five members elected from the Zanzibar House of Representatives). The number of directly elected members exceeds the number of nominated members. The Electoral Commission may review and, if necessary, increase the number of electoral constituencies before every general election. The National Assembly has a term of five years.

President

The President is the Head of State, Head of the Government and Commander-in-Chief of the Armed Forces. The President has no power to legislate without recourse to Parliament. The assent of the President is required before any bill passed by the National Assembly becomes law. Should the President withhold his assent and the bill be repassed by the National Assembly by a two-thirds' majority, the President is required by law to give his assent within 21 days unless, before that time, he has dissolved the National Assembly, in which case he must stand for re-election.

The President appoints a Vice-President to assist him in carrying out his functions. The President presides over the Cabinet, which comprises a Prime Minister and other ministers who are appointed from among the members of the National Assembly.

JUDICIARY

The independence of the judges is secured by provisions which prevent their removal, except on account of misbehaviour or incapacity when they may be dismissed at the discretion of the President. The Constitution also makes provision for a Permanent Commission of Enquiry, which has wide powers to investigate any abuses of authority.

CONSTITUTIONAL AMENDMENTS

The Constitution can be amended by an act of the Parliament of the United Republic, when the proposed amendment is supported by the votes of not fewer than two-thirds of all the members of the Assembly.

The Government

HEAD OF STATE

President: Lt-Col (Retd) JAKAYA MRISHO KIKWETE (took office 21 December 2005).
Vice-President: Dr ALI MOHAMMED SHENI.

CABINET
(April 2006)

President and Commander-in-Chief of the Armed Forces: Lt-Col (Retd) JAKAYA MRISHO KIKWETE.
Prime Minister: EDWARD LOWASSA.
Minister of Foreign Affairs and International Relations: Dr ASHA ROSE MIGIRO.
Minister of East African Co-operation: ANDREW JOHN CHENGE.
Minister of Finance: ZAKIA MEGHJI.
Minister of Planning, Economy and Empowerment: Dr JUMA NGASONGWA.
Minister of Industry, Trade and Marketing: NAZIR M. KARAMGI.
Minister of Agriculture, Food Security and Co-operatives: JOSEPH J. MUNGAI.
Minister of Natural Resources and Tourism: ANTONY MWANDU DIALLO.
Minister of Water: STEPHEN MASATO WASIRA.
Minister of Energy and Minerals: Dr IBRAHIM SAID MSABAHA.
Minister of Infrastructure Development: BASIL PESAMBILI MRAMBA.
Minister of Health and Social Welfare: Prof. DAVID HOMELI MWAKYUSA.
Minister of Education and Vocational Training: MARGARETH SIMWANZA SITTA.
Minister of Science, Technology and Higher Education: Prof. PETER MAHAMUDU MSOLLA.
Minister of Labour, Employment and Youth Development: Prof. JUMANNE ABDALLAH MAGHEMBE.
Minister of Land and Human Settlements: JOHN POMBE MAGUFULI.
Minister of Information, Culture and Sports: MUHAMMED SEIF KHATIB.
Minister of Defence and National Service: Prof. JUMA ATHUMAN KAPUYA.
Minister of Public Safety and Security: BAKARI HARITH MWAPACHU.
Minister of Home Affairs: JOHN ZEFANIA CHILIGATI.
Minister of Justice and Constitutional Affairs: Dr MARY MICHAEL NAGU.
Minister of Community Development: SOFIA MATTAYO SIMBA.
Minister of Livestock Development: SHUKURU JUMANNE KAWAMBWA.
Ministers of State in the President's Office: HAWA ABDULRAHMAN GHASIA (Public Service Management), PHILIP SANKA MARMO (Good Governance), KINGUNGE NGOMBALE MWIRU (Politics and Social Relations).
Ministers of State in the Vice-President's Office: Dr HUSSEIN MWINYI (Union Affairs), Prof. MARK MWANDOSYA (Environment).
Ministers of State in the Prime Minister's Office: MIZENGO PETER PINDA (Regional Administration and Local Governments), JUMA J. AKUKWETI (Parliamentary Affairs).

MINISTRIES

Office of the President: State House, POB 9120, Dar es Salaam; tel. (22) 2116679; fax (22) 2113425.
Office of the Vice-President: POB 5380, Dar es Salaam; tel. (22) 2113857; fax (22) 2113856; e-mail makamu@twiga.com.
Office of the Prime Minister: POB 980, Dodoma; tel. (26) 233201.
Ministry of Agriculture, Food Security and Co-operatives: POB 9192, Dar es Salaam; tel. (22) 2862480; fax (22) 2862077; e-mail psk@kilimo.go.tz.
Ministry of Community Development: POB 3448, Dar es Salaam; tel. (22) 2115074; fax (22) 2132647.
Ministry of Defence and National Service: POB 9544, Dar es Salaam; tel. (22) 2117153; fax (22) 2116719.
Ministry of East African Co-operation: Dar es Salaam.
Ministry of Education and Vocational Training: POB 9121, Dar es Salaam; tel. (22) 2110146; fax (22) 2113271; e-mail ps-moec@twiga.com.
Ministry of Energy and Minerals: POB 2000, Dar es Salaam; tel. (22) 2117153; fax (22) 2116719; e-mail madini@africaonline.co.tz.
Ministry of Finance: POB 9111, Dar es Salaam; tel. (22) 2111174; fax (22) 2138573.
Ministry of Foreign Affairs and International Relations: POB 9000, Dar es Salaam; tel. (22) 2111906; fax (22) 2116600.
Ministry of Health and Social Welfare: POB 9083, Dar es Salaam; tel. (22) 2120261; fax (22) 2139951; e-mail moh@cats-net.com.
Ministry of Home Affairs: POB 9223, Dar es Salaam; tel. (22) 2112034; fax (22) 2139675.
Ministry of Industry, Trade and Marketing: POB 9503, Dar es Salaam; tel. (22) 2181397; fax (22) 2182481.

TANZANIA

Ministry of Information, Culture and Sports: Dar es Salaam.

Ministry of Infrastructure Development: Dar es Salaam.

Ministry of Justice and Constitutional Affairs: POB 9050, Dar es Salaam; tel. (22) 2117099.

Ministry of Labour, Employment and Youth Development: POB 1422, Dar es Salaam; tel. (22) 2120419; fax (22) 2113082.

Ministry of Lands and Human Settlements: POB 9132, Dar es Salaam; tel. (22) 2121241; fax (22) 2113224; e-mail ps-ardhi@africaonline.co.tz.

Ministry of Livestock Development: Dar es Salaam.

Ministry of Natural Resources and Tourism: POB 9372, Dar es Salaam; tel. (22) 2111061; fax (22) 2110600; e-mail nature.tourism@mnrt.org; internet www.mnrt.org.

Ministry of Planning, Economy and Empowerment: Dar es Salaam.

Ministry of Public Safety and Security: Dar es Salaam.

Ministry of Science, Technology and Higher Education: POB 2645, Dar es Salaam; tel. (22) 2666376; fax (22) 2666097; e-mail msthe@msthe.go.tz.

Ministry of Water: POB 9153, Dar es Salaam; tel. (22) 2117153; fax (22) 37138; e-mail dppmaj@raha.com.

SUPREME REVOLUTIONARY COUNCIL OF ZANZIBAR
(April 2006)

President and Chairman: AMANI ABEID KARUME.

Chief Minister: SHAMSI VUAI NAHODHA.

Minister of Health and Social Welfare: SALUM JUMA OTHMAN.

Minister of Education, Culture and Sports: HAROUN ALI SULEIMAN.

Minister of Trade, Industry, Marketing and Tourism: MUSA AME SILIMA.

Minister of Agriculture, Natural Resources, the Environment, Livestock and Co-operatives: MOHAMMED ABOUD MOHAMED.

Minister of Water, Works, Energy and Land Development: BURHAN SAADAT HAJI.

Minister of Transport and Communications: Brig.-Gen. (retd) ADAM C. MWAKANJUKI.

Minister of Youth, Employment, Women's Development and Children: SAMIA SULUHU HASSAN.

Ministers of State in the President's Office: MWINYIAHJI MAKAME MWADINI (Finance and Economic Affairs), SULEIMAN OTHMAN NYANGA (Regional Administration and Special Forces), AHMED HASSAN DIRIA (Constitutional Affairs and Good Governance).

MINISTRIES

Office of the President: POB 776, Zanzibar; tel. (24) 2230814; fax (24) 2233722.

Office of the Chief Minister: POB 239, Zanzibar; tel. (24) 2311126; fax (24) 233788.

Ministry of Agriculture, Natural Resources, the Environment, Livestock and Co-operatives: Zanzibar; tel. (24) 232662.

Ministry of Education, Culture and Sports: POB 394, Zanzibar; tel. (24) 232827.

Ministry of Finance and Economy: POB 1154, Zanzibar; tel. (24) 231169.

Ministry of Health and Social Welfare: POB 236, Zanzibar; tel. (24) 232640.

Ministry of Information, Culture, Tourism and Youth: POB 772, Zanzibar; tel. (24) 232321.

Ministry of Trade, Industry, Marketing and Tourism: POB 772, Zanzibar; tel. (24) 232321.

Ministry of Transport and Communications: POB 266, Zanzibar; tel. (24) 2232841.

Ministry of Water, Works, Energy and Land Development: Zanzibar.

Ministry of Youth, Employment, Women's Development and Children: POB 884, Zanzibar; tel. (24) 30808.

President and Legislature

PRESIDENT

Election, 14 December 2005

Candidate	Votes	% of votes
Lt-Col (Retd) Jakaya Mrisho Kikwete (CCM)	9,123,952	80.28
Prof. Ibrahim Haruna Lipumba (CUF)	1,327,125	11.68
Freeman Mbowe (Chadema)	668,756	5.88
Augustine Lyatonga Mrema (TLP)	84,901	0.75
Sengondo Mvungi (NCCR—Maguezi)	55,819	0.49
Others	104,924	0.92
Total	**11,365,477**	**100.00**

NATIONAL ASSEMBLY

Speaker: SAMUEL SITTA.

Election, 14 December 2005

Party	Seats*
Chama Cha Mapinduzi (CCM)	266
Civic United Front (CUF)	28
Chama Cha Demokrasia na Maendeleo (Chadema)	11
Tanzania Labour Party (TLP)	1
United Democratic Party (UDP)	1
Total	**307**

*In addition to the 232 elective seats, 75 seats are reserved for women (included in the figures above). Furthermore, 10 seats are reserved for presidential nominees and five for members of the Zanzibar House of Representatives; the Attorney-General is also an *ex-officio* member of the National Assembly.

ZANZIBAR PRESIDENT

Election, 30 October 2005

Candidate	Votes	% of votes
Amani Abeid Karume	239,832	53.18
Seif Sharif Hamad	207,733	46.06
Haji Mussa Kitole	2,110	0.47
Others	1,293	0.29
Total	**450,968**	**100.00**

ZANZIBAR HOUSE OF REPRESENTATIVES

Speaker: (vacant).

Election, 30 October 2005

Party	Seats*
Chama Cha Mapinduzi (CCM)	31
Civic United Front (CUF)	18
Total	**49**

*In addition to the 50 elective seats, five seats are reserved for regional commissioners, 10 for presidential nominees, 15 for women (on a party basis in proportion to the number of elective seats gained) and one for the Attorney-General. Results in one constituency were invalidated; a fresh ballot was held on 14 December 2005 for which results were yet to be released.

Election Commission

National Election Commission of Tanzania (NEC): Posta House, POB 10923, Ghana/Ohio St, 6th and 7th Floor, Dar es Salaam; tel. (22) 2114963; fax (22) 2116740; e-mail info@nec.go.tz; internet www.nec.go.tz; f. 1993; Chair. LEWIS M. MAKAME; Dir of Elections R. R. KIRAVU.

Political Organizations

Bismillah Party: Pemba; seeks a referendum on the terms of the 1964 union of Zanzibar with mainland Tanzania.

Chama Cha Amani na Demokrasia Tanzania (CHADETA): House No. 41, Sadan St Ilala, POB 15809, Dar es Salaam; tel. (744) 889453; granted temporary registration in 2003.

TANZANIA

Chama Cha Demokrasia na Maendeleo (Chadema—Party for Democracy and Progress): House No. 170 Ufipa St., POB 31191, Dar es Salaam; tel. (22) 2182544; supports democracy and social development; Chair. EDWIN I. M. MTEI; Sec.-Gen. BOB NYANGA MAKANI.

Chama Cha Haki na Usitawi (Chausta—Party for Justice and Development): Drive Inn Oysterbay, POB 5450, Dar es Salaam; tel. 741247266; f. 1998; officially regd 2001; Chair. JAMES MAPALALA.

Chama Cha Mapinduzi (CCM) (Revolutionary Party of Tanzania): Kuu St, POB 50, Dodoma; tel. 2180575; e-mail katibumkuu@ccmtz.org; internet www.ccmtz.org; f. 1977 by merger of the mainland-based Tanganyika African National Union (TANU) with the Afro-Shirazi Party, which operated on Zanzibar and Pemba; sole legal party 1977–92; socialist orientation; Chair. BENJAMIN WILLIAM MKAPA; Vice-Chair. JOHN S. MALECELA, AMANI A. KARUME; Sec.-Gen. PHILIP MANGULA.

Civic United Front (CUF): Mtendeni St at Malindi, POB 3637, Zanzibar; tel. (24) 2237446; fax (24) 2237445; e-mail headquarters@cuftz.org; internet www.cuftz.org; f. 1992 by merger of Zanzibar opposition party Kamahuru and the mainland-based Chama Cha Wananchi; commands substantial support in Zanzibar and Pemba, for which it demands increased autonomy; Chair. Prof. IBRAHIM HARUNA LIPUMBA; Sec.-Gen. SEIF SHARIFF HAMAD.

Democratic Party (DP): Mchikichini Hala, POB 63102, Dar es Salaam; tel. 741430516; Leader Rev. CHRISTOPHER MTIKILA.

Movement for Democratic Alternative (MDA): Zanzibar; seeks to review the terms of the 1964 union of Zanzibar with mainland Tanzania; supports democratic institutions and opposes detention without trial and press censorship.

Demokrasia Makini (MAKINI): Kibo Ubungo, POB 75636, Dar es Salaam; tel. (744) 295670; officially regd 2001.

Forum for Restoration of Democracy (FORD): House No. 6, Rufiji St., Kariakoo, POB 15587, Dar es Salaam; tel. (741) 292271; f. 2002.

National Convention for Construction and Reform (NCCR—Mageuzi): Plot No. 2 Kilosa St., Ilala, POB 72444, Dar es Salaam; tel. (744) 318812; f. 1992; Chair. Dr KASSIM MAGUTU; Sec.-Gen. MABERE MARANDO.

National League for Democracy (NLD): Plot No. 7310 Sinza, POB 352, Dar es Salaam; f. 1993; Chair. EMMANUEL J. E. MAKAIDI; Sec.-Gen. MICHAEL E. A. MHINA.

National Reconstruction Alliance (NRA): Bububu St, Tandika Kilimahewa, POB 45197, Dar es Salaam; tel. (744) 496724; f. 1993; Chair. ULOTU ABUBAKAR ULOTU; Sec.-Gen. SALIM R. MATINGA.

Popular National Party (PONA): Plot 104, Songea St, Ilala, POB 21561, Dar es Salaam; Chair. WILFREM R. MWAKITWANGE; Sec.-Gen. NICOLAUS MCHAINA.

Tanzania Democratic Alliance Party (TADEA): Buguruni Malapa, POB 482, Dar es Salaam; tel. (22) 2865244; f. 1993; Pres. FLORA M. KAMOONA; Sec.-Gen. JOHN D. LIFA-CHIPAKA.

Progressive Party of Tanzania (PPT-Maendeleo): Plot No. 11, Kawawa Rd Morocco, POB 31932, Dar es Salaam; tel. (744) 300302; f. 2003.

Tanzania Labour Party (TLP): Argentina Manzese, POB 7273, Dar es Salaam; tel. (22) 2443237; f. 1993; Chair. LEO LWEKAMWA.

Tanzania People's Party (TPP): Mbezi Juu, Kawe, POB 60847, Dar es Salaam; removed from register of political parties 2002; Chair. ALEC H. CHE-MPONDA; Sec.-Gen. GRAVEL LIMO.

United Democratic Party (UDP): Mbezi Juu, SLP 5918, Dar es Salaam; tel. (748) 613723; f. 1994; Leader JOHN MOMOSE CHEYO.

United People's Democratic Party (UPDP): Mtaa wa Shariff Muss, POB 3121, Zanzibar; tel. (744) 753075; f. 1993; Chair. KHALFANI ALI ABDULLAH; Sec.-Gen. AHMED M. RASHID.

Union for Multi-Party Democracy (UMD): House No. 84, Plot No. 630, Block No. 5, Kagera St. Magomeni, POB 2985, Dar es Salaam; tel. (744) 478153; f. 1993; Chair. ABDALLAH FUNDIKIRA.

Diplomatic Representation

EMBASSIES AND HIGH COMMISSIONS IN TANZANIA

Algeria: 34 Ali Hassan Mwinyi Rd, POB 2963, Dar es Salaam; tel. (22) 2117619; fax (22) 2117620; e-mail algemb@twiga.com; Ambassador (vacant).

Angola: Plot 78, Lugalo Rd, POB 20793, Dar es Salaam; tel. (22) 2117674; fax (22) 2132349; e-mail angola@cats-net.com; Ambassador BRITO SOZINHO.

Belgium: Blacklines House, 5 Ocena Rd, POB 9210, Dar es Salaam; tel. (22) 2112688; fax (22) 2117621; e-mail daressalaam@diplobel.org; internet www.diplomatie.be/dar-es-salaam; Ambassador PETER MADDENS.

Burundi: Plot 1007, Lugalo Rd, POB 2752, Upanga, Dar es Salaam; tel. (22) 238608; e-mail burundemb@raha.com; Ambassador (vacant).

Canada: 38 Mirambo St, Garden Ave, POB 1022, Dar es Salaam; tel. (22) 2163300; fax (22) 2116897; e-mail dslam@international.gc.ca; internet www.dfait-maeci.gc.ca/tanzania; High Commissioner ANDREW MCALISTER.

Congo, Democratic Republic: 438 Malik Rd, POB 97, Upanga, Dar es Salaam; tel. (22) 2150282; fax (22) 2153341; e-mail drcemba@intafrica.com; Chargé d'affaires a.i. NSINGI ZI LUBAKI.

Cuba: Plot 313, Lugalo Rd, POB 9282, Upanga, Dar es Salaam; tel. (22) 2115928; fax (22) 2115927; e-mail embacuba.tz@raha.com; Ambassador FELIPE RUIZ O'FARRILL.

Denmark: Ghana Ave, POB 9171, Dar es Salaam; tel. (22) 2113887; fax (22) 2116433; e-mail daramb@um.dk; internet www.ambdaressalaam.um.dk; Ambassador CARSTEN NILAUS PEDERSEN.

Egypt: 24 Garden Ave, POB 1668, Dar es Salaam; tel. (22) 2117622; fax (22) 2112543; e-mail egypt.emb.tz@intafrica.com; Ambassador BAHER M. EL-SADEK.

Finland: Mirambo St and Garden Ave, POB 2455, Dar es Salaam; tel. (22) 2196565; fax (22) 2196573; e-mail sanomat.dar@formin.fi; internet www.finland.or.tz; Ambassador JORMA PAUKKU.

France: Ali Hassan Mwinyi Rd, POB 2349, Dar es Salaam; tel. (22) 2666021; fax (22) 2668435; e-mail ambfrance@africaonline.co.tz; internet www.ambafrance-tz.org; Ambassador EMMANUELLE D'ACHON.

Germany: Umoja House, Mirambo St/Garden Ave, 2nd Floor, Dar es Salaam; tel. (22) 2117409; fax (22) 2112944; e-mail german.emb.dar@raha.com; internet www.daressalam.diplo.de; Ambassador WOLFGANG RINGE.

Holy See: Oyster Bay, Plot 146, Haile Selassie Rd, POB 480, Dar es Salaam (Apostolic Nunciature); tel. (22) 2666422; fax (22) 2668059; e-mail nunzio@cats-net.com; Apostolic Nuncio Most Rev. LUIGI PEZZUTO (Titular Archbishop of Turris in Proconsulari).

Indonesia: 299 Ali Hassan Mwinyi Rd, POB 572, Dar es Salaam; tel. (22) 2119119; fax (22) 2115849; e-mail kbridsm@raha.com; Ambassador TRIJONO MARJONO.

Ireland: 353 Toure Dr., Oysterbay, Dar es Salaam; tel. (22) 2602355; fax (22) 2602362; e-mail ireland@cats-net.com; Chargé d'affaires a.i. JOHN MCCULLAGH.

Italy: Plot 316, Lugalo Rd, POB 2106, Dar es Salaam; tel. (22) 2115935; fax (22) 2115938; e-mail ambasciatore@italdipldar.org; Ambassador MARCELLO GRICCIOLI.

Japan: 1018 Ali Hassan Mwinyi Rd, POB 2577, Dar es Salaam; tel. (22) 2115827; fax (22) 2115830; Ambassador KATSUYA IKEDA.

Kenya: NIC Investment House, 14th Floor, Samora Machel Ave, POB 5231, Dar es Salaam; tel. (22) 2112955; fax (22) 2113098; e-mail khc@raha.com; High Commissioner ZACHARY DOMINIC MUBURI-MUITA.

Korea, Democratic People's Republic: Plot 5, Ursino Estate, Kawawa Rd, Msasani, POB 2690, Dar es Salaam; tel. (22) 2775395; fax (22) 2700838; Ambassador RO MIN SU.

Korea, Republic: Plot 8/1, Tumbawe Rd, Oyster Bay, POB 154, Dar es Salaam; tel. (22) 2600496; fax (22) 2600559; e-mail rok@intafrica.com; Ambassador AHN HYO-SEUNG.

Libya: 386 Mtitu St, POB 9413, Dar es Salaam; tel. (22) 2150188; fax (22) 2150068; Secretary of People's Bureau BASHIR ABDA AL-DA'IM BASHIR.

Malawi: Plot 38, Ali Hassan Mwinyi Rd, POB 7616, Dar es Salaam; tel. (22) 2666284; fax (22) 2668161; e-mail mhc@africaonline.co.tz; High Commissioner L. B. MALUNGA.

Mozambique: 25 Garden Ave, POB 9370, Dar es Salaam; tel. and fax (22) 2116502; High Commissioner PEDRO DAVANE.

Netherlands: Umoja House, 4th Floor, Garden Ave, POB 9534, Dar es Salaam; tel. (22) 2110000; fax (22) 2110044; e-mail nlgovdar@intafrica.com; internet www.netherlands-embassy.go.tz; Ambassador B. S. M. BERENDSEN.

Nigeria: 83 Haile Selassie Rd, POB 9214, Oyster Bay, Dar es Salaam; tel. (22) 2666000; fax (22) 2668947; e-mail nhc-dsm@raha.com; High Commissioner AHMED M. USMAN.

Norway: 160 Mirambo St, POB 2646, Dar es Salaam; tel. (22) 2113366; fax (22) 2116564; e-mail emb.daressalaam@mfa.no; internet www.norway.go.tz; Ambassador JORUNN MÆHLUM.

Poland: 63 Alykhan Rd, Upanga, POB 2188, Dar es Salaam; tel. (22) 2115271; fax (22) 2115812; e-mail polamb@wingrouptz.com; Chargé d'affaires a.i. EUGENIUSZ RZEWUSKI.

TANZANIA   *Directory*

Russia: Plot No. 73, Ali Hassan Mwinyi Rd, POB 1905, Dar es Salaam; tel. (22) 2666005; fax (22) 2666818; e-mail embruss@bol.co.tz; Ambassador LEONARD ALEKSEEVIC.

Rwanda: Plot 32, Ali Hassan Mwinyi Rd, POB 2918, Dar es Salaam; tel. (22) 2115889; fax (22) 2115888; e-mail ambarwa.dsm@raha.com; Ambassador ZEPHYR MUTANGUHA.

South Africa: Plot 1338/1339, Mwaya Rd, Msaski, POB 10723, Dar es Salaam; tel. (22) 2601800; fax (22) 2600684; e-mail highcomm@sahc-tz.com; High Commissioner S. G. MFENYANA.

Spain: 99B Kinondoni Rd, POB 842, Dar es Salaam; tel. (22) 2666936; fax (22) 2666938; e-mail embesptz@mail.mae.es; Ambassador JOSÉ MARÍA CASTROVIEJO Y BOLIBAR.

Sudan: 'Albaraka', 64 Ali Hassan Mwinyi Rd, POB 2266, Dar es Salaam; tel. (22) 2117641; fax (22) 2115811; e-mail sudan.emb.dar@raha.com; Ambassador ELMUGHIRA ALI OMAR.

Sweden: Mirambo St and Garden Ave, POB 9274, Dar es Salaam; tel. (22) 2111235; fax (22) 2113420; e-mail ambassaden.dar.es.salaam@sida.se; internet www.swedenabroad.se; Ambassador TORVALD ÅKESSON.

Switzerland: 79 Kinondoni Rd/Mafinga St, POB 2454, Dar es Salaam; tel. (22) 2666008; fax (22) 2666736; e-mail vertretung@dar.rep.admin.ch; Ambassador THOMAS FÜGLISTER.

Syria: 246 Alykhan Rd, Upanga, POB 2442, Dar es Salaam; tel. (22) 2117656; fax (22) 2115860; Chargé d'affaires a.i. M. B. IMADI.

Uganda: Extelcom Bldg, 7th Floor, Samora Ave, POB 6237, Dar es Salaam; tel. (22) 2667391; fax (22) 2667224; e-mail ugadar@intafrica.com; High Commissioner KATENTA APUULI.

United Kingdom: Umoja House, Garden Ave, POB 9200, Dar es Salaam; tel. (22) 2110101; fax (22) 2110102; e-mail bhc.dar@fco.gov.uk; internet www.britishhighcommission.gov.uk/tanzania; High Commissioner Dr ANDREW JOHN POCOCK.

USA: 686 Old Bagamoyo Rd, Msasani, POB 9123, Dar es Salaam; tel. (22) 2668001; fax (22) 2668238; e-mail embassyd@state.gov; internet tanzania.usembassy.gov; Ambassador MICHAEL L. RETZER.

Yemen: 353 United Nations Rd, POB 349, Dar es Salaam; tel. (22) 2117650; fax (22) 2115924; Chargé d'affaires a.i. MOHAMED ABDULLA ALMAS.

Zambia: 5–6 Ohio St/Sokoine Dr. Junction, POB 2525, Dar es Salaam; tel. and fax (22) 2112977; e-mail zhcd@raha.com; High Commissioner JOHN KASHONKA CHITAFU.

Zimbabwe: 2097 East Upanga, off Ali Hassan Mwinyi Rd, POB 20762, Dar es Salaam; tel. (22) 2116789; fax (22) 2112913; e-mail zimdares@cats-net.com; Ambassador J. M. SHAVA.

Judicial System

Permanent Commission of Enquiry: POB 2643, Dar es Salaam; tel. (22) 2113690; fax (22) 2111533; Chair. and Official Ombudsman Prof. JOSEPH F. MBWILIZA; Sec. A. P. GUVETTE.

Court of Appeal
Consists of the Chief Justice and four Judges of Appeal.

Chief Justice of Tanzania: BARNABAS SAMATTA.

Chief Justice of Zanzibar: HAMID MAHMOUD HAMID.

High Court: headquarters at Dar es Salaam, but regular sessions held in all Regions; consists of a Jaji Kiongozi and 29 Judges.

District Courts: situated in each district and presided over by either a Resident Magistrate or District Magistrate; limited jurisdiction, with a right of appeal to the High Court.

Primary Courts: established in every district and presided over by Primary Court Magistrates; limited jurisdiction, with a right of appeal to the District Courts and then to the High Court.

Attorney-General: ANDREW CHENGE.

Director of Public Prosecutions: KULWA MASSABA.

People's Courts were established in Zanzibar in 1970. Magistrates are elected by the people and have two assistants each. Under the Zanzibar Constitution, which came into force in January 1985, defence lawyers and the right of appeal, abolished in 1970, were reintroduced.

Religion

Religious surveys were eliminated from all government census reports after 1967. However, religious leaders and sociologists generally believe that the country's population is 30%–40% Christian and 30%–40% percent Muslim, with the remainder consisting of practitioners of other faiths, traditional indigenous religions and atheists. Foreign missionaries operate in the country, including Roman Catholics, Lutherans, Baptists, Seventh-day Adventists, Mormons, Anglicans and Muslims.

ISLAM

The Muslim population is most heavily concentrated on the Zanzibar archipelago and in the coastal areas of the mainland. There are also large Muslim minorities in inland urban areas. 99% of the population of Zanzibar is estimated to be Muslim. Between 80% and 90% of the country's Muslim population is Sunni; the remainder consists of several Shi'a groups, mostly of Asian descent. A large proportion of the Asian community is Isma'ili.

Ismalia Provincial Church: POB 460, Dar es Salaam.

National Muslim Council of Tanzania: POB 21422, Dar es Salaam; tel. (22) 234934; f. 1969; supervises Islamic affairs on the mainland only; Chair. Sheikh HEMED BIN JUMA BIN HEMED; Exec. Sec. Alhaj MUHAMMAD MTULIA.

Supreme Muslim Council: Zanzibar; f. 1991; supervises Islamic affairs in Zanzibar; Mufti Sheikh HARITH BIN KALEF.

Wakf and Trust Commission: POB 4092, Zanzibar; f. 1980; Islamic affairs; Exec. Sec. YUSUF ABDULRAHMAN MUHAMMAD.

CHRISTIANITY

The Christian population is composed of Roman Catholics, Protestants, Pentecostals, Seventh-day Adventists, members of the Church of Jesus Christ of Latter-day Saints (Mormons) and Jehovah's Witnesses.

Jumuiya ya Kikristo Tanzania (Christian Council of Tanzania): Church House, POB 1454, Dodoma; tel. (26) 2321204; fax (26) 2324445; f. 1934; Chair. Rt Rev. JOHN ACLAND RAMADHANI (Bishop of the Anglican Church); Gen. Sec. Dr WILSON LWEGANWA MTEBE.

The Anglican Communion

Anglicans are adherents of the Church of the Province of Tanzania, comprising 16 dioceses.

Archbishop of the Province of Tanzania and Bishop of Ruaha: Most Rev. DONALD LEO MTETEMELA, POB 1028, Iringa; fax (26) 2702479; e-mail ruaha@maf.or.tz.

Provincial Secretary: Dr R. MWITA AKIRI (acting), POB 899, Dodoma; tel. (26) 2321437; fax (26) 2324265; e-mail cpt@maf.org.

Greek Orthodox

Archbishop of East Africa: NICADEMUS OF IRINOUPOULIS (resident in Nairobi, Kenya); jurisdiction covers Kenya, Uganda and Tanzania.

Lutheran

Evangelical Lutheran Church in Tanzania: POB 3033, Arusha; tel. (57) 8855; fax (57) 8858; 1.5m. mems; Presiding Bishop Rt Rev. Dr SAMSON MUSHEMBA (acting); Exec. Sec. AMANI MWENEGOHA.

The Roman Catholic Church

Tanzania comprises five archdioceses and 25 dioceses. There were an estimated 10,476,621 adherents at 31 December 2003, equivalent to about 26.7% of the total population.

Tanzania Episcopal Conference

Catholic Secretariat, Mandela Rd, POB 2133, Dar es Salaam; tel. (22) 2851075; fax (22) 2851133; e-mail tec@cats-net.com; internet www.rc.net/tanzania/tec; f. 1980; Pres. Mgr SEVERINE NIWEMUGIZI (Bishop of Rulenge).

Archbishop of Arusha: Most Rev. JOSAPHAT LOUIS LEBULU, Archbishop's House, POB 3044, Arusha; tel. (27) 2544361; fax (27) 2548004; e-mail archbishoplebulu@habari.co.tz.

Archbishop of Dar es Salaam: Cardinal POLYCARP PENGO, Archbishop's House, POB 167, Dar es Salaam; tel. (22) 2113223; fax (22) 2125751; e-mail nyumba@cats-net.com.

Archbishop of Mwanza: Most Rev. ANTHONY MAYALA, Archbishop's House, POB 1421, Mwanza; tel. and fax (68) 501029; e-mail mwanza-archdiocese@cats-net.com.

Archbishop of Songea: Most Rev. NORBERT WENDELIN MTEGA, Archbishop's House, POB 152, Songea; tel. (65) 602004; fax (65) 602593; e-mail songea-archdiocese@cats-net.com.

Archbishop of Tabora: Most Rev. MARIO EPIFANIO ABDALLAH MGULUNDE, Archbishop's House, Private Bag, PO Tabora; tel. (62) 2329; fax (62) 4536; e-mail archbishops-office@yahoo.co.uk.

Other Christian Churches

Baptist Mission of Tanzania: POB 9414, Dar es Salaam; tel. (22) 2170130; fax (22) 2170127; f. 1956; Admin. FRANK PEVEY.

Christian Missions in Many Lands (Tanzania): German Branch, POB 34, Tunduru, Ruvuma Region; f. 1957; Gen. Sec. KARL GERHARD WARTH.

TANZANIA

Moravian Church: POB 377, Mbeya; 113,656 mems; Gen. Sec. Rev. SHADRACK MWAKASEGE.
Pentecostal Church: POB 34, Kahama.
Presbyterian Church: POB 2510, Dar es Salaam; tel. (22) 229075.

BAHÁ'Í FAITH

National Spiritual Assembly: POB 585, Dar es Salaam; tel. and fax (22) 2152766; e-mail bahaitz@africaonline.tz; mems resident in 2,301 localities.

OTHER RELIGIONS

Many people follow traditional beliefs. There are also some Hindu communities.

The Press

NEWSPAPERS

Daily

The African: Sinza Rd, POB 4793, Dar es Salaam; e-mail dimba@africaonline.co.tz; Editor-in-Chief JOHN KULEKANA.
Alasiri: POB 31042, Dar es Salaam; Swahili; Editor LUCAS MNUBI.
Daily News: POB 9033, Dar es Salaam; tel. (22) 2110165; fax (22) 2112881; f. 1972; govt-owned; Man. Editor SETHI KAMUHANDA; circ. 50,000.
The Democrat: Dar es Salaam; independent; Editor IDRISS LUGULU; circ. 15,000.
The Guardian: POB 31042, Dar es Salaam; tel. (22) 275250; fax (22) 273583; e-mail guardian@ipp.co.tz; internet www.ippmedia.com; f. 1994; English and Swahili; Man. Dir VUMI URASA; Man. Editor PASCAL SHIJA.
Kipanga: POB 199, Zanzibar; Swahili; publ. by Information and Broadcasting Services.
Majira: POB 71439, Dar es Salaam; tel. (22) 238901; fax (22) 231104; independent; Swahili; Editor THEOPHIL MAKUNGA; circ. 15,000.
Nipashe: POB 31042, Dar es Salaam; Swahili; Editor HAMISI MZEE.
Uhuru: POB 9221, Dar es Salaam; tel. (22) 2182224; fax (22) 2185065; e-mail uhuru@intafrica.com; f. 1961; official publ. of CCM; Swahili; Man. Editor SAIDI NGUBA; circ. 100,000.

Weekly

Business Times: POB 71439, Dar es Salaam; tel. (22) 238901; fax (22) 231104; e-mail majira@bcsmedia.com; internet www.bcstimes.com; independent; English; Editor ALLI MWAMBOLA; circ. 15,000.
The Express: Bakwata Bldg, 2nd Floor, POB 20588, Dar es Salaam; tel. (22) 2180058; fax (22) 2182659; e-mail express@raha.com; internet www.theexpress.com; independent; English; Editor FAYAZ BHOJANI; circ. 20,000.
Gazette of the United Republic: POB 9142, Dar es Salaam; tel. (22) 231817; official announcements; Editor H. HAJI; circ. 6,000.
Government Gazette: POB 261, Zanzibar; f. 1964; official announcements.
Kasheshe: POB 31042, Dar es Salaam; Swahili; Editor VENANCE MLAY.
Mfanyakazi (The Worker): POB 15359, Dar es Salaam; tel. (22) 226111; Swahili; trade union publ; Editor NDUGU MTAWA; circ. 100,000.
The Family Mirror: Faru/Nyamwezi St, Karikoo Area, POB 6804, Dar es Salaam; tel. (22) 181331; Editor ZEPHANIAH MUSENDO.
Mzalendo: POB 9221, Dar es Salaam; tel. (22) 2182224; fax (22) 2185065; e-mail uhuru@intafrica.com; f. 1972; publ. by CCM; Swahili; Man. Editor SAIDI NGABA; circ. 115,000.
Leta Raha: POB 31042, Dar es Salaam; Swahili; Editor EDMOND MSANGI.
Nipashe Jumapili: POB 31042, Dar es Salaam; Swahili.
Sunday News: POB 9033, Dar es Salaam; tel. (22) 2116072; fax (22) 2112881; f. 1954; govt-owned; Man. Editor SETHI KAMUCHANDA; circ. 50,000.
Sunday Observer: POB 31042, Dar es Salaam; e-mail guardian@ipp.co.tz; Man. Dir VUMI URASA; Man. Editor PETER MSUNGU.
Taifa Letu: POB 31042, Dar es Salaam; Swahili.

PERIODICALS

The African Review: POB 35042, Dar es Salaam; tel. (22) 243500; 2 a year; journal of African politics, development and international affairs; publ. by the Dept of Political Science, Univ. of Dar es Salaam; Chief Editor Dr C. GASARASI; circ. 1,000.

Directory

Eastern African Law Review: POB 35093, Dar es Salaam; tel. (22) 243254; f. 1967; 2 a year; Chief Editor N. N. N. NDITI; circ. 1,000.
Elimu Haina Mwisho: POB 1986, Mwanza; monthly; circ. 45,000.
Habari za Washirika: POB 2567, Dar es Salaam; tel. (22) 223346; monthly; publ. by Co-operative Union of Tanzania; Editor H. V. N. CHIBULUNJE; circ. 40,000.
Jenga: POB 2669, Dar es Salaam; tel. (22) 2112893; fax (22) 2113618; journal of the National Development Corpn; circ. 2,000.
Kiongozi (The Leader): POB 9400, Dar es Salaam; tel. (22) 229505; f. 1950; fortnightly; Swahili; Roman Catholic; Editor ROBERT MFUGALE; circ. 33,500.
Kweupe: POB 222, Zanzibar; weekly; Swahili; publ. by Information and Broadcasting Services.
Mlezi (The Educator): POB 41, Peramiho; tel. 30; f. 1970; every 2 months; Editor Fr DOMINIC WEIS; circ. 8,000.
Mwenge (Firebrand): POB 1, Peramiho; tel. 30; f. 1937; monthly; Editor JOHN P. MBONDE; circ. 10,000.
Nchi Yetu (Our Country): POB 9142, Dar es Salaam; tel. (22) 2110200; f. 1964; govt publ; monthly; Swahili; circ. 50,000.
Nuru: POB 1893, Zanzibar; f. 1992; bi-monthly; official publ. of Zanzibar Govt; circ. 8,000.
Safina: POB 21422, Dar es Salaam; tel. (22) 234934; publ. by National Muslim Council of Tanzania; Editor YASSIN SADIK; circ. 10,000.
Sikiliza: POB 635, Morogoro; tel. (56) 3338; fax (56) 4374; quarterly; Seventh-day Adventist; Editor MEL H. M. MATINYI; circ. 100,000.
Taamuli: POB 899, Dar es Salaam; tel. (22) 243500; 2 a year; journal of political science; publ. by the Dept of Political Science, Univ. of Dar es Salaam; circ. 1,000.
Tantravel: POB 2485, Dar es Salaam; tel. (22) 2111244; fax (22) 2116420; e-mail safari@ud.co.tz; internet www.tanzaniatouristboard.com; quarterly; publ. by Tanzania Tourist Board; Editor STEVE FISHER.
Tanzania Education Journal: POB 9121, Dar es Salaam; tel. (22) 227211; f. 1984; 3 a year; publ. by Institute of Education, Ministry of Education; circ. 8,000.
Tanzania Trade Currents: POB 5402, Dar es Salaam; tel. (22) 2851706; fax (22) 851700; e-mail betis@intafrica.com; bi-monthly; publ. by Board of External Trade; circ. 2,000.
Uhuru na Amani: POB 3033, Arusha; tel. (57) 8855; fax (57) 8858; quarterly; Swahili; publ. by Evangelical Lutheran Church in Tanzania; Editor ELIZABETH LOBULU; circ. 15,000.
Ukulima wa Kisasa (Modern Farming): Farmers' Education and Publicity Unit, POB 2308, Dar es Salaam; tel. (22) 2116496; fax (22) 2122923; e-mail fepu@twiga.com; f. 1955; bi-monthly; Swahili; publ. by Ministry of Food and Agriculture; Editor H. MLAKI; circ. 15,000.
Ushirika Wetu: POB 2567, Dar es Salaam; tel. (22) 2184081; e-mail ushirika@covision2000.com; monthly; publ. by Tanzania Federation of Co-operatives; Editor SIMON J. KERARYO; circ. 40,000.
Wela: POB 180, Dodoma; Swahili.

NEWS AGENCIES

Press Services Tanzania (PST) Ltd: POB 31042, Dar es Salaam; tel. and fax (22) 2119195.

Foreign Bureaux

Inter Press Service (IPS) (Italy): 304 Nkomo Rd, POB 4755, Dar es Salaam; tel. (22) 229311; Chief Correspondent PAUL CHINTOWA.
Newslink Africa (UK): POB 5165, Dar es Salaam; Correspondent NIZAR FAZAL.
Rossiyskoye Informatsionnoye Agentstvo—Novosti (RIA—Novosti) (Russia): POB 2271, Dar es Salaam; tel. (22) 223897; Dir ANATOLII TKACHENKO.
Xinhua (New China) News Agency: 72 Upanga Rd, POB 2682, Dar es Salaam; tel. (22) 223967; Correspondent HUAI CHENGBO.
Reuters (UK) is also represented in Tanzania.

Publishers

Central Tanganyika Press: POB 1129, Dodoma; tel. (26) 23000; fax (26) 2324565; e-mail ctzpress@maf.or.tz; f. 1954; religious; Man. PETER MAKASSI MANGATI.
DUP (1996) Ltd: POB 7028, Dar es Salaam; tel. and fax (22) 2410137; e-mail director@dup.udsm.ac.tz; f. 1979; educational, academic and cultural texts in Swahili and English; Dir Dr N. G. MWITTA.

TANZANIA

Eastern Africa Publications Ltd: POB 1002 Arusha; tel. (57) 3176; f. 1979; general and school textbooks; Gen. Man. ABDULLAH SAIWAAD.

Inland Publishers: POB 125, Mwanza; tel. (68) 40064; general non-fiction, religion, in Kiswahili and English; Dir Rev. S. M. MAGESA.

Oxford University Press: Maktaba Rd, POB 5299, Dar es Salaam; tel. (22) 229209; f. 1969; literature, literary criticism, essays, poetry; Man. SALIM SHAABAN SALIM.

Tanzania Publishing House: 47 Samora Machel Ave, POB 2138, Dar es Salaam; tel. (22) 2137402; e-mail tphhouse@yahoo.com; f. 1966; educational and general books in Swahili and English; Gen. Man. PRIMUS ISIDOR KARUGENDO.

GOVERNMENT PUBLISHING HOUSE

Government Printer: POB 9124, Dar es Salaam; tel. (22) 220291; Dir JONAS OFORO.

Broadcasting and Communications

TELECOMMUNICATIONS

Tanzania Communications Regulatory Authority (TCRA): POB 474, Dar es Salaam; tel. (22) 2118947; fax (22) 2116664; e-mail moa@tcc.go.tz; internet www.tcc.go.tz; f. 1993; licenses postal and telecommunications service operators; manages radio spectrum; acts as ombudsman.

MIC Tanzania Ltd: POB 2929, Dar es Salaam; tel. (22) 2126510; fax (741) 123014; e-mail mobitel@mobitel.co.tz; internet www.mobitel.co.tz; operates mobile cellular telecommunications services through Mobitel network.

Tanzania Telecommunications Co Ltd (TTCL): POB 9070, Dar es Salaam; tel. (22) 2110055; fax (22) 2113232; e-mail ttcl@ttcl.co.tz; 35% sold to consortium of Detecon (Germany) and Mobile Systems International (Netherlands) in Feb. 2001; Man. Dir ASMATH N. MPATWA.

Tritel Tanzania Ltd: POB 1853, Dar es Salaam; tel. (22) 2862191; fax (22) 2862710; e-mail info@tritel.co.tz; internet www.tritel.co.tz; mobile cellular telephone operator.

Vodacom (Tanzania) Ltd: POB 2369, Dar es Salaam; tel. (744) 702220; fax (744) 704014; e-mail care@vodacom.co.tz; internet www.vodacom.co.tz; mobile cellular telephone operator.

Zanzibar Telecom (Zantel): Zanzibar; f. 1999; mobile cellular telephone operator for Zanzibar; CEO MOHAMMED AHMED SALIM.

CelTel Ltd also provides telecommunications services.

BROADCASTING

Radio

Radio FM Zenj 96.8: Zanzibar; f. 2005; owned by Zanzibar Media Corpn; broadcasts to 60% of Zanzibar, to be extended to all of Zanzibar and mainland coast from southern Tanzania to Kenya; Gen. Man. AUSTIN MAKANI.

Radio Kwizera: N'Gara.

Radio One: POB 4374, Dar es Salaam; tel. (22) 275914; e-mail ipptech@ipp.co.tz; internet www.ippmedia.com.

Radio Tanzania Dar es Salaam (RTD): POB 9191, Dar es Salaam; tel. (22) 2860760; fax (22) 2865577; f. 1951; state-owned; domestic services in Swahili; external services in English; Dir ABDUL NGARAWA.

Radio Tanzania Zanzibar: state-owned.

Radio Tumaini (Hope): 1 Bridge St, POB 167, Dar es Salaam; tel. (22) 2117307; fax (22) 2112594; e-mail tumaini@africaonline.co.tz; broadcasts in Swahili within Dar es Salaam; operated by the Roman Catholic Church; broadcasts on religious, social and economic issues; Dir Fr JEAN-FRANÇOIS GALTIER.

Sauti Ya Tanzania Zanzibar (The Voice of Tanzania Zanzibar): POB 1178, Zanzibar; f. 1951; state-owned; broadcasts in Swahili on three wavelengths; Dir SULEIMAN JUMA.

Television

Dar Television (DTV): POB 21122, Dar es Salaam; tel. (22) 2116341; fax (22) 2113112; e-mail franco.dtv@raha.com; Man. Dir FRANCO TRAMONTANO.

Independent Television (ITV): Dar es Salaam.

Television Zanzibar: POB 314, Zanzibar; f. 1973; Dir JAMA SIMBA.

Finance

(cap. = capital; res = reserves; dep. = deposits; m. = million; brs = branches; amounts in Tanzanian shillings, unless otherwise indicated)

BANKING

Central Bank

Bank of Tanzania (Benki Kuu Ya Tanzania): 10 Mirambo St, POB 2939, Dar es Salaam; tel. (22) 2110946; fax (22) 2113325; e-mail info@hq.bot-tz.org; internet www.bot.tz.org; f. 1966; bank of issue; cap. 10,000m., res 302,889m., dep. 935,508m. (June 2003); Gov. and Chair. Dr DAUDI T. S. BALLALI; Dep. Gov. M. H. MBAYE; 4 brs.

Principal Banks

African Banking Corpn (Tanzania) Ltd: Barclays House, 1st Floor, Ohio St, POB 31, Dar es Salaam; tel. (22) 2119303; fax (22) 2112402; e-mail abct@africanbankingcorp.com; internet www.africanbankingcorp.com; wholly owned by African Banking Corpn Holdings Ltd; cap. 5,404m. (Dec. 2003); Chair. Dr JONAS KIPOKOLA.

Akiba Commercial Bank Ltd: TDFL Bldg, Ali Hassan Mwinyi Rd, POB 669, Dar es Salaam; tel. (22) 2118340; fax (22) 2114173; e-mail akiba@cctz.com; cap. 2,962m. (Dec. 2003); Chair. D. M. MOSHA; Man. Dir TOM KORE.

Azania Bancorp Ltd: POB 9271, Dar es Salaam; tel. (22) 2117997; fax (22) 2118010; e-mail info@azaniabank.co.tz; internet www.azaniabank.co.tz; 55% owned by National Social Security Fund, 31% owned by Parastatal Pension Fund, 9% owned by East African Development Bank, 5% owned by individuals; cap. 6,168m. (Dec. 2003); Chair. N. NSEMWA; CEO CHARLES SINGILI.

Barclays Bank (Tanzania) Ltd: Barclays House, Ohio St, POB 5137, Dar es Salaam; tel. (22) 2129381; fax (22) 2129757; e-mail karl.stumke@barclays.com; 99.9% owned by Barclays PLC (United Kingdom), 0.1% owned by Ebbgate Holdings Ltd; cap. 18,750m. (Dec. 2003); Chair. J. K. CHANDE; Man. Dir KARL STUMKE.

Capital Finance Ltd: TDFL Bldg, 5th Floor, 1008 Ohio St/Upanga Rd, POB 9032, Dar es Salaam; tel. (22) 2135152; fax (22) 2135150; e-mail mail@cfl.co.tz; wholly owned by Tanzania Development Finance Co Ltd; cap. 4,000m. (Dec. 2003); Chair. H. K. SENKORO; CEO J. H. MCGUFFOG.

CF Union Bank Ltd: Jivan Hirji Bldg, Indira Gandhi/Mosque St, POB 1509, Dar es Salaam; tel. (22) 2110212; fax (22) 2118750; e-mail cfunionbank@raha.com; f. 2002 by merger of Furaha Finance Ltd and Crown Finance & Leasing Ltd; cap. 2m. (Dec. 2003); Chair. MUNIR ASGARALI BHARWANI; Man. Dir G. R. MWAMUKONDA.

Citibank Tanzania Ltd: Ali Hassan Mwinyi Rd, POB 71625, Dar es Salaam; tel. (22) 2117575; fax (22) 2113910; 99.98% owned by Citibank Overseas Investment Corpn; Chair. EMEKA EMUWA.

CRDB Bank: Azikiwe St, POB 268, Dar es Salaam; tel. (22) 2117442; fax (22) 2116714; e-mail crdb@crdb.com; internet www.crdb.com; f. as Co-operative and Rural Development Bank in 1947, transferred to private ownership and current name adopted 1996; 30% owned by DANIDA Investment; provides commercial banking services and loans for rural development; cap. 8,234m., res 6,160m., dep. 269,767m. (Dec. 2003); Chair JERRY SOLOMON; Man. Dir Dr CHARLES S. KIMEI; 31 brs.

Dar es Salaam Community Bank Ltd (DCB): Arnautoglu Bldg, Bibi Titi Mohamed St, POB 19798, Dar es Salaam; tel. (22) 2180253; fax (22) 2180239; e-mail dcb@africaonline.co.tz; f. 2001; cap. 1,796m. (Dec. 2003); Chair. PAUL MILVANGE RUPIA; Man. Dir EDMUND PANCRAS MKWAWA.

Diamond Trust Bank Tanzania Ltd: POB 115, cnr of Mosque St and Jamaat St, Dar es Salaam; tel. (22) 2114888; fax (22) 2114210; f. 1946 as Diamond Jubilee Investment Trust; converted to bank and adopted current name in 1996; 33.4% owned by Diamond Trust Bank Kenya Ltd, 31.2% owned by Aga Khan Fund for Economic Development SA (Switzerland); cap. 1,108m., dep. 27,583m. (Dec. 2003); Chair. MAHEDI KANJI; CEO SANJEEV KUMAR.

Eurafrican Bank (Tanzania) Ltd: NDC Development House, cnr Kivukoni Front and Ohio St, POB 3054, Dar es Salaam; tel. (22) 2111229; fax (22) 2113740; e-mail eab@eurafricanbank-tz.com; f. 1994; 78.8% owned by Belgolaise/Fortis Bank Group; other shareholders: FMO-Netherlands Development Co (9.83%), Tanzania Development Finance (9.41%), others (1.96%); cap. 6,478m. (Dec. 2002); Chair. FULGENCE M. KAZAURA; Man. Dir JUMA KISAAME.

EXIM Bank (Tanzania) Ltd: NIC Investment House, Samora Ave, POB 1431, Dar es Salaam; tel. (22) 2113091; fax (22) 2119737; e-mail enquiry@eximbank-tz.com; internet www.eximbank-tz.com; cap. 3,500m., dep. 90,091m. (Dec. 2003); Chair. YOGESH MANEK; Man. Dir S. M. J. MWAMBENJA.

Federal Bank of the Middle East Ltd: POB 8298, Samora Ave, Dar es Salaam; tel. (22) 2126000; fax (22) 2126006; e-mail headoffice@fbme.com; internet www.fbme.com; f. 1982 in Cyprus as subsidiary of Federal Bank of Lebanon SAL (Lebanon); changed country of incorporation to Cayman Islands in 1986, and to Tanzania in 2003; cap. 46,000m. (Dec. 2003); Chair. AYOUB-FARID M. SAAB, FADI M. SAAB; Gen. Man. (Tanzania) JAN VAN JAAREN.

Habib African Bank Ltd: India St, POB 70086, Dar es Salaam; tel. (22) 2111107; fax (22) 2111014; cap. 1,300m. (Dec. 2003); Chair. HABIB MOHAMMED D. HABIB; Man. Dir MANZAR A. KAZMI.

International Bank of Malaysia (Tanzania) Ltd: Upanga/Kisutu St, POB 9363, Dar es Salaam; tel. (22) 2110518; fax (22) 2110196; e-mail ibm@afsat.com; Chair. JOSEPHINE PREMLA SIVARETNAM; CEO M. RAHMAT.

Kenya Commercial Bank (Tanzania) Ltd: National Audit House, Samora/Ohio St, POB 804, Dar es Salaam; tel. (22) 2115386; fax (22) 2115391; e-mail kbctanzania@kcb.co.tz; internet www.kcb.ke; cap. 6,000m. (Dec. 2003); Chair. S. MUDHUME; Man. Dir BAZRA TABULO.

Kilimanjaro Co-operative Bank Ltd: Mawenzi Rd, POB 1760, Moshi; tel. (27) 54470; fax (27) 53570; Chair. A. P. KAVISHE; Gen. Man. J. KULAYA.

Mufindi Community Bank: POB 147, Mafinga; tel. and fax (26) 2772165; e-mail mucoba@africaonline.co.tz; cap. 100m. (Dec. 2003); Chair. J. J. MUNGAI; Gen. Man. DANY MPOGOLE.

Mwanga Community Bank: Mwanga Township, POB 333, Mwanga, Kilimanjaro; tel. and fax (27) 2754235; Man. Dir CHRIS HALIBUT.

National Microfinance Bank Ltd (NMB): Samora Ave, POB 9213, Dar es Salaam; tel. (22) 2124048; fax (22) 2110077; e-mail ceo@nmbtz.com; internet www.nmbtz.com; f. 1997 following disbandment of The National Bank of Commerce; Chair. M. NGATUNGA; CEO JOHN R. GILES.

NBC (1997) Ltd (National Bank of Commerce Ltd): NBC House, Sokoine Drive, POB 1863, Dar es Salaam; tel. (22) 2112082; fax (22) 2112887; e-mail nbcltd@nbctz.com; f. 1997 following disbandment of National Bank of Commerce; 55% owned by ABSA Group Ltd (South Africa), 30% by Govt and 15% by International Finance Corpn; cap. 10,000m., res 30,290m., dep. 351,815m. (Dec. 2003); Chair. HAIDAR K. R. AMAN; Man. Dir GERALD JORDAAN; 32 brs.

People's Bank of Zanzibar Ltd (PBZ): POB 1173, Stone Town, Zanzibar; tel. (24) 2231119; fax (24) 2231121; e-mail pbzltd@zanlik.com; f. 1966; controlled by Zanzibar Govt; cap. 16m. (June 1991); Chair. M. ABOUD; Gen. Man. N. S. NASSOR; 3 brs.

Savings & Finance Ltd: Mission St/Samora Ave, POB 20268, Dar es Salaam; tel. (22) 2118625; fax (22) 2116733; Man. Dir SURANJAN GHOSH.

Stanbic Bank Tanzania Ltd: Sukari House, cnr Ohio St and Sokoine Drive, POB 72647, Dar es Salaam; tel. (22) 2112195; fax (22) 2113742; e-mail tanzaniainfo@stanbic.com; internet www.stanbic.co.tz; f. 1993; wholly owned by Standard Africa Holdings PLC; cap. 2,000m., dep. 154,776m. (Dec. 2002); Chair OWEN TIDBURY; Gen. Man. ADAM MCKINLAY; 4 brs.

Standard Chartered Bank Tanzania Ltd: International House, 1st Floor, cnr Shaaban Robert St and Garden Ave, POB 9011, Dar es Salaam; tel. (22) 2122160; fax (22) 2113770; f. 1992; wholly owned by Standard Chartered Holdings (Africa) BV, Netherlands; cap. 1,000m., res 21,551m., dep. 233,198m. (Dec. 2002); Chair. M. HART; Man. Dir S. TSIKIRAYI.

Tanzania Development Finance Co Ltd (TDFL): TDFL Bldg, Plot 1008, cnr Upanga Rd and Ohio St, POB 2478, Dar es Salaam; tel. (22) 2116417; fax (22) 2116418; e-mail mail@tdfl.co.tz; f. 1962; owned by Govt (32%), govt agencies of the Netherlands and Germany (5% and 26% respectively), the Commonwealth Development Corpn (26%) and the European Investment Bank (11%); cap. 3,303m. (Dec. 2001); Chair. H. K. SENKORO; CEO J. MCGUFFOG.

Tanzania Investment Bank (TIB): cnr Zanaki St and Samora Machel Ave, POB 9373, Dar es Salaam; tel. (22) 2111708; fax (22) 2113438; e-mail rtwalib@tib.co.tz; internet www.tib.co.tz; f. 1970; provides finance, tech. assistance and consultancy, fund administration and loan guarantee for economic devt; 99% govt-owned; cap. 7,641m. (Dec. 2003); Chair. FULGENECE M. KAZURA; Man. Dir WILLIAM A. MLAKI.

Tanzania Postal Bank (TPB): Extelecoms Annex Bldg, Samora Ave, POB 9300, Dar es Salaam; tel. (22) 2112358; fax (22) 2114815; e-mail md@postalbank.co.tz; internet www.postalbank.co.tz; f. 1991; state-owned; cap. 1,041m. (Dec. 2003); Chair. PAUL JUSTIN MKANGA; Man. Dir and CEO ALPHONSE R. KIHWELE; 4 brs and 113 agencies.

Ulc (Tanzania) Ltd: POB 31, Dar es Salaam; tel. (22) 2118888; fax (22) 2118953; e-mail dtbank@intafrica.com; cap. 2,204m. (Dec. 1999); Chair. Dr JONAS KIPOKOLA; CEO JAMES MACHARIA.

United Bank of Africa Ltd: PPF House, Ground/Mezzanine Floors, Samora Ave/Morogoro Rd, POB 9640, Dar es Salaam; tel. (22) 2130113; fax (22) 2130116; e-mail uba@cats-net.com; cap. 2,532m. (Dec. 2002); Chair. N. N. KITOMARI; Man. Dir I. J. MITCHELL.

STOCK EXCHANGE

Dar es Salaam Stock Exchange: Twigga Bldg, 4th Floor, Samora Ave, POB 70081, Dar es Salaam; tel. (22) 2133659; fax (22) 2122421; e-mail des@cats-net.com; internet www.darstockexchange.com; f. 1998; Chair. GABINUS MAGANGA; Chief Exec. Dr HAMISI S. KIBOLA.

INSURANCE

Jubilee Insurance Co of Tanzania Ltd (JICT): Dar es Salaam; 40% owned by Jubilee Insurance Kenya, 24% by local investors, 15% by the IFC, 15% by the Aga Khan Fund for Economic Devt, 6% by others; cap. US $2m.

National Insurance Corporation of Tanzania Ltd (NIC): POB 9264, Dar es Salaam; tel. (22) 2113823; fax (22) 2113403; f. 1963; state-owned; all classes of insurance; Chair. Prof. J. L. KANYWANYI; Man. Dir OCTAVIAN W. TEMU; 30 brs.

Trade and Industry

GOVERNMENT AGENCIES

Board of External Trade (BET): POB 5402, Dar es Salaam; tel. (22) 2851706; fax (22) 2851700; e-mail betis@intafrica.com; f. 1978; trade and export information and promotion, market research, marketing advisory and consultancy services; Dir-Gen. MBARUK K. MWANDORO.

Board of Internal Trade (BIT): POB 883, Dar es Salaam; tel. (22) 228301; f. 1967 as State Trading Corpn; reorg. 1973; state-owned; supervises seven national and 21 regional trading cos; distribution of general merchandise, agricultural and industrial machinery, pharmaceuticals, foodstuffs and textiles; shipping and other transport services; Dir-Gen. J. E. MAKOYE.

Parastatal Sector Reform Commission (PSRC): Sukari House, POB 9252, Dar es Salaam; tel. (22) 2115482; fax (22) 2113065; e-mail masalla@raha.com.

Tanzania Investment Centre (TIC): POB 938, Dar es Salaam; tel. (22) 2116328; fax (22) 2118253; e-mail information@tic.co.tz; internet www.tic.co.tz; f. 1997; promotes and facilitates investment in Tanzania; Exec. Dir SAMUEL SITTA.

CHAMBERS OF COMMERCE

Dar es Salaam Chamber of Commerce: Kelvin House, Samora Machel Ave, POB 41, Dar es Salaam; tel. (744) 270438; fax (22) 2112754; e-mail dcc1919@yahoo.com; f. 1919; Exec. Dir Y. P. MSEKWA.

Tanzania Chamber of Commerce, Industry and Agriculture: POB 9713, Dar es Salaam; tel. and fax (22) 2119437; e-mail tccia.info@cats-net.com; internet www.tccia.co.tz; f. 1988; Pres. E. MUSIBA.

Zanzibar Chamber of Commerce: POB 1407, Zanzibar; tel. (24) 2233083; fax (24) 2233349.

DEVELOPMENT CORPORATIONS

Capital Development Authority: POB 1, Dodoma; tel. (26) 2324053; f. 1973 to develop the new capital city of Dodoma; govt-controlled; Dir-Gen. EVARIST BABISI KEWBA.

Economic Development Commission: POB 9242, Dar es Salaam; tel. (22) 2112681; f. 1962 to plan national economic development; state-controlled.

National Development Corporation: Kivukoni Front, Ohio St, POB 2669, Dar es Salaam; tel. (22) 2112893; fax (22) 2113618; e-mail epztz@ndctz.com; internet www.ndctz.com; f. 1965; state-owned; cap. Ts. 30.0m.; promotes progress and expansion in production and investment.

Small Industries Development Organization (SIDO): POB 2476, Dar es Salaam; tel. (22) 2151946; fax (22) 2152070; e-mail sido-dg@africaonline.co.tz; internet www.sido.go.tz; f. 1973; promotes and assists development of small-scale enterprises in public, co-operative and private sectors, aims to increase the involvement of women in small businesses; Chair. JAPHET S. MLAGALA; Dir-Gen. MIKE LAISOR.

Sugar Development Corporation: Dar es Salaam; tel. (22) 2112969; fax (22) 230598; Gen. Man. GEORGE G. MBATI.

Tanzania Petroleum Development Corporation (TPDC): POB 2774, Dar es Salaam; tel. (22) 2181407; fax (22) 2180047; f. 1969; state-owned; oversees petroleum exploration and undertakes autonomous exploration, imports crude petroleum and distributes refined products; Man. Dir YONA S. M. KILLAGANE.

There is also a development corporation for textiles.

TANZANIA

INDUSTRIAL AND TRADE ASSOCIATIONS

Cashewnut Board of Tanzania: POB 533, Mtwara; tel. (59) 333445; fax (59) 333536; govt-owned; regulates the marketing, processing and export of cashews; Chair. Galus Abeid; Gen. Man. Dr Ali F. Mandali.

Confederation of Tanzania Industries (CTI): POB 71783, Dar es Salaam; tel. (22) 2123802; fax (22) 2115414; e-mail cti@raha.com; Dir Juma Mwapachu.

National Coconut Development Programme: POB 6226, Dar es Salaam; tel. (22) 2700552; fax (22) 275549; e-mail arim@arim.africaonline.co.tz; f. 1979 to revive coconut industry; processing and marketing via research and devt in disease and pest control, agronomy and farming systems, breeding and post-harvest technology; based at Mikocheni Agricultural Research Inst; Dir Dr Alois K. Kullaya.

Tanganyika Coffee Growers' Association Ltd: POB 102, Moshi.

Tanzania Association of Floriculture (TAFA): POB 11123, Arusha; tel. (57) 4432; fax (57) 4214; e-mail aru.cut@kabari.co.tz; Sec. Matthias Ole Kissambu.

Tanzania Coffee Board (TCB): POB 732, Moshi; tel. (55) 52324; fax (55) 53033; e-mail coffee@eoltz.com; internet www.newafrica.com; Man. Dir Leslie Omari.

Tanzania Cotton Board: Pamba House, Garden Ave, POB 9161, Dar es Salaam; tel. (22) 2122565; fax (22) 2112894; e-mail tclb@tancotton.co.tz; internet www.tancotton.co.tz; f. 1984; regulates, develops and promotes the Tanzanian cotton industry; Dir Gen. Dr J. C. B. Kabissa.

Tanzania Exporters' Association: Plot No. 139, Sembeti Rd, POB 1175, Dar es Salaam; tel. (22) 2781035; fax (22) 2112752; e-mail smutabuz@hotmail.com.

Tanzania Pyrethrum Board: POB 149, Iringa; f. 1960; Chair. Brig. Luhanga; CEO P. B. G. Hangaya.

Tanzania Sisal Authority: POB 277, Tanga; tel. (53) 44401; fax (53) 42759; Chair. W. H. Shellukindo; Man. Dir S. Shamte.

Tanzania Tobacco Board: POB 227, Mazimbu Rd, Morogoro; tel. (56) 4517; fax (56) 4401; Chair. S. Galinoma; CEO Hamisi Hasani Liana.

Tanzania Wood Industry Corporation: POB 9160, Dar es Salaam; Gen. Man. E. M. Mnzava.

Tea Association of Tanzania: POB 2177, Dar es Salaam; tel. (22) 2122033; e-mail trit@twiga.com; f. 1989; Chair. Dr Norman C. Kelly; Exec. Dir David E. A. Mgwassa.

Tea Board of Tanzania: POB 2663, Dar es Salaam; tel. and fax (22) 2114400; Chair. A. Mdee; Exec. Dir H. S. Mijinga.

Zanzibar State Trading Corporation: POB 26, Zanzibar; govt-controlled since 1964; sole exporter of cloves, clove stem oil, chillies, copra, copra cake, lime oil and lime juice; Gen. Man. Abdulrahman Rashid.

UTILITIES

Electricity

Tanzania Electric Supply Co Ltd (TANESCO): POB 9024, Dar es Salaam; tel. (22) 2112891; fax (22) 2113836; e-mail mdtan@intafrica.com; internet www.tenesco.com; state-owned; placed under private management in May 2002; privatization pending; Chair. Fulgence M. Kazaura; Man. Dir Rudy Huysen.

Gas

Enertan Corpn Ltd: POB 3746, Dar es Salaam.

Songas Ltd: POB 6342, Dar es Salaam; tel. (22) 2117313; fax (22) 2113614; internet www.songas.com; f. 1998; Gen. Man. Jim McCardle.

Water

Dar es Salaam Water and Sanitation Authority: POB 1573, Dar es Salaam; e-mail dawasapiu@raha.com; privatization pending.

National Urban Water Authority: POB 5340, Dar es Salaam; tel. (22) 2667505.

CO-OPERATIVES

There are some 1,670 primary marketing societies under the aegis of about 20 regional co-operative unions. The Co-operative Union of Tanzania is the national organization to which all unions belong.

Co-operative Union of Tanzania Ltd (Washirika): POB 2567, Dar es Salaam; tel. (22) 223346; f. 1962; Sec.-Gen. D. Holela; 700,000 mems.

Department of Co-operative Societies: POB 1287, Zanzibar; f. 1952; promotes formation and development of co-operative societies in Zanzibar.

Principal Societies

Bukoba Co-operative Union Ltd: POB 5, Bukoba; 74 affiliated societies; 75,000 mems.

Kilimanjaro Native Co-operative Union (1984) Ltd: POB 3032, Moshi; tel. (27) 2752785; fax (27) 2754204; e-mail kncu@kicheko.com; f. 1984; 88 regd co-operative societies.

Nyanza Co-operative Union Ltd: POB 9, Mwanza.

TRADE UNIONS

Union of Tanzania Workers (Juwata): POB 15359, Dar es Salaam; tel. (22) 226111; f. 1978; Sec.-Gen. Joseph C. Rwegasira; Dep. Secs-Gen. C. Manyanda (mainland Tanzania), I. M. Issa (Zanzibar); 500,000 mems (1991).

Agricultural Workers: Sec. G. P. Nyindo.

Central and Local Government and Medical Workers: Sec. R. Utukulu.

Commerce and Construction: Sec. P. O. Olum.

Communications and Transport Workers: Sec. M. E. Kaluwa.

Domestic, Hotels and General Workers: Sec. E. Kazoka.

Industrial and Mines Workers: Sec. J. V. Mwambuma.

Railway Workers: Sec. C. Sammang' Ombe.

Teachers: Sec. W. Mwenura.

Principal Unaffiliated Unions

Organization of Tanzanian Trade Unions (OTTU): Dar es Salaam; Sec.-Gen. Bruno Mpangal.

Workers' Department of Chama Cha Mapinduzi: POB 389, Vikokotoni, Zanzibar; f. 1965.

Transport

RAILWAYS

Tanzania Railways Corporation (TRC): POB 468, Dar es Salaam; tel. and fax (22) 2110599; e-mail ccm_shamte@trctz.com; f. 1977 after dissolution of East African Railways; privatization pending; operates 2,600 km of lines within Tanzania; Chair. J. K. Chande; Dir-Gen. Linford Mboma.

Tanzania-Zambia Railway Authority (Tazara): POB 2834, Dar es Salaam; tel. (22) 2860340; fax (22) 2865338; e-mail acistz@twiga.com; jtly owned and administered by the Tanzanian and Zambian Govts; operates a 1,860-km railway link between Dar es Salaam and New Kapiri Mposhi, Zambia, of which 969 km are within Tanzania; Chair. Salim Msoma; Man. Dir K. Mkandawire; Regional Man. (Tanzania) A. F. S. Nalitolela.

ROADS

In 2004 Tanzania had an estimated 85,000 km of classified roads, of which some 5,169 km were paved. A 1,930-km main road links Zambia and Tanzania, and there is a road link with Rwanda. A 10-year Integrated Roads Programme, funded by international donors and co-ordinated by the World Bank, commenced in 1991. Its aim was to upgrade 70% of Tanzania's trunk roads and to construct 2,828 km of roads and 205 bridges, at an estimated cost of US $650m.

The island of Zanzibar has 619 km of roads, of which 442 km are bituminized, and Pemba has 363 km, of which 130 km are bituminized.

INLAND WATERWAYS

Steamers connect with Kenya, Uganda, the Democratic Republic of the Congo, Burundi, Zambia and Malawi. A joint shipping company was formed with Burundi in 1976 to operate services on Lake Tanganyika. A rail ferry service operates on Lake Victoria between Mwanza and Port Bell.

SHIPPING

Tanzania's major harbours are at Dar es Salaam (eight deep-water berths for general cargo, three berths for container ships, eight anchorages, lighter wharf, one oil jetty for small oil tankers up to 36,000 gross tons, offshore mooring for oil supertankers up to 100,000 tons, one 30,000-ton automated grain terminal) and Mtwara (two deep-water berths). There are also ports at Tanga (seven anchorages and lighterage quay), Bagamoyo, Zanzibar and Pemba. A programme to extend and deepen the harbour entrance at Dar es Salaam commenced in 1997.

Tanzania Harbours Authority (THA): POB 9184, Dar es Salaam; tel. (22) 2110371; fax (22) 232066; internet www.bandari.com; privatization pending; Exec. Chair. J. K. Chande; Gen. Man. A. S. M. Janguo; 3 brs.

Chinese-Tanzanian Joint Shipping Co: POB 696, Dar es Salaam; tel. (22) 2113389; fax (22) 2113388; f. 1967; services to People's Republic of China, South East Asia, Eastern and Southern Africa, Red Sea and Mediterranean ports.

National Shipping Agencies Co Ltd (NASACO): POB 9082, Dar es Salaam; f. 1973; state-owned shipping co; Man. Dir D. R. M. LWIMBO.

Tanzania Central Freight Bureau (TCFB): POB 3093, Dar es Salaam; tel. (22) 2114174; fax (22) 2116697; e-mail tcfb@cats-net.com.

Tanzania Coastal Shipping Line Ltd: POB 9461, Dar es Salaam; tel. (22) 237034; fax (22) 2116436; regular services to Tanzanian coastal ports; occasional special services to Zanzibar and Pemba; also tramp charter services to Kenya, Mozambique, the Persian (Arabian) Gulf, Indian Ocean islands and the Middle East; Gen. Man. RICHARD D. NZOWA.

CIVIL AVIATION

There are 53 airports and landing strips. The major international airport is at Dar es Salaam, 13 km from the city centre, and there are also international airports at Kilimanjaro, Mwanza and Zanzibar. The management of Kilimanjaro International Airport was privatized in 1998. In 2005 it was reported that privatization was to be extended to the management of airports at Dar es Salaam, Mtware and Mwanza.

Tanzania Civil Aviation Authority (TCAA): IPS Bldg, cnr Samora Machel Ave and Azikiwe St, POB 2819, Dar es Salaam; tel. (22) 2115079; fax (22) 2118905; e-mail tcaa@tcaa.go.tz; internet www.tcaa.go.tz; f. 2003; replaced Directorate of Civil Aviation (f. 1977); ensures aviation safety and security, provides air navigation services; Dir-Gen. MARGARET T. MUNYAGI.

Air Tanzania Corporation: ATC House, Ohio St/Garden Ave, POB 543, Dar es Salaam; tel. (22) 2110245; fax (22) 2113114; f. 1977; operates an 18-point domestic network and international services to Africa, the Middle East and Europe; Chair. ABBAS SYKES; CEO JOSEPH S. MARANDUS; Dir-Gen. MELKIZEDECK SANARE.

Air Zanzibar: POB 1784, Zanzibar; f. 1990; operates scheduled and charter services between Zanzibar and destinations in Tanzania, Kenya and Uganda.

New ACS Ltd: Peugeot House, 36 Upanga Rd, POB 21236, Dar es Salaam; fax (22) 237017; operates domestic and regional services; Dir MOHSIN RAHEMTULLAH.

Precisionair: New Safari Hotel Bldg, Boma Rd, POB 1636, Arusha; tel. (27) 2502818; fax (27) 2508204; e-mail jgwaseko@precisionairtz.com; internet www.precisionairtz.com; f. 1993; operates scheduled and charter domestic and regional services.

Tanzanair: Royal Palm Hotel, POB 364, Dar es Salaam; tel. (22) 2843131; fax (22) 2844600; e-mail info@tanzanair.com; internet www.tanzanair.com; f. 1969; operates domestic and regional charter services, offers full engineering and maintenance services for general aviation aircraft.

Tourism

Mount Kilimanjaro is a major tourist attraction. Tanzania has set aside about one-quarter of its land area for 12 national parks, 17 game reserves, 50 controlled game areas and a conservation area. Other attractions for tourists include beaches and coral reefs along the Indian Ocean coast, and the island of Zanzibar (which received 86,495 tourists in 1997 and is expanding and upgrading its tourism facilities). Visitor arrivals totalled 576,198 in 2003, and in that year revenue from tourism was US $450m. (excluding revenue from passenger transport).

Tanzania Tourist Board: IPS Bldg, cnr Azikiwe St and Samora Machel Ave, POB 2485, Dar es Salaam; tel. (22) 2111244; fax (22) 2116420; e-mail safari@ud.co.tz; internet www.tanzania-web.com; state-owned; supervises the development and promotion of tourism; Man. Dir PETER J. MWENGUO.

Tanzania Wildlife Corporation: POB 1144, Arusha; tel. (57) 8830; fax (57) 8239; e-mail tawico@marie.gn.apc.org; organizes safaris; also exports and deals in live animals, birds and game-skin products; Gen. Man. DAVID S. BABU.

Zanzibar Tourist Corporation: POB 216, Zanzibar; tel. (24) 2238630; fax (24) 2233417; e-mail ztc@zanzinet.com; f. 1985; operates tours and hotel services; Gen. Man. SABAAH SALEH ALI.

THAILAND

Introductory Survey

Location, Climate, Language, Religion, Flag, Capital

The Kingdom of Thailand lies in South-East Asia. It is bordered to the west and north by Myanmar (Burma), to the north-east by Laos and to the south-east by Cambodia. Thailand extends southward, along the isthmus of Kra, to the Malay Peninsula, where it borders Malaysia. The isthmus, shared with Myanmar, gives Thailand a short coastline on the Indian Ocean, and the country also has a long Pacific coastline on the Gulf of Thailand. The climate is tropical and humid, with an average annual temperature of 29°C (85°F). There are three main seasons: hot, rainy and cool. Temperatures in Bangkok are generally between 20°C (68°F) and 35°C (95°F). The national language is Thai. There are small minorities of Chinese, Malays and indigenous hill peoples. The predominant religion is Buddhism, mainly of the Hinayana (Theravada) form. About 4% of the population, predominantly Malays, are Muslims, and there is also a Christian minority, mainly in Bangkok and the north. The national flag (proportions 2 by 3) has five horizontal stripes, of red, white, blue, white and red, the central blue stripe being twice as wide as each of the others. The capital is Bangkok.

Recent History

Formerly known as Siam, Thailand took its present name in 1939. Under the leadership of Marshal Phibul Songkhram, Thailand entered the Second World War as an ally of Japan. Phibul was deposed in 1944, but returned to power in 1947 after a military coup. His influence declined during the 1950s, and in 1957 he was overthrown in a bloodless coup, led by Field Marshal Sarit Thanarat. Elections took place, but in 1958 martial law was declared and all political parties were dissolved. Sarit died in 1963 and was succeeded as Prime Minister by Gen. (later Field Marshal) Thanom Kittikachorn, who had served as Deputy Prime Minister since 1959. Thanom continued the combination of military authoritarianism and economic development instituted by his predecessor. A Constitution was introduced in 1968, and elections to a National Assembly took place in 1969, but in November 1971, following an increase in communist insurgency and internal political unrest, Thanom annulled the Constitution, dissolved the National Assembly and imposed martial law.

During 1972 there were frequent student demonstrations against the military regime, and in October 1973 the Government was forced to resign, after the army refused to use force to disperse student protesters, and King Bhumibol withdrew his support from the administration. An interim Government was formed under Dr Sanya Dharmasakti, the President of the Privy Council. In October 1974 a new Constitution, legalizing political parties, was promulgated, and in January 1975 elections were held to the new House of Representatives. A coalition Government was formed in February by Seni Pramoj, the leader of the Democratic Party (DP), but it was defeated by a vote of 'no confidence' in the following month.

A new right-wing coalition Government, headed by the leader of the Social Action Party (SAP), Kukrit Pramoj (brother of Seni), was unable to maintain its unity, and Kukrit resigned in January 1976. After further general elections in April, a four-party coalition Government was formed, with Seni as Prime Minister. However, following violent student demonstrations in October during which the security forces killed hundreds of demonstrators, the Seni Government was dissolved, and a right-wing military junta, the National Administrative Reform Council (NARC), seized power. Martial law was declared, the Constitution was annulled, political parties were banned and strict press censorship was imposed. A new Constitution was promulgated, and a new Cabinet was announced, with Thanin Kraivixien, a Supreme Court judge, as Prime Minister.

Under the Thanin Government there was considerable repression of students and political activists. In October 1977 the Government was overthrown in a bloodless coup by a Revolutionary Council (later known as the National Policy Council—NPC) of military leaders, most of whom had been members of the NARC. The 1976 Constitution was abrogated, and the Secretary-General of the NPC (who was also the Supreme Commander of the Armed Forces), Gen. Kriangsak Chomanan, became Prime Minister. Many detainees were released, censorship was partially relaxed and the King nominated a National Assembly on the advice of the NPC. In December 1978 the National Assembly approved a new Constitution, and elections to a new House of Representatives were held in April 1979. Members of the Senate, however, were all nominated by the Prime Minister, and were almost all military officers. Kriangsak remained Prime Minister and formed a new Council of Ministers, after which the NPC was dissolved. However, Kriangsak resigned in March 1980, and was replaced by Gen. Prem Tinsulanonda, the Commander-in-Chief of the Army and the Minister of Defence. A new coalition Government, composed largely of centre-right politicians acceptable to the armed forces, was formed.

Although Prem's administration initially appeared to lack authority, it survived an abortive coup attempt in April 1981. In December of that year Prem effected a ministerial reshuffle, reincorporating members of the SAP (who had been excluded from the Government in March), in order to repulse a challenge from the new National Democracy Party (NDP), established by Kriangsak. In April 1983 no single party won an overall majority in elections to the House of Representatives, and a coalition Government was formed by the SAP, Prachakorn Thai, the DP and the NDP, despite Chart Thai being the party with the largest number of seats. Prem was again appointed Prime Minister.

In September 1985 a group of military officers, dissatisfied with the decline of the role of the armed forces in politics, staged a coup attempt in Bangkok. Troops loyal to the Government quickly suppressed the revolt, but at least five people were killed and about 60 were injured during the fighting. The leader of the revolt, Col Manoon Roopkachorn (who had also led the coup attempt in 1981), fled the country, but 40 others, including Kriangsak, were put on trial in October, accused of inciting sedition and rebellion. Gen. Arthit Kamlang-ek, the Supreme Commander of the Armed Forces and Commander-in-Chief of the Army (who was believed to have been sympathetic to the aims of the coup leaders), was replaced in his posts by Gen. Chavalit Yongchaiyudh, hitherto the army Chief of Staff.

In September 1985 and January 1986 there were extensive changes in the Government, including the replacement of all members of the SAP, following the resignation of Kukrit as the party's leader, and the introduction of members of the Progress Party into the coalition. In May 1986, following a parliamentary defeat for the Government over proposed vehicle taxation, the House of Representatives was dissolved. A general election for an enlarged legislature was held in July, when the DP won 100 of the 347 seats (compared with 56 of the 324 seats at the previous election). A coalition Government was formed, including members of the DP, Chart Thai, the SAP, Rassadorn and seven 'independent' ministers. Prem remained as Prime Minister.

In April 1988 dissident members of the DP voted to reject proposed legislation on copyright, which would have banned the counterfeiting of foreign manufactures and intellectual property, and 16 ministers belonging to the DP resigned for failing to maintain party unity. The King dissolved the House of Representatives, at Prem's request, and new elections were held in July. Internal disputes weakened support for the DP (25 dissidents had resigned in May), and Chart Thai won the largest number of seats (87). Gen. Chatichai Choonhavan, the leader of Chart Thai, was appointed Prime Minister in August, after Prem declined an invitation to remain in the post. A new Council of Ministers was formed, comprising members of Chart Thai, the DP, the SAP, Rassadorn, the United Democratic Party and the Muan Chon party.

Chatichai introduced reforms to encourage private enterprise and greater foreign investment, and also assumed an active role in foreign affairs. In an abrupt change of Thai policy, he sought to improve relations with Laos, Cambodia and Viet Nam. In April 1989 Ruam Thai, the Community Action Party, the Prachachon Party and the Progressive Party merged to form an opposition grouping called Ekkaparb (Solidarity). Nine members of the Prachachon Party subsequently defected to Chart Thai, giving the ruling coalition control of 229 of the 357 seats in the House of Representatives.

In March 1990 Chavalit resigned as acting Supreme Commander of the Armed Forces; he also resigned as Commander-in-Chief of the Army, in which post he was succeeded by Gen. Suchinda Kraprayoon, hitherto his deputy. In July, despite growing criticism of Chatichai's administration, following a number of corruption scandals and labour unrest, the House of Representatives overwhelmingly rejected an opposition motion of 'no confidence' in the Government. In August, however, Chatichai reorganized the Council of Ministers, incorporating Puangchon Chao Thai in the ruling coalition, and reducing the influence of the SAP, following the implication of many of its members in allegations of corruption.

In November 1990 Chatichai demoted the leader of the Muan Chon party, Chalerm Yoobamrung, an outspoken critic of the armed forces, from his position as Minister to the Prime Minister's Office. The leadership of the armed forces had demanded Chalerm's dismissal, threatening unspecified intervention if government changes did not take place. In early December Chatichai resigned as Prime Minister; he was reappointed on the next day and subsequently formed a coalition Government comprising Chart Thai, Rassadorn, Puangchon Chao Thai and former opposition parties Prachakorn Thai and Ekkaparb, which provided him with reduced support (227 of the 357 seats) in the House of Representatives.

On 23 February 1991 Chatichai's Government was ousted in a bloodless military coup. Gen. Sunthorn Kongsompong, the Supreme Commander of the Armed Forces, assumed administrative power as the Chairman of the newly created National Peace-keeping Council (NPC). The NPC was actually dominated by the effective head of the armed forces, Gen. Suchinda Kraprayoon, who was appointed joint Deputy Chairman of the NPC together with the Commanders-in-Chief of the Air Force and Navy and the Director-General of the Police. The coup leaders cited government corruption and abuse of power to justify their action; however, the coup was also widely believed to have been organized in response to the recent erosion of military influence.

Under the NPC, the Constitution was abrogated, the House of Representatives, the Senate and the Council of Ministers were dissolved, and martial law was imposed. The NPC won unprecedented royal approval, and in March 1991 an interim Constitution, approved by the King, was published. Anand Panyarachun, a business executive and former diplomat, was appointed acting Prime Minister pending fresh elections. Anand appointed a predominantly civilian 35-member interim Cabinet, composed mainly of respected technocrats and former ministers. Chatichai and Arthit, who had been arrested at the time of the coup, were released after two weeks. The NPC appointed a 292-member National Legislative Assembly, which included 149 serving or former military personnel, as well as many civilians known to have connections with the armed forces.

In May 1991 martial law was repealed in most areas, and political activity was permitted to resume. The New Aspiration Party (NAP—formed in October 1990 by Gen. Chavalit) gathered support as the traditional parties were in disarray, largely owing to investigations of corruption by the newly created Assets Examination Committee. In June 1991 a new party, Samakkhi Tham, was created to compete with the NAP. It was sponsored by the Commander-in-Chief of the Air Force, Air Chief Marshal Kaset Rojananin, and led by Narong Wongwan, a former leader of Ekkaparb. In August Suchinda assumed, in addition to the post of Commander-in-Chief of the Army, the role of Supreme Commander of the Armed Forces.

In November 1991 the Constitution Scrutiny Committee, which had been effectively nominated by the NPC, presented a draft Constitution to the National Legislative Assembly. Following public criticism of the draft (including a demonstration by 50,000 protesters in Bangkok), the document was amended to reduce the number of nominated senators from 360 to 270, and to abolish provisions that allowed the Senate the right to participate in the selection of the Prime Minister. Opposition parties, including the NAP and Palang Dharma (led by the popular and influential Governor of Bangkok, Maj.-Gen. Chamlong Srimuang), continued to oppose the draft, claiming that it perpetuated the power of the NPC. The National Legislative Assembly approved the new Constitution in December, but campaigners continued to express concern over certain provisional clauses (which were to remain in effect for four years), under which the NPC was to appoint the Prime Minister and the Senate, and regarding the Senate's right to vote jointly with the elected House on motions of 'no confidence', thus enabling the Senate to dismiss a government with the support of only 46 elected representatives.

The general election took place on 22 March 1992, when 2,185 candidates, representing 15 parties, contested the 360 seats; 59.2% of the electorate voted. Despite the establishment of an independent organization, Poll Watch, to monitor the elections, the practice of 'vote-buying' persisted in the poorer northern and north-eastern regions. Samakkhi Tham and Chart Thai secured the largest number of seats, 79 and 74 respectively. The NAP secured 72 seats and Palang Dharma won 41 seats, 32 of which were in Bangkok. On the day of the election the NPC appointed the 270 members of the Senate, 154 of whom were officers of the armed forces or police.

In late March 1992 it was announced that Narong Wongwan would lead a coalition government comprising his own party (Samakkhi Tham), Chart Thai, Prachakorn Thai, the SAP and Rassadorn, which together controlled 195 seats in the House of Representatives. US allegations of Narong's involvement in illicit drugs-trafficking, however, caused the nomination to be rescinded. In early April 1992 Suchinda was named as Prime Minister, despite his assurances before the election that he would not accept the post. He was replaced as Supreme Commander of the Armed Forces by Kaset and as Commander-in-Chief of the Army by his brother-in-law, Gen. Issarapong Noonpakdi, hitherto his deputy. Suchinda's accession to the premiership prompted an immediate popular protest by more than 50,000 demonstrators against the appointment of an unelected Prime Minister. Later in April Suchinda appointed eight other unelected members to a new Cabinet, retaining several technocrats from Anand's interim Government. The 49-member Council of Ministers also included three ministers who had been found guilty of 'possessing unusual wealth' by the Assets Examination Committee.

In early May 1992 Chamlong announced, at a rally attended by 100,000 demonstrators, that he would fast until death unless Suchinda resigned. The demonstrations continued uninterrupted for one week until the government parties agreed to amend the Constitution to prevent an unelected Prime Minister (including the incumbent Suchinda, who would have to resign) from taking office, and to limit the power of the unelected Senate. Chamlong abandoned his hunger strike, and temporarily suspended the demonstration. However, violent anti-Government demonstrations erupted in Bangkok when it appeared that the Government might renege on its commitments. The Government declared a state of emergency in Bangkok and neighbouring provinces, introducing a curfew and banning any large gatherings. Chamlong was arrested and more than 3,000 people were detained by security forces in a brutal attempt to suppress the riots, which continued for several days.

Following unprecedented intervention by King Bhumibol, Suchinda ordered the release of Chamlong, announced a general amnesty for those involved in the protests and pledged to introduce amendments to the Constitution. On 24 May 1992 Suchinda resigned, after failing to retain the support of the five coalition parties. On 10 June the National Assembly approved constitutional amendments, whereby the Prime Minister was required to be a member of the House of Representatives, the authority of the Senate was restricted and the President of the House of Representatives was to be the President of the National Assembly. On the same day the King, contrary to expectations, named Anand as Prime Minister. Anand appointed a politically neutral, unelected Cabinet, which included many of the figures from his previous administrations, and dissolved the National Assembly in preparation for a general election.

At the end of June 1992 the four parties that had opposed the military Government (the DP, the NAP, Palang Dharma and Ekkaparb) formed an alliance, the National Democratic Front (NDF), to contest the forthcoming elections. In July, in an effort to dissociate himself from the traditional coalition parties that had supported the Suchinda regime, Chatichai declined the leadership of Chart Thai and formed a new party, Chart Pattana, which quickly gained widespread support.

During June and July 1992 Anand introduced measures to curb the political power of the armed forces, reduce military control of state enterprises, and remove the authority of the armed forces to intervene in situations of social unrest. In August Kaset and Issarapong were dismissed from their positions at the head of the armed forces and demoted to inactive posts. A more extensive military reshuffle took place in September. The new Commander-in-Chief of the Army, Gen. Wimol Wongwanit,

THAILAND

pledged that the army would not interfere in politics under his command.

The general election took place on 13 September 1992, when 12 parties contested the 360 seats in the House of Representatives; 62.1% of the electorate voted. Poll Watch reported that 'vote-buying' and violence persisted, especially in the north-eastern region. The DP won the largest number of seats (79), while Chart Thai and Chart Pattana secured 77 and 60 seats respectively. The DP was able to form a coalition, with the NAP, Palang Dharma and Ekkaparb, which commanded 185 of the 360 seats. Despite its participation in the previous administration, the SAP (with 22 seats) was also subsequently invited to join the Government. On 23 September Chuan Leekpai, the leader of the DP, was formally approved as Prime Minister. Chuan declared his intention to eradicate corrupt practices, to decentralize government, to enhance rural development and to reduce the powers of the Senate.

Although Chuan's integrity as Prime Minister remained unquestioned, widespread dissatisfaction with his style of leadership began to emerge in early 1993. The SAP was critical of Chuan's alleged indecisiveness and slow progress in the implementation of national policy. In June, however, two motions of 'no confidence' in the Cabinet, introduced by Chart Pattana and Chart Thai, were rejected by a considerable margin, consolidating the Government's position. In September the SAP announced that it was to merge with four opposition parties, including Chart Pattana, under the leadership of Chatichai, while remaining in the ruling coalition. This appeared to be an attempt to secure the premiership for Chatichai, as the new SAP would command more seats than any other member of the coalition. However, four days later the SAP was expelled from the Government and replaced by the Seritham Party.

In September 1994 Chamlong resumed the leadership of Palang Dharma in party elections, and subsequently persuaded the party executive committee to approve the replacement of all 11 of the party's cabinet members. Chamlong's nominations for inclusion in the Cabinet included Thaksin Shinawatra, a prominent business executive, and Vichit Surapongchai, a banking executive, as Minister of Foreign Affairs and Minister of Transport and Communications respectively. Despite some opposition to the selection of unelected candidates, the appointments were confirmed in a cabinet reorganization in October, when Chamlong was named a Deputy Prime Minister.

In December 1994 the NAP withdrew from the ruling coalition over a constitutional amendment providing for the future election of local government representatives, including village headmen. The NAP voted against the Government to protect the vested interests of incumbent local administrators who would control many votes at the next election. In order to secure a parliamentary majority, Chuan was obliged to include Chatichai's Chart Pattana in the governing coalition, although this severely compromised the Government's claims to represent honesty and reform.

In January 1995 Chuan finally obtained the approval of the National Assembly for a series of amendments to the Constitution to expand the country's democratic base. Attempts in the previous year had been obstructed by the opposition, with the support of the majority of senators (who were mostly appointees of the 1991 coup leaders). The reforms adopted in 1995 included a reduction in the size of the appointed Senate to two-thirds of that of the elective House of Representatives, the lowering of the eligible voting age from 20 years to 18, equality for women, the establishment of an administrative court, the introduction of parliamentary ombudsmen and the prohibition of senators and members of the Government from holding monopolistic concessions with government or state bodies. This last amendment necessitated the resignation of Thaksin as Minister of Foreign Affairs, owing to his extensive business interests.

In May 1995 the opposition tabled a motion of 'no confidence' in the Government, in connection with a land reform scandal, which had prompted the resignation of the Minister of Agriculture and Co-operatives in December 1994. During a government investigation allegations that the land reform programme had been used to benefit wealthy landowners were substantiated. In April 1995, in what was regarded by the opposition as an inadequate response, land titles were removed from seven deed-holders and a senior official was dismissed from the land reform department. Following an announcement by Chamlong that Palang Dharma would not support the coalition in the 'no confidence' vote, Chuan dissolved the House of Representatives on 19 May and scheduled a general election for early July.

Introductory Survey

At elections to an enlarged House of Representatives, which took place on 2 July 1995, 12 political parties contested 391 seats; 62.0% of eligible voters participated in the election. Chart Thai won the largest number of seats (92), followed by the DP (86) and the NAP (57). Support for these parties was based on provincial patronage politics and allegations of 'vote-buying' were widespread. The leader of Chart Thai, Banharn Silapa-Archa (who was among those accused of 'possessing unusual wealth' by the military junta in 1991), formed a coalition Government comprising Chart Thai, the NAP, Palang Dharma, the SAP, Prachakorn Thai, Muan Chon and later Nam Thai (a business-orientated party formed in 1994 by Amnuay Viravan, a former minister). Thaksin (who had relinquished majority control of his company) had been elected to the leadership of Palang Dharma in May, following the resignation of Chamlong. Banharn appointed all the leaders of the coalition parties (except for the Muan Chon party) as Deputy Prime Ministers. Banharn assumed responsibility for the interior portfolio pending the findings of a commission established to investigate US allegations of drugs-trafficking by two leaders of powerful factions within Chart Thai who demanded control of the ministry. The composition of Banharn's Cabinet was widely criticized, owing to the lack of technocrats and the predominance, despite pre-election assurances, of professional politicians (who were often subject to allegations of corruption and 'vote-buying'). There was also dissatisfaction at the appointment of the inexperienced Surakiart Sathirathai, a lawyer, as Minister of Finance while the country was undergoing a process of financial liberalization.

In early 1996 the stability of the ruling coalition was jeopardized by an armed forces' plan to launch a US $1,000m. satellite system. Thaksin opposed the unnecessary expenditure, while Chavalit, the Minister of Defence, threatened to withdraw the NAP from the coalition if the project were cancelled. Chavalit had already consolidated his position with the armed forces in September 1995 by appointing a close associate, Gen. Pramon Phalasin, as Commander-in-Chief of the Army, contrary to the recommendations for promotions of the outgoing Commander-in-Chief, which were traditionally observed.

In March 1996 Banharn announced the composition of the new Senate, the first to be appointed by a democratically elected Prime Minister. In contrast to the previous Senate, only 39 active military officers were named as senators; other appointees included academics and business executives.

In May 1996 10 government ministers, including the Prime Minister, survived motions of 'no confidence', despite opposition revelations of financial irregularities at the Bangkok Bank of Commerce, including loans extended without collateral to members of the Thai Cabinet, notably the Deputy Minister of the Interior, Suchart Tancharoen, and the Deputy Minister of Finance, Newin Chidchob, both members of Chart Thai. Palang Dharma refused to support Suchart in the debate, probably in an attempt to dissociate itself from government corruption prior to the gubernatorial election in Bangkok. In order to pre-empt the withdrawal of Palang Dharma from the ruling coalition, five members of Chart Thai, including Suchart and Newin, resigned from their government positions. Palang Dharma subsequently agreed to remain in the coalition but announced the resignation of all five of its ministers from the Cabinet. In the ensuing cabinet reorganization at the end of May Surakiart, who had failed to take action to prevent huge losses at the Bangkok Bank of Commerce, was replaced by a former official in the Ministry of Finance, Bodi Chunnananda, Amnuay was appointed Minister of Foreign Affairs and the Palang Dharma ministers all agreed to return to their positions in the Cabinet.

In the gubernatorial election in Bangkok that took place in June 1996, Bhichit Rattakul, an environmental activist who contested the election as an independent, defeated Chamlong and the incumbent, Krisda Arunvongse Na Ayutthya. Krisda, who had won the governorship as a Palang Dharma representative, was supported by Prachakorn Thai following Palang Dharma's decision to support Chamlong's candidacy. Palang Dharma was severely weakened by the defeat. Chamlong sub-sequently announced that he was retiring from politics.

In July 1996 Vijit Supinit resigned from his position as Governor of the Bank of Thailand following a series of financial scandals. In August the Government suffered a set-back following the withdrawal of Palang Dharma from the ruling coalition. This defection, which was the apparent result of a cabinet dispute over alleged bribery in the awarding of bank licences, reduced the Government's legislative majority by 23 seats. In September Banharn was able to secure the support of his coalition partners in a scheduled motion of 'no confidence' in his administration only by undertaking to resign from the premiership. However, the inability of the coalition partners to agree on the appointment of a new Prime Minister led to the dissolution of the House of Representatives on 27 September.

In the general election, which was held on 17 November 1996 and was marred by violence and alleged extensive ballot-rigging, the NAP won 125 of the 393 seats, while the DP secured 123 seats. The majority of NAP seats were gained through provincial patronage politics, while the more politically-aware electorate of Bangkok returned the DP to 29 of the city's 37 seats. Chavalit, the leader of the NAP, was appointed Prime Minister, heading a coalition that incorporated Chart Pattana, the SAP, Prachakorn Thai, Muan Chon and the Seritham Party. The ruling coalition thus held 221 seats in the House of Representatives. Chatichai was appointed as the Chairman of the Prime Minister's special advisory group on economic and foreign affairs, and the majority of the other influential cabinet posts were assigned to other members of Chart Pattana and the NAP. Thaksin resigned as leader of Palang Dharma following the party's failure to win more than one seat in the House of Representatives.

As evidence of Chavalit's avowed intention to revive the economy, he allocated the finance portfolio and the deputy premiership with responsibility for economic affairs to Amnuay, a respected technocrat. However, Chavalit subsequently failed to give Amnuay the necessary support to overcome the obstacles imposed by other coalition members anxious to prevent the implementation of austere fiscal policies. In June 1997 Amnuay resigned and was replaced by the little-known Thanong Bidaya, the President of the Thai Military Bank. The Government's indecisive handling of the economy contributed to a financial crisis in mid-1997, following a series of sustained assaults on the Thai baht by currency speculators, which led to the baht's effective devaluation in early July. At the end of July the Governor of the Central Bank, Rerngchai Marakanonda, also resigned, citing political interference. The deterioration in the state of the economy in 1997 was reflected in an increase in popular protests. The most significant of these was an encampment of about 15,000 representatives of the Assembly of the Poor (a non-governmental organization campaigning for the improvement of conditions for impoverished farmers and landless agricultural labourers) outside the Prime Minister's office in January. The protesters dispersed in May, following the establishment of a fund to compensate villagers for relocation and destruction caused by government infrastructure projects. The Government introduced measures in June to constrain media attacks on the authorities and to limit mass protests.

In August 1997 Chavalit implemented a cabinet reorganization in an attempt to regain public confidence. On the advice of former Prime Minister Prem, the former Minister of Finance, Virabongsa Ramangkura, an outspoken critic of the Government's handling of the economic crisis, was appointed Deputy Prime Minister with responsibility for economic affairs, while Thaksin joined the Cabinet as Deputy Prime Minister with responsibility for regional development and trade. Despite the announcement of strict austerity measures and the intervention of the IMF, the economic situation continued to deteriorate.

Meanwhile, in January 1997 an assembly of 99 members was elected by the legislature to draft a new constitution following the unanimous approval of a constitution amendment bill by the National Assembly in September 1996. Uthai Pimchaichon, a former Minister of Commerce and advocate of the eradication of the influence of money in politics, was appointed Chairman of the Constitution Drafting Assembly. The draft Constitution included provisions for: a directly elected Senate; the replacement in the House of Representatives of 393 deputies from multi-member constituencies by 400 deputies from single-member constituencies and 100 deputies elected by proportional representation; the resignation of cabinet ministers from the legislature; the establishment of a minimum educational requirement for members of the National Assembly; the formation of an Election Commission to supervise elections (in place of the Ministry of the Interior); the centralization of vote-counting; compulsory voting; and the guarantee of press freedom. Although the draft gained the support of opposition parties and the media, there was considerable opposition to the new charter from within the ruling administration. Chavalit himself reneged on his pledge to support the draft, but then finally gave it his endorsement following the application of pressure by both business representatives and the armed forces.

Chavalit ensured his survival of a 'no confidence' motion tabled by the opposition by scheduling the censure debate prior to the vote on the draft Constitution. If defeated, Chavalit could thus dissolve the National Assembly rather than resign, delaying the vote on the draft Constitution and forcing fresh elections under the existing Constitution. In the event the Government won the 'no confidence' vote and the draft Constitution was approved on 27 September 1997, with 578 votes in favour, 16 opposed, 17 abstentions and 40 absences. Chavalit was allowed 240 days to complete enabling legislation for the new Constitution, prior to a general election. The new Constitution was promulgated on 11 October.

In October 1997 Thanong resigned as Minister of Finance, citing obstruction of his attempts to implement the extensive economic reforms required. Following popular demonstrations demanding the resignation of Chavalit, a cabinet reorganization was announced at the end of October. The new appointments, however, which included that of the Executive Vice-President of Bangkok Bank and a former minister, Khosit Panpiamrat, as the Minister of Finance, failed to restore public or investor confidence in the Government, and the Thai currency continued to depreciate. At the beginning of November Chavalit's announcement that he would resign from the premiership on 6 November, following the adoption of important electoral and financial legislation, caused a slight recovery of the Thai baht. Both Prem and Chatichai rejected approaches by members of the ruling coalition to prevent its collapse by assuming the leadership. Finally, on 9 November Chuan, who maintained his reputation for integrity, assumed the premiership, following the formation of a coalition comprising Chuan's DP, Chart Thai, the SAP, Ekkaparb, the Seritham Party, Palang Dharma and the Thai Party (as well as 12 of the 18 members of Prachakorn Thai), which commanded the support of 210 of the 393 seats in the House of Representatives.

The transfer of power to Chuan, under the terms of the new Constitution, without the intervention of the armed forces or resort to a non-elected leader, received widespread approval and represented significant democratic progress. The new Cabinet included Tarrin Nimmanhaeminda as Minister of Finance (a post he had occupied in Chuan's previous administration) and the former Deputy Prime Minister, Supachai Panichpakdi, as Minister of Commerce. However, the baht continued to depreciate, causing intermittent social unrest. In March a vote of 'no confidence' in Chuan's Government, which retained popular support, was defeated.

In May 1998 the Governor of the Central Bank, Chaiyawat Wibulsawadi, resigned, shortly before the publication of an independent report into the alleged mismanagement of the economy preceding the devaluation of the baht in July 1997 and the onset of the subsequent financial crisis. The report attributed much blame for the country's difficulties to the economic strategy followed by Chaiyawat, his predecessor Rerngchai Marakanonda, the former Prime Minister, Chavalit, and the former Minister of Finance, Amnuay Viravan. Chaiyawat was replaced by Chatu Mongol Sonakul, a former permanent secretary of finance. Also in May new electoral legislation was approved, enabling polls to be held six months later. However, despite pressure from the opposition, Chuan stated that elections would not be held until specific economic reforms had been put in place. At the same time there were fears that, under the new legislation, the 12 members of the ruling coalition who had defected from Prachakorn Thai to help form the Government in November 1997 might lose their legal status as legislators. (The 12 were formally expelled from Prachakorn Thai in October 1998 but continued to form part of the coalition Government.) In July a new political party, Thai Rak Thai, was established by the former Deputy Prime Minister, Thaksin Shinawatra.

By August 1998 Thailand's economy appeared to have stabilized, and Chuan received rare public praise from Queen Sirikit. However, the Government was beset by allegations of corruption. In October Chuan reorganized his Government, bringing the Chart Pattana party into the ruling coalition and thereby increasing to 257 the number of seats held by the coalition in the House of Representatives. Five new ministers were appointed to the Cabinet, including the Secretary-General of Chart Pattana, Suwat Liptapanlop, who was assigned the industry portfolio; however, many of the most influential portfolios were retained by the DP. In December the opposition filed a motion to remove Chuan and Tarrin from office, on the grounds that they had allegedly acted in breach of the Constitution by submitting four Letters of Intent to the IMF without first securing the approval of the House of Representatives; the motion was unsuccessful. In January 1999 the opposition filed a censure motion against three DP ministers (the Deputy Prime Minister and Minister of the Interior, Maj.-Gen. Sanan Kajornprasart, the Minister of Transport and Communications, Suthep Thaungsuban, and Tarrin), who were accused by the opposition of corruption, nepotism, incompetence and dishonesty. All three ministers survived the vote on the motion.

A series of minor bombings of government buildings, which occurred in December 1998 and January 1999, and included an attack on the DP headquarters in mid-January, were believed by a number of observers to be politically motivated. The Government reportedly attributed blame for the bombings to a group of unidentified opposition sympathizers.

In July 1999 the SAP withdrew from the governing coalition, reportedly as a result of intense disputes within the party concerning the allocation of cabinet positions, prompting a reorganization of the Cabinet. By August, however, public approval of the Government appeared to be in decline, and the coalition faced increasing demands from the opposition that the House of Representatives be dissolved and that elections be called. Thai Rak Thai intensified its recruitment campaign from mid-1999; a public debate on the alleged use of financial inducements by Thai Rak Thai to recruit members of other parties was initiated by members of the DP. In November Chavalit pledged his willingness to support Thai Rak Thai in the forthcoming general election in the event of his own NAP performing poorly at the polls.

In August 1999 a report on the state-owned Krung Thai Bank, which exposed the bank's dubious loan policies and other irregularities, was disclosed to the Senate and the press. The report led to criticism of the Government and to allegations of corruption being made against Tarrin, whose brother, Sirin Nimmanhaeminda, had been the President of Krung Thai Bank until his resignation in January. Although the Government was reported in October to have exonerated a number of senior Krung Thai executives, including Sirin, of allegations of inefficiency and dishonesty, the controversy surrounding the bank continued and constituted the main focus of a joint 'no confidence' motion filed by three main opposition parties against the Government in December, in which the ruling coalition was accused of mismanagement of the economy and of condoning corruption. Although the Government survived the censure debate, the proceedings exposed divisions within the governing coalition (particularly between the DP and Chart Thai), and also proved particularly damaging to Tarrin and to the Deputy Prime Minister and Minister of the Interior, Maj.-Gen. (retd) Sanan Kajornprasart.

The DP fared badly in provincial elections held in February 2000, possibly owing to discontent among the rural population with the Government's refusal to subsidize crop prices. In late January, however, the opposition NAP had also suffered a serious reverse when as many as 40 of its members of the House of Representatives, led by the former NAP Secretary-General, Sano Thianthong, boycotted a gathering intended to reaffirm their allegiance to the party in the approach to the anticipated elections. Sano, who had been forcibly removed from the party leadership in March 1999, was subsequently reported to have claimed that the dissident legislators were seeking a merger with Thai Rak Thai, which was enjoying increasing public support. Allegations of corruption against the ruling coalition re-emerged in 2000. In March Sanan was accused by the National Anti-Corruption Committee (NACC) of having falsified his assets declaration statement (recently required of all cabinet ministers). Although he denied the allegations, Sanan swiftly resigned from his ministerial positions and from his membership of the legislature, pending a ruling on the NACC's report by Thailand's Constitutional Court. (Sanan did, however, retain his position as Secretary-General of the DP.) A reorganization of the Cabinet was effected on 11 April; Banyat Bantadtan was appointed to replace Sanan as Deputy Prime Minister and Minister of the Interior. In August Sanan was convicted of corruption by the Constitutional Court.

On 4 March 2000, in the first significant test of the country's new reformist Constitution, elections to the new 200-member Senate were contested by more than 1,500 candidates. The level of voter participation was reported at 70%, with voting being compulsory for the first time. Although an increased focus on the suitability of the candidates themselves was reported, the widespread practice of 'vote-buying' persisted, and on 21 March the Election Commission (EC) disqualified 78 of the 200 winning candidates (including the wives of two cabinet ministers). A second round of polling was held in the 78 affected constituencies on 29 April, in which all but two of the disqualified contestants were permitted to stand again. However, there were further allegations of electoral fraud following the second round of voting, with 34 of the previously disqualified candidates being accused of various electoral violations. The EC responded by declaring that a second rerun of the polls would be held in at least nine of the affected constituencies, rejecting appeals for the dismissal of the allegations of fraud in the interest of political continuity. (While the final results of the elections remained in dispute, none of the declared winners were able to assume their seats as they lacked the necessary quorum, resulting in a backlog of legislation and obliging the outgoing Senate to remain in office in an interim capacity.) Although in May it was reported that 22 senatorial candidates had been cleared of allegations of fraud by the EC owing to lack of evidence, a third round of polling was scheduled to be held in June in a number of constituencies. The EC also announced that a number of prominent individuals were likely to be prosecuted for their involvement in electoral misconduct. Further allegations of electoral fraud necessitated a fourth and fifth round of polling in June and July respectively. Despite the resignation of almost 100 NAP deputies from the House of Representatives in June and July in support of an early dissolution of the House, Chuan reiterated his intention to dissolve the House in October. The SAP also withdrew from the House of Representatives in July in a similar attempt to gain an early dissolution. On 1 August Thailand's first-ever democratically elected Senate was formally inaugurated.

In November 2000 it was announced that elections to the House of Representatives would be held in January 2001. In December 2000 the NACC recommended that Thaksin Shinawatra should be indicted for having violated the Constitution by concealing financial assets and seeking to avoid the payment of taxes. One notable feature of Thai Rak Thai's electoral campaign was its targeting of rural votes by pledging grants of 1m. baht for each of Thailand's 70,000 villages and offering a debt-relief scheme for farmers. At the legislative elections held on 6 January 2001 Thai Rak Thai won 248 of the 500 seats in the House of Representatives, thereby almost gaining an unprecedented absolute majority. However, the elections were marred by widespread allegations of malpractice; indeed, many domestic and international observers declared that, despite the vigilance of the EC, they had been the most corrupt ever held in Thailand. In late January repolling was held in more than 60 constituencies where the EC had found evidence of fraudulent practice. In February a new cabinet nominated by Thaksin was formally approved by the King. All but five of the appointees were members of Thai Rak Thai, with which the Seritham Party had merged since the election, thus affording Thai Rak Thai an absolute majority in the House of Representatives. With the support of its coalition partners, the NAP and Chart Thai, the incoming Thai Rak Thai administration controlled 339 of the 500 seats in the House.

In April 2001 the Constitutional Court formally commenced hearing charges of corruption brought against the Prime Minister, as recommended by the NACC. In the same month two bombs exploded in southern Thailand, killing a child and injuring 42 people. The involvement of a militant Islamist separatist organization, the Pattani United Liberation Organization (PULO), was suspected. The PULO belonged to Bersatu, an umbrella organization of three separatists movements, which, the Government claimed, was seeking to establish a Muslim state in southern Thailand. In June there was a bomb attack on the Vietnamese embassy. It was believed to have been perpetrated by members of the Free Vietnam Movement. Three men from the USA were arrested shortly afterwards in connection with the incident.

Meanwhile, in May 2001 Prime Minister Thaksin dismissed the Governor of the Central Bank, Chatu Mongol Sonakul, following a dispute over monetary policy. Pridiyathorn Davakula was appointed as his replacement. The incident raised questions about the extent of governmental interference in the bank's affairs.

On 30 June 2001 by-elections were held in seven constituencies to fill seats in the House of Representatives vacated by members disqualified for breaches of campaign rules after the January elections. However, the polls were again marred by allegations of corruption. In July King Bhumibol appointed the former Deputy Interior Permanent Secretary, Palakorn Suwannarat, and the former Minister of Education, Kasem Watana-

THAILAND

chai, to the Privy Council. Watanchai had resigned from his post in the previous month; he was succeeded by Suwit Khunkitti in September.

The Prime Minister was acquitted of the charges against him regarding concealment of his assets in August 2001. The judges ruled by a narrow eight-to-seven majority in his favour. His exoneration was welcomed by his many supporters, who had conducted a popular campaign that was thought to have exerted some influence over the court's verdict.

In October 2001 the Government introduced a plan to provide low-cost health care for the nation's poorest people, thus implementing one of the Prime Minister's election pledges. Doubts remained over the quality of the service provided. Later in the same month the limits to the Government's reform efforts were highlighted when army Sub-Lt Duangchalerm Yoobamrung, son of Chalerm Yoobamrung, an influential NAP member of the House of Representatives, allegedly murdered a police officer during a fight in a night-club. Duangchalerm subsequently fled to Cambodia. As a result of his son's actions and subsequent popular criticism of the Government for its ineffectual attempts to bring him to justice, Chalerm was forced to resign from the deputy leadership of the NAP, although he retained an influential position within the Government. In May 2002 Duangchalerm surrendered himself to the Thai embassy in Malaysia, having entered the country illegally, and agreed to return home, where he entered a plea of not guilty to the charges against him. In March 2004 Duangchalerm was acquitted of all the charges against him, allegedly owing to insufficient evidence.

In November 2001 a panel of judges acting for the Public Prosecutor recommended that the former Governor of the Central Bank, Rerngchai Marakanonda, face a civil lawsuit for the part that he had played in precipitating the 1997 financial crisis. The hearing began in February 2002. In November 2003, however, the Administrative Court ruled in favour of a petition submitted by Rerngchai requesting that the civil lawsuit against him be dismissed. Meanwhile, in December 2002 King Bhumibol made a speech to mark his birthday in which he publicly criticized the Prime Minister, commenting that his Government's 'double standards' were effectively leading Thailand towards 'catastrophe'. His criticism was thought to be linked to his reported disapproval of the business relationship that existed between the Prime Minister and the King's son, Crown Prince Vajiralongkorn.

Prime Minister Thaksin's apparent sensitivity to criticism was reflected in his Government's increasingly repressive policies towards the media. In January 2002 an edition of the *Far Eastern Economic Review*, a Hong Kong-based publication, was banned for its inclusion of an article that suggested that tensions existed in the relationship between King Bhumibol and the Prime Minister. Meanwhile, it was reported that the Ministry of Defence had ordered the Nation Media Group to cease its provision of news programmes to a Bangkok radio station. The ban followed the broadcast of an interview with a senior opposition figure that was deemed to have been critical of the Prime Minister. The armed forces, which controlled all Thai radio frequencies, claimed that the decision had been taken for commercial reasons. The Prime Minister rebuffed allegations that his Government was attempting to impose restraints upon media freedom by commenting that the media were permitted to report freely but that any criticism should be constructive.

In January 2002 the NAP voted to merge with its coalition partner, Thai Rak Thai. Despite opposition from several NAP politicians, the party was legally dissolved in March. In the same month the Government was further strengthened when Chart Pattana joined the ruling coalition; a minor cabinet reorganization took place shortly afterwards in which Suwat Liptapanlop, Secretary-General of Chart Pattana, was allocated a ministerial position. Meanwhile, by-elections were held in 14 constituencies where the January 2001 general election results had been invalidated owing to substantiated allegations of electoral fraud and corruption. Thai Rak Thai lost five seats as a result, but retained its commanding majority in the National Assembly. Shortly afterwards six policemen died after gunmen attacked three security outposts—two in Pattani province and one in Yala province. The attacks were suspected to have been carried out by one of the militant Islamist separatist organizations known to exist in the area. Two bombs later exploded in Yala province, coinciding with a tour of the region by the Minister of the Interior. Further outbreaks of violence against the Thai police occurred in the area throughout the month. A Thai military official attributed the attacks to the Guragan Mujahideen Islam Pattani, a constituent group of Bersatu thought to be linked to the international terrorist network al-Qa'ida. In April the Constitutional Court formally granted the NAP's request that it be permitted to merge with Thai Rak Thai.

In May 2002 the Government succeeded in defeating 'no confidence' motions that had been brought by the opposition against 15 of its ministers, including nine members of the Cabinet. In October Prime Minister Thaksin implemented an extensive cabinet reorganization, in which, amongst other changes, Chavalit Yongchaiyudh was replaced as Minister of Defence by Thammarak Isarangura, while former Minister of Transport Wan Muhamad Nor Matha became Minister of the Interior. Six ministers were also appointed to take responsibility for new ministries that had been created as part of the Government's ongoing bureaucratic reforms. Later in the month a bomb exploded in the province of Yala, while in the neighbouring province of Songkhla five schools were subjected to arson attacks.

In February 2003 a further redistribution of cabinet portfolios took place. The Minister of Finance, Somkid Jatusripitak, and the Minister of Justice, Purachai Piemsomboon, were both appointed Deputy Prime Ministers; Somkid was replaced by his deputy, Suchart Jaovisidha, while Purachai was succeeded by former Minister of Energy Pongthep Thepkanjana. Deputy Prime Minister Prommin Lertsuridej was awarded the energy portfolio. Meanwhile, the Government announced the commencement of an intensive anti-drugs campaign intended to eliminate Thailand's drug problem within three months. As the campaign continued, the huge number of suspected drug dealers being killed prompted criticism from both local and international human rights groups, which claimed that the Thai authorities were operating an illegal 'shoot to kill' policy and effectively condoning extra-judicial violence. The Government rejected a request from the Office of the UN High Commissioner for Human Rights (OHCHR, see p. 45) that it be permitted to send a representative to the country to investigate the killings. In March Thaksin acknowledged that mistakes had been made during the campaign, but denied that the police had been responsible for any extra-judicial killings. However, later in that month Thaksin ordered that the campaign should henceforth be concentrated upon provinces along the border with Myanmar, where the majority of drugs-smuggling activity was believed to take place. By mid-April 2003, according to a statement issued by police, as a result of the campaign some 2,275 people had been killed, of whom the police admitted to shooting 51 fatally for reasons of self-defence. At the end of April Thaksin stated that the campaign had eradicated 'about 90%' of the country's drugs problem and, later in that year, declared it to have been a success. Meanwhile, two attacks on army bases in the south of the country were reportedly carried out by the PULO. In the following month, owing to the success of the anti-drugs offensive, Thaksin announced the commencement of a 'war on dark influences' intended to eradicate criminal networks operating in the country.

In April 2003 the DP elected Banyat Bantadtan as its new leader, following the retirement of Chuan Leekpai. In May, after a two-day 'no confidence' debate in the House of Representatives, five cabinet ministers evaded censure, following the tabling of an opposition motion accusing them of corruption. In the following month Thai Rak Thai defeated the DP at a by-election in Si Sa Ket. Later in June three men were arrested on suspicion of being members of the regional terrorist organization Jemaah Islamiah; they later confessed to having plotted to attack embassies and tourist destinations in the country. A further suspect was arrested in July. In the following month, in response to the perceived terrorist threat to Thailand, the Cabinet approved two anti-terrorism laws by decree, circumventing the legislature owing to the reported gravity of the threat. Shortly afterwards, the alleged former operational head of Jemaah Islamiah, the Indonesian citizen Riduan Isamuddin, also known as Hambali, was apprehended in Thailand; he was later taken into custody by the USA. In September the four suspected members of Jemaah Islamiah arrested earlier in the year were officially charged with membership of the organization and with plotting terrorist attacks in Thailand. Those charged, together with a fifth man being detained in Singapore, pleaded not guilty to the charges against them. Their trials began in November.

In October 2003, following the conclusion of its anti-drugs offensive five months previously, the Government announced the commencement of a 60-day campaign intended to rid Thailand of 'social evils' such as drug addiction, poverty and organized crime. In November a cabinet reorganization took place, which resulted in the removal of Chart Pattana from the Government. In consequence, Deputy Prime Minister Korn Dabbaransi and Minister of Labour and Social Welfare Suwat Liptapanlop were ousted from the Cabinet; they were succeeded by, respectively, Bhokin Bhalakula and Uraiwan Tiengthong.

In January 2004 an outbreak of violence in the south of the country, which resulted in the deaths of several members of the security forces and included arson attacks on several schools, prompted the Government to declare martial law in the predominantly Muslim provinces of Pattani, Yala and Narathiwat, on the border with Malaysia. The violence was suspected by the Government to have been perpetrated by Guragan Mujahideen Islam Pattani, although involvement by militants affiliated to Jemaah Islamiah was not discounted as a possibility. Two suspects arrested in January were believed to be members of Bersatu. The unrest continued into the following months, resulting in the temporary closure of approximately 1,000 schools in the area. Meanwhile, the Government responded by arresting local Islamic leaders and conducting army raids on *madrasahs* (Islamic religious schools), angering many members of the local Muslim population. In mid-February Prime Minister Thaksin proposed the construction of a security fence along the border, in order to prevent militants from taking refuge in Malaysia.

In March 2004 a further cabinet reorganization was implemented, in which the Ministers of Finance, Defence and the Interior—Suchart Jaovisidha, Thammarak Isarangura and Wan Muhamad Nor Matha—were replaced by, respectively, Somkid Jatusripitak, Chettha Thanajaro and Bhokin Bhalakula. Korn Dabbaransi returned to the Cabinet as Minister of Science and Technology. The changes were believed to have been made in response to the ongoing deterioration in the security situation in the south of the country, together with a decline in the performance of the Stock Exchange of Thailand and public protests at the Government's planned privatization of the Electricity Generating Authority of Thailand. Candidates supported by Thai Rak Thai performed well in local elections in mid-March, securing control of 47 of 74 newly created Provincial Administrative Organizations.

In mid-March 2004, following further arson attacks in the south, which had destroyed some 36 government buildings, Prime Minister Thaksin dismissed the national police chief and the army commander for the southern region. Later that month a bomb explosion in Sungai Kolok, in Narathiwat province, which injured 29 people, including 10 Malaysian tourists, prompted the Government to suspend a US $300m. development aid programme intended for Narathiwat, Pattani and Yala. Thaksin claimed that those responsible for the attack had crossed into Malaysia. A few days later a group of suspected militants stole a large quantity of explosives from a quarry in Yala province. In early April four police officers were arrested in connection with the recent disappearance of Somchai Neelapaijit, a prominent Muslim human rights lawyer who was defending the men charged in September 2003 with plotting attacks for Jemaah Islamiah.

The violence in the south escalated at the end of April 2004, when more than 100 suspected Islamic militants staged a series of raids on police and army bases. The security forces suppressed the attacks, killing 108 of the insurgents, including 32 who had taken refuge in a mosque in Pattani. Five security officials also died in the fighting. After the UN, human rights groups and some Muslim leaders questioned the level of force used by the security forces to quash the attacks, in early May the Government established an independent commission to investigate the incident at the mosque. Bomb explosions at three Buddhist temples in Narathiwat caused minor damage in mid-May. Meanwhile, a censure motion tabled by the DP against eight cabinet ministers on the grounds of alleged incompetence, corruption and abuse of power was rejected by the House of Representatives.

In late May 2004 the Government announced that it had established unofficial contact with the leader of Bersatu, Wan Kadir Che Man, with the aim of holding peace talks. Wan Kadir, who was living in exile in Malaysia, had recently stated that he was willing to abandon Bersatu's demand for a separate homeland in southern Thailand. None the less, religious tension in the south persisted, as the body of a Buddhist farmer was found decapitated and a Buddhist shrine in Pattani was ransacked. The proposed talks with Wan Kadir were indefinitely suspended at the end of the month, following strong opposition from Deputy Prime Minister Chavalit Yongchaiyudh, who feared the meeting could be regarded as formal recognition of Bersatu and its leader.

In mid-June some 3,000 teachers attended a rally in Pattani in support of demands for improved security following the killing of a colleague. At the end of the month more than 4,000 teachers in Narathiwat commenced strike action after a further shooting, but returned to work after two days in response to assurances of increased protection from the security forces.

At the end of June 2004 Chart Pattana rejoined the Government in a reshuffle, with Suwat Liptapanlop appointed as a Deputy Prime Minister, in what was regarded as an attempt by Thaksin to consolidate support ahead of the legislative elections due to be held in early 2005. A number of deputies from Chart Thai and the DP subsequently defected to Thai Rak Thai, and in August 2004 Chart Pattana merged into Thaksin's party. Meanwhile, several former senior members of the DP formed a new party, Mahachon. In early August, in its first report since its establishment in 2001, the National Human Rights Commission claimed that human rights violations had increased under Thaksin's administration, notably during the anti-drugs campaign in 2003, and accused the Government of becoming increasingly authoritarian. Thaksin rejected the report's criticisms, and declared a second anti-drugs offensive in October, which was to last for one year. The election of the DP candidate, Apirak Kosayodhin, as Governor of Bangkok in late August represented a set-back for Thaksin, who had favoured the candidature of Paveena Hongsakul, the former Secretary-General of Chart Pattana, who had stood as an independent.

More than 300 suspected insurgents had surrendered to the authorities by mid-July 2004 in response to a government campaign; they were transferred to a detention facility at a military camp to undergo a re-education programme. Nevertheless, violent attacks and minor bomb explosions continued to occur in the southern provinces, with killings of public officials, police officers, Buddhist monks and civilians regularly reported. In early August the independent commission investigating the deaths at the mosque in April released its report, which criticized the security forces for using grenades and concluded that troops had used disproportionate force. The Government announced that unspecified compensation would be paid to the families of those killed. At the end of August Thaksin visited Narathiwat, Pattani and Yala provinces, one day after a bomb had exploded at a market in Sukhirin, in Narathiwat, killing one person and injuring 31. The Government conceded that it had failed to control the violence in the south, and pledged to develop new strategies to quell the unrest.

In September 2004 a preliminary hearing was heard in the case of media rights activist Supinya Klangnarong and the owners and editors of the *Thai Post* newspaper, who were being sued for defamation by the Shin Corporation. The telecommunications and media company, founded by Thaksin and in which his family retained a controlling interest, objected to an article written by Supinya in July 2003 that suggested that the Shin Corporation had unfairly benefited under Thaksin's premiership. The court set the opening date for the criminal trial for 19 July 2005. In addition to the criminal charges, the Shin Corporation had filed a civil lawsuit seeking 400m. baht in damages. The lawsuit, which attracted considerable attention, was regarded as a test case for press freedom in Thailand.

In early October 2004 Thaksin effected a cabinet reshuffle that included the replacement of the Minister of Defence and the Minister of Agriculture and Co-operatives in an apparent response to the ongoing crisis in the south and an outbreak of avian influenza. The violence in southern Thailand continued throughout late 2004. One of the most serious incidents occurred in late October when troops fired tear gas to disperse more than 2,000 Muslim protesters who were demonstrating in Tak Bai, in Narathiwat province, against the detention of six suspected militants. Seven of the protesters were killed in the ensuing clashes and 78 of 1,300 demonstrators who were arrested later died, many from suffocation, as they were transported in overcrowded trucks to an army barracks. Amid increasing international concern at events in southern Thailand and at the Government's response to the unrest, Prime Minister Thaksin ordered an independent inquiry into the deaths. Most of those detained in connection with the protests were later released. A few days later two people were killed and 20 injured in a bomb attack in Sungai Kolok. Shortly afterwards, as tensions continued to rise, a further 20 people, including 15 police officers, were injured in two bomb explosions in Yala province. The deteriorating security situation prompted rare interventions from the monarchy. King Bhumibol urged the Government to use more restraint in the southern provinces, and Queen Sirikit called for an end to the violence. In the first two weeks of November around 30 Buddhists were killed in apparent revenge attacks by suspected Islamic militants. The PULO had earlier vowed to retaliate for the deaths in Tak Bai. Later that month an alleged leader of Bersatu was killed in a gunfight with the security forces in Panare, in the province of Pattani.

In a campaign devised by Prime Minister Thaksin, an estimated 100m. paper origami birds, folded and inscribed with peace messages by people in northern Thailand, were dropped by military planes over the southern provinces of Narathiwat, Pattani and Yala in early December 2004. However, critics dismissed the gesture, urging the Government to address the underlying problems behind the violence in the south, where more than 500 people had died since the beginning of the year. Shortly afterwards suspected Islamic militants shot dead a former prosecutor in Pattani, and two bomb explosions in Narathiwat injured five soldiers. In mid-December four Islamic teachers, who were suspected of being leaders of the separatist group Barisan Revolusi Nasional (part of Bersatu), were charged with terrorism and treason. Meanwhile, the inquiry into the incident at Tak Bai in October, in which 85 protesters died, concluded that the deaths had not been caused deliberately, but that the dispersal of the crowd and the transport of the prisoners had been mishandled and that senior officials had been negligent; the Ministry of Defence established a panel to consider disciplinary action against three army commanders, and they were subsequently transferred to inactive posts. The Cabinet later approved compensation worth more than 30m. baht for families of the dead and those injured. In late December at least two people were killed and several injured after a bomb exploded in Sungai Kolok. Following the fatal shooting of two of their colleagues, thousands of teachers in the south went on indefinite strike, urging the authorities to do more to protect them from attacks by Muslim militants.

The west coast of Thailand, in particular the province of Phang Nga, was severely affected by a series of tsunamis caused by a massive earthquake in the Indian Ocean on 26 December 2004. More than 5,300 people, including at least 1,700 foreigners from some 36 countries, were killed, and a further 2,900 were reported missing. The Thai Government largely refused international relief aid, but did accept considerable technical assistance in identifying the dead, a task that was made more difficult by the large number of foreign victims. At the end of January 2005 the UN World Tourism Organization held an emergency meeting on the Thai island of Phuket to discuss how to attract visitors back to areas devastated by the tsunamis. Many hotels and resorts had been badly damaged or destroyed in the disaster.

Thai Rak Thai won an overwhelming victory in legislative elections held on 6 February 2005, securing a large majority with 377 of the 500 seats in the House of Representatives. Although 20 parties contested the elections, fielding 2,289 candidates, only three other parties secured representation: the DP took 96 seats, Chart Thai 25 and Mahachon only two. The rate of voter participation was reported at 72%. Thai Rak Thai's success, which enabled it to form a single-party government for the first time, was widely attributed to Thaksin's prompt response to the devastation caused by the tsunamis in December and the strong performance of the economy under his premiership. As in previous election campaigns, however, there were allegations of widespread 'vote-buying', and numerous complaints of electoral malpractice were made. The election results prompted the immediate resignation of Banyat Bantadtan as leader of the DP; Abhisit Vejjajiva was elected as his replacement in March. Anek Laothamatas also subsequently resigned as leader of Mahachon, amid speculation that the party might merge with Thai Rak Thai; he was replaced, in an acting capacity, by Sanan Kajornprasart, pending a leadership election in late April. Prime Minister Thaksin began an unprecedented second consecutive term in office in March, following his formal re-election to the premiership by the House of Representatives. Somkid Jatusripitak retained his position as Minister of Finance in the new Cabinet, and was also appointed as a Deputy Prime Minister, while Kantathee Supamongkol, hitherto a trade representative, was allocated the foreign affairs portfolio, replacing Surakiart Sathirathai, who became a Deputy Prime Minister. Thammarak Isarangura, who had served as Minister of Defence during part of Thaksin's first term before being appointed as a Deputy Prime Minister, reassumed the defence portfolio.

The violence in southern Thailand continued unabated throughout early 2005, and by early March more than 690 people had died since January 2004. In February 2005 the Government approved the formation of a new 12,000-strong army regiment to be stationed in the south. The troops were to focus on development work, as well as on improving security. However, local Islamic leaders warned that an increased military presence in the region (where Thai Rak Thai had failed to secure a single seat in the recent elections) would only heighten disillusionment with the Government. During a three-day visit to the south in mid-February Thaksin announced controversial proposals to allocate development aid to villages in the region depending on the degree of violence found there. Some 1,580 villages had already been surveyed and categorized as red, yellow or green. The 358 villages where violent incidents were deemed to occur frequently were classified as 'red zones' and were to be deprived of funding. However, Thaksin later appeared to have abandoned the plans, which were widely criticized. As the Prime Minister's visit came to an end, a car bomb in Sungai Kolok killed six people and injured more than 40. In late March suspected Islamic militants ambushed a train in Narathiwat province, injuring some 19 people, including 10 police officers. Meanwhile, Thaksin indicated that he was considering adopting a more moderate approach towards the insurgency in the south. He appointed former Prime Minister Anand Panyarachun to chair a 48-member National Reconciliation Commission (NRC), which was charged with restoring peace, and announced his intention to reduce the number of troops deployed in the region. None the less, in early April two people were killed and more than 60 injured in three bomb explosions in the southern province of Songkhla, the first major attacks to occur outside the provinces of Narathiwat, Pattani and Yala.

In May 2005 a major corruption scandal was revealed concerning Minister of Transport Suriya Jungrungreangkit's alleged improprieties during the purchase of baggage-scanning equipment for the new Suvarnabhumi International Airport. The details surrounding the case remained, to those outside of the Government, largely unclarified; none the less, Suriya was the subject of a 'no-confidence' motion instigated by the DP, which, although easily defeated by the Government on account of its large majority in the House of Representatives, caused considerable damage to the reputation of the ruling party, in particular with regard to its stance on vice. In a cabinet reorganization effected in August, Suriya was transferred to the less prominent position of Minister of Industry.

Meanwhile, in June 2005 a delegation from the Organization of the Islamic Conference (OIC, see p. 340) was dispatched to Thailand on a fact-finding mission, at the invitation of Prime Minister Thaksin. In their subsequent report, the members of the delegation concluded, contrary to the claims of Islamic nations and rights groups, that religious issues were not the predominant factor in the ongoing militant attacks in the south of the country.

In late January 2006, in the largest corporate take-over in Thailand's history, Prime Minister Thaksin's family sold its 49.6% holding stake in national telecommunications firm Shin Corporation Public Co Ltd (Shin Corp) to Singapore's state investment wing, Temasek Holdings, at a price of 70,000m. baht (US $1,900m.). The transaction took place on the same day on which a new law raising the limit on foreign ownership in telecommunication firms from 25% to 49% came into effect. The sale provoked outrage within Thailand. Many Thais were angered by the massive tax-free gains made by the Shinawatra family; there were demands for the Prime Minister to donate to the state the 26,000m. baht that had been waived in tax, rather than to profit in this way and thus effectively condone tax evasion. Considerable suspicion was also aroused by the fact that Thaksin's son and daughter had purchased shares in Shin Corp from Ample Vision (an investment company established by the Prime Minister in the British Virgin Islands) at a cost of one baht per share and yet had been able to sell them, just three days later, at a price of 49.25 baht per share. Furthermore, there was widespread concern about the sale of a telecommunications firm to a foreign company on account of the potential threat to national security. Thaksin denied any wrongdoing.

In early February 2006 the Minister of Culture, Uraiwan Thienthong, tendered her resignation from the Cabinet, citing 'the decline in political morality' as the reason for her decision. Later that month, and without prior warning, Prime Minister Thaksin announced that the House of Representatives was being dissolved in preparation for an early election; it was subsequently declared that the poll was to be held in early April. While there was little doubt that the ruling Thai Rak Thai would win the election, the question of whether the party would attract a sufficient proportion of the vote to ease the pressure on Thaksin to resign was less certain. The premier's tactics were countered in an unexpected manner by the three main opposition parties—DP, Chart Thai and Mahachon—all of which announced that they were to boycott the proceedings. In an attempt to defuse the political tension, Thaksin offered to include the three parties within a national coalition government, regardless of whether or not they participated in the election; the offer was, however, rejected. Thaksin also declared his intention to resign if Thai Rak Thai failed to secure more than 50% of the votes cast. During the period prior to the election there were numerous protest rallies in the capital, with angry demonstrators demanding the removal from power of Thaksin. The political tension was accompanied by an intensification of violence in the southern regions. Hundreds of schools in Yala were closed temporarily following the killing of three Buddhist teachers, allegedly by Muslim militants. In March the Prime Minister's son, Phantongtae Shinawatra, was adjudged to have been guilty of securities violations relating to the sale of Shin Corp, and was fined 5.98m. baht (US $153,000), by the Securities and Exchange Commission (SEC); Phantongtae was deemed to have failed fully to disclose transactions pertaining to his stock-holdings.

On 2 April 2006 the legislative election was held and, as expected, Thai Rak Thai secured victory, winning approximately 57% of votes cast. Turn-out was an estimated 64.8% of registered voters. However, 33.1% of those who voted selected the 'no vote' option on ballot papers. Owing to the boycott of the poll by the three main opposition parties, the House of Representatives was unable to convene by the end of the month as a significant number of seats remained vacant, despite the holding of several by-elections. In May the Constitutional Court annulled the results of the election, declaring that they were invalid as the poll had been organized too quickly following the dissolution of the House of Representatives. The Election Commission subsequently announced that a new legislative election would take place in October.

Thailand is a member of the Association of South East Asian Nations (ASEAN, see p. 172) and generally maintains good relations with the other member states. Its former dependence on the USA has been greatly reduced by the increasing importance of regional trade and diplomatic relations. In the late 1980s Prime Minister Chatichai adopted a new business-orientated policy towards Cambodia, Laos, Viet Nam and Myanmar, encouraging investment in their developing economies; a policy successfully pursued by subsequent premiers. In April 1995, following lengthy discussions with Viet Nam, Cambodia and Laos, the four countries established the Mekong River Commission (see p. 387) to promote the joint development of the Mekong's resources. Relations with the People's Republic of China also improved as Thailand became one of China's most significant trading partners. In October 1993 Thailand was accepted as a full member of the Non-aligned Movement (see p. 397).

In January 1993, despite its previous reluctance to do so, Thailand officially closed its border with Cambodia to trade with areas controlled by the communist Cambodian insurgent group, the Party of Democratic Kampuchea (known as the Khmers Rouges), in compliance with UN sanctions against the movement. Nevertheless, violations of the embargo (mainly exports of logs and gems from Cambodia through Thailand) were widely reported during 1993. Accusations by representatives of the Cambodian Government that Thai complicity with the Khmers Rouges was undermining Cambodian attempts to end the insurgency were substantiated by reports from UN peace-keeping troops that members of the Thai armed forces were providing transport, medical care and other support for the Khmers Rouges. Official Thai government policy was to support the elected Government of Cambodia, but the armed forces controlled the border and were unwilling to jeopardize their lucrative business relations with the Khmers Rouges.

In January 1994 Chuan Leekpai made an official visit to Cambodia (the first such visit by a Thai premier) to improve bilateral relations, which had been adversely affected by the continuing allegations. Following this visit more strenuous efforts were made to control illicit border trade and to prevent members of the armed forces from co-operating with the Khmers Rouges. However, clashes between Thai and Cambodian troops continued as a result of incursions into Thai territory by Cambodian government forces in pursuit of the Khmers Rouges. In September 1995 Thailand and Cambodia signed an agreement to establish a border co-ordination committee. At its first meeting in November three border checkpoints, which had been closed in April, were reopened. In the latter half of 1997 intense fighting in Cambodia between forces loyal to the First Prime Minister, Hun Sen, and those of the former Second Prime Minister, Prince Norodom Ranariddh, led to further incursions, across Thailand's eastern border with Cambodia, and resulted in an influx of refugees to Thailand. In May 1998 Hun Sen visited Bangkok to hold discussions with Prime Minister Chuan. In January 1997, meanwhile, the Thai Government adopted a potentially controversial resolution unilaterally to extend Thailand's maritime jurisdiction over waters that were also claimed by Cambodia and Viet Nam. The Thai Government, however, insisted that its decision was legal under international practice.

In January 2003 Thai-Cambodian relations were severely strained when the Thai embassy and several Thai businesses situated in the Cambodian capital, Phnom-Penh, were attacked by Cambodian demonstrators. Those who perpetrated the attacks were protesting against remarks, allegedly made by a Thai actress, claiming that the temples at Angkor Wat in Cambodia in fact belonged to Thailand. In response to the rioting, Prime Minister Thaksin downgraded diplomatic relations with Cambodia and announced plans to evacuate all Thai citizens from the country and to expel illegal Cambodian immigrants living in Thailand; the joint border was subsequently closed. The Cambodian Government issued a formal apology for the incident and promised compensation for those who had been affected by the violence. The Thai Government permitted a limited reopening of the border for commercial reasons in February. In early March Cambodia's Prime Minister, Hun Sen, ordered the border to be closed again, owing to alleged security concerns and in protest at the economic inequality between the two countries. However, later in that month the border was fully reopened and, in April, diplomatic relations were upgraded. In the following month the Thai and Cambodian Cabinets held a joint meeting intended further to improve bilateral relations.

Following a military coup in Burma (now Myanmar) in September 1988, thousands of Burmese students fled to Thailand to avoid government repression. A prominent human rights group, Amnesty International, subsequently accused the Thai Government of coercing the students to return (resulting in their arrest and, in some cases, execution). In 1990 Myanma soldiers achieved unprecedented success in attacks on the strongholds of ethnic minorities on the Thai–Myanma border, since they were able to launch offensives from inside Thailand. The attacks resulted in a new influx of Myanma students and members of rebel ethnic groups seeking refuge in Thailand. The Thai Government refused to recognize those fleeing from Myanmar as refugees or to offer them aid. This refusal was motivated by its wish not to jeopardize the preferential treatment that it received from the Myanma Government, which had recently granted many licences to Thai businesses for the exploitation of Myanmar's natural resources.

In 1992 Myanma forces intensified their attacks on rebel bases near the Thai border. In March the Myanma Government warned Thai armed forces to withdraw from nearby border areas, but later in the month Thai troops clashed with Myanma forces which had entered Thailand to attack a nearby rebel base. In early December King Bhumibol appealed for a peaceful agreement to end the tension caused by the continued occupation by Myanma forces of Hill 491 in Chumphan province. In accordance with a bilateral agreement signed shortly afterwards, Myanma troops were withdrawn from the hill by late December. In February 1993 the two countries resolved to demarcate their common border. In April 1994 Thailand invited Myanmar to attend the annual ASEAN meeting of ministers responsible for foreign affairs in Bangkok. In early 1995, however, relations with Myanmar were strained by the persistent border incursions into Thailand by forces of the Myanma Government during their offensive to capture the headquarters of the rebel Karen (Kayin) National Union (KNU) and subsequent attacks on disarmed Kayin refugees held in Thai camps along the border. In August Myanmar closed its land border with Thailand in protest at the alleged killing of a substantial number of Myanma seamen by Thai fishermen. A visit by Prime Minister Chavalit to Yangon, the capital of Myanmar, in September failed to resolve the situation and further discussions were held in November. In October 1996 the Thai Government approved the opening of three border checkpoints.

In late 1996 and early 1997 attacks allegedly carried out by breakaway Kayin rebels on Kayin refugee camps in Thailand resulted in a number of minor clashes between the Thai army and the rebels. In December 1997 the Thai and Myanma Governments agreed jointly to establish a panel to determine the legitimacy of an estimated 98,000 Kayin refugees sheltered along Thailand's border with Myanmar. In the same month, relief agencies operating along the border accused the Thai military authorities of using oppressive tactics to encourage the refugees to return to Myanmar, although the Thai military had earlier denied reports of its involvement in the forced repatriation of Kayin refugees. In March 1998 the Thai Government announced plans for the forced repatriation of several hundred thousand Myanma immigrants working illegally in Thailand, in response to the economic crisis afflicting the country. In the same month one of the largest Kayin refugee camps along the Thai–Myanma border was destroyed in a cross-border attack by the pro-Government grouping, the Democratic Karen (Kayin) Buddhist Organization.

Relations between Thailand and Myanmar were placed under some strain in late 1999 when a group of armed Myanma student activists seized control of the Myanma embassy in Bangkok in early October, taking 89 people hostage and demanding the release of all political prisoners in Myanmar and the opening of a dialogue between the military Government and the opposition. All the hostages were released by the gunmen within 24 hours, in exchange for the Thai Government's provision of helicopter transport to give the hostage-takers safe passage to the Thai–Myanma border. The Thai Government's release of the hostage-takers angered the ruling military junta in Myanmar, prompting the country to close its border with Thailand. In November, in a further indication of a deterioration in relations between the two countries, Thai forces expelled thousands of illegal Myanma migrant workers from the town of Mai Sot on the Thai–Myanma border, despite threats made by Myanma government troops to shoot the returnees. Although the border was reopened to commerce in late November, relations between the two countries remained fraught.

In January 2000 10 armed Myanma rebels took control of a hospital in Ratchaburi, Thailand, holding hundreds of people hostage. The hostage-takers, reported by some sources to be linked to the Kayin insurgent group, God's Army (a small breakaway faction of the KNU—the main KNU denied any connection with the gunmen), issued several demands, including that the shelling of their base on the Thai–Myanma border by the Thai military be halted, that co-operation between Thai and Myanma government forces against the Kayins should cease, and that their people be allowed to seek refuge in Thailand. However, in contrast to its peaceful handling of the siege of the Myanma embassy in Bangkok in October 1999, the response of the Thai Government to this second hostage crisis (which raised doubts about Thailand's national security and provoked further criticism from both the Thai political opposition and the general population of the Thai Government's relative tolerance of Myanma dissident activity in Thailand) was severe: government forces stormed the hospital, killing all 10 of the hostage-takers and releasing all of the hostages unharmed. This uncompromising resolution of the incident was praised by the military Government in Myanmar, and was regarded by many observers as the signal of a broader campaign by the Thai authorities against dissident activity by ethnic Myanma opposition groups operating in Thailand.

In February 2001 a border incident erupted between Thailand and Myanmar after Myanma forces pursued rebels belonging to the Shan State Army (SSA) into the northern Thai province of Chiang Rai, prompting reprisals by Thai troops. Despite the agreement of a cease-fire, Thailand sealed its border with Myanmar, and the situation was aggravated by Myanmar's assertion that Thailand was assisting the SSA. In April officials belonging to a non-governmental organization in Thailand claimed that the number of refugees of Myanma origin in Thailand had been underestimated and that, as of early April, they totalled almost 131,000. In May the Minister of Foreign Affairs, Surakiart Sathirathai, visited Myanmar in an effort to resolve the ongoing border tensions, but with little success. In the same month the United Wa State Army (UWSA), a Myanma ethnic militia, captured Hua Lone Hill near Chiang Mai; Thai troops recaptured the hill following a four-day battle in which at least 20 members of the UWSA were killed. The Government later lodged a formal protest with the Myanma Government after its forces allegedly bombed a Thai outpost situated near the hill. The Myanma Government responded by accusing the Thai armed forces of having launched air strikes into its territory. The problems were exacerbated when an article appeared in a Myanma newspaper that the Thai authorities claimed was insulting to the monarchy. In June 2001, after repeatedly denying reports that he intended to visit Myanmar, Thaksin Shinawatra became the first Thai Prime Minister to visit Yangon since 1997. While the subsequent discussions succeeded in defusing the immediate tensions, the two sides failed to come to any firm agreement as to how they would overcome the problems affecting bilateral relations. In July the Minister of Defence, Chavalit Yongchaiyudh, also visited Myanmar, and the two countries agreed to work together to expedite the repatriation of refugees on the common border. In September Gen. Khin Nyunt of Myanmar visited Thailand on a trip considered by many to constitute a starting point for a new era of improved relations. In January 2002 a joint Thai-Myanma commission met for the first time since 1999 to discuss plans to establish a task force that would aid in the repatriation of illegal Myanma immigrants. Further talks were held in February, intended to facilitate bilateral co-operation in controlling the cross-border narcotics trade.

In March 2002 Thai-Myanma relations were placed under severe strain when Thai soldiers clashed with members of the UWSA in Chiang Mai. Following the incident, in which one Thai soldier and 12 UWSA guerrillas were killed, the Thai Government lodged a formal protest with Myanmar's ruling military junta. In April a bomb exploded on the so-called 'Friendship Bridge' linking the two countries, resulting in the deaths of at least seven people. Later in the same month the Vice-Chairman of Myanmar's ruling State Peace and Development Council (SPDC) visited Thailand to hold talks with the Government concerning drugs-smuggling and the continued border tensions. However, in May fresh fighting broke out along the joint border between Myanmar government troops, together with their UWSA allies, and the SSA; subsequently, the SPDC again accused the Thai Government of supporting the SSA, following which it closed the shared border, owing to the deterioration of bilateral relations. Meanwhile, following the commencement of a Myanma military campaign on the border, intended to reclaim outposts and camps in the country's Shan State, Thai troops fired across the frontier when two Thai soldiers were allegedly injured by Myanma shells. The Government denied that it supported Myanma insurgent ethnic militias but admitted that it had allowed refugees from Myanmar to cross into Thailand. Shortly afterwards Thaksin claimed that bilateral relations had deteriorated to a new low point and that only an apology from Myanmar would improve the situation. In August the Thai Minister of Foreign Affairs stated that the two countries had agreed to hold talks in an effort to resolve the ongoing bilateral tensions; the joint border finally reopened in October. Relations continued to improve in 2003 and, in February, Thaksin paid a visit to Myanmar, during which the possibility of bilateral co-operation to address the problems posed by the cross-border narcotics trade and illegal immigration were discussed. In July the Thai Government announced plans to relocate all Myanma political refugees resident in Thailand to refugee camps near the joint border, where it was believed they could more easily be controlled and would thus present less of a threat to Thailand's relations with Myanmar. In early 2004 Myanmar announced that it was to award Thailand fishing concessions in its waters for one year. Fishing rights had been terminated in May 2001 following tensions on the joint border. In June 2004 Prime Minister Gen. Khin Nyunt of Myanmar visited Thailand and discussed various economic, development and border issues with Prime Minister Thaksin. In December Thaksin paid a visit to Myanmar, his first since the ousting of Khin Nyunt in October, and held talks with the new Prime Minister, Lt-Gen. Soe Win. In January 2005 Thailand increased security along the border with Myanmar, amid concerns that fighting between Myanma troops and insurgents might encroach upon Thai territory. At the end of March the Thai Government ordered the relocation of about 3,000 Myanma political refugees to camps near the joint border. Around 1,000 of the refugees failed to meet a deadline to register with the Thai authorities, however, and were to be detained and deported to Myanmar. In April Thailand again increased security along the border with Myanmar, in response to renewed fighting between rival Myanma ethnic rebel groups close to Thai territory.

Relations with Malaysia were adversely affected in November 1995 by the killing of two Thai fishermen by a Malaysian patrol vessel. In December an understanding was reached on the issue and it was agreed to establish a joint committee to resolve a long-standing dispute over fishing rights. Relations were also strained in early 1996 by Thai opposition to the Malaysian construction of a wall along the countries' common border. In late 1996 and early 1997 Thailand co-operated with Malaysia to prevent illegal Bangladeshi workers from entering Malaysia. Relations between the two countries continued to improve during 1998: by April, Prime Minister Chuan and his Malaysian counterpart, Mahathir Mohamad, had met five times in as many months to discuss bilateral issues. In January the Malaysian authorities arrested, and transferred to the Thai authorities, three alleged Muslim separatist leaders wanted in Thailand in connection with terrorist activities in the southern provinces of the country. In February 1997 Malaysia and Thailand established the Kolok river as the border demarcation between the two countries. In April 2001 the two countries agreed to co-operate to find those responsible for two bomb attacks in southern Thailand. In the same month Prime Minister Thaksin paid an official visit to Malaysia, during which the two countries discussed border demarcation issues and agreed that the planned construction of a gas pipeline between Thailand and Malaysia would proceed as originally intended. Relations remained cordial and, in December 2002, the cabinets of the two countries held an historic joint meeting, during which trade and security issues were discussed. In early 2004 the Malaysian Government co-operated with Thailand in an attempt to bring an end to the escalating violence in the south of the country. In February the Thai Government mooted plans to construct a security fence along parts of the joint border, in the hope of preventing militants from seeking refuge in Malaysia. As unrest in southern Thailand continued, Prime Minister Thaksin visited Malaysia in April for talks with his counterpart, Abdullah Badawi, on security along the border and the economic development of the surrounding area. None the less, the Malaysian Government rejected suggestions that the suspected perpetrators of the violence in southern Thailand had escaped to Malaysia. Bilateral relations were strained in December, when the Thai Government claimed to have photographic evidence that militants in southern Thailand had received training in Malaysia. In January 2005 the Malaysian authorities arrested Abdul Rahman Ahmad, whom Thailand held responsible for organizing much of the separatist violence in the south. A diplomatic dispute arose between the two countries in October concerning the fate of 131 Muslim asylum-seekers, who had fled from the violence-stricken southern province of Narathiwat to neighbouring Malaysia (see the chapter on Malaysia). Although the issue was eventually resolved in February 2006 when the Thai Government announced that it was to allow the refugees to remain in Malaysia, relations between the two countries had by that stage descended to their lowest point in recent years. In November former Malaysian Prime Minister Mahathir Mohamad visited Thailand for discussions with Prime Minister Thaksin regarding the ongoing insurgency in southern Thailand. The negotiations made some progress towards easing the tension that had been caused by Thai security officials' accusations that the Malaysian authorities were failing to prevent insurgents from crossing the border into Thailand. Thaksin and Mahathir agreed that the two countries should cease their 'war of words' and Mahathir was to stop advocating autonomy for Thailand's southern regions. In December Manasae Saeloh, a suspected leader of PULO, was arrested in Malaysia and relinquished to the Thai authorities, by which he was wanted in connection with numerous bomb attacks and other acts of violence.

In November 1996 the Government approved a proposal for the establishment of a Joint Thai-Lao Border Committee. In December 1997 it was announced by the office of the UN High Commissioner for Refugees (UNHCR) that the review of the status of the last remaining group of Laotian refugees at the Ban Napho refugee camp in the Nakhan Phanom province of Thailand was scheduled to be completed by January 1998, after which the refugees were to be either allowed to settle in a third country or repatriated. In September 1999 282 Laotian refugees who had been residing at the camp were compulsorily repatriated by Thai officials and UNHCR after having been refused refugee status; a further 291 Laotian refugees were repatriated in December. In December 2003 the USA agreed to accept around 15,000 Laotian Hmong refugees living in refugee camps in Thailand. The first group of refugees was resettled in the USA in June 2004, under the aegis of the International Organization for Migration. Meanwhile, in August 2000 a border dispute arose between Thailand and Laos after Laos apparently attempted to assert sovereignty over all islands in the Mekong river, as it claimed was its right under the Siam-Franco treaty of 1926. The occupation by Laotian armed forces of the Mano I and Mano II islands took place during the demarcation of the river boundary (due to be completed by the end of 2000) between the two countries. In March 2002 a Thai court convicted 28 people, including 17 Laotian nationals, of charges relating to the dispute. Despite the existence of a bilateral extradition treaty, concluded in 2001, it was thought unlikely that Thailand would comply with a Lao Government request to extradite its citizens to Laos. In March 2004 the Thai and Laotian Governments held a joint cabinet meeting to discuss bilateral co-operation. In December Laos and Thailand agreed to complete the demarcation of their land border in the following year to mark the 55th anniversary of the establishment of diplomatic relations between the two countries.

In February 1998 it was reported that, owing to the country's ongoing economic crisis, Thailand was to reduce financial aid to neighbouring countries, including Cambodia, Laos, Myanmar and Viet Nam. In October the Vietnamese President, Tran Duc Luong, paid an official visit to Thailand, the first visit to the country by a Vietnamese head of state since the establishment of diplomatic relations more than 20 years previously. At the 31st annual ASEAN ministerial meeting in July, Thailand's Minister of Foreign Affairs, Surin Pitsuwan, proposed the modification of ASEAN's long-standing policy of non-interference in the internal affairs of member countries in favour of a policy of 'flexible engagement'; however, the proposal met with a generally negative response from most other ASEAN members. In November 2004, ahead of a summit meeting of ASEAN leaders in Vientiane, Laos, Prime Minister Thaksin Shinawatra threatened to walk out of the summit if other members raised concerns over his Government's handling of the unrest in Thailand's southern provinces. In the event Thaksin held separate talks with the leaders of Malaysia and Indonesia on regional security co-operation.

In 1999 Thailand contributed 1,500 troops to the multinational peace-keeping force in the UN-administered territory of East Timor (now Timor-Leste), following the territory's vote for independence from Indonesia in a referendum held in August. The country also maintained a cordial bilateral relationship with Indonesia, affirmed when the Thai Prime Minister visited Jakarta in February 2002.

In December 2001 the Prime Minister paid an official visit to the USA. During his stay he held talks with US President George W. Bush and assured him that Thailand would remain a strong ally in the US-led war on terrorism in the aftermath of the September terrorist attacks (see the chapter on the USA). In response, the US President praised the Thai Government for its consistent support throughout the campaign. In June 2003 Thaksin met with President Bush again in Washington, DC, to discuss counter-terrorism issues. In October President Bush attended a summit meeting of the Asia-Pacific Economic Co-operation (APEC, see p. 164) in Bangkok, having paid an official state visit to Thailand in the days preceding the summit. The two heads of state announced that they were to enter into formal negotiations with regard to the signing of a bilateral free-trade agreement. The terms of the deal were expected to be comprehensive, including measures intended to liberalize trade in consumer goods, agricultural products, services and investment, as well as intellectual property rights. However, following the completion of the sixth round of talks between the two countries, held in January 2006, scant progress had been made. Furthermore, the political upheaval precipitated by the sale of the Shinawatras' holding stake in Shin Corp, culminating in Thaksin's resignation in early April (see above), was expected significantly to delay further Thai-US negotiations.

Following the terrorist attack on the Indonesian island of Bali in October 2002 (see the chapter on Indonesia), the Thai Government increased security in the country owing to speculation that Thailand, and in particular the tourist resort of Phuket, might be the target of further regional terrorist activity. Evidence was discovered that suggested southern Thailand as one of the locations used by those responsible for planning the Bali attack. Meanwhile, several foreign governments issued advisories warning against unnecessary travel to the country. However, the Thai Government expressed its concern that such warnings were excessive and called for them to be rescinded.

Government

In December 1991 a new Constitution was promulgated, which provided for a National Assembly (comprising an elected House of Representatives and an appointed Senate) and a Cabinet headed by a Prime Minister. In June 1992 the National Assembly approved a constitutional amendment requiring the Prime

THAILAND

Introductory Survey

Minister to be a member of the House of Representatives. In January 1995 the National Assembly approved a constitutional charter, which provided for a number of amendments; these included lowering the voting age from 20 to 18 years and reducing the membership of the Senate to two-thirds of that of the House of Representatives.

A new draft Constitution was promulgated on 11 October 1997 (see Constitution, below): enabling legislation for the new Constitution was completed within 240 days.

Defence

In August 2005 the Thai armed forces had a total strength of 306,600: 190,000 in the army, 70,600 in the navy and an estimated 46,000 in the air force. Military service is compulsory for two years between the ages of 21 and 30. Paramilitary forces, including a volunteer irregular force, numbered an estimated 113,700. The defence budget was 78,000m. baht for 2005.

Economic Affairs

In 2004, according to estimates by the World Bank, Thailand's gross national income (GNI), measured at average 2002–04 prices, was US $158,703m., equivalent to $2,540 per head (or $8,020 per head on an international purchasing-power parity basis). During 1995–2004, it was estimated, the population increased at an annual average rate of 0.7%, while gross domestic product (GDP) per head increased, in real terms, by an average of 1.8% per year. Overall GDP increased, in real terms, at an average annual rate of 2.5% in 1995–2004. According to the Asian Development Bank (ADB), GDP increased by 6.2% in 2004 and by 4.5% in 2005.

Agriculture (including forestry, hunting and fishing) contributed an estimated 10.1% of GDP in 2004. In that year 42.3% of the employed labour force were engaged in the sector. Thailand's staple crop and principal agricultural export commodity is rice (Thailand became the world's largest exporter of rice in 1981). Rice exports accounted for 2.8% of the total value of exports in 2004. Other major crops include sugar cane, cassava (tapioca), oil palm fruit, maize, natural rubber, bananas, mangoes and pineapples. Timber was formerly a major source of export revenue, but a ban on uncontrolled logging was imposed in 1989. A reafforestation programme, initiated in the late 1980s, recommenced during 1993. Fisheries products and livestock (mainly cattle, buffaloes, pigs and poultry) are also important. Thailand is one of the world's largest exporters of farmed shrimp. During 1995–2004, according to figures from the ADB, agricultural GDP increased by an estimated annual average of 2.2%. In 2004, however, agricultural GDP contracted by 4.8%, owing to the effects of prolonged drought in much of the country, combined with an outbreak of avian influenza ('bird flu') in the region in late 2003 and early 2004; the latter development resulted in the imposition of bans by the European Union (EU) and Japan on imports of Thai poultry. The re-emergence of avian influenza in late 2004 further hindered growth; in 2005 agricultural GDP was estimated to have contracted by 2.4%.

Industry (including mining, manufacturing, construction and utilities) provided an estimated 43.5% of GDP in 2004. In that year 20.5% of the employed labour force were engaged in industrial activities. During 1995–2004, according to figures from the ADB, industrial GDP increased at an annual average rate of 3.4%. The GDP of the industrial sector increased by 8.0% in 2004 and by 5.7% in 2005.

Mining and quarrying contributed an estimated 2.7% of GDP in 2004 and engaged less than 0.1% of the employed labour force in that year. Gemstones, notably diamonds, are the principal mineral export, with jewellery accounting for 2.3% of the total value of exports in 2004. Natural gas and, to a lesser extent, petroleum are also exploited, and production of these fuels increased substantially from the late 1990s onwards. Tin, lignite, gypsum, tungsten, lead, antimony, manganese, gold, zinc, iron and fluorite are also mined. In 2001 licences were granted to permit the exploitation of a large deposit of potash at Somboon; it was eventually expected to yield up to 2m. metric tons per year, making it the world's second largest potash mine. However, in 2002 protests against the development of the mine, owing to concerns about its potential environmental impact, threatened to delay its development. In late 2001 a new gold mine was opened in Pichit province, the first to have been opened since the country ceased gold production in 1996. During 1995–2004, according to figures from the ADB, the GDP of the mining sector increased at an estimated average annual rate of 6.8%. Mining GDP increased by 6.8% in 2003 and by an estimated 5.4% in 2004.

Manufacturing provided an estimated 34.5% of GDP in 2004. In that year 14.9% of the employed labour force were engaged in the sector. In 1999 manufacturing's contribution to export earnings was 80%. Textiles and garments and electronics and electrical goods (particularly semiconductors) constitute Thailand's principal branches of manufacturing. Other manufacturing activities include the production of cigarettes, chemicals, cement and beer, sugar and petroleum refining, motor vehicle production, rubber production and the production of iron and steel. During 1995–2004, according to figures from the ADB, manufacturing GDP increased by an estimated annual average of 4.5%. The GDP of the sector increased by 10.4% in 2003 and by 8.3% in 2004.

Energy is derived principally from hydrocarbons. At the end of 2004 there were estimated proven gas reserves of some 430,000m. cu m, sufficient to sustain production at that year's level for 21 years. Estimated proven petroleum reserves were some 500m. barrels, enough to sustain production at 2004 levels for less than 7 years. In 2004 9.0m. metric tons of petroleum were produced and 18.2m. metric tons of natural gas. In 2003 petroleum accounted for 52.3% of total fuel consumption, natural gas for 32.3%, coal for 13.1% and hydroelectricity for 2.3%. Lignite is also exploited. Solar and wind energy account for about 1% of electric power. Thailand remains, however, heavily dependent on imported petroleum and electricity. In 2000 approximately 86% of its petroleum requirements were met by imports. In February 1996 licences were awarded by the state-owned Electricity Generating Authority of Thailand to two companies to provide an additional generating capacity of 1,380 MW by 2000 under the Independent Power Producers programme, Asia's largest scheme for private-sector electricity supply. A further 2,000 MW were to be produced by independent producers by 2002 and an additional 4,000 MW by 2006. In 2005 imports of mineral fuels comprised 17.6% of the value of merchandise imports.

Services (including transport and communications, commerce, banking and finance, public administration and other services) contributed an estimated 46.4% of GDP in 2004; 37.2% of the employed labour force were engaged in the services sector in that year. Tourism has become a major source of foreign exchange, and in the early 2000s was estimated to account for 6% of the country's GDP. The number of tourist arrivals rose to 11.7m. in 2004, and receipts increased to 384,360m. baht. However, the tourism sector's recovery from the regional repercussions of the terrorist attack on the Indonesian island of Bali in October 2002 was then jeopardized by the effects of the tsunami disaster of December 2004 and also by the ongoing unrest in southern Thailand (see Recent History). In April 2005 a series of bombings in Songkhla province included an attack on Hat Yai International Airport, and in October a second major terrorist attack on Bali was expected further to impede sectoral performance in that year. During 1995–2004, according to the ADB, the GDP of the services sector expanded by an estimated annual average of 1.6%. The GDP of the sector increased by 6.9% in 2004 and by 4.6% in 2005.

In 2004 Thailand recorded a visible trade surplus of US $10,582.8m.; in the same year there was a surplus of $6,632.4m. on the current account of the balance of payments. In 2005 the principal source of imports (22.0%) was Japan; other major suppliers in that year were the People's Republic of China, the USA and Malaysia. The principal market for exports in 2005 was the USA (15.4%); other important purchasers were Japan (13.6%), the People's Republic of China, Singapore and Hong Kong. The principal imports in 2005 were machinery and transport equipment (40.2%), basic manufactures, mineral fuels and lubricants and chemical products. The principal exports were machinery and transport equipment (45.3%), basic manufactures, food and live animals, miscellaneous manufactured goods (including clothing and accessories) and chemicals and related products.

There was an estimated overall budgetary surplus of 4,300m. baht in 2004, when expenditure of 1,109,300m. baht was envisaged. According to the ADB, Thailand's external debt totalled US $50,871m. at the end of 2005; in that year the cost of debt-servicing was equivalent to 9.8% of the value of exports of goods and services. The annual rate of inflation averaged 3.1% in 1995–2004. Consumer prices increased by 2.8% in 2004 and by 4.5% in 2005. In 2005 1.4% of the labour force were unemployed.

Thailand is a member of the UN Economic and Social Commission for Asia and the Pacific (ESCAP, see p. 33), the Asian Development Bank (ADB, see p. 169), the Association of South East Asian Nations (ASEAN, see p. 172), the Colombo Plan (see

p. 385) and the Asia-Pacific Economic Co-operation (APEC, see p. 164). In January 1993 the establishment of the ASEAN Free Trade Area (AFTA) commenced; the reduction of tariffs to between 0% and 5% was originally to be implemented by 2008 but this was subsequently brought forward to 2002. The target date for zero tariffs was advanced from 2015 to 2010 in November 1999. AFTA was formally established on 1 January 2002.

Thailand's emergence from the regional economic crisis precipitated, in 1997, by the collapse of the Thai baht, was mainly export-driven. In 2001, however, the deceleration of the global economy, in particular the economies of the USA and Japan, exacerbated by the September terrorist attacks on the USA, significantly curbed this recovery. Nevertheless, in July 2003, two years prior to the scheduled date of May 2005, the Government repaid the final instalment on an outstanding loan of US $4,800m. that had been awarded by the IMF and other international donors in the aftermath of the 1997 economic crisis. Following Thailand's instigation of a campaign to create an Asian Bond Fund (ABF) in 2002, foreign investment rose to $1,466m. in 2003, but declined to $1,289m. in 2004, before increasing substantially to reach $3,289m. in 2005. In order to encourage the liberalization of trade, in 2003 Thailand began to negotiate a number of bilateral free-trade agreements (FTAs). The Thailand-China FTA framework was implemented in October 2003, and a similar agreement with India took effect in September 2004. The Thai-Australian FTA, effective from January 2005, was comprehensive in scope, and was expected to be of particular benefit to the industrial goods export sector. Imports from Australia in 2005 rose sharply, increasing by 47.1% compared with 2004; exports to Australia also increased, by 28.6%. In April 2005 an FTA with New Zealand was signed, which came into effect in July of that year. The so-called Thailand-New Zealand Closer Economic Partnership provided for the elimination of 71% of tariffs upon implementation, and this percentage was expected to increase to 84% by 2010, with a view to achieving in subsequent years the total elimination of tariffs on all goods between the two countries. The implementation of these FTAs contributed to the significant increase in foreign direct investment recorded in 2005, which increased by $2,000m. compared with the previous year (see above). Negotiations concerning FTAs with Japan and the USA were expected to be concluded by mid-2005. However, at early 2006 significant progress had yet to be made before agreement with either nation was likely to be reached. Furthermore, the political upheaval precipitated by the sale of the Shinawatra family's holding stake in Shin Corp, which jeopardized the position of Prime Minister Thaksin in April (see Recent History), was widely expected significantly further to delay both sets of negotiations. In early 2004 the Government introduced plans to increase the competitiveness of the Thai financial sector by encouraging a number of mergers within the banking system, in order to improve its efficiency. In addition, $37,000m. was to be spent on infrastructure projects, scheduled for completion over the following five years, although independent analysts questioned whether the Government would be able to acquire sufficient funds for the undertaking. The re-emergence of avian influenza in the latter stages of 2004 resulted in another sub-standard year for the agricultural sector in 2005. By April 2006 the virus had claimed its 108th reported human fatality world-wide since late 2003, 14 of which had occurred in Thailand; although at that stage no confirmed incidents of human-to-human transmission had been reported, it was feared that the virus might in future combine with human influenza and lead to a human pandemic. In January 2006 the Government removed restrictions on foreign companies seeking to invest in state megaprojects. However, the political instability of early 2006, combined with the ongoing violence in the southernmost provinces of the country and the continued threat of regional terrorist activity, was expected to diminish the country's attractiveness as a destination for foreign investment. Fuel subsidies, which had been implemented by the Government in early 2004, were ended in July 2005. The substantial increase in international petroleum prices during 2005/06, however, was expected to have a negative impact on the Thai economy. The ADB projected growth of 4.7% for 2006 and of 5.5% for 2007.

Education

From January 2003, education became officially compulsory for 10 years, to be undertaken between the ages of seven and 16 years. In October 2002 12 years of free basic education was granted to students throughout the country for the first time, and in May 2004 this was expanded to 14 years, with the two years of pre-primary schooling henceforth also being offered free to all. Primary education begins at six years of age and lasts for six years. In 2001 86.3% of the total number of children in the relevant age group were enrolled within primary education. Secondary education, beginning at 12 years of age, also lasts for six years, divided into two equal cycles. In 2002 total secondary enrolment was equivalent to 84% of males and 80% of females in the relevant age-group. In 1996 the total enrolment at primary and secondary schools was equivalent to 71% of all school-age children. There were 20 state universities (12 of which were in Bangkok) and 26 private universities and colleges in 1995. In 2003 a total of approximately 1.9m. students were enrolled within the tertiary education sector. Budgetary expenditure on education by the central Government was 251,200m. baht (24.4% of total spending and equivalent to 4.0% of GDP) in the financial year ending 30 September 2004.

Public Holidays

2006: 1 January (New Year's Day), 12 February* (Makhabuja), 6 April (Chakri Day), 13–15 April (Songkran Festival), 1 May (Labour Day), 5 May (Coronation Day), 7 May* (Royal Ploughing Ceremony Day), 12 May* (Visakhabuja), 1 July (Half Year Bank Holiday), 10 July (Asalhabuja), 11 July* (Khao Phansa, beginning of Buddhist Lent), 12 August (Queen's Birthday), 23 October (Chulalongkorn Day), 5 December (King's Birthday), 10 December (Constitution Day), 31 December (New Year's Eve).

2007: 1 January (New Year's Day), February* (Makhabuja), 6 April (Chakri Day), 13–15 April (Songkran Festival), 1 May (Labour Day), 5 May (Coronation Day), May* (Royal Ploughing Ceremony Day), 31 May* (Visakhabuja), July* (Asalhabuja), 1 July (Half Year Bank Holiday), 21 July* (Khao Phansa, beginning of Buddhist Lent), 12 August (Queen's Birthday), October (Chulalongkorn Day), 5 December (King's Birthday), 10 December (Constitution Day), 31 December (New Year's Eve).

* Regulated by the Buddhist lunar calendar.

Weights and Measures

The metric system is in force, but a number of traditional measures are also used.

THAILAND

Statistical Survey

Source (unless otherwise stated): National Statistical Office, Thanon Larn Luang, Bangkok 10100; tel. (2) 281-0333; fax (2) 281-3815; e-mail onsoadm@nso.gov.th; internet www.nso.go.th.

Area and Population

AREA, POPULATION AND DENSITY

Area (sq km)	513,120*
Population (census results)†	
1 April 1990	54,548,530
1 April 2000	
Males	29,844,870
Females	30,762,077
Total	60,606,947
Population (official projected estimates at mid-year)	
2003	63,655,000
2004	64,197,000
2005	64,763,000
Density (per sq km) at mid-2005	126.2

* 198,117 sq miles.
† Excluding adjustment for underenumeration.

REGIONS
(projected estimates at mid-2005)

	Area (sq km)	Population ('000)	Density (per sq km)
Bangkok and vicinities	7,761.6	11,372	1,465.2
Bangkok	1,568.7	6,796	4,332.2
Sub-central Region	16,593.5	3,049	183.7
Eastern Region	36,502.5	4,401	120.6
Western Region	43,047.1	3,606	83.8
Northern Region	169,644.3	11,655	68.7
Northeastern Region	168,855.3	21,903	129.7
Southern Region	70,715.2	8,777	124.1
Total	513,119.5	64,763	126.2

PRINCIPAL TOWNS
(population at 2000 census)

Bangkok Metropolis*	6,320,174	Pak Kret	141,788
Samut Prakan	378,694	Si Racha	141,334
Nanthaburi	291,307	Khon Kaen	141,034
Udon Thani	220,493	Nakhon Pathom	120,657
Nakhon Ratchasima	204,391	Nakhon Si Thammarat	118,764
Hat Yai	185,557	Thanya Buri	113,818
Chon Buri	182,641	Surat Thani	111,276
Chiang Mai	167,776	Rayong	106,585
Phra Padaeng	166,828	Ubon Ratchathani	106,552
Lampang	147,812	Khlong Luang	103,282

* Formerly Bangkok and Thonburi.

Mid-2003 (UN estimate, incl. suburbs): Bangkok 6,486,401 (Source: UN, *World Urbanization Prospects: The 2003 Revision*).

BIRTHS, MARRIAGES AND DEATHS*

	Registered live births		Registered marriages		Registered deaths	
	Number	Rate (per 1,000)	Number	Rate (per 1,000)	Number	Rate (per 1,000)
1994	960,248	16.4	n.a.	n.a.	305,526	5.2
1995	963,678	16.2	470,751	7.9	324,842	5.5
1996	944,118	15.7	436,831	7.3	342,645	5.7
1997	897,604	14.8	396,928	6.5	303,918	5.0
1998	897,495	14.7	324,262	5.3	317,793	5.2
1999	754,685	12.3	348,803	5.7	362,607	5.9
2000	773,009	12.5	339,443	5.4	365,741	5.9
2001	790,425	12.7	324,661	n.a.	369,493	6.0

* Registration is incomplete. According to UN estimates, the average annual rates in 1990–95 were: Births 19.4 per 1,000; Deaths 6.0 per 1,000; in 1995–2000: Births 17.3 per 1,000; Deaths 6.6 per 1,000; in 2000–05: Births 16.3 per 1,000; Deaths 7.3 per 1,000 (Source: UN, *World Population Prospects: The 2004 Revision*).

Sources: mainly Ministry of Public Health, Ministry of the Interior, Bangkok.

Expectation of life (WHO estimates, years at birth): 70 (males 67; females 73) in 2003 (Source: WHO, *World Health Report*).

ECONOMICALLY ACTIVE POPULATION*
('000 persons aged 13 years and over, August of each year)

	2002	2003	2004
Agriculture, hunting and forestry	15,311	15,146	14,719
Fishing	488	415	396
Mining and quarrying	37	40	35
Manufacturing	5,040	5,086	5,313
Electricity, gas and water	95	105	99
Construction	1,620	1,614	1,878
Wholesale and retail trade; repair of motor vehicles, motorcycles and personal and household goods	4,739	5,057	5,452
Hotels and restaurants	1,988	2,103	2,206
Transport, storage and communications	965	988	1,068
Financial intermediation	263	279	303
Real estate, renting and business activities	499	567	634
Public administration and defence; compulsory social security	957	903	1,015
Education	947	957	1,083
Health and social work	471	518	535
Other community, social and personal service activities	602	621	713
Private households with employed persons	222	255	239
Extra-territorial organizations and bodies	5	1	1
Activities not adequately defined	15	21	23
Total employed	34,263	34,677	35,712
Unemployed	616	544	549
Total labour force	34,879	35,221	36,261
Males	19,244	19,397	20,023
Females	15,635	15,825	16,238

* Excluding the armed forces.
Source: ILO.

THAILAND

Health and Welfare

KEY INDICATORS

Total fertility rate (children per woman, 2003)	1.9
Under-5 mortality rate (per 1,000 live births, 2004)	21
HIV/AIDS (% of persons aged 15–49, 2003)	1.5
Physicians (per 1,000 head, 1999)	0.30
Hospital beds (per 1,000 head, 1995)	1.99
Health expenditure (2002): US $ per head (PPP)	321
Health expenditure (2002): % of GDP	4.4
Health expenditure (2002): public (% of total)	69.7
Access to water (% of persons, 2002)	85
Access to sanitation (% of persons, 2002)	99
Human Development Index (2003): ranking	73
Human Development Index (2003): value	0.778

For sources and definitions, see explanatory note on p. vi.

Agriculture

PRINCIPAL CROPS
('000 metric tons)

	2002	2003	2004
Rice (paddy)	26,057	27,241	26,948
Maize	4,230	4,160	4,094
Sorghum	132	137	200*
Cassava (Manioc, Tapioca)	16,868	18,430	20,400
Sugar cane	60,013	74,258	67,900
Dry beans	216	222	217
Soybeans (Soya beans)	260	270	271*
Groundnuts (in shell)	112	120*	130*
Coconuts	1,418	1,432	1,450†
Oil palm fruit	4,002	4,590	4,600†
Kapok fruit	139*	139*	140†
Cabbages†	220	260	260
Tomatoes	242	248†	248†
Pumpkins, squash, gourds†	220	226	226
Cucumbers and gherkins†	220	222	222
Dry onions	211	239	293
Garlic	125	105	100*
Green corn (maize)	252	280†	280†
Other vegetables†	1,216	1,236	1,236
Watermelons†	410	420	420
Bananas†	1,800	1,900	1,900
Oranges†	340	340	340
Tangerines, mandarins, clementines, satsumas†	668	668	668
Mangoes†	1,700	1,700	1,700
Pineapples	1,739	1,900†	1,900†
Papayas†	120	125	125
Other fruits†	1,130	1,123	1,123
Tobacco (leaves)	76	81	80†
Natural rubber	2,456	2,506	3,030*

* Unofficial figure.
† FAO estimate(s).

Source: FAO.

LIVESTOCK
('000 head, year ending September)

	2002	2003	2004
Horses	8	9*	9*
Cattle	4,820	5,048	5,000*
Buffaloes	1,613	1,650*	2,000*
Pigs	6,879	7,059	7,159
Sheep	39	42†	42*
Goats	178	178†	178*
Chickens	235,233	177,114	170,000*
Ducks	25,034	20,000*	17,000*
Geese*	260	260	270

* FAO estimate(s).
† Unofficial figure.

Source: FAO.

LIVESTOCK PRODUCTS
('000 metric tons)

	2002	2003	2004
Beef and veal	178.3*	180.0*	114.7
Buffalo meat	58.2*	59.5*	37.7
Pig meat*	646.1	642.2	656.5
Chicken meat	1,320†	1,227	878.5
Duck meat	93†	72†	85
Cows' milk	660.3	731.9	842.6
Hen eggs†	538	554	393
Other poultry eggs*	304	304	305
Cattle hides (fresh)*	45	45	45
Buffalo hides (fresh)*	6.9	7.0	7.1

* FAO estimate(s).
† Unofficial figure(s).

Source: FAO.

Forestry

ROUNDWOOD REMOVALS
('000 cubic metres, excl. bark)

	2002	2003*	2004*
Sawlogs, veneer logs and logs for sleepers	300	300	300
Other industrial wood	5,500	5,500	5,500
Fuel wood*	20,250	20,113	19,985
Total	26,050	27,913	25,785

* FAO estimates.

Source: FAO.

SAWNWOOD PRODUCTION
('000 cubic metres, incl. railway sleepers)

	2000	2001	2002
Coniferous (softwood)	17	18	18*
Broadleaved (hardwood)	203	215	270
Total	220	233	288

* FAO estimate.

2003–04: Production assumed to be unchanged from 2002 (FAO estimates).

Source: FAO.

Fishing

('000 metric tons, live weight)

	2001	2002	2003
Capture	2,833.7	2,842.4	2,817.5
Sardinellas	145.0	128.9	148.6
Anchovies, etc.	145.5	151.7	157.6
Indian mackerels	173.3	179.2	190.1
Aquaculture	714.3	621.5*	773.0
Giant tiger prawn	276.0	160.0*	176.0
Total catch	3,548.0	3,463.9*	3,590.5

* FAO estimate.

Source: FAO.

THAILAND

Statistical Survey

Mining

(production in metric tons, rounded, unless otherwise indicated)

	2002	2003	2004
Lignite ('000 metric tons)	19,572	18,843	20,060
Crude petroleum ('000 barrels)	27,582	34,990	31,158
Natural gas—gross production (million cu m)	20,527	21,677	22,366
Iron ore—gross weight	570,110	9,675	135,580
Iron ore—metal content	285,000	4,800	68,000
Lead ore—metal content	3,200	—	—
Zinc ore—metal content*	33,600	37,100	43,400
Tin concentrates—metal content	1,130	793	586
Manganese ore—metal content*	—	—	2,180
Tungsten concentrates—metal content*	31	208	180
Tantalum—metal and oxide powder	102	168	317
Antimony ore—metal content	1	38	52
Silver (kilograms)	18,018	12,496	10,700
Gold (kilograms)	4,950	4,269	4,500
Marble—dimension stone ('000 cu m)	461.3	339.2	236.6
Granite—dimension stone ('000 cu m)	7.6	9.9	10.0*
Granite—industrial ('000 metric tons)	3,370	3,107	3,500
Limestone ('000 metric tons)	110,440	112,941	133,196*
Dolomite ('000 metric tons)	933.2	865.7	992.9
Calcite ('000 metric tons)	172.8	232.0	436.6
Silica sand ('000 metric tons)	781.0	1,293.9	587.7
Ball clay ('000 metric tons)	450.8	579.4	610.2
Kaolin—marketable production ('000 metric tons)	299.2	559.3	631.0
Phosphate rock, crude	3,680	13,870	2,580
Fluorspar—metallurgical grade ('000 metric tons)	783.7	825.0	1,001.1
Feldspar	2,270	2,368	2,375
Barite	137.5	115.6	211.3
Perlite	7,600	5,700	6,000*
Gypsum ('000 metric tons)	6,326	7,291	7,619
Gemstones ('000 carats)	1,597	716	911

* Estimate(s).

Source: US Geological Survey.

Industry

SELECTED PRODUCTS
('000 metric tons, unless otherwise indicated)

	2003	2004	2005*
Raw sugar	7,766	7,100	4,633
Beer (million litres)	1,933	2,050	2,273
Spirits (million litres)	564	645	600
Synthetic fibre	830.7	893.9	809.0
Wood pulp	981.0	920.0	925.5
Petroleum products (million litres)	44,585	48,323	48,133
Cement	32,530	35,626	37,872
Galvanized iron sheets	462.1	436.1	283.6
Integrated circuits (million units)	8,223	9,848	11,378
Computer monitors ('000 units)	3,979	4,465	2,210
Computer keyboards ('000 units)	27,371	14,314	7,454
Hard disk drives ('000 units)	54,173	75,685	120,614
Printers ('000 units)	14,979	21,269	19,241

* Preliminary figures.

Source: Bank of Thailand, Bangkok.

Finance

CURRENCY AND EXCHANGE RATES

Monetary Units
100 satangs = 1 baht.

Sterling, Dollar and Euro Equivalents (30 December 2005)
£1 sterling = 70.65 baht;
US $1 = 41.03 baht;
€1 = 48.40 baht;
1,000 baht = £14.15 = $24.37 = €20.66.

Average Exchange Rate (baht per US $)
2003   41.485
2004   40.222
2005   40.220

Note: Figures refer to the average mid-point rate of exchange available from commercial banks. In July 1997 the Bank of Thailand began operating a managed 'float' of the baht. In addition, a two-tier market was introduced, creating separate exchange rates for purchasers of baht in domestic markets and those who buy the currency overseas.

BUDGET
(million baht, year ending 30 September)

Revenue	2001	2002	2003
Tax revenue	694,462	785,574	902,579
Taxes on income and profits	254,089	286,019	346,608
Personal	97,033	104,912	116,099
Corporate	140,098	162,415	208,211
Petroleum income tax	16,957	18,691	22,298
Taxes on consumption	327,802	379,716	421,466
General business tax	133	101	86
Value-added tax	126,804	147,228	150,457
Specific business tax	13,143	12,960	12,727
Excise taxes	187,722	219,426	258,196
Taxes on international trade	91,496	98,291	109,842
Import duties	91,403	98,116	109,628
Export duties	93	175	214
Other taxes	21,075	21,549	24,663
Non-tax revenue	81,340	91,327	110,009
State enterprises	52,271	56,108	54,532
Other	29,069	35,218	55,476
Total	**775,802**	**876,901**	**1,012,588**

Expenditure*	2001	2002	2003
General public services	42,733	53,084	51,906
Defence	75,413	76,724	77,774
Public order and safety	57,782	58,224	62,776
Education	222,035	223,622	240,979
Health	87,069	70,211	79,584
Social security and welfare	60,590	81,015	121,133
Housing and community amenities	36,496	50,237	22,508
Recreational, cultural and religious activities	6,870	6,918	5,481
Economic affairs and services	201,481	204,454	198,992
Fuel and energy	2,003	1,617	1,443
Agriculture, forestry and fisheries	75,115	75,279	68,612
Mining, manufacturing and construction	6,891	6,301	7,109
Transportation and communication	75,698	69,543	49,823
Other economic activities	41,774	51,714	72,005
Miscellaneous and unclassified items	117,766	130,919	132,964
Total	**908,235**	**955,408**	**994,097**
Current	717,577	751,783	827,204
Capital	190,658	203,625	166,893

* Excluding net lending (million baht): 378 in 2001; 96 in 2002; 2,101 in 2003.

Source: Bank of Thailand, Bangkok.

THAILAND

INTERNATIONAL RESERVES
(US $ million at 31 December)

	2003	2004	2005
Gold*	1,071	1,167	1,374
IMF special drawing rights	0	1	1
Reserve position in IMF	111	165	188
Foreign exchange	40,965	48,498	50,502
Total	42,147	49,831	52,065

* Revalued annually on the basis of the London market price.

Source: IMF, *International Financial Statistics*.

MONEY SUPPLY
('000 million baht at 31 December)

	2003	2004	2005
Currency outside banks	546.9	613.8	648.0
Demand deposits at deposit money banks	215.5	232.2	261.3
Total money (incl. others)	869.2	950.0	1,290.0

Source: IMF, *International Financial Statistics*.

COST OF LIVING
(Consumer Price Index; base: 2000 = 100)

	2002	2003	2004
Food (incl. beverages)	101.0	104.7	109.4
Fuel and light	109.3	111.1	116.0
Clothing (incl. footwear)	101.4	101.5	101.7
Rent	99.1	97.8	97.2
All items (incl. others)	102.3	104.1	107.0

Source: ILO.

NATIONAL ACCOUNTS
(million baht at current prices)

National Income and Product

	2002	2003	2004*
Compensation of employees	1,671,353	1,775,135	1,929,036
Operating surplus	2,400,813	2,648,221	3,012,022
Domestic factor incomes	4,072,166	4,423,356	4,941,058
Consumption of fixed capital	790,921	824,230	868,625
Gross domestic product (GDP) at factor cost	4,863,087	5,247,586	5,809,683
Indirect taxes	614,613	714,305	775,730
Less Subsidies	27,057	32,916	81,925
GDP in market prices	5,450,643	5,928,975	6,503,488
Net factor income from abroad	−88,632	−111,028	−126,197
Gross national product	5,362,011	5,817,947	6,377,291

Expenditure on the Gross Domestic Product
('000 million baht)

	2002	2003	2004*
Government final consumption expenditure	603,891	635,251	721,314
Private final consumption expenditure	3,119,979	3,388,461	3,687,551
Changes in inventories	54,146	53,598	75,029
Gross fixed capital formation	1,243,188	1,423,909	1,686,841
Total domestic expenditure	5,021,204	5,501,219	6,170,735
Exports of goods and services	3,499,004	3,886,566	4,587,860
Less Imports of goods and services	3,134,265	3,485,272	4,281,857
Statistical discrepancy	64,700	26,462	26,750
GDP in market prices	5,450,643	5,928,975	6,503,488
GDP at constant 1988 prices	3,237,042	3,464,701	3,678,511

Gross Domestic Product by Economic Activity

	2002	2003	2004*
Agriculture, hunting and forestry	406,809	498,684	543,418
Fishing	107,448	109,179	111,392
Mining and quarrying	135,851	154,582	175,020
Manufacturing	1,836,083	2,063,242	2,243,898
Electricity, gas and water	175,595	191,006	210,896
Construction	165,719	174,967	198,537
Wholesale and retail trade; repair of motor vehicles, motorcycles and personal and household goods	866,332	903,413	981,686
Hotels and restaurants	309,622	299,565	334,168
Transport, storage and communications	449,278	459,350	496,565
Financial intermediation	170,036	202,096	234,899
Real estate, renting and business activities	171,751	178,367	189,508
Public administration and defence; compulsory social security	244,783	262,187	295,638
Education	211,278	221,109	248,356
Health and social work	107,654	106,898	116,823
Other community, social and personal service activities	84,949	96,508	114,462
Private households with employed persons	7,455	7,822	8,222
GDP in market prices	5,450,643	5,928,975	6,503,488

* Preliminary figures.

Source: National Economic and Social Development Board, Bangkok.

BALANCE OF PAYMENTS
(US $ million)

	2002	2003	2004
Exports of goods f.o.b.	66,089.0	78,083.3	94,978.5
Imports of goods f.o.b.	−57,008.2	−66,908.7	−84,395.8
Trade balance	9,080.8	11,174.6	10,582.8
Exports of services	15,390.6	15,798.3	19,040.2
Imports of services	−16,720.4	−18,168.8	−23,116.4
Balance on goods and services	7,751.1	8,804.1	6,506.5
Other income received	3,356.1	3,015.2	3,119.3
Other income paid	−4,696.2	−4,807.4	−5,141.6
Balance on goods, services and income	6,410.9	7,011.9	4,484.1
Current transfers received	978.4	1,325.7	2,479.3
Current transfers paid	−375.0	−384.8	−331.0
Current balance	7,014.3	7,952.8	6,632.4
Direct investment abroad	−105.7	−487.9	−125.8
Direct investment from abroad	953.4	1,949.3	1,411.5
Portfolio investment assets	−913.3	−939.2	1,214.3
Portfolio investment liabilities	−694.4	851.0	240.4
Other investment assets	4,135.3	−409.7	−1,455.5
Other investment liabilities	−6,262.5	−8,589.7	−1,986.0
Net errors and omissions	1,409.7	191.4	−221.4
Overall balance	5,536.7	517.9	5,709.9

Source: IMF, *International Financial Statistics*.

External Trade

PRINCIPAL COMMODITIES
(distribution by SITC, '000 million baht)

Imports c.i.f.	2003	2004	2005
Food and live animals	102.1	116.2	133.7
Crude materials (inedible) except fuels	144.2	164.8	177.5
Mineral fuels, lubricants, etc.	372.9	529.0	839.3
Chemicals and related products	326.1	401.8	457.2
Basic manufactures	597.1	756.8	900.5
Machinery and transport equipment	1,404.9	1,589.6	1,910.6
Total (incl. others)	3,138.8	3,801.2	4,756.0

THAILAND

Exports f.o.b.	2003	2004	2005
Food and live animals	457.4	486.1	504.5
Crude materials (inedible) except fuels	165.3	199.9	220.1
Chemicals and related products	200.1	264.8	337.4
Basic manufactures	526.5	629.8	732.7
Machinery and transport equipment	1,471.7	1,742.9	2,008.6
Miscellaneous manufactured articles	313.3	340.0	358.9
Total (incl. others)	3,325.6	3,874.8	4,436.7

Source: Bank of Thailand, Bangkok.

PRINCIPAL TRADING PARTNERS
('000 million baht)

Imports c.i.f.	2003	2004	2005
Australia	65.6	88.8	130.6
China, People's Republic	251.1	329.7	449.0
France	41.7	42.0	75.4
Germany	105.1	114.4	128.7
Hong Kong	44.5	53.6	60.4
India	36.4	45.8	51.2
Indonesia	73.6	93.6	125.9
Italy	34.0	40.7	45.6
Japan	755.9	901.1	1,048.2
Korea, Republic	120.6	144.3	155.8
Malaysia	187.8	223.5	325.5
Philippines	56.0	62.4	75.7
Russia	24.2	41.1	64.4
Singapore	135.3	167.4	216.5
Switzerland	29.5	34.0	53.0
Taiwan	133.7	160.1	181.1
United Arab Emirates	84.6	149.5	229.2
United Kingdom	38.5	51.2	51.4
USA	296.3	291.2	349.4
Total (incl. others)	3,138.8	3,801.2	4,756.0

Exports f.o.b.	2003	2004	2005
Australia	89.7	99.1	127.4
Belgium	47.0	47.9	51.4
Canada	39.0	42.6	41.6
China, People's Republic	236.1	285.8	368.0
France	39.5	48.4	52.0
Germany	74.4	72.4	80.0
Hong Kong	179.1	198.3	246.9
Indonesia	94.2	129.2	159.6
Italy	39.7	53.7	49.9
Japan	472.1	541.8	605.6
Korea, Republic	65.8	74.5	90.7
Malaysia	160.5	213.3	229.1
Netherlands	98.2	104.1	110.6
Philippines	67.2	73.6	82.6
Singapore	243.1	282.0	300.5
Switzerland	36.4	28.1	27.1
Taiwan	107.2	104.6	108.5
United Arab Emirates	31.5	38.9	47.4
United Kingdom	107.1	121.8	112.4
USA	565.1	622.7	683.1
Viet Nam	52.4	75.4	95.0
Total (incl. others)	3,325.6	3,874.8	4,436.7

Source: Bank of Thailand, Bangkok.

Transport

RAILWAYS
(year ending 30 September)

	2000/01	2001/02	2002/03
Passengers carried ('000)	56,325	55,748	54,130
Passenger-kilometres (million)	10,321	10,378	10,251
Freight carried ('000 metric tons)	n.a.	9,917	11,356

ROAD TRAFFIC
('000 motor vehicles in use at 31 December)

	2001	2002	2003
Passenger cars	2,280.7	2,651.4	2,880.9
Buses and trucks	803.9	822.9	809.2
Vans and pick-ups	3,341.4	3,543.5	3,631.0
Motorcycles	15,236.1	16,581.2	18,210.5
Total (incl. others)	22,589.2	24,517.3	26,378.9

SHIPPING
Merchant Fleet
(registered at 31 December)

	2002	2003	2004
Number of vessels	629	671	751
Total displacement ('000 grt)	1,879.6	2,268.7	2,889.9

Source: Lloyd's Register-Fairplay, *World Fleet Statistics*.

International Sea-borne Freight Traffic
(Ports of Bangkok and Laem Chabang, year ending 30 September)

	2001/02	2002/03	2003/04
Goods loaded ('000 metric tons)	14,803	16,400	18,872
Goods unloaded ('000 metric tons)	24,755	26,965	28,656
Vessels entered	7,000	6,741	7,060

Source: Port Authority of Thailand.

CIVIL AVIATION
(traffic on scheduled services)

	1999	2000	2001
Kilometres flown (million)	163	172	182
Passengers carried ('000)	15,950	17,392	17,662
Passenger-km (million)	38,345	42,236	44,142
Total ton-km (million)	5,184	5,571	5,702

Sources: UN, *Statistical Yearbook*.

Tourism

FOREIGN TOURIST ARRIVALS BY COUNTRY OF RESIDENCE*

Country of origin	2002	2003	2004
Australia	358,616	284,749	396,959
China, People's Republic	763,708	624,923	780,050
France	254,610	220,659	252,458
Germany	412,968	389,293	449,765
Hong Kong	533,798	657,458	664,988
India	253,475	230,790	300,634
Japan	1,233,239	1,026,287	1,194,480
Korea, Republic	717,361	695,034	910,891
Malaysia	1,297,619	1,340,193	1,391,379
Singapore	687,982	633,805	737,677
Sweden	222,154	210,882	223,031
Taiwan	678,511	525,916	560,198
United Kingdom	574,007	550,087	634,750
USA	519,668	469,165	566,726
Total (incl. others)	10,872,976	10,082,109	11,737,413

* Includes Thai nationals resident abroad.

Receipts from tourism (million baht): 323,484 in 2002; 309,269 in 2003; 384,360 in 2004.

Source: Tourism Authority of Thailand.

Communications Media

	2002	2003	2004
Telephones ('000 main lines in use)	6,499.8	6,600.0	6,724.0
Mobile cellular telephones ('000 subscribers)	16,117	n.a.	28,000
Personal computers ('000 in use)	2,461	n.a.	3,716
Internet users ('000)	4,800.0	6,971.5	6,972.0

Radio receivers ('000 in use): 13,959 in 1997.

Television receivers ('000 in use): 18,400 in 2001.

Facsimile machines ('000 in use): 150 in 1997.

Book production (titles, excluding pamphlets): 8,142 in 1996.

Daily newspapers: 35 (with average circulation of 2,766,000 copies) in 1994; 35 (with average circulation of 2,700,000* copies) in 1995; 30 (with average circulation of 3,808,000 copies) in 1996.

Non-daily newspapers: 280 in 1995; 320 in 1996.

* Provisional.

Sources: International Telecommunication Union; UNESCO, *Statistical Yearbook*; UN, *Statistical Yearbook*.

Education

(2004)

	Institutions	Teachers	Students
Ministry of Education:			
Office of the Permanent Secretary:	4,769	119,918	3,880,370
Office of the Basic Education Commission	32,413	418,880	8,823,849
Office of the Higher Education Commission	166	46,190	1,891,693
Office of Vocational Education commission	412	16,913	631,700
Mahidol Wittayanusorn School	1	83	701
Mahamakut Buddist University	8	150	6,436
Mahachulalongkornrajavidyalaya University	12	373	8,999
Bangkok Metropolitan Education Department	433	13,012	347,638
Royal Thai Police	191	1,933	28,386
Department of Local Administration	516	17,829	393,487
Ministry of Social Development and Human Security	18	30	626
Ministry of Public Health	39	1,743	18,084
Merchant Marine Training Centre	1	45	911
Civil Aviation Training Centre	1	37	760
National Bureau of Buddhism	400	5,147	51,950
Fine Arts Department	16	1,011	9,831
Office of Sports and Recreational Development	27	921	16,883
Armed Forces	9	1,378	7,336
Total	39,432	645,593	16,119,640

Source: Ministry of Education.

Adult literacy rate (UNESCO estimates): 92.6% (males 94.9%; females 90.5%) in 2003 (Source: UN Development Programme, *Human Development Report*).

Directory

The Constitution

On 27 September 1997 the National Assembly approved a new Constitution, which was endorsed by the King and promulgated on 11 October. The main provisions are summarized below.

GENERAL PROVISIONS

Sovereignty resides in the people. The King as Head of State exercises power through the National Assembly, the Council of Ministers (Cabinet) and the Courts in accordance with the provisions of the Constitution. The human dignity, rights and liberty of the people shall be protected. The people, irrespective of their origin, sex or religion, shall enjoy equal protection under the Constitution. The Constitution is the supreme law of the State.

THE KING

The King is a Buddhist and upholder of religions. He holds the position of Head of the Thai Armed Forces. He selects and appoints qualified persons to be the President of the Privy Council and not more than 18 Privy Councillors to constitute the Privy Council. The Privy Council has a duty to render such advice to the King on all matters pertaining to His functions as He may consult. Whenever the King is absent from the Kingdom or unable to perform His functions, He will appoint a Regent. For the purposes of maintaining national or public safety or national economic security, or averting public calamity, the King may issue an Emergency Decree which shall have the force of an Act.

RIGHTS, LIBERTIES AND DUTIES OF THE THAI PEOPLE

All persons are equal before the law and shall enjoy equal protection under the law. Men and women shall enjoy equal rights. Unjust discrimination against a person on the grounds of origin, race, language, sex, age, physical or health condition, personal status, economic or social standing, religious belief, education or constitutionally political view, shall not be permitted. A person shall enjoy full liberty to profess a religion, a religious sect or creed, and observe religious precepts or exercise a form of worship in accordance with his or her belief, provided that it is not contrary to his or her civic duty, public order or good morals. A person shall enjoy the liberty to express his or her opinion, make speeches, write, print, publicize, and make expression by other means. A person shall enjoy an equal right to receive the fundamental education for the duration of not less than 12 years which shall be provided by the State without charge. A person shall enjoy the liberty to assemble peacefully and without arms, to unite and form an association, a union, league, co-operative, farmer group, private organization or any other group, and to unite and form a political party. A person shall enjoy an equal right to receive standard public health service, and the indigent shall have the right to receive free medical treatment from public health centres of the State. Every person shall have a duty to exercise his or her right to vote at an election. Failure to vote will result in the withdrawal of the right to vote as provided by law.

THE NATIONAL ASSEMBLY

The National Assembly consists of the House of Representatives and the Senate. The President of the House of Representatives is President of the National Assembly. The President of the Senate is Vice-President of the National Assembly. A bill approved by the National Assembly is presented by the Prime Minister to the King to be signed within 20 days from the date of receipt, and shall come into force upon its publication in the Government Gazette. If the King refuses his assent, the National Assembly must re-deliberate such bill. If the National Assembly resolves to reaffirm the bill with a two-thirds' majority, the Prime Minister shall present such bill to the King for signature once again. If the King does not sign and return the bill within 30 days, the Prime Minister shall cause the bill to be promulgated as an Act in the Government Gazette as if the King had signed it.

The House of Representatives consists of 500 members, 100 of whom are from the election on a party-list basis and 400 of whom are from the election on a constituency basis. Election is by direct suffrage and secret ballot. The list of any political party receiving votes of less than 5% of the total number of votes throughout the country shall be regarded as one for which no person listed therein is elected and such votes shall not be reckoned in the determination of the proportional number of the members of the House of Representatives. A person seeking election to the House of Representatives must be of Thai nationality by birth, be not less than 25 years of age, have graduated with not lower than a Bachelor's degree or its equivalent, except for the case of having been a member of the House of Representatives or a Senator before, and be a member of any and only one political party, for a consecutive period of not less than 90 days, up to the date of applying for candidacy in an election. The term of the House of Representatives is four years from the election day. The King has the prerogative power to dissolve the House of Representatives for a new election of members of the House. Members of the House may not renounce their party affiliation without resigning their seats.

The Senate consists of 200 members, elected by direct suffrage and secret ballot. A person seeking election to the Senate must be of Thai nationality by birth, of not less than 40 years of age, and have graduated with not lower than a Bachelor's degree or its equivalent. The term of the Senate is six years as from the election day.

When it is necessary for the interests of the State, the King may convoke an extraordinary session of the National Assembly.

The Election Commission consists of a Chairman and four other Commissioners appointed, by the King with the advice of the Senate, from persons of apparent political impartiality and integrity. Election Commissioners shall hold office for a term of seven years.

The National Human Rights Commission consists of a President and 10 other members appointed, by the King with the advice of the Senate, from persons having apparent knowledge and experiences in the protection of rights and liberties of the people. The term of office of members of the National Human Rights Commission is six years. The National Human Rights Commission has the duty to examine and report the commission or omission of acts which violate human rights or which do not comply with obligations under international treaties to which Thailand is a party.

THE COUNCIL OF MINISTERS

The King appoints the Prime Minister and not more than 35 other Ministers to constitute the Council of Ministers (Cabinet) having the duties to carry out the administration of state affairs. The Prime Minister must be appointed from members of the House of Representatives and must receive the approval of more than half the total number of members of the House. No Prime Minister or Ministers shall be members of the House of Representatives or Senators simultaneously. A Minister must be of Thai nationality by birth, of not less than 35 years of age and be a graduate with not lower than a Bachelor's degree or its equivalent.

The State shall establish the National Economic and Social Council to be charged with the duty to give advice and recommendations to the Council of Ministers on economic and social problems. A national economic and social development plan and other plans as provided by law shall obtain opinions of the National Economic and Social Council before they can be adopted and published.

LOCAL GOVERNMENT

Any locality which meets the conditions of self-government shall have the right to be formed as a local administrative organization as provided by law. A local administrative organization shall have a local assembly and a local administrative committee or local administrators. Members of a local assembly shall be elected by direct suffrage and secret ballot. A local administrative committee or local administrators shall be directly elected by the people or by the approval of a local assembly. Members of a local assembly, local administrative committee or local administrators shall hold office for a period of four years. A member of a local administrative committee or local administrator shall not be a government official holding a permanent position or receiving a salary, or an official or an employee of a state agency, state enterprise or local administration.

AMENDMENT OF THE CONSTITUTION

A motion for amendment must be proposed either by the Council of Ministers or by not less than one-fifth of the total number of members of the House of Representatives or the National Assembly as a whole. A motion for amendment must be proposed in the form of a draft Constitution Amendment and the National Assembly shall consider it in three readings. Promulgation must be approved by the votes of more than half of the total number of members of both Houses.

The Government

HEAD OF STATE

King: HM King BHUMIBOL ADULYADEJ (King Rama IX—succeeded to the throne June 1946).

PRIVY COUNCIL

Members: Gen. (retd) PREM TINSULANONDA (President), Dr SANYA DHARMASAKTI, M. L. CHIRAYU NAVAWONGS, Dr CHAOVANA NASYLVANTA, THANIN KRAIVIXIEN, Rear-Adm. M. L. USNI PRAMOJ, Air Vice-Marshal KAMTHON SINDHAVANANDA, Air Chief Marshal SIDDHI SAVETSILA, CHULANOPE SNIDVONGS, M. R. ADULKIT KITIYAKARA, Gen. PICHITR KULLAVANIJAYA, AMPOL SENANARONG, CHAMRAS KEMACHARU, M. L. THAWISAN LADAWAN, M. R. THEP DEVAKULA, SAKDA MOKKAMAKKUL, PALAKORN SUWANNARAT, KASEM WATANACHAI.

CABINET
(April 2006)

Prime Minister: THAKSIN SHINAWATRA.

Deputy Prime Ministers: SOMKID JATUSRIPITAK, CHIDCHAI WANNASATHIT, SUWAT LIPTAPANLOP, WISSANU KREA-NGAM, SURAKIART SATHIRATHAI, PINIJ JARUSOMBAT, SURIYA JUNGRUNGREANKIT.

Minister of Defence: Gen. THAMMARAK ISARANGURA.

Minister of Finance: THANONG BIDAYA.

Minister of Foreign Affairs: KANTATHEE SUPAMONGKOL.

Minister of Tourism and Sports: PRACHA MALEENONT.

Minister of Social Development and Human Security: WATANA MUANGSOOK.

Minister of Agriculture and Co-operatives: SUDARAT KEYURAPHAN.

Minister of Education: CHATURON CHAISANG.

Minister of the Interior: KONGSAK WATHANA.

Minister of Justice: CHITCHAI WANNASATHIT.

Minister of Culture: (vacant).

Minister of Natural Resources and Environment: YONGYUTH TIYAPAIRAT.

Minister of Energy: VISET CHOOPIBAN.

Minister of Transport: PONGSAK RAKTAPONGPAISAL.

Minister of Commerce: SOMKID JATUSRIPITAK.

Minister of Public Health: SUCHAI CHAROENRATHANAKUL.

Minister of Industry: SURIYA JUNGRUNGREANGKIT.

Minister of Information and Communications Technology: SORA-AT KLINPRATUM.

Minister of Labour: SOMSAK THEPSUTHIN.

Minister of Science and Technology: PRAVICH RATTANAPIEN.

Ministers in the Prime Minister's Office: SURANAND VEJJAJIVA, NEWIN CHIDCHOB.

MINISTRIES

Office of the Prime Minister: Government House, Thanon Nakhon Pathom, Bangkok 10300; tel. (2) 280-3526; fax (2) 282-8792; e-mail webmaster@opm.go.th; internet www.opm.go.th.

Ministry of Agriculture and Co-operatives: Thanon Ratchadamnoen Nok, Bangkok 10200; tel. (2) 281-5955; fax (2) 282-1425; e-mail webmaster@moac.go.th; internet www.moac.go.th.

Ministry of Commerce: 44/100 Thanon Nonthaburi 1, Amphur Muang, Nonthaburi, Bangkok 11000; tel. (2) 507-8000; fax (2) 507-7717; e-mail webmaster@moc.go.th; internet www.moc.go.th.

Ministry of Culture: Thanalongkorn Bldg, Thanon Boromrachanonnee, Bangplud, Bangkok 10700; tel. (2) 522-8888; e-mail webmaster@m-culture.go.th; internet www.m-culture.go.th.

Ministry of Defence: Thanon Sanamchai, Bangkok 10200; tel. (2) 222-1121; fax (2) 226-3117; e-mail webmaster@mod.go.th; internet www.mod.go.th.

Ministry of Education: Wang Chankasem, Thanon Ratchadamnoen Nok, Bangkok 10300; tel. (2) 281-9809; fax (2) 281-9241; e-mail website@emisc.moe.go.th; internet www.moe.go.th.

Ministry of Energy: 17 Kasatsuk Bridge, Thanon Rama I, Rong Mueng, Pathumwan, Bangkok 10330; tel. (2) 223-3344; fax (2) 222-3785; e-mail moen@energy.go.th; internet www.energy.go.th.

Ministry of Finance: Thanon Rama VI, Samsennai, Phaya Thai, Rajatevi, Bangkok 10400; tel. (2) 273-9021; fax (2) 273-9408; e-mail prinya@mof.go.th; internet www.mof.go.th.

Ministry of Foreign Affairs: Thanon Sri Ayudhya, Bangkok 10400; tel. (2) 643-5000; fax (2) 225-6155; e-mail information@mfa.go.th; internet www.mfa.go.th.

Ministry of Industry: 75/6 Thanon Rama VI, Ratchathewi, Bangkok 10400; tel. (2) 202-3000; fax (2) 202-3048; internet www.industry.go.th.

Ministry of Information and Communications Technology: Bangkok 10210; tel. (2) 238-5422; fax (2) 238-5423; e-mail pr@mict.go.th; internet www.mict.go.th.

Ministry of the Interior: Thanon Atsadang, Bangkok 10200; tel. (2) 222-1141; fax (2) 223-8851; e-mail webteam@moi.go.th; internet www.moi.go.th.

THAILAND

Ministry of Justice: Thanon Ratchadaphisek, Chatuchak, Bangkok 10900; tel. (2) 502-8051; fax (2) 502-8059; e-mail webmaster@moj.go.th; internet www.moj.go.th.

Ministry of Labour: Thanon Mitmaitri, Dindaeng, Huay Kwang, Bangkok 10400; tel. (2) 232-1421; fax (2) 246-1520; e-mail webmaster@mol.go.th; internet www.mol.go.th.

Ministry of Natural Resources and Environment: 92 Phaholyothin Soi 7, Samsen Nai, Bangkok 10400; tel. (2) 298-2754; fax (2) 298-2020; e-mail web@mnre.go.th; internet www.monre.go.th.

Ministry of Public Health: Thanon Tiwanon, Amphoe Muang, Nonthaburi 11000; tel. (2) 590-1000; fax (2) 591-8492; e-mail eng-webmaster@health.moph.go.th; internet www.moph.go.th.

Ministry of Science and Technology: Thanon Rama VI, Ratchathewi, Bangkok 10400; tel. (2) 246-0064; fax (2) 246-5146; internet www.most.go.th.

Ministry of Social Development and Human Security: Bangkok 10100; tel. (2) 659-6399; e-mail society@m-society.go.th; internet www.m-society.go.th.

Ministry of Tourism and Sports: Thanon Rama I, Pathumwan, Bangkok 10330; tel. (2) 283-1500; fax (2) 356-0746; e-mail webmaster@mots.go.th; internet www.mots.go.th.

Ministry of Transport: 38 Thanon Ratchadamnoen Nok, Khet Pom Prab Sattruphai, Bangkok 10100; tel. (2) 281-3871; fax (2) 283-3049; e-mail mot@mot.go.th; internet www.mot.go.th.

Legislature

RATHA SAPHA
(National Assembly)

Woothi Sapha
(Senate)

A constitutional amendment was enacted in January 1995, limiting the membership of the Senate to two-thirds of that of the House of Representatives.

On 22 March 1996 the Prime Minister appointed a new Senate, comprising 260 members, only 39 of whom were active members of the armed forces. (Under the new Constitution promulgated in October 1997, the Senate was to comprise 200 directly elected members.) Elections to the new 200-member Senate were held on 4 March 2000; however, owing to the repeated incidence of electoral fraud, a second round of voting took place in April and a third round was held in a number of constituencies in June, by which time only 197 members had been elected to the new Senate, which had yet to take office pending the election of its three remaining members. A fourth round of polling was held in June/July, which resulted in the election of a further two members to the Senate. At a fifth round of voting held later that month the final member was elected to the Senate. The 200-member Senate was subsequently sworn in on 1 August 2000.

President of the Senate: SUCHON CHALEEKURE.

Sapha Poothaen Rassadorn
(House of Representatives)

Speaker of the House of Representatives and President of the National Assembly: BHOKIN BHALAKULA.

General Election, 6 February 2005

Party	Seats
Thai Rak Thai	377
Democrat Party	96
Chart Thai	25
Mahachon	2
Total	**500***

* A total of 400 candidates contested the election in single-member constituencies and 100 through a party-list system.

Note: The results of the general election that took place on 2 April 2006 were subsequently annulled. A new election was provisionally scheduled to be held in October 2006.

Election Commission

Election Commission of Thailand (ECT): Srijullasup Bldg, 19th Floor, 44 Thanon Rama I, Pathumwan, Bangkok 10330; tel. (2) 613-7333; fax (2) 219-3411; e-mail dav@ect.go.th; internet www.ect.go.th; Chair. VASANA PUEMLARP.

Political Organizations

Chart Thai (Thai Nation): 1 Thanon Pichai, Dusit, Bangkok 10300; tel. (2) 243-8070; fax (2) 243-8074; e-mail chartthai@chartthai.or.th; internet www.chartthai.or.th; f. 1981; right-wing; founded political reform policy; includes mems of fmr United Thai People's Party and fmr Samakkhi Tham (f. 1991); Leader BANHARN SILAPA-ARCHA.

Democrat Party (DP) (Prachatipat): 67 Thanon Setsiri, Samsen Nai, Phyathai, 10400 Bangkok; tel. (2) 270-0036; fax (2) 279-6086; e-mail admin@democrat.or.th; internet www.democrat.or.th; f. 1946; liberal; Leader ABHISIT VEJJAJIVA; Sec.-Gen. SUTHEP THUAGSUBAN.

Ekkaparb (Solidarity): 670/104 Soi Thepnimit, Thanon Jaransanitwong, Bangpaid, Bangkok 10700; tel. (2) 424-0291; fax (2) 424-8630; f. 1989; opposition merger by the Community Action Party, the Prachachon Party, the Progressive Party and Ruam Thai; Leader CHAIYOS SASOMSAP; Sec.-Gen. NEWIN CHIDCHOB.

Mahachon: c/o House of Representatives, Bangkok; internet www.mahachon.or.th; f. 2004 following split in Democrat Party; Leader ANEK LAOTHAMMATHAT.

Muan Chon (Mass Party): 630/182 Thanon Prapinklao, Bangkok 10700; tel. and fax (2) 424-0851; f. 1985; dissolved after defection of leader Capt. Chalerm Yoobamrung to New Aspiration Party (NAP); re-formed in 2002 following merger of NAP with Thai Rak Thai; Leader Gen. VORAVIT PIBOONSILP; Sec.-Gen. KAROON RAKSASUK.

Palang Dharma (PD) (Righteous Force): 445/15 Ramkhamhaeng, 39 Bangkapi, Bangkok 10310; tel. (2) 718-5626; fax (2) 718-5634; internet www.pdp.or.th; f. 1988; Leader CHAIWAT SINSUWONG; Sec.-Gen. RAVEE MASCHAMADOL.

Prachakorn Thai (Thai Citizens Party): 1213/323 Thanon Srivara, Bangkapi, Bangkok 10310; tel. (2) 559-0008; fax (2) 559-0016; f. 1981; right-wing; monarchist; Leader SAMAK SUNDARAVEJ; Sec.-Gen. YINGPAN MANSIKARN.

Social Action Party (SAP) (Kij Sangkhom): 126 Soi Ongkarak Samsen, 28 Thanon Nakhon Chaisi, Dusit, Bangkok 10300; tel. (2) 243-0100; fax (2) 243-3224; f. 1981; conservative; Leader MONTREE PONGPANIT; Sec.-Gen. SUWIT KHUNKITTI.

Thai Freedom Party: Bangkok; f. 2002; Leader NIT SORASIT.

Thai Party: 193 Thanon Amnauy Songkram, Dusit, Bangkok; tel. and fax (2) 669-4367; f. 1997; Leader THANABORDIN SANGSATHAPORN; Gen. Sec. Rear-Adm. THAVEEP NAKSOOK.

Thai Rak Thai (Thais Love Thais): c/o House of Representatives, Bangkok; tel. (2) 668-7000; fax (2) 668-7100; e-mail spokesman@thairakthai.or.th; internet www.thairakthai.or.th; f. 1998; merged with New Aspiration Party (NAP) and Seritham Party following 2001 general election and with Chart Pattana in Aug. 2004; Leader THAKSIN SHINAWATRA.

Thon Trakul Thai (First Thai Nation): Bangkok; f. 2003; Leader CHUWIT KAMONVISIT.

Groupings in armed conflict with the Government include:

Barasan Revolusi Nasional (BRN) (National Revolutionary Front): Yala; Muslim secessionists.

Pattani United Liberation Organization (PULO): e-mail p_u_l_@hotmail.com; internet www.pulo.org; advocates secession of the five southern provinces (Satun, Narathiwat, Yala, Pattani and Songkhla); Leader HAYI DAO THANAM.

Diplomatic Representation

EMBASSIES IN THAILAND

Argentina: 16th Floor, Suite 1601, Glas Haus Bldg, 1 Soi Sukhumvit 25, Klongtoey, Bangkok 10110; tel. (2) 259-0401; fax (2) 259-0402; e-mail embtail@mozart.inet.co.th; Ambassador CARLOS FAUSTINO GARCÍA.

Australia: 37 Thanon Sathorn Tai, Bangkok 10120; tel. (2) 344-6300; fax (2) 344-6301; e-mail austembassy.bangkok@dfat.gov.au; internet www.austembassy.or.th; Ambassador BILL PATERSON.

Austria: 14 Soi Nandha, off Thanon Sathorn Tai, Soi 1, Bangkok 10120; tel. (2) 303-6057; fax (2) 287-3925; e-mail bangkok-ob@bmaa.gv.at; Ambassador ARNO RIEDEL.

Bangladesh: 727 Thanon Thonglor Sukhumvit, Soi 55, Bangkok 10110; tel. (2) 392-9437; fax (2) 391-8070; e-mail bdoot@samart.co.th; Ambassador SHAHED AKHTAR.

Belgium: 17th Floor, Sathorn City Tower, 175 Thanon Sathorn Tai, Tungmahamek, Sathorn, Bangkok 10120; tel. (2) 679-5454; fax (2) 679-5467; e-mail bangkok@diplobel.org; internet www.diplomatie.be/bangkok; Ambassador JAN MATTHYSEN.

THAILAND

Belize: 10th Floor, Pilot Pen Bldg, 331/1–3 Thanon Silom, Bangrak, Bangkok 10500; tel. (2) 636-8377; fax (2) 235-7653; e-mail belize@embelizeth.com; Ambassador DAVID A. K. GIBSON.

Bhutan: 375/1 Soi Ratchadanivej, Thanon Pracha-Uthit, Huay Kwang, Bangkok 10320; tel. (2) 274-4740; fax (2) 274-4743; e-mail bht_emb_bkk@yahoo.com; Ambassador CHENKYAB DORJI.

Brazil: 34th Floor, Lumpini Tower, 1168/101 Thanon Rama IV, Sathorn, Bangkok 10120; tel. (2) 679-8567; fax (2) 679-8569; e-mail embrasbkk@inet.co.th; internet www.brazilembassy.or.th; Ambassador MARCO ANTÔNIO DINIZ BRANDÃO.

Brunei: 132 Sukhumvit, Soi 23, Thanon Sukhumvit, Bangkok 10110; tel. (2) 204-1476; fax (2) 204-1486; Ambassador Dato' Paduka Haji MOHD YUNOS bin Haji MOHD HUSSEIN.

Bulgaria: 64/4 Soi Charoenmitr, Sukhumvit 63, Wattana, Bangkok 10110; tel. (2) 391-6180; fax (2) 391-6182; e-mail bulgemth@asianet.co.th; Ambassador ROUMEN IVANOV SABEV.

Cambodia: 185 Thanon Ratchadamri, Lumpini, Bangkok 10330; tel. (2) 254-6630; fax (2) 253-9859; e-mail recanbot@loxinfo.co.th; Ambassador UNG SEAN.

Canada: Abdulrahim Bldg, 15th Floor, 990 Thanon Rama IV, Bangrak, Bangkok 10500; tel. (2) 636-0540; fax (2) 636-0565; e-mail bngkk@international.gc.ca; internet www.international.gc.ca/bangkok; Ambassador DENIS COMEAU.

Chile: UBC II Bldg, 591 Thanon Sukhumvit, Soi 33, Klongtoey Nua, Wattana, Bangkok 10110; tel. (2) 260-3870; fax (2) 260-4328; e-mail embajada@chile-thai.com; internet www.chile-thai.com; Ambassador LUIS ALBERTO SEPÚLVEDA.

China, People's Republic: 57 Thanon Ratchadaphisek, Bangkok 10310; tel. (2) 245-7043; fax (2) 246-8247; e-mail chinaemb_th@mfa.gov.cn; internet www.chinaembassy.or.th; Ambassador ZHANG JIUHUAN.

Czech Republic: 71/6 Soi Ruamrudi 2, Thanon Ploenchit, Bangkok 10330; tel. (2) 255-3027; fax (2) 253-7637; e-mail bangkok@embassy.mzv.cz; internet www.mfa.cz/bangkok; Ambassador Dr JIŘÍ SITLER.

Denmark: 10 Soi Attakarn Prasit, Thanon Sathorn Tai, Bangkok 10120; tel. (2) 343-1100; fax (2) 213-1752; e-mail bkkamb@um.dk; internet www.ambbangkok.um.dk; Ambassador ULRIK HELWEG-LARSEN.

Egypt: 6 Las Colinas Bldg, 42nd Floor, Sukhumvit 21, Wattana, Bangkok 10110; tel. (2) 661-7184; fax (2) 262-0235; e-mail egyptemb@loxinfo.co.th; Ambassador TAMER AL-AZIZ ABDALLA KHALIL.

Finland: Amarin Tower, 16th Floor, 500 Thanon Ploenchit, Bangkok 10330; tel. (2) 256-9306; fax (2) 256-9310; e-mail Sanomat.BAN@formin.fi; Ambassador HEIKKI TUUANEN.

France: 35 Soi Rong Phasi Kao, Thanon Charoenkrung, Bangkok 10500; tel. (2) 657-5100; fax (2) 657-5135; e-mail press@ambafrance-th.org; internet www.ambafrance-th.org; Ambassador LAURENT AUBLIN.

Germany: 9 Thanon Sathorn Tai, Bangkok 10120; tel. (2) 287-9000; fax (2) 287-1776; e-mail info@german-embassy.or.th; internet www.bangkok.diplo.de; Ambassador Dr CHRISTOPH BRÜMMER.

Greece: Thai Wah Tower II, 30th Floor, 21/159 Thanon Sathorn Tai, Bangkok 10120; tel. (2) 679-1462; fax (2) 679-1463; e-mail embgrbkk@ksc.th.com; Ambassador MILTIADIS HISKAKIS.

Holy See: 217/1 Thanon Sathorn Tai, POB 12–178, Bangkok 10120 (Apostolic Nunciature); tel. (2) 212-5853; fax (2) 212-0932; e-mail vatemb@mozart.inet.co.th; Apostolic Nuncio Most Rev. SALVATORE PENNACCHIO (Titular Archbishop of Montemarano).

Hungary: Oak Tower, 20th Floor, President Park Condominium, 95 Sukhumvit Soi 24, Prakhanong, Bangkok 10110; tel. (2) 661-1150; fax (2) 661-1153; e-mail huembbgk@mozart.inet.co.th; Ambassador Dr ANDRAS BALOGH.

India: 46 Soi Prasarnmitr, 23 Thanon Sukhumvit, Bangkok 10110; tel. (2) 258-0300; fax (2) 258-4627; e-mail indiaemb@mozart.inet.co.th; Ambassador VIVEK KATJU.

Indonesia: 600–602 Thanon Phetchburi, Phyathai, Bangkok 10400; tel. (2) 252-3135; fax (2) 255-1267; e-mail kukbkk@ksc11.th.com; internet www.kbri-bangkok.com; Ambassador IBRAHIM YUSUF.

Iran: 602 Thanon Sukhumvit, between Soi 22–24, Bangkok 10110; tel. (2) 259-0611; fax (2) 259-9111; e-mail emb@mozart.inet.co.th; Ambassador RASOUL ESLAMI.

Israel: Ocean Tower II, 25th Floor, 75 Sukhumvit, Soi 19, Thanon Asoke, Bangkok 10110; tel. (2) 204-9200; fax (2) 204-9255; e-mail bangkok@israel.org; Ambassador GERSHON ZOHAR.

Italy: 399 Thanon Nang Linchee, Thungmahamek, Yannawa, Bangkok 10120; tel. (2) 285-4090; fax (2) 285-4793; e-mail ambasciata.bangkok@esteri.it; internet www.italian-embassy.org.ae/Ambasciata_Bangkok; Ambassador IGNAZIO DI PACE.

Japan: 1674 Thanon Phetchburi Tadmai, Bangkok 10320; tel. (2) 252-6151; fax (2) 253-4153; internet embjp-th.org; Ambassador ATSUSHI TOKINOYA.

Kazakhstan: Suite 3E1–3E2, 3rd Floor, 139 Rimco House, Sukhumvit 63, Klongton Nua, Wattana, Bangkok 10110; tel. (2) 714-9890; fax (2) 714-7588; e-mail kzdipmis@asianet.co.th; Chargé d'affaires a.i. SAKEN SEIDUALIYEV.

Korea, Democratic People's Republic: 14 Mooban Suanlaemthong 2, Thanon Pattanakarn, Suan Luang, Bangkok 10250; tel. (2) 319-2686; fax (2) 318-6333; Ambassador O SONG CHOL.

Korea, Republic: 23 Thanon Thiam-Ruammit, Huay Kwang, Bangkok 10320; tel. (2) 247-7537; fax (2) 247-7535; e-mail korea_emb_th@yahoo.co.kr; Ambassador JEE-JOON YOON.

Kuwait: 100/44 Sathorn Nakhon Tower, 24th Floor, Thanon Sathorn Nua, Bangrak, Bangkok 10500; tel. (2) 636-6600; fax (2) 636-7360; e-mail kwembasy@inet.co.th; Ambassador KHALED MOHAMMAD AHMAD AL-SHAIBANI.

Laos: 520/502/1–3 Soi Sahakarnpramoon, Thanon Pracha Uthit, Wangthonglang, Bangkok 10310; tel. (2) 539-6667; fax (2) 539-3827; e-mail sabaidee@bkklaoembassy.com; internet www.bkklaoembassy.com; Ambassador HIEM PHOMMACHANH.

Malaysia: 35 Thanon Sathorn, Tungmahamek, Sathorn, Bangkok 10120; tel. (2) 679-2190; fax (2) 679-2208; e-mail mwbngkok@samart.co.th; Ambassador Dato' SYED NORULZAMAN SYED KAMARULZAMAN.

Mexico: 20/60–62 Thai Wah Tower I, 20th Floor, Thanon Sathorn Tai, Bangkok 10120; tel. (2) 285-0995; fax (2) 285-0667; e-mail mexthai@loxinfo.co.th; internet www.sre.gob.mx/tailandia; Ambassador JAVIER RAMÓN BRITO MONCADA.

Mongolia: 251 Soi Rojana, Thanon Sukhumvit 21, Klongtoey Nua, Wattana, Bangkok 10110; tel. (2) 640-8017; fax (2) 258-3849; e-mail mongemb@loxinfo.co.th; Ambassador LUVSANDORJ DAWAGIV.

Morocco: One Pacific Place, 19th Floor, 140 Thanon Sukhumvit, between Soi 4–6, Bangkok 10110; tel. (2) 653-2444; fax (2) 653-2449; e-mail sifambkk@mweb.co.th; Ambassador EL HASSANE ZAHID.

Myanmar: 132 Thanon Sathorn Nua, Bangkok 10500; tel. (2) 233-2237; fax (2) 236-6898; e-mail mebkk@asianet.co.th; Ambassador U YE WIN.

Nepal: 189 Soi 71, Thanon Sukhumvit, Prakanong, Bangkok 10110; tel. (2) 390-2280; fax (2) 381-2406; e-mail nepembkk@asiaaccess.net.th; Ambassador JANAK BAHADUR SINGH.

Netherlands: 15 Soi Tonson, Thanon Ploenchit, Lumpini, Pathumwan, Bangkok 10330; tel. (2) 309-5200; fax (2) 309-5205; e-mail ban@minbuza.nl; internet www.netherlandsembassy.in.th; Ambassador PIETER J. TH. MARRES.

New Zealand: M Thai Tower, 14th Floor, All Season's Place, 87 Thanon Witthayu, Lumpini, Pathumwan, Bangkok 10330; tel. (2) 254-2530; fax (2) 253-9045; e-mail nzembbkk@loxinfo.co.th; Ambassador PETER RIDER.

Nigeria: 412 Thanon Sukhumvit 71, Prakhanong, Wattana, Bangkok 10110; tel. (2) 711-3076; fax (2) 392-6398; e-mail info@embnigeriabkk.com; internet www.embnigeriabkk.com; Ambassador THOMPSON SUNDAY OLUFUNSO OLUMOKO.

Norway: UBC II Bldg, 18th Floor, 591 Thanon Sukhumvit, Soi 33, Bangkok 10110; tel. (2) 204-6500; fax (2) 262-0218; e-mail emb.bangkok@mfa.no; internet www.emb-norway.or.th; Ambassador MERETTE FJELD BRATTESTED.

Oman: 82 Saeng Thong Thani Tower, 32nd Floor, Thanon Sathorn Nua, Bangkok 10500; tel. (2) 639-9380; fax (2) 639-9390; Chargé d'affaires a.i. Dr ADIL SALIM AHMED AL-SHANFARI.

Pakistan: 31 Soi Nana Nua, Thanon Sukhumvit, Bangkok 10110; tel. (2) 253-0288; fax (2) 253-0290; e-mail parepbkk@ji-net.com; Ambassador HUSSAIN BAKHSH BANGULZAI.

Panama: 14 Sarasin Bldg, 7th Floor, 14 Thanon Surasak, Bangrak, Bangkok 10500; tel. (2) 237-9008; fax (2) 237-9009; e-mail ptybkk@ksc.th.com; Ambassador RICARDO ANTONIO QUIJANO JIMÉNEZ.

Peru: Glas Haus Bldg, 16th Floor, 1 Soi Sukhumvit 25, Khet Wattana, Bangkok 10110; tel. (2) 260-6243; fax (2) 260-6244; e-mail peru@peruthai.or.th; internet www.peru.org.pe; Ambassador CARLOS MANUEL VELASCO MENDIOLA.

Philippines: 760 Thanon Sukhumvit, cnr Soi 30/1, Klongtan, Klongtoey, Bangkok 10110; tel. (2) 259-0139; fax (2) 259-2809; e-mail inquiry@philembassy-bangkok.net; internet www.philembassy-bangkok.net; Ambassador ANTONIO V. RODRIGUEZ.

Poland: Sriyukon Bldg, 84 Sukhumvit, Soi 5, Bangkok 10110; tel. (2) 251-8891; fax (2) 251-8895; Ambassador BOGDAN GORALCZYK.

Portugal: 26 Bush Lane, Thanon Charoenkrung, Bangkok 10500; tel. (2) 234-2123; fax (2) 238-4275; e-mail portemb@loxinfo.co.th; Ambassador JOÃO LIMA PIMENTEL.

Romania: 20/1 Soi Rajakhru, Phaholyothin Soi 5, Thanon Phaholyothin, Phayathai, Bangkok 10400; tel. (2) 617-1551; fax (2) 617-1113; e-mail romembnk@ksc.th.com; Ambassador CRISTIAN TEODORESCU.

THAILAND

Russia: 78 Thanon Sap, Bangrak, Bangkok 10500; tel. (2) 234-9824; fax (2) 237-8488; e-mail consulru@cscoms.com; internet www.thailand.mid.ru; Ambassador YEVGENY V. AFANASIEV.

Saudi Arabia: Sathorn Thani Bldg, 10th Floor, 82 Thanon Sathorn Nua, Bangkok 10500; tel. (2) 639-2999; fax (2) 639-2950; Chargé d'affaires HANI ABDULLAH MOMINAH.

Singapore: 129 Thanon Sathorn Tai, Bangkok 10120; tel. (2) 286-2111; fax (2) 287-2578; e-mail singemb_bkk@sgmfa.gov.sg; internet www.mfa.gov.sg/bangkok; Ambassador CHAN HENG WING.

Slovakia: Thai Wah Tower II, 22nd Floor, 21/144 Thanon Sathorn Tai, Bangkok 10120; tel. (2) 677-3445; fax (2) 677-3447; e-mail slovakemb@actions.net; Ambassador VASIL PYTEL.

South Africa: The Park Place, 6th Floor, 231 Soi Sarasin, Lumpini, Bangkok 10330; tel. (2) 253-8473; fax (2) 253-8477; e-mail saembbkk@loxinfo.co.th; Ambassador PEARL NOMVUME MAGAQA.

Spain: Lake Rajada Office Complex, Piso 23, 193 Thanon Rajadapisek, Klongtoey, Bangkok 10110; tel. (2) 661-8284; fax (2) 255-2388; e-mail embespth@mail.mae.es; internet www.embesp.or.th; Ambassador JUAN MANUEL LÓPEZ NADAL.

Sri Lanka: Ocean Tower II, 13th Floor, 75/6–7 Sukhumvit, Soi 19, Bangkok 10110; tel. (2) 261-1934; fax (2) 261-1936; e-mail slemb@ksc.th.com; Ambassador J. D. A. WIJEWARDENA.

Sweden: First Pacific Place, 20th Floor, 140 Thanon Sukhumvit, Bangkok 10110; tel. (2) 263-7200; fax (2) 263-7260; e-mail ambassaden.bangkok@foreign.ministry.se; internet www.swedenabroad.com/bangkok; Ambassador JONAS HAFSTRÖM.

Switzerland: 35 Thanon Witthayu, Lumpini, Pathumwan, Bangkok 10330; tel. (2) 253-0156; fax (2) 255-4481; e-mail vertretung@ban.rep.admin.ch; internet www.eda.admin.ch/bangkok_emb; Ambassador RODOLPHE S. IMHOOF.

Turkey: 61/1 Soi Chatsan, Thanon Suthisarn, Huay Kwang, Bangkok 10310; tel. (2) 274-7262; fax (2) 274-7261; e-mail tcturkbe@mail.cscoms.com; Ambassador MUMIN ALANAT.

Ukraine: 87 All Seasons Place, CRC Tower, 33rd Floor, Thanon Witthayu, Lumpini, Pathumwan, Bangkok 10330; tel. (2) 685-3216; fax (2) 686-3217; e-mail ukremb@asianet.co.th; Ambassador IHOR V. HUMENNYI.

United Arab Emirates: 82 Seng Thong Thani Bldg, 25th Floor, Thanon Sathorn Nua, Bangkok 10500; tel. (2) 639-9820; fax (2) 639-9818; Ambassador SALIM ISSA ALI AL-KATTAM AZ-ZAABI.

United Kingdom: 14 Thanon Witthayu, Lumpini, Pathumwan, Bangkok 10330; tel. (2) 305-8333; fax (2) 255-8619; e-mail info.bangkok@fco.gov.uk; internet www.britishembassy.gov.uk/Thailand; Ambassador DAVID WILLIAM FALL.

USA: 95 Thanon Witthayu, Lumpini, Pathumwan, Bangkok 10330; tel. (2) 205-4000; fax (2) 254-1171; e-mail acsbkk@state.gov; internet www.usa.or.th; Ambassador RALPH (SKIP) BOYCE.

Viet Nam: 83/1 Thanon Witthayu, Lumpini, Pathumwan, Bangkok 10330; tel. (2) 251-3551; fax (2) 251-7203; e-mail vnembassy@bkk.a-net.net.th; Ambassador NGUYEN QUOC KHANH.

Judicial System

SUPREME COURT

(Sarn Dika)

Thanon Ratchadamnoen Nai, Bangkok 10200; tel. (2) 221-3161; e-mail supremc@judiciary.go.th; internet www.supremecourt.or.th.

The final court of appeal in all civil, bankruptcy, labour, juvenile and criminal cases. Its quorum consists of three judges. However, the Court occasionally sits in plenary session to determine cases of exceptional importance or where there are reasons for reconsideration or overruling of its own precedents. The quorum, in such cases, is one-half of the total number of judges in the Supreme Court.

President (Chief Justice): ATTHANITI DISAMNART.

Vice-President: SUPRADIT HUTASINGH.

COURT OF APPEALS

(Sarn Uthorn)

Thanon Ratchadaphisek, Chatuchak, Bangkok 10900.

Appellate jurisdiction in all civil, bankruptcy, juvenile and criminal matters; appeals from all the Courts of First Instance throughout the country, except the Central Labour Court, come to this Court. Two judges form a quorum.

Chief Justice: KAIT CHATANIBAND.

Deputy Chief Justices: PORNCHAI SMATTAVET, CHATISAK THAMMASAKDI, SOMPOB CHOTIKAVANICH, SOMPHOL SATTAYA-APHITARN.

COURTS OF FIRST INSTANCE

Civil Court
(Sarn Pang)

Thanon Ratchadaphisek, Chatuchak, Bangkok 10900.

Court of first instance in civil and bankruptcy cases in Bangkok. Two judges form a quorum.

Chief Justice: PENG PENG-NITI.

Criminal Court
(Sarn Aya)

Thanon Ratchadaphisek, Kwaeng Jompol, Khet Jatujak, Bangkok 10900; tel. (2) 541-2274; fax (2) 541-2273; e-mail crim1@judiciary.go.th.

Court of first instance in criminal cases in Bangkok. Two judges form a quorum.

Chief Justice: PRADIT EKMANEE.

Central Juvenile and Family Court
(Sarn Yaowachon Lae Krobkrow Klang)

Thanon Rachini, Bangkok 10200; fax (2) 224-1546.

Original jurisdiction over juvenile delinquency and matters affecting children and young persons. Two judges and two associate judges (one of whom must be a woman) form a quorum.

Chief Justice: JIRA BOONPOJANASUNTHON.

Central Labour Court
(Sarn Rang Ngan Klang)

404 Thanon Phra Ram IV, Bangkok 10500.

Jurisdiction in labour cases throughout the country.

Chief Justice: CHAVALIT PRAY-POO.

Central Tax Court
(Sarn Phasi-Arkorn Klang)

Thanon Ratchadaphisek, Chatuchak, Bangkok 10900.

Jurisdiction over tax cases throughout the country.

Chief Justice: SANTI TAKRAL.

Provincial Courts (Sarn Changwat): Exercise unlimited original jurisdiction in all civil and criminal matters, including bankruptcy, within their own district, which is generally the province itself. Two judges form a quorum. At each of the five Provincial Courts in the south of Thailand (i.e. Pattani, Yala, Betong, Satun and Narathiwat) where the majority of the population are Muslims, there are two Dato Yutithum or Kadis (Muslim judges). A Kadi sits with two trial judges in order to administer *Shari'a* (Islamic) laws and usages in civil cases involving family and inheritance where all parties concerned are Muslims. Questions on Islamic laws and usages that are interpreted by a Kadi are final.

Thon Buri Civil Court (Sarn Pang Thon Buri): Civil jurisdiction over nine districts of metropolitan Bangkok.

Thon Buri Criminal Court (Sarn Aya Thon Buri): Criminal jurisdiction over nine districts of metropolitan Bangkok.

South Bangkok Civil Court (Sarn Pang Krungthep Tai): Civil jurisdiction over southern districts of Bangkok.

South Bangkok Criminal Court (Sarn Aya Krungthep Tai): Criminal jurisdiction over southern districts of Bangkok.

Magistrates' Courts (Sarn Kwaeng): Adjudicate in minor cases with minimum formality and expense. Judges sit singly.

Religion

Buddhism is the predominant religion, professed by more than 95% of Thailand's total population. About 4% of the population are Muslims, being ethnic Malays, mainly in the south. Most of the immigrant Chinese are Confucians. The Christians number about 305,000, of whom about 75% are Roman Catholic, mainly in Bangkok and northern Thailand. Brahmins, Hindus and Sikhs number about 85,000.

BUDDHISM

Sangha Supreme Council

The Religious Affairs Dept, Thanon Ratchadamnoen Nok, Bangkok 10300; tel. (2) 281-6080; fax (2) 281-5415.

Governing body of Thailand's 350,000 monks, novices and nuns.

Supreme Patriarch of Thailand: SOMDEJ PHRA YANSANGWARA.

The Buddhist Association of Thailand: 41 Thanon Phra Aditya, Bangkok 10200; tel. (2) 281-5693; fax (2) 281-9564; f. 1934; under royal patronage; 7,139 mems; Pres. NUTTAPASH INTUPUTI.

THAILAND

CHRISTIANITY

The Roman Catholic Church

For ecclesiastical purposes, Thailand comprises two archdioceses and eight dioceses. At 31 December 2003 there were an estimated 298,009 adherents in the country, representing about 0.5% of the population.

Catholic Bishops' Conference of Thailand
122/11 Soi Naksuwan, Thanon Nonsi, Yannawa, Bangkok 10120; tel. (2) 681-3900; fax (2) 681-5370; e-mail cbct_th@hotmail.com; f. 1969; Pres. Cardinal MICHAEL MICHAI KITBUNCHU (Archbishop of Bangkok).

Archbishop of Bangkok: Cardinal MICHAEL MICHAI KITBUNCHU, Assumption Cathedral, 51 Thanon Oriental, Charoenkrung 40, Bangrak, Bangkok 10500; tel. (2) 237-1031; fax (2) 237-1033; e-mail arcdibkk@loxinfo.co.th.

Archbishop of Tharé and Nonseng: Bishop LOUIS CHAMNIERN SANTISUKNIRAN, POB 6, Amphoe Muang, Sakon Nakhon 47000; tel. (42) 711718; fax (42) 712023.

The Anglican Communion

Thailand is within the jurisdiction of the Anglican Bishop of Singapore (q.v.).

Other Christian Churches

Baptist Church Foundation (Foreign Mission Board): 90 Soi 2, Thanon Sukhumvit, Bangkok 10110; tel. (2) 252-7078; Mission Admin. TOM WILLIAMS. (POB 832, Bangkok 10501).

Church of Christ in Thailand: 238 Thanon Phayathai, Khet Phayathai, Bangkok 10400; tel. (2) 236-9400; fax (2) 238-3520; e-mail cctecume@loxinfo.co.th; f. 1934; 132,440 communicants; Moderator Rev. Dr BOONRATNA BOAYEN; Gen. Sec. Rev. Dr SINT KIMHACHANDRA.

ISLAM

Office of the Chularajmontri: 100 Soi Prom Pak, Thanon Sukhumvit, Bangkok 10110; Sheikh Al-Islam (Chularajmontri) Haji SAWASDI SUMALAYASAK.

BAHÁ'Í FAITH

National Spiritual Assembly: 1415 Sriwara Soi 94, Wangthonglang, Bangkapi, Bangkok 10310; tel. (2) 530-7417; fax (2) 935-6515; e-mail nsathai@ksc.th.com; internet www.thai-bahais.org; mems resident in 76 provinces.

The Press

DAILIES

Thai Language

Baan Muang: 1 Soi Pluem-Manee, Thanon Vibhavadi Rangsit, Bangkok 10900; tel. (2) 513-3101; fax (2) 513-3106; Editor MANA PRAEBHAND; circ. 200,000.

Daily News: 1/4 Thanon Vibhavadi Rangsit, Laksi, Bangkok 10210; tel. (2) 561-1456; fax (2) 940-9875; internet www.dailynews.co.th; f. 1964; Editor PRACHA HETRAKUL; circ. 800,000.

Dao Siam: 60 Mansion 4, Thanon Rajdamnern, Bangkok 10200; tel. (2) 222-6001; fax (2) 222-6885; f. 1974; Editor SANTI UNTRAKARN; circ. 120,000.

Khao Panich (Daily Trade News): 22/27 Thanon Ratchadaphisek, Bangkok 10900; tel. (2) 511-5066; Editor SAMRUANE SUMPHANDHARAK; circ. 30,000.

Khao Sod (Fresh News): 12 Thanon Tethsaban Naruaman, Prachanivate 1, Chatuchak, Bangkok 10900; tel. (2) 580-0021; fax (2) 580-2301; e-mail matisale@matichon.co.th; internet www.matichon.co.th; Editor-in-Chief KIATICHAI PONGPANICH; circ. 650,000.

Kom Chad Luek: 44 Moo 10, Thanon Bangna Trad, Km 4.5, Bang Na, Bangkok 10260; tel. (2) 325-5555; fax (2) 317-2071; internet www.komchadluek.com; Editor ADISAL LIMPRUNGPATAKIT.

Krungthep Turakij Daily: Nation Multimedia Group Public Co Ltd, 44 Moo 10, Thanon Bangna-Trad, Bangna, Prakanong, Bangkok 10260; tel. (2) 317-0042; fax (2) 317-1489; e-mail ktwebeditor@nationgroup.com; internet www.bangkokbiznews.com; f. 1987; Publr and Group Editor SUTHICHAI YOON; Editor ADISAK LIMPRUNGPATANAKIT; circ. 75,882.

Matichon: 12 Thanon Tethsaban Naruaman, Prachanivate 1, Chatuchak, Bangkok 10900; tel. (2) 580-0021; fax (2) 580-2301; e-mail matisale@matichon.co.th; internet www.matichon.co.th; f. 1977; Man. Editor PRASONG LERTRATANAVISUTH; circ. 550,000.

Naew Na (Frontline): 96 Moo 7, Thanon Vibhavadi Rangsit, Bangkok; tel. (2) 521-4647; fax (2) 552-3800; Editor WANCHAI WONGMEECHAI; circ. 200,000.

Siam Daily: 192/8–9 Soi Vorapong, Thanon Visuthikasat, Bangkok; tel. (2) 281-7422; internet www.aiamdaily.com; Editor NARONG CHARUSOPHON.

Siam Post: Bangkok; Man. Dir PAISAL SRICHARATCHANYA.

Siam Rath (Siam Nation): 12 Mansion 6, Thanon Rajdamnern, Bangkok 10200; tel. (2) 622-1810; fax (2) 224-1982; e-mail siamrath@siamrath.co.th; internet www.siamrath.co.th; f. 1950; Editor ASSIRI THAMMACHOT; circ. 120,000.

Sue Tuakij: Bangkok; f. 1995; evening; business news.

Thai: 423–425 Thanon Chao Khamrop, Bangkok; tel. (2) 223-3175; Editor VICHIEN MANA-NATHEETHORATHAM.

Thai Rath: 1 Thanon Vibhavadi Rangsit, Bangkok 10900; tel. (2) 272-1030; fax (2) 272-1324; e-mail feedback@thairath.co.th; internet www.thairath.co.th; f. 1948; Editor MANICH SOOKSOMJITRA; circ. 800,000.

English Language

Bangkok Post: Bangkok Post Bldg, 136 Soi Na Ranong, Klongtoey, Bangkok 10110; tel. (2) 240-3700; fax (2) 671-3174; e-mail editor@bangkokpost.co.th; internet www.bangkokpost.net; f. 1946; morning; Editor KOWIT SANANDANG; circ. 49,378 (Dec. 1999).

Business Day: Olympia Thai Tower, 22nd Floor, 444 Thanon Ratchadaphisek, Huay Kwang, Bangkok 10310; tel. (2) 512-3579; fax (2) 512-3565; e-mail info@bday.net; internet www.biz-day.com; f. 1994; business news; Man. Editor CHATCHAI YENBAMROONG.

The Nation: 44 Moo 10, Editorial Bldg, 6th Floor, Thanon Bangna Trad, Km 4.5, Bang Na, Phra Khanong, Bangkok 10260; tel. (2) 325-5555; fax (2) 751-4446; e-mail info@nationgroup.com; internet www.nationmultimedia.com; f. 1971; morning; Publr and Group Editor SUTHICHAI YOON; Editor PANA JANVIROJ; circ. 55,000.

Thailand Times: 88 Thanon Boromrajachonnee, Taling Chan, Bangkok; tel. (2) 434-0330; Editor WUTHIPONG LAKKHAM.

Chinese Language

Kia Hua Tong Huan: 108 Thanon Suapa, Bangkok; tel. (2) 221-4182; f. 1959; Editor SURADECH KORNKITTICHAI; circ. 80,000.

New Chinese Daily News: 1022–1030 Thanon Charoenkrung, Talad-Noi, Bangkok 10110; tel. and fax (2) 234-0684; Editor PUSADEE KEETAWORANART; circ. 72,000.

Sing Sian Yit Pao Daily News: 267 Thanon Charoenkrung, Talad-Noi, Bangkok 10100; tel. (2) 222-6601; fax (2) 225-4663; e-mail singpau@loxinfo.co.th; f. 1950; Man. Dir NETRA RUTHAIYANONT; Editor TAWEE YODPETCH; circ. 70,000.

Tong Hua Daily News: 877/879 Thanon Charoenkrung, Talad-Noi, Bangkok 10100; tel. (2) 236-9172; fax (2) 238-5286; Editor CHART PAYONITHIKARN; circ. 85,000.

WEEKLIES

Thai Language

Bangkok Weekly: 533–539 Thanon Sri Ayuthaya, Bangkok 10400; tel. (2) 245-2546; fax (2) 247-3410; Editor VICHIT ROJANAPRABHA.

Mathichon Weekly Review: 12 Thanon Tethsaban Naruaman, Prachanivate 1, Chatuchak, Bangkok 10900; tel. (2) 580-0021; fax (2) 580-2301; e-mail weekly@matichon.co.th; internet www.matichon.co.th/weekly; Editor RUANGCHAI SABNIRAND; circ. 300,000.

Satri Sarn: 83/35 Arkarntrithosthep 2, Thanon Prachathipatai, Bangkok 10300; tel. (2) 281-9136; f. 1948; women's magazine; Editor NILAWAN PINTONG.

Siam Rath Weekly Review: 12 Mansion 6, Thanon Rajdamnern, Bangkok 10200; Editor PRACHUAB THONGURAI.

Skul Thai: 58 Soi 36, Thanon Sukhumvit, Bangkok 10110; tel. (2) 258-5861; fax (2) 258-9130; Editor SANTI SONGSEMSAWAS.

Wattachak: 88 Thanon Boromrajachonnee, Talingchan, Bangkok 10170; tel. (2) 434-0330; fax (2) 435-0900; e-mail rattanasingha@wattachak.com; Editor PRAPHAN BOONYAKIAT; circ. 80,000.

English Language

Bangkok Post Weekly Review: U-Chuliang Bldg, 3rd Floor, 968 Thanon Phra Ram Si, Bangkok 10500; tel. (2) 233-8030; fax (2) 238-5430; f. 1989; Editor ANUSSORN THAVISIN; circ. 10,782.

Business Times: Thai Bldg, 1400 Thanon Phra Ram IV, Bangkok 10110.

THAILAND

FORTNIGHTLIES
Thai Language

Darathai: 9-9/1 Soi Sri Ak-Sorn, Thanon Chuapleung, Tungmahamek, Sathorn, Bangkok 10120; tel. (2) 249-1576; fax (2) 249-1575; f. 1954; television and entertainment; Editor USA BUKKAVESA; circ 80,000.

Dichan: 1400 Thai Bldg, Thanon Phra Ram Si, Bangkok; tel. (2) 249-0351; fax (2) 249-9455; e-mail dichan@pacific.co.th; Man. Editor KHUNYING TIPYAVADI PRAMOJ NA AYUDHYA.

Lalana: 44 Moo 10, Thanon Bangna-Trad, Bang Na, Bangkok 10260; tel. (2) 317-1400; fax (2) 317-1409; f. 1972; Editor NANTAWAN YOON; circ. 65,000.

Praew: 65/101–103 Thanon Chaiyaphruk, Taling Chan, Bangkok; tel. (2) 422-9999; fax (2) 434-3555; e-mail praew@amarin.co.th; internet www.amarin.com; f. 1979; women and fashion; Editorial Dir SUPAWADEE KOMARADAT; Editor NUANCHAN SUPANIMIT; circ. 150,000.

MONTHLIES

Bangkok 30: 98/5–6 Thanon Phra Arthit, Bangkok 10200; tel. (2) 282-5467; fax (2) 280-1302; f. 1986; Thai; business; Publr SONCHAI LIMTHONGKUL; Editor BOONSIRI NAMBOONSRI; circ. 65,000.

Chao Krung: 12 Mansion 6, Thanon Rajdamnern, Bangkok 10200; Thai; Editor NOPPHORN BUNYARIT.

The Dharmachaksu (Dharma-vision): Foundation of Mahamakut Rajavidyalai, 241 Thanon Phra Sumeru, Bangkok 10200; tel. (2) 629-1417; fax (2) 629-4015; e-mail books@mahamakuta.inet.co.th; internet www.mahamakuta.inet.co.th; f. 1894; Thai; Buddhism and related subjects; Editor WASIN INDASARA; circ. 5,000.

Grand Prix: 4/299 Moo 5, Soi Ladplakhao 66, Thanon Ladplakhao, Bangkhen, Bangkok 10220; tel. (2) 971-6450; fax (2) 971-6469; e-mail pinyo@grandprixgroup.com; internet www.grandprixgroup.com/gpi/maggrandprix/grandprix.asp; f. 1970; Editor PINYO SILPASARTDUMRONG; circ. 80,000.

The Investor: Pansak Bldg, 4th Floor, 138/1 Thanon Petchburi, Bangkok 10400; tel. (2) 282-8166; f. 1968; English language; business, industry, finance and economics; Editor TOS PATUMSEN; circ. 6,000.

Kasikorn: Dept of Agriculture, Catuchak, Bangkok 10900; tel. (2) 561-4677; fax (2) 579-5369; e-mail pannee@doa.go.th; f. 1928; Thai; agriculture and agricultural research; Editor-in-Chief PAIROJ SUWANJINDA; Editor PANNEE WICHACHOO.

Look: 1/54 Thanon Sukhumvit 30, Pra Khanong, Bangkok 10110; tel. (2) 258-1265; Editor KANOKWAN MILINDAVANIJ.

Look East: 52/38 Soi Saladaeng 2, Silom Condominium, 12th Floor, Thanon Silom, Bangkok 10500; tel. (2) 235-6185; fax (2) 236-6764; f. 1969; English; Editor ASHA SEHGAL; circ. 30,000.

Metro Magazine: 109 Moo 8, 7th Floor, Srithepthai Bldg, Thanon Bangna-Trad, Bangna, Bangkok 10260; tel. (2) 746-7250; fax (2) 746-7266; e-mail mon@bkkmetro.com; internet www.bkkmetro.com; f. 1996; English language; lifestyle, events listings and consumer-oriented articles; Publr and Editor-in-Chief MUNINTRA SAENGSUVIMOL; circ. 35,000.

Motorcycle Magazine: 4/299 Moo 5, Soi Ladplakhao 66, Thanon Ladplakhao, Bangkhan, Bangkok 10220; tel. (2) 522-1731; fax (2) 522-1730; e-mail motorcycle@grandprixgroup.com; internet www.grandprixgroup.com/gpi/magmotor/motorcycle.asp; Publr PRACHIN EAMLAMNOW; circ. 70,000.

Saen Sanuk: 50 Soi Saeng Chan, Thanon Sukhumvit 42, Bangkok 10110; tel. (2) 392-0052; fax (2) 391-1486; English; travel and tourist attractions in Thailand; Editor SOMTAWIN KONGSAWATKIAT; circ. 85,000.

Sarakadee Magazine: Bangkok 12000; tel. (2) 281-6110; fax (2) 282-7003; e-mail admin@sarakadee.com; internet www.sarakadee.com; Thai; events, culture and nature.

Satawa Liang: 689 Thanon Wang Burapa, Bangkok; Thai; Editor THAMRONGSAK SRICHAND.

Villa Wina Magazine: Chalerm Ketr Theatre Bldg, 3rd Floor, Bangkok; Thai; Editor BHONGSAKDI PIAMLAP.

NEWS AGENCIES
Foreign Bureaux

Agence France-Presse (AFP): 18th Floor, Alma Link Bldg, 25 Soi Chidlom, Thanon Ploenchit, Lumpini Patumwan, Bangkok 10330; tel. (2) 650-3230; fax (2) 650-3234; e-mail afpbgk@samart.co.th; Bureau Chief PHILIPPE AGRET.

Associated Press (AP) (USA): Charn Issara Tower, 14th Floor, 942/51 Thanon Phra Ram IV, POB 775, Bangkok; tel. (2) 234-5553; Bureau Chief DENIS D. GRAY.

Bloomberg News (USA): All Season Place, 12th Floor, M. Thai Tower, 87 Thanon Witthayu, Bangkok 10330; tel. (2) 654-0255; fax (2) 654-0265.

Inter Press Service (IPS) (Italy): POB 180, Dusit Post Office, Dusit, Bangkok 10300; tel. (2) 243-2300; fax (2) 668-5090; e-mail ipsasia@ipsnews.net; Regional Dir JOHANNA SON.

Jiji Tsushin (Jiji Press) (Japan): Boonmitr Bldg, 8th Floor, 138 Thanon Silom, Bangkok; tel. (2) 236-8793; fax (2) 236-6800; Bureau Chief JUNICHI ISHIKAWA.

Kyodo News Service (Japan): U Chuliang Bldg, 2nd Floor, 968 Thanon Phra Ram IV, Bangkok 10500; tel. (2) 236-6822; Bureau Chief YOSHISUKE YASUO.

Reuters (UK): Maneeya Centre Bldg, 518/5 Thanon Ploenchit, 10330 Bangkok; tel. (2) 637-5500; Man. (Myanmar, Thailand and Indo-China) GRAHAM D. SPENCER.

United Press International (UPI) (USA): U Chuliang Bldg, 968 Thanon Phra Ram IV, Bangkok; tel. (2) 238-5244; Bureau Chief JOHN B. HAIL.

Viet Nam News Agency (VNA): 3/81 Soi Chokchai Ruamit, Bangkok; Bureau Chief NGUYEN VU QUANG.

Xinhua (New China) News Agency (People's Republic of China): Room 407, Capital Mansion, 1371 Thanon Phaholyothin, Saphan Kwai, Bangkok 10400; tel. and fax (2) 271-1413; Chief Correspondent YU ZUNCHENG.

PRESS ASSOCIATIONS

Confederation of Thai Journalists: 538/1 Thanon Sarnsan, Dusit, Bangkok 10300; tel. (2) 668-9422; fax (2) 668-7505; internet www.ctj.in.th; Pres. SMARN SUDTO; Sec.-Gen. SUWAT THONGTHANAKUL.

Press Association of Thailand: 299 Thanon Ratchasima, Dusit, Bangkok 10300; tel. (2) 537-3777; fax (2) 537-3888; e-mail webmaster@thaipressasso.com; internet www.thaipressasso.com; f. 1941; Pres. PREECHA SAMAKKIDHAM.

There are also regional press organizations and journalists' organizations.

Publishers

Advance Media: 1400 Rama IV Shopping Centre, Klongtoey, Bangkok 10110; tel. (2) 249-0358; Man. PRASERTSAK SIVASAHONG.

Amarin Printing and Publishing Public Co Ltd: 65/101–103 Moo 4 Thanon Chaiyaphruk, Taling Chan, Bangkok 10170; tel. (2) 422-9999; fax (2) 434-3555; e-mail info@amarin.co.th; internet www.amarin.com; f. 1976; general books and magazines; CEO METTA UTAKAPAN.

Bhannakij Trading: 34 Thanon Nakornsawan, Bangkok 10100; tel. (2) 282-5520; fax (2) 282-0076; Thai fiction, school textbooks; Man. SOMSAK TECHAKASHEM.

Chalermnit Publishing Co Ltd: 108 Thanon Sukhumvit, Soi 53, Bangkok 10110; tel. (2) 662-6264; fax (2) 662-6265; e-mail chalermnit@hotmail.com; internet www.chalermnit.com; f. 1937; dictionaries, history, literature, guides to Thai language, works on Thailand and South-East Asia; Man. Dir Dr PARICHART JUMSAI.

Dhamabuja: 5/1–2 Thanon Asadang, Bangkok; religious; Man. VIROCHANA SIRI-ATH.

Graphic Art Publishing: 105/19–2 Thanon Naret, Bangkok 10500; tel. (2) 233-0302; f. 1972; textbooks, science fiction, photography; CEO Mrs ANGKANA SAJJARAKTRAKUL.

Prae Pittaya Ltd: POB 914, 716–718 Wangburabha, Bangkok 10200; tel. (2) 221-4283; fax (2) 222–1286; general Thai books; Man. CHIT PRAEPANICH.

Praphansarn: Siam Sq., Soi 2, Thanon Phra Ram I, Bangkok; tel. (2) 434-1347; fax (2) 434-6812; e-mail editor@praphansarn.com; internet www.praphansarn.com; Thai pocket books; Man. Dir SUPHOL TAECHATADA.

Ruamsarn (1977): 864 Wangburabha, Thanon Panurangsri, Bangkok 10200; tel. (2) 221-6483; fax (2) 222-2036; f. 1951; fiction and history; Man. PITI TAWEWATANASARN.

Sermvitr Barnakarn: 222 Werng Nakorn Kasem, Bangkok 10100; general Thai books; Man. PRAVIT SAMMAVONG.

Silkworm Books: 6 Thanon Sukkasem, T. Suthep, Muang, Chiang Mai 50200; tel. (53) 226-161; fax (53) 226-163; e-mail silkworm@silkwormbooks.info; internet www.silkwormbooks.info; f. 1991; South-East Asian studies; English language.

Suksapan Panit (Business Organization of Teachers' Institute): 128/1 Thanon Ratchasima, Bangkok 10300; tel. (2) 416-7403; e-mail ssp@suksapan.or.th; internet www.suksapan.or.th; f. 1950; general, textbooks, children's, pocket books; Pres. PANOM KAW KAMNERD.

THAILAND

Suriyabarn Publishers: 14 Thanon Pramuan, Bangkok 10500; tel. (2) 234-7991; f. 1953; religion, literature, Thai culture; Man. Dir PRASIT SAETANG.

Thai Watana Panich: 905 Thanon Rama 3, Yannawa, Bangkok 10120; tel. (2) 683-3333; fax (2) 683-2000; e-mail webmaster@twp.co.th; internet www.twp.co.th; children's, school textbooks; Man. Dir INTIRA BUNNAG.

Watana Panit Printing and Publishing Co Ltd: 31/1–2 Soi Siripat, Thanon Mahachai, Samranrat, Pranakorn, Bangkok 10120; tel. (2) 222-1016; fax (2) 225-6556; school textbooks; Man. ROENGCHAI CHONGPIPATANASOOK.

White Lotus Co Ltd: 11/2 Soi 58, Thanon Sukhumvit, POB 1141, Bangkok 10501; tel. (2) 332-4915; fax (2) 331-4575; e-mail ande@loxinfo.co.th; internet whitelotusbooks.com; f. 1972; regional interests; Publisher DIETHARD ANDE.

PUBLISHERS' ASSOCIATION

Publishers' and Booksellers' Association of Thailand (PUBAT): 83/159 Moo 6, Thanon Ngam Wong Wan, Thung Song Hong, Lak Si, Bangkok 10210; tel. (2) 954-9560; fax (2) 954-9565; e-mail info@pubat.or.th; internet www.pubat.or.th; f. 1960; organizes national book fairs and provides promotional opportunities for publishers; Pres. THANACHAI SANTICHAIKUL; Gen. Sec. PLEARNPIT PRAEPANIT.

Broadcasting and Communications

TELECOMMUNICATIONS

National Telecommunications Commission (NTC): 87 Thanon Promprasitm, Bangkok 10400; tel. (2) 272-7054; fax (2) 278-1736; e-mail prntc@ntc.or.th; internet www.ntc.or.th; f. 2004; responsible for regulation and administration of telecommunications industry; Chair. Gen. CHOOCHART PROMPRASITM; Exec. Dir. WAJANA CHUENTONGKAM.

Post and Telegraph Department: Thanon Phaholyotin, Phayathai, Bangkok 10400; tel. (2) 271-0151; fax (2) 271-3511; e-mail office@ptd.go.th; internet www.ptd.go.th/ptdmain_eng; interim regulator of telecommunications sector pending creation of National Telecommunications Commission; Dir-Gen. SETHAPORN CUSRIPITUCK.

Advanced Info Service Public Co Ltd: 414 Thanon Phaholyothin, Shinawatra Tower I, Phayathai, Bangkok 10400; tel. (2) 299-5000; fax (2) 299-5719; e-mail callcenter@ais.co.th; internet www.ais900.com; mobile telephone network operator providing 3G (third generation) cellular services; Pres. YINGLUCK SHINAWATRA; Chair. SOMPRASONG BOONYACHAI.

CAT Telecom Public Co Ltd: 99 Thanon Changwattana, Laksi, Bangkok 10002; tel. (2) 573-0099; fax (2) 574-6054; e-mail pr@cattelecom.co.th; internet www.cattelecom.com; state-owned; f. 2003 following division of Communications Authority of Thailand (CAT); telephone operator; privatized in 2004; Chair. WISUDHI SRISUPHAN.

Samart Corpn Public Co Ltd: 99/1 Moo 4, Software Park Bldg, 35th Floor, Thanon Chaengwattana, Klong Gluar, Pak-kred, Nonthaburi 11120; tel. (2) 502-6000; fax (2) 502-6043; e-mail nikhila@samartcorp.com; internet www.samartcorp.com; telecommunications installation and distribution; cap. and res 700m. baht (1996), sales 11,597m. baht (2003); Chair. PICHAI VASANASONG; Exec. Chair. CHAROENRATH VILAILUCK.

True Move: 18 True Tower, Thanon Ratchadaphisek, Huai Khwang, Bangkok 10310; tel. (2) 647-5000; internet www.truemove.com; f. 2002; fmrly TA Orange Co Ltd; name changed as above in 2005; mobile telephone network operator; subsidiary of True Corpn PCL; Chief Exec. SUPACHAI CHEARAVANONT; 2,800 employees.

Telecomasia Corpn Public Co Ltd: Telecom Tower, 18 Thanon Ratchadaphisek, Huay Kwang, Bangkok 10320; tel. (2) 643-1111; fax (2) 643-9669; e-mail iroffice@asianet.co.th; internet www.telecomasia.co.th; telecommunications services; Chair. DHANIN CHEARAVANONT; Pres. and CEO SUPACHAI CHEARAVANONT.

Thai Telephone and Telecommunication Public Co Ltd (TT&T): Muang Thai Phatra Complex Tower 1, 24th Floor, 252/30 Thanon Ratchadaphisek, Huay Kwang, Bangkok; tel. (2) 693-2100; fax (2) 693-2126; e-mail webeditor@ttt.co.th; internet www.ttt.co.th; f. 1992; distributors of telecommunications equipment and services; Chair. DHONGCHAI LAMSAM; Pres. and CEO PRACHUAB TANTINON.

TOT Public Co Ltd: 89/2 Moo 3, Thanon Chaengwattana, Thungsonghong, Laksi, Bangkok 10210; tel. (2) 505-1000; e-mail prtot@tot.co.th; internet www.tot.co.th; state-owned; f. 2002; fmrly Telephone Organization of Thailand; name changed to TOT Corpn Public Co Ltd; name changed as above in 2005; telephone operator; de facto regulator; scheduled for transfer to private sector; Chair. Dr SATHIT LIMPONGPAN; Pres. TEERAWIT CHARUWAT.

Directory

Total Access Communications Public Co Ltd: Chai Bldg, 19th Floor, 333/3 Moo 4, Thanon Vibhavadi Rangsit, Ladyao Chatuchak, Bangkok 10900; tel. (2) 202-87000; fax (2) 202-8102; e-mail feedback@dtac.co.th; internet www.dtac.co.th; f. 1989; mobile telephone network operator; 41.46% owned by United Communication Industry Public Co Ltd; 29.94% owned by Telenor Asia Pte Ltd; Chair. BOONCHAI BENCHARONGKUL; CEOs VICHAI BENCHARONGKUL, SIGVE BREKKE.

United Communication Industry Public Co Ltd (UCOM): 499 Moo 3, Benchachinda Bldg, Thanon Vibhavadi Rangsit, Ladyao, Chatuchak, Bangkok 10900; tel. (2) 953-1111; fax (2) 953-2321; e-mail ir@ucom.co.th; internet www.ucom.co.th; telecommunications service provider; Chair. SRIBHUMI SUKHANETR; Pres. and Chief Exec. BOONCHAI BENCHARONGKUL.

BROADCASTING

Regulatory Authority

National Broadcasting Commission (NBC): Bangkok; f. 2005; 7-member independent regulatory body.

Radio and Television Executive Committee (RTEC): Programme, Administration and Law Section, Division of RTEC Works, Government Public Relations Dept, Thanon Ratchadamnoen Klang, Phra Nakhon Region, Bangkok 10200; constituted under the Broadcasting and TV Rule 1975, the committee consists of 17 representatives from 14 government agencies and controls the administrative, legal, technical and programming aspects of broadcasting in Thailand; regulatory functions were assumed by the National Broadcasting Commission.

Radio

Radio Thailand (RTH): National Broadcasting Services of Thailand, Government Public Relations Dept, Soi Aree Sampan, Thanon Phra Ram VI, Khet Phayathai, Bangkok 10400; tel. (2) 618-2323; fax (2) 618-2340; internet www.prd.go.th/mcic/radio.htm; f. 1930; govt-controlled; educational, entertainment, cultural and news programmes; operates 109 stations throughout Thailand; Dir of Radio Thailand SOMPHONG VISUTTIPAT.

> **Home Service:** 12 stations in Bangkok and 97 affiliated stations in 50 provinces; operates three programmes; Dir CHAIVICHIT ATISAB.
>
> **External Services:** f. 1928; in Thai, English, French, Vietnamese, Khmer, Japanese, Burmese, Lao, Malay, Chinese (Mandarin), German and Bahasa Indonesia; Dir AMPORN SAMOSORN.

Ministry of Education Broadcasting Service: Centre for Innovation and Technology, Ministry of Education, Bangkok; tel. (2) 246-0026; f. 1954; morning programmes for schools (Mon.–Fri.); afternoon and evening programmes for general public (daily); Dir of Centre PISAN SIWAYABRAHM.

Pituksuntirad Radio Stations: stations at Bangkok, Nakorn Rachasima, Chiangmai, Pitsanuloke and Songkla; programmes in Thai; Dir-Gen. PAITOON WAIJANYA.

Radio Saranrom: Thanon Ratchadamnoen, POB 2-131, Bangkok 10200; tel. (2) 224-4904; fax (2) 226-1825; f. 1968; as Voice of Free Asia; name changed as above in 1998; operated by the Ministry of Foreign Affairs; broadcasts in Thai; Dir of Broadcasting PAIBOON KUSKUL.

Television

Bangkok Broadcasting & TV Co Ltd (Channel 7): 998/1 Soi Sirimitr, Phaholyothin, Talad Mawchid, POB 456, Bangkok 10900; tel. (2) 272-0201; fax (2) 272-0010; e-mail prdept@ch7.com; internet www.ch7.com; commercial.

Bangkok Entertainment Co Ltd (Channel 3): Emporium Tower Bldg, 7th, 15th and 16th Floors, 622 Thanon Sukhumvit, Klongtoey, Bangkok 10110; tel. (2) 204-3333; fax (2) 204-1384; e-mail internet@thaitv3.com; internet www.thaitv3.com; Programme Dir PRAVIT MALEENONT.

Independent Television (ITV): 19 SCB Park Plaza, East Tower 3, Thanon Rachadapisek, Bangkok 10900; tel. (2) 791-1000; fax (2) 791-1010; e-mail webmaster@itv.co.th; internet www.itv.co.th; f. 1996; owned by a consortium including Nation Publishing Co, Siam Commercial Bank Public Co Ltd and Daily News media group.

The Mass Communication Organization of Thailand (Channel 9): 222 Thanon Asoke-Dindaeng, Bangkok 10300; tel. (2) 201-6000; fax (2) 245-1855; e-mail webmaster@mcot.net; internet www.mcot.net; f. 1952 as Thai Television Co Ltd; colour service; Dir-Gen. MINGKWAN SANGSUWAN.

The Royal Thai Army Television HSA-TV (Channel 5): 210 Thanon Phaholyothin, Sanam Pao, Bangkok 10400; tel. (2) 278-1770; fax (2) 279-0430; e-mail webadmin@tv5.co.th; internet www.tv5.co.th; f. 1958; operates channels nation-wide; Dir-Gen. Maj.-Gen. VIJIT JUNAPART.

THAILAND   *Directory*

Television of Thailand (Channel 11): Public Relations Dept, Fortune Town Bldg, 26th Floor, Thanon Ratchadaphisek, Huay Kwang, Bangkok 10310; tel. and fax (2) 248-1601; internet thailand.prd.go.th/about_prd_view.php?id=5; f. 1985; operates 16 colour stations; Dir-Gen. (vacant).

Thai TV Global Network: c/o Royal Thai Army HSA-TV, 210 Thanon Phaholyothin, Sanam Pao, Bangkok 10400; tel. (2) 278-1697; fax (2) 615-2066; e-mail tgn@tv5.co.th; established with the co-operation of all stations; distributes selected news, information and entertainment programmes from domestic stations for transmission to 170 countries world-wide via five satellite networks; Chair. Maj.-Gen. SOONTHORN SOPHONSIRI.

Finance

(cap. = capital; p.u. = paid up; res = reserves; dep. = deposits; m. = million; brs = branches; amounts in baht)

BANKING

Central Bank

Bank of Thailand: 273 Thanon Samsen, Bangkhunprom, Bangkok 10200; tel. (2) 283-5353; fax (2) 280-0449; e-mail webmaster@bot.or.th; internet www.bot.or.th; f. 1942; bank of issue; cap. 20m., res 29,860m., dep. 762,846m. (Dec. 2003); Gov. PRIDIYATHORN DAVAKULA; 4 brs.

Commercial Banks

Bangkok Bank Public Co Ltd: 333 Thanon Silom, Bangrak, Bangkok 10500; tel. (2) 231-4333; fax (2) 231-4742; e-mail info@bangkokbank.com; internet www.bangkokbank.com; f. 1944; cap. 1,399,935m., res 62,842m., dep. 1,186,111m. (Dec. 2004); 49% foreign-owned; Chair. CHARTRI SOPHONPANICH; Pres. CHARTSIRI SOPHONPANICH; 648 local brs, 22 overseas brs.

Bank of Asia Public Co Ltd: 191 Thanon Sathorn Tai, Khet Sathorn, Bangkok 10120; tel. (2) 287-2211; fax (2) 287-2973; e-mail webmaster@boa.co.th; internet www.bankasia4u.com; f. 1939; cap. 50,954m., res –9,376m., dep. 147,431m. (Dec. 2003); 78.85%-owned by ABN AMRO Bank NV; Chair. WEE CHO YAW; Pres. and CEO WONG KIM CHOONG; 127 local brs, 1 overseas br.

Bank of Ayudhya Public Co Ltd: 1222 Thanon Rama III, Bang Phongphang, Yan Nawa, Bangkok 10120; tel. (2) 296-2000; fax (2) 683-1275; e-mail webmaster@krungsri.com; internet www.krungsri.com; f. 1945; cap. 28,503m., res 36,623m., dep. 436,503m. (Dec. 2003); Chair. KRIT RATANARAK; Pres. PONGPINIT TEJAGUPTA; 384 local brs, 3 overseas brs.

BankThai Public Co Ltd: 44 Thanon Sathorn Nua, Silom, Bangrak, Bangkok 10500; tel. (2) 638-8000; fax (2) 633-9026; e-mail webmaster@bankthai.co.th; internet www.bankthai.co.th; f. 1998; cap. 14,935m., res –4,249m., dep. 214,269m. (Dec. 2002); Chair. TAWEE BUTSUNTORN; Pres. PHIRASILP SUBHAPHOLSIRI; 86 brs.

Kasikorn Bank Public Co Ltd: 1 Soi Kasikornthai, Thanon Ratburana, Bangkok 10140; tel. (2) 222-0000; fax (2) 470-1144; e-mail webmaster@kasikornbank.com; internet www.kasikornbank.com; f. 1945; fmrly Thai Farmers Bank Public Co Ltd; name changed as above April 2003; cap. 23,636m., res 39,068m., dep. 705,984m. (Dec. 2004); 48.98% foreign-owned; Chair. BANYONG LAMSAM; CEO BANTHOON LAMSAM; Pres. PRASARN TRAIRATVORAKUL; 495 local brs, 4 overseas brs.

Kiatnakin Bank Public Co Ltd: Amarin Tower, 12th Floor, 500 Thanon Ploenchit, Pathumwan, Bangkok 10330; tel. (2) 680-3333; fax (2) 256-9933; internet www.kiatnakinbank.com; f. 1971 under the name Kiatnakin Finance and Securities Co Ltd; name changed in 1999 to Kiatnakin Finance Public Co Ltd following separation of its finance and securities businesses; name changed as above in 2005; Chair. SUPHON WATTHANAVEKHIN; Pres. TAWATCHAI SUDTIKITPISAIN; 16 brs.

Krung Thai Bank Public Co Ltd (State Commercial Bank of Thailand): 35 Thanon Sukhumvit, Klongtoey, Bangkok 10110; tel. (2) 255-2222; fax (2) 255-9391; e-mail ptsirana@ktb.co.th; internet www.ktb.co.th; f. 1966; cap. 57,602.8m., res 9,014.1m., dep. 1,046,222.4m. (Dec. 2003); taken under the control of the central bank in 1998, pending transfer to private sector; merged with First Bangkok City Bank Public Co Ltd in 1999; Chair. SUPHACHAI PHISITVANICH; Pres. VIROJ NUALKHAIR; 610 local brs, 7 overseas brs.

Siam City Bank Public Co Ltd: 1101 Thanon Petchburi Tadmai, Bangkok 10400; tel. (2) 208-5000; fax (2) 253-1240; e-mail pr@scib.co.th; internet www.scib.co.th; f. 1941; cap. 21,128m., res 7,245m., dep. 426,425m. (Dec. 2003); taken under the control of the central bank in Feb. 1998; merged with Bangkok Metropolitan Bank Public Co Ltd in April 2002; Chair. SOMPOL KIATPHAIBOOL; Pres. and CEO APISAK TANTIVORAWONG ; 365 local brs, 1 overseas br.

Siam Commercial Bank Public Co Ltd: 9 Thanon Ratchadaphisek, Lardyao, Chatuchak, Bangkok 10900; tel. (2) 544-1111; fax (2) 937-7754; e-mail webmaster@telecom.scb.co.th; internet www.scb.co.th; f. 1906; cap. 31,305m., res 91,337m., dep. 612,697m. (Dec. 2001); Exec. Chair. VICHIT SURAPHONGCHAI; Pres. and CEO KHUNYING JADA WATTANASIRITHAM; 477 local brs, 4 overseas brs.

Standard Chartered Bank (Thai) Public Co Ltd: 90 Thanon Sathorn Nua, Silom, Bangkok 10500; tel. (2) 233-2111; fax (2) 236-1968; e-mail suteel@samart.co.th; internet www.standardcharterednakornthon.co.th; f. 1933 as Wang Lee Bank Ltd, renamed 1985; cap. 7,003m., res 255m., dep. 57,174m. (Dec. 2002); taken under the control of the central bank in July 1999, 75% share sold to Standard Chartered Bank (United Kingdom); name changed to Standard Chartered Nakornthon Bank PCL in 1999; name changed as above in 2005; Chair. DAVID GEORGE MOIR; CEO ANNE-MARIE DURBIN; 67 brs.

Thai Military Bank Public Co Ltd: 3000 Thanon Phahon Yothin, Bangkok 10900; tel. (2) 299-1111; fax (2) 273-7121; e-mail tmbir@tmb.co.th; f. 1957; merged with DBS Thai Danu Bank Public Co Ltd and Industrial Finance Corpn of Thailand Sept. 2004; cap. 104,080m., res –19,883m., dep. 338,646m. (Dec. 2003); Pres. and CEO SUBHAK SIWARAKSA; 367 local brs, 3 overseas brs.

Thanachart Bank Public Co Ltd: 1st, 2nd, 14th and 15th Floors, Thonson Bldg, 900 Thanon Phoenchit, Lumpini, Patumwan, Bangkok 10330; tel. (2) 655-9000; fax (2) 655-9001; e-mail nfs_rb@nfs.co.th; internet www.thanachart.com; f. 2002; Man. Dir SUVARNAPHA SUVARNAPRATHIP.

United Overseas Bank (Thai) PCL (UOBT): 191 Thanon Sathorn Tai, Bangkok 10120; tel. (2) 343-3000; fax (2) 287-2973; e-mail webmaster@uob.co.th; internet www.uob.co.th; f. 1998 as the result of the merger of Laem Thong Bank Ltd with Radanasin Bank; name changed to UOB Radanasin Bank Public Co Ltd in Nov. 1999; name changed as above in 2005; cap. 9,847m., res 58m., dep. 51,340m. (Dec. 2003); Man. Dir and CEO GAN HUI BENG; 37 brs.

Foreign Banks

ABN AMRO Bank NV (Netherlands): Bangkok City Tower, 3rd–4th Floors, 179/3 Thanon Sathorn Tai, Bangkok 10120; tel. (2) 679-5900; fax (2) 679-5901; e-mail wholesale.clients.internet@nl.abnamro.com; Country Man. BURNO SCHRIEKE.

Bank of America, NA (USA): Bank of America Centre, 2/2 Thanon Witthayu, Bangkok 10330; tel. (2) 251-6333; fax (2) 253-1905; f. 1949; cap. p.u. 2,000m. (May 1998); Man. Dir and Country Man. FREDERICK CHIN.

Bank of China (People's Republic of China): Bangkok City Tower, 179 Thanon Sathorn Tai, Bangkok 10120; tel. (2) 268-1010; fax (2) 268-1020.

Bank of Nova Scotia (Canada): Ground Floor, Ploenchit Tower, 898 Thanon Ploenchit, Bangkok 10330; tel. (2) 263-0303; fax (2) 263-0150; e-mail bbangkok@scotiabank.com; Vice-Pres. and Country Head KOBSAK DUANGDEE; Branch Man. NOEL SINGH.

Bank of Tokyo-Mitsubishi UFJ Ltd (Japan): Harindhorn Tower, 54 Thanon Sathorn Nua, Bangrak, Bangkok 10500; tel. (2) 266-3011; fax (2) 266-3055; cap. p.u. 3,100m., dep. 17,213m. (March 1996); Dir and Gen. Man. HIROSHI MOTOMURA.

Bharat Overseas Bank Ltd (India): 221 Thanon Rajawongse, Sumpphanthawongse, Bangkok 10100; tel. (2) 224-5412; fax (2) 224-5405; f. 1974; cap. p.u. 225m., dep. 1,254m. (March 1996); Man. K. S. GANAPATHY.

BNP Paribas (France): 29th Floor, Abdulrahim Place, 990 Thanon Rama IV, Silom, Bangrak, Bangkok 10500; tel. (2) 636-1900; fax (2) 636-1935.

Citibank, NA (USA): Sangtongtanee Bldg, 82 Thanon Sathorn Nua, Bangrak, Bangkok 10500; tel. (2) 232-2000; fax (2) 639-2564; internet www.citibank.com/thailand; cap. p.u. 3,849m., dep. 9,483m. (Feb. 1996); Man. DAVID L. HENDRIX.

Crédit Agricole Indosuez (France): CA Indosuez House, 152 Thanon Witthayu, POB 303, Bangkok 10330; tel. (2) 624-8000; fax (2) 651-4586; cap. p.u. 3,000m., dep. 7,896m. (Dec. 2003); Man. FRANÇOIS RAMEAU.

Deutsche Bank AG (Germany): 208 Thanon Witthayu, Bangkok 10330; tel. (2) 651-5000; fax (2) 651-5151; cap. p.u. 1,200m., dep. 3,703m. (March 1996); Man. GERHARD HEIGL.

Hongkong and Shanghai Banking Corpn (HSBC) (Hong Kong): HSBC Bldg, 968 Thanon Rama IV, Silom, Bangkok 10500; tel. (2) 614-4000; fax (2) 632-4818; cap. p.u. 2,000m., dep. 8,328m. (March 1996); Man. R. J. O. CROMWELL.

International Commercial Bank of China (Taiwan): 36/12 P. S. Tower Asoke, 21 Thanon Sukhumvit, Phrakhanong, Bangkok 10110; tel. (2) 259-2000; fax (2) 259-1330; e-mail accdept@icbc.co.th; cap. p.u. 500m., dep. 1,344m. (Feb. 1996); Vice-Pres. and Gen. Man. CHIA-NAN WANG.

JP Morgan Chase Bank (USA): Bubhajit Bldg, 2nd Floor, 20 Thanon Sathorn Nua, Silom, Bangrak, Bangkok 10500; tel. (2) 234-5992; fax (2) 234-8386; Man. Dir RAYMOND C. C. CHANG.

Mizuho Corporate Bank Ltd (Japan): 18th Floor, Tisco Tower, 48 Thanon Sathorn Nua, Silom, Bangrak, Bangkok 10500; tel. (2) 638-0200; fax (2) 638-0218.

Oversea-Chinese Banking Corpn Ltd (Singapore): Charn Issara Tower, 2nd Floor, 942/80 Thanon Rama IV, Suriwongse, Bangkok 10500; tel. (2) 236-6730; fax (2) 237-7390; cap. p.u. 651m., dep. 455m. (Feb. 1996); Gen. Man. NEW JING YAN.

RHB Bank Bhd (Malaysia): Liberty Sq. Bldg, 10th Floor, 287 Thanon Silom, Bangrak, Bangkok 10500; tel. (2) 631-2000; fax (2) 631-2018; e-mail rhbbkbk@asianet.co.th; internet www.rhbbank.com.my/cbob/thailand.shtm; Man. LEH THIAM GUAN.

Standard Chartered Bank (UK): Sathorn Nakorn Tower, 100 Thanon Sathon Nua, Silom, Bangrak, Bangkok 10500; tel. (2) 724-4000; fax (2) 636-0536; e-mail th.standardchartered-service@th.standardchartered.com; internet www.stanchart.com/th; cap. p.u. 1,200m., dep. 5,585m. (March 1996); CEO VISHNU MOHAN.

Sumitomo Mitsui Banking Corpn (Japan): Boon-Mitr Bldg, 138 Thanon Silom, Bangkok 10500; tel. (2) 353-8000; fax (2) 353-8100; cap. p.u. 3,200m., dep. 8,343m. (Feb. 1996); Gen. Rep. YOSHIHIRO YOSHIMURA.

Development Banks

Bank for Agriculture and Agricultural Co-operatives (BAAC): 469 Thanon Nakorn Sawan, Dusit, Bangkok 10300; tel. (2) 280-0180; fax (2) 280-0442; e-mail train@baac.or.th; internet www.baac.or.th; f. 1966 to provide credit for agriculture; cap. 22,761m., dep. 180,563m. (Dec. 2000); Exec. Chair. VARATHEP RATANAKORN; Pres. TEERAPONG TUNGTEERASUNUN; 491 brs.

Export-Import Bank of Thailand (EXIM THAILAND): EXIM Bldg, 1193 Thanon Phaholyothin, Phayathai, Bangkok 10400; tel. (2) 271-3700; fax (2) 271-3204; e-mail info@exim.go.th; internet www.exim.go.th; f. 1993; provides financial services to Thai exporters and Thai investors investing abroad; cap. 6,500m., res 2,060m., dep. 13,424m. (Dec. 2003); Chair. VIRABONGSA RAMANGKURA; Pres. SATAPORN JINICHITRA; 7 brs.

Government Housing Bank: 63 Thanon Rama IX, Huay Kwang, Bangkok 10310; tel. (2) 645-9000; fax (2) 246-1789; e-mail crm@ghb.co.th; internet www.ghb.co.th; f. 1953 to provide housing finance; cap. 9,483m., assets 152,973m., dep. 80,251m. (Dec. 1995); Chair. WISUDHI SRISUPHAN; Pres. KHAN PRACHUABMOH; 120 brs.

Small and Medium Enterprise Development Bank of Thailand: 9th Floor, Siripinyo Bldg, 475 Thanon Sri Ayudhaya, Rajtavee, Bangkok 10400; tel. (2) 201-3700; fax (2) 201-3723; e-mail sme@smebank.co.th; internet www.smebank.co.th; f. under above name in 2002; fmrly Small Industries Finance Office, which became Small Industrial Finance Co Ltd in 1991; Pres. CHOTISAK ASAPAVIRIYA.

Savings Bank

Government Savings Bank: 470 Thanon Phaholyothin, Phayathai, Bangkok 10400; tel. (2) 299-8000; fax (2) 299-8490; e-mail vicheal@gsb.or.th; internet www.gsb.or.th; f. 1913; cap. 0.1m., res 8,040m., dep. 522,824m. (Dec. 2002); Chair. SOMCHAINUK ENGTRAKUL; Dir-Gen. Dr CHARNCHAI MUSIGNISARKORN; 578 brs.

Bankers' Association

Thai Bankers' Association: Lake Rachada Office Complex, Bldg 2, 4th Floor, 195/5–7 Thanon Ratchadaphisek, Klongtoey, Bangkok 10110; tel. (2) 264-0883; fax (2) 264-0888; e-mail infodesk@tba.or.th; internet www.tba.or.th; f. 1958; Chair. CHARTSIRI SOPHONPANICH.

STOCK EXCHANGE

Stock Exchange of Thailand (SET): The Stock Exchange of Thailand Bldg, 62 Thanon Ratchadaphisek, Klongtoey, Bangkok 10110; tel. (2) 229-2000; fax (2) 654-5649; e-mail infoproducts@set.or.th; internet www.set.or.th; f. 1975; 27 mems; Pres. KITTIRAT NA RANONG; Chair. CHAVALIT THANACHANAN.

Securities and Exchange Commission: Diethelm Towers B, 10th/13th–16th Floors, 93/1 Thanon Witthayu, Lumpini, Patumwan, Bangkok 10330; tel. (2) 695-9999; fax (2) 256-7711; e-mail info@sec.or.th; internet www.sec.or.th; f. 1992; supervises new share issues and trading in existing shares; chaired by Minister of Finance; Sec.-Gen. THIRACHAI PHUVANAT NARANUBULA.

INSURANCE

In March 1997 the Government granted licences to 12 life assurance companies and 16 general insurance companies, bringing the total number of life insurance companies to 25 and non-life insurance companies to 83.

Selected Domestic Insurance Companies

American International Assurance Co Ltd: American International Tower, 181 Thanon Surawongse, Bangkok 10500; tel. (2) 634-8888; fax (2) 236-6452; e-mail bkk.group@aig.com; internet www.aia.co.th; f. 1983; ordinary and group life, group and personal accident, credit, life; Exec. Vice-Pres. and Gen. Man. DHADOL BUNNAG.

Ayudhya Insurance Public Co Ltd: Ploenchit Tower, 7th Floor, Thanon Ploenchit, Pathumwan, Bangkok 10330; tel. (2) 263-0335; fax (2) 263-0589; e-mail info@ayud.co.th; internet www.ayud.co.th; non-life; Chair. VERAPHAN TEEPSUWAN; Pres. ADISORN TANTIANANKUL.

Bangkok Insurance Public Co Ltd: Bangkok Insurance Bldg, 25 Thanon Sathorn Tai, Bangkok 10120; tel. (2) 285-8888; fax (2) 677-3737; e-mail corp.comm1@bki.co.th; internet www.bki.co.th; f. 1947; non-life; Chair. and Pres. CHAI SOPHONPANICH.

Bangkok Union Insurance Public Co Ltd: 175–177 Thanon Surawongse, Bangkok 10500; tel. (2) 233-6920; fax (2) 237-1856; f. 1929; non-life; Chair. MANU LIEWPAIROT.

China Insurance Co (Siam) Ltd: 36/68–69, 20th Floor, PS Tower, Thanon Asoke, Sukhumvit 21, Bangkok 10110; tel. (2) 259-3718; fax (2) 259-1402; f. 1948; non-life; Chair. JAMES C. CHENG; Man. Dir FANG RONG-CHENG.

Indara Insurance Public Co Ltd: 364/29 Thanon Si Ayutthaya, Ratchthewi, Bangkok 10400; tel. (2) 247-9261; fax (2) 247-9260; e-mail contact@indara.co.th; internet www.indara.co.th; f. 1949; non-life; Chair. PRATIP WONGNIRUND; Man. Dir SOPHON DEJTHEVAPORN.

International Assurance Co Ltd: 488/7–9 Thanon Henri Dunant, Patumwan, Bangkok 10330; tel. (2) 658-1919; fax (2) 254-7881; f. 1952; non-life, fire, marine, general; Chair. PICHAI KULAVANICH; CEO V. S. SAMAN.

Mittare Insurance Co Ltd: 295 Thanon Si Phraya, Bangrak, Bangkok 10500; tel. (2) 237-4646; fax (2) 236-1376; internet www.mittare.com; f. 1947; life, fire, marine, health, personal accident, automobile and general; fmrly Thai Prasit Insurance Co Ltd; Chair. SURACHAN CHANSRICHAWLA; Man. Dir SUKHATHEP CHANSRICHAWLA.

Ocean Life Insurance Co Ltd: 170/74–83 Ocean Tower I Bldg, Thanon Rachadapisek, Klongtoey, Bangkok 10110; tel. (2) 261-2300; fax (2) 261-3344; e-mail info@oli.co.th; internet www.oli.co.th; f. 1949; life; Chair. and Man. Dir KIRATI ASSAKUL.

Paiboon Insurance Co Ltd: Thai Life Insurance Bldg, 19th–20th Floors, 123 Thanon Ratchadapisek, Bangkok 10310; tel. (2) 246-9635; fax (2) 246-9660; f. 1927; non-life; Chair. ANUTHRA ASSAWANONDA; Pres. VANICH CHAIYAWAN.

Prudential TS Life Assurance Public Co Ltd: Sengthong Thani Tower, 28th, 30th and 31st Floors, 82 Thanon Sathorn Nua, Bangkok 10500; tel. (2) 639-9500; fax (2) 639-9699; e-mail customer.service.ptsl@ibm.net; internet www.prudential.co.th; f. 1983; Chair. Prof. BUNCHANA ATTHAKOR; Vice-Chair. DAN R. BARDIN.

Siam Commercial New York Life Insurance Public Co Ltd: 4th Floor, SCB Bldg 1, 1060 Thanon Petchburi, SCB Chidlom, Ratchathewi, Bangkok 10330; tel. (2) 655-3000; fax (2) 256-1517; e-mail don@scnyl.com; internet www.scnyl.com; f. 1976; life; Pres. and CEO C. DONALD CARDEN.

Southeast Insurance (2000) Co Ltd (Arkanay Prakan Pai Co Ltd): Southeast Insurance Bldg, 315G, 1–3 Thanon Silom, Bangrak, Bangkok 10500; tel. (2) 631-1331; f. 1946; life and non-life; Chair. CHAYUT CHIRALERSPONG; Gen. Man. NATDANAI INDRASUKHSRI.

Syn Mun Kong Insurance Public Co Ltd: 279 Thanon Srinakarin, Bangkapi, Bangkok 10240; tel. (2) 379-3140; fax (2) 731-6590; e-mail info@smk.co.th; internet www.smk.co.th; f. 1951; fire, marine, automobile and personal accident; Chair. THANAVIT DUSADEESURAPOJ; Man. Dir RUENGDEJ DUSADEESURAPOJ.

Thai Commercial Insurance Public Co Ltd: Sathorn Nakorn Tower, 25th Floor, 100/48–49 Thanon Sathorn Nua, Silom, Bangrak, Bangkok 10500; tel. (2) 236-5987; fax (2) 236-5990; f. 1940; automobile, fire, marine and casualty; Chair. SUKIT WANGLEE; Exec. Dir SUCHIN WANGLEE; Man. Dir SURAJIT WANGLEE.

Thai Health Insurance Co Ltd: 31st Floor, RS Tower, 121/89 Thanon Ratchadaphisek, Ding-Daeng, Bangkok 10400; tel. (2) 642-3100; fax (2) 642-3130; e-mail info@thaihealth.co.th; internet www.thaihealth.co.th; f. 1979; Chair. APIRAK THAIPATANAGUL; Man. Dir VARANG SRETHBHAKDI.

Thai Insurance Public Co Ltd: 34/3 Soi Lang Suan, Thanon Ploenchit, Lumpini, Pathumwan, Bangkok 10330; tel. (2) 652-2880; fax (2) 652-2870; e-mail tic@thaiins.com; internet www.thaiins.com; f. 1938; non-life; Chair. KAVI ANSVANANDA.

Thai Life Insurance Co Ltd: 123 Thanon Ratchadaphisek, Din-Daeng, Bangkok 10400; tel. (2) 247-0247; fax (2) 246-9945; e-mail corpcomm@thailife.com; internet www.thailife.com; f. 1942; life; Chair. and CEO VANICH CHAIYAWAN; Pres. APIRAK THAIPATANAGUL.

THAILAND

Directory

ThaiSri Insurance Co Ltd: 126/2 Thanon Krunthonburi, Klongsam, Bangkok 10600; tel. (2) 878-7111; fax (2) 860-7365; e-mail info@thaisri.com; internet www.thaisri.com; f. 1997; personal accident, automobile, fire, marine; jt venture between Thai Metropole Insurance and Zurich Financial Services Group (Switzerland); Chair. Sirin Nimmanahaeminda; Pres. Chartchai Panichewa.

Viriyah Insurance Co Ltd: RS Tower, 121/7 Thanon Ratchadaphisek, Din-Daeng, Bangkok 10320; tel. (2) 239-1000; fax (2) 641-3902; e-mail info@viriyah.co.th; internet www.viriyah.co.th; f. 1947; Man. Dir Suvaporn Thongthew.

Wilson Insurance Co Ltd: 18th Bangkok Insurance/YMCA Bldg, 25 Thanon Sathorn Tai, Thungmahamek, Sathorn, Bangkok 10120; tel. (2) 677-3999; fax (2) 677-3978; e-mail wilson@wilsonins.co.th; f. 1951; fire, marine, motor car, general; Chair. Chote Sophonpanich; Pres. Susumu Yukawa.

Associations

General Insurance Association: 223 Soi Ruamrudee, Thanon Witthayu, Bangkok 10330; tel. (2) 256-6032; fax (2) 256-6039; e-mail general@thaigia.com; internet www.thaigia.com; Exec. Dir Chalaw Fuangaromya.

Thai Life Assurance Association: 36/1 Soi Sapanku, Thanon Rama IV, Thungmahamek, Sathorn, Bangkok 10120; tel. (2) 287-4596; fax (2) 679-7100; e-mail tlaa@tlaa.org; internet www.tlaa.org; Pres. Apirak Thaipatanagul.

Trade and Industry

GOVERNMENT AGENCIES

Board of Investment (BOI): 555 Thanon Vipavadee Rangsit, Chatuchak, Bangkok 10900; tel. (2) 537-8111; fax (2) 537-8177; e-mail head@boi.go.th; internet www.boi.go.th; f. 1958; formed to publicize investment potential and encourage economically and socially beneficial investments and also to provide investment information; chaired by the Prime Minister; Sec.-Gen. Satit Chanjavanakul.

Board of Trade of Thailand: 150/2 Thanon Rajbopit, Bangkok 10200; tel. (2) 622-1860; fax (2) 225-3372; e-mail bot@tcc.or.th; internet www.thaiechamber.com; f. 1955; mems: chambers of commerce, trade asscns, state enterprises and co-operative societies (large and medium-sized companies have associate membership); Chair. Aiva Taulananda.

Central Sugar Marketing Centre: Bangkok; f. 1981; responsible for domestic marketing and price stabilization.

Financial Sector Restructuring Authority (FSRA): 130–132 Tower 3, Thanon Witthayu, Patumwan, Bangkok 10330; tel. (2) 263-2620; fax (2) 650-9872; e-mail webmaster@fra.or.th; internet www.fra.or.th; f. 1997 to oversee the restructuring of Thailand's financial system; Chair. Kamol Juntima; Sec.-Gen. Montri Chenvidayakam.

Forest Industry Organization: 76 Thanon Ratchadamnoen Nok, Bangkok 10100; tel. (2) 282-3243; fax (2) 282-5197; e-mail info@fio.co.th; internet www.fio.co.th; f. 1947; oversees all aspects of forestry and wood industries; Man. Col M. R. Aduldej Chakrabandhu.

Office of the Cane and Sugar Board: Ministry of Industry, Thanon Phra Ram Hok, Bangkok 10400; tel. (2) 202-3291; fax (2) 202-3293; e-mail wimonlak@narai.oie.go.th.

Rubber Estate Organization: Nabon Station, Nakhon Si Thammarat Province 80220; tel. (75) 411554; Man. Dir Somphol Isarathanachai.

DEVELOPMENT AGENCIES

National Economic and Social Development Board: 962 Thanon Krung Kasem, Bangkok 10100; tel. (2) 282-8454; fax (2) 628-2871; e-mail mis@nesdb.go.th; internet www.nesdb.go.th; economic and social planning agency; Sec.-Gen. Chakramon Phasukavanich.

Royal Developments Projects Board: Office of the Prime Minister, Bangkok; e-mail webmaster@rdpb.go.th; internet www.rdpb.go.th; Sec.-Gen. Dr Sumet Tantivejkul.

CHAMBER OF COMMERCE

Thai Chamber of Commerce: 150 Thanon Rajbopit, Bangkok 10200; tel. (2) 622-1880; fax (2) 225-3372; e-mail echam@thaiechamber.com; internet www.thaiechamber.com; f. 1946; 2,000 mems, 10 assoc. mems (1998); Chair. Pramon Sutivong; Pres. Vichien Tejaphaiboon.

INDUSTRIAL AND TRADE ASSOCIATIONS

Bangkok Rice Millers' Association: 14/3 Thanon Sathorn Tai, Bangkok 10120; tel. (2) 286-8298.

The Federation of Thai Industries: Queen Sirikit National Convention Center, Zone C, 4th Floor, 60 Thanon Ratchadaphisek Tadmai, Klongtoey, Bangkok 10110; tel. (2) 345-1000; fax (2) 345-1296; e-mail information@off.fti.or.th; internet www.fti.or.th; f. 1987; fmrly The Association of Thai Industries; 4,800 mems; Chair. Tawee Butsuntorn.

Mining Industry Council of Thailand: Soi 222/2, Thai Chamber of Commerce University, Thanon Vibhavadi Rangsit, Dindaeng, Bangkok 10400; tel. (2) 275-7684; fax (2) 692-3321; e-mail miningthai@miningthai.org; internet www.miningthai.org; f. 1983; intermediary between govt organizations and private mining enterprises; Chair. Yongyoth Petchsuwan; Sec.-Gen. Punya Adulyapichit.

Rice Exporters' Association of Thailand: 37 Soi Ngamdupli, Thanon Phra Rama IV, Tungmahamek, Sathorn, Bangkok 10120; tel. (2) 287-2674; fax (2) 287-2678; e-mail contact@riceexporters.or.th; Pres. Vichai Sriprasert; Sec.-Gen. Lt Chareon Laothamatas.

Rice Mill Association of Thailand: 81–81/1 Trok Rongnamkheng, 24 Thanon Charoenkrung, Talat Noi, Sampanthawong, Bangkok 10100; tel. (2) 235-7863; fax (2) 234-7286; Pres. Niphon Wongtragarn.

Sawmills Association: 101 Thanon Amnuaysongkhram, Dusit, Bangkok 10300; tel. (2) 243-4754; fax (2) 243-8629; e-mail smassoc@mail.cscoms.com; Pres. Vitoon Pongpasit.

Thai Coffee Exporters Association: 1302–06 Thanon Songwad, Samphantawong, Bangkok 10100; tel. (2) 221-1264; fax (2) 225-1962; e-mail cofexpo@cscoms.com.

Thai Contractors' Association: 110 Thanon Witthayu, Bangkok 10330; tel. (2) 251-0697; fax (2) 255-3990; e-mail webmaster@tca.or.th; internet www.tca.or.th; f. 1928 under the name The Engineering Association of Siam; name changed to The Engineering Contractors Assocn in 1967 and as above in 1983; Pres. Poomson Rojlertjanya; Sec.-Gen. Pradit Arphorn.

Thai Diamond Manufacturers Association: 116/1 Thanon Silom, Bangkok 10500; tel. (2) 238-2718; fax (2) 266-4830; e-mail odtcbkk@loxinfo.co.th; 11-mem. board; Pres. Chirakitti Tangkathac.

Thai Food Processors' Association: Tower 1, Ocean Bldg, 9th Floor, 170/21–22 Thanon Rajchadapisaktadmai, Klongtoey, Bangkok 10110; tel. (2) 261-2684; fax (2) 261-2996; e-mail thaifood@thaifood.org; internet www.thaifood.org.

Thai Jute Mill Association: Sivadol Bldg, 10th Floor, Rm 10, 1 Thanon Convent, Silom, Bangrak, Bangkok 10500; tel. (2) 234-1438; fax (2) 234-1439.

Thai Lac Association: 66 Soi Chalermkhetr 1, Thanon Yukul, Pomprab, Bangkok 10100; tel. (2) 233-8331.

Thai Maize and Produce Traders' Association: Sathorn Thani II Bldg, 11th Floor, 92/26–27 Thanon Sathorn Nua, Bangrak, Bangkok 10500; tel. (2) 234-4387; fax (2) 236-8413.

Thai Pharmaceutical Manufacturers Association: 188/107 Thanon Charansanitwongs, Banchanglaw, Bangkoknoi, Bangkok 10700; tel. (2) 863-5106; fax (2) 863-5108; e-mail tpma@asiaaccess.net.th; f. 1969; Pres. Chernporn Tengamnuay.

Thai Rubber Traders' Association: 57 Thanon Rongmuang 5, Pathumwan, Bangkok 10500; tel. (2) 214-3420; f. 1951; Pres. Sang Udomjarumance.

Thai Silk Association: Textile Industry Division, Soi Trimitr, Thanon Rama IV, Klongtoey, Bangkok 10110; tel. (2) 712-4328; fax (2) 258-8769; e-mail thsilkas@thaitextile.org; internet www.thaitextile.org/tsa; f. 1962; Pres. Setr Vanijvongse.

Thai Sugar Manufacturing Association: 78 Keatnakin Bldg, Captain Bush Lane, Thanon Charoenkrung, Bangkok 10500; tel. (2) 233-5858; fax (2) 233-4156; e-mail tsma2000@cscoms.com.

Thai Sugar Producers' Association: 8th Floor, Thai Ruam Toon Bldg, 794 Thanon Krung Kasem, Pomprap, Bangkok 10100; tel. (2) 282-0990; fax (2) 281-0342.

Thai Tapioca Trade Association: Sathorn Thani II Bldg, 20th Floor, 92/58 Thanon Sathorn Nua, Silom, Bangkok 10500; tel. (2) 234-4724; fax (2) 236-6084; e-mail ttta@loxinfo.co.th; internet www.ttta-tapioca.org; f. 1963; Pres. Sunai Sathaporn.

Thai Textile Manufacturing Association: 454–460 Thanon Sukhumvit, Klongton, Klongtoey, Bangkok 10110; tel. (2) 258-2023; fax (2) 260-1525; e-mail ttma@thaitextile.org; internet www.thaitextile.org/ttma; f. 1960; Pres. Phongsak Assakul.

Thai Timber Exporters' Association: Ratchada Trade Centre, 4th Floor, 410/73–76 Thanon Ratchadaphisek, Bangkok 10310; tel. (2) 287-3229; fax (2) 259-0481.

Timber Merchants' Association: 4 Thanon Yen-Arkad, Thung-Mahamek, Yannawa, Bangkok 10120; tel. (2) 249-5565.

Union Textile Merchants' Association (Thai Textile Merchants' Association): 562 Espreme Bldg, 4th Floor, Thanon Rajchawong,

Samphanthawong, Bangkok 10100; tel. (2) 622-6711; fax (2) 622-6714; e-mail tma@thaitextile.org; internet www.thaitextile.org/tma; Chair. THAVON TANTISIRIVIT.

UTILITIES
Electricity

Cogeneration Public Co Ltd: Grand Amarin Tower, 29th Floor, 1550 Thanon Petchburi Tadmai, Rachtavee, Bangkok 10320; tel. (2) 207-0970; fax (2) 207-0910; generation and supply of co-generation power; cap. and res 5,634m., sales 3,424m. (1996/97); Chair. PIERRE CHARLES E. SWARTENBROEK; Pres. CHANCHAI JIVACATE.

Electricity Generating Authority of Thailand (EGAT): 53 Thanon Charan Sanit Wong, Bang Kruai, Nothaburi, Bangkok 11130; tel. (2) 436-0000; fax (2) 436-4723; e-mail webmaster@egat.co.th; internet www.egat.co.th; f. 1969; scheduled for transfer to the private sector in 2004; Gov. SITTHIPORN RATANOPAS; Chair. CHERDPONG SIRIWIT.

Electricity Generating Public Co Ltd (EGCO): EGCO Tower, 222 Moo 5, Thanon Vibhavadi Rangsit, Tungsonghong, Laksi, Bangkok 10210; tel. (2) 998-5000; fax (2) 955-0956; e-mail pr@egco.com; internet www.egco.com; a subsidiary of the Electricity Generating Authority of Thailand (EGAT); 59% transferred to the private sector in 1994–96; 14.9%-owned by China Light and Power Co (Hong Kong); Chair. CHAI-ANAN SAMUDAVANIJA; Pres. VISIT AKARAVINAK.

The Metropolitan Electricity Authority: 30 Soi Chidlom, Thanon Ploenchit, Lumpini, Pathumwan, Bangkok 10330; tel. (2) 254-9550; fax (2) 251-9586; internet www.mea.or.th; f. 1958; one of the two main power distribution agencies in Thailand; Gov. SAROCH KUTCHAMATH.

The Provincial Electricity Authority: 200 Thanon Ngam Wongwan, Chatuchak, Bangkok 10900; tel. (2) 589-0100; fax (2) 589-4850; e-mail webmaster@pea.co.th; internet www.pea.co.th; f. 1960; one of the two main power distribution agencies in Thailand; Chair. PRACHERD SOOK-KAEW.

Water

Metropolitan Waterworks Authority: 18/137 Thanon Prachachuen, Don Muang, Bangkok 10210; tel. (2) 504-0123; fax (2) 503-9493; e-mail pubrela@mwa.co.th; internet english.mwa.co.th; f. 1967; state-owned; provides water supply systems in Bangkok; scheduled for transfer to private sector in 2004; Chair. SUJARIT PATCHIMNAN.

Provincial Waterworks Authority: 72 Thanon Chaengwattana, Don Muang, Bangkok 10210; tel. (2) 551-1020; fax (2) 552-1547; e-mail pr@pwa.co.th; internet www.pwa.co.th; f. 1979; provides water supply systems except in Bangkok Metropolis; scheduled for transfer to private sector in 2005; Gov. Dr PRASERT CHUAPHANIT; Chair. PHICHET SATHIRACHAWAN.

CO-OPERATIVES

In 1992 there were 4m. members of co-operatives, including 1.6m. in agriculture.

TRADE UNIONS

Under the Labour Relations Act (1975), a minimum of 10 employees are required in order to form a union; by August 1997 there were an estimated 1,028 such unions.

Confederation of Thai Labour (CTL): 25/20 Thanon Sukhumvit, Viphavill Village, Tambol Paknam, Amphur Muang, Samutprakarn, Bangkok 10270; tel. (2) 756-5346; fax (2) 323-1074; represents 44 labour unions; Pres. AMPORN BANDASAK.

Labour Congress of Thailand (LCT): 420/393–394 Thippavan Village 1, Thanon Teparak, Samrong-Nua, Muang, Samutprakarn, Bangkok 10270; tel. and fax (2) 384-6789; e-mail lct_org@hotmail.com; f. 1978; represents 224 labour unions, four labour federations and approx. 140,000 mems; Pres. PRATNENG SAENGSANK; Gen. Sec. SAMAM THOMYA.

National Congress of Private Employees of Thailand (NPET): 142/6 Thanon Phrathoonam Phrakanong, Phrakanong, Klongtoey, Bangkok 10110; tel. and fax (2) 392-9955; represents 31 labour unions; Pres. BANJONG PORNPATTANANIKOM.

National Congress of Thai Labour (NCTL): 1614/876 Samutprakarn Community Housing Project, Sukhumvit Highway Km 30, Tai Baan, Muang, Samutprakarn, Bangkok 10280; tel. (2) 389-5134; fax (2) 385-8975; represents 171 unions; Pres. PANAS THAILUAN.

National Free Labour Union Congress (NFLUC): 277 Moo 3, Thanon Ratburana, Bangkok 10140; tel. (2) 427-6506; fax (2) 428-4543; represents 51 labour unions; Pres. ANUSSAKDI BOONYAPRANAI.

National Labour Congress (NLC): 586/248–250 Moo 2, Mooban City Village, Thanon Sukhumvit, Bang Phu Mai, Mueng, Samutprakarn, Bangkok 10280; tel. and fax (2) 709-9426; represents 41 labour unions; Pres. CHIN THAPPHLI.

Thai Trade Union Congress (TTUC): 420/393–394 Thippavan Village 1, Thanon Teparak, Tambol Samrong-nua, Amphur Muang, Samutprakarn, Bangkok 10270; tel. and fax (2) 384-0438; f. 1983; represents 172 unions; Pres. PANIT CHAROENPHAO.

Thailand Council of Industrial Labour (TCIL): 99 Moo 4, Thanon Sukhaphibarn 2, Khannayao, Bungkum, Bangkok; tel. (2) 517-0022; fax (2) 517-0628; represents 23 labour unions; Pres. TAVEE DEEYING.

Transport
RAILWAYS

Thailand has a railway network of 4,041 km, connecting Bangkok with Chiang Mai, Nong Khai, Ubon Ratchathani, Nam Tok and towns on the isthmus.

State Railway of Thailand: 1 Thanon Rong Muang, Rong Muang, Pathumwan, Bangkok 10330; tel. (2) 220-4567; fax (2) 225-3801; e-mail info@railway.co.th; internet www.railway.co.th; f. 1897; 4,041 km of track in 2002; responsible for licensing a 4,044-km passenger and freight rail system, above ground; Chair. PRINYA JINDAPRASERT; Gov. CHITSANTI DHANASOBHON.

Bangkok Mass Transit System Public Co Ltd: 1000 Thanon Phahonyothin, Lad Yao, Chatuchak, Bangkok 10900; tel. (2) 617-7300; fax (2) 617-7133; f. 1992; responsible for the construction and management of the Skytrain, a two-line, 23.5-km elevated rail system, under the supervision of the Bangkok Metropolitan Area, the initial stage of which was opened in December 1999; Chair. KASAME CHATIKAVANIJ; Exec. Chair. and CEO KEEREE KANJANAPAS.

Mass Rapid Transit Authority of Thailand: 175 Thanon Rama IX, Huay Kwang, Bangkok 10320; tel. (2) 612-2444; fax (2) 612-2436; e-mail pr@mrta.co.th; internet www.mrta.co.th; a 20-km subway system was opened in Bangkok in July 2004; assigned to construct three new lines totalling 94 km in length, including: 27-km Blue Line (Hua Lamphong–Bang Khae; Bang Sue–Tha Phra); 24-km Orange Line (Bang Kapi–Bang Bumru); and 43-km Purple Line (Bang Yai–Rat Burana); Gov. PRAPAT CHONGSANGUAN.

ROADS

The total length of the road network was an estimated 53,436 km in 2001. A network of toll roads has been introduced in Bangkok in an attempt to alleviate the city's severe congestion problems.

Bangkok Mass Transit Authority (BMTA): 131 Thanon Thiam Ruammit, Huay Kwang, Bangkok 10310; tel. (2) 246-0973; fax (2) 247-2189; e-mail cnai.bmta@motc.go.th; internet www.bmta.co.th; controls Bangkok's urban transport system; Chair. JARUPONG REUNGSUWAN; Dir and Sec. POKSAK SETHABUTR.

Department of Highways: Thanon Sri Ayudhaya, Ratchathevi, Bangkok 10400; tel. (2) 245-9912; e-mail doh_pr@yahoo.com; internet www.doh.mot.go.th; Dir-Gen. TERDSAK SEDTHAMANOP.

Department of Land Transport: 1032 Thanon Phaholyothin, Chatuchak, Bangkok 10900; tel. (2) 272-5671; fax (2) 272-5680; e-mail admin@dlt.go.th; internet www.dlt.go.th; Dir-Gen. PREECHA ORPRASIRTH.

Express Transportation Organization of Thailand (ETO): 485/1 Thanon Sri Ayudhaya, Ratchathevi, Bangkok 10400; tel. (2) 245-3231; e-mail eto_001@mot.go.th; internet www.eto.mot.go.th; f. 1947; Pres. KOVIT THANYARATTAKUL.

SHIPPING

There is an extensive network of canals, providing transport for bulk goods. The port of Bangkok is an important shipping junction for South-East Asia, and consists of 37 berths for conventional and container vessels.

Marine Department: 1278 Thanon Yotha, Talardnoi, Samphanthawong, Bangkok 10100; tel. (2) 233-1311; fax (2) 236-7148; e-mail marine@md.go.th; internet www.md.go.th; Dir-Gen. TAWALYARAT ONSIRA.

Office of the Maritime Promotion Commission: 19 Thanon Phra Atit, Bangkok 10200; tel. (2) 281-9367; e-mail motc@motc.go.th; internet www.ompc.moto.go.th; f. 1979; Sec.-Gen. SOMSAK PIENSAKOOL.

Port Authority of Thailand: 444 Thanon Tarua, Klongtoey, Bangkok 10110; tel. (2) 269-3000; fax (2) 249-0885; e-mail patonline@port.or.th; internet www.port.or.th; 18 berths at Bangkok Port, 12 berths at Laem Chabang Port; scheduled for transfer to private sector in 2005; Chair. SATHIRAPAN KEYANONT; Dir-Gen. TAWANLYARAT ONSIRA.

THAILAND

Principal Shipping Companies

Jutha Maritime Public Co Ltd: Mano Tower, 2nd Floor, 153 Soi 39, Thanon Sukhumvit, Bangkok 10110; tel. (2) 260-0050; fax (2) 259-9825; e-mail jutha@loxinfo.co.th; services between Thailand, Malaysia, Korea, Japan and Viet Nam; Chair. Rear-Adm. CHANO PHENJATI; Man. Dir CHANET PHENJATI.

Precious Shipping Public Co Ltd: Cathay House, 7th Floor, 8/30 Thanon Sathorn Nua, Khet Bangrak, Bangkok 10500; tel. (2) 696-8800; fax (2) 633-8460; e-mail psl@preciousshipping.com; internet www.preciousshipping.com; Chair. Adm. AMNARD CHANDANAMATTHA; Man. Dir HASHIM KHALID MOINUDDIN.

Regional Container Lines Public Co Ltd: Panjathani Tower, 30th Floor, 127/35 Thanon Ratchadaphisek, Chongnonsee Yannawa, Bangkok 10120; tel. (2) 296-1088; fax (2) 296-1098; e-mail rclbkk@rclgroup.com; Chair. KUA PHEK LONG; Pres. SUMATE TANTHUWANIT.

Siam United Services Public Co Ltd: 30 Thanon Ratburana, Bangprakok, Ratburana, Bangkok 10140; tel. (2) 428-0029; fax (2) 427-6270; f. 1977; Chair. and Man. Dir MONGKHOL SIMAROJ.

Thai International Maritime Enterprises Ltd: Sarasin Bldg, 5th Floor, 14 Thanon Surasak, Bangkok 10500; tel. (2) 236-8835; services from Bangkok to Japan; Chair. and Man. Dir SUN SUNDISAMRIT.

Thai Maritime Navigation Co Ltd: Manorom Bldg, 15th Floor, 51 Thanon Rama IV, Klongtoey, Bangkok 10110; tel. (2) 672-8690; fax (2) 249-0108; e-mail tmn@tmn.co.th; internet www.tmn.co.th; services from Bangkok to Japan, the USA, Europe and ASEAN countries; Chair. VORASUGDI VORAPAMORN; Vice-Chair. ORMSIN CHIVAPRUCK.

Thai Mercantile Marine Ltd: 599/1 Thanon Chua Phloeng, Klongtoey, Bangkok 10110; tel. (2) 240-2582; fax (2) 249-5656; e-mail tmmbkk@asiaaccess.net.th; f. 1967; services between Japan and Thailand; Chair. SUTHAM TANPHAIBUL; Man. Dir TANAN TANPHAIBUL.

Thai Petroleum Transports Co Ltd: 355 Thanon Sunthornkosa, POB 2172, Klongtoey, Bangkok 10110; tel. (2) 249-0255; Chair. C. CHOWKWANYUN; Man. Capt. B. HAM.

Thoresen Thai Agencies Public Co Ltd: 26/26–27 Orakarn Bldg, 8th Floor, 26–27 Soi Chidlom, Thanon Ploenchit, Kwang Lumpinee, Khet Pathumwan, Bangkok 10330; tel. (2) 254-8437; fax (2) 655-5631; e-mail tta@thoresen.com; shipowner, liner operator, shipping agent in Thailand and Viet Nam; ship repairs, offshore and diving services; Chair. M. R. CHANDRAM S. CHANDRATAT; Man. Dir M. L. CHANDCHUTHA CHANDRATAT.

Unithai Group: 11th Floor, 25 Alma Link Bldg, Soi Chidlom, Thanon Ploenchit, Pathumwan, Bangkok 10330; tel. (2) 254-8400; fax (2) 253-3093; e-mail gerrit.d@unithai.com; internet www.unithai.com; regular containerized/break-bulk services to Europe, Africa and Far East; also bulk shipping/chartering; Chair. SIVAVONG CHANGKASIRI; CEO NARONG BOONYASAQUAN.

CIVIL AVIATION

Bangkok, Chiang Mai, Chiang Rai, Hat Yai, Phuket and Surat Thani airports are of international standard. U-Tapao is an alternative airport. In May 1991 plans were approved to build a new airport at Nong Ngu Hao, south-east of Bangkok, at an estimated cost of US $1,200m. Construction began in 1995, and the project was scheduled for completion in 2000. In January 1997, however, it was announced that, owing to the Government's financial problems, the Nong Ngu Hao project was to be suspended; priority was, instead, to be given to the existing airport at Don Muang in Bangkok, which was to be expanded to handle 45m. passengers annually by 2007, compared with 25m. in 1997. In December 2001 construction of the passenger terminal complex of Bangkok's second airport, Suvarnabhumi International Airport, commenced. The project was scheduled for completion in 2005; however, it was subsequently announced that construction was unlikely to be completed before July 2006.

Airports of Thailand Public Co Ltd (AOT): 333 Thanon Cherdwutagard, Don Muang, Bangkok 10210; tel. (2) 535-1111; fax (2) 531-5559; e-mail aotpr@airportthai.co.th; internet www.airportthai.co.th; f. 1998; Pres. BANCHA PATTANAPORN (acting).

Department of Civil Aviation: 71 Soi Ngarmduplee, Thanon Rama IV, Tung Mahamek, Sathorn District, Bangkok 10120; tel. (2) 287-0320; fax (2) 286-3373; e-mail dca@aviation.go.th; internet www.aviation.go.th; f. 1963; Dir-Gen. CHAISAK ANGKASUWAN.

Air Andaman: 87 Nailert Bldg, 4th Floor, Unit 402A, Thanon Sukhumvit, Bangkok; tel. (2) 251-4905; fax (2) 655-2378; internet www.airandaman.com; f. 2000; regional, scheduled passenger and charter services; Pres. ATICHART ATHAKRAVISUNTHORN.

Bangkok Airways: 99 Mu 14, Thanon Vibhavadirangsit, Chom Phon, Chatuchak, Bangkok 10900; tel. (2) 265-5678; fax (2) 265-5500; e-mail reservation@bangkokair.com; internet www.bangkokair.com; f. 1968 as Sahakol Air; name changed as above in 1989; privately owned; scheduled and charter passenger services to regional and domestic destinations; Pres. and CEO Dr PRASERT PRASARTTONG-OSOTH.

Kampuchea Airlines (OX): 138/70 Jewellery Centre, 17th Floor, Thanon Nares, Bangrak, Bangkok 10500; tel. (2) 267-3210; fax (2) 267-3216; e-mail bondmx@yahoo.com; f. 1997; owned by Cambodian govt (51%) and Orient Thai Airlines (49%); regional passenger flights from Phnom-Penh to Hong Kong and Bangkok; CEO UDOM TANTIPRASONGCHAI.

Nok Air: 89 Thanon Vibhavadi Rangsit, Bangkok 10900; tel. (2) 513-0121; fax (2) 513-0203; e-mail public.info@thaiairways.co.th; f. 2004; 39%-owned by Thai Airways International Public Co Ltd; flights to six domestic destinations; CEO PATEE SARASIN.

One-Two-Go: 138/70 17th Floor, Jewellery Centre, Thanon Nares, Bangrak, Bangkok 10500; tel. (2) 267-3210; fax (2) 267-3216; e-mail info@orient-thai.com; internet www.onetwo-go.com; f. 2003; subsidiary of Orient Thai Airlines; low-cost domestic flights; CEO UDOM TANTIPRASONGCHAI.

Orient Thai Airlines: 138/70 17th Floor, Jewellery Centre, Thanon Nares, Bangrak, Bangkok 10500; tel. (2) 267-2999; fax (2) 267-3217; e-mail info@orient-thai.com; internet www.orient-thai.com; f. 1993 as Orient Express Air; domestic and international flights; CEO and Man. Dir UDOM TANTIPRASONGCHAI.

PB Air: 101 Thanon Samsen, Bangkok 10300; tel. (2) 261-0271; fax (2) 261-0229; e-mail admin@pbair.com; internet www.pbair.com; f. 1990; scheduled domestic passenger services; Chair. PIYA BHIROM BHAKDI.

Phuket Airlines: 1168/102, 34th Floor, Lumpini Tower Bldg, Thanon Rama IV, Thungmahamek, Bangkok 10120; tel. (62) 679-8999; fax (62) 679-8236; e-mail info@phuketairlines.com; internet www.phuketairlines.com; f. 1999; domestic passenger services linking Ranong to Bangkok, Had Yai and Phuket; Pres. VIKROM AISIRI.

Thai AirAsia Co Ltd: Bangkok; internet www.airasia.com; f. 2004; jt venture between Shin Corpn Public Co Ltd (51%) and Malaysia's Air Asia Sdn Bhd (49%); low-cost domestic flights; CEO TASSAPON BIJLEVELD.

Thai Airways International Public Co Ltd (THAI): 89 Thanon Vibhavadi Rangsit, Bangkok 10900; tel. (2) 513-0121; fax (2) 513-0203; e-mail public.info@thaiairways.co.th; internet www.thaiair.com; f. 1960; 93% govt-owned; shares listed in July 1991, began trading in July 1992; merged with Thai Airways Co in 1988; scheduled for partial privatization in late 2000; domestic services from Bangkok to 20 cities; international services to over 50 destinations in Australasia, Europe, North America and Asia; Chair. THANONG BHIDAYA; Pres. KANOK ABHIRADEE.

Tourism

Thailand is a popular tourist destination, noted for its temples, palaces, beaches and islands. In 2004 tourist arrivals totalled 11,737,413. Tourism is Thailand's largest single source of foreign exchange. Revenue from tourism was an estimated 384,360m. baht in 2004.

Tourism Authority of Thailand (TAT): 1600 Thanon New Phetburi, Makkasan, Rachathewi, Bangkok 10400; tel. (2) 250-5500; fax (2) 250-5511; e-mail center@tat.or.th; internet www.tat.or.th; f. 1960; Chair. SONTHAYA KHUNPLERM; Gov. JUTHAMAS SIRIWAN.

Tourist Association of Northern Thailand: 51/20 Thanon Mahidol (Northern Tour), Chiang Mai 50100; tel. (53) 276-848; fax (53) 272-394; Pres. AURAWAN NIMANANDA.

TIMOR-LESTE
(EAST TIMOR)
Introductory Survey

Location, Climate, Language, Religion, Flag, Capital

The Democratic Republic of Timor-Leste, which is styled Timor Loro Sa'e (Timor of the rising sun) in the principal indigenous language, Tetum, occupies the eastern half of the island of Timor, which lies off the north coast of Western Australia. The western half of the island is Indonesian territory and constitutes part of the East Nusa Tenggara Province. In addition to the eastern half of Timor island, the territory also includes an enclave around Oecusse (Oekussi) Ambeno on the north-west coast of the island, and the islands of Ataúro (Pulo Cambing) and Jaco (Pulo Jako). Timor's climate is dominated by intense monsoon rain, succeeded by a pronounced dry season. The north coast of the island has a brief rainy season from December to February; the south coast a double rainy season from December to June, with a respite in March. The mountainous spine of the island has heavy rains that feed torrential floods. Tetum and Portuguese are the official languages. More than 30 languages are in use in Timor-Leste. The predominant religion is Christianity; 86% of the population were adherents of Roman Catholicism in 1997. Islam and animism are also practised. A national flag was officially adopted on 20 May 2002. The flag (proportions 1 by 2) displays a black triangle at the hoist (approximately one-third of the length of the flag) overlapping a yellow triangle (approximately one-half of the length of the flag) on a red background. The black triangle bears a five-pointed white star with one point aimed at the upper hoist corner. The capital is Dili.

Recent History

The Portuguese began trading in Timor in about 1520, principally for sandalwood, and they later established settlements and several ports on the island. They were forced to move to the north and east of the island by the Dutch, who had arrived in the early part of the 18th century and had established themselves at Kupana in the south-west. The division of the island between Portugal and the Netherlands was formalized in a treaty of 1859, although the boundaries were modified slightly in 1904. Portuguese Timor and Macao were administered as a single entity until 1896, when Portuguese Timor became a separate province. The eastern half remained a Portuguese overseas province when the Dutch recognized the western area as part of Indonesia in 1949.

The military coup in Portugal in April 1974 was followed by increased political activity in Portuguese Timor. In August 1975 the União Democrática Timorense (UDT, Timorese Democratic Union) demanded independence for Timor. The UDT allied with two other parties, the Associação Popular Democrática de Timor (APODETI) and Kota, against the alleged threat of a Communist regime being established by the Frente Revolucionária do Timor Leste Independente (Fretilin, Revolutionary Front for an Independent East Timor), and fighting broke out. The UDT forces were supported by the Indonesians. Gains on both sides were uneven, with Fretilin in control of Dili in mid-September. In the same month the Portuguese administration abandoned the capital and moved to the offshore island of Ataúro. A Portuguese attempt to arrange peace talks was rejected in October. The Indonesians intervened directly and by the beginning of December Indonesian troops controlled the capital. Portuguese-Indonesian peace talks in Rome in November were unsuccessful, and diplomatic relations were suspended after Indonesian military involvement. Two meetings of the UN Security Council voted for immediate withdrawal of Indonesian troops. Fretilin's unilateral declaration of independence in November was recognized in December by the People's Republic of China. In December the enclave of Oecusse (Oekussi) Ambeno in West Timor was declared part of Indonesian territory. In May 1976 the People's Representative Council of East Timor voted for integration with Indonesia. The UN did not recognize the composition of the Council as being representative, however, and by mid-1976 the Portuguese had not formally ceded the right to govern, although they had no remaining presence in the territory.

In July 1976 East Timor was declared the 27th province of Indonesia. Human rights organizations claimed that as many as 200,000 people, from a total population of 650,000, might have been killed by the Indonesian armed forces during the annexation. In February 1983 the UN Commission on Human Rights adopted a resolution affirming East Timor's right to independence and self-determination. In September, following a five-month cease-fire (during which government representatives negotiated with Fretilin), the armed forces launched a major new offensive. The rebels suffered a serious set-back in August 1985, when the Australian Government recognized Indonesia's incorporation of East Timor. In November 1988 Gen. Suharto, the President of Indonesia, visited East Timor, prior to announcing that travel restrictions (in force since the annexation in 1976) were to be withdrawn. The territory was opened to visitors in December. In October 1989 the Pope visited East Timor, as part of a tour of Indonesia, and made a plea to the Government to halt violations of human rights. In November 1990 the Government rejected proposals by the military commander of Fretilin, José Alexandre (Xanana) Gusmão, for unconditional peace negotiations aimed at ending the armed struggle in East Timor.

In 1991 tension in East Timor increased prior to a proposed visit by a Portuguese parliamentary delegation. Some Timorese alleged that the armed forces had initiated a campaign of intimidation to discourage demonstrations during the Portuguese visit. The mission, which was to have taken place in November, was postponed, owing to Indonesia's objection to the inclusion of an Australian journalist who was a prominent critic of Indonesia's policies in East Timor. In November the armed forces fired on a peaceful demonstration (believed to have been originally organized to coincide with the Portuguese visit) at the funeral of a separatist sympathizer in Dili. The Indonesian Armed Forces (ABRI), which admitted killing 20 civilians, claimed that the attack had been provoked by armed Fretilin activists. Independent observers and human rights groups refuted this and estimated the number of deaths at between 100 and 180. There were also subsequent allegations of the summary execution of as many as 100 witnesses. Under intense international pressure, Suharto established a National Investigation Commission. The impartiality of the Commission was challenged, however, on the grounds that it excluded non-governmental organizations, and Fretilin announced that it would boycott the investigation. Despite this, the Commission's findings received cautious foreign approbation, as they were mildly critical of ABRI and stated that 50 people had died, and 90 disappeared, in the massacre. The senior military officers in East Timor were replaced, and 14 members of the armed forces were tried by a military tribunal. The most severe penalty received by any of the soldiers involved was 18 months' imprisonment; this contrasted starkly with the sentences of convicted demonstrators, which ranged from five years' to life imprisonment.

In July 1992 Indonesia and Portugal agreed to resume discussions on East Timor under the auspices of the UN Secretary-General (although without a representative from Fretilin, which had indicated in May that it was prepared to take part in the negotiations). In August the UN General Assembly adopted its first resolution condemning Indonesia's violations of fundamental human rights in East Timor. In September the appointment of Abílio Soares as Governor of East Timor provoked widespread criticism in the province; although Soares was a native of East Timor, he was a leading advocate of the Indonesian occupation. In October the US Congress suspended defence training aid to Indonesia, in protest at the killing of separatist demonstrators in November 1991. In October 1992, prior to the anniversary of the massacre, Amnesty International reported that hundreds of suspected supporters of independence had been arrested and tortured to prevent a commemorative demonstration.

In November 1992 Xanana Gusmão was arrested. He was subsequently taken to Jakarta, where he was to be tried in February 1993 on charges of subversion and illegal possession of firearms. Xanana Gusmão's detention provoked international concern, and his replacement as leader of Fretilin, António Gomes da Costa (Mau Huno—who was himself arrested in April), claimed that his predecessor had been tortured. Two weeks after his capture, Xanana Gusmão publicly recanted his opposition to Indonesian rule in East Timor and advised Fretilin members to surrender. It transpired, however, that he was only co-operating with the authorities in order to gain the opportunity to speak publicly at a later date. During his trial, he was prevented from reading a prepared statement; the document was, however, illicitly conveyed to the press and was widely disseminated. In May Xanana Gusmão was found guilty of rebellion, conspiracy, attempting to establish a separate state and illegal possession of weapons, and was condemned to life imprisonment. The sentence was commuted to 20 years by Suharto in August. During the same month it was announced that all government combat forces were to be withdrawn from East Timor, leaving only troops involved in development projects. In September, however, the new acting leader of Fretilin, Konis Santana, declared that, contrary to announcements, the Indonesians were renewing their forces in East Timor and that killings and atrocities continued.

In December 1993 Xanana Gusmão managed to convey letters to the Portuguese Government and the International Commission of Jurists demanding an annulment of his trial, owing to the lack of impartiality of his defence lawyer. The Government subsequently banned Xanana Gusmão from receiving visitors. Also in December the first reconciliation talks took place in the United Kingdom between an Indonesian government official and a former leader of Timorese exiles opposed to Indonesia's occupation of East Timor. In January 1994 Indonesia announced to the UN Secretary-General's envoy that it would facilitate access to East Timor by human rights and UN organizations. In May, however, a privately-organized human rights conference being held in the Philippines, entitled the Asia-Pacific Conference on East Timor, provoked diplomatic tension with the Indonesian Government, which had attempted to force the abandonment of the conference. The outcome of the conference was the establishment of an Asia-Pacific coalition on East Timor, which consisted mainly of non-governmental organizations active in the region.

In July 1994 the Indonesian authorities suppressed a demonstration in Dili, following weeks of increasing tension in the capital; at least three people were reportedly killed during the protest. In August it was reported that the armed forces had held talks with Xanana Gusmão, included in which was the discussion of the possibility of holding a referendum under the auspices of the UN to determine the future status of the disputed territory. A second round of reconciliation talks between Indonesian officials and East Timorese exiles was held between late September and early October in the United Kingdom, and was attended by a UN envoy, although the main East Timorese opposition groups opposed the discussions, on the grounds that the participating East Timorese exiles were mostly in favour of Indonesian rule. The Indonesian Minister of Foreign Affairs, Ali Alatas, also held discussions in October in New York, USA, with José Ramos Horta, the Secretary for International Relations of Fretilin, the first such talks to be officially recognized. At the beginning of November President Suharto agreed to hold talks with exiled East Timorese dissidents. The Government's increasingly conciliatory position on East Timor was, however, reported largely to be a superficial attempt to improve the country's human rights image prior to the holding of the Asia-Pacific Economic Co-operation (APEC, see p. 164) summit meeting in Bogor, 60 km south of Jakarta, in mid-November.

In January 1995 Alatas, the Portuguese Minister of Foreign Affairs and the UN Secretary-General met in Geneva, Switzerland, for the fifth round of talks on East Timor. Agreement was reached to convene a meeting between separatist and pro-integrationist Timorese activists under the auspices of the UN, called the All-Inclusive Intra-East Timorese Dialogue (AETD). The AETD, which was held in June 1995, March 1996 and October 1997, failed to achieve any conclusive progress. The sixth and seventh rounds of talks between the Portuguese and Indonesian ministers responsible for foreign affairs took place in July 1995 and January 1996, again with little progress.

In September 1995 the worst rioting that year took place in protest against Indonesian Muslim immigrants, following an Indonesian prison official's alleged insult to Roman Catholicism. Mosques and Muslim businesses were burned, and some Muslims were forced to flee the island. Further riots erupted in October, in which rival groups of separatists and integrationists clashed on the streets. The Roman Catholic Apostolic Administrator in Dili, the Rt Rev. Carlos Filipe Ximenes Belo, persuaded the rioters to return home following an agreement with ABRI; however, the agreement was subsequently broken by the armed forces, who arrested more than 250 alleged rioters.

From September 1995 East Timorese activists began forcing entry into foreign embassies in Jakarta and appealing for political asylum. They were granted asylum by the Portuguese, who were still officially recognized by the UN as the administrative power in East Timor. The Indonesian Government permitted the asylum-seekers to leave, but denied that there was any persecution in East Timor. The culmination of the successful campaign was the storming in December of the Dutch and Russian embassies by 58 and 47 activists respectively. The demonstrators, some of whom were non-Timorese and belonged to a radical group called the People's Democratic Union, demanded unsuccessfully a meeting with the UN High Commissioner for Human Rights, José Ayala Lasso, who was visiting Indonesia and who, following a brief visit to East Timor, confirmed the occurrence of severe violations of human rights in the province.

In February 1996 President Suharto and the Portuguese Prime Minister met in Bangkok, Thailand (the first meeting on East Timor by heads of government). During the negotiations Portugal offered to re-establish diplomatic links in return for the release of Xanana Gusmão and the guarantee of human rights in East Timor. International awareness of East Timor was heightened in October, when Belo and José Ramos Horta were jointly awarded the Nobel Prize for Peace. The Indonesian Government, displeased with the Nobel committee's choice, declared that there would be no change in its policy on East Timor. Four days after the announcement of the award, Suharto visited East Timor for the first time in eight years.

Following the announcement of the Nobel Peace Prize, Bishop Belo repeated demands that the Government conduct a referendum on the issue of autonomy for East Timor. In November 1996 he became involved in a controversy regarding an interview that he had given to a German periodical, Der Spiegel, which quoted several controversial remarks, allegedly made by Belo, about the treatment of the East Timorese people by the Indonesian Government and ABRI. Belo denied having made the remarks, but was requested to appear before a parliamentary commission in Jakarta to explain the matter. This controversy, and the temporary confiscation of Belo's passport by the Indonesian authorities (which threatened to prevent Belo's visit to Norway to receive the Nobel award), prompted five days of demonstrations in his support in Dili. The rallies were reportedly the largest since 1975, but were conducted peacefully.

The award of the Nobel Peace Prize to José Ramos Horta proved even more controversial. The Governor of East Timor accused Ramos Horta of ordering the torture and killing of East Timorese people. Ramos Horta himself declared that the award should have been made to Xanana Gusmão and invited the Indonesian Government to enter into serious negotiations on the future of East Timor. Ramos Horta was banned from visiting the Philippines for the duration of an APEC summit meeting which took place there in late 1996; this ban was subsequently extended.

In November 1996 the Indonesian Government withdrew permission for foreign journalists to visit East Timor, where they had planned to attend a press conference conducted by Belo. In December Ramos Horta and Belo attended the Nobel Prize ceremony in Oslo, Norway. Riots in Dili (following a gathering of Belo's supporters to welcome him upon his return) resulted in the death of a member of ABRI; it was reported later in the month that at least one East Timorese citizen had been killed by the Indonesian authorities in a raid to capture those believed to be responsible for the soldier's death. (It was, however, generally recognized by non-governmental organizations working in East Timor that the Indonesian authorities had become more lenient about allowing demonstrations in 1996.)

Following an increase in clashes between resistance forces and ABRI prior to the general election, in June 1997 a military commander of Fretilin, David Alex, was apprehended by the Indonesian armed forces. His subsequent death in custody was highly controversial; resistance groups rejected the official explanation that he had been fatally injured in a clash with security forces and claimed that he had been tortured to death. Guerrilla activity subsequently intensified and in September at least seven Indonesian soldiers were killed in a clash with resistance forces. Further fighting took place in November and December.

In July 1997 the President of South Africa, Nelson Mandela, met Xanana Gusmão, with the approval of Suharto. Mandela subsequently announced that he had written to Suharto to request the prisoner's release. In September Mandela continued his attempts to mediate in the Timorese conflict by holding talks with Bishop Belo; despite international optimism, however, Mandela's initiative ultimately proved fruitless.

In November 1997 the Australia-East Timor Association released a report cataloguing human rights abuses perpetrated by members of the Indonesian armed forces against Timorese women; abuses cited in the report included enforced prostitution, rape and compulsory sterilization programmes. Also in November shots were fired when Indonesian troops stormed the campus of the University of East Timor in Dili, following a vigil held by students to commemorate the massacre in Dili in 1991. According to reports, at least one student was killed in the incident, a number of others were injured and many were arrested. Belo accused the Indonesian security forces of having used 'excessive force', and this was confirmed by a report made by the Indonesian National Commission on Human Rights in early December. Also in December the Commission demanded the abolition of the country's anti-subversion legislation. In the same month two Timorese were sentenced to death under the legislation for their part in an ambush of election security officials earlier in the year, prompting threats of increased guerrilla activities by separatist forces, and a further four were sentenced to 12 years' imprisonment for taking part in armed resistance operations. Meanwhile, Abílio Soares, who had been re-elected as Governor of East Timor in September, ordered the arrest of the leaders of the recently formed Movement for the Reconciliation and Unity of the People of East Timor (MRUPT), which he declared to be a proscribed movement.

In January 1998 Ramos Horta attempted to exploit the Government's economic difficulties by urging Suharto to agree to a cease-fire and to co-operate with the UN in creating protection zones to ensure the safety of disarmed resistance fighters; the Government, however, failed to respond to his requests. In the same month it was announced that a Timorese resistance congress that was due to be held in Portugal in March was to be replaced by a national convention to ensure the participation of the UDT. The convention, held in April, unanimously approved the 'Magna Carta' of East Timor, a charter intended to provide the basis for the constitution of future self-determination within the territory, and ratified plans for the establishment of the National Council of Timorese Resistance (CNRT), a body intended to give the Timorese resistance movement a single national structure and to bring together representatives of the defunct National Council of Maubere Resistance (CNRM), Fretilin and the UDT. Xanana Gusmão was appointed President of the new CNRT, and Ramos Horta was named as Vice-President. In March 1998, meanwhile, Konis Santana, the acting military leader of Fretilin, died following an accident; Taur Matan Ruak was appointed as his successor.

The accession of B. J. Habibie to the Indonesian presidency in May 1998 raised hopes that independence for East Timor might be granted in the near future. However, while President Habibie publicly suggested that the territory might be given a new 'special' status within Indonesia and that troops might be withdrawn, there was no initial indication that the Government was contemplating independence for the territory. While a number of prominent political prisoners were released soon after Habibie replaced Suharto as President, Xanana Gusmão's 20-year sentence was reduced by a mere four months. Following the killing of an East Timorese youth by Indonesian soldiers in June, the Government renewed efforts to demonstrate its conciliatory position and, in late July, effected a much-publicized withdrawal of a limited number of troops from the territory. However, opposition groups subsequently claimed that fresh troops were being sent by the Indonesian Government to replace those leaving (a claim denied by Indonesian military leaders).

In August 1998 it was announced that Indonesia and Portugal had agreed to hold discussions on the possibility of 'wide-ranging' autonomy for East Timor, and in early November the UN was reported to be opening discussions with the two countries regarding a UN plan for extensive autonomy for the territory. Following an outbreak of severe violence in the Alas region of East Timor later that month, in which 82 people were reported to have been killed, Portugal suspended its involvement in the talks; however, in January 1999 it was announced that the talks were to resume. During his visit to East Timor in December 1998, UN special envoy Jamsheed Marker held talks with both Xanana Gusmão and Belo; in the same month, Xanana Gusmão reportedly advocated that the Timorese people should consider the UN's proposal for autonomy, but only as a transitional stage prior to the holding of a referendum (the possibility of which, in December, was still ruled out by the Indonesian Government).

In January 1999 the Australian Government announced a significant change in its policy on East Timor, stating that it intended actively to promote 'self-determination' in the territory (although the precise intended meaning of 'self-determination' remained unclear). Later the same month, total independence for East Timor in the near future emerged as an apparent possibility when, in its boldest move to date to appease the East Timorese and the international community, the Indonesian Government suggested that a vote might be held in the national legislature, the Majelis Permusyawaratan Rakyat (MPR, People's Consultative Assembly), following the election to the House of Representatives (part of the MPR) scheduled for June, on the issue of Indonesia's granting independence to the territory. As a result of a request from the UN Secretary-General, Kofi Annan, the Government also announced that it was to allow Xanana Gusmão to serve the remainder of his 20-year prison sentence under house arrest in Jakarta. Following the Government's announcement regarding the possibility of independence for East Timor, a number of outbreaks of violence, attributed to supporters of the territory's integration with Indonesia, were reported to have occurred.

On 27 January 1999 the Indonesian Government unexpectedly announced that, if the East Timorese voted to reject Indonesia's proposals for autonomy, it would consider granting independence to the province. Although the Indonesian Government was initially opposed to a referendum on the issue of independence for East Timor, it signed an agreement with Portugal on 5 May, giving its assent to a process of 'popular consultation' taking the form of a UN-supervised poll to determine the future status of East Timor. The UN Mission in East Timor (UNAMET) was established by the UN Security Council in June to organize the poll in which the East Timorese could opt for a form of political autonomy or for independence. The 'popular consultation' was initially scheduled to be held on 8 August, and all East Timorese, including those living in exile, were to be allowed to participate in the ballot.

Following the announcement of the scheduled referendum, violence in the territory escalated. Anti-independence militia groups based within East Timor initiated a campaign of violence and intimidation in advance of the poll, which included summary killings, kidnappings, harassment and the forced recruitment of young East Timorese. The Indonesian military itself was discovered to be not only supporting but also recruiting, training and organizing many of the militias. Violence continued to escalate throughout the territory during April and May 1999. In one incident in April anti-independence militia members massacred 57 people in a churchyard in the town of Liquiça (Likisia); further massacres were reported to have occurred in other areas, including Dili. Also in April Xanana Gusmão (who in February had been moved from Cipinang prison in Jakarta to serve the remainder of his 20-year sentence under effective house arrest in the capital) responded to the increasing violence from anti-independence militias by reversing his previous position and urging guerrillas in Fretilin's military wing, the Forças Armadas Libertação Nacional de Timor Leste (Falintil), to resume their struggle. Although rival pro-independence and integrationist factions signed a peace accord in June supporting a cease-fire and disarmament in advance of the scheduled referendum, the violence continued unabated.

The escalating violence in the territory, together with logistical difficulties, led the UN to postpone the referendum to 21 August 1999 and then to 30 August. Although intimidation and violence by the militias continued, the referendum proceeded on 30 August. About 98.5% of those eligible to vote participated in the poll, which resulted in an overwhelming rejection, by 78.5% of voters, of the Indonesian Government's proposals for autonomy and in the endorsement of independence for East Timor. The announcement of the result of the referendum, however, precipitated a rapid descent into anarchy. Pro-Jakarta militias embarked upon a campaign of murder and destruction in which hundreds of civilians were killed; as many as 500,000 (according to the UN) were forced to flee their homes, and many buildings were destroyed in arson attacks. While many of those who were displaced from their homes sought refuge in the hills, about one-half were estimated by the UN to have left the territory (a large number having entered West

Timor), some involuntarily. In one incident during the campaign of extreme violence that followed the announcement of the result of the referendum, anti-independence militia members stormed the residence of Bishop Belo, evicting at gunpoint some 6,000 refugees who had sought shelter in the compound; the home of the bishop was burned down and dozens of East Timorese were reported to have been killed in the attack. Bishop Belo was evacuated to Australia, while Xanana Gusmão (who was released from house arrest in Jakarta by the Indonesian Government on 7 September) took refuge in the British embassy in Jakarta. Thousands of civilians besieged the UN compound in Dili, the premises of other international agencies, churches and police stations, seeking protection from the indiscriminate attacks of the militias. On 7 September martial law was declared in the territory, and a curfew was imposed. The violence continued unabated, however, and in mid-September, following international condemnation of the situation and intense diplomatic pressure, the Indonesian Government reversed its earlier opposition to a proposal by the Australian Government and agreed to permit the deployment of a multi-national peace-keeping force. As the massacre of civilians continued, thousands of refugees were airlifted to safety in northern Australia, along with the remaining employees of the UN (many local staff members of UNAMET were among the victims of the violence); shortly after the UN withdrew its staff, anti-independence militia members set fire to the UN compound in Dili. Meanwhile, aid agencies warned that as many as 300,000 East Timorese people would starve if humanitarian assistance were not urgently provided.

The first contingent of several thousand UN peace-keeping troops, forming the International Force for East Timor (Interfet), was deployed in the territory on 20 September 1999. Led by Australia, which committed 4,500 troops, the force gradually restored order. A week later the Indonesian armed forces formally relinquished responsibility for security to the multi-national force. At the end of October, after 24 years as an occupying force, the last Indonesian soldiers left East Timor. In late September Indonesia and Portugal reiterated their agreement for the transfer of authority in East Timor to the UN. On 19 October the result of the referendum was ratified by the MPR, thus permitting East Timor's accession to independence to proceed. Shortly thereafter, on 25 October, the UN Security Council established the UN Transitional Administration in East Timor (UNTAET—subsequently the UN Mission of Support in East Timor—UNMISET) as an integrated peace-keeping operation fully responsible for the administration of East Timor during its transition to independence. UNTAET, with an initial mandate until 31 January 2001, was to exercise all judicial and executive authority in East Timor, to undertake the establishment and training of a new police force, and to assume responsibility for the co-ordination and provision of humanitarian assistance and emergency rehabilitation; the transfer of command of military operations in the territory from Interfet to the UNTAET peace-keeping force was completed on 23 February 2000. Meanwhile, the UN also began a large-scale emergency humanitarian relief effort; however, many displaced and homeless East Timorese remained without access to adequate food supplies, shelter and basic health-care facilities.

Following reports that in mid-October 1999 Indonesian troops and militias had entered the isolated East Timorese enclave of Oecusse (situated within West Timor) and allegedly massacred around 50 people, Interfet troops were deployed in Oecusse; most of the enclave's population of 57,000 were believed to have been removed to refugee camps in West Timor, and by early November only 10,000 of its citizens had been accounted for. Following his popularly-acclaimed return to Dili in October, Xanana Gusmão met with the UNTAET Transitional Administrator, Sérgio Vieira de Mello, in November, and reportedly communicated the concerns of local East Timorese organizations that they were being marginalized by UNTAET officials. In late November he visited Jakarta in order to establish relations with the Indonesian Government, and in early December he visited Australia, where he met with representatives of the Australian Government to discuss the Timor Gap Treaty. (The Treaty, which had been concluded between Australia and Indonesia in 1991, provided a framework for petroleum and gas exploration in the maritime zone between Australia and East Timor and for the division of any resulting royalties between Australia and Indonesia. Indonesia ceased to be party to the original Treaty when it relinquished control of East Timor in October 1999, however, and the transitional administration in East Timor subsequently expressed a desire to renegotiate the terms of the Treaty, which the UN considered to have no legal standing, as Indonesian sovereignty over East Timor had never been recognized by the international body. In February 2000 a memorandum of understanding (MOU) relating to the Treaty was signed by the Australian Government and East Timor's UN administrators, temporarily maintaining the arrangement for the division of royalties (although between Australia and East Timor rather than Australia and Indonesia). East Timor received its first payment of royalties from Australia under the MOU in October 2000. In the same month, however, the formal renegotiation of the Treaty began, with East Timor requesting the redrawing of the boundaries covered by the Treaty and a larger share of petroleum and gas royalties. Following independence in May 2002 both countries formally signed the Treaty. However, owing to prolonged negotiations over the division of royalties, Australia did not ratify the agreement until March 2003.)

On 1 December 1999 José Ramos Horta returned to East Timor after 24 years of exile. Ramos Horta, who commanded much popular support, urged the East Timorese people to show forgiveness towards their former oppressors and called for reconciliation between Indonesia and East Timor. On 11 December Vieira de Mello convened the first meeting of the National Consultative Council (NCC) in Dili; the 15-member Council, comprising members of the CNRT and other East Timorese political representatives as well as UNTAET officials, was established in late 1999 to advise UNTAET.

A number of mass graves containing the bodies of suspected victims of the violence perpetrated by the anti-independence militias both before and after the holding of the referendum in August 1999 were discovered in East Timor (including two in the Oecusse enclave) in late 1999 and early 2000. In December 1999 Sonia Picado Sotela, the Chair of the International Commission of Inquiry in East Timor, confirmed that the team of UN investigators had discovered evidence of 'systematic killing'.

In January 2000 a panel appointed by the Indonesian Government to investigate human rights abuses in East Timor delivered its report to the Indonesian Attorney-General. The panel reportedly named 24 individuals whom it recommended should be prosecuted for their alleged involvement in violations of human rights in the territory. One of those named was the former Minister of Defence and Security and Commander-in-Chief of the Indonesian armed forces, Gen. Wiranto, who had since been appointed Co-ordinating Minister for Politics and Security in the Indonesian Government; also named were a number of senior military officers, as well as leaders of the pro-Jakarta militias responsible for the extreme violence perpetrated during the period following the referendum. However, pro-independence leaders in East Timor strongly criticized the report as inadequate. In the same month the International Commission of Inquiry in East Timor recommended that the UN establish an independent international body to investigate allegations of human rights violations in East Timor, and an international tribunal to deal with the cases of those accused by the investigators. In February the recently-appointed President of Indonesia, Abdurrahman Wahid, visited East Timor and publicly apologized for the atrocities committed by the Indonesian armed forces during the Republic's occupation of the territory. Wahid reaffirmed the commitment of the Indonesian Government to the prosecution of any individuals implicated in the violation of human rights in East Timor. In the same month Wahid suspended Gen. Wiranto from the Indonesian Government. (Wiranto subsequently resigned in May.) The UN Secretary-General, Kofi Annan, made an official visit to East Timor in mid-February, during which he pledged that investigations into violations of human rights in the territory would be carried out.

In April 2000 UNTAET signed an agreement with the Indonesian Government regarding the extradition to East Timor of Indonesian citizens facing charges relating to the violence of 1999, and in July 2000 a team from the Indonesian Attorney-General's Office visited East Timor to investigate a limited number of cases of human rights violations. However, relations between East Timor and Indonesia remained tense, and the introduction in August 2000 (in the closing stages of the annual session of the country's principal legislative body, the MPR) of an amendment to Indonesia's Constitution providing for the exclusion of military personnel from retroactive prosecution prompted fears among many international observers that the possibility of the prosecution of members of the Indonesian military believed responsible for recent human rights abuses in East Timor would be placed in serious jeopardy (despite the suggestions of senior

Indonesian legislators that the amendment would probably not apply to crimes such as genocide, war crimes and terrorism). In September the Indonesian Attorney General's Office named 19 people whom it suspected of involvement in the violence of 1999. Whilst human rights groups in both East Timor and Indonesia welcomed the publication of the list, which included the names of several former high-ranking members of the Indonesian armed forces, there was widespread disappointment that Gen. Wiranto was not among those named.

In June 2000 an agreement was reached between UNTAET and East Timorese leaders on the formation of a new transitional coalition Government, in which the two sides were to share political responsibility. The Cabinet of the new transitional Government, which was formally appointed in July, initially included four East Timorese cabinet ministers: João Carrascalão, President of the UDT and a Vice-President of the CNRT, who was allocated responsibility for infrastructure; Mari Alkatiri, Secretary-General of Fretilin, who was appointed Minister for Economic Affairs; Father Filomeno Jacob, who was appointed to oversee social affairs; and Ana Pessôa, who was placed in charge of internal administration. The new Cabinet also included four international representatives. Mariano Lopes da Cruz, an East Timorese national, was appointed as Inspector-General. It was reported that Xanana Gusmão, whilst holding no formal position in the new Government, was to be consulted on an informal basis by Sérgio Vieira de Mello (who was to retain ultimate control over the approval of any draft legislation proposed to the Cabinet) with respect to all political decisions. In October the Cabinet was expanded to nine members, with the appointment of José Ramos Horta as Minister of Foreign Affairs.

In mid-July 2000 UNTAET approved the establishment of a 'National Council' to advise the new Cabinet. The East Timorese National Council, the membership of which was expanded from 33 to 36 in October, consisted of a selection of East Timorese representatives from the political, religious and private sectors. The new National Council was inaugurated on 23 October and replaced the 15-member NCC. In the same month Xanana Gusmão was elected to lead the National Council.

In August 2000, meanwhile, Xanana Gusmão retired as the Military Commander of Falintil, in order to concentrate on his political role in the process of guiding East Timor towards full independence. Xanana Gusmão relinquished control of the guerrilla army to his deputy, Taur Matan Ruak. Initially, Falintil faced an uncertain future, and the refusal of the UN to allow the active involvement of the unit in attempts to combat incursions by Indonesian paramilitaries into East Timor led Xanana Gusmão to voice indirect criticism of the international organization in his resignation speech. In February 2001, however, a new East Timorese Defence Force (ETDF) was established, consisting of an initial 650 recruits drawn exclusively from the ranks of Falintil, which was itself to be dissolved. The former Military Commander of the guerrilla army, Taur Matan Ruak, was promoted to the rank of Brigadier-General and appointed to command the new force. Meanwhile, a fund was established to finance the support and retraining of an estimated 1,000 Falintil veterans who were to be demobilized. Training of the new Defence Force was to be conducted by Portugal and Australia; its role was described as that of 'policing', with the defence of the territory remaining the responsibility of UNTAET peace-keeping troops.

In December 2000 four of the five East Timorese members of the transitional Cabinet threatened to resign, reportedly in protest at their treatment by the UN. The ministers, who allegedly claimed that they were merely 'puppet ministers' in the new coalition Government, demanded further clarification of the legal status of the Cabinet and of their authority as individual cabinet ministers, and called for the establishment of a more clearly defined relationship between UNTAET and the Cabinet. Further complaints about UNTAET's treatment of East Timorese officials were voiced at a donors' conference for East Timor held in the same month, and press reports suggested the existence of a level of public resentment of the UN's presence in East Timor. However, in January 2001 Ramos Horta warned that any attempt to scale down the UN's presence in East Timor would destabilize the territory's progression towards independence. In late January 2001 the UN Security Council extended UNTAET's mandate (which had initially been scheduled to expire on 31 January 2001) until 31 January 2002. It was acknowledged, however, that modifications of the mandate might be necessary to take into account developments in East Timor's progression towards full independence and, in January

2002, the mandate was extended until 20 May 2002, the date set for independence. From August 2000, meanwhile, in a move that allowed for greater formal East Timorese influence in the governing of the territory during the period preceding the territory's accession to full independence, a process commenced whereby the transitional Government began to be redefined as the East Timorese Transitional Administration (ETTA). Consisting of both UNTAET and East Timorese staff, ETTA was composed of the transitional Cabinet, the National Council and the judiciary. Final authority over ETTA rested with the Special Representative of the UN Secretary-General and Transitional Administrator, Sérgio Vieira de Mello.

In February 2001 legislation providing for an election to an 88-seat Constituent Assembly, to be conducted on 30 August, was approved. The single chamber was to comprise 75 deputies elected on a national basis, using proportional representation, and one elected delegate from each of East Timor's 13 districts, chosen on a 'first-past-the-post' basis. The members of the Constituent Assembly were to be responsible for the preparation and adoption of a constitution, which would require the endorsement of at least 60 members. Meanwhile, a National Constitutional Commission, comprising representatives of various groups, was to be established in order to facilitate consultation with the people of East Timor.

In March 2001 Xanana Gusmão tendered his resignation as Speaker of the National Council, having become disaffected by the stagnation of the political process. At the same time he announced that he would not stand for President in the forthcoming elections for the post, despite commanding an overwhelming level of public support for his candidacy. In April UNTAET announced that José Ramos Horta would serve as Gusmão's replacement on the National Council, prompting his resignation as the Minister for Foreign Affairs (the two posts could not be held simultaneously). However, in the 9 April election for the post of Speaker, Manuel Carrascalão emerged victorious, defeating Ramos Horta, and criticized UNTAET for supporting his rival. Two weeks later José Ramos Horta resigned from the National Council and resumed his position in the transitional Cabinet. In June the CNRT announced its dissolution, reportedly in order to enable the groups of which it was comprised to evolve into fully independent political parties, and, in August, Xanana Gusmão finally yielded to immense popular pressure and international encouragement and announced his intention to stand for the presidency in 2002.

On 30 August 2001 91.3% of the eligible populace turned out to vote in the country's first free parliamentary election. Fretilin secured 55 of the 88 seats available in the Constituent Assembly, commanding 57% of the votes cast. In second place, with seven seats, was the Partido Democrático (PD). The Partido Social Democrata (PSD) and the Associação Social-Democrata Timorense (ASDT) won six seats each. In September Sérgio Vieira de Mello swore in the members of the Constituent Assembly, and five days later the second transitional Government was appointed. Mari Alkatiri of Fretilin was appointed leader of the Cabinet and retained the economy portfolio. José Ramos Horta continued as Minister for Foreign Affairs. Of 20 available government positions, nine were allocated to Fretilin, two to the PD and the remaining nine to independents and various experts. In October the Constituent Assembly appointed a committee to oversee the drafting of the Constitution, taking into account the views of over 36,000 East Timorese summarized in reports presented by 13 Constitutional Commissions. In November 2001 the Assembly approved the structure of the draft Constitution.

In December 2000 UNTAET issued its first indictments for crimes committed against humanity in connection with the violence that had surrounded the referendum in 1999, charging 11 people (including an officer of the Indonesian special forces) with the murder of nine civilians in September 1999. In January 2001 an East Timor court sentenced a former pro-Jakarta militia member to 12 years' imprisonment for the murder of a village chief in September 1999, marking the first successful prosecution related to the violence of 1999. In September 2001 the UN filed 'extermination' charges against nine militiamen and two Indonesian soldiers accused of murdering 65 people two years previously. In October, in the first civil case of its kind, a US federal court awarded six East Timorese a total of US $66m. in damages after Indonesian Gen. Johny Lumintang was found to bear responsibility for human rights abuses. In December 2001 a UN tribunal took the first step in bringing those responsible for the atrocities committed in 1999 to justice. Of the 11 individuals indicted in December 2000, 10 were convicted of crimes against humanity and sentenced to prison terms of up to 33 years. However, the Jakarta authorities resisted the extradition of the indicted Indonesian Special Forces Officer to face trial.

In February 2000, meanwhile, the Australian Government announced that all 470 East Timorese refugees remaining in Australia were expected to be returned to East Timor by the end of the month. Also in February, however, the UN expressed its concern that very few of the estimated 90,000 East Timorese refugees remaining in camps across the border in West Timor were returning to East Timor; it had earlier been reported that pro-Jakarta militias had been intimidating the refugees in West Timor and preventing them from returning home. In September the UN temporarily suspended its relief work among East Timorese refugees in West Timor, following the murder by pro-Jakarta militias of three UN aid workers in the territory earlier in the month. The murders prompted international criticism of the Indonesian Government for its failure to control the militia groups operating in West Timor. In November Ramos Horta alleged that estimates of the number of East Timorese refugees residing in West Timor (reported by some sources to be as high as 130,000) were being deliberately exaggerated by the Indonesian Government, and estimated the actual number of refugees to be no higher than 60,000–70,000. In December 2000 and January 2001, in an attempt to dispel the fears of refugees remaining in West Timor about the security situation in East Timor, UNTAET arranged for a number of groups of refugees to visit their homeland. The visits resulted in a number of refugees opting to return permanently to East Timor.

In June 2001 refugees from East Timor participated in a process of registration through which they were permitted to decide whether or not they wished to return to the newly independent state. Of the 113,791 refugees who took part, 98% wished to remain in Indonesia. However, it was thought that intimidation by pro-Indonesia militias might have influenced the result and that the survey did not necessarily reflect the participants' long-term intentions. In the same month the six men accused of the murder of the three UN aid workers in September 2000 were found guilty of violence against people and property rather than murder and given light sentences. The UN criticized the verdicts and pressed for a review.

Following the formal declaration of the election results, the families of former East Timorese militiamen began returning to their homeland in mid-September 2001. In October the Indonesian authorities announced the imminent halting of aid to an estimated 80,000 East Timorese who remained in refugee camps in West Timor and in November Xanana Gusmão visited West Timor in an effort to promote reconciliation and encourage thousands of the remaining refugees to return home.

In October 2001 the newly elected Constituent Assembly requested that the UN formally grant East Timor independence on 20 May 2002. Xanana Gusmão reluctantly lent his support to the request, although he commented that the choice of date was too politically partisan as it commemorated the 28th anniversary of the founding of the country's first political party. However, the UN Security Council endorsed the Assembly's request, and agreed to maintain a peace-keeping presence in the region for between six months and two years after the granting of independence.

On 22 March 2002 the Constituent Assembly finally promulgated East Timor's first Constitution, which was to become effective upon independence on 20 May of that year. The document provided for the adoption of Tetum and Portuguese as the country's official languages.

On 14 April 2002 East Timor held its first presidential election, which resulted in an overwhelming victory for Xanana Gusmão, who secured almost 83% of the votes cast. The only other candidate was Francisco Xavier do Amaral. Later in the same month Madalena Brites Boavida was sworn in as Minister of Finance and Planning in the second transitional Government, following the resignation of Fernando Borges.

On 20 May 2002 East Timor celebrated its formal accession to independence, upon which it became known officially as the Democratic Republic of Timor-Leste. The tenure of the UN interim administration was officially terminated and UNTAET was replaced by a smaller mission, the UN Mission of Support in East Timor (UNMISET), which was to remain in the country for two years to support administrative development and to assist in the maintenance of law and order, whilst downsizing its military presence as rapidly as possible. Xanana Gusmão was officially inaugurated as President and swore in the country's first Government. Parliament then held its inaugural session. Prime Minister Alkatiri stressed that the new Government would give priority to spending on health and education. The President of Indonesia, Megawati Sukarnoputri, attended the independence day celebrations, despite criticism from several members of the Indonesian legislature. On the following day Sérgio Vieira de Mello left the country; he was succeeded by Kamalesh Sharma, the head of UNMISET. Tension developed between Gusmão and Alkatiri after the latter was seen to have used Fretilin's parliamentary majority to secure the passage of a new Constitution that rendered Gusmão a largely symbolic head of state. The ill feeling persisted and in November 2002 Gusmão called for the resignation of one of Alkatiri's firmest allies, Rogerio Lobato, Minister for Internal Administration. However, Gusmão eventually retreated from his position, following which relations between the President and the Prime Minister appeared to improve somewhat.

In July 2002 President Gusmão visited Indonesia on his first official trip abroad since assuming the presidency. In September Timor-Leste became the 191st member of the UN. In the same month the Indonesian Government announced that the remaining refugee camps in West Timor would be closed at the end of 2002 and, in November, Gusmão visited the province in an effort to encourage the estimated 30,000 refugees who remained there to return to their homeland. In the following month Bishop Belo announced that he was leaving his position in Dili for health reasons. In the same month the Government declared a state of alert in the country following an outbreak of rioting in Dili during which two people were killed. The protests had begun when a police officer allegedly shot at a student participating in a peaceful demonstration outside the police headquarters in the city. The violence was the worst to have occurred in the country since independence. In January 2003 further violence ensued when a group of armed men attacked villages near the town of Atsabe in the Ermera district, resulting in the deaths of five people. In the following month a bus travelling to Dili was ambushed by a group of armed men; two people subsequently died. It was feared that the violence reflected the possible establishment of several militias and insurgent groups intent on undermining the stability of the new nation.

In March 2003 Prime Minister Alkatiri announced the appointment of Ana Pessôa to the newly created post of Deputy Prime Minister. The justice portfolio, formerly held by Pessôa, was allocated to her deputy, Domingos Sarmento. In the following month, owing to the apparent increase of violence in Timor-Leste in the preceding months, the UN Security Council announced that UNMISET would no longer follow its original downsizing plan (under which the phased withdrawal of UN troops from the country would have commenced in July 2003) and would instead implement an alternative two-phase plan. Under the new strategy, UNMISET would retain primary responsibility for national security until December 2003, maintaining its peace-keeping force at its existing level, before preparing to hand over full responsibility for national defence to Falintil-ETDF (see Defence) on 20 May 2004. In May 2003 the UN Security Council formally extended the mandate of UNMISET until 20 May 2004. In October 2003 the Timorese authorities assumed responsibility for the administration of border crossings in the country from the UN. However, in February 2004 UN Secretary-General Kofi Annan recommended that the mandate of UNMISET be extended, in a modified form and with a considerably reduced military presence, for a further six months following its expiry in May, in order to allow for consolidation of the progress that had been made in the country. In May 2004 the UN Security Council voted unanimously to renew UNMISET's mandate for an additional period of six months, extending the mission until 20 May 2005. In March 2005 Annan recommended that UNMISET be deployed for an additional year, extending the mandate until 20 May 2006, a suggestion that both the USA and Australia opposed, insisting that peace-keeping forces were no longer required in the country.

From mid-2002, at a specially created court in Jakarta (the Ad Hoc Indonesian Human Rights Tribunal on East Timor), the trials took place of 18 officers, government officials and militiamen believed to have participated in the violence that had surrounded the referendum for independence in 1999. In August 2002 Abílio Soares, the former governor of East Timor, was found guilty of two charges of 'gross rights violations'; he was sentenced to a three-year prison term. The sentence was widely criticized for its apparent leniency. In the same month the former chief of police in East Timor, Timbul Silaen, was acquitted of charges of failing to control his subordinates; five other Indonesian police and army officers were also acquitted shortly afterwards. In November former Indonesian militia leader Eurico Guterres was sentenced to 10 years in prison, having been convicted of crimes against humanity. In the following month the former military chief of Dili, Lt-Col Soedjarwo, was sentenced to a five-year prison term for his role in the violence. In March 2003 the court sentenced Brig.-Gen. Noer Muis, a former army chief in East Timor, to five years in prison for crimes against humanity. In August Indonesian armed forces officer Maj.-Gen. Adam Damiri, the last and most senior official to be tried by the tribunal, was convicted of having failed to prevent atrocities in East Timor and sentenced to three years in prison. The court was subjected to widespread international criticism, owing to the fact that only six of those tried were convicted of the charges against them. In April 2004, following an appeal, the Indonesian Supreme Court upheld the conviction of Abílio Soares. However, in July the Jakarta High Court overturned the guilty verdicts of Lt-Col Soedjarwo, Brig.-Gen. Muis, Maj.-Gen. Damiri and Col Gultom (a former Dili police chief), and also halved the sentence of Eurico Guterres to five years. The decision meant that all of the police and military officials indicted by the Tribunal had been released, leaving only the two civilians (Soares and Guterres) serving sentences. The USA and the European Union (EU) denounced the acquittals as massive failings of justice.

In early 2003 a UN-sponsored Special Panel for Serious Crimes (SPSC) that had been established in Dili began to issue indictments for crimes against humanity against several military officials in relation to the violence surrounding the referendum in 1999, including the former chief of the Indonesian armed forces, Gen. Wiranto, who faced prosecution for the first time. Wiranto denied the charges against him. The Indonesian Government, however, stated that it would refuse to permit the extradition of those charged to face trial. In April 2003 the SPSC sentenced José Cardosa Fereira, an East Timorese militia leader, to a 12-year prison term following his conviction for crimes against humanity. In June Quelo Mauno, a former leader of a pro-Indonesia militia, was convicted of the murder of an independence supporter in Oecusse in 1999 and sentenced to seven years in prison. In the following month the Dili court found a further two former pro-Indonesia militia leaders guilty of crimes against humanity and, by February 2004, some 47 people had been convicted of crimes relating to the referendum period. Meanwhile, the total number of people indicted by the court had risen to approximately 350, many of whom were resident in Indonesia; the Indonesian Government continued to refuse to extradite those indicted to face trial. In May 2004 the SPSC finally issued an arrest warrant for Wiranto, who had been nominated in the previous month as a candidate for Indonesia's presidential election, the first round of which was scheduled for July. Fearing a breach in relations with Indonesia, President Gusmão and the Prosecutor-General, Longuinhos Monteiro, both moved to distance themselves from the warrant, insisting that a good rapport with neighbouring countries should take precedence over court proceedings to hold people accountable for crimes committed during the emergence of their nation. In December 2004 Timor-Leste and Indonesia agreed to establish the joint Commission of Truth and Friendship (CTF) to investigate the killings carried out during the period of the Timorese vote for independence, and this was formally approved by their respective Governments in March 2005. However, the CTF was rapidly dismissed by the international community; none of the crimes committed during Indonesian occupation prior to 1999 was to be investigated, and the CTF process was not intended to lead to prosecution. Furthermore, offenders who co-operated 'fully in revealing the truth' were to be guaranteed impunity, irrespective of the nature of their crimes. In August 2005, despite the overwhelmingly negative response to the Commission, the 10-member panel was formally sworn in. Meanwhile, in February of that year the UN established the Commission of Experts, which was to review the judicial processes of the Ad Hoc Indonesian Human Rights Tribunal on East Timor, as well as the Serious Crimes Investigation Unit and the SPSC in Timor-Leste

In February 2004, as sporadic outbreaks of violence, reportedly perpetrated by rebel militias based in rural areas, continued to occur in Timor-Leste, Cristiano da Costa, the leader of the Popular Council for the Defence of the Democratic Republic of East Timor (Conselho Popular pela Defesa da República Democrática de Timor Leste—CPD-RDTL), announced that his organization intended to challenge the legitimacy of the established Government in Timor-Leste following the planned withdrawal of UNMISET in May 2004. However, UNMISET's mandate was subsequently extended for an additional year, although its presence was reduced to a mere 604 officers, while responsibility for law and order in the capital and for external security was transferred to the Government in advance of the formal full transfer of power. It was feared that the methods employed by the Government to suppress insurgents might result in further instability in the country. The use of the police to suppress political opposition was a particular cause for concern. In July 2004 the National Union of Resistance Staff and Veterans held a rally in Dili, demanding a cabinet reshuffle and the dismissal of the unpopular Rogerio Lobato. Police officers were drafted in, and resorted to beatings and the use of tear gas to disperse the crowd; some witnesses also claimed that guns were fired. Dili was the scene of another disturbance in December of the same year, when a group of 20 armed soldiers attacked a police station, injuring two officers and causing damage to the premises. There were also numerous reported sightings of alleged ex-militia groups, especially within border areas. In January 2005, in an operation intended to verify the accuracy of one such reported sighting in the Bobonaro district, police encountered six armed men and, following the resultant exchange of gunfire, one of the group was arrested. Prime Minister Alkatiri was quick to assert that it should not be assumed that the men were necessarily acting at the behest of the Indonesian army.

In December 2004 the first local elections since Timorese independence were held in Bobonaro and in the enclave of Oecusse. In order to promote female participation, a minimum of three women were to be elected to each village council. There was a high turnout, exceeding 90% in some areas, and voters were able to cast their ballots in a calm and orderly manner, free from intimidation. However, there were numerous logistical problems, including errors on the electoral roll, which prohibited some people from casting their vote and delayed the outcome of the elections from being determined. By October 2005 elections had been held in the remaining 11 districts. While local councils held extremely limited authority, the election results revealed a considerable decline in popular support for FRETILIN. Timor-Leste's principal party still maintained a sizeable majority, but its share of the vote decreased to less than 50% in some regions, representing a marked decline from previous levels of support.

Meanwhile, on 20 May 2005 the mandate of UNMISET was officially concluded, and the last remaining UN troops were withdrawn from Timor-Leste in the following month. The UN Office in Timor-Leste (UNOTIL) was established to facilitate the transfer of complete power to the Timorese authorities; its mandate was due to be concluded on 19 May 2006.

In July 2005 Prime Minister Alkatiri effected a cabinet reorganization, providing for an enlarged government comprising 17 ministries, with 15 deputy ministers and 11 state secretaries. Four state secretary portfolios, including those of defence and of public works, were transformed into full ministries. Alkatiri relinquished the role of Minister of Development and assumed control of the natural resources, minerals and energy policy portfolio. Abel Ximenes was selected to be the new Minister of Development; Antoninho Bianco was appointed as the inaugural Minister of Defence; and Odete Victor became Minister for Public Works.

In February 2006 an estimated 400 soldiers (approximately one-quarter of Timor-Leste's 1,600-strong army) staged a protest about living conditions in their barracks and about alleged discrimination against soldiers from western regions of the country; they claimed that army officers, who were predominantly from Timor-Leste's eastern regions, frequently passed over for promotion soldiers from western regions in favour of those from their own localities. Having deserted their duties, the protesting soldiers presented a petition to President Gusmão, who promised a government inquiry into their complaints and urged them to return to their barracks. The military leadership issued an ultimatum, demanding that they return to duty or be dismissed; when they had still failed to return by March, the Commander-in-Chief of the Army, Brig.-Gen. Taur Matan Ruak, sanctioned their dismissal.

In the conduct of its foreign affairs, Timor-Leste accorded high priority to the development of cordial relations with Indonesia. In June 2003 Prime Minister Alkatiri paid his first official visit to Indonesia, holding talks with President Megawati Sukarnoputri. However, despite an agreement between the two countries to co-operate in resolving outstanding border demarcation issues, in early 2004 Indonesia caused tensions by announcing that it planned to deploy security forces on the disputed islet of Sinai, located off Oecusse. The Government had previously protested when Indonesia had conducted military exercises on the islet in late 2003. In June 2004 the Timorese Minister for Foreign Affairs, José Ramos Horta, and his Indonesian counterpart, Hassan Wirayuda, signed an agreement that resolved 90% of the border demarcation question. The remaining nine disputed land segments included territory in the Oecusse enclave; however, six of the nine segments were subsequently agreed upon in October, leaving merely three areas still to be resolved. A formal border agreement between the two countries was signed by the respective heads of state during a visit by Indonesian President Susilo Bambang Yudhoyono to Dili in April 2005. During his stay Yudhoyono paid his respects at the cemetery in which victims from the 1991 Dili massacre (see above) were buried. It was hoped that the visit would facilitate the forging of closer relations. In October, however, tensions arose between the two countries after clashes in the Oecusse enclave, allegedly involving gangs that were supported by Indonesian troops. Both the Timorese and the Indonesian Ministers of Foreign Affairs dismissed the violence as mere civilian land disputes arising from confusion over the delineation of the border. Relations were further sullied by a report published in January 2006 by the Commission for Reception, Truth and Reconciliation (a national body created in 2002, charged with investigating alleged human rights violations during Indonesia's occupation of Timor-Leste). The report documented a catalogue of abuses allegedly carried out by Indonesian security forces in Timor-Leste between April 1974 and October 1999, claiming that as many as 180,000 Timorese civilians had died as a result of the Indonesian army's alleged deliberate policy of starvation. Later that month a scheduled meeting between Presidents Gusmão and Yudhoyono was cancelled; no official reason was given for the decision, but it was widely perceived to be as a result of Yudhoyono's displeasure with the findings of the report.

Meanwhile, Timor-Leste's relations with Australia were strained by ongoing discussions relating to the Timor Sea Treaty. In November bilateral negotiations began concerning the demarcation of the maritime boundary between the two countries, an important issue owing to its ramifications for the allocation of revenues from petroleum and gas fields in the Timor Sea. Australia refused to recognize the boundary delineated by the UN Convention on the Law of the Sea. Prime Minister Alkatiri accused Australia of deliberately attempting to stall the negotiations, following its refusal to agree to the holding of monthly discussions in order to bring about a more rapid resolution to the boundary issues. Months of acrimonious dispute ensued, during which numerous aid agencies, including the British-based Oxfam, accused Australia of pushing Timor-Leste to the point of ruin; Oxfam declared that if a maritime boundary were established between the two countries under international law, 'most, if not all' of the petroleum reserves would be allocated to Timor-Leste. In September 2004 the two countries appeared finally to have agreed upon a revenue-sharing arrangement, which over a period of 30 years would afford Timor-Leste $A5,000m. in tax and royalty payments from the natural-gas project in the Timor Sea. However, the negotiations again broke down, principally owing to the two countries' failure to agree on the contentious boundary issues. In February 2005 further acrimony ensued when the Australian Government agreed to a mid-point boundary with New Zealand but still refused to consider a similar arrangement with Timor-Leste, provoking widespread accusations of blatant hypocrisy. Instead, Australia proposed that the decision with Timor-Leste be deferred for up to 100 years while the major petroleum and gas deposits were exhausted, dismissing Timor-Leste's bid for a mid-point boundary as an 'ambit claim'. In late November a deal was finally reached, with both countries agreeing to share equally the oil and gas revenues from the disputed region, which included the Greater Sunrise Project; a final decision on the contentious issue of the delineation of a maritime boundary was deferred for 50 years in order to allow petroleum and gas projects to proceed. The agreement was formally signed in the Australian city of Sydney in January 2006.

Government

On 25 October 1999 the UN Security Council established the UN Transitional Administration in East Timor (UNTAET) as an integrated, multi-dimensional peace-keeping operation responsible for the administration of East Timor during its transition to independence. Under the terms of UN Security Council Resolution 1272 of 25 October 1999, UNTAET was empowered to exercise all legislative and executive authority in East Timor, including the administration of justice. Under the guidance of UNTAET, an 88-member Constituent Assembly, which was responsible for drafting a new constitution for East Timor, was elected in August 2001. A total of 75 deputies were elected nationally by proportional representation, the remaining members being elected by each of East Timor's 13 districts. On 22 March 2002 the Constituent Assembly promulgated East Timor's first Constitution and, on 14 April, the territory held its first presidential election. The President serves a five-year term. Upon the territory's accession to independence on 20 May 2002, the Constituent Assembly transformed itself into the National Parliament and the Government, which was largely composed of the same Cabinet members who had constituted the pre-independence Council of Ministers, was formally inaugurated by the President. UNTAET formally relinquished its responsibility for the administration of the country and was succeeded by the UN Mission of Support in East Timor (UNMISET), which remained in the country, in a supporting role, ultimately for three years. UNMISET was replaced in May 2005 by the UN Office in Timor-Leste (UNOTIL).

Defence

Within the framework of its mandate, the UN Transitional Administration in East Timor (UNTAET) was required to provide security and to maintain law and order throughout East Timor. (The authorized maximum strength of UNTAET was 8,950 troops, 200 military observers and 1,640 civilian police.) In early February 2001 a new East Timorese Defence Force (Falintil-ETDF) was established; the force was initially to fulfil a 'policing' role, with the defence of the territory remaining the responsibility of UNTAET troops. The first 650 recruits for the new Defence Force, which was ultimately to consist of 1,500 regulars and 1,500 reservists, were drawn from the ranks of the former guerrilla army, Falintil. The new force was trained by Portugal and Australia, and the first troops from Falintil-ETDF were deployed into the peace-keeping structure in early August 2001. In December Timor-Leste's navy was founded with the acquisition of two armed patrol boats from Portugal. The UN Mission of Support in East Timor (UNMISET), which replaced UNTAET in May 2002, had an authorized maximum strength of up to 5,000 troops, including 120 military observers, 1,250 police officers and 100 civilian experts. Provision was also made for 455 international civilian staff, 100 experts for a Civilian Support Group, 977 locally recruited staff and 241 UN Volunteers. In January 2004 UNMISET comprised 1,666 troops, 78 military observers and 319 civilian police, supported by 381 international and 678 local civilians. The peace-keeping force was gradually replaced, through a two-year process of phased withdrawal, by Falintil-ETDF. In July 2002 the first battalion of Falintil-ETDF assumed responsibility from UNMISET's peace-keeping force for the district of Lautem. The last remaining UN peace-keeping troops withdrew from Timor-Leste in June 2005, following the official completion of UNMISET's mandate in the previous month. In August 2005, according to Western estimates, Falintil-ETDF comprised 1,250 army personnel, including 30 women and a naval element of 36.

Economic Affairs

In 2004, according to estimates by the World Bank, Timor-Leste's gross national income (GNI), measured at average 2002–04 prices, was US $506m. GNI was equivalent to $550 per head in 2004. During 1995–2004, it was estimated, the population increased at an average annual rate of 1.1%, while gross domestic product (GDP) per head, in real terms, declined by 6.0% in 1998–2004. Overall GDP decreased, in real terms, at an average annual rate of 4.4% during 1998–2004. According to the Asian Development Bank (ADB), GDP decreased by 6.2% in 2003, but increased by 1.8% in 2004 and by 2.5% in 2005.

The economy of Timor-Leste is based principally on the agricultural sector, which in 2005 engaged approximately 75% of the Timorese population. In 2004 the agricultural sector (including forestry and fishing) contributed an estimated 31.6% of GDP. Coffee is a significant export commodity. Revenue from coffee exports, which constituted 48% of total export receipts in 2002, increased from US $4.0m. in 2003 to $6.6m. in 2004; however, coffee's contribution to total export earnings in 2004 declined to 6.2%. In September 2004 Café Cooperative Timor (CCT), a major exporter representing 20,000 farmers, signed an agreement with a leading US retailer of speciality coffee; the arrangement was expected to increase CCT farmers' earnings by between 150% and 300%. However, the coffee sector remained extremely susceptible to climatic conditions, which, combined with poor irrigation systems, were primarily responsible for significant fluctuations in annual output. There are small plantations of coconut, cloves and cinnamon. Subsistence crops include rice, maize and cassava. Livestock raised includes cattle and water buffalo. The forestry sector possesses potential. By 2000 UNTAET had announced that a comprehensive survey of Timor-Leste's forestry resources was to be conducted, and work had commenced on a sandalwood replanting project. In addition to ocean fishing, there is also some small-scale aquaculture. Between 2000 and 2003, according to figures from the ADB, in real terms the GDP of the agricultural sector increased at an estimated average annual rate of 3.6%. In 2001 favourable climatic conditions and the implementation of efforts to increase crop production contributed to a sustained agricultural recovery; in that year the GDP of the sector increased by 8.7%. The recovery continued throughout 2002, owing in part to the greater availability of seed and to the ongoing restoration of farming equipment in the country. However, a drought that began later in that year and continued throughout 2003 and into 2004 adversely affected agricultural production, resulting in crop failure and a severe food shortage in the country. The sector's GDP growth slowed to 6.0% in 2002, and in the following year agricultural GDP was estimated to have contracted by 0.4%. In 2004 the sector recovered strongly, with growth measured at 10.1% in that year.

The industrial sector (including mining and quarrying, manufacturing, utilities and construction) contributed 14.9% of GDP in 2004. According to figures from the ADB, industrial GDP increased at an average annual rate of 3.0% between 2000 and 2003. The industrial sector's GDP was estimated to have increased by 18.6% in 2001; however, GDP contracted by 3.4% in 2002 and by 4.9% in 2003, but increased by 2.2% in the following year.

There is a small manufacturing sector, which is mainly concerned with the production of textiles, the bottling of water and the processing of coffee. In 2004 the manufacturing sector provided 3.7% of GDP. In May of that year one of the world's largest wet-processing coffee factories was opened in Estado, which, together with expanded production at the existing Maubisse factory, was expected to increase significantly Timor-Leste's annual coffee output. Between 2000 and 2003, according to figures from the ADB, manufacturing GDP expanded at an average annual rate of 4.0%. The GDP of the manufacturing sector increased by 3.2% in 2002 and by 1.0% in 2003.

The mining sector contributed 0.8% of GDP in 2004. Mineral resources include high-grade marble, as well as offshore petroleum and gas. In the 1990s sizeable natural gas fields were discovered in and around the Timor Gap zone, and petroleum reserves in the region were estimated by some sources to total a potential 500m. barrels, valued at more than US $17,000m. in early 2001. The GDP of the mining sector was was estimated to have increased at an average annual rate of 3.1% in 2000–03. The sector's GDP increased by 3.1% in 2002 and by 3.0% in 2003.

The construction sector contributed 9.4% of GDP in 2004. According to figures from the ADB, the construction sector's GDP rose at an average annual rate of 2.8% in 2000–03. In 2002 the GDP of the sector increased by 0.4%, but in 2003 it contracted by 6.0%.

Timor-Leste's generating capacity amounted to some 40 MW prior to the civil conflict in 1999, of which about 50% was contained in two power stations at Dili. However, the territory's power facilities suffered extensive damage in the conflict. In October 2002 the Government elected to transfer control of the national power authority, Electricidade de Timor-Leste (EDTL), to external management, owing to a continuing deterioration in the financial position of the authority. The rehabilitation of the power sector was ongoing in 2006, although the physical rehabilitation of rural power facilities was largely complete by April 2003. Approximately one-half of budgetary capital expenditure in 2003 was allocated to the introduction of a pre-paid electricity meter system in Timor-Leste. However, in 2005 supplies of electricity remained intermittent; in some rural areas access to the electricity supply decreased to only 10% of households. According to figures from the ADB, the GDP of the utilities sector rose at an average annual rate of 3.7% in 2000–03. The sector's GDP remained constant in 2002 and contracted by 3.3% in 2003.

The services sector (including trade, transport and communications, finance, public administration and other services) contributed 53.5% of GDP in 2004. According to figures from the ADB, the services sector's GDP rose at an average annual rate of 5.8% in 2000–03. The GDP of this sector decreased by 8.5% in 2003 and by 1.8% in 2004. In 2004 public administration and defence accounted for an estimated 27.3% of GDP. Tourism remained negligible, owing to a lack of basic infrastructure, as well as to prohibitively high air fares from Indonesia and Australia. However, Timor-Leste's first commercial airline, Kakoak Air, was launched in March 2005; although initially offering only one twice-weekly service, to West Timor, it was hoped that the airline might in future expand to offer flights to and from a greater number of destinations, thereby encouraging more tourists to visit the country.

In 2004 Timor-Leste recorded a visible trade deficit of an estimated US $194m., while there was a surplus of $119m. on the current account of the balance of payments. In the early 2000s substantial official aid continued to dominate the country's trade flows. Although this aid contributed towards the rehabilitation and reconstruction of the economy, it also resulted initially in a deterioration in the country's trade and current-account deficits. Exports declined sharply following the violence of 1999. The ADB estimated export earnings, including those from coffee, to be only $4.0m. in 2001; however, total export revenue, excluding receipts from the oil and gas sector, rose to an estimated $6.0m. in 2002, to $7.0m. in 2003 and further to $8.0m in 2004.

In 2004/05 budgetary expenditure was estimated at US $78.7m. Total government revenue was projected to rise from $192.2m. (including grants of $30.8m.) in 2004/05 to $206.0m. in 2005/06. The ADB envisaged that the country's fiscal surplus would increase from the equivalent of 9.8% of GDP in 2004 to 32.4% in 2005. According to the ADB, consumer prices increased by 3.6% in 2001, by 4.8% in 2002 and by 7.1% in 2003. In the following year the inflation rate decreased to 3.2% and further to 1.8% in 2005. In 2001 the rate of unemployment was estimated by the ADB at 5.3%.

Following independence on 20 May 2002, Timor-Leste became a member of the Asian Development Bank (ADB, see p. 169), the Comunidade dos Países de Língua Portuguesa (Community of Portuguese-Speaking Countries, see p. 395) and the UN Economic and Social Commission for Asia and the Pacific (ESCAP, see p. 33). The country also holds observer status in the Association of South East Asian Nations (ASEAN, see p. 172). It attended the third Summit of the African, Caribbean and Pacific group of states (ACP), held in Fiji in July 2002, as an observer.

Upon independence Timor-Leste's first National Development Plan (NDP), drafted following a nation-wide process of popular consultation in the preceding months, came into operation. The Plan's principal objectives, over an 18-year period, were the reduction of poverty and the promotion of economic growth in Timor-Leste. It proposed the implementation of a phased programme of economic development, under which priority would be given in the short term to the creation of a legislative framework, the enlargement of institutional capacity and further infrastructural growth, following which it was hoped that more sustainable development might be achieved. By late 2002 preparations had been made to introduce into the National Parliament key economic legislation that would enable the development of a legal framework to regulate business activity in the new nation. The banking sector remained primarily localized in nature, although the level of deposits within the developing banking system continued to rise. The initial use of the US dollar as the official currency was not as widespread as had been anticipated. By the end of 2002, however, the process of 'dollarization' had been largely completed. In November 2003 Timor-Leste introduced its own, low-denomination coins (centavos) into the economy. In 2003 financial sector development accelerated and, by the end of that year, three commercial banks were operating in the country. In the immediate post-independence period external aid continued to be of absolutely vital importance to the Timorese economy, and the IMF cautioned that sound economic management would be critical to the preservation of macroeconomic stability, along with the provision of reasonable assurances to donors and other parties that the resources made available to Timor-Leste were being used effectively and accounted for properly. Moreover, by 2004 aid was becoming increasingly more difficult to attract. Following the contraction of 2003, the economy made a slight recovery in the following year, owing largely to enhanced agricultural performance in the latter half of 2004; with further growth being recorded in 2005. Notwithstanding the improvements in agricultural production, it was widely perceived that the Timorese Government was allocating insufficient resources to a sector in which the vast majority of the country's workers were engaged. The rehabilitation of irrigation systems along the southern-coastal rice-growing areas continued, but the process was gen-

TIMOR-LESTE

erally considered to be unsystematic. The Timor Sea Arrangement, relating to the sharing of petroleum and gas royalties with Australia (see Recent History), was signed upon Timorese independence in May 2002, and in December of that year the agreement was ratified by the National Parliament of Timor-Leste. The revenues that the Arrangement would provide were expected to constitute the new nation's primary source of income. However, disputes with Australia over the delineation of maritime boundaries in the Timor Sea resulted in a delay to the release of revenues from those fields affected by the negotiations. The Government was forced to request an additional US $126m. from international donors for 2004–06 in order to offset a shortfall in projected budget revenues. Meanwhile, in June 2003 a US company was granted permission to develop the Bayu-Undan liquefied natural gas (LNG) field in the Timor Sea. The agreement signed by Timor-Leste and Australia in January 2006 regarding the allocation of revenue from the Greater Sunrise gas project (see Recent History) was a significant boost for the country's hopes of achieving long-term economic stability, although the crucial issue of the delineation of a maritime boundary remained unresolved, with a final decision being deferred for 50 years under the terms of the accord. Prime Minister Alkatiri, however, warned against the dangers of developing a one-product economy. Nevertheless, the effective development and use of Timor-Leste's natural gas resources appeared to be the most promising path to self-sufficiency. In June 2005 the Government approved the creation of a Petroleum Fund, which was to serve as a long-term repository for all petroleum revenues and was intended to preserve the value of Timor-Leste's petroleum wealth for subsequent generations; to improve transparency; and to enforce accountability within the sector. The ADB projected GDP growth of 5.0% for 2006 and of 4.0% for 2007, thus anticipating much improvement on the 2.5% growth recorded in 2005. However, in a report published by the IMF in March 2006 it was estimated that annual growth of 7.0% or more was needed if significant progress were to be made by the Timorese Government in its effort to alleviate poverty.

Education

Prior to the civil conflict in 1999 there were 167,000 primary students, 32,000 junior secondary students and 19,000 senior secondary students. Primary school enrolment included 70% of those in the relevant age-group and secondary enrolment about 39%. Some 4,000 students were engaged in further education at the university and the polytechnic in Dili, while in addition several thousand East Timorese were following courses at Indonesian universities. It was estimated that, as a result of the civil conflict in 1999, 75%–80% of primary and secondary schools were either partially or completely destroyed. A total of 240,000 students registered for the 2000/01 academic year, however, a much higher number than anticipated. Literacy rates were reported to have reached only 41% by 1998, with lower rates recorded for women than for men. In January 2001, however, the reopening of the university improved the country's tertiary education facilities, enabling the enrolment of 4,500 students on degree courses and 3,000 on bridging programmes. Following East Timor's accession to nationhood in May 2002, the Government accorded priority to the development of education in Timor-Leste. In June 2002 the Emergency Schools Readiness Project, funded by the Trust Fund for East Timor (TFET), was completed, having effected the renovation of 535 schools and 2,780 classrooms since August 2000. It was succeeded by the Fundamental School Quality Project, under which 65 primary schools were to be constructed during 2002/03. The budget of the Central Fund for East Timor (CFET) allocated an estimated US $17.1m. to the education sector in 2002/03, 24.2% of total expenditure.

Public Holidays

2006: 1 January (New Year's Day), 14 April (Good Friday), 1 May (Labour Day), 20 May (Independence Day), 15 August (Assumption), 30 August (Constitution Day), 20 September (Liberation Day), 1 November (All Saints' Day), 12 November (Santa Cruz Day), 8 December (Immaculate Conception), 25 December (Christmas Day).

2007: 1 January (New Year's Day), 6 April (Good Friday), 1 May (Labour Day), 20 May (Independence Day), 15 August (Assumption), 30 August (Constitution Day), 20 September (Liberation Day), 1 November (All Saints' Day), 12 November (Santa Cruz Day), 8 December (Immaculate Conception), 25 December (Christmas Day).

Statistical Survey

Sources (unless otherwise stated): Indonesian Central Bureau of Statistics, Jalan Dr Sutomo 6–8, Jakarta 10710, Indonesia; tel. (21) 3507057; fax (21) 3857046; e-mail bpshq@bps.go.id; internet www.bps.go.id.

AREA AND POPULATION

Area: 14,609 sq km (5,641 sq miles).

Population: 747,750 (males 386,939, females 360,811) at census of 31 October 1990; 924,642 (males 467,757, females 456,885) at census of 31 July 2004.

Density (at 2004 census): 63.3 per sq km.

Principal Towns (population in 2000): Dili (capital) 48,200; Dare 17,100; Baucau 14,200; Maliana 12,300; Ermera 12,000. Source: Stefan Helders, *World Gazetteer* (internet www.world-gazetteer.com). *Mid-2003* (UN estimate, incl. suburbs): Dili 48,731. Source: UN, *World Urbanization Prospects: The 2003 Revision*.

Births and Deaths (UN estimates, annual averages): Birth rate per 1,000: 36.8 in 1990–95; 31.1 in 1995–2000; 47.4 in 2000–05. Death rate per 1,000: 15.5 in 1990–95; 12.1 in 1995–2000; 12.6 in 2000–05. Source: UN, *World Population Prospects: The 2004 Revision*.

Expectation of Life (WHO estimates, years at birth): 58 (males 55; females 61) in 2003. Source: WHO, *World Health Report*.

Economically Active Population (survey, persons aged 10 years and over, August 1993): Total employed 336,490; Unemployed 5,397; Total labour force 341,887. *Mid-2003* (estimates, '000): Agriculture, etc. 340; Total labour force 418. Source: FAO.

HEALTH AND WELFARE

Key Indicators

Total Fertility Rate (children per woman, 2003): 3.8.

Under-5 Mortality Rate (per 1,000 live births, 2004): 80.

Health Expenditure (2002): US $ per head: 195.

Health Expenditure (2002): % of GDP: 9.7.

Health Expenditure (2002): public (% of total): 63.9.

Access to Water (% of persons, 2002): 52.

Access to Sanitation (% of persons, 2002): 33.

Human Development Index (2003): ranking: 140.

Human Development Index (2003): value: 0.513.

For sources and definitions, see explanatory note on p. vi.

AGRICULTURE, ETC.

Principal Crops (FAO estimates, '000 metric tons, 2004): Rice (paddy) 65; Maize 70; Cassava (Manioc) 42; Sweet potatoes 26; Dry beans 5; Groundnuts (in shell) 4; Coconuts 14; Mangoes 3; Coffee (green) 14.

Livestock (FAO estimates, '000 head, 2004): Cattle 170; Sheep 25; Goats 80; Pigs 346; Horses 48; Buffaloes 70; Chickens 2,100.

Livestock Products (FAO estimates, '000 metric tons, 2004): Pig meat 10.1; Beef and buffalo meat 1.7; Chicken meat 1.8; Hen eggs 1.6.

Fishing (metric tons): Total catch 356 in 2001; 350 in 2002 (FAO estimate); 350 in 2003 (FAO estimate).

Source: FAO.

FINANCE

Currency and Exchange Rate: US currency is used: 100 cents = 1 US dollar ($). *Sterling and Euro Equivalents* (30 December 2005): £1 sterling = US $1.722; €1 = US $1.180; US $100 = £58.08 = €84.77.

Budget (estimates, US $ million, year ending 30 June 2005): *Revenue*: Domestic revenue 31.6 (Direct taxes 7.5, Indirect taxes 19.5, Non-tax revenue 4.6); Oil and gas revenues 129.8 (Tax revenues 93.9, Royalties and interest 35.9); Total 161.4 (excl. Grants 30.8). *Expenditure*: Recurrent expenditure 67.8 (Salaries and wages 28.2, Goods and services 39.6); Capital expenditure 10.9; Total 78.7. Source: IMF, *Timor-Leste: Selected Issues and Statistical Appendix* (May 2005).

Money Supply (estimates, US $ million, 31 December 2004): Demand deposits 49.4; Savings deposits 27.8; Time deposits 6.8; Total broad money 84.0. Source: IMF, *Timor-Leste: Selected Issues and Statistical Appendix* (May 2005).

Cost of Living (Consumer Price Index; base: year ending April 2000 = 100): 118.9 in 2002; 127.4 in 2003; 131.5 in 2004. Source: IMF, *Timor-Leste: Selected Issues and Statistical Appendix* (May 2005).

Gross National Product (US $ million at current prices): 363.4 in 2002; 371.1 in 2003; 481.7 in 2004. Source: IMF, *Timor-Leste: Selected Issues and Statistical Appendix* (May 2005).

Gross Domestic Product by Economic Activity (US $ million at current prices, 2004): Agriculture, forestry and fishing 107.1; Mining and quarrying 2.8; Manufacturing 12.5; Electricity, gas and water 3.3; Construction 31.9; Trade, restaurants and hotels 25.4; Transport and communications 31.8; Finance, rents and business services 29.4; Public administration and defence 92.7; Private services 2.1; *GDP in purchasers' values* 339.0. Source: IMF, *Timor-Leste: Selected Issues and Statistical Appendix* (May 2005).

Balance of Payments (estimates, US $ million, 2004): Exports of goods 8; Imports of goods −202; *Trade balance* −194; Services and other income (net) −4; *Balance on goods, services and income* −198; Current transfers (net) 317; *Current balance* 119; Capital transfers 47; Other capital flows (net) −40; Net errors and omissions −4; *Overall balance* 122. Source: IMF, *Timor-Leste: Selected Issues and Statistical Appendix* (May 2005).

EXTERNAL TRADE

Principal Commodities (US $ million, 1998): *Imports*: Rice 13; Other foodstuffs 22; Petroleum products 14; Construction materials 20; Total (incl. others) 135. *Exports*: Products of agriculture, forestry and fishing 51 (Food crops 8, Other crops 28, Livestock 12); Products of manufacturing 3; Total (incl. others) 55. *2004*: Total imports 146.1; Total exports 105.7 (Coffee 6.6). Source: Asian Development Bank, partly *Key Indicators of Developing Asian and Pacific Countries*.

Principal Trading Partner (US $ million, 1998): *Imports*: Indonesia 135. *Exports*: Indonesia 53.

Oil/Gas Receipts (estimates, US $ million): 29.5 in 2002; 41.4 in 2003; 129.8 in 2004. Source: IMF, *Timor-Leste: Selected Issues and Statistical Appendix* (May 2005).

TOURISM

Tourist Arrivals ('000 foreign visitors, excl. Indonesians, at hotels): 0.8 in 1996; 1.0 in 1997; 0.3 in 1998. Figures exclude arrivals at non-classified hotels: 204 in 1996; 245 in 1997; 41 in 1998.

COMMUNICATIONS MEDIA

Daily Newspapers: 2 in 1999; 1 in 2000.

Non-daily Newspapers: 1 in 1999; 1 in 2000.

Source: UNESCO, *Statistical Yearbook*.

EDUCATION

(2001/02)

Pre-primary: Infants 3,935.

Primary: Teachers 3,612; Infants 183,626.

Lower Secondary: Teachers 1,069; Students 29,685.

Upper Secondary: Teachers 577; Students 16,995.

Tertiary (estimates): Teachers 123; Students 6,349.

Adult Literacy Rate (UNESCO estimate): 58.6% in 2003. Sources: UNESCO Institute for Statistics and UN Development Programme, *Human Development Report*.

Directory

The Constitution

The Constitution of the Democratic Republic of East Timor was promulgated by the Constituent Assembly on 22 March 2002 and became effective on 20 May 2002, when the nation formalized its independence. (From this date the country elected to be known by its official name, the Democratic Republic of Timor-Leste.) The main provisions of the Constitution are summarized below:

FUNDAMENTAL PRINCIPLES

The Democratic Republic of East Timor is a democratic, sovereign, independent and unitary state. Its territory comprises the historically defined eastern part of Timor island, the enclave of Oecussi, the island of Ataúro and the islet of Jaco. Oecussi Ambeno and Ataúro shall receive special administrative and economic treatment.

The fundamental objectives of the State include the following: to safeguard national sovereignty; to guarantee fundamental rights and freedoms; to defend political democracy; to promote the building of a society based on social justice; and to guarantee the effective equality of opportunities between women and men.

Sovereignty is vested in the people. The people shall exercise the political power through universal, free, equal, direct, secret and periodic suffrage and through other forms stated in the Constitution.

In matters of international relations, the Democratic Republic of East Timor shall establish relations of friendship and co-operation with all other peoples. It shall maintain privileged ties with countries whose official language is Portuguese.

The State shall recognize and respect the different religious denominations, which are free in their organization. Tetum and Portuguese shall be the official languages.

FUNDAMENTAL RIGHTS, DUTIES, LIBERTIES AND GUARANTEES

All citizens are equal before the law and no one shall be discriminated against on grounds of colour, race, marital status, gender, ethnic origin, language, social or economic status, political or ideological convictions, religion, education and physical or mental condition. Women and men shall have the same rights and duties in family, political, economic, social and cultural life. Rights, freedoms and safeguards are upheld by the State and include the following: the right to life; to personal freedom, security and integrity; to habeas corpus; to the inviolability of the home and of correspondence; to freedom of expression and conscience; to freedom of movement, assembly and association; and to participate in political life. Freedom of the press is guaranteed.

Rights and duties of citizens include the following: the right and the duty to work; the right to vote (at over 17 years of age); the right to petition; the right and duty to contribute towards the defence of sovereignty; the freedom to form trade unions and the right to strike; consumer rights; the right to private property; the duty to pay taxes; the right to health and medical care; the right to education and culture.

ORGANIZATION OF THE POLITICAL POWER

Political power lies with the people. The organs of sovereignty shall be the President of the Republic, the National Parliament, the Government and the Courts. They shall observe the principle of separation and interdependence of powers. There shall be free, direct, secret, personal and regular universal suffrage. No one shall hold political office for life.

PRESIDENT OF THE REPUBLIC

The President of the Republic is the Head of State and the Supreme Commander of the Defence Force. The President symbolizes and guarantees national independence and unity and the effective functioning of democratic institutions. The President of the Republic shall be elected by universal, free, direct, secret and personal suffrage. The candidate who receives more than half of the valid votes shall be elected President. Candidates shall be original citizens of the Democratic Republic of East Timor, at least 35 years of age, in possession of his/her full faculties and have been proposed by a minimum of 5,000 voters. The President shall hold office for five years. The President may not be re-elected for a third consecutive term of office.

The duties of the President include the following: to preside over the Supreme Council of Defence and Security and the Council of State; to set dates for elections; to convene extraordinary sessions of the National Parliament; to dissolve the National Parliament; to promulgate laws; to exercise the functions of the Supreme Commander of the Defence Force; to veto laws; to appoint and dismiss the Prime Minister and other Government members; to apply to the Supreme Court of Justice; to submit relevant issues of national interest to a referendum; to declare a State of Emergency following the authorization of the National Parliament; to appoint and dismiss diplomatic representatives; to accredit foreign diplomatic representatives; to declare war and make peace with the prior approval of the National Parliament.

COUNCIL OF STATE

The Council of State is the political advisory body of the President of the Republic. It is presided over by the President of the Republic and comprises former Presidents of the Republic who were not removed from office, the Speaker of the National Parliament, the Prime Minister, five citizens elected by the National Parliament and five citizens nominated by the President of the Republic.

NATIONAL PARLIAMENT

The National Parliament represents all Timorese citizens, and shall have a minimum of 52 and a maximum of 65 members, elected by universal, free, direct, equal, secret and personal suffrage for a term of five years. The duties of the National Parliament include the following: to enact legislation; to confer legislative authority on the Government; to approve plans and the Budget and monitor their execution; to ratify international treaties and conventions; to approve revisions of the Constitution; to propose to the President of the Republic that issues of national interest be submitted to a referendum. The legislative term shall comprise five legislative sessions, and each legislative session shall have the duration of one year.

GOVERNMENT

The Government is the supreme organ of public administration and is responsible for the formulation and execution of general policy. It shall comprise the Prime Minister, the Ministers and the Secretaries of State, and may include one or more Deputy Prime Ministers and Deputy Ministers. The Council of Ministers shall comprise the Prime Minister, the Deputy Prime Ministers, if any, and the Ministers. It shall be convened and presided over by the Prime Minister. The Prime Minister shall be appointed by the President of the Republic. Other members of the Government shall be appointed by the President at the proposal of the Prime Minister. The Government shall be responsible to the President and the National Parliament. The Government's programme shall be submitted to the National Parliament for consideration within 30 days of the appointment of the Government.

JUDICIARY

The Courts are independent organs of sovereignty with competence to administer justice. There shall be the Supreme Court of Justice and other courts of law, the High Administrative, Tax and Audit Court, other administrative courts of first instance and military courts. There may also be maritime courts and courts of arbitration.

It is the duty of the Public Prosecutors to represent the State. The Office of the Prosecutor-General shall be the highest authority in public prosecution and shall be presided over by the Prosecutor-General, who is appointed and dismissed by the President of the Republic. The Prosecutor-General shall serve for a term of six years.

ECONOMIC AND FINANCIAL ORGANIZATION

The economic organization of East Timor shall be based on the co-existence of the public, private, co-operative and social sectors of ownership, and on the combination of community forms with free initiative and business management. The State shall promote national investment. The State Budget shall be prepared by the Government and approved by the National Parliament. Its execution shall be monitored by the High Administrative, Tax and Audit Court and by the National Parliament.

NATIONAL DEFENCE AND SECURITY

The East Timor defence force—Falintil-ETDF—is composed exclusively of national citizens and shall be responsible for the provision of military defence to the Democratic Republic of East Timor. There shall be a single system of organization for the whole national territory. Falintil-ETDF shall act as a guarantor of national independence, territorial integrity and the freedom and security of the population against any external threat or aggression. The police shall guarantee the internal security of the citizens.

The Superior Council for Defence and Security is the consultative organ of the President of the Republic on matters relating to defence and security. It shall be presided over by the President of the Republic and shall include a higher number of civilian than military entities.

GUARANTEE AND REVISION OF THE CONSTITUTION

Declaration of unconstitutionality may be requested by: the President of the Republic; the Speaker of the National Parliament; the Prosecutor-General; the Prime Minister; one-fifth of the Members of the National Parliament; the Ombudsman.

Changes to the Constitution shall be approved by a majority of two-thirds of Members of Parliament and the President shall not refuse to promulgate a revision statute.

FINAL AND TRANSITIONAL PROVISIONS

Confirmation, accession and ratification of bilateral and multilateral conventions, treaties, agreements or alliances that took place before the Constitution entered into force shall be decided by the respective bodies concerned; the Democratic Republic of East Timor shall not be bound by any treaty, agreement or alliance not thus ratified. Any acts or contracts concerning natural resources entered into prior to the entry into force of the Constitution and not subsequently confirmed by the competent bodies shall not be recognized.

Indonesian and English shall be working languages, together with the official languages, for as long as is deemed necessary.

Acts committed between 25 April 1974 and 31 December 1999 that can be considered to be crimes of humanity, of genocide or of war shall be liable to criminal proceedings within the national or international courts.

The Government

Until 20 May 2002 all legislative and executive authority in East Timor was exercised by the UN Transitional Administration in East Timor (UNTAET). Under its guidance, the Constituent Assembly promulgated a new Constitution on 22 March 2002 and the people of East Timor elected their first President on 14 April. Having satisfied both these preconditions, East Timor was formally granted independence on 20 May, at which time the Constituent Assembly transformed itself into East Timor's first Parliament and the Government was formally inaugurated by the President. The Government was largely composed of the same cabinet members who had constituted the pre-independence Council of Ministers.

Upon independence UNTAET was succeeded by the UN Mission of Support in East Timor (UNMISET), which was to remain in the country for an initial period of one year. UNMISET's mandate comprised the following elements: to provide support to core administrative structures critical to the political stability and viability of the new country; to assist in interim law enforcement and public security; to aid in the development of a new law enforcement agency—the East Timor Police Force (ETPF); and to contribute to the maintenance of internal and external security. Downsizing of the mission was to take place as rapidly as possible and it was intended that, over a period of two years, all operational responsibilities would be fully devolved to the East Timorese authorities. In May 2003 the UN Security Council extended the mandate of UNMISET for one further year and, in May 2004, for an additional year. In May 2005 UNMISET officially concluded its mission and was replaced by the new UN Office in Timor-Leste (UNOTIL), which was to conduct a one-year follow-on mission, intended to effect an efficient transference of skills and knowledge so as to facilitate the development of Timor-Leste's public institutions and rule of law. In early 2006 President Gusmão requested that, following the completion of UNOTIL's mission in May of that year, the UN Security Council retain a small political office in Timor-Leste to assist the national authorities during preparations for the legislative elections, due by August 2006, and presidential elections, due by April 2007.

HEAD OF STATE

President: José Alexandre (Xanana) Gusmão (took office 20 May 2002).

CABINET
(April 2006)

Prime Minister and Minister for Natural Resources, Minerals and Energy Policy: Mari bin Amude Alkatiri.

Deputy Prime Minister and Minister for State and Internal Administration: Ana Maria Pessôa Pereira da Silva Pinto.

Senior Minister for Foreign Affairs and Co-operation: José Ramos Horta.

Minister for Justice: Domingos Maria Sarmento.

Minister for Planning and Finance: Maria Madalena Brites Boavida.

TIMOR-LESTE

Minister for Interior Affairs: ROGÉRIO TIAGO LOBATO.
Minister for Health: RUI MARIA DE ARAÚJO.
Minister for Transport, Communications and Public Works: OVÍDIO DE JESUS AMARAL.
Minister for Education, Culture, Youth and Sport: ARMINDO MAIA.
Minister for Agriculture, Forestry and Fisheries: ESTANISLAU ALEIXO DA SILVA.
Minister for Development: ABEL XIMENES.
Minister for Defence: ROQUE RODRIGUES.
Minister for Labour and Solidarity: ARSÊNIO PAIXÃO BANO.
Minister for the Council of Ministers: ANTONINHO BIANCO.
Minister for Public Works: ODETE VICTOR.
Secretary of State for Commerce and Industry: ARLINDO RANGEL.
Secretary of State for Tourism, Environment and Investment and Acting Secretary of State for Mineral Resources and Power Policy: JOSÉ TEXEIRA.
Secretary of State for Parliamentary Affairs: ANTONINHO BIANCO.
Secretary of State for Education, Culture, Youth and Sports: VIRGILIO SMITH.
Secretary of State for Water and Sanitation: EGÍDIO DE JESÚS.
There are, in addition, 10 Vice-Ministers.

MINISTRIES

Office of the President: Palácio das Cinzas, Kaikoli, Dili; tel. 3339011; e-mail presidente-tl@easttimor.minihub.org.
Office of the Prime Minister: Palácio do Governo, Av. Presidente Nicolau Lobato, Dili; tel. 7243559; fax 3339503; e-mail mail@primeministerandcabinet.gov.tp; internet www.pm.gov.tp.
Ministry of Agriculture, Forestry and Fisheries: Dili; e-mail agriculture@gov.east-timor.org; internet www.gov.east-timor.org.
Ministry of Development and the Environment: Dili.
Ministry of Education, Culture, Youth and Sport: Dili; e-mail education@gov.east-timor.org.
Ministry of Foreign Affairs and Co-operation: Edif. GPA 1, Ground Floor, Rua Av. Presidente Nicolau Lobato, POB 6, Dili; tel. 3339600; fax 3339025; e-mail administration@mnec.gov-tl.net; internet www.mfac.gov.tp.
Ministry of Health: Palácio das Repartições, Edif. 3, Unit 4, POB 374, Dili; tel. 3322467; fax 3325189; e-mail health@gov.east-timor.org.
Ministry of the Interior: Dili.
Ministry of Justice: Av. Jacinto Candido, Dili; e-mail moj@moj.gov.tl.
Ministry of Planning and Finance: Palácio do Governo, Edif. 5, Av. Presidente Nicolau Lobato, Dili; tel. 3339546; e-mail itds@mopf.gov.tl; internet www.mopf.gov.tl.
Ministry of State Administration: Dili.
Ministry of Transport, Communications and Public Works: Av. Bispo de Madeiros, Dili; tel. 3339354; fax 3339350; e-mail info@mtcop.gov.tl; internet www.mtc.gov.tl.

President and Legislature

PRESIDENT

Presidential Election, 14 April 2002

Candidate	Votes	%
José Alexandre Gusmão	301,634	82.69
Francisco Xavier do Amaral	63,146	17.31
Total	364,780	100.00

NATIONAL PARLIAMENT

A single-chamber Constituent Assembly was elected by popular vote on 30 August 2001. Its 88 members included 75 deputies elected under a national system of proportional representation and one representative from each of Timor-Leste's 13 districts, elected under a 'first-past-the-post' system. Upon independence on 20 May 2002 the Constituent Assembly became the National Parliament; it held its inaugural session on the same day.

Speaker: FRANCISCO GUTERRES.

Directory

General Election, 30 August 2001

	Seats
Frente Revolucionária do Timor Leste Independente (Fretilin)	55
Partido Democrático (PD)	7
Associação Social-Democrata Timorense (ASDT)	6
Partido Social Democrata (PSD)	6
Klibur Oan Timor Asuwain (KOTA)	2
Partido Democrata Cristão (PDC)	2
Partido Nacionalista Timorense (PNT)	2
Partido do Povo de Timor (PPT)	2
União Democrática Timorense (UDT)	2
Partido Democrata Cristão de Timor (UDC/PDC)	1
Partido Liberal (PL)	1
Partido Socialista de Timor (PST)	1
Independent	1
Total	**88**

Election Commission

Commission for National Elections (CNE): Dili; f. 2004; govt body; Chair. MARIA DO CEU.

Political Organizations

Associação Popular Democrática de Timor Pro Referendo (Apodeti Pro Referendo) (Pro-Referendum Popular Democratic Association of Timor): c/o Frederico Almeida Santos Costa, CNRT Office, Balide, Dili; tel. 3324994; f. 1974 as Apodeti; adopted present name in August 2000; fmrly supported autonomous integration with Indonesia; Pres. FREDERICO ALMEIDA SANTOS COSTA.
Associação Social-Democrata Timorense (ASDT) (Timor Social Democratic Association): Av. Direitos Humanos Lecidere, Dili; tel. 3983331; f. 2001; Pres. FRANCISCO XAVIER DO AMARAL.
Barisan Rakyat Timor Timur (BRTT) (East Timor People's Front): fmrly supported autonomous integration with Indonesia; Pres. FRANCISCO LOPES DA CRUZ.
Conselho Popular pela Defesa da República Democrática de Timor Leste (CPD-RDTL) (Popular Council for the Defence of the Democratic Republic of East Timor): opp. the Church, Balide, Dili; tel. 3481462; f. 1999; promotes adoption of 1975 Constitution of Democratic Republic of East Timor; Spokesperson CRISTIANO DA COSTA.
Frente Revolucionária do Timor Leste Independente (Fretilin) (Revolutionary Front for an Independent East Timor): Rua dos Mártires da Pátria, Dili; tel. 3321409; f. 1974 to seek full independence for East Timor; entered into alliance with the UDT in 1986; Pres. FRANCISCO GUTERRES; Sec. for International Relations JOSÉ RAMOS HORTA.
Klibur Oan Timor Asuwain (KOTA) (Association of Timorese Heroes): Rua dos Mártires da Pátria, Fatuhada, Dili; tel. 3324661; e-mail clementinoamaral@hotmail.com; f. 1974 as pro-integration party; currently supports independence with Timorese traditions; Pres. MANUEL TILMAN.
Movement for the Reconciliation and Unity of the People of East Timor (MRUPT): f. 1997; Chair. MANUEL VIEGAS CARRASCALÃO.
Partai Liberal (PL) (Liberal Party): Talbessi Sentral, Dili; tel. 3786448; Pres. ARMANDO JOSÉ DOURADO DA SILVA.
Partido Democrata Cristão (PDC) (Christian Democrat Party): Former Escola Cartilha, Rua Quintal Kiik, Bairo Economico, Dili; tel. 3324683; e-mail arlindom@octa4.net.au; f. 2000; Pres. ANTÓNIO XIMENES.
Partido Democrático (PD) (Democratic Party): 1 Rua Democracia, Pantai Kelapa, Dili; tel. 3608421; e-mail flazama@hotmail.com; Pres. FERNANDO DE ARAÚJO.
Partido Democratik Maubere (PDM) (Maubere Democratic Party): Blk B II, 16 Surikmas Lama Kraik, Fatumeta, Dili; tel. 3184508; e-mail pdm_party@hotmail.com; f. 2000; Pres. PAOLO PINTO.
Partido Nacionalista Timorense (PNT) (Nationalist Party of Timor): Dili; tel. 3323518; Pres. Dr ABÍLIO ARAÚJO.
Partido do Povo de Timor (PPT) (Timorese People's Party): Dili; tel. 3568325; f. 2000; pro-integration; supported candidacy of Xanana Gusmão for presidency of East Timor; Pres. Dr JACOB XAVIER.
Partido Republika National Timor Leste (PARENTIL) (National Republic Party of East Timor): Perumnar Bairopite Bob

TIMOR-LESTE

Madey Ran, Fahan Jalam, Ailobu Laran RTK; tel. 3361393; Pres. FLAVIANO PEREIRA LOPEZ.

Partido Social Democrata Timor Lorosae (PSD) (Social Democrat Party of East Timor): Apartado 312, Correios de Dili, Dili; tel. 3357027; e-mail psdtimor@hotmail.com; f. 2000; Pres. MÁRIO VIEGAS CARRASCALÃO.

Partido Socialista de Timor (PST) (Socialist Party of Timor): Rua Colegio das Madras, Balide, Dili; tel. 3560246; e-mail kaynaga@hotmail.com; Marxist-Leninist Fretilin splinter group; Pres. AVELINO DA SILVA.

Partido Trabalhista Timorense (PTT) (Timor Labour Party): 2B Rua Travessa de Befonte, 2 Bairro Formosa, Dili; tel. 3322807; f. 1974; Pres. PAULO FREITAS DA SILVA.

União Democrata-Cristão de Timor (UDC/PDC) (Christian Democratic Union of Timor): 62 Rua Americo Thomaz, Mandarin, Dili; tel. 3325042; f. 1998; Pres. VINCENTE DA SILVA GUTERRES.

União Democrática Timorense (UDT) (Timorese Democratic Union): Palapagoa Rua da India, Dili; tel. 3881453; e-mail joaocarrascalao@email.msn.com; internet fitini.net/udttimor; f. 1974; allied itself with Fretilin in 1986; Pres. JOÃO CARRASCALÃO; Sec.-Gen. DOMINGOS OLIVEIRA.

Diplomatic Representation

EMBASSIES IN TIMOR-LESTE

Australia: Av. dos Mártires da Pátria, Dili; tel. 3322111; fax 3322247; e-mail dima-dili@dfat.gov.au; internet www.embassy.gov.au/tp.html; Ambassador MARGARET TWOMEY.

Brazil: Av. Governador Serpa Rosa, POB 157, Farol, Dili; tel. 3324203; fax 3324620; e-mail esctimor@office.net.au; Ambassador Dr KYWAL DE OLIVEIRA.

China, People's Republic: Av. Governador Serpa Rosa, Farol, Dili; tel. 3325168; fax 3325166; e-mail chinaemb_tp@mfa.gov.cn; Ambassador SU JIAN.

Indonesia: Farol, Palapaco, POB 207, Dili; tel. 3317107; fax 3312332; e-mail kukridil@hotmail.com; Ambassador AHMED BEY SOFWAN.

Japan: Av. de Portugal, Pantai Kelapa, POB 175, Dili; tel. 3323131; fax 3323130; e-mail japrepet@yahoo.co.jp; Ambassador HIDEAKI ASAHI.

Korea, Republic: Av. de Portugal, Motael, Dili; tel. 3321635; fax 3323636; e-mail koreadili@mofat.go.kr; Ambassador RYU JIN-KYU.

Malaysia: Rua Almirante Américo Thomás, Mandarin, Dili; tel. 3311141; fax 3321805; e-mail mwdili@timortelecom.tp; Ambassador ABDULLAH FAIZ BIN MOHD ZAIN.

Portugal: Edif. ACAIT, Av. Presidente Nicolau Lobato, Dili; tel. 3312533; fax 3312526; e-mail embaixada.portugal@embpor.tp; Ambassador JOÃO RAMOS PINTO.

Thailand: Suite 355–357, Central Maritime Hotel, Av. dos Direitos Humanos, Dili; tel. 3311605; fax 3311607; e-mail diliemb@mfa.go.th; Ambassador KULKUMUT SINGHARA NA AYUDHAYA.

United Kingdom: Av. de Portugal, Pantai Kelapa, Dili; tel. 3322838; fax 3312652; e-mail britishembassydili@fco.gov.uk; Ambassador TINA REDSHAW.

USA: Av. de Portugal, Praia dos Coqueiros, Dili; tel. 3324684; fax 3313206; e-mail larsonta@state.gov; Ambassador GROVER JOSEPH REES.

Judicial System

Until independence was granted on 20 May 2002 all legislative and executive authority with respect to the administration of the judiciary in East Timor was vested in UNTAET. During the transitional period of administration a two-tier court structure was established, consisting of District Courts and a Court of Appeal. The Constitution, promulgated in March 2002, specified that Timor-Leste should have three categories of courts: the Supreme Court of Justice and other law courts; the High Administrative, Tax and Audit Court and other administrative courts of first instance; and military courts. The judiciary would be regulated by the Superior Council of the Judiciary, the function of which would be to oversee the judicial sector and, in particular, to control the appointment, promotion, discipline and dismissal of judges. The effectiveness of the newly established judicial system was severely impaired by Timor-Leste's lack of human and material resources. In July 2002 there were only 22 judges in Timor-Leste, none of whom possessed more than two years of legal experience. In July 2003 the Court of Appeal was reconstituted. However, in the same month a ruling by its President that Timor-Leste's law should be based on that of Portugal and not Indonesia (as was currently the case) threatened to have serious consequences for the legal system.

Court of Appeal: Dili; Pres. CLAUDIO XIMENES.
Office of the Prosecutor-General: Dili; Prosecutor-General LONGUINHOS MONTEIRO; Dep. Prosecutor-General AMANDIO BENEVIDES.

Religion

In 2001 it was estimated that about 93.1% of the total population were Roman Catholic.

CHRISTIANITY

The Roman Catholic Church

Timor-Leste comprises the dioceses of Dili and Baucau, directly responsible to the Holy See. In December 2001 it had an estimated 767,209 Roman Catholics.

Bishop of Baucau: Most Rev. BASILIO DO NASCIMENTO, Largo da Catedral, Baucau 88810; tel. 4121209; fax 4121380.

Bishop of Dili: Most Rev. ALBERTO RICARDO DA SILVA, Av. dos Direitos Humanos, Bidau Lecidere, CP 4, Dili 88010; tel. 3324850.

Protestant Church

Igreja Protestante iha Timor Lorosa'e: Jl. Raya Comoro, POB 1186, Dili 88110; tel. and fax 3323128; f. 1988 as Gereja Kristen Timor Timur (GKTT); adopted present name 2000; Moderator Rev. FRANCISCO DE VASCONCELOS; 30,000 mems.

The Press

The Constitution promulgated in March 2002 guarantees freedom of the press in Timor-Leste.

Lalenok (Mirror): Rua Gov. Celestino da Silva, Farol, Dili; tel. 3321607; e-mail lalenok@hotmail.com; f. 2000; publ. by Kamelin Media Group; Tetum; 3 a week; Dir-Gen. and Chief Editor VIRGÍLIO DA SILVA GUTERRES; Editor JOSÉ MARIA POMPELA; circ. 300.

Lian Maubere: Dili; f. 1999; weekly.

The Official Gazette of East Timor: Dili; f. 1999 by UNTAET; forum for publication of all govt regulations and directives, acts of organs or institutions of East Timor and other acts of public interest requiring general notification; published in English, Portuguese and Tetum, with translations in Bahasa Indonesia available on request.

Suara Timor Lorosae: 7 Av. Martinez da Patria, Dili; tel. 322823; fax 322821; e-mail redaksi@suaratimorlorosae.com; internet www.suaratimorlorosae.com; f. 2000; daily; Editor-in-Chief and Publr SALVADOR J. XIMENES SOARES.

Tais Timor: Dili; f. 2000; fmrly published by the Office of Communication and Public Information (OCPI) of the UN; Tetum, English, Portuguese and Bahasa Indonesia; every fortnight; distributed free of charge; circ. 75,000.

Timor Post: Rua D. Aleixo Corte Real No. 6, Dili; f. 2000; managed by editors and staff of the former Suara Timor Timur; Bahasa Indonesia, Tetum, Portuguese and English; daily; Man. Editor OTELIO OTE; Chief Editor HUGO DE COSTA; circ. 600.

PRESS ASSOCIATION

Sindicato dos Jornalistas de Timor-Leste (SJTL): Rua Dom-Alexio Corte-Real, Bebora, Dili; tel. 7248549; e-mail sjti@yahoo.com; f. 2001; Pres. RODOLFO DE SOUSA.

Timor Lorosae Journalists' Association (TLJA): Rua de Caicoli, Dili; tel. 3324047; fax 3327505; e-mail ajtl_tlja@hotmail.com; f. 1999; Co-ordinator OTELIO OTE; Pres. VIRGÍLIO DA SILVA GUTERRES.

Broadcasting and Communications

TELECOMMUNICATIONS

Prior to the civil conflict in 1999, East Timor's telephone lines totalled about 12,000. Telecommunications transmission towers were reported to have suffered significant damage in the civil conflict. Indonesia withdrew its telecommunication services in September. A cellular telephone network service was subsequently provided by an Australian company, Telstra. In July 2002 the Government granted a consortium led by Portugal Telecom a 15-year concession permitting it to establish and operate Timor-Leste's telecommunications systems. Under the terms of the concession the consortium agreed to provide every district in Timor-Leste with telecommunications services at the most inexpensive tariffs viable within 15 months. At the expiry of the concession in 2017 the telecommunications system was to be transferred to government control. In February 2003 Timor-Leste Telecom assumed control of the country's cellular telephone network from Telstra.

Timor-Leste Telecom (TT): Sala No. 7, Hotel Timor, Av. dos Mártires da Pátria, Dili; tel. 3322245; fax 3303419; e-mail info@timortelecom.tp; internet www.timortelecom.tp; f. 2003; jt venture mainly operated by Portugal Telecom; provides telecommunications services in Timor-Leste.

BROADCASTING

Following independence UNMISET transferred control of public television and radio in Timor-Leste to the new Government. In 2003 a Public Broadcasting Service was established, controlled by an independent board of directors.

Radio

There are 18 radio stations operating in Timor-Leste, including community radio stations for each of the country's 13 districts. The Roman Catholic Church operates a radio station, Radio Kamanak, while a third populist station, Voz Esperança, broadcasts in Dili. A fourth radio station, Radio Falintil FM, also operates in Dili and, in October 2003, the Christian station Voice FM was established. In 2000 the US radio station, Voice of America, began broadcasting to Timor-Leste seven days a week in English, Portuguese and Bahasa Indonesia.

Radio Timor-Leste (RTL): Caicoli, Dili; tel. 3321826; e-mail radio@rttl.org; internet www.rttl.org; fmrly Radio UNTAET; name changed as above in 2002; broadcasts mainly in Bahasa Indonesia, but also in English, Portuguese and Tetum, to an estimated 90% of Timor-Leste's population; Man. PAULA RODRIGES.

Television

TV Timor-Leste (TVTL): Caicoli, Dili; tel. 3321825; e-mail tv@rttl.org; internet www.rttl.org; f. 2000 as Televisaun Timor Lorosa'e by UNTAET; adopted present name in May 2002; broadcasts in Tetum and Portuguese; Gen. Man. ANTONIO DIAZ.

Finance

In January 2000 a Central Fiscal Authority was established by the UNTAET Transitional Administrator. This later became the country's Ministry of Planning and Finance. On 24 January the National Consultative Council formally adopted the US dollar as Timor-Leste's transitional currency; the process of dollarization had been largely completed by early 2003. In November 2003 a new local currency was introduced, in the form of low-denomination coins (*centavos*), which were intended to facilitate transactions by the Timorese population and were fully exchangeable with the dollar. The new coins could not, however, be used outside Timor-Leste.

BANKING

Timor-Leste's banking system collapsed as a result of the violent unrest that afflicted the territory in 1999. In late 1999 Portugal's main overseas bank, Banco Nacional Ultramarino, opened a branch in Dili. In January 2001 the Australia and New Zealand Banking Group also opened a branch in the capital. During 2003 PT Bank Mandiri of Indonesia became the third foreign bank operating in the country. In February 2001 the East Timor Central Payments Office was officially opened. This was succeeded in November of that year by the Banking and Payments Authority, which was intended to function as a precursor to a central bank.

Banking and Payments Authority (BPA): Av. Bispo Medeiros, POB 59, Dili; tel. 3313718; fax 3313716; e-mail info@bancocentral.tl; internet www.bancocentral.tl; inaugurated Nov. 2001; regulates and supervises Timor-Leste's financial system, formulates and implements payments system policies, provides banking services to Timor-Leste's administration and foreign official institutions, manages fiscal reserves; fmrly Central Payments Office; cap. 7.4m., res 0.5m., dep. 46.3m; Chair. and Gen. Man. ABRAÃO F. DE VASCONSELOS; Dep. Gen. Mans MARIA JOSÉ DE JESUS SARMENTO, NUR AINI DJAFAR ALKATIRI.

Foreign Banks

Australia and New Zealand Banking Group Ltd (ANZ) (Australia): Cnr Av. Presidente Nicolau Lobato and Rua Belarmino Lobo, Bidau Lecidere, Dili; tel. 3324800; fax 3324822; e-mail anzeasttimor@anz.com; internet www.anz.com/TimorLeste; retail and commercial banking services; Gen. Man. PETER BOUTCHER; Group CEO JOHN MCFARLANE.

Banco Nacional Ultramarino (Portugal): Edif. BNU, Av. Presidente Nicolau Lobato 12/13, Dili; tel. 3323385; fax 3323678; e-mail cgd.timor@mail.timortelecom.tp; internet www.cgd.pt; Gen. Man. Dr CORREIA PINTO; 8 brs.

PT Bank Mandiri (Persero) (Indonesia): Dili.

Trade and Industry

GOVERNMENT AGENCIES

Investment and Export Promotion Agency: Dili; f. 2005; established to encourage the development of entrepreneurship within Timor-Leste.

The Timor Sea Designated Authority (TSDA): Av. de Portugal, POB 113, Farol, Dili; tel. 3324098; fax 3324082; e-mail dilioffice@timorseada.org; internet www.timorseada.org; f. 2003; responsible for regulating all petroleum activities and for securing new exploration and production contracts within the Joint Petroleum Development Area, on behalf of the respective govts of Timor-Leste and Australia; also has an office in Darwin, Australia; Exec. Sec. MARIA PIRES.

UTILITIES

In the early 2000s Timor-Leste's total generating capacity amounted to some 40 MW. As a result of the civil conflict in 1999, some 13–23 power stations were reported to require repairs ranging from moderate maintenance to almost complete rehabilitation. The rehabilitation of the power sector was ongoing in 2006, with funding largely provided by foreign donors. By July 2003 31 generators had been restored, supplying electricity to Dili, as well as to 12 districts and 33 subdistricts.

Electricidade de Timor-Leste (EDTL): EDTL Bldg, Rua Estrada de Balide, Caicoli, Dili; tel. 3339254; fax 7230095; e-mail virgiliofguterres@hotmail.com; govt dept; responsible for power generation, distribution and financial management of power sector in Timor-Leste; transferred to external management in 2002; Dir. VIRGILIO GUTERRES.

CO-OPERATIVE

Cooperativa Café Timor (CCT): 16 Rua Barros Gomes, Dili; f. 2000 under the Timor Economic Rehabilitation and Development Project; produces, markets and distributes organic coffee; also provides information and advisory services for member farmers; Operational Dir SISTO MONIZ PIEDADE; 19,000 mems.

TRADE UNIONS

Konfederasaun Sindikatu Timor-Leste (KSTL) (Trade Union Confederation of Timor-Leste): Rua Sebastiao da Costa, Colmera, Dili; f. 2001; represents nine unions, comprising approximately 4,700 workers within the press, teaching, nursing, and the construction, agricultural, maritime and transport sectors; Pres. JOSÉ DA CONCEIÇÃO DA COSTA.

Labour Advocacy Institute of East Timor (LAIFET): Rua Abílio Monteiro Palapaso, Dili; tel. 3317243; e-mail laifet@easttimor.minihub.org; Dir DOMINGOS BAPTISTA DE ARAUJO.

Serikat Buruh Socialis Timor (SBST) (Timor Socialist Workers' Union): Dili; controlled by Partido Socialista de Timor; Dir Dr LUCIANO DA SILVA.

Transport

ROADS

The road network in Timor-Leste is poorly designed and has suffered from long-term neglect. In December 1999 the World Bank reported that some 57% of the country's 1,414 km of paved roads were in poor or damaged condition. Many gravel roads are rough and potholed and are inaccessible to most vehicles. Some repair and maintenance work on the road network was carried out in 2005, using funding supplied by external donors.

SHIPPING

Timor-Leste's maritime infrastructure includes ports at Dili, Carabela and Com, smaller wharves at Oecusse (Oekussi) and Liquiça (Likisia), and slip-landing structures in Oecusse, Batugade and Suai. In November 2001, following its reconstruction, the management of the port at Dili was transferred to the Government. The port was expected to be a significant source of revenue.

Port Authority of Timor-Leste (APORTIL): 2 America Thomas Rd, Dili; f. 2003.

Principal Shipping Companies

Everise Freight Forwarding Inc: 2 Rua Belarminolobo, Dili; tel. 3324844; fax 3312856; e-mail everisedili@yahoo.com.

SDV Logistics (East Timor): Av. Presidente Nicolau Lobato, Bairo dos Grilos, POB 398, Dili; tel. 3322818; fax 3324077; e-mail dili@sdv.com; internet www.sdveasttimor.com; f. 1999; freight forwarder, shipping agent and customs broker; Man. Dir ERIC MANCINI.

CIVIL AVIATION

Timor-Leste has two international airports and eight grass runways. At mid-2000 operators of international flights to East Timor included Qantas Airways and Air North of Australia. In June 2001 Dili Express Pte was the first Timor-based company to begin international flights, with a service to Singapore. In 2005 Timor-Leste's first national carrier, Kakoak Air, commenced operations.

Civil Aviation Division (CAD): Dili; tel. 3317110; fax 3317111; e-mail henriques_sabino@yahoo.com; internet www.timor-leste.gov.tl/CAA/index.html; arm of the Ministry of Transport, Communications and Public Works; responsible for overall planning, implementation and operation of aviation services in Timor-Leste; Dir JULIAO X. CARLOS.

Kakoak Air: Dili; internet www.kakoakair.tp; f. 2005; operates twice-weekly passenger service between Dili and Kupang, Indonesia; Gen. Dir JORGE SERANNO.

Tourism

Turismo de Timor-Leste: Apartado 194, Dili; tel. 3310371; fax 3339179; e-mail info@turismotimorleste.com; internet www.turismotimorleste.com; Dir MIGUEL LOBATO.

TOGO

Introductory Survey

Location, Climate, Language, Religion, Flag, Capital

The Togolese Republic lies in West Africa, forming a narrow strip stretching north from a coastline of about 50 km (30 miles) on the Gulf of Guinea. It is bordered by Ghana to the west, by Benin to the east, and by Burkina Faso to the north. The climate in the coastal area is hot and humid, with an average annual temperature of 27°C (81°F), rainfall in this zone averages 875 mm (34.4 ins) per year, and is heaviest during May–October. Precipitation in the central region is heaviest in May–June and in October, and in the north, where the average annual temperature is 30°C (86°F), there is a rainy season from July–September. The official languages are French, Kabiye and Ewe. About one-half of the population follows animist beliefs, while about 35% are Christians and 15% Muslims. The national flag (approximate proportions 3 by 5) has five equal horizontal stripes, alternately green and yellow, with a square red canton, containing a five-pointed white star, in the upper hoist. The capital is Lomé.

Recent History

Togoland, of which modern Togo was formerly a part, became a German colony in 1894. Shortly after the outbreak of the First World War, the colony was occupied by French and British forces. After the war, a League of Nations mandate divided Togoland into two administrative zones, with France controlling the larger eastern section, while the United Kingdom governed the west. The partition of Togoland split the homeland of the Ewe people, who inhabit the southern part of the territory, and this has been a continuing source of friction. After the Second World War, French and British Togoland became UN Trust Territories. In May 1956 a UN-supervised plebiscite in British Togoland produced, despite Ewe opposition, majority support for a merger with the neighbouring territory of the Gold Coast, then a British colony, in an independent state. The region accordingly became part of Ghana in the following year. In October 1956, in another plebiscite, French Togoland voted to become an autonomous republic, with internal self-government, within the French Community. Togo's foremost political parties at that time were the Comité de l'unité togolaise (usually known as the Unité togolaise—UT), led by Sylvanus Olympio, and the Parti togolais du progrès (PTP), led by Nicolas Grunitzky, Olympio's brother-in-law. In 1956 Grunitzky became Prime Minister in the first autonomous Government, but in April 1958 a UN-supervised election was won by the UT. Olympio became Prime Minister and led Togo to full independence on 27 April 1960.

At elections in April 1961 Olympio became Togo's first President, while the UT was elected (unopposed) to all 51 seats in the Assemblée nationale. At the same time a referendum approved a new Constitution. On 13 January 1963 the UT regime was overthrown by a military revolt, in which Olympio was killed. Grunitzky subsequently assumed the presidency on a provisional basis. A referendum in May approved another Constitution, confirmed Grunitzky as President and elected a new legislature from a single list of candidates, giving equal representation to the four main political parties.

President Grunitzky was deposed by a bloodless military coup, led by Lt-Col (later Gen.) Etienne (Gnassingbé) Eyadéma, the Army Chief of Staff, on 13 January 1967. Eyadéma, a member of the Kabiye ethnic group, who had taken a prominent part in the 1963 rising and was reputedly Olympio's assassin, assumed the office of President in April. Political parties were banned, and the President ruled by decree. In November 1969 a new ruling party, the Rassemblement du peuple togolais (RPT), was founded, led by Eyadéma. Comprehensive government changes in January 1977 left Eyadéma as the sole representative of the armed forces in the Council of Ministers.

In Togo's first elections for 16 years, held on 30 December 1979, Eyadéma (the sole candidate) was confirmed as President of the Republic for a seven-year term. At the same time a new Constitution was overwhelmingly endorsed, while the list of 67 candidates for a single-party Assemblée nationale was approved by 96% of votes cast. On 13 January 1980 Eyadéma proclaimed the 'Third Republic'. In December 1986 President Eyadéma was re-elected, unopposed, for a further seven-year term. In the same month 13 people were sentenced to death for complicity in an attempted *coup d'état* staged in September 1985 (the exiled opposition leader, Gilchrist Olympio, son of the former President, was sentenced *in absentia*), although most of the death sentences were subsequently commuted.

In March 1990 some 230 candidates, all loyal to the RPT, contested elections to the Assemblée nationale's 77 seats. In October a commission was established to draft a new constitution, to be submitted to a national referendum in late 1991. In December 1990 the constitutional commission presented a draft document, which envisaged, *inter alia*, a plurality of political parties. Meanwhile, several recently formed, unofficial opposition movements formed a co-ordinating organization, the Front des associations pour le renouveau (FAR), led by Yawovi Agboyibo, to campaign for the immediate introduction of a multi-party political system. Eyadéma subsequently agreed to implement a general amnesty for political dissidents and to permit the legalization of political organizations. Following instances of violent unrest in April 1991, Eyadéma, fearing a civil conflict between the Kabiye and Ewe ethnic groups (the Government and armed forces were composed overwhelmingly of members of the first group, while opposition groups for the most part represented the Ewe people), announced that a new constitution would be introduced within one year, and that multi-party legislative elections would be organized. At the end of the month it was announced that the FAR was to be disbanded. Agboyibo subsequently formed his own party, the Comité d'action pour le renouveau (CAR), which in May became one of 10 parties to enter into a Front de l'opposition démocratique (FOD, later renamed the Coalition de l'opposition démocratique—COD).

Following the organization of a general strike by the FOD, the Government agreed, in June 1991, that a 'national conference' would be held, with the power to choose a transitional Prime Minister and to establish a transitional legislative body. The conference opened in July, attended by some 1,000 delegates, representing the organs of state, political parties, and religious and professional groups, although the armed forces boycotted the conference. Gilchrist Olympio returned from exile to participate. When the conference adopted resolutions suspending the Constitution, dissolving the Assemblée nationale and giving the conference sovereign power, government representatives withdrew. Subsequently the conference resolved to 'freeze' the assets of the RPT, to transfer most of the powers of the President to a Prime Minister, and to prevent Eyadéma from contesting future elections. In defiance of a decree issued by Eyadéma temporarily suspending proceedings, the conference elected a Prime Minister, Joseph Kokou Koffigoh (a senior lawyer and prominent human rights activist), announced the dissolution of the RPT and the formation of a transitional legislature, the Haut Conseil de la République (HCR). Eyadéma capitulated, signing a decree that proclaimed Koffigoh as transitional Prime Minister. In September Koffigoh formed a transitional Government, most of whose members had not previously held office: he himself assumed the defence portfolio.

In October 1991 members of the armed forces seized control of the national broadcasting station, demanding that full executive powers be restored to Eyadéma. They returned to barracks on Eyadéma's orders. Koffigoh confirmed that a constitutional referendum and elections would be held in 1992. In November 1991, following the adoption of legislation by the HCR confirming the dissolution of the RPT, troops seized the broadcasting headquarters and surrounded the Prime Minister's residence, demanding that Eyadéma nominate a new government and that the HCR be abolished. At least 20 people were killed in the fighting that ensued. In December troops captured Koffigoh during an attack on his residence, killing several of his guards. Koffigoh agreed to form a new government. At the end of December the reconvened HCR restored legal status to the RPT and announced the formation of a transitional 'Government of National Union', which comprised many of the members of the previous transitional administration, but also two close associates of Eyadéma.

In January 1992 an electoral schedule was announced; the constitutional referendum and local, legislative and presidential elections were to be held by June of that year. In May the attempted assassination of Gilchrist Olympio, who was regarded as a potential presidential candidate, and the murder of another prominent member of the opposition provoked renewed unrest. In late May the Council of Ministers abandoned the electoral timetable. In July the HCR adopted the draft Constitution and an electoral code, and the constitutional referendum was scheduled for August, although it was subsequently postponed. Meanwhile, a report published by the International Federation of Human Rights concluded that members of the armed forces had been responsible for the attempted murder of Olympio, implicating Eyadéma's son, Capt. Ernest Gnassingbé (a military officer), of involvement. Later in July Tavio Ayao Amorin, a member of the HCR regarded as a radical was shot and fatally wounded. In response, the recently formed Collectif de l'opposition démocratique (COD-2), an alliance of some 25 political organizations and trade unions, called a general strike, which was widely observed. In August agreement was reached on opposition access to the state-controlled media, and on the extension until 31 December of the transition period. In late August the HCR restored to Eyadéma the power to preside over the Council of Ministers, and to represent Togo abroad; furthermore, his agreement would henceforth be necessary in the appointment of members of the Government. The draft Constitution was amended so that members of the armed forces would no longer be obliged to resign their commissions before seeking election to public office.

The transitional Government was dissolved on 1 September 1992. Later that month a new transitional Government, led by Koffigoh, was appointed, including representatives of 10 parties; the most influential ministries were allocated to members of the RPT. On 27 September the new Constitution was approved in a referendum by 98.1% of the votes cast. At the end of the month, however, it was announced that the local, legislative and presidential elections were to be further postponed. In October eight opposition parties announced the formation of a 'Patriotic Front', to be led by the leader of the Union togolaise pour la démocratie (UTD), Edem Kodjo, and Agboyibo. In November Koffigoh dismissed two ministers (both adherents of the RPT) for their conduct during an attack on the HCR by members of the armed forces in October, but Eyadéma overruled this decision.

In January 1993 Eyadéma dissolved the Government, reappointing Koffigoh as Prime Minister, and stated that he would appoint a new government of national unity to organize elections. His action provoked protests by the opposition parties, who claimed that, according to the Constitution, the HCR should appoint a Prime Minister since the transition period had now expired. In the same month two ministers representing the French and German Governments visited Togo to offer mediation in the political crisis. During their visit at least 20 people were killed when police opened fire on anti-Government protesters. Thousands of Togolese subsequently fled from Lomé, many seeking refuge in Benin or Ghana. In February inter-Togolese discussions organized by the French and German Governments in France failed when the presidential delegation withdrew after one day. In that month the French, German and US Governments suspended their programmes of aid to Togo. A new Government, in which supporters of Eyadéma retained the principal posts, was formed in February. In March COD-2 member parties stated that they now regarded Koffigoh as an obstacle to democratization, and nominated a 'parallel' Prime Minister, Jean-Lucien Savi de Tové.

In April 1993 a new electoral schedule was announced. As subsequently modified, it envisaged elections to the presidency and the legislature in July and August, respectively. The RPT designated Eyadéma as its presidential candidate. In May the COD-2 declared that it would boycott the elections, alleging that they would not be fairly conducted, and that opposition politicians had no guarantee of their safety. In July, however, the Togolese Government and the COD-2 signed an agreement establishing 25 August as the date for the first round of presidential voting. The agreement stipulated that the Togolese armed forces should be confined to barracks during the election period, and that international military observers should be present to confirm this, while international civilian observers should also be present for the election. An independent, nine-member Commission électorale nationale (CEN) was to be established, to include three members nominated by the opposition parties. Gilchrist Olympio, who remained outside Togo, denounced the agreement, stating that Togolese refugees abroad (now estimated to number as many as 350,000) should be allowed to return home in safety before the poll. Later in July the COD-2 nominated Kodjo as its presidential candidate; however, in the same month two other candidates—Agboyibo and Abou Djobo Boukari—were nominated by parties affiliated to the COD-2. The Supreme Court rejected the candidacy of Gilchrist Olympio, as the candidate of the Union des forces de changement (UFC) on technical grounds. Prime Minister Koffigoh expressed support for Eyadéma's re-election. In August Boukari, Kodjo and Agboyibo announced their withdrawal from the election, expressing dissatisfaction with electoral preparations. Three candidates contested the presidential election held on 25 August at which Eyadéma was reported to have obtained 96.49% of the votes cast. French election observers concluded that the poll had not been satisfactorily conducted; observers from the USA and Germany had withdrawn from Togo shortly before the elections took place.

In the legislative elections, finally held, on 6 and 20 February 1994, some 347 candidates contested 81 seats. Despite the murder of an elected CAR representative after the first round, and violent incidents at polling stations during the second round, international observers expressed themselves satisfied with the conduct of the elections. The opposition won a narrow victory in the polls, with the CAR winning 36 seats and the UTD seven; the RPT obtained 35 seats and two other smaller pro-Eyadéma parties won three. During March Eyadéma consulted the main opposition parties on the formation of a new government. In late March the CAR and the UTD reached an agreement on the terms of their alliance and jointly proposed the candidacy of Agboyibo for Prime Minister. In March and April the Supreme Court declared the results of the legislative elections invalid in three constituencies (in which the CAR had won two seats and the UTD one) and ordered by-elections. In April Eyadéma nominated Kodjo as Prime Minister. The CAR subsequently declared that it would not participate in an administration formed by Kodjo. Kodjo took office on 25 April; his Government, formed in May, comprised eight members of the RPT and other pro-Eyadéma parties, three members of the UTD, and eight independents.

In November 1994 the CAR suspended its participation in the Assemblée nationale, and indicated that it would return only when agreement had been reached with the Government on the conduct of the by-elections, which were consequently postponed. In early 1995 the Government and the major opposition parties reached an agreement providing for the Government and the legislative opposition to have equal representation on national, district and local electoral commissions. In August the CAR officially resumed participation in the legislature. In April 1996 a deputy of the CAR resigned from the party. In May the CAR withdrew from the by-elections, following the rejection by the Government of its demands that the elections be conducted in the presence of an international monitoring committee. In the same month a UTD deputy was dismissed from the party.

At the by-elections, conducted on 4 and 18 August 1996 in the presence of 22 international observers, the RPT won control of all three constituencies. Consequently, the RPT and its allies were able to command a majority in the legislature, thus precipitating the resignation of the Kodjo administration. On 20 August Eyadéma appointed Kwassi Klutse, hitherto Minister of Planning and Territorial Development, as Prime Minister, and the new Council of Ministers, appointed in late August, comprised almost exclusively supporters of Eyadéma. In October a further CAR deputy resigned from the party, to join the RPT. In November the Union pour la justice et la démocratie, which held two seats in the legislature, announced that it was officially to merge with the RPT, thus giving the RPT an overall majority, with 41 seats.

In September 1997 a new electoral code was approved, providing for a CEN comprising nine members, chaired by the President of the Court of Appeal and including four members appointed by the opposition. The CAR, however, boycotted the legislative session in protest at the Government's refusal to reveal the findings of a report by a mission of the European Union (EU, see p. 228) on the country's electoral process. Later that month opposition parties, led by the CAR and the UFC, organized a demonstration in Lomé in protest at the new electoral law and condemned as fraudulent the Government's preparations for the forthcoming presidential election.

During campaigning for the presidential election, scheduled for 21 June 1998, Eyadéma permitted rival candidates to make brief campaign speeches on state television. Shortly before the election, however, the Government refused to permit the presence of 500 national observers trained by the EU. The election proceeded amid accusations of electoral malpractice, and on the following day counting of votes was halted without explanation, reportedly when the early returns showed Eyadéma to be in second place. Four members of the CEN resigned the same day, alleging intimidation. The Minister of the Interior and Security, Gen. Seyi Memene, announced that he assumed responsibility for the ballot count, and that Eyadéma had been re-elected President with 52.1% of the valid votes cast. Gilchrist Olympio, who had contested the election from exile in Ghana, was officially stated to have won 34.1%. Following the announcement of the result, violent protests erupted throughout Lomé. The USA condemned the conduct of the election, and called on the Government to respect its own laws and electoral code, while the EU decided not to recognize the result, which was, none the less, confirmed by the Constitutional Court.

In September 1998 Klutse announced his new Council of Ministers. Despite Eyadéma's stated intention to form a government of national unity, no opposition figures were willing to be included. Among the few new appointments was Koffigoh, as Minister of State, responsible for Foreign Affairs and Co-operation. In November the Government survived a legislative vote of censure tabled by the CAR and the UTD. In the same month Olympio urged Eyadéma to resign, offering to concede defeat at the June presidential election, and not to stand in future elections, if he did so.

In January 1999 the Government announced that the first round of legislative elections would be held in March. Elections to the Assemblée nationale took place on 21 March, contested only by the RPT and by two small parties loyal to Eyadéma, including Koffigoh's Coordination nationale des forces nouvelles, as well as by 12 independent candidates. (The principal opposition parties had boycotted the polling.) The Constitutional Court ruled that the RPT had won 77 seats, and that independent candidates had taken two seats. By-elections were to take place in two constituencies in which voting had been invalidated. (Both of these seats were subsequently won by the RPT.) The Court estimated turn-out at 66%, although the opposition stated that it was little more than 10%. Despite international criticism, Eyadéma rejected demands for fresh elections, declaring that the opposition had been afforded ample opportunity to participate. In April Klutse tendered his Government's resignation; in May Eugene Koffi Adogboli was appointed Prime Minister. Adogboli subsequently nominated a Council of Ministers dominated by long-standing supporters of Eyadéma.

In May 1999 Amnesty International published a report detailing numerous abuses of human rights committed by Togolese security forces, alleging that hundreds of political opponents of Eyadéma had been killed following the 1998 presidential election. In late July 1999 Eyadéma (who rejected the validity of the report) urged the UN and the Organization of African Unity (now the African Union—AU, see p. 153) to assist in the establishment of an international commission of inquiry into the allegations; such a commission was established in June 2000.

Discussions between the Government and opposition began in Lomé in July 1999, with the assistance of four international facilitators, representing France, Germany, the EU and La Francophonie (see p. 396). Eyadéma's announcement that he would not stand for re-election in 2003 and that new legislative elections would be held, was widely credited with breaking the deadlock in negotiations, and, after the opposition had agreed to accept Eyadéma's victory in the presidential election, an accord was signed on 29 July 1999 by all the parties involved in negotiations. The accord made provision for the creation of an independent electoral body and for the creation of a code of conduct to regulate political activity.

The first meeting took place in August 1999 of the 24-member Comité paritaire de suivi (CPS) responsible for the implementation of the accord, composed of an equal number of opposition and pro-Eyadéma representatives, and also including intermediaries from the EU. Harry Octavianus Olympio, the Minister for the Promotion of Democracy and the Rule of Law (and a cousin of Gilchrist Olympio), was appointed to head the CPS. Despite the reservations of the UFC, a compromise agreement on announcing election results was reached in September, and in December agreement was reached on a revised electoral code, providing for the establishment of an independent electoral commission. In April 2000 Eyadéma obliged the Assemblée nationale to accept the new electoral code. The EU expressed its satisfaction at the adoption of the electoral code, and subsequently offered to provide financial support for the elections, which were scheduled to be held later in 2000. The 20 members of the new Commission électorale nationale indépendante (CENI) were named in June, and in July Arthème Ahoomey-Zounou of the Convergence patriotique panafricaine (CPP—formed in 1999 by the amalgamation of the UTD and three smaller parties, and headed by Edem Kodjo) was elected as president of the CENI.

In August 2000 Adogboli was overwhelmingly defeated in a legislative vote of 'no confidence'; he therefore presented his resignation and that of his Government to Eyadéma. In late August Eyadéma appointed Agbéyomè Kodjo, hitherto the President of the Assemblée nationale, and regarded as a close ally of the President, as Prime Minister. A government reshuffle was effected in October. In December Eyadéma requested that the CENI publish a new electoral calendar. In January 2001 the four international facilitators of inter-Togolese dialogue expressed disappointment at the continued failure of the commission to establish a date for the repeatedly postponed legislative elections. Shortly afterwards the CENI announced that the legislative elections would be held in two rounds, on 14 and 28 October 2001, and that the disputed electoral registers from the 1998 presidential election would be used in these polls.

In February 2001 the report of the joint UN-OAU commission was published. The report concluded that 'systematic violations of human rights' had occurred in Togo in 1998 and stated that allegations of extra-judicial executions could not be disproven. Both the Government and the President of the Assemblée nationale, Ouattara Fambaré Natchaba, dismissed the report's conclusions, emphasizing that the commission had been unable to substantiate some of its findings.

In August 2001 Agboyibo was jailed for six months and fined 100,000 francs CFA, having been convicted of libelling Prime Minister Agbéyomè Kodjo. Several opposition groups withdrew from the CPS in protest at Agboyibo's detention, and two protest marches in support of his release were prohibited by the authorities. In late August the Kodjo announced that the legislative elections would be further postponed until 2002, and declared his support for a proposed constitutional change that would allow Eyadéma to contest a further term of office as President. In late November 2001 Eyadéma implied that he would be prepared to offer a pardon to Agboyibo, should he request one. Agboyibo, however, launched an appeal against his conviction. Although the appeals court found in favour of Agboyibo in mid-January 2002, he was immediately rearrested on charges of conspiring to commit violence during the 1998 presidential election campaign; Agboyibo was finally released from prison in mid-March 2002, on the orders of Eyadéma, who stated that the release was intended to facilitate national reconciliation; the charges against Agboyibo of conspiring to commit violence were also withdrawn.

In February 2002 the Assemblée nationale approved amendments to electoral legislation and to the remit and constitution of the CENI; notably, henceforth all candidates for legislative elections were required to have been continuously resident in Togo for six months prior to elections, with presidential candidates to have been resident for a continuous 12 months. The CENI was also to be reduced in size from 20 to 10 members, and decisions were henceforth to be taken by a two-thirds' majority, instead of the four-fifths' majority required hitherto; these amendments led to a further postponement of the elections, which had been scheduled to take place in March. These measures attracted international disapproval, notably prompting the EU to suspend aid intended to finance the legislative elections. In mid-February five opposition parties, including the CAR, the CPP and the UFC, issued a joint communiqué accusing the Government of having broken the conditions of the accord signed in July 1999, and in early March 2002 they rejected an invitation by Kodjo to nominate representatives to the CENI. The Government consequently announced that no date for the legislative elections could be announced until a complete electoral commission had been formed. In late March 10 opposition parties, which had not been party to the accord signed in 1999 and were therefore excluded from the CPS, announced the formation of a Coordination des partis de l'opposition constructive, headed by Harry Octavianus Olympio, who had also assumed the leadership of the Rassemblement pour le soutien de la démocratie et du développement (RSDD). In mid-May 2002 a committee of seven judges (the Comité de sept magistrats—C-7), charged with monitoring the electoral process at the proposed legislative elections, was appointed, in accordance with a provision of the revised electoral code that permitted the appointment of such a committee in the event that the CENI could not be formed by consensus. Several opposition parties, including the CAR, the CPP and the UFC condemned this decision, and announced their intention to boycott any elections organized by the C-7. At the end of May the EU announced that it would not renew funding for the three facilitators it supported in Togo, in view of the continued lack of progress towards democracy.

In late June 2002 Eyadéma dismissed Kodjo as Prime Minister and appointed Koffi Sama, the Secretary-General of the RPT, as Prime Minister; a new Government, which included several principal members of the former administration, was appointed in early July. Kodjo subsequently issued a statement criticizing the 'monarchic, despotic' regime of Eyadéma, and (in contrast to his former stated position) called for measures to ensure that Eyadéma would be unable to amend the Constitution to stand for a further term of office. The state prosecutor filed a suit against Kodjo on charges of disseminating false information and demeaning the honour of the President; Kodjo subsequently left Togo, taking up residence in France. In August Kodjo was expelled from the RPT, and in September an international arrest warrant, on charges of fraud, was issued against him. However, in October Kodjo's bank accounts in France were 'unfrozen', after a judicial inquiry failed to establish that the accounts had been used fraudulently.

Meanwhile, in early August 2002 four parties, including the CAR, announced the formation of an opposition alliance, the Front uni de l'opposition (Le Front), headed by Agboyibo. In late August renewed concern about the freedom of the press in Togo arose, following the approval by the Council of Ministers of a draft text of modifications to the press code; notably, journalists convicted of insulting the President could be sentenced to five years' imprisonment under the new proposed legislation. In mid-September the authorities announced that the legislative elections were to be held on 27 October. In late September the Secretary-General of the UFC, Jean-Pierre Fabre, was arrested, following a ban on public meetings by the party imposed by the Minister of the Interior, Security and Decentralization, who stated that the UFC's meetings frequently resulted in violence and disruption to public order.

In October 2002 the Assemblée nationale was dissolved, pending fresh elections. In late October nine opposition parties that had declined to participate in the elections announced the formation of a new alliance, the Coalition des forces démocrates (CFD); members of the grouping included the CAR, the CPP and the UFC, in addition to a faction of 'renovators' within the RPT (which subsequently became the Pacte socialiste pour le renouveau—PSR, led by Maurice Dahuku Pere). Meanwhile, a group of 'constructive opposition' parties (including the RSDD), which were prepared to participate in the electoral process and form alliances with the RPT, formed the Coordination des partis politiques de l'opposition constructive (CPOC). The elections proceeded as scheduled, without the participation of the principal opposition parties, on 27 October. The 81 seats of the Assemblée nationale were contested by 126 candidates, comprising 118 candidates nominated by 15 parties and eight independent candidates, although the RPT was the sole party to contest every seat. The RPT won 72 seats (in 46 of which they had been unopposed) and the RSDD three, while three other parties won a total of five seats, and one independent candidate was elected. The C-7, which now comprised six judges (following the resignation of one member of the committee on the day before the elections), estimated electoral turn-out at 67.43%, although the CFD claimed that only 10% of the electorate had voted.

Eyadéma reappointed Sama as Prime Minister in mid-November 2002; a new Government was formed in early December. Gen. Walla was replaced as Minister of the Interior, Security and Decentralization by Maj. Akila Esso Boco, and the former chief administrator of the port of Lomé, Katari Foli Bazi, was appointed as Keeper of the Seals, Minister of Justice responsible for the Promotion of Democracy and the Rule of Law. Roland Yao Kpotsra, a former ambassador to Belgium, was appointed as Minister of Foreign Affairs and Co-operation. All ministers were members of the RPT, with the exception of Harry Octavianus Olympio, who was appointed Minister responsible for Relations with Parliament.

In December 2002 the Assemblée nationale approved several constitutional amendments regarding the eligibility of presidential candidates. The restriction that had limited the President to serving two terms of office was to be removed, and the age of eligibility was to be reduced from 45 to 35 years. (It was widely believed that these measures were intended to permit Eyadéma to serve a further term of office, and also to permit the possible presidential candidacy of Eyadéma's son, Faure Gnassingbé.) Candidates were henceforth to be required to hold solely Togolese citizenship. Although these measures were adopted unanimously by the 80 members of the legislature present at the vote, they were vociferously denounced by the extra-parliamentary opposition; in particular, the UFC announced its intention of commencing a campaign of civil disobedience in response to the amendments. In February 2003 the UFC announced its withdrawal from the CFD, after other parties within the grouping agreed to appoint representatives to the CENI prior to the holding of a presidential election later in the year. In March Gilchrist Olympio announced that he intended to contest the presidential election as the candidate of the UFC, although it appeared that his candidacy would not meet residency requirements. In mid-April the Government announced that the presidential election was to be held on 1 June and later that month Eyadéma confirmed that he was to seek re-election. In May the CENI rejected the candidacy of Olympio, who had recently returned to Togo. (This rejection was confirmed by the Constitutional Court later in the month.) By mid-May six opposition candidates (including four representatives of the constituent parties of the CFD) had emerged. Emmanuel Bob Akitani, the First Vice-President of the UFC, was announced as his party's candidate, following Olympio's debarment.

Eyadéma was returned to office in the presidential election held on 1 June 2003, receiving 57.79% of the votes cast. His nearest rivals was Bob Akitani, with 33.69% of votes. Several of the defeated candidates declared that the election had been conducted fraudulently, although observers from the Economic Community of West African States (ECOWAS), the AU and the Conseil de l'Entente refuted these claims, stating that only minor irregularities had been witnessed. (The EU had been unable to reach agreement with the Togolese authorities on the provision of electoral observers.) Eyadéma was inaugurated for a further term of office on 20 June. Sama resigned as Prime Minister later in the month, but was reappointed as premier on 1 July, apparently with instructions from Eyadéma to form a government of national unity. However, most opposition parties reportedly declined representation in the administration, and the new Government, formed on 29 July, included only two representatives of the 'constructive opposition'. Faure Gnassingbé received his first ministerial posting, as Minister of Equipment, Mines, Posts and Telecommunications. In December Dama Dramani was elected as Secretary-General of the RPT, replacing Sama.

Talks between the EU and the Government on the conditions for a resumption of economic co-operation commenced in April 2004 in Brussels, Belgium; the government delegation, led by Sama, pledged to implement 22 measures such as introducing more transparent conditions for fair elections, revising the press code and guaranteeing political parties the freedom to conduct their activities without fear of harassment. Under pressure from the EU to strengthen democracy, President Eyadéma officially opened talks between the Government and opposition parties in May, despite a boycott of the ceremony by the CAR, the UFC and the CDPA—BT, which criticized the lack of preparations prior to the discussions; the UFC also deplored the exclusion of Gilchrist Olympio, who, it claimed, had been denied entry into Togo. In early June an EU mission charged with assessing Togo's progress in implementing democratic reforms held meetings with the Government, political and religious leaders and human rights organizations. Later that month Sama commenced a series of separate consultations with leaders of several opposition parties, including the UFC, and representatives of civil society organizations as part of the national dialogue opened in late May by Eyadéma. However, the CAR, the UFC and the CDPA—BT refused to participate in a multi-party commission established in mid-July to consider the revision of the electoral code and the funding of political parties. In early August it was reported that Gilchrist Olympio had been provided with a Togolese passport. Later that month the Assemblée nationale adopted amendments to the press code, notably abolishing prison sentences for offences such as defamation and repealing the powers of the Ministry of the Interior, Security and Decentralization to order the closure or seizure of newspapers.

In November 2004 the EU announced that it was to resume partial economic co-operation with Togo, in view of progress towards fulfilment of the 22 conditions established in April. It was emphasized, however, that the full resumption of development aid was dependent on the holding of free and fair elections within six months. In December Eyadéma announced that legislative elections would be held during the first half of

2005. In anticipation of the proposed elections, in January 2005 the Assemblée nationale adopted legislation introducing several amendments to the electoral code in accordance with the demands of the EU, notably strengthening the powers of the CENI and increasing its membership to 13, to include two representatives of civil society.

On 5 February 2005 Prime Minister Sama announced that President Eyadéma had died while being transported out of the country for medical treatment. The Togolese military closed the country's borders, thus preventing Natchaba, the President of the Assemblée nationale, who according to the Constitution was to assume the functions of head of state pending elections to be held within 60 days, from returning to Togo from a visit to Europe. Two hours after Sama's broadcast, Gen. Zakari Namdza, the Chief of Staff of the Armed Forces, announced on national television that the Constitution had been suspended and that the armed forces had pledged their allegiance to Eyadéma's son, Faure Gnassingbé, as the new head of state. The following day an extraordinary session of the Assemblée nationale was convened, at which deputies voted to remove Natchaba from his post as President of the legislature and appoint Gnassingbé in his place. The Assemblée also approved a constitutional amendment authorizing an interim president to serve the remainder of the deceased predecessor's term, rather than arranging elections within 60 days (Eyadéma's term was due to expire in June 2008).

Gnassingbé was formally sworn in as President of Togo on 7 February. The circumstances of his succession provoked domestic and international condemnation: the inauguration ceremony was boycotted by diplomats from Nigeria, the EU, the USA and the UN, while the AU and ECOWAS denounced the events following the death of Eyadéma as a *coup d'état* and demanded that Gnassingbé stand down to allow fair and democratic elections to be held. Meanwhile, the Togolese opposition called a two-day strike for 8 and 9 February, in protest at the perceived *coup d'état*; however, the strike was only partially observed. Subsequent protests, concentrated in the Lomé suburb of Bè, reportedly a stronghold of opposition support, resulted in at least four deaths and several injuries from clashes with security forces, who allegedly used tear gas and live ammunition to disperse protesters. There were reports that protesting crowds were gathering to prevent the closure of independent media outlets: nine private radio stations and two independent television stations were shut down by the Government in the week following Gnassingbé's accession to power, variously on the grounds of inciting civil disobedience and non-payment of taxes (all were subsequently permitted to resume broadcasting). A second opposition call to strike in Lomé on February 14 was largely unobserved outside Bè, where a further death was reported.

Following intense diplomatic pressure from ECOWAS, and from Nigeria in particular, Gnassingbé announced in a televised address to the nation on 18 February that elections would be held within 60 days—however, he declined to stand down before that time. Following this announcement, on 21 February the Assemblée nationale voted to reverse the constitutional amendments adopted on 6 February. Judging these concessions to be insufficient, ECOWAS imposed an arms embargo on Togo and travel restrictions on members of the Government, while the ambassadors of ECOWAS states were withdrawn from Lomé. The AU declared its support for the imposition of sanctions, while the USA announced that it would terminate all military assistance to Togo unless Gnassingbé stood down. On 24 February Gnassingbé, who was prohibited from travelling to neighbouring ECOWAS states, made brief visits to President Omar Bongo Ondimba of Gabon and the Libyan leader Col Muammar al-Qaddafi; reports speculated that he consulted these long-serving African heads of state for advice on his political situation. On 25 February it was revealed that Gnassingbé had been appointed President of the RPT, and endorsed as the party's candidate in the forthcoming presidential election. Later that day, Gnassingbé announced on national television that he was resigning from the post of President of the Assemblée nationale, and hence from the position of interim President, stating that he did not wish to compromise the transparency and fairness of the election. Abbas Bonfoh, Vice-President of the Assemblée nationale, became the acting head of state. The announcement was welcomed by ECOWAS, whose sanctions were immediately lifted; opposition groups, however, continued to demand that Natchaba (who returned to Togo in early March) should assume the post of interim President, and sporadic protests continued, concentrated once more in Bè (it was subsequently reported that five further deaths had occurred in connection with these demonstrations).

In early March 2005 the date of the election was subsequently set for 24 April; ECOWAS approved the date, although the opposition protested that it would be impossible to organize fair and transparent elections in such a brief period of time. (The EU also expressed doubts that fair elections could be held so promptly, and declined to send electoral observers.) Nevertheless, the radical opposition, which had grouped itself into a coalition of six parties (including, in addition to the four parties of the Front uni de l'opposition, the PSR and the UFC), subsequently announced that it would present a single candidate, Bob Akitani, to stand against Gnassingbé. Two members of the 'constructive opposition'—Harry Octavianus Olympio and the leader of the Parti du renouveau et de la rédemption, Nicolas Lawson—announced their candidacies; Gnassingbé's candidature was supported by five small parties of the 'constructive opposition' as well as by the RPT.

The period immediately before the presidential election was characterized by heightened social and political tensions. On 8 April 2005 the former Prime Minister, Agbéyomè Kodjo, returned to Togo, when he was arrested upon his entry into the country. (Following a court ruling on 26 April, all charges against Kodjo were withdrawn, and he was released from custody in mid-May.) Also on 8 April security forces shot dead one participant in a demonstration by supporters of the opposition in Tabligbo, north of Lomé. On 11 April a peaceful demonstration in the capital was reported to have been attended by several thousand supporters of the opposition, who protested against what was described as the 'repression' exercised by the authorities, and demanded that polling be postponed. On 16 April at least seven people were reported to have been killed, and some 150 injured, in clashes between supporters of the opposition and supporters of the youth wing of the RPT in Lomé. Bob Akitani refused to attend a meeting in Niamey, Niger on 20 April convened by the Nigerien President, Mamadou Tandja under the auspices of ECOWAS, to discuss the recent political violence in Togo, although Gnassingbé and the two candidates of the 'constructive opposition' attended. On 22 April Bonfoh dismissed the Minister of the Interior, Security and Decentralization, Maj. François Akila Esso Boko, after Boko had called for the presidential election to be postponed and for the appointment of a temporary premier from the opposition, citing the risk of civil war if the elections went ahead; following his dismissal, Esso Boko sought asylum in the German embassy in Lomé. On 23 April Lawson announced the withdrawal of his candidacy, in protest at Esso Boko's dismissal.

The Presidential elections were held, as scheduled, on 24 April 2005, amid ongoing tensions. Although widespread violence was not reported on polling day, the seizure of ballot boxes, following the closure of polls, in areas of Lomé in which the opposition was known to have considerable support, and in other areas of the interior, was reported. Preliminary results, issued by the CENI on 26 April, indicated that Gnassingbé had been elected as President by a significant majority. Although Gnassingbé announced that he envisaged the establishment of a government of national unity, the announcement of his victory precipitated widespread rioting, particularly in Lomé and in southern regions, with some reports suggesting that as many as 100 people had died in the violence. (According to official figures, 22 people were killed in the rioting.) Meanwhile, Gilchrist Olympio, who had returned to Togo in March, declared that Bob Akitini had been the legitimate winner of polling, claiming that the opposition candidate had received more than 70% of the votes cast. However, on 27 April ECOWAS observers issued a report on the elections, stating that the irregularities in the conduct of the election had not been such as to invalidate or draw into question the declared results. At least eight deaths were reported in clashes in Aného on 28 April, and the residences of prominent members of the RPT, as well as a German cultural centre, were reported to have been subject to arson attacks in Lomé. (Reports had circulated in Togo that the German authorities had provided support to the opposition.) By early May more than 20,000 Togolese were reported to have fled the country for either Benin or Ghana. On 3 May the Constitutional Court announced the final results of the elections, which were not substantially different from the preliminary figures declared by the CENI; Gnassingbé was attributed 60.16% of the votes cast, compared with the 38.25% awarded to Bob Akitani; Lawson (despite the formal withdrawal of his candidacy) and Harry Octavianus Olympio each received around 1%. Some 63% of the electorate were reported to have voted. Gnassingbé was inaugurated as President on 4 May. In mid-May an independent Togolese human rights organization claimed that around 800 people had been killed and more than 4,300 injured between late March and early May. (Another human rights group, aligned to the Government, reported 58 deaths during this period.) Gnassingbé later appointed a national commission of inquiry into the violence, headed by Koffigoh. Meanwhile, although the European Parliament adopted a resolution criticizing the conduct of the election, the election result was generally accepted by the international community.

On 19 May 2005 President Olusegun Obasanjo of Nigeria chaired a reconciliation summit in Abuja, the Nigerian capital, under the aegis of ECOWAS and the AU, which was attended by Gnassingbé, Gilchrist Olympio and other opposition leaders, as well as the Heads of State of Benin, Burkina Faso, Gabon, Ghana and Niger. (Bob Akitani was unable to participate owing to ill health.) The talks ended without agreement, however, as the radical opposition continued to reject the legitimacy of Gnassingbé's victory and demanded a full investigation of alleged election irregularities as a precondition for entering into any power-sharing arrangement. None the less, Gnassingbé subsequently held meetings with a number of opposition leaders to discuss the formation of what he termed a government of national unity. While the UFC upheld its refusal to participate in negotiations, most of the other opposition parties decided to join the talks. In late May the AU removed sanctions against Togo, declaring that it considered conditions in Togo to be constitutional. Meanwhile, refugees continued to flee Togo, amid reports that opposition supporters were being arrested or kidnapped by the security forces, and by late May 34,416 Togolese refugees (19,272 in Benin and 15,144 in Ghana) had been registered by the office of the UN High Commissioner for Refugees (UNHCR). It was estimated that a further 10,000 people had been internally displaced within Togo. Several thousand more people were reported to have fled Togo in subsequent months.

On 8 June 2005 Gnassingbé announced the appointment of Edem Kodjo, regarded as a member of the moderate opposition, as Prime Minister. Negotiations between the President and five 'radical' opposition parties had been unsuccessful, as Gnassingbé refused to accede to several principal opposition demands, including the scheduling of fresh presidential elections and the transfer of some presidential powers to the Prime Minister. Later in June the formation of a 30-member Council of Ministers, dominated by the RPT, but also including several representatives of the opposition and of civil society, was announced. Notably, Tchessa Abi of the PSR, was appointed as Keeper of the Seals, Minister of Justice; the other five members of the six-party coalition refused to participate and later condemned Abi's acceptance of a ministerial position, deciding to expel the PSR from the coalition. (The Minister of Culture, Tourism and Leisure, Gabriel Sassouvi Dosseh-Anyroh was expelled from the UFC, following his acceptance of a post in the administration.) Zarifou Ayéva, the leader of the moderate opposition Parti pour la démocratie et le renouveau (which party was absorbed into the RPT later in the year), was appointed as Minister of State, Minister of Foreign Affairs and African Integration, while an elder brother of the President, Kpatcha Gnassingbé, became Minister-delegate at the Presidency of the Republic, responsible for Defence and Veterans.

The return of the refugees was discussed by Gnassingbé and Gilchrist Olympio at a meeting in Rome, Italy, in July 2005, at which the two men also condemned violence and agreed that political prisoners arrested during the electoral process should be released. (Another meeting between the two men was held in Rome in November.) In August Gnassingbé ordered the release from custody of 14 men, including a former member of the élite presidential guard, who had been suspected of plotting a *coup d'état* in 2003, while 42 supporters of the opposition, who had been detained after the 2005 election, were also released. Agbéyomè Kodjo returned to Togo in early September and later that month, with Pere, announced the formation of a new opposition political party, the Alliance démocratique pour la Patrie. In late September Gnassingbé announced that the holding of legislative elections was to be expedited (although no date was specified), and that, in a measure intended to promote national unity, the country's first President, Sylvanus Olympio, was to be officially rehabilitated. Later in the month UNHCR published a report stating that between 400 and 500 people had been killed in the post-election violence in Togo earlier in the year, although the Togolese Government rejected this figure; the report issued by the Government's independent commission of enquiry in the following month put the death toll at 154, while an independent human rights organization reported that up to 1,000 deaths had occurred in pre- and post-election violence. In early November, as a further gesture of reconciliation, some 460 political prisoners were released from gaol in Lomé; the release of political prisoners was also expected to take place in other cities and regions.

In mid-March 2006 the Government announced, that, to encourage Togolese refugees to return to their country (at least 19,000 Togolese refugees were believed to be resident in Benin at the end of 2005) no legal proceedings were to be taken against opposition activists suspected of involvement in the unrest in 2005, excepting those involved in 'bloody crimes'; moreover, President Gnassingbé called for a formal resumption of the national dialogue between the authorities and the opposition.

Relations with neighbouring Ghana have frequently become strained, as the common border with Togo has periodically been closed in an effort to combat smuggling and to curb political activity by exiles on both sides. In March 1993 and January 1994 the Togolese Government accused Ghana of supporting armed attacks on Eyadéma's residence, reflecting earlier accusations of Ghanaian involvement in unrest in Togo in early 1991. Full diplomatic relations between the two countries, suspended since 1982, were formally resumed in November 1994, and various joint commissions were subsequently reactivated. The newly elected President of Ghana, John Kufuor, visited Togo to mark the celebrations for Liberation Day on 13 January 2001, and a *rapprochement* in relations between the two countries was subsequently reported.

Relations with fellow ECOWAS members were jeopardized by the perceived *coup d'état* by which Gnassingbé assumed power following the death of his father Eyadéma (see above). Relations with Nigeria, in particular, were further compromised when the Togolese authorities refused to grant an aeroplane carrying the advance delegation of President Olusegun Obasanjo permission to land in Lomé. Nigeria withdrew its ambassador to Togo and imposed restrictions on visits of Togolese officials to Nigeria following the incident, anticipating the sanctions imposed by ECOWAS after Gnassingbé initially declined to stand down as interim President in advance of presidential elections. Following Gnassingbé's resignation on 25 February, Nigeria and the other ECOWAS member states lifted their sanctions, returned their ambassadors to Lomé and resumed co-operation with Togo, approving the 24 April date for the presidential election and pledging to provide assistance to ensure the fairness and transparency of the poll.

Government

Under the terms of the Constitution that was approved in a national referendum on 27 September 1993, and subsequently modified, executive power is vested in the President of the Republic, who is directly elected, by universal adult suffrage, for a period of five years. The legislature is the unicameral Assemblée nationale, whose 81 members are also elected, by universal suffrage, for a five-year period. The Prime Minister is appointed by the President from among the majority in the legislature, and the Prime Minister, in consultation with the President, nominates other ministers. For administrative purposes, the country is divided into five regions. It is further divided into 30 prefectures and sub-prefectures.

Defence

In August 2005 Togo's armed forces officially numbered about 8,550 (army around 8,100, air force 250, navy 200). Paramilitary forces comprised a 750-strong gendarmerie. Military service is by selective conscription and lasts for two years. Togo receives assistance with training and equipment from France. The defence budget was estimated at 20,000m. francs CFA in 2005.

Economic Affairs

In 2004, according to estimates by the World Bank, Togo's gross national income (GNI), measured at average 2002–04 prices, was US $1,868m., equivalent to $380 per head (or $1,690 on an international purchasing-power parity basis). During 1995–2004, it was estimated, the population increased at an average annual rate of 2.8%, while gross domestic product (GDP) per head increased by an average of 0.6% per year. Overall GDP increased, in real terms, at an average annual rate of 3.5% in 1995–2004. Real GDP increased by 3.0% in 2004.

Agriculture (including forestry and fishing) contributed 41.2% of GDP in 2004; in the previous year 57.9% of the working population were employed in the sector. The principal cash crops are cotton (which contributed 15.9% of earnings from merchandise exports in 2002), coffee and cocoa. Togo has generally been self-sufficient in basic foodstuffs: the principal subsistence crops are cassava, yams, maize, millet and sorghum. Imports of livestock products and fish are necessary to satisfy domestic needs. During 1995–2004, according to the World Bank, agricultural GDP increased at an average annual rate of 3.1%; agricultural GDP declined by 0.9% in 2003, but increased by 3.2% in 2004.

Industry (including mining, manufacturing, construction and power) contributed 22.8% of GDP in 2004, and employed 10.1% of the working population in 1990. During 1995–2004, according to the World Bank, industrial GDP increased by an average of 3.6% per year; industrial GDP increased by 7.3% in 2004.

Mining and quarrying contributed 3.7% of GDP in 2003. Togo has the world's richest reserves of first-grade calcium phosphates. Concerns regarding the high cadmium content of Togolese phosphate rock have prompted interest in the development of lower-grade carbon phosphates, which have a less significant cadmium content; exports of crude fertilizers and crude minerals provided 16.6% of earnings from merchandise exports in 2002. Limestone and marble are also exploited. There are, in addition, smaller deposits of iron ore, gold, diamonds, zinc, rutile and platinum. In 1998 marine exploration revealed petroleum and gas deposits within Togo's territorial waters. In October 2002 the Togolese Government, the Hunt Oil Co of the USA and Petronas Carigali of Malaysia signed a joint-venture oil-production agreement, providing for the first offshore drilling in Togolese territorial waters. The GDP of the mining sector was estimated to have declined at an average annual rate of 3.2% in 1991–95.

Manufacturing contributed 9.4% of GDP in 2004. About 6.6% of the labour force were employed in the sector in 1990. Major companies are engaged notably in agro-industrial activities, the processing of phosphates, steel-rolling and in the production of cement. An industrial 'free zone' was inaugurated in Lomé in 1990, with the aim of attracting investment by local and foreign interests by offering certain (notably fiscal) advantages in return for guarantees regarding export levels and employment; a second 'free zone' has since opened, and provision has been made for 'free zone' terms to apply to certain businesses operating outside the regions. According to the World Bank, manufacturing GDP increased by an average of 5.5% per year in 1995–2004; manufacturing GDP increased by 6.5% in 2004.

Togo's dependence on imports of electrical energy from Ghana was reduced following the completion, in 1988, of a 65-MW hydroelectric installation (constructed in co-operation with Benin) at Nangbeto, on the Mono river. In early 2004 the Togolese and Beninois authorities announced that the Adjaralla hydroelectric installation, also on the Mono river, was to be modernized, and its production capacity increased markedly. None the less, in 2002 some 94.3% of electricity produced in Togo was generated from petroleum. In 2003 fuel imports constituted 18.8% of all merchandise imports by value. It was planned to connect the electricity grids of Togo and Benin, and to construct further power stations in both countries. A pipeline to supply natural gas from Nigeria to Togo (and also to Benin and Ghana) was expected to come on stream in the first half of 2006.

The services sector contributed 36.0% of GDP in 2004, and engaged 24.4% of the employed labour force in 1990. Lomé has been of considerable importance as an entrepôt for the foreign trade of land-locked countries of the region. However, political instability in the early 1990s and in 2005 resulted in the diversion of a large part of this activity to neighbouring Benin and undermined the tourism industry (previously an important source of foreign exchange). According to the World Bank, the GDP of the services sector increased by an average of 3.7% per year in 1995–2004; services GDP increased by 0.5% in 2004.

In 2003 Togo recorded a visible trade deficit of US $156.8m., while there was a estimated deficit of $161.9m. on the current account of the balance of payments. In 2002 the principal source of imports was France (20.4%); other major suppliers were Côte d'Ivoire, Canada, Belgium and Germany. The principal market for exports in that year was Ghana (which took 21.5% of Togo's exports); other significant purchasers were Benin and Burkina Faso. The principal exports in 2002 were cement, crude fertilizers and crude minerals, food and live animals, cotton, and iron and steel. The principal imports in that year were refined petroleum products, cereals and cereal preparations, road vehicles, iron and steel, and cement.

Togo's overall budget deficit for 2002 was 15,900m. francs CFA (equivalent to 1.6% of GDP). Togo's total external debt was US $1,707m. at the end of 2003, of which $1,489m. was long-term public debt. In that year the cost of debt-servicing was equivalent to 1.9% of the value of exports of goods and services. Annual inflation averaged 2.6% in 1990–93. Following the devaluation of the CFA franc in January 1994, inflation in that year averaged 39.2%. Consumer prices increased by an annual average of 1.8% in 1996–2004. Consumer prices decreased by 0.9% in 2003, before increasing by 0.3% in 2004.

Togo is a member of the Economic Community of West African States (see p. 217), of the West African organs of the Franc Zone (see p. 282), of the International Cocoa Organization (see p. 382), of the International Coffee Organization (see p. 382) and of the Conseil de l'Entente (see p. 385). Togo was admitted to the Islamic Development Bank (see p. 303) in 1998.

Following the devaluation of the CFA franc in early 1994, the IMF approved a series of credits in support of Togo's 1994–97 economic adjustment programme. During this period Togo recorded a decline in inflation, a decrease in its external debt and budget deficit, and an increase in GDP per head. From the late 1990s the Togolese economy was adversely affected by a number of economic and political factors. A sharp and sustained decline in the output of phosphates, historically one of Togo's major sources of export earnings, persistently low international prices for another of Togo's principal exports, cotton, and high international prices for a principal import, petroleum, had a negative impact on the trade balance. The construction of a new facility at Lomé's port, financed by the World Bank, in the first half of the 2000s was successful, reportedly in attracting container trade that previously had been routed through ports in neighbouring Ghana, while the port has also been a beneficiary of entrepôt trade displaced from Côte d'Ivoire as a result of the civil conflict in that country from late 2002. The European Union (EU) suspended development aid to Togo in 1993, citing the lack of a functioning democratic system within the country, while further external sources of aid were suspended in the wake of the internationally criticized presidential election of 1998. Although repeatedly delayed legislative elections were held in October 2002, both the USA and the EU declared themselves dissatisfied with the conduct of the polls, and therefore much international aid remained suspended. In April 2004, in talks with EU representatives in Brussels, Belgium, the Togolese authorities agreed a series of conditions that would have to be met in order for EU aid to resume (see above). Following the fulfilment of a number of these conditions, partial EU assistance to Togo was resumed in November. Continuing good relations with the EU and other sources of economic assistance were subsequently jeopardized by the accession to the presidency of Faure Gnassingbé in early 2005, widely denounced as a *coup d'état* and the consequent unrest, that resulted in more than 30,000 Togolese citizens fleeing the country (see above). While the presidential elections held in April of that year, which resulted in Gnassingbé obtaining an electoral mandate, were generally recognized by the international community, the resumption of financial assistance from external donors, perceived as an important factor in Togo's future economic development, remained largely dependent on the maintenance of political stability and on measures intended to ensure reconciliation between the Government and the opposition. Growth in 2005 was estimated at 2.7%, according to the Union économique et monetaire ouest-africaine.

Education

Primary education, which begins at six years of age and lasts for six years, is (in theory) compulsory. Secondary education, beginning at the age of 12, lasts for a further seven years, comprising a first cycle of four years and a second of three years. In 2000/01 enrolment at primary schools included 91% of children in the relevant age-group (100% of boys; 82% of girls). In the same year secondary enrolment was equivalent to 39% of the appropriate age group (boys 54%; girls 24%), according to UNESCO estimates. Proficiency in the two national languages, Ewe and Kabiye, is compulsory. Mission schools are important, educating almost one-half of all pupils. In 1998 15,028 students were enrolled in institutions providing higher education. The Université du Lomé (formerly the University du Bénin) had about 14,000 students in the early 2000s, and scholarships to French universities are available. A second university opened in Kara, in the north of Togo, in early 2004. Current expenditure on education was an estimated 23,800m. francs CFA in 1995 (16.2% of total expenditure by the central Government), and a further

TOGO

3,700m. francs CFA was allocated to scholarships and training (2.5% of total expenditure).

Public Holidays

2006: 1 January (New Year's Day), 10 January*† (Tabaski, Feast of the Sacrifice), 13 January (Liberation Day, anniversary of the 1967 coup), 24 January (Day of Victory, anniversary of the failed attack at Sarakawa), 17 April (Easter Monday), 24 April (Day of Victory), 27 April (Independence Day), 1 May (Labour Day), 25 May (Ascension Day), 5 June (Whit Monday), 15 August (Assumption), 23 September (anniversary of the failed attack on Lomé), 23 October* (Id al-Fitr, end of Ramadan), 1 November (All Saints' Day), 25 December (Christmas), 31 December*† (Tabaski, Feast of the Sacrifice).

2007: 1 January (New Year's Day), 13 January (Liberation Day, anniversary of the 1967 coup), 24 January (Day of Victory, anniversary of the failed attack at Sarakawa), 9 April (Easter Monday), 24 April (Day of Victory), 27 April (Independence Day), 1 May (Labour Day), 17 May (Ascension Day), 28 June (Whit Monday), 15 August (Assumption), 23 September (anniversary of the failed attack on Lomé), 13 October* (Id al-Fitr, end of Ramadan), 1 November (All Saints' Day), 20 December* (Tabaski, Feast of the Sacrifice), 25 December (Christmas).

* These holidays are dependent on the Islamic lunar calendar and may vary by one or two days from the dates given.

† This festival occurs twice (in the Islamic years AH 1426 and 1427) within the same Gregorian year.

Weights and Measures

The metric system is in force.

Statistical Survey

Source (except where otherwise indicated): Direction de la Statistique, BP 118, Lomé; tel. 221-22-87.

Area and Population

AREA, POPULATION AND DENSITY

Area (sq km)	56,785*
Population (census results)	
1 March–30 April 1970	1,997,109
22 November 1981	2,703,250
Population (UN estimates at mid-year)†	
2002	5,684,000
2003	5,836,000
2004	5,988,000
Density (per sq km) at mid-2004	105.5

* 21,925 sq miles.
† Source: UN, *World Population Prospects: The 2004 Revision.*

Ethnic Groups (percentage of total, 1995): Kabré 23.7; Ewe 21.9; Kabiyé 12.9; Watchi 10.1; Guin 6.0; Tem 6.0; Mobamba 4.9; Gourmantché 3.9; Lamba 3.2; Ncam 2.4; Fon 1.2; Adja 0.9; Others 2.9 (Source: La Francophonie).

PRINCIPAL TOWNS
(official estimates in 1997)

Lomé (capital, incl. suburbs)	700,000	Kpalimé		30,000
Sokodé	51,000	Kara		30,000

Mid-2003 (UN estimate, incl. suburbs): Lomé 799,122 (Source: UN, *World Urbanization Prospects: The 2003 Revision*).

BIRTHS AND DEATHS
(UN estimates, annual averages)

	1990–95	1995–2000	2000–05
Birth rate (per 1,000)	43.1	41.2	39.5
Death rate (per 1,000)	11.3	11.9	12.3

Source: UN, *World Population Prospects: The 2004 Revision.*

Expectation of life (WHO estimates, years at birth): 52 (males 50; females 54) in 2003 (Source: WHO, *World Health Report*).

ECONOMICALLY ACTIVE POPULATION
(census of 22 November 1981)

	Males	Females	Total
Agriculture, hunting, forestry and fishing	324,870	254,491	579,361
Mining and quarrying	2,781	91	2,872
Manufacturing	29,307	25,065	54,372
Electricity, gas and water	2,107	96	2,203
Construction	20,847	301	21,148
Trade, restaurants and hotels	17,427	87,415	104,842
Transport, storage and communications	20,337	529	20,866
Financing, insurance, real estate and business services	1,650	413	2,063
Community, social and personal services	50,750	12,859	63,609
Activities not adequately defined	14,607	6,346	20,953
Total employed	484,683	387,606	872,289
Unemployed	21,666	7,588	29,254
Total labour force	506,349	395,194	901,543

Mid-2003 (estimates in '000): Agriculture, etc. 1,210; Total labour force 2,091 (Source: FAO).

Health and Welfare

KEY INDICATORS

Total fertility rate (children per woman, 2003)	5.3
Under-5 mortality rate (per 1,000 live births, 2004)	140
HIV/AIDS (% of persons aged 15–49, 2003)	4.1
Physicians (per 1,000 head, 2001)	0.06
Hospital beds (per 1,000 head, 1990)	1.51
Health expenditure (2002): US $ per head (PPP)	163
Health expenditure (2002): % of GDP	10.5
Health expenditure (2002): public (% of total)	10.8
Access to water (% of persons, 2002)	51
Access to sanitation (% of persons, 2002)	34
Human Development Index (2003): ranking	143
Human Development Index (2003): value	0.512

For sources and definitions, see explanatory note on p. vi.

TOGO
Statistical Survey

Agriculture

PRINCIPAL CROPS
('000 metric tons)

	2002	2003	2004
Rice (paddy)	69.2	68.1	68.1*
Maize	510.1	516.3	485.0†
Millet	51.7	50.0	50.0*
Sorghum	169.0	177.3	180.0*
Cassava (Manioc)	727.7	724.0	725.0*
Taro (Coco Yam)	39.9	25.0	25.0*
Yams	574.9	568.9	570.0*
Dry beans	44.7	44.5	44.5*
Groundnuts (in shell)	35.7	36.7	33.0†
Coconuts*	14.0	14.5	14.5
Oil palm fruit*	115	115	115
Cottonseed†	90	90	100
Vegetables*	136.0	136.0	136.0
Bananas*	18	18	18
Oranges*	12.1	12.1	12.1
Other fruit*	20.6	20.6	20.6
Cotton (lint)†	70.0	71.0	76.0
Coffee (green)†	18.0	13.5	13.5
Cocoa beans	6.0†	7.0†	8.5*

* FAO estimate(s).
† Unofficial figure(s).
Source: FAO.

LIVESTOCK
(FAO estimates, '000 head, year ending September)

	2002	2003	2004
Cattle	279	279	279
Sheep	1,700	1,800	1,850
Pigs	300	310	320
Goats	1,460	1,470	1,480
Horses	2	2	2
Asses	3	3	3
Poultry	8,500	8,500	9,000

Source: FAO.

LIVESTOCK PRODUCTS
(FAO estimates, '000 metric tons)

	2002	2003	2004
Beef and veal	5.7	5.7	5.7
Mutton and lamb	3.7	3.9	4.1
Goat meat	3.7	3.7	3.7
Pig meat	4.6	4.8	4.9
Poultry meat	10.4	10.4	11.2
Game meat	4.5	4.5	4.5
Cows' milk	9.1	9.2	9.2
Hen eggs	6.3	6.3	6.4

Source: FAO.

Forestry

ROUNDWOOD REMOVALS
('000 cubic metres, excluding bark)

	2002	2003	2004*
Sawlogs, veneer logs and logs for sleepers	43	43	43
Other industrial wood	165	165	165
Fuel wood	5,600*	5,653*	5,707
Total	5,808	5,861	5,915

* FAO estimate(s).
Source: FAO.

Fishing

('000 metric tons, live weight)

	2001	2002	2003
Capture	23.2	20.9	27.5
Tilapias	3.5	3.5	3.5
Other freshwater fishes	1.5	1.5	1.5
West African ilisha	0.8	0.7	0.5
Bigeye grunt	0.8	1.1	0.4
Round sardinella	3.1	1.8	4.0
European anchovy	6.7	6.9	11.5
Atlantic bonito	0.7	0.8	1.7
Marlins, sailfishes	0.2	0.2	0.9
Carangids	3.0	1.7	1.3
Aquaculture	0.1	1.0	1.2
Total catch	23.3	22.0	28.7

Source: FAO.

Mining

('000 metric tons)

	2002	2003	2004
Limestone*	2,400	2,400	2,400
Phosphate rock (gross weight)	1,271	1,471	1,115
Phosphate content	460*	530*	418

* Estimate(s).
Source: US Geological Survey.

Industry

SELECTED PRODUCTS
('000 metric tons, unless otherwise indicated)

	2000	2001	2002
Palm oil	7.7*	7.7*	7.0†
Cement	700	800	800
Electric energy (million kWh)	68	85	n.a.

* FAO estimate.
† Unofficial figure.
Sources: FAO; UN, *Industrial Commodity Statistics Yearbook*.
2003 ('000 metric tons): Palm oil 7.0 (Unofficial figure) (Source: FAO).

Finance

CURRENCY AND EXCHANGE RATES

Monetary Units
100 centimes = 1 franc de la Communauté financière africaine (CFA).

Sterling, Dollar and Euro Equivalents (30 December 2005)
£1 sterling = 957.440 francs CFA;
US $1 = 556.037 francs CFA;
€1 = 655.957 francs CFA;
10,000 francs CFA = £10.44 = $17.98 = €15.24.

Average Exchange Rate (francs CFA per US $)
2003   581.20
2004   528.29
2005   527.47

Note: An exchange rate of 1 French franc = 50 francs CFA, established in 1948, remained in force until January 1994, when the CFA franc was devalued by 50%, with the exchange rate adjusted to 1 French franc = 100 francs CFA. This relationship to French currency remained in effect with the introduction of the euro on 1 January 1999. From that date, accordingly, a fixed exchange rate of €1 = 655.957 francs CFA has been in operation.

TOGO

BUDGET
('000 million francs CFA)

Revenue*	2000	2001	2002
Tax revenue	103.9	108.3	120.4
Direct tax revenue	26.6	24.6	28.3
Indirect tax revenue	n.a.	83.7	92.1
Taxes on international trade	n.a.	56.2	58.9
Other current revenue	13.0	19.3	20.0
Total	116.9	127.6	140.4

Expenditure†	2000	2001	2002
Current expenditure	139.4	128.2	144.1
Salaries and wages	56.0	55.2	55.3
Other operational expenses	61.6	55.2	69.5
Interest payments on public debt	21.8	17.8	19.3
External	19.6	16.3	15.4
Capital expenditure	28.3	22.8	24.8
Externally financed	25.1	20.1	21.3
Total	167.7	151.0	168.9

* Excluding grants received ('000 million francs CFA): 4.3 in 2000; 4.6 in 2001; 12.6 in 2002.
† Excluding lending minus repayments ('000 million francs CFA): −3.3 in 2000; 0.8 in 2001; 0.0 in 2002.

Source: Banque centrale des états de l'Afrique de l'ouest.

INTERNATIONAL RESERVES
(excluding gold, US $ million at 31 December)

	2002	2003	2004
IMF special drawing rights	0.3	0.2	—
Reserve position in IMF	0.4	0.5	0.5
Foreign exchange	204.4	204.2	359.2
Total	205.1	204.9	359.7

Source: IMF, *International Financial Statistics*.

MONEY SUPPLY
('000 million francs CFA at 31 December)

	2002	2003	2004
Currency outside banks	64.0	48.6	73.3
Demand deposits at deposit money banks	82.4	103.3	116.9
Total money (incl. others)	148.4	154.7	192.9

Source: IMF, *International Financial Statistics*.

COST OF LIVING
(Consumer Price Index for Lomé; base: 1996 = 100)

	2002	2003	2004
Food, beverages and tobacco	109.3	104.4	103.0
Clothing	103.0	108.1	114.9
Housing, water, electricity and gas	107.8	109.0	109.1
All items (incl. others)	115.9	114.9	115.3

Source: Banque centrale des états de l'Afrique de l'ouest.

NATIONAL ACCOUNTS
('000 million francs CFA at current prices)

Expenditure on the Gross Domestic Product

	2001	2002	2003
Final consumption expenditure	974.8	1,006.7	1,005.3
Households			
Non-profit institutions serving households	753.0	791.0	753.2
General government	221.8	215.7	252.1
Gross capital formation	158.6	164.8	175.3
Gross fixed capital formation	147.9	158.0	168.7
Changes in inventories			
Acquisitions, less disposals, of valuables	10.7	6.8	6.6
Total domestic expenditure	1,133.4	1,171.5	1,180.6
Exports of goods and services	314.5	358.4	441.7
Less Imports of goods and services	473.5	504.4	618.9
GDP at market prices	974.4	1,025.5	1,003.4

Gross Domestic Product by Economic Activity

	2001	2002	2003
Agriculture, hunting, forestry and fishing	368.4	389.1	349.8
Mining and quarrying	26.6	35.0	34.0
Manufacturing	86.5	93.5	97.8
Electricity, gas and water	32.3	38.9	42.1
Construction	22.3	23.0	21.3
Trade, restaurants and hotels	120.9	120.8	122.4
Transport, storage and communications	49.0	51.4	52.8
Non-market services	121.6	121.0	125.0
Other services	76.3	80.6	78.8
Sub-total	903.9	953.3	924.0
Import duties and taxes	70.5	72.1	79.3
GDP in purchasers' values	974.4	1,025.5	1,003.4

Source: Banque centrale des états de l'Afrique de l'ouest.

BALANCE OF PAYMENTS
(US $ million)

	2001	2002	2003
Exports of goods f.o.b.	357.2	424.2	597.7
Imports of goods f.o.b.	−516.1	−575.6	−754.5
Trade balance	−158.9	−151.4	−156.8
Exports of services	71.8	90.0	94.8
Imports of services	−129.9	−148.1	−204.2
Balance on goods and services	−217.0	−209.5	−266.3
Other income received	25.9	26.2	26.8
Other income paid	−55.2	−47.8	−50.2
Balance on goods, services and income	−246.3	−231.1	−289.6
Current transfers received	88.3	113.0	161.4
Current transfers paid	−11.1	−21.8	−33.8
Current balance	−169.1	−139.9	−161.9
Capital account (net)	21.4	13.6	20.6
Direct investment abroad	7.3	−2.7	6.3
Direct investment from abroad	63.6	53.7	33.7
Portfolio investment assets	5.3	−1.1	−4.7
Portfolio investment liabilities	5.8	13.0	18.6
Other investment assets	8.2	−3.8	−28.7
Other investment liabilities	61.0	91.7	117.7
Net errors and omissions	−5.4	5.0	−10.2
Overall balance	−2.0	29.6	−8.6

Source: IMF, *International Financial Statistics*.

External Trade

PRINCIPAL COMMODITIES
(US $ million)

Imports c.i.f.	2000	2001	2002
Food and live animals	46.2	64.5	65.4
Fish, crustaceans and molluscs and preparations thereof	11.8	13.5	6.9
Fish, fresh, chilled or frozen	11.3	12.7	6.0
Fish, frozen, excl. fillets	8.7	12.3	5.8
Cereals and cereal preparations	17.3	33.4	39.5
Wheat and meslin, unmilled	10.5	23.2	29.2
Mineral fuels, lubricants, etc.	61.0	56.3	61.0
Petroleum products, refined	60.4	55.7	60.4
Motor spirit, incl. aviation spirit	—	25.3	—
Gas oils	—	17.8	—
Animal and vegetable oils, fats and waxes	4.1	6.8	12.6
Chemicals and related products	34.0	36.8	42.4
Medicinal and pharmaceutical products	10.3	11.5	15.4
Basic manufactures	83.6	95.7	102.6
Textile yarn, fabrics, made-up articles and related products	21.5	12.6	14.4
Cotton fabrics, woven*	18.1	8.9	9.4
Other woven fabrics, 85% plus of cotton, bleached, etc., finished	17.7	8.5	8.5
Non-metallic mineral manufactures	24.4	34.9	36.8
Lime, cement and fabricated construction materials	21.5	32.4	30.3
Cement	20.5	31.4	29.0
Iron and steel	21.8	31.1	31.0
Iron and steel bars, rods, shapes and sections	8.6	16.4	15.6
Iron and steel bars, rods, shapes and sections, of other than high carbon or alloy steel	8.1	15.9	14.9
Machinery and transport equipment	60.1	55.2	76.8
Telecommunications, sound recording and reproducing equipment	7.0	11.7	9.2
Telecommunication equipment, parts and accessories	6.3	11.1	8.6
Road vehicles	26.2	20.4	33.1
Passenger motor vehicles (excl. buses)	15.6	9.6	11.0
Miscellaneous manufactured articles	17.6	21.4	22.6
Total (incl. others)	323.6	355.0	405.3

Exports f.o.b.	2000	2001	2002
Food and live animals	30.2	31.1	41.7
Cereals and cereal preparations	5.4	9.6	11.8
Coffee, tea, cocoa, spices, and manufactures thereof	16.7	9.7	10.5
Coffee, not roasted; coffee husks and skins	11.4	4.7	2.9
Crude materials, inedible, except fuels	96.9	73.2	86.6
Textile fibres and their waste†	42.1	22.3	40.0
Cotton	42.1	22.3	39.9
Raw cotton, excl. linters, not carded or combed	23.9	3.4	26.4
Cotton, carded or combed	18.0	18.6	13.4
Crude fertilizers and crude minerals	48.7	44.8	41.7
Crude fertilizers and crude minerals (unground)	48.2	43.7	41.4

Exports f.o.b.—continued	2000	2001	2002
Basic manufactures	45.1	93.9	93.9
Non-metallic mineral manufactures	29.3	64.9	66.8
Cement	29.1	64.9	66.3
Iron and steel	6.9	18.9	18.5
Iron and steel bars, rods, shapes and sections	5.2	9.5	8.4
Bars, rods (not wire rod), from iron or steel; hollow mining drill	4.9	8.7	7.6
Universals, plates and sheets, of iron or steel	0.4	7.3	7.2
Universals, plates and sheets, of iron or steel, of other than high carbon or alloy steel (excl. tinned)	0.3	6.7	7.1
Machinery and transport equipment	7.4	5.2	5.9
Total (incl. others)	191.7	220.2	250.6

* Excluding narrow or special fabrics.
† Excluding wool tops and wastes in yarn.

Source: UN, *International Trade Statistics Yearbook*.

PRINCIPAL TRADING PARTNERS
(US $ million)

Imports c.i.f.	2000	2001	2002
Belgium	16.1	12.0	20.5
Canada	9.1	23.2	23.6
China, People's Repub.	9.3	10.1	11.8
Côte d'Ivoire	38.0	20.4	25.5
Denmark	3.8	1.6	—
France (incl. Monaco)	75.5	67.8	82.5
Germany	14.0	15.8	20.5
Ghana	8.0	7.2	8.1
Hong Kong	5.5	6.4	7.3
India	4.5	5.4	4.8
Indonesia	3.7	4.8	7.8
Italy	7.9	21.5	14.6
Japan	10.4	8.1	7.8
Korea, Republic	2.5	8.1	1.1
Mauritania	9.9	7.7	4.5
Netherlands	20.8	7.3	13.0
Nigeria	5.0	5.1	4.6
Russia	9.3	7.0	6.2
Senegal	3.8	6.4	5.5
South Africa	2.5	7.3	8.1
Spain	5.3	11.8	10.7
Thailand	2.8	4.5	3.4
Turkey	1.4	1.1	10.7
Ukraine	2.1	4.0	12.9
United Kingdom	11.7	8.2	6.8
USA	5.0	10.1	18.6
Total (incl. others)	323.6	355.0	405.3

Exports f.o.b.	2000	2001	2002
Australia	—	4.4	9.2
Belgium	2.9	2.6	1.2
Benin	18.9	37.2	33.1
Brazil	6.0	1.5	0.6
Burkina Faso	2.8	22.8	32.6
France (incl. Monaco)	8.5	4.4	2.3
Germany	2.1	1.8	1.2
Ghana	31.8	49.4	53.8
Greece	3.4	1.9	4.2
India	9.0	4.2	5.0
Indonesia	5.7	3.0	2.9
Iran	10.1	—	—
Italy	5.2	4.7	4.5
Malaysia	0.9	1.0	5.0
Morocco	1.7	2.0	2.7
Netherlands	4.9	1.8	4.9

TOGO

Exports f.o.b.—continued	2000	2001	2002
New Zealand	—	2.9	8.5
Niger	2.1	9.8	11.6
Nigeria	8.3	4.3	5.0
Philippines	12.0	13.8	—
Poland	5.4	5.6	5.9
South Africa	10.8	6.4	5.9
Spain	4.0	2.1	n.a.
Thailand	1.4	1.2	4.3
USA	0.5	5.2	0.9
Total (incl. others)	191.7	220.2	250.6

Source: UN, *International Trade Statistics Yearbook*.

Transport

RAILWAYS
(traffic)

	1997	1998	1999
Passengers carried ('000)	152.0	35.0	4.4
Freight carried ('000 metric tons)	250	759	1,090
Passenger-km (million)	12.7	3.4	0.4
Freight ton-km (million)	28.8	70.6	92.4

Source: Société Nationale des Chemins de Fer du Togo, Lomé.

ROAD TRAFFIC
(motor vehicles registered at 31 December)

	1994	1995	1996*
Passenger cars	67,936	74,662	79,200
Buses and coaches	529	547	580
Goods vehicles	31,457	32,514	33,660
Tractors (road)	1,466	1,544	1,620
Motorcycles and scooters	39,019	52,902	59,000

* Estimates.

Source: IRF, *World Road Statistics*.

SHIPPING

Merchant Fleet
(registered at 31 December)

	2002	2003	2004
Number of vessels	17	20	26
Total displacement ('000 grt)	13.3	15.3	19.5

Source: Lloyd's Register-Fairplay, *World Fleet Statistics*.

International Sea-borne Freight Traffic
('000 metric tons)

Port Lomé	1997	1998	1999
Goods loaded	432.4	794.6	1,021.4
Goods unloaded	1,913.9	1,912.9	1,812.4

Source: Port Autonome de Lomé.

CIVIL AVIATION
(traffic on scheduled services)*

	1999	2000	2001
Kilometres flown (million)	3	3	1
Passengers carried ('000)	84	77	46
Passenger-km (million)	235	216	130
Total ton-km (million)	36	32	19

* Including an apportionment of the traffic of Air Afrique.

Source: UN, *Statistical Yearbook*.

Tourism

FOREIGN TOURIST ARRIVALS*

	2001	2002	2003
Benin	6,251	5,371	5,111
Burkina Faso, Mali and Niger	7,896	5,988	5,953
Côte d'Ivoire	3,438	3,071	4,134
France	8,480	12,764	14,154
Ghana	2,167	1,755	1,585
Nigeria	4,976	3,919	3,152
USA	1,592	1,626	1,384
Total (incl. others)	56,629	57,539	60,592

* Arrivals at hotels and similar establishments.

Receipts from Tourism (US $ million, incl. passenger transport): 11 in 2000; 14 in 2001; 16 in 2002.

Source: World Tourism Organization.

Communications Media

	2002	2003	2004
Telephones ('000 main lines in use)	51.2	60.6	n.a.
Mobile cellular telephones ('000 subscribers)	170	220	n.a.
Personal computers ('000 in use)	150	160	171
Internet users ('000)	200.0	210.0	221.0

Television receivers ('000 in use): 150 in 2000.

Radio receivers ('000 in use): 940 in 1997.

Facsimile machines ('000 in use): 17 in 1997.

Daily newspapers: 1 (average circulation 10,000 copies) in 1999; 1 (average circulation 10,000 copies) in 2000.

Book production (number of titles): 5 in 1998.

Sources: International Telecommunication Union; UNESCO, *Statistical Yearbook*, UNESCO Institute for Statistics; UN, *Statistical Yearbook*.

Education

(2002/03, unless otherwise indicated)

	Institutions*	Teachers	Males	Females	Total
Pre-primary	319	692	6,443	6,330	12,773
Primary	4,701	27,504	553,920	441,143	995,063
Secondary	n.a.	8,366†	181,246†	79,631†	260,877†
Tertiary	n.a.	384*	12,607†	2,564†	15,171†

* 1998/99.
† 1999/2000.

Source: UNESCO Institute for Statistics.

Adult literacy rate (UNESCO estimates): 53.0% (males 68.5%; females 38.3%) in 2003 (Source: UN Development Programme, *Human Development Report*).

Directory

The Constitution

The Constitution that was approved in a national referendum on 27 September 1992, and subsequently amended, defines the rights, freedoms and obligations of Togolese citizens, and defines the separation of powers among the executive, legislative and judicial organs of state.

Executive power is vested in the President of the Republic, who is elected, by direct universal adult suffrage, with a five-year mandate. The legislature, the Assemblée nationale, is similarly elected for a period of five years, its 81 members being directly elected by universal suffrage. The President of the Republic appoints a Prime Minister who is able to command a majority in the legislature, and the Prime Minister, in consultation with the President, appoints other government ministers. A Constitutional Court is designated as the highest court of jurisdiction in constitutional matters.

Constitutional amendments, approved by the Assemblée nationale in late December 2002, removed the previous restriction limiting the President to serving two terms of office; reduced the minimum age for presidential candidates from 45 to 35 years; and required presidential candidates holding dual or multiple citizenships to renounce their non-Togolese nationality or nationalities.

An amendment authorizing an interim President to serve the remainder of a deceased predecessor's term was approved by the Assemblée nationale in February 2005; later that month, however, the amendment was reversed.

The Government

HEAD OF STATE

President: FAURE GNASSINGBÉ (inaugurated 4 May 2005).

COUNCIL OF MINISTERS
(April 2006)

Prime Minister, Head of the Government: EDEM KODJO.
Minister of State, Minister of Foreign Affairs and African Integration: ZARIFOU AYÉVA.
Minister of State, Minister of Agriculture, Stockbreeding and Fisheries: CHARLES KONDI AGBA.
Minister of Primary and Secondary Education: KOMI KLASSOU.
Minister of the Environment and Forest Resources: ISSIFOU OKOULOU-KANTCHATI.
Minister of Trade, Industry and Crafts: JEAN-LUCIEN SAVI DE TOVÉ.
Minister of Communication and Civic Training: KOKOU TOZOUN.
Minister of Territorial Administration and Decentralization: KATARI FOLI-BAZI.
Keeper of the Seals, Minister of Justice: TCHESSA ABI.
Minister of Health: SUZANNE AHO ASSOUMA.
Minister of the Economy, Finance and Privatization: PAYADOWA BOUKPESSI.
Minister of Security: Col PITALOUNA-ANI LAOKPESSI.
Minister of Human Rights, Democracy and Reconciliation: Me LORETA MENSAH AKUÉTÉ.
Minister of Development and Land Management: YENDJA YENTCHABRÉ.
Minister of Youth and Sports: AGOUTA OUYENGA.
Minister of Relations with the Institutions of the Republic: COMLANGAN MAWUTOÈ D'ALMEIDA.
Minister of Population, Social Affairs and the Promotion of Women: SAYO BOYOTI.
Minister of Higher Education and Research: Prof. FIDÈL COMLAN.
Minister of Capital Works, Transport, Posts and Telecommunications: KOKOUVI DOGBÉ.
Minister of Towns: MARC AKLESSOU AKITÈM.
Minister of Labour, Employment and the Civil Service: YVES MADO NAGOU.
Minister of Mines, Energy and Water: KOKOU SOLÉTÉ AGBÉMADON.
Minister of Technical Education and Professional Training: ANTOINE AGBÉWANOU EDOU.
Minister of Culture, Tourism and Leisure: GABRIEL SASSOUVI DOSSEH-ANYROH.
Minister-delegate at the Presidency of the Republic, responsible for Defence and Veterans: KPATCHA GNASSINGBÉ.
Minister-delegate to the Prime Minister, responsible for the Private Sector and the Development of the Free Zone: IDRISSA DERMANE.
Minister-delegate to the Minister of State, Minister of Foreign Affairs and African Integration, responsible for Co-operation: GILBERT BAWARA.
Minister-delegate to the Minister of State, Minister of Agriculture, Stockbreeding and Fisheries, responsible for Water Supplies to Villages: KASSÉGNÉ ADJONOU.
Secretary of State to the Minister of the Population, Social Affairs and the Promotion of Women, responsible for the Protection of Children and Elderly Persons: AGNÉLÉ CHRISTINE MENSAH.
Secretary of State to the Minister of Youth and Sports, responsible for the Promotion of Young Persons: GILBERT KODJO ATSU.

MINISTRIES

Office of the President: Palais Présidentiel, ave de la Marina, Lomé; tel. 221-27-01; fax 221-18-97; e-mail presidence@republicoftogo.com; internet www.republicoftogo.com.
Office of the Prime Minister: Palais de la Primature, BP 1161, Lomé; tel. 221-15-64; fax 221-37-53.
Ministry of Agriculture, Stockbreeding and Fisheries: ave de Sarakawa, BP 341, Lomé; tel. 221-04-82; fax 221-87-92.
Ministry of Capital Works, Transport, Posts and Telecommunications: ave de Sarakawa, BP 389, Lomé; tel. 223-14-00; fax 221-68-12; e-mail eco@republicoftogo.com.
Ministry of Communication and Civic Training: BP 40, Lomé; tel. 221-29-30; fax 221-43-80; e-mail info@republicoftogo.com.
Ministry of Culture, Tourism and Leisure: 47 ave des Nations Unies, BP 3146, Lomé; tel. and fax 222-41-97.
Ministry of Defence and Veterans: Lomé; tel. 221-28-12; fax 221-88-41.
Ministry of Development and Land Management: Lomé.
Ministry of the Economy, Finance and Privatization: CASEF, ave Sarakawa, BP 387, Lomé; tel. 221-00-37; fax 221-25-48; e-mail eco@republicoftogo.com.
Ministry of the Environment and Forest Resources: Lomé; tel. 221-56-58; fax 221-03-33.
Ministry of Foreign Affairs and African Integration: place du Monument aux Morts, BP 900, Lomé; tel. 221-36-01; fax 221-39-74; e-mail diplo@republicoftogo.com.
Ministry of Health: rue Branly, BP 386, Lomé; tel. 221-35-24; fax 222-20-73.
Ministry of Higher Education and Research: rue Colonel de Roux, BP 12175, Lomé; tel. 222-09-83; fax 222-07-83.
Ministry of Human Rights, Democracy and Reconciliation: Lomé.
Ministry of Justice: ave de la Marina, rue Colonel de Roux, Lomé; tel. 221-26-53; fax 222-29-06.
Ministry of Labour, Employment and the Civil Service: angle ave de la Marina et rue Kpalimé, BP 372, Lomé; tel. 221-41-83; fax 222-56-85.
Ministry of Mines, Energy and Water: Lomé.
Ministry of Population, Social Affairs and the Promotion of Women: Lomé.
Ministry of Primary and Secondary Education: Lomé.
Ministry of Relations with the Institutions of the Republic: Lomé.
Ministry of Security: rue Albert Sarraut, Lomé; tel. 222-57-12; fax 222-61-50; e-mail info@republicoftogo.com.
Ministry of Technical Education and Professional Training: BP 398, Lomé; tel. 221-20-97; fax 221-89-34.
Ministry of Territorial Administration and Decentralization: Lomé.
Ministry of Trade, Industry and Crafts: 1 ave de Sarakawa, face au Monument aux Morts, BP 383, Lomé; tel. 221-20-25; fax 221-05-72; e-mail eco@republicoftogo.com.
Ministry of Youth and Sports: BP 40, Lomé; tel. 221-22-47; fax 222-42-28.

President and Legislature

PRESIDENT

Presidential Election, 24 April 2005

Candidate	Votes	% of votes
Faure Gnassingbé (RPT)	1,323,622	60.16
Emmanuel Bob Akitani (UFC)	841,642	38.25
Nicolas Lawson (PRR)	22,979	1.04
Harry Octavianus Olympio (RSDD)	12,033	0.55
Total	**2,200,276**	**100.00**

LEGISLATURE

Assemblée nationale

Palais des Congrès, BP 327, Lomé; tel. 222-57-91; fax 222-11-68; e-mail assemblee.nationale@syfed.tg.refer.org.

President: El Hadj ABASS BONFOH.

General Election, 27 October 2002

Party	Seats
Rassemblement du peuple togolais (RPT)	72
Rassemblement pour le soutien de la démocratie et du développement (RSDD)	3
Union pour la démocratie et le progrès social (UDPS)	2
Juvento—Mouvement de la jeunesse togolaise	2
Mouvement des croyants pour l'égalité et la paix (MOCEP)	1
Independents	1
Total	**81**

Election Commission

Commission électorale nationale indépendante (CENI): rue des Ekis, Lomé; tel. 222-39-61; Pres. KISSEM TCHANGAI-WALLA.

Political Organizations

In late 2005 there were around 70 registered political parties. Of those active in early 2006, the following were among the most influential:

Alliance démocratique pour la Patrie (ADP): Lomé; f. 2006; opposed to regime of Pres. Faure Gnassingbé; Leaders AGBEYOME KODJO, MAURICE DAHUKU PERE.

Alliance togolaise pour la démocratie (ATD): Lomé; Leader ADANI IFÉ ATAKPAMEVI.

Coalition des forces démocrates (CFD): Lomé; f. Oct. 2002 by nine parties that boycotted legislative elections held in that month; opposed the administration of fmr Pres. Eyadéma; the UFC left the coalition in Feb. 2003; Chair. EDEM KODJO (acting).

In mid-2003 constituent parties and groupings included:

Convergence patriotique panafricaine (CPP): BP 12703, Lomé; tel. 221-58-43; f. 1999 by merger of the Parti d'action pour la démocratie (PAD), the Parti des démocrates pour l'unité (PDU), the Union pour la démocratie et la solidarité (UDS) and the Union togolaise pour la démocratie (UTD); did not participate in legislative elections in 2002; Pres. EDEM KODJO; First Vice-Pres. JEAN-LUCIEN SAVI DE TOVÉ.

Front uni de l'opposition (Le Front): Lomé; f. 2002; Co-ordinator Me YAWOVI AGBOYIBO.

Alliance des démocrates pour le développement intégral (ADDI): Lomé; tel. 221-47-90; Leader Dr NAGBANDJA KAMPATIBE.

Comité d'action pour le renouveau (CAR): 58 ave du 24 janvier, BP06, Lomé; tel. 222-05-66; fax 221-62-54; e-mail yagboyibo@bibway.com; moderately conservative; Leader Me YAWOVI AGBOYIBO; Sec.-Gen. DODJI APEVON; 251,349 mems (Dec. 1999).

Convention démocratique des peuples africains—Branche togolaise (CDPA—BT): 2 rue des Cheminots, BP 13963, Lomé; tel. 221-71-75; fax 226-46-55; e-mail cdpa-bt@cdpa-bt.org; internet www.cdpa-bt.org; f. 1991; socialist; Gen.-Sec. LÉOPOLD GNININVI; First Sec. Prof. EMMANUEL Y. GU-KONU.

Union pour la démocratie et la solidarité—Togo (UDS—Togo): 276 blvd Circulaire, BP 8580, Lomé; tel. 222-55-64; fax 221-81-95; e-mail uds-togo@wanadoo.fr; Leader ANTOINE FOLLY.

Pacte socialiste pour le renouveau (PSR): Lomé; f. 2003 by fmr 'renovationist' mems of RPT; Leader TCHESSA ABI.

Coordination des partis politiques de l'opposition constructive (CPOC): Lomé; f. 2002; alliance of 'constructive opposition' parties that favoured working with the regime of fmr Pres. Eyadéma.

In mid-2003 members included:

Juvento—Mouvement de la jeunesse togolaise: Lomé; f. 2001; nationalist youth movement; Leaders MONSILIA DJATO, ABALO FIRMIN.

Mouvement des croyants pour l'égalité et la paix (MOCEP): Lomé; Leader COMLANGAN MAWUTOË D'ALMEIDA.

Union pour la démocratie et le progrès social (UDPS): Lomé; Sec.-Gen. SEKODONA SEGO.

Coordination nationale des forces nouvelles (CFN): Lomé; f. 1993; centrist; Pres. Me JOSEPH KOKOU KOFFIGOH.

Parti démocratique togolais (PDT): Lomé; Leader M'BA KABASSÉMA.

Parti du renouveau et de la rédemption (PRR): Lomé; Pres. NICOLAS LAWSON.

Parti des travailleurs (PT): 49 ave de Calais, BP 13974, Nyekonapoe, Lomé; tel. 913-65-54; socialist; Co-ordinating Sec. CLAUDE AMEGANVI.

Rassemblement du peuple togolais (RPT): place de l'Indépendance, BP 1208, Lomé; tel. 226-93-83; e-mail rpttogo@yahoo.fr; f. 1969; sole legal party 1969–91; Pres. FAURE GNASSINGBÉ; Sec.-Gen. DAMA DRAMANI.

Rassemblement pour le soutien de la démocratie et du développement (RSDD): Lomé; tel. 222-38-80; expelled from the CPOC (q.v.) in August 2003; Leader HARRY OCTAVIANUS OLYMPIO.

Union des forces de changement (UFC): 59 rue Koudadzé, Lom-Nava, BP 62168 Lomé; tel. and fax 221-33-32; e-mail contact@ufctogo.com; internet www.ufctogo.com; f. 1992; social-democratic; First Vice-Pres Emmanuel Bob Akitani contested presidential election in June 2003 under the designation Parti des forces de changement—Union des forces de changement; Pres. GILCHRIST OLYMPIO; First Vice-Pres. EMMANUEL BOB AKITANI; Sec.-Gen. JEAN-PIERRE FABRE.

Union des libéraux indépendants (ULI): f. 1993 to succeed Union des démocrates pour le renouveau; Leader KWAMI MENSAN JACQUES AMOUZOU.

Diplomatic Representation

EMBASSIES IN TOGO

China, People's Republic: 1381 rue de l'Entente, BP 2690, Lomé; tel. 222-38-56; fax 221-40-75; e-mail chinaemb_tg@mfa.gov.cn; Ambassador ZHANG SHIXIAN.

Congo, Democratic Republic: Lomé; tel. 221-51-55; Ambassador LOKOKA IKUKELE BOMOLO.

Egypt: 1163 rue de l'OCAM, BP 8, Lomé; tel. 221-24-43; fax 221-10-22; Ambassador RAGAA ALI HASSAN.

France: 13 ave du Golfe, BP 337, Lomé; tel. 221-25-71; fax 221-87-60; e-mail ambafrance-lome@tg.refer.org; internet www.ambafrance-tg.org; Ambassador ALAIN HOLLEVILLE.

Gabon: Lomé; tel. 222-18-93; fax 222-18-92; Ambassador (vacant).

Germany: blvd de la République, BP 1175, Lomé; tel. 221-23-38; fax 222-18-88; e-mail amballtogo@cafe.tg; Ambassador KLAUS GÜNTER GROHMANN.

Ghana: 8 rue Paulin Eklou, Tokoin-Ouest, BP 92, Lomé; tel. 221-31-94; fax 221-77-36; e-mail ghmfa01@cafe.tg; Ambassador KWABENA MENSA-BONSU.

Guinea: Lomé; tel. 221-74-98; fax 221-81-16.

Korea, Democratic People's Republic: Lomé; Ambassador KIL MUN YONG.

Libya: blvd du 13 janvier, BP 4872, Lomé; tel. 221-40-63; Chargé d'affaires a.i. AHMED M. ABDULKAFI.

Nigeria: 311 blvd du 13 janvier, BP 1189, Lomé; tel. and fax 221-59-76; Ambassador THOMAS AGUIYI-IRONSI.

USA: rue Kouenou, angle rue 15 Beniglato, BP 852, Lomé; tel. 221-29-94; fax 221-79-52; e-mail RobertsonJJ2@state.gov; internet togo.usembassy.gov; Ambassador DAVID BERNARD DUNN.

Judicial System

Justice is administered by the Constitutional Court, the Supreme Court, two Appeal Courts and the Tribunaux de première instance, which hear civil, commercial and criminal cases. There is a labour tribunal and a tribunal for children's rights. In addition, there are two exceptional courts, the Cour de sûreté de l'Etat, which judges crimes against internal and external state security, and the Tribunal spécial chargé de la répression des détournements de deniers publics, which deals with cases of misuse of public funds.

Constitutional Court: 32 ave Augustino de Souza, Lomé; tel. 221-72-98; fax 221-07-40; f. 1997; seven mems; Pres. ATSU KOFFI AMEGA.

Supreme Court: BP 906, Lomé; tel. 221-22-58; f. 1961; consists of three chambers (judicial, administrative and auditing); Chair. FESSOU LAWSON; Attorney-General KOUAMI AMADOS-DJOKO.

State Attorney: ATARA NDAKENA.

Religion

It is estimated that about 50% of the population follow traditional animist beliefs, some 35% are Christians and 15% are Muslims.

CHRISTIANITY

The Roman Catholic Church

Togo comprises one archdiocese and six dioceses. At 31 December 2003 there were an estimated 1,487,243 adherents in the country, representing about 24.9% of the total population.

Bishops' Conference

Conférence Episcopale du Togo, 561 rue Aniko Palako, BP 348, Lomé; tel. 221-22-72; fax 222-48-08; Statutes approved 1979; Pres. Most Rev. PHILIPPE FANOKO KOSSI KPODZRO (Archbishop of Lomé).

Archbishop of Lomé: Most Rev. PHILIPPE FANOKO KOSSI KPODZRO, Archevêché, 561 rue Aniko Palako, BP 348, Lomé; tel. 221-22-72; fax 222-48-08; e-mail archlome@lome.ocicnet.net.

Protestant Churches

There are about 250 mission centres, with a personnel of some 250, affiliated to European and US societies and administered by a Conseil Synodal, presided over by a moderator.

Directorate of Protestant Churches: 1 rue Maréchal Foch, BP 378, Lomé; Moderator Pastor AWUME (acting).

Eglise Evangélique Presbytérienne du Togo: 1 rue Tokmake, BP 2, Lomé; tel. 221-46-69; fax 222-23-63; Moderator Rev. Dr KODJO BESSA.

Fédération des Evangéliques du Togo: Lomé; Co-ordinator HAPPY AZIADEKEY.

BAHÁ'Í FAITH

Assemblée spirituelle nationale: BP 1659, Lomé; tel. 221-21-99; e-mail asnbaha@yahoo.fr; Sec. ALLADOUM NGOMNA; 18,788 adherents (2005).

The Press

DAILY

Togo-Presse: BP 891, Lomé; tel. 221-53-95; fax 222-37-66; f. 1961; official govt publ; French, Kabiye and Ewe; political, economic and cultural; circ. 8,000.

PERIODICALS

L'Aurore: Lomé; tel. 222-65-41; fax 222-65-89; e-mail aurore37@caramail.com; weekly; independent; Editor-in-Chief ANKOU SALVADOR; circ. 2,500.

Carrefour: 596 rue Ablogame, BP 6125, Lomé; tel. 944-45-43; e-mail carrefour1@caramail.com; f. 1991; pro-opposition; weekly; Dir HOLONOU HOUKPATI; circ. 3,000 (2000).

Cité Magazine: 50 ave Pas de Souza, BP 6275, Lomé; tel. and fax 222-67-40; e-mail citemag@cafe.tg; internet www.cafe.tg/citemag; monthly; Editor-in-Chief GAËTAN K. GNATCHIKO.

Le Citoyen: Lomé; tel. 221-73-44; independent.

La Colombe: Lomé; f. 2001; weekly.

Le Combat du Peuple: 62 rue Blagogee, BP 4682, Lomé; tel. 904-53-83; fax 222-65-89; e-mail combat@webmails.com; f. 1994; pro-opposition weekly; Editor LUCIEN DJOSSOU MESSAN; circ. 3,500 (2000).

Le Courrier du Golfe: rue de l'OCAM, angle rue Sotomarcy, BP 660, Lomé; tel. 221-67-92.

Crocodile: 299 rue Kuévidjin, no 27 Bé-Château, BP 60087, Lomé; tel. 221-38-21; fax 226-13-70; e-mail crocodile@caramail.com; f. 1993; pro-opposition; weekly; Dir VIGNO KOFFI HOUNKANLY; Editor FRANCIS-PEDRO AMAZUN; circ. 3,500 (2000).

Le Débat: BP 8737, Lomé; tel. 222-42-84; f. 1991; 2 a month; Dir PROSPER ETEH.

La Dépêche: BP 20039, Lomé; tel. and fax 221-09-32; e-mail ladepeche@hotmail.com; f. 1993; 2 a week; Editor ESSO-WE APPOLINAIRE MÈWÈNAMÈSSÈ; circ. 3,000.

Echos d'Afrique: CDPA-BT, BP 13963, Lomé; e-mail cdpa-bt@cdpa-bt.org; internet www.cdpa-bt.org/c_fra/c_echo.html; weekly; published by the CDPA—BT; Editor RIGOBERT BASSADOU.

L'Etoile du matin: S/C Maison du journalisme, Casier no 50, Lomé; e-mail wielfridsewa18@hotmail.com; f. 2000; weekly; Dir WIELFRID SÉWA TCHOUKOULI.

Etudes Togolaises: Institut National de la Recherche Scientifique, BP 2240, Lomé; tel. 221-57-39; f. 1965; quarterly; scientific review, mainly anthropology.

L'Eveil du Peuple: Lomé; weekly; re-established in 2002, having ceased publication in 1999.

L'Evénement: 44–50 rue Douka, Kotokoucondji, BP 1800, Lomé; tel. 222-65-89; f. 1999; independent; weekly; Dir MENSAH KOUDJODJI; circ. 3,000 (2000).

L'Exilé: Maison du journalisme, Casier no 28, Lomé; e-mail jexil@hotmail.com; f. 2000; weekly; independent; Editor HIPPOLYTE AGBOH.

Game su/Tev Fema: 125 ave de la Nouvelle Marché, BP 1247, Lomé; tel. 221-28-44; f. 1997; monthly; Ewe and Kabiye; govt publ. for the newly literate; circ. 3,000.

Hébdo-forum: 60 rue Tamakloe, BP 3681, Lomé; weekly.

Journal Officiel de la République du Togo (JORT): BP 891, Lomé; tel. 221-37-18; fax 222-14-89; government acts, laws, decrees and decisions.

Kpakpa Désenchanté: BP 8917, Lomé; tel. 221-37-39; weekly; independent; satirical.

Kyrielle: BP 81213, Lomé; e-mail noel@journaliste.org; f. 1999; monthly; culture, sport; Dir CREDO TETTEH; circ. 3,000 (2000).

Libre Togovi: BP 81190, Lomé; tel. 904-43-36; e-mail libretogovi@mail.com; 2 a week; pro-democracy, opposed to Govt of fmr Pres. Eyadéma; distributed by the Comité presse et communication de la concertation nationale de la société civile.

La Matinée: Tokoin Nkafu, rue Kpoguédé, BP 30368, Lomé; tel. 226-69-02; f. 1999; monthly; Dir KASSÉRÉ PIERRE SABI.

Le Miroir du Peuple: 48 rue Defale, BP 81231, Lomé; tel. 946-60-24; e-mail nouveau90@hotmail.com; f. 1998; fmrly Le Nouveau Combat; weekly; independent; Dir ELIAS EDOH HOUNKANLY; circ. 1,000 (2000).

Motion d'Information: Lomé; f. 1997; weekly; pro-opposition.

Nouvel Echo: BP 3681, Lomé; tel. 947-72-40; f. 1997; pro-opposition; weekly; Dir ALPHONSE NEVAME KLU; Editor JULIEN AYIH.

Nouvel Eclat: Lomé; tel. 945-55-42; e-mail nouvel.eclat@caramail.com; f. 2000; weekly; Dir CHARLES PASSOU; circ. 2,500 (2000).

Nouvel Horizon: Maison du journalisme, Casier no 38, BP 81213, Lomé; tel. 222-09-55; f. 2000; weekly; Dir DONNAS A. AMOZOUGAN; circ. 3,000 (2000).

La Nouvelle République: Lomé; tel. 945-55-43; e-mail nouvelle.republique@caramail.com; f. 1999; Dir WIELFRID SÉWA TCHOUKOULI; circ. 2,500 (2000).

La Parole: Lomé; tel. 221-55-90.

Politicos: Lomé; tel. 945-32-66; fax 226-13-70; e-mail politicos@hotmail.com; f. 1993; weekly; Editor ELVIS A. KAO; circ. 1,500 (2000).

Le Regard: BP 81213, Lomé; tel. 222-65-89; fax 226-13-70; e-mail leregard@webmails.com; f. 1996; weekly; pro-opposition; supports promotion of human rights; Editor ABASS MIKAÏLA SAIBOU; circ. 3,000 (2000).

Le Reporter des Temps Nouveaux: Maison du journalisme, Casier no 22, BP 1800, Lomé; tel. 945-40-45; fax 226-18-22; e-mail le_reporter@hotmail.com; f. 1998; weekly; independent; political criticism and analysis; Man. Editor ROMAIN ATTISO KOUDJODJI; circ. 3,000 (2000).

Le Scorpion—Akéklé: S/C Maison du journalisme, BP 81213, Lomé; tel. 944-43-80; fax 226-13-70; e-mail lescorpion@webmails.com; f. 1998; opposition weekly; Dir DIDIER AGBLETO; circ. 3,500 (2000).

Le Secteur Privé: angle ave de la Présidence, BP 360, Lomé; tel. 221-70-65; fax 221-47-30; monthly; publ. by Chambre de Commerce et d'Industrie du Togo.

Le Soleil: Lomé; tel. 944-41-97; e-mail joel12@dromadaire.com; f. 1999; weekly; Dir ARISTO GABA; circ. 2,000 (2000).

Témoin de la Nation: Maison du journalisme, Casier no 48, BP 434, Lomé; tel. 221-24-92; f. 2000; weekly; Dir ELIAS EBOH.

Tingo Tingo: 44–50 rue Douka, Kotokoucondji, BP 80419, Lomé; tel. 222-17-53; e-mail jtingo-tingo@yahoo.fr; f. 1996; weekly; independent; Editor AUGUSTIN ASIONBO; circ. 3,500 (2000).

Togo-Images: BP 4869, Lomé; tel. 221-56-80; f. 1962; monthly series of wall posters depicting recent political, economic and cultural events in Togo; publ. by govt information service; Dir AKOBI BEDOU; circ. 5,000.

Togo-Presse: BP 891, Lomé; tel. 221-53-95; fax 22-37-66; f. 1962; publ by Govt in French, Ewe and Kabre; political, economic and cultural affairs; Dir WIYAO DADJA POUWI; circ. 5,000 (2000).

La Tribune du Peuple: Lomé; weekly; pro-opposition; Dir KODJO AFATSAO SILIADIN.

PRESS ASSOCIATION

Union des Journalistes Indépendants du Togo: BP 81213, Lomé; tel. 226-13-00; fax 226-13-70; e-mail maison-du-journalisme@ids.tg; also operates Maison de Presse; Sec.-Gen. GABRIEL AYITÉ BAGLO.

NEWS AGENCY

Agence Togolaise de Presse (ATOP): 35 rue des Medias, BP 891, Lomé; tel. 221-53-95; fax 222-37-66; f. 1975; Dir-Gen. SEEDEM ABASSA.

Publishers

Centre Togolais de Communication Evangélique—Editions Haho (CTCE—Editions Haho): 1 rue de Commerce, BP 378, Lomé; tel. 221-45-82; fax 221-29-67; e-mail ctcte@cafe.tg; f. 1983; general literature, popular science, poetry, school textbooks, Christian interest; Dir KODJO MAWULI ETSÉ.

Editions Akpagnon: BP 3531, Lomé; tel. and fax 222-02-44; e-mail yedogbe@yahoo.fr; f. 1978; general literature and non-fiction; Man. Dir YVES-EMMANUEL DOGBÉ.

Editions de la Rose Bleue: BP 12452, Lomé; tel. 222-93-39; fax 222-96-69; e-mail dorkenoo_ephrem@yahoo.fr; general literature, poetry; Dir EPHREM SETH DORKENOO.

Les Nouvelles Editions Africaines du Togo (NEA-TOGO): 239 blvd du 13 janvier, BP 4862, Lomé; tel. and fax 222-10-19; e-mail neatogo@yahoo.fr; general fiction, non-fiction and textbooks; Dir-Gen. KOKOU A. KALIPE; Editorial Dir TCHOTCHO CHRISTIANE EKUE.

Les Presses de l'Université du Lomé: BP 1515, Lomé; tel. 225-48-44; fax 225-87-84.

Société Nationale des Editions du Togo (EDITOGO): BP 891, Lomé; tel. 221-61-06; f. 1961; govt-owned; general and educational; Pres. BIOSSEY KOKOU TOZOUN; Man. Dir WIYAO DADJA POUWI.

Broadcasting and Communications

TELECOMMUNICATIONS

Télécel Togo: Cité Maman N'Danida, route de Kpalimé, BP 14511, Lomé; tel. 225-82-50; fax 225-82-51; e-mail telecel@telecel.tg; internet www.telecel.tg; operates mobile cellular telecommunications network in Lomé and six other towns.

Togo Télécom: ave N. Grunitzky, BP 333, Lomé; tel. 221-44-01; fax 221-03-73; e-mail contact@togotel.net.tg; internet www.togotel.net.tg; Dir-Gen. KOSSIVI PAUL AYIKOE.

   Togo Cellulaire—Togocel: Lomé; tel. 004-05-06; e-mail togocel@togocel.tg; internet www.togocel.tg; f. 2001; provides mobile cellular communications services to more than 70% of the territory of Togo.

BROADCASTING

Radio

Legislation providing for the liberalization of radio broadcasting was ratified in November 1990. However, no definitive licences for radio stations had been issued by mid-2002, when 11 private stations were, nevertheless, in operation.

Radiodiffusion du Togo (Internationale)—Radio Lomé: BP 434, Lomé; tel. 221-24-93; fax 221-24-92; e-mail radiolome@yahoo.fr; f. 1953; state-controlled; radio programmes in French, English and vernacular languages; Dir AMÉVI DABLA.

Radiodiffusion du Togo (Nationale): BP 21, Kara; tel. 660-60-60; f. 1974 as Radiodiffusion Kara (Togo); state-controlled; radio programmes in French and vernacular languages; Dir M'BA KPENOUGOU.

Radio Avenir: BP 20183, 76 blvd de la Kara, Doumassessé, Lomé; tel. 221-20-88; fax 221-03-01; f. 1998; broadcasts in French, English, Ewe and Kotokoli; Dir KPÉLE-KOFFI AHOOMEY-ZUNU.

Radio Carré Jeunes: BP 2550, Adidogomé, Lomé; tel. 225-77-44; e-mail carrejeunes@yahoo.fr; f. 1999; community radio stn; popular education, cultural information; broadcasts in French, Ewe, Kabyè and other local languages; Dir FOLY ALODÉ GLIDJITO AMAGLI.

Radio de l'Evangile-Jésus Vous Aime (JVA): Klikamé, Bretelle Atikoumé BP 2313, Lomé; tel. 225-44-95; fax 225-92-81; e-mail radio.jva@fatad.org; f. 1995; owned by the West Africa Advanced School of Theology (Assemblies of God); Christian; education and development; broadcasts on FM frequencies in Lomé and Agou in French, English and 12 local languages; Dir Pastor DOUTI LALLEBILI FLINDJA.

Radio Galaxy: BP 20822, 253 rue 48, Doumassessé, Lomé; tel. and fax 221-63-18; e-mail radiogalaxy@yahoo.fr; f. 1996; broadcasts in French, English, Ewe and Kabyè; Dir PAUL S. TCHASSOUA.

Radio Kanal FM: Immeuble Decor, blvd du 13 janvier, BP 61554, Lomé; tel. 221-33-74; fax 220-19-68; e-mail kanalfm@cafe.tg; f. 1997; broadcasts in French and Mina; independent; Dir MODESTE MESSAVUSSUA-KUE.

Radio Maria Togo: BP 30162, 155 de la rue 158, Hédzranawoé, Lomé; tel. 226-11-31; fax 226-35-00; e-mail rmariatg@ids.tg; f. 1997; Roman Catholic; broadcasts in French, English and six local languages; Dir R. P. GUSTAVE SANVEE.

Radio Metropolys: 157 rue Missahoé, Tokoin Hôpital, derrière Pharmacie Ave Marie, Lomé; tel. 222-86-81; e-mail metropolys.lome@voila.fr; internet site.voila.fr/metropolys; f. 2000; secular and apolitical broadcasts in French only; Dir NOËLIE ASSOGBAVI.

Radio Nana FM: BP 6035, Immeuble du Grand Marché du Lomé, Lomé; tel. 221-02-63; e-mail petdog2@yahoo.fr; f. 1999; broadcasts in French and Mina; community stn; political, economic and cultural information; Dir PETER DOGBE.

Radio Nostalgie: 14 ave de la Victoire, Quartier Tokoin-Hôpital, BP 13836, Lomé; tel. 222-25-41; fax 221-07-82; e-mail nostalgietogo@yahoo.fr; internet www.nostalgie.tg; f. 1995; broadcasts in French, Ewe and Mina; Pres. and Dir-Gen. FLAVIEN JOHNSON.

Radio Tropik FM: BP 2276, Quartier Wuiti, Lomé; tel. 226-11-11; e-mail tropikfm@nomade.fr; f. 1995; broadcasts in French, Kabyè and Tem; Dir BLAISE YAO AMEDODJI.

Radio Zion: BP 13853, Adidogomé, Lomé; tel. 225-64-99; f. 1999; religious; broadcasts in French, Ewe and Kabyè; Dir LUC ADJAHO.

Television

Télévision Togolaise: BP 3286, Lomé; tel. 221-53-57; fax 221-57-86; e-mail televisiontogolaise@yahoo.fr; internet www.tvt.tg; f. 1973; state-controlled; three stations; programmes in French and vernacular languages; Dir PITANG TCHALLA.

Broadcasting Association

Organisation Togolaise des Radios et Télévisions Indépendantes (ORTI): Lomé; tel. 221-33-74; e-mail kawokou@syfed.tg.refer.org; Pres. RAYMOND AWOKOU KOUKOU.

Finance

(cap. = capital; res = reserves; dep. = deposits; m. = million; br. = branch; amounts in francs CFA, unless otherwise indicated)

BANKING

Central Bank

Banque Centrale des Etats de l'Afrique de l'Ouest (BCEAO): ave de Sarakawa, BP 120, Lomé; tel. 221-53-83; fax 221-76-02; e-mail ocourrier@lome.bceao.int; internet www.bceao.int; HQ in Dakar, Senegal; f. 1962; bank of issue for the mem. states of the Union économique et monétaire ouest-africaine (UEMOA, comprising Benin, Burkina Faso, Côte d'Ivoire, Guinea-Bissau, Mali, Niger, Senegal and Togo); cap. and res 859,313m., total assets 5,671,675m. (Dec. 2002); Gov. CHARLES KONAN BANNY; Dir in Togo AYÉWANOU AGETOHO GBEASOR; br. at Kara.

Commercial Banks

Banque Togolaise pour le Commerce et l'Industrie (BTCI): 169 blvd du 13 janvier, BP 363, Lomé; tel. 221-46-41; fax 221-32-65; e-mail btci@btci.tg; f. 1974; 48.5% by Groupe BNP Paribas (France) 24.8% owned by Société Financière pour les Pays d'Outre-mer; cap. and res 3,147m., total assets 75,143m. (Dec. 2003); Pres. BARRY MOUSSA BARQUÉ; Dir-Gen. YAO PATRICE KANEKATOUA; 8 brs.

Banque Internationale pour l'Afrique au Togo (BIA—Togo): 13 rue de Commerce, BP 346, Lomé; tel. 221-32-86; fax 221-10-19; e-mail bia-togo@cafe.tg; f. 1965; fmrly Meridien BIAO—Togo; 57.5% owned by Banque Belgolaise (Belgium); cap. and res 567m., total assets 51,793m. (Dec. 2003); Pres. KOMLA ALIPUI; Dir-Gen. JEAN-PAUL LE CALM; 7 brs.

Ecobank Togo (Ecobank-T): 20 rue de Commerce, BP 3302, Lomé; tel. 221-72-14; fax 221-42-37; e-mail ecobanktg@ecobank.com; internet www.ecobank.com; f. 1988; 80.7% owned by Ecobank

Transnational Inc (operating under the auspices of the Economic Community of West African States), 14.0% by Togolese private investors; cap. and res 4,843.1m., total assets 75,136.0m. (Dec. 2003); Dir-Gen. ROGER DAHA CHINAMON; 2 brs.

Ecobank Transnational Inc: 20 rue du Commerce, BP 3261, Lomé; tel. 221-03-03; fax 221-51-19; e-mail info@ecobank.com; internet www.ecobank.com; f. 1985; holding co for banking cos in Benin, Burkina Faso, Cameroon, Côte d'Ivoire, Ghana, Guinea, Liberia, Mali, Niger, Nigeria, Senegal and Togo, Ecobank Development Corpn and EIC Bourse; cap. and res US $105.5m., total assets $1,523.1m. (Dec. 2003); Pres. and Dir-Gen. PHILIP C. ASIODU.

Financial Bank Togo: 11 ave du 24 janvier, Lomé; tel. 271-32-71; fax 271-48-51; e-mail jean-yves.le-paulmier@financial-bank.com; f. 2004; cap. 1,500m. (2004); Pres. MENSAVI LULU MENSAH.

Société Interafricaine de Banque (SIAB): 14 rue de Commerce, BP 4874, Lomé; tel. 221-28-30; fax 221-58-29; e-mail siab@bibway.com; f. 1975; fmrly Banque Arabe Libyenne-Togolaise du Commerce Extérieur; 86% owned by Libyan Arab Foreign Bank, 14% state-owned; cap. and res 181m., total assets 6,999m. (Dec. 2003); Pres. ESSOWÉDÉOU AGBA; Dir-Gen. KHALIFA ACHOUR ETTLUAA.

Union Togolaise de Banque (UTB): blvd du 13 janvier, Nyékonakpoè, BP 359, Lomé; tel. 221-64-11; fax 221-22-06; e-mail utbsg@cafe.tg; f. 1964; 100% state-owned; transfer to majority private ownership proposed; cap. and res −12.3m., total assets 49.0m. (Dec. 2003); Pres. ESSOWÉDÉOU AGBA; Dir-Gen. YAOVI ATTIGBÉ ITOU; 11 brs.

Development Banks

Banque Ouest-Africaine de Développement (BOAD): 68 ave de la Libération, BP 1172, Lomé; tel. 221-42-44; fax 221-72-69; e-mail boadsiege@boad.org; internet www.boad.org; f. 1973; promotes West African economic development and integration; cap. 682,100m., total assets 849,993m. (Dec. 2004); Pres. (vacant).

Banque Togolaise de Développement (BTD): ave des Nîmes, angle ave N. Grunitzky, BP 65, Lomé; tel. 221-36-41; fax 221-44-56; e-mail togo_devbank@bibway.com; f. 1966; 43% state-owned, 20% owned by BCEAO, 13% by BOAD; transfer to majority private ownership pending; cap. and res 10,111m., total assets 33,418m. (Dec. 2003); Pres. ESSO KANDJA; Dir-Gen. ZAKARI DAROU-SALIM; 8 brs.

Société Nationale d'Investissement et Fonds Annexes (SNI & FA): 11 ave du 24 janvier, BP 2682, Lomé; tel. 221-62-21; fax 221-62-25; e-mail sni@ids.tg; f. 1971; fmrly Société Nationale d'Investissement et Fonds Annexes; 23% state-owned; cap. 2,600m., total assets 13,219m. (Dec. 2001); Pres. PALOUKI MASSINA; Dir-Gen. RICHARD K. ATTIPOE.

Savings Bank

Caisse d'Epargne du Togo (CET): 23 ave de la Nouvelle Marché, Lomé; tel. 221-20-60; fax 221-85-83; e-mail cet@ids.tg; internet www.cet.tg; state-owned; privatization proposed; cap. and res −3,617m., total assets 18,961m. (Dec. 2003); Pres. GNANDI SEMONDJI.

Credit Institution

Société Togolaise de Crédit Automobile (STOCA): 3 rue du Mono, BP 899, Lomé; tel. 221-37-59; fax 221-08-28; e-mail stoca@ids.tg; f. 1962; 93.3% owned by SAFCA; cap. and res −112m., total assets 1,677m. (Dec. 2003); Pres. DIACK DIAWAR; Dir-Gen. DÉLALI AGBALE.

Bankers' Association

Association Professionnelle des Banques et Etablissements Financiers du Togo: Lomé; tel. 221-24-84; fax 221-85-83.

STOCK EXCHANGE

Bourse Régionale des Valeurs Mobilières (BRVM): BP 3263, Lomé; tel. 221-23-05; fax 221-23-41; e-mail natcholi@brvm.org; internet www.brvm.org; f. 1998; national branch of BRVM (regional stock exchange based in Abidjan, Côte d'Ivoire, serving the member states of UEMOA); Man. in Togo NATHALIE BITHO ATCHOLI.

INSURANCE

Colina Togo: 10 rue du Commerce, BP 1349, Lomé; tel. 221-79-91; fax 221-73-58; e-mail c-togo@colina-sa.com; internet www.colina-sa.com; affiliated to Colina SA (Côte d'Ivoire); Dir-Gen. MARCUS LABAN.

Compagnie Commune de Réassurance des Etats Membres de la CICA (CICA—RE): ave du 24 janvier, BP 12410, Lomé; tel. 221-62-69; fax 221-49-64; e-mail cicare@cafe.tg; f. 1981; reinsurance co operating in 12 west and central African states; cap. 1,500m.; Chair. LÉON-PAUL N'GOULAKIA; Gen. Man. DIGBEU KIPRE.

Groupement Togolais d'Assurances (GTA): route d'Atakpamé, BP 3298, Lomé; tel. 225-60-75; fax 225-26-78; f. 1974; 62.9% state-owned; all classes of insurance and reinsurance; Pres. Minister of the Economy, Finance and Privatization; Man. Dir KOSSI NAMBEA.

Sicar Gras Savoye Togo: 140 blvd du 13 janvier, BP 2932, Lomé; tel. 221-35-38; fax 221-82-11; e-mail sicargs@sicargs.tg; internet www.grassavoye.com; affiliated to Gras Savoye (France); Dir GUY BIHANNIC.

UAT: Immeuble BICI, 169 blvd du 13 janvier, BP 495, Lomé; tel. 221-10-34; fax 221-87-24.

Trade and Industry

ECONOMIC AND SOCIAL COUNCIL

Conseil Economique et Social: Lomé; tel. 221-53-01; f. 1967; advisory body of 25 mems, comprising five trade unionists, five reps of industry and commerce, five reps of agriculture, five economists and sociologists, and five technologists; Pres. KOFFI GBODZIDI DJONDO.

GOVERNMENT AGENCIES

Direction Générale des Mines et de la Géologie: BP 356, Lomé; tel. 221-30-01; fax 221-31-93; organization and administration of mining in Togo; Dir-Gen. ANKOUME P. AREGBA.

EPZ Promotion Board: BP 3250, Lomé; tel. 221-13-74; fax 221-52-31; promotes the Export Processing Zone at Lomé internationally.

Société d'Administration des Zones Franches (SAZOF): BP 2748, Lomé; tel. 221-07-44; fax 221-43-05; administers and promotes free zones; Dir Gen. YAZAZ EGBARÉ.

Société Nationale de Commerce (SONACOM): 29 blvd Circulaire, BP 3009, Lomé; tel. 221-31-18; f. 1972; cap. 2,000m. francs CFA; importer of staple foods; Dir-Gen. JEAN LADOUX.

Société Nationale d'Investissement et Fonds Annexes (SNI & FA): 11 ave du 24 janvier, BP 2682, Lomé; tel. 221-62-21; fax 221-62-25; e-mail martialg@cafe.tg; f. 1971; state-owned investment co.; cap. 2,600m. francs CFA (Dec. 2000); Pres. PALOUKI MASSINA; Dir-Gen. RICHARD K. ATTIPOE.

DEVELOPMENT ORGANIZATIONS

Agricultural development is under the supervision of five regional development authorities, the Sociétés régionales d'aménagement et de développement.

Agence Française de Développement (AFD): 437 ave de Sarakawa, BP 33, Lomé; tel. 221-04-98; fax 221-79-32; e-mail afdlome@groupe-afd.org; internet www.afd.fr; Country Dir GENEVIÈVE JAVALOYES.

Association Française des Volontaires du Progrès (AFVP): BP 1511, Lomé; tel. 221-09-45; fax 221-85-04; e-mail afvp@togo-imet.com; internet www.afvp.org; f. 1965; Nat. Del. MARC LESCAUDRON.

Association Villages Entreprises: BP 23, Kpalimé; tel. and fax 441-00-62; e-mail averafp@hotmail.com; Dir KOMI AFELETE JULIEN NYUIADZI.

Office de Développement et d'Exploitation des Forêts (ODEF): 15 rue des Conseillers Municipaux, BP 334, Lomé; tel. 221-71-28; fax 221-34-91; f. 1971; develops and manages forest resources; Man. Dir KOFFI AGOGNO.

Recherche, Appui et Formation aux Initiatives d'Autodéveloppement (RAFIA): BP 43, Dapaong; tel. 770-80-89; fax 770-82-37; f. 1992; Dir NOIGUE TAMBILA LENNE.

Service de Coopération et d'Action Culturelle: BP 91, Lomé; tel. 221-21-26; fax 221-21-28; e-mail scac-lome@tg.refer.org; administers bilateral aid from the French Ministry of Foreign Affairs; Dir HENRI-LUC THIBAULT.

Société d'Appui a la Filière Café-Cacao-Coton (SAFICC): Lomé; f. 1992; development of coffee, cocoa and cotton production.

CHAMBER OF COMMERCE

Chambre de Commerce et d'Industrie du Togo (CCIT): ave de la Présidence, angle ave Georges Pompidou, BP 360, Lomé; tel. 221-70-65; fax 221-47-30; e-mail ccit@rdd.tg; f. 1921; Pres. ALEXIS LAMSEH LOOKY; Sec.-Gen. YAZAS EGBARÈ TCHOHOU; br. at Kara.

EMPLOYERS' ORGANIZATIONS

Conseil National du Patronat: 55 ave N. Grunitzky, BP 12429, Lomé; tel. and fax 221-08-30; f. 1989; Pres. A. J. KOUDOYOR.

Groupement Interprofessionnel des Entreprises du Togo (GITO): BP 345, Lomé; Pres. CLARENCE OLYMPIO.

Syndicat des Commerçants Importateurs et Exportateurs du Togo (SCIMPEXTO): BP 1166, Lomé; tel. 222-59-86; Pres. C. SITTERLIN.

Syndicat des Entrepreneurs de Travaux Publics, Bâtiments et Mines du Togo: BP 12429, Lomé; tel. 221-19-06; fax 221-08-30; Pres. JOSÉPHE NAKU.

UTILITIES

Electricity

Communauté Electrique du Bénin: ave de la Kozah, BP 1368, Lomé; tel. 221-61-32; fax 221-37-64; e-mail dg@cebnet.org; f. 1968 as a jt venture between Togo and Benin to exploit the energy resources in the two countries; Chairs KOFFI DJERI, Z. MARIUS HOUNKPATIN; Man. CYR M'PO KOUAGOU.

Togo Electricité: 426 ave du Golfe, BP 42, Lomé; tel. 221-27-43; fax 221-64-98; e-mail m.ducommun@ids.tg; f. 2000; to replace Compagnie Energie Electrique du Togo; production, transportation and distribution of electricity; Man. Dir MARC DUCOMMUN-RICOUX.

Gas

Société Togolaise de Gaz SA (Togogaz): BP 1082, Lomé; tel. 221-44-31; fax 221-55-30; 71% privatization pending; Dir-Gen. JOËL POMPA.

Water

Société Togolaise des Eaux (STE): 53 ave de la Libération, BP 1301, Lomé; tel. 221-34-81; fax 221-46-13; f. 2003 to replace Régie Nationale des Eaux du Togo; production and distribution of drinking water.

TRADE UNIONS

Collectif des Syndicats Indépendants (CSI): Lomé; f. 1992 as co-ordinating org. for three trade union confederations.

Confédération Nationale des Travailleurs du Togo (CNTT): Bourse du Travail, BP 163, 160 blvd du 13 janvier, Lomé; tel. 222-02-55; fax 221-48-33; f. 1973; Sec.-Gen. DOUEVI TCHIVIAKOU.

Confédération Syndicale des Travailleurs du Togo (CSTT): 14 rue Van Lare, BP 3058, Lomé; tel. 222-11-17; fax 222-44-41; e-mail cstt-tg@cstt-togo.org; f. 1949, dissolved 1972, re-established 1991; comprises 36 unions and 7 professional federations (Agro-Alimentation, Education, General Employees, Industry, Public Services, Transport, Woodwork and Construction); Sec.-Gen. BELIKI ADRIEN AKOUETE; 50,000 mems.

Union Nationale des Syndicats Indépendants du Togo (UNSIT): Tokoin-Wuiti, BP 30082, Lomé; tel. 221-32-88; fax 221-95-66; e-mail unsit@netcom.tg; f. 1991; Sec.-Gen. NORBERT GBIKPI-BENISSAN; 17 affiliated unions.

Transport

RAILWAYS

Société Nationale des Chemins de Fer du Togo (SNCT): BP 340, Lomé; tel. 221-43-01; fax 221-22-19; f. 1900; owned by West African Cement (Wacem) since Jan. 2002; total length 355 km, incl. lines running inland from Lomé to Atakpamé and Blitta (280 km); a coastal line, running through Lomé and Aného, which links with the Benin railway system, was closed to passenger traffic in 1987 (a service from Lomé to Palimé—119 km—has also been suspended); passengers carried (1999): 4,400 (compared with 628,200 in 1990); freight handled (1999): 1.9m. metric tons; Gen. Man. ROY GEMMELL.

ROADS

In 1996 there were an estimated 7,520 km of roads, of which 2,376 km were paved. The rehabilitation of the 675-km axis road that links the port of Lomé with Burkina Faso, and thus provides an important transport corridor for land-locked West African countries, was considered essential to Togo's economic competitiveness; in 1997 the World Bank provided a credit of US $50m. for the rehabilitation of a severely deteriorated 105-km section of the road between Atakpamé and Blitta. In 1998 Kuwait awarded Togo a loan of 6,000m. francs CFA francs to improve the Notse-Atakpamé highway. Other principal roads run from Lomé to the borders of Ghana, Nigeria and Benin.

Africa Route International (ARI—La Gazelle): Lomé; tel. 225-27-32; f. 1991 to succeed Société Nationale de Transports Routiers; Pres. and Man. Dir BAWA S. MANKOUBI.

SHIPPING

The major port, at Lomé, generally handles a substantial volume of transit trade for the land-locked countries of Mali, Niger and Burkina Faso, although political unrest in Togo, in the early 1990s, resulted in the diversion of much of this trade to neighbouring Benin. In 1995 the Banque ouest-africaine de développement approved a loan of 5,000m. francs CFA to help finance the rehabilitation of the infrastructure at Lomé port. The project aimed to re-establish Lomé as one of the principal transit ports on the west coast of Africa, and further upgrading of the port's facilities, including the computerization of port operations and the construction of a new container terminal, was implemented in the late 1990s, with private-sector funding. By 1999 freight traffic had recovered to 2.8m. metric tons, compared with only 1.1m. tons in 1993. There is another port at Kpémé for the export of phosphates.

Port Autonome de Lomé: BP 1225, Lomé; tel. 227-47-42; fax 227-26-27; e-mail togoport@togoport.tg; internet www.togoport.tg; f. 1968; transferred to private management in Jan. 2002; Pres. ASSIBA AMOUSSOU-GUENOU; Man. Dir Intendant Mil. AWA BELEYI; 1,600 employees (2003).

Conseil National des Chargeurs Togolais (CNCT): BP 2991, Lomé; tel. 223-71-00; fax 227-08-37; e-mail cnct@cnct.tg; internet www.cnct.tg; f. 1980; restructured 2001; Dir-Gen. MAGUÉNANI KOMOU.

Ecomarine International (Togo): Immeuble Ecomarine, Zone Portuaire, BP 6014, Lomé; tel. 227-48-04; fax 227-48-06; e-mail kegbeto@ecomarineint.com; f. 2001 to develop container-handling facility at Lomé Port; operates maritime transport between Togo, Senegal and Angola; Chief Exec. KOFI I. J. EGBETO.

Société Ouest-Africaine d'Entreprises Maritimes Togo (SOAEM—Togo): Zone Industrielle Portuaire, BP 3285, Lomé; tel. 221-07-20; fax 221-34-17; f. 1959; forwarding agents, warehousing, sea and road freight transport; Pres. JEAN FABRY; Man. Dir JOHN M. AQUEREBURU.

Société Togolaise de Navigation Maritime (SOTONAM): place des Quatre Etoiles, rond-point du Port, BP 4086, Lomé; tel. 221-51-73; fax 227-69-38; state-owned; privatization pending; Man. PAKOUM KPEMA.

SOCOPAO—Togo: 18 rue du Commerce, BP 821, Lomé; tel. 221-55-88; fax 221-73-17; f. 1959; freight transport, shipping agents; Pres. GUY MIRABAUD; Man. Dir HENRI CHAULIER.

SORINCO—Marine: 110 rue de l'OCAM, BP 2806, Lomé; tel. 221-56-94; freight transport, forwarding agents, warehousing, etc.; Man. AHMED EDGAR COLLINGWOOD WILLIAMS.

Togolaise d'Armements et d'Agence de Lignes SA (TAAL): 21 blvd du Mono, BP 9089, Lomé; tel. 222-02-43; fax 221-06-09; f. 1992; shipping agents, haulage management, crewing agency, forwarding agents; Pres. and Man. Dir LAURENT GBATI TAKASSI-KIKPA.

CIVIL AVIATION

There are international airports at Tokoin, near Lomé (Gnassingbé Eyadéma International Airport), and at Niamtougou. In addition, there are smaller airfields at Sokodé, Sansanné-Mango, Dapaong and Atakpamé.

Air Togo—Compagnie Aérienne Togolaise: Aéroport International de Lomé-Tokoin, BP 20393, Lomé; tel. 226-22-11; fax 226-22-30; e-mail airtogo@airtogo.net; internet www.airtogo.net; f. 1963; cap. 5m. francs CFA; scheduled internal services; Man. Dir AMADOU ISAAC ADE.

Peace Air Togo (PAT): Lomé; tel. and fax 222-71-40; internal services and services to Burkina Faso, Côte d'Ivoire and Ghana; Man. Dir PELSSEY NORMAN.

Société aéroportuaire de Lomé-Tokoin (SALT): Aéroport International de Lomé-Tokoin, BP 10112, Lomé; tel. 223-60-60; fax 226-88-95; e-mail salt@cafe.tg; Dir-Gen. Dr AKRIMA KOGOE.

Transtel Togo: Lomé; f. 2001; flights between Togo and France and Belgium; Gen. Man. M. MOROU.

Tourism

Togo's tourist industry declined precipitously in the wake of the political instability of the early 1990s; occupancy rates in the capital's hotels dropped from 33% in 1990 to 10% in 1993. The tourist industry did, however, recover in the late 1990s. Some 69,818 foreign tourist arrivals were reported in 1999, although numbers declined to 60,592 in 2003. In 2002 receipts from tourism totalled US $16m. In 1998 hotel occupancy rates were estimated at 20%. In that year there were 2,258 hotel rooms and 4,289 hotel beds available.

Office National Togolais du Tourisme (ONTT): BP 1289, Lomé; tel. 221-43-13; fax 221-89-27; internet www.togo.tourisme.com; f. 1963; Dir FOLEY DAHLEN (acting).

TONGA

Introductory Survey

Location, Climate, Language, Religion, Flag, Capital

The Kingdom of Tonga comprises 170 islands in the south-western Pacific Ocean, about 650 km (400 miles) east of Fiji. The Tonga (or Friendly) Islands are divided into three main groups: Vava'u, Ha'apai and Tongatapu. Only 36 of the islands are permanently inhabited. The climate is mild (16°–21°C or 61°–71°F) for most of the year, though usually hotter (27°C or 81°F) in December and January. The languages are Tongan, which is a Polynesian language, and English. Tongans are predominantly Christians of the Wesleyan faith, although there are some Roman Catholics and Anglicans. The national flag (proportions 1 by 2) is red, with a rectangular white canton, containing a red cross, in the upper hoist. The capital is Nuku'alofa, on Tongatapu Island.

Recent History

The foundations of the constitutional monarchy were laid in the 19th century. The kingdom was neutral until 1900, when it became a British Protected State. The treaty establishing the Protectorate was revised in 1958 and 1967, giving Tonga increasing control over its affairs. Prince Tupouto'a Tungi, who had been Prime Minister since 1949, succeeded to the throne as King Taufa'ahau Tupou IV in December 1965 and appointed his brother, Prince Fatafehi Tu'ipelehake, to be Prime Minister. Tonga achieved full independence, within the Commonwealth, on 4 June 1970.

Elections to the Legislative Assembly held in May 1981 resulted unexpectedly in the new Assembly becoming dominated by traditionalist conservatives. In March 1982 the Minister of Finance, Mahe Tupouniua, resigned at the King's request after refusing to grant him extrabudgetary travel funds. Further elections to the Legislative Assembly took place in May 1984. In September 1985 the King declared his support for the French Government's programme of testing nuclear weapons in the South Pacific, on the grounds that it was in the broader interests of the Western alliance. However, he upheld his former statement of opposition to the tests in French Polynesia.

Elections were held in February 1987 to the nine commoner seats in the Legislative Assembly; among the six newcomers to the legislature were reported to be some of the Government's harshest critics. In July 1988 the Supreme Court awarded 26,500 pa'anga in damages to 'Akilisi Pohiva, the editor of a local independent journal and an elected member of the Legislative Assembly, after the Government had been found guilty of unfairly dismissing him from his job in the Ministry of Education in 1985, because he had reported on controversial issues. The court ruling intensified opposition demands for the abolition of perceived feudal aspects within Tongan society.

In September 1989 the commoner members of the Legislative Assembly boycotted the Assembly, leaving it without a quorum, in protest at the absence of the Minister of Finance when they had wanted to question him about the proceeds of the Government's sale of Tongan passports to foreign nationals, a process which had begun in 1983 as a means of acquiring revenue. Upon resuming their seats in the Assembly later in the month, the commoners introduced a motion demanding the reform of the Assembly to make it more accountable to the people. The motion proposed the creation of a more balanced legislature by increasing elected representation from nine to 15 seats and reducing noble representation to three seats (the Cabinet's 12 members also sit in the Assembly). In March 1990 a group of Tongan conservatives submitted an electoral petition, alleging bribery and corruption against Pohiva, the leader of the pro-reform commoners, and his colleagues, who had been re-elected by substantial majorities in the February general election. (In July 1988 the King had indicated his opposition to majority rule, claiming that the monarchical Government reacted more quickly to the needs of the people than the Government of a parliamentary democracy.)

In October 1990 Pohiva initiated a court case against the Government, claiming that its controversial sale of passports to foreign citizens was unconstitutional and illegal. The passports were sold mainly in Hong Kong, for as much as US $30,000 each, allowing the purchasers, in theory, to avoid travel restrictions imposed on Chinese passport-holders. In February 1991, however, a constitutional amendment to legalize the naturalization of the new passport-holders was adopted by an emergency session of the Legislative Assembly, and the case was therefore dismissed. In March a large demonstration was held in protest at the Government's actions, and a petition urging the King to invalidate the 426 passports in question, and to dismiss the Minister of Police (who was responsible for their sale), was presented by prominent commoners and church leaders. In the following month the Government admitted that the former President of the Philippines, Ferdinand Marcos, and his family had been given Tongan passports as gifts, after his fall from power in 1986. The events that ensued from the sale of passports were widely viewed as indicative of the growing support for reform and for greater accountability in the government of the country. By 1996, however, most of the 6,600 passports sold under the scheme had expired.

In August 1991 the Prime Minister, Prince Fatafehi Tu'ipelehake, retired from office, owing to ill health (the Prince died in April 1999), and was succeeded by the King's cousin, Baron Vaea of Houma, who had previously held the position of Minister of Labour, Commerce and Industries.

Plans by campaigners for democratic reform to establish a formal political organization were realized in November 1992, when the Pro-Democracy Movement was founded. The group, led by Fr Seluini 'Akau'ola (a Roman Catholic priest), organized a constitutional convention in the same month, at which options for the introduction of democratic reform were discussed. The Government, however, refused to recognize or to participate in the convention, prohibiting any publicity of the event and denying visas to invited speakers from abroad. Nevertheless, the pro-democracy reformists appeared to be enjoying increased public support, and, at elections in February 1993, won six of the nine elective seats in the Legislative Assembly. However, Pohiva's position was undermined when, in December 1993 and February 1994, he lost two defamation cases in the Supreme Court, following the publication of allegations of fraudulent practice in his journal, *Kele'a*. In August 1994 Tonga's first political party was formed when the Pro-Democracy Movement (which had been recognized in 1992, the group having been formed in the early 1970s as the Human Rights and Democracy Movement in Tonga) launched its People's Party, under the chairmanship of a local businessman, Huliki Watab.

In May 1995 the Minister of Finance, Cecil Cocker, resigned from the Cabinet following allegations that he had sexually harassed three women while attending a regional conference in Auckland. Cocker received an official reprimand for his conduct from New Zealand's acting Prime Minister, Don McKinnon.

Elections took place on 24 January 1996, at which pro-democracy candidates retained six seats in the Legislative Assembly. In March three journalists, including the editor of *The Times of Tonga*, were arrested and imprisoned in connection with an article in the newspaper that criticized the newly appointed Minister of Police, Fire Services and Prisons, Clive Edwards, for unfavourable remarks that he had made regarding the People's Party. All three were subsequently released, but were found guilty in April under a law against angering a civil servant.

In July 1996 the Legislative Assembly voted to resume the sale of Tongan passports to Hong Kong Chinese, despite the controversy caused by a similar scheme in the early 1990s. As many as 7,000 citizenships were to be made available for between 10,000 and 20,000 pa'anga, granting purchasers all the rights of Tongan nationality, except ownership of land.

In September 1996 a motion to impeach the Minister of Justice and Attorney-General, Tevita Topou, was proposed in the Legislative Assembly. The motion alleged that Topou had continued to receive his daily parliamentary allowance during an unauthorized absence from the Assembly. Moreover, the publication of details of the impeachment motion, which had been reported to *The Times of Tonga* by Pohiva, before it had been submitted to the Legislative Assembly, resulted in the imprisonment of Pohiva and of the newspaper's editor, Kalafi Moala, and deputy editor, Filakalafi Akau'ola, for contempt of parliament. The three were subsequently released, although in October Moala was found guilty on a further charge of contempt. In the same month the King closed the Assembly (which had been expected to sit until mid-November) until further notice. He denied that he had taken this decision in order to prevent further impeachment proceedings against Topou. Furthermore, in February 1997 the Speaker of the Legislative Assembly was found guilty of contempt of court for criticizing the Chief Justice's decision to release the three journalists imprisoned in September of the previous year. The Government rejected accusations made in early 1997 by journalists in Tonga and media organizations throughout the region that it was attempting to force the closure of *The Times of Tonga*, despite forbidding Moala (who was resident in New Zealand) to enter Tonga without written permission from the Government, banning all government-funded advertising in the publication and forbidding all government employees to give interviews to its journalists.

Parliament reopened in late May 1997. In June Akau'ola was arrested once again and charged with sedition for publishing a letter in *The Times of Tonga* that questioned government policy. However, in the same month the Government suffered a significant reverse when the Court of Appeal ruled that the imprisonment of Pohiva and the two journalists in late 1996 had been unlawful. In August the Prime Minister of New Zealand, Jim Bolger, paid an official visit to Tonga. Following the visit, Pohiva, who had unsuccessfully sought a meeting with Bolger, criticized New Zealand's relationship with Tonga, claiming that financial assistance from the country hindered democratic reform.

In September 1997, following a formal apology from Topou, the Legislative Assembly voted to abandon impeachment proceedings against him. In October Pohiva announced that he was helping to prepare a proposed draft Constitution for presentation to the Legislative Assembly; the document's principal recommendation was to be the direct election of all 30 members of the Assembly.

In March 1998 Fakafanua, a former Minister of Lands, Survey and Natural Resources, was arrested and remanded on bail in connection with charges of fraud, extortion and accepting bribes. He was released by the Supreme Court later in the month after he accused the police of unlawful imprisonment. One police-officer was convicted of this charge in April, while five other men, including Edwards, were acquitted.

In mid-September 1998 the King closed the Legislative Assembly in response to a petition, signed by more than 1,000 people, which sought the removal from office of the Speaker, Eseta Fusitu'a. A parliamentary committee was forced to conduct an inquiry into the activities of Fusitu'a, who was accused of misappropriating public funds and of abusing his position. Pohiva and other pro-democracy activists commended the king for his decisive action in response to the petition. Legislation presented to the legislature later that month, which proposed that in future the Legislative Assembly should appoint cabinet ministers (a responsibility hitherto reserved for the King), was seen as further evidence of the increasing influence of the pro-democracy lobby in the political life of the country.

At the general election held on 11 March 1999 five members of the reformist Tonga Human Rights and Democracy Movement (formerly the Pro-Democracy Movement/People's Party) were returned to the Legislative Assembly, compared with six at the previous election. In April Veikune was appointed as Speaker and Chairman of the Legislative Assembly, replacing Eseta Fusitu'a, who had lost his seat at the general election. In late 1999 the former Minister for Lands, Survey and Natural Resources, Fakafanua, appeared in court on charges of forgery and bribery.

On 3 January 2000 the King appointed his youngest son, Prince 'Ulukalala-Lavaka-Ata, as Prime Minister, replacing Baron Vaea who had in 1995 announced his desire to retire. It had been expected that Crown Prince Tupouto'a would take up the position, but his support for constitutional reform in Tonga (notably the abolition of life-time terms for the and ministers) contrasted with the King's more conservative approach. In March of that year a report published by the US State Department claimed that Tonga's system of Government, whereby the Legislative Assembly is not directly elected, was in breach of UN and Commonwealth human rights guide-lines. The report was welcomed by 'Akilisi Pohiva, the leader of the Tonga Human Rights and Democracy Movement, who reiterated the party's demands for greater democracy, set out in a draft constitution completed in late 1999.

In November 2000 the Tonga Human Rights and Democracy Movement condemned the Government's decision to co-operate with an Australian biotechnology company wishing to carry out research into the genetic causes of a range of diseases. Tonga's extended family structures and the genetic isolation of its ethnically homogenous Polynesian population were cited as providing a rare opportunity for research. In return for its co-operation in the project, Tonga was to receive a share of the royalties from the sale of any drugs developed.

In January 2001 the Prime Minister announced a reallocation of cabinet positions in which he assumed responsibility for the newly created telecommunications portfolio. In the same month claims which appeared in a newspaper report that members of the pro-democracy movement had been involved in a plot to assist a prison break-out, to seize weapons from the army and to assassinate a cabinet minister were vehemently denied by representatives of the group. A spokesperson for the movement stated that the allegations were merely the latest in a series of claims aimed at discrediting the organization. Meanwhile, ongoing concerns for the freedom of the media in Tonga were renewed following the arrest of the deputy editor of *The Times of Tonga* on charges of criminal libel.

In February 2001 the Tonga Human Rights and Democracy Movement launched a public petition to amend Tonga's Nationality Act to allow Tongans who had taken up citizenship in other countries to retain Tongan citizenship. Their stated objective in undertaking the petition was to acknowledge Tonga's dependence on remittances from Tongans living overseas.

In September 2000, meanwhile, protests took place in Nuku'alofa, prompted by concerns that Chinese immigrant businesses, encouraged by the Government to establish themselves in Tonga, were creating unfavourable economic conditions for Tongan businesses. The Tonga Human Rights and Democracy Movement appealed to the Government to cease issuing work permits to foreign (predominantly Chinese) business people and to end the sale of Tongan passports, which had raised an estimated US $30m. during the 1980s. In order to protect this money from his ministers, whom he feared would squander it on unsuitable public works projects should it enter Tonga, the King requested that the funds be placed in the Tonga Trust Fund, held in a cheque account at the San Francisco, CA, branch of the Bank of America. In June 1999 Jesse Bogdonoff, a Bank of America employee, successfully sought royal approval to invest the money in a company in Nevada called Millennium Asset Management, where Bogdonoff was named as the Fund's Advising Officer. Bogdonoff later claimed that he had made a profit of about $11m., which so impressed the King that he appointed Bogdonoff as Court Jester. The balance of the Fund and the interest it had accrued (altogether some $40m.) was due to be returned to Tonga on 6 June 2001; instead the money appeared to have vanished, along with Millennium Asset Management, which had ceased to exist. In September Princess Pilolevu, acting as Regent in the absence of the King and the Crown Prince, dismissed Kinikinilau Tutoatasi Fakafanua, currently Minister of Education but who at the time of the incident had been Minister of Finance, along with the Deputy Prime Minister and Minister of Justice, Tevita Tupou, both of whom were trustees of the fund. She appointed the Minister of Police, Fire Services and Prisons, Clive Edwards, as Acting Deputy Prime Minister. Parliament created a committee to investigate the crime and tabled a motion to impeach Fakafanua and Tupou. There were no apparent reprisals, or legal action, against Bogdonoff, who claimed that he had been deliberately misled as to the value of the funds. In October the Acting Deputy Prime Minister denied that the Privy Council had directed the transfers from the Fund or that any ministers were implicated. He stressed that at least $2.1m. of the fund, invested in Tongan banks, was duly accounted for. In June 2002, however, the Government admitted that about $26m. had been lost as a result of Bogdonoff's actions and that legal proceedings had been initiated in the USA. It was announced in February 2003 that the case would be heard in December of that year; also in February the Legislative Assembly began impeachment proceedings against the ministers implicated in the matter. In February 2004 it was reported that the Government had agreed to settle out of court with Bogdonoff, who was to pay just US $1m. in compensation to the Tongan authorities.

In January 2002 Pohiva published allegations that the King held a secret offshore bank account containing US $350m., some of which was believed to be the proceeds of gold recovered from an

18th century shipwreck. He claimed to possess a letter written to the King from within the palace referring to the account. The Government dismissed the letter as a forgery. Nevertheless, Pohiva was briefly held in custody in February, whilst police searched the offices of the Tonga Human Rights and Democracy Movement and confiscated the hard drives of its computers in an attempt to find the source material of the allegations. Later that month New Zealand's Minister of Foreign Affairs and Trade condemned Tonga as being endemically corrupt, implying that New Zealand's annual $NZ6m. profited the élite rather than the Tongan people as a whole. In February the King admitted that he did possess an overseas account, with the Bank of Hawaii, but it contained the profits of vanilla sales from his own plantation. Nevertheless, Pohiva was formally charged with the use and publication of a forged document. In May 2002 he was acquitted of charges of sedition.

A general election was held on 6–7 March 2002, at which 52 candidates competed for the nine commoners' seats in the Legislative Assembly. The Tonga Human Rights and Democracy Movement won seven seats. In September, having repeatedly failed since 1998 to secure government approval for the group's registration under this name, the organization once again became known as the Human Rights and Democracy Movement in Tonga (HRDMT). In November 2005, however, the Government gave approval for a licence to be granted under the Incorporated Societies Act as Friendly Islands Human Rights and Democracy Movement Inc (FIHRDM Inc).

In late July 2002 it was reported that Pohiva, Moala and Akau'ola were seeking damages from the Tongan Government for wrongful imprisonment, following their incarceration in 1996 on charges of contempt of parliament.

Concerns for the freedom of the media re-emerged in February 2003 when the Government declared *The Times of Tonga*, the twice-weekly newspaper printed in New Zealand, to be a 'prohibited import', describing it as a foreign publication with a political agenda. The ban was challenged, and in April Tonga's Chief Justice, Gordon Ward, ruled that it was both illegal and unconstitutional. However, within hours of the ruling the Government ordered a new ban under different legislation. Ward overruled the ban in the following month, describing it as 'an ill-disguised attempt to restrict the freedom of the press'. However, on arrival from New Zealand 2,000 copies of the paper were seized by the Tongan customs authorities. Moreover, a few days later legislation was proposed that aimed to limit the power of the Supreme Court by excluding laws and ordinances approved by the Legislative Assembly and the Privy Council from judicial review. In early June the Supreme Court granted an injunction to *The Times of Tonga* ordering the Government to allow its distribution. The Government once again defied the order, stating that it would appeal. In mid-June the newspaper (which had been banned in Tonga since February) was finally allowed to go on sale within the country, after Gordon Ward had threatened each individual member of the Cabinet with contempt of court if they did not permit its distribution.

One of the most vocal critics of the affair was the King's nephew, Prince 'Uluvalu Tu'ipelehake, who in June 2003 expressed concern that the attempts to legislate against the freedom of the press and to restrict the right to seek judicial review would bring Tonga into disrepute. In mid-July it was reported that the Government had abandoned its proposals to limit the powers of the Supreme Court as a result of strong opposition to the plans. However, later that month the Legislative Assembly approved the Media Operators' Bill, which introduced restrictions on the involvement of foreign nationals in Tonga's media. The legislation was widely viewed as a further attempt to ban *The Times of Tonga*, the editor of which resided in New Zealand. In early October Tonga's Roman Catholic bishop led a march by some 8,600 people to the government buildings in Nuku'alofa. The demonstration, which was the largest of its kind in Tonga's history, aimed to persuade the Government not to introduce any further restrictions on media freedom in the country. However, a few days later the Legislative Assembly voted in favour of a constitutional amendment allowing for greater control of the media, and shortly afterwards introduced the Newspaper Act, which gave the Government increased powers to regulate the content of newspapers in the country. It was reported that the legislation had been approved by 16 votes to 11, with virtually all of the elected members voting against the proposals and virtually all of the appointed members voting in favour.

The introduction of legislation restricting media freedom in the country in late 2003 threatened to jeopardize Tonga's international relations, and in November the New Zealand Government announced that it was to review its relationship with Tonga as a result of these developments. The Tongan Government reacted angrily to the announcement, summoning New Zealand's ambassador to the islands to register its displeasure. However, in January 2004 Prince 'Uluvalu Tu'ipelehake appealed to Australia's Minister for Foreign Affairs, Alexander Downer, to encourage political reform and to support attempts to increase democratic representation in Tonga.

In February 2004 the King of Tonga's second son Ma'atu Fatafehi Alaivahamama'o Tuku'aho died of a heart attack at 48 years of age. Some 6,000 people attended his funeral and the King and Queen announced that they would undertake a period of mourning lasting 100 nights.

Serious and ongoing financial problems with the national airline, Royal Tongan Airlines, culminated in April 2004 with the grounding and repossession of the company's passenger jet in Auckland, New Zealand, and the consequent suspension of all international flights. Domestic flights continued to be operated by the airline, but in the following month the entire company ceased all operations when its last remaining domestic aircraft broke down and it was announced that no funds were available to repair it. The collapse of the airline caused considerable disquiet throughout Tonga, particularly among those involved in the islands' increasingly important tourist industry, which had relied heavily on the carrier's international services. Tourism officials estimated an almost immediate loss of bookings worth 1.2m. pa'anga, in addition to the loss of 261 jobs and a possible further 585. At the opening session of the Legislative Assembly in late May seven of the nine elected representatives staged a boycott, demanding the resignation of the Prime Minister, who they claimed had allowed millions of pa'anga to be wasted during his tenure as chairman of the airline. Alternative flight arrangements were subsequently made (see Economic Affairs).

A legal challenge to the constitutional amendments governing media freedom, introduced by the Government in 2003, was begun in the Supreme Court in August 2004. Shortly before the legal hearing began the Prime Minister announced the dismissal of three cabinet ministers, including the Minister of Police, Fire Services and Prisons, Clive Edwards, who had been one of the principal proponents of the constitutional amendments. No reasons were given for the dismissals, however, prompting expressions of concern for the stability of the Government and an appeal from the royalist Kotoa Movement for the Prime Minister to resign on the grounds that he had become too isolated from the people. At a public meeting in early September the King and Queen led several hundred Tongans in communal prayers for the guidance of their leaders.

In November 2004 the Prime Minister announced that four new cabinet ministers would be appointed from among the elected members of the Legislative Assembly (two from the Nobles and two from the People's Representatives) following the elections in March 2005. The announcement, which represented a departure from the usual procedure whereby ministers were selected from outside parliament, was seen by many, including members of the pro-democracy movement, as a welcome concession towards democratic reform. However, former cabinet minister Clive Edwards criticized the proposals, claiming that they were anti-democratic, as they required two members of the Legislative Assembly, elected by the people, to relinquish their seats in order to assume the new positions from which they could be dismissed at the discretion of the King.

Elections for the nine Nobles' seats took place on 16 March and for the nine commoners' seats on 17 March 2005. The latter were contested by a record number of 60 candidates. Two newly elected members from each group were appointed to positions in the Cabinet, and a by-election for the four vacated seats took place on 3–5 May. The Minister of Defence, 'Aloua Fetu'utolu Tupou, died suddenly in mid-April. One of the new representatives elected at the subsequent by-election was the former cabinet minister and member of the newly formed People's Democratic Party (PDP), Clive Edwards. The PDP had been launched in April by a breakaway group from the HRDMT, which had stated its intention to pursue political reform in a more aggressive manner. The new organization was registered in early July, despite fears that this might be deemed illegal, as no provision existed in the Constitution for the establishment of political parties.

In late May 2005 some 8,000 people marched to Tonga's Royal Palace in one of the largest demonstrations of its kind to take place in the country. The protesters presented a petition to the King expressing discontent at high electricity prices charged by the Shoreline Power Group and the elevated salaries reportedly paid to the company's executives and urging the Government to renationalize the generation and distribution of power supply in Tonga.

In July 2005 public servants voted to approve the first national strike in Tonga's history, following the Government's rejection of a request by the Public Service Association (PSA) to reconsider large disparities in salary increases awarded to public-sector workers in the recent budget. Almost all of the country's teachers, numerous healthcare workers and employees from many other public services, initially totalling some 3,000 workers, joined the strike. Accusations of government attempts to restrict the PSA's access to the media were made when the power supply of a private television station was cut shortly before a statement by the PSA was due to be broadcast. During the third week of the strike some 10,000 people marched to the Royal Palace in support of the PSA in a demonstration that constituted the largest ever to take place in Tonga. Striking public servants expressed the hope that the King might overrule the Cabinet, which had hitherto rejected their demands. Subsequent reports of vandalism against school property and government vehicles were received, and an attempt had apparently been made to burn down the house of a senior executive of the Shoreline Power Group. Moreover, an unoccupied house belonging to the King on the island of Tongatapu was destroyed by fire in an incident believed by some to be related to recent events in the country. A range of measures, including a new salary scale, subsequently proposed by the Government, was again rejected by the PSA. However, the strike ended in early September when the two sides signed an agreement allowing for salary increases of between 60% and 80%. More significantly, the agreement also provided for the establishment of a commission to review the country's Constitution and to examine possibilities for a more democratic form of government. This represented a major victory for the PSA, which had maintained throughout the dispute that the basic cause of its grievances lay in Tonga's political system. Shortly afterwards a further demonstration by more than 10,000 people took place, appealing to the King to dismiss the entire Government and to conduct a constitutional review within 12 months. Protesters also reiterated their demands for the renationalization of government assets, particularly power generation, but also Tonga's orbital satellite positions and its internet domain address. In October the King agreed to the establishment of a parliamentary committee to examine the issue of constitutional reform.

In February 2006, following the Cabinet's consideration of measures to permit a significant reduction in the number of public servants, the PSA threatened further strike action, stating that the Government's proposals breached the agreement signed in September 2005. Also in February 2006, Prime Minister 'Ulukalala-Lavaka-Ata resigned from office, relinquishing all his portfolios. People's Representative Dr Feleti (Fred) Sevele, a commoner and advocate of constitutional reform, was appointed acting Prime Minister. Sevele also assumed temporary responsibility for the the Prince's other ministerial portfolios (including civil aviation, telecommunications, marine and ports). Prince 'Ulukalala had faced increasing demands for his resignation, amid accusations of incompetence and inefficiency. In view of his pro-democracy stance, the appointment of Sevele was widely welcomed. He was expected to be influential in the establishment of democratic government in Tonga, partly owing to his close relationship with the progressive Crown Prince.

In March 2006 the proposals relating to the reduction in the number of government departments were hastily approved by the Cabinet in order to meet final deadlines for submission. The consultation period lasted only two weeks; the new structure of government departments was required to be agreed and implemented by 30 June, the date upon which the two-year contracts of the incumbent heads of departments were due to expire. It was agreed that most ministries would remain in place, although some were to merge, thereby reducing the existing 16 ministries to 14. In May, during the course of his first official visit to New Zealand, Prime Minister Feleti Sevele confirmed that about one-quarter of posts in the civil service were to be abolished, as part of the Government's commitment to the reduction of budgetary expenditure. The National Committee for Political Reform, chaired by Prince 'Uluvalu Tu'ipelehake, was due to present its findings in August 2006.

A major earthquake, the strongest ever recorded in the country's history, struck Tonga in May 2006. Many buildings and facilities, including the country's main hospital and wharves at the port of Nuku'alofa, suffered serious damage. Following his confirmation in the position of Prime Minister at the end of March, Dr Feleti Sevele retained responsibility for the portfolios of labour, commerce, industries, disaster relief and communications in a reallocation of cabinet portfolios in mid-May. Other changes included the replacement of Cecil Cocker as Deputy Prime Minister by Dr Viliami Tangi and the appointment of 'Alisi Taumoepeau, the country's first female minister, who became Attorney-General and Minister of Justice.

A friendship treaty that Tonga signed with the USA in July 1988 provided for the safe transit within Tongan waters of US ships capable of carrying nuclear weapons. Tonga was virtually alone in the region in failing to condemn the French Government for its decision to resume nuclear-weapons tests in the South Pacific in mid-1995. However, in May 1996 it was announced that Tonga was finally to accede to the South Pacific Nuclear-Free Zone Treaty (see p. 352).

In September 1990 Tongasat, a Tongan telecommunications company founded earlier that year by Tongan citizens jointly with a US entrepreneur, laid claim to the last 16 satellite positions remaining in the earth's orbit that were suitable for trans-Pacific communications. Despite the protests of leading member nations of Intelsat (the international consortium responsible for most of the world's satellite services), the International Telecommunication Union (see p. 125), was obliged to approve the claim, and Tongasat was subsequently granted six positions. A dispute with Indonesia, concerning that country's use of satellite positions reserved by Tonga in 1990, was resolved by the signing of an agreement in December 1993. In May of the following year the two countries established diplomatic relations at ambassadorial level.

In November 1998 Tonga announced that it had decided to terminate its diplomatic links with Taiwan and to establish relations with the People's Republic of China. Tonga opened a consulate in China in May 2005.

In January 2002, in the Red Sea, Israeli commandos seized a ship that was allegedly transporting weapons to Palestinians. The ship was flying a Tongan 'flag of convenience' and had been registered in the Kingdom, although its ownership was uncertain. The reformist politician 'Akilisi Pohiva criticized Tonga's policy of international ship registration, which generated income through sales of flags of convenience. (The issue of international shipping registration had never been debated in Parliament.) Following the seizure, the registration system was closed in June. However, in September another Tongan-registered ship was seized off the coast of Italy and its crew arrested on suspicion of plotting an al-Qa'ida-sponsored terrorist attack in Europe. Furthermore, it was reported in early October that the Greek businessman in charge of the Tongan International Registry of Ships, Pelopidas Papadopoulos, had absconded with the proceeds of the operation owed to the Tongan Government, totalling some US $0.3m.

Government

Tonga is a hereditary monarchy. The King is Head of State and Head of Government. He appoints, and presides over, the Privy Council which acts as the national Cabinet. Apart from the King, the Council includes 14 ministers (increased from 10 in 2005), appointed for life and led by the Prime Minister, and the Governors of Ha'apai and Vava'u. The unicameral Legislative Assembly comprises the King and 30 members: the Privy Council, nine hereditary nobles (chosen by their peers) and nine representatives elected by all adult Tongan citizens. Elected members hold office for three years. There are no official political parties, although opposition groupings continue to campaign for democratic reform.

Defence

Tonga has its own defence force, consisting of both regular and reserve units. Projected government expenditure on defence in the financial year 1999/2000 was 3.3m. pa'anga (5.0% of total budgetary expenditure); in the same year estimated expenditure on law and order was 4.6m. pa'anga (6.9% of total current expenditure).

Economic Affairs

In 2004, according to estimates by the World Bank, Tonga's gross national income (GNI), measured at average 2002–04 prices, was US $186.2m., equivalent to $1,830 per head (or $7,220 per head on an international purchasing-power parity basis). During 1995–2004, it was estimated, the population increased at an average annual rate of 0.5%, while gross domestic product (GDP) per head increased, in real terms, by an average of 1.5% per year. Overall GDP increased, in real terms, at an average annual rate of 2.1% in 1995–2004. The GDP growth rate was estimated by the Asian Development Bank (ADB) at 1.6% in 2004 and at 2.5% in 2005.

Agriculture (including forestry and fishing) contributed 28.0% of GDP in 2002/03, and engaged 31.8% of the employed labour force in 2003. According to the ADB, agricultural GDP increased at an average annual rate of 1.0% in 1995–2003. The principal cash crops are coconuts, vanilla and squash (pumpkin), which normally form the major part of Tonga's exports. In 2000/01 exports of squash provided almost half of total export earnings (some 45%), although this figure declined to 10.8% in the calendar year 2002, owing to over-production, which resulted in the depression of the crop's price on the important Japanese market. In 2003 the percentage of export earnings accounted for by squash rose again, to reach 40.4%. Vanilla beans acquired comparable significance, accounting for 13.4% in 1995/96; however, production subsequently declined and accounted for only 1.5% of total export earnings in 2003. Yams, taro, sweet potatoes, watermelons, tomatoes, cassava, lemons and limes, oranges, groundnuts and breadfruit are also cultivated as food crops, while the islanders keep pigs, goats, poultry and cattle. Food and live animal imports accounted for more than 13%% of total import costs in 2003. The fishing industry is of increasing importance. Exports of fish rose from 3.2m. pa'anga in 2002 to 12.4m. pa'anga in 2003, when they contributed some 35.6% of total export earnings. The ADB estimated that agricultural GDP increased by 3.8% in 2003 before declining by 3.3% in 2004.

Industry (including mining, manufacturing, construction and utilities) provided 14.6% of GDP in 2002/03 and engaged 26.4% of the employed labour force in 1996. According to the ADB, industrial GDP expanded at an average annual rate of 1.9% in 1995–2003. Compared with the previous year, industrial GDP was calculated by the ADB to have expanded by 2.4% in 2003 but to have contracted by 1.0% in 2004. Manufacturing contributed 4.1% of GDP in 2002/03, and (with mining) employed 22.8% of the labour force in 1996. Output of food products and beverages dominates the manufactured sector. The food and textile sectors of manufacturing registered the largest increases in 1999/2000, raising the value of their production by 14.6% and 56.8% respectively. Other industrial activities are the production of concrete blocks, small excavators, furniture, handicrafts, leather goods, sports equipment (including small boats), brewing and coconut oil. There is also a factory for processing sandalwood. In early 2003 permission was granted for a Chinese businessman to establish a cigarette factory in the islands.

In an attempt to reduce fuel imports, a 2-MW wave-energy power plant was constructed in the early 1990s, and would, it was hoped, supply one-third of the islands' total electricity requirements when in full operation. A project to provide all the outer islands with solar power by 2000 was begun in 1996. Imports of mineral fuels accounted for more than 19% of total import costs in 2003.

Service industries contributed 57.4% of GDP in 2002/03 and engaged 39.5% of the employed labour force in 1996. According to the ADB, the GDP of the services sector increased at an average annual rate of 2.8% in 1995–2003. The ADB estimated that the GDP of the services sector expanded by 3.0% in 2003 and by 4.8% in 2004. Tourism makes a significant contribution to the economy. Tourism receipts rose from US $9m. in 2002 to $15m. in 2003. The trade, restaurants and hotels sector contributed 15.1% of GDP in 2002/03 and engaged 8.5% of the employed labour force in 1996. Visitor arrivals were estimated at 41,208 in 2004 (compared with 30,883 in 1999). However, the collapse of Royal Tongan Airlines in mid-2004 (see Recent History) resulted in severe losses for the tourism industry. In November 2005, furthermore, the monopoly of the domestic airline, Air Peau 'o Vava'u, was ended, following criticism of its service and its majority ownership by Crown Prince Tupouto'a. Following a review, Tonga's 'single airline' policy was officially terminated in April 2006 when a second carrier, Airlines Tonga (a joint venture with Air Fiji), was permitted to continue its operations on a long-term basis.

In 2005, according to the ADB, Tonga recorded a visible trade deficit of US $90m., and a deficit of US $10m., on the current account of the balance of payments. The latter was equivalent to 4.2% of GDP in 2004. In 2004 the principal sources of imports were New Zealand (46.7%) and Fiji (21.1%), while Japan and the USA were the principal markets for exports (purchasing 51.4% and 24.9% respectively). The principal exports in that year were foodstuffs. The principal imports were foodstuffs, machinery and transport equipment, basic manufactures and mineral fuels.

According to ADB figures, in the financial year ending 30 June 2004 an overall budgetary surplus was estimated at the equivalent to 1.4%. Tonga's total external debt reached US $81m. in 2005. In 2002 the cost of debt-servicing was equivalent to 5.9% of the total revenue from exports of goods and services. At March 2005 total debt, most of which was external, was calculated at approximately 42% of GDP. Official development assistance totalled US $22.3m. in 2002, of which US $16.7m. was bilateral aid. In 2005/06 official development assistance from Australia totalled $A14.2m. and aid from New Zealand in the same year amounted to $NZ6.1m. According to ADB figures, the annual rate of inflation averaged 6.7% in 1995–2004. Consumer prices increased by an average of 11.0% in 2004 and 8.0% in 2005. Some 5.5% of the labour force were unemployed in 2003, according to the ADB.

Tonga is a member of the Pacific Community (see p. 350), the Pacific Islands Forum (see p. 352), the Asian Development Bank (ADB, see p. 169) and the UN Economic and Social Commission for Asia and the Pacific (ESCAP, see p. 33). The country is a signatory of the Lomé Conventions and the successor Cotonou Agreement (see p. 277) with the European Union (EU). The Working Party on the Accession of Tonga to the World Trade Organization (WTO, see p. 370) was established in 1995. In December 2005 Tonga's Schedule of Specific Commitments in Services was adopted and the country's membership of the organization was approved.

The constraints on Tonga's economic development have included inclement weather, inflationary pressures, large-scale emigration and over-reliance on the agricultural sector. The country remains vulnerable to fluctuations in prices for squash on the international market. The diversification of the country's sources of income has been an important issue for Tonga. In 1999 Tonga signed a bilateral trade agreement with the People's Republic of China, and a trade delegation from that country visited the islands in the following year. It was thought that China hoped to use Tonga as a base for the production of export goods (including garments and agricultural items) for the Australian and New Zealand markets. A delegation of senior Chinese trade officials visited Tonga in August 2004 to assess investment opportunities in agriculture, information technology and the power supply industry. In November of that year Tonga's King returned from a private visit to China and announced that the Chinese Government had approved a programme of aid worth some US $20m. for economic development in Tonga over the next few years. A bilateral trade agreement between the two countries was signed in January 2005. It was reported in early 2002 that the Tongan Government had reached an agreement with a US company to develop the island of 'Eua as a rocket-launching site for the purposes of 'space tourism'. In late 2005 it was announced that the first launch was expected to take place in 2008. The Tongan economy was weakened in 2003 by the continuing decline in the value of the pa'anga, which had lost some 54% against the New Zealand dollar since 2001. The currency recovered somewhat in 2004–05. Remittances from Tongans resident overseas (estimated to number at least 35,000) remained an important source of income, totalling 200m. pa'anga in 2004/05. In 2002, supported by a loan and technical assistance from the ADB, the Economic Public Sector Reform Programme (EPSRP) was initiated. The programme aimed to improve the performance of the civil service and of public enterprises while decreasing costs, to implement a comprehensive reform of the country's tax system and reduce opportunities for tax evasion, and to develop better investment conditions. The Government introduced a form of value-added tax in April 2005. Levied at a rate of 15%, the new consumption tax replaced various existing taxes. It was hoped that its introduction would permit a decrease in rates of individual and corporate tax. After several consecutive years of fiscal deficits, a small budgetary surplus was achieved in 2003/04, mainly as a result of an improvement in tax collection and reductions in capital expenditure. This process of fiscal consolidation continued in 2004/05, but a budget deficit of at least 3.7m. pa'anga (equivalent to 2.8%

of GDP) was projected for 2005/06. The ADB anticipated that GDP growth would decline to 1.6% in 2006. Budgetary and inflationary pressures were expected to increase following the implementation of increases of 60%–80% in public-sector salaries (see Recent History). The salary increases envisaged for 2007 and 2008 were expected to reach the equivalent of 11.0% and 7.8% respectively of GDP. Moreover, Tonga's terms of accession to the WTO, concluded in December 2005, were criticized by some observers on the grounds that the country would be forced to implement drastic reductions in trade tariffs, hitherto a vital source of revenue for the financing of areas such as health and education.

Education

Free state education is compulsory for children between five and 14 years of age, while the Government and other Commonwealth countries offer scholarship schemes enabling students to go abroad for higher education. In 1999 there were 117 primary schools, with a total of 17,105 pupils in 2003. There was a total of 14,567 pupils in secondary education in 2003 and secondary schools numbered 69 in 1999. There were also four technical and vocational colleges in 1999, with a total of 467 students, and one teacher-training college, with 288 students. In 1990 there were 230 Tongans studying overseas. Some degree courses are offered at the university division of 'Atenisi Institute. A new establishment offering higher education, the 'Unuaki 'o Tonga Royal Institute (UTRI), opened in 2004. Recurrent government expenditure on education in 1999/2000 was an estimated 10.9m. pa'anga (equivalent to 16.5% of total recurrent budgetary expenditure).

Public Holidays

2006: 1 January (New Year's Day), 14–17 April (Easter), 25 April (ANZAC Day), 4 May (HRH the Crown Prince's Birthday), 4 June (Independence Day), 4 July (HM the King's Birthday), 4 November (Constitution Day), 4 December (Tupou I Day), 25–26 December (Christmas Day and Boxing Day).

2007: 1 January (New Year's Day), 6–9 April (Easter), 25 April (ANZAC Day), 4 May (HRH the Crown Prince's Birthday), 4 June (Independence Day), 4 July (HM the King's Birthday), 4 November (Constitution Day), 4 December (Tupou I Day), 25–26 December (Christmas Day and Boxing Day).

Weights and Measures

In 1980 Tonga adopted the metric system of weights and measures in place of the imperial system.

Statistical Survey

Source (unless otherwise indicated): Tonga Government Department of Statistics, POB 149, Nuku'alofa; tel. 23300; fax 24303; e-mail statdept@tongatapu.net.to.

AREA AND POPULATION

Area: 748 sq km (289 sq miles).

Population: 94,649 at census of 28 November 1986; 97,784 (males 49,615, females 48,169) at census of 30 November 1996; 101,800 at mid-2004 (estimate from Asian Development Bank, *Key Indicators of Developing Asian and Pacific Countries. By Group* (1996 census, provisional): Tongatapu 66,577; Vava'u 15,779; Ha'apai 8,148; 'Eua 4,924; Niuas 2,018.

Density (mid-2004): 136.1 per sq km.

Principal Towns (population in '000, 1986): Nuku'alofa (capital) 21.3; Mu'a 4.1; Neiafu 3.9. Source: Stefan Helders, *World Gazetteer* (internet www.world-gazetteer.com). *Mid-2003* (UN estimate, incl. suburbs): Nuku'alofa (capital) 34,654. Source: UN, *World Urbanization Prospects: The 2003 revision*.

Births, Marriages and Deaths (2000): Registered live births 2,471 (birth rate 24.6 per 1,000); Registered marriages 747 (marriage rate 7.4 per 1,000); Registered deaths 653 (death rate 6.5). Source: UN, *Demographic Yearbook*.

Expectation of Life (WHO estimates, years at birth): 71 (males 71; females 71) in 2003. Source: WHO, *World Health Report*.

Economically Active Population (persons aged 15 years and over, 1996): Agriculture, forestry and fishing 9,953; Mining and quarrying 43; Manufacturing 6,710; Electricity, gas and water 504; Construction 500; Trade, restaurants and hotels 2,506; Transport, storage and communications 1,209; Financing, insurance, real estate and business services 657; Public administration and defence 3,701; Education 1,721; Health and social work 510; Other community, social and personal services 1,320; Extra-territorial organizations 72; *Total employed* 29,406 (males 18,402, females 11,004); Unemployed 4,502 (males 3,293, females 1,209); *Total labour force* 33,908 (males 21,695, females 12,213). *Mid-2003* (estimates): Agriculture, etc. 12,000; Total labour force 38,000 (Source: FAO).

HEALTH AND WELFARE

Key Indicators

Total Fertility Rate (children per woman, 2003): 3.7.
Under-5 Mortality Rate (per 1,000 live births, 2004): 25.
Physicians (per 1,000 head, 2001): 0.34.
Health Expenditure (2002): US $ per head (PPP): 292.
Health Expenditure (2002): % of GDP: 6.9.
Health Expenditure (2002): public (% of total): 73.5.
Access to Water (% of persons, 2002): 100.
Access to Sanitation (% of persons, 2002): 97.
Human Development Index (2003): ranking 54.

Human Development Index (2003): value 0.810.

For sources and definitions, see explanatory note on p. vi.

AGRICULTURE, ETC.

Principal Crops (FAO estimates, '000 metric tons, 2004): Sweet potatoes 6; Cassava 9; Taro 4; Yams 4; Copra 1,500; Coconuts 58; Pumpkins, squash and gourds 20,000; Bananas 1; Plantains 3; Oranges 1; Lemons and limes 3; Other fruits 3.

Livestock (FAO estimates, '000 head, year ending September 2004): Pigs 81; Horses 11; Cattle 11; Goats 13; Chickens 300.

Livestock Products (FAO estimates, metric tons, 2004): Pig meat 1,496; Other meat 684; Hen eggs 28; Honey 12; Cattle hides 40; Cow's milk 370.

Forestry (FAO estimates, '000 cu m, 2004): *Roundwood Removals* (excl. bark): 2; *Sawnwood Production:* 2.

Fishing (metric tons, live weight, 2003): Capture 4,435 (Albacore 611; Marine crustaceans 386); Aquaculture 23; *Total catch* 4,458..

Source: FAO.

INDUSTRY

Production (2004): Electric energy 41 million kWh. Source: Asian Development Bank, *Key Indicators of Developing Asian and Pacific Countries*.

FINANCE

Currency and Exchange Rates: 100 seniti (cents) = 1 pa'anga (Tongan dollar or $T). *Sterling, US Dollar and Euro Equivalents* (30 November 2005): £1 sterling = $T3.4882; US $1 = $T2.0198; €1 = $T2.3771; $T100 = £28.67 = US $49.51 = €42.07. *Average Exchange Rate* (pa'anga per US $): 2.1952 in 2002; 2.1420 in 2003; 1.9716 in 2004.

Budget (estimates, million pa'anga, year ending 30 June 2003): *Revenue:* Taxation 76.2; Other current revenue 20.7; Capital receipts 0.4; Total 97.3 (excl. grants received from abroad 3.5). *Expenditure:* Current expenditure 91.0; Capital expenditure 10.1; Total 101.1 (excl. net lending –0.6). Source: Asian Development Bank, *Key Indicators of Developing Asian and Pacific Countries*.

International Reserves (US $ million at 31 December 2004): IMF special drawing rights 0.38; Reserve position in the IMF 2.66; Foreign exchange 55.25; Total 58.29. Source: IMF, *International Financial Statistics*.

Money Supply ('000 pa'anga at 31 December 2004): Currency outside banks 17,292; Demand deposits at deposit money banks 54,554; Total money 71,846. Source: IMF, *International Financial Statistics*.

TONGA
Directory

Cost of Living (Consumer Price Index, excl. rent; base: 2000 = 100): 119.5 in 2002; 133.4 in 2003; 148.1 in 2004. Source: IMF, *International Financial Statistics*.

Gross Domestic Product at Constant 2000/01 Prices (million pa'anga, year ending 30 June): 285.5 in 2000/01; 293.0 in 2001/02; 302.0 in 2002/03. Source: Asian Development Bank, *Key Indicators of Developing Asian and Pacific Countries*.

Gross Domestic Product by Economic Activity (million pa'anga at current prices, year ending 30 June 2003): Agriculture, forestry and fishing 85.4; Mining and quarrying 1.1; Manufacturing 12.4; Electricity, gas and water 5.3; Construction 25.9; Trade, restaurants and hotels 46.0; Transport, storage and communications 22.6; Finance and real estate 33.1; Public administration and other 73.4; *Sub-total* 305.3; *Less* Imputed bank service charges 10.3; *Gross value added in basic prices* 295.1; Indirect taxes, *less* subsidies 65.9; *GDP at market prices* 361.0. Source: Asian Development Bank, *Key Indicators of Developing Asian and Pacific Countries*.

Balance of Payments (US $ million, year ending 30 June 2004): Exports of goods f.o.b. 13.9; Imports of goods f.o.b. −82.9; *Trade balance* −69.0; Exports of services and income 28.6; Imports of services and income −31.8; *Balance on goods, services and income* −72.2; Current transfers (net) 80.0; *Current balance* 7.8; Direct investment 27.7; Portfolio investment 4.4; Other long-term capital 16.3; Other short-term capital 2.6; Net errors and omissions −18.9; Statistical discrepancy −14.0; *Overall balance* 25.9. Source: Asian Development Bank, *Key Indicators of Developing Asian and Pacific Countries*.

EXTERNAL TRADE

Principal Commodities ('000 pa'anga, 2003): *Imports:* Food and live animals 26,881; Beverages and tobacco 28,021; Crude materials (inedible) except fuels 22,732; Mineral fuels 38,518; Chemicals 9,693; Basic manufactures 15,652; Machinery and transport equipment 30,395; Miscellaneous manufactured articles 8,119; Total (incl. others) 201,678. *Exports:* Food and live animals 36,576; Manufactured goods 437; Total (incl. others) 37,301. *Revised Totals* ('000 pa'anga, 2003): Imports 199,214; Exports 34,865.

Principal Trading Partners (US $ million, 2004): *Imports:* Australia 11.2; China, People's Repub. 2.4; Fiji 23.0; Indonesia 1.3; Japan 2.8; New Zealand 50.8; USA 7.3; Total (incl. others) 108.8. *Exports:* India 1.0; Japan 12.5; USA 6.1; Total (incl. others) 24.4.

Source: Asian Development Bank, *Key Indicators of Developing Asian and Pacific Countries*.

TRANSPORT

Road Traffic (registered vehicles in use, 2000): Passenger cars 4,800; Commercial vehicles 4,400. Source: UN, *Statistical Yearbook*.

Shipping (international traffic, '000 metric tons, 1998): Goods loaded 13.8; Goods unloaded 80.4. 1991: Vessels entered ('000 net registered tons) 1,950 (Source: UN, *Statistical Yearbook*). *Merchant Fleet* (registered at 31 December 2004): Vessels 77; Total displacement ('000 grt) 109.2 (Source: Lloyd's Register-Fairplay, *World Fleet Statistics*).

Civil Aviation (traffic on scheduled services, 2001): Passengers carried 57,000; Passenger-km 13 million; Total ton-km 1 million. Source: UN, *Statistical Yearbook*.

TOURISM

Foreign Tourist Arrivals: 36,585 in 2002; 40,110 in 2003 (estimate); 41,208 in 2004 (estimate).

Tourist Arrivals by Country (2003, estimates): Australia 8,272; New Zealand 14,682; USA 7,565; Fiji 2,012; United Kingdom 1,385; Germany 979; Japan 790; Total (incl. others) 40,110.

Tourism Receipts (US $ million, excl. passenger transport): 6 in 2001; 8 in 2002; 15 in 2003.

Sources: IMF, *Tonga: Statistical Appendix* (February 2003); World Tourism Organization.

COMMUNICATIONS MEDIA

Radio Receivers (1997): 61,000 in use.

Television Receivers (1997): 2,000 in use.

Telephones ('000 main lines, 2002): 11.2 in use.

Mobile Cellular Telephones (2002): 3,354 subscribers.

Personal Computers (2002): 2,000.

Internet Users (2002): 2,900.

Facsimile Machines (1996): 250 in use.

Daily Newspapers (1996): 1; estimated circulation 7,000.

Non-daily Newspapers (2001): 2; estimated circulation 13,000.

Sources: UNESCO, *Statistical Yearbook*; UN, *Statistical Yearbook*; Audit Bureau of Circulations, Australia; and International Telecommunication Union.

EDUCATION

Primary (2003): 117 schools (1999); 773 teachers; 17,105 pupils.

General Secondary (2003): 39 schools (1999); 1,012 teachers; 14,567 pupils.

Technical and Vocational (1999): 4 colleges; 45 teachers (1990); 467 students.

Teacher-training (1999): 1 college; 22 teachers (1994); 288 students.

Universities, etc. (1985): 17 teachers; 85 students.

Other Higher Education (1985): 36 teachers (1980); 620 students. In 1990 230 students were studying overseas on government scholarships.

Directory

The Constitution

The Constitution of Tonga is based on that granted in 1875 by King George Tupou I. It provides for a government consisting of the Sovereign; a Privy Council, which is appointed by the Sovereign and consists of the Sovereign and the Cabinet; the Cabinet, which consists of a Prime Minister, a Deputy Prime Minister, several other ministers (formerly eight but increased to 12 in 2005) and the Governors of Ha'apai and Vava'u; a Legislative Assembly and a Judiciary. Limited law-making power is vested in the Privy Council and any legislation passed by the Executive is subject to review by the Legislative Assembly. The unicameral Legislative Assembly comprises the King, the Cabinet, nine hereditary nobles (chosen by their peers) and nine representatives elected by all adult Tongan citizens. Elected members hold office for three years.

The Government

HEAD OF STATE

The Sovereign: HM King TAUFA'AHAU TUPOU IV (succeeded to the throne 15 December 1965).

CABINET
(May 2006)

Prime Minister and Minister of Labour, Commerce, Industries, of Disaster Relief and Activities and of Communications: Dr FELETI (FRED) SEVELE.

Deputy Prime Minister and Minister of Health: Dr VILIAMI TANGI.

Minister of Finance: SIOSIUA 'UTOIKAMANU.

Minister of Foreign Affairs, Acting Minister of Defence and Acting Governor of Vava'u: TU'A TAUMOEPEAU TUPOU.

Minister of Education, Women's Affairs and Culture: Dr TEVITA HALA PALEFAU.

Governor of Ha'apai: MALUPO.

Minister of Lands, Survey, Natural Resources and Environment: TUITA.

Minister of Police, Fire Services and Prisons: SIAOSI TAIMANI 'AHO.

Minister of Training, Employment, Youth and Sports: TU'IVAKANO.

Minister of Works: NUKU.

Minister of Agriculture, Forestry and Fisheries: PEAUAFI HAUKINIMA.

TONGA

Directory

Attorney-General and Minister of Justice: Malia Viviena 'Alisi Numia Afeaki Taumoepeau.
Minister of Civil Aviation, Marine and Ports: Paul Karalus.
Minister of Tourism: Fineasi Funaki.

GOVERNMENT MINISTRIES AND OFFICES

Office of the Prime Minister: POB 62, Taufa'ahau Rd, Kolofo'ou, Nuku'alofa; tel. 24644; fax 23888; e-mail fttuita@pmo.gov.to; internet www.pmo.gov.to.
Palace Office: Salote Rd, Kolofo'ou, Nuku'alofa; tel. 21000; fax 24102.
Ministry of Agriculture and Fisheries: Administration Office, Vuna Rd, Kolofo'ou, Nuku'alofa; tel. 23038; fax 23039; e-mail maf-holo@candw.to.
Ministry of Civil Aviation: POB 845, Salote Rd, Nuku'alofa; tel. 24144; fax 24145; e-mail info@mca.gov.to; internet www.mca.gov.to.
Ministry of Education: POB 61, Vuna Rd, Kolofo'ou, Nuku'alofa; tel. 23511; fax 23596; e-mail moe@kalianet.to.
Ministry of Finance: Treasury Building, POB 87, Vuna Rd, Kolofo'ou, Nuku'alofa; tel. 23066; fax 21010; e-mail minfin@candw.to.
Ministry of Foreign Affairs: National Reserve Bank Building, Salote Rd, Kolofo'ou, Nuku'alofa; tel. 23600; fax 23360; e-mail secfo@candw.to.
Ministry of Health: POB 59, Taufa'ahau Rd, Tofoa, Nuku'alofa; tel. 23200; fax 24921.
Ministry of Internal Affairs: POB 110, Salote Rd, Fasi-moe-afi, Nuku'alofa; tel. 23688; fax 23880.
Ministry of Justice: POB 130, Railway Rd, Kolofo'ou, Nuku'alofa; tel. 21055; fax 23098.
Ministry of Lands, Survey and Natural Resources: POB 5, Vuna Rd, Kolofo'ou, Nuku'alofa; tel. 23611; fax 23216.
Ministry of Marine and Ports: POB 397, Vuna Rd, Ma'ufanga, Nuku'alofa; tel. 22555; fax 26234; e-mail marine@kalianet.to.
Ministry of Telecommunications: Nuku'alofa.
Ministry of Works and Disaster Relief Activities: 'Alaivahamama'o Rd, Vaololoa, Nuku'alofa; tel. 23100; fax 25440; e-mail mowtonga@kalianet.to.
Department of Civil Aviation: Salote Rd, Fasi-moe-afi; tel. 24144; fax 24145.

Legislative Assembly

The Legislative Assembly consists of the Speaker, the members of the Cabinet, nine nobles chosen by the 33 Nobles of Tonga, and nine representatives elected by all Tongans over 21 years of age. There are elections every three years, and the Assembly is required to meet at least once every year. The most recent election was held on 16–17 March 2005, when seven of the nine elected representatives were members of the reformist Tonga Human Rights and Democracy Movement (which was subsequently renamed the Friendly Islands Human Rights and Democracy Movement Inc). By-elections were held on 3 May for the seats vacated by two Nobles and on 5 May for two commoners' seats, following the appointment of these four members to the Cabinet.
Speaker and Chairman of the Legislative Assembly: Tu'iha'angana.

Political Organizations

Although the Constitution of Tonga does not provide for the official establishment of political parties, the following groups have been active:
Friendly Islands Human Rights and Democracy Movement Inc (FIHRDM Inc): POB 843, Nuku'alofa; tel. 25501; fax 26330; e-mail demo@kalianet.to; f. late 1970s; est. and recognized in 1992 as the Pro-Democracy Movement; application in 1998 for incorporation under new name of Tonga Human Rights and Democracy Movement refused by the Govt; reverted to the name of Human Rights and Democracy Movement in Tonga (HRDMT) in 2002; assumed present name in Nov. 2005; campaigns for democratic reform and increased parliamentary representation for the Tongan people; Sec. 'Akilisi Pohiva.
Kotoa Movement: f. 2001; campaigns in support of monarchy; Sec. Semisi Kailahi.
People's Democratic Party: Nuku'alofa; f. 2005; breakaway group from HRDMT; Pres. Sione Tesina Fuko; Vice-Pres. Sione Tu'alau Mangisi; Sec. Semisi Tapueluelu.

Diplomatic Representation

EMBASSY AND HIGH COMMISSIONS IN TONGA

Australia: Salote Rd, Private Bag 35, Nuku'alofa; tel. 23244; fax 23243; e-mail ahctonga@kalianet.to; internet www.embassy.gov.au/to.html; High Commissioner Colin Hill.
China, People's Republic: Vuna Rd, POB 877, Nuku'alofa; tel. 24554; fax 24595; e-mail chinaemb_to@mfa.gov.cn; Ambassador Hu Yeshun.
New Zealand: cnr Taufa'ahau and Salote Rds, POB 830, Nuku'alofa; tel. 23122; fax 23487; e-mail nzhcnuk@kalianet.to; High Commissioner Michael McBryde.

Judicial System

There are eight Magistrates' Courts, the Land Court, the Supreme Court and the Court of Appeal.

Appeal from the Magistrates' Courts is to the Supreme Court, and from the Supreme Court and Land Court to the Court of Appeal (except in certain matters relating to hereditary estates, where appeal lies to the Privy Council). The Chief Justice and Puisne Judge are resident in Tonga and are judges of the Supreme Court and Land Court. The Court of Appeal is presided over by the Chief Justice and consists of three judges from other Commonwealth countries. In the Supreme Court the accused in criminal cases, and either party in civil suits, may elect trial by jury. In the Land Court the judge sits with a Tongan assessor. Proceedings in the Magistrates' Courts are in Tongan, and in the Supreme Court and Court of Appeal in Tongan and English.

Supreme Court

POB 11, Nuku'alofa; tel. 23599; fax 22380; e-mail cj_tonga@kalianet.to.
Chief Justice: Robin M. Webster.
Puisne Judge: Tony Ford.
Chief Registrar: Manakovi Pahulu.

Religion

The Tongans are almost all Christians, and about 36% of the population belong to Methodist (Wesleyan) communities. There are also significant numbers of Roman Catholics (15%) and Latter-day Saints (Mormons—15%). Anglicans (1%) and Seventh-day Adventists (5%) are also represented. Fourteen churches are represented in total.

CHRISTIANITY

Kosilio 'ae Ngaahi Siasi 'i Tonga (Tonga National Council of Churches): POB 1205, Nuku'alofa; tel. 23291; fax 27506; e-mail tncc@kalianet.to; f. 1973; three mem. churches (Free Wesleyan, Roman Catholic and Anglican); Chair. Rt Rev. Soane Lilo Foliaki; Gen. Sec. Rev. Simote M. Vea.

The Anglican Communion

Tonga lies within the diocese of Polynesia, part of the Church of the Province of New Zealand. The Bishop of Polynesia is resident in Fiji.
Archdeacon of Tonga and Samoa: The Ven. Sam Koy, The Vicarage, POB 31, Nuku'alofa; tel. 22136.

The Roman Catholic Church

The diocese of Tonga, directly responsible to the Holy See, comprises Tonga and the New Zealand dependency of Niue. At 31 December 2003 there were an estimated 15,767 adherents in the diocese. The Bishop participates in the Catholic Bishops' Conference of the Pacific, based in Fiji.
Bishop of Tonga: Dr Soane Lilo Foliaki, Toutai-mana Catholic Centre, POB 1, Nuku'alofa; tel. 23822; fax 23854; e-mail cathbish@kalianet.to.

Other Churches

Church of Jesus Christ of Latter-day Saints (Mormon): Mission Centre, POB 58, Nuku'alofa; tel. 26007; fax 23763; 50,735 mems; Pres. Douglas W. Banks.
Church of Tonga: Nuku'alofa; f. 1928; a branch of Methodism; 6,912 mems; Pres. Rev. Finau Katoanga.
Free Constitutional Church of Tonga: POB 23, Nuku'alofa; tel. 23966; fax 24458; f. 1885; 15,941 mems (1996); Pres. Rev. Semisi Fonua; brs in Australia, New Zealand and USA.

TONGA
Directory

Free Wesleyan Church of Tonga (Koe Siasi Uesiliana Tau'ataina 'o Tonga): POB 57, Nuku'alofa; tel. 23522; fax 24020; e-mail fwc@kalianet.to; f. 1826; 36,500 mems; Pres. Rev. Dr 'ALIFALETI MONE.

Tokaikolo Christian Fellowship: Nuku'alofa; f. 1978; breakaway group from Free Wesleyan Church; 5,000 mems.

BAHÁ'Í FAITH

National Spiritual Assembly: POB 133, Nuku'alofa; tel. 21568; fax 23120; e-mail nsatonga@oceanoflight.to; mems resident in 142 localities.

The Press

Eva, Your Guide to Tonga: POB 958, Nuku'alofa; tel. 25779; fax 24749; e-mail vapress@kalianet.to; internet www.matangitonga.to; f. 1989; 4 a year; publication suspended under media restrictions in Jan. 2004; Editor PESI FONUA; circ. 4,500.

Ko e Kele'a (Conch Shell): POB 1567, Nuku'alofa; tel. 25501; fax 26330; f. 1986; monthly; activist-oriented publication, economic and political; Editor TAVAKE FUSIMALOHI; circ. 3,500.

Lali: Nuku'alofa; f. 1994; monthly; English; national business magazine; Publr KALAFI MOALA.

Lao and Hia: POB 2808, Nuku'alofa; tel. 14105; weekly; Tongan; legal newspaper; Editor SIONE HAFOKA.

Matangi Tonga: POB 958, Nuku'alofa; tel. 25779; fax 24749; e-mail vapress@matangitonga.to; internet www.matangitonga.to; f. 1986; monthly; national news magazine ceased publication following suspension of licence in Jan. 2004 and subsequently published solely on internet; Editor PESI FONUA.

'Ofa ki Tonga: c/o Tokaikolo Fellowship, POB 2055, Nuku'alofa; tel. 24190; monthly; newspaper of Tokaikolo Christian Fellowship; Editor Rev. LIUFAU VAILEA SAULALA.

Taumu'a Lelei: POB 1, Nuku'alofa; tel. 27161; fax 23854; e-mail tmlcath@kalianet.to; f. 1931; monthly; Roman Catholic; Editor Dr SOANE LILO FOLIAKI.

The Times of Tonga/Koe Taimi'o Tonga: POB 880, Hala Velingatoni, Kolomotu'a; tel. 23177; fax 23292; e-mail times@kalianet.to; internet www.tongatimes.com; f. 1989; twice-weekly; English edition covers Pacific and world news, Tongan edition concentrates on local news; licence suspended in Feb. 2004; Publr KALAFI MOALA; Editor MATENI TAPUELUELU; circ. 8,000.

Tohi Fanongonongo: POB 57, Nuku'alofa; tel. 26533; fax 24020; e-mail fwctf@kalianet.to; monthly; Wesleyan; Editor Rev. TEVITA PAUKAMEA TIUETI.

Tonga Chronicle/Kalonikali Tonga: POB 197, Nuku'alofa; tel. 23302; fax 23336; e-mail chroni@kalianet.to; internet www.netstorage.com/kami/tonga/news/; f. 1964; govt-sponsored; weekly; Editor MATEAKI-KIHE-IOTU HEIMULI; circ. 6,000 (Tongan and English).

Publisher

Vava'u Press Ltd: POB 958, Nuku'alofa; tel. 25779; fax 24749; e-mail vapress@matangitonga.to; internet www.matangitonga.to; f. 1980; books and magazines; Pres. PESI FONUA.

Broadcasting and Communications

TELECOMMUNICATIONS

Tonga Communications Corporation: Private Bag 4, Nuku'alofa; tel. 26700; fax 26701; internet www.tcc.to; responsible for domestic and international telecommunications services; Gen. Man. STEPHEN TUSLER.

Tongasat—Friendly Islands Satellite Communications Ltd: POB 2921, Nuku'alofa; tel. 24160; fax 23322; e-mail panuve@tongasat.com; 80% Tongan-owned; private co but co-operates with Govt in management and leasing of orbital satellite positions; Chair. Princess PILOLEVU TUITA; Man. Dir SEMISI PANUVE; Sec. CLIVE EDWARDS.

BROADCASTING

Radio

Tonga Broadcasting Commission: POB 36, Tungi Rd, Fasi-moe-afi, Nuku'alofa; tel. 23555; fax 24417; independent statutory board; commercially operated; manages two stations, A3Z Radio Tonga 1 and Radio Tonga 2, with programmes in Tongan and English; Gen. Man. TAVAKE FUSIMALOHI.

93FM: Pacific Partners Trust, POB 478, Nuku'alofa; tel. 23076; fax 24970; broadcasts in English, Tongan, German, Mandarin and Hindi.

A3V The Millennium Radio 2000: POB 838, Nuku'alofa; tel. 25891; fax 24195; e-mail a3v@tongatapu.net.to; broadcasts on FM; musical programmes; Gen. Man. SAM VEA.

Tonga News Association: Nuku'alofa; Pres. PESI FONUA.

Television

Oceania Broadcasting Inc started relaying US television programmes in 1991. The Tonga Broadcasting Commission launched the country's first television service in July 2000. The studios and broadcasting facilities are located near Nuku'alofa, providing local news and sport.

Oceania Broadcasting Network: POB 91, Nuku'alofa; tel. 23314; fax 23658.

Finance

(cap. = capital; res = reserves; dep. = deposits; m. = million; amounts in Tongan dollars)

BANKING

Australia and New Zealand Banking Group Ltd: Cnr of Salote and Railway Rds, POB 910, Nuku'alofa; tel. 24944; fax 23870; internet www.candw.to/banks; Gen. Man. MARK DAWSON.

Bank of Tonga: POB 924, Nuku'alofa; tel. 23933; fax 23634; e-mail bot-gm@kalianet.to; f. 1974; owned by Govt of Tonga (40%) and Westpac Banking Corpn (60%); cap. 3.0m., res 10.6m., dep. 88.6m. (Sept. 2003); Chair. ALAN WALTER; Gen. Man. MISKA TU'IFA; 4 brs.

MBf Bank Ltd: POB 3118, Nuku'alofa; tel. 24600; fax 24662; e-mail info@mbfbank.to; internet www.mbfbank.to; f. 1993; 93.35% owned by MBf Asia Capital Corpn Holdings Ltd, 4.75% owned by Crown Prince Tupouto'a, 0.95% owned by Tonga Investments Ltd, 0.95% owned by Tonga Co-operative Federation Society; Gen. Man. H. K. YEOH.

National Reserve Bank of Tonga: POB 25, Post Office, Nuku'alofa; tel. 24057; fax 24201; e-mail nrbt@reservebank.to; internet www.reservebank.to; f. 1989; to assume central bank functions of Bank of Tonga; issues currency; manages exchange rates and international reserves; cap. 1.0m., res 0.7m., dep. 61.9m. (June 2002); Gov. SIOSI C. MAFI; Chair. Prince 'ULUKALALA-LAVAKA-ATA.

Tonga Development Bank: Fatafehi Rd, POB 126, Nuku'alofa; tel. 23333; fax 23775; e-mail tdevbank@tdb.to; internet www.tdb.to; f. 1977; to provide credit for developmental purposes, mainly in agriculture, fishery, tourism and housing; cap. 10.5m., res 7.7m. (Dec. 2004); Man. Dir 'OTENIFI AFU'ALO MATOTO; 5 brs.

Westpac Banking Corporation: c/o Bank of Tonga, Railway Rd, Nuku'alofala; tel. 23933; fax 24048; Gen. Man. MISKA TU'IFUA.

Trade and Industry

DEVELOPMENT ORGANIZATIONS

Tonga Investments Ltd: POB 27, Nuku'alofa; tel. 24388; fax 24313; f. 1992; to replace Commodities Board; govt-owned; manages five subsidiary companies; Chair. Baron VAEA OF HOUMA; Man. Dir ANTHONY WAYNE MADDEN.

Tonga Association of Small Businesses: Nuku'alofa; f. 1990; to cater for the needs of small businesses; Chair. SIMI SILAPELU.

CHAMBER OF COMMERCE

Tonga Chamber of Commerce and Industries: Tungi Arcade, POB 1704, Nuku'alofa; tel. 25168; fax 26039; e-mail chamber@kalianet.to; Pres. AISAKE EKE.

TRADE ASSOCIATIONS

Tonga Kava Council: Nuku'alofa; to promote the development of the industry both locally and abroad; Chair. TOIIMOANA TAKATAKA.

Tonga Squash Council: Nuku;alofa; promotes the development of the industry; introduced a quota system for exports in 2004; Pres. TSUTOMU NAKAO; Sec. STEVEN EDWARDS.

UTILITIES

Shoreline Power Group: POB 47, Taufa'ahau Rd, Kolofo'ou, Nuku'alofa; tel. 23311; fax 23632; provides electricity via diesel motor generation, took over operations from the Tonga Electric

Power Board in 2004; CEO SOANE RAMANLAL; Chair. Prince TUPOUTO'A.

Tonga Water Board: POB 92, Taufa'ahau Rd, Kolofo'ou, Nuku'alofa; tel. 23298; fax 23518; operates four urban water systems, serving about 25% of the population; Man. SAIMONE P. HELU.

CO-OPERATIVES

In April 1990 there were 78 registered co-operative societies, including the first co-operative registered under the Agricultural Organization Act.

Tonga Co-operative Federation Society: Tungi Arcade, Nuku'alofa.

TRADE UNIONS

Association of Tongatapu Squash Pumpkin Growers: Nuku'alofa; f. 1998.

Public Service Association (PSA): Nuku'alofa; Pres. FINAU TUTONE; Sec. VUNA FA'OTUSIA.

Tonga Nurses' Association and Friendly Islands Teachers' Association (TNA/FITA): POB 150, Nuku'alofa; tel. 23200; fax 24291; Pres. FINAU TUTONE; Gen. Sec. 'ANA FOTU KAVAEFIAFI.

Transport

ROADS

Total road length was estimated at 680 km in 1999, of which some 27% were all-weather paved roads. Most of the network comprises fair-weather-only dirt or coral roads.

SHIPPING

The chief ports are Nuku'alofa, on Tongatapu, and Neiafu, on Vava'u, with two smaller ports at Pangai and Niuatoputapu.

Shipping Corporation of Polynesia Ltd: Queen Salote Wharf, Vuna Rd, POB 453, Nuku'alofa; tel. 23853; fax 23250; e-mail info@scptonga.com; internet www.scptonga.com; regular inter-islands passenger and cargo services; Chair. CECIL COCKER; Gen. Man. MOSESE FAKATOU.

Uata Shipping Lines: 'Uliti Uata, POB 100, Nuku'alofa; tel. 23855; fax 23860.

Warner Pacific Line: POB 93, Nuku'alofa; tel. 21088; services to Samoa, American Samoa, Australia and New Zealand; Man. Dir MA'AKE FAKA'OSIFOLAU.

CIVIL AVIATION

Tonga is served by Fua'amotu International Airport, 22 km from Nuku'alofa, and airstrips at Vava'u, Ha'apai, Niuatoputapu, Niuafo'ou and 'Eua. The country's international airline, Royal Tongan Airlines, collapsed in May 2004 (see Recent History). A new domestic carrier, Air Peau 'o Vava'u, was established in June 2004 to provide limited internal air services (see below). Air New Zealand provides a regular service to Australia and New Zealand and a regional carrier, Reef Air, operates between Tonga, Niue and Fiji. The New Zealand-based low-cost airline, Pacific Blue, was to begin two direct flights per week between Sydney and Tonga and three per week between Auckland and Tonga in November 2005. In the same month the monopoly of Air Peau 'o Vava'u was ended. Following a review, Tonga's 'single airline' policy was officially terminated in April 2006 when a second carrier, Airlines Tonga, a joint venture between Air Fiji and Teta Tours (a Tongan travel company), was permitted to continue its operations on a long-term basis.

Air Peau 'o Vava'u: Vava'u; f. 2004; began operating domestic flights in June 2004 following the collapse of Royal Tongan Airlines in May 2004; operates a fleet of two DC-3s and one 10-seat Islander aircraft with technical support from Pion Air of New Zealand; CEO BRIAN PENTECOST; Man. MOSIKAKA MOENGANGONGO.

Tourism

Tonga's attractions include scenic beauty and a mild climate. There were an estimated 41,208 visitors to the islands in 2004. In addition, in 2003 some 6,500 cruise-ship passengers visited the islands. In 2002 revenue from the industry earned US $9m. (an increase of some 14% compared with the previous year). The majority of tourists were from New Zealand, the USA and Australia.

Tonga Tourist Association: POB 74, Nuku'alofa; tel. 23344; fax 23833; e-mail royale@kalianet.to; Pres. PAPILOA FOLIAKI; Sec. KOLOLIANA NAUFAHU.

Tonga Visitors' Bureau: Vuna Rd, POB 37, Nuku'alofa; tel. 25334; fax 23507; e-mail tvb@kalianet.to; internet www.tongaholiday.com; f. 1978; Dir VA'INGA PALU.

TRINIDAD AND TOBAGO

Introductory Survey

Location, Climate, Language, Religion, Flag, Capital

The Republic of Trinidad and Tobago consists of Trinidad, the southernmost of the Caribbean islands, and Tobago, which is 32 km (20 miles) to the north-east. Trinidad, which accounts for 94% of the total area, lies just off the north coast of Venezuela, on the South American mainland, while the country's nearest neighbour to the north is Grenada. The climate is tropical, with a dry season from January to May. Rainfall averages 1,561 mm (61.5 ins) per year. Annual average daytime temperatures range between 32°C (90°F) and 21°C (70°F). The official and main language is English, but French, Spanish, Hindi and Chinese are also spoken. In 2000 some 55% of the population were Christians, mainly Roman Catholics (30%) and Anglicans (25%), while 23% were Hindus and 6% Muslims. The national flag (proportions 3 by 5) is deep red, divided by a white-edged black diagonal stripe from upper hoist to lower fly. The capital is Port of Spain, on the island of Trinidad.

Recent History

Trinidad was first colonized by the Spanish in 1532, but was ceded to the British in 1802. Africans were transported to the island to work as slaves, but slavery was abolished in 1834. Shortage of labour led to the arrival of large numbers of Indian and Chinese immigrants, as indentured labourers, during the second half of the 19th century. In 1888 the island of Tobago, which had finally been ceded to the British in 1814, was joined with Trinidad as one political and administrative unit, and the territory remained a British colony until its independence on 31 August 1962.

Modern politics emerged in the 1930s with the formation of a trade union movement. The first political party, the People's National Movement (PNM), was founded in 1956 by Dr Eric Williams. It campaigned successfully at the elections to the Legislative Council in September 1956, and Williams became the colony's first Chief Minister in October. In 1958 the territory became a member of the newly established Federation of the West Indies, and in the following year achieved full internal self-government, with Williams as Premier. The Federation collapsed in 1961, however, following the secession of Jamaica and, subsequently, Trinidad and Tobago. After independence, in 1962, Williams was restyled Prime Minister, and the Governor became Governor-General. In 1967 Trinidad and Tobago became the first member of the Commonwealth (see p. 193) to join the Organization of American States (OAS, see p. 333).

In April 1970 the Government declared a state of emergency, following violent demonstrations, lasting several weeks, by supporters of 'Black Power', protesting against foreign influence in the country's economy and demanding solutions to the problem of unemployment, which was particularly severe among Trinidadians of African descent. On the day that the emergency was proclaimed, part of the Trinidad and Tobago Regiment (the country's army) mutinied. The mutiny collapsed after only three days, and some officers and soldiers who participated were subsequently imprisoned. At a general election in May 1971, the PNM won all 36 seats in the House of Representatives.

A new Constitution came into effect on 1 August 1976, whereby Trinidad and Tobago became a republic, within the Commonwealth. The first parliamentary elections of the republic were held in September, when the PNM won 24 of the 36 seats in the House of Representatives. The United Labour Front (ULF), a newly formed party led by trade unionists, won 10 seats, while the Democratic Action Congress (DAC) won the two Tobago seats. The former Governor-General, Ellis Clarke, was sworn in as the country's first President in December 1976. A parliamentary resolution in 1977 to grant Tobago self-rule resulted, after long resistance from the Government, in the formation in 1980 of a Tobago House of Assembly, giving the island limited autonomy. Tobago was granted full internal self-government in January 1987.

Williams died in March 1981, having consistently refused to nominate a successor. The President selected George Chambers, a deputy leader of the PNM and Minister of Agriculture, to assume the leadership on an interim basis. He was formally adopted as party leader in May and confirmed as Prime Minister. The PNM increased its majority in the House of Representatives by two seats in a general election in November. The ULF, the DAC and the Tapia House Movement, campaigning jointly as the Trinidad and Tobago National Alliance, succeeded in retaining only 10 seats. The newly formed Organization for National Reconstruction (ONR), led by a former PNM minister, Karl Hudson-Phillips, secured 22% of the total vote but no seats.

Co-operation between the four opposition parties increased, and, at local elections in August 1983, they successfully combined to inflict electoral defeat on the PNM. In August 1984 the National Alliance and the ONR established a common front, to be known as the National Alliance for Reconstruction (NAR). At elections to the Tobago House of Assembly in November 1984, the DAC achieved a convincing victory, reducing the PNM's representation to one seat. In September 1985 Arthur Napoleon Raymond (A. N. R.) Robinson, leader of the DAC and a former Deputy Prime Minister in the PNM Government, was elected leader of the NAR. In February 1986 the four parties merged to form one opposition party, still known as the NAR.

The stringent economic policies of the PNM Government undermined its public support and provoked labour unrest over wage restraint, notably in a bitter strike at Trinidad's petroleum refineries during May 1984. The next general election, held in December 1986, resulted in a decisive victory for the NAR. Robinson was appointed Prime Minister. Chambers was among those members of the PNM who lost their seats, and in January 1987 Patrick Manning, the former Minister of Energy, was appointed leader of the parliamentary opposition. In March Noor Mohammed Hassanali, formerly a senior judge, took office as President, following the retirement of Ellis Clarke.

Although the NAR increased its majority of borough and county council seats at local elections held in Trinidad in September, the party experienced internal difficulties during 1987 and 1988. In June 1987 former members of the Tapia House Movement announced that they were to leave the NAR. In February 1988 more than 100 NAR members met to discuss the leadership of the alliance and the direction of its policies. Two cabinet ministers (including Basdeo Panday, the Minister of External Affairs) and one junior minister were subsequently dismissed from the Government. All three were former members of the ULF, which derived most of its support from the 'East' Indian community. Despite their accusations of racism against the NAR leadership, they were expelled from the party in October. In April 1989 Panday and the other dissidents announced the formation of a left-wing opposition party, the United National Congress (UNC). In July 1990 Panday was elected leader of the UNC at the party's first national assembly. In September President Hassanali confirmed Panday as the leader of the parliamentary opposition, replacing Manning. The UNC, with six seats in the House of Representatives, replaced the PNM, with only three seats, as the principal opposition party.

In July 1990 members of the Jamaat al Muslimeen, a small Muslim group led by Yasin Abu Bakr, attempted to seize power. The rebels destroyed the capital's police headquarters and took control of the parliament building and the state television station. Some 45 people were taken hostage, among them Robinson and several cabinet ministers. The rebels demanded Robinson's resignation, elections within 90 days and an amnesty for those taking part in the attempted coup. On 28 July a state of emergency was declared and a curfew was imposed: police preoccupation with the political crisis had resulted in widespread looting in the capital. On 31 July the Prime Minister, who had sustained gunshot wounds, was released from captivity by the rebels. On 1 August the attempted coup, in which some 30 people were killed and another 500 injured, ended after the rebels surrendered unconditionally. An amnesty pardoning them, signed by the President of the Senate, Joseph Emmanuel Carter, in his capacity as acting Head of State, was proclaimed invalid, on the grounds that it had been signed under duress. In mid-August Bakr and his followers were charged with treason, a capital offence.

In November 1991 the imprisoned Jamaat al Muslimeen rebels won an appeal to the Judicial Committee of the Privy Council in the United Kingdom (the final court of appeal for Trinidad and Tobago), which ruled that the validity of the presidential pardon issued during the attempted coup in July 1990 should be determined before the rebels were brought to trial, and that an application for their release should be heard by the High Court of Trinidad and Tobago immediately. On 30 June 1992 the High Court ruled that the pardon was valid, and ordered the immediate release of the 114 defendants. The Government announced that it would pursue all legal means of appeal against the decision, which it deemed to be of great constitutional significance. In March 1993 delays in the payment of compensation to the rebels, for what the High Court ruled was their wrongful imprisonment, led Bakr to threaten 'action' against the Government. In October the Court of Appeal ruled to uphold the decision of the High Court. In October 1994 the Privy Council ruled to overturn the decisions of the High Court and the Court of Appeal, declaring the pardon invalid. As a result, the Jamaat al Muslimeen would be unable to claim compensation for wrongful imprisonment. However, it was also ruled that to rearrest the rebels and try them for offences committed during the insurrection would constitute an abuse of the legal process. However, the Jamaat al Muslimeen was subsequently awarded some TT $2.1m. in compensation for the destruction of its buildings following the coup attempt.

A general election, held on 16 December 1991, resulted in a decisive victory for the PNM, which secured 45% of the votes and won 21 seats in the House of Representatives. The implementation of unpopular austerity measures was widely acknowledged as the main cause of the defeat of the NAR, which lost all but two of its legislative seats. As a result of his party's defeat, Robinson resigned as leader. A notable feature of the elections was the re-emergence of ethnic voting, with the vast majority of the votes divided between the Afro-Trinidadian-orientated PNM and the largely Indo-Trinidadian UNC, which secured 13 seats in the House of Representatives. Patrick Manning was sworn in as Prime Minister the day after the ballot. A promise made by the PNM in its election manifesto to settle a public-sector claim for salaries and allowances withheld during the austerity programme of the outgoing NAR Government was honoured in the budget submitted to Parliament in January 1992. However, the Government's continued failure to effect a settlement led to escalating industrial unrest. In February 1993 several thousand public-sector employees joined protests against the delay in payments and at the Government's plans to restructure inefficient state enterprises, involving some 2,600 redundancies. In early 1994 a government offer of a settlement of the public-sector claim was rejected by the majority of employees. In mid-1995 the Government introduced a new plan to settle the claim, involving the issue of bonds with tax credits, which was accepted by the Trinidad and Tobago Unified Teachers' Association. However, industrial action resumed in September, when some 25,000 public-sector employees observed a 24-hour strike in support of demands for a more favourable settlement. In March 1996, following a further 48-hour stoppage, agreement was finally reached on a settlement involving the issue, over a period of four years, of bonds worth TT $1,000m. Meanwhile, industrial unrest persisted in opposition to continuing government plans for the rationalization and privatization of unproductive public utilities.

At elections to the Tobago House of Assembly, held on 7 December 1992, the NAR retained control, securing 11 seats, with the remaining elective seat won by the PNM. In July 1993 the Government and the Tobago House of Assembly agreed to begin discussions concerning the upgrading of Tobago's constitutional status. Measures subsequently submitted for consideration by the legislature included the establishment of an executive council on Tobago and the appointment of an independent senator to represent the island.

Appeals for the restoration of capital punishment, prompted by growing public concern at the increasing rate of murder and violent crime in Trinidad and Tobago, gained considerable impetus in August 1993 following the murder of the country's Prison Commissioner. Warrants issued shortly afterwards for the execution of two convicted murderers were suspended following protests by human rights organization Amnesty International. In July 1994 Trinidad and Tobago conducted its first execution since 1979. However, the convicted murderer, Glen Ashby, was hanged only minutes before a facsimile transmission from the Privy Council in the United Kingdom was sent to the Court of Appeal in Trinidad granting a stay of execution. Reportedly, an undertaking had been given by the Attorney-General, Keith Sobion, that the execution would not be conducted until all applications for a stay had been exhausted. In July 1994 the Privy Council issued a conservatory order whereby, in the case of two men due to be heard by the Trinidad Court of Appeal, should their execution be ordered, it could not be conducted until the case had been heard by the Privy Council itself. This decision provoked protest from the Chief Justice of Trinidad and Tobago, who accused the Privy Council of pre-empting the Court of Appeal's exercise of its jurisdiction. Subsequently, the Government announced its intention to introduce legislation establishing the Court of Appeal as the final appeal court for criminal cases, pending regional agreement on a Caribbean appeal court. In March 1995 an international jurists' inquiry found that the execution of Ashby was illegal and that sufficient evidence existed to cite Sobion for contempt of court. However, the report was non-binding, and no action was taken.

In July 1995 the Speaker of the House of Representatives, Occah Seapaul, was accused by the Government of bringing her office into disrepute; an unsuccessful attempt by Seapaul to sue a former business partner, Victor Jattan, had led the court to question the veracity of Seapaul's testimony. Seapaul refused to accede to demands for her resignation, and rejected as unconstitutional the proposal, by the Attorney-General, to conduct a confidence motion on the matter. Lacking the necessary two-thirds' majority in the legislature to unseat Seapaul, the Government introduced draft legislation to amend the Constitution in order to allow the removal of the Speaker by means of a simple majority. The proposal was approved by the Senate, but debate of the bill was obstructed in the House of Representatives by Seapaul, who adjourned the session and ordered the suspension of the leader of the House, Ken Valley, for six months, on a charge of contempt. (Valley subsequently secured a High Court order reinstating him.) In August acting President Joseph Emmanuel Carter declared a limited state of emergency in the capital, thus empowering the Government to place Seapaul under house arrest and facilitating the prompt approval in the House of Representatives of the constitutional amendment. In protest at the Government's action, Seapaul's brother, Ralph Maraj, resigned as the Minister of Public Utilities. Maraj subsequently relinquished his seat in the legislature and his membership of the PNM, later joining the UNC. The state of emergency was ended after four days, and Seapaul was released from detention, having agreed to vacate her position pending a High Court ruling on constitutional motions filed by her against the Government.

A general election was held on 6 November 1995. The PNM and the UNC each secured 17 seats, while the NAR won the remaining two. Following discussions between the leader of the UNC, Basdeo Panday, and Robinson, who had resumed the leadership of the NAR in October, a coalition Government was established, with Panday as Prime Minister. The Cabinet included Robinson as Minister Extraordinaire and Adviser to the Cabinet, with special responsibility for Tobago. It was widely understood that the NAR's support for the UNC in forming the Government had been dependent on undertakings concerning the prompt upgrading of Tobago's constitutional status.

At elections to the Tobago House of Assembly, held on 9 December 1996, the NAR secured 10 of the 12 elective seats; the PNM obtained one seat, and the remaining seat was won by an independent candidate.

On 14 February 1997 Robinson was elected President to replace Noor Mohammed Hassanali on his retirement from the position in March. However, the appointment (by an electoral college comprising the members of the Senate and the House of Representatives) was, for the first time, contested: traditionally, all parties support the nominee of the Government for the presidency, which is a ceremonial position only. On this occasion the PNM, which objected to the Government's nomination of Robinson (owing to his status as an active politician with party affiliation), presented its own candidate, a High Court Judge, Anthony Lucky. Lucky received 18 votes, compared with the 46 votes obtained by Robinson, who was inaugurated on 19 March.

In March 1998 militia of the Jamaat al Muslimeen prevented employees of the Ministry of Works and Transport from establishing a barrier around land inhabited by the Jamaat al Muslimeen, in order to halt further expansion of settlements. Bakr denounced the Government for attempting to provoke a violent reaction from the militants. A fence was eventually constructed after Government employees resumed their task, under the protection of the police force. In December 1999 the

Jamaat al Muslimeen repeated their warning that they would not permit building work to take place adjacent to their headquarters.

In early January 2000 Hanraj Sumairsingh, a member of the UNC, was found murdered. It was subsequently reported that Sumairsingh had written to the Prime Minister several times regarding threats by the Minister of Local Government, Dhanraj Singh, following Sumairsingh's revelation of alleged corruption in the unemployment relief programme administered by Singh's ministry. In a separate incident, a petrol bomb was thrown at the house of a member of a regional development corporation, which had also recently reported corruption in the unemployment scheme. A full investigation was initiated and in October Singh was dismissed from his government post and replaced by Carlos John. Singh was charged with the murder of Sumairsingh, but in October 2003 he was found not guilty of ordering the killing.

In mid-January 2000 two government-appointed Tobagan senators were dismissed from their posts, following their earlier failure to support a government-sponsored bill. President Robinson refused, however, to revoke their appointments, stating that their dismissal would damage relations between the two islands. In late January Robinson publicly announced that Panday had ceased to attend their weekly discussions of current affairs. Following mediation by the Archbishop of Port of Spain, Robinson announced that, having brought the state of relations between the two islands to the public's attention, he would agree to revoke the senators' appointments.

In October 1997 it was announced that the Government had approved a proposal by the Attorney-General to expedite executions of persons convicted of murder, whereby the Government would allow only 18 months for completion of a hearing before the UN Human Rights Committee (UNHRC) and the Inter-American Commission on Human Rights (IACHR), in the event of the Privy Council rejecting an appeal. The Government hoped, by imposing a time limit on the UNHRC and the IACHR, to complete the appeals process within the five years allowed by the Privy Council as the maximum length of time between sentencing and execution. In April 1998 the Government refused to grant leave for the hearing of appeals against the death penalty made by nine men convicted of murder (the so-called 'Chadee gang'). The nine subsequently appealed to the UNHRC. In late May 1998 the Government announced that it was withdrawing from the UNHRC and the IACHR, as neither body had been able to guarantee to hear appeals within the 18 months requested by the Government. Many Caribbean states expressed their support for Trinidad and Tobago, although the opposition PNM criticized the withdrawals as damaging the islands' international reputation, while the Roman Catholic Church and Amnesty International also criticized the move on humanitarian grounds. In June 1998 the IACHR ordered Trinidad and Tobago not to execute five people whose cases it had been scheduled to review; however, the authorities announced that the IACHR no longer had any jurisdiction over the cases, and that the executions would be carried out.

In October 1998, in what was considered a landmark case, the Privy Council rejected the appeals of two convicted murderers, who had claimed that their constitutional rights had been infringed by the conditions in which they had been imprisoned. In January 1999, in a further landmark judgment, the Privy Council ruled that, even though Trinidad and Tobago had withdrawn from the IACHR, two convicted killers could not be executed while their appeals were being considered by the Commission, since the appeals had been made prior to the withdrawal. In April the Privy Council ordered the release of three prisoners who had spent almost four years awaiting execution.

In May 1999 the Privy Council rejected an appeal for clemency made by the nine members of the Chadee gang, who had claimed that they were being held in cruel and degrading conditions. However, the Privy Council granted a stay of execution on the grounds that the Court of Appeal in Trinidad and Tobago had been hurried into a decision by the Government, in order to allow time to consider the legality of hanging as a means of administering the death penalty. At the end of May the Privy Council ruled that Trinidad and Tobago could legally proceed with the nine executions, which, despite international protests, were carried out in early June.

In April 2000 the Government announced that it was to withdraw from the first optional protocol to the International Covenant on Civil and Political Rights, following a judgment from the UNHRC that Trinidad and Tobago could not continue to adhere to the resolution while differing on the subject of the death sentence. The announcement attracted widespread international condemnation. The Government, however, stated that the withdrawal was intended purely to prevent condemned murders from addressing lengthy appeals to the UNHRC. The Government also announced the introduction of a constitutional amendment, which would allow executions to proceed before the IACHR and the UNHRC had ruled on the cases. On 14 February 2001, at a Caribbean Community and Common Market (CARICOM, see p. 183) summit in Barbados, the leaders of 11 Caribbean states signed an agreement to establish the Caribbean Court of Justice (CCJ). The Court was to replace the Privy Council as the final court of appeal, and was to be based in Trinidad and Tobago. The CCJ would be financed by a US $100m. trust fund raised by the Caribbean Development Bank. In February Parliament voted to accept the authority of the new Court to settle CARICOM matters. The Court was eventually inaugurated on 16 April 2005. However, owing to UNC opposition to adopting the appellate jurisdiction of the CCJ, the new Court was likely only to have jurisdiction over CARICOM matters.

At the general election of 11 December 2000 the UNC secured 19 of the 36 seats in the House of Representatives, while the PNM won 16 seats and the NAR secured one. On 20 December, following a delay owing to a recount of votes, Panday was inaugurated as Prime Minister for the second time. At elections to the Tobago House of Assembly, held on 29 January 2001, the PNM secured eight of the 12 elective seats, ending the traditional domination of the House by the NAR, which obtained the remaining four seats. In the same month Panday announced his Cabinet and his nominations to the Senate. However, President Robinson refused to approve the senate nominations of seven UNC members, declaring them to be unconstitutional, as they had been defeated as candidates in the election. The Jamaat al Muslimeen threatened to hold widespread demonstrations should the seven nominations be approved. Nevertheless, on 14 February the President reluctantly approved all of Panday's nominations (as he was constitutionally obliged to do), although he urged the Prime Minister not to appoint any of the seven controversial senators to the Cabinet.

The Government was beset by allegations of corruption in mid-2001. In July a report in the *Sunday Express* newspaper claimed that government ministers, including the former Minister of Energy, Finabar Gangar, had received payments in exchange for supporting various tenders for contracts with the state-owned oil company, Petrotrin. Furthermore, in mid-July a report by the Auditor-General on the North West Regional Health Authority (NWRHA) claimed to have discovered irregularities in the health authority's accounts and accused three of its executives of corruption. In July the Minister of Communications and Information Technology, Ralph Maraj, threatened to resign if Panday did not act to curb corruption. Panday responded by divesting Maraj of responsibility for the National Broadcasting Network and Freedom of Information Act. Panday's party rival, Attorney-General Ramesh Maharaj, also was relinquished of some of his responsibilities. Relations between the Attorney-General and the Prime Minister continued to deteriorate throughout September. Maharaj, with Maraj and two other cabinet members formed a faction within the UNC. This faction, which was known as Team Unity, subsequently gained control of the party's national executive. Despite attempts by Team Unity to prevent UNC constituent elections from taking place on 9 September, supporters of Panday were victorious in 30 of the 34 constituencies.

On 1 October 2001 it was confirmed that Maharaj and Sudama had been dismissed from their government posts for their continued criticism of the Prime Minister. Maraj subsequently also resigned from his position. The Government's legislative majority was effectively lost when the three ministers subsequently formed a coalition with the PNM and the NAR and obstructed attempts by Panday to approve the budget. Amid increasing pressure from the opposition for his resignation and threats of a vote of 'no confidence' in his Government, on 10 October Panday asked President Robinson to dissolve Parliament. Parliament was duly suspended and it was announced that elections were to be held on 10 December. The opposition parties indicated in mid-October 2001 that their alliance with the three dissident UNC ministers would not extend to the election, however. Maharaj and his allies subsequently challenged Panday for control of the UNC and petitioned the Elections and Boundaries Commission (EBC) for an injunction to prevent Panday from issuing the party's list of electoral candidates under the UNC name. The action was rejected by the EBC in early November, and a further appeal by Team Unity was similarly unsuccessful.

Meanwhile, in September 2001 a report published by the independent Personnel Management Services into the allegations of corruption at the NWRHA recommended the dismissal of four senior executives. In mid-November Dr Tim Gopeesingh, the former Chairman of the NWRHA, admitted to charges of fraud. In late November the Director of Public Prosecutions announced that police were investigating the case of a cheque for US $50,000 issued to Panday by Gopeesingh in his capacity as leader of UNC's Northwest Liaison Office, at the time of the 2000 elections. Panday maintained that the cheque was paid into a constituency bank account, but this was disputed by a UNC treasurer. In December Panday and other government ministers were implicated in alleged instances of misconduct relating to contracts given to the US-owned power company Inncogen Ltd, to supply electricity to four new factories in Trinidad, which had failed to be built.

In the general election of 10 December 2001 the UNC and the PNM secured an equal number (18) of seats in the House of Representatives while no other party gained legislative representation. Following a recount of votes in two marginal constituencies, in mid-December the EBC announced that the UNC had secured 49.7% of votes cast, while the PNM had won 46.3%. In mid-December the two party leaders announced they had reached an agreement on political collaboration in government, although not a coalition arrangement, that would allow the President to appoint the Prime Minister and Speaker in the House of Representatives and to reform the electoral process. However, following the appointment of Manning as Prime Minister on 24 December and PNM nominee Max Richards as Speaker of the House of Representatives, the UNC withdrew from the post-election agreement.

Panday's refusal to be sworn in as leader of the opposition and to agree to elect a Speaker in the House of Representatives (Richards had withdrawn from the position after his impartiality was questioned) prevented the convening of the new Parliament in early January 2002. Panday announced the UNC's intention to prevent Parliament from sitting for the next six months, thereby forcing Manning to call a new election, according to the provisions of the Constitution. Following concern expressed by the business community at the effect of the political impasse on the country's economy, at the end of January Manning and Panday met for discussions. However, neither these meetings, nor negotiations mediated by CARICOM leaders in February, provided a solution to the dispute. Later in February Manning agreed to put the UNC's proposals for an executive comprising equal numbers of PNM and UNC representatives to the PNM party council. The UNC accused the Prime Minister of deliberately delaying the process and warned of civil unrest if a date for a fresh election was not set. In the following month controversy also arose over Robinson's continued occupation of the position of President. His tenure expired on 18 March, but, as the legislature had not been convened, Robinson obtained Manning's permission to remain in office. The first session of the new House of Representatives was reconvened on 5 April; however, owing to the failure of the two parties to elect a Speaker, proceedings were adjourned.

Meanwhile, in mid-March 2002 Panday's former finance minister, Brian Kuei Tung, and several senior government officials and prominent businessmen were arrested on charges of fraud and misbehaviour in public office with regard to the construction of a new terminal at Piarco Airport. Manning ordered a Commission of Inquiry into the project. Panday himself was also questioned by the authorities regarding his failure to declare a joint bank account held with his wife in the United Kingdom, and on 20 September he was officially charged with fraud. In late March doctors in public hospitals went on strike for three days in protest at the delay of several months in the payment of their salaries. Doctors staged a further strike in late April, to demand better pay and working conditions. The conflict between the UNC and PNM continued throughout mid-2002. In July two more UNC members of parliament were accused of criminal activity by the Commission of Inquiry into the airport project. The former works minister Carlos John was accused of ignoring tender procedures during his time in office and in the same month cocaine worth US $246,000 and two missiles were apparently found at the home of the former housing minister Sadiq Baksh.

A report by the Commission of Inquiry into the EBC in early June 2002 documented countless flaws in its practices and recommended that all its members should resign. However, its members failed to relinquish their posts, despite Manning's pledge to implement the recommended reforms. In late July Manning announced that if Parliament failed to elect a Speaker by 31 October, further elections would be held. Manning made a final attempt to convene Parliament on 28 August; however, the members again failed to elect a Speaker, some UNC representatives resorting deliberately to voting against their own candidate. The following day Manning dissolved Parliament and announced that elections would take place on 7 October. In early September a new political party, the Citizens' Alliance, was formed. It was led by a former PNM finance minister, Wendell Mottley, and aimed to prevent another tied election.

In elections held on 7 October 2002 the PNM won 50.7% of votes cast and 20 seats in the House of Representatives, while the UNC secured 46.6% of votes and 16 seats. Voter turn-out was estimated at 69.6%. Manning again acceded to the office of Prime Minister, stating his intention to seek solutions to issues that divided the nation's political and racial communities. He appointed a new Cabinet, which included most of the members of the previous administration in their former positions. One of the new Government's first acts was the proposal of legislation aimed at preventing abduction and acts of terrorism, as well as a planned increase in penalties for acts of corruption committed by holders of public office.

In January 2003 Panday caused controversy by accusing Manning of associating with the Jamaat al Muslimeen group, which, he claimed, had links with the al-Qa'ida (Base) organization, a network of fundamentalist Islamist militants, held to be responsible for terrorist attacks. Later in January two newspaper reporters claimed that they had been taken to a chemical weapons laboratory owned by a radical Islamist group which had threatened to attack US and British visitors to the country. The claims prompted warnings from the US and British Governments and led to the cancellation of trips to the islands by some cruise-ship operators. In August the Jamaat al Muslimeen leader, Yasin Abu Bakr, was charged with conspiracy to murder two former Jamaat al Muslimeen members in June 2003. However, in March 2005 the failure of the jury in the trial to reach a majority verdict resulted in the judge ordering a retrial.

The Government's preferred candidate, Maxwell Richards, was elected President on 14 February 2003. In early April the UNC proposed a motion of 'no confidence' in the President of the Senate, Linda Baboolal, whom the party accused of exploiting her office to restrict criticism of government policies. In August the Government inaugurated a Committee on Race Relations to promote understanding and mutual respect among the various sectors of the population. In early November Manning carried out a cabinet reorganization; notable among the reallocation of portfolios was the appointment of Howard Lee Chin, hitherto Minister of National Security, to the newly established tourism portfolio. The new ministry had been established in an attempt to increase growth in the sector. On 12 March 2004 Lawrence Achong resigned as Minister of Labour and Small and Micro Enterprise Development. He was replaced at the end of the month by Anthony Roberts. Achong's resignation reportedly followed a disagreement with Manning over the implementation of a minimum wage for construction workers in his Point Fortin constituency. Around 1,900 construction workers on the Atlantic Liquefied Natural Gas (LNG) expansion project had gone on strike in February over salary levels. Employees returned to work on 19 April having secured salary increases of up to 22% and a potential completion bonus.

Despite government efforts, in 2003 and 2004 there were increasing concerns over the continuing rise in crime rates, particularly kidnapping and murder. The number of kidnappings for ransom totalled 51 in 2004, compared with 27 in 2002, while the number of murders rose from 172 in 2002 to 260 in 2004. In June 2003 the Senate approved legislation imposing a minimum 25-year prison sentence on those convicted of kidnap. In October opposition groups held a demonstration in the capital in protest at the increasing crime rates. Two UNC deputies were arrested during the protest, which coincided with the announcement in Parliament of the 2004 budget. In an effort to address the rising violent crime, in February 2004 the Government initiated a joint military-police unit. Manning pledged to invest in new technology to increase intelligence and surveillance capabilities.

In a landmark ruling, on 20 November 2003 the Privy Council ruled that Trinidad and Tobago's mandatory death sentence for convicted murderers was unconstitutional and inconsistent with the country's international obligations. The ruling followed an appeal brought by Balkissoon Roodal, who had been sentenced to death in July 1999. However, in July 2004 the Privy Council overturned its earlier ruling. A panel of nine judges, rather than the customary five, decreed that the Trinidadian Constitution did not allow outside intervention to abolish the mandatory death penalty. However, the judges further ruled that this would not apply to the estimated 100 prisoners who had benefited from the November judgment.

In October 2004 Manning announced that the Integrity Commission would investigate allegations that the Minister of Housing, Dr Keith Rowley, had used materials designated for a state hospital for a private-sector project. However, the Prime Minister dismissed opposition demands that Rowley resign. In April 2005 a parliamentary inquiry cleared Rowley of assaulting a UNC member of parliament in the tearoom of the legislature in the previous September. However, the UNC criticized the inquiry and urged members not to sign the report exonerating Rowley. Two UNC deputies, Gillian Lucky and Dr Fuad Khan, responded by declaring themselves to be independent members of parliament. In April it was disclosed that an independent tribunal was to investigate allegations that Chief Justice Satnarine Sharma had tried to pervert the course of justice. The Attorney-General and the Director of Public Prosecutions claimed that Sharma attempted to prevent a doctor being charged with the murder of his wife. Sharma subsequently filed a lawsuit against Manning, claiming that the Prime Minister's recommendation for an investigation into the allegations was biased.

Despite continuing concerns about the rise in criminal activity and allegations of government corruption, at an election to the Tobago House of Assembly on 17 January 2005 the governing PNM increased its majority from eight to 11 of the 12 seats, while the NAR, which had campaigned on a pro-devolution platform, secured just one legislative seat.

Allegations of political corruption persisted throughout 2005. In May corruption charges were filed against Panday, his wife, and the former UNC Minister of Works and Transport, Carlos John, in relation to the construction project at Piarco Airport. In April 2006 Panday was found guilty of charges, brought in 2002, of failing fully to declare his income while Prime Minister. He was sentenced to two years' imprisonment. Also in May 2005 the Minister of Works and Transport, Franklyn Khan, tendered his resignation pending an inquiry into corruption allegations against him. Allegations against the Minister of Energy and Energy Industries, Eric Williams, also prompted an investigation; however, Williams remained in office. In November Khan was charged with six counts of corruption, while in January 2006 Williams was charged with accepting bribes from a potential contractor. Both Williams and Khan denied the charges, and Williams stepped down from government. Responsibility for the Ministry of Energy and Energy Industries was subsequently added to the portfolio of the Minister of Public Administration and Information, Lenny Saith.

In July–October 2005 a series of bombs exploded in Port of Spain. The first, on 11 July, was placed in a dustbin and injured 15 people. Two small explosions occurred in August and September, then a fourth bomb exploded in a bar on 14 October, injuring at least 14 people, followed by a fifth device on 27 October. Two minor explosions in Moriah, Tobago were thought to be unrelated. The bombs in Port of Spain were believed to be criminal, rather than terrorist, attacks; police suggested that they may have been planted to distract attention from drugs-related activities. Following the fourth explosion five people, including Yasin Abu Bakr, were arrested, but were subsequently released without being charged. The Jamaat al Muslimeen denied responsibility for the attacks. The authorities' perceived failure to find the perpetrators prompted widespread anger throughout the country. Mounting public pressure on the Government to curb the deterioration in law and order culminated on 22 October in a demonstration in the capital, attended by thousands of protesters.

In September 2005 Manning pledged to reduce unemployment, which, he claimed, was a major cause of the high crime rate. In a further measure to control the rising levels of violent crime, in the same month the Prime Minister also announced that he had invited the British Metropolitan Police Service and the USA's Federal Bureau of Investigation to establish specialist units in Trinidad and Tobago. (Some 39 police-officers from the United Kingdom arrived in April 2006. They were expected to be incorporated into the Special Anti-Crime Unit for at least two years.) In October 2005 the Minister of National Security, Martin Joseph, admitted that the murder rate and the rate of detection were unacceptable. He declared that the increase in drugs- and arms-trafficking was largely responsible for the rise in kidnappings and killings. The total number of murders in 2005 rose to 389, while the rate of detection declined from 44% in 2002 to 21% in mid-2005. Some 80% of murders were committed with illegal guns. The number of kidnappings also rose in 2005.

In November 2005 the Government made a number of proposals aimed at stemming the rise in violent crime. Proposed reforms to the police force increased Parliament's role in selecting members of the Police Service Commission and the Police Commissioner, while removing the Prime Minister's right to veto the appointment of the latter. The reforms also conferred on the Commissioner of Police greater powers of discipline and management. Another proposal was the establishment of a court expressly for hearing cases involving gun-related crime and kidnapping. Furthermore, legislation would prevent kidnappers and alleged perpetrators of more than three violent crimes from securing bail, and would allow suspected kidnappers to held for up to 60 days before being charged.

On 7 November 2005 Yasin Abu Bakr was re-arrested and charged with seditious speech, incitement and terrorism, after allegedly preaching a sermon that called for a war on affluent Muslims who refused to pay *zakat*, a tithe for the poor, to his organization. In February 2006 the Attorney-General sought high court authorization for the state to confiscate 12 properties from members of the Jamaat al Muslimeen in compensation for damaged caused during the attempted coup in 1990.

In July 1991 Trinidad and Tobago ratified with Venezuela a joint declaration on maritime boundaries, under which Trinidad and Tobago's maritime boundary was to be extended from 200 nautical miles (370 km) to 350 nautical miles (648 km). Relations with Venezuela deteriorated in late 1996 and early 1997 owing to a series of incidents involving Trinidadian fishing vessels. In May 1997 a two-year fishing agreement was completed for approval by both Governments. However, tensions were revived later in the month after 15 Trinidadian fishermen were arrested by Venezuelan coast-guards. The Trinidadian Government referred the issue to the OAS and in response, Venezuela briefly withdrew its ambassador from the country. A revised two-year treaty was endorsed in December, permitting an unlimited number of vessels from each country into a shared fishing area. A joint fisheries commission was also re-established. In October 1998 it was agreed that the two countries would negotiate treaties on free trade and on co-operation against drugs-trafficking. In August 2003 the two countries signed a memorandum of understanding on the joint exploitation of cross-border oil and gas fields. The negotiations were suspended in mid-2004 but recommenced in January 2006. The discussions stalled temporarily following Trinidad and Tobago's refusal to sign Venezuela's PetroCaribe energy accord, launched the previous year, which offered oil concessions and favourable financing terms to Caribbean nations. The accord was expected adversely to affect, at least initially, Trinidad and Tobago's energy sector. However, negotiations resumed in March.

In July 2000 talks were held to find a solution to the maritime border dispute between Trinidad and Barbados. Despite further talks being held over the next two years, little progress was made. In January 2004 the Prime Minister of Trinidad and Tobago indicated he would refer the matter to the CARICOM (see p. 183). Bilateral relations deteriorated in February after several Barbadian fishermen were arrested in Trinidad and Tobago's waters; Barbados subsequently imposed economic sanctions on imports from Trinidad and Tobago, which they were later ordered to lift by CARICOM's Council for Trade and Economic Development. Meanwhile, in early February Barbados announced plans to seek UN arbitration under the UN Convention on the Law of the Seas. This move was criticized by the Trinidad and Tobago Government, which claimed it undermined the proposed CCJ. None the less, hearings on the boundary dispute commenced in October 2005 at the International Dispute Resolution Centre.

Government

Legislative power is vested in the bicameral Parliament, consisting of the Senate, with 31 members, and the House of Representatives, with 36 members. Representatives are elected for a five-year term by universal adult suffrage. The President is a constitutional Head of State, chosen by an electoral college of members of both the Senate and the House of Representatives.

Members of the Senate are nominated by the President in consultation with, and on the advice of, the Prime Minister and the Leader of the Opposition. The Cabinet has effective control of the Government and is responsible to Parliament. Tobago Island was granted its own House of Assembly in 1980 and given full internal self-government in January 1987. The Tobago House of Assembly has 15 members, of whom 12 are elected. The remaining three are selected by the majority party.

Defence

In August 2005 the defence forces consisted of an army estimated at 2,000 men, and a coastguard of 700, with 12 patrol craft. Included in the coastguard is an air force of 50. The defence budget for 2004 was an estimated TT $197m. (US $32.0m.)

Economic Affairs

In 2004, according to estimates by the World Bank, Trinidad and Tobago's gross national income (GNI), measured at average 2002–04 prices, was US $11,359.8m., equivalent to US $8,580 per head (or US $11,180 on an international purchasing-power parity basis). During 1995–2004, it was estimated, the population increased at an average annual rate of 0.5%, while gross domestic product (GDP) per head increased, in real terms, by an average of 5.1% per year. Overall GDP increased, in real terms, at an average annual rate of 5.6% in 1995–2004; according to the IMF, economic growth was 6.2% in 2004.

Agriculture (including forestry, hunting and fishing) contributed an estimated 0.9% of GDP and employed an estimated 5.0% of the working population in 2004. The principal cash crops are sugar cane, coffee, cocoa and citrus fruits. The fishing sector is small-scale, but is an important local source of food. In 2001 the Government allocated TT $5m. to create an Agriculture Disaster Relief Fund, designed to alleviate the effects of natural disasters upon the agricultural sector. During 2000–04, according to official estimates, agricultural GDP declined by an average of 6.5% per year. The sector contracted by 18.2% in 2003 and by a further, estimated 21.1% in 2004.

Industry (including mining and quarrying, manufacturing, construction and power) provided an estimated 51.3% of GDP and employed an estimated 30.8% of the working population in 2004. During 2000–04, according to the IMF, industrial GDP increased at an average annual rate of 12.4%. Industrial GDP increased by 25.9% in 2003 and by an estimated 9.0% in 2004.

The petroleum sector provided an estimated 36.8% of GDP in 2004. In that year the mining and quarrying sector (including petroleum production) employed some 3.4% of the working population. The petroleum industry is the principal sector of Trinidad and Tobago's economy. According to the IMF, the GDP of the petroleum sector increased at an estimated annual average rate of 14.1% during 2000–04. The sector grew by 31.3% in 2003 and by an estimated 7.9% in 2004. Trinidad has the world's largest deposits of natural asphalt, and substantial reserves of natural gas. In 2005 Trinidad and Tobago was the world's second largest producer (after Chile) of methanol, a by-product of natural gas. Cement, limestone and sulphur are also mined.

Manufacturing contributed an estimated 6.6% of GDP in 2004 and employed 10.4% of the working population. The principal branches in 2003 (measured by value of output) were petroleum-refining, fertilizers, iron and steel, food products, paper and paperboard, and cement, lime and plaster. During 2000–04, manufacturing GDP increased at an average annual rate of 6.8%. Manufacturing GDP increased by 4.2% in 2003 and by an estimated 9.5% in 2004.

Almost all of the country's energy is derived from natural gas (it provided 99.5% of total electricity production in 2002). Natural gas is also used as fuel for the country's two petroleum refineries and several manufacturing plants. In 2002 16 international companies were involved in petroleum and gas exploration in Trinidad and Tobago's offshore areas. Imports of fuel products comprised only 0.4% of the value of merchandise imports in 1995, but the proportion increased to an estimated 22.8% in 2004. In that year exports of gas accounted for an estimated 31.7% of total exports, while exports of petroleum and petroleum products accounted for an estimated 26.3%.

The services sector contributed an estimated 47.8% of GDP and employed some 63.4% of the working population in 2004. Tourism is a major source of foreign exchange; in 2002 receipts from tourism totalled US $224m. and in 2003 some 409,069 foreign tourists visited the islands. However, there were fears that the increasing rates of violent crime would adversely affect tourism revenues. In February 2004 Prime Minister Manning announced a series of initiatives to promote leisure and 'eco-tourism' in Tobago and business tourism in Trinidad. According to official estimates, the GDP of the services sector increased at an average annual rate of 3.5% in 2000–04. Sectoral GDP increased by 4.0% in 2003 and by an estimated 4.8% in 2004.

In 2004 Trinidad and Tobago recorded a visible trade surplus of an estimated US $1,272m., and there was a surplus of US $919m. on the current account of the balance of payments. In 2004 the principal source of imports was the USA (34.0%); other major suppliers were Brazil (10.4%) and Venezuela (3.1%). The USA was also the principal market for exports (69.8%) in that year; other important purchasers were Jamaica (3.8%) and Barbados (3.3%). The principal exports in 2004 were fuels (58.1%), chemicals (24.4%) and basic manufactures (10.8%). The principal imports were fuels (22.8%), foodstuffs (7.1%) and transport equipment (4.5%).

In 2004/05 there was an estimated budgetary surplus of TT $2,896m., equivalent to 3.7% of GDP. At the end of 2003 Trinidad and Tobago's total external debt was US $2,751m., of which US $1,861m. was long-term public debt. In that year the cost of debt-servicing was equivalent to 4.1% of the value of exports of goods and services. The annual rate of inflation averaged 4.3% in 2000–04. Consumer prices increased by an estimated average of 3.9% in 2003 and by 3.6% in 2004. According to the IMF, some 7.8% of the labour force were unemployed in 2004.

Trinidad and Tobago is a member of the Caribbean Community and Common Market (CARICOM, see p. 183), the Inter-American Development Bank (IDB, see p. 284), the Latin American Economic System (SELA, see p. 386), and the Association of Caribbean States (ACS, see p. 384). In November 2005 a bilateral free trade agreement was signed with Costa Rica, enabling duty-free access to markets for more than 90% of goods. Trinidad and Tobago was one of the six founder members of CARICOM's Caribbean Single Market and Economy (CSME), which was inaugurated on 1 January 2006. It was anticipated that the CSME would facilitate the free movement of goods, services and labour throughout most of the CARICOM region.

The discovery of significant petroleum and natural gas deposits in the 1990s, combined with substantial foreign investment, meant that by the early 21st century the energy sector was a major contributor to Trinidad and Tobago's economy. The development of a major liquefied natural gas (LNG) plant at Point Fortin from 2001 would eventually make Trinidad and Tobago one of the world's leading suppliers of LNG. In April 2003 Atlantic LNG's third train was commissioned and a fourth train, the largest single gas train in the world, with an annual capacity of 5.2m. metric tons, began operations in December 2005. In September 2003 BP Energy Company of Trinidad and Tobago (formerly BP Amoco) announced the discovery of the country's largest ever natural gas deposit. Substantial foreign investment allowed increased industrialization, which, combined with high international fuel prices, contributed to rapid economic expansion and a substantial trade surplus between 2002–05. However, the strong economic performance of the energy sector was not representative of the economy as a whole. In July 2003 the loss-making state sugar company Caroni closed, making 8,000 employees redundant (an additional 10,000 had lost their jobs the previous October). The company reopened in the following month under the new name Sugar Manufacturing Company Ltd, but with a vastly reduced work-force and operating at the Sainte Madeleine plant only. Moreover, concerns about rising crime rates damaged investor confidence, increased security costs for businesses and threatened the tourism industry. Furthermore, although some progress had been made to liberalize certain sectors of the economy (namely gas), further reform was overdue, particularly in telecommunications. Also of concern was the standard of public services and infrastructure, as well as the increasing public-sector debt. Nevertheless, overall GDP increased by an estimated 7.0% in 2005. While the energy sector continued to lead growth, expansion in the non-energy sector rose from 3.2% in 2004 to 4.0% in 2005. The Central Bank forecast growth of 9.5% in 2006, partly owing to the commission of the fourth LNG train in late 2005. The persistently high average rate of unemployment was forecast to decline to 6.5% by 2006.

Education

Primary and secondary education is provided free of charge. Attendance at school is officially compulsory for children between five and 12 years of age. Primary education begins at the age of five and lasts for seven years. Secondary education, beginning at 12 years of age, lasts for up to five years, comprising a first cycle of three years and a second of two years. Entrance to secondary schools is determined by the Common Entrance Examination. Many schools are administered jointly by the state and religious bodies. In 2002/03 enrolment at primary schools included 90.6% of children in the relevant age-group (males 90.9%; females 90.3%), while enrolment at secondary schools was equivalent to 72.0% of children in the relevant age-group (males 69.4%; females 74.7%). In 2000 the Government announced an education reform programme to improve access to, and levels of, education. A school-to-work apprenticeship programme was also to be established.

The Trinidad campus of the University of the West Indies (UWI), at St Augustine, offers undergraduate and postgraduate programmes. The UWI Institute of Business offers postgraduate courses, and develops programmes for local companies. Other institutions of higher education are the Eric Williams Medical Sciences complex, the Polytechnic Institute and the East Caribbean Farm Institute. The country has one teacher training college and three government-controlled technical institutes and vocational centres, including the Trinidad and Tobago Hotel School. In the late 1990s the Government established the Trinidad and Tobago Institute of Technology, and the College of Science, Technology and Applied Arts of Trinidad and Tobago. In March 2004 a Steering Committee was appointed to conduct a strategic review of tertiary education, and distance and lifelong learning, in an attempt to improve consistency within the tertiary sector and in relation to the education system as a whole. Budgeted expenditure on education by the central Government in 2005 was TT $3,140.3m., equivalent to 11.2% on total government expenditure.

Public Holidays

2006: 1 January (New Year's Day), 30 March (Spiritual Baptist Shouters' Liberation Day), 14–17 April (Easter), 30 May (Indian Arrival Day), 15 June (Corpus Christi), 19 June (Labour Day), 1 August (Emancipation Day), 31 August (Independence Day), 21 October† (Divali), 23 October* (Id al-Fitr, end of Ramadan), 25–26 December (Christmas).

2007: 1 January (New Year's Day), 30 March (Spiritual Baptist Shouters' Liberation Day), 6–9 April (Easter), 30 May (Indian Arrival Day), 7 June (Corpus Christi), 19 June (Labour Day), 1 August (Emancipation Day), 31 August (Independence Day), 13 October* (Id al-Fitr, end of Ramadan), 9 November† (Divali), 25–26 December (Christmas).

* These holidays are dependent on the Islamic lunar calendar and may vary by one or two days from the dates given.

† Dependent on lunar sightings.

Weights and Measures

The metric system is replacing the imperial system of weights and measures.

Statistical Survey

Sources (unless otherwise stated): Central Statistical Office, National Statistics Bldg, 80 Independence Sq., POB 98, Port of Spain; tel. 623-6945; fax 625-3802; e-mail info@cso.gov.tt; internet www.cso.gov.tt; Central Bank of Trinidad and Tobago, POB 1250, Port of Spain; tel. 625-4835; fax 627-4696; e-mail info@central-bank.org.tt; internet www.central-bank.org.tt

Area and Population

AREA, POPULATION AND DENSITY

Area (sq km)	5,128*
Population (census results)	
2 May 1990	1,213,733
15 May 2000	
Males	633,051
Females	629,315
Total	1,262,366
Population (official estimates at September)	
2000	1,262,400
2001	1,266,800
2002	1,275,700
Density (per sq km) at September 2002	248.8

* 1,980 sq miles. Of the total area, Trinidad is 4,828 sq km (1,864 sq miles) and Tobago 300 sq km (116 sq miles).

POPULATION BY ETHNIC GROUP
(1990 census*)

	Males	Females	Total	%
African	223,561	221,883	445,444	39.59
Chinese	2,317	1,997	4,314	0.38
'East' Indian	226,967	226,102	453,069	40.27
Lebanese	493	441	934	0.08
Mixed	100,842	106,716	207,558	18.45
White	3,483	3,771	7,254	0.64
Other	886	838	1,724	0.15
Unknown	2,385	2,446	4,831	0.43
Total	**560,934**	**564,194**	**1,125,128**	**100.00**

* Excludes some institutional population and members of unenumerated households, totalling 44,444.

ADMINISTRATIVE DIVISIONS
(population at 2000 census)

	Population	Capital
Trinidad	1,208,282	Port of Spain
Port of Spain (city, capital)	49,031	—
San Fernando (city)	55,419	—
Arima (borough)	32,278	Arima
Chaguanas (borough)	67,433	Chaguanas
Point Fortin (borough)	19,056	Point Fortin
Diego Martin	105,720	Petit Valley
San Juan/Laventille	157,295	Laventille
Tunapuna/Piarco	203,975	Tunapuna
Couva/Tabaquite/Talparo	162,779	Couva
Mayaro/Rio Claro	33,480	Rio Claro
Sangre Grande	64,343	Sangre Grande
Princes Town	91,947	Princes Town
Penal/Debe	83,609	Penal
Siparia	81,917	Siparia
Tobago	54,084	Scarborough

BIRTHS AND DEATHS
(UN estimates, annual averages)

	1990–95	1995–2000	2000–05
Birth rate (per 1,000)	17.6	14.1	14.2
Death rate (per 1,000)	6.6	6.9	7.9

Source: UN, *World Population Prospects: The 2004 Revision.*

Expectation of life (WHO estimates, years at birth): 70 (males 67; females 73) in 2003 (Source: WHO, *World Health Report*).

TRINIDAD AND TOBAGO

EMPLOYMENT
('000 persons aged 15 years and over, October–December)

	2003	2004
Agriculture, forestry, hunting and fishing*	25.9	29.1
Mining and quarrying†	17.7	19.6
Manufacturing‡	58.7	60.4
Electricity, gas and water	5.6	7.4
Construction	74.5	91.4
Wholesale and retail trade, restaurants and hotels	100.5	102.1
Transport, storage and communication	41.0	45.6
Finance, insurance, real estate and business services	45.7	45.7
Community, social and personal services	168.7	174.8
Activities not adequately defined	3.4	4.4
Total employed	541.8	580.7
Males	334.1	348.6
Females	207.7	232.1
Unemployed	61.3	48.8
Total labour force	603.1	629.5

* Includes sugar manufacture.
† Includes oil manufacture.
‡ Excludes sugar and oil manufacture.

Health and Welfare

KEY INDICATORS

Total fertility rate (children per woman, 2003)	1.6
Under-5 mortality rate (per 1,000 live births, 2004)	20
HIV/AIDS (% of persons, aged 15–49, 2003)	3.2
Physicians (per 1,000 head, 1997)	0.79
Hospital beds (per 1,000 head, 1996)	5.11
Health expenditure (2002): US $ per head (PPP)	428
Health expenditure (2002): % of GDP	3.7
Health expenditure (2002): public (% of total)	37.3
Access to water (% of persons, 2002)	91
Access to sanitation (% of persons, 2002)	100
Human Development Index (2003): ranking	57
Human Development Index (2003): value	0.801

For sources and definitions, see explanatory note on p. vi.

Agriculture

PRINCIPAL CROPS
('000 metric tons)

	2002	2003	2004*
Rice (paddy)	3.9	2.9	3.0
Maize	3.3	3.0	3.0
Taro (Coco yam)	6.9	4.7	4.8
Sugar cane	1,339.0	873.0	680.0
Pigeon peas	2.8	2.9	2.9
Coconuts*	21.0	16.5	18.0
Cabbages	1.8	1.7	1.8
Lettuce	1.4	1.4	1.4
Tomatoes	1.2	1.7	1.8
Pumpkins, squash and gourds	5.8	5.9*	6.1
Cucumbers and gherkins	3.6	3.7*	3.8
Aubergines	1.9	2.0*	2.1
Other fresh vegetables*	4.9	5.1	5.4
Watermelons	0.9	1.0*	1.2
Bananas*	6.5	6.7	6.8
Plantains*	4.3	4.4	4.5
Oranges	5.0	5.0*	5.1
Lemons and limes*	1.4	1.5	1.5
Grapefruit and pomelo	2.5	2.6*	2.7
Pineapples*	3.6	3.8	4.2
Other fruit*	39.7	40.7	41.9
Coffee (green)	0.2	0.6	0.6
Cocoa beans	1.6	1.0	1.3

* FAO estimate(s).
Source: FAO.

LIVESTOCK
('000 head, year ending September)

	2002	2003	2004
Horses*	1.1	1.2	1.2
Mules*	1.8	1.9	1.9
Asses*	2.1	2.2	2.2
Cattle	31.6*	29.0	29.0
Buffaloes*	5.6	5.7	5.7
Pigs	80.0*	75.7	78.0*
Poultry	31,016	27,500*	28,200*
Sheep*	3.5	3.4	3.4
Goats*	58.5	58.6	59.0

* FAO estimate(s).
Source: FAO.

LIVESTOCK PRODUCTS
('000 metric tons)

	2002	2003	2004
Beef and veal	0.9	0.8	0.8*
Pig meat	2.9	2.8	2.9*
Poultry meat	60.0	56.5	57.6
Cows' milk	10.0	8.9	10.0*
Hen eggs	3.7†	3.7†	3.7*

* FAO estimate.
† Unofficial figure.
Source: FAO.

Forestry

ROUNDWOOD REMOVALS
('000 cubic metres, excl. bark)

	2002	2003	2004*
Sawlogs, veneer logs and logs for sleepers	57.0	60.0	60.0
Fuel wood*	35.7	35.3	34.9
Total	92.7	95.3	94.9

* FAO estimates.
Source: FAO.

SAWNWOOD PRODUCTION
('000 cubic metres, incl. railway sleepers)

	2002	2003	2004
Total (all broadleaved)	43	43	43*

* FAO estimate.
Source: FAO.

Fishing

('000 metric tons, live weight of capture)

	2001	2002	2003
Demersal percomorphs	2.3	2.5	2.4
King mackerel	0.6	1.5	0.9
Serra Spanish mackerel	2.7	2.5	2.0
Tuna-like fishes	0.7	0.8	0.6
Sharks, rays, skates, etc.	0.8	1.0	0.9
Other marine fishes	2.6	3.0	2.0
Penaeus shrimps	0.9	0.9	0.7
Total catch (incl. others)	10.8	12.6	9.7

Source: FAO.

TRINIDAD AND TOBAGO

Mining

('000 barrels, unless otherwise indicated)

	2001	2002	2003
Crude petroleum	41,374	47,684	48,947
Natural gas liquids	7,521	8,505	10,500*
Natural gas (million cu m)†	16,599	19,172	26,810

* Estimate.
† Figures refer to the gross volume of output; marketed production (in million cu m) was: 15,173 in 2001; 17,777 in 2002; 26,046 in 2003.
Source: US Geological Survey.

Industry

SELECTED PRODUCTS
('000 metric tons, unless otherwise indicated)

	2001	2002	2003
Raw sugar	91	98	68
Fertilizers	4,209	4,721	4,965
Methanol	2,789	2,829	2,846
Cement	697	744	766
Iron (direct reduced)	2,187	2,316	2,275
Steel:			
billets	668	817	896
wire rods	605	705	641
Electric energy (million kWh)*	5,460	5,643	n.a.

* Source: UN Economic Commission for Latin America and the Caribbean.

Finance

CURRENCY AND EXCHANGE RATES

Monetary Units
100 cents = 1 Trinidad and Tobago dollar (TT $).

Sterling, US Dollar and Euro Equivalents (30 December 2005)
£1 sterling = TT $10.8091;
US $1 = TT $6.2774;
€1 = TT $7.4055;
TT $1,000 = £92.52 = US $159.30 = €135.04.

Average Exchange Rate (TT $ per US $)
2003   6.2951
2004   6.2990
2005   6.2842

CENTRAL GOVERNMENT BUDGET
(TT $ million)

Revenue	2002/03	2003/04	2004/05*
Energy sector	6,717	8,422	14,101
Corporation tax	5,102	6,598	11,569
Withholding tax (oil)	157	144	328
Royalties	1,008	1,095	1,230
Unemployment levy	291	410	750
Green Fund levy	94	139	183
Excise duties	34	37	40
Signature bonuses	31	—	—
Non-energy sector	10,629	12,202	13,796
Taxes	9,541	10,975	12,020
Taxes on income	4,674	4,937	5,743
Taxes on property	78	85	64
Taxes on goods and services	3,546	4,484	4,548
Value-added tax	2,121	3,021	2,948
Other	1,425	1,463	1,600
Taxes on international trade	1,070	1,243	1,434
Other	175	226	232
Non-tax revenue of non-oil sector	1,088	1,227	1,776
Capital revenue and grants	20	4	19
Total	17,366	20,628	27,916

Expenditure	2002/03	2003/04	2004/05*
Current expenditure	15,096	17,499	22,287
Wages and salaries	4,548	4,849	5,446
Goods and services	2,038	2,375	3,365
Interest payments	2,592	2,364	2,594
Domestic	1,834	1,638	1,874
External	758	726	720
Transfers and subsidies	5,918	7,911	10,883
Households	2,046	2,154	2,690
Public sector bodies	1,937	3,035	3,380
Other	1,935	2,722	4,813
Capital expenditure and net lending	998	1,601	2,734
Total	16,094	19,100	25,020

* Preliminary estimates.

INTERNATIONAL RESERVES
(US $ million at 31 December)

	2003	2004	2005
Gold (national valuation)	25.5	26.8	31.4
IMF special drawing rights	1.1	2.7	3.7
Reserve position in IMF	192.2	172.5	71.3
Foreign exchange	2,257.8	2,993.0	4,781.4
Total	2,476.6	3,195.0	4,887.8

Source: IMF, *International Financial Statistics*.

MONEY SUPPLY
(TT $ million at 31 December)

	2003	2004	2005
Currency outside banks	1,708.6	1,957.4	2,425.4
Demand deposits at commercial banks	5,108.0	5,795.3	9,358.6
Total money (incl. others)	7,723.0	8,375.4	13,292.6

Source: IMF, *International Financial Statistics*.

COST OF LIVING
(Consumer Price Index; base: 2000 = 100)

	2001	2002
Food	114.0	125.6
Heat and light	100.3	101.2
Clothing	98.7	96.4
Rent	101.1	102.5
All items (incl. others)	105.6	109.9

All items: 114.2 in 2003; 118.3 in 2004.
Source: ILO.

TRINIDAD AND TOBAGO

NATIONAL ACCOUNTS
(TT $ million at current prices)

National Income and Product

	1998	1999	2000
Compensation of employees	17,864.3	19,087.3	20,004.0
Operating surplus	11,918.8	13,569.3	24,233.0
Domestic factor incomes	29,783.1	32,656.6	44,237.0
Consumption of fixed capital	4,562.8	4,787.0	6,063.0
Gross domestic product (GDP) at factor cost	34,345.9	37,443.6	50,300.0
Indirect taxes	4,070.4	3,989.3	1,379.0*
Less Subsidies	379.6	398.9	807.0
GDP in purchasers' values	38,036.7	41,034.0	50,872.0
Net factor income	−2,527.0	−2,518.0	−3,953.0
Gross national income (GNI)	35,509.7	38,516.0	46,919.0
Less Consumption of fixed capital	4,410.0	5,177.0	6,063.0
National income at market prices	31,099.7	33,339.0	40,856.0

* Figure obtained as a residual.

Source: UN, Economic Commission for Latin America and the Caribbean, *Statistical Yearbook*.

Gross national income (TT $ million at current prices): 51,604.0 (GDP in purchasers' values 55,009.1, Net factor income −3,402.2) in 2001; 56,456.6 (GDP in purchasers' values 59,486.9, Net factor income −3,030.3) in 2002; 65,402.8 (GDP in purchasers' values 67,692.2, Net factor income −2,289.4) in 2003 (preliminary figures).

Expenditure on the Gross Domestic Product

	2002	2003	2004*
Government final consumption expenditure	7,652	8,956	10,643
Private final consumption expenditure	33,771	35,245	34,614
Gross capital formation	10,826	11,908	12,951
Total domestic expenditure	52,249	56,108	58,208
Exports of goods and services	28,299	36,872	45,990
Less Imports of goods and services	25,182	26,812	32,320
Statistical discrepancy	1,127	1,587	5,703
GDP in purchasers' values	56,493	67,755	77,581

* Preliminary figures.

Gross Domestic Product by Economic Activity

	2002	2003	2004*
Agriculture, hunting, forestry and fishing	787	713	669
Petroleum	14,765	22,711	28,563
Manufacturing	4,494	4,701	5,125
Construction	4,092	5,156	6,239
Distribution	9,287	9,902	10,624
Hotels	255	243	263
Finance, insurance and, real estate	8,890	9,182	9,732
Government	4,333	5,560	5,718
Other services	9,376	9,709	10,804
Sub-total	56,279	67,877	77,737
Less Imputed bank service charges	2,187	2,486	3,018
Value-added tax	2,401	2,364	2,864
GDP in purchaser's values	56,493	67,755	77,581

* Preliminary figures.

BALANCE OF PAYMENTS
(US $ million)

	2002	2003	2004*
Exports of goods f.o.b.	3,920	5,256	6,523
Imports of goods f.o.b.	−3,682	−3,922	−5,251
Trade balance	238	1,334	1,272
Services (net)	264	313	353
Balance on goods and services	502	1,647	1,625
Other income (net)	−480	−362	−773
Balance on goods, services and income	22	1,285	852
Current transfers (net)	55	66	68
Current balance	76	1,351	919
Direct investment abroad	−106	−225	−200
Direct investment from abroad	791	1,234	1,826
Official, medium and long-term disbursements	18	101	251
Official, medium and long-term amortization	−79	−130	−241
Commercial banks (net)	−79	92	—
Other private sector capital (incl. net errors and omissions)	−572	−2,089	−2,072
Overall balance	49	334	483

* Estimates.

Source: IMF, *Trinidad and Tobago: 2004 Article IV Consultation—Staff Report; Staff Statement; Public Information Notice on the Executive Board Discussion; and Statement by the Executive Director for Trinidad and Tobago* (January 2005).

External Trade

PRINCIPAL COMMODITIES
(US $ million)

Imports c.i.f.	2002	2003	2004
Imports for processing	9.8	12.7	14.9
Consumer goods	511.1	538.1	640.4
Non-durable	302.7	350.0	399.2
Food	270.7	306.4	349.4
Other	32.0	43.6	49.7
Durable	208.4	188.1	241.2
Raw materials and intermediate goods	1,895.3	2,071.9	2,338.3
Fuels	1,018.6	1,064.2	1,118.0
Construction materials	124.9	159.5	181.9
Other	751.8	848.2	975.4
Capital goods	1,275.9	1,256.7	1,796.0
Transport equipment	169.0	174.1	218.0
Oil and mining machinery	87.0	85.3	102.6
Other	1,019.9	997.3	1,475.4
Total (incl. others)	3,682.3	3,991.7	4,894.2

Exports f.o.b.	2002	2003	2004
Food and live animals	169.4	149.3	161.4
Sugar	24.8	24.1	20.4
Beverages and tobacco	101.1	101.1	83.1
Fuels	2,064.2	3,355.7	3,621.0
Crude petroleum	586.0	814.9	821.6
Refined petroleum products	1,182.0	1,571.1	821.4
Liquefied natural gas	274.9	676.3	1,750.7
Natural gas liquids	184.3	274.4	227.3
Chemicals	647.1	906.6	1,522.0
Anhydrous ammonia	338.0	490.0	919.0
Urea	63.0	101.1	102.7
Methanol	192.0	257.0	441.5
Other	54.1	58.5	58.8
Manufactures	564.7	443.1	671.8
Steel	332.0	321.1	412.1
Machinery	93.9	72.1	129.7
Miscellaneous manufactured articles	60.2	63.1	66.7
Total (incl. others)*	3,604.2	5,090.3	6,236.3

* Excluding re-exports (US $ million): 40.8 in 2002; 114.6 in 2003; 166.6 in 2004.

TRINIDAD AND TOBAGO

PRINCIPAL TRADING PARTNERS
(US $ million)

Imports c.i.f.	2002	2003	2004
Barbados	30.7	22.2	22.7
Brazil	210.2	352.5	511.1
Canada	104.1	116.9	107.9
Central American Common Market (CACM)	25.6	23.5	21.6
European Free Trade Association (EFTA)	40.3	40.7	37.6
European Union (EU)	586.7	697.1	1,080.2
Guyana	15.8	22.4	26.0
Jamaica	17.4	16.8	14.2
USA	1,236.5	1,179.7	1,662.2
Venezuela	399.2	364.5	153.5
Total (incl. others)	3,682.3	3,911.7	4,894.2

Exports f.o.b.	2002	2003	2004
Barbados	179.5	203.7	213.8
Brazil	18.5	30.8	36.9
Canada	92.4	95.4	83.8
European Union (EU)	259.4	214.9	223.2
Guyana	83.0	149.9	122.4
Jamaica	294.2	353.6	245.6
USA	1,803.5	2,785.2	4,471.8
Venezuela	24.1	42.2	17.9
Total (incl. others)	3,875.0	5,204.9	6,402.9

Transport

ROAD TRAFFIC
(estimated motor vehicles in use)

	1994	1995	1996
Passenger cars	122,000	122,000	122,000
Lorries and vans	24,000	24,000	24,000

Source: IRF, *World Road Statistics*.

Total number of registered vehicles: 292,908 in 1999; 316,163 in 2000; 331,595 in 2001 (provisional figure).

SHIPPING
Merchant Fleet
(registered at 31 December)

	2002	2003	2004
Number of vessels	69	76	95
Total displacement ('000 grt)	26.8	28.1	33.5

Source: Lloyd's Register-Fairplay, *World Fleet Statistics*.

International Sea-borne Freight Traffic
(estimates, '000 metric tons)

	1988	1989	1990
Goods loaded	7,736	7,992	9,622
Goods unloaded	4,076	4,091	10,961

Source: UN, *Monthly Bulletin of Statistics*.

1998: Port of Spain handled 3.3m. metric tons of cargo.

CIVIL AVIATION
(traffic on scheduled services)

	1999	2000	2001
Kilometres flown (million)	25	28	29
Passengers carried ('000)	1,112	1,254	1,388
Passenger-km (million)	2,720	2,765	2,723
Total ton-km (million)	309	300	288

Source: UN, *Statistical Yearbook*.

Tourism

FOREIGN TOURIST ARRIVALS

Country of origin	2001	2002	2003
Barbados	27,878	33,989	37,320
Canada	43,291	41,506	43,036
Germany	11,371	5,659	7,491
Grenada	15,130	16,539	19,220
Guyana	20,062	22,299	22,783
Saint Vincent and Grenadines	8,405	9,636	11,041
United Kingdom	48,570	51,688	57,566
USA	118,962	133,565	138,935
Venezuela	10,207	11,107	10,273
Total (incl. others)	383,101	384,212	409,069

Tourism receipts (US $ million, incl. passenger transport): 371 in 2000; 361 in 2001; 402 in 2002.

Sources: World Tourism Organization.

Communications Media

	2002	2003	2004
Telephones ('000 main lines in use)	325.1	n.a.	321.3
Mobile cellular telephones ('000 subscribers)	361.9	520.0	647.9
Personal computers ('000 in use)	104	n.a.	137
Internet users ('000)	138	n.a.	160.0

Radio receivers (1997, '000 in use): 680.
Facsimile machines (1998, number in use): 5,024.
Daily newspapers: 4 in 1997 (average circulation: 191,000 in 2001).
Non-daily newspapers: 5 in 1997 (average circulation 167,000 in 2001).
Television receivers ('000 in use): 449 in 2001.

Sources: International Telecommunication Union; UN, *Statistical Yearbook*; UNESCO, *Statistical Yearbook*.

Education

(2001/02, unless otherwise indicated)

	Institutions	Teachers	Males	Females	Total
Pre-primary	50*	1,790	13,702	8,398	22,100
Primary	480	7,975	79,023	75,924	154,947
Secondary	101†	5,443	47,150	49,075	96,225
University and equivalent	3	550	3,931	5,935	9,866

* Government schools and assisted schools only, in 1992/93.
† 1993/94.

Source: UNESCO.

Adult literacy rate (UNESCO estimates): 98.5% (males 99.0%; females 97.9%) in 2002 (Source: UN Development Programme, *Human Development Report*).

Directory

The Constitution

Trinidad and Tobago became a republic, within the Commonwealth, under a new Constitution on 1 August 1976. The Constitution provides for a President and a bicameral Parliament comprising a Senate and a House of Representatives. The President is elected by an Electoral College of members of both the Senate and the House of Representatives. The Senate consists of 31 members appointed by the President: 16 on the advice of the Prime Minister, six on the advice of the Leader of the Opposition and nine at the President's own discretion from among outstanding persons from economic, social or community organizations. The House of Representatives consists of 36 members who are elected by universal adult suffrage. The duration of a Parliament is five years. The Cabinet, presided over by the Prime Minister, is responsible for the general direction and control of the Government. It is collectively responsible to Parliament.

The Government

HEAD OF STATE

President: Prof. GEORGE MAXWELL RICHARDS (took office 17 March 2003).

THE CABINET
(April 2006)

Prime Minister, Minister of Finance and of Tobago Affairs: PATRICK MANNING.
Attorney-General: JOHN JEREMIE.
Minister of Legal Affairs: CHRISTINE KANGALOO.
Minister of Community Development, Culture and Gender Affairs: JOAN YUILLE-WILLIAMS.
Minister of Social Development: ANTHONY ROBERTS.
Minister of Education: HAZEL ANNE MARIE MANNING.
Minister of Agriculture, Land and Marine Resources: JARRETTE NARINE.
Minister of Foreign Affairs: KNOWLSON GIFT.
Minister of Health: JOHN RAHAEL.
Minister of Housing: Dr KEITH ROWLEY.
Minister of Local Government: RENNIE DUMAS.
Minister of Planning and Development: CAMILLE ROBINSON REGIS.
Minister of Public Utilties and the Environment: PENELOPE BECKLES.
Minister of Labour and Small and Micro Enterprise Development: DANNY MONTANO.
Minister of National Security: MARTIN JOSEPH.
Minister of Public Administration and Information and of Energy and Energy Industries: LENNY SAITH.
Minister of Science, Technology and Tertiary Education: MUSTAPHA ABDUL HAMID.
Minister of Sport and Youth Affairs: ROGER BOYNES.
Minister of Tourism: HOWARD CHIN LEE.
Minister of Trade and Industry: KENNETH VALLEY.
Minister of Works and Transport: COLM IMBERT.

MINISTRIES

Office of the President: President's House, Circular Rd, St Ann's, Port of Spain; tel. 624-1261; fax 625-7950; e-mail presoftt@carib-link.net.
Office of the Prime Minister: Whitehall, Maraval Rd, Port of Spain; tel. 622-1625; fax 622-0055; e-mail opm@ttgov.gov.tt; internet www.opm.gov.tt.
Ministry of Agriculture, Land and Marine Resources: St Clair Circle, St Clair, Port of Spain; tel. 622-1221; fax 622-8202; e-mail apdmalmr@trinidad.net; internet www.agriculture.gov.tt.
Ministry of the Attorney-General: Cabildo Chambers, 23–27 St Vincent St, Port of Spain; tel. 623-7010; fax 625-0470; e-mail ag@ag.gov.tt; internet www.ag.gov.tt.
Ministry of Community Development, Culture and Gender Affairs: ALGICO Bldg, Jerningham Ave, Belmont, Port of Spain; tel. 625-3012; fax 625-3278; e-mail cdcga@tstt.net.tt.
Ministry of Education: Alexandra St, St Clair; tel. 622-2181; fax 622-4892; e-mail mined@tstt.net.tt.
Ministry of Energy and Energy Industries: Level 9, Riverside Plaza, Cnr Besson and Piccadilly Sts, Port of Spain; tel. 623-6708; fax 623-2726; e-mail admin@energy.gov.tt; internet www.energy.gov.tt.
Ministry of Finance: Eric Williams Finance Bldg, Independence Sq., Port of Spain; tel. 627-9700; fax 627-6108; e-mail mofcmu@tstt.net.tt; internet www.finance.gov.tt.
Ministry of Foreign Affairs: Knowsley Bldg, 10–14 Queen's Park West, Port of Spain; tel. 623-4116; fax 624-4220; e-mail permanentsecretary@foreign.gov.tt.
Ministry of Health: IDC Bldg, 10–12 Independence Sq., Port of Spain; tel. 627-0012; fax 623-9528; e-mail scdda@carib-link.net; internet www.healthsectorreform.gov.tt.
Ministry of Housing: 44–46 South Quay, Port of Spain; tel. 624-5058; fax 625-2793; e-mail info@housing.gov.tt; internet www.housing.gov.tt.
Ministry of Labour and Small and Micro Enterprise Development: Level 11, Riverside Plaza, Cnr Besson and Piccadilly Sts, Port of Spain; tel. 623-4451; fax 624-4091; e-mail rplan@tstt.net.tt; internet www.labour.gov.tt.
Ministry of Legal Affairs: Registration House, Huggins Bldg, South Quay, Port of Spain; tel. 623-7163; fax 625-9805; e-mail mlalr@tstt.net.tt.
Ministry of Local Government: Kent House, Maraval Rd, Port of Spain; tel. 622-1669; fax 622-4783; e-mail molg2@carib-link.net.
Ministry of National Security: Temple Court, 31–33 Abercromby St, Port of Spain; tel. 623-2441; fax 627-8044; e-mail mns@tstt.net.tt.
Ministry of Planning and Development: Telly Paul Bldg, St Vincent St, Port of Spain; tel. 627-0403; fax 623-0341.
Ministry of Public Administration and Information: 45A-C St Vincent St, Port of Spain; tel. 623-8578; fax 623-6027; e-mail secretariat@nict.gov.tt; internet nict.gov.tt.
Ministry of Public Utilities and the Environment: Sacred Heart Bldg, 16–18 Sackville St, Port of Spain; tel. 625-6083; fax 625-7003; e-mail environment@tstt.net.tt.
Ministry of Science, Technology and Tertiary Education: Cnr Agra and Patna Sts, St James; tel. 628-9925; fax 622-0775; e-mail stte@stte.gov.tt; internet www.stte.gov.tt.
Ministry of Social Development: Ansa McAl Bldg, 69 Independence Sq., Port of Spain; tel. 625-8565; fax 627-4853; e-mail infor@msd.gov.tt; internet www.msd.gov.tt.
Ministry of Sport and Youth Affairs: ISSA Nicholas Bldg, Cnr Frederick and Duke Sts, Port of Spain; tel. 625-8874; fax 623-5006.
Ministry of Tobago Affairs: Whitehall, Queens Park West, Port of Spain; tel. 622-1625; fax 622-0055; e-mail opm@ttgov.gov.tt.
Ministry of Tourism: 51–55 Frederick St, Port of Spain; tel. 624-1403; fax 625-0437; e-mail mintourism@tourism.gov.tt.
Ministry of Trade and Industry: Level 15, Riverside Plaza, Cnr Besson and Piccadilly St, Port of Spain; tel. 623-2931; fax 627-8488; e-mail info@tradeind.gov.tt; internet www.tradeind.gov.tt.
Ministry of Works and Transport: Cnr Richmond and London Sts, Port of Spain; tel. 625-1225; fax 625-8070.

Legislature

PARLIAMENT

Senate
President: Dr LINDA BABOOLAL.

House of Representatives
Speaker: BARENDRA SINANAN.
Election, 7 October 2002

Party	% of votes	Seats
People's National Movement	50.7	20
United National Congress	46.6	16
National Alliance for Reconstruction	1.1	—
Citizens' Alliance	1.0	—
Total (incl. others)	100.0	36

TOBAGO HOUSE OF ASSEMBLY

The House is elected for a four-year term of office and consists of 12 elected members and three members selected by the majority party.
Chief Secretary: ORVILLE LONDON.

TRINIDAD AND TOBAGO

Election, 17 January 2005

Party	Seats
People's National Movement	11
Democratic Action Congress	1
Total	**12**

Election Commission

Elections and Boundaries Commission (EBC): Scott House, 134–138 Frederick St, Port of Spain; tel. 623-4622; fax 627-7881; Chair. Dr NORBERT MASSON.

Political Organizations

Citizens' Alliance: 2 Gray St, St Clair, Port of Spain; f. to contest the October 2002 elections; Leader WENDELL MOTTLEY.

Democratic Action Congress: Scarborough; f. Jan. 2003 by faction of National Alliance for Reconstruction (q.v.); only active in Tobago; Leader HOCHOY CHARLES.

Democratic Party of Trinidad and Tobago (DPTT): Port of Spain; f. March 2002; Leader STEVE ALVAREZ.

Lavantille Out-Reach for Vertical Enrichment: L. P. 50, Juman Dr., Morvant; tel. 625-7840; f. 2000; Leader LENNOX SMITH; Gen. Sec. VAUGHN CATON.

National Alliance for Reconstruction (NAR): 71 Dundonald St, Port of Spain; tel. 627-6163; f. 1983 as a coalition of moderate opposition parties; reorganized as a single party in 1986; Leader CARSON CHARLES; Chair. CHRISTO GIFT.

National Democratic Organization (NDO): L. P. 2, Freedom St, Enterprise, Chaguanas; tel. 750 9063; e-mail ndotrini@yahoo.com; f. 2000; Leader ENOCH JOHN; Sec. RICHARD JOODEEN.

National Democratic Party (NDP): Port of Spain; Leader CARSON CHARLES.

National Joint Action Committee (NJAC): Point Fortin; tel. 648-2749; Leader MAKANDAL DAAGA.

People's Empowerment Party (PEP): Miggins Chamber, Young St, Scarborough; tel. 639-3175; f. by independent mems of the Tobago House of Assembly; Leader DEBORAH MOORE-MIGGINS; Gen. Sec. RICHARD ALFRED.

People's National Movement (PNM): Balisier House, 1 Tranquility St, Port of Spain; tel. 625-1533; e-mail pnm@carib-link.net; internet www.pnm.org.tt; f. 1956; moderate nationalist party; Leader PATRICK MANNING; Chair. FRANKLIN KHAN; Gen. Sec. MARTIN JOSEPH.

Republican Party: Port of Spain; Leader NELLO MITCHELL.

United National Congress (UNC): Rienzi Complex, 78–81 Southern Main Rd, Couva; tel. 636-8145; e-mail info@unc.org.tt; internet www.unc.org.tt; f. 1989; social democratic; Leader WINSTON DOOKERAN; Chair. BASDEO PANDAY; CEO TIM GOPEESINGH.

Diplomatic Representation

EMBASSIES AND HIGH COMMISSIONS IN TRINIDAD AND TOBAGO

Argentina: TATIL Bldg, 4th Floor, 411 Maraval Rd, POB 162; Port of Spain; tel. 628-7557; fax 628-7544; e-mail embargen-pos@carib-link.net; Ambassador JOSÉ LUIS VIGNOLO.

Brazil: 18 Sweet Briar Rd, St Clair, POB 382, Port of Spain; tel. 622-5779; fax 622-4323; e-mail contact@brazilembtt.org; internet www.brazilembtt.org; Ambassador LUIZ FERNANDO DE ATHAYDE.

Canada: Maple House, 3–3A Sweet Briar Rd, St Clair, POB 1246, Port of Spain; tel. 622-6232; fax 628-1830; e-mail pspan@dfait-maeci.gc.ca; internet www.portofspain.gc.ca; High Commissioner HOWARD STRAUSS.

China, People's Republic: 39 Alexandra St, St Clair, Port of Spain; tel. 622-6976; fax 622-7613; e-mail tian@wow.net; Ambassador HUANG XING.

Cuba: Furness Bldg, 2nd Floor, 90 Independence Sq., Port of Spain; tel. 627-1306; fax 627-3515; e-mail embajador@tstt.net.tt; Ambassador SERGIO OLIVA GUERRA.

Dominican Republic: Suite 8, 1 Dere St, Queen's Park West, Port of Spain; tel. 624-7930; fax 623-7779; e-mail embadom@tstt.net.tt; Ambassador JOSÉ MANUEL CASTILLO BETANCES.

France: TATIL Bldg, 6th Floor, 11 Maraval Rd, Port of Spain; tel. 622-7447; fax 628-2632; e-mail francett@wow.net; internet www.ambafrance-tt.org; Ambassador CHARLEY CAUSERET.

Germany: 7–9 Marli St, Newtown, POB 828, Port of Spain; tel. 628-1630; fax 628-5278; e-mail germanembassy@tstt.net.tt; internet www.port-of-spain.diplo.de; Ambassador Dr HELMUT OHLRAUN.

Holy See: 11 Mary St, St Clair, POB 854, Port of Spain; tel. 622-5009; fax 628-5457; e-mail apnun@trinidad.net; Apostolic Nuncio Most Rev. THOMAS E. GULLICKSON (Titular Archbishop of Bomarzo).

India: 6 Victoria Ave, POB 530, Port of Spain; tel. 627-7480; fax 627-6985; e-mail hcipos@tstt.net.tt; internet www.hcipos.com; High Commissioner J. S. SAPRA.

Jamaica: 2 Newbold St, St Clair, Port of Spain; tel. 622-4995; fax 628-9043; e-mail jhctnt@tstt.net.tt; High Commissioner (vacant).

Japan: 5 Hayes St, St Clair, POB 1039, Port of Spain; tel. 628-5991; fax 622-0858; e-mail jpemb@wow.net; Ambassador YOSHIO YAMAGISHI.

Mexico: ALGICO Bldg, 4th Floor, 91–93 St Vincent St, Port of Spain; tel. 627-7047; fax 627-1028; e-mail embamex@carib-link.net; Ambassador LUZ ELENA INÉS BUENO ZIRIÓN.

Netherlands: Life of Barbados Bldg, 3rd Floor, 69–71 Edward St, POB 870, Port of Spain; tel. 625-1210; fax 625-1704; e-mail info@holland.tt; internet www.holland.tt; Chargé d'affaires a.i. ANDRÉ VERKADE.

Nigeria: 3 Maxwell-Phillip St, St Clair, Port of Spain; tel. 622-4002; fax 622-7162; High Commissioner NNE FURO KURUBO.

Panama: Suite 6, 1A Dere St, Port of Spain; tel. 623-3435; fax 623-3440; e-mail embapatt@wow.net; Ambassador GERARDO MALONEY.

Suriname: Tatil Bldg, 5th Floor, 11 Maraval Rd, Port of Spain; tel. 628-0704; fax 628-0086; e-mail surinameembassy@tstt.net.tt; Ambassador NEVILLE J. VEIRA.

United Kingdom: 19 St Clair Circle, St Clair, POB 778, Port of Spain; tel. 622-2748; fax 622-4555; e-mail csbbhc@opus.co.tt; High Commissioner RONALD NASH.

USA: 15 Queen's Park West, POB 752, Port of Spain; tel. 622-6371; fax 625-5462; e-mail usispos@trinidad.net; internet usembassy.state.gov/trinidad; Ambassador Dr ROY L. AUSTIN.

Venezuela: 16 Victoria Ave, POB 1300, Port of Spain; tel. 627-9821; fax 624-2508; e-mail embaveneztt@carib-link.net; Ambassador HECTOR AZOCAR.

Judicial System

The Chief Justice, who has overall responsibility for the administration of justice in Trinidad and Tobago, is appointed by the President after consultation with the Prime Minister and the Leader of the Opposition. The President appoints and promotes judges on the advice of the Judicial and Legal Service Commission. The Judicial and Legal Service Commission, which comprises the Chief Justice as chairman, the chairman of the Public Service Commission, two former judges and a senior member of the bar, appoints all judicial and legal officers. The Judiciary comprises the higher judiciary (the Supreme Court) and the lower judiciary (the Magistracy). In February 2005 Parliament voted to accept the authority of the Caribbean Court of Justice (CCJ) to settle international trade disputes. The Court was formally inaugurated in Port of Spain on 16 April 2005.

Chief Justice: SATNARINE SHARMA.

Supreme Court of Judicature: Knox St, Port of Spain; tel. 623-2417; fax 627-5477; e-mail ttlaw@wow.net; internet www.ttlawcourts.org; the Supreme Court consists of the High Court of Justice and the Court of Appeal. The Supreme Court is housed in three locations: Port of Spain, San Fernando and Tobago. There are 23 Supreme Court Puisne Judges who sit in criminal, civil, and matrimonial divisions; Registrar EVELYN PETERSEN.

Court of Appeal: The Court of Appeal hears appeals against decisions of the Magistracy and the High Court. Further appeals are directed to the Judicial Committee of the Privy Council of the United Kingdom, sometimes as of right and sometimes with leave of the Court. The Court of Appeal consists of the Chief Justice, who is President, and six other Justices of Appeal.

The Magistracy and High Court of Justice

The Magistracy and the High Court exercise original jurisdiction in civil and criminal matters. The High Court hears indictable criminal matters, family matters where the parties are married, and civil matters involving sums over the petty civil court limit. High Court judges are referred to as either Judges of the High Court or Puisne Judges. The Masters of the High Court, of which there are four, have the jurisdiction of judges in civil chamber courts. The Magistracy (in its petty civil division) deals with civil matters involving sums of less than TT $15,000. It exercises summary jurisdiction in criminal

TRINIDAD AND TOBAGO

matters and hears preliminary inquiries in indictable matters. The Magistracy, which is divided into 13 districts, consists of a Chief Magistrate, a Deputy Chief Magistrate, 13 Senior Magistrates and 29 Magistrates.

Chief Magistrate: SHERMAN MCNICHOLLS, Magistrates' Court, St Vincent St, Port of Spain; tel. 625-2781.
Director of Public Prosecutions: GEOFFREY HENDERSON.
Attorney-General: JOHN JEREMIE.

Religion

In 2000 it was estimated that 24.6% of the population was Protestant, including Anglican (7.8%), Pentecostal (6.8%), Seventh-day Adventist (4%) and Presbyterian (3.3%), while some 22.5% of the population was Hindu, 5.8% Muslim and 5.4% Shouter Baptist.

CHRISTIANITY

Caribbean Conference of Churches: 8 Gallus St, Woodbrook, POB 876, Port of Spain; tel. 623-0588; fax 624-9002; e-mail ccchq@tstt.net.tt; internet www.ccc-caribe.org; f. 1973; Gen. Sec. GERARD GRANADO.

Christian Council of Trinidad and Tobago: Hayes Court, 21 Maraval Rd, Port of Spain; tel. 637-9329; f. 1967; church unity organization formed by the Roman Catholic, Anglican, Presbyterian, Methodist, African Methodist, Spiritual Baptist and Moravian Churches, the Church of Scotland and the Salvation Army, with the Ethiopian Orthodox Church and the Baptist Union as observers; Pres. The Rt Rev. CALVIN BESS (Anglican Bishop of Trinidad and Tobago); Sec. GRACE STEELE.

The Anglican Communion

Anglicans are adherents of the Church in the Province of the West Indies, comprising eight dioceses. The Archbishop of the West Indies is the Bishop of Nassau and the Bahamas.

Bishop of Trinidad and Tobago: The Rt Rev. CALVIN WENDELL BESS, Hayes Court, 21 Maraval Rd, Port of Spain; tel. 622-7387; fax 628-1319; e-mail bessc@tstt.net.tt; internet www.trinidad.anglican.org.

Protestant Churches

Presbyterian Church in Trinidad and Tobago: POB 187, Paradise Hill, San Fernando; tel. and fax 652-4829; e-mail pctt@tstt.net.tt; f. 1868; Moderator Rt Rev. RAWLE C. SUKHU; 45,000 mems.

Baptist Union of Trinidad and Tobago: 104 High St, Princes Town; tel. 655-2291; f. 1816; Pres. Rev. ALBERT EARL-ELLIS; Gen. Sec. Rev. JOHN S. C. BRAMBLE; 24 churches, 3,300 mems.

The Roman Catholic Church

For ecclesiastical purposes, Trinidad and Tobago comprises the single archdiocese of Port of Spain. At 31 December 2003 there were some 383,302 adherents in the country, representing about 30% of the total population.

Antilles Episcopal Conference: 9A Gray St, Port of Spain; tel. 622-2932; fax 628-3688; e-mail aec@carib-link.net; internet www.catholiccaribbean.org; f. 1975; 21 mems from the Caribbean and Central American regions; Pres. Most Rev. LAWRENCE ALOYSIUS BURKE (Archbishop of Kingston, Jamaica); Gen. Sec. Rev. GERARD E. FARFAN.

Archbishop of Port of Spain: EDWARD J. GILBERT, 27 Maraval Rd, Port of Spain; tel. 622-1103; fax 622-1165; e-mail abishop@carib-link.net.

HINDUISM

Hindu immigrants from India first arrived in Trinidad and Tobago in 1845. The vast majority of migrants, who were generally from Uttar Pradesh, were Vishnavite Hindus, who belonged to sects such as the Ramanandi, the Kabir and the Sieunaraini. The majority of Hindus currently subscribe to the doctrine of Sanathan Dharma, which evolved from Ramanandi teaching.

Arya Pratinidhi Sabha of Trinidad Inc (Arya Samaj): Seereeram Memorial Vedic School, Old Southern Main Rd, Montrose Village, Chaguanas; tel. 663-1721; e-mail sadananramnarine@hotmail.com; internet www.trinidadaryasamaj.org; Pres. LAKHRAM VIJAY BACHAN.

Pandits' Parishad (Council of Pandits): Maha Sabha Headquarters, Eastern Main Rd, St Augustine; tel. 645-3240; works towards the co-ordination of temple activities and the standardization of ritual procedure; affiliated to the Maha Sabha; 200 mems.

Sanathan Dharma Maha Sabha of Trinidad and Tobago Inc: Maha Sabha Headquarters, Eastern Main Rd, St Augustine; tel. 645-3240; e-mail mahasabha@ttemail.com; internet www.websitetech.com/mahasabha; f. 1952; Hindu pressure group and public organization; organizes the provision of Hindu education; Pres. Dr D. OMAH MAHARAJH; Sec. Gen. SATNARAYAN MAHARAJ.

The Press

DAILIES

Newsday: 19–21 Chacon St, Port of Spain; tel. 623-2459; fax 657-5008; internet www.newsday.co.tt; f. 1993; CEO and Editor-in-Chief THERESE MILLS; circ. 2,200,000.

Trinidad Guardian: 22 St Vincent St, POB 122, Port of Spain; tel. 623-8871; fax 625-5702; e-mail letters@ttol.co.tt; internet www.guardian.co.tt; f. 1917; morning; independent; Editor-in-Chief DOMINIC KALIPERSAD; circ. 52,617.

Trinidad and Tobago Express: 35 Independence Sq., Port of Spain; tel. 623-1711; fax 627-1451; e-mail express@trinidadexpress.com; internet www.trinidadexpress.com; f. 1967; morning; CEO KEN GORDON; Editor KEITH SMITH; circ. 55,000.

PERIODICALS

The Boca: Crews Inn Marina and Boatyard, Village Sq., Chaguaramas; tel. 634-2055; fax 634-2056; e-mail boca@boatersenterprise.com; internet www.boatersenterprise.com/boca; monthly; magazine of the sailing and boating community; Man. Dir JACK DAUSEND.

The Bomb: Southern Main Rd, Curepe; tel. 645-2744; weekly.

Caribbean Beat: 6 Prospect Ave, Maraval, Port of Spain; tel. 622-3821; fax 628-0639; e-mail info@meppublishers.com; internet www.caribbean-beat.com; 6 a year; distributed by BWIA International Airways Ltd; Editor JEREMY TAYLOR; Ma. HELEN SHAIR-SINGH.

Catholic News: 31 Independence Sq., Port of Spain; tel. 623-6093; fax 623-9468; e-mail cathnews@trinidad.net; internet www.catholicnews-tt.net; f. 1892; weekly; Editor JUNE JOHNSTON; circ. 16,000.

Economic Bulletin: 35–41 Queen St, POB 98, Port of Spain; tel. 623-7069; fax 625-3802; e-mail statinfo@wow.net; f. 1950; issued 3 times a year by the Central Statistical Office.

Energy Caribbean: 6 Prospect Ave, Maraval, Port of Spain; tel. 622-3821; fax 628-0639; e-mail dchin@meppublishers.com; internet www.meppublishers.com; f. 2002; bimonthly; Editor DAVID RENWICK.

Showtime: Cnr 9th St and 9th Ave, Barataria; tel. 674-1692; fax 674-3228; circ. 30,000.

Sunday Express: 35 Independence Sq., Port of Spain; tel. 623-1711; fax 627-1451; e-mail express@trinidadexpress.com; internet www.trinidadexpress.com; f. 1967; Editor OMATIE LYDER; circ. 51,405.

Sunday Guardian: 22 St Vincent St, POB 122, Port of Spain; tel. 623-8870; fax 625-7211; e-mail esunday@ttol.co.tt; internet www.guardian.co.tt; f. 1917; independent; morning; Editor-in-Chief DOMINIC KALIPERSAD; circ. 48,324.

Sunday Punch: Cnr 9th St and 9th Ave, Barataria; tel. 674-1692; fax 674-3228; internet www.tntmirror.com; weekly; Editor ANTHONY ALEXIS; circ. 40,000.

Tobago News: Milford Rd, Scarborough; tel. 639-5565; fax 625-4480; f. 1985; weekly; Editor COMPTON DELPH.

Trinidad and Tobago Gazette: 2–4 Victoria Ave, Port of Spain; tel. 625-4139; weekly; official govt paper; circ. 3,300.

Trinidad and Tobago Mirror: Cnr 9th St and 9th Ave, Barataria; tel. 674-1692; fax 674-3228; internet www.tntmirror.com; 2 a week; Editors KEN ALI, KEITH SHEPHERD; circ. 35,000.

Tropical Agriculture: Faculty of Agriculture and Natural Sciences, University of the West Indies, St Augustine; tel. and fax 645-3640; e-mail tropicalagri@fans.uwi.tt; f. 1924; journal of the School of Agriculture (fmrly Imperial College of Tropical Agriculture); quarterly; Editor-in-Chief Prof. FRANK A. GUMBS.

Weekend Heat: Southern Main Rd, Curepe; tel. 625-4583; weekly; Editor STAN MORA.

Publishers

Caribbean Children's Press: 7 Coronation St, St James; tel. and fax 628-4248; e-mail caripres@tstt.net.tt; f. 1987; educational publishers for primary schools.

Caribbean Educational Publishers: Gulf View Link Rd, La Romaine; tel. 657-9613; fax 652-5620; e-mail mbscep@tstt.net.tt; Pres. TEDDY MOHAMMED.

Charran Publishing House Ltd: 60 South Quay, Port of Spain; tel. 625-9821; fax 623-6597; e-mail publishing@charran.com; Man. RICO CHARRAN.

TRINIDAD AND TOBAGO
Directory

Lexicon Trinidad Ltd: 48 Boundary Rd, San Juan; tel. 675-3395; fax 675-3360; e-mail lexicon@tstt.net.tt; Dir KEN JAIKARANSINGH.

Morton Publishing: 97 Saddle Rd, Maraval; tel. 348-37777; fax 762-9923; e-mail morton@morton-pub.com; internet www.morton-pub.com; f. 1977; educational books; Pres. DOUG MORTON; Dir JULIE MORTON.

Prospect Press (Media and Editorial Projects): 6 Prospect Ave, Maraval, Port of Spain; tel. 622-3821; fax 628-0639; e-mail meppublishers@meppublishers.com; internet www.meppublishers.com; f. 1991; magazine and book publishing; Man. Dir JEREMY TAYLOR.

Royards Publishing Co: 7A Macoya Industrial Estate, Macoya; tel. 663-6002; fax 663-6316; e-mail sales@royards.com; internet www.royards.com; f. 1984; educational publishers.

Trinidad Publishing Co Ltd: 22–24 St Vincent St, Port of Spain; tel. 623-8870; fax 625-7211; e-mail business@ttol.co.tt; internet www.guardian.co.tt; f. 1917; Man. Dir GRENFELL KISSOON.

Broadcasting and Communications

TELECOMMUNICATIONS

Regulatory Body

Telecommunications Authority of Trinidad and Tobago (TATT): Suites 3–5, BEN Court, 76 Boundary Rd, San Juan; tel. 675-8288; fax 674-1055; e-mail info@tatt.org.tt; internet www.tatt.org.tt; f. 2001 to oversee the liberalization of the telecommunications sector; Chair. Dr KHALID HASSANALI.

Major Companies

bmobile: 114 Frederick St, Port of Spain; fax 625-5807; e-mail service@tstt.co.tt; internet www.bmobile.co.tt; f. 1991 as TSTT Cellnet; name changed as above 2006; 51% state-owned, 49% by Cable & Wireless (United Kingdom); mobile cellular telephone operator.

Columbus Communications Trinidad Ltd (CCTL): Port of Spain; digital cable television, internet and local telephone service providers; mobile cellular telephone licence granted in 2006.

Digicel Trinidad and Tobago: 11–13 Victoria Ave, Port of Spain; tel. 628-7000; fax 622-0887; e-mail tt.customer.care@digicelgroup.com; internet www.digiceltrinidadandtobago.com; owned by an Irish consortium; mobile cellular telephone licence granted in 2005; Chair. DENIS O'BRIEN; CEO STEPHEN BREWER.

LaqTel Ltd: Sackville St, Port of Spain; tel. and fax 624-2437; e-mail learnmore@laqtel.net; internet laqtel.info; f. 2002; awarded mobile cellular telephone licence in 2005; Chair. ANTHONY JACELON.

One Caribbean Media Ltd (OCM): 35 Independence Sq., Port of Spain; tel. 623-1711; fax 625-5712; e-mail tjohnson@trinidadexpress.com; internet www.onecaribbeanmedia.net; f. 2006 by merger of Caribbean Communications Network (CCN) and The Nation Corpn (Barbados); Chair. Sir FRED GOLLOP; CEO CRAIG REYNALD.

Open Telecom Ltd: 88 Edward St, Port of Spain; tel. 622-6736; e-mail sales@opentelecom.com; internet www.gillettegroup.com/opentelecom/index.htm; Chair. PETER GILLETTE.

Telecommunication Services of Trinidad and Tobago (TSTT) Ltd: 1 Edward St, POB 3, Port of Spain; tel. 625-4431; fax 627-0856; e-mail tsttceo@tstt.net.tt; internet www.tstt.co.tt; 51% state-owned, 49% by Cable & Wireless (United Kingdom); 51% privatization pending; CEO CARLOS ESPINAL.

BROADCASTING

Radio

Central Radio 90.5: 1 Morequito Ave, Valsayn, Port of Spain; tel. 662-4309.

Hott 93 FM: Cumulus Broadcasting Inc, 3A Queens Park West, Port of Spain; tel. 623-4688; fax 624-3234; e-mail studio@hott93.com.

Homeviewtnt.com: Port of Spain; e-mail customerservice@homeviewtnt.com; internet www.homeviewtnt.com; operates 6 commercial radio stations: Radio 90.5 FM; Sangeet 106 FM; 103 FM; Ebony 104 FM; Vibe CT105 FM; Radio Trinbago 94.7 FM.

Love 94.1 and Power 102 FM: 88–90 Abercromby St, Port of Spain; tel. 627-6937; fax 624-8223; internet www.power102fm.com; CEO LENNOX TOUSSAINT; Gen. Man. RUEBEN MOHAMMED.

Music Radio 97 FM: Long Circular Rd, St James; tel. 622-9797; fax 624-3234.

National Broadcasting Network Ltd (FM 100, Yes 98.9 FM, Swar Milan 91.1, Radio 610): 11A Maraval Rd, Port of Spain; tel. 662-4141; fax 622-0344; e-mail bdesilva@nbn.co.tt; f. 1957; AM and FM transmitters at Chaguanas, Cumberland Hill, Hospedales and French Fort, Tobago; govt-owned; CEO DOMINIC BEAUBRUN; Man. BRENDA DE SILVA; est. regular audience 105,000.

Trinidad Broadcasting Co Ltd (Radio Trinidad, Radio Nine Five): Broadcasting House, 11B Maraval Rd, POB 716, Port of Spain; tel. 622-1151; fax 622-2380; commercial.

Trinidad Broadcasting Company (Radio Trinidad 730 AM, Rhythm Radio, Caribbean Tempo and WEFM 96.1 FM): 22 St Vincent St, Port of Spain; tel. 623-9202; fax 622-2380; f. 1947; commercial; four programmes; Man. Dir GRENFELL KISSOON.

Trinidad and Tobago Radio Network: 35 Independence Sq., Port of Spain; tel. 624-7078.

Television

National Broadcasting Network Ltd: 11A Maraval Rd, POB 665, Port of Spain; tel. 622-4141; fax 622-0344; e-mail bdesilva@nbn.co.tt; f. 1962; state-owned commercial station; operates channels 2, 4, 13, 16, TIC and The Information Channel; CEO DOMINIC BEAUBRUN.

TV6: 35 Express House, Independence Sq., Port of Spain; tel. 627-8806; fax 627-1451; e-mail tjohnson@trinidadexpress.com; internet www.onecaribbeanmedia.net; f. 1991; operates channels 6 and 18; owned by One Caribbean Media Ltd (OCM); CEO CRAIG REYNALD; Gen. Man. RASHIDAN BOLAI.

Finance

(cap. = capital; dep. = deposits; res = reserves; m. = million; brs = branches; amounts in TT $ unless otherwise stated)

BANKING

Central Bank

Central Bank of Trinidad and Tobago: Eric Williams Plaza, Brian Lara Promenade, POB 1250, Port of Spain; tel. 625-4835; fax 627-4696; e-mail info@central-bank.org.tt; internet www.central-bank.org.tt; f. 1964; cap. 100.0m., res 100.0m., dep. 10,637.2m. (Sept. 2003); Gov. EWART S. WILLIAMS.

Commercial Banks

Citibank (Trinidad and Tobago) Ltd: 12 Queen's Park East, POB 1249, Port of Spain; tel. 625-1046; fax 624-8131; internet www.citicorp.com; f. 1983; fmrly The United Bank of Trinidad and Tobago Ltd; name changed as above 1989; owned by Citicorp Merchant Bank Ltd; cap. 30.0m., res 14.7m., dep. 455.5m. (Dec. 1996); Chair. IAN E. DASENT; Man. Dir STEVE BIDESHI; 2 brs.

Citicorp Merchant Bank Ltd: 12 Queen's Park East, POB 1249, Port of Spain; tel. 623-3344; fax 624-8131; cap. 57.1m., res 28.5m., dep 473.6m. (Dec. 2002); owned by Citibank Overseas Investment Corpn; Chair. IAN E. DASENT; Man. Dir KAREN DARBASIE.

First Citizens Bank Ltd: 62 Independence Sq., Port of Spain; tel. 625-2893; fax 623-3393; e-mail itc@firstcitizenstt.com; internet www.firstcitizenstt.com; f. 1993 following merger of National Commercial Bank of Trinidad and Tobago Ltd, Trinidad Co-operative Bank Ltd and Workers' Bank of Trinidad and Tobago; state-owned; cap. 340.0m., res 907.3m., dep. 3,237.5m. (Sept. 2002); Chair. SAMUEL A. MARTIN; CEO LARRY HOWAI; 22 brs.

RBTT Ltd: Royal Court, 19–21 Park St, POB 287, Port of Spain; tel. 623-1322; fax 625-3764; e-mail royalinfo@rbtt.co.tt; internet www.rbtt.com; f. 1972 as Royal Bank of Trinidad and Tobago to take over local brs of Royal Bank of Canada; present name adopted April 2002; cap. 403.9m., res 219.3m., dep. 5,184.0m. (March 2003); Chair. PETER J. JULY; CEO TERRENCE A. J. MARTINS; 21 brs.

Republic Bank Ltd: 9–17 Park St, POB 1153, Port of Spain; tel. 623-1056; fax 624-1323; e-mail email@republictt.com; internet www.republictt.com; f. 1837 as Colonial Bank; became Barclays Bank in 1972; name changed as above 1981; merged with Bank of Commerce Trinidad and Tobago Ltd 1997; cap. 481.2m., res 252.5m., dep. 21,123.3m. (Sept. 2003); Chair. and Man. Dir RONALD HARFORD; Exec. Dir GREGORY I. THOMSON; 47 brs.

Republic Finance & Merchant Bank Ltd: 9–17 Park St, POB 1153, Port of Spain; tel. 623-1056; fax 624-1323; e-mail email@republictt.com; internet www.republictt.com; f. 1965; owned by Republic Bank Ltd (q.v.); cap. 30.0m., res 35.0m., dep. 2,066.1m. (Sept. 2002); Chair. RONALD HARFORD; Man. Dir DAVID J. DULAL-WHITEWAY.

Scotiabank Trinidad and Tobago Ltd: Cnr of Park and Richmond Sts, POB 621, Port of Spain; tel. 625-3566; fax 627-5278; e-mail scotiamain@carib.link.net; internet www.scotiabanktt.com; cap. 117.6m., res 207.9m., dep. 5,690.5m. (Oct. 2003); Chair. ROBERT H. PITFIELD; Man. Dir RICHARD P. YOUNG; 23 brs.

TRINIDAD AND TOBAGO   *Directory*

Development Banks

Agricultural Development Bank of Trinidad and Tobago: 87 Henry St, POB 154, Port of Spain; tel. 623-6261; fax 624-3087; e-mail adbceo@tstt.net.tt; f. 1968; provides long-, medium- and short-term loans to farmers and the agri-business sector; Chair. HUBERT ALLEYNE; CEO JACQUELINE RAWLINS.

DFL Caribbean: 10 Cipriani Blvd, POB 187, Port of Spain; tel. 623-4665; fax 624-3563; e-mail dfl@dflcaribbean.com; internet www.dflcaribbean.com; provides short- and long-term finance, and equity financing for projects in manufacturing, agro-processing, tourism, industrial and commercial enterprises; total assets US $84.2m. (Dec. 1998); Chair. AUDLEY WALKER; Man. Dir GERARD M. PEMBERTON.

Credit Unions

Co-operative Credit Union League of Trinidad and Tobago Ltd: 32–34 Maraval Rd, St Clair; tel. 622-3100; fax 622-4800; e-mail culeague@tstt.net.tt; internet www.ccultt.org; Chair. GARY CROSS.

Hindu Credit Union Co-operative Society Ltd: Ramlals Bldg, Main Rd, Chaguanas; tel. 671-3718; e-mail e-mail@hinducreditunion.com; internet www.hinducreditunion.com/hcu.html; Pres. HARRY HARNARINE.

STOCK EXCHANGE

Trinidad and Tobago Stock Exchange Ltd: Nicholas Tower, 10th Floor, 63-65 Independence Square, Port of Spain; tel. 625-5107-9; fax 623-0089; e-mail ttstockx@tstt.net.tt; internet www.stockex.co.tt; f. 1981; 39 companies listed (2006); electronic depository system came into operation in 2003; Chair. ANDREW MC EACHRANE; CEO HUGH EDWARDS.

INSURANCE

American Life and General Insurance Co (Trinidad and Tobago) Ltd: ALGICO Plaza, 91–93 St Vincent St, POB 943, Port of Spain; tel. 625-4425; fax 623-6218; e-mail algico@wow.net; Man. Dir GORDON DEANE.

Bankers Insurance Co of Trinidad and Tobago Ltd: 177 Tragarete Rd, Port of Spain; tel. 622-4613; fax 628-6808; e-mail bankersinsurance@hcu.co.tt; internet www.hinducreditunion.com; subsidiary of Hindu Credit Union.

Barbados Mutual Life Assurance Society: The Mutual Centre, 16 Queen's Park West, POB 356, Port of Spain; tel. 628-1636; Gen. Man. HUGH MAZELY.

Capital Insurance Ltd: 38–42 Cipero St, San Fernando; tel. 657-8077; fax 652-7306; f. 1958; motor and fire insurance; total assets TT $65m.; 10 brs and 9 agencies.

Colonial Life Insurance Co (Trinidad) Ltd: Colonial Life Bldg, 29 St Vincent St, POB 443, Port of Spain; tel. 623-1421; fax 627-3821; e-mail info@clico.com; internet www.clico.com; f. 1936; Chair. LAWRENCE A. DUPREY; CEO CLAUDIUS DACON.

CUNA Caribbean Insurance Society Ltd: 37 Wrightson Rd, POB 193, Port of Spain; tel. 623-7963; fax 623-6251; e-mail cunains@trinidad.net; internet www.cunacaribbean.com; f. 1991; marine aviation and transport; motor vehicle, personal accident, property; Gen. Man. ANTHONY HALL; 3 brs.

Furness Anchorage General Insurance Ltd: 11–13 Milling Ave, Sea Lots, POB 283, Port of Spain; tel. 623-0868; fax 625-1243; e-mail furness@wow.net; internet www.furnessgroup.com; f. 1979; general; Chair. WILLIAM A. FERREIRA.

GTM Fire Insurance Co Ltd: 95–97 Queen St, Port of Spain; tel. 623-1525.

Guardian General Insurance Ltd: Princes Court, Keate St, Port of Spain, Port of Spain; tel. 623-4741; fax 623-4320; e-mail info@guardiangenerallimited.com; internet www.guardiangenerallimited.com; founded by merger of NEMWIL and Caribbean Home; Chair. HENRY PETER GANTEAUME; CEO RICHARD ESPINET.

Guardian Life of the Caribbean: 1 Guardian Dr., West Moorings, Port of Spain; tel. 625-5433; internet www.guardianlife.co.tt; Chair. ARTHUR LOK JACK; Pres. and CEO DOUGLAS CAMACHO.

Gulf Insurance Ltd: 1 Gray St, St Clair, Port of Spain; tel. 622-5878; fax 628-0272; e-mail gulf@wow.net; f. 1974; general.

Maritime Financial Group: Maritime Centre, 10th Ave, POB 710, Barataria; tel. 674-0130; fax 638-6663; f. 1978; property and casualty; CEO JOHN SMITH.

Motor and General Insurance Co Ltd: 1–3 Havelock St, St Clair, Port of Spain; tel. 622-2637; fax 622-5345.

New India Assurance Co (T & T) Ltd: 22 St Vincent St, Port of Spain; tel. 623-1326; fax 625-0670; e-mail newindia@wow.net.

Presidential Insurance Co Ltd: 54 Richmond St, Port of Spain; tel. 625-4788; e-mail pic101@tstt.net.tt.

Trinidad and Tobago Export Credit Insurance Co Ltd: 30 Queen's Park West, Port of Spain; tel. and fax 628–2762; e-mail eximbank@wow.net; internet www.eximbankttt.com; Gen. Man. JOSEPHINE IBLE.

Trinidad and Tobago Insurance Ltd (TATIL): 11 Maraval Rd, POB 1004, Port of Spain; tel. 622-5351; fax 628-0035; e-mail info@tatil.co.tt; internet www.tatil.co.tt; Chair. JOHN JARDIM; CEO RELNA VIRE.

INSURANCE ORGANIZATIONS

Association of Trinidad and Tobago Insurance Companies: 28 Sackville St, Port of Spain; tel. 624-2817; fax 625-5132; e-mail jsc-attic@trinidad.net; internet www.attic.org.tt; Chair. INEZ SINANAN.

National Insurance Board: Cipriani Pl., 2A Cipriani Blvd, Port of Spain; tel. 625-2171-8; fax 627-1787; e-mail nib@nibtt.co.tt; internet www.nibtt.co.tt; f. 1971; statutory corporation; Chair. CALDER HART; Exec. Dir JEFFREY MCFARLANE.

Trade and Industry

GOVERNMENT AGENCIES

Cocoa and Coffee Industry Board: 27 Frederick St, POB 1, Port of Spain; tel. 625-0298; fax 627-4172; e-mail ccib@tstt.net.tt; f. 1962; marketing of coffee and cocoa beans, regulation of cocoa and coffee industry; Man. KENT VILLAFANA.

Export-Import Bank of Trinidad and Tobago Ltd (EXIMBANK): 30 Queen's Park West, Port of Spain; tel. 628-2762; fax 622-3545; e-mail eximbank@wow.net; internet www.eximbankttt.com; Chair. CLARRY BENN; CEO BRIAN AWANG.

Trinidad and Tobago Forest Products Ltd (TANTEAK): Connector Rd, Carlsen Field, Chaguanas; tel. 665-0078; fax 665-6645; f. 1975; harvesting, processing and marketing of state plantation-grown teak and pine; privatization pending; Chair. RUSKIN PUNCH; Man. Dir CLARENCE BACCHUS.

DEVELOPMENT ORGANIZATIONS

National Energy Corporation of Trinidad and Tobago Ltd: PLIPDECO House, Orinoco Dr., POB 191, Point Lisas, Couva; tel. 636-4662; fax 679-2384; e-mail infocent@carib-link.net; internet www.ngc.co.tt; owned by the National Gas Co of Trinidad and Tobago Ltd (q.v.); f. 1979; Chair. KENNETH BIRCHWOOD; Pres. FRANK LOOK KIN.

National Housing Authority: 44–46 South Quay, POB 555, Port of Spain; tel. 627-1703; fax 625-3963; e-mail info@housing.gov.tt; internet www.housing.gov.tt; f. 1962; Chair. ANDRE MONYEIL; CEO NOEL GARCIA.

Point Lisas Industrial Port Development Corporation Ltd (PLIPDECO): PLIPDECO House, Orinoco Dr., POB 191, Point Lisas, Couva; tel. 636-2201; fax 636-4008; e-mail plipdeco@plipdeco.com; internet www.plipdeco.com; f. 1966; privatized in the late 1990s; deep-water port handling general cargo, liquid and dry bulk, to serve adjacent industrial estate, which now includes iron and steel complex, methanol, ammonia, urea and related downstream industries; Chair. Commdr KAYAM MOHAMMED; CEO Capt. RAWLE BADDALOO.

CHAMBERS OF COMMERCE

South Trinidad Chamber of Industry and Commerce: Suite 311, Cross Crossing Shopping Centre, Lady Hailes Ave, San Fernando; tel. 652-5613; e-mail execoffice@southchamber.org; internet www.southchamber.org; f. 1956; Pres. RAMPERSAD MOTILAL; CEO Dr THACKWRAY DRIVER.

Trinidad and Tobago Chamber of Industry and Commerce (Inc): Chamber Bldg, Columbus Circle, Westmoorings, POB 499, Port of Spain; tel. 637-6966; fax 637-7425; e-mail chamber@chamber.org.tt; internet www.chamber.org.tt; f. 1891; Pres. CHRISTIAN MOUTTET; CEO JOAN FERREIRA; 600 mems.

INDUSTRIAL AND TRADE ASSOCIATIONS

Agricultural Society of Trinidad and Tobago: 1st Floor, Henry St, Port of Spain; tel. 623-7797; fax 623-3087; e-mail agrisoc@tstt.net.tt.

Coconut Growers' Association (CGA) Ltd: Eastern Main Rd, POB 229, Laventille, Port of Spain; tel. 623-5207; fax 623-2359; e-mail cgaltd@tstt.net.tt; f. 1936; 354 mems; Chair. PHILLIP AGOSTINI.

Co-operative Citrus Growers' Association of Trinidad and Tobago Ltd: Eastern Main Rd, POB 174, Laventille, Port of Spain; tel. 623-2255; fax 623-2487; e-mail ccga@wow.net; internet www

TRINIDAD AND TOBAGO

.ccga.co.tt; f. 1932; 437 mems; Pres. AINSLEY NICHOLS; Gen. Man. MUMTAZ ALI.

Pan Trinbago: Victoria Park Suites, 14–17 Park St, Port of Spain; tel. 623-4486; fax 625-6715; e-mail admin@pantrinbago.co.tt; internet www.pantrinbago.co.tt; f. 1971; official body for Trinidad and Tobago steelbands; Pres. PATRICK LOUIS ARNOLD; Sec. RICHARD FORTEAN.

Shipping Association of Trinidad and Tobago: 15 Scott Bushe St, Port of Spain; tel. 623-3355; fax 623-8540; e-mail agm@shipping.co.tt; internet www.shipping.co.tt; f. 1938; Pres. NOEL JENVEY; Gen. Man. JENNIFER GONZÁLEZ.

Sugar Association of the Caribbean: Brechin Castle, Couva; tel. 636-2449; fax 636-2847; f. 1942; promotes and protects sugar industry in the Caribbean; 6 mem. asscns; Chair. IAN MCDONALD; Sec. A. MOHAMMED.

Trinidad and Tobago Contractors' Association: Morequito Ave, Valsayn Park, Valsayn; tel. 637-2967; fax 637-2963; e-mail sec@ttca.com; internet www.ttca.com; f. 1968; represents contractors and manufacturers and suppliers to the sector; Pres. HUGH SCHAMBER.

Trinidad and Tobago Manufacturers' Association: 122–124 Frederick St, Port of Spain; tel. 623-1029; fax 623-1031; e-mail ttmagm@opus.co.tt; internet www.ttma.com; f. 1956; 260 mems; Pres. ANTHONY ABOUD.

EMPLOYERS' ORGANIZATION

Employers' Consultative Association of Trinidad and Tobago (ECA): 43 Dundonald St, POB 911, Port of Spain; tel. 625-4723; fax 625-4891; e-mail ecatt@tstt.net.tt; internet www.ecatt.org; f. 1959; Chair. CLARENCE RAMBHARAT; CEO LINDA BESSON; 156 mems.

STATE HYDROCARBONS COMPANIES

National Gas Company of Trinidad and Tobago Ltd (NGC): Orinoco Dr., Point Lisas Industrial Estate, POB 1127, Port of Spain; tel. 636-4662; fax 679-2384; e-mail ngc@ngc.co.tt; internet www.ngc.co.tt; f. 1975; purchases, sells, compresses, transmits and distributes natural gas to consumers; Chair. KEITH AWONG; Pres. FRANK LOOK KIN.

Petroleum Company of Trinidad and Tobago Ltd (Petrotrin): Petrotrin Administration Bldg, Cnr Queen's Park West and Cipriani Blvd, Port of Spain; tel. 625-5240; fax 624-4661; e-mail kharnanan@petrotrin.com; internet www.petrotrin.com; f. 1993 following merger between Trinidad and Tobago Oil Company Ltd (Trintoc) and Trinidad and Tobago Petroleum Company Ltd (Trintopec); govt-owned; petroleum and gas exploration and production; operates refineries and a manufacturing complex, producing a variety of petroleum and petrochemical products; Chair. MALCOLM JONES; Gen. Man. WAYNE BERTRAND; Vice-Pres KAIN LOOK YEE, KELVIN HARNANAN.

Petrotrin Trinmar Operations: Petrotrin Administration Bldg, Point Fortin; tel. 648-2127; fax 648-2519; f. 1962; owned by Petrotrin; marine petroleum and natural gas co; Gen. Man. VICTOR MICHELLE; 705 employees.

Trintomar Ltd: Petrotrin Administration Bldg, Pointe-à-Pierre; tel. 649-5500; e-mail lisle.ramyad@petrotrin.com; 80% owned by Petrotrin, 20% owned by NGC; develops offshore petroleum sector; Sec. ADRIAN JEFFERS.

UTILITIES

Regulatory Authority

Regulated Industries Commission: 90 Independence Sq., Port of Spain; tel. 627-0821; fax 624-2027; e-mail ricoffice@ric.org.tt; internet www.ric.org.tt; Chair. DENNIS PANTIN; Exec. Dir HARJINDER S. ATWAL.

Electricity

Inncogen Ltd: 10 Marine Villas, Columbus Blvd, West Moorings by the Sea; tel. 632-7339; fax 632-7341; internet www.centennialenergy.com/inncogen.html; 49.9% share bought by Centennial Energy in Feb. 2004; Chair. ROBERT PALEDINE.

Power Generation Co of Trinidad and Tobago (PowerGen): 6A Queen's Park West, Port of Spain; tel. 624-0383; fax 625-3759; owned by Mirant (USA); Gen. Man. GARTH CHATOOR.

Trinidad and Tobago Electricity Commission (TTEC): 63 Frederick St, POB 121, Port of Spain; tel. 623-2611; fax 623-3759; e-mail ttecisd@trinidad.net; internet www.ttec.co.tt; state-owned electricity transmission and distribution company; 51% owned by Power Generation Company of Trinidad and Tobago, 49% owned by Southern Electric Int./Amoco; Chair. DEVANAND RAMLAL; Gen. Man. DENIS SINGH.

Gas

National Gas Company of Trinidad and Tobago Ltd: see State Hydrocarbons Companies..

Water

Water and Sewerage Authority (WASA): Farm Rd, St Joseph; tel. 662-9272; fax 652-1253; internet www.wasa.gov.tt; CEO ERROL GRIMES; Gen. Man. JERRY N. JOHNSON.

TRADE UNIONS

National Trade Union Centre (NATUC): 16 New St, Port of Spain; tel. 625-3023; fax 627-7588; e-mail natuc@carib-link.net; f. 1991 as umbrella org. unifying entire trade-union movt, incl. former Trinidad and Tobago Labour Congress and Council of Progressive Trade Unions; Pres. ROBERT GIUSEPPI; Gen. Sec. VINCENT CARBERA.

Principal Affiliates

Airline Superintendent's Association: c/o Data Centre Bldg, BWIA, Piarco; tel. 664-3401; fax 664-3303; Pres. JEFFERSON JOSEPH; Gen. Sec. THEO OLIVER.

All-Trinidad Sugar and General Workers' Trade Union (ATSGWTU): Rienzi Complex, Exchange Village, Southern Main Rd, Couva; tel. 636-2354; fax 636-3372; e-mail atsgwtu@tstt.net.tt; f. 1937; Pres. RUDRANATH INDARSINGH; Gen. Sec. SYLVESTER MARAJH; 2,000 mems.

Amalgamated Workers' Union: 16 New St, Port of Spain; tel. 627-6717; fax 627-8993; f. 1953; Pres.-Gen. CYRIL LOPEZ; Sec. FLAVIUS NURSE; c. 7,000 mems.

Association of Technical, Administrative and Supervisory Staff: Brechin Castle, Couva; Pres. Dr WALLY DES VIGNES; Gen. Sec. ISAAC BEEPATH.

Aviation, Communication and Allied Workers' Union: Aero Services Bldg, Orange Grove Rd, Tacarigua; tel. and fax 640-6518; f. 1982; Pres. CHRISTOPHER ABRAHAM; Gen. Sec. SIEUNARINE BALROOP.

Banking, Insurance and General Workers' Union: 27 Borde St, Woodbrook, Port of Spain; tel. 627-0278; fax 627-3931; e-mail bgwu@carib-link.net; internet www.bigwu.org; f. 1974 as Bank and General Workers' Union; name changed as above following merger with Bank Employees' Union in 2003; Pres. VINCENT CABRERA; Dep. Pres. WAYNE CORBIE.

Communication, Transport and General Workers' Trade Union: Aero Services Credit Union Bldg, Orange Grove Rd, Tacarigua; tel. and fax 640-8785; e-mail cattu@tstt.net.tt; Pres. JAGDEO JAGROOP; Gen. Sec. RAYMOND SMALL.

Communication Workers' Union: 146 Henry St, Port of Spain; tel. 623-5588; fax 625-3308; e-mail cwutdad@tstt.net.tt; f. 1953; Pres. PATRICK HALL; Gen. Sec. LYLE TOWNSEND; c. 2,100 mems.

Contractors' and General Workers' Trade Union (CGWTU): 37 Rushworth St, San Fernando; tel. 657-8072; fax 657-6834; Pres. OWEN HINDS; Gen. Sec. AINSLEY MATTHEWS.

Customs and Excise Extra Guard Association: Nicholas Court, Abercromby St, Port of Spain; tel. 625-3311; Pres. ALEXANDER BABB; Gen. Sec. NATHAN HERBERT.

Fire Services Association (FSA): 52 Lewis St, Woodbrook, Port of Spain; tel. 628-1033; Pres. LENNOX LONDON; Sec. JULES MOORE.

National Farmers' and Workers' Union: 25 Coffee St, San Fernando; tel. 652-4348; Pres. Gen. RAFFIQUE SHAH; Gen. Sec. DOOLIN RANKISSOON.

National General Workers' Union: c/o 143 Charlotte St, Port of Spain; tel. 623-0694; Pres. JIMMY SINGH; Gen. Sec. CHRISTOPHER ABRAHAM.

National Union of Domestic Employees (NUDE): 53 Wattley Circular Rd, Mount Pleasant Rd, Arima; tel. 667-5247; fax 664-0546; e-mail domestic@tstt.net.tt; Gen. Sec. IDA LE BLANC.

National Union of Government and Federated Workers: 145–147 Henry St, Port of Spain; tel. 623-4591; fax 625-7756; e-mail headoffice@nugfw.org.tt; internet nugfw.org.tt; f. 1937; Pres. Gen. ROBERT GUISEPPI; Gen. Sec. JACQUELINE JACK; c. 20,000 mems.

Oilfield Workers' Trade Union (OWTU): Paramount Bldg, 99A Circular Rd, San Fernando; tel. 652-2701; fax 652-7170; e-mail owtu@owtu.org; internet www.owtu.org; f. 1937; Pres. ERROL MCLEOD; Gen. Sec. WENDY JOY WHITE; 9,000 mems.

Public Services Association: 89–91 Abercromby St, POB 353, Port of Spain; tel. 623-7987; fax 627-2980; e-mail psa@tstt.net.tt; f. 1938; Pres. JENNIFER BAPTISTE; Sec. PATRICK ROUSSEAU; c. 15,000 mems.

Seamen and Waterfront Workers' Trade Union: 1D Wrightson Rd, Port of Spain; tel. 625-1351; fax 625-1182; e-mail swwtu@tstt.net

TRINIDAD AND TOBAGO

.tt; f. 1937; Pres.-Gen. MICHAEL ANNISETTE; Sec.-Gen. ROSS ALEXANDER; c. 3,000 mems.

Steel Workers' Union of Trinidad and Tobago: c/o ISPAT, Point Lisas, Couva; tel. 679-4666; fax 679-4175; e-mail swutt@tstt.net.tt; Pres. GRAFTON WOODLEY; Gen. Sec. WAYNE ROBERTS.

Transport and Industrial Workers' Union: 114 Eastern Main Rd, Laventille, Port of Spain; tel. 623-4943; fax 623-2361; f. 1962; Pres. ALDWYN BREWSTER; Gen Sec. JUDY CHARLES; c. 5,000 mems.

Trinidad and Tobago Airline Pilots' Association (TTALPA): 35A Brunton Rd, St James; tel. 628-6556; fax 628-2418; e-mail info@ttalpa.org; internet www.ttalpa.org; Chair. Capt. ANTHONY WIGHT; Man. CHRISTINE DAVIS.

Trinidad and Tobago Postal Workers' Union: c/o General Post Office, Wrightson Rd, POB 692, Port of Spain; tel. 625-2121; fax 642-4303; Pres. KENNETH SOOKOO; Gen. Sec. EVERALD SAMUEL.

Trinidad and Tobago Unified Teachers' Association: Cnr Fowler and Southern Main Rd, Curepe; tel. 645-2134; fax 662-1813; e-mail ttuta@trinidad.net; Pres. CLYDE PERMELL; Gen. Sec. DAVID LEWIS.

Union of Commercial and Industrial Workers: TIWU Bldg, 114 Eastern Main Rd, POB 460, Port of Spain; tel. and fax 626-2285; f. 1951; Pres. KELVIN GONZALES; Gen. Sec. ROSALIE FRASER; c. 1,500 mems.

Transport

RAILWAYS

The railway service was discontinued in 1968. However, in 2005 the Ministry of Works and Transport announced plans to reintroduce a railway service. Construction on the project was scheduled to begin in 2007 and was expected to take 10–15 years, costing an estimated TT $15,000m.

ROADS

In 1999 there were 7,900 km (4,910 miles) of roads in Trinidad and Tobago. In 2005 the Ministry of Works and Transport announced plans to invest some TT $140m. in building a 40 km highway to connect Princes Town to Mayaro. In the same year the US Agency for International Development allocated US $3.2m. to fund the repair of roads damaged by 'Hurricane Ivan' in 2004.

Public Transport Service Corporation: Railway Bldgs, South Quay, POB 391, Port of Spain; tel. 623-2341; fax 625-6502; f. 1965; to operate national bus services; CEO EDISON ISAAC; operates a fleet of buses.

SHIPPING

The chief ports are Port of Spain, Pointe-à-Pierre and Point Lisas in Trinidad and Scarborough in Tobago. Port of Spain handles 85% of all container traffic, and all international cruise arrivals. In 1998 Port of Spain handled 3.3m. metric tons of cargo. Port of Spain and Scarborough each have a deep-water wharf. Port of Spain possesses a dedicated container terminal, with two large overhead cranes. Plans were put in place in 2002 for an expansion of operations, through the purchase of an additional crane, the computerization of operations, and the deepening of the harbour (from 9.75 m to 12 m).

Caribbean Drydock Ltd: Port Chaguaramas, Western Main Rd, Chaguaramas; tel. 634-4226; fax 625-1215; e-mail info@ttdockyard.com; internet www.caridoc.org; ship repair, marine transport, barge and boat construction.

Point Lisas Industrial Port Development Corporation Ltd (PLIPDECO): see Development Organizations.

Port Authority of Trinidad and Tobago: Dock Rd, POB 549, Port of Spain; tel. 623-2901; fax 627-2666; e-mail vilmal@patnt.com; internet www.patnt.com; f. 1962; Chair. DEREK HUDSON; CEO CHRISTOPHER MENDEZ.

Shipping Association of Trinidad and Tobago: 15 Scott Bushe St, Port of Spain; tel. 623-3355; fax 623-8570; e-mail satt@wow.net; internet shipping.co.tt; Pres. SONJA VOISIN-TOM; Gen. Man. JENNIFER GONZÁLEZ.

CIVIL AVIATION

Piarco International Airport is situated 25.7 km (16 miles) south-east of Port of Spain and is used by numerous airlines. The airport was expanded and a new terminal was constructed in 2001. Piarco remains the principal air transportation facility in Trinidad and Tobago. However, following extensive aerodrome development at Crown Point Airport (located 13 km from Scarborough) in 1992 the airport was opened to jet aircraft. It is now officially named Crown Point International Airport. There is a domestic service between Trinidad and Tobago.

Airports Authority of Trinidad and Tobago (AATT): Airport Administration Centre, Piarco International Airport; tel. 669-8047; fax 669-2319; e-mail airport@tntairports.com; internet www.airporttnt.com; administers Piarco and Crown Point International Airports; Chair. LINUS ROGERS.

BWIA West India Airways Ltd (Trinidad and Tobago): Administration Bldg, Golden Grove Rd, Piarco International Airport, POB 604, Port of Spain; tel. 669-3000; fax 669-1865; e-mail mail@bwee.com; internet www.bwee.com; f. 1980 by merger of BWIA International (f. 1940) and Trinidad and Tobago Air Services (f. 1974); state-owned; operates scheduled passenger and cargo services linking destinations in the Caribbean region, South America, North America and Europe; operates Tobago Express service between Trinidad and Tobago; Chair. ARTHUR LOK JACK; CEO NELSON TOM YEW.

Tourism

The climate and coastline attract visitors to Trinidad and Tobago. The latter island is generally believed to be the more beautiful and is less developed. The annual pre-Lenten carnival is a major attraction. In 2003 there were an estimated 409,069 foreign visitors, excluding cruise-ship passengers, and tourist receipts in 2002 were estimated at US $402m. In 2000 there were an estimated 82,859 cruise-ship passenger arrivals. There were 4,532 hotel rooms in Trinidad and Tobago in that same year. The Government announced plans to increase first-class hotel room accommodation by 8,000 in 2001, marketing the islands as a sophisticated cultural destination. There were additional tourism developments in Chaguaramas and Toco Bay.

Tourism Development Company of Trinidad and Tobago (TDC): 10–14 Philipps St, POB 222, Port of Spain; tel. 623-6022; fax 624-3848; f. 1993 as Tourism and Industrial Devt Co of Trinidad and Tobago; restructured and renamed as above in 2005.

Trinidad Hotels, Restaurants and Tourism Association (THRTA): c/o Trinidad & Tobago Hospitality and Tourism Institute, Airway Rd, Chaguaramas; tel. 634-1174; fax 634-1176; e-mail info@tnthotels.com; internet www.tnthotels.com; Pres. ERNEST LITTLES; Exec. Dir GREER ASSAM.

Tobago Hotel and Tourism Association: Goddard's Bldg, Auchenskeoch, Carnbee; tel. and fax 639-9543; e-mail tthtatob@tstt.net.tt; Pres. RENE SEEPERSADSINGH.

TUNISIA

Introductory Survey

Location, Climate, Language, Religion, Flag, Capital

The Republic of Tunisia lies in North Africa, bordered by Algeria to the west and by Libya to the south-east. To the north and east, Tunisia has a coastline on the Mediterranean Sea. The climate is temperate on the coast, with winter rain, but hot and dry inland. Temperatures in Tunis are generally between 6°C (43°F) and 33°C (91°F). The country's highest recorded temperature is 55°C. Average annual rainfall is up to 1,500 mm in the north, but less than 200 mm in the southern desert. The official language is Arabic, and there is a small Berber Tamazight-speaking minority. French is widely used as a second language. Islam is the state religion, and almost all of the inhabitants are Muslims. There are small minorities of Christians and Jews. The national flag (proportions 2 by 3) is red, with a white disc, containing a red crescent moon and a five-pointed red star, in the centre. The capital is Tunis.

Recent History

Formerly a French protectorate, Tunisia was granted internal self-government by France in September 1955 and full independence on 20 March 1956. Five days later elections were held for a Constitutional Assembly, which met in April and appointed Habib Bourguiba as Prime Minister in a Government dominated by members of his Néo-Destour (New Constitution) Party. In July 1957 a republic was established, with Bourguiba as Head of State, and a new Constitution was promulgated in June 1959. At elections held in November Bourguiba was elected unopposed to the new office of President, and the Néo-Destour Party won all 90 seats in the new National Assembly.

By 1964 the Néo-Destour Party had become the only legal political organization and in November of that year it was renamed the Parti socialiste destourien (PSD). A moderate socialist economic programme was introduced, which began with the expropriation of foreign-owned lands. However, attempts to introduce agricultural collectivization in 1964–69, under the direction of Ahmad Ben Salah, Minister of Finance and Planning, were abandoned in September 1969 because of resistance from the rural population. Ben Salah was dismissed, arrested and subsequently sentenced to 10 years' hard labour. He escaped in 1973 and fled to Europe, from where he organized the radical Mouvement de l'unité populaire (MUP). In 1970 Hédi Nouira, hitherto Governor of the Banque Centrale de Tunisie, was appointed Prime Minister. He began to reverse Ben Salah's socialist economic policies, with the introduction of liberal economic reforms in the sectors of industry and agriculture.

Liberalization of the economy was not accompanied by political reform, and the extensive powers of Nouira and Bourguiba were increasingly challenged by younger PSD members in the early 1970s. However, at the 1974 PSD Congress, Bourguiba was elected President-for-Life of the PSD and Nouira was confirmed as Secretary-General. In March 1975, after approving the necessary amendments to the Constitution, the National Assembly elected Bourguiba President-for-Life of Tunisia. Political differences emerged concerning economic policy, and the previously loyal trade union movement, the Union Générale Tunisienne du travail (UGTT), led by Habib Achour, began to assert its independence from the PSD. In January 1978, for the first time since independence, a 24-hour general strike took place, organized by the UGTT. In violent clashes between troops and strikers, at least 50 people were killed and many trade union leaders, including Achour, were arrested. Subsequently Achour was sentenced to 10 years' hard labour and a new Secretary-General of the UGTT, Tijani Abid, declared the willingness of trade unions to co-operate with the Government.

In April 1980 Nouira resigned, owing to ill health, and was succeeded as Prime Minister and Secretary-General of the PSD by Muhammad Mzali. Under Mzali, signs of greater political tolerance became apparent. The one-party system ended in mid-1981, when the Parti communiste tunisien (PCT), which had been proscribed in 1963, was granted legal status. The Government announced that any political group that gained more than 5% of the votes cast in the forthcoming legislative elections would also be officially recognized. Many of the UGTT leaders imprisoned after the 1978 disturbances were pardoned, and Achour was reappointed Secretary-General of the UGTT. At elections to the National Assembly in November 1981 the PSD and the UGTT formed an electoral alliance, the Front national, which received 94.6% of the total votes cast and won all 126 seats in the new Assembly.

In July 1986 Mzali was replaced as Prime Minister by Rachid Sfar (hitherto Minister of Finance), and was dismissed as Secretary-General of the PSD. Mzali subsequently fled to Algeria, and was sentenced *in absentia* to terms of imprisonment and hard labour for defamatory comments against Tunisian leaders and mismanagement of public funds. Elections to the National Assembly, in November, were boycotted by the opposition parties, with the result that the PSD, opposed only by 15 independent candidates, won all 125 seats.

During late 1987 President Bourguiba's behaviour became increasingly erratic. In October he revoked several of his recent appointments of leading state officials, and dismissed Sfar from the premiership. Zine al-Abidine Ben Ali was appointed Prime Minister and Secretary-General of the PSD; he retained the interior portfolio, which he had held since 1986. In early November 1987 a disagreement between Bourguiba and Ben Ali was reported, apparently concerning the recent trial of 90 Islamists accused of plotting against the Government. On 7 November seven doctors declared that President Bourguiba was unfit to govern, owing to senility and ill health. In accordance with the Constitution, Ben Ali was sworn in as President. Hédi Baccouche (previously Minister of Social Affairs) was appointed Prime Minister, and a new Council of Ministers was formed, which excluded several close associates of Bourguiba. Ben Ali announced plans to reform the Constitution and to permit greater political freedom. In the same month the Government permitted the publication of previously suspended opposition newspapers, and by early 1988 some 3,000 political and non-political detainees had been released. In February the PSD was renamed the Rassemblement constitutionnel démocratique (RCD), in order to reflect the new administration's commitment to democratic reform.

In April 1988 legislation was enacted by the National Assembly to institute a multi-party political system, and in July the Assembly approved a series of proposals to reform the Constitution. The office of President-for-Life was abolished, and the President was, henceforth, to be elected by universal suffrage every five years and limited to two consecutive terms of office. In the same month there was a significant reorganization of the Government, notably affecting ministers who had served under Bourguiba. In September two further opposition parties, the left-wing Rassemblement socialiste progressiste and the liberal Parti social pour le progrès (renamed the Parti social libéral—PSL—in 1993 and the Parti social démocratique libéral—PSDL—in 2005) were legalized. In November the Government claimed that there were no longer any political prisoners in Tunisia, a total of 8,000 people having been released during the first year of Ben Ali's regime.

Ben Ali was nominated as the sole candidate (supported by all the officially recognized parties) for the presidential election of 2 April 1989, and was duly elected President, receiving 99.3% of the votes cast. In legislative elections, the RCD won all 141 seats in the National Assembly, with some 80% of the votes cast. The fundamentalist Hizb an-Nahdah or the Parti de la renaissance (whose candidates contested the election as independents, since the party was not officially recognized), won some 13% of the votes cast, but failed to win any seats under an electoral system that favoured the ruling party. In September Ben Ali dismissed Prime Minister Baccouche, following a disagreement concerning the Government's economic policy, and appointed Hamed Karoui, the former Minister of Justice, in his place.

In May 1990 the National Assembly approved a reformed electoral code, introducing a system of partial proportional representation for forthcoming municipal elections. The winning party was to receive 50% of the seats, while the remainder were to be distributed among all the parties, according to the number of votes received by each one. However, the six legal opposition parties boycotted the elections, held in June, arguing that they were neither free nor fair. Consequently, the RCD won control of all but one of the 245 municipal councils.

Ben Ali stated in December 1991 that changes to the electoral system, to be formulated in consultation with opposition parties, would be implemented during 1992, with the aim of ensuring greater representation at the national level for parties other than the RCD. In December 1992 Ben Ali announced a revision of the electoral code, to include the introduction of partial proportional representation at legislative elections scheduled for March 1994. However, this apparent willingness to co-operate with the legalized opposition was accompanied by further repression of the Islamist movement, with increased censorship of publications sympathetic to their cause, and the harassment of suspected activists.

In March 1992 the human rights organization Amnesty International published a report which detailed the arrests of some 8,000 suspected an-Nahdah members over an 18-month period, and cited 200 cases of the torture and ill-treatment of detainees. It also claimed that at least seven Islamists had died while in custody. The Government initially denied the allegations, but later conceded that some violations of human rights had occurred. In mid-March it was announced that human rights 'units' were to be established within the Ministries of Foreign Affairs, Justice and the Interior, although new restrictions were imposed on the activities of unofficial, quasi-political groups such as the Ligue tunisienne des droits de l'homme (LTDH). In the same month an amnesty was granted to more than 1,000 detainees. In July and August the trials were held in Tunis of 171 alleged members of an-Nahdah, and of 108 alleged members of the organization's military wing, who were all accused of conspiring to overthrow the Government; 46 of the defendants were sentenced to life imprisonment, 16, including Rachid Ghannouchi, the leader of an-Nahdah, *in absentia*. (In 1993 Ghannouchi was granted political asylum in the United Kingdom.) Prison sentences of between one and 24 years were imposed on the remainder. In October appeals on behalf of 265 of those convicted were rejected, and another 20 an-Nahdah sympathizers were reportedly arrested and quantities of weapons and explosives seized in police raids.

There were indications in 1993 of a revival of political activity, and in April a new political organization, the Mouvement du renouveau (MR—Ettajdid), held its first Congress. In November Ben Ali announced that presidential and legislative elections were to take place in March 1994. His candidacy for the presidency was supported not only by the RCD, but also by most of the legal opposition parties. In January 1994 the National Assembly adopted reforms to the electoral code: thenceforth 19 of the 163 seats in the enlarged Assembly were to be allocated to opposition parties in proportion to their overall national vote. At the presidential election, which took place concurrently with the legislative elections on 20 March 1994, Ben Ali was re-elected President, receiving 99.9% of the votes cast. The RCD received 97.7% of the total votes cast in the legislative elections, securing all 144 seats that were contested under a simple majority system. Of the 19 seats reserved for opposition candidates, the Mouvement des démocrates socialistes (MDS) secured 10, the MR four, the Union démocratique unioniste (UDU) three and the Parti de l'unité populaire (PUP) two. The rate of voter participation was officially estimated at 95.5%.

In October 1995 Muhammad Mouada, the MDS Secretary-General, was arrested and accused of having received money from an unnamed foreign country. The previous day Mouada had, in an open letter to the President, criticized the lack of political freedom in Tunisia; however, government officials denied any connection between the letter and Mouada's arrest. In late October the Tunisian authorities prevented Khemais Chamari, an MDS member of the National Assembly, from travelling to Malta to attend an international conference on human rights. In the following month Chamari's parliamentary immunity was withdrawn, in order to allow judicial charges (relating to Mouada's trial) to be brought against him. Meanwhile, in an apparently conciliatory gesture towards the opposition, Ben Ali pardoned the leader of the Parti des ouvriers communistes tunisiens (POCT), Hamma Hammani, who had been imprisoned in April 1994, and his associate Muhammad Kilani, the former editor of the POCT journal. (Nevertheless, Hammani apparently remained the object of official harassment and in March 1996 his passport was confiscated. He was given a nine-year prison sentence *in absentia* in July 1999 for belonging to an illegal organization and finally surrendered to the authorities in early 2002. However, having commenced a hunger strike to protest against his subsequent imprisonment, Hammani was finally released on health grounds in September.) In February 1996 Mouada was sentenced to two years' imprisonment for 'illegal detention of currency'. Although a court of appeal subsequently reduced his term by one year, at the end of the month Mouada was sentenced to 11 years' imprisonment for maintaining links with and receiving money from Libya. In July Chamari was sentenced to five years' imprisonment for breaching security proceedings relating to Mouada's trial. Human rights organizations protested at the severity of the sentence and appealed to the Tunisian authorities to release all political detainees. In December Mouada and Chamari were released conditionally on humanitarian grounds.

In June 1996 President Ben Ali reorganized the Government and appointed Abd al-Aziz Ben Dhia as Secretary-General of the RCD. Wide-ranging ministerial changes were effected in January 1997, and Ben Ali again reorganized the Council of Ministers in October—notably appointing Saïd Ben Mustapha as Minister of Foreign Affairs and Ali Chaouch as Minister of the Interior. In December 1996 Ben Ali announced plans to amend the electoral law, which, *inter alia*, would lower the minimum eligible age of candidates for the National Assembly (from 25 to 23 years) and increase the representation of legal opposition parties in the Assembly and in municipal councils. Political parties would not be permitted to be based on religion, language, race or region, nor to have foreign links. The scope of referendums was also to be widened. In December 1997 the Council of Ministers reached consensus on draft legislation to amend the electoral law.

In January 1999 draft legislation was presented to the National Assembly to introduce extraordinary provisions to the Constitution in order to allow pluralism in the presidential election scheduled to be held that year. The amendments, which were approved in March, allowed for the leaders of all political parties to contest the presidency provided that they had held their current leadership position for at least five consecutive years, and that their party was represented by one or more deputies in the legislature. (Hitherto opposition parties had been unable to present candidates, owing to the requirement that they be supported by at least 30 deputies in the Assembly.) Despite the new provisions, only two leaders of opposition parties were eligible to contest the presidency, namely Abderrahmane Tlili (UDU) and Muhammad Belhadj Amor (PUP). Ben Ali had himself been re-elected Chairman of the RCD at a party congress in July 1998, when he had been formally nominated as the party's presidential candidate.

The first contested presidential election since independence was held on 24 October 1999. As expected, Ben Ali comprehensively defeated his two rivals, securing 99.5% of the vote. Voter participation was officially estimated at 91.4%. At concurrent elections to the National Assembly the RCD won all of the 148 seats contested under a simple majority system. Of the 34 seats reserved for opposition candidates, 13 were won by the MDS, the UDU and the PUP both took seven seats, the MR won five, and the PSL two. Some 91.5% of the electorate voted, according to official sources. In November the President effected a major government reorganization: Hamed Karoui was replaced as Prime Minister by Muhammad Ghannouchi (previously Minister of International Co-operation and Foreign Investment) and Abdallah Kallel succeeded Ali Chaouch as Minister of the Interior. At municipal elections held in May 2000 the RCD won more than 94% of the 4,128 seats being contested, and maintained control over all local councils.

In June 2000 the President of the Conseil national pour les libertés en Tunisie (CNLT), Moncef Marzouki, visited London, United Kingdom, where he declared that a national democratic conference was to be held later in the year. Marzouki reportedly held talks with the leader of an-Nahdah, Rachid Ghannouchi, and proposed future co-operation between secular and Islamist factions of the Tunisian opposition. In September it was reported that the Secretary-General of the UGTT, Ismail Sahbani, had resigned his post; he was replaced in an acting capacity by Abdessalem Djerad. In June 2001 Sahbani was sentenced to a total of 13 years' imprisonment after he was found guilty of two separate cases of embezzlement and forgery.

In early November 2000 President Ben Ali announced a number of initiatives aimed at furthering the democratization process and promoting human rights in Tunisia. The measures included: state compensation for detainees held in police custody without reasonable grounds; the transfer of responsibility for the prison system from the Ministry of the Interior to the Ministry of Justice; new legislation to improve conditions in prisons and to reduce censorship of the press; and an increase, by 50%, in government subsidies allocated for other political parties and their publications. In late November 14 alleged members of an illegal Islamist organization were sentenced to prison terms of between two and 17 years. In December Marzouki received a one-year prison sentence, having been convicted of belonging to an illegal group and of disseminating false information. In September 2001 the court of appeal announced the suspension of Marzouki's sentence, although his civil rights were not restored. Marzouki, who had been prevented from travelling abroad on several occasions during 2001, finally had the ban on him leaving Tunisia lifted in early December, and he departed for France later that month.

Meanwhile, at the fifth congress of the LTDH, held in October 2000, a new executive board was elected, with Mokhtar Trifi, an outspoken critic of the Ben Ali regime, as President. Four former members of the board subsequently filed a suit against the new leadership, claiming that, owing to procedural irregularities, it was invalid, and in late November a court imposed a moratorium on the activities of the LTDH. The Tunisian Government denied having ordered the ruling, but was strongly criticized by international and local human rights groups for its perceived role in the affair. Trial proceedings against the LTDH began at the end of January 2001, and in mid-February a judgment was issued that the results of the October congress should be invalidated. In March Trifi was charged with dissemination of false information and violation of the recent court ruling; however, in mid-June the court of appeal ruled that the LTDH could resume its activities and ordered it to hold another congress within a year.

President Ben Ali effected a significant reorganization of the Government in late January 2001. Muhammad Ghannouchi remained as Prime Minister, but several portfolios were reallocated. The most notable change in the enlarged Government (which included 19 new ministers) was the promotion of the former Government Secretary-General, Abdallah Kaâbi, to become Minister of the Interior. There was a minor reorganization of the Council of Ministers in October.

In March 2001 more than 250 human rights activists in Tunisia produced a petition that demanded wide-ranging democratic reforms in the country prior to the presidential and legislative elections scheduled for 2004. Also in March 2001 some 100 moderate figures in civil society signed a separate petition accusing Ben Ali of corruption and nepotism and denouncing his plans to amend the Constitution so as to permit him to seek a fourth term in office. In April an-Nahdah released a joint communiqué with Mouada's faction of the MDS, proposing the formation of an opposition coalition to unite Islamists and liberals against the Ben Ali regime. Later that month the President instructed the Ministry of the Interior to investigate all alleged abuses by the security forces against Tunisian citizens and to ensure that those found guilty were punished. In May he made a series of conciliatory gestures, including the release of a number of political prisoners; however, the detention and imprisonment of several leading opponents of the regime continued. Meanwhile, in late April the National Assembly approved revisions to the press code under which the offence of 'defamation of public order' was abolished. The amendments also removed the threat of prison sentences for certain violations of the code. The changes were, however, condemned as inadequate by the Association des journalistes tunisiens.

The central committee of the ruling RCD announced in September 2001 that it would formally propose changes to the country's Constitution in order to enable Ben Ali to seek a fourth presidential term. In April 2002 members of the National Assembly overwhelmingly approved a constitutional reform bill, and at a referendum held on 26 May, according to official figures, the constitutional changes were approved by 99.5% of voters; the rate of voter participation was officially recorded at 95.6%. The amendments raised the age limit for presidential candidates from 70 to 75 years, and removed the limit on the number of terms that could be served by a President. In August 2003 the changes were promulgated and Ben Ali formally announced his intention to stand for a fourth term at elections scheduled for late 2004. Provision was also made for the creation of a second legislative chamber, for the establishment of a two-round presidential election system, and for a number of measures that would improve civil liberties and public freedoms.

In early April 2002 a tanker lorry exploded outside a synagogue on the island of Djerba. More than 20 people were killed in the incident, most of them German tourists, and a similar number suffered injuries. The Tunisian authorities initially claimed that the explosion had been an accident, but a spokesman for the Israeli Ministry of Foreign Affairs insisted that it was an anti-Semitic 'terrorist' attack. The Tunisian authorities subsequently confirmed that the explosion had been a 'premeditated criminal act'. A number of Arabic newspapers immediately carried claims that the al-Qa'ida (Base) organization of Osama bin Laden—the principal suspect in the September 2001 attacks on New York and Washington, DC—was responsible, and in late June 2002 the Qatar-based satellite television station Al-Jazeera broadcast a statement by a spokesman for al-Qa'ida, asserting that the attack had been perpetrated in the name of al-Qa'ida, in protest against Israel's recent military offensive against Palestinian-controlled areas of the West Bank.

Later in April 2002, apparently in response to the Djerba attack, Abdallah Kaâbi was replaced as Minister of the Interior by Hédi M'henni, hitherto Minister of Social Affairs. A new Director-General of National Security was also appointed. In May 13 senior military officers, including the army Chief of Staff, Brig.-Gen. Abdelaziz Skik, were killed when the helicopter in which they were travelling crashed to the west of Tunis. Col Rachid Ammar was named as Skik's successor.

In September 2002 President Ben Ali implemented a major reorganization of the Council of Ministers. In an attempt to improve efficiency in government operations, a number of ministries were merged or abolished, although most strategic posts remained unaltered. In early November eight people were arrested in Lyon, France, in connection with the Djerba explosion. Among those detained was the brother of the man suspected of having driven the lorry, and later that month he was one of three people to be questioned further in Paris by a senior French judge as part of ongoing anti-terrorism investigations. The other five suspects were released without charge. In early March 2003 five people were arrested in Spain in connection with the incident, and another person was detained in France shortly afterwards; in the following month police in Saudi Arabia arrested a German citizen who had been briefly detained by the authorities in that country following the explosion.

Meanwhile, in January 2003 Ben Ali announced the merger of a number of ministries, reducing them in number from 29 to 25. The most notable changes were the creation of a Ministry of Justice and Human Rights and of a Ministry of Employment. In August a minor reorganization of the Council of Ministers was effected, although the most strategic posts were unaffected. Earlier that month the leader of the UDU, Abderrahmane Tlili, was arrested and charged with the abuse of power and the embezzlement of funds from the Office de l'Aviation Civile et des Aéroports, of which he had previously been the President and Director-General.

During 2003–04 the Tunisian authorities continued to take stern action against opponents of the Ben Ali regime. In July 2003 Abdallah Zouari, an Islamist journalist, who had been released from detention in June 2002, having served an 11-year sentence for 'belonging to an illegal organization', was sentenced to four months' imprisonment for libel; in August 2003 Zouari received a further nine-month term for 'failing to obey an administrative order'. In October Radhia Nasraoui, a prominent Tunisian human rights lawyer, commenced a hunger strike in protest against her alleged harassment by the authorities, claiming that she had been targeted because she had defended political prisoners and had accused the Government of using torture against opposition activists. Nasraoui ended her hunger strike in December.

President Ben Ali carried out a further minor reshuffle of the Council of Ministers in January 2004. The Minister of Finance, Taofik Baccar, was appointed Governor of the Banque Centrale de Tunisie and his vacated ministerial portfolio was assumed by Munir Jeidan, hitherto Secretary of State to the Minister of Finance, in charge of the Budget. New Ministers of Sport, of Trade, and of Tourism and Handicrafts were also appointed. Later that month it was announced that women would constitute at least 25% of the RCD's candidates at the legislative elections scheduled for October. A further limited reorganization of the Government took place in late March, with Muhammad Rachid Kechiche being appointed Minister of Finance in place of Jeidan. Jeidan assumed Kechiche's previous post of Government Secretary-General in charge of Relations with the Chamber of Deputies and the Chamber of Advisers.

TUNISIA

In the months prior to the presidential election, a group of opposition figures, including Moncef Marzouki, now the leader of the Congrès pour la République, launched an appeal calling for President Ben Ali to step down and for the amendment of the Constitution to prevent the President from remaining in office indefinitely. Ben Ali responded by addressing members of the RCD in July 2004 and assuring them that the elections would be held 'within a context of transparency and the respect of law', while requesting that foreign observers be present at the elections. By mid-September four candidates had officially registered to run for President—namely Ben Ali, Muhammad Bouchiha of the PUP, Mounir Béji of the PSL and Muhammad Ali Halouani of the MR. The Parti démocratique progressiste announced in mid-October that it was withdrawing its candidates for the legislative elections in protest at what it considered an illegitimate electoral process in which it was denied access to the media and faced serious delays in having its manifesto approved. The presidential election took place on 24 October; Ben Ali received 94.49% of the votes cast, while Bouchiha secured 3.78%, Halouani 0.95% and Béji 0.79%. Voter turn-out was officially estimated at 91.5%. At the legislative elections, which took place concurrently, the RCD won all of the 152 seats contested under a simple majority system, 25% of which would be occupied by women under new legislation, while of the 37 reserved for the opposition, the MDS won 14 seats, the PUP 11, the UDU seven, and the MR and PSL three and two seats, respectively. On 10 November Ben Ali announced a major reshuffle of the Council of Ministers, appointing new Ministers of National Defence, of Foreign Affairs and of the Interior and Local Development, and creating new Ministries of Transport and of Environment and Land Planning.

In 2004–05 there was increased concern on the part of international human rights organizations regarding the holding of political prisoners and claims of abuse in Tunisian gaols. In early April 2004 eight young people were arrested and sentenced to between 19 and 26 years' imprisonment for using the internet to plan terrorist activities, although in August six of the prisoners had their sentences reduced to 13 years. In early June the leader of the UDU, Abderrahmane Tlili, was imprisoned for nine years after being convicted of abusing his position while he was head of the Office de l'Aviation Civile et des Aéroports. A report published in early July by the organization Human Rights Watch criticized the Government's handling of political prisoners, many of whom, it claimed, had spent several years in solitary confinement, and urged the Tunisian authorities to allow domestic and international monitors to inspect prison standards. In early November President Ben Ali pardoned 80 Islamist prisoners, including two leaders of the banned group an-Nahdah.

In late February 2005, at a meeting of the Central Committee of the RCD, Ben Ali announced plans to create a national electoral observatory in time for the municipal elections scheduled for May. He also reiterated his determination to see women occupying at least 25% of the electoral lists for these elections. In mid-April it was announced that elections would take place in early July for the new Chamber of Advisers. The second legislative chamber would be composed of 126 members, of whom 43 would be indirectly elected by municipal councillors and deputies, and 42 by the main professional federations and trade unions. The remaining 41 members were to be appointed by the President. At the municipal elections held on 8 May 2005, the RCD won 4,098 of the 4,366 council seats contested, and in early July councillors and deputies elected 43 members (as representatives of the regions) to the Chamber of Advisers, all of whom were RCD candidates. In mid-August Ben Ali effected a major reshuffle of the Council of Ministers: Abdelwahab Abdallah, a former principal adviser to the President, was appointed as Minister of Foreign Affairs and Kamel Morjane received the defence portfolio. Ali Chaouch assumed the post of Minister of Social Affairs, Solidarity and Tunisians Abroad and was succeeded as Secretary-General of the RCD by Morjane's predecessor, Hédi M'henni. The Chamber of Advisers held its inaugural session in mid-October and Abdullah Kallel was elected as Speaker. However, 14 seats remained vacant after the UGTT refused to elect its members to the new chamber.

Meanwhile, in early July 2005 five men who had been convicted in April of crimes related to terrorism were released from gaol following an appeal; the prison sentences of six others were reduced. The men had been convicted of belonging to the Base of Holy War in Mesopotamia organization in Iraq (Tanzim Qa'idat al-Jihad fi Bilad ar-Rafidain—also known as al-Qa'ida in Iraq) and of planning to attend terrorist training camps abroad.

Relations with the other countries of the Maghreb improved considerably in the 1980s. A meeting between President Bourguiba and President Ben Djedid Chadli of Algeria in March 1983 led to the drafting of the Maghreb Fraternity and Co-operation Treaty, which envisaged the eventual creation of a Greater Maghreb Union, and was signed by Mauritania in December. In January 1988 Tunisia and Algeria held further discussions on the establishment of a greater Arab Maghreb, and in April border restrictions between Tunisia and Libya were removed. In February 1989, at a meeting of North African Heads of State in Morocco, a treaty was concluded that proclaimed the Union of the Arab Maghreb (Union du Maghreb arabe—UMA, see p. 388), comprising Algeria, Libya, Mauritania, Morocco and Tunisia. The treaty envisaged: the establishment of a council of heads of state; regular meetings of ministers responsible for foreign affairs; and, eventually, the free movement of goods, people, services and capital throughout the countries of the region.

In 1982 President Bourguiba permitted the Palestine Liberation Organization (PLO) to establish its headquarters near Tunis. In October 1985 Israeli aircraft attacked the PLO headquarters, causing the deaths of some 72 people, including 12 Tunisians. US support for the right of Israel to retaliate (the attack was a reprisal for the murder of three Israeli citizens in Cyprus) severely strained relations between Tunisia and the USA. In April 1988 Abu Jihad, the military commander of the PLO, was assassinated at his home in Tunis. The Tunisian Government blamed Israel for the murder, and complained to the UN Security Council. The PLO transferred its offices to Gaza in mid-1994, following the signing of the PLO-Israeli Cairo Agreement on implementing Palestinian self-rule in the Gaza Strip and in Jericho.

In January 1988 the Tunisian Government announced that diplomatic relations with Egypt, which had been severed in 1979, would be resumed. In March 1990 Ben Ali made the first visit to Cairo by a Tunisian President since 1965, and signed several agreements on bilateral co-operation. In September 1990 a majority of members of the League of Arab States (the Arab League, see p. 306) resolved to move the League's headquarters from Tunis (where it had been established 'temporarily' in 1979) to its original site in Cairo: the Tunisian Government protested at the decision.

Tunisia assumed the annual presidency of the UMA in January 1993. The Government made clear its determination to reactivate the process of Maghreb union, as well as dialogue with the European Community (now European Union—EU, see p. 228). In April 1994 the UMA ratified 11 agreements designed to improve co-operation and trade within the Maghreb. However, tensions between the UMA's member states subsequently undermined the activities of the Union. In March 1999 Ben Ali made his first official visit to Morocco, during which he pledged to strengthen relations with that country, and to revive the UMA. A summit meeting of ministers responsible for foreign affairs of the five UMA member states was arranged, and proceeded in the Algerian capital in March 2001. However, the meeting, which was to have made preparations for the first summit meeting of UMA Heads of State since 1995, quickly broke down following disagreements between Moroccan and Algerian representatives.

Relations with Algeria improved appreciably after the second round of Algerian elections, at which the fundamentalist Front islamique du salut (FIS) had been expected to secure victory, was suspended in January 1992, and Tunisia welcomed the appointment of Muhammad Boudiaf as Chairman of the High Council of State, as well as the suppression of the FIS. During a visit to Tunis in February 1993, Boudiaf's successor, Ali Kafi, exchanged letters with Ben Ali to ratify the official demarcation of the 1,000-km border between Tunisia and Algeria, which had been the subject of dispute since Algerian independence. Ben Ali and Kafi also pledged to co-operate in countering the threat of terrorism in the region. In early 1995 six Tunisian border guards were killed in an attack perpetrated by Algerian Islamists in protest at the Tunisian authorities' alleged support for the Algerian security forces. Another serious incident occurred at the joint border in May 2000, when Tunisian security forces responded to an attack by Algerian Islamists; three of the Islamists were killed and two Tunisian soldiers wounded. The attack followed the signing of a bilateral customs agreement aimed at ending cross-border smuggling, considered by the Algerian Government to facilitate the activities of Islamist groups in Algeria. A number of bilateral agreements were signed during a visit to Algeria by Ben Ali in February 2002; most notably, the two countries pledged to formalize delineation of their maritime border.

In December 2003 Tunisia hosted the '5+5 Dialogue Summit', attended by the Heads of State of the five UMA countries and Portugal, Spain, Italy, France and Malta, at which discussions focused on political stability, economic co-operation, immigration and the continued crisis between the Israelis and the Palestinians. At the conclusion of the summit the 10 countries issued a declaration, which provided a working blueprint for future economic, political and cultural co-operation within the Euro-Mediterranean region.

In October 1994 Tunisia and Israel signalled the beginning of the normalization of bilateral relations with the announcement of plans to establish interests offices in the Belgian embassies in Tunis and Tel-Aviv. The offices opened in April and May 1996, respectively. Relations between the two countries were strained in early 1997, following Tunisia's criticism of Israel's alleged failure to implement agreements concluded with the PLO; although the two countries' respective interests offices remained open, Tunisia suspended the process of normalizing relations with Israel. The Tunisian Government installed a liaison office in the Gaza Strip in April 1995; a second office was planned for Jericho. In February 2000 a senior-level delegation from Tunisia visited Israel, where it was agreed, *inter alia*, that the two countries would establish a joint committee for advancing trade and tourism. However, in October, in response to the escalating Israeli–Palestinian crisis, Tunisia announced that it had severed all diplomatic ties with Israel. As violence continued to escalate in the Palestinian territories in early 2002, the Tunisian authorities again denounced Israeli aggression and urged international organizations to take firm action to end the crisis. In November 2003 it was reported that representatives from the Tunisian and Israeli Ministries of Foreign Affairs had held talks in Tunis with regard to the possible reopening of the interests offices in Tel-Aviv and Tunis. In late March 2004 Tunisia postponed a summit meeting of the Arab League, scheduled to be held in Tunis, citing differences among member states concerning an agenda for the talks (reportedly to include an appropriate Arab response to US pressure for political reform in the Middle East and to recent Israeli actions in the Palestinian territories). The summit eventually commenced in Tunis in late May; however, conflicts over the summit's agenda remained and no agreement was reached on an Arab-Israeli peace initiative.

In June 1993 President Ben Ali, addressing the European Parliament in Strasbourg, advocated the establishment of a Euro-Maghreb Development Bank, which, by stimulating economic growth in North Africa, would alleviate illegal immigration into Europe. In July 1995 Tunisia concluded an association agreement with the EU, designed to foster closer commercial and political co-operation between the two. In October the new French President, Jacques Chirac, made an official visit to Tunisia. Chirac and Ben Ali agreed that henceforth they would meet annually, in order to consolidate bilateral relations. Ben Ali made an official visit to France in October 1997, during which he countered criticisms regarding his country's record on human rights by claiming that there were currently no political prisoners in Tunisia. Several Tunisian deputies demanded a suspension of the association agreement in June 2000, after EU member states (particularly France) criticized the Tunisian authorities' failure to protect human rights. Relations between France and Tunisia deteriorated further during 2001 when the French Government again criticized the growing use of violence against human rights activists and voiced its concern at gaol sentences imposed upon prominent opposition figures. Relations improved, however, during 2002–04 and in December 2003 Chirac again visited Tunisia. The two countries signed a number of co-operation agreements relating to tourism and bilateral social security arrangements. In late January 2005 the French Prime Minister, Jean-Pierre Raffarin, visited Tunisia and encouraged democratic reform in the country and closer relations with the EU. In mid-November the EU made an official complaint to the Tunisian Government days before the UN-sponsored World Summit on the Information Society was scheduled to begin in Tunis. Tunisian security forces had prevented a group of international delegates, including the German ambassador to the UN and representatives of international human rights bodies and non-governmental organizations, from entering the German cultural institute in the Tunisian capital. In a separate incident, a journalist for the French daily newspaper *Libération* was later stabbed by unknown assailants.

In December 2003 the US Secretary of State, Colin Powell, visited Tunisia for talks with President Ben Ali and the Tunisian Minister of Foreign Affairs, Habib Ben Yahia. Powell praised the excellent relations between the two countries and Tunisia's contribution to the 'war on terror'; however, he urged the Tunisian Government to pursue further political and economic reforms. In February 2004 Ben Ali visited Washington, DC, where he met with the US President, George W. Bush, to discuss a number of trade-related issues. During the talks Bush also stressed that, while the USA applauded Tunisia's efforts to liberalize its society, it remained critical of the country's poor human rights record and the continued oppression of the Tunisian media.

Government

Under the 1959 Constitution (with subsequent amendments), legislative power is held by the unicameral National Assembly, with 189 members who are elected by universal adult suffrage for a five-year term. (Of the 189 members, 152 are elected under a simple majority system, while 37 seats are reserved for the opposition, allotted according to the proportion of votes received nationally by each party.) In 1988 a multi-party system was officially permitted by law. Executive power is held by the President, elected for five years by popular vote at the same time as the Assembly. The President, who is Head of State and Head of Government, appoints a Council of Ministers, led by a Prime Minister, which is responsible to him. Constitutional amendments relating to the presidency and legislature were approved at a national referendum in May 2002 (see Recent History). For local administration the country is divided into 24 governorates.

Defence

In August 2005 total armed forces numbered an estimated 35,300 (including some 22,700 conscripts), consisting of an army of 27,000, a navy of about 4,800 and an air force of 3,500. Paramilitary forces included a 12,000-strong national guard. From 2003 women were required to complete military service. Officer-training is undertaken in the USA and France as well as in Tunisia. The defence budget for 2005 totalled an estimated TD 550m.

Economic Affairs

In 2004, according to estimates by the World Bank, Tunisia's gross national income (GNI), measured at average 2002–04 prices, was US $26,301m., equivalent to $2,630 per head (or $7,310 per head on an international purchasing-power parity basis). During 1995–2004, it was estimated, the population increased at an average annual rate of 1.2%, while gross domestic product (GDP) per head increased, in real terms, by an average of 3.8%. Overall GDP increased, in real terms, at an average annual rate of 5.1% per year in 1995–2004; it grew by 5.8% in 2004 and by 4.0% in 2005.

Agriculture (including forestry and fishing) contributed 12.8% of GDP and employed 18.7% of the working population in 2005. The principal crops are wheat, barley, tomatoes, watermelons, potatoes and olives. However, Tunisia imports large quantities of cereals, dairy produce, meat and sugar. The country's main agricultural export is olive oil; olives, citrus fruit and dates are also grown for export. During 1995–2004 agricultural GDP increased at an average annual rate of 5.9%. Agricultural GDP increased by 9.0% in 2004, but decreased by 5.0% in 2005.

Industry (including mining, manufacturing, construction and power) contributed 30.8% of GDP and engaged 32.3% of the employed labour force in 2005. During 1995–2004 industrial GDP increased by an average of 4.3% per year. Growth in industrial GDP was recorded at 4.2% in 2004 and at 1.2% in 2005.

Mining (excluding hydrocarbons) contributed 0.6% of GDP in 2005. In 1994 mining (with gas, electricity and water) employed 1.6% of the working population. In 2000 the principal mineral export was petroleum (which accounted for 10.4% of total export earnings). Tunisia's proven published oil reserves at the end of 2004 were estimated at 600m. barrels, sufficient to maintain production (at 2004 levels—averaging an estimated 69,000 barrels per day) for just over 25 years. Iron, zinc, lead, barite, gypsum, phosphate, fluorspar and sea salt are also mined. In addition, Tunisia possesses large reserves of natural gas. The GDP of the mining sector (excluding hydrocarbons) decreased by 4.9% in 2005.

Manufacturing (excluding hydrocarbons) contributed 18.9% of GDP in 2005, and employed 19.6% of the working population in 1994. Manufacturing is based on the processing of the country's principal agricultural and mineral products. Other important sectors include textiles, construction materials, machinery, chemicals, and paper and wood. In 1995–2004 manufacturing

GDP increased at an average annual rate of 4.5%. Manufacturing GDP grew by 4.6% in 2004 and (excluding hydrocarbons) by 0.7% in 2005.

Energy is derived principally from gas (which contributed 89.0% of total electricity output in 2002) and petroleum (10.2%), although Tunisia also has several hydroelectric plants. Imports of mineral fuels and lubricants comprised 6.9% of the value of total imports in 2003. In the late 1990s a project was under way to link the Tunisian electricity grid to that of Libya; the task was scheduled to be completed by 2006.

The services sector accounted for 56.4% of GDP and employed 49.0% of the working population in 2005. Tourism represents an important source of revenue: receipts from tourism in 2003 totalled US $1,935m. dinars, and there were 5.11m. tourist arrivals. The GDP of the services sector increased by an average of 5.0% per year in 1995–2004. Growth in the sector's GDP was recorded at 5.0% in 2004 and at 9.0% in 2005.

In 2004 Tunisia recorded a visible trade deficit of US $2,434m., and a deficit of $555m. on the current account of the balance of payments. In 2005 the principal sources of imports were France (accounting for 23.5% of the total), Italy (20.9%), Germany and Spain. The principal markets for Tunisian exports in that year were also France (taking 32.9%), Italy (24.0%) and Germany. The member states of the European Union (EU, see p. 228) accounted for 80.5% of Tunisia's exports and 71.4% of its imports in 1999. Tunisia's principal exports in 2005 were textiles, manufactured garments and leather products; machinery, electrical products and transport equipment; energy and lubricants; and agricultural and food products. The principal imports in that year were machinery, electrical products and transport equipment; textiles, manufactured garments and leather products; miscellaneous manufactured articles; and energy and lubricants.

In 2003 there was a budgetary deficit of TD 584m. (equivalent to 2.0% of GDP). At the end of 2003 Tunisia's total external debt was US $15,502m., of which $13,134m. was long-term public debt. In that year the cost of debt-servicing was equivalent to 13.0% of the value of exports of goods and services. The average annual rate of inflation was 2.6% in 2000–05; consumer prices increased by 3.6% in 2004 and by 2.1% in 2005. A reported 14.2% of the labour force were unemployed in 2005.

Tunisia is a member of the Arab Fund for Economic and Social Development (AFESD, see p. 161), the Arab Monetary Fund (see p. 163) and the Union of the Arab Maghreb (Union du Maghreb arabe—UMA, see p. 388).

From the mid-1990s Tunisia experienced strong economic growth, low inflation and declining poverty as a result of sound macroeconomic policies and improvements to the country's regulatory framework. Although in 2002 economic growth stagnated and the privatization programme, which had previously reduced government debt levels significantly, slowed (with just three of a possible 26 companies given over to private control), the Government remained committed to further privatization of state-owned enterprises. The sale of 33.5% of the Banque du Sud did not take place as expected in 2004 as the Government failed to secure any bids; however, the divestment was completed in November 2005, raising revenue of some US $80m. The sale of a 35% stake in the state-owned Tunisie Télécom was under way in 2005, and was initially expected to be completed by the latter part of 2006 (although there were reports in early 2006 that the sale might be delayed since fewer serious bids than anticipated had been received by this time). The 10th development plan (for 2002–06) aimed to increase international trade and accelerate structural reforms in order to create a more competitive economy and encourage private investment. Tunisia's tourism industry, which provides an estimated 7% of total GDP, was adversely affected by the recession in global travel following the suicide attacks against the USA in September 2001, as well as the terrorist attack at Djerba in April 2002. However, by mid-2003 the industry had begun to recover, with visitor numbers to Tunisia increasing once again; the Government proceeded apace with its ambitious programme to develop the sector, which aims to double the number of visitors to the country to 10m. by 2010. Meanwhile, the Tunisian economy continued to become more closely integrated with those of the EU member states, in preparation for the removal of all trade barriers between Tunisia and the EU in 2008. In early 2006 the IMF praised Tunisia's economic performance in 2005, which followed sustained economic growth in 2004. The Fund noted that GDP growth in 2005 remained at some 4%, while inflation was low (at 2.1%). The Tunisian authorities were notably commended for having maintained macroeconomic stability despite rising international petroleum prices. However, although GDP was forecast to increase by some 5.8% in 2006, the IMF considered that further efforts were required to reduce unemployment (which was rising especially fast among university graduates) and to improve the business climate for potential investors in Tunisian markets. Moreover, optimism regarding the prospects for the Tunisian economy was tempered by the large civil service wage bill, as well as the high level of public debt—officially recorded at 67.8% of GDP in 2004.

Education

Education is compulsory in Tunisia for a period of nine years between the ages of six and 16. Primary education begins at six years of age and normally lasts for six years. Secondary education begins at the age of 12 and lasts for seven years, comprising a first cycle of three years and a second cycle of four years. In 2002/03, according to UNESCO estimates, the total enrolment at primary schools was equivalent to 97% of the school-age population (97% of boys; 97% of girls). In that year the total enrolment at secondary schools was equivalent to 64% of children in the relevant age-group (61% of boys; 68% of girls). Arabic is the first language of instruction in primary and secondary schools, but French is also used. The University of Tunis was divided in 1988 to form separate institutions, one for the arts, the other for the sciences, and two new universities were opened in 1986, at Monastir and Sfax. In 2004/05 a total of 311,569 students were enrolled at higher educational establishments in Tunisia. Public expenditure on education was equivalent to 18.2% of total government spending in 2001/02.

Public Holidays

2006: 1 January (New Year's Day), 10 January*† (Aid el-Kebir, Feast of the Sacrifice), 20 March (Independence Day), 21 March (Youth Day), 9 April (Martyrs' Day), 1 May (Labour Day), 25 July (Republic Day), 13 August (Women's Day), 15 October (Evacuation of Bizerta), 23 October* (Aid es-Seghir, end of Ramadan), 7 November (accession of President Ben Ali), 31 December*† (Aid el-Kebir, Feast of the Sacrifice).

2007: 1 January (New Year's Day), 20 March (Independence Day), 21 March (Youth Day), 9 April (Martyrs' Day), 1 May (Labour Day), 25 July (Republic Day), 13 August (Women's Day), 13 October* (Aid es-Seghir, end of Ramadan), 15 October (Evacuation of Bizerta), 7 November (accession of President Ben Ali), 20 December* (Aid el-Kebir, Feast of the Sacrifice).

* These holidays are dependent on the Islamic lunar calendar and may differ by one or two days from the dates given.

† This festival occurs twice (in the Islamic years AH 1426 and 1427) within the same Gregorian year.

Weights and Measures

The metric system is in force.

TUNISIA   *Statistical Survey*

Statistical Survey

Source (unless otherwise stated): Institut National de la Statistique, Ministère du Développement Economique, 70 rue al-Cham, 1002 Tunis; tel. (71) 891-002; fax (71) 792-559; e-mail ins@e-mail.ati.tn; internet www.ins.nat.tn.

Area and Population

AREA, POPULATION AND DENSITY

Area (sq km)	
Land	154,530
Inland waters	9,080
Total	163,610*
Population (census results)	
20 April 1994	
Males	4,447,341
Females	4,338,023
Total	8,785,364
28 April 2004	9,910,872
Population (official estimate at 1 July)	
2005	10,031,100
Density (per sq km) at 1 July 2005	64.9†

* 63,170 sq miles.
† Land area only.

GOVERNORATES
(at 1 July 2005)

	Area (sq km)	Population (estimates)	Density (per sq km)
Tunis	346	986,100	2,850.0
Ariana	498	436,700	876.9
Ben Arous	761	521,100	684.8
Manouba	1,060	342,000	322.6
Nabeul	2,788	705,300	253.0
Zaghouan	2,768	163,300	59.0
Bizerte	3,685	529,400	143.7
Béja	3,558	303,800	85.4
Jendouba	3,102	418,000	134.8
Le Kef	4,965	258,300	52.0
Siliana	4,631	233,700	50.5
Kairouan	6,712	547,700	81.6
Kasserine	8,066	415,500	51.5
Sidi Bouzid	6,994	398,100	56.9
Sousse	2,621	557,700	212.8
Monastir	1,019	466,700	458.0
Mahdia	2,966	382,400	128.9
Sfax	7,545	869,700	115.3
Gafsa	8,990	325,900	36.3
Tozeur	4,719	98,500	20.9
Kébili	22,084	144,400	6.5
Gabès	7,175	346,000	48.2
Médenine	8,588	437,000	50.9
Tataouine	38,889	144,000	3.7
Total	**163,610**	**10,031,100**	**61.3**

PRINCIPAL TOWNS
(2004, census results)

Tunis (capital)	728,453	Ettadhamen		118,487
Sfax (Safaqis)	265,131	Kairouan (Qairawan)		117,930
Ariana	240,749	Gabès		116,323
Sousse	173,047	Bizerta (Bizerte)		114,371

Source: Thomas Brinkhoff, *City Population* (internet www.citypopulation.de).

BIRTHS, MARRIAGES AND DEATHS

	Registered live births		Registered marriages		Registered deaths	
	Number	Rate (per 1,000)	Number	Rate (per 1,000)	Number	Rate (per 1,000)
1990	205,345	25.4	55,612	6.8	45,700	5.6
1991	207,455	25.2	59,010	7.1	46,500	5.6
1992	211,649	25.2	64,700	7.6	46,300	5.5
1993	207,786	24.1	54,120	6.3	49,400	5.7
1994	200,223	22.7	52,431	5.9	50,300	5.7
1995	186,416	20.8	53,726	6.0	52,000	5.8
1996	178,801	19.7	56,349	6.2	40,817	5.5
1997	173,757	18.9	57,861	6.3	42,426	5.6

Birth rate (per 1,000): 16.7 in 2002; 17.1 in 2003; 16.8 in 2004.
Death rate (per 1,000): 5.8 in 2002; 6.1 in 2003; 6.0 in 2004.
Expectation of life (WHO, estimates, years at birth): 72 (males 70; females 74) in 2003 (Source: WHO, *World Health Report*).

EMPLOYMENT
('000 persons aged 15 years and over at 20 April 1994)

	Males	Females	Total
Agriculture, forestry and fishing	393.7	107.3	501.0
Manufacturing	244.7	211.0	455.7
Electricity, gas and water*	34.4	2.4	36.8
Construction	302.6	3.2	305.8
Trade, restaurants and hotels†	277.8	37.8	315.6
Community, social and personal services‡	503.9	163.2	667.1
Activities not adequately defined	28.6	10.0	38.6
Total employed	**1,785.7**	**534.9**	**2,320.6**

* Including mining and quarrying.
† Including financing, insurance, real estate and business services.
‡ Including transport, storage and communications.

Mid-2003 (estimates in '000): Agriculture, etc. 966; Total labour force 4,110 (Source: FAO).

Health and Welfare

KEY INDICATORS

Total fertility rate (children per woman, 2003)	2.0
Under-5 mortality rate (per 1,000 live births, 2004)	25
HIV/AIDS (% of persons aged 15–49, 2003)	0.1
Physicians (per 1,000 head, 1997)	0.70
Hospital beds (per 1,000 head, 1997)	1.70
Health expenditure (2002): US $ per head (PPP)	415
Health expenditure (2002): % of GDP	5.8
Health expenditure (2002): public (% of total)	49.9
Access to water (% of persons, 2002)	82
Access to sanitation (% of persons, 2002)	80
Human Development Index (2003): ranking	89
Human Development Index (2003): value	0.753

For sources and definitions, see explanatory note on p. vi.

Agriculture

PRINCIPAL CROPS
('000 metric tons)

	2002	2003	2004
Wheat	422	1,984	1,722
Barley	90	290	395
Potatoes	310	310	375
Broad beans (dry)	22	48	46
Other pulses*	36	45	46
Almonds	19	36	44
Olives	350	1,200*	350*
Artichokes	16	10	15*
Tomatoes	907	992	970
Pumpkins, squash and gourds*	35	35	35
Cucumbers and gherkins	31	30*	30*
Chillies and green peppers	210	193	255
Green onions and shallots†	135	131	105
Dry onions	120	110†	85†
Green peas	15	15*	15*
Green broad beans	23	23*	23*
Carrots*	50	50	50
Watermelons	400	395	450
Oranges	106	106*	106*
Tangerines, mandarins, clementines and satsumas	42	42*	42*
Lemons and limes	25	25*	25*
Grapefruit and pomelos	72†	72*	72*
Other citrus fruit	68	68*	68*
Apples	100	99	121
Pears	68	60	62
Apricots	25	26	27
Peaches and nectarines	82	92	92*
Grapes	114	107	115*
Figs	18	18*	18*
Dates	115	111	122

* FAO estimate(s).
† Unofficial figure(s).

Source: FAO.

LIVESTOCK
('000 head, year ending September)

	2002	2003*	2004*
Horses*	57	57	57
Mules*	81	81	81
Asses*	230	230	230
Cattle	753	760	760
Camels*	231	231	231
Sheep	6,833	6,850	6,850
Goats	1,449	1,400	1,400
Chickens*	62,000	62,000	62,000
Turkeys	4,370	4,400	4,400

* FAO estimate(s).
Source: FAO.

LIVESTOCK PRODUCTS
('000 metric tons)

	2002	2003	2004
Beef and veal	59.8	62.7	63.0*
Mutton and lamb	58.3	59.6	60.0*
Poultry meat	118.1	115.0	120.6
Cows' milk	943.0	941.0	864.0
Sheep's milk*	17.0	17.3	17.3
Goats' milk*	12.2	12.2	12.2
Cheese*	3.9	3.9	3.9
Hen eggs*	83.0	78.0	83.0
Wool: greasy*	8.8	8.8	8.8
Wool: scoured*	6.0	6.0	6.0
Cattle hides*	5.3	5.3	5.3
Sheepskins*	7.9	8.0	8.0

* FAO estimate(s).
Source: FAO.

Forestry

ROUNDWOOD REMOVALS
(FAO estimates, '000 cu m, excl. bark)

	2002	2003	2004
Sawlogs, veneer logs and logs for sleepers	21	21	21
Pulpwood	75	75	75
Other industrial wood	118	118	118
Fuel wood	2,116	2,126	2,138
Total	2,329	2,340	2,352

Source: FAO.

SAWNWOOD PRODUCTION
('000 cu m, incl. sleepers)

	1992	1993	1994
Coniferous (softwood)	2.2	5.8	6.8
Broadleaved (hardwood)	4.0	13.6	13.6
Total	6.2	19.4	20.4

1995–2004: Production as in 1994 (FAO estimates).
Source: FAO.

Fishing

('000 metric tons, live weight)

	2001	2002	2003
Capture	98.5	96.7	90.3
Mullets	3.0	3.0	3.2
Common pandora	3.2	2.7	2.8
Sargo breams	3.2	3.2	0.4
Bogue	2.9	3.2	3.4
Jack and horse mackerels	4.2	4.7	4.1
Sardinellas	12.9	12.5	11.8
European pilchard	14.0	13.3	12.1
Chub mackerel	3.7	2.5	4.5
Caramote prawn	3.4	2.5	2.3
Common cuttlefish	7.1	8.0	7.2
Aquaculture	1.9	2.0	2.1
Total catch (incl. others)	100.4	98.7	92.5

Source: FAO.

Mining

('000 metric tons, unless otherwise indicated)

	2002	2003	2004*
Crude petroleum ('000 barrels)	26,800	24,300	25,700
Natural gas (million cu m)	2,149	2,167	2,530
Iron ore: gross weight	198	164	244
Iron ore: metal content	105	97	128
Lead concentrates (metric tons)†	5,081	5,000	5,500‡
Zinc concentrates (metric tons)†	35,692	36,000	29,011
Phosphate rock§	7,461	7,890	7,954
Barite (Barytes) (metric tons)	5,539	3,000	1,813
Salt (marine)	616	700	608
Gypsum (crude)‡	125	110	130

* Preliminary figures.
† Figures refer to metal content of concentrates.
‡ Estimated production.
§ Figures refer to gross weight. The estimated phosphoric acid content (in '000 metric tons) was: 2,240 in 2002; 2,370 in 2003.

Source: US Geological Survey.

TUNISIA

Industry

SELECTED PRODUCTS
('000 metric tons, unless otherwise indicated)

	2002	2003	2004
Superphosphates	796	875	872*
Phosphoric acid	1,219	1,164	1,241*
Cement	6,022	6,038	7,124*
Electric power (million kWh)	11,281	n.a.	n.a.
Beer ('000 hectolitres)	1,100	997	n.a.
Wine ('000 hectolitres)	271	246	n.a.
Olive oil	30	70	n.a.
Flour	753	786	n.a.
Refined sugar	126	131	n.a.
Crude steel	200	86	70*
Quicklime	471	446	450*
Motor gasoline ('000 barrels)	3,380	3,600	3,700*
Kerosene ('000 barrels)	1,590	1,270	1,300*
Diesel oil ('000 barrels)	3,500	3,780	4,000*
Residual fuel oil ('000 barrels)	4,020	4,050	3,200*

* Preliminary figure.

Sources: partly UN, *Industrial Commodity Statistics Yearbook*; US Geological Survey.

Finance

CURRENCY AND EXCHANGE RATES

Monetary Units
1,000 millimes = 1 Tunisian dinar (TD).

Sterling, Dollar and Euro Equivalents (30 December 2005)
£1 sterling = 2.348 dinars;
US $1 = 1.363 dinars;
€1 = 1.608 dinars;
100 Tunisian dinars = £42.60 = $73.35 = €62.17.

Average Exchange Rate (dinars per US $)
2003 1.2885
2004 1.2455
2005 1.2974

BUDGET
(million dinars)*

Revenue†	2001	2002	2003‡
Tax revenue	6,222	6,429	6,654
Taxes on income, profits, etc.	1,828	2,025	2,177
Value-added tax	1,930	1,895	2,006
Taxes on trade	655	595	554
Non-tax revenue	683	854	960
Capital revenue	—	7	19
Total	6,904	7,290	7,632

Expenditure§	2001	2002	2003‡
Current expenditure	5,659	5,997	6,317
Wages and salaries	3,392	3,645	3,937
Goods and services	623	627	658
Interest payments	885	915	904
Domestic	396	380	359
External	489	535	546
Transfers and subsidies	758	809	819
Capital expenditure	2,228	2,233	2,305
Direct investment	1,337	1,322	1,335
Capital transfers and equity	891	912	970
Total	7,886	8,230	8,622

* Figures refer to the consolidated accounts of the central Government, including administrative agencies and social security funds. The data exclude the operations of economic and social agencies with their own budgets.
† Excluding grants from abroad (million dinars): 79 in 2001; 118 in 2002; 77 (estimated figure) in 2003. Also excluded are receipts from privatization (million dinars): 11 in 2001; 339 in 2002; 8 in 2003.
‡ Estimated figures.
§ Excluding net lending (million dinars): 102 in 2001; 96 in 2002; 130 (estimated figure) in 2003.

Source: IMF, *Tunisia: Preliminary findings of the 2004 Article IV Consultation Mission* (July 2004).

CENTRAL BANK RESERVES
(US $ million at 31 December)

	2003	2004	2005
Gold (national valuation)	3.6	3.7	3.2
IMF special drawing rights	2.5	9.3	2.2
Reserve position in IMF	30.0	31.4	28.9
Foreign exchange	2,912.9	3,895.0	4,341.1
Total	2,949.0	3,939.4	4,375.4

Source: IMF, *International Financial Statistics*.

MONEY SUPPLY
(million dinars at 31 December)

	2002	2003	2004
Currency outside banks	2,518	2,664	2,968
Demand deposits at commercial banks	3,918	4,178	4,589
Total money (incl. others)	6,892	7,265	8,036

Source: IMF, *International Financial Statistics*.

COST OF LIVING
(Consumer Price Index; base: 2000 = 100)

	2003	2004	2005
Food	109.7	115.1	115.2
Housing	106.3	109.2	112.4
Clothing	104.1	105.8	108.9
Transport	109.1	112.8	118.3
All items (incl. others)	107.6	111.5	113.8

NATIONAL ACCOUNTS
(million dinars at current prices)

Expenditure on the Gross Domestic Product

	2002	2003	2004
Government final consumption expenditure	4,793	5,266	5,560
Private final consumption expenditure	18,727	20,131	22,025
Increase in stocks	87	531	649
Gross fixed capital formation	7,607	7,531	8,023
Total domestic expenditure	31,214	33,459	36,257
Exports of goods and services	13,542	14,094	15,659
Less Imports of goods and services	14,823	15,341	16,812
GDP in purchasers' values	29,933	32,212	35,104
GDP at constant 1990 prices	18,332	19,350	20,481

Source: IMF, *International Financial Statistics*.

TUNISIA

Gross Domestic Product by Economic Activity

	2003	2004	2005
Agriculture and fishing	3,879.1	4,450.3	4,351.7
Mining (excluding hydrocarbons)	228.3	200.4	196.1
Manufacturing (excluding hydrocarbons)	5,753.0	6,207.6	6,431.8
Hydrocarbons, electricity and water	1,369.4	1,633.5	1,832.6
Construction and public works	1,702.8	1,839.9	2,004.4
Transport and telecommunications	2,822.0	3,224.7	3,799.4
Hotels and restaurants	1,794.1	2,000.4	2,199.3
Trade, finance, etc.	6,970.5	7,413.2	8,046.7
Non-market services	4,587.9	4,742.6	5,120.3
Sub-total	29,107.4	31,712.6	33,982.3
Less Imputed bank service charges	759.9	823.6	924.5
GDP at factor cost	28,347.2	30,889.0	33,057.8
Indirect taxes, *less* subsidies	3,864.8	4,259.0	4,532.1
GDP in purchasers' values	32,211.9	35,148.0	37,589.9

BALANCE OF PAYMENTS
(US $ million)

	2002	2003	2004
Exports of goods f.o.b.	6,857	8,027	9,679
Imports of goods f.o.b.	−8,981	−10,297	−12,114
Trade balance	−2,123	−2,269	−2,434
Exports of services	2,681	2,937	3,629
Imports of services	−1,450	−1,612	−1,986
Balance on goods and services	−893	−945	−791
Other income received	72	81	114
Other income paid	−1,056	−1,173	−1,412
Balance on goods, services and income	−1,877	−2,037	−2,088
Current transfers received	1,156	1,343	1,564
Current transfers paid	−25	−36	−31
Current balance	−746	−730	−555
Capital account (net)	75	59	108
Direct investment abroad	−4	−2	−2
Direct investment from abroad	795	541	593
Portfolio investment liabilities	6	14	24
Other investment assets	−882	−428	−283
Other investment liabilities	942	985	1,123
Net errors and omissions	−46	−56	−32
Overall balance	140	383	977

Source: IMF, *International Financial Statistics*.

External Trade

PRINCIPAL COMMODITIES
(million dinars)

Imports c.i.f.	2003	2004	2005
Agricultural and food products	1,261.6	1,526.6	1,626.7
Energy, lubricants, etc.	1,456.2	1,658.0	2,267.7
Minerals, phosphates and related products	318.7	369.5	421.1
Textiles, manufactured garments, leather and leather products	3,409.6	3,326.6	3,303.5
Machinery, electrical products and transport equipment	5,404.7	6,528.5	6,641.1
Transport equipment	998.8	1,210.5	1,265.7
Other industrial machinery, equipment and parts	2,716.9	3,310.6	3,306.4
Electrical machinery, apparatus, etc.	1,689.0	2,007.5	2,068.9
Miscellaneous manufactured articles	2,188.1	2,551.1	2,841.5
Total	14,038.9	15,960.3	17,101.5

Exports f.o.b.	2003	2004	2005
Agricultural and food products	749.9	1,368.9	1,452.6
Energy, lubricants, etc.	1,032.6	1,151.0	1,757.3
Minerals, phosphates and related products	685.9	864.9	953.5
Textiles, manufactured garments, leather and leather products	4,880.6	5,111.8	5,133.1
Machinery, electrical products and transport equipment	2,149.7	2,597.9	3,141.7
Transport equipment	221.4	284.7	351.9
Other industrial machinery, equipment and parts	730.2	806.0	869.0
Electrical machinery, apparatus, etc.	1,198.2	1,507.1	1,920.8
Miscellaneous manufactured articles	843.8	960.5	1,169.4
Total	10,342.6	12,054.9	13,607.7

PRINCIPAL TRADING PARTNERS
(million dinars)*

Imports c.i.f.	2003	2004	2005
Algeria	167.5	93.5	175.7
Belgium	413.8	444.9	449.4
China, People's Republic	238.7	362.5	494.6
France	3,653.0	3,978.1	4,015.8
Germany	1,267.8	1,339.3	1,402.8
Italy	2,804.7	3,011.1	3,578.7
Japan	255.9	317.6	276.4
Libya	460.4	526.9	661.9
Netherlands	285.3	284.3	318.2
Spain	748.8	839.1	879.3
Sweden	166.1	226.5	130.7
Switzerland	165.0	175.8	185.3
United Kingdom	314.1	345.5	376.2
USA	345.4	445.7	424.7
Total (incl. others)	14,038.9	15,960.3	17,101.5

Exports f.o.b.	2003	2004	2005
Algeria	133.4	135.6	237.2
Belgium	405.9	358.9	373.8
France	3,365.5	3,986.7	4,474.8
Germany	1,105.6	1,105.2	1,148.2
India	59.7	106.9	126.7
Italy	2,281.4	3,051.4	3,260.6
Libya	453.8	432.6	612.9
Netherlands	239.1	265.7	292.8
Spain	481.8	729.4	747.0
Switzerland	218.2	49.0	62.6
United Kingdom	337.3	346.6	362.2
Total (incl. others)	10,342.6	12,054.9	13,607.7

* Imports by country of production; exports by country of last destination.

Transport

RAILWAYS
(traffic)

	2001	2002	2003
Passengers carried ('000)	36,827.0	36,560.0	35,725.0
Passenger-kilometres (million)	1,285.0	1,265.0	1,243.0
Freight carried ('000 metric tons)	12,047.0	11,929.0	11,605.0
Freight net ton-kilometres (million)	2,279.1	2,250.0	2,174.0

TUNISIA

ROAD TRAFFIC
(estimates, motor vehicles in use at 31 December)

	2000	2001	2002
Passenger cars	516,525	552,897	585,194
Buses and coaches	11,143	11,973	12,181
Lorries and vans	240,421	253,760	266,499
Road tractors	8,307	9,165	9,605

Source: International Road Federation, *World Road Statistics*.

SHIPPING

Merchant Fleet
(vessels registered at 31 December)

	2002	2003	2004
Number of vessels	75	73	73
Total displacement ('000 grt)	185.5	174.3	175.3

Source: Lloyd's Register-Fairplay, *World Fleet Statistics*.

International Sea-borne Freight Traffic
('000 metric tons)

	2001	2002	2003
Goods loaded*	6,777	6,730	6,717
Goods unloaded	14,971	15,287	13,917

* Excluding Algerian crude petroleum loaded at La Skhirra.

CIVIL AVIATION
(traffic on scheduled services)

	1999	2000	2001
Kilometres flown (million)	27	27	26
Passengers carried ('000)	1,923	1,908	1,926
Passenger-km (million)	2,762	2,690	2,696
Total ton-km (million)	282	284	283

Source: UN, *Statistical Yearbook*.

Tourism

FOREIGN TOURIST ARRIVALS BY NATIONALITY
('000)

	2001	2002	2003
Algeria	623.1	728.3	811.5
Austria	114.8	77.2	70.0
Belgium	150.7	122.1	132.6
France	1,047.4	885.2	834.0
Germany	934.7	613.7	488.5
Italy	398.3	375.2	379.8
Libya	1,016.6	1,280.7	1,325.7
Switzerland	114.2	93.9	85.8
United Kingdom	314.7	257.8	223.2
Total (incl. others)	5,387.3	5,063.5	5,114.3

Receipts from tourism (US $ million, incl. passenger transport): 2,061 in 2001; 1,831 in 2002; 1,935 in 2003.

Source: partly World Tourism Organization.

Communications Media

	2002	2003	2004
Telephones ('000 main lines in use)	1,200.0	1,153.8	1,203.5
Mobile cellular telephones ('000 subscribers)	389.2	1,899.9	3,735.7
Personal computers ('000 in use)	255	400	472
Internet users ('000)	505.5	630.0	835.0

Radio receivers ('000 in use): 2,060 in 1997.

Facsimile machines (number in use): 31,000 in 1997.

Book production (titles): 1,260 in 1999.

Daily newspapers: 7 (average circulation 180,000) in 2000.

Non-daily newspapers: 29 (average circulation 940,000) in 2000.

Periodicals (titles): 182 in 2000 (average circulation 525,000).

Television receivers ('000 in use): 1,900 in 2000.

Sources: UNESCO, *Statistical Yearbook*; UN, *Statistical Yearbook*; and International Telecommunication Union.

Education

(2004/05)

	Institutions	Teachers	Students
Primary	4,494	58,342	1,171,019
Secondary	1,191	59,123	1,084,878
Higher	175	16,671*	311,569*

* Full-time equivalent.

Adult literacy rate (UNESCO estimates): 74.3% (males 83.4%; females 65.3%) in 2003 (Source: UNDP, *Human Development Report*).

Directory

The Constitution

A new Constitution for the Republic of Tunisia was promulgated on 1 June 1959 and amended on 12 July 1988; further amendments were approved by national referendum on 26 May 2002. Its main provisions are summarized below:

NATIONAL ASSEMBLY

Legislative power is exercised by a bicameral parliament: the Chamber of Deputies and the Chamber of Advisers, which was established by the constitutional amendments approved in May 2002. Every citizen who has had Tunisian nationality for at least five years and who has attained 20 years of age has the right to vote. The Chamber of Deputies, which is elected (at the same time as the President) every five years, shall hold two sessions every year, each session lasting not more than three months. Additional meetings may be held at the demand of the President or of a majority of the deputies. The Chamber of Advisers currently consists of 126 members; while this number is revised every six years, it must never exceed two-thirds of the number of members of the Chamber of Deputies. One-third of the members of the Chamber of Advisers is composed of representatives of the main professional unions and federations, one-third by representatives of the 24 governorates (one or two from each governorate, depending on the size of its popula-

TUNISIA

tion), and the remainder are appointed by the President. The members of the Chamber of Advisers serve a six-year term; one-half of its members are replaced every three years.

HEAD OF STATE

The President of the Republic is both Head of State and Head of the Executive. He must be not less than 40 years of age and not more than 75 (not more than 70, prior to the May 2002 amendments). The President is elected by universal suffrage for a five-year term. The amendments approved in May 2002 removed restrictions on the renewal of the presidential mandate (previously, this was renewable twice consecutively). The President is also the Commander-in-Chief of the army and makes both civil and military appointments. The Government may be censured by the National Assembly, in which case the President may dismiss the Assembly and hold fresh elections. If censured by the new Assembly thus elected, the Government must resign. Should the presidency fall vacant for any reason before the end of a President's term of office, the President of the National Assembly shall take charge of affairs of the state for a period of 45 to 60 days. At the end of this period a presidential election shall be organized. The President of the National Assembly shall not be eligible as a presidential candidate.

COUNCIL OF STATE

Comprises two judicial bodies: an administrative body dealing with legal disputes between individuals and state or public bodies, and an audit office to verify the accounts of the state and submit reports.

ECONOMIC AND SOCIAL COUNCIL

Deals with economic and social planning and studies projects submitted by the National Assembly. Members are grouped in seven categories representing various sections of the community.

The Government

HEAD OF STATE

President: ZINE AL-ABIDINE BEN ALI (took office on 7 November 1987; elected 2 April 1989; re-elected 20 March 1994, 24 October 1999 and 24 October 2004).

COUNCIL OF MINISTERS
(April 2006)

Prime Minister: MUHAMMAD GHANNOUCHI.
Minister to the Prime Minister, in charge of Civil Service and Administrative Development: ZOUHAIR MDHAFFER.
Minister of State, Special Adviser to the President and Spokesman for the Presidency: ABD AL-AZIZ BEN DHIA.
Minister of Foreign Affairs: ABDELWAHAB ABDALLAH.
Minister of the Interior and Local Development: RAFIK BELHAJ KACEM.
Minister of National Defence: KAMEL MORJANE.
Minister of Justice and Human Rights: BÉCHIR TEKKARI.
Minister of Religious Affairs: RIDHA AL-AKHZOURI.
Minister Director of the Presidential Office: AHMAD IYADH OUEDERNI.
Minister of Family, Women's, Children's and Elderly Affairs: SALOUA AYACHI LABBEN.
Minister of Social Affairs, Solidarity and Tunisians Abroad: ALI CHAOUCH.
Minister of Education and Training: SADOK KORBI.
Minister of Scientific Research, Technology and Competence Development: TAÏEB HADHRI.
Minister of Culture and Heritage Preservation: MUHAMMAD AL-AZIZ BEN ACHOUR.
Minister of Public Health: RIDHA KECHRID.
Minister of Youth, Sports and Physical Education: ABDALLAH AL-KAÂBI.
Minister of Employment and Professional Integration of Youth: CHADLI LAROUSSI.
Minister of Finance: MUHAMMAD RACHID KECHICHE.
Minister of Agriculture and Water Resources: MUHAMMAD HABIB HADDAD.
Minister of Transport: ABDERRAHIM ZOUARI.
Minister of Tourism: TIJANI HADDAD.
Minister of Trade and Handicrafts: MONDHER ZENAÏDI.
Minister of Equipment, Housing and Territorial Development: SAMIRA KHAYACH BELHAJ.
Minister of Development and International Co-operation: MUHAMMAD NOURI JOUINI.
Minister of State Property and Land Affairs: RIDHA GRIRA.
Minister of Communications and Relations with Parliament: RAFAÂ DKHIL.
Minister of Higher Education: LAZHAR BOU OUNI.
Minister of Industry, Energy and Small and Medium Enterprises: AFIF CHELBI.
Government Secretary-General in charge of Relations with the Chamber of Deputies and the Chamber of Councillors: MUNIR JEIDAN.

There are, in addition, 18 Secretaries of State.

MINISTRIES

Ministry of Agriculture and Water Resources: 30 rue Alain Savary, 1002 Tunis; tel. (71) 786-833; e-mail mag@ministeres.tn.
Ministry of Communication Technologies: 3 bis rue d'Angleterre, 1000 Tunis; tel. (71) 359-000; fax (71) 352-353; e-mail communications@ministeres.tn; internet www.infocom.tn.
Ministry of Culture and Heritage Preservation: 8 rue 2 Mars 1934, la Kasbah, 1006 Tunis; tel. (71) 562-661; fax (71) 574-580; e-mail mcu@ministeres.tn; internet www.culture.tn.
Ministry of Development and International Co-operation: place Ali Zouaoui, 1069 Tunis; tel. (71) 240-133; e-mail boce@mdci.gov.tn.
Ministry of Education and Training: ave Bab Benat, 1030 Tunis; tel. (71) 568-768; e-mail med@ministeres.tn.
Ministry of Employment and Professional Integration of Youth: 10 ave Ouled Haffouz, 1005 Tunis; tel. (71) 790-838; fax (71) 794-615; e-mail mfpe@ministeres.tn.
Ministry of the Environment and Land Planning: Centre Urbain Nord, Ariana, 2080 Tunis; tel. (71) 704-000; fax (71) 702-431; e-mail meat@ministeres.tn; internet www.environnement.nat.tn.
Ministry of Equipment, Housing and Territorial Development: 10 blvd Habib Chita, Cité Jardin, 1002 Tunis; tel. (71) 842-244; fax (71) 780-397; e-mail meh@ministeres.tn.
Ministry of Family, Women's, Children's and Elderly Affairs: 2 rue d'Alger, 1000 Tunis; tel. (71) 336-721; fax (71) 349-900; e-mail maffe@email.ati.tn.
Ministry of Finance: place du Gouvernement, 1008 Tunis; tel. (71) 571-888; fax (71) 963-959; e-mail mfi@ministeres.tn.
Ministry of Foreign Affairs: ave de la Ligue des états arabes, Tunis; tel. (71) 847-500; e-mail mae@ministeres.tn.
Ministry of Higher Education: ave Ouled Haffouz, 1030 Tunis; tel. (71) 786-300; fax (71) 786-711; e-mail mes@mes.rnu.tn; internet www.universites.tn.
Ministry of Industry, Energy and Small and Medium Enterprises: 37 ave Kheireddine Pacha, 1002 Tunis; tel. (71) 289-368; fax (71) 892-350; e-mail mind@ministeres.tn; internet www.tunisieindustrie.nat.tn.
Ministry of the Interior and Local Development: ave Habib Bourguiba, 1000 Tunis; tel. (71) 333-000; fax (71) 340-888; e-mail mint@ministeres.tn.
Ministry of Justice and Human Rights: 31 ave Bab Benat, 1006 Tunis; tel. (71) 561-440; fax (71) 586-106; e-mail mju@ministeres.tn.
Ministry of National Defence: blvd Bab Menara, 1030 Tunis; tel. (71) 560-240; fax (71) 561-804; e-mail mdn@ministeres.tn.
Ministry of Public Health: Bab Saâdoun, 1006 Tunis; tel. (71) 560-545; fax (71) 567-100; e-mail msp@ministeres.tn.
Ministry of Religious Affairs: 176 ave Bab Benat, 1009 Tunis; tel. (71) 570-147; fax (71) 570-283; e-mail mar@ministeres.tn.
Ministry of Scientific Research, Technology and Competence Development: Lotissement en-Nassim, HBC 13, Montplaisir, 1073 Tunis; tel. (71) 796-827; fax (71) 796-165; e-mail mrstdc@ministeres.tn; internet www.mrstdc.gov.tn.
Ministry of Social Affairs, Solidarity and Tunisians Abroad: 25 ave Bab Benat, 1006 Tunis; tel. (71) 567-502; fax (71) 568-722; e-mail mas@ministeres.tn.
Ministry of State Property and Land Affairs: 19 ave de Paris, 1000 Tunis; tel. (71) 341-644; fax (71) 342-410; e-mail mdeaf@ministeres.tn.
Ministry of Tourism: 1 ave Muhammad V, 1001 Tunis; tel. (71) 341-077; fax (71) 332-070; e-mail mta@ministeres.tn; internet www.tunisietourisme.com.
Ministry of Trade and Handicrafts: 37 ave Kheireddine Pacha, 1002 Tunis; tel. (71) 892-313; fax (71) 792-420; e-mail mcmr@ministeres.tn; internet www.artisanat.nat.tn.

Ministry of Transport: 13 rue Montplaisir par l'ave Med V, 1002 Tunis; tel. (71) 285-048; e-mail mtr@ministeres.tn.

President and Legislature

PRESIDENT

Presidential Election, 24 October 2004

Candidate	Votes	% of votes
Zine al-Abidine Ben Ali	4,204,292	94.49
Muhammad Bouchiha	167,986	3.78
Muhammad Ali Halouani	42,213	0.95
Mounir Béji	35,067	0.79
Total*	4,449,558	100.00

* Excluding 14,779 invalid votes.

LEGISLATURE

Majlis an-Nuab
(Chamber of Deputies)

President: FOUAD MEBAZAÂ.

Election, 24 October 2004

Party	Votes	%	Seats
Rassemblement constitutionnel démocratique	3,678,645	87.62	152
Mouvement des démocrates socialistes	194,829	4.64	14
Parti de l'unité populaire	152,987	3.64	11
Union démocratique unioniste	92,708	2.21	7
Mouvement du renouveau	43,268	1.03	3
Parti social libéral	25,261	0.60	2
Others	10,473	0.25	0
Total*	4,198,171	100.00	189†

* Excluding 15,305 spoilt ballot papers.
† Under the terms of an amendment to the electoral code adopted by the National Assembly in 1998, 20% of the seats in the National Assembly (and thus 37 in the current legislature) were reserved for candidates of opposition parties. These were allotted according to the proportion of votes received nationally by each party.

Majlis al-Mustasharin
(Chamber of Advisers)

Speaker: ABDULLAH KALLEL.

Election, 3 July 2005

	Seats*
Representatives of the main professional unions and federations	42
Representatives of the governorates†	43
Appointed by the President‡	41
Total	126

* Members of the Chamber of Advisers serve a six-year term; one-half of its members are replaced every three years.
† One or two members are elected from each of the 24 governorates, depending on the size of its population.
‡ Appointed on 1 August 2005.

Political Organizations

Congrès pour la République: Tunis; e-mail webmaster@tunisie2004.net; internet www.tunisie2004.net/new; f. 2001; Leader MONCEF MARZOUKI.

Forum démocratique pour le travail et les libertés (FDTL): Tunis; internet www.fdtl.org; f. 2002; Leader Dr MUSTAPHA BEN JAFAÂR.

Mouvement des démocrates socialistes (MDS): Tunis; in favour of a pluralist political system; participated in 1981 election and was officially recognized in Nov. 1983; Political Bureau of 11 mems, National Council of 60 mems, normally elected by the party Congress; Sec.-Gen. ISMAIL BOULAHYA.

Mouvement du renouveau (MR—Ettajdid): 6 rue Métouia, 1000 Tunis; tel. (71) 256-400; fax (71) 240-981; f. 1993; successor to Parti communiste tunisien; legal; Sec.-Gen. MUHAMMAD HARMEL; Pres. of Nat. Council MUHAMMAD ALI HALOUANI.

Mouvement de l'unité populaire (MUP): Tunis; supports radical reform; split into two factions, one led by Ahmad Ben Salah living in exile until 1988; the other became the Parti de l'unité populaire (see below); Co-ordinator BRAHIM HAYDER.

Parti démocratique progressiste (PDP): Tunis; e-mail admin@pdpinfo.org; internet pdpinfo.org; f. 1983; as Rassemblement socialiste progressiste, officially recognized in Sept. 1988; changed name as above in 2001; leftist; Sec.-Gen. AHMAD NEJIB CHEBBI.

Parti de la renaissance—Hizb an-Nahdah: Tunis; e-mail nahdha@ezzeitouna.org; internet www.nahdha.net; formerly Mouvement de la tendance islamique (banned in 1981); Leader RACHID GHANNOUCHI; Sec.-Gen. Sheikh ABD AL-FATHA MOUROU.

Parti des ouvriers communistes tunisiens (POCT): Tunis; e-mail pcot@albadil.org; internet www.albadil.org; illegal; Leader HAMMA HAMMANI.

Parti social démocratique libéral (PSDL): 38 rue Gandhi, 1001 Tunis; tel. and fax (71) 812-007; e-mail psl@meet-u.com; f. 1988; officially recognized in Sept. 1988 as the Parti social pour le progrès; renamed Parti social libéral in 1993; adopted present name in 2005; liberal; Pres. MOUNIR BÉJI; Vice-Pres. HOSNI LAHMAR.

Parti de l'unité populaire (PUP): 7 rue d'Autriche, 1002 Tunis; tel. (71) 289-678; fax (71) 796-031; split from MUP (see above); officially recognized in Nov. 1983; Leader MUHAMMAD BOUCHIHA.

Parti des verts pour le progrès (PVP): f. 2006; seeks to promote awareness of the environment; Sec.-Gen. MONGI KHAMASSI.

Rassemblement constitutionnel démocratique (RCD): blvd 9 avril 1938, Tunis; e-mail info@rcd.tn; internet www.rcd.tn; f. 1934 as the Néo-Destour Party, following a split in the Destour (Constitution) Party; renamed Parti socialiste destourien in 1964; adopted present name in Feb. 1988; moderate left-wing republican party, which achieved Tunisian independence; Political Bureau of nine mems, and a Cen. Cttee of 200, elected by the party Congress; Chair. ZINE AL-ABIDINE BEN ALI; First Vice-Chair. HAMED KAROUI; Second Vice-Chair. MUHAMMAD GHANNOUCHI; Sec.-Gen. HÉDI M'HENNI.

Rassemblement national arabe: Tunis; banned in 1981; Leader BASHIR ASSAD.

Union démocratique unioniste (UDU): Tunis; officially recognized in Nov. 1988; supports Arab unity; Sec.-Gen. ABDERRAHMANE TLILI.

Diplomatic Representation

EMBASSIES IN TUNISIA

Algeria: 18 rue de Niger, 1002 Tunis; tel. (71) 783-166; fax (71) 788-804; Ambassador ABDELAZIZ MAOUI.

Argentina: 10 rue al-Hassan et Houssaine, BP 9, al-Menzah IV, 1002 Tunis; tel. (71) 231-222; fax (71) 750-058; e-mail etune@emb_argentina.intl.tn; Ambassador JESÚS FERNANDO TABOADA.

Austria: 16 rue ibn Hamdiss, BP 23, al-Menzah, 1004 Tunis; tel. (71) 751-091; fax (71) 767-824; e-mail autriche@ambassade_autriche.intl.tn; Ambassador Dr WERNER HELMUTH EHRLICH.

Bahrain: 72 rue Mouaouia ibn Soufiane, al-Menzah VI, Tunis; tel. (71) 750-865.

Belgium: 47 rue du 1er juin, BP 24, 1002 Tunis; tel. (71) 781-655; fax (71) 792-797; e-mail tunis@diplobel.org; internet www.diplomatie.be/tunis; Ambassador ROBERT DEVRIESE.

Brazil: 5 rue Sufétula, BP 83, 1002 Tunis; tel. (71) 893-569; fax (71) 846-995; e-mail brasemb.tunis@gnet.tn; Ambassador SÉRGIO BARCELLOS TELLES.

Bulgaria: 5 rue Ryhane, BP 6, Cité Mahragène, 1082 Tunis; tel. (71) 798-962; fax (71) 791-667; e-mail bgtunis.amb@planet.tn; Ambassador TCHAVDAR TCHERVENKOV.

Canada: 3 rue du Sénégal, place d'Afrique, BP 31, Belvédère, 1002 Tunis; tel. (71) 104-000; fax (71) 104-190; e-mail tunis@dfait-maeci.gc.ca; internet www.dfait-maeci.gc.ca/tunisia; Ambassador WILFRID-GUY LICARI.

China, People's Republic: 22 rue Dr Burnet, 1002 Tunis; tel. (71) 780-064; fax (71) 792-631; e-mail chinaemb_tn@mfa.gov.cn; Ambassador LIU YUHE.

Congo, Democratic Republic: 11 rue Tertullien, Notre Dame, Tunis; tel. (71) 281-833; Ambassador MBOLADINGA KATAKO.

Côte d'Ivoire: 17 rue el-Mansoura, BP 21, Belvédère, 1002 Tunis; tel. (71) 755-911; fax (71) 755-901; e-mail ambassade-cotivoire@net.tn; Ambassador KOUASSI GUSTAVE OUFFOUÉ.

Cuba: 1 rue Amilcar, al-Menzah VIII, 1004 Tunis; tel. (71) 767-235; fax (71) 755-922; e-mail embacuba@planet.tn; Ambassador ROLANDO GONZÁLEZ TELLEZ.

TUNISIA

Czech Republic: 98 rue de Palestine, BP 53, Belvédère, 1002 Tunis; tel. (71) 780-456; fax (71) 793-228; e-mail tunis@embassy.msv.cz; internet www.mzv.cz/tunis; Ambassador JAROMÍR PŘIVRATSKÝ.
Denmark: 5 rue de Mauritanie, BP 254, Belvédère, 1002 Tunis; tel. (71) 792-600; fax (71) 790-797; e-mail dannebrog@planet.tn; Ambassador HERLUF HANSEN.
Djibouti: Tunis; Ambassador ALI ABDOU MUHAMMAD.
Egypt: ave Muhammad V, Quartier Montplaisir, rue 8007, Tunis; tel. (71) 792-233; fax (71) 794-389; Ambassador SHADIA FARRAQ.
France: 2 place de l'Indépendence, 1000 Tunis; tel. (71) 105-122; fax (71) 105-190; e-mail presse@ambassadefrance-tn.com; internet www.ambassadefrance-tn.org; Ambassador SERGE DEGALLAIX.
Germany: 1 rue al-Hamra, BP 35, Mutuelleville, 1002 Tunis-Mutuelleville; tel. (71) 786-455; fax (71) 788-242; e-mail reg1@tunis.diplo.de; internet www.tunis.diplo.de; Ambassador Dr PETER SCHMIDT.
Greece: 6 rue Saint Fulgence, Notre Dame, 1082 Tunis; tel. (71) 288-411; fax (71) 789-518; e-mail amb.grec@planet.tn; Ambassador OURAMIA ARVANITI.
Hungary: 12 rue Achtart, Nord Hilton, Tunis; tel. (71) 780-544; fax (71) 781-264; e-mail huembtun@planet.tn; Ambassador Dr GYÖRGY SZATHMÀRY.
India: 4 place Didon, Notre Dame, 1002 Tunis; tel. (71) 787-819; fax (71) 783-394; e-mail amb.tunis@mea.gov.in; Chargé d'affaires a.i. J. P. MEENA.
Indonesia: BP 63, al-Menzah, 1004 Tunis; tel. (71) 860-377; fax (71) 861-758; e-mail kbritun@gnet.tn; Ambassador HERTOMO REKSODIPUTRO.
Iran: 10 rue de Docteur Burnet, Belvédère, 1002 Tunis; tel. (71) 790-084; fax (71) 793-177; Ambassador SAYED BAGHER SAKHAEE.
Iraq: ave Tahar B. Achour, route X2 m 10, Mutuelleville, Tunis; tel. (71) 962-480; fax (71) 963-737; e-mail tunemb@iraqmofamail.net; Ambassador HATIM ABBAS MUHAMMAD ALI.
Italy: 3 rue de Russie, 1002 Tunis; tel. (71) 321-811; fax (71) 324-155; e-mail ambitalia.tunis@email.ati.tn; internet ambitalia-tn.bo.cnr.it; Ambassador ARTURO OLIVIERI.
Japan: 9 rue Apollo XI, BP 163, Cité Mahrajène, 1082 Tunis; tel. (71) 791-251; fax (71) 786-625; Ambassador YASUAKI ONO.
Jordan: 10 Nahj ash-Shankiti, 1002 Tunis; tel. (71) 785-760; fax (71) 786-461; e-mail emb.jordan@planet.tn; Ambassador NAYEF AL-HADID.
Korea, Republic: 16 rue Caracalla, BP 297, Notre Dame, 1082 Tunis; tel. (71) 799-905; fax (71) 791-923; e-mail tunisie@mofat.go.kr; Ambassador CHOE IN-SOP.
Kuwait: 40 route Ariane, al-Menzah, Tunis; tel. (71) 236-811; Ambassador MEJREN AHMAD AL-HAMAD.
Libya: 48 bis rue du 1er juin, Tunis; tel. (71) 236-666; Ambassador ABD AL-ATTI OBEIDI.
Mauritania: 17 rue Fatma Ennechi, BP 62, al-Menzah, Tunis; tel. (71) 234-935; Ambassador MOHAMED LAMINE OULD YAHYA.
Morocco: 39 ave du 1er juin, 1002 Tunis; tel. (71) 782-775; fax (71) 787-103; e-mail sifamatunis@emb_maroc.intl.tn; Ambassador NAJIB ZEROUALI EL-OUARITI.
Netherlands: 6–8 rue Meycen, BP 47, Belvédère, 1082 Tunis; tel. (71) 797-724; fax (71) 785-557; e-mail nlgovtun@planet.tn; internet www.hollandembassy-tunisia.com; Ambassador RITA DULCI RAHMAN.
Norway: BP 124, Les Berges du Lac, 1053 Tunis; tel. (71) 861-777; fax (71) 961-080; e-mail emb.tunis@mfa.no; internet www.norvege-tunisie.org; Ambassador PER KRISTIAN PEDERSEN.
Pakistan: 7 rue Ali ibn Abi Talib, BP 142, al-Menzah VI, 1004 Tunis; tel. (71) 234-366; fax (71) 752-477; e-mail parep@pakemb.intl.tn; Ambassador MOEEN JAN NAEEM.
Poland: 5 Impasse No. 1, rue de Cordoue, El Manar I, Tunis; tel. (71) 873-837; fax (71) 872-987; e-mail polamba.tunis@email.ati.tn; Ambassador ZDZISŁAW RACZYŃSKI.
Portugal: 2 rue Sufétula, Belvédère, 1002 Tunis; tel. (71) 893-981; fax (71) 791-008; e-mail embportunes@embport.intl.tn; Ambassador ARISTIDES VIEIRA GONÇALVES.
Qatar: rue Alhadi Krai, Northern al-Omran Quarter, 1082 Tunis; tel. (71) 849-600; fax (71) 781-620; e-mail tunis@mofa.gov.qa; Ambassador HAMAD BIN HAMAD AL-ATTIYA.
Romania: 18 ave d'Afrique, al-Menzah V, 1004 Tunis; tel. (71) 766-926; fax (71) 767-695; e-mail ambroum@planet.tn; Chargé d'affaires a.i. NICOLAE DUMITRU.
Russia: 4 rue Bergamotes, BP 48, El Manar I, 2092 Tunis; tel. (71) 882-446; fax (71) 882-478; e-mail russie@emb_rus.intl.tn; Ambassador VENYAMIN V. POPOV.
Saudi Arabia: 16 rue d'Autriche, Belvédère, Tunis; tel. (71) 281-295; Ambassador Sheikh ABBAS FAIK GHAZZAOUI.

Senegal: 122 ave de la Liberté, Tunis; tel. (71) 802-397; fax (71) 780-770; Ambassador ABDOURAHMANE SOW.
Serbia and Montenegro: 4 rue de Libéria, 1002 Tunis; tel. (71) 783-057; fax (71) 796-482; e-mail yuamb.1@gnet.tn; Ambassador MILORAD JOVANOVIĆ.
Somalia: 6 rue Hadramout, Mutuelleville, Tunis; tel. (71) 289-505; Ambassador AHMAD ABDALLAH MUHAMMAD.
South Africa: 7 rue Achtart, Nord Hilton, 1082 Tunis; tel. (71) 800-311; fax (71) 796-742; e-mail sa@emb-safrica.intl.tn; internet www.southafrica.intl.tn; Ambassador DANIEL NICHOLAAS MEYER.
Spain: 22-24 ave Dr Ernest Conseil, Cité Jardin, 1002 Tunis; tel. (71) 782-217; fax (71) 786-267; e-mail emb.tunez@mae.es; Ambassador JUAN MANUEL CABRERA HERNÁNDEZ.
Sudan: 30 ave d'Afrique, Tunis; tel. (71) 238-544; fax (71) 750-884.
Switzerland: BP 56, Les Berges du Lac, 1053 Tunis; tel. (71) 962-997; fax (71) 965-796; e-mail vertretung@tun.rep.admin.ch; Ambassador PETER VON GRAFFENRIED.
Syria: 119 Azzouz Ribai-Almanar 3, Tunis; tel. (71) 888-188; Ambassador Dr SAMI GLAIEL.
Turkey: Lot 4, ave Hédi Karray, Centre Urban Nord, 1082 Tunis; tel. (71) 750-668; fax (71) 767-045; e-mail tunus.be@planet.tn; Ambassador H. SELAH KORUTÜRK.
Ukraine: 7 rue Saint Fulgence, Notre Dame, 1002 Tunis; tel. (71) 845-861; fax (71) 840-866; e-mail ambassade.ukraine@planet.tn; Chargé d'affaires a.i. OLEKSANDR DEMYANYUK.
United Arab Emirates: 9 rue Achtart, Nord Hilton, Belvédère, 1002 Tunis; tel. (71) 783-522; e-mail emirates.embassy@planet.tn; Ambassador MUHAMMAD HAMAD OMRANE.
United Kingdom: Rue du Lac Windermere, Les Berges du Lac, 1053 Tunis; tel. (71) 108-700; fax (71) 108-769; e-mail british.emb@planet.tn; internet www.britishembassy.gov.uk/tunisia; Ambassador ALAN GOULTY.
USA: Les Berges du Lac, 1053 Tunis; tel. (71) 107-000; fax (71) 107-090; e-mail tuniswebsitecontact@state.gov; internet tunis.usembassy.gov; Ambassador WILLIAM J. HUDSON.
Yemen: rue Mouaouia ibn Soufiane, al-Menzah VI, Tunis; tel. (71) 237-933; Ambassador RASHID MUHAMMAD THABIT.

Judicial System

The **Cour de Cassation** in Tunis has three civil and one criminal sections. There are three **Cours d'Appel** at Tunis, Sousse and Sfax, and 13 **Cours de Première Instance**, each having three chambers, except the **Cour de Première Instance** at Tunis which has eight chambers. **Justices Cantonales** exist in 51 areas.

Religion

The Constitution of 1956 recognizes Islam as the state religion, with the introduction of certain reforms, such as the abolition of polygamy. An estimated 99% of the population are Muslims. Minority religions include Judaism (an estimated 2,000 adherents in 1993) and Christianity. The Christian population comprises Roman Catholics, Greek Orthodox, and French and English Protestants.

ISLAM

Grand Mufti of Tunisia: Sheikh KAMAL AD-DIN JA'EIT.

CHRISTIANITY

The Roman Catholic Church

There were an estimated 20,000 adherents in Tunisia in December 2003.

Bishops' Conference: 4 rue d'Alger, 1000 Tunis; tel. (71) 335-831; fax (71) 335-832; e-mail eveche.tunisie@evechetunisie.org; f. 1964; Pres. Bishop of Tunis Most Rev. FOUAD TWAL; Sec.-Gen. RAMÓN ECHEVERRÍA.

The Protestant Church

Reformed Church of Tunisia: 36 rue Charles de Gaulle, 1000 Tunis; tel. (71) 327-886; e-mail eglisereformee@yahoo.fr; f. 1880; c. 220 mems; Pastor WILLIAM BROWN.

The Press

DAILIES

Ach-Chourouk (Sunrise): 10 rue ach-Cham, Tunis; tel. (71) 331-000; fax (71) 253-024; e-mail directiongenerale@alchourouk.com; internet www.alchourouk.com; Dir SLAHEDDINE AL-AMRI; circ. 70,000.

El-Horria: 8 rue de Rome, Tunis; tel. (71) 351-719; internet www.tunisieinfo.com/alhorria; Arabic; organ of the RCD; Dir MUHAMMAD HÉDI TRIKI; circ. 50,000.

La Presse de Tunisie: 6 rue Ali Bach-Hamba, 1000 Tunis; tel. (71) 341-066; fax (71) 349-720; e-mail contact@lapresse.tn; internet www.lapresse.tn; f. 1936; French; Dir-Gen. ZOHRA BEN ROMDHANE; circ. 40,000.

Le Quotidien: 25 rue Jean Jaurès, 1000 Tunis; tel. (71) 331-000; fax (71) 235-024; e-mail directiongenerale@lequotidien-tn.com; internet www.lequotidien-tn.com; f. 2001; French; Dir SLAHEDDINE AL-AMRI; circ. 20,000.

Le Renouveau: 8 rue de Rome, 1000 Tunis; tel. (71) 352-498; fax (71) 351-927; internet www.tunisieinfo.com/LeRenouveau; f. 1988; organ of the RCD; French; Dir and Editor-in-Chief NEJIB OUERGHI.

As-Sabah (The Morning): blvd du 7 novembre, BP 441, al-Menzah, 1004 Tunis; tel. (71) 723-361; fax (71) 717-222; e-mail info@assabah.com.tn; internet www.assabah.com.tn; f. 1951; Arabic; Dir HABIB CHEIKHROUHOU; circ. 50,000.

As-Sahafa: 6 rue Ali Bach-Hamba, Tunis; tel. (71) 341-066; fax (71) 349-720; internet www.sahafa.com; f. 1936; Arabic; Dir MONCEF GUUJA.

Le Temps: ave 7 novembre 1987, al-Menzah, 1004 Tunis; tel. (71) 717-222; fax (71) 723-361; e-mail letemps@gnet.tn; internet www.letemps.com.tn; f. 1975; French; Dir HABIB CHEIKHROUHOU; circ. 42,000.

PERIODICALS

Afrique Economie: 16 rue de Rome, BP 61, 1015 Tunis; tel. (71) 347-441; fax (71) 353-172; e-mail iea@planet.tn; f. 1970; monthly; Dir MUHAMMAD ZERZERI.

Al-Akhbar (The News): 1 passage d'al-Houdaybiyah, Tunis; tel. (71) 344-100; internet www.akhbar.tn; f. 1984; weekly; general; Dir MUHAMMAD BEN YOUSUF; circ. 75,000.

Les Annonces: 6 rue de Sparte, BP 1343, Tunis; tel. (71) 350-177; fax (71) 347-184; f. 1978; 2 a week; French/Arabic; Dir MUHAMMAD NEJIB AZOUZ; circ. 170,000.

Al-Anouar at-Tounissia (Tunisian Lights): 10 rue ach-Cham, 1002 Tunis; tel. (71) 331-000; fax (71) 340-600; Dir SLAHEDDINE AL-AMRI; circ. 165,000.

L'Avenir: 26 rue Gamal Abd an-Nasser, BP 1200, Tunis; tel. (71) 258-941; f. 1980; weekly; organ of Mouvement des démocrates socialistes (MDS).

Al-Bayan (The Manifesto): 87 ave Jughurta, Belvédère, 1002 Tunis; tel. (71) 791-098; fax (71) 796-400; e-mail darelbayane@fnet.tn; f. 1977; weekly; general; Dir HÉDI DJILANI; Editorial Dir HÉDI BÉHI; circ. 100,000.

Al-Biladi (My Country): 15 rue 2 mars 1934, Tunis; f. 1974; Arabic; political and general weekly for Tunisian workers abroad; Dir HÉDI AL-GHALI; circ. 90,000.

Bulletin Mensuel de Statistiques: Institut National de la Statistique, 70 rue al-Cham, BP 265, 1080 Tunis; tel. (71) 891-002; fax (71) 792-559; e-mail ins@mdci.gov.tn; internet www.ins.nat.tn; monthly.

Conjoncture: 37 ave Kheireddine Pacha, 1002 Tunis; tel. (71) 891-826; fax (71) 574-112; e-mail conjoncture2003@yahoo.fr; f. 1974; monthly; economic and financial surveys; Dir HABIB BEDHIAFI; circ. 5,000.

Démocratie: Tunis; f. 1978; monthly; French; organ of the MDS; Dir HASSIB BEN AMMAR; circ. 5,000.

Dialogue: 15 rue 2 mars 1934, Tunis; tel. (71) 264-899; f. 1974; weekly; French; cultural and political organ of the RCD; Dir NACEUR BECHEKH; circ. 30,000.

Etudiant Tunisien: Tunis; f. 1953; French and Arabic; Chief Editor FAOUZI AOUAM.

Al-Fajr (Dawn): Tunis; f. 1990; weekly; Arabic; publ. of the Hizb an-Nahdah movement; Dir HAMADI JEBALI (imprisoned Jan. 1991).

Al-Falah: rue Alain Savary, al-Khadra, 1003 Tunis; tel. (71) 800-800; fax (71) 798-598; weekly; agricultural; Dir ABD AL-BAKI BACHA; Editor GHARBI HAMOUDA; circ. 7,000.

Al-Fikr (Thought): Tunis; f. 1955; monthly; Arabic; cultural review.

L'Hebdo Touristique: rue 8601, 40, Zone Industrielle, La Charguia 2, 2035 Tunis; tel. (71) 786-866; fax (71) 794-891; f. 1971; weekly; French; tourism; Dir TIJANI HADDAD; circ. 5,000.

IBLA: Institut des Belles Lettres Arabes, 12 rue Jemaâ el-Haoua, 1008 Tunis; tel. (71) 560-133; fax (71) 572-683; e-mail ibla@gnet.tn; internet www.iblatunis.org; 2 a year; French; social and cultural review on Maghreb and Muslim-Arab affairs; Dirs J. FONTAINE, D. BOND; circ. 800.

Al-Idhaa wa Talvaza (Radio and Television): 71 ave de la Liberté, Tunis; tel. and fax (71) 796-691; f. 1956; fortnightly; Arabic language broadcasting magazine; Dir MUSTAPHA KHAMMARI; Editor JAMEL KARMAOUI.

Irfane (Children): 6 rue Muhammad Ali, 1000 Tunis; tel. (71) 256-877; fax (71) 351-521; f. 1965; monthly; Arabic; Dir-Gen. RIDHA EL OUADI; circ. 100,000.

Jeunesse Magazine: 6 rue Muhammad Ali, 1000 Tunis; tel. (71) 256-877; fax (71) 351-521; f. 1980; monthly; Arabic; Dir-Gen. RIDHA EL OUADI; circ. 30,000.

Journal Officiel de la République Tunisienne: ave Farhat Hached, 2040 Radès; tel. (71) 299-914; fax (71) 297-234; f. 1860; the official gazette; French and Arabic editions published twice weekly by the Imprimerie Officielle (The State Press); Pres. and Dir-Gen. ROMDHANE BEN MIMOUN; circ. 20,000.

Al-Maoukif: Tunis; e-mail mawkef_21@yahoo.fr; weekly; organ of the Parti démocratique progressiste; Dir AHMAD NEJIB CHABI; Editor-in-Chief RASHID KHASHANA.

Al-Maraa (The Woman): 56 blvd Bab Benat, 1006 Tunis; tel. (71) 567-845; fax (71) 567-131; e-mail unft@email.a.t.i.tn; f. 1961; monthly; Arabic/French; political, economic and social affairs; issued by the Union Nationale de la Femme Tunisienne; Pres. AZIZA HABIRA; circ. 10,000.

Le Mensuel: Tunis; f. 1984; monthly; economic, social and cultural affairs.

Al-Moussawar: 10 rue ach-Cham, Tunis; tel. (71) 289-000; fax (71) 289-357; weekly; circ. 75,000.

Outrouhat: Tunis; monthly; scientific; Dir LOTFI BEN AÏSSA.

Ar-Rai (Opinion): Tunis; f. 1977; by MDS; weekly; opposition newspaper; Dir HASSIB BEN AMMAR; circ. 20,000.

Réalités: 85 rue de Palestine, Belvédère, BP 227, 1002 Tunis; tel. (71) 788-313; fax (71) 893-489; e-mail sof@realites.com.tn; internet www.realites.com.tn; f. 1979; weekly; French/Arabic; Dir TAÏEB ZAHAR; circ. 25,000.

At-Tariq al-Jadid (New Road): 6 rue Metouia, Tunis; tel. (71) 256-400; fax (71) 350-748; f. 1981; organ of the Mouvement du renouveau; Editor MUHAMMAD HARMEL.

Tounes al-Khadra: rue Alain Savary, 1003 Tunis; tel. (71) 800-800; fax (71) 798-598; f. 1976; monthly; agricultural, scientific and technical; Dir ABD AL-BAKI BACHA; Editor GHARBI HAMOUDA; circ. 5,000.

Tunis Hebdo: 1 passage d'al-Houdaybiyah, Tunis; tel. (71) 344-100; fax (71) 355-079; e-mail tunishebdo@tunishebdo.com.tn; internet www.tunishebdo.com.tn; f. 1973; weekly; French; general and sport; Dir MUHAMMAD BEN YOUSUF; circ. 35,000.

Tunisia News: rue 8601, 40, Zone Industrielle, La Charguia 1, 2035 Tunis; tel. (71) 786-866; fax (71) 794-891; e-mail haddad.tijani@planet.tn; f. 1993; weekly; English; Dir TIJANI HADDAD; circ. 5,000.

NEWS AGENCIES

Tunis Afrique Presse (TAP): 7 ave Slimane Ben Slimane, al-Manar, 2092 Tunis; tel. (71) 889-000; fax (71) 883-500; e-mail desk.intern@email.ati.tn; internet www.tap.info.tn; f. 1961; Arabic, French and English; offices in Algiers, Rabat, Paris and New York; daily news services; Chair. and Gen. Man. MUHAMMAD BEN EZZEDDINE.

Foreign Bureaux

Agence France-Presse (AFP): 45 ave Habib Bourguiba, Tunis; tel. (71) 337-896; fax (71) 352-414; e-mail pvro.afp@gnet.tn; Chief PATRICK VAN ROEKEGHEM.

Agencia EFE (Spain): 126 rue de Yougoslavie, 1000 Tunis; tel. (71) 321-497; fax (71) 325-976; e-mail manostos@gnet.tn; Chief MANUEL OSTOS LÓPEZ.

Agenzia Nazionale Stampa Associata (ANSA) (Italy): Tunis; Chief MANUELA FONTANA.

Informatsionnoye Telegrafnoye Agentstvo Rossii—Telegrafnoye Agentstvo Suverennykh Stran (ITAR—TASS) (Russia): Tunis; Chief VIKTOR LEBEDEV.

Inter Press Service (IPS) (Italy): 80 ave Tahar Ben Ammar, al-Menzah IX, 1013 Tunis; tel. (71) 880-182; fax (71) 880-848; f. 1976; Chief ABD AL-MAJID BEJAR.

Kuwait News Agency (KUNA): Tunis; tel. (71) 717-624; fax (71) 718-062.

TUNISIA

Reuters (United Kingdom): 3 rue ibn Rachiq, BP 369, Belvédère, 1002 Tunis; tel. (71) 787-711; fax (71) 787-454; Senior Correspondent ABD AL-AZIZ BARROUHI.

Rossiiskoye Informatsionnoye Agentstvo—Novosti (RIA—Novosti) (Russia): 102 ave de la Liberté, Tunis; tel. (71) 283-781; Chief NICOLAS SOLOGUBOVSKII.

Saudi Press Agency (SPA): Tunis.

Xinhua (New China) News Agency (People's Republic of China): 6 rue Smyrne, Notre Dame, Tunis; tel. (71) 281-308; Dir XIE BINYU.

Publishers

Ad-Dar al-Arabia Lil Kitab: 4 ave Mohieddine el-Klibi, al-Manar, BP 32, al-Manar 2, 2092 Tunis; tel. (71) 888-255; fax (71) 888-365; f. 1975; general literature, children's books, non-fiction; Dir-Gen. MUSTAPHA ATTIA.

Bouslama Editions: 15 ave de France, 1000 Tunis; tel. (71) 243-745; fax (71) 381-100; f. 1960; history, children's books; Man. Dir ALI BOUSLAMA.

Centre de Publications Universitaires: Campus Universitaire, BP 255, 1080 Tunis; tel. (71) 874-000; fax (71) 871-677; e-mail cpu@cpu.rnu.tn; internet www.mes.tn/cpu.

Cérès Editions: 6 rue Alain Savary, Belvédère, 1002 Tunis; tel. (71) 280-550; fax (71) 287-216; e-mail info@ceres-editions.com; internet www.ceres-editions.com; f. 1964; art books, literature, novels; Pres. MUHAMMAD BEN SMAIL.

Dar Cheraït: Centre Culturel et Touristique Dar Cheraït, Route Touristique, 2200 Tozeur; tel. (76) 452-100; fax (76) 452-329; e-mail darcherait@planet.tn; internet www.darcherait.com.tn.

Dar al-Kitab: 5 ave Bourguiba, 4000 Sousse; tel. (73) 25097; f. 1950; literature, children's books, legal studies, foreign books; Pres. TAÏEB KACEM; Dir FAYÇAL KACEM.

Dar as-Sabah: Centre Interurbain, BP 441, al-Menzah, 1004 Tunis; tel. (71) 717-222; fax (71) 718-366; f. 1951; 200 mems; publishes daily and weekly papers which circulate throughout Tunisia, North Africa, France, Belgium, Luxembourg and Germany; Dir-Gen. MONCEF CHEIKHROUHOU.

Editions Apollonia: 4 rue Claude Bernard, 1002 Tunis; tel. (71) 786-381; fax (71) 799-190; e-mail hannibal@apollonia.com.tn; internet www.apollonia.com.tn.

Institut National de la Statistique: 70 rue al-Cham, BP 265, 1080 Tunis; tel. (71) 891-002; fax (71) 792-559; e-mail ins@mdci.gov.tn; internet www.ins.nat.tn; publishes a variety of annuals, periodicals and papers concerned with the economic policy and devt of Tunisia.

Librairie al-Manar: 60 ave Bab Djedid, BP 179, 1008 Tunis; tel. (71) 253-224; fax (71) 336-565; e-mail librairie.almanar@planet.tn; f. 1938; general, educational, Islam; Man. Dir HABIB M'HAMDI.

Maison Tunisienne d'Edition: Tunis; f. 1966; all kinds of books, magazines, etc.; Dir ABDELAZIZ ACHOURI.

Société d'Arts Graphiques, d'Edition et de Presse: 15 rue 2 mars 1934, La Kasbah, Tunis; tel. (71) 264-988; fax (71) 569-736; f. 1974; prints and publishes daily papers, magazines, books, etc.; Chair. and Man. Dir HASSAN FERJANI.

Sud Editions: 79 rue de Palestine, 1002 Tunis; tel. (71) 785-179; fax (71) 848-664; f. 1976; Arab literature, art and art history, history, sociology, religion; Man. Dir M. MASMOUDI.

GOVERNMENT PUBLISHING HOUSE

Imprimerie Officielle de la République Tunisienne: ave Farhat Hached, 2040 Radès; tel. (71) 434-211; fax (71) 434-234; f. 1860; Man. Dir ROMDHANE BEN MIMOUN.

Broadcasting and Communications

TELECOMMUNICATIONS

Société Tunisienne d'Entreprises des Télécommunications (SOTETEL): rue des Entrepreneurs, Zone Industrielle, BP 640, La Charguia 2, 1080 Tunis; tel. (71) 941-100; fax (71) 940-584; e-mail sotetel@email.ati.tn; internet www.sotetel.com.tn; transferred to private ownership in 1998; Dir-Gen. MHÉDI DRIDI.

Orascom Telecom Tunisia: 11 rue 8607, Zone Industrielle, La Charguia 1, 2035 Tunis; internet www.otelecom.com; Chair. and CEO NAGUIB SAWIRIS.

Tunisie Télécom: 41 rue Asdrubal, 1002 Tunis; tel. (71) 801-717; fax (71) 800-777; e-mail actel.virtuelle@ttnet.tn; internet www.tunisietelecom.tn; Pres. and Gen. Man. AHMED MAHJOUB.

BROADCASTING

Radio

Etablissement de la Radiodiffusion-Télévision Tunisienne (ERTT): 71 ave de la Liberté, 1002 Tunis; tel. (71) 847-300; fax (71) 781-058; e-mail info@radiotunis.com; internet www.radiotunis.com; govt service; broadcasts in Arabic, French, German, Italian, Spanish and English; radio stations at Gafsa, El-Kef, Monastir, Sfax, Tataouine and Tunis (three); television stations Tunis 7 and Canal 21; Pres. MUSTAPHA KHAMMARI.

Radio Mosaïque: Tunis; e-mail dg@mosaiquefm.net; internet www.mosaiquefm.net; f. 2003; first privately-owned radio station when launched in 2003; broadcasts in Arabic and French to Tunis and the north-east of the country; Dir-Gen. NOUREDDINE BOUTAR.

Television

Television was introduced in northern and central Tunisia in January 1966, and by 1972 transmission covered the country. A relay station to link up with European transmissions was built at al-Haouaria in 1967, and a second channel was introduced in 1983.

Etablissement de la Radiodiffusion-Télévision Tunisienne: see Radio..

Office National de la Télédiffusion (ONT): 13 rue de Bizerte, 1006 Tunis; tel. (71) 794-609.

Finance

(cap. = capital; dep. = deposits; res = reserves; m. = million; brs = branches; amounts in dinars unless otherwise stated)

BANKING

Central Bank

Banque Centrale de Tunisie (BCT): 25 rue Hédi Nouira, BP 777, 1080 Tunis; tel. (71) 340-588; fax (71) 354-214; e-mail boc@bct.gov.tn; internet www.bct.gov.tn; f. 1958; cap. 6.0m., res 32.8m.,dep. 2,526.7m., total assets 4,666.8m. (Dec. 2001); Gov. TAOUFIK BACCAR; 10 brs.

Commercial Banks

AMEN Bank: ave Muhammad V, 1002 Tunis; tel. (71) 835-500; fax (71) 833-517; e-mail amen.bank@amenbank.com.tn; internet www.amenbank.com.tn; f. 1967 as Crédit Foncier et Commercial de Tunisie; changed name as above in 1995; cap. 70.0m., res 91.9m., dep. 1,604.1m. (Dec. 2003); Chair. and Pres. RACHID BEN YEDDER; Gen. Man. AHMAD EL-KARM; 73 brs.

Arab Banking Corpn Tunisie: ABC Building, rue du Lac d'Annecy, Les Berges du Lac, 1053 Tunis; tel. (71) 861-861; fax (71) 860-427; e-mail abc.tunis@arabbanking.com; internet www.arabbanking.com; f. 2000; cap. 18m., dep. 83m. (Dec. 2004); Chair. AGELI ABDESSALEM BRENI; Gen. Man. SADOK ATTIA; 4 brs.

Arab Tunisian Bank: 9 rue Hédi Nouira, POB 520, 1001 Tunis; tel. (71) 351-155; fax (71) 342-852; e-mail atbbank@atb.com.tn; internet www.atb.com.tn; f. 1982; cap. 35m., res 50.9m., dep. 858.9m. (Dec. 2001); Pres. ABDELHAMEED ABDELMAJEED SHOMAN; Gen. Man. MUHAMMAD FERID BEN TANFOUS; 32 brs.

Banque de l'Habitat: 21 ave Kheireddine Pacha, BP 242, 1002 Tunis; tel. (71) 785-277; fax (71) 784-417; e-mail banquehabitat@bh.fin.tn; internet www.bh.com.tn; f. 1984; 57.4% govt-owned; cap. and res 79.3m., total assets 1,590.7m. (Dec. 1998); Pres. and Gen. Dir ABOU HAFS AMOR NAJÏ; 49 brs.

Banque Internationale Arabe de Tunisie (BIAT): 70–72 ave Habib Bourguiba, BP 520, 1080 Tunis; tel. (71) 340-733; fax (71) 342-820; e-mail abderrazak.lahiani@biat.com.tn; internet www.biat.com.tn; f. 1976; cap. 100.0m., res 128.2m., dep. 2,659.4m. (Dec. 2004); Pres. and Dir-Gen. CHÉKIB NOUIRA; 102 brs.

Banque Nationale Agricole: rue Hédi Nouira, 1001 Tunis; tel. (71) 831-000; fax (71) 835-551; f. 1989 by merger of the Banque Nationale du Développement Agricole and the Banque Nationale de Tunisie; cap. 100.0m., res 236.3m., dep. 2,786.4m. (Dec. 2002); Pres. and Gen. Man. MONCEF DAKHLI; Gen. Sec. FAOUZIA OUNIS; 140 brs.

Banque du Sud: 95 ave de la Liberté, 1002 Tunis; tel. (71) 849-400; fax (71) 790-945; e-mail courier@banksud.com.tn; internet www.banksud.com.tn; f. 1968; cap. 100.0m., res 50.8m., dep. 1,418.1m. (Dec. 2002); consortium of Attijariwafa Bank (Morocco) and Banco Santander (Spain) bought a 33.54% interest in Dec. 2005; Pres. MONCEF CHEFFAR; Dir-Gen. MUHAMMAD HAITAMI; 93 brs.

Banque de Tunisie SA: 2 rue de Turquie, BP 289, 1001 Tunis; tel. (71) 332-188; fax (71) 349-401; e-mail finance@bt.com.tn; f. 1884; cap. 50.0m., res 172.8m., dep. 1,053.2m. (June 2005); Chair. and Man. Dir FAOUZI BEL KAHIA; 5 brs and 82 agencies.

Citibank N.A.: 55 ave Jugurtha, BP 72, Belvédère, 1001 Tunis; tel. (71) 785-136; fax (71) 785-556; e-mail lilia.benyahya@citigroup.com; f. 1989; cap. 10m., total assets 387m. (Dec. 1998); Gen. Man. NAYERA N. AMIN; 2 brs.

Société Tunisienne de Banque (STB): rue Hédi Nouira, BP 638, 1001 Tunis; tel. (71) 340-477; fax (71) 348-400; e-mail stb@stb.com.tn; internet www.stb.com.tn; f. 1957; 50% govt-owned; merged with Banque Nationale de Développement Touristique and Banque de Développement Economique de Tunisie in 2000; cap. 124.4m., res 280.1m., dep. 2,613.4m. (Dec. 2002); Chair. MUHAMMAD EL-BÉJI HAMDA; Pres. LAROUSSI BAYOUDH; 116 brs.

Union Bancaire pour le Commerce et l'Industrie: 139 ave de la Liberté, Belvédère, 1002 Tunis; tel. (71) 842-000; fax (71) 346-737; e-mail dg@ubci.com.tn; internet www.ubci.com.tn; f. 1961; cap. 35.0m., res 106.2m., dep. 813.3m. (Dec. 2002); affiliated to Banque Nationale de Paris Intercontinentale; Pres. and Gen. Man. SLAHEDDINE BOUGERRA; 39 brs.

Union Internationale de Banques SA: 65 ave Habib Bourguiba, BP 109, 1000 Tunis; tel. (71) 347-000; fax (71) 353-090; e-mail lilia.meddeb@uib.fin.tn; internet www.uib.com.tn; f. 1963 as a merging of Tunisian interests by the Société Tunisienne de Banque with Crédit Lyonnais (France) and other foreign banks, including Banca Commerciale Italiana; cap. 70.0m., res 40.9m., dep. 1,441.8m. (Dec. 2001); Gen. Man. ALI KOOLI; 94 brs.

Merchant Banks

Banque d'Affaires de Tunisie (BAT): 32 rue Hédi Karray, 1082 Tunis; tel. (71) 703-175; fax (71) 703-6804; e-mail bat@bat.com.tn; internet www.bat-tunisie.com; f. 1997; cap. 4.5m.; Gen. Man. HABIB KARAOUL.

International Maghreb Merchant Bank (IM Bank): Immeuble Maghrebia, Bloc B, 2035 Tunis; tel. (71) 860-816; fax (71) 860-057; f. 1995; auth. cap. 3m., total assets 3.1m. (Dec. 1995); Pres. MONCEF CHEIKH-ROUHOU; CEO KACEM BOUSNINA.

Development Banks

Banque Arabe Tuniso-Libyenne de Développement et de Commerce Extérieur: 25 ave Kheireddine Pacha, BP 102, Belvédère, 1002 Tunis; tel. (71) 781-500; fax (71) 782-818; f. 1983; promotes trade and devt projects between Tunisia and Libya, and provides funds for investment in poorer areas; cap. 100.0m., res 21.4m., dep. 63.3m. (Dec. 2001); Pres. and Man. Dir SAÏD M'RABET.

Banque de Tunisie et des Emirats d'Investissement: 5 bis blvd Muhammad Badra, 1002 Tunis; tel. (71) 783-600; fax (71) 783-756; scheduled to merge with Union Internationale de Banques; Dir-Gen. MONCEF DAKHLI.

Banque Tunisienne de Solidarité (BTS): 56 ave Muhammad V, 1002 Tunis; tel. (71) 844-040; fax (71) 845-537; e-mail bts@email.ati.tn; f. 1997; provides medium- and short-term finance for small-scale projects; cap. 40m.; Pres. NAÏJA AHMED; 25 brs.

Banque Tuniso-Koweïtienne de Développement: 10 bis ave Muhammad V, BP 49, 1001 Tunis; tel. (71) 340-000; fax (71) 343-106; e-mail ask@btkd-bank.com; internet www.btkd-bank.com; f. 1981; provides long-term finance for devt projects; cap. 100m., res 74.9m. (Dec. 2000); Dir-Gen. ANOUAR BELARBI.

Société Tuniso-Séoudienne d'Investissement et de Développement (STUSID): 32 rue Hédi Karray, BP 20, 1082 Tunis; tel. (71) 718-233; fax (71) 719-233; e-mail commercial@stusid.com.tn; internet www.stusid.com.tn; f. 1981; provides long-term finance for devt projects; cap. 100.0m., res 84.4m., dep. 10.5m. (Dec. 2002); Chair. Dr ABD AL-AZIZ A. AN-NASRALLAH; Pres. and Dir-Gen. ABD AL-WAHEB NACHI.

'Offshore' Banks

Alubaf International Bank: rue Montplaisir, BP 51, Belvédère, 1002 Tunis; tel. (71) 793-500; fax (71) 793-905; e-mail alub.tn@gnet.tn; f. 1985; cap. US $25.0m., res $5.5m., dep. $62.5m. (Dec. 2002); Chair. Dr AHMAD MNEISSI; Gen. Man. BASHIR MUHAMMAD EL-AGHEL.

Beit Ettamwil Saudi Tounsi (BEST): 88 ave Hédi Chaker, 1002 Tunis; tel. (71) 790-000; fax (71) 780-235; f. 1983; cap. US $50m., total assets $156.0m. (Dec. 1996); Pres. Dr SALAH JEMIL MALAIKA.

North Africa International Bank: ave Kheireddine Pacha, 1002 Tunis; tel. (71) 950-800; fax (71) 950-840; e-mail naib@planet.tn; f. 1984; cap. US $30.0m., res $17.0m., dep. $85.3m. (2003); Chair. and Gen. Man. SADDIK M. HIJJAJI.

Tunis International Bank: 18 ave des Etats-Unis d'Amérique, BP 81, 1002 Tunis; tel. (71) 782-411; fax (71) 782-223; e-mail tib1.tib@planet.tn; internet www.tib.com.tn; f. 1982; cap. US $25.0m., res $10.1m., dep. $234.1m. (Dec. 2002); Chair. ZOUHAIR KHOURI; 3 brs.

STOCK EXCHANGE

Bourse de Tunis: Centre Babel, Bloc E, Zone Montplaisir, 1002 Tunis; tel. (71) 799-414; fax (71) 789-189; e-mail hamdi.bannour@bvmt.com.tn; internet www.bvmt.com.tn; Chair. AHMED HADDOUEJ.

INSURANCE

Caisse Tunisienne d'Assurances Mutuelles Agricoles: 6 ave Habib Thameur, 1069 Tunis; tel. (71) 340-933; fax (71) 332-276; f. 1912; Pres. MOKTAR BELLAGHA; Dir-Gen. MEZRI JELIZI.

Cie d'Assurances Tous Risques et de Réassurance (ASTREE): 45 ave Kheireddine Pacha, BP 780, 1002 Tunis; tel. (71) 792-211; fax (71) 794-723; e-mail courrier@astree.com.tn; internet www.astree.com.tn; f. 1950; cap. 4m.; Pres. and Dir-Gen. MUHAMMAD HACHICHA.

Cie Tunisienne pour l'Assurance du Commerce Extérieur (COTUNACE): ave Muhammad V/Montplaisir I, rue 8006, 1002 Tunis; tel. (71) 783-000; fax (71) 782-539; e-mail cotunace2@email.ati.tn; internet www.cotunace.com.tn; f. 1984; cap. 5m.; 65 mem. cos; Pres. and Dir-Gen. MONCEF ZOUARI.

Lloyd Tunisien: Lloyd Bldg, ave Tahan Haddad, Les Berges du Lac, 1053 Tunis; tel. (71) 962-777; fax (71) 962-440; f. 1945; fire, accident, liability, marine, life; cap. 1m.; Chair. and Man. Dir MUHAMMAD AZIZ MAULOUK.

Société Tunisienne d'Assurance et de Réassurance (STAR): ave de Paris, Tunis; tel. (71) 340-866; fax (71) 340-835; internet www.star.com.tn; f. 1958.

Tunis-Ré (Société Tunisienne de Réassurance): ave Muhammad V, Montplaisir 1, BP 133, 1082 Tunis; tel. (71) 844-011; fax (71) 787-573; e-mail tunis.re@email.ati.tn; f. 1981; various kinds of reinsurance; cap. 24.4m.; Chair. and Gen. Man. MUHAMMAD EL-FATEH MAHERZI.

Trade and Industry

GOVERNMENT AGENCIES

Centre de Promotion des Exportations (CEPEX): Centre Urbain, BP 225, 1080 Tunis; tel. (71) 350-344; fax (71) 353-683; e-mail cepexedpuc@attmail.com; internet www.cepex.nat.tn; f. 1973; state export promotion org.; Pres. and Gen. Man. FERID TOUNSI.

Foreign Investment Promotion Agency (FIPA): Centre Urbain Nord, 1004 Tunis; tel. (71) 702-140; fax (71) 702-600; e-mail fipa.tunisia@mci.gov.tn; internet www.investintunisia.tn; f. 1995; Dir-Gen. ABDESSALEM MANSOUR.

Office du Commerce de la Tunisie (OCT): 65 rue de Syrie, 1002 Tunis; tel. (71) 800-040; fax (71) 788-974; e-mail OCT@Email.ati.tn; f. 1962; CEO BELGACEM NAFTI; Sec.-Gen. MUSTAPHA DEBBABI.

CHAMBERS OF COMMERCE AND INDUSTRY

Chambre de Commerce et d'Industrie de Tunis: 1 rue des Entrepreneurs, 1000 Tunis; tel. (71) 350-300; fax (71) 354-744; e-mail ccitunis@planet.tn; internet www.ccitunis.org.tn; f. 1885; 25 mems; Pres. JILANI BENM'BAREK.

Chambre de Commerce et d'Industrie du Centre: rue Chadli Khaznadar, 4000 Sousse; tel. (73) 225-044; fax (73) 224-227; f. 1895; 25 mems; Pres. KABOUDI MONCEF; Dir FATEN BASLY.

Chambre de Commerce et d'Industrie du Nord-Est: Tom Bereaux Bizerte Center, angle rues 1er mai, Med Ali, 7000 Bizerte; tel. (72) 431-044; fax (72) 431-922; f. 1903; 5 mems; Pres. KAMEL BELKAHIA; Dir MOUFIDA CHAKROUN.

Chambre de Commerce et d'Industrie de Sfax: Rue du Lieutenant Hammadi Tej, BP 794, 3000 Sfax; tel. (74) 296-120; fax (74) 296-121; e-mail ccis@ccis.org.tn; internet www.ccis.org.tn; f. 1895; 35,000 mems; Dir IKRAM MAKNI.

INDUSTRIAL AND TRADE ASSOCIATIONS

Agence de Promotion de l'Industrie (API): 63 rue de Syrie, 1002 Tunis; tel. (71) 792-144; fax (71) 782-482; e-mail api@api.com.tn; internet www.tunisieindustrie.nat.tn; f. 1987 by merger; co-ordinates industrial policy, undertakes feasibility studies, organizes industrial training and establishes industrial zones; overseas offices in Belgium, France, Germany, Italy, the United Kingdom, Sweden and the USA; 24 regional offices; Gen. Man. MUHAMMAD BEN ABDALLAH.

Centre Technique du Textile (CETTEX): ave des Industries, Zone Industrielle, Bir el-Kassaâ, BP 279, Ben Arous, 2013 Tunis; tel. (71) 381-133; fax (71) 382-558; e-mail cettex@textiletunisia.com.tn; responsible for the textile industry; Dir KHALED TOUIBI.

Cie des Phosphates de Gafsa (CPG): Cité Bayech, 2100 Gafsa; tel. (76) 226-022; fax (76) 224-132; e-mail cpg@cpg.com.tn; internet www.cpg.com.tn; f. 1897; production and marketing of phosphates; Pres. KAÏS DALY.

Entreprise Tunisienne d'Activités Pétrolières (ETAP): 27 ave Kheireddine Pacha, BP 367, 1002 Tunis; tel. (71) 782-288; fax (71) 786-141; e-mail dexprom@etap.com.tn; internet www.etap.com.tn; responsible for exploration and investment in hydrocarbons.

Office des Céréales: Ministry of Agriculture, 30 rue Alain Savary, 1002 Tunis; tel. (71) 790-351; fax (71) 789-573; f. 1962; responsible for the cereals industry; Chair. and Dir-Gen. A. SADDEM.

Office National des Mines: 24 rue 8601, BP 215, 1080 Tunis; tel. (71) 787-366; fax (71) 794-016; f. 1963; mining of iron ores; research and study of mineral wealth; Chair. and CEO MOHAMMED FADHEL ZERELLI.

Office National des Pêches (ONP): Le Port, La Goulette, Tunis; tel. (71) 275-093; marine and fishing authority; Dir-Gen. L. HALAB.

Office des Terres Domaniales (OTD): 30 rue Alain Savary, 1002 Tunis; tel. (71) 800-322; fax (71) 795-026; e-mail otd@email.ati.tn; f. 1961; responsible for agricultural production and the management of state-owned lands; Dir BÉCHIR BEN SMAÏL.

UTILITIES
Electricity and Gas

Société Tunisienne de l'Electricité et du Gaz (STEG): 38 rue Kemal Atatürk, BP 190, 1080 Tunis; tel. (71) 341-311; fax (71) 349-981; e-mail dpsc@steg.com.tn; internet www.steg.com.tn; f. 1962; responsible for generation and distribution of electricity and for production of natural gas; Pres. and Gen. Man. MUHAMMAD MONCEF BOUSSEN; 35 brs.

Water

Société Nationale d'Exploitation et de Distribution des Eaux (SONEDE): ave Slimane ben Slimane, el-Manar 2, 2092 Tunis; tel. (71) 887-000; fax (71) 871-000; e-mail sonede@sonede.com.tn; internet www.sonede.com.tn; f. 1968; production and supply of drinking water; Chair. and Man. Dir ABDELAZIZ MABROUK.

TRADE AND OTHER UNIONS

Union Générale des Etudiants de Tunisie (UGET): 11 rue d'Espagne, Tunis; f. 1953; 600 mems; Pres. MEKKI FITOURI.

Union Générale Tunisienne du Travail (UGTT): 29 place Muhammad Ali, 1001 Tunis; tel. (71) 332-400; fax (71) 332-439; e-mail ugtt.tunis@email.ati.tn; internet www.ugtt.org.tn; f. 1946 by Farhat Hached; affiliated to ICFTU; mems 360,000 in 24 affiliated unions; 18-member exec. bureau; Sec.-Gen. ABDESSALEM DJERAD.

Union Nationale des Agriculteurs (UNA): 6 ave Habib Thameur, 1000 Tunis; tel. (71) 246-920; fax (71) 349-843; f. 1955; Pres. BACHA ABD AL-BAKI.

Union Nationale de la Femme Tunisienne (UNFT): 56 blvd Bab Benat, 1008 Tunis; tel. (71) 560-178; fax (71) 567-131; e-mail unft@email.ati.tn; internet www.unft.org.tn; f. 1956; 100,000 mems; promotes the rights of women; 28 regional delegations, 199 professional training centres, 13 professional alliances; Pres. AZIZA HATIRA; Vice-Pres. FAÏZA AZOUZ; 23 brs abroad.

Union Tunisienne de l'Industrie, du Commerce et de l'Artisanat (UTICAL): 103 ave de la Liberté, Belvédère, 1002 Tunis; tel. (71) 780-366; fax (71) 782-143; internet www.utica.org.tn; f. 1946; mems: 15 national federations and 170 syndical chambers at national levels; Pres. HÉDI JILANI.

Transport

RAILWAYS

In 2002 the total length of railways was 2,257 km. A total of 35.7m. passengers travelled by rail in Tunisia in 2003.

Société Nationale des Chemins de Fer Tunisiens (SNCFT): Bâtiment La Gare Tunis Ville, place Barcelona, 1001 Tunis; tel. (71) 345-680; fax (71) 344-045; f. 1956; state org. controlling all Tunisian railways; Pres. and Dir-Gen. ALI CHEIKH KHALLFALLAH.

Société des Transports de Tunis: 1 ave Habib Bourgiba, BP 660, 1025 Tunis; tel. (71) 259-422; fax (71) 342-727; internet www.snt-smlt.com.tn; f. 2003 following merger of the Société Nationale des Transports and the Société du Métro Léger de Tunis; operates 5 light train routes with 136 trains, and 206 local bus routes with 1,050 buses; also operates in the suburbs of Tunis-Goulette-Marsa, with 18 trains; Chair. and Man. Dir CHEDLY HAJRI.

ROADS

In 1996 there were an estimated 23,100 km of roads. Of these, 6,240 km were main roads and 7,900 km secondary roads.

Société Nationale de Transport Interurbain (SNTRI): ave Muhammad V, BP 40, Belvédère, 1002 Tunis; tel. (71) 784-433; fax (71) 786-605; e-mail drn@sntri.com.tn; f. 1981; Dir-Gen. SASSI YAHIA.

Société des Transports de Tunis: see above.

There are 12 **Sociétés Régionales des Transports**, responsible for road transport, operating in different regions in Tunisia.

SHIPPING

Tunisia has seven major ports: Tunis-La Goulette, Radès, Bizerta, Sousse, Sfax, Gabès and Zarzis. There is a special petroleum port at La Skhirra.

Office de la Marine Marchande et des Ports: Bâtiment Administratif, Port de la Goulette, 2060 La Goulette; tel. (71) 735-300; fax (71) 735-812; maritime port administration; Pres. and Dir-Gen. ALI LABIEDH.

Cie Générale Maritime: Résidence Alain Savary, Bloc D7, Apt 74, 1003 Tunis; tel. and fax (71) 860-430; e-mail logwan.girgen@gnet.tn; Chair. ELIAS MAHERZI.

Cie Méditerranéenne de Navigation: Tunis; tel. (71) 331-544; fax (71) 332-124.

Cie Tunisienne de Navigation SA (CTN): 5 ave Dag Hammarskjöold, BP 40, 1001 Tunis; tel. (71) 341-777; fax (71) 345-736; e-mail cotunav@ctn.com.tn; internet www.ctn.com.tn; f. 1959; state-owned; brs at Bizerta, La Goulette, Sfax and Sousse; Chair. M. YONSAÂ.

Gabès Marine Tankers: Immeuble SETCAR, route de Sousse, km 13, 2034 Tunis; tel. (71) 445-644; fax (71) 454-650; e-mail gabesmarine@gmt.com.tn; Chair. FÉRID ABBÈS.

Gas Marine: Immeuble SETCAR, route de Sousse, km 13, 2034 ez-Zahra; tel. (71) 454-644; fax (71) 454-650; Chair. HAMMADI ABBÈS.

Hannibal Marine Tankers: 2ème Etage, Residence Lakeo, rue du Lac Michigan, Les Berges du Lac, 1053 Tunis; tel. (71) 960-037; fax (71) 960-243; e-mail hannibal.tankers@gnet.tn; Gen. Man. AMEUR MAHJOUB.

Société Tunisienne de Navigation Petrolière (PETRONAV): Residence Raoudha, Les Berges du Lac, 1053 Tunis; tel. (71) 861-965; fax (71) 861-780; Chair. HICHEM KHATTECH.

SONOTRAK: 179 ave Muhammad Hédi Khefacha, Gare Maritime de Kerkenna, 3000 Sfax; tel. (74) 498-216; fax (74) 497-496; e-mail jabeur.m@planet.tn; Chair. TAOUFI JRAD.

Tunisian Shipping Agency: Zone Industrielle, Radès 2040, BP 166, Tunis; tel. (71) 448-379; fax (71) 448-410; e-mail tsa.rades@planet.tn; Chair. MUHAMMAD BEN SEDRINE.

CIVIL AVIATION

There are international airports at Tunis-Carthage, Sfax, Djerba, Monastir, Tabarka, Gafsa and Tozeur. In January 2000 it was announced that a new airport was to be built at Enfidha, 100 km south of Tunis. Construction of the airport commenced in March 2005 and the airport was scheduled to be operational by the end of 2008. There were also plans to construct a new airport in Tunis, designed to handle 5m. passengers, by the end of 2006.

Office de l'Aviation Civile et des Aéroports: BP 137 and 147, Aéroport International de Tunis-Carthage, 1080 Tunis; tel. (71) 755-000; fax (71) 755-133; e-mail relations.exterieures@oaca.nat.tn; internet www.oaca.nat.tn; f. 1972; civil aviation and airport administration; Pres. and Dir-Gen. MEHREZ BECHEIKH.

Nouvelair Tunisie: Zone Touristique Dkhila, 5065 Monastir; tel. (73) 520-600; fax (73) 520-666; e-mail info@nouvelair.com.tn; internet www.nouvelair.com; f. 1989 as Air Liberté Tunisie; name changed as above in 1996; Tunisian charter co; flights from Tunis, Djerba and Monastir airports to Scandinavia and other European countries; Chair. AZIZ MILAD; Gen. Man. SAMI ZITOUNI.

Tuninter: Immeuble Securas, Zone Industrielle, BP 1080, La Charguia 11, 1080 Tunis; tel. (71) 701-717; fax (71) 712-193; e-mail tuninter@mail.gnet.tn; f. 1992; Tunisian charter co; Man. Dir ABD AL-KARIM OUERTANI.

TunisAir (Société Tunisienne de l'Air): blvd du 7 novembre 1987, 2035 Tunis; tel. (71) 700-100; fax (71) 700-897; e-mail mail@tunisair.com.tn; internet www.tunisair.com; f. 1948; 45.2% govt-owned; 20% of assets privatized in 1995; flights to Africa, Europe and the Middle East; Pres. and Dir-Gen. YOUSSEF NÉJI.

Tunisavia (Société de Transports, Services et Travaux Aériens): blvd du leader Yasser Arafat, 2035 Tunis-Carthage International Airport, Tunis; tel. (71) 280-555; fax (71) 281-333; e-mail siege@tunisavia.com.tn; internet www.tunisavia.com.tn; f. 1974; helicopter and charter operator; Pres. AZIZ MILAD; Dir-Gen. MOHSEN NASRA.

Tourism

The main tourist attractions are the magnificent sandy beaches, Moorish architecture and remains of the Roman Empire. Tunisia contains the site of the ancient Phoenician city of Carthage. Tourism, a principal source of foreign exchange, has expanded rapidly,

TUNISIA

following extensive government investment in hotels, improved roads and other facilities. The number of hotel beds increased from 71,529 in 1980 to 188,600 in 1999. Foreign tourist arrivals totalled 5.1m. in 2003 (compared with 4.7m. in 1998). Receipts from tourism in 2003 totalled US $1,935m.

Office National du Tourisme Tunisien: 1 ave Muhammad V, 1001 Tunis; tel. (71) 341-077; fax (71) 350-997; e-mail ontt@email.ati.tn; internet www.tunisietourisme.com.tn; f. 1958; Dir-Gen. KHALED CHEIKH.

TURKEY

Introductory Survey

Location, Climate, Language, Religion, Flag, Capital

The Republic of Turkey lies partly in south-eastern Europe and partly in western Asia. The European and Asian portions of the country (known, respectively, as Thrace and Anatolia) are separated by the Sea of Marmara, linking the Black Sea and the Aegean Sea. Turkey has an extensive coastline: on the Black Sea, to the north; on the Mediterranean Sea, to the south; and on the Aegean Sea, to the west. Most of Turkey lies in Asia, the vast Anatolian peninsula being bordered to the east by Armenia, Georgia, the Nakhichevan Autonomous Republic (part of Azerbaijan) and Iran, and to the south by Iraq and Syria. The smaller European part of the country is bordered to the west by Greece and Bulgaria. In the Asian interior the climate is one of great extremes, with hot dry summers and cold, snowy winters on the plateau. Temperatures in Ankara are generally between −4°C (25°F) and 30°C (86°F). On the Mediterranean coast it is more equable, with mild winters and warm summers. The principal language is Turkish, spoken by 90% of the population. About 7% speak Kurdish, mainly in the south-east. In 1928 the Arabic characters of the written Turkish language were superseded by Western-style script. Islam is the religion of 99% of the population. The national flag (proportions 2 by 3) is red, with a white crescent and a five-pointed white star to the left of centre. The capital is Ankara.

Recent History

Turkey was formerly a monarchy, ruled by a Sultan, with his capital in Constantinople (now Istanbul). At its zenith, the Turkish Empire, under the Osmanlı (Ottoman) dynasty, extended from the Persian (Arabian) Gulf to Morocco, including most Arab regions and south-eastern Europe. Following the dissolution of the Ottoman Empire after the First World War, political control of Turkey itself passed to the nationalist movement led by Mustafa Kemal, a distinguished army officer. On 23 April 1920, in defiance of the Sultan, a newly elected assembly established a provisional Government, led by Kemal, in Ankara, then a minor provincial town. Kemal's forces waged war against the Greek army in 1920–22, forcing the Greeks to evacuate Smyrna (İzmir) and eastern Thrace (the European portion of Turkey). The new regime abolished the sultanate in November 1922 and declared Turkey a republic, with Ankara as its capital and Kemal as its first President, on 29 October 1923. The Ottoman caliphate (the former monarch's position as Islamic religious leader) was abolished in March 1924.

Kemal remained President of Turkey, with extensive dictatorial powers, until his death in 1938. He vigorously pursued a radical programme of far-reaching reform and modernization, including the secularization of the state (in 1928), the abolition of Islamic courts and religious instruction in schools, the emancipation of women (enfranchised in 1934), the banning of polygamy, the development of industry, the introduction of a Latin alphabet, the adoption of the Gregorian (in place of the Islamic) calendar, and the encouragement of European culture and technology. Another Westernizing reform was the introduction of surnames in 1934: Kemal assumed the name Atatürk ('Father of the Turks'). His autocratic regime attempted, with considerable success, to replace the country's Islamic traditions by the principles of republicanism, nationalism, populism and state control.

Following Atatürk's death, his Cumhuriyet Halk Partisi (CHP—Republican People's Party), the only authorized political grouping, remained in power under his close associate, İsmet İnönü, who had been Prime Minister in 1923–24 and from 1925 to 1937. İnönü was President from 1938 to 1950, and maintained Turkey's neutrality during most of the Second World War (Turkey declared war on Germany in February 1945). After the war İnönü introduced some liberalization of the regime. The one-party system was ended in 1946, when opposition leaders, including Celâl Bayar and Adnan Menderes, registered the Demokratik Parti (DP—Democratic Party). Numerous other parties were subsequently formed. The DP won Turkey's first free election in 1950, and ruled for the next decade. Bayar became President, with Menderes as Prime Minister.

In May 1960 the Government was overthrown by a military coup, led by Gen. Cemal Gürsel, who assumed the presidency, claiming that the DP regime had betrayed Atatürk's principle of secularism. A series of coalition governments, mostly led by İnönü, held office from November 1961 until October 1965, when an election was won by the conservative Adalet Partisi (Justice Party), led by Süleyman Demirel, which appealed to supporters of the former DP. The Demirel Government remained in power until March 1971, when escalating student and labour unrest caused the armed forces to demand its resignation. 'Guided democracy', under military supervision, continued until October 1973, with a succession of right-wing 'non-party' administrations, martial law and the rigorous suppression of all left-wing activities.

The return to civilian rule began in April 1973, when the Turkish Grand National Assembly (TGNA—the legislative body established in 1961) chose Adm. Fahri Korutürk as President, in preference to a candidate supported by the armed forces. Military participation in government was ended by an election in October 1973. No single party received sufficient support to form a government, and negotiations on the creation of a coalition continued until January 1974, when Bülent Ecevit, leader of the CHP (which had become a left-of-centre party), took office as Prime Minister, having negotiated a coalition with the Milli Selamet Partisi (MSP—National Salvation Party), a pro-Islamic right-wing group. Deteriorating relations with Greece were exacerbated by the Greek-backed coup in Cyprus (q.v.) in July 1974, when Turkey responded by dispatching troops, and occupying the northern part of the island, to protect the Turkish Cypriot population. Despite the failure of the coup, Turkish forces kept control of northern Cyprus, and the island remained effectively partitioned.

A long period of political instability was fostered by a succession of unsuccessful coalitions, headed by either Ecevit or Demirel, and prompted an escalation in political violence, mainly involving clashes between left-wing and right-wing groups. On 12 September 1980, as the violence neared the scale of a civil war, the armed forces, led by Gen. Kenan Evren, Chief of the General Staff, seized power in a bloodless coup; a five-member National Security Council (NSC) was formed, which appointed a mainly civilian Cabinet. Martial law was declared throughout the country. In December the NSC published a decree endowing the military regime with unlimited powers. During 1981–83 a campaign to eradicate all possible sources of political violence was undertaken. In April 1981 former politicians were banned from future political activity, and in October all political parties were disbanded.

The new Government succeeded in reducing the level of political violence in Turkey and in restoring law and order. However, that this had been achieved at the expense of respect for human rights caused concern among Western Governments: Turkey was banned from the Parliamentary Assembly of the Council of Europe (see p. 211), aid from the European Community (EC, now European Union—EU, see p. 228) was suspended, and fellow members of NATO urged Turkey to return to democratic rule as soon as possible. In October 1981 a Consultative Assembly was established to draft a new constitution, which was approved by referendum in November 1982; objections were widely expressed that the President was to be accorded excessive powers while judicial powers and the rights of trade unions and the press were to be curtailed. An appended 'temporary article' installed Evren as President for a seven-year term.

In May 1983 the NSC revoked the ban on political organizations, permitting the formation of parties, subject to strict rules, in preparation for the first election to be held under the new Constitution. All the former political parties remained proscribed, and 723 former members of the TGNA and leading party officials were banned from political activity for up to 10 years. Followers of the former political parties regrouped under new names and with new leaders. Of the 15 new parties, however, only three were allowed to take part in the election: the Milliyetçi Demokrasi Partisi (MDP—Nationalist Democracy Party) and the Halkçı Partisi (HP—Populist Party), both of which had the tacit support of the NSC, and the conservative Anavatan Partisi (ANAP—Motherland Party), led by Turgut Özal, the former Deputy Prime Minister for Economic Affairs. In the November general election ANAP won 211 of the 400 seats in the unicameral legislature. Accordingly, Özal was appointed Prime Minister in December. Although this result suggested a decisive rejection of military rule, martial law was still in operation in almost one-half of the provinces a year after the election.

In November 1985 the HP and the Sosyal Demokrasi Partisi (Social Democratic Party), respectively the main opposition parties within and outside the National Assembly, merged to form the Sosyal Demokrat Halkçı Parti (SHP—Social Democratic Populist Party). However, the left-wing opposition was split as a result of the immediate formation of the Demokratik Sol Parti (DSP—Democratic Left Party), which drew support from the former CHP. The MDP voted to disband in May 1986.

At a national referendum in September 1987 a narrow majority approved the repeal of the ban on participation in political affairs imposed on more than 200 politicians in 1981. This enabled Ecevit to assume the leadership of the DSP, while Demirel was elected as leader of the Doğru Yol Partisi (DYP—True Path Party). In a general election conducted in November 1987 ANAP obtained 292 of the 450 seats in the enlarged TGNA, while the SHP won 99 seats and the DYP 59.

Özal succeeded Evren as President in November 1989, having secured the support of the simple majority required in a third round of voting by the TGNA at the end of October. Yıldırım Akbulut, the Speaker of the TGNA and a former Minister of the Interior, was subsequently appointed Prime Minister. At an ANAP party congress convened in June 1991 Akbulut was defeated by former Minister of Foreign Affairs Mesut Yılmaz in a contest for the party leadership. Akbulut subsequently resigned as Prime Minister, and, in accordance with the Constitution, President Özal invited Yılmaz, the leader of ANAP's liberal faction, to head a new administration.

In a general election held on 20 October 1991 the DYP, under the leadership of Demirel, received an estimated 27.3% of the votes cast, narrowly defeating ANAP (with 23.9%) and the SHP (with 20.6%). Demirel formed a coalition administration with the SHP (who with the DYP accounted for 266 of the 450 newly elected deputies in the TGNA), with Erdal İnönü, the SHP party leader, as deputy premier. The coalition set out a programme for political and economic reform, and international observers were impressed by Demirel's apparent commitment to human rights. The implementation of amendments designed to discourage torture were, however, impeded by a lack of consensus within the Government, and the problems were exacerbated during 1992 by a succession of political defections from the SHP, which by September had reduced the representation of the coalition parties in the TGNA to 229. Although the DYP and the SHP performed well at municipal elections in early June, the reactivation of the CHP in September (following a relaxation of guidelines for the formation of political parties) threatened to undermine left-wing support for the Government.

At a special ANAP party conference in December 1992, concern was expressed that right-wing extremism had become the dominant force behind the party leadership, prompting the emergence of a dissident, more conservative faction of the party. Subsequently some 70 deputies announced their intention to leave ANAP in order to form a new party headed by President Özal. In April 1993, however, Özal died of heart failure. In May Süleyman Demirel was elected to the presidency, with a simple majority in a third round of voting by the TGNA. Minister of State Tansu Çiller was elected to the DYP party leadership in early June and promptly assumed the premiership. Çiller (Turkey's first female Prime Minister) formed a new Cabinet, retaining the 12 SHP members of the previous Government but replacing 17 former DYP ministers, notably several Demirel loyalists. The Prime Minister's personal support was consolidated in December when five DYP ministers were replaced.

The new administration was strained by a sharp escalation of violence on the part of the outlawed Partiya Karkeren Kurdistan (PKK—Kurdistan Workers' Party). Plans to extend cultural and educational rights to the Kurds were abandoned following strong opposition from Demirel, right-wing members of the DYP and military leaders, who, in October, effectively resisted a proposal to discuss the establishment of local autonomy for the Kurdish population in the south-east of the country.

In early 1994 Çiller's political standing was damaged by a devaluation of the Turkish lira, following a loss of confidence in the currency on the part of international credit agencies. The DYP performed unexpectedly well in municipal elections in March, however, obtaining 24% of the national vote; Çiller was thus able to pursue her programme of economic austerity, although in July the Constitutional Court halted her accelerated privatization plans. In October an attempt to introduce new legislation on privatization revealed serious political differences within the coalition Government. Proposals for the democratization of the Constitution also provoked disagreements concerning the extent to which should be enshrined freedoms of expression and movement. In late November the TGNA approved legislation enabling the sale of some 100 state enterprises, prompting a protest organized by trade unions in Ankara.

In February 1995 a special conference of the SHP voted to merge with the CHP, consequently increasing the Government's parliamentary majority but forcing a renegotiation of the conditions of the coalition. Agreement was reached by Çiller and Hikmet Çetin, the CHP leader, in March, and an extensive reorganization of the Government was undertaken in order to accommodate the party. Çetin became Deputy Prime Minister and Minister of State; İnönü assumed the foreign affairs portfolio.

In June 1995 the DYP obtained 39% of votes cast in municipal elections, a result that Çiller claimed to be a vindication of her personal standing as leader and of her Government's policies, in particular the pursuit of closer relations with the EU. However, efforts by Çiller to extend democratic rights within the Constitution encountered considerable opposition, both from conservative elements within her own party and from the fundamentalist Islamist Refah Partisi (RP—Welfare Party). Certain constitutional reforms, including the removal of restrictions on political associations and trade unions, the lowering of the age of eligibility to vote from 21 to 18 years, and the expansion of the TGNA by 100 parliamentary seats to 550, were finally approved at the end of July. Çiller, however, failed to obtain sufficient support for the amendment of the 'anti-terrorism' legislation, which was expected to be crucial in securing the European Parliament's ratification of the EU-Turkish customs union (see below).

Deniz Baykal was elected leader of the CHP in September 1995. All CHP ministers subsequently resigned their cabinet positions, and ensuing coalition negotiations with Çiller failed as it became apparent that the political differences between the two leaders were insurmountable. Later in September Demirel was forced to accept the Prime Minister's resignation, but Çiller was immediately invited to form a new government. An attempt by Çiller to form a coalition with ANAP was unsuccessful, and in October a minority DYP administration failed to secure a parliamentary vote of confidence. A significant obstacle to a new DYP-CHP agreement was removed when Çiller conceded the necessity of holding an early general election. A DYP-CHP Government, headed by Çiller, with Baykal as Deputy Prime Minister and Minister of Foreign Affairs, took office in early November.

At the general election, in December 1995, the RP, which had campaigned to strengthen political and economic relations with other Islamic countries, to withdraw from NATO and the EU customs union, and to increase state involvement in the economy, secured the largest number of parliamentary seats (158), with 21.4% of the votes cast. The DYP won 135 seats, with 19.2% of the votes, while ANAP took 132, with 19.7% of the votes. Since no party had an absolute majority, the two other parties securing parliamentary representation, the DSP and the CHP, were expected to have considerable political leverage in the new parliament. (Under the new electoral arrangements, eight other parties secured no seats in the legislature, having failed to reach the minimum requirement of 10% of support.) Although during the election campaign the DYP and ANAP leaders had both declared their opposition to participating in a coalition administration with the RP, in January 1996 President Demirel invited RP leader Necmettin Erbakan to attempt to form a government. Despite Erbakan's declared willingness to negotiate an agreement with any of the four main parties, as well as to compromise on the RP's main policies, no coalition partner could be found. Subsequent efforts by Çiller to form a government through an agreement with ANAP also failed, and in early February Demirel invited Mesut Yılmaz, of ANAP, to establish a new administration. Following protracted negotiations, Yılmaz and Çiller reached a coalition agreement, which was signed and approved by Demirel in March; Çiller conceded the premiership to Yılmaz, under a rotating arrangement. The new Government secured a parliamentary vote of confidence by 257 votes to 207, but was soon strained by tensions between the two leaders, and allegations of corruption against Çiller. In April and May ANAP deputies failed to support Çiller, following votes in the TGNA to establish commissions to investigate her alleged illegal involvement in the sale of the TEDAŞ state electricity company and of a Turkish car manufacturer. Members of the DYP accused Yılmaz of further undermining Çiller's position, by passing information to the media detailing evidence of the misappropriation of secret security funds under her premiership, in order to force her resignation before her scheduled assumption of the office of Prime Minister in 1997. Meanwhile, opposition parties questioned the credibility of the Government after the Constitutional Court annulled the March 1996 vote of confidence. At the end of May Çiller announced the withdrawal of her party's support for the Government and publicly called for Yılmaz's resignation. Political tensions were heightened in that month by an assassination attempt on President Demirel.

In early June 1996 the RP renewed its demands for a general election, after it won 34% of the votes cast in municipal elections. At the same time the RP secured the DYP's support for a censure motion against the Government to be considered in the TGNA. This was withdrawn when Yılmaz announced the resignation of his Government, following the official publication of the Constitutional Court's ruling. Necmettin Erbakan was subsequently invited to form a government, and at the end of June the RP concluded an agreement with the DYP; Erbakan was to lead the new coalition administration, with Çiller assuming the deputy premiership and foreign affairs portfolio. The leaders asserted that the objective of the new Government was to secure political and economic stability, and they guaranteed that Turkey would adhere to its existing international and strategic agreements. Eight DYP deputies in the TGNA resigned from the party in protest at the coalition with the RP, and a further 15 DYP deputies failed to endorse the new administration in a parliamentary vote of confidence conducted in July. Although the Government secured a narrow majority, it was immediately confronted by local demonstrations and mounting international concern regarding several hundred left-wing prisoners who had initiated a hunger strike in May, in protest at their treatment and conditions of confinement. At the end of July, following the deaths of 12 protesters and widespread unrest within many prisons, the Government concluded an agreement with the prisoners to end their action in return for guarantees that included the transfer of 102 activists from a high-security prison in Anatolya and greater access to medical care.

The contradictions inherent in the new RP-DYP administration became evident in many aspects of government policy. In foreign affairs, the Government attempted to reassure its Western allies of its continued support. At the end of July 1996 the mandate for the use of Turkish airbases by allied forces engaged in 'Operation Provide Comfort' (see below) was extended, and in August a new military co-operation agreement was signed with Israel, expanding on an accord concluded in February. In addition, there was evidence of the military's asserting its authority by dismissing 13 officers in August on disciplinary charges relating to Islamist practices (50 officers had been dismissed on similar grounds in December 1995). At the same time, however, Prime Minister Erbakan embarked on a tour of Asian and Middle Eastern Muslim countries in order to strengthen bilateral relations and co-operation. In August Turkey and Iran finalized an economic agreement, shortly after legislation had been ratified in the USA that threatened punitive measures against countries undertaking investments in Iran. A visit by Erbakan to Libya in October became politically damaging when the Libyan leader, Col Muammar al-Qaddafi, expressed opposition to Turkey's relations with NATO and the EU and, moreover, advocated the establishment of a Kurdish homeland. Turkey's ambassador to Libya was temporarily recalled. However, censure motions brought against Erbakan's administration by three opposition parties were defeated in a single vote in the TGNA. In January 1997 the TGNA cleared Çiller of the final corruption charges against her. In the same month Hüsamettin Cindoruk, who had been expelled from the DYP in October 1995, established a new breakaway party, the Demokrat Türkiye Partisi (DTP—Democratic Turkey Party).

In November 1996, meanwhile, the Government was confronted by allegations of state involvement in criminal activities, following a traffic accident at Susurluk, in the north-west, in which a senior police-officer and a wanted criminal were killed. The resignation a few days later of the Minister of the Interior, Mehmet Agar, was said to be unconnected to the incident. Details subsequently emerged of the activities of the alleged mafia member, Abdullah Catli, which included drugs-trafficking as well as intelligence work for the state (which some commentators suspected included the assassination of left-wing activists during the 1980s), while there was evidence that Agar had held meetings with members of organized criminal groups and had secured Catli a gun licence. In December 1996 Istanbul's Director of Security and five other senior officers were suspended during investigation proceedings into the death, in July, of a casino owner, in which Catli was a leading suspect. In January 1997 a report on the Susurluk incident by the Prime Minister's office recommended that judicial inquiries be initiated into the conduct of some 35 people, including Agar and the former Istanbul security director. A series of popular protests staged against corruption in government and to demand full judicial consideration of the Susurluk case was initiated in the following month.

There were civil disturbances in early February 1997 following an Islamist rally in the Sincan district of Ankara, at which Iran's ambassador to Turkey criticized Turkey's relations with Israel and its NATO allies and advocated the introduction of *Shari'a* law. The RP district mayor, who had organized the rally, was suspended. At the same time pressure from the military and DYP members of the Government forced the RP to withdraw proposals to extend Muslim education and to allow religious garments to be worn by public workers. In late February the Government defeated a censure motion in the TGNA, proposed by the DSP and CHP in protest at the Government's alleged undermining of the secular state. At a meeting of the NSC held at the end of February, the military leadership presented a list of 18 measures that would ensure the secular state traditions, including greater supervision of Islamic financial and media operations, the removal of Islamists from public administration and closure of all unauthorized Islamic groupings; the military warned of punitive action if the proposals were not implemented. Political tension was defused when Erbakan, who had initially criticized the NSC for attempting to impose laws on the Government, signed a memorandum endorsing the NSC measures and declared that the leaders of all the main political parties were unanimous in their view that the Constitution must be upheld. The Council of Ministers agreed in March to implement the NSC proposals, but concern subsequently arose that the failure of the Government to act on the measures would result in the collapse of the administration, owing to increasing pressure from the military on the DYP to withdraw from the coalition arrangement, as well as pressure from extreme elements within the governing parties. Two dissident DYP government ministers resigned in protest at Erbakan's leadership, and demanded an early election on the grounds that their party leader, Çiller, had failed to restrain the Islamist tendencies of the RP. At a meeting of the NSC held in late April the political crisis was again temporarily resolved when Erbakan agreed to pursue the military's demands, including restrictions on Islamic education. At the end of April 122 members of an Islamist sect were sentenced to up to four years' imprisonment for forming an illegal group and contravening a ban on Islamic dress, and in May Erbakan approved the dismissal of 161 army officers for allegedly demonstrating Islamist sympathies. Although the Government defeated an opposition attempt in that month to pursue a censure motion in the TGNA, the political situation remained critical, and charges from the military, opposition parties and dissident members of the DYP that the Government was undermining the modern secular tradition were reinforced when the country's chief prosecutor initiated legal proceedings to ban the RP (on the grounds that the party had violated the Constitution). By June the coalition had lost its majority in the TGNA as a result of defections principally from the DYP. Erbakan announced that he would seek an early election, but the military continued to exert pressure on the Government, and the Prime Minister finally resigned in mid-June. President Demirel asked the ANAP leader, Mesut Yılmaz, to form a new administration, and a coalition with the DSP and the DTP was inaugurated at the beginning of July; the coalition controlled only a minority of seats in the TGNA, and was dependent on the support of the CHP. The tripartite Government pledged to improve law and order, implement previously proposed changes to the education system, and vigorously pursue EU membership. Defections from the DYP continued through July, and by the end of the month its representation in the TGNA had been reduced from 135 to 93.

In August 1997 the TGNA approved legislation extending compulsory education from five to eight years. This was intended to raise the entry age to Islamic schools from 11 to 14, thus reducing attendance at such schools and lessening Islamic influence. The RP organized popular demonstrations in protest against the legislation (which constituted a principal demand of the military) during July and August and, following the implementation of the measures, in September. In August a further 73 members of the armed forces were expelled, owing to suspected affiliation to Islamist organizations. Further public demonstrations were prompted by the military's insistence on the strict enforcement of the ban on wearing Islamic dress in public buildings, notably educational establishments. The largest of these demonstrations was attended by 10,000 people in İstanbul at the end of February 1998. In early March the University of İstanbul temporarily annulled the ban and the Government stated that it would not be strictly enforced. In mid-March the Government survived its third censure motion, which was presented against the Minister for Education for his handling of the issue of Islamic dress. A few days later 20 members of a proscribed Islamic organization were arrested for inciting the demonstrations. At the end of the month the NSC criticized the Government for advocating a relaxation of the enforcement of anti-Islamic legislation; the Government subsequently proposed further measures to curb Islamist radicalism, and the universities announced their decision to enforce the dress code.

Meanwhile, Çiller's participation in the coalition with the RP and her opposition to a possible ban on the party had caused offence to the secular establishment, causing a deterioration in the previously good relations between Çiller and the armed forces. In March 1998 the Court of Appeals ruled that Çiller could not be prosecuted in connection with a particular allegation that she had misused government funds during her premiership owing to the threat to national security interests. However, in April her loss of support in the TGNA led to a vote in favour of the commencement of an investigation into alleged irregularities in Çiller's accumulation of wealth between 1991 and 1996. In October 1997 Çiller's husband, Ozer Çiller, had been charged with forgery.

In January 1998 the Constitutional Court ordered the dissolution of the RP on the grounds that it was responsible for undermining the secular regime, and banned seven of its members, including Erbakan, from holding political office for five years. The ban attracted widespread international criticism and human rights organizations condemned the decision. The ruling took effect in February; many former RP deputies joined the Fazilet Partisi (FP—Virtue Party), which had been established in December 1997. By March 1998 the FP's representation in the TGNA had risen to 140 seats, making it the largest parliamentary party (ANAP controlled 139 seats). In April the mayor of İstanbul, Reçep Tayyip Erdoğan, who was expected to assume the leadership of the FP, was sentenced to 10 months' imprisonment for inciting hatred; he was released pending an appeal. Erdoğan's conviction and the investigation of hundreds of civil servants, teachers and government officials for their alleged support of Islamist organizations was widely criticized.

The stability of Yılmaz's minority Government was threatened by the demands of the CHP for an early general election. The CHP demonstrated its power in April 1998 by voting with the opposition in favour of an investigation into allegations of corruption against the Prime Minister. Following an agreement signed by Yılmaz and CHP leader Deniz Baykal, the Prime Minister announced in June 1998 that he was to resign at the end of the year; he was to be succeeded by an interim government which would call early elections for April 1999.

It was announced in May 1998 that former Minister of the Interior Mehmet Agar was to be tried for his involvement in the Susurluk incident. In that month Çiller's husband was found guilty of misleading a parliamentary commission; his sentence, of five months' imprisonment, was later commuted to a fine. In August 12 former RP politicians, including Erbakan and FP leader Recai Kutan, were charged with illegally diverting funds from the party prior to its dissolution. An investigation into Çiller's assets was begun in September. Further investigations were launched in that month into Çiller and the former Minister of Finance for financial irregularities, and the immunity of the former TGNA Speaker was revoked, to allow an investigation, at his request, into his conduct following corruption allegations.

In September 1998 the Court of Appeal upheld the prison sentence on the mayor of İstanbul. Public demonstrations were held in protest at the sentence. As a result of his conviction Erdoğan was deprived of his position of mayor; he also resigned from the FP. In December new charges were filed against him for insulting the judiciary in a speech following his sentencing in September. In November corruption charges against Çiller were dismissed by a parliamentary commission, owing to insufficient evidence, while Erbakan was acquitted on charges of slandering the judiciary, and Minister of State Güneş Taner was removed from office, following a parliamentary censure motion arising from corruption allegations. In December Ozer Çiller was acquitted on charges of falsifying documents.

The Government resigned in November 1998, after the TGNA approved a motion of 'no confidence' submitted by the CHP in response to accusations of corruption against Yılmaz. In December Bülent Ecevit of the DSP was invited to form an administration. He abandoned the task after three weeks of negotiations, primarily with the DYP, failed to reach an agreement. Yalım Erez, the Minister of Trade and Industry, was subsequently offered the premiership. In early January 1999, however, the DYP indicated that it would support Ecevit. Erez relinquished his mandate, and in mid-January Ecevit formed a Government, comprising DSP and independent deputies, which was to govern until the elections in April; the administration subsequently secured a vote of confidence in the TGNA. Also in January a motion was filed for the dissolution of the pro-Kurdish nationalist Halkın Demokrasi Partisi (HADEP—People's Democracy Party), owing to its alleged links with the Kurdish separatist PKK (see below); in March, however, the Constitutional Court ruled that HADEP was to be allowed to contest the elections.

In February 1999 the trial began of 79 alleged Islamists, including Erbakan. Hasan Celal Güzel, the leader of the Yeniden Doğuş Partisi (YDP—Rebirth Party), was sentenced to one year's imprisonment in February for inciting hatred in a speech at a meeting in Kayseri province; he received a further one-year sentence in May for insulting the President, and was imprisoned for five months from December for incitement to vengeance and hostility. In February the Minister of Finance and Customs resigned in order to stand for election as mayor of İstanbul. Meanwhile, the High Election Council ruled that former RP deputies would not be allowed to take part in the forthcoming elections as independent candidates.

Despite pressure to postpone the elections, voting proceeded as scheduled on 18 April 1999. No party won an outright majority in the TGNA; the DSP won 136 of the 550 seats, and subsequently formed a coalition with the Milliyetçi Hareket Partisi (MHP—Nationalist Movement Party), which had won 129 seats, and ANAP, which had won 86 seats. The remaining seats in the TGNA were won by the FP (111), and the DYP (85), with three seats won by independent candidates. HADEP performed strongly in the south-east, but failed to secure the 10% of the national vote necessary for a seat in the TGNA. The CHP leader, Deniz Baykal, resigned following the poor performance of his party. The new Government, led by Bülent Ecevit, won a parliamentary vote of confidence on 9 June. In May the Chief Prosecutor instituted a court case against the FP, with the aim of dissolving the party.

In late August 1999 some 17,100 people were killed in an earthquake measuring 7.8 on the Richter scale, which struck near İzmit, in north-west Turkey. Both the Government and the armed forces were criticized for the lack of co-ordination and the slowness of the response to the crisis. A second earthquake, measuring 7.2 on the Richter scale, resulted in a further 800 deaths in the same region in November. In that month Turkey enacted legislation to allow conscripts to pay to shorten their military service in order to raise funds for reconstruction after the earthquake.

In August 1999 several articles of a political parties act relating to the closure of parties were approved: no party would be permitted to reform, even under a different name, party officials would be prohibited from active politics for five years and would be forbidden from standing as candidates for the party, although they would be permitted to stand as independent candidates. In September the FP submitted its preliminary defence against the motion to ban it. In October the assets of Erbakan and nine other former RP officials were frozen as part of the continuing trial of a case brought by the Treasury demanding the repayment of aid given to the RP in 1997, as well as the repayment of allegedly unregistered party funds. In March 2000 Erbakan was sentenced to one year in prison and a lifetime ban from politics for provoking animosity and hatred in a speech made in 1994; his conviction was upheld by an appeals court in July. (In January 2001, however, his sentence was suspended, under penal legislation allowing conditional release for certain convictions.) In December 1999, meanwhile, 300 people were detained following protests over the ban on wearing headscarves in universities and in that month the Court of Appeals ruled that the prerogative to wear Islamic headscarves was not a democratic right.

Internal power struggles within the FP became increasingly evident from 1999. In July, following the appointment of a new Secretary-General, a number of members, including the deputy leader, resigned in protest at these appointments, which they claimed had been made without their knowledge, and in March 2000 Abdullah Gül announced his intention to challenge Kutan for the leadership of the party. However, Gül was narrowly defeated in a vote in May. In February the party was again threatened with closure, following its accusations that the army had links with Hezbollah, a fundamentalist guerrilla organization (see below).

In January 2000, following a lack of agreement within the TGNA on a suitable presidential candidate (Demirel's term of office was to end in May), Ecevit announced plans for a constitutional amendment that would allow Demirel to renew his term. Despite the agreement of the governing coalition for the proposal, a vote in the TGNA failed to achieve the necessary level of support for the amendment to be carried. In April the parties of the governing coalition agreed to nominate the Chairman of the Constitutional Court, Ahmet Necdet Sezer, as their joint candidate for the presidency; he was elected in a third round of voting.

In June 2000 the TGNA rejected a recommendation to indict former Prime Minister Mesut Yılmaz on corruption charges related to the sale of state-owned land. The rejection came after Yılmaz indicated that ANAP could be forced to withdraw its support from the governing coalition, and thereby cause the collapse of the Government. In July, as part of a minor reorganization, Yılmaz joined the Government as Minister of State, also replacing Cumhur Ersümer, the Minister of Energy and Natural Resources, as Deputy Prime Minister. Yılmaz's inclusion in Government was welcomed by the FP.

Ecevit spoke out in June 2000 in favour of abolishing capital punishment, emphasizing this as a prerequisite for Turkey if it was to be fully integrated with the EU; he also stated that the extradition of offenders to Turkey would be facilitated by the abolition. The issue was one which was said to divide the ruling coalition. In August the military claimed that thousands of civil servants were trying to destroy the secular system and urged the TGNA to enact measures enabling their removal. The Government had already attempted to change by cabinet decree laws which would authorize the dismissal of civil servants suspected of supporting radical Islamist or Kurdish groups, but Sezer twice vetoed the measures, insisting that the proposals had to be introduced by parliamentary legislation.

At HADEP's national conference in November 2000 Murat Bozlak was elected unopposed as leader, replacing Ahmet Turan Demir. Deniz Baykal was re-elected leader of the CHP in the same month. In December the case was brought before the Constitutional Court seeking the closure of the FP, on the grounds of its being a focus for fundamentalist activities and an illegally established successor to RP.

Under the relative stability of the Ecevit Government, the Turkish economy appeared to be making significant improvements throughout most of 2000, with the implementation of structural reform measures. In November, however, a severe banking crisis was provoked by an investigation by the Banking and Supervision Agency into 10 failed banks. The investigation exposed the vulnerability of the banking sector and the lack of confidence of foreign investors in the Turkish economy, as a result of a widening current-account deficit and delays to the structural reform programme. The IMF and the World Bank agreed to emergency loans in order to support the programme. In February 2001 a second economic crisis was precipitated following a dispute between the President and Prime Minister: Sezer had accused Ecevit of not responding adequately to allegations of government corruption. Opposition parties and the business community had demanded the dismissal of Deputy Prime Minister Hüsamettin Özkan, the Minister of Energy, Cumhur Ersümer, and the Minister of Public Works, Koray Aydın, and the initiation of a parliamentary investigation into the affairs of Ersümer and Aydın. The precarious balance of power within the governing coalition was, however, thought to have dissuaded Ecevit from undertaking any action against the alleged corruption. Later in February Turkey, with the support of the IMF, abandoned its exchange-rate controls and allowed the lira to float, while empowering the central bank to pursue a rigorous monetary policy to control inflation.

Following the crisis, in March 2001 Ecevit replaced the Minister of Finance, Reçep Onal, with Kemal Derviş, a senior economist at the World Bank, in an attempt to salvage Turkey's economic reforms and restore confidence in the financial markets. He also replaced the Governor of the Central Bank, Gazi Erçel, with Süreyya Serdegeçti. Following Derviş's appointment, the head of the Banking and Supervision Agency resigned. Derviş announced an emergency plan for economic stabilization, which included the restructuring of three state-owned banks under one supervisory board, and succeeded in securing the financial support of the IMF and the World Bank.

The political implications of the financial crisis continued to be felt throughout April 2001, as anti-Government demonstrations involving tens of thousands of people degenerated into riots in Ankara and İzmir, which were dispersed by security forces. However, Ecevit rejected demands for his Government to resign. Later in the month it was announced that 15 officials and business executives were to be tried on conspiracy and bribery charges, following a high-profile investigation into corruption in the state energy sector. The testimonies of the defendants resulted in the resignation of the Minister of Energy and Natural Resources, Cumhur Ersümer, who was succeeded by Zeki Cakan of the ANAP in early May.

In May 2001 the TGNA approved legislation designed to meet conditions demanded by the IMF before the latter was to release US $10,000m. in financial aid. A major condition was the privatization of Turkey's telecommunications sector, which was widely opposed by TGNA members. At the end of the month the Minister of State for Privatization, Yuksel Yalova, resigned, owing to disagreements within the Government over the liberalization of the tobacco industry stipulated by the IMF. Prime Minister Ecevit attempted to replace Yalova with the Minister of the Interior, Sadettin Tantan, but the latter refused the transfer and resigned from his cabinet and ANAP posts in early June, following disagreements with Mesut Yılmaz. Tantan was succeeded as Minister of the Interior by Rüştü Kazim Yücelen, hitherto State Minister in charge of human rights. In late July the Minister of Communications, Enis Öksüz, resigned, owing to his opposition to the planned IMF-imposed reforms in the telecommunications sector. In early September the Minister of Public Works and Housing, Koray Aydın, resigned from his government post and from the TGNA, after corruption charges were brought against him in respect of his alleged receipt of funds from contracts relating to reconstruction in the aftermath of the 1999 earthquake damage.

In late June 2001 the Constitutional Court banned the FP, on the grounds that it was essentially a continuation of the banned Islamist RP and was thus regarded as seeking to undermine the secular system. The Court expelled two FP members from the TGNA; however, it refrained from ordering the mass expulsions of the 100 remaining FP members from the legislature, who were allowed to remain in place as independents or join two planned successor parties. The ban was, nevertheless, opposed by most TGNA members, who were reportedly concerned that it would lead to more political instability. In July the European Court of Human Rights (ECHR) upheld the Government's 1998 decision to ban the RP. In July 2001 former FP leader Recai Kutan established a new Islamist party, Saadet Partisi (SP—Felicity Party), incorporating about one-half of the former members of the FP (mainly from the conservative wing); the new party pledged to defend religious rights without challenging the secular State. It was believed that, as with the FP, Erbakan was the main force in the party. In mid-August the remaining members of the FP joined the new reformist Islamist Adalet ve Kalkınma (AK) Partisi (Justice and Development Party), established by the former mayor of İstanbul, Reçep Tayyip Erdoğan, and FP member Gül as an alternative to the SP. Shortly afterwards Erdoğan came under investigation for comments he had reportedly made in 1994 that allegedly insulted the Turkish State.

In early October 2001 the TGNA overwhelmingly approved a number of constitutional amendments designed to facilitate Turkey's admission to the EU. The changes largely pertained to political freedoms and civil liberties, including minority rights (notably regarding the use of the Kurdish language); however, amendments to articles concerning the death penalty refrained from abolishing capital punishment outright. Significantly, the number of civilians on the powerful NSC would rise from five to nine, thereby lessening the power of the military (which would retain five members). Improved rights for women were approved in late November.

In January 2002 the Constitutional Court imposed restrictions on the political activities of AK Partisi leader Erdoğan, owing to his earlier allegedly seditious activities. The Court banned him from contesting the elections to the TGNA, and ordered his party to remove him from its leadership within six months. In early March Ankara's Higher Criminal Court sentenced Erbakan to two years and four months in prison for embezzling party funds. (In December 2003 the Court of Appeals in Ankara upheld this sentence, although it was deferred for one year on medical grounds.)

In early February 2002 the TGNA approved additional laws on freedom of thought and expression by means of a 'mini-reform' programme designed to satisfy EU standards. In subsequent weeks the ruling coalition experienced increasing disagreement over the possible execution of PKK leader Abdullah Öcalan, and on broadcasting and education in the Kurdish language, with the MHP taking an uncompromising stance on these issues in opposition to ANAP. The discord prompted rumours of a possible general election, which intensified towards mid-2002 as it became apparent that the Prime Minister was in poor health. In late June, none the less, Ecevit, who was reportedly under pressure from members of his own party to resign, discounted the possibility of an early election, on the grounds that this would undermine the economic recovery programme.

In July 2002, however, Ecevit was finally forced to call early elections to the TGNA for November, after several of his ministers and numerous DSP party legislators resigned, thereby denying the ruling coalition a majority in the TGNA. The MHP had earlier that month publicly called for an early election. Notable resignations included those of Deputy Prime Minister and Minister of State Hüsamettin Özkan, Minister of Foreign Affairs İsmail Cem and Minister of Culture İstemihan Talay. Cem formed a new party, the Yeni Türkiye Partisi (YTP—New Turkey Party), with 62 defectors from the DSP, whose representation in the TGNA had fallen from 128 seats to 65 seats. Ecevit appointed DSP member Şükrü Sina Gürel as Deputy Prime Minister and Minister of State, and concurrently Minister of Foreign Affairs. In early August the Minister of Finance, Kemal Derviş, also resigned, having offered to resign in July, but remaining in office at President Sezer's request. Derviş initially indicated that he would join the YTP, but subsequently agreed to co-operate with the CHP. The Minister of Labour and Social Security also resigned in August, demonstrating the disintegration of Ecevit's Government. Meanwhile, at the end of August the notably pro-EU and strongly secularist commander of the army's ground forces, Gen. Hilmi Özkök, was appointed to the powerful position of Chief of the General Staff for a four-year term.

In late September 2002 the AK Partisi, which was leading in opinion polls, underwent a reverse, when Turkey's highest election board confirmed the Constitutional Court's decision to ban Erdoğan from holding public office. Although he had publicly professed secular and pro-European views, Erdoğan retained the distrust of the secularist military and judiciary, and in October the chief prosecutor sought to obtain an outright ban on the AK Partisi, although this was not implemented. Attempts by several political parties to delay the election also failed.

The elections to the TGNA, held on 3 November 2002, significantly transformed the Turkish political landscape. With voter participation of 79.0%, the AK Partisi won 34.3% of the votes cast, securing 363 seats in the TGNA. Only one other party, the CHP, achieved the 10% of the vote required for representation in the TGNA, winning 19.4% of the votes cast and securing 178 seats. The DSP, which had won the majority of seats in the April 1999 election, won just 1.2% of the votes cast, while its coalition partners, the MHP and ANAP, won 8.3% and 5.1% of the vote, respectively. The new Genç Partisi (Youth Party), established in 2002 by the millionaire businessman, Cem Uzan, won 7.3% of the votes cast. Following the election, President Sezer appointed AK Partisi deputy leader Abdullah Gül as Prime Minister, since Erdoğan was ineligible for the position. (None the less, Erdoğan acted as *de facto* Prime Minister, exerting a strong influence on the new Government and making a number of foreign official visits.) The new Council of Ministers largely consisted of technocrats from the AK Partisi. Three Deputy Prime Ministers, Abdüllatif Şener, Mehmet Ali Şahin and Ertuğrul Yalçınbayır, were appointed, while Ali Babacan became Minister of State with responsibility for the Economy and Kemal Unakıtan acquired the financial portfolio. Mehmet Vecdi Gönül was appointed Minister of National Defence. Owing to the fact that AK Partisi's representation in the TGNA was only four seats less than the two-thirds' majority needed to amend the Constitution, and the party commanded the support of several independents, in early December the legislature approved constitutional reforms allowing Erdoğan to contest a forthcoming by-election. Initially vetoed by Sezer, these changes were subsequently re-endorsed by the TGNA, forcing the President to accept them.

In January 2003 Erdoğan was re-elected leader of the AK Partisi and immediately announced plans to contest the by-election for the TGNA, membership of which would allow him to become Prime Minister. In February the electoral commission endorsed his candidacy, and Erdoğan was elected to the TGNA on 9 March. Two days later President Sezer appointed Erdoğan as Prime Minister, after Gül relinquished the post, as expected. Erdoğan appointed a new Council of Ministers, which retained most ministers from the incumbent Government. Gül replaced Yalçınbayır as Deputy Prime Minister and also assumed the foreign affairs portfolio. In June the TGNA adopted a further series of human rights reforms, including additional legislation to permit education and broadcasting in Kurdish and other minority languages, and to amend the existing legal definition of terrorism, in order to qualify for accession negotiations with the EU. At the end of that month Sezer vetoed one of the amendments, under which peaceful advocacy of an independent Kurdish state would no longer be illegal (on the grounds that it posed a threat to the Turkish state). However, the TGNA utilized its power to overrule the veto by returning the legislation to the President without amendment. Further reforms approved by the TGNA (in accordance with EU requirements) at the end of July included the reconstitution of the predominantly military NSC as an entirely advisory body and the offer of a qualified amnesty to KADEK supporters, with the specific exclusion of those believed to have committed acts of violence; these measures were formally approved by Sezer on 6 August. At the end of September a decision by the Court of the Appeals over the November 2002 elections confirming the disqualification of DEHAP (as HADEP had become reconstituted in March 2003—see below) for malpractice prompted concern that the results would be annulled, thereby ending the majority of the AK Partisi. On 4 October 2003 the High Electoral Council upheld the election results. In the same month an independent parliamentary deputy joined the Liberal Demokratik Parti, which consequently secured one seat in the TGNA.

On 15 November 2003 some 25 people were killed and about 300 injured in two suicide bombings outside two of İstanbul's largest synagogues. On 20 November a further two suicide bombs exploded outside the Hong Kong and Shanghai Banking Corporation and the British consulate in İstanbul, killing some 31 people (including the Consul-General) and injuring more than 450. Although several extremist Turkish Islamist groups, including the Great Eastern Islamic Raiders' Front (IBDA-C), claimed responsibility for the attacks, the involvement of the militant Islamist al-Qa'ida (Base) network (see below) was immediately suspected. Erdoğan condemned all acts of terrorism in a national statement, and demonstrations were staged in Turkey against the bombings, although popular sentiment also attributed blame to the US-led military action in Iraq. By the end of that month a total of 62 had been killed in the four bomb attacks, and 159 had been arrested on suspicion of involvement, of whom a number had been charged. The Turkish authorities announced that the bombings had been organized by a 'cell' of Turkish nationals connected to al-Qa'ida, all of whom had been trained outside Turkey; one principal suspect was repatriated from Syria, while another was arrested on Turkey's south-eastern border with Iran.

Local government elections, which were held on 28 March 2004, resulted in a strong increase in support for the AK Partisi, which secured 42% of the votes cast and 58 of the country's 81 provinces. The CHP, having become subject to internal factional divisions, won only 18% of the votes. In May, as part of the series of reforms intended to bring Turkey into conformity with EU human rights and democratic standards, the TGNA adopted draft constitutional amendments to abolish the death penalty and anti-terrorist state security courts, to guarantee equality for women and to establish full parliamentary control over the budget of the armed forces. The approval in the same month of new education legislation, ending restrictions on university entrance for those trained in religious schools, was viewed with concern by defendants of Turkey's official secularism. Consequently, the Government's decision at the beginning of June, following a veto by President Sezer, to suspend the introduction of the legislation was generally welcomed. Security concerns shortly before a NATO summit, attended by US President George Bush, in June were heightened by further explosions in İstanbul, including a suicide bombing, in which four people were killed. In the same month Turkey's stated commitment to new human rights standards, in compliance with EU requirements, was demonstrated by the Supreme Court's decision to order the release of the four Kurdish former parliamentary deputies, who had been sentenced to 15 years' imprisonment in 1994 for supporting the PKK. Following their release, a court in July 2004 overturned their convictions and ordered retrials. The most celebrated of the four, Leyla Zana, after her release, urged the organization to reinstate the cease-fire ended by the organization in September 2003 (see below). In a further significant measure, the TGNA in July 2004 authorized the prosecution for corruption of former Prime Minister Mesut Yılmaz and three other former ministers. In mid-August a further three bombs exploded at hotels in İstanbul, killing two people, and were again attributed by the authorities to Kurdish militants.

In January 2005, following the provisional offer by the EU in December 2004 for the commencement of accession negotiations, Islamist party leaders criticized the conditions imposed and demanded that the Government organize a referendum on EU membership; protests were organized in İstanbul and in İzmit. In early February 2005 the Chairman of the Human Rights Consultative Council tendered his resignation, citing continuing impediments posed by the Government (which had rejected a previous critical report of the Council over the stance on human rights). Later in February the Minister of Culture and Tourism, a reformist member of the AK Partisi, also resigned.

Turkey's new penal code, adopted as a precondition for the commencement of EU accession talks (see below), entered into force at the beginning of June 2005, after a two-month postponement. Sezer subsequently vetoed an amendment reducing the penalties for anti-secular teaching in illegal religious schools. However, at the end of June the TGNA overruled the President's veto, which was supported by the ruling AK Partisi. In the same month a minor government reorganization was effected.

In late 2005 the Government's announcement that the renowned Turkish writer, Orhan Pamuk, had been charged with denigrating the Turkish state, after he made a reference in an interview to a Swiss newspaper to the massacre of some 1.5m. Armenians by Turks between 1915 and 1923, prompted international criticism. Pamuk's trial began, amid nationalist protests, in December but was immediately adjourned, after the municipal court in İstanbul ruled that, under the terms of the unrevised penal code, the Ministry of Justice should decide whether or not it proceed. In January 2006 the charges against Pamuk were abandoned, after the Minister of Justice referred the case back to the court, which refused to uphold it. (It was reported, however, that some 60 journalists were on trial at that time on charges of insulting the Turkish state.) In February the trial began of five prominent journalists, including the editor of a principal Armenian newspaper, who had been charged with denigrating the judiciary, after criticizing a September 2005 court decision to prohibit a university conference in İstanbul on the massacre of Armenians in 1915–23.

In March 2006 controversy emerged over the appointment of a new Central Bank Governor, following the expiry of Serdegeçti's term in office. The Government's selection of Adnan Buyukdeniz, the manager of a financial enterprise that operated according to Islamic law, proved controversial, raising concern over the continuation of the authorities' economic policy, and was finally rejected by Sezer. In April Sezer approved the nomination of Durmuş Yılmaz, a long-standing Central Bank director, who pledged commitment to the IMF-supported policy of monetary restraint. In the same month the trial of two Syrian nationals, including a suspected member of al-Qa'ida, was merged with that of 71 defendants charged with involvement in the bombings in İstanbul in November 2003. In March 2006 three people were killed when a bomb exploded near the Governor's office in the south-eastern town of Van, and in early April a further bomb attack was staged at the offices of the AK Partisi in İstanbul.

Although Turkey was readmitted to the Parliamentary Assembly of the Council of Europe in May 1984, the Assembly continued to advocate the establishment of full democracy and political freedom in the country. In July 1987 all martial law decrees were repealed when martial law was replaced with a state of emergency in several provinces. The Government's signing, in January 1988, of UN and Council of Europe agreements denouncing torture, however, met with a cynical response from both the domestic and international media. Turkey's human rights record has continued to be a focus of international scrutiny.

In July 1999 the ECHR found Turkey guilty of 13 counts of violating rights of free speech and ordered it to pay some 110,000m. lira in damages. In August amnesty legislation was approved by the TGNA to ease the extreme overcrowding in Turkish prisons, with the release of some 26,500 prisoners (of a total prison population of 69,000) and the reduction in sentence for a further 32,000. Although the legislation was initially intended to encourage Kurdish rebels to surrender, it was subsequently altered so that prisoners serving sentences for terrorism would not benefit from the law. However, the bill received widespread criticism and was vetoed by President Demirel in early September. Unrest broke out in that month in prisons across the country as a result of the poor conditions and overcrowding; 10 prisoners were killed and a number of guards were taken hostage. The Minister of Justice later announced that a special force was to be established to ensure prison security. In September some 100 people were arrested in İstanbul while trying to issue a press release on the prison incidents. Prison unrest continued, and in February 2000 a protocol was signed providing for the education of prison inmates. During April and May a number of prison officials were dismissed for improper conduct and contacts with prisoners.

In December 1999 the ECHR found Turkey guilty of breaking the European Convention on Human Rights by its closure of the pro-Kurdish Demokrasi Partisi (DEP—Democracy Party, see below) and ordered it to pay compensation of 70,000 French francs. It was also announced that a human rights consultation committee was to be established to provide information and to act on any complaints received. A report published by the Turkish Human Rights Foundation in June 2000 asserted that as many as 1m. people had been victims of torture over the preceding decade. The report criticized the fact that perpetrators of torture were not subjected to due investigation.

In November 2000 hundreds of political prisoners throughout Turkey (mainly members of left-wing organizations) embarked on a hunger strike, in protest against plans to transfer them to high-security prisons where they would be held in isolation cells. Following attempts to force-feed the prisoners, in violation of international medical ethics, confrontations ensued between the prisoners and the authorities. In December Turkish security forces raided some 20 prisons in an attempt to end the hunger strikes. The three-day action resulted in the deaths of 30 prisoners and two soldiers. After the authorities regained control of the prisons, over 1,000 prisoners were transferred to the isolation cells. There were widespread allegations, supported by human rights organizations Human Rights Watch and Amnesty International, that many prisoners had been subjected to torture both before and after their transfer to these cells, where many prisoners resumed their hunger strike. Also in December the TGNA approved legislation granting an amnesty to as many as 35,000 prisoners by reducing their sentences by 10 years; the legislation was, however, rejected by President Sezer on the grounds that it was divisive and would not serve the cause of justice. By the end April the number of deaths resulting from the hunger strike had reached 20, with some 30 more seriously ill. The Government refused to open negotiations with the prisoners, although the Minister of Justice announced an initiative to improve prison inspections. In May EU officials warned that failure to resolve the issue could jeopardize Turkey's candidacy for the EU. During the remainder of 2001 many of the strikers were released or hospitalized; of these, some subsequently ended their strike. In November police stormed the houses of some of the released strikers in an attempt forcibly to end the strikes; four protesters reportedly died of self-immolation during the police operation. By January 2003 a total of 104 people had died as a result of the ongoing hunger strikes, but no compromise had been reached on the issue of prison accommodation.

Meanwhile, during 2001 the TGNA introduced new legislation, including constitutional amendments, designed to improve the country's human rights and civil liberties in preparation for eventual EU accession (see above). In March the Government had announced a new programme aimed at facilitating EU membership that entailed, *inter alia*, the eventual abolition of the death penalty and ending restrictions on freedom of expression, as well as improving the rights of minorities, but EU officials criticized the programme for its lack of specifics. Despite such plans, the TGNA approved a four-month extension of the state of emergency in the predominantly Kurdish south-east of the country, and in May the Turkish Radio and Television Supreme Council ordered the closure of 89 radio and television stations for broadcasting separatist and disruptive programmes. In October the TGNA approved wide-ranging constitutional amendments embracing improvements in civil liberties and human rights; further liberalizing reforms were approved in February 2002 (see above). Meanwhile, in November women were granted new rights, including equal status to men in several key areas.

In June 2002 the Government proposed additional reforms that abolished the death penalty and removed a ban on broadcasting and education in the Kurdish language. In early August the TGNA formally abolished the death penalty in peacetime; in September, however, Amnesty International released a report alleging the widespread use of torture by police, citing testimony from more than 60 individuals during the first half of 2002. In mid-October a court in İstanbul sentenced 10 police-officers to prison terms ranging from five to 10 years for beating, torturing and sexually abusing 15 teenage suspects in 1995. The case had received considerable publicity both in Turkey and abroad, and the police-officers had been acquitted on two previous occasions, resulting in strong condemnation by human rights groups. The officers launched an appeal against their verdict, but in early April 2003 the Court of Appeals upheld the sentences. Following his appointment as Prime Minister in March, Erdoğan immediately pledged to bring about major improvements in Turkey's human rights record and to eliminate the use of torture. A series of reforms, approved by the TGNA in July (see above), included provisions for the prompt investigation of allegations of torture and for prohibiting the trial of civilians in military courts in peacetime. In May 2004 the TGNA approved a number of constitutional amendments, in accordance with EU requirements, which included the removal of references to the death penalty and the abolition of the country's system of State Security Courts (used to try dissidents).

The Government's position on the Kurdish situation remained a major element of its human rights policy. In September 2001 hundreds of Kurds were reportedly arrested to prevent their attending a mass rally in Ankara. In January 2002 the Government acted against a campaign to allow the Kurdish language to be taught in schools and universities by arresting hundreds of activists. In February an İstanbul court acquitted a publisher, Fatih Tas, for disseminating 'separatist' articles, written by US academic and linguist Noam Chomsky, which criticized US support for Turkish military operations aimed at suppressing Kurdish nationalism. Chomsky himself attended the trial in support of Tas. In March the Government postponed the trial of an expatriate Kurdish novelist, who had been charged with violating the ban on the Kurdish language. Later that month clashes between security forces and Kurds at a HADEP-organized Kurdish new year celebration in Mersin resulted in the death of two policemen and one demonstrator. The decision by the AK Partisi Government in November to permit a maximum of 30 minutes per day of Kurdish language programmes on state television and a maximum of 45 minutes on state radio was greeted with disappointment by Kurdish groups, who had long sought unlimited broadcasting of Kurdish programmes on commercial and local radio and television stations. In mid-March 2003 a ruling by Turkey's Constitutional Court banned HADEP from political activity on the grounds that it had been aiding the PKK (a charge which the party denied). Some 46 members of the party were also subjected to a five-year ban. Shortly afterwards HADEP became reconstituted as the Democratik Halkın Partisi (DEHAP—Democratic People's Party).

A significant increase in outbreaks of urban terrorism in early 1990, together with a perceived increase in the influence of fundamentalist thought, led to widespread fears of a return to the extremist violence of the late 1970s. The increase in terrorist attacks by Islamist and left-wing groups, especially the Dev-Sol (Revolutionary Left), was exacerbated by the Government's stance in the Gulf crisis of 1990–91 (see below), and both factions unleashed a series of attacks against Western targets in Turkey, including US civilians, diplomatic missions and offices of several national airlines and banks in İstanbul and Ankara. The leader of Dev-Sol, Dursun Karatas, was detained in France in September 1994, and diplomatic efforts began to ensure his extradition. Two weeks later a former Minister of Justice, Mehmet Topaç, was shot dead by Dev-Sol members in Ankara. In August 1995 several bombs exploded in İstanbul (killing two civilians), at least one of which was reported to have been placed by a previously unknown Islamist group. In January 1996 a left-wing faction of Dev-Sol, Devrimci Halk Kurtuluş Partisi—Cephesi (DHKP—C, the Revolutionary People's Liberation Party—Front), claimed responsibility for the murder of two leading Turkish business executives in İstanbul. At the end of the year it was reported that Dev-Sol had been subsumed by the DHKP—C.

In January 2000 the Government launched a major operation against the fundamentalist guerrilla group Hezbollah (apparently sponsored by fundamentalist elements in Iran but unrelated to the Lebanese group of the same name). An armed confrontation between police and Hezbollah members resulted in the death of its leader, Hüseyin Velioğlu, and the capture of two of his closest associates; information provided by these associates led to the discovery of the bodies of nine men, believed to have been abducted by the group in İstanbul. In early 2000 the operation succeeded in detaining some 690 suspected Hezbollah members and the bodies of more than 50 people, believed to have been victims of the group, were discovered. At that time the Government denied that it had tolerated the activities of Hezbollah, owing to its anti-PKK activities, and the office of the Chief of the General Staff strongly denied allegations of links between Hezbollah and the army. In February Çiller denied that the state had supplied weapons to Hezbollah during her time as Prime Minister and in March two regional FP staff were arrested on suspicion of membership of Hezbollah; the FP said it would expel them if found guilty. In October Turkish security forces captured Mehmet Sudan, Velioğlu's successor, and the Ministry of the Interior reported that since January some 1,600 people with ties to Hezbollah had been arrested.

In December 2000 two police-officers were killed and a further three were injured, following an attack on a police bus in İstanbul. In January 2001 the DHKP—C claimed responsibility for a suicide bomb attack on a police building, which killed two people. In April Sahil Izzet Erdis, the leader of the outlawed IBDA—C, was sentenced to death on charges of seeking to overthrow the secular state. In early September a suicide bomber, believed to be acting on behalf of the DHKP—C, killed two policemen and a foreign tourist in central İstanbul. In May 2002 the EU designated the DHKP—C as a terrorist organization. In November 2004 security forces arrested several members of DHKP—C, in two attempted military operations.

In 1984 the outlawed PKK, seeking the creation of a Kurdish national homeland in Turkey, launched a violent guerrilla campaign against the Turkish authorities in the south-eastern provinces. The Government responded by arresting suspected Kurdish leaders, sending in more security forces, establishing local militia groups, and imposing martial law (and later states of emergency) in the troubled provinces. Violence continued to escalate, however, and in April and May 1990 clashes between rebel Kurds, security forces and civilians resulted in the deaths of 140 people. The conflict entered a new phase when in August and October 1991, and March 1992 (in retaliation for continuing cross-border attacks on Turkish troops), government fighter planes conducted numerous sorties into northern Iraq in order to attack suspected PKK bases there. In the course of these raids many civilians and refugees (including Iraqi Kurds) were reportedly killed, prompting international observers and relief workers publicly to call into question the integrity of the exercises. The Iraqi Government lodged formal complaints with the UN, denouncing Turkish violations of Iraq's territorial integrity.

Violence in the south-eastern provinces, resulting from ethnic tension, persisted throughout 1992 and 1993, despite the stated commitment of the Demirel administration to foster new initiatives for improved relations with ethnic minorities. In late 1992 Turkish air and ground forces (in excess of 20,000 troops), conducted further attacks upon PKK bases inside northern Iraq, hoping to take advantage of losses inflicted on the Kurdish rebels by an offensive in October initiated by Iraqi Kurdish *peshmerga* forces, aimed at forcing the PKK from Iraq. Hopes that a negotiated resolution to the conflict might be achieved, following the unilateral declaration of a cease-fire by the PKK in March 1993, were frustrated by renewed fighting in May and an intensification of the conflict in June. The bombing of several coastal resorts and of tourist attractions in central İstanbul confirmed the PKK's intention to disrupt the country's economy and to attract international attention to the conflict. PKK activists and supporters also conducted protests and attacked Turkish property throughout Europe.

In November 1993 a 10,000-strong élite anti-terrorist force was created to counter the PKK forces, in addition to the estimated 150,000–200,000 troops already positioned in the area of conflict. In early 1994 the security forces mounted a heavy offensive against the separatists, and again conducted air attacks on suspected PKK strongholds in south-eastern Turkey and in northern Iraq. Reports that an estimated 6,000 Kurds were forcibly displaced into northern Iraq as a result of the destruction of their villages by security forces were denied by the Minister of Foreign Affairs. Further air offensives against Kurdish targets in northern Iraq were undertaken in August, while clashes between the PKK and security forces were reported in south-eastern Turkey. In late September security forces initiated an operation in the eastern Munzur mountains to destroy PKK stores and supply routes. In November a Kurdish proposal for a cease-fire, accompanied by international mediation, to achieve a peaceful settlement to the conflict was rejected by the Government, which emphasized the success of its anti-terrorist campaign.

On 20 March 1995 a massive offensive, involving 35,000 air and ground force troops, was initiated against PKK targets in northern Iraq. Turkish forces advanced some 40 km across the border, prompting protests from Iraq, as well as concern on the part of the USA and the EU that the military intervention should not be consolidated into a permanent occupation force. The Turkish Government insisted that the offensive was designed to destroy PKK base camps and to force the separatists from northern Iraq (where, it claimed, the PKK had taken advantage of a power vacuum in the region to become securely established). The UN assisted in the evacuation of several thousand Kurds from the northern Iraqi town of Zakho, amid reports of intimidation by the occupying Turkish troops. Under increasing international pressure, Turkey undertook a complete withdrawal of its troops by May. Official figures stated that 555 Kurdish separatists and 58 Turkish soldiers were killed as a result of the operation. Earlier, in April, the PKK had obtained permission to convene in the Netherlands, in an attempt to establish a Kurdish parliament-in-exile, prompting Turkey to temporarily recall its ambassador to the Netherlands. Fighting was again resumed in the south-east of the country in June, and in July a further week-long offensive was conducted against Kurdish bases in northern Iraq. In December the PKK leader, Abdullah Öcalan, announced a unilateral cease-fire on the part of his organization. By March 1996, having received no assurances of a cease-fire from the Turkish authorities, Öcalan advised tourists against visiting the country, warning of possible renewed attacks against major tourist sites. During April an estimated 400 PKK members were killed in the renewed military operation. In the following months PKK activists were frequently pursued into northern Iraq by Turkish ground and air forces, provoking protests from the Iraqi Government, and fighting in the south-eastern provinces escalated. At the end of June five soldiers were killed in a suicide bomb attack in Tunceli, eastern Turkey. A further two suicide attacks, reportedly by PKK members, were perpetrated in October, killing 10 people. In response Turkish security forces conducted air raids against PKK targets in northern Iraq, which continued into early 1997. An estimated 2,800 PKK activists were killed during 1996 as a result of the conflict, in addition to 532 members of the security forces and 145 civilians.

In May 1997 Turkey again launched a massive military offensive against the PKK in northern Iraq, involving the mobilization of 50,000 troops. Turkey claimed that the incursion was in response to an appeal by the Iraqi-based Kurdistan Democratic Party (KDP), which co-operated with the Turkish attack. The operation elicited rigorous condemnation from Iraq, Iran and Syria, but the response from members of NATO was muted. Turkish military officials claimed that the attack, which continued through June, had achieved its objectives of destroying several PKK bases in northern Iraq and estimated that more than 3,000 PKK troops had been killed. A further offensive, launched in September, was speculated to be part of a Turkish plan to establish a security zone in northern Iraq to prevent cross-border attacks by the PKK. This assumption was apparently confirmed by the lifting of the state of emergency in three of the nine south-eastern provinces at the beginning of October.

Despite PKK threats to extend the separatist struggle throughout Turkey, if the Turkish Government refused to seek a political solution to the conflict, further Turkish troops entered northern Iraq in February 1998. Further operations against the PKK took place in April, including the capture of a former PKK commander, Semdin Sakik. Sakik had surrendered to the DPK in March, following a disagreement with Öcalan, which fuelled speculation concerning internal dissent within the movement. The Government undertook heavy offensive action in northern Iraq in late May and early June. At the end of August the PKK declared a unilateral cease-fire; this was, however, rejected by the Government.

Relations with Syria, which had already deteriorated in July 1998 (owing to Syria's repeated claim to the Hatay region of Turkey), worsened in early October, after Turkey threatened the use of force if Syria did not expel Öcalan and close down terrorist training camps in both Syria and the Beka'a valley in Lebanon. It was reported that 10,000 Turkish troops had been deployed near the border; the Turkish ambassador to Syria was also recalled. Egypt and, later, Iran both attempted to mediate in the dispute, and, following a meeting of Turkish and Syrian officials in late October, an agreement was signed under which Syria would not allow the PKK to operate on its territory; Öcalan was thus forced to leave the country, and he arrived in Italy in November. Turkey had already temporarily recalled its ambassador to Italy in October, after a meeting of the Kurdish parliament-in-exile was hosted there. Relations deteriorated further when Italy refused to extradite Öcalan to Turkey and Öcalan applied for asylum. Demonstrations were held in Turkey against Italy, and Italian goods were boycotted; Turkey also threatened to end diplomatic relations with Italy if Öcalan's asylum request was granted. PKK attacks in the south-east were reported during November, and government operations against the PKK continued. In January 1999 Öcalan was reported to have left Italy after his asylum application was turned down. His whereabouts were unclear, until, in February, Öcalan was captured at the Greek embassy in Kenya and returned to Turkey. Widespread Kurdish protests were held throughout Europe.

At the end of February 1999 Öcalan was formally charged, in the absence of defence counsel, and the first hearing was set for late March. PKK violence in protest at the trial continued in that month, and there were also threats of violence against tourists in Turkey. A series of bomb attacks in İstanbul were later attributed to a new Kurdish group, the Nationalist Kurdish Revenge Teams. In early March Turkey conveyed information to the ECHR regarding Öcalan's trial; at that time it was reported that he had appointed two lawyers. In April a further operation was launched against the PKK, involving the deployment of some 15,000 Turkish troops in northern Iraq. Semdin Sakik, the former PKK commander who had been captured in March 1998, was sentenced to death in May 1999; his sentence was upheld by the Supreme Court in October. In late June Öcalan was convicted on treason charges and sentenced to death; violent demonstrations were held in protest at his sentence. A third PKK leader, Cevat Soysal, was arrested in Moldova in July.

The PKK agreed to a cease-fire in early August 1999, and at that time Öcalan announced that the PKK was prepared to surrender its arms in exchange for Kurdish rights; PKK fighters withdrew from Turkey at the end of the month. However, the Government insisted that the PKK cease hostilities entirely in order for Turkey to reassess the situation. Following a statement issued by Öcalan in September in which he urged PKK rebels to show their commitment to the end of hostilities by surrendering to Turkish forces, two eight-member PKK delegations travelled to Ankara where they were arrested and detained by the authorities.

In September 1999 the Kurdish parliament-in-exile convened in Brussels, where it voted to dissolve and to join the Kurdistan National Congress. Following the cease-fire, the number of armed confrontations in the south-east had declined substantially and in October the Government reduced the number of check-points in the region. In November Öcalan's death sentence was upheld on appeal and the chief prosecutor rejected his application for a final appeal; his lawyers referred the case to the ECHR. A second trial against Öcalan, together with 101 other defendants, began in Ankara in December for a series of offences including extortion and murder allegedly carried out in the 1970s; the trial was adjourned until February 2000. In January 2000 the parties of the governing coalition announced that they had agreed to delay Öcalan's execution until a ruling had been given by the ECHR.

In February 2000 the PKK announced formally the end to its war against Turkey and stated that it would campaign for Kurdish rights within a framework of peace and democracy. In February three HADEP mayors were arrested and charged with aiding the PKK; they were released on bail, following protests both from within Turkey and internationally, including from the EU. Relations with the EU further deteriorated in February, when Turkey denied EU politicians permission to visit Öcalan in prison. At that time 18 people, including the HADEP leader, Ahmet Turan Demir, were sentenced to almost four years' imprisonment for organizing demonstrations in support of Öcalan. Despite the PKK's cease-fire declaration, Turkish troops continued to push into Kurdish strongholds throughout the year. In September at least 38 civilians were reported to have been killed, following sorties by Turkish fighter planes into northern Iraq targeting suspected PKK bases and in early 2001 Turkish troops advanced into Kurdish northern Iraq, in an attempt to suppress PKK activities. Some 2,500 PKK rebels were believed to be based along the Iran–Iraq border at this time.

In June 2000 there were a number of reports of increased tension within the PKK leadership, with some members, including, according to some sources, Öcalan's brother, Osman, no longer acknowledging Abdullah Öcalan as leader of the organization. In September Selahattin Celik, a founder member of the PKK, formed a breakaway group, styling itself 'the Initiative', to continue the PKK's military campaign. However, Celik, who was based in Germany, lacked the resources and forces to wage a guerrilla war. The hearing of the appeal against Öcalan's death sentence began at the ECHR in November. Öcalan's appeal was based on the grounds that he had not received a fair trial in Turkey under the terms of the European Convention on Human Rights.

In April 2002 the PKK formally announced a change of name to the Congress for Freedom and Democracy in Kurdistan (KADEK), under the leadership of Öcalan, and asserted its wish to campaign peacefully for Kurdish rights. Although the movement had abandoned its initiative for an independent Kurdish state, the announcement was received with scepticism on the part of the Turkish Government. However, KADEK was not included in the EU's list of organizations designated as 'terrorist', and it was believed that its agenda had been designed to win support from the EU. In June the ECHR awarded compensation to 13 Kurdish former members of the TGNA who had been imprisoned by the Government in 1994 for supporting the PKK. At the end of November 2002, in a sign that the Government had acknowledged the conversion of the PKK, the state of emergency that prevailed in the two remaining south-eastern provinces of Diyarbakır and Sirnak was finally ended.

In early October 2002, meanwhile, the State Security Court officially commuted Öcalan's death sentence to life imprisonment, in accordance with the abolition of the death penalty in peacetime by the TGNA in August. The court's decision was controversial, since Öcalan was widely despised by the Turkish public for his armed insurrections during the 1980s and 1990s. In March 2003 the ECHR issued a non-binding ruling that Öcalan had not received a fair trial, and criticized Turkey for violating some of Öcalan's rights; however, the ECHR rejected accusations by Öcalan's lawyers of inhumane treatment and illegal detention. Turkey immediately appealed against the ECHR, fearing renewed pressure from the EU to hold a retrial if the ruling was upheld. Despite its success in defeating Kurdish separatism, the Government continued to fear the possible emergence of a Kurdish state in northern Iraq after the USA's successful war against Iraqi President Saddam Hussain's regime in March–April 2003 (see below). A partial amnesty offered to supporters of KADEK by the Government in July failed, apparently owing to the effective exclusion of the movement's leadership, with only eight members accepting the terms by the end of August. On 1 September, following renewed KADEK attacks in eastern Turkey, KADEK formally ended the cease-fire declared in February 2000, accusing the authorities of failing to address demands for improved Kurdish rights and freedom of expression. In November 2003 KADEK was reconstituted as the Kongreya Gelê Kurdistanê (KONGRA-GEL—Kurdistan People's Congress). In January 2004 the US Administration added KONGRA-GEL to its list of designated 'terrorist' organizations.

After revoking its cease-fire, KONGRA-GEL organized sporadic attacks throughout 2004. In late July government troops launched an offensive against KONGRA-GEL positions at the border with Iraq. In November further clashes between security forces and KONGRA-GEL militants, in which six rebels were killed, were reported in south-eastern Turkey. In early 2005 security forces repelled an attack staged from northern Iraq by suspected KONGRA-GEL members, and also arrested two KONGRA-GEL militants who had been planning a bomb attack in Mersin. In April the KONGRA-GEL leadership announced that the organization was to revert to its original name, PKK (although it appeared that not all elements of the movement did so). In May the ECHR ruled that the trial of Öcalan had been unfair, on the grounds that he had not been tried by an independent tribunal (owing to the presence of a military judge on the panel); the Turkish Government indicated that a further trial would be conducted.

A series of bomb attacks in July and August 2005 were attributed to Kurdish militants (although the PKK denied responsibility), including one on a tourist bus in the Aegean Sea resort of Kuşadası, in which five people died, and another against an army unit in south-eastern Turkey. In September some 88 PKK supporters were arrested in İstanbul, after protesting at being prevented from attending a rally in support of Öcalan (who had, it was reported, been placed under solitary confinement), while Turkish nationalists clashed with PKK demonstrators in the western town of Bozüyük. Despite the PKK's extension until early October of a unilateral cease-fire, which it had declared in late August, clashes between rebels and government forces continued in the east of the country. Later in October Kurdish protests erupted in the north-western town of Eskişehir, where the trial was in process of four security officers accused of killing two civilians, including a minor, while in pursuit of rebels. In November rioting erupted in the south-eastern town of Şemdinli, after three suspected perpetrators of a bomb attack apparently aimed against a PKK supporter, in which one person was killed, were discovered to be police intelligence agents. The Government subsequently pledged that an investigation would be conducted into the incident. Security forces continued to stage operations in the east of the country against members of the PKK and its re-emerged military wing, Hezên Parastina Gel (HPG—People's Defence Forces). In March 2006 some 50 suspected militants were detained after a security operation in central Turkey. At the end of that month the funeral of 14 suspected PKK supporters in the south-eastern town of Viranşehir precipitated large-scale Kurdish rioting; some 12 people were killed in the region in April, following clashes between protesters and security forces, while three civilians were killed when Kurdish protesters attacked a bus in İstanbul.

Turkey has been a member of NATO since 1952, and is widely considered to have fulfilled a crucial role in NATO defence strategy in south-eastern Europe. During the 1990s Turkey's importance to its key ally, the USA, increased as its strategic location allowed it to co-operate with the USA in regional security issues. The Turkish Government responded positively to requests from the USA for logistical aid, following the forcible annexation of Kuwait by Iraq in August 1990, and complied with UN proposals for economic sanctions against Iraq by closing its border to all non-essential trade and, later, to traffic. In September Turkey and the USA extended an agreement to allow the USA access to more than 25 military establishments, in return for military and economic aid, that had been initially signed in 1980, and renewed in 1987. In mid-January 1991 a resolution to extend the war powers of the Government and effectively endorse the unrestricted use of Turkish air bases by coalition forces was agreed by the TGNA. On the following day US aircraft embarked upon bombing missions into north-east Iraq from NATO bases inside south-east Turkey. In February and March the US Government announced substantial increases in military and economic aid to Turkey. In April an estimated 600,000 Kurds attempted to flee northern Iraq into Turkey. Following a massive international relief effort and the subsequent repatriation of the majority of refugees, the Turkish Government agreed to the deployment in south-east Turkey of a 3,000-strong multinational 'rapid reaction force', which would respond to any further acts of aggression by Iraq against the Kurds in the newly created 'safe havens'. While all ground forces were withdrawn in October, the Turkish Government agreed to the continued use of its air bases by a small allied air-strike force to conduct patrols of northern Iraq under the mandate of 'Operation Provide Comfort'. The mandate was granted six-month extensions, despite increasing unease on the part of the Turkish authorities that the Kurdish enclave was providing a refuge for PKK separatists. Difficulties in Turkey's relations with the USA arose in 1994, following a decision by the US Congress to withhold some military and economic aid in order to encourage greater respect for human rights in the Turkish Government's treatment of Kurdish separatists.

In March 1996 the Turkish Government assured the TGNA that the mandate for the use of Turkish bases for allied aircraft engaged in 'Operation Provide Comfort' would be terminated, following the approval of a final three-month extension. At the end of July, however, the new RP Prime Minister, Necmettin Erbakan, in spite of his earlier election pledge to conclude the arrangement, secured a final extension of the operation's mandate until the end of the year. In September the Turkish Government refused permission for the use of its air bases for a US military operation against Iraqi forces that had violated the Kurdish area in northern Iraq. Turkey amassed an estimated additional 20,000 troops along the border and revealed proposals to establish a temporary security zone in the region in order to stem any influx of refugees from Iraq and to prevent the PKK from exploiting the situation. The Government also undertook to relocate the military co-ordination centre of 'Operation Provide Comfort' from Zakho in northern Iraq to Silopi in south-eastern Turkey. ('Operation Provide Comfort' was superseded by the more limited aerial surveillance operation 'Northern Watch' in January 1997.) In October 1996 the Turkish Government was actively involved in negotiations between the conflicting Kurdish factions in northern Iraq to secure a peace agreement, not least in an attempt to end the power vacuum in that region which threatened Turkey's security. A second round of talks, following the conclusion of a preliminary agreement at the end of October, was initiated in November. During 1996 Turkey pursued diplomatic efforts to secure the reopening of the petroleum pipeline from Kirkuk in northern Iraq to Yumurtalik in Turkey, which had been closed since August 1990 as a result of UN-imposed economic sanctions. The pipeline was finally reactivated in December, in accordance with a UN agreement permitting the export of US $2,000m. of petroleum by Iraq over a six-month period, in order to fund the purchase of essential medical and other humanitarian supplies. As relations between Iraq and the UN deteriorated from the end of 1997, Turkey announced that it opposed the use of its Incirlik air base for potential US-led strikes against Iraq and urged a peaceful solution to the crisis. Relations deteriorated further in late 1998, and Turkey again urged a diplomatic solution. Although Turkey was informed of the airstrikes against Iraq in December, in January 1999 it announced that Turkish air bases would not be used in any new operation against Iraq.

Following the terrorist attacks on the USA in September 2001, perpetrated by Osama bin Laden's al-Qa'ida (Base) network of fundamentalist Islamist militants, Turkey emerged as a crucial ally in the former's 'war on terror', immediately pledging its co-operation. In October the TGNA agreed in principle to send troops to Afghanistan and allow foreign forces to be stationed in Turkey, and in December US Secretary of State Colin Powell visited Turkey to discuss security and bilateral trade issues. (It was believed that, in return for assisting in the US-led campaign, Turkey would gain financial assistance from the USA and persuade the Administration to pressure the EU into accepting Turkey's membership.) Meanwhile, hundreds of Turkish commandos were deployed in Uzbekistan in preparation for possible combat in Afghanistan, and 90 of these entered northern Afghanistan to train the opposition United National Islamic Front for the Salvation of Afghanistan (the United Front—UF, or 'Northern Alliance'). Turkey had for some years had contacts with the UF's Gen. Abdulrashid Dostam, having given him asylum in the late 1990s. Turkey assumed command of the International Security Assistance Force (ISAF) in Afghanistan in June 2002, raising its troop presence in that country to 1,000. (Turkish command of the ISAF ended in February 2003, whereupon control of the force passed to Germany and the Netherlands.)

Throughout 2002 Turkish leaders became increasingly concerned about the possibility that the USA would open a 'second front' in its military campaign to overthrow the regime of Saddam Hussain. In particular, the Government feared a break-up of the Iraqi state and the creation of a Kurdish state in northern Iraq that could be used to foster Kurdish nationalism in its own territory, and the possible mass exodus of Iraqi Kurds into Turkey. There were also concerns about the disruption to Turkish-Iraqi trade and economic co-operation that any US-led attack would bring. Ecevit's illness and the subsequent preparations for elections to the TGNA in November meant that no agreements between Turkey and the USA were reached over the latter's planned invasion of Iraq. Relations between the two countries were further complicated by the victory of the AK Partisi in the elections, and overwhelming public opposition to war against Iraq. By January 2003 a number of senior US officials had visited Turkey to persuade the Government to accept the deployment of 62,000 US troops in the south-east of the country, and the use of the region as a staging post for a 'northern front' in the planned conflict. Following lengthy negotiations, the US Government offered a financial package of US $6,000m. in direct grants and an additional $20,000m. in loans and trade concessions in compensation for any economic losses incurred during the war; however, the Turkish authorities considered this sum to be insufficient. President Sezer in late February warned that US forces could only be deployed in Turkey if the USA obtained a second UN resolution from the UN Security Council authorizing the use of force against Iraq. On 1 March 2003 the TGNA rejected a motion allowing the USA to deploy troops in Turkey. (Although 264 members of the TGNA had voted in favour of the deployment, with 250 against, the motion was four votes short of a majority of deputies in attendance.) As many as 50 AK Partisi legislators voted against the Government, underscoring the level of opposition to US plans for a military campaign to oust the Iraqi regime. On 20 March the TGNA voted only to allow the use of Turkish airspace for the conflict, but endorsed the deployment of Turkish troops in Iraq if considered necessary. The US-led coalition forces initiated attacks against the Iraqi regime on 20 March, and shortly thereafter abandoned attempts to negotiate the use of Turkish bases. The aid package was withdrawn following the TGNA vote, but in early April the USA offered a new, reduced package totalling a loan of US $8,500m. in order to repair bilateral relations. The US Secretary of State, Colin Powell, visited Ankara at that time and secured Turkish permission for humanitarian aid and US logistical supplies to be delivered to US and coalition troops in Iraq via Turkish territory.

In September 2003 the Turkish and US Governments signed an agreement approving the US $8,500m. loan to compensate for the adverse effects of the March–April conflict in Iraq. In early October a motion proposed by the Council of Ministers in favour of contributing peace-keeping troops to the US-led coalition in Iraq was endorsed by the TGNA. Following widespread protests in both Turkey and Iraq, however, Erdoğan announced that he would consider reversing this decision, and in early November the planned deployment of Turkish forces in Iraq was cancelled. In February 2005, at the same time as an official visit to Turkey by the US Secretary of State, demonstrations were staged in Ankara in protest at US foreign policy, including the continuing US military presence in Iraq.

Although Turkey and Greece are both members of NATO, long-standing disputes over sovereignty in the Aegean Sea and concerning Cyprus have strained relations between the two countries, and tension was exacerbated when Turkey granted recognition to the 'Turkish Republic of Northern Cyprus' ('TRNC'), proclaimed in November 1983 (see the chapter on Cyprus). In April 1988 the Greek Prime Minister, Andreas Papandreou, officially accepted Turkey's status as an associate of the EC by signing the Protocol of Adaptation (consequent on Greece's accession to the EC) to the EC-Turkey Association Agreement, which the Greek Government had hitherto refused to do, and in June Turgut Özal became the first Turkish Prime Minister to visit Greece for 36 years. In February 1990 relations deteriorated again, following violent clashes between Christians and the Muslim minority in western Thrace, in Greece. Throughout the early 1990s Turkey and Greece maintained strong support for their respective communities in Cyprus during the ongoing, but frequently interrupted, negotiations to resolve the issue.

The issue of the demarcation of territorial waters in the Aegean re-emerged as a source of tension with Greece in 1994. Turkey insisted that it would retaliate against any expansion of territorial waters in the region, as provided for under the terms of the UN Convention on the Law of the Sea (UNCLOS), which entered into force in November. Military exercises in the region were undertaken, by both Turkish and Greek naval vessels, and resumed in June 1995 following ratification of UNCLOS by the Greek Parliament. Relations between the two countries, which remained strained during 1995 over the issue of the treatment of the Muslim minority in western Thrace, deteriorated sharply in early 1996, owing to a series of incidents in the Aegean in which both countries claimed sovereignty of Imia (Kardak), a small, uninhabited island. Turkey's claim was based on a concession granted by Italy prior to the 1947 settlement that awarded the main Dodecanese islands to Greece. The dispute was exploited by nationalist media in both countries; however, the threat of military action was averted in February 1996 when the two sides agreed to a petition of the US Government to withdraw naval vessels from the region and to pursue efforts to conclude a diplomatic solution. Differences remained on the means of achieving a settlement, with Greece proposing to take the dispute to international arbitration, an option endorsed by the EU Council of Ministers, and Turkey advocating bilateral negotiations. Throughout 1996 relations between the two countries remained strained as a result of several minor confrontations between Greek and Turkish patrol vessels in the Aegean, persistent Greek allegations of violations of its airspace by Turkish aircraft and Turkish concern at the treatment of the ethnic population in western Thrace. From mid-1996 an escalation in intercommunal tension in Cyprus emphasized divisions between the two countries. Turkey remained committed in its support for the 'TRNC' authorities and resolved to respond with military action to the proposed deployment of an anti-aircraft missile system in the Greek Cypriot territory. A joint defence doctrine was agreed by the Turkish and 'TRNC' authorities in January 1997, and in March a co-operation accord, providing for some US $250m. in economic assistance to the 'TRNC', was ratified by the two sides.

In April 1997, following Greece's continued refusal to conduct bilateral discussions with Turkey over sovereignty rights in the Aegean, Turkey rejected proposals to refer the dispute over Imia (Kardak) to the International Court of Justice (ICJ). At the end of April the Greek and Turkish ministers responsible for foreign affairs held bilateral talks in Malta under EU auspices, during which it was agreed that each country would establish a committee of experts to help resolve bilateral disputes. The two committees were to be separate and independent and were to communicate through the EU. In July, at a NATO summit in Madrid, Spain, direct talks took place between Demirel and the Greek Prime Minister, Konstantinos Simitis (the first such meeting for three years). An agreement, known as the Madrid agreement, was signed in which both sides pledged to respect the other's sovereign rights and to renounce violence, and the threat of violence, in their dealings with each other. Later in July, following earlier statements from Turkey expressing the hope that Greece would revoke its veto on EU aid, Greece stated that the veto would not be removed unless Turkey agreed to international arbitration over the disputed islet of Imia (Kardak).

In July 1997 Turkey announced the formation of a joint committee to implement partial integration between Turkey and the 'TRNC', in response to the EU's agreement to commence accession talks with Cyprus. Turkey also declared in September that should the EU continue to conduct membership talks with the Greek Cypriot Government, then it would seek further integration with the 'TRNC'. Shortly afterwards Turkey banned all Greek Cypriot ships from entering Turkish ports. Following the involvement of Greece in Greek Cypriot military exercises in October, in November Turkish forces engaged in military manoeuvres in the 'TRNC'. However, Yılmaz and Simitis held a cordial meeting later in November and agreed to explore confidence-building measures. Throughout 1997 and early 1998 relations were strained by accusations of violations of airspace and territorial waters, made by both Greece and Turkey. The most serious incident occurred in October 1997 when Greece accused Turkey of harassing a plane carrying the Greek Minister of Defence. In January 1998 Turkey declared that a Greek plan to extend its territorial waters from six to 12 miles under UNCLOS was unacceptable, as were plans to open several Aegean islets for settlement. Turkey also protested to the UN that the proposed opening of an airbase at Paphos in southern Cyprus would destabilize the military situation on the island. In April Greece again vetoed the release of aid promised to Turkey under the Turkish-EU customs union.

Relations deteriorated in 1998 as a result of a purchase agreement between the Greek-Cypriot Government and Russia for anti-aircraft missiles. Turkey maintained that their deployment would be a threat to its territory and in July announced that it planned to deploy missiles in the 'TRNC' if the missiles deal proceeded. In December, however, the Greek Cypriot Government announced that it would not be deploying the missiles in Cyprus and that they would be deployed on Crete, Greece. In January 1999 Turkey refused to pay compensation which had been awarded by the ECHR to a Greek Cypriot woman for land lost as a result of the Turkish occupation of northern Cyprus.

Relations with Greece deteriorated in early 1999, following repeated Turkish accusations of Greek support for the PKK; Greece denied the accusations, although Öcalan was later captured at the Greek embassy in Kenya. In March Turkey alleged that Greece had unilaterally suspended 'confidence-building' talks on the dispute in the Aegean, and denied a claim that Turkish aircraft had violated Greek airspace. At the end of August relations between the two countries improved markedly, following the Greek response to the earthquake that occurred in north-west Turkey at the end of that month. Greek rescue teams were among the first to arrive in Turkey, and Greece agreed to lift its veto on EU development loans and aid to Turkey; Turkey reciprocated the gesture by sending a rescue team to Greece following a smaller-scale earthquake in Athens in September. A joint business council announced it was to resume its activities in September and in that month the Turkish and Greek ministers responsible for foreign affairs met for discussions in Brussels. Train services linking Greece and Turkey were introduced in November. In January 2000 the Greek Minister of Foreign Affairs made the first official visit to Turkey by a Greek foreign minister in 38 years, during which it was agreed that direct talks would be held to reduce military tensions in the Aegean. In February the Turkish Minister of Foreign Affairs made an equally historic visit, becoming the first Turkish foreign minister to visit Greece in 40 years. In October, however, relations with Greece were strained once again, when Greece withdrew from a joint NATO military exercise in the Aegean, after it accused Turkey of preventing Greek aircraft from flying over the disputed islands of Limnos and Ikaria. This followed a joint NATO military exercise with Greek and Turkish troops on a Greek beach in June, which had been considered to be a mark of considerable progress in Greek-Turkish relations. In February 2001 the Greek parliament decreed a 'Genocide Day' to commemorate the Turkish assault on the Greek community in eastern Turkey by Atatürk's forces in 1922. However, in April 2001 both Turkey and Greece announced major reductions in their weapons-procurement programmes, and in May Greece announced measures to improve the rights of its ethnic Turks (mainly in Thrace). In June the two countries discussed the possibility of allowing Turkish nationals to visit Greek islands in the Aegean for day trips without the need for visas, and the Minister of Foreign Affairs, Ismail Cem, received his Greek counterpart, Georgios Papandreou, to discuss friendship-building measures such as the demining of their mutual border and co-hosting the 2008 European Football Championship. In November 2001 Turkey and Greece signed an agreement that allowed Greece to repatriate illegal Turkish immigrants.

None the less, Cyprus continued to overshadow bilateral relations, and in May 2001 Cem warned that there would be 'no limits' to Turkey's response were Cyprus to be admitted to EU membership before a political settlement had been reached; in early November Ecevit warned that Turkey could annex the 'TRNC' if this were to occur. In February 2002 the Turkish and Greek foreign ministers recommenced talks, following the resumption of negotiations between the Greek and Turkish Cypriot sides on the island. In mid-March Turkey and Greece discussed ongoing disputes over the Aegean Sea, including the control of the continental shelves and the resources beneath them. Later in the month the two Governments signed an agreement to build a 285-km natural gas pipeline from Ankara to Komotini, Greece, thereby allowing Iranian gas to flow to the EU via the existing Tabriz (Iran)–Ankara pipeline. In late April the Turkish and Greek foreign ministers announced that they would send a joint mission to the Middle East to support efforts to end the Israeli–Palestinian violence. In September a series of meetings took place between Turkish and Greek officials and government ministers, and in October Greece offered its support for the scheduling of EU accession negotiations with Turkey.

Following the elections to the TGNA in November 2002, Reçep Tayyip Erdoğan stated that a final peace agreement over Cyprus would accelerate Turkey's chances of joining the EU. Erdoğan, whose political priority was Turkey's membership of the EU, was increasingly in conflict with Turkish Cypriot leader Rauf Denktaş's unyielding stance on reaching a political solution. In January 2003 Erdoğan publicly criticized Denktaş and stated that he was in favour of a new policy for Cyprus, with a view to achieving a solution by 28 February 2003 in order to allow the 'TRNC' to join the EU in 2004 at the same time as the Greek part of the island. During late 2002 and early 2003 the Turkish- and Greek-Cypriot leaders had made significant progress towards reaching a final agreement, which would permit the entire island to accede to the EU on 1 May 2004. However, negotiations on the peace plan failed in March 2003 (see the chapter on Cyprus). Following further UN-sponsored discussions in New York, on

13 February 2004 agreement was reached on a reunification plan based on proposals drafted by the UN Secretary-General, Kofi Annan. The Greek Cypriot President, Tassos Papadopoulos, and Denktaş, resumed UN-sponsored negotiations in the Cypriot capital, Nicosia, on 19 February. Greece and Turkey joined the negotiations later in March; however, both Papadopoulos and Denktaş subsequently opposed a final resolution, which was to be submitted for approval by both the Greek- and Turkish-Cypriot communities at a referendum. On 24 April the reunification plan was endorsed by Turkish Cypriots by 64.9% of votes cast at the referendum, but rejected by Greek Cypriots by an overwhelming majority of 75.8% of the votes; consequently, only the Greek part of Cyprus was admitted to the EU on 1 May. EU officials subsequently announced measures to alleviate the economic sanctions in force against the 'TRNC'. In April 2005 the Turkish Cypriot Prime Minister, Mehmet Ali Talat, who strongly supported reunification of the island and full participation in the EU, was elected to the 'TRNC' presidency, replacing Denktaş.

Following the 1980 military coup, the EC-Turkish Association Council (which had been established in 1963) was suspended, together with all community aid to the country. Turkey was readmitted to associate membership of the EC in September 1986, but failed to gain access to the suspended EC aid or to extend the rights of the large number of Turkish workers in Europe. In April 1987 Turkey made a formal application to become a full member of the EC. In December 1989 the application was effectively rejected, at least until 1993, by the Commission of the European Communities. The Commission cited factors including Turkey's unsatisfactory human rights record, high rate of inflation, dependence upon the rural population and inadequate social security provisions as falling short of EC expectations. During informal discussions in 1993 representatives of the EC reiterated their concern at abuses of human rights in Turkey and the lack of progress in the political negotiations regarding Cyprus; however, they recognized the strategic importance of Turkey's role as a stable regional influence. The Turkish Government began to implement measures to construct a customs union with the EU, which was to become effective on 1 January 1995. Human rights issues remained the main obstacle to securing an agreement, and in December 1994 the customs union was postponed on these grounds. An attempt to conclude the agreement in January 1995 was unsuccessful, owing to opposition from the Greek Government. (The negotiations were complicated by Greek demands concerning EU relations with Cyprus.) In February Greece withdrew its veto on the customs union, having received assurance on the accession of Cyprus to the EU, and the agreement was signed in March; however, it was to be subject to ratification by the European Parliament. The Turkish Government subsequently pursued efforts to introduce new democratization legislation and to secure the support of European leaders for the customs union by extending guarantees on human rights and treatment of its Kurdish population. The final terms of the arrangement were agreed at a meeting of the EU-Turkish Association Council in October, and were approved by the European Parliament in December. The EU was expected to provide a total of ECU 1,800m. over a five-year period, in order to assist the implementation of the new trade regime and to alleviate any initial hardships resulting from the agreement. The customs union came into effect on 1 January 1996. Its implementation was, however, delayed, owing to Greek opposition to the release of ECU 375m. in aid, claiming that Turkish action in the Aegean was a violation of the agreement. In July Greece withdrew its opposition to Turkey's participation in an EU-Mediterranean assistance programme, although the block on funds from the customs union remained in effect. Throughout 1996 the Turkish Government criticized the EU for its failure to adhere to the terms of the economic agreement. In January 1997 Turkey warned that it would disrupt any expansion of NATO if the EU refused to consider the Turkish membership application. Previously, Turkey had prevented the use of NATO facilities by members of Western European Union, owing to Greek opposition to Turkey's full participation in the regional defence grouping.

Relations with the EU were tense in 1997 as the next group of EU applicants was selected. In December, following EU announcements that Turkey would not be invited to join the EU, but that it would be invited to a newly created EU Conference, which was to include both EU and non-EU states, Turkey stated that it would not attend such a conference and that it would also cease negotiations on Cyprus, human rights and the Aegean disputes. It further threatened to boycott EU goods and to withdraw its application to the EU if it was not included in a list of candidates by June. On 20 December Turkey announced a six-month freeze in relations with the EU. The EU later announced it was withholding all aid to Turkey for 1998, owing to the situation in the south-east of the country and its human rights problems. Turkey officially declined its invitation to the EU Conference in March 1998 and in May Turkey declined to attend a scheduled meeting of the EU-Turkish Association Council. Relations with France deteriorated in May when the French National Assembly adopted a motion recognizing the Turkish 'genocide' against the Armenians in 1915–23; a number of bilateral military and commercial contracts were suspended as a result. Relations with France temporarily improved in February 2000, following a decision by the French Senate not to place the draft law recognizing the Armenian 'genocide' (approved by the National Assembly in 1998) on its agenda for discussion.

In October 1999 an EU report declared Turkey to be a suitable candidate to join that body, although at that time Turkey said that it would not accept any extraordinary conditions attached to such a candidacy, particularly with relation to Öcalan and the Kurdish problem. A number of EU members declared their support for Turkey in late 1999, including Greece and Italy; Turkish relations with both countries had improved in that year. In December Turkey was invited to attend the EU summit in Helsinki, Finland, and to accept formal status as a candidate for membership. Turkey initially objected, owing to attached conditions concerning Cyprus and the Aegean dispute with Greece, but following a visit to Turkey by Javier Solana, the Secretary-General of the Council of the European Union, Turkey accepted. It announced at that time that it would seek an end to its territorial disputes with Greece by 2004, the deadline set by the EU for a review.

In August 2000 Turkey signed the International Covenant of Civil and Political Rights and the International Covenant on Economic, Social and Cultural Rights. This was described as a positive step by the EU in its progress to accession report on Turkey in November 2000, although it pointed out that Turkey had not yet acceded to a number of other major human rights instruments, such as the abolition of the death penalty and the Convention on the Elimination of All Forms of Racial Discrimination. The report concluded that Turkey did not yet meet the Copenhagen criteria (which state that a country must have achieved 'stability of institutions guaranteeing democracy, the rule of law, human rights and respect for and protection of minorities'), thus making accession negotiations impossible, and described the overall human rights record in Turkey as worrying. It also stated that although Turkey had the basic features of a democratic system, it was slow to implement institutional reforms. Accession was also conditional on a satisfactory settlement of the Cyprus problem. This condition led to the Turkish withdrawal from the UN-sponsored proximity talks in protest. Prime Minister Ecevit accused the EU of 'deception' over Turkey's membership application, stating that the EU had reneged on a promise not to link Turkey's application to a resolution of the Cyprus problem and disputes with Greece over territorial rights in the Aegean Sea. A rewording of the Cyprus condition was later approved by Turkey; however, further tension was caused by Turkey's obstruction of an EU-NATO agreement enabling the EU's planned Rapid Reaction Force to use NATO assets, despite Turkey's offer to contribute up to 6,000 troops to the Rapid Reaction Force.

In 2000 and 2001 the Armenian 'genocide' question also continued to provoke tension between Turkey and the international community. In April 2000 Turkey complained to Israel after the Israeli education minister stated that he believed school pupils should be taught of the 'genocide' of the Armenians; the minister was speaking at a meeting to mark the 85th anniversary of the massacre. In October the Turkish parliament threatened not to renew the USA's mandate to use a Turkish airbase if the US Congress backed a draft resolution which referred to the killing of the 1.5m. Armenians by Turkey in 1915–23 as 'genocide'. Following intervention by President Bill Clinton, the House of Representatives agreed to withdraw the resolution. The European Parliament adopted a resolution in mid-November which formally accused Turkey of genocide against Armenians in 1915 (at the same time it also called on Turkey to pull its forces out of the 'TRNC'). Turkey reacted angrily, with the FP proposing a legislative investigation 'with the aim of removing wrong and biased opinions'. Relations with France were, however, more seriously damaged in January 2001, after the French National Assembly unanimously voted to recognize the 1915–23 massacre of Armenians under the Ottoman Empire as 'genocide', against the wishes of the Government. In November 2000 the French Senate had already voted to recognize the massacre as genocide; none the less, the French Government attempted to reassure Turkey that relations between the two countries remained intact. Following the National Assembly vote, however, Ecevit stated that the French action would damage relations between the two countries and recalled Turkey's ambassador to France immediately after the vote for consultations. In late January 2001 Turkey cancelled a surveillance satellite contract with a French firm. Another French company was barred from tendering for a major defence contract and the Minister of Health threatened to ban French medical imports. Turkey also removed a French telecommunications group from the list of bidders for the privatization of the state-owned telecommunications company. The Government further announced plans to erect a 'genocide' monument to the 1.5m. Algerians killed in the 1954–62 war of independence against the French.

Relations between Turkey and the EU received a set-back in early May 2001 when the ECHR ruled that Turkey had grossly violated the human rights of thousands of Greek Cypriots during its invasion, and subsequent occupation of northern Cyprus since 1974. The court highlighted the failure of the Turkish Government to investigate the fate of missing Greek Cypriots, and their forcible eviction from the north and the subsequent confiscation of their property.

In late May 2001 Turkey nominally agreed to grant the EU's Rapid Reaction Force access to NATO assets for future operations. Although Turkey would be consulted on such matters, it would not have the same participation rights or veto powers as the existing 15 EU members. However, Turkish officials remained dissatisfied at the arrangements, having lobbied strongly for a greater influence in EU security planning. Turkey also feared that an upsurge of violence in Cyprus would necessitate the deployment of the Rapid Reaction Force on the island, placing the EU directly against itself, and had unsuccessfully sought guarantees against such an eventuality. In early December Turkey finally reached agreement with the EU regarding the Rapid Reaction Force after months of British diplomacy.

In August 2001, meanwhile, the ECHR ruled that the Government's decision to ban the Islamist FP did not violate human rights laws. In October the TGNA passed constitutional amendments designed to facilitate EU membership but stopped short of abolishing the death penalty, a crucial EU demand. The issue of capital punishment placed the EU at odds with the ultra-nationalist MHP in the ruling coalition, which had pledged to exact the death penalty imposed on PKK leader Abdullah Öcalan.

In August 2002 the EU welcomed the TGNA's vote to abolish the death penalty in peacetime, as part of a broader package of reforms, and, similarly, reacted positively to the commutation of Öcalan's death sentence to life imprisonment in October of that year (see above). The new AK Partisi Government elected in November pledged to accelerate efforts to join the EU. However, in that month Valéry Giscard d'Estaing, the Chairman of the Convention on the Future of Europe, made controversial remarks when he publicly stated that Turkey should never be allowed to join the EU, and that its accession would mean the 'end of the European Union'. Senior EU officials distanced themselves from the remarks, which were also dismissed by Erdoğan. At the EU summit in Copenhagen, Denmark, in December, EU leaders agreed to delay negotiations on Turkish membership until after December 2004, and to resume discussions then only if Turkey had fulfilled all the entry obligations. Several EU members, notably France and Germany, remained less enthusiastic about Turkish membership, citing its poor human rights record, which Turkey again pledged to improve. The delays angered the Turkish Government, and Erdoğan warned that continuing delays to negotiations and attempts to exclude Turkey from the EU could cause increased anti-Muslim sentiments against the organization.

A further complication to Turkish ambitions for EU membership emerged with the failure of a UN plan for the reunification of Cyprus in April 2004 (see above). The resultant accession of only Greek Cypriot Cyprus to the EU on 1 May presented complications for Turkey's EU aspirations, although the Greek Cypriot Government declared that it would not veto Turkey's membership application, provided that it met the standards stipulated by the EU. An official visit to Greece by Erdoğan in early May (the first by a Turkish premier in 16 years) reflected the improvement in relations between the two countries; bilateral discussions particularly concerned Turkey's application for EU membership. An EU summit in Brussels in June reaffirmed that a decision would be taken in December on whether Turkey had made sufficient progress on the EU's criteria for membership and that formal accession negotiations would be initiated if standards were considered to have been met. However, severe doubts about Turkey's qualifications had been presented in a European Parliament resolution, which had been adopted overwhelmingly in April, drawing attention to Turkey's continued use of torture, to the persecution of minorities and other contraventions. In September the European Commission indicated that proposals to make adultery a criminal offence under a revised penal code would adversely affect Turkey's prospects of satisfying EU membership requirements. Later that month the TGNA approved a version of the penal reforms from which the adultery clause had been omitted, thereby increasing the likelihood that Turkey would be permitted to begin formal accession talks.

In early October 2004 the European Commission announced its approval of Turkey's qualification for accession negotiations, on condition that reforms continued. In many EU member states, however, there was increasing popular opposition to the admission of Turkey, especially in Germany and France, where the opposition was believed to reflect concern over the accession of a predominantly Muslim country; some favoured an option that Turkey be offered 'privileged member' status, rather than full membership. On 17 December the EU extended a provisional invitation to Turkey to commence accession negotiations on 3 October 2005, subject to the Turkish Government's fulfilment of a number of criteria, including continued progress in political and economic reforms. Erdoğan accepted an EU requirement to sign a customs accord with member states by that date, but insisted that the protocol would not constitute official Turkish recognition of the authorities of Greek Cyprus; instead he agreed to a compromise arrangement, whereby Turkey made a commitment for future recognition. The British Prime Minister welcomed the agreement; however, both the French and Austrian Governments pledged to conduct national referendums on Turkish entry, while a demonstration in protest at Turkish membership was conducted in Italy. In June 2005 the German Bundestag (Federal Assembly) became the latest EU legislature to attract Turkish anger by condemning the Armenian 'genocide' and accusing the Turkish Government of failing to address the issue.

In late July 2005, pending an EU decision on the opening of accession negotiations in October, the Turkish Government signed the requisite customs protocol with Cyprus and the other nine new EU member states, but appended a declaration reaffirming that the accord did not constitute official recognition of Greek Cyprus. In September EU member states adopted a draft declaration stating that Turkish recognition of Cyprus was necessary to the accession process, but without stipulating a date for this (thereby posing no obstacle to the beginning of negotiations). At the beginning of October intensive debate took place between EU member states to resolve the impasse over Austria's insistence that Turkey be offered the lesser option of 'privileged partnership' (to which the Turkish Government remained opposed), rather than full membership. Austria withdrew its veto to the admission of Turkey, after Croatia was unexpectedly declared eligible to enter into membership negotiations (see the chapter on Croatia). Turkey's accession negotiations with the EU were officially approved on 3 October, and opened on the following day. In early November an EU report, while welcoming Turkey's economic performance (see Economic Affairs), criticized a lack of progress in political reforms, citing continued human rights violations, including torture, and the necessity for further judicial reforms. Furthermore, the subsequent reluctance of the Turkish authorities to open ports and airports to Greek Cypriot-registered traffic by the end of 2006, in adherence to the customs protocol and as a condition to progress in the accession negotiations, prompted criticism from EU officials and repeated threats from the Greek Cypriot Government to veto Turkey's membership.

Following the formal dissolution of the USSR in December 1991, the Turkish Government sought to further its political, economic and cultural influence in the Caucasus and Central Asia, in particular with Azerbaijan, Kazakhstan, Kyrgyzstan, Turkmenistan and Uzbekistan, all of which share ethno-linguistic ties with Turkey. Following the outbreak of war between Armenia and Azerbaijan in 1991, Turkey blockaded Armenia and provided support to its 'Turkic' ally, Azerbaijan. In April 1992 Prime Minister Demirel undertook an official visit to several former Soviet republics, pledging aid of more than US $1,000m. in the form of credits for the purchase of Turkish goods and contracts. At the same time programmes broadcast by the Turkish national television company began to be relayed, by satellite, to the region. In June leaders of 11 nations, including Turkey, Greece, Albania and six former Soviet republics, established the Organization of the Black Sea Economic Co-operation (see p. 339), and expressed their commitment to promoting greater co-operation with regard to transport, energy, information, communications and ecology. In October 1994 a meeting of the Heads of State of Turkey, Azerbaijan, Turkmenistan, Uzbekistan, Kazakhstan and Kyrgyzstan took place in İstanbul, in an effort to develop and improve relations among the 'Turkic' republics. Summit meetings have subsequently been convened each year. In the late 1990s Turkey sought to encourage Western firms to build a new petroleum pipeline from Baku, Azerbaijan, to the Turkish port of Ceyhan, thereby allowing the transportation of petroleum from the Caspian Sea to the Mediterranean, via Azerbaijan and Georgia. Such a scheme would also increase Turkey's importance to the EU by making it the centre of the Transport Corridor Europe–Caucasus–Asia (TRACECA) project. Despite the cost of the pipeline, construction began in June 2002. In October 2000 President Sezer signed military co-operation pacts with Kyrgyzstan and Uzbekistan, allowing Turkey to train and equip their armed forces. In mid-2001 work began on a new natural gas pipeline from Dzhubga, Russia, to Samsun, Turkey, beneath the Black Sea, which would increase Turkey's dependency on Russian natural gas. During a significant visit to Turkey in December 2004 the Russian President, Vladimir Putin, signed co-operation agreements in the fields of trade, defence and finance.

In late 1995 a long-standing dispute with Syria and Iraq concerning the water supply from the Euphrates and Tigris rivers re-emerged as a major source of tension in Turkey's external relations. (Hostilities with Syria had already intensified during the year over that country's apparent support for the PKK, with the Turkish Government accusing Syria of supplying armaments to the separatist organization.) In December Syria issued a formal protest at the construction of a new hydroelectric dam on the Euphrates river (as part of the extensive southern Anatolia project—GAP) arguing that it would adversely affect the supply of water flowing into Syria. Further protests by Syria and Iraq that Turkey was storing their share of water from the two rivers and restricting flow, in contravention of previous agreements, resulted in a ruling, in March 1996, by the Council of the Arab League that the waters of the rivers should be shared equally between the three countries. In September 1997, President Demirel appealed for talks with Syria and Iraq on the use of the waters of the Euphrates. In August 1998, however, the Government refused to revive water talks with Syria and Iraq, citing issues that had first to be improved between the countries, primarily that of terrorism. Relations between Syria and Turkey improved during 1999 and in October officials from the two countries reportedly agreed to open a new border crossing. However, in January 2000 Turkey appealed to the USA not to remove Syria from its list of nations accused of sponsoring terrorism, until such time as all PKK bases had been removed from Syria, and in that month Turkey ruled out any concessions on the water issue in order to aid talks between Israel and Syria. In March Turkey and Syria announced a new framework for bilateral relations and discussed the basic principles which would apply to them, although in that month Turkey warned against the use of a map, prepared by Syria for use at a trade fair, which showed the Turkish region of Hatay as Syrian territory. A major improvement in relations materialized in early 2002 when Turkey signed an agreement with Syria allowing for joint military exercises. In early 2003 Turkey and Syria agreed to co-operate in bringing about a peaceful solution to the crisis over Iraq's alleged weapons of mass destruction and the US pursuit of regime change in Iraq. President Bashar al-Assad became the first Syrian Head of State to undertake an official visit to Turkey in early January 2004; the visit appeared to demonstrate the continuing *rapprochement* between the two countries.

In early 1996 Turkey signed a new military and intelligence co-operation agreement with Israel, which permitted the use of Turkish airbases and airspace for military training purposes. The pact stemmed from common concerns about Iran, Iraq, and Syria, and received support from the USA, a strong ally of both Turkey and Israel. The Arab League denounced the agreement as 'an act of aggression'. Business deals quickly followed, especially those concerning the supply of Turkish water to Israel. However, the gradual improvement in Turkey's relations with its Arab neighbours from 2000 made the pact with Israel less significant, and, in response to the increasing violence between Israelis and Palestinians in the West Bank and Gaza, Prime Minister Ecevit in April 2002 accused Israel of 'genocide' against the Palestinians. None the less, in August 2002 Turkey signed an agreement with Israel according to which it would sell the latter 50m. cu m of water every year for the next 20 years. In May 2004 relations with Israel became further strained, when Prime Minister Erdoğan condemned an Israeli offensive in Gaza. In January 2005, however, the Turkish Deputy Prime Minister and Minister of Foreign Affairs made an official visit to Israel (the first by a Turkish politician since the AK Partisi Government was elected in November 2002).

In April 1996 the Turkish and Iranian authorities ordered the expulsion of diplomatic personnel following accusations of Iranian involvement in Islamic terrorist attacks committed in Turkey in the early 1990s. In August relations with Iran were strengthened by the conclusion of an agreement providing for the construction of a 320-km pipeline between the two countries and the export of substantial supplies of natural gas from Iran by 1999 (later revised to 1998). In December 1996 the Presidents of Turkey and Iran agreed to pursue greater economic and security co-operation. A trade agreement was concluded granting each other the status of most favoured nation. In February 1997 the Iranian ambassador to Turkey provoked a diplomatic crisis by advocating the introduction of Islamic law in Turkey. Criticism of the actions of the Turkish military by an Iranian consul-general later in that month resulted in both men being asked to leave the country. Iran responded by expelling two Turkish diplomats. However, both countries immediately undertook diplomatic initiatives to restore relations, and in March it was agreed that all bilateral agreements were to be pursued. Following negotiations, it was announced at the end of September that full diplomatic relations were to be resumed.

In October 1998 Iran and Turkey established a committee to demarcate their joint border; they later signed a memorandum to increase customs co-operation at their main border crossing. In February 1999 the two countries agreed to implement measures aimed at more effective co-operation on border security. In June a meeting of the Turkish-Iranian border committee was held for the first time since 1994; a number of issues were discussed and it was agreed that the committee should meet every year. In July, however, the Turkish chargé d'affaires was twice summoned to the Iranian Ministry of Foreign Affairs following the alleged bombing of an Iranian border region by Turkey in which five people died, although Turkey claimed that its air force had bombed Kurdish targets in Iraq not Iran. In August a meeting of the Turkish-Iranian security commission ended with the signing of a memorandum of understanding in which the two countries agreed to combat illegal organizations within their respective territories. In October Turkey announced it would contribute to compensation for the Iranian bomb damage; a Turkish report into the incident concluded that Turkey had bombed Iraq not Iran, although some people with Iranian citizenship, living in northern Iraq, might have been affected. In October Iran's President Muhammad Khatami welcomed the improvement in ties with Turkey, although in that month Iran expressed concern about Turkey's co-operation with Israel. In December Turkey protested to Iran following the death of a soldier in a clash on the border. In January 2000 the Iranian and Turkish ministers responsible for foreign affairs held talks in Ankara and signed a memorandum of understanding to promote bilateral co-operation. During 2001 both countries sought to improve co-operation in combating drugs-trafficking and organized crime. However, rising tensions between Azerbaijan and Iran over claims to the Caspian Sea, Turkey's strong support for Azerbaijan, its continuing alliance with Israel, and competition for influence in the Caucasus and Central Asia, threatened to bring occasional tensions to the relationship. In early 2003 both Turkey and Iran were seeking to increase their influence in Iraq during the build-up of US military forces in the region, and after the subsequent collapse of the regime of Saddam Hussain, Turkey sought to develop ties with Iraq's ethnic Turkoman minority, with Iran favouring the majority Shi'a population of Iraq.

Government

Under the Constitution approved by referendum in November 1982 (with subsequent amendments), legislative power is vested in the unicameral Turkish Grand National Assembly (TGNA), with 550 deputies, who are elected by universal adult suffrage for a five-year term. Executive power is vested in the President, to be elected by the TGNA for a seven-year term and empowered to appoint a Prime Minister and senior members of the judiciary, the Central Bank and broadcasting organizations; to dissolve the TGNA; and to declare a state of emergency entailing rule by decree. For administrative purposes, Turkey comprises 81 provinces and 2,074 municipalities.

Defence
Turkey joined the North Atlantic Treaty Organization (NATO) in 1952. Military service in the army lasts for 18 months. The total strength of the active armed forces at 1 August 2005 was 514,850 (including 391,000 conscripts), comprising an army of 402,000, a navy of 52,750 and an air force of 60,100. There was a gendarmerie numbering 150,000 and a coast guard of 3,250 (including 1,400 conscripts). Reserve forces totalled 378,700 in the armed forces and 50,000 in the gendarmerie. In April 2005 the Governments of Greece and Turkey announced military co-operation measures, including the establishment of direct communications between two air force bases, in an effort to ease tension over air space violations over the Aegean Sea. Defence expenditure for 2005 was budgeted at about US $9,810m.

Economic Affairs
In 2004, according to estimates by the World Bank, Turkey's gross national income (GNI), measured at average 2002–04 prices, was US $268,741m., equivalent to $3,750 per head (or $7,680 per head on an international purchasing-power parity basis). During 1995–2004, it was estimated, the population increased at an average annual rate of 1.7%, while gross domestic product (GDP) per head rose, in real terms, by an average of 2.1% per year. Overall GDP increased, in real terms, by an annual average of 3.8% in 1995–2004. GDP increased by 5.8% in 2003 and by 8.9% in 2004.

Agriculture (including forestry and fishing) contributed 11.5% to GDP and engaged 34.0% of the employed population in 2004. The country is self-sufficient in most basic foodstuffs. The principal agricultural exports are cotton, tobacco, wheat, fruit and nuts. Other important crops are barley, sunflower and other oilseeds, maize, sugar beet, potatoes, tea and olives. The raising of sheep, goats, cattle and poultry is also an important economic activity. During 1995–2004 agricultural GDP increased by an annual average of 1.4%; growth in the agricultural sector was 4.3% in 2004.

Industry (including mining, manufacturing, construction and power) contributed 29.0% to GDP and engaged 23.0% of the employed population in 2004. During 1995–2004 industrial GDP increased by an annual average of 3.3%; growth in the industrial sector was 10.5% in 2004.

Mining contributed 1.2% to GDP and engaged 0.5% of the employed population in 2004. Chromium, copper and borax are the major mineral exports. Coal, petroleum, natural gas, bauxite, iron ore, manganese and sulphur are also mined. In the late 1990s the country's first gold mine, near Bergama on the Aegean coast, was being developed. During 1990–2001 mining GDP increased by an annual average of 0.8%.

Manufacturing contributed 20.7% to GDP and employed 17.4% of the employed population in 2004. The most important branches, measured by gross value of output, are textiles, food-processing, petroleum refineries, iron and steel, and industrial chemicals. During 1995–2004 manufacturing GDP increased by an annual average of 4.4%; growth in the manufacturing sector was 12.7% in 2004.

Energy is derived principally from thermal power plants. In 2002 40.6% of energy was derived from natural gas, 24.8% from coal, 26.0% from hydroelectric power, and a further 8.3% from petroleum. The energy sector contributed 4.1% to GDP and employed 0.5% of the employed population in 2002. Total domestic output of crude petroleum and natural gas accounts for some 12% of the country's hydrocarbon requirements. Imports of crude petroleum comprised 12.5% of the value of total imports in 2003. A major development project for south-east Anatolia, scheduled for completion in 2010, was to increase Turkey's energy production by 70% and to irrigate 1.6m. ha of uncultivable or inadequately irrigated land, by constructing dams and hydroelectric plants on the Tigris and Euphrates rivers and their tributaries. In June 2000 the construction of a petroleum pipeline between Baku, Azerbaijan, and the Turkish terminal at Ceyhan was approved. In mid-2001 construction began of a new 'blue stream' natural gas pipeline running between Russia and Turkey under the Black Sea. In early 2006 the Government confirmed that the country's first nuclear installation was to be constructed in the Black Sea province of Sinop, with its completion envisaged for 2012.

The services sector contributed 59.6% of GDP and engaged 43.0% of the employed population in 2004. Tourism is one of Turkey's fastest growing sources of revenue. Total tourist arrivals increased to about 13.3m. in 2003, generating some US $13,203m. in revenue. Remittances from Turkish workers abroad also make an important contribution to the economy, amounting to $2,835m. in 2001. During 1995–2004 the GDP of the services sector increased by an annual average of 4.2%; growth in the sector was 10.4% in 2004.

In 2004 Turkey recorded a visible trade deficit of US $23,924m., and there was a deficit of $15,543m. on the current account of the balance of payments. In 2003 the principal source of imports (13.6%) was Germany; other major suppliers were Russia, France, the United Kingdom and the USA. Germany was also the principal market for exports in that year (15.8%); other important purchasers were the USA, the United Kingdom, Italy and France. The UN restrictions on trade with Iraq reversed Turkey's previously strong trading relations with that country. Exports in 2003 were dominated by basic manufactures (mainly textiles), machinery and transport equipment, and clothing and accessories. In that year the principal imports were machinery and transport equipment, basic manufactures, chemical products and mineral fuels (particularly crude petroleum).

In 2004 there was a budgetary deficit of 30,300m. new Turkish liras. Turkey's external debt at the end of 2003 was US $145,662m., of which $64,758m. was long-term public debt. In that year the cost of debt-servicing was equivalent to 38.5% of the value of exports of goods and services. The annual rate of inflation averaged 56.2% in 1992–2005. Consumer prices increased by 8.6% in 2004 and by 8.2% in 2005. In 2004 the rate of unemployment was estimated at 10.3%.

Turkey is a member of numerous international and regional organizations, including the Developing Eight (D-8, see p. 385), the Economic Co-operation Organization (ECO, see p. 223), and the Organization of the Black Sea Economic Co-operation (see p. 339). Turkey was accepted as a candidate for membership of the European Union (EU, see p. 228) in December 1999.

Turkey's economy has been afflicted by persistently high rates of inflation, an expanding public-sector deficit, ongoing political instability and a poor rate of tax collection. In December 1999 the Government reached a stand-by credit agreement with the IMF, which was to finance the implementation of strict fiscal and monetary policies, and of structural reforms. A privatization programme resumed in early 2000, and envisaged the divestment of 74 state enterprises. However, the country experienced a severe financial crisis in November 2000 and again in February 2001 (see Recent History), resulting in soaring interest rates and an effective devaluation of the lira. As part of a recovery strategy announced in March, the Turkish Government reasserted its commitment to the privatization programme, as a precondition to the extension of funds from the IMF and the World Bank. In February 2002 the IMF commended the progress made by the Turkish authorities in the restructuring of the banking sector, public-sector reform, and preparations for privatization, and renewed the stand-by credit arrangement, which was to support the 2002–04 economic programme. The AK Partisi Government, elected in November 2002, pledged to continue to meet the IMF's conditions. In May 2003, however, the IMF refused to release funds due to Turkey under the stand-by credit agreement until the Government demonstrated its commitment to meeting reform programme objectives. In July the authorities announced the adoption of corrective measures, including significant reductions in state budgetary expenditure, in an effort to meet IMF requirements. At the end of July the TGNA approved further extensive human rights reforms in order to qualify for accession negotiations with the EU. By the end of 2003 the economy demonstrated strong recovery, and inflation had been reduced to the lowest level reached for some 30 years. The Turkish Government continued to gain approbation from the international community for its stated commitment to human rights reforms, and on 17 December the EU extended a provisional invitation to Turkey to commence accession negotiations in October 2005, subject to the continued fulfilment of a number of political and economic conditions (see Recent History). Economic growth remained exceptionally strong in 2004, while the rate of inflation declined further, productivity was significantly

TURKEY

improved, and measures to reduce the extremely high level of external debt had also proved successful. At the end of that year it was announced that the authorities aimed to secure IMF support for a new three-year economic programme of continuing fiscal discipline. At the beginning of 2005 the Government established a new monetary unit, the new Turkish lira, as part of ongoing efforts to restrain inflation (the old currency remained in circulation until the end of the year). A number of major privatization agreements were concluded during 2005. In May a new three-year stand-by arrangement was approved with the IMF to support the Government's economic and financial programme. Despite increasing controversy, Turkey's accession negotiations with the EU were officially approved, as scheduled, on 3 October (see Recent History). Later that month the Government announced the 2006 budget, which projected a fiscal deficit within EU-required limits and a further reduction in the rate of inflation, prompting the IMF to disburse delayed loans. In early November 2005 an EU report granted Turkey the status of a functioning market economy, a declaration that contributed to stimulating investor confidence. In December the IMF concluded the first and second reviews under the stand-by credit arrangement, continuing to commend Turkey's economic performance, while waiving the non-observance of certain criteria, particularly those relating to the implementation of banking and pension reform legislation. The Government had continued to restrain the rate of inflation and had also succeeded in further reducing public debt; however, an increasing current-account deficit, resulting, in part, from a higher international price of petroleum and strengthening of the lira, was perceived as the greatest cause of concern. A severe outbreak of a lethal strain (H5N1) of highly contagious avian influenza, which was first reported in October 2005, prompted the authorities to order the cull of about 2m. poultry and the EU, in an effort to contain the disease, to impose a ban on poultry exports from Turkey. By January 2006 some 21 human cases of the H5N1 virus were also confirmed, with a potential adverse impact on revenue from trade and tourism; at the end of February, however, it was announced that the measures taken by the authorities had succeeded in containing the outbreak. In March the IMF criticized a government proposal to extend tax relief to certain industrial sectors, which was perceived as failure to adhere to the terms of the credit agreement. In April the new Governor of the Central Bank pledged commitment to the continuation of the policy of monetary restraint.

Education

Legislation took effect in September 1997 to increase the duration of compulsory primary education from five to eight years, for children between six and 14 years of age. All state education up to University or Higher Institute levels is co-educational and provided free of charge. The number of primary schools reached 36,117 in 2003/04, compared with 12,511 in 1950. Secondary education, which lasts for at least three years, may be undertaken in general high schools, open high schools or vocational and technical high schools. In 2002/03 some 86% of children in the relevant age-group were enrolled in primary education (males 89%; females 84%), while secondary enrolment in that year was equivalent to 79% (males 90%; females 67%) of children in the appropriate age-group. In 2003/04 some 1.8m. students attended 1,248 higher education institutes. Government expenditure on education was budgeted at about US $6,700m in 2004.

Public Holidays

2006: 1 January (New Year's Day), 10–13 January*† (Kurban Bayram—Feast of the Sacrifice), 23 April (National Sovereignty and Children's Day), 19 May (Commemoration of Atatürk, and Youth and Sports Day), 30 August (Victory Day), 23–25 October* (Şeker Bayram—End of Ramadan), 29 October (Republic Day), 31 December–3 January 2007*† (Kurban Bayram—Feast of the Sacrifice).

2007: 1 January (New Year's Day), 23 April (National Sovereignty and Children's Day), 19 May (Commemoration of Atatürk, and Youth and Sports Day), 30 August (Victory Day), 13–15 October* (Şeker Bayram—End of Ramadan), 29 October (Republic Day), 20–23 December* (Kurban Bayram—Feast of the Sacrifice).

* These holidays are dependent on the Islamic lunar calendar and may vary by one or two days from the dates given.

† This festival occurs twice (in the Islamic years AH 1426 and 1427) within the same Gregorian year.

Weights and Measures

The metric system is in force.

Statistical Survey

Sources (unless otherwise stated): T.C. Başbakanlık Devlet İstatistik Enstitüsü (State Institute of Statistics), Necatibey Cad. 114, 06580-Yücetepe/Ankara; tel. (312) 4176440; fax (312) 4253387; internet www.die.gov.tr.

Area and Population

AREA, POPULATION AND DENSITY

Area (sq km)	
Land	769,604
Inland water	13,958
Total	783,562*
Population (census results)	
21 October 1990	56,473,035
22 October 2000	
Males	34,346,735
Females	33,457,192
Total	67,803,927
Population (official estimates at mid-year)	
2003	70,712,000
2004	71,789,000
2005	72,844,000
Density (per sq km) at mid-2005	94.7

* 302,535 sq miles.

PROVINCES
(2000 census)

	Area (sq km)	Population	Density (per sq km)
Adana	14,046	1,849,478	131.7
Adıyaman	7,606	623,811	82.0
Afyon	14,719	812,416	55.2
Ağri	11,499	528,744	46.0
Aksaray	7,966	396,084	49.7
Amasya	5,704	365,231	64.0
Ankara	25,402	4,007,860	157.8
Antalya	20,791	1,719,751	82.7
Ardahan	4,968	133,756	26.9
Artvin	7,367	191,934	26.1
Aydın	7,904	950,757	120.3
Balıkesir	14,473	1,076,347	74.4
Bartın	2,080	184,178	88.5
Batman	4,659	456,734	98.0
Bayburt	3,739	97,358	26.0
Bilecik	4,307	194,326	45.1
Bingöl	8,254	253,739	30.7
Bitlis	7,095	388,678	54.8
Bolu	8,323	270,654	32.5
Burdur	7,135	256,803	36.0
Bursa	10,886	2,125,140	195.2
Çanakkale	9,950	464,975	46.7
Çankırı	7,492	270,355	36.1
Çorum	12,796	597,065	46.7
Denizli	11,804	850,029	72.0

TURKEY

Statistical Survey

—continued	Area (sq km)	Population	Density (per sq km)
Diyabakır	15,204	1,362,708	89.6
Düzce	2,593	314,266	121.2
Edirne	6,098	402,606	66.0
Elazığ	9,281	569,616	61.4
Erzincan	11,728	316,841	27.0
Erzurum	25,331	937,389	37.0
Eskişehir	13,902	706,009	50.8
Gaziantep	6,845	1,285,249	187.8
Giresun	6,832	523,819	76.7
Gümüşhane	6,437	186,953	29.0
Hakkari	7,179	236,581	33.0
Hatay	5,831	1,253,726	215.0
Iğdir	3,588	168,634	47.0
Isparta	8,871	513,681	57.9
İçel	15,512	1,651,400	106.5
İstanbul	5,315	10,018,735	1,885.0
İzmir	12,016	3,370,866	280.5
Kahramanmaraş	14,457	1,002,384	69.3
Karabük	4,109	225,102	54.8
Karaman	8,869	243,210	27.4
Kars	10,139	325,016	32.1
Kastamonu	13,158	375,476	28.5
Kayseri	17,109	1,060,432	62.0
Kırıkkale	4,570	383,508	83.9
Kırklareli	6,300	328,461	52.1
Kırşehir	6,530	253,239	38.8
Kilis	1,428	114,724	80.3
Kocaeli	3,625	1,206,085	332.7
Konya	40,814	2,192,166	53.7
Kütahya	12,014	656,903	54.7
Malatya	12,103	853,658	70.5
Manisa	13,229	1,260,169	95.3
Mardin	8,806	705,098	80.1
Muğla	12,949	715,328	55.2
Muş	8,067	453,654	56.2
Nevşehir	5,392	309,914	57.5
Niğde	7,365	348,081	47.3
Ordu	5,952	887,765	149.2
Osmaniye	3,196	458,782	143.5
Rize	3,922	365,938	93.3
Sakarya	4,880	756,168	155.0
Samsun	9,364	1,209,137	129.1
Siirt	5,473	263,676	48.2
Sinop	5,817	225,574	38.8
Sivas	28,567	755,091	26.4
Şanlıurfa	19,336	1,443,422	74.6
Şırnak	7,152	353,197	49.4
Tekirdağ	6,342	623,591	98.3
Tokat	10,073	828,027	82.2
Trabzon	4,664	975,137	209.1
Tunceli	7,686	93,584	12.2
Uşak	5,363	322,313	60.1
Van	22,983	877,524	38.2
Yalova	850	168,593	198.3
Yozgat	14,074	682,919	48.5
Zonguldak	3,310	615,599	186.0
Total	783,562	67,803,927	86.5

PRINCIPAL TOWNS
(population at census of 22 October 2000, within municipal boundaries)

İstanbul	8,803,468		Erzurum	361,235
Ankara (capital)	3,203,362		Kahramanmaraş	326,198
İzmir (Smyrna)	2,232,265		Van	284,464
Bursa	1,194,687		Sakarya	283,752
Adana	1,130,710		Denizli	275,480
Gaziantep	853,513		Elazığ	266,495
Konya	742,690		Gebze	253,487
Antalya	603,190		Sivas	251,776
Diyarbakır	545,983		Batman	246,678
Mersin (İçel)	537,842		Tarsus	216,382
Kayseri	536,392		Balıkesir	215,436
Eskişehir	482,793		Trabzon	214,949
Şanlıurfa	385,588		Manisa	214,345
Malatya	381,081		Kinkkale	205,078
Samsun	363,180			

Mid-2003 (UN estimates, incl. suburbs): İstanbul 9,371,163; Ankara 3,428,420; İzmir 2,387,686; Bursa 1,319,898; Adana 1,199,016.

Source: UN, *World Urbanization Prospects: The 2003 Revision*.

BIRTHS, MARRIAGES AND DEATHS

	Registered live births		Registered deaths	
	Number*	Rate (per 1,000)	Number*	Rate (per 1,000)
2000	1,494,000	22.2	477,000	7.1
2001	1,486,000	21.7	485,000	7.1
2002	1,482,000	21.3	491,000	7.0
2003	1,479,000	20.9	498,000	7.0
2004	1,478,000	20.6	506,000	7.1

* Rounded figures.

Marriages: 461,417 in 2000; 453,213 in 2001; 447,820 in 2002; 477,451 in 2003 (provisional).

Expectation of life (WHO estimates, years at birth): 70 (males 68; females 73) in 2003 (Source: WHO, *World Health Report*).

ECONOMICALLY ACTIVE POPULATION*
(sample surveys, '000 persons aged 15 years and over)

	2002	2003	2004
Agriculture, hunting and forestry	7,438	7,152	7,373
Fishing	19	13	27
Mining and quarrying	120	83	104
Manufacturing	3,731	3,664	3,801
Electricity, gas and water	103	100	83
Construction	958	965	1,029
Wholesale and retail trade; repair of motor vehicles, motorcycles and personal and household goods	3,154	3,205	3,307
Restaurants and hotels	826	847	872
Transport, storage and communications	1,004	1,022	1,100
Financial intermediation	238	229	237
Real estate, renting and business activities	460	509	549
Public administration and defence	1,151	1,177	1,252
Education	850	867	818
Health and social work	506	522	469
Other community, social and personal services	620	618	583
Private households with employed persons	174	174	182
Extra-territorial organizations and bodies	1	2	4
Total employed	21,354	21,147	21,791
Unemployed	2,464	2,493	2,498
Total labour force	23,818	23,640	24,289
Males	17,058	17,086	17,901
Females	6,760	6,554	6,388

* Excluding armed forces.

Source: ILO.

WORKERS ABROAD

	2000	2001	2002
Turkish citizens working abroad (number)	1,170,226	1,178,412	1,200,725
Workers' remittances from abroad (US $ million)	4,560	2,786	1,936

Turkish citizens working abroad (number): 1,197,968 in 2003; 1,195,612 in 2004.

Sources: Undersecretariat of the Prime Ministry for Foreign Trade; Secretariat of the State Planning Organization.

TURKEY

Health and Welfare

KEY INDICATORS

Total fertility rate (children per woman, 2003)	2.4
Under-5 mortality rate (per 1,000 live births, 2004)	32
HIV/AIDS (% of persons aged 15–49, 2001)	<0.1
Physicians (per 1,000 head, 2002)	1.3
Hospital beds (per 1,000 head, 2000)	2.6
Health expenditure (2002): US $ per head (PPP)	420
Health expenditure (2002): % of GDP	6.5
Health expenditure (2002): public (% of total)	65.8
Access to water (% of persons, 2002)	93
Access to sanitation (% of persons, 2002)	83
Human Development Index (2003): ranking	94
Human Development Index (2003): value	0.750

For sources and definitions, see explanatory note on p. vi.

Agriculture

PRINCIPAL CROPS
('000 metric tons)

	2002	2003	2004
Wheat	19,508	19,008	21,000
Rice (paddy)	360	372	490
Barley	8,300	8,100	9,000
Maize	2,100	2,800	3,000
Rye	255	240	270
Oats	290	270	275
Potatoes	5,200	5,300	4,800
Sugar beet	16,523	12,623	13,514
Dry beans	250	250	250
Chick peas	650	600	620
Lentils	565	540	540
Vetch	132	123	124*
Walnuts	120	130	126
Hazelnuts (Filberts)	600	480	350
Olives	1,800	850	1,600
Sunflower seed	850	800	900
Cottonseed	1,457	1,308	1,390†
Cabbages	720	721	700
Lettuce	345	340	362
Spinach	220	220	213
Tomatoes	9,450	9,820	9,440
Cauliflower	90	108	110
Pumpkins, squash and gourds	345	368	374
Cucumbers and gherkins	1,670	1,780	1,725
Aubergines (Eggplants)	955	935	900
Green chillies and peppers	1,750	1,790	1,700
Green onions and shallots	210	220	220*
Dry onions	2,050	1,750	2,040
Garlic	96	125	109
Leeks and other alliacious vegetables	290	305	305*
Green beans	515	545	582
Carrots	235	405	438
Other vegetables	503	501	506*
Watermelons	4,575	4,250	3,825
Cantaloupes and other melons	1,820†	1,700†	1,700*
Bananas	95	110	130
Oranges	1,250	1,250	1,300
Tangerines, mandarins, etc.	590	550	670
Lemons and limes	525	550	600
Grapefruit and pomelo	125	135	135
Apples	2,200	2,600	2,100
Pears	340	370	320
Quinces	110	110	110*
Apricots	352	499	350†
Cherries	210	265	245
Sour cherries	100	145	138
Peaches and nectarines	455	470	372
Plums	200	210	210

—continued	2002	2003	2004
Strawberries	145	150	155
Grapes	3,500	3,600	3,500
Figs	250	280	275
Other fruits and berries	162	187	187*
Cotton (lint)	988	900	925†
Tea (made)	135	154	202
Pimento, allspice*	20	20	20
Anise, badian and fennel	13	12	12*
Other spices	81	62	62*
Tobacco (leaves)	153	160	157

* FAO estimate(s).
† Unofficial figure.

Source: FAO.

LIVESTOCK
('000 head, year ending September)

	2002	2003	2004
Horses	271	249	271*
Mules	97	95	97*
Asses	462	417	462*
Cattle	10,548	9,804	9,789
Buffaloes	138	121	113
Camels	1	1	1
Pigs	3	4	7
Sheep	26,972	25,174	25,431
Goats	7,022	6,780	6,772
Chickens	217,575	245,776	277,533
Ducks	914	832	800*
Geese	1,398	1,400	1,400*
Turkeys	3,254	3,092	3,994

* FAO estimate.

Source: FAO.

LIVESTOCK PRODUCTS
('000 metric tons)

	2002	2003	2004
Beef and veal	327.6	290.5	365.0
Buffalo meat	1.6	1.7	1.9
Mutton and lamb*	286	267	273
Goat meat*	46.5	45.0	45.0
Horse meat*	2.0	1.7	2.0
Poultry meat	710.9	887.0	894.8
Cows' milk	7,490.6	9,514.3	9,609.3
Buffalo milk	50.9	48.8	39.3
Sheep milk	657.4	770.0	771.7
Goats' milk	209.6	278.1	259.1
Butter and ghee	99.1	124.4	124.8
Cheese	113.5	129.9	130.6
Hen eggs	722.2	791.7	770.0*
Honey	74.6	69.5	73.9
Wool: greasy	38.2	46.5	46.0
Wool: scoured	15.3	18.6	18.8
Cattle hides (fresh)*	30.2	27.0	34.5
Sheepskins (fresh)*	50.7	47.3	48.4
Goatskins (fresh)*	6.0	5.8	5.8

* FAO estimate(s).

Source: FAO.

TURKEY

Forestry

ROUNDWOOD REMOVALS
('000 cubic metres, excl. bark)

	2002	2003	2004
Sawlogs, veneer logs and logs for sleepers	5,606	5,137	5,235
Pulpwood	3,684	3,650	4,278
Other industrial wood	1,901	1,942	1,712
Fuel wood	4,931	5,081	5,278
Total	16,122	15,810	16,503

Source: FAO.

SAWNWOOD PRODUCTION
('000 cubic metres, incl. railway sleepers)

	2002	2003	2004
Coniferous (softwood)	3,015	2,986	3,625
Broadleaved (hardwood)	2,564	2,629	2,590
Total	5,579	5,615	6,215

Source: FAO.

Fishing

('000 metric tons, live weight)

	2001	2002	2003
Capture	527.7	566.7	507.8
Blue whiting	20.8	10.5	7.5
Mullets	38.6	27.6	26.0
European anchovy	320.0	373.0	295.0
Bluefish	13.1	25.0	22.0
Mediterranean horse mackerel	15.5	19.5	16.4
Striped venus	7.5	10.0	19.7
Aquaculture	67.2	61.2	79.9
Trout	38.1	34.6	40.9
Seabasses	15.5	14.3	21.0
Total catch	595.0	627.8	587.7

Note: Figures exclude aquatic plants and aquatic mammals (the capture of 80 toothed whales was recorded in 2002).
Source: FAO.

Mining

('000 metric tons, unless otherwise indicated)

	2002	2003	2004[1]
Hard coal	3,313	3,090	2,843
Lignite	49,627	43,749	43,754
Crude petroleum ('000 barrels)	17,579	16,980	16,270
Natural gas ('000 cu m)[2]	268,000[3]	275,947	344,196
Iron ore: gross weight	3,433	3,429	3,857
Iron ore: metal content[3]	1,830	1,830	2,060
Copper[4]	48.3	58.0[3]	49.0[3]
Bauxite[5]	287.4	364.3	365.8
Lead: mine output[4]	17.4	17.5	18.7
Lead: concentrates[3,4]	8.5	8.5	9.1
Chromium[6]	313.6	229.3	506.4
Silver (kilograms)[4,7]	79,000	95,000	73,000[3]
Gold (kilograms)[3,4,7]	5,000	6,500	4,500
Marble ('000 cu m)	557.6	544.6	669.0
Limestone[8]	30,261	28,609	30,963
Quartzite	2,006.7	2,908.6	2,961.9
Dolomite	976.0	1,158.5	2,109.4
Bentonite	559.6	831.1	850.0[3]
Kaolin	372.3	370.5	536.0
Silica sand[9]	1,274	1,283	1,188

—continued	2002	2003	2004[1]
Gypsum[8]	264.0	196.7	250.1
Magnesite: mine output	3,044.4	3,224.3	3,733.0
Feldspar: mine output	1,766.4	1,862.3	1,983.3
Borate minerals: mine output	2,214.1	2,207.1	2,878.9
Borate minerals: concentrates	1,368.0	1,399.0	1,697.0
Nitrogen[10]	300.5	289.3	329.4
Perlite: mine output	151.9	136.7	133.8
Pumice	820.3	895.6	1,036.0
Pyrites[9]	952.1	1,103.9	765.4
Sodium sulphate: concentrates	562.7	556.6	523.3

[1] Preliminary figures.
[2] Marketed production only.
[3] Estimate(s).
[4] Figures refer to metal content of ores and concentrates.
[5] Figures refer to public sector production only. Data for private sector production are not available, but production is estimated to have been 30,000 metric tons in each year.
[6] Figures refer to gross weight of ores.
[7] Figures include estimated output from the by-products of refining other base metals.
[8] Excluding production used for making cement.
[9] Figures refer to gross weight of minerals.
[10] Nitrogen content of ammonia.

Source: US Geological Survey.

Industry

SELECTED PRODUCTS
('000 metric tons, unless otherwise indicated)

	2001	2002	2003
Newsprint	88	54	20
Paper for packaging	43	37	15
Beer and raki (million litres)	764	796	841
Cigarettes	126	131	112
Crude steel*	14,382	16,046	18,298
Pig-iron*	248	158	181
Cement*	30,125	32,576	35,077
Copper (refined)*†	58	41	45
Polyethylene	207	201	191
Polyvinyl chloride compositions§	147	157	140
Coke and semi-coke*‖	1,890	2,080	2,543
Motor spirit (petrol, '000 barrels)*	24,993	31,634	28,800
Naphthas ('000 barrels)*	16,656	11,947	10,700
Jet fuel ('000 barrels)*	9,496	9,368	13,300
Distillate fuel oils ('000 barrels)*	58,901	59,281	53,800
Residual fuel oils ('000 barrels)*	56,323	53,077	38,600
Domestic refrigerators ('000)	2,332	3,165	4,127
Domestic washing machines ('000)	1,022	1,685	2,412
Domestic gas cookers ('000)	665	906	1,468
Vacuum cleaners ('000)	590	782	614
Dishwashers ('000)	224	352	399
Television receivers ('000)¶	8,025	12,463	15,035
Tractors (number)	15,054	10,371	29,288
Passenger motor cars (number)	226,795	259,812	425,409
Lorries (number)	7,056	12,223	18,707
Buses and minibuses (number)	12,446	15,506	43,227
Electricity (million kWh)	122,725	129,367	140,129

* Data from US Geological Survey.
† Estimate(s).
‡ Excluding potassic fertilizers.
§ Including precipitated calcium carbonate.
‖ Including semi-coke.
¶ Colour televisions only.

Source (unless otherwise indicated): Secretariat of the State Planning Organization.

2004 ('000 metric tons, provisional figures, unless otherwise indicated): Pig iron 213; Refined copper 50,000 (estimate); Coke and semi-coke 2,855; Motor spirit (petrol, '000 barrels) 27,350; Naphthas ('000 barrels) 12,700; Jet fuel ('000 barrels) 14,000; Distillate fuel oils ('000 barrels) 53,660; Residual fuel oils ('000 barrels) 40,270 (Source: US Geological Survey).

TURKEY

Finance

CURRENCY AND EXCHANGE RATES

Monetary Units
100 kuruş = 1 new Turkish lira.

Sterling, Dollar and Euro Equivalents (30 December 2005)
£1 sterling = 2.316 new liras;
US $1 = 1.345 new liras;
€1 = 1.587 new liras;
1,000 new Turkish liras = £431.77 = US $743.47 = €630.22.

Average Exchange Rate (new Turkish liras per US $)
2003 1.5009
2004 1.4255
2005 1.3436

Note: A new currency, the new Turkish lira, equivalent to 1,000,000 of the former units, was introduced on 1 January 2005. Figures in this survey have been converted retrospectively to reflect this development.

CONSOLIDATED BUDGET
(million new Turkish liras)

Revenue	2001	2002	2003
General budget	50,890.5	74,603.7	98,558.7
Taxation	39,735.9	59,631.9	84,316.2
Taxes on income	15,647.6	19,343.2	25,716.0
Taxes on wealth	433.3	734.3	2,092.1
Taxes on goods and services	18,103.2	30,064.0	43,927.0
Taxes on foreign trade	5,551.1	9,487.2	12,578.7
Non-tax revenue	7,418.4	10,874.5	10,222.8
Special revenue and funds	3,736.2	4,097.3	4,019.8
Annexed budget revenues	652.5	988.6	1,691.7
Total	51,543.0	75,592.3	100,250.4

Expenditure	2001	2002	2003
Current expenditure	20,448.0	31,108.0	38,513.9
Personnel	15,211.9	23,089.2	30,209.5
Other current expenditure	5,236.1	8,018.8	8,304.4
Investment expenditure	4,149.6	6,891.8	7,179.7
Transfers	55,981.5	77,682.6	94,761.3
Interest payments	41,062.2	51,870.7	58,609.2
Domestic debt interest	37,494.3	46,807.0	52,718.9
Foreign debt interest	3,567.9	5,063.6	5,890.3
Transfers to state-owned economic enterprises	1,107.1	2,170.0	1,881.0
Tax rebates	2,918.2	5,665.8	8,335.9
Social security payments	5,112.0	11,205.0	15,922.0
Other transfers	5,268.8	6,746.1	9,973.2
Total	80,579.1	115,682.4	140,454.8

2004 (million new Turkish liras): Total revenue 110,720.9; Total expenditure 141,020.9.

2005 (million new Turkish liras): Total revenue 134,819.2; Total expenditure 144,562.3.

Source: Ministry of Finance, İstanbul.

INTERNATIONAL RESERVES
(US $ million at 31 December)

	2003	2004	2005
Gold (national valuation)	1,558	1,583	1,912
IMF special drawing rights	30	14	16
Reserve position in IMF	168	175	161
Foreign exchange	33,793	35,480	50,402
Total	35,549	37,252	52,491

Source: IMF, *International Financial Statistics*.

MONEY SUPPLY
(million new Turkish liras at 31 December)

	2002	2003	2004
Currency outside banks	6,899	9,775	12,444
Demand deposits at deposit money banks	7,860	11,358	14,168
Total money (incl. others)	14,814	21,194	26,782

Source: IMF, *International Financial Statistics*.

COST OF LIVING
(Consumer Price Index for urban areas; base: 2000 = 100)

	2002	2003	2004
Food (incl. tobacco)	225.3	290.0	316.1
Clothing	231.3	293.9	305.3
Rent (incl. fuel and light)	217.4	268.9	310.1
All items	223.8	280.4	310.1

Source: ILO.

NATIONAL ACCOUNTS
(million new Turkish liras at current prices)

National Income and Product

	2002	2003	2004
Compensation of employees*	72,923.6	93,978.0	n.a.
Operating surplus*	138,723.3	179,960.2	n.a.
Domestic factor incomes	211,646.8	273,938.2	325,106.6
Consumption of fixed capital	23,982.2	27,294.2	32,323.1
Gross domestic product (GDP) at factor cost	235,629.0	301,232.4	357,429.7
Indirect taxes	43,185.6	59,481.0	73,633.0
Less Subsidies	1,240.5	950.5	551.1
GDP in purchasers' values	277,574.1	359,762.9	430,511.5
Factor income received from abroad	8,030.3	8,415.6	10,040.1
Less Factor income paid abroad	10,572.0	11,497.7	11,619.2
Gross national product (GNP)	275,032.4	356,680.9	428,932.3
Less Consumption of fixed capital	23,982.2	27,294.2	32,323.1
National income in market prices	251,050.2	329,386.7	396,609.3

* Provisional figures.

Expenditure on the Gross Domestic Product

	2002	2003	2004
Government final consumption expenditure	38,722.0	49,004.5	56,775.5
Private final consumption expenditure	184,420.2	239,585.9	284,631.3
Increase in stocks	13,133.8	26,328.9	33,973.7
Gross fixed capital formation	46,043.0	55,618.3	76,722.4
Total domestic expenditure	282,318.9	370,537.7	452,102.9
Exports of goods and services	81,134.1	98,496.3	124,348.2
Less Imports of goods and services	85,232.4	110,334.4	149,299.1
Sub-total	278,220.6	358,699.6	427,151.9
Statistical discrepancy	–646.6	1,063.3	3,359.5
GDP in purchasers' values	277,574.1	359,762.9	430,511.5
GDP at constant 1987 prices	118.6	125.5	136.7

TURKEY

Statistical Survey

Gross Domestic Product by Economic Activity

	2002	2003	2004
Agriculture, forestry and fishing	32,114.9	42,126.2	48,394.7
Mining and quarrying	2,914.1	3,858.1	5,174.4
Manufacturing	55,764.4	71,910.8	87,609.6
Electricity, gas and water	11,355.9	13,044.4	14,277.2
Construction	11,398.7	12,662.0	15,380.7
Wholesale and retail trade	45,271.1	58,491.4	72,769.1
Hotels and restaurants	10,664.1	12,838.4	15,945.0
Transport, storage and communications	41,820.6	53,846.2	62,009.2
Financial institutions	12,944.7	17,884.6	21,603.6
Ownership of dwellings	11,637.8	14,653.0	18,398.6
Other private services	9,753.6	12,429.1	14,889.3
Government services	27,838.4	36,561.5	42,548.5
Private non-profit institutions	1,664.0	3,610.4	3,530.1
Sub-total	275,142.2	353,916.0	422,529.9
Import duties	10,527.4	13,758.6	18,802.9
Less Imputed bank service charges	8,095.6	7,911.7	10,821.3
GDP in purchasers' values	277,574.1	359,762.9	430,511.5

BALANCE OF PAYMENTS
(US $ million)

	2002	2003	2004
Exports of goods f.o.b.	40,124	51,206	67,001
Imports of goods f.o.b.	−47,407	−65,216	−90,925
Trade balance	−7,283	−14,010	−23,924
Exports of services	14,802	19,086	24,047
Imports of services	−6,922	−8,581	−11,274
Balance on goods and services	597	−3,505	−11,151
Other income received	2,486	2,246	2,651
Other income paid	−7,040	−7,805	−8,170
Balance on goods, services and income	−3,957	−9,064	−16,670
Current transfers received	2,482	1,088	1,165
Current transfers paid	−46	−61	−38
Current balance	−1,521	−8,037	−15,543
Direct investment abroad	−176	−499	−858
Direct investment from abroad	1,063	1,753	2,733
Portfolio investment assets	−2,096	−1,386	−1,388
Portfolio investment liabilities	1,503	3,851	9,411
Other investment assets	−777	−986	−7,352
Other investment liabilities	1,642	4,365	14,493
Net errors and omissions	148	5,026	2,812
Overall balance	−214	4,087	4,308

Source: IMF, *International Financial Statistics*.

External Trade

PRINCIPAL COMMODITIES
(distribution by SITC, US $ million, excl. military goods)

Imports c.i.f.	2001	2002	2003
Crude materials (inedible) except fuels	2,409.8	3,620.2	5,103.6
Metalliferous ores and metal scrap	608.4	1,231.3	2,106.4
Mineral fuels, lubricants, etc.	6,176.3	7,216.5	8,647.6
Petroleum, petroleum products, etc.	4,710.6	5,355.9	6,640.8
Crude petroleum and bituminous oils	3,878.0	4,087.8	4,776.5
Chemicals and related products	6,103.1	7,613.0	10,052.7
Organic chemicals	1,397.9	1,546.4	1,952.2
Medicinal and pharmaceutical products	1,345.3	1,717.2	2,302.1
Artificial resins, plastics, etc.	1,376.3	1,921.2	2,673.0
Basic manufactures	6,699.2	8,838.7	11,719.2
Textile yarn, fabrics, etc.	1,945.4	2,882.2	3,499.3
Iron and steel	1,813.6	2,173.7	3,298.9

Imports c.i.f.—*continued*	2001	2002	2003
Machinery and transport equipment	12,625.1	15,582.7	21,495.8
Power-generating machinery and equipment	1,957.1	2,030.9	2,031.4
Machinery specialized for particular industries	1,623.9	2,852.7	3,993.6
Textile and leather machinery (incl. parts)	660.0	1,700.5	2,352.1
General industrial machinery, equipment and parts	1,820.2	2,204.6	2,730.4
Road vehicles	1,814.3	2,296.6	5,342.0
Passenger motor vehicles (excl. buses)	586.8	813.3	2,219.7
Miscellaneous manufactured articles	2,500.3	2,931.7	3,832.9
Non-monetary gold, unwrought or semi-manufactured	989.4	1,406.2	2,598.4
Total (incl. others)	41,399.1	51,270.2	69,339.7

Exports f.o.b.	2001	2002	2003
Food and live animals	3,309.8	3,056.0	3,929.9
Vegetables and fruit	2,142.7	2,031.2	2,570.2
Fruit and nuts	1,178.3	1,145.0	1,349.3
Chemicals and related products	1,187.4	1,301.8	1,608.0
Basic manufactures	9,535.3	10,562.7	13,357.4
Textile yarn, fabrics, etc.	3,943.2	4,244.8	5,263.3
Non-metallic mineral manufactures	1,151.4	1,329.6	1,623.2
Iron and steel	2,546.9	2,839.2	3,428.2
Iron and steel bars, rods, shapes, etc.	1,233.4	1,221.3	1,686.6
Machinery and transport equipment	7,094.8	8,555.3	12,344.1
Colour television receivers	865.0	1,453.6	1,820.2
Road vehicles	2,296.7	3,165.7	4,946.3
Passenger motor vehicles (excl. buses)	972.9	1,072.9	2,197.5
Miscellaneous manufactured articles	8,152.2	9,898.3	12,632.6
Clothing and accessories (excl. footwear)	6,661.2	8,056.8	9,963.3
Total (incl. others)	31,333.9	35,762.2	47,252.8

Source: UN, *International Trade Statistics Yearbook*.

PRINCIPAL TRADING PARTNERS
(US $ million, excl. military goods*)

Imports c.i.f. (excl. grants)	2001	2002	2003
Algeria	1,064.0	1,079.5	1,081.6
Austria	417.5	587.4	969.1
Belgium	984.5	1,147.1	1,523.6
China, People's Republic	925.8	1,365.9	2,610.3
France (incl. Monaco)	2,283.9	3,047.5	4,164.1
Germany	5,335.4	7,014.7	9,453.0
India	354.9	564.1	722.9
Iran	839.8	920.5	1,860.7
Israel	529.5	541.3	459.5
Italy	3,484.1	4,132.1	5,471.6
Japan	1,307.4	1,462.8	1,927.1
Korea, Republic	759.5	900.0	1,312.4
Libya	847.8	754.0	1,072.5
Netherlands	1,051.6	1,308.3	1,656.7
Romania	481.1	656.6	956.0
Russia	3,435.7	3,863.2	5,451.3
Saudi Arabia	729.6	788.0	969.1
Spain	1,066.1	1,388.8	2,003.8
Sweden	543.9	534.0	822.2
Switzerland	1,227.4	2,138.1	2,970.3
Syria	463.5	506.2	413.3
Ukraine	757.6	978.1	1,331.5
United Kingdom	1,913.8	2,430.4	3,500.0
USA	3,261.4	3,067.9	3,496.6
Total (incl. others)	41,399.1	51,270.2	69,339.7

TURKEY

Statistical Survey

Exports f.o.b.	2001	2002	2003
Algeria	422.0	510.8	573.0
Austria	341.3	363.0	473.2
Belgium	688.3	689.4	885.6
Bulgaria	299.4	378.3	621.7
China, People's Republic	199.4	265.5	504.6
Denmark	271.7	362.9	454.0
Egypt	421.5	325.1	345.8
France	1,895.3	2,123.5	2,826.1
Germany	5,366.7	5,835.2	7,484.9
Greece	476.1	582.8	920.4
Iran	360.5	308.1	533.8
Israel	805.2	850.9	1,083.0
Italy	2,342.2	2,361.2	3,194.8
Netherlands	892.4	1,043.9	1,525.9
Poland	241.2	340.9	486.0
Romania	392.0	560.4	873.3
Russia	924.1	1,168.3	1,367.6
Saudi Arabia	500.6	547.3	741.5
Spain	950.4	1,115.2	1,792.2
United Arab Emirates	380.1	452.4	702.9
United Kingdom	2,174.9	3,005.8	3,670.1
USA	3,125.8	3,336.8	3,753.9
Total (incl. others)	31,333.9	35,762.0	47,252.8

* Imports by country of origin, exports by country of last consignment.

Source: UN, *International Trade Statistics Yearbook*.

Transport

RAILWAYS
(traffic)

	2001	2002	2003*
Passengers carried ('000)	76,323	73,088	76,993
Passenger-km (million)	5,568	5,204	5,878
Freight carried ('000 metric tons)†	14,362	14,424	15,755
Freight ton-km (million)	7,562	7,224	8,669

* Provisional figures.
† Excluding parcels and departmental traffic.

ROAD TRAFFIC
(motor vehicles at end of February)

	2001	2002	2003
Passenger cars	4,534,803	4,600,140	4,700,343
Minibuses	239,381	241,700	245,394
Buses and coaches	119,306	120,097	123,500
Small trucks	833,175	875,381	973,457
Trucks	396,493	399,025	405,034
Motorcycles and mopeds	1,031,221	1,046,907	1,073,415
Special purpose vehicles	57,490	58,790	60,511

SHIPPING

Merchant Fleet
(registered at 31 December)

	2002	2003	2004
Number of vessels	1,147	1,113	1,114
Total displacement ('000 grt)	5,658.8	4,950.6	4,678.9

Source: Lloyd's Register-Fairplay, *World Fleet Statistics*.

International Sea-borne Traffic

	1999	2000	2001
Vessels entered (number)	23,097	25,199	20,431
Passengers disembarked (number)	482,715	600,948	590,454
Goods unloaded ('000 metric tons)*	71,453	79,337	68,342
Vessels cleared (number)	18,097	18,385	18,916
Passengers embarked (number)	484,244	593,493	599,474
Goods loaded ('000 metric tons)*	25,075	25,477	34,137

* Including timber.

CIVIL AVIATION
(scheduled services)

	2001	2002	2003
Domestic services:			
Kilometres flown ('000)	32,126	28,553	28,180
Number of passengers	5,161,634	4,922,619	4,991,517
Passenger-km ('000)	2,858,614	2,705,316	2,751,910
Freight handled (metric tons)	439,942	29,263	29,146
Total ton-km ('000)	284,968	274,807	275,681
International services:			
Kilometres flown ('000)	105,701	102,485	101,738
Number of passengers	4,753,464	4,993,176	4,802,897
Passenger-km ('000)	12,211,712	13,020,432	12,223,997
Freight handled (metric tons)	263,960	89,836	88,993
Total ton-km ('000)	1,540,588	1,714,432	1,617,729

Tourism

TOURISTS BY COUNTRY OF ORIGIN

Country	2001	2002	2003
Austria	351,111	369,866	370,306
Belgium	302,079	306,911	299,583
Bulgaria	539,425	832,220	1,005,684
France	489,488	510,381	444,142
Germany	2,818,888	3,421,112	3,231,115
Greece	173,264	255,867	364,571
Iran	326,931	432,083	497,189
Israel	282,631	263,867	302,920
Netherlands	616,110	848,771	921,704
Romania	179,322	177,397	184,366
Russia	750,173	937,298	1,272,140
United Kingdom	684,102	917,872	935,765
USA	255,405	197,402	162,198
Total (incl. others)	10,782,673	12,789,827	13,340,956

Tourism receipts (million US $, excl. passenger transport, incl. expenditure of Turkish nationals residing abroad): 10,067 in 2001; 11,901 in 2002; 13,203 in 2003.

Source: World Tourism Organization.

Communications Media

	2002	2003	2004
Telephones ('000 main lines in use)	18,914.9	18,916.7	19,125.2
Mobile cellular telephones ('000 subscribers)	23,374.4	27,887.5	34,707.5
Personal computers ('000 in use)	3,000	n.a.	3,703
Internet users ('000)	4,300	6,000	10,220

Radio receivers ('000 in use): 11,300 in 1997.
Television receivers ('000 in use): 21,152 in 2001.
Facsimile machines (number in use): 108,014 in 1997.
Book production (titles): 2,920 in 1999.
Daily newspapers (number): 542 in 2000.
Non-daily newspapers (number): 688 in 2000.
Sources: International Telecommunication Union; UNESCO Institute for Statistics; UN, *Statistical Yearbook*.

Education

(2003/04, provisional figures)

	Institutions	Teachers	Students
Pre-primary	13,692	19,122	358,499
Primary	36,117	384,029	10,479,538
Secondary:			
general	2,831	86,051	1,963,998
vocational and teacher training	3,681	73,998	1,050,394
Higher	1,248	78,804	1,841,546

Adult literacy rate (UNESCO estimates): 88.3% (males 95.7%; females 81.1%) in 2003 (Source: UN Development Programme, *Human Development Report*).

Directory

The Constitution

In October 1981 the National Security Council (NSC), which took power in September 1980, announced the formation of a Consultative Assembly to draft a new constitution, replacing that of 1961. The Assembly consisted of 40 members appointed directly by the NSC and 120 members chosen by the NSC from candidates put forward by the governors of the 67 provinces; all former politicians were excluded. The draft Constitution was approved by the Assembly in September 1982 and by a national referendum in November. Its main provisions are summarized below:

Legislative power is vested in the unicameral Grand National Assembly, which (following an amendment in July 1995) comprises 550 deputies. The election of deputies is by universal adult suffrage for a five-year term. Executive power is vested in the President, who is elected by the Grand National Assembly for a seven-year term and is empowered to appoint a Prime Minister and senior members of the judiciary, the Central Bank and broadcasting organizations; to dissolve the Assembly; and to declare a state of emergency entailing rule by decree. Strict controls on the powers of trades unions, the press and political parties were also included. An appended 'temporary article' automatically installed the incumbent President of the NSC as Head of State for a seven-year term, assisted by a Presidential Council comprising members of the NSC.

In July 2003 the Grand National Assembly approved an amendment reducing the number of NSC members from 13 to six. The NSC was henceforth to be a predominantly civilian advisory body, comprising the President, Prime Minister, Chief of General Staff, and Ministers of Foreign Affairs, National Defence and Internal Affairs. Amendments approved by the Assembly in May 2004 included guarantees of equal rights between men and women, the removal of references to capital punishment and the abolition of State Security Courts.

The Government

HEAD OF STATE

President: AHMET NECDET SEZER (took office 16 May 2000).

COUNCIL OF MINISTERS
(April 2006)

All ministers were members of the Adalet ve Kalkınma (AK) Partisi.

Prime Minister: REÇEP TAYYIP ERDOĞAN.
Deputy Prime Minister and Minister of Foreign Affairs: ABDULLAH GÜL.
Deputy Prime Ministers: Dr ABDÜLLATIF ŞENER, MEHMET ALI ŞAHIN.
Ministers of State: Prof. BEŞIR ATALAY, ALI BABACAN, Prof. MEHMET AYDIN, NIMET ÇUBUKÇU, KÜRŞAT TÜZMEN.
Minister of Justice: CEMIL ÇIÇEK.
Minister of National Defence: MEHMET VECDI GÖNÜL.
Minister of Internal Affairs: ABDÜLKADIR AKSU.
Minister of Finance: KEMAL UNAKITAN.
Minister of National Education: Dr HÜSEYIN ÇELIK.
Minister of Public Works and Settlement: FARUK NAFIZ ÖZAK.
Minister of Health: Prof. REÇEP AKDAĞ.
Minister of Transport: BINALI YILDIRIM.
Minister of Agriculture and Rural Affairs: MEHMET MEHDI EKER.
Minister of Labour and Social Security: MURAT BAŞESKIOĞLU.
Minister of Industry and Trade: ALI COŞKUN.
Minister of Energy and Natural Resources: Dr MEHMET HILMI GÜLER.
Minister of Culture and Tourism: ATILLA KOÇ.
Minister of the Environment and Forestry: OSMAN PEPE.

MINISTRIES

President's Office: Cumhurbaşkanlığı Köşkü, Çankaya, Ankara; tel. (312) 4685030; fax (312) 4271330; e-mail cumhurbaskanligi@tccb.gov.tr; internet www.cankaya.gov.tr.

Prime Minister's Office: Başbakanlık, Bakanlıklar, Ankara; tel. (312) 4189056; fax (312) 4180476; e-mail info@basbakanlik.gov.tr; internet www.basbakanlik.gov.tr.

Deputy Prime Minister's Office: Başbakan yard. ve Devlet Bakanı, Bakanlıklar, Ankara; tel. (312) 4191621; fax (312) 4191547.

Ministry of Agriculture and Rural Affairs: Tarım ve Köyişleri Bakanlığı, Kampüsü Eskişehir Yolu 9km Lodumlu, Ankara; tel. (312) 2865385; fax (312) 2863964; e-mail admin@tarim.gov.tr; internet www.tarim.gov.tr.

Ministry of Culture and Tourism: Kültür ve Turizm Bakanlığı, Atatürk Bul. 29, 06050 Opera, Ankara; tel. (312) 3090850; fax (312) 3124359; e-mail info@kulturturizm.gov.tr; internet www.kulturturizm.gov.tr.

Ministry of Energy and Natural Resources: Enerji ve Tabii Kaynaklar Bakanlığı, İnönü Bul. 27, Ankara; tel. (312) 2126420; fax (312) 2156586; e-mail webmaster@enerji.gov.tr; internet www.enerji.gov.tr.

Ministry of the Environment and Forestry: Gevre Bakanlığı, Atatürk Bulvarı 153 Bakanlıklar, Ankara; tel. (312) 4176000; fax (312) 2150094; internet www.cevreorman.gov.tr.

Ministry of Finance: Maliye Bakanlığı, Dikmen Cad., Ankara; tel. (312) 4250018; fax (312) 4250058; e-mail bshalk@maliye.gov.tr; internet www.maliye.gov.tr.

Ministry of Foreign Affairs: Dişişleri Bakanlığı, Yeni Hizmet Binası, 06100 Balgat, Ankara; tel. (312) 2921000; fax (312) 2873869; internet www.mfa.gov.tr.

Ministry of Health: Sağlık Bakanlığı, Mithatpasa Cad. 3 Sihhiye, Ankara; tel. (312) 4356440; fax (312) 4339885; e-mail info@saglik.gov.tr; internet www.saglik.gov.tr.

Ministry of Industry and Trade: Sanayi ve Ticaret Bakanlığı, Eskişehir yolu üzeri 7 km Ankara; tel. (312) 2860365; internet www.sanayi.gov.tr.

TURKEY

Ministry of Internal Affairs: İçişleri Bakanlığı, Bakanlıklar, Ankara; tel. (312) 4181368; fax (312) 4181795; internet www.icisleri.gov.tr.

Ministry of Justice: Adalet Bakanlığı, 06659 Kizilay, Ankara; tel. (312) 4177770; fax (312) 4173954; internet www.adalet.gov.tr.

Ministry of Labour and Social Security: Çalışma ve Sosyal Güvenlik Bakanlığı, İnönü Bul. 42, 06100 Emek, Ankara; tel. (312) 2966000; fax (312) 4179765; tel. webmaster@csgb.gov.tr; internet www.calisma.gov.tr.

Ministry of National Defence: Milli Savunma Bakanlığı, 06100 Ankara; tel. (312) 4254596; fax (312) 4184737; e-mail meb@meb.gov.tr; internet www.msb.gov.tr.

Ministry of National Education: Milli Eğitim Bakanlığı, Atatürk Bul., Bakanlıklar, Ankara; tel. (312) 4191410; fax (312) 4177027; internet www.meb.gov.tr.

Ministry of Public Works and Settlement: Bayındırlık ve İskan Bakanlığı, Vekaletler Cad. 1, 06100 Ankara; tel. (312) 4186443; fax (312) 4251288; e-mail webadmin@bayindirlik.gov.tr; internet www.bayindirlik.gov.tr.

Ministry of Transport: Ulaştırma Bakanlığı, Hakkı Turayliç Cad. 5, 06338 Emek, Ankara; tel. (312) 5501000; fax (312) 2124930; internet www.ubak.gov.tr.

Legislature

BÜYÜK MILLET MECLISI
(Grand National Assembly)

Speaker: BÜLENT ARINÇ.

General Election, 3 November 2002

Party	% of votes	Seats
Adalet ve Kalkınma (AK) Partisi	34.28	363
Cumhuriyet Halk Partisi (CHP)	19.40	178
Doğru Yol Partisi (DYP)	9.55	0
Milliyetçi Hareket Partisi (MHP)	8.34	0
Genç Partisi (GP)	7.25	0
Demokratik Halk Partisi (DHP)*	6.23	0
Anavatan Partisi (ANAP)	5.13	0
Saadet Partisi (SP)	2.48	0
Demokratik Sol Parti (DSP)	1.22	0
Yeni Türkiye Partisi (YTP)	1.15	0
Büyük Birlik Partisi (BBP)	1.02	0
Independents	0.99	9
Others	2.96	0
Total	**100.00**	**550**

* Alliance based on Halkın Demokrasi Partisi (HADEP).

Election Commission

Yüksek Seçim Kurulu (YSK) (Higher Council of Elections): Bayındır Şakak, 3 Kızılny, Ankara; tel. (312) 4344900; independent; Chair. TUFAN ALGAN.

Political Organizations

Political parties were banned from 1980–83. Legislation enacted in March 1986 stipulated that a party must have organizations in at least 45 provinces, and in two-thirds of the districts in each of these provinces, in order to take part in an election. A political party is recognized by the Government as a legitimate parliamentary group only if it has at least 20 deputies in the Grand National Assembly.

In mid-1992, following the adoption of less restrictive legislation concerning the formation of political parties, several new parties were established, and the left-wing CHP, dissolved in 1981, was reactivated.

Adalet ve Kalkınma (AK) Partisi (Justice and Development Party): internet www.akparti.org.tr; f. 2001; Islamist-orientated; Leader RECEP TAYYIP ERDOĞAN.

Anavatan Partisi (ANAP) (Motherland Party): 13 Cad. 3, Balgat, Ankara; tel. (312) 2865000; fax (312) 2865019; e-mail anavatan@anap.org.tr; internet www.anap.org.tr; f. 1983; supports free-market economic system, moderate nationalist and conservative policies, rational social justice system, integration with the EU and closer ties with the Islamic world; Chair. NESRIN NAS; Sec.-Gen. YAŞAR OKUYAN.

Büyük Birlik Partisi (BBP) (Great Unity Party): Tuna Cad. 28, Yenişehir, Ankara; tel. (312) 4340923; fax (312) 4355818; e-mail bbp@bbp.org.tr; internet www.bbp.org.tr; f. 1993; Chair. MUHSIN YAZICIOĞLU.

Cumhuriyet Halk Partisi (CHP) (Republican People's Party): Çevre Sok. 38, Ankara; tel. and fax (312) 4685969; e-mail chpbim@chp.org.tr; internet www.chp.org.tr; f. 1923; by Kemal Atatürk, dissolved in 1981 and reactivated in 1992; merged with Sosyal Demokrat Halkçı Parti (Social Democratic Populist Party) in Feb. 1995; left-wing; Leader DENIZ BAYKAL; Sec.-Gen. TARHAN ERDEM.

Değişen Türkiye Partisi (DEPAR) (Changing Turkey Party): Aşağlı Öveçler 6, Cad. 78, Sok. 15/2, Dikmen, Ankara; tel. (312) 4794875; fax (312) 4795964; e-mail webmaster@depar.org; internet www.depar.org; f. 1998; Chair. GÖKHAN ÇAPOĞLU.

Demokrasi ve Barış Partisi (DBP) (Democracy and Peace Party): Menekşe 1, Sok. 10-A/7, Kızılay, Ankara; tel. (312) 4173587; f. 1996; pro-Kurdish; Leader REFIK KARAKOÇ.

Demokratik Toplum Partisi (DTP) (Democratic Society Party): Barışmanço Cad. 32, Sok. 37 Balgat, Ankara; tel. (12) 2863200; fax (12) 2851819; e-mail dtpgm@dtpgm.org.tr; internet www.dth-web.com; f. Oct. 2004 as Democratic Society Movement; registered as pol. party Nov. 2005; Pres LEYLA ZANA, AYSEL TUĞLUK, AHMET TÜRK.

Demokrat Türkiye Partisi (DTP) (Democratic Turkey Party): Mesnevi Sok. 27, Ankara; tel. (312) 4420151; fax (312) 4421263; e-mail sevginazlioglu@dtp.org.tr; internet www.dtp.org.tr; Leader İSMET SEZGIN.

Demokratik Sol Partisi (DSP) (Democratic Left Party): Fevzi Çakmak Cad. 17, Ankara; tel. (312) 2124950; fax (312) 2213474; e-mail akguvercinist@dsp.org.tr; internet www.dsp.org.tr; f. 1985; centre-left; drawing support from members of the fmr Republican People's Party; Chair. BÜLENT ECEVIT; Sec.-Gen. ZEKI SEZER.

Doğru Yol Partisi (DYP) (True Path Party): Çetýn Emeç Bul. 117, Balgat, Ankara; tel. (312) 4441946; fax (312) 2898783; e-mail dyp@dyp.org.tr; internet www.dyp.org.tr; f. 1983; centre-right; replaced the Justice Party (f. 1961 and banned in 1981); Chair. MEHMET AĞAR; Sec.-Gen. Dr KAMIL TURAN.

Emeğin Partisi (EMEP) (Labour Party): Ulufeci Sok. Fındıkoba Ishani 2/2, Kocamustafapaşa, İstanbul; tel. (212) 5884332; fax (212) 5884341; e-mail info@emep.org; internet www.emep.org; Pres. LEVENT TÜZEL.

Emekci Halk Partisi (EHP) (Working People's Party): f. Jan. 2004.

Genç Partisi (GP) (Youth Party): internet www.gp.org.tr; f. 2002; populist, nationalist; Leader CEM UZAN.

İşçi Partisi (IP) (Workers' Party): Toros Sok. 9, Sıhhıye, Ankara; tel. (312) 2318111; fax (312) 2292994-95; e-mail ip@ip.org.tr; internet www.ip.org.tr; f. 1992; Chair. DOĞU PERINÇEK.

Liberal Demokratik Parti (LDP) (Liberal Democratic Party): Gazi Mustafa Kemal Bul., 108/18 Maltepe, 06570 Ankara; tel. (312) 2323374; fax (312) 4687597; e-mail info@ldp.org.tr; internet www.ldp.org.tr; f. 1994; Chair. BESIM TIBUK.

Millet Partisi (MP) (Nation Party): İstanbul Cad., Rüzgarlı Gayret Sok. 2, Ankara; tel. (312) 3127626; fax (312) 3127651; internet www.mp.org.tr; f. 1992; Chair. AYKUT EDIBALI.

Milliyetçi Hareket Partisi (MHP) (Nationalist Movement Party): Karanfil Sok. 69, 06640 Bakanlıklar, Ankara; tel. (312) 4195956; fax (312) 2311424; e-mail mhp@mhp.org.tr; internet www.mhp.org.tr; f. 1983; fmrly the Democratic and Conservative Party; Leader DEVLET BAHÇELI; Sec.-Gen. FARUK BAL.

Özgürlük ve Dayanisma Partisi (ODP) (Freedom and Solidarity Party): Necatibey Cad. 23/11, Ankara; e-mail ozgurluk@odp.org.tr; internet www.odp.org.tr; f. 1996; Leader UFUK URAZ.

Özgür Toplum Parti (OTP) (Free Society Party): f. June 2003; assoc. with Halkın Demokrasi Partisi; Leader AHMET TURAN DEMIR.

Saadet Partisi (SP) (Felicity Party): f. 2001; replaced conservative wing of Islamic fundamentalist and free-market advocating Fazilet Partisi (Virtue Party), which was banned in June 2001; Leader NECMETTIN ERBAKAN.

Türkiye Komünist Partisi (TKP) (Communist Party of Turkey): Osmanağa Mahallesi Nüzhet Efendi Sok. 38, Kadıköy, İstanbul; tel. (216) 4185351; fax (216) 3461137; e-mail tkp@tkp.org.tr; internet www.tkp.org.tr; f. 1981 as the Party of Socialist Power, name changed as above in 2001; Gen. Sec. KEMAL OKUYAN.

Türkiye Partisi (TP) (Turkish Party): f. Feb. 2004; Chair. TEKIN ENEREM.

Yeniden Doğuş Partisi (YDP) (Rebirth Party): Sağlık Sok. 3, Sıhhıye, Ankara; tel. (312) 4356565; fax (312) 4356564; f. 1992; Chair. HASAN CELAL GÜZEL.

Yeni Parti (YP) (New Party): Rabat Sok 27, Gaziosmanpaşa, Ankara; tel. (312) 4469254; fax (312) 4469579; f. 1993; Leader YUSUF BOZKURT ÖZAL.

Yeni Türkiye Partisi (YTP) (New Turkey Party): f. 2002; comprised of former DSP politicians; Leader İSMAIL CEM.

The following proscribed organizations were engaged in an armed struggle against the Government:

Devrimici Halk Kurtuluş—Cephesi (DHKP—C) (Revolutionary People's Liberation Party—Front): e-mail dhkc@ozgurluk.org; internet www.ozgurluk.org/dhkc; left-wing faction of Dev-Sol; subsumed parent organization in 1996.

Partiya Karkeren Kurdistan (PKK) (Kurdistan Workers' Party): e-mail kgnetorg@kongra-gel.com; internet www.kongra-gel.org; f. 1978; 57-member directorate; launched struggle for an independent Kurdistan in 1984; declared cease-fire 2000; renamed Congress for Freedom and Democracy in Kurdistan (KADEK) April 2002; renamed KONGRA-GEL Nov. 2003; return to fmr name, PKK, announced April 2005, following resumption of armed struggle; name KONGRA-GEL continued to be used by some elements; re-emerged military wing, Hezên Parastina Gel (HPG—People's Defence Forces); Leader ABDULLAH ÖCALAN; Chair. ZÜBEYIR AYDAR.

Diplomatic Representation

EMBASSIES IN TURKEY

Afghanistan: Cinnah Cad. 88, 06551 Çankaya, Ankara; tel. (312) 4422523; fax (312) 4426256; Ambassador ABDUL GHAFOOR POYA FARYABI.

Albania: Ebuziya Tevfik Sok. 17, Çankaya, Ankara; tel. (312) 4416103; fax (312) 4416104; e-mail realemtr@hotmail.com; Ambassador JONUZ BEGAJ.

Algeria: Şehit Ersan Cad. 42, 06680 Çankaya, Ankara; tel. (312) 4687719; fax (312) 4687619; Ambassador SMAIL ALLAOUA.

Argentina: Uğar Mumcu Cad. 60/3, 06700 Gaziosmanpaşa, Ankara; tel. (312) 4462062; fax (312) 4462063; e-mail embarg@kablonet.com.tr; Ambassador SEBASTIAN BRUGO MARCO.

Australia: Nenehatun Cad. 83, 06700 Gaziosmanpaşa, Ankara; tel. (312) 4599500; fax (312) 4464827; e-mail info@embaustralia.org.tr; internet www.embaustralia.org.tr; Ambassador JONATHAN PHILP.

Austria: Atatürk Bul. 189, Kavaklıdere, Ankara; tel. (312) 4190431; fax (312) 4189454; e-mail austroambtr@superonline.com; Ambassador Dr MARIUS CALLIGARIS.

Azerbaijan: Baku Sok. 1, Oran, Ankara; tel. (312) 4911681; fax (312) 4920430; e-mail azer-tr@tr.net; internet www.azembassy.org.tr; Ambassador ZAKIR HASHIMOV.

Bangladesh: Cinnah Cad. 78/7–10, Çankaya, Ankara; tel. (312) 4392750; fax (312) 4392408; Ambassador NAZRUL ISLAM.

Belarus: Abidin Daver Sok. 17, 065550 Çankaya, Ankara; tel. (312) 4416769; fax (312) 4416674; e-mail turkey@belembassy.org; Ambassador NATALLIA ZHYLEVICH.

Belgium: Mahatma Gandhi Cad. 55, Gaziosmanpaşa, Ankara; tel. (312) 4468247; fax (312) 4468251; e-mail ankara@diplobel.org; Ambassador JAN MATTHYSEN.

Bosnia and Herzegovina: Turan Emeksiz Sok. 3/9, Park Evleri B Blok, Gaziosmanpaşa, Ankara; tel. (312) 4273602; fax (312) 4273604; e-mail bh_emb@ttnet.net.tr; Ambassador NERKEZ ARIFHODŽIĆ.

Brazil: Reşit Galip Cad., İlkadım Sok. 1, Ankara; tel. (312) 4481840; fax (312) 4481838; e-mail brasemb@brasembancara.org; Ambassador BRIAN MICHAEL FRASER NEELE.

Bulgaria: Atatürk Bul. 124, 06680 Kavaklıdere, Ankara; tel. (312) 4672071; fax (312) 4672574; e-mail bulemb@superonline.com; Ambassador BRANIMIR MLADENOV.

Canada: Nenehatun Cad. 75, 06700 Gaziosmanpaşa, Ankara; tel. (312) 4599200; fax (312) 4599361; e-mail ankra@dfait-maeci.gc.ca; Ambassador MICHAEL LEIR.

Chile: Reşit Galip Cad., İrfanli Sok. 14/1–3, 06700 Gaziosmanpaşa, Ankara; tel. (312) 4473418; fax (312) 4474725; e-mail echiletr@ttnet.net.tr; Ambassador PEDRO BARROS.

China, People's Republic: Gölgeli Sok. 34, 06700 Gaziosmanpaşa, Ankara; tel. (312) 4360628; fax (312) 4464248; Ambassador SONG AIGUO.

Croatia: Kelebek Sok. 15/A, Gaziosmanpaşa, Ankara; tel. (312) 4469460; fax (312) 4464700; e-mail hrvelank@marketweb.net.tr; Ambassador AMIR MUHAREMI.

Cuba: Şölen Sok. 8, 06550 Çankaya, Ankara; tel. (312) 4428970; fax (312) 4414007; e-mail conscuba@ato.org.tr; Ambassador MIGUEL ANDRÉS LAMAZARES PUELLO.

Czech Republic: Kaptanpaşa Sok. 15, 06700 Gaziosmanpaşa, Ankara; tel. (312) 4056955; fax (312) 4477395; e-mail ankara@embassy.mzv.cz; Ambassador EVA FILIPI.

Denmark: Mahatma Gandhi Cad. 74, 06700 Ankara; tel. (312) 4466141; fax (312) 444724986; e-mail ankamb@um.dk; internet www.danimarka.org.tr; Ambassador CHRISTIAN HOPPE.

Egypt: Atatürk Bul. 126, 06680 Kavaklıdere, Ankara; tel. (312) 4684647; fax (312) 4270099; Ambassador AHMAD AMIN FATHALLA.

Estonia: Reşit Galip Cad. 128/5, 06700 Gaziosmanpaşa, Ankara; tel. (312) 4056970; fax 4056976; e-mail linda.kolk@estemb.org.tr; Ambassador ANDRES TOMASBERG.

Finland: Kader Sok. 44, 06700 Gaziosmanpaşa, Ankara; tel. (312) 4261930; fax (312) 4680072; Ambassador BJÖRN EKBLOM.

France: Paris Cad. 70, 06540 Kavaklıdere, Ankara; tel. (312) 4554545; fax (312) 4554527; e-mail ambafr@ada.net.tr; internet www.ambafrance-tr.org; Ambassador BERNARD GARCIA.

Georgia: Hilal 1 Mahallesi, 7 Cad., 31 Yıldız-Çankaya; Ankara; tel. (312) 4426508; fax (312) 4426507; e-mail geoemb@ada.net.tr; Ambassador GRIGOL MGALOBLISHVILI.

Germany: Atatürk Bul. 114, 06680 Kavaklıdere, Ankara; tel. (312) 4555100; fax (312) 4266959; e-mail infomail@germanembassyank.com; internet www.germanembassyank.com; Ambassador Dr WOLF-RUTHART BORN.

Greece: Zia ür-Rahman Cad. 9–11, 06670 Gaziosmanpaşa, Ankara; tel. (312) 4368860; fax (312) 4463191; e-mail greekembassy@ttnet.net.tr; Ambassador MICHAEL B. CHRISTIDES.

Holy See: Birlik Mah. 3, Cad. 37, PK 33, 06552 Çankaya, Ankara (Apostolic Nunciature); tel. (312) 4953514; fax (312) 4953540; e-mail vatican@tr.net; Apostolic Nuncio Most Rev. ANTONIO LUCIBELLO (Titular Archbishop of Thurio).

Hungary: Sancak Mah. Layoş, Koşut Cad. 2, Yıldız, Çankaya, Ankara; tel. (312) 4422273; fax (312) 4415049; e-mail huembtur@isnet.net.tr; Ambassador Dr ZSOLT G. SZALAY.

India: Cinnah Cad. 77/A, 06680 Çankaya, Ankara; tel. (312) 4382195; fax (312) 4403429; e-mail chancery@indembassy.org.tr; Ambassador ALOKE SEN.

Indonesia: Abdullah Cevdet Sok. 10, 06680 Çankaya, Ankara; tel. (312) 4382190; fax (312) 4382193; e-mail indoank@marketweb.net.tr; Ambassador AMIN RIANOM.

Iran: Tahran Cad. 10, Kavaklıdere, Ankara; tel. (312) 4682821; fax (312) 4682823; Ambassador FIROOZ DOWLATABADI.

Iraq: Turan Emeksiz Sok. 11, 06700 Gaziosmanpaşa, Ankara; tel. (312) 4687421; fax (312) 4684832; Ambassador MUNTHIR N. ABDULLA.

Ireland: Uğur Mumcu Cad. 88, MNG Binası B Blok Kat 3, Gaziosmanpaşa 06700 Ankara; tel. (312) 4466172; fax (312) 4468061; e-mail ireland@superonline.com; Ambassador ANTONY MANNIX.

Israel: Mahatma Gandhi Cad. 85, 06700 Gaziosmanpaşa, Ankara; tel. (312) 4463605; fax (312) 4261533; e-mail israel@marketweb.net.tr; Ambassador PINHAS AVIVI.

Italy: Atatürk Bul. 118, Kavaklıdere, Ankara; tel. (312) 4265460; fax (312) 4265800; e-mail itaamb@superonline.com; internet www.italian-embassy.org.ae/Ambasciata_Ankara; Ambassador Dr VITTORIO CLAUDIO SORDO.

Japan: Reşit Galip Cad. 81, 06700 Gaziosmanpaşa, Ankara; tel. (312) 4460500; fax (312) 4372504; e-mail japonbe@ada.net.tr; Ambassador TOMOYUKI ABE.

Jordan: Dede Korkut Sok. 18 Mesnevi, 06690 Çankaya, Ankara; tel. (312) 4402054; fax (312) 4404327; Ambassador (vacant).

Kazakhstan: Kiliç Ali Sok. 6, 06450 Or An Diplomatik Sitesi, Ankara; tel. (312) 4919100; fax (312) 4914455; e-mail kazank@ada.net.tr; Ambassador Dr BEIBIT ISABAYEV.

Korea, Republic: Cinnah Cad., Alaçam Sok 5, 06690 Çankaya, Ankara; tel. (312) 4684821; fax (312) 4682279; Ambassador KIM YOUNG-KI.

Kuwait: Reşit Galip Cad. Kelebek Sok. 110, Gaziosmanpaşa, Ankara; tel. (312) 4450576; fax (312) 4464510; e-mail kuwait@ada.net.tr; Ambassador ABDULLAH ABD AL-AZIZ AD-DUWAIKH.

Kyrgyzstan: Turan Güneş Bul. 15 Cad. 21, Oran-Yıldız, Ankara; tel. (312) 9613506; fax (312) 9613513; e-mail kirgiz-o@tr.net; Ambassador MAMBETJUNUS ABYLOV.

Lebanon: Kızkulesi Sok. 44, Gaziosmanpaşa, Ankara; tel. (312) 4467485; fax (312) 4461023; e-mail lebembas@ttnet.net.tr; Ambassador GEORGES H. SIAM.

Libya: Cinnah Cad. 60, 06690 Çankaya, Ankara; tel. (312) 4381110; fax (312) 4403862; e-mail ashaabiankara@hotmail.com; Ambassador MUHAMMAD A. MANGUSH.

Lithuania: Mahatma Gandhi Cad. 17/8–9, 06700 Gaziosmanpaşa, Ankara; tel. (312) 4470766; fax (312) 4470663; e-mail lrambasd@ada.net.tr; Ambassador VYTAUTAS NAUDUŽAS.

Macedonia, former Yugoslav republic: Filistin Sok. 30/2, 06700 Gaziosmanpaşa, Ankara; tel. (312) 4469204; fax (312) 4469206; e-mail macemb@ttnet.net.tr; Ambassador MUHEDIN RUSTEMI.

Malaysia: Mahatma Gandhi Cad. 58, 06700 Gaziosmanpaşa, Ankara; tel. (312) 4463547; fax (312) 4464130; e-mail mwankara@isnet.net.tr; Ambassador AHMAD MOKHTAR SELAT.

TURKEY

Mexico: Kırkpınar Sok. 18/6, 06540 Çankaya, Ankara; tel. (312) 4423033; fax (312) 4420221; e-mail mexico@embamextur.com; internet www.mexico.org.tr; Ambassador AMANDA MIREYA TERÁN MUNGUIA.
Moldova: Kaptanpaşa Sok. 49, 06700 Gaziosmanpaşa, Ankara; tel. (312) 4465527; fax (312) 4465816; Ambassador VICTOR TVIRCUN.
Mongolia: Koza Sok. 109, 06700 Gaziosmanpaşa, Ankara; tel. (312) 4467977; fax (312) 4467791; Ambassador PANIDJUNAI KHALIUN.
Morocco: Reşit Galip Cad., Rabat Sok. 11, 06700 Gaziosmanpaşa, Ankara; tel. (312) 4376020; fax (312) 4471405; e-mail sifamtatr@tr.net; Ambassador ABDELLAH ZAGOUR.
Netherlands: Hollanda Cad. 3, 06550 Yıldız, Ankara; tel. (312) 4091800; fax (312) 4091898; e-mail ank@minbuza.nl; internet www.nl.org.tr; Ambassador SJOERD I. H. GOSSES.
New Zealand: PK 162, İran Cad. 13/4, 06700 Kavaklıdere, Ankara; tel. (312) 4679054; fax (312) 4679013; e-mail newzealand@superonline.com; Ambassador JANE HENDERSON.
Nigeria: Uğur Mumcu Sok. 56, 06700 Gaziosmanpaşa, Ankara; tel. (312) 4481077; fax (312) 4481082; Chargé d'affaires a.i. MUHAMMAD K. NDANUSA.
Norway: Kirkpinar Sok. 18/3–4, 06540 Çankaya, Ankara; tel. (312) 4058010; fax (312) 4430544; e-mail emb.ankara@mfa.no; Ambassador HANS WILHELM LONGVA.
Oman: Mahatma Gandhi Cad. 63, 06700 Gaziosmanpaşa, Ankara; tel. (312) 4470630; fax (312) 4470632; e-mail oman@superonline.com; Ambassador MUHAMMAD NASSER AL-WOHAIBI.
Pakistan: İran Cad. 37, 06700 Gaziosmanpaşa, Ankara; tel. (312) 4271410; fax (312) 4671023; e-mail parepankara@hotmail.com; Ambassador Lt-Gen (retd) SYED IFTIKHAR HUSSAIN SHAH.
Philippines: Mahatma Gandhi Cad. 56, 06700 Gaziosmanpaşa, Ankara; tel. (312) 4465831; fax (312) 4465733; e-mail ankarape@marketweb.net.tr; Ambassador OFELIA B. CASTAÑO.
Poland: Atatürk Bul. 241, 06650 Kavaklıdere, Ankara; tel. (312) 4572000; fax (312) 4572001; e-mail polamb@superonline.com; internet www.polonya.org.tr; Chargé d'affaires a.i. GRZEGORZ MICHALSKI.
Portugal: Kuleli Sok 26, 06700 Gaziosmanpaşa, Ankara; tel. (312) 4461890; fax (312) 4461892; e-mail embport@domi.com.tr; Ambassador ANTÓNIO MONTEIRO PORTUGAL.
Qatar: Bakü Sok. 6, Diplomatik Site, Oran, Ankara; tel. (312) 4411365; fax (312) 4411544; e-mail ankara@mofa.gov.qa; Ambassador Dr MUHAMMAD HASSAN AN-NUAIMI.
Romania: Bükreş Sok. 4, 06680 Çankaya, Ankara; tel. (312) 4271243; fax (312) 4271530; e-mail romania@attglobal.net; internet www.roembtr.org; Ambassador CONSTANTIN MIHAIL GRIGORIE.
Russia: Karyağdı Sok. 5, 06692 Çankaya, Ankara; tel. (312) 4392122; fax (312) 4383952; e-mail rfembassy@fromru.com; internet www.turkey.mid.ru; Ambassador Dr PETR V. STEGNIY.
Saudi Arabia: Turan Emeksiz Sok. 6, 06700 Gaziosmanpaşa, Ankara; tel. (312) 4685540; fax (312) 4274886; Ambassador MUHAMMAD A. AL-BASSAM.
Serbia and Montenegro: Paris Cad. 47, 06450 Kavaklıdere, Ankara; tel. (312) 4260236; fax (312) 4278345; e-mail yugoslav@tr.net; Ambassador ZORAN S. POPOVIĆ.
Slovakia: Atatürk Bul. 245, 06692 Kavaklıdere, Ankara; tel. (312) 4675075; fax (312) 4682689; e-mail slovak@superonline.com; Ambassador VIKTOR BAUER.
Slovenia: Küpe Sok. 1/3, 06700 Gaziosmanpaşa, Ankara; tel. (312) 4056007; fax (312) 4466887; Ambassador ANDREJ GRASSELLI.
South Africa: Filistin Cad. 27, 06700 Gaziosmanpaşa, Ankara; tel. (312) 4464056; fax (312) 4466434; e-mail saembassy@ada.net.tr; internet www.southafrica.org.tr; Ambassador SOBIZANA MNGQIKANA.
Spain: Abdullah Cevdet Sok. 8, 06680 Çankaya, Ankara; tel. (312) 4380392; fax (312) 4426991; e-mail embesptr@mail.mae.es; Ambassador MANUEL DE LA CÁMARA.
Sudan: Sancak Mah. 12 Cad. 16, 06550 Çankaya, Ankara; tel. (312) 4413885; fax (312) 4413886; e-mail sudani@superonline.com.tr; Ambassador Dr BAHA'ALDIN HANAFI.
Sweden: Katip Çelebi Sok. 7, 06692 Kavaklıdere, Ankara; tel. (312) 4664558; fax (312) 4685020; e-mail swedemb@ada.net.tr; Ambassador ANNE DISMORR.
Switzerland: Atatürk Bul. 247, 06692 Kavaklıdere, Ankara; tel. (312) 4675555; fax (312) 4671199; e-mail vertretung@ank.rep.admin.ch; Ambassador WALTER B. GYGER.
Syria: Sedat Simavi Sok. 40, 06680 Çankaya, Ankara; tel. (312) 4409657; fax (312) 4385609; Ambassador KHALED RAAD.
Tajikistan: Mahatma Gandhi Cad. 36, Gaziosmanpaşa, Ankara; tel. (312) 4461602; fax (312) 4463621; Chargé d'affaires a.i. ROUSTAM DODOJONOV.
Thailand: Çankaya Cad. Kader Sok. 45/3–4, 06700 Gaziosmanpaşa, Ankara; tel. (312) 4673059; fax (312) 4277284; e-mail thaiank@kablonet.com.tr; Ambassador KAROON RUECHUYOTHIN.
Tunisia: Kuleli Sok. 12, 06700 Gaziosmanpaşa, Ankara; tel. (312) 4377812; fax (312) 4377100; e-mail at.ankara@superonline.com; Ambassador MOHAMED LESSIR.
'Turkish Republic of Northern Cyprus': Rabat Sok. 20, 06700 Gaziosmanpaşa, Ankara; tel. (312) 4462920; fax (312) 4465238; e-mail kktcbe@superonline.com; Ambassador TAMER GAZIOĞLU.
Turkmenistan: Koza Sok. 28, Çankaya, Ankara; tel. (312) 4417122; fax (312) 4417125; Ambassador NURBERDY AMANMURADOV.
Ukraine: Sancak Mahallesi 206 Sok. 17, 06550 Yıldız, Çankaya, Ankara; tel. (312) 4415499; fax (312) 4406815; e-mail ukremb_tr@kablonet.com.tr; internet web.ttnet.net.tr/ukremb; Ambassador OLEKSANDR MISHCHENKO.
United Arab Emirates: Reşit Galip Cad. Şairler Sok. 28, 06700 Gaziosmanpaşa, Ankara; tel. (312) 4476861; fax (312) 4475545; e-mail uaeemb@superonline.com; Ambassador KHALID GHANIM AL-GAITH.
United Kingdom: Şehit Ersan Cad. 46/A, Çankaya, Ankara; tel. (312) 4553344; fax (312) 4553351; e-mail britembinf@turk.net; internet www.britishembassy.org.tr; Ambassador Sir PETER WESTMACOTT.
USA: Atatürk Bul. 110, Kavaklıdere 06100, Ankara; tel. (312) 4555555; fax (312) 4670019; e-mail ozbagd@state.gov; internet ankara.usembassy.gov; Ambassador ROSS WILSON.
Uzbekistan: Sancak Mah. 211 Sok. 3, 06550 Çankaya, Ankara; tel. (312) 4413871; fax (312) 4427058; e-mail uzbekembassy@superonline.com; Ambassador RUSTAM ISAYEV.
Venezuela: Cinnah Cad. 78/2, Çankaya, Ankara; tel. (312) 4387135; fax (312) 4406619; e-mail embveank@ttnet.net.tr; Ambassador KALDONE G. NWEIHED.
Yemen: Fethiye Sok. 2, 06700 Gaziosmanpaşa, Ankara; tel. (312) 4462637; fax (312) 4461778; e-mail yememb@superonline.com; Ambassador AHMAD HUSSEIN AL-BASHA.

Judicial System

Until the foundation of the Turkish Republic, a large part of the Turkish civil law—the laws affecting the family, inheritance, property, obligations, etc.—was based on the Koran, and this holy law was administered by special religious (*Shari'a*) courts. The legal reform of 1926 was not only a process of secularization, but also a radical change of the legal system. The Swiss Civil Code and the Code of Obligation, the Italian Penal Code and the Neuchâtel (Cantonal) Code of Civil Procedure were adopted and modified to fit Turkish customs and traditions.

According to current Turkish law, the power of the judiciary is exercised by judicial (criminal), military and administrative courts. These courts render their verdicts in the first instance, while superior courts examine the verdict for subsequent rulings.

SUPERIOR COURTS

Constitutional Court: Consists of 11 regular and four substitute members, appointed by the President. Reviews the constitutionality of laws, at the request of the President of the Republic, parliamentary groups of the governing party or of the main opposition party, or of one-fifth of the members of the National Assembly, and sits as a high council empowered to try senior members of state. The rulings of the Constitutional Court are final. Decisions of the Court are published immediately in the Official Gazette, and shall be binding on the legislative, executive and judicial organs of the state; Chief Justice TÜLAY TUĞCU.

Court of Appeals: The court of the last instance for reviewing the decisions and verdicts rendered by judicial courts. It has original and final jurisdiction in specific cases defined by law. Members are elected by the Supreme Council of Judges and Prosecutors; Chief Justice OSMAN ARSLAN.

Council of State: An administrative court of the first and last instance in matters not referred by law to other administrative courts, and an administrative court of the last instance in general. Hears and settles administrative disputes and expresses opinions on draft laws submitted by the Council of Ministers. Three-quarters of the members are appointed by the Supreme Council of Judges and Public Prosecutors, the remaining quarter is selected by the President of the Republic.

Military Court of Appeals: A court of the last instance to review decisions and verdicts rendered by military courts, and a court of first and last instance with jurisdiction over certain military persons, stipulated by law, with responsibility for the specific trials of these

TURKEY

persons. Members are selected by the President of the Republic from nominations made by the Military Court of Appeals.

Supreme Military Administrative Court: A military court for the judicial control of administrative acts concerning military personnel. Members are selected by the President of the Republic from nominations made by the Court.

Court of Jurisdictional Disputes: Settles disputes among judicial, administrative and military courts arising from disagreements on jurisdictional matters and verdicts.

Court of Accounts: A court charged with the auditing of all accounts of revenue, expenditure and government property, which renders rulings related to transactions and accounts of authorized bodies on behalf of the National Assembly.

Supreme Council of Judges and Public Prosecutors: The President of the Council shall be the Minister of Justice, and the Under-Secretary to the Minister of Justice shall serve as an *ex-officio* member of the Council. Three regular and three substitute members from the Court of Appeals, together with two regular and two substitute members of the Council of State, shall be appointed to the Supreme Council by the President of the Republic for a four-year term. Decides all personnel matters relating to judges and public prosecutors.

Public Prosecutor: The law shall make provision for the tenure of public prosecutors and attorneys of the Council of State and their functions. The Chief Prosecutor of the Republic, the Chief Attorney of the Council of State and the Chief Prosecutor of the Military Court of Appeals are subject to the provisions applicable to judges of higher courts.

Military Trial: Military trials are conducted by military and disciplinary courts. These courts are entitled to try the military offences of military personnel and those offences committed against military personnel or in military areas, or offences connected with military service and duties. Military courts may try non-military persons only for military offences prescribed by special laws.

Religion

ISLAM

More than 99% of the Turkish people are Muslims. However, Turkey is a secular state. Although Islam was stated to be the official religion in the Constitution of 1924, an amendment in 1928 removed this privilege. After 1950 subsequent Governments have tried to re-establish links between religion and state affairs, but secularity was protected by the revolution of 1960, the 1980 military takeover and the 1982 Constitution.

Diyanet İşleri Reisi: Head of Religious Affairs in Turkey Prof. MUSTAFA SAIT YAZICIOĞLU.

CHRISTIANITY

The town of Antioch (now Antakya) was one of the earliest strongholds of Christianity, and by the the 4th century had become a patriarchal see. Formerly in Syria, the town was incorporated in Turkey in 1939. Constantinople (now İstanbul) was also a patriarchal see, and by the 6th century the Patriarch of Constantinople was recognized as the Ecumenical Patriarch in the East. Gradual estrangement from Rome developed, leading to the final breach between the Catholic West and the Orthodox East, usually assigned to the year 1054.

In 1986 there were about 100,000 Christians in Turkey.

The Orthodox Churches

Armenian Patriarchate: Ermeni Patrikliği, 34130 Kumkapı, İstanbul; tel. (212) 5170970; fax (212) 5164833; e-mail patriarchate@post.com; f. 1461; 67,000 adherents (2004); Patriarch MESROB II.

Bulgarian Orthodox Church: Bulgar Ortodoks Kilisesi, Halâskâr Gazi Cad. 319, Şişli, İstanbul; Rev. Archimandrite GANCO ÇOBANOF.

Greek Orthodox Church: The Ecumenical Patriarchate (Rum Ortodoks Patrikhanesi), Sadrazam Ali Paşa Cad. 35, 34220 Fener-Haliç, İstanbul; tel. (212) 5319670; fax (212) 5319014; e-mail patriarchate@ec-patr.org; internet www.ec-patr.org; Archbishop of Constantinople (New Rome) and Ecumenical Patriarch BARTHOLOMEW I.

The Roman Catholic Church

At 31 December 2003 there were an estimated 29,145 adherents in the country.

Bishops' Conference: Conferenza Episcopale di Turchia, Satırcı Sok 2, Harbiye, 34373 İstanbul; tel. (212) 2190089; fax (212) 2411543; f. 1987; Pres. Most Rev. RUGGERO FRANCESCHINI (Archbishop of İzmir).

Armenian Rite

Patriarchate of Cilicia: f. 1742; Patriarch NERSES BEDROS TARMOUNI XIX (resident in Beirut, Lebanon).

Archbishopric of İstanbul: Sakızağacı Cad. 31, PK 183, 80072 Beyoğlu, İstanbul; tel. (212) 2441258; fax (212) 2432364; f. 1830; Archbishop HOVHANNES TCHOLAKIAN.

Byzantine Rite

Apostolic Exarchate of İstanbul: Hamalbaşı Cad. 44, PK 259, 80070 Beyoğlu, İstanbul; tel. (212) 2497104; fax (212) 2411543; f. 1861; Vicar Delegate LOUIS PELÂTRE (Titular Bishop of Sasima).

Bulgarian Catholic Church: Bulgar Katolik Kilisesi, Eski Parmakkapı Sok. 15, Galata, İstanbul.

Latin Rite

Metropolitan See of İzmir: Church of St Polycarp, Necatibey Bul. 2, PK 267, 35212 İzmir; tel. (232) 4840531; fax (232) 4845358; e-mail padrestefano@hotmail.com; Archbishop of İzmir GIUSEPPE GERMANO BERNARDINI.

Apostolic Vicariate of Anatolia: Uray Cad. 85, PK 35, 33001 Mersin; tel. (324) 2320578; fax (324) 2320595; e-mail curiaves@future.net.tr; e-mail vic.ap@softhome.com; f. 1990; Vicar Apostolic RUGGERO FRANCESCHINI (Titular Bishop of Sicilibba).

Apostolic Vicariate of İstanbul: Papa Roncalli Sok. 83, 80230 Harbiye, İstanbul; tel. (212) 2480775; fax (212) 2411543; e-mail vapostolique@yahoo.fr; f. 1742; Vicar Apostolic LOUIS PELÂTRE (Titular Bishop of Sasima).

Maronite Rite

The Maronite Patriarch of Antioch, Cardinal Nasrallah Pierre Sfeir, is resident in Lebanon.

Melkite Rite

The Greek Melkite Patriarch of Antioch, Gregoire III Laham, is resident in Damascus, Syria.

Syrian Rite

The Syrian Catholic Patriarch of Antioch, Ignace Pierre VIII Abdel Ahad, is resident in Beirut, Lebanon.

Patriarchal Vicariate of Turkey: Sarayarkası Sok 15, PK 84, 80090 Ayazpaşa, İstanbul; tel. (212) 2432521; fax (212) 2490261; Vicar Patriarchal Rev. YUSUF SAĞ.

The Anglican Communion

Within the Church of England, Turkey forms part of the diocese of Gibraltar in Europe. The Bishop is resident in England.

Archdeacon of the Aegean: Canon JEREMY PEAKE (resident in Vienna, Austria).

JUDAISM

In 1996 it was estimated that there were about 25,000 Jews in Turkey.

Jewish Community of Turkey: Türkiye Hahambaşılığı, Yemenici Sok 23, Beyoğlu, 34430 Tünel, İstanbul; tel. (212) 2938794; fax (212) 2441980; e-mail jcommnty@atlas.net.tr; Chief Rabbi ISAK HALEVA.

The Press

Almost all İstanbul papers are also printed in Ankara and İzmir on the same day, and some in Adana. Among the most serious and influential papers are the dailies *Milliyet* and *Cumhuriyet*. The weekly *Gırgır* is noted for its political satire. The most popular dailies are the İstanbul papers *Sabah*, *Hürriyet*, *Milliyet* and *Zaman*; *Yeni Asır*, published in İzmir, is the best-selling quality daily of the Aegean region. There are numerous provincial newspapers with limited circulation.

PRINCIPAL DAILIES

Adana

Yeni Adana: Abidinpaşa Cad. 56, Adana; tel. (322) 3599006; fax (322) 3593655; e-mail yeniadana@ttnet.net.tr; internet www.yeniadana.net; f. 1918; political; Propr ÇETIN REMZI YÜREĞIR; Chief Editor YALÇIN REMZI YÜREĞIR; circ. 2,000.

TURKEY

Ankara

Ankara Ticaret: Rüzgârlı Caddesi, Ibrahim Müteferrika Sok. 2/10, Ankara; tel. (312) 3112131; fax (312) 3116690; f. 1954; commercial; Chief Editor ZEKI OCAK; Gen. Man. ISTIKLAL YARADILIŞ; circ. 2,470.

Belde: Rüzgarlı Gayret Sok. 7/1, Ulus, Ankara; tel. (312) 3106820; f. 1968; Propr İLHAN İŞBILEN; circ. 3,399.

Tasvir: Ulus Meydanı, Ulus İş Hanı, Kat 4, Ankara; tel. (312) 4111241; f. 1960; conservative; Editor ENDER YOKDAR; circ. 3,055.

Turkish Daily News: Hŭlya Sok. 45, 06700 GOP, Ankara; tel. (312) 4475647; fax (312) 4468374; e-mail tdn-f@tr.net; internet www.turkishdailynews.com; f. 1961; English language; Publr ILHAN ÇEVIK; Editor-in-Chief ILNUR ÇEVIK; circ. 54,500.

Türkiye Ticaret Sicili: Karanfil Sok. 56, Bakanlıklar, Ankara; f. 1957; commercial; Editor YALÇIN KAYA AYDOS.

Vakit: Konya Yolu 8 km, 68 Balgat, Ankara; tel. (312) 2877906; f. 1978; Man. Editor NALI ALAN; circ. 3,384.

Yeni Tanin: Ankara; f. 1964; political; Propr BURHANETTIN GÖĞEN; Man. Editor AHMET TEKEŞ; circ. 3,123.

Yirmidört Saat: Gazeteciler Cemiyeti Çevre Sok. 35, Çankaya, Ankara; tel. (312) 1682384; f. 1978; Propr BEYHAN CENKÇI.

Eskişehir

Istikbal: Köprübaşı Değirmen Cad. 19/4, Eskişehir; tel. (222) 2318975; fax (222) 2345888; f. 1950; morning; Editor VEDAT ALP.

Gaziantep

Olay (Event): Olay Medya Plaza, Topraklik, Gaziantep; tel. (342) 2206666; fax (342) 2206670; e-mail olay@olaymedya.com; internet www.olaymedya.com; f. 1992; Man. EROL MARAS.

İstanbul

Akşam: Davutpapa Cad. 34, Zeytinburnu, İstanbul; tel. (212) 4493000; fax (212) 4819571; e-mail iletisim@aksam.com.tr; internet www.aksam.com.tr; Man. Dir NERMI KARACABEYLI.

Apoyevmatini: İstiklâl Cad., Suriye Pasajı 348, Beyoğlu, İstanbul; tel. (212) 2437635; f. 1925; Greek language; Publr Dr Y. A. ADAŞOĞLU; Editor İSTEFAN PAPADOPOULOS; circ. 1,200.

Bugün: Medya Plaza Basın Ekspres Yolu, 34540 Güneşli, İstanbul; tel. (212) 5504850; fax (212) 5023340; f. 1989; Propr ÖNAY BILGIN; circ. 184,884.

Cumhuriyet (Republic): Türkocağı Cad. 39, 34334 Cağaloğlu, İstanbul; tel. (212) 5120505; fax (212) 5138595; internet www.cumhuriyet.com.tr; f. 1924; morning; liberal; Man. Editor HIKMET ÇETINKAYA; circ. 75,000.

Dünya (World): Yil Mahallesi 100, 34440 Bağcilar, İstanbul; tel. (212) 4402424; fax (212) 4402033; internet www.dunya.com; f. 1952; morning; economic; Editor-in-Chief OSMAN S. AROLAT; circ. 60,000.

Fotomaç: Medya Plaza Basın Ekspres Yolu, 34540 Güneşli, İstanbul; tel. (212) 5504900; fax (212) 5028217; f. 1991; Chief Officer İBRAHIM SETEN; circ. 250,000.

Günaydın-Tan: Alayköşkü, Cad. Eryilmaz Sok. 13, Cağaloğlu, İstanbul; tel. (212) 5120050; fax (212) 5260823; f. 1968; Editor-in-Chief SECKIN TURESAY.

Hürriyet: Babiali Cad. 15–17, Guneslikoy, 34540 Bakırköy, İstanbul; tel. (212) 5550050; fax (212) 5156705; internet www.hurriyet.com.tr; f. 1948; morning; independent political; Propr AYDIN DOĞAN; Chief Editor ERTUĞRUL ÖZKÖK; circ. 542,797.

Meydan (Nationalism): Yüzyıl Mahallesi, Mahmutbey Viyadüğü Altı, İkitelli, 34410 Cağaloğlu, İstanbul; tel. (212) 5056111; fax (212) 5056436; f. 1990; Propr REFIK ARAS; Ed. UFUK GULDEMIR.

Milli Gazete: Çayhane Sok. 1, 34040 Topkapı, İstanbul; tel. (212) 5674775; fax (212) 5674024; f. 1973; pro-Islamic; right-wing; Editor-in-Chief EKREM KIZILTAŞ; circ. 51,000.

Milliyet: Doğan Medya Center, Bağcilar, 34554 İstanbul; tel. (212) 5056111; fax (212) 5056233; internet www.milliyet.com.tr; f. 1950; morning; political; Publr AYDIN DOĞAN; Editor-in-Chief DERYA SAZAK; circ. 630,000.

Nor Marmara: İstiklâl Cad., Solakzade Sok. 5, PK 507, İstanbul; tel. (212) 2444736; f. 1940; Armenian language; Propr and Editor-in-Chief ROBER HADDELER; Gen. Man. ARI HADDELER; circ. 2,200.

Sabah (Morning): Medya Plaza, Basın Ekspres Yolu, Güneşli, İstanbul; tel. (212) 5504810; fax (212) 5028143; internet www.sabah.com.tr; Propr DINÇ BILGIN; Editor ZAFER MUTLU; circ. 550,000.

Tercüman: Sercekale Sok. 4, 34370 Topkapı, İstanbul; tel. (212) 5017505; fax (212) 5446562; f. 1961; right-wing; Propr SEDAT COLAK; Chief Editor NAZIF OKUMUS; circ. 32,869.

Türkiye (Turkey): Çatalçeşme Sok. 17, 34410 Cağaloğlu, İstanbul; tel. (212) 5139900; fax (212) 5209362; e-mail bulend@ihlas.net.tr; internet www.turkiyegazetesi.com; f. 1970; Editor-in-Chief KENAN AKIN; circ. 450,000.

Yeni Nesil (New Generation): Sanayi Cad., Selvi Sok. 5, Yenibosna, Bakırköy, İstanbul; tel. (212) 5846261; fax (212) 5567289; f. 1970; as Yeni Asya; political; Editor-in-Chief UMIT SIMSEK.

Yeni Şafak: Yenidoğan Mah., Şenay Sok. 2, Kat 1, Bayrampaşa, İstanbul; tel. (212) 6122390; fax (212) 6121944; internet www.yenisafak.com.tr.

Yeniyüzyıl: Medya Plaza Basın Ekspres Yolu, 34540 Güneşli, İstanbul; tel. (212) 5028877; fax (212) 5028295; Editor KEREM ÇALISKAN.

Zaman (Time): Çobançeşme, Kalendar Sok. 21, 34530 Yenibosna, İstanbul; tel. (212) 6393450; fax (212) 6522423; e-mail okurhatti@zaman.com.tr; internet www.zaman.com.tr; f. 1962; morning; political, independent; Man. Editor ADEM KALAC; circ. 210,000.

İzmir

Rapor: Gazi Osman Paşa Bul. 5, İzmir; tel. (232) 4254400; f. 1949; Owner DINÇ BILGIN; Man. Editor TANJU ATEŞER; circ. 9,000.

Ticaret Gazetesi: 1571 Sok 16, 35110 Çınarlı, 35110 İzmir; tel. (232) 4619642; fax (232) 4619646; e-mail ticinfo@unimedya.net.tr; internet www.ticaretgazetesi.com; f. 1942; commercial news; Editor-in-Chief AHMET SÜKUTI TÜKEL; Man. Editor CEMAL M. TÜKEL; circ. 5,009.

Yeni Asır (New Century): Yeni Asır Plaza, Ankara Cad. 3, İzmir; tel. (232) 4615000; fax (232) 4610757; e-mail yeniasır@yeniasır.com.tr; internet www.yeniasir.com.tr; f. 1895; political; Man. Editor AYDIN BILGIN; Editorial Dir HAMDI TÜRKMEN; circ. 60,000.

Konya

Yeni Konya: Mevlâna Cad. 4, Konya; tel. (332) 2112594; f. 1945; political; Man. Editor M. NACI GÜCÜYENER; Chief Editor ADIL GÜCÜYENER; monthly circ. 1,657.

Yeni Meram: Abidinpapa Cad. Yüregir Ýphaný Kat 3; tel. (332) 3599006; fax (332) 3593655; e-mail yeniadana@ttnet.net.tr; internet www.yeniadana.net; f. 1949; political; Propr ÇETÝN REMZY YÜREDÝR; Chief Editor YALÇIN REMZY YÜREDÝR; monthly circ. 44,000.

WEEKLIES

Ankara

EBA Briefing: Bestekar Sok. 21/8, Kavaklıdere, Ankara; tel. (312) 4180628; fax (312) 4180432; f. 1975; publ. by Ekonomik Basın Ajansı (Economic Press Agency); political and economic survey; Publrs ORHAN TOLUN, YAVUZ TOLUN.

Ekonomi ve Politika: Kavaklıdere, Ankara; f. 1966; economic and political; Publr ZIYA TANSU.

Türkiye İktisat Gazetesi: Karanfil Sok 56, 06582 Bakanlıklar, Ankara; tel. (312) 4184321; fax (312) 4183268; f. 1953; commercial; Chief Editor MEHMET SAĞLAM; circ. 11,500.

Turkish Economic Gazette: Atatürk Bul. 149, Bakanlıklar, Ankara; tel. (312) 4177700; publ. by UCCET.

Turkish Probe: Hülya Sok. 45, 06700 GOP, Ankara; tel. (312) 4475647; fax (312) 4468374; English language; Publr A. ILHAN ÇEVIK; Editor-in-Chief ILNUR ÇEVIK; circ. 2,500.

Antalya

Pulse: PK 7, Kemer, Antalya; tel. and fax (242) 8180105; e-mail uras@ada.net.tr; internet www.turkpulse.com; politics and business; English; published online; Publr VEDAT URAS.

İstanbul

Aktüel: Medya Plaza Basın Ekspres Yolu, 34540 Güneşli, İstanbul; tel. (212) 5504870; e-mail aktuel@birnumara.com.tr; internet aktuel.birnumara.com.tr; f. 1991; Gen. Man. GÜLAY GÖKTÜRK; Man. Editor ALEV ER.

Bayrak: Çatalçeşme Sok. 50/5, 34410 Cağaloğlu, İstanbul; tel. (212) 5275575; fax (212) 5268363; f. 1970; political; Editor MEHMET GÜNGÖR; circ. 10,000.

Elegans: Valikonağı Cad. Y.K.V. Binası K:5 D:3 34363 Nişantaşı 80220 İstanbul; tel. (212) 2336506; fax (212) 2312878; e-mail elegans@elegans.com.tr; internet www.elegans.com.tr; f. 1985; social, economic and global issues; Editor-in-Chief OMER TOYFUN YUMAK.

Ekonomik Panaroma: Büyükdere Cad. Ali Kaya Sok. 8, 80720 Levent, İstanbul; tel. (212) 2696680; f. 1988; Gen. Man. AYDIN DEMIRER.

Ekonomist: Hürgüç Gazetecilik AŞ Hurriyet Tesisleri, Kireçocaği Mevkii, Evren Mah., Güneşli Köy, İstanbul; tel. (212) 5500050; f. 1991; Gen. Man. ADIL ÖZKOL.

Gırgır: Alayköşkü Cad., Çağaloğlu, İstanbul; tel. (212) 2285000; satirical; Propr and Editor OĞUZ ARAL; circ. 500,000.

İstanbul Ticaret: İstanbul Chamber of Commerce, Ragip Gümüşpala Cad. 84, 34378, Eminönü, İstanbul; tel. (212) 5114150; fax (212) 5131565; f. 1958; commercial news; Publr MEHMET YILDIRIM.

Nokta: Gelisim Yayinlari, Büyükdere Cad., Ali Kaya Sok. 8, 80720 Levent, İstanbul; tel. (212) 2782930; fax (212) 2794378; Editor ARDA USKAN; circ. 60,000.

Tempo: Hürgüç Gazetecilik AŞ Hürriyet Tesisleri, Güneşli, İstanbul; tel. (212) 5500081; f. 1987; Dir SEDAT SIMAVI; Gen. Man. MEHMET Y. YILMAZ.

Türk Dünyası Araştırmalar Dergisi: Hürgüç Gazetecilik AŞ Hürriyet Tesisleri, Güneşli, İstanbul; tel. (212) 5500081; Dir SEDAT SIMAVI; Gen. Man. MEHMET Y. YILMAZ.

PERIODICALS
Ankara

Azerbaycan Türk Kültür Dergisi: Vakıf İş Hanı 324, Anafartalar, Ankara; f. 1949; literary and cultural periodical of Azerbaijani Turks; Editor Dr AHMET YAŞAT.

Bayrak Dergisi: Bestckar Sok. 44/5, Kavaklıdere, Ankara; f. 1964; Publr and Editor HAMI KARTAY.

Bilim ve Teknik: Bilim ve Teknik Dergisi Tübitak, Atatürk Bul. 221, Kavaklıdere, 06100 Ankara; tel. (312) 4270625; fax (312) 4276677; e-mail bteknik@tubitak.gov.tr; internet www.biltek.tubitak.gov.tr; f. 1967; monthly; science; Propr Prof. NÜKET YETIS; Man. Editor RAŞIT GÜRDILEK.

Devlet Opera ve Balesi Genel Müdürlüğü: Ankara; tel. (312) 3241476; fax (312) 3107248; f. 1949; state opera and ballet; Gen. Dir. RENGIM GOKMEN.

Devlet Tiyatrosu: Devlet Tiyatrosu Um. Md., Ankara; f. 1952; art, theatre.

Eğitim ve Bilim: Kızılırmak Sok. 8, Kocatepe, Ankara; tel. (312) 4180614; fax (312) 4175365; e-mail ipekt@ted.org.tr; f. 1928; quarterly; education and science; publ. by the Turkish Educational Asscn (TED); Editors Prof. AYDAN ERSÖZ, Dr GÜLTEKIN ÖZDEMIR, ANDREW DAVENTRY; circ. 500.

Karınca: Türk Kooperatifçilik Kurumu, Mithatpaşa Cad. 38/A, 06420 Kızılay, Ankara; tel. (312) 4359899; fax (312) 4304292; f. 1934; monthly review publ. by the Turkish Co-operative Asscn; Editor Prof. Dr RASIH DEMIRCI; circ. 5,000.

Maden Tetkik Arama Genel Müdürlüğü: İnönü Bul., Ankara; f. 1935; 2 a year; publ. by Mineral Research and Exploration Institute of Turkey; English Edition *Bulletin of Mineral Research and Exploration* (2 a year).

Mimarlık (Architecture): Konur Sok. 4/2, Kızılay, Ankara; tel. (312) 4173727; fax (312) 4180361; e-mail mimarlikdergisi@mimarlarodasi.org.tr; internet www.mimarlarodasi.org.tr; f. 1963; every 2 months; publ. by the Chamber of Architects of Turkey; Editor N. MÜGE CENGIZKAN; circ. 20,000.

Mühendis ve Makina: Sümer 2 Sok. 36/1-A, 06640 Demirtepe, Ankara; tel. (312) 2313159; fax (312) 2313165; f. 1957; engineering; monthly; Publr Chamber of Mechanical Engineers; Propr MEHMET SOĞANCI; Editor YÜKSEL KÖKEN; circ. 30,000.

Teknik ve Uygulama: Konur Sok. 4/4, 06442 Kızılay, Ankara; tel. (312) 4182374; f. 1986; engineering; every 2 months; publ. by the Chamber of Mechanical Engineers; Propr İSMET RIZA ÇEBI; Editor UĞUR DOĞAN; circ. 3,000.

Türk Arkeoloji ve Etnoğrafya Dergisi (General Directorate of Monuments and Museums): Kültür ve Turizm Bakanlığı, Kültür Varlıkları ve Müzeler Genel Müdürlüğü-II. Meclis Binası Ulus, 06100 Ankara; tel. (312) 3104960; fax (312) 3118248; e-mail kulturvarlikmuze@kulturturizm.gov.tr; internet www.kulturturizm.gov.tr; archaeological.

Türk Dili: Türk Dil Kurumu, Atatürk Bul. 217, 06680 Kavaklıdere, Ankara; tel. (312) 4286100; fax (312) 4285288; e-mail tdili@tdk.gov.tr; internet www.tdk.gov.tr; f. 1951; monthly; Turkish literature and language; Editor Prof. Dr ŞÜKRÜ HALUK AKALIN.

Turkey—Economic News Digest: Karanfil Sok. 56, Ankara; f. 1960; Editor-in-Chief BEHZAT TANIR; Man. Editor SADIK BALKAN.

Türkiye Bankacılık: PK 121, Ankara; f. 1955; commercial; Publisher MUSTAFA ATALAY.

Türkiye Bibliyografyası: Milli Kütüphane Başkanlığı, 06490 Bahçelievler, Ankara; tel. (312) 2126200; fax (312) 2230451; e-mail katalog@mkutup.gov.tr; internet www.mkutup.gov.tr; f. 1928; monthly; Turkish national bibliography; publ. by the Turkish National Library, Cataloguing and Classification Dept; Dir AHMET ÇELENKOĞLU.

Türkiye Makaleler Bibliyografyası (Bibliography of Articles in Turkish Periodicals): Milli Kütüphane Başkanlığı, 06490 Bahçelievler, Ankara; tel. (312) 2126200; fax (312) 2230451; e-mail bibliografya@mkutup.gov.tr; internet www.mkutup.gov.tr; f. 1952; monthly; Turkish articles, bibliography; publ. by the Turkish National Library, Bibliography Preparation Dept; Dir SEMA AKINCI.

İstanbul

Arkeoloji ve Sanat Dergisi (Archaeology and Art Magazine): Hayriye Cad. 3/5 Çorlu Apt., Beyoğlu 80060, İstanbul; tel. (212) 2456838; fax (212) 2456877; e-mail info@arkeolojisanat.com; internet arkeolojisanat.com; f. 1978; bi-monthly; publ. by Archaeology and Art Publications; Publr and Editor NEZIH BAŞGELEN; English-Language Submissions Editor BRIAN JOHNSON.

Bankacılar: Nışpetıye Cad. Akmerkez, B3 Blok. Kat 13–14, 80630 Etiler, İstanbul; tel. (212) 2820973; fax (212) 2820946; publ. by Banks' Asscn of Turkey; quarterly.

İstanbul Ticaret Odası Mecmuası: Gümüşpala Cad. 84, 34378 Eminönü, İstanbul; tel. (212) 5114150; fax (212) 5131565; f. 1884; quarterly; journal of the Istanbul Chamber of Commerce (ICOC); English; Editor-in-Chief CENGIZ ERSUN.

Musiki Mecmuası (Music Magazine): Sem'i Bey Sok. 19/3, Yıldızbakkal, Kadıköy 81130, İstanbul; tel. (216) 3306299; e-mail etemungor@hotmail.com; f. 1948; monthly; music and musicology; Editor ETEM RUHI ÜNGÖR.

Nûr (The Light): Nuruosmaniye Cad., Sorkun Han 28/2, 34410, Cağaloğlu, İstanbul; tel. (212) 5277607; fax (212) 5208231; e-mail sozler@ihlas.net.tr; internet www.sozler.com.tr; f. 1986; religion; Publr MEHMET NURI GÜLEÇ; Editor CEMAL UŞAK; circ. 10,000.

Pirelli Mecmuası: Büyükdere Cad. 117, Gayrettepe, İstanbul; tel. (212) 2663200; fax (212) 2520718; e-mail bilyay@ibm.net; f. 1964; monthly; Publr Türk-Pirelli Lastikleri AŞ; Editor UĞUR CANAL; circ. 24,500.

Ruh ve Madde Dergisi (Spirit and Matter): Ruh ve Madde Publications and Health Services Co., PK 9, 80072 Beyoğlu, İstanbul; tel. (212) 2431814; fax (212) 2520718; e-mail bilyay@bilyay.org.tr; internet www.ruhvemadde.com; f. 1959; organ of the Foundation for Spreading the Knowledge to Unify Humanity; Editor HALUK HACALOGLU.

Sevgi Dünyası (World of Respect): Aydede Cad. 4/5, 80090 Taksimi, İstanbul; tel. (212) 2504242; fax (212) 2702252; e-mail editor@dostlik.org; internet www.dostluk.org; f. 1963; monthly; social, psychological and spiritual; Publr and Editor Dr REFET KAYSERILIOĞLU.

Turkey: Ihlas Holding Merkez Binası, Ekim Cad. 29, 34520 Yenibosna, İstanbul; tel. (212) 4542530; fax (212) 4542555; e-mail img@img.com.tr; internet www.img.com.tr; f. 1982; monthly; English language, economics; Editor MEHMET SOZTUTAN; circ. 43,000.

Varlık: Ayberk Ap. Piyerloti Cad. 7–9, Çemberlitaş, 34400 İstanbul; tel. (212) 5162004; fax (212) 5162005; e-mail varlik@isbank.net.tr; internet www.varlik.com.tr; f. 1933; monthly; literary; Editors FILIZ NAYIR DENIZTEKIN, ENVER ERCAN; circ. 4,000.

İzmir

İzmir Ticaret Odası Dergisi: Atatürk Cad. 126, 35210 İzmir; tel. (232) 4417777; fax (232) 4837853; f. 1927; every 2 months; publ. by Chamber of Commerce of İzmir; Sec.-Gen. Prof. Dr İLTER AKAT; Man. ÜMIT ALEMDAROĞLU.

NEWS AGENCIES

Anadolu Ajansı: Mustafa Kemal Bul. 128/C, Tandogan, Ankara; tel. (312) 2317000; fax (312) 2312174; e-mail disyayin@anadoluajansi.com.tr; internet www.anadoluajansi.com.tr; f. 1920; Chair. ALI AYDIN DUNDAR; Gen. Dir BEHIÇ EKŞI.

ANKA Ajansı: Büklüm Sok. 20–22, Kavaklıdere, Ankara; tel. (312) 4172500; fax (312) 4180254; e-mail anka@ankaajansi.com.tr; Dir-Gen. MÜŞERREF HEKIMOĞLU.

Bagımsız Basın Ajansı (BBA): Saglam Fikir Sok. 11, Esentepe, İstanbul; tel. (212) 2122936; fax (212) 2122940; e-mail bba@bba.tv; internet www.bba.tv; f. 1971; provides camera crewing, editing and satellite services in Turkey, the Balkans, the Middle East and the former Soviet republics to broadcasters world-wide.

EBA Ekonomik Basın Ajansı (Economic Press Agency): Bestekar Sok 21/8, Kavaklıdere, 06680 Ankara; tel. (312) 4180628; fax (312) 4180432; e-mail ebainfo@ttnet.net.tr; internet www.ebanews.com; f. 1969; private economic news service; Propr ORHAN TOLUN; Editor YAVUZ TOLUN.

Hürriyet Haber Ajansı: Hürriyet Medya Towers, Güneşli, 34544 İstanbul; tel. (212) 6770365; fax (212) 6770372; e-mail ucebeci@hurriyet.com.tr; f. 1963; Dir-Gen. UĞUR ÇEBECI.

İKA Haber Ajansı (Economic and Commercial News Agency): Atatürk Bul. 199/A-45, Kavaklıdere, Ankara; tel. (312) 1267327; f. 1954; Dir ZIYA TANSU.

Milha News Agency: Doğan Medya Center, Bağcılar, 34554 İstanbul; tel. (212) 5056111; fax (212) 5056233.

TURKEY

Ulusal Basın Ajansı (UBA): Meşrutiyet Cad. 5/10, Ankara; Man. Editor Oğuz Seren.

Foreign Bureaux

Agence France-Presse (AFP): And Sok. 8/13, Çankaya, Ankara; tel. (312) 4689680; fax (312) 4689683; e-mail sinan.fisek@afp.com; Correspondent Sinan Fişek.

Agenzia Nazionale Stampa Associata (ANSA) (Italy): Sedat Simavı Sok. 30/5, Ankara; tel. (312) 4406084; fax (312) 4405029; Correspondent Romano Damiani.

Associated Press (AP) (USA): Tunus Cad. 87/3, Kavaklıdere, Ankara; tel. (312) 4282709; Correspondent Emel Anıl.

Bulgarska Telegrafna Agentsia (BTA) (Bulgaria): Hatır Sok. 25/6, Gaziosmanpaşa, Ankara; tel. (312) 4273899; Correspondent Lubomir Gabrovski.

Deutsche Presse-Agentur (dpa) (Germany): Yesil Yalı Sok, Liman Apt 6/6 Yesilköy, İstanbul; tel. (212) 5738607; Correspondent Bahadettin Güngör.

Informatsionnoye Telegrafnoye Agentstvo Rossii—Telegrafnoye Agentstvo Suverennykh Stran (ITAR—TASS) (Russia): Romşu Sok. 7/7, Ankara; tel. (312) 4405781; fax (312) 4391955; e-mail tassankara@superonline.com; Correspondent Andrei Palaria.

Reuters: Emirhan Cad. 145/A, Dikilitaş Beşiktaş, 80700 İstanbul; tel. (212) 2750875; fax (212) 2116794; e-mail turkey.marketing@reuters.com; internet about.reuters.com/turkey; Gen. Man. Sameeh ed-Din.

United Press International (UPI) (USA): Cağaloğlu, İstanbul; tel. (212) 2285238; Correspondent Ismet Imset.

Xinhua (New China) News Agency (People's Republic of China): Horasan Sok. 16/4, Gaziosmanpaşa, Ankara; tel. (312) 4361456; fax (312) 4465229; Correspondent Wang Qiang.

Zhongguo Xinwen She (China News Agency); People's Republic of China: Nenehatun Cad. 88-2, Ata Apartmanı, Gaziosmanpaşa, Ankara; tel. (312) 4362261; Correspondent Chang Chiliang.

AFP also has representatives in İstanbul and İzmir; AP is also represented in İstanbul.

JOURNALISTS' ASSOCIATION

Gazeteciler Cemiyeti: Cağaloğlu, İstanbul; tel. (212) 5138300; fax (212) 5268046; f. 1946; Pres. Necmi Tanyolaç; Sec. Rıdvan Yele.

Publishers

Altın Kitaplar Yayınevi Anonim ŞTİ: Celal Ferdi Gökçay Sok., Nebioğlu Han, Kat. 1, Cağaloğlu, İstanbul; tel. (212) 5268012; fax (212) 5268011; e-mail info@altinkitaplar.com.tr; internet www.altinkitaplar.com; f. 1959; fiction, non-fiction, biography, children's books, encyclopaedias, dictionaries; Publrs Fethi Ul, Turhan Bozkurt; Chief Editor Mürsit Ul.

Arkadas Co Ltd: Mithatpaşa Cad. 28c, 06441 Yenisehir, Ankara; tel. (312) 4344624; fax (312) 4356057; e-mail info@arkadas.com.tr; internet www.arkadas.com.tr; f. 1980; fiction, educational and reference books; Gen. Man. Cumhur Ozdemir.

Arkeoloji ve Sanat Yayınları (Archaeology and Art Publications): Hayriye Cad. 3/4 Çorlu Apt., Beyoğlu, 80060 İstanbul; tel. (212) 2456838; fax (212) 2456877; e-mail info@arkeolojisanat.com; internet www.arkeolojisanat.com; f. 1978; classical, Byzantine and Turkish studies, art and archaeology, numismatics and ethnography books; Publr Nezih Basgelen; Senior Editor Brian Johnson.

Bilgi Yayınevi: Meşrutiyet Cad. 46/A, Yenişehir, 06420 Ankara; tel. (312) 4318122; fax (312) 4317758; e-mail info@bilgiyayinevi.com.tr; internet www.bilgiyayinevi.com.tr.

IKI NOKTA (Research Press & Publications Industry & Trade Ltd): Moda Cad. 180/10, Kadıköy, 81300 İstanbul; tel. (216) 3490141; fax (216) 3376756; e-mail info@ikinokta.com; internet www.ikinokta.com; humanities; Pres. Yücel Yaman.

Iletisim Yayınları: Klodfarer Cd Iletisim Han 7/2, Cağaloğlu, 34400 İstanbul; tel. (212) 5162263; fax (212) 5161258; e-mail iletisim@iletisim.com.tr; internet www.iletisim.com.tr; f. 1984; fiction, non-fiction, encyclopaedias, reference; Gen. Man. Nihat Tuna.

Inkilap Kitabevi: Ankara Cad. 99, Sirkeci, İstanbul; tel. (212) 5140610; fax (212) 5140612; e-mail posta@inkilap.com; internet www.inkilap.com; f. 1935; general reference and fiction; Man. Dir A. Fıkri; Dir of Foreign Rights S. Diker.

Kabalci Yayınevi: Himaye-i Etfal Sok. 8-B, 34110 Cağaloğlu, İstanbul; tel. (212) 5226305; fax (212) 5268495; e-mail info@kabalci.com.tr; internet www.kabalci.com.tr; art, history, literature, social sciences; Pres. Sabri Kabalci.

Metis Yayınları: Ipek Sok. 9, 80060 Beyoğlu, İstanbul; tel. (212) 2454509; fax (212) 2454519; e-mail metis@turk.net; internet www.metisbooks.com; f. 1982; fiction, literature, non-fiction, social sciences; Dir Semih Sökmen.

Nurdan Yayınları Sanayi ve Ticaret Ltd Sti; Prof. Kâzim Ismail Gürkan Cad. 13, Kati 1, 34410 Cağaloğlu, İstanbul; tel. (212) 5225504; fax (212) 5125186; e-mail info@nurdan.com.tr; internet www.nurdan.com.tr; f. 1980; children's and educational; Dir Nurdan Tüzüner.

Parantez Yayınları AŞ: Istikal Cad. 212 Alt Kat 8, Beyoğlu, İstanbul; tel. and fax (212) 2528567; e-mail parantez@yahoo.com; internet www.planet.com.tr/bilisim/parantez; f. 1991; Publr Metin Zeynioğlu.

Payel Yayınevi: Cağaloğlu Yokusu Evren han Kat 3/51, 34400 Cağaloğlu, İstanbul; tel. (212) 5284409; fax (212) 5118233; f. 1966; science, history, literature; Editor Ahmet Öztürk.

Remzi Kitabevi AŞ: Selvili Mescit Sok 3, 34440 Cağaloğlu, İstanbul; tel. (212) 5139424; fax (212) 5229055; e-mail post@remzi.com.tr; internet www.remzi.com.tr; f. 1927; general and educational; Dirs Erol Erduran, Ömer Erduran, Ahmet Erduran.

Saray Medikal Yayın Tıc Ltd Sti: 168 Sok. 5/1, Bornova, İzmir; tel. (232) 3394969; fax (232) 3733700; e-mail eozkarahan@novell.cs.eng.dev.edu.tr; f. 1993; medicine, social sciences.

Seckin Yayınevi: Saglik Sok. 19B, 06410 Sihhiye, Ankara; tel. (312) 4353030; fax (312) 4352472; e-mail yayin@seckin.com.tr; internet www.seckin.com.tr; f. 1959; accounting, computer science, economics, law; Dir Koray Seçkin.

Türk Dil Kurumu (Turkish Language Institute): Atatürk Bul. 217, 06680 Kavaklıdere, Ankara; tel. (312) 4268124; fax (312) 4285288; e-mail bilgi@tdk.gov.tr; internet tdk.gov.tr; f. 1932; non-fiction, research, language; Pres. Prof. Dr Şükrü Haluk Akalın.

Varlık Yayınları: Ayberk Ap. Piyerloti Cad. 7–9, Çemberlitaş, 34400 İstanbul; tel. (212) 5162004; fax (212) 5162005; e-mail varlik@isbank.net.tr; internet www.varlik.com.tr; f. 1946; fiction and non-fiction books; Dirs Filiz Nayir Deniztekin, Osman Deniztekin.

GOVERNMENT PUBLISHING HOUSE

Ministry of Culture and Tourism: Directorate of Publications, Necatibey Cad. 55, 06440 Kızılay, Ankara; tel. (312) 2315450; fax (312) 2315036; e-mail yayimlar@kutuphanelergm.gov.tr; internet www.kultur.gov.tr; f. 1973; Dir Ali Osman Güzel.

PUBLISHERS' ASSOCIATION

Türkiye Yayıncılar Birliği Derneği (The Publishers' Association of Turkey): Kazım Ismail Gürkan Cad. 12, Ortaklar Han Kat 3/17, Cağaloğlu, İstanbul; tel. (212) 5125602; fax (212) 5117794; e-mail info@turkyaybir.com.tr; internet www.turkyaybir.org.tr; f. 1985; Pres. Çetin Tüzüner; Sec. Metin Celal Zeynioğlu; 230 mems.

Broadcasting and Communications

TELECOMMUNICATIONS

General Directorate of Communications: 90 Str. no. 5, 06338 Ankara; tel. (312) 2128088; fax (312) 2121775; regulatory authority; Dir-Gen. Hayrettin Soytas.

Telekomünikayson Kurumu: Yeşilırmak Sok., 16 Demirtepe, 06430 Ankara; tel. (312) 5505095; fax (312) 5505145; e-mail info@tk.gov.tr; internet www.tk.gov.tr; 45% privatized in 2001; bidding in 55% share tender completed in June 2005; provides telecoms services throughout Turkey; 19m. subscribers; Dir-Gen. Mehmet C. Ekinalan.

Turkcell: Mesrutiyet Cad. 153, 80050 Tepebasi, Istanbul; tel. (312) 3131000; e-mail musteri.hizmetleri@turkcell.com.tr; internet www.turkcell.com.tr; provides mobile cellular services; 40.3% held by the Cukurova Group, 37.1% by Sonera Holding; 25.6m. subscribers at June 2005; CEO Muzaffer Akpinar.

BROADCASTING

Regulatory Authority

Türkiye Radyo ve Televizyon Üst Kurulu (Turkish Radio and Television Supreme Council): Bilkent Plaza B2 Blok, Bilkent, 06530 Ankara; tel. (312) 2975000; fax (312) 2661985; e-mail rtuk@rtuk.org.tr; internet www.rtuk.org.tr; responsible for assignment of channels, frequencies and bands, controls transmitting facilities of radio stations and TV networks, draws up regulations on related matters, monitors broadcasting and issues warnings in case of violation of the Broadcasting law; Chair. Zahid Akman.

TURKEY

Radio

Türkiye Radyo ve Televizyon Kurumu (TRT) (Turkish Radio and Television Corpn): Oran Sitesi, B Blok Kat 9, 06450 Oran, Ankara; tel. (312) 4901797; fax (312) 4905936; internet www.trt.net.tr; f. 1964; controls Turkish radio and television services, incl. four national radio channels; Dir-Gen. YÜCEL YENER; Head of Radio ÇETIN TEZCAN.

Voice of Turkey: PK 333, 06443 Yenişehir, Ankara; tel. (312) 4909800; fax (312) 4909845; e-mail englishservice@tsr.gov.tr; internet www.tsr.gov.tr; foreign service of the TRT; Man. Dir DANYAL GÜRDAL.

There are also more than 50 local radio stations, an educational radio service for schools and a station run by the Turkish State Meteorological Service. The US forces have their own radio and television service.

Television

Türkiye Radyo ve Televizyon Kurumu (TRT): (Turkish Radio and Television Corpn): Oran Sitesi Turan Günes Bul. A Block Kat 6, 06450 Oran, Ankara; e-mail nilgun.artun@trt.net.tr; internet www.trt.net.tr; five national channels in 2000 and two satellite channels broadcasting to Europe; Head of Television NILGÜN ARTUN; Dir Ankara TV GÜRKAN ELÇI.

In addition there are also 11 other television stations, including cable networks. These are: ATV (www.atv.com.tr), Cine 5 (www.cine5.com.tr), Kanal D (www.kanald.com.tr), Kanal 6 (www.kanal6.com.tr), Kral TV (www.kraltv.com.tr), No1 TV (www.levi.com.tr/no1tv), NTV Online (www.ntv.co.tr), Show TV (www.showtv.net), Star (www.star.com.tr), TGRT (www.tgrt.com.tr) and NTVMSNBC (www.ntvmsnbc.com).

Finance

(cap. = capital; res = reserves; dep. = deposits; m. = million; brs = branches; amounts in Turkish liras unless otherwise stated)

The Central Bank of the Republic of Turkey was founded in 1931, and constituted in its present form in 1970. The Central Bank is the bank of issue and is also responsible for the execution of monetary and credit policies, the regulation of the foreign and domestic value of the Turkish lira jointly with the Government, and the supervision of the credit system. In 1987 a decree was issued to bring the governorship of the Central Bank under direct government control.

The largest of the private-sector Turkish banks is the Türkiye İş Bankası, which operates 871 branches.

There are several credit institutions in Turkey, including the Türkiye Sınai Kalınma Bankası (Industrial Development Bank), which was founded in 1950, with the assistance of the World Bank, to encourage private investment in industry by acting as underwriter in the issue of share capital.

There are numerous co-operative organizations, including agricultural co-operatives in rural areas. There are also a number of savings institutions.

In 1990 the Turkish Government announced plans to establish a structure for offshore banking. A decree issued in October 1990 exempted foreign banks, operating in six designated free zones, from local banking obligations.

In June 1999 an independent supervisory body, the Regulatory and Supervisory Board for Banking, was established by law to monitor the financial sector. The treasury, the Ministry of Finance, the Central Bank, the state planning organization, the Capital Markets Board and the Banks' Association of Turkey were each to nominate one member to the Board for a six-year term. The Board was operational from mid-2000. Other legislation passed in June 1999 incorporated core principles of the Basle Committee on Banking Supervision relating to risk-based capital requirements, loan administration procedures, auditing practices and credit risk issues.

At the end of 1999 the number of banks operating in Turkey (excluding the Central Bank) totalled 81, of which seven were state owned. Following a number of liquidations, mergers and acquisitions in the banking system after 2000, the number of banks had been reduced to 48 by the end of 2004. Of this total, 13 were development and investment banks and the remainder commercial banks; the number of state-owned banks had been reduced to six and there were 13 foreign banks.

BANKING

Regulatory Authority

Bancacılık Düzenleme ve Denetleme Kurumu (BDDK) (Banking Regulation and Supervisory Agency): Atatürk Bulvari 191, 06680 Kavaklidere, Ankara; tel. (312) 4556500; fax (312) 4240877; e-mail bilgi@bddk.org.tr; internet www.bddk.org.tr; Chair. ENGIN AKCAKOCA.

Central Bank

Türkiye Cumhuriyet Merkez Bankası AŞ (Central Bank of the Republic of Turkey): Head Office, İstiklal Cad. 10 Ulus, 06100 Ankara; tel. (312) 3103646; fax (312) 3107434; e-mail iletisimbilgi@tcmb.gov.tr; internet www.tcmb.gov.tr; f. 1931; bank of issue; cap. 25,000.0m., res 879,326,105m., dep. 72,325,452,364m. (Dec. 2005); Gov. DURMUŞ YILMAZ; 21 brs.

State Banks

Bayindirbank AŞ: Buyukdere Cad. 143, 34394 Esentepe, İstanbul; tel. (212) 3401000; fax (212) 3473217; internet www.bayindirbank.com.tr; control passed to Savings Deposit Insurance Fund in 2001.

Türkiye Cumhuriyeti Ziraat Bankası (Agricultural Bank of the Turkish Republic): Bankalar Cad. 42, 06107 Ulus, Ankara; tel. (312) 3103750; fax (312) 3101134; e-mail zbmail@ziraatbank.com.tr; internet www.ziraatbank.com.tr; f. 1863; absorbed Türkiye Emlâk Bankası AŞ (Real Estate Bank of Turkey) in July 2001; cap. 7,965,933,000m., res 2,308,576,000m., dep. 35,410,775,000m. (Dec. 2003); Chair. Prof. Dr İLHAN ULUDAĞ; Gen. Man. CAN AKIN ÇAĞLAR; 1,177 brs.

Türkiye Halk Bankası AŞ: Esikişehir Yolu, 2 Cad. 63, Söğütözü, 06520 Ankara; tel. (312) 2892000; fax (312) 2893875; e-mail info@halkbank.com.tr; internet www.halkbank.com.tr; f. 1938; absorbed Türkiye Öğretmenler Bankası TAŞ in 1992; acquired 96 branches of Türkiye Emlak Bankası in 2001; merged with Pamukbank TAŞ in 2004; cap. 3,554,378,000m., dep. 12,350,614,000m. (Dec. 2002); Chair. MEHMET ZEKI SAYIN; Gen. Man. HASAN LEBCCI; 899 brs.

Türkiye İhracat Kredi Bankası AŞ (Türk Eximbank) (Export Credit Bank of Turkey): Milli Müdafa Cad. 20, 06100 Bakanlıklar, Ankara; tel. (312) 4171300; fax (312) 4257896; e-mail ankara@eximbank.gov.tr; internet www.eximbank.gov.tr; f. 1987; fmrly Devlet Yatırım Bankası AŞ (f. 1964); cap. 1,065m. new Turkish liras, res 34m. new Turkish liras, total assets 2,612m. new Turkish liras (Dec. 2005); state owned; extends credit to exporters, insures and guarantees export transactions; Chair. TUNCER KAYALAR; Gen. Man. H. AHMET KILIÇOĞLU; 2 brs.

Türkiye Vakıflar Bankası TAO (Foundation Bank of Turkey): Camlik Cad. Cayir Cimen Sok. 2, 80620 1 Levent, İstanbul; tel. (212) 3167116; fax (212) 3167126; e-mail international@vakifbank.com.tr; internet www.vakifbank.com.tr; f. 1954; cap. 1,323,082,000m., res 111,599,000m., dep. 10,397,935,000m. (Dec. 2002); Chair. YUSUF BEYAZIT; Gen. Man. BILAL KARAMAN; 297 brs.

Principal Commercial Banks

Akbank TAŞ: Sabancı Center, 34330 4 Levent, 80745 İstanbul; tel. (212) 2700044; fax (212) 2697787; e-mail investor.relations@akbank.com; internet www.akbank.com.tr; f. 1948; cap. 1,200,000,000m., res 2,518,162,000m., dep. 19,706,097,000m. (Dec. 2003); Chair. and Man. Dir EROL SABANCI; Pres. and CEO ZAFER KURTUL; 623 brs.

Alternatifbank AŞ: Cumhuriyet Cad. 22–24, Elmadağ, 34367 İstanbul; tel. (212) 3156500; fax (212) 2331500; e-mail sakir.somek@abank.com.tr; internet www.abank.com.tr; Anadolu Group; cap. 508,407,000m., dep. 604,725,000m. (March 2004); Chair. TUNCAY ÖZILHAN; CEO MURAT ARIG; 22 brs.

Denizbank AŞ: Büyükdere Cad. 106, 34394 Esentepe, İstanbul; tel. (212) 3550800; fax (212) 2747993; e-mail info@denizbank.com; internet www.denizbank.com; f. 2004; cap. US $407.3m., res $150.0m., dep. $4,267.1m. (Dec. 2004); Pres. and CEO HAKAN ATEŞ; Chair. Dr YEYSI SEVIG.

Finansbank AŞ: Büyükdere Cad. 129, 80300 Mecidiyeköy, İstanbul; tel. (212) 3185000; fax (212) 2161742; e-mail fi@finansbank.com.tr; internet www.finansbank.com; f. 1987; sold to Banque National de Paris in mid-2001; cap. 354,905,000m., res 8,135,000m., dep. 3,692,454,000m. (Dec. 2002); Chair. HÜSNÜ ÖZYEĞIN; Man. Dir Dr ÖMER ARAS; 173 brs.

Koçbank AŞ: Barbaros Bulvari, Morbasan Sok., Koza İş Merkezi-C Blok, 80700 Balmumcu, Beşiktaş, İstanbul; tel. (212) 2747777; fax (212) 2746549; e-mail fim@kocbank.com.tr; internet www.kocbank.com.tr; f. 1986; cap. 1,067,492,000m., res 74,714,000m., dep. 4,609,183,000m. (Dec. 2002); CEO KEMAL KAYA; Gen. Man. HALIL ERGÜR; 143 brs.

Oyak Bank AŞ: Eski Büyükdere Cad., Ayazaga Köyyolu 6, Maslak, 34398 İstanbul; tel. (212) 4440600; fax (212) 4440600; e-mail contactcenter@oyakbank.com.tr; internet www.oyakbank.com.tr; f. 1990; cap. 338,198,000m., res 38,272,000m., dep. 2,975,538,000m. (Dec. 2002); Chair. ŞERIF COŞKUN ULUSOY; Gen. Man. E. HAKAN EMINSOY; 306 brs.

Şekerbank TAŞ: Büyükdere Cad. 171 Metrocity İş Merkezi A-Blok 34330 1 Levent, İstanbul; tel. (212) 3197000; fax (212) 2456837; e-mail intdiv@sekerbank.com.tr; internet www.sekerbank.com.tr; f. 1953; cap. 76,000,000m., res 187,690,000m., dep. 2,249,287,000m.

TURKEY

(Dec. 2003); Rabobank owns 51%; Chair. and Gen. Man. Hasan Basri Göktan; 197 brs.

Tekfenbank AŞ: Tekfen Tower, 34394 4 Levent, İstanbul; tel. (212) 3570202; fax (212) 3570231; e-mail sehnaz.gunay@tefkenbank.com; internet www.tefkenbank.com; f. 1989; name changed as above 2001, when Bank Ekspres merged with Tekfen Yatirim ve Finansman Bankasi AŞ; cap. 117,431,000m., res 51,061,000m. dep. 487,365,000m. (Dec. 2002); Chair. Ercan Kumcu; Pres. and CEO Mehmet Erten; 31 brs.

Tekstilbank AŞ: Büyükdere Cad. 63, 34398 Maslak, İstanbul; tel. (212) 3355335; fax (212) 3281328; internet www.tekstilbank.com.tr; f. 1986; cap. 125,500,000m., dep. 834,982,000m. (Dec. 2002); GSD Holdings owns 75%; Chair. Osman Tunaboylu; Gen. Man. Cim Güzelaydınlı; 26 brs.

Türk Ekonomi Bankası AŞ: Meclisı Mebusan Cad. 35, 34427 Fındıklı, İstanbul; tel. (212) 2512121; fax (212) 2525058; internet www.teb.com.tr; f. 1927; fmrly Kocaeli Bankası TAŞ; cap. 55,125,000m., res 202,107,000m., dep. 2,842,719,000m. (Dec. 2002); Chair. Yavuz Canevi; Man. Dir and Gen. Man. Varol Civil; 73 brs.

Türkiye Garanti Bankası AŞ (Garantibank): Nispetiye Mah, Aytar Cad. 2, 34340 Levent Beşiktaş, İstanbul; tel. and fax (212) 3181818; fax (212) 3181888; e-mail mutlus@garanti.com.tr; internet www.garantibank.com; f. 1946; Doğuş Group; cap. 11,522,305,000m., dep. 15,646,110,000m. (Dec. 2001); Chair. Ferit Faik Şahenk; Pres., CEO and Gen. Man. Ergun Özen; 403 brs.

Türkiye İş Bankası AŞ (İşbank): İş Kuleleri, 34330 Levent, İstanbul; tel. (212) 3160000; fax (212) 3160900; e-mail halkla.iliskiler@isbank.com.tr; internet www.isbank.com.tr; f. 1924; cap. 810,573,000m., res 3,126,147,000m., dep. 17,022,996,000m. (Dec. 2002); Chair. Dr Ahmet Kirman; CEO and Gen. Man. Ersin Özince; 871 brs.

Yapı ve Kredi Bankası AŞ: Yapı Kredi Plaza, Blok D, Büyükdere Cad., Levent 34330 İstanbul; tel. (212) 3397000; fax (212) 3396000; e-mail yi@ykb.com; internet www.ykb.com.tr; f. 1944; cap. 2,122,665,000m., res 994,242,000m., dep. 11,408,578,000m. (Dec. 2001); Cukurova Group is main shareholder; Chair. Mehmet Çekinmez; CEO Reha Yolalan; 420 brs.

Development and Investment Banks

Sınai Yatırım Bankası AŞ (Industrial Investment Bank): Büyükdere Cad. 129, Esentepe, 80300 İstanbul; tel. (212) 2131600; fax (212) 2131303; e-mail form@syb.com.tr; internet www.syb.com.tr; f. 1963; cap. 22,500,000m., res 30,166,236m., dep. 15,123,746m. (Dec. 2000); Chair. Cahit Kocaömer; Pres. and Gen. Man. Halil Eroğlu.

Türkiye Kalkınma Bankası AS (Development Bank of Turkey): İzmir Cad. 35, Kızılay, 06440 Ankara; tel. (312) 4171220; fax (312) 4183967; e-mail tkbhaberlesme@tkb.com.tr; internet www.tkb.com.tr; f. 1975; cap. 100,000,000m., res 61,868,664.5m., dep. 51,753,881.1m. (Dec. 2001); Pres. and Gen. Dir Tacı Bayhan; 6 brs.

Türkiye Sınai Kalkınma Bankası AŞ (Industrial Development Bank of Turkey): Meclisi Mebusan Cad. 161, Findikli, 34427 İstanbul; tel. (212) 3345050; fax (212) 2432975; e-mail info@tskb.com.tr; internet www.tskb.com.tr; f. 1950; cap. 38,500,000m., res 13,236,000m., total assets 525,824,000m. (Dec. 2001); Chair. Cahıt Kocaömer; Pres. Halil Eroğlu; 2 brs.

Foreign Banks

ABN AMRO NV (Netherlands): Tamburi Ali Efendi Sok. 13, 80630 Etiler, İstanbul; tel. (212) 3594040; fax (212) 3595050; f. 1921; Gen. Man. Albert Meijer; 1 br.

Arap Türk Bankası AŞ (Arab Turkish Bank): Vali Konağı Cad. 10, 34367 Nişantaşı, İstanbul; tel. (212) 2250500; fax (212) 2250526; e-mail webmaster@arabturkbank.com; internet www.arabturkbank.com; f. 1977; dep. 20,000,000m., res 25,011,000m., dep. 193,748,000m. (Dec 2002); 54% owned Arabbanks; Chair. A. Aykut Demiray; Gen. Man. Muhammad Najib Hmida el-Jamal; 3 brs.

Banca di Roma (Italy): Büyükdere Cad. Üç Yol Mevlik, Noramin İş Merkezi Kat 5, Maslak, 80670 İstanbul; tel. (212) 2859310; fax (212) 2769425; e-mail istanbul@tr.bdroma.com; f. 1911; Gen. Man. Fabio Lucheroni.

Bank Mellat (Iran): Abide-i Hürriyet Cad. Geçit 10, 34381 İstanbul; tel. (212) 2963120; fax (212) 2964505; e-mail mellat@mellatbank.com; f. 1982; cap. and res US $13.9m., dep. US $16.6m. (Dec. 2004); Chair. Younes Hormozi; 3 brs.

BNP-AK-Dresdner Bank AŞ: 1 Levent Plaza, Büyükdere Cad. 173, A Blok Kat. 8, Levent, İstanbul; tel. (212) 3395700; fax (212) 3395705; e-mail fininst@bnp-ak-dresdner.com.tr; f. 1985; cap. 98,632,731m., res 85,050,364m., dep. 19,454,587m. (Dec. 2003); Pres. and Chair. Akın Kozanoğlu; Gen. Man. Philippe Ditisheim.

Citibank NA (USA): Büyükdere Cad. 100, Maya Akar Centre, 24th Floor, 80280 Esentepe, İstanbul; tel. (212) 2887700; fax (212) 2887760; e-mail dardo.sabarots@citicorp.com; internet www.citibank.com.tr; f. 1981; Gen. Man. Sebastian Parades; 3 brs.

CALYON Bank Türk AŞ (France): Büyükdere Cad. Plaza C Blok K Yapı Kredi Plaza, Levent, 80620 İstanbul; tel. (212) 3393700; fax (212) 2826301; internet www.calyon.com; f. 2004; created by the transfer of Crédit Lyonnais's Corporate and Investment Banking division to Crédit Agricole Indosuez; Chair. Jean Laurent; CEO Edouard Esparbes.

Habib Bank Ltd (Pakistan): Abide-i Hürriyet Cad. 12, PK 8, 80222 Şişli, İstanbul; tel. (212) 2460235; fax (212) 2340807; e-mail habibbank@fornet.net.tr; f. 1983; cap. 50,000m., res 2,125m., dep. 158,207m. (Dec. 1998); Gen. Man. A. B. Türkay; 1 br.

HSBC Bank AŞ: Ayazaoa Mah. Ahi Evren Cad. Dereboyu Sok. Maslak 34398 İstanbul; tel. (212) 3663000; fax (212) 3663383; internet www.hsbc.com.tr; f. 1990 as Midland Bank AŞ, name changed as above in 1999; acquired Demirbank TAŞ (f. 1953) in 2001; Chair. Keith R. Whitson; CEO Piraye Y. Antika; 159 brs.

JPMorgan Chase Bank (USA): Kat 10, Atakule A Blok, Emirhan Cad. 145, Dikilitaş, 80700 İstanbul; tel. (212) 3268300; fax (212) 3268384; f. 1984; Gen. Man. M. Megalli; 1 br.

Kuwait Turkish Evkaf Finance House: Büyükdere Cad. 129, 34594 Esentepe/Sisli, İstanbul; tel. (212) 3541111; fax (212) 3541212; e-mail kuveytturk@kuveytturk.com.tr; internet www.kuveytturk.com.tr; f. 1988; cap. 95,310,000m., res 12,407,111m., dep. 600,812,373m. (Dec. 2002); Chair. Muhammad S. al-Omar; CEO Ufuk Uyan; brs 51.

Société Générale SA (France): Akmerkez E-3, Nispetiye Cad., Blok Kat. 9, Eitler, 80600 İstanbul; tel. (212) 2821942; fax (212) 2821848; f. 1990; Pres. and Dir-Gen. Daniel Bouton; 1 br.

Turkish Bank AŞ ('TRNC'): Valikonağı Cad. 7, 34371 Nişantaşı, İstanbul; tel. (212) 2250330; fax (212) 2250353; e-mail dmm@turkishbank.com; internet www.turkishbank.com; f. 1982; cap. 8,000,000m., res 15,687,000m., dep. 186,360,000m. (Dec. 2001); 60% Özyol Holding, 39% Türk Bankası Ltd; Chair. Hamit B. Belli; 15 brs.

Westdeutsche Landesbank Girozentrale (Germany): Ebulula Mardin Cad., Maya Park Towers, 80630 İstanbul; tel. (212) 3392500; fax (212) 3522258; internet www.westlb.de; f. 1990; Gen. Man. Andreas Schröter; 2 brs.

Banking Organization

Banks' Association of Turkey: Nıspetıye Cad. Akmerkez B3 Blok. Kat 13–14, 34340 Etiler, İstanbul; tel. (212) 2820973; fax (212) 2820946; e-mail gensek@tbb.org.tr; internet www.tbb.org.tr; f. 1958; Chair. Ersin Özince (acting); Sec.-Gen. Dr Ekrem Keskin.

STOCK EXCHANGE

İstanbul Menkul Kıymetler Borsası (İMKB): Resitpaşa Mah., Tuncay Artun Cad., 34467 Emirgan, İstanbul; tel. (212) 2982100; fax (212) 2982500; e-mail info@ise.org; internet www.ise.org; f. 1866; revived in 1986 after being dormant for about 60 years; 114 mems of stock market, 138 mems of bond and bills market; Chair. and CEO Osman Birsen; Senior Vice-Chair. Arıl Seren.

INSURANCE

AKSigorta: Meclis-i Mebusan Cad. 147 Fındıklı 34427 İstanbul; tel. (212) 2519400; fax (212) 2430861; e-mail info@aksigorta.com.tr; internet www.aksigorta.com.tr; f. 1960; Chair. M. Akın Kozanoğlu; Gen. Man. I. Ragıp Yergin.

Anadolu Sigorta TAŞ (Anadolu Insurance Co): Rıhtım Cad. 57, 80030 Karaköy, İstanbul; tel. (212) 2516540; fax (212) 2432690; internet www.anadolusigorta.com.tr; f. 1925; Chair. Burhan Karagöz; Gen. Man. Ahmet Yavuz.

Ankara Sigorta TAŞ (Ankara Insurance Co): Bankalar Cad. 80, 80020 Karaköy, İstanbul; tel. (212) 2521010; fax (212) 2524744; internet www.ankarasigorta.com.tr; f. 1936; Chair. Dr Muhsın Mengütürk; Gen. Man. Yusuf Cemil Satoğlu.

Destek Reasürans TAŞ: Abdi İpekçi Cad. 75, 80200 Maçka, İstanbul; tel. (212) 2312832; fax (212) 2415704; f. 1945; reinsurance; Pres. Onur Ökten; Gen. Man. İbrahim Yaycıoğlu.

AXA Oyak AŞ: Büyükdere Cad. Imtaş Han 116, Zincirlikuyu, İstanbul; tel. (212) 2747000; fax 2720837; internet www.axaoyak.com.tr.

Başak Sigorta AŞ: Halaskargazi Cad. 15, 34373 Harbiye, İstanbul; tel. (212) 2316000; fax (212) 2307604; e-mail basak_sigorta@basak.com.tr; internet www.basak.com.tr; Gen. Man. Enis Basım.

Güven Sigorta TAŞ: Bankalar Cad. 81, 34420 Karaköy, İstanbul; tel. (212) 2547900; fax (212) 2551360; e-mail info@guvensigorta.com.tr; internet www.guvensigorta.com.tr; f. 1924; owned by Turkish Agricultural Credit Co-operatives Central Union; all branches of insurance; Gen. Man. A. Kadir Simsek.

Finans Sigorta AS: Rüzgalıbahçe Mah. Cumhuriyet Cad. Acarlar İş Merkezi 10 C Blok, 34805 Kavacık, Beykoz İstanbul; tel. (212) 5386000; fax (212) 5386290; internet www.finanssigorta.com.tr; Pres. YENER DINÇMEN.

Garanti Sigorta: Mete Cad. Parkhan 40, Taksim İstanbul; tel. (212) 3931000; fax (212) 2490104; internet www.garantisigorta.com.tr; f. 1989; Doğuş Group; Gen. Man. HASAN GÜLLER.

Güneş Sigorota: Güneş Plaza, Büyükdere Cad. 110, 80280 Esentepe, İstanbul; tel. (212)3556565; fax (212)3556464; e-mail gunes@gunessigorta.com.tr; internet www.gunessigorta.com.tr; f. 1957.

Hür Sigorta AŞ: Büyükdere Cad., Hür Han 15/A, 80260 Şişli, İstanbul; tel. (212) 2322010; fax (212) 2463673; e-mail hursigorta@hursigorta.com.tr; internet www.hursigorta.com.tr; Chair. BÜLENT SEMILER; Gen. Man. GÜNER YALÇINER.

Işik Sigorta AŞ: Gülsuyu Kavşağı, Işık Plaza, Maltepe 81560 İstanbul; tel. (216) 4274757; fax (216) 4274774; e-mail bilgi@isiksigorta.com; internet www.isiksigorta.com.

İstanbul Reasürans AŞ: Güneş Plaza, Büyükdere Caddesi No. 110 Kat 9, 80280 Esentepe-Şişli/İstanbul; tel. (212) 3556891; fax (212) 2173723; f. 1979; Chair. HASAN ALTANER; Gen. Man. GÜLGÜN ÜNLÜOĞLU.

İsviçre Sigorta AŞ: Kısıklı Cad. 30, Altunizade 34662, İstanbul; tel. (216) 4742000; fax (216) 4742000; internet www.isvicre-sigorta.com .tr; f. 1926; as La Suisse Umum Sigorta; 1981 taken over by İsviçre; Fire, Accident, Marine, Engineering, Agricultural; Chair and Man. Dir OKAN BALCI; 7 regional brs.

Koç Allianz Sigorta AŞ: Bağlarbaşı, Kısıklı Cad. 11, Altunizade 34662 İstanbul; tel. (216) 5566666; fax (216) 5566777; e-mail info@kocallianz.com.tr; internet www.kocallianz.com.tr; f. 1923; Chair. M. RAHMI KOÇ.

Milli Reasürans TAŞ: Teşvikiye Cad. 43–57, 34368 Teşvikiye, İstanbul; tel. (212) 2314730; fax (212) 2308608; e-mail info@millire .com.tr; internet www.millire.com.tr; f. 1929; premium income 575,963,764m., total assets 616,430,830m. (Dec. 2004); Chair. Prof. Dr AHMET KIRMAN; Dir and Gen. Man. CAHIT NOMER.

Ray Sigorta: Kefelıköy Cad. 35, Tarabya 34457 Sarıyer,İstanbul; tel. (212) 3632500; fax (212) 2994849; e-mail info@raysigorta.com.tr; internet www.raysigorta.com.tr; f. 1958; Doğan Group is major shareholder.

Şeker Sigorta AŞ: Meclisi Mebusan Cad. 87, Karaköy, İstanbul; tel. (212) 2514035; fax (212) 2491046; e-mail info@sekersigorta.com.tr; internet www.sekersigorta.com.tr; f. 1954; Chair. HASAN BASRI GÖKTAN; Gen. Man. KAMIL YIĞIT.

TEB Sigorta: Meclis-i Mebusan Cad. 127/6, Findikli 34427, Istanbul; tel. (212) 2519600; fax (212) 2922571; e-mail info@tebsigorta .com.tr; internet info@raysigorta.com.tr.

Türkiye Genel Sigorta AŞ: Meclisi Mebusan Cad. 91, Salıpazarı, 34433 İstanbul; tel. (212) 3349000; fax (212) 3349019; e-mail genel@genelsigorta.com; internet www.genelsigorta.com; f. 1948; Chair. MEHMET E. KARAMEHMET; Gen. Man. HULUSI TAŞKIRAN.

Yapi Kredi Sigorta AŞ: Yapi Kredi Plaza, Blok A, Büyükdere Cad., 34330 Levent, Istanbul; tel. (212) 3360606; fax (212) 3360808; e-mail yksigorta@yksigorta.com.tr; internet www.yksigorta.com.tr; f. 1944; Chair. ALI IHSAN KARACAN; Gen. Man. MURAT GUVENEL.

Trade and Industry

GOVERNMENT AGENCY

Özelleştirme İdaresi Başkanlığı (Privatization Administration): Ziya Gökalp Cad. 80, Kurtuluş Ankara; tel. (312) 4304560; fax (312) 4403271; e-mail info@oib.gov.tr; internet www.oib.gov.tr; co-ordinates privatization programme; Pres. UGUR BAYAR.

Rekabet Kurumu (Turkish Competition Authority): Bilkent Plaza B3 Blok PK, 06800 Bilkent, Ankara; tel. (312) 2914444; fax (312) 2667920; e-mail rek@rekabet.gov.tr; internet www.rekabet.gov.tr; f. 1997; prevents restriction of competition, oversees mergers, and monitors state aid; Pres. and Chair. MUSTAFA PARLAK.

DEVELOPMENT ORGANIZATIONS

Turkish Atomic Energy Authority: Prime Minister's Office, Eskişehir yolu 9.km Lodumlu, 06530 Ankara; tel. (312) 2871529; fax (312) 2871224; e-mail ali.alat@taek.gov.tr; internet www.taek .gov.tr; f. 1956; controls the development of peaceful uses of atomic energy; 11 mems; Pres. OKAY ÇAKIROĞLU; Vice-Pres. ALI ALAT.

Turkish Electricity Authority (TEAS) (Nuclear Power Plants Department): İnönü Bul. 27, 06440 Ankara; tel. (312) 2229855; fax (312) 2127853; state enterprise to supervise the construction and operation of nuclear power plants; attached to the Ministry of Energy and Natural Resources; Head of Dept NEVZAT ŞAHIN.

CHAMBERS OF COMMERCE AND INDUSTRY

Union of Chambers of Commerce, Industry, Maritime Commerce and Commodity Exchanges of Turkey (UCCET) (Türkiye Odalar Borsalar Birliği—TOBB): Atatürk Bul. 149, 06640 Bakanlıklar, Ankara; tel. (312) 4138000; fax (312) 4183268; e-mail info@info.tobb.org.tr; internet www.tobb.org.tr; f. 1952; represents 335 chambers and commodity exchanges; Pres. RIFAT HISARCIKLIOĞLU.

Ankara Chamber of Commerce (Ankasa Tabip Odasi—ATO): Mithatpaşa Cad. 62/18 Kızılay, Ankara; tel. (312) 4188700; fax (312) 4187794; e-mail ato@ato.org.tr; internet www.ato.org.tr.

Ankara Chamber of Industry: Atatürk Bul. 193, 06680 Kavaklıdere, Ankara; tel. (312) 4171200; fax (312) 4174370; e-mail aso@aso .org.tr; internet www.aso.org.tr; f. 1963; Chair. ZAFER ÇAĞLAYAN.

İstanbul Chamber of Commerce (ICOC): Reşadiye Cad. 34112 Eminönü, İstanbul; tel. (212) 4556000; fax (212) 5131565; e-mail ito@ito.org.tr; internet www.ito.org.tr; f. 1882; more than 230,000 mems; Chair. MEHMET YILDIRIM.

İstanbul Chamber of Industry: Meşrutiyet Cad. 118, Tepebaşı, İstanbul; tel. (212) 2522900; fax (212) 2493963; internet www.iso.org .tr; Pres. HÜSAMETTIN KAVI.

İzmir Chamber of Commerce: Atatürk Cad. 126, 35210 İzmir; tel. (232) 4417777; fax (232) 4837853; e-mail info@izto.org.tr; internet www.izto.org.tr; f. 1885; Pres. EKREM DEMIRTAŞ; Sec.-Gen. HALIT SOYDAN.

EMPLOYERS' ASSOCIATIONS

Türk Sanayicileri ve İşadamları Derneği (TÜSİAD) (Turkish Industrialists' and Businessmen's Association): Meşrutiyet Cad. 74, 80050 Tepebaşı, İstanbul; tel. (212) 2495448; fax (212) 2491350; e-mail webmaster@tusiad.org; internet www.tusiad.org; f. 1971; 451 mems; Pres. ÖMER SABANCI; Sec.-Gen. Dr HALUK R. TÜKEL.

Türkiye İşveren Sendikaları Konfederasyonu (TİSK) (Turkish Confederation of Employer Associations): Hoşdere Cad. Reşat Nuri Sok. 108, 06540 Çankaya Ankara; tel. (312) 4397717; fax (312) 4397592; e-mail tisk@tisk.org.tr; internet www.tisk.org.tr; f. 1962; represents (on national level) 21 employers' associations, with 8,300 affiliated enterprises; official representative in labour relations; Pres. TUĞRUL KUDATGOBILIK; Sec.-Gen. BÜLENT PIRLER.

UTILITIES

Electricity

Elektrik Üretim-İletim AŞ (EÜAŞ-Electricity Authority): İnönü Bul. 27, 06490 Ankara; tel. (312) 2229885; fax (312) 2131305; e-mail sedat.duman@euas.gov.tr; attached to Ministry of Energy and Natural Resources; Man. SEDAT DUMAN.

TRADE UNIONS

Confederations

DİSK (Türkiye Devrimci İşçi Sendikaları Konfederasyonu) (Confederation of Progressive Trade Unions of Turkey): Cad. Abide-I Hürriyet 117, Kat. 5-6-7, Şişli, İstanbul; tel. (212) 2910005; fax (212) 2342075; e-mail disk-f@tr.net; internet www.disk.org.tr; f. 1967; member of ICFTU, ETUC and TUAC; 26 affiliated unions; Pres. SÜLEYMAN ÇELEBI; Sec.-Gen. MUSA CAM.

Türk-İş (Türkiye İşçi Sendikaları Konfederasyonu Genel Başkanlığı) (Confederation of Turkish Trade Unions): Bayındır Sok 10, Kiziiay, Ankara; tel. (312) 4333125; fax (312) 4336809; e-mail intdept@turkis.org.tr; internet www.turkis.org.tr; f. 1952; member of ICFTU, ETUC, ICFTU-APRO and OECD/TUAC; 32 national unions and federations with 1.7m. mems; Pres. SALIH KILIÇ; Gen. Sec. MUSTAFA KUMLU.

Principal DİSK Trade Unions

BASS (Türkiye Devrimci Banka ve Sigorta İşçileri Sendikası) (Bank and Insurance Employees Unionı): Sumer 2 Sok. 29 Kat. 4, 06640 Kizilay, Ankara; tel. (312) 2325009; fax (312) 2316730; e-mail bass-w@tr.net; internet www.bass-sen.org.tr; Pres. TURGUT YILMAZ; 15,000 mems.

Basın-İş (Türkiye Basın İşçileri Sendikası) (Press Workers' Union): İstanbul; e-mail basinis@basin-is.org; internet www .basin-is.org; f. 1964; Gen. Man. YAKUP AKKAYA; Gen. Sec. ISMAIL HAKKI KÜTÜKÇÜ; 5,000 mems.

Birlesik Metal-İs (Birlesik Metal İşçileri Sendikası): Tünel Yolu Cad. 2, 81110 Bostancı, Kadıköy, İstanbul; tel. (216) 3622091; fax (216) 3736502; e-mail info@birlesikmetal.com; Gen. Sec. MUZAFFER ŞAHIN; 58,800 mems.

Demiryol-İş (Türkiye Demiryolu İşçileri Sendikası) (Railway Workers): Necatibey Cad., Sezenler Sok 5, 06430 Yenişehir, Ankara; tel. (312) 2318029; fax (312) 2318032; internet www.sendikaonline

.com; f. 1952; Pres. Ergün Atalay; Gen. Sec. Hüseyin Demir; 25,000 mems.

Deri-İş (Türkiye Deri İşçileri Sendikası) (Leather Industry): Ahmet Kutsi Tecer Cad. 12/6, Merter, İstanbul; tel. (212) 5048083; fax (212) 5061079; f. 1948; Pres. Nusrettin Yilmaz; Gen. Sec. Ali Sel; 11,000 mems.

Dev. Sağlık-İş (Türkiye Devrimci Sağlık İşçileri Sendikası) (Health Employees): İstanbul; f. 1961; Pres. Doğan Halis; Gen. Sec. Sabri Tanyeri; 15,000 mems.

Genel-İş (Türkiye Genel Hizmet İşçileri Sendikası) (Municipal Workers): Çankırı Cad. 28, Kat 5–9, Ulus, Ankara; tel. (312) 3091547; fax (312) 3091046; f. 1983; Pres. Mahmut Seren; Gen. Sec. Kani Beko; 50,000 mems.

Gıda-İş (Türkiye Gıda Sanayii İşçileri Sendikası): Ahmet Kutsi Tecer Cad. 12/3, 34010 Merter, İstanbul; tel. (212) 5751540; fax (212) 5753099; Pres. Mehmet Muhlaci; Gen. Sec. Yurdakul Gözde; 31,000 mems.

Koop-İş (Türkiye Kooperatif ve Büro İşçileri Sendikası) (Co-operative and Office Workers): İzmir Cad. Fevzi Çakmak Sok. 15/11–12, Yenişehir, Ankara; tel. (312) 4300855; f. 1964; Pres. Ahmet Balaman; Gen. Sec. Ahmet Güven; 29,000 mems.

Limter-İş (Liman, Tersane Gemi Yapım Onarım İşçileri Sendikası) (Harbour, Shipyard, Ship Building and Repairs): İcmeler Tren İstasyonu Yanı 12/1, Tuzla, İstanbul; tel. (216) 3955271; f. 1947; Pres. Emir Babakuş; Gen. Sec. Asker Şit; 7,000 mems.

Nakliyat-İş (Nakliye İşçileri Sendikası) (Transportation Workers): Guraba Hüseyin Ağa Mah. Kakmacı Sok. 10, Daire 11 Vatan Cad. Tranvay, Durağı Karşısı, Aksaray, İstanbul; tel. (212) 5332069; Pres. Şemsi Ercan; Gen. Sec. Nedim Firat.

OLEYİS (Otel, Lokanta, Eğlence Yerleri İşçileri Sendikası) (Hotel, Restaurant and Places of Entertainment Workers' Union): Necatibey Cad. 96/1-3, Kızılay, Ankara; tel. (312) 2308624; fax (312) 2308626; e-mail oleysis@oleyis.org.tr; internet www.oleyis.org.tr; f. 1947; Pres. Kamer Aktaş; Gen. Sec. Erdoğan Yahya; 4,000 mems.

Petkim-İş (Türkiye Petrol, Kimya ve Lastik Sanayii İşçileri Sendikası): İzmir Cad., Fevzi Çakmak Sok. 7/13, Ankara; tel. (312) 2300861; fax (312) 2299429; Pres. Mustafa Karadayi; 18,000 mems.

Sosyal-İş (Türkiye Sosyal Sigortalar, Eğitim, Büro, Ticaret Kooperatif Banka ve Güzel Sanatlar İşçileri Sendikası) (Banking, Insurance and Trading): Necatibey Cad. Sezenler Sok. Lozan Apt. 2/14, Yenişehir, Ankara; tel. (312) 2318178; fax (312) 2294638; Pres. Özcan Kesgeç; Gen. Sec. H. Bedri Doğanay; 31,000 mems.

Tekstil İşçileri Sendikası: Ahmet Kutsi Tecer Cad. 12/1, Merter, İstanbul; tel. (212) 6429742; fax (212) 5044887; Pres. Ridvan Budak; 45,000 mems.

Tümka-İş (Türkiye Tüm Kağıt Selüloz Sanayii İşçileri Sendikası): Gündoğdu Sok. 19/3, Merter, İstanbul; tel. (212) 5750843; Pres. Sabri Kaplan; 3,000 mems.

Other Principal Trade Unions

Denizciler (Türkiye Denizciler Sendikası) (Seamen): Rıhtım Cad., Denizciler Sok. 7, Tophane, İstanbul; tel. (212) 2929081; fax (212) 2933938; e-mail kul@cakakul.av.tr; f. 1959; Pres. Turhan Uzun; Gen. Sec. Çemil Yeniay; 4,272 mems.

Fındık-İş (Fiskobirlik İşçileri Sendikası) (Hazelnut producers): Giresun; Pres. Akçın Koç; Gen. Sec. Ersait Şen.

Hava-İş (Türkiye Sivil Havacılık Sendikası) (Civil Aviation): İncirli Cad., Volkan Apt., 68/1 Bakırköy, İstanbul; tel. (212) 6602095; fax (212) 5719051; e-mail havais@havais.org.tr; internet www.havais.org.tr; Pres. Atilay Ayçin; Gen. Sec. Mustafa Yağci; 9,451 mems.

Liman-İş (Türkiye Liman ve Kara Tahmil İşçileri Sendikası) (Longshoremen): Necatibey Cad., Sezenler Sok. 4, Kat. 5, Sıhhıye, Ankara; tel. (312) 2317418; fax (312) 2302484; e-mail liman-is@tr-net.net.tr; f. 1963; Pres. Raif Kiliç; Gen. Sec. Erding Çakir; 5,000 mems.

Şeker-İş (Türkiye Şeker Sanayii İşçileri Sendikası) (Sugar Industry): Karanfil Sok. 59, Bakanlıklar, Ankara; tel. (312) 4184273; fax (312) 4259258; f. 1952; Pres. Ömer Çelik; Gen. Sec. Fethi Tekin; 35,000 mems.

Tarım-İş (Türkiye Orman, Topraksu, Tarım ve Tarım Sanayii İşçileri Sendikası) (Forestry, Agriculture and Agricultural Industry Workers): Bankacı Sok. 10, 06700 Kocatepe, Ankara; tel. (312) 4190456; fax (312) 4193113; e-mail tarim-is@tr.net; internet www.tarimis.org.tr; f. 1961; Pres. Bedrettin Kaykaç; Gen. Sec. İ. Sabri Keskin; 16,000 mems.

Tekgıda-İş (Türkiye Tütün, Müskirat Gıda ve Yardımcı İşçileri Sendikası) (Tobacco, Drink, Food and Allied Workers' Union of Turkey): 4 Levent Konaklar Sok., İstanbul; tel. (212) 2644996; fax (212) 2789534; e-mail bilgi@tekgida.org.tr; internet www.tekgida.org.tr; f. 1952; Pres. Hüseyin Karakoç; Gen. Sec. Mustafa Türkel; 176,000 mems.

Teksif (Türkiye Tekstil, Örme ve Giyim Sanayii İşçileri Sendikası) (Textile, Knitting and Clothing): Ziya Gökalp Cad. Aydoğmuş Sok. 1, Kurtuluş, Ankara; tel. (312) 4312170; fax (312) 4357826; f. 1951; Pres. Zeki Polat; 80,000 mems.

Tez-Koop-İş (Türkiye, Ticaret, Kooperatif, Eğitim, Büro ve Güzel Sanatlar İşçileri Sendikası) (Commercial and Clerical Employees): Üç Yıldız Cad. 29, Subayevleri, Ayınlıkevler, 06130 Ankara; tel. (312) 3183979; fax (312) 3183988; f. 1962; Pres. Sadik Özben; Gen. Sec. Hüseyin Hamurcu; 30,000 mems.

Türk Harb-İş (Türkiye Harb Sanayii ve Yardımcı İşkolları İşçileri Sendikası) (Defence Industry and Allied Workers): İnkılap Sok. 20, Kızılay, Ankara; tel. (312) 4175097; fax (312) 4171364; f. 1956; Pres. Osman Çimen; Gen. Sec. Ahmet Tunbak; 35,000 mems.

Türk-Metal (Türkiye Metal, Çelik, Mühimmat, Makina ve Metalden Mamul, Eşya ve Oto, Montaj ve Yardımcı İşçileri Sendikası) (Auto, Metal and Allied Workers): Kızılırmak Mah., Adalararası Sok. 3, Eskişehir Yolu 1 km, 06560 Söğütözü, Ankara; tel. (312) 2844010; fax (312) 2844018; e-mail bilgiislem@turkmetal.org.tr; f. 1963; Pres. Mustafa Özbek; 247,000 mems.

Yol-İş (Türkiye Yol, Yapı ve İnşaat İşçileri Sendikası) (Road, Construction and Building Workers' Unions): Sümer 1 Sok. 18, Kızıloy, Ankara; tel. (312) 2324687; fax (312) 2324810; f. 1963; Pres. Bayram Meral; Gen. Sec. Fikret Barin; 170,000 mems.

Transport

RAILWAYS

The total length of the railways operated within the national frontiers was 10,922 km in 2000, of which 8,671 km were main lines, 2,122 km were electrified, and 2,505 km were signalled. A new direct rail link between Ankara and İstanbul, reducing the distance from 577 km to 416 km, was under construction. There are direct rail links with Bulgaria to Iran and Syria. A new line connecting Turkey with Georgia was also planned. İstanbul operates an 18-km light railway system, and opened its first metro line in September 2000. Both systems are being expanded. Ankara and İzmir both operate metro railways.

Türkiye Cumhuriyeti Devlet Demiryolları İşletmesi Genel Müdürlüğü (TCDD) (Turkish Republic State Railways): Talatpaşa Bul., 06330 Gar, Ankara; tel. (312) 3090515; fax (312) 3123215; e-mail tcddapk@tcdd.gov.tr; internet www.tcdd.gov.tr; f. 1924; operates all railways and connecting ports (see below) of the State Railway Administration, which acquired the status of a state economic enterprise in 1953, and a state economic establishment in 1984; 470 main-line diesel locomotives, 74 main-line electric locomotives, 965 passenger coaches and 16,070 freight wagons; Chair. of Bd and Gen. Dir Süleyman Karaman.

ROADS

In 2002 the total road network was estimated at 354,421 km of classified roads, of which 31,318 km were highways and 30,050 km were secondary roads; about 41.6% of the network was paved.

Bayındırlık ve İskan Bakanlığı, Karayolları Genel Müdürlüğü (KGM) (General Directorate of Highways): Yücetepe, 06100 Ankara; tel. (312) 4158000; fax (312) 4186996; e-mail info@kgm.gov.tr; internet www.kgm.gov.tr; f. 1950; Dir-Gen. Hicabi Ece.

SHIPPING

At the end of 2004 Turkey's merchant fleet comprised 1,114 vessels and had an aggregate displacement of 4,678,885 grt.

General-purpose public ports are operated by two state economic enterprises. The ports of Bandırma, Derince, Haydarpaşa (İstanbul), İskenderun, İzmir, Mersin and Samsun, all of which are connected to the railway network, are operated by Turkish State Railways (TCDD) (see above), while the smaller ports of Antalya, Giresun, Hopa, Tekirdağ and Trabzon are operated by the Turkish Maritime Organization (TDI).

Turkish Maritime Organization (TDI): Genel Müdürlüğü, Karaköy, İstanbul; tel. (212) 2515000; fax (212) 2495391.

Port of Bandırma: TCDD Liman İşletme Müdürlüğü, Bandırma; tel. (266) 2234966; fax (266) 2236011; Port Man. Okkes Demirel; Harbour Master Rusen Okan.

Port of Derince: TCDD Liman İşletme Müdürlüğü, Derince; Port Man. Ali Arif Aytaç; Harbour Master Haydar Doğan.

Port of Haydarpaşa (İstanbul): TCDD Liman İşletme Müdürlüğü Haydarpaşa, İstanbul; tel. (212) 3379988; fax (312) 3451705; Port Man. Nedim Ozcan; Harbour Master İsmail Safaer.

Port of İskenderun: TCDD Liman İşletme Müdürlüğü, İskenderun; tel. (326) 6140047; fax (326) 6132424; Port Man. Hilmi Sönmez; Harbour Master İshak Özdemir.

Port of İzmir: TCDD Liman İşletme Müdürlüğü, İzmir; tel. (232) 4632252; fax (232) 4632248; Port Man. GÜNGÖR ERKAYA; Harbour Master MEHMET ONGEL.

Port of Mersin: TCDD Liman İşletme Müdürlüğü, Mersin; tel. (324) 2330687; fax (324) 2311350; Port Man. FAHRI SAYILI; Harbour Master RACI TARHUSOĞLU.

Port of Samsun: TCDD Liman İşletme Müdürlüğü, Samsun; tel. (362) 4357616; fax (362) 4317849; Port Man. SAFFET YAMAK; Harbour Master Capt. ARIF H. UZUNOĞLU.

Private Companies

Deniz Nakliyatı TAŞ (Turkish Cargo Lines): Meclisı Mebusan Cad. 151, 80040 Fındıklı, İstanbul; tel. (212) 2522600; fax (212) 2512696; f. 1955; regular liner services between Turkey and Mediterranean, Adriatic, Red Sea, US Atlantic, and Indian and Far East ports; Gen. Man. NEVZAT BILICAN; 17 general cargo ships, 4 roll-on, roll-off, 8 bulk/ore carriers.

İstanbul Deniz Otobusleri Sanayi ve Ticaret AŞ: POB 81110, Bostanci, İstanbul; tel. (216) 3628013; fax (216) 3620443; ferry company; Chair. MUSTAFA ACIKALIN; Man. Dir BINALI YILDIRIM; 23 vessels.

Kiran Shipping Group of Companies: Fahrettin Kerim Gorkay Cad. 22, Denizcilar İş Merkezi B Blok Kat 2, 81190 Altunizade, İstanbul; tel. (216) 3916150; fax (216) 3916168; Chair. TURGUT KIRAN; Man. Dir TAMER KIRAN; 16 vessels.

Ozsay Seatransportation Co Inc: Güzelyalı, E-5 Üzeri 18, 34903 Pendik, İstanbul; tel. (216) 4933610; fax (216) 4930306; e-mail ozsay@tnn.net; Pres. RECEP KALKAVAN; Man. Dir OMER KALKAVAN; 10 vessels.

Pinat Gida Sanayi ve Ticaret AŞ: Pak Ismerkezi Prof. Dr Bulent Tarcan Sok 5/3, 80290 Gayrettepe, İstanbul; tel. (212) 2747533; fax (212) 2750317; e-mail pinat@pinat.com.tr; Pres. ENGIN PAK; Man. Dir ALPAY CITAK; 7 vessels.

T.D.I Sehir Hatlan İşletmesi: Mayis Han, Bahcekapi 27, 34420 Sirkeci, İstanbul; tel. (212) 5264020; fax (212) 2495391; 14 vessels.

Türkiye Denizcilik İşletmeleri Denizyolları İşletmesi Müdürlüğü (TDI): Meclisı Mebusan Cad. 18, 80040 Salıpazarı, İstanbul; tel. (212) 2521700; fax (212) 2515767; internet www.tdi.com.tr; ferry company; Chair. ERKAN ARIKAN; Man. Dir KADIR KURTOĞLU; 5 vessels.

Vakif Deniz Finansal Kiralama AŞ: Rihtim Cad. 201 Tahir Han kat 6, PK 853, 80040 Karaköy, İstanbul; 15 vessels.

Yardimci Shipping Group of Companies: Aydintepe Mah. Tersaneler Cad. 50 Sok 7, 81700 Tuzla, İstanbul; tel. (216) 4938000; fax (216) 4928080; e-mail moliva@turk.net; Chair. KEMAL YARDIMCI; Man. Dir HUSEYIN YARDIMCI; 11 vessels.

Shipping Associations

SS Gemi Armatörleri Motorlu Taşıyıcılar Kooperatifi (Turkish Shipowners' Asscn): Meclisı Mebusan Cad., Dursun Han, Kat. 7, No 89, Salıpazarı İstanbul; tel. (212) 2510945; fax (212) 2492786; f. 1960; Pres. GÜNDÜZ KAPTANOĞLU; Man. Dir A. GÖKSU; 699 vessels; 5,509,112 dwt (1993).

Türk Armatörler Birliği (Turkish Shipowners' Union): Meclisı Mebusan Cad. Dursun Han, Kat. 7 No. 89, Salıpazarı, İstanbul; tel. (212) 2453022; fax (212) 2492786; f. 1972; 460 mems; Pres. ŞADAN KALKAVAN; Co-ordinator HAKAN ÜNSALER; 8,780,436 dwt (1997).

Vapur Donatanları ve Acenteleri Derneği (Turkish Shipowners' and Shipping Agents' Asscn): Mumhane Cad. Emek İş Hanı Kat. 3 No. 31, Karaköy, İstanbul; tel. (212) 2443294; fax (212) 2432865; e-mail vapurd@vda.org.tr; internet www.vda.org.tr; f. 1902; worldwide agency service; Pres. Capt. M. LEBLEBICIOĞLU; Man. Dir C. KAPLAN.

CIVIL AVIATION

There are airports for scheduled international and internal flights at Atatürk (İstanbul), Esenboğa (Ankara), Adnan Menderes (İzmir and Trabzon), while international charter flights are handled by Adana, Dalaman and Antalya. Fifteen other airports handle internal flights only.

Alfa Hava Yolları AŞ (Alfa Airlines Inc.): Fatih Cad. 21, Günesli, 34540 İstanbul; tel. (212) 6303348; fax (212) 6575869; e-mail hkeser@airalfa.com.tr; internet www.airalfa.com.tr; f. 1992; charter services to Europe; Man. Dir NECMETTIN METINER.

Eurosun Airlines (ESN): Fener Mah, Bul. Ozgurluk, Melda 2/7, Antalya 07134; tel. (242) 3235060; fax (242) 3241252; f. 1999 as Air Rose, assumed present name in June 2000; charter flights to European destinations; Man. Dir MESUT SENER.

İstanbul Hava Yolları AŞ (Istanbul Airlines): Firuzköy Yolu, Bağlar İçi Mevzii 26, 34850 Avcılar, İstanbul; tel. (212) 5092100; fax (212) 5938742; internet www.istanbulairlines.com.tr; f. 1985; charter services from major Turkish cities to European destinations; Gen. Man. SAFI ERGIN.

Onur Air Taşımacılık AŞ: Senlik Mahallesi, Gatal Sok. 3, 34810 Florya, İstanbul; tel. (212) 6632300; fax (212) 6632319; internet www.onurair.de; f. 1992; regional and domestic passenger and cargo charter services; Chair. CANKUT BAGANA.

Pegasus Hava Taşımacılığı AŞ: İstasyon Cad. 24, Kat. 1, 34800 Yeşilyurt, İstanbul; tel. (212) 6632934; fax (212) 5739627; internet www.pgtair.com; f. 1989; charter services; Chair. S. ALTUN; Gen. Man. L. J. LOWTH.

Sky Airlines: Jalan Cad., Suite 41, Baranaklar-Anatalya 07100; tel. (242) 3237576; fax (242) 3237567; f. 2000; regional passenger charter flights; CEO TALHA GORGULU.

Sonmez Hava Yolları: 9 km Yakova Yolu, PK 189, Bursa; tel. (224) 2610440; fax (224) 2465445; f. 1984; scheduled flights and dedicated freight; Chair. ALI OSMAN SÖNMEZ.

SunExpress: Fener Mahallesi Sinanoghu Cad., Oktay Airport, PK 28, 07100 Antalya; tel. (242) 3234047; fax (242) 3234057; e-mail sunexpress@condor.de; internet www.sunexpress.de; f. 1990; charter and scheduled passenger and freight; serves European destinations; Man. Dir PAUL SCHWAIGER.

Top Air: Atatürk Havalimani, E-Kapısı, Polis Okulu Arkası, 34640 Sefaköy, İstanbul; tel. (212) 5416040; fax (212) 5985060; e-mail info@topair.com.tr; internet www.topair.com.tr; f. 1990; charter and scheduled flights for tour operators.

Türk Hava Yolları AO (THY) (Turkish Airlines Inc.): Genel Müdürlük Binas, Atatürk Hava Limanı, 34830 Yeşilköy, İstanbul; tel. (212) 6636300; fax (212) 6634744; e-mail turkishairlines@thy.com; internet www.thy.com.tr; f. 1933; 23% of shares floated late 2004, further privatization pending; extensive internal network and scheduled and charter flights to destinations in the Middle East, Africa, the Far East, Central Asia, the USA and Europe; Chair. CANDAN KARLITEKIN.

Tourism

Visitors to Turkey are attracted by the climate, fine beaches and ancient monuments. With government investment, the country has rapidly become a leading holiday destination for European tourists (particularly from the United Kingdom and Germany). In 2003 the number of tourists increased to 13.3m. (compared with 7.5m in 1999), while receipts from tourism reached US $13,203m.

Ministry of Culture and Tourism: Kültür Bakanlığı ve Turizm, Atatürk Bul. 29, 06050 Opera, Ankara; tel. (312) 3090850; fax (312) 3124359; e-mail info@kulturturizm.gov.tr; internet www.kulturturizm.gov.tr; f. 1963; Dir-Gen. of Information MUSTAFA SYAHHAN; Dir-Gen. of Investments and Establishments KUDRET ASLAN.

TURKMENISTAN

Introductory Survey

Location, Climate, Language, Religion, Flag, Capital

Turkmenistan, formerly the Turkmen Soviet Socialist Republic, is situated in the south-west of Central Asia. It is bordered to the north by Uzbekistan, to the north-west by Kazakhstan, to the west by the Caspian Sea, to the south by Iran and to the south-east by Afghanistan. The climate is severely continental, with extremely hot summers and cold winters. The average temperature in January is −4°C (25°F), but winter temperatures can fall as low as −33°C (−27°F). In summer temperatures often reach 50°C (122°F) in the south-east Kara-Kum desert; the average temperature in July is 28°C (82°F). Precipitation is slight throughout much of the country: average annual rainfall ranges from only 80 mm (3.1 ins) in the north-west to about 300 mm (11.8 ins) in mountainous regions. In 1990 Turkmen, a member of the Southern Turkic group, was declared the official language of the republic. Most of the population are Sunni Muslims. Islam in Turkmenistan has traditionally featured elements of Sufi mysticism and shamanism, and pilgrimages to local religious sites are reported to be common. The national flag (proportions 2 by 3) consists of three unequal vertical stripes (proportions 4–6–23), of green, maroon and green; the maroon stripe bears a vertical design of five different carpet patterns above an orange wreath of olive branches, while the green stripe nearest the fly has in its upper dexter corner five white five-pointed stars framed by a narrow white crescent moon. The capital is Aşgabat.

Recent History

In 1877 Russia began a campaign against the Turkmen, which culminated in the battle of Gök Tepe in 1881, at which some 20,000 Turkmen are estimated to have been killed. In 1895 the Russian conquest was confirmed by agreement with the British; the international boundary thus established divided some Turkmen under Russian rule from others in the British sphere of influence. In 1917 the Bolsheviks attempted to take power in the region, but there was little support from among the local population. An anti-Bolshevik Russian Provisional Government of Transcaspia was formed, and a Turkmen Congress was also established. Soviet forces were sent to Aşgabat, and a Turkestan Autonomous Soviet Socialist Republic, which included Transcaspia, was declared on 30 April 1918. In July, however, nationalists, aided by British forces, ousted the Bolshevik Government and established an independent Government in Aşgabat, protected by a British garrison. After the British withdrew, however, the Government was soon removed, and by 1920 Red Army troops, led by Gen. Mikheil Frunze, were in control of Aşgabat. As part of the National Delimitation of Central Asia, the Turkmen Soviet Socialist Republic (SSR) was established on 27 October 1924. In May 1925 it became a constituent republic of the USSR. Political power in the republic became the preserve of the Communist Party of Turkmenistan (CPT).

The Soviet agricultural collectivization programme, which was begun in 1929 and entailed the forcible settlement of traditionally nomadic people in collective farms, provoked military resistance, and guerrilla warfare against Soviet power continued until 1936. In 1928 a campaign against the practice of religion in Turkmenistan was launched: almost all Islamic institutions were closed, including schools, courts and mosques. In the early 1930s there was a campaign among the Turkmen intelligentsia for greater political autonomy for Turkmenistan. As a result, many Turkmen intellectuals were imprisoned or executed. The scope of the purges widened in the late 1930s to include government and CPT officials, notably the Chairman of the republican Supreme Soviet (Supreme Council—legislature), Nederbai Aitakov, who was executed in c. 1937.

After the early 1930s there was little development in the industrial sector. Agriculture was encouraged and irrigation extended. Irrigation projects such as the Kara-Kum Canal, the largest such scheme in the USSR, enabled rapid development of cotton-growing, especially after 1945. The immigration of Russians into the urban areas of Turkmenistan, from the 1920s, gradually diminished the proportion of Turkmen in leading posts in the republic. In 1958 the First Secretary (leader) of the CPT, Sukhan Babayev, proposed that Turkmen should occupy more senior positions. He was dismissed, together with many of his colleagues in government.

In the late 1980s Turkmenistan's role as a provider of raw materials (mainly natural gas and cotton) to more developed regions of the USSR provoked strong criticism of the relationship between republican and the all-Union authorities. The environmental and health hazards connected with intensive agriculture were also widely discussed in the republican media. However, the geographical remoteness of the republic and its poor level of communications with other parts of the USSR inhibited its involvement in the political changes occurring in other Soviet republics. Moreover, the lack of any history as a unified nation, together with continuing tribal divisions, did not engender any mass movement for national autonomy, as occurred elsewhere.

In the absence of any significant pro-democracy movement, the CPT dominated the republic's elections to the all-Union Congress of People's Deputies in the Soviet and Russian capital, Moscow, in early 1989. In September, however, Turkmen intellectuals formed Unity (Agzybirlik), a 'popular front' organization concerned with the status of the Turkmen language, indigenous arts, environmental matters and economic issues. In the following month it was officially registered. However, after support for the movement increased, it was banned in January 1990. Nevertheless, Unity's founding congress took place in the following month. As a result of the official animosity towards the nascent democratic movement, only the CPT and its approved organizations were permitted to participate in elections to the republican Supreme Soviet on 7 January, at which CPT members won the majority of the 175 seats. When the new Supreme Soviet convened, Saparmyrat Niyazov, the First Secretary of the CPT since 1985, was elected Chairman of the Supreme Soviet, the highest government office in the republic.

Despite the continuing dominance of the CPT, some concessions were made to popular pressure. In May 1990 Turkmen officially became the state language, replacing Russian; Turkmenistan was the last of the Soviet republics to introduce such legislation. On 22 August the Turkmen Supreme Soviet adopted a declaration of sovereignty, which asserted the right of the republic to determine its own political and social system and to secede from the USSR. On 27 October Niyazov was elected, by direct ballot, to the new post of executive President of Turkmenistan. He was unopposed in the election and reportedly received 98.3% of the votes cast.

In late 1990 and early 1991 Turkmenistan participated in negotiations towards a new Union Treaty, which was to redefine the status of the republics within the structure of the USSR. The underdeveloped state of the economy, and the republic's dependence on the central Government for subsidies, ensured that the republic's leadership was one of the most enthusiastic proponents of the preservation of the USSR. At the all-Union referendum on the status of the USSR in March 1991, 95.7% of eligible voters in Turkmenistan approved the preservation of the USSR as a 'renewed federation', the highest proportion of any Soviet republic.

President Niyazov made no public announcements either opposing or supporting the attempted coup by conservative communist elements in Moscow of August 1991. However, opposition groups, including Unity, publicly opposed the coup, which led to the arrest of several of their leaders. Following the failure of the coup attempt, Niyazov remained in power and announced that the CPT would be retained as the ruling party, unlike in other republics, where the communist parties had been suspended or dissolved; however, in December the CPT changed its name to the Democratic Party of Turkmenistan (DPT), with Niyazov as its Chairman. On 18 October Turkmenistan was among the signatories of the treaty establishing an economic community of eight republics. This was followed on 26 October by a national referendum at which, according to the official results, 94.1% of the electorate voted for independence. On the following day the Turkmen Supreme Soviet adopted a law on independence. The name of the republic was changed from the Turkmen SSR to Turkmenistan, and a new state emblem, flag and national anthem were adopted. On 21 December Turkmenistan became a signatory, with 10 other republics, of the Alma-Ata (Almaty) Declaration, which formally established the Commonwealth of Independent States (CIS, see p. 201); this decision was subsequently ratified by the Turkmenistani Supreme Council.

In the first half of 1992 Turkmenistan's state structures remained unchanged, with the DPT dominant both in the Council of Ministers and the Supreme Council. However, ultimate power resided with Niyazov, in his capacity as President of the Republic and leader of the DPT. Although Niyazov reportedly continued to enjoy widespread popular support, there was some criticism of his increasingly authoritarian style of leadership, which involved rigid control of the media, the restriction of opposition activity and the promotion of a presidential 'cult of personality'. (It was reportedly the last ambition that prompted the resignation, in mid-1992, of the Minister of Foreign Affairs, Abdy Kuliyev.) The new Constitution, adopted on 18 May, further enhanced presidential authority, making Niyazov Head of Government (Prime Minister), as well as Head of State, and giving him certain legislative prerogatives. He was also to act concurrently as the Supreme Commander of the Armed Forces. In June Niyazov was re-elected, unopposed, to the presidency, receiving a purported 99.5% of the votes cast in a direct ballot.

Other significant structural changes were introduced under the new Constitution. The Supreme Council was to be replaced as Turkmenistan's legislature by a 50-member Majlis (Assembly); however, until the expiry of its five-year term, the Supreme Soviet elected in 1990 (although renamed the Majlis), was to be retained as the republican legislature. The Khalk Maslakhaty (People's Council) was established as the 'supreme representative body of popular power'. The Khalk Maslakhaty was to act in a supervisory capacity, and would not diminish the authority of the President or the Majlis; however, it was to debate and decide important political and economic issues, and would also be empowered to demand changes to the Constitution and to vote to express 'no confidence' in the President, if it found his actions to be at variance with the law. The Khalk Maslakhaty was to comprise the 50 deputies of the Majlis in addition to 50 elected and 10 appointed representatives from the electoral districts of Turkmenistan (the former were directly elected in November–December 1992); it was also to include other members of local government and prominent figures of Turkmen society, including the members of the Government and the Chairman of the Supreme Court, and was to be headed by the President. At its first session, in mid-December, the Khalk Maslakhaty awarded Niyazov the rank of General, further enhancing his authority.

After the new Constitution was adopted, there were fears that the rights of Turkmenistan's ethnic minorities (the largest, Russians and Uzbeks, represented some 10% and 9%, respectively, of the total population in the early 1990s) were in jeopardy, as the document stipulated that only ethnic Turkmen would be eligible for employment in state enterprises. Moreover, the Russian language was no longer to be used as the means of inter-ethnic communication (the status that it had held since 1990, when Turkmen replaced Russian as the official language). Nevertheless, Turkmenistan did not experience inter-ethnic violence or religious conflict, such as occurred in some other former republics of the USSR. Although the population is predominantly Muslim, Turkmenistan's Constitution guaranteed state secularism, a principle that was strongly emphasized by President Niyazov.

The presidential 'personality cult' was strengthened during 1993, with numerous institutions, streets and public buildings being named after Niyazov—the Caspian Sea port of Krasnovodsk was renamed Türkmenbaşi ('Head of the Turkmen', a recently introduced mode of address for Niyazov). The construction also continued of a number of extravagantly furbished palaces for Niyazov. In December the Majlis voted to extend Niyazov's term of office until 2002, on the grounds that the republic's political and economic stability depended on the realization of Niyazov's '10 Years of Prosperity' programme of gradual reforms. The extension of Niyazov's presidency was endorsed by a reported 99.99% of the electorate in a referendum held on 15 January 1994.

Elections to the new, 50-member Majlis were held in December 1994, officially with the participation of 99.8% of the registered electorate. It was reported that 49 of the 50 deputies had been elected unopposed. The Majlis convened for the first time in late December; the overwhelming majority of the deputies were believed to be members of the DPT.

Despite the result of the referendum of January 1994, elements of opposition to Niyazov were believed to be active in Turkmenistan. Anti-Niyazov activists were also based in exile, in other republics of the CIS, in particular Russia, where Abdy Kuliyev led one branch of the opposition, the so-called Turkmenistan Foundation. In June 1995 the Turkmenistani Supreme Court sentenced two opposition leaders to respective terms of 12 and 15 years' imprisonment in a labour colony, having found them guilty of involvement in an alleged plot to assassinate Niyazov. (Two leading members of the Turkmenistani opposition-in-exile had been arrested in Moscow in 1994 by Russian security forces, in connection with the alleged coup attempt, but had been released following protests by Russian human rights groups.) In July 1995 a protest rally took place in Aşgabat (reportedly the first to be held in Turkmenistan since independence), at which up to 1,000 demonstrators criticized Niyazov's leadership and the continuing economic hardships. In August, in what was interpreted as a response to the previous month's unrest, Niyazov dismissed 10 of Turkmenistan's 50 local etrap (district or raion) administrative leaders. In October the President also dismissed several senior members of the Council of Ministers. The Institute for Democracy and Human Rights was inaugurated in Aşgabat in October 1996, with Niyazov as its director.

In 1996 and 1997 Niyazov effected widespread dismissals of government officials, as well as local administrative leaders and members of the judiciary. In February 1998 the President revealed that he planned to amend the Constitution after the legislative elections of December 1999, devolving certain presidential powers to the Majlis and relinquishing the post of Prime Minister (a post that he retained, however, in 2006). In April 1998 elections to the Khalk Maslakhaty were held, with the reported participation of 99.5% of the electorate.

Turkmenistan continued to attract the censure of international human rights organizations during the late 1990s. In April 1998 a delegation of the Organization for Security and Co-operation in Europe (OSCE, see p. 327) appealed to Niyazov to release eight political prisoners who had been detained since the Aşgabat demonstration of July 1995. Niyazov agreed to their release, following which he made his first official visit to the USA where, it was reported, President Bill Clinton discussed with him the question of human rights in Turkmenistan, as well as the need for political and economic reforms.

Niyazov's systematic purging of government and other officials continued in May 1998. An attempted military rebellion that occurred in western Turkmenistan in September was followed by the dismissal of the Minister of Defence, and the comprehensive reorganization of senior personnel of the armed forces and border troops. In the same month a number of regional governors were removed from office, and in October Niyazov dismissed the Chairman of the National Television and Radio Company. In the wake of public disorder outside an Aşgabat bank in December, wide-ranging dismissals of municipal police and security officials were effected, as well as personnel changes within the Ministry of the Economy and Finance.

The promotion of the presidential 'personality cult' appeared to intensify during 1998: in October Niyazov was honoured with his third 'hero of Turkmenistan' award (the country's highest honour), and in December a giant ceremonial arch, the 'Arch of Independence', surmounted by a revolving gold-plated statue of the President, was inaugurated in central Aşgabat. In the same month Niyazov was unanimously re-elected Chairman of the DPT. In what was interpreted as an effort to counter growing international accusations of dictatorial methods, the President declared, in December, that the elections to the Majlis scheduled for late 1999 would be contested on a multi-party basis, and that the establishment of new political parties would be permitted in advance of the poll. In early 1999, in a further attempt to prove his commitment to human rights, the President declared a moratorium on the death penalty. (In December the Khalk Maslakhaty voted to abolish the death penalty; Turkmenistan thus became the first Central Asian republic to proscribe capital punishment.)

Elections to the Majlis were conducted on 12 December 1999. According to official reports, some 99% of the registered electorate participated in the poll. In the event, the DPT was the only party represented and the OSCE declined an invitation to monitor the poll, claiming that there was little evidence of a genuinely democratic process. In late December the new Majlis approved an amendment to the Constitution whereby Niyazov's presidential term was extended indefinitely. Niyazov had made repeated claims that the success of democratic and economic reform would be dependent on the continuity of successive 10-year plans. Following the Majlis' endorsement of the amendment, Niyazov announced that the creation of opposition political parties would not be contemplated before 2010, when, he explained, the 'political conscience' of the Turkmen people would be fully formed. These developments further aroused the concerns of the international community, and there was considerable outrage when, in March 2000, the leader of the unofficial popular opposition front, Unity, Nurberdy Nurmamedov, was sentenced to five years' imprisonment on charges of hooliganism and intent to murder, after he protested that the December 1999 amendment to the Constitution was undemocratic.

On 1 January 2000 Turkmenistan formally adopted a revised form of the Latin script, replacing the Cyrillic script that had been introduced for the Turkmen language in the 1920s. In early 2000 Niyazov enacted a law that detailed the first phase of extensive reforms to administrative, economic and social structures. The reform programme was to be considered by the Majlis, which had been granted new legislative and regulatory powers following the December 1999 elections. In January 2000 the Majlis announced the creation of four permanent parliamentary committees to examine: legislation; science, education and culture; economy and social policy; and international and inter-parliamentary relations.

In January and June 2000 President Niyazov dismissed a number of prominent government officials, including three Deputy Prime Ministers. Meanwhile, in June the President approved the founding of a joint Council for the Supervision of Foreigners, which gave Turkmenistan's security services the power to monitor the movements of foreigners arriving or temporarily residing in the country. Niyazov also instructed Turkmenistani citizens and government organizations to close any bank accounts held abroad, in order to curtail the flow of capital outside Turkmenistan. In July Niyazov issued an order declaring that, henceforth, knowledge of the Turkmen language would be a mandatory requirement for all government officials; heads of state organizations, ministries and higher-education institutions were given 30 days to learn the language or lose their positions. Furthermore, all candidates for leadership posts were to have their genealogies over the previous three generations verified. At the end of July the President dismissed Boris Shikhmuradov, the Minister of Foreign Affairs; he was replaced by Batyr Berdiyev. All officials were, henceforth, to be appointed for a six-month probation period.

In the early 2000s Niyazov oversaw the introduction of a number of policies intended to develop a strong Turkmen national identity. In April 2001 the President closed the opera and ballet theatre in Aşgabat, which he denounced as 'alien' to Turkmen culture; it was replaced with a national music and drama theatre instructed to produce the works of contemporary Turkmen authors. A principal element of Niyazov's developments to promote a Turkmen national culture was the publication of the *Ruhnama*, or national code of spiritual conduct, a volume purportedly written by the President. This text became a key element of the school curriculum, and was in effect elevated to the status of a holy text, with display of the volume required in mosques and citations from the work included in inscriptions in religious and public buildings. (A second volume of the *Ruhnama* was published in September 2004.)

In July 2001 Berdiyev was dismissed as Minister of Foreign Affairs, and replaced by Rashid Merepov. In late October Shikhmuradov was dismissed as ambassador to the People's Republic of China. He fled to exile in Moscow from where, in early November, he issued a statement condemning President Niyazov's rule. Meanwhile, it was reported that a warrant for Shikhmuradov's arrest on charges of the misappropriation of state property had been issued by the Prosecutor-General, Gurbanbibi Atajanova, along with a request for his extradition from Russia. Although Shikhmuradov denied the charges, Turkmenistani officials claimed that his actions were an attempt to avoid prosecution; it was also widely speculated that Shikhmuradov intended to replace Niyazov by means of a *coup d'état*, possibly with foreign support. In January 2002 he established the People's Democratic Movement of Turkmenistan, with the aim of deposing Niyazov. In early February Nurmukhammed Khanamov resigned as ambassador to Turkey in order to join the opposition movement. In mid-February a former Deputy Prime Minister, Khudayberdy Orazov, announced his support for the opposition-in-exile. The Turkmenistani authorities subsequently issued a request for the extradition of Khanamov and accused Orazov of embezzling state funds. By May there had been several further high-level defections to the opposition movement. Meanwhile, in March Niyazov dismissed a number of senior officials from the defence, intelligence and security services (including the Minister of Defence), whom he accused of plotting to remove him from power. In addition, the State Border Service was placed under the direct control of the President. A new Minister of Internal Affairs was appointed in May, and in the same month Seitbay Gandimov was dismissed as Deputy Prime Minister and Chairman of the Central Bank, following allegations of links to Orazov. A further cabinet reshuffle followed in August. Government changes in September included the appointment of three new ministers and the creation of a Ministry of National Security, under Batyr Busakov, to replace the Committee for National Security. In late September the recently appointed Chairman of the Central Bank was dismissed, following the theft from the Bank of US $41.5m. In the same month Niyazov announced the creation of so-called 'labour armies', comprising 20,000 men under the age of 35, which were to be drafted to work without remuneration on public projects; the term of service was to be two years, irrespective of previous army service. Further government changes took place in mid-November, and Ovezgeldy Atayev was elected Chairman of the Majlis.

On 25 November 2002 it was widely reported that an assassination attempt had been made against the presidential motorcade, as it travelled through Aşgabat. An emergency cabinet meeting was held, and Niyazov publicly accused former officials Shikhmuradov and Khanamov, among others, of an attempted coup. An official announcement the following day reported the arrest of 16 suspects, although international human rights organizations reported hundreds of detentions in subsequent days. Also on 25 November Shikhmuradov, who had clandestinely returned to Turkmenistan, was arrested in Aşgabat. Following a televised confession, a one-day trial at the Supreme Court on 30 December found Shikhmuradov guilty of the attempt on Niyazov's life, and he was sentenced to 25 years' imprisonment (subsequently increased to a life sentence by the Majlis). Orazov and Khanamov were also convicted *in absentia*, and former Minister of Foreign Affairs Batyr Berdiyev was detained and sentenced in early 2003 to 25 years' imprisonment for his alleged involvement in the assassination attempt; the opposition-in-exile subsequently indicated that Berdiyev may have died. Meanwhile, opposition leader Murad Esenov, in exile in Sweden, claimed that the assassination attempt had been staged as a pretext for the arrest of Shikhmuradov and other members of the opposition, and the OSCE, concerned at the circumstances surrounding Shikhmuradov's trial and confession, sent a fact-finding mission to Aşgabat. In late December the Uzbek ambassador to Turkmenistan (whose embassy had been searched, in violation of the UN's Vienna Convention on Diplomatic Relations) was expelled from the country, having been accused of harbouring Shikhmuradov immediately after the attack (see below). In June 2003 Orazov reportedly stated that Shikhmuradov and his opposition allies had intended to stage a *coup d'état*, but that they had no intention of killing Niyazov.

In early January 2003 the International Crisis Group, based in Brussels, Belgium, warned of persistent human rights abuses in Turkmenistan and claimed that the country had become a transit route for drugs-trafficking and a refuge for members of the deposed Taliban regime fleeing neighbouring Afghanistan. Niyazov issued decrees in February that temporarily reinstated the requirement for exit visas (which had been abolished in December 2001), and imposed severe restrictions on the exchange of Turkmenistani currency. (The requirement for exit visas was abolished again in March 2004.) The import of foreign periodicals was prohibited, and more severe restrictions were imposed on journalists. Meanwhile, on 6 April 2003 elections to the Khalk Maslakhaty and to district and village councils took place, with the participation of some 89.3% of the electorate. The OSCE, which had accused the authorities of widespread human rights abuses in a report issued in March, questioned the legitimacy of the electoral process.

On 15 August 2003 amendments to the Constitution elevated the Khalk Maslakhaty, which was henceforth to comprise 2,507 members, to the status of a 'permanently functioning supreme representative body of popular authority', and required it to remain in continuous session. The Khalk Maslakhaty was also accorded a number of legislative powers, which enabled it to pass constitutional laws, thus effectively displacing the Majlis as the country's leading legislative body. Other changes to the Constitution forbade Turkmenistani citizens from holding dual nationality, superseding an agreement on dual nationality reached with Russia in December 1993 (see below).

Government changes in September 2003 included the appointment of Maj.-Gen. Agageldy Mamatgeldiyev as Minister of Defence. As part of further restructuring in November, two new Deputy Prime Ministers and a new Minister of National Security were appointed. Also in November a new law was passed restricting the activities of religious groups by criminalizing any confession not registered with the Ministry of Justice (at that time the only state-registered faiths were Sunni Islam and Russian Orthodox Christianity). The formation of political parties on religious grounds was also prohibited. In the same month a new law came into force, which severely restricted the activities of NGOs, imposing fines, prison sentences and periods of 'corrective labour' for those convicted under the new guide-lines. In late November the UN General Assembly adopted a resolution (which was, notably, supported by Russia), expressing grave concerns over human rights violations in Turkmenistan. At the end of the month Niyazov pardoned more than 7,000 prisoners.

Meanwhile, in late September 2003 opposition leaders meeting in Prague, Czech Republic, announced the formation of the Union of Democratic Forces of Turkmenistan (UDFT), comprising the United Democratic Opposition of Turkmenistan (ODOT) of Abdy Kuliyev, the Fatherland (Vatan) movement (based in Sweden), the Revival Social Political Movement and Nurmukhammed Khanamov's Republican Party of Turkmenistan. A further meeting of senior UDFT members took place in late November in Vienna, Austria.

In December 2003 President Niyazov reorganized the state broadcasting organizations. Further government changes were made in January 2004, including the appointment of a new Minister of Petroleum, Natural Gas and Mineral Resources. In February Niyazov replaced 15,000 medical workers with army conscripts, in an attempt to reduce government expenditure on health care. Registration requirements for religious communities were made more flexible by a presidential decree issued in March, although communities remained subject to strict control and supervision. In late April the Minister of the Economy and Finance, the Minister of Education and the heads of two state-controlled banks were dismissed. In mid-May Niyazov signed a decree prohibiting the use of child labour in the cotton industry. A further presidential decree, issued in early June, invalidated all higher-education degrees received abroad; all teachers with such degrees were to be dismissed. Niyazov implemented further government changes in mid-July, dismissing the Minister of Trade and Foreign Economic Relations, Charymammed Gayibov, who was replaced by Gurbangeldi Melekeyev. Another significant government change occurred in mid-August, with the appointment of Geldimukhammet Ashirkulov as Minister of Internal Affairs. (In early December Ashirkulov was, in turn, replaced by Akmamed Rahmanov.) Meanwhile, in October Niyazov removed Enebai Atayeva as Deputy Prime Minister and Governor of the cotton-producing Ahal Velayat (Region). This dismissal reportedly reflected dissatisfaction with the nationwide cotton harvest; the regional deputy governor and four heads of cotton-producing associations were also replaced. In early November President Niyazov passed what was apparently Turkmenistan's first law preventing the illegal use and trafficking of drugs. In the same month the UN General Assembly adopted a second resolution criticizing human rights violations in Turkmenistan; Russia abstained from voting, having voted in support of the November 2003 resolution (see above), while Uzbekistan voted against the resolution, despite its explicit condemnation of discrimination by the Government of Turkmenistan against ethnic Russians, Uzbeks and other minorities.

In October 2004 the Khalk Maslakhaty declined a request, reportedly submitted by Niyazov, that a presidential election (which the incumbent President would not contest) be permitted to take place in 2008 or 2009. Elections to the Majlis were conducted on 19 December 2004. According to official reports, 76.9% of the registered electorate participated in the poll. In the event, the DPT was the only party represented and, despite the assertion of Turkmenistan's Central electoral commission that the elections were conducted on a wholly democratic basis, in accordance with the Constitution and with international norms, no international observers had been invited to monitor the poll. (A second round of voting took place on 9 January 2005 in seven districts, where candidates had failed to obtain the required 50% plus one of the votes cast.) In April 2005 Niyazov declared that a multi-candidate presidential election would be conducted in 2009, following elections for district governors in 2006, regional governors in 2007 and parliamentary deputies in 2008. However, in October 2005 President Niyazov was the only member of the Khalk Maslakhaty to vote in favour of retaining on the Council's agenda a discussion of his proposal to hold a presidential election in 2009.

Meanwhile, in February 2005 Niyazov announced plans to close all hospitals outside Aşgabat, stating that the provision of hospitals outside the capital was unnecessary, particularly given the shortage of doctors. Niyazov also ordered the closure of rural libraries, asserting that the rural Turkmen population was largely illiterate and therefore made limited use of the existing facilities. The President imposed further restrictions in April, prohibiting the import and circulation of all foreign print media, including those produced in neighbouring countries, and refusing to renew the licences of international shipping firms and express couriers, asserting that their services were more costly and less reliable than the state's postal service. In June a report published by the London School of Hygiene and Tropical Medicine (United Kingdom) expressed concern at the 'systematic dismantling' of Turkmenistan's health-care system, asserting that people were dying because they could not afford health-care fees; the report urged the international community to apply pressure on Turkmenistan to improve services.

Throughout 2005 and in the first months of 2006 President Niyazov frequently replaced state officials; many of those dismissed were accused of corruption or other abuses of office, and sentenced to long custodial terms. Notably, in late May 2005 the Deputy Prime Minister for the Fuel and Energy Sector, Yolly Gurbanmuradov, was dismissed, having been accused of 'serious shortcomings' and of abusing his position for personal gain while serving as head of the State Bank for Foreign Economic Activities in 1993–2001. Despite conflicting reports that Gurbanmuradov had either hanged himself in prison or been killed during interrogation, in late July 2005 it was reported that he had been sentenced to 25 years' imprisonment. Meanwhile, at the end of May Niyazov also removed Shekersoltan Mukhammedova from the chairmanship of the Central Bank, accusing her of corruption. She was replaced by Jumaniyaz Annaorazov, hitherto the Minister of the Economy and Finance. Niyazov further reorganized the energy sector in August and September of that year. In mid-April 2006 Niyazov appointed Muhammatyuly Ogshukov, previously First Deputy Prosecutor-General, to replace Gurbanbibi Atajanova as Prosecutor-General. Although Niyazov initially stated that Atajanova was to retire (having occupied the post since 1997), later in the month Atajanova admitted to charges made by Niyazov that she had taken bribes and stolen state property while serving as Prosecutor-General. In early May Niyazov declared invalid the presidential decree relieving her of her post in connection with her retirement, instead decreeing that she was relieved of her duties for 'shameful' deeds and damaging the title of her office.

One of the fundamental principles of Turkmenistan's foreign policy is that of 'permanent neutrality', a concept that is enshrined in the Constitution. The republic's neutral status was recognized by the UN General Assembly in December 1995, two months after Turkmenistan became the first of the former Soviet republics to join the Non-aligned Movement (see p. 397). The policy of neutrality has led Turkmenistan to adopt a somewhat equivocal attitude towards its membership of the CIS. President Niyazov has consistently expressed opposition to centralized structures within the Commonwealth, preferring to regard it as a 'consultative body'. Moreover, the republic has refused to sign a number of CIS agreements on closer political, military and economic integration, and at the beginning of September 2005 Niyazov confirmed that Turkmenistan intended to withdraw from the CIS, remaining an associate member.

None the less, Turkmenistan's most important political ally and economic partner remains Russia, the leading CIS state. In December 1993 Turkmenistan became the first of the former Soviet republics to sign an agreement on dual citizenship with Russia; it was hoped that this would further strengthen bilateral relations, while helping to stem the exodus of ethnic Russians from the republic. However, at a meeting in Moscow in April 2003, Niyazov and President Vladimir Putin of Russia agreed to rescind the agreement (which was believed to have facilitated the ability of Niyazov's opponents to operate from exile). Later in April Niyazov decreed that the estimated 95,000 dual passport holders in Turkmenistan should renounce either their Russian or Turkmenistani citizenship within two months, prompting protests from the Russian Ministry of Foreign Affairs, which insisted that the new agreement was not meant to apply retroactively and, moreover, had not yet been ratified by Russia. In June the Russian Gosudarstvennaya Duma (State Duma) adopted a resolution condemning Niyazov's unilateral revocation of dual citizenship, and the Russian Government subsequently deemed Turkmenistan unsafe for its citizens. Nevertheless, in August the Khalk Maslakhaty passed constitutional amendments forbidding Turkmenistani citizens from holding dual citizenship, and placing any dual citizens remaining in the country in breach of the law. (The 1995 treaty on Turkmen-Russian dual citizenship expired *de jure* in May 2005.)

Meanwhile, Turkmenistan's natural gas exports were a persistent cause of friction between the two countries. Transport of natural gas from Turkmenistan was dependent on the use of the former Soviet pipeline system, which remained largely under Russian control. In 1993 Turkmenistan's access to European markets via this system was effectively curbed by Russia's decision to direct Turkmenistani gas exports to Ukraine and Transcaucasia. However, as a result of the recipient countries' delay in paying for their gas imports, Turkmenistan suspended all deliveries in 1993–95, which in turn was severely detrimental to the Turkmenistani economy. Although gas exports to Ukraine and Transcaucasia were resumed in 1996, in March 1997 Niyazov announced the dissolution of the Turkmenistani-Russian company, Türkmenrosgaz—which held a monopoly on the sale and export of Turkmenistani gas—because the company was in severe debt. In response, the Russian Government denied Turkmenistan access to the regional pipeline system. Although Ukraine began to repay its outstanding debt to Turkmenistan, delivery was hampered by Russia's refusal to lower its transport tariffs to the level demanded by Turkmenistan. However, in December 1998 Turkmenistan reached an agreement with Russia regarding the transport of natural gas, and deliveries to Ukraine were resumed in January 1999, only to be suspended again in May, owing to further payment problems. In May 2000 the Turkmenistani authorities agreed to increase its deliveries of natural gas to Russia annually for the following three to four years. At the beginning of 2001 Turkmenistan halted its deliveries to Russia, owing to the failure of the two sides to agree on a mutually acceptable price; agreement was finally reached in February with Itera, an affiliate of the Russian gas monopoly, Gazprom. Turkmenistan also signed an agreement with Itera and a Russian energy company, Zarubezhneft, for the development of Turkmenistan's onshore and offshore hydrocarbons deposits.

Meanwhile, Turkmenistan resumed natural gas deliveries to Ukraine in November 2000, and in May 2001 Turkmenistan agreed to supply Ukraine with 250,000m. cu m of natural gas in 2002–06. In April 2003 Turkmenistan agreed to supply Russia with more than 2,000,000m. cu m of natural gas over 25 years; a similar agreement was reached with Ukraine in late 2003. However, in early January 2005 Turkmenistan stopped supplying Russia with natural gas, in an attempt to force Gazprom to agree to an increase in the price of gas sold by Turkmenistan. Russia refused to negotiate gas prices until 2007, under the terms of the bilateral agreement signed in 2003, and Turkmenistan resumed gas supplies to Russia after 10 days. However, Turkmenistan did manage to persuade Ukraine to accept an increase in the price of gas from US $44 per 1,000 cu m to $58, after Niyazov briefly suspended gas supplies to that country. The impasse between Russia and Turkmenistan was resolved in April 2005, when Gazprom agreed to make all payments for gas from Turkmenistan in cash, abandoning the previous partial barter system. In late 2005 Turkmenistan attempted to secure a new agreement on gas prices, and at the end of the year Gazprom agreed to purchase 30,000m. cu m of natural gas in 2006 at $65 per 1,000 cu m. Meanwhile, after Ukraine increased the price of the goods it used as barter in part-exchange for Turkmenistani gas, in June Niyazov threatened to halt supplies to the country. The two states subsequently signed a new, 18-month contract, which required Ukraine to pay for its gas in cash only. Ukraine was to purchase 59,500m. cu m of gas at $44 per 1,000 cu m (lower than the rate agreed to in January 2005), and to repay its arrears for past exports in commodities, without increasing their prices. In March 2006 Ukraine confirmed that it owed Turkmenistan $169.6m. ($46.8m. in cash, and $122.8m. in commodities) for gas supplied in 2003–05, and the two countries agreed a schedule of repayment. However, it was unclear how Turkmenistan would continue to export gas to Ukraine beyond 2006, without a significant increase in pipeline and production capacity. Niyazov increased the price of Turkmenistani gas to $65 per 1,000 cu m for 2006 for all other countries, and in February 2006 he announced plans to increase the price further, to $100 per 1,000 cu m, later in the year.

Of the remaining CIS member states, Turkmenistan has concentrated on developing closer relations with the neighbouring Central Asian republics of Kazakhstan, Kyrgyzstan, Tajikistan and Uzbekistan. However, unlike Kazakhstan, Kyrgyzstan and Uzbekistan, Turkmenistan remained neutral regarding the civil war in Tajikistan (q.v.), and it did not contribute troops to the joint CIS peace-keeping forces in the region. None the less, Aşgabat did become one of the venues for the Tajikistani peace negotiations. In July 2001 Turkmenistan and Kazakhstan signed a treaty demarcating their shared border. In September 2000 Turkmenistan and Uzbekistan had signed a treaty defining their 1,867 km border and, under President Niyazov's orders, a 1,700-km fence was installed along the border in 2001 (although increased control of the border was reported to have led to local tensions). Relations with Uzbekistan deteriorated sharply in December 2002, following the alleged coup attempt of 25 November (see above). In mid-December the Uzbek embassy in Aşgabat was searched for evidence, and Uzbekistan's ambassador to Turkmenistan was subsequently declared *persona non grata*, on the grounds that he supported the alleged instigator of the coup, Boris Shikhmuradov. The Uzbekistani authorities reacted with hostility, and troops from both countries were deployed along their common border. Stricter border controls were subsequently implemented. In mid-November 2004 President Niyazov and President Islam Karimov of Uzbekistan met for their first presidential summit in more than four years in Buxoro, Uzbekistan, where they signed three bilateral agreements, pledging friendship between the two countries, mutual trust, and co-operation; simplifying regulations concerning cross-border travel for residents of border zones (where cross-border smuggling and related shooting incidents had become increasingly prevalent); and agreeing on a framework for sharing regional water resources. The Presidents declared that all bilateral issues had been resolved, and in early December they celebrated the demarcation of the border between the two countries. A new Uzbekistani ambassador to Turkmenistan was appointed in January 2005.

The legal status of the Caspian Sea, and the ownership of the extensive deposits of petroleum and natural gas beneath it, provoked controversy from the mid-1990s between Turkmenistan and the other littoral states (Azerbaijan, Russia, Kazakhstan and Iran). Although the Sea had been divided into national economic zones during the Soviet period, after 1992 some states demanded a new demarcation. At a special conference on the Sea's status, held in Aşgabat in November 1996, the Ministers of Foreign Affairs of all five countries established a working group to formulate a new convention. Nevertheless, in early 1997 Turkmenistan and Azerbaijan were engaged in a dispute over the status of two Caspian oilfields (the Azeri and Chirag fields—known as the Khazar and Kaverochkin fields to the Turkmen), which were being developed by Azerbaijan and a consortium of international companies. The situation deteriorated in July 1997, when Azerbaijan announced its intention to develop, in conjunction with a consortium of Russian companies, a third oilfield, which both countries laid claim to, known as Kyapaz to the Azeris and as Serdar to the Turkmen. Although Russia subsequently withdrew from the project, Azerbaijan refused to abandon its claim to the field. Apparently in response, in September Turkmenistan launched its first international tender for petroleum and gas exploration in the Caspian Sea, and announced that it expected Azerbaijan to compensate it for developing the Azeri and Chirag fields. The commercial exploitation of the latter field began in November. Although Kazakhstan and Russia signed an agreement in October 2000 defining the legal status of the Caspian Sea, the remaining littoral states (Azerbaijan, Iran and Turkmenistan) made limited progress. In November 2003 representatives of the five littoral states, meeting in Tehran, Iran, signed a UN-sponsored framework Convention for the Protection of the Marine Environment of the Caspian Sea, which sought to alleviate environmental damage in the Caspian Sea region. In mid-January 2005 President Niyazov approved a proposal from a Canadian company, Buried Hill Energy and Petroleum, to develop the Serdar oilfield, prompting protests from Azerbaijan. In November Niyazov agreed that a production-sharing agreement would be signed with Buried Hill Energy and Petroleum for the development of the Turkmenistani sector of the Caspian Sea.

Iran plays the most important role in Turkmenistan's foreign relations outside the CIS. In 1992 a number of agreements on closer political, economic and cultural integration were signed, including an accord to construct a railway line between Iran and

Turkmenistan. The line, which linked the Turkmenistani city of Tejen with the northern Iranian city of Mashad, was opened in May 1996, thus affording Turkmenistan access both to the Persian (Arabian) Gulf and to Istanbul, Turkey. Turkmenistan and Iran also signed an agreement on the construction of a 140-km gas pipeline between the Korpeje natural gas deposit in south-western Turkmenistan and the city of Kord Kuy in northern Iran. The pipeline was to be the first segment on a route, which, it was envisaged, would eventually transport Turkmenistani gas via Iran to Turkey and thence to western Europe. The inauguration of the pipeline in December 1997 opened the first alternative export route for Turkmenistan's natural gas, and thus promised greater economic independence for the republic from Russia. In April 2006 Iran reached agreement with Turkmenistan on gas imports, which were expected to total some 6,000m. cu m in 2006 and some 8,000m. cu m in 2007.

In March 2003 work on a project, conceived in 1999, to construct an underwater trans-Caspian gas export pipeline to Turkey, via Azerbaijan and Georgia, was suspended indefinitely, owing to disagreement between Turkmenistan and Azerbaijan over the division of the pipeline's anticipated throughput. Meanwhile, in late April 2002 President Niyazov requested UN support for the construction of a proposed 1,680-km gas pipeline from Turkmenistan to Fazilka, a village on the Pakistan–India border, via Afghanistan, led by the US company Unocal. (The project had been suspended in 1998, owing to conflict in Afghanistan, but was resurrected following the removal of the Taliban regime in Afghanistan in late 2001.) The Afghan Interim Administration supported the proposal, and at the end of May the leaders of Turkmenistan, Afghanistan and Pakistan signed a memorandum of understanding on a feasibility study for the project. In December 2002 an agreement was signed on the construction of the pipeline, which was expected to be able to carry some 708,000m. cu m of gas per year. Construction was expected to begin in late 2006. In February 2006 Pakistan and Turkmenistan signed a memorandum of understanding, according to which Turkmenistan agreed to supply Pakistan with some 90.6m. cu m of gas per day for 30 years. Also in February, India, which had expressed an interest in participating in the project, was asked to announce its decision on the matter by mid-May. If the Indian Government decided to participate, a 640-km extension was to be added to the pipeline, at a cost of some $600m.

President Niyazov confirmed his country's neutrality by developing equal relations with the Taliban and their opposition, the United National Islamic Front for the Salvation of Afghanistan, commonly known as the United Front, in the late 1990s. Turkmenistan was central in organizing peace negotiations between the Taliban and United Front in both July 1999 and December 2000. Niyazov maintained the country's neutrality following the large-scale suicide attacks in the USA in September 2001, which were attributed to the Saudi Arabian-born leader of the Islamist militant al-Qa'ida (Base) organization, Osama bin Laden, who had developed a close association with the Taliban. However, Niyazov expressed general support for attempts to form a US-led international coalition to combat global terrorism, although he declared that its formation should be co-ordinated by the UN, rather than the USA. None the less, the President gave his consent to the use of Turkmenistan's ground and air transport 'corridors' for the delivery of humanitarian aid to Afghanistan during airstrikes against al-Qa'ida and its Taliban hosts; Niyazov refused US troops access to Turkmenistan's military bases, however, reaffirming the country's policy of non-interference. In November 2003 Turkmenistan and Russia agreed to supply Afghanistan with natural gas for a period of one year.

In April 2006 Turkmenistan and the People's Republic of China signed an agreement to construct a natural gas pipeline from Turkmenistan to China; details of the pipeline's construction, under consideration since 1997, were to be finalized by the end of the year. According to the agreement, China was to purchase 30,000m. cu m of Turkmenistani gas per year for 30 years from 2009.

Turkmenistan enjoys close relations with Turkey (which has been regarded as competing with Iran for political and economic influence in the region), not least owing to the Turkmens' ethnic and linguistic ties with the Turks. Turkmenistan is a member, with both Turkey and Iran (among others), of the Economic Co-operation Organization (ECO, see p. 223).

Government
Under the terms of the 1992 Constitution, the President of the Republic is directly elected, by universal adult suffrage, for five years, although in December 1993 the legislature voted to extend President Niyazov's mandate—due to expire in 1997—until 2002 (this was endorsed in a national referendum in January 1994). In December 1998 the Khalk Maslakhaty endorsed an amendment to the Constitution whereby Niyazov's mandate was extended indefinitely. The President is both Head of State and Head of Government (Prime Minister in the Council of Ministers), holding executive power in conjunction with the Council of Ministers (which is appointed by the President), and is concurrently Supreme Commander of the Armed Forces. The supreme legislative body is the Majlis (Assembly), the 50 members of which are directly elected for a term of five years. The deputies of the Majlis also sit on the Khalk Maslakhaty (People's Council), a supervisory organ, which includes 65 directly elected and 10 appointed representatives from all districts of Turkmenistan, the members of the Council of Ministers and other prominent figures, and is headed by the President of the Republic. In August 2003 a constitutional law and a constitutional amendment were passed elevating the Khalk Maslakhaty to the status of 'permanently functioning supreme representative body of popular authority', and requiring it to remain in continuous session. The constitutional changes ascribed to the Khalk Maslakhaty, which was, henceforth, to comprise 2,507 members, a number of legislative powers, including the passing of constitutional laws, thereby effectively displacing the Majlis as the country's leading legislative body. Turkmenistan is divided into five velayats (regions), which are subdivided into 50 etraps (districts).

Defence
In mid-1992 Turkmenistan began the establishment of national armed forces, based upon the former Soviet military units still stationed in the republic; under an agreement with Russia, these forces were initially under joint Turkmenistani and Russian command. Since 1993 Turkmenistan has co-operated with Russia and Kazakhstan in the operation of the Caspian Sea Flotilla, another former Soviet force, based, under Russian command, at Astrakhan, Russia. In May 1994 Turkmenistan became the first Central Asian republic of the former USSR to join the North Atlantic Treaty Organization's 'Partnership for Peace' (see p. 316) programme. However, one of the fundamental principles of Turkmenistan's foreign policy is that of 'permanent neutrality', which is enshrined in the Constitution. The republic's neutrality was recognized by the UN General Assembly in December 1995, two months after Turkmenistan became the first former Soviet republic to join the Non-aligned Movement (see p. 397). In August 2005 the armed forces numbered 26,000, comprising an army of 21,000, an air force of 4,300 and a navy (largely coastguard units) of 700. Military service lasts for 24 months. The budget for 2005 allocated 899,000m. manat (US $173m.) to defence.

Economic Affairs
In 2004, according to estimates by the World Bank, Turkmenistan's gross national income (GNI), measured at average 2002–04 prices, was US $6,615m., equivalent to $1,340 per head (or $6,910 per head on an international purchasing-power parity basis). During 1995–2004, it was estimated, the population increased at an average annual rate of 1.8%, while gross domestic product (GDP) per head increased, in real terms, by an average of 8.3% per year. Overall GDP increased, in real terms, at an average annual rate of 10.3% per year in 1995–2004. According to the Asian Development Bank (ADB, see p. 169), GDP increased by 21.0% in 2004 and by 10.0% in 2005.

Agriculture contributed an estimated 21.0% of GDP in 2003, according to the World Bank. The sector employed 48.2% of the employed labour force in that year, according to figures from the ADB. Although the Kara-Kum desert covers some 80% of the country's territory, widespread irrigation has enabled rapid agricultural development; however, over-intensive cultivation of the principal crop, cotton, together with massive irrigation projects, have led to serious ecological damage. In 1996 cotton contributed an estimated 11.5% of GDP, although the Government planned to reduce cotton production in favour of food production by 2010. Other important crops include grain, vegetables and fruit (in particular grapes and melons), although the country remains heavily dependent on imports of foodstuffs. Livestock husbandry (including the production of astrakhan and karakul wools) plays a central role in the sector, and silkworms are bred. According to the World Bank, agricultural production increased, in real terms, by an annual average of 5.8% in 1995–2003. Real agricultural GDP increased by 9.5% in 2002 and by 9.9% in 2003.

Industry (including mining, manufacturing, construction and power) contributed an estimated 44.6% of GDP in 2003, when 13.8% of the employed labour force were engaged in the sector. During 1995–2003, according to the World Bank, industrial GDP increased, in real terms, at an average annual rate of 10.1%. However, real industrial GDP increased by 13.2% in 2002 and by 16.2% in 2003.

Turkmenistan is richly endowed with mineral resources, in particular natural gas and petroleum (recoverable reserves of which were estimated at some 2,900,000m. cu m and 100m. metric tons, respectively, at the end of 2004). In 2004 Turkmenistan produced approximately 54,600m. cu m of gas, and production of petroleum averaged 202,000 barrels per day. Plans to improve the refinery at Seidi were announced in early 2004. In addition, Turkmenistan has large deposits of iodine, bromine, sodium sulphate, clay, gypsum and different types of salt.

The manufacturing sector contributed 20.7% of GDP in 2003. The principal branches of manufacturing are the processing of mineral resources (predominantly petroleum and natural gas) and textiles (mainly cotton products). Petroleum is refined at three refineries, at Türkmenbaşi, Seidi and Türkmenabat. According to the World Bank, manufacturing GDP increased by 24.0% in 1998–2003. Sectoral growth was estimated at 25.6% in 2002 and 34.7% in 2003.

In 2002 the country's electricity was produced by thermal power stations (fuelled by domestically produced natural gas). In 2003 an estimated 10,800m. kWh of electricity was produced; of electricity produced in 1994, some 20% was reported to have been exported, while a proportion of the remainder was distributed free of charge to domestic users. (Some charges for domestic electricity use were introduced in 1996; however, the 2006 budget provided for free distribution.) In 2003 mineral fuels accounted for just 0.7% of the value of merchandise imports, according to ADB estimates.

In 2003 the services sector provided an estimated 34.4% of GDP, and employed some 38.0% of the working population. Trade and catering services form the major part of the sector, providing some 6% of employment in 1998. According to the World Bank, services GDP increased, in real terms, at an average annual rate of 11.7% in 1995–2003. Real services GDP increased by 34.1% in 2002 and by 22.2% in 2003.

According to the ADB, in 2005 Turkmenistan recorded a visible trade surplus of US $1,301m. In 2004 the ADB estimated that there was a surplus of $82m. on the current account of the balance of payments. In 2004 the principal source of imports (accounting for 14.0% of the total) was Russia; other major suppliers were Ukraine (13.8%), the USA (11.1%), the United Arab Emirates (8.1%), Turkey (8.0%) and Germany (6.8%). The principal market for exports (49.8%) was Ukraine; other major purchasers were Iran (17.2%) and Italy (5.3%). In 2003 the principal exports were basic manufactures. The principal imports in that year were machinery and transport equipment, basic manufactures, chemicals, miscellaneous manufactured articles, and food and live animals.

In 2003 the budgetary deficit was estimated at 496,000m. manats (equivalent to some 0.8% of GDP). At the end of 1999 Turkmenistan's total external debt was US $2,015m., of which $1,678m. was long-term public debt. In that year the cost of debt-servicing was equivalent to 31.1% of the value of exports of goods and services. According to the ADB, the country's external debt totalled $1,273m. in 2004. Consumer prices increased by an annual average of 1,150% in 1993 and by 1,748% in 1994, but the inflation rate declined to 1,005% in 1995, to 992% in 1996 and to an estimated 84% in 1997. Average prices rose by 16.8% in 1998 and by 24.2% in 1999. The inflation rate declined again in 2000, to an annual average of 7.4%, and in 2001, to 4.0%. According to estimates by the European Bank for Reconstruction and Development (EBRD, see p. 224), deflation of 3.5% in 2002 and 1.9% in 2003 was recorded. In 2003 some 57,000 people were registered as unemployed (about 2.5% of the labour force); however, unofficial sources estimated the rate to be considerably higher.

Turkmenistan became a member of the IMF and the World Bank in 1992. It also joined the EBRD as a 'Country of Operations' and, with five other former Soviet republics, the Economic Co-operation Organization (ECO, see p. 223). In 1994 Turkmenistan became a member of the Islamic Development Bank (IDB, see p. 303), and it joined the ADB in 2000.

The disruptions in inter-republican trade that followed the dissolution of the USSR in December 1991 damaged Turkmenistan's industrial sector, which relied heavily on imported finished and intermediate goods. Moreover, the failure, or delay, of many of Turkmenistan's CIS trading partners to pay for imports of natural gas (the mainstay of the republic's economy) resulted in huge arrears, and Turkmenistan was forced to suspend deliveries several times throughout the 1990s and early 2000s, with adverse consequences for the economy. The opening of a new gas pipeline to Iran in late 1997 did, however, contribute to some revival in the economically crucial gas sector. In 2003 Turkmenistan concluded major agreements with both Russia and Ukraine to supply them with natural gas for 25 years. In 2005–06 Turkmenistan renegotiated arrangements for the supply of natural gas to these countries (see Recent History). The rate of inflation decreased significantly and GDP grew strongly from 2000, largely owing to the export of natural gas, petroleum and cotton, and, in particular, to an increase in international prices of natural gas, and a sustained increase in output (although a small decline in production, of 0.9%, was recorded in 2004). However, there were concerns that Turkmenistan's economy was over-dependent on the hydrocarbons sector. From the mid-1990s the Government sought to increase the value of the country's traditional exports, based on natural resources and crops, and the production of cotton textiles and yarn for export increased markedly during the second half of that decade. However, an inefficient tax system and a poorly regulated banking sector, largely under state control, continued to hinder economic stability, and estimates of the private sector's contribution to GDP in 2003 varied between 20% and 30%, reflecting the lack of structural reform or market liberalization. Moreover, despite Turkmenistan's membership of the IMF and the World Bank, the Government has had only minimal contact with these and other international agencies, while the political environment and the country's international isolation have deterred foreign investment. Although growth of 21.0% was recorded in 2004, it slowed to some 10.0% in 2005 and was expected to decline to 6.5% in 2006. A balanced budget of some $15,600m. was approved for 2006, with projected expenditure allowing for the provision of free gas, electricity, water and salt supplies.

Education

A state-funded education system was introduced under Soviet rule. Although some schools provided instruction in Russian, Uzbek and Kazakh, President Niyazov pledged to eradicate teaching in languages other than Turkmen. Primary and secondary education lasts for nine years. In 1990 the total enrolment at higher schools was equivalent to 21.8% of the relevant age-group. The 1999 budget allocated 26.9% of total expenditure (1,048,700m. manats) to education. Free education at Turkmenistan's 16 universities was apparently abolished in 2003, while it was reported that the number of places for students in educational establishments had been sharply reduced since the mid-1990s. In 2004 a presidential decree invalidating all higher-education degrees received abroad came into effect; all teachers with such degrees were to be dismissed.

Public Holidays

2006: 1 January (New Year's Day), 10 January (Memorial Day; Kurban Bairam—Id al-Adha, Feast of the Sacrifice*†), 19 February (National Flag Day; President Niyazov's Birthday), 8 March (International Women's Day), 21 March (Novrus Bairam, Turkmen New Year), 8–9 May (Victory Day), 18 May (Revival and Unity Day), 6 October (Remembrance Day), 24 October* (Oraza Bairam—Id al-Fitr, end of Ramadan), 27–28 October (Independence Day), 12 December (Turkmenistan Neutrality Day), 31 December*† (Kurban Bairam—Id al-Adha, Feast of the Sacrifice).

2007: 1 January (New Year's Day), 12 January (Memorial Day), 19 February (National Flag Day; President Niyazov's Birthday), 8 March (International Women's Day), 21 March (Novrus Bairam, Turkmen New Year), 8–9 May (Victory Day), 18 May (Revival and Unity Day), 6 October (Remembrance Day), 13 October* (Oraza Bairam—Id al-Fitr, end of Ramadan), 27–28 October (Independence Day), 12 December (Turkmenistan Neutrality Day), 20 December* (Kurban Bairam—Id al-Adha, Feast of the Sacrifice).

* These holidays are dependent on the Islamic calendar and may vary by one or two days from the dates given.

† This festival occurs twice (in the Islamic years AH 1426 and 1427) within the same Gregorian year.

Weights and Measures

The metric system is in force.

TURKMENISTAN

Statistical Survey

Principal sources (unless otherwise stated): IMF, *Turkmenistan, Economic Review, Turkmenistan—Recent Economic Developments* (December 1999); World Bank, *Statistical Handbook: States of the Former USSR*.

Area and Population

AREA, POPULATION AND DENSITY

Area (sq km)	488,100*
Population (census results)	
12 January 1989	3,533,925
10 January 1995	
Males	2,225,331
Females	2,257,920
Total	4,483,251
Population (UN estimates at mid-year)†	
2002	4,630,000
2003	4,698,000
2004	4,766,000
Density (per sq km) at mid-2004	9.8

* 188,456 sq miles.
† Source: UN, *World Population Prospects: The 2004 Revision*.

Population (official estimate): 6,525,800 at 1 December 2004 (Source: National Institute of State Statistics and Information).

POPULATION BY ETHNIC GROUP
(official estimates at 1 January 1993)

	Number	%
Turkmen	3,118,000	73.3
Russian	419,000	9.8
Uzbek	382,000	9.0
Kazakh	87,000	2.0
Tatar	39,000	0.9
Ukrainian	34,000	0.8
Azeri	34,000	0.8
Armenian	32,000	0.8
Belarusian	9,000	0.2
Others	100,000	2.4
Total	**4,254,000**	**100.0**

Ethnic groups (percentage of total, at census of 1995): Turkmen 77.0; Uzbek 9.2; Russian 6.7; Kazakh 2.0; Other 5.1 (Source: US Embassy in Turkmenistan).

PRINCIPAL TOWNS
(estimated population at 1 January 1999)

Aşgabat (capital)	605,000	Türkmenbaşi‡	70,000
Türkmenabat*	203,000	Bayramaly	60,000
Daşoguz	165,000	Tejen	54,000
Mari	123,000	Serdar§	51,000
Balkanabat†	119,000		

* Formerly Charjew (Chardzhou).
† Formerly Nebit-Dag.
‡ Formerly Krasnovodsk.
§ Formerly Gyzylarbat (Kizyl-Arvat).

1 July 2002 (official estimate): Aşgabat 743,000.

Mid-2003 (UN estimate, incl. suburbs): Aşgabat 573,924 (source: UN, *World Urbanization Prospects: The 2003 Revision*).

BIRTHS, MARRIAGES AND DEATHS

	Registered live births		Registered marriages		Registered deaths	
	Number	Rate (per 1,000)	Number	Rate (per 1,000)	Number	Rate (per 1,000)
1987	126,787	37.2	31,484	9.2	26,802	7.9
1988	125,887	36.0	33,008	9.4	27,317	7.8
1989	124,992	34.9	34,890	9.8	27,609	7.7

Registered deaths: 25,755 (death rate 7.0 per 1,000) in 1990; 27,403 (7.3 per 1,000) in 1991; 27,509 (6.8 per 1,000) in 1992; 31,171 (7.2 per 1,000) in 1993; 32,067 (7.3 per 1,000) in 1994.

1998 (provisional): Live births 98,461 (birth rate 20.3 per 1,000); Marriages 26,361 (marriage rate 5.4 per 1,000); Deaths 29,628 (death rate 6.1 per 1,000).

Source: UN, *Demographic Yearbook*.

Births (UN estimates, annual averages): Birth rate (per 1,000): 35.7 in 1985–90; 32.5 in 1990–95; 24.5 in 1995–2000 (Source: UN, *World Population Prospects: The 2004 Revision*).

Deaths (UN estimates, annual averages): Death rate (per 1,000): 8.2 in 1985–90; 8.4 in 1990–95; 8.0 in 1995–2000 (Source: UN, *World Population Prospects: The 2004 Revision*).

2002: Birth rate 22.2 per 1,000; death rate 6.4 per 1,000 (Source: UN, *Statistical Yearbook for Asia and the Pacific*).

Expectation of life (WHO estimates, years at birth): 60 (males 56; females 65) in 2003 (Source: WHO, *World Health Report*).

EMPLOYMENT
('000 persons at 31 December)

	1996	1997	1998*
Agriculture	769.8	778.8	890.5
Forestry	2.5	2.9	1.9
Industry†	172.0	188.1	226.8
Construction	136.2	122.8	108.2
Trade and catering	91.8	101.2	115.8
Transport and communications	77.7	77.9	90.7
Information-computing services	1.3	1.0	1.2
Housing and municipal services	50.2	46.9	48.3
Health care and social security	97.4	100.4	89.2
Education, culture and arts	183.8	185.9	190.5
Science, research and development	9.2	6.9	5.2
General administration	24.7	25.3	28.8
Finance and insurance	8.7	9.6	12.6
Other activities	41.5	28.3	29.0
Total	**1,666.8**	**1,675.9**	**1,838.7**

* Provisional.
† Comprising manufacturing (except printing and publishing), mining and quarrying, electricity, gas, water, logging and fishing.

2003 ('000 persons at 31 December, estimates): Employed 2,065 (Agriculture 995, Industry 285, Other 785); Unemployed 57; Total labour force (incl. those not registered) 2,320 (Source: Asian Development Bank, *Key Indicators of Developing Asian and Pacific Countries*).

TURKMENISTAN

Health and Welfare

KEY INDICATORS

Total fertility rate (children per woman, 2003)	2.7
Under-5 mortality rate (per 1,000 live births, 2004)	103
HIV/AIDS (% of persons aged 15–49, 2003)	<0.1
Physicians (per 1,000 head, 1997)	3.17
Hospital beds (per 1,000 head, 1997)	7.11
Health expenditure (2002): US $ per head (PPP)	182
Health expenditure (2002): % of GDP	4.3
Health expenditure (2002): public (% of total)	70.7
Access to water (% of persons, 2002)	71
Access to sanitation (% of persons, 2002)	62
Human Development Index (2003): ranking	97
Human Development Index (2003): value	0.738

For sources and definitions, see explanatory note on p. vi.

Agriculture

PRINCIPAL CROPS
('000 metric tons)

	2002	2003	2004
Wheat	2,326*	2,487*	2,600
Rice (paddy)	80	110	110
Barley	40*	51*	60
Potatoes	140	160	150†
Sugar beet†	220	255	230
Cottonseed*	300	420	445
Cabbages	45*	49*	50†
Tomatoes	225*	247*	250†
Dry onions	79*	87*	85†
Carrots	48*	53*	53†
Other vegetables	22*	57*	57†
Watermelons†	240	250	230
Grapes†	165	175	180
Apples	35*	40*	40†
Other fruits and berries†	56	59	58
Cotton (lint)*	148	205	218

* Unofficial figure(s).
† FAO estimate(s).
Source: FAO.

LIVESTOCK
('000 head at 1 January)

	2002	2003	2004
Horses*	17	16	16
Asses*	25	25	25
Camels*	40	40	40
Cattle	1,750*	1,900	2,000
Pigs	30*	30	30
Sheep	10,350*	12,570†	13,150†
Goats	650*	730†	750†
Chickens†	6,500	6,800	7,000
Turkeys*	200	200	200

* FAO estimate(s).
† Unofficial figure(s).
Source: FAO.

LIVESTOCK PRODUCTS
('000 metric tons)

	2002	2003	2004
Beef and veal	92†	101†	106
Mutton and lamb	83†	90†	95
Goat meat	6†	6†	7
Poultry meat	11†	12†	14
Other meat	1†	1†	2
Cows' milk	1,398	1,529	1,400
Cheese*	1.6	1.6	1.6
Butter	2.8	3.1	3.0
Hen eggs	28†	35†	35
Honey*	8	8	8
Raw silk (incl. waste)*	4.5	4.5	4.5
Wool: greasy*	21.0	20.0	20.0
Wool: scoured*	12.6	12.0	12.0
Cattle hides (fresh)*	9.6	10.5	11.0
Sheepskins (fresh)*	11	12	13

* FAO estimate(s).
† Unofficial figure(s).
Source: FAO.

Fishing

(metric tons, live weight)

	2001	2002	2003
Capture	12,749	12,812	14,543
Azov sea sprat	12,300	12,418	14,276
Aquaculture	43	38	24
Silver carp	42	37	23
Total catch	12,792	12,850	14,567

Source: FAO.

Mining

('000 metric tons, unless otherwise indicated)

	2002	2003	2004
Crude petroleum*	9,000	10,000	10,100
Natural gas (million cu metres)*	49,900	55,100	54,600
Bentonite†	50	50	50
Salt (unrefined)†	215	215	215
Gypsum (crude)†	100	100	100

* Source: BP, *Statistical Review of World Energy*.
† Estimates from US Geological Survey.

TURKMENISTAN

Industry

SELECTED PRODUCTS
('000 metric tons, unless otherwise indicated)

	2000	2001	2002
Cottonseed oil	48	45	26
Wheat flour	544	579	400
Woven cotton fabrics (million sq metres)	34	61	78
Woven silk fabrics ('000 sq metres)	216	115	283
Blankets	14	7	10
Knotted wool carpets and rugs ('000 sq metres)	1,040	1,434	1,475
Footwear, excl. rubber ('000 pairs)	478	444	253
Nitric acid (100%)	192	151	212
Ammonia (nitrogen content)	117	99	130
Nitrogenous fertilizers (a)*	89	72	103
Phosphate fertilizers (b)*†	11	11	17
Soap	3.0	2.5	1.6
Motor spirit (petrol)	1,132	1,283	n.a.
Gas-diesel (distillate fuel) oil	2,247	2,547	n.a.
Residual fuel oils	2,365	2,681	n.a.
Clay building bricks (million)	309	269	279
Quicklime	17	17	15
Cement	420	448	486
Electric energy (million kWh)	9,845	10,825	n.a.

* Production in terms of (a) nitrogen or (b) phosphoric acid.
† Official figures.

Source: mainly UN, *Industrial Commodity Statistics Yearbook*.

Woven woollen fabrics (million sq metres): 2.8 in 1996; 3.2 in 1997; 2.5 in 1998 (Source: UN, *Industrial Commodity Statistics Yearbook*).

Ethyl alcohol ('000 hectolitres): 2 in 1997; 1 in 1998; 1 in 1999 (Source: UN, *Industrial Commodity Statistics Yearbook*).

2003 ('000 metric tons, unless otherwise indicated, estimates): Wheat flour 503; Nitrogenous fertilizers 96; Gas-diesel (distillate fuel) oil 1,750; Cement 239; Electric energy (million kWh) 10,800 (Source: Asian Development Bank, *Key Indicators of Developing Asian and Pacific Countries*).

Finance

CURRENCY AND EXCHANGE RATES

Monetary Units
100 tenge = 1 Turkmen manat.

Sterling, Dollar and Euro Equivalents (30 November 2005)
£1 sterling = 8,980.4 manats;
US $1 = 5,200.0 manats;
€1 = 6,119.6 manats;
10,000 Turkmen manats = £1.11 = $1.92 = €1.63.

Note: The Turkmen manat was introduced on 1 November 1993, replacing the Russian (formerly Soviet) rouble at a rate of 1 manat = 500 roubles. Following the introduction of the Turkmen manat, a multiple exchange rate system was established. The foregoing information refers to the official rate of exchange. This rate was maintained at US $1 = 4,165 manats between May 1997 and April 1998. It was adjusted to $1 = 5,200 manats in April 1998. In addition to the official rate, there was a commercial bank rate of exchange until this market was closed in December 1998. There is also a 'parallel' market rate, which averaged $1 = 6,493 manats in 1998 and reached $1 = 14,200 manats at mid-1999.

BUDGET
('000 million manats)

Revenue*	1997	1998	1999†
State budget	2,067.3	1,867.5	2,382.3
Personal income tax	108.3	157.4	224.9
Profit tax	579.6	412.0	422.0
Value-added tax	797.9	714.9	946.3
Natural resources tax	231.2	43.1	201.1
Excise tax	92.4	221.3	377.8
Other receipts*	257.9	318.8	210.1
Pension and Social Security Fund	471.0	711.0	832.5
Medical Insurance Fund	32.7	8.2	0.0
Repayments on rescheduled gas debt	246.6	474.1	478.3
Total	**2,817.6**	**3,060.8**	**3,693.1**

Expenditure	1997	1998	1999‡
National economy	843.9	461.1	623.3
Agriculture	632.5	331.4	223.2
Transport and communications	121.1	63.4	190.0
Other	90.3	66.3	210.1
Socio-cultural services†	975.7	1,850.0	1,907.9
Education	435.3	919.2	1,048.7
Health	443.1	493.8	550.6
Communal services	9.1	337.9	188.6
Culture, recreation and other purposes	88.2	99.1	120.0
Defence§	440.2	435.8	582.0
Pension and Social Security Fund	387.8	511.5	605.9
Interest payments	72.1	11.1	18.0
Public administration and other purposes	94.3	153.4	157.2
Total	**2,814.0**	**3,422.8**	**3,894.3**

* Including grants received and road fund revenues.
† Approved budget.
‡ Excluding expenditure of the Pension and Social Security Fund.
§ Variable coverage, owing to changes in classification.

2001 (estimates, '000 million manats): Revenue 5,363.0; Expenditure 5,642.0 (Source: Asian Development Bank, *Key Indicators of Developing Asian and Pacific Countries*).

2002 ('000 million manats): Revenue 8,243.1; Expenditure 8,165.0 (Source: Asian Development Bank, *Key Indicators of Developing Asian and Pacific Countries*).

2003 ('000 million manats): Revenue 11,026.0; Expenditure 11,522.0 (Source: Asian Development Bank, *Key Indicators of Developing Asian and Pacific Countries*).

INTERNATIONAL RESERVES
(US $ million at 31 December)

	1999	2000	2001
Total	1,607.0	1,854.0	1,935.0

Source: Asian Development Bank, *Key Indicators of Developing Asian and Pacific Countries*.

MONEY SUPPLY
(million manats at 31 December)

	1995	1996	1997
Currency in circulation	56,629	270,248	408,000
Demand deposits at banks	48,475	408,000	401,000

Total money ('000 million manats at 31 December): 2,651.1 in 2000; 3,061.6 in 2001 (Source: Asian Development Bank, *Key Indicators of Developing Asian and Pacific Countries*).

COST OF LIVING
(Consumer Price Index; base: previous year at 31 December = 100)

	2002*	2003*	2004†
All items	107.8	105.7	110.0

* Estimate.
† Projection.

Source: European Bank for Reconstruction and Development.

TURKMENISTAN

NATIONAL ACCOUNTS
('000 million manats at current prices)

Expenditure on the Gross Domestic Product

	2001	2002	2003
Government final consumption expenditure	4,496.7	4,963.0	7,560.0
Private final consumption expenditure	15,741.5	22,191.1	31,904.5
Increase in stocks	1,068.9	—	—
Gross fixed capital formation	12,144.5	12,468.0	15,100.0
Total domestic expenditure	33,451.6	39,622.1	54,564.5
Exports of goods and services	14,423.9	31,237.9	35,553.9
Less Imports of goods and services	12,221.3	24,161.0	30,944.5
Sub-total	35,654.2	46,699.0	59,174.0
Statistical discrepancy	–241.4	—	—
GDP in purchasers' values	35,412.8	46,699.0	59,174.0

Gross Domestic Product by Economic Activity
('000 million manats, at current prices)

	2000	2001	2002*
Agriculture	5,885.9	8,327.6	9,646.3
Mining and quarrying } Manufacturing } Electricity, gas and water }	8,985.5	12,996.7	15,880.8
Construction	1,736.6	2,136.8	2,289.4
Trade	900.7	2,363.9	2,056.3
Transport and communications	1,701.3	1,919.2	2,094.8
Finance	353.5	422.0	
Public administration	735.2	912.8	} 10,887.0
Other activities	5,349.2	6,333.8	
Total	25,647.9	35,412.8	42,854.6

* Estimates.

Gross domestic product ('000 million manats at current prices): 46,699 in 2002 (revised); 59,174 in 2003; 63,480 in 2004 (estimate).

Source: Asian Development Bank, *Key Indicators of Developing Asian and Pacific Countries*.

BALANCE OF PAYMENTS
(US $ million)

	1996	1997	1998
Exports of goods f.o.b.	1,692.0	774.0	614.1
Imports of goods f.o.b.	–1,388.3	–1,005.0	–1,137.1
Trade balance	303.7	–230.9	–523.0
Services (net)	–323.4	–402.5	–471.0
Balance on goods and services	–19.7	–633.5	–994.0
Other income (net)	16.7	84.8	32.6
Balance on goods, services and income	–3.0	–548.7	–961.4
Current transfers (net)	4.8	–31.2	26.9
Current account	1.8	–579.9	–934.5
Direct investment	108.1	102.4	64.1
Trade credit (net)	60.8	–266.5	56.5
Other (net)	–211.6	1,035.9	749.7
Net errors and omissions	46.4	–71.4	33.9
Overall balance	5.4	220.6	–30.3

2001 (US $ million): Exports of goods f.o.b. 2,620.2; Imports of goods f.o.b. –2,348.8; Trade balance 271.4 (Source: Asian Development Bank, *Key Indicators of Developing Asian and Pacific Countries*).

2002 (US $ million): Exports of goods f.o.b. 2,855.6; Imports of goods f.o.b. –2,119.4; Trade balance 736.2 (Source: Asian Development Bank, *Key Indicators of Developing Asian and Pacific Countries*).

2003 (US $ million; estimates): Exports of goods f.o.b. 3,720.0; Imports of goods f.o.b. –2,450.0; Trade balance 1,270.0 (Source: Asian Development Bank, *Key Indicators of Developing Asian and Pacific Countries*).

External Trade

PRINCIPAL COMMODITIES
(US $ million)

Imports c.i.f.	2001	2002	2003
Food and live animals	129.4	114.3	130.3
Beverages and tobacco	56.8	70.1	67.4
Mineral fuels, lubricants, etc.	39.1	25.7	17.7
Chemicals	178.6	210.8	271.2
Basic manufactures	448.7	394.2	487.7
Machinery and transport equipment	1,204.7	857.6	1,125.6
Miscellaneous manufactured articles	128.1	112.7	165.2
Total (incl. others)	2,348.8	2,119.4	2,450.0*

Exports f.o.b.	2001	2002	2003
Food and live animals	4.7	3.4	2.9
Beverages and tobacco	—	0.6	0.3
Mineral fuels, lubricants, etc.	123.7	83.8	152.4
Chemicals	7.0	28.4	55.0
Basic manufactures	141.6	150.6	169.6
Machinery and transport equipment	14.5	17.1	16.9
Miscellaneous manufactured articles	52.8	74.1	80.8
Total (incl. others)	2,620.2	2,855.6	3,320.0*

* Estimate.

Source: Asian Development Bank, *Key Indicators of Developing Asian and Pacific Countries*.

PRINCIPAL TRADING PARTNERS
(US $ million)

Imports	2002	2003	2004
France	32.6	82.6	136.4
China, People's Repub.	109.7	104.9	87.6
Germany	103.7	106.3	201.9
Iran	80.9	93.3	116.8
Japan	8.3	3.4	56.2
Russia	360.9	538.9	413.3
Turkey	233.5	236.6	236.3
Ukraine	213.3	382.7	406.7
United Arab Emirates	181.9	190.7	238.8
USA	137.3	47.1	326.9
Total (incl. others)	2,127.9	2,510.7	2,950.3

Exports	2002	2003	2004
Afghanistan	28.6	73.8	92.4
Germany	4.0	11.6	40.1
Iran	355.6	507.9	583.5
Italy	486.8	624.8	179.7
Russia	22.9	27.0	34.8
Switzerland	3.8	18.3	20.3
Turkey	168.1	224.7	159.7
Ukraine	1,346.1	1,353.0	1,694.4
United Arab Emirates	33.9	95.2	109.4
USA	49.0	56.5	79.2
Total (incl. others)	2,815.8	3,449.1	3,400.5

Source: Asian Development Bank, *Key Indicators of Developing Asian and Pacific Countries*.

TURKMENISTAN   *Directory*

Transport

RAILWAYS
(traffic)

	1996	1997	1999*
Passenger journeys (million)	7.8	6.4	3.1
Passenger-km (million)	2,104	958	701
Freight transported (million metric tons)	15.9	18.5	17.2
Freight ton-km (million)	6,779	7,445	7,337

* Data for 1998 were not available.

Source: *Railway Directory*.

SHIPPING

Merchant Fleet
(registered at 31 December)

	2002	2003	2004
Number of vessels	41	43	41
Total displacement ('000 grt)	45.7	47.4	42.9

Source: Lloyd's Register-Fairplay, *World Fleet Statistics*.

CIVIL AVIATION
(estimated traffic on scheduled services)

	1999	2000	2001
Kilometres flown (million)	9	20	22
Passengers carried ('000)	220	1,284	1,407
Passenger-kilometres (million)	640	1,466	1,608
Total ton-kilometres (million)	74	144	156

Source: UN, *Statistical Yearbook*.

Tourism

FOREIGN VISITOR ARRIVALS
(incl. excursionists)

Country of nationality	1995	1996	1997
Afghanistan	11,803	18,301	n.a.
Azerbaijan	n.a.	10,642	114
Iran	82,925	82,386	171,071
Kazakhstan	n.a.	9,466	4,971
Kyrgyzstan	n.a.	15,798	22,066
Pakistan	7,000	5,837	3,075
Russia	n.a.	3,916	6,979
Tajikistan	n.a.	10,623	11,310
Turkey	46,414	52,230	62,915
Uzbekistan	n.a.	45,259	31,784
Total (incl. others)	232,832	281,988	332,425

Foreign visitor arrivals: 300,000 in 1998.

Tourism receipts (US $ million): 66 in 1996; 74 in 1997; 192 in 1998.

Source: World Tourism Organization.

Communications Media

	2000	2001	2002
Television receivers ('000 in use)	875	880	n.a.
Telephones ('000 main lines in use)	364.4	387.6	374.0
Mobile cellular telephones ('000 subscribers)	9.5	8.2	8.2
Internet users ('000)	6	8	n.a.

Internet users (2004): 36,000.

Telephones (2003): 376,100 main lines in use.

Book production (including pamphlets): 450 titles (5,493,000 copies) in 1994.

Radio receivers ('000 in use): 1,225 in 1997.

Personal computers ('000 in use): 2 in 1999.

Sources: International Telecommunication Union; UNESCO, *Statistical Yearbook*.

Education

(1984/85)

	Institutions	Students
Secondary schools	1,900	800,000
Secondary specialized schools	35	36,900
Higher schools (incl. universities)	9	38,900

1990/91: 76,000 students at higher schools (Source: UNESCO, *Statistical Yearbook*).

Institutions (2005): Secondary schools 1,704; Secondary specialized schools 15; Higher schools (incl. universities) 16 (Source: Permanent Mission of Turkmenistan to the United Nations).

Students enrolled at universities (2003): 14,859 (Source: UNICEF).

Adult literacy rate (UNESCO estimates): 98.8% (males 99.3%; females 98.3%) in 1995–99 (Source: UN Development Programme, *Human Development Report*).

Directory

The Constitution

A new Constitution was adopted on 18 May 1992. The Constitution was organized into eight sections (detailing: fundamentals of the constitutional system; fundamental human and civil rights, freedoms and duties; the system of state governmental bodies; local self-government; the electoral system and provisions for referendum; judicial authority; the office of the prosecutor-general; and final provisions), and included the following among its main provisions:

The President of the Republic is directly elected by universal adult suffrage for a five-year term. A President may hold office for a maximum of two terms. The President is not only Head of State, but also head of Government (Prime Minister in the Council of Ministers) and Supreme Commander of the Armed Forces. The President must ratify all parliamentary legislation and in certain circumstances may legislate by decree. The President appoints the Council of Ministers and chairs sessions of the Khalk Maslakhaty (People's Council).

Supreme legislative power resides with the 50-member Majlis, a unicameral parliament which is directly elected for a five-year term. Sovereignty, however, is vested in the people of Turkmenistan, and the supreme representative body of popular power is the Khalk

TURKMENISTAN

Maslakhaty. This is described as a supervisory organ with no legislative or executive functions, but it is authorized to perform certain duties normally reserved for a legislature or constituent assembly. Not only does it debate and approve measures pertaining to the political and economic situation in the country, but it examines possible changes to the Constitution and may vote to express 'no confidence' in the President of the Republic, on grounds of unconstitutionality. The Khalk Maslakhaty is comprised of all the deputies of the Majlis, a further 50 directly elected and 10 appointed representatives from all districts of the country, the members of the Council of Ministers, the respective Chairmen of the Supreme Court and the Supreme Economic Court, the Prosecutor-General and the heads of local councils.

The Constitution, which defines Turkmenistan as a democratic state, also guarantees the independence of the judiciary and the basic human rights of the individual. The age of majority is 18 years (parliamentary deputies must be aged at least 21). Ethnic minorities are granted equality under the law, although Turkmen is the only official language. A central tenet of Turkmenistan's foreign policy is that of 'permanent neutrality'.

Note: On 15 January 1994 a referendum confirmed President Saparmyrat Niyazov's exemption from the need to be re-elected in 1997. An amendment to the Constitution, approved by the Khalk Maslakhaty in December 1999, extended the term of Niyazov's presidency indefinitely. In February 2001, following Niyazov's announcement that he would retire by 2010, the Khalk Maslakhaty endorsed a resolution to hold open presidential elections in 2008–10, following his retirement. In August 2003 a constitutional law and a constitutional amendment were passed elevating the Khalk Maslakhaty to the status of 'permanently functioning supreme representative body of popular authority', and requiring it to remain in continuous session. The constitutional changes ascribed to the Khalk Maslakhaty a number of legislative powers, including the passing of constitutional laws, thereby effectively displacing the Majlis as the country's leading legislative body. The Khalk Maslakhaty was to comprise 2,507 members.

The Government

HEAD OF STATE

President of the Republic: Gen. SAPARMYRAT A. NIYAZOV (directly elected 27 October 1990; re-elected 21 June 1992. Term extended by referendum held on 15 January 1994; a constitutional amendment of 28 December 1999 extended his term of office indefinitely).

COUNCIL OF MINISTERS
(May 2006)

Prime Minister: Gen. SAPARMYRAT A. NIYAZOV.
Deputy Prime Minister and Minister of Health and the Medical Industry: GURBANGULY BERDYMUKHAMMETOV.
Deputy Prime Minister and Minister of Construction and Building-materials Production: ORAZMURAD ESENOV.
Deputy Prime Minister and Minister of Power Engineering and Industry: YUSUP DAVUDOV.
Deputy Prime Minister and Co-ordinator of Relations with the CIS: AGANIYAZ AKIYEV.
Deputy Prime Minister: JUMANIYAZ ANNAORAZOV.
Minister of Agriculture: ESENMYRAT ORAZGELDIYEV.
Minister of Communications: RESULBERDY KHOZHAGURBANOV.
Minister of Culture, Television and Radio Broadcasting: ENEBAI ATAYEVA.
Minister of Defence: Maj.-Gen. AGAGELDY MAMATGELDIYEV.
Minister of the Economy and Finance: (vacant).
Minister of Education: SHEMSHAT ANNAGYLYJOVA.
Minister of Environmental Protection: MAGTYMGULY AKMURADOV.
Minister of Foreign Affairs: RASHID MEREDOV.
Minister of Internal Affairs: AKMAMED RAHMANOV.
Minister of Justice: ASYRGELDI GULGARAYEV.
Minister of National Security: GELDIMUHAMMET ASHIRMUHAMMEDOV.
Minister of Petroleum, Natural Gas and Mineral Resources: GURBANMURAT ATAYEV.
Minister of Railways: ORAZBERDY HADAYBERDIYEV.
Minister of Road Transport and Highways: BAYMUKHAMMET KELOV.
Minister of Social Security: BIBITACH VEKILOVA.
Minister of the Textile Industry: YKLYMBERDY PAROMOV.
Minister of Trade and Foreign Economic Relations and Turkmen Consumers' Union: GURBANGELDI MELEKEYEV.
Minister of Water Resources: TEKEBAI ALTYYEV.

MINISTRIES

Office of the President and the Council of Ministers: 744000 Aşgabat, ul. 2001 24, Presidential Palace; tel. (12) 35-45-34; fax (12) 35-51-12.
Ministry of Agriculture: 744000 Aşgabat, ul. 2011 63; tel. (12) 35-66-91; fax (12) 35-01-18; e-mail minselhoz@online.tm.
Ministry of Communications: 744000 Aşgabat, ul. 2002 40; tel. (12) 35-21-52; fax (12) 35-05-95; e-mail mincom@telecom.tm; internet www.mct.gov.tm.
Ministry of Construction and Building-materials Production: 744000 Aşgabat, ul. 2049; tel. (12) 51-23-59.
Ministry of Culture, Television and Radio Broadcasting: 744000 Aşgabat, ul. 1984 14; tel. (12) 35-30-61; fax (12) 35-35-60.
Ministry of Defence: 744000 Aşgabat, ul. 1995 4; tel. (12) 35-22-59.
Ministry of the Economy and Finance: 744000 Aşgabat, ul. 2008 4; tel. (12) 51-05-63; fax (12) 51-18-23.
Ministry of Education: 744000 Aşgabat, ul. 2002 2; tel. (12) 35-58-03; fax (12) 39-88-11.
Ministry of Environmental Protection: 744000 Aşgabat, ul. 2035 102; tel. (12) 35-43-17; fax (12) 51-16-13; e-mail ministr@nature-tm.org; internet www.grida.no/enrin/htmls/turkmen/soe2/index.htm.
Ministry of Foreign Affairs: 744000 Aşgabat, pr. 2076 83; tel. (12) 26-62-11; fax (12) 35-42-41; e-mail mfatm@online.tm.
Ministry of Health and the Medical Industry: 744000 Aşgabat, pr. 2076 90; tel. (12) 35-60-47; fax (12) 35-50-32.
Ministry of Internal Affairs: 744000 Aşgabat, pr. 2076 85; tel. (12) 35-59-23.
Ministry of Justice: 744000 Aşgabat, ul. 2022 86; tel. (12) 38-04-11.
Ministry of National Security: 744000 Aşgabat, pr. Magtymguly 91; fax (12) 51-07-55.
Ministry of Petroleum, Natural Gas and Mineral Resources: 744000 Aşgabat, ul. 2002 28; tel. (12) 39-38-27; fax (12) 39-38-21; e-mail ministryoilgas@online.tm.
Ministry of Power Engineering and Industry: 744000 Aşgabat, ul. 2008 6; tel. (12) 35-38-70; fax (12) 39-06-82; e-mail kuwwat@online.tm.
Ministry of Railways: Aşgabat, ul. Saparmurat Turkmenbashi 9.
Ministry of Road Transport and Highways: 744000 Aşgabat, ul. 1916 141; tel. (12) 35-02-36; fax (12) 35-18-43; e-mail tcentr@online.tm.
Ministry of Social Security: 744007 Aşgabat, ul. 2003 3; tel. (12) 25-30-03.
Ministry of the Textile Industry: 744000 Aşgabat, ul. 2026 52; tel. (12) 51-03-03.
Ministry of Trade and Foreign Economic Relations and Turkmen Consumers' Union: 744000 Aşgabat, ul. 2002 1; tel. (12) 35-10-47; fax (12) 35-73-24; e-mail mtfer@online.tm.
Ministry of Water Resources: 744000 Aşgabat, ul. 2005 1; tel. (12) 39-06-15; fax (12) 39-85-39.

Legislature

Khalk Maslakhaty
(People's Council)

744000 Aşgabat.

Under the Constitution of May 1992, the Khalk Maslakhaty was established as the supreme representative body in the country. Formally, it is neither a legislative nor an executive body, although its decisions supersede those of both parliament and presidency. The 2,507-member body consists of the President, the Majlis deputies, the Chairman of the Supreme Court, the Prosecutor-General, the members of the Council of Ministers, the hakims (governors) of the five velayats (regions) and the hakim of the city of Aşgabat; the elected people's representatives of each district; the chairpersons of parties, the Youth Union, trade unions, and the Women's Union, who are members of the All-national Galkynyş National Revival Movement of Turkmenistan; the chairpersons of public organizations; representatives of the Council of Elders; the hakims of cities that are the administrative centres of the velayats and etraps (districts); and the heads of the local councils (archins) of the cities and villages that are the administrative centres of the districts. It is headed by the President of the Republic. Elections for the 50 district representatives were held in November and December 1992; the Council

TURKMENISTAN

convened for the first time later in December. Fresh elections were held in April 1998 and on 6 April 2003. On the latter occasion, according to official reports, 99.8% of eligible voters participated. It was also reported that all candidates were members of the Democratic Party of Turkmenistan. A constitutional law and constitutional amendment passed in August 2003 elevated the Khalk Maslakhaty to the status of 'permanently functioning supreme representative body of popular authority'. The Khalk Maslakhaty was henceforth required to remain in continuous session, and effectively displaced the Majlis as the country's leading legislative body.

Life Chairman: Gen. SAPARMYRAT A. NIYAZOV.

Majlis
(Assembly)

744000 Aşgabat, ul. Bitarap Turkmenistan 17; tel. (12) 35-31-25; fax (12) 35-31-47.

Chairman: OVEZGELDY ATAYEV.

The 50-member Majlis is directly elected for a term of five years. Elections to the Majlis were held on 19 December 2004, officially with the participation of 76.88% of the registered electorate. A second round of voting took place in seven districts on 9 January 2005, where candidates had failed to obtain an absolute majority of votes. All contestants were believed to be members of the ruling party, the Democratic Party of Turkmenistan. The deputies of the Majlis also form part of the Khalk Maslakhaty.

Election Commission

Central Commission for Elections and Referendums: Aşgabat; comprises a chairman, two vice-chairmen, a secretary and 12 mems, all elected by the President of the Republic; Chair. MYRAT KARRYYEV; Sec. JEREN TAIMOVA.

Political Organizations

Democratic Party of Turkmenistan: 744014 Aşgabat, ul. 2002 28; tel. (12) 25-12-12; name changed from Communist Party of Turkmenistan in 1991; Chair. Gen. SAPARMYRAT A. NIYAZOV.

Unity (Agzybirlik): Aşgabat; e-mail agzybirlik@hotmail.com; internet hem.lidnet.se/~agzybirlik/; f. 1989; popular front organization; denied official registration except from Oct. 1991 to Jan. 1992; Leader NURBERDY NURMAMEDOV.

Turkmenistan is effectively a one-party state, with the Democratic Party of Turkmenistan (led by the President of the Republic) dominant in all areas of government. The President of the Republic is also the leader of the National Revival Movement of Turkmenistan (Galknyş). There are, however, several unregistered opposition groups, such as Agzybirlik (Unity). A Social Democratic Party was reportedly established in Aşgabat in August 1996, upon the merger of several small unofficial groups.

Other opposition elements are based in other republics of the Commonwealth of Independent States, in particular Russia. A leading opposition figure in exile is a former Minister of Foreign Affairs, ABDY KULIYEV, whose United Democratic Opposition of Turkmenistan (ODOT) is based in Moscow, Russia. In January 1996 several of the Turkmenistan Fund's leaders left to form the Movement for Democratic Reform (based in Sweden). The Fatherland (Watan) movement (also based in Sweden; e-mail info@watan.ru; internet watan.ru) comprises Turkmen and other Central Asian oppositionists. In January 2002 a former Minister of Foreign Affairs, BORIS SHIKHMURADOV, established the opposition People's Democratic Movement of Turkmenistan (PDMT; internet gundogar.org); however, he was imprisoned in December, having been convicted of orchestrating the attempted assassination of President Saparmyrat Nizayov in November. Another opposition leader accused of conspiring with Shikhmuradov was NURMUKHAMMED KHANAMOV, founder of the Republican Party of Turkmenistan (RPT; internet tmrepublican.org; Co-Chair. NURMUKHAMMET HANAMOV; SAPAR YKLYMOV).

Opposition leaders met in Prague, Czech Republic, in September 2003 and announced the formation of the Union of Democratic Forces of Turkmenistan (UDFT), comprising four main groups: the RPT; Fatherland; the ODOT; and the Revival Social Political Movement.

Diplomatic Representation

EMBASSIES IN TURKMENISTAN

Afghanistan: 744000 Aşgabat, ul. 2009 94; tel. (12) 48-07-57; fax (12) 48-07-26; Ambassador ABDUL KARIM KHADAM.

Armenia: 744000 Aşgabat, ul. 2002 14; tel. (12) 35-44-18; fax (12) 39-55-38; e-mail eat@online.tm; Ambassador ARAM V. GRIGORIAN.

Azerbaijan: Aşgabat, ul. Prosveshcheniya 44; tel. (12) 36-46-08; fax (12) 36-46-10; e-mail azsefir_ashg@online.tm; Ambassador ELKHAN BAKHADUR OGLY GUSEYINOV.

Belarus: 744000 Aşgabat; tel. (12) 27-37-94; fax (12) 27-37-99; Ambassador YURIY MALUMOV.

China, People's Republic: 744036 Aşgabat, Berzengi raion, Hotel 'Kuwwat'; tel. (12) 51-81-31; fax (12) 51-88-78; e-mail chemb@cat.glasnet; Ambassador LU GUICHENG.

France: 744000 Aşgabat, Four Points Ak Altin Hotel, Office Bldg, pr. 2076 141/1; tel. (12) 36-35-50; fax (12) 36-35-46; e-mail cad.achgabat-amba@diplomatie.gouv.fr; Ambassador JEAN-CLAUDE RICHARD.

Georgia: 744000 Aşgabat, ul. 2011 139A; tel. (12) 34-48-38; fax (12) 34-32-48; e-mail georgia@online.tm; Ambassador GIA MACHARADZE.

Germany: 744000 Aşgabat, Four Points Ak Altin Hotel, pr. 2076; tel. (12) 36-35-15; fax (12) 36-35-22; e-mail grembtkm@online.tm; Ambassador HANS MONDORF.

India: Aşgabat, Imperial International Business Centre, Y. Emre 1, Mir 2/1, POB 80; tel. (12) 45-61-52; fax (12) 45-61-56; e-mail indembinfo@online.tm; Ambassador Prof. RAM PAL KAUSHIK.

Iran: 744000 Aşgabat, ul. 2072 3; tel. (12) 35-02-37; fax (12) 35-05-65; e-mail isroiref@online.tm; Ambassador GHOLAM-REZA ANSARI.

Japan: 744000 Aşgabat, Four Points Ak Altin Hotel, Office Bldg, pr. 2076 141/1; tel. (12) 36-35-07; Ambassador YASUO SAITO (resident in Moscow, Russia).

Kazakhstan: Aşgabat, Garashsyzlyk Shayoly, International Ustay Compound, ul. 1986 13/11; tel. and fax (12) 48-04-68; e-mail turemb@online.tm; Ambassador MURAT ATANOV.

Kyrgyzstan: Aşgabat, ul. 2009 Gegorly 85; tel. and fax (12) 35-55-06; e-mail kyrgtm@by.ru; internet kyrgtm.by.ru; Ambassador ZARYLBEK A. AKMATBEKOV.

Libya: Aşgabat, ul. 2011 17A; tel. (12) 35-49-17; fax (12) 39-35-26; Chargé d'affaires a.i. RAGAB BEN KHAMADI.

Pakistan: Aşgabat, ul. Garashsyzlyk 4/1; tel. (12) 48-21-28; fax (12) 48-21-30; e-mail parepashgabat@online.tm; Ambassador SAID AKBAR AFRIDI.

Romania: Aşgabat, ul. 1997 43A; tel. (12) 34-76-55; fax (12) 34-76-20; e-mail ambromas@online.tm; Ambassador TASIN GEMIL.

Russia: 744004 Aşgabat, ul. 1966 11; tel. (12) 35-39-57; fax (12) 39-84-66; e-mail emb-rus@online.tm; Ambassador IGOR BLATOV.

Saudi Arabia: Aşgabat, ul. 1951 2/1, Internal Imperial Centre for Business; tel. (12) 45-49-63; fax (12) 45-49-70; e-mail tmemb@mofa.gov.sa; Ambassador ABD AL-AZIZ IBRAHIM AL-GHADEER.

Tajikistan: 744000 Aşgabat, ul. 2002 14; tel. (12) 35-56-96; fax (12) 39-31-74; e-mail embtd@online.tm; Ambassador KOZIDAVLAT KOIMDODOV.

Turkey: 744007 Aşgabat, ul. 2009 9; tel. (12) 35-41-18; fax (12) 39-19-14; e-mail askabat.be@mfa.gov.tr; Ambassador HAKKI AKIL.

Ukraine: 744001 Aşgabat, ul. 2011 49; tel. (12) 39-13-73; fax (12) 39-10-28; e-mail ukremb@online.tm; Ambassador VIKTOR MAYKO.

United Arab Emirates: 744000 Aşgabat, Khalifa Centre, ul. 1966 124; tel. (12) 45-69-15; fax (12) 45-69-16; Ambassador HASSAN ABDULLAH AL-ADHAB.

United Kingdom: 744001 Aşgabat, Four Points Ak Altin Hotel, 3rd Floor, Office Bldg, pr. 2076; tel. (12) 36-34-62; fax (12) 36-34-65; e-mail beasb@online.tm; internet www.britishembassy.gov.uk/turkmenistan; Ambassador PETER BUTCHER.

USA: 744000 Aşgabat, ul. 1984 9; tel. (12) 35-00-45; fax (12) 39-26-14; e-mail irc-ashgabat@iatp.edu.tm; internet turkmenistan.usembassy.gov; Ambassador TRACEY ANN JACOBSON.

Uzbekistan: Aşgabat, pr. Türkmenbaşi 124; tel. (12) 34-24-34; fax (12) 34-23-37; e-mail emuzbek@online.tm; Ambassador ALISHER KODIROV.

Judicial System

Chairman of the Supreme Court: YAGSHIGELDY ESENOV.

Prosecutor-General: MUHAMMATYULY OGSHUKOV, Aşgabat, ul. Seidi 4; fax (12) 35-44-82.

Religion

The majority of the population are adherents of Islam. In June 1991 the Turkmen Supreme Soviet adopted a Law on Freedom of Conscience and Religious Organizations. In April 1994 a council (Gengeş) for religious affairs was established, within the office of the President; it was chaired by the Kazi of Turkmenistan and his deputy was the head of the Orthodox Church in Turkmenistan. In November 2003 new legislation, which replaced that approved in 1991, was passed, restricting the activities of religious groups, although registration requirements for religious communities were made more flexible by a presidential decree, issued in early 2004, and further legislation, approved in March of that year, reduced the membership threshold required for a group to register from 500 to five. Prior to these amendments, only Sunni Muslim and Russian Orthodox Christian groups had been permitted to register. However, by mid-2004 groups of Seventh-day Adventist and Baptist Christians, Hare Krishnas and Baha'is had also registered.

ISLAM

Turkmen are traditionally Sunni Muslims, but with elements of Sufism. Islam, the religion of the Turkmen for many centuries, was severely persecuted by the Soviet regime from the late 1920s. Until July 1989 Aşgabat was the only Central Asian capital without a functioning mosque. The Muslims of Turkmenistan are officially under the jurisdiction of the Muslim Board of Central Asia, based in Tashkent, Uzbekistan, but, in practice, the Government permits little external influence in religious affairs. The Board is represented in Turkmenistan by a *kazi*, who is responsible for appointing Muslim clerics in all rural areas.

Kazi of Turkmenistan: ROVSHEN ALLABERDIYEV.

CHRISTIANITY

Roman Catholic Church

The Church is represented in Turkmenistan by a Mission, established in September 1997. There were an estimated 50 adherents at 31 December 2003.

Superior: Fr ANDRZEJ MADEJ, 744000 Aşgabat, ul. 2009 20A, POB 98; tel. (12) 39-11-40; fax (12) 35-36-83; e-mail amadej@mail.ru.

The Russian Orthodox Church (Moscow Patriarchate)

The Church in Turkmenistan comes under the jurisdiction of the Eparchy of Tashkent and Central Asia (Metropolitan of Tashkent and Central Asia, VLADIMIR (IKIM), Uzbekistan.

JUDAISM

Leader: LYUBOV GARBUZOVA.

The Press

All publications listed below are in Turkmen, except where otherwise stated.

PRINCIPAL NEWSPAPERS

Adalat (Justice): 744005 Aşgabat, ul. 2033/1 4; tel. (12) 39-79-04; weekly; Editor-in-Chief DOVLET HOJAMUHAMMEDOVIC GURBANGELDIYEV; circ. 42,575.

Aşgabat/Ashkhabad: 744004 Aşgabat, ul. 1995 20; tel. (12) 22-33-04; f. 1960; 3 a week; journal of the Union of Writers of Turkmenistan; popular; in Turkmen and Russian; Editor-in-Chief SAPARMYRAT GARAKHANOV; Deputy Editor-in-Chief ORAZ AKGAYEV; circ. 6,832.

Beyik Türkmenbaşiyn Nesli (Generation of Turkmenbashi the Great): 744064 Aşgabat, ul. 1995 20; tel. (12) 39-17-64; f. 1922; 3 a week; for young people; Editor ANNAGUL NARLIEVA; circ. 21,591.

Dogry ÿol (True Path): ; internet www.dogryyol.com; daily; Russian and English; online only; opposition.

Edebiyat we sungat (Literature and Art): 744004 Aşgabat, ul. 1995 20; tel. (12) 35-30-34; f. 1958; weekly; Editor ANNAMYRAT POLADOV; circ. 19,111.

Esger (Soldier): 744004 Aşgabat, ul. 2038 29; tel. (12) 35-68-09; f. 1993; weekly; organ of the Council of Ministers; military newspaper; Editor-in-Chief KAKAMURAT BALLYEV; circ. 40,200.

Galkynyş (Revival): 744604 Aşgabat, ul. 1995 20; tel. (12) 22-34-23; weekly; Editor-in-Chief KHUDAIBERDI DIVANGULIYEV; circ. 44,586.

Habarlar: 744004 Aşgabat, ul. 1995 20; tel. (12) 46-84-70; weekly; in Russian and Turkmen; television and radio; business; advertisements; Editor-in-Chief R. BALABAN; circ. 3,596.

Mugallymlar gazeti (Teachers' Newspaper): 744004 Aşgabat, ul. 1976 20; tel. (12) 35-09-66; f. 1952; 3 a week; organ of the Ministry of Education; Editor REJEPNUR GURBANNAZAROV; circ. 75,226.

Neitralnyi Turkmenistan (Neutral Turkmenistan): 744004 Aşgabat, ul. 1995 20; tel. and fax (12) 39-42-76; fax (12) 22-34-37; e-mail nt@online.tm; internet www.tmpress.gov.tm; f. 1924; 6 a week; organ of the Majlis and the Council of Ministers; in Russian; Editor-in-Chief VIKTOR MIHAYLOV; circ. 30,091.

Novosti Turkmenistana (Turkmenistan News): 744000 Aşgabat, ul. 2002 24A; tel. (12) 39-12-21; fax (12) 51-02-34; f. 1994; weekly; in Russian, English and Turkmen; publ. by Dowlet Khabarlar Gullugy news agency; circ. 500.

Syyasy sokhbetdeş (Political Symposium): 744604 Aşgabat, ul. 1995 20; tel. (12) 25-10-84; f. 1992; weekly; organ of the Democratic Party of Turkmenistan; Editor AKBIBI YUSUPOVA; circ. 14,500.

Turkmenistan: Zolotoi Vek (Turkmenistan: The Golden Age): Aşgabat; internet www.turkmenistan.gov.tm; online only; in Russian; publ. by Democratic Union of Journalists of Turkmenistan.

Türkmening yupekyoli (Turkmen Railwayman): 744007 Aşgabat, ul. Chary Nurymov 3; tel. (12) 35-06-52; f. 1936; weekly; organ of the Turkmenistan State Railways; covers transport and communications; Editor BAYRAM SAHEDOV; circ. 7,000.

Türkmenistan: 744004 Aşgabat, ul. 1995 20; tel. (12) 39-14-55; f. 1920; 6 a week; organ of the Council of Ministers and the Majlis; Editor KAKABAY ILIYASOV; circ. 25,591.

Watan (Fatherland): 744604 Aşgabat, ul. 1995 20; tel. (12) 22-34-56; f. 1925; 3 a week; Editor-in-Chief AMANMUHAMMET REPOW; circ. 25,419.

PRINCIPAL PERIODICALS

Monthly, unless otherwise indicated.

Diller duniesi (World of Languages): 744014 Aşgabat, ul. 1960 22; tel. (12) 29-15-41; f. 1972; 6 a year; publ. by the Ministry of Education; in Russian and Turkmen.

Diyar: 744604 Aşgabat, ul. 1995 20; tel. (12) 35-53-97; f. 1992; foreign policy and international relations; publ. by the President of the Republic and the Council of Ministers; Editor-in-Chief ASHIRBERDY GURBANOV; circ. 12,881.

Finansovye vesti (Financial News): 744004 Aşgabat, ul. 1995 20; tel. (12) 29-42-76; f. 1994; in Russian, English and Turkmen; publ. by the Ministry of the Economy and Finance.

Garagum (Kara-Kum): 744005 Aşgabat, ul. 1995 20; tel. (12) 35-11-15; f. 1928; literary; Editor SAPAR ORAYEV; circ. 2,546.

Guneş (The Sun): 744000 Aşgabat, ul. 1995 20; tel. (12) 22-33-05; for children; Editor-in-Chief SHADURDY CHARYGYLLYEV; circ. 44,696.

Gurbansoltan Eje: 744604 Aşgabat, ul. 1995 20; tel. (12) 22-33-09; f. 1931; fmrly *Ovadan* (Beautiful); for women; Editor AKBIBI YUSUBOVA; circ. 56,626.

Izvestiya Akademii Nauk Turkmenistana (Academy of Sciences of Turkmenistan News): 744000 Aşgabat, ul. 2011 59; f. 1946; 6 a year; in Russian and Turkmen.

Politicheskii sobesednik (Political Symposium): 744604 Aşgabat, ul. 1995 20; tel. (12) 25-10-84; f. 1937; in Russian; publ. by the Democratic Party of Turkmenistan; circ. 2,300.

Saglyk (Health): 744000 Aşgabat, ul. 2020 39/57; tel. (12) 39-16-21; f. 1990; 6 a year; publ. by the Ministry of Health and the Medical Industry; Editor-in-Chief BAYRAMAMMED TACHMAMEDOV; circ. 35,071.

Türkmen dili khem edebiyati (Turkmen Language and Literature): Aşgabat; tel. (12) 41-88-03; f. 1991; 6 a year; publ. by the Ministry of Education.

Türkmen dunyasi: 744004 Aşgabat, ul. 2011 20; tel. (12) 47-81-18; organ of the Humanitarian Association of World Turkmen; Editor-in-Chief ANNABERDY AGABAYEV; circ. 11,956.

Türkmen medeniyeti (Turkmen Culture): 744007 Aşgabat, ul. 1960 21; tel. (12) 25-37-22; f. 1993; 2 a year; publ. by the Ministry of Culture, Television and Radio Broadcasting; Editor GELDYMYRAT NURMUKHAMMEDOV.

Türkmen sporty (Sport Turkmenistana—Turkmen Sport): Aşgabat 744004, ul. 1995 20; tel. (12) 22-33-72; weekly; in Turkmen and Russian; Editor-in-Chief VIKTOR MIHAYLOV; circ. 2,500.

Türkmenistanyn Lukmancykygy: 74404 Aşgabat, ul. A. Gulmammedov 4A; tel. (12) 35-25-40; every two months; health-care policy; Editor-in-Chief O. SERDAROV.

Türkmenistanyn oba khozhalygy (Agriculture of Turkmenistan): 744000 Aşgabat, ul. 2011 63; tel. (12) 35-19-38; f. 1929; Editor BYASHIM TALLYKOV; circ. 3,500.

Türkmenistanyng Mejlisining Maglumatlary (Bulletin of the Majlis of Turkmenistan): 744000 Aşgabat, ul. 1986 110; tel. (12) 35-50-39; fax (12) 35-31-47; e-mail mejlis@online.tm; f. 1960; 4 a year; in Russian and Turkmen.

TURKMENISTAN
Directory

Vozrozhdeniye (Rebirth): 744604 Aşgabat, ul. 1995 20; tel. (12) 35-10-84; in Russian; political; Editor-in-Chief H. DIVANGULYEV; circ. 1,500.

NEWS AGENCIES

Türkmen Dowlet Khabarlar Gullugy (Turkmen State News Service): 744000 Aşgabat, ul. 2002 24A; tel. (12) 39-12-21; fax (12) 51-02-34; e-mail tpress@online.tm; f. 1967; Dir JEREN TAIMOVA.

Foreign Bureau

Anadolu Ajansı (Turkey): Aşgabat, ul. 2009 41A/110; tel. (12) 51-07-50; e-mail askabat@anadoluajansi.com.tr.

Publishers

Magaryf Publishing House: Aşgabat; Dir N. ATAYEV.

Turkmenistan State Publishing Service: 744000 Aşgabat, ul. 1995 20; tel. (12) 46-90-13; f. 1965; politics, science and fiction; Dir A. M. JANMURADOV.

Ylym Publishing House: 744000 Aşgabat, ul. 2011 59; tel. (12) 29-04-84; f. 1952; desert development, science; Dir N. I. FAIZULAYEVA.

Broadcasting and Communications

TELECOMMUNICATIONS

Türkmentelekom: 744000 Aşgabat, ul. 2010 36; tel. (12) 51-12-77; fax (12) 51-02-40; e-mail admin@telecom.tm; internet www.telecom.tm; f. 1993; Dir-Gen. ANNALY CH. BERDINOBATOV.

BROADCASTING

Turkmen State Information Agency (Turkmen Dovlet Habarlary): 744004 Aşgabat, ul. 2002; tel. (12) 39-12-21; fax (12) 51-02-34; e-mail tpress@online.tm; Head JEREN TAIMOVA.

Radio

Turkmen National Radio Co: 744000 Aşgabat, ul. Navoi 5; tel. (12) 39-25-20; Chair. MURAD ORAZOV.

Char Tarapdan (From All Sides): tel. (12) 39-86-72; Dir CHARY REJEPOV.

Miras (Heritage): tel. (12) 35-68-50; Dir GURBANDURDY REJEPOV.

Watan (Fatherland): tel. (12) 51-12-96; Dir YAILIM I. ORAZOV.

Television

Turkmen National Television Co: 744000 Aşgabat, ul. Navoi 5; tel. (12) 39-25-20; Chair. MURAD ORAZOV.

Altyn Asyr (Golden Age): tel. (12) 39-85-06; Dir SHADURDY A. ALOLOV.

Miras (Heritage): tel. (12) 35-20-43; Dir BYAGUL CH. NURMURADOVA.

Türkmenistan: tel. (12) 35-00-86; Dir MURAD A. ORAZOV.

Yaşlyk (Youth): tel. (12) 35-00-86; Dir (vacant).

Finance

(cap. = capital; res = reserves; dep. = deposits; m. = million; brs = branches; amounts in Turkmen manats)

BANKING

Long-standing lack of confidence in the banking sector, together with a regional financial crisis, prompted a restructuring of the sector, in December 1998, by presidential decree. Government ownership of banks was increased, while restrictions on lending by the Central Bank were intensified and the merger of smaller banks was encouraged. By late 2002 there were 12 commercial banks.

Central Bank

Central Bank of Turkmenistan: 744000 Aşgabat, ul. 2002 36; tel. (12) 38-10-27; fax (12) 51-08-12; e-mail merkez3@online.tm; f. 1991; central monetary authority, issuing bank and supervisory authority; Chair. GELDIMURAT ABILOV; 5 brs.

Other Banks

Daykhanbank: Aşgabat, ul. 2067 60; tel. and fax (12) 41-98-68; e-mail daybank@online.tm; f. 1989 as independent bank, Agroprombank, reorganized 1999; specializes in agricultural sector; Chair. of Bd NURBERDY BAYRAMOV; 70 brs.

Garagum International Joint-Stock Bank: 744000 Aşgabat, ul. 1960 3; tel. (12) 35-22-01; fax (12) 35-38-54; f. 1993 as International Bank for Reconstruction, Development and Support of Entrepreneurship, name changed 2000; Chair. BEKMAMED SOLTANMEMEDOV.

Garaşyslyk Bank: Aşgabat, ul. 2009 30A; tel. (12) 35-48-75; fax (12) 39-01-24; e-mail garash@cbtm.net; f. 1999 following merger of Gas Bank and Aşgabat Bank; cap. US $5m. (Oct. 2003); Chair. (vacant); 5 brs.

President Bank: 744000 Aşgabat, ul. 2002 22; tel. (12) 35-79-43; fax (12) 51-08-12; e-mail presidentbank@cbtm.net; f. 2000; cap. US $60m.; Exec. Dir (vacant).

Savings Bank of Turkmenistan (Sberbank): 744000 Aşgabat, pr. 2076 86; tel. (12) 35-46-71; fax (12) 35-40-04; f. 1923, reorganized 1989; wholly state-owned; Chair. BEGENCH BAYMUKHAMEDOV; 120 brs.

Senagatbank: 744013 Aşgabat, ul. 1966 42; tel. (12) 45-31-33; fax (12) 45-44-09; e-mail senagat@online.tm; f. 1989; cap. 31,200m., res 1,394m., dep. 32,547m. (Feb. 2005); Chair. GELDYMURAD CHAPAYEV; 5 brs.

Turkmenvnesheconombank—State Bank for Foreign Economic Affairs of Turkmenistan: 744000 Aşgabat, ul. 2010 22; tel. (12) 35-02-52; fax (12) 39-79-82; e-mail tveb@online.tm; f. 1992 as independent bank, from Soviet Vneshekonombank; wholly state-owned; cap. 125,863m., res 149,156m., dep. 1,185,747m. (Dec. 2003); Chair. GUVANCH B. GEOKLENOV; 5 brs.

Türkmenbank—State Commercial Bank 'Türkmenistan': 744000 Aşgabat, ul. 2002 10A; tel. (12) 51-07-21; fax (12) 39-67-35; e-mail turkmenbank@ctbm.net; f. 1992; Chair. (vacant).

Türkmenbaşi Bank: 744000 Aşgabat, ul. 2026 54; tel. (12) 51-24-50; fax (12) 51-11-11; e-mail mail@investbank.org; f. 1992 as Investbank, renamed in 2000; Chair. AMANMURAT PAJAYEV; 23 brs.

Foreign and Joint-Venture Banks

Bank Saderat Iran: Aşgabat, pr. 2076 181; tel. (12) 34-67-67; fax (12) 34-20-70; Man. ALI AMOLI.

Kreditbank: 744000 Aşgabat, pr. 2076; tel. (12) 35-02-22; fax (12) 35-03-09; e-mail kreditbank@online.tm; f. 1995; fmrly Rossiiskii Kredit; Chair. BATYR BAYRIYEV.

National Bank of Pakistan: 744000 Aşgabat, ul. 2002 7, Hotel 'Emperyal Grand Turkmen'; tel. (12) 35-35-16; fax (12) 35-04-65; e-mail nbptm@online.tm; Gen. Man. SHAKHZAD JAKHANGIR KHOKAR.

Turkmen Turkish Commercial Bank: 744014 Aşgabat, pr. 2076 111/2, POB 15; tel. (12) 51-14-07; fax (12) 51-11-23; e-mail ttcb@online.tm; f. 1993, with 50% Turkish ownership; cap. 28,923m., res 7,390m., dep. 54,367m. (Oct. 2003); Chair. NUBERDI BAYRAMOV.

COMMODITY EXCHANGE

State Commodity and Raw Materials Exchange of Turkmenistan: 744000 Aşgabat, pr. 2076 111; tel. (12) 35-43-21; fax (12) 51-03-04; e-mail info@exchange.gov.tm; internet www.turkmenbusiness.org; f. 1994; Chair. KHOJAMUKHAMMET MUKHAMMEDOV.

Trade and Industry

GOVERNMENT AGENCIES

National Institute of State Statistics and Information on Turkmenistan (Türkmenmillihasabat): 744000 Aşgabat, ul. 2033 72; tel. (12) 39-42-65; fax (12) 35-43-79; e-mail staff@natstat.gov.tm; f. 1997; Dir JUMADURDY BAIRAMOV.

State Agency for Foreign Investment (SAFI): 744000 Aşgabat, ul. 2011 53; tel. and fax (12) 35-04-16; e-mail saffi@online.tm; f. 1996; monitors and regulates all foreign investment in Turkmenistan; registers foreign cos in Turkmenistan; Dir (vacant).

DEVELOPMENT ORGANIZATION

Small and Medium Enterprise Development Agency (SMEDA): 744000 Aşgabat, ul. 2015 8; tel. (12) 34-42-59; fax (12) 34-51-49; e-mail smeda@cat.glasnet.ru; jt venture between Turkmen Govt and the European Union (EU); Dir SERDAR BABAYEV.

CHAMBER OF COMMERCE

Chamber of Commerce and Industry of Turkmenistan: 744000 Aşgabat, ul. 2037 17; tel. (12) 35-64-03; fax (12) 35-13-52; e-mail mission@online.tm; f. 1959; Chair. ARSLAN F. NEPESOV.

UTILITIES

Electricity

Kuvvat Turkmen State Energy Technology Corpn: 744000 Aşgabat, 2008 6; tel. (12) 35-68-04; fax (12) 39-06-82; e-mail kuvvat@online.tm; state electrical power generation co and agency; Chair. YUSUP DAVYDOV.

STATE HYDROCARBONS COMPANIES

Türkmenbaşi Oil Refinery: 745000 Balkan Velayat, Türkmenbaşi, POB 5; tel. (00222) 7-45-45; fax (00222) 7-45-44; production and refining of petroleum; sales of petroleum and liquefied natural gas; Dir TACHBERDY TAGIYEV.

Türkmengaz: 744036 Aşgabat, ul. 1939 56; tel. (12) 40-32-00; fax (12) 40-32-54; e-mail annam@online.tm; f. 1996; govt agency responsible for natural gas operations, inc. development of system of extraction, processing of gas and gas concentrate and gas transportation and sale; Chair. BAGTIYAR HAJIGURBANOV.

Türkmengeologiya: 744000 Aşgabat, ul. 2023 7/32; tel. (12) 35-13-46; fax (12) 35-50-15; govt agency responsible for natural gas and petroleum exploration; Chair. SAPARGELDI JUMAYEV.

Türkmenneft: 745100 Balkan Velayat, Balkanabat, pr. Magtymguly 49; tel. (00243) 2-19-45; govt agency responsible for petroleum operations and production; Chair. KARYAGDY TASHLIYEV; Gen. Dir KHAKIM IMAMOV.

Türkmenneftegazstroi: 744036 Aşgabat, ul. Arçabil 56; tel. (12) 40-35-01; fax (12) 40-35-01; e-mail tngg@online.tm; govt agency for construction projects in the hydrocarbons sector; Chair. GURBANBERDI ORAZMURADOV.

TRADE UNIONS

Federation of Trade Unions of Turkmenistan: 744000 Aşgabat, ul. 1966 13; tel. (12) 35-62-08; fax (12) 35-21-30; Chair. ENEBAY G. ATAYEVA.

Committee of Trade Unions of Ahal Velayat: 744000 Ahal Velayat, pos. Anau, Gyaver etrap; tel. 41-39-19; Dir A. TAGANOV.

Committee of Trade Unions of Daşoguz Velayat: 746311 Daşoguz Velayat, Niyazovsk, Saparmyrat Türkmenbaşi shayoly 8; Dir SH. IGAMOV.

Transport

RAILWAYS

The main rail line in the country runs from Türkmenbaşi (formerly Krasnovodsk), on the Caspian Sea, in the west, via Aşgabat and Mari, to Türkmenabat (formerly Charjew) in the east. From Türkmenabat one line runs further east, to the other Central Asian countries of the former USSR, while another runs north-west, via Uzbekistan and Kazakhstan, to join the Russian rail network. In 2005 the total length of rail track in use in Turkmenistan was 2,516 km. A 203-km rail link from Türkmenabat to Atamarut was opened in 1999. In 1996 a rail link was established with Iran (on the route Tejen–Serakhs–Mashhad), thus providing the possibility of rail travel and transportation between Turkmenistan and Istanbul, Turkey, as well as giving access to the Persian (Arabian) Gulf. A 540-km railway line, running south–north across the country from Aşgabat to Daşoguz, via Garagum, was completed in early 2006.

Turkmenistan State Railways (Türkmendemorjollari): 744007 Aşgabat, ul. 1966 7; tel. (12) 35-55-45; fax (12) 51-06-32; f. 1992; Pres. B. P. REDJEPOV.

ROADS

In 1999 there was an estimated total of 24,000 km of roads, of which some 19,500 km were hard-surfaced. In 2000 construction began on a 600-km road linking Aşgabat and Daşoguz.

SHIPPING

Shipping services link Türkmenbaşi (formerly Krasnovodsk) with Baku (Bakı—Azerbaijan), Makhachkala (Dagestan, Russia) and the major Iranian ports on the Caspian Sea. The Amu-Dar'ya river is an important inland waterway. From 2000 Türkmenbaşi port was undergoing an extensive process of modernization.

Shipowning Companies

Neftec: Balkan Velayat, Türkmenbaşi; tel. (2) 765-81; fax (2) 766-89.

Turkmen Maritime Steamship Co: Balkan Velayat, Türkmenbaşi, ul. Shagadama 8; tel. (2) 767-34.

Turkmen Shipping Co: Balkan Velayat, Türkmenbaşi, ul. Shagadama 8; tel. (2) 972-67; fax (2) 767-85.

Türkmenderyayollary: 746000 Lebap Velayat, Türkmenabat, ul. Gyamichiler 8; tel. (2) 223-12; fax (2) 23-46-88; f. 1992 as Turkmen River Shipping Co; renamed as above in 1998.

Türkmennefteflot: Balkan Velayat, Türkmenbaşi, POB 6; tel. (2) 762-62.

CIVIL AVIATION

Turkmenistan's international airport is at Aşgabat.

National Civil Aviation Authority of Turkmenistan (Türkmenhovayollary): 744000 Aşgabat, ul. 2007 3A; tel. (12) 35-10-52; fax (12) 35-44-02; e-mail aviahead@online.tm; f. 1992; Chief Exec. BAIMURAD BAIRIYEV.

Turkmenistan Airlines: 744000 Aşgabat, pr. 2033 80; tel. (12) 35-10-52; fax (12) 35-44-02; f. 1992; domestic and international scheduled and charter passenger flights, incl. services to Europe, Central and South-East Asia, and the Middle East; three divisions: Ahal Air Co, Khazar Air Co and Lebap Air Co; Gen. Dir ALEKSEI P. BONDAREV.

Tourism

Although the tourism sector in Turkmenistan remains relatively undeveloped, owing, in part, to the vast expanse of the Kara-Kum desert (some 80% of the country's total area), the Government has made efforts to improve the standard of visitor accommodation (there are a number of new luxury hotels in Aşgabat) and to improve the capacity and efficiency of the capital's international airport). The scenic Kopet Dagh mountains, the Caspian Sea coast, the archaeological sites and mountain caves of Kugitang, and the hot subterranean mineral lake at Kov-Ata are among the country's natural attractions, while the ancient cities of Mari and Nisa—former capitals of the Seljuk and Parthian empires, respectively—are of considerable historical interest. In addition, Kunya-Urgench is an important site of Muslim pilgrimage. In 1998, according to the World Tourism Organization, there were approximately 300,000 visitors from abroad, and receipts from tourism totalled US $192m.

State Committee for Tourism and Sport: 744000 Aşgabat, ul. 1984 17; tel. (12) 35-47-77; fax (12) 39-67-40; e-mail travel@online.tm; internet www.tourism-sport.gov.tm; founded on the basis of the State Tourist Corpn Turkmensyyakhat; f. 2000; Dir ATAMYRAT BERDIYEV.

National Institute of Sport and Tourism: 744001 Aşgabat, ul. 2038 15A; tel. (12) 36-25-40; fax (12) 36-24-56; f. 1981; activities include the provision of training in 15 types of sport, catering and tourism; Rector AŞIR MOMMADOV.

TUVALU

Introductory Survey

Location, Climate, Language, Religion, Flag, Capital

Tuvalu is a scattered group of nine small atolls (five of which enclose sizeable lagoons), extending about 560 km (350 miles) from north to south, in the western Pacific Ocean. Its nearest neighbours are Fiji to the south, Kiribati to the north and Solomon Islands to the west. The climate is warm and pleasant, with a mean annual temperature of 30°C (86°F), and there is very little seasonal variation. The average annual rainfall is about 3,500 mm (140 ins), the wettest months being November to February. The inhabitants speak Tuvaluan and English. Almost all of them profess Christianity, and about 98% are Protestants. The national flag (proportions 1 by 2) is light blue with the United Kingdom flag as a rectangular canton in the upper hoist, occupying one-quarter of the area, and nine five-pointed yellow stars (arranged to symbolize a map of the archipelago) in the fly. The flag was reintroduced in February 1997 to replace a design, adopted in October 1995, omitting the British union flag. The capital is on Funafuti Atoll.

Recent History

Tuvalu was formerly known as the Ellice (or Lagoon) Islands. Between about 1850 and 1875 many of the islanders were captured by slave-traders and this, together with European diseases, reduced the population from about 20,000 to 3,000. In 1877 the United Kingdom established the Western Pacific High Commission (WPHC), with its headquarters in Fiji, and the Ellice Islands and other groups were placed under its jurisdiction. In 1892 a British protectorate was declared over the Ellice Islands, and the group was linked administratively with the Gilbert Islands to the north. In 1916 the United Kingdom annexed the protectorate, which was renamed the Gilbert and Ellice Islands Colony (GEIC). During the Japanese occupation of the Gilbert Islands in 1942–43, the administration of the GEIC was temporarily moved to Funafuti in the Ellice Islands. (For more details of the history of the GEIC, see the chapter on Kiribati.)

A series of advisory and legislative bodies prepared the GEIC for self-government. In May 1974 the last of these, the Legislative Council, was replaced by the House of Assembly, with 28 elected members (including eight Ellice Islanders) and three official members. A Chief Minister was elected by the House and chose between four and six other ministers, one of whom had to be from the Ellice Islands.

In January 1972 the appointment of a separate GEIC Governor, who assumed most of the functions previously exercised by the High Commissioner for the Western Pacific, increased the long-standing anxiety of the Ellice Islanders over their minority position as Polynesians in the colony, dominated by the Micronesians of the Gilbert Islands. In a referendum held in the Ellice Islands in August and September 1974, more than 90% of the voters favoured separate status for the group, and in October 1975 the Ellice Islands, under the old native name of Tuvalu ('eight standing together', which referred to the eight populated atolls), became a separate British dependency. The Deputy Governor of the GEIC took office as Her Majesty's Commissioner for Tuvalu. The eight Ellice representatives in the GEIC House of Assembly became the first elected members of the new Tuvalu House of Assembly. They elected one of their number, Toaripi Lauti, to be Chief Minister. Tuvalu was completely separated from the GEIC administration in January 1976. The remainder of the GEIC was renamed the Gilbert Islands and achieved independence, as Kiribati, in July 1979.

Tuvalu's first separate elections took place in August 1977, when the number of elective seats in the House of Assembly was increased to 12. An independence Constitution was finalized at a conference in London in February 1978. After five months of internal self-government, Tuvalu became independent on 1 October 1978, with Lauti as the first Prime Minister. The pre-independence House of Assembly was redesignated Parliament. In September 2000 Tuvalu was formally admitted to the UN.

In 1983 the USA formally renounced its claim, dating from 1856, to the four southernmost atolls. Following elections to Parliament in September 1981, Lauti was replaced as Prime Minister by Dr Tomasi (later Sir Tomasi) Puapua. Puapua was re-elected Prime Minister following subsequent elections in September 1985.

In February 1986 a nation-wide poll was conducted to establish public opinion as to whether Tuvalu should remain an independent constitutional monarchy, with the British monarch at its head, or become a republic. Only on one atoll did the community appear to be in favour of the adoption of republican status. In March Tupua (later Sir Tupua) Leupena, a former Speaker of Parliament, was appointed Governor-General, replacing Sir Penitala Teo, who had occupied the post since independence in 1978.

At a general election in September 1989 supporters of Puapua were reported to have been defeated in the election, and an opponent, Bikenibeu Paeniu (who had been appointed Minister of Community Services within the previous year), was elected Prime Minister. In October 1990 Toaripi Lauti succeeded Sir Tupua Leupena as Governor-General.

Legislation approved by Parliament in mid-1991, which sought to prohibit all new religions from the islands and to establish the Church of Tuvalu as the State Church, caused considerable controversy and extensive debate. A survey showed the population to be almost equally divided over the matter, although Paeniu firmly opposed the motion, describing it as incompatible with basic human rights.

In August 1991 the Government announced that it was to prepare a compensation claim against the United Kingdom for the allegedly poor condition of Tuvalu's economy and infrastructure at the time of the country's achievement of independence in 1979. Moreover, Tuvalu was to seek additional compensation for damage caused during the Second World War when the United Kingdom gave permission for the USA to build airstrips on the islands (some 40% of Funafuti is uninhabitable because of large pits created by US troops during the construction of an airstrip on the atoll). Relations with the United Kingdom deteriorated further in late 1992, when the British Government harshly criticized the financial policy of Paeniu's Government. Paeniu defended his Government's policies, and stated that continued delays in the approval of aid projects from the United Kingdom meant that Tuvalu would not be seeking further development funds from the British Government.

At a general election held in September 1993, three of the 12 incumbent members of Parliament lost their seats. At elections to the premiership held in the same month, however, Paeniu and Puapua received six votes each. When a second vote produced a similar result, the Governor-General dissolved Parliament, in accordance with the Constitution. Paeniu and his Cabinet remained in office until the holding of a further general election in November. At elections to the premiership in the following month Kamuta Latasi defeated Paeniu by seven votes to five. Puapua, who had agreed not to challenge Paeniu in the contest in favour of supporting Latasi, was elected Speaker of Parliament. In June 1994 Latasi removed the Governor-General, Toomu Malaefono Sione, from office, some seven months after he had been appointed to the position, and replaced him with Tulaga (later Sir Tulaga) Manuella. Latasi alleged that Paeniu's appointment of Sione had been politically motivated.

In December 1994, in what was widely regarded as a significant rejection of its political links with the United Kingdom, the Tuvaluan Parliament voted to remove the British union flag from the Tuvalu national flag. A new design was selected and the new flag was inaugurated in October 1995. Speculation that the British monarch would be removed as Head of State intensified during 1995, following the appointment of a committee to review the Constitution. The three-member committee was to examine the procedure surrounding the appointment and removal of the Governor-General, and, particularly, to consider the adoption of a republican system of government.

In late 1996 the Deputy Prime Minister, Otinielu Tausi, and the parliamentary Speaker, Dr Tomasi Puapua, both announced their decision to withdraw their support for Latasi's Government, thereby increasing the number of opposition members in Parliament from five to seven. This reversal appeared to be in response to increasing dissatisfaction among the population with Latasi. This had been perceived firstly with his unpopular initiative to replace the country's national flag, and was exacerbated by revelations that the leasing of Tuvalu's telephone code to a foreign company had resulted in the use of the islands' telephone system for personal services considered indecent by the majority of islanders. (It was announced by the Government in October 2000 that the lease was to be terminated by the end of the year.) Opponents of the Prime Minister submitted a parliamentary motion of 'no confidence' in his Government in December, which was approved by seven votes to five. Paeniu subsequently defeated Latasi, by a similar margin, to become Prime Minister, and a new Cabinet was appointed. The new premier acted promptly to restore the country's original flag, by proposing a parliamentary motion in February 1997, which was approved by seven votes to five.

A total of 35 candidates contested a general election on 26 March 1998. The period prior to the election had been characterized by a series of bitter disputes between Paeniu and Latasi, in which both had made serious accusations of sexual and financial misconduct against the other. Five members of the previous Parliament were returned to office, although Latasi unexpectedly failed to secure re-election. Paeniu was subsequently re-elected Prime Minister by 10 votes to two. In June the new Government announced a series of development plans and proposals for constitutional reform, including the introduction of a code of conduct for political leaders and the creation of an ombudsman's office. Paeniu stated that his administration intended to consult widely with the population before any changes were implemented. Also in 1998 Puapua was appointed Governor-General, replacing Manuella.

On 13 April 1999 Paeniu lost a parliamentary vote of confidence and was forced to resign. Later in the month Ionatana Ionatana, hitherto the Minister of Health, Education, Culture, Women and Community Affairs, was elected by Parliament as the new Prime Minister. On his appointment Ionatana immediately effected a reshuffle of the Cabinet.

Potentially the most significant new source of revenue for many years was established in September 1998 when the Government signed an agreement to lease the country's national internet suffix '.tv' to a Canadian information company. The company, which defeated several other business interests to secure the deal, was expected to market the internet address to international television companies. Although that arrangement subsequently failed, it was announced in February 2000 that a US $50m. deal on the sale of the '.tv' suffix had been concluded with a US company. The sale was expected to generate some US $10m. annually in revenue. The funds generated from the sale enabled Tuvalu officially to join the UN, and participate in the 55th annual UN General Assembly Meeting, held in September 2000.

In March 2000 18 schoolgirls and their supervisor were killed in a fire in a school dormitory on Vaitupu atoll. A government inquiry was established into the disaster, which was reportedly the worst in independent Tuvalu's history.

In early December 2000 Prime Minister Ionatana Ionatana died unexpectedly. The Deputy Prime Minister, Lagitupu Tuilimu was immediately appointed as interim Prime Minister, pending the election of a replacement. In late February 2001 Parliament elected as Prime Minister the Minister of Internal Affairs and Rural and Urban Development, Faimalaga Luka; he assumed responsibility for the additional portfolios of foreign affairs, finance and economic planning, and trade and commerce, and immediately named a new cabinet.

A vote of 'no confidence' was upheld against Luka in December 2001 while he was in New Zealand for a medical examination. Koloa Talake, a former Minister of Finance, was elected Prime Minister in the same month, winning eight of the 15 votes cast (the number of parliamentary seats having been increased from 12 to 15). He appointed an entirely new Cabinet.

Talake announced in March 2002 that lawyers were preparing evidence for further legal action against the United Kingdom, seeking compensation for the alleged inequality of the division of assets between Tuvalu and Kiribati when the two nations had achieved independence in the late 1970s. Following the general election held on 25 July 2002, Saufatu Sopoanga, a former Minister of Finance, defeated Amasone Kilei, the opposition candidate, by eight votes to seven to become the new Prime Minister. Sopoanga subsequently announced his intention to hold a referendum on the adoption of a republican system of Government in Tuvalu.

In May 2003 two by-elections resulted in the loss of the Government's one-seat majority. The Government's subsequent refusal to convene Parliament (allegedly in order to evade a vote of 'no confidence') was strongly criticized by the opposition. The Government maintained that it would regain its majority with an imminent defection from the opposition and would then convene Parliament. In July, however, the situation remained unchanged and the opposition consequently sought a court order obliging Sopoanga to convene Parliament. The appointment, in early September, of Faimalaga Luka, hitherto Speaker and a member of Parliament, as the country's new Governor-General necessitated an additional by-election, which resulted in a further delay to Parliament's being convened. However, following the success of its candidate at the by-election, and (as anticipated) the defection of an opposition member, the Government regained its majority in mid-October. Parliament was finally convened in early November.

In April 2004 the Government announced that a team of officials was touring the outer islands to canvas opinion on the adoption of republican status for Tuvalu. If islanders indicated sufficient support for the proposal, it was thought that a referendum might be held in June 2005. In March 2005 the Prime Minister indicated that he expected the referendum to go ahead, stating that he had encountered widespread concern among Tuvaluans that the British Government was failing to meet its financial obligations to the islands. By mid-2006, however, a referendum had not taken place.

In August 2004 the Prime Minister, Saufatu Sopoanga, was ousted by nine parliamentary votes to five in a vote of 'no confidence' after a member of the Government crossed the floor to vote with the opposition and was joined by the Speaker. The election of a new Prime Minister, however, was delayed by Sopoanga's decision to relinquish his seat, thus necessitating the organization of a by-election before Parliament could select a premier. Deputy Prime Minister Maatia Toafa assumed the role of acting Prime Minister in the interim. Sopoanga regained his seat in a by-election in early October, and on 11 October acting Prime Minister Maatia Toafa was elected to the premiership, defeating Sopoanga by eight votes to seven.

In April 2005 it was announced that Sio Patiale, a member of Parliament, was to resign on grounds of ill health. The consequent by-election was expected to be very significant, owing to the possibility that it might result in a majority for the opposition in Parliament. In the same month the Governor-General, Faimalaga Luka, resigned, having reached the maximum permitted age for the post of 65, and was replaced by Filiomea Telito. Luka died in August of that year. A further by-election in September, caused by the resignation of another member of Parliament, was won by a candidate who decided to support the Government, thus consolidating its majority.

In May 2005 the President of Taiwan visited three countries in the Pacific, including Tuvalu, in an attempt to improve diplomatic relations. During his brief visit, the Prime Minister signed a joint communiqué with his Tuvaluan counterpart.

Tuvalu's annual visitor arrival numbers were greatly increased by a meeting of ministers which the country hosted in Funanfuti in June 2005. Some 80 delegates from 14 Pacific island countries attended the meeting to discuss issues concerned with economic development in the region.

In early 2006 it was announced that the next legislative election was to be conducted on 3 August. The Prime Minister declared his intention to seek re-election.

In 1989 a UN report on the 'greenhouse effect' (the heating of the earth's atmosphere) listed Tuvalu as one of the island groups which would completely disappear beneath the sea in the 21st century, unless drastic action were taken. At the UN World Climate Conference, held in Geneva in November 1990, Paeniu appealed for urgent action by developed nations to combat the environmental changes caused by the 'greenhouse effect', which were believed to include a 10-fold increase in cyclone frequency (from two in 1940 to 21 in 1990), an increase in salinity in ground water and a considerable decrease in the average annual rainfall. The Government remained critical, however, of the inertia with which it considered certain countries had reacted to its appeal for assistance and reiterated the Tuvaluan people's fears of physical and cultural extinction. The subsequent Prime Minister, Kamuta Latasi, was similarly critical of the industrial world's apparent disregard for the plight of small island nations vulnerable to the effects of climate change, particularly when Tuvalu was struck by tidal waves in 1994 (believed to be the first experienced by the islands). Attempts during the mid-1990s to secure approval for resettlement plans for Tuvaluans to other countries, including Australia and New Zealand, were largely unsuccessful. The Government of Tuvalu was strongly critical of Australia's refusal to reduce its emission of pollutant gases (known to contribute to the 'greenhouse effect') at the Conference of the Parties to the Framework Convention on Climate Change (UN Environment Programme, see p. 58) in Kyoto, Japan, in late 1997. In July 2001, however, Australia adopted the Kyoto Protocol, which urged industrial nations to reduce carbon-dioxide emissions by 5.2% from 1990 levels by 2012. In March 2001 Tuvalu, Kiribati and the Maldives announced their decision to take legal action against the USA for its refusal to sign the Kyoto Protocol. In August Tuvalu was one of six states at the Pacific Islands Forum to demand a meeting with US President George W. Bush to try to enlist his support for the Kyoto Protocol. (The USA produced nearly one-third of the industrialized countries' carbon-dioxide emissions and had repeatedly refused to adopt the Protocol.)

The installation of a new sea-level monitoring station began in December 2001 as part of the South Pacific Sea Level and Climate Monitoring Project administered by the Australian aid agency, AusAID. In January 2002 it was reported that the Government had engaged a US law firm to prosecute the USA and other nations for failing to meet their commitments to the United Nations Framework Convention on Climate Change (UNFCC). In September 2003 Tuvalu's Prime Minister addressed the 58th session of the UN General Assembly in New York and appealed for collective action to mitigate the impact of climate change and rising sea-levels on the islands. He once again urged all industrialized nations, particularly the USA, to sign the Kyoto Protocol. In the following month the Government of Niue, which had for many years suffered from a decline in population owing to the migration of its inhabitants to New Zealand, officially invited the residents of Tuvalu to resettle on Niue. The feasibility of this offer, however, was in question following the devastation caused to Niue by a cyclone in January 2004. The option of resettling on other neighbouring islands, including Fiji, was to be considered but only as a last resort. In March 2006 it was reported that the people of Tuvalu were unhappy at the prospect of leaving their homeland, fearing that it would mean the loss of their identity. The Prime Minister was also considering the purchase of land in other countries for economic reasons, while declaring that this might be a useful long-term solution should the problems caused by climate change worsen.

Tuvalu was subject to considerable international criticism in mid-2004 regarding its decision to join the International Whaling Commission (IWC, see p. 378). Environmental and animal welfare groups accused the Tuvaluan Government of accepting financial incentives from Japan in return for agreeing to use its vote to support a removal of the ban on commercial whaling at the commission's annual meeting in Italy in July 2004. In May 2006, furthermore, prior to the IWC's annual meeting in Japan, Tuvalu reiterated its stance. During a visit to Funafuti the New Zealand Minister of Conservation had hoped to persuade Tuvalu to reverse its policy. New Zealand had agreed to finance and conduct a training and survey programme of the whales and dolphins in Tuvaluan waters.

Government

Tuvalu is a constitutional monarchy. Executive authority is vested in the British sovereign, as Head of State, and is exercisable by her representative, the Governor-General, who is appointed on the recommendation of the Prime Minister and acts, in almost all cases, on the advice of the Cabinet. Legislative power is vested in the unicameral Parliament, with 12 members elected by universal adult suffrage for four years (subject to dissolution). The Cabinet is led by the Prime Minister, who is elected by and from the members of Parliament. On the Prime Minister's recommendation, other ministers are appointed by the Governor-General. The Cabinet is responsible to Parliament. Each of the inhabited atolls has its own elected Island Council, which is responsible for local government.

Economic Affairs

In 2002 the Asian Development Bank (ADB) estimated Tuvalu's gross domestic product (GDP) at current prices to be $A26.9m., equivalent to $A2,478 per head. During 1995–2004, it was estimated, the population increased at an average annual rate of 1.8%. According to figures from the ADB, overall GDP increased, in real terms, at an average annual rate of 4.5% in 1995–2004. Compared with the previous year, GDP rose by 4.0% in 2004 and by 2.0% in 2005.

Agriculture (including fishing) is, with the exception of copra production, of a basic subsistence nature. The sector contributed some 16.6% of GDP in 2002. According to ADB figures, the GDP of the agricultural sector declined at an average annual rate of 1.6% in 1995–2002. Compared with the previous year, agricultural GDP decreased by 2.6% in 2001 and by 9.4% in 2002. In 2003, according to FAO, the sector engaged some 25% of the labour force. Coconuts (the source of copra) are the only cash crop; exports of copra were worth $A6,000 in 1997. Pulaka, taro, papayas, the screw-pine (*Pandanus*) and bananas are cultivated as food crops and honey is produced. In the late 1990s and early 2000s agriculture became increasingly affected by climate change and rising sea-levels. More frequent high tides caused flooding which damaged crops, particularly the important taro crop, and killed tree roots, which reduced the harvest of coconuts and other fruits. Livestock comprises pigs, poultry and goats. Fish and other sea products are staple constituents of the islanders' diet. The sale of fishing licences to foreign fleets is an important source of income and earned $A11.8m. in 2001 (compared with $A3.6m. in 1997), equivalent to 50.3% of current revenue. Revenue from this source, however, declined in subsequent years.

Industry (including mining, manufacturing, construction and utilities) accounted for 14.8% of GDP in 2002. In 1995–2002, according to ADB figures, industrial GDP expanded at an average annual rate of 7.2%. Compared with the previous year, the sector's GDP increased by 10.3% in 2001 and by 6.5% in 2002. Manufacturing is confined to the small-scale production of coconut-based products, soap and handicrafts. The manufacturing sector contributed some 3.7% of GDP in 2002.

Energy is derived principally from a power plant (fuelled by petroleum) and, on the outer islands, solar power. In 1989 mineral fuels accounted for almost 13% of total import costs.

The Government is an important employer (engaging 1,185 people in 2001, equivalent to about one-half of the labour force) and consequently the services sector makes a relatively large contribution to Tuvalu's economy (providing some 68.6% of GDP in 2002). In 1995–2002, according to ADB figures, the GDP of the services sector increased at an average annual rate of 7.3%. Compared with the previous year, the sector's GDP expanded by 6.3% in 2001 and by 3.4% in 2002. The islands' remote situation and lack of amenities have hindered the development of a tourist industry. Visitor arrivals totalled 1,496 in 2003 and only 1,214 in 2004. An important source of revenue has been provided by remittances from Tuvaluans working abroad. Remittances from some 450 Tuvaluan seafarers employed on foreign (predominantly German) merchant ships were estimated at $A5m. in 2003 (equivalent to some 20% of GDP). In 2001 receipts from the leasing of the islands' internet domain address reached US $1.6m., while revenue from telecommunication licence fees totalled US $0.31m.

Tuvalu recorded a visible trade deficit of US $23.9m. in 2003; in that year the cost of imports exceeded $24.0m., while export revenue totalled only $147,100. The principal source of imports in 2003 was Fiji (47.9%). The principal market for exports were Australia and Fiji. The principal imports in 2003 were machinery, mechanical appliances and electrical equipment, mineral products, transport equipment and prepared foodstuffs.

According to ADB figures, the 2004 budget allowed for current expenditure of $A20.7m. and for capital spending of $0.4m. Revenue totalled $A15.4m. in the same year (some 62% lower than in 2002). With the support of the Consolidated Investment Fund (a depository of the TTF), in 2005 the budget deficit was reduced to $A1.2m., equivalent to 4.0% of GDP (compared with a deficit equivalent to 9.0% of GDP in 2004). The fiscal deficit for 2006, however, was expected to reach $A2.9m. and to increase further in 2007, to $A6.3m. In 1987 the Tuvalu Trust Fund (TTF) was established, with assistance from New Zealand, Australia and the United Kingdom, to generate funding, through overseas investment, for development projects. By 2005 the endowment value of the TTF was estimated to total $A99.4m. In 2005 the TTF contributed 18% of fiscal expenditure. Official development assistance in 2002 totalled US $11.7m., of which US $11.2m. was bilateral aid. In 2005/06 New Zealand budgeted for bilateral assistance worth $NZ2.05m. Aid from Australia was budgeted at $A5m. for the same year. Tuvalu also receives significant financial assistance from Taiwan since its establishment of diplomatic relations with that island. The annual rate of inflation averaged 2.6% in 1995–2004. According to the ADB, the average inflation rate increased from 2.1% in 2004 to 2.8% in 2005.

Tuvalu is a member of the Pacific Community (see p. 350), the Pacific Islands Forum (see p. 352) and the UN Economic and Social Commission for Asia and the Pacific (ESCAP, see p. 33). In May 1993 the country was admitted to the Asian Development Bank (ADB, see p. 169).

According to international criteria, Tuvalu is one of the world's least developed nations. Its economic development has been adversely affected by inclement weather and constrained by inadequate infrastructure. Tuvalu's vulnerability to fluctuations in the price of copra on the international market and the country's high dependence on imports have resulted in a persistent visible trade deficit. Tuvalu has also remained reliant on income from overseas and has continued to depend on foreign assistance for its development budget. Owing to a high rate of population growth and a drift from the outer islands to the capital, there is a serious problem of overcrowding on Funafuti. In August 1999 a US $4m. loan was secured to establish an outer islands development fund. The Island Development Programme aimed not only to decentralize administration but also to raise the standards of local public services and to encourage the development of small businesses. The capital assets of the Falekaupule Trust Fund, which was established in July 1999 and charged with promoting sustainable increases in funding for the development of the outer islands, reached US $8.2m. in 2001. In February 2000, meanwhile, the sale of the '.tv' internet suffix (see Recent History) substantially increased the islands' income (revenue from the sales totalled $A24.9m. in 2000, although this declined to some $A3m. in the following year). Proceeds from the sale were used to develop the country's infrastructure and were channelled largely into improving roads and the education system, also allowing the Government to investigate the possibility of buying land in Fiji, should the resettlement of Tuvalu's population become necessary. In an attempt to ensure the continuity of flights to Tuvalu, the Government committed itself to the purchase of majority shares in Air Fiji in March 2002, using a loan from the National Bank of Tuvalu. Meanwhile, the economy continued to suffer from the increasing impact of climate change on the islands, with high tides flooding homes, government buildings and the airport, and causing damage to agricultural produce in February 2005. Two major projects were expected to revitalize Tuvalu's economy: with assistance from the Japanese Government, the electricity network on Funafuti was to be rebuilt during 2005–06; and, in an effort to raise remittances from overseas workers, the Tuvalu Maritime Training Institute was to be substantially upgraded. However, the expansion of the institute was delayed pending the next round of accreditation assessments by the International Maritime Organization, which was due to take place by November 2006. The upgrade was aimed at significantly increasing the number of graduates of the institute. The Government's short-term development strategy has been formulated within a programme known as Te Kakeega II, eight strategic areas of focus being identified. The achievement of these aims, however, was largely dependent upon the performance of the TTF, funds from which accounted for 17% of the Government's recurrent budgetary receipts in 2005. Revenue from the sale of fishing licences was becoming more vulnerable to the fluctuations in fish stocks caused by the increasing frequency of the climatic phenomena known as El Niño and La Niña. Receipts from fish licences and revenue from the '.tv' internet domain facility together were projected to reach $A11m. in 2006. Although a substantial increase in the country's budget deficit was envisaged for 2007, a slight reduction in the deficit was anticipated for 2008. The transfer of some government enterprises to the private sector, in order to finance the country's budget deficits, was under consideration. The Government was investigating the possibilities of raising further income through taxation and user charges.

Education

Education is provided by the Government, and is compulsory between the ages of six and 15 years. In 2001 there were 10 primary schools, with a total of 1,798 pupils and 102 teachers. There was one secondary school in 2001, with 32 teachers and 558 pupils. The only tertiary institution is the Maritime Training School at Amatuku on Funafuti. Further training or vocational courses are available in Fiji and Kiribati. The University of the South Pacific (based in Fiji) has an extension centre on Funafuti. A programme of major reforms in the education system in Tuvalu, begun in the early 1990s, resulted in the lengthening of primary schooling (from six to eight years) and a compulsory two years of secondary education, as well as the introduction of vocational, technical and commerce-related courses at the Maritime Training School. Adult literacy was estimated at 98% at the 1991 census. Total government expenditure on education in 2001 was equivalent to some 35% of total budgetary expenditure. The education sector received funding US $10.5m. in 2005, as part of a joint grant provided by the New Zealand Government and the World Bank.

Public Holidays

2006: 1 January (New Year's Day), 13 March (Commonwealth Day), 14–17 April (Easter), 5 June (Queen's Official Birthday), 5 August (National Children's Day), 1–2 October (Tuvalu Day, anniversary of independence), 11 November (Prince of Wales's Birthday), 25 December (Christmas Day), 26 December (Boxing Day).

2007: 1 January (New Year's Day), 13 March (Commonwealth Day), 6–9 April (Easter), 4 June (Queen's Official Birthday), 5 August (National Children's Day), 1–2 October (Tuvalu Day, anniversary of independence), 11 November (Prince of Wales's Birthday), 25 December (Christmas Day), 26 December (Boxing Day).

Statistical Survey

AREA AND POPULATION

Land Area: 26 sq km (10 sq miles).

Population: 9,043 at census of 17 November 1991; 9,561 (males 4,729, females 4,832) at census of 1 November 2002; 10,764 (official estimate) at mid-2004. *By Atoll* (1996): Funafuti 3,836; Vaitupu 1,205; Niutao 749; Nanumea 818; Nukufetau 756; Nanumaga 644; Nui 608; Nukulaelae 370; Niulakita 75. *Mid-2004* (official estimate): Funafuti 5,394.

Density (mid-2004): 414.0 per sq km.

Principal Town (population at mid-2000): Vaiaku (capital) 4,590.

Births and Deaths (2000): Birth rate 21.8 per 1,000; Death rate 7.7 per 1,000. Source: UN, *Statistical Yearbook for Asia and the Pacific*.

Expectation of Life (WHO estimates, years at birth): 61 (males 61; females 62) in 2003. Source: WHO, *World Health Report*.

Economically Active Population: In 1979 there were 936 people in paid employment, 50% of them in government service. In 1979 114 Tuvaluans were employed by the Nauru Phosphate Co, with a smaller number employed in Kiribati and about 255 on foreign ships. At the 1991 census the total economically active population (aged 15 years and over) stood at 2,383 (males 1,605, females 778). *Mid-2003* (estimates): Agriculture, etc. 1,000; Total labour force 4,000 (Source: FAO).

HEALTH AND WELFARE

Key Indicators

Total Fertility Rate (children per woman, 2003): 2.8.

Under-5 Mortality Rate (per 1,000 live births, 2004): 51.

Health Expenditure (2002): US $ per head (PPP): 77.

Health Expenditure (2002): % of GDP: 6.9.

Health Expenditure (2002): public (% of total): 46.7.

Access to Water (% of persons, 2002): 93.

Access to Sanitation (% of persons, 2002): 88.

For sources and definitions, see explanatory note on p. vi.

AGRICULTURE, ETC.

Principal Crops (FAO estimates, metric tons, 2004): Coconuts 1,600; Copra 150; Bananas 270; Other fruit (excl. melons) 465.

Livestock (FAO estimate, '000 head, 2004): Pigs 13.5.

Livestock Products (FAO estimates, metric tons, 2004): Poultry meat 45; Pig meat 93; Hen eggs 22; Honey 3.

Fishing (FAO estimates, metric tons, live weight, 2003): Total catch 1,500 (Skipjack tuna 800; Yellowfin tuna 100).

Source: FAO.

FINANCE

Currency and Exchange Rates: Australian and Tuvaluan currencies are both in use. Australian currency: 100 cents = 1 Australian dollar ($A). *Sterling, US Dollar and Euro Equivalents* (30 December 2005): £1 sterling = $A2.3469; US $1 = $A1.3630; €1 = $A1.6079; $A100 = £42.61= US $73.37 = €61.19. *Average Exchange Rate ($A per US dollar)*: 1.5419 in 2003; 1.3598 in 2004; 1.3095 in 2005.

Budget ($A '000, 2004): Current revenue 15,419 (Revenue from taxation 5,777, Non-tax revenue 9,642); Expenditure 21,094 (Current expenditure 20,697, Capital expenditure 397). Source: Asian Development Bank, *Key Indicators of Developing Asian and Pacific Countries*.

Official Development Assistance (US $ million, 2001): Bilateral 3.8; Multilateral 0.2; Total 4.0 (all grants). Source: UN, *Statistical Yearbook for Asia and the Pacific*.

Cost of Living (Consumer Price Index for Funafuti; base: July–Sept. 2003 = 100): 95.8 in 2002; 99.0 in 2003; 101.8 in 2004. Source: Asian Development Bank, *Key Indicators of Developing Asian and Pacific Countries*.

Gross Domestic Product at Constant 1988 Prices ($A '000 at factor cost): 16,947 in 2002; 17,286 in 2003 (estimate); 17,805 in 2004 (estimate).

Gross Domestic Product by Economic Activity ($A '000 at current prices, 2002): Agriculture 4,565; Mining 237; Manufacturing 1,016; Electricity, gas and water 1,433; Construction 1,370; Trade, restaurants and hotels 3,700; Transport, storage and communications 3,429; Finance and real estate 4,055; Public administration 7,188; Community and personal services, *less* imputed bank charges 500; *Total* 27,490. Source: Asian Development Bank, *Key Indicators of Developing Asian and Pacific Countries*.

Balance of Payments ($A '000, 1996): Exports of goods f.o.b. 361; Imports of goods f.o.b. −10,740; *Trade balance* −10,379; Exports of services and other income 10,502; Imports of services and other income −8,758; *Balance on goods, services and income* −8,635; Unrequited transfers (net) 9,082; *Current balance* 447; Capital account (net) 2,088; Net errors and omissions −55; *Overall balance* 2,480. Source: Asian Development Bank, *Key Indicators of Developing Asian and Pacific Countries*.

EXTERNAL TRADE

Principal Commodities ($A '000, 2002): *Imports:* Animals and animal products 1,418.9; Vegetable products 1,061.6; Prepared foodstuffs 2,156.6; Mineral products 2,815.2; Base metals and articles thereof 1,794.2; Machinery, mechanical appliances and electrical equipment 2,515.4; Transportation equipment 1,488.8; Total (incl. others) 20,362. *Exports:* Vegetable products 23.4; Chemical products 2.5; Plastics and rubber 13.6; Base metals and articles thereof 19.3; Machinery, mechanical appliances and electrical equipment 127.6; Optical, photographic and medical equipment 54.3; Miscellaneous manufactured articles 2.7; Total (incl. others) 252.5. *2003* ($A '000): Total imports 24,043; Total exports 147.1. *2005* ($A '000): Total imports 16,908. Source: Tuvalu Central Statistics Division.

Principal Trading Partners (US $ million, 2003): *Imports:* Australia 3.42; Fiji 10.62; Japan 2.41; New Zealand 1.82; Germany 1.71 Total (incl. others) 22.16. *Exports:* Australia 0.20; Fiji 0.11; Germany 0.05; Italy 0.08; Poland 0.06; Total (incl. others) 1.45.

Source: Asian Development Bank, *Key Indicators of Developing Asian and Pacific Countries*.

TRANSPORT

Shipping: *Merchant Fleet* (registered at 31 December 2004): Vessels 48; Total displacement ('000 grt) 138.2. Source: Lloyd's Register-Fairplay, *World Fleet Statistics*.

TOURISM

Tourist Arrivals: 1,236 in 2002; 1,496 in 2003; 1,214 in 2004. Source: South Pacific Tourism Organization.

Tourist Arrivals by Country of Residence (2001): Australia 445; Fiji/Kiribati 861; Germany 68; Japan 317; New Zealand 232; United Kingdom 67; USA 101; Total (incl. others) 2,813. Source: *Tuvalu 2002 Economic and Public Sector Review*.

COMMUNICATIONS MEDIA

Non-daily Newspapers (1996): 1; estimated circulation 300*.

Telephones (main lines, 2001): 1,000 in use†.

Internet Users (2002): 1,250.

Radio Receivers (1997): 4,000 in use*.

Facsimile Machines (1993): 10 in use‡.

* Source: UNESCO, *Statistical Yearbook*.
† Source: International Telecommunication Union.
‡ Source: UN, *Statistical Yearbook*.

EDUCATION

Primary (2001): 9 government schools, 1 private school; 102 teachers; 1,798 pupils.

General Secondary (2001): 1 government school; 32 teachers; 558 pupils. A maritime school offers training for 60 merchant seamen per year, with vocational, technical and commerce-related courses. The University of the South Pacific has an extension centre in Funafuti offering diploma and vocational courses and the first two years of degree courses (the latter requiring completion in Suva, Fiji).

Directory

The Constitution

A new Constitution came into effect at independence on 1 October 1978. Its main provisions are as follows:

The Constitution states that Tuvalu is a democratic sovereign state and that the Constitution is the Supreme Law. It guarantees protection of all fundamental rights and freedoms and provides for the determination of citizenship.

The British sovereign is represented by the Governor-General, who must be a citizen of Tuvalu and is appointed on the recommendation of the Prime Minister. The Prime Minister is elected by Parliament, and up to four other ministers are appointed by the Governor-General from among the members of Parliament, after consultation with the Prime Minister. The Cabinet, which is directly responsible to Parliament, consists of the Prime Minister and the other ministers, whose functions are to advise the Governor-General upon the government of Tuvalu. The Attorney-General is the principal legal adviser to the Government. Parliament is composed of 15 members directly elected by universal adult suffrage for four years, subject to dissolution, and is presided over by the Speaker (who is elected by the members). The Constitution also provides for the operation of a Judiciary (see Judicial System) and for an independent Public Service. Under a revised Constitution that took effect on 1 October 1986, the Governor-General no longer has the authority to reject the advice of the Government.

The Government

HEAD OF STATE

Sovereign: HM Queen ELIZABETH II.

Governor-General: FILOIMEA TELITO (took office 15 April 2005).

CABINET
(April 2006)

Prime Minister and Minister of Foreign Affairs and Labour: MAATIA TOAFA.

Deputy Prime Minister and Minister of Works and Energy and of Communications and Transport: SAUFATU SOPOANGA.

Minister of Finance, Economic Planning and Industries: BIKENIBEU PAENIU.

Minister of Health and of Education and Sports: Dr ALESANA KLIES SELUKA.

Minister of Natural Resources: SAMUELU PENITALA TEO.

TUVALU

Minister of Home Affairs and Rural Development: LETI PELESALA.

MINISTRIES

Ministry of Communications and Transport: Vaiaku, Funafuti; tel. 20051.

Ministry of Education and Sports: Vaiaku, Funafuti; tel. 20416; fax 20832.

Ministry of Finance, Economic Planning and Industries: PMB, Vaiaku, Funafuti; tel. 20408; fax 20210.

Ministry of Foreign Affairs and Labour: Vaiaku, Funafuti; tel. 20100; fax 20820.

Ministry of Health: Vaiaku, Funafuti; tel. 20416; fax 20832.

Ministry of Home Affairs and Rural Development: Vaiaku, Funafuti; tel. 20172; fax 20821.

Ministry of Natural Resources: Vaiaku, Funafuti; tel. 20160; fax 20826.

Ministry of Works and Energy: PMB, Vaiaku, Funafuti; tel. 20051; fax 20772.

Legislature

PARLIAMENT

Parliament has 15 members, who hold office for a term of up to four years. A general election was held on 25 July 2002. The next election was scheduled to be held on 3 August 2006. There are no political parties.

Speaker: OTINIELU TAUTELEIMALAE TAUSI.

Diplomatic Representation

There are no embassies or high commissions in Tuvalu. The British High Commissioner in Fiji is also accredited as High Commissioner to Tuvalu. Other Ambassadors or High Commissioners accredited to Tuvalu include the Australian, New Zealand, US, French and Japanese Ambassadors in Fiji.

Judicial System

The Supreme Law is embodied in the Constitution. The High Court is the superior court of record, presided over by the Chief Justice, and has jurisdiction to consider appeals from judgments of the Magistrates' Courts and the Island Courts. Appeals from the High Court lie with the Court of Appeal in Fiji or, in the ultimate case, with the Judicial Committee of the Privy Council in the United Kingdom.

There are eight Island Courts with limited jurisdiction in criminal and civil cases.

High Court: Vaiaku, Funafuti; tel. 20837.
Chief Justice: VINCENT LUNABEK.
Attorney-General: IAKOBA ITALELEI TAEIA.

Religion

CHRISTIANITY

Te Ekalesia Kelisiano Tuvalu (The Christian Church of Tuvalu): POB 2, Funafuti; tel. 20755; fax 20651; f. 1861; autonomous since 1968; derived from the Congregationalist foundation of the London Missionary Society; some 98% of the population are adherents; Pres. Rev. TOFIGA FALANI; Gen. Sec. Rev. KITIONA TAUSI.

Roman Catholic Church: Catholic Centre, POB 58, Funafuti; tel. and fax 20527; e-mail cathcent@tuvalu.tv; 122 adherents (31 Dec. 2003); Superior Fr CAMILLE DESROSIERS.

Other churches with adherents in Tuvalu include the Church of Jesus Christ of Latter-day Saints (Mormons), the Jehovah's Witnesses, the New Apostolic Church and the Seventh-day Adventists.

BAHÁ'Í FAITH

National Spiritual Assembly: POB 48, Funafuti; tel. 20860; mems resident in 8 localities.

The Press

Tuvalu Echoes: Broadcasting and Information Office, Vaiaku, Funafuti; tel. 20138; fax 20732; f. 1984; fortnightly; English; Editor MELAKI TAEPE; circ. 250.

Te Lama: Ekalesia Kelisiano Tuvalu, POB 2, Funafuti; tel. 20755; fax 20651; quarterly; religious; Pres. Rev. ETI KINE; Editor Rev. KITIONA TAUSI; circ. 1,000.

Broadcasting and Communications

TELECOMMUNICATIONS

Tuvalu Telecommunications Corporation: Vaiaku, Funafuti; tel. 20001; fax 20800; e-mail media@tuvalu.tv; f. 1994.

BROADCASTING

Tuvalu Media Corporation: PMB, Vaiaku, Funafuti; tel. 20731; fax 20732; e-mail media@tuvalu.tv; f. 1999; govt-owned; Chief Broadcasting and Information Officer PUSINELLI LAAFAI.

Radio

Radio Tuvalu: Broadcasting and Information Office, PMB, Vaiaku, Funafuti; tel. 20138; fax 20732; f. 1975; daily broadcasts in Tuvaluan and English, 43 hours per week; Programme Producer RUBY S. ALEFAIO.

Finance

BANKS

Development Bank of Tuvalu: PMB 9, Vaiaku, Funafuti; tel. 20199; fax 20850; f. 1993; replaced the Business Development Advisory Bureau.

National Bank of Tuvalu: POB 13, Vaiaku, Funafuti; tel. 20803; fax 20802; e-mail nbt@tuvalu.tv; f. 1980; commercial bank; govt-owned; ($A '000) cap. 471.0, res 3,128.9, dep. 21,547.4 (Dec. 2002); Chair. SEVE PAENIU; Gen. Man. IONATANA PEIA; brs on all atolls.

Trade and Industry

GOVERNMENT AGENCIES

National Fishing Corporation of Tuvalu (NAFICOT): POB 93, Funafuti; tel. 20724; fax 20152; fishing vessel operators; seafood processing and marketing; agents for diesel engine spare parts, fishing supplies and marine electronics; Gen. Man. SEMU SOPOANGA TAAFAKI.

Tuvalu Philatelic Bureau: POB 24, Funafuti; tel. 20224; fax 20712; e-mail philatelic@tuvalu.tv.

CHAMBER OF COMMERCE

Tuvalu Chamber of Commerce: POB 27, Vaiaku, Funafuti; tel. 20917; fax 20646; e-mail tpasefika@hotmail.com; Chair. MATANILE IOSEFA; Sec. TEO PASEFIKA.

UTILITIES

Electricity

Tuvalu Electricity Corporation (TEC): POB 32, Vaiaku, Funafuti; tel. 20352; fax 20351; e-mail thomas@tuvalu.tv.

CO-OPERATIVES

Tuvalu Co-operative Society Ltd: POB 11, Funafuti; tel. 20747; fax 20748; e-mail mlaafai@tuvalu.tv; f. 1979; by amalgamation of the eight island socs; controls retail trade in the islands; Gen. Man. MONISE LAAFAI; Registrar SIMETI LOPATI.

Tuvalu Coconut Traders Co-operative: Contact TAAI KATALAKE.

TRADE UNION

Tuvalu Overseas Seamen's Union (TOSU): POB 99, Funafuti; tel. 20609; fax 20610; e-mail tosu@tuvalu.tv; f. 1988; Gen. Sec. TOMMY ALEFAIO.

Transport

ROADS
Funafuti has some impacted-coral roads totalling some 8km in length; elsewhere, tracks exist.

SHIPPING
There is a deep-water lagoon at the point of entry, Funafuti, and ships are able to enter the lagoon at Nukufetau. Irregular shipping services connect Tuvalu with Fiji and elsewhere. The Government operates an inter-island vessel.

CIVIL AVIATION
In 1992 a new runway was constructed with EU aid to replace the grass landing strip on Funafuti. Air Marshall Islands operates a three-weekly service between Funafuti, Nadi (Fiji) and Majuro (Marshall Islands). In June 1995 Tuvalu, Kiribati, the Marshall Islands and Nauru agreed to begin discussions on the establishment of a joint regional airline. The Government of Tuvalu purchased a substantial shareholding (estimated at some US $2m.) in Air Fiji in 2001.

Tourism

In 2004 there was one hotel, with 16 rooms, on Funafuti and three guest houses. There were 1,214 tourist arrivals in 2004. On average a similar number of people visit the islands on official business each year, although this figure was increased in 2005 by Tuvalu's hosting of a regional meeting of Ministers of Finance. The majority of visitors are from Fiji, Kiribati, Australia, Japan and New Zealand.

Tuvalu Tourism Office: Ministry of Finance, Economic Planning and Industries, PMB, Funafuti; tel. 20840; fax 20210; e-mail lleneuoti@yahoo.com; internet www.timelesstuvalu.com; Tourism Officer LONO LENEUOTI.

UGANDA

Introductory Survey

Location, Climate, Language, Religion, Flag, Capital

The Republic of Uganda is a land-locked equatorial country in East Africa, bordered by Sudan to the north, the Democratic Republic of the Congo to the west, Kenya to the east and Rwanda, Tanzania and Lake Victoria to the south. The climate is tropical, with temperatures, moderated by the altitude of the country, varying between 15°C and 30°C. The official language is English and there are many local languages, the most important of which is Luganda. About 75% of the population follow Christian beliefs, while some 15% are Muslims. The national flag (proportions 2 by 3) has six horizontal stripes: black, gold, red, black, gold and red. In the centre is a white disc containing a crested crane. The capital is Kampala.

Recent History

Formerly a British protectorate, Uganda became an independent member of the Commonwealth on 9 October 1962. The Government was led by Dr Milton Obote, leader of the Uganda People's Congress (UPC) from 1960 and Prime Minister from April 1962. At independence the country comprised four regions, including the kingdom of Buganda, which had federal status. Exactly one year after independence Uganda became a republic, with Mutesa II, Kabaka (King) of Buganda, as first President. In February 1966 Obote led a successful coup against the Kabaka, and in April he became executive President. In September 1967 a new Constitution was introduced, establishing a unitary republic, and Buganda was brought under the control of the central Government. After an assassination attempt on President Obote in December 1969 all opposition parties were banned.

Obote was overthrown in January 1971 by the army, led by Maj.-Gen. (later Field Marshal) Idi Amin Dada, who assumed full executive powers and suspended political activity. The National Assembly was dissolved in February, when Amin declared himself Head of State, took over legislative powers and suspended parts of the 1967 Constitution. In August 1972 Amin, proclaiming an 'economic war' to free Uganda from foreign domination, undertook a mass expulsion of non-citizen Asians (who comprised the majority of the resident Asian population), thereby incurring widespread international condemnation.

Amin's regime was characterized by the ruthless elimination of suspected opponents, mass flights of refugees to neighbouring countries and periodic purges of the army (which, in turn, perpetrated numerous atrocities). Relations within the East African Community (EAC), comprising Uganda, Kenya and Tanzania, deteriorated during the 1970s. In February 1976 Amin claimed that large areas of western Kenya were historically part of Uganda, and in November 1978 Uganda annexed the Kagera salient from Tanzania. In early 1979 an invasion force comprising Tanzanian troops and the Uganda National Liberation Army (UNLA), formed by Ugandan exiles, gained control of the southern region of Uganda. Amin's forces capitulated, and in April a Tanzanian assault force entered Kampala. The remaining pro-Amin troops were defeated in June. Amin fled initially to Libya, and in 1980 took up permanent residence in Saudi Arabia. He remained in exile there until his death in August 2003.

A provisional Government, the National Executive Council (NEC), was established in April 1979 from the ranks of the Uganda National Liberation Front (UNLF, a coalition of 18 previously exiled groups), with Dr Yusuf Lule, a former vice-chancellor of Makerere University, as President. When Lule attempted to reshuffle the NEC in June, opposition from within the UNLF forced his resignation. Lule was succeeded by Godfrey Binaisa (a former Attorney-General), who was, in turn, overthrown by the Military Commission of the UNLF in May 1980, after he had decided to allow only UNLF members to stand in parliamentary elections and attempted to reorganize the leadership of the UNLA. The elections, in December, were contested by four parties and won by the UPC, with Obote, who remained its leader, becoming President for the second time. The defeated parties complained of gross electoral malpractice by UPC supporters.

The Obote Government was subject to constant attack from guerrilla groups operating inside the country. Hundreds of Obote's opponents were detained, including Democratic Party (DP) members of the National Assembly, and several newspapers were banned. Following the withdrawal of Tanzanian troops in June 1981, there were reports from the West Nile Region of further atrocities by Ugandan soldiers. In January 1982 the Uganda Popular Front was formed to co-ordinate, from abroad, the activities of the main opposition groups in exile: the Uganda Freedom Movement (UFM), the Uganda National Rescue Front and the National Resistance Movement (NRM), led by Lule and his former Minister of Defence, Lt-Gen. Yoweri Museveni. The NRM had a military wing, the National Resistance Army (NRA), led by Museveni. Lule died in 1985, whereupon Museveni became sole leader of the NRM and NRA. From 1982 thousands of Ugandans were reported to have fled the country, to escape fighting between guerrilla forces and UNLA troops. In March 1983, during a campaign by the UNLA to repel an NRA offensive, attacks on refugee camps resulted in the deaths of hundreds of civilians, and more than 100,000 people were displaced. The NRA denied involvement in the massacres.

In July 1985 Obote was overthrown in a military coup, led by Brig. (later Lt-Gen.) Basilio Okello. (Obote was subsequently granted political asylum by Zambia.) A Military Council, headed by Lt-Gen. (later Gen.) Tito Okello, the Commander-in-Chief of the army, was established to govern the country, pending elections to be held one year later. In subsequent months groups that had been in opposition to Obote, with the exception of the NRA and the NRM (see below), reached agreement with the new administration, and accepted positions on the Military Council. An amnesty was declared for exiles who had supported Amin. The UNLA allegedly continued to perpetrate atrocities under the Okello regime.

In August 1985 the NRA, led by Museveni, entered into negotiations with the Government (under the auspices of President Daniel arap Moi of Kenya), while conducting a simultaneous military campaign to overthrow Okello. During the following two months the NRA gained control of large areas of the country. In December the NRA and the Government signed a peace agreement; the terms of the accord were never implemented, however, and on 26 January 1986 the NRA took control of Kampala by force and dissolved the Military Council. Okello fled to Sudan, and then to Tanzania. On 29 January Museveni was sworn in as President, and in February he announced the formation of a new Cabinet, comprising mainly members of the NRA and NRM, but also representatives of other political groups including the DP, the UPC, the UFM, the Federal Democratic Movement (FEDEMO), and three members of the previous administration. A National Resistance Council (NRC) was formed to act in place of a legislature for an indefinite period. All party political activity was banned in March, although political organizations were not proscribed. At a summit meeting in March the Heads of State of all the countries adjoining Uganda pledged their support for Museveni.

Initial attempts to integrate defeated rebel forces into the NRA were only partially successful, and guerrilla groups remained active in northern Uganda. An association of opposition groups, the Uganda People's Democratic Movement (UPDM), was formed in May 1986.

In June 1987 the NRC offered an amnesty to rebels (except those accused of murder or rape). In August, however, the UPDM joined with a faction of the FEDEMO and another opposition group, the United National Front, to form an alliance seeking Museveni's overthrow. The most widespread source of disruption during 1987 was a rebellion that had arisen in northern and eastern Uganda in late 1986 by the cultish 'Holy Spirit' movement; between December 1986 and November 1987 some 5,000 ill-equipped 'Holy Spirit' fighters were reportedly killed in clashes with the NRA. By December 1987 the rebellion had been suppressed, and its leader had escaped to Kenya. Surviving members of the movement, however, regrouped as the Lord's Resistance Army (LRA—see below). In early 1988 the NRC extended the period of its amnesty to guerrilla groups: by mid-April it was reported that almost 30,000 rebels had surrendered. Many of these were integrated into the NRA.

In February 1989 the first national election since 1980 was held. The NRC, hitherto composed solely of presidential nominees, was expanded from 98 to 278 members, to include 210 elected representatives. While 20 ministerial posts were reserved for nominated members of the NRC, 50 were allocated to elected members. Also in February Museveni appointed a constitutional commission to assess public opinion on Uganda's political future and to draft a new constitution.

In October 1989 (despite opposition from the DP) the NRC approved draft legislation to prolong the Government's term of office by five years from January 1990 (when its mandate had been due to expire): the NRM justified seeking to extend its rule by claiming that it required further time in which to prepare a new constitution, organize elections, eliminate guerrilla activity, improve the judiciary, police force and civil service and rehabilitate the country's infrastructure. In March 1990 the NRM extended the national ban on party political activity (imposed in March 1986) for a further five years. In July the leader of the UPDM, Eric Otema Allimadi, signed a peace accord with the Government. During April 1991 the NRA initiated a campaign to combat continuing rebel activity in the north and east: by July it was reported that at least 1,500 guerrillas had been killed and more than 1,000 arrested. In May Museveni formally invited all former resident Asians expelled at the time of the Amin regime to return, pledging the restitution of expropriated property.

In December 1992 the Constitutional Commission presented its draft Constitution to the Government. The draft was published in March 1993, and in the following month the NRC passed legislation authorizing the establishment of a Constituent Assembly (see below). In July the NRC adopted a constitutional amendment revoking the abolition of traditional rulers, as provided for under the 1967 Constitution. Restored traditional rulers would, however, have only ceremonial significance.

In January 1994 the Ugandan National Democratic Alliance and the Ugandan Federal Army agreed to suspend their armed struggle, under the provisions of a government amnesty, and in March the surrender of senior members of the Ruwenzururu Kingdom Freedom Movement in the south-west signified the end of a conflict dating from independence. During January the Government took part in negotiations with the LRA. However, following the collapse of the discussions, the LRA intensified guerrilla activities in northern Uganda. From 1994 large numbers of security forces were deployed in the region, representing a considerable burden on national resources; they failed, however, to suppress the rebellion (see below).

At elections to the 288-member Constituent Assembly, which took place on 28 March 1994, more than 1,500 candidates contested the 214 elective seats. Although the elections were officially conducted on a non-party basis, NRM members were believed to have secured the majority of votes in the centre, west and south-west of the country, whereas UPC and DP members, who advocated an immediate return to multi-party politics, secured the most seats in the north and east. The Constituent Assembly, which also comprised nominated representatives of the armed forces, political parties, trade unions, and youth and disabled organizations, debated and amended the draft Constitution, finally enacting it in September 1995. The Constitution, under whose terms a national referendum on the future introduction of a multi-party political system took place in 2000 (see below), was promulgated in October 1995.

A presidential election took place in May 1996, at which Museveni was returned to office, winning 74.2% of the votes cast. The election was pronounced free and fair by international observers. Museveni's main rival, Paul Ssemogerere (the Chairman of the DP, who had resigned as Second Deputy Prime Minister and Minister of Public Service in June 1995), took 23.7% of the votes. As the unofficial representative of an electoral alliance between the DP and the UPC, Ssemogerere was widely perceived to be associated with the UPC's exiled leader, Dr Milton Obote. Legislative elections took place in June 1996. The total membership of the NRC, redesignated the Parliament under the new Constitution, was reduced from 278 to 276, comprising 214 elected and 62 nominated representatives. Also in June elections were held for new local councils (to replace the resistance committees). In July Museveni appointed an enlarged Government.

From the mid-1990s the Museveni administration was greatly preoccupied with combating insurrections perpetrated by three main rebel groups in northern and western Uganda. In the north the LRA (reportedly backed by Sudan) was becoming increasingly disruptive. During 1993–98 the LRA was alleged to have killed as many as 10,000 people, while some 220,000 sought refuge in protected camps; economic activity in the region was devastated. The LRA's use of abducted children as soldiers (reportedly some 10,000 by early 1999) attracted widespread international condemnation. The Government strongly resisted pressure to resume negotiations with the LRA, prompting some speculation that Museveni (a southerner) might be prepared to profit from the disablement of opposition strongholds in the northern region. In May 1999, however, the Government appeared to modify its policy towards the LRA by offering it an amnesty and promising its leader, Joseph Kony, a cabinet post in the event of his being democratically elected. In the west, meanwhile, the Uganda People's Defence Forces (UPDF, as the NRA had become) fought intermittently with two rebel groups: the Allied Democratic Front (ADF), mainly comprising Ugandan Islamic fundamentalist rebels, exiled Rwandan Hutu militiamen and former soldiers from Zaire (which became the Democratic Republic of the Congo—DRC—in May 1997), and the West Nile Bank Front (WNBF). Although WNBF activities subsided in mid-1997, following the killing of several hundred of its members by Sudanese rebels, the ADF mounted a persistent terror campaign from mid-1997 against western Ugandan targets, threatening tourism to the region and disrupting economic activity. In May 1999 Roman Catholic leaders in the Ruwenzori region offered to mediate between the Ugandan Government and the ADF, which was believed to bear the main responsibility for a series of bomb attacks on civilian targets in Kampala from 1998. In August 1999, confronted by escalating security problems on various fronts, the Government was reported to have recalled for military service some 10,000 demobilized troops, and in September the command structure of the UPDF was reorganized. In October the High Court dismissed charges of treason against some 340 alleged members of the now defunct WNBF who had been detained for more than two years. In November the UPDF launched a new offensive against the ADF in the Ruwenzori region. In December the Parliament adopted legislation that extended (not without conditions, in some cases) an amnesty to all rebels in opposition to President Museveni. The ADF's response was apparently to intensify its struggle. In February 2000 President Museveni was reported to be personally co-ordinating military operations against the ADF in western Uganda, and to have renewed his appeal to the rebels to avail themselves of the new amnesty legislation.

In July 1999 legislation was enacted providing for the proposed referendum on a multi-party political system to take place in 2000 as planned. However, most political parties announced that they would boycott the referendum on the grounds that it would be manipulated by the NRM for its own objectives. In October a US-based human rights organization, Human Rights Watch, criticized Uganda's political system and claimed that the country was moving away from democracy. Ugandan political leaders had criticized the readiness of some Western donors (in particular those that formed the Referendum 2000 Group in December 1999) to support the referendum process, claiming that by so doing they were legitimizing the prevailing suspension of active political opposition. In February 2000 Uganda's Multi-Party National Referendum Committee appealed for a postponement of the referendum on the grounds that the Electoral Commission had not made funds available to some advocates of a return to political pluralism. In the same month the Referendum 2000 Group expressed concern at the Government's failure to implement measures on which it had made conditional its support of the referendum process. At the referendum, which proceeded on 29 June, 90.7% of participants voted in favour of retaining the existing 'no-party' political system. However, the result was effectively nullified by the Constitutional Court in 2004 (see below).

A presidential election was held on 12 March 2001. The election had been scheduled for 7 March, but was delayed to allow the Electoral Commission time to check and amend the electoral register after it was found to contain about 2.5m. more voters than there were citizens eligible to vote. At the election, which had a participation rate of 70%, Museveni was re-elected President, winning 69.3% of the votes cast. His main challenger, Kizza Besigye, won 27.8%. There were some allegations of electoral malpractice and intimidation of opposition politicians, but international observers held that this did not affect the overall result. Besigye, who had served with Museveni during the civil war as his personal physician, represented the first real challenge to Museveni's authority.

Legislative elections were held on 26 June 2001, at which 50 parliamentarians, including 10 ministers, failed to secure re-election. The rate of voter participation was reported as being low. The total number of seats in Parliament was increased to 292 (comprising 214 elected and 78 nominated representatives), of which the NRM reportedly secured more than 70%. In July Museveni appointed a new Cabinet, which included the 10 ministers who had failed to retain their parliamentary seats in June. Notably, Amama Mbabazi was appointed as Minister of Defence, a portfolio hitherto held by Museveni.

In May 2002 Parliament approved the Political Parties and Organizations Act 2002, which severely curtailed the activities of political parties, while classifying the NRM as a 'political system' rather than a party. The Act also provided for the dissolution of all parties not registered by 17 January 2003. However, in March 2003 opposition leaders successfully challenged two clauses of the Act in the Constitutional Court, which ruled that the NRM was not a system, but a political party, and suspended the section of the Act that required parties to register, pending the outcome of a further petition against the Act. (The Attorney-General later clarified that parties would still be obliged to register, but not by a particular time.) The ruling allowed political parties to operate nationally for the first time in 17 years. The NRM became the first party to apply for registration, in June 2003, under the modified name of the National Resistance Movement Organisation (NRM-O); some opposition parties remained reluctant to register under a law that they still regarded as restrictive. Meanwhile, in late May Museveni effected a cabinet reorganization, notably appointing Prof. Gilbert Bukenya as Vice-President, following the resignation of the incumbent, Dr Speciosa Kazibwe, and dismissing a number of ministers who had recently expressed opposition to a proposal to revoke the current two-term limit on the presidential mandate. This proposal was endorsed by the Cabinet in August. By April 2004 some 60 new political parties had emerged, although only 13 had applied for registration. Also in April Museveni was promoted to the rank of General, before formally retiring from the military in order to comply with legislation barring serving members of the armed forces from active membership of a political party. Museveni retained his position as Commander-in-Chief of the armed forces.

In June 2004 the Constitutional Court issued a ruling that annulled the Referendum (Political System) Act of 2000 and effectively nullified the June 2000 referendum at which a return to a multi-party system had been rejected. Thus, legislative elections, scheduled to be held concurrently with the presidential election in 2006, would be held under the new system—subject to approval at a referendum, which was to be held in July 2005 (see below). The referendum appeared to be unnecessary, however, as in November 2004 the Constitutional Court repealed legislation preventing political parties from contesting elections. The Court also rejected an appeal from opposition parties against mandatory registration, and ruled that parties would have six months to register prior to the 2006 elections.

Meanwhile, it was reported in August 2004 that a new opposition party, the Forum for Democratic Change (FDC), had been formed by a merger of Reform Agenda, the Parliamentary Advocacy Forum and the National Democratic Forum. Several parliamentarians affiliated to the UPC had apparently joined the new party.

In February 2005 the Constitution (Amendment) Bill, which provided for a return to multi-party democracy, was presented to the Parliament. The Bill also contained a provision for the removal of the two-term limit on the presidency. Museveni had yet to publicly declare whether he intended to stand for a third term of office, however, it was widely accepted that he would. Throughout 2004 Museveni had engaged in what amounted to a tacit campaign for re-election: he abolished an unpopular local tax on 'boda bodas' (motorcycle taxis) in Kampala and offered deputies who openly supported his re-election funds to be used ostensibly to enable them to consult with their constituents on the Constitution (Amendment) Bill. Furthermore, in mid-January 2005 Museveni effected a cabinet reshuffle, in which several ministers who had advocated a third presidential term for Museveni were promoted. Parliament approved the removal of the two-term limit on the presidency in June, and voted in favour of the holding of a national referendum on the restoration of multi-party democracy. At the referendum, which took place on 28 July, 92.5% of participants approved the motion. The rate of voter participation was low, however, at just 47%. The opposition had called for a boycott of the referendum.

In October 2005 Besigye returned from four years of self-imposed exile in South Africa in order to contest the presidential election as the FDC's candidate. (He had left Uganda following the presidential elections of 2001 claiming to fear for his safety.) Besigye was arrested in November 2005 and charged with rape and treason. He was also accused of belonging to the People's Redemption Army—a rebel group allegedly based in eastern DRC. Besigye denied any link to the movement, although he had previously threatened to attempt to overthrow the Government. Besigye was also accused of association with the LRA. The FDC claimed the charges against Besigye were politically motivated and designed to prevent him from contesting the election. Large numbers of his supporters gathered to demonstrate outside the police station where he was being detained and two days of violence ensued, with the security forces resorting to the use of tear gas in order to disperse the crowds. Later that month 14 people who, with Besigye, were also being tried for treason were granted bail by the High Court. However, a group of armed men, not in regular army uniform, arrived and waited for them outside court and the 14 opted to remain in custody. The following week Besigye and a number of others appeared before a military tribunal and were charged with terrorism and illegally possessing weapons. Besigye's lawyers contested the tribunal's jurisdiction and refused to enter a plea. His trial by court martial was to begin following the conclusion of his civil trial. In December Besigye pleaded not guilty to the treason charge at the High Court; his trial was postponed until early January, raising fears that it might not conclude in time for the election. The High Court ruled that the military should suspend its trial until the Constitutional Court had examined its legality; however, the military stated its intention to proceed, noting that it was not subordinate to the High Court. (Although the High Court had granted Besigye bail, he remained in military custody.) In January 2006 the High Court ruled that the military tribunal's authority to detain Besigye had expired and ordered his release. The Constitutional Court judged that the military did not have the jurisdiction to try Besigye, and that the charges related to terrorism and the illegal possession of weapons could only be heard by the High Court. It also ruled that the deployment of troops to the High Court in November was unconstitutional. In February a High Court jury found Besigye not guilty of rape. Under Ugandan law a jury can advise a judge but its decision is not binding. The High Court adjourned Besigye's trial until after the election.

Meanwhile, in mid-November 2005 President Museveni confirmed his intention to stand for a third term in office. He was subsequently elected unopposed as the NRM-O candidate.

At the presidential election, held on 23 February 2006, Museveni won 59.3% of the valid votes cast and was elected for a third term. Besigye was the only other candidate to mount a credible challenge, receiving 37.4% of the votes. While international observers did not condemn the process outright, they reported a number of serious flaws and concluded that a law passed in 1997 that effectively granted the NRM-O access to public funds for campaigning did not provide a fair basis for multi-party elections. (Parliamentary elections were held concurrently with the presidential election, although results were not immediately made available.)

In March 2006 Besigye was acquitted of rape. The military conceded that Besigye would not have to face a court martial while on trial for treason, but did not drop the charges against him and appealed against the ruling that the terrorism and weapons charges must be heard in the High Court. In April Besigye challenged the results of the presidential election in the Supreme Court. The Court unanimously decided that the Electoral Commission had not conducted the election in compliance with the Constitution and other relevant legislation. However, it further ruled (by four votes to three) that this had not substantially affected the final outcome of the election. Besigye's trial for treason commenced in April; he and his 22 co-defendants denied the charges.

Meanwhile, in April 2005 it was reported that the former President, Apollo Milton Obote, was considering a return from exile in Zambia. However, the Ugandan Government stated that it had yet to receive a formal request from Obote for permission to re-enter Uganda, and that until it did so it would not declare its position on the issue. Obote died in October, still in exile. His body was returned to Uganda where he was accorded a state funeral.

During 1987 Uganda's relations with neighbouring Kenya deteriorated, with the Museveni Government accusing the regime of President Moi of sheltering and supporting Ugandan rebels. When, in October, Uganda stationed troops at the two countries' common border, Kenya threatened to retaliate with force against any attempts by Ugandan military personnel to cross the frontier in pursuit of rebels. In December there were clashes between Kenyan and Ugandan security forces, and the border was temporarily closed. In late December, following the intervention of the Organization of African Unity (now the African Union, see p. 153), discussions between the Heads of State of the two countries led to a resumption of normal traffic across the border. However, several incursions into Kenya by Ugandan troops were subsequently reported. In November 1994 the Presidents of Uganda, Kenya and Tanzania met in Arusha, Tanzania, and established a permanent commission for co-operation between the three countries. During early 1995 Kenya protested strongly to the UN following the granting of refugee status in Uganda to an alleged Kenyan guerrilla leader; the Ugandan Government subsequently claimed to have deported the dissident to an unspecified third country. In March 1996 Museveni, Moi and President Benjamin Mkapa of Tanzania, meeting in Nairobi, Kenya, formally inaugurated the Secretariat of the Permanent Tripartite Commission for East African Co-operation, which aimed to revive the EAC (see p. 385). A treaty for the re-establishment of the EAC, providing for the creation of a free trade area (with the eventual introduction of a single currency), for the development of infrastructure, tourism and agriculture within the Community and for the establishment of a regional legislature and court was ratified by the three Heads of State in November 1999. Museveni, Mkapa and President Mwai Kibaki of Kenya signed a protocol in March 2004 on the creation of a customs union, whereby most duties on goods within the EAC would be eliminated. The customs union was established on 1 January 2005.

During 1988 tension arose along Uganda's border with Zaire (now the DRC—see above), owing to a number of attacks by Zairean troops on NRA units; further border clashes occurred in 1992. In November 1996 Ugandan rebels were reportedly operating from within Zaire with the support of Zairean troops. In late 1996 and early 1997 the Ugandan authorities repeatedly denied allegations that Ugandan forces were occupying territory in eastern Zaire; however, it was widely reported that the Museveni Government supplied armaments and tactical support to Laurent-Désiré Kabila's Alliance des forces démocratiques pour la libération du Congo-Zaïre, which took power in Zaire in May 1997. The Museveni administration, however, subsequently withdrew its support from the new regime in the DRC, as President Kabila made no attempt to sever the ongoing supply of armaments to Ugandan guerrilla groups operating in the DRC–Uganda border region. In August 1998 the Museveni administration, in co-operation with the Rwandan Government, deployed troops in the eastern part of the DRC, avowedly to protect Ugandan and Rwandan security interests; the two Governments formed a joint military command in November 1998. The Kabila regime accused Uganda and Rwanda of creating, with DRC rebels, a Tutsi-dominated alliance with expansionist ambitions; it was also alleged that the DRC's two eastern neighbours were illegally exploiting mineral interests in the area occupied by their forces. In July 1999 a comprehensive cease-fire agreement was concluded in Lusaka, Zambia, by the Heads of State of all the countries engaged militarily in the civil war in the DRC, including those of Angola, Namibia and Zimbabwe, who had supported the DRC Government. Under the terms of the Lusaka accord, the cease-fire was to be monitored by a joint military commission, while a UN peace-keeping force was to be deployed on the withdrawal from the DRC of all foreign troops. However, the implementation of the Lusaka accord did not proceed smoothly. In May tensions arose between Uganda and Rwanda when the DRC rebel group that they had been jointly supporting divided into two factions, backed, respectively, by the Ugandan and Rwandan Governments. In mid-August these tensions escalated into hostilities between Ugandan and Rwandan armed forces around the city of Kisangani, in the DRC. In November President Museveni and President Bizimungu of Rwanda met in Uganda and reaffirmed their commitment to the Lusaka accord. In May 2000 the DRC Government signed an agreement in which it consented to the deployment of 500 UN military observers and 5,000 support troops, the UN Mission in the Democratic Republic of the Congo (MONUC, see p. 77), to monitor the frequently violated cease-fire that had been inaugurated by the Lusaka accord. Almost immediately afterwards, however, hostilities erupted again between Ugandan and Rwandan troops in Kisangani. In mid-May Uganda and Rwanda withdrew their troops in Kisangani to positions some 100 km from the city, to prepare the way for its eventual cession to the control of MONUC. In September Uganda claimed to have withdrawn all its troops from zones declared as demilitarized under the Lusaka accord. In December all parties in the conflict signed an agreement under which all forces would withdraw 15 km from positions of military engagement by January 2001, to allow UN peace-keepers to ensure the observance of the cease-fire. In January 2001 President Kabila was assassinated by one of his bodyguards; he was succeeded by his son, Joseph Kabila, who immediately engaged in international efforts to end the conflict. In mid-March the groups involved in the conflict, under the aegis of the UN Security Council, commenced the military disengagement of their forces. However, factions subsequently refused to proceed with the withdrawal from military positions until MONUC guaranteed security in the region. Following the publication of a UN report, in April, alleging that Burundi, Rwanda and Uganda were illegally exploiting the DRC's mineral reserves, Museveni announced that Uganda would withdraw its remaining troops from the DRC and pull out of the UN-sponsored Lusaka accord. In late 2001 Rwandan troops occupied positions in the eastern DRC that had been vacated by the UPDF in June of that year, prompting fears that clashes would again erupt between Rwandan and Ugandan forces. Furthermore, each side accused the other of supporting rebel groups. In October it was reported that a new rebel group, known as the People's Redemption Army, had been formed in the Rwanda-controlled part of the DRC by dissident UPDF officers who had defected earlier in the year. However, following negotiations between Museveni and Kagame (now the President of Rwanda), which were held in London, United Kingdom, in November, both sides exchanged delegations of inspectors to verify that the dissidents based in their respective countries were not receiving government support, and relations began to stabilize once more. Despite the redeployment of Ugandan troops in the north-east of the DRC in January 2002, to prevent escalating fighting between the rebel factions from reaching the border with Uganda, negotiations between Uganda and Rwanda continued, with British mediation, and in April the two countries signed a peace agreement in Kigali. In September a peace accord was signed by Uganda and the DRC in Luanda, Angola, providing for the normalization of relations between the two countries and the complete withdrawal of Ugandan troops from the DRC. Uganda subsequently began the withdrawal of its troops, although the UN permitted some of them to remain near the north-eastern town of Bunia to assist with maintaining security. In March 2003 skirmishes between Ugandan forces and a local rebel group were reported near Bunia. The Governments of Uganda and the DRC and local rebel groups subsequently signed a cease-fire agreement, although later that month the Rwandan Government threatened to resume military engagement in eastern DRC if the UN failed to secure the withdrawal of all Ugandan troops. In response to the continuing violence around Bunia, which was in contravention of the peace agreement, the UN Security Council issued a resolution calling for increased numbers of military and humanitarian observers to be stationed in the DRC under the MONUC mandate, and the immediate withdrawal of Ugandan troops. The Ugandan Government subsequently pledged to withdraw forces from the DRC, and all remaining Ugandan troops left the north-east of the country in May. In April 2005 the International Criminal Court (ICC, see p. 291), based in The Hague, Netherlands, began proceedings against Uganda following accusations by the DRC Government that Ugandan troops had violated human rights and massacred Congolese civilians while deployed in the country. The DRC also demanded reparations for destruction and looting allegedly carried out by the UPDF. The Ugandan Government denied the claims. In 1999 the DRC had asked the ICC to halt acts of aggression from Uganda; in a provisional ruling in 2000 the ICC ordered both sides to refrain from conflict. (The DRC filed a similar case against Rwanda in the World Court in 2002.)

From the late 1980s Sudanese troops reportedly made repeated incursions into Ugandan territory in pursuit of Sudanese rebels. In early 1992 nearly 80,000 Sudanese refugees fled to Uganda, followed by a further 50,000 in August 1993. Relations between the two countries deteriorated seriously in 1994, when each Government accused the other of harbouring and supporting their respective outlawed guerrilla groups; in April 1995

Uganda severed diplomatic relations with Sudan. In October 1995 intense fighting between Sudanese rebels and government forces resulted in the displacement of several thousand Ugandans residing in the border region. In November the Ugandan Government dispatched troops to protect the area. In the following month Museveni threatened to launch military assaults into Sudan in retaliation for the Sudanese Government's alleged continuing support for the LRA. Sudanese troops shelled the border area for three consecutive days in April 1996, provoking strong protest from the Ugandan Government. In September Sudan and Uganda resumed diplomatic relations, and in the following month a preliminary accord was signed in the Iranian capital, Tehran. Relations between the two countries did not, however, improve: in September 1996 and in February 1997 it was alleged that Sudanese aircraft had once again attacked northern Uganda, and in April, despite a continuing dialogue mediated by Iran and Libya, the Sudanese authorities claimed that their forces had killed several hundred Ugandan soldiers who had been assisting Sudanese rebels from within Sudanese territory. In February 1998 Uganda deployed troops along the Uganda–Sudan border, with the aim of preventing LRA rebels from taking captives over the frontier into Sudan. In December, in Kenya, the Presidents of Uganda and Sudan unexpectedly signed an accord that set out a comprehensive resolution of the two countries' differences. The Nairobi Agreement, which had been mediated by former US President Jimmy Carter, committed Uganda and Sudan to the renunciation of force as a means of settling disputes; to the disarmament and disbandment of terrorist groups and the cessation of support for rebel groups; to the repatriation of prisoners of war; and to the restoration of full diplomatic relations by the end of February 2000. Joint committees were to be established to oversee the implementation of the Agreement from January 2000. In June negotiations to uphold the peace process were held in the USA. Further meetings were held in Kampala in September, during which Uganda and Sudan agreed to disarm the LRA, which had been active throughout 2000, and to relocate it at least 1,000 km deeper within Sudanese territory. It was also agreed that the Governments of Uganda, Sudan, Libya and Egypt, in collaboration with the Carter Center, Canada, the UN Children's Fund and the office of the UN High Commissioner for Refugees (UNHCR), would set up a body to find and repatriate all children abducted from Sudan by rebel groups. Rebel attacks continued in northern Uganda, however, and in January 2001 President Museveni threatened to send troops to pursue rebel groups into Sudanese territory. In February Museveni deployed troops in northern Uganda, reportedly to defend against possible LRA attacks during the presidential election. In mid-May the Sudanese President, Omar al-Bashir, attended Museveni's presidential inauguration in Kampala. Following a Libyan diplomatic initiative in that month, Sudan and Uganda agreed to restore diplomatic relations. In August the Ugandan embassy reopened in the Sudanese capital, Khartoum, and a chargé d'affaires was appointed; relations were upgraded to an ambassadorial level in April 2002. In August 2001 al-Bashir announced that his Government would no longer provide support for the LRA, and in December bank accounts used by the LRA in London, United Kingdom, were frozen. Negotiations between Sudan and Uganda continued successfully throughout early 2002, with both countries remaining committed to implementing the Nairobi Agreement. In March it was announced that Sudan was to allow the UPDF to deploy forces within its borders in order to pursue operations against the LRA, and later that month the Ugandan Government announced that its troops had captured all four main bases in Sudan belonging to the LRA. In November the Sudanese authorities agreed to extend permission for Ugandan troops to remain on its territory for as long as Uganda deemed necessary.

Between late 2002 and early 2004, after having been largely driven from its bases in southern Sudan, the LRA was estimated to have abducted some 10,000 children—almost as many as it had kidnapped over the entire previous decade. In early 2003 Museveni agreed to a cease-fire and appointed a delegation to commence peace negotiations with the LRA, but these soon collapsed. The Government ordered 800,000 people in northern Uganda to enter refugee camps for their protection; however, the LRA continued to attack the camps. In October LRA attacks, which had begun to spread further south and east, intensified, and a counter-offensive by the UPDF in December had little success. Nevertheless, Museveni claimed in January 2004 that the LRA had been 'defeated decisively' and that his forces were on the verge of killing its leader, Kony. Also in January the ICC announced that it was to initiate plans for an investigation into the activities of the LRA, referred for consideration by the Court in the previous month by Museveni. In late February, in one of the worst attacks in recent years, the LRA massacred more than 200 civilians sheltering in a refugee camp near Lira, in northern Uganda. The camp had been guarded by a local self-defence militia group, but this force was quickly overwhelmed; some rebels were reported to be wearing militia uniforms. In the following weeks the UPDF launched assaults on two LRA groups in two villages near the camp, killing 16 rebels in one attack and five in the other. Thousands demonstrated in Lira against the Government's failure to protect civilians, and the protests rapidly became violent. The UPDF commenced a new offensive in southern Sudan, and in March killed more than 50 rebels entering Uganda from Sudan. Despite the UPDF's continued claims of imminent victory, the LRA attacks continued unabated. Museveni offered to agree a cease-fire with the LRA in April, on condition that peace negotiations were opened. However, an interview with Kony in a Sudanese publication suggested that he was opposed to negotiations and in May attacks were carried out on refugee camps by the LRA. The Government introduced legislation in mid-2004 that allowed the prosecution by the ICC of Ugandans suspected of war crimes. In June it was reported that at least 12 high-ranking LRA commanders had taken advantage of an amnesty offered by the Government and surrendered; among them was Kony's personal secretary. In July the ICC investigation into the activities of the LRA began; in April 2005 it was reported that the ICC was to establish a field office in Kampala in order to expedite its investigation.

Meanwhile, in November 2004 an LRA spokesman stated that the group no longer believed a military end to the conflict was possible, and that the LRA was thus willing to negotiate towards a peace accord. A cease-fire was agreed, although fighting continued outside the cease-fire zone. Delegations representing the Government and the LRA met in December in Kitgum, in northern Uganda, and Museveni subsequently extended the cease-fire until the end of December. Although there were indications at the end of December that the Government and LRA were close to agreeing a permanent truce, the LRA postponed the signing of a memorandum of understanding in order to continue internal consultations. Shortly afterwards a UPDF force was ambushed, for which Museveni blamed the LRA. The Government refused to extend the cease-fire, and UPDF troops re-occupied the cease-fire zone in order to prevent attacks on civilians. A cease-fire was agreed in February 2005, during which an amnesty was offered to LRA fighters who wished to surrender. Later that month Brig. Sam Kolo, the LRA's chief negotiator in the recent peace talks, escaped an attack by LRA combatants with the help of the UPDF, to whom he surrendered. The UPDF stated that Kolo's life was in danger following a dispute with the LRA's deputy leader, Vincent Otti. The Government's chief negotiator confirmed that Otti would take Kolo's place in any future negotiations. However, many observers regarded Kolo as one of the LRA's most rational commanders, and attributed to him the success of recent negotiations. In March, following a government request, the ICC agreed to delay issuing arrest warrants for LRA commanders after concerns were raised that they would be reluctant to negotiate if they feared arrest once peace had been established. The cease-fire agreed in February lapsed in March, and fighting resumed. The UPDF began an offensive against LRA bases, while the LRA, in turn, attacked villages and resumed its abduction of children. In August one of Kony's several 'wives' was captured by the UPDF. She and hundreds of other LRA members had been persuaded to surrender (or at least to not resist capture) by radio broadcasts of messages from rescued former members of the LRA urging their friends to return home without fear of prosecution under the five-year amnesty. It was thought that the LRA had dwindled from 3,000 to just 300 fighters; that assistance from the Sudanese military had ceased; and that the group was short of food and arms.

In September 2005 two groups of LRA fighters, one led by Otti, entered the DRC from southern Sudan. Representatives of the UN met for first time with the LRA and urged the group to disarm. The meeting was also attended by senior members of DRC military. In October the ICC issued arrest warrants for Kony, Otti and three other LRA commanders. Kony was indicted on 12 counts of crimes against humanity, including sexual enslavement, and 21 counts of war crimes. The UPDF claimed to have recently killed one of the five indicted LRA commanders.

Shortly after the warrants were issued the LRA altered its tactics and began to attack humanitarian workers. In November it killed two UN mine clearance experts in southern Sudan. Later that month Otti offered to enter into peace negotiations, stating he was willing to be tried by the ICC, but added that the UPDF had also committed crimes during the conflict for which the Government should be tried. In April 2006 it was announced that refugee camps in the Lango and Teso sub-regions were to close (but not those in the Acholi sub-region). Also in that month the Ugandan Parliament approved legislation that enabled the Government to exclude Kony and others from the amnesty offered to the LRA.

During the late 1980s an estimated 250,000 Rwandan refugees were sheltering in Uganda. Relations with Rwanda deteriorated in October 1990, following the infiltration of northern Rwanda by an invasion force of some 4,000 Rwandan rebels who had been based in Uganda; their leader, Maj.-Gen. Fred Rwigyema (who was killed by the Rwandan armed forces), was a deputy commander of the NRA and a former Ugandan Deputy Minister of Defence. In November President Museveni dismissed all non-Ugandan members of the NRA. In February 1991 a conference was held on the Rwandan security situation; an amnesty was agreed for all Rwandans who were exiled abroad, and the rebels were urged to observe a cease-fire. Nevertheless, the allegedly Uganda-based Rwandan rebels continued to operate in northern Rwanda during 1991–93. In January 1992 it was reported that 64,000 Ugandans residing near the two countries' common border had been displaced, owing to cross-border shelling by Rwandan troops. In August 1993 the UN Observer Mission Uganda-Rwanda (subsequently disbanded) stationed troops on the Ugandan side of the border to verify that no military assistance reached Rwandan rebels. In May 1994 the Ugandan authorities appealed for emergency assistance, claiming that the corpses of thousands of victims of massacres taking place in Rwanda were contaminating the water supply of districts abutting Lake Victoria. The victory in Rwanda of the Front patriotique rwandais (FPR) in mid-1994 brought about a significant change in bilateral relations; Maj.-Gen. Paul Kagame, Rwandan Vice-President and Minister of National Defence, had previously served in the Ugandan NRA, as had other members of the FPR administration. In August 1995 Museveni made an official visit to Rwanda, and both countries made commitments to enhance economic and social co-operation. In August 1998 Uganda and Rwanda jointly deployed troops in the DRC (see above). Relations between the two countries worsened again during their involvement in the hostilities in the DRC; there were frequent reports of fighting, especially around the town of Kisangani. However, this tension eased when both armies withdrew from Kisangani during May 2000 (see above), and in July Museveni and Kagame met to discuss relations between their respective countries. In January 2001 at least 15,000 Rwandan refugees, most of them Hutu, entered Uganda following an order in Tanzania to expel all non-citizens. A further 7,000 Rwandan refugees had entered Uganda through Tanzania by July. In July 2003 the Rwandan Government signed a tripartite agreement with the Ugandan authorities and UNHCR, providing for the voluntary repatriation of some 26,000 Rwandans resident in refugee camps in western Uganda. In February 2004 an improvement in diplomatic relations between Rwanda and Uganda (following progress in the situation in the DRC) was demonstrated by a bilateral agreement to strengthen co-operation in several fields.

At the end of 2004, according to UNHCR, the number of refugees in Uganda totalled 250,482, including 214,673 from Sudan, 18,902 from Rwanda and 14,982 from the DRC.

President George W. Bush of the USA visited Uganda as part of a tour of five sub-Saharan countries in July 2003. During his visit Bush praised Uganda's efforts to combat the spread of HIV/AIDS, which had resulted in a decline in the infection rate from some 14% in the early 1990s to an estimated 5% in 2001. Presidents Museveni and Bush also discussed the African Growth and Opportunity Act, approved by the US Congress in 2000, which granted African countries satisfying certain criteria preferential trade access to the US market until 2008. In November 2003 it was reported that the USA had resumed military aid to Uganda, following a four-year suspension in response to the deployment of Ugandan troops in the DRC.

Government

Following the January 1986 coup, power was vested in a broad-based interim Government, headed by an executive President. A National Resistance Council (NRC) was formed to legislate by decree. In addition, resistance committees were formed at local and district level. Political activity was suspended, although political parties were not banned. National elections were held in February 1989. Representatives were elected directly to local-level resistance committees; these elected representatives to district-level resistance committees, and these, in turn, elected representatives to the NRC. The NRC was expanded from 98 members, all nominated by the President, to 278 members, of whom 68 were nominated by the President and 210 were elected. In October 1989 the NRC approved legislation prolonging the Government's term of office by five years from January 1990, when its mandate had been due to expire. A new Constitution was enacted by an elected Constituent Assembly in September 1995 and came into force in the following month. The first direct presidential election was held in May 1996, and national legislative elections took place in the following month to a 276-member Parliament, as the NRC became—comprising 214 directly elected and 62 nominated members. Voting also took place in June for local councils (which replaced the resistance committees). Further local elections were held in November 1997 and January 2002. Under the terms of the new Constitution, a national referendum on the future introduction of a multi-party political system took place in June 2000, at which voters overwhelmingly endorsed the retention of the existing 'no-party' system (this was nullified by the Constitutional Court in 2004—see Recent History). Following legislative elections in June 2001, the number of seats in Parliament stood at 292, comprising 214 directly elected representatives and 78 nominated members. Legislation to amend the Constitution in order to allow multi-party politics, and to remove the two-term limit on the presidency, was approved by the Parliament in early 2005 and by 92.5% of voters at a referendum held on 28 July 2005.

Defence

In August 2005 the Uganda People's Defence Forces was estimated to number 40,000–45,000 men, including paramilitary forces (a border defence unit of about 600 men, a police air wing of about 800 men, about 400 marines and local defence units of about 3,000 men, with a further 7,000 reportedly under training). Defence was allocated an estimated 348,000m. shillings by the central Government in 2005. The Lord's Resistance Army (LRA) was thought to have about 1,500 members, with about 600 in Uganda and the remainder in Sudan. The Allied Democratic Front was believed to comprise some 200 men. The West Nile Bank Front was thought to number 1,000, but had not launched any attacks in the previous 12 months and was therefore considered dormant.

Economic Affairs

In 2004, according to estimates by the World Bank, Uganda's gross national income (GNI), measured at average 2002–04 prices, was US $6,911m., equivalent to $270 per head (or $1,520 per head on an international purchasing-power parity basis). During 1995–2004, it was estimated, the population increased at an average annual rate of 2.8%, while gross domestic product (GDP) per head increased, in real terms, by an average of 3.3% per year. Overall GDP increased, in real terms, at an average annual rate of 6.2% in 1995–2004; growth was 5.7% in 2004.

Agriculture (including hunting, forestry and fishing) contributed 23.4% of GDP in the financial year 2003/04 and engaged 78.7% of the employed labour force at the census of 12 September 2002. The principal cash crops are coffee (which provided 18.8% of export earnings in 2003), tobacco, tea and cotton. Maize, sugar cane and cocoa are also cultivated, and the production of cut flowers is an important activity. The main subsistence crops are plantains, cassava, sweet potatoes, millet, sorghum, maize, beans, groundnuts and rice. In addition, livestock (chiefly cattle, goats, sheep and poultry) are reared, and freshwater fishing is an important rural activity. Agricultural GDP increased by an average of 3.8% per year in 1995–2004, according to the World Bank; it increased by 5.2% in 2004.

Industry (including mining, manufacturing, construction and power) contributed 25.2% of GDP in 2003/04, and employed 4.4% of the working population at the 2002 census. Industrial GDP increased at an average annual rate of 9.0% in 1995–2004, according to the World Bank; it increased by 5.6% in 2004.

Mining has made a negligible contribution to GDP since the 1970s (0.9% in 2003/04) and at the 2002 census employed just 0.3% of the working population. The Government aims to encourage renewed investment in the sector. Output of copper, formerly an important export, virtually ceased during the late

1970s. However, the state-owned Kilembe copper mine in western Uganda was transferred to private ownership and the first phase of preparations to reopen the mine was expected to be completed during 2005; the second phase was expected to take a further 10 months to complete. The production of cobalt from stockpiled copper pyrites commenced in 1999. Uganda is believed to possess the world's second largest deposit of gold, which began to be exploited again in the mid-1990s. Apatite and limestone are also mined. There are, in addition, reserves of iron ore, magnetite, tin, tungsten, beryllium, bismuth, asbestos, graphite, phosphate and tantalite. Mining GDP increased by 8.9% in 1998/99.

Manufacturing contributed 11.0% of GDP in 2003/04 and at the 2002 census employed 2.3% of the working population. The most important manufacturing activities are the processing of agricultural commodities, brewing, vehicle assembly and the production of textiles, cement, soap, fertilizers, paper products, metal products, shoes, paints, matches and batteries. Manufacturing GDP increased by an average of 9.4% per year in 1995–2004, according to the World Bank; it increased by 4.0% in 2004.

Energy is derived principally from hydroelectric power. In 1998 Uganda generated only about two-thirds of national energy requirements. However, plans are under way to expand hydroelectric production. Imports of petroleum and petroleum products accounted for 13.6% of the value of Uganda's merchandise imports in 2003.

The services sector contributed 51.4% of GDP in 2003/04, and engaged 16.9% of the employed labour force at the 2002 census. Trade is the most important aspect of the sector. Services GDP increased by an average of 7.2% per year in 1995–2004, according to the World Bank. GDP in the sector increased by 6.3% in 2004.

In 2004 Uganda recorded a visible trade deficit of US $753.6m., and there was a deficit of $199.8m. on the current account of the balance of payments. In 2003 the principal sources of imports were Kenya (26.0%), India, South Africa, Japan and the United Kingdom, the United Arab Emirates, the USA and the People's Republic of China; Kenya (14.7%), Switzerland, the Netherlands, the United Kingdom and South Africa were the main markets for exports in that year. The Common Market for Eastern and Southern Africa (COMESA, see p. 191) and the European Union (EU, see p. 228) are important trading partners: in 2003 they took 28.3% and 17.7%, respectively, of total imports and provided 27.7% and 26.3%, respectively, of total exports. The principal exports in 2003 were coffee, fish, tobacco, gold and tea; the main imports in that year were petroleum products, road vehicles, cereals and cereal preparations, iron and steel and medical and pharmaceutical products.

In the financial year ending 30 June 2004 Uganda's central government budgetary deficit was an estimated 85,400m. shillings, equivalent to 0.6% of GDP. Uganda's external debt totalled US $4,553m. at the end of 2003, of which $4,168m. was long-term public debt. In that year the cost of debt-servicing was equivalent to 7.1% of the value of exports of goods and services. The annual average rate of inflation was 3.8% in 1995–2004; consumer prices increased by 8.9% in 2003 and by 4.0 in 2004.

Uganda is a member of the COMESA, the African Development Bank (see p. 151) and the East African Community (EAC, see p. 385).

Uganda is regarded as having an open, deregulated economy, with conditions favourable to investment. Inflation has remained low since the late 1990s, the foreign exchange regime has been liberalized since the mid-1990s and privatization is well advanced. As such, Uganda has enjoyed good relations with international donors. In February 1995 international creditor Governments agreed to cancel some two-thirds of Uganda's bilateral government-guaranteed debt. During 1998–2000 Uganda secured international aid and debt-relief, including assistance under the IMF's initiative for heavily indebted poor countries (HIPC), to the value of US $1,500m. It was estimated that these funds would reduce Uganda's annual debt-servicing obligations by about 65%–75%. In March 2000 donor countries commended Uganda for having focused its economic policies on the reduction of poverty and for its commitment to reduce defence spending to 2% of GDP. However, a large part of Uganda's GDP growth is offset by the rapid annual increase in population. Moreover, the ongoing conflict with the LRA in the north of the country has led to continued high expenditure on defence and has hampered growth in the region. In September 2002 the IMF approved a three-year arrangement for Uganda under its Poverty Reduction and Growth Facility (PGRF), worth some $17.8m, which expired in September 2005. Following its expiration the IMF announced that Uganda's economy had improved to the point where it no longer qualified for aid. The IMF would, however, continue to offer support and advice on reforms. Nevertheless, Uganda remains one of poorest nations in the world, with GDP per head of just $270 in 2004, and the country's economy faces two main challenges. Firstly, to sustain growth (which is still largely dependent on agricultural exports) at a sufficient level to enable the reduction of poverty, with income distributed more evenly throughout the country; and secondly to reduce its reliance on foreign aid, which finances around one-half of the country's expenditure. This second challenge became a priority in 2005–06 as foreign governments withheld aid to Uganda in protest at President Museveni's increasingly autocratic rule. In response the Government enacted measures to improve tax collection and increased the level of value-added tax.

Education

Education is not compulsory. Most schools are supported by the Government, although a small proportion are sponsored by missions. Traditionally all schools have charged fees. In 1997, however, the Government introduced an initiative known as Universal Primary Education (UPE), whereby free primary education was to be phased in for up to four children per family. Primary education begins at six years of age and lasts for seven years. Secondary education, beginning at the age of 13, lasts for a further six years, comprising a first cycle of four years and a second of two years. In 2002/03, according to UNESCO, enrolment at pre-primary level was 3% (for both boys and girls). In that year, 141% of children in the appropriate age-group (males 142%; females 139%) were enrolled at primary schools. According to UNESCO estimates, enrolment at secondary schools was 16% (males 17%; females 16%), while just 3% of those in the relevant age group (males 4%; females 2%) were enrolled in tertiary education. In addition to Makerere University in Kampala there is a university of science and technology at Mbarara, and a small Islamic university is located at Mbale. In 2001 30,243 students were enrolled at state universities. Education expenditure in the financial year ending 30 June 1997 accounted for 24.9% of government current expenditure.

Public Holidays

2006: 1 January (New Year's Day), 10 January*† (Id al-Adha, Feast of the Sacrifice), 26 January (Liberation Day), 8 March (International Women's Day), 14–17 April (Easter), 1 May (Labour Day), 3 June (Martyrs' Day), 9 June (National Heroes' Day), 9 October (Independence Day), 23 October* (Id al-Fitr, end of Ramadan), 25 December (Christmas), 26 December (Boxing Day), 31 December*† (Id al-Adha, Feast of the Sacrifice).

2007: 1 January (New Year's Day), 26 January (Liberation Day), 8 March (International Women's Day), 6–9 April (Easter), 1 May (Labour Day), 3 June (Martyrs' Day), 9 June (National Heroes' Day), 9 October (Independence Day), 13 October* (Id al-Fitr, end of Ramadan), 20 December* (Id al-Adha, Feast of the Sacrifice), 25 December (Christmas), 26 December (Boxing Day).

* These holidays are dependent on the Islamic lunar calendar and the exact dates may vary by one or two days from those given.

† This festival occurs twice (in the Islamic years AH 1426 and 1427) within the same Gregorian year.

Weights and Measures

The metric system is in force.

UGANDA

Statistical Survey

Sources (unless otherwise stated): Uganda Bureau of Statistics, POB 13, Entebbe; tel. (41) 320165; fax (41) 320147; e-mail ubos@infocom.co.ug; internet www.ubos.org; Statistics Department, Ministry of Finance, Planning and Economic Development, POB 8147, Kampala.

Area and Population

AREA, POPULATION AND DENSITY

Area (sq km)	
Land	197,097
Inland water	43,941
Total	241,038*
Population (census results)	
12 January 1991	16,671,705
12 September 2002	
Males	11,929,803
Females	12,512,281
Total	24,442,084
Population (official estimates at mid-year)	
2003	24,426,200
2004	26,302,000
Density (per sq km) at mid-2004	133.4†

* 93,065 sq miles.
† Land area only.

PRINCIPAL ETHNIC GROUPS
(at census of 12 September 2002)*

Acholi	1,145,357		Basoga	2,062,920
Baganda	4,126,370		Iteso	1,568,763
Bagisu	1,117,661		Langi	1,485,437
Bakiga	1,679,519		Lugbara	1,022,240
Banyakole	2,330,212			

* Ethnic groups numbering more than 1m. persons, excluding population enumerated in hotels.

DISTRICTS
(population, official estimates at mid-2004)

Central	7,015,300		Northern	5,812,700
Kalangala	41,400		Adjumani	225,100
Kampala	1,290,500		Apac	716,800
Kayunga	306,800		Arua	915,500
Kiboga	249,200		Gulu	491,000
Luwero	496,100		Kitgum	307,500
Masaka	777,300		Kotido	705,400
Mpigi	424,300		Lira	805,200
Mubende	742,400		Moroto	185,500
Mukono	845,800		Moyo	229,800
Nakasongola	129,200		Nakapiripirit	170,500
Rakai	485,700		Nebbi	453,500
Sembabule	190,700		Pader	315,300
Wakiso	1,035,800		Yumbe	291,500
Eastern	6,712,400		Western	6,761,500
Bugiri	464,800		Bundibugyoi	232,900
Busia	239,500		Busheny	746,400
Iganga	757,300		Hoima	380,000
Jinja	436,100		Kabale	479,400
Kaberamaido	130,600		Kabarole	368,300
Kamuli	753,200		Kamwenge	312,300
Kapchorwa	208,600		Kanungu	212,300
Katakwi	343,800		Kasese	568,600
Kumi	417,500		Kibaale	454,100
Mayuge	346,800		Kisoro	224,300
Mbale	760,800		Kyenjojo	405,700
Pallisa	552,000		Masindi	512,900
Sironko	305,700		Mbarara	1,142,500
Soroti	406,800		Ntungamo	400,000
Tororo	589,300		Rukungiri	322,000
			Total	**26,302,000**

PRINCIPAL TOWNS
(population according to provisional results of census of 12 September 2002)*

Kampala (capital)	1,208,544		Entebbe	57,518
Gulu	113,144		Kasese	53,446
Lira	89,971		Njeru	52,514
Jinja	86,520		Mukono	47,305
Mbale	70,437		Arua	45,883
Mbarara	69,208		Kabale	45,757
Masaka	61,300		Kitgum	42,929

* According to administrative divisions of 2002.

BIRTHS AND DEATHS
(UN estimates, annual averages)

	1990–95	1995–2000	2000–05
Birth rate (per 1,000)	49.8	49.6	50.2
Death rate (per 1,000)	18.7	18.8	16.1

Source: UN, *World Population Prospects: The 2004 Revision*.

Expectation of life (WHO estimates, years at birth): 49 (males 47; females 50) in 2003 (Source: WHO, *World Health Report*).

EMPLOYMENT
(persons aged 10 years and over, census of 12 September 2002)*

	Males	Females	Total
Agriculture, hunting and forestry	2,545,962	2,649,779	5,195,741
Fishing	102,043	16,743	118,786
Mining and quarrying	13,613	6,127	19,740
Manufacturing	108,653	45,594	154,247
Electricity, gas and water supply	12,860	1,509	14,369
Construction	105,769	2,939	108,708
Wholesale and retail trade, repair of motor vehicles, motorcycles and personal and household goods	191,191	143,145	334,336
Hotels and restaurants	23,741	64,099	87,840
Transport, storage and communications	119,437	5,798	125,235
Financial intermediation / Real estate, renting and business activities	14,539	7,562	22,101
Public administration and defence, compulsory social security	146,319	27,278	173,597
Education	124,167	85,015	209,182
Health and social work	54,327	53,108	107,435
Other community, social and personal service activities	22,736	26,734	49,470
Private households with employed persons	14,019	19,115	33,134
Not classifiable by economic activity	120,219	76,167	196,386
Total employed	**3,719,595**	**3,230,712**	**6,950,307**

* Excluding population enumerated at hotels.

UGANDA

Health and Welfare

KEY INDICATORS

Total fertility rate (children per woman, 2003)	7.1
Under-5 mortality rate (per 1,000 live births, 2004)	138
HIV/AIDS (% of persons aged 15–49, 2003)	4.1
Physicians (per 1,000 head, 2002)	0.05
Hospital beds (per 1,000 head, 1991)	0.92
Health expenditure (2002): US $ per head (PPP)	77
Health expenditure (2002): % of GDP	7.4
Health expenditure (2002): public (% of total)	27.9
Access to water (% of persons, 2002)	56
Access to sanitation (% of persons, 2002)	41
Human Development Index (2003): ranking	144
Human Development Index (2003): value	0.508

For sources and definitions, see explanatory note on p. vi.

Agriculture

PRINCIPAL CROPS
('000 metric tons)

	2002	2003	2004
Rice (paddy)	120	109	140
Maize	1,217	1,207	1,350
Millet	590	640	700
Sorghum	427	443	420
Potatoes	546	567	573
Sweet potatoes	2,592	2,558	2,650
Cassava (Manioc)	5,373	5,265	5,500
Sugar cane*	1,600	1,600	1,600
Dry beans	535	481	545
Cow peas, dry*	64	64	64
Pigeon peas	82	84	84
Soybeans	166	187	158
Groundnuts (in shell)	148	130	155
Sesame seed	106	110*	110*
Seed cotton*	67	67	67
Onions, dry*	147	147	147
Vegetables and melons*	409	409	409
Bananas*	615	615	615
Plantains	9,888	9,605	9,900
Other fruit*	53	53	53
Coffee (green)	189	151	186*
Tea (made)	34	37	36*
Tobacco (leaves)	34	34	33*
Cotton (lint)	22	22*	22*

* FAO estimate(s).

Source: FAO.

LIVESTOCK
('000 head, year ending September)

	2002	2003	2004*
Asses*	18	18	18
Cattle	6,328	6,558	6,100
Sheep	1,141	1,603	1,600
Goats	6,852	7,821	7,700
Pigs	1,710	1,226	1,300
Chickens	32,638	23,032	24,000

* FAO estimates.

Source: FAO.

LIVESTOCK PRODUCTS
(FAO estimates, '000 metric tons)

	2002	2003	2004
Beef and veal	106	110	106
Mutton and lamb	6	8	8
Goat meat	25	29	29
Pig meat	84	60	60
Poultry meat	54	38	38
Other meat	18	18	18
Cows' milk	700	700	700
Poultry eggs	20	20	20
Cattle hides	15	15	15

Source: FAO.

Forestry

ROUNDWOOD REMOVALS
(FAO estimates, '000 cubic metres, excl. bark)

	2002	2003	2004
Sawlogs, veneer logs and logs for sleepers	1,055	1,055	1,055
Other industrial wood	2,120	2,120	2,120
Fuel wood	35,142	35,683	36,235
Total	38,317	38,858	39,410

Source: FAO.

SAWNWOOD PRODUCTION
('000 cubic metres, incl. railway sleepers)

	1997	1998	1999
Coniferous (softwood)	57	61	67
Broadleaved (hardwood)	172	184	197
Total	229	245	264

2000–04: Production assumed to be unchanged from 1999 (FAO estimates).

Source: FAO.

Fishing

('000 metric tons, live weight)

	2001	2002	2003
Capture	220.7	221.9	239.9
Cyprinids	12.2	12.0	8.3
Tilapias	96.2	98.0	97.3
Characins	10.3	7.1	9.5
Nile perch	88.9	90.7	112.8
Aquaculture	2.4	4.9	5.5
Total catch	223.1	226.8	245.4

Note: Figures exclude aquatic mammals, recorded by number rather than by weight. The number of Nile crocodiles caught was: 900 in 2001; 0 in 2002; 2 in 2003.

Source: FAO.

UGANDA

Statistical Survey

Mining

('000 metric tons, unless otherwise indicated)

	2002	2003	2004
Cement (hydraulic)	506.0	507.1	520.0*
Tantalum and niobium (columbium) concentrates (kilograms)	6,463	16,240	4,200
Cobalt (metric tons)	450*	0	436
Gold (kilograms)	3	40	178
Limestone	140.0	226.4	272.3
Salt (unrefined)*	5	5	5

* Estimate(s).

Source: US Geological Survey.

Industry

SELECTED PRODUCTS
('000 metric tons, unless otherwise indicated)

	2000	2001	2002
Beer (million litres)	126.1	114.0	98.9
Soft drinks (million litres)	72.7	81.1	94.3
Cigarettes (million)	1,244	1,066	1,092
Sugar	137.8	133.9	167.7
Soap	75.2	90.8	92.2
Cement	368.8	433.8	502.2
Paint ('000 litres)	2,792	2,424	2,384
Edible oil and fat	45.9	51.7	45.6
Animal feed	31.7	13.1	30.5
Footwear ('000 pairs)	1,696	1,979	978
Wheat flour	12.2	52.0	52.8
Electricity (million kWh)	1,638.9	—	—

Source: Bank of Uganda.

Finance

CURRENCY AND EXCHANGE RATES

Monetary Units
100 cents = 1 new Uganda shilling.

Sterling, Dollar and Euro Equivalents (30 December 2005)
£1 sterling = 3,128.45 new Uganda shillings;
US $1 = 1,816.86 new Uganda shillings;
€1 = 2,143.35 new Uganda shillings;
10,000 new Uganda shillings = £3.20 = $5.50 = €4.67.

Average Exchange Rate (new Uganda shillings per US $)
2003 1,963.7
2004 1,810.3
2005 1,780.7

Note: Between December 1985 and May 1987 the official exchange rate was fixed at US $1 = 1,400 shillings. In May 1987 a new shilling, equivalent to 100 of the former units, was introduced. At the same time, the currency was devalued by 76.7%, with the exchange rate set at $1 = 60 new shillings. Further adjustments were implemented in subsequent years. Foreign exchange controls were mostly abolished in 1993.

BUDGET
(million new shillings, year ending 30 June)

Revenue	2001/02	2002/03	2003/04*
Revenue†	1,251,000	1,434,000	1,672,400
Grants	797,700	819,800	1,224,100
Total	2,048,700	2,253,800	2,896,500

Expenditure	2001/02	2002/03	2003/04*
Recurrent expenditure	1,436,050	1,586,500	1,786,800
Wages and salaries	546,250	612,300	675,100
Interest payments	150,800	174,100	249,500
Development expenditure	1,043,500	1,142,000	1,175,300
External expenditure	605,500	682,100	680,000
Domestic expenditure	438,000	459,900	485,300
Net lending and arrears	−4,700	41,600	19,800
Total	2,474,850	2,770,100	2,981,900

* Projections.
† Tax revenue excludes tax refunds and government payments.

INTERNATIONAL RESERVES
(US $ million at 31 December)

	2002	2003	2004
IMF special drawing rights	3.0	4.8	0.7
Foreign exchange	931.1	1,075.5	1,307.4
Total	934.0	1,080.3	1,308.1

2005: IMF special drawing rights US $1.1m.

Source: IMF, *International Financial Statistics*.

MONEY SUPPLY
(million new shillings at 31 December)

	2002	2003	2004
Currency outside banks	466,610	546,232	588,608
Demand deposits at commercial banks	632,834	688,683	752,630
Total money	1,099,444	1,252,915	1,341,238

Source: IMF, *International Financial Statistics*.

COST OF LIVING
(Consumer Price Index for all urban households; base: 2000 = 100)

	2002	2003	2004
Food	92.5	106.7	111.4
Clothing	100.5	102.7	101.0
Rent, fuel and light	110.7	116.5	121.0
All items (incl. others)	101.6	110.5	114.5

Source: ILO.

NATIONAL ACCOUNTS
(million new shillings at current prices, year ending 30 June)

Expenditure on the Gross Domestic Product

	2001/02	2002/03	2003/04
Government final consumption expenditure	1,590,832	1,799,058	2,078,490
Private final consumption expenditure	8,273,674	9,245,061	10,225,752
Increase in stocks	40,438	46,168	50,886
Gross fixed capital formation	1,986,539	2,406,625	2,822,496
Total domestic expenditure	11,891,483	13,496,912	15,177,624
Exports of goods and services	1,208,796	1,471,686	1,798,454
Less Imports of goods and services	2,771,728	3,169,844	3,734,057
Statistical discrepancy	−23,123	85,639	−359
GDP in purchasers' values	10,305,427	11,884,394	13,241,662
GDP at constant 1997/98	9,690,038	10,191,543	10,798,720

UGANDA

Gross Domestic Product by Economic Activity
(at factor cost)

	2001/02	2002/03	2003/04
Agriculture, hunting, forestry and fishing	1,652,722	2,018,500	2,317,635
Mining and quarrying	80,343	87,557	92,240
Manufacturing	938,103	1,012,814	1,090,129
Electricity, gas and water	135,566	148,943	166,087
Construction	820,042	995,006	1,146,587
Wholesale and retail trade	1,076,943	1,215,342	1,359,812
Hotels and restaurants	268,215	304,618	351,832
Transport, storage and communications	579,690	697,667	835,955
General government services	494,105	524,622	537,242
Education	642,427	754,160	849,063
Health	231,811	266,251	272,407
Other services	785,643	858,300	883,326
Total monetary GDP	7,705,609	8,883,779	9,902,317
Non-monetary GDP			
Agriculture	1,261,353	1,498,428	1,691,695
Construction	54,958	60,084	65,347
Owner-occupied dwellings	390,397	428,491	462,102
Total GDP at factor cost	9,412,317	10,870,782	12,121,461

BALANCE OF PAYMENTS
(US $ million)

	2002	2003	2004
Exports of goods f.o.b.	480.7	563.0	705.3
Imports of goods f.o.b.	−1,054.5	−1,240.9	−1,458.9
Trade balance	−573.8	−677.8	−753.6
Exports of services	232.8	294.4	447.4
Imports of services	−543.2	−523.6	−695.5
Balance on goods and services	−884.2	−907.1	−1,001.7
Other income received	24.2	27.6	35.7
Other income paid	−148.1	−170.7	−207.9
Balance on goods, services and income	−1,008.2	−1,050.2	−1,174.0
Current transfers received	1,015.3	893.9	1,150.7
Current transfers paid	−367.1	−195.9	−176.5
Current balance	−360.0	−352.2	−199.8
Direct investment from abroad	184.6	202.2	222.0
Portfolio investment liabilities	0.7	21.0	−16.9
Other investment assets	−59.1	−124.9	0.2
Other investment liabilities	50.1	265.3	121.5
Net errors and omissions	7.1	−9.9	−4.4
Overall balance	−175.1	−2.8	122.5

Source: IMF, *International Financial Statistics*.

External Trade

PRINCIPAL COMMODITIES
(distribution by SITC, US $ '000)

Imports c.i.f.	2001	2002	2003
Food and live animals	89,819	106,142	144,836
Cereals and cereal preparations	54,421	73,039	106,698
Crude materials (inedible) except fuels	35,533	37,547	47,703
Mineral fuels, lubricants, etc.	162,899	174,828	188,770
Petroleum, petroleum products and related materials	161,851	173,791	187,255
Animal and vegetable oils, fats and waxes	30,630	41,242	64,523
Chemicals and related products	130,106	130,066	180,354
Medicinal and pharmaceutical products	49,394	48,173	74,920
Basic manufactures	189,010	208,302	270,623
Paper, paperboard, and articles of paper pulp, paper or paperboard	32,411	33,419	37,660
Non-metallic mineral manufactures	34,080	40,970	51,862
Iron and steel	44,927	55,448	77,755
Machinery and transport equipment	285,291	284,751	344,098
Machinery specialized for particular industries	21,446	36,704	40,070
Telecommunications and sound recording/reproducing apparatus	60,199	39,512	48,936
Electrical machinery, apparatus, etc.	47,095	40,337	52,178
Road vehicles (incl. air-cushion vehicles) and parts (excl. tyres, engines and electrical parts)	89,211	105,074	115,096
Miscellaneous manufactured articles	80,339	88,022	130,046
Total (incl. others)	1,006,557	1,073,732	1,375,106

Exports f.o.b.	2001	2002	2003
Food and live animals	236,676	245,442	272,838
Fish, crustaceans, molluscs and preparations thereof	75,430	85,805	84,649
Coffee, tea, cocoa, spices and manufactures	132,999	138,679	157,646
Beverages and tobacco	34,449	47,534	45,764
Tobacco and tobacco manufactures	32,402	45,286	43,212
Crude materials (inedible) except fuels	75,869	52,439	61,726
Hides, skins and furskins, raw	25,205	9,448	4,844
Textile fibres (not wool tops) and their wastes (not in yarn)	15,934	12,721	22,180
Crude animal and vegetable materials n.e.s.	19,937	21,474	29,845
Mineral fuels, lubricants and related materials	22,825	26,438	41,664
Petroleum, petroleum products and related materials	12,271	10,787	27,884
Electric current	10,554	15,645	13,779
Gold, non-monetary (excl. gold ores and concentrates)	49,224	60,722	33,726
Total (incl. others)	451,765	467,605	534,106

UGANDA

PRINCIPAL TRADING PARTNERS
(US $ '000)

Imports c.i.f.	2001	2002	2003
Belgium	15,938	16,587	23,087
China, People's Repub.	36,227	44,026	70,248
France	24,450	11,693	15,596
Germany	38,212	30,306	39,151
Hong Kong	19,652	17,447	16,805
India	66,555	71,913	102,160
Italy	17,748	20,050	23,320
Japan	75,018	87,312	90,361
Kenya	281,472	312,870	357,327
Malaysia	23,161	32,058	42,062
Netherlands	14,840	18,842	25,015
Sweden	18,105	9,148	8,811
South Africa	72,850	83,665	98,984
United Arab Emirates	56,258	61,917	80,416
United Kingdom	72,252	67,738	86,411
USA	28,133	35,842	78,129
Total (incl. others)	1,006,557	1,073,732	1,375,106

Exports f.o.b.	2001	2002	2003
Australia	5,404	4,644	9,214
Belgium	16,085	21,902	12,899
Congo, Democratic Repub.	8,832	7,554	12,891
Egypt	5,278	1,948	2,673
France	4,057	6,844	5,116
Germany	12,134	13,399	12,024
Hong Kong	26,505	13,360	12,300
Japan	8,032	13,354	10,006
Kenya	59,063	61,504	78,432
Netherlands	52,803	56,000	48,955
Rwanda	16,617	12,873	20,803
Singapore	7,278	8,719	13,859
South Africa	24,076	42,997	29,632
Spain	7,961	17,732	14,526
Sudan	9,152	5,763	13,765
Switzerland	70,674	69,011	72,993
Tanzania	6,689	5,774	5,832
United Arab Emirates	6,119	6,914	345
United Kingdom	28,806	30,015	33,883
USA	6,743	9,190	12,693
Total (incl. others)	451,764	467,605	534,106

Transport

RAILWAYS
(traffic)

	1994	1995	1996
Passenger-km (million)	35	30	28
Freight ton-km (million)	208	236	187

Freight traffic ('000 ton-km): 219,491 in 2001; 217,476 in 2002; 212,616 in 2003.

ROAD TRAFFIC
(vehicles in use)

	2001	2002	2003
Passenger cars	53,105	54,173	56,837
Buses and coaches	17,993	18,842	20,572
Lorries and vans	59602	61,187	64,650
Motorcycles	66,984	71,229	80,088

CIVIL AVIATION
(traffic on scheduled services)

	1999	2000	2001
Kilometres flown (million)	2	2	2
Passengers carried ('000)	36	39	41
Passenger-km (million)	198	215	235
Total ton-km (million)	37	40	42

Source: UN, *Statistical Yearbook*.

Tourism

FOREIGN TOURIST ARRIVALS

Country of residence	2001	2002	2003
Congo, Democratic Repub.	5,974	7,586	5,915
India	4,588	5,708	6,639
Kenya	64,933	80,518	114,499
Norway	7,090	1,480	1,528
Rwanda	39,597	52,431	50,143
Tanzania	16,863	23,584	30,534
United Kingdom	13,626	15,171	17,181
USA	10,550	11,922	13,179
Total (incl. others)	205,287	254,219	305,719

Tourism receipts (US $ million, incl. passenger transport): 193 in 2001; 201 in 2002; 221 in 2003 (Source: World Tourism Organization).

Communications Media

	2002	2003	2004
Telephones ('000 main lines in use)	55.0	61.0	71.6
Mobile cellular telephones ('000 subscribers)*	393.3	776.2	1,165.0
Personal computers ('000 in use)	82	103	121
Internet users ('000)	100	125	200

Source: International Telecommunication Union.

Television receivers ('000 in use, 2000): 610.

Radio receivers ('000 in use, 1997): 2,600.

Facsimile machines (number in use, 1996): 3,000 (estimate)*.

Book production (titles, excl. pamphlets and govt publications, 1996): 288.

Daily newspapers (1996): titles 2; average circulation ('000 copies) 40.

*Year ending 30 June.

Sources: mainly UNESCO, *Statistical Yearbook*; UN, *Statistical Yearbook*.

Education

(2001)

	Institutions	Teachers	Students
Primary	12,280	127,038	6,900,916
Secondary	2,400	30,425	539,786
Teacher training colleges	n.a.	n.a.	13,285
Technical schools and institutes	58	605	5,452
Universities (state)	2	n.a.	30,243
Universities (private)	10	n.a.	n.a.

In addition, in 2001, there were 10 national teacher colleges, 5 Uganda technical colleges and 5 Uganda commercial colleges.

Primary schools (2003): Institutions 13,353; Teachers 145,587; Pupils 7,633,314.

Secondary schools (2003): Institutions 2,055; Teachers 38,549; Pupils 683,609.

Adult literacy rate (UNESCO estimates): 68.9% (males 78.8%; females 59.2%) in 2002 (Source: UN Development Programme, *Human Development Report*).

Directory

The Constitution

Following the military coup in July 1985, the 1967 Constitution was suspended, and all legislative and executive powers were vested in a Military Council, whose Chairman was Head of State. In January 1986 a further military coup established an executive Presidency, assisted by a Cabinet of Ministers and a legislative National Resistance Council (NRC). In September 1995 a Constituent Assembly (comprising 214 elected and 74 nominated members) enacted a draft Constitution. The new Constitution was promulgated on 8 October 1995. Under its terms, a national referendum on the introduction of a multi-party political system was to take place in 2000. The referendum produced an overwhelming vote in favour of retaining the existing 'no-party' system; however, the referendum was annulled by the Constitutional Court in 2004. A direct presidential election took place in May 1996, followed in June of that year by legislative elections to the Parliament. This body, comprising 214 elected members and 62 nominated members, replaced the NRC. At the general election of June 2001 the number of nominated members was increased to 78. Legislation outlining the transition to multi-party politics was passed by the Parliament on 28 June 2005 and approved by 92.5% of voters in a national referendum held on 28 July 2005. The legislation also removed the two-term limit on the presidency.

The Government

HEAD OF STATE

President: Gen. (retd) YOWERI KAGUTA MUSEVENI (took office 29 January 1986; elected 9 May 1996, re-elected 12 March 2001 and 23 February 2006).

Vice-President: Prof. GILBERT BALIBASEKA BUKENYA.

THE CABINET
(January 2006)

A new Government was to be appointed following legislative elections held on 23 February 2006.

Prime Minister and Leader of Government Business in Parliament: Prof. APOLLO NSIBAMBI.

First Deputy Prime Minister and Minister of Relief and Disaster Preparedness: Lt-Gen. MOSES ALI.

Second Deputy Prime Minister and Minister of Public Service: HENRY MUGANWA KAJURA.

Minister in Charge of the Presidency: BEATRICE WABUDEYA.

Minister in the Office of the Prime Minister: Prof. MONDO GEORGE KAGONYERA.

Minister of Defence: AMAMA MBABAZI.

Minister of Internal Affairs: Dr RUHAKANA RUGUNDA.

Minister of Finance, Planning and Economic Development: Dr EZRA SURUMA.

Minister in Charge of Security: BETTY AKECH.

Minister of Works, Housing and Communications: JOHN NASASIRA.

Minister of Agriculture, Animal Industry and Fisheries: Capt. JANAT BALUNZI MUKWAYA.

Minister of Energy and Mineral Development: SYDA NAMIREMBE BBUMBA.

Minister of Education and Sports: NAMIREMBE BITAMAZIRE.

Minister of Justice and Constitutional Affairs and Attorney General: GERALD KIDDU MAKUBUYA.

Minister of Gender, Labour and Social Services: ZOE BAKOKO BAKORU.

Minister of Trade, Industry, Tourism, Wildlife and Antiquities: DAUDI MIGEREKO.

Minister of Water, Lands and Environment: Col KAHINDA OTAFIRE.

Minister of Health: Brig. JIM KATUGUGU MUWHEZI.

Minister without Portfolio and National Political Commissar: Dr CRISPUS W. C. B. KIYONGA.

Minister of Foreign Affairs: SAM KUTESA.

Minister of Local Government: Prof. TARSIS KABWEGYERE.

In addition to the Cabinet Ministers, there are 45 Ministers of State.

MINISTRIES

Office of the President: Parliament Bldg, POB 7168, Kampala; tel. (41) 2258441; fax (41) 2256143; e-mail info@gouexecutive.net; internet www.gouexecutive.net.

Office of the Prime Minister: POB 341, Kampala; tel. (41) 2259518; fax (41) 2242341.

Ministry of Agriculture, Animal Industry and Fisheries: POB 102, Entebbe; tel. (41) 2320987; fax (41) 2321255; e-mail psmaaif@infocom.co.ug; internet www.agriculture.go.ug.

Ministry of Defence: Bombo, POB 7069, Kampala; tel. (41) 2270331; fax (41) 2245911.

Ministry of Education and Sports: Embassy House and Development Bldg, Plot 9/11, Parliament Ave, POB 7063, Kampala; tel. (41) 2234451; fax (41) 2230437; e-mail pro@education.go.ug; internet www.education.go.ug.

Ministry of Energy and Mineral Development: Amber House, Kampala Rd, Kampala; tel. (41) 2311111; e-mail psmemd@energy.go.ug; internet www.energyandminerals.go.ug.

Ministry of Finance, Planning and Economic Development: Appollo Kaggwa Rd, Plot 2/4, POB 8147, Kampala; tel. (41) 2234700; fax (41) 2230163; e-mail webmaster@finance.go.ug; internet www.finance.go.ug.

Ministry of Foreign Affairs: Embassy House, POB 7048, Kampala; tel. (41) 2345661; fax (41) 2258722; e-mail info@mofa.go.ug; internet www.mofa.go.ug.

Ministry of Gender, Labour and Social Development: Udyam House, Jinja Rd, POB 7168, Kampala; tel. (41) 2258334.

Ministry of Health: Plot 6, Lourdel Rd, Wandegeya, POB 7272, Kampala; tel. (41) 2340884; fax (41) 2340887; e-mail info@health.go.ug; internet www.health.go.ug.

Ministry of Internal Affairs: Jinja Rd, POB 7191, Kampala; tel. (41) 2231103; fax (41) 2231188; e-mail psmia@infocom.co.ug.

Ministry of Justice and Constitutional Affairs: Parliament Bldg, POB 7183, Kampala; tel. (41) 2230538; fax (41) 2254829; e-mail mojca@africaonline.co.ug; internet www.justice.go.ug.

Ministry of Local Government: Uganda House, 8/10 Kampala Rd, POB 7037, Kampala; tel. (41) 2341224; fax (41) 2258127; e-mail info@molg.go.ug; internet www.molg.go.ug.

Ministry of Public Service: 12 Nakasero Hill Rd, POB 7003, Kampala; tel. (41) 2251003; fax (41) 2255363; e-mail info@publicservice.go.ug; internet www.publicservice.go.ug.

Ministry of Tourism, Trade and Industry: 6/8 Parliament Ave, POB 7103, Kampala; tel. (41) 2232971; fax (41) 2242188; e-mail ps@mintrade.org.

Ministry of Water, Lands and Environment: POB 7096, Kampala; tel. (41) 2342931; e-mail mwle@mwle.go.ug; internet www.mwle.go.ug.

Ministry of Works, Transport, Housing and Communications: POB 10, Entebbe; tel. (42) 2320101; fax (42) 2320135; e-mail mowhc@utlonline.co.ug; internet www.miniworks.go.ug.

President and Legislature

PRESIDENT

Election, 23 February 2006

Candidate	Votes	% of votes
Gen. (Retd) Yoweri Kaguta Museveni (NRM-O)	4,078,677	59.28
Kizza Besigye (FDC)	2,570,572	37.36
John Ssebaana Kizito (DP)	109,055	1.59
Abed Bwanika (Ind.)	65,344	0.95
Miria Obote Kalule (UPC)	56,584	0.82
Total	6,880,232	100.00

PARLIAMENT

Speaker: EDWARD SSEKANDI.

Deputy Speaker: REBECCA KADAGA.

The National Resistance Movement, which took office in January 1986, established a National Resistance Council (NRC), initially comprising 80 nominated members, to act as a legislative body. National elections were held on 11–28 February 1989, at which 210 members of an expanded NRC were elected by members of district-

UGANDA

level Resistance Committees (themselves elected by local-level Resistance Committees, who were directly elected by universal adult suffrage). The remaining 68 seats in the NRC were reserved for candidates nominated by the President (to include 34 women and representatives of youth organizations and trades unions). Political parties were not allowed to participate in the election campaign. In October 1989 the NRC approved legislation extending the Government's term of office by five years from January 1990, when its mandate was to expire. The Constituent Assembly (see Constitution) extended further the NRM's term of office in November 1994. Under the terms of the Constitution that was promulgated in October 1995, the NRC was restyled as the Ugandan Parliament. Legislative elections to the Parliament took place in June 1996 (again officially on a 'no-party' basis). The total membership of the Parliament was reduced from 278 to 276, comprising 214 elected and 62 nominated representatives. A national referendum on the future introduction of a multi-party political system was staged in June 2000, at which 90.7% of participants voted in favour of retaining the 'no-party' political system—the referendum was nullified in mid-2004 (see Recent History). A general election was held on 26 June 2001, following which the number of seats in Parliament stood at 292, comprising 214 directly elected representatives, 53 nominated female representatives, 10 nominated representatives from the UPDF, five nominated representatives for workers, five for people with disabilities and five for young people. Legislation was adopted by the Parliament in June 2005, and ratified by a national referendum on 28 July of that year, restoring multi-party politics and lifting the two-term limit on the presidency. Multi-party legislative elections were held on 23 February 2006; results were not immediately made available.

Election Commission

Electoral Commission: 53–56 Jinja Rd, POB 22678, Kampala; tel. (41) 2337500; fax (41) 2337595; e-mail info@ec.or.ug; internet www.ec.or.ug; independent; Chair. Dr BADRU M. KIGGUNDU.

Political Organizations

Political parties were ordered to suspend active operations, although not formally banned, in March 1986. At a referendum on the future restoration of a plural political system, which took place on 29 June 2000, the retention of the existing 'no-party' system was overwhelmingly endorsed by voters. However, the result was nullified by the Constitutional Court in mid-2004. Following a successful challenge to the Political Parties and Organisations Act 2002, political parties were permitted to resume their activities nationally from March 2003. Discussions on a proposed transition to multi-party politics commenced in 2004. By April of that year some 60 new political parties had emerged, but only 13 had sought registration. In mid-2005 legislation was passed allowing for a return to full multi-party democracy; the legislation was approved by 92.5% of voters in a national referendum held on 28 July 2005.

Bazzukulu ba Buganda (Grandchildren of Buganda): Bagandan separatist movement.

Buganda Youth Movement: f. 1994; seeks autonomy for Buganda; Leader STANLEY KATO.

Conservative Party (CP): f. 1979; Leader JEHOASH MAYANJA-NKANGI.

Democratic Party (DP): City House, Plot 2/3 William St, POB 7098, Kampala; tel. and fax (41) 2252536; e-mail info@dpuganda.org; internet www.dpuganda.org; f. 1954; main support in southern Uganda; seeks a multi-party political system; Pres. JOHN SSEBAANA KIZITO; Vice-Pres. ZACHARY OLUM.

Federal Democratic Movement (FEDEMO): Kampala.

Forum for Democratic Change: f. 2004 by a merger of the Reform Agenda, the Parliamentary Advocacy Forum and the National Democratic Forum; Leader REAGAN OKUMU.

Forum for Multi-Party Democracy: Kampala; Gen. Sec. JESSE MASHATTE.

Movement for New Democracy in Uganda: based in Zambia; f. 1994 to campaign for multi-party political system; Leader DAN OKELLO-OGWANG.

National Resistance Movement Organisation (NRM-O): f. as National Resistance Movement to oppose the UPC Govt 1980–85; also opposed the mil. Govt in power from July 1985 to Jan. 1986; its fmr mil. wing, the National Resistance Army (NRA), led by Lt-Gen. (later Gen. retd) Yoweri Kaguta Museveni, took power in Jan. 1986; name changed as above on registration in 2003; Chair. Dr SAMSON KISEKKA.

Directory

Nationalist Liberal Party: Kampala; f. 1984 by a breakaway faction of the DP; Leader TIBERIO OKENY.

Uganda Democratic Alliance: Leader APOLO KIRONDE.

Uganda Democratic Freedom Front: Leader Maj. HERBERT ITONGA.

Uganda Freedom Movement (UFM): Kampala; mainly Baganda support; withdrew from NRM coalition Govt in April 1987; Sec.-Gen. (vacant).

Uganda Independence Revolutionary Movement: f. 1989; Chair. Maj. OKELLO KOLO.

Uganda Islamic Revolutionary Party (UIRP): Kampala; f. 1993; Chair. IDRIS MUWONGE.

Uganda National Unity Movement: Chair. Alhaji SULEIMAN SSALONGO.

Uganda Patriotic Movement: Kampala; f. 1980; Sec.-Gen. JABERI SSALI.

Uganda People's Congress (UPC): POB 1951, Kampala; internet www.members.home.net/upc; f. 1960; socialist-based philosophy; mainly northern support; ruling party 1962–71 and 1980–85, sole legal political party 1969–71; Nat. Leader Dr JAMES RWANYARARE.

Ugandan People's Democratic Movement (UPDM): seeks democratic reforms; support mainly from north and east of the country; includes mems of fmr govt armed forces; signed a peace accord with the Govt in 1990; Chair. ERIC OTEMA ALLIMADI; Sec.-Gen. EMMANUEL OTENG.

Uganda Progressive Union (UPU): Kampala; Chair. ALFRED BANYA.

New parties seeking registration in 2004 included the **Forum for Integrity in Leadership (FIL)**, the **Movement for Democratic Change (MDC)**, the **National Peasant Party (NPP)**, the **National Progressive Movement (NPM)**, the **People's Independent Party (PIP)** and the **Republic Women and Youth Party (RWYP)**.

The following organizations are in armed conflict with the Government:

Alliance of Democratic Forces (ADF): active since 1996 in south-eastern Uganda; combines Ugandan Islamic fundamentalist rebels, exiled Rwandan Hutus and guerrillas from the Democratic Republic of the Congo; Pres. Sheikh JAMIL MUKULU.

Lord's Resistance Army (LRA): f. 1987; claims to be conducting a Christian fundamentalist 'holy war' against the Govt; forces est. to number up to 1,500, operating mainly from bases in Sudan; Leader JOSEPH KONY; a breakaway faction (LRA—Democratic) is led by RONALD OTIM KOMAKECH.

Uganda National Rescue Front Part Two (UNRF II): based in Juba, Sudan; Leader ALI BAMUZE.

Uganda People's Freedom Movement (UPFM): based in Tororo and Kenya; f. 1994 by mems of the fmr Uganda People's Army; Leader PETER OTAI.

West Nile Bank Front (WNBF): operates in northern Uganda.

Diplomatic Representation

EMBASSIES AND HIGH COMMISSIONS IN UGANDA

Algeria: 14 Acacia Ave, Kololo, POB 4025, Kampala; tel. (41) 2232918; fax (41) 2341015; e-mail ambalgka@imul.com; Ambassador ABDELKADER AZIRIA.

Belgium: Rwenzori House, 3rd Floor, 1 Lumumba Ave, POB 7043, Kampala; tel. (41) 2345559; fax (41) 2347212; e-mail kampala@diplobel.org; internet www.diplomatie.be/kampala; Ambassador KOENRAAD ADAM.

China, People's Republic: 37 Malcolm X Ave, Kololo, POB 4106, Kampala; tel. (41) 2259881; fax (41) 2235087; e-mail chinaemb_ug@mfa.gov.cn; Ambassador FAN GUIJIN.

Congo, Democratic Republic: 20 Philip Rd, Kololo, POB 4972, Kampala; tel. (41) 2250099; fax (41) 2340140; Chargé d'affaires a.i. BISELELE WA MUTSHIPAYI.

Cuba: KAR Dr., 16 Lower Kololo Terrace, POB 9226, Kampala; tel. (41) 2233742; fax (41) 2233320; e-mail ecuba@africaonline.co.ug; Ambassador RICARDO ANTONIO DANZA SIGAS.

Denmark: Plot 3, Lumumba Ave, POB 11243, Kampala; tel. (31) 2263211; fax (31) 2264624; e-mail kmtamb@um.dk; internet www.ambkampala.um.dk; Ambassador STIG BARLYNG.

Egypt: 33 Kololo Hill Dr., POB 4280, Kampala; tel. (41) 2254525; fax (41) 2232103; e-mail egyembug@utlonline.co.ug; Ambassador REDA ABDEL RAHMAN.

UGANDA

Ethiopia: 3L Kitante Close, off Kira Rd, POB 7745, Kampala; tel. (41) 2348340; fax (41) 2341885; e-mail ethiokam@starcom.co.ug; Ambassador TESFAYE HABISSO.

France: 16 Lumumba Ave, Nakasero, POB 7212, Kampala; tel. (41) 2342120; fax (41) 2341252; e-mail ambafrance.kampala@diplomatie.gouv.fr; internet www.ambafrance.or.ug; Ambassador BERNARD GARANCHER.

Germany: 15 Philip Rd, Kololo, POB 7016, Kampala; tel. (41) 2501111; fax (41) 2501115; e-mail germemb@africaonline.co.ug; Ambassador Dr ALEXANDER MÜHLEN.

Holy See: Chwa 11 Rd, Mbuya Hill, POB 7177, Kampala (Apostolic Nunciature); tel. (41) 2505619; fax (41) 2221774; e-mail nuntius@utlonline.co.ug; Apostolic Nuncio Most Rev. CHRISTOPHE PIERRE (Titular Archbishop of Gunela).

India: 11 Kyaddondo Rd, Nakasero, POB 7040, Kampala; tel. (41) 2257368; fax (41) 2254943; e-mail hc@hicomindkampala.org; High Commissioner SIBARATA TRIPATHI.

Iran: 9 Bandali Rise, Bugolobi, POB 24529, Kampala; tel. (41) 2221689; fax (41) 2223590; Ambassador ABOUTALEBI MORTEZA.

Ireland: 25 Yusuf Lule Rd, Nakasero, POB 7791, Kampala; tel. (41) 2344348; fax (41) 2344353; e-mail irishaid@starcom.co.ug; Chargé d'affaires a.i. AINE HEARNS.

Italy: 10 Lourdel Rd, Nakasero, POB 4646, Kampala; tel. (41) 2250442; fax (41) 250448; e-mail ambkamp@imul.com; internet www.imul.com/embitaly; Ambassador Dr MAURIZIO TEUCCI.

Japan: EADB Bldg, Nile Ave, POB 23553, Kampala; tel. (41) 2349542; fax (41) 2349547; e-mail jembassy@jembassy.co.ug; Ambassador RYUUZI KIKUCHI.

Kenya: 41 Nakasero Rd, POB 5220, Kampala; tel. (41) 2258235; fax (41) 2258239; e-mail kenhicom@africaonline.co.ug; High Commissioner JAPHETH R. GETUGI.

Korea, Democratic People's Republic: 10 Prince Charles Dr., Kololo, POB 5885, Kampala; tel. (41) 2546033; fax (41) 2250224; Chargé d'affaires KANG YONG DOK.

Libya: 26 Kololo Hill Dr., POB 6079, Kampala; tel. (41) 2344924; fax (41) 2344969; e-mail l.a.p.b.@utlonline.co.ug; Sec. of People's Bureau ABDALLA ABDULMAULA BUJELDAIN.

Netherlands: Rwenzori Courts, 4th Floor, Plot 2, Nakasero Rd, POB 7728, Kampala; tel. (41) 2346000; fax (41) 2231861; e-mail kam@minbuza.nl; internet www.netherlandsembassyuganda.org; Ambassador JOHANNA MARIA GEERTRUI BRANDT.

Nigeria: 33 Nakasero Rd, POB 4338, Kampala; tel. (41) 2233691; fax (41) 2232543; e-mail nighicom-sgu@africaonline.co.ug; High Commissioner CHUKUDI DIXON ORIKE.

Norway: 8A John Babiiha Ave, Kololo, POB 22770, Kampala; tel. (41) 2343621; fax (41) 2343936; e-mail emb.kampala@norad.no; internet www.norway.go.ug; Ambassador BJØRG SCHONHOWD LEITE.

Russia: 28 Malcolm X Ave, Kololo, POB 7022, Kampala; tel. (41) 2345698; fax (41) 2345798; e-mail russemb@imul.com; Ambassador VALERY I. UTKIN.

Rwanda: 2 Nakaima Rd, POB 2468, Kampala; tel. (41) 2344045; fax (41) 2258547; e-mail ambakampala@minaffet.gov.rw; Ambassador IGNACE KAMALI KAREGESA.

Saudi Arabia: 3 Okurut Close, Kololo, POB 22558, Kampala; tel. (41) 2340614; fax (41) 2254017; e-mail reskala@infocom.co.ug; Chargé d'affaires MAJED ABDULRAHMAN M. MARTHA AL-OTAIBI.

South Africa: 2B Nakasero Hill Lane, POB 22667, Kampala; tel. (41) 2343543; fax (41) 2348216; e-mail sahc@infocom.co.ug; High Commissioner THANDUYISE HENRY CHILIZA.

Sudan: 21 Nakasero Rd, POB 3200, Kampala; tel. (41) 2230001; fax (41) 2346573; e-mail sudanikampala@africaonline.co.ug; Ambassador HASSAN IBRAHIM GADKARIM.

Sweden: 24 Lumumba Ave, Nakasero, POB 22669, Kampala; tel. (41) 2340970; fax (41) 2340979; e-mail ambassaden.kampala@sida.se; internet www.swedenabroad.com/kampala; Ambassador ERIK ABERG.

Tanzania: 6 Kagera Rd, Nakasero, POB 5750, Kampala; tel. (41) 2256272; fax (41) 2343973; e-mail tzrepkla@utlonline.co.ug; High Commissioner RAJAB H. GAMAHA.

United Kingdom: 10–12 Parliament Ave, POB 7070, Kampala; tel. (31) 2312000; fax (41) 2257304; e-mail bhcinfo@starcom.co.ug; internet www.britain.or.ug; High Commissioner FRANCOIS GORDON.

USA: Plot 1577, Ggaba Rd, POB 7007, Kampala; tel. (41) 2259791; fax (41) 2259794; e-mail ambkampala@state.gov; internet kampala.usembassy.gov; Ambassador STEVEN A. BROWNING.

Judicial System

Courts of Judicature: POB 7085, Kampala; tel. (41) 2233420; e-mail hclib@imul.com; internet www.judiciature.go.ug.

The Supreme Court
Kabaka Anjagala Rd, Mengo.
Hears appeals from the Court of Appeal. Also acts as a Constitutional Court.
Chief Justice: BENJAMIN ODOKI.
Deputy Chief Justice: L. E. M. MUKASA-KIKONYOGO.
The Court of Appeal: 5 Parliament Ave, Kampala; hears appeals from the High Court; the Court of Appeal consists of the Deputy Chief Justice and no fewer than seven Justices of Appeal, the number thereof being prescribed by Parliament.

The High Court
POB 7085, Kampala; tel. (41) 2233422.
Has full criminal and civil jurisdiction and also serves as a Constitutional Court. The High Court consists of the Principal Judge and 27 Puisne Judges.
Principal Judge: JAMES OGOOLA.

Magistrates' Courts: These are established under the Magistrates' Courts Act of 1970 and exercise limited jurisdiction in criminal and civil matters. The country is divided into magisterial areas, presided over by a Chief Magistrate. Under the Chief Magistrate there are two categories of Magistrates. The Magistrates preside alone over their courts. Appeals from the first category of Magistrates' Court lie directly to the High Court, while appeals from the second categories of Magistrates' Court lie to the Chief Magistrate's Court, and from there to the High Court. There are 27 Chief Magistrates' Courts, 52 Magistrates' Grade I Courts and 428 Magistrates' Grade II Courts.

Religion

Christianity is the majority religion—its adherents constitute approximately 75% of the population. Muslims account for approximately 15% of the population. A variety of other religions, including traditional indigenous religions, several branches of Hinduism, the Bahá'í Faith and Judaism, are practised freely and, combined, make up approximately 10% of the population. There are few atheists in the country. In many areas, particularly in rural settings, some religions tend to be syncretistic: deeply held traditional indigenous beliefs are blended into or observed alongside the rites of recognized religions, particularly in areas that are predominantly Christian. Missionary groups of several denominations are present and active in the country, including the Pentecostal Church, the Baptist Church, the Episcopal Church/Church of Uganda, the Church of Christ and the Mormons.

CHRISTIANITY

The Roman Catholic and Anglican Churches claim approximately the same number of followers, accounting for approximately 90% of the country's professed Christians. The Seventh-day Adventist Church, the Church of Jesus Christ of Latter-day Saints (Mormons), the Orthodox Church, Jehovah's Witnesses, the Baptist Church, the Unification Church and the Pentecostal Church, among others, are also active.

The Anglican Communion
Anglicans are adherents of the Church of the Province of Uganda, comprising 29 dioceses. In 2002 there were about 8m. adherents.
Archbishop of Uganda and Bishop of Kampala: Most Rev. LIVINGSTONE MPALANYI-NKOYOYO, POB 14123, Kampala; tel. (41) 2270218; fax (41) 2251925; e-mail couab@uol.co.ug.

Greek Orthodox Church
Archbishop of East Africa: NICADEMUS OF IRINOUPOULIS (resident in Nairobi, Kenya); jurisidiction covers Kenya, Tanzania and Uganda.

The Roman Catholic Church
Uganda comprises four archdioceses and 15 dioceses. At 31 December 2003 there were an estimated 11,225,908 adherents (equivalent to some 42.3% of the total population).

Uganda Episcopal Conference
Uganda Catholic Secretariat, POB 2886, Kampala; tel. (41) 2510398; fax (41) 2510545; f. 1974; Pres. Most Rev. PAUL BAKYENGA (Archbishop of Mbarara).

Archbishop of Gulu: Most Rev. JOHN BAPTISTE ODAMA, Archbishop's House, POB 200, Gulu; tel. (471) 232026; fax (471) 223593; e-mail metrog@africaonline.co.ug.

UGANDA

Archbishop of Kampala: Cardinal EMMANUEL WAMALA, Archbishop's House, POB 14125, Mengo, Kampala; tel. (41) 2270183; fax (41) 2345441; e-mail rubaga@africaonline.co.ug.
Archbishop of Mbarara: Most Rev. PAUL BAKYENGA, POB 184, Mbarara; tel. (485) 220052; fax (485) 221249; e-mail mbarch@utlonline.co.ug.
Archbishop of Tororo: Most Rev. JAMES ODONGO, Archbishop's House, POB 933, Mbale; tel. (45) 22233269; fax (45) 22233754; e-mail tororoad@africaonline.co.ug.

ISLAM

Muslims are mainly Sunni, although there are Shi'a followers of the Aga Khan among the Asian community.

The Uganda Muslim Supreme Council: POB 3247, Kampala; Mufti of Uganda IBRAHIM SAID LUWEMBA; Chief Kadi and Pres. of Council HUSAYN RAJAB KAKOOZA.

BAHÁ'Í FAITH

National Spiritual Assembly: POB 2662, Kampala; tel. (41) 2540511; fax (41) 2530147; e-mail bahai@spacenetuganda.com; mems resident in 2,721 localities.

JUDAISM

There is a small Jewish community, the Abayudaya, in central Uganda, with 600 members and six synagogues.

The Press

DAILY AND OTHER NEWSPAPERS

The Citizen: Kampala; official publ. of the Democratic Party; English; Editor JOHN KYEYUNE.
The Economy: POB 6787, Kampala; weekly; English; Editor ROLAND KAKOOZA.
Financial Times: Plot 17/19, Station Rd, POB 31399, Kampala; tel. (41) 2245798; bi-weekly; English; Editor G. A. ONEGI OBEL.
Focus: POB 268, Kampala; tel. (41) 2235086; fax (41) 2242796; f. 1983; publ. by Islamic Information Service and Material Centre; 4 a week; English; Editor HAJJI KATENDE; circ. 12,000.
Guide: POB 5350, Kampala; tel. (41) 2233486; fax (41) 2268045; f. 1989; weekly; English; Editor-in-Chief A. A. KALIISA; circ. 30,000.
The Monitor: POB 12141, Kampala; tel. (41) 2232367; fax (41) 2232369; e-mail info@monitor.co.ug; internet www.monitor.co.ug; f. 1992; daily; English; Man. Dir CONRAD NKUTU; Exec. Editor Dr PETER MWESIGE; circ. 22,000 (Mon.–Sat.), 24,000 (Sun.).
Mulengera: POB 6787, Kampala; weekly; Luganda; Editor ROLAND KAKOOZA.
Munnansi News Bulletin: POB 7098, Kampala; f. 1980; weekly; English; owned by the Democratic Party; Editor ANTHONY SGEKWEYAMA.
Munno: POB 4027, Kampala; f. 1911; daily; Luganda; publ. by the Roman Catholic Church; Editor ANTHONY SSEKWEYAMA; circ. 7,000.
New Vision: POB 9815, Kampala; tel. (41) 2235846; fax (41) 2235221; e-mail wpike@newvision.co.ug; internet www.newvision.co.ug; f. 1986; official govt newspaper; daily; English; Editor WILLIAM PIKE; circ. 34,000 (Mon.–Sat.), 42,000 (Sun.).

  Bukedde: daily; Luganda; Editor MAURICE SSEKWAUNGU; circ. 16,000.
  Etop: weekly; vernacular; Editor KENNETH OLUKA; circ. 5,000.
  Ormuri: tel. (485) 221265; e-mail visionmb@infocom.co.ug; weekly; vernacular; Editor JOSSY MUHANGI; circ. 11,000.
  Rupiny: weekly; vernacular; Editor CHRIS BANYA; circ. 5,000.

Ngabo: POB 9362, Kampala; tel. (41) 2242637; f. 1979; daily; Luganda; Editor MAURICE SEKAWUNGU; circ. 7,000.
The Star: POB 9362, Kampala; tel. (41) 2242637; f. 1980; revived 1984; daily; English; Editor SAMUEL KATWERE; circ. 5,000.
Taifa Uganda Empya: POB 1986, Kampala; tel. (41) 2254652; f. 1953; daily; Luganda; Editor A. SEMBOGA; circ. 24,000.
Weekly Topic: POB 1725, Kampala; tel. (41) 2233834; weekly; English; Editor JOHN WASSWA; circ. 13,000.

PERIODICALS

Eastern Africa Journal of Rural Development: Dept of Agricultural Economics and Agribusiness, Makerere University, POB 7062, Kampala; tel. (77) 2616540; fax (41) 2530858; e-mail bkiiza@infocom.co.ug; annual; Editor BARNABAS KIIZA; circ. 800.
The Exposure: POB 3179, Kampala; tel. (41) 2267203; fax (41) 2259549; monthly; politics.

Leadership: POB 2522, Kampala; tel. (41) 2221358; fax (41) 2221576; f. 1956; 6 a year; English; Roman Catholic; circ. 7,400.
Mkombozi: c/o Ministry of Defence, Republic House, POB 3798, Kampala; tel. (41) 2270331; f. 1982; military affairs; Editor A. OPOLOTT.
Musizi: POB 4027, Mengo, Kampala; f. 1955; monthly; Luganda; Roman Catholic; Editor F. GITTA; circ. 30,000.
Pearl of Africa: POB 7142, Kampala; monthly; govt publ.
Uganda Confidential: POB 5576, Kampala; tel. (41) 2250273; fax (41) 2255288; e-mail ucl@swiftuganda.com; internet www.swiftuganda.com/~confidential; f. 1990; monthly; Editor TEDDY SSEZI-CHEEYE.

NEWS AGENCIES

Uganda News Agency (UNA): POB 7142, Kampala; tel. (41) 2232734; fax (41) 2342259; Dir CRISPUS MUNDUA (acting).

Foreign Bureaux

Inter Press Service (IPS) (Italy): Plot 4, 3rd St, Industrial Area, POB 16514, Wandegeya, Kampala; tel. (41) 2235846; fax (41) 2235211; Correspondent DAVID MUSOKE.
Newslink Africa (United Kingdom): POB 6032, Kampala.
Rossiiskoye Informatsionnoye Agentstvo—Novosti (RIA—Novosti) (Russia): POB 4412, Kampala; tel. (41) 2232383; Correspondent Dr OLEG TETERIN.
Xinhua (New China) News Agency (People's Republic of China): Plot 27, Prince Charles Dr., Kampala; tel. (41) 2347109; fax (41) 2254951; Chief Correspondent WANG SHANGZHI.

Publishers

Centenary Publishing House Ltd: POB 6246, Kampala; tel. (41) 2241599; fax (41) 2250427; f. 1977; religious (Anglican); Man. Dir Rev. SAM KAKIZA.
Fountain Publishers Ltd: POB 488, Kampala; tel. (41) 2259163; fax (41) 2251160; e-mail fountain@starcom.co.ug; internet www.fountainpublishers.co.ug; f. 1989; general, school textbooks, children's books, academic, scholarly; Man. Dir JAMES TUMUSIIME.
Longman Uganda Ltd: POB 3409, Kampala; tel. (41) 2242940; f. 1965; Man. Dir M. K. L. MUTYABA.
Uganda Printing and Publishing Corporation: POB 33, Entebbe; tel. (41) 2220639; fax (41) 2220530; f. 1993; Man. Dir P. A. BAKER.

Broadcasting and Communications

TELECOMMUNICATIONS

CelTel Ltd: POB 6771, Kampala; tel. (41) 2230110; fax (41) 2230106; e-mail celmail@imul.com; Man. Dir A. K. SSEMMANDA.
MTN Uganda Ltd: POB 24624, Kampala; tel. (31) 2212053; fax (31) 2212333; internet www.mtn.co.ug; f. 1998.
Uganda Communications Commission: Communications House, 12th Floor, 1 Colville St, POB 7376, Kampala; tel. (41) 2348830; fax (41) 2348832; e-mail ucc@ucc.co.ug; internet www.ucc.co.ug; f. 1998; regulatory body; Chair. Dr A. M. S. KATAHOIRE; Exec. Dir PATRICK MASAMBU.
Uganda Telecom Ltd (UTL): POB 7171, Kampala; tel. (41) 2258855; fax (41) 2345907; f. 1998; state-owned; privatization pending.

BROADCASTING

Regulatory Body

Uganda Broadcasting Council (UBC): Broadcasting Council Secretariat, Worker's House, Northern wing, 6th Floor, Plot 1 Pilkington Rd, POB 27553, Kampala; tel. (41) 2251452; fax (41) 2250612; e-mail info@broadcastug.com; internet www.broadcastug.com; f. 1998; statutory body enacted by the Electronic Media Act of 2000; main functions include licensing and regulating radio and television stations, video and cinema operators and libraries for hiring out video recordings or cinema films; consists of 12 mems appointed by the Minister of Information; Chair. GODFREY MUTABAAZI; Dir.-Gen EDGAR TABAARO.

Radio

91.3 Capital FM: POB 7638, Kampala; tel. (41) 2235092; fax (41) 2344556; e-mail capital@imul.com; f. 1993; independent music

UGANDA *Directory*

station broadcasting from Kampala, Mbarara and Mbale; Chief Officers WILLIAM PIKE, PATRICK QUARCOO.

Central Broadcasting Service (CBS): POB 12760, Kampala; tel. (41) 2272993; fax (41) 2340031; e-mail cbs@imul.com; f. 1996; independent station broadcasting in local languages and English to most of Uganda.

Radio One: POB 4589, Kampala; tel. (41) 2348211; fax (41) 2348311.

Radio Uganda: POB 7142, Kampala; tel. (41) 2257256; fax (41) 2256888; f. 1954; state-controlled; broadcasts in 24 languages, including English, Swahili and Ugandan vernacular languages; Commr for Broadcasting JACK TURYAMWIJUKA.

Sanyu Radio: Katto Plaza, Nkrumah Rd, Kampala; f. 1993; independent station broadcasting to Kampala and its environs.

Voice of Toro: POB 2203, Kampala.

Television

Sanyu Television: Naguru; f. 1994; independent station broadcasting to Kampala and its environs.

Uganda Television (UTV): POB 7142, Kampala; tel. (41) 2254461; f. 1962; state-controlled commercial service; programmes mainly in English, also in Swahili and Luganda; transmits over a radius of 320 km from Kampala; five relay stations are in operation, others are under construction; Controller of Programmes FAUSTIN MISANVU.

Finance

(cap. = capital; res = reserves; dep. = deposits; m. = million; brs = branches; amounts in new Uganda shillings, unless otherwise indicated)

BANKING

Central Bank

Bank of Uganda: 37–43 Kampala Rd, POB 7120, Kampala; tel. (41) 2258441; fax (41) 2255983; e-mail info@bou.or.ug; internet www.bou.or.ug; f. 1966; bank of issue; cap. 20,000m., res 437,957m., dep. 2,666,070m. (June 2003); Gov. EMMANUEL TUMUSIIME-MUTEBILE; Dep. Gov. Dr LOUIS KASEKENDE.

State Bank

Uganda Development Bank: UDB Towers, 22 Hannington Rd, POB 7210, Kampala; tel. (41) 2230446; fax (41) 2258571; e-mail udb@afsat.com; f. 1972; state-owned; reorg. 2001; privatization pending; cap. 11m. (Dec. 1993); Chair. JOHN R. DOWNER.

Commercial Banks

Allied Bank International (Uganda) Ltd: 24 Jinja Rd, POB 2750, Kampala; tel. (41) 2236535; fax (41) 2230439; e-mail allied@alliedbank.co.ug; internet www.alliedbank.co.ug; reorg. in 1996; 78% owned by Banque Belgolaise SA, 22% by Netherlands govt agency; cap. 4,001m., res 2,638m., dep. 42,020m. (Dec. 2004); Chair. JOHN CARRUTHERS; Man. Dir KWAME AHADZI; 3 brs.

Cairo International Bank: 30 Kampala Rd, POB 7052, Kampala; tel. (41) 2235666; fax (41) 2230130; e-mail cib@spacenetuganda.com; 44.4% owned by Banque du Caire, 36.1% owned by Kato Aromatics SAE, 6.5% each owned Bank of Egypt, Bank Misr and Bank of Alexandria; cap. 7,135m. (Dec. 2003); Chair. Dr IBRAHIM KAMEL; Man. Dir NABIL GHANEM.

Crane Bank Ltd: Crane Chambers, 38 Kampala Rd, POB 22572, Kampala; tel. (41) 2231337; fax (41) 2231578; e-mail cranebnk@cranebanklimited.com; internet www.cranebanklimited.com; 33% owned by Anglo Universal Holdings Ltd, 17% by M/S Meera Investments Ltd, remainder owned by private investors; cap. 5,000m. (Dec. 2003); Chair. SAMSON MUWANGUZI; Man. Dir ROBERT WARLOW.

Diamond Trust Bank (Uganda) Ltd: Diamond Trust Bldg, Plot 17–19, Kampala Rd, POB 7155, Kampala; tel. (41) 2259331; fax (41) 2342286; e-mail info@dtbuganda.co.ug; 40% owned by The Diamond Jubilee Investment Trust, 33.3% owned by Aga Khan Fund for Economic Development, 26.7% owned by Diamond Trust Bank Kenya Ltd; cap. 4,000m. (Dec. 2003); Chair. R. A. BIRD; CEO BALIVADA V. G. RAO.

DFCU Bank Ltd: Impala House, 13 Kimathi Ave, POB 70, Kampala; tel. (41) 2231784; fax (41) 2231687; e-mail dfcubank@dfcugroup.com; internet www.dfcugroup.com; f. 1984 as Gold Trust Bank Ltd; current name adopted 2000; cap. and res 8,500m., dep. 29,801m. (Dec. 2001); Chair. Dr WILLIAM KALEMA; Man. Dir COLIN MCCORMACK.

International Credit Bank Ltd: Katto Plaza, Plot 11/13, Nkrumah Rd, POB 22212, Kampala; tel. (41) 2342291; fax (41) 2230408; f. 1977; cap. and res 2,060m., dep. 9,794m. (June 1996); Chair. THOMAS I. KATTO; Gen. Man. S. BALARAMAN.

Mercantile Credit Bank Ltd: Plot 10, Old Port Bell Rd, POB 620, Kampala; tel. and fax (41) 2235967; e-mail mcb@afsat.com; cap. 1,000m. (Dec. 2003); Chair. PALLE MOELLER; Man. NELSON LUGOLOBI.

National Bank of Commerce (Uganda) Ltd: Cargen House, Plot 13A, Parliament Ave, POB 23232, Kampala; tel. (41) 2347699; fax (41) 2347701; e-mail nbc@swiftuganda.com; cap. 4,631m. (Dec. 2003); Chair. AMOS NZEYI; Man. Dir G. BANGERA.

Nile Bank Ltd: Spear House, Plot 22, Jinja Rd, POB 2834, Kampala; tel. (41) 2346904; fax (41) 2257779; e-mail info@nilebank.co.ug; internet www.nilebank.co.ug; f. 1988; 15.88% owned by East African Development Bank, remainder owned by private investors; cap. 4,000m. (Dec. 2003); Chair. J. B. BYAMUGISHA; Man. Dir RICHARD P. BYARUGABA; 3 brs.

Orient Bank Ltd: Orient Plaza, Plot 6/6A, Kampala Rd, POB 3072, Kampala; tel. (41) 2236012; fax (41) 2236066; e-mail mail@orient-bank.com; internet www.orient-bank.com; f. 1993; cap. 5,000m., dep. 61,012m. (Dec. 2003); Chair. KETAN MORJARIA; Man. Dir SAMWIRI H. K. NJUKI; 6 brs.

Post Bank Uganda Ltd: Plot 11/13, Nkrumah Rd, POB 7189, Kampala; tel. (41) 2258551; fax (41) 2347107; e-mail postbank@imul.com; wholly state-owned; cap. 2,000m. (Dec. 2003); Chair. STEPHEN MWANJE.

Development Banks

Capital Finance Corpn Ltd: 4 Pilkington Rd, POB 21091, Kampala; tel. (41) 2345200; fax (41) 2258310; e-mail cfc@starcom.co.ug; 70% owned by City Credit Bank Ltd; Chair. KEMAL LALANI; Man. Dir and CEO GHULAM HAIDER DAUDANI.

Centenary Rural Development Bank: 7 Entebbe Rd, POB 1892, Kampala; tel. (41) 2251276; fax (41) 2251273; e-mail crdb@imul.com; cap. 4,110m. (Dec. 2003); Chair. Dr JOHN DDUMBA SSENTAMU; CEO HUNG LIHN.

Development Finance Co of Uganda Ltd: Rwenzori House, 1 Lumumba Ave, POB 2767, Kampala; tel. (41) 2231215; fax (41) 2259435; e-mail dfcu@dfcugroup.com; internet www.dfcugroup.com; owned by Commonwealth Devt Corpn (60%), Uganda Devt Corpn (18.5%) and International Finance Corpn (21.5%); cap. 3,978m. (Dec. 2003); Chair. WILLIAM S. KALEMA; Man. Dir C. MCCORMACK.

East African Development Bank (EADB): East African Development Bank Bldg, 4 Nile Ave, POB 7128, Kampala; tel. (41) 2230021; fax (41) 2259763; e-mail dg@eadb.org; internet www.eadb.org; f. 1967; Govts of Kenya, Uganda and Tanzania 25.46% each; remaining 23.62% shared between FMO (Netherlands); Deutsche Investitions- und Entwicklungs-GmbH (Germany); SBIC—Africa Holdings; Commercial Bank of Africa (Kenya); Nordea AB (Sweden); Standard Chartered Bank (United Kingdom); Barclays Bank PLC (United Kingdom); provides financial and tech. assistance to promote industrial development within Uganda, Kenya and Tanzania; regional offices in Nairobi and Dar es Salaam; cap. SDR 37.5m., res SDR −0.4m. (Dec. 2002); Dir Gen. GODFREY TUMUSIIME.

Housing Finance Co Uganda Ltd: Investment House, 25 Kampala Rd, POB 1539, Kampala; tel. (41) 2341227; fax (41) 2341429; e-mail hfcultd@infocom.co.ug; 50% owned by Govt, 50% owned by National Social Security Fund; cap. 1,000m. (Dec. 2003); Chair. ALOYSIUS SEMANDA; CEO J. OKWIR.

Foreign Banks

Bank of Baroda (Uganda) Ltd (India): 18 Kampala Rd, POB 7197, Kampala; tel. (41) 2233680; fax (41) 2230781; e-mail bobho@spacenetuganda.com; internet www.bankofbaroda.com; f. 1969; wholly owned by Bank of Baroda (India); cap. 16,919m., dep. 106,743m. (Dec. 2003); Chair. M. L. RATHI; Man. Dir P. L. KAGALWALA; 6 brs.

Barclays Bank of Uganda Ltd (United Kingdom): 16 Kampala Rd, POB 2971, Kampala; tel. (41) 2232594; fax (41) 2259467; e-mail barclays-uganda@barclays.com; internet www.barclays.com/uganda.htm; f. 1969; wholly owned by Barclays Bank PLC (United Kingdom); cap. 2,000m., res 10,619m., dep. 147,428m. (Dec. 2001); Chair. and Man. Dir FRANK GRIFFITHS; 4 brs.

Citibank (Uganda) Ltd (USA): Plot 4, Centre Court, Ternan Ave, Nakasero, POB 7505, Kampala; tel. (41) 2340951; fax (41) 2340624; internet www.citibank.com/eastafrica/uganda.htm; 99.9% owned by Citicorp Overseas Investment Corpn, 0.1% owned by Foremost Investment; cap. 21,285m. (Dec. 2003); Chair. Prof. J. M. L. SSEBUWUUFU; Man. Dir NADEEM LODHI.

Stanbic Bank Uganda Ltd (United Kingdom): Crested Towers, Short Tower, 17 Hannington Rd, POB 7131, Kampala; tel. (41) 2231152; fax (41) 2231116; e-mail ugandainfo@stanbic.com; internet www.stanbic.co.ug; f. 1906 as National Bank of India Uganda; adopted present name 1993; wholly owned by Stanbic Africa Holdings Ltd (United Kingdom); merged with Uganda Commercial

UGANDA
Directory

Bank Ltd 2002; cap. 5,119m. (Dec. 2003); Chair. Dr M. ALIKER; Man. Dir KITILI MBATHI; 2 brs.

Standard Chartered Bank Uganda Ltd (United Kingdom): 5 Speke Rd, POB 7111, Kampala; tel. (41) 2258211; fax (41) 2231473; e-mail sbc.uganda@ug.standardchartered.com; internet www.standardchartered.com/ug; f. 1969; wholly owned by Standard Chartered Bank Africa PLC; cap. 2,000m. (Dec. 2003); Chair. J. MULWANA; Man. Dir R. ETEMESI.

Tropical Africa Bank Ltd (Libya): Plot 27, Kampala Rd, POB 9485-7292, Kampala; tel. (41) 2341408; fax (41) 2232296; e-mail tabu10@calva.com; f. 1972; 50% govt-owned, 50% owned by Libyan Arab Foreign Bank; cap. 7,000m. (Dec. 2003); Chair. C. M. KASSAMI; Gen. Man. and CEO MOHAMED A. WAHRA.

STOCK EXCHANGE

Uganda Securities Exchange: Workers' House, 2nd Floor, Northern Wing, 1 Pilkington Rd, POB 23552, Kampala; tel. (41) 2343297; fax (41) 2343841; e-mail info@use.or.ug; internet www.use.or.ug; f. 1997; Chair. GEOFFREY A. ONEGI-OBEL; Chief Exec. SIMON RUTEGA.

INSURANCE

East Africa General Insurance Co Ltd: Plot 14, Kampala Rd, POB 1392, Kampala; tel. (3 1) 2262221; fax (41) 2343234; e-mail vkrishna@eagen.co.ug; internet www.eagen.co.ug; f. 1949; fire, life, motor, marine and accident; CEO VYASA KRISHNA.

National Insurance Corporation: Plot 3, Pilkington Rd, POB 7134, Kampala; tel. (41) 2258001; fax (41) 2259925; f. 1964; general and life; Man. Dir S. SEBUUFU.

Pan World Insurance Co Ltd: POB 7658, Kampala; tel. (41) 2341618; fax (41) 2341593; e-mail pwico@imul.com; Gen. Man. GORDON SENTIBA.

Uganda American Insurance Co Ltd: POB 7077, Kampala; tel. and fax (41) 2533781; f. 1970; Man. Dir STAN MENSAH.

Uganda Co-operative Insurance Ltd: Plot 10, Bombo Rd, POB 6176, Kampala; tel. (41) 2241836; fax (41) 2258231; f. 1982; general; Chair. EPHRAIM KAKURU; Gen. Man. (vacant).

Trade and Industry

GOVERNMENT AGENCIES

Capital Markets Authority: East African Development Bank Bldg, 4 Nile Ave, POB 24565, Kampala; tel. (41) 2342788; fax (41) 2342803; e-mail cma@starcom.co.ug; f. 1996 to develop, promote and regulate capital markets sector; Chair. TWAHA KIGONGO KAAWAASE.

Enterprise Development Unit (EPD): Kampala; oversees privatization programme; Exec. Dir LEONARD MUGANWA.

Export and Import Licensing Division: POB 7000, Kampala; tel. (41) 2258795; f. 1987; advises importers and exporters and issues import and export licences; Prin. Commercial Officer JOHN MUHWEZI.

Uganda Advisory Board of Trade: POB 6877, Kampala; tel. (41) 2233311; f. 1974; issues trade licences and service for exporters.

Uganda Export Promotion Board: POB 5045, Kampala; tel. (41) 2230233; fax (41) 2259779; e-mail uepc@starcom.co.ug; internet www.ugandaexportsonline.com; f. 1983; provides market intelligence, organizes training, trade exhbns, etc.; Exec. Dir FLORENCE KATE.

Uganda Investment Authority: Investment Centre, Plot 28, Kampala Rd, POB 7418, Kampala; tel. (41) 2251561; fax (41) 2342903; e-mail info@ugandainvest.com; internet www.ugandainvest.com; f. 1991; promotes foreign and local investment, assists investors, provides business information, issues investment licences; Exec. Dir Dr MAGGIE KIGOZI.

DEVELOPMENT ORGANIZATIONS

Agriculture and Livestock Development Fund: f. 1976; provides loans to farmers.

National Housing and Construction Corpn: Crested Towers, POB 659, Kampala; tel. (41) 2257461; fax (41) 2258708; e-mail nhcc@imul.com; internet www.nhcc.ug.com; f. 1964; govt agent for building works; also develops residential housing; Chair. Dr COLIN SENTONGO; Gen. Man. M. S. KASEKENDE.

Uganda Industrial Development Corpn Ltd (ULDC): 9–11 Parliament Ave, POB 7042, Kampala; f. 1952; Chair. SAM RUTEGA.

CHAMBER OF COMMERCE

Uganda National Chamber of Commerce and Industry: Plot 17/19, Jinja Rd, POB 3809, Kampala; tel. (41) 2258792; fax (41) 2258793; e-mail uma@starcom.co.ug; Chair. BONEY KATATUMBA.

INDUSTRIAL AND TRADE ASSOCIATIONS

CMB Ltd (Coffee Marketing Board): POB 7154, Kampala; tel. (41) 2254051; fax (41) 2230790; state-owned; privatization pending; purchases and exports coffee; Chair. Dr DDUMBA SSENTAMU; Man. Dir SAM KIGGUNDU.

Cotton Development Organization: POB 7018, Kampala; tel. (41) 2232968; fax (41) 2232975; Man. Dir JOLLY SABUNE.

Produce Marketing Board: POB 3705, Kampala; tel. (41) 2236238; Gen. Man. ESTHER KAMPAMPARA.

Uganda Coffee Development Authority: Coffee House, Plot 35, Jinja Rd, POB 7267, Kampala; tel. (41) 2256940; fax (41) 2256994; e-mail ucdajc@ugandacoffee.org; internet www.ugandacoffee.org; f. 1991; enforces quality control and promotes coffee exports, maintains statistical data, advises Govt on local and world prices and trains processors and quality controllers; Man. Dir HENRY NGABIRANO.

Uganda Importers', Exporters' and Traders' Association: Kampala.

Uganda Manufacturers' Association (UMA): POB 6966, Kampala; tel. (41) 2221034; fax (41) 2220285; e-mail uma@starcom.co.ug; internet www.uganda.co.ug/uma.htm; promotes mfrs' interests; Chair. JAMES MULWANA.

Uganda Tea Authority: POB 4161, Kampala; tel. (41) 2231003; state-owned; controls and co-ordinates activities of the tea industry; Gen. Man. MIRIA MARGARITA MUGABI.

EMPLOYERS' ORGANIZATION

Federation of Uganda Employers: POB 3820, Kampala; tel. (41) 2220201; fax (41) 2221257; e-mail fue@infocom.co.ug; internet www.employers.co.ug; Chair. ALOYSIUS K. SSEMMANDA; Exec. Dir ROSEMARY N. SSENABULYA.

UTILITIES

Electricity

Uganda Electricity Board: POB 7059, Kampala; tel. (41) 2254071; fax (41) 2235119; e-mail okumu@infocom.co.ug; f. 1948; privatization pending; Chair. J. E. N. KAGULE-MAGAMBO; 36 brs.

Water

National Water & Sewerage Corpn: Plot 39, Jinja Rd, POB 7053, Kampala; tel. (41) 2256596; fax (41) 2346532; e-mail nwscmd@infocom.co.ug; internet www.nwsc.co.ug; f. 1972; privatization pending; Man. Dir WILLIAM TSIMWA MUHAIRWE; 12 brs.

CO-OPERATIVES

In 2000 there were 6,313 co-operative societies, grouped in 34 unions. There is at least one co-operative union in each administrative district.

Uganda Co-operative Alliance: Kampala; co-ordinating body for co-operative unions, of which the following are among the most important:

Bugisu Co-operative Union Ltd: Palisa Rd, Private Bag, Mbale; tel. (45) 2233027; f. 1954; processors and exporters of Bugisu arabica coffee; 226 mem. socs; Gen. Man. WOMUTU.

East Mengo Growers' Co-operative Union Ltd: POB 7092, Kampala; tel. (41) 2270383; fax (41) 2243502; f. 1968; processors and exporters of coffee and cotton; 280 mem. socs; Chair. FRANCIS MUKAMA; Man. JOSEPH SSEMOGERERE.

Kakumiro Growers' Co-operative Union: POB 511, Kakumiro; processing of coffee and cotton; Sec. and Man. TIBIHWA-RUKEERA.

Kimeeme Livestock Co-operative Society: Mwanga II Rd, POB 6670, Kampala; f. 1984; farming and marketing of livestock; Chair. SAMUSI LUKIMA.

Lango Co-operative Union: POB 59, Lira; f. 1956; ginning and exporting of conventional and organic cotton produce; Gen. Man. PATRICK ORYANG.

Masaka Co-operative Union Ltd: POB 284, Masaka; tel. (481) 220260; f. 1951; coffee, dairy farming, food processing, carpentry; 245 primary co-operative socs; Chair. J. M. KASOZI; Gen. Man. EDWARD C. SSERUUMA.

Nyakatonzi Growers Co-operative Union: Fort Portal Rd, POB 32, Kasese; tel. (483) 244370; fax (483) 244135; f. 1957; processors and exporters of coffee and cotton; Gen. Man. ADAM BWAMBALE.

South Bukedi Co-operative Union: 6 Busia Rd, POB 101, Tororo; tel. (45) 2244327; f. 1952; ginning and export of cotton lint; Gen. Man. MICHAEL O. OGUNDY.

UGANDA

South-west Nile Co-operative Union: POB 33, Pakwach, Nebbi; f. 1958; ginning and export of cotton; Gen. Man. PHILIP UPAKRWOTH.

Uganda Co-operative Savings and Credit Society: 62 Parliament Ave, POB 9452, Kampala; tel. (41) 2257410; f. 1973; Chair. PATRICK KAYONGO.

Uganda Co-operative Transport Union: 41 Bombo Rd, POB 5486, Kampala; tel. (41) 2567571; f. 1971; general transport, imports of motor vehicles, vehicle repair and maintenance; Gen. Man. STEPHEN TASHOBYA.

Wamala Growers' Co-operative Union Ltd: POB 99, Mityana; tel. (46) 2222036; f. 1968; coffee and cotton growers, real estate agents, cattle ranchers, printers, mfrs of edible oils, bricks, tiles and clay products; 250 mem. socs; Gen. Man. HERBERT KIZITO.

West Mengo Growers' Co-operative Union Ltd: POB 7039, Kampala; tel. (41) 2567511; f. 1948; cotton growing and buying, coffee buying and processing, maize milling; 250 mem. socs; Chair. H. E. KATABALWA MIIRO.

West Nile Tobacco Co-operative Union: Wandi, POB 71, Arua; f. 1965; growing, curing and marketing of tobacco; Gen. Man. ANDAMAH BABWA.

TRADE UNION

National Organization of Trade Unions (NOTU): POB 2150, Kampala; tel. (41) 2256295; f. 1973; Chair. E. KATURAMU; Sec.-Gen. MATHIAS MUKASA.

Transport

RAILWAYS

In 1992 there were 1,241 km of 1,000-mm-gauge track in operation. A programme to rehabilitate the railway network is under way.

Uganda Railways Corporation: Nasser Rd, POB 7150, Kampala; tel. (41) 2254961; fax (41) 2344405; f. 1977 following the dissolution of East African Railways; Man. Dir D. C. MURUNGI.

ROADS

Uganda's road network consists of approximately 10,000 km of national or trunk roads (of which some 2,200 km are bituminized, the rest being gravel), 25,000 km of district or feeder roads, 2,800 km of urban roads (comprising roads in Kampala City, the 13 municipal councils and the 50 town councils in the country) and 30,000 km of community roads. There are also private roads, some of which are open to the general travelling public. Road transport remains the dominant mode of transport in terms of scale of infrastructure and the volume of freight and passenger movement. The National (Trunk) Road Network carries 80% of Uganda's passenger and freight traffic and includes international routes linking Uganda to neighbouring countries and to the sea (via Kenya and Tanzania), and internal roads linking areas of high population and large administrative and commercial centres. It provides the only form of access to most rural communities. The Government is implementing a programme of continuous upgrading of key gravel roads to bitumen standard.

INLAND WATERWAYS

A rail wagon ferry service connecting Jinja with the Tanzanian port of Tanga, via Mwanza, was inaugurated in 1983, thus reducing Uganda's dependence on the Kenyan port of Mombasa. In 1986 the Uganda and Kenya Railways Corporations began the joint operation of Lake Victoria Marine Services, to ferry goods between the two countries via Lake Victoria.

CIVIL AVIATION

The international airport is at Entebbe, on Lake Victoria, some 40 km from Kampala. There are also several small airfields.

Civil Aviation Authority (CAA): Passenger Terminal Bldg, 2nd floor, Entebbe International Airport, POB 5536, Kampala; tel. (41) 220516; fax (41) 2321401; e-mail aviation@caa.co.ug; internet www.caa.co.ug; Man. Dir AMBROSE AKANDONDA.

Principal Airlines

Dairo Air Cargo Services: 24 Jinja Rd, POB 5480, Kampala; tel. (41) 2257731.

Eagle Air Ltd: Entebbe International Airport, POB 7392, Kampala; tel. (41) 2344292; fax (41) 2344501; e-mail eagle@swiftuganda.com; internet www.eagleuganda.com; f. 1994; domestic services, charter flights to neighbouring countries; Man. Dir Capt. ANTHONY RUBOMBORA.

East African Airlines: Airways House, 6 Colville St, POB 5740, Kampala; tel. (41) 2232990; fax (41) 2257279; f. 2002; services to Africa and the Middle East; CEO BENEDICT MUTYABA.

Inter Air: Nile Ave, POB 22658, Kampala; tel. (41) 2255508.

Tourism

Uganda's principal attractions for tourists are the forests, lakes, mountains and wildlife and an equable climate. A programme to revive the tourist industry by building or improving hotels and creating new national parks began in the late 1980s. There were 305,179 tourist arrivals in 2003 (compared with 12,786 in 1983). Revenue from the sector in 2003 was estimated at US $221m., including revenue from the transport of passengers

Uganda Tourist Board: Impala House, 13/15 Kimatti Ave, POB 7211, Kampala; tel. (41) 2342196; fax (41) 2342188; e-mail utb@visituganda.com; internet www.visituganda.com; Chair. PETER KAMYA; Gen. Man. IGNATIUS NAKISHERO.

UKRAINE

Introductory Survey

Location, Climate, Language, Religion, Flag, Capital

Ukraine is situated in east-central Europe. It is bordered by Poland, Slovakia, Hungary, Romania and Moldova to the west, by Belarus to the north and by Russia to the north-east and east. To the south lie the Black Sea and the Sea of Azov. The climate is temperate, especially in the south. The north and north-west share many of the continental climatic features of Poland or Belarus, but the Black Sea coast is noted for its mild winters. Droughts are not infrequent in southern areas. Average temperatures in Kyiv (Kiev) range from −6.1°C (21°F) in January to 20.4°C (69°F) in July, and average annual rainfall is 615 mm (24 ins). The official state language is Ukrainian, although Russian is widely spoken, except in the west. Most of the population are adherents of Orthodox Christianity (which has three separate jurisdictions in Ukraine) and there are many adherents to the Roman Catholic Church (mostly 'Greek' Catholics, followers of the Eastern rites) in western regions. There are also a number of Protestant churches and small communities of Jews and Muslims, the latter principally comprising Crimean Tatars. The national flag (proportions 2 by 3) has two equal horizontal stripes, of pale blue over yellow. The capital is Kyiv.

Recent History

The original East Slavic state, Kyivan (Kievan) Rus, founded in the late 10th century, was based in what is now Ukraine ('the Borderlands'), and is claimed as the precursor of Russia, Belarus and Ukraine. Following the fall of the Rus principalities, in the 13th and 14th centuries, during the Mongol invasions, the Ukrainians (sometimes known as Little Russians or Ruthenians) developed distinctively from the other Eastern Slavs, mainly under Polish and Lithuanian rulers. Ukrainians first entered the Russian Empire in 1654, when a Cossack state east of the Dnipro (Dniepr) river, led by Hetman Bohdan Khmelnytsky, sought Russian protection from Polish invasion. In 1667 Ukraine was divided: the regions east of the Dnipro became part of Russia, while Western Ukraine was annexed by Poland. Russia gained more Ukrainian lands as a result of subsequent partitions of Poland (1793 and 1795) and, in the south, from the Ottoman Empire; the western regions were acquired by Austria.

When the Russian Empire collapsed, in 1917, Ukrainian nationalists set up a central Rada (council or soviet) in Kyiv and demanded autonomy from the Provisional Government in Petrograd (St Petersburg). After the Bolshevik coup, in November, the Rada proclaimed a Ukrainian People's Republic. In December the Bolsheviks established a rival Government in Kharkiv, and by February 1918 much of Ukraine was occupied by Soviet forces. In March, however, the Bolsheviks were forced to cede Ukraine to Germany, under the terms of the Treaty of Brest-Litovsk. Ukraine was the battleground for much of the fighting in the Civil War over the next two years, but in December 1920 a Ukrainian Soviet Socialist Republic (SSR) was established.

The Treaty of Rīga, which formally ended the Soviet–Polish War in 1921, assigned territories in western Ukraine to Poland, Czechoslovakia and Romania. Eastern and central lands formed the Ukrainian SSR, one of the founding members of the Union of Soviet Socialist Republics (USSR), in December 1922. The collectivization of agriculture from 1929 had severe consequences for the republic; at least 5m. Ukrainians were estimated to have died in a famine in 1933, which resulted from collectivization. In the 1930s advocates of the wider Ukrainian cultural or political autonomy were arrested, and by the late 1930s almost the entire Ukrainian cultural and political élite had been imprisoned, killed or exiled. Ukraine also suffered greatly during the Second World War, which resulted in an estimated 6m. deaths in the republic.

Soviet victory in the war, and the annexing of territories from Czechoslovakia, Poland and Romania resulted in the uniting of the western and eastern areas of Ukraine, and the republic gained representation, nominally separate from that of the USSR, at the UN. In 1954 Crimea (formerly part of Russia), the Tatar inhabitants of which had been deported *en masse* to Soviet Central Asia in 1944, was transferred to Ukrainian control.

During the 1960s there was an increase in covert opposition to the regime, manifested in the production of independent publications, known as *samvydav* (*samizdat*—self-publishing). In 1973 Petro Shelest, First Secretary (leader) of the CPU was dismissed and replaced by Vladimir Shcherbitsky, a loyal ally of the Soviet leader, Leonid Brezhnev.

The accession of the reformist Mikhail Gorbachev to the Soviet leadership, in 1985, had little initial effect in Ukraine, largely owing to the conservatism of the Shcherbitsky administration. On 26 April 1986 a serious explosion occurred at the Chornobyl (Chernobyl) nuclear power station, in northern Ukraine. Only after unusually high levels of radiation were reported in other European countries did Soviet officials admit that large amounts of radioactivity had leaked into the atmosphere. Some 135,000 people were evacuated from a 50-km (30-mile) exclusion zone around Chornobyl (including large areas within neighbouring Belarus). Thirty-one people were killed in the initial explosion, but in 1996 it was reported that an estimated 2,500 deaths in Ukraine may have been caused by the accident, while a further 3.2m. people had been affected by the disaster, as a result of increased numbers of cancers and other related illnesses.

Official secrecy surrounding the Chornobyl accident led to greater public support for opposition movements in Ukraine. In 1988, moreover, the liberal nationalist Ukrainian People's Movement for Restructuring (Rukh) was founded by a group of prominent writers and intellectuals. Rukh's manifesto was published in 1989, and local branches were established throughout the republic. Furthermore, economic problems contributed to a growing militancy among mining communities in the Donbass region (around Donetsk, in eastern Ukraine), producing 11 strikes in the first three months of 1989. The revival of hitherto 'underground' religious groups from 1988 also assumed a national character in Ukraine. Notably, the Ukrainian (Byzantine rite) Catholic Church was legalized in December 1989, when Gorbachev met Pope John Paul II.

Shcherbitsky was dismissed in September 1989; he was replaced by Volodymyr Ivashko. In local and republican elections, held on 4 March 1990, candidates supported by the Democratic Bloc, a coalition led by Rukh (which had been registered in February), won 108 of the 450 seats in the Verkhovna Rada (Supreme Council—republican legislature). Independents supported by the Bloc won about 60 seats, although an estimated 280 supported the CPU leadership. The Bloc was particularly successful in western Ukraine, but performed poorly in the Russian-speaking regions of eastern and southern Ukraine.

In June 1990 Ivashko was elected Chairman of the Verkhovna Rada (the highest state post in the republic). In response to protests by deputies of the Democratic Bloc, he resigned later in the month as First Secretary of the CPU. On 16 July the Verkhovna Rada adopted a declaration of sovereignty. Ivashko was obliged to resign as Chairman of the Verkhovna Rada later in the month, following his appointment as Deputy General Secretary of the Communist Party of the Soviet Union. He was replaced by Leonid Kravchuk, hitherto Second Secretary of the CPU.

In October 1990 Vitaliy Masol resigned as Chairman of the Council of Ministers (Prime Minister); he was succeeded by Vitold Fokin, who was regarded as a moderate reformist. The Government participated in negotiations on a new union treaty and signed the protocol to a draft treaty in March 1991. The Government also agreed to conduct the all-Union referendum on the future of the USSR (see the chapter on the Russian Federation), but appended a further question to the referendum, asking if Ukraine's declaration of sovereignty should form the basis for participation in a renewed federation. Of the electorate, 84% participated in the referendum, 70% of whom approved Gorbachev's proposal to preserve the USSR as a 'renewed federation'. However, Ukraine's own question received greater support (80%), and an additional question in certain western regions, which asked voters if they supported a fully independent Ukraine, secured the support of 90% of those voting.

Following the attempted *coup d'état* by conservative communists in Moscow, the Russian and Soviet capital, on 19 August 1991, the Verkhovna Rada, on 24 August, adopted a declaration of independence, pending confirmation by a referendum on 1 December, when direct presidential elections were also scheduled. The CPU was banned at the end of August.

Despite his background in the CPU, Kravchuk's support for Ukrainian independence ensured his election as President of the Republic on 1 December 1991, with 62% of the votes cast. His closest rival, Vyacheslav Chornovil, a member of Rukh and a former dissident, received 23%. In the referendum, held concurrently with the presidential election, some 90% of the electorate voted in favour of independence (84% of the electorate participated), which thereby took effect. Outwith Crimea, where 54% voted in favour of Ukrainian independence, more than 80% of the electorate voted for independence in every administrative region of Ukraine. In early December an independent Ukrainian armed forces was established. In January 1992 a new interim currency coupon, which retained the Ukrainian name of the Soviet currency, the karbovanets, was introduced.

Criticism of the Government intensified as inflation increased sharply following the withdrawal of subsidies from foodstuffs in July 1992, and it resigned in September, having been conclusively defeated in a vote of 'no confidence'. In October Leonid Kuchma, hitherto director-general of a missile factory in Dnipropetrovsk, was appointed Prime Minister, and a new Government was formed. In November the Verkhovna Rada granted Kuchma special powers to rule by decree for a period of six months. He proposed an extensive programme of economic reform. These measures were strongly opposed by left-wing groups, including the Socialist Party of Ukraine (SPU), which had been formed from elements of the CPU and which, in association with other left-wing groups, began a campaign to rescind the ban on the CPU. In January 1993 Viktor Yushchenko, a leading exponent of market reform, was appointed Governor of the National Bank of Ukraine (NBU). In May, following the refusal of the legislature to renew the special powers granted to him in November 1992, Kuchma offered to resign, although this proposal was rejected by the legislature. As Ukraine began to experience 'hyperinflation', more than 2m. miners and factory workers, mainly in the Donbass region, joined a strike, in June 1993, to protest at the declining standard of living, demanding a referendum of confidence in the President and in the Verkhovna Rada.

Viktor Pynzenyk's resignation as Deputy Prime Minister, in August 1993, was regarded as marking the departure from the Government of the last serious advocate of economic reform. In September Kuchma again tendered his resignation, which was accepted by the legislature; Yufym Zvyahylsky, hitherto First Deputy Prime Minister and a former Mayor of Donetsk and coal-mine director (in which capacity he had been a prominent leader of the protests earlier in the year), was appointed as Prime Minister, in an acting capacity, although after several days President Kravchuk assumed direct control of the Government. The proposed referendum on confidence in the President and legislature was cancelled and early legislative elections were scheduled.

The elections to the new, 450-member Verkhovna Rada were held on 27 March 1994, with two subsequent rounds of voting in April, in constituencies where candidates had failed to secure 50% of the votes cast. The CPU (which had been permitted to contest the elections in advance of its subsequent re-legalization, pending the outcome of parliamentary discussion) won 86 seats, more than any other group, and, in alliance with the SPU and the Peasants' Party of Ukraine (PPU), formed the largest bloc in the Verkhovna Rada; 170 nominally independent candidates were elected. Rukh won 20 seats, and other moderate nationalist parties received 13. A notable political division between eastern Ukraine (where left-wing parties obtained greater support) and the west of the country (where moderate nationalist parties won the greatest share of the votes) was evident in the election results. Further rounds of voting, held in late 1994 to fill the 112 vacant seats, failed to elect candidates in more than 50 seats, which thus remained empty. In May Oleksandr Moroz, the leader of the SPU, was elected Chairman of the Verkhovna Rada, which in June elected Masol as Prime Minister.

A presidential election, held on 26 June 1994, proved inconclusive, as no candidate secured the minimum 50% of the votes necessary for election. Kravchuk received the greatest share of votes cast, with 37.7%, followed by Kuchma, with 31.3%. In a second round of voting, held on 10 July, Kuchma was elected President, securing 52.1% of the votes. A continuing polarity in voting patterns was recorded between the east, where voters largely supported Kuchma, and the west, where Kravchuk secured a majority of votes cast. In October Pynzenyk was appointed as First Deputy Prime Minister, responsible for Economic Reform. In March 1995 Masol resigned as Prime Minister; he was replaced, in an acting capacity, by Yevhen Marchuk, hitherto Deputy Prime Minister and Chairman of the State Security Service. In June the President and the Verkhovna Rada signed a Constitutional Agreement, announcing the cancellation of a referendum of confidence in the President and the legislature, previously announced by Kuchma, but granting the President additional powers, including the right to appoint leading officials without the approval of the Verkhovna Rada, and to issue decrees with the force of legislation. These provisions were to remain in effect until the adoption of a new Constitution. The President was to retain the prerogative to legislate economic reform by decree until the expiry of his term in 1999.

In July 1995 a major government reshuffle was initiated, in which several reformist ministers were demoted, and more conservative politicians were appointed, including Pavlo Lazarenko, as First Deputy Prime Minister. In November the Verkhovna Rada voted to suspend the privatization of petroleum and gas enterprises. In May 1996 Kuchma dismissed Marchuk as premier, appointing Lazarenko in his place. Following lengthy discussions, the new Constitution was adopted on 28 June. It confirmed the extensive new powers of appointment granted to the President in the interim Constitutional Agreement, including the right to nominate the Prime Minister.

In July 1996 the Cabinet of Ministers resigned; Lazarenko retained the premiership in the new Government. As unrest in the coal-mining industry continued, the Government commenced a structural reorganization of the sector, and in mid-July an agreement was reached with the trade unions to end an ongoing strike. The attempted assassination of Lazarenko, shortly after the signing of the agreement, was linked by some observers to his role in resolving the dispute. The introduction of a new currency, the hryvnya, in the same month, was regarded as an indication that the serious economic difficulties that had affected Ukraine for several years were beginning to relent. In December Kuchma issued a decrees stipulating that, henceforth, the Ministries of Internal Affairs, Foreign Affairs, Defence and Information were to be directly subordinated to the President. Kuchma dismissed Lazarenko in June. In July the legislature approved Valeriy Pustovoytenko, latterly Minister without Portfolio, as the new Prime Minister. In a subsequent government reorganization several ministries were transformed into state committees, which were to be directly answerable to the President. In September the legislature approved a new electoral law, which provided for 225 seats in the 450-member Verkhovna Rada to be allocated by proportional representation on the basis of party lists, subject to a minimum threshold of 4% of the total votes cast, and for the remaining 225 to be elected from single-seat constituencies. Meanwhile, it was announced that Lazarenko was to be prosecuted on charges of embezzlement.

A total of 30 parties and electoral blocs contested the legislative elections to the Verkhovna Rada held on 29 March 1998, in which 70.8% of the electorate participated. The CPU obtained 123 seats, becoming the largest party in the legislature. Eight parties secured representation on the basis of party lists and some 136 independent deputies were elected. In order to comply with a ruling by the Constitutional Court, preventing ministers from simultaneously sitting in the Verkhovna Rada, several ministers resigned from the Government following their election to the legislature. In June Kuchma declared that legislation on economic reform would be introduced by presidential decree. Oleksandr Tkachenko, the leader of the PPU, was elected as Chairman of the legislature in July. Lazarenko was arrested in early December as he attempted to enter Switzerland, and charged with money 'laundering'. In February 1999 the Verkhovna Rada endorsed a resolution allowing for Lazarenko to be charged, and shortly afterwards he was detained in the USA. During 1999–2000 a number of ministers were dismissed, resulting in a high turnover of government members.

In the first round of voting in the presidential election, held on 31 October 1999, Kuchma won the largest proportion of the votes cast for any candidate, with 36.5%; his opponent in the second round was Petro Symonenko of the CPU, who had obtained 22.2% of the first-round votes. The rate of participation was 70%. In early November Kuchma undertook a number of measures that were regarded as being intended to ensure his re-election in the second round. The governors of three oblasts (regions) in which the popular vote had supported Symonenko or the third-placed candidate, Moroz, were dismissed. Shortly afterwards Kuchma appointed Marchuk, another left-wing candidate in the first round of the election, as Chairman of the National Security and Defence Council. In the second ballot on 14 November Kuchma retained the presidency, receiving some 57.7% of the votes cast. Notably, the regional division in voting patterns evident in earlier presidential and parliamentary elections was not repeated. International observers stated that the election campaign and voting in the second round had been flawed, but that the overall result, none the less, adequately represented the will of the people. Kuchma was inaugurated on 30 November.

Having rejected a proposal to re-appoint Pustovoytenko as premier, the Verkhovna Rada endorsed the nomination of Yushchenko in mid-December 1999. His appointment was widely welcomed, in particular by centre-right factions and internationally, as he had obtained a reputation as a competent and trustworthy economic reformer during his tenure as Governor of the NBU; Yushchenko's appointment, however, precipitated discontent within left-wing factions in the legislature. Following the formation in January 2000 of a centrist parliamentary majority, led by Kravchuk (in which position he remained until September), left-wing opposition compelled the new majority to hold a separate session in an exhibition centre near the parliamentary building, where it voted unanimously to remove Tkachenko and his deputy from the chairmanship of the legislature. The opposition continued to meet in the Verkhovna Rada building, although the faction was insufficient to constitute a quorum. In February the majority faction elected Ivan Plyushch, an ally of Pustovoytenko, as legislative Chairman. After several days deputies of the centre-right grouping forced their way into the parliamentary building, and normal activity resumed.

Meanwhile, a presidential decree issued in January 2000, scheduling a referendum on proposed constitutional amendments for 16 April, was widely condemned; more than 3m. signatures had reportedly been collected in favour of this proposal, which appeared to be intended to strengthen the constitutional position of the President. Of the six questions initially intended to feature in the referendum, two were excluded from the plebiscite by the Constitutional Court. The four remaining questions—on the dissolution of the Verkhovna Rada should deputies fail to approve the state budget within three months of its submission; the reduction of the number of deputies from 450 to 300; the establishment of a bicameral legislature; and the placing of limitations on the immunity enjoyed by deputies—were approved by a majority of the 81% of the electorate that participated in the referendum. There was, however, no indication that the proposals were to be implemented, and it thus appeared that the referendum had served primarily to increase the President's authority over the legislature.

In June 2000 Lazarenko was convicted *in absentia* of money 'laundering' by a court in Switzerland, and given an 18-month suspended prison sentence. In July the Deputy Prime Minister, responsible for Energy Issues, Yuliya Tymoshenko, a prominent instigator of reforms in the energy sector and the leader of the Fatherland party, was charged with corruption, as a result of investigations into her former ally, Lazarenko, in the USA. In late September Kuchma dismissed the Minister of Foreign Affairs, Boris Tarasyuk, and appointed Anatoliy Zlenko in his place.

In early November 2000 a decapitated corpse, believed to be that of an investigative journalist, Heorhiy Gongadze, missing since mid-September, was discovered by police, near Kyiv. Gongadze, who had edited an internet news site, *Ukrainska Pravda* (Ukrainian Truth), which had investigated incidents of high-level political corruption, had been a vocal critic of Kuchma; he had also made allegations of harassment by state officials. In late November Moroz released tape recordings in which Kuchma, the head of the presidential administration, Volodymyr Lytvyn, and the Minister of Internal Affairs, Yuriy Kravchenko, were alleged to discuss possible means of killing Gongadze. Over subsequent months several hours of audio recordings were released, precipitating a serious political crisis. Controversy surrounded the authenticity of the recordings, which a former presidential security adviser, Maj. Mykola Melnychenko, claimed to have made over a period of several months, prior to fleeing Ukraine. (Melnychenko was subsequently granted asylum in the USA.) In late December 2000 demonstrations urging the resignation of Kuchma began in a number of cities, and continued throughout early 2001.

In January 2001 Kuchma dismissed Tymoshenko, as an investigation into her alleged involvement in tax evasion and the smuggling of Russian gas proceeded. In February further audio recordings were made public. After initially denying the authenticity of the recordings, Kuchma admitted that the recordings were of his voice, but stated that they had been edited in an attempt to incriminate him. Demonstrations in Kyiv to demand Kuchma's resignation continued for several weeks, of which Tymoshenko, leading a loose coalition of opposition movements, the National Salvation Forum (NSF), was one of the most prominent leaders. In February, in an apparent concession to the demands of the protesters, Kuchma dismissed the head of the national security service, Gen. Leonid Derkach, and the head of the presidential bodyguard. In mid-February Tymoshenko was arrested on charges of tax evasion. In late February the Prosecutor-General's office formally identified the body discovered in November as that of Gongadze, and opened a murder inquiry. In May Gongadze's death was attributed to a criminal attack, with no political motives, and it was announced that the investigation into his death was to be closed. Meanwhile, in early March a demonstration by up to 18,000 anti-Kuchma protesters in Kyiv degenerated into violent clashes and was dispersed by police with tear-gas; several prominent members of the extreme nationalist Ukrainian National Assembly-Ukrainian National Self-Defence Organization (UNA-UNSO), including its leader, Andriy Shkil, were arrested and subsequently charged with provoking unrest. In late March, in an apparent conciliatory gesture towards the opposition, Kuchma dismissed Kravchenko as Minister of Internal Affairs, replacing him with Yuriy Smirnov. At the end of the month Tymoshenko was released from prison, and all charges against her were dismissed; in April the Supreme Court suspended Tymoshenko's re-arrest, although the charges against her remained a subject of investigation (several of the charges against her were abandoned in September).

In late April 2001 the Verkhovna Rada approved a motion of 'no confidence' in the Prime Minister and his Cabinet of Ministers. Yushchenko's position had been regarded as particularly vulnerable, as a result of his increasing unpopularity with both members of the Verkhovna Rada and with so-called 'oligarchs' (politically influential businessmen); this was despite the economic growth achieved during his premiership—in 2000 economic growth had been recorded for the first time since independence. In May Anatoliy Kinakh, hitherto First Deputy Prime Minister, responsible for Economic Policy, was appointed as Prime Minister; this appointment was widely regarded as an indication that the measures towards economic reform associated with Yushchenko were unlikely to be continued.

In the latter half of 2001 a number of electoral blocs were formed in preparation for the forthcoming legislative elections. In late September Tymoshenko issued an appeal for other opposition groupings to join the NSF, but rejected the suggestion that the NSF unite with the Our Ukraine bloc of centrist and nationalist parties headed by Yushchenko; her supporters subsequently become known as the Yuliya Tymoshenko Bloc (YuTB). Meanwhile, supporters of Kuchma formed the For a United Ukraine (FUU) bloc, headed by Lytvyn, which incorporated five parties, including several generally regarded as sympathetic to the interests of the oligarchs: among the members of the FUU were: Kinakh's Party of Industrialists and Entrepreneurs of Ukraine; the Party of the Regions (PR) and Working Ukraine.

In mid-October 2001 the Minister of Defence, Col-Gen. Oleksandr Kuzmuk, resigned, following the accidental shooting down, during military exercises over the Black Sea, of a passenger aircraft, as a result of which all 78 people on board were killed. Kuzmuk was replaced by Gen. Volodymyr Shkidchenko. (A similar incident, in which a missile hit an apartment block near Kyiv in 2000, had resulted in 20 deaths.)

In February 2002 Ukrainian prosecutors charged Lazarenko, *in absentia*, with having ordered the murders of two parliamentary deputies in 1996 and 1998; in March 2002 the Prosecutor-General was reported to have rejected a motion approved by the Verkhovna Rada for the initiation of a legal investigation into Kuchma's alleged role in the case. In March the Government's director of arms exports, Valeriy Malev, was killed in an automobile collision. It subsequently emerged that several days before Malev's death Kuchma had been informed of the discovery of audio recordings made by Melnychenko, in which Kuchma and

Malev were allegedly heard to discuss the sale of air-defence equipment to Iraq, in violation of UN sanctions.

In the legislative elections, held on 31 March 2002, Our Ukraine, which by this time comprised 10 moderate and nationalist parties, including two factions of Rukh, obtained both the largest share of the votes (23.6%) and the largest number of seats to be won by any party, receiving 112; FUU received the second largest number of seats (101), but only 11.8% of the votes cast. The CPU obtained 20.0% of the votes cast, but received only 66 seats, compared with the 123 it had obtained in 1998. The Social-Democratic Party of Ukraine—United (SDPU—U) received 24 seats and 6.3% of the votes cast, the SPU 23 seats and 6.9% of the votes and the YuTB 22 seats, and 7.3% of the votes. A total of 93 independent candidates were elected. Opposition spokesmen alleged that incidents of electoral fraud had been perpetrated, and a report by observers from the Organization for Security and Co-operation in Europe (OSCE, see p. 327) indicated 'important flaws' in the organization of the elections. In the subsequent formation of parliamentary factions, supporters of Kuchma were able to establish a larger grouping than those of Yushchenko. Neither grouping was sufficiently large to constitute a parliamentary majority in its own right, and attempts to form a coherent majority in the legislature continued throughout 2002. After the elections Viktor Medvedchuk, the Chairman of the SDPU—U, was appointed to head the presidential administration, following the election of the incumbent, Lytvyn, as Chairman of the Verkhovna Rada.

In August 2002 Kuchma announced that a Constitutional Commission was to be formed to investigate the possibility of introducing constitutional reforms, with the intention of surmounting the executive–parliamentary tensions that had characterized much of Ukrainian politics since independence; in particular, Kuchma expressed support for the introduction of a bicameral parliament and for a wider usage of proportional representation in the election of deputies. In mid-October a senior judge in Kyiv opened a criminal investigation into Kuchma, who was charged with violating 11 articles of the criminal code, including charges of corruption, abuse of power and the sale of military radar equipment to Iraq. In late October the Supreme Court rejected an appeal by the Office of the Prosecutor-General declaring the case to be illegal. However, in early November, an ally of Kuchma, Vasyl Malyarenko, was elected as Chairman of the Supreme Court, replacing Vitaliy Boyko, and in late December the Court ruled that the investigation into Kuchma had, indeed, been opened illegally.

In mid-November 2002 Kuchma dismissed Kinakh as Prime Minister; he was replaced, on 16 November, by Viktor Yanukovych, latterly Governor of Donetsk Oblast; a new Government, in which several principal positions remained unchanged, was appointed later in the month. In early December a stable pro-presidential majority was finally established in the Verkhovna Rada. Later in the month the legislature voted, at the second attempt, to dismiss Volodymyr Stelmakh as Governor of the NBU, and to approve Tihipko as his replacement.

In February 2003 Yushchenko issued a public statement, addressed to Kuchma, Yanukovych and Lytvyn, urging an end to what was described as 'political terror', including alleged physical assaults against a number of political activists and the unsolved murders of several journalists. Later in the month anti-Kuchma demonstrations were held in several major cities; attendance at a rally in Kyiv, at which Yushchenko, Tymoshenko and Symonenko issued addresses, was estimated at up to 15,000, according to police figures, or up to 150,000, according to the organizers of the rally. Meanwhile, in mid-February 2003 the Verkhovna Rada rejected draft legislation on constitutional reform, presented by deputies of the SDPU—U and SDU, providing for the election of all 450 deputies by proportional representation on the basis of party lists, within the existing 225 constituencies; the draft, which was supported by deputies of Our Ukraine, the CPU and the YuTB, in addition to allies of the Government, was again rejected by the Verkhovna Rada in April. However, in March Kuchma submitted a draft on constitutional reform to the legislature: the draft envisaged that the Verkhovna Rada be replaced with a 300-seat State Assembly elected under a party-list system, and an 81-member House of the Regions; moreover, the parliament was to be granted the power to dismiss the Prime Minister, and the President the power to dissolve parliament. In late April 2003 the two highest-ranking members of the Government were elected to senior positions in the PR: Yanukovych was elected as party Chairman and the First Deputy Prime Minister and Minister of Finance, Mykola Azarov, became the Chairman of the party's Political Council. In mid-May an appeals court in Kyiv ordered the closure of all cases that had been opened by the Office of the Prosecutor-General against Tymoshenko. However, in mid-June the Supreme Court annulled the ruling, and investigations into the cases recommenced.

In June 2003 Lazarenko was released on bail in the USA (in mid-May a team of US lawyers had travelled to Ukraine to conduct investigations, and Lazarenko's trial, on charges of money laundering, commenced in mid-March 2004). Also in June 2003 Shkidchenko resigned as Minister of Defence, following criticism of the efficiency of the military by Kuchma (78 people had been killed in July 2002 when a military plane crashed into a crowd of spectators at an airshow; Kuchma had rejected Shkidchenko's offer to resign on that occasion); he was replaced by Marchuk. In mid-June Kuchma submitted revised draft legislation on constitutional reform to the Verkhovna Rada; notably, proposals for the introduction of a bicameral legislature had been withdrawn. However, following the failure of the Verkhovna Rada to support either the constitutional amendments proposed by Kuchma or those presented by a group of opposition deputies, the President stated that he was prepared to co-operate with members of the legislative opposition. In early September a new draft, prepared by members of the pro-presidential and CPU legislative factions (widely known as the Medvedchuk-Symonenko draft), was presented to the Verkhovna Rada; the draft envisaged the extension of the mandate of the existing legislature by one year, until 2007, when its replacement would be elected by a system of proportional representation. The draft also provided for the direct election, in 2004, of an interim president with reduced powers, until 2006, when a president would be elected by the Verkhovna Rada.

Meanwhile, in August 2003 Kuchma dismissed Col-Gen. Yuriy Smirnov from his position as Minister of Internal Affairs; he was replaced by Mykola Bilokon. In September Zlenko retired from the post of Minister of Foreign Affairs. He was replaced by Kostyantyn Hryshchenko, hitherto Ukraine's ambassador to the USA. In October Kuchma dismissed the Prosecutor-General, Svyatoslav Pyskun, nominating Hennadiy Vasilyev, hitherto the First Deputy Chairman of the Verkhovna Rada and a former Chief Prosecutor in Donetsk Oblast, as his replacement, and the legislature approved the appointment in mid-November. There were renewed concerns about the use of force to inhibit political debate, after Our Ukraine was prevented from holding a conference in Donetsk at the end of October. Reports stated that as many as 2,000 people had prevented members and supporters of the grouping from entering the building where the meeting was to have been held, and that propaganda material linking Yushchenko with Nazi symbols and ideology had been disseminated around the city. Our Ukraine, the YuTB and the SPU subsequently issued a statement accusing the Kuchma administration of dictatorial methods. In mid-November members of Our Ukraine were refused permission to hold a meeting in Sumy, and the electricity supply to the offices of a newspaper in the town was reportedly disconnected for the duration of a visit by Yushchenko. (In late October Kuchma had ordered the Ministry of Internal Affairs and the State Security Service to investigate allegations made by Yushchenko that he was the target of an assassination plot.)

In an apparent attempt to encourage the legislature to approve constitutional reforms, in November 2003 Kuchma requested that the Constitutional Court rule on the circumstances under which the President could dissolve the Verkhovna Rada. In December Andriy Klyuyev, a Deputy Chairman of the PR and former Vice-Governor of Donetsk Oblast, was appointed as a Deputy Prime Minister. On 24 December the Verkhovna Rada gave provisional approval to the Medvedchuk-Symonenko draft on constitutional reform (however, the 274 votes cast in favour of the proposals, although sufficient to enable the bill to receive a second reading in the legislature, fell short of the 300 votes required for the approval of a constitutional amendment). The leadership of the Our Ukraine, YuTB and SPU factions did not support the proposals. On 30 December the Constitutional Court ruled that Kuchma would be eligible to seek re-election upon the expiry of his term of office in October 2004, as the constitutional provision that prevented the President from holding more than two consecutive mandates had been introduced during Kuchma's first term and did not apply retroactively. However, Kuchma denied that he intended to seek re-election. In early January 2004 Valeriy Khoroshkovskyi resigned as Minister of the Economy and Progress Towards European Integration; he was replaced by Mykola Derkach. On 3 February 2004 the Verkhovna Rada voted to amend the Medvedchuk-Symonenko draft on constitutional reform, removing those proposals pertaining to the election of the president by the legislature, which had attracted international criticism. This amendment, which was approved by 304 votes, was supported by the SPU, although Our Ukraine and the YuTB refused to participate in the voting.

In March 2004 the Verkhovna Rada approved legislation, supported by the SPU and the CPU, which introduced a proportional-representation system for the election of all 450 parliamentary deputies, within the existing 225 constituencies; the percentage of the votes required for a party to obtain election was to be reduced from 4% to 3%. The vote was boycotted by the Our Ukraine and YuTB factions; it was signed into law by Kuchma in early April. Also in March a bill to modify the presidential-election procedure, in accordance with which candidates would be required to collect the signatures of 500,000 eligible voters, rather than the 1m. required under legislation adopted in 1999, was approved. On 7 April the Verkhovna Rada failed to approve the competing proposals for reform embodied in the amended Medvedchuk-Symonenko draft, after 289 votes were cast in its favour, fewer than the 300 required. In accordance with the Constitution, the draft could not be reintroduced to the legislature for the period of one year.

In April 2004 Serhiy Tulub was appointed as Minister of Fuel and Energy (a position from which he had resigned in 2000). In June Lazarenko was convicted of money laundering, fraud and extortion by a federal court in Los Angeles, CA, USA. In September Kuchma accepted the resignation of Marchuk as Minister of Defence. His replacement was Kuzmuk, who had resigned from the position in 2001.

Politics in 2004 were dominated by preparations for the presidential election. In April Yanukovych was named as the candidate for the pro-presidential bloc, while Yushchenko's candidacy was officially registered in August; a total of 24 candidates were eventually registered to contest the poll. On 20 August two bombs exploded in a Kyiv market, and a further explosion occurred on 3 September; the authorities suggested that the explosions were connected to members of Our Ukraine, while the opposition claimed that the secret services had orchestrated the attacks in an attempt to discredit the opposition. In September Yushchenko was admitted to a clinic in Vienna, Austria, and subsequently emerged with his face severely scarred by lesions; his supporters claimed this was the result of poisoning during a meal with senior members of the secret services, and Yushchenko himself accused the incumbent administration of seeking to murder him. Shortly before the first round of the election Yanukovych, in his capacity as Prime Minister, announced that the rate of state pensions was to be increased. In his capacity as presidential candidate, meanwhile, Yanukovych pledged to grant Russian the status of a joint official language and work towards permitting dual Ukrainian-Russian citizenship. Yushchenko, conversely, made it clear that he would, if elected, seek the closer integration of Ukraine into the European Union (EU, see p. 228) and the North Atlantic Treaty Organization (NATO, see p. 314). Meanwhile, concerns (which had first emerged following Yanukovych's appointment as Prime Minister, in 2002) were expressed that Yanukovych had reportedly been imprisoned on two occasions in 1967–72, apparently on charges of theft and assault, although both charges had been subsequently annulled.

The first round of voting, held on 31 October 2004, failed to supply any one candidate with a majority of votes cast. The Central Electoral Committee (CEC) published the final results of the poll, awarding Yushchenko 39.9% of the votes cast, and Yanukovych 39.3%, on 10 November. Yushchenko and Yanukovych were, therefore, to proceed to a second round on 21 November. The CEC initially indicated that Yanukovych led by nearly 3% in the second round, with more than 99% of the votes counted, contradicting several exit polls endorsed by the opposition. Large-scale protests at the allegedly fraudulent conduct of the count, and in support of both Yushchenko and Tymoshenko, commenced in central Kyiv on 22 November, focused around the central Maidan Nezalezhnosti (Independence Square). The youth group Pora! (Enough!) played a principal role in the organization of the protests. The demonstrators established a tent settlement along Kyiv's main thoroughfare, and adopted the colour orange as a unifying symbol, leading what became known as the 'orange revolution'. Protests were almost entirely peaceful, with several hundred thousand people reportedly present at the height of the demonstrations. Meanwhile, a number of local administrations, including the city councils of Kyiv and Lviv, declared that they did not accept the results announced by the CEC and that they regarded Yushchenko as the legitimate Head of State, while demonstrations against the conduct of the election were reported across the country. The OSCE condemned the conduct of both rounds of voting. On 23 November Yushchenko took a symbolic oath of office in front of the Verkhovna Rada. On 24 November the CEC officially announced the preliminary results of the second round: Yanukovych was declared the winner, with 49.5% of the votes cast, while Yushchenko was deemed to have received 46.6%. Opposition protests persisted, however, with demands for a general strike the following day, and speeches and demonstrations continued in freezing conditions in central Kyiv, led by Yushchenko and Tymoshenko; protesters blockaded numerous government buildings. Smaller protests in favour of Yanukovych were also held, principally in eastern Ukraine, where the administrations of several oblasts (notably Donetsk and Luhansk) expressed their intention to hold referendums on autonomy or secession should Yushchenko be declared president.

Following an appeal to the Supreme Court regarding the conduct of the second round of voting, on 25 November 2004 the Court announced that it would suspend the publication of the election results until the opposition's complaints could be considered. A significant shift in the allegiances of the mass media was also observed, with staff at state-owned broadcasting outlets, which had hitherto been reported to demonstrate a clear pro-Yanukovych bias, announcing that they would begin 'full and impartial' coverage of the events surrounding the disputed vote. On 27 November the Verkhovna Rada voted to declare the 21 November ballot invalid and to express a lack of confidence in the CEC, while a subsequent motion of 'no confidence' in Yanukovych's Government was passed on 1 December (these resolutions, however, carried no legal force, as they required the signature of President Kuchma to be binding). On 29 November it was reported that Tihipko, hitherto the manager of Yanukovych's presidential campaign, had resigned from the position of Governor of the NBU, and considered his role within Yanukovych's campaign to have concluded (he was replaced as head of the bank by his predecessor, Stelmakh). Meanwhile, Polish President Aleksander Kwaśniewski, Lithuanian President Valdas Adamkus and the EU High Representative for Common Foreign and Security Policy, Javier Solana Madariaga, arrived in Kyiv to attempt mediation between the two parties in the crisis (Yushchenko had rejected Kuchma's offer of mediation). Yushchenko repeatedly stated that the only resolution that he considered acceptable was a repeat run of the second round of voting, a course of action described by Kuchma as lacking domestic or international precedent. On 3 December the Supreme Court ruled that the results of the second round of voting as announced by the CEC on 24 November were invalid, and ordered that a repeat election be conducted within three weeks.

Following extensive negotiations, on 8 December 2004 the Verkhovna Rada voted to support a series of amendments to the Constitution and electoral law, with some 420 deputies voting in favour of the proposals. The constitutional amendments included several of the changes included in the Medvedchuk-Symonenko draft of amendments, among them the transfer of several powers of appointment from the President to the Prime Minister and the legislature. The amendments also foresaw the expulsion from the legislature of any deputy who left the party or bloc on whose list he or she had been elected. Immediately after the vote, Kuchma signed the amendments into law, although they were not fully to take effect until after the legislative elections due to be held in March 2006. Kuchma also announced the dismissal of the Prosecutor-General, Hennadiy Vasilyev (who was replaced by his predecessor, Pyskun, who had recently won a court case declaring his dismissal in 2003 to be illegal), and approved a substantial reconstitution of the CEC. Yanukovych was granted leave from his position as Prime Minister in order to campaign for the repeated second round of voting; he was replaced in an acting capacity by Azarov. The repeat ballot was held on 26 December. Preliminary results suggested a victory for Yushchenko; however, Yanukovych lodged complaints against the conduct of the election with the CEC and, subsequently, the Supreme Court, thus causing the official publication of the results to be delayed until all legal means of protest had been exhausted. Meanwhile, on 27 December, Minister of Transport and Communications Heorhiy Kirpa was found dead, apparently as a result of multiple bullet wounds.

Earlier in the month, Yuriy Lyakh, Chairman of the Ukrainian Credit Bank, had been found dead in his office, from neck wounds apparently inflicted with a paper knife. Both cases were officially described as suicide, despite widespread speculation that both deaths had been political assassinations. On 31 December Yanukovych resigned as Prime Minister and on 6 January 2005 Kuchma signed a decree dismissing the Cabinet of Ministers. On that date Yanukovych's complaints were rejected by the Supreme Court, and four days later Yushchenko was officially declared to have won the ballot of 26 December 2004, receiving 52.0% of the votes cast, compared with the 44.2% awarded to Yanukovych. A clear regional divide was evident in the results: in 16 of the 27 primary administrative divisions of Ukraine, the most popular candidate in that region had obtained more than 75% of the votes cast; Yushchenko obtained such support in 12 administrative divisions, mainly in western and central Ukraine, including Kyiv City, while Yanukovych received similarly majorities in four districts: the eastern oblasts of Donetsk and Luhansk, the Autonomous Republic of Crimea, and in Sevastopol City. A final appeal, lodged by Yanukovych with the Supreme Court, was rejected on 20 January 2005, and Yushchenko was inaugurated as President on 23 January.

On 4 February 2005 the Verkhovna Rada voted to approve Yushchenko's nomination of Tymoshenko as Prime Minister. The composition of an entirely new Cabinet of Ministers was subsequently announced. Notably, Kinakh (who had announced his support for Yushchenko after the first round of voting) was appointed as First Deputy Prime Minister. Three further Deputy Prime Minister positions were created. Yuriy Latsenko was appointed Minister of Internal Affairs, and Anatoliy Hritsenko became Minister of Defence. Yushchenko also appointed many new regional governors, and named Petro Poroshenko, a prominent 'oligarch', as Chairman of the National Security and Defence Council. Yanukovych, meanwhile, expressed his intention of leading a 'harsh opposition' to Yushchenko's administration. The new Government declared a priority to be combating corruption. Several privatizations conducted during Kuchma's presidency were regarded as constituting a principal form of corrupt practice, and the extent to which they should be investigated became a significant source of tension between the various parties and elements represented within the new administration (see Economic Affairs). Similar tensions existed over other policy matters between the three main political groupings represented within the Government: nationalists and populists, associated chiefly with Tymoshenko; statist socialists linked with the SPU; and those elements regarded as more sympathetic to business interests, associated more closely with Yushchenko. The latter formed a new political party, People's Union Our Ukraine (also known as Our Ukraine, particularly after the Reforms and Order party, led by Pynzenyk, which had adopted the name 'Our Ukraine' in 2004, was ordered to revert to its previous name in July 2005); Yushchenko was named as the Honorary Chairman of the party, Roman Bezsmertnyi (Yushchenko's electoral campaign manager and a Deputy Prime Minister) became the Chairman of the party's Council, and Yuriy Yekhanurov (a former First Deputy Prime Minister and Minister of the Economy, and the recently appointed Governor of Dnipropetrovsk Oblast) the Chairman of the party's Executive Committee. Yushchenko also endorsed a reopening of the investigation into the death of Gongadze. On 4 March former Minister of the Interior Kravchenko, who was alleged to be one of the officials who had discussed the killing of Gongadze on the audio recordings released in 2000, was found dead, reportedly as the result of suicide, shortly before he had been due to be questioned at the office of the Prosecutor-General. It was subsequently announced that four people were to be charged in connection with Gongadze's death. The trial of three people commenced in January 2006; the fourth man, suspected of being Gongadze's killer, was believed to have fled Ukraine. However, it soon became apparent that some of the new administration's policy decisions had been instrumental in reducing the hitherto strong rate of economic growth. Increases in social spending (introduced by both the new Government, and by the Yanukovych administration prior to the first round of voting in late 2004), introduced as part of an anti-poverty campaign, led to heightened inflation. Moreover, Tymoshenko's decision, in April, to maintain at existing levels the retail prices of petroleum (for which Ukraine was heavily dependent on Russia) resulted in several Russian companies limiting their supplies to Ukraine, purportedly in order to carry out repairs to pipelines, causing a severe shortfall relative to demand. However, in mid-May Tymoshenko alleged that fuel deliveries to Ukraine had been suspended as part of an attempt to exert political pressure on the country. Later in May Yushchenko issued a decree criticizing the Government's action in restraining prices as incompatible with the principles of market economics, and ordered that the limits imposed be rescinded as a matter of urgency. Meanwhile, inter-factional disagreements in the Verkhovna Rada meant that several items of legislation, which had been intended to expedite Ukraine's application for membership of the World Trade Organization (WTO, see p. 370) were not approved by the legislature before the beginning of its summer recess. In mid-July, as part of anti-corruption measures, Yushchenko announced that the national traffic police (which was renowned for demanding bribes from motorists) was to be disbanded with immediate effect.

The growing tensions between the constituent groupings that had supported the 'orange revolution' resulted in a series of resignations in early September 2005, amid accusations of corruption. On 1 September an adviser to Tymoshenko, Mykola Brodsky, alleged that elements close to Yushchenko were engaged in corrupt practices (during the previous month there had been widespread press coverage of the apparently extravagant lifestyle of Yushchenko's son, as well as concern that Tymoshenko's official declaration of wealth and income did not appear to be complete); one day later the Chief of the Presidential Staff, Oleksandr Zinchenko, announced his resignation, criticizing the corrupt actions of Poroshenko, in particular. On 8 September Mykola Tomenko announced his resignation as Deputy Prime Minister. Later the same day Yushchenko dismissed Tymoshenko and her Government, and also announced that Poroshenko had resigned from the National Security and Defence Council. In a statement generally understood to pertain specifically to Tymoshenko, Yushchenko stated that the Government had been dismissed because it had failed to operate cohesively, having been undermined by factionalism and machinations. Tymoshenko subsequently gave a lengthy televised interview in which she expressed regret at her dismissal, criticized several close associates of Yushchenko, and stated that, as a result of her dismissal, the YuTB would effectively go into opposition and present its own list of candidates, separate from those of Our Ukraine, at the 2006 elections to the Verkhovna Rada.

The split between the YuTB and Our Ukraine was demonstrated on 20 September 2005, when the Verkhovna Rada narrowly failed to approve Yushchenko's nomination of Yekhanurov as Prime Minister. Consequently, in order to obtain support for Yekhanurov's nomination from the sizable PR faction within the legislature, Yushchenko and Yanukovych agreed a 10-point memorandum; among the controversial measures provided for by the document were an amnesty for all those involved in electoral fraud at the annulled second round of presidential voting in 2004, and an extension of the immunity from prosecution enjoyed by legislative deputies to members of regional and local councils. Having thereby obtained support for what would effectively be an interim administration, on 22 September Yekhanurov was confirmed as Prime Minister, having received 289 votes in favour of his nomination in the Verkhovna Rada, compared with the 223 votes obtained prior to the signature of the memorandum. Several ministers holding principal positions in the former administration retained their portfolios. New appointments included that of Arseniy Yatsenyuk as Minister of the Economy, replacing Serhiy Terokhin, and that of Serhiy Holovatyi as Minister of Justice, replacing Roman Zvarych (whose position in the Government had become untenable, as a result of revelations that he did not possess the legal qualifications indicated by his official biography). Stanislav Stashevskyi was appointed as First Deputy Prime Minister, replacing Kinakh, who became the Chairman of the National Security and Defence Council. The dismissal of Pyskun as Prosecutor-General, on 14 October, was a further significant personnel change; his replacement, in an acting capacity, was Serhiy Vynokurov, who subsequently announced that all criminal charges against Poroshenko had been abandoned. On 31 October the Verkhovna Rada approved the appointment of Oleksandr Medvedko as Prosecutor-General.

The issue of Ukraine's dependence on other countries, and particularly Russia, for energy supplies assumed renewed significance in late 2005, as a result of demands issued by the Russian state-controlled gas monopoly, Gazprom, that Ukraine pay market prices (US $230 per 1,000 cu m) for the supply of natural gas, rather than the heavily subsidized rate (of $50 per 1,000 cu m) that it had paid hitherto. Following the failure of the

Ukrainian authorities and Gazprom to reach agreement, on 1 January 2006 Gazprom suspended supplies to Ukraine, a measure that, combined with sub-zero temperatures, caused considerable hardship in Ukraine, as well as resulting in the loss of supplies to other central and western European countries which accessed gas from pipelines traversing Ukraine. On 4 January supplies of natural gas to Ukraine were restored, after Ukraine agreed to pay $95 per 1,000 cu m for a mixture of Russian and Turkmenistani natural gas, which was to be supplied to Ukraine by a Swiss-registered company, Ukrtransgaz. This agreement was to be subject to renegotiation after six months.

The new arrangements for the purchase of natural gas were a source of considerable controversy within Ukraine and were instrumental in bringing about a vote of 'no confidence' in the Government on 10 January 2006, which was approved by 250 votes to 50 against. (Tymoshenko stated that she would withdraw from the agreement in the event of her again becoming Prime Minister.) Although such a vote should, theoretically, have resulted in the Government's removal from office, the constitutional position at this time was obscure (the transfer of many of the powers of appointment from the president to the prime minister and the chairman of the Verkhovna Rada agreed in late 2004 had taken effect on 1 January 2006), and in the absence of a functioning Constitutional Court President Yushchenko requested that the Yekhanurov administration remain in office until after the forthcoming legislative elections.

The legislative elections proceeded, as scheduled, on 26 March 2006, contested by 45 parties and blocs. The changes that had taken place in Ukrainian politics since the previous elections in 2002, and the introduction of a system of full proportional representation and the exclusion of nominally independent deputies, meant that the new Verkhovna Rada had a very different composition to the one that it replaced. The results of voting did, however, confirm the persistence of the division in support for parties between, on one hand, eastern and southern, and on the other hand, central and western regions. Yanukovych's PR became the largest party in the new legislature, with 32.1% of the total votes cast, receiving 186 seats. The YuTB was placed second, with 22.3% and 129 seats, while the Our Ukraine bloc (comprising several smaller, generally liberal or nationalist parties, in addition to Our Ukraine) obtained 14.0% and 81 seats, considerably less, in both percentage and seat terms, than the Our Ukraine electoral alliance of 2002 had received. Only two other groupings—the SPU, with 5.7% (33 seats) and the CPU, with 3.7% (21 seats)—surpassed the 3% quota required to obtain representation. (Three other blocs that had been associated with the 'orange revolution', including one led by Lytvyn, obtained less than 3% of the votes cast, as did several groups based around various centrist parties that had held substantial parliamentary representation during the Kuchma presidency.) Although there were some suspicions of malpractice in the concurrent elections to the Crimean Supreme Council (see below), and some other minor flaws, the elections to the Verkhovna Rada were described by international monitors as free and fair. The failure of any party or bloc to obtain a majority of legislative seats necessitated the formation of a coalition government, although by mid-May the members of the coalition, or indeed, whether any sustainable coalition could be created, remained unclear.

Despite the political differences between the Ukrainian-speaking western regions and the Russian-speaking eastern regions that were evident during the 1990s and 2000s, only in the Crimean peninsula did any significant movement for re-unification with Russia emerge. (Speculation that several eastern and southern regions would hold referendums for autonomy in late 2004 appeared to be largely transient, and associated with the disputed presidential election, rather than representing any long-term political aspirations.) The situation was further complicated by the status of the Crimean Tatars, who had been forcibly deported to Soviet Central Asia in 1944, and who began to return to Crimea from late 1989. In a referendum held in January 1991, residents of Crimea (which then had the status of an ordinary oblast) voted to restore it to the status of a nominally autonomous republic. The decision, although it had no legal basis, was ratified by the Verkhovna Rada. In June Crimean Tatars established 'parallel' institutions to those of the state, without any constitutional or legal status. The Kurultay was a popular assembly that was intended to convene once a year, the Mejlis was a national assembly that was to meet throughout the year, and a number of local assemblies were also established. In February 1992 the Crimean Supreme Council, the regional legislature, voted to transform the region into the Republic of Crimea, and in May declared Crimea an independent state, adopting a new Constitution. However, following threats from the Verkhovna Rada to impose an economic blockade and direct rule on Crimea, the independence declaration was rescinded. In June the Ukrainian Government confirmed Crimea's status as an autonomous republic within Ukraine, which was otherwise to remain a unitary state. (The city of Sevastopol was not, however, to form part of the autonomous republic.) Meanwhile, relations between the local leadership and Crimean Tatars, some 250,000 of whom had returned to Crimea by late 1992, deteriorated steadily, primarily as a result of disputes over the ownership of land and property, and the right to gain Ukrainian citizenship. In October a Tatar encampment was dispersed on the orders of the Crimean Government, and in response some 6,000 Tatars stormed the Crimean parliament building.

With the election of Yurii Meshkov as President of Crimea in January 1994, it appeared likely that the region would renew efforts towards sovereignty, as well as establish closer links with Russia. In response, the Verkhovna Rada approved constitutional amendments, according to which the Ukrainian President could nullify any measures taken by the Crimean authorities that he deemed to be illegal. In March a referendum was held in Crimea, simultaneously with the Ukrainian legislative elections; 70% of those voting in the referendum supported broader autonomous powers for Crimea. In May, following a vote by the Crimean parliament to restore the suspended Constitution of May 1992, the Ukrainian Government ordered the Crimean legislature to rescind its decision; the crisis appeared to have been defused by June 1994, when delegations from the Ukrainian and Crimean parliaments met in Simferopol, the Crimean capital, where it was agreed that Crimea would continue to be subject to Ukrainian law. In September the Crimean legislature voted to restrict the Crimean President's executive authority, in response to which Meshkov temporarily suspended parliament. Meanwhile, the Verkhovna Rada approved a constitutional amendment, permitting it to nullify any legislation adopted by the Crimean parliament that contravened the Ukrainian Constitution. In March 1995 the Ukrainian legislature voted to abolish both the Crimean Constitution of May 1992 and the Crimean presidency, and in April 1995 Kuchma imposed direct rule on Crimea.

In October 1995 the Crimean legislature approved a new Constitution. Before its final adoption by the Verkhovna Rada in December 1996, the Constitution underwent several amendments; notably, Ukrainian was recognized as the state language, although Russian was to be the language of all official correspondence of the autonomous republic. In February 1997, contrary to national law, which stipulates that the appointment of the Crimean Prime Minister is the prerogative of the Ukrainian President, the Crimean parliament arrogated to itself the power to appoint the regional Government. In April it appointed Anatolii Franchuk as the new Crimean premier, in place of Arkadii Demydenko. Kuchma suspended this resolution, declaring it to be a violation of the Ukrainian Constitution but, following the approval of a second motion of 'no confidence' in Demydenko, in June Kuchma consented to his dismissal. A new Council of Ministers headed by Franchuk was subsequently approved by the Crimean legislature. In October 1997 Kuchma exercised his veto over items of legislation approved by the Crimean Supreme Council—the adoption of Russian as the peninsula's official language of business communication, and the realignment of Crimea's time zone with that of Moscow—that were regarded as an assertion of the primacy of Crimea's links with Russia. Further conflict arose between the national Government and the Crimean legislature in February 1998, following the approval of legislation by the Verkhovna Rada, whereby all Ukrainian citizens were to be eligible to contest the seats in the Crimean legislature—hitherto, only citizens resident in Crimea had been eligible. In addition, the new legislation stated that elections to the Crimean parliament were to be held simultaneously with the elections to the Verkhovna Rada in March and not in September, as previously decided by the Crimean Supreme Council.

Elections to the Crimean legislature in March 1998 brought the issue of the status of the Crimean Tatars to the fore, when demonstrations were staged by Tatars appealing for the right to vote. The OSCE estimated that about one-half of the 165,000 Tatars resident in Crimea did not have Ukrainian citizenship and were, therefore, ineligible to vote. Leonid Grach, the leader of the CPU in Crimea, was elected Chairman of the new Crimean

Supreme Council. In May a new Council of Ministers was appointed, with Sergei Kunitsyn as Chairman. In January 1999 a new Crimean Constitution came into effect, which granted the Crimean authorities the right to manage its own property and to pass a budget. Although citizenship had recently been granted to a number of Crimean Tatars, representatives of the group held a demonstration in May in Simferopol, demanding constitutional changes to ensure better representation and rights for Crimean Tatars and for the Crimean Tatar language to be recognized as a state language, and subsequent protests culminated in a 20,000-strong demonstration in Simferopol in May 2000. In mid-July 2001 the Supreme Council dismissed Kunitsyn from the premiership for the third time. Although Kuchma had refused to recognize the previous dismissals, in late July Kuchma accepted Kunitsyn's removal from office, and expressed support for the new premier elected by the Crimean Supreme Council, Valerii Gorbatov of the Working Ukraine party.

As campaigning for the concurrent elections to the Verkhovna Rada and the Crimean Supreme Council, to be held on 31 March 2002, commenced, controversy was provoked at the end of February by the invalidation of Grach's candidacy for a seat in the Supreme Council, on technical grounds. Despite his disqualification, Grach's name appeared on ballot papers, and he was re-elected to the Supreme Council in defiance of the decision of the Crimean Court of Appeal. The elections to the Crimean Supreme Council demonstrated a sizeable shift in support away from the communists, towards centrists, whose grouping, known as the Kunitsyn Team, after its leader, won 39 of the 100 seats in the Council; a pro-communist electoral alliance known as the Grach bloc received 28 seats; three other parties obtained representation, and 29 independent candidates were elected. In late April the Ukrainian Supreme Court approved Grach's appeal, thereby serving to legitimize his status as a deputy of the Crimean legislature. However, Grach was unsuccessful in his campaign for re-election as Chairman of the Crimean legislature, being defeated by a former deputy Chairman, Boris Deich. The new parliament also voted for the dismissal of Gorbatov and the re-appointment of Kunitsyn as Prime Minister, and reformists loyal to Kunitsyn were successful in establishing a majority in the legislature. None the less, in the concurrent elections to the Verkhovna Rada, the CPU remained the most popular party on the peninsula. Notably, for the first time, Crimean Tatar deputies were elected to the Verkhovna Rada, within the Our Ukraine bloc. Russian nationalists only successfully attracted votes in the Crimean city of Sevastopol.

In early 2004 concern was expressed by ethnic Russians resident in Crimea that a measure, approved by the Crimean Government in 2000, which ordered foreign citizens resident in Crimea to pay higher rates for utilities and accommodation than those paid by Ukrainian citizens, were being applied to Russian citizens resident in the Republic. Meanwhile, an increase in ethnic tensions between Crimean Tatars and the Slavic inhabitants of the peninsula was reported in early 2004. Although it appeared that disputes over land were the principal source of tensions, some reports suggested that violence had been provoked by groups of Russian right-wing extremists and militant Cossack groups resident in neighbouring regions of Russia. In the first few months of the year, in advance of the 60th anniversary of the deportation of the Tatars from the peninsula, several clashes and violent incidents occurred, and in early April a petition, signed by over 35,000 Crimean Tatars, which alleged that the police force in Crimea were ignoring incidents of inter-ethnic violence against Tatars, was presented to President Kuchma. The continuing tension in Crimean society was reflected in the allegiances displayed in the presidential election of late 2004, when the peninsula's Russophone majority overwhelmingly supported Yanukovych, while the Crimean Tatar minority were reported to have voted principally for the victorious candidate, Yushchenko, in the hope that he would act to address their grievances regarding land distribution and greater ethnic autonomy. In late April 2005 Kunitsyn resigned as Prime Minister of Crimea, following his appointment as an adviser to President Yushchenko; the Crimean Supreme Council voted to approve Anatolii Matviyenko as his replacement. Matviyenko's appointment caused some controversy on the peninsula, both because he had never held any position of responsibility in Crimea and because of his affiliations with both Ukrainian nationalists and the YuTB, which did not enjoy significant support in the Republic. Matviyenko was subject to frequent criticism as Prime Minister, particularly for failing to resolve concerns about widespread corruption or the issue of land allocation to returning Crimean Tatars, and his premiership proved short-lived. Following the dismissal of Tymoshenko as Prime Minister of Ukraine, in early September, the Crimean Supreme Council voted to dismiss the republican Government; Matviyenko duly resigned on 20 September. On 23 September the Crimean Supreme Council approved the appointment of Anatolii Burdyugov, the leader of the Crimean branch of Yushchenko's People's Union Our Ukraine party, as Prime Minister, and a new Government was formed at the end of the month. In late February 2006 the Crimean legislature voted to hold a referendum on the proposed introduction of Russian as a state language within the peninsula; however, President Yushchenko stated that the referendum would be unconstitutional, and this ruling was subsequently confirmed by the CEC.

Elections to the Crimean Supreme Council, held concurrently with local elections and with those to the Verkhovna Rada on 26 March 2006, were marred by allegations of electoral fraud; moreover, one candidate was killed on polling day and, in early April, the body of a local councillor was found in unexplained circumstances, after his apparent abduction (however, police stated that the latter killing did not appear to have a political motive). At the end of March the President's Representative in Crimea, Volodomyr Kulich, announced that a commission comprising senior officials of several ministries and law-enforcement bodies was to be established to investigate the apparent electoral violations. Meanwhile, protesters outside the Crimean Parliament demanded that elections in districts where violations were found be declared null and void. (No official results of the Crimean elections had been released by this time.) The national Prosecutor-General and Matviyenko (in his role as deputy head of the presidential secretariat, to which he had been appointed in November 2005) also became involved in the investigation of the alleged irregularities. The results of the elections were finally announced on 19 April. The For Yanukovych bloc (principally comprising the Party of the Regions) obtained the largest proportion of the votes cast, with 32.6%; it was awarded 44 of the 100 seats in the Supreme Council. The second-placed party was the pro-Russian Union party, with 7.6% of the votes and 10 seats. The Kunitsyn bloc obtained 10 seats, the CPU nine, the People's Movement of Ukraine-Rukh and the YuTB each obtained eight seats, the Nataliya Vitrenko People's Opposition bloc obtained seven seats, and the 'Ne Tak' Opposition bloc (which comprised several centrist parties associated with allies of former President Kuchma, most notably the SDPU—U) obtained four.

Following the collapse of the USSR in 1991, the Ukrainian leadership was notably reluctant to sign any union agreement with the other former Soviet republics that might compromise its declaration of independence. It was this reluctance to enter into a renewed political union that led to the establishment of the CIS by President Kravchuk, and the leaders of Russia and Belarus, on 8 December. Although relations with Russia, as Ukraine's major trading partner and a country with close ethnic, historic, cultural and familial links with Ukraine, remained generally good following independence, tensions existed between those who sought to renew closer relations with Russia and countries of 'Eurasia', and those who sought to emphasize Ukraine's independence and 'European' status. Ukraine agreed to a unified command for the strategic (principally nuclear-armed) forces of the former USSR, but began to establish its own conventional armed forces. In January 1994 a trilateral agreement on the removal of nuclear weapons from Ukraine was signed by Ukraine, Russia and the USA, and in November the Verkhovna Rada voted to ratify the Treaty on the Non-Proliferation of Nuclear Weapons (see p. 98). In December Kuchma formally signed the Treaty, and the Strategic Arms' Reduction Treaty (START) I entered into force. The transfer to Russia of Ukraine's nuclear weapons was completed by June 1996.

Throughout the 1990s Ukraine consistently refused to participate in organizations that it perceived as being dominated by Russia, although it became an associate member of the CIS Air Defence Agreement in 1995. In 1997 Ukraine initiated the establishment of the GUAM (Georgia-Ukraine-Azerbaijan-Moldova) grouping. In 2001 a permanent office of the grouping was opened in Yalta, Crimea. However, as the Kuchma administration became increasingly isolated internationally in the early 2000s, particularly in response to allegations that it had illegally sold military equipment to the Iraqi regime of Saddam Hussain, Ukraine's relationship with Russia appeared to strengthen. Notably, in January 2003 Kuchma was elected as Chairman of the CIS, becoming the first non-Russian to hold that post. (Kuchma was replaced by Russian President Vladimir Putin in 2004.) Later in 2003, proposals to form a 'single economic zone' with Belarus, Kazakhstan and Russia became increasingly popular, and were approved by the Verkhovna Rada in September, on the condition that participation did not contravene the Ukrainian Constitution. The future of the 'single economic zone' was, however, uncertain following the election of Yushchenko to the Ukrainian presidency in late 2004. In August 2005 President Yushchenko and President Mikheil Saakashvili of Georgia, meeting in Borjomi, Georgia, signed the Borjomi Declaration, on the creation of a new Community of Democratic Choice, an alliance that intended to remove divisions and resolve conflicts in the Baltic, Black Sea and Caspian regions. The new, nine-country grouping was officially launched in December, at a meeting in Kyiv; some Russian observers expressed concern that the grouping might serve to weaken its influence.

The principal controversy between Ukraine and Russia concerned ownership of the former Soviet Black Sea Fleet, based in Sevastopol, on the Crimean peninsula. Although both countries agreed in July 1992 to exercise joint control over the fleet for a transitional period of three years, in April 1995 the Russian parliament imposed a moratorium on plans to divide the fleet. Nevertheless, in June Russian President Boris Yeltsin and Kuchma agreed to the equal division of the fleet, with separate Ukrainian and Russian bases. The main Russian base was to be at Sevastopol, although the exact legal status of the city was left unresolved. Yeltsin and Kuchma signed an agreement on 31 May 1997, in accordance with which the Russian fleet was to lease three bays in Sevastopol for 20 years, while the Ukrainian fleet was to use the remainder. Upon expiry, the treaty could be renewed for five years, but would then be subject to renegotiation. A bilateral Treaty of Friendship, Co-operation and Partnership was also signed, in which, significantly, Russia for the first time recognized the sovereignty of Ukraine. Russia finally ratified the treaty in February 1999, and in June of that year and in March 2000 further agreements were signed between Russia and Ukraine pertaining to the fleet and the operations and services of jointly used facilities. In January 2003 a treaty delineating the land boundary between Russia and Ukraine (which remained largely unmarked and unregulated) was signed by Kuchma and President Vladimir Putin of Russia, although discussions on the status of the Sea of Azov, which lies between the two countries, remained unresolved. Work on the construction of a dam in the Sea precipitated considerable controversy, and raised concerns that the territorial integrity of Ukraine was being violated. In December Presidents Kuchma and Putin signed an agreement on the use of the Sea of Azov, the entirety of which was defined as comprising the internal waters of both countries. Agreement was also reached on the maritime state boundary of Russia and Ukraine in the region.

The Ukrainian presidential election of 2004 caused considerable upheaval in diplomatic relations with Russia. During the course of the campaign, the Russian Government was accused by the Ukrainian opposition and external commentators of interference in favour of Yanukovych; notably, President Putin visited Ukraine before each round of voting to appear publicly with Yanukovych and Kuchma, and telephoned Yanukovych to congratulate him on his apparent victory after the second round before the official (and subsequently annulled) results had been announced. Some US $300m. were reported to have been donated to the Yanukovych campaign by the Russian authorities, and Putin described the demonstrations that resulted in the election being re-run as constitutionally illegitimate. Symbolically, and in accordance with promises made during his election campaign, President Yushchenko visited Moscow one day after his inauguration in January 2005, and emphasized the importance of maintaining co-operative relations with Russia. However, further diplomatic tension was caused by the appointment of Tymoshenko as Prime Minister in February, in part as a result of a warrant existing in Russia for her arrest on charges of the attempted bribery of Russian officials during her time as head of a Ukrainian natural gas trading company in the 1990s.

Ukraine sought to counterbalance its close relations with Russia by a policy of engagement with Western nations and organizations, as part of what was termed a 'multi-vector' foreign policy. In 1994 Ukraine joined NATO's 'Partnership for Peace' (see p. 316) programme; a 'Charter on a Distinctive Relationship' was signed with the Organization in 1997, envisaging enhanced co-operation with the Alliance. In April 1999, in protest at NATO airstrikes against Yugoslavia (now Serbia and Montenegro), the Verkhovna Rada voted to withdraw from the 'Partnership for Peace' programme. When the conflict ended Ukraine rejoined the programme, and in July sent troops to form part of the peace-keeping force in the Serbian province of Kosovo (Kosovo and Metohija).

Following pressure from the USA, in 1998 Ukraine cancelled an agreement to supply turbines to Bushehr nuclear power station in Iran. The USA, in return, pledged to allocate additional investment to the development of Ukraine's energy sector. In March 2000 the USA, one of the major aid donors to Ukraine in the mid-1990s, became concerned about allegations that Ukraine had misused IMF funds, and demanded a full audit of the central bank before any more assistance would be forthcoming. During a visit to Ukraine in June, US President Bill Clinton pledged aid towards the decommissioning of the Chornobyl reactor, which was closed in December. Relations with the USA deteriorated somewhat during 2002, following allegations that Ukraine, with the complicity of President Kuchma, had transferred military equipment to Iraq. In October a joint British-US inquiry failed to determine the veracity of the allegations, which the Ukrainian Government continued to deny. However, in March 2003, following the commencement of US-led military action in Iraq, Ukraine agreed to a request by the USA to dispatch an anti-nuclear, anti-biological and anti-chemical warfare unit, comprising 448 troops, to Kuwait. The Verkhovna Rada approved this measure in mid-March, although it also approved a motion condemning the US-led intervention. In June the Verkhovna Rada approved proposals to dispatch up to 1,800 troops to serve in the Polish-administered stabilization zone in southern Iraq; some 1,650 Ukrainian troops entered service in the zone from September. The participation of Ukrainian forces in Iraq appeared to lead to an improvement in relations with the USA, and in October Prime Minister Viktor Yanukovych visited Washington, DC, and met Vice-President Richard B. Cheney and Secretary of State Colin Powell. Yushchenko's inauguration as President was widely expected to lead to an improvement in US-Ukrainian relations, and the 'orange revolution' that had brought Yushchenko to power was generally regarded favourably in the USA. In early April 2005 Yushchenko visited the USA, meeting President George W. Bush and addressing the US Senate. Relations with the USA did not appear to be affected negatively by Yushchenko's approval, later that month, of a decree authorizing the withdrawal of Ukrainian peace-keeping troops from Iraq by the end of the year, as had been approved by the Verkhovna Rada in the previous year.

Ukraine signed a trade agreement with the EU in June 1995, and was formally admitted to the Council of Europe (see p. 211) in November. The Ukrainian leadership had long expressed an intention to pursue full membership of the EU; however, the failure to abolish capital punishment (which is prohibited by the conditions of membership of the organization) before March 2000 was a source of tension, as was the slow pace of political and economic reform and, in particular, concerns that President Kuchma may have been implicated in the murder of investigative journalist Heorhiy Gongadze in 2000. President Yushchenko, who was elected in late 2004, emphasized in his earliest diplomatic pronouncements that he regarded the integration of Ukraine into both the EU and NATO as fundamental goals of his presidency.

In recent years Ukraine has provided troops to UN peace-keeping missions in several countries.

Government

Executive power is vested in the President and the Prime Minister, and legislative power is the prerogative of the 450-member Verkhovna Rada. The President is elected by direct, popular vote for a five-year term. Prior to constitutional amendments agreed in late 2004, the President appointed the Prime Minister and the members of the Cabinet of Ministers. However, with effect from 2006 several presidential powers of appointment were to be transferred to the Prime Minister, who was to be elected by the Verkhovna Rada. The President was to retain the right to appoint certain principal ministers, and, in certain circumstances, to dissolve the legislature. Ukraine is a unitary state, divided for administrative purposes into 24 oblasts (regions), one Autonomous Republic (Crimea), and two metropolitan areas (Kyiv and Sevastopol). The Constitution guarantees local self-government to regions, cities, settlements and villages. Regional governors are appointed by the President.

Defence

In December 1991 the Verkhovna Rada adopted legislation establishing independent Ukrainian armed forces. In August 2005 there 187,600 active personnel in the Ukrainian armed forces (excluding the Black Sea Fleet and some 95,000 active civilian personnel), including 125,000 ground forces, 49,100 in the air force, and an estimated 13,500 in the navy. There were also paramilitary forces, comprising 45,000 in the Border Guard and an estimated 39,900 serving under the Ministry of Internal Affairs. In addition, 14,000 were serving in the Coast Guard and some 9,500 were serving in civil defence troops answerable to the Ministry for Emergency Situations and Protection of the Population from the Consequences of the Chornobyl Catastrophe. There were, additionally, some 1m. reserves. Military service is compulsory for males over 18 years of age, for a period of 18 months in the ground forces and air forces, and two years in the navy. Legislation approved in March 2005 provided for the reduction by six months of the terms of conscription to the ground forces and the navy. The 2005 budget allocated an estimated 5,530m. hryvnyas to defence. In 1998 proposals to end conscription by 2015 were announced as part of a programme of military reforms.

Economic Affairs

In 2004, according to the World Bank, Ukraine's gross national income (GNI), measured at average 2002–04 prices, was US $60,297m., equivalent to $1,260 per head (or $6,250 per head on an international purchasing-power parity basis). During 1995–2004 gross domestic product (GDP) per head increased, in real terms, at an average rate of 3.5% per year. Over the same period, the population decreased by an annual average of 0.8%. Ukraine's GDP increased, in real terms, by an average of 2.7% annually during 1995–2004. Real GDP increased by 9.4% in 2003 and by 12.1% in 2004.

Agriculture (including forestry and fishing) contributed 13.7% of GDP in 2004, according to estimates by the World Bank, and it provided 18.9% of employment in 2003. Ukraine has large areas of extremely fertile land, forming part of the 'black earth' belt, and the country is self-sufficient in almost all aspects of agricultural production. The principal crops are grain, potatoes, sugar beet and other vegetables. A programme to transfer state collective farms to private ownership was initiated in 1991. In January 1997 only 14% of land was managed by private farms, although in that year private farms contributed some 46% of total agricultural output. During 1995–2004, according to the World Bank, agricultural GDP increased by an annual average of 0.3%, in real terms. Following a severe winter in 2002, there was a significantly reduced harvest in 2003: wheat production decreased by 82.5%, according to the FAO, and overall agricultural GDP declined by 9.9%. In 2004 the GDP of the sector increased by 18.0%.

Industry (including mining, manufacturing, construction and power) contributed an estimated 40.1% of GDP in 2004, according to the World Bank, and it provided 29.9% of employment in 2003. Heavy industry dominates the sector, particularly metalworking, mechanical engineering, chemicals and machinery products. The mining and metallurgical sector accounted for 27.2% of industrial output in 1997. Defence-related industrial activity, traditionally important, was being converted to non-military production, and by 1997 some 80% of defence-industry factories had been transformed. According to the World Bank, industrial GDP increased by an average of 3.9% annually, in real terms, in 1995–2004. Real industrial GDP increased by 15.0% in both 2003 and 2004.

In 2003 3.7% of the work-force were engaged in mining and quarrying. Ukraine has large deposits of coal (mainly in the huge Donbass coal basin) and high-grade iron ore, and there are also significant reserves of manganese, titanium, graphite, natural gas and petroleum. Production of coal declined by some 53% in 1989–95, and in 1996 the Government implemented a major reorganization of the coal-mining industry, including the closure of several loss-making mines.

The manufacturing sector contributed 25.2% of GDP in 2004, according to the World Bank, and the sector provided 17.6% of employment in 2003. During 1990–2003 manufacturing GDP decreased by an annual average of 4.7%, in real terms. However, the GDP of the sector increased by 7.0% in 2002 and by 16.0% in 2003.

Ukraine is highly dependent on imports of energy products, of which Russia and Turkmenistan are the principal suppliers. Imports of mineral fuels comprised 29.5% of the value of total imports in 2005. Ukraine is also vitally important as an energy transit country, situated as it is between the mineral resource-rich countries of the former USSR and the developed economies of Europe. A pipeline from a new oil terminal at Odesa, on the Black Sea coast, to Brody, near the border with Poland, which was originally intended to carry petroleum from the Caspian Sea to central and western Europe, was completed in 2001; however, following Ukraine's failure to secure petroleum suppliers from the Caspian region, the pipeline entered operation in reverse direction, permitting Russian companies to pump their petroleum to the Black Sea for export. Ukraine has five nuclear power stations. However, following the accident at the Chornobyl station in 1986, the viability of the country's nuclear power programme was called into question. Nevertheless, two new nuclear reactors, the first to be completed since the Chornobyl accident, began energy production in 2004. In 2002 nuclear power accounted for 44.9% of Ukraine's electricity production; coal accounted for 17.2%, and natural gas for 31.6%.

The services sector contributed an estimated 46.3% of GDP in 2004, according to the World Bank, and employed 51.2% of the labour force in 2003. During 1995–2004 the GDP of the sector increased by an average of 1.6% annually, in real terms. The real GDP of the sector increased by 11.1% in 2003 and 9.3% in 2004.

In 2004 Ukraine recorded a trade surplus of US $3,741m., while there was a surplus of $6,809m. on the current account of the balance of payments. In 2005 the principal markets for exports were Russia (accounting for 21.9%), Turkey (5.9%) and Italy (5.5%). The principal source of imports in that year was Russia (providing 35.5% of all imports), followed by Germany (9.4%), Turkmenistan (7.4%) and the People's Republic of China (5.0%). The principal imports in 2005 were mineral products (which accounted for 32.0% of the total), machinery, mechanical and electrical equipment, vehicles and transportation equipment, chemical products, base metals, and plastics and rubbers. The principal exports in that year were base metals (some 41.0% of the total, comprising principally iron and steel), mineral products, chemical products, and machinery, mechanical and electrical equipment.

In 2003, according to preliminary figures, a budgetary deficit of 162m. hryvnyas was recorded, equivalent to 0.1% of GDP. Ukraine's total external debt was US $16,309m. at the end of 2003, of which $8,893m. was long-term public debt. In that year the cost of debt-servicing was equivalent to 12.5% of the value of exports of goods and services. In 1995–2004 the average annual inflation rate was 18.8%. Consumer prices increased by 12.3% in 2004 and by 10.3% in 2005. Some 9.1% of the labour force were unemployed in 2003.

Ukraine became a member of the IMF and the World Bank in 1992. It also joined the European Bank for Reconstruction and Development (EBRD, see p. 224) as a 'Country of Operations'. In June 1994 Ukraine signed an agreement of partnership and co-operation with the European Union (EU, see p. 228), which was ratified in 1998. An interim trade accord was signed with the EU in June 1995. Ukraine is a member of the Organization of the Black Sea Economic Co-operation (see p. 339), and is seeking membership of the World Trade Organization (see p. 370).

Ukraine experienced severe economic problems following the dissolution of the USSR, and by 2001 recorded GDP was equivalent to just 44% of the level recorded in 1991. The economy showed significant signs of improvement from 2000, when GDP registered positive growth for the first time since the USSR's collapse. As part of a programme of proposed fiscal reforms, in May 2003 the Verkhovna Rada approved a uniform rate of income tax of 13% for individuals, to take effect from 2004, modelled on a system successfully introduced in Russia, which had been credited with reducing the rate of tax evasion. In February 2004 Ukraine was removed from the list of 'non-compliant' countries and territories of the Financial Action Task Force on Money Laundering (FATF), in response to the introduction in 2003 of measures to combat flaws in the financial regulatory system, which had led to the imposition of economic sanctions by the USA and Canada. The disruption to the national economy caused by the disputed presidential election of late 2004 caused widespread concern, as did the apparent economic mismanagement that followed the 'orange revolution'. Moreover, tensions over economic policy rapidly became evident in the Government formed in February 2005; growth in the first nine months of 2005 was reported to have slowed to some 3%, compared with the 12.1% recorded for 2004. In March 2005 President Viktor Yushchenko approved an amended state budget for 2005, which, notably, envisaged an increase of 50% in

UKRAINE

welfare spending. The investigation of the circumstances of the numerous disputed privatizations of the post-Soviet period were also designated a priority for the government. One of the most controversial privatizations to be carried out under the regime of President Leonid Kuchma, that of Kryvorizhstal, Ukraine's largest steel plant, was among the first to be annulled. A 90% stake in the company, which had been sold for US $800m. in June 2004, to a consortium headed by Viktor Pinchuk (son-in-law of President Kuchma) and Renat Akhmetov (believed to be Ukraine's richest person, and a close ally of defeated presidential candidate Viktor Yanukovych), was returned to state control. The conditions of the initial sale had been widely condemned as having unfairly favoured this consortium over foreign bidders, and suggestions that the company had been sold for significantly less than its actual worth appeared to be confirmed when the stake was sold to Mittal Steel (of the Netherlands) for $4,800m. in October 2005. It was hoped that proposed measures intended to combat corruption would increase the economy's attractiveness to foreign investment; however by the end of 2005 foreign investment in the country had not increased markedly, and concerns remained that the country had the potential to experience prolonged periods of political instability, particularly following the transfer of numerous presidential powers to the legislature and prime minister in early 2006.

Education

After Ukrainian was decreed the state language, in 1990, policies were adopted to ensure that all pupils were granted the opportunity of tuition in Ukrainian. In 2001 there was also tuition in Russian, as well as in Romanian, Hungarian, Moldovan, Crimean Tatar and Polish. In the early 1990s there were significant changes to the curriculum, with a greater emphasis on Ukrainian history and literature. Some religious and private educational institutions were established in the early 1990s. Education is officially compulsory between seven and 15 years of age. Primary education begins at seven years of age and lasts for four years. Secondary education, beginning at 11, lasts for a maximum of seven years, comprising a first cycle of five years and a second of two years. In 1998/99 72% of children in the relevant age-group were enrolled in primary education. In 1993 enrolment in secondary education was 91%. In 2003/04 there were 2,269,800 students enrolled in higher education. Combined enrolment at the primary, secondary and tertiary levels was some 78% in 1998. In 2003 government expenditure on education totalled 11,901m. hryvnyas (12.1% of the total budgetary expenditure), according to preliminary figures.

Public Holidays

2006: 1 January (New Year), 7 January (Orthodox Christmas), 8 March (International Women's Day), 24 April (Orthodox Easter Monday), 1–2 May (Labour Day), 9 May (Victory Day), 28 June (Constitution Day), 24 August (Independence Day).
2007: 1 January (New Year), 7 January (Orthodox Christmas), 8 March (International Women's Day), 9 April (Orthodox Easter Monday), 1–2 May (Labour Day), 9 May (Victory Day), 28 June (Constitution Day), 24 August (Independence Day).

Weights and Measures

The metric system is in force.

Statistical Survey

Principal source (unless otherwise stated): State Committee for Statistics, 01023 Kyiv, vul. Sh. Rustaveli 3; tel. (44) 226-20-21; fax (44) 235-37-39; e-mail info@ukrstat.gov.ua; internet www.ukrstat.gov.ua.

Area and Population

AREA, POPULATION AND DENSITY

Area (sq km)	603,700*
Population (census results)	
12 January 1989	51,706,742
5 December 2001	
Males	22,441,344
Females	26,015,758
Total	48,457,102
Population (official estimates)	
2004	47,622,436†
2005	47,280,800‡
2006	46,886,356§
Density (per sq km) at 1 February 2006	77.7

* 233,090 sq miles.
† Estimate at 1 January.
‡ Rounded figure, estimate at 1 January.
§ Estimate at 1 February.

POPULATION BY ETHNIC GROUP
(permanent inhabitants, census of 5 December 2001)

	'000	%
Ukrainian	37,541.7	78.13
Russian	8,334.1	17.34
Belarusian	275.8	0.57
Moldovan	258.6	0.54
Crimean Tatar	248.2	0.52
Bulgarian	204.6	0.43
Hungarian	156.6	0.33
Romanian	151.0	0.31
Polish	144.1	0.30
Jewish	103.6	0.22
Armenian	99.9	0.21
Others	534.1	1.11
Total	**48,052.3**	**100.00**

ADMINISTRATIVE DIVISIONS

	Area ('000 sq km)	Population (at 1 February 2006)*	Density (per sq km)
Regions			
Cherkasy	20.9	1,339,788	64.1
Chernihiv	31.9	1,166,599	36.6
Chernivtsi	8.1	907,620	112.1
Dnipropetrovsk	31.9	3,443,666	108.0
Donetsk	26.5	4,617,016	174.2
Ivano-Frankivsk	13.9	1,388,334	99.9
Kharkiv	31.4	2,826,169	90.0
Kherson	28.5	1,125,251	39.5
Khmelnytsky	20.6	1,372,134	66.6
Kirovohrad	24.6	1,065,647	43.3
Kyiv	28.1	1,762,109	62.7
Luhansk	26.7	2,405,854	90.1
Lviv	21.8	2,575,177	118.1
Mykolayiv	24.6	1,218,618	49.5
Odesa	33.3	2,400,012	72.1
Poltava	28.8	1,553,231	53.9
Rivne	20.1	1,155,983	57.5
Sumy	23.8	1,224,676	51.5
Ternopil	13.8	1,111,249	80.5
Transcarpathia	12.8	1,244,937	97.3
Vinnytsia	26.5	1,699,632	64.1
Volyn	20.2	1,039,798	51.5
Zaporizhzhia	27.2	1,859,141	68.4
Zhytomyr	29.9	1,328,491	44.4
Cities			
Kyiv	0.8	2,693,802	3,367.3
Sevastopol	0.9	378,941	421.0
Autonomous Republic			
Crimea	26.1	1,982,481	76.0
Total	**603.7**	**46,886,356**	**77.7**

* Official estimates.

UKRAINE

PRINCIPAL TOWNS
(population at census of 5 December 2001, rounded)

Kyiv (Kiev, capital)	2,611,000	Poltava		318,000
Kharkiv	1,470,000	Chernihiv		305,000
Dnipropetrovsk	1,065,000	Cherkasy		295,000
Odesa	1,029,000	Sumy		293,000
Donetsk	1,016,000	Horlivka		292,000
Zaporizhzhia	815,000	Zhytomyr		284,000
Lviv	733,000	Dniprodzerzhynsk		256,000
Kryvyi Rih	669,000	Khmelnytsky		254,000
Mykolayiv	514,000	Kirovohrad		254,000
Mariupol*	492,000	Rivne		249,000
Luhansk†	463,000	Chernivtsi		241,000
Makiyivka	390,000	Kremenchuk		234,000
Vinnytsia	357,000	Ternopil		228,000
Simferopol	344,000	Ivano-Frankivsk		218,000
Sevastopol	342,000	Lutsk		209,000
Kherson	328,000	Bila Tserkva		200,000

* Known as Zhdanov from 1948 to 1989.
† Known as Voroshylovhrad from 1935 to 1958 and from 1970 to 1989.

BIRTHS, MARRIAGES AND DEATHS*

	Registered live births Number	Rate (per 1,000)	Registered marriages Number	Rate (per 1,000)	Registered deaths Number	Rate (per 1,000)
1997	442,581	8.8	345,013	6.8	754,152	15.0
1998	419,238	8.4	310,504	6.2	719,955	14.3
1999	389,208	7.8	344,888	6.9	739,170	14.8
2000	385,126	7.8	274,523	5.5	758,082	15.3
2001	376,479	7.8	309,602	6.4	745,953	15.4
2002	390,687	8.1	317,228	6.6	754,911	15.7
2003	408,591	8.5	370,966	7.8	765,408	16.0
2004†	427,300	9.0	278,200	5.9	761,300	16.0

* Rates for 1996–2000 are based on unrevised population estimates.
† Rounded figures.

Expectation of life (WHO estimates, years at birth): 67 (males 62; females 73) in 2003 (Source: WHO, *World Health Report*).

IMMIGRATION AND EMIGRATION

	2003	2004	2005
Immigrants	39,849	38,567	39,580
Emigrants	63,699	46,182	34,997

ECONOMICALLY ACTIVE POPULATION
(annual averages, '000 persons aged 15–70 years)

	2001	2002	2003
Agriculture, hunting and forestry	3,965.0	4,019.5	3,860.8
Fishing	28.2	29.8	21.7
Mining and quarrying	814.9	797.6	769.5
Manufacturing	3,739.8	3,782.7	3,607.4
Electricity, gas and water supply	678.6	741.1	723.6
Construction	992.0	966.4	1,047.3
Wholesale and retail trade; repair of motor vehicles, motorcycles and personal and household goods	2,448.2	2,516.2	2,711.9
Hotels and restaurants	330.0	343.2	358.6
Transport, storage and communications	1,427.7	1,428.5	1,494.2
Financial intermediation	211.7	216.6	232.6
Real estate, renting and business activities	555.4	611.4	622.1
Public administration and defence; compulsory social security	1,139.9	1,113.5	1,188.0

—continued	2001	2002	2003
Education	1,797.5	1,709.5	1,769.9
Health and social work	1,545.8	1,567.1	1,544.5
Other community, social and personal service activities	557.3	546.2	584.9
Private households with employed persons	6.1	11.4	16.2
Extra-territorial organizations and bodies	—	—	1.5
Total employed	20,238.1	20,400.7	20,554.7
Total unemployed	2,516.9	2,301.0	2,059.5
Total labour force	22,755.0	22,701.7	22,614.2
Males	11,678.5	11,612.9	n.a.
Females	11,076.5	11,088.8	n.a.

Source: ILO.

Health and Welfare

KEY INDICATORS

Total fertility rate (children per woman, 2003)	1.2
Under-5 mortality rate (per 1,000 live births, 2004)	18
HIV/AIDS (% of persons aged 15–49, 2003)	1.4
Physicians (per 1,000 head, 2001)	2.97
Hospital beds (per 1,000 head, 2001)	8.74
Health expenditure (2002): US $ per head (PPP)	210
Health expenditure (2002): % of GDP	4.7
Health expenditure (2002): public (% of total)	71.1
Access to water (% of persons, 2002)	98
Access to sanitation (% of persons, 2002)	99
Human Development Index (2003): ranking	78
Human Development Index (2003): value	0.766

For sources and definitions, see explanatory note on p. vi.

Agriculture

PRINCIPAL CROPS
('000 metric tons)

	2002	2003	2004
Wheat	20,556.0	3,599.3	17,520.2
Barley	10,363.8	6,833.2	11,084.4
Maize	4,180.3	6,875.1	8,866.8
Rye	1,511.2	624.0	1,592.5
Oats	924.9	940.7	1,007.0
Millet	111.5	340.9	458.8
Buckwheat	209.4	310.9	293.6
Potatoes	16,619.5	18,453.0	20,754.8
Sugar beet	14,452.5	13,391.9	16,600.4
Dry peas	613.2	371.2	636.3
Sunflower seed	3,270.5	4,254.4	3,050.1
Cabbages	1,162.7	1,541.0	1,559.3
Tomatoes	1,311.7	1,265.2	1,145.7
Pumpkins, squash and gourds	792.4	893.7	543.6
Cucumbers and gherkins	650.9	816.1	712.6
Chillies and green peppers	130.6	131.8	128.2
Dry onions	513.5	521.6	721.7
Garlic	132.0	103.2	130.7
Carrots	445.4	529.7	674.9
Watermelons	347.4	331.7	307.1
Other vegetables and melons*	343.6	407.3	542.2
Apples	522.3	871.3	716.9
Pears	131.1	149.5	151.7
Apricots	68.5	110.5	99.3
Cherries (incl. sour cherries)	218.8	220.0	263.8
Plums	94.7	135.2	173.3
Grapes	359.3	540.9	374.0
Other fruits and berries (excl. melons)*	107.7	120.4	128.6

* Unofficial figures.

Source: FAO.

UKRAINE

LIVESTOCK
('000 head at 1 January)

	2002	2003	2004
Horses	693	684	637
Cattle	9,421	9,108	7,712
Pigs	8,370	9,204	7,322
Sheep	967	950	893
Goats	998	1,034	965
Chickens*	115,000	124,000	121,200

* Unofficial figures.
Source: FAO.

LIVESTOCK PRODUCTS
('000 metric tons)

	2002	2003	2004
Beef and veal	703.8	722.9	613.8
Pig meat	599.3	630.9	558.8
Poultry meat	299.7	324.0	375.5
Other meat	45.1	47.0	44.2
Cows' milk	13,846.7	13,340.4	13,457.6
Sheep's milk	19.0	17.6	30.4
Goats' milk	261.4	293.1	289.0
Cheese	145.2	185.3	242.9
Butter	131.3	148.0	138.0
Poultry eggs	656.6	657.4	683.6
Hen eggs	646.8	648.6	677.3
Honey	51.1	53.6	57.9
Cattle hides (fresh)*	102	115	103

* FAO estimates.
Source: FAO.

Forestry

ROUNDWOOD REMOVALS
('000 cubic metres, excl. bark)

	2002	2003	2004
Sawlogs, veneer logs and logs for sleepers	3,325	3,892	4,570
Pulpwood	510	793	954
Other industrial wood*	1,022	951	941
Fuel wood*	7,423	8,118	8,396
Total	12,280	13,754	14,862

* Unofficial figures.
Source: FAO.

SAWNWOOD PRODUCTION
('000 cubic metres, incl. railway sleepers)

	2001	2002*	2003*
Coniferous (softwood)	1,097	1,072	1,110
Broadleaved (hardwood)	898	877	909
Total	1,995	1,950	2,019

* Unofficial figures.
2004: Production assumed to be unchanged from 2003 (FAO estimates).
Source: FAO.

Fishing
('000 metric tons, live weight)

	2001	2002	2003
Capture	360.9	265.6	222.3
Azov sea sprat	19.0	13.3	11.1
Blue grenadier	1.3	0.0	10.6
Snoek	3.0	3.8	7.5
Sardinellas	10.6	13.7	5.5
European pilchard (sardine)	27.9	19.8	20.1
European sprat	49.0	45.5	31.4
European anchovy	16.7	12.9	13.1
Greenback horse mackerel	7.6	5.7	25.0
Other jack and horse mackerels	40.9	13.5	9.4
Chub mackerel	19.0	8.0	4.8
Antarctic krill	14.0	32.0	17.7
Wellington flying squid	8.6	11.2	10.4
Aquaculture	31.0	30.8	25.6
Common carp	20.0	20.0	15.0
Total catch	392.0	296.4	248.0

Source: FAO.

Mining
('000 metric tons, unless otherwise indicated)

	2000	2001	2002
Hard (incl. coking) coal	63,050	63,000	66,400
Brown coal (incl. lignite)	1,067	1,000	1,000
Crude petroleum	3,692.9	3,700.0	3,720.0
Natural gas (million cu m)	17,847.1	18,200.0	18,400.0
Iron ore: gross weight	55,883.2	54,650.0	58,900.0
Iron ore: metal content*	30,600	30,000	32,300
Manganese ore*†	930	930	940
Ilmenite concentrate	576.7	650.0	670.0*
Rutile concentrate	58.6	60.0	70.0
Zirconium concentrates*	30.0	33.6	34.3
Uranium concentrate (metric tons)†	600	750	800
Bentonite*	300	300	300
Kaolin	225	225	225
Potash salts (crude)*‡	85	75	60
Native sulphur*	80	80	80
Salt (unrefined)	2,286.5	2,300.0*	2,300.0*
Graphite (metric tons)	7,431	7,500*	7,500*
Peat*	1,000	1,000	1,000

* Estimated production.
† Figures refer to the metal content of ores and concentrates.
‡ Figures refer to potassium oxide content.
Source: US Geological Survey.

Industry

SELECTED PRODUCTS
('000 metric tons, unless otherwise indicated)

	2000	2001	2002
Margarine	140	167	168
Flour	2,710	2,686	2,699
Raw sugar*	1,780	1,947	1,621
Ethyl alcohol ('000 hectolitres)	1,968	2,643	2,840
Wine ('000 hectolitres)	948	1,425	2,081
Beer ('000 hectolitres)	10,765	13,059	14,999
Cigarettes (million)	58,774	69,731	n.a.
Wool yarn: pure and mixed	3.8	3.7	3.5
Cotton yarn: pure and mixed	8.5	11.0	10.7
Flax yarn	1.0	1.3	0.8
Woven cotton fabrics (million sq metres)	37	46	57
Woven woollen fabrics (million sq metres)	8.2	7.4	7.0
Linen fabrics (million sq metres)	3.5	5.7	4.1
Footwear, excl. rubber ('000 pairs)	16,417	18,929	19,200

UKRAINE

Statistical Survey

—continued	2000	2001	2002
Hydrochloric acid	58.1	66.8	60.5
Sulphuric acid	1,036	1,040	935
Nitric acid	9	6	4
Phosphoric acid	41.2	30.9	18.5
Caustic soda (Sodium hydroxide)	134	134	133
Soda ash (Sodium carbonate)	575	651	679
Nitrogenous fertilizers (a)†	2,202	2,153	2,311
Phosphatic fertilizers (b)†	82	61	28
Potassic fertilizers (c)†	20	20	8
Rubber tyres ('000)‡	6,508	6,862	6,244
Rubber footwear ('000 pairs)	2,170	2,527	2,665
Clay building bricks (million)	1,405	1,382	1,462
Quicklime	3,631	4,367	4,456
Cement	5,311	5,786	7,157
Pig-iron	26,052	26,536	27,764
Crude steel: for castings	482	500	872
Crude steel: ingots	31,782	33,523	34,543
Tractors (number)§	4,034	3,640	2,980
Household refrigerators ('000)	451	509	583
Household washing machines ('000)	125	166	232
Radio receivers ('000)	36	26	33
Television receivers ('000)	62	148	159
Passenger motor cars ('000)	17	26	44
Buses and motor coaches (number)	3,582	2,474	2,102
Lorries (number)	11,185	6,747	2,343
Bicycles ('000)‖	n.a.	109	245
Electric energy (million kWh)	171,445	172,972	n.a.

* Production from home-grown sugar beet.
† Production of fertilizers is in terms of (a) nitrogen; (b) phosphoric acid; or (c) potassium oxide.
‡ Tyres for road motor vehicles.
§ Tractors of 10 horse-power and over, excluding industrial tractors and road tractors for tractor-trailer combinations.
‖ Excluding children's bicycles.

Source: UN, *Industrial Commodity Statistics Yearbook*.

2003 ('000 metric tons, unless otherwise indicated): Raw sugar (production from home-grown sugar beet) 2,486; Cement 8,900; Household refrigerators ('000) 788; Passenger motor cars ('000) 106; Electric energy (million kWh) 180.

Finance

CURRENCY AND EXCHANGE RATES

Monetary Units
100 kopiykas = 1 hryvnya.

Sterling, Dollar and Euro Equivalents (30 December 2005)
£1 sterling = 8.6956 hryvnyas;
US $1 = 5.0500 hryvnyas;
€1 = 5.9575 hryvnyas;
100 hryvnyas = £11.50 = $19.80 = €16.79.

Average Exchange Rate (hryvnyas per US $)
2003   5.3327
2004   5.3192
2005   5.1247

Note: Following the dissolution of the USSR in December 1991, Russia and several other former Soviet republics retained the rouble (known as the karbovanets—KRB in Ukraine) as their monetary unit. In November 1992 this currency ceased to be legal tender in Ukraine, and was replaced (initially at par) by a currency coupon, also known as the karbovanets, or kupon, for a transitional period. Following the introduction of the transitional currency, Ukraine operated a system of multiple exchange rates, but in October 1994 the official and auction rates were merged. The unified exchange rate at 31 December 1995 was US $1 = 179,400 KRB. On 2 September 1996 Ukraine introduced a new currency, the hryvnya, at a rate of 100,000 KRB per hryvnya (1.750 hryvnyas per $).

GENERAL BUDGET
(million hryvnyas)*

Revenue†	2001	2002	2003‡
Current revenue	67,761	80,260	95,861
Tax revenue	55,982	67,957	80,454
Taxes on income, profits and capital gains	17,759	21,098	27,770
Social security contributions	15,047	18,465	21,239
Pension fund	13,115	15,749	17,994
Domestic taxes on goods and services	19,716	24,310	25,585
General sales tax, turnover tax and value-added tax	11,308	13,762	12,754
Value-added tax	10,348	13,471	12,598
Excises	2,654	4,098	5,246
Taxes on natural resources	3,682	4,463	5,274
Land tax	1,619	1,806	2,032
Taxes on international trade and transactions	2,422	2,853	4,404
Import duties	1,938	2,358	3,271
Other current revenue	11,779	12,303	15,407
Entrepreneurial and property income	3,428	2,798	5,284
Gas transit fee	1,943	1,531	2,009
Administration fees and charges	6,507	8,334	7,350
Fines and forfeits	1,413	689	476
Capital revenue	453	1,097	1,838
Total	**68,214**	**81,357**	**97,699**

Expenditure and net lending	2001	2002	2003‡
General public services	4,420	5,087	6,631
Executive and legislative organs	3,168	3,499	4,497
Defence	3,337	3,217	4,942
Public order and safety	3,717	4,825	5,576
Law enforcement	3,512	4,552	5,166
Education	7,798	9,784	11,901
Health	5,403	6,697	8,706
Social security and welfare	30,293	37,094	40,715
Social security	11,049	n.a.	n.a.
Pension fund	15,547	19,968	22,045
Housing and community services	1,746	1,859	2,424
Recreational, cultural and religious affairs	1,319	1,319	1,931
Economic services	7,424	7,620	12,705
Fuel and energy	2,374	2,373	3,558
Coal mines	1,198	2,140	2,646
Mineral resources extraction	1,442	1,037	2,278
Transportation and communication	1,778	2,250	3,212
Road transport	1,174	1,585	2,419
Interest payments	3,931	2,789	2,543
Foreign	2,281	2,125	2,242
Domestic	1,650	664	301
Other expenditure	924	15	—
Total	**70,312**	**80,306**	**98,074**

* Figures refer to the consolidated accounts of central government and those of local government.
† Excluding grants received (million hryvnyas): 221 in 2001; 292 in 2002; 213 in 2003.
‡ Preliminary figures.

INTERNATIONAL RESERVES
(US $ million at 31 December)

	2003	2004	2005
Gold (national valuation)	206.5	222.3	275.9
IMF special drawing rights	21.2	1.2	1.0
Foreign exchange	6,709.5	9,301.2	19,113.5
Total	**6,937.2**	**9,524.7**	**19,390.4**

Source: IMF, *International Financial Statistics*.

UKRAINE

MONEY SUPPLY
(million hryvnyas at 31 December)

	2003	2004	2005
Currency outside banks	33,119.3	42,344.9	60,231.4
Demand deposits at banks	19,968.3	25,765.4	40,102.6
Total money (incl. others)	53,129.4	68,186.6	100,432.2

Source: IMF, *International Financial Statistics*.

COST OF LIVING
(Consumer Price Index; base: previous year = 100)

	2003	2004	2005
Food and beverages	110.9	115.3	110.7
Other consumer goods	101.5	105.4	104.0
Services	105.4	107.9	115.8
All goods and services	108.2	112.3	110.3

NATIONAL ACCOUNTS

National Income and Product
(million hryvnyas at current prices)

	2001	2002	2003
Compensation of employees	86,440	103,117	122,188
Net operating surplus and mixed income	56,183	58,894	76,024
Domestic primary incomes	142,623	162,011	198,212
Consumption of fixed capital	34,303	36,160	38,885
Gross domestic product (GDP) at factor cost	176,926	198,171	237,097
Taxes on production and imports	30,720	30,764	34,277
Less Subsidies	3,456	3,125	4,030
GDP in market prices	204,190	225,810	267,344
Primary incomes received from abroad	898	850	1,335
Less Primary incomes paid abroad	4,478	4,075	4,432
Gross national income (GNI)	200,610	222,585	264,247
Less Consumption of fixed capital	34,303	36,160	38,885
Net national income	166,307	186,425	225,362
Current transfers from abroad	8,304	10,671	12,299
Less Current transfers paid abroad	322	299	592
Net national disposable income	174,289	196,797	237,069

Expenditure on the Gross Domestic Product
(million hryvnyas at current prices)

	2001	2002	2003
Final consumption expenditure	156,344	170,325	201,624
Households	112,260	124,560	146,301
Non-profit institutions serving households	4,017	4,226	4,493
General government	40,067	41,539	50,830
Gross capital formation	44,525	45,594	58,851
Gross fixed capital formation	40,211	43,289	55,075
Changes in inventories	4,229	2,209	3,661
Acquisitions, less disposals, of valuables	85	96	115
Total domestic expenditure	200,869	215,919	260,475
Exports of goods and services	113,245	124,392	154,394
Less Imports of goods and services	109,924	114,501	147,525
GDP in market prices	204,190	225,810	267,344

2004 (million hryvnyas, preliminary figure): GDP in market prices 345,943.

Gross Domestic Product by Economic Activity
(million hryvnyas at current prices)

	2001	2002	2003
Agriculture, hunting, forestry and fishing	29,421	29,418	29,059
Mining and quarrying	8,513	10,016	10,854
Manufacturing	35,592	40,386	49,702
Electricity, gas and water supply	11,232	11,425	12,270
Construction	7,291	7,653	10,268
Wholesale and retail trade; repair of motor vehicles, motorcycles and personal goods	22,409	24,593	31,622
Transport, storage and communication	24,587	27,523	35,092
Education	8,904	10,819	13,781
Health and social work	6,011	7,361	9,137
Other economic activities	29,336	35,148	42,712
Sub-total	183,296	204,342	244,497
Less Financial intermediation services indirectly measured	2,806	3,148	4,280
Gross value added in basic prices	180,490	201,194	240,217
Taxes on products	25,060	25,484	28,205
Less Subsidies on products	1,360	868	1,078
GDP in market prices	204,190	225,810	267,344

BALANCE OF PAYMENTS
(US $ million)

	2002	2003	2004
Exports of goods f.o.b.	18,669	23,739	33,432
Imports of goods f.o.b.	−17,959	−23,221	−29,691
Trade balance	710	518	3,741
Exports of services	4,682	5,214	6,287
Imports of services	−3,535	−4,444	−5,155
Balance on goods and services	1,857	1,288	4,873
Other income received	165	254	389
Other income paid	−769	−835	−1,034
Balance on goods, services and income	1,253	707	4,228
Current transfers received	1,967	2,270	2,671
Current transfers paid	−46	−86	−95
Current balance	3,174	2,891	6,804
Capital account (net)	17	−17	7
Direct investment abroad	5	−13	−4
Direct investment from abroad	693	1,424	1,715
Portfolio investment assets	2	1	−6
Portfolio investment liabilities	−1,718	−923	−70
Other investment assets	−781	−940	−10,065
Other investment liabilities	734	715	4,196
Net errors and omissions	−895	−965	−54
Overall balance	1,231	2,173	2,523

Sources: IMF, *International Financial Statistics*.

UKRAINE

External Trade

PRINCIPAL COMMODITIES
(distribution by Harmonized System, US $ million)

Imports f.o.b.	2003	2004	2005
Vegetable products	776.3	439.5	525.5
Prepared food, beverages, spirits, tobacco	1,098.8	1,004.6	1,454.9
Mineral products	8,479.1	10,845.4	11,567.8
Mineral fuels, oils, waxes and bituminous substances	7,856.9	10,160.9	10,661.9
Coal	449.5	900.3	714.3
Crude petroleum	3,678.4	4,837.4	4,500.4
Natural gas	3,190.0	3,591.4	3,946.0
Chemicals and related products	1,771.6	2,248.4	3,097.9
Plastics, rubbers, and articles thereof	1,034.6	1,406.6	1,938.1
Plastic and articles thereof	791.7	1,070.9	1,497.5
Wood pulp, paper, paperboard, scrap and waste paper and articles thereof	824.6	785.2	1,004.1
Paper and paperboard, articles of paper pulp	709.0	664.8	866.6
Textiles and textile articles	851.9	992.2	1,406.2
Base metals and articles thereof	1,196.8	1,752.9	2,468.8
Iron and steel	505.4	814.7	1,151.2
Machinery and mechanical appliances, electrical equipment and appliances, parts and accessories	3,478.3	4,740.7	6,342.3
Machinery and mechanical appliances, computers, etc.	2,468.4	3,214.3	4,051.8
Electrical machinery, equipment and parts, etc.	1,009.8	1,526.4	2,290.5
Vehicles, aircraft, vessels and associated transportation equipment	1,874.3	2,493.6	3,219.7
Vehicles other than railway or tramway rolling stock	1,698.0	2,246.1	3,023.1
Total (incl. others)	2,302.1	28,996.0	36,141.1

Exports f.o.b.	2003	2004	2005
Vegetable products	745.8	1,137.4	1,695.9
Cereals	402.3	844.3	1,384.1
Prepared food, beverages, spirits, tobacco	904.3	1,140.7	1,291.7
Mineral products	3,500.0	4,323.7	4,708.0
Ores, slag and ash	539.8	679.4	1,045.4
Mineral fuels, oils, waxes and bituminous substances	2,753.0	3,386.7	3,344.9
Chemicals and related products	1,943.0	2,782.0	2,990.2
Textiles, textile articles, etc.	851.9	882.6	914.0
Base metals and articles thereof	8,500.8	13,050.8	14,047.2
Iron and steel	6,729.9	10,768.3	11,485.9
Articles of iron and steel	1,078.1	1,448.0	1,852.0
Machinery and mechanical appliances, electrical equipment and appliances, parts and accessories	2,326.1	3,031.0	2,841.8
Machinery and mechanical appliances, computers, etc.	1,426.1	1,801.9	1,924.5
Electrical machinery, equipment and parts, etc.	899.9	1,229.1	917.3
Vehicles, aircraft, vessels and associated transportation equipment	984.1	2,037.3	1,655.9
Railway or tramway locomotives, rolling stock, track fixtures and fittings, signals, etc.	549.8	1,492.8	965.0
Total (incl. others)	23,080.2	32,672.3	34,286.7

PRINCIPAL TRADING PARTNERS
(US $ million)

Imports f.o.b.	2003	2004	2005
Austria	324.2	344.4	458.6
Belarus	343.6	538.2	939.9
Brazil	360.5	264.0	312.5
China, People's Republic	519.0	733.3	1,810.4
Czech Republic	314.3	419.7	594.1
Finland	295.1	255.7	351.3
France (incl. Monaco)	530.2	653.0	799.0
Germany	2,273.5	2,731.8	3,384.2
Hungary	270.1	362.3	647.9
Italy	645.1	806.0	1,030.3
Japan	377.7	422.0	548.2
Kazakhstan	492.5	388.5	186.4
Korea, Rep.	228.7	322.0	648.5
Netherlands	280.9	352.2	464.2
Poland	802.4	968.7	1,406.7
Russia	8,645.7	11,811.8	12,843.4
Sweden	246.8	418.4	547.5
Switzerland	175.9	300.0	253.6
Turkey	312.3	368.4	607.7
Turkmenistan	1,746.2	1,953.7	2,678.1
United Kingdom	564.7	733.6	502.7
USA	498.3	763.6	710.1
Total (incl. others)	23,020.8	28,996.0	36,141.1

Exports f.o.b.	2003	2004	2005
Algeria	351.2	593.8	618.3
Belarus	340.4	550.8	892.0
Bulgaria	325.5	498.5	543.5
China, People's Republic	1,003.2	831.4	711.2
Cyprus	272.6	168.4	217.5
Czech Republic	216.4	299.1	377.4
Egypt	291.6	367.6	802.5
Estonia	364.0	278.4	125.1
Germany	1,423.8	1,891.0	1,286.2
Hungary	849.9	807.6	690.7
India	202.8	481.8	736.9
Iran	295.6	434.8	577.0
Italy	1,268.5	1,620.4	1,893.9
Kazakhstan	306.9	622.9	668.0
Korea, Republic	182.2	358.4	202.2
Latvia	266.6	377.3	311.6

UKRAINE

Statistical Survey

Exports f.o.b.—continued

	2003	2004	2005
Lithuania	237.7	468.6	209.5
Moldova	486.0	659.8	679.1
Netherlands	481.4	525.0	515.1
Poland	763.2	997.9	1,010.9
Romania	497.5	731.7	489.8
Russia	4,311.4	5,888.7	7,495.8
Saudi Arabia	236.7	241.6	386.5
Singapore	132.2	286.4	489.6
Slovakia	289.1	398.1	508.6
Spain	211.5	521.8	573.6
Switzerland	439.8	472.9	396.4
Syria	281.8	603.8	676.2
Turkey	901.9	1,869.2	2,035.0
United Arab Emirates	137.1	426.1	345.7
United Kingdom	310.0	346.6	358.4
USA	718.6	1,506.9	956.5
Total (incl. others)	23,080.2	32,672.3	34,286.7

Transport

RAILWAYS
(traffic)

	2003	2004	2005
Passengers carried ('000 journeys)	476,700	452,200	447,000
Freight carried ('000 metric tons)	443,500	460,900	448,700
Passenger-km (million)	52,200	51,800	52,400
Freight ton-km (million)	224,900	233,600	223,400

ROAD TRAFFIC
(motor vehicles in use)

	1998	1999	2000
Passenger cars	4,877,787	5,210,774	5,250,129
Motorcycles and mopeds	2,609,201	2,432,787	2,251,505

Source: IRF, *World Road Statistics*.

INLAND WATERWAYS

	2003	2004	2005
Passengers carried ('000 journeys)	9,100	11,800	13,600
Freight carried ('000 metric tons)	18,800	20,600	21,400
Passenger-km (million)	100	100	100
Freight ton-km (million)	14,700	14,900	15,900

SHIPPING

Merchant Fleet
(registered at 31 December)

	2002	2003	2004
Number of vessels	828	829	647
Total displacement ('000 grt)	1,349.9	1,378.8	1,144.8

Source: Lloyd's Register-Fairplay, *World Fleet Statistics*.

International Sea-borne Freight Traffic
('000 metric tons, incl. transit departures)

	2002	2003	2004
Goods loaded	62,196	55,704	65,424
Goods unloaded	6,648	7,860	11,400

Source: UN, *Monthly Bulletin of Statistics*.

CIVIL AVIATION
(traffic on scheduled services)

	1999	2000	2001
Kilometres flown (million)	31	32	30
Passengers carried ('000)	891	951	986
Passenger-kilometres (million)	1,312	1,387	1,418
Total ton-kilometres (million)	138	145	149

Source: UN, *Statistical Yearbook*.

Tourism

TOURIST ARRIVALS
('000 non-resident persons)

Country of residence	2001	2002	2003
Belarus	752.7	1,045.1	1,595.4
Hungary	357.2	776.2	1,182.0
Moldova	2,194.1	2,259.4	2,557.0
Poland	366.9	556.0	1,239.2
Russia	4,857.6	5,170.3	5,026.2
Total (incl. others)	9,174.2	10,516.7	12,513.9

Tourism receipts (US $ million, incl. passenger transport): 759 in 2001; 1,001 in 2002; 1,204 in 2003.

Sources: World Tourism Organization.

Communications Media

	2002	2003	2004
Book production (titles)	12,444	13,805	14,790
Newspapers (titles)	3,047	2,891	3,014
Magazines and other periodicals (titles)	1,923	2,246	2,385
Telephones ('000 main lines in use)	10,833.3	11,109.5	12,142.0
Mobile cellular telephones ('000 subscribers)	3,692.7	6,466.5	13,735.0
Personal computers ('000 in use)	951	n.a.	1,327
Internet users ('000)	900	n.a.	3,750

Radio receivers ('000 in use): 45,050 in 1997.
Television receivers ('000 in use): 23,000 in 2000.
Facsimile machines (number in use): 42,161 in 2000.

Sources: mainly UNESCO, *Statistical Yearbook*; International Telecommunication Union.

Education

(2004/05, unless otherwise indicated)

	Institutions	Teachers	Students
Pre-primary	14,900*	191,500†	996,000
Primary and General secondary	21,700	547,000	5,731,000
Specialized secondary: vocational	1,011	n.a.	507,300
Higher	1,007‡	121,300†	2,269,800‡

* Including some 2,200 with activities suspended.
† 1993/94 figure.
‡ 2003/04 figure.

Adult literacy rate (UNESCO estimates): 99.4% (males 99.7%; females 99.2%) in 2003 (Source: UN Development Programme, *Human Development Report*).

Directory

Constitution

The Constitution of Ukraine, summarized below, was adopted at the Fifth Session of the Verkhovna Rada on 28 June 1996. It replaced the Soviet-era Constitution (Fundamental Law), originally approved on 12 April 1978, but amended several times after Ukraine gained independence in 1991, and entered into force the day of its adoption. On 8 December 2004, following the disputed (and subsequently annulled) second round of voting in the presidential election, the Verkhovna Rada approved a number of constitutional amendments, principally concerned with transferring a number of presidential powers, including the appointment of the majority of ministerial posts, to the Prime Minister and to the Verkhovna Rada. These amendments, which were signed into law on the same day by the outgoing President, Leonid Kuchma, were scheduled to take effect either conditionally on 1 September 2005 (subject to various reforms to local government having been approved by that date) or unconditionally on 1 January 2006. As the reforms to local government had not been agreed, the constitutional amendments took effect from the latter date, excepting those pertaining to the Verkhovna Rada or Prime Minister, which were to be implemented following the assembly of a legislature after the general election held in March 2006.

FUNDAMENTAL PRINCIPLES

Ukraine is a sovereign and independent, unitary and law-based state, in which power is exercised directly by the people through the bodies of state power and local self-government. The life, honour, dignity and health of the individual are recognized as the highest social value. The Constitution is the highest legal authority; the power of the State is divided between the legislative, the executive and the judicial branches. The state language is Ukrainian. The use and protection of Russian and other languages of national minorities, and the development of minorities' ethnic and cultural traditions is guaranteed. The State ensures protection of all forms of ownership rights and management, as well as the social orientation of the economy. The state symbols of Ukraine, its flag, coat of arms and anthem, are established.

THE RIGHTS, FREEDOMS AND DUTIES OF CITIZENS

The rights and freedoms of individuals are declared to be unalienable and inviolable regardless of race, sex, political or religious affiliation, wealth, social origin or other characteristics. Fundamental rights, such as the freedoms of speech and association and the right to private property, are guaranteed. Citizens have the right to engage in political activity and to own private property. All individuals are entitled to work and to join professional unions to protect their employment rights. The Constitution commits the State to the provision of health care, housing, social security and education. All citizens have the right to legal assistance. Obligations of the citizenry include military service and taxes. The age of enfranchisement for Ukrainian citizens is 18 years. Elections to organs of state authority are declared to be free and conducted on the basis of universal, equal and direct suffrage by secret ballot.

THE VERKHOVNA RADA

The Verkhovna Rada (Supreme Council) is the sole organ of legislative authority in Ukraine. It consists of 450 members, elected for a four-year term on the basis of proportional representation. The constitutional reforms approved in late 2004 prohibit deputies from leaving the party or bloc for whom they have been elected during the term of their elective mandate. Only Ukrainian citizens aged over 21 years, who have resided in Ukraine for the five previous years are eligible for election to parliament. The Verkhovna Rada is a permanently acting body, which elects its own Chairman and Deputy Chairmen.

The most important functions of the legislature include: the enactment of laws; the approval of the state budget and other state programmes; the scheduling of presidential elections; the removal (impeachment) of the President; appointment of the Prime Minister; the declaration of war or conclusion of peace; the foreign deployment of troops; and consenting to international treaty obligations within the time-limit prescribed by law. Within 15 days of a law passed by the Verkhovna Rada being received by the President, the President shall officially promulgate it or return it for repeat consideration by parliament. If, during such consideration, the legislature re-adopts the law by a two-thirds' majority, the President is obliged to sign it and officially promulgate it within 10 days. The President of Ukraine may terminate the authority of the Verkhovna Rada if, within 30 days of a single, regular session a plenary session cannot be convened, except within the last six months of the President's term of office.

THE PRESIDENT

The President of Ukraine is the Head of State, and is guarantor of state sovereignty and the territorial integrity of Ukraine. The President is directly elected for a period of five years. A presidential candidate must be aged over 35 years and a resident of the country for the 10 years prior to the election. The President may hold office for no more than two consecutive terms.

The President's main responsibilities include: the scheduling of elections and of referendums on constitutional amendments; the conclusion of international treaties; and the promulgation of laws. The President appoints certain senior members of the Cabinet of Ministers; the constitutional reforms agreed in late 2004 transferred responsibility for the appointment of the majority of Ministers to the Prime Minister.

The President is the Supreme Commander of the Armed Forces of Ukraine and chairs the National Security and Defence Council. The President may be removed from office by the Verkhovna Rada by impeachment, for reasons of state treason or another crime. The decision to remove the President must be approved by at least a three-quarters' majority in the Verkhovna Rada. In the event of the termination of the authority of the President, the Prime Minister executes the duties of the President until the election and entry into office of a new President.

THE CABINET OF MINISTERS

The principal organ of executive government is the Cabinet of Ministers, which is responsible before the President and accountable to the Verkhovna Rada. The Cabinet supervises the implementation of state policy and the state budget and the maintenance of law and order. The Cabinet of Ministers is headed by the Prime Minister. The duties of the Prime Minister include the submission of proposals to the President on the creation, reorganization and liquidation of ministries and other central bodies of executive authority. The Cabinet of Ministers must resign when a new President is elected, or in the event of the adoption of a vote of 'no confidence' by the Verkhovna Rada.

JUDICIAL POWER

Justice in Ukraine is administered by the Constitutional Court and by courts of general jurisdiction. The Supreme Court of Ukraine is the highest judicial organ of general jurisdiction. Judges hold their position permanently, except for justices of the Constitutional Court and first judicial appointments, which are made by the President for a five-year term. Other judges, with the exception of justices of the Constitutional Court, are elected by the Verkhovna Rada. Judges must be at least 25 years of age, have a higher legal education and at least three years' work experience in the field of law, and have resided in Ukraine for no fewer than 10 years. The Procuracy of Ukraine is headed by the General Procurator, who is appointed with the consent of parliament and dismissed by the President. The term of office of the General Procurator is five years.

A Superior Justice Council, responsible for the submission of proposals regarding the appointment or dismissal of judges, functions in Ukraine. The Council consists of 20 members. The Chairman of the Supreme Court of Ukraine, the Minister of Justice, and the General Procurator are *ex-officio* members of the Superior Justice Council.

LOCAL SELF-GOVERNMENT

The administrative and territorial division of Ukraine consists of the Autonomous Republic of Crimea, 24 provinces (oblasts), the cities of Kyiv and Sevastopol (which possess special status), districts (raions), cities, settlements and villages. Local self-government is the right of territorial communities. The principal organs of territorial communities are the district and provincial councils, which, with their chairmen, are directly elected for a term of four years. The chairmen of district and provincial councils are elected by the relevant council and head their executive structure. Provincial and district councils monitor the implementation of programmes of socio-economic and cultural development of the relevant provinces and districts, and adopt and monitor the implementation of district and provincial budgets, which are derived from the state budget.

UKRAINE

THE AUTONOMOUS REPUBLIC OF CRIMEA

The Autonomous Republic of Crimea is an inseparable, integral part of Ukraine. It has its own Constitution, which is adopted by the Supreme Council of the Autonomous Republic of Crimea (the representative organ of Crimea) and approved by the Verkhovna Rada. Legislation adopted by the Autonomous Republic's Supreme Council and the decisions of its Council of Ministers must not contravene the Constitution and laws of Ukraine. The Chairman of the Council of Ministers is appointed and dismissed by the Supreme Council of the Autonomous Republic of Crimea with the consent of the President of Ukraine. Justice in Crimea is administered by courts belonging to the single court system of Ukraine. An Office of the Representative of the President of Ukraine functions in Crimea.

The jurisdiction of the Autonomous Republic of Crimea includes: organizing and conducting local referendums; implementing the republican budget on the basis of the state policy of Ukraine; ensuring the function and development of the state and national languages and cultures; participating in the development and fulfilment of programmes for the return of deported peoples.

THE CONSTITUTIONAL COURT

The Constitutional Court consists of 18 justices, six of whom are appointed by the President, six by the Verkhovna Rada and six by the assembly of judges of Ukraine. Candidates must be citizens of Ukraine, who are at least 40 years of age and have resided in Ukraine for the previous 20 years. Justices of the Constitutional Court serve a term of nine years, with no right to reappointment. A Chairman is elected by a secret ballot of the members for a single three-year term.

The Constitutional Court provides binding interpretations of the Constitution. It rules on the constitutionality of: parliamentary legislation; acts of the President and the Cabinet of Ministers; the official interpretation of the Constitution of Ukraine; international agreements; and the impeachment of the President of Ukraine.

CONSTITUTIONAL AMENDMENTS AND THE ADOPTION OF A NEW CONSTITUTION

A draft law on amending the Constitution may be presented to the Verkhovna Rada by the President or at least one-third of the constitutional composition of the parliament. A draft law on amending the Constitution, which has been given preliminary approval by a majority of the constitutional composition of the Verkhovna Rada, is considered adopted if it receives the support of at least a two-thirds' parliamentary majority. In the case of its approval it is confirmed by a nation-wide referendum designated by the President.

The Government

HEAD OF STATE

President: VIKTOR A. YUSHCHENKO (elected 26 December 2004; inaugurated 23 January 2005).

CABINET OF MINISTERS
(April 2006)

Prime Minister: YURIY I. YEKHANUROV.
First Deputy Prime Minister: STANISLAV T. STASHEVSKYI.
Deputy Prime Minister: ROMAN P. BEZSMERTNYI.
Deputy Prime Minister: VYACHESLAV A. KYRYLENKO.
Deputy Prime Minister: YURIY F. MELNYK.
Minister of Internal Affairs: YURIY V. LUTSENKO.
Minister of Foreign Affairs: BORIS I. TARASYUK.
Minister of the Coal Industry: VIKTOR S. TOPOLOV.
Minister of Culture and Tourism: IHOR D. LIKHOVYI.
Minister of Defence: ANATOLIY S. HRYTSENKO.
Minister of the Economy: ARSENIY P. YATSENYUK.
Minister of Education and Science: STANISLAV M. NIKOLAYENKO.
Minister of Fuel and Energy: IVAN V. PLACHKOV.
Minister of Labour and Social Policy: IVAN YA. SAKHAN.
Minister of Construction, Architecture and Housing and Communal Services: PAVLO S. KACHUR.
Minister for the Protection of Health: YURIY V. POLYACHENKO.
Minister of Agrarian Policy: OLEKSANDR P. BARANIVSKYI.
Minister for Industrial Policy: VOLODYMYR M. SHANDRA.
Minister for the Protection of the Environment: PAVLO M. IHNATENKO.
Minister of Transport and Communications: VIKTOR V. BONDAR.
Minister for Emergency Situations and the Protection of the Population from the Consequences of the Chornobyl Catastrophe: VIKTOR I. BALOGA.
Minister for the Family, Youth and Sport: YURIY O. PAVLENKO.
Minister of Finance: VIKTOR M. PYNZENYK.
Minister of Justice: SERHIY P. HOLOVATYI.
Minister of the Cabinet of Ministers: BOHDAN YE. BUTS.

MINISTRIES

Office of the President: 01220 Kyiv, vul. Bankova 11; tel. (44) 291-53-33; fax (44) 293-61-61; e-mail president@adm.gov.ua; internet www.president.gov.ua.

Office of the Cabinet of Ministers: 01008 Kyiv, vul. M. Hrushevskoho 12/2; tel. (44) 293-21-71; fax (44) 293-20-93; e-mail web@kmu.gov.ua; internet www.kmu.gov.ua.

Ministry of the Agrarian Policy: 01001 Kyiv, vul. Khreshchatyk 24; tel. (44) 226-34-66; fax (44) 229-87-56; e-mail ministr@minapk.kiev.ua; internet www.minagro.gov.ua.

Ministry of the Coal Industry: Kyiv.

Ministry of Construction, Architecture and Housing and Communal Services: Kyiv.

Ministry of Culture and Tourism: 01601 Kyiv, vul. Ivana Franka 19; tel. (44) 226-26-45; fax (44) 235-32-57; e-mail zovn@mincult.gov.ua; internet www.mincult.gov.ua.

Ministry of Defence: 03168 Kyiv, Povitroflotskyi pr. 6; tel. (44) 226-26-56; fax (44) 226-20-15; e-mail pressmou@pressmou.kiev.ua; internet www.mil.gov.ua.

Ministry of the Economy: 01008 Kyiv, vul. M. Hrushevskoho 12/2; tel. (44) 253-93-94; fax (44) 226-31-81; e-mail meconomy@me.gov.ua; internet www.me.gov.ua.

Ministry of Education and Science: 01135 Kyiv, pr. Peremohy 10; tel. (44) 226-26-61; fax (44) 274-10-49; e-mail vgk@ministry.edu-ua.net; internet www.mon.gov.ua.

Ministry of Emergency Situations and the Protection of the Population from the Consequences of the Chornobyl Catastrophe: 01030 Kyiv, vul. O. Honchara 55a; tel. (44) 247-30-54; fax (44) 247-31-44; e-mail main@mns.gov.ua; internet www.mns.gov.ua.

Ministry of the Family, Youth and Sport: 01019 Kyiv, vul. Esplanadna 42; tel. (44) 289-12-64; fax (44) 289-12-94; e-mail correspond@mms.gov.ua.

Ministry of Finance: 01008 Kyiv, vul. M. Hrushevskoho 12/2; tel. (44) 293-74-66; fax (44) 293-21-78; e-mail infomf@minfin.gov.ua.

Ministry of Foreign Affairs: 01018 Kyiv, pl. Mykhailivska 1; tel. (44) 221-28-33; fax (44) 226-31-69; internet www.mfa.gov.ua.

Ministry of Fuel and Energy: 01601 Kyiv, vul. Khreshchatik 30; tel. (44) 239-41-64; fax (44) 462-05-61; e-mail kanc@mintop.energy.gov.ua; internet mpe.energy.gov.ua.

Ministry of Industrial Policy: 03035 Kyiv, vul. Surikova 3; tel. (44) 246-33-30; fax (44) 246-32-36; e-mail minister@industry.gov.ua.

Ministry of Internal Affairs: 01024 Kyiv, vul. Akademika Bohomoltsya 10; tel. (44) 256-03-33; fax (44) 256-16-33; e-mail mail@centrmia.gov.ua; internet mvs.gov.ua.

Ministry of Justice: 01001 Kyiv, vul. Horodetskoho 13; tel. and fax (44) 228-37-23; e-mail themis@minjust.gov.ua; internet www.minjust.gov.ua.

Ministry of Labour and Social Policy: 01023 Kyiv, vul. Esplanadna 8/10; tel. (44) 220-90-97; fax (44) 220-90-64; e-mail public@subs-mspp.kiev.ua; internet www.minpraci.gov.ua.

Ministry for the Protection of the Environment: 01601 Kyiv, vul. Khreshchatyk 5; tel. (44) 228-06-44; fax (44) 229-83-83; e-mail menr@menr.gov.ua; internet www.menr.gov.ua.

Ministry for the Protection of Health: 01021 Kyiv, vul. M. Hrushevskoho 7; tel. (44) 253-24-39; fax (44) 253-69-75; internet www.moz.gov.ua.

Ministry of Transport and Communications: 01135 Kyiv, pr. Peremohy 14; tel. (44) 226-22-04; fax (44) 216-72-06; e-mail info@mintrans.gov.ua; internet www.mintrans.gov.ua.

UKRAINE

President and Legislature

PRESIDENT

Presidential Election, First Ballot, 31 October 2004

Candidates	Votes	%
Viktor A. Yushchenko (Independent)	11,188,675	39.91
Viktor F. Yanukovych (Party of the Regions)	11,008,731	39.27
Oleksandr O. Moroz (Socialist Party of Ukraine)	1,632,098	5.82
Petro M. Symonenko (Communist Party of Ukraine)	1,396,135	4.98
Nataliya M. Vitrenko (Progressive Socialist Party of Ukraine)	429,794	1.53
Anatoliy K. Kinakh (Party of Industrialists and Entrepreneurs of Ukraine)	262,530	0.94
Oleksandr M. Yakovenko (Communist Party of Workers and Peasants)	219,191	0.78
Oleksandr O. Omelchenko (Unity)	136,830	0.49
Leonid M. Chernovetskiy (Independent)	129,066	0.46
Others	240,746	0.86
Against all candidates	556,962	1.99
Total*	28,035,184	100.00

* Including 834,426 invalid votes (2.98% of the total).

Second Ballot, 26 December 2004*

Candidates	Votes	%
Viktor A. Yushchenko (Independent)	15,115,712	52.00
Viktor F. Yanukovych (Party of the Regions)	12,848,528	44.20
Against all candidates	682,239	2.35
Total†	29,068,971	100.00

* The results of an initial second round of voting, conducted on 21 November 2004, in which the Central Electoral Commission had declared Yanukovych the winner, were annulled by the Supreme Court.
† Including 422,492 invalid votes (1.45% of the total).

LEGISLATURE

General Election, 26 March 2006

Parties and blocs	Votes	% of votes	Seats
Party of the Regions	8,148,745	32.14	186
Yuliya Tymoshenko bloc*	5,652,876	22.30	129
Our Ukraine bloc†	3,539,140	13.96	81
Socialist Party of Ukraine	1,444,224	5.70	33
Communist Party of Ukraine	929,591	3.67	21
Nataliya Vitrenko People's Opposition bloc‡	743,704	2.93	—
Lytvyn's People's bloc§	619,905	2.45	—
Kostenko and Plyushch's Ukrainian People's Bloc‖	476,155	1.88	—
Assembly	441,912	1.74	—
Enough!-Reforms and Order Party civil bloc¶	373,478	1.47	—
'Ne Tak' Opposition bloc[1]	257,106	1.01	—
Others	1,785,299	7.04	—
Against all lists	449,650	1.77	—
Total[2]	25,352,380	100.00	450

* Electoral bloc principally comprising Fatherland and the Ukrainian Social Democratic Party.
† Electoral bloc principally comprising the the Christian Democratic Union Party, the Congress of Ukrainian Nationalists, the People's Movement of Ukraine-Rukh, the Party of Industrialists and Entrepreneurs of Ukraine, People's Union Our Ukraine and the Synod Ukrainian Republican Party.
‡ Electoral bloc principally comprising the Russian-Ukrainian Union Party (Rus) and the Progressive Socialist Party of Ukraine.
§ Electoral bloc principally comprising the People's Party, the All-Ukrainian Justice party and the Ukrainian Peasants' Democratic Party.
‖ Electoral bloc principally comprising the Party of Free Farmers and Entrepreneurs of Ukraine, the Synodal Ukraine Party and the Ukrainian People's Party.
¶ Electoral bloc principally comprising Enough! and the Party of Reforms and Order.
[1] Electoral bloc principally comprising the All-Ukrainian Centre Association, the Republican Party of Ukraine, the Social Democratic Party of Ukraine (United) and Women For The Future.
[2] Including 490,595 invalid votes (1.94% of the total).

Election Commission

Central Electoral Commission of Ukraine (CEC) (Tsentralna vyborcha Komisiya Ukrainy): 01196 Kyiv, pl. L. Ukrainky 1; tel. (44) 286-84-62; e-mail post@cvk.gov.ua; internet www.cvk.gov.ua; Head YAROSLAV V. DAVYDOVYCH.

Political Organizations

Since the 1990s Ukrainian political life has been characterized by frequent changes of formation and allegiance within and between various factions or blocs. In November 2005 there were 126 political parties registered in Ukraine, of which the following were among the most important:

Assembly (Viche): 01004 Kyiv, vul. Tereshchenkivska 11A/5; tel. (44) 461-97-22; e-mail party@viche.com.ua; internet www.viche.org.ua; f. 1993 as Constitutional-Democratic Party; present name adopted 2005; supports democracy, private property rights, free market economics and freedom of speech; Chair. INNA H. BOHOSLOVSKA.

Brotherhood (Bratstvo): 04111 Kyiv, vul. Chernyakhivskoho 36; tel. (44) 237-10-43; fax (44) 449-94-31; e-mail bratstvo@bratstvo.info; internet www.bratstvo.info; f. 2003; extreme right-wing, Orthodox Christian; opposed to democracy and to Ukraine integrating with NATO and other Western institutions; boycotted 2006 legislative elections; Chair. DMRYTRO O. KORCHYNSKYI.

Christian Democratic Party of Ukraine (Khrystyyansko-Demokratychna Partiya Ukrainy): 01004 Kyiv, vul. Baseyna 1/2A; tel. (44) 235-39-96; fax (44) 234-19-49; e-mail fil@hdpu.org.ua; internet www.xdpress.com.ua; f. 1992; centrist democratic party; Chair. VITALIY S. ZHURAVSKIY; 42,000 mems.

Communist Party of Ukraine (CPU) (Komunistychna Partiya Ukrainy): 04070 Kyiv, vul. Borysohlibska 7; tel. (44) 425-54-87; fax (44) 416-31-37; e-mail press@kpu.net.ua; internet www.kpu.net.ua; banned 1991–93; advocates state control of economy and confederation with Russia; Sec. of Cen. Cttee PETRO M. SYMONENKO.

Enough! (Pora!): 01025 Kyiv, vul. Desyatynna 1/3; tel. (44) 461-41-58; e-mail info@pora.org.ua; internet www.pora.org.ua; f. 2005 on the basis of the 'Yellow Pora' civil organization; supports expansion of democratic freedoms and greater integration with the West; contested 2006 legislative elections as mem. of the Enough!-Party of Reforms and Order civic bloc; Chair. of Political Council VLADYSLAV V. KASKIV.

Fatherland (Batkivshchyna): 01133 Kyiv, bulv. Lesi Ukrainki 26/916; tel. (44) 284-52-21; e-mail sector@byti.com.ua; internet www.tymoshenko.com.ua; f. 1999; merged with Conservative Republican Party (led by STEPAN KHMARA) in 2002, and with Yabloko party in 2004; nationalist, populist, supportive of socially-orientated economics; contested 2006 legislative elections as mem. of Yuliya Tymoshenko bloc; Chair. YULIYA V. TYMOSHENKO; 221,000 mems (2005).

Green Party of Ukraine (Partiya Zelenykh Ukrainy): 01030 Kyiv, vul. Chapayeva 2/16; tel. (44) 224-91-06; fax (44) 220-66-94; e-mail office@greenparty.org.ua; internet www.greenparty.org.ua; f. 1990 as political wing of environmental organization, Green World (f. 1987), registered 1991; Pres. VITALIY M. KONONOV.

Party of Industrialists and Entrepreneurs of Ukraine (Partiya promyslovtsiv i pidpryyemtsiv Ukrainy): 01023 Kyiv, vul. Sh. Rustaveli 11; tel. and fax (44) 590-17-44; e-mail pppu@iptelecom.net.ua; internet pppu.com.ua; f. 2000; contested 2006 legislative elections as mem. of Our Ukraine bloc; Chair. ANATOLIY K. KINAKH.

Party of the Regions (PR) (Partiya Regioniv): 04053 Kyiv, vul. Kudryavska 3/5; tel. (44) 254-29-20; fax (44) 212-55-83; e-mail presscenter@partyofregions.org.ua; internet www.partyofregions.org.ua; f. 1997 as the Workers' Solidarity Party of Regional Rebirth of Ukraine; present name adopted 2001; Chair. VIKTOR F. YANUKOVYCH; 460,000 mems (Dec. 2001).

People's Democratic Party (PDP) (Narodno-Demokratychna Partiya—NDP): 03150 Kyiv, vul. Antonovicha 107; tel. (44) 522-84-18; fax (44) 522-87-26; e-mail zagal@sndp.kiev.ua; internet www.ndp.org.ua; f. 1996; contested 2006 legislative elections as mem. of the People's Democratic Party bloc; centrist; Leader VALERIY P. PUSTOVOYTENKO; 281,110 mems (2003).

People's Movement of Ukraine-Rukh (PMU-R) (Narodnyi Rukh Ukrainy): 01034 Kyiv, vul. O. Honchara 33; tel. (44) 246-47-67; fax (44) 531-30-42; e-mail org@nru.org.ua; internet www.nru.org.ua; f. 1989 as popular movement (Ukrainian People's Movement for Restructuring); registered as political party in 1993; contested 2006 legislative elections as mem. of Our Ukraine bloc; national democratic party; Chair. BORIS I. TARASYUK.

People's Party (Narodna Partiya): 01034 Kyiv, vul. Reitarska 6A; tel. (44) 270-61-84; fax (44) 270-65-91; e-mail info@narodapartiya

.info; internet www.narodna.info; f. 1996 as Agrarian Party of Ukraine; renamed People's Agrarian Party of Ukraine in mid-2004; present name adopted 2005; contested 2006 legislative elections as mem. of Lytvyn's People's bloc; centrist; Leader VOLODYMYR M. LYTVYN.

People's Union Our Ukraine (Our Ukraine) (Narodnyi Soyuz Nasha Ukraina) (Nasha Ukraina): 04070 Kyiv, vul. Borychiv Tik 22A; tel. (44) 206-60-95; e-mail tak@ua.org.ua; internet www.razom.org.ua; f. 2005 to support administration of Pres. Yushchenko; contested 2006 legislative elections as mem. of the Our Ukraine bloc; Hon. Pres. VIKTOR A. YUSHCHENKO; Chair. of Council ROMAN P. BEZSMERTNYI; Chair. of Exec. Cttee YURIY I. YEKHANUROV; 7,789 mems (April 2005).

Progressive Socialist Party of Ukraine (Prohresyvna Sotsialistychna Partiya Ukrainy): 01021 Kyiv, vul. Panas Mirnoho 27/51; tel. (44) 254-18-40; fax (44) 278-54-91; e-mail pspu@svitonline.com; internet www.vitrenko.org; f. 1996 by members of the Socialist Party of Ukraine; contested 2006 legislative elections as mem. of the Nataliya Vitrenko People's Opposition bloc; favours extension of Belarus-Russia Union to incorporate Ukraine; opposed to Ukraine seeking membership of NATO; Chair. NATALIYA M. VITRENKO.

Rebirth (Vidrodzheniya): 03049 Kyiv, pr. Povitroflotskiy 25; tel. (44) 486-36-39; f. 2004; supports measures intended to guarantee social justice and strengthen family life, and closer co-operation with Ukraine's strategic partners, including the USA, Russia and the European Union; Leader VASYL HLADKIKH.

Reforms and Order Party (Partiya 'Reformy i poryadok'): 01021 Kyiv, vul. Instytutska 28; tel. (44) 585-41-16; fax (44) 585-41-17; e-mail ref_ord@i.com.ua; internet www.prp.org.ua; f. 1997 as Reforms and Order Party; changed name to Our Ukraine in mid-2004; in July 2005 the Ministry of Justice ruled that the party had acted unlawfully in adopting the name 'Our Ukraine', and the party reverted to its original name; contested 2006 legislative elections as part of the Enough!-Party of Reforms and Order civic bloc; Chair. VIKTOR M. PYNZENYK.

Russian Movement of Ukraine (Russkoye Dvizheniye Ukrainy): 79000 Lviv, vul. Novakivskoho 8/4; tel. and fax (322) 75-80-59; e-mail rdu@rdu.org.ua; f. 2001 as For A United Rus; seeks by moderate means to re-establish a political union of Belarus, Russia and Ukraine, and to restore the status of Russian as an official language of Ukraine, alongside Ukrainian; Chair. OLEKSANDR H. SVISTUNOV.

Social-Democratic Party of Ukraine (United) (SDPU—U) (Sotsial-Demokratychna Partiya Ukrainy—Obyednana): 01030 Kyiv, vul. Ivano-Franko 18; tel. (44) 536-15-71; fax (44) 536-15-78; e-mail sdpuo@sdpuo.com; internet www.sdpuo.com; f. 1995; contested 2006 legislative elections as mem. of the 'Ne Tak' Opposition bloc; Chair. VIKTOR V. MEDVEDCHUK; 385,000 mems (2004).

Socialist Party of Ukraine (SPU) (Sotsialistychna Partiya Ukrainy): 01025 Kyiv, vul. Vorovskoho 45; tel. (44) 554-17-13; fax (44) 573-58-97; e-mail pravozahist2003@ukr.net; internet www.socpart.info; f. 1991; formed as partial successor to CPU; advocates democratic socialism; Leader OLEKSANDR O. MOROZ; c. 69,000 mems.

Synod Ukrainian Republican Party (Ukrainska respublikanska partiya 'Sobor'—Sobor): 03150 Kyiv, vul. Laboratorna 1/62A; e-mail office@urpsobor.ln.ua; internet www.sobor.org.ua; f. 2002 by merger of Synod Ukrainian People's Party (Sobor) and the Ukrainian Republican Party; right-wing, nationalist; contested 2006 legislative elections as mem. of Our Ukraine bloc; Leader LEVKO H. LUKYANENKO.

Ukrainian People's Party (UPP) (Ukrainska Narodna Partiya): 01601 Kiev, vul. Pushkinska 28A; tel. (44) 234-59-17; fax (44) 234-10-30; e-mail office@unp-ua.org; internet www.unp-ua.org; f. 1999 as breakaway faction of People's Movement of Ukraine-Rukh by fmr leader Vyacheslav Chornovil; fmrly Ukrainian People's Movement-Rukh; present name adopted 2003; contested 2006 legislative elections as mem. of Kostenko and Plyushch's Ukrainian People's bloc; Chair. YURIY I. KOSTENKO.

Union Party (Partiya 'Soyuz'): 04070 Kyiv, vul. Pochainynska 28A; tel. (44) 467-76-61; e-mail office@partsouz.org; internet www.partsouz.org; f. 1997; affiliated to Russian Movement of Ukraine; supports interests of Russian-speakers within Ukraine (notably in Crimea), including the introduction of Russian as a state language, and the creation of a common market between Belarus, Russia and Ukraine; Head LEV MURYMSKIY.

CRIMEAN POLITICAL ORGANIZATIONS

Like its Ukrainian counterpart, the Communist Party of Crimea was banned in August 1991. In September 1993, however, a new organization of that name was registered. Several other political groups emerged in 1993–94. The 'Russia' bloc consisted of various pro-Russian parties, including the Republican Party of Crimea, the former leader of which, YURII MESHKOV, won the Crimean presidential election in January 1994. Several parties promoting business interests were formed, including the Party for the Economic Rebirth of Crimea. The dominant political party among the Crimean Tatars was the Organization of the Crimean Tatar Movement (OCTM—f. 1991), which advocates the restoration of Tatar statehood in the Crimea. The OCTM also organized a Crimean Tatar representative body, the Mejlis, led by MUSTAFA CEMILEV (DZHEMILEV). The National Movement of the Crimean Tatars is a more moderate organization, committed to co-operation with the existing political structures in Crimea, and in March 2002 seven Crimean Tatars were elected to the Crimean Supreme Council, compared with just one in 1998. The National Party (Milli Firka) is a radical nationalist group. In the elections to the Verkhovna Rada held concurrently with elections to the Crimean Supreme Council in March 2006, the Party of the Regions was the most popular party, as was the case nation-wide, although the share of the vote that it received in the Autonomous Republic (58.01%) was markedly higher than that recorded throughout Ukraine. Although the second-placed Our Ukraine received only 7.62% of the votes cast in the Republic, it was believed to have received particular support from Crimean Tatars, partly because of the inclusion of MUSTAFA CEMILEV and another leader of the Mejlis, REFAT ÇUBAROV (CHUBAROV), on the party's national list; both men were duly elected to the Verkhovna Rada

Diplomatic Representation

EMBASSIES IN UKRAINE

Afghanistan: 01037 Kyiv, pr. Chervonozoryanyi 42; tel. and fax (44) 245-81-04; e-mail sm_kh2003@yahoo.com; Ambassador (vacant).

Algeria: 01001 Kyiv, vul. B. Khmelnytskoho 64; tel. (44) 216-70-79; fax (44) 216-70-08; e-mail ambkv@ksv.net.ua; Ambassador MOKADDEM BAFDAL.

Argentina: 01901 Kyiv, vul. Ivana Franka 36; tel. (44) 490-25-16; fax (44) 238-69-22; e-mail eucra@mrecic.gov.ar; internet www.argamb.ukrpack.net; Chargé d'affaires a.i. JORGE DANIEL ABADES.

Armenia: 01901 Kyiv, vul. Volodymyrska 45; tel. (44) 224-90-05; fax (44) 224-05-00; e-mail despanut@visti.com; Ambassador ARMEN KHACHATRIAN.

Austria: 01030 Kyiv, vul. Ivana Franka 33; tel. (44) 244-39-43; fax (44) 230-23-52; e-mail kiew-ob@bmaa.gv.at; internet www.aussenministerium.at/kiew; Ambassador Dr MICHAEL MIESS.

Azerbaijan: 04050 Kyiv, vul. Hlubochytska 24; tel. (44) 244-69-40; fax (44) 244-69-46; e-mail dmin@azembass.kiev.ua; Ambassador TALYAT MUSEIB OĞLU ALIYEV.

Belarus: 01030 Kyiv, vul. M. Kotsyubynskogo 3; tel. (44) 537-52-05; fax (44) 537-52-13; e-mail ukraine@belembassy.org; internet www.belembassy.org.ua; Ambassador VALENTYN V. VELICHKO.

Belgium: 01030 Kyiv, vul. Leontovicha 4; tel. (44) 238-26-00; fax (44) 238-26-01; e-mail kiev@diplobel.org; Ambassador PIERRE COLOT.

Brazil: 01010 Kyiv, bulv. Suvorova 14/12; tel. (44) 290-63-01; fax (44) 290-95-68; e-mail kivbrem@brazil.kiev.ua; Ambassador RENATO LUIZ RODRIGUEZ MARQUES.

Bulgaria: 01023 Kyiv, vul. Hospitalna 1; tel. (44) 235-52-96; fax (44) 224-99-29; e-mail embbul@carrier.kiev.ua; Ambassador ANGEL GANEV.

Canada: 01901 Kyiv, vul. Yaroslaviv Val 31; tel. (44) 590-31-00; fax (44) 590-31-57; e-mail kyiv@international.gc.ca; internet www.kyiv.gc.ca; Ambassador ABINA DANN.

China, People's Republic: 01901 Kyiv, vul. M. Hrushevskoho 32; tel. and fax (44) 253-73-71; e-mail cxjl@ukrpack.net; Ambassador YAO PEISHENG.

Croatia: 01091 Kyiv, vul. Artema 51/50; tel. (44) 216-58-62; fax (44) 224-69-43; e-mail croemb@carrier.kiev.ua; Ambassador Dr MARIO MIKOLIĆ.

Cuba: 01901 Kyiv, prov. Bekhterevskyi 5; tel. (44) 216-57-43; fax (44) 216-19-07; e-mail embacuba@naverex.kiev.ua; Ambassador JULIO GARMENDIA PEÑA.

Czech Republic: 01901 Kyiv, vul. Yaroslaviv Val 34A; tel. (44) 272-04-31; fax (44) 272-62-04; e-mail kiev@embassy.mzv.cz; internet www.mzv.cz/kiev; Ambassador Dr KAREL STINDL.

Egypt: 01901 Kyiv, vul. Observatorna 19; tel. (44) 212-13-27; fax (44) 216-94-28; e-mail boustan@egypt-emb.kiev.ua; Ambassador YOUSSEF MOUSTAFA ZADA.

Estonia: 01901 Kyiv, vul. Volodymyrska 61/11; tel. (44) 590-07-80; fax (44) 590-07-81; e-mail saatkond@estemb.kiev.ua; internet www.estemb.kiev.ua; Ambassador PAUL LETTENS.

Finland: 01901 Kyiv, vul. Striletska 14; tel. (44) 278-70-49; fax (44) 278-20-32; e-mail sanomat.kio@formin.fi; internet www.finland.org.ua; Ambassador LAURA REINILÄ.

France: 01034 Kyiv, vul. Reitarska 39; tel. (44) 590-36-00; fax (44) 590-36-30; e-mail pressefr@carrier.kiev.ua; internet www.ambafrance.kiev.ua; Ambassador JEAN-PAUL VEZIANT.

UKRAINE

Georgia: 04119 Kyiv, vul. Melnikov 83D/4; tel. (44) 451-43-53; fax (44) 451-43-56; e-mail gruzll@i.kiev.ua; Ambassador GRIGOL KATAMADZE.

Germany: 0901 Kyiv, vul. B. Khmelnytskoho 25; tel. (44) 247-68-00; fax (44) 247-68-18; e-mail kanzlei@german-embassy.kiev.ua; internet www.kiew.diplo.de; Ambassador DIETMAR GERHARD STÜDEMANN.

Greece: 01901 Kyiv, vul. Sofiyisvka 19; tel. (44) 254-54-71; fax (44) 254-39-98; e-mail greece@kiev.relc.com; Ambassador PANAYOTIS GOUMAS.

Holy See: 01901 Kyiv, vul. Turhenyevska 40; tel. (44) 482-35-57; fax (44) 482-35-53; e-mail nuntius@visti.com; Apostolic Nuncio Most Rev. IVAN JURKOVIČ (Titular Archbishop of Corbavia).

Hungary: 01034 Kyiv, vul. Reitarska 33; tel. (44) 230-80-01; fax (44) 272-20-90; e-mail hungary@kiev.farlep.net; internet www.hungaryemb.kiev.ua; Ambassador JÁNOS TÓTH.

India: 01901 Kyiv, vul. Teryokhina 4; tel. (44) 468-66-61; fax (44) 468-66-19; e-mail india@public.ua.net; internet www.indianembassy.org.ua; Ambassador SHEHKHOLEN KIPGEN.

Indonesia: 04107 Kyiv, vul. Nahirna 27B; tel. (44) 206-54-46; fax (44) 206-54-40; e-mail kbri@indo.ru.kiev.ua; internet www.kbri.kiev.ua; Ambassador ALBERTUS EMANUEL ALEXANDER LATURIUW.

Iran: 01901 Kyiv, vul. Kruhlouniversytetska 12; tel. (44) 229-44-63; fax (44) 229-32-55; Ambassador SEYYED MUSSA KAZEMI.

Israel: 01901 Kyiv, bulv. L. Ukrainky 34; tel. (44) 284-81-08; fax (44) 284-97-48; e-mail ambass-sec@kiev.mfa.gov.il; internet kiev.mfa.gov.il; Ambassador NAOMI BEN-AMI.

Italy: 01901 Kyiv, vul. Yaroslaviv Val 32B; tel. (44) 464-05-31; fax (44) 464-05-38; e-mail ambital.kiev@utel.net.ua; internet sedi.esteri.it/kiev; Ambassador FABIO FABBRI.

Japan: 01901 Kyiv, Muzeiniy prov. 4; tel. (44) 490-55-00; fax (44) 490-55-02; e-mail jpembua@sovamua.com; internet www.ua.emb-japan.go.jp; Ambassador MUTSUO MABUCHI.

Kazakhstan: 01901 Kyiv, vul. Melnykova 26; tel. and fax (44) 483-11-98; e-mail post@kazakh.kiev.ua; internet www.kazembassy.com.ua; Ambassador AMANGELDY ZH. ZHUMABAYEV.

Korea, Republic: 01034 Kyiv, vul. Volodymyrska 43; tel. (44) 246-37-59; fax (44) 246-37-57; e-mail korea@koremb.kiev.ua; Ambassador LEE SUNG-JOO.

Kuwait: 04053 Kyiv, vul. Kudryavska 13–19; tel. (44) 238-27-32; fax (44) 238-63-94; Ambassador HAFEEZ MOHAMMED AL-AJMI.

Kyrgyzstan: 04053 Kyiv, vul. Artema 51/50; tel. (44) 219-13-97; fax (44) 246-88-89; e-mail chukik@public.ua.net; Ambassador ESENGUL K. OMURALIYEV.

Latvia: 01901 Kyiv, vul. Sichnevoho Povstannya 6B; tel. (44) 490-70-30; fax (44) 490-70-35; e-mail embassy.ukraine@mfa.gov.lv; Ambassador ANDRIS VILCĀNS.

Libya: 04050 Kyiv, vul. Ovrutska 6; tel. (44) 238-60-70; fax (44) 238-60-68; Sec. of People's Bureau (Ambassador) SEDDYK MOHAMED AL-SHIBANI AL-GWERI.

Lithuania: 01901 Kyiv, vul. Buslivska 21; tel. (44) 254-09-20; fax (44) 254-09-28; e-mail amb.ua@urm.lt; Ambassador VIKTORAS BAUBLYS.

Macedonia, former Yugoslav republic: 03150 Kyiv, vul. I. Fedorova 12; tel. (44) 238-66-16; fax (44) 238-66-17; e-mail embmac@carrier.kiev.ua; Ambassador Dr MARTIN GULESKI.

Moldova: 01010 Kyiv, vul. Sichnevoho Povstannya 6; tel. (44) 290-77-21; fax (44) 290-77-22; Ambassador MIHAIL LAUR.

Netherlands: 01901 Kyiv, Kontraktova pl. 7; tel. (44) 490-82-00; fax (44) 490-82-09; e-mail kie@minbuza.nl; internet www.holland.com.ua; Ambassador Dr RON KELLER.

Nigeria: 015 Kyiv, bulv. Panfiliovtsiv 36; tel. (44) 254-58-50; fax (44) 254-53-71; Ambassador IGNATIUS KHEKAYRE ADGURU.

Norway: 01901 Kyiv, vul. Striletska 15; tel. (44) 590-04-70; fax (44) 234-06-55; e-mail emb.kiev@mfa.no; internet www.norway.com.ua; Ambassador JOSTEIN HELGE BERNHARDSEN.

Pakistan: 01015 Kyiv, pr. Panfilovtsiv 7; tel. and fax (44) 280-25-77; fax (44) 254-45-30; e-mail parepkyiv@mail.kar.net; Ambassador TAJ UL HAQ.

Poland: 01034 Kyiv, vul. Yaroslaviv Val 12; tel. (44) 230-07-00; fax (44) 270-63-36; e-mail ambasada@polska.com.ua; internet www.polska.com.ua; Ambassador JACEK KLUCZKOWSKI.

Portugal: 01901 Kyiv, vul. V. Vasylkivska 9/2/12; tel. (44) 227-24-42; fax (44) 230-26-25; e-mail embport@svtonline.com; Ambassador JOSÉ MANUEL DA ENCARNAÇÃO PESSANHA VIEGAS.

Romania: 01030 Kyiv, vul. M. Kotsyubynskoho 8; tel. (44) 234-52-61; fax (44) 235-20-25; e-mail romania@iptelecom.net.ua; Ambassador TRAIAN LAURENTIU HRISTEA.

Russia: 03049 Kyiv, Povitroflotskyi pr. 27; tel. (44) 244-09-63; fax (44) 246-34-69; e-mail embrus@public.icyb.kiev.ua; internet www.embrus.org.ua; Ambassador VIKTOR S. CHERNOMYRDIN.

Serbia and Montenegro: 04070 Kyiv, vul. Voloska 4; tel. (44) 425-60-60; fax (44) 425-60-47; e-mail ambascg@adamant.net; Ambassador GORAN ALEKSIC.

Slovakia: 01901 Kyiv, vul. Yaroslaviv Val 34; tel. (44) 212-03-10; fax (44) 272-32-71; e-mail embassy@kiev.mfa.sk; internet www.kiev.mfa.sk; Ambassador URBAN RUSNÁK.

South Africa: 01004 Kyiv, vul. V. Vasylkivska 9/2, POB 7; tel. (44) 287-71-72; fax (44) 287-72-06; e-mail saemb@utel.net.ua; Ambassador ASHRAF SENTSO.

Spain: 01901 Kyiv, vul. Dekhtyarivska 38–44/7; tel. (44) 213-18-58; fax (44) 213-00-31; e-mail embespua@mail.mae.es; Ambassador LUIS JAVIER GIL CATALINA.

Sweden: 01901 Kyiv, vul. Ivana Franka 34/33; tel. (44) 494-42-70; fax (44) 494-42-71; e-mail ambassaden.kiev@foreign.ministry.se; internet www.sweemb.kiev.ua; Ambassador JOHN-CHRISTER AHLANDER.

Switzerland: 01901 Kyiv, vul. I. Fedorova 12; tel. (44) 220-54-73; fax (44) 246-65-13; e-mail vertretung@kie.rep.admin.ch; internet www.eda.admin.ch/kiev; Ambassador CHRISTIAN FAESSLER.

Turkey: 01901 Kyiv, vul. Arsenalna 18; tel. (44) 284-99-64; fax (44) 285-64-23; e-mail kiev.be@mfa.gov.tr; Ambassador ALI BILGE CANKOREL.

Turkmenistan: 01901 Kyiv, vul. Pushkinska 6; tel. (44) 229-34-49; fax (44) 229-30-34; e-mail ambturkm@ukrpack.net; Ambassador AMANGELDY O. BAYRAMOV.

United Kingdom: 01025 Kyiv, vul. Desyatynna 9; tel. (44) 490-36-60; fax (44) 490-36-62; e-mail ukembinf@sovamua.com; internet www.britemb-ukraine.net; Ambassador ROBERT BRINKLEY.

USA: 01901 Kyiv, vul. Yu. Kotsyubynskoho 10; tel. (44) 490-40-00; fax (44) 490-40-85; e-mail press@usembassy.kiev.ua; internet kiev.usembassy.gov; Ambassador WILLIAM B. TAYLOR, Jr (designate).

Uzbekistan: 01901 Kyiv, vul. Volodymyrska 16; tel. (44) 228-12-46; fax 229-55-09; Ambassador ILHOM O. HAYDAROV.

Viet Nam: 01011 Kyiv, vul. Leskova 5; tel. (44) 254-45-89; fax (44) 294-80-87; e-mail dsq@dsqvn.kiev.ua; Ambassador VU DUONG HUAN.

Judicial System

Constitutional Court of Ukraine (Konstytutsiyniy sud Ukraini): 01220 Kyiv, vul. Zhylianska 14; tel. (44) 289-05-53; fax (44) 287-20-01; e-mail idep@ccu.gov.ua; internet www.ccu.gov.ua; f. 1996; Chair. PAVLO B. YEVHRAFOV (acting).

Supreme Court (Verkhovnyi sud Ukraini): 01024 Kyiv, vul. P. Orlyka 4; tel. (44) 253-63-08; e-mail interdep@scourt.gov.ua; internet www.scourt.gov.ua; Chair. VASYL MALYARENKO.

Supreme Economic Court (Vyshyi hospodarskyi sud Ukraini): 01011 Kyiv, vul. Kopylenka 6; tel. (44) 536-05-00; fax (44) 536-18-18; e-mail kantselariya@usu.arbitr.gov.ua; internet www.arbitr.gov.ua; f. 1991; Chief Justice DMYTRO M. PRYTYKA.

Office of the Prosecutor-General: 01011 Kyiv, vul. Riznytska 13/15; tel. (44) 226-20-27; fax (44) 280-28-51; e-mail ilrd@gp.gov.ua; internet www.gp.gov.ua; Prosecutor-General OLEKSANDR MEDVEDKO.

Religion

State Department for Religion (Derzhavnyi departament u spravakh religii): 01601 Kiev, vul. Prorizna 15/5; tel. (44) 279-37-16; fax (44) 279-36-43; e-mail ddeprelig@kv.ukrtel.net; internet www.derzhdeprelig.gov.ua; Chair. IHOR V. BONDARCHUK.

CHRISTIANITY

The Eastern Orthodox Church

Eastern Orthodoxy is the principal religious affiliation in Ukraine. Until 1990 all legally constituted Orthodox church communities in Ukraine were part of the Ukrainian Exarchate of the Russian Orthodox Church (Moscow Patriarchate). In that year the Russian Orthodox Church in Ukraine was renamed the Ukrainian Orthodox Church (UOC), partly to counter the growing influence of the previously prohibited Ukrainian Autocephalous Orthodox Church (UAOC). In the early 1990s there was considerable tension between the UOC and the UAOC over the issue of church property seized in 1930. A new ecclesiastical organization was formed in June 1992, when Filaret (Denisenko), the disgraced former Metropolitan of Kyiv, united with a faction of the UAOC to form the Kyiv Patriarchate. The UOC (Kyiv Patriarchate) elected a Patriarch, Volody-

UKRAINE

Directory

myr (Romaniuk), in October. Following Volodymyr's death in July 1995, Filaret was elected as Patriarch, prompting some senior clergy to leave the church and join the UAOC. In the mid-2000s the UOC (Moscow Patriarchate) remained the largest church organization in Ukraine.

Ukrainian Autocephalous Orthodox Church: 01001 Kyiv, vul. Tryokhsvyatytelska 8A; e-mail uapc-ptr@uapc-ptr.kiev.ua; internet www.uaoc.kiev.ua; f. 1921, forcibly incorporated into the Russian Orthodox Church (Moscow Patriarchate) in 1930; continued to operate clandestinely; formally revived in 1990; 1,172 parishes, five monasteries and convents in 2005; Administrator Archbishop IHOR (ISICHENKO).

Ukrainian Orthodox Church (Moscow Patriarchate): 01015 Kyiv, vul. Sichnevoho Povstannya 25/49; tel. (44) 255-12-04; fax (44) 254-53-01; e-mail mitropolia@svitonline.com; internet www.pravoslavye.org.ua; exarchate of the Russian Orthodox Church (Moscow Patriarchate); 10,783 parishes, 158 monasteries and convents in 2005; Metropolitan of Kyiv and All-Ukraine VLADIMIR (SABODAN).

Ukrainian Orthodox Church (Kyiv Patriarchate): 01004 Kyiv, vul. Pushkinska 36; tel. (44) 234-10-96; fax (44) 234-30-55; internet www.kievpatr.org.ua; f. 1992 by factions of the Ukrainian Orthodox Church (Moscow Patriarchate) and Ukrainian Autocephalous Orthodox Church; 3,484 parishes, 36 monasteries and convents in 2005; 'Patriarch of Kyiv and all Rus-Ukraine' FILARET (DENISENKO).

Russian Orthodox Old Belief (Old Ritual) Church (Russkaya Pravoslavnaya Staroobryadcheskaya Tserkov): 49017 Dnipropetrovsk, pr. K. Marksa 60/8; tel. (562) 52-17-75; internet www.staroobryad.narod.ru; f. 1652 by separation from the Moscow Patriarchate; divided into two main branches: the *popovtsi* (which have priests) and the *bespopovtsi* (which reject the notion of ordained priests and the use of all sacraments, other than that of baptism). Both branches are further divided into various groupings. The largest group of *popovtsi* are those of the Belokrinitskii Concord; 52 parishes, two monasteries and convents of the Belokrinitskii Concord in Ukraine in 2005, and 10 parishes of *bezpopovtsi* at that time; Bishop of Kyiv and all Ukraine SAVVATIYE .

The Roman Catholic Church

Most Roman Catholics in Ukraine are adherents of the Byzantine Rites, the so-called 'Greek' Catholic Church, which is based principally in Western Ukraine and Transcarpathia. Some controversy arose, in August 2005, when the seat of the head of the Byzantine-rite Church, was relocated from Lviv to the Ukrainian capital, Kyiv. In 2005 there were 3,386 parishes of the Byzantine rites in Ukraine, 870 Roman Catholic parishes of the Latin rite and 20 parishes of the Armenian rite. Ukraine comprises three archdioceses (including one each for Catholics of the Latin, Byzantine and Armenian rites) and 14 dioceses (of which one is directly responsible to the Holy See). At 31 December 2003 there were an estimated 4,399,344 adherents (excluding adherents of the Armenian rite, for whom figures were not available), equivalent to some 9.9% of the population. Of that number, more than 75% followed the Byzantine rites. Adherents of Latin-rite Catholicism in Ukraine are predominantly ethnic Poles.

Bishops' Conference: Bishops' Conference of Ukraine, 79008 Lviv, pl. Katedralna 1; tel. (322) 76-94-15; fax (322) 96-61-14; f. 1992; Pres. Cardinal MARIAN JAWORSKI (Metropolitan Archbishop of Lviv).

Byzantine Ukrainian Rite

Archbishop-Major of Kyiv and Halych: Cardinal LUBOMYR HUSAR, c/o 79000 Lviv, pl. Sv. Yura 5; tel. (322) 97-11-21; fax (322) 72-25-24; e-mail press@ugcc.org.ua; internet www.ugcc.org.ua; head of Ukrainian Greek Catholic Church; established in 1596 by the Union of Brest, which permitted Orthodox clergymen to retain the Eastern rite, but transferred their allegiance to the Roman Pontiff in 1946, at the self-styled Synod of Lvov (Lviv Sobor); the Catholics of the Byzantine rite were forcibly integrated into the Russian Orthodox Church (Moscow Patriarchate), but continued to function in an 'underground' capacity; relegalized in 1989; in 2005 the seat of the head of the Church was relocated from Lviv, in western Ukraine, to Kyiv.

Latin Rite

Metropolitan Archbishop of Lviv: Cardinal MARIAN JAWORSKI, 79008 Lviv, pl. Katedralna 1; tel. (322) 76-94-15; fax (322) 96-61-14; e-mail k@rkc.lviv.ua; internet www.rkc.lviv.ua.

Armenian Rite

Archbishop of Lviv: (vacant).

Protestant Churches

There were 6,578 Protestant communities registered in Ukraine in 2001. These comprised both those churches that had been repressed and forced to operate clandestinely during the period of Soviet rule, the largest of which were the All-Ukrainian Union of United Evangelical Christians-Baptists, and the All-Ukrainian Union of Christians of the Evangelical Faith—Pentacostalists, and a number of confessions introduced to Ukraine during the 1990s by missionaries, primarily from Europe and North America.

All-Ukrainian Union of Christians of the Evangelical Faith—Pentecostalists: 01033 Kyiv, vul. Karyerna 44; 1,364 parishes in 2005.

All-Ukrainian Union of Associations of Evangelical Christians-Baptists: 01004 Kyiv, vul. L. Tolstoho 3B; tel. (44) 234-82-41; fax (44) 234-16-76; e-mail union@baptist.kiev.ua; 2,394 parishes in 2005, 131,950 adherents in 2001; affiliated to the Euro-Asiatic Federation of the Union of Evangelical Christians-Baptists; Pres. HRIHORIY I. KOMENDANT.

Ukrainian Lutheran Church: 01004 Kyiv, vul. V. Vasylkivska 14/15; tel. (44) 235-77-21; fax (44) 234-08-00; e-mail vhorpynchuk@yahoo.com; internet www.ukrlc.org; 39 parishes in 2005; Leader of Church Bishop Dr VYACHESLAV HORPYNCHUK.

ISLAM

In 2005 there were 455 Islamic communities officially registered in Ukraine, of which 342 were located in the Autonomous Republic of Crimea. In 2001 there were an estimated 2m. adherents of Islam in Ukraine. The return of Crimean Tatars to Crimea from Central Asia, to where they were exiled at Stalin's behest during the Second World War, has had a significant impact upon the growth of Islamic communities in the republic since the early 1990s. An Islamic University was established in Donetsk in 1998.

Independent Federation of Muslim Social Organizations of Ukraine (Arraid): 04119 Kyiv, vul. Dekhtyarivska 25A; tel. (44) 490-99-00; fax (44) 490-99-22; e-mail office@arraid.org; internet www.arraid.org; f. 1997; brs in Dnipropetrovsk, Donetsk, Kharkiv, Luhansk, Lviv, Odesa, Simferopol, Vinnytsya and Zaporizhzhya; publishes periodical *Arraid (Pioneer)* in Arabic and Russian and educational material in Russian, Tatar and Ukrainian; undertakes charitable and educational work; Chair. FAROUK ASHOUR.

Religious Administration of Muslims in Crimea: 95000 Crimea, Simferopol, Kebir Çami Mosque; 320 communities in 2005; Mufti AJE NURALI ABLAIYEV.

Religious Administration of Muslims in Ukraine: 04071 Kyiv, vul. Lukyanovska; tel. (44) 465-18-77; fax 456-17-70; e-mail islam@i.kiev.ua; f. 1992; 60 communities in 2005; Mufti Sheikh TAMIN AHMED MUHAMED MUTAH.

JUDAISM

In 2001 there were 103,600 Jews in Ukraine (according to census results), despite high levels of emigration from the 1970s. From 1989 there was a considerable revival in the activities of Jewish communities. In 2005 there were 251 Jewish communities in Ukraine, compared with 12 synagogues in 1989.

All-Ukrainian Jewish Congress: 01023 Kyiv, vul. Mechnykova 14/1; tel. (44) 235-71-20; fax (44) 235-10-67; e-mail vek@i.kiev.ua; internet www.jewish.kiev.ua; f. 1997; affiliated to the Federation of Jewish Communities of the CIS and the Baltic states; unites 183 communities; Chief Rabbi of Ukraine AZRIEL CHAIKIN.

Jewish Confederation of Ukraine: 04071 Kyiv, vul. Shekavystka 29; tel. (44) 536-12-21; e-mail eku@jewukr.org; internet www.jewukr.org; Chief Rabbi of Kyiv and All Ukraine YAAKOV DOV BLEICH.

BAHÁ'Í FAITH

National Spiritual Assembly: Kyiv; tel. (44) 442-33-46; fax (44) 449-66-86; e-mail secretariat@bahai.org.ua.

The Press

In 1996 there were an estimated 44 daily newspapers published in Ukraine. In 2004 there were a total of 3,014 newspapers and 2,385 periodicals published in the country. In addition to newspapers published in Ukraine, several newspapers and magazines published in Russia have a large circulation in Ukraine.

The publications listed below are in Ukrainian, except where otherwise stated.

PRINCIPAL NEWSPAPERS

Demokratychna Ukraina (Democratic Ukraine): 03047 Kyiv, pr. Peremohy 50; tel. (44) 454-88-30; fax (44) 456-91-21; e-mail du@uct.ua; internet www.dua.com.ua; f. 1918; fmrly *Radyanska Ukraina* (Soviet Ukraine); 4 a week; Editor VITALIY ADAMENKO; circ. 62,400 (2005).

Den (The Day): 04212 Kyiv, vul Marshala Tymoshenka 2L; tel. (44) 414-40-66; fax (44) 414-49-20; e-mail master@day.kiev.ua; internet www.day.kiev.ua; f. 1998; in Ukrainian and Russian; 5 a week; publ. by the Presa Ukrainy (Press of Ukraine) Publishing House; Editor-in-Chief LARYSA IVSHYNA; circ. 62,500 (2001).

Fakty i Kommentarii (Facts and Commentaries): 04116 Kyiv, vul. V. Vasylevskoy 27–29; tel. (44) 244-57-81; fax (44) 246-85-50; e-mail info@facts.kiev.ua; internet www.facts.kiev.ua; daily; politics, economics, sport, law, culture; in Russian.

Holos Ukrainy/Golos Ukrainy (Voice of Ukraine): 03047 Kyiv, vul. Nesterova 4; tel. (44) 441-88-11; fax (44) 224-72-54; e-mail mail@golos.com.ua; f. 1991; organ of the Verkhovna Rada; in Ukrainian and Russian; 5 a week; Editor SERHIY M. PRAVDENKO; circ. 150,000 (2002).

Kiyevskiye Vedomosti (Kyiv Gazette): 04086 Kyiv, vul. Olzhycha 29; tel. (44) 238-28-07; internet www.kv.com.ua; f. 1992; in Russian; national daily; Dir-Gen. VLADIMIR P. DERIKIT; Editor-in-Chief NIKOLAI V. ZAKREVSKII; circ. 138,300 (2002); also weekly edition (Fridays), in Ukrainian, *Kyivski Vidomosti*.

Kommersant-Ukraina (Businessman-Ukraine): Kyiv; internet www.kommersant.ua; f. 2005; owned by Kommersant Publishing House (Russia); in Russian; Dir-Gen. KAZBEK BEKTURSUNOV; Editor-in-Chief ANDREI VALILYEV.

Kyiv Post: 01133 Kyiv, vul. L. Ukrainky 34/501; tel. and fax (44) 496-11-11; e-mail editor@kyivpost.com; internet www.kyivpost.com; f. 1995; weekly, in English; Publr JED SUNDEN; Chief Editor ANDREY SLIVKA; circ. 25,000 (2003).

Literaturna Ukraina (Literary Ukraine): 01061 Kyiv, bulv. L. Ukrainky 20; tel. (44) 296-36-39; e-mail lit_ukraine@ukr.net; f. 1927; weekly; organ of Union of Writers of Ukraine; Editor PETRO PEREBYJNIS; circ. 6,340 (2004).

Molod Ukrainy (The Youth of Ukraine): 03047 Kyiv, pr. Peremohy 50; tel. (44) 454-83-83; fax (44) 235-31-52; e-mail mu@pressa.com.ua; f. 1925; 3 a week; Editor-in-Chief V. I. BODENCHUK; circ. 27,042 (2005).

News from Ukraine: Kyiv; tel. and fax (44) 244-58-45; f. 1964; weekly; in English, for an international audience; Editor VOLODYMYR KANASH.

Pravda Ukrainy (The Truth of Ukraine): 03047 Kyiv, pr. Peremohy 50; tel. (44) 441-85-34; f. 1938; deregistered Jan. 1998, re-registered Jan. 1999; 5 a week; in Russian; Editor-in-Chief OLHA PRONINA; circ. 40,000.

Robitnycha Hazeta/Rabochaya Gazeta (Workers' Gazette): 03047 Kyiv, pr. Peremohy 50; tel. (44) 441-83-33; fax (44) 446-68-85; f. 1957; 5 a week; publ. by the Cabinet of Ministers and Inter-regional Association of Manufacturers; editions in Russian and Ukrainian; Editor-in-Chief IVAN G. LITVIN; circ. 113,666 (2001).

Silski Visti (Rural News): 03047 Kyiv, pr. Peremohy 50; tel. (44) 441-86-32; fax (44) 446-93-71; e-mail silvis@visti.com; internet www.silskivisti.kiev.ua; f. 1920; 3 a week; Editor I. V. SPODARENKO; circ. 572,262 (2002).

Ukraina Moloda (Ukraine The Young): 03047 Kyiv, pr. Peremohy 50; tel. and fax (44) 454-83-92; e-mail post@umoloda.kiev.ua; 5 a week; independent; Editor MYKHAYLO DOROSHENKO; circ. 103,171 (2002).

Ukrainska Pravda (Ukrainian Truth): Kyiv; e-mail oradim@yahoo.com; internet www2.pravda.com.ua; online only; in English, Russian and Ukrainian; Editor-in-Chief OLENA PRYTULA.

Ukrainske Slovo (The Ukrainian Word): 01010 Kyiv, vul. Sichnevoho Povstannya 6; tel. (44) 280-17-30; fax (44) 280-70-59; e-mail info@ukrslovo.gu.ua; internet www.ukrslovo.com.ua; f. 1933; weekly; nationalist; Editor-in-Chief WOLODYMYR HAPTAR.

Uryadoviy Kuryer (Official Courier): 01008 Kyiv, vul. Sadova 1; tel. (44) 253-12-95; fax (44) 253-39-50; e-mail letter@ukcc.com.ua; internet www.ukcc.com.ua; f. 1990; 5 a week; organ of the Cabinet of Ministers; Editor-in-Chief MYKHAYLO M. SOROKA; circ. 125,000 (2002).

Vechirniy Kiev (Evening Kiev): 04136 Kyiv, vul. Marshala Hrechka 13; tel. (44) 434-61-09; fax (44) 443-96-09; e-mail office@vechirka.kiev.ua; internet www.vechirka.kiev.ua; f. 1906; 5 a week; Editor-in-Chief OLEKSANDR BALABKO; circ. 45,000 (2005).

Vlada i Polityka/Vlast i Politika (Power and Politics): 01042 Kyiv, vul. P. Lumumby 4v/200; tel. (44) 201-01-28; fax (44) 201-01-29; e-mail vip@vipnews.com.ua; internet www.vipnews.com.ua; f. 2001; weekly; in Ukrainian and Russian; Dir-Gen. ANDRIY V. NAKONECHNYI; Editor-in-Chief YURIY L. UZDEMYR; circ. 22,000 (2002).

Za Vilnu Ukrainu (For a Free Ukraine): 79000 Lviv, vul. Voronoho 3; tel. (322) 97-92-49; fax (322) 72-95-27; e-mail zwuky@mail.lviv.ua; f. 1990; 5 a week; independent; Editor-in-Chief MYKHAYLO SIRKIV; circ. 30,058 (2001).

PRINCIPAL PERIODICALS

Avto-Tsentr (Autocentre): 03047 Kyiv, pr. Peremohy 50, POB 2; tel. (44) 206-56-01; fax (44) 458-44-04; e-mail info@autocentre.ua; internet www.autocentre.ua; f. 1997; weekly; motoring; in Russian; Editor-in-Chief SERGEI TARNAVSKII; circ. 200,000.

Barvinok (Periwinkle): 04119 Kyiv, vul. Dekhtyarivska 38–44; tel. (44) 213-99-13; fax (44) 211-04-36; e-mail barvinok@kievweb.com.ua; f. 1928; fortnightly; illustrated popular fiction for school-age children; in Ukrainian; Editor VASYL VORONOVYCH; circ. 40,000.

Berezil: 61002 Kharkiv, vul. Chernyshevskoho 59; tel. (57) 700-32-23; fax (57) 700-54-37; f. 1956; fmrly Prapor; monthly; journal of Union of Writers of Ukraine; fiction and socio-political articles; Editor-in-Chief VOLODYMYR NAUMENKO; circ. 5,000.

Delovaya Stolitsya (Capital City Business): 01135 Kyiv, vul. Pavlovska 29; tel. (44) 461-91-32; fax (44) 461-91-40; e-mail dsnews@dsnews.com.ua; internet www.dsnews.com.ua; f. 2001; weekly; in Russian; Editor-in-Chief INNA KOVTUN; circ. 46,700 (2003).

Delovaya Ukraina (Business Ukraine): 01133 Kyiv, vul. Kutuzova 18/7/2; tel. and fax (44) 201-03-90; e-mail delukr@email.kiev.ua; internet www.delukr.kiev.ua; f. 1992; 2 a week; business issues; in Ukrainian and Russian; Editor ALLAL KOVTUM.

Dnipro (The Dnieper): 04119 Kyiv, vul. Dekhtyarivska 38–44; tel. (44) 446-11-42; f. 1927; 2 a month; novels, short stories, essays, poetry; social and political topics; Editor MYKOLA LUKIV.

Donbas/Donbass: 83055 Donetsk, vul. Artema 80A; tel. (622) 93-82-26; f. 1923; monthly; journal of Union of Writers of Ukraine; fiction; in Ukrainian and Russian; circ. 20,000 (1991).

Dzerkalo Tyzhnya/Zerkalo Nedyeli (Mirror of the Week): 03680 Kyiv, vul. Tverska 5; tel. (44) 536-02-44; fax (44) 269-74-52; e-mail info@mirror.kiev.ua; internet www.zerkalo-nedeli.com; weekly; politics, economics, the arts; Ukrainian and Russian edns; also English edition (online only); Editor-in-Chief VLADIMIR MOSTOVOI; circ. 30,000 (Russian edn), 12,000 (Ukrainian edn).

Dzvin (Bell): 79005 Lviv, vul. Kn. Romana 6; tel. (322) 72-36-20; f. 1940; monthly; journal of Union of Writers of Ukraine; fiction; Editor ROMAN FEDORIV; circ. 152,500.

Interesna Hazeta (Interesting Magazine): 03047 Kyiv, pr. Peremohy 50; tel. (44) 441-82-59; e-mail postmail@avkpress.kiev.ua; 2 a month; general; circ. 700,000.

Kompanyon (Companion): 01103 Kyiv, vul. Kykbydze 39; tel. (44) 494-25-01; fax (44) 494-25-05; e-mail komp@companion.ua; internet www.companion.ua; f. 1996; weekly; in Russian; economics, politics, business; Editor-in-Chief A. POHORELOV; circ. 25,000 (2004).

Kyiv: 01025 Kyiv, vul. Desyatinna 11; tel. (44) 229-02-80; f. 1983; monthly; journal of the Union of Writers of Ukraine and the Kyiv Writers' Organization; fiction; Editor-in-Chief PETRO M. PEREBYJNIS.

Malyatko (Child): 04119 Kyiv, vul. Dekhtyarivska 38–44; tel. and fax (44) 483-98-91; e-mail malyatko_1@online.com.ua; f. 1960; monthly; illustrated; for pre-school children; Editor-in-Chief ZINAIDA LESHENKO; circ. 35,780 (2005).

Nataly: 02156 Kyiv, vul. Kyoto 25; tel. (44) 519-34-33; fax (44) 518-77-90; internet www.nataly.com.ua; monthly; women's interest; Editor-in-Chief ZHANNA LAVROVA; circ. 679,115 (2002).

Natsionalna Bezpeka i Oborona (National Security and Defence): 01034 Kyiv, vul. Volodymyrska 46, Olekander Razumkov Ukrainian Centre for Economic and Political Studies; tel. (44) 201-11-98; fax (44) 201-11-99; e-mail info@uceps.com.ua; internet www.uceps.com.ua; f. 2000; monthly; politics, economics, international relations; in Ukrainian and English; Pres. ANATOLIY GRYTSENKO.

Obrazotvorche Mistetstvo (Fine Arts): 04655 Kyiv, vul. Sichovykh Striltsiv 1–5; tel. (44) 272-02-86; fax (44) 272-14-54; e-mail spilka@nbi.com.ua; f. 1933; 4 a year; publ. by the National Union of Artists of Ukraine; fine arts; Editor-in-Chief MYKOLA MARYCHEVSKIY; circ. 1,500.

Perets (Pepper): 03047 Kyiv, pr. Peremohy 50; tel. (44) 454-82-14; fax (44) 234-35-82; e-mail prudnyk@bigmir.net; f. 1922; monthly; publ. by the Presa Ukrainy Publishing House; satirical; Editor MYKHAYLO PRUDNYK; circ. 15,000 (2003).

Politychna Dumka/Politicheskaya Mysl/Political Thought: 01030 Kyiv, vul. Leontovycha 5; tel. and fax (44) 235-02-29; e-mail politdumka@bigmir.net; internet www.politdumka.kiev.ua; f. 1993; current affairs and political analysis; Ukrainian, Russian and English edns; Editor-in-Chief VOLODYMYR POLOKHALO.

Polityka i Chas/Politics and the Times: 02160 Kyiv, pr. Vozyednanya 15–17; tel. and fax (44) 550-31-44; e-mail times@uct.kiev.ua; f. 1994 to replace *Pid praporam Lenina* (Under the Banner of Lenin); monthly; organ of the Ministry of Foreign Affairs; international relations and foreign affairs; in Ukrainian (monthly) and English (quarterly); Editor-in-Chief LEONID BAIDAK; circ. 6,000 (2003).

Ukraina (Ukraine): 03047 Kyiv, pr. Peremohy 50; tel. and fax (44) 446-63-16; internet uamedia.visti.net/ukraine/; f. 1941; monthly;

UKRAINE

social and political life in Ukraine; illustrated; Editor-in-Chief YURIY PERESUNKO; circ. 70,000.

Ukraina Business (Ukraine Business): 01004 Kyiv, vul. Pushkinska 20/24; tel. and fax (44) 224-25-55; e-mail malva@ukrbus.kiev.ua; f. 1990; weekly; Editor-in-Chief YURIY VASYLCHUK; circ. 22,000 (2001).

Ukrainskiy Teatr (Ukrainian Theatre): Kyiv; tel. (44) 228-24-74; f. 1936; 6 a year; publ. by the Mistetstvo (Fine Art) Publishing House; journal of the Ministry of Art and Culture, and the Union of Theatrical Workers of Ukraine; Editor-in-Chief YURIY BOHDASHEVSKIY; circ. 4,100.

Visti z Ukrainy (News from Ukraine): 01034 Kyiv, vul. Zolotovoritska 6; tel. (44) 228-56-42; fax (44) 228-04-28; f. 1960; weekly; aimed at Ukrainian diaspora; Editor VALERIY STETSENKO; circ. 50,000.

Vitchyzna (Fatherland): 01021 Kyiv, vul. M. Hrushevskoho 34; tel. (44) 253-28-51; f. 1933; 6 a year; Ukrainian prose and poetry; Editor OLEKSANDR HLUSHKO; circ. 50,100.

Vsesvit (The Whole World): 01021 Kyiv, vul. M. Hrushevskoho 34/1; tel. (44) 253-13-18; fax (44) 253-06-13; e-mail myk@vsesvit-review.kiev.ua; internet www.vsesvit-journal.com; f. 1925; monthly; foreign fiction, critical works and reviews of foreign literature and art; Editor-in-Chief OLEH MYKYTENKO; circ. 3,000.

Yeva (Eve): 04050 Kyiv, vul. Melnykova 12A/8; tel. (44) 568-59-53; fax (44) 568-58-96; e-mail info@evamag.com; f. 1998; 6 a year; fashion, design; Editor-in-Chief IRYNA B. DANYLEVSKA; circ. 10,000 (2002).

Zhinka (Woman): 03047 Kyiv, pr. Peremohy 50; tel. and fax (44) 446-90-34; e-mail zhinka@cki.ipri.kiev.ua; f. 1920; monthly; publ. by Presa Ukrainy Publishing House; social and political subjects; fiction; for women; Editor LIDIYA MAZUR; circ. 250,000.

NEWS AGENCIES

Interfax-Ukraina (Interfax-Ukraine): 01034 Kyiv, vul. Reitarska 8/5 A; tel. (44) 464-04-65; fax (44) 464-05-69; e-mail news@interfax.kiev.ua; internet www.interfax.kiev.ua; f. 1992; Dir OLEKSANDR MARTYNENKO.

Respublika Ukrainian Independent Information Agency (UNIAR): 02005 Kyiv, vul. Mechnykova 14/1; tel. (44) 246-46-34; e-mail naboka@uniar.kiev.ua; internet www.uniar.com.ua; independent press agency; Dir S. NABOKA.

Ukrainian Independent Information and News Agency (UNIAN): 01001 Kyiv, vul. Khreshchatyk 4; tel. (44) 229-33-53; fax (44) 461-91-11; e-mail info@unian.net; internet www.unian.net; f. 1993; press agency and monitoring service; selected services are provided in Ukrainian, Russian and English; Gen. Dir OLEH I. NALIVAIKO; Editor-in-Chief OLEKSANDR A. KHARCHENKO.

Ukrainski Novyni Informatsyonnoye Ahentstvo (Ukrainian News Information Agency): 01033 Kyiv, vul. Volodymyrska 61/11/41; tel. (44) 494-31-60; fax (44) 494-31-67; e-mail office@ukranews.com; internet www.ukranews.com; f. 1993; economic and political news; in Ukrainian, Russian and English.

UkrInform–Ukrainian National Information Agency: 01001 Kyiv, vul. B. Khmelnytskoho 8/16B; tel. (44) 229-22-42; fax (44) 229-81-52; e-mail chiefadm@ukrinform.com; internet www.dinau.com; f. 1918; until 1990 Ukrainian branch of TASS (State Information Agency of the Soviet Union).

Foreign Bureaux

Agenzia Nazionale Stampa Associata (ANSA) (Italy): Kyiv, vul. Chitadelna 5–9/45; tel. and fax (44) 290-21-38; internet www.ansa.it; Correspondent ALESSANDRO PARONE.

Česká tisková kancelář (ČTK) (Czech Republic): 01042 Kyiv, vul. I. Kudri 41/22/49; tel. and fax (44) 295-91-61; internet www.ctk.cz.

Deutsche Presse-Agentur (dpa) (Germany): 01001 Kyiv, vul. Khreshchatyk 29/32; tel. (44) 225-57-60; internet www.dpa.de.

Magyar Távirati Iroda (MTI) (Hungary): 01030 Kyiv, vul. Ivana Franka 24A/8; tel. and fax (44) 235-62-04; e-mail mti@gu.kiev.ua; internet www.mti.ua; Correspondent KATALIN BENKONE OZE.

Reuters (United Kingdom): 01001 Kyiv, vul. B. Khmelnytskoho 8–16/112; tel. (44) 244-91-50; fax (44) 244-91-53; e-mail kiev.newsroom@reuters.com; internet www.reuters.com; Chief Correspondent T. RODDAM.

RIA—Novosti (Russian Information Agency—News); Russia: 03150 Kyiv, vul. V. Vasylivska 134/49; tel. and fax (44) 434-48-45.

Publishers

In 1996 there were 6,460 book titles (including pamphlets and brochures) published in Ukraine (total circulation 50.9m.). By 2004 the number of book titles published in Ukraine had increased to 14,790.

Budivelnik (Builder): 04053 Kyiv, vul. Observatorna 25; tel. (44) 212-10-90; f. 1947; books on building and architecture; in Ukrainian and Russian; Dir S. N. BALATSKII.

Dnipro (The Dnieper): 01034 Kyiv, vul. Volodymyrska 42; tel. (44) 224-31-82; e-mail dnipro-pbl@svitonline.com; internet www.dnipro-publ.kiev.ua; f. 1919; classics, fiction, art and popular editions, in Ukrainian and Russian; Dir TARAS I. SERGIYCHUK.

Donbas/Donbass: 83002 Donetsk, vul. B. Khmelnytskoho 102; tel. (622) 93-25-84; fiction and criticism; in Ukrainian and Russian; Dir B. F. KRAVCHENKO.

Folio: Kharkiv; tel. and fax (572) 47-61-25; e-mail foliosp@kharkov.ukrpack.net; internet folio.com.ua; f. 1992; classic and contemporary fiction in Russian, Ukrainian and French; Gen. Man. ALEKSANDR V. KRASOVITSKII.

Kamenyar (Stonecrusher): 79000 Lviv, vul. Pidvalna 3; tel. (322) 72-19-49; fax (322) 72-19-49; e-mail vyd_kamenyar@mail.lviv.ua; fiction and criticism; in Ukrainian; Dir DMYTRO I. SAPIGA.

Karpaty (The Carpathians): 88000 Transcarpathian obl., Uzhhorod, Radyanska pl. 3; tel. (312) 23-25-13; fiction and criticism; in Ukrainian and Russian; Dir V. I. DANKANICH.

Konsum: 61057 Kharkiv, POB 9123; tel. (572) 17-01-19; fax (572) 23-76-75; e-mail book@konsum.kharkov.ua; internet konsum.kharkov.ua; politics, economics, human rights, legal and medical books.

Lybid (Swan): 01001 Kyiv, vul. Pushkinska 32; tel. (44) 228-10-93; fax (44) 229-11-71; e-mail info@lybid.org.ua; internet www.lybid.org.ua; f. 1835; University of Kyiv press; Dir OLENA A. BOIKO.

Mayak (Beacon): 65026 Odesa, vul. Zhukovskoho 14; tel. and fax (482) 22-35-95; e-mail majak@farlep.net; fiction and criticism; in Ukrainian and Russian; Dir D. A. BUKHANENKO.

Medytsyna Svitu (Medicines of the World): 79071 Lviv, vul. Kulparkivska 131; tel. (32) 263-34-65; fax (32) 297-80-49; e-mail msvitu@mail.lviv.ua; internet www.msvitu.lviv.ua; f. 1997; medical journals and books, books pertaining to history, art and religion; Dirs VOLODYMYR PAVLIUK, ZENON MATCHAK.

Mystetstvo: 01034 Kyiv, vul. Zolotovoritska 11; tel. (44) 235-53-92; fax (44) 279-05-64; e-mail mystetstvo@ukr.net; f. 1932; fine art criticism, theatre and screen art, tourism, Ukrainian culture; in Ukrainian, Russian, English, French and German; Dir NINA PRYBEHA.

Molod (Youth): 04119 Kyiv, vul. Dekhtyarivska 38–44; tel. (44) 213-11-60; fax (44) 213-11-92; in Ukrainian; Dir O. I. POLONSKA.

Muzichna Ukraina (Musical Ukraine): 01034 Kyiv, vul. Pushkinska 32; tel. (44) 225-63-56; fax (44) 224-63-00; f. 1966; books on music; in Ukrainian; Dir N. P. LINNIK; Editor-in-Chief B. R. VERESHCHAGIN.

Naukova Dumka (Scientific Thought): 01601 Kyiv, vul. Tereshchenkivska 3; tel. (44) 234-40-68; fax (44) 234-70-60; e-mail ndumka@i.kiev.ua; internet www.ndumka.kiev.ua; f. 1922; scientific books and periodicals in all branches of science; research monographs; Ukrainian literature; dictionaries and reference books; in Ukrainian, Russian and English; Dir I. R. ALEKSEYENKO.

Osvita (Education): 04053 Kyiv, vul. Yu. Kotsyubynski 5; tel. and fax (44) 216-54-44; e-mail osvita@kv.ukrtel.net; internet www.osvitapublish.com.ua; f. 1920; state-owned; educational books for schools of all levels; Dir-Gen. IRAYIDA PODOLYUK.

Prapor (Flag): 61002 Kharkiv, vul. Chubarya 11; tel. (572) 47-72-52; fax (572) 43-07-21; fmrly Berezil; general; in Ukrainian and Russian; Dir V. S. LEBETS.

Prosvita (Enlightenment): 01032 Kyiv, bulv. Shevchenka 46; tel. (44) 234-15-86; fax (44) 234-95-23; e-mail office@prosvita.kiev.ua; internet www.prosvita.kiev.ua; f. 1990; textbooks for all levels of education from pre-school to higher education.

Rodovid: 01001 Kyiv, POB 548; tel. and fax (44) 220-48-29; e-mail rodovid@ln.ua; internet www.rodovid.net; history, ethnography, poetry, cultural history.

Sich (Camp): 49070 Dnipropetrovsk, pr. K. Marksa 60; tel. (562) 45-22-01; fax (562) 45-44-04; f. 1964; fiction, juvenile, socio-political, criticism; in Ukrainian, English, German, French and Russian; Dir V. A. SIROTA; Editor-in-Chief V. V. LEVCHENKO.

Tavria: 95000 Crimea, Simferopol, vul. Gorkogo 5; tel. (652) 27-45-66; fax (652) 27-65-74; e-mail ingvi@ukr.net; fiction, criticism, folklore and geography; in Ukrainian, Russian and Crimean Tatar; Dir Y. IVANICHENKO.

Tekhnika (Technologyi): Kyiv; tel. (44) 228-22-43; f. 1930; industry and transport books, popular science, posters and booklets; in Ukrainian and Russian; Dir M. G. PISARENKO.

Tsentr Yevropy (The Centre of Europe): 79000 Lviv, vul. Kostyushko 18/317; tel. (322) 72-35-66; fax (322) 72-76-71; e-mail centrevr@is.lviv.ua; internet www.centrevr@is.lviv.ua; f. 1994;

books related to the history and culture of Halychyna (Galicia); Dir SERHIY E. FRUKHT.

Ukraina: 01054 Kyiv, vul. Hoholivska 7H; tel. (44) 216-36-02; fax (44) 216-97-35; e-mail ua@alfacom.net; internet www.ua.alfacom.net; f. 1922; humanities, science, reference and literary works; Dir MYKOLA V. STETYUHA; Editor-in-Chief OLEKSANDR P. KOSYUK.

Ukrainska Ensyklopedia (Ukrainian Encyclopedia): 01030 Kyiv, vul. B. Khmelnytskoho 51; tel. (44) 224-80-85; encyclopedias, dictionaries and reference books; Dir A. V. KUDRITSKIY.

Ukrainskiy Pysmennyk (Ukrainian Writer): 01054 Kyiv, vul. O. Honshara 52; tel. (44) 486-25-92; e-mail ukps@ln.ua; f. 1933; publishing house of the National Union of Writers of Ukraine; fiction; in Ukrainian; Dir A. O. SAVCHUK.

Urozhai (Harvest): 03035 Kyiv, vul. Uritskoho 45; tel. (44) 220-16-26; f. 1925; books and journals about agriculture; Dir V. G. PRIKHODKO.

Veselka (Rainbow): 04050 Kyiv, vul. Melnikova 63; tel. (44) 213-95-01; fax (44) 213-33-59; e-mail veskiev@iptelecom.net.ua; f. 1934; books for pre-school and school-age children; in Ukrainian and foreign languages; Dir YAREMA HOYAN.

Vyscha Shkola (High School): 01054 Kyiv, vul. Hoholivska 7; tel. and fax (44) 216-33-05; f. 1968; educational, scientific, reference, etc.; Dir V. P. KHOVKHUN; Editor-in-Chief V. V. PIVEN.

Zdorovya (Health): 01054 Kyiv, vul. O. Honshara 65; tel. (44) 216-89-08; books on medicine, physical fitness and sport; in Ukrainian; Dir A. P. RODZIYEVSKIY.

Znannya (Knowledge): 01034 Kyiv, vul. Striletska 28; tel. (44) 234-80-43; fax (44) 238-82-65; e-mail znannia@society.kiev.ua; internet www.znannia.com.ua; f. 1948; general non-fiction; Dir VOLODYMYR KARASOV.

Broadcasting and Communications

TELECOMMUNICATIONS

Regulatory Authorities

State Committee for Communication and Information: 01001 Kyiv, vul. Khreshchatyk 22; tel. (44) 228-15-00; fax (44) 228-61-41; e-mail mailbox@stc.gov.ua; internet www.stc.gov.ua; Chair. IHOR V. KRAVETS.

Major Service Providers

Astelit: 03110 Kyiv, vul. Solomyanska 11 A; internet www.life.com.ua; f. 2005; 51% owned by TurkCell (Turkey); provides mobile cellular telecommunications services under the brand name 'Life'.

Golden Telecom GSM: 01021 Kyiv, vul. Mechnikova 14/1; tel. (44) 247-56-65; internet www.goldentele.com; mobile cellular telephone services; Gen. Man. YURIY BEZBORODIV.

KyivStar GSM: Kyiv, vul. Sichnevoho Povstannya 24; tel. (44) 466-04-66; internet www.kyivstar.net; f. 1997; 54.2% owned by Telenor (Norway); provides mobile cellular telecommunications services under the brand names 'Ace & Base' and 'Djuice' in major cities and other regions across Ukraine; Pres. IHOR LITOVCHENKO; 15.1m. subscribers (May 2006).

Ukrainian Mobile Communications: 01010 Kyiv, vul. Moskovska 21; tel. (44) 311-95-59; fax (44) 314-22-48; e-mail slavik@umc.com.ua; internet www.umc.com.ua; f. 1991; 51% owned by Ukrtelecom; Deutsche Telekom AG (Germany), TDC Tele Danmark (Denmark) and Royal KPN NV (Netherlands) each own 16.3% of shares; operates mobile cellular telephone network under the brand names 'Jeans (Dzhyns)', SimSim' and 'UMC'; Gen. Man. MARTIN DIRKS; 10.5m. subscribers (Aug. 2005).

UkrTelecom: 01030 Kyiv, bulv. Shevchenka 18; tel. (44) 226-25-41; fax (44) 234-39-57; e-mail ukrtelecom@ukrtelecom.net; internet www.ukrtelecom.ua; f. 1993; national fixed telecommunications network operator; provides national and international telecommunications services; Chair. of Bd HEORHIY B. DZEKON.

BROADCASTING

Regulatory Authorities

State Committee for Television and Radio Broadcasting (Derzhavnyi komitet telebachennya i radiomovlennya Ukrainy): 01001 Kyiv, vul. Khreshchatyk 26/206; tel. (44) 239-63-89; internet comin.kmu.gov.ua; responsibilities include the supervision of 27 state-controlled television and radio companies; Chair. IVAN S. CHYZH.

National Council of Ukraine for Television and Radio Broadcasting: 01025 Kyiv, vul. Desyatynna 14; tel. (44) 228-74-11; fax (44) 228-75-75; e-mail tvr@i.com.ua; internet www.nradatvr.kiev.ua; f. 1994; monitoring and supervisory functions; issues broadcasting licences; Chair. BORYS KHOLOD.

Radio

Ukrainian State Television and Radio Co (Derzhavna Teleradiomovna Kompaniya Ukrainy): 01001 Kyiv, vul. Khreshchatyk 26; Chair. ZYNOVIY V. KULYK.

Hromadske (Community) Radio: Kyiv, vul. Volodymyrska 61/11/50; tel. (44) 494-40-14; e-mail roman@radio.org.ua; internet www.radio.org.ua; information, news and discussion programmes; Pres. (vacant).

National Radio Co of Ukraine-Ukrainian Radio (Natsionalna Radiokompaniya Ukrainy-Ukrainske Radio): 01001 Kyiv, vul. Khreshchatyk 26; tel. (44) 279-33-79; fax (44) 279-34-77; e-mail krutouz@nrcu.gov.ua.

Radio Ukraine International: 01001 Kyiv, vul. Khreshchatyk 26; tel. (44) 229-45-86; e-mail vsru@nrcu.gov.ua; internet www.nrcu.gov.ua; broadcasts in English, German, Romanian and Ukrainian; Pres. VIKTOR I. NABRUSKO; Dir OLEKSANDR DYKYS.

There were, in addition, several independent radio stations broadcasting to the major cities of Ukraine.

Television

Ukrainian State Television and Radio Co (Derzhavna Teleradiomovna Kompaniya Ukrainy): see Radio (above); Chair. of Television OLEKSANDR M. SAVENKO.

1+1: 01001 Kyiv, vul. Khreshchatyk 7/11; tel. and fax (44) 490-01-01; e-mail contact@1plus1.tv; internet www.1plus1.tv; f. 1995; independent; broadcasts for 24 hours daily to 95% of Ukrainian population; Chair. of Bd of Dirs OLEKSANDR YU. RODNYANSKY.

5 Kanal: 04176 Kyiv, vul. Elektrykiv 26; tel. (44) 239-16-86; internet 5.ua; terrestrial broadcasts to 14 cities, and cable and satellite broadcasts; 24-hour news broadcasts; Dir-Gen. IVAN ADAMCHUK.

Inter: 01601 Kyiv, vul. Dmitriyevska 30; tel. and fax (44) 490-67-65; e-mail pr@inter.ua; internet www.inter.kiev.ua; f. 1996.

Novy Kanal (New Channel): 04107 Kyiv, vul. Nahorna 24/1; tel. (44) 238-80-28; fax (44) 238-80-20; e-mail post@novy.tv; internet www.novy.tv; f. 1998; broadcasts in Ukrainian and Russian; Chair. OLEKSANDR M. TKACHENKO.

Pershyi Natsionalnyi (First National): 04119 Kyiv, vul. Melnykova 42; tel. (44) 241-39-09; fax (44) 246-88-48; e-mail office@firstnational.kiev.ua; internet www.ntu.org.ua; state-owned.

STB: 03113 Kyiv, vul. Shevtsova 1; tel. (44) 501-98-99; e-mail y@stb.ua; internet stb.ua; Dirs VLAD STAROVOYTOV, KYRYL BYSTRYAKOV.

Finance

(cap. = capital; res = reserves; dep. = deposits; brs = branches; m. = million; amounts in hryvnyas, unless otherwise indicated)

In June 2004 there were 158 banks registered in Ukraine, of which two were state-owned, and 18 were majority or wholly foreign-owned. Some 127 of the banks had assets worth less than US $150m., and the largest 25 banks accounted for 72.3% of the total banking assets.

BANKING

Central Bank

National Bank of Ukraine: 01008 Kyiv, vul. Institutska 9; tel. (44) 253-44-78; fax (44) 230-20-33; e-mail postmaster@bank.gov.ua; internet www.bank.gov.ua; f. 1991; cap. 10m., res 4,575m., dep. 9,820m. (Dec. 2003); Gov. VOLODYMYR S. STELMAKH.

Other State Banks

Republican Bank of Crimea: 95000 Crimea, Simferopol, ul. Gorkogo; tel. (652) 51-09-46; e-mail webmaster@rbc.crimea.ua.

UkrExImBank—State Export-Import Bank of Ukraine: 03150 Kyiv, vul. Horkoho 127; tel. (44) 247-80-70; fax (44) 247-80-82; e-mail bank@eximb.com; internet www.eximb.com; f. 1992; fmrly br. of USSR Vneshekonombank (External Trade Bank); cap. 909.2, dep. 2,651.0m., total assets 2,937.2m. (Dec. 2002); Chair. of Bd OLEKSANDR N. SOROKIN; 29 brs.

Commercial Banks

AVAL Bank: 01011 Kyiv, vul. Leskova 9; tel. (44) 490-88-01; fax (44) 490-87-55; e-mail info@aval.ua; internet www.aval.ua; f. 1992; acquired by Raiffeisen International Bank AG (Austria) in 2005; cap. US $187.6m., net assets $2,131.3m. (July 2004); Pres. FEDIR I. SHPIG; Chair. of Bd OLEKSANDR V. DERKACH; 1,381 brs.

Bank Pekao (Ukraine): 43016 Volyn obl., Lutsk, vul. Halytskoho 14; tel. (332) 77-62-10; fax (332) 72-03-57; e-mail pekao@pekao.com

.ua; internet www.pekao.com.ua; f. 1997; present name adopted 2000; 100% owned by Polish interests; cap. 22.5m., res 1.7m., dep. 8.7m. (Dec. 1999); Chair. of Bd JANUSZ DEDO.

BIG-Energiya (BIG-Energy): 01032 Kyiv, vul. Kominterna 15; tel. (44) 256-59-42; fax 246-63-32; e-mail inter@bigenergy.com.ua; internet www.bigenergy.com.ua; f. 1993 as ZEVS; present name adopted 2001; cap. 100.0m., res 24.5m., dep. 320.2m. (Dec. 2002); Chair. of Council ALESKANDR V. SAGURA; Chair. of Bd VIKTOR V. STETSENKO.

Brokbiznesbank: 03057 Kyiv, pr. Peremohy 41; tel. (44) 231-18-60; fax (44) 459-67-80; e-mail bank@bankbb.com; internet www.bankbb.com; f. 1991; cap. 70.5m., res 59.7m., dep. 916.6m. (Dec. 2002); Chair. of Council VLADIMIR STELMAH; Chair. of Bd SERGEI P. MISHTA.

Calyon Bank Ukraine: 01034 Kyiv, vul. Volodymyrska 23A; tel. (44) 490-14-01; fax (44) 490-14-02; e-mail jacques.mounier@ua.calyon.com; internet www.creditlyonnais.kiev.ua; f. 1993; fmrly Crédit Lyonnais Bank Ukraine, present name adopted 2004; cap. 31.2m., res 13.7m., dep. 402.5m. (Dec. 2003); Chair. HERVÉ LEQUITTE; Dir-Gen. JACQUES MOUNIER.

Crimea-Bank: 95000 Crimea, Simferopol, vul. Krylova 37; tel. (652) 27-04-76; fax (652) 27-04-56.

Donghorbank: 83086 Donetsk, vul. Artema 38; tel. and fax (62) 332-73-24; e-mail pr_financing@dongorbank.com; internet www.dongorbank.com; f. 1992; present name adopted 2002; cap. 202.2m., dep. 666.5m., total assets 1014.94m. (July 2004); Head of Supervisory Bd MAXIM TIMCHENKO; Head of Management Bd VLADIMIR POPOVICH.

EnergoBank: 01001 Kyiv, vul. Luteranska 9/9; tel. (44) 201-69-02; fax (44) 228-39-54; e-mail bank@energobank.com.ua; internet www.energobank.com.ua; f. 1991; cap. 26.5m., res 6.2m., dep. 226.9m. (July 2004); Chief Officer VITALIY MYGASHKO; 9 brs.

Fiatbank: 29000 Khmelnytsky, vul. Proskurovska 19; tel. (382) 26-47-18; fax (382) 226-91-18; Gen. Dir VALERIY BEZVERKHNIY.

Finance and Credit Bank: 04050 Kyiv, vul. Sichovykh Striltsiv 60; tel. (44) 490-68-70; fax (44) 238-24-65; e-mail common@fc.kiev.ua; internet www.fc.kiev.ua; f. 1990; present name adopted 1995; cap. 54.6m., res 28.5m., dep. 861.4m. (Dec. 2002); Chair. VLADIMIR G. KHLYVNYUK; 11 brs.

First Ukrainian International Bank/Pershyi Ukrainskyi Mizhnarodnyi Bank (FUIB): 83000 Donetsk, vul. Universitetska 2A; tel. (623) 32-45-03; fax (623) 32-47-00; e-mail info@fuib.com; internet www.fuib.com; f. 1991; 48.99% owned by AzovStal Iron and Steel Works, 20% by Fortis Bank (Netherlands); cap. US $29.2m., res $18.3m., dep. $177.8m. (Dec. 2003); Chair. of Council IRVING KUCZYNSKI; Chair. of Bd A. I. DOVGOPOLYUK (acting).

Inko Joint-Stock Bank: 01021 Kyiv, vul. Mechnikova 18; tel. (44) 573-92-19; fax (44) 293-87-90.

Inprombank (Innovational-Industrial Bank): 61003 Kharkiv, vul. Klochkivska 3; tel. (572) 23-58-68; fax (57) 719-19-79; e-mail bank@inprombank.ua; internet www.inprombank.ua; f. 1992; fmrly Ukrainian Bank for Trade Co-operation (Bank Torhovoho Spivrobitnytstva); present name adopted 2003; cap. 8.2m., res 0.2m., dep. 10.6m. (Jan. 2004); Pres. OLEG TOKAR; Chair. of Bd VIKTOR STEPHANIV; 3 brs.

Khreshchatyk Bank: 01001 Kyiv, vul. Khreshchatyk 8A; tel. and fax (44) 464-12-28; e-mail bank@xbank.com.ua; internet www.xcitybank.com.ua; f. 1993; present name adopted 1998; 51% owned by Central Financial Dept of Kyiv City State Administration; cap. 140.0m., total assets 1,820.6m. (July 2005); Chair. of Bd DMYTRO M. GRYDZHYK; 51 brs.

Kredyt Bank (Ukraina): 79026 Lviv, vul. Sakharova 78; tel. (322) 97-23-20; fax (322) 97-08-37; e-mail office@wucb.lviv.net; internet www.kredytbank.com.ua; f. 1990; fmrly West Ukrainian Commercial Bank—Zakhidno-Ukrainskyi Komertsiinyi Bank; present name adopted 2001; 66.7% owned by PKO Bank Polski SA (Poland), 28.25% owned by European Bank for Reconstruction and Development (United Kingdom); cap. 143.4m., res −19.4m., dep. 720.0m. (Dec. 2002); Chair. STEPAN I. KUBIV.

Kredytprombank: 01014 Kyiv, bulv. Druzhby Narodiv 38; tel. and fax (44) 490-27-79; fax (44) 490-72-28; e-mail kpb@kreditprombank.com; internet www.kreditprombank.com; f. 1997, as Inkombank-Ukraina; present name adopted 1999; 49.6% owned by Homerton Trading Ltd (Ireland); cap. 136.2m., res 1.5m., dep. 1,026.2m. (Dec. 2003); Chair. of Bd NIKOLAI P. ROZHKO; Chief Exec. LYUDMILA V. RASPUTNA.

Legbank: 01033 Kyiv, vul. Zhylyanska 27; tel. (44) 227-95-00; fax (44) 227-95-19; e-mail legbank@legbank.kiev.ua; internet www.legbank.kiev.ua; f. 1989; 11 brs.

Lesbank: 88000 Transcarpathian obl., Uzhhorod, vul. Voloshina 52; tel. (312) 23-31-01; fax (312) 23-25-04; Pres. and Chair. VASYLIY D. SIVULYA.

Megabank: 61002 Kharkiv, vul. Artema 30; tel. (572) 14-33-63; fax (572) 47-20-79; e-mail mega@megabank.net; internet www.megabank.net; f. 1990; present name adopted 2001; cap. 34.9m., res 24.3m., dep. 333.4m. (Dec. 2003); Chair. of Bd VIKTOR G. SUBOTIN; Pres. OLEKSIY S. LOHVINENKO; 8 brs.

Mriya Bank: 01601 Kyiv, vul. Hoholevska 22–24; tel. (44) 216-04-90; e-mail post@mriya.com; internet www.mriya.com; f. 1992; cap. 60.8m., res 36.5m., dep. 678.8m. (Jan. 2005); Chair. of Bd KONSTANTIN VORUSHILIN; 20 brs.

Nadra Bank: 04053 Kyiv, vul. Sichovykh Striltsiv 15; tel. (44) 238-84-00; fax (44) 246-48-40; e-mail pr@nadrabank.kiev.ua; internet www.nadra.com.ua; f. 1993; cap. 221.1m., res 128.3m. (Jan. 2003); Pres. IGOR V. GILENKO; 152 brs.

Pivdennyi Bank (Southern Bank): 65014 Odesa, Sabanskii per. 2; tel. (482) 34-43-98; fax (482) 34-75-56; e-mail daa@pivdenny.odessa.ua; f. 1993; cap. 108.9m., dep. 1,029.0m., total assets 1,167.2m. (Dec. 2003); Chair. of Bd and Dir-Gen. VADYM V MOROKHOVSKIY; 4 brs.

Praveks-Bank: 01021 Kyiv, uzviz Klovskyi 9/2; tel. (44) 294-81-80; fax (44) 294-81-03; e-mail bank@pravex.com; internet www.pravex.com; f. 1992; cap. 60.0m., res 11.9m., dep. 799.1m. (Dec. 2002); Chair. of Council LEONID CHERNOVETSKIY; Chair. of Bd ANATOLIY KHILCHEVSKIY; 300 brs and sub-brs.

Premierbank: 49000 Dnipropetrovsk, vul. Mechnykova 18; tel. (56) 770-44-00; fax (56) 770-02-71; e-mail post@premierbank.dp.ua; internet www.premierbank.dp.ua; f. 1994; present name adopted 1999; cap. 45.0m., res 13.3m., dep. 189.5m. (Dec. 2002); Pres. VOLODYMYR M. HAVRYLOV; Chair. of Bd IGOR N. FOMIN; 5 brs.

PrivatBank: 49094 Dnipropetrovsk, nab. Peremohy 50; tel. (562) 39-05-11; fax (56) 778-54-74; e-mail privatbank@pbank.dp.ua; internet www.privatbank.com.ua; cap. 513.3m., res 61.0m., dep. 5,336.0m. (Dec. 2002); Chair. of Supervisory Council GENNADII BOGOLYUBOV; Chair. of Bd ALEXANDER DUBILET.

Prominvestbank (Industrial-Investment Bank): 01001 Kyiv, prov. Shevchenka 12; tel. (44) 201-51-20; fax (44) 201-50-44; e-mail bank@pib.com.ua; internet www.pib.com.ua; f. 1922 as Stroibank, name changed 1992; cap. 1,368.2m., total assets 14,590.3m. (Dec. 2005); Chair. VOLODYMYR P. MATVYENKO; 600 brs.

Raiffeisenbank Ukraine: 01033 Kyiv, vul. Zhylyanska 43; tel. (44) 490-05-00; fax (44) 490-05-01; e-mail infobox.rbu@rbu-kiev.raiffeisen.at; internet www.raiffeisenbank.com.ua; f. 1998; 100% owned by Austrian interests; cap. 166.2m., res 2.4m., dep. 2,495.7m. (Dec. 2003); Chair. of Bd IHOR FRANTSKEVYCH.

Real Bank: 61200 Kharkiv, pr. Lenina 60A; tel. (57) 333-27-14; fax (57) 333-31-06; e-mail bank@realbank.com.ua; internet www.realbank.com.ua; f. 1990; cap. 50.3m., dep. 53.5m., total assets 179.3m. (Jan. 2005); Chair. YURIY M. SHRAMKO; 3 brs and sub-brs.

Rodovid Bank: 04070 Kyiv, vul. P. Sahaidachniy 17; tel. (44) 255-86-47; fax (44) 255-86-54; e-mail info@rodovidbank.com; internet www.rodovidbank.com; f. 1990; fmrly Perkom—Personal Computer Bank; cap. 100.0m., res 57.2m., dep. 259.0m. (Jan. 2005); Chair. of Bd DENIS V. GORBUNENKO; 2 brs.

Rostok Bank: 03680 Kyiv, bulv. I. Lepse 4; tel. (44) 484-50-35; fax (44) 488-74-21; e-mail rostok_bank@svitonline.com; internet www.rostok-bank.kiev.ua; f. 1994; cap. US $3.4m., res $0.8m., dep. $2.6m. (Dec. 2002); Pres. IHOR MASOL; Chair. ANATOLIY KOSMIN; 3 brs.

Skhidno-Yevropeyskiy Bank (East European Bank): 01042 Kyiv, bulv. Druzhby Narodiv 17/5; tel. (44) 205-42-70; fax (44) 205-42-78; e-mail eebank@eebank.com.ua; internet www.eebank.com.ua; f. 1993; present name adopted 1998; cap. 40.0m., res 3.5m., dep. 199.1m. (Dec. 2004); Pres. MYKHAYLO HONCHAROV; Dir-Gen. VALERIY NOSOVETS; 31 brs and 3 sub-brs.

Tavrika Bank: 99028 Sevastopol, ul. Repina 1; tel. and fax (692) 45-41-46; e-mail oleg@tavrika.com; internet www.tavrika.com; f. 1991; cap. 60.5m., res 6.3m., dep. 246.9m. (Feb. 2004); Chair. of Bd SERGEI A. BOGATYREV; 10 brs.

Transbank: 03150 Kyiv, vul. Fizkultury 9; tel. (44) 227-27-83; fax (44) 220-45-88; e-mail common@transbank.kiev.ua; internet www.transbank.kiev.ua; f. 1991; cap. 25.0m., res 3.8m., dep. 35.7m. (Dec. 2002); Pres. RUSTEM VALEYEV; Chair. of Bd MYKOLA LASKOV (acting); 3 brs.

Ukrainian Credit Bank: 03056 Kyiv, pr. Peremohy 37; tel. (44) 236-96-31; fax (44) 230-23-86; e-mail roleg@viaduk.net; internet www.ucb.com.ua; f. 1992; cap. 28.2m., res 29.4m., dep. 501.2m. (Dec. 2002); Pres. VALENTIN A. ZHURSKIY; 1 br..

Ukrainian Innovation Bank—Ukrinbank: 04053 Kyiv, vul. Smirnova-Lastochkina 10A; tel. (44) 247-20-02; fax (44) 247-21-18; e-mail ukrinbank@ukrinbank.com; internet www.ukrinbank.com; f. 1989; long-term investment credits; commercial and foreign exchange transactions; cap. 40.0m., res 49.6m., dep. 429.5m. (Dec. 2003); Chair. SERHIY MESCHERYAK; 29 brs.

UkrGazPromBank: 02098 Kyiv, Dniprovska nab. 13; tel. (44) 553-65-45; fax (44) 553-29-39; e-mail ukrgazprombank@ugpb.com;

UKRAINE

internet www.ugpb.com; f. 1996; cap. 34.7m., res 44.1m., dep. 172.0m. (Dec. 2003); Chair. LEONID STOVBCHATII.

UkrSibbank: 04070 Kyiv, vul. Andriyevksa 2/12; tel. (572) 23-04-90; fax (572) 23-08-88; e-mail office@ukrsibbank.com; internet www.ukrsibbank.com; f. 1990; present name adopted 1992; commercial and investment banking, non-banking financial services; cap. 1,543.7m. (Dec. 2004), res 13.0m., dep. 3,251.2m. (Dec. 2003); Chair. of Bd OLEKSANDR E. ADARYCH; 646 brs and sub-brs.

UkrSotsBank—Bank for Social Development: 03150 Kyiv, vul. Kovpak 29; tel. (44) 230-32-24; fax (44) 230-32-23; e-mail info@ukrsotsbank.com; internet www.usb.com.ua; f. 1990; cap. US $106m., res $90m., dep. $825m. (July 2004); Chair. of Supervisory Council VALERIY KHOROSHKOVSKIY; Chair. of Bd BORIS TIMONKIN; over 500 brs.

VA Bank-Vseukrainsky Aktsionerny Bank (All-Ukrainian Share Bank): 04119 Kyiv, vul. Zoolohichna 5; tel. (44) 490-06-09; fax (44) 216-00-33; e-mail bank@vabank.ua; internet www.vabank.ua; f. 1992; cap. 108.4m., res 25.1m., dep. 320.6m. (Sept. 2003); Pres. SERHIY MAKSIMOV; Chair. YURIY BLASHCHUK; 7 brs.

Savings Bank

State Savings Bank of Ukraine—Oschadbank (Derzhavnyi Oshchadnyi Bank Ukrainy): 01023 Kyiv, vul. Hospitalna 12 H; tel. (44) 247-85-69; fax (44) 247-85-68; internet www.oschadnybank.com; f. 1922; cap. 100m., res 117m., dep. 1,705m. (April 2001); Pres. ANDRIY PYSHNIY (acting).

Banking Association

Association of Ukrainian Banks (Asotsiatsiya Ukrainskykh Bankiv): 02002 Kyiv, vul. M. Raskova 15/703; tel. (44) 516-87-75; fax (44) 516-87-76; e-mail aub@carrier.kiev.ua; internet www.aub.com.ua; fmrly Commercial Bank Asscn; Pres. OLEKSANDR SUGONIAKO.

COMMODITY EXCHANGES

Carpathian Commodity Exchange: 78200 Ivano-Frankivsk obl., Kolomiya, vul. Vahylevycha 1, POB 210; tel. and fax (343) 32-19-61; f. 1996; Gen. Man. IVAN P. VATUTIN.

Crimea Universal Exchange: 95050 Crimea, Simferopol, vul. L. Chaikinoy 1/421; tel. (652) 22-04-32; fax (652) 22-12-73; f. 1923 as Simferopol Commodity Exchange; present name adopted 1991; Pres. NATALIYA S. SYUMAK.

Dnipro (Pridniprovska) Commodity Exchange: 49094 Dnipropetrovsk, vul. Nab. Lenina 15A; tel. (562) 35-77-45; fax (56) 744-27-16; e-mail ptb@pce.dp.ua; internet www.pce.dp.ua; originally 1908 as Katerinoslav Commodity Exchange; re-established with present name in 1991; brs in Dniprodzerzhynsk, Kryvyi Rih, Marhanets, Pavlohrad and Synelnykove; Gen. Man. VADYM F. KAMEKO.

Donetsk Commodity Exchange: 83086 Donetsk, vul. Pershotravnevska 12; tel. (62) 338-10-93; fax (62) 335-92-91; e-mail oltradex@pub.dn.ua; f. 1991; Gen. Man. PETRO O. VYSHNEVSKYI.

Kharkiv Commodity Exchange: 61003 Kharkiv, vul. Universytetska 5; tel. (572) 12-33-21; fax (572) 12-74-95; e-mail ss@htb.kharkov.ua; f. 1993; Pres. IHOR V. ZOTOV.

Kyiv Universal Exchange: 01103 Kyiv, Zaliznychne shose 57; tel. (44) 295-11-29; fax (44) 295-44-36; e-mail nva@iptelecom.net.ua; internet www.kue.kiev.ua; f. 1990; Pres. KONSTANTIN LAPUSHEN.

Odesa Commodity Exchange: 65114 Odesa, vul. Lyustdorfska doroha 140A; tel. (482) 61-89-92; fax (482) 47-72-84; e-mail yuri@oce.odessa.ua; f. 1796; re-established 1990; Gen. Man. MYKOLA O. NIKOLISHEN.

Dnipro (Pridniprovska) Commodity Exchange: 49094 Dnipropetrovsk, vul. Nab. Lenina 15A; tel. (562) 35-77-45; fax (56) 744-27-16; e-mail ptb@pce.dp.ua; internet www.pce.dp.ua; originally 1908 as Katerinoslav Commodity Exchange; re-established with present name in 1991; brs in Dniprodzerzhynsk, Kryvyi Rih, Marhanets, Pavlohrad and Synelnykove; Gen. Man. VADYM F. KAMEKO.

Ukrainian Universal Commodity Exchange: 03680 Kyiv, pr. Akadmika Hlushkova 1/6; tel. (44) 251-94-90; fax (44) 251-95-40; e-mail birga@uutb.kiev.ua; internet www.uutb.com.ua; f. 1991; Pres. OLEKSANDR M. BORKOVSKYI.

Zaporizhzhya Commodity Exchange 'Hileya': 69037 Zaporizhzhya, vul. 40 rokiv Radyanskoyi Ukrainy 41; tel. (612) 33-32-73; fax (612) 34-76-62; f. 1991; re-established 1996; Gen. Man. ANTON A. KHULAKHSIZ.

INSURANCE

In March 2004 there were 360 insurance companies operating in Ukraine, of which the following were among the most important.

State Insurance Companies

Crimean Insurance Co: 99011 Sevastopol, vul. Butakov 4; tel. (692) 55-31-28; fax (692) 54 23 00; e-mail ksk@stel.sebastopol.ua; f. 1993; Dir ISABELLA BILDER.

DASK UkrinMedStrakh: 01601 Kyiv, vul. O. Honshara 65; tel. (44) 216-30-21; fax (44) 216-96-92; e-mail ukrmed@ukrpack.com; f. 1999; provides compulsory medical insurance to foreigners and stateless persons temporarily resident in Ukraine.

Oranta Insurance Co: 01015 Kyiv, vul. Sichnevogo Povstannya 34B; tel. (44) 537-58-00; fax (44) 537-58-83; e-mail oranta@oranta.ua; internet www.oranta.ua; f. 1921; Chair. of Bd OLEG SPILKA.

Commercial Insurance Companies

AIG Ukraine: 01004 Kyiv, vul. Shovkovychna 42–44; tel. (44) 490-65-50; fax (44) 490-65-48; e-mail reception@aig.com.ua; internet www.aig.com.ua; f. 2000; affiliated to American International Group (USA); Gen. Man. IHOR KOVALENKO.

AKB Garant Insurance Co: 03062 Kyiv, pr. Peremohy 67; tel. (44) 459-52-00; fax (44) 459-52-07; e-mail akb@garant.kiev.ua; internet www.garant.kiev.ua; f. 1994; general insurance services; Gen. Man. OLEKSANDR I. DYACHENKO.

Alcona Insurance Co: 03150 Kyiv, vul. V. Vasylivska 102; tel. (44) 247-44-77; e-mail alcona@alcona.kiev.ua; internet www.insurance.kiev.ua/alcona/; f. 1992; insurance and reinsurance.

Aska Insurance Co: 03186 Kyiv, vul. Antonova 5; tel. (44) 241-11-67; e-mail office@aska.com.ua; internet www.aska.com.ua; life and non-life insurance; Chair. HALINA N. TRETYAKOVA; Gen. Man. A. SOSYS.

Dask Insurance Co: 49000 Dnipropetrovsk, vul. K. Libkhnekhta 4D; tel. (562) 32-09-75; fax (562) 32-09-81; e-mail dask@dask.dp.ua; internet www.dask.com.ua; f. 1993; affiliated to Dask Insurance Group; Dir IRINA MURASCHKO.

Disco Insurance Co: 49000 Dnipropetrovsk, vul. K. Lybknekhta 4D; tel. (562) 32-09-78; fax (562) 32-09-81; e-mail disco@disco.dp.ua; internet www.disco.dp.ua; f. 1992; affiliated to Dask Insurance Group.

ECCO Insurance Co: 01034 Kyiv, vul. Prorizna 4/23; tel. (44) 228-10-82; e-mail insurance@ecco-alpha.kiev.ua; internet www.ecco-insurance.at; f. 1991; affiliated to ECCO (Austria); life and non-life insurance.

EnergoPolis Insurance Co: 03049 Kyiv, vul. Bohdanivska 10; tel. (44) 244-02-36; fax (44) 244-05-94; e-mail office@enpolis.com.ua; internet www.enpolis.com.ua; Chair. of Bd and Dir-Gen. VIKTOR MYKOLAYCHUK.

Galinstrakh Insurance Co: 79012 Lviv, vul. Ak. Sakharova 34; tel. (322) 75-70-30; fax (322) 97-10-40; e-mail gis@is.lviv.ua; internet www.gis.com.ua; f. 1991; general insurance services; Chair. of Bd STEPHAN SOVINSKIY.

Ingo—Ukraina Insurance Co: 01054 Kyiv, vul. Vorovskogo 33; tel. (44) 490-27-44; fax (44) 490-27-48; internet www.ingo.com.ua; f. 1994; fmrly Ostra-Kyiv Insurance Co; re-insurance, medical, travel, property and cargo insurance; Chair. of Bd IHOR N. HORDYENKO.

Inter-Policy Insurance Co: 01033 Kyiv, vul. Volodymyrska 69; tel. (44) 227-70-96; fax (44) 220-74-45; e-mail office@inter-policy.com; f. 1993.

Kyiv Insurance Co: 04053 Kyiv, vul. Yu. Kotsubynskoho 20; tel. (44) 461-92-41; fax (44) 461-92-43; e-mail info@kic.kiev.ua; internet www.kic.kiev.ua; f. 1998.

Ostra Insurance Co: 65026 Odesa, vul. Pushkinska 13; tel. (482) 22-38-87; fax (482) 24-18-37; e-mail main@ostra.com.ua; internet www.ostra.com.ua; f. 1990; non-life insurance; Chair. KHYRACH MAHDYEV.

QBE Ukraina Insurance: 01033 Kyiv, vul. Saksahanskoho 36D; tel. (44) 537-53-90; fax (44) 537-53-99; e-mail insurance@qbe-ukraine.com; internet www.qbe-ukraine.com; f. 1998; affiliate of QBE Insurance (New Zealand).

Skide Insurance Co: 04050 Kyiv, vul. Hlybochytska 72; tel. (44) 417-40-04; fax (44) 228-40-33; e-mail skide@iptelecom.net.ua; f. 1991; Pres. VOLODYMYR BESARAB.

Skide-West Insurance Co: 04053 Kyiv, vul. Sichovykh Striltsiv 40; tel. (44) 238-62-38; fax (44) 246-96-25; e-mail mail@skide-west.com; internet www.skide-west.com; f. 1993; cap. US $389.1m. (2004); Pres. ANDRIY PERETYAZHKO; 37 brs and representative offices.

Sun Life Ukraine: 01032 Kyiv, vul. Starovokzalna 17; tel. (44) 235-20-02; fax (44) 235-89-17; e-mail office@sunlife.com.ua; internet www.sunlife.com.ua; f. 1993; life insurance; Pres. ROSTYSLAV B. TALSKYI.

UkrGazPromPolis Insurance Co: 01034 Kyiv, vul. O. Honshara 41; tel. (44) 235-25-00; e-mail office@ugpp.com.ua; internet www

.ugpp.com.ua; f. 1996; jointly owned by UkrGazProm, UkrGazProm-Bank and KyivTransGaz; Pres. KONSTANTYN O. YEFYMENKO.

Insurance Association

League of Insurance Organizations of Ukraine: 02002 Kyiv, vul. M. Roskovoyi 11; tel. and fax (44) 516-82-30; e-mail liga@uainsur.com; internet www.uainsur.com; f. 1992; non-profit asscn of insurance cos; Pres. ALEKSANDR FILONYUK.

Trade and Industry

GOVERNMENT AGENCY

State Property Fund of Ukraine (Fond Derzhavnoho Maina Ukrainy): 01133 Kyiv, vul. Kutuzova 18/9; tel. (44) 200-33-33; fax (44) 286-79-85; e-mail marketing@spfu.kiev.ua; internet www.spfu.gov.ua; Head VALENTYNA P. SEMENYUK.

NATIONAL CHAMBER OF COMMERCE

Ukrainian Chamber of Commerce and Industry (Torgovo-Promyslova Palata Ukrainy/Torgovo-Promyshlennaya Palata Ukrainy): 01601 Kyiv, vul. V. Zhytomyrska 33; tel. (44) 272-29-11; fax (44) 212-33-53; e-mail ucci@ucci.org.ua; internet www.ucci.org.ua; f. 1972; Chair. SERHIY P. SKRYPCHECNKO; 28 brs.

REGIONAL CHAMBERS OF COMMERCE

Chambers of Commerce are located in every administrative region of Ukraine, including the following:

Chamber of Commerce and Industry of Crimea: 95013 Crimea, Simferopol, ul. Sevastopolskaya 45; tel. (652) 44-93-70; fax (652) 44-58-13; e-mail cci@cci.crimea.ua; internet www.cci.crimea.ua; 1974; sub-brs in Armyansk, Dzhankoi, Feodosiya, Kerch, Yalta and Yevpatoriya; Pres. NEONILA M. GRACHEVA.

Dnipropetrovsk Chamber of Commerce: 49044 Dnipropetrovsk, vul. Shevchenka 4; tel. (562) 36-22-58; fax (562) 36-22-59; e-mail miv@dcci.dp.ua; internet www.dcci.dp.ua; brs at Kryvyi Rih and Dniprodzerzhynsk; Pres. VYTALIY H. ZHMURENKO.

Donetsk Chamber of Commerce: 83007 Donetsk, pr. Kyivskyi 87; tel. (62) 387-80-00; fax (62) 387-80-01; e-mail dcci@dttp.donetsk.ua; internet www.cci.donbass.com; f. 1964; brs at Artemovsk, Horlivka, Kramatorsk and Mariupol; Pres. GENNADII D. CHIZHIKOV.

Kharkiv Chamber of Commerce: 61012 Kharkiv, vul. Katsarsksa 3A; tel. (57) 714-96-90; fax (572) 28-21-36; e-mail info@kcci.kharkov.ua; internet www.kcci.kharkov.ua; Pres. VIKTOR I. LOBODA.

Kyiv Chamber of Commerce and Industry: 01504 Kyiv-54, vul. B. Khmelnytskoho 55; tel. (44) 246-83-01; fax (44) 246-99-66; e-mail info@kiev-chamber.org.ua; internet www.kiev-chamber.org.ua; Pres. MYKOLA V. ZASULSKIY.

Lviv Chamber of Commerce and Industry: 79011 Lviv, Stryiskiy park 14; tel. (322) 76-46-13; fax (322) 97-07-49; e-mail lcci@cci.com.ua; internet www.lcci.com.ua; f. 1850; Pres. OLEH M. KHUSTOCHKA.

Odesa Chamber of Commerce: 65011 Odesa, vul. Bazarna 47; tel. (48) 777-20-96; fax (482) 49-63-07; e-mail oav@orcci.odessa.ua; internet www.orcci.odessa.ua; f. 1924; brs at Illichivsk, Izmayil and Reni; Pres. SERHIY SHUVALOV.

Sevastopol Chamber of Commerce and Industry: 99011 Sevastopol, ul. B. Morskaya 34; tel. (692) 54-35-36; fax (692) 54-06-44; e-mail stpp@optima.com.ua; internet www.stpp.org.ua; f. 1963; Pres. LYUDMILA I. VISHNYA.

Transcarpathian (Zakarpatska) Chamber of Commerce and Industry: 88015 Transcarpathian obl., Uzhhorod, vul. Hrushevskoho 62; tel. (312) 66-22-14; fax (312) 66-44-77; e-mail tpp@tpp.uzhgorod.ua; internet www.tpp.uzhgorod.ua; br. at Mukachevo; Pres. OTTO O. KOVCHAR.

Zaporizhzhya Chamber of Commerce: 69000 Zaporizhzhya, bulv. Tsentralnyi 4; tel. (612) 13-50-24; fax (612) 33-11-72; e-mail cci@cci.zp.ua; internet www.cci.zp.ua; brs at Berdyansk and Melitopol; Pres. VOLODYMYR I. SHAMYLOV.

EMPLOYERS' ORGANIZATION

Congress of Business Circles of Ukraine: 01061 Kyiv, vul. Prorizna 15; tel. (44) 228-64-81; fax (44) 229-52-84; Pres. VALERIY G. BABICH.

UTILITIES

Regulatory Bodies

National Electricity Regulatory Commission of Ukraine: 03057 Kyiv, vul. Smolenska 19; tel. (44) 241-90-01; fax (44) 241-90-47; e-mail box@nerc.gov.ua; f. 1994; promotion of competition and protection of consumer interests; Chair. YURIY PRODAN.

State Committee for Nuclear Regulation (Derzhavnyi komitet yadernoho rehulyuvannya Ukrainy): 01011 Kyiv, vul. Arsenalna 9/11; tel. (44) 254-33-47; fax (44) 254-33-11; e-mail pr@hq.snrc.gov.ua; internet www.snrc.gov.ua; Chair. OLENA A. MYKOLAICHUK.

Electricity

EnergoAtom: 71500 Zaporizhzhya obl., Energodar; tel. (44) 294-48-89; e-mail pr@nae.atom.gov.ua; f. 1996; responsible for scientific and technical policy within the nuclear-power industry; manages all five nuclear-power producing installations in Ukraine; Pres. (vacant).

There were 27 electricity distribution companies in Ukraine, including Dniproenergo (serving Dnipropetrovsk), Kyivenergo (serving Kyiv) and Zaporizhoblenergo (serving Zaporizhzhya). These companies were previously grouped in the Unified Energy Systems of Ukraine. Thirteen regional distribution companies were privatized in 1998–2001.

Kyivenergo: 01001 Kyiv, 1 pl. Ivana Franka 5; tel. (44) 201-03-37; fax (44) 201-03-38; e-mail pubrel@me-press.kiev.ua; internet www.kievenergo.com.ua; power generation and distribution; Chair. IVAN PLACHKOV.

Zakhidenergo (West Energy): 79011 Lviv, vul. Sventitskoho 2; tel. (322) 79-89-41; fax (322) 78-90-59; e-mail z_vtv@rdc.west.energy.gov.ua; f. 1995; power generation; Pres. and Gen. Dir VOLODYMYR PAVLYUK.

Gas

Naftogaz Ukrainy (Oil and Gas of Ukraine): 01001 Kyiv, vul. B. Khmelnytskoho 6B; tel. (44) 461-25-37; fax (44) 220-15-26; e-mail ngu@naftogaz.net; internet www.naftogaz.com; f. 1998; state-owned; production and distribution of gas and petroleum; storage of gas; gas- and condensate-processing; Chair. of Bd (vacant).

TRADE UNION FEDERATIONS

Confederation of Free Trade Unions of Ukraine (CFTUU) (Konfederatsiya Vilnykh Profspilok Ukrainy—KVPU): 03150 Kyiv, vul. V. Vasylkivska 54; tel. (44) 227-33-38; fax (44) 227-72-83; e-mail info@kvpu.org.ua; internet www.kvpu.org.ua; independent; Chair. MYKHAYLO VOLYNETS.

Federation of Trade Unions of Ukraine (FTUU): 01012 Kyiv, Maidan Nezalezhnosti 2; tel. (44) 228-87-88; fax (44) 229-80-57; e-mail belova@uprotel.net.ua; f. 1990; fmr Ukrainian branch of General Confederation of Trade Unions of the USSR; affiliation of 40 trade union brs; Chair. OLEKSANDR M. STOYAN.

Transport

RAILWAYS

In 2002 there were 22,078 km of railway track in use, of which more than 9,000 km were electrified. Lines link most towns and cities in the country. There are direct lines linking Ukraine with Berlin (Germany), Bucharest (Romania), Bratislava (Slovakia), Budapest (Hungary), Chişinău (Moldova), Minsk (Belarus), Moscow (Russia), Vienna (Austria) and Warsaw (Poland).

State Railway Transport Administration—Ukrzaliznytsia: 03680 Kyiv, vul. Tverska 5; tel. (44) 223-00-10; fax (44) 258-80-11; e-mail ci@uz.gov.ua; internet www.uz.gov.ua; Dir-Gen. Minister of Transport and Communications.

Ukrreftrans: 03049 Kyiv, vul. Furmanova 1/7; tel. (44) 245-47-22; e-mail sekretar@interntrans.com.ua; internet www.intertrans.com.ua; state-owned freight transportation service.

City Underground Railways

Dnipropetrovsk Metro: 49038 Dnipropetrovsk, vul. Kurchatova 8; tel. (562) 42-37-68; fax (56) 778-65-33; e-mail metrodp@ukr.net; internet gorod.dp.ua/metro; f. 1995; one line with six stations; total length 8 km; total planned network of 74 km.

Kharkiv Metro: 61012 Kharkiv, vul. Engelsa 29; tel. (572) 12-59-83; fax (572) 23-21-41; e-mail metro@tender.kharkov.com; internet www.metro.kharkov.ua; f. 1975; three lines with 26 stations, total length 34 km; Gen. Man. LEONID A. ISAYEV.

Kyiv Metro: 03055 Kyiv, pr. Peremohy 35; tel. (44) 238-44-21; fax (44) 238-44-46; e-mail nto@metro.kiev.ua; internet www.metro.kiev.ua; f. 1960; three lines with 45 stations; Dir MYKOLA M. SHAVLOVSKIY.

ROADS

At 31 December 2002 there were 169,678 km of roads, of which 96.8% were paved. In December 2000 there were 13,081 km of main or national roads, and 156,410 km of secondary or regional roads.

UKRAINE

INLAND WATERWAYS

The length of navigable inland waterways in Ukraine declined notably during the 1990s, from 4,405 km in 1990 to 2,281 km in 2001. The Dnipro (Dniepr—Dnieper) river, which links Kyiv, Cherkasy, Dnipropetrovsk and Zaporizhzhya with the Black Sea, is the most important route for river freight.

SHIPPING

The main ports are Yalta and Yevpatoriya in Crimea, and Odesa. In addition to long-distance international shipping lines, there are services to the Russian ports of Novorossiisk and Sochi, and Batumi and Sukhumi in Georgia. Although many passenger routes on the Black Sea ceased to operate in the 1990s, there are regular passenger services from Odesa to Haifa (Israel) and İstanbul (Turkey), and, in the summer months, between Odesa and Crimea. At December 2004 Ukraine's merchant fleet (647 vessels) had a total displacement of 1.1m. grt.

Port Authority

Port of Odesa Authority: 65026 Odesa, pl. Mytna 1; tel. (48) 729-35-55; fax (48) 729-36-27; e-mail bev@port.odessa.ua; internet www.port.odessa.ua; cargo handling and storage; Gen. Man. OLEKSANDR S. SOBOROV.

Shipping Companies

Azov Shipping Co: 87510 Donetsk obl., Mariupol, pr. Admirala Lunina 89; tel. (629) 31-15-00; fax (629) 31-12-25; e-mail admin@c2smtp.azsco.anet.donetsk.ua; f. 1871; Pres. SERHIY V. PRUSIKOV.

State Black Sea Shipping Co: 65026 Odesa, vul. Lanzheronovska 1; tel. (482) 25-21-60; fax (482) 60-57-33; Pres. BORIS SCHERBAK.

Ukrainian Danube Shipping Co: 68600 Odesa obl., Izmayil, vul. Chervonaflotska 28; tel. (4841) 2-55-50; fax (4841) 2-53-55; e-mail udp_t@udp.izmail.uptel.net; f. 1944; cargo and passenger services; Pres. PETR S. SUVOROV.

Ukrainian Shipping Co (UkrShip): 65014 Odesa, vul. Marazlyevska 8; tel. (48) 734-73-50; fax (48) 777-07-00; e-mail admin@ukrship.odessa.ua; f. 1996; Pres. A. SAVITSKIY.

Ukrrechflot Co: 04071 Kyiv, Nizhny val. 51; tel. (44) 416-88-79; fax (44) 417-86-82; jt-stock co; Pres. NIKOLAY A. SLAVOV.

Yugreftransflot: 99014 Crimea, Sevastopol, ul. Rybakov 5; tel. (692) 41-25-41; fax (692) 42-39-19; e-mail jsc@urtf.com; jt-stock co; Chair. VOLODYMYR ANDREYEV.

CIVIL AVIATION

Ukraine has air links with cities throughout the former USSR and with major European, North American, Asian and African cities. The principal international airport is at Boryspil (Kyiv), but several other airports, including those at Dnipropetrovsk and Odesa, also service international flights.

AeroSvit Airlines: 01032 Kyiv, bulv. Shevchenko 58A; tel. (44) 246-50-70; fax (44) 246-50-46; e-mail av@aswt.kiev.ua; internet www.aerosvit.com; f. 1994; operates scheduled and charter passenger services to domestic and international destinations; Chief Exec. and Dir-Gen. GRYGORIY GURTOVOY.

Air Urga: 25005 Kirovograd, vul. Dobrovolskoho 1A; tel. (522) 35-11-25; fax (522) 35-11-52; e-mail office@urga.com.ua; internet www.urga.com.ua; f. 1993; regional and international passenger and cargo flights; Dir-Gen. LEONID SHMAYEVICH.

ARP 410—Kyiv Aircraft Repair Plant (ARP 410—Kyivsky Aviyaremontny Zavod): 03151 Kyiv, Vozdukhoflotsky pr. 94; tel. (44) 246-26-64; fax (44) 243-40-33; e-mail arp410-cs@svitonline.com; internet www.arp410.com.ua; f. 1999; domestic passenger and international cargo flights; Dir-Gen. ANATOLIY P. KUDRIN.

Donbassaero Airlines (Donbass-Vostochnye Aviyalinii Ukrainy—Donbassaero): 83021 Donetsk, Donetsk International Airport; tel. (062) 385-61-68; fax (0622) 332-00-55; e-mail info@donbass.aero; internet www.donbass.aero; f. 1991; present name adopted 2003; passenger and cargo flights between Donetsk and domestic and international destinations in the CIS, central Europe and the Middle East; Dir-Gen. ALEKSANDR HRECHKO.

Khors Air Company: 01133 Kyiv, vul. L. Ukrainki 34; tel. (44) 294-94-11; fax (44) 573-86-72; e-mail aircargo@khors.com.ua; internet www.khors.com.ua; f. 1990; operates international, regional and domestic cargo and passenger services; Gen. Dir ANATOLIY VYSOCHANSKIY.

Ukraine International Airlines (Mizhnarodni Avialinyi Ukraini): 01054 Kyiv, ul. B. Khmelnytskogo 63A; tel. (44) 461-56-56; fax (44) 230-88-66; e-mail uia@ps.kiev.ua; internet www.ukraine-international.com; f. 1992; 61.6% state-owned, 22.5% owned jointly by SAir (Switzerland) and Austrian Airlines (Austria); operates domestic services, and international services to European and Middle Eastern destinations from Kyiv, Dnipropetrovsk, Kharkiv, Lviv, Odesa and Simferopol; Pres. VITALIY M. POTEMSKIY.

UM Air—Ukrainian Mediterranean Airlines (UM Air—Ukrainsko-Sredizemnomorskiye Aviyalinii): 01055 Kyiv, vul. Shlyavska 7; tel. (44) 238-20-02; fax (44) 238-20-43; e-mail umair@umairlines.com; internet www.umairlines.com; f. 2000; scheduled and charter flights between Kyiv and international destinations, including Azerbaijan, Belarus, Bulgaria, Egypt, Finland, Georgia, Greece, Iran, Lebanon, Slovakia, Slovenia, Spain and Turkey; Pres. RODRIG MERKHEZH.

Tourism

The Black Sea coast of Ukraine has several popular resorts, including Odesa and Yalta. The Crimean peninsula is a popular tourist centre in both summer and winter, owing to its temperate climate. Kyiv, Lviv and Odesa have important historical attractions and there are many archaeological monuments on the Black Sea coast, including the remains of ancient Greek and Ottoman settlements. However, the tourist industry remains little developed outside Kyiv, Lviv and the Black Sea resorts. There were 12.5m. foreign tourist arrivals in Ukraine in 2003, when receipts from tourism totalled US $1,204m. In 2005 the requirement that tourist visitors from European Union countries and Switzerland obtain a visa to visit Ukraine was waived, initially for an experimental six-month period.

Ministry of Culture and Tourism: see The Government (Ministries).

Ministry of Health Resorts and Tourism of the Autonomous Republic of Crimea: 95005 Crimea, Simferopol, pr. Kirova 13; tel. (652) 54-46-68; fax (652) 25-94-38; e-mail tourism_crimea@ukr.net; internet www.tourism.crimea.ua; Minister ALEKSANDR I. TARYANIK.

State Tourism Adminstration of Ukraine (Derzhavna turystychna administratsiya Ukrainy): 01034 Kyiv, vul. Yaroslaviv val 36; tel. (44) 272-42-15; fax (44) 272-42-77; e-mail info@tourism.gov.ua; internet www.tourism.gov.ua; f. 1999; Chair. VALERIY I. TSYBUKH.

THE UNITED ARAB EMIRATES

Introductory Survey

Location, Climate, Language, Religion, Flag, Capital

The United Arab Emirates (UAE) lies in the east of the Arabian peninsula. It is bordered by Saudi Arabia to the west and south, and by Oman to the east. In the north the UAE has a short frontier with Qatar and a coastline of about 650 km on the southern shore of the Persian (Arabian) Gulf, separated by a detached portion of Omani territory from a small section of coast on the western shore of the Gulf of Oman. The climate is exceptionally hot in summer, with average maximum temperatures exceeding 40°C, and humidity is very high. Winter is mild, with temperatures ranging from 17°C to 20°C. Average annual rainfall is very low: between 100 mm and 200 mm. The official language is Arabic, spoken by almost all of the native population. Arabs are, however, outnumbered by non-Arab immigrants, mainly from India, Pakistan, Bangladesh and Iran. According to official estimates, UAE nationals represented about 25% of the total population in 1994. Most of the inhabitants are Muslims, mainly of the Sunni sect. The national flag (proportions 1 by 2) has three equal horizontal stripes, of green, white and black, with a vertical red stripe at the hoist. The capital is Abu Dhabi.

Recent History

Prior to independence, the UAE was Trucial Oman, also known as the Trucial States, and the component sheikhdoms of the territory were under British protection. Although, from 1892, the United Kingdom assumed responsibility for the sheikhdoms' defence and external relations, they were otherwise autonomous and followed the traditional form of Arab monarchy, with each ruler having virtually absolute power over his subjects.

In 1952 the Trucial Council, comprising the rulers of the seven sheikhdoms, was established in order to encourage the adoption of common policies in administrative matters, possibly leading to a federation of the states. Petroleum, the basis of the area's modern prosperity, was first discovered in 1958, when deposits were located beneath the coastal waters of Abu Dhabi, the largest of the sheikhdoms. Onshore petroleum was found in Abu Dhabi in 1960. Commercial exploitation of petroleum began there in 1962, providing the state with greatly increased revenue. However, Sheikh Shakhbut bin Sultan an-Nahyan, the Ruler of Abu Dhabi since 1928, failed to use the income from petroleum royalties to develop his domain. As a result, the ruling family deposed him in August 1966 and installed his younger brother, Sheikh Zayed bin Sultan. Under the rule of Sheikh Zayed, Abu Dhabi was transformed, with considerable income from the petroleum industry allocated for public works and the provision of welfare services. In 1966 petroleum was discovered in neighbouring Dubai (the second largest of the Trucial States), which also underwent a rapid development.

In January 1968 the United Kingdom announced its intention to withdraw British military forces from the area by 1971. In March 1968 the Trucial States joined nearby Bahrain and Qatar (which were also under British protection) in what was named the Federation of Arab Emirates. It was intended that the Federation should become fully independent, but the interests of Bahrain and Qatar proved to be incompatible with those of the smaller sheikhdoms, and both seceded from the Federation in August 1971 to become separate independent states. In July six of the Trucial States (Abu Dhabi, Dubai, Sharjah, Umm al-Qaiwain, Ajman and Fujairah) had agreed on a federal Constitution for achieving independence as the United Arab Emirates (UAE). The United Kingdom accordingly terminated its special treaty relationship with the States, and the UAE became independent on 2 December 1971. The remaining sheikhdom, Ras al-Khaimah, joined the UAE in February 1972. At independence Sheikh Zayed of Abu Dhabi took office as the first President of the UAE. Sheikh Rashid bin Said al-Maktoum, the Ruler of Dubai since 1958, became Vice-President, while his eldest son, Sheikh Maktoum bin Rashid al-Maktoum (Crown Prince of Dubai), became Prime Minister in the Federal Council of Ministers. A 40-member consultative assembly, the Federal National Council, was also inaugurated.

In January 1972 the Ruler of Sharjah, Sheikh Khalid bin Muhammad al-Qasimi, was killed by rebels under the leadership of his cousin, Sheikh Saqr bin Sultan, who had been deposed as the sheikhdom's Ruler in June 1965. However, the rebels were defeated, and Sheikh Khalid was succeeded by his brother, Sheikh Sultan bin Muhammad al-Qasimi.

In August 1976 Sheikh Zayed, disappointed with progress towards centralization, reportedly announced that he was not prepared to accept another five-year term as President. In November, however, the highest federal authority, the Supreme Council of Rulers (comprising the Rulers of the seven emirates), re-elected him unanimously, following agreements granting the Federal Government greater control over defence, intelligence services, immigration, public security and border control.

Owing to a dispute over a senior appointment in February 1978, the forces of Dubai and Ras al-Khaimah refused to accept orders from the Federal Defence Force. Although Ras al-Khaimah later reintegrated with the Federal Defence Force, Dubai's armed forces effectively remained a separate entity. In March 1979 a 10-point memorandum from the National Council, containing proposals for increased unity, was rejected by Dubai, which, together with Ras al-Khaimah, boycotted a meeting of the Supreme Council. In April Sheikh Maktoum resigned as Prime Minister; he was replaced by his father, Sheikh Rashid, who formed a new Council of Ministers in July, while retaining the post of Vice-President. Sheikh Ahmad bin Rashid al-Mu'alla, the Ruler of Umm al-Qaiwain (the smallest of the emirates) since 1929, died in February 1981, and was succeeded by his son, Rashid. Sheikh Rashid bin Humaid an-Nuaimi, the Ruler of Ajman since 1928, died in September 1981, and was succeeded by his son, Humaid.

The UAE was a founder member of the Co-operation Council for the Arab States of the Gulf (the Gulf Co-operation Council—GCC, see p. 205) in May 1981. The GCC aims to achieve greater political and economic integration between Gulf countries (for further details, see below).

There was an attempted coup in Sharjah in June 1987, when Sheikh Abd al-Aziz, a brother of Sheikh Sultan, announced (in his brother's absence) the abdication of the Ruler, on the grounds that he had mismanaged the economy. The Supreme Council of Rulers intervened to endorse Sheikh Sultan's claim to be the legitimate Ruler of Sharjah, effectively restoring him to power. Sheikh Abd al-Aziz was given the title of Crown Prince and was granted a seat on the Supreme Council. In February 1990, however, Sheikh Sultan removed his brother from the post of Crown Prince and revoked his right to succeed him as Ruler. In July Sheikh Sultan appointed Sheikh Ahmad bin Muhammad al-Qasimi, the head of Sharjah's petroleum and mineral affairs office, as Deputy Ruler of Sharjah, although he was not given the title of Crown Prince.

In October 1990, upon the death of his father, Sheikh Maktoum acceded to the positions of Ruler of Dubai and Vice-President and Prime Minister of the UAE.

Meanwhile, in July 1991 the UAE became involved in a major international financial scandal, when regulatory authorities in seven countries abruptly closed down the operations of the Bank of Credit and Commerce International (BCCI), in which the Abu Dhabi ruling family and agencies had held a controlling interest (77%) since April 1990. The termination of the bank's activities followed the disclosure of systematic, large-scale fraud by BCCI authorities prior to April 1990. By the end of July 1991 BCCI's activities had been suspended in all 69 countries in which it had operated. At the conclusion of fraud trials in May 1994 all but one of the defendants were sentenced to terms of imprisonment ranging from three to 14 years. (In June 1995 a court of appeal overturned the guilty verdicts of two of those imprisoned.) New legislation was subsequently prepared to strengthen the role of the Central Bank and to enforce stricter regulation of the Emirates' financial sector.

In January 1995 the Ruler of Dubai, Sheikh Maktoum, issued a decree naming Sheikh Muhammad bin Rashid al-Maktoum as Crown Prince, and Sheikh Hamdan bin Rashid al-Maktoum as Deputy Ruler of Dubai. In June 1996 legislation designed to make the provisional Constitution permanent was endorsed by the Federal National Council, following its approval by the

Supreme Council of Rulers. At the same time Abu Dhabi was formally designated capital of the UAE.

In April 2001 Dubai's Director-General of Ports and Customs, Dr Obeid Saqer bin Busit, was sentenced to 27 years' imprisonment, having been convicted on two charges of corruption arising from abuse of his position; bin Busit was the highest ranking civil servant ever to have been tried for corruption in the UAE. Six other defendants (three UAE nationals and three Pakistani expatriates) were also convicted. The arrests had been ordered personally by Dubai's Crown Prince in February, following a two-year investigation, and it was subsequently reported that the federal Minister of Justice and Islamic Affairs and Awqaf (Religious Endowments) had proposed the establishment of an anti-corruption commission and the institution of more stringent legislation to counter corruption. There were, however, subsequent reports that those convicted of the customs fraud had been pardoned.

Industrial safety concerns emerged during 2002 after 27 workers were killed when the Dubai dry docks flooded in March and an unknown number of construction workers were killed and injured when the roof of a new power plant under construction at the Jebel Ali industrial centre near Dubai city collapsed in August. Further concerns over the safety of the rapidly expanding construction industry emerged in September 2004 when five workers were killed in an accident during building works at Dubai International Airport.

In October 2003 Sheikh Zayed appointed Sheikh Hamdan bin Zayed an-Nayhan as a Deputy Prime Minister, in addition to his existing responsibilities as Minister of State for Foreign Affairs. Sheikh Zayed also, in November, issued a decree installing Sheikh Muhammad bin Zayed an-Nahyan, the Chief of Staff of Federal Armed Forces, as Deputy Crown Prince of Abu Dhabi. Meanwhile, in mid-June 2003 Sheikh Saqr bin Muhammad al-Qasimi, the ruler of Ras al-Khaimah, deposed his eldest son, Khalid, as Crown Prince and appointed a younger son, Sa'ud, in his place. Sheikh Khalid, a noted reformist, was said to have protested against the decision, which he claimed had been influenced by his father's ill health. Tanks from the federal UAE armed forces arrived in Ras al-Khaimah city on 15 June, apparently in an attempt to prevent supporters of Sheikh Khalid from demonstrating against the decision. Tension in the emirate eased on 16 June, however, after the departure of the deposed Sheikh to Oman. In January 2004 Sheikh Sa'ud continued his brother's reform programme by ordering the release of 124 prisoners, including several of the protesters who had demonstrated against his appointment.

Sheikh Zayed died on 2 November 2004, following several years of health problems, including a kidney transplant in 2000. His son, Sheikh Khalifa bin Zayed an-Nahyan, automatically succeeded him as Ruler of Abu Dhabi and was elected by the Supreme Council to the presidency on the following day. Sheikh Zayed's death was preceded, on 1 November 2004, by a rare restructuring of the Council of Ministers (the first such reorganization since 1997); the most significant changes were the appointment as Minister of Economy and Planning of Sheikha Lubna al-Qasimi, who thus became the first woman to hold a cabinet position in the UAE, and the combining of the petroleum and mineral resources ministry with the electricity and water portfolio to form a new Ministry of Energy, headed by Muhammad bin Dhaen al-Hamili. On 8 December Sheikh Khalifa announced a similarly unusual restructuring of the Abu Dhabi Executive Council, to be chaired by the new Crown Prince, Sheikh Muhammad, who also remained the Chief of Staff of Federal Armed Forces.

On 4 January 2006 Sheikh Maktoum, who had reportedly suffered from heart problems, died suddenly while in Australia. He was immediately succeeded as Ruler of Dubai by his brother, Sheikh Muhammad bin Rashid al-Maktoum, who had been Dubai's Crown Prince since 1995. It was announced on 5 January 2006 that, as expected, Sheikh Muhammad had also replaced Sheikh Maktoum as Vice-President and Prime Minister of the federation. Sheikh Muhammad's first Council of Ministers, approved by the President on 9 February, contained nine new ministers (including a second female minister—Mariam Muhammad Khalfan ar-Roumi at the Ministry of Social Affairs) and several new portfolios; however, most of the major ministries remained unchanged. Sheikh Muhammad retained control of the Ministry of Defence, a position he has held since 1971.

The UAE's slow progress towards electoral democracy showed signs of accelerating on 1 December 2005, when Sheikh Khalifa announced tentative proposals to open one-half of the 40 seats in the Federal National Council to indirect election via new national councils in each of the emirates. The President envisaged that this represented the first step towards wider participatory democracy and the federation's first general election. Officials indicated that the steady democratization of the GCC states had created both external and internal pressure on the Government to adopt constitutional change. Abu Dhabi had a first opportunity to experiment with direct democracy when elections were held for 15 of the 21 seats on the board of the Abu Dhabi Chamber of Commerce and Industry (ADCCI) on 5 December. About 50,000 ADCCI company members were eligible to vote in the election.

Meanwhile, reports in 2004 indicated that Dubai was considering tabling a bid for the 2016 Olympic Games. The construction of a US $2,000m. complex, to be named Sports City, was scheduled for completion in 2007 and intended to provide much of the infrastructure required for a successful bid. Work on the complex commenced in 2004.

Conflict arose between the UAE and Iran in 1992 concerning the sovereignty of Abu Musa, an island situated between the states in the Persian (Arabian) Gulf. The island had been administered since 1991 under a joint agreement between Iran and Sharjah, in accordance with which an Iranian garrison was stationed on the island. In that year Iran had also seized the smaller neighbouring islands of Greater and Lesser Tunb. In April 1992 the Iranian garrison on Abu Musa was said to have seized civilian installations on the island. There were further allegations that Iranian officials were attempting to force expatriate workers employed by the UAE to leave the island, preventing the entry of other expatriates, and increasing the number of Iranian nationals there. However, in April 1993 all those who had been expelled from or refused entry to Abu Musa in 1992 were reportedly permitted to return. In October 1993 Sheikh Zayed announced the introduction of a federal law standardizing the limits of the UAE's territorial waters to 12 nautical miles (22.2 km) off shore, in response to a similar announcement by the Iranian authorities. In December 1994 the UAE announced its intention to refer the dispute to the International Court of Justice in The Hague, Netherlands, and in February 1995 it was alleged that Iran had deployed air defence systems on the islands. In November officials from the UAE and Iran, meeting in Qatar, failed to reach agreement on establishing an agenda for ministerial-level negotiations. In March 1996 bilateral relations deteriorated further when Iran opened an airport on Abu Musa; in the following month Iran established a power station on Greater Tunb. In February 1999 the UAE protested at the construction by Iran of municipal facilities on Abu Musa and at recent Iranian military exercises near the disputed islands. Iran subsequently complained to the UN that, in disputing the location of its military exercises, the UAE was interfering in Iranian internal affairs. During 1999 the UAE was increasingly critical of the *rapprochement* between Saudi Arabia and Iran, claiming that it was at the expense of Saudi relations with the UAE. In November a tripartite committee, established by the GCC and comprising representatives of Oman, Qatar and Saudi Arabia, announced that it would continue efforts to facilitate a settlement. At the end of the month Sheikh Zayed boycotted a meeting of GCC leaders in Saudi Arabia, in protest at the lack of attention given to the dispute with Iran by the other GCC members at a time when they were increasingly moving towards improved relations with Iran. In December the UAE renewed its request for Iran to enter into direct negotiations or to agree to international arbitration over the islands. In March 2000, following a statement by Iran that it would be prepared to negotiate over the islands, the UAE asserted that it would refer it to the GCC tripartite committee. By early 2006 no significant progress had been reached concerning a resolution of the territorial dispute.

In response to Iraq's occupation of Kuwait in August 1990, the UAE (which supported the US-led multinational effort against Iraq) announced that foreign armed forces opposing the Iraqi invasion would be provided with military facilities in the Emirates. By the mid-1990s, however, the UAE was among those states questioning the justification for the continued maintenance of international sanctions (imposed in 1990) against Iraq, in view of the resultant humanitarian consequences for the Iraqi population. In June 1998 the UAE reiterated its support for an end to the economic blockade against Iraq, and in August it was announced that the UAE was to restore diplomatic ties with Iraq. The UAE reopened its embassy in the Iraqi capital in April 2000. However, the Ruler of Fujairah was criticized in Iraq following a speech, at the UN Millennium Summit in New York in September, in which he called on Iraq to apply all pertinent UN Security Council resolutions, particularly those related to the issue of prisoners of war. Although Iraq's Minister of Trade visited Abu Dhabi in December, where he was received by Sheikh Zayed, the UAE lent its support to a declaration of the GCC annual summit meeting that urged Iraq to conform with UN resolutions: it was generally considered that the Emirates had been compelled to endorse the declaration in return for GCC support for the UAE in its territorial dispute with Iran. Addressing the Arab Inter-Parliamentary Union in February 2001, Sheikh Zayed none the less urged Arab states to work jointly towards an end to the sanctions regime in force against Iraq. In November the UAE and Iraq signed a free-trade agreement, which was ratified by Sheikh Zayed in May 2002.

The UAE severed diplomatic relations with the Taliban regime in Afghanistan in late September 2001, in response to the suicide attacks against New York and Washington, DC, on 11 September. Hitherto, the UAE had been one of only three states to maintain ties with the Taliban (the Emirates' relations with the Taliban being at chargé d'affaires level). The Saudi-born Osama bin Laden, whose al-Qa'ida (Base) organization was at that time based in Afghanistan, was the USA's principal suspect in having orchestrated the September 2001 attacks. After diplomatic relations were severed, the UAE's Minister of Foreign Affairs stated that the Emirates had sought to persuade the Taliban to hand over bin Laden so that he might stand trial in an international court. In common with other GCC members, the UAE pledged support for the US Administration in its efforts to bring to justice the perpetrators of terrorism, swiftly extraditing a suspected militant Islamist wanted for questioning in France. None the less, the UAE emphasized that the success of the US-led 'coalition against terror' must be linked to a resumption of the Arab-Israeli peace process, and expressed concerns that military action should not target any Arab state. The UAE's banking sector came under international scrutiny after US investigators claimed to have evidence of transactions between banks in the UAE and the USA linking bin Laden with the terrorist attacks. At the end of September the Emirates' Central Bank ordered that the assets in the UAE of 27 individuals and organizations accused by the USA of involvement in terrorism be 'frozen'; in early November the Central Bank reportedly ordered a 'freeze' on the assets of a further 62 entities. Following the swift defeat of the Taliban regime in the US-led military offensive, which began in early October, and the inauguration of a new Afghan interim administration in late December 2001, in early February 2002 the Afghan embassy in the UAE was reopened; the opening of the Emirates' embassy in Kabul was announced in mid-March. In November the Central Bank tightened regulations on an informal money-transfer system known as *hawala*, after the practice was criticized by Western law enforcement agencies as an important element in the financing of terrorism.

At the summit meeting of the Council of the League of Arab States (the Arab League, see p. 306) convened in Beirut, Lebanon, in late March 2002, the Minister of State for Foreign Affairs, Sheikh Hamdan bin Zaid an-Nahyan, declared the UAE to be opposed to any future US-led campaign to oust the regime of Saddam Hussain in Iraq as a potential second phase in the USA's declared 'war on terror'. The UAE continued to urge a diplomatic solution to the crisis, and promoted a plan for the Iraqi leader to go into exile in order to prevent a war to oust his regime; however, in March 2003 the UAE disregarded calls by some members of the Arab League to refuse to provide facilities for military action in Iraq. At the commencement of the conflict later in the same month some 3,000 US air force personnel and 72 combat aircraft were stationed in the UAE. Following the overthrow of Iraq's Baathist regime by the US-led coalition in early April and the announcement later in that month that US forces were to be withdrawn from Saudi Arabia, the US Government stated that it would develop the adh-Dhafra airport in Abu Dhabi for use by its military aircraft. In the immediate aftermath of the main period of conflict, the UAE provided significant humanitarian aid to Iraq, and also intended to secure a stake in its reconstruction. After the US envoy, James Baker, visited the country in January 2004, the UAE agreed to write off most of Iraq's US $3,800m. debt.

In July 2004 the UAE signed a Trade and Investment Framework Agreement with the USA—regarded as a preliminary step on the path towards a bilateral free-trade agreement (FTA). Negotiations with the USA over an FTA duly commenced in March 2005. However, the talks were postponed in March 2006 following a sustained disagreement between the two countries over the acquisition of the United Kingdom-based ports and ferries operator, P&O, which owned six US ports (among a total portfolio of 51 terminals), by the state-owned Dubai Ports World (DP World). DP World agreed to divest the six US ports after the US Congress, in opposition to the US executive, threatened to block the deal owing to security fears.

Meanwhile, relations between the UAE and Saudi Arabia, which had argued that the GCC should negotiate a trade deal as a single body, had also become strained by the Emirates' trade negotiations with the USA. In December 2005 the Saudi–UAE relationship was weakened further by a border dispute relating to the Shaybah oilfield in the Rub al-Khali desert region.

Government

The highest federal authority is the Supreme Council of Rulers, comprising the hereditary rulers of the seven emirates, each of whom is virtually an absolute monarch in his own domain. Decisions of the Supreme Council require the approval of at least five members, including the rulers of both Abu Dhabi and Dubai. From its seven members, the Supreme Council elects a President and a Vice-President. The President appoints the Prime Minister and the Federal Council of Ministers, responsible to the Supreme Council, to hold executive authority. The legislature is the Federal National Council, a consultative assembly (comprising 40 members appointed for two years by the emirates) which considers laws proposed by the Council of Ministers. There are no political parties.

Defence

In August 2005 the armed forces totalled an estimated 50,500 men (of whom some 30% were thought to be expatriates): an army of 44,000, an air force of 4,000 and a navy of around 2,500. The Union Defence Force and the armed forces of Abu Dhabi, Dubai, Ras al-Khaimah and Sharjah were formally merged in 1976, although Dubai still maintains a degree of independence (as to a lesser extent do other emirates). Military service is voluntary. The defence budget for 2005 was estimated at AED 9,740m. A US air force, numbering 1,300 at August 2005, was also stationed in the UAE.

Economic Affairs

In 1998, according to estimates by the World Bank, the UAE's gross national income (GNI), measured at average 1996–98 prices, was US $49,205m., equivalent to $18,060 per head (or $19,410 on an international purchasing-power parity basis). During 1995–2004, it was estimated, the population increased by an average annual rate of 6.6%, while gross domestic product (GDP) per head decreased, in real terms, by an average of 1.4% per year during 1995–2002. Overall GDP increased, in real terms, by an average annual rate of 5.0% in 1995–2002; according to Central Bank figures, growth was 11.9% in 2003 and an estimated 9.7% in 2004.

Agriculture (including livestock and fishing) contributed an estimated 2.6% of GDP and engaged 6.9% of the employed population in 2004. The principal crops are dates, tomatoes and cabbages. The UAE imports some 70% of food requirements, but is self-sufficient in salad vegetables, eggs and poultry. Some agricultural products are exported, on a small scale. Livestock-rearing and fishing are also important. During 1993–2002 agricultural GDP increased at an average annual rate of 9.0%; the sector grew by 0.3% in 2003 and by 9.7% in 2004.

Industry (including mining, manufacturing, construction and power) contributed an estimated 54.2% of GDP and engaged 35.9% of the working population in 2004. During 1993–2002 industrial GDP increased by an average of 3.6% per year; the sector expanded by 12.7% in 2003 and by 7.3% in 2004.

Mining and quarrying contributed an estimated 32.2% of GDP and employed 2.3% of the working population in 2004. Petroleum production is the most important industry in the UAE, with exports of crude petroleum and related products providing an estimated 40.0% of total export revenues in 2005. At the end of 2004 the UAE's proven recoverable reserves of petroleum were 97,800m. barrels, representing 8.2% of world reserves. Production levels in 2004 averaged 2.67m. barrels per day (b/d). From July 2005 the UAE's production quota within the Organization of the Petroleum Exporting Countries (OPEC, see p. 344) was 2,444,000 b/d. The UAE has large natural gas reserves, estimated at 6,060,000m. cu m at the end of 2004 (3.4% of world reserves). Most petroleum and natural gas reserves are concentrated in Abu Dhabi. Dubai is the second largest producer of petroleum in the UAE. Marble and sand are also quarried.

THE UNITED ARAB EMIRATES

Introductory Survey

The major heavy industries in the UAE are related to hydrocarbons, and activities are concentrated in the Jebel Ali Free Zone (in Dubai) and the Jebel Dhanna-Ruwais industrial zone in Abu Dhabi. The most important products are liquefied petroleum gas, distillate fuel oils and jet fuels. There are two petroleum refineries in Abu Dhabi, and the emirate has 'downstream' interests abroad. Manufacturing contributed an estimated 12.9% of GDP and employed 13.0% of the working population in 2004. The most important sectors are aluminium, steel and chemicals. During 1993–2002 manufacturing GDP increased at an average annual rate of 9.1%; the sector's GDP expanded by 7.9% in 2003 and by 16.3% in 2004.

Electric energy is generated largely by thermal power stations, utilizing the UAE's own petroleum and natural gas resources. Each of the emirates is responsible for its own energy production.

The services sector contributed an estimated 43.2% of GDP and engaged 57.3% of the working population in 2004. The establishment of the Jebel Ali Free Zone in 1985 enhanced Dubai's reputation as a well-equipped entrepôt for regional trade, and significant growth in both re-exports and tourism has been recorded in recent years. Following a sharp decline in values on the informal stock exchange in mid-1998, an official stock exchange was inaugurated in Dubai in March 2000; a second exchange was subsequently opened in Abu Dhabi. During 1993–2002 the GDP of the services sector increased by an average of 6.2% per year; the sector's GDP increased by 11.3% in 2003 and by 12.6% in 2004.

In 2004, according to preliminary estimates, the UAE recorded a visible trade surplus of AED 99,910m., and there was a surplus of AED 37,930m. on the current account of the balance of payments. In 2004 the principal source of imports was India, with 12.8% of the total. Other important suppliers in that year were China, Japan, the USA, Germany and the United Kingdom. The principal market for non-petroleum exports in 2004 was also India, with 16.0% of the total. Other important markets in that year were Iran, Saudi Arabia, China and Bahrain. Much of the UAE's petroleum is exported to Far East Asian countries. The principal exports in 2004, excluding hydrocarbons, were base metals and articles of base metal, plastics, rubber and related articles, and pearls, precious or semi-precious stones and precious metals. The principal imports in that year were machinery and electrical equipment, pearls, precious or semi-precious stones and precious metals, and vehicles and other transport equipment.

A deficit of AED 855m. was estimated for the consolidated government budget of 2004. In the same year there was an estimated federal budgetary deficit of AED 2,160m. The federal budget, to which Abu Dhabi is the major contributor, reflects only about one-quarter of the country's total public expenditure, as the individual emirates also have their own budgets for municipal expenditure and local projects. Annual inflation averaged 2.3% in 1995–2002. Consumer prices rose by 3.1% in 2003 and by 4.7% in 2004. Some 2.3% of the labour force were recorded as unemployed in 2000. About 80% of the work-force are estimated to be non-UAE nationals.

In addition to its membership of OPEC (see p. 344) and the Co-operation Council for the Arab States of the Gulf (GCC, see p. 205), the UAE also belongs to the Organization of Arab Petroleum Exporting Countries (OAPEC, see p. 338) and the Arab Fund for Economic and Social Development (AFESD, see p. 161). The UAE, and Abu Dhabi in particular, is a major aid donor. Abu Dhabi disburses loans through the Abu Dhabi Fund for Development (ADFD). GCC member states established a unified regional customs tariff in January 2003 and agreed to create a single market and currency no later than January 2010. The economic convergence criteria for the monetary union were agreed at a GCC summit in Abu Dhabi in December 2005.

Abu Dhabi and Dubai, the principal petroleum producers, dominate the economy of the UAE, while the northern emirates remain relatively undeveloped. (In January 2005, for example, the federal Government announced that the northern emirates would receive an extra US $408m. from the state budget.) There is little co-ordination in the economic affairs of the emirates, and the relationship between Abu Dhabi and Dubai in particular is not always cordial. The UAE is less dependent than other petroleum-producing countries on the hydrocarbons sector (crude oil accounted for some 32.0% of GDP in 2004), and Dubai is of particular importance as an entrepôt for regional trade. Following a period of reduced income from petroleum in the late 1990s (owing to the decline in international petroleum prices), the Emirates have sought different ways of maximizing government revenue; Abu Dhabi has continued with its privatization programme, divesting the electricity and water sector along with telecommunications; Dubai has encouraged self-reliance and greater profitability among its state enterprises; and the northern emirates have continued to expand non-oil-sector activities. In recent years, the federal economy has recorded a sustained high performance. Although the UAE was concerned that its tourism sector (which enjoyed particularly strong growth in Dubai during the 1990s) would be severely affected by renewed conflict in the Gulf, the repercussions of the US-led military campaign to oust the regime of Saddam Hussain in Iraq and further regional instability related to Iran pushed oil prices to very high levels, leading to a strong export performance in 2003–05. The 2006 budget, approved by the Council of Ministers in February, anticipated a fiscal balance that was almost certain to result in an actual surplus due to petroleum prices remaining at a higher level than projected. Economic growth was estimated at 9.7% in 2004, and further impressive increases in real GDP, of about 8%, were forecast for 2005 and 2006. It was, however, regarded as important that the UAE address its rapidly increasing inflation rate, which was reported to have reached some 15% at the end of 2005. Another disadvantage of the rapid economic expansion driven by the huge petroleum revenues was the insulation it provided to the administration from incentives to reform, either politically (in terms of democratization) or economically (in terms of diversification).

Education

Primary education is compulsory, beginning at six years of age and lasting for six years. Secondary education, starting at the age of 12, also lasts for six years, comprising two equal cycles of three years. As a proportion of all school-age children, the total enrolment at primary schools was equivalent to 83% in 2002/03 (males 84%; females 82%). Secondary enrolment included 71% of children in the relevant age-group in the same year (males 70%; females 72%). Most of the teachers are from other Arab countries. In September 1988 four higher colleges of technology (two for male and two for female students) opened, admitting a total of 425 students, all of whom were citizens of the UAE; by 2002/03 71,194 students were enrolled in university and other higher education. In 2002/03 16,128 students were enrolled at the University at Al-Ain in Abu Dhabi. Many other students currently receive higher education abroad. Federal government expenditure provided to the Ministries of Education and of Higher Education and Scientific Research in the 2002/03 fiscal year totalled AED 5,383m. (25.3% of total expenditure by the central Government). The Sorbonne University, based in Paris, France, signed an agreement in February 2006 with the Ministry of Higher Education and Scientific Research to open a branch in Abu Dhabi.

Public Holidays

2006: 1 January (New Year's Day), 10 January*† (Id al-Adha, Feast of the Sacrifice), 31 January* (Muharram, Islamic New Year), 10 April* (Mouloud, Birth of Muhammad), 21 August* (Leilat al-Meiraj, Ascension of Muhammad), 24 September* (first day of Ramadan), 23 October* (Id al-Fitr, end of Ramadan), 2 December (National Day), 25 December (Christmas Day), 31 December*† (Id al-Adha, Feast of the Sacrifice).

2007: 1 January (New Year's Day), 20 January* (Muharram, Islamic New Year), 31 March* (Mouloud, Birth of Muhammad), 10 August* (Leilat al-Meiraj, Ascension of Muhammad), 13 September* (first day of Ramadan), 13 October* (Id al-Fitr, end of Ramadan), 2 December (National Day), 20 December* (Id al-Adha, Feast of the Sacrifice), 25 December (Christmas Day).

* These holidays are dependent on the Islamic lunar calendar and may vary slightly from the dates given.

† This festival occurs twice (in the Islamic years AH 1426 and 1427) within the same Gregorian year.

Weights and Measures

The imperial, metric and local systems are all in use.

THE UNITED ARB EMIRATES

Statistical Survey

Source (unless otherwise stated): Planning Sector, Ministry of Economy and Planning, POB 901, Abu Dhabi; tel. (2) 6265000; fax (2) 6215339; e-mail mop@uae.gov.ae; internet www.uae.gov.ae/mop.

Area and Population

AREA, POPULATION AND DENSITY

Area (sq km)	77,700*
Population (census results)	
December 1985	1,622,464
17 December 1995	
Males	1,606,804
Females	804,237
Total	2,411,041
Population (official estimates at mid-year)	
2002	3,754,000
2003	4,041,000
2004	4,320,000
Density (per sq km) at mid-2004	55.6

* 30,000 sq miles.

POPULATION BY EMIRATE
(preliminary figures, mid-2003)

	Area (sq km)	Population	Density (per sq km)
Abu Dhabi	67,350	1,591,000	23.6
Dubai	3,900	1,204,000	308.7
Sharjah	2,600	636,000	244.6
Ajman	250	235,000	940.0
Ras al-Khaimah	1,700	195,000	114.7
Fujairah	1,150	118,000	102.6
Umm al-Qaiwain	750	62,000	82.7
Total	77,700	4,041,000	52.0

PRINCIPAL TOWNS
(estimated population at mid-2003)

Dubai	1,171,000	Ras al-Khaimah	102,000
Abu Dhabi (capital)	552,000	Fujairah	54,000
Sharjah	519,000	Umm Al-Quwain	38,000
Al-Ain	348,000	Khor-Fakkan	32,000
Ajman	225,000		

BIRTHS, MARRIAGES AND DEATHS

	Live births Number	Rate (per 1,000)	Marriages* Number	Rate (per 1,000)	Deaths Number	Rate (per 1,000)
1996	47,050	18.9	6,275	2.5	4,785	1.9
1997	46,360	17.5	6,573	2.5	4,878	1.8
1998	48,136	17.0	6,920	2.4	5,033	1.8
1999	49,659	16.4	10,182	3.4	5,194	1.7
2000	53,686	16.5	8,965	2.8	5,396	1.7
2001	56,136	16.1	9,697	2.8	5,758	1.8
2002	58,070	15.5	11,285	3.0	5,994	1.6
2003	61,165	15.1	12,277	3.0	6,002	1.5

* Muslim marriages only.

Expectation of life (WHO estimates, years at birth): 73 (males 72; females 75) in 2003 (Source: WHO, *World Health Report*).

EMPLOYMENT
(persons aged 15 years and over)

	2002	2003	2004*
Agriculture, hunting, forestry and fishing	163,192	166,428	168,574
Mining and quarrying	31,702	32,911	35,575
Oil and gas	27,197	28,073	30,015
Manufacturing	276,476	299,064	319,384
Electricity, gas and water supply	26,591	28,359	28,848
Construction	420,896	473,577	497,974
Wholesale and retail trade; repair of motor vehicles, motorcycles and personal and household goods	415,974	450,208	478,716
Hotels and restaurants	94,930	98,509	109,931
Transport, storage and communications	130,923	142,548	147,807
Financial intermediation	25,724	26,368	27,011
Real estate, renting and business activities	63,664	67,107	73,817
Public administration and defence; compulsory social security	237,368	250,174	264,568
Community, social and personal service activities	91,035	99,328	106,700
Private households with employed persons	197,825	199,731	200,240
Total employed	2,176,300	2,334,312	2,459,145

* Preliminary figures.

Health and Welfare

KEY INDICATORS

Total fertility rate (children per woman, 2003)	2.8
Under-5 mortality rate (per 1,000 live births, 2004)	8
HIV/AIDS (% of persons aged 15–49, 1994)	0.18
Physicians (per 1,000 head, 1997)	1.81
Hospital beds (per 1,000 head, 1996)	2.64
Health expenditure (2002): US $ per head (PPP)	750
Health expenditure (2002): % of GDP	3.1
Health expenditure (2002): public (% of total)	73.4
Access to sanitation (% of persons, 2002)	100
Human Development Index (2003): ranking	41
Human Development Index (2003): value	0.849

For sources and definitions, see explanatory note on p. vi.

Agriculture

PRINCIPAL CROPS
('000 metric tons)

	2002	2003	2004*
Potatoes	10.0	7.1	7.1
Cabbages	29.9	14.3	15.0
Lettuce	1.7	0.8	0.9
Spinach	0.8	1.0*	1.0
Tomatoes	231.1	134.0	240.0
Cauliflower	12.5	5.5	10.0
Pumpkins, squash and gourds	20.5	19.8	20.0
Cucumbers and gherkins	25.9	11.3	15.0
Aubergines (Eggplants)	18.1	14.1	20.0
Chillies and green peppers	5.3	5.4	5.4
Green onions and shallots	13.2	15.9	15.9

THE UNITED ARAB EMIRATES

—continued

	2002	2003	2004*
Green beans	2.2	1.1	1.2
Carrots	2.0	1.1	2.0
Other vegetables	140.6	150.0*	150.0
Watermelons	6.7	2.3	3.0
Cantaloupes and other melons	12.3	4.7	7.0
Lemons and limes	15.3	11.3	11.3
Other citrus fruit	5.9	4.9	4.9
Mangoes	9.3	4.3	4.3
Dates	757.6	757.6	760.0
Other fruit	6.8	5.3	5.6

* FAO estimate(s).
Source: FAO.

LIVESTOCK
('000 head, year ending September)

	2002	2003	2004*
Cattle	107	113	115
Camels	246	259	250
Sheep	554	583	590
Goats	1,430	1,495	1,450
Chickens*	12,000	18,000	13,000

* FAO estimates.
Source: FAO.

LIVESTOCK PRODUCTS
('000 metric tons)

	2002	2003	2004*
Beef and veal*	9.2	9.5	9.8
Camel meat*	14.6	15.4	15.4
Mutton and lamb*	17.1	7.2	9.0
Goat meat*	11.2	10.4	10.4
Poultry meat*	28.6	41.0	30.0
Cows' milk	10.9	11.5	11.5
Camels' milk	37.3	39.2	39.4
Sheep's milk	11.0	11.6	12.0
Goats' milk	33.1	34.8	35.0
Hen eggs	17.7†	16.7†	17.0

* FAO estimates.
† Unofficial figure.
Source: FAO.

Fishing
('000 metric tons, live weight of capture)

	2001	2002	2003
Capture	112.6	97.6	95.2
Groupers and seabasses	27.7	22.8	18.8
Grunts and sweetlips	4.8	4.5	3.8
Emperors (Scavengers)	22.6	21.1	20.3
King soldier bream	4.1	4.8	5.9
Sardinellas	4.2	3.5	4.1
Stolephorus anchovies	4.0	6.4	3.5
Narrow-barred Spanish mackerel	7.7	3.8	5.7
Other seerfishes	2.9	—	—
Jacks and crevalles	2.8	4.8	1.6
Carangids	4.1	1.2	3.3
Indian mackerel	2.0	2.1	2.9
Aquaculture	—	—	2.3
Total catch (incl. others)	112.6	97.6	97.5

Source: FAO.

Mining

	2002	2003	2004
Crude petroleum (million barrels)	750	920	970
Natural gas (million cu metres)*	42,000	45,000	46,000

* On a dry basis.
Source: US Geological Survey.

Industry

SELECTED PRODUCTS
(estimates, '000 barrels, unless otherwise indicated)

	2002	2003	2004
Cement ('000 metric tons)	7,000	9,000	8,000
Aluminium ('000 metric tons)	536	560	683
Motor spirit (petrol)	11,400	11,000	12,000
Kerosene	39,000	40,000	40,000
Gas-diesel (distillate fuel) oil	34,900	33,800	36,000
Residual fuel oils	11,300	7,800	13,000
Liquefied petroleum gas	81,000	87,000	88,000

Source: US Geological Survey.

Electric energy (million kWh): 42,957 in 2002; 48,163 in 2003 (preliminary).

Finance

CURRENCY AND EXCHANGE RATES

Monetary Units
   100 fils = 1 UAE dirham (AED).

Sterling, Dollar and Euro Equivalents (30 December 2005)
   £1 sterling = 6.324 dirhams;
   US $1 = 3.673 dirhams;
   €1 = 4.332 dirhams;
   100 UAE dirhams = £15.81 = $27.23 = €23.08.

Exchange Rate: The Central Bank's official rate was set at US $1 = 3.671 dirhams in November 1980. This remained in force until December 1997, when the rate was adjusted to $1 = 3.6725 dirhams.

BUDGET OF THE CONSOLIDATED GOVERNMENTS
(million UAE dirhams)

Revenue	2002	2003	2004*
Tax revenue	6,881	7,044	9,255
Custom revenue	1,663	2,449	3,040
Non-tax revenue	50,337	69,968	85,160
Revenue from petroleum and natural gas	40,926	56,738	73,322
Profit of joint stock corporations	3,357	2,935	3,322
Total	57,218	77,012	94,415

Expenditure	2002	2003	2004*
Current expenditure	72,602	74,253	79,986
Salaries and wages	14,612	15,159	15,484
Goods and services	22,187	23,801	24,260
Subsidies and transfers	14,782	10,408	11,281
Development expenditure	12,470	16,028	15,551
Loans and equity	1,544	1,152	−267
Total	86,616	91,433	95,270

* Preliminary.
Source: Central Bank of the United Arab Emirates.

THE UNITED ARAB EMIRATES

Statistical Survey

INTERNATIONAL RESERVES
(US $ million at 31 December)

	2002	2003	2004
Gold*	90.7	—	—
IMF special drawing rights	1.5	0.7	5.4
Reserve position in IMF	320.6	355.6	315.5
Foreign exchange†	14,897.2	14,731.5	18,209.0
Total	15,310.0	15,087.8	18,529.9

* Valued at US $228 per troy ounce.
† Figures exclude the Central Bank's foreign assets and accrued interest attributable to the governments of individual emirates.

Source: IMF, *International Financial Statistics*.

MONEY SUPPLY
(million UAE dirhams at 31 December)

	2002	2003	2004
Currency outside banks	11,938	13,785	15,778
Demand deposits at commercial banks	35,116	44,477	65,040
Total money	47,054	58,262	80,818

Source: IMF, *International Financial Statistics*.

COST OF LIVING
(Consumer Price Index; base: 2000 = 100)

	2002	2003	2004*
Food, beverages and tobacco	102.4	104.7	110.2
Clothing and footwear	104.9	106.6	108.5
Housing (incl. rent)	107.1	112.7	120.2
Furniture, etc.	102.8	104.4	106.8
Medical care and health services	112.5	115.3	118.8
Transport and communications	103.8	106.6	112.9
Recreation and education	113.2	114.7	116.2
All items (incl. others)	105.8	109.1	114.2

* Preliminary figures.

NATIONAL ACCOUNTS
(million UAE dirhams at current prices)

National Income and Product

	2002	2003	2004*
Compensation of employees	79,102	88,926	94,395
Operating surplus	157,785	193,950	242,972
Domestic factor incomes	236,887	282,876	337,367
Consumption of fixed capital	35,969	38,876	41,394
Gross domestic product (GDP) at factor cost	272,856	321,752	378,761
Indirect taxes, *less* subsidies	2,430	3,396	3,928
GDP in purchasers' values	275,286	325,148	382,689
Net factor income from abroad	−11,805	−16,261	−16,135
Gross national income	263,481	308,887	366,554
Less Consumption of fixed capital	35,969	38,876	41,394
National income in market prices	227,512	270,011	325,160
Less Net current transfers from abroad	1,050	1,000	1,500
National disposable income	226,462	269,011	323,660

* Preliminary figures.

Expenditure on the Gross Domestic Product

	2002	2003	2004*
Government final consumption expenditure	41,818	46,057	48,221
Private final consumption expenditure	142,829	158,047	184,677
Increase in stocks	2,870	2,950	3,392
Gross fixed capital formation	62,404	73,105	81,255
Total domestic expenditure	249,921	280,159	317,545
Exports of goods and services	201,076	256,775	314,988
Less Imports of goods and services	175,711	211,786	249,844
GDP in purchasers' values	275,286	325,148	382,689

* Preliminary figures.

Gross Domestic Product by Economic Activity

	2002	2003	2004*
Agriculture, hunting, forestry and fishing	9,105	9,152	10,100
Mining and quarrying	73,277	92,901	124,089
Oil and gas	72,552	92,136	123,261
Manufacturing	37,710	42,215	49,546
Electricity and water	4,930	6,009	6,720
Construction	21,478	26,072	28,468
Wholesale and retail trade, and repairs	28,894	35,460	38,682
Restaurants and hotels	6,025	6,525	7,343
Transport, storage and communications	21,742	24,692	27,263
Financial institutions and insurance	17,314	19,902	22,318
Real estate and business services	22,524	25,355	29,540
Government services	27,864	30,737	32,201
Community, social and personal services	5,663	6,492	6,951
Private households with employed persons	2,030	2,065	2,126
Sub-total	278,556	327,577	385,347
Less Imputed bank service charge	5,700	5,825	6,586
Net indirect taxes	2,430	3,396	3,928
GDP in purchasers' values	275,286	325,148	382,689

* Preliminary figures.

BALANCE OF PAYMENTS
(preliminary, '000 million UAE dirhams)

	2002	2003	2004
Exports of goods f.o.b.	191.57	246.56	332.87
Imports of goods f.o.b.	−137.84	−168.29	−232.96
Trade balance	53.73	78.26	99.91
Services (net)	−28.36	−33.27	−44.35
Income (net)	3.40	−0.14	0.93
Balance on goods, services and income	28.77	44.85	56.49
Current transfers (net)	−16.25	−17.12	−18.57
Current balance	12.51	27.73	37.93
Capital and financial accounts (net)	−5.50	−24.59	−19.30
Net errors and omissions	−8.53	1.59	−5.81
Overall balance	−1.52	4.73	12.83

Source: Central Bank of the United Arab Emirates.

THE UNITED ARAB EMIRATES

External Trade

PRINCIPAL COMMODITIES
(million UAE dirhams)

Imports c.i.f.	2001	2002	2003
Vegetable products	5,400.1	6,394.8	5,767.6
Prepared foodstuffs, beverages, spirits and tobacco	2,974.8	3,481.2	4,942.1
Chemical products, etc.	6,696.3	7,180.6	8,927.5
Plastics, rubber and articles thereof	4,325.1	4,693.0	5,573.9
Textiles and textile articles	10,083.1	10,572.3	11,262.2
Pearls, precious or semi-precious stones, precious metals, etc.	16,462.9	17,357.9	21,181.2
Base metals and articles of base metal	8,226.5	9,887.7	13,305.1
Machinery and electrical equipment	26,236.3	29,804.7	34,072.8
Vehicles and other transport equipment	14,915.6	14,866.7	21,537.8
Total (incl. others)	112,175.7	122,582.5	147,775.8

Exports f.o.b.*	2001	2002	2003
Vegetable products	237.2	213.5	225.6
Prepared foodstuffs, beverages, spirits and tobacco	319.8	469.5	1,080.7
Mineral products	536.4	1,288.8	1,258.2
Chemical products, etc.	359.3	422.7	441.3
Plastics, rubber and articles thereof	215.1	690.9	1,093.8
Textiles and textile articles	908.1	822.3	719.3
Stone, plaster, cement, ceramic and glassware	394.5	490.0	922.5
Base metals and articles of base metal	3,475.9	3,286.8	3,221.1
Machinery and electrical equipment	271.6	155.2	195.8
Vehicles and other transport equipment	247.2	41.0	582.1
Total (incl. others)†	7,536.0	8,649.5	10,588.6

* Excluding petroleum exports and excluding re-exports; re-exports amounted to 31,444.0m. dirhams in 2001, 41,124.9m. dirhams in 2002 and 50,696.7m. dirhams in 2003.
† Excluding free-zone exports.

PRINCIPAL TRADING PARTNERS
(million UAE dirhams)

Imports	2002	2003	2004
Australia	2,415.1	2,594.0	3,319.4
Belgium	2,009.1	2,205.1	3,262.8
Brazil	969.7	1,492.1	2,363.9
China, People's Republic	12,560.7	15,753.6	19,514.6
Finland	714.8	1,362.4	2,110.7
France (incl. Monaco)	5,921.1	9,859.8	9,990.0
Germany	9,254.0	11,593.6	12,970.9
Hong Kong	1,401.0	1,683.0	2,229.6
India	7,665.8	12,037.1	26,070.4
Indonesia	1,879.6	2,103.2	2,384.3
Iran	1,433.1	1,974.7	4,035.7
Italy (incl. San Marino)	5,275.3	6,260.5	7,821.7
Japan	10,145.1	12,775.1	16,262.8
Korea, Republic	5,914.5	4,703.2	6,059.9
Malaysia	1,725.2	2,612.6	4,166.9
Netherlands	1,918.0	2,132.6	2,229.3
Pakistan	1,283.9	1,539.7	1,643.1
Saudi Arabia	4,121.1	5,036.0	6,539.3
Singapore	2,605.8	2,482.5	2,969.4
Spain	1,521.2	1,661.6	1,975.0
Switzerland-Liechtenstein	1,093.2	4,878.8	7,046.6
Taiwan	1,872.8	1,967.0	2,516.0
Thailand	1,928.9	2,036.4	2,586.0
Turkey	1,624.2	2,627.0	4,102.4
United Kingdom	7,904.2	8,144.2	10,864.2
USA	9,606.2	9,687.5	13,875.2
Total (incl. others)	122,582.5	147,775.8	202,896.4

Exports*	2002	2003	2004
Afghanistan	106.8	92.3	143.4
Australia	84.4	117.7	199.7
Bahrain	682.6	925.1	607.0
Belgium	71.0	101.5	341.2
Canada	182.2	156.1	130.6
China, People's Republic	372.9	465.0	667.0
Egypt	96.8	141.3	228.4
Germany	154.8	96.8	112.4
India	480.8	567.4	2,335.0
Indonesia	172.5	233.9	282.8
Iran	295.4	941.6	1,265.9
Iraq	67.8	282.7	591.6
Italy	120.8	98.6	123.4
Japan	542.8	440.2	315.2
Korea, Republic	406.8	321.5	213.5
Kuwait	401.5	563.2	475.5
Malaysia	133.2	95.2	169.4
Netherlands	287.2	263.7	155.6
Oman	109.3	92.8	160.8
Pakistan	174.2	324.3	436.8
Qatar	202.2	237.7	323.9
Saudi Arabia	403.8	503.1	692.9
Singapore	96.7	105.4	170.0
Somalia	72.6	328.1	334.6
Sri Lanka	50.1	61.9	157.4
Sudan	105.5	120.5	188.6
Syria	103.9	125.2	124.7
Taiwan	183.1	243.7	354.9
Thailand	129.7	201.5	170.2
United Kingdom	316.1	259.6	289.9
USA	610.2	485.0	521.6
Yemen	273.3	278.5	402.0
Total (incl. others)	8,649.5	10,588.6	14,615.2

* Excluding petroleum exports.

Transport

ROAD TRAFFIC
('000 registered motor vehicles in use)

	2000	2001	2002
Passenger cars (incl. taxis)	561.9	654.2	606.1
Trucks (incl. public)	83.3	66.2	66.2
Buses (incl. public)	14.7	13.3	16.0
Other	13.2	11.2	13.1
Total	701.4	745.0	673.0

Total vehicles in use ('000 registered): 767 in 2002 (revised); 792 in 2003.

SHIPPING

Merchant Fleet
(registered at 31 December)

	2002	2003	2004
Number of vessels	356	363	384
Total displacement ('000 grt)	703.3	799.0	799.2

Source: Lloyd's Register-Fairplay, *World Fleet Statistics*.

International Sea-borne Shipping
(estimated freight traffic, '000 metric tons)

	1988	1989	1990
Goods loaded	63,380	72,896	88,153
Crude petroleum	54,159	63,387	78,927
Other cargo	9,221	9,509	9,226
Goods unloaded	8,973	8,960	9,595

Source: UN, *Monthly Bulletin of Statistics*.

THE UNITED ARAB EMIRATES

CIVIL AVIATION
(traffic on scheduled services)*

	1999	2000	2001
Kilometres flown (million)	106	123	136
Passengers carried ('000)	5,848	6,893	7,676
Passenger-km (million)	18,154	22,691	26,202
Total ton-km (million)	2,950	3,649	4,148

* Figures include an apportionment (one-quarter) of the traffic of Gulf Air, a multinational airline with its headquarters in Bahrain.

Source: UN, *Statistical Yearbook*.

Tourism

FOREIGN TOURIST ARRIVALS*

Country	2001	2002	2003
Canada	36,742	95,878	55,297
Egypt	96,002	111,822	121,221
France	69,620	90,735	98,624
Germany	194,079	236,660	235,147
India	246,335	336,046	357,941
Iran	194,140	270,350	334,453
Jordan	58,844	73,140	76,553
Lebanon	61,133	74,225	83,137
Pakistan	117,116	154,711	183,724
Russia	205,126	267,655	324,484
United Kingdom	384,443	491,604	496,147
USA	98,893	123,112	175,116
Total (incl. others)†	4,133,531	5,445,367	5,871,023

* Figures refer to international arrivals at hotels and similar establishments.
† Total includes domestic tourists.

Receipts from tourism (US $ million, incl. passenger transport): 1,200 in 2001; 1,332 in 2002; 1,439 in 2003.

Source: World Tourism Organization.

Communications Media

	2002	2003	2004
Telephones ('000 main lines in use)	1,093.7	1,135.8	1,187.7
Mobile cellular telephones ('000 subscribers)	2,428.1	2,972.3	3,683.1
Personal computers ('000 in use)	450	n.a.	450
Internet users ('000)	1,016.8	1,110.2	1,348.8
Daily newspapers	9	n.a.	n.a.

1996: Combined circulation of 7 daily newspapers 384,000 copies.
1997 ('000 in use): Radio receivers 820; Facsimile machines 50.
2001 ('000 in use): Television receivers 780.

Sources: partly UNESCO, *Statistical Yearbook*; UN, *Statistical Yearbook*; International Telecommunication Union.

Education

(Government schools only)

	2000/01	2002/03	2003/04
Institutions	740	744	755
Teachers*	27,616	27,954	27,855
Students			
Pre-primary	22,219	22,596	20,561
Primary	204,760	214,235	218,739
Secondary	65,195	65,202	64,618
Other schools	3,487	4,607	5,154

* Includes administrative and technical staff.

Adult literacy rate (UNESCO estimates): 77.3% (males 75.6%; females 80.7%) in 2002 (Source: UNDP, *Human Development Report*).

Directory

The Constitution

A provisional Constitution for the UAE took effect in December 1971. This laid the foundation for the federal structure of the Union of the seven emirates, previously known as the Trucial States.

The highest federal authority is the Supreme Council of Rulers, which comprises the rulers of the seven emirates. It elects the President and Vice-President from among its members. The President appoints a Prime Minister and a Council of Ministers. Proposals submitted to the Council require the approval of at least five of the Rulers, including those of Abu Dhabi and Dubai. The legislature is the Federal National Council, a consultative assembly comprising 40 members appointed by the emirates for a two-year term.

In July 1975 a committee was appointed to draft a permanent federal constitution, but the National Council decided in 1976 to extend the provisional document for five years. The provisional Constitution was extended for another five years in December 1981, and for further periods of five years in 1986 and 1991. In November 1976, however, the Supreme Council amended Article 142 of the provisional Constitution so that the authority to levy armed forces was placed exclusively under the control of the federal Government. Legislation designed to make the provisional Constitution permanent was endorsed by the Federal National Council in June 1996, after it had been approved by the Supreme Council of Rulers.

The Government

HEAD OF STATE

President: Sheikh KHALIFA BIN ZAYED AN-NAHYAN (Ruler of Abu Dhabi, elected by the Supreme Council of Rulers as President of the UAE on 3 November 2004).

Vice-President: Sheikh MUHAMMAD BIN RASHID AL-MAKTOUM (Ruler of Dubai).

SUPREME COUNCIL OF RULERS
(with each Ruler's date of accession)

Ruler of Abu Dhabi: Sheikh KHALIFA BIN ZAYED AN-NAHYAN (2004).
Ruler of Dubai: Sheikh MUHAMMAD BIN RASHID AL-MAKTOUM (2006).
Ruler of Sharjah: Sheikh SULTAN BIN MUHAMMAD AL-QASIMI (1972).
Ruler of Ras al-Khaimah: Sheikh SAQR BIN MUHAMMAD AL-QASIMI (1948).
Ruler of Umm al-Qaiwain: Sheikh RASHID BIN AHMAD AL-MU'ALLA (1981).
Ruler of Ajman: Sheikh HUMAID BIN RASHID AN-NUAIMI (1981).
Ruler of Fujairah: Sheikh HAMAD BIN MUHAMMAD ASH-SHARQI (1974).

COUNCIL OF MINISTERS
(April 2006)

Prime Minister and Minister of Defence: Sheikh MUHAMMAD BIN RASHID AL-MAKTOUM.
Deputy Prime Ministers: Sheikh SULTAN BIN ZAYED AN-NAHYAN, Sheikh HAMDAN BIN ZAYED AN-NAHYAN.
Minister of Finance and Industry: Sheikh HAMDAN BIN RASHID AL-MAKTOUM.
Minister of the Interior: Lt-Gen. Sheikh SAIF BIN ZAYED AN-NAHYAN.
Minister of Presidential Affairs: Sheikh MANSOUR BIN ZAYED AN-NAHYAN.
Minister of Foreign Affairs: Sheikh ABDULLAH BIN ZAYED AN-NAHYAN.

THE UNITED ARAB EMIRATES

Minister of Higher Education and Scientific Research: Sheikh NAHYAN BIN MUBARAK AN-NAHYAN.
Minister of Public Works: Sheikh HAMDAN BIN MUBARAK AN-NAHYAN.
Minister of Economy: Sheikha LUBNA BINT KHALID AL-QASIMI.
Minister of Justice: MUHAMMAD BIN NAKHIRA ADH-DHAHERI.
Minister of Energy: MUHAMMAD BIN DHAEN AL-HAMILI.
Minister of Labour: Dr ALI BIN ABDULLAH AL-KA'ABI.
Minister of Governmental Sector Development: SULTAN BIN SAID AL-MANSOUR.
Minister of Social Affairs: Dr MARIAM MUHAMMAD KHALFAN AR-ROUMI.
Minister of Education: Dr HANIF HASSAN ALI.
Minister of Health: HUMAID MUHAMMAD OBAID AL-QATTAMI.
Minister of the Environment and Water: Dr MUHAMMAD SAID AL-KINDI.
Minister of Culture, Youth and Community Development: ABD AR-RAHMAN MUHAMMAD AL-OWAIS.
Minister of State for Financial and Industrial Affairs: Dr MUHAMMAD KHALFAN BIN KHARBASH.
Minister of State for Cabinet Affairs: MUHAMMAD ABDULLAH AL-GARGAWI.
Minister of State for Foreign Affairs: MUHAMMAD HUSSAIN ASH-SHAALI.
Minister of State for Federal National Council Affairs: Dr ANWAR MUHAMMAD GARGASH.

FEDERAL MINISTRIES

Office of the Prime Minister: POB 12848, Dubai; tel. (4) 3534550; fax (4) 3530111.
Office of the Deputy Prime Minister: POB 831, Abu Dhabi; tel. (2) 4451000; fax (2) 4450066.
Ministry of Culture, Youth and Community Development: POB 17, Abu Dhabi.
Ministry of Defence: POB 46616, Abu Dhabi; tel. (4) 4461300; fax (4) 4463286.
Ministry of Economy: POB 901, Abu Dhabi; tel. (2) 6265000; fax (2) 6215339; e-mail economy@emirates.net.ae; internet www.uae.gov.ae/mop.
Ministry of Education: POB 295, Abu Dhabi; tel. (2) 6213800; fax (2) 6313778; e-mail moe@uae.gov.ae; internet www.moe.gov.ae.
Ministry of Energy: POB 59, Abu Dhabi; tel. (2) 6262288; fax (2) 6272291; e-mail moew@uae.gov.ae; internet www.uae.gov.ae/moew.
Ministry of the Environment and Water: POB 899, Abu Dhabi.
Ministry of Finance and Industry: POB 433, Abu Dhabi; tel. (2) 6726000; fax (2) 6768414; e-mail mofi@uae.gov.ae; internet www.uae.gov.ae/mofi.
Ministry of Foreign Affairs: POB 1, Abu Dhabi; tel. (2) 6652200; fax (2) 6668015; e-mail mofa@uae.gov.ae.
Ministry of Governmental Sector Development: POB 899, Abu Dhabi.
Ministry of Health: POB 848, Abu Dhabi; tel. (2) 6330000; fax (2) 6726000; e-mail postmaster@moh.gov.ae; internet www.moh.gov.ae/intro.
Ministry of Higher Education and Scientific Research: POB 45253, Abu Dhabi; tel. (2) 6428000; fax (2) 6427262; e-mail mohe@uae.gov.ae; internet www.uae.gov.ae/mohe.
Ministry of the Interior: POB 398, Abu Dhabi; tel. (2) 4414666; fax (2) 4414938; e-mail moi@uae.gov.ae; internet moi.uae.gov.ae.
Ministry of Justice: POB 260, Abu Dhabi; tel. (2) 6814000; fax (2) 6810680; e-mail moj@uae.gov.ae; internet www.uae.gov.ae/moj.
Ministry of Labour: POB 809, Abu Dhabi; tel. (2) 6671700; fax (2) 6665889; e-mail mol@uae.gov.ae; internet www.mol.gov.ae.
Ministry of Presidential Affairs: Abu Dhabi.
Ministry of Public Works: POB 878, Abu Dhabi; tel. (2) 6651778; fax (2) 6665598; e-mail mpwh@uae.gov.ae.
Ministry of Social Affairs: POB 809, Abu Dhabi.
Ministry of State for Cabinet Affairs: POB 899, Abu Dhabi; tel. (2) 6811106; fax (2) 6812968; e-mail moca@uae.gov.ae; internet www.uae.gov.ae/moca.
Ministry of State for Federal National Council Affairs: POB 899, Abu Dhabi.
Ministry of State for Financial and Industrial Affairs: POB 433, Abu Dhabi; tel. (2) 771133; fax (2) 793255.
Ministry of State for Foreign Affairs: POB 1, Abu Dhabi; tel. (2) 6660888; fax (2) 6652883.

Legislature
FEDERAL NATIONAL COUNCIL

Formed under the provisional Constitution, the Council is composed of 40 members from the various emirates (eight each from Abu Dhabi and Dubai, six each from Sharjah and Ras al-Khaimah, and four each from Ajman, Fujairah and Umm al-Qaiwain). Each emirate appoints its own representatives separately. The Council studies laws proposed by the Council of Ministers and can reject them or suggest amendments.
Speaker: SAID MUHAMMAD SAID AL-GHANDI.

Diplomatic Representation
EMBASSIES IN THE UNITED ARAB EMIRATES

Afghanistan: POB 5687, Abu Dhabi; tel. (2) 6655560; fax (2) 6655576; Ambassador FARID ZEKRIA.
Algeria: POB 3070, Abu Dhabi; tel. (2) 448943; fax (2) 447068; Ambassador HAMID CHEBIRA.
Argentina: POB 3325, Abu Dhabi; tel. (2) 4436838; fax (2) 4431392; e-mail embar@emirates.net.ae; Ambassador RUBÉN EDWARDO CARO.
Australia: POB 32711, Level 14, Al-Muhairy Centre, Abu Dhabi; tel. (2) 6346100; fax (2) 6393525; e-mail abudhabi.embassy@dfat.gov.au; internet www.uae.embassy.gov.au; Ambassador JEREMY CHRISTOPHER.
Austria: POB 35539, Al-Khazna Tower, Abu Dhabi; tel. (2) 6766611; fax (2) 6715551; e-mail abu-dhabi-ob@bmaa.gv.at; internet www.austrianembassy.ae; Ambassador Dr GERALD KRIECHBAUM.
Azerbaijan: Plot N-297, Villa Sector W/16, Al-Bateen Area, Abu Dhabi; tel. (2) 6662848; fax (2) 6663150; e-mail azembassy@emirates.net.ae; Ambassador ELDAR SALIMOV.
Bahrain: POB 3367, Abu Dhabi; tel. (2) 6657500; fax (2) 6674141; e-mail bahrain1@emirates.net.ae; Ambassador Sheikh AHMAD BIN KHALIFA AL-KHALIFA.
Bangladesh: POB 2504, Abu Dhabi; tel. (2) 4465100; fax (2) 4464733; e-mail banglaad@emirates.net.ae; Ambassador MIRZA SHAMSUZZAMAN.
Belarus: POB 30337, Villa 434, 26th St, Ar-Rouda Area, Abu Dhabi; tel. (2) 4453399; fax (2) 4451131; e-mail uae@belembassy.org; Ambassador VLADIMIR SULIMSKY.
Belgium: POB 3686, Abu Dhabi; tel. (2) 6319449; fax (2) 6319353; e-mail abudhabi@diplobel.org; internet www.diplomatie.be/abudhabi; Ambassador PHILIPPE DARTOIS.
Belize: POB 43432, Abu Dhabi; tel. (2) 6333554; fax (2) 6330429; Ambassador ELHAM S. FREIHA.
Bosnia and Herzegovina: POB 43362, Abu Dhabi; tel. (2) 6444164; fax (2) 6443619; e-mail embhad@emirates.net.ae; Ambassador MILUTIN VASILJEVIĆ.
Brazil: POB 3027, Abu Dhabi; tel. (2) 6665352; fax (2) 6654559; e-mail abubrem@emirates.net.ae; Ambassador JOSÉ FERREIRA LOPES.
Brunei: POB 5836, Abu Dhabi; tel. (2) 6817755; fax (2) 6813433; e-mail kbdauh98@emirates.net.ae; Ambassador Haji ADNAN BIN Haji ZAINAL.
Canada: POB 6970, Abu Dhabi; tel. (2) 4071300; fax (2) 4071399; e-mail abdbi@dfait-maeci.gc.ca; internet www.dfait-maeci.gc.ca/abudhabi/menu-en.asp; Ambassador W. DAVID HUTTON.
China, People's Republic: POB 2741, Abu Dhabi; tel. (2) 4434276; fax (2) 4436835; e-mail chinaemb_ae@mfa.gov.cn; internet ae.chineseembassy.org; Ambassador ZHANG ZHIJUN.
Czech Republic: POB 27009, Abu Dhabi; tel. (2) 6782800; fax (2) 6795716; e-mail abudhabi@embassy.mzv.cz; Ambassador ROMAN LESZCZYŃSKI.
Egypt: POB 4026, Abu Dhabi; tel. (2) 4445566; fax (2) 4449878; e-mail alaa1@emirates.net.ae; Ambassador MUHAMMAD SAID OBAID.
Eritrea: POB 2597, Abu Dhabi; tel. (2) 6331838; fax (2) 6346451; Ambassador OSMAN MUHAMMAD OMAR.
Finland: POB 3634, Abu Dhabi; tel. (2) 6328927; fax (2) 6325063; e-mail sanomat.abo@formin.fi; internet www.finland.ae; Ambassador RAIMO ANTTOLA.
France: POB 4014, Abu Dhabi; tel. (2) 4435100; fax (2) 4434158; e-mail ambafr@emirates.net.ae; internet www.ambafrance-eau.org; Ambassador PATRICE PAOLI.
The Gambia: Abu Dhabi; Ambassador KEBBA NJIE.
Germany: POB 2591, Abu Dhabi; tel. (2) 6446693; fax (2) 6446942; e-mail info@abu-dhabi.diplo.de; internet www.abu-dhabi.diplo.de; Ambassador JÜRGEN STELTZER.

Greece: POB 5483, Abu Dhabi; tel. (2) 6654847; fax (2) 6656008; e-mail grembauh@emirates.net.ae; Ambassador PANAGIOTIS THEODORAKOPOULOS.
Hungary: POB 44450, Abu Dhabi; tel. (2) 6660107; fax (2) 6667877; e-mail hungexad@emirates.net.ae; Chargé d'affaires a.i. ZSIGMOND DVORZSÁNSZKI.
India: POB 4090, Abu Dhabi; tel. (2) 6664800; fax (2) 6651518; e-mail infowing@indembassyuae.org; internet www.indembassyuae.org; Ambassador C. M. BHANDARI.
Indonesia: POB 7256, Abu Dhabi; tel. (2) 4454448; fax (2) 4455453; e-mail indonemb@emirates.net.ae; internet www.indonesianembassy.ae; Ambassador FAISAL BAFADAL.
Iran: POB 4080, Abu Dhabi; tel. (2) 4447618; fax (2) 4448714; e-mail iranemb@emirates.net.ae; internet www.iranembassy.org.ae; Ambassador MUHAMMAD ALI HADI.
Iraq: Manhal St, Haoudh 55, St 32, Abu Dhabi; tel. (2) 6655152; fax (2) 6655214; e-mail adbemb@iraqmofamail.net; Ambassador MUSTAFA KAMIL ABOOD.
Italy: POB 46752, Abu Dhabi; tel. (2) 4435622; fax (2) 4434337; e-mail info@italia.ae; internet www.ambabudhabi.esteri.it; Ambassador DOMENICO PEDATA.
Japan: POB 2430, Abu Dhabi; tel. (2) 4435969; fax (2) 4434219; e-mail embjpn@emirates.net.ae; internet www.uae.emb-japan.go.jp; Ambassador TOSHIO MOCHIZUKI.
Jordan: POB 4024, Abu Dhabi; tel. (2) 4447100; fax (2) 4449157; e-mail embjoad1@emirates.net.ae; Ambassador EID KAMAL AR-RODAN.
Kenya: POB 3854, Abu Dhabi; tel. (2) 6666300; fax (2) 6652827; e-mail kenyarep@emirates.net.ae; internet www.kenyaembassy-uae.org; Ambassador BISHAR A. HUSSEIN.
Korea, Republic: POB 3270, Abu Dhabi; tel. (2) 4435337; fax (2) 4435348; e-mail keauhlee@emirates.net.ae; Ambassador JOON-JAE LEE.
Kuwait: POB 926, Abu Dhabi; tel. (2) 4446888; fax (2) 4444990; Ambassador IBRAHIM AL-MANSOUR.
Lebanon: POB 4023, Abu Dhabi; tel. (2) 4492100; fax (2) 4493500; e-mail libanamb@emirates.net.ae; Ambassador HASSAN BERRO.
Libya: POB 5739, Abu Dhabi; tel. (2) 4450030; fax (2) 4450033; e-mail libyandh@emirates.net.ae; Chargé d'affaires ABD AL-HAMID ALI SHAIKHY.
Malaysia: POB 3887, Abu Dhabi; tel. (2) 4482775; fax (2) 4482779; e-mail mwadhabi@emirates.net.ae; Ambassador Dato' ABD. MUBIN RAZALI.
Mauritania: POB 2714, Abu Dhabi; tel. (2) 4462724; fax (2) 4465772; Ambassador MUHAMMAD AL-MUKHTAR OULD M. YAHAYA.
Morocco: POB 4066, Abu Dhabi; tel. (2) 4433963; fax (2) 4433917; e-mail sifmaabo@emirates.net.ae; Ambassador ABDELKADER ZAOUI.
Netherlands: POB 46560, Abu Dhabi; tel. (2) 6321920; fax (2) 6313158; e-mail abu.dhabi@minbuza.nl; internet www.netherlands.ae; Ambassador D. P. M. DE WAAL.
Norway: POB 47270, Abu Dhabi; tel. (2) 6211221; fax (2) 6213313; e-mail web.abudhabi@mfa.no; internet www.norway.ae; Ambassador ULF CHRISTIANSEN.
Oman: POB 2517, Abu Dhabi; tel. (2) 4463333; fax (2) 4464633; Ambassador Sheikh MUHAMMAD BIN MARHOON AL-MAMARI.
Pakistan: POB 846, Abu Dhabi; tel. (2) 4447800; fax (2) 4447172; e-mail pakem@emirates.net.ae; Ambassador (vacant).
Philippines: Abu Dhabi; tel. (2) 6345664; fax (2) 6313559; e-mail philemae@emirates.net.ae; Ambassador JOSEPH GERARD B. ANGELES.
Poland: POB 2334, Abu Dhabi; tel. (2) 4465200; fax (2) 4462967; e-mail polcon99@emirates.net.ae; internet www.plembassy.gov.ae; Ambassador ROMAN CHAKACZKIEWICZ.
Qatar: POB 3503, 26th St, Al-Minaseer, Abu Dhabi; tel. (2) 4493300; fax (2) 4493311; e-mail abudhabi@mofa.gov.qa; Ambassador ABDULLAH M. AL-UTHMAN.
Romania: 9 POB 70416, Abu Dhabi; tel. (2) 6666346; fax (2) 6651598; e-mail romaniae@emirates.net.ae; Ambassador IOAN EMIL VASILIU.
Russia: POB 8211, Abu Dhabi; tel. (2) 6721797; fax (2) 6788731; e-mail eastpoint@geocities.com; Ambassador OLEG DERKOVSKII.
Saudi Arabia: POB 4057, Abu Dhabi; tel. (2) 4445700; fax (2) 4448491; internet www.mofa.gov.sa/detail.asp?InServiceID=266&intemplatekey=MainPage; Ambassador SALEH MUHAMMAD AL-GHUFAILI.
Somalia: POB 4155, Abu Dhabi; tel. (2) 6669700; fax (2) 6651580; e-mail somen@emirates.net.ae; Ambassador HUSSEIN MUHAMMAD BULLALEH.
South Africa: POB 29446, Madinat Zayed, an-Najdah St, 8th St, Villa 12A, Abu Dhabi; tel. (2) 6337565; fax (2) 6333909; e-mail saemb@emirates.net.ae; internet www.southafrica.ae; Ambassador DIKGANG FRANS MOOPELOA.
Spain: POB 46474, Abu Dhabi; tel. (2) 6269544; fax (2) 6274978; e-mail embespae@mail.mae.es; Ambassador MANUEL PIÑEIRO.
Sri Lanka: POB 46534, Abu Dhabi; tel. (2) 6426666; fax (2) 6428289; e-mail lankemba@emirates.net.ae; Ambassador MUHAMMAD NABAVI JUNAID.
Sudan: POB 4027, Abu Dhabi; tel. (2) 6666788; fax (2) 6654231; e-mail sudembll@emirates.net.ae; Chargé d'affaires MOHIEDDIN SLAIM AHMED.
Sweden: POB 31867, Abu Dhabi; tel. (2) 6210162; fax (2) 6394941; e-mail ambassaden.abudhabi@foreign.ministry.se; internet www.swedenabroad.com/abudhabi; Ambassador BRUNO S. BEIJER.
Switzerland: POB 46116, Abu Dhabi; tel. (2) 6274636; fax (2) 6269627; e-mail vertretung@adh.rep.admin.ch; internet www.eda.admin.ch/uae; Ambassador PETER VOGLER.
Syria: POB 4011, Abu Dhabi; tel. (2) 4448768; fax (2) 4449387; Ambassador (vacant).
Thailand: POB 47466, Abu Dhabi; tel. (2) 6421772; fax (2) 6421773; e-mail thaiauh@emirates.net.ae; Ambassador SOMSAKDI SURIYAWONGSE.
Tunisia: POB 4166, Abu Dhabi; tel. (2) 6811331; fax (2) 6812707; e-mail ambtunad@emirates.net.ae; Ambassador AHMAD BEN MUSTAPHA.
Turkey: POB 3204, Abu Dhabi; tel. (2) 6655466; fax (2) 6662691; e-mail tcabudbe@emirates.net.ae; Ambassador SELIM KANAOSMANOĞLU.
Ukraine: POB 45714, Abu Dhabi; tel. (2) 6327586; fax (2) 6327506; e-mail embukr@emirates.net.ae; Ambassador IHOR TIMOFEYEV.
United Kingdom: POB 248, Abu Dhabi; tel. (2) 6326600; fax (2) 6345968; e-mail chancery.abudhabi@fco.gov.uk; internet www.britishembassy.gov.uk/uae; Ambassador RICHARD MAKEPEACE.
USA: POB 4009, Abu Dhabi; tel. (2) 4142200; fax (2) 4142469; e-mail webmasterabudhabi@state.gov; internet uae.usembassy.gov; Ambassador MICHELE J. SISON.
Yemen: POB 2095, Abu Dhabi; tel. (2) 4448457; fax (2) 4447978; e-mail yememenb@emirates.net.ae; Ambassador Dr ABDULWAHED MUHAMMAD FAREA.

Judicial System

The 95th article of the Constitution of 1971 provided for the establishment of the Union Supreme Court and Union Primary Tribunals as the judicial organs of State.

The Union has exclusive legislative and executive jurisdiction over all matters that are concerned with the strengthening of the federation, such as foreign affairs, defence and Union armed forces, security, finance, communications, traffic control, education, currency, measures, standards and weights, matters relating to nationality and emigration, Union information, etc.

The late President Sheikh Zayed signed the law establishing the new federal courts on 9 June 1978. The new law effectively transferred local judicial authorities into the jurisdiction of the federal system.

Primary tribunals in Abu Dhabi, Sharjah, Ajman and Fujairah are now primary federal tribunals, and primary tribunals in other towns in those emirates have become circuits of the primary federal tribunals.

The primary federal tribunals may sit in any of the capitals of the four emirates and have jurisdiction on all administrative disputes between the Union and individuals, whether the Union is plaintiff or defendant. Civil disputes between Union and individuals will be heard by primary federal tribunals in the defendant's place of normal residence.

The law requires that all judges take a constitutional oath before the Minister of Justice and that the courts apply the rules of *Shari'a* (Islamic religious law) and that no judgment contradicts the *Shari'a*. All employees of the old judiciaries will be transferred to the federal authority without loss of salary or seniority.

In February 1994 President Sheikh Zayed ordered that an extensive range of crimes, including murder, theft and adultery, be tried in *Shari'a* courts rather than in civil courts.

Chief Shari'a Justice: AHMAD ABD AL-AZIZ AL-MUBARAK.

Religion

ISLAM

Most of the inhabitants are Muslims of the Sunni sect, while about 16% of Muslims are Shi'ites.

THE UNITED ARAB EMIRATES

CHRISTIANITY
Roman Catholic Church

Apostolic Vicariate of Arabia: POB 54, Abu Dhabi; tel. (2) 4461895; fax (2) 4465177; e-mail vicarpar@emirates.net.ae; responsible for a territory covering most of the Arabian peninsula (including Saudi Arabia, the UAE, Oman, Qatar, Bahrain and Yemen), containing an estimated 1,300,500 Catholics (31 December 2003); Vicar Apostolic Fr PAUL HINDER (Titular Bishop of Macon, Georgia).

The Anglican Communion

Within the Episcopal Church in Jerusalem and the Middle East, the UAE forms part of the diocese of Cyprus and the Gulf. The Anglican congregations in the UAE are entirely expatriate. The Bishop in Cyprus and the Gulf resides in Cyprus, while the Archdeacon in the Gulf is resident in Qatar.

Chaplain, St Andrew's Church: Rev. CLIVE WINDEBANK, St Andrew's Church, POB 262, Abu Dhabi; tel. (2) 4461631; fax (2) 4465869; e-mail standrew@emirates.net.ae.

The Press

The former Ministry of Information and Culture placed a moratorium on new titles.

ABU DHABI

Abu Dhabi Magazine: POB 662, Abu Dhabi; tel. (2) 6214000; fax (2) 6348954; f. 1969; Arabic, some articles in English; monthly; Editor ZUHAIR AL-QADI; circ. 18,000.

Adh-Dhafra: POB 4288, Abu Dhabi; tel. (2) 6328103; Arabic; weekly; independent; publ. by Dar al-Wahdah.

Emirates News: POB 791, Abu Dhabi; tel. (2) 4451446; fax (2) 4453662; e-mail emrtnews@emirates.net.ae; f. 1975; English; daily; publ. by Al-Ittihad Press, Publishing and Distribution Corpn; Chair. Sheikh ABDULLAH BIN ZAYED AN-NAHYAN; Man. Editor PETER HELLYER; circ. 21,150.

Al-Fajr (The Dawn): POB 505, Abu Dhabi; tel. (2) 4488300; fax (2) 4488436; e-mail info@alfajrnews.ae; Arabic; daily; Man. Editor OBEID AL-MAZROUI; circ. 28,000.

Hiya (She): POB 2488, Abu Dhabi; tel. (2) 4474121; Arabic; weekly for women; publ. by Dar al-Wahdah.

Al-Ittihad (Unity): POB 791, Abu Dhabi; tel. (2) 4452206; fax (2) 4455126; f. 1972; Arabic; daily and weekly; publ. by Al-Ittihad Press, Publishing and Distribution Corpn; Man. Editor OBEID SULTAN; circ. 58,000 daily, 60,000 weekly.

Majed: POB 791, Abu Dhabi; tel. (2) 4451804; fax (2) 4451455; e-mail majid-magazine@emi.co.ae; internet www.emi.co.ae; Arabic; f. 1979; weekly; children's magazine; Man. Editor AHMAD OMAR; circ. 145,300.

Ar-Riyada wa-Shabab (Sport and Youth): POB 2710, Dubai; tel. (4) 4444400; fax (4) 4445973; Arabic; weekly; general interest.

UAE and Abu Dhabi Official Gazette: POB 899, Abu Dhabi; tel. (2) 6660604; Arabic; daily; official reports and papers.

UAE Press Service Daily News: POB 2035, Abu Dhabi; tel. (2) 4444292; f. 1973; English; daily; Editor RASHID AL-MAZROUI.

Al-Wahdah (Unity): POB 2488, Abu Dhabi; tel. (2) 4478400; fax (2) 4478937; f. 1973; daily; independent; Man. Editor RASHID AWEIDHA; Gen. Man. KHALIFA AL-MASHWI; circ. 20,000.

Zahrat al-Khaleej (Splendour of the Gulf): POB 791, Abu Dhabi; tel. (2) 4461600; fax (2) 4451653; f. 1979; Arabic; weekly; publ. by Al-Ittihad Press, Publishing and Distribution Corpn; women's magazine; circ. 10,000.

DUBAI

Akhbar Dubai (Dubai News): Department of Information, Dubai Municipality, POB 1420, Dubai; f. 1965; Arabic; weekly.

Al-Bayan (The Official Report): POB 2710, Dubai; tel. (4) 6688222; fax (4) 6688222; f. 1980; owned by Dubai authorities; Arabic; daily; Editor-in-Chief Sheikh HASHER MAKTOUM; circ. 82,575.

Emirates Woman: POB 2331, Dubai; tel. (4) 2824060; fax (4) 2827593; e-mail annabel@motivate.co.ae; f. 1979; Motivate Publishing; English; monthly; fashion, health and beauty; Editor ANNABEL KANTARIA; circ. 18,690.

Gulf News: POB 6519, Dubai; tel. (4) 4447100; fax (4) 4441627; e-mail editorial@gulf-news.co.ae; internet www.gulf-news.co.ae; f. 1978; An-Nisr Publishing; English; daily; two weekly supplements, Junior News (Wednesday), Gulf Weekly (Thursday); Editor-in-Chief OBAID HUMAID AT-TAYER; Editor FRANCIS MATTHEW; circ. 86,900.

Al-Jundi (The Soldier): POB 2838, Dubai; tel. (4) 3433033; fax (4) 3433343; e-mail mod5@emirates.net.ae; f. 1973; Arabic; monthly; military and cultural; Editor Col MUHAMMAD ALI AL-EASSA; circ. 5,000–7,000.

Khaleej Times: POB 11243, Dubai; tel. (4) 4382400; fax (4) 4390519; e-mail ktimes@emirates.net.ae; internet www.khaleejtimes.com; f. 1978; a Galadari enterprise; English; daily; free weekly supplement, Weekend(Friday); Man. Dir QASSIM MUHAMMAD YOUSUF; Editor S. NIHAL SINGH; circ. 70,000.

Trade and Industry: POB 1457, Dubai; tel. (4) 2280000; fax (4) 2211646; e-mail dcciinfo@dcci.org; internet www.dcci.org; f. 1975; Arabic and English; monthly; publ. by Dubai Chamber of Commerce and Industry; circ. 26,000.

Viva: POB 500024, Dubai; tel. (4) 2108000; fax (4) 2108080; e-mail viva-enquiries@itp.com; internet www.vivamagazine.ae; f. 2004; publ. by ITP; Editor MANDIE GOWER; circ. 23,000.

What's On: POB 2331, Dubai; tel. (4) 2824060; fax (4) 2824436; e-mail editor-wo@motivate.co.ae; f. 1979; Motivate Publishing; English; monthly; Exec. Editor IAN FAIRSERVICE; circ. 17,905.

RAS AL-KHAIMAH

Akhbar Ras al-Khaimah (Ras al-Khaimah News): POB 87, Ras al-Khaimah; Arabic; monthly; local news.

Al-Ghorfa: POB 87, Ras al-Khaimah; tel. (7) 2333511; fax (7) 2330233; f. 1970; Arabic and English; free monthly; publ. by Ras al-Khaimah Chamber of Commerce; Editor ZAKI H. SAQR.

Ras al-Khaimah Magazine: POB 200, Ras al-Khaimah; Arabic; monthly; commerce and trade; Chief Editor AHMAD AT-TADMORI.

SHARJAH

Al-Azman al-Arabia (Times of Arabia): POB 5823, Sharjah; tel. (6) 5356034.

The Gulf Today: POB 30, Sharjah; tel. (6) 5591919; fax (6) 5532737; e-mail tgtmkt@alkhaleej.co.ae; f. 1995; English; daily; circ. 38,000.

Al-Khaleej (The Gulf): POB 30, Sharjah; tel. (6) 5625304; fax (6) 5598547; f. 1970; Arabic; daily; political, independent; Editor GHASSAN TAHBOUB; circ. 82,750.

Sawt al-Khaleej (Voice of the Gulf): Sharjah; tel. (6) 5358003.

Ash-Sharooq (Sunrise): POB 30, Sharjah; tel. (6) 5598777; fax (6) 5599336; f. 1970; Arabic; weekly; general interest; Editor YOUSUF AL-HASSAN.

At-Tijarah (Commerce): Sharjah Chamber of Commerce and Industry, POB 580, Sharjah; tel. (6) 5116600; fax (6) 5681119; e-mail scci@sharjah.gov.ae; internet www.sharjah.gov.ae; f. 1970; Arabic/English; monthly magazine; circ. 50,000; annual trade directory; circ. 100,000.

UAE Digest: Sharjah; tel. (6) 5354633; fax (6) 5354627; English; monthly; publ. by Universal Publishing; commerce and finance; Man. Dir FARAJ YASSINE; circ. 10,000.

NEWS AGENCIES

Emirates News Agency (WAM): POB 3790, Abu Dhabi; tel. (2) 4454545; fax (2) 4454694; f. 1977; operated by the Ministry of Information and Culture; Dir IBRAHIM AL-ABED.

UAE Press Service: POB 2035, Abu Dhabi; tel. (2) 6820424.

Foreign Bureaux

Agenzia Nazionale Stampa Associata (ANSA) (Italy): POB 44106, Abu Dhabi; tel. (2) 4454545.

Kuwait News Agency (KUNA): Apartment 907, 9th Floor, Bldg No. 728, Zayed I St, Khalidiya, Abu Dhabi; tel. (2) 6666994; fax (2) 6666935.

Reuters (UK): POB 7872, Abu Dhabi; tel. (2) 6328000; fax (2) 6333380; Man. JEREMY HARRIS.

Publishers

All Prints: POB 857, Abu Dhabi; tel. (2) 6338235; publishing and distribution; Partners BUSHRA KHAYAT, TAHSEEN S. KHAYAT.

ITP: POB 500024, Dubai; tel. (4) 2108000; fax (4) 2108080; e-mail info@itp.com; internet www.itp.com.

Al-Ittihad Press, Publishing and Distribution Corpn: POB 791, New Airport Rd, Abu Dhabi; tel. (2) 4455555; fax (2) 4451653; Chair. KHALFAN BIN MUHAMMAD AR-ROUMI.

Motivate Publishing: POB 2331, Dubai; tel. (4) 2824060; fax (4) 2824436; e-mail motivate@motivate.ae; internet www.motivatepublishing.com; f. 1979; books and magazines; Man. Partner and Group Editor IAN FAIRSERVICE.

THE UNITED ARAB EMIRATES

Broadcasting and Communications

TELECOMMUNICATIONS

Telecommunications Regulatory Authority (TRA): Abu Dhabi; f. 2004; Dir-Gen. MUHAMMAD AL-GHANEM.

Emirates Telecommunications Corpn (Etisalat): POB 300, Abu Dhabi; tel. (2) 6333111; fax (2) 6344432; e-mail prd@etisalat.co.ae; internet www.etisalat.co.ae; provides telecommunications services throughout the UAE; Pres. and CEO MUHAMMAD OMRAN.

BROADCASTING

Radio

Abu Dhabi Radio: Abu Dhabi; tel. (2) 4451111; fax (2) 4451155; f. 1968; broadcasts in Arabic over a wide area; also broadcasts in French, Bengali, Filipino and Urdu; Dir-Gen. ABD AL-WAHAB AR-RADWAN.

Capital Radio: POB 63, Abu Dhabi; tel. (2) 4451000; fax (2) 4451155; English-language FM music and news station, operated by the Ministry of Information and Culture; Station Man. AIDA HAMZA.

Dubai Radio and Colour Television: POB 1695, Dubai; tel. (4) 3370255; fax (4) 3374111; broadcasts domestic Arabic and European programmes; Chair. Sheikh HASHER MAKTOUM; Dir-Gen. ABD AL-GHAFOOR SAID IBRAHIM.

Ras al-Khaimah Broadcasting Station: POB 141, Ras al-Khaimah; tel. (7) 2851151; fax (7) 2353441; two transmitters broadcast in Arabic and Urdu; Dir Sheikh ABD AL-AZIZ BIN HUMAID.

Sharjah Broadcasting Station: POB 155, Sharjah; broadcasts in Arabic and French.

Umm al-Qaiwain Broadcasting Station: POB 444, Umm al-Qaiwain; tel. (6) 7666044; fax (6) 7666055; e-mail uaqfm@emirates.net.ae; f. 1978; broadcasts music and news in Arabic, Malayalam, Sinhala and Urdu; Gen. Man. ALI JASSEM.

UAE Radio and Television—Dubai: POB 1695, Dubai; tel. (4) 3369999; fax (4) 3374111; e-mail dubairtv@emirates.net.ae; broadcasts in Arabic and English to the USA, India and Pakistan, the Far East, Australia and New Zealand, Europe and North and East Africa; Chair. Sheikh HASHEM MAKTOUM; Dir-Gen. AHMED SAID AL-GAOUD; Controller of Radio HASSAN AHMAD.

Television

Dubai Radio and Colour Television: see Radio..

UAE Radio and Television-Dubai: see Radio; Controller of Programmes NASIB BITAR.

UAE TV—Abu Dhabi: POB 637, Abu Dhabi; tel. (2) 4452000; fax (2) 4451470; internet www.ecssr.ac.ae/05uae.6television.html; f. 1968; broadcasts programmes incorporating information, entertainment, religion, culture, news and politics; Dir-Gen. ALI OBAID.

UAE Television—Sharjah: POB 111, Sharjah; tel. (6) 5361111; fax (6) 5541755; f. 1989; broadcasts in Arabic and Urdu in the northern emirates; Executive Dir MUHAMMAD DIAB AL-MUSA.

Finance

(cap. = capital; res = reserves; dep. = deposits; m. = million; brs = branches; amounts in dirhams, unless otherwise indicated)

BANKING

Central Bank

Central Bank of the United Arab Emirates: POB 854, Abu Dhabi; tel. (2) 6652220; fax (2) 66652504; e-mail uaccbadm@emirates.net.ae; internet www.uaecb.gov.ae; f. 1973; acts as issuing authority for local currency; superseded UAE Currency Board December 1980; cap. 300m., res 1,260m., dep. 36,868m. (Dec. 2003); Chair. MUHAMMAD EID AL-MURAIKHI; Gov. SULTAN NASSER AS-SUWAIDI; 6 brs.

Principal Banks

Abu Dhabi Commercial Bank (ADCB): POB 939, Abu Dhabi; tel. (2) 6962222; fax (2) 6776499; internet www.adcb.com; f. 1985 by merger; 65% govt-owned, 35% owned by private investors; cap. 1,250.0m., res 3,216.4m., dep. 22,731.8m. (Dec. 2003); Chair. SAID MUBARAK RASHID AL-HAJERI; CEO and Man. Dir KHALIFA MUHAMMAD HASSAN; 32 brs.

Abu Dhabi Islamic Bank: POB 313, As-Sultan Tower, Baniyas St (Najda), Abu Dhabi; tel. (2) 6343000; fax (2) 6342222; e-mail adib@adib.co.ae; internet www.e-adib.com; f. 1997; cap. 1,000.0m., res 228.3m., dep. 7,708.6m. (Dec. 2003); Chair. MUHAMMAD BIN HUMOUDA BIN ALI; CEO ABD AL-AZIZ AHMAD AL-MEHAIRI (acting).

Arab Bank for Investment and Foreign Trade (ARBIFT): POB 46733, ARBIFT Bldg, Hamdan St, Tourist Club Area, Abu Dhabi; tel. (2) 6721900; fax (2) 6777550; e-mail arbiftho@emirates.net.ae; internet www.arbift.com; f. 1976; jointly owned by the UAE Govt, the Libyan Arab Foreign Bank and the Banque Extérieure d'Algérie; cap. 570.0m., res 731.3m., dep. 3,442.4m. (Dec. 2003); Chair. Dr ABD AL-HAFID ZLITNI; Gen. Man. IBRAHIM NASSER LOOTAH; 5 brs in Abu Dhabi.

Arab Emirates Investment Bank PJSC: POB 5503, Office 904, Twin Towers, Baniyas St, Deira, Dubai; tel. (4) 2222191; fax (4) 2274351; e-mail aeibank@emirates.net.ae; f. 1976 as Arab Emirate Investment Bank Ltd, name changed as above in 2000; cap. 40.9m., res 95.4m., dep. 238.8m. (Dec. 2003); Chair. KHALID MUHAMMAD SAID AL-MULLA; Gen.-Man. SAJJAD AHMAD.

Bank of Sharjah Ltd: POB 1394, Sharjah; tel. (6) 5694411; fax (6) 5694422; e-mail bankshj@emirates.net.ae; internet www.bank-of-sharjah.com; f. 1973; cap. 1,000m., res 176.4m., dep. 2,354m. (Dec. 2004); Chair. AHMAD AN-NOMAN; Gen. Man. VAROUJ NERGUIZIAN; brs in Abu Dhabi and Dubai.

Commercial Bank of Dubai PSC: POB 2668, Mankhool St, Dubai; tel. (4) 3523355; fax (4) 3520444; e-mail cbd-ho@cbd.co.ae; internet www.cbd.co.ae; f. 1969; 20% owned by Govt of Dubai; cap. 496.0m., res 1,148.6m., dep. 6,917.2m. (Dec. 2003); Chair. AHMAD HUMAID AT-TAYER; CEO OMAR ABD AR-RAHIM LEYAS; 16 brs.

Commercial Bank International PSC: POB 4449, Ar-Riqah St, Dubai; tel. (4) 2275265; fax (4) 2279038; e-mail cbiho@emirates.net.ae; internet www.cbiuae.com; f. 1991; cap. 267.1m., res 111.3m., dep. 2,472.3m. (Dec. 2002); Chair. and Man. Dir SALEH AHMAD ASH-SHALL.

Dubai Bank PJSC: POB 65555, Sheikh Zayed Rd, Dubai; e-mail info@dubaibank.ae; internet www.dubaibank.ae; tel. (4) 3328929; fax (4) 3290071; f. 2002 by Emaar Properties, a real-estate developer; cap. 300.0m; Chair. Sheikh HAMDAN BIN MUHAMMAD BIN RASHID AL-MAKTOUM; CEO ZIAD MAKKAWI.

Dubai Islamic Bank PLC: POB 1080, Dubai; tel. (4) 2953000; fax (4) 2954000; e-mail contactus@alislami.ae; internet www.alislami.co.ae; f. 1975; cap. 1,000.0m., res 694.2m., dep. 20,204.0 (Dec. 2003); Chair. Dr MUHAMMAD KHALFAN BIN KHARBASH; CEO SAAD ABD AR-RAZAK; 9 brs.

Emirates Bank International PJSC: POB 2923, Beniyas Rd, Deira, Dubai; tel. (4) 2256256; fax (4) 2268005; e-mail nadeyar@emiratesbank.com; internet www.emiratesbank.com; f. 1977 by merger; 77% owned by Govt of Dubai; cap. 1,148.0m., res 3,640.2m., dep. 22,818.2m. (Dec. 2003); Chair. AHMAD HUMAID AT-TAYER; Man. Dir and CEO RICK PUDNER; 26 brs.

Emirates Islamic Bank PJSC: POB 5547, Beniyas Rd, Deira, Dubai; tel. (4) 2256256; fax (4) 2255322; e-mail nadeyar@emiratesbank.com; internet www.emiratesbank.com; f. 1976 as Middle East Bank; became a Public Joint Stock Co (PJSC) in 1995; changed name as above in 2004; subsidiary (99.8% owned) of Emirates Bank Int.; cap. 500.0m., res 176.7m., dep. 1,209.2m. (Dec. 2002); Vice-Chair. FARDAN BIN ALI AL-FARDAN; 10 brs.

First Gulf Bank: POB 6316, Sheikh Zayed St, Abu Dhabi; tel. (2) 6394000; fax (2) 6217721; e-mail fgbabd@emirates.net.ae; f. 1979; cap. 389.4m., res 281.2m., dep. 6,309.4m. (Dec. 2003); Chair. Sheikh TAHNOON BIN ZAYED AN-NAHYAN; Gen. Man. ABD AL-HAMID SAID; 5 brs.

Investbank PSC: Al-Borj Ave, POB 1885, Sharjah; tel. (6) 5694440; fax (6) 5694442; e-mail sharjah@invest-bank.com; internet www.invest-bank.com; f. 1975; cap. 401.0m., res 204.3m., dep. 2,593.5m. (Dec. 2003); Chair. Dr ABDULLAH OMRAN TARYAM; Gen. Man. SAMI FARHAT; 5 brs.

Mashreqbank PSC: POB 1250, Omer bin al-Khattab St, Deira, Dubai; tel. (4) 2229131; fax (4) 2226061; internet www.mashreqbank.com; f. 1967 as Bank of Oman; adopted present name 1993; cap. 715.9m., res 1,151.9m., dep. 21,049.3m. (Dec. 2003); Chair. ABDULLAH AHMAD AL-GHURAIR; Man. Dir and CEO ABD AL-AZIZ AL-GHURAIR; 36 brs.

National Bank of Abu Dhabi (NBAD): POB 4, Tariq ibn Ziad St, Abu Dhabi; tel. (2) 6666800; fax (2) 6655329; internet www.nbad.com; f. 1968; owned jointly by Abu Dhabi Investment Authority and UAE citizens; cap. 941.6m., res 3,413.5m., dep. 38,153.8m. (Dec. 2003); Chair. Sheikh MUHAMMAD BIN HABROUSH AS-SUWAIDI; CEO MICHAEL H. TOMALIN; 56 brs.

National Bank of Dubai PJSC: POB 777, Baniyas St, Deira, Dubai; tel. (4) 2222111; fax (4) 2283000; e-mail contactus@nbd.co.ae; internet www.nbd.co.ae; f. 1963; cap. 1,080.6m., res 4,165.9m., dep. 29,776.2m. (Dec. 2003); Chair. Dr KHALIFA MUHAMMAD AHMAD SULAYMAN; Gen. Man. R. DOUGLAS DOWIE; 38 brs.

National Bank of Fujairah PSC: POB 887, Hamad bin Abdullah St, Fujairah; tel. (9) 2224513; fax (9) 2224516; e-mail nbfho@nbf.co.ae; internet www.nbf.com; f. 1982; owned jointly by Govt of Fujairah (36.78%), Govt of Dubai (9.78%), and UAE citizens and cos

THE UNITED ARAB EMIRATES

(51.25%); cap. 531.4m., res 226.6m., dep. 2,473.3m. (Dec. 2003); Chair. Sheikh SALEH BIN MUHAMMAD ASH-SHARQI; Gen. Man. MICHAEL H. WILLIAMS; 5 brs.

National Bank of Ras al-Khaimah PSC: POB 5300, Rakbank Bldg, Oman St, al-Nakheel, Ras al-Khaimah; tel. (7) 2281127; fax (7) 2283238; e-mail nbrakho@emirates.net.ae; internet www.rakbank.co.ae; f. 1976; cap. 275.0m., res 268.1m., dep. 3,055.3m. (Dec. 2003); Chair. Sheikh KHALID BIN SAQR AL-QASIMI; Gen. Man. J. G. HONEYBILL; 14 brs.

National Bank of Umm al-Qaiwain PSC: POB 800, Umm al-Qaiwain Private Properties Dept Bldg, King Faisal St, Umm al-Qaiwain; tel. (6) 7655225; fax (4) 7655440; e-mail edpnbuaq@emirates.net.ae; f. 1982; cap. 250.0m., res 169.8m., dep. 1,363.3m. (Dec. 2003); Chair. Sheikh SA'UD BIN RASHID AL-MU'ALLA; Man. Dir, CEO and Gen. Man. Sheikh NASSER BIN RASHID AL-MU'ALLA; 10 brs.

Sharjah Islamic Bank: POB 4, Al-Borj Ave, Sharjah; tel. (6) 5681000; fax (6) 5680101; e-mail nbsmail@emirates.net.ae; internet www.nbs.ae; f. 1976 as National Bank of Sharjah; name changed as above in 2005, reflecting the bank's conversion to *Shari'a*-compliant operations; commercial bank; cap. 385.7m., res 286.1m., dep. 1,895.9m. (Dec. 2003); Chair. Sheikh SULTAN BIN MUHAMMAD BIN SULTAN AL-QASSIMI; Gen. Man. HUSSAIN AL-QEMZI; 9 brs.

Union National Bank: POB 3865, Salam St, Abu Dhabi; tel. (2) 6741600; fax (2) 6786080; e-mail feedback@unb.co.ae; internet www.unb.co.ae; f. 1983; fmrly Bank of Credit and Commerce (Emirates); cap. 904.3m., res 523.7m., dep. 13,946.3m. (Dec. 2003); Chair. Sheikh NAHYAN BIN MUBARAK AN-NAHYAN; CEO MUHAMMAD NASR ABDEEN; 12 brs in Abu Dhabi, 7 brs in Dubai, 2 each in Sharjah and al-Ain, and one each in Ras al-Khaimah, Ajman and Fujairah.

United Arab Bank: POB 25022, 6th Floor, HE Sheikh Abdullah bin Salem al-Qassimi Bldg, al-Qassimi St, Sharjah; tel. (6) 5733900; fax (6) 5733907; e-mail uarbae@emirates.net.ae; internet www.uab.ae; f. 1975; affiliated to Société Générale, France; cap. 302.6m., res 210.1m., dep. 2,138.3m. (Dec. 2003); Chair. Sheikh FAISAL BIN SULTAN AL-QASSIMI; Gen. Man. BERTRAND GIRAUD; 9 brs.

Development Banks

Emirates Industrial Bank: POB 2722, Abu Dhabi; tel. (2) 6339700; fax (2) 6319191; f. 1982; offers low-cost loans to enterprises with at least 51% local ownership; 51% state-owned; cap. 200m.; Chair. MUHAMMAD KHALFAN KHIRBASH; Gen. Man. MUHAMMAD ABD AL-BAKI MUHAMMAD.

United Arab Emirates Development Bank: Abu Dhabi; tel. (2) 6344986; f. 1974; participates in development of real estate, agriculture, fishery, livestock and light industries; cap. 500m.; Gen. Man. MUHAMMAD SALEM AL-MELEHY.

Foreign Banks

ABN AMRO Bank NV (Netherlands): Istiqlal St, POB 22401, Abu Dhabi; tel. (2) 6335400; fax (2) 6330182; POB 2567, Deira, Dubai; tel. (4) 3512200; fax (4) 3511555; POB 1971, Sharjah; tel. (6) 5093101; fax (6) 5360099; internet www.abnamro-uae.com; f. 1974; cap. 223m., total assets 3,677m. (1999); Man. (Abu Dhabi) BRICE ROPION.

Al-Ahli Bank of Kuwait KSC: POB 1719, Deira, Dubai; tel. (4) 2681118; fax (4) 2684445; e-mail abkdub@emirates.net.ae; Chair. MURAD YOUSUF BEHBEHANI.

Arab-African International Bank (Egypt): POB 1049, Dubai; tel. (4) 2223131; fax (4) 2222257; e-mail aaibdxb@emirates.net.ae; internet www.aaibank.com; POB 928, Abu Dhabi; tel. (2) 6323400; fax (2) 6323400; e-mail aaib@emirates.net.ae; f. 1970; Chair. Dr FAHD AR-RASHID; Gen. Man. (Dubai) MUHAMMAD FARAMAOUI.

Arab Bank PLC (Jordan): POB 875, Abu Dhabi; tel. (2) 6392225; fax (2) 6212370; POB 11364, Dubai; tel. (4) 2221231; fax (4) 2233749; POB 130, Sharjah; tel. (6) 5613995; fax (6) 5618887; POB 4972, Ras al-Khaimah; tel. (7) 2288437; fax (7) 2282337; POB 300, Fujairah; tel. (9) 2222050; fax (9) 2224024; POB 17, Ajman; tel. (6) 7422431; fax (6) 7426871; f. 1970; Man. NAIM KHUSHASHI; 8 local brs.

Banca Intesa SpA: POB 3839, Abu Dhabi; tel. (2) 6274224; fax (2) 6273709; Dep. Chief Man. DANIÈLE PANIN.

Bank of Baroda (India): POB 3162, Dubai; tel. (2) 3536962; fax (2) 3531955; e-mail barbaead@emirates.net.ae; f. 1974; Chair. K. KANNAN; CEO PAR KASH SINGH; also brs in Abu Dhabi, al-Ain, Deira (Dubai), Sharjah and Ras al-Khaimah.

Bank Melli Iran: Regional Office and Main Branch, POB 1894, Dubai; tel. (4) 2221462; fax (4) 2269157; e-mail bmirodxb@emirates.net.ae; f. 1969; Regional Dir AZIZ AZIMI NOBAR; brs in Dubai, Abu Dhabi, al-Ain, Sharjah, Fujairah and Ras al-Khaimah.

Bank Saderat Iran: POB 700, Abu Dhabi; tel. (2) 6225155; fax (2) 6225062; POB 4182, Dubai; tel. (4) 2220920; fax (4) 2270593; also Sharjah, Ajman, Fujairah and al-Ain; Man. ALI VERDI.

Banque Banorabe (France): POB 4370, Dubai; tel. (4) 2284655; fax (4) 2236260; POB 5803, Sharjah; tel. (6) 5736100; fax (6) 5736080; e-mail banorabe@emirates.net.ae; internet www.banorabe.com; f. 1974; fmrly Banque de l'Orient Arabe et d'Outre Mer; Chair. and Gen. Man. SAMER AZHARI; UAE Regional Man. BASSEM M. AL-ARISS.

Banque du Caire (Egypt): POB 533, Abu Dhabi; tel. (2) 6224900; fax (2) 6225881; POB 1502, Dubai; tel. (4) 3715175; fax (4) 3713013; POB 254, Sharjah; tel. (6) 5739222; fax (6) 5739292; POB 618, Ras al-Khaimah; tel. (7) 2332245; fax (7) 2334202; Gulf Regional Man. FOUAD ABD AL-KHALEK TAHOON.

Banque Libanaise pour le Commerce SA (France): POB 3771, Abu Dhabi; tel. (2) 6270909; fax (2) 6268851; e-mail blcad@emirates.net.ae; POB 854, Sharjah; tel. (6) 5724561; fax (6) 5727843; e-mail blcdxbrm@emirates.net.ae; POB 4207, Dubai; tel. (4) 2222291; fax (4) 2279861; POB 771, Ras al-Khaimah; UAE Regional Man. ELIE N. SALIBA.

Barclays Bank PLC (UK): POB 2734, Abu Dhabi; tel. (2) 6275313; fax (2) 6268060; POB 1891, Zabeel, Dubai; tel. (4) 3344156; fax (4) 3366700; Corporate Dir of Gulf JONATHAN PINE.

BNP Paribas (France): POB 2742, Abu Dhabi; tel. (2) 6267800; fax (2) 6268638; POB 7233, Dubai; tel. (4) 2225200; fax (4) 2225849; Gen. Man. (Abu Dhabi) LUC FICHTER; Gen. Man. (Dubai) MICHEL DUBOIS.

Citibank NA (USA): POB 749, Dubai; tel. (4) 3522100; fax (4) 3524942; POB 346, Sharjah; tel. (6) 5354511; POB 999, Abu Dhabi; tel. (2) 6742484; fax (2) 6334524; POB 294, Ras al-Khaimah; POB 1430, al-Ain; f. 1963; Gen. Man. AHM BIN BREK.

Credit Agricole Indosuez Gulf (France): POB 9256, Dubai; tel. (4) 3314211; fax (4) 3313201; POB 46786, Abu Dhabi; tel. (2) 6267500; fax (2) 6275581; f. 1975; f. 1981; Regional Man. FRANÇOIS RIVIER.

El Nilein Industrial Development Bank (Sudan): POB 46013, Al-Lulu St, Abu Dhabi; tel. (2) 6269995; fax (2) 6275551; e-mail nilienau@emirates.net.ae; internet www.nilienuae.com; f. 1977; Man. DIRAR M. HAMZA.

Habib Bank AG Zurich (Switzerland): POB 2681, Abu Dhabi; tel. (2) 6322838; fax (2) 6351822; POB 1166, Sharjah; POB 3306, Dubai; f. 1974; Joint Pres. H. M. HABIB; Vice-Pres. HATIM HUSSAIN; 8 brs.

Habib Bank Ltd (Pakistan): POB 888, Dubai; tel. (4) 3597799; fax (4) 3594172; POB 897, Abu Dhabi; tel. (2) 6325665; fax (2) 6333620; f. 1967; Regional Gen. Man. AMAN AZIZ SIDDIQUI; 8 brs.

HSBC Bank Middle East (UK): POB 66, Dubai; tel. (4) 3535000; fax (4) 35315641; e-mail hsbcuae@emirates.net.ae; internet www.banking.middleeast.hsbc.com; f. 1946; total assets US $7,832m. (1999); Dep. Chair. ANDREW DIXON; CEO MUKHTAR HUSSAIN; 8 brs throughout UAE.

Janata Bank (Bangladesh): POB 2630, Abu Dhabi; tel. (2) 6344542; fax (2) 6348749; POB 3342, Dubai; tel. (4) 2281442; fax (4) 2246023; Chair. MUHAMMAD ALI; Man. Dir M. A. HASHEM; brs in al-Ain, Dubai and Sharjah.

Lloyds TSB Bank PLC (UK): POB 3766, Al-Wasr Rd, Jumeira, Dubai; tel. (4) 3422000; fax (4) 3422660; e-mail ltsbbank@emirates.net.ae; f. 1977; Area Man. RICHARD STOCKDALE.

National Bank of Bahrain BSC: POB 46080, Abu Dhabi; tel. (2) 6335288; fax (2) 6333783; Sr Man. FAROUK KHALAF.

National Bank of Oman SAOG: POB 3822, Abu Dhabi; tel. (2) 6348111; fax (2) 6321043; Man. O. R. QUADRI.

Rafidain Bank (Iraq): POB 2727, Abu Dhabi; tel. (2) 6335882; fax (2) 6326996; Gen. Man. ZANAIB TALEB.

Standard Chartered Bank (UK): POB 240, Abu Dhabi; tel. (2) 6330077; fax (2) 6341511; POB 999, Dubai; tel. (4) 3520455; fax (4) 3525054; POB 5, Sharjah; tel. (6) 5357788; fax (6) 5543604; POB 1240, al-Ain; tel. (3) 7641253; fax (3) 7654824; Gen. Man. COLIN AVERY.

United Bank Ltd (Pakistan): POB 1367, Dubai; tel. (4) 3552020; fax (4) 3514525; e-mail deira_branch@ublme.com; POB 237, Abu Dhabi; tel. (2) 6391507; fax (2) 6315052; e-mail muroor_branch@ublme.com; f. 1959; Gen. Man. SHAUKAT MIR; 8 brs in UAE.

Bankers' Association

United Arab Emirates Bankers' Association: POB 44307, Abu Dhabi; tel. (2) 6272541; fax (2) 6274155; e-mail ebauae@emirates.net.ae; internet www.eba_ae.com; f. 1983.

STOCK EXCHANGES

Abu Dhabi Securities Market (ADSM): POB 54500, Abu Dhabi; tel. (2) 6277777; fax (2) 6128782; e-mail info@adsm.co.ae; internet www.adsm.co.ae; f. 2000; Chair. HAREB MASOUD AD-DARMAKI.

Dubai Financial Market (DFM): POB 9700, Dubai; tel. (4) 3055555; fax (4) 3314922; e-mail helpdesk@dfm.co.ae; internet www.dfm.co.ae; f. 2000; 14 listed cos, two bonds, six mutual funds; market capitalization AED 61,370m. (Feb. 2004); Dir-Gen. ESSA ABD AL-FATTAH KAZIM.

THE UNITED ARAB EMIRATES *Directory*

INSURANCE

Abu Dhabi National Insurance Co (ADNIC): POB 839, Abu Dhabi; tel. (2) 6264000; fax (2) 6268600; e-mail adnic@emirates.net.ae; f. 1972; subscribed 25% by the Govt of Abu Dhabi and 75% by UAE nationals; all classes of insurance; Chair. and Gen. Man. KHALAF A. AL-OTAIBA.

Al-Ahlia Insurance Co: POB 128, Ras al-Khaimah; tel. (7) 2221479; f. 1977; Chair. Sheikh OMAR BIN ABDULLAH AL-QASSIMI; 3 brs.

Al-Ain Ahlia Insurance Co: POB 3077, Abu Dhabi; tel. (2) 4459900; fax (2) 4456685; e-mail alainins@emirates.net.ae; internet www.alaininsurance.com; f. 1975; Chair. MUHAMMAD BIN J. R. AL-BADIE ADH-DHAHIRI; Gen. Man. MUHAMMAD MAZHAR HAMADEH; brs in Dubai, Sharjah, Tarif, Ghouifat and al-Ain.

Dubai Insurance Co PSC: POB 3027, Dubai; tel. (4) 2693030; fax (4) 2693727; e-mail dubins@emirates.net.ae; f. 1970; Chair. MAJID AL-FUTTAIM.

Sharjah Insurance Co: POB 792, Sharjah; tel. (6) 5686690; fax (6) 5686545; e-mail sirco@emirates.net.ae; internet www.sharjahinsurance.co.ae; f. 1970; Gen. Man. MUHAMMAD FAWZI NAJI.

Union Insurance Co: POB 3196, Abu Dhabi; POB 460, Umm al-Qaiwain; POB 4623, Dubai; tel. (6) 666223; Gen. Man. L. F. DOKOV.

Trade and Industry

DEVELOPMENT ORGANIZATIONS

Abu Dhabi Development Finance Corpn: POB 814, Abu Dhabi; tel. (2) 6441000; fax (2) 6440800; e-mail opadfdmn@emirates.net.ae; provides finance to the private sector; Chair. Sheikh KHALIFA BIN ZAYED AN-NAHYAN; Dir-Gen. SAID KHALFAN MATAR AR-ROMAITHI.

Abu Dhabi Fund for Development (ADFD): POB 814, as-Salam St, Abu Dhabi; tel. (2) 6441000; fax (2) 6440800; e-mail opadfdmn@emirates.net.ae; f. 1971; offers economic aid to other Arab states and other developing countries in support of their development; cap. AED 4,000m.; Dir-Gen. SAID KHALFAN MATAR AR-ROMAITHI.

Abu Dhabi Investment Authority (ADIA): POB 3600, Abu Dhabi; tel. (2) 6213100; f. 1976; responsible for co-ordinating Abu Dhabi's investment policy; Chair. Sheikh KHALIFA BIN ZAYED AN-NAHYAN; Pres. Sheikh MUHAMMAD HABROUSH AS-SUWAIDI; 1 br. overseas.

Abu Dhabi Investment Company (ADIC): POB 46309, Abu Dhabi; tel. (2) 6658100; fax (2) 6650575; e-mail adic@emirates.net.ae; internet www.adic.co.ae; f. 1977; investment and merchant banking activities in the UAE and abroad; 98% owned by ADIA and 2% by National Bank of Abu Dhabi; total assets AED 5,947m. (1997); Chair. HAREB MASOOD AD-DARMAKI; Gen. Man. HUMAID DARWISH AL-KATBI.

Abu Dhabi Planning Department: POB 12, Abu Dhabi; tel. (2) 6727200; fax (2) 6727749; f. 1974; supervises Abu Dhabi's Development Programme; Chair. MUSALLAM SAID ABDULLAH AL-QUBAISI; Under-Sec. AHMAD M. HILAL AL-MAZRUI.

Dubai Development and Investment Authority (DDIA): Dubai; CEO MUHAMMAD AL-GARGAWI.

Dubai Holding: Dubai; f. 2004; supervises major construction projects in Dubai; cap. AED 25,000m. (Oct. 2004); CEO MUHAMMAD AL-GURGAWI.

General Industry Corpn (GIC): POB 4499, Abu Dhabi; tel. (2) 6214900; fax (2) 6325034; e-mail info@gic.co; internet www.gic.co.ae; f. 1979; responsible for the promotion of non-petroleum-related industry; Chair. Sheikh HAMAD BIN TAHNOON AN-NAHYAN; Dep. Dir-Gen. SUHAIL MUHAMMAD AL-AMERI.

International Petroleum Investment Co (IPIC): POB 7528, Abu Dhabi; tel. (2) 6336200; fax (2) 6216045; f. 1984; cap. US $200m.; state-owned venture to develop overseas investments in energy and energy-related projects; Chair. Sheikh MANSUR BIN ZAYED AN-NAHYAN; Man. Dir KHALIFA MUHAMMAD ASH-SHAMSI.

Sharjah Economic Development Corpn (SHEDCO): Sharjah; tel. (6) 5371212; industrial investment co; jt venture between Sharjah authorities and private sector; auth. cap. AED 1,000m.; Gen. Man. J. T. PICKLES.

CHAMBERS OF COMMERCE

Federation of UAE Chambers of Commerce and Industry: POB 3014, Abu Dhabi; tel. (2) 6214144; fax (2) 6339210; e-mail fcciauh@emirates.net.ae; POB 8886, Dubai; tel. (4) 2212977; fax (4) 2235498; e-mail fccidxb@emirates.net.ae; internet www.fcci-uae.com; f. 1976; seven mem. chambers; Pres. SAID SAIF BIN JABER AS-SUWAIDI; Sec.-Gen. ABDULLAH SULTAN ABDULLAH.

Abu Dhabi Chamber of Commerce and Industry: POB 662, Abu Dhabi; tel. (2) 6214000; fax (2) 6215867; e-mail services@adcci.gov.ae; internet www.adcci-uae.com; f. 1969; 45,000 mems; Pres. SAID SEIF BIN JABER AS-SUWAIDI; Dir-Gen. MUHAMMAD OMAR ABDULLAH.

Ajman Chamber of Commerce and Industry: POB 662, Ajman; tel. (6) 7422177; fax (6) 7427591; e-mail ajmchmbr@emirates.net.ae; internet www.ajcci.co.ae; f. 1977; Pres. HAMAD MUHAMMAD ABU SHIHAB; Dir-Gen. MUHAMMAD BIN ABDULLAH AL-HUMRANI.

Dubai Chamber of Commerce and Industry: POB 1457, Dubai; tel. (4) 2280000; fax (4) 2211646; e-mail dcci@dcci.gov.ae; internet www.dcci.org; f. 1965; 40,000 mems; Pres. HASSAN BIN ASH-SHEIKH; Dir-Gen. ABD AR-RAHMAN GHANEM AL-MUTAIWEE.

Fujairah Chamber of Commerce, Industry and Agriculture: POB 738, Fujairah; tel. (9) 2222400; fax (9) 2221464; e-mail fujccia@emirates.net.ae; Pres. SAID ALI KHAMAS; Dir-Gen. SHAHEEN ALI SHAHEEN.

Ras al-Khaimah Chamber of Commerce, Industry and Agriculture: POB 87, Ras al-Khaimah; tel. (7) 2333511; fax (7) 2330233; e-mail rakchmbr@emirates.net.ae; f. 1967; 800 mems; Pres. ALI ABDULLAH MUSSABEH; Dir-Gen. ALI MUHAMMAD ALI AL-HARANKI.

Sharjah Chamber of Commerce and Industry: POB 580, Sharjah; tel. (6) 5116600; fax (6) 5681119; e-mail scci@sharjah.gov.ae; internet www.sharjah.gov.ae; f. 1970; 33,500 mems; Chair. AHMAD MUHAMMAD AL-MIDFA'A; Dir-Gen. SAID OBAID AL-JARWAN.

Umm al-Qaiwain Chamber of Commerce and Industry: POB 436, Umm al-Qaiwain; tel. (6) 7656915; fax (6) 7657056; Pres. ABDULLAH RASHID AL-KHARJI; Man. Dir SHAKIR AZ-ZAYANI.

STATE HYDROCARBONS COMPANIES

Abu Dhabi

Supreme Petroleum Council: POB 898, Abu Dhabi; tel. (2) 602000; fax (2) 6023389; f. 1988; assumed authority and responsibility for the administration and supervision of all petroleum affairs in Abu Dhabi; Chair. Sheikh KHALIFA BIN ZAYED AN-NAHYAN; Sec.-Gen. YOUSUF BIN OMEIR BIN YOUSUF.

Abu Dhabi National Oil Co (ADNOC): POB 898, Abu Dhabi; tel. (2) 6020000; fax (2) 6023389; e-mail adnoc@adnoc.com; internet www.adnoc.com; f. 1971; cap. AED 7,500m.; state company; deals in all phases of oil industry; owns two refineries: one on Umm an-Nar island and one at Ruwais; Habshan Gas Treatment Plant (scheduled for partial privatization); gas pipeline distribution network; a salt and chlorine plant; holds 60% participation in operations of ADMA-OPCO and ADCO, and 88% of ZADCO; has 100% control of Abu Dhabi National Oil Co for Oil Distribution (ADNOC-FOD), Abu Dhabi National Tanker Co (ADNATCO), National Drilling Co (NDC) and interests in numerous other companies, both in the UAE and overseas; ADNOC is operated by Supreme Petroleum Council, Chair. Sheikh KHALIFA BIN ZAYED AN-NAHYAN; Gen. Man. YOUSUF BIN OMEIR BIN YOUSUF.

Subsidiaries include:

Abu Dhabi Co for Onshore Oil Operations (ADCO): POB 270, Abu Dhabi; tel. (2) 6040000; fax (2) 6669785; shareholders are ADNOC (60%), British Petroleum, Shell and Total (9.5% each), Exxon and Mobil (4.75% each) and Partex (2%); oil exploration, production and export operations from onshore oilfields; average production (1990): 1.2m. b/d; Chair. YOUSUF BIN OMEIR BIN YOUSUF; Gen. Man. ANDRE VAN STRIJP.

Abu Dhabi Drilling Chemicals and Products Ltd (ADDCAP): POB 46121, Abu Dhabi; tel. (2) 6029000; fax (2) 6029010; e-mail addcap@emirates.net.ae; f. 1975; production of drilling chemicals and provision of marine services; wholly-owned subsidiary of ADNOC; Chair. YOUSUF BIN OMEIR BIN YOUSUF; Gen. Man. MAHFOUD A. DARBOUL ASH-SHEHHI.

Abu Dhabi Gas Co (ATHEER): POB 345, Abu Dhabi; tel. (2) 6020000; fax (2) 6027150; processing and distribution of natural gas.

Abu Dhabi Gas Industries Co (GASCO): POB 665, Abu Dhabi; tel. (2) 6030000; fax (2) 6037414; e-mail info@gasco.ae; internet www.gasco.ae; f. 1978; started production in 1981; recovers condensate and LPG from Asab, Bab and Bu Hasa fields for delivery to Ruwais natural gas liquids fractionation plant; capacity of 22,000 metric tons per day; ADNOC has a 68% share; Total, Shell Gas and Partex have a minority interest; Chair. YOUSUF OMAIR BIN YOUSUF; Gen. Man. MUHAMMAD A. SAHOO.

Abu Dhabi Gas Liquefaction Co (ADGAS): POB 3500, Abu Dhabi; tel. (2) 6061111; fax (2) 6065456; f. 1973; owned by ADNOC, 51%; British Petroleum (BP), 16%; Total, 8%; Mitsui and Co, 22%; Mitsui Liquefied Gas Co, 3%; operates LGSC and the LNG plant on Das Island which uses natural gas produced in association with oil from offshore fields and has a design capacity of approx. 2.3m. metric tons of LNG per year and 1.29m. tons of LPG per year; the liquefied gas is sold to the Tokyo Electric Power Co, Japan; Chair. A. N. AS-SUWEIDI; Gen. Man. P. J. CARR.

Abu Dhabi Marine Operating Co (ADMA-OPCO): POB 303, Abu Dhabi; tel. (2) 6060000; fax (2) 6065062; operates a concession 60%

THE UNITED ARAB EMIRATES

owned by ADNOC, 40% by Abu Dhabi Marine Areas Ltd; f. 1977 as an operator for the concession; production (1984): 67,884,769 barrels (8,955,721 metric tons); Chair. YOUSUF BIN OMEIR BIN YOUSUF; Gen. Man. HENRY BACCONNIER.

Abu Dhabi Oil Refining Co (TAKREER): POB 3593, Abu Dhabi; tel. (2) 6027000; fax (2) 6065062; refining of crude oil; production of chlorine and related chemicals.

ADNOC Distribution: POB 4188, Abu Dhabi; tel. (2) 6771300; fax (2) 6722322; e-mail adnoc-fod@adnoc-fod.co.ae; internet www .adnoc-fod.co.ae; 100% owned by ADNOC; distributes petroleum products in UAE and world-wide; Chair. YOUSUF BIN OMEIR BIN YOUSUF; Gen. Man. JAMAL JABER ADH-DHAREEF.

National Drilling Co (NDC): POB 4017, Abu Dhabi; tel. (2) 6316600; fax (2) 6317045; e-mail ndcisc@emirates.net.ae; drilling operations; Chair. ABDULLAH NASSER AS-SUWAIDI; Gen. Man. NAJEEB HASSAN AZ-ZAABI.

National Petroleum Construction Co (NPCC): POB 2058, Abu Dhabi; tel. (2) 5549000; fax (2) 5549111; e-mail npccnet@emirates .net.ae; f. 1973; 'turnkey' construction and maintenance of offshore facilities for the petroleum and gas industries; cap. AED 100m.; Chair. MUHAMMAD BUTTI K. AL-QUBAISI; Gen. Man. AQEEL A. MADHI.

Ajman

Ajman National Oil Co (AJNOC): POB 410, Ajman; tel. (6) 7421218; f. 1983; 50% govt-owned, 50% held by Canadian and private Arab interests.

Dubai

DUGAS (Dubai Natural Gas Co Ltd): POB 4311, Dubai (Location: Jebel Ali); tel. (4) 3846000; fax (4) 3846118; wholly owned by Dubai authorities; Dep. Chair. and Dir SULTAN AHMAD BIN SULAYEM.

Dubai Petroleum Co (DPC): POB 2222, Dubai; tel. (4) 3846000; fax (4) 3846118; holds offshore concession, which began production in 1969; wholly owned by Dubai authorities; Pres. S. L. CORNELIUS.

Emirates General Petroleum Corpn (Emarat): POB 9400, Dubai; tel. (4) 3444444; fax (4) 3444292; f. 1981; wholly owned by Ministry of Finance and Industry; distribution of petroleum; Gen. Man. AHMAD MUHAMMAD AL-KAMDA.

Emirates National Oil Co (ENOC): POB 6442, Enoc House, 4th Floor, al-Qutaeyat Rd, Dubai; tel. (4) 3374400; fax (4) 3031221; e-mail webmaster@enoc.co.ae; f. 1993; responsible for management of Dubai-owned cos in petroleum-marketing sector; Chief Exec. HUSSAIN M. SULTAN.

Emirates Petroleum Products Co Pvt. Ltd: POB 5589, Dubai; tel. (4) 372131; fax (4) 3031605; f. 1980; jt venture between Govt of Dubai and Caltex Alkhaleej Marketing; sales of petroleum products, bunkering fuel and bitumen; Chair. Sheikh HAMDAN BIN RASHID AL-MAKTOUM.

Sedco-Houston Oil Group: POB 702, Dubai; tel. (4) 3224141; holds onshore concession of over 400,000 ha as well as the offshore concession fmrly held by Texas Pacific Oil; Pres. CARL F. THORNE.

Sharjah

A Supreme Petroleum Council was established in Sharjah in 1999; it was to assume the responsibilities of the Petroleum and Mineral Affairs Department.

Petroleum and Mineral Affairs Department: POB 188, Sharjah; tel. (6) 5541888; Dir ISMAIL A. WAHID.

Sharjah Liquefied Petroleum Gas Co (SHALCO): POB 787, Sharjah; tel. (6) 5286333; fax (6) 5286111; e-mail shalco@shalco.ae; f. 1984; gas processing; producer of liquified commercial propane and commercial butane; 60% owned by Sharjah authorities, 25% BP Sharjah LPG Co, 7.5% each Itochu Corpn and Tokyo Boeki of Japan; Gen. Man. SALEH ALI.

Umm al-Qaiwain

Petroleum and Mineral Affairs Department: POB 9, Umm al-Qaiwain; tel. (6) 7666034; Chair. Sheikh SULTAN BIN AHMAD AL-MU'ALLA.

UTILITIES
Abu Dhabi

A decree issued in late February 1998 restructured the Abu Dhabi utilities sector in preparation for its privatization.

Abu Dhabi Water and Electricity Authority (ADWEA): POB 6120, Abu Dhabi; tel. (2) 6943333; fax (2) 6943491; e-mail webmaster@adwea.gov.ae; internet www.adwea.gov.ae; f. 1999 to oversee the privatization of the water and electricity sectors; Chair. Sheikh DIAB BIN ZAYED AN-NAHYAN.

Abu Dhabi Distribution Co: POB 219, Abu Dhabi; tel. (2) 642300; fax (2) 6426033; e-mail customerservice@addc.co.ae; internet www.adwea.gov.ae/addc; f. 1999; distribution of water and electricity.

Abu Dhabi National Energy Co (Taqa): Abu Dhabi; f. 2005; owns assets in power, water, petroleum and mineral sectors in the UAE and abroad.

Abu Dhabi Transmission and Dispatch Co: POB 173, Abu Dhabi; tel. (2) 6414000; fax (2) 6426333; internet www.adwea.gov .ae/transco; f. 1999.

Abu Dhabi Water and Electricity Co (ADWEC): POB 51111, Abu Dhabi; tel. (2) 6943333; fax (2) 6425773; internet www.adwec .ae; f. 1999.

Al-Ain Distribution Co: POB 1065, al-Ain; tel. (3) 7636000; fax (3) 7632025; e-mail aadc@aadc.cc; internet www.adwea.gov.ae/aadc; f. 1999; distribution of water and electricity.

Bayounah Power Co: POB 3477, Abu Dhabi; tel. (2) 6731100; fax (2) 6730403; internet www.adwea.gov.ae/bpc; f. 1999.

Al-Mirfa Power Co: POB 32277, Abu Dhabi; tel. (2) 8833044; fax (2) 8833011; e-mail mirfa@emirates.net.ae; internet www.adwea .gov.ae/ampc; f. 1999; to control Mirfa and Madinat Zayed plants; capacity 300 MW electricity per day, 37m. gallons water per day; Chair. ABDULLAH AL-AHBABI; Gen. Man. PHILIP GRAHAM TILSON.

Al-Taweelah Power Co: POB 32255, Abu Dhabi; tel. (2) 5627000; fax (2) 5627055; internet www.adwea.gov.ae/atpc; f. 1999.

Emirates CMS Power Co: POB 47688, Abu Dhabi; tel. (2) 5067100; fax (2) 5067157; e-mail zgdesouza@cmsenergy.com; internet www.adwea.gov.ae/ecpc; f. 1999; owns and operates the Al-Taweelah plant; Man. Dir BRIAN S. JACKSON.

Umm an-Nar Power Co: POB 33488, Abu Dhabi; tel. (2) 5582700; fax (2) 5582405; internet www.adwea.gov.ae/uanpc; f. 1999.

Dubai

Dubai Electricity and Water Authority (DEWA): POB 564, Dubai; tel. (4) 3244444; fax (4) 3248111; e-mail dewa@dewa.gov .ae; internet www.dewa.gov.ae; Gen. Man. SAID MUHAMMAD AHMAD AL-TAYER.

Northern Emirates (Ajman, Fujairah, Ras al-Khaimah and Umm al-Qaiwain)

Ministry of Energy: see Ministries, above.

Sharjah

Sharjah Electricity and Water Authority (SEWA): Sharjah; tel. (2) 5288888; fax (2) 5288000; internet www.sewa.gov.ae.

Transport

RAILWAYS

In mid-2005 Dubai Municipality awarded the construction contract for an urban light-railway system, provisionally known as Dubai Metro, to Mitsubishi Corpn of Japan; completion of the project was expected to take five years. Further railway proposals, including a 700-km rail network linked to the growing Saudi network and a monorail on the Palm Jumeirah development, were under consideration in 2006.

ROADS

Roads are rapidly being developed in the UAE, and Abu Dhabi and Dubai are linked by a good road which is dual carriageway for most of its length. This road forms part of a west coast route from Shaam, at the UAE border with the northern enclave of Oman, through Dubai and Abu Dhabi to Tarif. An east coast route links Dibba with Muscat. Other roads include the Abu Dhabi–al-Ain highway and roads linking Sharjah and Ras al-Khaimah, and Sharjah and Dhaid. An underwater tunnel links Dubai Town and Deira by dual carriageway and pedestrian subway. Plans for the construction of a causeway between the UAE and Qatar were announced in December 2004. In 2003 there was a total paved-road network of 4,030 km.

SHIPPING

Dubai has been the main commercial centre in the Gulf for many years. Abu Dhabi has also become an important port since the opening of the first section of its artificial harbour, Port Zayed. There are smaller ports in Sharjah, Fujairah, Ras al-Khaimah and Umm al-Qaiwain. Dubai possesses two docks capable of handling 500,000-ton tankers, seven repair berths and a third dock able to accommodate 1,000,000-ton tankers. The Dubai port of Mina Jebel Ali, which was to be expanded at a cost of some US $1,362m., has the largest man-made harbour in the world.

Abu Dhabi

Abu Dhabi Seaport Authority: POB 422, Port Zayed, Abu Dhabi; tel. (2) 6730600; fax (2) 6731023; e-mail mrktdept@emirates.net.ae; internet www.portzayed.gov.ae; f. 1972; administers Port Zayed under the ownership of Dubai Ports World; facilities at the port include 21 deep-water berths and five container gantry cranes of 40 metric tons capacity; cold storage 20,500 tons; in 2000 Port Zayed handled 315,810 20-ft equivalent units (TEUs); Chair. Sheikh SAID BIN ZAYED AN-NAHYAN; Asst Under-Sec. for Operations MUBARAK MUHAMMAD AL-BU AINAIN.

Abu Dhabi National Tanker Co (ADNATCO): POB 2977, Abu Dhabi; tel. (2) 6277733; fax (2) 6272940; subsidiary co of ADNOC, operating owned and chartered tankships, and transporting crude petroleum, refined products and sulphur; Chair. NASSER AHMAD AS-SUWAIDI; Gen. Man. BADER M. AS-SUWAIDI.

Abu Dhabi Petroleum Ports Operating Co (ADPPOC): POB 61, Abu Dhabi; tel. (2) 6333500; fax (2) 6333567; e-mail adppoc@emirates.net.ae; f. 1979; manages Jebel Dhanna, Ruwais, Das Island, Umm an-Nar and Zirku Island SPM terminal, Mubarraz; cap. AED 50m.; 60% owned by ADNOC, 40% by LAMNALCO Kuwait; Chair. YOUSUF BIN OMEIR BIN YOUSUF; Gen. Man. KHALIFA M. AL-GOBAISI.

National Marine Services Co (NMS): POB 7202, Abu Dhabi; tel. (2) 6339800; fax (2) 6211239; operate, charter and lease specialized offshore support vessels; cap. AED 25m.; owned 60% by ADNOC and 40% by Jackson Marine Corpn USA; Chair. SOHAIL FARES AL-MAZRUI; Gen. Man. Capt. HASSAN A. SHARIF.

Dubai

Dubai Ports World (DP World): POB 17000, Dubai; tel. (4) 8815000; fax (4) 8816093; e-mail mktg@dpa.ae; internet www.dpa.ae; f. 2005 by the merger of Dubai Ports Authority (DPA, f. 1991 by the merger of Mina Jebel Ali and Mina Rashid) and Dubai Ports International (DPI, f. 1999); state-owned; storage areas and facilities for loading and discharge of vessels; operates ports of Mina Jebel Ali and Mina Rashid in Dubai, Port Zayed in Abu Dhabi, Fujairah Port and numerous other int. facilities; handled 6m. TEUs in 2004 (as DPA); Exec. SULTAN AHMAD BIN SULAYEM; CEO MUHAMMAD SHARAF.

Dubai Drydocks: POB 8988, Dubai; tel. (4) 3450626; fax (4) 3450116; e-mail drydocks@drydocks.gov.ae; internet www.drydocks.gov.ae; f. 1983; state-owned; dry-docking and repairs, tank cleaning, construction of vessels and floating docks, conversions, galvanizing, dredging, etc.; Chief Exec. GEOFF TAYLOR.

Sea Bridge Shipping: POB 8458, Dubai; tel. (4) 3379858; fax (4) 3372600; cargo ships; Chair. S. RAMAKRISHNAN; Man. Dir L. B. CULAS.

Vela International Marine: POB 26373, City Towers 2, Sheikh Zayed Rd, Dubai; tel. (4) 3312800; fax (4) 3315675; operates tankships; Chair. DHAIFALLAH F. ALUTAIBI; Man. Dir ADEL M. AD-DULAIJIN.

Fujairah

Fujairah Port: POB 787, Fujairah; tel. (9) 2228800; fax (9) 2228811; f. 1982; operated by Dubai Ports World; offers facilities for handling container, general cargo and 'roll on, roll off' traffic; handled 565,723 TEUs in 1999; Chair. Sheikh SALEH BIN MUHAMMAD ASH-SHARQI; Gen. Man. Capt. MOUSA MURAD; Harbour Master Capt. TAMER MASOUD.

Ras al-Khaimah

Mina Saqr Port Authority: POB 5130, Ras al-Khaimah; tel. (7) 2668444; fax (7) 2668533; port operators handling bulk cargoes, containers, general cargo and 'roll on, roll off' traffic; govt-owned; Chair. Sheikh MUHAMMAD BIN SAQR AL-QASIMI; Man. DAVID ALLAN.

Sharjah

Sharjah Ports and Customs Department: POB 510, Sharjah; tel. (6) 5281666; fax (6) 5281425; e-mail shjports@emirates.net.ae; internet www.sharjahports.gov.ae; the authority administers Port Khalid, Hamriyah Port and Port Khor Fakkan and offers specialized facilities for container and 'roll on, roll off' traffic, reefer cargo and project and general cargo; in 2003 Port Khalid handled 145,482 TEUs of containerized shipping, and Port Khor Fakkan 1,444,451 TEUs; Port Khalid and Hamriyah Port together handled over 4m. metric tons of non-containerized cargo; Chair. (Ports and Customs) Sheikh KHALID BIN ABDULLAH AL-QASIMI; Dir-Gen. ISSA JUMA AL-MUTAWA.

Fal Shipping Co Ltd: POB 6600, Sharjah; tel. (6) 5286666; fax (6) 5280861; operates tankships; Chair. ABDULLA JUMA AS-SARI; Gen. Man. MUHAMMAD OSMAN FADUL.

Umm al-Qaiwain

Ahmed bin Rashid Port and Free Zone Authority: POB 279, Umm al-Qaiwain; tel. (6) 7655882; fax (6) 7651552; e-mail abrpaftz@emirates.net.ae.

CIVIL AVIATION

There are six international airports at Abu Dhabi, al-Ain (Abu Dhabi), Dubai (DIA), Fujairah and Ras al-Khaimah, and a smaller one at Sharjah, which forms part of Sharjah port, linking air, sea and overland transportation services. Owing to space constraints at DIA, plans for the construction of a huge new airport with a capacity of 120m. passengers per year at Jebel Ali, in Dubai, were in progress in 2006. A project to redevelop Sharjah International Airport, at a cost of US $61m., was scheduled for completion by late 2006. In 1995 a total of 11.6m. passengers used the six UAE airports, 3.3m. of them passing through Abu Dhabi airports; in 2005 a record 23m. passengers used Dubai airport alone. Abu Dhabi withdrew from Gulf Air, which it had owned jointly with Bahrain and Oman (and previously with Qatar), in September 2005.

Civil Aviation Department: POB 20, Abu Dhabi; tel. (2) 6757500; responsible for all aspects of civil aviation; Chair. HAMDAN BIN MUBARAK AN-NAHYAN.

Abu Dhabi Aviation: POB 2723, Abu Dhabi; tel. (2) 4449100; fax (2) 4449081; f. 1976; domestic charter flights; Chair. HAMDAN BIN MUBARAK AN-NAHYAN; Gen. Man. MUHAMMAD IBRAHIM AL-MAZROUI.

 Emirates Air Service: POB 2723, Abu Dhabi; tel. (2) 6757021; fax (2) 4449100; f. 1976; as Abu Dhabi Air Services; overhaul, engine and avionics servicing, component repairs and complete refurbishment.

Air Arabia: Sharjah; f. 2003; owned by the Sharjah Govt; low-fare airline; operates three aircraft and serves 16 destinations; CEO ADAL ALI.

Emirates Airline: POB 686, Dubai; tel. (4) 2951111; fax (4) 2955817; e-mail corpcom@emiratesairline.com; internet www.emiratesairline.com; f. 1985; services to 78 destinations in 55 countries; owned by the Dubai Govt; the airline carried 12.5m. passengers in 2004/05 and 401,500 metric tons of freight in 2004/05; Group Chair. Sheikh AHMAD BIN SAID AL-MAKTOUM; Vice-Chair. and Group Pres. MAURICE FLANAGAN; Pres., Emirates Airline TIM CLARK.

Etihad Airways: Abu Dhabi; f. 2003; owned by the Abu Dhabi Govt; operates 34 aircraft serving 16 short- and long-haul destinations; Chair. Sheikh AHMAD BIN SAIF AN-NAHYAN.

Falcon Express Cargo Airlines: Dubai International Airport, POB 93722, Dubai; tel. (4) 2826886; fax (4) 2823125; e-mail feca@emirates.net.ae; f. 1995; dedicated courier freight.

RAK Airways: Ras al-Khaimah; f. 2005; owned by the Ras al-Khaimah Government; operates from Ras al-Khaimah Int. Airport; to serve destinations in Middle East, North Africa and the South Asia.

Tourism

Tourism is an established industry in Dubai and Sharjah, and plans are being implemented to foster tourism in other emirates, notably in Abu Dhabi. In 2003 foreign visitors to the UAE totalled almost 5.9m., compared with 616,000 in 1990.

Abu Dhabi Tourism Authority: Abu Dhabi; f. 2004; Chair. Sheikh SULTAN BIN TAHNUN AN-NAHYAN.

Department of Tourism and Commerce Marketing: POB 594, Dubai; tel. (4) 2230000; fax (4) 2230022; e-mail info@dubaitourism.co.ae; internet www.dubaitourism.co.ae.

Dubai Information Department: POB 1420, Dubai; Dir OMAR DEESI.

Fujairah Tourism Bureau: POB 829, Fujairah; tel. (9) 2231554; fax (9) 2231006; e-mail fujtourb@emirates.net.ae; internet www.fujairah-tourism.ae; f. 1995; Chair. Sheikh SAID ASH-SHARQI; Dir WAHID BIN YOUSSEF.

National Corporation for Tourism and Hotels (NCTH): Abu Dhabi; 20% owned by Government of Abu Dhabi.

Ras al-Khaimah Information and Tourism Department: POB 141, Ras al-Khaimah; tel. (7) 2751151; Chair. Sheikh ABD AL-AZIZ BIN HUMAID AL-QASIMI.

Sharjah Commerce and Tourism Development Authority: POB 26661, 11th Floor, Crescent Tower, Buheirah Corniche, Sharjah; tel. (6) 5562777; fax (6) 5563000; e-mail sctda@sharjahcommerce-tourism.gov.ae; internet www.sharjah-welcome.com; f. 1980; Dir. MUHAMMAD SAIF AL-HAJRI.

THE UNITED KINGDOM

Introductory Survey

Location, Climate, Language, Religion, Flag, Capital

The United Kingdom of Great Britain and Northern Ireland lies in north-western Europe, occupying the major portion of the British Isles. The country's only land boundary is with the Republic of Ireland. Great Britain, consisting of one large island and a number of smaller ones, comprises England, Scotland to the north and Wales to the west. It is separated from the coast of western Europe by the English Channel to the south and by the North Sea to the east. The northern and western shores are washed by the Atlantic Ocean. Ireland lies to the west across the Irish Sea. Northern Ireland, which is a constitutionally distinct part of the United Kingdom, is situated in the north-east of Ireland and is composed of six of the nine counties in the Irish province of Ulster, with the rest of the island comprising the Republic of Ireland. The climate of the United Kingdom is generally temperate but variable. The average temperature is about 15°C (59°F) in summer and about 5°C (41°F) in winter. Average annual rainfall is 900–1,000 mm (35–40 ins). The language is English, but Welsh is spoken by about one-fifth of the Welsh population. The Church of England is the established church in England. Other large Christian denominations are Roman Catholicism, Methodism, the United Reformed Church and the Baptists. The national flag (proportions 1 by 2), known as the Union Jack, is a superimposition of the red cross of Saint George of England, the white saltire of Saint Andrew of Scotland and the red saltire of Ireland, all on a blue background. The capital is London.

Recent History

At the end of the Second World War the United Kingdom still ruled a vast overseas empire, and successive British Governments, in response both to nationalist aspirations and world pressure, gradually granted independence to the colonies; almost all of these became members of the Commonwealth (see p. 193). Britain's dominance diminished over the Commonwealth, which became a free association of states, and by the end of the 1970s the country looked exclusively to the North Atlantic Treaty Organization (NATO, see p. 314) and to the European Community (EC—now European Union—EU, see p. 228) for its future security.

In 1951 a Conservative Government was formed by Winston Churchill, the wartime Prime Minister. The Conservatives remained in power for 13 years, led successively by Churchill, Sir Anthony Eden (1955–57), Harold Macmillan (1957–63) and Sir Alec Douglas-Home (1963–64). The election of 1964 gave a small parliamentary majority to the Labour Party, led by Harold Wilson. The Labour Party was re-elected in 1966, but in 1970 a Conservative Government, under Edward Heath, was returned.

After the general election of February 1974 Wilson formed a minority Government; at a further election in October the Labour Party achieved a small majority in the House of Commons. Wilson resigned as Prime Minister in April 1976, and was succeeded by James Callaghan. His Labour Government immediately encountered a serious monetary crisis and, following a series of by-election defeats, became a minority Government again.

In the general election of May 1979 the Conservative Party won a parliamentary majority. A Government was formed under Margaret Thatcher, who became the United Kingdom's first female Prime Minister. Thatcherite policy proved controversial, owing to the austerity of certain economic measures and an accompanying increase in unemployment. New legislation restricted the power of the trade unions.

Michael Foot was elected Leader of the Labour Party in November 1980. The increasing prominence of extreme left-wing members caused serious rifts in the Labour Party, and in March 1981 four former ministers from the right wing of the party formed the Social Democratic Party (SDP). The SDP formed a political alliance with the Liberals in 1981.

In April 1982 Argentine forces invaded the British dependency of the Falkland Islands (q.v.). The successful military campaign to recover the islands in June increased the Government's popularity, despite rising unemployment and strict monetary control of the economy. In the general election of June 1983 the Conservative Party increased its majority in the House of Commons to 146 seats. The Labour Party's parliamentary representation fell and Neil Kinnock subsequently replaced Foot as the Labour Leader.

At a general election in June 1987 the Conservative Party won an overall majority of 102 seats in the House of Commons. In March 1988 the SDP-Liberal Alliance formally merged as the Social and Liberal Democrats (SLD—later known as the Liberal Democrats), and in July Paddy Ashdown (of the former Liberal Party) was elected sole Leader of the SLD.

In mid-1990 the introduction of a local tax, the community charge (or 'poll tax'), in conjunction with an economic recession, and the unpopularity of changes to the education system and of proposed reforms to the National Health Service (NHS), contributed to considerable national dissatisfaction with the Thatcher administration. The Government was also divided, chiefly over policy on integration with the EC. In November Sir Geoffrey Howe resigned as the Lord President of the Council, Leader of the House of Commons and Deputy Prime Minister, in protest against Thatcher's hostility towards economic and political union within the EC. Michael Heseltine (who had resigned as Secretary of State for Defence in 1986) announced that he would challenge Thatcher for the leadership of the Conservative Party. In the first ballot of the leadership election (conducted among Conservative Members of Parliament—MPs) Thatcher failed to achieve an outright victory and subsequently withdrew her candidacy. John Major, Chancellor of the Exchequer since October 1989, finally won the contest and was officially appointed Prime Minister in November 1990.(The community charge was replaced with a local 'council tax', based on property values, in April 1993.)

In a general election held on 9 April 1992 the Conservative Party was re-elected with an overall, but substantially reduced, majority in the House of Commons. The Conservative Party obtained 336 (of 651) seats and 41.9% of the votes cast, the Labour Party 271 seats and 34.4% of the votes, and the Liberal Democrats 21 seats and 17.9% of the votes.

Economic recession continued, and the Government's economic policies were criticized not only by political opponents, but also by industrial and business leaders. Divisions within the Conservative Party over the provisions of the Treaty on European Union (the Maastricht Treaty) were exacerbated by the United Kingdom's departure from the exchange rate mechanism (ERM) of the European Monetary System (see p. 265) in September 1992. The Treaty was endorsed by the House of Lords, the non-elected upper chamber, in July 1993, despite fierce opposition from some Conservatives. However, in a vote to ratify the Treaty, by adopting a motion on its so-called 'social chapter', conducted in the House of Commons later in July, 'rebel' Conservatives joined the Opposition to defeat the motion. The Prime Minister introduced a confidence motion the following day, and speculation that Major would call a general election in the event of a defeat for the Government ensured the support of dissident MPs.

Following the Labour Party's fourth successive general election defeat, in April 1992, Kinnock announced his resignation as Leader of the party. In July John Smith was elected to replace him. Prior to his death, in May 1994, Smith reformed the relationship between the Labour Party and the trade unions, reducing the unions' influence over policy formulation and the election of party chiefs and parliamentary candidates. In July Anthony (Tony) Blair, Labour's parliamentary spokesman on home affairs, was elected Leader by the party's electoral college. John Prescott became Deputy Leader. Blair's initiative to abandon Labour's socialist commitment to common ownership of the means of production provoked a much-publicized reassessment of party ideology, and became a test of support for the new leadership. In April 1995 a special party conference endorsed a draft text to replace the relevant clause of the party's constitution.

At local elections held in Scotland in April 1995 the Conservative Party obtained only 11% of the votes cast. The Labour

Party, which had disclosed proposals for devolution in the event of its forming a government, won 47% of the votes, and the Scottish National Party (SNP) 27%. By May the Government's majority in the House of Commons had been reduced to 10 members. In June Major announced his resignation as Leader of the Conservative Party, asserting that speculation regarding a challenge to his leadership was undermining both his authority as Prime Minister and that of the Government. The Secretary of State for Wales, John Redwood, resigned from the Cabinet in order to challenge Major as party Leader. In the ballot for the leadership, held in July, Major obtained 218 of the 329 votes of the parliamentary party (compared with Redwood's 89). By April 1996 the Government's majority in the House of Commons had declined to a single seat.

In March 1996 the imposition by the EU of a comprehensive trade ban on British beef products, in response to a major public health alert (see below), reinforced the position of those Conservative MPs demanding a limitation in the country's convergence with the EU. In April Major committed a future Conservative administration to conducting a popular referendum on the country's participation in a European single currency. In June more than 70 Conservative MPs declared their support for a wider referendum on EU membership, demonstrating the increasingly organized strength of the so-called Eurosceptic faction of the party.

In December 1996 the Government officially lost its majority in the House of Commons when the Labour Party won a by-election for a previously Conservative-held seat. In February 1997 the Labour Party attempted to force a government defeat, in order to prompt a general election, by introducing a parliamentary censure motion against the Minister of Agriculture, Fisheries and Food, Douglas Hogg, for his administration of the bovine spongiform encephalopathy (BSE) crisis (see below). However, the Ulster Unionists upheld the Government's position by abstaining. By March the Conservatives' parliamentary minority had deepened, following a further Labour by-election victory and the defection of a Eurosceptic MP.

At a general election held on 1 May 1997 the Labour Party (now frequently referred to as New Labour, emphasizing the reforms undertaken under Blair's leadership) secured an overwhelming victory, winning 418 of the 659 parliamentary seats, with 44.3% of the votes cast in Britain. The Conservative Party won only 165 seats, with 31.5% of the vote. Moreover, for the first time in its history, the Conservative Party failed to win any parliamentary representation in Scotland or Wales. The Liberal Democrats increased their number of seats to 46, although with a slightly reduced share of the votes (17.2%, compared with 17.9% in 1992). Major immediately announced his resignation as Leader of the Conservative Party: William Hague, hitherto Secretary of State for Wales, was elected to the post (and thus as Leader of the Opposition) by Conservative MPs in June.

In the new Labour Government Gordon Brown was named as Chancellor of the Exchequer, Robin Cook became the new Secretary of State for Foreign and Commonwealth Affairs, while John Prescott, appointed Deputy Prime Minister, assumed additional responsibility for the environment, transport and the regions. Peter Mandelson, one of Blair's closest advisers and regarded as highly influential in the organization of Labour's election campaign, was appointed Minister without Portfolio, with responsibility for co-ordinating government policy (a non-Cabinet post). The new administration announced a series of radical policy proposals and government reforms, including an employment initiative, aimed initially at long-term unemployed 18–24 year olds, which was to be financed by a single taxation levy on the profits of privatized industries. Brown announced changes to the management and regulation of the economy and the financial sector (including a transfer of operational responsibility for monetary policy to the Bank of England), while Cook defined the Government's broad approach to foreign affairs, with greater emphasis on the country's role in international organizations and the incorporation of human rights concerns into foreign policy and trade decisions. A new Department for International Development was established, to assume the functions of the former Overseas Development Administration (previously under the authority of the Foreign and Commonwealth Office) at cabinet level. The Government's parliamentary programme included additional legislation for improved standards in education, the adoption of a national minimum wage, and constitutional reform.

In July 1997 the Government formally published its proposals for the establishment of devolved legislative authorities in Scotland and Wales. For Scotland a proposed new elected Parliament was envisaged as having powers to legislate on all domestic matters, including education, health, local government, law and order, and the possible mandate to vary taxes set by the United Kingdom Government. An executive level of government was to be headed by a First Minister. The 129 Members of the Scottish Parliament (MSPs) were to be elected every four years by a combined system of direct voting and a form of proportional representation. The Welsh Assembly, like the Scottish body, was envisaged as assuming control of the annual block grant for the region from central government, and as undertaking responsibility for issues covered by the Welsh Office. The 60-member Assembly was to be elected under the same system as in Scotland. In a referendum held in Scotland in September, 74.3% of voters supported a new Parliament, while 63.5% approved its having tax-raising powers. The results, although representing only an estimated 44.7% and 38.1% of eligible voters, respectively, were considered by the Government as being an endorsement of its proposals. The referendum in Wales, held one week later, was less conclusive, with only 50.3% of voters (or some 25% of eligible voters) endorsing the Assembly. None the less, the Government declared its intention of implementing the majority decision. The political settlement on the future governance of Northern Ireland (see below), concluded in April, provided for new constitutional arrangements regarding the status of Northern Ireland within the United Kingdom and for the establishment of a British-Irish Council.

In October 1998 the Leader of the Government in the House of Lords, Baroness Jay of Paddington, announced that legislation was to be introduced to remove the voting rights of hereditary peers, and that a Royal Commission was to be appointed to consider options for a definitive reform of the second chamber. Opposition from within the House of Lords was appeased in December when a compromise agreement was reached under which 92 hereditary peers were to retain their seats in an interim second chamber pending the definitive reform. Draft legislation for the abolition of hereditary peers and the establishment of an interim chamber was published in January 1999. In October the upper chamber approved the House of Lords Bill, and in November it received royal assent. In January 2000 the Royal Commission published its proposals for the definitive reform of the upper house, recommending that the new chamber should comprise some 550 members, the majority of whom would be chosen by an independent commission, while a 'significant minority' (between 65 and 195) would be elected by regional proportional representation.

At elections to the new legislative authorities in Scotland and Wales, held in May 1999, the Labour Party, while securing the greatest number of seats, failed to gain an overall majority in either assembly. In Scotland the Labour Party obtained 56 of the total 129 seats, while the SNP won 35 seats, the Conservative Party 18 seats, and the Liberal Democrats 17 seats; the remaining three seats were won by independent candidates. The Labour Party and the Liberal Democrats subsequently formed a coalition administration, headed by Donald Dewar as First Minister. In Wales the Labour Party secured 28 of the total 60 seats, while Plaid Cymru obtained 17 seats, the Conservative Party nine seats and the Liberal Democrats six seats. Despite Labour's lack of an overall majority, in mid-May the Welsh First Minister, Alun Michael, opted to form a minority administration rather than a formal coalition. Powers were transferred to both the Scottish and the Welsh legislatures on 1 July 1999.

During 2000 there was considerable political upheaval in both Wales and Scotland. In February Rhodri Morgan succeeded Alun Michael as Welsh First Minister. Michael had resigned shortly before the Welsh Assembly adopted a vote of no confidence in his leadership. In May the Leader of Plaid Cymru, Dafydd Wigley, resigned owing to ill health; he was replaced by Ieuan Wyn Jones in August. In October the ruling Labour Party entered into a coalition agreement with the Liberal Democrats, who obtained two portfolios, including that of Deputy First Minister, in the reorganized nine-member Welsh Cabinet. Meanwhile, in Scotland the unexpected resignation of Alex Salmond as Leader of the SNP in July precipitated a leadership contest in which John Swinney was elected as Salmond's successor. Following the death in October of the First Minister, Dewar, the Labour Party in Scotland elected Henry McLeish to succeed him as their Leader. Later that month McLeish, hitherto Minister for Enterprise and Lifelong Learning, was also elected to succeed Dewar as First Minister.

THE UNITED KINGDOM

Introductory Survey

In August 1999 the Liberal Democrats elected Charles Kennedy to succeed Paddy Ashdown as their Leader. In October Blair conducted a government reorganization in which Peter Mandelson replaced Marjorie (Mo) Mowlam as Secretary of State for Northern Ireland. Mandelson had been appointed President of the Board of Trade and Secretary of State for Trade and Industry in July 1998 but had resigned in December following allegations of financial impropriety.

In September 2000 the Labour administration suffered its most serious domestic crisis since coming to power when protesters (primarily road hauliers and farmers) angered by rising fuel prices, blockaded the country's major petroleum refineries and distribution depots. In November the Government announced concessions aimed at road hauliers and motorists, notably a small reduction in the price of petroleum and the freezing of duty on fuel until at least April 2002.

In January 2001 the Government suffered another reverse when Mandelson resigned as Secretary of State for Northern Ireland after his initial denial of any direct involvement in an enquiry to the Home Office in June 1998 regarding the application for British citizenship of an Indian business executive, Srichand Hinduja, appeared to be false. Dr John Reid, hitherto Secretary of State for Scotland, was appointed to succeed Mandelson, thus becoming the first Roman Catholic to hold the Northern Ireland portfolio.

In February 2001 incidences of foot-and-mouth disease (FMD—a non-fatal yet highly contagious virus carried by cloven-hoofed animals) in south-east England prompted the European Commission to impose a temporary ban on the export of live animals, meat and dairy products from the United Kingdom. It had been widely anticipated (though not officially confirmed) that a general election would be conducted concurrently with local elections scheduled for 3 May. However, a continuing rise in the number of cases of FMD, mounting pressure from agricultural interest groups and popular opposition to the timing of the polls, led the Government to announce in April that emergency legislation would be introduced to provide for a five-week postponement of the local elections (the first time such legislation had been required during peacetime).

In early May 2001 Blair announced that a general election (as well as the postponed local elections) would be conducted on 7 June, although new incidences of FMD continued to be discovered. In August the Government announced the establishment of three separate independent inquiries into the outbreak of FMD, but rejected opposition calls for a full public inquiry into the crisis. The last case of FMD was identified in September and in January 2002 the Government announced that the United Kingdom was free of the disease. In February the European Commission agreed to lift remaining restrictions on the import and export of British meat, animal products and livestock. A report published by the National Audit Office in June 2002 confirmed that the losses to the British economy resulting from the FMD crisis totalled some £5,000m. In July the inquiry into the Government's handling of the crisis was published and was highly critical of the Government's response to the outbreak, stating that FMD spread far wider than it should have as a result of inadequate contingency plans and the Government's sluggish response.

At the general election held on 7 June 2001 the Labour Party won a further comprehensive victory, securing 413 of the 659 parliamentary seats with 40.7% of the votes cast. The Conservative Party won 166 seats with 31.7% of the votes cast, while the Liberal Democrats increased their parliamentary representation to 53 seats, with 18.3% of the votes cast. The election was, however, marred by the lowest rate of voter participation, 59.4%, since 1918. Following his party's poor performance, Hague announced his intention to resign the leadership of the Conservative Party; in September Iain Duncan Smith, hitherto the Conservative Party's parliamentary spokesman on defence, was elected to replace Hague as Leader of the Conservative Party and thus of the Opposition. Meanwhile, in a major reorganization of the Cabinet, Jack Straw, hitherto Secretary of State for the Home Department, replaced Cook as Secretary of State for Foreign and Commonwealth Affairs and David Blunkett, formerly Secretary of State for Education, assumed Straw's vacated portfolio. The Ministry of Agriculture, Fisheries and Food, which had been heavily criticized for its handling of the FMD outbreak, was replaced by the Department for Environment, Food and Rural Affairs and a new Department for Work and Pensions was created. Furthermore, Blair removed the responsibility for transport, environment and the regions from the Deputy Prime Minister, John Prescott, appointing Stephen Byers, previously Secretary of State for Trade and Industry, as head of the newly formed Department for Transport, Local Government and the Regions (DTLR).

Upon their release in November 2001, the Government's proposals for the reform of the House of Lords encountered fierce opposition from both Labour and opposition MPs concerning the number of directly elected members envisaged in the plans. The public consultation process on the proposals ended in January 2002 and the President of the Council and the Leader of the House of Commons, Robin Cook, announced that there would be an extended period of reflection. In May the Government effectively abandoned the recommendations produced in November 2001, and in December 2002 a new joint committee of MPs and peers presented seven options for the future proportion of elected members in the House of Lords, ranging from a wholly elected chamber to a wholly appointed house. However, in February 2003 all seven options were rejected by MPs voting in the House of Commons.

In December 2001 a Labour MP defected to the Liberal Democrats in protest at the Government's continued failure to improve public services. Furthermore, Blair also encountered criticism for allegedly neglecting domestic issues and increasingly concentrating on foreign policy, in particular the war in Afghanistan (see below). Also in December anti-terrorism legislation was introduced in response to the events of 11 September in the USA (see below), which, most notably, provided for the detention of suspected international terrorists without trial if their deportation was not deemed possible. However, in July 2002 the legislation was declared unlawful and in breach of the European Convention on Human Rights by the Special Immigration Appeals Committee (SIAC). In October the British Court of Appeal ruled against the July decision and in May 2003 Blunkett announced proposals that would allow police to hold terrorist suspects without charge for up to 14 days. In October the SIAC rejected appeals by 10 foreign nationals who had been detained indefinitely without trial.

The resignation in May 2002 of Byers as Secretary of State for Transport, Local Government and the Regions (see below) precipitated a major reorganization of several government departments. The DTLR was abolished and a new Department for Transport, to be headed by Alistair Darling, hitherto Secretary of State for Work and Pensions, was created. Most of the other responsibilities of the former DTLR were transferred to the Office of the Deputy Prime Minister.

In mid-March 2003 Clare Short announced her intention to resign as Secretary of State for International Development if Blair approved British participation in the US-led campaign to oust the regime of Saddam Hussain in Iraq (see below) without a pertinent UN resolution. Following failure to secure a second UN resolution authorizing military action in Iraq and the announcement that British troops would be deployed as part of the US-led coalition to remove Hussain, Cook resigned as Leader of the House of Commons, citing his unwillingness to accept collective responsibility for the decision to commit the United Kingdom to military action without international agreement or domestic support. Two ministers of state and a number of ministerial aides also resigned in protest at Blair's decision. Short's revised intention, to remain in her post, attracted criticism from across the political spectrum. Blair suffered another major reverse when 139 Labour MPs voted in favour of a motion stating that there was no moral justification for an attack in Iraq, although another motion endorsing his strategy was approved by 412 votes to 149. In April Blair appointed Reid to replace Cook. Ian McCartney, hitherto Secretary of State for Work and Pensions, succeeded Reid as Minister without Portfolio and Party Chair. Short finally resigned from the Cabinet in May, accusing Blair of reneging on assurances he had made to her concerning the need for a UN mandate to establish a legitimate Iraqi government. She was succeeded by Baroness Amos of Brondesbury, who became Britain's first black female cabinet minister.

At elections to the Scottish and Welsh legislative authorities held on 1 May 2003 the Labour Party again won the largest number of seats in both assemblies. In Wales Labour secured 30 of the 60 available seats, Plaid Cymru won 12 seats, the Conservatives 11, and the Liberal Democrats six; the remaining seat was taken by an independent candidate. Morgan subsequently unveiled a nine-member, all-Labour Cabinet. In Scotland the Labour Party obtained 50 of the total 129 seats, while the SNP took 27, the Conservatives 18, the Liberal Democrats 17, the Scottish Green Party seven, and the Scottish Socialist Party six;

the remaining four seats were won by independent candidates. Labour and the Liberal Democrats afterwards agreed to continue their coalition and in mid-May Jack McConnell, who had succeeded McLeish as Leader of the Labour Party in Scotland and First Minister in November 2001, announced a new 11-member administration comprising eight Labour and three Liberal Democrat ministers.

In May 2003 Straw indicated that evidence that Iraq had possessed weapons of mass destruction might never be found, prompting allegations from a number of anti-war MPs that the perceived threat posed by that country had been exaggerated, and that the House of Commons had been misled. Attacks on the Government's integrity centred on the claim in a dossier—*Iraq's Weapons of Mass Destruction*, published by the British Government in September 2002 to outline its case for the removal of the Iraqi regime—that Iraq had 'existing and active military plans for the use of chemical and biological weapons, which could be activated in 45 minutes'. A journalist of the British Broadcasting Corporation (BBC), Andrew Gilligan, alleged that the Government had 'sexed up' the dossier against the wishes of the intelligence services and 'probably...knew that the 45-minute claim was wrong'. Blair denied the accusations and stated that the evidence had been compiled and approved by the Joint Intelligence Committee (JIC). The JIC's Chairman, John Scarlett, later testified that neither the Office of the Prime Minister nor the Prime Minister's Director of Communications and Strategy, Alastair Campbell, had requested that the '45-minute claim' be included in the dossier.

In early June 2003 Cook called for the Prime Minister to sanction an independent inquiry into the circumstances surrounding the publication of the dossier, while Short accused Blair of presenting false information to the Cabinet and of entering into a secret pact in September 2002 with the US President, George W. Bush, to take military action in Iraq by February 2003. The following day it was announced that the all-party Foreign Affairs Select Committee (FASC) would conduct an independent inquiry into whether the Government had presented 'accurate and complete information to Parliament in the period leading up to military action in Iraq, particularly in relation to Iraq's weapons of mass destruction' and that Parliament's Intelligence and Security Committee (ISC) would investigate the role played by intelligence agencies in providing the Government with information. It also transpired that the 45-minute claim had been provided by a single source from within the Iraqi military and that the JIC had been unable to corroborate it; furthermore, it emerged that documents used to compile a claim in the dossier that Iraq had sought significant quantities of uranium from African countries had been forged. In mid-June the ISC censured the Prime Minister's Office for publishing a second dossier in early February, which had contained intelligence material combined with plagiarized and outdated material taken from an academic paper publicly available on the internet.

In late June 2003 a disagreement broke out between Campbell and the BBC over the allegations that the first dossier had been 'sexed up'. Gilligan had claimed in a newspaper article just days after his initial broadcast that Campbell had been personally responsible for the changes that had been made to the dossier, against the wishes of the intelligence agencies. In early July the FASC concluded that Campbell had not exerted or sought to exert improper influence on the drafting of the first dossier; however, it was critical of the undue prominence given to the 45-minute claim and also of Campbell's role in the production of the second dossier, which had led Blair unwittingly to misinform Parliament that 'further intelligence' existed on Iraq's strategy of hiding weapons of mass destruction. The BBC, however, while refusing to reveal its source, rejected Campbell's demand that it retract the story.

On 18 July 2003 the dispute between the Government and the BBC intensified after Dr David Kelly, a senior adviser to the Proliferation and Arms Control Secretariat at the Ministry of Defence (MoD), whose identity as Gilligan's source had been confirmed earlier that month by the MoD, was found dead, apparently having committed suicide. There were calls for the resignations of Campbell and the Secretary of State for Defence, Geoffrey Hoon, and Blair immediately ordered an independent judicial inquiry into Kelly's death, to be chaired by Lord Hutton of Bresagh. On 20 July the BBC admitted that Dr Kelly had been the source for its story and it was also reported that Hoon had authorized the MoD's strategy vis-à-vis Kelly, which dictated that officials would not volunteer Kelly's name but would confirm his identity if it was suggested by journalists. Blair steadfastly denied authorizing the disclosure of Kelly's name to journalists, while Hoon maintained that he and his department had striven to ensure Kelly's anonymity.

On 19 August 2003 Campbell appeared before the Hutton inquiry and admitted that the Government had mishandled the naming of Dr Kelly and had failed adequately to support him. However, he again denied having any influence over the first dossier. He was also critical of the MoD for its 'naming strategy' with regard to Kelly. When Hoon was called before the inquiry later that month he again denied direct responsibility for the naming of Kelly. Furthermore, he revealed that the Prime Minister's Office had requested he write to the BBC naming Kelly as the Government's suspected source for the story. The following day Blair appeared before the inquiry and insisted that he took full responsibility for the decisions leading to the unmasking of Dr Kelly and that if Gilligan's allegations had been true he would have resigned. On 30 August Campbell announced his resignation as Director of Communications and Strategy, although he denied the decision was related to the recent events.

In September 2003 the ISC published its report and criticized Blair for not revealing to the House of Commons prior to its vote on whether to support military action in Iraq in March that he had been informed by the JIC in February that any such action would heighten the terrorist threat to the United Kingdom. The ISC was also critical of Hoon's evidence, but its report cleared Campbell of 'sexing up' the first dossier and exonerated the Government of any political interference in the assessment of secret intelligence. The report also concluded that there was convincing evidence to suggest that Iraq had active nuclear, chemical and biological programmes and the capability to produce chemical and biological weapons.

On 28 January 2004 Lord Hutton released the report of his inquiry into the apparent suicide of Dr David Kelly. Hutton's main findings were that Kelly had taken his own life; that Gilligan's allegations that the Prime Minister's Office had inserted the 45-minute claim knowing it to be wrong and that the first dossier had been 'sexed up' were unfounded; that there had been no dishonourable or duplicitous strategy on behalf of the Government to reveal Dr Kelly's name to the media, but that the MoD had erred by failing to inform Kelly that his name would be confirmed if journalists suggested it, and that its handling of Kelly after his public exposure had been unsatisfactory; that the BBC's editorial system was defective; that the BBC management had not fully investigated the Government's complaints; and that the organization's Board of Governors had failed comprehensively to scrutinize the dispute before publicly supporting the management's defence of Gilligan. Gavyn Davies immediately announced his resignation as Chairman of the Board of Governors; the following day the Director-General of the BBC, Greg Dyke, also resigned, and Gilligan tendered his resignation on 30 January.

In early February 2004 Blair announced the establishment of a further inquiry, under Lord Butler of Brockwell, into the accuracy of the intelligence gathered on Iraqi weapons of mass destruction, which would examine any discrepancies between the information collected, evaluated and used by the Government before the conflict in Iraq and intelligence discovered by the Iraq Survey Group (see below) since the end of major combat operations in May 2003. In July 2004 Lord Butler published the findings from his inquiry, which revealed that intelligence surrounding the compilation of the first dossier was 'seriously flawed' and criticized the intelligence services for using unreliable sources of information within Iraq. It also disclosed that before the start of the war there was no proof that Iraq had any significant stocks of weapons of mass destruction. While it suggested that the next Chairman of the JIC should be a person 'with experience of dealing with ministers in a senior role', it stressed that there was no evidence of 'deliberate distortion or culpable negligence' on the part of the JIC.

In June 2003, meanwhile, an extensive reorganization of the Cabinet included plans to effect major changes to the British legal and judicial system. Under the proposals the post of Lord Chancellor, which had been in existence for some 1,400 years, was to be abolished and a US-style supreme court was to replace the judicial function of the House of Lords as the United Kingdom's highest court of appeal. The Lord Chancellor's Office was replaced by a newly created Department for Constitutional Affairs, which also assumed responsibility for the abolished Scottish and Welsh Offices. Officials from those offices were located within the new department, although Darling assumed the position of Secretary of State for Scotland in addition to the transport portfolio and Peter Hain, who replaced Reid as Leader of the House of Commons, retained the post of Secretary of State for Wales. Reid subsequently replaced Alan Milburn as Secretary of State for Health. Lord Falconer of Thoroton was appointed to head the Department for Constitutional Affairs whilst also assuming temporarily the functions of the Lord Chancellor—although he would not sit as a judge—pending the full implementation of the reforms. Furthermore, responsibility for appointing judges would no longer rest with the Lord Chancellor but would pass to a proposed independent judicial appointments commission. The reshuffle and, in particular, the decision to abolish such a historic position without prior consultation, was heavily criticized by a number of MPs and Lords, and Blair was requested by the Speaker of the House of Commons to appear before the chamber to clarify the decisions and their repercussions. Consultation papers regarding the further reform of the House of Lords, which proposed the removal of the remaining 92 hereditary peers and the creation of a wholly appointed upper chamber with unchanged revising powers, and the abolition of the position of Lord Chancellor and the creation of a supreme court, were published by the Government in September 2003. On 8 March 2004 the House of Lords determined by 216 votes to 183 to refer the Constitutional Reform Bill to a Lords select committee for further scrutiny. The Government announced later that month that it was postponing plans to abolish the remaining 92 hereditary peers; it intended, however, to continue with plans to establish a supreme court and remove the post of Lord Chancellor. In early July the Lords select committee revealed that it had made several amendments to the bill; however, the clause providing for the removal of the Lord Chancellor was rejected by the House of Lords later that month by 240 votes to 208. The Government subsequently agreed only to modify the Lord Chancellor's role. In March 2005 an attempt by the Government to separate the Lord Chancellor's roles as supreme judge, Speaker of the House of Lords and government minister failed when a new amendment to the bill, proposing that the Lord Chancellor need not be a member of the House of Lords or a lawyer, was rejected by the upper house. However, the House of Lords subsequently voted by a majority of 12 to allow an MP who was not necessarily a lawyer to take on the role of Lord Chancellor, and the Constitutional Reform Bill received royal assent in late March. As part of the reform of the role of Lord Chancellor, in January 2006 the House of Lords formally agreed to elect a Speaker, the Lord Chancellor having hitherto traditionally presided over debates; a vote was to take place by 30 June. In April the Constitutional Reform Act came into force, and the Lord Chief Justice of England and Wales, Lord Phillips of Worth Matravers, assumed control of the judiciary in England and Wales from the Lord Chancellor. However, the new Supreme Court was not scheduled to commence operations until October 2009.

Meanwhile, in September 2003 Blair came under increasing pressure after the Labour Party candidate at a by-election in a previously safe Labour constituency was defeated by the Liberal Democrats' candidate. In early October 2003 Blair effected a minor reshuffle of the Cabinet, following the death of the Leader of the House of Lords, Lord Williams of Mostyn. Baroness Amos was appointed to replace Lord Williams and Hilary Benn was promoted from his position as Minister of State for International Development to succeed Amos as the head of that department. In late October Duncan Smith announced his resignation as Leader of the Conservative Party after Conservative MPs approved a vote of no confidence in his leadership. He was replaced by Michael Howard, a former Secretary of State for the Home Department, who was elected Leader unopposed.

Dissent from within the Labour Party continued to threaten to undermine Blair's authority and in November 2003 the Government's controversial health and social care legislation, which would allow a number of high-performing hospitals to become foundation trusts (allowing hospital managers greater autonomy), secured passage through Parliament with a majority of just 17 votes. In January 2004, in the most notable Labour revolt since Blair became Prime Minister, 72 Labour MPs voted against the Government's Higher Education Bill, which would introduce repayable and variable university tuition fees from 2006. Only intense lobbying from a number of cabinet ministers secured the passage of the Bill—by five votes. In April the Minister of State for Citizenship, Immigration and Counter-Terrorism, Beverley Hughes, resigned after it had been revealed that she had approved an immigration process in which rigorous tests for granting British citizenship were not carried out.

On 10 June 2004, at elections to the European Parliament and at local elections, the Labour Party suffered significant losses. In the local elections Labour lost 464 seats and eight councils, leaving them with control of 39 councils, while the Conservatives gained 263 seats and 13 councils, increasing their total to 51 councils, and the Liberal Democrats suffered a net loss of two councils, leaving them with control of nine. The Conservatives won 37% of the votes cast, the Liberal Democrats 27% and the Labour Party 26%. The Labour Party's poor performance was widely attributed to popular dissatisfaction with the Government's decisions surrounding the Iraq war. In the European elections the Conservatives won 27 of the 78 seats allocated to the United Kingdom (compared with 36 in 1999) and Labour won 19 (a decline of 10 seats). The Liberal Democrats gained two seats, while the Eurosceptic UK Independence Party increased its representation in the European Parliament from three seats to 12. Electoral participation was registered at 38.2%, compared with 24% in 1999.

In a cabinet reorganization in September 2004 Alan Milburn was reinstated to the Cabinet as Chancellor of the Duchy of Lancaster and given responsibility for general election strategy and Alan Johnson replaced Andrew Smith (who had resigned shortly before the reshuffle) as Secretary of State for Work and Pensions. In early November, in a referendum, 77.9% of people rejected the proposed establishment of an elected regional assembly for north-east England; voter turn-out was registered at 47.7%.

In late November 2004 an inquiry led by Sir Alan Budd was set up to investigate accusations that the Secretary of State for the Home Department, David Blunkett, had fast-tracked a visa application for the employee of his former lover, Kimberly Quinn—an accusation that he initially vehemently denied. In early December the report of the inquiry revealed a 'chain of events' linking Blunkett to the dispatch of the application, although no evidence was uncovered of his direct intervention. Although he continued to assert his innocence of any deliberate wrongdoing, Blunkett resigned from the Cabinet. Charles Clarke, hitherto Secretary of State for Education and Skills, was appointed to replace him, while Ruth Kelly, the former Minister for the Cabinet Office, was allocated Clarke's role. Also in December the Law Lords ruled that the detention without trial under the 2001 Anti-Terrorism, Crime and Security Act of the remaining nine foreign suspects who could not be deported was discriminatory and in breach of their human rights, overturning an earlier ruling by SIAC. Clarke presented a new anti-terrorism bill to Parliament in February 2005 since the powers of detention under the 2001 Act were due to expire in March, as a result of the legal ruling. The new bill encountered strong criticism from human rights groups, which claimed it infringed civil liberties. The House of Lords adopted the bill in mid-March after the Government had made significant amendments to it in response to its repeated rejection by the upper house.

In late March 2004 eight men were arrested and large amounts of bomb-making equipment were seized in a major anti-terrorism operation in south-east England. In early April five of the men were charged with terrorism-related offences. Later in April 10 people were arrested in Manchester in another major police operation, and further police raids across England in early August resulted in the arrests of 12 suspected terrorists. By early May 2004 562 people had been detained in the United Kingdom under anti-terrorism laws since September 2001. Of those, 97 had been charged with terrorism offences and 14 deported.

In early April 2005 Blair announced that a general election would take place on 5 May. Prior to this announcement a Labour candidate, Stephen Wilkinson, had defected to the Liberal Democrats, having become disillusioned with Blair's 'increasingly authoritarian' style of Government. The following day, however, a Liberal Democrat MP, Paul Marsden, defected to Labour, having left the party four years earlier in protest at its decision to approve military action in Afghanistan (see below). The Labour Party focused its election campaign on the economy, the Conservatives on crime and immigration and the Liberal Democrats on replacing the council tax with a local income tax and on the party's opposition to the war in Iraq. Blair's credibility was adversely affected by continuing controversy about Iraq, which was exacerbated by the publication of the initial (previously undisclosed) advice of the Attorney-General on the legality of the war.

At the general election on 5 May 2005 the Labour Party was re-elected for a third term, albeit with a substantially reduced majority, securing 356 of the 645 parliamentary seats contested, with 35.2% of the votes cast. The Conservative Party and the Liberal Democrats both increased their representation in the House of Commons, securing 197 seats (with 32.3% of the votes cast) and 62 seats (with 22.0%), respectively. Voting in one further constituency was postponed, owing to the death of a candidate. The rate of participation by eligible voters was 61.3%. Following the election, the Leader of the Ulster Unionist Party, David Trimble, resigned, in view of the party's poor performance (Trimble had himself lost his seat), while Michael Howard also announced his intention to step down as Leader of the Conservative Party. Blair commenced a major reorganization of ministerial portfolios on 6 May. David Blunkett returned to the Cabinet as Secretary of State for Work and Pensions, John Reid was named as the new Secretary of State for Defence, replacing Hoon (who became Lord Privy Seal and Leader of the House of Commons), while Patricia Hewitt (hitherto Secretary of State for Trade and Industry and Minister for Women) took on Reid's former post as Secretary of State for Health. Alan Johnson was allocated the trade and industry portfolio, while David Miliband assumed the newly created post of Minister of Communities and Local Government.

On 7 July 2005 52 people were killed and more than 700 injured in four attacks—three on London Underground trains and one on a bus—perpetrated by suicide bombers in London. Of the four bombers, all of whom also died in the attacks, three were subsequently discovered to have been native British Muslims of Pakistani descent, while the fourth was a convert to Islam of Jamaican origin. Responsibility for the attacks was claimed on the same day, via the internet, by a group that styled itself the 'Secret Organisation of al-Qa'ida of Jihad Organisation in Europe'. Other claims of responsibility included that, made later in July, of the Abu Hafs al-Masri Brigade, which had likewise asserted its responsibility for bomb attacks carried out in Madrid, Spain, in 2004. In September 2005 Al-Jazeera, a Qatar-based television station, broadcast a videotaped communiqué, supplied to it by al-Qa'ida, in which Mohammad Sidique Khan, who had been identified as one of the four 7 July bombers, cited the United Kingdom's participation in the invasion of Iraq in 2003 as one of the motivations for the attacks. In a separate part of the communiqué al-Qa'ida claimed responsibility for the attacks. On 21 July 2005 at least four further attempts to attack London Underground trains and a bus with bombs were unsuccessful owing to the failure of the bombs to explode. By 29 July four men suspected of involvement in the 21 July attacks had been arrested, including one who had fled to Italy. Of the four initial detainees, all of whom were reported to be of African origin, two had obtained British citizenship in recent years, while a third had been granted indefinite leave to remain in the United Kingdom in 2000. On 8 August four suspects were remanded in custody for their alleged involvement in the attempted attacks of 21 July. A further 10 people, meanwhile, were remanded in custody between 3 and 10 August for offences allegedly committed in connection with the 21 July attacks. In September Italy agreed to extradite a fifth man suspected of direct involvement in the attacks to the United Kingdom.

The Security Service—known as MI5—was criticized for its failure to prevent the attacks of July 2005 and, in particular, for its decision, in June, to reduce its estimation of the threat to the United Kingdom from international terrorism to its lowest level since 11 September 2001. For its part, in response to the attacks, the Government sought the support of both the Conservatives and the Liberal Democrats for proposed new legislation to counter terrorism; and requested the assistance of mainstream Muslim leaders in the United Kingdom to combat Islamic radicalism. In mid-September 2005 the Government published a new Terrorism Bill. The draft legislation sought to establish new offences of preparing terrorist acts or assisting others to commit them; attendance at terrorist training facilities in any part of the world or providing such training; and 'direct or indirect encouragement' of terrorist acts and the release of communications that 'glorify, exalt or celebrate' acts of terrorism committed over the past 20 years. It was further proposed that the maximum period for which suspected terrorists could be detained without charge should be extended from 14 to 90 days. While a number of the bill's provisions were supported by both the Conservatives and the Liberal Democrats, representatives of those parties claimed that the Government had failed to justify the proposed extension of the maximum period of detention without charge to 90 days. Civil liberties organizations, meanwhile, claimed that such an extension would infringe on suspects' human rights. In November the 90-day extension was emphatically rejected by the House of Commons, by 322 votes to 291. The rejection of the proposed legislation, which 49 Labour MPs had also refused to support, marked the first defeat that the Labour Government had suffered in the Commons since it assumed power in 1997. The defeat was followed by a vote in favour of extending the maximum permissible period of detention of terrorist suspects without charge to 28 days. Meanwhile, later in September the Secretary of State for the Home Department, Charles Clarke, announced a proposal to create a so-called inter-faith commission that would seek to advise the Government on ways to overcome obstacles to the better integration of the various communities in the United Kingdom. On the following day most of the recommendations put forward by Muslim working groups that had been established following the July attacks in London, including the proposed establishment of a national advisory council that would aim to counter the use of mosques by extremists and to lessen reliance on preachers from overseas, were welcomed by Clarke.

In mid-October 2005 the Government's contentious Identity Cards Bill secured passage through the House of Commons by 309 votes to 284, 25 Labour MPs having voted against it. In late October, however, the House of Lords adopted, by 260 votes to 111, wide-ranging amendments to the Government's Racial and Religious Hatred Bill, with a view to guaranteeing freedom of speech in respect of religion. The proposed legislation was intended to afford to Muslims and other religious groups legal safeguards similar to those already enjoyed by ethnic groups—thus anticipating a reported increase in assaults on Muslims and attacks on mosques that had occurred following the July bombings in London. Also in late October the Government published a white paper in which it detailed proposals for the reform of the state school system. Strong opposition to the proposed reforms was expressed by elements within the Labour Party: in January 2006, as the Government prepared to present the proposed reforms as draft legislation, it was reported that parts of them were opposed by as many as 100 Labour MPs, who feared they would have a damaging effect on comprehensive secondary school education.

In mid-October 2005 the Secretary of State for Trade and Industry, Alan Johnson, announced that he had concluded an agreement with public-sector trade unions whereby a retirement age of 65 would apply for civil servants, nurses and teachers who joined those professions from April 2007, while the retirement age of those already so employed at April 2007 would remain fixed at 60. The reform was intended to reduce the Government's unfunded public-sector pension deficit, which had been estimated at £400,000m.–£700,000m. At the end of November a government-appointed commission led by Lord Turner of Ecchinswell published recommendations on the longer-term reform of state pension arrangements, which included, notably, a proposed raising of the state pensionable age from 65 to 68 by 2050.

In early November 2005 David Blunkett resigned as Secretary of State for Work and Pensions after it transpired that aspects of his tenure of appointments by private companies after he had resigned from the Cabinet in December 2004 had contravened guide-lines for former ministers accepting such positions within two years of relinquishing office. Blunkett was succeeded by John Hutton, who had been appointed to the Cabinet in May 2005 as Chancellor of the Duchy of Lancaster and Minister for the Cabinet Office. On 6 December members of the Conservative Party elected David Cameron to be the new Leader of the party and, thus, of the Opposition. In early January 2006, two days after he had issued a statement in which he admitted that he had received treatment for alcoholism, Charles Kennedy resigned as Leader of the Liberal Democrats. Sir Menzies Campbell, the Deputy Leader of the party under Kennedy, was elected as the Liberal Democrats' new Leader in March.

In December 2005 Blair dismissed calls that had been made by human rights organizations for a public inquiry into allegations that the United Kingdom's airspace and air transport facilities had been used in the transfer ('extraordinary rendition') of detainees, in particular terrorist suspects, by the US Central Intelligence Agency (CIA) to third countries where it was possible that they might be subjected to torture during interrogation. At a press conference in December Blair insisted that he had no evidence to suggest that anything illegal had occurred in connection with the so-called rendition flights. In January

2006, however, the *New Statesman* magazine published a Foreign and Commonwealth Office memorandum it had obtained in which it was stated that rendition flights were probably illegal under international law. The memorandum further stated that the Office's own investigations had discovered at least two instances of such flights across British airspace, but that there 'could be more'. In February the foreign affairs committee of the House of Commons stated in its annual report on human rights that the Government had been too slow to investigate allegations that as many as 200 rendition flights had crossed British airspace. According to the committee, the Government was obliged, under the UN Convention against Torture and Other Cruel, Inhuman or Degrading Treatment or Punishment, to investigate such allegations, together with other claims that the USA had established secret camps in third countries for the purpose of interrogating detainees. Also in February Blair referred to the US camp for detained 'enemy combatants' at Guantánamo Bay, Cuba, as an anomaly that would eventually have to be addressed. On the previous day the High Court had granted three former residents of the United Kingdom who were detained at Guantánamo Bay permission to seek through the courts a petition by the British Government for their release, as it had already done in nine previous cases.

In late January 2006 two clauses of the Government's Racial and Religious Hatred Bill were rejected by the House of Commons when MPs voted, by margins of 288 votes to 279 and 283 votes to 282, in favour of amendments to the bill that had been introduced by the House of Lords with the aim of guaranteeing freedom of speech in respect of religion. The bill received royal assent in the following month. Also in January the House of Lords introduced five amendments to the Government's Identity Cards Bill, including, notably, one that stipulated that the new cards should not become compulsory without new primary legislation; and voted to remove the section of the Government's Terrorism Bill that sought to criminalize the glorification of terrorism. In February the House of Commons rejected one of the amendments introduced by the House of Lords that would have made identity cards wholly voluntary, while accepting the requirement for new primary legislation before the proposed identity cards could be made compulsory. Following a series of votes in which the House of Lords repeatedly rejected the Government's proposals, returning the bill to the Commons, in late March both chambers accepted a compromise whereby all passport applicants would have their details placed on a national identity register from 2008, but could choose not to be issued an identity card until 2010. In mid-February, meanwhile, the House of Commons voted to restore the clause of the Terrorism Bill that sought to criminalize the glorification of terrorism, but the House of Lords voted again, at the end of the month, to delete it. In late March the House of Lords finally approved the bill, including the clause outlawing the glorification of terrorism, and the Terrorism Act came into force in mid-April.

The defeat of the Labour Party candidate by the candidate of the Liberal Democrats in a by-election to the previously safe Labour seat of Dunfermline and West Fife in Scotland on 9 February 2006 acquired additional significance in the context of Blair's eventual replacement as Leader of the Labour Party. (As long ago as October 2004 Blair had indicated that he would seek a third mandate as Labour Leader, as secured in May 2005, but not a fourth.) The result of the by-election, as well as being an embarrassment for Labour and a fillip for the Liberal Democrats, was interpreted by many observers as reflecting adversely on Chancellor Gordon Brown, who was regarded as Blair's likely successor before the next general election, in view of the prominent role he had played in Labour's campaign to retain the seat, which neighboured his own constituency of Kirkcaldy and Cowdenbeath.

In March 2006, after the House of Lords Appointments Commission had expressed concern over a number of Labour nominations for peerages, it was revealed that four of the nominees had made unpublicized loans totalling at least £4.5m. to the Labour Party. A police investigation was subsequently launched into whether, effectively, the Labour Party had illegally sold 'titles of honour'. While it appeared that no law had been broken and the police investigation was widened to examine the funding of both the Conservatives and the Liberal Democrats, the nominations undermined the Labour Party's commitment to transparency in political party funding, the reform of which it had begun after its election in 1997. Labour had in fact been under no legal obligation—as it would have been had they been donations—to declare the loans, but the fact that the party's treasurer, Jack Dromey, had been unaware of them strengthened the impression of duplicity. In February the Secretary of State for Culture, Media and Sport, Tessa Jowell, had been the subject of allegations of corruption owing to an investigation in Italy of the financial affairs of her husband. In March, following an inquiry conducted by the Cabinet Secretary, Sir Gus O'Donnell, Blair cleared Jowell of breaching the ministerial code of conduct.

At local elections held on 4 May 2006 the Labour Party performed poorly, most notably in London, losing 319 seats and 17 councils, leaving them in overall control of 30 councils. The Conservative Party gained 316 seats and 11 councils, increasing their total to 68 councils. The Liberal Democrats failed to make any significant impact with net gains of two seats and one council, giving them control of 13 councils. On 5 May Blair effected a major reorganization of the Cabinet. Clarke was dismissed as Secretary of State for the Home Department, following the revelation in late April that a number of foreign nationals convicted and imprisoned for crimes committed while living in Britain had not been considered for deportation following their release. Reid was appointed to the vacant position, and was replaced as Secretary of State for Defence by Des Browne (previously Chief Secretary to the Treasury). Margaret Beckett (hitherto Secretary of State for the Environment, Food and Rural Affairs) was appointed Secretary of State for Foreign and Commonwealth Affairs, succeeding Straw, who took the title of Lord Privy Seal and Leader of the House of Commons. Prescott remained as Deputy Prime Minister, although most of his policy responsibilities were allocated to a new Department for Communities and Local Government.

Following four major rail accidents in and around London in 1997–2002 in which some 50 people were killed (the most serious was the Paddington rail crash of October 1999 in which 31 people died), the Government initiated major reviews of the British rail network. In October 2001 the Secretary of State for Transport, Local Government and the Regions, Stephen Byers, controversially placed the heavily indebted rail infrastructure operating company, Railtrack, into administration and announced plans to replace it with a 'not-for-profit' company to be formed by train operators, freight companies, passenger groups and trade unions. The following day Railtrack's Chief Executive denounced the Government's treatment of the company and its shareholders and announced his resignation. Nevertheless, Byers insisted that he was not prepared to use public money to reimburse shareholders in the failed company despite coming under increasing pressure from financial institutions in the City of London. In late March 2002 a £500m. bid for Railtrack was tabled by Network Rail, a company that had been formed by Byers in October 2001 and had no shareholders, and thus pledged to reinvest any operating surplus in the rail infrastructure. Network Rail's offer included a government grant worth £300m., although Byers stressed that this sum would only be payable to the company if it succeeded in swiftly removing the rail system from administration. Shortly after the Network Rail offer was received, Railtrack announced that it would no longer seek to proceed with legal action to recover losses for shareholders (as they would be receiving a return on their investment if Network Rail's bid was successful). Byers' handling of the affair was nevertheless severely criticized by both Labour and opposition MPs, who accused him of reneging on his earlier pledge not to use public money to compensate Railtrack shareholders. Byers resigned in May 2002 following a rail crash in Potters Bar, in which seven people were killed. In early October Railtrack was released from administration and Network Rail assumed the responsibility for running the United Kingdom's railway infrastructure. In January 2003 more than 30,000 former shareholders in Railtrack commenced collective legal action against the Government to seek compensation for losses allegedly incurred when the company had been placed in administration. In October 2005 collective legal action by some 49,000 former private shareholders in Railtrack, who sought payment of damages to compensate for the Government's alleged 'malfeasance' in respect of Railtrack's bankruptcy in 2001, was rejected by the High Court. Among the testimony the High Court had heard was an admission by Byers that he had made an inaccurate statement to a committee of the House of Commons in 2001 regarding Railtrack. In February 2006 Byers apologized to the House of Commons for the inaccurate statement.

In January 2004 the Secretary of State for Transport, Alistair Darling, announced a comprehensive review of the structure of the railway industry, although it was stressed that the review would not question the future of Network Rail nor seek to alter the involvement of the private sector in the railways. In July, as a result of the comprehensive rail review announced in January, a Government white paper was published that set out several major reforms for the British rail network. In September 2005 five executives of the companies involved in the Hatfield rail crash of October 2000 were acquitted of having breached health and safety legislation. Network Rail, however, was convicted of contravening the Health and Safety Act in respect of the accident. In October 2005 Network Rail and maintenance company Balfour Beatty were fined, respectively, £10m. and £3.5m. for contraventions of the Act that had played a part in the Hatfield rail crash. In December the Crown Prosecution Service announced that Network Rail would be prosecuted for contraventions of the Health and Safety Act that had allegedly contributed to the rail crash in Paddington in 1999.

In 1920, faced with mounting popular support for independence in Ireland, where a guerrilla campaign was being waged by the clandestine Irish Republican Army (IRA), in an attempt to force British withdrawal, the British Government conceded to demands for Home Rule, but only to a limited extent, since this was strongly opposed by Protestants in the province of Ulster, who did not wish to become part of a Catholic-dominated all-Ireland state. The Government of Ireland Act (1920) thus provided for two parliaments in Ireland: one in Dublin, for 26 of the 32 counties of Ireland, which obtained dominion status as the Irish Free State, now the Republic of Ireland (q.v.), in 1922, and one in Belfast, for the remaining six counties, which collectively became known as Northern Ireland and remained an integral part of the United Kingdom.

With the support of the Protestant majority in Northern Ireland, the Ulster Unionist Council (UUC), which had campaigned for the continuation of union with Great Britain, retained permanent control of the Belfast Parliament. The province was governed by a one-party administration, with an all-unionist Cabinet headed by a provincial Prime Minister. The British monarch was represented by a Governor. Since Catholics were not only effectively excluded from political power, but also suffered discrimination in civil matters, a state of sectarian tension continued.

During the late 1960s an active civil rights movement emerged, which sought to end the Catholics' grievances by non-violent means. However, Protestant extremists viewed the movement as a republican threat, and resorted to violence against Catholic activists. The IRA was originally a small element in the civil rights movement, but, after increasingly serious disturbances, a breakaway group, calling itself the Provisional IRA, embarked on a campaign of violence with the aim of reuniting Ireland on its own terms. In April 1969 the Northern Ireland Government requested that British army units be assigned to protect important installations and in August the British and Northern Ireland Governments agreed that all security forces in the province would be placed under British command. In March 1972, as a result of increased violence, the British Government assumed direct responsibility for law and order. Finding this unacceptable, the Northern Ireland Government resigned. The British Government prorogued the Northern Ireland Parliament and introduced direct rule from London, thus alienating many Protestants.

In 1973 new legislation abolished the office of Governor and the Northern Ireland Parliament, and provided for new constitutional arrangements. In June elections were conducted for a 78-member Northern Ireland Assembly, and an Executive was subsequently constituted from its members. An important part of this new 'power-sharing' arrangement was the establishment of a limited role for the Irish Government in Northern Ireland's affairs. Accordingly, in December, at Sunningdale (in southern England), the British and Irish Governments and the Northern Ireland Executive finalized an agreement to form a Council of Ireland (with members drawn from the Governments of Northern Ireland and the Republic), which would have a range of economic and cultural responsibilities in both parts of Ireland. However, the 'Sunningdale Agreement' and the new devolved authority in Northern Ireland were rejected by many Protestants, and led, in 1974, to a general strike. A state of emergency was declared and the Executive was forced to resign. The Assembly was prorogued, and the province returned to direct rule by the British Government. The collapse of the Sunningdale Agreement led to a rise in popularity of the more extreme Democratic Unionist Party (DUP—founded in 1971, and led by Rev. Dr Ian Paisley), which established itself as the main rival to the previously dominant Ulster Unionist Party (UUP—the 'official' Unionists).

Throughout the 1970s the Provisional IRA and the Irish National Liberation Army (INLA, which emerged in 1975) continued their terrorist attacks on both British military and civilian targets, while Protestant 'loyalist' paramilitary groups engaged in indiscriminate bombings and killings of Roman Catholics.

Discussions between the Governments of the United Kingdom and the Republic of Ireland in 1984–85 culminated in the signing of the Anglo-Irish Agreement in November 1985. The Agreement established the Intergovernmental Conference, through which British and Irish ministers were to meet regularly to discuss political, security, legal and cross-border matters relating to Northern Ireland. While giving the Irish Government a formal consultative role in the affairs of Northern Ireland, the Agreement recognized that the constitutional status of Northern Ireland remained unchanged and would not be altered without the consent of a majority of the province's population. The Agreement had the support of the predominantly Catholic Social Democratic and Labour Party (SDLP), and was approved by the Irish and British Parliaments. However, it was strongly opposed by most unionist politicians, who organized mass demonstrations and violent protests against the Agreement. In June 1986 the Northern Ireland Assembly was dissolved.

The Provisional IRA's campaign of violence in Northern Ireland escalated during 1987 and in 1988 IRA members conducted a successful campaign against British military targets, particularly in Western Europe. Between late 1988 and early 1991 a series of terrorist attacks took place against British Army personnel and politicians in both mainland Britain and in continental Europe.

In September 1989 the Irish Government demanded a review of the Ulster Defence Regiment (UDR), the main security force in the province, following allegations that intelligence had been passed to loyalist paramilitary groups by the UDR, and subsequently used by them to target and murder members of the IRA. In May 1990 the alleged breaches of security were confirmed. During the resulting prosecution of a member of the Ulster Defence Association (UDA) in January 1992, fresh evidence emerged of collusion between the security forces and loyalist paramilitary organizations, and details of events leading to the murder by the UDA in 1989 of a republican lawyer, Patrick Finucane, were revealed. In June 1999 a former British soldier, William Stobie, was charged with Finucane's murder. He subsequently claimed to have been working as a police informer at the time and to have warned them of the impending killing. Furthermore, it was revealed that Stobie had confessed to his involvement in the murder to the Royal Ulster Constabulary (RUC—the Northern Ireland police force) nine years earlier. The revelation prompted calls for a judicial inquiry into the original investigation of the killing. In September 2000 it was reported that an investigation into Finucane's murder, which had been established in April 1999 and was led by Sir John Stevens, the Commissioner of the Metropolitan Police Force, had revealed evidence of 'institutional collusion' between undercover army agents and loyalist paramilitaries. In November 2001 Stobie was acquitted of any involvement in Finucane's murder, after it was ruled that, owing to medical reasons, the main prosecution witness was incapable of testifying. In August 2002, at the behest of the British Government, a former Canadian supreme court judge, Peter Cory, began investigating whether six cases where collusion between the security forces and paramilitary organizations had been alleged (including the Finucane murder) would be subject to public inquiries. Meanwhile, in December 2001 Stobie was assassinated by loyalist paramilitaries.

In April 2003 Stevens published the interim results of his inquiry, in which he stated that he had found evidence of 'widespread collusion' between the security forces and loyalist paramilitaries in the murder of innocent civilians, and that the murders of Finucane and Adam Lambert, who had been killed by the UDA in 1987, could have been prevented. The report concluded that the RUC's investigation of Finucane's murder should have resulted in the early detection and arrest of his killers, and it was highly critical of the withholding of intelligence and evidence by the RUC and the British army's Force Research Unit (FRU)—a secret agency that recruited and controlled agents within loyalist and republican paramilitary organizations. In addition, it was revealed that the RUC had failed to warn or protect nationalists known to be at risk from attack by loyalist paramilitaries. Stevens also announced that a number of investigations remained ongoing and that 57 files, among them one on the former head of the FRU, Brig. Gordon Kerr, had been sent to the Northern Ireland Director of Public Prosecutions. In May 2003 Kenneth Barrett, a senior member of the UDA, was arrested and charged with Finucane's murder. In early July the European Court of Human Rights in Strasbourg, France, ruled that the United Kingdom was guilty of a serious breach of the Human Rights Convention for failing to carry out an adequate investigation into the death of Finucane. In March 2004 the Finucane family launched a court action against the British Government to force it to publish the Cory report and to set up a public inquiry into the murders of Patrick Finucane and three other people in the late 1990s. The report was published on 1 April and inquiries were immediately set up into the deaths of these people. However, a public investigation into Finucane's killing was delayed until Barrett's trial had been completed. In September Barrett was convicted of Finucane's murder, having pleaded guilty; he was sentenced to 22 years' imprisonment. Following the conclusion of the trial, pressure was again placed on the Government to open a public inquiry. In late September Reid's successor as Secretary of State for Northern Ireland, Paul Murphy, announced that an inquiry would be held under restrictions after the introduction of new legislation intended to address national security requirements. The Finucane family, however, insisted that a public investigation should take place. When the proposed bill on inquiries was announced in November, the Finucane family expressed concern that a large proportion of evidence in the case would have to be considered in private under its terms. The bill was also criticized by Cory and human rights organizations. Nevertheless, the Inquiries Act received royal assent in April 2005, and the Government intended to proceed with its plans for a restricted inquiry into Finucane's murder in 2006.

In January 1990, meanwhile, the British Government launched an initiative to convene meetings between representatives from the major political parties in Northern Ireland and the British and Irish Governments to discuss devolution in Northern Ireland and the future of its relations with the Republic of Ireland. Sinn Féin (the political wing of the Provisional IRA) was to be excluded from the talks because of its refusal to denounce the IRA's campaign of violence. Bilateral discussions between the British Government and the DUP, the UUP, the SDLP and the Alliance Party eventually began in April 1991, and talks subsequently commenced between all the Northern Ireland parties and the Irish Government. The principal point of contention was the unionists' demand that Ireland hold a referendum on Articles 2 and 3 of its Constitution, which lay claim to the territory of Northern Ireland. The Irish Government, however, remained unwilling to make such a concession except as part of an overall settlement. With no progress made on this, nor on the subject of Ireland's role in the administration of Northern Ireland, the negotiations formally ended in November 1992, and the Anglo-Irish Conference resumed.

In August 1992 the British Government announced the proscription of the UDA under the Emergency Provisions Act, a measure that was widely regarded as long overdue in the light of the UDA's paramilitary activities from the early 1970s onwards (some committed under the name of Ulster Freedom Fighters—UFF). In late 1993 and early 1994 police on the mainland made several large seizures of explosives, which the Government claimed to be evidence of improving anti-terrorist surveillance. During this period frequent discoveries of IRA devices and bomb alerts caused much disruption, especially to public transport services.

In October 1993 the British and Irish Prime Ministers, John Major and Albert Reynolds, issued a joint statement setting out the principles on which future negotiations were to be based. The statement emphasized the precondition that Sinn Féin permanently renounce violence before being admitted to the negotiations. In December the Prime Ministers made a joint declaration, known as the 'Downing Street Declaration', which provided a specific framework for a peace settlement. The initiative, which was widely supported by opposition parties in Britain and Ireland, referred to the possibility of a united Ireland and accepted the legitimacy of self-determination, while insisting on majority consent within Northern Ireland. The DUP, the UUP and Sinn Féin rejected the document, which effectively removed any confidence of achieving an imminent peace settlement. However, the British and Irish Governments reiterated their intention to pursue the peace process.

On 31 August 1994 the IRA announced 'a complete cessation of violence'. On 13 October the loyalist paramilitary groups declared a suspension of military activity, which was effectively to be linked to that of the IRA. Later that month Major announced new measures to restart the peace process, adopting the 'working assumption' that the IRA cease-fire was permanent. The first public meeting between Sinn Féin and government officials was held in December, marking the start of exploratory talks between the two sides. In February 1995 John Major and the new Irish Prime Minister, John Bruton, presented a Framework Document, together with a separate British government paper on a new Northern Ireland Assembly. The Framework Document reaffirmed the principles of the Downing Street Declaration, and included provisions for the co-operation and involvement of both Governments in the peace settlement. In addition, the Document proposed the establishment of a cross-border body in which elected representatives of the Irish Parliament and a Northern Ireland Assembly might create and implement policy on issues agreed by the two Governments, in consultation with the Northern Irish parties. The proposals for the Northern Ireland Assembly envisaged an elected authority with wide legislative and executive responsibility (except, initially, over taxation, and law and order), although it was to be monitored by a three-member elected panel. Both Governments emphasized that the proposals were to form the basis of negotiations and public consideration, and any final agreement was to be subject to parliamentary approval and popular consent by means of a referendum.

Despite a positive Sinn Féin response to the Framework Document, the issue of decommissioning paramilitary weapons remained the major obstacle to peace negotiations. The Government repeatedly objected to Sinn Féin's linking of IRA decommissioning with the demilitarization of Northern Ireland. In May 1995, having agreed that these would be discussed as separate issues, the Secretary of State for Northern Ireland, Sir Patrick Mayhew, and the Sinn Féin President, Gerry Adams, met (the highest-level encounter of the two sides in 20 years) at an investment conference for Northern Ireland, held in Washington, DC, USA. Further political dialogue was hindered by Sinn Féin's opposition to the British Government's insistence that decommissioning by paramilitary organizations be a precondition to conducting all-party negotiations.

In November 1995 the British and Irish Governments agreed to initiate preliminary talks (provisionally scheduled to commence in February 1996) with all the parties in Northern Ireland and to establish an international commission to assess the practicalities of the decommissioning of armaments and other aspects of the peace process. US President Bill Clinton endorsed this 'twin-track' initiative during a visit later that month, and the commission, chaired by one of Clinton's advisers, George Mitchell, began meetings with all sides involved in the peace process in December. The final report of the international commission was issued in January 1996, and recommended proceeding with all-party talks on the condition that all sides endorse the eventual complete disarmament of paramilitary organizations, the renunciation of violence and the cessation of paramilitary 'punishment' attacks. According to the report, arms' decommissioning was to be considered in parallel with the negotiations, while the eventual surrender of weaponry was to be conducted under international supervision, with those involved free from prosecution. The report was generally supported by all sides.

In February 1996 the IRA abruptly terminated its cease-fire by exploding a large bomb in London. The organization blamed the British Government for the resumption of hostilities, citing its inflexible response to the Mitchell report. Later in February a man killed in a second explosion in London was found to be an IRA activist, and the security forces subsequently uncovered details of a revived mainland bombing campaign. Bruton and Major declared that they would suspend all ministerial dialogue with Sinn Féin, but would intensify efforts to achieve a peaceful settlement. At the end of the month the leaders announced an initiative to pursue the peace process, incorporating nationalist and unionist demands. Consultations were to commence immediately on an electoral format to establish a forum for intersectoral dialogue prior to the initiation of comprehensive political negotiations, to be based on the 1995 Framework Document. In March the British Cabinet approved a 'hybrid' electoral system for the Northern Ireland forum, in an attempt to accommodate demands from all sides and to ensure a wide representation of the region's political groupings. Participants in the all-party negotiations were to be selected from among the 110 forum members. In the election, held on 30 May, the UUP secured 24% of the votes cast and the largest number of seats (30), while the DUP and the SDLP took 21 and 17 seats respectively. Sinn Féin's 15% share of the votes secured the party 17 seats. In addition, seven seats were won by the Alliance Party, three by the United Kingdom Unionist Party (UKUP) and two each by the Progressive Unionist Party (PUP), the Ulster Democratic Party (UDP), the Women's Coalition of Northern Ireland and representatives of Labour (a coalition of left-wing individuals and associations). The multi-party discussions, which commenced on 10 June, were undermined by Sinn Féin's exclusion, in the absence of a new IRA cease-fire declaration, and by unionist opposition to the appointment of George Mitchell as Chairman of the plenary session of the proceedings, which they claimed was part of a nationalist agenda. Despite tentative progress in the peace discussions, further political uncertainty followed the explosion of an IRA bomb in Manchester in June and both the British and Irish Governments undertook to review their relations with Sinn Féin.

In July 1996 political events in Northern Ireland were dominated by sectarian disputes regarding the organization of traditional Protestant marches. The peace process suffered a further reverse when the SDLP announced that it was to withdraw from the recently elected forum, owing to the British Government's management of the crisis to which the disputes gave rise. In July and September raids by the security forces against suspected IRA bases in southern England resulted in the seizure of explosives, and were reported by the police to have averted planned attacks on infrastructural and political targets.

In October 1996 the UUP and the SDLP agreed on a draft agenda, based on the provisions of the Mitchell report, to enable substantive multi-party talks to proceed without being dominated by the issue of weapons' decommissioning. In November Sinn Féin revealed a set of proposals, formulated with the SDLP in order to bolster the peace process, which included the implementation by the British Government of confidence-building measures, such as the release of IRA prisoners, and a guarantee that Sinn Féin would be admitted to the talks in the event of a renewed IRA cease-fire. In response, John Major defined the terms by which the party could join the talks, namely, a credible and lasting restoration of the IRA cease-fire and an end to all paramilitary training activities and punishment beatings. However, the Irish Government urged a more flexible response to any eventual cease-fire announcement. In January 1997 all-party talks resumed, but were suspended in March until after the general election to the United Kingdom Parliament, scheduled to be held in May. Prior to the poll the IRA undertook a co-ordinated programme of disruption in mainland Britain, while sectarian tensions increased in Northern Ireland.

In the general election, held on 1 May 1997, the UUP secured 10 of the 18 seats available, with 32.7% of the votes cast in Northern Ireland. Sinn Féin regained a parliamentary mandate, winning two seats (with 16.1% of the votes). The SDLP won three seats, with 24.1% of the votes. The DUP lost two of its previously held seats, securing two seats (13.6%), and the UKUP won its first seat in a general election (1.6%).

The newly elected Labour Government generated renewed optimism that a peace settlement could be achieved. Prime Minister Blair proposed a timetable for the talks, and reiterated that he envisaged their conclusion no later than May 1998—when the results were to be put to a popular referendum. In late June 1997 the British and Irish Governments announced a new initiative to accelerate the peace process, whereby the decommissioning of paramilitary weapons, together with other confidence-building measures, would be undertaken concurrently with political negotiations, in an attempt to facilitate Sinn Féin's participation in the process, and clarified that Sinn Féin would be eligible to join substantive negotiations six weeks after a new IRA cease-fire announcement.

On 19 July 1997 the IRA announced a restoration of its cease-fire. A few days later the Irish and British Governments issued a joint statement that the all-party negotiations would commence on 15 September, with the participation of Sinn Féin. At the same time, however, the unionist parties rejected the measures for weapons' decommissioning that had been formulated by the two Governments. At the end of August the new Secretary of State for Northern Ireland, Mo Mowlam, concluded that the restoration of the IRA cease-fire was 'unequivocal' and invited Sinn Féin to join the talks. Accordingly, in September Sinn Féin endorsed the so-called Mitchell principles, which committed participants to accepting the outcome of the peace process and renouncing violence as a means of punishment or resolving problems. The UUP, together with the DUP and UKUP, which had already declared their boycott of any discussions with Sinn Féin, and other loyalist representatives, failed to attend the opening session of the talks when they resumed in September, owing partly to a statement by the IRA that undermined Sinn Féin's endorsement of the Mitchell principles. The talks were further jeopardized by the explosion of a republican bomb in Co Armagh for which the dissident paramilitary faction, the Continuity Army Council, which along with the Loyalist Volunteer Force (LVF) had been proscribed in June, claimed responsibility. Nevertheless, the UUP rejoined the peace negotiations a few days later. In late September all eight parties to the talks signed a procedural agreement to pursue substantive negotiations. At the same time the Independent International Commission on Decommissioning (IICD) was inaugurated, under the chairmanship of the former head of the Canadian armed forces, Gen. John de Chastelain. The first meeting between a British Prime Minister and Sinn Féin leaders in more than 70 years took place at the talks in October, when Blair held private discussions with Adams and Martin McGuinness. In December the murder of the convicted LVF Leader, Billy Wright, by INLA prisoners prompted an escalation of sectarian violence throughout Northern Ireland. In January 1998 Mowlam took the unprecedented action of meeting loyalist paramilitary prisoners within Belfast's Maze prison, which secured their continued endorsement of PUP and UDP participation in the peace discussions.

In mid-January 1998 Blair and the Irish Prime Minister, Bertie Ahern, published a document outlining a framework for negotiations. The so-called Propositions on Heads of Agreement envisaged 'balanced constitutional change' by both Governments and proposed wide-ranging institutional reform providing for a devolved form of government within Northern Ireland. On 25 March George Mitchell announced that the multi-party peace talks were to be concluded by 9 April. The deadline was preceded by intensive negotiations. Finally, on 10 April a settlement was announced. The so-called Good Friday Agreement envisaged radical reform of the political structures of Northern Ireland, its relations with Ireland, and its constitutional standing within the United Kingdom. The main provisions of the Agreement were as follows: the establishment of a 108-member elected Northern Ireland Assembly, with authority to legislate on all domestic matters currently administered by the Northern Ireland Office; an Executive Committee, to be elected by the Assembly and headed by a First Minister and Deputy First Minister; an obligation that the Assembly establish, within one year, a North/South Ministerial Council (which had been one of the most contentious issues of the talks) at which representatives of the Irish Government and the executive authority in Northern Ireland might consider issues of cross-border concern; regular meetings of representatives of the Irish Government with members of the British Parliament, the Northern Ireland Assembly and other regional assemblies of the United Kingdom, under a new British-Irish Council, with the objective of promoting co-operation, information exchange and agreement on issues of mutual interest; amendment of Articles 2 and 3 of the Irish Constitution; replacement of the 1985 Anglo-Irish Agreement with a new bilateral accord, incorporating a British-Irish Inter-governmental Council to oversee the Assembly and North/South Council; and a commitment by all parties to achieve the decommissioning of paramilitary weapons within two years. David Trimble, the Leader of the UUP, secured the critical support of his party for the settlement, although several dissident UUP politicians later joined the DUP and UKUP in their campaign to prevent an endorsement of the accord, and the Protestant Orange Order urged its 80,000 members to oppose the Agreement. Sinn Féin approved the accord. Some 71.1% of voters in Northern Ireland and 94.4% of voters in the Republic approved the proposed peace settlement in popular referendums conducted on 22 May, securing its immediate future. Parties in Northern Ireland began almost immediately to prepare for the elections to the Northern Ireland Assembly, which were scheduled to be held on 25 June. Voting was to be conducted using the single transferable vote system of proportional representation, providing for six members to be elected from each of the 18 Westminster parliamentary constituencies, with a broad representation of political preferences.

In the elections to the Northern Ireland Assembly, conducted on 25 June 1998, the UUP won 28 of the 108 seats, while the SDLP took 24, despite having won the largest share of first-preference votes under the new voting system. Sinn Féin won 18 Assembly seats. Those opposed to the Good Friday Agreement secured a total of 28 seats, including 20 representatives of the DUP, five of the UKUP and three dissident UUP politicians. The remaining seats were won by the Alliance Party (six), the PUP (two) and the Women's Coalition (two). Following the election, Lord Alderdice resigned as Leader of the Alliance Party, owing to its decline in popular support, and was subsequently appointed as the presiding officer of the new Assembly. At the inaugural meeting of the Assembly, on 1 July, Trimble was elected as First Minister of the executive body, while Seamus Mallon of the SDLP was elected as Deputy First Minister. Sectarian violence soon threatened to disrupt the peace process following confrontations between the security forces and members of the Orange Order who, in defiance of the newly established Parades Commission, sought to march its traditional route along the predominantly Roman Catholic Garvaghy Road in Drumcree. However, following the deaths of three young Roman Catholics in a petrol bomb attack in Ballymoney, Co Antrim, in mid-July the majority of the loyalists in Drumcree abandoned their protest. In August the peace process again came under threat when 29 people in Omagh, Co Tyrone, were killed by an explosive device, planted by a republican splinter group, the Real IRA. Later that month Ahern announced a series of anti-terrorism measures in an effort to facilitate convictions against terrorists based in the Republic of Ireland. Similarly, Blair announced legislation, which was approved in September, including heightened powers to convict anyone conspiring within the United Kingdom to commit terrorist offences.

Progress in the peace process continued to be obstructed throughout late 1998 by a dispute between unionists and Sinn Féin concerning the decommissioning of paramilitary weapons, with Trimble insisting that the admittance of Sinn Féin representatives to the Executive Committee be conditional on progress in the demilitarization of the IRA. For its part, Sinn Féin insisted that the Good Friday Agreement did not specify when decommissioning should begin, only that it should be completed by May 2000. As a result of the dispute the deadline of 21 October 1998 for the formation of the Executive Committee and the North/South bodies was not met. In December agreement was finally reached on the responsibilities of the 10 government departments of the Executive Committee and of six North/South 'implementation' bodies. This was endorsed by the Northern Ireland Assembly in February 1999.

In early March 1999 the date for the devolution of powers to the new Northern Ireland institutions, envisaged as 10 March in the Good Friday Agreement, was postponed until 2 April. However, despite strenuous efforts by Blair and Ahern to end the impasse, the April deadline was not met. An 'absolute deadline' for devolution was subsequently set for 30 June 1999, after which date, Blair asserted, he would suspend the Northern Ireland Assembly if agreement had not been reached. On 25 June the two Prime Ministers presented a compromise plan that envisaged the immediate establishment of the Executive Committee prior to the surrender of paramilitary weapons, with the condition that Sinn Féin guarantee that the IRA complete decommissioning by May 2000. Negotiations continued beyond the June deadline but collapsed in mid-July when Trimble announced that the UUP would not participate in a devolved administration with Sinn Féin until some decommissioning had taken place. Consequently the devolution of powers from Westminster was postponed until after the summer recess. A review of the peace process, headed by George Mitchell, began in September. That month the former Chairman of the Conservative Party, Chris Patten, who had been appointed in April 1998 to head an independent commission charged with conducting a review of policing in Northern Ireland, published his report. Recommended changes to the RUC included the establishment of an elected body of representatives drawn from all sections of the community to which the new force would be accountable, the aggressive recruitment of Roman Catholic officers in order that the force should achieve a balanced representation, and a reduction in the number of serving officers from 13,500 to 7,500, subject to the successful conclusion of the peace process. The report provoked anger from unionists, who particularly objected to plans to change the force's name, oath and symbols. Sinn Féin, meanwhile, renewed its demand that the force be disbanded.

In November 1999 Mitchell concluded the review of the peace process, producing an agreement providing for the devolution of powers to the Executive Committee. The agreement followed a statement by the IRA that it would appoint a representative to enter discussions with the IICD. Trimble persuaded his party to approve the agreement. On 29 November the Northern Ireland Assembly convened to appoint the 10-member Executive Committee. On 2 December power was officially transferred from Westminster to the new Northern Ireland executive at Stormont Castle and, in accordance with the Good Friday Agreement, the Irish Government removed from the Republic's Constitution its territorial claim over Northern Ireland. In mid-December the inaugural meeting was held of the North/South Ministerial Council. The British-Irish Council met for the first time later that month. In late December Peter Mandelson, the new Secretary of State for Northern Ireland, announced a review of security procedures in Northern Ireland and the withdrawal of some 2,000 troops from the province, and in January 2000 he adopted the majority of the recommendations contained in the Patten report, provoking an angry response from unionists. That month Adams dismissed the possibility of immediate IRA decommissioning, and a report by the IICD confirmed that there had been no disarmament. With the prospect of the collapse of the peace process, the British and Irish Governments engaged in intensive negotiations. On 1 February the IRA released a statement giving assurances that its cease-fire would not be broken and expressing support for the peace process. However, it failed to comply with an 11 February deadline to begin decommissioning, and legislation came into effect on that day suspending the new executive, legislative and co-operative institutions and returning Northern Ireland to direct rule. The IRA subsequently announced its withdrawal from discussions with the IICD. Adams refused to participate in any further review of the peace process until the suspended institutions had been restored.

Direct talks between the British and Irish Governments and the principal parties resumed in early May 2000, with the Government promising to restore the Northern Ireland institutions on 22 May and postpone the deadline for decommissioning until June 2001, subject to a commitment by the IRA on the arms issue. On 6 May the IRA responded by offering to 'initiate a process that will completely and verifiably put arms beyond use'. Under the offer a number of IRA arms depositories were to be regularly inspected by two independent international figures, Martii Ahtisaari, the former President of Finland, and Cyril Ramaphosa, a principal figure in the South African peace process. Trimble narrowly succeeded in securing the approval of the UUP of a return to power sharing, and on 30 May power was once again transferred from Westminster to the new Northern Ireland institutions. In accordance with their continued policy of attempting to impede the functioning of the Assembly, DUP ministers agreed to retake their places in the Assembly but announced their intention periodically to resign their posts in order to disrupt parliamentary business. In June the IRA allowed three arms depositories to be inspected by Ramaphosa and Ahtisaari and announced that it had also resumed contact with the IICD. The two inspectors affirmed that the arms they had seen were 'safely and adequately stored' and that they had installed devices at the depositories, which would enable them to detect if the weapons were subsequently tampered with.

In July 2000 the decision again to prohibit the Orange Order from marching along the Garvaghy Road in Drumcree provoked renewed sectarian violence and numerous attacks on the security forces. Later that month, under the terms of the Good Friday Agreement, the final group of 86 convicted terrorists was freed from prison in Northern Ireland. Their release was widely criticized as it had been conditionally linked to the commencement of IRA arms' decommissioning, which had yet to begin. In August Mandelson warned feuding loyalist paramilitary groups that they risked further delaying IRA decommissioning if they continued their retaliatory attacks. In an attempt to quell unrest, troops were once again deployed on the streets of Belfast, and John Adair, the Leader of the UFF, who was widely believed to be responsible for many of the incidents, was arrested and imprisoned; he had been released under the provisions of the Good Friday Agreement in September 1999. Nevertheless, revenge attacks continued throughout late 2000. In mid-December, however, the feud was declared to be at an end by three of the four groups involved.

Meanwhile, in November 2000 unionist attempts to postpone the passing of the Northern Ireland Policing Bill, by proposing an amendment to the element of it that would ensure equal recruitment of both Protestants and Roman Catholics, were narrowly defeated in the House of Lords. The following week the bill received royal assent and later that month the House of

Lords approved controversial legislation that would enable members of the Irish Parliament to stand for election to the Northern Ireland Assembly as well as to the British Parliament.

In early March 2001 the IRA unexpectedly announced that it had re-established contact with the IICD. Following talks with Ahern in Belfast Blair maintained that whilst a comprehensive settlement to the decommissioning issue remained some distance away the differences between the two sides were 'narrowing'. Earlier in March a bomb, suspected to have been planted by the Real IRA, intent on further disrupting peace negotiations, exploded outside the British Broadcasting Corporation (BBC) building in London. The incident was widely condemned by all parties democratically involved in the peace process. A further bombing in the British capital took place in April. The Real IRA had also been responsible for four previous attacks on mainland Britain during 2000 and early 2001. In May 2001 the US Government designated the Real IRA as a foreign terrorist organization and froze its assets in the USA. In April 2003 five members of the Real IRA were sentenced to terms of imprisonment ranging from 16 to 22 years for their roles in the London bombings.

At the general election to the British Parliament held on 7 June 2001 the UUP won six seats (compared with 10 in 1997), with 26.8% of the votes cast in Northern Ireland. The DUP secured five seats, gaining three at the expense of the UUP, with 22.5% of the votes cast. Sinn Féin increased its parliamentary representation, winning four seats, with 21.7% of the votes, while the SDLP took only three seats, with 21.0% of the votes. The UUP suffered a further significant reverse at local elections held in Northern Ireland later in June, with Sinn Féin and the DUP making substantial gains at the UUP's expense.

Following Trimble's announcement of his intention to resign as First Minister on 1 July 2001 if the IRA had not commenced a process of decommissioning, Blair and Ahern held emergency talks with representatives from the UUP, Sinn Féin and the SDLP in London in mid-June. Despite further discussions between the parties in Belfast later that month, on 1 July Trimble duly resigned. The administrative functions of the office of the First Minister were assumed on a caretaker basis by the Minister of Enterprise, Trade and Investment, Sir Reg Empey. (Mallon's position of Deputy First Minister became vacant, although he continued to exercise the functions of his office.) Trimble's resignation triggered a six-week period at the end of which, barring the resolution of the impasse between the parties and the election of a First Minister and Deputy First Minister, new elections to the Assembly would have to be held. Days later the IICD stated that the IRA had yet to decommission a single weapon, nor had it outlined how it intended to put its arms beyond use.

The prospects of a resolution to the continuing deadlock over the issues of decommissioning, police reform and demilitarization deteriorated further following renewed sectarian violence in the Ardoyne area of north Belfast in June 2001. The rioting continued into July and early that month a Catholic youth was killed by loyalist paramilitaries. Later in July at least 10 civilians and 113 police officers were injured after nationalists staged a series of protests to coincide with traditional Orange Order celebrations. The RUC subsequently claimed that the IRA had fomented the unrest.

In early August 2001 the British and Irish Governments unveiled their joint 'Proposals for the Implementation of the Good Friday Agreement', which they maintained were non-negotiable, and granted the parties involved in the peace process five days in which to respond to them. The proposals stipulated that while decommissioning was not a precondition of the Agreement, it remained indispensable to a political resolution and must be resolved in a manner 'acceptable to and verified by the IICD'. However, while Trimble stated that he would 'carefully consider' the proposals, he remained adamant that in the continued absence of IRA decommissioning of weapons there would be no progress. Although the five-day deadline for responding to the proposals was not met, on 8 August both the IICD and the IRA issued statements confirming that they had agreed upon a confidential decommissioning scheme, and de Chastelain announced that he was satisfied that the IRA had begun a process that would put arms 'completely and verifiably' beyond use. Trimble described the announcement as a 'step forward', but insisted that it was not sufficient for him to retract his resignation and demanded evidence of the destruction of weapons. Faced with the impending collapse of the Northern Irish institutions, on 10 August the British Government suspended the Northern Ireland institutions for a 24-hour period. Under a legal loophole contained within the Good Friday Agreement, this decision allowed for a six-week extension to the previously imposed deadline for the election of a First Minister and Deputy. In response to the suspension, the IRA withdrew the offer to commence the process of decommissioning. Notably, the withdrawal was announced just hours after the arrest of three suspected IRA members in Colombia on suspicion of collaborating with the left-wing guerrilla movement, Fuerzas Armadas Revolucionarias de Colombia (FARC, now Fuerzas Revolucionarias de Colombia—Ejército del Pueblo), on illegal paramilitary training methods and bomb-making techniques. The three men were subsequently charged with training guerrillas to construct bombs and travelling on false documents, and were transferred to a high security prison in Bogotá.

Also in August 2001 speculation that the RUC (which was renamed the Police Service of Northern Ireland—PSNI—in November) had ignored warnings of an imminent bomb attack in Omagh, prior to the atrocity in August 1998 (see above), prompted an inquiry by the Police Ombudsman for Northern Ireland, Nuala O'Loan, into the police force's investigation of the bombing. O'Loan's report, which was published in December 2001, stated that the RUC's Special Branch had failed to pass on two separate warnings from informants, and that a number of grave errors were made during the subsequent police investigation into the attack. In mid-August the British Government had announced revised policing proposals, which envisaged the equal division of recruitment to the PSNI between Protestants and Roman Catholics and allowed for the possibility of ex-paramilitary prisoners sitting on the 29 District Police Partnership Boards, providing they relinquished their support for terrorist organizations. Sinn Féin had rejected the proposals before their publication and insisted that they would refuse to nominate members to the new 19-member Northern Ireland Policing Board (NIPB), which would be responsible for overseeing the PSNI. On 4 November the RUC was officially renamed the PSNI and three days later the NIPB held its inaugural meeting. The two vacant Sinn Féin seats on the board were allocated to the DUP and the UUP. In early February 2002 the Chairman of the NIPB issued a joint statement on behalf of the NIPB, O'Loan and the Chief Constable of the PSNI, Sir Ronnie Flanagan (who had been criticized in O'Loan's report), which recognized that 'on the basis of the information available the Omagh bombing could not have been prevented'. Later that month Flanagan announced his resignation. Meanwhile, in late January Colm Murphy, the only person to have been charged in relation to the bomb attack, was sentenced to 14 years' imprisonment by the Special Criminal Court in Dublin for conspiracy to cause an explosion. In September Hugh Orde was appointed Chief Constable of the PSNI. In August 2003 the Leader of the Real IRA, Kevin McKevitt, was sentenced to 20 years' imprisonment by the Special Criminal Court in Dublin for directing a terrorist organization. Shortly afterwards the British Government undertook to provide funds totalling some £800,000 to enable the families of the victims of the Omagh bombing to pursue their civil court case for damages against McKevitt, Murphy and three other Real IRA members who were allegedly involved in the atrocity. Investigations into the Omagh bombing continued in 2003 and 2004 and in March 2004 one of the five men being sued by the relatives of the Omagh victims was sentenced to three and a half years' imprisonment for membership of the Real IRA.

Meanwhile, on 22 September 2001 Dr John Reid, who had succeeded Mandelson as Secretary of State for Northern Ireland earlier that year (see above), announced a further 24-hour suspension of the Assembly, thus granting the parties a further six weeks in which to overcome the continuing impasse. Trimble subsequently announced that the UUP would table a motion in the Assembly to exclude the two Sinn Féin ministers from the Executive, and that if, as was almost certain, the motion was defeated and there was still no progress on the decommissioning issue by the IRA, UUP ministers would begin to withdraw from the Executive, thus precipitating its collapse. Following continued sectarian clashes in late September (for which Reid held the UDA responsible) and the murder of a journalist in Co Armagh, for which the LVF claimed responsibility, the Secretary of State announced that the British Government no longer recognized the UDA/UFF and LVF cease-fires.

On 8 October 2001 the UUP exclusion motion was defeated and on 18 October the three UUP ministers and the two DUP ministers resigned. On 23 October the IRA and the IICD issued separate statements, which affirmed that the IRA had taken the unprecedented step of putting a significant quantity of arms, ammunition and explosives beyond use. The move prevented the imminent collapse of the Northern Irish institutions and was widely welcomed by all pro-Agreement parties. Trimble immediately announced that he would reappoint the three UUP ministers to the Executive and seek re-election to the post of First Minister. On 24 October the UUP ministers reassumed their posts and the following day the DUP reassumed its two portfolios. Later in October Trimble received approval from the UUP Executive to retake his post as First Minister with the SDLP Leader-elect, Mark Durkan, announcing his intention to stand for the position of Deputy First Minister. On 2 November, however, Trimble failed in his attempt to be re-elected as First Minister. Although he secured 70.6% of the total votes cast (including all 38 nationalist votes), two anti-Agreement members of the UUP voted against Trimble, thus preventing him from obtaining the constitutionally required majority of unionists in favour of his re-election. Following intensive negotiations, three members of the independent Alliance Party and one member of the Women's Coalition agreed to redesignate themselves temporarily as unionists and on 6 November Trimble finally regained the post of First Minister. Durkan was returned as Deputy First Minister.

In December 2001 the British Government provoked considerable controversy when it announced that it had agreed to grant Sinn Féin MPs access to the facilities of the House of Commons and that they would receive their full parliamentary allowances and travel expenses, despite the fact that they still refused to take their seats in Parliament or participate in debates, and would not swear allegiance to the Queen. In January 2002 Sinn Féin MPs occupied offices in the House of Commons for the first time.

In mid-2002, despite the announcement in April that the IRA had put a further quantity of arms, ammunition and explosives beyond use, the fragility of the peace process was underscored by unprecedented levels of street violence in north and east Belfast and by the ongoing detention and investigation in Colombia of the three Irishmen accused of collaborating with FARC rebels in that country. The three detainees were subsequently discovered to have strong links with Sinn Féin, and in April a US congressional investigation heard testimonies of further evidence of current IRA links to left-wing rebels in Colombia. Adams' refusal to testify before the US investigation, allied with alleged IRA involvement in the theft of documents from PSNI Special Branch offices in Belfast in March and the discovery, in June, of an IRA intelligence database listing details of more than 200 judges, politicians and members of the security forces, provoked unionist demands that Sinn Féin ministers be removed from the power-sharing Executive and further 'crisis' meetings between the British and Irish Governments.

In July 2002 the IRA apologized for the deaths and injuries of 'non-combatants' caused as a result of its actions over the previous 30 years. The sincerity of the apology was questioned by Trimble, and senior unionists were sceptical that the IRA remained committed to the peace process in the light of continued sectarian violence in Belfast, for which the UUP maintained that the IRA was primarily responsible. Earlier in July, during talks between the British and Irish Governments and the pro-Agreement parties in Belfast, Trimble had implied that UUP ministers would resign from the Executive by the end of that month if the IRA did not clearly demonstrate its commitment to a 'full transition from violence to democracy'.

Violent sectarian disturbances continued in Belfast during August 2002. Early that month the Real IRA was suspected to have been responsible for detonating a bomb that killed a Protestant man—the first fatality caused by the organization since the Omagh bombing in August 1998—and in mid-August a Roman Catholic was murdered in an apparent revenge act for the earlier wounding of a young Protestant. The situation was exacerbated by the escalation of a feud between rival loyalist paramilitary groups, which resulted in a number of shootings, and unionists called for the establishment of an independent body to monitor the paramilitary cease-fires. Later that month the ruling council of the UUP, the UUC, announced that it would withdraw the party's ministers from the Northern Ireland Executive on 18 January 2003 if the IRA and Sinn Féin had not demonstrated a complete transition to democracy and non-violence.

In early October 2002 Northern Ireland was once again plunged into political crisis after Sinn Féin's offices at the Northern Ireland Assembly were raided by police, who, as part of a major investigation into intelligence-gathering by republicans, suspected that the IRA had infiltrated the Northern Ireland Office (NIO) and gained access to large numbers of confidential documents. Among a number of people detained was Sinn Féin's Head of Administration, Denis Donaldson, who was charged with possession of documents likely to be of assistance to terrorist organizations. Trimble accused Sinn Féin of a 'massive political conspiracy' and threatened to withdraw from the Executive unless the British Government proposed the expulsion of Sinn Féin from the Assembly. Emergency talks between the British and Irish Governments and the Northern Ireland political leaders followed; however, Blair's demands for IRA concessions on the arms issue were not met. On 11 October the two DUP ministers resigned from the Executive, and on 14 October Reid suspended the Assembly and returned Northern Ireland to direct rule. In a joint statement, Blair and Ahern announced that the devolved institutions would only be restored if Sinn Féin ended its link with paramilitary organizations and Blair subsequently called on the IRA to disband itself. Later that month the IRA announced the suspension of all contact with the IICD and claimed that the British Government was to blame for the current crisis, having failed to honour its commitments under the Good Friday Agreement.

Also in October 2002 the trial commenced in Bogotá of the three suspected IRA members who were charged with 'instructing guerillas in the manufacture of bombs, detonation of explosive artefacts and the planning of terrorist attacks'. However, the three accused refused to attend the hearing, claiming they would not receive a fair trial. Upon resumption of the trial in December the Irishmen did not appear in court, asserting their right to remain silent and the trial was again adjourned after two key witnesses failed to attend the hearing. The trial resumed in March 2003 but was subjected to numerous delays. In April 2004 the three men were acquitted of training guerillas, although they were fined for travelling on false passports. The Colombian Attorney-General sucessfully appealed against their acquittal, however, and the three were each sentenced to 17 years' imprisonment in December. They subsequently fled Colombia, and in August 2005 it was revealed that they had returned to Ireland.

Talks aimed at resolving the impasse continued between the major parties during late 2002 and early 2003; however, relations between unionists and nationalists remained strained. Further talks in January and February were overshadowed by a severe escalation of the feud between rival loyalist paramilitary organizations in Belfast. In April US President George W. Bush held talks with Ahern and the pro-Agreement parties at which he urged their leaders to 'seize the opportunity for peace'. Despite these efforts, plans to publish proposals for reinstating the Northern Ireland institutions were abandoned just days later, after Blair and Ahern announced that a statement issued by the IRA informing the two Governments of its 'future intentions' had failed to meet their demands for a definitive cessation of paramilitary activities.

In early May 2003 Adams stated that the IRA leadership was determined 'that there will be no activities which will undermine in any way the peace process or the Good Friday Agreement'; however, Blair cited the refusal of the IRA to give him 'absolute clarity' that it had ceased all paramilitary activity as the reason for his decision again to postpone the elections. Nevertheless, the British and Irish Governments published their Joint Declaration, which included plans to reduce the security forces from 14,500 to 5,000 by April 2005; to repeal anti-terrorist legislation specific to Northern Ireland; to establish an independent international monitoring body to assess any breaches of the Good Friday Agreement; to transfer policing and judicial powers to the devolved government; and provision that terrorists who had committed crimes for which they had not yet been convicted would have their cases heard at 'special judicial tribunals'. The Declaration also called for a full and permanent cessation of all paramilitary activity, including military attacks, intelligence gathering, weapons procurement and punishment attacks.

In June 2003 Trimble secured a narrow victory at an emergency meeting of the UUC over UUP MP Jeffrey Donaldson, who had attempted to persuade the party to support a motion to reject the Joint Declaration. Donaldson, Rev. Martin Smyth (the party's President) and David Burnside subsequently resigned the UUP Westminster whip, provoking further speculation about a split within the party. Days later the three dissident MPs were suspended from the party. In July the High Court in

Belfast ruled that their suspension was 'unlawful, invalid and of no force or effect', and Trimble suffered a further reverse when more than 37% of the members of his constituency association expressed their lack of confidence in his leadership of the party. In September Trimble succeeded narrowly in passing a motion at the UUC which urged Donaldson, Smyth and Burnside to retake the party whip at Westminster; however, the three MPs insisted they would remain outside the parliamentary party and continue their opposition to the Joint Declaration.

Talks between the British and Irish Governments and the major Northern Irish political parties continued during late 2003, and in September the four members of the International Monitoring Commission (IMC) were appointed. Trimble and Adams met with Ahern and Blair in London in mid-October, and on 21 October it was revealed that elections to the Northern Ireland Assembly would take place on 26 November. However, later on 21 October Trimble issued a statement in which he maintained that the acts of decommissioning of IRA weapons, witnessed by de Chastelain earlier that day, had lacked the transparency the UUP required to be convinced of the IRA's genuine desire to commit to a lasting peace. Trimble announced that the peace process would be put on hold pending the convening of the UUC, thus preventing the devolution of powers to the Northern Ireland institutions; however, both Blair and Ahern insisted that the elections would proceed on 26 November. The British Government acknowledged in late October that the devolved institutions would not be restored following the elections and that a review of the Good Friday Agreement would take place in early 2004, although Blair stressed that the fundamental principles of the Agreement were not a matter for negotiation. A statement issued by the IRA on 29 October maintained that it had honoured its commitments and that there would be no more acts of decommissioning until the UUP agreed to support the restoration of power sharing.

At the elections to the Northern Ireland Assembly, held on 26 November 2003, the anti-Good Friday Agreement DUP secured 30 of the 108 seats, thus becoming the largest party in the province. The UUP won 27 seats, while Sinn Féin increased its parliamentary representation to 24 seats. The SDLP suffered a significant loss of support, winning just 18 seats. The remaining seats were won by the Alliance Party (six) and the PUP, the UKUP and an independent candidate, all of which secured one seat. The rate of voter participation was officially recorded at 63.1%. The election results increased the pressure on Trimble from anti-Agreement factions of the UUP, which again called for his resignation. Furthermore, the DUP demanded a full renegotiation of the Good Friday Agreement. However, both Ahern and Blair reiterated that the 'principles and values' of the Agreement would not be changed. In December an independent report into a series of car bombs detonated in Dublin and Monaghan, Ireland, in May 1974 in which 33 people were killed and some 300 were injured, concluded that there were 'grounds for suspecting' that British security forces had helped loyalist paramilitaries to carry out the atrocities. Families of the victims repeated their demands for a public inquiry into the incidents. Later that month Donaldson resigned from the UUP; two other UUP deputies also left the party and in early January 2004 they confirmed that they would join the DUP. Days later, however, Burnside and Smyth announced that they had retaken the UUP whip at Westminster.

In January 2004 the DUP Leader, Ian Paisley, met Ahern at the Irish embassy in London for talks. While Ahern highlighted the significance of the discussions, the DUP remained insistent that it would not conduct face-to-face talks with Sinn Féin until the IRA had disbanded. The review of the Good Friday Agreement commenced in early February with Paisley setting out his party's own proposals for power sharing. Whilst acknowledging that the proposals signalled progress on the part of the DUP they were generally negatively received by Sinn Féin, which feared that they would lead to a return to unionist majority rule. The talks were stalled in early March as Trimble withdrew his party in protest at the alleged IRA involvement in the kidnapping of a dissident republican in Belfast in late February. Later that month Ahern and Blair met to hold talks with political groups and reiterated their commitment to the conclusion of a power-sharing deal. In late March Trimble was re-elected to the leadership of the UUP. In April the IMC issued its first report in which it highlighted the levels of ongoing paramilitary activity by both loyalist and republican groups in Northern Ireland. The British Government subsequently announced that it would impose financial sanctions on Sinn Féin and the PUP.

The review of the Good Friday Agreement resumed at Leeds Castle in England in September 2004, having been put on hold for the European elections. As the talks began de Chastelain announced that the IRA would be prepared to decommission its weapons if a political deal were agreed upon; however, the talks ended with no agreement. In early October Paisley and Ahern held an unprecedented meeting in Dublin to try to break the impasse. Paisley subsequently announced his desire to adhere to the Good Friday Agreement but signalled that this could only be achieved if the IRA disbanded. Later in the month in its second report, however, the IMC again highlighted the high level of paramilitary violence in Northern Ireland and the unlikelihood of the IRA disarming.

In late 2004 the process showed real signs of progressing to a successful conclusion. In mid-November the UDA indicated its intention to end violence and demilitarize following an announcement by the Secretary of State for Northern Ireland, Paul Murphy, that the UDA cease-fire of February 2004 would be officially recognized by the Government. On 17 November the British and Irish Governments passed their proposals for restoring the power-sharing executive to the DUP and Sinn Féin for consultation. One week later Paisley met with Blair and stated that the disarming of the IRA would only be an acceptable starting point for the power-sharing agreement if it was verified by photographic evidence. At the end of the month Adams met the Northern Ireland Chief Constable, Hugh Orde, to discuss decommissioning, while Paisley met de Chastelain in Belfast to review issues surrounding the destruction of the IRA's weapons. The following day Paisley gave an ultimatum to the IRA that if the peace accord were not restored in the current situation it would become an almost impossible task in the future and also called for the IRA to repent its past actions. Adams declared Paisley's comments to be offensive and stated that Sinn Féin would go no further in negotiations. On 8 December, despite being resigned to the collapse of the peace process, Blair and Ahern met in Belfast to reveal their final proposals to restore devolution. The following day the IRA declared that photographic proof of decommissioning had never been an option and that although the IRA was committed to the peace process, it would not be subjected to a process of humiliation.

In December 2004 an estimated £26.5m. was stolen from the Belfast headquarters of Northern Bank. The PSNI immediately set up an investigation into the robbery and on 7 January 2005 Orde stated that the IRA had been responsible for the robbery. In a report published in mid-February the IMC implicated not only the IRA but also Sinn Féin leaders (these accusations were vehemently denied by Adams). In early February Ahern and Blair warned the IRA that its failure to demilitarize was the only obstacle to reaching an agreement on power sharing; the following day the IRA withdrew its commitment to decommissioning its weapons. In March, responding to Sinn Féin's alleged involvement in the robbery of the Northern Bank, the British Parliament voted to withdraw from the party its entitlement to an allowance payable to Northern Irish political parties, and from Sinn Féin's four MPs their entitlement to personal parliamentary allowances. Early in April, in an initiative that aimed to break the deadlock over the restoration of devolution, Adams urged the IRA to embrace the political alternative to armed struggle that now existed. In May Sean Gerard Hoey, who had already been detained on charges of terrorism and membership of the Real IRA, was charged with the murder of the 29 people who had been killed in the Omagh bombing in 1998; his trial was expected to commence in September 2006.

At the general election to the British Parliament held on 5 May 2005 the UUP recorded its worst electoral performance since the formation of Northern Ireland's first government in 1921, retaining only one of the five seats it had previously held, with 17.8% of the votes cast in Northern Ireland. The DUP secured nine seats, gaining four at the expense of the UUP, with 33.7% of the votes cast. Sinn Féin increased its parliamentary representation, winning five seats (compared with four at the previous election), with 24.3% of the votes, while the representation of the SDLP, which took three seats with 17.5% of the votes, remained unchanged. Following the election, in which he had himself lost his seat, Trimble resigned as Leader of the UUP. (In June the UUP elected Sir Reg Empey, former Minister for Enterprise, Trade and Investment in the Northern Ireland Executive, as its new Leader.) In a major reorganization of ministerial portfolios on 6 May Peter Hain replaced Paul Murphy as the Secretary of State for Northern Ireland. Hain's retention of the office—Secretary of State for Wales—he had held in the outgoing

Cabinet was criticized by the DUP, which claimed that the status of the Northern Ireland portfolio had thereby been diminished.

In May 2005, after he had held seemingly fruitless discussions with, separately, Sinn Féin and unionist leaders in London, Hain emphasized that progress in the peace process could only be achieved on the basis of the Good Friday Agreement. Paisley, however, described the Good Friday Agreement as 'dead', stating that progress would only be achieved through comprehensive, verifiable weapons' decommissioning by the IRA and its abandonment of its criminal activities. Meanwhile, on 10 May the European Parliament adopted a resolution that accused members of the IRA of the murder of a Catholic man, Robert McCartney, in Belfast in January. Towards the end of the month a report by the IMC highlighted the IRA's continued military readiness and its recruitment and training campaign. In mid-June the House of Commons voted to extend for one year the withdrawal of parliamentary allowances from Sinn Féin and its MPs.

In late July 2005 the IRA issued a communiqué in which it formally renounced its armed struggle and committed itself to the pursuit of its objectives, including the goal of a united Ireland, through peaceful means only. At the same time the IRA undertook to conclude the process of comprehensive, verifiable weapons' decommissioning. Welcoming the IRA's communiqué in a joint statement, Blair and Ahern emphasized that the commitments it contained must be authenticated in action. Leading unionists, including Paisley and Empey, together with US President George W. Bush, responded to the IRA's announcement in a similar fashion. Unionist uncertainty over the good faith of the IRA's statement was reflected in the DUP's condemnation of the Government's decision to begin removing security facilities in South Armagh on the day after it had been issued. Hain's announcement, on 1 August, of a plan to reduce within two years the number of British army personnel in Northern Ireland by 50%, and to repeal anti-terrorism measures exclusive to Northern Ireland, likewise provoked condemnation by unionists. On 4 August Blair asssured Paisley, who had threatened to impede the restoration of devolution the previous day in a meeting with Hain, that power sharing remained dependent on the fulfilment by the IRA of the undertaking it had made to disarm. Loyalist violence that broke out that day in Belfast and continued sporadically throughout the month was attributed to a feud between the paramilitary Ulster Volunteer Force (UVF) and the LVF. On 10 September the most serious sectarian violence for 10 years erupted in Belfast and continued for three days after the route of a march by the Orange Order had been diverted away from a nationalist area in the west of the city. On 14 September, in view of incontrovertible evidence of the UVF's involvement in the unrest, Hain withdrew the United Kingdom's recognition of the UVF's 11-year cease-fire.

In late September 2005 the IRA formally declared in a communiqué that it had completed the process of verifiable weapons' decommissioning. De Chastelain, who together with two clergymen, one Catholic and one Protestant, had witnessed the decommissioning, announced at the same time that he was satisfied that the arms decommissioned represented the totality of the IRA's arsenal. Both Blair and Ahern welcomed the IRA's statement as a significant step towards peace and Hain stated that negotiations on the restoration of devolution should commence in early 2006. Paisley, however, objected that the alleged completion of decommissioning had lacked transparency and declared that he would not participate in power sharing with Sinn Féin. In early October the DUP presented Blair with a list of conditions that it insisted must be met to ensure that the unionist community received equal treatment with the IRA, and without whose fulfilment it would refuse to negotiate with Sinn Féin on power sharing. Later in October Paisley criticized a decision to restore to Sinn Féin from 1 November its entitlement to the allowance payable to Northern Irish political parties as a concession to the IRA. Unionists condemned the Government's intention, announced by Hain in late October, to grant an amnesty to certain categories of suspects who remained at large, claiming that the Government had secretly offered the amnesty to the IRA as an inducement for it to abjure violence. At the end of October the LVF responded to weapons' decommissioning by the IRA by disbanding all of its paramilitary units.

The DUP absented itself from talks held in mid-November 2005 between Hain, the Irish Minister of Foreign Affairs, Dermot Ahern, and representatives of Sinn Féin, including Martin McGuinness, the party's chief negotiator, who challenged Paisley to keep his word that he would share power with Sinn Féin after the IRA had decommissioned its arms. On 23 November the Government's Northern Ireland (Offences) Bill secured passage through the House of Commons. As a result of the legislation thus approved, the cases of some 150 people—including members of the security forces as well as republican and unionist paramilitaries—sought for crimes committed before the conclusion of the Good Friday Agreement would be heard by a special tribunal, but those convicted would be freed on licence. The DUP renewed its condemnation of the legislation as insulting to the victims of terrorism. During the debate of the bill in the House of Commons Hain acknowledged that the legislation was part of a commitment made to Sinn Féin prior to the IRA's formal renunciation of its armed struggle in July. In December Sinn Féin itself ceased to endorse the legislation after discovering that the amnesty contained within it would also be extended to members of the British armed forces. In January 2006 Hain announced that the proposed legislation was to be withdrawn.

In early December 2005, in a further response to the IRA's abandonment of its armed struggle, the Government announced that British military strength in Northern Ireland would be reduced to below 9,000 in the following month. On 8 December the Public Prosecution Service retracted allegations that the IRA had infiltrated the NIO in 2002 (see above). After Denis Donaldson, former Head of Administration of Sinn Féin, had confessed to having been an informer working for the British security services for some 20 years and, on 16 December 2005, been expelled from the party, Adams asserted that the allegations of infiltration had been part of an attempt by those within the security services who opposed Sinn Féin's participation in government to wreck the Northern Ireland Assembly. On 19 December, however, Hain dismissed calls for an inquiry into the affair.

In late January 2006 Blair and Irish Prime Minister Bertie Ahern announced that multi-party discussions would recommence on 6 February. In a report published days before the talks were due to begin the IMC alleged that the process of decommissioning IRA weapons had not been completed in September 2005 as the IRA had claimed and the IICD had verified. The IMC's report also lent support to a claim made in January by a senior detective in the PSNI that the IRA was still involved in organized crime, by accusing some of it members of organized criminal activity and asserting that the IRA continued to gather intelligence. At the same time, however, the IMC's report stated that the IRA no longer committed acts of terrorism. For its part, the IICD reaffirmed its claim that the IRA had completed the process of weapons' decommissioning in September. At a conference of the DUP on 4 February 2006 Paisley described as a 'blatant lie' the claim that the IRA had completely disarmed and dismissed any question of sharing power with Sinn Féin before it did so. Despite these set-backs, multi-party talks seeking to restart the peace process were initiated on schedule on 6 February near Belfast.

In mid-February 2006 Hain presented to the House of Commons the Northern Ireland (Miscellaneous Provisions) Bill which, if adopted, would allow the Government to transfer responsibility for policing and justice to Northern Irish politicians. The bill also provided for the organization of immediate elections to the Northern Ireland Assembly, in the event of political agreement being reached, rather than waiting until 2007 for such elections to be held. However, the discovery of the body of the former Sinn Féin Head of Administration at the Northern Ireland Assembly and self-confessed former agent for the British security services, Denis Donaldson, in Co Donegal, Ireland, in early April 2006 appeared likely to impede progress in the stalled peace process. Despite Sinn Féin's condemnation of the apparent murder and the Provisional IRA's claim that it had had 'no involvement whatsoever' in Donaldson's death, prominent unionists, including Paisley, blamed republicans for his death.

Two days after Donaldson's body had been discovered Blair and Ahern issued a major joint statement that sought to clarify the course that the renewed peace process should take in 2006. The two Prime Ministers stated their conviction that the IRA no longer represented a terrorist threat and that all parties should engage in political dialogue; and stated that their aim was to set out a practical framework and reasonable timescale for progress in the restoration of devolution. In order to counter the danger of a political vacuum, the Northern Ireland Assembly was recalled on 15 May. The Assembly's primary responsibility was to elect a First Minister and a Deputy First Minister as soon as possible, to allocate ministerial portfolios, and to make other preparations for government. Once the Assembly had elected a First Minister and a Deputy First Minister on a cross-community basis and formed an Executive, power would automatically be devolved to the Assembly and at that point the British Government's power to suspend the Assembly would lapse definitively. In the event of the Assembly's being unable to elect First and Deputy First Ministers within the normal six-week period, Blair and Ahern stated that they would be prepared to allow a further period of 12 weeks after the summer recess for the formation of an Executive. However, if by 24 November the Assembly had failed to achieve this, the Prime Ministers' joint view was that no further purpose would be served by another election at that point or in May 2007. They would be obliged, therefore, to cancel salaries and allowances payable to members of the Assembly and to defer restoration of the Assembly and the Executive until a clear political willingness to exercise devolved power existed. Such a deferral would have immediate implications for the British and Irish Governments' joint stewardship of the peace process and detailed work was stated to have already begun on British-Irish partnership arrangements that would become necessary under such circumstances.

In November 1988 the European Court of Human Rights ruled in favour of four men who were protesting against being detained without charge in Northern Ireland for more than four days, under the Prevention of Terrorism Act (which allows detention for up to seven days). In December the Government responded to the ruling by announcing a derogation from the European Convention for the Protection of Human Rights. In November 1991 the UN Committee Against Torture expressed concern over cases of alleged ill-treatment of terrorist suspects in detention and other abuses of human rights in Northern Ireland, which had been detailed in a report compiled by a prominent human rights organization, Amnesty International. In September 1995 the European Court of Human Rights unexpectedly overturned an earlier decision of the European Commission of Human Rights and ruled that the killing of three IRA activists in Gibraltar, in 1988, was in breach of Article 2 of the Convention, defining the 'right of life'. While clearing the Government of operating a 'shoot-to-kill' policy, the Court insisted that excessive and unlawful force had been used. In May 1997 the newly elected Labour Government announced that the European Convention was to be incorporated into United Kingdom law and applied in full in Northern Ireland and that the jurisdiction of British courts would be extended to cover the rights guaranteed in the Convention. The Human Rights Act received royal assent in November 1998 and came into force in October 2000. Meanwhile, in April 1998 a report of a special inquiry of the UN Human Rights Commission, initiated in October 1997, upheld complaints by human rights groups regarding the RUC's intimidation of lawyers defending terrorist suspects and the failure to extend adequate legal rights to those detained under emergency legislation. In particular, the report recommended a new inquiry into the allegations that the RUC failed to prevent the murder, by UDA activists, of the republican lawyer Patrick Finucane in Belfast in 1989 (see above). In May 2001 the European Court of Human Rights awarded compensation to the families of 10 IRA members killed by security forces in Northern Ireland during the 1980s and 1990s, after it agreed that the Government had breached Article 2 of the Convention. It also criticized the investigation into the shootings of eight of those 10 IRA members for its lack of independence.

A new official inquiry into the fatal shooting of 14 republican demonstrators by the security forces in Derry (Londonderry) in January 1972, conducted by Lord Saville of Newdigate, began hearing evidence in March 2000. The destruction by the British army, prior to the inquiry, of rifles required as evidence prompted lawyers representing the families of the victims to accuse the Ministry of Defence of deliberately attempting to frustrate the process. In a significant development in November the lawyer acting for the 440 soldiers involved in the case accepted, in contrast to the findings of an original inquiry, that none of the civilians officially listed as killed or wounded in the incident had been armed. He did, however, maintain that a second list of at least 34 'untraced or unidentified casualties' who were never publicly acknowledged as injured in the incident could have included in their number gunmen who had fired on the soldiers. In May 2001 Martin McGuinness survived a motion of 'no confidence' in the Northern Ireland Assembly, after he admitted in a written statement presented to the Saville inquiry that he was the IRA's adjutant (effectively second-in-command) in Derry in January 1972. McGuinness, however, denied that IRA gunmen had been involved in the exchanges of fire with security forces and rejected the claim of an eyewitness that he had fired the first shot. In January 2003 Sir Edward Heath, British Prime Minister in 1972, appeared before the inquiry and dismissed allegations that the shootings had been premeditated as 'absurd'. In November 2003 McGuinness appeared before the inquiry but refused to disclose the names of IRA comrades who had been with him in Derry on 'Bloody Sunday', despite being warned by Lord Saville that he could face further legal action. McGuinness insisted that the IRA had not conducted any military operations in Derry that day and that no IRA members had been killed or injured during the shootings. The inquiry concluded in November 2004 with the tribunal retiring to compile its report.

In June 2005 the Government published reports compiled, respectively, by the Council of Europe's Commissioner for Human Rights and the European Committee for the Prevention of Torture and Inhuman or Degrading Treatment or Punishment (CPT) that contained strong criticism of the United Kingdom's policies on terrorist suspects and those seeking political asylum in the country. Fault was found in particular with the Anti-Terrorism, Crime and Security Act (2001) because it enabled the Secretary of State for Home Affairs to subject suspects to control orders without trial. The report of the Commissioner also claimed that there were deficiencies in the procedures governing legal appeals by unsuccessful political asylum seekers against deportation. The Government strongly denied a claim by the CPT that detainees had been mistreated. Later in June human rights groups, with the support of opposition parties and some Labour MPs, sought to persuade the Government not to repatriate Zimbabwean asylum seekers whose applications had failed on the grounds that they risked mistreatment on their return to Zimbabwe. Also in June a report published by Amnesty International alleged that, by detaining them prior to deportation, the Government had infringed the human rights of as many as 25,000 failed applicants for political asylum in the United Kingdom in 2004. In July the Government announced that it had suspended its policy of deporting failed Zimbabwean applicants for political asylum pending a High Court's consideration of its legality. In October, in a 'test case', the Asylum and Immigration Tribunal ruled that an unsuccessful Zimbabwean applicant for political asylum could not be repatriated to Zimbabwe as he would be at risk of mistreatment there. On the following day, in response to the likelihood that British courts would uphold appeals by foreign nationals against deportation to countries where they risked persecution, the Government announced that it would seek to overrule a majority decision by the European Court of Human Rights in 1996 that national security interests could not take precedence over an individual's inalienable human rights.

The United Kingdom became a full member of the EC in January 1973. A referendum in 1975 endorsed British membership by a large majority. The first direct election of British representatives to the European Parliament took place in June 1979. During the 1980s the Thatcher Government demanded controls on spending by the EC, and particularly reform of the Common Agricultural Policy (CAP), and expressed scepticism regarding proposals for greater European economic unity, on the grounds that this was likely to entail a loss of national sovereignty. In October 1990, however, the United Kingdom joined the ERM. Following Major's assumption of the British premiership, relations with individual members of the EC (particularly Germany) improved, and the Government adopted a more pragmatic approach towards European developments. Nevertheless, the British Government agreed to the terms of the Treaty on European Union only after substantial concessions had been granted for the United Kingdom. In particular, the United Kingdom's participation in the final stage of European Economic and Monetary Union (EMU), including the adoption of a single EC currency by 2000, was made optional. Following the implementation of the Maastricht Treaty in November 1993, proposals to extend membership of the EU (as the EC became) to other European countries provoked concern on the part of the British Government over voting rights for larger countries within the EU's Council of Ministers; however, a compromise agreement effectively permitting new members to join the EU was concluded in March 1994. In December, despite objections on the part of the United Kingdom, EU ministers approved a new fisheries agreement, which permitted controlled access for Spanish trawlers to an area of water around Ireland.

British relations with the EU were adversely affected by concerns over the safety of beef from British cattle. In March 1996 a report by a government health advisory committee recognized a possible link between BSE, evident in cattle herds in all parts of the country, and a new strain of Creutzfeldt-Jakob disease (CJD), a degenerative disease affecting humans. The findings of the report provoked a serious crisis of consumer confidence within the United Kingdom and abroad, and several countries announced a ban on all imports of beef and related products from the United Kingdom. At the end of March comprehensive restrictions on the export from the United Kingdom of all live cattle, beef and derivatives were imposed by the European Commission. EU ministers of agriculture undertook to support the British Government in compensating farmers for any necessary slaughter of cattle herds, on condition that adequate measures were adopted to eradicate BSE.

The election, in May 1997, of the Labour Government generated expectations of a significant improvement of relations between the United Kingdom and the EU. The Blair administration immediately announced its intention to withdraw the country's option not to participate in the 'social chapter' of the Maastricht Treaty, and to promote completion of the internal economic market and enlargement of the EU. However, the Government's opposition to greater EU authority over national borders and immigration controls, and its demands for reform of the CAP, remained potential obstacles to a successful conclusion of the negotiations to review the implementation of the Maastricht Treaty. In June 1997 EU Heads of Government signed the Treaty of Amsterdam, amending the Maastricht Treaty. The new agreement incorporated the social chapter, given the Labour Government's willingness to subscribe to the protocol, although it was not expected to be enforced in the United Kingdom until the new Treaty had been ratified by all members. The United Kingdom, together with Ireland, secured an exemption from obligations with regard to immigration, asylum and visa policies; however, Blair negotiated an option to participate in certain co-operative aspects of the border arrangements.

In July 1997 the European Commission criticized the Government for failing to prevent illegal exports of beef. The Minister of Agriculture, Fisheries and Food, Jack Cunningham, agreed to tighten measures to act against meat-processing plants and suppliers who were breaching the EU ban. The Government's efforts to restore confidence in British beef products included pursuing the selective slaughter of cattle, agreed under the previous administration, developing the certified herd scheme to allow for the export of beef from herds where computerized records could prove there had been no cases of BSE for at least eight years, and promoting a date-based scheme to export meat from animals born since August 1996 (when the last stocks of contaminated animal feed had been destroyed). In March 1998 a public inquiry was established in the United Kingdom to review the emergence and identification of BSE and the new variant of CJD over the 10 years prior to March 1996. Sir Nicholas Phillips, a judge of the Court of Appeal, was appointed to lead the inquiry. In October 2000 the long-delayed report of the Phillips inquiry into the BSE crisis was finally published. In the 16-volume report Lord Phillips attributed the BSE crisis to intensive farming and the practice of feeding cattle and sheep remains to cows, yet stated that neither the BSE epidemic nor the infection of consumers could have been prevented because, owing to the long incubation period of the disease, it had taken hold before the first cattle were identified as suffering from the disease.

In July 1999 the European Commission formally ended the ban on British beef exports, with effect from 1 August, subject to the provision that all beef was de-boned and came from animals whose pedigree could be traced. However, despite the Commission's ruling, France announced that it would maintain its embargo on British beef pending a report by its own food safety agency on the advisability of ending restrictions. Similarly, Germany delayed ending the ban pending a decision by its parliament. In November, in the light of continued French intransigence, the European Commission announced its intention to initiate legal proceedings to secure French compliance with the lifting of the ban. In January 2000 the European Commission formally began legal proceedings against France at the European Court of Justice (ECJ) in Luxembourg. However, the legal process was complicated by a French counter-claim already submitted to the court asserting that the European Commission had breached EU law by failing to protect public health when it rejected the French submission that it was unsafe to end the ban on British beef. Later that month the European Commission announced that it would not seek an interim judgment to force France to lift its ban pending a ruling by the ECJ, which, it was envisaged, could take up to two years. Legal action was also initiated by the Commission against Germany, which continued to uphold its ban. In September 2001 the ECJ issued a preliminary ruling, which stated that the French ban on British beef was illegal; that initial ruling was upheld at a subsequent ECJ hearing in December. In March 2002 the European Commission issued France with a letter of formal notice identifying France's failure to end the embargo on British beef and to which the French Government was expected to respond within 30 days. However, the French Minister of Agriculture and Fisheries insisted that the ban would remain in place at least until after the legislative elections in that country, scheduled to be held in June. In October the French Government removed the ban on British beef. (In November 2005 the British Department for Environment, Food and Rural Affairs lifted the ban on sales for human consumption of meat from cattle aged over 30 months, and in March 2006 the EU removed the remaining restrictions on the United Kingdom's foreign sales of live cattle and beef products.) Later in October 2002 relations between France and the United Kingdom were again strained following disagreements between Blair and the French President, Jacques Chirac, over EU agricultural policy reform. Bilateral relations deteriorated further after France invited the President of Zimbabwe, Robert Mugabe, to attend a summit of African leaders in Paris. Sanctions prohibiting Mugabe and other Zimbabwean political leaders from travelling to EU countries had been imposed in February 2002 in response to Zimbabwe's prevention of the deployment of an EU observation mission which was to monitor elections in that country. Relations between the United Kingdom and France were also strained by their differing views on the necessity of military action in Iraq (see below). In October 2003 Chirac visited London for talks with Blair, at which Chirac expressed his reservations over US-British policies in Iraq; however, they agreed to enhance co-operation to combat illegal immigration. In mid-November 2004 Chirac again visited London to mark the 100th anniversary of the *entente cordiale* agreement, which had settled outstanding colonial disputes between the two countries. Whilst praising the close relationship between the two countries and their joint determination to fight terrorism, he reiterated his reservations towards military action in Iraq.

At the end of October 1997 the Chancellor of the Exchequer, Gordon Brown, attempted to clarify the Government's stance on the European single currency, following a period of intense speculation. He identified five key principles for participation in EMU, relating to its impact on the British economy and employment, and insisted that membership would have to be preceded by a sustained period of economic stability. In December 1997 Blair objected to a decision of other EU leaders to establish a new economic policy group comprising representatives of countries adopting the single currency from 1 January 1999. None the less, the Government emphasized its commitment to the successful introduction of the euro (as the currency was designated). In May 1999 Blair expressed his intention to end what he termed Britain's 'ambivalence' towards the EU and to make the country a 'leading partner' in the bloc. Earlier in the year he had predicted that the relevant conditions for participation in EMU would be in place shortly after the next general election. In June 2003 Brown announced that four of the five key principles for deciding British participation in EMU had not yet been fulfilled. Nevertheless, he stated that the Government remained in favour of joining the single currency when the conditions were in place.

Despite his previously vehement stance opposing such a move, in mid-April 2004 Blair announced plans to hold a referendum on the proposed new draft EU constitutional treaty. The draft had been prepared by a convention, headed by the former French President, Valéry Giscard d'Estaing, during 2002–03, and was finally approved by the leaders of the 25 member states of the EU in mid-June 2004. A bill was published in late January 2005 to allow for a referendum on the treaty. In June, however, following the failure of the French and Dutch electorates to endorse the treaty in referendums, Straw announced that the Government would not proceed with a second reading of the bill in the House of Commons. At the same time Straw emphasized the Government's view that the treaty represented 'a sensible new set of rules for the enlarged EU'.

Following Iraq's forcible annexation of Kuwait in August 1990, the British Government promptly supported the efforts of the

USA in defending Saudi Arabia from potential Iraqi aggression and deployed some 42,000 personnel in the subsequent engagement in hostilities against Iraq, under the auspices of the UN. British troops also participated in subsequent humanitarian efforts to protect the Kurdish population within Iraq from persecution by the Iraqi armed forces. In January 1993 British fighter aircraft participated in US-led attacks on military targets in Iraq, launched in response to renewed Iraqi incursions into Kuwait and obstruction of a UN investigation into a suspected Iraqi nuclear weapons programme. In September 1996 the British Government awarded political and logistical support to a series of air-strikes by the USA against targets in Iraq. In December 1998, following Iraq's refusal to co-operate with weapons inspections by the UN Special Commission (UNSCOM, see p. 15), the USA and the United Kingdom conducted a further series of air-strikes in an effort to 'degrade' Iraq's military capabilities. Further airborne attacks were conducted in early 1999 and mid-2000 in response to alleged violations by Iraq of the UN air exclusion zone. In February 2001 the United Kingdom and the USA were again involved in the bombardment of a number of targets in Iraq, in response to a reportedly increased threat to aircraft from those countries in the preceding weeks. The action was, however, condemned by several Western and Arab countries.

In March 2002 Blair faced opposition from within the Labour Party as speculation mounted about the possibility of further military action against Iraq. Blair indicated in July that he had 'tremendous concerns' about any possible military strikes on Iraq and subsequently announced his support for the UN Security Council's proposal that UN weapons inspectors be readmitted to Iraq. He did, however, stress in late August that the British Government was determined to deal with the threat posed by Iraq's possession of weapons of mass destruction. In early September, in response to mounting public opposition to possible military action in Iraq, Blair insisted that no decision on such moves had yet been taken but stated that he would publish a dossier outlining the 'real and unique threat' posed by the regime of the Iraqi President, Saddam Hussain, by the end of the month. Following a meeting with the US President, George W. Bush, Blair announced that the United Kingdom and the USA would attempt to secure a new UN Security Council resolution that would approve military action in Iraq, should that country fail to comply with UN weapons inspectors. Both British and US officials greeted with scepticism Iraq's declaration, made on 16 September, of its willingness to readmit weapons inspectors 'without conditions'; however, the People's Republic of China, France and Russia cautiously welcomed the move. In late September the British Government published the dossier outlining its case against the Iraqi regime and the perceived threat posed by that country's 'illicit weapons programmes' to the security of both the West and the Middle East (see above). However, it appeared that the United Kingdom and the USA were becoming increasingly isolated in their attempts to secure approval for the use of military force against Iraq. On 8 November, after a compromise had been reached between the five permanent members, the UN Security Council unanimously adopted Resolution 1441, which demanded, *inter alia*, that Iraq permit weapons inspectors from UNSCOM's replacement UNMOVIC and the International Atomic Energy Agency (IAEA, see p. 98) unrestricted access to sites suspected of holding illegal weapons and required the Iraqi leadership to make a full declaration of its chemical, biological, nuclear and ballistic weapons, as well as related materials used in civilian industries, within 30 days. The resolution warned that this represented a 'final opportunity' for the Iraqi authorities to comply with their disarmament obligations under previous UN resolutions, affirming that Iraq would face 'serious consequences' in the event of non-compliance with the UN inspectors or of any 'false statements and omissions' in its weapons declaration. Later in November the Liberal Democrats' parliamentary motion proposing that no military action should be taken against Iraq without a fresh mandate from the UN and a vote in the House of Commons was defeated by 452 votes to 85; 32 Labour MPs voted in favour of the motion.

In mid-December 2002 the British Secretary of State for Foreign and Commonwealth Affairs, Jack Straw, denounced Hussain's claims that he had destroyed all weapons of mass destruction as an 'obvious falsehood'. The USA also stated that Iraq was in 'material breach' of UN Resolution 1441 since it had failed to give a complete account of its weapons capabilities, citing in particular Iraq's failure to account for stocks of biological weapons such as anthrax. During January 2003 Blair, while asserting that conflict was not inevitable if Iraq complied with the UN's disarmament terms and insisting that UNMOVIC and the IAEA be granted sufficient time in order to complete their inspections, ordered large numbers of troops to the Persian (Arabian) Gulf region to join the increasing number of US forces already in position there. However, it also became apparent that month that disagreements over policy on Iraq within the Government, the Labour Party and Parliament as a whole were increasing, particularly following Blair's refusal in mid-January to guarantee that British troops would not be involved in a military campaign in Iraq should there be no UN resolution approving such action. On 27 January, 60 days after the resumption of UN weapons inspections in Iraq (as stipulated under Resolution 1441), the head of UNMOVIC, Hans Blix, and the Director-General of the IAEA, Muhammad el-Baradei, briefed the UN Security Council on the progress of inspections. El-Baradei stated that IAEA inspectors had found no evidence that Iraq had restarted its nuclear weapons programme, but requested more time for the organization to complete its research. Blix, for his part, claimed that there was no evidence that Iraq had destroyed known stocks of illegal chemical and long-range ballistic weapons, and announced that he was sceptical about Baghdad's willingness to disarm. Following the briefing, Straw declared Iraq to be in 'material breach' of Resolution 1441.

In late January 2003, as the likelihood of a US-led military response to the crisis increased, the United Kingdom was one of eight European countries to sign a joint statement expressing support for the USA's stance on Iraq. The following month increasing British popular opposition to military action against Iraq precipitated nation-wide 'anti-war' demonstrations, including a march in London attended by some 1m. people. Blair continued with his efforts to secure a second UN Security Council resolution authorizing a US-led campaign in Iraq should inspectors from UNMOVIC continue to report Baghdad's non-compliance; however, on 26 February he suffered a damaging reverse when 122 Labour MPs supported an all-party motion in the House of Commons stating that the case for military action against Iraq was 'as yet unproven'. Earlier in February the USA had presented to the Security Council what it claimed to be overwhelming evidence of Iraq's possession of weapons of mass destruction, its attempts to conceal such weapons from the UN inspectorate and its links with international terrorism, including the al-Qa'ida network. Despite signs of progress being reported by Blix in mid-February in his report to the UN Security Council, on 24 February the United Kingdom, the USA and Spain presented a draft resolution to the Security Council effectively authorizing a US-led military campaign against Hussain's regime, in response to Iraq's failure to disarm peacefully. The resolution stated that a deadline of 17 March would be set, by which time Iraq should prove that it was disarming; however, no specific mention was made of consequent military action in the event of the deadline not being met by Iraq, apparently in an effort by the US-led coalition to persuade France, Russia and China not to exercise their right of veto. Officials from France, Russia and Germany responded to the draft resolution by presenting an alternative proposal involving an extended timetable of weapons inspections in order to avert a war. On 7 March Straw submitted an amended draft resolution to the Security Council which concluded that Iraq would have 'failed to take the final opportunity to disarm unless on or before 17 March the Council concludes that Iraq has demonstrated full, unconditional, immediate and active co-operation with its disarmament obligations under resolution 1441'. On 12 March Blair proposed six new conditions that Iraq must meet in order to prove that it was serious about disarmament: this was seen as an attempt at a compromise that might encourage wavering countries in the Security Council to support an amended resolution. The British proposals came a day after President Bush had rejected a suggested 45-day postponement of any decision to go to war by six countries that had the power to influence the Security Council vote, although Blair also indicated that British forces would participate in the anticipated US-led campaign in Iraq without the passing of a second UN resolution.

On 16 March 2003 Blair attended a summit meeting in the Azores, Portugal, along with President Bush and the Spanish Prime Minister, José María Aznar López. The following day the United Kingdom, the USA and Spain withdrew their resolution from the UN, stating that they reserved the right to take their own action to ensure Iraqi disarmament. Later that day Bush issued an ultimatum giving Saddam Hussain and his two sons 48 hours to leave Baghdad or face military action. Shortly after the expiry of Bush's 48-hour deadline, on 19 March US and British armed forces launched a 'broad and concerted campaign' (codenamed 'Operation Iraqi Freedom') to oust the regime of Saddam Hussain. US-led coalition forces crossed into Iraq from Kuwait and began a steady advance towards the capital. At the same time a campaign of massive air-strikes was launched against the key symbols of the Iraqi regime in and around Baghdad, including selected military bases, communications sites, government buildings and broadcasting headquarters. The US and British forces adopted a simultaneous campaign of issuing leaflets and broadcasting radio messages, in an effort to persuade Iraqi citizens to abandon their support for the incumbent regime: their declared intention was that Operation Iraqi Freedom would precipitate the disintegration of the regime 'from within'. British troops were principally engaged in securing towns in southern Iraq, including Iraq's second city of Basra, after the US-led coalition had seized control of the key southern port of Umm Qasr and the Al-Faw Peninsula. During the campaign Blair frequently stressed his desire that the UN should play a central role in the future of Iraq. Baghdad was captured by US forces on 9 April and, following the seizure by US troops of Saddam Hussain's birthplace and power base, Tikrit (to the north of Baghdad), on 14 April, the Iraqi regime appeared to have collapsed. Although the whereabouts of Saddam Hussain and his sons remained unknown, by late April a number of senior Iraqi officials had been captured and on 1 May President Bush officially declared an end to 'major combat operations' in Iraq. Hussain's sons Uday and Qusay were killed in late July following an exchange of gunfire with US special forces in Mosul and Saddam Hussain was captured by US special forces on 14 December near Tikrit.

Meanwhile, on 22 May 2003 the UN Security Council approved Resolution 1483, which recognized the US- and British-led Coalition Provisional Authority (CPA), headed by US diplomat L. Paul Bremer, III, as the legal occupying power in Iraq, and mandated the CPA to establish a temporary Iraqi governing authority. UN sanctions imposed on Iraq in 1990 were also lifted. However, it soon became clear that the arrest or elimination of the main figures of the old regime was not diminishing the level of armed resistance to coalition forces. In July the British Government formally assumed command of the multinational task force for south-eastern Iraq, with its headquarters in Basra, comprising some 16,000 troops of which 11,000 were British. In early September the British Government agreed to dispatch a further 1,200 troops to Iraq while placing another 1,800 soldiers on stand-by. In January 2004 Blair pledged that British troops would remain in Iraq for a minimum of a further two years and that there would be no reduction in the strength of British forces in the country until the transfer of power to a provisional Iraqi administration, scheduled for July that year.

Meanwhile, there appeared to be little sign of the chemical, biological and nuclear weapons which had been the *raison d'être* of the US-led campaign and in early October 2003 the Iraq Survey Group (ISG), a group of more than 1,000 experts established by the US-led coalition in May to investigate the presence of illegal weapons in Iraq, which had been given the task of locating supplies of these weapons, published its interim report. This indicated that while no such weapons themselves had been found, there was evidence of weapons-related programmes and of Iraqi attempts to gain nuclear technology on the international black market. In January 2004 the 400-member Joint Captured Material Exploitation Group, led by an Australian brigadier, was withdrawn from Iraq, leading to suggestions that the coalition had failed to locate conventional weapons or sites, such as missiles and launchers, that might be used in conjunction with banned weapons. In mid-September a draft report compiled by the ISG in Washington, DC, USA revealed that no weapons of mass destruction had been found in Iraq. Later that month at a Labour Party conference Blair apologized for the intelligence claim that Iraq possessed weapons of mass destruction; however, he refused to apologize for sending British troops to Iraq, stating that the removal of Saddam Hussain was sufficient justification.

Following a week of intense violence in Iraq in April 2004 in which 74 people were killed and five British troops were injured in suicide bomb attacks, the Government announced plans to deploy more troops and in late May a further 370 troops were sent to Iraq bringing the number of British soldiers there to around 8,900. On 28 June, two days ahead of schedule, the USA formally transferred sovereignty to Iraq and the interim Prime Minister Dr Ayad Allawi and his cabinet ministers were sworn in. A further 400 British troops were sent to Iraq in preparation for the country's first multi-party elections for over 50 years, which took place on 30 January 2005. By the end of January 2006, according to official figures, 100 British soldiers had been killed while serving in Iraq. Earlier that month the Ministry of Defence reported that 230 British soldiers had been injured in Iraq since the invasion in 2003, 40 of them seriously.

Meanwhile, following the publication in late April 2004 of photographs showing abuse by US soldiers of Iraqi detainees, the *Daily Mirror* newspaper in early May printed photographs of alleged abuse of Iraqi prisoners by British troops. The photographs were eventually revealed to be fake and led to the removal of the newspaper's editor, Piers Morgan. In the same month it was revealed that the International Committee of the Red Cross had voiced its concern over the treatment of Iraqi prisoners by coalition forces in a report published in February; however the Government claimed it had no knowledge of such a report until much later. In May the Secretary of State for Defence, Geoffrey Hoon, admitted that British forces had taken part in incidents of assault in Iraq in the form of the forced hooding of detainees and stated that investigations were taking place into 33 incidents of alleged abuse. The Government encountered further criticism in early June when it was revealed that the Ministry of Defence was in fact investigating 75 claims of abuse. In June the House of Commons defence committee announced plans to form a cross-party parliamentary committee to investigate the role of British troops in Iraq, particularly following the transfer of power to Iraq at the end of the month. In mid-June it was announced that four British soldiers from the Royal Regiment of Fusiliers would be tried before a court martial on charges of assault and indecent assault following the emergence of personal photographs depicting incidents of abuse. They were tried in Osnabrück, Germany, in January 2005, convicted and sentenced to terms of imprisonment ranging from four months to two years. In July the Attorney-General announced that 11 British soldiers would appear before a court martial on charges, including unlawful killing, manslaughter and inhuman treatment of persons, that had been brought by the Army Prosecution Authority in connection with military operations in Iraq in 2003. In September 2005 the trial before a court martial began of four serving and three former members of the Parachute Regiment who were charged with murder and violent disorder in connection with a military operation in Iraq in 2003. All seven were acquitted in November on the grounds of insufficient evidence.

In early 1999 the United Kingdom was one of the principal participants in a NATO air offensive against the Federal Republic of Yugoslavia (now Serbia and Montenegro). The campaign, which began in March, was intended to end the atrocities committed by Serb forces against ethnic Albanians in the Serbian province of Kosovo (see the chapter on Serbia and Montenegro). Although NATO did not have a direct mandate from the UN Security Council for the offensive, it insisted that earlier UN resolutions provided ample justification for the use of force on humanitarian grounds. However, although NATO's stated targets were to be exclusively military, the campaign was widely criticized for the number of civilian casualties caused by NATO errors. It was also widely held that NATO was failing in its stated aim of averting a humanitarian disaster in Kosovo, because the air offensive had prompted Serbia to intensify its attacks on Kosovans, provoking a severe refugee crisis as hundreds of thousands of Kosovans attempted to flee the province. In late March Blair announced the establishment of a cross-departmental group to respond to the refugee crisis, and pledged £10m. in aid. Following a visit to Kosovan refugee encampments in the former Yugoslav republic of Macedonia (FYRM) in May, Blair promised to increase aid to £40m. and announced that the United Kingdom would receive 1,000 refugees a week. The Government had earlier been criticized by its NATO partners for its reluctance to accept the refugees. As the military campaign developed Blair was perceived as the most determined of NATO's leaders in his effort to force the Yugoslav President, Slobodan Milošević, to accept the alliance's terms for a cessation of hostilities. In early June Milošević conceded to these demands, and by the end of that month Serb forces had withdrawn from Kosovo. British troops formed part of the force that entered the province to enforce the peace process. In November diplomatic relations between the two countries were restored.

In late August 2001 some 2,000 British troops were deployed in the FYRM as part of a multinational 3,500-strong NATO mission (Operation Essential Harvest) mandated to disarm members of the ethnic Albanian National Liberation Army and destroy their weapons during a 30-day period. The large proportion of British troops involved in the operation provoked criticism from opposition parties and the death under fire of a British member of the mission later that month led to increased popular opposition in the United Kingdom to the British forces' presence in the FYRM. Nevertheless, following the successful completion of Operation Essential Harvest some 3,900 British troops remained in the Balkans as part of NATO's Kosovo Force. In July 2002 it was announced that the majority of the remaining 2,000 British troops in Kosovo would be withdrawn by the end of August.

The terrorist attacks on New York and Washington, DC, on 11 September 2001, for which the USA held the al-Qa'ida (Base) organization of Osama bin Laden responsible and in which 78 British citizens were killed, were denounced by Blair as an attack on the democratic world. The Prime Minister pledged that the United Kingdom would stand 'shoulder to shoulder' with the USA in its quest to bring the perpetrators of the attacks to justice and offered to provide military and diplomatic assistance to the US Government. Blair, who by late October had held talks with more than 50 foreign heads of government, played a significant role in strengthening the international coalition against terrorism and obtaining support for military action against the Islamist Taliban regime in Afghanistan, which was suspected of harbouring senior al-Qa'ida figures, including bin Laden.

On 4 October 2001 the British Government released documents detailing evidence of al-Qa'ida's responsibility for the attacks on the USA, and three days later US and British armed forces commenced the aerial bombardment of suspected al-Qa'ida camps and strategic Taliban positions in Afghanistan. Blair stressed, however, that military strikes were part of a wider, lengthy campaign against terrorism involving diplomatic, economic and political action. In mid-October British military leaders agreed to deploy up to 1,000 ground troops in Afghanistan and the following month the Secretary of State for Defence, Geoffrey Hoon, confirmed that British troops were involved in ground operations in Afghanistan. In mid-November 100 British soldiers, belonging to the Special Boat Service unit, seized control of Bagram airbase outside the Afghanistan capital, Kabul, and the number of British troops on 48-hour stand-by was raised from 4,000 to 6,000. By the end of November, however, only 400 of 6,000 troops remained on high alert.

In mid-December 2001 it was announced that the United Kingdom had agreed to lead the International Security Assistance Force (ISAF), which was granted a six-month mandate by the UN to provide security in Kabul and its environs. ISAF was expected to comprise as many as 5,000 troops from 17 countries, some 2,000 of whom would be from the United Kingdom. The first British peace-keeping troops arrived in Afghanistan later in December. In March 2002 a separate force of 1,700 British combat troops was deployed in Afghanistan to assist US special forces with their pursuit of the remaining Taliban and al-Qa'ida fighters, and later that month Hoon stated that British troops would not be withdrawn from Afghanistan until the threat of al-Qa'ida and the Taliban had been eradicated. In April 2006 around 2,000 British troops remained stationed in Afghanistan, either participating in ISAF or assisting US special forces. An additional 3,300 British troops were to be deployed in Afghanistan by June, mainly in the south of the country.

In November 1991 the United Kingdom and the USA demanded that Libya extradite for trial, either in the United Kingdom or the USA, two suspected intelligence agents who were alleged to be responsible for an explosion that destroyed a US passenger aircraft over Lockerbie, Scotland, in 1988. The United Kingdom subsequently supported the imposition, by the UN, of economic and political sanctions against Libya. In view of Libya's continued refusal to allow the suspects to be tried in Scotland, in August 1998 the United Kingdom and the USA conceded to a Libyan proposal, subsequently endorsed by the UN Security Council, that they be tried on neutral territory in the Netherlands. In March 1999 Libya finally agreed to the extradition of the suspects, who arrived for trial at Camp Zeist, near The Hague, in early April. The UN sanctions against Libya were subsequently suspended. The trial of Abd al-Baset Ali Muhammad al-Megrahi and Al-Amin Khalifa Fhimah, which was heard under Scottish law by a panel of Scottish judges in the presence of international observers, commenced in May 2000. At the end of January 2001 the judges announced that they had unanimously found al-Megrahi guilty of the murder of 270 people and sentenced him to life imprisonment. Fhimah was, however, acquitted, owing to lack of evidence of his involvement in the bombing, and freed to return to Libya. Despite mounting pressure from Arab League states, the British Secretary of State for Foreign and Commonwealth Affairs, Robin Cook, maintained that sanctions against Libya would not be permanently revoked until Libya accepted responsibility for the bombing and paid 'substantial' compensation. In mid-March 2002, following an appeal that was unanimously rejected by the five judges, al-Megrahi was transferred to a prison in Scotland to begin his sentence; it was ruled in November 2003 that he would serve 27 years in prison before becoming eligible for parole. Also in March 2002 Libya appointed an ambassador to the United Kingdom for the first time in 17 years. In early August 2002 a minister of the British Foreign and Commonwealth Office visited Libya for talks with Libyan leader Col al-Qaddafi, representing the first visit by a British government minister to Libya for some 20 years.

In March 2003 it was reported that, following negotiations in London, Libya had agreed to accept civil responsibility for the actions of its officials in the Lockerbie case and would pay US $10m. in compensation to the families of the victims. Payment of the compensation was to be a three-stage process: $4m. would be paid to each family on the permanent lifting of UN sanctions; a further $4m. would follow upon the removal of unilateral US sanctions; and a final payment of $2m. would be made when Libya was removed from the list of countries that the USA deemed to support international terrorism. However, Libya would pay only an additional $1m. to each family if the USA did not complete the second and third stages. On 16 August Libya delivered a letter to the President of the UN Security Council stating that it accepted 'responsibility for the actions of its officials' in the Lockerbie bombing; agreed to pay compensation to the families of the victims; pledged co-operation in any further Lockerbie inquiry; and agreed to continue its co-operation in the 'war against terror' and to take practical measures to ensure that such co-operation was effective. Following the transfer of $2,700m. in compensation to the International Bank of Settlements, the United Kingdom submitted a draft resolution to the Security Council requesting the formal lifting of UN sanctions against Libya. On 12 September 13 of the 15 members of the UN Security Council approved the lifting of the sanctions imposed against Libya; France and the USA abstained from the vote.

In mid-December 2003 Blair announced that Libya had agreed to disclose and dismantle its programme to develop weapons of mass destruction and long-range ballistic missiles. The statement was the culmination of nine months of clandestine negotiations between Qaddafi and British and US diplomats during which the Libyan authorities had reportedly shown evidence of a 'well advanced' nuclear weapons programme, as well as the existence of large quantities of chemical weapons and bombs designed to carry poisonous gas. Libya also agreed to adhere to the Chemical Weapons Convention and to sign an additional protocol allowing the IAEA to carry out random inspections of its facilities. In February 2004 the first meeting between cabinet-level ministers of the United Kingdom and Libya for more than 20 years took place in London. However, later that month the Secretary of the Libyan General People's Congress, Shukri Muhammad Ghanem, caused controversy when he claimed that compensation was being paid to the families of the Lockerbie victims in order to 'buy peace' and avoid sanctions, and that the country did not accept responsibility for the Lockerbie bombing; he also denied any Libyan involvement in the murder of Yvonne Fletcher, the British police officer who was shot outside the Libyan People's Bureau in London in 1984. The following day the Libyan Secretary for Foreign Liaison and International Co-operation issued a statement in which he announced his regret at Ghanem's comments and reiterated that Libya stood by its acceptance of responsibility for the Lockerbie bombing. In March 2004 Blair visited Tripoli and held talks with Qaddafi, after which the British Prime Minister stated that there was genuine hope for a 'new relationship', while Qaddafi insisted that he was willing to join the international 'war against terror'. It was also announced that British police officers would travel to Libya in early April to continue investigations into the murder of Fletcher. In September Qaddafi announced that Libya had dismantled its weapons of mass destruction programme and in December, with the unilateral sanctions imposed upon Libya by the USA having consequently been lifted, Libya paid the second instalment of its compensation to the families of those killed in the Lockerbie bombing. In May 2006 Libya was removed from the US list of states deemed to support international terrorism, paving the way for the payment of the final instalment of compensation. In October 2005 a memorandum of understanding signed by Libya and the United Kingdom guaranteed that

Libya would not subject to torture or execute any person who was repatriated to it from the United Kingdom.

In February 1990 diplomatic relations (severed in 1982) were restored between the United Kingdom and Argentina. While both countries continued to indicate that their respective claims to sovereignty over the Falkland Islands were not negotiable, political dialogue was able to proceed under a mutual arrangement to circumvent the issue of sovereignty. In September 1995 the two sides concluded an accord to allow exploration for offshore petroleum and gas deposits in the disputed waters around the Islands. A joint commission was to be established to supervise licensing and revenue-sharing. (The first licences were awarded in October 1996.) In October 1995 Major met with the Argentine President, Carlos Menem (the first meeting at this level since the 1982 war) at the UN headquarters in New York, USA. In October 1998 Menem made an official visit to the United Kingdom, the first by an Argentinian President in almost 40 years. In June 2000 relatives of the 323 Argentinians who were killed when a British submarine sank an Argentinian battleship during the Falklands conflict in 1982 announced their intention to take their claim for compensation from the British Government to the European Court of Human Rights. However, the claim was judged inadmissible the following month owing to the amount of time that had elapsed between the incident and the claim being lodged. In July 2001 Blair became the first serving British Prime Minister to visit Argentina.

The long-standing dispute with Spain over the sovereignty of Gibraltar has frequently strained relations between the two countries (see the chapters on Spain and Gibraltar). Dialogue between the United Kingdom and Spain over the future of Gibraltar resumed in July 2001 for the first time since 1998, and further discussions were held in Luxembourg in October 2001, although Gibraltar's Chief Minister, Peter Caruana, refused to attend either meeting. In November the British Government announced it would be willing to consider joint sovereignty of the territory with Spain. This statement angered Caruana, who again boycotted talks between the British and Spanish Foreign Ministers, held in Barcelona, Spain, later that month at which the British and Spanish Governments concluded that they would reach an agreement on the future of the territory by mid-2002. In January Caruana agreed to attend discussions scheduled for the following month, on the condition that Gibraltar was granted equal status at the meeting and that Britain and Spain guaranteed that any proposal regarding British-Spanish joint sovereignty of the territory would be withdrawn if rejected at a referendum. Caruana's conditions were not met and he was again absent from talks held in early February. In March some 25,000 people protested in Gibraltar against the proposed power-sharing arrangement; nevertheless, both the Spanish and British Governments reiterated their determination to proceed with plans for a joint sovereignty agreement. However, in April, just days before talks on the future of Gibraltar were scheduled to recommence, the Spanish Prime Minister stated that Spain would never cede its claim to sovereignty over the territory. In response to this announcement, Caruana insisted that if the British Government entered an agreement with Spain granting concessions over sovereignty, the Gibraltar Government would organize its own referendum, thus making it even more difficult for the British and Spanish Governments to secure popular approval for their proposals. In May Jack Straw, the British Secretary of State for Foreign and Commonwealth Affairs, visited Gibraltar and stated that he would not enter into an agreement with Spain that was not in the best interests of the citizens of Gibraltar. In July Straw confirmed that the United Kingdom was willing to share sovereignty of the territory with Spain, subject to approval by the residents of Gibraltar at a referendum, provoking angry protests in Gibraltar, and later in July Caruana announced that Gibraltar would conduct its own referendum on the sovereignty issue by the end of October. Both the Spanish and the British Governments condemned Caruana's decision to hold a referendum and stated that it would lack any validity. The Gibraltar referendum held on 7 November, which explicitly asked if Gibraltarians approved 'of the principle that Britain and Spain should share sovereignty over Gibraltar' resulted in an overwhelming rejection of the Spanish and British proposals. Of the electorate, 99.0% voted against shared sovereignty; the rate of voter participation was recorded at 87.9%. In June 2003 the British Government announced that talks with Spain regarding the possibility of sharing the sovereignty of Gibraltar had failed and suspended any further negotiations over the issue indefinitely. In December 2004 a tripartite meeting between the United Kingdom, Spain and Gibraltar was held in the United Kingdom, and it was subsequently announced that henceforth decisions on the territory's future must be agreed by all three parties. In March 2006 Straw sought to reassure Spain that, in the view of the British Government, Spanish rights over Gibraltar would not be affected by a proposed new constitution for the territory, despite the inclusion of references to the right to self-determination of Gibraltarians.

Relations with Iran, which had improved during the early 2000s, were strained following the arrest in August 2003 in northern England of Hade Soleimanpour, a former Iranian ambassador to Argentina, on suspicion of involvement in a terrorist attack in Buenos Aires in 1994 in which 85 people were killed. In September 2003 the Iranian ambassador to the United Kingdom, Morteza Sarmadi, was recalled to Tehran for consultations and the following day the British embassy in Iran was temporarily closed after shots were fired at the building. Sarmadi returned to the United Kingdom later that week; however, the British embassy in Tehran came under fire on two further occasions, prompting the Foreign and Commonwealth Office to protest strongly to the Iranian authorities. In November the United Kingdom rejected Argentina's request for extradition and Soleimanpour, who had earlier been released on bail, subsequently returned to Iran. Later that month there was a further attack on the British embassy in Tehran. In May 2004 demonstrators demanded the closure of the embassy and the removal of the ambassador, in protest against British policy in Iraq, and threw petrol bombs at the building. Diplomatic relations were further strained in June when three British patrol crafts and eight Royal Navy personnel were captured on the Shatt al-Arab waterway by Iranian authorities who claimed the servicemen had entered Iranian territorial waters. After intense negotiations between British and Iranian diplomats the men were released four days later and claimed that they had been forcibly escorted into Iranian waters. In 2005–06 there remained tensions between the two countries regarding Iran's uranium enrichment projects, which the United Kingdom claimed it was developing in order to build atomic weapons.

Government

The United Kingdom is a constitutional monarchy. The Sovereign is the Head of State and the monarchy is hereditary. Parliament consists of the House of Commons and the House of Lords. The 646 members of the Commons are elected for a maximum of five years by direct suffrage by all citizens of 18 years and over, using single-member constituencies. The House of Lords is composed of hereditary Peers of the Realm and Life Peers and Peeresses created by the Sovereign for outstanding public service. Legislation may be initiated in either House but it usually originates in the Commons. Each bill has three readings in the Commons and it is then passed to the House of Lords who may return it to the Commons with amendments or suggestions. The House of Lords may delay, but cannot prevent, any bill from becoming law once it has been passed by the Commons. Executive power is held by the Cabinet, headed by the Prime Minister. The Cabinet is responsible to the House of Commons.

The Northern Ireland Act 1974 made the Secretary of State for Northern Ireland and his ministers answerable to Parliament at Westminster for the government of Northern Ireland, under a parliamentary order which is renewable annually. In October 1982 a 78-member Northern Ireland Assembly was elected, in accordance with the Northern Ireland Act 1982: its role was primarily consultative, pending the devolution of executive power. The 1985 Anglo-Irish Agreement, signed by the Prime Ministers of the United Kingdom and of the Republic of Ireland in November, left the constitutional status of Northern Ireland unaltered, but gave the Republic of Ireland a consultative role in Northern Irish affairs, through an Intergovernmental Conference. In June 1986 the British Government announced the dissolution of the Northern Ireland Assembly, four months before the end of its four-year term, following a boycott of meetings by some members, in protest at the Anglo-Irish Agreement. Elections to a new 108-member Assembly were held on 25 June 1998, as part of the multi-party agreement on the future governance of Northern Ireland, approved by a popular referendum in May. An Executive Committee, headed by a First Minister, was constituted from among the legislative members. Responsibility for all matters formerly implemented by the Northern Ireland Office was transferred to the devolved authority under new parliamentary legislation implemented in December 1999. The 1998 Agreement also provided for the establishment of a North/South Ministerial Council, to facilitate co-operation between the Irish Government and representatives of the Northern Ireland executive on specific cross-border and all-island concerns, and of a British-Irish Council, comprising representatives of British and Irish Governments, members of the devolved authorities in Northern Ireland, Scotland and Wales, and representatives of the Isle of Man and the Channel Islands. The arrangements of the Anglo-Irish Agreement were replaced by a British-Irish Intergovernmental Conference, with responsibility to oversee the new political institutions. The new Northern Ireland institutions were suspended in February 2000, owing to a political impasse concerning the decommissioning of paramilitary weapons and Northern Ireland was returned to direct rule. On 30 May, following an agreement on the issue of decommissioning, power was once again transferred from Westminster to the new Northern Ireland institutions. The Northern Ireland Executive was suspended again on 14 October 2002 and Northern Ireland was returned to direct rule from Westminster.

In 1999 devolved legislative authorities were established in Scotland and Wales. In Scotland a new elected parliament, based in Edinburgh, was established with powers to legislate on all domestic matters (incl. education, health, local government and law and order) and with a mandate to vary taxes set by the Government of the United Kingdom by 3%. The Assembly has 129 members, elected every four years by a combined system of direct voting, on the basis of Westminster parliamentary constituencies, and a form of proportional representation, whereby additional members are elected from a party list on the basis of the larger constituencies used for elections to the European Parliament. The Welsh Assembly, located in Cardiff, undertook responsibility for issues covered by the Welsh Office of the Government of the United Kingdom. The 60-member Assembly was elected under the same system as in Scotland. Elections to the two Assemblies took place simultaneously in May 1999 and the transfer of powers took place on 1 July.

Legislation providing for the abolition of all but 92 hereditary peers and the establishment of an interim second chamber pending a definitive reform of the House of Lords was passed in November 1999.

Defence

The United Kingdom is a member of the North Atlantic Treaty Organization (NATO, see p. 314) and maintains a regular army. The total strength of the armed forces at 1 August 2005, including those enlisted outside Britain (3,740), was 205,890 (army 116,760, navy 40,630, air force 48,500). In November 2000 the United Kingdom pledged to contribute 12,500 troops to a European Union (EU) rapid reaction force, which was to be ready to be deployed by 2003. In November 2004 the United Kingdom committed troops to two of 13 EU 'battle groups' (one comprising solely British troops and one in conjunction with the Netherlands). All battle groups were to be ready for deployment to crisis areas in 2007, but the British battle group was to be prepared for duties in 2005–06. There is no compulsory military service. The United Kingdom possesses its own nuclear weapons. Government budgeted defence expenditure for 2005 totalled £27,500m.

Economic Affairs

In 2004, according to estimates by the World Bank, the United Kingdom's gross national income (GNI), measured at average 2002–04 prices, was US $2,016,393m., equivalent to $33,940 per head (or $31,640 per head on an international purchasing-power parity basis). During 1995–2004, it was estimated, the population increased at an average annual rate of 0.2%, while gross domestic product (GDP) per head increased, in real terms, by an average of 2.5% per year. Overall GDP increased, in real terms, at an average annual rate of 2.8% in 1995–2004; it increased by 2.5% in 2003 and by 3.2% in 2004, according to official figures.

Agriculture (including hunting, forestry and fishing) contributed 0.9% of GDP and engaged 1.4% of the employed labour force in 2004. The principal crops include wheat, sugar beet, potatoes and barley. Livestock-rearing (particularly poultry and cattle) and animal products are important, as is fishing. In 2001 the agricultural sector was adversely affected by the outbreak of foot-and-mouth disease, which resulted in the slaughter of more than 6.5m. animals. The GDP of the agricultural sector increased, in real terms, by an average of 0.7% per year during 1995–2004; it declined by 2.1% in 2003, but increased by 1.7% in 2004.

Industry (including mining, manufacturing, construction and power) contributed 24.8% of GDP and engaged 19.3% of the employed labour force in 2004. Industrial GDP increased, in real terms, at an average annual rate of 0.8% during 1995–2004; it increased by 0.9% in 2003 and by 1.1% in 2004.

Mining (including petroleum and gas extraction) contributed 2.8% of GDP in 2004 and engaged 0.8% of the employed labour force in 1990. Natural gas, sand and gravel, limestone, crude petroleum, igneous rock and coal are the principal minerals produced. The GDP of the mining sector decreased, in real terms, at an average annual rate of 0.8% during 1995–2003; it declined by 0.2% in 2002 and by 5.4% in 2003.

Manufacturing provided 14.3% of GDP and engaged 11.5% of the employed labour force in 2004. Measured by the value of output, the principal branches of manufacturing in 1997 were transport equipment (accounting for 12.5% of the total), food products (11.8%), machinery (10.8%), chemical products (10.0%) and metals and metal products (7.6%). In real terms, the GDP of the manufacturing sector increased at an average annual rate of 0.3% during 1995–2003; manufacturing GDP declined by 2.6% in 2002, but increased by 0.4% in 2003.

Energy is derived principally from natural gas, petroleum and coal, although natural gas is increasingly favoured in preference to coal. Of the United Kingdom's total consumption of energy in 2004, 40.9% was derived from natural gas, 32.6% from petroleum, 16.7% from solid fuels and 8.3% from primary electricity (including nuclear power, hydroelectric power and imports). In March 2006 23 nuclear power reactors were operating in the United Kingdom. In 2005 mineral fuels accounted for about 8.9% of the value of total merchandise imports. In mid-2003 plans were announced for the construction of three new offshore wind farms, which would provide sufficient energy to power 15% of British homes upon their completion. It was anticipated that they would supply some 5% of the United Kingdom's electric power by 2010.

Services accounted for 74.3% of GDP and engaged 79.2% of the employed labour force in 2004. The United Kingdom is an important international centre for business and financial services. Financial intermediation and other business services (including renting and real estate) contributed 30.0% of GDP in 2004. Receipts from tourism totalled £12,805m. in 2000. However, the tourism industry suffered badly in 2001 as a result of the foot-and-mouth crisis and the events of 11 September, and tourism receipts declined by almost 12%, to £11,306m. In 2002 the sector recovered slightly; receipts from tourism increased to £11,737m. in that year and to £11,855m. in 2003. A significant increase, to £13,047m., was recorded in 2004. Transport and communications are also important, and the sector contributed 7.2% of GDP in 2004. In real terms, the GDP of the services sector increased at an average annual rate of 3.6% during 1995–2004; it increased by 2.6% in 2003 and by 3.8% in 2004.

In 2004 the United Kingdom recorded a visible trade deficit of £58,614m., and there was a deficit of £22,975m. on the current account of the balance of payments. In 2005 the principal source of imports (13.9%) was Germany, while the principal market for exports in that year was the USA (14.7%). Other major trading partners include France, the Netherlands, Ireland and Belgium-Luxembourg. The principal imports in 2005 were mechanical and electrical machinery and road vehicles. These items also constituted the United Kingdom's principal exports, together with petroleum and petroleum products.

In 2004/05 there was an estimated budgetary deficit of £19,400m. (equivalent to 1.6% of GDP). The annual rate of inflation averaged 2.6% in 1995–2004; it increased to 3.0% in 2004, but slowed to 2.8% in 2005. The rate of unemployment was 5.1% in the final quarter of 2005.

The United Kingdom is a member of the European Union (EU, see p. 228). It is also a member of the Organisation for Economic Co-operation and Development (OECD, see p. 320).

In the early 1990s the British economy experienced a recession; however, by 1994 the economy had recovered and strong GDP growth was recorded during the late 1990s. In May 1997 the newly elected Labour Government confirmed its commitment to restricting the inflation rate to 2.5%, and granted the Bank of England operational independence for monetary policy to achieve the target within the framework of long-term economic stability. Following the announcement in mid-2003 that four of the five key principles for British participation in European Economic and Monetary Union (EMU, see p. 265) had not yet been fulfilled, the Chancellor of the Exchequer, Gordon Brown, stated that the United Kingdom would adopt the harmonized index of consumer prices method (HICP), used by other EMU members and the USA, to calculate inflation. This came into force in December 2003, and the annual inflation target under HICP was reduced to 2.0%. Annual HICP inflation was 2.5% in the year to November 2005, mainly as a result of higher petroleum and transport prices. In the early 2000s Brown effected a number of substantial increases in expenditure on public services, made possible by the continuing expansion of the economy, with total managed expenditure scheduled to rise to £552,000m. in the financial year 2006/07. From early 2002 the global economic slowdown, partly caused by the effects of the terrorist attacks on the USA in September 2001 (see Recent History), prompted the Bank of England to introduce a series of interest rate reductions in order to stimulate the stagnating economy, and in July 2003 the interest rate was cut to just 3.5%—the lowest level since 1964. Between November 2003 and August 2004, however, the Bank of England gradually increased the interest rate to 4.75% in an attempt to slow the housing market, where the low cost of borrowing had fuelled rapid price increases. In August 2005, in response to evidence of a renewed weakening of the economy, the rate was cut by 0.25%. Nevertheless, the British economy has remained one of the more robust in the western world, with unemployment and inflation lower than in most European countries. In September 2004 the number of unemployed Britons fell to its lowest level since records began in 1984, with just 4.6% of the population seeking employment, although by January 2006 this figure had increased to 5.0%. The major cause for concern, however, became the significantly higher Treasury borrowing figures that were required in order to meet government spending requirements. The IMF warned in December 2003 that Brown would have to reduce expenditure by £1,200m. per year over the next five years or raise taxes in order to stay within his desired limits of borrowing (1% of national income). Public-sector borrowing remained high, however, reaching an estimated £37,000m. in 2005/06, despite constant reassurances from the Treasury that reductions were in sight. In March 2006 Brown announced that net borrowing would fall to £23,000m. by 2010/11. There were also fears concerning the rapidly widening current-account deficit, which reached an unprecedented £31,900m. in 2005. Meanwhile, GDP growth declined to 1.8% in 2005 and was forecast at 2.0%–2.5% for 2006.

Education

Education in the United Kingdom is compulsory for all children between the ages of five (four in Northern Ireland) and 16 and takes place in several stages: nursery (now part of the foundation stage in England), primary, secondary, further and higher education. Further education, the non-compulsory fourth stage, covers non-advanced education, which can be taken at both further (including tertiary) education colleges, higher education institutions and increasingly in secondary schools. Higher education, the fifth stage, is study beyond the General Certificate of Education (GCE) Advanced Level (A Level) and its equivalent, which, for most full-time students, takes place in higher education institutions.

Educational establishments in the United Kingdom are administered and financed in several ways. Most schools are controlled by local education authorities (LEAs), which are part of the structure of local government, but some are 'assisted', receiving grants direct from central government sources and being controlled by governing bodies, which have a substantial degree of autonomy. Alongside the state system, there are independent schools, which do not receive grants from public funds but are financed by fees and endowments; many of these schools are administered by charitable trusts and church organizations.

The Learning and Skills Council (LSC) is responsible for funding the further education sector in England and the National Council for Education and Training for Wales (part of Education and Learning Wales—ELWa) does so for Wales. The LSC in England is also responsible for funding provision for non-prescribed higher education in further education sector colleges and further education provided by LEA maintained and other institutions, referred to as 'external institutions'. In Wales, ELWa funds further education provision made by further education institutions via a third party or sponsored arrangements. The Scottish Further Education Funding Council (SFEFC) funds further education colleges in Scotland, while the Department for Employment and Learning funds further education colleges in Northern Ireland.

Government finance for publicly funded higher education institutions (to help meet the costs of teaching, research and related activities) is distributed by the Higher Education Funding Councils (HEFC) in England and Scotland, the Higher Education Council (ELWa) in Wales, and the Department of Employment and Learning in Northern Ireland. In addition, some designated higher education (mainly Higher National Diplomas/Higher National Certificates and Certificates of Higher Education) is also funded by these sources. The further education sources mentioned above fund the remainder.

Student loans are the main form of support for assistance with living costs for higher education students. The maximum loan in 2005/06 for full-time students was £5,175. The amount of loan depends on where a student lives or studies, the length of the academic year, the course of study and the year of the course. The amount of loan paid also depends on the student's and their family's income. Loans are repaid on the basis of income after the student has left their course, and only when they start earning over £15,000. Most students who began full-time undergraduate courses at publicly funded higher academic institutions in or after 1998/99, or their parents or spouse, have to contribute towards the tuition fees for each year of the course. The level of the contribution is means-tested. Those on lower family incomes get free tuition. From September 2004 a full-time undergraduate would have to pay up to £1,150 a year towards their tuition fees. From 2006, it is envisaged that universities in England will be entitled to set variable fees for individual courses, up to a maximum of £3,000, which will rise in line with inflation. However, any rise above the current (2005/06) level of £1,175 will be subject to an access agreement in partnership with the Office for Fair Access. Since the academic year 2000/01, eligible full-time Scottish-domiciled or EU students who are studying in Scotland no longer pay tuition fees. Other additional forms of student support include dependant's allowances, young and mature student bursaries, hardship funds, disabled students' allowance and care leavers' grant, and the Higher Education (HE) Grant, introduced in September 2004.

Responsibility for education is substantially devolved: the Secretary of State for Education and Skills is responsible, in principle, for all sectors of education in England (the individual LEAs have substantial autonomy over the education system in their area), while the Secretary of State for Wales is responsible for all non-university education in Wales and, since April 1993, for the college of the University of Wales. The Secretaries of State for Scotland and Northern Ireland have full educational responsibilities. Assessment of the quality of schools is undertaken in England by an inspectorate, the Office for Standards in Education, in Wales by Her Majesty's Chief Inspectorate For Education and Training in Wales, in Scotland by Her Majesty's Inspectorate of Education and in Northern Ireland by the Education and Training Inspectorate.

In recent years there has been a major expansion of pre-school education. Many children under the age of five attend state nursery schools or nursery schools attached to primary schools. Others may attend playgroups in the voluntary sector or privately run nurseries. In England and Wales many primary schools also operate an early admission policy where they admit children under the age of five into 'reception classes'. The primary stage covers three age ranges: nursery (under five), infant (five to seven or eight) and junior (up to 11 or 12) but in Scotland and Northern Ireland there is generally no distinction between infant and junior schools. Most public-sector primary schools take both boys and girls in mixed classes.

Secondary education generally begins at the age of 11, although in England many areas have 'middle schools' for children aged eight to 12 years or nine to 13 years. In most areas, the state-maintained system of comprehensive schools prevails. Pupils are admitted to such schools without reference to ability. Some localities, however, retain a system of grammar and secondary modern schools, to which admission is determined through a test of ability. Specialist schools covering 10 areas (arts, business and enterprise, engineering, humanities, language, mathematics and computing, music, science, sports and technology) also operate in England. The Specialist Schools Programme helps schools, in partnership with private-sector sponsors and supported by additional government funding, to establish distinctive identities through their chosen specialisms and achieve their target to raise standards. Specialist schools have a special focus on their chosen subject area, but must meet the National Curriculum requirements and deliver a broad and balanced education to all pupils. Schools can also combine any two specialisms. Special schools (day or boarding) are provided by LEAs for certain children with special educational needs, although the vast majority are educated in ordinary schools. All children attending special schools are offered a curriculum designed to overcome their learning difficulties and to enable them to become self-reliant.

Examinations for the single-system General Certificate of Secondary Education (GCSE) may be taken (usually at the age of 16) in as many subjects as a candidate wishes. In 1989 the Government implemented legislation introduced under the Education Reform Act (1988), which provided for a National Curriculum and national testing of pupils aged seven, 11 and 14 years in state schools in England and Wales (Key Stages 1, 2 and 3, respectively). All state schools in England, Wales and Northern Ireland must conform to the national curricula, which set out which subjects pupils should study, what they should be taught and what standards they should achieve. In Scotland the curriculum in state schools is not prescribed by statute, however the Secretary of State for Scotland issues national advice and guidance to schools and Scottish Local Authorities. The Qualifications and Curriculum Authority is the statutory body which advises the Government on all matters concerned with the curriculum and all aspects of school examinations and assessment in state schools in England. It is also responsible for vocational qualifications. Similar arrangements operate for Wales, Scotland and Northern Ireland. The A Level, generally taken at the age of 18, was introduced in the early 1950s, and serves as a qualification for entrance to higher education. Over the years there have been attempts to broaden the curriculum and experience of those taking A Levels (e.g. the Advanced Supplementary examination in 1989). In September 2000, however, a completely revised approach to A Level was introduced, based entirely on a modular approach. Candidates are now able to take modules as they proceed through the course, rather than being examined in a single session at the end of the course. The new A Level qualification consists of two parts, the AS (Advanced Subsidiary), which can also be taken as a free-standing qualification, and A2. All students now take the AS and then, where appropriate, proceed to the more challenging A2 to complete their A level. In 1999/2000 National Qualifications (NQ) were introduced in Scotland. NQs include Standard Grades, Intermediate 1 and 2 and Higher Grades. Pupils study for the Scottish Certificate of Education (SCE)/NQ Standard Grade, approximately equivalent to GCSE, in their third (S3) and fourth (S4) years of secondary schooling (roughly ages 14 and 15), with courses taking two years to complete. Each subject has several elements, some of which are internally assessed in school, and Standard Grade courses are offered at three levels: Credit (grades 1–2), General (grades 3–4) and Foundation (grades 5–6). The Higher Grade requires one further year of study and for the more able candidates the range of subjects taken may be as wide as at Standard Grade with as many as five or six subjects spanning both arts and science. Three or more Highers are regarded as being approximately the equivalent of two or more A Levels.

Since 1986 the National Council for Vocational Qualifications (NCVQ) has established a framework of National Vocational Qualifications (NVQ) in England, Wales and Northern Ireland. The framework is based on five defined levels of achievement, ranging from Level 1, broadly equating to foundation skills in semi-skilled occupations, to Level 5, equating to professional/senior management occupations. The competence-based system has also been extended in Scotland through a system of Scottish Vocational Qualifications (SVQ) along similar lines to the NVQs. General National Vocational Qualifications (GNVQ), along with General Scottish Vocational Qualifications (GSVQ) have also been introduced. GNVQs, which are normally studied in school or college, aim to incorporate skills required by employers and are designed to develop the skills and understanding needed in vocational areas such as business, engineering or health and social care, in order to provide an introduction into both further education and employment. They are awarded at Foundation and Intermediate levels and through Vocational Certificates of Education (VCEs—more commonly known as vocational A levels), which replaced the Advanced level GNVQ. GSVQs are awarded on the basis of a modular framework of National Certificate Units, which give candidates practical and knowledge-based vocational skills and are taken in secondary schools and colleges.

Further and higher education may be pursued through vocational or academic courses, on a full-time, part-time or 'sandwich' basis. The decision to admit students is made by each institution according to its own entrance requirements. The term 'further education' may be used in a general sense to cover all non-advanced courses taken after the period of compulsory education, but more commonly it excludes those staying on at secondary school and those in higher education, i.e. courses in universities and colleges leading to qualifications above A Level, SCE Higher Grade, GNVQ/NVQ level three, and their equivalents. Since 1 April 1993 sixth-form colleges have been included in the further education sector.

Higher education is defined as courses that are of a standard that is higher than A Level, the SCE Higher Grade of the SCE, GNVQ/NVQ Level 3 or the Edexcel (formerly BTEC) or SQA National Certificate/Diploma. Higher education students are most likely to be working towards one of the following qualifications. An Honours degree: the most common of these is Bachelor of Arts (BA Hons) and Bachelor of Science (BSc Hons). These are usually full-time three-year courses but can also be taken as longer part-time courses and may be available through distance learning. In Scotland, where students usually start a year earlier, a full-time first-degree generally takes four years for Honours and three years for the broad-based Ordinary degree. A Foundation degree: this is a new vocationally focused higher education qualification. It aims to increase the number of people qualified at higher technician and associate professional level (e.g. legal executives, engineering technicians, personnel officers, laboratory technicians, teaching assistants). Both full- and part-time courses are offered in a variety of work-related subjects and offer progression to a full Honours degree. A Higher National Diploma (HND) or Diploma of Higher Education (Dip HE): these take two years full-time, and there is the option of turning them into an Honours degree by studying for a further year. Some students go on to do postgraduate studies, usually leading to a masters degree, such as a Master of Arts (MA), or Master of Science (MSc), or to a Doctorate (PhD). A Masters degree usually lasts one year full-time or two years part-time. A PhD usually lasts three years full-time or six years part-time.

In 2003/04 there were 89 universities (including the Open University) and 60 other higher education institutions in the United Kingdom, together with the privately funded University of Buckingham, offering courses of higher education. The Open University, founded in 1969, and funded directly by the Department for Education and Skills, provides degree courses by means of television, radio, audio/video cassettes, correspondence tuition, online (using interactive CD-ROM or computer software) and short residential schools. No formal qualifications are required for entry to its courses. Some British universities and colleges also now offer study through distance learning, usually learning at home or work.

Budgetary expenditure on education and training in 2004/05 totalled an estimated £65,300m, representing 13.5% of total expenditure.

Public Holidays

2006: 1 January (New Year's Day), 2 January* (Scotland only), 17 March (St Patrick's Day, Northern Ireland only), 14 April* (Good Friday), 17 April† (Easter Monday), 1 May* (Early May Holiday), 29 May (Spring Holiday), 12 July (Battle of the Boyne, Northern Ireland only), 7 August* (Summer Bank Holiday, Scotland only), 28 August† (Late Summer Bank Holiday), 25 December (Christmas Day), 26 December* (Boxing Day).

2007: 1 January (New Year's Day), 2 January* (Scotland only), 19 March (St Patrick's Day, Northern Ireland only), 6 April* (Good Friday), 9 April† (Easter Monday), 7 May* (Early May Holiday), 28 May (Spring Holiday), 12 July (Battle of the Boyne, Northern Ireland only), 6 August* (Summer Bank Holiday, Scotland only), 27 August† (Late Summer Bank Holiday), 25 December (Christmas Day), 26 December* (Boxing Day).

* Bank Holidays but not national holidays in Scotland.
† Excluding Scotland.

Weights and Measures

The metric system of weights and measures is now the primary system in force, although the imperial system is still used in limited areas.

Weight

1 pound (lb) = 16 ounces (oz) = 453.59 grams.
14 pounds = 1 stone = 6.35 kilograms.
112 pounds = 1 hundredweight (cwt) = 50.8 kilograms.
20 hundredweights = 1 ton = 1,016 kilograms.

Length

1 yard (yd) = 3 feet (ft) = 36 inches (ins) = 0.9144 metre.
1,760 yards = 1 mile = 1.609 kilometres.

Capacity

1 gallon = 4 quarts = 8 pints = 4.546 litres.

THE UNITED KINGDOM

Statistical Survey

Source (unless otherwise stated): Office for National Statistics, 1 Drummond Gate, London SW1V 2QQ; internet www.statistics.gov.uk.

Statistics refer to the United Kingdom unless otherwise indicated.

Area and Population

AREA, POPULATION AND DENSITY

Area (sq km)	242,514*
Population usually resident (census results)	
21 April 1991	56,466,700
29 April 2001	
Males	28,581,233
Females	30,207,961
Total	58,789,194
Population (official estimates at mid-year)	
2002	59,321,700†
2003	59,553,800
2004	59,834,300
Density (per sq km) at mid-2004	246.7

* 93,638 sq miles.
† Figure revised on basis of local authority population studies.

DISTRIBUTION OF POPULATION
(at mid-2004, '000)

	Area (sq km)	Population	Density (per sq km)
Great Britain	228,937	58,124.0	253.9
England	130,281	50,093.1	384.5
Wales	20,732	2,952.5	142.4
Scotland	77,925	5,078.4	65.2
Northern Ireland	13,576	1,710.3	126.0
Total	242,514	59,834.3	246.7

ADMINISTRATIVE AREAS
(population estimates at mid-2003, '000)

England

Greater London	7,387.8
Metropolitan Counties:	
Greater Manchester	2,531.0
Merseyside	1,364.2
South Yorkshire	1,272.6
Tyne and Wear	1,083.2
West Midlands	2,578.4
West Yorkshire	2,095.9
Unitary Authorities:	
Bath and North-east Somerset	171.0
Blackburn with Darwen	139.8
Blackpool	142.4
Bournemouth	163.6
Bracknell Forest	110.1
Brighton and Hove	251.5
Bristol	391.5
Darlington	98.2
Derby	233.2
East Riding of Yorkshire	321.3
Halton	118.4
Hartlepool	90.2
Herefordshire	176.9
Isle of Wight	136.2
Kingston upon Hull	247.9
Leicester	283.9
Luton	185.2
Medway	251.1
Middlesbrough	139.0
Milton Keynes	215.7
North Lincolnshire	155.1
North Somerset	191.4
Stoke-on-Trent	238.0
Swindon	181.2
Telford and Wrekin	160.2
Thurrock	145.3
Torbay	131.2
Warrington	193.2
West Berkshire	144.2
Windsor and Maidenhead	135.3
Wokingham	151.2
York	183.1
Non-Metropolitan Counties:	
Bedfordshire	388.6
Buckinghamshire	478.0
Cambridgeshire	571.0
Cheshire	678.7
Cornwall/Isles of Scilly	513.5
Cumbria	489.8
Derbyshire	743.0
Devon	714.9
Dorset	398.2
Durham	494.2
East Sussex	496.1
Essex	1,324.1
Gloucestershire	568.5
Hampshire	1,251.0
Hertfordshire	1,040.9
Kent	1,348.7
Lancashire	1,147.0
Leicestershire	619.3
Lincolnshire	665.3
Norfolk	810.7
North Yorkshire	576.1
North-east Lincolnshire	157.4
Nottingham	273.9
Peterborough	158.8
Plymouth	241.5
Poole	137.5
Portsmouth	188.8
Reading	144.2
Redcar and Cleveland	139.1
Rutland	35.7
Slough	118.8
South Gloucestershire	246.9
Southampton	221.1
Southend-on-Sea	160.3
Stockton-on-Tees	186.2
Northamptonshire	642.7
Northumberland	309.3
Nottinghamshire	755.5
Oxfordshire	615
Shropshire	286.8
Somerset	507.5
Staffordshire	811.0
Suffolk	678.1
Surrey	1,064.6
Warwickshire	519.3
West Sussex	759
Wiltshire	440.8
Worcestershire	549.3

Wales

Unitary Authorities:

Blaenau Gwent	68.9
Bridgend	129.9
Caerphilly	170.2
Cardiff	315.1
Carmarthenshire	176.0
Ceredigion	77.2
Conwy	110.9
Denbighshire	94.9
Flintshire	149.4
Gwynedd	117.5
Isle of Anglesey	68.4
Merthyr Tydfil	55.4
Monmouthshire	86.2
Neath Port Talbot	135.3
Newport	139.3
Pembrokeshire	116.3
Powys	129.3
Rhondda Cynon Taff	231.6
Swansea	224.7
Torfaen	90.7
Vale of Glamorgan	121.0
Wrexham	129.7

Scotland

Unitary Authorities:

Aberdeen City	206.6
Aberdeenshire	229.4
Angus	107.5
Argyll and Bute	91.3
Clackmannanshire	47.7
Dumfries and Galloway	147.2
Dundee City	143.1
East Ayrshire	119.5
East Dunbartonshire	107.0
East Lothian	91.1
East Renfrewshire	89.7
Edinburgh, City of	448.4
Eilean Siar	26.1
Falkirk	145.9
Fife	352.0
Glasgow City	577.0
Highland	209.1
Inverclyde	83.1
Midlothian	79.7
Moray	87.5
North Ayrshire	136.0
North Lanarkshire	321.9
Orkney Islands	19.3
Perth and Kinross	136.0
Renfrewshire	171.0
Scottish Borders	108.3
Shetland Islands	21.9
South Ayrshire	111.6
South Lanarkshire	303.0
Stirling	86.4
West Dunbartonshire	92.3
West Lothian	161.0

Northern Ireland

Unitary Authorities:

Antrim	49.2
Ards	74.4
Armagh	55.4
Ballymena	59.6
Ballymoney	27.8
Banbridge	43.1
Belfast	271.6
Carrickfergus	38.5
Castlereagh	66.1
Coleraine	56.0
Cookstown	33.4
Craigavon	82.2
Derry	106.4
Down	65.2
Dungannon	48.7
Fermanagh	58.7
Larne	30.9
Limavady	33.6
Lisburn	109.6
Magherafelt	40.9
Moyle	16.3
Newry and Mourne	89.6
Newtownabbey	80.3
North Down	77.1
Omagh	49.5
Strabane	38.6

Sources: Office for National Statistics; General Register Office for Scotland; Northern Ireland Statistics and Research Agency.

THE UNITED KINGDOM

Statistical Survey

PRINCIPAL LOCALITIES*
(population estimates at mid-2003, '000)

Locality	Population	Locality	Population
Greater London (capital)	7,387.8	Belfast	271.6
Birmingham	992.1	Newcastle upon Tyne	266.6
Leeds	715.2	Bolton	263.8
Glasgow City	577.0	Walsall	252.4
Sheffield	512.5	Rotherham	251.5
Bradford	477.8	Brighton and Hove	251.5
Edinburgh	448.4	Medway	251.1
Liverpool	441.9	Kingston upon Hull	247.9
Manchester	432.4	South Gloucestershire	246.9
Bristol	391.5	Plymouth	241.5
Kirklees	391.4	Wolverhampton	238.9
Fife	352.1	Stoke-on-Trent	238.0
North Lanarkshire	321.9	Derby	233.2
East Riding of Yorkshire	321.3	Rhondda, Cynon, Taff	231.6
Wakefield	318.3	Aberdeenshire	229.4
Cardiff	315.1	Swansea	224.7
Wirral	313.8	Southampton	221.1
Coventry	305.0	Barnsley	220.1
Dudley	304.7	Oldham	218.0
Wigan	303.9	Salford	216.5
South Lanarkshire	303.0	Milton Keynes	215.7
Doncaster	288.4	Tameside	213.5
Sandwell	285.0	Trafford	211.7
Leicester	283.9	Highland	209.1
Sunderland	283.1	Rochdale	206.6
Stockport	282.5	Aberdeen City	206.6
Sefton	281.6	Solihull	200.3
Nottingham	273.9		

* Local authority areas with populations greater than 200,000.

Sources: Office for National Statistics; General Register Offices for Scotland and Northern Ireland.

BIRTHS, MARRIAGES AND DEATHS*

	Registered live births Number	Rate (per 1,000)	Registered marriages Number	Rate (per 1,000)	Registered deaths Number	Rate (per 1,000)
1997	726,622	12.5	310,218	5.3	632,517	10.8
1998	716,888	12.3	304,797	5.2	627,592	10.7
1999	699,976	12.0	310,083	5.3	629,476	10.7
2000	697,029	11.6	305,912	5.2	610,579	10.4
2001	669,123	11.4	286,133	4.9	604,393	10.2
2002	668,777	11.3	293,021	4.9	608,045	10.2
2003	695,549	11.7	308,620	5.1	612,085	10.3
2004†	716,000	12.1	311,180	5.2	583,100	9.7

* In England and Wales, figures for births are tabulated by year of occurrence, while figures for Scotland and Northern Ireland are tabulated by year of registration. Births to non-resident mothers in Northern Ireland are excluded from the figures for the United Kingdom.
† Provisional figures.

Sources: Office for National Statistics; General Register Office for Scotland; Northern Ireland Statistics and Research Agency.

Expectation of life (WHO estimates, years at birth): 79 (males 76; females 81) in 2003 (Source: WHO, *World Health Report*).

IMMIGRATION AND EMIGRATION*

Immigrants
('000)

Nationality and country†	2001	2002	2003
EU‡	86	89	101
Commonwealth countries	199	191	207
Australia, New Zealand, Canada	77	61	68
South Africa	22	27	28
Bangladesh, India, Sri Lanka	32	36	45
Pakistan	18	10	13
Caribbean	3	5	4
Other	47	52	49
Other territories	194	232	205
USA	24	28	28
Middle East	30	32	27
Total	**480**	**513**	**513**

Emigrants
('000)

Nationality and country†	2001	2002	2003
EU‡	94	125	122
Commonwealth countries	114	123	131
Australia, New Zealand, Canada	80	84	90
South Africa	8	10	14
Bangladesh, India, Sri Lanka	8	7	7
Pakistan	3	4	4
Caribbean	2	2	1
Other	13	16	15
Other territories			
USA	28	37	27
Middle East	9	12	7
Total	**308**	**359**	**362**

* Figures are derived from a small sample of passengers and refer to long-term migration only, excluding all movements between the UK and the Republic of Ireland and short-term visitors who are granted extensions of stay in the UK or abroad. Long-term migrants are defined as persons who have resided (or intend to reside) for one year or more in the UK and intend to reside (or have resided) outside the UK for one year or more.
† Figures refer to the country of immigrants' last permanent residence or emigrants' intended future residence.
‡ Figures for all years show the EU as it was constituted on 1 January of year shown (excluding the UK).

Source: International Passenger Survey, Office for National Statistics.

WORK-FORCE JOBS BY INDUSTRY
('000)

	2002	2003	2004
Agriculture, hunting, forestry and fishing	423	414	441
Energy and water	216	213	190
Manufacturing	3,881	3,752	3,517
Construction	1,866	1,943	2,194
Distribution, hotels and restaurants	6,856	6,883	7,094
Transport, storage and communications	1,806	1,787	1,805
Banking, finance, insurance, etc.	5,672	5,772	5,975
Public administration, education and health	6,969	7,165	7,438
Other services	1,805	1,791	1,878
Total	**29,495**	**29,721**	**30,531**
Males	15,663	15,788	16,426
Females	13,832	13,934	14,105

THE UNITED KINGDOM

Health and Welfare

KEY INDICATORS

Total fertility rate (children per woman, 2003)	1.6
Under-5 mortality rate (per 1,000 live births, 2004)	6
HIV/AIDS (% of persons aged 15–49, 2003)	0.2
Physicians (per 1,000 head, 2002)	2.1
Hospital beds (per 1,000 head, 2000)	4.1
Health expenditure (2002): US $ per head (PPP)	2,160
Health expenditure (2002): % of GDP	7.7
Health expenditure (2002): public (% of total)	83.4
Access to water (% of persons, 2000)	100
Access to sanitation (% of persons, 2000)	100
Human Development Index (2003): ranking	15
Human Development Index (2003): value	0.939

For sources and definitions, see explanatory note on p. vi.

Agriculture

PRINCIPAL CROPS
('000 metric tons)

	2002	2003	2004
Wheat	15,973	14,288	15,473
Barley	6,128	6,370	5,815
Oats	753	749	630
Rye	29	25	32
Triticale (wheat-rye hybrid)	65	61	63
Potatoes	6,966	5,918	6,316
Sugar beet	9,557	9,168	8,850
Rapeseed	1,468	1,771	1,609,
Dry peas	292	288	242*
Dry broad beans	96*	158*	160†
Other pulses	536*	488*	520†
Dry onions	283.4	373.6	340.9
Mushrooms	84.7	81.0	74.0
Carrots	731.2	617.8	619.3
Cabbages	244.0	229.2	265.6
Cauliflowers	115.8	122.4	165.3
Green peas	406.0	399.0	313.3
Linseed	18	59	54
Lettuce	125.9	142.2	136.4
Tomatoes	100.9	75.6	78.5
Cucumbers and gherkins	73.6	77.0	61.4
Apples	179.4	143.9	174.1
Pears	34.2	29.6	22.7
Strawberries	38.5	44.8	50.2

* Unofficial estimate.
† FAO estimate.
Source: FAO.

LIVESTOCK
('000 head, year ending September)

	2002	2003	2004
Cattle	10,343	10,517	10,603
Sheep and lambs	35,834	35,846	35,890
Pigs	5,588	5,047	5,161
Chickens	145,200	157,000	157,780
Ducks and geese*	2,220	2,010	2,075
Turkeys*	8,850	8,050	8,300

* Unofficial figures.
Source: FAO.

LIVESTOCK PRODUCTS
('000 metric tons, unless otherwise indicated)

	2002	2003	2004
Beef and veal	694	699	712
Mutton and lamb	307	306	314
Pigmeat	774	687	679
Poultry meat	1,556.3	1,569.5	1,556.3
Offal	256	257	n.a.
Butter	136	131	122
Cheese	380	363	373
Cows' milk	14,869	15,010	14,555*
Milk, evaporated and condensed	118.0	169.8	143.8†
Hen eggs	551.9	550.5	551.9
Wool: greasy	60	60	60
Wool: scoured	42	42	42†
Cattle hides (fresh)	65	63	66

* Unofficial figure.
† FAO estimate.
Source: FAO.

Forestry

ROUNDWOOD REMOVALS
('000 cubic metres, excl. bark)

	2002	2003	2004
Sawlogs, veneer logs and logs for sleepers	4,720	4,912	5,030
Pulpwood	2,465	2,555	2,617
Other industrial wood	386	377	395
Fuel wood	231	231	231
Total	7,802	8,075	8,273

Source: FAO.

SAWNWOOD PRODUCTION
('000 cubic metres, incl. railway sleepers)

	2002	2003	2004
Coniferous (softwood)	2,640	2,687	2,722
Broadleaved (hardwood)	91	81	61
Total	2,731	2,768	2,783

Source: FAO.

Fishing

('000 metric tons, live weight)

	2001	2002	2003
Capture	741.0	689.9	635.5
Atlantic cod	32.8	31.5	21.5
Haddock	42.9	52.9	41.4
Blue whiting	51.9	28.7	29.4
Atlantic herring	81.4	72.9	90.3
Atlantic mackerel	199.0	200.4	183.0
Norway lobster	28.5	28.5	27.8
Aquaculture	170.5	179.0*	181.8*
Atlantic salmon	138.5	145.6	145.6
Total	911.6	869.0*	817.3*

* FAO estimate.

Note: Figures exclude aquatic mammals, recorded by number rather than weight. The number of whales caught was: 87 in 2001; 68 in 2002; 142 in 2003.

Source: FAO.

THE UNITED KINGDOM

Mining and Quarrying

('000 metric tons, unless otherwise indicated)

	2002	2003	2004
Hard coal (incl. slurries)	29,989	28,259	25,096
Natural gas and petroleum:			
Methane—colliery	60	90	n.a.
Methane—North Sea[1]	105,880	105,125	95,919
Crude petroleum	108,023	98,998	88,708
Condensates and others[2]	8,514	8,238	7,858
Iron ore[3]	0	1*	1*
China clay (sales)[4]	2,163	2,097	1,995
Ball clay (sales)	921	885	965
Fireclay[5]	491	528	600
Fuller's earth (sales)[6]	44	34	28
Common clay and shale[5]	10,306	10,680	11,000
Slate[7]	742	832	1,000
Limestone[8]	80,688	78,935	90,000
Dolomite[8]	12,946	12,167	n.a.
Chalk[5]	8,587	8,066	8,000
Sandstone[9]	18,362	18,259	18,500
Common sand and gravel[10]	94,424	91,803	90,500
Igneous rock	51,225	51,356	52,000
Gypsum*	1,700	1,700	1,700
Rock salt*	1,500	1,700	2,000
Salt from brine	1,000	1,000	1,000
Salt in brine[11]*	3,200	3,200	3,200
Fluorspar*	53	56	52
Barytes*	59	57	61
Talc	6	6	4
Potash[12]	540	621	540

* Estimate(s).
[1] 2004 figure refers to all methane.
[2] Includes ethane, propane and butane, in addition to condensates (pentane and hydrocarbons).
[3] Figures refer to gross weight. The estimated iron content is 55%.
[4] Dry weight.
[5] Excluding production in Northern Ireland.
[6] Estimates based on data from producing companies.
[7] Including waste used for constructional fill and powder and granules used in industry.
[8] Dolomite included with limestone for 2004.
[9] Including grit and conglomerate.
[10] Including marine-dredged sand and gravel for both home consumption and export.
[11] Used for purposes other than salt-making.
[12] Chloride (K_2O content).

Source: British Geological Survey.

Industry

SELECTED PRODUCTS
('000 metric tons, unless otherwise indicated)

	2001	2002	2003
Wheat flour	5,667	5,616	5,572
Refined sugar[1]	1,222	1,430	1,368
Margarine and other table spreads	409	415	442
Crude seed and nut oil[2]	786	805	769
Beer ('000 hectolitres)	56,802	56,672	58,014
Cigarettes ('000 million)	47.7	49.6	49.1
Butane and propane[3]	1,764	2,157	n.a.
Petroleum naphtha[3]	3,405	3,090	n.a.
Motor spirit (petrol)[3]	21,455	23,178	n.a.
Aviation turbine fuel[3]	5,910	5,603	n.a.
Burning oil[3]	3,088	3,344	n.a.
Diesel fuel and gas oil[3]	26,746	28,383	n.a.
Fuel oil[3]	10,119	8,621	n.a.
Lubricating oils[3]	656	516	n.a.
—continued	2001	2002	2003
Petroleum bitumen (asphalt)[3]	1,707	1,909	n.a.
Cement	11,090	11,089	11,215
Pig-iron[4]	9,870	8,561	10,228
Crude steel (usable)	13,543	11,667	13,268
Aluminium—unwrought	589.4	551.5	549.2
Refined lead—unwrought[5]	366.3	374.6	356.2
Zinc—unwrought: primary	99.6	99.6	16.6
Passenger motor cars ('000)	1,492.4	1,629.7	1,657.6
Road goods vehicles ('000)	192.9	191.3	188.9
Electric energy (million kWh)	377,069	384,683	387,142

[1] Production from home-grown sugar beet only.
[2] Including maize oil.
[3] Refinery production only (excluding supplies from other sources).
[4] Including blast-furnace ferro-alloys.
[5] Excluding hard lead.

Finance

CURRENCY AND EXCHANGE RATES

Monetary Units
100 pence (pennies) = 1 pound sterling (£).

Dollar and Euro Equivalents (30 December 2005)
US $1 = 58.07 pence;
€1 = 68.51 pence;
£100 = $172.19 = €145.96.

Average Exchange Rate (pound sterling per US $)
2003   0.6125
2004   0.5462
2005   0.5500

BUDGET
(general government transactions, non-cash basis, year ending 31 March, £ '000 million)

Summary of Balances

	2002/03	2003/04	2004/05
Revenue	396.0	421.8	451.4
Less Expense	409.1	443.1	470.7
Net operating balance	−13.1	−21.3	−19.4
Less Net acquisition of non-financial assets	12.2	14.5	20.6
Net lending/borrowing	−25.2	−35.8	−40.0

Source: HM Treasury, *Public Sector Finances Databank* (February 2006).

Revenue

	2002/03	2003/04	2004/05
Inland revenue	215.9	227.8	250.1
Income tax (net)	109.3	113.5	122.4
Corporation tax	29.5	28.3	34.1
National insurance contributions	64.6	72.5	78.1
Customs and excise	108.7	115.7	120.9
Value added tax	63.5	69.1	73.0
Fuel duties	22.1	22.8	23.3
Business rates	18.5	18.4	18.7
Council tax	16.9	18.8	19.9
Other taxes and royalties	14.7	15.9	17.0
Interest and dividends	4.9	4.9	5.7
Gross operating surplus and rent	18.9	19.5	19.2
Other receipts and adjustments	−2.5	0.9	−0.2
Total	396.0	421.8	451.4

Source: HM Treasury, *Public Sector Finances Databank* (February 2006).

THE UNITED KINGDOM

Expense/Outlays

Expense by economic type	2002/03	2003/04	2004/05*
Compensation of employees	112.4	118.8	} 230.6
Use of goods and services	87.3	100.2	
Consumption of fixed capital	13.9	14.0	14.6
Interest	21.5	22.8	24.4
Subsidies	7.4	9.1	9.6
Social benefits and grants	145.5	156.6	163.8
Current transfers abroad	2.4	2.5	6.4
Accounting adjustments	16.0	16.6	16.3
Total†	406.4	440.6	465.8

* Estimates.
† Unrevised totals; see Summary of Balances for revised aggregates.
Source: HM Treasury, *Public Expenditure Statistical Analyses* (July 2005).

Outlays by function of government*	2002/03	2003/04	2004/05†
General public services	11.0	12.0	13.4
EU transactions	−1.9	−2.2	−0.7
International services	4.7	5.2	5.4
Public-sector debt interest	21.6	22.9	24.5
Defence	26.1	27.4	28.2
Public order and safety	24.7	26.8	28.7
Enterprise and economic development	5.9	6.4	7.0
Science and technology	1.9	2.2	2.3
Employment policies	3.2	3.4	3.5
Agriculture, fisheries and forestry	4.9	5.5	5.7
Transport	13.6	16.6	18.1
Environment protection	6.5	6.7	7.6
Housing and community amenities	4.9	5.9	7.0
Health	66.3	74.9	81.5
Recreation, culture and religion	6.7	6.8	6.9
Education and training	54.9	60.9	65.3
Social protection	144.8	154.9	162.7
Accounting adjustments	18.0	18.0	18.4
Total‡	418.0	454.2	485.5

* Including net acquisition of non-financial assets.
† Estimates.
‡ Unrevised totals; see Summary of Balances for revised aggregates.
Source: HM Treasury, *Public Expenditure Statistical Analyses* (July 2005).

OFFICIAL RESERVES
(US $ million at 31 December)*

	2003	2004	2005
Gold	4,202	4,397	5,126
IMF special drawing rights	379	328	287
Foreign currencies	33,105	35,564	37,349
Reserve position in IMF	6,332	5,533	1,765
Other reserve assets	2,042	3,918	3,569
Total	46,060	49,740	48,096

* Reserves are revalued at 31 March each year.
Source: Bank of England.

CURRENCY IN CIRCULATION
(£ million)

	2002	2003	2004
Annual averages:			
Bank of England notes*	30,431	32,922	34,850
Scottish bank notes	2,304	2,460	2,577
Northern Ireland bank notes	1,240	1,325	1,407
Total bank notes	33,975	36,707	38,835
Estimated coin*	3,175	3,314	3,446
Total outstanding	37,150	40,020	42,281
of which:			
In public circulation†	30,713	33,072	34,865
At 31 December:			
Currency in public circulation†	34,987	36,252	39,237

* Average of Wednesdays. Includes amounts held by Scottish and Northern Irish banks as backing for their own note issues.
† Outside of monetary financial institutions.
Source: Bank of England.

COST OF LIVING
(General Index of Retail Prices, annual averages; base: January 1987 = 100)

	2003	2004	2005
Food	151.1	152.0	153.8
Catering	226.3	232.3	239.2
Alcoholic drink	199.8	203.7	207.7
Tobacco	304.1	315.0	328.7
Housing	244.1	267.9	287.5
Fuel and light	131.4	140.7	159.8
Household goods	143.0	144.2	145.2
Household services	173.9	180.1	184.3
Clothing and footwear	100.8	98.0	95.7
Personal goods and services	198.3	199.8	203.6
Motoring expenditure	181.2	183.0	184.2
Fares and other travel costs	209.7	217.0	225.9
Leisure goods	103.0	99.1	94.5
Leisure services	248.1	253.0	261.2
All items	181.3	186.7	192.0

NATIONAL ACCOUNTS
(£ million at current prices)

National Income and Product

	2002	2003	2004
Compensation of employees	588,591	617,641	648,734
Gross operating surplus	258,750	277,165	293,494
Mixed income	66,149	69,771	73,116
Gross domestic product (GDP) at factor cost	913,490	964,577	1,015,344
Taxes on production and imports	143,086	150,430	158,104
Less Subsidies	8,120	9,088	9,712
Statistical discrepancy	—	—	703
GDP at market prices	1,048,456	1,105,919	1,164,439
Primary incomes received from abroad	} 21,774	} 22,353	} 25,184
Less Primary incomes paid abroad			
Gross national income	1,070,230	1,128,272	1,189,623
Less Consumption of fixed capital	111,956	115,323	121,577
Net national income	958,274	1,012,949	1,068,046
Current transfers from abroad	} −6,711	} −8,135	} −9,752
Less Current transfers paid abroad			
Net national disposable income	951,563	1,004,814	1,058,294

Expenditure on the Gross Domestic Product

	2002	2003	2004
Final consumption expenditure	904,326	956,789	1,007,488
Households	667,361	697,764	731,768
Non-profit institutions serving households	25,998	27,248	28,910
General government	210,967	231,777	246,810
Gross capital formation	175,681	180,112	194,798
Gross fixed capital formation	172,558	175,946	190,066
Changes in inventories	2,909	4,203	4,769
Acquisitions, less disposals, of valuables	214	−37	−37
Total domestic expenditure	1,080,007	1,136,901	1,202,286
Exports of goods and services	274,945	282,231	289,959
Less Imports of goods and services	306,496	313,213	328,384
Statistical discrepancy	—	—	578
GDP in purchasers' values	1,048,456	1,105,919	1,164,439
GDP at constant 2002 prices	1,048,456	1,074,858	1,109,574

THE UNITED KINGDOM

Statistical Survey

Gross Domestic Product by Economic Activity

	2002	2003	2004
Agriculture, hunting, forestry and fishing	9,213	10,127	9,381
Mining and quarrying	22,718	22,282	29,849
Manufacturing	147,901	146,127	154,636
Electricity, gas and water supply	16,480	17,112	16,322
Construction	54,783	60,891	67,619
Wholesale and retail trade; repair of motor vehicles, motorcycles and personal and household goods	115,044	121,514	128,382
Hotels and restaurants	31,191	32,633	33,757
Transport, storage and communication	74,366	78,332	78,279
Financial intermediation	63,261	71,499	70,258
Real estate, renting and business activities*	223,599	239,380	254,669
Public administration and defence	47,027	50,266	53,483
Education	55,396	59,032	62,610
Health and social work	62,643	66,657	69,308
Other community, social and personal services	48,378	51,801	54,236
Sub-total	972,000	1,027,653	1,082,789
Less Financial intermediation services indirectly measured	41,207	45,921	49,464
Gross value added at basic prices	930,796	981,732	1,033,324
Value added taxes on products	71,374	77,665	81,747
Other taxes on products	52,890	53,584	56,892
Less Subsidies on products	6,604	7,062	7,524
GDP in purchasers' values	1,048,456	1,105,919	1,164,439

* Including imputed rents of owner-occupied dwellings.

Note: Totals may not be equal to the sum of component parts, owing to rounding.

BALANCE OF PAYMENTS
(£ million)

	2002	2003	2004
Exports of goods f.o.b.	186,511	188,615	190,859
Imports of goods f.o.b.	−233,598	−236,479	−249,473
Trade balance	−47,087	−47,864	−58,614
Exports of services	88,434	93,616	99,100
Imports of services	−72,898	−76,734	−78,911
Balance on goods and services	−31,551	−30,982	−38,425
Other income received	124,762	126,085	139,656
Other income paid	−101,083	−101,893	−113,493
Balance on goods, service and income	−7,872	−6,790	−12,262
Current transfers received	12,701	12,368	12,819
Current transfers paid	−21,316	−22,329	−23,532
Current balance	−16,487	−16,751	−22,975
Capital account (net)	868	1,296	1,980
Direct investment abroad	−34,466	−39,943	−43,996
Direct investment from abroad	16,782	12,838	39,566
Portfolio investment abroad	−1,011	−36,267	−142,425
Portfolio investment from abroad	51,010	95,891	93,346
Financial derivatives (net)	1,001	−5,401	−7,875
Other investment abroad	−96,934	−259,170	−319,241
Other investment from abroad	71,186	252,826	392,859
Net errors and omissions	7,592	−6,878	8,957
Overall balance	−459	−1,559	196

GROSS PUBLIC EXPENDITURE ON OVERSEAS AID
(£ million, year ending 31 March)

	2002/03	2003/04	2004/05
Total bilateral aid*	2,516.3	2,597.7	2,800.5
DFID† bilateral programmes	1,791.5	1,960.6	2,144.8
Poverty reduction budget support	215.4	339.3	422.9
Other financial aid	307.1	366.9	328.6
Technical co-operation	558.0	482.1	508.3
Grants and other aid in kind	395.9	448.5	526.0
Humanitarian assistance	294.7	308.3	344.0
DFID debt relief	20.4	15.5	14.9
Other bilateral programmes	724.8	637.1	655.7
CDC investments	237.3	350.4	233.3
Debt relief	408.1	175.5	281.8
Other‡	79.5	111.2	140.5
Total multilateral aid	1,475.9	1,865.5	1,797.6
DFID multilateral programmes	1,422.5	1,787.9	1,503.6
European Community	870.7	1,031.4	898.2
World Bank Group	221.9	382.6	206.5
International Monetary Fund	11.4	9.4	1.8
Global Environmental Assistance	27.3	61.1	52.4
HIPC Trust Fund	17.9	19.9	42.1
Regional development banks	90.6	80.4	82.2
UN agencies	166.9	187.9	194.1
Commonwealth	7.6	6.7	8.6
International research organizations	8.1	8.4	17.8
Other multilateral programmes	53.4	77.6	294.0
EC/EU	30.3	54.2	272.3
Global Environmental Assistance	0.1	0.1	0.1
UN agencies	22.0	22.3	20.6
Commonwealth	0.8	0.8	0.8
International research organizations	0.2	0.2	0.2
Administrative costs	154.8	249.7	224.8
Total gross expenditure on aid	4,147.0	4,712.9	4,822.8

* Excluding official advances to Commonwealth Development Corporation.
† Department for International Development; assumed the responsibilities of the Overseas Development Administration in May 1997.
‡ Mainly non-DFID debt relief.

Source: Department for International Development, *Statistics on International Development*.

External Trade

(Note: Figures include the Isle of Man and the Channel Islands)

PRINCIPAL COMMODITIES
(£ million)

Imports c.i.f.	2003	2004	2005
Food and live animals	16,459	17,208	18,499
Mineral fuels, lubricants, etc.	11,563	16,824	24,423
Petroleum, petroleum products, etc.	10,484	14,584	20,474
Chemicals and related products	26,168	27,927	29,158
Basic manufactures*	29,921	32,299	33,187
Machinery and transport equipment	101,645	104,183	113,792
Mechanical machinery and equipment	18,993	19,725	21,680
Electrical machinery, apparatus, etc.	43,747	45,797	52,927
Road vehicles and parts†	29,959	30,732	31,241
Other transport equipment	8,946	7,929	7,944
Miscellaneous manufactured articles	38,235	39,820	42,056
Clothing and footwear	12,719	13,087	13,850
Scientific and photographic apparatus	7,067	7,256	7,403
Total (incl. others)	236,479	251,347	274,828

THE UNITED KINGDOM

Exports f.o.b.	2003	2004	2005
Food and live animals	6,481	6,462	6,589
Mineral fuels, lubricants, etc.	16,558	17,941	21,523
Petroleum, petroleum products, etc.	14,608	16,256	19,804
Chemicals and related products	31,403	32,008	33,001
Organic chemicals	6,076	6,040	6,515
Medicinal products	11,908	12,326	12,147
Basic manufactures*	23,136	24,458	26,548
Machinery and transport equipment	79,815	78,377	87,766
Mechanical machinery and equipment	24,302	23,810	25,434
Electrical machinery, apparatus, etc.	30,706	28,623	36,003
Road vehicles and parts†	17,513	18,489	19,322
Other transport equipment	7,294	7,455	7,007
Miscellaneous manufactured articles	22,612	22,919	24,708
Scientific and photographic apparatus	7,302	7,041	7,235
Total (incl. others)	188,615	190,933	209,308

*Sorted industrial diamonds, usually classified with natural abrasives (under 'crude materials'), are included with 'basic manufactures'.
† Excluding tyres, engines and electrical parts.

PRINCIPAL TRADING PARTNERS
(£ million)

Imports c.i.f.	2003	2004	2005
Austria	2,772	2,356	2,376
Belgium-Luxembourg	13,169	13,860	14,939
Canada	3,645	4,154	4,072
China, People's Republic	8,321	10,360	12,853
Denmark	3,394	3,360	4,233
Finland	2,660	2,340	2,398
France	20,360	20,155	21,823
Germany	33,620	35,417	38,165
Hong Kong	5,486	5,745	6,546
India	2,088	2,280	2,755
Ireland	9,908	10,145	10,218
Italy	11,466	12,197	12,404
Japan	8,062	8,066	8,576
Korea, Republic	2,556	3,063	3,029
Netherlands	16,672	18,214	20,078
Norway	6,441	8,470	12,021
Russia	2,449	3,496	5,124
Singapore	2,663	3,367	3,794
South Africa	2,940	3,262	3,906
Spain (excl. Canary Is)	9,236	9,128	10,491
Sweden	4,565	5,125	5,295
Switzerland	3,768	3,436	3,869
Turkey	2,622	3,239	3,499
USA	22,746	21,892	21,740
Total (incl. others)	236,479	251,347	274,828

Exports f.o.b.	2003	2004	2005
Australia	2,298	2,457	2,583
Belgium-Luxembourg	11,373	10,512	11,131
Canada	3,249	3,340	3,278
China	1,931	2,372	2,813
Denmark	2,180	2,042	2,259
France	18,885	18,567	19,682
Germany	20,805	21,673	23,002
Hong Kong	2,490	2,635	3,091
India	2,293	2,236	2,804
Ireland	12,224	14,137	16,244
Italy	8,603	8,401	8,678
Japan	3,723	3,864	3,906
Netherlands	13,597	12,032	12,379
Norway	1,894	1,937	2,204
Spain (excl. Canary Is)	8,943	9,102	9,992
Sweden	3,823	4,355	4,511
Switzerland	2,798	2,840	4,969
USA	28,780	28,591	30,682
Total (incl. others)	188,615	190,933	209,308

Transport

RAILWAYS

	2002/03	2003/04	2004/05
Passenger journeys (million):			
Great Britain national railways	976	1,014	1,088
Northern Ireland railways	6.3	6.9	6.9
Underground railways (London and Glasgow)	955	961	989
Light rail	142	147	159
Passenger-kilometres (million):			
Great Britain national railways	39,678	40,937	42,369
Northern Ireland railways	236.3	233.0	225.2
Underground railways (London and Glasgow)	7,410	7,383	7,649
Light rail	878	903	990
Freight carried (million metric tons)*	87.0	88.9	102.0
Freight ton-kilometres ('000 million)*	18.7	18.9	20.7

* Great Britain only. Figures exclude parcels and materials for rail infrastructure. From 2004/05, figures for for freight carried are not strictly comparable with previous years.

Sources: Department for Transport (Great Britain); Department for Regional Development (Northern Ireland).

ROAD TRAFFIC
('000 licensed vehicles in Great Britain at 31 December)

	2002	2003	2004
Private motor cars	24,543	24,985	25,754
Motorcycles, scooters and mopeds	941	1,005	1,060
Light goods vehicles*	2,622	2,730	2,900
Heavy goods vehicles	425	426	434
Public passenger vehicles	92	96	100

* Goods vehicles less than 3,500 kg in weight.

Source: Department for Transport.

THE UNITED KINGDOM

SHIPPING

Merchant Fleet
(registered at 31 December)

	2002	2003	2004
Number of vessels	1,525	1,594	1,569
Total displacement ('000 grt)	8,045.1	10,843.7	11,122.9

Source: Lloyd's Register-Fairplay, *World Fleet Statistics*.

International Sea-borne Freight Traffic
('000 metric tons)

	2002	2003	2004
Goods imported	320,800	323,800	342,400
Goods exported	237,500	231,900	230,600

Source: Department for Transport.

CIVIL AVIATION
(United Kingdom airlines)

	2002	2003	2004
All scheduled services:			
Aircraft stage flights (number)	911,518	895,095	927,040
Aircraft-kilometres flown (million)	1,047.1	1,088.0	1,138.0
Passengers carried (million)	72.2	76.3	82.8
Passenger-kilometres flown (million)	156,493.9	164,806.3	173,816.0
Total cargo carried (metric tons)	768,736	800,645	842,993
Total metric ton-kilometres (million)	4,997.0	5,242.0	5,371.8
Freight metric ton-kilometres (million)	4,940.5	5,187.0	5,297.0
Mail metric ton-kilometres (million)	56.6	54.5	74.8
Domestic scheduled services:			
Aircraft stage flights (number)	359,400	345,954	373,858
Aircraft-kilometres flown (million)	126.0	123.0	134.5
Passengers carried (million)	19.8	20.8	21.9
Passenger-kilometres flown (million)	8,321.9	8,903.7	9,262.6
Total cargo carried (metric tons)	16,755	17,248	14,862
Total metric ton-kilometres (million)	6.4	6.5	5.2
Freight metric ton-kilometres (million)	3.6	3.4	2.6
Mail metric ton-kilometres (million)	2.8	3.1	2.6
International scheduled services:			
Aircraft stage flights (number)	552,118	549,141	553,182
Aircraft-kilometres flown (million)	921.1	965.0	1,003.4
Passengers carried (million)	52.4	55.5	60.8
Passenger-kilometres flown (million)	148,172.1	155,902.6	164,553.4
Total cargo carried (metric tons)	751,975	783,397	828,132
Total metric ton-kilometres (million)	4,990.7	5,235.1	5,366.6
Freight metric ton-kilometres (million)	4,936.9	5,183.6	5,294.4
Mail metric ton-kilometres (million)	53.8	51.5	72.2

Source: Civil Aviation Authority.

Tourism

FOREIGN VISITORS BY REGION OF ORIGIN
('000)

	2002	2003	2004
EU	14,799	15,699	17,738
Other Europe	1,418	1,508	1,686
North America	4,272	3,997	4,356
Other countries	3,691	3,511	3,975
Total	24,180	24,715	27,755
Total expenditure (£ million)	11,737	11,855	13,047

Source: International Passenger Survey, Office for National Statistics, *Travel Trends*.

VISITS BY COUNTRY OF PERMANENT RESIDENCE
('000)

	2002	2003	2004
Belgium-Luxembourg	1,010	978	1,167
France	3,077	3,073	3,254
Germany	2,556	2,611	2,968
Ireland	2,439	2,488	2,578
Italy	977	1,168	1,348
Netherlands	1,419	1,549	1,620
Poland	188	325	528
Scandinavia and Finland	1,477	1,507	1,727
Spain	1,010	1,206	1,465
Switzerland	593	564	597
Other Europe	1,239	1,738	2,172
USA	3,611	3,346	3,616
Canada	660	652	740
Japan	368	314	347
Australia/New Zealand	839	867	961
South Africa	276	266	269
Latin America	240	246	229
Middle East	541	494	538
Other countries	1,660	1,323	1,631
Total	24,180	24,715	27,755

Source: International Passenger Survey, Office for National Statistics, *Travel Trends*.

Communications Media

	2002	2003	2004
Telephones ('000 main lines in use)	34,898	n.a.	33,700
Mobile cellular telephones ('000 subscribers)	49,677	52,984	61,100
Personal computers ('000 in use)	23,972	n.a.	35,890
Internet users ('000)	25,000	n.a.	37,600

1996: Facsimile machines (number in use) 1,992,000.

1997: Radio receivers ('000 in use) 84,500.

1999: Book production (titles) 110,965.

2000: Daily newspapers 108 (average circulation 19,159,000); Non-daily newspapers 467 (average circulation 6,246,000).

Sources: UNESCO, *Statistical Yearbook*; UN, *Statistical Yearbook* and International Telecommunication Union.

THE UNITED KINGDOM

Education

ENGLAND AND WALES

	2001/02[1]	2002/03[1]	2003/04
Number of schools (at January)	27,634	27,470	27,526
Teachers ('000, at January):[2]			
Maintained primary schools[3]	200.3	196.9	195.3
Maintained secondary schools[3]	205.9	207.4	209.0
Other schools	79.3	81.3	84.6
Total	485.5	485.6	488.9
Full-time pupils ('000, at January):			
Nursery schools	9.2	9.1	8.9
Maintained primary schools[3]	4,325.2	4,279.4	4,224.9
Maintained secondary schools[3]	3,476.1	3,520.4	3,540.1
All Special schools	96.0	95.4	93.3
Pupil referral units[4]	10.4	12.4	13.5
Independent schools[5,6]	574.9	584.3	595.5
Total	8,491.8	8,501.0	8,476.1
Part-time pupils ('000, at January)	387.9	374.9	364.5
Further education establishments	420	404	403
Students in further education ('000)[7,8]			
Full-time students	958.2	959.3	962.0
Part-time students	3,269.8	3,318.4	3,237.7

[1] Includes revised figures.
[2] Qualified teachers only. Full-time teachers and the full time equivalent of part-time teachers. Excluding Pupil Referral Unit.
[3] Including middle schools deemed either primary or secondary.
[4] Excluding pupils registered elsewhere.
[5] Including Direct Grant nursery schools.
[6] Including City Technology Colleges and, from 2002/03, City Academies.
[7] Whole year counts. Figures for 2003/04 are provisional estimates.
[8] Further education institution figures for England have been revised to include Learning and Skills Council funded students only.

Sources: Department for Education and Skills; National Assembly for Wales; Scottish Executive; Northern Ireland Department of Education; Northern Ireland Department for Employment and Learning; Higher Education Statistics Authority.

SCOTLAND*

	2003/04	2004/05	2005/06
Education authority and grant-aided:			
schools:			
primary	2,248	2,217	2,194
secondary	386	386	385
special	194	192	190
Total	2,8282	2,795	2,769
teachers:†			
primary	22,321	22,577	n.a.
secondary	24,881	24,984	n.a.
special	2,027	1,993	n.a.
Total	49,230	49,554	n.a.
pupils:			
primary	406,015	398,100	390,260
secondary	318,427	317,900	315,840
special	7,680	7,389	7,140
Total	732,122	723,389	713,240
Further education day colleges:			
establishments	46	46	46
full-time academic staff†	n.a.	n.a.	n.a.
full-time students	n.a.	74,685	n.a.

* Response rates to data collections vary.
† The figures quoted are for full-time teaching staff.

Source: Scottish Executive.

NORTHERN IRELAND

	2002/03	2003/04	2004/05
Pre-school education centres:*			
number of centres	363	383	365
children in funded places	5,804	5,913	5,952
Controlled and maintained schools:			
establishments:			
nursery	294	100	99
primary	897	892	894
secondary	164	163	162
grammar:			
preparatory	20	19	18
secondary	71	70	70
special	47	47	45
hospital schools	3	3	3
independent schools	22	17	17
pupils:			
nursery	14,092	6,238	6,121
primary	166,328	171,561	169,422
secondary	92,645	92,047	90,085
grammar:			
preparatory	2,651	2,606	2,576
secondary	63,102	63,347	63,364
special	4,879	4,834	4,669
hospital schools	236	298	317
independent schools	948	835	802
Total	344,881	341,766	337,356
teachers (full-time equivalent):			
nursery	206	198	193
primary	8,753	8,481	8,353
secondary	6,722	6,523	6,527
grammar:			
preparatory	154	154	149
secondary	4,118	4,157	4,171
special	819	823	805
Total	20,772	20,335	20,198
Further education establishments:			
institutions	16	16	16
students on vocational courses:			
full-time	24,826	n.a.	n.a.
part-time	62,200	n.a.	n.a.
students on non-vocational courses	n.a.	n.a.	n.a.
teaching staff:			
full-time	1,770	n.a.	n.a.
part-time	3,096	n.a.	n.a.

* Voluntary and private centres funded under the Pre-School Education Expansion Programme, which began in 1998/99.

HIGHER EDUCATION INSTITUTIONS
('000 United Kingdom—academic years)*

	2001/02	2002/03	2003/04
Number of universities†	90	89	89
Number of other higher education institutes	58	60	60
Full-time teaching and research staff	119.9	120.8	n.a.
Students taking higher education courses:			
full-time students	1,326.2	1,386.7	n.a.
part-time students	961.7	988.2	n.a.

* Generally annual 'snapshots' at November/December each year. From 2001/02, however, figures for higher education institutions are based on the Higher Education Statistics Authority 'Standard Registration' count in July and are not directly comparable with previous years.
† Including the Open University.

Sources: Department for Education and Skills; National Assembly for Wales; Scottish Executive; Northern Ireland Department of Education; Northern Ireland Department for Employment and Learning; Higher Education Statistics Agency.

Directory

The Constitution

The United Kingdom is a constitutional monarchy. In the ninth century, when England was first united under a Saxon King, the monarchy was the only central power and the Constitution did not exist. Today, the Sovereign acts on the advice of her Ministers which she cannot, constitutionally, ignore; power, which has been at various times and in varying degrees in the hands of kings, feudal barons, ministers, councils and parliaments, or of particular groups or sections of society, is vested in the people as a whole, and the Sovereign is an essential part of the machinery of government which has gradually been devised to give expression to the popular will.

Both the powers of the Government and the functions of the Sovereign are determined by the Constitution, by the body of fundamental principles on which the State is governed and the methods, institutions and procedures which give them effect. But the United Kingdom has no written Constitution: there is no document, no one law or statute, to which reference can be made. The Constitution is an accumulation of convention, precedent and tradition which, although continually changing as the times change, is at any one moment binding and exact.

Some of the principles and many of the practices are secured by Statute, some are avowed by Declaration or Manifesto and many are incorporated in the Common Law. Magna Carta, in 1215, began the process by which the law of the land acquired a status of its own, independent of King and Parliament; the Bill of Rights of 1689 ended the long era of rivalry between Crown and Parliament and began the story of their co-operation; and the Reform Act of 1832 dramatically broadened the basis of representative government and prepared the way for further changes. The Constitution is, above all, based on usage. It has been modified to match changing customs and to meet successive situations. Any one Parliament could, if it chose, revise or repeal every law and disown every convention that has constitutional significance. It could destroy the whole fabric of political and social existence, including its own; because, according to the Constitution, Parliament, which represents the people, is supreme. The work of one Parliament is not binding on its successors, except in so far as changes must be made by constitutional means. Parliament cannot disobey the law, but it can change it.

It would be impossible to enumerate the principles which are extant in the British Constitution. In constitutional as in legal practice, the way has been to admit the general principle in quite practical terms related to specific practical problems: the Habeas Corpus Act, for example, which establishes the principle of no imprisonment without trial, makes no mention of the principle itself but lays down in most concrete terms the punishments that shall be inflicted on a judge, or other law officer, if he fails to issue the Writ (commanding the prisoner to be brought before the court) when applied for. The principles of the Constitution and constitutional practice are in fact inherent in the Common Law on the one hand and in the structure, functions and procedures of the various instruments of government on the other: of the Crown, of Parliament, of the Privy Council, of the Government and the Cabinet and of the government departments.

THE SOVEREIGN

The monarchy is hereditary, descending to the sons of the Sovereign in order of seniority or, if there are no sons, to the daughters.

The constitutional position of the Queen as head of the State, quite apart from her position as head of the Commonwealth, demands that she keep herself informed on all aspects of the life of her subjects, that she maintain absolute impartiality and that she should personally visit the different parts of her realm as often as it is possible for her to do so, but she has also quite specific functions, all exercised on ministerial advice: she summons, prorogues and dissolves Parliament; she must give Royal Assent to a Bill which has passed through both Houses of Parliament, before it becomes law; she is head of the judiciary (although the judiciary is now quite independent of the executive); she appoints all important state officials, including judges, officers of the forces and representatives abroad, and she confers honours and awards. Her formal consent is necessary before a Minister can take up office or a Cabinet be formed; and before a treaty may be concluded, war declared or peace made. These are some of the more essential functions. However, the Queen also has many residuary responsibilities, such as the guardianship of infants and persons of unsound mind, the creation of corporations, granting of printing rights for the Bible and Prayer Book and for state documents; and her signature and consent are necessary to many important state papers. Constitutional government cannot in fact be carried on without the Sovereign, so much so that provision has been made by Act of Parliament for the appointment of a Regent should the Sovereign be incapacitated or under age and for Counsellors of State to act in the temporary absence of the Queen.

PARLIAMENT

The Queen in Parliament—the House of Commons and the House of Lords—is the supreme legislative authority in the United Kingdom. Under the Parliament Act of 1911 the maximum life of one Parliament was fixed at five years: if, that is, Parliament has not meanwhile been dissolved for any other reason, such as the fall of the Government, then a general election is at the end of five years necessary by law. During its lifetime, the power of Parliament is theoretically absolute; it can make or unmake any law. In practice, of course, it must take account of the electorate. Parliament is prorogued at intervals during its life, which therefore consists of a number of sessions; by present custom, a session has normally 160 sitting days and is divided into five periods: from November (when the session is opened) until Christmas (about 30 days), from January till Easter (50), from Easter till Whitsun (30), from Whitsun until the end of July (40) and 10 days in October.

The House of Commons has 646 members, each elected for one geographical constituency. The Speaker, who is elected by the members immediately a new parliament meets, presides. Members of Parliament may be elected either at a general election or at a by-election (held in the event of the death, resignation or expulsion of the sitting member) and in either case hold their seats during the life of the existing parliament. All British subjects who are more than 18 years of age (and subjects of any Commonwealth country and of the Republic of Ireland who are resident in the United Kingdom) have the vote unless legally barred (e.g. for insanity). Anyone who has the vote may stand as a candidate for election except clergymen of the Church of England, the established Churches of Scotland and Northern Ireland and the Roman Catholic Church, and certain officers of the Crown; civil servants must resign from the service if they wish to stand as a Member of Parliament.

There are over 700 members of the House of Lords, including 12 Lords of Appeal in Ordinary (appointed for life to carry out the judicial duties of the House); the two archbishops and the 24 senior diocesan bishops of the Church of England are also members. The House of Lords Act 1999 ended the right of hereditary peers to sit and vote in the House of Lords. An amendment to the Act provided for 92 of the existing hereditary peers to remain as members until the next stage of reform.

Members of Parliament whose views coincide form parties which agree in each case to support the policies put forward by their chosen leaders, and to present a common front on all important issues both in Parliament and to the electorate. This system evolved during the 17th and 18th centuries and is now essential to the working of the British Constitution. Under the party system, the Queen sends for the leader of the party which wins the majority of seats (although not necessarily of votes) at a general election and asks him or her to form a government. The party with the second largest number of seats forms the Opposition, which has quite specific functions. Members of other minority parties and independents may support the Government or Opposition as they choose. Each party has its own Whips, officials whose duty it is to arrange, (in consultation with the Whips of other parties), matters of procedure and organization; to ensure that members attend debates; and to muster for their party its maximum voting strength. In addition, each party has its own national and local organizations outside Parliament.

Parliamentary procedure, like the Constitution itself, is determined by rules, customs, forms and practices which have accumulated over many centuries. The Speaker is responsible for their application, and generally for controlling the course of business and debates in the house.

It is the duty of Parliament to make the laws which govern the life of the community, to appropriate the necessary funds for the various services of state and to criticize and control the Government. Parliament is also consulted before the ratification of certain international treaties and agreements.

Legislation may (with some exceptions) be initiated in either House and on either side of the House. In practice, most Public Bills are introduced into the House of Commons by the Government in power (the chief exceptions are Private Members' Bills) as the result of Cabinet decisions. Each Bill which is passed by the Commons at its third reading is sent to the House of Lords, who either accept it or return it to the Commons with suggested amendments. The Lords cannot in any instance prevent Bills passed by the Commons from becoming law: over Money Bills or Bills affecting the duration of Parliament they have no power at all, and by the Parliament Act of 1949 any other Bill passed by the Commons in two successive sessions may be presented for Royal Assent without the consent of the Lords, provided one year has elapsed between the date of the second reading in the Commons and the date of its final passing. In practice, the House of Lords is extremely unlikely to delay matters thus far, and its main function is to scrutinize the work of the

THE UNITED KINGDOM

Commons, to caution and suggest. Bills of a non-controversial kind are sometimes introduced initially in the House of Lords.

Northern Ireland

Following the prorogation of the Northern Ireland Parliament in 1972, responsibility for the Government of Northern Ireland rested with the Secretary of State for Northern Ireland. Direct rule continued until 1973, when the Northern Ireland Executive was established under the provisions of the Northern Ireland Constitution Act (1973). The Northern Ireland Executive assumed responsibility for the administration of Northern Ireland and was answerable to the Northern Ireland Assembly, elected in June 1973. The Executive collapsed in May 1974, and the Secretary of State resumed control of the Northern Ireland departments.

In October 1982 a new Northern Ireland assembly was elected under the provisions of the Northern Ireland Act 1982. Under the Act, the Assembly was eventually to resume legislative and executive functions, provided that it produced proposals for the resumption of its powers, deemed to be acceptable to the people of Northern Ireland by Parliament. In June 1986 the Assembly was dissolved.

In November 1985 the Anglo-Irish Agreement was signed by the Prime Ministers of the United Kingdom and the Republic of Ireland, leaving the status of Northern Ireland unaltered and confirming that the status of Northern Ireland would not be altered without the consent of a majority of its inhabitants. The Agreement provided for the establishment of an intergovernmental conference, through which the Government of the Republic of Ireland was permitted to make proposals on matters relating to Northern Irish affairs.

New constitutional arrangements for Northern Ireland were agreed by the leaders of Northern Ireland's political parties (with the exception of the Democratic Unionist Party and the United Kingdom Unionist Party) and by the British and Irish Governments in April 1998, and were approved in a popular referendum conducted in May. Accordingly, legislation was introduced into the United Kingdom Parliament to provide for the transfer of responsibility for the administration of Northern Ireland to an elected Assembly and Executive. A North/South Ministerial Council was established by the Assembly to undertake consideration of all-Ireland issues. Representatives of the Irish and British Governments, of the devolved authorities in Northern Ireland, Scotland and Wales and of the Channel Islands and Isle of Man were to convene under a British-Irish Council, to consider the development of the islands and formulate common policies, although with no legislative or administrative powers. A new bilateral agreement between the United Kingdom and the Republic of Ireland subsumed the 1985 accord and established a new British-Irish Intergovernmental Conference. The new Northern Ireland institutions were suspended in February 2000, owing to a political impasse concerning the decommissioning of paramilitary weapons and Northern Ireland was returned to direct rule. In May, following an agreement on the issue of decommissioning, power was once again transferred from Westminster to the new Northern Ireland institutions. The Northern Ireland Assembly and Executive were suspended again in October 2002 and Northern Ireland was returned to direct rule from Westminster. The Assembly was recalled on 15 May 2006.

Scotland and Wales

In 1999 devolved legislative authorities were established in Scotland and Wales. In Scotland a new elected parliament, based in Edinburgh, was established with powers to legislate on all domestic matters (incl. education, health, local government and law and order) and with a mandate to vary taxes set by the Government of the United Kingdom by 3%. The Assembly has 129 members, elected every four years by a combined system of direct voting, on the basis of Westminster parliamentary constituencies, and a form of proportional representation, whereby additional members are elected from a party list on the basis of the larger constituencies used for elections to the European Parliament. The Welsh Assembly, located in Cardiff, undertook responsibility for issues covered by the Welsh Office of the Government of the United Kingdom. The 60-member Assembly was elected under the same system as in Scotland. Elections to the two Assemblies took place simultaneously in May 1999 and the transfer of powers took place on 1 July.

THE PRIVY COUNCIL

The power of the Privy Council has declined with the development of the Cabinet and its main function today is to give effect to decisions made elsewhere. There are at present over 500 Privy Counsellors, including Cabinet Ministers (who are automatically created Privy Counsellors), and people who have reached eminence in some branch of public affairs. Meetings are presided over by the Queen, and the responsible minister is the Lord President of the Council, an office which, since 1600, has always been held by a member of the party in power, who is usually also a leading member of the Cabinet. The Privy Council is responsible for making Orders in Council, of which there are two kinds: those made in virtue of the Royal prerogative, e.g. the ratification of treaties, and those which are authorized by Act of Parliament and are, in fact, a form of delegated legislation. It has also various advisory functions which cover such subjects as scientific, industrial, medical and agricultural research. An important organ of the Privy Council is the Judicial Committee.

HER MAJESTY'S GOVERNMENT

The Government is headed by the Prime Minister, who is also the leader of the party which holds the majority in the House of Commons. It includes ministers who are in charge of government departments and those who hold traditional offices which involve no special departmental duties; the Chancellor of the Exchequer and the Lord Chancellor, who are specially responsible for financial and economic and legal affairs respectively; the law officers of the Crown (the Attorney-General and Solicitor-General, the Lord Advocate for Scotland and the Solicitor-General for Scotland); the Ministers of State, who are usually appointed to assist Ministers in charge of departments; and Parliamentary Secretaries and Under-Secretaries.

The cabinet system developed during the 18th century from the informal meetings of Privy Counsellors who were also ministers, and who formed a committee of manageable size which could take decisions far more quickly and simply than larger bodies. The Cabinet today has between 15–25 members at the discretion of the Prime Minister—its main duty is to formulate policy for submission to Parliament.

The doctrine of ministerial responsibility has also evolved gradually, but was generally accepted by the middle of the last century. Each Minister must take full responsibility, particularly in Parliament, for the work of his own department; if his department fails over any important matter, he will be expected to resign. Ministers also assume collective responsibility for the work of the Government and for any advice which it may offer to the Crown.

The Government

HEAD OF STATE

Sovereign: Her Majesty Queen ELIZABETH II (succeeded to the throne 6 February 1952).

THE MINISTRY
(May 2006)

The Cabinet

Prime Minister, First Lord of the Treasury and Minister for the Civil Service: ANTHONY (TONY) BLAIR.

Deputy Prime Minister: JOHN PRESCOTT.

Chancellor of the Exchequer: GORDON BROWN.

Secretary of State for Foreign and Commonwealth Affairs: MARGARET BECKETT.

Secretary of State for the Home Department: Dr JOHN REID.

Secretary of State for the Environment, Food and Rural Affairs: DAVID MILIBAND.

Secretary of State for Transport and Secretary of State for Scotland: DOUGLAS ALEXANDER.

Secretary of State for Health: PATRICIA HEWITT.

Chancellor of the Duchy of Lancaster: HILARY ARMSTRONG.

Secretary of State for Northern Ireland and Secretary of State for Wales: PETER HAIN.

Secretary of State for Defence: DES BROWNE.

Secretary of State for Culture, Media and Sport: TESSA JOWELL.

Parliamentary Secretary to the Treasury and Chief Whip: JACQUELINE (JACQUI) SMITH.

Secretary of State for Education and Skills: ALAN JOHNSON.

Chief Secretary to the Treasury: STEPHEN TIMMS.

Lord Privy Seal and Leader of the House of Commons: JOHN (JACK) STRAW.

Minister without Portfolio: HAZEL BLEARS.

Leader of the House of Lords and Lord President of the Council: Baroness AMOS OF BRONDESBURY.

Secretary of State for Constitutional Affairs and Lord Chancellor for the transitional period: Lord FALCONER OF THOROTON.

Secretary of State for International Development: HILARY BENN.

Secretary of State for Work and Pensions: JOHN HUTTON.

Secretary of State for Trade and Industry: ALISTAIR DARLING.

Secretary of State for Communities and Local Government: RUTH KELLY.

THE UNITED KINGDOM

Also attending Cabinet

Lords Chief Whip and Captain of the Gentlemen at Arms: Lord GROCOTT OF TELFORD.
Attorney-General: Lord GOLDSMITH OF ALLERTON.
Minister of State for Europe in the Foreign and Commonwealth Office: GEOFFREY (GEOFF) HOON.
Minister for Trade, Foreign and Commonwealth Office and Department of Trade and Industry: IAN MCCARTNEY.

Law Officers

Attorney-General: Lord GOLDSMITH OF ALLERTON.
Solicitor-General: MIKE O'BRIEN.
Advocate-General for Scotland: Lord DAVIDSON OF GLEN CLOVA.

Ministers not in the Cabinet

Minister of State for Local Government, Department for Communities and Local Government: PHIL WOOLAS.
Minister of State for Housing and Planning, Department for Communities and Local Government: YVETTE COOPER.
Paymaster-General: DAWN PRIMAROLO.
Financial Secretary to the Treasury: JOHN HEALEY.
Economic Secretary to the Treasury: ED BALLS.
Minister of State for the Middle East, Foreign and Commonwealth Office: Dr KIM HOWELLS.
Minister of State for Crime Reduction, Policing, Community Safety and Counter-Terrorism, Home Office: TONY MCNULTY.
Minister of State for the Criminal Justice System and Law Reform, Home Office: Baroness SCOTLAND OF ASTHAL.
Minister of State for Citizenship, Immigration and Nationality, Home Office: LIAM BYRNE.
Minister of State, Department for Constitutional Affairs: HARRIET HARMAN.
Minister of State for Climate Change and Environment, Department for Environment, Food and Rural Affairs: IAN PEARSON.
Minister of State for Pensions Reform, Department for Work and Pensions: JAMES PURNELL.
Minister of State for Employment and Welfare Reform, Department for Work and Pensions: JIM MURPHY.
Minister of State for Transport, Department for Transport: Dr STEPHEN LADYMAN.
Ministers of State for Health, Department for Health: ROSIE WINTERTON, ANDY BURNHAM, Lord WARNER OF BROCKLEY, CAROLINE FLINT.
Ministers of State, Northern Ireland Office: DAVID HANSON, Lord ROOKER.
Minister of State, Ministry of Defence: ADAM INGRAM.
Minister for Energy, Department of Trade and Industry: MALCOLM WICKS.
Minister of State for Industry and the Regions, Department of Trade and Industry: MARGARET HODGE.
Minister of State for Children and Families, Department for Education and Skills: BEVERLEY HUGHES.
Minister of State for Schools, Department for Education and Skills: JIM KNIGHT.
Minister of State for Higher Education and Lifelong Learning, Department for Education and Skills: BILL RAMMELL.
Minister of State, Department for Culture, Media and Sport: RICHARD CABORN.

MINISTRIES

Prime Minister's Office: 10 Downing St, London, SW1A 2AA; tel. (20) 7270-3000; fax 020 7295-0918; internet www.number-10.gov.uk.
Cabinet Office and the Office of the Chancellor of the Duchy of Lancaster: 70 Whitehall, London, SW1A 2AS; tel. (20) 7276-1234; internet www.cabinet-office.gov.uk.
Department for Communities and Local Government: Office of the Deputy Prime Minister, Eland House, Bressenden Place, London, SW1E 5DU; tel. (20) 7944-4400; fax (20) 7944-9645; e-mail enquiryodpm@odpm.gsi.gov.uk; internet www.odpm.gov.uk.
Department for Constitutional Affairs: Selborne House, 54 Victoria St, London, SW1E 6QW; tel. (20) 7210-8500; fax (20) 7210-0647; e-mail general.queries@dca.gsi.gov.uk; internet www.dca.gov.uk.
Department for Culture, Media and Sport: 2–4 Cockspur St, London SW1Y 5DH; tel. (20) 7211-6200; fax (20) 7211-6032; e-mail enquiries@culture.gov.uk; internet www.culture.gov.uk.

Ministry of Defence: Main Bldg, Whitehall, London, SW1A 2HB; tel. (20) 7218-9000; e-mail public@ministers.mod.uk; internet www.mod.uk.
Department for Education and Skills: Sanctuary Bldgs, Great Smith St, London, SW1P 3BT; tel. (870) 000-2288; fax (20) 7925-6000; e-mail info@dfes.gsi.gov.uk; internet www.dfes.gov.uk.
Department for Environment, Food and Rural Affairs (DEFRA): Lower Ground Floor, Ergon House, c/o Nobel House, 17 Smith Sq., London, SW1P 3JR; tel. (20) 7238-3000; fax (20) 7238-6609; e-mail helpline@defra.gsi.gov.uk; internet www.defra.gov.uk.
Foreign and Commonwealth Office: King Charles St, London, SW1A 2AH; tel. (20) 7008-1500; internet www.fco.gov.uk.
Department of Health: Richmond House, 79 Whitehall, London, SW1A 2NS; tel. (20) 7210-4850; fax (20) 7210-5523; e-mail dhmail@dh.gsi.gov.uk; internet www.dh.gov.uk.
Home Office: 50 Queen Anne's Gate, London, SW1H 9AT; tel. (20) 7035-4848; fax (20) 7035-4745; e-mail public.enquiries@homeoffice.gsi.gov.uk; internet www.homeoffice.gov.uk.
Department for International Development: 1 Palace St, London, SW1E 5HE; tel. (20) 7023-0000; fax (20) 7023-0019; e-mail enquiry@dfid.gov.uk; internet www.dfid.gov.uk.
Northern Ireland Office: 11 Millbank, London, SW1P 4PN; tel. (20) 7210-0260; fax (20) 7210-0213; e-mail press.nio@nics.gov.uk; internet www.nio.gov.uk.
Scotland Office: Dover House, Whitehall, London, SW1A 2AU; tel. (20) 7270-6754; fax 20 7270-6812; e-mail scottish.secretary@scotland.gsi.gov.uk; internet www.scotlandoffice.gov.uk.
Department of Trade and Industry: 1 Victoria St, London, SW1H 0ET; tel. (20) 7215-5000; e-mail dti.enquiries@dti.gsi.gov.uk; internet www.dti.gov.uk.
Department for Transport: Great Minster House, 76 Marsham St, London, SW1P 4DR; tel. (20) 7944-8300; fax (20) 7944-9643; internet www.dft.gov.uk.
HM Treasury: 1 Horse Guards Rd, London, SW1A 2HQ; tel. (20) 7270-4558; fax (20) 7270-4861; e-mail public.enquiries@hm-treasury.gov.uk; internet www.hm-treasury.gov.uk.
Wales Office: Gwydyr House, Whitehall, London, SW1A 2ER; tel. (20) 7270-0534; e-mail wales.office@walesoffice.gsi.gov.uk; internet www.walesoffice.gov.uk.
Department for Work and Pensions: Richmond House, 79 Whitehall, London, SW1A 2NS; tel. (20) 7712-2171; fax (20) 7712-2386; internet www.dwp.gov.uk.

Legislature

PARLIAMENT

House of Commons

Speaker: MICHAEL MARTIN.
Chairman of Ways and Means: SIR ALAN HASELHURST.
Leader of the House: JOHN (JACK) STRAW.

General Election, 5 May 2005

	Votes	% of votes	Seats
Labour Party	9,556,183	35.2	356*
Conservative Party	8,772,598	32.3	198†
Liberal Democrats	5,982,045	22.0	62
Democratic Unionist Party	241,856	0.9	9
Scottish National Party	412,267	1.5	6
Sinn Féin	174,530	0.6	5
Plaid Cymru (Party of Wales)	174,838	0.6	3
Social Democratic and Labour Party	125,626	0.5	3
Ulster Unionist Party	127,314	0.5	1
Others	1,565,070	5.9	3
Total	**27,132,327**	**100.0**	**646†**

* Including the Speaker.
† Including the representative for the South Staffordshire constituency, for which the election was postponed until 24 June 2005, owing to the death of the Liberal Democrat candidate.

House of Lords
(May 2006)

Lord High Chancellor: Lord FALCONER OF THOROTON.
Lord Chairman of Committees: Lord BRABAZON OF TARA.
Leader of the House: Baroness AMOS OF BRONDESBURY.

THE UNITED KINGDOM

	Seats
Archbishops and Bishops	26
Life Peers under the Appelate Jurisdiction Act 1876	26
Life Peers under the Life Peerages Act 1958	581
Peers under the House of Lords Act 1999	92
Total	**725**

The Legislative Authorities and Executive Bodies of Northern Ireland, Scotland and Wales

New constitutional arrangements for Northern Ireland were agreed by the leaders of Northern Ireland's political parties (with the exception of the Democratic Unionist Party and the United Kingdom Unionist Party) and by the British and Irish Governments in April 1998, and were approved in a popular referendum conducted in May. Accordingly, legislation was introduced into the United Kingdom Parliament to provide for the transfer of responsibility for the administration of Northern Ireland to an elected Assembly and Executive. Elections to a new 108-member Assembly were held on 25 June 1998. An Executive Committee, headed by a First Minister, was constituted from among the legislative members. Responsibility for all matters formerly implemented by the Northern Ireland Office was transferred to the devolved authority under new parliamentary legislation implemented in December 1999. The new Northern Ireland institutions were suspended in February 2000, owing to a political impasse concerning the decommissioning of paramilitary weapons and Northern Ireland was returned to direct rule. On 30 May, following an agreement on the issue of decommissioning, power was once again transferred from Westminster to the new Northern Ireland institutions. However, the Northern Ireland Executive was suspended again on 14 October 2002 and Northern Ireland was returned to direct rule from Westminster.

In 1999 devolved legislative authorities were established for Scotland and Wales. An executive level of government, headed by a First Minister, was also established for each country. The Scottish Assembly assumed powers to legislate on all domestic matters, including education, health, local government and law and order. It also had a mandate to vary taxes set by the United Kingdom Government by 3%. The Welsh Assembly (Cynulliad Cenedlaethol Cymru) assumed responsibility for issues covered by the Welsh Office of the United Kingdom Government. Both Assemblies were elected, for a term of four years, by a combined system of direct voting, on the basis of Westminster parliamentary constituencies, and a form of proportional representation, whereby additional members were elected from a party list on the basis of the larger constituencies used for election to the European Parliament. The transfer of powers to both the Scottish and the Welsh authorities took place on 1 July.

NORTHERN IRELAND

Legislature

Northern Ireland Assembly

On 14 October 2002 the Assembly was suspended and Northern Ireland was returned to direct rule from Westminster. Elections, scheduled to have taken place in May 2003, were subsequently postponed until November. Following the elections, the Assembly remained suspended. The Assembly was recalled on 15 May 2006, under temporary rules that precluded the enacting of legislation, in order to elect a multi—party devolved executive by the deadline imposed by the British Government of 24 November. Failure to meet this deadline would result in the cancellation of salaries and allowances payable to the members of the Assembly and the introduction of partnership arrangements between the British and Irish Governments to govern Northern Ireland.

Presiding Officer: EILEEN BELL.

Election, 26 November 2003

	First preference votes	% of first preference votes	Seats
Democratic Unionist Party	177,944	25.7	30
Sinn Féin	162,758	23.5	24
Ulster Unionist Party	156,931	22.7	27
Social Democratic and Labour Party	117,547	17.0	18
Alliance Party	25,372	3.7	6
Independents	19,256	2.8	1
Progressive Unionist Party	8,032	1.2	1
United Kingdom Unionist Party	5,700	0.8	1
Total (incl. others)	**692,028**	**100.0**	**108**

Note: In January 2004 three assembly members resigned from the Ulster Unionist Party (UUP) and joined the Democratic Unionist Party (DUP), increasing the DUP's total number of seats to 33 and reducing that of the UUP to 24

Northern Ireland Executive
(May 2006)

On 14 October 2002 the Executive was suspended and Northern Ireland was returned to direct rule from Westminster.

Secretary of State for Northern Ireland: PETER HAIN; responsible for the overall conduct of the Northern Ireland political process, policing, security policy, prisons, criminal justice and international relations for which the British Government remains responsible; also represents Northern Ireland's interest in the British Cabinet.

Minister of State: DAVID HANSON; responsible for political development, criminal justice and human rights and equality; also assumes responsibility for the Department for Social Development, and the Department of Culture, Arts and Leisure.

Minister of State: Lord ROOKER; assumes responsibility for the Office of the First Minister and Deputy First Minister, the Department of Finance and Personnel, the Department of Agriculture and Rural Development and the Department of Environment.

Parliamentary Under-Secretary of State: PAUL GOGGINS; responsible for prisons; also assumes responsibility for the Department of Health, Social Services and Public Safety and the Department for Regional Development.

Parliamentary Under-Secretary of State: MARIA EAGLE; assumes responsibility for the Department of Enterprise, Trade and Investment, the Department of Education and the Department for Employment and Learning.

SCOTLAND

Legislature

Scottish Parliament

Presiding Officer: GEORGE REID.

Election, 1 May 2003

	Total votes	%	Seats
Labour Party	1,225,464	33.1	50
Scottish National Party	855,381	23.1	27
Conservative Party	615,208	16.6	18
Liberal Democrats	520,157	14.1	17
Green Party	132,138	3.6	7
Scottish Socialist Party	244,139	6.6	6
Others	108,895	3.1	4
Total	**3,701,382**	**100.0**	**129**

Cabinet
(April 2006)

First Minister: JACK MCCONNELL.
Deputy First Minister and Minister for Enterprise and Lifelong Learning: NICOL STEPHEN.
Minister for Justice: CATHY JAMIESON.
Minister for Education and Young People: PETER PEACOCK.
Minister for Health and Community Care: ANDY KERR.
Minister for Environment and Rural Development: ROSS FINNIE.
Minister for Finance and Public Services: TOM MCCABE.
Minister for Communities: MALCOLM CHISHOLM.

THE UNITED KINGDOM

Minister for Parliamentary Business: MARGARET CURRAN.
Minister for Tourism, Culture and Sport: PATRICIA FERGUSON.
Minister for Transport and Telecommunication: TAVISH SCOTT.
Lord Advocate: COLIN BOYD.
Solicitor-General: ELISH ANGIOLINI.

WALES
Legislature
Welsh Assembly

Presiding Officer: Lord DAFYDD ELIS-THOMAS.
Election, 1 May 2003

	Total votes	%	Seats
Labour Party	647,073	41.0	30
Plaid Cymru	347,838	22.0	12
Conservative	336,657	21.3	11
Liberal Democrats	228,263	14.4	6
Others	19,757	1.3	1
Total	1,579,588	100.0	60

Cabinet
(April 2006)

First Minister: RHODRI MORGAN.
Minister for Finance, Local Government and Public Services: SUE ESSEX.
Minister for Assembly Business, Equality and Children: JANE HUTT.
Minister for Social Justice and Regeneration: EDWINA HART.
Minister for Health and Social Services: Dr BRIAN GIBBONS.
Minister for Enterprise, Innovation and Networks: ANDREW DAVIES.
Minister for Education and Lifelong Learning: JANE DAVIDSON.
Minister for the Environment, Planning and Countryside: CARWYN JONES.
Minister for Culture, the Welsh Language and Sports: ALAN PUGH.

Election Commission

The Electoral Commission: Trevelyan House, Great Peter St, London SW1P 2HW; tel. (20) 7271-0500; fax (20) 7271-0505; e-mail info@electoralcommission.org.uk; internet www.electoralcommission.org.uk; f. 2000; independant; Chair. SAM YOUNGER; Chief Exec. PETER WARDLE.

Political Organizations

Alliance Party: 88 University St, Belfast, BT7 1HE; tel. (28) 9032-4274; fax (28) 9033-3147; e-mail alliance@allianceparty.org; internet www.allianceparty.org; f. 1970; non-sectarian and non-doctrinaire party of the centre, attracting support from within both Catholic and Protestant sections of the community in Northern Ireland; 3,000 mems; Leader DAVID FORD; Gen. Sec. ALLAN LEONARD.

British National Party: POB 287, Waltham Cross, Hertfordshire, EN8 8ZU; tel. (870) 757-6267; e-mail enquiries@bnp.org.uk; internet www.bnp.org.uk; f. 1982 as a breakaway faction from the National Front; National Chair. NICK GRIFFIN.

Communist Party of Britain: Ruskin House, 23 Coombe Road, Croydon, CR0 1BD; tel. (20) 7428-9300; fax (20) 7517-9733; e-mail office@communist-party.org.uk; internet www.communist-party.org.uk; f. 1920; re-established 1988; militant Marxist-Leninist; Gen.-Sec. ROBERT GRIFFITHS.

Conservative and Unionist Party: 25 Victoria St, London, SW1H 0DL; tel. (20) 7222-9000; fax (20) 7222-1135; internet www.conservatives.com; f. 1870 as Conservative Central Office; aims to uphold the Crown and the Constitution; to build a sound economy based on freedom and enterprise; to encourage personal responsibility and a wider spread of ownership of property; to look after those most in need; to ensure respect for law and order; to improve educational standards and widen parents' choice; to strengthen Britain's defences, maintain its interests and increase its influence abroad, not least through commitment to the European Union; member of the International Democrat Union and the European Democrat Union; in the European Parliament part of the European People's Party-European Democrat Group; 320,000 mems (adherent on a local, rather than national, basis); Leader DAVID CAMERON; Chair. FRANCIS MAUDE.

Co-operative Party: 77 Weston St, London, SE1 3SD; tel. (20) 7357-0230; fax (20) 7407-4476; e-mail p.hunt@party.coop; internet www.party.coop; f. 1917; under an Agreement with the Labour Party it is recognized as the political party representing the co-operative movement, and fields candidates, jointly with the Labour Party, who are Labour and Co-operative candidates at local and British parliamentary elections; promotes the principles of the co-operative movement; seeks to extend co-operative enterprise and cares for the interests of the consumer; individual mems in 269 brs; 47 societies are affiliated; Chair. G. THOMAS; Sec. PETER HUNT.

Democratic Unionist Party: 91 Dundela Ave, Belfast, BT4 3BU; tel. (28) 9047-1155; fax (28) 9065-4480; e-mail info@dup.org.uk; internet www.dup.org.uk; f. 1971; pro-British party of Northern Ireland; Leader Rev. Dr IAN R. K. PAISLEY; Chief Executive ALLAN EWART; Party Sec. NIGEL DODDS.

Green Party: 1a Waterlow Rd, London, N19 5NJ; tel. (20) 7272-4474; fax (20) 7272-6653; e-mail office@greenparty.org.uk; internet www.greenparty.org.uk; f. 1973 as People, adopted the name Ecology Party in 1975; present name adopted in 1985; campaigns for the protection of the environment and the promotion of social justice; approx. 6,000 mems; Chair. RICHARD MALLENDER; Principal Speakers Dr CAROLINE LUCAS, KEITH TAYLOR.

Labour Party: 16 Old Queen St, London, SW1H 9HP; tel. (8705) 900200; fax (20) 7802-1234; e-mail info@new.labour.org.uk; internet www.labour.org.uk; f. 1900; a democratic socialist party affiliated to the Socialist International and the Party of European Socialists; aims to achieve a dynamic economy, serving the public interest, with a strong private sector and high quality public services; a just society, with full equality of opportunity; an open democracy, guaranteeing fundamental human rights and governmental accountability; and a healthy environment. The Labour Party is committed to co-operating with European institutions, the UN, the Commonwealth and other international bodies to secure peace, freedom, democracy, economic security and environmental protection for all; also committed to pursuing these aims with trade unions, co-operative societies, voluntary organizations, consumer groups and other representative bodies. The party has been a member of the Socialist Group in the European Parliament since 1973; supports European economic and political union; 208,000 individual mems (2004), total individual and affiliated membership 3,965,000 (1995); Leader ANTHONY (TONY) BLAIR; Chair. HAZEL BLEARS; Gen. Sec. PETER WATT.

Liberal Democrats: 4 Cowley St, London, SW1P 3NB; tel. (20) 7222-7999; fax (20) 7799-2170; e-mail info@libdems.org.uk; internet www.libdems.org.uk; f. 1988 following the merger of the Liberal Party (f. 1877) and the Social Democratic Party (f. 1981, disbanded 1990); c. 100,500 mems; Leader Sir MENZIES CAMPBELL; Pres. SIMON HUGHES.

Plaid Cymru—Party of Wales: Tŷ Gwynfor, 18 Park Grove, Cardiff, CF10 3BN; tel. (29) 2064-6000; fax (29) 2064-6001; e-mail post@plaidcymru.org; internet www.plaidcymru.org; f. 1925; promotes Welsh interests and seeks independence for Wales; formed a parliamentary alliance with the SNP in April 1986; 10,000 mems; Leader IEUAN WYN JONES; Dep. Leader JILL EVANS.

Progressive Unionist Party: 299 Newtownards Rd, Belfast, BT4 1AG; tel. (28) 9022-5040; e-mail central@pup-ni.org.uk; internet www.pup-ni.org.uk; loyalist party in Northern Ireland; Leader DAVID ERVINE.

Scottish Liberal Democrats: 4 Clifton Terrace, Edinburgh, EH12 5DR; tel. (131) 337-2314; fax (131) 337-3566; e-mail administration@scotlibdems.org.uk; internet www.scotlibdems.org.uk; Leader NICOL STEPHEN.

Scottish National Party (SNP): 107 McDonald Rd, Edinburgh, EH7 4NW; tel. (131) 525-8900; fax (131) 525-8901; e-mail snp.hq@snp.org; internet www.snp.org; f. 1934; advocates independence for Scotland as a member of the EU and Scottish control of national resources; Leader ALEX SALMOND; Pres. IAN HUDGHTON; Nat. Sec. Dr ALASDAIR ALLAN.

Scottish Socialist Party: 70 Stanley Street, Glasgow, G41 1JB; tel. (141) 429-8200; fax (141) 429-8040; e-mail ssp.glasgow@btconnect.com; internet www.scottishsocialistparty.org; f. 1998; Convener TOMMIE SHERIDAN.

Sinn Féin ('Ourselves Alone'): 51–55 Falls Rd, Belfast, BT12 4PD; tel. (28) 9022-3000; fax (28) 9022-3001; e-mail sfadmin@eircom.net; internet www.sinnfein.ie; f. 1905; political wing of the Provisional IRA; seeks the reunification of Ireland and the establishment of a 32-county democratic socialist state; engages in community politics; Chair. MARY LOU MCDONALD; Pres. GERRY ADAMS; Gen. Sec. MITCHELL MCLAUGHLIN.

Social Democratic and Labour Party (SDLP): 121 Ormeau Rd, Belfast, BT7 1SH; tel. (28) 9024-7700; fax (28) 9023-6699; e-mail sdlp@indigo.ie; internet www.sdlp.ie; f. 1970; radical, left-of-centre principles with a view to the eventual reunification of Ireland by popular consent; Leader MARK DURKAN.

Socialist Labour Party: 9 Victoria Rd, Barnsley, South Yorkshire, S70 2BB; tel. and fax (1226) 770957; e-mail info@socialist-labour-party.org.uk; internet www.socialist-labour-party.org.uk; supports renationalization of industry, constitutional reform, withdrawal from the European Union; Gen. Sec. ARTHUR SCARGILL; Pres. PAUL HARDMAN.

Socialist Workers' Party (SWP): POB 42184, London, SW8 2WD; tel. (20) 7819-1170; fax (20) 7819-1179; e-mail enquiries@swp.org.uk; internet www.swp.org.uk; f. 1950; advocates workers' control through revolution, not reform; c. 9,000 mems; Nat. Sec. MARTIN SMITH.

Ulster Unionist Party: Cunningham House, 429 Holywood Rd, Belfast, BT4 2LN; tel. (28) 9076-5500; fax (28) 9076-9419; e-mail uup@uup.org; internet www.uup.org; f. 1905; governed Northern Ireland 1921–72; supports parity and equality for Northern Ireland within the United Kingdom; Pres. JOHN WHITE; Leader Sir REG EMPEY.

UK Independence Party: POB 9876, Birmingham, B6 4DN; tel. (121) 333-7737; fax (121) 333-1520; e-mail webmail@ukip.org; internet www.ukip.org; f. 1993; advocates withdrawal from the European Union; 27,000 mems; Leader ROGER KNAPMAN; Chair. DAVID CAMPBELL-BANNERMAN.

United Kingdom Unionist Party: Parliament Buildings Stormont, Belfast; tel. (28) 9052-1482; fax (28) 9052-1483; e-mail info@ukup.org; seeks to preserve the union between Great Britain and Northern Ireland; Leader ROBERT MCCARTNEY.

Veritas: 109–110 Bolsover St, London, W1W 5NT; tel. (20) 7631-3757; e-mail mail@veritasparty.com; internet www.veritasparty.com; f. 2005; advocates withdrawal from the European Union; Leader PATRICK ESTON; Chief Exec. JONATHAN LOCKHART.

The following paramilitary organizations in Northern Ireland are proscribed under Schedule 2 of the Emergency Provisions Act 1978: (nationalist) the Irish Republican Army, the Irish National Liberation Army, Cumann na mBan (women's section of the IRA), Fianna na hEireann (youth section of the IRA), Saor Eire and the Irish People's Liberation Organization; (loyalist) the Ulster Freedom Fighters, the Ulster Volunteer Force and the Red Hand Commandos. In August 1992 the loyalist Ulster Defence Association (UDA) was proscribed by the British Government. The Loyalist Volunteer Force (LVF) and the Continuity Army Council (CAC) were proscribed in 1997.

Diplomatic Representation

EMBASSIES AND HIGH COMMISSIONS IN THE UNITED KINGDOM

Afghanistan: 31 Prince's Gate, London, SW7 1QQ; tel. (20) 7589-8891; fax (20) 7584-4801; e-mail info@afghanembassy.co.uk; internet www.afghanembassy.co.uk; Ambassador AHMAD WALI MASOUD.

Albania: 2nd Floor, 24 Buckingham Gate, London, SW1E 6LB; tel. (20) 7828-8897; fax (20) 7828-8869; e-mail amblonder@hotmail.com; Ambassador KASTRIOT ROBO.

Algeria: 54 Holland Park, London, W11 3RS; tel. (20) 7221-7800; fax (20) 7221-0448; e-mail algerianembassy@btconnect.com; Ambassador MUHAMMAD SALAH DEMBRI.

Andorra: 63 Westover Rd, London, SW18 2RF; tel. (20) 8874-4806; fax (20) 8874-4902; Chargé d'affaires a.i. MARIA ROSA PICART DE FRANCIS.

Angola: 22 Dorset St, London, W1U 6QY; tel. (20) 7299-9850; fax (20) 7486-6397; e-mail embassy@angola.org.uk; internet www.angola.org.uk; Ambassador ANA MARIA TELES CARREIRA.

Antigua and Barbuda: 2nd Floor, 15 Crawford Pl., London, W1H 4LP; tel. (20) 7258-0070; fax (20) 7258-7486; e-mail enquiries@antigua-barbuda.com; internet www.antigua-barbuda.com; High Commr Dr CARL ROBERTS.

Argentina: 65 Brook St, London, W1K 4AH; tel. (20) 7318-1300; fax (20) 7318-1301; e-mail embar.ru@btconnect.com; internet www.argentine-embassy-uk.org; Ambassador FEDERICO MIRRÉ.

Armenia: 25A Cheniston Gdns, London, W8 6TG; tel. (20) 7938-5435; fax (20) 7938-2595; e-mail armemb@armenianembassyuk.com; Ambassador Dr VAHE GABRIELYAN.

Australia: Australia House, Strand, London, WC2B 4LA; tel. (20) 7379-4334; fax (20) 7240-5333; internet www.australia.org.uk; High Commr RICHARD ALSTON.

Austria: 18 Belgrave Mews West, London, SW1X 8HU; tel. (20) 7344-3250; fax (20) 7344-0292; e-mail london-ob@bmaa.gv.at; internet www.bmaa.gv.at/london; Ambassador Dr GABRIELE MATZ-NER-HOLZER.

Azerbaijan: 4 Kensington Court, London, W8 5DL; tel. (20) 7938-3412; fax (20) 7937-1783; e-mail sefir@btinternet.com; Ambassador RAFAEL IBRAHIMOV.

Bahamas: 10 Chesterfield St, London, W1J 5JL; tel. (20) 7408-4488; fax (20) 7499-9937; e-mail information@bahamashclondon.net; internet www.bahamas.co.uk; High Commr BASIL G. O'BRIEN.

Bahrain: 30 Belgrave Sq., London, SW1X 8QB; tel. (20) 7201-9170; fax (20) 7201-9183; Chargé d'affaires a.i. YOUSUF JAMEEL.

Bangladesh: 28 Queen's Gate, London, SW7 5JA; tel. (20) 7584-0081; fax (20) 7581-7477; e-mail bhclondon@btconnect.com; internet www.bangladeshhighcommission.org.uk; High Commr SABIHUDDIN AHMED.

Barbados: 1 Great Russell St, London, WC1B 3ND; tel. (20) 7631-4975; fax (20) 7323-6872; e-mail london@foreign.gov.bb; High Commr L. EDWIN POLLARD.

Belarus: 6 Kensington Court, London, W8 5DL; tel. (20) 7937-3288; fax (20) 7361-0005; e-mail uk@belembassy.org; internet www.belembassy.org/uk; Ambassador Dr ALYAKSEI MAZHUKHOU.

Belgium: 17 Grosvenor Cres., London, SW1X 7EE; tel. (20) 7470-3700; fax (20) 7470-3795; e-mail london@diplobel.org; internet www.diplobel.org/uk; Ambassador Baron THIERRY DE GRUBEN.

Belize: 3rd Floor, 45 Crawford Pl., London, W1H 4LP; tel. (20) 7723-3603; fax (20) 7723-9637; e-mail bzhc-lon@btconnect.com; internet www.belizehighcommission.com; High Commr ALEXIS ROSADO.

Bolivia: 106 Eaton Sq., London, SW1W 9AD; tel. (20) 7235-4248; fax (20) 7235-1286; e-mail info@embassyofbolivia.co.uk; internet www.embassyofbolivia.co.uk; Ambassador GONZALO MONTENEGRO.

Bosnia and Herzegovina: 5–7 Lexham Gardens, London, W8 5JJ; tel. (20) 7373-0867; fax (20) 7373-0871; e-mail mensur@jusic.fsnet.co.uk; Ambassador TANJA MILASINOVIĆ.

Botswana: 6 Stratford Pl., London, W1C 1AY; tel. (20) 7499-0031; fax (20) 7495-8595; High Commr ROY BLACKBEARD.

Brazil: 32 Green St, London, W1K 7AT; tel. (20) 7399-9000; fax (20) 7399-9100; e-mail info@brazil.org.uk; internet www.brazil.org.uk; Ambassador JOSÉ MAURICIO BUSTANI.

Brunei: 19–20 Belgrave Sq., London, SW1X 8PG; tel. (20) 7581-0521; fax (20) 7235-9717; e-mail bhcl@brunei-high-commission.co.uk; High Commr Pengiran Dato' MAIDIN HASHIM.

Bulgaria: 186–188 Queen's Gate, London, SW7 5HL; tel. (20) 7584-9400; fax (20) 7584-4948; e-mail info@bulgarianembassy.org.uk; internet www.bulgarianembassy.org.uk; Ambassador NIKOLOV MATEV.

Cambodia: 28-32 Wellington Rd, London, NW8 9SP; tel. (20) 7483-9063; fax (20) 7483-9061; e-mail cambodianembassy@btconnect.com; internet www.cambodianembassy.org.uk; Ambassador HOR NAMBORA.

Cameroon: 84 Holland Park, London, W11 3SB; tel. (20) 7727-0771; fax (20) 7792-9353; High Commr SAMUEL LIBOCK MBEI.

Canada: 1 Grosvenor Sq., London, W1K 4AB; tel. (20) 7258-6600; fax (20) 7258-6533; e-mail ldn@dfait-maeci.gc.ca; internet www.dfait-maeci.gc.ca/london; High Commr MEL CAPPE.

Chile: 12 Devonshire St, London, W1G 7DS; tel. (20) 7580-6392; fax (20) 7436-5204; e-mail embachile@embachile.co.uk; internet www.echileuk.demon.co.uk; Ambassador MARIANO FERNÁNDEZ.

China, People's Republic: 49–51 Portland Pl., London, W1B 4JL; tel. (20) 7299-4049; fax (20) 7636-5578; e-mail press@chinese-embassy.org.uk; internet www.chinese-embassy.org.uk; Ambassador ZHA PEIXIN.

Colombia: 3 Hans Cres., London, SW1X OLN; tel. (20) 7589-9177; fax (20) 7589-4718; e-mail mail@colombianembassy.co.uk; internet www.colombianembassy.co.uk; Ambassador Dr ALFONSO LÓPEZ CABALLERO.

Congo, Democratic Republic: 281 Gray's Inn Rd, London, WC1X 8QF; tel. (020) 7278-9825; fax (020) 7833-9967; e-mail info@ambardcongo.org.uk; internet www.ambardcongo.org.uk; Ambassador EUGÉNIE TSHIELA.

Costa Rica: Flat 1, 14 Lancaster Gate, London, W2 3LH; tel. (20) 7706-8844; fax (20) 7706-8655; e-mail costaricanembassy@btconnect.com; Chargé d'affaires a.i. SYLVIA UGALDE.

Côte d'Ivoire: 2 Upper Belgrave St, London, SW1X 8BJ; tel. (20) 7235-6991; fax (20) 7259-5320; Ambassador YOUSSOUFU BAMBA.

Croatia: 21 Conway St, London, W1T 6BN; tel. (20) 7387-2022; fax (20) 7387-0310; e-mail croemb.london@mvp.hr; internet uk.mfa.hr; Ambassador JOŠKO PARO.

Cuba: 167 High Holborn, London, WC1V 6PA; tel. (20) 7240-2488; fax (20) 7836-2602; e-mail embacuba@cubaldn.com; internet www.cubaldn.com; Ambassador RENÉ JUAN MUJICA CANTELAR.

Cyprus: 93 Park St, London, W1K 7ET; tel. (20) 7499-8272; fax (20) 7491-0691; e-mail cyphclondon@dial.pipex.com; High Commr PETROS EFTYCHIOU.

THE UNITED KINGDOM
Directory

Czech Republic: 26 Kensington Palace Gdns, London, W8 4QY; tel. (20) 7243-1115; fax (20) 7727-9654; e-mail london@embassy.mzv.cz; internet www.mzv.cz/london; Ambassador JAN WINKLER.

Denmark: 55 Sloane St, London, SW1X 9SR; tel. (20) 7333-0200; fax (20) 7333-0270; e-mail lonamb@um.dk; internet www.amblondon.um.dk; Ambassador TOM RISDAHL JENSEN.

Dominica: 1 Collingham Gdns, London, SW5 0HW; tel. (20) 7370-5194; fax (20) 7373-8743; e-mail dominicahighcom@btconnect.com; High Commr AGNES ADONIS (acting).

Dominican Republic: 139 Inverness Terrace, London, W2 6JF; tel. (20) 7727-6285; fax (20) 7727-3693; e-mail info@dominicanembassy.org.uk; internet www.dominicanembassy.org.uk; Ambassador ANIBAL DE CASTRO.

Ecuador: Flat 3B, 3 Hans Cres, Knightsbridge, London, SW1X 0LS; tel. (20) 7584-1367; fax (20) 7823-9701; e-mail ecugranbretania@mmrree.gov.ec; Chargé d'affaires a.i. DÉBORAH SALGADO CAMPAÑA.

Egypt: 26 South St, London, W1K 1DW; tel. (20) 7499-3304; fax (20) 7491-1542; e-mail etembuk@hotmail.com; internet www.egyptianconsulate.co.uk; Ambassador GEHAD MADI.

El Salvador: Mayfair House, 39 Great Portland St, London, W1W 7JZ; tel. (20) 7436-8282; fax (20) 7436-8181; e-mail evilanova@rree.gob.sv; Ambassador Dr VLADIMIRO P. VILLALTA.

Equatorial Guinea: 13 Park Place, St. James's, London, SW1A 1LP; tel. (20) 7499-6867; fax (20) 7499-6782; internet www.embarege-londres.org; Ambassador AGUSTIN NZE NFUMU.

Eritrea: 96 White Lion St, London, N1 9PF; tel. (20) 7713-0096; fax (20) 7713-0161; e-mail eriemba@erimbauk.com; Ambassador NEGASSI SENGAL GHEBREZGHI.

Estonia: 16 Hyde Park Gate, London, SW7 5DG; tel. (20) 7589-3428; fax (20) 7589-3430; e-mail embassy.london@estonia.gov.uk; internet www.estonia.gov.uk; Ambassador Dr MARGUS LAIDRE.

Ethiopia: 17 Prince's Gate, London, SW7 1PZ; tel. (20) 7589-7212; fax (20) 7584-7054; e-mail info@ethioembassy.org.uk; internet www.ethioembassy.org.uk; Ambassador BERHANU KEBEDE.

Fiji: 34 Hyde Park Gate, London, SW7 5DN; tel. (20) 7584-3661; fax (20) 7584-2838; e-mail fijirepuk@compuserve.com; High Commr EMITAI LAUSIKI BOLADUADUA.

Finland: 38 Chesham Pl., London, SW1X 8HW; tel. (20) 7838-6200; fax (20) 7235-3680; e-mail sanomat.lon@formin.fi; internet www.finemb.org.uk; Ambassador JAAKKO LAAJAVA.

France: 58 Knightsbridge, London, SW1X 7JT; tel. (20) 7073-1000; fax (20) 7073-1004; e-mail presse.londres-amba@diplomatie.fr; internet www.ambafrance-uk.org; Ambassador GÉRARD ERRERA.

Gabon: 27 Elvaston Pl., London, SW7 5NL; tel. (20) 7823-9986; fax (20) 7584-0047; Ambassador ALAIN MENSAH-ZAGUELET.

The Gambia: 57 Kensington Court, London, W8 5DG; tel. (20) 7937-6316; fax (20) 7937-9095; e-mail gambia@gamhighcom.fsnet.co.uk; High Commr TAMSIR JALLOW (acting).

Georgia: 4 Russell Gardens, London, W14 8EZ; tel. (20) 7603-7799; fax (20) 7603-6682; e-mail embassy@geoemb.plus.com; internet www.geoemb.org.uk; Ambassador GELA CHARKVIANI.

Germany: 23 Belgrave Sq., London, SW1X 8PZ; tel. (20) 7824-1300; fax (20) 7824-1449; e-mail mail@german-embassy.org.uk; internet www.german-embassy.org.uk; Ambassador WOLFGANG FRIEDRICH ISCHINGER.

Ghana: 13 Belgrave Sq., London, SW1X 8PN; tel. (20) 7235-4142; fax (20) 7245-9552; e-mail enquiries@ghana-com.co.uk; internet www.ghana-com.co.uk; High Commr ISAAC OSEI.

Greece: 1A Holland Park, London, W11 3TP; tel. (20) 7229-3850; fax (20) 7229-7221; e-mail political@greekembassy.org.uk; internet www.greekembassy.org.uk; Ambassador ANASTASE SCOPELITIS.

Grenada: 5 Chandos St, London, W1G 9DG; tel. (20) 7631-4277; fax (20) 7631-4274; e-mail grenada@high-commission.demon.co.uk; High Commr JOSEPH STEPHEN CHARTER.

Guatemala: 13 Fawcett St, London, SW10 9HN; tel. (20) 7351-3042; fax (20) 7376-5708; e-mail embaguate.gtm@btconnect.com; Ambassador EDMUNDO RENÉ URRUTIA GARCIA.

Guinea: 48 Onslow Gardens, London, SW7 3PY; tel. (20) 7594-4809; e-mail ambaguineeuk@yahoo.uk; Ambassador LANSANA KEÏTA.

Guyana: 3 Palace Court, Bayswater Rd, London, W2 4LP; tel. (20) 7229-7684; fax (20) 7727-9809; e-mail ghc.l@ic24.net; High Commr LALESHWAR K. N. SINGH.

Holy See: 54 Parkside, London, SW19 5NE (Apostolic Nunciature); tel. (20) 8944-7189; fax (20) 8947-2494; e-mail nuntius@globalnet.co.uk; Apostolic Nuncio Most Rev. FAUSTINO SAINZ MUÑOZ (Titular Archbishop of Novaliciana).

Honduras: 115 Gloucester Pl., London, W1U 6JT; tel. (20) 7486-4880; fax (20) 7486-4550; e-mail hondurasuk@lineone.net; Chargé d'affaires a.i. IVAN ROMERO-NASSER.

Hungary: 35 Eaton Pl., London, SW1X 8BY; tel. (20) 7235-5218; fax (20) 7823-1348; e-mail office@huemblon.org.uk; internet www.huemblon.org.uk; Ambassador BÉLA SZOMBATI.

Iceland: 2A Hans St, London, SW1X 0JE; tel. (20) 7259-3999; fax (20) 7245-9649; e-mail icemb.london@utn.stjr.is; internet www.iceland.org/uk; Ambassador SVERRIR HAUKUR GUNNLAUGSSON.

India: India House, Aldwych, London, WC2B 4NA; tel. (20) 7836-8484; fax (20) 7836-4331; e-mail info@hclondon.net; internet www.hclondon.net; High Commr KAMALESH SHARMA.

Indonesia: 38 Grosvenor Sq., London, W1X 2HW; tel. (20) 7499-7661; fax (20) 7491-4993; e-mail kbri@btconnect.com; internet www.indonesianembassy.org.uk; Ambassador RADEN MUHAMMAD MARTY MULIANA NATALEGAWA.

Iran: 16 Prince's Gate, London, SW7 1PT; tel. (20) 7225-3000; fax (20) 7589-4440; e-mail info@iran-embassy.org.uk; internet www.iran-embassy.org.uk; Chargé d'affaires a.i. HAMID REZA NAFEZ AREFI.

Iraq: 169 Knightsbridge, London, SW7 1DW; tel. (20) 7581-2264; fax (20) 7589-3356; e-mail lonemb@iraqmofa.net; Ambassador Dr SALAH AL SHAIKHLY.

Ireland: 17 Grosvenor Pl., London, SW1X 7HR; tel. (20) 7235-2171; fax (20) 7245-6961; Ambassador DÁITHÍ O'CEALLAIGH.

Israel: 2 Palace Green, Kensington, London, W8 4QB; tel. (20) 7957-9500; fax (20) 7957-9555; e-mail info1@london.mfa.gov.il; internet london.mfa.gov.il; Ambassador ZVI HEIFETZ.

Italy: 14 Three Kings Yard, London, W1K 4EH; tel. (20) 7312-2200; fax (20) 7312-2230; e-mail ambasciata.londra@esteri.it; internet www.amblondra.esteri.it; Ambassador GIANCARLO ARAGONA.

Jamaica: 1–2 Prince Consort Rd, London, SW7 2BZ; tel. (20) 7823-9911; fax (20) 7589-5154; e-mail jamhigh@jhcuk.com; internet www.jhcuk.com; High Commr GAIL MATHURIN.

Japan: 101–104 Piccadilly, London, W1J 7JT; tel. (20) 7465-6543; fax (20) 7491-9347; e-mail info@jpembassy.org.uk; internet www.uk.emb-japan.go.jp; Ambassador YOSHIJI NOGAMI.

Jordan: 6 Upper Phillimore Gdns, London, W8 7HA; tel. (20) 7937-3685; fax (20) 7937-8795; e-mail info@jordanembassyuk.org; internet www.jordanembassyuk.org; Ambassador Dr ALIA BOURAN.

Kazakhstan: 33 Thurloe Sq., London, SW7 2SD; tel. (20) 7581-4646; fax (20) 7584-8481; e-mail london@kazakhstan-embassy.org; internet www.kazakhstan-embassy.org.uk; Ambassador ERLAN IDRISSOV.

Kenya: 45 Portland Pl., London, W1N 4AS; tel. (20) 7636-2371; fax (20) 7323-6717; e-mail info@kenyahighcommission.com; High Commr JOSEPH KIRUGUMI MUCHEMI.

Korea, Democratic People's Republic: 73 Gunnersbury Ave, London, W5 4LP; tel. (20) 8992-4965; fax (20) 8992-2053; Ambassador RI YONG HO.

Korea, Republic: 60 Buckingham Gate, London, SW1E 6AJ; tel. (20) 7227-5500; fax (20) 7227-5503; internet korea.embassyhomepage.com/index.htm; Ambassador Dr YOON-JE CHO.

Kuwait: 2 Albert Gate, London, SW1X 7JU; tel. (20) 7590-3400; fax (20) 7823-1712; e-mail kuwait@dircon.co.uk; internet www.kuwaitinfo.org.uk; Ambassador KHALID AL-DUWAISAN.

Kyrgyzstan: Ascot House, 119 Crawford St, London, W1U 6BJ; tel. (20) 7935-1462; fax (20) 7935-7449; e-mail embassy@kyrgyz-embassy.org.uk; Chargé d'affaires a.i. MAYA SABIRDINA.

Latvia: 45 Nottingham Pl., London, W1U 5LY; tel. (20) 7312-0040; fax (20) 7312-0042; e-mail embassy.uk@mfa.gov.lv; internet www.london.mfa.gov.lv; Ambassador INDULIS BĒRZIŅŠ.

Lebanon: 15–21 Kensington Palace Gardens, London, W8 4RB; tel. (20) 7229-7265; fax (20) 7243-1699; e-mail emb.leb@btinternet.com; Ambassador JIHAD MORTADA.

Lesotho: 7 Chesham Pl., London, SW1 8HN; tel. (20) 7235-5686; fax (20) 7235-5023; e-mail lhc@lesotholondon.org.uk; internet www.lesotholondon.org.uk; High Commissioner MORENA SEEISO BERENG SEEISO.

Liberia: 23 Fitzroy Sq., London, W1 6EW; tel. (20) 7388-5489; fax (20) 7380-1593; Ambassador WESLEY MOMO JOHNSON.

Libya: 15 Knightsbridge, London, SW1X 7LY; tel. (20) 7201-8280; fax (20) 7245-0588; Sec. of the People's Bureau MUHAMMAD ABU AL-QASSIM AZWAI.

Lithuania: 84 Gloucester Pl., London, W1U 6AU; tel. (20) 7486-6401; fax (20) 7486-6403; e-mail amb.uk@urm.lt; internet amb.urm.lt/jk; Ambassador AURIMAS TAURANTAS.

Luxembourg: 27 Wilton Cres., London, SW1X 8SD; tel. (20) 7235-6961; fax (20) 7235-9734; e-mail embassy@luxembourg.co.uk; Ambassador JEAN-LOUIS WOLZFELD.

Macedonia, former Yugoslav republic: Suites 2.1 and 2.2, 2nd Floor, Buckingham Court, Buckingham Gate, London, SW1E 6PE; tel. (20) 7976-0535; fax (20) 7976-0539; e-mail info@

macedonianembassy.org.uk; internet www.macedonianembassy.org.uk; Ambassador GJORGJI SPASOV.

Madagascar: 118 Piccadilly, London, W1J 7NW; tel. (20) 7569-6721; fax (20) 7569-6722; e-mail embamadlon@yahoo.co.uk; Chargé d'affaires a.i. IARY BERTHINE RAVAOARIMANANA.

Malawi: 33 Grosvenor St, London, W1K 4QT; tel. (20) 7491-4172; fax (20) 7491-9916; e-mail kwacha@malawihighcomm.prestel.co.uk; High Commr Dr FRANCIS MOTO.

Malaysia: 45 Belgrave Sq., London, SW1X 8QT; tel. (20) 7235-8033; fax (20) 7235-5161; e-mail mwlon@btconnect.com; High Commr Dato' ABDUL AZIA MOHAMMED.

Maldives: 22 Nottingham Pl., London, W1U 5NJ; tel. (20) 7224-2135; fax (20) 7224-2157; e-mail maldives.high.commission@virgin.net; internet www.maldiveshighcommission.org; High Commr HASSAN SOBIR.

Malta: Malta House, 36–38 Piccadilly, London, W1V 0PQ; tel. (20) 7292-4800; fax (20) 7734-1831; e-mail maltahighcommission.london@gov.mt; High Commr Dr MICHAEL REFALO.

Mauritania: 8 Carlos Pl., London, W1K 3AS; tel. (20) 7478-9323; fax (20) 7478-9339; e-mail ambarim@aol.com; Ambassador OULD MOCTAR NECHE MÉLAÏNINE.

Mauritius: 32–33 Elvaston Pl., London, SW7 5NW; tel. (20) 7581-0294; fax (20) 7823-8437; e-mail londonmhc@btinternet.com; High Commr ABHIMANU MAHENDRA KUNDASAMY.

Mexico: 16 St George St, Hanover Square, London, W1S 1LX; tel. (20) 7499-8586; fax (20) 7495-4035; e-mail mexuk@easynet.co.uk; internet www.embamex.co.uk; Ambassador JUAN JOSÉ BREMER DE MARTINO.

Moldova: 5 Dolphin Square, Edensor Road, London, W4 2ST; tel. (20) 8995-6818; fax (20) 8995-6927; e-mail mail@moldovanembassy.org.uk; internet www.moldovanembassy.org.uk; Ambassador MARIANA DURLEŞTEANU.

Mongolia: 7 Kensington Court, London, W8 5DL; tel. (20) 7937-0150; fax (20) 7937-1117; e-mail office@embassyofmongolia.co.uk; internet www.embassyofmongolia.co.uk; Ambassador DALRAIN DAVAASAMBUU.

Morocco: 49 Queen's Gate Gdns, London, SW7 5NE; tel. (20) 7581-5001; fax (20) 7225-3862; e-mail mail@sifamaldn.org; Ambassador MOHAMMED BELMAHI.

Mozambique: 21 Fitzroy Sq., London, W1T 6EL; tel. (20) 7383-3800; fax (20) 7383-3801; e-mail agumende@mozambiquehc.co.uk; internet www.mozambiquehc.org.uk; High Commr ANTONIO GUMENDE.

Myanmar: 19A Charles St, London, W1J 5DX; tel. (20) 7499-4340; fax (20) 7409-7043; e-mail memblondon@aol.com; Ambassador U NAY WIN.

Namibia: 6 Chandos St, London, W1G 9LU; tel. (20) 7636-6244; fax (20) 7637-5694; e-mail namibia.hicom@btconnect.com; High Commr RINGO FESTUS ABED.

Nepal: 12A Kensington Palace Gdns, London, W8 4QU; tel. (20) 7229-1594; fax (20) 7792-9861; e-mail info@nepembassy.org.uk; internet www.nepembassy.org.uk; Ambassador PRABAL SHUMSHERE JUNG BAHADUR RANA.

Netherlands: 38 Hyde Park Gate, London, SW7 5DP; tel. (20) 7590-3200; fax (20) 7225-0947; e-mail london@netherlands-embassy.org.uk; internet www.netherlands-embassy.org.uk; Ambassador Count JAN M. V. A. DE MARCHANT ET D'ANSEMBOURG.

New Zealand: New Zealand House, 80 Haymarket, London, SW1Y 4TQ; tel. (20) 7930-8422; fax (20) 7839-4580; e-mail aboutnz@newzealandhc.org.uk; internet www.nzembassy.com/uk; High Commr JONATHAN HUNT.

Nicaragua: Suite 31, Vicarage House, 58–60 Kensington Church St, London, W8 4DB; tel. (20) 7938-2373; fax (20) 7937-0952; e-mail embanic1@yahoo.co.uk; Ambassador PIERO PAOLO COEN UBILLA.

Nigeria: Nigeria House, 9 Northumberland Ave, London, WC2N 5BX; tel. (20) 7839-1244; fax (20) 7839-8746; e-mail chancery@nigeriahc.org.uk; internet www.nigeriahc.org.uk; High Commr Dr CHRISTOPHER KOLADE.

Norway: 25 Belgrave Sq., London, SW1X 8QD; tel. (20) 7591-5500; fax (20) 7245-6993; e-mail emb.london@mfa.no; internet www.norway.org.uk; Ambassador BJARNE LINDSTRØM.

Oman: 167 Queen's Gate, London, SW7 5HE; tel. (20) 7225-0001; fax (20) 7589-2505; Ambassador HUSSAIN ALI ABDULLATIF.

Pakistan: 34–36 Lowndes Sq., London, SW1X 9JN; tel. (20) 7664-9200; fax (20) 7664-9224; e-mail pareplondon@supanet.com; internet www.pakmission-uk.gov.pk; Ambassador MALEEDHA LODHI.

Panama: 40 Hertford St, London, W1J 7SH; tel. (20) 7493-4646; fax (20) 7493-4333; e-mail panama1@btconnect.com; Ambassador LILIANA FERNÁNDES.

Papua New Guinea: 3rd Floor, 14 Waterloo Pl., London, SW1R 4AR; tel. (20) 7930-0922; fax (20) 7930-0828; internet www.pnghighcomm.org.uk; High Commr JEAN L. KEKEDO.

Paraguay: 3rd Floor, 344 Kensington High St, London, W14 8NS; tel. (20) 7610-4180; fax (20) 7371-4279; e-mail embapar@btconnect.com; internet www.paraguayembassy.co.uk; Chargé d'affaires a.i. MARIA CHRISTINA ACOSTA ALVAREZ.

Peru: 52 Sloane St, London, SW1X 9SP; tel. (20) 7235-1917; fax (20) 7235-4463; e-mail postmaster@peruembassy-uk.com; internet www.peruembassy-uk.com; Ambassador LUIS SOLARI TUDELA.

Philippines: 9A Palace Green, London, W8 4QE; tel. (20) 7937-1600; fax (20) 7937-2925; e-mail embassy@philemb.org.uk; internet www.philemb.org.uk; Ambassador EDGARDO B. ESPIRITU.

Poland: 47 Portland Pl., London, W1B 1JH; tel. (870) 774-2700; fax (20) 7291-3575; e-mail polishembassy@polishembassy.org.uk; internet www.polishembassy.org.uk; Chargé d'affaires a. i. CEZARY KRÓL.

Portugal: 11 Belgrave Sq., London, SW1X 8PP; tel. (20) 7235-5331; fax (20) 7235-0739; e-mail london@portembassy.co.uk; Ambassador FERNANDO ANDRESEN-GUIMARÃES.

Qatar: 1 South Audley St, London, W1K 1NB; tel. (20) 7493-2200; fax (20) 7493-2661; Ambassador KHALID BIN RASHID BIN SALIM AL-HAMOUDI AL-MANSOURI.

Romania: Arundel House, 4 Palace Green, London, W8 4QD; tel. (20) 7937-9666; fax (20) 7937-8069; e-mail roemb@roemb.co.uk; internet www.roemb.co.uk; Ambassador DAN GHIBERNEA.

Russia: 13 Kensington Palace Gdns, London, W8 4QX; tel. (20) 7229-2666; fax (20) 7229-5804; e-mail office@rusemblon.org; internet www.great-britain.mid.ru; Ambassador YURII VIKTOROVICH FEDOTOV.

Rwanda: 120–122 Seymour Pl., London, W1H 1NR; tel. (20) 7724-9832; fax (20) 7724-8642; e-mail uk@ambarwanda.org.uk; internet www.ambarwanda.org.uk; Ambassador CLAVER GATETE.

Saint Christopher and Nevis: 2nd Floor, 10 Kensington Court, London, W8 5DL; tel. (20) 7937-9718; fax (20) 7937-7484; e-mail sknhighcomm@btconnect.com; High Commr JAMES E. WILLIAMS.

Saint Lucia: 1 Collingham Gdns, London, SW5 0HW; tel. (20) 7370-7123; fax (20) 7370-1905; e-mail hcslu@btconnect.com; High Commr EMMANUEL H. COTTER.

Saint Vincent and the Grenadines: 10 Kensington Court, London, W8 5DL; tel. (20) 7565-2874; fax (20) 7937-6040; e-mail info@svghighcom.co.uk; High Commr CENIO E. LEWIS.

Saudi Arabia: 30 Charles St, London, W1J 5DZ; tel. (20) 7917-3000; fax (20) 7917-3330; e-mail ukemb@mofa.gov.sa; internet www.saudiembassy.org.uk; Ambassador Prince MUHAMMAD BIN NAWAF BIN ABDULAZIZ.

Senegal: 39 Marloes Rd, London, W8 6LA; tel. (20) 7937-7237; fax (20) 7938-2546; e-mail email@senegalembassy.co.uk; internet www.senegalembassy.co.uk; Ambassador Gen. MAMADOU NIANG.

Serbia and Montenegro: 28 Belgrave Sq., London, SW1X 8QB; tel. (20) 7235-9049; fax (20) 7235-7092; internet www.yugoslavembassy.org.uk; Ambassador Dr DRAGIŠA BURZAN.

Sierra Leone: 41 Eagle St, London, WC1R 4TL; tel. (20) 7404-0140; fax (20) 7430-9862; e-mail info@slhc-uk.org.uk; internet www.slhc-uk.org.uk; High Commr Alhaji SULAIMAN TEJAN-JALLOH.

Singapore: 9 Wilton Cres., London, SW1X 8SP; tel. (20) 7235-8315; fax (20) 7245-6583; e-mail info@singaporehc.org.uk; High Commr MICHAEL ENG CHENG TEO.

Slovakia: 25 Kensington Palace Gdns, London, W8 4QY; tel. (20) 7313-6470; fax (20) 7313-6481; e-mail mail@slovakembassy.co.uk; internet www.slovakembassy.co.uk; Chargé d'affaires a.i. RADOVAN JAVORČIK.

Slovenia: 10 Little College St, London, SW1P 3SH; tel. (20) 7222-5400; fax (20) 7222-5277; e-mail vlo@mzz-dkp.gov.si; internet www.gov.si/mzz-dkp/vlo/eng; Ambassador IZTOK MIROŠIČ.

South Africa: South Africa House, Trafalgar Sq., London, WC2N 5DP; tel. (20) 7451-7299; fax (20) 7451-7284; e-mail webdesk@southafricahouse.com; internet www.southafricahouse.com; High Commr Dr LINDIWE MABUZA.

Spain: 39 Chesham Pl., London, SW1X 8SB; tel. (20) 7235-5555; fax (20) 7259-5392; e-mail embespuk@mail.mae.es; Ambassador CARLOS MIRANDA Y ELÍO.

Sri Lanka: 13 Hyde Park Gdns, London, W2 2LU; tel. (20) 7262-1841; fax (20) 7262-7970; e-mail mail@slhc-london.co.uk; internet www.slhclondon.org; High Commr KSHENUKA SENEWIRATNE.

Sudan: 3 Cleveland Row, St James's, London, SW1A 1DD; tel. (20) 7839-8080; fax (20) 7839-7560; e-mail admin@sudanembassy.co.uk; internet www.sudanembassy.co.uk; Ambassador Dr HASAN ABDIN.

Swaziland: 20 Buckingham Gate, London, SW1E 6LB; tel. (20) 7630-6611; fax (20) 7630-6564; e-mail swaziland@swaziland.btinternet.com; Ambassador MARY MADZANDZA KANYA.

THE UNITED KINGDOM

Directory

Sweden: 11 Montagu Pl., London, W1H 2AL; tel. (20) 7917-6400; fax (20) 7724-4174; e-mail ambassaden.london@foreign.ministry.se; internet www.swedenabroad.com/london; Ambassador STAFFAN CARLSSON.

Switzerland: 16–18 Montagu Pl., London, W1H 2BQ; tel. (20) 7616-6000; fax (20) 7724-7001; e-mail swissembassy@lon.rep.admin.ch; internet www.swissembassy.org.uk; Ambassador ALEXIS P. LAUTENBERG.

Syria: 8 Belgrave Sq., London, SW1X 8PH; tel. (20) 7245-9012; fax (20) 7235-4621; e-mail info@syrianembassy.co.uk; internet www.syrianembassy.co.uk; Ambassador Dr SAMI KHIYAMI.

Tanzania: 3 Stratford Pl., London, WIC 1AS; tel. (20) 7569-1470; fax (20) 7491-3710; e-mail balozi@tanzania-online.gov.uk; internet www.tanzania-online.gov.uk; High Commr HASSAN OMAR GUMBO KIBELLOH.

Thailand: 29–30 Queen's Gate, London, SW7 5JB; tel. (20) 7589-2944; fax (20) 7823-7492; e-mail thaiduto@btinternet.com; internet www.thaiembassyuk.org.uk; Ambassador VIKROM KOOMPIROCHANA.

Tonga: 36 Molyneux St, London, W1H 5BQ; tel. (20) 7724-5828; fax (20) 7723-9074; e-mail fetu@btinternet.com; High Commr Dr SIONE NGONGO KIOA.

Trinidad and Tobago: 42 Belgrave Sq., London, SW1X 8NT; tel. (20) 7245-9351; fax (20) 7823-1065; e-mail tthc.info@btconnect.net; High Commr GLENDA P. MOREAN-PHILLIP.

Tunisia: 29 Prince's Gate, London, SW7 1QG; tel. (20) 7584-8117; fax (20) 7584-3205; Ambassador MUHAMMAD GHARIANI.

Turkey: 43 Belgrave Sq., London, SW1X 8PA; tel. (20) 7393-0202; fax (20) 7393-0066; e-mail turkishconsulate@btconnect.com; internet www.turkishconsulate.org.uk; Ambassador AKIN ALPTUNA.

Turkmenistan: 2nd Floor South, St George's House, 14–17 Wells St, London, W1P 3FP; tel. (20) 7255-1071; fax (20) 7323-9184; Ambassador YAZMURAD SERYAEV.

Uganda: Uganda House, 58/59 Trafalgar Sq., London, WC2N 5DX; tel. (20) 7839-5783; fax (20) 7839-8925; internet www.ugandahighcommission.co.uk; High Commr JOAN KAKIMA NYAKATUURA RWABYOMERE.

Ukraine: 60 Holland Park, London, W11 3SJ; tel. (20) 7727-6312; fax (20) 7792-1708; internet www.ukremb.org.uk; Ambassador IHOR KHARCHENKO.

United Arab Emirates: 30 Princes Gate, London, SW7 1PT; tel. (20) 7581-1281; fax (20) 7581-9616; e-mail information@uaeembassyuk.net; internet www.uaeembassyuk.net; Ambassador ISSA SALEH AL-GURG.

USA: 24–32 Grosvenor Sq., London, W1A 1AE; tel. (20) 7499-9000; fax (20) 7629-9124; internet www.usembassy.org.uk; Ambassador ROBERT HOLMES TUTTLE.

Uruguay: 2nd Floor, 140 Brompton Rd, London, SW3 1HY; tel. (20) 7589-8835; fax (20) 7581-9585; e-mail emb@urubri.demon.co.uk; Ambassador RICARDO VARELA.

Uzbekistan: 41 Holland Park, London, W11 2RP; tel. (20) 7229-7679; fax (20) 7229-7029; e-mail info@uzbekembassy.org; internet www.uzbekembassy.org; Ambassador TUKHTAPULAT RISKIEV.

Venezuela: 1 Cromwell Rd, London, SW7 2HW; tel. (20) 7584-4206; fax (20) 7589-8887; e-mail info@venezlon.co.uk; internet www.venezlon.co.uk; Ambassador ALFREDO TORO-HARDY.

Viet Nam: 12–14 Victoria Rd, London, W8 5RD; tel. (20) 7937-1912; fax (20) 7937-6108; e-mail embassy@vietnamembassy.org.uk; internet www.vietnamembassy.org.uk; Ambassador TRINH DUC DZU.

Yemen: 57 Cromwell Rd, London, SW7 2ED; tel. (20) 7584-6607; fax (20) 7589-3350; e-mail yemenembassy@btconnect.com; internet www.yemenembassy.org.uk; Ambassador a.i. MUHAMMAD TAHA MUSTAFA.

Zambia: 2 Palace Gate, London, W8 5NG; tel. (20) 7589-6655; fax (20) 7581-1353; internet www.zhcl.org.uk; High Commr ANDERSON KASEBA CHIBWA.

Zimbabwe: Zimbabwe House, 429 Strand, London, WC2R 0QE; tel. (20) 7836-7755; fax (20) 7379-1167; e-mail zimlondon@yahoo.co.uk; Ambassador GABRIEL MHARADZE MACHINGA.

Judicial System

There are, historically, three sources of the law as administered in the law courts today: Statute Law, which is written law and consists mainly of Acts of Parliament; Common Law, which originated in ancient usage and has not been formally enacted; and Equity, which was the system evolved by the Lord Chancellor's court (Court of Chancery) to mitigate the strictness of some of the common law rules. The law of the European Community has now been added to these.

Scottish common and statute law differ in some respects from that current in the rest of the United Kingdom, owing to Scotland's retention of its own legal system under the Act of Union with England of 1707.

Three factors help to ensure a fair trial: the independence of judges, who, in the case of High Court Judges, are outside the control of the executive and can be removed from office only after an address from Parliament to the Sovereign (Circuit Judges can be removed by the Lord Chancellor); the participation of private citizens in all important criminal and some civil cases, in the form of a summoned jury of 12 persons, who judge, if necessary by a majority, the facts of a case, questions of law being decided by the judge; and the system of appeals to a higher court, including the Criminal and Civil Divisions of the Court of Appeal, and, thereafter, the House of Lords.

The Courts and Legal Services Act 1990 provided for radical change in the legal profession, including legislation permitting solicitors to appear in higher courts, and extensive reform of the civil courts, whereby the civil cases formerly heard in the High Court, could be transferred to the county courts.

In June 2003 the Government announced its intention to create a new free-standing Supreme Court to take over the judicial functions of the House of Lords and the Judicial Committee of the Privy Council. The proposed legislation was adopted in March 2005, although the Supreme Court was not expected to commence operations until October 2009.

MAGISTRATES' COURTS OR PETTY SESSIONS

The criminal courts of lowest jurisdiction are presided over by Justices of the Peace, who are unpaid lay people appointed by the Lord Chancellor. They have power to try all non-indictable offences, and some of the less serious indictable offences, if the defendant agrees. The trial of nearly all criminal offences begins in the magistrates' court. Approximately 95% of all criminal offences are dealt with solely by magistrates' courts. In the vast majority of committals for trial in the Crown Court magistrates are not required to consider evidence.

In London and in certain other large towns there are a small number of professional salaried magistrates, known as metropolitan stipendiary magistrates in London and as stipendiary magistrates in the provinces, who sit alone, whereas lay justices normally sit in threes when acting judicially.

Youth Courts, composed of specially trained justices selected by the justices of each petty sessional division (in London, by the Lord Chancellor), have power to try most charges against children under 18 years. The general public is excluded and there are restrictions on newspaper reports of the proceedings.

Magistrates also have power to grant, renew, transfer or remove or order the forfeiture of licences for the sale of alcoholic drinks, and to control the structural design of premises where alcohol is sold for consumption on the premises. They also control the licensing of betting shops, and grant bookmakers' permits.

COUNTY COURTS

A high proportion of civil actions are tried in these courts, which are presided over by a circuit judge, or, in some cases, a district judge, sitting alone. From 1 July 1991 county courts were granted unlimited jurisdiction.

THE CROWN COURT

The Crown Court came into being on 1 January 1972, under the Courts Act 1971, replacing Quarter Sessions and Assizes, to deal with serious criminal cases where trial by jury is required. The Crown Court sits at various centres throughout England and Wales. Court centres have been administratively divided into three tiers. The most serious offences are tried at first and second tier centres presided over by High Court Judges, Circuit Judges or Recorders. Circuit Judges or Recorders preside over third tier centres, where the less serious offences are tried. The Crown Court for the City of London is the Central Criminal Court (the Old Bailey).

HIGH COURT OF JUSTICE

Certain civil cases are heard in the three divisions of this court— Chancery, Queen's Bench and Family. The Chancery Division deals with litigation about property, patents, family trusts, companies, dissolution of partnerships and disputed estates. The Queen's Bench Division hears cases involving damage to property, personal injuries, etc. and also includes the Commercial and Admiralty Courts. The Family Division hears contested or complex divorce and separation cases and matters relating to children such as adoption, wardship or guardianship of minors.

Chancery Division

President: Sir ROBERT ANDREW MORRITT (Chancellor).

Judges: Sir JOHN EDMUND FREDERIC LINDSAY, Sir EDWARD CHRISTOPHER EVANS-LOMBE, Sir WILLIAM ANTHONY BLACKBURNE, Sir GAVIN ANTHONY LIGHTMAN, Sir COLIN PERCY FARQUHARSON RIMER, Sir ANDREW EDWARD WILSON PARK, Sir NICHOLAS RICHARD PUMFREY,

THE UNITED KINGDOM

Sir Michael Christopher Campbell Hart, Sir Lawrence Anthony Collins, Sir Nicholas John Patten, Sir Terrence Michael Elkan Barnet Etherton, Sir Peter Winston Smith, Sir Kim Martin Jordan Lewison, Sir David Anthony Stewart Richards, Sir George Anthony Mann, Sir Nicholas Roger Warren, Sir David James Tyson Kitchin, Sir David James Tyson Kitchin.

Queen's Bench Division

President: Sir Igor Judge.

Judges: Sir Stuart Neil McKinnon, Sir Peter John Cresswell, Sir Christopher John Holland, Sir Anthony David Colman, Sir John Thayne Forbes, Sir Thomas Richard Atkin Morison, Sir Andrew David Collins, Sir Alexander Neil Logie Butterfield, Sir George Michael Newman, Sir David Anthony Poole, Sir Gordon Julian Hugh Langley, Sir Robert Franklyn Nelson, Sir Roger Grenfell Toulson (also Chairman of the Law Commission), Sir David Eady, Sir Jeremy Mirth Sullivan, Sir David Herbert Penry-Davey, Sir David William Steel, Sir Charles Anthony St John Gray, Sir Nicolas Dušan Bratza (Judge of the European Court of Human Rights), Sir Michael John Burton, Sir Rupert Matthew Jackson, Sir Patrick Elias, Sir Richard John Pearson Aikens, Sir Stephen Robert Silber, Sir John Bernard Goldring, Sir Peter Francis Crane, Dame Anne Judith Rafferty, Sir Geoffrey Douglas Grigson, Sir Richard John Hedley Gibbs, Sir Richard Henry Quixano Henriques, Sir Stephen Miles Tomlinson, Sir Andrew Charles Smith, Sir Stanley Jeffrey Burnton, Sir Patrick James Hunt, Sir Christopher John Pitchford, Sir Brian Henry Leveson, Sir Duncan Brian Walter Ouseley, Sir Richard George Bramwell McCombe, Sir Raymond Evan Jack, Sir Robert Michael Owen, Sir Colin Crichton Mackay, Sir John Edward Mitting, Sir David Roderick Evans, Sir Nigel Anthony Lamert Davis, Sir Peter Henry Gross, Sir Brian Richard Keith, Sir Jeremy Lionel Cooke, Sir Richard Alan Field, Sir Christopher John Pitchers, Sir Colman Maurice Treacy, Sir Peregrine Charles Hugo Simon, Sir Roger John Royce, Dame Laura Mary Cox, Sir Adrian Bruce Fulford, Sir Jack Beatson, Sir Michael George Tugendhat, Sir David Clive Clarke, Dame Elizabeth Gloster, Sir David Michael Bean, Sir Alan Fraser Wilkie, Dame Linda Penelope Dobbs, Sir Henry Egar Garfield Hodge, Sir Paul James Walker, Sir David Calvert-Smith, Sir Christopher Simon Courtenay Stephenson Clarke, Dame Caroline Jane Swift, Sir Brian Frederick James Langstaff, Sir David Lloyd Jones, Sir Charles Peter Lawford Openshaw, Sir Vivian Arthur Ramsay, Sir Nicholas Edward Underhill, Sir Stephen John Irwin.

Family Division

President: Sir Mark Howard Potter.

Judges: Dame Joyanne Winifred Bracewell, Sir Jan Peter Singer, Sir Andrew Tristam Hammett Kirkwood, Sir Hugh Peter Derwyn Bennett, Sir Edward James Holman, Dame Mary Claire Hogg, Sir Christopher John Sumner, Sir Arthur William Hessin Charles, Sir David Roderick Lessiter Bodey, Dame Jill Margaret Black, Sir James Lawrence Munby, Sir Paul James Duke Coleridge, Sir Mark Hedley, Dame Anna Evelyn Hamilton Pauffley, Sir Roderic Lionel James Wood, Dame Florence Jacquelene Baron, Sir Ernest Nigel Ryder, Sir Andrew Ewart McFarlane, Dame Julia Wendy Macur.

COURT OF APPEAL

An appeal lies in civil cases to this court from County Courts and the High Court of Justice and in criminal cases from the Crown Courts. The Master of the Rolls is the effective head of the court.

Ex-Officio Judges

Lord Chief Justice of England and Wales: Lord Phillips of Worth Matravers.
Master of the Rolls: Sir Anthony Peter Clarke.
President of the Queen's Bench Division: Sir Igor Judge.
President of the Family Division: Sir Mark Howard Potter.
Chancellor of the High Court: Sir (Robert) Andrew Morritt.
Lords Justices of Appeal: Sir Robin Ernest Auld, Sir Malcolm Thomas Pill, Sir Alan Hylton Ward, Sir Mathew Alexander Thorpe, Sir Henry Brooke (Vice-President Civil Division of the Court of Appeal), Sir George Mark Waller, Sir John Frank Mummery, Sir John Murray Chadwick, Sir Richard Joseph Buxton, Sir Anthony Tristam Kenneth May (Vice-President Queen's Bench Division of the High Court), Sir Simon Lane Tuckey, Sir Anthony Peter Clarke, Sir John Grant McKenzie Laws, Sir Stephen John Sedley, Sir David Nicholas Ramsey Latham, Sir Bernard Anthony Rix, Sir Jonathan Frederic Parker, Dame Mary Howarth Arden, Sir David Wolfe Keene, Sir John Anthony Dyson (Deputy Head of Civil Justice), Sir Andrew Centlivres Longmore, Sir Robert John Anderson Carnwath, Sir Thomas Scott Gillespie Baker, Dame Janet Hilary Smith, Sir Roger John Laugharne Thomas, Sir Robert Raphael Hayim Jacob, Sir Nicholas Peter Rathbone Wall, Sir David Edmond Neuberger, Sir Maurice Ralph Kay, Sir Anthony Hooper, Sir William Marcus Gage, Sir Martin James Moore-Bick, Sir Timothy Andrew Wigram Lloyd, Sir Nicholas Allan Roy Wilson, Sir Alan George Moses, Sir Stephen Price Richards, Dame Heather Carol Hallett, Sir Anthony Phillip Gilson Hughes.

HOUSE OF LORDS

In civil and criminal cases this is the final court of appeal.
Lord High Chancellor: Lord Falconer of Thoroton.
Lords of Appeal in Ordinary: Lord Bingham of Cornhill, Lord Nicholls of Birkenhead, Lord Hoffmann, Lord Hope of Craighead, Lord Saville of Newdigate, Lord Scott of Foscote, Lord Rodger of Earlsferry, Lord Walker of Gestingthorpe, Baroness Hale of Richmond, Lord Carswell, Lord Brown of Eaton-under-Heywood, Lord Mance.

JUDICIAL COMMITTEE OF THE PRIVY COUNCIL

Final court of appeal for appeals from certain Commonwealth territories; also exercises domestic jurisdiction in ecclesiastical matters and appeals from disciplinary tribunals of certain professions.

Northern Irish Judicial System

The judicial system of Northern Ireland, so far as the Supreme Court is concerned, is a miniature of the English system, and is based on the Judicature (Northern Ireland) Act 1978. It consists, as in England, of the High Court, the Court of Appeal, and the Crown Court (which has jurisdiction in criminal matters). The jurisdiction of the Magistrates' Courts (Courts of Summary Jurisdiction) is exercised by a permanent judiciary of legally qualified resident magistrates.

COUNTY COURTS

The county court system corresponds to its English counterpart, but there is no system of pleadings, as is found in the English county court. There are also variations in jurisdiction levels. County court judges share with the judges of the High Court the exercise of the jurisdiction of the Crown Court.

HIGH COURT

The Lord Chief Justice of Northern Ireland: Sir Brian Kerr (President), Royal Courts of Justice, Chichester St, Belfast, BT1 3JF; tel. (28) 9072-4603; fax (28) 9031-3508; e-mail adminoffice@courtsni.gov.uk; internet www.courtsni.gov.uk.

Judges: Sir Malachy Higgins, Sir Paul Frederick Girvan, Sir Patrick Coghlin, Sir John Gillen, Sir Ronald Weatherup, Sir Reginald Weir, Sir Charles Morgan, Sir Donnell Deeny, Sir Anthony Ronald Hart.

COURT OF APPEAL

President: The Lord Chief Justice of Northern Ireland

Judges: Sir John Sheil, Sir Michael Nicholson, Sir Anthony Campbell.

Scottish Judicial System

CRIMINAL COURTS

Minor offences are dealt with in District courts.

Sheriff Court

Most criminal actions, including all but the most serious offences, are tried in this court. Each of the six sheriffdoms of Scotland has a Sheriff Principal and a number of Sheriffs, who hear the cases.

High Court of Justiciary

This is the supreme criminal court in Scotland: all the most serious cases are taken there. Appeal may be made to it from the Sheriff Court and from the District courts; there is, however, no further appeal to the House of Lords.

The 32 judges of this court are known as Lords Commissioners of Justiciary and are headed by the Lord Justice General and the Lord Justice Clerk. Apart from their criminal jurisdiction in this court, these judges are also judges of the Court of Session (see below) in civil cases. The Lord Justice General is also the President of the Court of Session.

THE UNITED KINGDOM

CIVIL COURTS

Sheriff Court

This court hears civil as well as criminal cases, and in civil cases its jurisdiction is practically unlimited. It has concurrent jurisdiction with the Court of Session in divorce actions. Appeal may be made to the Court of Session or the Sheriff Principal.

Court of Session

This is the supreme civil court in Scotland. It has an Inner House and an Outer House.

The Inner House has two divisions of equal standing, each consisting of four judges (the quorum is three although due to pressure of business an extra division of three judges frequently sits) under the presidency of the Lord President and the Lord Justice Clerk respectively; it is mainly an appeal court, whence further appeal may be made to the House of Lords.

First Division

Lord Justice General and President of the Court of Session: Lord HAMILTON.

Judges: Lady COSGROVE, Lord PHILLIP, Lord NIMMO SMITH.

Second Division

Lord Justice Clerk: Lord GILL.

Judges: Lord MACFAYDEN, Lord OSBORNE, Lord ABERNETHY, Lord JOHNSTON.

The Outer House deals with the major civil cases and divorce actions. The judges are those of the High Court of Justiciary, sitting in a civil capacity as judges of the Court of Session.

Judges: Lord DAWSON, Lord KINGARTH, Lord EASSIE, Lord REED, Lord WHEATLEY, Lady PATON, Lord CARLOWAY, Lord CLARKE, Lord HARDIE, Lord MACKAY OF DRUMADOON, Lord McEWAN, Lord MENZIES, Lord DRUMMOND YOUNG, Lord EMSLIE, Lady SMITH, Lord BRODIE, Lord BRACADALE, Lady DORRIAN, Lord HODGE, Lord MACPHAIL, Lord GLENNIE, Lord KINCLAVEN.

Religion

CHRISTIANITY

Churches Together in Britain and Ireland: Bastille Court, 2 Paris Garden, London, SE1 8ND; tel. (20) 7654-7254; fax (20) 7654-7222; e-mail gensec@ctbi.org.uk; internet www.ctbi.org.uk; f. 1990 as successor to the British Council of Churches; co-ordinates the activities of its 32 member churches and liaises with ecumenical bodies in Britain and Ireland. Its work divisions include Church Life, Church and Society and International Affairs, Spirituality, Racial Justice, Mission and Inter-faith Relations. It provides a forum for joint decision-making and enables the churches to take action together; Gen. Sec. Rev. Canon BOB FYFFE.

Action of Churches Together in Scotland (ACTS): Scottish Churches' House, Dunblane, Perthshire, FK15 0AJ; tel. (1786) 823588; fax (1786) 825844; e-mail ecumenical@acts-scotland.org; internet www.acts-scotland.org; aims to encourage and express unity of Christian Churches in Scotland; Convener Dr ALISON ELLIOT; Gen. Sec. Rev. KEVIN FRANZ.

Churches Together in England (CTE): 27 Tavistock Sq., London, WC1H 9HH; tel. (20) 7529-8141; fax (20) 7529-8134; e-mail office@cte.org.uk; internet www.churches-together.org.uk; 23 mem. bodies; Pres Most Rev. and Rt Hon. Dr ROWAN WILLIAMS, Rev. DAVID COFFEY, Rt Rev. NATHAN HOVHANNISIAN, H.E. Cardinal CORMAC MURPHY-O'CONNOR; Gen. Sec. Rev. BILL SNELSON.

Churches Together in Wales (CYTÛN): 58 Richmond Rd, Cardiff, CF24 3UR; tel. (29) 2046-4204; fax (29) 2045-5427; e-mail post@cytun.org.uk; internet www.cytun.org.uk; fmrly the Council of Churches for Wales; 11 mem. bodies; Gen Sec. (vacant).

Irish Council of Churches: Inter-Church Centre, 48 Elmwood Ave, Belfast, BT9 6AZ; tel. and fax (28) 9066-3145; fax (28) 9066-4160; e-mail irish.churches@btconnect.com; internet www.irishchurches.org; f. 1922 (present name adopted 1966); 15 mem. churches; the organization of the churches in Ireland takes no account of the partition of the island into two separate political entities, with the Republic of Ireland and Northern Ireland thus subject to a unified jurisdiction for ecclesiastical purposes; Pres. Rt Rev. PETER BARRETT; Gen. Sec. MICHAEL EARLE.

The Anglican Communion

The Church of England

The Church of England is the Established Church, and as such acknowledges the authority of Parliament in matters in which secular authority is competent to exercise control. Queen Elizabeth I was declared 'supreme Governor on Earth' of the Church of England, and the Sovereign is consecrated to this office at coronation.

In England, there are two Provinces, Canterbury and York. The former contains 30, the latter 14, dioceses. Each Province has its ancient Convocations, the Upper and Lower House. By the Enabling Act the Constitution of the National Assembly of the Church of England ('Church Assembly') received statutory recognition in 1920, with power, subject to the control and authority of Parliament, of initiating legislation on all matters concerning the Church of England. Measures passed by the Assembly and approved by Parliament were submitted for the Royal Assent, having the force of Acts of Parliament.

In 1970, by the Synodical Government Measure (1969), the Church Assembly was reconstituted as the General Synod and was also given authority to exercise most of the functions of the Convocations. The House of Bishops consists of members of the Upper House of the Convocations (53 persons). The House of Clergy consists of the Lower Houses (a maximum of 259 persons). The House of Laity consists almost entirely of representatives of the dioceses elected by the deanery synods (a maximum of 258 persons).

In 2001 there were 1,372,000 people on the Church's electoral rolls.

The Archbishops and the 24 senior Bishops sit in the House of Lords.

Archbishop of Canterbury, Primate of All England and Metropolitan: Most Rev. and Rt Hon. ROWAN WILLIAMS, Lambeth Palace, London, SE1 7JU; tel. (20) 7898-1200; fax (20) 7261-1765; internet www.archbishopofcanterbury.org.

Archbishop of York, Primate of England and Metropolitan: Rt Rev. JOHN SENTAMU, Bishopthorpe Palace, Bishopthorpe, York, YO23 2GE; tel. (1904) 707021; fax (1904) 709204; e-mail office@bishopthorpe.u-net.com; internet www.bishopthorpepalace.co.uk.

General Synod of the Church of England: Church House, Great Smith St, London, SW1P 3NZ; tel. (20) 7898-1000; fax (20) 7898-1369; e-mail synod@c-of-e.org.uk; internet www.cofe.anglican.org; Sec.-Gen. WILLIAM FITTALL.

The Church of Ireland

The See House, Cathedral Close, Armagh, BT61 7EE; tel. (28) 3752-7144; fax (28) 3752-7823; internet www.ireland.anglican.org.

Ireland (including Northern Ireland) comprises two archdioceses and 10 dioceses; according to census results, 15.3% of the population of Northern Ireland were members of the Church of Ireland in 2001.

Archbishop of Armagh and Primate of All Ireland: Most Rev. Lord ROBIN EAMES, The See House, Cathedral Close, Armagh, BT61 7EE; tel. (28) 3752-7144; fax (28) 3752-7823; e-mail archbishop@armagh.anglican.org.

The Church in Wales

39 Cathedral Rd, Cardiff, CF11 9XF; tel. (29) 2034-8200; fax (29) 2038-7835; e-mail information@churchinwales.org.uk; internet www.churchinwales.org.uk.

The Province of Wales was created as a result of the Welsh Church Act of 1914, which took effect on 31 March 1920 and separated the four Welsh Dioceses from the Province of Canterbury. It is divided into six Dioceses served by 620 stipendiary clerics. The number of Easter communicants is approximately 75,000. The Church in Wales has an administrative governing body which is a legislative assembly composed of bishops, clergy and laity, and a representative body incorporated by Royal Charter, which holds and manages the property and central funds of the Church; Provincial Sec. JOHN SHIRLEY.

Archbishop of Wales: Most Rev Dr. BARRY C. MORGAN, Llys Esgob, Cathedral Green, Llandaff, Cardiff, CF5 2YE; tel. (29) 2056-2400; fax (29) 2056-8410; e-mail archbishop@churchinwales.org.uk; internet wales.anglican.org.

The Scottish Episcopal Church

21 Grosvenor Cres., Edinburgh, EH12 5EE; tel. (131) 225-6357; fax (131) 346-7247; e-mail office@scotland.anglican.org; internet www.scotland.anglican.org.

Formerly the Established Church of Scotland, was disestablished and disendowed in 1689; is in full communion with all branches of the Anglican Communion; seven dioceses: Aberdeen and Orkney, Argyll and The Isles, Brechin, Edinburgh, Glasgow and Galloway, Moray, Ross and Caithness, and St Andrews, Dunkeld and Dunblane. There is a Bishop in each diocese; one of them is elected by the other Bishops as the Primus; Churches, mission stations, etc. 310, clergy 402, communicants 29,810; Sec.-Gen. to the General Synod JOHN STUART.

Primus: Most Rev. BRUCE CAMERON (Bishop of Aberdeen and Orkney), The Diocesan Office, 39 King's Cres., Aberdeen, AB24 3HP; tel. (1224) 636653; fax (1224) 636186; e-mail office@aberdeen.anglican.org.

The Roman Catholic Church

For ecclesiastical purposes Great Britain comprises seven archdioceses and 23 dioceses. There is also an apostolic exarchate for the Ukrainian Rite. Ireland (including Northern Ireland) comprises four archdioceses and 22 dioceses. The dioceses of Down and Connor and Dromore are completely in Northern Ireland, while the archdiocese of Armagh and the dioceses of Derry and Clogher are partly in Northern Ireland and partly in the Republic of Ireland. At 31 December 2003 there were an estimated 4,090,383 adherents in England and Wales, of whom about 15,000 were of the Ukrainian Rite, and an estimated 694,285 adherents in Scotland. At the 2001 census 40.3% of the population of Northern Ireland gave their religion as Catholic or Roman Catholic.

Latin Rite

Bishops' Conference of England and Wales

39 Eccleston Sq., London, SW1V 1BX; tel. (20) 7630-8220; fax (20) 7901-4821; e-mail secretariat@cbcew.org.uk; internet catholic-ew.org.uk.
President H.E. Cardinal CORMAC MURPHY-O'CONNOR (Archbishop of Westminster).

Archbishop of Westminster: H.E. Cardinal CORMAC MURPHY-O'CONNOR, Archbishop's House, Westminster, London, SW1P 1QJ; tel. (20) 7798-9033; fax (20) 7798-9077; e-mail archbishop@rcdow.org.uk; internet www.rcdow.org.uk/archbishop.

Archbishop of Birmingham: Most Rev. VINCENT NICHOLS, Archbishop's House, 8 Shadwell St, Queensway, Birmingham, B4 6EY; tel. (121) 236-9090; fax (121) 212-0171; e-mail archbishop@rc-birmingham.org; internet www.birminghamdiocese.org.uk.

Archbishop of Liverpool: Most Rev. PATRICK ALTHAM KELLY, Archbishop's House, Lowood, Carnatic Road, Mossley Hill, Liverpool, L18 8BY; tel. (151) 724-6398; fax (151) 724-6405; e-mail archbishop.liverpool@rcaolp.co.uk; internet www.archdiocese-of-liverpool.co.uk.

Archbishop of Southwark: Most Rev. KEVIN JOHN MCDONALD, Archbishop's House, 150 St George's Rd, Southwark, London, SE1 6HX; tel. (20) 7928-2495; fax (20) 7928-7833; internet www.rcsouthwark.co.uk.

Archbishop of Cardiff: Most Rev. PETER SMITH, Archbishop's House, 41–43 Cathedral Rd, Cardiff, South Glamorgan, CF11 9HD; tel. (29) 2037-9036; fax (29) 2034-5950; e-mail arch@rcacd.org; internet www.rcacd.org.

Archbishop of Armagh and Primate of All Ireland: Most Rev. SEÁN BRADY, Ara Coeli, Armagh, BT61 7QY; tel. (28) 3752-2045; fax (28) 3752-6182; e-mail admin@aracoeli.com; internet www.archdioceseofarmagh.org.

Bishops' Conference of Scotland

64 Aitken St, Airdrie, ML6 6LT; tel. (1236) 764061; fax (1236) 762489; e-mail gensec@bpsconfscot.com; internet www.scmo.org.uk.
President Most Rev. KEITH MICHAEL PATRICK CARDINAL O'BRIEN; Gen. Sec. Right Rev. HENRY DOCHERTY.

Archbishop of St Andrews and Edinburgh: Most Rev. KEITH MICHAEL PATRICK CARDINAL O'BRIEN, Archbishop's House, 42 Greenhill Gdns, Edinburgh, EH10 4BJ; tel. (131) 447-3337; fax (131) 447-0816; e-mail archkp@lineone.net.

Archbishop of Glasgow: Most Rev. MARIO JOSEPH CONTI, Curial Offices, 196 Clyde St, Glasgow, G1 4JY; tel. (141) 226-5898; fax (141) 225-2600; e-mail info@rcag.org.uk; internet www.rcag.org.uk.

Ukrainian Rite

Apostolic Exarch: (vacant), Bishop's House, 22 Binney St, London, W1K 5BQ; tel. (20) 7629-1534; fax (20) 7355-3314; e-mail frben@catholic.org.

Protestant Churches

Association of Baptist Churches in Ireland: 19 Hillsborough Rd, Moira, Craigavon, County Armagh, BT67 0HG; tel. (28) 9261-9267; fax (28) 9261-0150; e-mail abc@thebaptistcentre.org; internet www.baptistireland.org; 111 churches; 93 ministers; 8,446 mems; Pres. Pastor HARRY DOWDS; Dir Pastor WILLIAM COLVILLE.

Baptist Union of Great Britain: Baptist House, POB 44, 129 Broadway, Didcot, Oxfordshire, OX11 8RT; tel. (1235) 517700; fax (1235) 517715; e-mail info@baptist.org.uk; internet www.baptist.org.uk; f. 1813; the Baptist form of church government is congregational; baptism by immersion of believers is practised; the Churches are grouped in associations; mems (2003) 140,918; Pres. (2005/06) Rev. ROY SEARLE; Gen. Sec. Rev. DAVID R. COFFEY.

Church of Scotland: 121 George St, Edinburgh, EH2 4YN; tel. (131) 225-5722; fax (131) 220-3113; e-mail lturnbull@cofscotland.org.uk; internet www.churchofscotland.org.uk; the national Church of Scotland was reformed in 1560, and became Presbyterian in doctrine and constitution. In 1921 the Church of Scotland Act was passed, by which the articles declaring the full spiritual freedom of the Church are recognized as lawful. In 1925 the Church of Scotland (Property and Endowments) Act became law, and made over to the Church of Scotland places of worship, manses and endowments in absolute property, vesting the future control of them in Trustees. The union of the Church of Scotland and the United Free Church was effected in 1929; Moderator of the General Assembly Rt Rev. DAVID W. LACY; Lord High Commr to the 2005 General Assembly Lord MACKAY OF CLASHFERN; 600,000 mems.

Elim Pentecostal Church: PO Box 38, Cheltenham, Glos, GL50 3HN; tel. (1242) 519904; fax (1242) 222279; e-mail info@elimhq.org.uk; internet www.elim.org.uk; f. 1915; c. 580 churches and 60,000 adherents in Great Britain; Gen. Superintendent Rev. J. J. GLASS.

Free Church of Scotland: The Mound, Edinburgh, EH1 2LS; tel. (131) 226-5286; fax (131) 220-0597; e-mail offices@freechurchofscotland.org.uk; internet www.freechurch.org; f. 1843; 103 congregations; Principal Clerk of Assembly Rev. JAMES MACIVER.

Free Churches Group, Churches Together in England: 27 Tavistock Sq., London, WC1H 9HH; tel. (20) 7529-8131; fax (20) 7529-8134; e-mail office@cte.org.uk; internet www.churches-together.org.uk; central body for the co-ordination of the work of the Free Churches throughout England and Wales; Moderator Rev. DAVID COFFEY; Gen. Sec. Rev. BILL SNELSON.

Lutheran Church in Great Britain: 30 Thanet St, London, WC1H 9QH; tel. (20) 7554-2900; fax (20) 7383-3081; e-mail enquiries@lutheran.org.uk; internet www.lutheran.org.uk; Gen. Sec. Rev. THOMAS BRUCH.

Methodist Church: Methodist Church House, 25 Marylebone Rd, London, NW1 5JR; tel. (20) 7467-5123; fax (20) 7467-3761; e-mail mediaoffice@methodistchurch.org.uk; internet www.methodistchurch.org.uk; f. 1739 by Rev. John Wesley, a priest of the Church of England; the governing body of the Church is the Annual Conference, which consists of ministers and lay representatives. The Church throughout Great Britain is divided into 33 Districts, and these hold their Synod Meetings in the autumn and the spring. The Districts are divided into Circuits, which hold regular Circuit Meetings, made up of representatives from the churches within the Circuit. There are also local Church Councils; 293,661 mems (2004); Pres. of the Methodist Conference (2005/06) Rev. THOMAS STUCKEY; Gen. Sec. of the Methodist Conference Rev. DAVID DEEKS.

Methodist Church in Ireland: 1 Fountainville Ave, Belfast, BT9 6AN; tel. (28) 9032-4554; fax (28) 9023-9467; e-mail secretary@irishmethodist.org; internet www.irishmethodist.org; 220 churches; 303 ministers; 53,990 mems; Sec. Rev. W. WINSTON GRAHAM.

Moravian Church: 5 Muswell Hill, London, N10 3TJ; tel. (20) 8883-3409; fax (20) 8365-3371; e-mail office@moravian.org.uk; internet www.moravian.org.uk; f. 1457; Sec. Provincial Board JACKIE MORTEN.

Moravian Church in Ireland: 37 Deramore Park South, Malone Rd, Belfast, BT9 5JY; tel. (28) 9068-1554; e-mail derick.woods@btinternet.com; f. 1749; Chair. of Conf. DERICK WOODS.

Non-Subscribing Presbyterian Church of Ireland: 41A Rosemary St, Belfast, BT1 1QB; tel. and fax (28) 9032-5365; e-mail info@nspresbyterian.org; internet www.nspresbyterian.org; Moderator Rt. Rev. COLIN CAMPBELL; Clerk Rev. NIGEL PLAYFAIR.

Presbyterian Church in Ireland: Church House, Fisherwick Pl., Belfast, BT1 6DW; tel. (28) 9032-2284; fax (28) 9041-7307; e-mail info@presbyterianireland.org; internet www.presbyterianireland.org; 545 churches; 497 ministers; 270,600 mems, 29,300 in 550 Sunday Schools; Moderator of the Gen. Assembly Rt Rev. Dr HARRY UPRICHARD; Clerk of Assembly and Gen. Sec. Rev. Dr DONALD WATTS.

Presbyterian Church of Wales: 81 Merthyr Rd, Whitchurch, Cardiff, CF14 1DD; tel. (29) 2062-7465; fax (29) 2061-6188; e-mail swyddfa.office@ebcpcw.org.uk; internet www.ebcpcw.org.uk; f. 1811; 832 churches, 77 full-time ministers, 34,819 mems (2005); Moderator of General Assembly Rev. R. BEBB; Gen. Sec. Rev. IFAN RH ROBERTS.

The Religious Society of Friends (Quakers) in Britain: Friends House, 173 Euston Rd, London, NW1 2BJ; tel. (20) 7663-1000; fax (20) 7663-1001; e-mail enquiries@quaker.org.uk; internet www.quaker.org.uk; f. mid-17th century by George Fox; the Quakers have 15,800 mems and 8,400 'attenders' in Great Britain; Recording Clerk (Sec.) ELSA DICKS.

Salvation Army: 101 Newington Causeway, London, SE1 6BN; tel. (20) 7367-4500; fax (20) 7367-4728; e-mail info@salvationarmy.org.uk; internet www.salvationarmy.org.uk; f. 1865; Territorial Commdr SHAW CLIFTON.

THE UNITED KINGDOM

Union of Welsh Independents: Tŷ John Penri, 5 Axis Court, Riverside Business Park, Swansea Vale, Swansea, SA7 0AJ; tel. (1792) 795888; fax (1792) 795376; e-mail undeb@annibynwyr.org; internet www.cwmeurope.org/uwi.htm; Pres. Rev. GERAINT TUDOR; Gen. Sec. Rev. DEWI MYRDDIN HUGHES.

United Free Church of Scotland: 11 Newton Place, Glasgow, G3 7PR; tel. (141) 332-3435; fax (141) 333-1973; e-mail office@ufcos.org.uk; internet www.ufcos.org.uk; f. 1900; 66 congregations, 40 ministers and pastors, 4,200 mems; Moderator of the General Assembly Rev. ANDREW MCMILLAN; Gen. Sec. Rev. JOHN O. FULTON.

United Reformed Church: United Reformed Church House, 86 Tavistock Pl., London, WC1H 9RT; tel. (20) 7916-2020; fax (20) 7916-2021; e-mail urc@urc.org.uk; internet www.urc.org.uk; f. 1972 by union of the Congregational Church in England and Wales and the Presbyterian Church of England; joined by the Churches of Christ 1981 and by the Scottish Congregational Church 2000; approx. 1,700 churches and 90,000 mems; Moderator Rev. Dr DAVID PEEL; Gen. Sec. Rev. Dr DAVID CORNICK.

Orthodox Churches

Council of Oriental Orthodox Churches: 34 Chertsey Rd, Church Sq., Shepperton, Middx, TW17 9LF; tel. and fax (1932) 232913; Sec. Deacon AZIZ M. A. NOUR.

Armenian Apostolic Church: The Armenian Vicarage, St Sarkis Church, Iverna Gdns, London, W8 6TP; tel. (20) 7937-0152; fax (20) 7937-9049; e-mail arajnortaran@aol.com; internet accc.org.uk; Bishop NATHAN HOVHANNISIAN.

Greek Orthodox Church (Archdiocese of Thyateira and Great Britain of the Oecumenical Patriarchate): Thyateira House, 5 Craven Hill, London, W2 3EN; tel. (20) 7723-4787; fax (20) 7224-9301; e-mail thyateiragb@yahoo.com; f. 1922; Archbishop of Thyateira and Great Britain GREGORIOS; Chancellor Bishop ATHANASIOS OF TROPAEOU.

Russian Orthodox Patriarchal Church in Great Britain: Cathedral of the Assumption and All Saints, Ennismore Gdns, London, SW7 1NH; tel. (20) 7584-0096; fax (20) 7584-9864; e-mail webdeacon@sourozh.org; internet www.sourozh.org; Archbishop INNOKENTY OF KORSUN (acting).

Serbian Orthodox Church: 131 Cob Lane, Bournville, Birmingham, B30 1QE; tel. (121) 458-5273; fax (121) 458-4986; Very Rev. MILENKO ZEBIĆ.

Other Christian Churches

First Church of Christ, Scientist: 8 Wright's Lane, Kensington, London, W8 6TA; tel. (20) 7937-3389; fax (20) 7937-3341; e-mail fccslon@tiscali.co.uk; internet www.ccs.org.uk; f. 1879; The Mother Church, The First Church of Christ, Scientist, in Boston, Mass (USA); approx. 150 churches in Great Britain; District Man. for Great Britain and Ireland TONY LOBL.

Church of Jesus Christ of Latter-day Saints (Mormon): Press Office, 751 Warwick Rd, Solihull, West Midlands, B91 3DQ; tel. (121) 712-1202; fax (121) 712-1126; e-mail mclavertymw@ldschurch.org; internet www.lds.org.uk; f. 1830; c. 181,000 mems (2004); Area Pres. HAROLD G. HILLAM.

General Assembly of Unitarian and Free Christian Churches: Essex Hall, 1–6 Essex St, London, WC2R 3HY; tel. (20) 7240-2384; fax (20) 7240-3089; e-mail ga@unitarian.org.uk; internet www.unitarian.org.uk; f. 1928; Gen. Sec. JEFFREY J. TEAGLE.

Jehovah's Witnesses: Watch Tower House, The Ridgeway, London, NW7 1RN; tel. (20) 8906-2211; fax (20) 8371-0051; internet www.watchtower.org; f. 1900; there were an estimated 125,000 Jehovah's Witnesses in the UK in 2005.

Seventh-day Adventist Church Headquarters: Stanborough Park, Watford, Herts, WD25 9JZ; tel. (1923) 672251; fax (1923) 893212; e-mail info@adventist.org.uk; internet www.adventist.org.uk; there were an estimated 25,000 mems. in approx. 300 congregations across the UK and Ireland in early 2006; Communication Dir JOHN SURRIDGE.

Spiritualists' National Union: Redwoods, Stansted Hall, Stansted Mountfitchet, Essex, CM24 8UD; tel. (845) 458-0768; fax (1279) 812034; e-mail snu@snu.org.uk; internet www.snu.org.uk; f. 1891 (and inc. 1901); for the advancement of Spiritualism as a religion and a religious philosophy, it is a trust corporation officially recognized as the central and national body representing the Spiritualists of Great Britain; conducts the Arthur Findlay College of Psychic Science; 400 Spiritualist churches, societies and 20,000 individual mems; Pres. D. P. GASCOYNE; 40 Newmarket, Otley, LS21 3AE; Gen. Sec. CHARLES S. COULSTON.

ISLAM

The Muslim community in the United Kingdom, which according to the 2001 census numbered 1.59m., consists mainly of people from the Indian sub-continent and their British-born descendants. The chief concentrations of Muslims are in London, the Midlands, South Wales, Lancashire and Yorkshire. There are more than 900 mosques in the United Kingdom; the oldest is the Shah Jehan Mosque in Woking, Surrey.

London Central Mosque Trust and Islamic Cultural Centre: 146 Park Rd, London, NW8 7RG; tel. (20) 7724-3363; fax (20) 7724-0493; e-mail info@iccuk.org; internet www.iccuk.org; Dir-Gen. Dr AHMAD AD-DUBAYAN.

Muslim Council of Britain: Boardman House, 64 Broadway, London, E15 1NT; tel. (20) 8432-0585; fax (20) 8432-0587; e-mail admin@mcb.org.uk; internet www.mcb.org.uk; Sec.-Gen. Sir IQBAL SACRANIE.

SIKHISM

According to the 2001 census, there were 336,000 Sikhs in the United Kingdom, who originally came from the Punjab region of the Indian sub-continent as well as from East Africa, although many are now British-born. Each gurdwara (temple) is independent, and there is no central national body.

Sikh Missionary Society, UK: 10 Featherstone Rd, Southall, Middx, UB2 5AA; tel. (20) 8574-1902; fax (20) 8574-1912; e-mail info@sikhmissionarysociety.org; internet www.gurmat.info; promotes Sikhism and acts as a resource centre for information and literature; Hon. Gen. Sec. SURINDER SINGH PUREWAL.

HINDUISM

There were, according to the 2001 census 559,000 Hindus in the United Kingdom, with their own origins in India, East Africa and Sri Lanka, although many are now British by birth. Hindus in the United Kingdom are concentrated in London, the Midlands and Yorkshire.

JUDAISM

The Jewish community in the United Kingdom numbered 267,000, according to the 2001 census. There are about 350 synagogues in the United Kingdom.

Chief Rabbi of the United Hebrew Congregations of the Commonwealth: Rabbi Prof. JONATHAN SACKS, Office of the Chief Rabbi, Alder House, 735 High Rd, London, N12 0US; tel. (20) 8343-6301; fax (20) 8343-6310; e-mail info@chiefrabbi.org; internet www.chiefrabbi.org.

Court of the Chief Rabbi (Beth Din): 735 High Rd, London, N12 0US; tel. (20) 8343-6270; fax (20) 8343-6257; e-mail info@bethdin.org.uk; Registrar D. FREI.

There is no comprehensive organization of synagogues covering the country as a whole. In London and the South-East there are the following major synagogue organizations:

Liberal Judaism: The Montagu Centre, 21 Maple St, London, W1T 4BE; tel. (20) 7580-1663; fax (20) 7631-9838; e-mail montagu@liberaljudaism.org; internet www.liberaljudaism.org; f. 1902; 9,300 mems, 31 affiliated synagogues, 3 assoc. communities; Chief-Exec. Rabbi DANNY RICH.

Movement for Reform Judaism: The Sternberg Centre for Judaism, 80 East End Road, Finchley, London N3 2SY; tel. (020) 8349-4731; e-mail admin@reformjudaism.org.uk; internet www.reformjudaism.org.uk; Chief-Exec. Rabbi TONY BAYFIELD.

Spanish and Portuguese Jews' Congregation: 2 Ashworth Rd, London, W9 1JY; tel. (20) 7289-2573; fax (20) 7289-2709; e-mail howardmiller@spsyn.org.uk; internet www.sandp.org; f. 1657; Pres. of the Bd of Elders BERNARD MOCATTA; Chief Exec. HOWARD MILLER.

Union of Orthodox Hebrew Congregations: 140 Stamford Hill, London, N16 6QT; tel. (20) 8802-6226; fax (20) 8809-6590; f. 1926; over 6,000 mems; Exec. Dir Rabbi ARON M. GRUNWALD.

United Synagogue: Adler House, 735 High Rd, London, N12 0US; tel. (20) 8343-8989; fax (20) 8343-6262; e-mail info@unitedsynagogue.org.uk; internet www.unitedsynagogue.org.uk; f. 1870 by Act of Parliament; Pres. Dr SIMON HOCHHAUSER; Chief Exec Rabbi SAUL ZNEIMER.

West London Synagogue of British Jews: 33 Seymour Pl., London, W1H 5AU; tel. (20) 7723-4404; fax (20) 7224-8258; e-mail admin@wls.org.uk; internet www.wls.org.uk; f. 1840; c. 4,000 mems; Senior Rabbi MARK L. WINER; Exec. Dir ALAN SHAPIRO.

BUDDHISM

According to the 2001 census, the Buddhist community in the United Kingdom numbered 152,000.

Buddhist Society: 58 Eccleston Sq., London, SW1V 1PH; tel. (20) 7834-5858; fax (20) 7976-5238; e-mail info@thebuddhistsociety.org; internet www.thebuddhistsociety.org; f. 1924; Registrar LOUISE MARCHANT.

THE UNITED KINGDOM

BAHÁ'Í FAITH

National Spiritual Assembly of the Bahá'ís of the United Kingdom: 27 Rutland Gate, London, SW7 1PD; tel. (20) 7584-2566; fax (20) 7584-9402; e-mail opi@bahai.org.uk; internet www.bahai.org.uk; f. 1923; Sec. Dr KISHAN MANOCHA; Chair. SHIRIN TAHZIB.

The Press

The United Kingdom has some of the highest circulation figures in the world for individual newspapers (*Daily Mail* 2.2m., *The Sun* 3.0m., *News of the World* 3.2m.). At 1 January 2004 there were more than 2,600 regional and local daily and weekly newspapers (including free titles) in the United Kingdom and the total weekly circulation of all newspapers was 136.4m.

There is no law which specifies the operations of the press but several items of legislation bear directly on press activities. Although exact reporting of legal proceedings appearing at the time of trial is protected from later charges of defamation, the freedom to report cases is subject to certain restrictions as defined in the Judicial Proceedings Act of 1926, in the Children's and Young Persons' Act of 1933 and in the Criminal Justice Act 1967. The strict laws of contempt of court and of libel somewhat limit the scope of the press. Journalists are subject to the former if they publish material liable to interfere with a matter which is *sub judice* but this law is qualified by the Administration of Justice Act of 1960 which declares an editor not guilty of contempt if, after taking reasonable care, he remained ignorant of the fact that proceedings were pending. The Scottish law of contempt is more severe than the English. Libel cases can involve the awarding of punitive damages against the press. The Defamation Act of 1952 lessened the possible repercussions of unintentional libel and made provision for the claim of fair comment by the defence.

The Official Secrets Act of 1911 prohibits the publication of secret information where this is judged not to be in the national interest. The Secretary of State for the Home Department is empowered to require a person with information about a violation of the Act to disclose his source. Journalists have no exemption here. The publication of morally objectionable and harmful material is treated in the Children's and Young Persons' (Harmful Publications) Act of 1955 and in the Obscene Publications Act.

Legislative measures have been taken to limit the excessive development of concentrations of newspaper ownership and the extent of the control by newspaper owners over other mass media such as the television. The Television Act of 1964 provided for intervention by the Postmaster-General or the Independent Broadcasting Authority where investments by newspaper owners in television companies are judged liable to lead to abuses. The Monopolies and Mergers Act of 1965 requires the written consent of the Department of Trade and Industry for the transfer of daily or weekly papers with an aggregate average of over 500,000 copies per day of publication. The Department's decision is based on the conclusions of the Monopolies Commission to which, with exception of cases of papers judged to be uneconomical and of papers with an average daily circulation of no more than 25,000 copies, all cases are referred for investigation.

The Press Complaints Commission, which replaced the Press Council in 1991, has an independent chairman and 16 members, drawn from the lay public and the press. It deals with complaints from the public and upholds an 18-point Code of Practice.

Among the most influential newspapers may be included: *The Times, The Guardian, The Independent, Daily Telegraph* and *Financial Times* (daily), *The Observer, The Independent on Sunday, The Sunday Times* and *Sunday Telegraph* (Sunday newspapers). Prominent among the popular press are: *Daily Mail, Daily Mirror, The Express* and *The Sun* (daily), *Sunday Mirror, News of the World* and *The People* (Sunday newspapers).

No important newspaper is directly owned by a political party. The great rate of news consumption has fostered the growth of large national groups or chains of papers controlled by a single organization or individual. The largest of these chains are as follows:

Daily Mail and General Trust PLC: Northcliffe House, 2 Derry St, London, W8 5TT; tel. (20) 7938-6747; fax (20) 7938-4626; e-mail webmaster@dmgt.co.uk; internet www.dmgt.co.uk; controls through Associated Newspapers one national daily, *Daily Mail*, one national Sunday, *The Mail on Sunday*, one London daily, *Evening Standard*; through the Northcliffe Newspapers Group Ltd controls 20 daily titles, 27 weekly titles and 50 free newspapers; Group Chair. Viscount ROTHERMERE; Group CEO CHARLES SINCLAIR.

Guardian Media Group PLC: 75 Farringdon Rd, London, EC1M 3JY; tel. (20) 7713-4452; fax (20) 7742-0679; internet www.gmgplc.co.uk; subsidiary publishing cos include Guardian Newspapers Ltd (controls The Guardian, The Observer) and Manchester Evening News Ltd; Chair. PAUL MYNERS; CEO Sir BOB PHILLIS (until 31 July 2006).

Independent Newspapers UK: Independent House, 191 Marsh Wall, London, E14 9RS; tel. (20) 7005-2000; internet www.inmplc.com; British subsidiary of Ireland's Independent News & Media PLC; publishes one national daily, *The Independent*, and one national Sunday paper, *The Independent on Sunday*; Chief Exec. Sir ANTHONY O'REILLY; Chair. Dr B. HILLERY.

News International PLC: 1 Virginia St, London, E98 1XY; tel. (20) 7782-6000; fax (20) 7782-6097; internet www.newsint.co.uk; British subsidiary of USA's News Corporation; subsidiary cos: News Group Newspapers Ltd (controls The Sun and News of the World), Times Newspapers Ltd (controls The Times and The Sunday Times); Exec. Chair. LESLIE HINTON.

Trinity Mirror PLC: 1 Canada Sq., Canary Wharf, London, E14 5AP; tel. (20) 7293-3000; fax (20) 7293-3280; internet www.trinitymirror.com; f. 1999; by merger of Mirror Group Newspapers Ltd and Trinity International Holdings; controls a total of over 250 newspapers, including one national daily paper, *Daily Mirror*, two national Sunday papers, *The People, Sunday Mirror* and two Scottish national papers *Daily Record* and *Sunday Mail* and numerous regional and local papers; Chair. Sir IAN GIBSON; Chief Exec. SYLVIA (SLY) BAILEY.

United Business Media PLC: Ludgate House, 245 Blackfriars Rd, London, SE1 9UY; tel. (20) 7921-5000; e-mail communications@unitedbusinessmedia.com; internet www.unitedbusinessmedia.com; f. 1996 by merger of United Newspapers and MAI group; international media and information group; three core business divisions—professional media, market research, news distribution; Chair. GEOFF UNWIN; CEO DAVID LEVIN.

PRINCIPAL NATIONAL DAILIES
(average net circulation figures (in the United Kingdom only) as at April 2006, unless otherwise stated)

Daily Express: The Northern & Shell Bldg, 10 Lower Thames St, London, EC3R 6EN; tel. (8714) 341010; e-mail expressletters@express.co.uk; internet www.express.co.uk; f. 1900; Propr Northern and Shell Group; Editor PETER HILL; circ. 792,194.

Daily Mail: Northcliffe House, 2 Derry St, London, W8 5TT; tel. (20) 7938-6000; fax (20) 7937-4463; e-mail news@dailymail.co.uk; internet www.dailymail.co.uk; f. 1896; inc. News Chronicle 1960 and Daily Sketch 1971; Propr Associated Newspaper Holdings; Editor-in-Chief PAUL DACRE; Man. Dir GUY ZITTER; circ. 2,225,441.

Daily Mirror: 1 Canada Sq., Canary Wharf, London, E14 5AP; tel. (20) 7293-3000; fax (20) 7293-3280; e-mail mailbox@mirror.co.uk; internet www.mirror.co.uk; f. 1903; Propr Trinity Mirror PLC; Editor RICHARD WALLACE; circ. 1,523,712.

Daily Star: The Northern & Shell Bldg, 10 Lower Thames St, London, EC3R 6EN; tel. (8714) 341010; fax (20) 7922-7960; e-mail news@dailystar.co.uk; internet www.dailystar.co.uk; f. 1978; Propr Express Newspapers PLC; Editor DAWN NEESOM; circ. 671,431.

Daily Telegraph: 1 Canada Sq., Canary Wharf, London, E14 5DT; tel. (20) 7538-5000; fax (20) 7513-2512; e-mail dtletters@telegraph.co.uk; internet www.telegraph.co.uk; Daily Telegraph, f. 1855, Morning Post, f. 1772; amalgamated 1937; Propr Barclay Bros; Chief Exec. MURDOCH MACLENNAN; Editor JOHN BRYANT (acting); circ. 860,103.

Financial Times: Number One Southwark Bridge, London, SE1 9HL; tel. (20) 7873-3000; fax (20) 7873-3076; internet www.ft.com; f. 1880; Propr Pearson PLC; Chair. Sir DAVID BELL; Editor LIONEL BARBER; circ. 132,647.

The Guardian: 119 Farringdon Rd, London, EC1R 3ER; and 164 Deansgate, Manchester, M3 3GG; tel. (20) 7278-2332; fax (20) 7837-2114; e-mail userhelp@guardian.co.uk; internet www.guardian.co.uk; tel. (161) 832-7200; fax (161) 832-5351; f. 1821; Propr Guardian Newspapers Ltd; Editor ALAN RUSBRIDGER; circ. 336,226.

The Independent: Independent House, 191 Marsh Wall, London, E14 9RS; tel. (20) 7005-2000; fax (20) 7005-2999; e-mail customerservices@independent.co.uk; internet www.independent.co.uk; f. 1986; Editor SIMON KELNER; circ. 216,801.

Racing Post: 1 Canada Sq., Canary Wharf, London, E14 5AP; tel. (20) 7293-3000; fax (20) 7293-3758; e-mail editor@racingpost.co.uk; internet www.racingpost.co.uk; f. 1986; covers national and international horse racing, greyhound racing, general sport and betting; Editor CHRIS SMITH; circ. 74,453.

The Sport: 19 Gt Ancoats St, Manchester, M60 4BT; tel. (161) 236-4466; fax (161) 236-4535; internet www.dailysport.net; f. 1988; Propr Sport Newspapers Ltd; Editor DAVID BEEVERS.

The Sportsman: Sports Betting Media Ltd, 1 Riverside, Manbre Rd., London W6 9WA; tel. (20) 8846-3000; fax (20) 8846-3014; e-mail letters@thesportsman.com; internet www.thesportsman.com; f. 2006; covers national and international sport and betting; Editor-in-Chief CHARLIE METHVEN.

The Sun: 1 Virginia St, London, E98 1SN; tel. (20) 7782-4000; fax (20) 7782-4108; e-mail news@the-sun.co.uk; internet www.thesun.co

.uk; f. 1921 as *Daily Herald*; present name since 1964; Propr News International PLC; Editor REBEKAH WADE; Man. Dir MIKE ANDERSON; circ. 2,966,432.

The Times: 1 Pennington St, London, E98 1XY; tel. (20) 7782-5000; fax (20) 7782-5046; internet www.timesonline.co.uk; f. 1785; Propr News International PLC; Editor ROBERT THOMSON; circ. 640,195.

LONDON DAILIES
(average net circulation figures as at April 2006, unless otherwise stated)

Evening Standard: Northcliffe House, 2 Derry St, London, W8 5TT; tel. (20) 7938-6000; fax (20) 7937-2648; internet www.thisislondon.co.uk; f. 1827; merged with Evening News 1980; Monday–Friday; evening; Propr Associated Newspaper Holdings PLC; Editor VERONICA WADLEY; Man. Dir BERT HARDY; circ. 324,123.

Metro: 1 Surrey Quays Rd, London, SE16 7ND; tel. (20) 7651-5200; fax (20) 7651-5342; e-mail editorial@ukmetro.co.uk; internet www.metro.co.uk; f. 1999; Monday–Friday; morning; also distributed in Bristol, Birmingham, Edinburgh, Glasgow, Nottingham, Leeds, Manchester, Newcastle and Sheffield; Propr Associated Newspaper Holdings PLC; Editor KENNY CAMPBELL; Man. Dir STEVE AUCKLAND; circ. 520,211 (London); 1,035,996 (total UK).

PRINCIPAL PROVINCIAL DAILIES
(average net circulation figures as at April 2006, unless otherwise stated)

Aberdeen

Evening Express: Aberdeen Journals Ltd, Lang Stracht, Mastrick, Aberdeen, AB15 6DF; tel. (1224) 690222; fax (1224) 699575; e-mail ee.news@ajl.co.uk; internet www.thisisaberdeen.co.uk; f. 1879; Editor DAMIAN BATES; circ. 56,868.

Press and Journal: POB 43, Lang Stracht, Mastrick, Aberdeen, AB15 6DF; tel. (1224) 690222; fax (1224) 663575; e-mail pj.editor@ajl.co.uk; internet www.thisisnorthscotland.co.uk; f. 1747; morning; Propr Northcliffe Newspapers Ltd; Editor DEREK TUCKER; circ. 17,092.

Belfast

Belfast Telegraph: 124–144 Royal Ave, Belfast, BT1 1EB; tel. (28) 9026-4000; fax (28) 9055-4506; e-mail newseditor@belfasttelegraph.co.uk; internet www.belfasttelegraph.co.uk; f. 1870; independent; evening; Proprs Independent News and Media PLC; Editor MARTIN LINDSAY; circ. 93,786.

Daily Ireland: Teach Basil, 2 Hannahstown Hill, Belfast, BT17 0LT; tel. (48) 9061-2345; fax (48) 9062-3885; internet www.dailyireland.com; f. 2005; morning; Editor COLIN O'CARROLL; circ. 10,017.

Irish News: 113–117 Donegall St, Belfast, BT1 2GE; tel. (28) 9032-2226; fax (28) 9033-7505; e-mail newsdesk@irishnews.com; internet www.irishnews.com; f. 1855; Irish nationalist; morning; Editor NOEL DORAN; circ. 48,323.

News Letter: 45–56 Boucher Cres., Belfast, BT12 6QY; tel. (28) 9068-0000; fax (28) 9066-9910; e-mail newsletter@mgn.co.uk; internet www.newsletter.co.uk; f. 1737; pro-Union; morning; Editor AUSTIN HUNTER; circ. 28,616.

Birmingham

Birmingham Post: 28 Colmore Circus, Queensway, Birmingham, B4 6AX; tel. (121) 234-5904; fax (121) 625-1105; e-mail thepost@mrn.co.uk; internet www.icbirmingham.co.uk; f. 1857; acquired by Mirror Group Newspapers Ltd in 1997; morning; independent; Editor FIONA ALEXANDER; circ. 13,002.

The Evening Mail: 28 Colmore Circus, Queensway, Birmingham, B4 6AX; tel. (121) 236-3366; fax (121) 233-0271; e-mail eveningmail@mrn.co.uk; internet www.icbirmingham.co.uk; f. 1870; acquired by Mirror Group Newspapers Ltd in 1997; evening; independent; Editor STEVE DYSON; circ. 85,074.

Bradford

Telegraph & Argus: Newsquest (Bradford) Ltd, Hall Ings, Bradford, BD1 1JR; tel. (1274) 729511; fax (1274) 723634; e-mail newsdesk@bradford.newsquest.co.uk; internet www.thisisbradford.co.uk; f. 1868; evening; Editor PERRY AUSTIN-CLARKE; circ. 42,044.

Brighton

The Argus: Newsquest (Sussex) Ltd, Argus House, Crowhurst Rd, Hollingbury, Brighton, BN1 8AR; tel. (1273) 544544; fax (1273) 566114; e-mail editor@theargus.co.uk; internet www.theargus.co.uk; f. 1880; Man. Dir MARTYN WILLIS; Editor MICHAEL BEARD; circ. 35,169.

Bristol

Evening Post: Temple Way, Bristol, BS99 7HD; tel. (117) 934-3000; fax (117) 934-3575; e-mail epnews@bepp.co.uk; internet www.thisisbristol.com; f. 1932; inc. the Evening World; Propr Northcliffe Newspapers; independent; Editor MIKE NORTON; Man. Dir TIM KITCHEN; circ. 56,250.

Western Daily Press: Temple Way, Bristol, BS99 7HD; tel. (117) 934-3000; fax (117) 934-3574; e-mail wdnews@bepp.co.uk; internet www.westpress.co.uk; f. 1858; Propr Bristol Evening Post and Press Ltd; morning; independent; Editor ANDY WRIGHT; circ. 47,306.

Cardiff

South Wales Echo: Havelock St, Cardiff, CF10 1XR; tel. (29) 2022-3333; fax (29) 2058-3624; e-mail echo.newsdesk@wme.co.uk; internet www.icwales.co.uk; f. 1884; Propr Trinity Mirror PLC; evening; independent; Editor RICHARD WILLIAMS; circ. 54,635.

The Western Mail: Havelock St, Cardiff, CF10 1XR; tel. (29) 2022-3333; fax (29) 2058-3652; e-mail readers@wme.co.uk; internet www.icwales.co.uk; f. 1869; independent; Man. Dir MARK HAYSOM; Editor ALAN EDMUNDS; circ. 42,956.

Coventry

Coventry Evening Telegraph: Corporation St, Coventry, CV1 1FP; tel. (24) 7663-3633; fax (24) 7655-0869; e-mail letters@coventry-telegraph.co.uk; internet www.iccoventry.co.uk; f. 1891 as *Midland Daily Telegraph*; Propr. Trinity Mirror PLC; independent; Man. Dir GERALDINE AITKEN; Editor ALAN KIRBY.

Darlington

Northern Echo: Newsquest (North East) Ltd, POB 14, Priestgate, Darlington, Co Durham, DL1 1NF; tel. (1325) 381313; fax (1325) 360756; e-mail newsdesk@nne.co.uk; internet www.thisisthenortheast.co.uk; f. 1869; morning; independent; Editor PETER BARRON; circ. 53,481.

Derby

Derby Evening Telegraph: Northcliffe House, Meadow Rd, Derby, DE1 2DW; tel. (1332) 291111; fax (1332) 253027; e-mail newsdesk@derbytelegraph.co.uk; internet www.thisisderbyshire.co.uk; f. 1932; inc. Derby Daily Telegraph, f. 1879, Derby Daily Express, f. 1884; Man. Dir PAUL KEARNEY; Editor STEVE HALL; circ. 47,809.

Dundee

Courier and Advertiser: Albert Sq., Dundee, DD1 9QJ; tel. (1382) 223131; fax (1382) 225511; e-mail editor@thecourier.co.uk; internet www.thecourier.co.uk; f. 1810; morning; Editor WILLIAM HUTCHEON; circ. 78,010.

Edinburgh

Edinburgh Evening News: Barclay House, 108 Holyrood Rd, Edinburgh, EH8 8AS; tel. (131) 620-8620; fax (131) 620-8696; e-mail jmclellan@edinburghnews.com; internet www.edinburghnews.com; f. 1873; Propr European Press Holdings; Editor JOHN MCLELLAN; circ. 56,646.

The Scotsman: Barclay House, 108 Holyrood Rd, Edinburgh, EH8 8AS; tel. (131) 620-8620; fax (131) 620-8616; e-mail enquiries@scotsman.com; internet www.scotsman.com; f. 1817; morning; Propr Johnston Press Plc; Editor JOHN MCGURK; circ. 64,686.

Glasgow

Daily Record: 1 Central Quay, Glasgow, G3 8DA; tel. (141) 309-3000; fax (141) 309-3340; internet www.dailyrecord.co.uk; morning; independent; f. 1895; Propr Trinity Mirror PLC; Editor-in-Chief BRUCE WADDELL; circ. 438,545.

The Express: Park House, Park Circus Place, Glasgow, G3 6AF; tel. (141) 332-9600; fax (141) 332-5448; internet www.express.co.uk; morning; regional edition of The Express; Propr Northern and Shell Group; Editor DAVID HAMILTON.

Glasgow Evening Times: 200 Renfield St, Glasgow, G2 3Q3; tel. (141) 302-7000; fax (141) 302-6600; e-mail times@eveningtimes.co.uk; internet www.eveningtimes.co.uk; f. 1876; independent; Propr Newsquest; Editor DONALD MARTIN; circ. 81,393.

The Herald: 200 Renfield St, Glasgow, G2 3QB; tel. (141) 302-7000; fax (141) 302-7171; e-mail news@theherald.co.uk; internet www.theherald.co.uk; f. 1783; morning; independent; Propr Newsquest; Editor CHARLES MCGHEE; circ. 75,998.

Grimsby

Grimsby Telegraph: 80 Cleethorpe Rd, Grimsby, DN31 3EH; tel. (1472) 360360; fax (1472) 372257; e-mail newsdesk@

THE UNITED KINGDOM

grimsbytelegraph.co.uk; internet www.thisisgrimsby.co.uk; f. 1898; evening; Editor MICHELLE LALOR; circ. 38,297.

Ipswich

East Anglian Daily Times: 30 Lower Brook St, Ipswich, IP4 1AN; tel. (1473) 324732; e-mail news@eadt.co.uk; internet www.eadt.co.uk; morning; Editor TERRY HUNT; circ. 37,338.

Kingston upon Hull

Hull Daily Mail: Blundell's Corner, Beverley Rd, Kingston upon Hull, HU3 1XS; tel. (1482) 327111; fax (1482) 584353; e-mail news@hdmp.co.uk; internet www.thisishull.co.uk; f. 1885; evening; Editor JOHN MEEHAN; circ. 67,860.

Leeds

Yorkshire Evening Post: POB 168, Wellington St, Leeds, LS1 1RF; tel. (113) 243-2701; fax (113) 238-8536; internet www.thisisleeds.co.uk; f. 1890; independent; Publr Johnston Press Plc; Editor NEIL HODGKINSON; circ. 63,265.

Yorkshire Post: POB 168, Wellington St, Leeds, LS1 1RF; tel. (113) 2432701; fax (113) 244-3430; internet www.yorkshireposttoday.co.uk; f. 1754; morning; Conservative; Publr Yorkshire Post Newspapers Ltd; Editor PETER CHARLTON; circ. 54,730.

Leicester

Leicester Mercury: St George St, Leicester, LE1 9FQ; tel. (116) 251-2512; fax (116) 253-0645; e-mail nickcarter@leicestermercury.co.uk; internet www.thisisleicestershire.co.uk; f. 1874; evening; Editor NICK CARTER; circ. 78,075.

Liverpool

Daily Post: POB 48, Old Hall St, Liverpool, L69 3EB; tel. (151) 227-2000; fax (151) 472-2474; e-mail newsdesk@dailypost.co.uk; internet www.icliverpool.co.uk; f. 1855; inc. Liverpool Mercury, f. 1811; morning; independent; Propr Trinity Mirror PLC; Editor JANE WOLSTENHOLME; circ. 18,741.

Liverpool Echo: POB 48, Old Hall St, Liverpool, L69 3EB; tel. (151) 227-2000; fax (151) 472-2474; e-mail letters@liverpoolecho.co.uk; internet www.icliverpool.co.uk; f. 1879; evening; independent; Propr Trinity Mirror PLC; Editor ALASTAIR MACHRAY; circ. 120,131.

Manchester

Manchester Evening News: 164 Deansgate, Manchester, M60 2RD; tel. (161) 832-7200; fax (161) 831-7418; e-mail newsdesk@men-news.co.uk; internet www.manchesteronline.co.uk/men; f. 1868; independent; Editor PAUL HORROCKS; circ. 128,445.

Middlesbrough

Evening Gazette: Borough Rd, Middlesbrough, TS1 3AZ; tel. (1642) 245401; fax (1642) 210565; e-mail editor@eveninggazette.co.uk; internet www.gazettelive.co.uk; f. 1869; Propr Trinity Mirror PLC; Man. Dir ALISTAIR MCCOLL; Editor DARREN THWAITES; circ. 55,545.

Newcastle upon Tyne

Evening Chronicle: Groat Market, Newcastle upon Tyne, NE1 1ED; tel. (191) 232-7500; fax (191) 232-2256; e-mail ec.news@ncjmedia.co.uk; internet www.icnewcastle.co.uk; f. 1885; Propr Trinity Mirror PLC; Editor PAUL ROBERTSON; circ. 83,425.

The Journal: Groat Market, Newcastle upon Tyne, NE1 1ED; tel. (191) 232-7500; fax (191) 230-4144; e-mail jnl.newsdesk@ncjmedia.co.uk; internet www.icnewcastle.co.uk; f. 1832; morning; Propr Trinity Mirror PLC; Editor BRIAN AITKEN; circ. 40,945.

Norwich

Eastern Daily Press: Prospect House, Rouen Rd, Norwich, NR1 1RE; tel. (1603) 628311; fax (1603) 612930; e-mail edp@archant.co.uk; internet www.edp24.co.uk; f. 1870; independent; Propr Archant Regional Ltd; Editor PETER FRANZEN; circ. 69,355.

Nottingham

Nottingham Evening Post: Castle Wharf House, Nottingham, NG1 7EU; tel. (115) 948-2000; fax (115) 964-4032; e-mail newsdesk@nottinghameveningpost.co.uk; internet www.thisisnottingham.co.uk; f. 1878; Editor GRAHAM GLEN; circ. 68,354.

Plymouth

Western Morning News: 17 Brest Rd, Derriford, Plymouth, PL6 5AA; tel. (1752) 765500; fax (1752) 765535; internet www.westernmorningnews.co.uk; f. 1860; Editor-in-Chief ALAN QUAL-

Directory

TROUGH; circ. 42,325; companion evening paper, Evening Herald; Editor BILL MARTIN; circ. 44,767.

Portsmouth

The News: The News Centre, Hilsea, Portsmouth, PO2 9SX; tel. (23) 9266-4488; fax (23) 9267-3363; e-mail newsdesk@thenews.co.uk; internet www.portsmouth.co.uk; f. 1877; evening; Editor MIKE GILSON.

Preston

Lancashire Evening Post: Oliver's Place, Preston, PR2 9ZA; tel. (1772) 254841; fax (1772) 880173; e-mail lep.newsdesk@rim.co.uk; internet www.prestononline.co.uk; f. 1886; Editor SIMON REYNOLDS; circ. 34,877.

Sheffield

The Star: York St, Sheffield, S1 1PU; tel. (114) 276-7676; fax (114) 272-5978; e-mail alan.powell@sheffieldnewspapers.co.uk; internet www.sheffieldtoday.co.uk; f. 1887; evening; independent; Propr Johnston Press; Editor ALAN POWELL.

Southampton

Southern Daily Echo: Newspaper House, Test Lane, Redbridge, Southampton, SO16 9JX; tel. (23) 8042-4777; fax (23) 8042-4545; e-mail newsdesk@soton-echo.co.uk; internet www.dailyecho.co.uk; f. 1888; Propr Newsquest; Editor IAN MURRAY; circ. 41,469.

Stoke-on-Trent

The Sentinel: Staffordshire Sentinel Newspapers Ltd, Sentinel House, Etruria, Stoke-on-Trent, ST1 5SS; tel. (1782) 602525; fax (1782) 602616; e-mail newsdesk@thesentinel.co.uk; internet www.thisisthesentinel.co.uk; f. 1854; Editor MIKE SASSI; circ. 70,486.

Sunderland

Sunderland Echo: Echo House, Pennywell, Sunderland, Tyne and Wear, SR4 9ER; tel. (191) 501-7111; fax (191) 534-3807; e-mail echo.news@northeast-press.co.uk; internet www.sunderlandtoday.co.uk; f. 1873; evening; Editor ROB LAWSON.

Swansea

South Wales Evening Post: Adelaide St, Swansea, SA1 1QT; tel. (1792) 510000; fax (1792) 514197; internet www.thisissouthwales.co.uk; f. 1930; Editor SPENCER FEENEY; circ. 54,682.

Telford

Shropshire Star: Ketley, Telford, Shropshire, TF1 5HU; tel. (1952) 242424; fax (1952) 254605; e-mail newsroom@shropshirestar.co.uk; internet www.shropshirestar.com; f. 1964; evening; Propr Shropshire Newspapers Ltd; Editor SARAH-JANE SMITH; circ. 77,457.

Wolverhampton

Express and Star: 51–53 Queen St, Wolverhampton, West Midlands, WV1 1ES; tel. (1902) 313131; fax (1902) 710106; e-mail newsdesk@expressandstar.co.uk; internet www.westmidlands.com; f. 1874; evening; Propr The Midland News Association Ltd; Editor ADRIAN FABER; circ. 150,533.

York

The Press: POB 29, 76–86 Walmgate, York, YO1 9YN; tel. (1904) 653051; fax (1904) 612853; e-mail newsdesk@ycp.co.uk; internet www.thisisyork.co.uk; Editor KEVIN BOOTH; circ. 35,761.

PRINCIPAL WEEKLY NEWSPAPERS
(average net circulation figures as at April 2006, unless otherwise stated)

Asian Times: Ethnic Media Group, 65 Whitechapel Rd, London, E1 1DU; tel. (20) 7650-2000; fax (20) 7650-2001; internet www.asiantimesonline.co.uk; Editor BURHAN AHMAD; Man. Dir WAYNE BOWER.

The Business: 292 Vauxhall Bridge Rd, London, SW1V 1AE; tel. (20) 7961-0000; fax (20) 7961-0101; e-mail rkidd@thebusiness.press.net; internet www.thebusinessonline.com; f. 1996; relaunched in 1998; Propr European Press Holdings; Editor-in-Chief ANDREW NEIL; Man. Dir PAUL WOOLFENDEN; circ. 151,093.

Daily Star Sunday: Ludgate House, 245 Blackfriars Rd, London, SE1 9UX; tel. (20) 7928-8000; fax (20) 7633-0244; e-mail dailystarnewsdesk@dailystar.co.uk; internet www.dailystar.co.uk; f. 1978; Propr Express Newspapers PLC; Editor GARETH MORGAN; circ. 316,719.

The Independent on Sunday: Independent House, 191 Marsh Wall, London, E14 9RS; tel. (20) 7005-2000; fax (20) 7005-2627; internet www.independent.co.uk; f. 1990; Propr Independent Newspapers UK; Editor Tristan Davies; circ. 200,064.

The Mail on Sunday: Northcliffe House, 2 Derry St, London, W8 5TS; tel. (20) 7938-3829; fax (20) 7937-1004; internet www.mailonsunday.co.uk; f. 1982; Propr Associated Newspaper Ltd; Editor Peter Wright; Man. Dir Stephen Miron; circ. 2,170,147.

News of the World: 1 Virginia St, London, E1 9XR; tel. (20) 7782-1000; fax (20) 7583-9504; e-mail newsdesk@news-of-the-world.co.uk; internet www.newsoftheworld.co.uk; f. 1843; Propr News International PLC; Sunday; Editor Andy Coulson; Man. Dir Mike Anderson; circ. 3,248,676.

The Observer: 3-7 Herbal Hill, London, EC1R 5EJ; tel. (20) 7278-2332; fax (20) 7713-4250; e-mail userhelp@guardian.co.uk; internet www.observer.co.uk; f. 1791; owned by Guardian Newspapers Ltd; Sunday; Editor Roger Alton; circ. 418,978.

The People: 1 Canada Sq., Canary Wharf, London, E14 5AP; tel. (20) 7293-3000; fax (20) 7293-3887; internet www.people.co.uk; f. 1881; Propr Trinity Mirror PLC; Editor Mark Thomas; circ. 783,684.

Scotland on Sunday: Barclay House, 108 Holyrood Rd, Edinburgh, EH8 8AS; tel. (131) 620-8620; fax (131) 620-8491; e-mail letters_sos@scotlandonsunday.com; internet www.scotlandonsunday.com; f. 1988; Propr Johnston Press Plc; Editor (vacant); circ. 77,615.

Sunday Express: Ludgate House, 245 Blackfriars Rd., London, SE1 9UX; tel. (8714) 341010; fax (20) 7620-1656; internet www.express.co.uk; f. 1918; inc. Sunday Despatch 1961; independent; Propr Northern and Shell Group; Editor-in-Chief Martin Townsend; circ. 846,506.

Sunday Herald: 200 Renfield St, Glasgow, G2 3QB; tel. (141) 302-7800; e-mail editor@sundayherald.com; internet www.sundayherald.com; f. 1999; Propr Newsquest Media Group; Editor Richard Walker; circ. 59,397.

Sunday Life: 124–144 Royal Ave, Belfast, BT1 1EB; tel. (28) 9026-4300; fax (28) 9054-4507; e-mail writeback@belfasttelegraph.co.uk; internet www.sundaylife.co.uk; f. 1988; Editor Martin Lindsay; circ. 77,688.

Sunday Mail: 40 Anderston Quay, Glasgow, G3 8DA; tel. (141) 309-3000; fax (141) 242-3587; e-mail mailbox@sundaymail.co.uk; internet www.sundaymail.co.uk; Propr Mirror Group Newspapers Ltd; Editor Allan Rennie; circ. 519,419.

Sunday Mercury: Weaman St, Birmingham, B4 6AY; tel. (121) 234-5567; e-mail sundaymercury@mrn.co.uk; internet www.icbirmingham.co.uk; Propr Trinity Mirror PLC; f. 1918; Editor David Brookes; circ. 66,007.

Sunday Mirror: 1 Canada Sq., Canary Wharf, London, E14 5AP; tel. (20) 7293-3000; fax (20) 7822-3587; e-mail mailbox@mirror.co.uk; internet www.sundaymirror.co.uk; f. 1915; Propr Trinity Mirror PLC; independent; Editor Tina Weaver; circ. 1,367,486.

The Sunday Post: 144 Port Dundas Rd, Glasgow, G4 OHZ; tel. (141) 332-9933; fax (141) 331-1595; e-mail mail@sundaypost.com; internet www.sundaypost.com; f. 1919; Propr D.C. Thomson & Co. Ltd; Editor David Pollington; circ. 468,414.

Sunday Sport: 19 Gt Ancoats St, Manchester, M60 4BT; tel. (161) 236-4466; fax (161) 236-4535; f. 1986; Editor Mark Harris; circ. 132,990.

Sunday Sun: Thomson House, Groat Market, Newcastle upon Tyne, NE1 1ED; tel. (191) 201-6251; fax (191) 230-0238; e-mail colin.patterson@ncjmedia.co.uk; internet www.sundaysun.co.uk; f. 1919; Propr Trinity Mirror PLC; independent; north-east England; Editor Colin Patterson; circ. 75,499.

Sunday Telegraph: 1 Canada Sq., Canary Wharf, London, E14 5DT; tel. (20) 7538-5000; fax (20) 7538-6242; e-mail stletters@telegraph.co.uk; internet www.telegraph.co.uk; f. 1961; Propr Barclay Bros; Editor Patience Wheatcroft; circ. 662,270.

The Sunday Times: 1 Pennington St, London, E98 1ST; tel. (20) 7782-5000; fax (20) 7782-5658; internet www.sunday-times.co.uk; f. 1822; Propr News International PLC; Editor John Witherow; circ. 1,190,867.

Wales on Sunday: Havelock St, Cardiff, CF1 1XR; tel. (29) 2058-3583; internet www.icwales.co.uk; f. 1991; Editor Tim Gordon; circ. 47,724.

SELECTED PERIODICALS
(circulation figures as at July 2005, unless otherwise stated)

Arts and Literature

Apollo Magazine: 20 Theobald's Rd, London, WC1X 8PF; tel. (20) 7430-1900; fax (20) 7404-7386; e-mail editorial@apollomag.com; internet www.apollo-magazine.com; f. 1925; monthly; fine and decorative art; Publr Paul Josefowitz; Editor Michael Hall.

Architects' Journal: EMAP Construct, 151 Rosebery Ave, London, EC1R 4GB; tel. (20) 7505-6700; fax (20) 7505-6701; e-mail isabel.allen@construct.emap.com; internet www.ajplus.co.uk; f. 1895; Thursday; Editor Isabel Allen; circ. 13,491.

Architectural Review: EMAP Construct, 151 Rosebery Ave, London, EC1R 4GB; tel. (20) 7505-6725; fax (20) 7505-6701; e-mail paul.finch@emap.com; internet www.arplus.com; f. 1896; monthly; Editor Paul Finch; circ. 19,915.

The Artist: Caxton House, 63–65 High St, Tenterden, Kent, TN30 6BD; tel. (1580) 763673; fax (1580) 765411; e-mail sally@tapc.co.uk; internet www.theartistmagazine.co.uk; f. 1931; monthly; Editor Sally Bulgin.

Art Review: 1 Sekforde St, London, EC1R 0BE; tel. (20) 7107-2760; fax (20) 7107-2761; e-mail info@art-review.co.uk; internet www.art-review.com; f. 1949; monthly; Editor Rebecca Wilson.

BBC Music Magazine: Origin Publishing Ltd, 14th Floor, Tower House, Fairfax St, Bristol, BS1 3BN; tel. (117) 927-9009; fax (117) 934-9008; e-mail musicmagazine@originpublishing.co.uk; internet www.bbcmusicmagazine.com; f. 1992; monthly; classical music; Editor Oliver Condy; circ. 56,096.

The Bookseller: Endeavour House, 189 Shaftesbury Ave, London, WC2H 8TJ; tel. (20) 7420-6006; fax (20) 7420-6103; e-mail letters.to.editor@bookseller.co.uk; internet www.thebookseller.com; f. 1858; incorporates Bent's Literary Advertiser (f. 1802); Friday; Propr VNU Entertainment Media UK Ltd; Man. Dir Christine Martin; Editor Neill Denny.

The Burlington Magazine: 14–16 Dukes Rd, London, WC1H 9SZ; tel. (20) 7388-1228; fax (20) 7388-1229; e-mail burlington@burlington.org.uk; internet www.burlington.org.uk; f. 1903; monthly; all forms of art, ancient and modern; Editor Richard Shone.

Classical Music: 241 Shaftesbury Ave, London, WC2H 8TF; tel. (20) 7333-1742; fax (20) 7333-1769; e-mail classical.music@rhinegold.co.uk; internet www.rhinegold.co.uk; f. 1976; Editor Keith Clarke; circ. 18,000.

Dancing Times: 45–47 Clerkenwell Green, London, EC1R 0EB; tel. (20) 7250-3006; fax (20) 7253-6679; e-mail dt@dancing-times.co.uk; internet www.dancing-times.co.uk; f. 1910; monthly; ballet and modern dance; Editor Mary Clarke.

Empire: 7th Floor, Endeavour House, Shaftesbury Ave, WC2H 8JG; tel. (20) 7437-9011; fax (20) 7859-8613; e-mail empire@emap.com; internet www.empireonline.com; monthly; film and video; Editor Colin Kennedy; circ. 205,981.

Film Review: Visual Imagination Ltd, 9 Blades Court, Deodar Rd, London, SW15 2NU; tel. (20) 8875-1520; fax (20) 8875-1588; e-mail filmreview@visimag.com; internet www.visimag.com/filmreview; f. 1954; monthly; international cinema and video; Editor Neil Corry.

Folklore: The Folklore Society, c/o The Warburg Institute, Woburn Sq., London, WC1H 0AB; tel. (20) 7862-8564; e-mail submissions@folklore-society.com; internet www.folklore-society.com; f. 1878; 3 a year; Editor Prof. Patricia Lysaght.

The Gramophone: Teddington Studios, Broom Rd, Teddington, Middlesex, TW11 9BE; tel. (20) 8267-5050; fax (20) 8267-5844; e-mail gramophone@haynet.com; internet www.gramophone.co.uk; f. 1923; monthly; Publr Simon Temlett; Editor James Inverne; circ. 45,791 (Dec. 2005).

Granta: 2/3 Hanover Yard, Noel Rd, London, N1 8BE; tel. (20) 7704-9776; fax (20) 7704-0474; e-mail editorial@granta.com; internet www.granta.com; quarterly; Editor Ian Jack; circ. 80,000.

Index on Censorship: 6–8 Amwell St, London, EC1R 1UQ; tel. (20) 7278-2313; fax (20) 7278-1878; e-mail contact@indexoncensorship.org; internet www.indexoncensorship.org; f. 1972; four a year; concerned with freedom of expression throughout the world; Editor Ursula Owen.

Jazz Journal International: Jazz Journal Ltd, 3 & 3A Forest Rd, Loughton, Essex IG10 1DR; tel. (20) 8532-0456; fax (20) 8532-0440; f. 1948; monthly; Editor Janet Cook.

Language Learning Journal: Association for Language Learning, 150 Railway Terrace, Rugby, CV21 3HN; tel. (1788) 546443; fax (1788) 544149; e-mail info@all-languages.org.uk; internet www.all-languages.org.uk; f. 1990; 2 a year; Editors Norbert Pachler, Douglas Allford; circ. 5,000.

mixmag: EMAP Metro Publications Ltd, 2nd Floor, Mappin House, 4 Winsley St, London, W1N 7AR; tel. (20) 7436-1515; fax (20) 7312-8977; e-mail mixmag@emap.com; internet www.mixmag.net; f. 1983; acquired by Development Hell Ltd in 2005; monthly; dance music and club culture; Editor Andrew Harrison; circ. 42,235.

Mojo: Mappin House, 4 Winsley St, London, W1W 8HF; tel. (20) 7436-1515; fax (20) 7312-8296; e-mail mojo@emap.com; internet www.mojo4music.com; f. 1993; monthly; popular music; Editor Phil Alexander; circ. 114,626.

NME: IPC Media Ltd, 25th Floor, King's Reach Tower, Stamford St, London, SE1 9LS; tel. (20) 7261-5000; fax (20) 7261–6022; e-mail conor_mcnicholas@ipcmedia.com; internet www.nme.com; f. 1952; Wednesday; popular music; Editor CONOR MCNICHOLAS; circ. 76,792 (Dec. 2005).

Opera: 36 Black Lion Lane, London, W6 9BE; tel. (20) 8563-8893; fax (20) 8563-8635; e-mail editor@opera.co.uk; internet www.opera.co.uk; f. 1950; monthly; Editor JOHN ALLISON.

Poetry Review: 22 Betterton St, London, WC2H 9BX; tel. (20) 7420-9880; fax (20) 7240-4818; e-mail poetryreview@poetrysoc.com; internet www.poetrysoc.com; f. 1909; quarterly; Editor FIONA SAMPSON.

Q Magazine: EMAP Metro Publications, Mappin House, 5th Floor, 4 Winsley St, London, W1W 8HF; tel. (20) 7182-8000; fax (20) 7182-8547; e-mail q@emap.com; internet www.q4music.com; f. 1986; monthly; music, general features; Editor PAUL REES; circ. 160,310.

Sight and Sound: British Film Institute, 21 Stephen St, London, W1T 1LN; tel. (20) 7255-1444; fax (20) 7436-2327; e-mail s&s@bfi.org.uk; internet www.bfi.org.uk/sightandsound; f. 1932; monthly; international film review; Editor NICK JAMES; circ. 22,616.

The Stage: Stage House, 47 Bermondsey St, London, SE1 3XT; tel. (20) 7403-1818; fax (20) 7403-1418; e-mail info@thestage.co.uk; internet www.thestage.co.uk; f. 1880; Thursday; theatre, light entertainment, television, opera, dance; Man. Dir CAROLINE COMERFORD; circ. 29,841.

The Times Literary Supplement: Admiral House, 66–68 East Smithfield, London, E1W 1BX; tel. (20) 7782-3000; fax (20) 7782-3100; e-mail letters@the-tls.co.uk; internet www.the-tls.co.uk; f. 1902; Friday; weekly journal of literary criticism; Editor Sir PETER STOTHARD; circ. 33,951.

Top of the Pops: Room A1136, Woodlands, 80 Wood Lane, London, W12 0TT; e-mail totp.magazine@bbc.co.uk; internet www.bbcmagazines.com/totp; fortnightly; popular music; Editor PETER HART; circ. 140,192.

Current Affairs and History

Antiquity: King's Manor, York, YO1 7EP; tel. and fax (1904) 433994; fax (1904) 433994; e-mail editor@antiquity.ac.uk; internet antiquity.ac.uk; f. 1927; quarterly; archaeological; Editor Prof. MARTIN CARVER.

The Big Issue: 1–5 Wandsworth Rd, London, SW8 2LN; tel. (20) 7526-3200; fax (20) 7526-3201; e-mail press@bigissue.com; internet www.bigissue.com; also offices based in Cardiff, Glasgow, Manchester, the Midlands and Bristol producing regional weekly editions; f. 1991; weekly; current affairs, social issues; Editor MATT FORD; total circ. 155,575.

Classical Quarterly: Journals Marketing, Oxford University Press, Great Clarendon St, Oxford, OX2 6DP; tel. (1865) 556767; fax (1865) 267835; e-mail cqeditor@classics.ox.ac.uk; internet www3.oup.co.uk/clquaj; f. 1906; 2 a year; language, literature, history and philosophy; Editors Dr MIRIAM T. GRIFFIN, JUDITH MOSSMAN.

Contemporary Review: POB 1242, Oxford, OX1 4FJ; tel. and fax (1865) 201529; e-mail editorial@contemporaryreview.co.uk; internet www.contemporaryreview.co.uk; f. 1866; monthly; publ by Contemporary Review Co Ltd; politics, international affairs, social subjects, the arts; Editor Dr RICHARD MULLEN.

English Historical Review: Oxford University Press, Gt Clarendon St, Oxford, OX2 6DP; e-mail ehr@oup.com; internet www3.oup.co.uk/enghis; f. 1886; 5 a year; learned articles and book reviews; Editors PHILIP WALLER, G. W. BERNARD.

The Historian: The Historical Association, 59A Kennington Park Rd, London, SE11 4JH; tel. (20) 7735-3901; fax (20) 7582-4989; e-mail enquiry@history.org.uk; internet www.history.org.uk; f. 1912; 4 a year; Editors Prof. BILL SPECK, IAN MASON; circ. 3,500.

History Today: 20 Old Compton St, London, W1D 4TW; tel. (20) 7534-8000; fax (20) 7534-8008; e-mail p.furtado@historytoday.com; internet www.historytoday.com; f. 1951; monthly; illustrated general historical magazine; Editor PETER FURTADO; circ. 27,919.

Illustrated London News: 20 Upper Ground, London, SE1 9PF; tel. (20) 7805-5555; fax (20) 7805-5911; e-mail iln@ilng.co.uk; internet www.ilng.co.uk; 4 a year; Group Editor ALISON BOOTH; Man. Dir LISA BARNARD.

International Affairs: Royal Institute of International Affairs, Chatham House, 10 St James's Sq., London, SW1Y 4LE; tel. (20) 7957-5724; fax (20) 7957-5710; e-mail csoper@chathamhouse.org.uk; internet www.chathamhouse.org.uk; f. 1922; six per year; publ. by Blackwell Publishing; original articles, and reviews of publications on international affairs; Editor CAROLINE SOPER.

Journal of Contemporary History: 4 Devonshire St, London, W1W 5BH; tel. (20) 7580-4330; fax (20) 7436-6428; e-mail jchoffice@sagepub.co.uk; internet jch.sagepub.com; f. 1966; quarterly; publ. by SAGE Publications Ltd; Editors RICHARD J. EVANS, NIALL FERGUSON, STANLEY PAYNE.

London Gazette: POB 7923, London, SE1 5ZH; tel. (870) 600-3322; fax (20) 7394-4581; e-mail london.gazette@tso.co.uk; internet www.london-gazette.co.uk; f. 1665; 5 a week; the oldest existing world newspaper; government journal of official, legal and public notices.

New Left Review: 6 Meard St, London, W1F 0EG; tel. (20) 7734-8830; fax (20) 7439-3869; e-mail mail@newleftreview.org; internet www.newleftreview.org; f. 1960; 6 a year; international politics, economics and culture; Editor PERRY ANDERSON.

New Statesman: 3rd Floor, 52 Grosvenor Gardens, London, SW1W 0AU; tel. (20) 7730-3444; fax (20) 7259-0181; e-mail info@newstatesman.co.uk; internet www.newstatesman.com; f. 1913; weekly; current affairs, politics and the arts; Editor JOHN KAMPFNER; circ. 23,267.

People in Power: Cambridge International Reference on Current Affairs Ltd (CIRCA), 13–17 Sturton St, Cambridge, CB1 2SN; tel. (1223) 568017; fax (1223) 354643; e-mail pip@circaworld.com; internet www.peopleinpower.com; f. 1987; bi-monthly; current worldwide government listings; Editor ROGER EAST.

The Political Quarterly: Blackwell Publishing Ltd, 9600 Garsington Rd, Oxford, OX4 2DQ; tel. (1865) 476303; fax (1865) 476770; internet www.blackwellpublishing.com; f. 1930; 5 a year; Editors ANDREW GAMBLE, ANTHONY WRIGHT.

Prospect: 2 Bloomsbury Pl., London, WC1A 2QA; tel. (20) 7255-1344; fax (20) 7255-1279; e-mail editorial@prospect-magazine.co.uk; internet www.prospect-magazine.co.uk; f. 1995; 12 a year; political and cultural; Editor DAVID GOODHART; circ. 26,533.

Race & Class: The Institute of Race Relations, 2–6 Leeke St, London, WC1X 9HS; tel. (20) 7837-0041; fax (20) 7278-0623; e-mail info@irr.org.uk; internet www.irr.org.uk; f. 1959; quarterly; journal on racism, empire and globalization; Editors A. SIVANANDAN, HAZEL WATERS.

The Spectator: 56 Doughty St, London, WC1N 2LL; tel. (20) 7405-1706; fax (20) 7242-0603; e-mail editor@spectator.co.uk; internet www.spectator.co.uk; f. 1828; Thursday; independent political and literary review; Editor MATTHEW D'ANCONA; circ. 67,120.

Tribune: 9 Arkwright Rd, London, NW3 6AN; tel. (20) 7433-6410; fax (20) 7433-6419; e-mail tribuneweb@btconnect.com; internet www.tribuneweb.co.uk; f. 1937; Friday; Labour's independent weekly; politics, current affairs, arts; Editor CHRIS MCLAUGHLIN; Commercial Dir FLETCHER DHEW.

Economics and Business

Accountancy Age: 32–34 Broadwick St, London, W1A 2HG; tel. (20) 7316-9000; fax (20) 7316-9250; e-mail news@accountancyage.com; internet www.accountancyage.co.uk; f. 1969; weekly; Man. Dir BRIN BUCKNOR; Editor DAMIAN WILD; circ. 70,092.

The Banker: Tabernacle Ct, 16–28 Tabernacle St, London, EC2A 4DD; tel. (20) 7382-8000; fax (20) 7382-8586; e-mail stephen.timewell@ft.com; internet www.thebanker.com; f. 1926; monthly; monetary and economic policy, international and domestic banking and finance, banking technology, country surveys; Editor-in-Chief STEPHEN TIMEWELL; circ. 26,089.

Campaign: Haymarket Marketing Publications Ltd, 174 Hammersmith Rd, London, W6 7JP; tel. (20) 8267-4656; fax (20) 8267-4915; e-mail campaign@haynet.com; internet www.campaignlive.com; f. 1968; advertising, marketing and media; Thursday; Editor CLAIRE BEALE; circ. 10,585.

Crops: Reed Farmers Publishing, Quadrant House, The Quadrant, Sutton, Surrey, SM2 5AS; tel. (20) 8652-4080; fax (20) 8652-8928; e-mail crops@rbi.co.uk; internet www.fwi.co.uk; f. 1984; fortnightly; Editor DEBBIE BEATON; circ. 24,368.

Economic Journal: Blackwell Publishing Ltd, 9600 Garsington Rd, Oxford, OX4 2QD; tel. (1865) 791100; fax (1865) 791347; e-mail philippa.sumner@oxon.blackwellpublishing.com; internet www.blackwellpublishing.com; f. 1891; eight a year; Editors MARIANNE BERTRAND, LEONARDO FELLI, JÖRN-STEFFEN PISCHKE, STEVE MACHIN, ANDREW SCOTT, JAUME VENTURA.

The Economist: 25 St James's St, London, SW1A 1HG; tel. (20) 7830-7000; fax (20) 7839-2968; e-mail inquiries@economist.com; internet www.economist.com; f. 1843; 50% owned by Pearson PLC, 50% by individual shareholders; Friday; Editor JOHN MICKELTHWAIT; Exec. Editor ANTHONY GOTTLIEB; circ. 155,371.

Euromoney: Nestor House, Playhouse Yard, London, EC4V 5EX; tel. (20) 7779-8888; fax (20) 7779-8653; e-mail hotline@euromoneyplc.com; internet www.euromoney.com; f. 1969; monthly; Editor CLIVE HORWOOD; circ. 27,712.

Farmers Weekly: Quadrant House, The Quadrant, Sutton, Surrey, SM2 5AS; tel. (20) 8652-4911; fax (20) 8652-4005; e-mail farmers.weekly@rbi.co.uk; internet www.fwi.co.uk; f. 1934; Friday; Editor JANE KING; circ. 73,890.

Investors Chronicle: FT Business, Tabernacle Ct, 16–28 Tabernacle St, London, EC2A 4DD; tel. (20) 7382-8000; fax (20) 7382-8105;

THE UNITED KINGDOM

e-mail ic.customer.services@ft.com; internet www.investorschronicle.co.uk; f. as Money Market Review 1860; amalgamated with Investors Chronicle 1914; amalgamated with the Stock Exchange Gazette 1967; Friday; independent financial and economic review; Editor MATTHEW VINCENT; circ. 38,171.

Management Today: 174 Hammersmith Rd, London, W6 7JP; tel. (20) 8267-4629; fax (20) 8267-4680; e-mail editorial@mtmagazine.co.uk; internet www.mtmagazine.co.uk; f. 1966; monthly; Editor MATTHEW GWYTHER; circ. 100,464.

Education

Higher Education Quarterly: Blackwell Publishing, 9600 Garsington Rd, Oxford, OX4 2DQ; tel. (1865) 776868; fax (1865) 714591; e-mail customerservices@oxon.blackwellpublishing.com; internet www.blackwellpublishing.com; f. 1946; quarterly; Editor Prof. HEATHER EGGINS.

The Teacher: Hamilton House, Mabledon Pl., London, WC1H 9BD; tel. (20) 7380-4708; fax (20) 7383-7230; e-mail teacher@nut.org.uk; internet www.teachers.org.uk/theteacher; f. 1872; magazine of the NUT; news, comments and articles on all aspects of education; eight times a year; Editor MITCH HOWARD.

The Times Educational Supplement: Admiral House, 66–68 East Smithfield, London, E1W 1BX; tel. (20) 7782-3000; fax (20) 7782-3200; e-mail editor@tes.co.uk; internet www.tes.co.uk; f. 1910; Friday; Editor JUDITH JUDD; circ. 85,383.

The Times Higher Education Supplement: Admiral House, 66–68 East Smithfield, London, E1W 1BX; tel. (20) 7782-3000; fax (20) 7782-3300; e-mail editor@thes.co.uk; internet www.thes.co.uk; f. 1971; Thursday; Editor JOHN O'LEARY; circ. 23,507.

Home, Fashion and General

Arena: Endeavour House, 189 Shaftesbury Ave, London, WC2H 8JG; tel. (20) 7437-9011; fax (20) 7520-6500; e-mail arenamag@emap.co.uk; monthly; men's interest; Editor ANTHONY NOGUERA; circ. 46,680.

B: 64 North Row, London W1K 7LL; tel. (20) 7150-7020; fax (20) 7150-7667; e-mail letters@bmagazine.co.uk; internet www.bmagazine.co.uk; f. 1997; monthly; fashion, beauty, lifestyle, travel; Editor NINA AHMAD; circ. 167,371.

Bella: H. Bauer Publishing Ltd, 1st Floor, 24–28 Oval Rd, London, NW1 7DT; tel. (20) 7241-8000; fax (20) 7241-8056; internet www.bauer.co.uk; f. 1987; weekly; fashion, beauty, health, cookery, handicrafts; Editor-in-Chief JAYNE MARSDEN; circ. 389,100.

Best: National Magazine Company, 72 Broadwick St, London, W1F 9EP; tel. (20) 7439-5000; fax (20) 7439-6886; e-mail best@natmags.co.uk; internet www.natmags.co.uk; f. 1987; weekly; women's interest; Editor LOUISE COURT; circ. 398,289.

Chat: IPC Connect Ltd, King's Reach Tower, Stamford St, London, SE1 9LS; tel. (20) 7261-6565; fax (20) 7261-6534; e-mail ingrid_millar@ipcmedia.com; internet www.ipcmedia.com; weekly; women's interest; Editor GILLY SINCLAIR; circ. 609,163.

Company: National Magazine House, 72 Broadwick St, London, W1F 9EP; tel. (20) 7439-5000; fax (20) 7439-6886; e-mail company.mail@natmags.co.uk; internet www.company.co.uk; monthly; Editor VICTORIA WHITE; circ. 302,127.

Cosmopolitan: National Magazine House, 72 Broadwick St, London, W1F 9EP; tel. (20) 7439-5000; fax (20) 7439-5016; e-mail contact@natmags.co.uk; internet www.cosmopolitan.co.uk; f. 1972; monthly; women's interest; Editor-in-Chief SAM BAKER; circ. 462,943.

Elle: 64 North Row, London, W1K 7LL; tel. (20) 7150-7000; fax (20) 7150-7001; e-mail lorraine.candy@hf-uk.com; internet www.hachettefilipacchiuk.co.uk; f. 1985; monthly; women's interest; Editor LORRAINE CANDY; circ. 203,584.

Esquire: National Magazine House, 72 Broadwick St, London, W1F 9EP; tel. (20) 7439-5000; fax (20) 7439-5675; e-mail contact@esquire.co.uk; internet www.esquire.co.uk; f. 1991; monthly; men's interest; Editor SIMON TIFFIN; circ. 63,605.

Eve: Griffin House, 161 Hammersmith Rd, London, W6 8BS; tel. (20) 8267-5000; fax (20) 8267-8222; e-mail evemagazine@haynet.com; internet www.evemagazine.co.uk; Editor SARA CREMER; circ. 162,077.

FHM: Mappin House, 4 Winsley Street, London, W1W 8HF; tel. (20) 7436-1515; fax (20) 7182-8021; e-mail help@fhm.com; internet www.fhm.com; f. 1987; monthly; men's interest; Editor ROSS BROWN; circ. 560,167.

Glamour: Vogue House, Hanover Sq., London, W1S 1JU; tel. (20) 7499-9080; e-mail glamour-editorial@condenast.co.uk; internet www.glamour.com; f. 2001; monthly; women's interest; Editor JO ELVIN; circ. 609,626.

Good Housekeeping: National Magazine House, 72 Broadwick St, London, W1F 9EP; tel. (20) 7439-5000; fax (20) 7437-6886; e-mail contact@goodhousekeeping.co.uk; internet www.goodhousekeeping.co.uk; f. 1922; monthly; Editor-in-Chief LOUISE CHUNN; circ. 475,838.

GQ: The Condé Nast Publications Ltd, Vogue House, Hanover Sq., London, W1S 1JU; tel. (20) 7499-9080; fax (20) 7495-1679; internet www.gq-magazine.co.uk; f. 1988; monthly; Editor DYLAN JONES; circ. 125,050.

Grazia: Endeavour House, 189 Shaftesbury Ave, London, WC2H 8JG; tel. (20) 7437-9011; internet www.emap.com; f. 2005; weekly; Editor JANE BRUTON; circ. 155,157.

Harpers & Queen: National Magazine House, 72 Broadwick St, London, W1F 9EP; tel. (20) 7439-5000; fax (20) 7437-6886; internet www.harpersandqueen.co.uk; f. 1929; Prprs National Magazine Co Ltd; monthly; international fashion, beauty, general features; Editor LUCY YEOMANS; circ. 100,102.

Heat: Endeavour House, 189 Shaftesbury Ave, London, WC2H 8JG; tel. (20) 7437-9011; e-mail heat@emap.com; internet www.emap.com; f. 1999; Tuesdays; celebrity news, TV, radio, films; Editor MARK FRITH; circ. 560,438.

Hello!: Hello! Ltd, Wellington House, 69–71 Upper Ground, London, SE1 9PQ; tel. (20) 7667-8700; fax (20) 7667-8716; e-mail hello@hellomagazine.com; internet www.hellomagazine.com; Propr. Hola S.A. (Spain); weekly; Publr SALLY CARTWRIGHT; Editor RONNIE WHELAN; circ. 392,480.

Homes and Gardens: King's Reach Tower, Stamford St, London, SE1 9LS; tel. (20) 7261-6202; fax (20) 7261-6247; internet www.homesandgardens.com; f. 1919; monthly; Editor DEBORAH BARKER; circ. 146,279.

House & Garden: The Condé Nast Publications Ltd, Vogue House, Hanover Sq., London, W1S 1JU; tel. (20) 7499-9080; fax (20) 7629-2907; e-mail harriet.milward@condenast.co.uk; internet www.houseandgarden.co.uk; f. 1920; monthly; Editor SUSAN CREWE; circ. 140,096.

Ideal Home: IPC Media Ltd, King's Reach Tower, Stamford St, London, SE1 9LS; tel. (20) 7261-6474; fax (20) 7261-6697; e-mail ideal_home@ipcmedia.com; internet www.idealhomemagazine.co.uk; f. 1920; 11 a year; Editor SUE ROSE; circ. 247,006.

InStyle: 12th Floor, King's Reach Tower, Stamford St, London, SE1 9LS; tel. (20) 7261-4747; fax (20) 7261-6664; internet www.ipcmedia.com/magazines/instyle; f. 2001; monthly; fashion, beauty; Editor (vacant); circ. 196,568.

The Lady: 39–40 Bedford St, London, WC2E 9ER; tel. (20) 7379-4717; fax (20) 7836-4620; e-mail editors@lady.co.uk; internet www.lady.co.uk; f. 1885; Tuesday; Editor ARLINE USDEN; circ. 34,582.

Loaded: IPC Media Ltd, King's Reach Tower, Stamford St, London, SE1 9LS; tel. (20) 7261-5562; fax (20) 7261-5557; e-mail lisa_langley@ipcmedia.com; internet www.loaded.co.uk; f. 1994; monthly; music, fashion, contemporary lifestyles; Editor MARTIN DAUBNEY; circ. 237,083.

Marie Claire: IPC Media Ltd, 13th Floor, King's Reach Tower, Stamford Street, London, SE1 9LS; tel. (20) 7261-5240; fax (20) 7261-5277; e-mail marieclaire@ipcmedia.com; internet www.marieclaire.co.uk; f. 1988; monthly; women's interest; Man. Editor MARIE O'RIORDAN; circ. 381,281.

Maxim: 30 Cleveland St, London, W1T 4JD; tel. (20) 7907-6000; fax (20) 7907-6020; e-mail editorial@maxim-magazine.co.uk; internet www.maxim-magazine.co.uk; f. 1995; monthly; health, fitness, fashion, finance; Editor GREG GUTFIELD; circ. 227,377.

My Weekly: D. C. Thomson & Co Ltd, 80 Kingsway East, Dundee, DD4 8SL; tel. (1382) 223131; fax (1382) 452491; e-mail myweekly@dcthomson.co.uk; f. 1910; Thursday; women's interest; Editor SALLY HAMPTON; circ. 225,914.

New Woman: EMAP Elan, Endeavour House, 189 Shaftesbury Ave, London, WC2H 8JG; tel. (20) 7437-9011; fax (20) 7208-3585; e-mail lizzi.hosking@emap.com; internet www.newwomanonline.co.uk; monthly; women's interest; Editor MARGI CONKLIN; circ. 270,686.

Now: King's Reach Tower, Stamford St, London, SE1 9LS; tel. (870) 444-5000; fax (20) 7261-6789; internet www.nowmagazine.co.uk; weekly; celebrity news, TV, radio, films; Editor JANE ENNIS; circ. 591,795.

Nuts: 26th Floor, King's Reach Tower, Stamford St, London, SE1 9LS; tel. (20) 7261-6174; e-mail nutsmagazine@ipcmedia.com; internet www.nutsmag.co.uk; f. 2004; weekly; Editor PHIL HILTON; circ. 304,751.

OK!: The Northern & Shell Building, 10 Lower Thames St, London, EC3R 6EN; tel. (871) 434-1010; e-mail editor@ok-magazine.com; internet www.ok-magazine.co.uk; weekly; Editor NICK McCARTHY; circ. 532,843.

The People's Friend: D. C. Thomson & Co Ltd, 80 Kingsway East, Dundee, DD4 8SL; tel. (1382) 223131; fax (1382) 452491; e-mail peoplesfriend@dcthomson.co.uk; f. 1869; Wednesday; women's fiction, home, crafts, general; Editor MARGARET McCOY; circ. 363,638.

Prima: 72 Broadwick St, London, W1F 9EP; tel. (20) 7439-5000; fax (20) 7312-4100; e-mail prima@natmags.co.uk; internet www.primamagazine.co.uk; f. 1986; English edition; monthly; Editor MAIRE FAHEY; circ. 331,715.

Private Eye: 6 Carlisle St, London, W1D 3BN; tel. (20) 7437-4017; fax (20) 7437-0705; e-mail strobes@private-eye.co.uk; internet www.private-eye.co.uk; f. 1961; fortnightly; satirical; Editor IAN HISLOP; circ. 209,981.

Reader's Digest: Reader's Digest Association Ltd, (British Edition) 11 Westferry Circus, Canary Wharf, London, E14 4HE; tel. (20) 7715-8000; fax (20) 7715-8716; e-mail theeditor@readersdigest.co.uk; internet www.readersdigest.co.uk; f. 1938; monthly; Editor KATHERINE WALKER; circ. 773,731.

The Scots Magazine: D. C. Thomson & Co. Ltd, 2 Albert Sq., Dundee, DD1 9QJ; tel. (1382) 223131; fax (1382) 322214; e-mail mail@scotsmagazine.com; internet www.scotsmagazine.com; f. 1739; monthly; Scottish interest; circ. 43,360.

She: 72 Broadwick St, London, W1F 9EP; tel. (20) 7439-5000; fax (20) 7437-6886; e-mail contact@she.co.uk; internet www.she.co.uk; f. 1955; monthly; Editor TERRY TAVNER; circ. 148,262.

Take a Break: Bauer Publishing Ltd, 24–28 Oval Rd, London, NW1 7DT; tel. (20) 7241-0000; fax (20) 7241-8052; e-mail tab.features@bauer.co.uk; internet www.bauer.co.uk; Thursday; Editor JOHN DALE; circ. 1,200,397.

Tatler: The Condé Nast Publications Ltd, Vogue House, Hanover Sq., London, W1S 1JU; tel. (20) 7499-9080; fax (20) 7409-0451; internet www.tatler.co.uk; f. 1709; monthly; Editor GEORDIE GREIG; circ. 87,193.

That's Life!: Academic House, 24–28 Oval Rd, London, NW1 7DT; tel. (20) 7241-8000; fax (20) 7241-8008; e-mail sales@tpc-london.com; internet www.bauer.co.uk; f. 1995; Thursday; Editor JO CHECKLEY; circ. 569,631.

Vanity Fair: The Condé Nast Publications Ltd, Vogue House, Hanover Sq., London, W1R 0AD; tel. (20) 7499-9080; fax (20) 7499-4415; internet www.vanityfair.co.uk; monthly; Editor HENRY PORTER; circ. 94,073.

Viz: Dennis Publishing Ltd, 30 Cleveland St, London, W1T 4JD; tel. (20) 7907-6000; fax (20) 7687-7099; e-mail viz@viz.co.uk; internet www.viz.co.uk; f. 1979; ten a year; Publr WILL WATT; Editor SIMON DONALD; circ. 125,154.

Vogue: The Condé Nast Publications Ltd, Vogue House, Hanover Sq., London, W1S 1JU; tel. (20) 7499-9080; fax (20) 7408-0559; internet www.vogue.co.uk; f. 1916; monthly; Editor ALEXANDRA SHULMAN; circ. 210,333.

The Voice: Blue Star House, 234–244 Stockwell Rd, London, SW9 9UG; tel. (20) 7737-7377; fax (20) 7274-8994; e-mail letters@gvmedia.co.uk; internet www.voice-online.co.uk; f. 1982; Monday; black interest; Group Editor DEIDRE FORBES.

Wallpaper*: King's Reach Tower, Stamford St, London, SE1 9LS; tel. (20) 7261-6830; fax (20) 7261-5419; e-mail marketing@wallpaper.com; internet www.wallpaper.com; f. 1996; 10 times a year; Editor JEREMY LANGMEAD; circ. 107,805.

Woman: King's Reach Tower, Stamford St, London, SE1 9LS; tel. (20) 7261-5000; fax (20) 7261-5997; e-mail woman@ipcmedia.com; internet www.ipcmedia.com/magazines/woman; f. 1937; Tuesday; Editor LISA BURROW; circ. 485,463.

Woman and Home: King's Reach Tower, Stamford St, London, SE1 9LS; tel. (20) 7261-5000; fax (20) 7261-7346; e-mail woman&home@ipcmedia.com; internet www.ipcmedia.com/magazines/womanhome; f. 1926; monthly; Editor SUE JAMES; circ. 327,554.

Woman's Own: King's Reach Tower, Stamford St, London, SE1 9LS; tel. (20) 7261-5500; fax (20) 7261-5346; internet www.ipcmedia.com/magazines/womansown; f. 1932; Tuesday; Editor-in-Chief ELSA MCALONAN; circ. 424,292.

Woman's Weekly: King's Reach Tower, Stamford St, London, SE1 9LS; tel. (20) 7261-5000; internet www.ipcmedia.com/magazines/womansweekly; f. 1911; Wednesday; Editor SHEENA HARVEY; circ. 425,568.

Zoo: Emap East Ltd, 8th Floor, Endeavour House, 189 Shaftesbury Ave, London, WC2H 8JG; tel. (20) 7208-3797; e-mail ben.wilson@emap.com; internet www.zooweekly.co.uk; f. 2004; weekly; Editor PAUL MERRILL; circ. 260,317.

Law

Law Quarterly Review: 100 Avenue Rd, London, NW3 3PF; tel. (02) 7393-7000; fax (20) 7393-7010; internet www.sweetandmaxwell.co.uk; f. 1885; quarterly; Editor Prof. FRANCIS M. B. REYNOLDS.

Law Society's Gazette: 113 Chancery Lane, London, WC2A 1PL; tel. (20) 7242-1222; e-mail gazette-editorial@lawsociety.org.uk; internet www.lawgazette.co.uk; f. 1903; weekly; Editor JONATHAN AMES; circ. 106,172 (Jun. 2004).

The Lawyer: 50 Poland St, London, W1V 4AX; tel. (20) 7970-4614; fax (20) 7970-4640; e-mail catrin.griffiths@thelawyer.com; internet www.thelawyer.com; weekly; Editor CATRIN GRIFFITHS; circ. 31,449.

Leisure Interests and Sport

Autocar Magazine: Haymarket Publishing Ltd, 60 Waldegrave Rd, Teddington, Middx, TW11 8LG; tel. (20) 8267-5630; fax (20) 8267-5759; e-mail autocar@haynet.com; internet www.autocar.co.uk; f. 1895; Wednesday; Editor CHAS HALLETT; circ. 66,245.

Autosport: Somerset House, Somerset Rd, Teddington, Middx, TW11 8RU; tel. (20) 8267-5000; fax (20) 8267-5922; e-mail autosport@haynet.com; internet www.autosport.com; f. 1950; Thursday; covers all aspects of motor sport; Editor-in-Chief LAWRENCE FOSTER; circ. 44,541.

Car: Media House, Peterborough Business Park, Peterborough, PE2 6EA; tel. (1733) 468000; fax (1733) 468660; e-mail car@emap.com; internet www.carmagazine.co.uk; f. 1962; monthly; Editor JASON BARLOW; circ. 95,537.

Country Life: 20th Floor, King's Reach Tower, Stamford St, London, SE1 9LS; tel. (20) 7261-7058; fax (20) 7261-5139; e-mail sally_smith@ipcmedia.com; internet www.countrylife.co.uk; f. 1897; Thursday; Editor CLIVE ASLET; circ. 42,693.

The Countryman: POB 5956, Sherbourne, Dorset, DT9 9AA; tel. and fax (1935) 812434; e-mail burford@countrymanmagazine.co.uk; internet www.countrymanmagazine.co.uk; f. 1927; monthly; independent; Editor BILL TAYLOR; circ. 22,870.

FourFourTwo: Somerset House, Somerset Rd, Teddington, TW11 8RT; tel. (20) 8267-5848; fax (20) 8267-5354; e-mail 442@haynet.com; internet www.fourfourtwo.com; f. 1994; monthly; football; Editor HUGH SLEIGHT; circ. 94,030.

BBC Gardeners' World Magazine: BBC Worldwide Ltd, 80 Wood Lane, London, W12 0TT; tel. (20) 8433-3959; fax (20) 8433-3986; e-mail adam.pasco@bbc.co.uk; internet www.gardenersworld.com; f. 1991; monthly; Editor ADAM PASCO; circ. 326,622.

Golf Monthly: King's Reach Tower, Stamford St, London, SE1 9LS; tel. (20) 7261-7237; fax (20) 7261-7240; e-mail golfmonthly@ipcmedia.com; internet www.golf-monthly.co.uk; monthly; Editor JANE CARTER; circ. 78,379.

BBC Good Food: BBC Worldwide Ltd, 80 Wood Lane, London, W12 0TT; tel. (20) 8433-2000; fax (20) 8433-3931; e-mail goodfoodrs@galleon.co.uk; internet www.bbcmagazines.com/goodfood; f. 1989; monthly; Editor GILLIAN CARTER; circ. 317,039.

Hi-Fi News: Leon House, 10th Floor, 233 High St, Croydon, Surrey, CR9 1HZ; tel. (20) 8726-8310; fax (20) 8726-8397; e-mail hi-finews@ipcmedia.com; internet www.hifinews.com; f. 1956; monthly; all aspects of high quality sound reproduction, record reviews; Editor STEVE FAIRCLOUGH; circ. 15,862.

Men's Health: 72 Broadwick St, London, W1F 9EP; tel. (20) 7339-4400; fax (20) 7339-4444; internet www.menshealth.co.uk; f. 1995; monthly; lifestyle, health, general features; Editor MORGAN REES; circ. 228,108.

Practical Photography: Bretton Ct, Bretton, Peterborough, PE3 8DZ; tel. (1733) 264666; fax (1733) 465246; e-mail practical.photography@emap.com; internet www.practicalphotography.co.uk; monthly; Editor ANDREW JAMES; circ. 56,202.

Radio Times: BBC Worldwide Ltd, Woodlands, 80 Wood Lane, London, W12 0TT; tel. 0870 608 4455; fax (20) 8433-3160; e-mail radio.times@bbc.co.uk; internet www.radiotimes.com; f. 1923; weekly; programme guide to television and radio broadcasts; Editor GILL HUDSON; circ. 1,080,199.

Rugby World: Room 2318, King's Reach Tower, Stamford St, London, SE1 9LS; tel. (20) 7261-6830; fax (20) 7261-5419; e-mail paul_morgan@ipcmedia.com; internet www.rugbyworld.com; monthly; Editor PAUL MORGAN; circ. 44,496 (Dec. 2004).

Time Out: Time Out Magazine Ltd, Universal House, 251 Tottenham Court Rd, London, W1T 7AB; tel. (20) 7813-3000; fax (20) 7813-6001; e-mail net@timeout.com; internet www.timeout.com; f. 1968; weekly; listings and reviews of events in London; Time Out Group also publishes city guides and specialized London guides; Editor GORDON THOMSON; circ. 88,851.

TVTimes: 10th Floor, King's Reach Tower, Stamford St, London, SE1 9LS; tel. (20) 7261-7000; fax (20) 7261-7777; e-mail tvtimes_letters@ipcmedia.com; internet www.ipcmedia.com/magazines/tvtimes; f. 1955; features and listings of all television broadcasts; Editor IAN ABBOTT; circ. 418,192.

What Car?: 60 Waldegrave Rd, Teddington, Middx, TW11 8LG; tel. (20) 8267-5688; fax (20) 8267-5750; e-mail whatcar@haynet.com; internet www.whatcar.com; f. 1973; Group Editor STEVE FOWLER; circ. 126,220.

What's On TV: King's Reach Tower, Stamford St, London, SE1 9LS; tel. (20) 7261-7535; fax (20) 7261-7739; e-mail wotv-postbag@ipcmedia.com; internet www.ipcmedia.com/magazines/whatsontv;

THE UNITED KINGDOM
Directory

f. 1991; weekly; television programme guide and features; Publr AMY CULLIGAN; Editor COLIN TOUGH; circ. 1,673,790.

The Wisden Cricketer: 1.4 Shepherds Bldg, Charecroft Way, London, W14 0EE; internet www.cricinfo.com; f. 1921; monthly; Editor JOHN STERN; circ. 35,682.

Zest: 72 Broadwick St, London, W1F 9EP; tel. (20) 7439-5000; fax (20) 7437-6886; e-mail contact@zest.co.uk; internet www.zest.co.uk; health, beauty, fitness and nutrition; Editor ALISON PYLKKANEN; circ. 111,981.

Medicine, Science and Technology

Biochemical Journal: Portland Press Ltd, 3rd Floor, Eagle House, 16 Procter St, London, WC1V 6NX; tel. (20) 7280-4100; fax (20) 7280-4170; e-mail editorial@portlandpress.com; internet www.biochemj.org; f. 1906; 2 a month; publ. by Portland Press on behalf of the Biochemical Society; Chair. Editorial Board GEORGE BANTING; Publr P. J. STARLEY.

British Journal of Psychiatry: 17 Belgrave Sq., London, SW1X 8PG; tel. (20) 7235-2351; fax (20) 7259-6507; e-mail publications@rcpsych.ac.uk; internet bjp.rcpsych.org; monthly; original articles, reviews and correspondence; publ. by the Royal College of Psychiatrists; Editor PETER TYRER; circ. 14,100.

British Journal of Psychology: St Andrew's House, 48 Princess Rd East, Leicester, LE1 7DR; tel. (116) 254-9568; fax (116) 247-0787; e-mail journals@bps.org.uk; internet www.bps.org.uk; f. 1904; quarterly; publ. by the British Psychological Society; Editor Prof. GEOFFREY UNDERWOOD.

British Journal of Sociology: 9600 Garsington Rd, Oxford, OX4 2DQ; tel. (1865) 776868; fax (1865) 714591; internet www.blackwellpublishing.com/bjos; f. 1950; quarterly; Editor BRIDGET HUTTER.

British Medical Journal: British Medical Asscn House, Tavistock Sq., London, WC1H 9JR; tel. (20) 7387-4499; fax (20) 7383-6418; e-mail bmj@bmj.com; internet www.bmj.com; f. 1840; Saturday; 10 overseas editions; Editor Dr FIONA GODLEE; circ. 122,982.

Computer Weekly: Reed Business Information, Quadrant House, The Quadrant, Sutton, Surrey, SM2 5AS; tel. (20) 8652-8642; fax (20) 8652-8979; e-mail cwnews@rbi.co.uk; internet www.computerweekly.com; f. 1966; Thursday; Editor HOOMAN BASSIRIAN.

Computing: VNU Business Publications BV, VNU House, 32–34 Broadwick St, London, W1A 2HG; tel. (20) 7316-9000; fax (20) 7316-9160; e-mail computing@vnu.co.uk; internet www.computing.co.uk; f. 1973; Thursday; Editor TOBY WOLPE; circ. 115,000.

The Ecologist: Unit 18, Chelsea Wharf, 15 Lots Rd, London, SW10 0QJ; tel. (20) 7351-3578; fax (20) 7351-3617; e-mail editorial@theecologist.org; internet www.theecologist.org; f. 1970; 10 per year; all aspects of ecology, the environment, etc.; Editor ZAC GOLDSMITH.

Flight International: Reed Business Information, Quadrant House, The Quadrant, Sutton, Surrey, SM2 5AS; tel. (20) 8652-3842; fax (20) 8652-3840; e-mail flight.international@rbi.co.uk; internet www.flightinternational.com; f. 1909; Tuesday; Editor MURDO MORRISON.

The Geographical Magazine: Winchester House, 259–269 Old Marylebone Rd, London, NW10 5RA; tel. (20) 7170-4360; fax (20) 7170-4361; e-mail magazine@geographical.co.uk; internet www.geographical.co.uk; f. 1935; monthly; Dep. Editor GEORDIE TORR; circ. 21,684.

Lancet: 32 Jamestown Rd, London, NW1 7BY; tel. (20) 7424-4910; fax (20) 7424-4911; e-mail editorial@lancet.com; internet www.lancet.com; f. 1823; Saturday; medical; Editor Dr RICHARD HORTON.

Nature: Macmillan Magazines Ltd, 4 Crinan St, London, N1 9XW; tel. (20) 7833-4000; fax (20) 7843-4596; e-mail nature@nature.com; internet www.nature.com/nature; f. 1869; Thursday; scientific; Editor-in-Chief Dr PHILIP CAMPBELL.

New Scientist: Lacon House, 84 Theobald's Rd, London, WC1X 8NS; tel. (20) 7611-1200; fax (20) 7611-1250; e-mail news@newscientist.com; internet www.newscientist.com; f. 1956; Thursday; science and technology; Editor JEREMY WEBB; circ. 161,506 (worldwide).

Nursing Times: EMAP Healthcare Ltd, Greater London House, Hampstead Rd, London, NW1 7EJ; tel. (20) 7874-0500; fax (20) 7874-0505; e-mail nt@emap.com; internet www.nursingtimes.net; f. 1905; Tuesday; professional nursing journal; Editor RACHEL DOWNEY; circ. 72,166.

The Practitioner: Ludgate House, 245 Blackfriars Rd, London, SE1 9UY; tel. (20) 7921-8113; fax (20) 7921-8135; e-mail gatkin@cmpinformation.com; f. 1868; 12 per year; medical journal for General Practitioners; Editor GAVIN ATKIN; circ. 35,840.

Religion and Philosophy

Catholic Herald: Herald House, Lambs Passage, Bunhill Row, London, EC1Y 8TQ; tel. (20) 7588-3101; fax (20) 7256-9728; e-mail editorial@catholicherald.co.uk; internet www.catholicherald.co.uk; f. 1888; Catholic weekly newspaper; Friday; Editor LUKE COPPEN.

Church Times: 33 Upper St, London, N1 0PN; tel. (20) 7359-4570; fax (20) 7226-3073; e-mail editor@churchtimes.co.uk; internet www.churchtimes.co.uk; f. 1863; Church of England and world-wide Anglican news; Friday; Editor PAUL HANDLEY.

Jewish Chronicle: Jewish Chronicle Newspaper Ltd, 25 Furnival St, London, EC4A 1JT; tel. (20) 7415-1500; fax (20) 7405-9040; e-mail jconline@thejc.com; internet www.thejc.com; f. 1841; Friday; Editor DAVID ROWAN; circ. 35,603.

Methodist Recorder: 122 Golden Lane, London, EC1Y 0TL; tel. (20) 7251-8414; fax (20) 7608-3490; e-mail editorial@methodistrecorder.co.uk; internet www.methodistrecorder.co.uk; f. 1861; Thursday; Man. Editor MOIRA SLEIGHT.

New Blackfriars: Blackfriars, Oxford, OX1 3LY; tel. (1865) 776868; fax (1865) 714591; e-mail nb.editor@english.op.org; internet www.blackwellpublishing.com; f. 1920; monthly; religious and cultural; Editor Rev. FERGUS KERR.

Philosophy: Royal Institute of Philosophy, 14 Gordon Sq., London, WC1H 0AR; tel. (20) 7387-4130; e-mail j.garvey@royalinstitutephilosophy.org; internet www.royalinstitutephilosophy.org; f. 1925; quarterly; Editor ANTHONY O'HEAR.

The Universe: 1st Floor, St James's Bldgs, Oxford St, Manchester, M1 6FP; tel. (161) 236-8856; fax (161) 236-8530; e-mail newsdesk@the-universe.net; internet www.the-universe.net; f. 1860; Sunday; illustrated Catholic newspaper and review; publ. by Gabriel Communications Ltd; Editor JOSEPH KELLY.

Woman Alive: Christian Publishing and Outreach, Garcia Estate, Canterbury Rd, Worthing, West Sussex, BN13 1BW; tel. (1903) 264556; fax (1903) 821081; e-mail womanalive@cpo.org.uk; internet www.womanalive.co.uk; f. 1982; monthly; Editor JACKIE STEAD.

PRESS ORGANIZATION

Press Complaints Commission: 1 Salisbury Sq., London, EC4Y 8JB; tel. (20) 7353-1248; fax (20) 7353-8355; e-mail complaints@pcc.org.uk; internet www.pcc.org.uk; f. 1991 to replace the Press Council, following the report of the Committee on Privacy and Related Matters; an independent organization established by the newspaper and magazine industry through the Press Standards Board of Finance to deal with complaints from the public about the contents and conduct of newspapers and magazines; the Commission has an independent chairman and 17 members, drawn from the lay public (who are in the majority) and the press. It upholds a 16-point Code of Practice, agreed by a committee of editors representing the newspaper and magazine industry. It aims to ensure that the British press maintains the highest professional standards, having regard to generally established press freedoms; Chair. Sir CHRISTOPHER MEYER; Dir TIM TOULMIN.

NEWS AGENCIES

Associated Press Ltd: Associated Press House, 12 Norwich St, London, EC4A 1BP; tel. (20) 7353-1515; fax (20) 7353-8118; f. 1931; British subsidiary of Associated Press of USA; delivers a world-wide foreign news and photographic service to Commonwealth and foreign papers; Chair. LOUIS D. BOCCARDI; Bureau Chief BARRY RENFREW.

Press Association Ltd: 292 Vauxhall Bridge Rd, London, SW1V 1AE; tel. (870) 120-3200; fax (870) 120-3201; e-mail info@pa.press.net; internet www.pa.press.net; f. 1868; national news agency of the United Kingdom and the Republic of Ireland; Chair. Sir HARRY ROCHE; CEO and Editor-in-Chief PAUL POTTS; Editor JONATHAN GRUN.

Reuters Group PLC: 30 The South Colonnade, Canary Wharf, London, E14 5EZ; tel. (20) 7250-1122; fax (20) 7324-5400; e-mail editor@reuters.com; internet www.reuters.co.uk; f. 1851; world-wide news and information service to media and business clients in 57,900 organizations and media clients in 157 countries; Chair. NIALL FITZGERALD; CEO TOM GLOCER.

United Press International (UPI): Empire House, Empire Way, Middlesex, HA9 0EW; tel. (20) 8970-2604; fax (20) 8970-2613; internet www.upi.com; supplies world-wide news and news-picture coverage in English and Arabic to newspapers, radio and television stations throughout the world; Editor-in-Chief MICHAEL MARSHALL.

Principal Foreign Bureaux

Agence France-Presse (AFP): 78 Fleet St, London, EC4Y 1NB; tel. (20) 7353-7461; fax (20) 7353-8359; e-mail london.bureau@afp.com; internet www.afp.com; Bureau Chief PIERRE LESOURD.

Agencia EFE (Spain): 6th Floor, 299 Oxford St, London, W1C 2DZ; tel. (20) 7493-7313; fax (20) 7493-7314; e-mail efelondon@btclick.com; internet www.efe.es; Bureau Chief JOAQUIN RABAGO.

THE UNITED KINGDOM

Agenzia Nazionale Stampa Associata (ANSA) (Italy): Essex House, 12–13 Essex St, London, WC2R 3AA; tel. (20) 7240-5514; fax (20) 7240-5518; internet www.ansa.it; Bureau Chief FRANCESCO BIANCHINI.

Australian Associated Press Ltd (AAP): 12 Norwich St, London, EC4A 1QJ; tel. (20) 7353-0153; fax (20) 7583-3563; e-mail news .london@aap.com.au; internet aap.com.au; Chief Correspondent PAUL MULVEY.

Canadian Press: Associated Press House, 12 Norwich St, London, EC4A 1QE; tel. (20) 7353-6355; fax (20) 7583-4238; Bureau Chief KEVIN WARD.

Česká tisková kancelář (ČTK) (Czech Republic): Glenhurst Ave, London, NW5 1PS; tel. (20) 7482-4995; e-mail czechnews@btinternet .com; Chief Correspondent JIŘÍ MAJSTR.

Cyprus News Agency: 23 Chase Way, London, N14 5EB; tel. and fax (20) 8368-1946; internet www.cyna.org.cy/corr.htm; Chief Correspondent KYRIACOS TSIOUPRAS.

Deutsche Presse-Agentur (dpa) (Germany): 30 Old Queen St, London, SW1H 9HP; tel. (20) 7233-2888; fax (20) 7233-3534; e-mail london@dpa.com; Bureau Chief THOMAS BURMEISTER.

Dow Jones Newswires (USA): 12 Norwich St, London, EC4A 1QN; tel. (20) 7842-9560; fax (20) 7842-9561; internet www.djnewswires .com; Senior Editor GABRIELLA STERN.

Informatsionnoye Telegrafnoye Agentstvo Rossii—Telegrafnoye Agentstvo Suverennykh Stran (ITAR—TASS) (Russia): Suite 12–20, Second Floor, Morley House, 314–320 Regent St, London, W1R 5AB; tel. (20) 7580-5543; fax (20) 7580-5547; internet www.itar-tass.com; Bureau Chief IGOR E. BORISENKO.

Jiji Press (Japan): International Press Centre, 76 Shoe Lane, London, EC4A 3JB; tel. (20) 7936-2847; fax (20) 7583-8353; e-mail jijildn2@ma.kew.net; internet www.jiji.com; Bureau Chief J. ANUMA.

Kyodo News (Japan): 5th Floor, 20 Orange St, London, WC2H 7EF; tel. (20) 7766-4400; fax (20) 7766-4411; e-mail london@kyodonews.jp; internet www.kyodo.co.jp; f. 1945; Bureau Chief HIDEO MIYAWAKI.

Maghreb Arabe Presse (Moroccan News Agency): 35 Westminster Bridge Rd, London, SE1 7JB; tel. (20) 7401-8146; fax (20) 7401-8148; e-mail maplon@aol.com; internet www.map.ma; Bureau Chief ALI BAHAIJOUB.

Press Trust of India (PTI): Room 310, 3rd Floor, Linen Hall, 162–168 Regent St, London, W1B 5TD; tel. (20) 7039-0112; fax (20) 7039-0114; e-mail ptilondon@aol.com; internet www.ptinews.com; Chief of Bureau H. S. RAO.

RIA—Novosti (Russian Information Agency—Novosti); Russia: 3 Rosary Gardens, London, SW7 4NW; tel. (20) 7370-3002; fax (20) 7244-7875; e-mail ria@novosti.co.uk; internet www.rian.ru; Bureau Chief SVETLANA BABAYEVA; Correspondent ALEXANDER SMOTROV.

Saudi Press Agency (SPA): 18 Seymour St, London W1H 7JR; tel. (20) 7486-8324; fax (20) 7935-7465.

Xinhua (New China) News Agency (People's Republic of China): 8 Swiss Terrace, Belsize Rd, Swiss Cottage, London, NW6 4RR; tel. (20) 7586-8271; fax (20) 7722-8512; Chief Correspondent LI ZHIGAO.

INSTITUTIONS

Chartered Institute of Journalists: 2 Dock Offices, Surrey Quays Rd, London, SE16 2XU; tel. (20) 7252-1187; fax (20) 7232-2302; e-mail memberservices@cioj.co.uk; internet www.cioj.co.uk; f. 1884; Pres. SANGITA SHAH; Gen. Sec. DOMINIC COOPER.

Newspaper Press Fund: Dickens House, 35 Wathen Rd, Dorking, Surrey, RH4 1JY; tel. (1306) 887511; fax (1306) 888212; f. 1864; charity for journalists and their dependants; Pres. Lord ROTHERMERE; Sec. D. J. ILOTT; 5,500 mems.

Newspaper Publishers' Association: 34 Southwark Bridge Rd, London, SE1 9EU; tel. (20) 7207-2200; fax (20) 7928-2067; f. 1906; comprises 8 national newspaper groups and 22 titles; Chair. ELLIS WATSON; Dir STEPHEN ORAM.

Newspaper Society: Bloomsbury House, 74–77 Great Russell St, London, WC1B 3DA; tel. (20) 7636-7014; fax (20) 7631-5119; e-mail ns@newspapersoc.org.uk; internet www.newspapersoc.org.uk; f. 1836; represents the regional and local press; Pres. Sir NICHOLAS HEWITT; Dir DAVID NEWELL.

Periodical Publishers' Association Ltd: Queen's House, 28 Kingsway, London, WC2B 6JR; tel. (20) 7404-4166; fax (20) 7404-4167; e-mail info1@ppa.co.uk; internet www.ppa.co.uk; f. 1913; trade association for the British magazine industry; Chair. NICHOLAS COLERIDGE; Chief Exec. IAN LOCKS; more than 350 mems.

> **Association of Publishing Agencies:** 55/56 Lincoln's Inn Fields, London, WC2A 3LJ; tel. (20) 7404-4166; fax (20) 7404-4167; e-mail info@apa.co.uk; internet www.apa.co.uk; f. 1993; trade association for the customer publishing industry; Chair. JASON FROST.

Directory

UK Association of Online Publishers: Queen's House, 28 Kingsway, London, WC2B 6JR; tel. (20) 7400-7562; fax (20) 7404-4167; e-mail alex.white@ukaop.org.uk; internet www .ukaop.org.uk; f. 2002; represents the interests of online content providers; Dir ALEXANDRA WHITE.

Scottish Daily Newspaper Society: 48 Palmerston Pl., Edinburgh, EH12 5DE; tel. (131) 220-4353; fax (131) 220-4344; e-mail info@sdns.org.uk; f. 1915; Dir JAMES B. RAEBURN.

Scottish Newspaper Publishers' Association: 48 Palmerston Pl., Edinburgh, EH12 5DE; tel. (131) 220-4353; fax (131) 220-4344; e-mail info@snpa.org.uk; internet www.snpa.org.uk; Dir JAMES B. RAEBURN.

See also under Employers' Organizations and Trade Unions.

Principal Publishers

Publishing firms in the United Kingdom are mainly located in London and many are members of large publishing groups, notably Reed Elsevier, Random House, the Pearson Group and the Thomson Corporation. Fiction remains the largest category. The United Kingdom publishes more new titles every year than any other European country. In 2002 125,390 new titles were issued.

Asean Academic Press Ltd: POB 13945, London, E5 0XY; fax (20) 8533-5856; e-mail aapub@attglobal.net; internet www .aseanacademicpress.com; educational, technical, professional and scientific books on Asia.

Ashgate Publishing Ltd: Gower House, Croft Rd, Aldershot, Hants, GU11 3HR; tel. (1252) 331551; fax (1252) 344405; e-mail info@ashgatepublishing.com; internet www.ashgate.com; f. 1967; social sciences and humanities, art, business and public sector management books; imprints: Ashgate, Gower, Lund Humphries, Variorum; Chair. N. FARROW.

Batsford: The Chrysalis Bldg, Bramley Rd, London, W10 6SP; tel. (20) 7314-1400; fax (20) 7314-1594; e-mail info@chrysalisbooks.co .uk; internet www.chrysalisbooks.co.uk; f. 1843; part of Chrysalis Books PLC; crafts, design, architecture, art techniques, fashion, film, chess, bridge, gardening, English heritage, historic Scotland; Chief Exec. MARCUS LEAVER.

BBC Worldwide Ltd: Woodlands, 80 Wood Lane, London, W12 0TT; tel. (20) 8433-2000; fax (20) 8749-0538; e-mail bbcworldwide@ bbc.co.uk; internet www.bbcworldwide.com; Chief Exec. JOHN SMITH.

Berlitz Publishing Co Ltd: 58 Borough High St, London, SE1 1XF; tel. (20) 7403-0284; fax (20) 7403-0290; e-mail publishing@berlitz.co .uk; internet www.berlitzpublishing.com; f. 1970; travel, languages, reference, leisure, children's books; acquired by Apa Publications in 2002; Group Man. Dir JEREMY WESTWOOD.

A. & C. Black Publishers Ltd: 37 Soho Sq., London, W1D 3QZ; tel. (20) 7758-0200; fax (20) 7758-0222; e-mail enquiries@acblack.com; internet www.acblack.com; f. 1807; inc. Adlard Coles Nautical, Christopher Helm, Herbert Press, Pica Press, T & AD Poyser, Thomas Reed; acquired by Bloomsbury Publishing PLC in 2001; children's and educational books, music, arts and crafts, drama, reference, sport, theatre, travel, sailing, ornithology; Chair. NIGEL NEWTON; Editorial Dir JANET MURPHY.

Blackwell Publishing: 9600 Garsington Rd, Oxford, OX4 2DQ; tel. (1865) 776868; fax (1865) 714591; e-mail customerservices@oxon .blackwellpublishing.com; internet www.blackwellpublishing.com; f. 1921; academic, professional, business, medical and science books and journals; Chair. NIGEL BLACKWELL; CEO RENÉ OLIVIERI.

Bloomsbury Publishing PLC: 36 Soho Sq., London, W1D 3DY; tel. (20) 7494-2111; fax (20) 7434-0151; e-mail csm@bloomsbury.com; internet www.bloomsbury.com; f. 1986; fiction, non-fiction and children's; Chair. and CEO NIGEL NEWTON; Editor-in-Chief ALEXANDRA PRINGLE.

Bowker (UK) Ltd: 1st Floor, Medway House, Cantalupe Rd, East Grinstead, West Sussex, RH19 3BJ; tel. (1342) 310450; fax (1342) 310486; e-mail sales@bowker.co.uk; internet www.bowker.co.uk; owned by the Cambridge Information Group; business information, general reference and bibliographies; Man. Dir DOUG MCMILLAN.

Marion Boyars Publishers Ltd: 24 Lacy Rd, London, SW15 1NL; tel. (20) 8788-9522; fax (20) 8789-8122; e-mail marion.boyars@talk21 .com; internet www.marionboyars.co.uk; fiction, plays, cinema, music, translations, literary criticism, sociology; Man. Dir CATHERYN KILGARRIFF.

Calder Publications Ltd: 51 The Cut, London, SE1 8LF; tel. (20) 7633-0599; fax (20) 7928-5930; e-mail info@calderpubublications .com; internet www.calderpublications.com; f. 1950; fiction, plays, music, opera, European classics, translations, general books, social science, politics; Calderbooks, Journal of Beckett Studies, English National Opera guides; Man. Dir JOHN CALDER.

Cambridge University Press: The Edinburgh Bldg, Shaftesbury Rd, Cambridge, CB2 2RU; tel. (1223) 325892; fax (1223) 325891; e-mail assist@cambridge.org; internet www.cambridge.org; f. 1534; academic and scientific monographs and textbooks, educational, English language teaching materials, microsoftware, bibles, prayer books and academic journals; Chief Exec. STEPHEN R. R. BOURNE.

Canongate: 14 High St, Edinburgh, EH1 1TE; tel. (131) 557-5111; fax (131) 557-5211; e-mail info@canongate.co.uk; internet www.canongate.net; Chair. JAMIE BYNG.

Jonathan Cape Ltd: Random House, 20 Vauxhall Bridge Rd, London, SW1V 2SA; tel. (20) 7840-8400; fax (20) 7233-6117; e-mail enquiries@randomhouse.co.uk; internet www.randomhouse.co.uk; f. 1921; imprint of The Random House Group Ltd; general, biography, travel, belles-lettres, fiction, history, poetry; subsidiary imprint: The Bodley Head (biography, current affairs, humour); Publishing Dir DAN FRANKLIN.

Carlton Books: 20 Mortimer St, London W1T 3JW; tel. (20) 7612-0400; fax (20) 7612-0401; e-mail sales@carltonbooks.co.uk; internet www.carltonbooks.co.uk; f. 1992; Chief Exec. JONATHAN GOODMAN.

Century: Random House, 20 Vauxhall Bridge Rd, London, SW1V 2SA; tel. (20) 7840-8400; fax (20) 7233-6127; e-mail enquiries@randomhouse.co.uk; internet www.randomhouse.co.uk; f. 1987; imprint of Random House Group Ltd; general, biography, travel, current affairs, fiction, memoirs, music, philosophy; Man. Dir RICHARD CABLE.

Chatto and Windus, Ltd: 20 Vauxhall Bridge Rd, London, SW1V 2SA; tel. (20) 7840-8400; fax (20) 7233-6117; internet www.randomhouse.co.uk; imprint of The Random House Group Ltd (see below); general, academic, biography, memoirs, politics, history, literary criticism, current affairs, cultural studies and fiction; imprint: Hogarth Press; Dir ALISON SAMUEL.

Chrysalis Books Group: The Chrysalis Building, Bramley Rd, London, W10 6SP; tel. (20) 7314-1400; fax (20) 7314-1594; e-mail sales@chrysalisbooks.co.uk; internet www.chrysalisbooks.co.uk; f. 1989; imprints: Batsford, Brassey's, Collins & Brown, Conway, National Trust Books, Paper Tiger, Pavilion, Putnam Aeronautical Books, Robson, Sterling; Chair. CHRIS WRIGHT; Group Chief Exec. RICHARD HUNTINGFORD.

Church House Publishing: Church House, Great Smith St, London, SW1P 3NZ; tel. (20) 7898-1451; fax (20) 7898-1449; e-mail publishing@c-of-e.org.uk; internet www.chpublishing.co.uk; Publ. Man. ALAN MITCHELL.

James Clarke and Co Ltd: POB 60, Cambridge, CB1 2NT; tel. (1223) 350865; fax (1223) 366951; e-mail publishing@jamesclarke.co.uk; internet www.jamesclarke.co.uk; f. 1859; religious, reference and academic; imprints: Acorn Editions, Lutterworth Press, Patrick Hardy Books; Man. Dir ADRIAN BRINK.

CMP Information Directories Division: Sovereign House, Sovereign Way, Tonbridge, Kent, TN9 1RW; tel. (1732) 377591; fax (1732) 367301; internet www.cmpdata.co.uk; reference and buyers' guides; Commercial Dir DUNCAN CLARK.

Collins Bartholomew: Westerhill Rd, Bishopbriggs, Glasgow, G64 2QT; tel. (141) 306-3752; fax (141) 306-3130; e-mail collinsbartholomew@harpercollins.co.uk; internet www.bartholomewmaps.com; f. 1826; cartographic division of HarperCollins Publishers; maps, atlases, guide books, bespoke mapping services and data; Man. Dir THOMAS WEBSTER; Cartographic Dir SHEENA BARCLAY.

Conran Octopus: 2–4 Heron Quays, London, E14 4JP; tel. (20) 7531-8400; fax (20) 7531-8627; e-mail info@conran-octopus.co.uk; internet www.conran-octopus.co.uk; illustrated reference books; imprint of Octopus Publishing Group; Man. Dir JANE ASPDEN.

Constable and Robinson Ltd: 3 The Lanchesters, 162 Fulham Palace Rd, London, W6 9ER; tel. (20) 8741-3663; fax (20) 8748-7562; e-mail enquiries@constablerobinson.com; internet www.constablerobinson.com; biography and autobiography, general and military history, current affairs, psychology and self-help, health, popular science, and crime fiction; Man. Dir NICHOLAS ROBINSON.

Continuum Publishing Group: The Tower Bldgs, 11 York Rd, London, SE1 7NX; tel. (20) 7922-0880; fax (20) 7922-0881; e-mail p.law@continuumbooks.com; internet www.continuumbooks.com; f. 1994; popular culture, religion, humanities, social sciences, philosophy and education; imprints: T&T Clark, Sheffield University Press, Thoemmes and The Handsel Press; Publ. Dir ROBIN BAIRD-SMITH.

James Currey Publishers: 73 Botley Rd, Oxford, OX2 0BS; tel. (1865) 246454; fax (1865) 246454; e-mail editorial@jamescurrey.co.uk; internet www.jamescurrey.co.uk; African and world anthropology; Chair. JAMES CURREY; Man. Dir DOUGLAS H. JOHNSON.

Darton, Longman and Todd Ltd: 1 Spencer Court, 140–142 Wandsworth High St, London, SW18 4JJ; tel. (20) 8875-0155; fax (20) 8875-0133; e-mail tradesales@darton-longman-todd.co.uk; internet www.darton-longman-todd.co.uk; f. 1959; theology, spirituality, religious biography and history, Bibles; Sales and Marketing Dir A. MORDUE.

David & Charles Ltd: Brunel House, Forde Close, Newton Abbot, Devon, TQ12 4PU; tel. (870) 990-8222; fax (870) 442-2034; e-mail postmaster@davidandcharles.co.uk; internet www.davidandcharles.co.uk; f. 1960; general, trade and reference; Man. Dir BUDGE WALLIS (acting).

André Deutsch Ltd: 20 Mortimer St, London, W1T 3JW; tel. (20) 7612-0400; fax (20) 7612-0401; e-mail enquiries@carltonbooks.co.uk; f. 1950; biography, memoirs, humour, art, politics, history, travel, sport; imprint of Carlton Books.

Dorling Kindersley PLC: 80 Strand, London, WC2R ORL; tel. (20) 7010-3000; fax (20) 7010-6060; internet uk.dk.com; f. 1974; acquired by Pearson PLC in 2000; illustrated reference books; Chief Exec. GARY JUNE; Man. Dir DEBORAH WRIGHT.

Gerald Duckworth and Co Ltd: 90–93 Cowcross St, London, EC1M 6BF; tel. (20) 7490-7300; fax (20) 7490-0080; e-mail info@duckworth-publishers.co.uk; internet www.ducknet.co.uk; f. 1898; fiction, academic; Propr PETER MAYER; COO GILLIAN HALKINS.

Edinburgh University Press: 22 George Sq., Edinburgh, EH8 9LF; tel. (131) 650-4218; fax (131) 662-0053; e-mail timothy.wright@eup.ed.ac.uk; internet www.eup.ed.ac.uk; learned books and journals; Chair. TIM RIX.

Edward Elgar Publishing Ltd: Glensanda House, Montpellier Parade, Cheltenham, GL50 1UA; tel. (1242) 226934; fax (1242) 262111; e-mail info@e-elgar.co.uk; internet www.e-elgar.com; f. 1986; economics, law, business and management; Man. Dir E. ELGAR.

Elsevier Ltd: The Boulevard, Langford Lane, Kidlington, Oxford, OX5 1GB; tel. (1865) 843000; fax (1865) 843010; e-mail directenquiries@elsevier.com; internet www.elsevier.com; f. 1958; academic and professional reference books; imprints: Academic Press, Architectural Press, Bailliere Tindall, Butterworth-Heinemann, Churchill Livingstone, Digital Press, Elsevier, Elsevier Advanced Technology, Focal Press, Gulf Professional, JAI, Made Simple Books, Morgan Kaufmann, Mosby, Newnes, North-Holland, Pergamon, Saunders; Man. Dir ANNA MOON.

Elsevier Ltd (Butterworth Heinemann): Linacre House, Jordan Hill, Oxford, OX2 8DP; tel. (1865) 314502; fax (1865) 314568; internet www.bh.com; books and electronic products across business, technical for students and professionals; Man. Dir PHILIP SHAW.

Elsevier Ltd (Health Sciences): 32 Jamestown Rd, London, NW1 7BY; tel. (20) 7424-4200; fax (20) 7483-2293; internet www.elsevierhealth.com; smedical books and journals; imprints: Bailliere Tindall, Churchill Livingstone, Elsevier, Mosby, Pergamon, Saunders; Man. Dir MARY GING.

Encyclopaedia Britannica UK Ltd: 2nd Floor, Unity Wharf, 13 Mill St, London, SE1 2BH; tel. (20) 7500-7800; fax (20) 7500-7878; e-mail enquiries@britannica.co.uk; internet www.britannica.co.uk; f. 1768; publs Encyclopaedia Britannica, Britannica Book of the Year, Great Books of the Western World, Britannica Learning Library, Britannica Almanac; Man. Dir LEAH MANSOOR.

Euromonitor plc: 60–61 Britton St, London, EC1M 5UX; tel. (20) 7251-8024; fax (20) 7608-3149; e-mail info@euromonitor.com; internet www.euromonitor.com; f. 1972; business and commercial reference; Chair. R. N. SENIOR; Man. Dir T. J. FENWICK.

Evans Brothers Ltd: 2A Portman Mansions, Chiltern St, London, W1U 6NR; tel. (20) 7487-0920; fax (20) 7487-0921; e-mail sales@evansbrothers.co.uk; internet www.evansbooks.co.uk; f. 1906; educational, children's, general and overseas books; Man. Dir S. T. PAWLEY; Publr SU SWALLOW.

Everyman's Library: Northburgh House, 10 Northburgh St, London, EC1V 0AT; tel. (20) 7566-6350; fax (20) 7490-3708; e-mail books@everyman.uk.com; internet www.everyman.uk.com; Publr DAVID CAMPBELL.

Faber and Faber Ltd: 3 Queen Sq., London, WC1N 3AU; tel. (20) 7465-0045; fax (20) 7465-0034; internet www.faber.co.uk; f. 1929; biography, autobiography, children's, film, drama, popular science, economics, fiction, history, music, poetry; Man. Dir STEPHEN PAGE.

The Folio Society Ltd: 44 Eagle St, London, WC1R 4FS; tel. (20) 7400-4200; fax (20) 7400-4242; internet www.foliosoc.co.uk; f. 1947; fine illustrated editions of fiction, history, biographies, drama and poetry; Editorial Dir SUE BRADBURY.

Footprint Handbooks Ltd: 6 Riverside Court, Lower Bristol Rd, Bath, BA2 3DZ; tel. (1225) 469141; fax (1225) 469461; e-mail discover@footprintbooks.com; internet www.footprintbooks.com; Dirs JAMES DAWSON, PATRICK DAWSON.

W. Foulsham & Co Ltd: The Publishing House, Bennetts Close, Slough, Berks, SL1 5AP; tel. (1753) 526769; fax (1753) 535003; e-mail reception@foulsham.com; internet www.foulsham.com; f. 1819; finance, reference; Man. Dir BARRY BELASCO.

Fourth Estate: 77–85 Fulham Palace Rd, London, W6 8JB; tel. (20) 8741-4414; fax (20) 8307-4466; e-mail general@4thestate.co.uk; internet www.4thestate.co.uk; f. 1984; literature, humour, general reference, current affairs; literary and commercial fiction; cookery; imprint of HarperCollins Publishers; Pub. Dir NICHOLAS PEARSON.

Samuel French Ltd: 52 Fitzroy St, London, W1T 5JR; tel. (20) 7387-9373; fax (20) 7387-2161; e-mail theatre@samuelfrench-london.co.uk; internet www.samuelfrench-london.co.uk; f. 1830; drama; Chair. CHARLES VAN NOSTRAND; Man. Dir VIVIEN GOODWIN.

Ginn and Co: Halley Court, Jordan Hill, Oxford, OX2 8EJ; tel. (1865) 888000; fax (1865) 134222; e-mail enquiries@ginn.co.uk; internet www.ginn.co.uk; f. 1924; imprint of Harcourt Education UK Ltd; educational; Chair. CHRIS JONES; Man. Dir PAUL SHUTER.

Victor Gollancz Ltd: Orion House, 5 Upper St Martin's Lane, London, WC2H 9EA; tel. (20) 7420-3444; fax (20) 7240-4823; internet www.orionbooks.co.uk; f. 1928; imprint of Orion Publishing Group Ltd; science fiction and fantasy; Dirs SIMON SPANTON, JO FLETCHER.

Granta Books: 2/3 Hanover Yard, Noel Rd, London, N1 8BE; tel. (20) 7704-9776; fax (20) 7704-0474; e-mail glynch@granta.com; internet www.granta.com; fiction, political non-fiction; Editorial Dir GEORGE MILLER.

Gresham Books Ltd: 46 Victoria Rd, Summertown, Oxford OX2 7QD; tel. (1865) 513582; fax (1865) 512718; e-mail info@gresham-books.co.uk; internet www.gresham-books.co.uk; f. 1978; hymn books, school histories, music folders; Chief Exec. P. A. LEWIS.

Guinness World Records Ltd: 338 Euston Rd, London, NW1 3BD; tel. (20) 7891-4567; fax (20) 7891-4501; e-mail info@guinnessrecords.com; internet www.guinnessworldrecords.com; f. 1954; acquired by Gullane Entertainment in 2001; music and general interest; CEO STEPHEN NELSON; Man. Dir CHRISTOPHER IRWIN.

Robert Hale Ltd: Clerkenwell House, 45–47 Clerkenwell Green, London, EC1R 0HT; tel. (20) 7251-2661; fax (20) 7490-4958; e-mail enquire@halebooks.com; internet www.halebooks.com; f. 1936; memoirs, biography, travel, sport, fiction, belles-lettres, general non-fiction; Man. Dir JOHN HALE.

Hamlyn Octopus: 2–4 Heron Quays, London, E14 4JP; tel. (20) 7531-8400; fax (20) 7531-8650; e-mail info-ho@hamlyn.co.uk; internet www.hamlyn.co.uk; imprint of Octopus Publishing Group; cookery, DIY, gardening, sports, health, animals; Man. Dir ALISON GOFF.

Harcourt Education International: Halley Court, Jordan Hill, Oxford, OX2 8EJ; tel. (1865) 311366; fax (1865) 314641; e-mail international@harcourteducation.co.uk; internet www.harcourteducation.co.uk; part of Reed Elsevier UK Ltd; imprints: Ginn, Heinemann, Rigby; Chief Exec. CHRIS JONES.

Harlequin Mills and Boon Ltd: Eton House, 18–24 Paradise Rd, Richmond, Surrey, TW9 1SR; tel. (20) 8288-2800; fax (20) 8288-2899; internet www.millsandboon.co.uk; f. 1908; romantic fiction; Man. Dir GUY HALLOWES.

HarperCollins Publishers Ltd: 77–85 Fulham Palace Rd, London, W6 8JB; tel. (20) 8307-4000; fax (20) 8307-4440; e-mail contact@harpercollins.co.uk; internet www.harpercollins.co.uk; f. 1819; bought by News International 1989; fiction and non-fiction of all classes, including biographies, history, travel, nature, sport, art, children's, classics, atlases, reference, religion; imprints: Armada, Bartholomew, Collins, Collins Bibles, Collins Cartographic, Collins Classics, Collins Crime, Collins English Dictionaries, Collins Liturgical, Flamingo, Fontana, HarperCollins, HarperCollins Audio, HarperCollins Paperbacks, HarperCollins Science Fiction and Fantasy, Jets, Lions, Marshall Pickering, Nicholson, Thorsons, Times Books, Tolkien, Tracks, Young Lions; CEO VICTORIA BARNSLEY.

The Harvill Press: The Random House Group Ltd, 20 Vauxhall Bridge Rd, London, SW1V 2SA; tel. (20) 7840-8400; fax (20) 7840-8664; e-mail enquiries@randomhouse.co.uk/harvill; internet www.randomhouse.co.uk/harvill; fiction, non-fiction, illustrated books; Publr CHRISTOPHER MACLEHOSE.

Haynes Publishing: Sparkford, Yeovil, Somerset, BA22 7JJ; tel. (1963) 440635; fax (1963) 440001; e-mail sales@haynes.co.uk; internet www.haynes.co.uk; f. 1960; transport, manuals etc.; Chair. J. H. HAYNES; Man. Dir J. HAYNES.

Headline Book Publishing Ltd: 338 Euston Rd, London, NW1 3BH; tel. (20) 7873-6000; fax (20) 7873-6124; e-mail headline.books@headline.co.uk; internet www.headline.co.uk; f. 1986; division of Hodder Headline Ltd; fiction, autobiography, biography, food and wine, gardening, popular science, sport and TV tie-ins; Chief Exec. TIM HELY HUTCHINSON; Man. Dir MARTIN NEILD.

Heinemann: Halley Court, Jordan Hill, Oxford, OX2 8EJ; tel. (1865) 311366; fax (1865) 310043; e-mail uk.schools@repp.co.uk; internet www.heinemann.co.uk; imprint of Harcourt Education International; educational textbooks for UK and abroad; Man. Dir BOB OSBORNE.

William Heinemann Ltd: Random House, 20 Vauxhall Bridge Rd, London, SW1V 2SA; tel. (20) 7840-8400; fax (20) 7233-6127; e-mail enquiries@randomhouse.co.uk; internet www.randomhouse.co.uk; arts, biography, fiction, history, science, travel; Publishing Dirs RAVI MIRCHANDANI, ANDY MCKILLOP.

Hodder Arnold: 338 Euston Rd, London, NW1 3BH; tel. (20) 7873-6000; fax (20) 7873-6325; e-mail feedback.arnold@hodder.co.uk; internet www.arnoldpublishers.com; f. 1890; imprint of Hodder Education; humanities, medical, nursing, health sciences, statistics; journals cover scientific, technical, engineering; Man. Dir PHILIP WALTERS.

Hodder Education: 338 Euston Rd, London, NW1 3BH; tel. (20) 7873-6000; fax (20) 7873-6299; e-mail educationenquiries@hodder.co.uk; internet www.hoddereducation.co.uk; division of Hodder Headline; imprints: Hodder Arnold, Hodder Gibson, Hodder Murray and Teach Yourself; Man. Dir PHILIP WALTERS.

Hodder Headline: 338 Euston Rd, London, NW1 3BH; tel. (20) 7873-6000; fax (20) 7873-6124; internet www.madaboutbooks.com; f. 1993; bought by achette Liure SA 2004; divisions: Hodder Education, John Murray Ltd, Headline Book Publishing Ltd, Hodder and Stoughton Ltd; Hachette Children's Books Group Chief Exec. TIM HELY HUTCHINSON.

Hodder and Stoughton: 338 Euston Rd, London, NW1 3BH; tel. (20) 7873-6000; fax (20) 7873-6024; internet www.hodderheadline.co.uk; f. 1868; imprints: Mobius, Sceptre; general, biography, travel, fiction, current affairs; Man. Dir JAMIE HODDER-WILLIAMS.

IOP Publishing Ltd: Dirac House, Temple Back, Bristol, BS1 6BE; tel. (117) 929-7481; fax (117) 929-4318; e-mail info@iop.org; internet www.iop.org; f. 1874; scientific and technical publishers; Man. Dir J. R. COWHIG.

Jane's Information Group: Sentinel House, 163 Brighton Rd, Coulsdon, Surrey, CR5 2YH; tel. (20) 8700-3700; fax (20) 8763-1006; e-mail info.uk@janes.com; internet www.janes.com; intelligence and analysis on national and international defence, security and risk developments; CEO ALFRED ROLINGTON.

Jordan Publishing Ltd: 21 St Thomas St, Bristol, BS1 6JS; tel. (117) 923-0600; fax (117) 923-0486; e-mail sue_hall@jordanpublishing.co.uk; internet www.jordanpublishing.co.uk; f. 1863; practical law books covering family law, litigation, company, property and private client law; Man. Dir Dr CAROLINE VANBRIDGE-AMES.

Michael Joseph Ltd: 80 Strand, London, WC2R 0RL; tel. (20) 7010-3000; fax (20) 7010-6060; internet www.penguin.co.uk; f. 1936; general, fiction; division of Penguin; Publishing Dir LOUISE MOORE.

Richard Joseph Publishers Ltd: POB 15, Torrington, EX38 8ZJ; tel. (1805) 625750; fax (1805) 625376; e-mail info@sheppardsworld.co.uk; internet www.sheppardsworld.co.uk; reference and directories; Man. Dir RICHARD JOSEPH.

Kenyon-Deane: 10 Station Rd, Industrial Estate, Malvern, Worcs., WR13 6RN; tel. and fax and fax. (1684) 540154; e-mail simonsmith@cressrelles4drama.fsbusiness.co.uk; f. 1971; owned by Cressrelles Publishing Company Ltd; incorporates Kenyon House Press, H. F. W. Deane Ltd; plays and drama textbooks, specialists in all-women plays and plays for young people; Man. Dir LESLIE SMITH.

Kingfisher Publications PLC: New Penderel House, 283–288 High Holborn, London, WC1V 7HZ; tel. (20) 7903-9999; fax (20) 7242-4979; e-mail sales@kingfisherpub.com; internet www.kingfisherpub.com; children's books; imprints: Kingfisher; Man. Dir JOHN RICHARDS.

Kogan Page Ltd: 120 Pentonville Rd, London, N1 9JN; tel. (20) 7278-0433; fax (20) 7837-6348; e-mail kpinfo@kogan-page.co.uk; internet www.kogan-page.co.uk; f. 1967; business, management, accountancy, textbooks, transport, careers, personal development, training, European studies, consumer, reference; Man. Dir PHILIP KOGAN.

Lawrence and Wishart Ltd: 99A Wallis Rd, London, E9 5LN; tel. (20) 8533-2506; fax (20) 8533-7369; e-mail lw@lwbks.co.uk; internet www.lwbks.co.uk; f. 1936; politics, history, feminism, race, economics, Marxist theory, cultural studies; Man. Dir SALLY DAVISON.

Letts Educational: The Chiswick Centre, 414 Chiswick High Rd, London, W4 5TF; tel. (20) 8996-3333; fax (20) 8742-8390; e-mail mail@lettsed.co.uk; internet www.letts-education.com; children's, educational, textbooks; Man. Dir NIGEL WARD.

Lexis Nexis Butterworths: Halsbury House, 35 Chancery Lane, London, WC2A 1EL; tel. (20) 7400-2500; fax (20) 7400-2842; internet www.lexisnexis.co.uk; f. 1818; law, tax, accountancy, banking books and journals; Pres. and CEO KURT P. SANFORD.

Frances Lincoln: 4 Torriano Mews, Torriano Ave, London, NW5 2RZ; tel. (20) 7284-4009; fax (20) 7485-0490; e-mail reception@frances-lincoln.com; internet www.franceslincoln.com; f. 1977; children's fiction and non-fiction; Man. Dir JOHN NICHOLL.

THE UNITED KINGDOM

Liverpool University Press: 4 Cambridge St, Liverpool, L69 7ZU; tel. (151) 794-2233; fax (151) 794-2235; e-mail j.m.smith@liverpool.ac.uk; internet www.liverpool-unipress.co.uk; f. 1899; European and American literature, social, political, economic and ancient history, planning, hispanic studies, population studies, architecture, art, art history, cultural studies, science fiction criticism series; Publr ROBIN BLOXSIDGE.

Lonely Planet Publications: 78–82 Rosebery Ave, London, EC1R 4RW; tel. (20) 7841-9000; fax (20) 7841-9001; e-mail go@lonelyplanet.co.uk; internet www.lonelyplanet.com; f. 1973; travel, languages; Publr KATHARINE LECK.

Lund Humphries: Gower House, Croft Rd, Aldershot, Hants, GU11 3HR; tel. (1252) 331551; fax (1252) 344405; e-mail info@lundhumphries.com; internet www.lundhumphries.com; f. 1969; arts, graphic arts, design, architecture, photography, scholarly, Arabic language; Dir NIGEL FARROW.

Lutterworth Press: POB 60, Cambridge, CB1 2NT; tel. (1223) 350865; fax (1223) 366951; e-mail sales@lutterworth.com; internet www.lutterworth.com; f. 1799; imprint of James Clarke & Co Ltd; the arts, crafts, biography, educational, environmental, history, theology, travel, sport, juvenile fiction and non-fiction; Man. Dir ADRIAN BRINK.

McGraw-Hill Education: McGraw-Hill House, Shoppenhangers Rd, Maidenhead, Berks., SL6 2QL; tel. (1628) 502500; fax (1628) 770224; internet www.mcgraw-hill.co.uk; technical, scientific, computer studies, professional reference, general and medical books; Snr Vice Pres. SIMON ALLEN.

Macmillan Education Ltd: Between Towns Rd, Oxford, OX4 3PP; tel. (1865) 405700; fax (1865) 405701; e-mail info@macmillan.com; internet www.macmillaneducation.com; a division of Macmillan Publishers Ltd; English Language Teaching and educational books; Chair. CHRISTOPHER PATERSON; Man. Dir CHRIS HARRISON.

Manchester University Press: Oxford Rd, Manchester, M13 9NR; tel. (161) 275-2310; fax (161) 274-3346; e-mail mup@manchester.ac.uk; internet www.manchesteruniversitypress.co.uk; f. 1904; all branches of higher education, arts, science and social sciences; Chief Exec. DAVID RODGERS.

Methuen Publishing Ltd: 11–12 Buckingham Gate, London, SW1E 6LB; tel. (20) 7798-1600; fax (20) 7828-2098; e-mail name@methuen.co.uk; internet www.methuen.co.uk; f. 1889; literature, fiction, non-fiction, biography, sport, theatre, drama, humour, music; imprint: Politico's Publishing; Man. Dir PETER TUMMONS; Publishing Dir MAX EILENBERG.

Mitchell Beazley: 2–4 Heron Quays, London, E14 4JP; tel. (20) 7531-8400; fax (20) 7531-8650; e-mail info-mb@mitchell-beazley.co.uk; internet www.mitchell-beazley.co.uk; f. 1969; imprint of Octopus Publishing Group Ltd; Miller's antiques, arts and design, interiors and style, gardening, reference, wine and food; Publr JANE ASPDEN.

John Murray Publishers Ltd: 338 Euston Rd, London, NW1 3BH; tel. (20) 7873-6000; fax (20) 7873-6446; internet www.hodderheadline.co.uk; f. 1768; acquired by Hodder Headline in 2002; biography, autobiography, memoir, history, travel, fiction, current affairs; Man. Dir ROLAND PHILIPPS.

Nelson Thornes Ltd: Delta Pl., 27 Bath Rd, Cheltenham, GL53 7TH; tel. (1242) 267100; fax (1242) 221914; e-mail mail@nelsonthornes.com; internet www.nelsonthornes.com; educational; Man. Dir FRED GRAINGER.

James Nisbet and Co Ltd: Pirton Ct, Priors Hill, Pirton, Hitchin, Herts., SG5 3QA; tel. and fax (1462) 713444; f. 1810; business management, educational; Chair. E. M. MACKENZIE-WOOD.

Novello and Co Ltd: 8/9 Frith St, London, W1D 3JB; tel. (20) 7434-0066; fax (20) 7287-6329; e-mail promotion@musicsales.co.uk; internet www.chester-novello.com; music; Man. Dir JAMES RUSHTON.

Octopus Publishing: 2–4 Heron Quays, London, E14 4JP; tel. (20) 7531-8400; fax (20) 7531-8650; internet www.octopus-publishing.co.uk; imprints: Bounty, Conran Octopus, Hamlyn, Mitchell Beazley, Philip's, Miller's, Baca; Chief Exec. DEREK FREEMAN.

Open University Press, McGraw-Hill Education: Shoppenhangers Rd, Maidenhead, SL6 2QL; tel. (1628) 502500; fax (1628) 770224; e-mail enquiries@openup.co.uk; internet www.openup.co.uk; academic, study skills, politics, sociology, psychology, education, higher education, media, film and cultural studies, health and social welfare, counselling and psychotherapy, management and public policy; Gen. Man. SHONA MULLEN.

Orion Publishing Group: Orion House, 5 Upper St Martin's Lane, London, WC2H 9EA; tel. (20) 7240-3444; fax (20) 7240-4822; e-mail info@orionbooks.co.uk; internet www.orionbooks.co.uk; f. 1991; imprints: Dolphin, Everyman Paperbacks, Orion, Phoenix, Gollancz, Cassell, Weidenfeld & Nicolson, Allen & Unwin, Halban; Chief Exec. ANTHONY CHEETHAM.

Peter Owen Ltd: 73 Kenway Rd, London, SW5 0RE; tel. (20) 7373-5628; fax (20) 7373-6760; e-mail admin@peterowen.com; internet www.peterowen.com; f. 1951; general publishers of fiction, autobiography, biography, translations, etc; publishers of books in the UNESCO series of Representative Works; Man. Dir PETER OWEN; Editorial Dir ANTONIA OWEN.

Oxford University Press: Gt Clarendon St, Oxford, OX2 6DP; tel. (1865) 556767; fax (1865) 556646; e-mail webenquiry.uk@oup.com; internet www.oup.com; f. c.1478; Bibles, prayer books, Oxford English Dictionary, the Dictionary of National Biography and many other dictionaries and books of reference, learned and general works from the humanities to the sciences, educational, electronic, music and children's books and audio-visual and English language teaching material; Sec. to the Delegates of the Press and Chief Exec. HENRY REECE.

Palgrave Macmillan Ltd: Houndmills, Basingstoke, Hants., RG21 6XS; tel. (1256) 329242; fax (1256) 479476; internet www.palgrave.com; academic, professional, textbooks and journals; Man. Dir D. J. G. KNIGHT.

Pan Macmillan Ltd: 20 New Wharf Rd, London, N1 9RR; tel. (20) 7014-6000; fax (20) 7014-6001; e-mail books@macmillan.co.uk; internet www.panmacmillan.com; fiction and non-fiction, children's, general reference; imprints: Macmillan, Pan, Picador, Sidgwick & Jackson, Boxtree, Tor, Macmillan Children's Books, Campbell Books, Young Picador, Rodale; Chief Exec. RICHARD CHARKIN.

Pavilion Books Ltd: Chrysalis Books, Chrysalis Bldg, Bramley Rd, London, W10 6SP; tel. (20) 7314-1400; fax (20) 7221-6455; e-mail info@pavilionbooks.co.uk; internet www.chrysalisbooks.co.uk; general; acquired by Chrysalis Group PLC in 2001; Chair. CHRIS WRIGHT; Editorial Dir KATE OLDFIELD.

Pearson Education Ltd: Edinburgh Gate, Harlow, Essex, CM20 2JE; tel. (1279) 623623; fax (1279) 431059; internet www.pearsoned.co.uk; Propr Pearson PLC; educational; CEO. JOHN FALLON.

Pearson Publishing Group: Pearson Publishing Group, Chesterton Mill, French's Rd, Cambridge, CB4 3NP; tel. (1223) 350555; fax (1223) 356484; e-mail info@pearson.co.uk; internet www.pearsonpublishing.co.uk; Chair. GLEN MORENO.

Penguin Books Ltd: 80 The Strand, London WC2R 0RL; tel. (20) 7010-3000; fax (20) 7416-3099; e-mail editor@penguin.co.uk; internet www.penguin.co.uk; f. 1936; holding co Pearson PLC; paperback imprints: Penguin and Puffin; reprints and original works of fiction and non-fiction including travel, biography, science and social studies, reference books, handbooks, plays, poetry, classics and children's books; Penguin Group UK is made up of Penguin Press (Allen Lane, Reference, Penguin Classics and Penguin Modern Classics), Penguin General (imprints: Penguin, Hamish Hamilton, Michael Joseph, Viking) and the children's division (imprints: Puffin, Ladybird, Warne); Chair. and Chief Exec. JOHN MAKINSON; Man. Dir (UK) HELEN FRASER.

Phaidon Press Ltd: Regent's Wharf, All Saints St, London, N1 9PA; tel. (20) 7843-1000; internet www.phaidon.com; art, architecture, contemporary culture, design, decorative arts, fashion, photography and music, film, fine art; Chair. RICHARD SCHLAGMAN.

Philip's: 111 Salusbury Rd, London, NW6 6RG; tel. (20) 7644-6940; fax (20) 7644-6986; e-mail philips@philips-maps.co.uk; internet www.philips-maps.co.uk; imprint of Octopus Publishing Group; maps, atlases, globes, astronomy, encyclopaedias; Publr JOHN GAISFORD.

Pluto Press: 345 Archway Rd, London, N6 5AA; tel. (20) 8348-2724; fax (20) 8348-9133; e-mail beech@plutobooks.com; internet www.plutobooks.com; academic, scholarly, current affairs and reference; Man. Dir ROGER VAN ZWANENBERG; Editorial Dir ANNE BEECH.

Proquest Information and Learning: The Quorum, Barnwell Rd, Cambridge, CB5 8SW; tel. (1223) 215512; fax (1223) 215514; e-mail mailmarketing@proquest.co.uk; internet www.proquest.co.uk; f. 1973; as Chadwyck-Healey Ltd; changed name as above in 2001; academic; Chair. ALAN ALDWORTH; Gen. Man. STEVEN HALL.

The Random House Group: Random House, 20 Vauxhall Bridge Rd, London, SW1V 2SA; tel. (20) 7840-8400; fax (20) 7233-6115; internet www.randomhouse.co.uk; imprints: Arrow, Cedar, Jonathan Cape, Century, Chatto & Windus, Ebury Press, William Heinemann, Hutchinson, Random House Business Books, Harvill Secker, Pimlico, Vintage, Random House Children's, Red Fox, Rider, Vermilion, Yellow Jersey; Chair. and Chief Exec. GAIL REBUCK.

Reader's Digest Association Ltd: 11 Westferry Circus, Canary Wharf, London, E14 4HE; tel. (20) 7715-8000; fax (20) 7715-8181; internet www.readersdigest.co.uk; various non-fiction, condensed and series fiction; Chair THOMAS RYDER; Man. Dir ANDREW LYNAM-SMITH.

Reed Business Information: Quadrant House, The Quadrant, Sutton, Surrey, SM2 5AS; tel. (20) 8652-3500; fax (20) 8652-8932; e-mail information@reedinfo.co.uk; internet www.reedbusiness.co.uk; f. 1866; business directories and online services; CEO KEITH JONES.

THE UNITED KINGDOM

Reed Elsevier plc: 1–3 Strand, London, WC2N 5JR; tel. (20) 7930-7077; fax (20) 7166-5799; internet www.reedelsevier.com; f. 1992; Chief Exec. Sir CRISPIN DAVIS.

Routledge: 2 Park Square, Milton Park, Abingdon, Oxfordshire OX14 4RN; tel. (20) 7017-6000; fax (20) 7017-6699; e-mail info@routledge.co.uk; internet www.routledge.com; f. 1988; member of Taylor and Francis Group; professional, academic, reference; Man. Dir JEREMY NORTH.

SAGE Publications Ltd: 1 Oliver's Yard, 55 City Rd, London, EC1Y 1SP; tel. (20) 7324-8500; fax (20) 7324-8600; e-mail info@sagepub.co.uk; internet www.sagepub.co.uk; f. 1971; academic and professional social sciences, sciences and humanities; imprint: Paul Chapman; Man Dir STEPHEN BARR.

Schofield and Sims Ltd: Dogley Mill, Penistone Rd, Fenay Bridge, Huddersfield, West Yorks., HD8 0NQ; tel. (1484) 607080; fax (1484) 606815; e-mail schofield_and_sims@compuserve.com; internet www.schofieldandsims.co.uk; f. 1901; educational; Chair. J. STEPHEN PLATTS.

Scholastic Ltd: Villiers House, Clarendon Ave, Leamington Spa, Warwickshire, CV32 5PR; tel. (1926) 887799; fax (1926) 883331; internet www.scholastic.co.uk; f. 1964; direct marketing, educational and children's books; Man. Dir KATE WILSON.

SCM-Canterbury Press Ltd: St Mary's Works, St Mary's Plain, Norwich, NR3 3BH; tel. (1603) 612914; fax (1603) 624483; e-mail admin@scm-canterburypress.co.uk; internet www.scm-canterburypress.co.uk; f. 1929; religious, theological; Group CEO ANDREW MOORE.

Scripture Union: 207–209 Queensway, Bletchley, Milton Keynes, Bucks, MK2 2EB; tel. (1908) 856000; fax (1908) 856111; e-mail info@scriptureunion.org.uk; internet www.scriptureunion.org.uk; f. 1867; Christian education and Bible reading aids.

Martin Secker and Warburg Ltd: Random House, 20 Vauxhall Bridge Rd, London, SW1V 2SA; tel. (20) 7840-8400; fax (20) 7233-6117; internet www.randomhouse.co.uk; imprint of Random House Group Ltd; f. 1936; history, music, political, biography, art, criticism, science, fiction; Editorial Dir GEOFFREY MULLIGAN.

Sidgwick and Jackson Ltd: 20 New Wharf Rd, London, N1 9RR; tel. (20) 7014-6000; fax (20) 7014-6023; internet www.panmacmillan.com; f. 1908; popular non-fiction, biography, autobiography, military history, music and popular culture, history; Publr RICHARD MILNER.

Simon and Schuster: Africa House, 64–78 Kingsway, London, WC2B 6AH; tel. (20) 7316-1900; fax (20) 7316-0331; e-mail enquiries@simonandschuster.co.uk; internet www.simonsays.com; f. 1986; owned by Gy Viacom; fiction, non-fiction, music, travel; imprints: Pocket Books, Touchstone, Scribner, Free Press; Man. Dir IAN S. CHAPMAN.

Society for Promoting Christian Knowledge: 36 Causton St, London, SW1P 4ST; tel. (20) 7592-3900; fax (20) 7592-3939; e-mail spck@spck.org.uk; internet www.spck.org.uk; f. 1698; religious; imprints: SPCK, Triangle, Azure, Sheldon Press; Dir of Publishing SIMON KINGSTON.

Souvenir Press Ltd: 43 Great Russell St, London, WC1B 3PD; tel. (20) 7580-9307; fax (20) 7580-5064; e-mail souvenirpress@ukonline.co.uk; general; Man. Dir ERNEST HECHT.

The Stationery Office: St Crispins, Duke St, Norwich, NR3 1PD; tel. (1603) 622211; e-mail book.enquiries@tso.co.uk; internet www.tso.co.uk; f. 1786 as His Majesty's Stationery Office (govt publishing house); privatized (acquired by National Publishing Group consortium) in 1996; business and publishing services; publishes Hansard, Highway Code, British Pharmacopoeia; Chair. RUPERT PENNANT-REA; Chief Exec. TIM HAILSTONE.

Sweet and Maxwell Ltd: 100 Avenue Rd, London, NW3 3PF; tel. (20) 7393-7000; fax (20) 7393-7010; e-mail customer.services@sweetandmaxwell.co.uk; internet www.sweetandmaxwell.co.uk; f. 1799; imprints: Stevens and Sons Ltd, W. Green, Round Hall, ESC Publishing, the European Law Centre; holding co Thomson Corporation; law books; Man. Dir WENDY BEECHAM.

Taylor and Francis Group Ltd: 4 Park Square, Milton Park, Abingdon, Oxfordshire, OX14 4RN; tel. (20) 7017-6000; fax (20) 7017-6699; e-mail info@tandf.co.uk; internet www.taylorandfrancisgroup.com; division of Informa PLC; imprints: Taylor and Francis, Routledge, Garland Science and Psychology Press; professional, academic, scientific, technical, reference; books and journals; Chief Exec. ROGER HORTON.

Thames and Hudson Ltd: 181A High Holborn, London, WC1V 7QX; tel. (20) 7845-5000; fax (20) 7845-5050; e-mail sales@thameshudson.co.uk; internet www.thamesandhudson.com; art, archaeology, history, etc.; Man. Dir T. NEURATH.

Time Warner Book Group UK: Brettenham House, Lancaster Pl., London, WC2E 7EN; tel. (20) 7911-8000; fax (20) 7911-8100; e-mail email.uk@twbg.co.uk; internet www.twbg.co.uk; subsidiary of AOL Time-Warner; imprints: Time-Warner, Abacus, Virago, Orbit, Little, Brown, Atom; Chief Exec. DAVID YOUNG.

Times Books: 77–85 Fulham Palace Rd, London, W6 8JB; tel. (20) 8741-7070; fax (20) 8307-4037; Proprs HarperCollins Publishers Ltd; atlases, maps and general reference; Man. Dir SARAH BAILEY.

Transworld Publishers Ltd: 61–63 Uxbridge Rd, London, W5 5SA; tel. (20) 8579-2652; fax (20) 8579-5479; e-mail info@transworld-publishers.co.uk; internet www.booksattransworld.co.uk; imprints: Corgi, Bantam Books, Black Swan, Bantam Press, Doubleday, Expert Books, Eden Project Books, Channel 4 Books; all types of fiction and non-fiction; Man. Dir LARRY FINLAY.

University of Wales Press: 10 Columbus Walk, Brigantine Pl., Cardiff, CF10 4UP; tel. (29) 2049-6899; fax (29) 2049-6108; e-mail press@press.wales.ac.uk; internet www.wales.ac.uk/press; f. 1922; academic and educational (Welsh and English); Dir ASHLEY DRAKE.

Usborne Publishing: Usborne House, 83–85 Saffron Hill, London, EC1N 8RT; tel. (20) 7430-2800; fax (20) 8636-3758; e-mail mail@usborne.co.uk; internet www.usborne.com; f. 1973; educational and children's publishing; Man. Dir T. P. USBORNE.

Viking: 80 Strand, London, WC2R 0RL; tel. (20) 7010-3000; fax (20) 7010-6060; literary imprint of Penguin Books; fiction, general non-fiction, biography, history, art, literature, science, popular culture; Publishing Dir VENETIA BUTTERFIELD.

Virgin Books: Thames Wharf Studios, Rainville Rd, London, W6 9HA; tel. (20) 7386-3300; fax (20) 7386-3360; e-mail info@virgin-books.co.uk; internet www.virginbooks.com; W. H. Allen and Co. f. before 1800; general, popular culture, film, music, humour, biography, fiction, non-fiction, erotica; imprints: Virgin, Black Lace and Nexus; Man. Dir K. T. FORSTER.

Frederick Warne (Publishers) Ltd: 80 Strand, London, WC2R 0RL; tel. (20) 7010-3000; fax (20) 7010-6707; e-mail peterrabbit@penguin.co.uk; internet www.peterrabbit.com; f. 1865; a division of Penguin Books since 1983; classic illustrated children's books (including Beatrix Potter); Man. Dir SALLY FLOYER.

Weidenfeld and Nicolson Ltd: Orion House, 5 Upper St Martin's Lane, London, WC2H 9EA; tel. (20) 7240-3444; fax (20) 7240-4822; e-mail info@orionbooks.co.uk; internet www.orionbooks.co.uk; f. 1947; imprint of Orion Publishing Group (see above); fiction and non-fiction covering wide range of subjects, biography, belles-lettres and art books; Chair. Lord WEIDENFELD; Man. Dir Adrian BOURNE.

The Women's Press: 27 Goodge St, London, W1T 2LD; tel. (20) 7636-3992; fax (20) 7637-1866; e-mail charlotteg@the-womens-press.com; internet www.the-womens-press.com; f. 1978; feminist; Man. Dir CHARLOTTE GASCOIGNE.

Yale University Press: 47 Bedford Sq., London, WC1B 3DP; tel. (20) 7079-4900; fax (20) 7079-4901; e-mail sales@yaleup.co.uk; internet www.yalebooks.co.uk; f. 1961; Man. Dir ROBERT BALDOCK.

Zed Books Ltd: 7 Cynthia St, London, N1 9JF; tel. (20) 7837-4014; fax (20) 7833-3960; e-mail zedbooks@zedbooks.demon.co.uk; internet www.zedbooks.co.uk; f. 1977; academic, scholarly, current affairs; Editors ROBERT MOLTENO, ANNA HARDMAN.

PUBLISHERS' ORGANIZATIONS

Booktrust: Book House, 45 East Hill, London, SW18 2QZ; tel. (20) 8516-2977; fax (20) 8516-2998; e-mail info@booktrust.org.uk; internet www.booktrust.org.uk; non-profit-making organization funded by voluntary donations and membership fees; f. 1945; originally f. 1925 as The National Book Council to extend the use and enjoyment of books; renamed Book Trust 1986; publishes annotated book lists; postal book information service; organizes book prizes, including the Booker Prize for Fiction; Young Book Trust inc the Centre for Children's Books (reference collection of the current two years' children's books); Chair. TREVOR GLOVER; Exec. Dir CHRIS MEADE.

Publishers' Association: 29B Montague St, London, WC1B 5BW; tel. (20) 7691-9191; fax (20) 7691-9199; e-mail mail@publishers.org.uk; internet www.publishers.org.uk; f. 1896; represents book and journal publishers in the UK and seeks to promote the sales of British books; Pres. RICHARD CHARKIN; Chief Exec. RONNIE WILLIAMS; 180 mems.

Scottish Publishers' Association: Scottish Book Centre, 137 Dundee St, Edinburgh, EH11 1BG; tel. (131) 228-6866; fax (131) 228-3220; e-mail carol.lothian@scottishbooks.org; internet www.scottishbooks.org; f. 1973; assists member publishers in the promotion and marketing of their books; offers export services, consultancy and training; Chair. JANIS ADAMS; Dir LORRAINE FANNIN.

THE UNITED KINGDOM

Broadcasting and Communications

REGULATORY AUTHORITY

Office of Communications (Ofcom): Riverside House, 2A Southwark Bridge Rd, London, SE1 9HA; tel. (20) 7981-3000; fax (20) 7981-3333; e-mail contact@ofcom.org.uk; internet www.ofcom.org.uk; f. 2003 to replace the Office of Telecommunications, the Broadcasting Standards Commission, the Radio Authority, the Radiocommunications Agency and the Independent Television Commission; the independent regulator for the British communications industries, with responsibilities across television, radio, telecommunications and wireless communications services; promotes choice, quality and value in electronic communications services, where appropriate, by encouraging competition between the providers of those services; ensures the most efficient use of the radiocommunications spectrum (the airwaves used for the transmission of all non-military wireless communications services); ensures that a wide range of electronic communications services, including broadband, is available across the United Kingdom; ensures that a wide range of television and radio programmes of high quality and wide appeal are broadcast; maintains plurality in the media by ensuring a sufficiently broad range of ownership; protects audiences against offensive or harmful material, unfairness or the infringement of piracy on television and radio; Chair. Lord CURRIE OF MARYLEBONE; Chief Exec. STEPHEN CARTER.

TELECOMMUNICATIONS

British Telecommunications PLC: BT Centre, 81 Newgate St, London, EC1A 7AJ; tel. (20) 7356-5000; fax (20) 7356-6630; internet www.bt.com; wholly owned subsidiary of BT Group PLC; Chair. Sir CHRISTOPHER BLAND; Chief Exec. BEN VERWAAYEN.

Cable and Wireless PLC: Lakeside House, Cain Rd, Bracknell, Berkshire, RG12 1XL; tel. (20) 7528-2000; fax (20) 7528-2181; internet www.cwcom.co.uk; acquired rival co Energis in mid-2005; Chair. RICHARD LAPTHORNE; UK Chair. and Joint Group Man. Dir. JOHN PLUTHERO; International Chair. and Joint Group Man. Dir. HARRIS JONES.

Kingston Communications: 37 Carr Lane, Hull, HU1 3RE; tel. (1482) 602100; fax (1482) 219289; e-mail publicrelations@kcom.com; internet www.kcom.com; Chair. MICHAEL ABRAHAMS; Chief Exec. MALCOLM FALLEN.

National Grid Wireless: Wireless House, Warwick Technology Park, Heathcote Lane, Warwick, CV34 6TN; tel. (1926) 416000; fax (20) 416600; e-mail marketinguk@ngridwireless.com; internet www.nationalgridwireless.com; wholly-owned subsidiary of National Grid Transco PLC; fmrly known as Crown Castle UK Ltd; name changed as above following acquisition of the firm by National Grid Transco PLC in June 2004; CEO STEVEN MARSHALL.

NTL UK: NTL Bldg, 280 Barclay Wood Business Park, Barclay Way, Hook, Reading, RG27 9XA; tel. (1256) 752000; fax (1256) 752100; internet www.ntl.com; merged with Telewest Communications PLC in March 2006; Chair. JAMES MOONEY; CEO STEPHEN BURCH.

O$_2$: 260 Bath Rd, Slough, Berks, SL1 4DX; tel. (1753) 504000; fax (1752) 565010; e-mail feedback@o2.com; internet www.o2.co.uk; formerly BT Cellnet; demerged from BT Group in October 2002 and became part of the mmO$_2$ group; acquired by Telefónica, SA in March 2006; Chair. and CEO PETER ERSKINE.

Orange: Gt Park Rd, Almondsbury Park, Bradley Stoke, Bristol, BS32 4QJ; tel. (870) 376-8888; internet www.orange.co.uk; f. 1994; acquired by France Telecom in 2000; part of the Orange SA (France) group; Chief Exec. SANJIV AHUJA; Group Chair DIDIER LOMBARD.

T-Mobile UK: Hatfield Business Park, Herts, AL10 9BW; tel. (1707) 315000; internet www.t-mobile.co.uk; owned by Deutsche Telekom AG; formerly One2One; Man. Dir BRIAN MCBRIDE.

TeleWest Communications PLC: Export House, Causeway, Woking, Surrey, GU21 1QX; tel. (1483) 750900; fax (1483) 750901; internet www.telewest.co.uk; merged with NTL UK in March 2006; Chair. JAMES MOONEY; CEO STEPHEN BURCH.

THUS PLC: 322 Regents Park Rd, London, N3 2QQ; tel. (845) 272-0666; e-mail thus.enquiries@thus.net; internet www.thus.co.uk; f. 1994 as Scottish Telecom; changed name as above in 1999; Chair. PHILIP ROGERSON; Chief Exec. BILL ALLAN.

Virgin Mobile: Willow Grove House, POB 2692, Trowbridge, West Wiltshire, BA14 0TQ; tel. (1225) 895555; fax (1225) 895881; internet www.virginmobile.com; f. 1999; Chair. CHARLES MARK GURASSA; CEO TOM ALEXANDER.

Vodafone Group PLC: The Connection, Newbury, Berks, RG14 2FN; tel. (1635) 33251; fax (1635) 676147; internet www.vodafone.com; Chair. Lord MACLAURIN OF KNEBWORTH; Chief Exec. ARUN SARIN.

BROADCASTING

British Broadcasting Corporation (BBC): Broadcasting House, London, W1A 1AA; tel. (20) 7580-4468; fax (20) 7637-1630; internet www.bbc.co.uk; f. 1922; operates under Royal Charter. It is financed by the television licence fees; Chair. MICHAEL GRADE; Dir-Gen. MARK THOMPSON; COO JOHN SMITH; Dir of Drama, Entertainment and CBBC ALAN YENTOB; Dir of Television JANA BENNETT; Dir of Marketing, Communications and Audiences TIM DAVIE; Dir of Nations and Regions PAT LOUGHREY; Dir of BBC People STEPHEN DANDO; Dir of Policy, Strategy, Legal and Distribution CAROLINE THOMSON; Dir of News HELEN BOADEN; Dir of BBC Global News RICHARD SAMBROOK; Dir of Radio and Music JENNY ABRAMSKY; Dir of Sport ROGER MOSEY; Dir of New Media and Technology ASHLEY HIGHFIELD.

Radio

British Broadcasting Corporation

BBC Radio provides a service of five national networks throughout the United Kingdom, 38 local radio stations in England and the Channel Islands, Radio Scotland, Radio Wales, Radio Cymru, broadcasting in Welsh, and Radio Ulster and Radio Foyle (in Northern Ireland); it also offers a number of specialist digital services; Dir of Radio and Music JENNY ABRAMSKY.

Radio 1: broadcasts 24 hours a day of contemporary music programmes; Controller ANDY PARFITT.

Radio 2: broadcasts popular music and culture; Controller LESLEY DOUGLAS.

Radio 3: provides 24-hour broadcasts of classical music, drama, talks and documentaries; Controller ROGER WRIGHT.

Radio 4: broadcasts news and current affairs and also provides a wide range of features, drama and discussions; Controller MARK DAMAZER.

Radio Five Live: began broadcasting in March 1994, replacing Radio 5; provides a 24-hour service of news and sports programmes; also operates **Five Live Sports Extra**, a part-time digital network for sports events not broadcast elsewhere on BBC Radio; Controller BOB SHENNAN.

6 Music: began broadcasting in 2002, digital station playing pop and rock music; Controller LESLEY DOUGLAS.

1Xtra: began broadcasting in 2002; digital station playing contemporary urban music for a young audience; Controller ANDY PARFITT.

Asian Network: began broadcasting in 2002, digital station aimed at the Asian communities in the United Kingdom.

BBC7: digital radio station featuring archive material, began broadcasting in 2002; Controller MARK DAMAZER.

BBC World Service: Bush House, Strand, London, WC2B 4PH; tel. (20) 7240-3456; fax (20) 7557-1258; e-mail worldservice@bbc.co.uk; internet www.bbc.co.uk/worldservice; the World Service in English is broadcast for 24 hours daily, in 32 languages, and is directed to all areas of the world. In addition, there are special services to: the Far East (in Mandarin, Cantonese, Indonesian, Thai and Vietnamese); the Indian sub-continent (in Bengali, Burmese, Hindi, Nepali, Pashto, Persian, Sinhala, Tamil and Urdu); the Caucasus and Central Asia (in Azeri, Kazakh, Kyrgyz, Uzbek and Russian); the Middle East and North Africa (in Arabic and French); Central, East, West and South Africa (in English, French, Hausa, Kinyarwanda/Kirundi, Portuguese, Somali and Swahili); and the Western Hemisphere (in Portuguese for Brazil and Spanish for Latin America). Services in the following languages are transmitted for listeners in Europe: Albanian, Bulgarian, Croatian, Czech and Slovak, Greek, Hungarian, Macedonian, Polish, Romanian, Russian, Serbian, Slovene and Turkish; Dir RICHARD SAMBROOK.

Independent National Radio

Classic FM: 30 Leicester Sq., London, WC2H 7LA; tel. (20) 7343-9000; fax (20) 7344-2703; e-mail enquiries@classicfm.com; internet www.classicfm.com; began broadcasting September 1992; popular classical music; Exec. Chair. RALPH BERNARD; Station Man. DARREN HENLEY.

Independent Radio News (IRN): 200 Gray's Inn Rd, London, WC1X 8XZ; tel. (20) 7430-4814; e-mail irn@itn.co.uk; internet www.irn.co.uk; f. 1973; produced by ITN Radio; news agency for the independent local radio network; Chair. TERRY SMITH; Man. Dir JOHN PERKINS.

The Local Radio Company: 11 Duke St, High Wycombe, Buckinghamshire, HP13 6EE; tel. (1494) 688200; fax (1494) 688201; internet www.thelocalradiocompany.com; owns and operates 26 local radio licences across the United Kingdom; f. 2004; to purchase the entire share capital of Radio Investments Ltd; Chief Exec. RICHARD WHEATLY.

TalkSport UK: 18 Hatfields, London, SE1 8DJ; tel. (20) 7959-7800; fax (20) 7959-7808; internet www.talksport.net; began broadcasting

THE UNITED KINGDOM

February 1995 as Talk Radio UK; name changed as above January 2000; Propr The Wireless Group; Chair. and Chief Exec. KELVIN MACKENZIE.

Virgin Radio (Virgin 1215): 1 Golden Sq., London, W1F 9DJ; tel. (20) 7434-1215; fax (20) 7434-1197; e-mail reception@ginger.com; internet www.virginradio.co.uk; began broadcasting April 1993; popular music; Propr Scottish Media Group; Chief Exec. JOHN PEARSON.

Television
British Broadcasting Corporation

BBC Television: Television Centre, Wood Lane, London, W12 7RJ; tel. (20) 8743-8000; internet www.bbc.co.uk; operates two terrestrial services, BBC-1 and BBC-2, and six digital channels, BBC-3, BBC-4, CBeebies, CBBC, BBC News 24 and BBC Parliament; Dir of Television JANA BENNETT.

BBC-1: internet www.bbc.co.uk/bbcone; provides a coverage of over 99% of the population of the United Kingdom. Colour service began in 1969; a breakfast-time television service began in 1983; Controller PETER FINCHAM.

BBC-2: internet www.bbc.co.uk/two; opened in 1964, and is available to 99% of the population. Colour service began in 1967; Controller ROLY KEATING.

BBC-3: internet www.bbc.co.uk/bbcthree; digital entertainment channel; Controller JULIAN BELLAMY.

BBC-4: internet www.bbc.co.uk/bbcfour; digital channel showing in-depth cultural programmes; Controller JANICE HADLOW.

CBBC: internet www.bbc.co.uk/cbbc; digital service for children aged six to 13; Controller RICHARD DEVERELL.

CBeebies: internet www.bbc.co.uk/cbeebies; digital service aimed at under-fives.

BBC News 24: internet www.bbc.co.uk/news24; 24 hour digital news service.

BBC Parliament: internet www.bbc.co.uk/parliament; provides coverage from the Houses of Parliament and the devolved Parliament and Assemblies in Scotland, Wales and Northern Ireland.

Independent Television

In October 1991 the Independent Television Commission (ITC), in accordance with the provisions of the Broadcasting Act of 1990, awarded the 16 licences that constituted the renamed Channel 3 (ITV 1). The franchises were allocated by a system of competitive tendering, although the ITC was empowered to select a company presenting a lower bid in 'exceptional circumstances'. The new licences came into force on 1 January 1993, when Channel 4 (q.v.) also became an ITC licensee. By the end of 1995 the ITC had also issued 183 non-domestic satellite and licensable programme service licences. In October 1995 the ITC awarded the licence for the fifth terrestrial channel to Channel 5 Broadcasting; broadcasting commenced in March 1997. In June the ITC awarded the British Digital Broadcasting consortium (ONdigital, later renamed ITV Digital) three licences to operate digital terrestrial television (DTT) services in the United Kingdom. Following the collapse of ITV Digital in April 2002, the ITC withdrew the consortium's licences and in May it announced that they were to be re-tendered; in August one licence was awarded to the BBC and two to Crown Castle International. DTV Services Ltd, a consortium of the BBC, Crown Castle International and BSkyB, subsequently announced its plans to launch Freeview, which would provide a wide range of free-to-view digital television channels. Freeview commenced broadcasting in late 2002. The ITC became part of Ofcom in late 2003. In early 2005 Ofcom published a provisional timetable outlining plans for the country to switch entirely from analogue to digital television region by region between 2008 and 2012.

Channel Four Television: 124 Horseferry Rd, London, SW1P 2TX; tel. (20) 7306-8333; internet www.channel4.com; f. 1980; began broadcasting 1982; national television service; available to 97% of the population; financed by advertising; in accordance with the Broadcasting Act (1990), Channel Four became a public corporation and ITC licensee, responsible for selling its own advertising, from January 1993; Chair. LUKE JOHNSON; Chief Exec. ANDY DUNCAN.

five: 22 Long Acre, London, WC2E 9LY; tel. (8457) 050505; e-mail customerservices@five.tv; internet www.five.tv; awarded licence for fifth national terrestrial channel in October 1995; commenced broadcasting on 30 March 1997 as Channel 5; renamed as above in 2002; solely owned by RTL; Chair. DAVID ELSTEIN; Chief Exec. JANE LIGHTING.

Independent Television News Ltd (ITN): 200 Gray's Inn Rd, London, WC1X 8XZ; tel. (20) 7833-3000; internet www.itn.co.uk; f. 1955; ITV PLC holds a 40% stake, with Daily Mail and General Trust PLC, Reuters Holdings and United Business Media each holding a 20% stake; provides all national and international news programming for ITV 1 and the London region, plus news programming for Channel 4 and Independent Radio News (IRN); also operates the ITN Archive, ITN Multimedia and ITN Factual; became a profit-making company in 1993; Chief Exec. MARK WOOD.

ITV PLC: The London Television Centre, Upper Ground, London, SE1 9LT; tel. (20) 7620-1620; internet www.itvplc.com; f. 2003 following the merger of Carlton and Granada; owns all of the regional Channel 3 licences in England and Wales; Chair. Sir PETER BURT; Chief Exec. CHARLES ALLEN.

Scottish Media Group PLC: 200 Renfield St, Glasgow, G2 3PR; tel. (141) 300-3300; e-mail corporate.affairs@smg.plc.uk; internet www.smg.plc.uk; Chair. CHRIS MASTERS; Chief Exec. ANDREW FLANAGAN.

S4C Welsh Fourth Channel Authority (Awdurdod Sianel Pedwar Cymru): Parc Ty Glas, Llanishen, Cardiff, CF14 5DU; tel. (29) 2074-7444; fax (29) 2075-4444; e-mail hotline@s4c.co.uk; internet www.s4c.co.uk; f. 1980; commenced broadcasting in 1982; television service for Wales; Chair. JOHN WALTER JONES; Chief Exec. IONA JONES.

Independent Television (ITV—Channel 3) Regional Licencees

Independent Television Association Ltd (ITV): ITV Network Centre, 200 Grays Inn Rd, London, WC1X 8HF; tel. (20) 7843-8000; fax (20) 7843-8158; e-mail info@itv.co.uk; internet www.itv.com; f. 1956; from 1992 the central co-ordinating body for Channel 3 (ITV 1); Dir of Television SIMON SHAPS.

Good Morning TV (GMTV): c/o London TV Centre, London, SE1 9TT; tel. (20) 7827-7000; fax (20) 7827-7001; internet www.gm.tv; nationwide breakfast-time service; began broadcasting in January 1993 (replacing TV-am PLC); 50% owned by ITV PLC; Chair. CHARLES ALLEN; Man. Dir PAUL CORLEY.

ITV Anglia: Anglia House, Norwich, NR1 3JG; tel. (1603) 615151; fax (1603) 631032; internet www.angliatv.com; East of England; Propr ITV PLC; began broadcasting in 1959; Man. Dir GRAHAM CREELMAN; Controller of Programmes and Regional News NEIL THOMPSON.

ITV Border: Television Centre, Carlisle, CA1 3NT; tel. (1228) 525101; fax (1228) 541384; internet www.border-tv.com; Borders and the Isle of Man; Propr ITV PLC; Chief Exec. PADDY MERRALL.

ITV Central: Duty Office, Gas St, Birmingham, B1 2JT; tel. (870) 600-6766; fax (121) 634-4898; internet www.itvregions.com/central; South, East and West Midlands; ITV PLC; Man. Dir IAN SQUIRES.

ITV Granada: Granada TV Centre, Quay St, Manchester, M60 9EA; tel. and fax (161) 832-7211; fax (161) 827-2180; internet www.itvregions.com/granada; north-west England; Propr ITV PLC; Man. Dir SUSAN WOODWARD.

ITV London: London Television Centre, Upper Ground, London, SE1 9LT; fax (20) 7261-8163; e-mail newsdesk@itvlondon.com; internet www.itvregions.com/london; London area, Monday to Thursday, Friday to 5.15 p.m; formed by a merger of Carlton and LWT in February 2004; Propr ITV PLC; Man. Dir CHRISTY SWORDS.

ITV Meridian: Solent Business Park, Whiteley, Hants, PO15 7PA; tel. and fax (1489) 442000; e-mail meridiannewssouth@itv.com; internet www.itvregions.com/meridian; south and south-east England; began broadcasting in January 1993; Propr ITV PLC; Man. Dir LYNDSAY CHARLTON.

ITV Tyne Tees: Television House, The Watermark, Gateshead, NE11 9SZ; tel. (191) 404-8700; fax (191) 404-8780; e-mail tyne.tees@itv.com; internet www.itvregions.com/tyne_tees; f. 1959; North-east England; Propr ITV PLC; Man. Dir and Controller of Programmes GRAEME THOMPSON.

ITV Wales: Television Centre, Culverhouse Cross, Cardiff, CF5 6XJ; tel. (29) 2059-0590; fax (29) 2059-7183; e-mail info@itvwales.com; internet www.itvregions.com/wales; fmrly HTV Wales; Propr ITV PLC; Man. Dir ROGER LEWIS.

ITV West: The Television Centre, Bath Rd, Bristol, BS4 3HG; tel. (117) 972-2722; fax (117) 971-7685; e-mail itvwestnews@itv.com; internet www.itvregions.com/west; fmrly HTV West; Propr ITV PLC; Man Dir MARK HASKELL.

ITV Westcountry: Langage Science Park, Western Wood Way, Plymouth, PL7 5BQ; tel. (1752) 333333; fax (1752) 333444; internet www.itvregions.com/westcountry; south-west England; began broadcasting in January 1993; Propr ITV PLC; Man. Dir MARK HASKELL.

ITV Yorkshire: Television Centre, Leeds, LS3 1JS; tel. (113) 243-8283; fax (113) 243-3655; internet www.itvregions.com/yorkshire; Propr ITV PLC; Man. Dir DAVID M. B. CROFT.

Grampian Television Ltd: Television Centre, Craigshaw Business Park, West Tullos, Aberdeen, AB12 3QH; tel. (1224) 848848; fax (1224) 848800; e-mail gtv@grampiantv.co.uk; internet www.grampiantv.co.uk; north Scotland; acquired by Scottish Media

Group in June 1997; Chair. Dr CALUM A. MACLEOD; Man. Dir DERRICK THOMSON.

Scottish Television PLC: 200 Renfield St, Glasgow, G2 3PR; tel. (141) 300-3000; fax (141) 300-3030; internet www.scottishtv.co.uk; f. 1957; central Scotland; Propr Scottish Media Group; Chair. BRIAN MARJORIBANKS; Chief Exec. DONALD ERNSLIE.

Ulster Television PLC: Havelock House, Ormeau Rd, Belfast, BT7 1EB; tel. (28) 9032-8122; fax (28) 9024-6695; internet www.u.tv; started transmission 1959; Chair. JOHN B. MCGUCKIAN; Chief Exec. JOHN MCCANN.

Satellite and Cable Broadcasting

By June 2003 there were 12,358,637 households in the United Kingdom receiving multi-channel satellite or cable television services. Of these, 6,559,000 were paying to subscribe to digital satellite television with a further 3,260,051 households subscribing to cable television (digital 2,188,375; analogue 1,071,676). The major satellite and cable television companies are listed below.

BBC Worldwide Television: Woodlands, 80 Wood Lane, London, W12 0TT; tel. (20) 8433-2000; fax (20) 8749-0538; internet www.bbcworldwide.com; began broadcasting in 1991; part of BBC Worldwide Ltd; broadcasts 24-hour news and information ('BBC World') and light entertainment programmes to Europe ('BBC Prime'); other news programmes broadcast to Africa, Asia (including a Japanese-language service to Japan), the Middle East, Australia and New Zealand; Chief Exec. JOHN SMITH.

British Sky Broadcasting Group PLC (BskyB): Grant Way, Isleworth, Middlesex, TW7 5QD; tel. (20) 7705-3000; fax (20) 7705-3030; internet www.sky.com; f. 1990 by merger of British Satellite Broadcasting (BSB) and Sky TV PLC (a subsidiary of News International); satellite broadcaster and programme provider; multi-channel digital television service SkyDigital (see below); Chair. RUPERT MURDOCH; Chief Exec. JAMES MURDOCH.

Cable News Network Inc (CNN): 16 Great Marlborough St, London, W1F 7HS; tel. (20) 7693-1000; fax (20) 7693-1550; internet www.cnn.com; Sr Vice-Pres. Europe, Middle East and Africa TONY MADDOX.

Eurosport UK: 55 Drury Lane, London, WC2B 5SQ; tel. (20) 7468-7777; fax (20) 7468-0023; e-mail network@eurosport.co.uk; internet www.eurosport.co.uk; began broadcasting in 1989; Dir E. FLORENT.

MTV Networks Europe: 180 Oxford St, London, W1D 1DS; tel. (20) 7478-6000; fax (20) 7284-7788; internet www.mtv.co.uk; began broadcasting in 1987; popular music; Pres. BRENT HANSEN.

NTL: NTL House, Bartley Way, Hook, Hants, RG27 9UP; tel. (118) 954-4000; fax (1256) 754100; internet www.ntl.com; Chair JAMES MOONEY; Chief Exec. STEPHEN BURCH.

UK TV: 160 Great Portland St, London, W1W 5QA; tel. (20) 7299-6200; fax (20) 7299-6000; internet www.uktv.co.uk; began broadcasting 1992; satellite, cable and DTT; Chief Exec. RICHARD EMERY.

Digital Television

The first digital television services became available in 1998. Digital television is envisaged as a replacement to existing analogue frequencies, available by cable, satellite and terrestrial operators. In April 2002, following the collapse of ITV Digital, the Independent Television Committee (ITC) invited tenders for the licences to operate digital terrestrial television services in the United Kingdom. In August the ITC awarded one licence to the BBC and two to Crown Castle, who combined to provide Freeview. By 31 December 2005 69.4% of households in the United Kingdom were receiving digital television services.

Freeview: Broadcast Centre, 201 Wood Lane, London, W12 7TP; tel. (8708) 809980; internet www.freeview.co.uk; f. 2002; a consortium of the BBC, Crown Castle and BSkyB providing Freeview, a digital service offering 39 television stations and additional interactive services; commenced transmission in late 2002.

SkyDigital: 6 Centaurs Business Park, Grant Way, Isleworth, Middlesex, TW7 5QD; tel. (20) 7705-3000; fax (20) 7705-3030; internet www.sky.com; owned by British Sky Broadcasting Group PLC; Chief Exec. JAMES MURDOCH.

Finance

The United Kingdom's central bank is the Bank of England, which was established by Act of Parliament and Royal Charter in 1694 and nationalized under the Bank of England Act 1946. The Scottish and Northern Ireland banks issue their own notes but these are largely covered by holdings of Bank of England notes.

The Bank of England holds the main government accounts, acts as registrar of government stocks and as agent of the Government for a number of financial operations. It is also banker to a number of commercial banks. The London clearing banks maintain a substantial proportion of their total cash holdings in the form of balances at the Bank and these are used in the settlement of daily cheque and credit clearings. The Bank has traditionally been responsible for advising the Government on the formulation of monetary policy and for its subsequent execution. A new Bank of England Act, which accorded the Bank statutory operational independence for monetary policy, within agreed government economic targets, received Royal Assent in April 1998, and entered into force on 1 June. The Act provided for the establishment of a Monetary Policy Committee (MPC), with responsibility for analysing and formulating monetary policy within the framework of maintaining price stability and supporting the Government's economic policies. The Treasury was to reserve the right to direct the Bank with respect to monetary decisions in extreme circumstances. The MPC was to comprise the Governor of the Bank, the two newly-created Deputy-Governors, two other Bank officials and four members appointed by the Chancellor of the Exchequer. The Bank's Court of Directors was to review the MPC's procedures and produce an annual report, to be presented to Parliament, under new measures to promote greater accountability and transparency of the Bank's operations. The 1998 Act also transferred, to the Financial Services Authority, the Bank's functions with regard to the supervision of banks.

The commercial banks may be divided into two broad categories: clearing banks and other banks. Clearing banks play the main part in operating the money transmission system throughout the United Kingdom. The other banks comprise accepting houses (taking their name from their business of accepting bills of exchange for payment) and other British-owned banks, overseas-owned banks and consortium banks. As the use of bills of exchange has declined, all accepting houses have assumed the specialist financial services of merchant banks, which include the management of investment trusts, foreign currency trading and company mergers and acquisitions. Since the late 1980s several merchant banks have been incorporated into larger banking organizations to provide a full range of financial, including retail, banking services.

Consortium banks have been formed in the United Kingdom by groups of banks, mostly from overseas, but including some British clearing banks. Initially they were set up to afford shareholders access to the Eurocurrency markets. More recently consortia have been formed as a means of combining institutions from similar geographical areas, when a London operation would be uneconomic for individual banks. Consortium banks are important participants in the major inter-bank markets in sterling and currency deposits and certificates of deposit.

The discount houses are a specialized group of institutions peculiar to London. They raise the greater part of their funds from within the banking sector. These funds are borrowed by the houses at call or short notice (thereby providing the lending banks with a highly liquid interest-bearing investment) and are used to purchase correspondingly liquid assets—mainly Treasury and commercial bills, short-dated government stocks, certificates of deposit, local authority debt, etc. The discount houses are now more generally incorporated as part of the group of banks authorized by the Bank as listed money market institutions under the 1986 Financial Services Act. The United Kingdom's official reserves, comprising gold, convertible currencies and special drawing rights on the International Monetary Fund, are held in the Exchange Equalization Account operated since 1932 by the Bank of England as agent for the Treasury.

The London Gold Market engages in the trading, transporting, refining, melting, assaying and vaulting of gold. The unique feature of the London market is the 'fixing', which determines the price of gold on a twice-daily basis by matching orders from customers and markets throughout the world. In September 1996 the London Commodity Exchange merged with the London International Financial Futures and Options Exchange (LIFFE), which has since become unique as an exchange trading options on individual equities and on financial, agricultural, soft commodity and equity index products. In October 2001 the French-based Euronext security market acquired LIFFE for a sum of £555m.

The building society movement is important both as a medium of savings (the largest in the United Kingdom) and for the finance of house purchase in a country where more than two-thirds of dwellings are owner-occupied. The expansion of building societies into banking was a characteristic of the late 1980s. This trend was furthered in the 1990s with several large building societies converting to banks through public share offers or opting to merge with similar institutions or with retail banks in order to provide a comprehensive range of financial services. In 2001 there were 48 societies registered in the United Kingdom, compared with 190 in 1984. By mid-2005 that number had increased to 63.

National Savings are administered by the Department for National Savings and the Trustee Savings Banks. Through the Department for National Savings the Government administers the National Savings Bank 'investment' and 'ordinary' accounts, National Savings certificates, Premium bonds and other securities, all aimed primarily at the small saver. The outlets for these services are some 16,000 post offices in the United Kingdom.

THE UNITED KINGDOM

There are certain institutions set up to provide finance for specific purposes; the more important of these are the 3i Group PLC (which provides investment capital to companies which do not have ready access to capital markets) and the Agricultural Mortgage Corporation (loans against mortgages on agricultural property).

The main capital market is the London Stock Exchange, and since October 1986 the volume of business transacted has greatly expanded with the introduction of the Stock Exchange Automated Quotations system (SEAQ), an electronic trading system which allows off-floor trading. The process of automating trading was completed in October 1997 when the Stock Exchange Electronic Trading Service (Sets) became operational.

The United Kingdom has a highly developed insurance market, located primarily in London. Lloyd's, with its unique system of underwriting syndicates (of which there were 62 in January 2005) has an international reputation for marine, aviation and reinsurance, as well as a significant share of the British motor insurance market. Much of Lloyd's premium income comes from outside the United Kingdom through Lloyd's 169 accredited brokers. There are over 800 authorized insurance companies in the United Kingdom, dealing with life and general insurance, as well as international reinsurance.

BANKING

(cap. = capital; p.u. = paid up; auth. = authorized; m. = million; dep. = deposits; res = reserves; subs. = subscribed; brs = branches; amounts in pounds sterling)

The 1987 Banking Act replaced the Banking Act of 1979 under which a statutory framework for the supervision of the banking sector was established. The 1987 Act defines new criteria by which an institution can be authorized to accept deposits. The administrative authority for the Act is the Bank of England.

The Financial Ombudsman Service: South Quay Plaza, 183 Marsh Wall, London, E14 9SR; tel. (20) 7964-1000; fax (20) 7964-1001; e-mail complaint.info@financial-ombudsman.org.uk; internet www.financial-ombudsman.org.uk; f. 2001 to replace The Personal Investment Authority Ombudsman Bureau, The Insurance Ombudsman Bureau, The Office of the Banking Ombudsman, The Office of the Building Societies Ombudsman, The Office of the Investment Ombudsman, The Securities and Futures Authority Complaints Bureau, The Financial Services Authority Complaints Unit and The Personal Insurance Arbitration Service; Chair. CHRISTOPHER KELLY; Chief Ombudsman WALTER MERRICKS.

Central Bank

Bank of England: Threadneedle St, London, EC2R 8AH; tel. (20) 7601-4444; fax (20) 7601-5460; e-mail enquiries@bankofengland.co.uk; internet www.bankofengland.co.uk; inc by Royal Charter in 1694, and nationalized by Act of Parliament on 1 March 1946; amended by 1998 Bank of England Act (see above); the Government's banker and on its behalf manages the note issue; also the bankers' bank; mem. of the Cheque and Credit Clearing Company; cash centre at Leeds and Debden; agencies in Belfast, Birmingham, Bristol, Cambridge, Cardiff, Exeter, Glasgow, Greater London, Leeds, Liverpool, Manchester, Newcastle upon Tyne, Nottingham and Southampton; capital stock amounting to 14.6m. is held by the Treasury; cap. 15m., res 151m., dep. 13,450m. (Feb. 2005); Gov. MERVYN KING; Dep. Govs Sir JOHN GIEVE, RACHEL LOMAX.

Principal Banks Incorporated in the United Kingdom

Abbey National Plc: Abbey National House, 2 Triton Sq., Regent's Place, London, NW1 3AN; tel. (870) 607-6000; e-mail feedback@abbey.com; internet www.abbey.com; f. 1944; as Abbey National Building Society; current status assumed in 1989; Banco Santander Central Hispano, SA; total assets 128,189m. (Jan. 2005); Chair. Lord BURNS; Chief Exec. FRANCISCO GÓMEZ-ROLDÁN; 793 brs.

Alliance & Leicester PLC: Carlton Park, Narborough, Leicester, LE19 0AL; tel. (116) 201-1000; fax (116) 200-4040; internet www.alliance-leicester.co.uk; fmrly a building society; assumed banking status in 1997; broad-based financial services provider incl. business banking services through wholly-owned subsidiary, Girobank; total assets 58,982m. (Dec. 2005); Chair. Sir DEREK HIGGS; Chief Exec. RICHARD A. PYM; 254 brs.

Barclays Bank PLC: 1 Churchill Place, London, E14 5HP; tel. (20) 7699-5000; fax (20) 7699-3463; internet www.barclays.co.uk; inc. 1896; clearing bank; principal operating co of Barclays PLC (group holding co); cap. 1,642m., res 6,332m., dep. 329,815m. (Dec. 2003); Group Chair. Sir MATTHEW BARRETT; Chief Exec. JOHN VARLEY; 3,500 brs in 76 countries.

Cheltenham and Gloucester PLC (C&G): Barnett Way, Gloucester, GL4 3RL; tel. (1452) 372372; fax (1452) 373955; internet www.cheltglos.co.uk; f. 1850; as Cheltenham and Gloucester Benefit Building Society; current name and status assumed in 1995; mem. of the Lloyds TSB Group; cap. 508.3m., res 1,725.7m., dep. 15,180m. (Dec. 2003); Chair. ROGER F. BURDEN; Man. Dir JON PAIN.

Clydesdale Bank PLC: 30 St Vincent Pl., Glasgow, G1 2HL; tel. (141) 248-7070; fax (141) 204-0828; internet www.cbonline.co.uk; f. 1838; wholly-owned by National Australia Bank Ltd; clearing bank; total assets 22,250.2m. (Dec. 2005); Chair. MALCOLM WILLIAMSON; Chief Exec. (Europe) LYNNE PEACOCK; 307 brs.

The Co-operative Bank PLC: POB 101, 1 Balloon St, Manchester, M60 4EP; tel. (161) 832-3456; fax (161) 829-4475; e-mail customerservice@co-operativebank.co.uk.; internet www.co-operativebank.co.uk; f. 1872; clearing bank; total assets 11,365.1m. (Jan. 2006); Chair. GRAHAM R. BENNETT; Chief Exec. DAVID ANDERSON; 119 brs.

Coutts and Co: 440 Strand, London, WC2R 0QS; tel. (20) 7753-1000; fax (20) 7753-1050; internet www.coutts.com; f. 1692; private clearing bank and asset management; parent co Royal Bank Of Scotland Group PLC; cap. 41.3m., dep. 7,390.8m. (Dec. 1996); Chair. Earl of Home DAVID DOUGLAS-HOMEEarl of Home ; Chief Exec. SARAH DEAVES; 22 brs.

HBOS PLC: POB 5, The Mound, Edinburgh, EH1 1YZ; tel. (131) 442-7777; fax (131) 243-5537; e-mail pressoffice@hbosplc.com; internet www.hbosplc.com; f. 2001 following merger between Bank of Scotland and Halifax PLC; total assets £540,873m. (Dec. 2005); Chair. Lord STEVENSON; Chief Exec. ANDY HORNBY.

HSBC Bank PLC: 8 Canada Sq., London, E14 5HQ; tel. (20) 7991-8888; internet www.hsbc.co.uk; f. 1836; from 1992 subsidiary of HSBC Holdings PLC; clearing bank; cap. 797m., res 12,226m., dep. 186,303m. (Dec. 2003); Chair. STEPHEN GREEN; Group Chief Exec. MICHAEL GEOGHEGAN; 1,700 brs.

Lloyds TSB Bank PLC: 25 Gresham St, London, EC2V 7HN; tel. (20) 7626-1500; fax (20) 7661-4790; internet www.lloydstsb.co.uk; f. 1995 by merger of Lloyds Bank PLC (f. 1765) and TSB Group (f. 1973), name changed as above June 1999; clearing bank; total assets 309,754m. (Dec. 2005); Chair. Sir VICTOR BLANK; Chief Exec. ERIC DANIELS; 2,500 brs.

Lloyds TSB Scotland PLC: POB 177, Henry Duncan House, 120 George St, Edinburgh, EH2 4LH; tel. (131) 225-4555; fax (131) 220-4217; internet www.lloydstsb.com/scotland; f. 1983 as TSB Bank Scotland PLC following merger of four Scottish TSBs; wholly-owned subsidiary of Lloyds TSB Group PLC; cap. 75m., dep. 5,376.28m. (Dec. 2003); Chair. Prof. EWAN BROWN; Chief Exec. S. RICE; 184 brs.

National Westminster Bank PLC: 135 Bishopsgate, London, EC2M 3UR; tel. (20) 7375-5000; fax (20) 7375-5050; internet www.natwest.co.uk; f. 1968; clearing bank; acquired by The Royal Bank of Scotland Group PLC in 2000; cap. 2,159m., res 1,686m., dep. 130,617m. (Dec. 2002); Chair. Sir GEORGE ROSS MATHEWSON; Group Chief Exec. FRED GOODWIN; 2,416 brs.

Northern Bank: Donegall Sq. West, Belfast, BT1 6JS; tel. (28) 9024-5277; fax (28) 9024-1790; internet www.nbonline.co.uk; f. 1960; owned by Danske Bank Group; Chair. PETER STRAARUP; Chief Exec. DON PRICE.

Northern Rock PLC: Northern Rock House, Gosforth, Tyne and Wear, NE3 4PL; tel. (845) 600-8401; fax (191) 284-8470; internet www.northernrock.co.uk; current status assumed in 1997; total assets 65,654.2 (Jan. 2005); Chair. Dr MATT W. RIDLEY; Chief Exec. ADAM APPLEGARTH.

The Royal Bank of Scotland PLC: POB 31, 36 St Andrew Sq., Edinburgh, EH2 2YB; tel. (131) 556-8555; fax (131) 557-6565; internet www.rbs.co.uk; f. 1985 as result of merger of Royal Bank of Scotland and Williams & Glyn's Bank. The Royal Bank of Scotland (est. by Royal Charter in 1727) merged with National Commercial Bank of Scotland in 1969. Williams & Glyn's Bank was result of merger of Glyn Mills & Co (est. 1753) and Williams Deacon's Bank (est. 1771); subsidiary of The Royal Bank of Scotland Group PLC; clearing bank; cap. 769m., res 19,482m., dep. 346,260m. (Dec. 2003); Chair. Sir TOM MCKILLOP; Group Chief Exec. Sir FRED GOODWIN; 680 brs.

Standard Chartered Bank: 1 Aldermanbury Sq., London, EC2V 7SB; tel. (20) 7280-7500; fax (20) 7280-7791; internet www.standardchartered.com; f. 1853; holding co Standard Chartered PLC; total assets US $215,096m. (Dec. 2005); Chair. BRYAN SANDERSON; Chief Exec. MERVYN DAVIES; 570 brs.

Ulster Bank Ltd: 11–16 Donegall Sq. East, Belfast, BT1 5UB; tel. (28) 9027-6000; fax (28) 9027-5661; e-mail morrow@ulsterbank.com; internet www.ulsterbank.co.uk; f. 1836; mem. of Royal Bank of Scotland Group; cap. 209m., res 56m., dep. 10,640m. (Dec. 2002); Chair. Dr ALAN GILLESPIE; Group Chief Exec. CORMAC MCCARTHY; 269 brs.

Woolwich Ltd: Watling St, Bexleyheath, Kent, DA6 7RR; tel. (20) 8298-5000; fax (1322) 555621; internet www.woolwich.co.uk; f. 1847 as Woolwich Building Society; assumed present status in July 1997; acquired by Barclays PLC in October 2000; cap. 150.6m. res 60.7m., dep. 35,828.9m. (Dec. 2001); Chair. MATTHEW BARRETT; Man. Dir IVO PHILIPPS (acting); 412 brs.

Yorkshire Bank PLC: 20 Merrion Way, Leeds, LS2 8NZ; tel. (113) 247-2000; fax (113) 242-0733; internet www.ybonline.co.uk; f. 1859; wholly owned by National Australia Bank Ltd; cap. 251.1m., res 91.4m., dep. 7,691.1m. (Sept. 2002); Chief Exec. (Europe) LYNNE PEACOCK; COO CHRIS BAYLISS; 260 brs.

Principal Merchant Banks

Ansbacher & Co Ltd: 2 London Bridge, London, SE1 9RA; tel. (20) 7089-4700; fax (20) 7089-4850; e-mail info@ansbacher.com; internet www.ansbacher.com; f. 1894; cap. 50.0m., res 1.3m., total assets 671.6m. (June 2003); Chair. MICHAEL BROGAN; Man. Dir HUGH TITCOMB.

Barclays Capital: 5 The North Colonnade, Canary Wharf, London, E14 4BB; tel. (20) 7623-2323; e-mail publisher@barclayscapital.com; internet www.barcap.com; investment banking division of Barclays PLC; Chief Exec. ROBERT E. DIAMOND, Jnr.

Brown, Shipley & Co Ltd: Founders Court, London, EC2R 7HE; tel. (20) 7606-9833; fax (20) 7282-3274; e-mail marketing@brownshipley.com; internet www.brownshipley.com; f. 1810; acquired by Kredietbank SA Luxembourgeoise in 1992; cap. issued 86.4m., dep. 573.7m. (Dec. 2001); Chair. DAVID ROUGH; Man. Dir S. BLANEY.

Butterfield Private Bank: 99 Gresham St, London, EC2V 7NG; tel. (20) 7776-6700; fax (20) 7776-6701; e-mail info@butterfieldprivatebank.co.uk; internet www.butterfieldprivatebank.co.uk; f. 1919; acquired by Bermuda's Bank of Butterfield in February 2004; cap. 5.4m., res 13.1m., dep. 453.3m. (March 2003); Pres. and CEO ALAN R. THOMPSON.

Cater Allen Ltd: 9 Nelson St, Bradford, BD1 5AN; tel. (114) 228-2407; e-mail info@caterallen.co.uk; internet www.caterallen.co.uk; f. 1981 by merger of Cater Ryder and Co Ltd (f. 1816) and Allen Harvey and Ross Ltd (f. 1888); acquired by Abbey National Treasury Services in 1997; cap. 100m., dep. 1,411.6m. (Dec. 2001); Chair. MALCOLM MILLINGTON; Man. Dir RICHARD J. DUNN.

Citibank International PLC: POB 49930, London, SE5 7XT; tel. (20) 7500-5000; fax (20) 7500-1695; internet www.citibank.co.uk; f. 1972; cap. 1,410.3m., res 200.6m., dep. 16,694.6m. (Dec. 2003); Chair. and Chief Exec. WILLIAM J. MILLS.

Citigroup: Victoria Plaza, 111 Buckingham Palace Rd, London, SW1W 0SB; tel. (20) 7721-2000; fax (20) 7222-7062; f. 2000; by merger of J. Henry Schroder & Co Ltd and Salomon Smith Barney, changed name to above in 2001; Chairs CHARLES McVEIGH, DAVID CHALLEN.

Close Brothers Ltd: 10 Crown Pl., London, EC2A 4FT; tel. (20) 7426-4000; e-mail enquiries@closebrothers.co.uk; internet www.closebrothers.co.uk; cap. 82.5m., res 165.9m., dep. 2,618.0m. (July 2004); Chair. DAVID SCHOLEY; Chief Exec. C. D. KEOGH.

DB UK Bank Ltd: 23 Great Winchester St, London, EC2P 2AX; tel. (20) 7545-8000; fax (20) 7545-6155; internet www.deutsche-bank.com; f. 1838; as George Peabody & Co; renamed Morgan Grenfell & Co Ltd in 1910; present name adopted 2004; acquired by Deutsche Bank Group in 1989; cap. 385m., res 2.8m., dep. 5,224.4m. (Dec. 2003); Chair. D. H. THOMAS; Chief Exec. D. G. PENFOLD; 1 br.

Dresdner Kleinwort Wasserstein Ltd: 20 Fenchurch St, London, EC3P 3DB; tel. (20) 7623-8000; fax (20) 7623-4069; e-mail website@drkw.com; internet www.drkw.com; wholly owned subsidiary of Kleinwort Benson Group; ultimate holding co Dresdner Bank AG; share cap. 548.6m., res 67.5m., dep. 963,012m. (Dec. 2003); Chair. ALLAN C. D. YARROW.

Investec Bank (UK) Ltd: 2 Gresham St, London, EC2V 7QP; tel. (20) 7597-4000; fax (20) 7597-4070; internet www.investec.com; f. 1977 as Allied Arab Bank Ltd, name changed as above 1997; acquired Guinness Mahon & Co Ltd 1998; cap. 354.0m., res 37.4m., dep. 2,991.3m. (March 2004); Chair. H. HERMAN; CEO B. FRIED.

N M Rothschild & Sons Limited: New Court, St Swithin's Lane, London, EC4P 4DU; tel. (20) 7280-5000; fax (20) 7929-1643; internet www.rothschild.com; f. 1804; cap. 50.0m., res 81.2m., dep. 2,947.9m. (March 2004). Chair. Baron DAVID DE ROTHSCHILD; 5 brs.

Singer & Friedlander Ltd: 21 New St, Bishopsgate, London, EC2M 4HR; tel. (20) 7623-3000; fax (20) 7623-2122; internet www.singer-friedlander.com; f. 1907; cap. 50m., res 2.9m., dep. 1,652.4m. (Dec. 2003); Chair. PAUL SELWAY-SWIFT; Chief Exec. TONY SHEARER; 2 brs.

UBS Limited: 1 Finsbury Ave, London, EC2M 2PP; tel. (20) 7567-8000; fax (20) 7568-4800; internet www.ubs.co.uk; Chair. MARCEL OSPEL; CEO PETER WUFFLI.

West Merchant Bank Ltd: 33–36 Gracechurch St, London, EC3V 0AX; tel. (20) 7623-8711; fax (20) 7626-1610; f. 1964 as Standard Chartered Merchant Bank Ltd; renamed Chartered West LB Ltd in 1990; present name adopted 1993; subsidiary of Westdeutsche Landesbank Girozentrale; cap. 90.0m., res 7.3m., dep. 5,148.4m. (Dec. 1997); Chief Exec. RICHARD BRIANCE.

Consortium Banks

Joint ventures are recognized banks or licensed deposit-taking institutions which are registered in the United Kingdom and which have more than one bank among their principal shareholders, a majority of which are foreign.

Ahli United Bank (UK) PLC: 7 Baker St, London, W1U 8EG; tel. (20) 7487-6500; fax (20) 7487-6808; internet www.ahliunited.com; f. 1966 as United Bank of Kuwait, changed name as above in 2003; owned by 11 Kuwaiti banks; cap. US $200.1m., res $6.2m., dep. $2,187.4m. (Dec. 2003); Chair. FAHAD MAZIAD AR-RAJAAN; Group Chief Exec. ADL A. AL-LABBAN.

Anglo-Romanian Bank: 3 Finsbury Sq., London, EC2A 1AE; tel. (20) 7826-4200; fax (20) 7628-1274; e-mail enquiries@anglorom.com; internet www.anglorom.com; f. 1973; owned by Banca Comerciala Romana; cap. 21.8m., dep. 39.1m. (Dec. 2003); Chair. M.G. WOOD; CEO THOMAS BUTLER.

British Arab Commercial Bank Ltd: 8–10 Mansion House Pl., London, EC4N 8BJ; tel. (20) 7648-7777; fax (20) 7600-3318; internet www.bacb.co.uk; f. 1972; owned by HSBC Bank Middle East, Libyan Arab Foreign Bank (Libya), Bank Al-Maghrib (Morocco), Central Bank of Egypt, Banque Extérieure d'Algérie, Rafidain Bank (Iraq); cap. 83.6m., dep. 1,275.0m. (Dec. 2005); Chair. ANDREW DIXON; Chief Exec. MICHAEL PARR.

Saudi International Bank (Al-Bank Al-Saudi Al-Alami Ltd): 1 Knightsbridge, London, SW1X 7XS; tel. (20) 7259-3456; fax (20) 7259-6060; f. 1975; total assets 2,991m. (Dec. 1998); Chair. Dr KHALED AL-FAYEZ; CEO MATTHEW C. SNYDER.

Savings Organization

National Savings & Investments: 375 Kensington High St, London, W14 8SD; tel. (845) 9645-0000; e-mail pressoffice@nationalsavings.co.uk; internet www.nsandi.com; govt department and Executive Agency of the Chancellor of the Exchequer; money placed in National Savings and Investments is used by the Treasury to help cost-effectively manage the national debt and contribute towards the Government's financing needs; Chief Exec. ALAN COOK; Man. Dir KAREN JONES.

National Savings regional offices: Glasgow, G58 1SB; Durham, DH99 1NS; Blackpool, FY3 9ZW; Lytham St Annes, Lancs., FY0 1YN; f. 1861; Chief Exec. PETER BAREAU.

Credit Institutions

ECI Ventures: 1st Floor, Brettenham House, Lancaster Pl., London, WC2E 7EN; tel. (20) 7606-1000; fax (20) 7240-5050; e-mail ecivmail@eciv.co.uk; internet www.eciv.co.uk; f. 1976; advises and manages ECI5 (£78m. UK Ltd Partnership), ECI6 (£100m. UK Ltd Partnership) and EC17 (£175m. UK Ltd Partnership) to provide equity capital, mainly for management buyouts; Chair. Sir JOHN BANHAM.

3i Group PLC: 91 Waterloo Rd, London, SE1 8XP; tel. (20) 7928-3131; fax (20) 7928-0058; e-mail general_enquiries@3i.com; internet www.3i.com; f. 1945 as the Industrial and Commercial Finance Corpn Ltd by the English and Scottish clearing banks, renamed Finance for Industry PLC, renamed Investors in Industry Group PLC in 1983, and renamed as above in 1988; provides long-term and permanent financial advice; cap. 292.1m., res 1,757.1m., dep. 1,385.0m. (March 1995); Chair. Baroness HOGG; Chief Exec. PHILIP YEA.

Banking and Finance Organizations

Association of Foreign Banks (AFB): 1 Bengal Ct, London, EC3V 9DD; tel. (20) 7283-8300; fax (20) 7283-8302; e-mail secretariat@foreignbanks.org.uk; internet www.foreignbanks.org.uk; f. 1947 in 1996 incorporated mems of the British Overseas and Commonwealth Banks' Association (f. 1917); changed name as above in 2002; approx. 185 mem. banks; Chair. MARK GARVIN; Man. Dir JOHN TREADWELL.

Banking Code Standards Board: 6 Frederick's Pl., London, EC2R 8BT; tel. (845) 230-9694; fax (20) 7600-6914; e-mail helpline@bcsb.org.uk; internet www.bankingcode.org.uk; fmrly Independent Review Body; self-regulatory body which monitors and enforces Banking Code (for personal customers) and Business Banking Code; Chair. GERARD LEMOS; Chief Exec. SEYMOUR FORTESCUE.

British Bankers' Association: Pinners Hall, 105–108 Old Broad St, London, EC2N 1EX; tel. (20) 7216-8800; fax (20) 7216-8811; internet www.bba.org.uk; f. 1919; Pres. Sir PETER MIDDLETON; Chief Exec. IAN MULLEN.

Building Societies Association (BSA): 3 Savile Row, London, W1S 3BP; tel. (20) 7347 0655; fax (20) 7734 6416; e-mail web.master@

THE UNITED KINGDOM

bsa.org.uk; internet www.bsa.org.uk; represents building societies; Chair. PHILIP WILLIAMSON; Dir-Gen. ADRIAN COLES.

The Chartered Institute of Bankers in Scotland: Drumsheugh House, 38B Drumsheugh Gardens, Edinburgh, EH3 7SW; tel. (131) 473-7777; fax (131) 473-7788; e-mail info@ciobs.org.uk; internet www.ciobs.org.uk; f. 1875; professional examinations, courses and publications; approx. 13,000 mems; Pres. DAVID THORBURN; Chief Exec. Prof. CHARLES W. MUNN.

Institute of Financial Services: 4–9 Burgate Lane, Canterbury, CT1 2XJ; tel. (1227) 818609; fax (1227) 784331; e-mail customerservices@ifslearning.com; internet www.ifslearning.com; f. 1879 as the Chartered Institute of Bankers, current name adopted 2001; a registered charity and one of the leading bodies for the provision of financial education and life-long career support to both the financial services industry and the wider community; Pres. MICHAEL KIRKWOOD; Chief Exec. GAVIN SHREEVE.

Investment Management Association: 65 Kingsway, London, WC2B 6TD; tel. (20) 7831-0898; fax (20) 7831-9575; e-mail ima@investmentuk.org; internet www.investmentuk.org; f. 2002 following merger of the Association of Unit Trusts and Investment Funds and the Fund Managers Association; represents the UK unit trust and investment management industry; Chair. SIMON DAVIES; Chief Exec. RICHARD SAUNDERS.

London Investment Banking Association: 6 Frederick's Pl., London, EC2R 8BT; tel. (20) 7796-3606; fax (20) 7796-4345; e-mail liba@liba.org.uk; internet www.liba.org.uk; mems c. 50 British and foreign banks and securities houses; Chair. A. C. D. YARROW; Dir-Gen. JONATHAN TAYLOR.

London Money Market Association: 2 Gresham St, London, EC2V 7QP; tel. (20) 7597-4485; fax (20) 7597-4491; e-mail rvardy@investec.co.uk; internet www.lmma.co.uk; f. 1998; mems include international banks, securities houses, building societies; 26 mems; Chair. IAN MAIR; Dep. Chair. R. J. VARDY, I. FOX.

Northern Ireland Bankers' Asscn: Stokes House, 17–25 College Sq. East, Belfast, BT1 6DE; tel. (28) 9032-7551; fax (28) 9033-1449; e-mail sharon@niba.demon.co.uk; Chair. A. HEGARTY; Sec. WILLIAM MCALISTER.

STOCK EXCHANGE

The London Stock Exchange: 10 Paternoster Sq., London, EC4M 7LS; tel. (20) 7797-1000; fax (20) 7334-8916; e-mail infosales@londonstockexchange.com; internet www.londonstockexchange.com; had its origins in the coffee houses of 17th-century London, when those wishing to invest or raise money bought and sold shares in joint-stock companies; formally constituted in 1802. By 1890 an association of stock exchanges had been formed. In 1965 a process of federation began which led to the amalgamation of all stock exchanges in the UK and Ireland in 1973. The Irish Stock Exchange officially ended its 200-year-old association with the London Stock Exchange in December 1995. In November 1986, the Exchange became a private limited company and member firms became shareholders of the Exchange with one vote each. In 1991, the 1875 Deed of Settlement was superseded as the Exchange's constitutional document by a Memorandum and Articles of Association. The governing council of the Exchange was replaced with a Board of Directors drawn from the Exchange's executive and from its customer and user base. In October 1996 an electronic quotation and trading system was introduced, which allowed for off-floor trading and direct global access to share price information. The old mandatory separation of the functions of brokers and jobbers and the system of fixed minimum commissions were then abolished. The Exchange regulates the operation of the market-place as a Recognised Investment Exchange and also regulates listed companies as the United Kingdom's Competent Authority for Listing. The Official List is the Exchange's main market. In June 1995 an Alternative Investment Market (AIM) was established to accommodate smaller and expanding companies. In March 2000 the member institutions voted to end 199 years of mutual status and convert the London Stock Exchange into a public limited company. Its own shares were fully listed from July 2001. In September 2000 plans for the proposed merger with its German counterpart, Deutsche Börse, were abandoned following a hostile takeover bid for the Exchange by the Swedish technology company Om Gruppen. The bid was rejected by shareholders in November. In October 2002 the London Stock Exchange opened a new derivatives trading platform, which would enable private investors to purchase covered warrants. In March 2006 there were 3,141 companies listed on the London Stock Exchange, including 1,336 UK-listed companies, 324 overseas-listed companies and 1,473 companies on AIM; Chair. CHRIS GIBSON-SMITH; Chief Exec. CLARA FURSE.

SUPERVISORY BODIES

In May 1997 the Government announced its intention to establish a single statutory supervisory authority for the financial services sector. Accordingly, in November the then Securities and Investment Board was transformed into a new Financial Services Authority (FSA). From 1 June 1998, when the new Bank of England Act entered into force, the FSA incorporated the Board of Banking Supervision, which advises on supervision policy. The FSA also assumed responsibility for the supervision of insurance companies from the Department of Trade and Industry. On 1 December 2001 the FSA formally incorporated the activities of the existing regulatory bodies as well as the Building Societies Commission, the Registry of Friendly Societies and the Friendly Societies Commission following the enactment of the 2000 Financial Services and Markets Act.

The Financial Ombudsman Service: (see p. 4548).

Financial Services Authority: 25 The North Colonnade, Canary Wharf, London, E14 5HS; tel. (20) 7066-1000; fax (20) 7066-1099; e-mail consumerhelp@fsa.gov.uk; internet www.fsa.gov.uk; f. 1998; to undertake supervision, regulation and market surveillance of all areas of financial activity as defined under the 2000 Financial Services and Markets Act; single statutory regulator responsible for regulating deposit taking, insurance and investment business, promoting public understanding of the financial system and reducing financial crime; Chair. CALLUM MCCARTHY; Chief Exec. JOHN TINER.

Securities Institute: Centurion House, 24 Monument St, London, EC3R 8AQ; tel. (20) 7645-0600; fax (20) 7645-0601; e-mail info@sii.org.uk; internet www.securities-institute.org.uk; f. 1992; aims to promote professional standards and ethics in the securities industry; Chair. SCOTT DOBBIE; Chief Exec. SIMON CULHANE.

INSURANCE

Lloyd's: 1 Lime St, London, EC3M 7HA; tel. (20) 7327-1000; fax (20) 7327-5229; e-mail helpdesk@lloyds.com; internet www.lloyds.com; had its origins in the coffee house opened c. 1688 by Edward Lloyd and was incorporated by Act of Parliament (Lloyd's Acts 1871–1982); an international insurance market and Society of Underwriters, consisting of about 1,497 individual and (since January 1994) 714 corporate members grouped into syndicates who accept risks on the basis of unlimited and limited liability respectively; business is effected through firms of accredited Lloyd's brokers who alone are permitted to place insurances either directly or by way of reinsurance, and some three-quarters of the annual premium income is from overseas business. Lloyd's accounts for approximately half of all international insurance premiums underwritten in the London market. The Lloyd's market is administered by the Corporation of Lloyd's through an 18-member Council, mostly elected by and from the underwriting membership. Lloyd's is regulated by the Financial Services Authority (FSA), under the Financial Services and Markets Act of 2000; capacity to accept insurance premiums of more than £14,800m. in 2006; 62 syndicates underwriting insurance in 2006, covering all classes of business from more than 190 countries and territories world-wide; Council Chair. Lord LEVENE; CEO RICHARD WARD.

Principal Insurance Companies

Allianz Cornhill Insurance PLC: 57 Ladymead, Guildford, Surrey, GU1 1DB; tel. (1483) 568161; fax (1483) 300952; internet www.allianzcornhill.co.uk; part of the Allianz Group (Germany); f. 1905, fmrly Cornhill Insurance Co PLC; Chair. Lord WALKER OF WORCESTER; Chief Exec. ANDREW TORRANCE.

AVIVA PLC: POB 420, St Helen's, 1 Undershaft, London, EC3P 3DQ; tel. (20) 7283-2000; e-mail aviva_info@aviva.com; internet www.aviva.com; formed by merger of Commercial Union and General Accident in 1998; merged with The Norwich Union PLC in 2000; renamed as above in 2002; Chair. Lord SHARMAN OF REDLYNCH; Group Chief Exec. RICHARD HARVEY.

AXA Insurance PLC: 1 Aldgate, London, EC3N 1RE; tel. (20) 7702-3109; fax (20) 7369-3909; e-mail customerservice@axa-insurance.co.uk; internet www.axa-insurance.co.uk; f. 1903; Chair. ANTHONY HAMILTON; CEO PETER HUBBARD.

Britannic Assurance PLC: 1 Wythall Green Way, Wythall, Birmingham, B47 6WG; tel. (870) 887-0001; fax (870) 887-0002; internet www.britannicassurance.co.uk; f. 1866; owned by Resolution PLC, which was created in September 2005 through the merger of Resolution Life Group Ltd and Britannic Group PLC; Chair. MALCOLM WILLIAMSON; Group CEO PAUL THOMPSON.

Co-operative Insurance Society Ltd (CIS): Miller St, Manchester, M60 0AL; tel. (161) 832-8686; fax (161) 837-4048; e-mail cis@cis.co.uk; internet www.cis.co.uk; f. 1867; Chair. SIMON BUTLER; Chief Exec. DAVID ANDERSON.

Direct Line Group: 3 Edridge Rd, Croydon, Surrey, CR9 1AG; tel. (20) 8686-3313; fax (20) 8681-0512; internet www.directline.com; wholly owned by The Royal Bank of Scotland; Man. Dir CHRIS MOAT.

Ecclesiastical Insurance Office PLC: Beaufort House, Brunswick Rd, Gloucester, GL1 1JZ; tel. (1452) 528533; fax (1452) 423557;

THE UNITED KINGDOM

e-mail marketing@eigmail.com; internet www.ecclesiastical.co.uk; f. 1887; Chair. NICHOLAS SEALY; Chief Exec. GRAHAM V. DOSWELL.

Equitable Life Assurance Society: Walton St, Aylesbury, Buckinghamshire, HP21 7QW; tel. (845) 603-6771; fax (1296) 386383; e-mail enquiries@equitable.co.uk; internet www.equitable.co.uk; f. 1762; Chair. VANNI TREVES; Chief Exec. CHARLES THOMSON.

Friends Provident PLC: 100 Wood St., London, EC2V 7AN; tel. (870) 608-3678; fax (1306) 740150; internet www.friendsprovident.co.uk; f. 1832; Chair. Sir ADRIAN A. MONTAGUE; Group CEO KEITH SATCHELL.

Legal and General Group PLC: Temple Court, 11 Queen Victoria St, London, EC4N 4TP; tel. (20) 7528-6200; fax (20) 7528-6222; internet www.legalandgeneral.com; f. 1836; Group CEO TIM BREEDON; Group Chair. ROB MARGETTS; Sec. DAVID BINDING.

  Legal and General Insurance Ltd: Temple Court, 11 Queen Victoria St, London, EC4N 4TP; tel. (20) 7528-6200; fax (20) 7528-6222; f. 1946 as British Commonwealth Insurance Co; Chair. TIM BREEDON; Sec. JEAN WEBB.

Liverpool Victoria Friendly Society Ltd: County Gates, Bournemouth, BH1 2NF; tel. (1202) 292333; fax (1202) 292253; internet www.liverpoolvictoria.co.uk; f. 1843; Chair. and Acting Chief Exec. JOHN WOOLHOUSE.

MGM Assurance (Marine and General Mutual Life Assurance Society): MGM House, Heene Rd, Worthing, Sussex, BN11 2DY; tel. (1903) 836067; fax (1903) 836004; e-mail customercentre@mgm-assurance.co.uk; internet www.mgm-assurance.co.uk; f. 1852; Chair. CHRISTOPHER REEVES; CEO GERARD P. N. HEALY.

The National Farmers Union Mutual Insurance Society Ltd: Tiddington Rd, Stratford upon Avon, Warwicks., CV37 7BJ; tel. (1789) 204211; fax (1789) 298992; internet www.nfumutual.co.uk; f. 1910; Chair. Sir DON CURRY; Group Chief Exec. IAN GEDEN.

Pearl: The Pearl Centre, Lynch Wood, Peterborough, Cambridgeshire, PE2 6FY; tel. (1733) 470470; fax (1733) 472300; internet www.pearl.co.uk; f. 1864; part of Pearl Group Limited; present name adopted Dec. 2003; Chair. JONATHAN EVANS.

Phoenix Life Group: 101 Old Hall Stm Liverpoolm L69 3HS; tel. (151) 703-5000; fax (151) 703-5001; internet www.phoenixlifegroup.co.uk; f. 2005 by a merger of Swiss Life UK and Royal & Sun Alliance UK life business; Exec. Chair. CLIVE COWDREY; Group CEO PAUL THOMPSON.

The Prudential Assurance Co Ltd: 250 Euston Rd, London, NW1 2PQ; tel. (20) 7405-9222; fax (20) 7548-3465; internet www.prudential.co.uk; f. 1848; holding co: Prudential Corpn PLC; Group Chair. Sir DAVID CLEMENTI; CEO MARK TUCKER.

Royal and Sun Alliance Insurance Group PLC: 9/F, 1 Plantation Place, 30 Venture St, London EC3M 3BD; tel. (20) 7111-7000; internet www.royalsunalliance.com; f. 1996 by merger of Royal Insurance Holdings PLC (f. 1845) and Sun Alliance Group PLC; Chair. JOHN NAPIER; CEO ANDY HASTE.

Royal Liver Assurance Ltd: Royal Liver Bldg, Pier Head, Liverpool, L3 1HT; tel. (151) 236-1451; fax (151) 236-2122; internet www.royal-liver.com; f. 1850; Chair. DAVID E. WOODS; Chief Exec. STEVE BURNETT.

The Royal London Mutual Insurance Society Ltd: 55 Gracechurch St, London, EC3V ORL; tel. (870) 850-6070; fax (1625) 605400; e-mail info@royal-london.co.uk; internet www.royal-london.co.uk; f. 1861; Chair. HUBERT REID; CEO MIKE YARDLEY.

  Scottish Life: POB 54, 19 St Andrew Sq., Edinburgh, EH2 1YE; tel. (131) 456-7777; fax (131) 456-7880; e-mail enquiries@scottishlife.co.uk; internet www.scottishlife.co.uk; f. 1881; re-inc as a Mutual Company 1968; became part of Royal London Mutual Insurance Society in July 2001; Chief Exec. BRIAN DUFFIN.

Scottish Widows' PLC: POB 17036, 69 Morrison St, Edinburgh, EH3 8YF; tel. (131) 655-6000; fax (131) 662-4053; internet www.scottishwidows.co.uk; f. 1815 as Scottish Widows' Fund and Life Assurance Society; name changed as above March 2000 following acquisition by Lloyds TSB; Chair. GAVIN GEMMELL; CEO ARCHIE KANE.

The Standard Life Assurance Co: Standard Life House, 30 Lothian Rd, Edinburgh EH1 2DH; tel. (845) 606-0100; e-mail customer_service@standardlife.com; internet www.standardlife.co.uk; f. 1825; assets under management £96,000m. (Feb. 2004); Chair. Sir BRIAN STEWART; Group CEO SANDY CROMBIE.

Swiss Re UK Ltd: 30 St Mary Axe, London, EC3A 8EP; tel. (20) 7933-3000; fax (20) 7933-5000; internet www.swissre.com; CEO (life and health) CRAIG THORNTON; CEO (property and casualty) PAUL MARTIN.

Wesleyan Assurance Society: Colmore Circus, Birmingham, B4 6AR; tel. (121) 335-3487; fax (121) 200-2971; internet www.wesleyan.co.uk; f. 1841; Chair. LOWRY D. MACLEAN; CEO CRAIG ERRINGTON.

Zurich Assurance Ltd: UK Life Centre, Station Rd, Swindon, SN1 1EL; tel. (1793) 511227; fax (1793) 506625; internet www.zurich.co.uk; f. 1872; Group Chair. MANFRED GENTZ; CEO JAMES SCHIRO.

Insurance Associations

Associated Scottish Life Offices: POB 25, Craigforth, Stirling, FK9 4UE; tel. (1786) 448844; fax (1786) 450427; constituted 1841 as an Association of General Managers of Scottish Offices transacting life assurance business; 7 full mems; Chair. GRAHAM POTTINGER; Dep. Chair. DAVID HENDERSON.

Association of British Insurers: 51 Gresham St, London, EC2V 7HQ; tel. (20) 7600-3333; fax (20) 7696-8999; e-mail info@abi.org.uk; internet www.abi.org.uk; f. 1985; principal trade association for insurance companies; protection, promotion, and advancement of the common interests of all classes of insurance business; c. 420 mems; Chair. KEITH SATCHELL; Dir-Gen. STEPHEN HADDRILL.

British Insurance Brokers' Association (BIBA): BIBA House, 14 Bevis Marks, London, EC3A 7NT; tel. (870) 950-1790; fax (20) 7626-9676; e-mail enquiries@biba.org.uk; internet www.biba.org.uk; f. 1977; Chair. MAX TAYLOR; Chief Exec. ERIC GALBRAITH.

Chartered Insurance Institute: 20 Aldermanbury, London, EC2V 7HY; tel. (20) 8989-8464; fax (20) 8530-3052; e-mail customer.serv@cii.co.uk; internet www.cii.co.uk; f. 1897; inc 1912; approx. 90,000 mems; Pres. MICHAEL BRIGHT; Dir-Gen. Dr A. SCOTT.

Fire Protection Association: London Rd, Moreton-in-Marsh, Gloucestershire, GL56 0RH; tel. (1608) 812500; fax (1608) 812501; e-mail fpa@thefpa.co.uk; internet www.thefpa.co.uk; f. 1946; Man. Dir JON O'NEILL.

Fire and Risk Services: BRE Garston, Watford, Herts., WD25 9XX; tel. (1923) 664000; fax (1923) 664910; e-mail enquiries@brecertification.co.uk; internet www.bre.co.uk/frs; f. 1986; incorporates the Loss Prevention Council, fire division of the Building Research Establishment; Dir CHRIS BROADBENT.

Insurance Institute of London: 20 Aldermanbury, London, EC2V 7HY; tel. (20) 7600-1343; fax (20) 7600-6857; e-mail iil.london@cii.co.uk; internet www.iilondon.co.uk; f. 1907; Pres. STEVE MCGILL.

International Underwriting Association (IUA): London Underwriting Centre, 3 Minster Ct, Mincing Lane, London, EC3R 7DD; tel. (20) 7617-4444; fax (20) 7617-4440; e-mail info@iua.co.uk; internet www.iua.co.uk; f. 1998 as Scottish Widows' Fund and Life Assurance Society; Chair. TONY MEDNIUK; Chief Exec. DAVE J. MATCHAM.

Advisory Body

The Financial Ombudsman Service: (see p. 4548).

Associations of Actuaries

Faculty of Actuaries: 18 Dublin St, Edinburgh, EH1 3PP; tel. (131) 240-1300; fax (131) 240-1313; e-mail faculty@actuaries.org.uk; internet www.actuaries.org.uk; f. 1856; 13 Honorary Fellows; Pres. HARVIE W. BROWN; Chief Exec. CAROLINE INSTANCE.

Institute of Actuaries: Staple Inn Hall, High Holborn, London, WC1V 7QJ; tel. (20) 7632-2100; fax (20) 7632-2111; e-mail institute@actuaries.org.uk; internet www.actuaries.org.uk; f. 1848; Royal Charter 1884; 13,000 mems; Pres. MICHAEL POMERY; Sec.-Gen. CAROLINE INSTANCE.

Trade and Industry

GOVERNMENT AGENCIES

Advisory, Conciliation and Arbitration Service (Acas): Brandon House, 180 Borough High St, London, SE1 1LW; tel. (20) 7210-3613; fax (20) 7210-3615; internet www.acas.org.uk; f. 1975; an independent organization, under the direction of a council comprising employers, trade union representatives and independent members, appointed by the Sec. of State for Trade and Industry. The service aims to improve organizations and working life through good employment relations. Acas provides collective conciliation, arbitration, mediation, advisory, training and information services, and conciliates in individual employment rights issues; Chair. RITA DONAGHY; Chief Exec. JOHN TAYLOR.

Central Arbitration Committee: POB 51547, London, SE1 1ZG; tel. (20) 7904-2300; fax (20) 7904-2301; e-mail enquiries@cac.gov.uk; internet www.cac.gov.uk; f. 1976 as an independent body under the 1975 Employment Protection Act, in succession to Industrial Court/Industrial Arbitration Board; arbitrates on trade disputes; adjudicates on disclosure of information complaints; determines claims for statutory trade union recognition under the 1999 Employment Relations Act and certain issues relating to the implementation of the European Works Council; Chair. Sir MICHAEL BURTON; Chief Exec. GRAEME CHARLES.

THE UNITED KINGDOM — Directory

Charity Commission for England and Wales: Harmsworth House, 13–15 Bouverie St, London, EC4Y 8DP; tel. (845) 300-0218; fax (20) 7674-2300; e-mail enquiries@charitycommission.gsi.gov.uk; internet www.charitycommission.gov.uk; statutory organization responsible for the regulation of registered charities; Chief Exec. ANDREW HIND; Chair. GERALDINE PEACOCK.

Competition Appeal Tribunal: Victoria House, Bloomsbury Pl., London, WC1A 2EB; tel. (20) 7979-7979; fax (20) 7979-7978; e-mail info@catribunal.org.uk; internet www.catribunal.org.uk; f. 2002; a specialist tribunal established to hear certain cases in the sphere of British competition and economic regulatory law; hears appeals against decisions of the Office of Fair Trading and the regulators in the telecommunications, electricity, gas, water, railways and air traffic services sectors under the Competition Act of 1998; reviews decisions of the Office of Fair Trading, the Competition Commission and the Secretary of State made pursuant to the merger control and market investigation provisions of the Enterprise Act of 2002; also has jurisdiction, under the Competition Act of 1998, to award damages in respect of infringements of EC or British competition law and, under the Communications Act of 2003, to hear appeals against decisions of OFCOM; headed by the President and a panel of Chairmen and 19 mems with backgrounds in law, economics, business, accountancy and regulation who sit with the President or a mem. of the panel of Chairmen to hear cases; Pres. Sir CHRISTOPHER BELLAMY; Registrar CHARLES DHANOWA.

Competition Commission: Victoria House, Southampton Row, London, WC1B 4AD; tel. (20) 7271-0100; fax (20) 7271-0367; e-mail info@competition-commission.gsi.gov.uk; internet www.competition-commission.org.uk; conducts in-depth inquiries into mergers, markets and the regulation of the major regulated industries; f. 1998; Chair (vacant); Chief Exec. MARTIN STANLEY.

Competition Service: Victoria House, Bloomsbury Pl., London, WC1A 2EB; tel. (20) 7979-7979; fax (20) 7979-7978; e-mail info@catribunal.org.uk; internet www.catribunal.org.uk; f. 2003 under the Enterprise Act 2002; a corporate and executive non-departmental public body, whose purpose is to fund and provide support services to the Competition Appeal Tribunal; Mems Sir CHRISTOPHER BELLAMY, JANET RUBIN, CHARLES DHANOWA; Dir of Operations JEREMY STRAKER.

Countryside Agency: John Dower House, Crescent Pl., Cheltenham, Gloucestershire, GL50 3RA; tel. (1242) 521381; fax (1242) 584270; e-mail info@countryside.gov.uk; internet www.countryside.gov.uk; f. 1999; advises Government and acts on issues relating to the environmental, economic and social well-being of the English countryside; Chair. STUART BURGESS; Chief Exec. GRAHAM GARBUTT.

Environment Agency: Rio House, Waterside Drive, Aztec West, Almondsbury, Bristol, BS32 4UD; tel. (8708) 506506; e-mail enquiries@environment-agency.gov.uk; internet www.environment-agency.gov.uk; f. 1996; incorporated former National Rivers Authority; Chair. of Board Sir JOHN HARMAN; Chief Exec. BARONESS YOUNG OF OLD SCONE.

Food Standards Agency: Aviation House, 125 Kingsway, London, WC2B 6NH; tel. (20) 7276-8000; fax (20) 7276-8004; e-mail helpline@foodstandards.gsi.gov.uk; internet www.food.gov.uk; f. 2000; Chair. DEIRDRE HUTTON; Chief Exec. Dr JON BELL.

Forestry Commission: Silvan House, 231 Corstorphine Rd, Edinburgh, EH12 7AT; tel. (131) 334-0303; fax (131) 334-3047; e-mail enquiries@forestry.gsi.gov.uk; internet www.forestry.gov.uk; government department responsible for protecting and expanding the forests and woodlands of England, Scotland and Wales and increasing their value to society and the environment; implements the Government's forestry policy within the framework of the Forestry Acts, administers the Woodland Grant Scheme, controls tree-felling through the issue of licences, administers plant health regulations to protect woodlands against tree-pests and diseases, and conducts research; responsible for the management of the national forests; Chair. Lord CLARK OF WINDEMERE; Dir-Gen. TIM ROLLINSON.

Health and Safety Executive: Caerphilly Business Park, Caerphilly, CF83 3GG; tel. (845) 345-0055; fax (845) 408-9566; e-mail hse.infoline@natbrit.com; internet www.hse.gov.uk; Chief Exec. GEOFFREY PODGER.

Learning and Skills Council: Cheylesmore House, Quinton Road, Coventry, CV1 2WT; tel. (845) 019-4170; fax (24) 7682-3675; e-mail info@lsc.gov.uk; internet www.lsc.gov.uk; Chair. CHRIS BANKS; Chief Exec. MARK HAYSOM.

National Audit Office: 157–197 Buckingham Palace Rd, London, SW1W 9SP; tel. (20) 7798-7000; fax (20) 7798-7070; e-mail enquiries@nao.gsi.gov.uk; internet www.nao.org.uk; audits the financial statements of all government departments and agencies, certain public bodies and international organizations; the Comptroller and Auditor-General is responsible for controlling receipts into, and issues from, the Consolidated and National Loans Funds and reports to Parliament on value for money issues or on important issues arising from the financial statements; Comptroller and Auditor-General Sir JOHN BOURN.

National Consumer Council: 20 Grosvenor Gdns, London, SW1W 0DH; tel. (20) 7730-3469; fax (20) 7730-0191; e-mail info@ncc.org.uk; internet www.ncc.org.uk; f. 1975; 12 mems; Chair. LARRY WHITTY.

Office of Fair Trading: Fleetbank House, 2–6 Salisbury Sq., London, EC4Y 8JX; tel. (20) 7211-8000; fax (20) 7211-8800; e-mail enquiries@oft.gsi.gov.uk; internet www.oft.gov.uk; f. 1973; monitors consumer affairs, competition policy, consumer credit, estate agencies, etc.; Chair. PHILIP COLLINS; Chief Exec. JOHN FINGLETON.

oneLondon: 28 Park St, London, SE1 9EQ; tel. (20) 7403-0300; fax (20) 7248-8877; e-mail info@one-london.com; internet www.one-london.com; f. 2001 following merger between London Enterprise Agency and Greater London Enterprise; Chair. AMANDA JORDAN; Man. Dir PETER THACKWRAY.

Postal Services Commission (Postcomm): Hercules House, 6 Hercules Rd, London, SE1 7DB; tel. (20) 7593-2100; fax (20) 7593-2142; e-mail info@psc.gov.uk; internet www.psc.gov.uk; f. 2000 under the Postal Services Act of 2000 to regulate Consignia PLC (formerly the Post Office, but renamed Royal Mail Group PLC in 2002); duties include the introduction of competition, ensuring a universal postal service, licensing postal operators (including Royal Mail) and controlling the uniformity of Royal Mail postal tariffs; Chair. NIGEL STAPLETON; Chief Exec. SARAH CHAMBERS.

Statistics Commission: Artillery House, 11–19 Artillery Row, London, SW1P 1RT; tel. (20) 7273-8008; fax (20) 7273-8019; e-mail statscom@statscom.org.uk; internet www.statscom.org.uk; f. 2000; advises on the quality, quality assurance and priority-setting for National Statistics and on the procedures designed to deliver statistical integrity, to ensure National Statistics are trustworthy and responsive to public needs; Chair. DAVID RHIND; Chief Exec. RICHARD ALLDRITT.

United Kingdom Atomic Energy Authority: Harwell International Business Centre, Didcot, Oxfordshire, OX11 0RA; tel. (1235) 820220; fax (1235) 434452; internet www.ukaea.org.uk; f. 1954; to take responsibility for British research and development into all aspects of atomic energy; separated into AEA Technology, which operated as the Authority's commercial division, and UKAEA; AEA Technology transferred to the private sector in 1996. UKAEA's core task is to manage the decommissioning of reactors and other facilities used for the nuclear research and development programme. It also carries out fusion research. These activities are conducted at sites at Windscale (Cumbria), Dounreay (Caithness), Harwell and Culham (Oxfordshire) and Winfrith (Dorset); Chair. BARBARA THOMAS; Chief Exec. DIPESH SHAH.

DEVELOPMENT ORGANIZATIONS

Economic Research Institute of Northern Ireland (ERINI): Pearl Assurance House, 1–3 Donegall Sq. East, Belfast, BT1 5HB; tel. (28) 9023-2125; fax (28) 9033-1250; e-mail info@niec.org.uk; internet www.niec.org.uk; f. 2004 to replace the Northern Ireland Economic Council (f. 1977); provides independent advice to the Government on the development of economic policy for Northern Ireland; 15 mems representing trade union, employer, and independent interests; Chair. JOHN BEATH; Dir VICTOR HEWITT.

Invest Northern Ireland (Invest NI): Bedford Sq., Bedford St, Belfast, BT1 4NN; tel. (28) 9023-9090; fax (28) 9043-6536; e-mail info@investni.com; internet www.investni.com; f. 2002 to assume responsibility for the activities of the Industrial Development Board for Northern Ireland, the Local Enterprise Development Unit, the Industrial Research and Technology Unit, the Company Development Programme and the business support activities of the Northern Ireland Tourist Board; Invest NI is the main economic development agency in Northern Ireland and, sponsored by the Dept of Enterprise, Trade and Investment, aims to accelerate economic growth in Northern Ireland; Chair. STEPHEN KINGON; Chief Exec. LESLIE MORRISON.

London First: 1 Hobhouse Court, Suffolk St, London, SW1Y 4HH; tel. (20) 7665-1500; fax (20) 7665-1501; e-mail staff@london-first.co.uk; internet www.london-first.co.uk; promotes London as a business centre; Chair. STEPHEN O'BRIEN; Pres. Lord SHEPPARD OF DIDGEMERE.

Overseas Development Institute: 111 Westminster Bridge Rd, London, SE1 7JD; tel. (20) 7922-0300; fax (20) 7922-0399; e-mail media@odi.org.uk; internet www.odi.org.uk; Chair. Baroness JAY; Dir SIMON MAXWELL.

Scottish Enterprise: 5 Atlantic Quay, 150 Broomielaw, Glasgow, G2 8LU; tel. (141) 248-2700; fax (141) 221-3217; e-mail network.helpline@scotent.co.uk; internet www.scottish-enterprise.com; economic development agency for lowland Scotland; Chair. Sir JOHN WARD; Chief Exec. JACK PERRY.

THE UNITED KINGDOM
Directory

CHAMBERS OF COMMERCE

British Chambers of Commerce (BCC): 65 Petty France, London, SW1H 9EU; tel. (20) 7654-5800; fax (20) 7654-5819; e-mail info@britishchambers.org.uk; internet www.chamberonline.co.uk; f. 1860; in January 1993 subsumed National Chamber of Trade (f. 1897); represents the new Approved Chamber Network in the United Kingdom (comprising 70 Chambers at August 2003); Pres. BILL MIDGLEY; Dir-Gen. DAVID FROST.

International Chamber of Commerce (ICC) United Kingdom: 12 Grosvenor Pl., London, SW1X 7HH; tel. (20) 7838-9363; fax (20) 7235-5447; e-mail info@iccorg.co.uk; internet www.iccuk.net; f. 1920; British affiliate of the world business org.; Dir ANDREW HOPE.

London Chamber of Commerce and Industry: 33 Queen St, London, EC4R 1AP; tel. (20) 7248-4444; fax (20) 7489-0391; e-mail lc@londonchamber.co.uk; internet www.londonchamber.co.uk; Pres. MICHAEL CASSIDY; Chief Exec. COLIN STANBRIDGE.

Northern Ireland Chamber of Commerce and Industry: Chamber of Commerce House, 22 Great Victoria St, Belfast, BT2 7BJ; tel. (28) 9024-4113; fax (28) 9024-7024; e-mail mail@northernirelandchamber.com; internet www.nicci.co.uk; f. 1783; Pres. Lord RANA; Chief Exec. FRANKN HEWITT; 4,000 mems.

INDUSTRIAL AND TRADE ASSOCIATIONS

Aluminium Federation: Broadway House, Calthorpe Rd, Five Ways, Birmingham, B15 1TN; tel. (870) 138-9714; fax (121) 456-2274; e-mail alfed@alfed.org.uk; internet www.alfed.org.uk; f. 1962; Pres. JOAN CHESNEY; Sec.-Gen. WILL SAVAGE.

Association of the British Pharmaceutical Industry: 12 Whitehall, London, SW1A 2DY; tel. (20) 7930-3477; fax (20) 7747-1411; e-mail abpi@abpi.org.uk; internet www.abpi.org.uk; f. 1930; Pres. VINCENT LAWTON; Dir-Gen. Dr RICHARD BARKER.

Association of Manufacturers of Domestic Appliances: Rapier House, 40–46 Lamb's Conduit St, London, WC1N 3NW; tel. (20) 7405-0666; fax (20) 7405-6609; e-mail info@amdea.org.uk; internet www.amdea.org.uk; f. 1969; 35 mem. cos; Dir-Gen. PETER CARVER.

BFM (British Furniture Manufacturers): 30 Harcourt St, London, W1H 2AA; tel. (20) 7724-0851; fax (20) 7706-1924; e-mail info@bfm.org.uk; internet www.bfm.org.uk; merged in January 1993 with BFM Exhibitions and BFM Exports; Man. Dir ROGER MASON.

British Beer and Pub Association: Market Towers, 1 Nine Elms Ln., London, SW8 5NQ; tel. (20) 7627-9191; fax (20) 7627-9123; e-mail enquiries@beerandpub.com; internet www.beerandpub.com; f. 1904; 73 mems; trade association for British brewing industry and multiple pub chains; Chief Exec. ROB HAYWARD.

British Cable Association: 37A Walton Rd, East Molesey, Surrey, KT8 0DH; tel. (20) 8941-4079; fax (20) 8783-0104; e-mail admin@bcauk.org; internet www.bcauk.org; f. 1958; fmrly British Cable Makers' Confederation; Sec.-Gen. PETER SMEETH.

British Cement Association: Riverside House, 4 Meadows Business Park, Station Approach, Blackwater, Camberley, Surrey, GU17 9AB; tel. (1276) 608700; fax (1276) 608701; e-mail info@bca.org.uk; internet www.bca.org.uk; Chair. M. J. LODGE; Chief Exec. MIKE GILBERT.

British Ceramic Confederation: Federation House, Station Rd, Stoke-on-Trent, Staffs., ST4 2SA; tel. (1782) 744631; fax (1782) 744102; e-mail bcc@ceramfed.co.uk; internet www.ceramfed.co.uk; f. 1984; 150 mems; Chief Exec. KEVIN FARRELL.

British Clothing Industry Association: 5 Portland Pl., London, W1B 1PW; tel. (20) 7636-7788; fax (20) 7636-7515; e-mail bcia@dial.pipex.com; f. 1980; Chair. JAMES MCADAM; Dir JOHN R. WILSON.

British Electrotechnical and Allied Manufacturers' Association (BEAMA Ltd): Westminster Tower, 3 Albert Embankment, London, SE1 7SL; tel. (20) 7793-3000; fax (20) 7793-3003; e-mail info@beama.org.uk; internet www.beama.org.uk; f. 1905 as British Electrical and Allied Manufacturers' Association Ltd, present name from 2002; 460 mems; Pres. and Chair. RICHARD DICK; CEO DAVID DOSSETT.

British Exporters' Association: Broadway House, Tothill St, London, SW1H 9NQ; tel. (20) 7222-5419; fax (20) 7799-2468; e-mail bexamail@aol.com; internet www.bexa.co.uk; Pres. Sir RICHARD NEEDHAM; Chair. SUE WALTON; Dir HUGH BAILEY.

British Footwear Association: 3 Burystead Place, Wellingborough, Northants, NN8 1AH; tel. (1933) 229005; fax (1933) 225009; e-mail info@britfoot.com; internet www.britfoot.com; Chief Exec. NIALL CAMPBELL.

British Glass: 9 Churchill Way, Chapeltown, Sheffield, S35 2PY; tel. (114) 290-1850; fax (114) 290-1851; e-mail info@britglass.co.uk; internet www.britglass.co.uk; over 100 mems; Dir-Gen. DAVID WORKMAN.

British Hospitality Association: Queen's House, 55/56 Lincoln's Inn Fields, London, WC2A 3BH; tel. (845) 880-7744; fax (20) 7404-7799; e-mail info@bha.org.uk; internet www.bha-online.org.uk; f. 1907; Pres. RAMON PAJARES; Chief Exec. ROBERT COTTON.

British Non-Ferrous Metals Federation: Broadway House, 60 Calthorpe Rd, Five Ways, Birmingham, B15 1TN; tel. (121) 456-6100; fax (121) 456-2274; e-mail bnfmf@copperuk.org.uk; Dir DAVID PARKER.

The British Precast Concrete Federation Ltd: 60 Charles St, Leicester, LE1 1FB; tel. (116) 253-6161; fax (116) 251-4568; e-mail info@britishprecast.org; internet www.britishprecast.org; f. 1918; approx. 125 mems; Chief Exec. MARTIN A. CLARKE.

British Printing Industries Federation: Farringdon Point, 29–35 Farringdon Rd, London, EC1M 3JF; tel. (870) 240-4085; fax (20) 7405-7784; e-mail cicely.brown@bpif.org.uk; internet www.britishprint.com; f. 1900; 2,500 mems; Pres. DOMINIC WALSH; Chief Exec. MICHAEL JOHNSON.

British Rubber Manufacturers' Association: 6 Bath Pl., Rivington St, London, EC2A 3JE; tel. (20) 7457-5040; fax (20) 7972-9008; e-mail mail@brma.co.uk; internet www.brma.co.uk; f. 1968; Pres. JAMES RICKARD; Dir A. J. DORKEN.

The Carpet Foundation: MFC Complex, 60 New Rd, Kidderminster, Worcs., DY10 1AQ; tel. (1562) 755568; fax (1562) 865405; internet www.comebacktocarpet.com; 18 mems; Chair. JOHN DUNCAN; Chief Exec. MIKE HARDIMAN.

CBI (The Voice of Business): Centre Point, 103 New Oxford St, London, WC1A 1DU; tel. (20) 7379-7400; fax (20) 7240-1578; internet www.cbi.org.uk; f. 1965 as the Confederation of British Industry, name changed as above in 2001; acts as a national point of reference for all seeking views of industry and is recognized internationally as the representative organization of British industry and management; advises the Government on all aspects of policy affecting the interests of industry; has a direct corporate membership employing more than 4m., and a trade association membership representing more than 6m. of the workforce; Pres. JOHN SUNDERLAND; Dir-Gen. Sir DIGBY JONES.

Chemical Industries Association: King's Buildings, Smith Sq., London, SW1P 3JJ; tel. (20) 7834-3399; fax (20) 7834-4469; e-mail enquiries@cia.org.uk; internet www.cia.org.uk; Pres. ALISTAIR STEEL; Dir-Gen. JUDITH HACKITT.

Construction Confederation: 55 Tufton St, London, SW1P 3QL; tel. (870) 8989090; fax (870) 8989095; e-mail enquiries@thecc.org.uk; internet www.constructionconfederation.co.uk; f. 1878; 5,000 mems; Chair. PETER COMMINS; Chief Exec. STEPHEN RATCLIFFE.

Dairy UK: 93 Baker St, London, W1U 6QQ; tel. (20) 7486-7244; fax (20) 7487-4734; e-mail info@dairy.org; internet www.dairyuk.org; f. 1933; Pres. DAVID CURRY; Dir-Gen. JIM BEGG.

Electrical Contractors' Association: ESCA House, 34 Palace Court, London, W2 4HY; tel. (20) 7313-4800; fax (20) 7221-7344; e-mail electricalcontractors@eca.co.uk; internet www.eca.co.uk; f. 1901; Pres. BILL WRIGHT; Dir DAVID R. J. POLLOCK.

Energy Networks Association: 18 Stanhope Pl., London, W2 2HH; tel. (20) 7706-5100; e-mail info@energynetworks.org; internet www.electricity.org.uk; f. 2003; represents British gas and electricity transmission and distribution licence holders; Chair. MARK HORSLEY; Chief Exec. NICK GOODALL.

Engineering Employers' Federation: Broadway House, Tothill St, London, SW1H 9NQ; tel. (20) 7222-7777; fax (20) 7222-2782; e-mail enquiries@eef-fed.org.uk; internet www.eef.org.uk; f. 1896; 5,700 mems through 14 associations; Pres. ALAN WOOD; Dir-Gen. MARTIN TEMPLE.

Farmers' Union of Wales: Llys Amaeth, Plas Gogerddan, Aberystwyth, Ceredigion, SY23 3BT; tel. (1970) 820820; fax (1970) 820821; e-mail headoffice@fuw.org.uk; internet www.fuw.org.uk; f. 1955; 14,000 mems; Pres. GARETH VAUGHAN.

Food and Drink Federation: 6 Catherine St, London, WC2B 5JJ; tel. (20) 7836-2460; fax (20) 7836-0580; e-mail generalenquiries@fdf.org.uk; internet www.fdf.org.uk; Dir-Gen. MELANIE LEECH.

Glass and Glazing Federation: 44–48 Borough High St, London, SE1 1XB; tel. (870) 042-4255; fax (870) 042-4266; e-mail info@ggf.org.uk; internet www.ggf.org.uk; f. 1977; trade organization for employers and cos in the flat glass, glazing, home improvement, plastic and window film industries; Chief Exec. NIGEL REES.

Institute of Export: Export House, Minerva Business Park, Lynch Wood, Peterborough, PE2 6FT; tel. (1733) 404400; fax (1733) 404444; e-mail institute@export.org.uk; internet www.export.org.uk; f. 1935; professional educational organization devoted to the development of British export trade and the interests of those associated with it; more than 6,000 mems; Pres. Sir MARTIN LAING; Chair. ANDY NEMES; Dir-Gen. MARIA MCCAFFERY.

Labour Relations Agency: 2-8 Gordon St, Belfast, BT1 2LG; tel. (28) 9032-1442; fax (28) 9033-0827; e-mail info@lra.org.uk; internet www.lra.org.uk; f. 1976; provides an impartial and confidential employment relations service to those engaged in industry,

www.europaworld.com

THE UNITED KINGDOM

commerce and the public services in Northern Ireland; provides advice on good employment practices and assistance with the development and implementation of employment policies and procedures; also active in resolving disputes through its conciliation, mediation and arbitration services.

National Association of British and Irish Millers Ltd: 21 Arlington St, London, SW1A 1RN; tel. (20) 7493-2521; fax (20) 7493-6785; e-mail info@nabim.org.uk; internet www.nabim.org.uk; trade assoc. of the British flour milling industry; f. 1878; Dir-Gen. ALEXANDER WAUGH; Sec. NIGEL BENNETT.

National Farmers' Union: Agriculture House, 164 Shaftesbury Ave, London, WC2H 8HL; tel. (20) 7331-7200; fax (20) 7331-7313; e-mail nfu@nfuonline.com; internet www.nfuonline.com; f. 1904 as Lincolnshire Farmers' Union, adopted present name in 1908; Pres. TIM BENNETT; Dir-Gen. RICHARD MACDONALD.

National Metal Trades Federation: Savoy Tower, 77 Renfrew St, Glasgow, G2 3BZ; tel. (141) 332-0826; fax (141) 332-5788; e-mail alex.shaw@nmtf.org.uk; internet www.nmtf.org.uk; Sec. ALEX SHAW.

Northern Ireland Hotels Federation: Midland Bldg, Whitla St, Belfast, BT15 1JP; tel. (28) 9035-1110; fax (28) 9035-1509; e-mail office@nihf.co.uk; internet www.nihf.co.uk; Pres. RODNEY WATSON; Chief Exec. JANICE GAULT.

Northern Ireland Textiles and Apparel Assen: 5C The Square, Hillsborough, BT26 6AG; tel. (28) 9268-9999; fax (28) 9268-9968; e-mail info@nita.co.uk; internet www.nita.co.uk; f. 1993; Dir LINDA MACHUGH; 30 mems.

Northern Ireland Trade Asscns Ltd: 10 Arthur St, Belfast, BT1 4DG; secretariat to 14 trade asscns; Dir LINDA MACHUGH.

Producers Alliance for Cinema and Television (PACT) Ltd: 2nd Floor, 1 Procter St, London, WC1V 6DW; tel. (20) 7067-4367; fax (20) 7067-4377; e-mail enquiries@pact.co.uk; internet www.pact.co.uk; film and TV producers; represents 1,000 companies; Chief Exec. JOHN MCVAY; Chair. ANDREW ZEIN.

Quarry Products Association: Gillingham House, 38–44 Gillingham St, London, SW1V 1HU; tel. (20) 7963-8000; fax (20) 7963-8001; e-mail info@qpa.org; internet www.qpa.org; fmrly British Ready Mixed Concrete Assoc., and the British Aggregate Construction Materials Industry Ltd; Chair LYNDA THOMPSON; Dir SIMON VAN DER BYL.

Scottish Building: Carron Grange, Carrongrange Ave, Stenhousemuir, FK5 3BQ; tel. (1324) 555550; fax (1324) 555551; e-mail info@scottish-building.co.uk; internet www.scottish-building.co.uk; Pres. DAVID SMITH; Gen. Man. DOUGLAS FERGUS.

Scottish Enterprise—Textiles: Apex House, 99 Haymarket Terrace, Edinburgh, EH12 5DH; tel. (131) 313-6243; fax (131) 313-4231; internet www.scottish-textiles.co.uk; present name since 1991.

Sea Fish Industry Authority (Seafish): 18 Logie Mill, Logie Green Rd, Edinburgh, EH7 4HG; tel. (131) 558-3331; fax (131) 558-1442; e-mail seafish@seafish.co.uk; internet www.seafish.org; non-departmental public body sponsored by the four United Kingdom Government fisheries departments and funded by a levy on seafood; works with all sectors of the British seafood industry to satify consumers, raise standards, improve efficiency and secure a sustainable future; Chair. ANDREW DEWAR-DURIE; Chief Exec. JOHN RUTHERFORD.

Society of British Aerospace Companies Ltd: Unit 7, Salamanca Sq, 9 Albert Embankment, London, SE1 7SP; tel. (20) 7091–4500; fax (20) 7091-4545; e-mail post@sbac.co.uk; internet www.sbac.co.uk; f. 1916; national trade association for the British aerospace industry; Pres. CHRIS GEOGHEGAN; Dir-Gen. Dr SALLY HOWES.

Society of Motor Manufacturers and Traders: Forbes House, Halkin St, London, SW1X 7DS; tel. (20) 7235-7000; fax (20) 7235-7112; e-mail smmt@smmt.co.uk; internet www.smmt.co.uk; Pres. ROGER PUTNAM; Chief Exec. CHRISTOPHER MACGOWAN.

The Sugar Bureau: Duncan House, Dolphin Sq., London, SW1V 3PW; tel. (20) 7828-9465; fax (20) 7821-5393; e-mail info@sugar-bureau.co.uk; internet www.sugar-bureau.co.uk; represents sugar companies in the UK, provides technical, educational and consumer information about sugar and health; Dir Dr R.C. COTTRELL.

Timber Trade Federation: Clareville House, 26/27 Oxendon St, London, SW1Y 4EL; tel. (20) 7839-1891; fax (20) 7930-0094; e-mail ttf@ttf.co.uk; internet www.ttf.co.uk; Chief Exec. JOHN WHITE.

Ulster Chemists' Asscn: 73 University St, Belfast, BT7 1HL; tel. (28) 9032-0787; fax (28) 9031-3737; e-mail adrienne@ulster-chemists.abelgratis.com; internet www.uca.org.uk; f. 1901; promotion and protection of interests of community pharmacies in Northern Ireland; Pres. PATRICK LANE.

Ulster Farmers' Union: Dunedin, 475 Antrim Rd, Belfast, BT15 3DA; tel. (28) 9037-0222; fax (28) 9037-1231; e-mail info@ufuhq.com; internet www.ufuni.org; f. 1918; Pres. CAMPBELL TWEED; Chief Exec. CLARKE BLACK; 12,500 mems.

United Kingdom Petroleum Industry Association: 9 Kingsway, London, WC2B 6XF; tel. (20) 7240-0289; fax (20) 7379-3102; e-mail info@ukpia.com; internet www.ukpia.com; Pres. DAVE BLAKEMORE; Dir-Gen. CHRIS HUNT.

EMPLOYERS' ASSOCIATIONS

British Retail Consortium: 2nd Floor, 21 Dartmouth St, London, SW1H 9BP; tel. (20) 7854-8900; fax (20) 7854-8901; e-mail info@brc.org.uk; internet www.brc.org.uk; f. 1975; represents retailers; Dir-Gen. KEVIN HAWKINS; Man. Dir JEREMY BEADLES.

Chartered Management Institute: Management House, Cottingham Rd, Corby, NN17 1TT; tel. (1536) 204222; fax (1536) 201651; e-mail enquiries@managers.org.uk; internet www.managers.org.uk; f. 1992 as the Institute of Management by amalgamation of British Institute of Management (f. 1947) and Institution of Industrial Managers (f. 1931); changed name as above in 2002; represents 71,000 individual mems and 450 corporate members; Pres. Sir PAUL JUDGE; Chief Exec. MARY CHAPMAN.

Federation of Small Businesses: Sir Frank Whittle Way, Blackpool Business Park, Blackpool, Lancashire FY4 2FE; tel. (1253) 336000; fax (1253) 348046; e-mail membership@fsb.org.uk; internet www.fsb.org.uk; f. 1974; represents the interests of British small businesses and the self employed; 185,000 mems; Policy Chair. JOHN WALKER.

Institute of Directors: 116 Pall Mall, London, SW1Y 5ED; tel. (20) 7766-8888; fax (20) 7766-8822; e-mail enquiries@iod.com; internet www.iod.com; f. 1903; 53,000 mems; Chair. CHRISTOPHER BEALE; Dir-Gen. MILES TEMPLEMAN.

UTILITIES

Electricity

Regulatory Authorities

Office of Gas and Electricity Markets (Ofgem): 9 Millbank, London, SW1P 3GE; tel. (20) 7901-7000; fax (20) 7901-7066; internet www.ofgem.gov.uk; f. 1999 following merger of Offer and Ofgas; regulates the gas and electricity industries in England, Scotland and Wales and aims to promote the interests of all gas and electricity customers by promoting competition and regulating monopolies; Chair. Sir JOHN MOGG; Chief Exec. ALISTAIR BUCHANAN.

Northern Ireland Authority for Energy Regulation: Queens House, 10–18 Queens Street, Belfast, BT1 6ED; tel. (28) 9031-1575; e-mail ofreg@nics.gov.uk; internet ofreg.nics.gov.uk; independent public body to regulate the electricity and natural gas industries in Northern Ireland; Chief Exec. DOUGLAS MCILDOON.

Principal Electricity Companies

British Energy PLC: Systems House, Alba Campus, Livingston, EH54 7EG; tel. (1506) 408700; fax (1506) 408888; e-mail john.mcnamara@british-energy.com; internet www.british-energy.com; Chair. Sir ADRIAN MONTAGUE; Chief Exec. BILL COLEY.

CE Electric UK: 98 Aketon Rd, Castleford, WF10 5DS; tel. (1977) 605934; fax (1977) 605944; internet www.ceelectricuk.com; wholly owned subsidiary of MidAmerican Energy Holdings Company; delivers electricity to 3.6m. homes in the North East of England, Yorkshire and Humberside; Dir J. M. FRANCE.

Central Networks: Herald Way, Pegasus Business Park, East Midlands Airport, Castle Donnington, DE74 2TU; tel. (1332) 393415; internet www.central-networks.co.uk; Propr Eon; formerly East Midlands Electricity PLC; merged with Midlands Electricity PLC in 2004 and name changed to above; Man. Dir BOB TAYLOR.

EDF Energy: 40 Grosvenor Pl., London, SW1X 7GN; tel. (20) 7242-9050; e-mail info@edfenergy.com; internet www.edfenergy.com; supplies electricity and gas through London Energy, SWEB Energy and Seeboard Energy; Chair. DANIEL CAMUS; Chief Exec. VINCENT DE RIVAZ.

Green Energy (UK) PLC: 190 Strand, London, WC2 8JN; e-mail newconnections@greenenergy.uk.com; internet www.greenenergy.uk.com; Chair. Sir PETER THOMPSON; CEO DOUGLAS STEWART.

National Grid PLC: 1–3 Strand, London, WC2N 5EH; tel. (20) 7004-3000; fax (20) 7004-3004; internet www.nationalgrid.com; Chair. Sir JOHN PARKER; CEO ROGER URWIN.

Northern Ireland Electricity PLC: 120 Malone Rd, Belfast, BT9 5HT; tel. (28) 9066-1100; e-mail customercontact@nie.co.uk; internet www.nie.co.uk; holding co Viridian Group; Chair. DIPESH SHAH; Man. Dir HARRY MCCRACKEN.

npower: Oak House, Bridgwater Rd, Warndon, Worcester, WR4 9FP; tel. (1793) 877777; fax (1793) 892525; internet www.npower.com; f. 1999 to combine the electricity and gas supply business of six companies; launched in 2000; CEO DAVID THRELFALL.

Powergen UK: Westwood Way, Westwood Business Park, Coventry, CV4 8LG; tel. (24) 7642-4000; fax (24) 7642-5432; internet www

.powergen.co.uk; wholly owned subsidiary of Eon; CEO Dr PAUL GOLBY.

RWE Npower plc: Windmill Hill Business Park, Whitehill Way, Swindon, Wiltshire, SN5 6PB; tel. (1793) 877777; fax (1793) 893861; internet www.rwenpower.com; Pres. and CEO HARRY ROELS; Group CEO ANDREW DUFF.

Scottish and Southern Energy PLC: Inveralmond House, 200 Dunkeld Rd, Perth, PH1 3AQ; tel. (1738) 456660; fax (1738) 455281; internet www.scottish-southern.co.uk; Chair. Sir ROBERT SMITH; CEO IAN MARCHANT.

ScottishPower PLC: Corporate Office, 1 Atlantic Quay, Glasgow, G2 8SP; tel. (141) 248-8200; fax (141) 248-8300; internet www.scottishpower.plc.uk; Chair. CHARLES MILLER SMITH; CEO PHILIP BOWMAN.

South Wales Electricity PLC: POB 7506, Perth, PH1 3QR; internet (800) 052-5252; internet www.swalec.co.uk; part of Scottish and Southern Energy Group; CEO JOHN ROBINS.

Gas
Regulatory Authorities

Office of Gas and Electricity Markets (Ofgem): see Electricity.
Northern Ireland Authority for Energy Regulation: see Electricity.

Principal Gas Suppliers

British Gas: POB 50, Leeds, LS1 1LE; tel. (113) 382-1022; e-mail house@house.co.uk; internet www.house.co.uk; Chair. Sir ROBERT WILSON; CEO FRANK CHAPMAN.

EDF Energy: see Electricity.

Midlands Gas Ltd: Birchfield House, Joseph St, Oldbury, West Midlands, B69 2AQ; tel. (121) 244-2988; fax (121) 544-2985; subsidiary co of Eon; Man. Dir PETER WEBSTER.

npower: see Electricity.

Phoenix Natural Gas Ltd: 197 Airport Rd West, Belfast, BT3 9ED; tel. (28) 9055-5555; fax (28) 9055-5500; e-mail info@phoenix-natural-gas.com; internet www.phoenix-natural-gas.com; f. 1997; CEO PETER DIXON.

ScottishPower: Energy 1 Atlantic Quay, Glasgow, G2 8SP; tel. (141) 248-8200; fax (141) 248-8300; internet www.scottishpower.plc.uk; Chair. CHARLES MILLER SMITH; CEO PHILIP BOWMAN.

Southern Electric Gas Ltd: Westacott Way, Littlewick Green, Maidenhead, Berks, SL6 3QB; tel. (1628) 822166; fax (1628) 584400; internet www.scottish-southern.co.uk; CEO JIM FORBES.

SWEB Energy: Freepost 3805, Plymouth, PL1 1WN; tel. (800) 365000; fax (01392) 4489111; internet www.sweb.co.uk; Chief Exec. VINCENT DE RIVAZ.

Water
Regulatory Authority

Office of Water Services (Ofwat): Centre City Tower, 7 Hill St, Birmingham, B5 4UA; tel. (121) 625-1300; fax (121) 625-1400; e-mail enquiries@ofwat.gsi.gov.uk; internet www.ofwat.gov.uk; independent economic regulator of the water and sewerage cos in England and Wales; ensures compliance with the functions specified in the Water Industry Act of 1991; protects consumer interests through 10 regional WaterVoice Committees, which represent the interests of water customers and investigate customer complaints, and a WaterVoice Council; Dir-Gen. PHILIP FLETCHER.

Principal Companies

Anglian Water Services Ltd: POB 770, Lincoln, LN5 7WX; tel. (8457) 919155; fax (1480) 326981; internet www.anglianwater.co.uk; Chair. JONSON COX; CEO PETER SIMPSON.

Department for Regional Development (Northern Ireland), Water Service: Northland House, 3 Frederick St, Belfast, BT1 2NR; tel. (8457) 440088; e-mail waterline@waterni.gov.uk; internet www.waterni.gov.uk; Chief Exec. KATHARINE BRYAN.

Mid-Kent Water PLC: Rocfort Rd, Snodland, Kent, ME6 5AH; tel. (1634) 873033; fax (1634) 242764; e-mail water@midkent.co.uk; internet www.midkentwater.co.uk; Hastings Fund Management; Chair. GORDON MAXWELL; Gen. Man. PAUL BUTLER.

Scottish Water: Castle House, 6 Castle Drive, Carnegie Campus, Dunfermline, KY11 8GG; tel. 0845 601 8855; e-mail customer.service@scottishwater.co.uk; internet www.scottishwater.co.uk; f. 2002; Chair. RONNIE MERCER (acting); Chief Exec. Dr JON HARGREAVES.

Severn Trent Water Ltd: 2297 Coventry Rd, Birmingham, B26 3PU; tel. (121) 722-4000; fax (121) 722-4800; internet www.stwater.co.uk; Propr Bouygues; Chair. Sir JOHN EGAN; Chief Exec. COLIN MATTHEWS.

South East Water Ltd: 3 Church Rd, Haywards Heath, West Sussex, RH16 3NY; tel. (845) 301-8045; e-mail contactcentre@southeastwater.co.uk; internet www.southeastwater.co.uk; owned by Macquarie Bank of Australia; Man. Dir MARGARET DEVLIN.

South Staffordshire Water PLC: POB 63, Walsall, WS2 7PJ; tel. (1922) 616239; internet www.south-staffs-water.co.uk; Exec. Chair. DAVID SANKEY; Man. Dir Dr JACK CARNELL.

South West Water Ltd: Peninsula House, Rydon Lane, Exeter, EX2 7HR; tel. (1392) 446688; fax (1392) 434966; internet www.southwestwater.co.uk; part of Pennon Group; Chair. KENNETH HARVEY; CEO ROBERT BATY (until June 2006).

Southern Water PLC: POB 41, Worthing, West Sussex, BN13 3NZ; tel. (1903) 264444; fax (1903) 691435; e-mail customerservices@southernwater.co.uk; internet www.southernwater.co.uk; Man. Dir STEWART DERWENT.

Thames Water Utilities Ltd: POB 286, Swindon, SN38 2RA; tel. (845) 920-0888; internet www.thameswateruk.co.uk; Propr RWE; COO JERRY ENGLAND; Man. Dir WERNER BÖTTCHER.

Three Valleys Water PLC: POB 48, Bishops Rise, Hatfield, Herts, AL10 9HL; tel. (1707) 268111; fax (1707) 277188; internet www.3valleys.co.uk; Chair. Sir ALAN THOMAS; Man. Dir PETER DARBY.

United Utilities PLC: Dawson House, Great Sankey, Warrington, WA5 3LW; tel. (1925) 237000; fax (1925) 237073; internet www.uuplc.co.uk; Chair. Sir RICHARD EVANS; Chief Exec. PHILIP GREEN.

Welsh Water (Dwr Cymru Cyfyngedig): Pentwyn Rd, Nelson, Treharris, Mid Glamorgan, CF46 6LY; tel. (1443) 452300; fax (1443) 452809; e-mail enquiries@dwrcymru.com; internet www.dwrcymru.com; f. 1989; Chair. Lord BURNS; Man. Dir NIGEL ANNETT.

Wessex Water Services Ltd: Claverton Down Rd, Bath, BA2 7WW; tel. (1225) 526000; e-mail info@wessexwater.co.uk; internet www.wessexwater.co.uk; Propr YTL (Malaysia); Chair. and CEO COLIN SKELLETT.

Yorkshire Water Services Ltd: POB 500, Bradford, BD6 2SZ; tel. (845) 1242424; fax (1274) 372800; internet www.yorkshirewater.com; Chair. JOHN NAPIER; Man. Dir KEVIN WHITEMAN.

CO-OPERATIVE ORGANIZATIONS

Co-operatives UK (The Union of Co-operative Enterprises): Holyoake House, Hanover St, Manchester, M60 0AS; tel. (161) 246-2900; fax (161) 831-7684; e-mail pauline.green@cooperatives-uk.coop; internet www.cooperatives-uk.coop; f. 1869; co-ordinates, informs and advises the 45 retail consumer co-operative societies and 700 worker co-operatives and employee-owned businesses; Chair. BEN REID; Society Sec. JOHN BUTLER; Chief Exec. Dame PAULINE GREEN.

Co-operative Group Ltd: New Century House, POB 53, Manchester, M60 4ES; tel. (161) 834-1212; fax (161) 834-4507; internet www.co-op.co.uk; f. 1863; Chair. BOB BURLTON; Chief Exec. MARTIN BEAUMONT.

National Association of Co-operative Officials: 6A Clarendon Pl., Hyde, Cheshire, SK14 2QZ; tel. (161) 351-7900; fax (161) 366-6800; Gen. Sec. L. W. EWING.

TRADE UNIONS
Central Organizations

Trades Union Congress (TUC): Congress House, Great Russell St, London, WC1B 3LS; tel. (20) 7636-4030; fax (20) 7636-0632; e-mail info@tuc.org.uk; internet www.tuc.org.uk; f. 1868; a voluntary association of trade unions, the representatives of which meet annually to consider matters of common concern to their members. A General Council of 57 members is elected at the annual Congress to keep watch on all industrial movements, legislation affecting labour and all matters touching the interest of the trade union movement, with authority to promote common action on general questions and to assist trade unions in the work of organization. Through the General Council and its Executive Committee, the TUC campaigns on issues of concern to employees and provides services for affiliated unions. It also makes nominations to various bodies such as the Health and Safety Commission, the Equal Opportunities Commission and the Advisory, Conciliation and Arbitration Service Council. In early 2006 65 unions, with a total membership of almost 6.4m., were affiliated to the TUC. The TUC is affiliated to the International Confederation of Free Trade Unions and the European Trade Union Confederation, and nominates the British Workers' Delegate to the International Labour Organization; Pres. GLORIA MILLS; Gen. Sec. BRENDAN BARBER.

Irish Congress of Trade Unions (Northern Ireland Committee): 4–6 Donegall Street Pl., Belfast, BT1 2FN; tel. (28) 9024-7940; fax (28) 9024-6898; e-mail info@ictuni.org; internet www.ictuni.org; 31 affiliated unions in Northern Ireland, with a membership of 208,079 (2004); Gen. Sec. DAVID BEGG.

THE UNITED KINGDOM
Directory

Scottish Trades Union Congress: 333 Woodlands Rd, Glasgow, G3 6NG; tel. (141) 337-8100; fax (141) 337-8101; e-mail info@stuc.org.uk; internet www.stuc.org.uk; f. 1897; 627,478 Scottish trade unionists affiliated through 45 trade unions and 30 trades union councils (2004); Gen. Sec. BILL SPEIRS.

Wales Trades Union Council: 1 Cathedral Rd, Cardiff; tel. (29) 2034-7010; fax (29) 2022-1940; e-mail wtuc@tuc.org.uk; internet www.wtuc.org.uk; f. 1973; Gen. Sec. FELICITY WILLIAMS.

General Federation of Trade Unions: Central House, Upper Woburn Pl., London, WC1H 0HY; tel. (20) 7388-0852; fax (20) 7383-0820; e-mail gftuhq@gftu.org.uk; internet www.gftu.org.uk; f. 1899; by the TUC; 30 affiliated organizations, with a total membership of 240,525; Pres. GARY OAKES.

Principal Trade Unions Affiliated to the TUC

Includes all affiliated unions whose membership is in excess of 10,000.

ACCORD: Simmons House, 46 Old Bath Rd, Charvil, Reading, Berkshire, RG10 9QR; tel. (118) 934-1808; fax (118) 932-0208; e-mail info@accordhq.org; internet www.accord-myunion.org; Gen. Sec. GED NICHOLS; 25,338 mems.

Amicus the Union: 35 King St, London, WC2E 8JG; tel. (20) 7420-8900; fax (20) 7420-8998; e-mail simon.dubbins@amicustheunion.org; internet www.amicustheunion.org.uk; f. 2002 by merger of Amalgamated Engineering and Electrical Union and Manufacturing, Science, Finance; merged with UNIFI in 2004; Gen. Sec. DEREK SIMPSON; 1,080,046 mems.

Associated Society of Locomotive Engineers and Firemen (ASLEF): 9 Arkwright Rd, London, NW3 6AB; tel. (20) 7317-8600; fax (20) 7794-6406; e-mail info@aslef.org.uk; internet www.aslef.org.uk; f. 1880; Gen. Sec. KEITH NORMAN; 16,571 mems.

Association of Teachers and Lecturers (ATL): 7 Northumberland St, London WC2N 5RD; tel. (20) 7930-6441; fax (20) 7930-1359; e-mail info@atl.org.uk; internet www.atl.org.uk; f. 1978; Pres. JANE BENNETT; Gen. Sec. Dr MARY BOUSTED; 113,161 mems.

Association of University Teachers (AUT): Egmont House, 25–31 Tavistock Place, London, WC1H 9UT; tel. (20) 7670-9700; fax (20) 7670-9799; e-mail hq@aut.org.uk; internet www.aut.org.uk; f. 1919; Pres. ANGELA ROGER; Gen. Sec. SALLY HUNT; 48,000 mems.

Bakers, Food and Allied Workers' Union (BFAWU): Stanborough House, Great North Rd, Stanborough, Welwyn Garden City, Herts., AL8 7TA; tel. (1707) 260150; fax (1707) 261570; e-mail bfawho@aol.com; internet www.bfawu.org; f. 1861; Pres. RONNIE DRAPER; Gen. Sec. JOSEPH MARINO; 28,426 mems.

British Actors' Equity Association: Guild House, Upper St Martin's Lane, London, WC2H 9EG; tel. (20) 7379-6000; fax (20) 7379-7001; e-mail info@equity.org.uk; internet www.equity.org.uk; Pres. HARRY LANDIS; Gen. Sec. IAN MCGARRY; 35,274 mems.

Broadcasting, Entertainment, Cinematograph and Theatre Union (BECTU): 373–377 Clapham Rd, London, SW9 9BT; tel. (20) 7346-0900; fax (20) 7346-0901; e-mail info@bectu.org.uk; internet www.bectu.org.uk; f. 1991 as a result of merger between Asscn of Cinematograph, Television and Allied Technicians (f. 1933) and the Broadcasting and Entertainment Trades Alliance (f. 1984); Pres. TONY LENNON; Gen. Sec. ROGER BOLTON; 17,604 mems.

Chartered Society of Physiotherapy (CSP): 14 Bedford Row, London, WC1R 4ED; tel. (20) 7306-6666; fax (20) 7306-6611; e-mail enquiries@csp.org.uk; internet www.csp.org.uk; Pres. Baroness FINLAY OF LLANDAFF; Chief Exec. PHIL GRAY; 47,500 mems.

Communications Workers' Union (CWU): 150 The Broadway, Wimbledon, London, SW19 1RX; tel. (20) 8971-7200; fax (20) 8971-7300; e-mail info@cwu.org; internet www.cwu.org; f. 1995 by merger of the National Communications Union and the Union of Communication Workers; Pres. PAT O'HARA; Gen. Sec. BILLY HAYES; 266,263 mems.

Community: Swinton House, 324 Gray's Inn Rd, London, WC1X 8DD; tel. (20) 7239-1200; fax (20) 7278-8378; e-mail info@community-tu.org; internet www.community-tu.org; f. 2004 by the merger of ISTC and the National Union of Knitwear, Footwear and Apparel Trades; Gen. Sec. MICHAEL J. LEAHY; 70,059 mems.

Connect: 30 St George's Rd, Wimbledon, London, SW19 4BD; tel. (20) 8971-6000; fax (20) 8971-6002; e-mail union@connectuk.org; internet www.connectuk.org; trade union for professioals in the communications industry; fmrly Society of Telecom Executives, name changed as above Jan. 2000; Pres. DENISE MCGUIRE; Gen. Sec. ADRIAN ASKEW; 20,000 mems.

Educational Institute of Scotland (EIS): 46 Moray Pl., Edinburgh, EH3 6BH; tel. (131) 225-6244; fax (131) 220-3151; e-mail enquiries@eis.org.uk; internet www.eis.org.uk; f. 1847; professional and trade union org. for teachers and lecturers in schools, colleges and universities; Pres. JACK BARNETT; Gen. Sec. RONALD A. SMITH; 54,269 mems.

FDA: 2 Caxton St, London, SW1H 0QH; tel. (20) 7343-1111; fax (20) 7343-1105; e-mail head-office@fda.org.uk; internet www.fda.org.uk; Pres. MARTIN FLETCHER; Gen. Sec. JONATHAN BAUME; 11,390 mems.

Fire Brigades Union (FBU): Bradley House, 68 Coombe Rd, Kingston upon Thames, Surrey, KT2 7AE; tel. (20) 8541-1765; fax (20) 8546-5187; e-mail office@fbu.org.uk; internet www.fbu.org.uk; f. 1918; Pres. RUTH WINTERS; Gen. Sec. MATT WRACK; 47,071 mems.

GMB—Britain's General Union: 22–24 Worple Rd, Wimbledon, London, SW19 4DD; tel. (20) 8947-3131; fax (20) 8944-6552; e-mail info@gmb.org.uk; internet www.gmb.org.uk; f. 1982; Pres. MARY TURNER; Gen. Sec. PAUL KENNY (acting); 600,106 mems.

Musicians' Union (MU): 60–62 Clapham Rd, London, SW9 0JJ; tel. (20) 7582-5566; fax (20) 7582-9805; e-mail info@musiciansunion.org.uk; internet www.musiciansunion.org.uk; f. 1893; Gen. Sec. JOHN F. SMITH; 31,283 mems.

NATFHE (The University & College Lecturers' Union) (formerly National Association of Teachers in Further and Higher Education): 27 Britannia St, London, WC1X 9JP; tel. (20) 7837-3636; fax (20) 7837-4404; e-mail hq@natfhe.org.uk; internet www.natfhe.org.uk; f. 1976; Pres. JOHN WILKIN; Gen. Sec. PAUL MACKNEY; 66,991 mems.

National Association of Schoolmasters Union of Women Teachers (NASUWT): Hillscourt Education Centre, Rose Hill, Rednal, Birmingham, B45 8RS; tel. (121) 453-6150; fax (121) 457-6208; e-mail nasuwt@mail.nasuwt.org.uk; internet www.teachersunion.org.uk; f. 1919; merged with UWT 1976; Pres. PETER MCLOUGHLIN; Gen. Sec. CHRIS KEATES; 236,005 mems.

National Union of Journalists (NUJ): Headland House, 308-312 Gray's Inn Rd, London, WC1X 8DP; tel. (20) 7278-7916; fax (20) 7837-8143; e-mail info@nuj.org.uk; internet www.nuj.org.uk; f. 1907; Pres. TIM LEZARD; Gen. Sec. JEREMY DEAR; 35,000 mems.

National Union of Marine Aviation and Shipping Transport Officers (NUMAST): Oceanair House, 750–760 High Rd, Leytonstone, London, E11 3BB; tel. (20) 8989-6677; fax (20) 8530-1015; e-mail enquiries@numast.org; internet www.numast.org; f. 1936; Sec. BRIAN ORRELL; 19,100 mems.

National Union of Rail, Maritime and Transport Workers (RMT): 39 Chalton Rd, London, NW1 1JD; tel. (20) 7387-4771; fax (20) 7387-4123; e-mail info@rmt.org.uk; internet www.rmt.org.uk; f. 1990 through merger of National Union of Railwaymen (f. 1872) and National Union of Seamen (f. 1887); Pres. TONY DONAGHY; Gen. Sec. BOB CROW; 67,476 mems.

National Union of Teachers (NUT): Hamilton House, Mabledon Pl., London, WC1H 9BD; tel. (20) 7388-6191; fax (20) 7387-8458; internet www.teachers.org.uk; Pres. JUDY MOORHOUSE; Gen. Sec. STEVE SINNOTT; 272,853 mems.

Nationwide Group Staff Union (NGSU): Middleton Farmhouse, 37 Main Rd, Middleton Cheney, Banbury, OX17 2QT; tel. (1295) 710767; fax (1295) 712580; e-mail ngsu@ngsu.org.uk; internet www.ngsu.org.uk; Gen. Sec. TIM POIL; 12,100 mems.

Prison Officers' Association (POA): Cronin House, 245 Church St, London, N9 9HW; tel. (20) 8803-0255; fax (20) 8803-1761; internet www.poauk.org.uk; f. 1939; Chair. COLIN MOSES; Gen. Sec. BRIAN CATON; 34,119 mems.

Prospect: 75–79 York Rd, London, SE1 7AQ; tel. (20) 7902-6600; fax (20) 7902-6667; e-mail paul.noon@prospect.org.uk; internet www.prospect.org.uk; f. 1919 as the Institution of Professionals, Managers and Specialists; changed name as above in 2001; Pres. ALAN GREY; Gen. Sec. PAUL NOON; 105,426 mems.

Prospect (Engineers' and Managers' Association Sector): Flaxman House, Gogmore Lane, Chertsey, Surrey, KT16 9JS; tel. (1932) 577007; fax (1932) 567707; e-mail chertsey@prospect.org.uk; internet www.prospect.org.uk; f. 1913; Pres. DAVID SIMPSON; Gen. Sec. PAUL NOON; 28,776 mems.

Public and Commercial Services Union (PCS): 160 Falcon Rd, London, SW11 2LN; tel. (20) 7924-2727; fax (20) 7924-1847; internet www.pcs.org.uk; f. 1998 by merger of Civil and Public Services Asscn (f. 1903) and Public Services, Tax and Commerce Union (f. 1996); Pres. JANICE GODRICH; Gen. Sec. MARK SERWOTKA; 320,000 mems.

Society of Radiographers (SoR): 207 Providence Sq., Mill St, London, SE1 2EW; tel. (20) 7740-7200; fax (20) 7740-7204; e-mail info@sor.org; internet www.sor.org; Pres. HAZEL HARRIES-JONES; Chief Exec. RICHARD EVANS; 17,383 mems.

Transport and General Workers' Union (TGWU): Transport House, 128 Theobalds Rd, London, WC1X 8TN; tel. (20) 7611-2500; fax (20) 7611-2555; e-mail tgwu@tgwu.org.uk; internet www.tgwu.org.uk; Gen. Sec. TONY WOODLEY; 820,118 mems.

Transport Salaried Staffs' Association (TSSA): Walkden House, 10 Melton St, London, NW1 2EJ; tel. (20) 7387-2101; fax (20) 7383-0656; e-mail enquiries@tssa.org.uk; internet www.tssa.org.uk; f. 1897; Pres. DAVID PORTER; Gen. Sec. GERRY DOHERTY; 31,034 mems.

THE UNITED KINGDOM

Union of Construction, Allied Trades and Technicians (UCATT): UCATT House, 177 Abbeville Rd, Clapham, London, SW4 9RL; tel. (20) 7622-2442; fax (20) 7720-4081; e-mail info@ucatt.org.uk; internet www.ucatt.org.uk; f. 1921; Pres. JOHN THOMPSON; Gen. Sec. ALAN RITCHIE; 110,886 mems.

Union of Shop, Distributive and Allied Workers (USDAW): 188 Wilmslow Rd, Manchester, M14 6LJ; tel. (161) 224-2804; fax (161) 257-2566; e-mail enquiries@usdaw.org.uk; internet www.usdaw.org.uk; Pres. MARGE CAREY; Gen. Sec. JOHN HANNETT; 331,703 mems.

UNISON: 1 Mabledon Pl., London, WC1H 9AJ; tel. (845) 355-0845; fax (20) 7551-1101; e-mail direct@unison.co.uk; internet www.unison.org.uk; f. 1993 through merger of Confederation of Health Service Employees (COHSE—f. 1910), National and Local Government Officers Asscn (NALGO—f. 1905) and National Union of Public Employees (NUPE—f. 1888); Pres. PAULINE GRANT; Gen. Sec. DAVE PRENTIS; 1,031,000 mems.

Unions not affiliated to the TUC

Irish National Teachers' Organization: 23 College Gardens, Belfast, BT9 6BS (headquarters in Dublin); tel. (28) 9038-1455; fax (28) 9066-2803; e-mail info@ni.into.ie; internet www.into.ie; f. 1868; affiliated to the Irish Congress of Trade Unions (Northern Ireland Committee); Northern Sec. F. BUNTING; 6,300 mems.

National Farmers' Union (NFU): (see p. 4554).

Northern Ireland Musicians' Asscn: Unit 4, Fortwilliam Business Park, Dargan Rd, Belfast, BT3 9JZ; tel. and fax (28) 9037-0037; Sec. H. HAMILTON; 1,003 mems.

Northern Ireland Public Service Alliance: Harkin House, 54 Wellington Park, Belfast, BT9 6DP; tel. (28) 9066-1831; fax (28) 9066-5847; e-mail info@nipsa.org.uk; internet www.nipsa.org.uk; affiliated to the Irish Congress of Trade Unions (Northern Ireland Committee); Pres. (2005/06) BILLY LYNN; Gen. Sec. JOHN COREY; 42,000 mems.

Services Industrial Professional Technical Union: 3 Antrim Rd, Belfast, BT15 2BE; tel. (28) 9031-4000; fax (28) 9031-4044; e-mail info@siptu.ie; internet www.siptu.ie; affiliated to the Irish Congress of Trade Unions (Northern Ireland Committee); Gen. Sec. JOE O'FLYNN; Regional Sec. JACK NASH; 7,001 members.

Ulster Teachers' Union: 94 Malone Rd, Belfast, BT9 5HP; tel. (28) 9066-2216; fax (28) 9068-3296; e-mail office@utu.edu; internet www.utu.edu; f. 1919; affiliated to the Irish Congress of Trade Unions (Northern Ireland Committee); Gen. Sec. AVRIL HALL-CALLAGHAN; 6,500 mems (Dec. 2004).

Union of Democratic Mineworkers (UDM): The Sycamores, Moor Rd, Bestwood, Nottingham, NG6 8UE; tel. (115) 976-3468; fax (115) 976-3474; f. 1986; Pres. and Gen. Sec. NEIL GREATREX; c. 4,000 mems.

United Road Transport Union: 76 High Lane, Manchester, M21 9EF; tel. (800) 526639; fax (161) 861-0976; e-mail info@urtu.com; internet www.urtu.com; f. 1890; Gen. Sec. ROBERT MONKS; 16,800 mems.

National Federations

Confederation of Shipbuilding and Engineering Unions: 140–142 Walworth Rd, London, SE17 1JW; tel. (20) 7703-2215; fax (20) 7252-7397; e-mail alan.robson@cseu.org.uk; 1,093,001 mems in 10 affiliated trade unions; Gen. Sec. ALAN ROBSON.

Federation of Entertainment Unions: 1 Highfield, Twyford, Hampshire, SO21 1QR; tel. (1962) 713134; fax (1962) 713134; e-mail harris.s@btconnect.com; f. 1990; Sec. STEVE HARRIS.

Transport

RAILWAYS

The Railways Act 1993, providing for a process of rail privatization, received royal assent in November 1993. A separate, government-owned company, Railtrack, was set up on 1 April 1994 to take responsibility for infrastructure (track, signals and stations) and levy charges on train operators for track access. British Rail was to remain in control of all businesses (except Railtrack) until their transfer to the private sector. As a result of the 1993 Railways Act, 25 Train Operating Units (TOUs) came into being on 1 April 1994. The Director of Passenger Rail Franchises was responsible for awarding franchises for the 25 TOUs as early as practicable and was to monitor the franchises to ensure compliance with the agreed contracts. The first passenger train franchises were awarded in December 1995, and two TOUs were transferred to private operators in February 1996; the final TOU transferred to private sector at the end of March 1997. Railtrack was transferred to the private sector in May 1996. In October 2001 the Government placed the heavily-indebted Railtrack in administration. In March 2002 Network Rail, a 'not-for-profit' Government-supported company, offered £500m. for Railtrack, and in July Railtrack shareholders voted to accept Network Rail's offer. Railtrack remained in administration until October 2002, when the final takeover by National Rail proceeded.

In July 1987 the Channel Tunnel Treaty was signed between the Governments of France and the United Kingdom, providing the constitutional basis for the construction of a cross-channel tunnel between the two countries, comprising a fixed link of two rail tunnels and one service tunnel, at an estimated cost of £4,700m. Of the total length of 31 miles (50 km), 23 miles are under the seabed. The tunnel was opened in May 1994. In late 2004 it was announced that the rail services provider, Eurostar UK, would move all London operations from the Waterloo International terminal to St Pancras station by 2007.

DfT Rail Group: Department for Transport, Great Minster House, 76 Marsham St, London SW1P 4DR; tel. (20) 7944-8300; fax (20) 7944-9643; e-mail rail@dft.gsi.gov.uk; internet http://www.dft.gov.uk/stellent/groups/dft_railways/documents/sectionhomepage/dft_railways_page.hcsp; f. 2005; strategic and financial responsibility for the railways, assumed many functions of the Strategic Rail Authority (SRA), which was dissolved in August 2005 following a national rail review in July 2004; Dir-Gen. MIKE MITCHELL.

Office of Rail Regulation: 1 Kemble St, London, WC2B 4AN; tel. (20) 7282-2000; fax (20) 7282-2040; e-mail rail.library@orr.gsi.gov.uk; internet www.rail-reg.gov.uk; Chair. CHRIS BOLT.

Network Rail Ltd: 40 Melton St, London, NW1 2EE; tel. (20) 7557-8000; fax (20) 7557-9000; e-mail enquiries@networkrail.com; internet www.networkrail.co.uk; f. 2002; as a 'not-for-profit' company by train operators, rail unions and passenger groups to take over responsibility for running the UK rail network from Railtrack PLC; Chair. IAN MCALLISTER; Chief Exec. JOHN ARMITT.

Northern Ireland Railways Co Ltd: Central Station, East Bridge St, Belfast, BT1 3PB; tel. (28) 9089-9400; fax (28) 9089-9401; internet www.nirailways.co.uk; f. 1967; subsidiary of Northern Ireland Transport Holding Co (see below) and part of the Translink rail and bus network; operates rail services for passenger traffic over 342 km and for freight traffic over 268 km of railway track; a high-speed passenger service between Belfast and Dublin, launched, in co-operation with Irish Rail, began operations in 1997; Chief Exec. KEITH MOFFATT.

Channel Tunnel

Eurotunnel Group: UK Terminal, Ashford Rd, Folkestone, Kent, CT18 8XX; tel. (1303) 282222; fax (1303) 850360; e-mail press@eurotunnel.com; internet www.eurotunnel.com; customer information; Anglo-French consortium contracted to design, finance and construct the Channel Tunnel under a concession granted for a period up to 2052 (later extended to 2086); receives finance exclusively from the private sector, including international commercial banks; the Channel Tunnel was formally opened in May 1994; operates a service of road vehicle 'shuttle' trains and passenger and freight trains through the Channel Tunnel; Chair. and Chief Exec. JAQCUES GOUNON.

Eurostar UK/Eurostar Group Ltd: Eurostar House, Waterloo Station, London, SE1 8SE; tel. (1777) 777879; e-mail press.office@eurostar.co.uk; internet www.eurostar.com; commenced international high-speed passenger rail services in 1994; provides services from London and Ashford, in Kent, direct to Paris, Brussels, Lille, Calais, Frethun, Disneyland Paris, Avignon and Bourg St Maurice; Chair. GUILLAUME PEPY; CEO RICHARD BROWN.

Metropolitan Transport

Docklands Light Railway: POB 154, Castor Lane, London, E14 0DS; tel. (20) 7363-9700; fax (20) 7363-9532; e-mail cservice@dlr.co.uk; internet www.dlr.co.uk; opened Sep. 1987; in 1992 responsibility for the Railway was transferred from London Transport to the London Docklands Development Corporation; in 1998 the Railway was again transferred to the Dept for Environment, Transport and the Regions and in July 2000 the Railway became part of Transport for London; franchised to a private co, Docklands Railway Management, in March 1997; comprises a 38-station system bounded by Bank, Tower Gateway, King George V (North Woolwich), Beckton, Stratford, Island Gardens (Isle of Dogs) and Lewisham; in June 2005 construction began on an extension from King George V to Woolwich Arsenal, due to be completed in February 2009; Chair. IAN BROWN; Dir JONATHAN FOX.

Transport for London (TFL): Windsor House, 42–50 Victoria St, London, SW1H 0TL; tel. (20) 7941-4500; fax (20) 7649-9121; e-mail enquire@tfl.gov.uk; internet www.tfl.gov.uk; f. 2000; executive arm of Greater London Authority responsible for activities of former London Transport; London's integrated transport body, responsible for all modes of transport, TFL is an executive arm of the Greater London Authority (GLA); Chair. KEN LIVINGSTONE; Commissioner PETER HENDY.

London Underground: 55 Broadway, London, SW1H 0BD; tel. (20) 7222-5600; internet www.tfl.gov.uk/tube; f. 1985; however, dates back to 1863; responsible for providing and securing the services of underground rail in Greater London; Man. Dir TIM O'TOOLE; COO MIKE BROWN.

Associations

Railway Industry Association: 22 Headfort Pl., London, SW1X 7RY; tel. (20) 7201-0777; fax (20) 7235-5777; e-mail ria@riagb.org.uk; internet www.riagb.org.uk; f. 1875; represents UK-based railway suppliers, with a free sourcing service for products and services; Chair. HAYDN ABBOTT; Dir-Gen. JEREMY CANDFIELD.

Association of Train Operating Companies: 3rd Floor, 40 Bernard St, London, WC1N 1BY; tel. (20) 7841-8000; e-mail atocnews@atoc.org; internet www.atoc.org; f. 1994; Chair. ADRIAN SHOOTER (acting); Dir-Gen. GEORGE MUIR.

ROADS

Total road length in Great Britain in 2004 was 387,674 km (243,777 miles), of which 3,523 km (2,160 miles) was motorway. In 2004 there were 24,880 km (15,460 miles) of roads of all classes in Northern Ireland, including some 110 km (68 miles) of motorway.

Highways Agency: 123 Buckingham Palace Rd, London, SW1W 9HA; tel. and fax (8457) 504030; e-mail ha_info@highways.gov.uk; internet www.highways.gov.uk; executive agency of the Department for Transport; responsible for maintaining, operating and improving the trunk road network in England; Chief Exec. ARCHIE ROBERTSON.

Exel PLC: Ocean House, The Ring, Bracknell, RG12 1AN; tel. (1344) 302000; fax (1344) 710031; internet www.exel.com; f. 1969; as the National Freight Corpn, a statutory body responsible to the Minister for Transport; became a limited company in 1980; bought by consortium of employees and former employees 1982; changed name from National Freight Consortium PLC 1989; merged with Ocean Group in 2000; Chair. NIGEL RICH; Chief Exec. JOHN ALLAN.

Northern Ireland Transport Holding Co: Chamber of Commerce House, 22 Great Victoria St, Belfast, BT2 7LX; tel. (28) 9024-3456; fax (28) 9033-3845; internet www.translink.co.uk/nithco.asp; publicly owned; three subsidiaries are part of the Translink rail and bus network; Chair. VERONICA PALMER; Chief Exec. KEITH MOFFATT.

Metro: Milewater Rd, Belfast, BT3 9BG; tel. (28) 9035-1201; fax (28) 9035-1474; internet www.translink.co.uk/Metro.asp; responsible for operating municipal transport in the City of Belfast; Chief Exec. KEITH MOFFATT.

Ulsterbus Ltd: Milewater Rd, Belfast, BT3 9BG; Central Station, Belfast, BT1 3PB; tel. (28) 9089-9400; fax (28) 9035-1474; internet www.translink.co.uk/atulsterbus.asp; responsible for almost all bus transport in Northern Ireland, except Belfast city; services into the Republic of Ireland; assoc. co Flexibus Ltd (minibus contract hire); Chief Exec. KEITH MOFFATT.

INLAND WATERWAYS

There are some 3,200 km (2,000 miles) of inland waterways in Great Britain under the control of the British Waterways Board, varying from the river navigations and wide waterways accommodating commercial craft to canals taking small holiday craft.

British Waterways: Willow Grange, Church Rd, Watford, Herts., WD17 4QA; tel. (1923) 201120; fax (1923) 201400; e-mail enquiries.hq@britishwaterways.co.uk; internet www.britishwaterways.co.uk; f. 1963; Chair. TONY HALES; Chief Exec. ROBIN EVANS.

SHIPPING

There are more than 400 ports in the United Kingdom, of which London (Tilbury), Milford Haven, the Tees and Hartlepool ports, the Forth ports, Grimsby and Immingham, Southampton, Sullom Voe, the Medway ports, Dover, Felixstowe and Liverpool are the largest (in terms of the tonnage of goods traffic handled). Twenty-one ports, including Southampton, Grimsby and Immingham, Hull and five ports in South Wales, are owned and administered by Associated British Ports. The majority of the other large ports are owned and operated by public trusts, including London, which is administered by the Port of London Authority, and Belfast, administered by the Belfast Harbour Commission. Under the Ports Act (1991), trust ports were permitted to become private, commercial enterprises. By mid-1995 five major trust ports, including the Port of London Authority and the Medway Ports Authority, had been transferred to the private sector. In May 1998 the Government announced that the port of Belfast was to be transferred to the private sector. Sullom Voe, Bristol and a number of smaller ports are under the control of local authorities, and there are more than 100 ports owned and administered by statutory or private companies; of these, Felixstowe, Liverpool (owned by Mersey Docks and Harbour Company) and Manchester are the largest.

Britain is linked to the rest of Europe by an extensive passenger and vehicle ship ferry service. There are also hovercraft services to Belgium and France for passengers and vehicles. There are regular freight services from Belfast, Warrenpoint and Larne, in Northern Ireland, to ports in Great Britain and Europe; passenger services operate daily between Northern Ireland and Great Britain.

Associated British Ports (ABR): 150 Holborn, London, EC1N 2LR; tel. (20) 7430-1177; fax (20) 7430-1384; e-mail pr@abports.co.uk; internet www.abports.co.uk; f. 1983; controls 21 UK ports; Chair. CHRIS CLARK; Chief Exec. BO LERENIUS.

The Baltic Exchange Ltd: 38 St Mary Axe, London, EC3A 8BH; tel. (20) 7623-5501; fax (20) 7369-1622; e-mail enquiries@balticexchange.co.uk; internet www.balticexchange.com; world market for chartering ships, charters aircraft, buys and sells ships and aircraft; Chair. ANTHONY COOKE; Chief Exec. JEREMY PENN.

British Ports Association (BPA): Africa House, 64–78 Kingsway, London, WC2B 6AH; tel. (20) 7242-1200; fax (20) 7430-7474; e-mail info@britishports.org.uk; internet www.britishports.org.uk; promotes and protects the general interests of port authorities, comments on proposed legislation and policy matters; Dir DAVID WHITEHEAD.

Port of London Authority: Bakers' Hall, 7 Harp Lane, London, EC3R 6LB; tel. (20) 7743-7900; fax (20) 7743-7999; internet www.portoflondon.co.uk; Chair. SIMON SHERRARD; Chief Exec. RICHARD EVERITT.

Principal Shipping Companies

Belfast Freight Ferries Ltd: Victoria Terminal 1, Dargan Rd, Belfast, BT3 9LJ; tel. (28) 9077-0112; fax (28) 9078-1217; roll-on, roll-off service to Heysham; Chair. ANGUS FRASER; Man. Dir ALAN PEACOCK.

BG Freightline: c/o TR Shipping Services, Victoria Terminal 3, West Bank Rd, Belfast, BT3 9JL; tel. (28) 9077-7968; fax (28) 9077-4299; e-mail rbarham@trshipping.co.uk; internet www.trshipping.co.uk; container service to Rotterdam.

Bibby Line Ltd: 105 Duke St, Liverpool, L1 5JQ; tel. (151) 708-8000; fax (151) 794-1000; e-mail enquiries@bibbyline.co.uk; internet www.bibbyline.co.uk; f. 1807; operates chemical carriers and shallow water accommodation units; Chair. S. P. SHERRARD; Man. Dir CY GREEN.

Boyd Line: 7 The Orangery, Hesslewood Country Office Park, Ferriby Rd, Hessle, HU13 0LH; tel. (1482) 324024; fax (1482) 323737; e-mail jon.carden@boydline.co.uk; internet www.boydline.co.uk; vessel owners and managers; Man. Dir JONATHAN CARDEN; 2 vessels.

BP Shipping Ltd: Breakspear Park, Breakspear Way, Hemel Hempstead, Herts., HP2 4UL; tel. (1442) 232323; fax (1442) 255893; internet www.bpshipping.co.uk; f. 1915; division of British Petroleum Ltd; Chief Exec. ROBERT MALONE; 28 vessels.

Caledonian MacBrayne Ltd: The Ferry Terminal, Gourock, Renfrewshire, PA19 1QP; tel. (1475) 650100; fax (1475) 637607; e-mail info@calmac.co.uk; internet www.calmac.co.uk; state-owned ferry co; extensive car and passenger services on Firth of Clyde, to Western Isles of Scotland and a service between Ballycastle, in Northern Ireland, and Rathlin Island; 30 roll-on/roll-off vessels; Chair. HAROLD MILLS; Man. Dir LAWRIE SINCLAIR.

Coastal Container Line Ltd: Coastal House, Victoria Terminal 3, West Bank Rd, Belfast, BT3 9JL; tel. (28) 9037-3200; fax (28) 9037-1444; container services to Liverpool and Cardiff; Operations Dir JOHN FORRESTER.

Condor Ferries Ltd: Condor House, New Harbour Rd South, Hamworthy, Poole, Dorset, BH15 4AJ; tel. (1202) 207207; fax (1202) 685184; e-mail reservations@condorferries.co.uk; internet www.condorferries.co.uk; services to the Channel Islands and France.

Crescent Marine Services: Brunswick House, 8–13 Brunswick Pl., Southampton, SO15 2AP; tel. (23) 8063-9777; fax (23) 8063-9888; e-mail info@crescentgroup.co.uk; internet www.crescentplc.com; f. 1899; purchased by Clipper Group in 1997; Group CEO KEVIN HOBBS.

Exel PLC: see Roads, above.

F. T. Everard & Sons Ltd: Blake House, Schooner Court, Admiral's Park, Crossways, Dartford, Kent, DA2 6QQ; tel. (1322) 394500; fax (1322) 311934; e-mail info@ft-everard.co.uk; internet www.ft-everard.co.uk; shipowners; forestry products service between Sweden, the UK and Ireland, tanker and dry cargo in Europe; 45 vessels; Chair. MICHAEL EVERARD.

James Fisher & Sons: Fisher House, POB 4, Barrow-in-Furness, Cumbria, LA14 1HR; tel. (1229) 615400; fax (1229) 835705; e-mail postmaster@james-fisher.co.uk; internet www.james-fisher.co.uk; f. 1847; provider of marine services operating in three sectors: Tankships, Cable Laying Vessels and Marine Support Services; Exec. Chair. TIMOTHY C. HARRIS; CEO NICHOLAS P. HENRY.

THE UNITED KINGDOM

Furness, Withy & Co Ltd: Furness House, 53 Brighton Rd, Redhill, Surrey, RH1 6YL; tel. (1737) 771122; fax (1737) 761234; Man. Dirs PAUL EDWARDS, A. MOUZOUROPOULOS.

Fyffes PLC: Houndmills Rd, Houndmills Industrial Estate, Basingstoke, Hampshire, RG21 6XL; tel. (1256) 383200; fax (1256) 383259; e-mail info@fyffes.com; internet www.fyffes.co.uk; f. 1901; Chair. CARL P. MCCANN; Chief Exec. DAVID V. MCCANN.

Geest Line: 3700 Parkway, Whiteley, Fareham, PO15 7AL; tel. (1489) 873575; fax (1489) 873562; e-mail quotes@geestline.com; internet www.geestline.com; Man. Dir W. SALMOND.

Gibson Gas Tankers Ltd: 1A Commercial Quay, 86 Commercial St, Leith, Edinburgh, EH6 6LX; tel. (131) 554-4466; fax (131) 554-3843; f. 1966; Man. Dir C. SPENCER.

Goulandris Bros Ltd: 34A Queen Anne's Gate, London, SW1H 9AB; tel. (20) 7222-5244; fax (20) 7222-6817; e-mail chartering@goulanbros.co.uk; internet www.goulanbros.co.uk; tankers and bulk carriers; Man. Dir BASIL GOULANDRIS.

Thos. & Jas. Harrison Ltd: Mersey Chambers, Covent Garden, Liverpool, L2 8UF; tel. (151) 236-5611; fax (151) 236-1200; e-mail mailroom@harrisons.co.uk; f. 1853; liner operators and UK agency, principally to the Caribbean and South America; Chair. MICHAEL A. SEAFORD.

Heyn Group Ltd: 1 Corry Pl., Belfast Harbour, Belfast, BT3 9AH; tel. (28) 9035-0035; fax (28) 9035-0011; e-mail info@heyn.co.uk; internet www.heyn.co.uk; Man. Dir DAVID CLARKE.

Holbud Ship Management Ltd: Hydery House, 66 Leman St, London, E1 8EU; tel. (20) 7488-4901; fax (20) 7265-0654; ship agents; Dir B. D. SABARWAL.

John Kelly Fuels (Ireland) Ltd: 1 Lombard St, Belfast, BT1 1BN; tel. (28) 9026-1500; fax (28) 9033-0032; e-mail info@kelly-fuels.co.uk; internet www.kellyfuels.co.uk; f. 1840; coal and petroleum distributors, shipping agent; Chair. and Man. Dir R. REIHILL.

Mobil Shipping Co Ltd: Mobil Court, 3 Clements Inn, London, WC2A 2EB; tel. (20) 7412-4000; fax (20) 7430-2150; tanker services; Man. Dir JOHN ENSTON.

Norfolkline Ferries: 12 Quays Terminal, Tower Rd, Birkenhead, Wirral, CH41 1FE; tel. (870) 600-4321; e-mail info@norsemerchant.com; internet www.norsemerchant.com; acquired by Norfolk Line Group in 2005; roll-on, roll-off freight, car and passenger services to Birkenhead; Dir PHILIP SHEPHERD.

Peninsular and Oriental Steam Navigation Co: 79 Pall Mall, London, SW1Y 5EJ; tel. (20) 7930-4343; fax (20) 7925-0384; e-mail communications@pogroup.com; internet www.pogroup.com; f. 1837; ferry operators; worldwide container shipping services; port management and development; also engaged in non-shipping activities incl. cold storage and road haulage; acquired by Dubai Ports World (DP World) in March 2006; Chair. Sir JOHN PARKER; Chief Exec. ROBERT WOODS.

P & O European Ferries (Irish Sea) Ltd: The Harbour, Larne, Co Antrim, BT40 1AW; tel. (28) 2887-2200 (freight); tel. (0870) 242-4777 (passenger); fax (28) 2887-2129 (freight); fax (28) 2887-2195 (passenger); e-mail callcentre@poefis.com; internet www.poirishsea.com; subsidiary of P & O Group; Gen. Man. G. MCCULLOUGH.

P & O Ferries Ltd: Channel House, Channel View Rd, Dover, Kent, CT17 9TJ; tel. (1304) 863000; fax (1304) 863223; e-mail customer.services@poferries.com; internet www.poferries.com; car and passenger services across the English Channel and North Sea; Chief Exec. RUSS PETERS.

Shell International Trading and Shipping Co Ltd: 80 Strand, London, WC2R 0ZA; tel. (20) 7546-5000; fax (20) 7546-2200; internet www.shell.co.uk; worldwide operations trading and transporting crude petroleum and supplying petroleum products; incorporates Shell Tankers (UK) Ltd; Pres. R. J. W. WALLIS.

Souter Shipping Ltd: Clayton House, Regent Centre, Gosforth, Newcastle upon Tyne, NE3 3HW; tel. (191) 285-0621; bulk carriers, parcels tankers, conventional tankers; Man. Dir R. I. D. SOUTER.

Stena Line: 1 Davy Court, Central Park, Castle Mound Way, Rugby, Warwickshire, CV23 0UZ; tel. (1788) 203333; fax (1788) 203302; e-mail info.uk@stenaline.com; internet www.stenaline.com; parent co Stena AB; services to Ireland and the Netherlands; Man. Dir GUNNAR BLOMDAHL.

Stephenson Clarke Shipping Ltd: Eldon Court, Percy St, Newcastle upon Tyne, NE99 1TD; tel. (191) 232-2184; fax (191) 261-1156; f. 1730; Man. Dir G. WALKER.

Andrew Weir Shipping Ltd: Dexter House, 2 Royal Mint Court, London, EC3N 4XX; tel. (20) 7575-6000; fax (20) 7481-4784; e-mail aws@aws.co.uk; internet www.aws.co.uk; f. 1885; shipowners, ship managers; Man Dir STEPHEN CORKHILL.

Shipping Associations

Chamber of Shipping Ltd: Carthusian Court, 12 Carthusian St, London, EC1M 6EZ; tel. (20) 7417-2800; fax (20) 7726-2080; e-mail postmaster@british-shipping.org; internet www.british-shipping.org; Pres. MAURICE STOREY (2006); Dir-Gen. MARK BROWNRIGG.

Passenger Shipping Association Ltd (PSA): 1st Floor, 41–42 Eastcastle St, London W1W 8DU; tel. (20) 7436-2449; fax (20) 7636-9206; e-mail h.tapping@psa-psara.org; internet www.the-psa.co.uk; formerly Ocean Travel Development (f. 1958); 50 mems; Chair. JOHN CRUMMIE; Dir WILLIAM GIBBONS.

CIVIL AVIATION

In addition to many international air services into and out of the country, an internal air network operates from more than 20 main commercial airports.

The principal airports are Heathrow and Gatwick serving London, and Manchester, Birmingham and Glasgow, which in 2004 handled 67.1m., 31.3m., 21.0m., 8.8m. and 8.6m. passengers, respectively. In March 1991 a new development was opened at Stansted, including a new terminal, cargo centre and rail link to central London. In 2004 Stansted handled 21.0m. passengers. A new £30m. London City Airport, in the Docklands, opened in October 1987, providing domestic and international flights to and from city centres for business travellers. In 2003 London City handled 1.4m. passengers. In November 2001 plans for the construction of a fifth terminal at Heathrow were approved by the Government. The first phase is scheduled for completion in 2007 and will increase capacity at the airport to some 90m. passengers a year.

BAA PLC: 130 Wilton Rd, London, SW1V 1LQ; tel. (20) 7834-9449; fax (20) 7932-6699; e-mail newsdesk@baa.com; internet www.baa.com; f. 1966 as British Airports Authority; privatized in 1987; propr of Heathrow, Stansted, Gatwick, Southampton, Glasgow, Aberdeen and Edinburgh airports; Chair. MARCUS AGIUS; Chief Exec. MIKE CLASPER.

Civil Aviation Authority (CAA): CAA House, 45–59 Kingsway, London, WC2B 6TE; tel. (20) 7379-7311; fax (20) 7453-6244; internet www.caa.co.uk; f. 1972; public service enterprise and a regulatory body responsible for economic and safety regulation of civil aviation; advises Government on aviation issues; conducts economic and scientific research; produces statistical data; regulates British airspace; represents consumer interests and manages airspace users' needs; Chair. Sir ROY MCNULTY.

National Air Traffic Services (NATS) Ltd: 5th Floor, Brettenham House South, Lancaster Pl., London, WC2E 7EN; tel. (20) 7309-8666; internet www.nats.co.uk; f. 1960 as National Air Traffic Control Services; name changed as above in 1972 when the org. became part of the CAA (q.v.); public private partnership between the Airline Group (a consortium of British Airways, BMI, Virgin Atlantic, Britannia, Monarch, easyJet and Airtours), British airport operator BAA plc, NATS employees and the British Government; provides air traffic control services over the UK and North Atlantic and at 14 British airports. It operates and maintains a nationwide communications, surveillance and navigation network; Chair. CHRIS GIBSON-SMITH; CEO PAUL BARRON.

Principal Private Airlines

Air Southwest: Plymouth City Airport, Crownhill, Plymouth, PL6 8BW; tel. (870) 241-8202; e-mail contactus@airsouthwest.com; internet www.airsouthwest.com; f. 2003; scheduled domestic services from Plymouth, Newquay and Bristol; Man. Dir MALCOLM NAYLOR.

British Airways PLC (BA): Waterside, Harmondsworth, POB 365, Middx, UB7 0GB; tel. (845) 779-9977; internet www.britishairways.com; f. 1972; operates extensive domestic, European and worldwide services, scheduled services to more than 250 destinations in 99 countries; Chair. MARTIN BROUGHTON; Chief Exec. WILLIE WALSH.

British Mediterranean Airways Ltd (BMED): Cirrus House, Bedfont Rd, London Heathrow Airport, Staines, Middlesex, TW19 7NL; tel. (1784) 266300; fax (1784) 266353; internet www.flybmed.com; f. 1994; scheduled passenger services to destinations in the Middle East, Africa and Central Asia; Chair. Lord HESKETH; Chief Exec. DAVID RICHARDSON.

bmi: Donington Hall, Castle Donington, Derby, DE74 2SB; tel. (1332) 854000; fax (1332) 854662; internet www.flybmi.com; f. 1938 as Air Schools Ltd; name changed to British Midland Airways Ltd in 1964 and as above in 2002; scheduled services to 30 destination in the UK, mainland Europe and North America; cargo and charter flights; Chair. Sir MICHAEL BISHOP; CEO NIGEL TURNER.

BmiBaby: Donington Hall, Castle Donington, Derby, DE74 2SB; tel. (1332) 854000; internet www.bmibaby.com; f. 2002; low-cost passenger services to 20 European destinations; Man. Dir DAVID BRYON.

THE UNITED KINGDOM

easyJet Airline: London Luton Airport, Easy Land, Luton, LU2 9LS; tel. (1582) 445566; fax (1582) 443355; internet www.easyjet.co.uk; f. 1995; low-cost scheduled domestic and European passenger services from 8 UK airports; Chair. Sir COLIN CHANDLER; Chief Exec. ANDREW HARRISON.

First Choice Airways: Commonwealth House, Chicago Ave, Manchester Airport, M90 3DP; tel. (870) 757-2757; fax (161) 908-2275; e-mail eteam@firstchoice.co.uk; internet www.firstchoice.co.uk; f. 1987 as air2000; name changed to above in 2004; scheduled services to the Mediterranean, the USA and the Caribbean; subsidiary of First Choice Holidays PLC; Man. Dir CHRIS BROWNE.

FlyBe: Jack Walker House, Exeter International Airport, Exeter, EX5 2HL; tel. (1392) 366669; fax (1392) 366151; e-mail customerrelationsadmin@flybe.com; internet www.flybe.com; f. 1979 as Jersey European Airways; name changed as above 2002; independent regional low fares airline providing low-cost domestic and European services from 19 British airports; Chair. and CEO JIM FRENCH.

FlyGlobespan: Colinton House, 10 West Mill Road, Colinton, Edinburgh, EH13 0NX; tel. (870) 556-1522; internet www.flyglobespan.com; f. 2003; low-cost scheduled European flights to 19 destinations, operating from Edinburgh, Glasgow and London Stansted airports; Chair. TOM DALRYMPLE.

KLM UK: Skyway House, Parsonage Rd, Takeley, Bishop Stortford, Herts, CM22 6PU; tel. (1279) 874066; fax (1279) 874067; internet www.klm.com; f. 1980 as Air UK; CEO L. M. VAN WIJK.

Loganair Ltd: St Andrews Drive, Glasgow Airport, Abbotsinch, Paisley, Renfrewshire, PA3 2TG; tel. (141) 848-7594; fax (141) 887-6020; internet www.loganair.co.uk; f. 1962; operating as British Airways franchisee; Scottish domestic services; Chair. SCOTT GRIER; Chief Exec. JIM CAMERON.

Monarch Airlines: Prospect House, Prospect Way, London Luton Airport, Luton, LU2 9NU; tel. (1582) 400000; fax (1582) 411000; internet www.flymonarch.com; f. 1967; scheduled and charter services to the Mediterranean; CEO PETER BROWN.

MyTravel Group PLC: Parkway One, 300 Princess Rd, Manchester, M14 7QU; tel. (161) 232-0066; fax (161) 232-6524; internet www.mytravelgroup.com; world-wide charter operations; operates scheduled, chartered and low-cost passenger service to European destinations; Chair. MICHAEL BECKETT; CEO PETER MCHUGH.

MyTravelLite: Holiday House, Sandbrook Park, Rochdale, OL11 1SA; tel. (8701) 564564; internet www.mytravellite.com; low-cost passenger services to 12 European destinations; Man. Dir JULIAN CARR.

Thomsonfly: London Luton Airport, Luton, LU2 9ND; tel. (870) 190-0737; e-mail kimberley_kay@tui-uk.co.uk; internet www.thomsonfly.com; f. 2004; propr TUI AG; operates scheduled services from Coventry, Sheffield and Bournemouth to domestic and European destinations; Chief Commercial Officer ALEX HUNTER.

Virgin Atlantic Airways: Manor Royal, Crawley, West Sussex, RH10 2NU; tel. (1293) 562345; fax (1293) 561721; internet www.virgin-atlantic.com; f. 1984; operates services to destinations in the USA, the Caribbean and the Far East; Chair. Sir RICHARD BRANSON.

Tourism

In 2004 there were an estimated 27.8m. arrivals by foreign visitors to the United Kingdom, generating £13,047m. in revenue.

Northern Ireland Tourist Board: 59 North St, Belfast, BT1 1NB; tel. (28) 9023-1221; fax (28) 9024-0960; e-mail info@nitb.com; internet www.discovernorthernireland.com; Chair. TOM MCGRATH; Chief Exec. ALAN CLARKE.

VisitBritain: Thames Tower, Black's Rd, London, W6 9EL; tel. (20) 8846-9000; fax (20) 8563-0302; e-mail corporatepr@visitbritain.org; internet www.visitbritain.com; markets Great Britain overseas and England to the British; Chair. Lord MARSHALL OF KNIGHTSBRIDGE; Chief Exec. TOM WRIGHT.

Visit London: 6th Floor, 2 More London Riverside, London, SE1 2RR; tel. (20) 7234-5751; fax (20) 7234-5800; e-mail enquiries@visitlondon.com; internet www.visitlondon.com; f. 1963; promotes and markets London to leisure and business visitors; Chair. TAMARA INGRAM; CEO DAVID CAMPBELL.

VisitScotland: Ocean Point One, 94 Ocean Drive, Leith, Edinburgh, EH6 6JH; tel. (131) 472-2222; e-mail info@visitscotland.com; internet www.visitscotland.com; Chair. PETER LEDERER; Chief Exec. PHILIP RIDDLE.

Visit Wales: Brunel House, 2 Fitzalan Rd, Cardiff, CF24 0UY; tel. (8708) 300306; fax (8701) 211259; e-mail info@visitwales.co.uk; internet www.visitwales.co.uk; Chair. PHILIP EVANS; Chief Exec. JONATHAN JONES.

UNITED KINGDOM CROWN DEPENDENCIES

The Channel Islands and the Isle of Man lie off shore from the United Kingdom but are not integral parts of the country. They are dependencies of the British Crown and have considerable self-government in internal affairs.

THE CHANNEL ISLANDS

The Channel Islands lie off the north-west coast of France to the west of Normandy, in the English Channel (la Manche). The bailiwicks of the Channel Islands (Guernsey and its dependencies, and Jersey) are the remnants of the Duchy of Normandy, which was in permanent union with the English (now British) Crown from 1106. They do not, however, form part of the United Kingdom. The islands have their own legislative assemblies and legal and administrative systems, their laws depending for their validity on Orders made by the Queen in Council. Her Majesty's Government in the United Kingdom is responsible for the defence and international relations of the islands, and the Crown is ultimately responsible for their good government. The bailiwicks do not form part of the European Union.

In addition to the British public holidays, the Channel Islands also celebrate 9 May (Liberation Day).

Guernsey

Introduction

The civil flag of Guernsey is white, bearing a red cross of St George, with a yellow couped cross superimposed on the cross. The capital is St Peter Port. English is the language in common use, but the Norman *patois* is spoken in some rural parishes. Dependencies of Guernsey are Alderney, Brecqhou, Sark, Herm, Jethou and Lihou.

Statistical Survey

(including Herm and Jethou)

Source (unless otherwise stated): Advisory and Finance Committee, Sir Charles Frossard House, La Charroterie, St Peter Port, Guernsey, GY1 1FH; tel. (1481) 717000; fax (1481) 717157; internet www.gov.gg/esu.

AREA AND POPULATION

Area: 63.1 sq km (24.3 sq miles).

Population (census of 29 April 2001): 59,807 (males 29,138, females 30,669).

Density (per sq km, 2001): 947.8.

Principal Towns (2001): St Peter Port 16,488; Vale 9,573; Castel 8,975; St Sampson 8,592; St Martin 6,267.

Births and Deaths (2000): Live births 644; Deaths 565.

Employment (September 2001): Total employed 32,293 (males 17,670, females 14,623); Total unemployed 338 (males 214, females 124).

Economically Active Population (2004): Horticulture and other primary 1,125; Manufacturing 1,383; Construction 3,214; Utilities 423; Transport 1,041; Hostelry 2,056; Supplier and wholesale selling 783; Retail 3,673; Personal services 845; Recreation and culture 460; Finance 7,158; Miscellaneous business 2,009; Information services 851; Health 2,033; Education 1,468; Public administration 2,637; Non-profit 252; Unallocated 25; *Total labour force* 31,436.

AGRICULTURE

The principal crops are flowers, much of which are grown under glass. About 16.3 sq km (6.2 sq miles) are cultivated.

FINANCE

Currency and Exchange Rates: 100 pence = 1 pound sterling (£). *Dollar and Euro Equivalents* (30 December 2005): US $1 = 58.07 pence; €1 = 68.51 pence; $100 = $172.19 = €145.96
Note: Guernsey is in monetary union with the United Kingdom. It has its own coins and notes but United Kingdom coins and notes are also legal tender

Budget (£ '000, 2003): *Revenue:* General revenue income: 287,969; *Expenditure:* General revenue expenditure: 254,390.

Cost of Living: (Retail Price Index at mid-year; base: 31 December 1999 = 100) All items 114.8 in 2003; 120.5 in 2004; 124.5 in 2005.

Gross Domestic Product by Economic Activity (estimates, £ '000, 2003): Horticulture 14,438; Other Primary 10,284; Manufacturing 36,337; Construction 105,962; Tourism 65,655; Retail, utilities, distribution and miscellaneous services 170,350; Financial services 438,055; Professional, business and personal services 176,889; Health, education and public administration 182,227; *Total factor incomes* 1,200,197; *Less* Pensions 28,000; *Total* 1,172,197 (excl. other income 213,865).

EXTERNAL TRADE

Principal Commodities: *Imports* (1999): Petroleum and oil 168,026,000 litres. *Exports* (1998, £ million): Light industry 47; Total flowers 34.0; Total vegetables 5.0.

TRANSPORT

Road Traffic (vehicles registered, 2004): Private vehicles 40,268; Commercial vehicles 7,673; Motorcycles 5,681.

Shipping (2004): Passenger movements 384,187.

Civil Aviation (2004): Passenger movements 907,661.

TOURISM

Number of Visitors (2004): 355,000.

COMMUNICATIONS MEDIA

Telephones (2004): 55,100 main lines in use.

Mobile Cellular Telephones (2004): 43,800.

Internet Users (2004): 36,000.

Source: International Telecommunication Union.

EDUCATION

Primary (2000): 4,977 pupils.

Secondary (2000): 3,900 pupils.

Directory

The Constitution

The Lieutenant-Governor and Commander-in-Chief of Guernsey is the personal representative of the Sovereign and the channel of communication between the Crown and the Insular Government. He is appointed by the Crown. He is entitled to sit and speak in the Assembly of the States, but not to vote.

The Bailiff is appointed by the Crown and is President both of the Assembly of the States (the insular legislature), where he has a casting vote, and of the Royal Court of Guernsey.

The government of the island is conducted by a Policy Council, 10 departments and five 'specialist' committees. The Chief Minister may nominate a Deputy Chief Minister and Ministers for each of the 10 departments. Ministers and committee chairmen are elected by the members of the States of Deliberation.

The States of Deliberation is composed of the following members:

(*a*) The Bailiff, who is President *ex officio*.

(*b*) HM Procureur (Attorney-General) and HM Comptroller (Solicitor-General) Law Officers of the Crown, who are appointed by the Crown. They are entitled to sit in the States and to speak, but not to vote.

(*c*) The 45 People's Deputies elected by popular franchise.

(*d*) The two Alderney Representatives elected by the States of Alderney.

Projets de Loi (Permanent Laws) require the sanction of Her Majesty in Council.

The function of the States of Election is to elect persons to the office of Jurat. It is composed of the following members:

(*a*) The Bailiff (President *ex officio*).

(*b*) The 12 Jurats or 'Jures-Justiciers'.

(*c*) The 10 Rectors of the Parishes.

(*d*) HM Procureur and HM Comptroller.

(*e*) The 45 People's Deputies.

(*f*) The 34 Douzaine Representatives.

Meetings of the States and of the Royal Court, formerly conducted in French, are now conducted in English, but the proceedings in both are begun and ended in French.

The Government

Lieutenant-Governor and Commander-in-Chief of the Bailiwick of Guernsey: Sir Fabian Malbon.
Secretary and ADC to the Lieutenant-Governor: Col R. H. Graham.
Bailiff of Guernsey: Geoffrey Robert Rowland.
Deputy Bailiff: Richard John Collas.
HM Procureur (Attorney-General): John Nikolas Van Leuven.
HM Comptroller (Solicitor-General): Howard Edward Roberts.
Chief Executive of the States: Mike Brown.

POLICY COUNCIL
(April 2006)

Chief Minister: Laurie Morgan.
Deputy Chief Minister and Minister of the Environment: Bernard Flouquet.
Minister of the Treasury and Resources: Lyndon Trott.
Minister of the Home Department: Michael Torode.
Minister of Education: Martin Ozanne.
Minister of Health and Social Services: Peter Roffey.
Minister of Housing: David Jones.
Minister of Public Services: William Bell.
Minister of Social Security: Mary Lowe.
Minister of Commerce and Employment: Stuart Falla.
Minister of Culture and Leisure: Peter Sirett.

Judicial System

Justice is administered in Guernsey by the Royal Court, which consists of the Bailiff and the 12 Jurats. The Royal Court also deals with a wide variety of non-contentious matters. A Stipendiary Magistrate deals with minor civil and criminal cases. The Guernsey Court of Appeal deals with appeals from the Royal Court.

Religion

CHRISTIANITY
The Church of England

The Church of England in Guernsey is the established church. The Deanery includes the islands of Alderney, Sark, Herm and Jethou; it forms part of the diocese of Winchester.

Dean of Guernsey: Very Rev. Canon K. Paul Mellor, The Deanery, Cornet St, St Peter Port, GY1 1BZ; tel. (1481) 720036; e-mail paul@townchurch.org.gg; internet www.townchurch.org.gg.

The Roman Catholic Church

The diocese of Portsmouth includes the Channel Islands and part of southern England. In Guernsey there are five Roman Catholic churches, of which the senior is St Joseph and St Mary, Cordier Hill, St Peter Port.

Catholic Dean of Guernsey: Canon Gerard Hetherington, Amphill House, Cordier Hill, St Peter Port, GY1 1JH; tel. (1481) 720196; fax (1481) 711247; e-mail sjoss.guernsey@virgin.net; internet www.catholicgsy.org.uk.

Other Christian Churches

The Presbyterian Church and the Church of Scotland are represented by St Andrew's Church, The Grange, St Peter Port. The Baptist, Congregational, Elim and Methodist Churches are also represented in the island.

The Press

Guernsey Press and Star: The Guernsey Press Co, POB 57, Braye Rd, Vale, GY1 3BW; tel. (1481) 240240; fax (1481) 240235; e-mail newsroom@guernsey-press.com; internet www.guernsey-press.com; f. 1897; daily; independent; Editor Richard Digard; circ. 16,189.

Guernsey Weekly Press: The Guernsey Press Co, POB 57, Braye Rd, Vale, GY1 3BW; tel. (1481) 240240; fax (1481) 240235; e-mail editorial@thisisguernsey.com; internet www.thisisguernsey.com; f. 1902; Thursday; independent; Editor Richard Digard.

Publisher

Toucan Press: The White Cottage, route de Carteret, Castel, GY5 7YG; tel. (1481) 257017; f. 1850; history, Thomas Hardy, Channel Islands; Man. Dir G. Stevens Cox.

Broadcasting and Communications

TELECOMMUNICATIONS

Cable and Wireless Guernsey: POB 3, St Peter Port, GY1 3AB; tel. (1481) 700700; fax (1481) 724640; e-mail customercare@cwguernsey.com; internet www.cw.com/guernsey; Chief Exec. Geoffrey Houston.

BROADCASTING
Radio

BBC: Radio and Television (see United Kingdom).
BBC Radio Guernsey: Television House, Bulwer Ave, St Sampsons, GY2 4LA; tel. (1481) 200600; fax (1481) 200361; e-mail radio.guernsey@bbc.co.uk; internet www.bbc.co.uk/guernsey; f. 1982; Man. Editor David Martin.

Island FM: 12 Westerbrook, St Sampsons, GY2 4QQ; tel. (1481) 242000; fax (1481) 241120; e-mail studio@islandfm.guernsey.net; internet www.islandfm.com; Programme Controller Gary Burgess.

Television

Channel Television: Television House, Bulwer Ave, St Sampson, GY2 4LA; tel. (1481) 241888; fax (1481) 241889; e-mail broadcast@channeltv.co.uk; internet www.channelonline.tv; Chair. Lord Iliffe; Chief Exec. Huw Davies.

(See also under Jersey.)

Finance

(cap. = capital; dep. = deposits; res = reserves; brs = branches; amounts in pounds sterling, unless otherwise indicated.)

Guernsey Financial Services Commission: POB 128, La Plaiderie Chambers, La Plaiderie, St Peter Port, GY1 3HQ; tel. (1481) 712706; fax (1481) 712010; e-mail info@gfsc.gg; internet www.gfsc.gg; regulates banking, investment, insurance and fiduciary activities; Dir-Gen. Peter Neville.

BANKING

In December 2005 total bank deposits in Guernsey were £80,728m. in 51 financial institutions.

British Clearing Banks

The banks listed below are branches of British banks, and details concerning directors, capital, etc. of the parent bank will be found under the appropriate section in the pages dealing with the United Kingdom.

Barclays Bank PLC: POB 41, Le Marchant House, Le Truchot, St Peter Port, GY1 3BE; tel. (1481) 705600; fax (1481) 713712; e-mail guernsey@internationalbanking.barclays.com; internet www.internationalbanking.barclays.com; Dir STEPHEN JONES; 2 brs.

HSBC Bank PLC: POB 31, HSBC House, Lefebvre St, St Peter Port, GY1 3AT; tel. (1481) 717717; fax (1481) 717700; internet www.hsbc.co.uk; Area Man. G. JOHN DAVIES; 5 brs.

Lloyds TSB Offshore Ltd: POB 13, 24 High St, St Peter Port, GY1 4BD; tel. (1481) 724061; fax (1481) 717468; 5 brs.

National Westminster Bank PLC: 35 High St, St Peter Port, GY1 4BE; tel. (1481) 703800; fax (1481) 727019; Dir PETER MARCHANT.

Other Banks

Adam and Company International Ltd: POB 402, St Andrew's House, Le Bordage, St Peter Port, GY1 3GB; tel. (1481) 715055; fax (1481) 726919; e-mail adamint@guernsey.net; internet www.adambank.com; f. 1990; cap. 0.5m., res 0.5m., dep. 91.5m. (Dec. 2003); Chair. RAY ENTWHISTLE; Man. Dir BARRY JOHN MILDON.

Banca Monte dei Paschi (Channel Islands) Ltd: St Julian's Court, St Julian's Ave, St Peter Port, GY1 4HA; tel. (1481) 723776; fax (1481) 728628; e-mail admin@bmpci.co; internet www.mps.it; f. 1973; cap. 1.0m., res 5.8m., dep. 75.3m. (Dec. 2002); Chair. P. BRIONI; Man. Dir I. C. LACEY.

Bank of Bermuda (Guernsey) Ltd: POB 208, Bermuda House, St Julian's Ave, St Peter Port, GY1 3NF; tel. (1481) 707000; fax (1481) 726987; internet www.bankofbermuda.bm; f. 1973; cap. 14.0m., res 8.9m., dep. 591.8m., (Dec. 2003); Man. Dir PETER LE NOURY.

Bank of Butterfield International (Guernsey) Ltd: POB 25, Regency Court, Glategny Esplanade, St Peter Port, GY1 3AP; tel. (1481) 711521; fax (1481) 714533; e-mail info@butterfield.gg; internet www.butterfieldbank.gg; Man. Dir BOB MOORE.

Bristol and West International Ltd: POB 611, Old Bank, St Peter Port, GY1 4NY; tel. (1481) 720609; fax (1481) 711658; e-mail info@bwi.co.gg; internet www.bwi.co.gg; f. 1964; cap. 6.2m., res 41.6m., dep. 805.7m. (March 2004); Chair. IAN BEVERIDGE.

BSI Generali Bank (CI) Ltd: POB 162, Generali House, Hirzel St, St Peter Port, GY1 4HA; tel. (1481) 714444; fax (1481) 734649; internet www.ch.bsibank.com; f. 1989; Chair. RETO KESSLER.

Clariden Bank: POB 581, Helvetia Court, South Esplanade, St Peter Port, GY1 6LJ; tel. (1481) 715333; fax (1481) 716569; internet www.clariden.com; cap. US $14.2m., res $8.0m., dep. $522.3m. (Dec. 2003); Chair. B. F. STALDER; CEO A. F. GOOD.

Close Bank Guernsey Ltd: POB 116, Admiral Park, St Peter Port, GY1 3EZ; tel. (1481) 726014; fax (1481) 726645; e-mail infogsy@closepb.com; internet www.closepb.com; cap. 1.0m., dep. 309.4m. (Jan. 2005); Chair. C. N. FISH; Man. Dir A. HENTON.

Crédit Suisse (Guernsey) Ltd: POB 368, Helvetia Court, South Esplanade, St Peter Port, GY1 3JY; tel. (1481) 719000; fax (1481) 724676; e-mail csguernsey.info@credit-suisse.com; internet www.credit-suisse.com/guernsey; f. 1986; cap. US $6.1m., res $126.3m., dep. $2,401.5m. (Dec. 2003); CEO A. F. GOOD.

EFG Private Bank (Channel Islands) Ltd: POB 603, EFG House, St Julian's Ave, St Peter Port, GY1 4NN; tel. (1481) 723432; fax (1481) 723488; internet www.efggroup.com; cap. 5.0m., res 28.3m., dep. 406.0m. (Dec. 2004); Man. Dir M. J. DE JERSEY.

SG Hambros Bank (Channel Islands) Ltd: POB 6, Hambro House, St Julian's Ave, St Peter Port, GY1 3AE; tel. (1481) 726521; fax (1481) 727139; e-mail channelislands@sghambros.com; internet www.sghambros.com; f. 1967; formerly SG Hambros Bank and Trust (Guernsey) Ltd; name changed in 2005 following merger with SG Hambros Bank and Trust (Jersey) Ltd; merchant bankers; cap. 2.5m., res 54.7m., dep. 523.2m. (Dec. 2003); Chair. W. J. NEWBURY; Chief Exec. R. A. OLLIVER.

HSBC Private Bank (Guernsey) Ltd: HSBC Republic Bldg, Rue du Pré, St Peter Port, GY1 1LU; tel. (1481) 710901; fax (1481) 711824; internet www.hsbcprivatebank.com; f. 1985; cap. US $22.0m., res $378.0m., dep. $5,833.7m. (Dec. 2003); CEO GARY MILLER; COO KULVINDER SINGH.

Investec Bank (Channel Islands) Ltd: POB 188, La Vieille Cour, St Peter Port, GY1 3LP; tel. (1481) 723506; fax (1481) 741147; e-mail enquiries@investec-ci.com; internet www.investec.com; f. 1977 as Guinness Mahon Guernsey Ltd, name changed as above in 1999; cap. 8.7m., res 22.8m., dep. 523.0m. (March 2003); Chair. H. HERMAN; Gen. Man. MORT MIRGHAVAMEDDIN.

Lloyds TSB Offshore Ltd Private Banking Office: POB 136, Sarnia House, Le Truchot, St Peter Port, GY1 4EN; tel. (1481) 708000; fax (1481) 727416; e-mail pvtbankingg@lloydstsb-offshore.com; internet www.privatebanking.lloydstsb-offshore.com; Head of Sales and Relationships MARK JACKSON.

MeesPierson Reads: POB 119, Martello Court, Admiral Park, St Peter Port, GY1 3HB; tel. (1481) 751000; fax (1481) 751001; e-mail international@meespiersonreads.com; internet www.meespiersonreads.com; cap. 3.2m., res 62.8m., dep. 835.0m. (Dec. 2003); Man. Dir MICHAEL AYRE.

N. M. Rothschild & Sons (CI) Ltd: POB 58, St Julian's Court, St Julian's Ave, St Peter Port; tel. (1481) 713713; fax (1481) 727705; e-mail private.banking@rothschild.co.uk; internet www.rothschild.gg; f. 1967; subsidiary of N. M. Rothschild & Sons Ltd, London; cap. 5m., res 66.9m., dep. 970.5m. (March 2005); Chair. PETER JOHNS; Man. Dir PETER ROSE.

Rothschilds Bank Switzerland (CI) Ltd: POB 330, St Julian's Court, St Julian's Ave, St Peter Port, GY1 3UA; tel. (1481) 710521; fax (1481) 711272; e-mail tom.odonnell@rothschildbank.com; internet www.rothschildbank.com; Dir TOM O'DONNELL.

Royal Bank of Canada (Channel Islands) Ltd: POB 48, Canada Court, St Peter Port, GY1 3BQ; tel. (1481) 744000; fax (1481) 744001; internet www.rbcprivatebanking.com; f. 1973; wholly-owned subsidiary of Royal Bank of Canada; cap. 5m., res 82.2m., dep. 218.5m. (Oct. 2003); Chair. M. LAGOPOULOS; Man. Dir J. P. BREWSTER.

Schroders (CI) Ltd: POB 334, Sarnia House, Le Truchot, St Peter Port, GY1 3UF; tel. (1481) 703700; fax (1481) 703600; internet www.schroders.com/ci; cap. 5m., res 24m., dep. 550m. (Dec. 2004); Man. Dir TRUDI CLARK.

Banking Organization

Association of Guernsey Banks: c/o HSBC Bank PLC, POB 31, Lefebvre St, St Peter Port, GY1 3AT; fax (1481) 717710; e-mail stevehogg@hsbc.com; internet www.agb.org.gg; f. 1988; Chair. STEVE HOGG.

STOCK EXCHANGE

Channel Islands Stock Exchange, LBG: 1 Lefebvre St, St Peter Port, GY1 4PJ; tel. (1481) 737151; e-mail info@cisx.com; internet www.cisx.com; 31 cos listed.

INSURANCE

There were 254 insurance companies with offices in Guernsey in 2002.

Generali International Ltd: POB 613, Generali House, Hirzel St, St Peter Port, GY1 4PA; tel. (1481) 714108; fax (1481) 712424; e-mail enquiries@generali-guernsey.com; internet www.generali-worldwide.com.

Heritage Group: POB 225, Polygon Hall, Le Marchant St, St Peter Port, GY1 4HY; tel. (1481) 716000; fax (1481) 712357; e-mail info@heritage.gg; internet www.heritage.co.gg.

Insurance Corpn of the Channel Islands Ltd: POB 160, Dixcart House, St Peter Port, GY1 4EY; tel. (1481) 713322; fax (1481) 729189; e-mail icci@insurancecorporation.com; internet www.insurancecorporation.com; mem. of the Royal Sun Alliance Group; Man. Dir PETER WALPOLE.

Islands' Insurance Co Ltd: Lancaster Court, Forest Lane, St Peter Port, GY1 1WJ; tel. (1481) 710731.

Norwich Union Insurance Group: Hirzel Court, St Peter Port; tel. (1481) 724864.

Trade and Industry

CHAMBER OF COMMERCE

Guernsey Chamber of Commerce: Suite 3, 16 Glategny Esplanade, St Peter Port, GY1 1WN; tel. (1481) 727483; fax (1481) 710755; e-mail director@chamber.guernsey.net; internet chamber.guernsey.net; f. 1808; Dir MIKE COLLINS.

UTILITIES

Electricity

Guernsey Electricity: POB 4, Electricity House, North Side, Vale, GY1 3AD; tel. (1481) 200700; fax (1481) 246942; e-mail admin@electricity.gg; internet www.electricity.gg; Chair. KEN GREGSON; Man. Dir IAN WATSON.

Gas

Guernsey Gas: POB 70, Rue du Commerce, St Peter Port, GY1 3BZ; tel. (1481) 724811; internet www.gsygas.com; Dir PAUL GARLICK.

Water

Guernsey Water: POB 30, South Esplanade, St Peter Port, GY1 3AS; tel. (1481) 724552; fax (1481) 715094; fmrly States of Guernsey Waterboard; name changed as above May 2004.

Transport

SHIPPING

Alderney Shipping Co Ltd: POB 77, St Peter Port, GY1 4BN; tel. (1481) 730981; fax (1481) 712081; e-mail alderneyshipping@aldshp.co.uk; internet www.aldshp.co.uk.

Condor Ferries Ltd: New Jetty, White Rock, St Peter Port; tel. (1481) 729666; fax (1481) 712555; internet www.condorferries.co.uk; f. 1964; regular passenger service operating between the Channel Islands and St Malo, and between the Channel Islands and Poole, Weymouth and Portsmouth; Man. Dir ROBERT PROVAN; Gen. Man. NICK DOBBS.

Condorferries Freight: POB 10, New Jetty Offices, White Rock, St Peter Port, GY1 3AF; tel. (1481) 728620; fax (1481) 728521; e-mail jeff.vidamour@condorferries.co.uk; internet www.condorferries.com; regular ro-ro freight services between Portsmouth, Guernsey, Jersey and St Malo; Freight Dir JEFF VIDAMOUR.

Herm Seaway Express: Albert Pier, St Peter Port; tel. (1481) 724161; fax (1481) 700226; Contact PETER WILCOX.

Isle of Sark Shipping Co Ltd: White Rock, St Peter Port, GY1 2LN; tel. (1481) 724059; fax (1481) 713999; e-mail info@sarkshipping.guernsey.net; internet www.sarkshipping.guernsey.net; operates daily services between Guernsey and Sark.

Trident Charter Co Ltd: Woodville, Les Dicqs, Vale, GY6 8JW; tel. (1481) 245253; fax (1481) 700226; Contact PETER WILCOX.

CIVIL AVIATION

Aurigny Air Services Ltd: States Airport, La Planque Lane, Forest, GY8 0DT; tel. (1481) 822886; fax (1481) 823344; e-mail marketing@aurigny.com; internet www.aurigny.com; f. 1968; scheduled passenger services from Guernsey to Alderney, Jersey, London, Dinard, Amsterdam, Manchester, East Midlands; freight services, tour operation, ambulance charters and third party handling; Man. Dir MALCOLM HART.

Tourism

An estimated 355,000 tourists visited Guernsey during 2004.

VisitGuernsey: POB 23, St Peter Port, GY1 3AN; tel. (1481) 723552; fax (1481) 714951; e-mail enquiries@visitguernsey.com; internet www.visitguernsey.com; Chief Exec. STUART PINNELL.

Islands of the Bailiwick of Guernsey

Alderney

The area of Alderney is 7.9 sq km (3.1 sq miles) and in 2001 the population was about 2,294. The principal town is St Anne's.

The President, who is elected for a four-year term, is the civic head of Alderney and has precedence on the island over all persons except the Lieutenant-Governor of Guernsey, and the Bailiff of Guernsey or his representative. He presides over meetings of the States of Alderney, which are responsible for the administration of the island with the exception of police, public health and education, which are administered by the States of Guernsey. The States consist of 10 members who hold office for four years and are elected by universal suffrage of residents.

President of the States: Sir NORMAN BROWSE.
Chief Executive of the States: DAVID JEREMIAH.
Clerk of the Court: SARAH KELLY.

Brecqhou and Lihou

Brecqhou (measuring 1.2 km by 0.5 km) is a dependency of Sark. Lihou (area 0.2 sq km) is, for administrative purposes, part of Guernsey.

Herm

Herm is a tourist and farming island and is held on long lease from the States of Guernsey by Wood of Herm Island Ltd, with a duty to preserve the island's outstanding natural beauty and peacefulness. The island has an area of 2.0 sq km (0.8 sq miles). In 2001 the combined population of Herm and Jethou was 97.

Tenant: Wood of Herm Island Ltd.

Herm Island Administration Office: tel. (1481) 722377; e-mail directors@herm-island.com; internet www.herm-island.com; Island Man. A. G. HEYWORTH.

Jethou

Jethou has an area of 0.2 sq km (0.07 sq mile) and is leased by the Crown to a tenant who has no official functions.

Sark

The area of the island is 5.5 sq km (2.1 sq miles) and in 2001 the population was 589. No motor vehicles are permitted apart from a small number of tractors. In summer a daily boat service runs between Guernsey and Sark, and in winter a limited service is provided. There are two harbours on the island.

The Seigneur of Sark is the hereditary civic head of the island and thereby entitled to certain privileges. The Seigneur is a member of the Chief Pleas of Sark, the island's parliament, and has a suspensory veto on its ordinances. The Seigneur has the right, subject to the approval of the Lieutenant-Governor of Guernsey, to appoint the Seneschal of Sark, who is President of the Chief Pleas and Chairman of the Seneschal's Court, which is the local Court of Justice.

In March 2006 the Chief Pleas approved legislation to reduce the number of its members from 52 to 28, of whom 14 were to be Tenants and the remaining 14 residents. Under the reformed system the members of the Chief Pleas would be elected by universal suffrage of residents. Legislative elections were due to be held by December 2006.

Seigneur of Sark: JOHN MICHAEL BEAUMONT.
Seneschal: Lt-Col R. J. GUILLE.
Greffier: T. P. HAMON.

Sark Committee Office: La Chasse Marette, GY9 0SF; tel. (1481) 832118; fax (1481) 833086; e-mail sarkcommsec@gtonline.net; internet www.sark.gov.gg.

Sark Tourism: Harbour Hill, Sark, GY9 0SB; tel. (1481) 832345; fax (1481) 832483; internet www.sarktourism.gov.gg.

Jersey

Introduction

Jersey, the largest of the Channel Islands, is situated to the southeast of Guernsey, from which it is separated by 27 km (17 miles) of sea. The official language of Jersey is English (since 1960), although French is still used in the courts. The state and civil flag is white with a red saltire and coat of arms bearing three yellow lions and surmounted by a yellow crown. The capital is St Helier.

Statistical Survey

Source (unless otherwise stated): States of Jersey Statistics Department, Cyril Le Marquand House, PO Box 140, JE4 8QT, Jersey; tel. (1534) 603423; fax (1534) 603644; e-mail d.millard@gov.je; internet www.gov.je/statistics.

AREA AND POPULATION

Area: 116.2 sq km (44.9 sq miles).
Population (census of 11 March 2001): 87,186 (males 42,484, females 44,702). *2004* (official estimate at 31 December): 87,700.
Density (per sq km, 2004): 754.7.
Principal Towns (2001): St Helier 28,310; St Saviour 12,491; St Brelade 10,134; St Clement 8,196.
Births and Deaths (2004): Live births 973 (11.1 per 1,000); Deaths 745 (8.5 per 1,000).
Economically Active Population (census of 11 March 2001): Total 48,104 (males 25,983, females 22,121).

AGRICULTURE, ETC.

Principal Crops: There are 32,046 vergees of land under cultivation and 2,490 vergees under glasshouses (1 vergee = 2,200 sq yards). The principal crops are potatoes, cauliflowers and tomatoes. Dairy and cattle farming are important activities.
Fishing ('000 metric tons, 2003): Capture 1,759 (Wet fish 363, Brown crab 540, Lobster 167, Spider crab 233, Crawfish 1, Scallops 312, Whelk 134, Others 9); Aquaculture 669 (Oysters 560, Scallops 1, Mussels 108); *Total catch* 2,428.

FINANCE

Currency and Exchange Rates: 100 pence = 1 pound sterling (£). *Dollar and Euro Equivalents* (30 December 2005): US $1 = 58.07 pence; €1 = 68.51 pence; £100 = $172.19 = €145.96
Note: Jersey is in monetary union with the United Kingdom. It has its own coins and notes but United Kingdom coins and notes are also legal tender.
Budget (£ million, 2004): Revenue 441; Expenditure 460.
Cost of Living (Retail Price Index; base June 2000 = 100, all items): 113.4 in 2003; 118.9 in 2004; 122.6 in 2005.

EXTERNAL TRADE

Exports (£ '000, 2000): Agricultural products 1,651,903.

TRANSPORT

Road Traffic (vehicles registered at 31 December 2001): Motor cars 71,059; Motorcycles 5,676; Mopeds 2,200; Buses and minibuses 691; Tractors 2,369; Vans 7,562; Trucks 3,617; Total (incl. others) 94,538.
Shipping: *Vessels Using St Helier Port:* Commercial vessel arrivals 2,924 (2004); Passenger arrivals 450,195 (2001).
Civil Aviation (2004): Aircraft movements 71,648; Total passengers carried 1,496,805 (Arrivals 748,565, Departures 748,240).

TOURISM

Tourist Arrivals (2004): *Holiday and Leisure Visitors* (staying in paid accommodation): 377,900 (UK mainland 301,460; Other Channel Islands 14,900; France 29,380; Germany 10,060); *Total Arrivals:* 731,310.

COMMUNICATIONS MEDIA

Telephones (2003): 73,200 main lines in use.
Mobile Cellular Telephones (2003): 79,200.
Internet Users (2001): 8,000.
Source: International Telecommunication Union.

EDUCATION

Pupils (2004): Primary 7,164 (State schools 5,842, Private 1,322); Secondary 6,038 (State schools 5,024, Private 1,014).

Directory

The Constitution

The Lieutenant-Governor and Commander-in-Chief of Jersey is the personal representative of the Sovereign, the Commander of the Armed Forces of the Crown, and the channel of communication between the Crown and the Insular Government. He is appointed by the Crown, and is entitled to sit and speak in the Assembly of the States of Jersey, but not to vote. He has a veto on certain forms of legislation.

The Bailiff is appointed by the Crown, and is President both of the Assembly of the States (the insular legislature) and the Royal Court of Jersey. In the States, he has a right of dissent and a casting vote.

The Deputy Bailiff is appointed by the Crown and, when authorized by the Bailiff to do so, he may discharge any function appertaining to the office of Bailiff.

The government of the island is conducted by a Council of Ministers, which consists of a Chief Minister and nine other ministers. The Chief Minister is elected by the States and nominates the other ministers, subject to the approval of the States. The States consist of 12 Senators (elected for six years, six retiring every third year), 12 Constables (triennial), and 29 Deputies (triennial). They are elected by universal suffrage. The Dean of Jersey, the Attorney-General and Solicitor-General are appointed by the Crown and are entitled to sit and speak in the States, but not to vote. Permanent laws passed by the States require the sanction of Her Majesty in Council, but Triennial Regulations do not.

The Government

Lieutenant-Governor and Commander-in-Chief of Jersey: Lt-Gen. ANDREW RIDGEWAY.
Secretary to the Lieutenant-Governor and ADC: Lt-Col A. J. C. WOODROW.
Bailiff: Sir PHILIP MARTIN BAILHACHE.
Deputy Bailiff: MICHAEL CAMERON ST JOHN BIRT.
Dean of Jersey: Very Rev. JOHN N. SEAFORD.
Attorney-General: WILLIAM JAMES BAILHACHE.
Solicitor-General: STEPHANIE CLAIRE NICOLLE.
Greffier of the States: MICHAEL NELSON DE LA HAYE.

COUNCIL OF MINISTERS
(April 2006)

Chief Minister: FRANK HARRISON WALKER.
Minister for the Treasury and Resources: TERENCE LE SUEUR.
Minister for Home Affairs: WENDY KINNARD.
Minister for Education, Sport and Culture: MICHAEL VIBERT.
Minister for Health and Social Services: STUART SYVRET.
Minister for Social Security: PAUL ROUTIER.
Minister for Economic Development: PHILLIP OZOUF.
Minister for Transport and Technical Services: GUY DE FAYE.
Minister for Housing: TERENCE LE MAIN.
Minister for Planning and the Environment: FREDERICK ELLYER COHEN.

Judicial System

Justice is administered in Jersey by the Royal Court, which consists of the Bailiff or Deputy Bailiff and 12 Jurats elected by an Electoral College. There is a Court of Appeal, which consists of the Bailiff (or Deputy Bailiff) and two Judges, selected from a panel appointed by the Crown. A final appeal lies to the Privy Council in certain cases.

A Stipendiary Magistrate deals with minor civil and criminal cases. He also acts as an Examining Magistrate in some criminal matters.

Religion

CHRISTIANITY

The Church of England
The Church of England is the established church. The Deanery of Jersey is an Ecclesiastical Peculiar, governed by its own canons, the Dean being the Ordinary of the Island; it is attached to the diocese of Winchester for episcopal purposes.

Dean of Jersey: Very Rev. JOHN N. SEAFORD, The Deanery, David Place, St Helier, JE2 4TE; tel. (1534) 720001; fax (1534) 617488; e-mail deanofjersey@jerseymail.co.uk.

The Roman Catholic Church
The diocese of Portsmouth includes the Channel Islands and part of southern England. The Episcopal Vicar for the Channel Islands resides at St Peter Port, Guernsey. In Jersey there are 12 Roman Catholic churches, including St Mary and St Peter's, Wellington Rd (English), and St Thomas, Val Plaisant, St Helier (French).

Other Christian Churches
The Baptist, Congregational New Church, Methodist and Presbyterian churches are also represented.

The Press

Jersey Evening Post: POB 582, JE4 8XQ; tel. (1534) 611611; fax (1534) 611622; e-mail editorial@jerseyeveningpost.com; internet www.thisisjersey.com; f. 1890; independent; progressive; Propr The Claverley Company; Editor CHRIS BRIGHT; Man. Dir JERRY RAMSDEN; circ. 22,037.

Jersey Weekly Post: POB 582, JE4 8XQ; tel. (1534) 611611; fax (1534) 611622; e-mail editorial@jerseyeveningpost.com; internet www.thisisjersey.com; Thursday; Propr The Claverley Company; Editor CHRIS BRIGHT; circ. 1,200.

Publishers

Ashton & Denton Publishing Co (CI) Ltd: 3 Burlington House, St Saviour's Rd, St Helier, JE2 4LA; tel. (1534) 735461; fax (1534) 875805; e-mail asden@supanet.com; f. 1957; local history, holiday guides, financial; Man. Dir A. MACKENZIE.

Barnes Publishing Ltd: 18 Great Union Rd, St Helier, JE2 3RD; tel. (1534) 618166; fax (1534) 607029; e-mail ian.barnes@barnespublishing.com; internet barnespublishing.com; f. 1993; as Apache Publishing; name changed to above in 1998; Man. Dir IAN BARNES.

Broadcasting and Communications

TELECOMMUNICATIONS

Jersey Telecom: POB 53, No. 1 The Forum, Grenville St, St Helier, JE4 8PB; tel. (1534) 882882; fax (1543) 882883; e-mail enquiries@jerseytelecom.com; internet www.jerseytelecom.com; Chair. JOHN HENWOOD; Man. Dir BOB LAWRENCE.

BROADCASTING

Radio
BBC: Radio and Television (see United Kingdom).

BBC Radio Jersey: 18 Parade Rd, St Helier, JE2 3PL; tel. (1534) 837228; e-mail jersey@bbc.co.uk; internet www.bbc.co.uk/jersey; f. 1982; broadcasts 77 hours a week; Editor DENZIL DUDLEY.

Channel 103 FM: 6 Tunnell St, St Helier, JE2 4LU; tel. (1534) 888103; fax (1534) 877177; e-mail admin@channel103.com; internet www.channel103.com; f. 1992; Man Dir LINDA BURNHAM.

Television
Channel Television: Television Centre, St Helier, JE1 3ZD; tel. (1534) 816816; fax (1534) 816817; e-mail broadcast@channeltv.co.uk; internet www.channelonline.tv; f. 1962; daily transmissions; Chair. FRANCIS HAMON; Group Chief Exec. HUW DAVIES.

Programmes are also received from the BBC, Channel 4 and five in the United Kingdom and also from France.

Finance

Jersey Financial Services Commission: POB 267, Nelson House, David Pl., St Helier, JE4 8TP; tel. (1534) 822000; fax (1534) 822001; e-mail info@jerseyfsc.org; internet www.jerseyfsc.org; f. 1998; financial services regulator; Dir-Gen. DAVID CARSE.

BANKING
(cap. = capital; auth. = authorized; m. = million; dep. = deposits; res = reserves; br./brs = branch(es); amounts in pounds sterling, unless otherwise indicated.)

In 2005 total bank deposits in Jersey were £184,641m. in 47 institutions.

British Clearing Banks
The banks listed below are branches of British banks, and details concerning directors, capital, etc. of the parent bank will be found under the appropriate section in the pages dealing with the United Kingdom.

Barclays Bank PLC: POB 8, 13 Library Pl., St Helier, JE4 8NE; tel. (1534) 812000; fax (1534) 813500; Jersey Man. MARTYN SCRIVEN; 4 brs.

National Westminster Bank PLC: POB 11, 16 Library Pl., St Helier, JE4 8NH; tel. (1534) 282828; fax (1534) 282730; Man. P. TAYLOR; 6 brs.

Other Banks

ABN AMRO Trust Company (Jersey) Ltd: POB 255, 7 Castle St, St Helier, JE4 8TB; tel. (1534) 604301; e-mail pbclients@uk.abnamro.com; internet www.abnamroprivatebanking.com/jersey; f. 1991; Gen. Man. MARK HENNY.

AIB Bank (CI) Ltd: POB 468, AIB House, Grenville St, St Helier, JE4 8WT; tel. (1534) 883000; fax (1534) 883112; e-mail business.development@aiboffshore.com; internet www.alliedirishoffshore.com; f. 1981; cap. 2.5m., res 63.6m., dep. 891.0m. (Dec. 2003); Man. Dir J. F. LYNES.

Ansbacher (Channel Islands) Ltd: POB 393, 7–11 Britannia Pl., Bath St, St Helier, JE4 8US; tel. (1534) 504504; fax (1534) 504575; e-mail info@ansbacher.co.je; internet www.ansbacher.com/channelislands.html; f. 1984 as Westpac Banking Corpn (Jersey) Ltd; acquired by Henry Ansbacher Group in 1995; cap. 2.5m., res 9.1m., dep. 353.9m. (Sept. 2002); Man. Dir ANDREW EVANS.

Bank of Ireland (Jersey) Ltd: POB 416, Bank of Ireland House, Francis St, St Helier, JE4 9WD; tel. (1534) 617453; fax (1534) 617815; internet www.bankofireland.ie; Man. Dir D. M. COSGRAVE.

Bank Leumi (Jersey) Ltd: POB 510, 27 Hill St, St Helier, JE4 5TR; tel. (1534) 702590; fax (1534) 702570; e-mail dlieberman@leumijersey.com; internet www.bankleumi.co.uk; f. 1993; cap. 2.5m., res 2.3m., dep. 136.0m. (Dec. 2004).

Bank of Nova Scotia Channel Islands Ltd: POB 60, Kensington Chambers, 46–50 Kensington Pl., St Helier, JE4 9PE; tel. (1534) 789898; fax (1534) 873327; e-mail mailbox@scotia-offshore.com; f. 1972; cap. US $1.3m., dep. $445.9m. (Sept. 2003); Chair. J. R. MACDONALD; Man. Dir J. D. MURPHY.

Bank of Scotland International Ltd: Halifax House, 31–33 New St, St Helier, JE4 8YW; tel. (1534) 613500; fax (1534) 759280; e-mail enquiry@bankofscotlandint.co.uk; internet www.bankofscotland-international.com; cap. 15.0m., dep. 822.8m. (Feb. 2001); f. 1986; Man. Dir GRAEME HALL.

Banque Transatlantique (Jersey) Ltd: POB 206, 47–49 La Motte St, St Helier, JE4 0XR; tel. (1534) 881471; fax (1534) 881473; e-mail btj@sboff.com; internet www.transat.tm.fr.

BBVA Privanza Bank (Jersey) Ltd: 2 Mulcaster St, St Helier, JE2 3NJ; tel. (1534) 511200; fax (1534) 511201; e-mail info@bbvajersey.com; cap. 6.5m., res 48.2m., dep. 976.9m. (Dec. 2000); Man. M. LOPEZ.

BHF-Bank (Jersey) Ltd: 6 Wests Centre, St Helier, JE2 4ST; tel. (1534) 879044; fax (1534) 879246; f. 1981; cap. €4m., res €6.7m., dep. €880.9m. (Dec. 2000); Man. J. M. ALCOCK.

Citibank (Channel Islands) Ltd: POB 104, 38 The Esplanade, St Helier, JE4 8QB; tel. (1534) 608010; fax (1534) 608190; internet www.citibank.com/privatebank/index.htm; f. 1969; cap. US $0.9m., res $7.6m., dep. $724.3m. (Dec. 2003); Chair. CLIVE JONES.

Coutts (Jersey) Ltd: POB 6, 23–25 Broad St, St Helier, JE4 8ND; tel. (1534) 282394; fax (1534) 282400; internet www.coutts.com; f. 1969; cap. 0.5m., dep. 18.5m.; Island Dir DAVID NEUSCHAFFER.

Deutsche Bank International Ltd: POB 727, St Paul's Gate, New St, St Helier, JE4 8ZB; tel. (1534) 889900; fax (1534) 889911; internet www.dboffshore.com; f. 1972; cap. 15.0m., res 154.2m., dep. 2,801.5m. (Dec. 2003); Man. Dir MARK WILDMAN; 3 brs.

Dexia Private Bank Jersey Ltd: POB 12, 2–6 Church St, St Helier, JE4 9NE; tel. (1534) 834400; fax (1534) 834411; e-mail dexiapbjsy@localdial.com; internet www.dexia-privatebank.je; Man. Dir DAVID G. SMITH.

Fairbairn Private Bank Ltd: 28 New St, St Helier, JE2 3TE; tel. (1534) 887889; fax (1534) 509725; e-mail jer@fairbairnpb.com; internet www.fairbairnpb.com; f. 1994 as Flemings (Jersey) Ltd, changed name as above in 2004; cap. 0.5m., res 17m., dep. 245m. (Dec. 2004); Man. Dir G. J. HORTON.

UNITED KINGDOM CROWN DEPENDENCIES

SG Hambros Bank (Channel Islands) Ltd: POB 78, 18 Esplanade, St Helier, JE4 8PR; tel. (1534) 815555; fax (1534) 815640; e-mail channelislands@sghambros.com; internet www.sghambros.com; f. 1967 as Hambros (Jersey) Ltd; previously SG Hambros Bank and Trust (Jersey) Ltd; name changed in 2005 following merger with SG Hambros Bank and Trust (Guernsey) Ltd; subsidiary of SG Hambros Bank and Trust Ltd, London; cap. 2.6m., res 5.8m., dep. 732.2m. (Dec. 2003); Chair. W. J. NEWBURY; Man. Dir RICHARD OLLIVER.

HSBC Bank International Ltd: HSBC House, St Helier, JE1 1HS; tel. (1534) 616000; fax (1534) 616001; e-mail offshore@hsbc.com; internet www.offshore.hsbc.com; cap. res. 146.4m. dep. 5,063.0m. (Dec. 2002); Chief Exec. GUY HAMILTON.

HSBC Bank Middle East: POB 315, St Helier, JE4 8UB; tel. (1534) 606511; fax (1534) 606149; e-mail mem.bpa@hsbc.com; internet www.banking.middleeast.hsbc.com; cap. US $331.4m., res $314.0m., dep. $9,158.8m. (Dec. 2003); Chair. STEPHEN GREEN.

HSBC Private Bank (Jersey) Ltd: POB 88, 1 Grenville St, St Helier, JE4 9PF; tel. (1534) 606500; fax (1534) 606504; internet www.hsbcprivatebank.com; fmrly HSBC Republic Bank (Jersey) Ltd; name changed as above in Jan. 2004; cap. 1.1m., res 47.3m., dep. 1,293.0m. (Dec. 2003); CEO JONATHAN WATSON.

ING Bank (Jersey) Ltd: Huguenot House, 28 La Motte St, St Helier, JE2 4SZ; tel. (1534) 880888; fax (1534) 880777; f. 1988; name changed as above in 2003; Man. J. FAVRE.

Kleinwort Benson (Channel Islands) Ltd: POB 76, Wests Centre, St Helier, JE4 8PQ; tel. (1534) 613000; fax (1534) 613141; f. 1962; mem. of the Dresdner Bank Group; cap. 5., res 113.0m., dep. 2,154.3m. (Dec. 2003); Man. Dir R. F. ROBINS.

Lloyds TSB Offshore Ltd: POB 311, 25 New St, St Helier, JE4 8ZU; tel. (800) 735-3408; fax (1534) 604830; e-mail jerseyoffc@lloydstsb-offshore.com; internet www.lloydstsb-offshore.com; part of Lloyds TSB banking group; cap. 120.0m., res 100.4m., dep. 2,767.5m. (Dec. 2003); Chair. DAVID JAMES OLDFIELD; 4 brs.

JP Morgan Chase Bank: POB 127, JP Morgan House, Grenville St, St Helier, JE4 8QH; tel. (1534) 626262; fax (1534) 626301; Gen. Man. L. C. WORTHAM.

JP Morgan Trust Co (Jersey): POB 127, JP Morgan House, Grenville St, St Helier; tel. (1534) 626262; fax (1534) 626300; cap. US $30m.; Chair. T. TODMAN; Man. Dir L. C. WORTHAM.

The Royal Bank of Scotland International Ltd: POB 64, 71 Bath St, St Helier, JE4 8PJ; tel. (1534) 285200; fax (1534) 285222; internet www.rbsint.com; cap. 86.5m., res 686.3m., dep. 14,216.7m. (Dec. 2002); Chief Exec. JIM PATON.

Standard Bank Jersey Ltd: POB 583, Standard Bank House, 47–49 La Motte St, St Helier, JE4 8XR; tel. (1534) 881188; fax (1534) 881133; e-mail sbj@standardbank.com; internet www.sboff.com; f. 1977; fmrly Brown Shipley (Jersey); cap. 10.0m., res 12.1m., dep. 611.6m. (Dec. 2004); Chair. R. A. G. LEITH; CEO IAN GIBSON.

Standard Chartered (Jersey) Ltd: 15 Castle St, St Helier, JE4 8PT; tel. (1534) 704000; fax (1534) 704600; e-mail ccc.jersey@uk.standardchartered.com; internet www.standardchartered.com/je; f. 1966; name changed as above in 2004; cap. & res US $332m. (Dec. 2004); CEO ALISON MCFADYEN.

INSURANCE

Jersey Mutual Insurance Soc., Inc: 74 Halkett Pl., St Helier, JE1 1BT; tel. (1534) 734246; fax (1534) 733381; e-mail info@jerseymutual.com; internet www.jerseymutual.com; f. 1869; fire; Pres. P. F. HANNING; Sec. S. J. MOREL.

Trade and Industry

CHAMBER OF COMMERCE

Chamber of Commerce: Chamber House, 25 Pier Rd, St Helier, JE1 4HF; tel. (1534) 724536; fax (1534) 734942; e-mail admin@jerseychamber.com; internet www.jerseychamber.com; f. 1768; Pres. KEVIN KEEN; Chief Exec. ANDREW GOODYEAR; 500 mems.

Utilities

Electricity

Jersey Electricity Co Ltd: POB 45, Queen's Rd, St Helier, JE4 8NY; tel. (1534) 505460; fax (1534) 505565; e-mail jec@jec.co.uk; internet www.jec.co.uk; f. 1924; Chair. DEREK MALTWOOD; CEO MIKE LISTON.

Gas

Jersey Gas Co Ltd: POB 169, Thomas Edge House, Tunnell St, St Helier, JE4 8RE; tel. (1534) 755500; fax (1534) 769822; e-mail jerseygas@jsy-gas.com; internet www.jsygas.com; Man. Dir ROBERT STADDON.

Water

Jersey New Waterworks Co Ltd: Mulcaster House, Westmount Rd, St Helier, JE4 9PN; tel. (1534) 707301; fax (1534) 707401; e-mail info@jerseywater.je; internet www.jerseywater.je; Chair. DAVID NORMAN.

Transport

SHIPPING

The harbour of St Helier has 1,400 m of cargo working quays, with 10 berths in dredged portion (2.29 m) and eight drying berths.

Condor Jersey Ltd: Elizabeth Terminal and Albert Quay, St Helier; tel. (1534) 607080; fax (1534) 280767; e-mail reservations@condorferries.co.uk; internet www.condorferries.co.uk; head office in Poole, England; daily services to mainland Britain; also regular services to Guernsey and St Malo (France); Gen. Man. NICK DOBBS.

CIVIL AVIATION

The States of Jersey Airport is at St Peter, Jersey.

Airline

FlyBe: States Airport, St Peter; tel. (871) 700-0123; internet www.flybe.com; f. 1983 as Jersey European Airways, changed name as above in 2004; services between Jersey and Guernsey, London, Exeter, Blackpool, Bristol, Leeds/Bradford, Birmingham, the Isle of Man, Belfast, Dublin, Derry, Amsterdam, Marseilles and Dinard; Chief Exec. BARRY PERROTT.

Tourism

In 2004 Jersey recorded some 731,310 tourists arrivals; 377,900 visitors stayed in paid accommodation.

Jersey Tourism: Liberation Sq., St Helier, JE1 1BB; tel. (1534) 500700; fax (1534) 500808; e-mail info@jersey.com; internet www.jersey.com; Dir DAVID DE CARTERET.

THE ISLE OF MAN

Introduction

The Isle of Man lies in the Irish Sea between the Cumbrian coast of England and Northern Ireland. It is a dependency of the Crown and does not form part of the United Kingdom. It has its own legislative assembly and legal and administrative systems, its laws depending for their validity on Orders made by the Queen in Council. Her Majesty's Government in the United Kingdom is responsible for the defence and international relations of the island, and the Crown is ultimately responsible for its good government. However, control of direct taxation is exercised by the Manx Government and, although most rates of indirect taxation are the same on the island as in the United Kingdom, there is some divergence of rates. The capital is Douglas. In addition to the British public holidays, the Isle of Man also celebrates 5 July (Tynwald Day).

Statistical Survey

Source: Isle of Man Government Offices, Douglas; internet www.gov.im.

AREA AND POPULATION

Area: 572 sq km (221 sq miles).

Population (census, 29–30 April 2001): 76,315 (males 37,372, females 38,943).

Density (per sq km, 2001): 133.4.

Principal Towns (2001): Douglas (capital) 25,347; Onchan 8,803; Ramsey 7,322; Peel 3,785; Port Erin 3,351; Castletown 3,100.

UNITED KINGDOM CROWN DEPENDENCIES

The Isle of Man

Births and Deaths (2004): Live births 862 (birth rate 11.3 per 1,000); Deaths 798 (death rate 10.5 per 1,000).

Employment (29–30 April 2001): 39,050 (males 21,299, females 17,751): Agriculture, etc. 543; Manufacturing 3,185; Construction 2,512; Transport and communication 2,970; Retail distribution 3,644; Banking and finance 8,959; Professional and scientific services 7,356; Public administration 3,105.

AGRICULTURE, ETC.

Crops (area in acres, 2004): Cereals and potatoes 10,666; Grass 66,743; Rough grazing 34,084.

Livestock (2004): Cattle 21,442; Sheep 85,134; Pigs 817; Poultry 14,871.

Fishing (2004): *Amount Landed* (metric tons): Scallops 1,106; Queen scallops 859; *Value of Landings:* Scallops £1.7m.; Queen scallops £0.45m.; Total first-hand sale value of all landings: £2.8m.

FINANCE

Currency and Exchange Rates: 100 pence = 1 pound sterling (£). *Dollar and Euro Equivalents* (30 December 2005): US $1 = 58.07 pence; €1 = 68.51 pence; £100 = $172.19 = €145.96

Note: The Isle of Man is in monetary union with the United Kingdom. It has its own coins and notes, but United Kingdom coins and notes are also legal tender.

Budget: (projections, year ending 31 March 2005): *Total Revenue* £476.6m. (Value-added tax £266.9m.; Resident income tax £95.9m.); *Total Expenditure* £467.5m.

Cost of Living: (Retail Price Index at September; base: January 2000 = 100) All items 109.1 in 2003; 114.7 in 2004; 119.5 in 2005.

TRANSPORT

Road Traffic (registered vehicles, 2001): Private 45,195; Engineering 385; Goods 4,489; Agricultural 931; Hackney 790; Public service 146; Motorcycles, scooters and tricycles 4,519.

Shipping (2003/04, unless otherwise indicated): Passengers handled 664,012; Registered merchant vessels 299; Other registered vessels 677; Total displacement ('000 grt, 2004) 7,341.

Civil Aviation: Passengers handled 773,743 (2004); Freight carried 4,594 metric tons (2003).

TOURISM

Tourist Arrivals (2004): Staying visitors 240,958; Day visitors 7,286; Business travellers 92,658.

COMMUNICATIONS MEDIA

Telephone Connections (2001): Fixed 56,000; Mobile 32,000.

Television Licences (2000): 28,601.

EDUCATION

State Primary (2004/05): 35 schools, 6,653 students.

State Secondary (2004/05): 5 schools, 4,788 students.

College (2004/05): 1 college, 8,300 students

There are, in addition, two private schools.

Directory

The Constitution

The legislature is Tynwald, comprising two branches, the Legislative Council and the House of Keys, sitting together as one body, but voting separately on all questions except in certain eventualities. The House of Keys has 24 members elected by adult suffrage for five years. The Legislative Council is composed of a President, the Lord Bishop of Sodor and Man, the Attorney-General and eight members elected by the House of Keys. The Head of State of the Isle of Man is the British monarch. The Lieutenant-Governor, who is the Crown's personal representative on the island, is appointed by the Head of State for a five-year term.

The Government

HEAD OF STATE

Lord of Mann: HM Queen ELIZABETH II.
Lieutenant-Governor: Sir PAUL HADDACKS.

COUNCIL OF MINISTERS
(April 2006)

Chief Minister: DONALD JAMES GELLING.
Minister of Agriculture, Fisheries and Forestry: PHIL GAWNE.
Minister of Transport: PHIL BRAIDWOOD.
Minister of the Treasury: ALLAN BELL.
Minister of Health and Social Security: STEVE RODAN.
Minister of Home Affairs: JOHN SHIMMIN.
Minister of Local Government and the Environment: JOHN RIMINGTON.
Minister of Trade and Industry: ALEX DOWNIE.
Minister of Tourism and Leisure: DAVID CRETNEY.
Minister of Education: DAVID M. ANDERSON.

GOVERNMENT OFFICES

Isle of Man Government: Bucks Rd, Douglas; tel. (1624) 685685; fax (1624) 685710; e-mail chiefsecs@gov.im; internet www.gov.im.

External Relations Division: Government Office, Bucks Rd, Douglas, IM1 3PN; tel. (1624) 685202; fax (1624) 685710; e-mail anne.shimmin@cso.gov.im; internet www.gov.im.

Legislature

TYNWALD

President: NOEL QUAYLE CRINGLE.
Deputy President: JAMES ANTHONY BROWN.

Legislative Council (Upper House)

President of the Council: NOEL QUAYLE CRINGLE.
Lord Bishop of Sodor and Man: Rt Rev. GRAEME PAUL KNOWLES.
Attorney-General: WILLIAM JOHN HOWARTH CORLETT.
Members appointed by the House of Keys: G. H. WAFT, D.J. GELLING, L.I. SINGER, E. G. LOWEY, C. M. CHRISTIAN, P.M. CROWE, D.M.W. BUTT, A.F. DOWNIE.
Clerk: MARILYN CULLEN.

House of Keys (Lower House)

Speaker: JAMES ANTHONY BROWN.
Deputy Speaker: HAZEL HANNAN.
Clerk of Tynwald, Secretary of the House and Counsel to the Speaker: MALACHY CORNWELL-KELLY.

The House of Keys consists of 24 members, elected by adult suffrage—eight for Douglas, two for Ramsey, one each for Peel and Castletown, and 12 for rural districts. The last general election was held in November 2001. There are no political parties as such on the Isle of Man.

Judicial System

The Isle of Man is, for legal purposes, an autonomous sovereign country under the British Crown, with its own legislature and its own independent judiciary administering its own common or customary and statute law. The law of the Isle of Man is, in most essential matters, the same as the law of England and general principles of equity administered by the English Courts are followed by the Courts of the Isle of Man unless they conflict with established local precedents. Her Majesty's High Court of Justice of the Isle of Man is based upon the English system but modified and simplified to meet local conditions. Justices of the Peace (JPs) are appointed by the Lord Chancellor of England usually on the nomination of the Lieutenant-Governor. The Deemsters (see below), the High Bailiff, the Mayor of Douglas, and the Chairmen of the Town and Village Commissioners are *ex-officio* JPs. The Manx Court of Appeal consists of the Deemsters and the Judge of Appeal.

First Deemster and Clerk of the Rolls: J.M. KERRUÍSH.
Second Deemster: D.C. DOYLE.
Judge of Appeal: G. F. TATTERSALL.

UNITED KINGDOM CROWN DEPENDENCIES   The Isle of Man

Religion

CHRISTIANITY

The Church of England

The Isle of Man forms the diocese of Sodor and Man, comprising 27 parishes. The parish church at Peel was designated a cathedral in 1980.

Lord Bishop of Sodor and Man: Rt Rev. GRAEME PAUL KNOWLES, Bishop's House, The Falls, Tromode Road, Cronkbourne, IM4 4PZ; tel. (1624) 622108; fax (1624) 672890; e-mail bishop-sodor@mcb.net.

Roman Catholic Church

The deanery of the Isle of Man is part of the archdiocese of Liverpool. There are eight Catholic churches on the island.

Dean of the Isle of Man: Very Rev. Canon BRENDAN ALGER, St Mary of the Isle, Douglas, IM1 3EG; tel. (1624) 675509.

Other Churches

There are also congregations of the following denominations: Baptist, Bethel Non-Denominational, Christadelphian, Congregational, Greek Orthodox, Independent Methodist, Methodist, Presbyterian, Elim Pentecostal, United Reform, and Society of Friends; also Christian Science, Jehovah's Witnesses and the Church of Jesus Christ of Latter-day Saints.

There are small Bahá'í, Jewish and Muslim communities on the island.

The Press

Isle of Man Church Leader: POB 9, Peel, IM99 9XA; tel. (1624) 843102; e-mail faulds@mcb.net; internet www.churchleader.co.im; monthly; Editor IAN FAULDS; circ. 15,000.

Isle of Man Courier: Publishing House, Peel Rd, Douglas, IM1 5PZ; tel. (1624) 695695; fax (1624) 661041; e-mail john.sherrocks@newsiom.co.im; internet www.iomonline.co.im; f. 1884; weekly; Editor JOHN SHERROCKS; circ. 36,018.

Isle of Man Examiner: Publishing House, Peel Rd, Douglas, IM1 5PZ; tel. (1624) 695695; fax (1624) 661041; e-mail john.sherrocks@newsiom.co.im; internet www.iomonline.co.im; f. 1880; weekly; Editor JOHN SHERROCKS; circ. 14,436.

The Manx Independent: Publishing House, Peel Rd, Douglas, IM1 5PZ; tel. (1624) 695695; fax (1624) 661041; e-mail john.sherrocks@newsiom.co.im; internet www.iomonline.co.im; f. 1987; Friday; Editor JOHN SHERROCKS; circ. 12,711.

Manx Tails Magazine: Media House, Cronkbourne, Douglas, IM4 4SB; tel. (1624) 696560; fax (1624) 625623; e-mail mail@manninmedia.co.im; internet www.manninmedia.co.im/tails.html; monthly; Editor SIMON RICHARDSON.

Sea Breezes Magazine: Media House, Cronkbourne, Douglas, IM4 4SB; tel. (1624) 696573; fax (1624) 661655; e-mail seabreezes@manninmedia.co.im; internet www.seabreezes.co.im; f. 1919; Editor ANDREW DOUGLAS.

Publishers

Amulree Publications: Glen Rd, Laxey, IM4 7AN; tel. (1624) 862238; e-mail amulree@ttwebsite.com; internet www2.mcb.net/amulree.

Electrochemical Publications Ltd: Asahi House, Church Rd, Port Erin, IM9 6AQ; tel. (1624) 834941; fax (1624) 835400; e-mail sales@elchempub.comt; internet www.elchempub.com; Man. Dir WILLIAM GOLDIE.

Grove Publishing Co: The Ballacrosha, Ballaugh, Sulby, IM7 5BP; tel. (1624) 897355.

Lily Publications Ltd: POB 33, Ramsey, IM99 4LP; tel. (1624) 898446; fax (1624) 898449; e-mail lilypubs@aol.com; Man. Dir MILES COWSILL.

Mannin Media Group Ltd: Media House, Cronkbourne, Douglas, IM4 4SB; tel. (1624) 696565; fax (1624) 662077; e-mail mail@manninmedia.co.im; internet www.manninmedia.co.im; Chief Exec. STEVEN BROWN.

The Manx Experience: 45 Slieau Dhoo, Tromode Park, Douglas; tel. (1624) 627727; fax (1624) 663627; e-mail manx@enterprise.net; Man. Dirs GWYNNETH AND COLIN BROWN.

Pines Press: The Pines, Ballelin, Maughold, Ramsey, IM7 1HJ; tel. (1624) 862030.

Keith Uren Publishing: 12 Manor Lane, Farmhill, Braddan, IM2 2NX; tel. and fax (1624) 611100; e-mail portfolio@manxe.net.

Vathek Publishing Ltd: Bridge House, Dalby, IM5 3BP; tel. (1624) 844056; fax (1624) 845043; e-mail mlw@vathek.com; internet www.vathek.com.

Broadcasting and Communications

TELECOMMUNICATIONS

Manx Telecom Ltd: POB 100, Douglas, IM99 1HX; tel. (1624) 633633; fax (1624) 636011; e-mail mail@manx-telecom.com; internet www.manx-telecom.com; wholly owned subsidiary of O_2 Plc; Man. Dir CHRIS HALL.

BROADCASTING

Isle of Man Communications Commission: Salisbury House, Victoria St, Douglas, IM1 2LW; tel. (1624) 677022; fax (1624) 626499; e-mail margaret.king@cc.gov.im; internet www.gov.im/government/boards/cc.xml; appointed by the Isle of Man Government to represent the island's interests in all matters of telecommunications, radio and television; Chair. of Comm. J. P. SHIMMIN; Dir ANTHONY R. HEWITT.

Radio and Television

BBC: Radio and Television (see United Kingdom).

ITV Border: Television (see United Kingdom).

Manx Radio: POB 1368, Douglas, IM99 1SW; tel. (1624) 682600; fax (1624) 682604; e-mail postbox@manxradio.com; internet www.manxradio.com; commercial station operated (by agreement with the Isle of Man Government) by Radio Manx Ltd; Chair. DAVID NORTH; Man. Dir ANTHONY PUGH.

The Isle of Man also receives television programmes from Channel 4 and five.

Finance

Isle of Man Government Financial Supervision Commission: POB 58, Finch Hill House, Bucks Rd, Douglas, IM99 1DT; tel. (1624) 689300; fax (1624) 689399; e-mail fsc@gov.im; internet www.fsc.gov.im; responsible for the licensing, authorization and supervision of banks, building societies, investment businesses, collective investment schemes and corporate service providers; also responsible for the Companies Registry; Chief Exec. JOHN ASPDEN.

Treasury: Government Office, Buck's Rd, Douglas, IM1 3PU; tel. (1624) 685586; fax (1624) 685662; e-mail treasuryadmin@gov.im; internet www.gov.im/treasury; Minister ALLAN BELL; Chief Financial Officer P. M. SHIMMIN.

BANKING

(cap. = capital; res = reserves; dep. = deposits; m. = million; brs = branches; amounts in pounds sterling)

At 31 December 2005 total bank deposits in the Isle of Man amounted to some £37,480m. and there were 48 licensed banks and three building societies. The Financial Supervision Commission may allow a major bank to establish a presence on the island on a managed bank basis, by awarding an offshore banking licence.

AIB Bank (Isle of Man) Ltd: POB 247, Douglas, IM99 2RD; tel. (845) 600-0639; fax (1624) 639636; e-mail one@aiboffshore.com; internet www.aiboffshore-online.com; f. 1977; cap. 7.5m., dep. 525.7m. (Dec. 2003); Chair. J. C. FARGHER; Man. Dir C. J. HOWLAND.

Alliance & Leicester (International) Ltd: POB 226, 19–21 Prospect Hill, Douglas, IM99 1RY; tel. (1624) 678285; fax (1624) 663577; e-mail marketing@alil.co.im; internet www.alil.co.im; Man. Dir SIMON HULL.

Anglo Irish Bank Corpn (IOM) PLC: Jubilee Bldgs, Victoria St, Douglas, IM1 2SH; tel. (1624) 698000; fax (1624) 698001; e-mail enquiries@angloirishbank.co.im; internet www.angloirishbank.co.im; Man. Dir MARK GAYWOOD.

Bank of Ireland (IOM) Ltd: POB 246, Christian Rd, Douglas, IM99 1XF; tel. (1624) 644222; fax (1624) 644298; e-mail info@boiiom.com; internet www.boiiom.com; Chief Operating Officer MICHAEL MCKAY.

Barclays Private Bank and Trust (Isle of Man) Ltd: POB 48, Queen Victoria House, Victoria St, Douglas, IM99 1DF; tel. (1624) 682828; fax (1624) 620905; internet www.barclays.co.uk/privatebank; Man. Dir LESLIE CUNLIFFE.

Barclays Private Clients International Ltd: POB 213, Eagle Court, 25 Circular Rd, Douglas, IM99 1RH; tel. (1624) 684000; fax (1624) 684321; international banking services; Man. Dir T. PARKES; 6 brs.

Britannia International Ltd: Britannia House, Athol St, Douglas, IM99 1SD; tel. (1624) 681100; fax (1624) 681105; e-mail enquiries@britanniainternational.com; internet www.britanniainternational.com; offshore subsidiary of Britannia Building Society; Man. Dir PETER MANSFIELD.

Cayman National Bank and Trust Co Ltd: 34 Athol St, Douglas, IM1 1RD; tel. (1624) 646900; fax (1624) 662192; e-mail mail@cnciom.com; internet www.cnciom.com; f. 1985; subsidiary of Cayman National Corpn, Cayman Islands; Man. Dir I. M. E. BANCROFT.

Celtic Bank Ltd: POB 114, Celtic House, Victoria St, Douglas, IM99 1JW; tel. (1624) 622856; fax (1624) 620926; f. 1977; issued cap. 6.8m., res 5.4m., dep. 503.2m. (March 2005); Chair. RICHARD G. DANIELSON; Chief Exec. SIMON YOUNG.

Close Private Bank (Isle of Man): POB 203, St George's Court, Upper Church St, Douglas, IM99 1RB; tel. (1624) 643200; fax (1624) 622039; e-mail infoiom@closepb.com; internet www.closepb.com; f. 1976; merchant bank; cap. 5.0m., res 0.1m., dep. 162.1m. (July 2001); Man. Dir ANDREW HENTON.

Conister Trust PLC: Conister House, 16–18 Finch Rd, Douglas, IM1 2PT; tel. (1624) 694694; fax (1624) 624278; e-mail info@conistertrust.com; internet www.conistertrust.com; f. 1935; specializes in asset finance; cap. 8m., dep. 47m.; Chair. PETER HAMMONDS; 1 br.

Duncan Lawrie (IOM) Ltd: 14–15 Mount Havelock, Douglas, IM1 2QG; tel. (1624) 620770; fax (1624) 676315; e-mail iom@duncanlawrie.com; internet www.duncan-lawrie.co.uk; cap. 6.0m., dep. 86.1m. (Dec. 2002); Chair. P. J. FIELD; Man. Dir ALAN M. MOLLOY.

Fairbairn Private Bank (IOM) Ltd: St Mary's Court, 20 Hill St, Douglas, IM1 1EU; tel. (1624) 645000; fax (1624) 627218; e-mail iom@fairbairnpb.com; internet www.fairbairnpb.com; cap. 5.0m., res 16.1m., dep. 455.1m. (Dec. 2003); Chair. F. LE ROEX; Man. Dir G. HORTON.

Habib European Bank Ltd: St James's House, Market St, Douglas, IM1 2PQ; tel. (1624) 622554; fax (1624) 627135; e-mail habibbank@manx.net; internet www.habibbank.com; wholly-owned subsidiary of Habib Bank AG Zurich; cap. 5.0m., dep. 66.5m. (Dec. 2004); Sr Vice-Pres. A. SHAIKH.

Lloyds TSB Offshore Ltd: Victory House, Prospect Hill, Douglas, IM99 1AH; tel. (1624) 638269; fax (1624) 673435; e-mail cbiom@lloydstsb-offshore.com; internet www.lloydstsb-offshore.com; 5 brs.

Nationwide International Ltd: POB 217, 5–11 St George's St, Douglas, IM99 1RN; tel. (1624) 696000; fax (1624) 696001; internet www.nationwideinternational.com; f. 1990; Man. Dir CARL GANDY.

Singer & Friedlander (Isle of Man) Ltd: POB 197, 5–11 St George's St, Douglas, IM99 1SN; tel. (1624) 699222; fax (1624) 699200; e-mail info@singers.co.im; internet www.singers-iom.co.im; f. 1971; merchant bank; cap. 5.0m., res 30.4m., dep. 257.9m. (Dec. 2003); Man. Dir R. JAMES.

Standard Bank Isle of Man Ltd: Standard Bank House, 1 Circular Rd, Douglas, IM1 1SB; tel. (1624) 643643; fax (1624) 643800; e-mail sbiom@standardbank.com; internet www.sboff.com; cap. 5.0m., res 9.4m., dep. 635.1m. (Dec. 2004); Man. Dir K. J. FODEN.

Zurich Bank International Ltd: POB 422, Lord St, Douglas, IM99 3AF; tel. (1624) 671666; fax (1624) 627526; internet www.zurichbankinternational.com; f. 1983; res 1.9m., dep. 125.8m.; Chair. CHRIS GIBSON; Man. Dir GRAHAM SHEWARD.

'Offshore' Banks

AbbeyInternational: POB 150, Abbey House, Circular Road, Douglas, IM99 1NH; tel. (1624) 644800; fax (1624) 644691; e-mail customerservices@abbeyinternational.com; internet www.abbeyinternational.com; Man. Dir P. BRACKPOOL.

Bank of Scotland International: POB 19, Prospect Hill, Douglas, IM99 1AT; tel. (1624) 613500; fax (1624) 759280; e-mail enquiries@bankofscotland.co.uk; internet www.bankofscotlandinternational.com; f. 1976; cap. 5m.

Bradford & Bingley International Ltd: 30 Ridgeway St, Douglas, IM1 1TA; tel. (1624) 695000; fax (1624) 695001; e-mail enquiries@bbi.co.im; internet www.bbi.co.im; f. 1989; wholly-owned subsidiary of Bradford & Bingley PLC, UK; cap. and res 207m.; Gen. Man. JOHN SHEATH.

Coutts (IOM) International Ltd: Coutts House, Summerhill Rd, Onchan, IM3 1RB; tel. (1624) 632222; fax (1624) 620988; Gen. Man. P. WEYNANDT.

The Derbyshire (Isle of Man) Ltd: POB 136, 64 Athol St, Douglas, IM99 1LR; tel. (1624) 663432; fax (1624) 615133; e-mail info@derbyshire.co.im; internet www.derbyshire.co.im; Man. Dir CLIVE D. PARRISH.

Isle of Man Bank Ltd: 2 Athol St, Douglas IM99 1AN; tel. (1624) 637000; fax (1624) 624686; internet www.natwestoffshore.com; f. 1865; cap. 7.5m., res 155.6m., dep. 1,308.2m. (Dec. 2003); bankers to Isle of Man Government; mem. of the Royal Bank of Scotland Group; Chair. J. L. MORRIS; 11 brs.

The Royal Bank of Scotland International Ltd: POB 151, Royal Bank House, 2 Victoria St, Douglas, IM99 1NJ; tel. (1624) 646464; fax (1624) 646497; e-mail marketingiom@rbsint.com; internet www.rbsint.com; Dir WILLIAM MCKAY.

Restricted Banks

Bermuda Trust (Isle of Man) Ltd: POB 34, 12/13 Hill St, Douglas, IM99 1BW; tel. (1624) 637777; Gen. Man. H. CALLOW.

Irish Permanent International: 12–14 Ridgeway St, Douglas, IM1 1EN; tel. (1624) 641641; fax (1624) 676795; e-mail info@irishpermanentintl.com; internet www.irishpermanentintl.com; Man. Dir PHILIP MURRAY.

Merrill Lynch Bank and Trust Co (Cayman) Ltd: Belgravia House, 34–44 Circular Rd, Douglas, IM1 1QW; tel. (1624) 688600; fax (1624) 688601; Man. N. ORDERS.

Nedbank Ltd: Samuel Harris House, St George's St, Douglas, IM1 1AJ; tel. (1624) 690800; fax (1624) 612836; e-mail nediom@nedbank.co.uk.

INSURANCE

There were 191 authorized insurance companies in the Isle of Man in 2004, including:

Canada Life International Ltd: St Mary's, The Parade, Castletown, IM9 1RJ; tel. (1624) 820200; fax (1624) 820201; e-mail customer.support@canadalifeint.com; internet www.canadalifeint.com; Man. Dir TONY PARRY.

CMI Insurance Co Ltd: Clerical Medical House, Victoria Rd, Douglas, IM99 1LT; tel. (1624) 638888.

Friends Provident International Ltd: Royal Court, Castletown, IM9 1RA; tel. (1624) 821212; fax (1624) 824405; e-mail servicedesk@fpiom.com; internet www.fpinternational.com; Man. Dir PAUL QUIRK.

Hansard International Ltd: POB 192, Harbour Court, Lord Street, Douglas, IM99 1QL; tel. (1624) 688000; fax (1624) 688008; e-mail enquiries@hansard.com; internet www.hansard.com; Chair. Dr LEONARD S. POLONSKY.

Isle of Man Assurance Ltd: IOMA House, Hope St, Douglas, IM1 1AP; tel. (1624) 681200; fax (1624) 681391; e-mail ioma@ioma.co.im; internet www.ioma.co.im; Chair. ROBIN BIGLAND; Man. Dir NIGEL WOOD.

Royal Insurance Service Co (IOM) Ltd: Jubilee Bldgs, 1 Victoria St, Douglas, IM99 1BF; tel. (1624) 645947; fax (1624) 620934; Man. DAVID STACEY.

Royal Skandia Life Assurance Ltd: POB 159, Skandia House, King Edward Rd, Onchan, IM99 1NU; tel. (1624) 655555; fax (1624) 611715; internet www.royalskandia.com.

Scottish Provident International Life Assurance Ltd: Provident House, Ballacottier Business Park, Cooil Rd, Douglas, IM2 2SP; tel. (1624) 681681; fax (1624) 677336; internet www.spila.com; f. 1991; Man. Dir LILLIAN BOYLE.

Tower Insurance Co Ltd: POB 27, Jubilee Bldgs, 1 Victoria St, Douglas, IM99 1BF; tel. (1624) 645900; fax (1624) 663864; e-mail tower.insurance@uk.royalsun.com; subsidiary of Royal and Sun Alliance PLC; Dir DAVID STACEY.

Zurich International Life Ltd: 45–51 Athol St, Douglas, IM99 1EF; tel. (1624) 662266; fax (1624) 662038; internet www.zurichintlife.com.

Insurance Association

Insurance and Pensions Authority: HSBC House, Ridgeway St, Douglas, IM1 1ER; tel. (1624) 646000; fax (1624) 646001; e-mail ipa.admin@ipa.gov.im; internet www.gov.im/ipa; Chief Exec. DAVID VICK.

Trade and Industry

CHAMBER OF COMMERCE

Isle of Man Chamber of Commerce: 17 Drinkwater St, Douglas, IM1 1PP; tel. (1624) 674941; fax (1624) 663367; e-mail enquiries@iomchamber.org.im; internet www.iomchamber.org.im; 400 mems; Pres. STUART MCCUDDEN; Chair. JOHN HOLLIS; Chief Exec. BARBARA O'HANLON.

UTILITIES

Electricity

Manx Electricity Authority: POB 177, Douglas, IM99 1PS; tel. (1624) 687687; fax (1624) 687612; e-mail hr@mea.gov.im; internet www.gov.im/mea; Chief Exec. ASHTON LEWIS.

Gas

Manx Gas Ltd: Murdoch House, South Quay, Douglas, IM1 5PA; tel. (1624) 644444; fax (1624) 626528; internet www.manxgas.com; Man. Dir C. J. SIDLEY.

UNITED KINGDOM CROWN DEPENDENCIES   The Isle of Man

Water

Isle of Man Water Authority: Drill Hall, Tromode Rd, Douglas, IM2 5PA; tel. (1624) 695949; fax (1624) 695956; e-mail water@gov.im; internet www.gov.im/water; Chief Exec. PATRICK HEATON-ARMSTRONG.

TRADE UNIONS

In 1991 the Trade Union Act was approved by Tynwald, providing for the registration of trade unions. Although trade unions had been active previously on the Isle of Man, they had not received legal recognition.

Manx Fish Producers' Organization Ltd: Heritage Centre, The Quay, Peel, IM5 1TA; tel. (1624) 842144; fax (1624) 844395; e-mail manx.fa@lineone.net.

Manx National Farmers' Union: Agriculture House, Ground Floor, Tromode, IM4 4QE; tel. (1624) 674191; fax (1624) 662204.

Transport and General Workers' Union: 25 Fort St, Douglas, IM1 2LJ; tel. (1624) 621156; fax (1624) 673115; Regional Industrial Organizer J. B. MOFFATT.

Transport

RAILWAYS

Isle of Man Transport: Transport Headquarters, Banks Circus, Douglas, IM1 5PT; tel. (1624) 662525; fax (1624) 663637; e-mail info@busandrail.dtl.gov.im; internet www.iombusandrail.info; 29 km (18 miles) of electric track; also 25 km (16 miles) of steam railway track, and Snaefell Mountain Railway (7 km of electric track); 85 buses; Dir of Public Transport DAVID R. HOWARD.

ROADS

There are over 640 km (400 miles) of country roads, excluding streets and roads in the four towns; about one-half are main roads.

Dept of Transport: Sea Terminal, Douglas, IM1 2RF; tel. (1624) 686600; fax (1624) 686617; e-mail enquiries@dot.gov.im; internet www.gov.im/transport; Chief Exec. IAN THOMPSON.

Isle of Man Transport: see above.

SHIPPING

Isle of Man Steam Packet Co Ltd: Imperial Bldgs, Douglas, IM1 2BY; tel. (1624) 645645; fax (1624) 645609; internet www.steam-packet.com; f. 1830; daily services operate all the year round between Heysham and Douglas; during the summer there are frequent services between the island and Dublin, Belfast and Liverpool; during the winter there is a weekend service to Liverpool; Chair. JUAN KELLY; Man. Dir HAMISH ROSS; fleet of 1 passenger/car ferry, 1 roll-on/roll-off passenger/freight ferry and 2 Seacat Fastcraft.

Mezeron Ltd: East Quay, Ramsey, IM8 1BG; tel. (1624) 812302; fax (1624) 815613; e-mail mezeron@mezeronuk.co.uk; f. 1983; cargo services; Man. Dir N. A. LEECE.

Ramsey Steamship Co Ltd: 8 Auckland Terrace, Parliament St, Ramsey, IM8 1AF; tel. (1624) 816202; fax (1624) 816206; e-mail tony@ramsey-steamship.com; internet www.ramsey-steamship.com; f. 1913; cargo services; Sec. and Man. A. G. KENNISH.

Tufton Oceanic Investments Ltd: 9 Myrtle St, Douglas, IM1 1ED; tel. (1624) 663616; fax (1624) 663918; e-mail tufton@tuftonoceanic.com; internet www.tuftonoceanic.com.

CIVIL AVIATION

Eastern Airways: Ronaldsway Airport, Ballasalla, IM9 2AS; tel. (1652) 680600; e-mail information@easternairways.com; internet www.easternairways.com; daily scheduled passenger services to Birmingham, Bristol, Leeds and Newcastle.

Emerald Airways Ltd: Ronaldsway Airport, Ballasalla, IM9 2AS; tel. (1624) 825608; fax (1624) 825723; internet www.flyjem.com; f. 1987; daily cargo and passenger services to Liverpool.

EuroManx: Ronaldsway Airport, Ballasalla, IM9 2AS; tel. (870) 7877879; internet www.euromanx.com; scheduled UK and European passenger services.

FlyBe: Ronaldsway Airport, Ballasalla, IM9 2AS; tel. (1624) 822162; internet www.flybe.com; daily services to Birmingham.

Island Aviation and Travel Ltd: Ronaldsway Airport, Ballasalla, IM9 2AS; tel. (1624) 824300; fax (1624) 824946; e-mail enquiries@iaat.co.uk; internet www.iaat.co.uk; provides executive charters to worldwide destinations, runs air-ambulance services, aircraft management, handling.

Tourism

In 2004 a total of 240,958 tourists stayed at least one night on the Isle of Man.

Dept of Tourism and Leisure, Tourism Division: Sea Terminal Buildings, Douglas, IM1 2RG; tel. (1624) 686801; fax (1624) 686800; e-mail tourism@gov.im; internet www.visitisleofman.com; responsibilities of tourist board, also operates modern and vintage transport systems, a Victorian theatre and an indoor and outdoor sport and leisure complex; f. 1896; CEO CAROL GLOVER.

UNITED KINGDOM OVERSEAS TERRITORIES

From February 1998 the British Dependent Territories were referred to as the United Kingdom Overseas Territories, following the announcement of the interim findings of a British government review of the United Kingdom's relations with the Overseas Territories. In March 1999 draft legislation confirming this change was published by the British Government: under the proposed legislation, the citizens of Overseas Territories would be granted the rights, already enjoyed by the citizens of Gibraltar and the Falkland Islands, to British citizenship and of residence in the United Kingdom. These entitlements were not reciprocal, and British citizens would not enjoy the same rights with regard to the Overseas Territories. The British Overseas Territories Act entered effect in May 2002. The British Government meanwhile announced its determination to ensure that legislation in the Overseas Territories adhered to British and European Union standards, particularly in the areas of financial regulation and human rights.

ANGUILLA

Introductory Survey

Location, Climate, Language, Religion, Flag, Capital

Anguilla, a coralline island, is the most northerly of the Leeward Islands, lying 113 km (70 miles) to the north-west of Saint Christopher (St Kitts) and 8 km (5 miles) to the north of St Maarten/St Martin. Also included in the Territory are the island of Sombrero, 48 km (30 miles) north of Anguilla, and several other uninhabited small islands. The climate is sub-tropical, the heat and humidity being tempered by the trade winds. Temperatures average 27°C (80°F) and mean annual rainfall is 914 mm (36 ins), the wettest months being September to December. English is the official language. Many Christian churches are represented, the principal denominations being the Anglican and Methodist Churches. The flag (proportions 3 by 5 on land, 1 by 2 at sea) has a dark blue field with the Union flag in the upper hoist corner and, in the centre of the fly, a white shield bearing three orange circling dolphins above a light blue base. The capital is The Valley.

Recent History

Anguilla, previously inhabited by Arawaks and Caribs, was a British colony from 1650 until 1967. From 1825 the island became increasingly associated with Saint Christopher (St Kitts) for administrative purposes (also see chapter on Saint Christopher and Nevis). The inhabitants of Anguilla petitioned for separate status in 1875 and 1958. In February 1967, however, St Christopher-Nevis-Anguilla assumed the status of a State in Association with the United Kingdom, as did four other former British colonies in the Eastern Caribbean. These Associated States became independent internally, while the British Government retained responsibility for external affairs and defence.

In May 1967 the Anguillans, under the leadership of Ronald Webster, a local businessman and head of the only political party, the People's Progressive Party (PPP), repudiated government from Saint Christopher. After attempts to repair the breach between Saint Christopher and Anguilla had failed, British security forces were deployed in Anguilla in March 1969 to install a British Commissioner. Members of London's Metropolitan Police Force remained on the island until the Anguilla Police Force was established in 1972. In July 1971 the British Parliament approved the Anguilla Act, one clause of which stipulated that, should Saint Christopher-Nevis-Anguilla decide to end its associated status, Anguilla could be separated from the other islands. In August the British Government's Anguilla Administration Order 1971 determined that the British Commissioner would continue to be responsible for the direct administration of the island, with the co-operation of a local elected council. The terms of this Order were superseded by the introduction of a new Constitution in February 1976. Anguilla formally separated from Saint Christopher-Nevis-Anguilla on 19 December 1980, assuming the status of British Dependent Territory. In accordance with the terms of the British Government's Anguilla Constitution Order of 1982, a new Constitution came into operation in Anguilla on 1 April 1982.

Legislative elections were held in March 1976, and Webster was appointed Chief Minister. In February 1977, following his defeat on a motion of confidence, he was replaced by Emile Gumbs as Chief Minister and as leader of the PPP (renamed the Anguilla National Alliance—ANA—in 1980). Webster was returned to power, to lead the recently formed Anguilla United Party (AUP), at a general election in May 1980. The dismissal of the Minister of Agriculture in May 1981 led to serious divisions within the Government, and the resignation in sympathy of another minister precipitated the collapse of Webster's administration. Webster subsequently formed a new political party, the Anguilla People's Party (APP), which won five of the seven seats in a general election in June. An early general election in March 1984 resulted in a conclusive defeat for the APP, including the loss of Webster's own seat. Gumbs became Chief Minister, and pursued a policy of revitalizing the island's economy, mainly through tourism and attracting foreign investment. Webster resigned from the leadership of the APP, which was renamed the Anguilla Democratic Party (ADP).

The majority of the population expressed no desire for independence, but the new Government appealed for wider powers for the Executive Council, and for more aid and investment from the United Kingdom in the island's economy and infrastructure. In October 1985 the Governor appointed a committee to review the Constitution, in response to an earlier unanimous request from the House of Assembly for modifications, particularly concerning the status of women and of persons born overseas of Anguillan parents. The amendments, which provided for the appointment of a Deputy Governor and designated international financial affairs (the 'offshore' banking sector) as the Governor's responsibility, came into effect in May 1990.

Gumbs remained Chief Minister following a general election in February 1989. The ANA won only three seats in the House of Assembly but was supported by the independent member, Osbourne Fleming, who retained his cabinet portfolio. The ADP secured one seat and the revived AUP won two.

In May 1991 the British Government abolished capital punishment for the crime of murder in Anguilla (as well as in several other British Dependent Territories).

A general election in March 1994 failed to produce a clear majority for any one party, and a coalition was subsequently formed by the ADP and the AUP, which had each won two seats and, respectively, secured 31% and 11% of total votes cast. The ANA, under the leadership of Eric Reid, won two seats with 36% of the vote, while the remaining seat was secured by Fleming. The AUP leader, Hubert Hughes, was subsequently appointed Chief Minister, replacing Sir Emile Gumbs (as he had become); on becoming Chief Minister, Hughes immediately stated that he might seek Anguilla's independence from the United Kingdom.

In October 1995 the island suffered severe damage from 'Hurricane Luis'. Destruction of buildings and infrastructure, as well as damage to the agricultural sector, was estimated to be worth some EC $72m. Hughes was highly critical of the British Government's response to the hurricane, which he alleged was inadequate. In May 1997 Robert Harris, hitherto Deputy Governor, assumed office as Governor.

The announcement by the British Government in January 1997 that it was considering the extension of its powers in the Dependent Territories of the Caribbean attracted further criticism from Hughes. The proposed reintroduction of reserve powers, whereby the Governor (with the consent of the British Government) can amend, veto or introduce legislation without the agreement of the local legislature, provoked accusations from Hughes that the United Kingdom hoped to create a situation in which Territories would be forced to seek independence. The British Government, however, maintained that the initiative had been prompted largely by a desire to secure Anguilla's financial services sector from exploitation by criminal organizations, particularly drugs-traffickers (which had remained a problem, owing to the territory's bank secrecy laws).

In September 1997 Hughes publicly denounced Robert Harris for being oblivious to his country's needs, and, furthermore, made allegations of corruption within the Civil Service Association (CSA). The CSA denied the claim and immediately requested a public apology. Meanwhile Osbourne Fleming pressed for Hughes' resignation, claiming that the remarks were unjustified and jeopardized public and investor confidence in the Government.

In May 1998 Hughes announced that public consultations would be undertaken on a proposal to reform Anguilla's constitutional status in the hope that a reformed Constitution could be in place before the general election, scheduled for March 1999. Hughes criticized the current Constitution for vesting executive authority in the Governor rather than in locally elected ministers. Hughes ruled out any prospect of creating a Senate on the grounds of the cost involved. In September 1998, however, the British Government announced that its Overseas Dependencies were to be renamed United Kingdom Overseas Territories. In March 1999 the British Government issued a policy document confirming the change of name, and guaranteeing citizens of Overseas Dependencies the right to British citizenship. The proposals also included the requirement that the Constitutions of Overseas Territories should be revised in order to conform to British and international standards. The process of revision of the Anguillan Constitution began in September 1999.

Following the general election of 4 March 1999 the composition of the legislature remained unaltered. The AUP-ADP coalition therefore kept control of the House of Assembly, and the four members of the Executive Council retained their portfolios.

In May 1999 the two ADP ministers threatened to withdraw from the coalition Government, accusing Hughes of excluding them from the decision-making process, and in June the ADP leader, Victor Banks, resigned his post as Minister of Finance and Economic Development, and withdrew from the ruling coalition. The other ADP minister, Edison Baird, refused, however, to resign his post, and was subsequently expelled from the party. Although Banks' resignation deprived the AUP-ADP coalition of its majority in the House of Assembly, Hughes announced that he did not intend to resign his position. Banks and the three members of the opposition ANA therefore withdrew from the House, demanding that fresh elections be held. Lacking the necessary quorum in the legislature, the Government was unable to implement policy or to introduce a budget for 1999/2000.

In January 2000 legal proceedings begun by Hughes, in an attempt to compel the Speaker to convene the House of Assembly, were rejected by the High Court. Hughes therefore announced that he would hold legislative elections in March 2000. At the elections, held on 3 March, the ANA won three seats, the AUP two, and the ADP one, while Edison Baird was elected as an independent. The ANA and the ADP, which had formed an electoral alliance, known as the Anguilla United Front, prior to the elections, therefore gained control of the House of Assembly. The leader of the ANA, Osbourne Fleming, was subsequently appointed the Chief Minister of an Executive Council that included two other ANA ministers, while Victor Banks was again appointed Minister of Finance, Economic Development, Investment and Commerce.

In February 2000 the Governor, Robert Harris, departed the island. Harris, who had reportedly been extremely frustrated by the island's political crisis, suggested that he had found it very difficult to work closely with the Government of Anguilla. Peter Johnstone replaced Harris as Governor, who, in turn, was replaced by Alan Huckle in May 2004.

Following Anguilla's inclusion on an Organisation for Economic Co-operation and Development (OECD, see p. 320) blacklist of tax 'havens' in 2000, the Government introduced a number of articles of legislation to combat money-laundering on the island, including the establishment of a 'Money Laundering Reporting Authority'. OECD removed Anguilla from the list in March 2002, declaring that the Government had made sufficient commitments to improve transparency and effective exchange of information on tax matters by the end of 2005. In late 2002, however, the burgeoning financial sector faced further disruption when the United Kingdom, under pressure from the European Union (EU, see p. 228), as part of its effort to investigate tax evasion, demanded that Anguilla disclose the identities and account details of Europeans holding private savings accounts on the island. Anguilla, along with some other British Overseas Territories facing similar demands, claimed it was being treated unfairly compared with more powerful European countries, such as Switzerland and Luxembourg. In February 2004 a new financial regulatory body, the Anguilla Financial Services Commission, commenced operations. The Commission replaced the Financial Services Department of the Ministry of Finance and represented a further commitment to transparency within the sector.

In June 2001 the Government officially approved the draft of its National Telecommunications Policy, which would liberalize the sector. Although the legislation still needed to pass through parliament, in April 2003 Cable & Wireless, the country's sole telecommunications provider, signed an agreement with the Government to open the market for competition. The opposition argued that a single operator was more suitable in a country as small as Anguilla, where economies of scale were not achievable. It was argued that the proposed legislation could lead to a reduction in investment and consequent job losses.

In August 2003 the Government sold 6m. shares at US $1 each in the Anguilla Electricity Company, a profit-making public utility, in order to raise funds for the US $20m. expansion and reconstruction of Wallblake Airport. The proceeds of the sale were to go towards lengthening the airport's runway in order to accommodate larger aircraft. The AUP leader Hubert Hughes criticized the sale as unnecessary and questioned the transparency of the process.

In May 2004 Edison Baird replaced Hubert Hughes as Leader of the Opposition after Albert Hughes resigned from the AUP and transferred his support to Baird. Baird later formed a new political party, the Anguilla National Strategic Alliance (ANSA), in advance of the general election, which was constitutionally due by June 2005.

At the general election, which was held on 21 February 2005, the Anguilla United Front (the AUF, comprising the ANA and the ADP) secured four seats and 38.9% of the votes cast; the remaining three seats were shared by the Anguilla United Movement (as the AUP had been renamed, with one seat and 19.4% of the votes) and the ANSA (two seats and 19.2% of the ballot). The remaining 23% of the votes were shared between independent candidates and the Anguilla Progressive Party. Turn-out was 74.6%—considerably higher than expected. Analysts were also surprised by the scale of the AUF's victory; a closer contest had been expected, but the alliance campaigned strongly on the success of its infrastructural improvements, particularly the expansion of Wallblake Airport, during its previous administration. Fleming announced a new Executive Council on 22 February. The only change was the replacement as Minister of Education, Health, Social Development and Lands of Eric Reid, who retired and did not contest the election. Evans Rogers succeeded him.

In December 2005 the Government announced its intention to establish a new Constitutional and Electoral Reform Commission, to build on the work done by the previous electoral commission in 2001–04 in ascertaining the views of the people of Anguilla. The Commission began work in February 2006; key issues to be addressed were the fundamental rights and freedoms outlined in the Constitution, the powers of the Governor and the size of the House of Assembly. An initial draft of the Commission's recommendations was expected in April.

In November 2005 it was announced that Andrew George was to succeed Alan Huckle as Governor in June 2006, when the latter was scheduled to leave to assume the governorship of the Falkland Islands.

In May 2002 the British Overseas Territories Act, having received royal assent in the United Kingdom in February, came into force and granted British citizenship to the people of its Overseas Territories, including Anguilla. Under the new law Anguillans would be able to hold British passports and work in the United Kingdom and anywhere else in the EU.

In July 2005 the Governments of Anguilla and the British Virgin Islands announced the formal establishment of the maritime boundary between the two territories. The boundary had been agreed in 2002 following discussions facilitated by the British Government.

Government

The Constitution vests executive power in a Governor, appointed by the British monarch. The Governor is responsible for external affairs, international financial affairs, defence and internal security. In most other matters the Governor acts on the advice of the Executive Council, led by the Chief Minister. Legislative power is held by the House of Assembly, comprising 11 members: two *ex officio*, two nominated by the Governor, and seven elected for five years by universal adult suffrage. The Executive Council is responsible to the House.

Economic Affairs

In 2004, according to the Government's provisional figures, the gross national income (GNI) of Anguilla, measured at current prices, was EC $377.82m., equivalent to EC $30,172 per head. During 1996–2004, it was estimated, the population increased at an average annual rate of 2.0%, while gross domestic product (GDP) per head increased, in real terms, by an average of 3.1% per year. Overall GDP increased, in real terms, at an average annual rate of 5.1% in 1996–2004; growth was 12.7% in 2004.

Agriculture (including crops, livestock and fishing) contributed an estimated 2.3% to GDP in 2004 and agriculture, fishing and mining engaged 3.3% of the employed labour force in 2002. Smallholders grow vegetables and fruit for domestic consumption; the principal crops are pigeon peas, sweet potatoes and maize. Livestock-rearing traditionally supplies significant export earnings, but the principal productive sector is the fishing industry (which is also a major employer). Real agricultural GDP increased by an annual average of 1.1% during 1996–2004, although growth was an estimated 7.1% in 2004.

Industry (including mining, manufacturing, construction, and power), which accounted for an estimated 19.5% of GDP in 2004 and (not including the small mining sector) engaged 18.8% of the employed labour force in 2001, is traditionally based on salt production and shipbuilding. Real industrial GDP increased by an annual average of 6.6% in 1996–2004; the sector expanded dramatically in 2004, by an estimated 31.0%.

The mining and quarrying sector, contributed an estimated 1.4% of GDP in 2004 and engaged only 0.2% of the working population in 1992. Anguilla's principal mineral product is salt. Mining GDP increased by an annual average of 13.1% during 1996–2004; growth was an estimated 35.0% in 2004.

The manufacturing sector, accounting for 2.4% of employment in 2003 and for only an estimated 0.9% of GDP in 2004, consists almost entirely of boat-building and fisheries processing. Real manufacturing GDP increased by an annual average of 6.0% in 1996–2004. Sectoral GDP decreased by an estimated 24.7% in 2004.

The construction industry, which engaged 14.9% of the employed labour force in 2001, accounted for an estimated 12.9% of GDP in 2004. Until a slowdown in the late 1990s, growth in the construction industry was very high, owing to reconstruction work necessitated by the effects of 'Hurricane Luis'. GDP in the construction sector increased at an annual average of 5.1% during 1996–2004, in real terms; the sector expanded dramatically in 2004, by an estimated 45.2%. Imported hydrocarbon fuels meet most energy needs.

The services sector accounted for an estimated 78.2% of GDP in 2004 and engaged 77.9% of the employed labour force in 2001. Tourism is increasingly the dominant industry of the economy, and is a catalyst for growth in other areas. The hotel and restaurant sector is the largest contributor to GDP, accounting for 25.6% of GDP in 2004. The contribution to GDP from the hotel and restaurant sector increased by 15.1% in 2004. In 2004 tourism expenditure totalled EC $187.3m. The USA provided 65.7% of visitors (excluding excursionists) in the same year. The scheduled opening of Anguilla's first championship-standard golf course in early 2006 was expected further to contribute to tourism revenues. The 'offshore' financial institutions are also important contributors to the GDP of the service industry, with the banking and insurance sector contributing 13.3% of GDP in 2004. The real GDP of the services sector increased at an annual average of 5.4% in 1996–2004; growth was 13.7% in 2004, in real terms.

In 2003 Anguilla recorded a merchandise trade deficit of EC $170.9m., and a deficit on the current account of the balance of payments of EC $110.3m. The trade deficit was partly offset by receipts from the 'invisibles' sector: tourism, financial services, remittances from Anguillans abroad and official assistance. The principal sources of imports are the USA, Puerto Rico and the Netherlands Antilles. The principal markets for exports are the USA and St Maarten. The main commodity exports are lobsters, fish, livestock and salt. Imports, upon which Anguilla is highly dependent, consist of foodstuffs, construction materials, manufactures, machinery and transport equipment. In late 2004 Anguilla began refining sugar for export, resulting in an increase in manufactured exports in the first six months of 2005.

In 2004, according to preliminary figures from the Eastern Caribbean Central Bank (ECCB, see p. 388), a budgetary deficit of EC $18.4m. was recorded (equivalent to 4.9% of GDP). Anguilla's external public debt totalled an estimated US $9.8m. in 2002. Development assistance was estimated to total US $3.1m. in 1998. Consumer prices increased by an annual average of 6.2% in 1995–2004; the average annual rate of inflation increased by 4.6% in 2004. Some 7.8% of the labour force were unemployed in July 2002 (compared with 26% in 1985).

In April 1987 Anguilla became the eighth member of the ECCB and in 2001 joined the regional stock exchange, the Eastern Caribbean Securities Exchange (based in Saint Christopher and Nevis), established in the same year. The Territory is also a member of the Organisation of Eastern Caribbean States (OECS, see p. 397) and an associate member of the Association of Caribbean States (ACS, see p. 384) and the Economic Community for Latin America and the Caribbean (ECLAC, see p. 36). As a dependency of the United Kingdom, Anguilla has the status of Overseas Territory in association with the EU (see p. 228). In 1999 Anguilla was granted associate membership of the Caribbean Community and Common Market (CARICOM, see p. 183).

Since its reversion to dependency on the United Kingdom, as a separate unit, the island has developed its limited resources. Both tourism, which has become the dominant industry, resulting in a high level of tourism-related activity in the construction industry during the 1990s, and the international financial sector have apparently benefited from the perceived stability of dependent status. However, Anguilla remains particularly vulnerable to adverse climatic conditions, as was demonstrated in October 1995, when 'Hurricane Luis' devastated the island, and again in November 1999, when damage caused by 'Hurricane Lenny' forced the temporary closure of the island's two largest tourist resorts. The Government of Osbourne Fleming, which took office in 2000, committed itself to increased expenditure and increased state investment in tourism, financial services and fisheries. The Government also hoped to establish the island as a centre for information technology and electronic commerce, and to raise revenue from the sale and leasing of internet domain names. A total of 3,041 new International Business Companies had been registered by the end of 2003. In February 2005 the Financial Services Commission introduced procedures, under the Anguilla Mutual Funds Act 2004, to allow the formation of mutual and hedge funds within 24 hours; it was hoped the new provisions would provide a further boost to the financial sector. In 2004 the banking and insurance sector expanded by an estimated 25.8%. The ECCB predicted an expansion in economic activity of around 5.1% in 2005, led by growth in the construction and tourism sectors.

Education

Education is free and compulsory between the ages of five and 16 years. Primary education begins at five years of age and lasts for six years. Secondary education, beginning at eleven years of age, lasts for a further six years. There are six government primary schools and one government secondary school. A 'comprehensive' secondary school education system was introduced in September 1986. Post-secondary education is undertaken abroad. According to the 2005 budget address, recurrent government expenditure on education in 2000–04 averaged 13.8% of total recurrent expenditure, the second largest government expenditure in a single sector after health.

Public Holidays

2006: 2 January (for New Year's Day), 14 April (Good Friday), 17 April (Easter Monday), 1 May (Labour Day), 30 May (Anguilla Day), 5 June (Whit Monday), 12 June (Queen's Official Birthday), 7 August (August Monday), 10 August (August Thursday), 11 August (Constitution Day), 19 December (Separation Day), 25–26 December (Christmas).

2007: 1 January (New Year's Day), 6 April (Good Friday), 9 April (Easter Monday), 1 May (Labour Day), 28 May (Whit Monday), 30 May (Anguilla Day), 11 June (Queen's Official Birthday), 6 August (August Monday), 9 August (August Thursday), 10 August (Constitution Day), 19 December (Separation Day), 25–26 December (Christmas).

Weights and Measures

The metric system has been adopted, although imperial weights and measures are also used.

Statistical Survey

Source: Government of Anguilla, The Secretariat, The Valley; tel. 497-2451; fax 497-3389; e-mail stats@gov.ai; internet www.gov.ai.

AREA AND POPULATION

Area (sq km): 96 (Anguilla 91, Sombrero 5).

Population: 11,561 (males 5,705, females 5,856) at census of 9 May 2001. *2003* (official estimate): 12,200 at 31 December 2003.

Density (at 31 December 2003): 127.1 per sq km.

Principal Towns (population at 2001 census): South Hill 1,495; North Side 1,195; The Valley (capital) 1,169; Stoney Ground 1,133. *Mid-2003* (UN estimate, incl. suburbs): The Valley 1,380 (Source: UN, *World Urbanization Prospects: The 2003 Revision*).

Births, Marriages and Deaths (2003): Registered live births 139; Birth rate 11.4 per 1,000; Registered marriages 75; Marriage rate 6.1 per 1,000; Registered deaths 65; Death rate 5.3 per 1,000.

Expectation of Life (official estimates, years at birth): 78.88 (males 76.52; females 81.11) in 2003.

Economically Active Population (persons aged 15 years and over, census of 9 May 2001): Agriculture, fishing and mining 183; Manufacturing 135; Electricity, gas and water 81; Construction 830; Trade 556; Restaurants and hotels 1,587; Transport, storage and communications 379; Finance, insurance, real estate and business services 433; Public administration, social security 662; Education, health and social work 383; Other community, social and personal services 164; Private households with employed persons 164; Activities not stated 871; *Total employed* 5,644 (males 3,014, females 2,630); Unemployed 406 (males 208, females 198); *Total labour force* 6,050 (males 3,222, females 2,828). *July 2002:* Total employed 5,496 (males 3,009, females 2,487); Unemployed 465 (males 204, females 261); Total labour force 5,961 (Source: ILO).

HEALTH AND WELFARE

Under-5 Mortality Rate (per 1,000 live births, 1997): 34.0.

Physicians (per 1,000 head, 2003): 1.2.

Health Expenditure (% of GDP, 1998): 4.92.

Sources: Caribbean Development Bank, *Social and Economic Indicators 2004* and Pan American Health Organization.

For definitions, see explanatory note on p. vi.

UNITED KINGDOM OVERSEAS TERRITORIES

Anguilla

AGRICULTURE, ETC.

Fishing (FAO estimates, metric tons, live weight, 2003): Marine fishes 180, Caribbean spiny lobster 60, Stromboid conchs 10; Total catch 250. Source: FAO.

INDUSTRY

Electric Energy (million kWh): 53.60 in 2001; 55.33 in 2002; 58.39 in 2003.

FINANCE

Currency and Exchange Rates: 100 cents = 1 Eastern Caribbean dollar (EC $). *Sterling, US Dollar and Euro Equivalents* (30 December 2005): £1 sterling = EC $4.679; US $1 = EC $2.700; €1 = EC $3.185; EC $100 = £21.51 = US $37.04 = €31.40. *Exchange Rate:* Fixed at US $1 = EC $2.70 since July 1976.

Budget (EC $ million, 2004, preliminary): *Revenue:* Tax revenue 95.2 (Taxes on domestic goods and services 47.1, Taxes on international trade and transactions 47.5, Taxes on property 0.6); Non-tax revenue 20.5; Total 115.7. *Expenditure:* Current expenditure 93.9 (Personal emoluments 36.3, Other goods and services 34.6, Transfers and subsidies 19.8, Interest payments 3.2); Capital expenditure 41.7; Total 135.6. Source: Eastern Caribbean Central Bank, *Annual Economic and Financial Review 2004*.

Cost of Living (Consumer Price Index; base: 2000 = 100): All items 102.9 in 2002; 106.1 in 2003; 111.0 in 2004. Source: ILO.

Expenditure on the Gross Domestic Product (EC $ million at current prices, 2004, preliminary): Government final consumption expenditure 59.72; Private final consumption expenditure 344.31; Gross fixed capital formation 138.32; *Total domestic expenditure* 542.35; Export of goods and services 229.20; *Less* Import of goods and services 376.08; *GDP in purchasers' values* 395.46. Source: Eastern Caribbean Central Bank.

Gross Domestic Product by Economic Activity (EC $ million at current prices, 2004, preliminary): Agriculture (including crops, livestock and fishing) 7.76; Mining and quarrying 4.73; Manufacturing 3.18; Electricity and water 14.14; Construction 43.16; Wholesale and retail 20.86; Hotels and restaurants 85.73; Transport and Communications 44.99; Banks and insurance 44.54; Real estate and housing 8.61; Government services 50.81; Other services 6.72; *Sub-total* 335.23; *Less* Imputed bank service charge 34.36; *GDP at factor cost* 300.87. Source: Eastern Caribbean Central Bank.

Balance of Payments (EC $ million, 2003): Export of goods f.o.b. 11.49; Imports of goods f.o.b. −182.42; *Trade balance* −170.93; Exports of services 192.06; Imports of services −116.37; *Balance on goods and services* −95.24; Other income received 4.98; Other income paid −19.82; *Balance on goods, services and income* −110.08; Current transfers received 23.28; Current transfers paid −23.50; *Current balance* −110.30; Capital account (net) 16.64; Direct investment (net) 76.66; Portfolio investment (net) −0.97; Other investment (net) 23.36; Net errors and omissions 13.72; *Overall balance* 19.11.

EXTERNAL TRADE

Principal Commodities (EC $ million, 2004): *Imports:* Food and live animals 41.1; Beverages and tobacco 17.2; Mineral fuels, lubricants, etc. 26.5; Chemicals and related products 19.9; Basic manufactures 50.6; Machinery and transport equipment 86.3; Miscellaneous manufactured articles 27.4; Total (incl. others) 276.6. *Exports* (incl. re-exports): Beverages and tobacco 1.0; Mineral fuels, lubricants, etc. 1.6; Basic manufactures 1.0; Machinery and transport equipment 6.8; Miscellaneous manufactured articles 4.8; Total (incl. others) 15.5.

Principal Trading Partners (EC $ million, 2004): *Imports:* Barbados 3.9; Canada 4.0; Guadeloupe 5.0; Netherlands Antilles 20.5; Puerto Rico 21.1; Trinidad and Tobago 19.2; United Kingdom 15.4; USA 140.7; US Virgin Islands 8.9; Total (incl. others) 276.6. *Exports* (incl. re-exports): British Virgin Islands 0.2; Guadeloupe 0.6; Guyana 0.6; Netherlands Antilles 7.4; Saint Christopher and Nevis 0.3; Saint Lucia 1.3; USA 2.4; US Virgin Islands 1.6; Total (incl. others) 15.5.

TRANSPORT

Road Traffic (motor vehicles licensed, 2003): Private cars 3,198; Hired cars 830; Buses/trucks/jeeps/pickups 2,002; Motor cycles 53; Tractors 5; Heavy equipment 168; Other 7.

Shipping: *Merchant Fleet* (registered at 31 December 2004): 3; Total displacement 701 grt. Source: Lloyd's Register-Fairplay, *World Fleet Statistics*.

TOURISM

Visitor Arrivals: 111,118 (Stop-overs 43,969, Excursionists 67,149) in 2002; 109,282 (Stop-overs 46,915, Excursionists 62,367) in 2003; 119,130 (Stop-overs 53,711. Excursionists 65,419) in 2004 (preliminary). Source: Eastern Caribbean Central Bank.

Visitor Arrivals by Country of Residence (2004, preliminary): Canada 1,526; Caribbean 7,269; Germany 1,097; Italy 1,061; United Kingdom 3,216; USA 35,295; Total (incl. others) 119,130. Source: Eastern Caribbean Central Bank.

Tourism Receipts (estimates, US $ million): 61.0 in 2001; 55.3 in 2002; 61.7 in 2003.

COMMUNICATIONS MEDIA

Radio Receivers (1997): 3,000 in use.
Television Receivers (1999): 1,000 in use.
Telephones (2002): 5,796 main lines in use.
Facsimile Machines (1993): 190 in use.
Mobile Cellular Telephones (2000): 15,000 subscribers.
Internet Connections (2002): 1,391.

Sources: partly UN, *Statistical Yearbook*; International Telecommunication Union.

EDUCATION

Pre-primary (2003): 11 schools; 38 teachers; 499 pupils.
Primary (2003): 8 schools; 92 teachers; 1,438 pupils.
General Secondary (2002/03): 1 school; 91 teachers; 1,102 pupils.
Adult Literacy Rate (UNESCO estimates): 95.4% (males 95.1%; females 95.7%) in 1995. Source: UNESCO, *Statistical Yearbook*.

Directory

The Constitution

The Constitution, established in 1976, accorded Anguilla the status of a British Dependent Territory. It formally became a separate dependency on 19 December 1980, and is administered under the Anguilla Constitution Orders of 1982 and 1990. British Dependent Territories were referred to as United Kingdom Overseas Territories from February 1998 and draft legislation confirming this change and granting citizens rights to full British citizenship and residence in the United Kingdom was published in March 1999. The British Overseas Territories Act entered into effect in May 2002. The British Government proposals also included the requirement that the Constitutions of Overseas Territories should be revised in order to conform to British and international standards. The process of revision of the Anguillan Constitution began in September 1999.

The British monarch is represented locally by a Governor, who presides over the Executive Council and the House of Assembly. The Governor is responsible for defence, external affairs (including international financial affairs), internal security (including the police), the public service, the judiciary and the audit. The Governor appoints a Deputy Governor. On matters relating to internal security, the public service and the appointment of an acting governor or deputy governor, the Governor is required to consult the Chief Minister. The Executive Council consists of the Chief Minister and not more than three other ministers (appointed by the Governor from the elected members of the legislative House of Assembly) and two *ex-officio* members (the Deputy Governor and the Attorney-General). The House of Assembly is elected for a maximum term of five years by universal adult suffrage and consists of seven elected members, two *ex-officio* members (the Deputy Governor and the Attorney-General) and two nominated members who are appointed by the Governor, one upon the advice of the Chief Minister, and one after consultations with the Chief Minister and the Leader of the Opposition. The House elects a Speaker and a Deputy Speaker.

The Governor may order the dissolution of the House of Assembly if a resolution of 'no confidence' is passed in the Government, and elections must be held within two months of the dissolution.

The Constitution provides for an Anguilla Belonger Commission, which determines cases of whether a person can be 'regarded as belonging to Anguilla' (i.e. having 'belonger' status). A belonger is someone of Anguillan birth or parentage, someone who has married a belonger, or someone who is a citizen of the United Kingdom Overseas Territories from Anguilla (by birth, parentage, adoption or naturalization). The Commission may grant belonger status to those

Anguilla

who have been domiciled and ordinarily resident in Anguilla for not less than 15 years.

The Government

Governor: ALAN HUCKLE (sworn in 28 May 2004).

Governor-designate: ANDREW GEORGE (scheduled to take office in June 2006).

EXECUTIVE COUNCIL
(April 2006)

Chief Minister and Minister of Home Affairs, Gender Affairs, Immigration, Labour, Lands and Physical Planning and Environment: OSBOURNE FLEMING (AUF).

Minister of Finance, Economic Development, Investment, Tourism and Commerce: VICTOR F. BANKS (AUF).

Minister of Education, Health, Sports and Youth and Culture: EVANS MCNEIL ROGERS (AUF).

Minister of Infrastructure, Communications, Public Utilities, and Housing: KENNETH HARRIGAN (AUF).

Attorney-General: RONALD SCIPIO.

Deputy Governor: HENRY MCCRORY.

Parliamentary Secretary with responsibility for Water, Agriculture and Fisheries: ALBERT HUGHES.

MINISTRIES

Office of the Governor: Government House, POB 60, The Valley; tel. 497-2622; fax 497-3314; e-mail govthouse@anguillanet.com.

Office of the Chief Minister: The Secretariat, The Valley; tel. 497-2518; fax 497-3389; e-mail chief-minister@gov.ai.

All ministries are based in The Valley, mostly at the Secretariat (tel. 497-2451; internet www.gov.ai).

Legislature

HOUSE OF ASSEMBLY

Speaker: DAVID CARLY.

Clerk to House of Assembly: Rev. JOHN A. GUMBS.

Election, 21 February 2005

Party	% of votes	Seats
Anguilla United Front (AUF)	38.9	4
Anguilla United Movement (AUM)	19.4	1
Anguilla National Strategic Alternative (ANSA)	19.2	2
Anguilla Progressive Party (APP)	9.5	—
Total (incl. others)	100.0	7

There are also two *ex-officio* members and two nominated members.

Political Organizations

Anguilla National Strategic Alliance (ANSA): The Valley; Leader EDISON BAIRD.

Anguilla Progressive Party (APP): The Valley.

Anguilla United Front (AUF): The Valley; internet www.unitedfront.ai; f. 2000; Leader OSBOURNE FLEMING; alliance comprising:

Anguilla Democratic Party (ADP): The Valley; f. 1981 as Anguilla People's Party; name changed 1984; Leader VICTOR F. BANKS.

Anguilla National Alliance: The Valley; f. 1980 by reconstitution of People's Progressive Party; Leader OSBOURNE FLEMING.

Anguilla United Movement (AUM): The Valley; f. 1979; revived 1984; previously known as the Anguilla United Party—AUP; conservative; Leader HUBERT B. HUGHES.

Judicial System

Justice is administered by the High Court, Court of Appeal and Magistrates' Courts. During the High Court sitting, the Eastern Caribbean Supreme Court provides Anguilla with a judge.

Religion

CHRISTIANITY

The Anglican Communion

Anglicans in Anguilla are adherents of the Church in the Province of the West Indies, comprising nine dioceses. Anguilla forms part of the diocese of the North Eastern Caribbean and Aruba.

Bishop of the North Eastern Caribbean and Aruba: Rt Rev. LEROY ERROL BROOKS, St Mary's Rectory, POB 180, The Valley; tel. 497-2235; fax 497-3012; e-mail brookx@anguilla.net.com.

The Roman Catholic Church

The diocese of St John's-Basseterre, suffragan to the archdiocese of Castries (Saint Lucia), includes Anguilla, Antigua and Barbuda, the British Virgin Islands, Montserrat and Saint Christopher and Nevis. The Bishop resides in St John's, Antigua.

Roman Catholic Church: St Gerard's, POB 47, The Valley; tel. 497-2405.

Protestant Churches

Methodist Church: South Hill; Minister Rev. LINDSAY RICHARDSON.

The Seventh-day Adventist, Baptist, Church of God, Pentecostal, Apostolic Faith and Jehovah's Witnesses Churches and sects are also represented.

The Press

Anguilla Life Magazine: Caribbean Commercial Centre, POB 109, The Valley; tel. 497-3080; fax 497-2501; 3 a year; circ. 10,000.

The Light: POB 1373, Herbert's Commercial Centre, The Valley; tel. 497-5058; fax 497-5795; e-mail thelight@anguillanet.com; f. 1993; weekly; newspaper; Editor GEORGE C. HODGE.

Official Gazette: The Valley; tel. 497-5081; monthly; govt newssheet.

What We Do in Anguilla: POB 1373, Herbert's Commercial Centre, The Valley; tel. 497-5641; fax 497-5795; e-mail thelight@anguillanet.com; f. 1987; monthly; tourism; Editor GEORGE C. HODGE; circ. 50,000.

Broadcasting and Communications

TELECOMMUNICATIONS

Cable & Wireless Anguilla: POB 77, The Valley; tel. 497-3100; fax 497-2501; internet www.cwwionline.com/buhome.asp?bu=Anguilla; Gen. Man. SUTCLIFFE HODGE.

Cingular Wireless: Hanna-Waver House, The Valley; tel. 497-8322; e-mail rhon.rogers@an.cingular.com; owned by Digicel Ltd (Bermuda); fmrly AT&T Wireless; commenced operations in 2005.

BROADCASTING

Radio

Caribbean Beacon Radio: POB 690, Long Rd, The Valley; Head Office: POB 7008, Columbus, GA 31908, USA; tel. 497-4340; fax 497-4311; f. 1981; privately owned and operated; religious and commercial; broadcasts 24 hours daily; Pres. Dr GENE SCOTT; CEO B. MONSELL HAZELL.

Heart Beat Radio: The Valley; tel. 497-3354; fax 497-5995; e-mail info@hbr1075.com; internet hbr1075.com; f. 2001; commercial.

Kool FM: North Side, The Valley; tel. 497-0103; fax 497-0104; e-mail kool@koolfm103.com; internet www.koolfm103.com; commercial.

Radio Anguilla: Dept of Information and Broadcasting, Treasury Dept, The Valley; tel. 497-2218; fax 497-5432; e-mail radioaxa@anguillanet.com; internet www.radioaxa.com; f. 1969; owned and operated by the Govt of Anguilla since 1976; 250,000 listeners throughout the north-eastern Caribbean; broadcasts 17 hours daily; Dir of Information and Broadcasting KENNETH HODGE; News Editor WYCLIFFE RICHARDSON.

Voice of Creation Station: The Valley; internet www.voiceofcreation.com; f. 2000; religious station with devotional and gospel music.

ZJF FM: The Valley; tel. 497-3157; f. 1989; commercial.

Television

Anguilla Television: terrestrial channels 3 and 9; 24-hour local and international English language programming.

Caribbean Cable Communications (Anguilla): POB 336, George Hill, The Valley; tel. 497-3600; fax 497-3602; e-mail alisland@anguillanet.com; internet www.caribcable.com.

Finance

(cap. = capital; res = reserves; dep. = deposits; m. = million; amounts in EC dollars)

CENTRAL BANK

Eastern Caribbean Central Bank: Fairplay Commercial Complex, POB 1385, The Valley; tel. 497-5050; fax 497-5150; e-mail eccbaxa@anguillanet.com; internet www.eccb-centralbank.org; HQ in Basseterre, Saint Christopher and Nevis; bank of issue and central monetary authority for Anguilla, Antigua and Barbuda, Dominica, Grenada, Montserrat, Saint Christopher and Nevis, Saint Lucia and Saint Vincent and the Grenadines; Gov. Sir K. DWIGHT VENNER.

COMMERCIAL BANKS

Caribbean Commercial Bank (Anguilla) Ltd: POB 23, The Valley; tel. 497-3917; fax 497-3570; e-mail service@ccb.ai; internet www.ccb.ai; f. 1976; Chair. OSBOURNE B. FLEMING; Man. Dir PRESTON B. BRYAN.

FirstCaribbean International Bank Ltd: The Valley; e-mail care@firstcaribbeanbank.com; internet www.firstcaribbeanbank.com; f. 2002 following merger of Caribbean operations of Barclays Bank PLC and CIBC; Exec. Chair. MICHAEL MANSOOR; CEO CHARLES PINK.

National Bank of Anguilla Ltd: POB 44, The Valley; tel. 497-2101; fax 497-3310; e-mail info@nba.ai; internet www.nba.ai; f. 1985; 5% owned by Govt of Anguilla; cap. 28.6m., res 10.1m., dep. 309.1m. (March 2002); Chair. JOSEPH N. PAYNE; CEO E. VALENTINE BANKS.

Scotiabank Anguilla Ltd: Fairplay Commercial Centre, POB 250, The Valley; tel. 497-3333; fax 497-3344; e-mail scotia@anguillanet.com; internet www.scotiabank.com; Man. WALTER MACCALMAN.

There are 'offshore', foreign banks based on the island, but most are not authorized to operate in Anguilla. There is a financial complex known as the Caribbean Commercial Centre in The Valley.

TRUST COMPANIES

Barwys Trust Anguilla Ltd: Caribbean Suite, The Valley; e-mail jbw@barwys.com; Man. BART WISJMULLER.

Codan Trust Co (Anguilla) Ltd: c/o Intertrust Offices, POB 147, The Valley; tel. 498-4126; fax 498-8423; e-mail anguilla@cdp.bm; internet www.cdp.bm.

Financial Services Co Ltd: POB 58, The Valley; tel. 497-3777; fax 497-5377; e-mail firstanguilla@anguillalaw.com.

First Anguilla Trust Co Ltd: Mitchell House, POB 174, The Valley; tel. and fax 498-8800; e-mail information@firstanguilla.com; internet www.firstanguilla.com; Mans JOHN DYRUD, PALMAVON WEBSTER.

Geneva Trust Corporation: National Bank Corporate Bldg, Airport Rd, The Valley; e-mail dekokera@soa.wits.ac.za; Man. AWYN DE KOKER.

Hansa Bank and Trust Co Ltd: Hansa Bank Bldg, POB 213, The Valley; tel. 497-3802; fax 497-3801; e-mail hansa@attglobal.net; internet www.hansa.net.

Intertrust (Anguilla) Ltd: POB 1388, The Valley; tel. 497-2189; fax 497-5007; e-mail anguilla@intertrustgroup.com; internet www.intertrust-group.com.

HWR Services (Anguilla) Ltd: Harlaw Chambers, POB 1026, The Valley; tel. 498-5000; fax 498-5001; e-mail heather.wallace@harneys.com; internet www.harneys.com.

Renaissance International Trust: POB 687, The Valley; tel. 498-7878; fax 498-7872; e-mail renaissance@anguillanet.com.

Sinel Trust (Anguilla) Ltd: Sinel Chambers, POB 1269, The Valley; tel. 497-3311; fax 497-5659; e-mail arichardson@sineltrust.com; internet www.sineltrust-anguilla.com.

Sterling Trust (Anguilla), Ltd: National Bank of Anguilla Bldg, St Mary's Rd, The Valley; tel. 497-2189; fax 497-5007; e-mail hwoltz@sterlinggroup.bs; Man. HOWELL W. WOLTZ.

REGULATORY AUTHORITY

Anguilla Financial Services Commission: The Secretariat, POB 60, The Valley; tel. 497-3881; fax 497-5872; e-mail lanston_c@anguillafsd.com; internet www.anguillafsc.com; f. 2004 to replace the Financial Services Department of the Ministry of Finance, Economic Development, Investment, Tourism and Commerce; Chair. JOHN LAWRENCE.

STOCK EXCHANGE

Eastern Caribbean Securities Exchange: based in Basseterre, Saint Christopher and Nevis; e-mail info@ecseonline.com; internet www.ecseonline.com; f. 2001; regional securities market designed to facilitate the buying and selling of financial products for the eight member territories—Anguilla, Antigua and Barbuda, Dominica, Grenada, Montserrat, Saint Christopher and Nevis, Saint Lucia and Saint Vincent and the Grenadines; Gen. Man. TREVOR BLAKE.

INSURANCE

A-Affordable Insurance Services Inc: Old Factory Plaza, POB 6, The Valley; tel. 497-5757; fax 497-2122.

Barbados Mutual Life Assurance Society: Herbert's Commercial Complex, The Valley, POB 492; tel. 497-3712; fax 497-3710.

British American Insurance Co Ltd: Herbert's Commercial Centre, POB 148, The Valley; tel. 497-2653; fax 497-5933; e-mail britam@anguillnet.com.

Caribbean General Insurance Ltd: POB 65, South Hill; tel. 497-6541.

D-3 Enterprises Ltd: Herbert's Commercial Centre, POB 1377, The Valley; tel. 497-3525; fax 497-3526; e-mail d-3ent@anguillanet.com; Man. CLEMENT RUAN.

Gulf Insurance Ltd: Blowing Point; tel. 497-6613; fax 497-6713.

Malliouhana Insurance Co Ltd: Herbert's Commercial Centre, POB 492, The Valley; tel. 497-3712; fax 497-3710; e-mail maico@anguillanet.com; Man. MONICA HODGE.

Nagico Insurance: POB 79, The Valley; tel. 497-2976; fax 497-3303; e-mail fairplay@anguillanet.com.

National Caribbean Insurance Co Ltd: Herbert's Commercial Centre, POB 323, The Valley; tel. 497-2865; fax 497-3783.

Nem West Indies Insurance Ltd (Nemwil): Old Factory Plaza, POB 6, The Valley; tel. 497-5757; fax 497-2122.

Trade and Industry

DEVELOPMENT ORGANIZATION

Anguilla Development Board: POB 285, Wallblake Rd, The Valley; tel. 497-3690; fax 497-2959.

CHAMBER OF COMMERCE

Anguilla Chamber of Commerce and Industry: POB 321, The Valley; tel. 497-2701; fax 497-5858; e-mail acoci@anguillanet.com; internet www.anguillachamber.com; Pres. JOHN BENJAMIN; Exec. Dir CALVIN BARTLETT.

INDUSTRIAL AND TRADE ASSOCIATION

Anguilla Financial Services Association (AFSA): POB 1071, The Valley; tel. 497-8367; fax 497-3096; e-mail pwebster@websterdyrud.com; internet online.offshore.com.ai/afsa; Pres. PAM WEBSTER; Exec. Dir ODELL MCCANTS, Jr.

UTILITIES

Electricity

Anguilla Electricity Co Ltd: POB 400, The Valley; tel. 497-5200; fax 497-5440; e-mail info@anglec.com; internet www.anglec.com; f. 1991; operates a power-station and generators; Chair. EVERET ROMNEY; Gen. Man. NEIL MCCONNIE.

Transport

ROADS

Anguilla has 140 km (87 miles) of roads, of which 100 km (62 miles) are tarred.

SHIPPING

The principal port of entry is Sandy Ground on Road Bay. There is a daily ferry service between Blowing Point and Marigot (St Martin).

Link Ferries: Little Harbour; tel. 497-2231; fax 497-3290; e-mail fbconnor@anguillanet.com; internet www.link.ai; f. 1992; daily services to Julianna International Airport (St Martin) and charter services; Owner FRANKLYN CONNOR.

CIVIL AVIATION

Wallblake Airport, 3.2 km (2 miles) from The Valley, has a bitumen-surfaced runway with a length of 1,100 m (3,600 ft). In 1996 Anguilla signed an agreement with the Government of Aruba providing for the construction of a new jet airport on the north coast of the island, with finance of some US $30m. from the Aruba Investment Bank. In May 2004 reconstruction and expansion of Wallblake Airport commenced. The project was to cost EC $49.2m., most of which was intended for the extension of the runway to a length of 1,470 m (4,900 ft).

Air Anguilla: POB 110, Wallblake; tel. 497-2643; fax 497-2982; scheduled services to St Thomas, St Martin/St Maarten, Saint

Christopher and Beef Island (British Virgin Islands); Pres. RESTORMEL FRANKLIN.

American Eagle: POB 659, Wallblake Airport; tel. 497-3131; fax 497-3502; operates scheduled flights from Puerto Rico three times a day (December to April) and once daily (May to November).

Caribbean Star Airlines: POB 1628W, Wallblake Airport; tel. 497-8690; fax 497-8689; e-mail ceo@flycaribbeanstar.com; internet www.flycaribbeanstar.com.

Tyden Air: POB 107, Wallblake Airport; tel. 497-3419; fax 497-3079; charter company servicing whole Caribbean.

Tourism

Anguilla's sandy beaches and unspoilt natural beauty attract tourists and also day visitors from neighbouring St Martin/St Maarten. In November 1999 'Hurricane Lenny' badly affected Anguilla, forcing the temporary closure of the island's two largest hotels. Tourism receipts totalled some US $61.7m. in 2003 and there were 759 hotel rooms on the island; in the same year 52.5% of visitors were from the USA, 9.2% were from other Caribbean countries, while most of the remainder were from the United Kingdom, Canada, Italy and Germany. Visitor numbers totalled 119,130 in 2004.

Anguilla Tourist Board: POB 1388, The Valley; tel. 497-2759; fax 497-2710; e-mail atbtour@anguillanet.com; internet www.anguilla-vacation.com.

Anguilla Hotel and Tourism Association: Coronation Ave, POB 1020, The Valley; tel. 497-2944; fax 497-3091; e-mail ahta@anguillanet.com; internet www.ahta.ai; f. 1981; Exec. Dir TRUDY NIXON.

BERMUDA

Introductory Survey

Location, Climate, Language, Religion, Flag, Capital

The Bermudas or Somers Islands are an isolated archipelago, comprising about 138 islands, in the Atlantic Ocean, about 917 km (570 miles) off the coast of South Carolina, USA. Bridges and causeways link seven of the islands to form the principal mainland. The climate is mild and humid. Temperatures are generally between 8°C (46°F) and 32°C (90°F), with an average annual rainfall of 1,470 mm (58 ins). The official language is English, but there is a small community of Portuguese speakers. Most of the inhabitants profess Christianity, and numerous denominations are represented, the principal one being the Anglican Church. The flag (proportions 1 by 2) is the British 'Red Ensign' (this usage being unique among the British colonies), with, in the fly, the colony's badge: a seated red lion holding a shield (with a gold baroque border), which depicts the wreck off Bermuda of the ship of the first settlers. The capital is Hamilton.

Recent History

Bermuda was first settled by the British in 1609. It has had a representative assembly since 1620 (and thus claims one of the oldest parliaments in the world), and became a British crown colony in 1684. Bermuda was granted internal self-government by the Constitution introduced in 1968, although the British Government retains responsibility in certain matters. Various amendments to the 1968 Constitution were made in 1973, the most important being the establishment of the Governor's Council, through which the Governor exercises responsibility for external affairs, defence, internal security and the police. In 1974 the Government Leader was restyled Premier and the Executive Council became the Cabinet.

The first general election under the new Constitution, which took place in May 1968 against a background of rioting and racial tension (some 60% of the population are of African origin, the rest mostly of European extraction), was won by the United Bermuda Party (UBP), a moderate, multi-racial party whose policies were based on racial co-operation and continued support for dependent status. The underlying racial tensions were emphasized in 1972 and 1973 by shooting incidents which resulted in the deaths of the Governor, the Commissioner of Police and three others. In December 1977 the Governor's assassin and another convicted murderer were executed, and further rioting and arson ensued. A state of emergency was declared, and British troops were flown to Bermuda to restore order.

At the general election of May 1976, the UBP was returned to power with a decreased majority, winning 26 of the 40 seats in the House of Assembly. The remaining seats were won by the mainly black, left-wing Progressive Labour Party (PLP), which campaigned for independence. In August 1977 Sir John Sharpe, Premier and leader of the UBP since December 1975, resigned both posts and was succeeded by David Gibbons, the Minister of Finance.

In February 1978 a Royal Commission was established to investigate the causes of racial violence, and in August the Commission published a report which suggested the redrawing of constituency boundaries to improve the PLP's prospects for winning seats. Despite this, the UBP won the December 1980 election. Gibbons resigned as Premier and UBP leader in January 1982 and was succeeded by John Swan, the Minister of Home Affairs. At a general election in February 1983, the UBP increased its majority in the House of Assembly. Internal divisions within the PLP led to the expulsion from the party of four PLP members of the House of Assembly. These members, after sitting as independents, formed a new centre party, the National Liberal Party (NLP), in August 1985. In October Swan called an early general election, hoping to take advantage of the divided opposition. The UBP was decisively returned to power, securing 31 of the 40 seats in the House of Assembly, while the PLP retained only seven seats and the NLP won two. Following a general election in February 1989, the UBP remained in power, but with a reduced representation in the House of Assembly. By contrast, the PLP increased its representation.

Constitutional amendments introduced in 1979 included provision for closer consultation between the Premier and the Leader of the Opposition on the appointment of members of the Public Service Commission and the Boundaries Commission, and on the appointment of the Chief Justice. The 1978 Royal Commission recommended early independence for Bermuda, but the majority of the population at that time seemed to oppose such a policy. Swan had declared himself in favour of eventual independence for the colony, but only with the support of the Bermudian people.

In August 1992 Lord Waddington (former leader of the British House of Lords) replaced Sir Desmond Langley as Governor. Waddington remained in office until June 1997, when he was succeeded by Thorold Masefield.

At a general election on 5 October 1993 (the first to be held since the voting age was lowered from 21 to 18 years in 1990), the UBP was returned to power, winning 22 seats in the House of Assembly, while the PLP secured 18. In February 1994 legislation providing for the organization of a referendum on independence for Bermuda was narrowly approved in the House of Assembly. The debate on independence was believed to have intensified as a result of the announcement in late 1993 that British and US forces would close their facilities and withdraw permanently from the island by April 1995 and September 1995, respectively. The PLP, which advocates independence for Bermuda, consistently opposed the organization of a referendum on the subject, believing that the independence issue should be determined by a general election. In May 1994 a PLP legislative motion to reject a proposed government inquiry into the possibilities for independence was narrowly approved, effectively halting further progress towards a referendum. However, the debate continued, and in October a government delegation travelled to London for official discussions on the subject. Further legislation regarding the proposed referendum was narrowly approved in March 1995, and it was subsequently announced that a vote would be held in August. The PLP encouraged its supporters to boycott the poll, which required not only a majority of votes, but also the approval of 40% of eligible voters in order to achieve a pro-independence result.

The referendum, which was delayed briefly owing to the passage of 'Hurricane Felix', took place on 16 August 1995. Some 59% of eligible voters participated in the poll (a relatively low level for Bermuda), of which 74% registered their opposition to independence from the United Kingdom, and 26% expressed their support for independence. The following day Swan resigned as Premier and as leader of the UBP. Factions within the governing party were perceived to have become considerably polarized during the independence debate, which had resulted in the division of opinion along racial lines. The Minister of Finance, Dr David Saul (who had remained neutral on the independence issue), was subsequently elected leader of the UBP, and Saul was therefore sworn in as Premier on 25 August. Saul stated that his principal objectives were to re-establish a climate of political stability (thus reassuring the international business community), to encourage the continued development of the financial services and tourism sectors and to reunite the UBP. However, under Saul's leadership divisions within the party appeared to deepen, culminating in June 1996 in the approval of a motion of censure against him in the House of Assembly. The motion, which was supported by five UBP members, had been prompted by disagreement with Saul's decision to authorize the establishment of a foreign-owned restaurant in the Territory, in contravention of a ruling by the Bermuda Monetary Authority regarding the granting of franchises to such businesses.

In an attempt to restore a measure of unity within the UBP, Saul announced a reallocation of cabinet portfolios in January 1997. In the reorganization three of the five party members who had supported a motion of censure against Saul in June of the previous year were appointed to positions in the Cabinet. In March, however, Saul announced his resignation as Premier, as a member of the House of Assembly and as the leader of the party. He was replaced by Pamela Gordon, who was elected to the party leadership (and thus as Premier) unopposed.

In May 1998 Pamela Gordon effected a major reorganization of the Cabinet with the expressed aim of making the Government 'more efficient and effective'. In the following month the Court of Appeal upheld the constitutionality of the Prohibited Restaurants Act, passed by the House of Assembly in response to a further attempt by a group of Bermudian entrepreneurs, including Sir John Swan, to introduce fast-food franchises to Bermuda. The debate on the bill in the House of Assembly had been highly contentious, and was reported to have caused deep divisions within the ruling UBP. The Supreme Court had previously ruled that the Act was contrary to the provisions of the Constitution, as it made no provision for compensation. In July 1999 the Judicial Committee of the Privy Council upheld the constitutionality of the Prohibited Restaurants Act, rejecting a final appeal by the consortium.

Elections to the House of Assembly took place on 9 November 1998. The PLP won its first ever majority in the House of Assembly, taking 26 seats, while the UBP obtained 14 seats. Turn-out was estimated at 81%. On 10 November a new Cabinet was appointed and party leader Jennifer Smith was sworn in as Bermuda's first PLP Premier. In her subsequent public address she sought to reassure the international business community that her Government would seek to enhance Bermuda's attraction as an international business centre, and that she would resist any attempts to alter the island's tax status. Smith further promised that, although independence for Bermuda remained a stated aim of her party, no immediate moves towards independence were planned.

In February 1999 Smith met members of the Organisation for Economic Co-operation and Development (OECD, see p. 320) to reassure them that Bermuda was determined to improve regulation of the 'offshore' financial services sector. In March the British Government published draft legislation re-designating its Dependencies as United Kingdom Overseas Territories, and guaranteeing their citizens' rights to a British passport and to residence in the United Kingdom. The document also stated, however, that the Overseas Territories would be obliged to reform their legislation to ensure compliance with European standards on human rights and on financial regulation. In October it was announced that in accordance with the proposed reforms, corporal and capital punishment were to be removed from the statute book.

A report by the Financial Action Task Force on Money Laundering (see p. 389) concluded in June 2000 that Bermuda appeared 'to have effective regulations and supervision' in place in its financial services sector. In the same month the Government agreed to co-operate with OECD in an international effort to reduce tax evasion, promising to end within five years the 'harmful' practices that had given the island a reputation as a tax 'haven'. Measures included a pledge to exchange information about tax in Bermuda with other nations, the introduction of legislation for companies to audit accounts and for these to be made available to the Bermudian authorities, and in the opening up of previously sheltered sectors of the economy to international companies. The Government had, however, pledged to maintain its existing tax system, which included no income tax. In December the members of the House of Assembly agreed, for the first time, to declare their assets and financial interests.

In October 2000 the opposition UBP boycotted the opening of parliament in protest at government plans to reduce the number of seats in the House of Assembly. Pamela Gordon claimed that there had not been adequate public consultation on the matter. Premier Smith had rejected calls for a constitutional conference or a referendum on the proposals, which included replacing the two-member constituencies with single-member ones, although she did announce that the Government would hold a public meeting to discuss the issue. The PLP believed that the existing system was weighted in favour of the UBP, which was considered the party of the white population. The UBP claimed that changes made without proper consultation and a referendum would mean a move towards a 'black dictatorship'. In December the House of Assembly approved a motion requesting the British Government to approve the establishment of a boundaries commission, which would recommend the size of the island's constituencies. Any changes would be subject to ratification by the United Kingdom's Foreign and Commonwealth Office (FCO). In January 2001 the UBP submitted an 8,500-signature petition to the British Government, demanding a constitutional conference or referendum before any changes were made. Gordon also claimed that some Bermudians had refused to sign the petition fearing recriminations. The FCO, however, stated that a constitutional conference was unnecessary, and in April it began consultations over the proposed changes. The commission recommended reducing the number of seats in the House of Assembly by four, to 36. In addition, whereas deputies had previously been elected from 20 two-member constituencies, under the proposed scheme each member of parliament would be elected by a separate constituency. The FCO approved the changes before the July 2003 general election.

In October 2001 the former Prime Minister, Pamela Gordon, resigned as leader of the UBP. The party elected Grant Gibbons as her successor. In November Sir John Vereker succeeded Sir Thorold Masefield as Governor of Bermuda.

In May 2002 the British Overseas Territories Act, having received royal assent in the United Kingdom in February, came into force and granted British citizenship to the people of its Overseas Territories, including Bermuda. Under the new law Bermudians would be able to hold British passports and work in the United Kingdom and anywhere else in the European Union (see p. 228).

In mid-2002 the issue of financial transparency and corporate governance in Bermuda re-emerged following the disastrous collapse of the US energy concern Enron and several other multinationals in late 2001 and early 2002. The indictment on tax-evasion charges of Dennis Kozlowski, the former CEO of Tyco International Ltd, a manufacturer of electronic security systems with a nominal headquarters on the island, fuelled a growing campaign in the US media and the US Congress against the perceived lack of financial regulation and scrutiny in Bermuda. The Corporate Patriot Enforcement Act of 2005, approved by the US Congress in that year, sought to discourage US corporations to relocate their headquarters from the USA to offshore sites such as Bermuda, by making them still liable to pay tax in the USA.

At an election to the smaller 36-seat House of Assembly on 24 July 2003, the PLP retained its parliamentary majority, securing 22 seats, but its share of the popular vote was reduced to 51.7% (compared with 48.0% for the UBP). Smith resigned as Premier following pressure from 11 'rebel' PLP MPs after it emerged that she had retained her seat, in what was regarded as a 'safe' PLP constituency, by just eight votes. She was replaced by the erstwhile Minister of Works and Engineering, William Alexander Scott. Eugene Cox, the Deputy Prime Minister, also resigned, and was succeeded by Dr Ewart Brown, also the Minister of Transport. Cox, however, retained his position as Minister of Finance. The election campaign was dominated by resentment towards wealthy foreign workers and criticism of the personal style of Smith, regarded by many as uncommunicative and aloof. Scott's first Cabinet, announced a few days after the elections, consisted of 12 members, despite the PLP's pre-election pledge to reduce the size of the executive to eight in order to reduce costs.

Following the death of Eugene Cox in January 2004, his daughter, Paula Ann Cox, the erstwhile Minister of Education and Justice and Attorney-General, was appointed as Minister of Finance. Several other changes were made to the Cabinet at the same time. In July Scott effected a further minor cabinet reshuffle after Maurine Webb resigned as Minister of Tourism, Telecommunications and E-Commerce. Responsibility for tourism transferred to Ewart Brown and Michael Scott, the erstwhile Minister of Legislative Affairs, was allocated Webb's other portfolios. The legislative affairs portfolio was added to the responsibilities of Mussenden, with the end result of reducing the size of the Cabinet by one. However, Walter Lister, former Deputy Speaker of the House of Assembly, was appointed to the Cabinet in August, although he was not allocated a portfolio.

In December 2004 Scott announced that a Bermuda Independence Commission would be established in order to foment debate regarding the island's future. This Commission was duly established in January 2005 and in November it submitted its report; however, its findings were criticized for being biased, as they failed to include contributions from the UBP, including only the ruling PLP's submission. In an attempt to quell the criticism, Scott declared that discussions would take place in 2006 regarding the future status of Bermuda. However, public opinion remained strongly in favour of maintaining links with the United Kingdom: according to opinion polls in early 2006, only 28% of the public supported independence. In March both the UN and the British Government indicated their support for a referendum on the issue; however, Scott maintained that the question of independence should be decided at the next general election, which was constitutionally due by 2008. The issue of independence created political tension between the population's black majority, from which the PLP drew much of its support, and the white minority. A UN report released in July 2005 said that Bermuda's history of segregation was still an issue among some people. Many of the older generation of African descent believed independence would bring closure to that period. However, some white Bermudians believed that the stability of the island was partly owing to British influence and that independence might be detrimental to Bermuda's economy.

Following increased drugs-smuggling and immigration violations by Jamaican nationals, in January 2003 it was announced that Jamaican visitors to Bermuda would henceforth require visas. In February 2005 a Supreme Court judge ruled as discriminatory and unlawful the Government's policy of deferring the right to apply for parole for prisoners convicted of drugs-smuggling until they had served one-half of their sentence. Prisoners convicted of non-drugs, non-sexual or non-violent offences were allowed to apply for parole after serving one-third of their sentence. In July the Misuse of Drugs Amendment Act introduced legislation allowing courts to fine those convicted of drugs offences up to US $1m. and to impose prison sentences of between 10 years and life.

Government

Bermuda is a crown colony of the United Kingdom, with a wide measure of internal self-government. An appointed Governor, responsible for external affairs, defence and internal security, represents the British monarch. The bicameral legislature comprises the Senate (11 nominated members) and the House of Assembly, with 36 members representing separate constituencies elected for five years by universal adult suffrage. The Governor appoints the majority leader in the House as Premier, and the latter nominates other ministers. The Cabinet is responsible to the legislature. For the purposes of local government, the island has long been divided into nine parishes (originally known as 'tribes', except for the 'public land' of St George's, the capital until 1815). The town of St George's and the city of Hamilton constitute the two municipalities of the Territory.

Defence

The local defence force is the Bermuda Regiment, with a strength of some 630 men and women in 1999. The Regiment employs selective conscription.

Economic Affairs

In 1997, according to estimates by the World Bank, Bermuda's gross national income (GNI), measured at average 1995–97 prices, was US $2,128m. During 1995–2004, it was estimated, the population increased at an average annual rate of 0.4%, while overall gross domestic product (GDP) increased, in real terms, at an average annual rate of 3.4% in 1996–2004; growth was estimated at 4.4% in 2003, but only 1.6% in 2004. In 2000 GDP per head was estimated to be equivalent to some US $34,600, one of the highest levels in the world.

Agriculture (including fishing, mining and quarrying) engaged only 1.7% of the employed labour force in 2003 and contributed 0.8% of GDP in 2004. The principal crops were potatoes, carrots, bananas, vegetables and melons. Flowers (notably lilies) are grown for export. Other vegetables and fruit are also grown, but Bermuda remains very dependent upon food imports, which, with beverages and tobacco, accounted for 18.1% of total imports in 2004. Livestock-rearing includes cattle and goats (both mainly for dairy purposes), pigs and poultry. There is a small fishing industry, mainly for domestic consumption. In 1996–2004 agricultural GDP increased by an annual average of 5.4%; the sector grew by 6.5% in 2003 and by a further 5.0% in 2004.

Industry (including manufacturing, construction, quarrying and public utilities) contributed 9.5% of GDP in 2004 and engaged an estimated 11.7% of the employed labour force in 2003. The main activities include ship repairs, boat-building and the manufacture of paints and pharmaceuticals. The principal industrial sector is construction (in which an estimated 7.9% of the total labour force were engaged in 2003). Most of Bermuda's water is provided by privately collected rainfall. Energy requirements are met mainly by the import of mineral fuels (fuels accounted for 10.9% of total imports in 2004). An explosion at Bermuda's only power plant in July 2005 reduced electricity production to just 85 MW from its full capacity of 165 MW. The cost of repairing the damage was estimated at B $10m. Industrial GDP increased by an average of 2.4% per year in 1996–2004; the sector expanded by 2.2% in 2003 and by 4.7% in 2004.

Bermuda is overwhelmingly a service economy, with service industries contributing an estimated 89.7% of GDP in 2004 and engaging 86.6% of the employed labour force in 2003. In 2003 18.0% of the employed labour force worked in restaurants and hotels, but tourism is estimated to account for some 60% of all employment, directly and indirectly. The total number of tourists, particularly of cruise-ship passengers, is strictly controlled, in order to maintain Bermuda's environment and its market for wealthier visitors. Most tourists come from the USA (some 75.7% of total arrivals by air in 2005). In 2005 517,196 tourists visited Bermuda, an increase of 8.3% on the previous year's figure. In September 2003 the impact of 'Hurricane Fabian' led to the cancellation of several cruise-ship visits and the temporary closure of the international airport to commercial aircraft. In addition, two leading hotels suffered extensive damage. Largely as a consequence of the hurricane, tourism revenue declined to B $342.5m. in 2003, from B $378.8m. the previous year, before recovering slightly to B $353.7m. in 2004. In 1996–2004 the GDP of the services sector increased by an annual average of 3.8%; services GDP increased by 4.0% in 2003 and by 1.9% in 2004.

There is a significant commercial and 'offshore' financial sector, and in 2000 Bermuda was the world's third largest insurance market, having doubled in size during the 1990s. In late 2001 the industry came under huge pressure from claims made in connection to the September terrorist attacks in the USA, although increased demand for insurance and reinsurance services led to a number of new companies being formed at the same time. It was estimated that, in 1995, the entire financial sector contributed more than one-third of foreign exchange earnings. An estimated 28.8% of the employed labour force were engaged directly in the finance, insurance, real estate and business sectors in 2003. International business was estimated to account for 20.4% of GDP in 2004. In 2003 the number of companies registered in Bermuda totalled 13,528. The GDP of the international business sector increased by an annual average of 10.0% in 1996–2004; the sector increased by 10.3% in 2003 and by a further 2.1% in 2004. Another important source of income is the 'free-flag' registration of shipping, giving Bermuda one of the largest fleets in the world. In 1999 Bermuda passed the Electronic Transactions Act, designed to create an infrastructure to support the country's burgeoning 'e-commerce' sector, which was intended to become Bermuda's third major service industry, alongside financial services and tourism.

Bermuda is almost entirely dependent upon imports, has very few commodity exports and, therefore, consistently records a large visible trade deficit (an estimated B $781m. in 2003). Receipts from the service industries normally ensure a surplus on the current account of the balance of payments (reportedly around $70m. in 2002). The USA is the principal source of imports (80% of total imports in 2003) and the principal market for exports. Other important trading partners include the United Kingdom, Canada and France. The main exports are rum, flowers, medicinal and pharmaceutical products and the re-export of petroleum products. The principal imports are machinery and food, beverages and tobacco.

In 2002/03 Bermuda recorded a provisional budgetary surplus of some B $29.7m. A deficit of some $78.9m. was forecast for the 2003/04 financial year. The average annual rate of inflation was 2.3% in 1993–2004. The rate averaged 3.2% in 2003 and 3.6% in 2004. In February 2001 government figures indicated that unemployment had fallen for the first time since 1993. In 2002 foreign workers comprised some 26.7% of those employed in the Territory.

Bermuda, the oldest colony of the United Kingdom, has the status of Overseas Territory in association with the European Union (see p. 228) and has also been granted Designated Territory status by the British Government (this allows Bermudian-based funds and unit trusts access to the British market). Bermuda's financial services also benefit from a special tax treaty with the USA. A similar agreement was signed in November 2005 with Australia, in which both parties would share tax information on a specific subject under investigation or audit. In 2000 Bermuda joined the Caribbean Tourism Organization. In July 2003 Bermuda became an associate member of the Caribbean Community and Common Market (CARICOM, see p. 183).

Bermudians enjoy a high standard of living, although addressing the inequality of the distribution of wealth is a key objective of the PLP Government that took office in 2003, as is local disquiet at the cost of property. The Government borrowed B $85m. to underpin the 2004/05 budget, which was mostly intended for expenditure on social projects, such as housing for the homeless and health services. Proximity to the USA and the parity of the US and Bermuda dollars help both tourism and financial industries, and Bermuda's status as a United Kingdom Overseas Territory remains a perceived contributor to political stability and financial integrity. The Territory's insurance industry has experienced a period of rapid expansion and remains the most important component of the financial sector. Following a decline in the tourism sector in 2001, partly owing to the repercussions of the terrorist attacks on the USA in September, the Bermuda Alliance for Tourism launched a rebranding of Bermuda as a luxury destination, in order to attract higher-spending visitors. Against expectations, however, tourism expenditures continued to decline, in part owing to 'Hurricane Fabian', which caused several million Bermudian dollars-worth of damage in late 2003. In January 2005 the Minister of Tourism and Transport, Dr Ewart Brown, announced plans to extend the tourist season into the winter months in order to increase tourism revenue by 7% over the following three years. One proposed measure to achieve this target was the revival of the African Diaspora Heritage Trail. In the long term, the Government will need to address the differences between the requirements of the international businesses domiciled on Bermuda and the needs of Bermudians employed in other sectors. Concerns were also raised over how much further the international business sector could expand without putting excessive strain on the local infrastructure. Furthermore, commentators regarded the island's continuing heavy dependence on the tourism and 'offshore' finance sectors as potentially risky; in particular, discussion of changes to

UNITED KINGDOM OVERSEAS TERRITORIES

Bermuda

Bermuda's tax exemption laws resulted in several international business companies indicating their intentions to move to other regimes if financial conditions were to deteriorate, an eventuality which the island's high inflation rate made more likely. According to official estimates, growth for 2005/06 was forecast at between 2.5%–3.0%.

Education

There is free compulsory education in government schools between the ages of five and 16 years, and a number of scholarships are awarded for higher education and teacher training. There are also seven private secondary schools which charge fees. The Bermuda College, founded in 1972, accepts students over the age of 16, and is the only post-secondary educational institution. Extramural degree courses are available through Queen's University, Canada, and Indiana and Maryland Universities, USA. A major programme to upgrade the education system, involving the establishment of five new primary and two secondary schools, was implemented between 1996 and 2002.

Public Holidays

2006: 1 January (New Year's Day), 14 April (Good Friday), 24 May (Bermuda Day), 12 June (Queen's Official Birthday), 3 August (Cup Match), 4 August (Somers' Day), 4 September (Labour Day), 11 November (Remembrance Day), 25–26 December (Christmas).

2007: 1 January (New Year's Day), 6 April (Good Friday), 24 May (Bermuda Day), 11 June (Queen's Official Birthday), 2 August (Cup Match), 3 August (Somers' Day), 3 September (Labour Day), 11 November (Remembrance Day), 25–26 December (Christmas).

Weights and Measures

The metric system has been widely adopted but imperial and US weights and measures are both used in certain fields.

Statistical Survey

Source: Dept of Statistics, POB HM 3015, Hamilton HM MX; tel. 297-7761; fax 295-8390; e-mail statistics@gov.bm; internet www.gov.bm.

AREA AND POPULATION

Area: 53.3 sq km (20.59 sq miles).

Population (civilian, non-institutional): 58,460 at census of 20 May 1991; 62,059 (males 29,802, females 32,257) at census of 20 May 2000.

Density (census of 2000): 1,164.3 per sq km.

Principal Towns (population at 1991 census): St George's 1,648; Hamilton (capital) 1,100.

Births, Marriages and Deaths (2002): Live births 830 (birth rate 13.4 per 1,000); Marriage rate 15.1 per 1,000; Deaths 404 (death rate 6.5 per 1,000).

Expectation of Life (years at birth, official estimates in 2002): Males 75.2; Females 79.3. Source: Pan American Health Organization.

Employment (excluding unpaid family workers, 2003): Agriculture, forestry, fishing, mining and quarrying 638; Manufacturing 1,063; Electricity, gas and water 405; Construction 2,959; Wholesale and retail trade 5,015; Restaurants 1,779; Hotels 2,981; Transport and communications 2,861; Financial intermediation 2,821; Real estate 507; Business activities 3,756; Public administration 3,982; Education, health and social services 2,916; Other community, social and personal services 2,222; International business activity 3,781; *Total employed* 37,686 (males 19,597, females 18,089).

HEALTH AND WELFARE

Physicians (per 1,000 head, 2003): 1.9.

Hospital Beds (per 1,000 head, 2003): 22.6.

Health Expenditure (% of GDP, 1997): 4.2.

Health Expenditure (public, % of total, 1995): 53.2.

Source: partly Pan American Health Organization.

For definitions, see explanatory note on p. vi.

AGRICULTURE, ETC.

Principal Crops (FAO estimates, metric tons, 2004): Potatoes 800; Carrots 340; Vegetables and melons 2,100; Bananas 330.

Livestock (FAO estimates, 2004): Cattle 600; Horses 900; Pigs 600.

Livestock Products (FAO estimates, metric tons, 2004): Cows' milk 1,350; Hen eggs 280.

Fishing (metric tons, live weight, 2003): Groupers 33; Snappers and jobfishes 31; Wahoo 88; Yellowfin tuna 47; Carangids 41; Caribbean spiny lobster 31; Total catch (incl. others) 358.

Source: FAO.

INDUSTRY

Electric Energy (consumption, million kWh): 590 in 2003.

FINANCE

Currency and Exchange Rates: 100 cents = 1 Bermuda dollar (B $). *Sterling, US Dollar and Euro Equivalents* (30 December 2005): £1 sterling = B $1.7219; US $1 = B $1.000; €1 = B $1.1797; B $100 = £58.08 = US $100.00 = €84.77. *Exchange Rate:* The Bermuda dollar is at par with the US dollar. Note: US and Canadian currencies are also accepted.

Budget (B $ million, 2002/03, provisional): *Total Revenue* 671.1 (Customs duties 185.0; Payroll tax 203.4; Hotel occupancy tax 10.9; Passenger tax 22.5; Land tax 40.5; International company tax 47.7; Stamp duties 34.9). *Total Expenditure* 641.4 (Salaries and wages 248.3; Other goods and services 151.3; Grants and contributions 140.2; Capital expenditure 70.8).

Cost of Living (Consumer Price Index; base: 1993 = 100): 119.6 in 2002; 123.4 in 2003; 127.8 in 2004.

Expenditure on the Gross Domestic Product (B $ million at current prices, year ending 31 March 2001): Government final consumption expenditure 367; Private final consumption expenditure 2,079; Gross fixed capital formation 679; *Total domestic expenditure* 3,125; Exports of goods and services 1,597; *Less* Imports of goods and services 1,325; *GDP in purchasers' values* 3,397. Source: UN, *National Accounts Statistics*.

Gross Domestic Product by Economic Activity (B $ million at current prices, 2004): Agriculture, forestry and fishing 37.5; Manufacturing 78.7; Electricity, gas and water 80.4; Construction and quarrying 272.4; Wholesale and retail trade and repair services 379.0; Restaurants and hotels 245.8; Transport and communications 270.4; Financial intermediation 536.0; Real estate and renting activities 712.0; Business activities 391.1; Public administration 218.2; Education, health and social work 304.4; Other community, social and personal services 94.5; International business activity 926.5; *Sub-total* 4,546.9; *Less* Imputed bank service charges 257.7; Indirect taxes, less subsidies 216.1; *GDP in purchasers' values* 4,505.3.

Balance of Payments (B $ million, 2004, estimates): Gross receipts 2,241 (Tourism 354; Professional services 1,300); Gross payments −2,069 (Imports 965); *Overall balance* (net) 172. Source: Bermuda Monetary Authority.

EXTERNAL TRADE

Principal Commodities (B $ million, 2004): *Imports:* Food, beverages and tobacco 175.0; Clothing 42.5; Fuels 105.4; Chemicals 108.4; Basic material and semi-manufacturing 144.4; Machinery 183.8; Transport equipment 64.6; Finished equipment 144.8; Miscellaneous 0.3; Total (incl. others) 969.1. *Exports* (2003, preliminary estimate): Total 52.0.

Principal Trading Partners (US $ million): *Imports* (1999): Canada 40.2; United Kingdom 34.5; USA 518.3; Total (incl. others) 712.1. *Exports* (1995): France 7.5; United Kingdom 3.9; USA 31.3; Total (incl. others) 62.9.

Source: partly UN, *International Trade Statistics Yearbook*.

TRANSPORT

Road Traffic (vehicles in use, 2003): Private cars 20,976; Motorcycles 20,331; Buses, taxis and limousines 794; Trucks and tank wagons 3,818; Other 764; Total 46,683.

Shipping: *Ship Arrivals* (1999): Cruise ships 140; Cargo ships 171; Oil and gas tankers 17. *Merchant Fleet** (registered at 31 December 2004): 122; Total displacement 6,166,162 grt. *International Freight Traffic†* ('000 metric tons, 1990): Goods loaded 130; Goods unloaded 470.

* Source: Lloyd's Register-Fairplay, *World Fleet Statistics*.
† Source: UN, *Monthly Bulletin of Statistics*.

Civil Aviation (1999): Aircraft arrivals 6,024; Passengers 354,026; Air cargo 4,761,444 kg; Air mail 422,897 kg.

TOURISM

Visitor Arrivals: 482,673 (arrivals by air 256,576, cruise-ship passengers 226,097) in 2003; 477,757 (arrivals by air 271,617, cruise-

UNITED KINGDOM OVERSEAS TERRITORIES   *Bermuda*

ship passengers 206,140) in 2004; 517,196 (arrivals by air 269,587, cruise-ship passengers 247,609) in 2005.

Tourism Receipts (B $ million, estimated): 378.8 in 2002; 342.5 in 2003; 353.7 in 2004.

COMMUNICATIONS MEDIA

Radio Receivers (1997): 82,000 in use.
Television Receivers (1999): 70,000 in use.
Telephones (2001): 56,300 main lines in use.
Mobile Cellular Telephones (2001): 13,300 subscribers.
Personal Computers (2001): 32,000 in use.
Internet Users (1999): 25,000.
Daily Newspapers (2000): 1 (estimated circulation 17,700).
Non-daily Newspapers (2000): 2 (estimated circulation 11,600).

Sources: mainly UNESCO, *Statistical Yearbook*; UN, *Statistical Yearbook*; International Telecommunication Union.

EDUCATION

Pre-primary (1999): 12 schools; 191 teachers; 429 pupils.
Primary (1999): 25 schools; 368 teachers; 4,980 pupils.
Senior (1999): 18 schools; 399 teachers; 2,335 pupils*.
Higher (2002): 1 institution; 544 students.
* Including six private schools.

Adult Literacy Rate (UNESCO estimates): 99% (males 98%; females 99%) in 1998 (Source: UNESCO, *Statistical Yearbook*).

Directory

The Constitution

The Constitution, introduced on 8 June 1968 and amended in 1973 and 1979, contains provisions relating to the protection of fundamental rights and freedoms of the individual; the powers and duties of the Governor; the composition, powers and procedure of the Legislature; the Cabinet; the judiciary; the public service and finance.

The British monarch is represented by an appointed Governor, who retains responsibility for external affairs, defence, internal security and the police.

The Legislature consists of the monarch, the Senate and the House of Assembly. Three members of the Senate are appointed at the Governor's discretion, five on the advice of the Government leader and three on the advice of the Opposition leader. The Senate elects a President and Vice-President. The House of Assembly, consisting of 36 members elected under universal adult franchise, elects a Speaker and a Deputy Speaker, and sits for a five-year term.

The Cabinet consists of the Premier and at least six other members of the Legislature. The Governor appoints the majority leader in the House of Assembly as Premier, who in turn nominates the other members of the Cabinet. They are assigned responsibilities for government departments and other business and, in some cases, are assisted by Permanent Cabinet Secretaries.

The Cabinet is presided over by the Premier. The Governor's Council enables the Governor to consult with the Premier and two other members of the Cabinet nominated by the Premier on matters for which the Governor has responsibility. The Secretary to the Cabinet, who heads the public service, acts as secretary to the Governor's Council.

Voters must be British subjects aged 18 years or over (lowered from 21 years in 1990), and, if not possessing Bermudian status, must have been registered as electors on 1 May 1976. Candidates for election must qualify as electors, and must possess Bermudian status.

Under the British Overseas Territories Act, which entered into effect in May 2002, Bermudian citizens have the right to United Kingdom citizenship and the right of abode in the United Kingdom. British citizens do not enjoy reciprocal rights.

The Government

Governor and Commander-in-Chief: Sir JOHN VEREKER (took office 21 November 2001).
Deputy Governor: NICK CARTER.

CABINET
(April 2006)

Premier: WILLIAM ALEXANDER SCOTT.
Deputy Premier, Minister of Tourism and Transport: Dr EWART FREDERICK BROWN.
Minister of Finance: PAULA ANN COX.
Minister of the Environment: NELETHA I. BUTTERFIELD.
Minister of Education and Development: TERRY E. LISTER.
Minister of Health and Family Services: PATRICE K. MINORS.
Minister of Labour, Home Affairs and Public Safety: K. H. RANDOLPH HORTON.
Minister of Telecommunications and E-Commerce: MICHAEL SCOTT.
Minister of Works, Engineering and Housing: ASHFIELD DEVENT.
Minister of Community Affairs and Sports: DALE D. BUTLER.
Attorney-General and Minister of Justice and Legislative Affairs: Sen. LARRY D. MUSSENDEN.

MINISTRIES

Office of the Governor: Government House, 11 Langton Hill, Pembroke HM 13; tel. 292-3600; fax 292-6831; e-mail depgov@ibl.bm; internet www.gov.bm.
Office of the Premier: Cabinet Office, Cabinet Bldg, 105 Front St, Hamilton HM 12; tel. 292-5501; fax 292-0304; e-mail ascott@gov.bm; internet www.gov.bm.
Ministry of Community Affairs and Sports: Old Fire Station Bldg, 81 Court St, Hamilton HM 12; tel. 295-0855; fax 295-6292.
Ministry of Education and Development: Dundonald Pl., 14 Dundonald St, POB HM 1185, Hamilton HM EX; tel. 278-3300; fax 278-3348; internet www.moe.bm.
Ministry of the Environment: Government Administration Bldg, 30 Parliament St, Hamilton HM 12; tel. 297-7590; fax 292-2349; e-mail browlinson@gov.bm.
Ministry of Finance: Government Administration Bldg, 30 Parliament St, Hamilton HM 12; tel. 295-5151; fax 295-5727.
Ministry of Health and Family Services: 7 Point Finger Rd, Paget DV 04, POB HM 380, Hamilton HM BX; tel. 236-0224; fax 236-3971; e-mail ejjoell@gov.bm; internet www.healthandfamily.gov.bm.
Ministry of Justice and Legislative Affairs and Attorney-General's Chambers: 1st Floor, Global House, 43 Church St, Hamilton HM 12; tel. 292-2463; fax 292-3608; e-mail agc@gov.bm.
Ministry of Labour, Home Affairs and Public Safety: Global House, 43 Church St, Hamilton HM 12; tel. 292-5998; fax 295-5267; e-mail lhaps@gov.bm.
Ministry of Telecommunications and E-Commerce: POB HM 101, Hamilton HM AX; tel. 292-4595; fax 295-1462; e-mail gtelecom@gov.bm; internet www.mtec.bm.
Ministry of Tourism and Transport: Global House, 43 Church St, Hamilton HM 12; tel. 295-3130; fax 295-1013.
Ministry of Works, Engineering and Housing: 3rd Floor, General Post Office Bldg, 56 Church St, POB HM 525, Hamilton HM 12; tel. 297-7699; fax 295-0170; e-mail nfox@bdagov.bm.

Legislature

SENATE

President: ALFRED OUGHTON.
Vice-President: Dr IDWAL WYN (WALWYN) HUGHES.
There are 11 nominated members.

HOUSE OF ASSEMBLY

Speaker: STANLEY W. LOWE.
Deputy Speaker: Dr JENNIFER M. SMITH.
Clerk to the Legislature: Y. MURIEL ROACH; tel. 292-7408; fax 292-2006; e-mail mroach@gov.bm.

General Election, 24 July 2003

Party	% of votes	Seats
Progressive Labour Party	51.6	22
United Bermuda Party	48.0	14
Total (incl. others)	100.0	36

Political Organizations

National Liberal Party (NLP): 53 Church St, Hamilton HM 12, POB HM 2190, Hamilton HM FX; tel. 236-9438; f. 1985; Leader DESSALINE WALDRON; Chair. GRAEME OUTERBRIDGE.

Progressive Labour Party (PLP): Alaska Hall, 16 Court St, POB 1367, Hamilton HM 12; tel. 292-2264; fax 295-7890; e-mail info@plp.bm; internet www.plp.bm; f. 1963; advocates the 'Bermudianization' of the economy, more equitable taxation, a more developed system of welfare and preparation for independence; Leader WILLIAM ALEXANDER SCOTT; Deputy Leader Dr EWART FREDERICK BROWN; Chair. RODERICK BURCHALL.

United Bermuda Party (UBP): Central Office, 3rd Floor, Bermudiana Arcade, 27 Queen St, Hamilton HM 12; tel. 295-0729; fax 292-7195; e-mail info@ubp.bm; internet www.ubp.bm; f. 1964; policy of participatory democracy, supporting system of free enterprise; Leader GRANT GIBBONS; Chair. AUSTIN B. WOODS.

Judicial System

Chief Justice: RICHARD GROUND.
President of the Court of Appeal: Sir JAMES ASTWOOD.
Registrar of Supreme Court and Court of Appeal: MICHAEL J. MELLO.
Attorney-General: Sen. LARRY MUSSENDEN.
Director of Public Prosecutions: VINETTE GRAHAM-ALLEN.
Solicitor-General: WILHELM C. BOURNE.

The Court of Appeal was established in 1964, with powers and jurisdiction of equivalent courts in other parts of the Commonwealth. The Supreme Court has jurisdiction over all serious criminal matters and has unlimited civil jurisdiction. The Court also hears civil and criminal appeals from the Magistrates' Courts. The three Magistrates' Courts have jurisdiction over all petty offences, and have a limited civil jurisdiction.

Religion

CHRISTIANITY

In 2000 it was estimated that 23% of the population were members of the Anglican Communion, 15% were Roman Catholics, 11% were African Methodist Episcopalians, 7% were Seventh-day Adventists and 4% were Wesleyan Methodists. The Presbyterian Church, the Baptist Church and the Pentecostal Church are also active in Bermuda.

The Anglican Communion

The Anglican Church of Bermuda consists of a single, extra-provincial diocese, directly under the metropolitan jurisdiction of the Archbishop of Canterbury, the Primate of All England. There are about 23,000 Anglicans and Episcopalians in Bermuda.

Bishop of Bermuda: Rt Rev. EWEN RATTERAY, Bishop's Lodge, 18 Ferrar's Lane, Pembroke HM 08, POB HM 769, Hamilton HM CX; tel. 292-6987; fax 292-5421; e-mail bishopratteray@ibl.bm; internet www.anglican.bm.

The Roman Catholic Church

Bermuda forms a single diocese, suffragan to the archdiocese of Kingston in Jamaica. At 31 December 2003 there were an estimated 9,275 adherents in the Territory. The Bishop participates in the Antilles Episcopal Conference (currently based in Port of Spain, Trinidad and Tobago).

Bishop of Hamilton in Bermuda: ROBERT JOSEPH KURTZ, 2 Astwood Rd, POB HM 1191, Hamilton HM EX; tel. 232-4414; fax 232-4447; e-mail rjkurtz@northrock.bm.

Protestant Churches

Baptist Church: Emmanuel Baptist Church, 35 Dundonald St, Hamilton HM 10; tel. 295-6555; fax 296-4461; Pastor RONALD K. SMITH.

Wesley Methodist Church: 41 Church St, POB HM 346, Hamilton HM BX; tel. 292-0418; fax 295-9460; e-mail info@wesley.bm; internet www.wesley.bm; Rev. JEFF CHANT.

The Press

Bermuda Homes and Gardens Magazine: Suite 16352, 48 Par-la-Ville Rd, Hamilton HM 11; tel. 295-5845; e-mail info@bdahomesandgardens.bm; monthly, free.

Bermuda Magazine: POB HM 283, Hamilton HM HX; tel. 295-0695; fax 295-8616; e-mail cbarclay@ibl.bm; f. 1990; quarterly; Editor-in-Chief CHARLES BARCLAY.

Bermudian Business Online: POB HM 283, Hamilton HM AX; tel. 295-0695; e-mail berpub@ibl.bm; internet www.bermudianbusiness.com; Publr TINA STEVENSON.

The Bermuda Sun: 19 Elliott St, POB HM 1241, Hamilton HM FX; tel. 295-3902; fax 292-5597; e-mail bdasun@ibl.bm; internet www.bermudasun.bm; f. 1964; 2 a week; official govt gazette; Editor TONY MCWILLIAM; circ. 12,500.

The Bermudian: 13 Addendum Lane, Pitt's Bay Rd, Pembroke HM07; POB HM 283, Hamilton HM AX; tel. 295-0695; fax 295-8616; e-mail berpub@ibl.bm; f. 1930; monthly; pictorial and resort magazine; Editor MEREDITH EBBIN; circ. 7,500.

Cable TV Guide: 41 Victoria St, Hamilton HM 12; tel. 295-3902; fax 295-5597.

The Mid-Ocean News: 2 Par-la-Ville Rd, POB HM 1025, Hamilton HM DX; tel. 295-5881; fax 295-1513; f. 1911; weekly with TV Guide; Editor TIM HODGSON; Gen. Man. KEITH JENSEN; circ. 14,500.

The Royal Gazette: 2 Par-la-Ville Rd, POB HM 1025, Hamilton HM DX; tel. 295-5881; fax 295-1513; internet www.theroyalgazette.com; f. 1828; morning daily; Editor WILLIAM J. ZUILL; Gen. Man. KEITH JENSEN; circ. 17,500.

TV Week: 2 Par-la-Ville Rd, Hamilton HM 08; tel. 295-5881.

The Worker's Voice: 49 Union Sq., Hamilton HM 12; tel. 292-0044; fax 295-7992; e-mail biu@ibl.bm; fortnightly; organ of the Bermuda Industrial Union; Editor Dr B. B. BALL.

Publisher

Bermudian Publishing Co: POB HM 283, Hamilton HM AX; tel. 295-0695; fax 295-8616; e-mail berpub@ibl.bm; social sciences, sociology, sports; Editor KEVIN STEVENSON.

Broadcasting and Communications

TELECOMMUNICATIONS

Bermuda Telephone Co (BTC): 30 Victoria St, POB 1021, Hamilton HM DX; tel. 295-1001; fax 295-1192; internet www.btc.bm; f. 1987; Pres. FRANCIS R. MUSSENDEN.

Bermuda Digital Communications: 22 Reid St, Hamilton HM 11; tel. 296-4010; fax 296-4020; e-mail info@bdc.bm; internet www.bdc.bm; mobile cellular telephone operator; f. 1998; Chair. and CEO KURT EVE.

Cable & Wireless (Bermuda) Ltd: 1 Middle Rd, Smith's FL 03, POB HM 151, Hamilton HM AX; tel. 297-7000; fax 295-8995; e-mail helpdesk@bda.cwplc.com; internet www.cw.com/bermuda; Gen. Man. EDDIE SAINTS.

TeleBermuda International (TBI) Ltd: Bermuda Commercial Bank Bldg, 2nd Floor, 43 Victoria St, Hamilton HM 12; tel. 296-9000; fax 296-9010; e-mail save@telebermuda.com; internet www.telebermuda.com; f. 1997; a division of GlobeNet Communications, provides an international service; owns a fibre-optic network connecting Bermuda and the USA; Gen. Man. JAMES FITZGERALD.

BROADCASTING

Radio

Bermuda Broadcasting Company: POB HM 452, Hamilton HM BX; tel. 295-2828; fax 295-4282; e-mail zbmzfb@bermudabroadcasting.com; internet www.bermudabroadcasting.com; f. 1982 as merger of ZBM (f. 1943) and ZFB (f. 1962); operates 4 radio stations; CEO ULRIC P. RICHARDSON; Operations Man. E. DELANO INGHAM.

DeFontes Broadcasting Co Ltd (VSB): POB HM 1450, Hamilton HM FX; tel. 292-0050; fax 295-1658; e-mail vsbnews@ibl.bm; internet www.vsb.bm; f. 1981 as St George's Broadcasting Co; commercial; 4 radio stations; Pres. KENNETH DEFONTES; Station Man. MIKE BISHOP.

Television

Bermuda Broadcasting Company: see Radio; operates 2 TV stations (Channels 7 and 9).

Bermuda Cablevision Ltd: 19 Laffan St, Hamilton; tel. 292-5544; fax 296-3023; e-mail info@cablevision.bm; internet www.cablevision.bm; f. 1988; 180 channels; Pres. DAVID LINES; Gen. Man. JEREMY ELMAS.

DeFontes Broadcasting Co Ltd (VSB): see Radio; operates 1 TV station.

Finance

(cap. = capital; res = reserves; dep. = deposits; m. = million; brs = branches; amounts in Bermuda dollars)

BANKING

Central Bank

Bermuda Monetary Authority: 31 Reid St, Hamilton, HM 12; tel. 295-5278; fax 292-7471; e-mail info@bma.bm; internet www.bma.bm; f. 1969; central issuing and monetary authority; cap. 10.6m., res 15.3m., total assets 117.0m. (Dec. 2002); Chair., CEO and Controller of Foreign Exchange CHERYL-ANN LISTER.

Commercial Banks

Bank of Bermuda Ltd: 6 Front St, POB HM 1020, Hamilton HM DX; tel. 295-4000; fax 295-7093; e-mail corpcom@ibl.bm; internet www.bankofbermuda.bm; f. 1889; acquired by HSBC in Feb. 2004; cap. 29.0m., res 390.4m., dep. 10,165.2m. (Dec. 2002); CEO PHILLIP BUTTERFIELD; COO ANDY GENT; 6 brs.

Bank of N. T. Butterfield & Son Ltd: 65 Front St, POB HM 195, Hamilton HM AX; tel. 295-1111; fax 292-4365; e-mail contact@bntb.bm; internet www.bankofbutterfield.com; f. 1858; inc. 1904; cap. 21.3m., res 143.0m., dep. 5,246.5m. (June 2002); Chair. Dr JAMES A. C. KING; Pres. and CEO ALAN R. THOMPSON; 4 brs.

Bermuda Commercial Bank Ltd: Bermuda Commercial Bank Bldg, 43 Victoria St, Hamilton HM 12; tel. 295-5678; fax 295-8091; e-mail enquiries@bcb.bm; internet www.bermuda-bcb.com; f. 1969; 48.06% owned by First Curaçao International Bank NV; cap. 10.3m., res 10.8m., dep. 533.2m. (Sept. 2002); Pres. JOHN CHR. M. A. M. DEUSS; Pres. and COO TIMOTHY W. ULRICH.

STOCK EXCHANGE

Bermuda Stock Exchange: 3rd Floor, Washington Mall, Church St, Hamilton HM FX; tel. 292-7212; fax 292-7619; e-mail info@bsx.com; internet www.bsx.com; f. 1971; 380 listed equities, funds, debt issues and depositary programmes; Chair. DAVID BROWN; Pres. and CEO GREG WOJCIECHOWSKI.

INSURANCE

Bermuda had a total of some 1,600 registered insurance companies in 2002, the majority of which are subsidiaries of foreign insurance companies, or owned by foreign industrial or financial concerns. Many of them have offices on the island.

Insurance Information Office: Cedarpark Centre, 48 Cedar Ave, POB HM 2911, Hamilton HM LX; tel. 292-9829; fax 295-3532; e-mail biminfo@bii.bm; internet www.bermuda-insurance.org.

Major Companies

ACE Bermuda: ACE Bldg, 30 Woodbourne Ave, POB HM 1015, Hamilton HM DX; tel. 295-5200; fax 295-5221; e-mail info@mail.ace.bm; internet www.ace.bm; total revenues US $3,017.0m. (Dec. 1999); Pres. EVAN GREENBERG; Chair. and CEO BRIAN DUPERREAULT.

Argus Insurance Co Ltd: Argus Insurance Bldg, 12 Wesley St, POB HM 1064, Hamilton HM EX; tel. 295-2021; fax 292-6763; e-mail insurance@argus.bm; internet www.argus.bm; Pres. and CEO GERALD D. E. SIMONS.

Bermuda Insurance Management Association (BIMA): POB HM 1752, Hamilton HM GX; tel. 295-4864; fax 292-7375.

Paumanock Insurance Co Ltd: POB HM 2267, Hamilton HM JX; tel. 292-2404; fax 292-2648.

X. L. Insurance Co Ltd: 1 Bermudiana Rd, Hamilton HM 11; tel. 292-8515; fax 295-5226; e-mail info@xl.bm; internet www.xlinsurance.com; Pres. and Chief Exec. BRIAN O'HARA.

Trade and Industry

GOVERNMENT AGENCY

Bermuda Registrar of Companies: Government Administration Bldg, 30 Parliament St, Hamilton HM 12; tel. 297-7574; fax 292-6640; e-mail jfsmith@gov.bm; internet www.roc.gov.bm; Registrar of Companies STEPHEN LOWE.

DEVELOPMENT ORGANIZATION

Bermuda Small Business Development Corpn: POB HM 637, Hamilton HM CX; tel. 292-5570; fax 295-1600; e-mail bdasmallbusiness@gov.bm; internet www.bsbdc.bm; f. 1980; funded jtly by the Govt and private banks; guarantees loans to small businesses; assets $2m. (March 2004); Gen. Man. LUCRECIA MING.

CHAMBER OF COMMERCE

Bermuda Chamber of Commerce: 1 Point Pleasant Rd, POB HM 655, Hamilton HM CX; tel. 295-4201; fax 292-5779; e-mail info@bermudacommerce.com; internet www.bermudacommerce.com; f. 1907; Pres. CHARLES GOSLING; Exec. Vice-Pres. DIANE GORDON; 750 mems.

INDUSTRIAL AND TRADE ASSOCIATION

Bermuda International Business Association (BIBA): Ground Floor, 20 Victoria St, Hamilton HM 12; tel. 292-0632; fax 292-1797; e-mail lrawlins@biba.org; internet www.biba.org; Chair. GREG HAYCOCK; CEO DEBORAH MIDDLETON.

EMPLOYERS' ASSOCIATIONS

Bermuda Employers' Council: Reid House, Ground Floor, 31 Church St, Hamilton HM 12; tel. 295-5070; fax 295-1966; e-mail emp.org@bec.bm; internet www.bec.bm; f. 1960; advisory body on employment and labour relations; Pres. GERALD SIMONS; Exec. Dir ANDREA MOWBRAY; 347 mems.

Construction Association of Bermuda: POB HM 238, Hamilton HM AX; tel. 236-5537; fax 236-5485; e-mail administrator@constructionbermuda.com; internet www.constructionbermuda.com; f. 1968; Pres. ALEX M. DECOUTO; 65 mems.

Hotel Employers of Bermuda: c/o Bermuda Hotel Asscn, 'Carmel', 61 King St, Hamilton HM 19; tel. 295-2127; fax 292-6671; e-mail johnh@ibl.bm; f. 1968; Pres. FRANK STOCEK; CEO JOHN HARVEY; 8 mems.

UTILITY

BELCO Holdings Ltd: 27 Serpentine Rd, POB HM 1026, Hamilton HM DX; tel. 295-5111; fax 292-8975; e-mail webmaster@belco.bhl.bm; internet www.belcoholdings.bm; f. 1908; holding co for Bermuda Electric Light Co Ltd, Bermuda Gas and Utility Co Ltd, and BELCO Energy Services Co; Chair. J. MICHAEL COLLIER; Pres. and CEO GARRY A. MADEIROS.

TRADE UNIONS

In 1997 trade union membership was estimated at 8,859. There are nine registered trade unions, the principal ones being:

Bermuda Federation of Musicians and Variety Artists: Reid St, POB HM 6, Hamilton HM AX; tel. 291-0138; Sec.-Gen. LLOYD H. L. SIMMONS; 318 mems.

Bermuda Industrial Union: 49 Union Sq., Hamilton HM 12; tel. 292-0044; fax 295-7992; e-mail biu@biu.bm; f. 1946; Pres. DERRICK BURGESS; Gen. Sec. HELENA BURGESS; 5,202 mems.

Bermuda Public Services Union: POB HM 763, Hamilton HM CX; tel. 292-6985; fax 292-1149; e-mail info@bpsu.bm; re-formed 1961; Pres. NIGEL A. D. PEMBERTON; Gen. Sec. EDWARD G. BALL, Jr; 3,454 mems.

Bermuda Union of Teachers: POB HM 726, Hamilton HM CX; tel. 292-6515; fax 292-0697; e-mail butunion@ibl.bm; f. 1919; Pres. ANTHONY E. WOLFFE; Gen. Sec. MICHAEL A. CHARLES; 700 mems.

Transport

ROADS

There are some 225 km (140 miles) of public highways and 222 km (138 miles) of private roads, with almost 6 km (4 miles) reserved for cyclists and pedestrians. Each household is permitted only one passenger vehicle, and visitors may only hire mopeds, to limit traffic congestion.

SHIPPING

The chief port of Bermuda is Hamilton, with a secondary port at St George's. Both are used by freight and cruise ships. There is also a 'free' port, Freeport, on Ireland Island. In 2000 it was proposed to enlarge Hamilton docks in order to accommodate larger cruise ships. There remained, however, fears that such an enlargement would place excessive strain on the island's environment and infrastructure. Bermuda is a free-flag nation, and at December 2004 the shipping register comprised 122 vessels, totalling 6,166,162 grt.

Department of Marine and Ports Services: POB HM 180, Hamilton HM AX; tel. 295-6575; fax 295-5523; e-mail marineports@bolagov.bm; Dir of Marine and Ports Services BARRY COUPLAND; Deputy Dir and Habour Master MICHAEL DOLDING.

Department of Maritime Administration: POB HM 1628, Hamilton HM GX; tel. 295-7251; fax 295-3718; e-mail maradros@gov.bm; Chief Surveyor DUNCAN CURRIE; Registrar of Shipping ANGELIQUE BURGESS.

UNITED KINGDOM OVERSEAS TERRITORIES

Principal Shipping Companies

A. M. Services Ltd: Belvedere Bldg, 69 Pitts Bay Rd, Pembroke HM 08; tel. 295-0850; fax 292-3704; e-mail amsl@northrock.bm.

Atlantic Marine Limited Partnership: Richmond House, 12 Par-la-Ville Rd, Hamilton HM HX; tel. 295-0614; fax 292-1549; e-mail management@amlp.bm; internet www.amlp.bm; f. 1970; Pres. Jens Alers.

B & H Ocean Carriers Ltd: 3rd Floor, Par-la-Ville Pl., 14 Par-la-Ville Rd, POB HM 2257 HM JX, Hamilton; tel. 295-6875; fax 295-6796; e-mail info@bhocusa.com; internet www.bhocean.com; f. 1987; Chair. Michael S. Hudner.

Benor Tankers Ltd: Cedar House, 41 Cedar Ave, HM 12 Hamilton; Pres. Carl-Erik Haavaldsen; Chair. Harry Rutten.

Bermuda International Shipping Ltd: Waverley Bldg, 35 Church St, Hamilton HM 12; tel. 296-9798; fax 295-4556; e-mail meyerfreight@ibl.bm; internet www.meyer.bm; Dir J. Henry Hayward.

Container Ship Management Ltd: 14 Par-la-Ville Rd, Hamilton HM 08; tel. 295-1624; fax 295-3781; e-mail csm@csm.bm; internet www.bcl.bm/csm; Pres. Geoffrey Frith.

Gearbulk Holding Ltd: Par-la-Ville Pl., 14 Par-la-Ville Rd, HM JX Hamilton; tel. 295-2184; fax 295-2234; internet www.gearbulk.com; Pres. Arthur E. M. Jones.

Golden Ocean Management: Par-la-Ville Pl., 14 Par-la-Ville Rd, POB HM 1593, Hamilton HM 08; tel. 295-6935; fax 295-3494; internet www.goldenocean.no; Man. Dir Herman Billung.

Norwegian Cruise Line: 3rd Floor, Reid House, Church St, POB 1564, Hamilton; internet www.ncl.com; Chair. Einar Kloster.

Shell Bermuda (Overseas) Ltd: Shell House, Ferry Reach, POB 2, St George's 1.

Unicool Ltd: POB HM 1179, HM EX Hamilton; tel. 295-2244; fax 292-8666; Pres. Mats Jansson.

Worldwide Shipping Managers Ltd: Suite 402, 7 Reid St, POB HM 1862, HM 11 Hamilton; tel. 295-3770; fax 295-3801.

CIVIL AVIATION

The former US Naval Air Station (the only airfield) was returned to the Government of Bermuda in September 1995, following the closure of the base and the withdrawal of US forces from the islands.

Department of Civil Aviation: POB GE 218, St George's GE BX; tel. 293-1640; fax 293-2417; e-mail info@dca.gov.bm; internet www.dca.gov.bm; responsible for all civil aviation matters; Dir of Civil Aviation Ian MacIntyre.

Bermuda International Airport: 3 Cahow Way, St George's GE CX; tel. 293-2470; e-mail dao@gov.bm; internet www.bermudaairport.com; Gen. Man. James G. Howes.

Delta Airlines: Kindley Field; tel. 293-2050; internet www.delta.com; passenger and air cargo service.

Tourism

Tourism is the principal industry of Bermuda and is government-sponsored. The great attractions of the islands are the climate, scenery, and facilities for outdoor entertainment of all types. In 2005 a total of 517,196 tourists (including 247,609 cruise-ship passengers) visited Bermuda. In 2004 the industry earned B $353.7m. In 2002 there were 6,523 hotel beds.

Bermuda Department of Tourism: Tulip House, Suite 9, 70 Borough High St; tel. 864-9924; fax 864-9966; e-mail ukEurope@bermudatourism.com; internet www.bermudatourism.com; Dir of Tourism Cherie-Lynn Whitter.

Bermuda Hotel Association: 'Carmel', 61 King St, Hamilton HM 19; tel. 295-2127; fax 292-6671; e-mail johnh@ibl.bm; internet www.experiencebermuda.com; Chair. Norman Mastalir; Exec. Dir John Harvey; Pres. Michael Winfield; 37 mem. hotels.

THE BRITISH ANTARCTIC TERRITORY

The British Antarctic Territory lies within the Antarctic Treaty area (i.e. south of latitude 60° S). The Territory, created by an Order in Council which came into force on 3 March 1962, consists of all islands and territories south of latitude 60° S, between longitudes 20° W and 80° W, and includes the South Orkney Islands, the South Shetland Islands, the Antarctic Peninsula and areas south and east of the Weddell Sea. With the island of South Georgia and the South Sandwich Islands (now forming a separate territory, q.v.), this area had been constituted by the United Kingdom as the Falkland Islands Dependencies in 1908. The flag of the British Antarctic Territory (proportions 1 by 2) has a white field bearing the union flag of the United Kingdom in the canton and, in the centre of the fly half of the flag, the arms of the territory, which consists of a white shield with three wavy blue horizontal lines at the top overlapped by a red triangle, apex downwards, bearing a brown and yellow torch with red-bordered yellow flames framed by golden rays, the shield supported by a golden lion and a black and white penguin with a yellow throat, both supporters surmounted by a scroll of yellow and light blue with a red reverse and the red inscription 'Research and Discovery'; above the shield, a helmet of grey, light blue and white supporting a torse, alternately of white and light blue, is depicted below a sailing ship of black flying the British Blue Ensign at the gaff. The Territory has its own legal system and postal administration, and is financially self-sufficient owing to revenue derived from income tax and the sale of postage stamps.

Area: Land covers about 1,709,400 sq km (660,003 sq miles).

Population: There is no permanent population, but scientists and support personnel (some 50 in the Antarctic winter, rising to about 400 in summer) staff the British Antarctic Survey stations.

Commissioner, Head of Overseas Territories Department: Tony Crombie, Polar Regions Unit, Overseas Territories Dept, Foreign and Commonwealth Office, King Charles St, London, SW1A 2AH, United Kingdom; tel. (20) 7008-2741.

Administrator, Head of Polar Regions Unit: Dr Mike Richardson, Polar Regions Unit, Overseas Territories Dept, Foreign and Commonwealth Office, King Charles St, London, SW1A 2AH, United Kingdom; tel. (20) 7008-2616.

British Antarctic Survey: High Cross, Madingley Rd, Cambridge, CB3 0ET, United Kingdom; tel. (1223) 221400; fax (1223) 362616; e-mail basweb@bas.ac.uk; internet www.antarctica.ac.uk; f. 1962 to replace Falkland Islands Dependencies Survey; responsible for almost all British scientific activities in Antarctica; operates two ice-strengthened ocean-going vessels (RRS *Ernest Shackleton* and RRS *James Clark Ross*), four de Havilland Twin Otter and one Dash-7 aircraft; Science Budget £32.678m. in 2003/04; Dir Prof. Chris G. Rapley.

RESEARCH STATIONS

	Latitude	Longitude
Halley	75° 34′ S	26° 32′ W
Rothera	67° 34′ S	68° 07′ W
Signy (summer only)	60° 43′ S	45° 36′ W

THE BRITISH INDIAN OCEAN TERRITORY (BIOT)

The British Indian Ocean Territory (BIOT) was formed in November 1965, through the amalgamation of the former Seychelles islands of Aldabra, Desroches and Farquhar with the Chagos Archipelago, a group of islands 1,930 km north-east of Mauritius, previously administered by the Governor of Mauritius. Aldabra, Desroches and Farquhar were ceded to Seychelles when that country was granted independence in June 1976. Since then BIOT has comprised only the Chagos Archipelago, including the coral atoll Diego Garcia, with a total land area of 60 sq km (23 sq miles), together with a surrounding area of some 54,400 sq km (21,000 sq miles) of ocean.

BIOT was established to meet British and US defence requirements in the Indian Ocean. Previously, the principal economic function of the islands was the production of copra: the islands, together with the coconut plantations, were owned by a private company. The copra industry declined after the Second World War, and, following the purchase of the islands by the British Crown in 1967, the plantations ceased to operate and the inhabitants were offered the choice of resettlement in Mauritius or in Seychelles. The majority (which numbered about 1,200) went to Mauritius, the resettlement taking place during 1969–73, prior to the construction of the military facility. Mauritius subsequently campaigned for the immediate return of the Territory, and received support from the Organization of African Unity (now the African Union, see p. 153) and from India. Mauritius supported the former island population in a protracted dispute with the United Kingdom over compensation for those displaced, which ended in 1982 when the British Government agreed to an *ex-gratia* payment of £4m. In early 1984, however, it was reported that people who had been displaced from Diego Garcia were seeking US $6m. from the US Government to finance their resettlement in Mauritius. In March 1999 a former resident of BIOT obtained leave from the High Court in London to seek a judicial review of the validity of the Immigration Ordinance of 1971, under which the islanders were removed from BIOT, and which continued to prevent them from resettling in the Territory; a review was instigated in July 2000. Later in March 1999 it was disclosed that the displaced islanders and their families, now estimated to number up to 4,000, were not to be included in the offer of full British citizenship, with the right of abode in the United Kingdom, that was to be extended to residents of other United Kingdom Overseas Territories by legislation pending in the British Parliament.

In November 2000 the High Court ruled that the Chagos islanders (Ilois) had been illegally evicted from the Chagos Archipelago, and quashed Section 4 of the 1971 Ordinance, which prevented the return of the Ilois to BIOT. During the case it became known that the British Government had received a subsidy of US $11m. on the purchase of Polaris submarines in the 1960s from the USA, in return for the lease of Diego Garcia for the US military. Furthermore, the Government had apparently termed the Ilois 'contract workers' in order to persuade the UN that the islanders were not an indigenous population with democratic rights. However, memorandums of the Foreign and Commonwealth Office revealed government knowledge of some of the Ilois living in the Chagos Archipelago for two generations. The British Secretary of State for Foreign and Commonwealth Affairs declined an appeal, thereby granting the islanders an immediate right to return to BIOT. Despite this, a new ordinance, issued in January 2001, allowed the residents to return to any of the islands in the Archipelago, except Diego Garcia, easing US fears of a population near its military base. The British Overseas Territories Act came into effect in May 2002, allowing the displaced islanders to apply for British citizenship. At that time the British Government was also examining the feasibility of a return to the Chagos Archipelago for the islanders, who continued to seek compensation. (However, a report had concluded that resettlement on the atolls of Salomon and Peros Banhos was logistically possible, if not necessarily economically viable.) In October 2003, at the British High Court, the islanders were told that, although they could claim to have been ill-treated, the British Government had not known at the time that its actions were unlawful and their claims for compensation were dismissed. Many of the islanders subsequently moved to the United Kingdom.

Meanwhile, a meeting of the Chagos Social Committee in November 2000 unanimously resolved to oppose any idea of independence for the Chagos islands. One month later the Ilois announced their intention to sue the US Government for US $6,000m. in compensation. The hearing of the case, in which the Ilois alleged genocide, torture and forced relocation, opened in December 2001. In mid-2002 the Chagos islanders initiated legal action against the recruitment consultancy that supplies civilian employees for the US naval base on Diego Garcia, alleging that the company had discriminated against them when appointing staff to the base; the consultancy was the first of 12 entities that the islanders intended to sue in the USA.

In June 2004 the British Government issued two decrees explicitly stating the country's control of immigration services within the archipelago and banning the Ilois from visiting. In a meeting with a British official in November, however, the Chagossian group reached agreement for some 100 people to visit Diego Garcia for the purpose of visiting the graves of relatives. In early April 2006 102 Chagossians commenced a 12-day visit to the archipelago. Meanwhile, a judicial review of the two decrees issued in June 2004 was ongoing.

A 1966 agreement between the United Kingdom and the USA provided for BIOT to be used by both countries over an initial period of 50 years, with the option of extending this for a further 20 years. The United Kingdom undertook to cede the Chagos Archipelago to Mauritius when it was no longer required for defence purposes. Originally the US military presence was limited to a communications centre on Diego Garcia. In 1972, however, construction of a naval support facility was begun, apparently in response to the expansion of the Soviet maritime presence in the Indian Ocean. Facilities on Diego Garcia include a communications centre, a runway with a length of 3,650 m, anchorage, refuelling and various ancillary services. In August 1987 the US navy began to use Diego Garcia as a facility for minesweeping helicopters taking part in operations in the Persian (Arabian) Gulf. Following Iraq's invasion of Kuwait in August 1990, Diego Garcia was used as a base for US B-52 aircraft, which were deployed in the Gulf region. Runway facilities on Diego Garcia were again used in September 1996 and December 1998 as a base for US support aircraft during US missile attacks on Iraq. In October 2001 US forces used the Diego Garcia base to launch strikes on Afghanistan with B-52 aircraft. In March–April 2003 the base was used to launch bombing raids on Iraq in the US-led military campaign to oust the regime of Saddam Hussein.

In January 1988 Mauritius renewed its campaign to regain sovereignty over the Chagos Archipelago, and reiterated its support for a 'zone of peace' in the Indian Ocean. In November 1989, following an incident in which a military aircraft belonging to the US air force accidentally bombed a US naval vessel near Diego Garcia, a demonstration was held outside the US embassy in Mauritius, demanding the withdrawal of foreign military forces from the area. The Mauritius Government announced that it would draw the attention of the UN Security Council to the dangers that it perceived in the execution of US military air exercises. However, the US Assistant Secretary of State for African Affairs reiterated during an official visit to Mauritius, in the same month, that the USA would maintain its military presence in the Indian Ocean. In December 2000, following the British High Court's ruling, Mauritius once again staked its claim for sovereignty over the Chagos Archipelago. In April 2004 Paul Bérenger, the recently installed Prime Minister of Mauritius, renewed the campaign to reclaim sovereignty after specialists in international law advised him that the decree by which the United Kingdom separated the Chagos Archipelago from Mauritius was illegal. An attempt was made to block the Mauritian Government from pursuing the case at the International Court of Justice on the basis of a long-standing ruling, whereby members of the Commonwealth could not take the United Kingdom to court; in July the ruling was extended to former members of the Commonwealth, in order to prevent Mauritius from circumventing the obstacle by withdrawing from that organization. Mauritius then announced that it would pursue the matter at the General Assembly of the UN.

The civil administration of BIOT is the responsibility of a non-resident commissioner in the Foreign and Commonwealth Office in London, represented on Diego Garcia by a Royal Naval commander and a small British naval presence. A chief justice, a senior magistrate and a principal legal adviser (who performs the functions of an attorney-general) are resident in the United Kingdom.

Land Area: about 60 sq km.

Population: There are no permanent inhabitants. In November 2004 there were about 4,000 US and British military personnel and civilian support staff stationed in the Territory.

Currency: The official currency is the pound sterling, but the US dollar is also accepted.

Commissioner: TONY CROMBIE, Head of Overseas Territories Dept, Foreign and Commonwealth Office, King Charles St, London SW1A 2AH United Kingdom; tel. (20) 7008–2890.

Administrator: TONY HUMPHRIES, Overseas Territories Dept, Foreign and Commonwealth Office, King Charles St, London SW1A 2AH United Kingdom; tel. (20) 7008–2890.

Commissioner's Representative: Commdr NEIL HINCH, RN, Diego Garcia, c/o BFPO Ships.

THE BRITISH VIRGIN ISLANDS

Introductory Survey

Location, Climate, Language, Religion, Flag, Capital

The British Virgin Islands consist of more than 60 islands and cays, of which only 16 are inhabited. The islands, most of which are mountainous and of volcanic origin (the only exception of any size is the coralline island of Anegada), lie at the northern end of the Leeward Islands, about 100 km (62 miles) to the east of Puerto Rico and adjoining the United States Virgin Islands. The climate is subtropical but extremes of heat are relieved by the trade winds. The average annual rainfall is 1,000 mm (39 ins). The official language is English. Most of the inhabitants profess Christianity. The flag is the British 'Blue Ensign', with the Territory's badge (a green shield, with a white-clad virgin and 12 oil lamps, above a scroll bearing the motto 'vigilate') in the fly. The capital, Road Town, is situated on the island of Tortola.

Recent History

Previously peopled by Caribs, and named by the navigator Christopher Colombus after St Ursula and her 11,000 fellow-martyrs, the islands were settled by buccaneers and the Dutch, but were finally annexed by the British in 1672. In 1872 they became part of the British colony of the Leeward Islands, which was administered under a federal system. The federation was dissolved in July 1956, but the Governor of the Leeward Islands continued to administer the British Virgin Islands until 1960, when an appointed Administrator (restyled Governor in 1971) assumed direct responsibility. Unlike the other Leeward Islands, the British Virgin Islands did not join the Federation of the West Indies (1958–62), preferring to develop its links with the US Virgin Islands.

A new Constitution was introduced in April 1967, when H. Lavity Stoutt became the islands' first Chief Minister. He was later replaced by Willard Wheatley. At an election in September 1975 Stoutt's Virgin Islands Party (VIP) and the United Party (UP) each won three of the seven elective seats on the Legislative Council. Wheatley, sitting as an independent member, held the balance of power and he continued in office, with Stoutt as Deputy Chief Minister.

An amended Constitution took effect in June 1977, giving more extensive internal self-government; some electoral changes were also made (see Constitution). In the first election to the enlarged Legislative Council to take place under the new Constitution, in November 1979, independent candidates won five of the nine elective seats, with the VIP winning the remainder. Stoutt secured enough support to be reinstated as Chief Minister. In the November 1983 election the VIP and the UP each secured four seats. The one successful independent candidate, Cyril Romney, became Chief Minister and formed a coalition Government with members of the UP.

In August 1986 the Governor dissolved the Legislative Council six days before a scheduled council debate on a motion of 'no confidence' against Romney (who had allegedly been involved with a company under investigation by the British police and the US Department of Justice's Drug Enforcement Administration). At a general election in the following month the VIP won five of the nine elective seats, with the UP and independent candidates (including Romney) taking two seats each. Stoutt was appointed Chief Minister.

The Deputy Chief Minister, Omar Hodge, was dismissed from the Executive Council in March 1988, following an official inquiry into allegations of financial malpractice (he continued to protest his innocence, and won a libel suit in January 1990). Hodge was replaced by Ralph O'Neal, formerly leader of the UP, who joined the VIP.

At a general election in November 1990 the VIP increased its majority, while the UP lost both its seats. Stoutt retained the post of Chief Minister.

The principal concern of the Stoutt administration in the early 1990s was the trade in, and increasing local use of, illicit drugs. In late 1990 the Stoutt administration introduced legislation to impose more stringent regulations governing the 'offshore' financial sector, while plans to review immigration policy were under discussion, in an attempt to reduce the number of illegal immigrants entering the Territory. Both areas had previously been considered to be insufficiently protected from exploitation by traffickers seeking to introduce illicit drugs into the islands or to divert funds from their sale through the financial sector.

In August 1993 the British Government appointed three commissioners to review the Territory's Constitution at the request of the Legislative Council. Proposed changes included the introduction of direct elections for the position of Chief Minister, the enlargement of the Legislative Council and the adoption of a bill of rights. The British Government's decision in early 1994 to accept the commission's proposal to enlarge the Legislative Council to 13 seats (by the creation of four seats representing the Territory 'at large') was strongly criticized by Stoutt. His opposition to the changes intensified in July, when he failed to obtain a deferral of the decision in order that the Legislative Council could debate the issue. Discussions on various recommendations in the review continued in 1995 and 1996.

At elections to the newly enlarged legislature on 20 February 1995 the VIP won six seats, the UP and the Concerned Citizens' Movement (CCM—formerly IPM) each secured two seats and independent candidates won the remaining three seats. One of the successful independents, Alvin Christopher, subsequently gave his support to the VIP, thus providing the party with the majority required to form a Government, again headed by Stoutt. However, in May, the Deputy Chief Minister, Ralph O'Neal, was appointed Chief Minister, following the sudden death of Stoutt.

In July 1996 the Governor, David Mackilligin, recommended that there should be a public debate on the continued use of judicial corporal punishment in the Territory (the British Virgin Islands being the only British Dependent Territory in which the practice remained in force). The issue was raised owing to concern that, as a signatory to the European Convention on Human Rights, the United Kingdom was potentially in violation of the accord every time that a sentence of corporal punishment was passed in the islands.

In May 1998 Frank Savage was appointed Governor. In September the Governments of the United Kingdom and of the British Virgin Islands signed a Memorandum of Co-operation and Partnership. The Memorandum was intended to foster a closer working relationship between the two countries, in particular in relation to the execution of public works and services.

In March 1999 the Government of the United Kingdom published draft legislation pertaining to its relationship with its Overseas Dependencies, which were to be renamed United Kingdom Overseas Territories (and had been referred to as such since February 1998). The legislation proposed the extension of British citizenship to the citizens of Overseas Territories, although it also required its Territories to amend their legislation on human rights and on the regulation of the financial services sector to meet international standards. In July the British Government appointed a consultant, Alan Hoole, a former Governor of Anguilla, to review the Constitution of the British Virgin Islands. In September Hoole proposed several changes to the Constitution, including the introduction of more frequent meetings of the Legislative Council and the removal of the Governor's powers to veto legislation. Under the terms of the proposed changes, the Governor was also to be obliged to consult with the Executive Council before implementing policy in his areas of special responsibility (foreign affairs, the civil service and defence). It was also suggested that members of the Legislative Council and senior civil servants should be obliged to declare their interests. In August the Governor outlined the Government's legislative programme. The main aim of the proposed legislation was to ensure that the regulation of the financial services sector conformed to international standards. Savage, who also announced the introduction of a comprehensive review of the education system, announced that the drafting of the proposed amendments to the Constitution would continue throughout the year.

Elections to the Legislative Council took place on 17 May 1999. The VIP retained control of the legislature, increasing its representation to seven seats. The recently founded National Democratic Party (NDP) took five seats, while the CCM retained one seat. The UP and several independent candidates also contested the elections. O'Neal subsequently re-appointed the members of the previous Executive Council.

In September 2000 the Legislative Council passed legislation abolishing judicial corporal punishment on the British Virgin Islands, in keeping with the United Kingdom's acceptance of the European Convention of Human Rights. In November the Legislative Council voted in favour of making 7 March, the birth date of Lavity Stoutt, a public holiday; this was to replace, from 2002, the public holiday of 14 November, the birthday of the Prince of Wales.

The Organisation for Economic Co-operation and Development (see p. 320) announced in April 2002 that the British Virgin Islands had made sufficient commitments to improve the transparency of its tax and regulatory systems to be removed from an updated list of un-co-operative tax 'havens', first published in 2000. Also in April, a tax information exchange agreement, designed to reduce the potential for abuse of the tax system, was signed with the USA. In the same month, the financial secretary, L. Allen Wheatley, was arrested in connection with the mishandling of government contracts relating to the Beef Island Airport development project, and in May the Government survived a motion of 'no confidence' brought against it in connection with the airport development project. In November 2002 some of the charges against Wheatley were dropped after the prosecution was unable to provide sufficient evidence of fraud or breach of trust; however, the presiding magistrate said there was enough evidence for Wheatley to answer related charges of theft and corruption. The trial of Wheatley and four other men began in November 2003; four of the five defendants pleaded guilty to approving an airport telecommunications contract based on inflated prices that cost the Government some US $450,000. In January 2004 Wheatley was sentenced to nine months in jail; in return for the guilty pleas, prosecutors withdrew theft charges, which carry much harsher jail terms. (Wheatley had already been sentenced to five years' imprisonment on separate corruption charges in February 2003.) Meanwhile, also in November 2003 it was reported that another former member of O'Neal's administration, Andrew Fahie, the erstwhile Minister of Education and Culture, was being investigated over money diverted from the airport development project.

In late 2002 the recovering financial sector faced further disruption when the United Kingdom, under pressure from a European Union (EU, see p. 228) investigation into tax evasion, demanded that the British Virgin Islands disclose the identities and account details of Europeans holding private savings accounts on the islands. The British Virgin Islands, along with some other British Overseas Territories facing similar demands, claimed it was being treated unfairly compared with more powerful European countries, such as Switzerland and Luxembourg. In January 2005 the Business Companies Act came into force, which eliminated the distinction between laws governing local and 'offshore' businesses. Further reform to the tax system also took place.

In May 2002 the British Overseas Territories Act, having received royal assent in the United Kingdom in February, came into force and granted British citizenship to the people of its Overseas Territories, including the British Virgin Islands. Under the new law British Virgin Islanders would be able to hold British passports and work in the United Kingdom and anywhere else in the EU.

In October 2002 Tom Macan succeeded Frank Savage as Governor.

A general election was held on 16 June 2003. The NDP secured eight seats compared with the VIP's five after a campaign that was dominated by the issues of alleged corruption, management of public-sector capital projects, and relations with the United Kingdom. The VIP demanded a recount in two constituencies, claiming not all the votes had been counted; however, the complaint was rejected by the High Court. The new Chief Minister, Orlando Smith, appointed Ronnie Skelton as Minister of Finance, and of Health and Social Development, Paul Wattley as Minister of Communications and Works, Lloyd Black as Minister of Education and Culture, and J. Alvin Christopher as Minister of Natural Resources and Labour. Following Wattley's death in July 2005, Christopher was appointed Minister of Communications and Works in September. Eileene L. Parsons succeeded Christopher as Minister for Natural Resources and Labour.

Following the scandal over the Beef Island Airport development scheme, and in an attempt to hold public offices more accountable for their expenditure and renew public trust in the executive, in late September 2003 the new Government passed an Audit Act. A commission for constitutional review was appointed in April 2004, which was to consider, *inter alia*, the criteria for qualification for residency status, the reserve powers of the Governor, the duties of the Attorney-General and the introduction of an article relating to human rights into the Constitution. A Constitutional Review Report was released in 2005, based on the commission's findings. Among the suggestions included in the report were the reform of the legal system (including the introduction of legal aid), and a move towards a cabinet system of government, with the title of Chief Minister changing to Premier. The possibility of renaming the Legislative Council a Parliament was also examined. A meeting to discuss the proposed constitutional reform, between representatives of the British Government and the Chief Minister, was held in Barbados in early May 2006.

In February 2005 the Legislative Council approved the Firearms Amendment Act designed to reduce levels of gun crime committed with illegal weapons. New proposed legislation regarding the liberalization of the telecommunications sector was under discussion in Parliament in early 2006; however, the bill was was subsequently withdrawn after disagreement over which members should vote. At the following parliamentary sitting, at the beginning of May, the bill was again presented for debate, but members voted for it to be removed from the order paper for a second time. The Minister for Communications and Works, J. Alvin Christopher, failed to vote in favour of withdrawing the proposed legislation, instead abstaining along with members of the opposition. The following week Christopher was dismissed from his government post; he was to be replaced by Elmore Stoutt.

On 18 April 2006 David Pearey was sworn in as Governor in succession to Tom Macan.

Government

Under the provisions of the 1977 Constitution, the Governor is appointed by the British monarch and is responsible for external affairs, defence and internal security. The Governor is also Chairman of the Executive Council, which comprises five other members.

The Legislative Council comprises 15 members: a Speaker, one *ex-officio* member, and 13 members elected by universal adult suffrage.

Defence

The United Kingdom is responsible for the defence of the islands. In September 1999 it was announced that Royal Air Force patrols were to be undertaken from the islands in order to intercept drugs-traffickers. Central government expenditure on defence totalled US $0.4m. in 1997.

Economic Affairs

In 2003, according to estimates by the Caribbean Development Bank (CDB), the British Virgin Islands' gross domestic product (GDP) was US $824.4m., equivalent to some $38,643 per head. The population doubled during 1984–94, to 17,903, primarily owing to a large influx of immigrants from other Caribbean Islands, the United Kingdom and the USA. During 1995–2004, it was estimated, the population increased at an average annual rate of 1.9%, while GDP increased, in real terms, by some 4% per year during 1995–99, according to reports. Estimated growth was some 3.6% in 2004.

Agriculture (including forestry and fishing) contributed 1.6% of GDP in 2002, and engaged 0.4% of those in paid employment in 2003. The Territory produces fruit and vegetables for domestic consumption or export to the US Virgin Islands, and some sugar cane (for the production of rum). Food imports accounted for 18.9% of total import costs in 1997. The fishing industry caters for local consumption and export, and provides a sporting activity for tourists, although the Government was looking to develop deep-sea fishing commercially for domestic and export markets.

Industry (including mining, manufacturing, construction and public utilities) accounted for 5.2% of GDP in 2002 and engaged 11.9% of the employed labour force in 2003. The mining sector is negligible, consisting of the extraction of materials for the construction industry and of some salt. Manufacturing, which provided 0.8% of GDP in 2002, consists mainly of light industry; there is one rum distillery, two factories for the production of ice, some plants producing concrete blocks and other construction materials, small boat manufacture and various cottage industries. Construction activity accounted for 2.4% of GDP in 2002. Most energy requirements must be imported (mineral fuels accounted for an estimated 8.5% of total imports in 1997).

Services, primarily tourism and financial services, constitute the principal economic sector of the British Virgin Islands, contributing 93.3% of GDP in 2001, and accounting for 87.7% of employment in 2003. The tourism industry earned some US $253.8m. in 2002, and employed about one-third of the working population, directly or indirectly. The British Virgin Islands is the largest 'bareboat' chartering centre in the Caribbean, and approximately 60% of stop-over visitors stay aboard yachts. Nevertheless, in 2002 the restaurants and hotels sector contributed 13.5% of GDP. The number of stop-over visitors reached 337,134 in 2005 (most of whom were from the USA), an 11.0% increase on the previous year's total; the ratio of tourists to local population is therefore higher than at any other Caribbean destination. The 2001 budget included $53m. to be spent on renovations to the Beef Island airport, in addition to further investment to the country's infrastructure, which was expected to provide a boost to tourism revenue in the second half of the decade.

Financial services expanded rapidly as a result of legislative measures adopted in 1984, and in 2004 the 'offshore' sector contributed over one-half of direct government revenue (some US $110m.). There were a cumulative total of 544,000 International Business Company (IBC) registrations in the islands in 1984–2004. The islands have also recorded significant growth in the establishment of mutual funds and of insurance companies. In January 2002 the Government created the Financial Services Commission, an independent regulatory authority for the sector, in order to meet international demands for a clear separation between the Government and financial services regulation.

In 2003, according to the CDB, the British Virgin Islands recorded a trade deficit of US $158.1m. The trade deficit is normally offset by receipts from tourism, development aid, remittances from islanders working abroad (many in the US Virgin Islands) and, increasingly, from the 'offshore' financial sector. The principal sources of imports (most of the islands' requirements must be imported) are the USA (which provided 56.9% of imports in 1997), Trinidad and Tobago, Antigua and Barbuda, and also the United Kingdom. The principal markets for the limited amount of exports are the US Virgin Islands and the USA and Puerto Rico; rum is exported to the USA. Machinery and transport equipment are the main imports (accounting for 28.3% of total imports in 1997), and fruit and vegetables, rum, sand and gravel are the main exports.

The budget for the 2004 financial year recorded revenue at US $204.7m. against recurrent and capital expenditure of $214.2m. In 1996/97 there was a surplus of $56m. on the current account of the balance of payments. British budgetary support ceased in 1977, but the United Kingdom grants assistance for capital development. In 2004 total external debt was calculated to be

UNITED KINGDOM OVERSEAS TERRITORIES

The British Virgin Islands

$44.1m. In 1998 the territory received $1.2m. in development assistance. Central Government debt to GDP ratio was estimated at 10.0% in the same year. The average annual rate of inflation was 3.1% in 1995–2005; consumer prices increased by an average 0.7% in 2004 and by 2.3% in 2005. The rate of unemployment was estimated to be 3.5% in 2005.

The British Virgin Islands became an associate member of the Caribbean Community and Common Market (CARICOM, see p. 183) in 1991; it is a member of CARICOM's Caribbean Development Bank (CDB, see p. 188) and an associate member of the Organisation of Eastern Caribbean States (OECS, see p. 397). In economic affairs the Territory has close affiliations with the neighbouring US Virgin Islands, and uses US currency. As a dependency of the United Kingdom, the islands have the status of Overseas Territory in association with the European Union (EU, see p. 228).

The economy of the British Virgin Islands is largely dominated by tourism and by the provision of international financial services. The 'offshore' financial sector, which developed rapidly in the last two decades of the 20th century, is an important source of employment and provided 54% of direct government revenue in 2004. Despite ongoing efforts to attract insurance and trust companies to the islands, it was estimated that in early 2000 IBCs still accounted for around 90% of government revenues from financial services. International attempts, notably by the Organisation for Economic Co-operation and Development (OECD, see p. 320), to encourage the reform of 'offshore' financial centres are therefore of great concern to the British Virgin Islands, particularly as IBCs, which are not taxed and which are not obliged to disclose their directors or shareholders, have been singled out for particular criticism. Nevertheless, revenue from annual licence fees paid by 'offshore' companies remained strong in the early 21st century. Despite the rise of the financial sector, tourism remains the most important sector of the economy, as the construction and retail sectors, amongst others, are to a certain extent dependent on its performance. In the long term, however, the Government hoped to encourage greater diversification of the economy, in order to reduce reliance on tourism and financial services, both of which remained vulnerable to external pressures. Although the aftermath of the September 2001 terrorist attacks in the USA adversely affected tourism revenues in 2002, which was only partially offset by increased activity in the 'offshore' banking sector, the economy performed strongly in 2003. In 2004 legislation was approved eliminating the distinction between 'onshore' and 'offshore' taxation regimes, in order to bring the economic structure of the Virgin Islands into confirmity with EU and OECD requirements; a transitional period was to end in January 2007. The budget for the 2005/06 allocated US $1m. for an emergency and disaster relief fund and some $2m. for a reserve fund. The economy was estimated to have grown by 2.3% in 2005, fuelled by growth in the tourism and 'offshore' banking sectors. GDP was forecast to increase by 6.5% in 2006.

Education

Primary education is free, universal and compulsory between the ages of five and 11. Secondary education is also free and lasts from 12 to 16 years of age. In 2002 some 628 pupils were enrolled in pre-primary schools and in 2003 there were 2,735 pupils attending primary schools. In that year some 1,633 were enrolled in secondary education. Higher education is available at the University of the Virgin Islands (St Thomas, US Virgin Islands) and elsewhere in the Caribbean, in North America and in the United Kingdom. Central government expenditure on education in 1997 was US $17.1m.

Public Holidays

2006: 1 January (New Year's Day), 6 March (Lavity Stoutt's Birthday), 13 March (Commonwealth Day), 14 April (Good Friday), 17 April (Easter Monday), 5 June (Whit Monday), 10 June (Queen's Official Birthday), 1 July (Territory Day), 7–9 August (Festival Monday, Tuesday and Wednesday), 21 October (Saint Ursula's Day), 25–26 December (Christmas).

2007: 1 January (New Year's Day), 5 March (Lavity Stoutt's Birthday), 12 March (Commonwealth Day), 6 April (Good Friday), 9 April (Easter Monday), 28 May (Whit Monday), 9 June (Queen's Official Birthday), 1 July (Territory Day), 6–8 August (Festival Monday, Tuesday and Wednesday), 21 October (Saint Ursula's Day), 25–26 December (Christmas).

Weights and Measures

The imperial system is used.

Statistical Survey

Source: Development Planning Unit, Central Administrative Complex, Road Town, Tortola; tel. 494-3701; fax 494-3947; e-mail dpu@dpu.org; internet www.dpu.gov.vg.

AREA AND POPULATION

Area: 153 sq km (59 sq miles). *Principal Islands* (sq km): Tortola 54.4; Anegada 38.8; Virgin Gorda 21.4; Jost Van Dyke 9.1.

Population: 16,644 (males 8,570, females 8,074) at census of 12 May 1991; 19,864 (males 10,234, females 9,630) in 1999; 21,689 (estimate) at mid-2004; *By Island* (1980): Tortola 9,119; Virgin Gorda 1,412; Anegada 164; Jost Van Dyke 134; Other islands 156; (1991) Tortola 13,568. Source: partly Caribbean Development Bank, *Social and Economic Indicators.*

Density (mid-2004): 141.7 per sq km.

Principal Town: Road Town (capital), population 12,000 (UN estimate, incl. suburbs, mid-2003). Source: UN, *World Urbanization Prospects: The 2003 Revision.*

Births, Marriages and Deaths (registrations, 2004): 316 live births (birth rate 14.7 per 1,000); 426 marriages (marriage rate 19.6 per 1,000); 120 deaths (death rate 5.5 per 1,000).

Expectation of Life (years at birth, estimates): 73.8 (males 69.9; females 78.5) in 2004.

Employment (2003): Agriculture, hunting and forestry 43; Fishing 13; Mining and quarrying 80; Manufacturing 283; Electricity, gas and water supply 196; Construction 1,208; Wholesale and retail trade 1,359; Hotels and restaurants 2,486; Transport, storage and communications 613; Financial 712; Real estate, renting and business activities 1,142; Public administration and social security 4,770; Education 981; Health and social work 124; Other community, social and personal service activities 416; Private households with employed persons 384; Not classifiable by economic activity 5; Total 14,815.

HEALTH AND WELFARE

Physicians (per 1,000 head, 1999): 1.15.

Hospital Beds (per 1,000 head, 2003): 2.0.

Health Expenditure (% of GDP, 1995): 3.9. *2003* (public expenditure only): 3.1.

Health Expenditure (public, % of total, 1995): 36.5.

Source: Pan American Health Organization.

For definitions, see explanatory note on p. vi.

AGRICULTURE, ETC.

Livestock (FAO estimates, '000 head, 2004): Cattle 2.4; Sheep 6.1; Goats 10.0; Pigs 1.5.

Fishing (FAO estimates, metric tons, live weight, 2003): Swordfish 2, Caribbean spiny lobster 3, Stromboid conchs 6; Total catch (incl. others) 50.

Source: FAO.

INDUSTRY

Electric Energy (production, million kWh): 43 in 1988; 44 in 1989; 45 in 1990. 1991–2001 annual production as in 1990 (UN estimates). Source: UN, *Industrial Commodity Statistics Yearbook.*

FINANCE

Currency and Exchange Rate: United States currency is used: 100 cents = 1 US dollar ($). *Sterling and Euro Equivalents* (30 December 2005): £1 sterling = US $1.7219; €1 = US $1.1797; US $100 = £58.08 = €84.77.

Budget ($ million, 2004): *Revenue:* Tax revenue 72.6 (Import duties 24.2, Income and property tax 41.7, Passenger and hotel tax 6.7); Non-tax revenue 132.1 (Financial services sector 109.8); Total recurrent revenue 204.7. *Expenditure:* Recurrent expenditure 180.4 (Goods and services 62.9; Wages and salaries 83.6; Subsidies and transfers 32.9); Capital expenditure 33.8; Total expenditure 214.2.

Cost of Living (Consumer Price Index; base: 1995 = 100): 131.8 in 2003; 132.7 in 2004; 135.7 in 2005.

Gross Domestic Product ($ million, at market prices): 798.0 in 2002; 873.0 in 2003; 943.0 in 2004. Source: UN, *National Accounts Statistics.*

Expenditure on the Gross Domestic Product ($ million at current prices, 2003): Government final consumption expenditure 101; Private final consumption expenditure 372; Gross capital formation 215; *Total domestic expenditure* 688; Exports of goods and services 894; *Less* Imports of goods and services 710; *GDP in purchasers' values* 873. Source: UN, *National Accounts Statistics.*

Gross Domestic Product by Economic Activity (rounded figures in current prices, $ million, 1999): Agriculture, hunting and forestry 4.1; Fishing 5.4; Mining and quarrying 0.4; Manufacturing 27.0;

Electricity, gas and water 11.1; Construction 49.0; Wholesale and retail trade 90.0; Hotels and restaurants 98.0; Transport, storage and communications 79.0; Financial intermediation 43.0; Real estate, renting and business services 188.0; Public administration 35.0; Education 13.6; Health and social work 9.5; Other community, social and personal services 15.8; Private households with employed persons 6.0; *Sub-total* 674.0; *Less* Imputed bank service charges 35.0; Indirect taxes, less subsidies 23.0; *GDP in purchasers' values* 662.0. Source: UN, *National Accounts Statistics*.

EXTERNAL TRADE

Principal Commodities ($ '000): *Imports c.i.f.* (1997): Food and live animals 31,515; Beverages and tobacco 8,797; Crude materials (inedible) except fuels 1,168; Mineral fuels, lubricants, etc. 9,847; Chemicals 8,816; Basic manufactures 31,715; Machinery and transport equipment 47,019; Total (incl. others) 116,379. *Exports f.o.b.* (1996): Food and live animals 368; Beverages and tobacco 3,967; Crude materials (inedible) except fuels 1,334; Total (incl. others) 5,862. *2001* (exports, $ million) Animals 0.1; Fresh fish 0.7; Gravel and sand 1.4; Rum 3.6; Total 28.13.

Principal Trading Partners ($ '000): *Imports c.i.f.* (1997): Antigua and Barbuda 1,807; Trinidad and Tobago 2,555; United Kingdom 406; USA 94,651; Total (incl. others) 166,379. *Exports f.o.b.* (1996): USA and Puerto Rico 1,077; US Virgin Islands 2,001; Total (incl. others) 5,862. *1999:* Imports 208,419; Exports 2,081.

Source: mainly UN, *International Trade Statistics Yearbook*.

TRANSPORT

Road Traffic (motor vehicles in use): 6,900 in 1992; 6,700 in 1993; 7,000 in 1994. *2004* (motor vehicles registered and licensed): 13,106 (private cars 9,106). Source: mainly UN, *Statistical Yearbook*.

Shipping: *International Freight Traffic* ('000 metric tons, 2002): Goods unloaded 145.6. *Cargo Ship Arrivals* (2002): 2,027. *Merchant Fleet* (vessels registered, at 31 December 2004): 14; Total displacement 2,520 grt (Sources: British Virgin Islands Port Authority, and Lloyd's Register-Fairplay, *World Fleet Statistics*).

Civil Aviation (passenger arrivals): 145,929 in 2000; 144,914 in 2001; 134,690 in 2002.

TOURISM

Visitor Arrivals ('000): 317.8 stop-over visitors, 300.4 cruise-ship passengers in 2003; 303.8 stop-over visitors, 466.6 cruise-ship passengers in 2004; 337.1 stop-over visitors, 449.2 cruise-ship passengers in 2005.

Visitor Expenditure (US $ million, estimates): 373.8 in 2001; 356.5 in 2002; 368.0 in 2003.

Source: Caribbean Development Bank, *Social and Economic Indicators*.

COMMUNICATIONS MEDIA

Radio Receivers (1997): 9,000 in use.
Television Receivers (1999): 4,000 in use.
Telephones (1996): 10,000 main lines in use.
Facsimile Machines (1996): 1,200 in use.
Non-daily Newspapers (1996): 2 (estimated circulation 4,000).

Sources: UNESCO, *Statistical Yearbook*; UN, *Statistical Yearbook*.

EDUCATION

Pre-primary: 5 schools (1994/95); 46 teachers (2001/02); 628 pupils (2001/02).
Primary: 20 schools (1993/94); 168 teachers (2001/02); 2,735 pupils (2003).
Secondary: 4 schools (1988); 166 teachers (UNESCO estimate, 2001/02); 1,633 pupils (2003).
Tertiary: 1,916 pupils enrolled (2003).

Source: UNESCO Institute for Statistics; Caribbean Development Bank, *Social and Economic Indicators*.

Directory

The Constitution

The British Virgin Islands have had a representative assembly since 1774. The present Constitution took effect from June 1977. Under its terms, the Governor is responsible for defence and internal security, external affairs, terms and conditions of service of public officers, and the administration of the Courts. The Governor also possesses reserved legislative powers in respect of legislation necessary in the interests of his special responsibilities. There is an Executive Council, with the Governor as Chairman, one *ex-officio* member (the Attorney-General), the Chief Minister (appointed by the Governor from among the elected members of the Legislative Council) who has responsibility for finance, and three other ministers (appointed by the Governor on the advice of the Chief Minister); and a Legislative Council consisting of a Speaker, chosen from outside the Council, one *ex-officio* member (the Attorney-General) and 13 elected members (nine members from one-member electoral districts and four members representing the Territory 'at large').

The division of the islands into nine electoral districts, instead of seven, came into effect at the November 1979 general election. The four 'at large' seats were introduced at the February 1995 general election. The minimum voting age was lowered from 21 years to 18 years.

Under the British Overseas Territories Act, which entered into effect in May 2002, British Virgin Islanders have the right to United Kingdom citizenship and the right of abode in the United Kingdom. British citizens do not enjoy reciprocal rights.

The Government

Governor: DAVID PEAREY (assumed office 18 April 2006).
Deputy Governor: DANCIA PENN.

EXECUTIVE COUNCIL
(April 2006)

Chairman: DAVID PEAREY (The Governor).
Chief Minister: Dr ORLANDO SMITH.
Deputy Chief Minister and Minister of Finance, and of Health and Social Development: RONNIE SKELTON.
Minister of Natural Resources and Labour: EILEENE L. PARSONS.
Minister of Education and Culture: LLOYD BLACK.
Minister of Communications and Works: ELMORE STOUTT.
Attorney-General: CHERNO JALLOW.

MINISTRIES

Office of the Governor: Government House, POB 702, Road Town, Tortola; tel. 494-2345; fax 494-5790; e-mail bvigovernor@gov.vg; internet www.bvi.gov.vg.

Office of the Deputy Governor: Central Administration Bldg, Road Town, Tortola; tel. 468-3701; fax 494-6481; e-mail dpenn@gov.vg; internet www.bvi.gov.vg.

Office of the Chief Minister: 33 Admin Dr., Wickham's Cay I, Road Town, Tortola; tel. 468-3701; fax 468-4435; e-mail cmo@caribsurf.com.

Ministry of Communications and Works: Road Town, Tortola; tel. 468-3701; e-mail mcw@gov.vg.

Ministry of Education and Culture: Road Town, Tortola; tel. 468-3701; e-mail bvimecgov@hotmail.com.

Ministry of Finance, Health and Social Development: Road Town, Tortola; tel. 468-3701; fax 468-6180; e-mail finance@gov.vg.

Ministry of Natural Resources and Labour: Road Town, Tortola; tel. 468-3701; e-mail nrl@gov.vg.

All ministries are based in Road Town, Tortola, mainly at the Central Administration Bldg (fax 494-4435; internet www.bvi.gov.vg).

LEGISLATIVE COUNCIL

Speaker: V. INEZ ARCHIBALD.
Clerk: JULIA LEONARD-MASSICOTT.
General Election, 16 June 2003

Party	% of vote	Seats
National Democratic Party	52.4	8
Virgin Islands Party	42.2	5
Other	5.4	—
Total	**100.0**	**13**

Political Organizations

Concerned Citizens' Movement (CCM): Road Town, Tortola; f. 1994 as successor to Independent People's Movt; Leader ETHLYN SMITH.

UNITED KINGDOM OVERSEAS TERRITORIES   The British Virgin Islands

National Democratic Party (NDP): Road Town, Tortola; f. 1998; Chair. RUSSELL HARRIGAN; Leader ORLANDO SMITH.

United Party (UP): POB 3348, Road Town, Tortola; tel. 495-2656; fax 494-1808; e-mail liberatebvi@msn.com; f. 1967; Chair. ULRIC SCATLIFFE; Pres. CONRAD MADURO.

Virgin Islands Party (VIP): Road Town, Tortola; Leader RALPH T. O'NEAL.

Judicial System

Justice is administered by the Eastern Caribbean Supreme Court, based in Saint Lucia, which consists of two divisions: the High Court of Justice and the Court of Appeal. There are two resident High Court Judges, and a visiting Court of Appeal which is comprised of the Chief Justice and two Judges of Appeal and which sits twice a year in the British Virgin Islands. There is also a Magistrates' Court, which hears prescribed civil and criminal cases. The final Court of Appeal is the Privy Council in the United Kingdom.

Resident Judges: STANLEY MOORE, KENNETH BENJAMIN.
Magistrate: DORIEN TAYLOR.
Registrar: GAIL CHARLES.
Magistrate's Office: Road Town, Tortola; tel. 494-3460; fax 494-2499.

Religion

CHRISTIANITY

The Roman Catholic Church

The diocese of St John's-Basseterre, suffragan to the archdiocese of Castries (Saint Lucia), includes Anguilla, Antigua and Barbuda, the British Virgin Islands, Montserrat and Saint Christopher and Nevis. The Bishop is resident in St John's, Antigua.

The Anglican Communion

The British and US Virgin Islands form a single, missionary diocese of the Episcopal Church of the United States of America. The Bishop of the Virgin Islands is resident on St Thomas in the US Virgin Islands.

Protestant Churches

Various Protestant denominations are represented, principally the Methodist Church. Others include the Seventh-day Adventist, Church of God and Baptist Churches.

The Press

The BVI Beacon: 10 Russell Hill Rd, POB 3030, Road Town, Tortola; tel. 494-3434; fax 494-6267; e-mail bvibeacn@surfbvi.com; internet www.bvibeacon.com; f. 1984; Thursdays; covers local and international news; Editor LINNELL M. ABBOTT; circ. 3,400.

The Island Sun: 112 Main St, POB 21, Road Town, Tortola; tel. 494-2476; fax 494-5854; e-mail issun@candwbvi.net; internet www.islandsun.com; f. 1962; Fridays; Editor VERNON W. PICKERING; circ. 3,000.

The BVI StandPoint: Wickhams Cay, POB 4311, Road Town, Tortola; tel. 494-8106; fax 494-8647; e-mail bvistandpoint@surfbvi.com; internet www.bvistandpoint.net; fmrly BVI PennySaver, adopted current name in 2001; Tuesdays; covers local and international news; Editor SUSAN HENIGHAN; circ. 18,000.

The Welcome: POB 133, Road Town, Tortola; tel. 494-2413; fax 494-4413; e-mail info@bviwelcome.com; internet www.bviwelcome.com; f. 1971; every 2 months; general, tourist information; Publr PAUL BACKSHALL; Editor CLAUDIA COLLI; annual circ. 172,000.

Publishers

Caribbean Publishing Co (BVI) Ltd: POB 3403, Road Town, Tortola; tel. 494-2060; fax 494-3060; e-mail bvi-sales@caribpub.com; Sales Man. ARTHUR RUBAINE.

Island Publishing Services Ltd: POB 133, Road Town, Tortola; tel. 494-2413; fax 494-658; e-mail cpcips@surfbvi.com; internet www.bviwelcome.com; publishes The British Virgin Islands Welcome Tourist Guide.

Broadcasting and Communications

TELECOMMUNICATIONS

Plans to liberalize the telecommunications sector were under way in early 2006.

Telephone Services Management Unit: Central Administration Bldg, Road Town, Tortola; tel. 494-4728; fax 494-6551; e-mail tsmu@bvigovernment.org; govt agency.

Cable & Wireless (WI) Ltd: Cutlass Bldg, Wickhams Cay 1, POB 440, Road Town, Tortola; tel. 494-4444; fax 494-2506; e-mail candw@candwbvi.net; internet www.candw.vg; f. 1967; CEO VANCE LEWIS.

CCT Boatphone: Geneva Pl., Road Town, Tortola; tel. 444-4444; e-mail info@bvicellular.com; internet www.bvicellular.com; mobile cellular telephone operator.

BROADCASTING

Radio

Caribbean Broadcasting System: POB 3049, Road Town, Tortola; tel. 494-4990; commercial; Gen. Man. ALVIN KORNGOLD.

Virgin Islands Broadcasting Ltd—Radio ZBVI: Baughers Bay, POB 78, Road Town, Tortola; tel. 494-2250; fax 494-1139; e-mail zbvi@caribsurf.com; internet www.zbvi.vi; f. 1965; commercial; Gen. Man. HARVEY HERBERT; Ops Man. SANDRA POTTER WARRICAN.

Television

BVI Cable TV: Fishlock Rd, POB 694, Road Town, Tortola; tel. 494-3205; fax 494-2952; programmes from US Virgin Islands and Puerto Rico; 53 channels; Man. Dir TODD KLINDWORTH.

Television West Indies Ltd (ZBTV): Broadcast Peak, Chawell, POB 34, Tortola; tel. 494-3332; commercial.

Finance

BANKING

Regulatory Authority

Financial Services Commission: internet www.bvifsc.vg; f. 2002; independent financial services regulator; Chair. MICHAEL RIEGELS; CEO ROBERT MATHAVIOUS.

Commercial Banks

Ansbacher (BVI) Ltd: International Trust Bldg, POB 659, Road Town, Tortola; tel. 494-3215; fax 494-3216.

Banco Popular de Puerto Rico: POB 67, Road Town, Tortola; tel. 494-2117; fax 494-5294; internet www.bancopopular.com; Man. SANDRA SCATLIFFE.

Bank of East Asia (BVI) Ltd: POB 901, Road Town, Tortola; tel. 495-5588; fax 494-4513; Man. ELIZABETH WILKINSON.

Bank of Nova Scotia (Canada): Wickhams Cay 1, POB 434, Road Town, Tortola; tel. 494-2526; fax 494-4657; e-mail Michael.Rolle@scotiabank.com; internet www.scotiabank.com; f. 1967; Man. Dir MICHAEL ROLLES.

Citco Bank (BVI) Ltd: Citco Bldg, Wickhams Cay, POB 662, Road Town, Tortola; tel. 494-2218; fax 494-3917; e-mail bvi-trust@citco.com; internet www.citco.com; f. 1978; Man. RENE ROMER.

DISA Bank (BVI) Ltd: POB 985, Road Town, Tortola; tel. 494-6036; fax 494-4980; Man. ROSA RESTREPO.

First Bank Virgin Islands: Wickham's Cay 1, Road Town, Tortola; tel. 494-2662; fax 494-5106; internet www.firstbankvi.com.

FirstCaribbean International Bank Ltd: Wickhams Cay 1, POB 70, Road Town, Tortola; tel. 494-2171; fax 494-4315; e-mail care@firstcaribbeanbank.com; internet www.firstcaribbeanbank.com; f. 2003 following merger of Caribbean operations of Barclays Bank PLC and CIBC; CEO CHARLES PINK; Exec. Dir SHARON BROWN.

HSBC Guyerzeller Bank (BVI) Ltd: POB 3162, Road Town, Tortola; tel. 494-5416; fax 494-5417; e-mail rhbvi@surfbvi.com; Dir KENNETH W. MORGAN.

Rathbone Bank (BVI) Ltd: POB 986, Road Town, Tortola; tel. 494-6544; fax 494-6532; e-mail rathbone@surfbvi.com; Man. CORNEL BAPTISTE.

VP Bank (BVI) Ltd: POB 3463, Road Town, Tortola; tel. 494-1100; fax 494-1199; e-mail vpbank@surfbvi.com; internet www.vpbank.com; Gen-Man. PETER REICHENSTEIN.

Development Bank

Development Bank of the British Virgin Islands: Wickhams Cay 1, POB 275, Road Town, Tortola; tel. 494-3737; fax 494-3119; state-owned; Chair. MEADE MALONE.

TRUST COMPANIES

Abacus Trust and Management Services Ltd: POB 3339, Road Town, Tortola; tel. 494-4388; fax 494-3088; e-mail mwmabacus@surfbvi.com; Man. MEADE MALONE.

UNITED KINGDOM OVERSEAS TERRITORIES

The British Virgin Islands

Aleman, Cordero, Galindo and Lee Trust (BVI) Ltd: POB 3175, Road Town, Tortola; tel. 494-4666; fax 494-4679; e-mail alcogalbvi@alcogal.com; Man. GABRIELLA CONTE.

AMS Trustees ltd: POB 116, Road Town, Tortola; tel. 494-3399; fax 494-3041; e-mail ams@amsbvi.com; Man. ROGER DAWES.

Belmont Trust Ltd: POB 3443, Road Town, Tortola; tel. 494-5800; fax 494-2545; e-mail belmont@kpmgbvi.net; Man. ANDREA DOUGLAS.

CCP Financial Consultants Ltd: POB 681, Road Town, Tortola; tel. 494-6777; fax 494-6787; e-mail mail@ccpbvi.com; internet www.ccpbvi.com; Man. JOSEPH ROBERTS.

Citco BVI Ltd: POB 662, Road Town, Tortola; tel. 494-2217; fax 494-3917; e-mail bvi-trust@citco.com; internet www.citco.com; Man. REINIER TEIXEIRA DE MATTOS.

Guardian Trust & Securities Ltd: POB 438, Road Town, Tortola; tel. 494-2616; fax 494-2704; e-mail infovg@equitytrust.com; Man. LINDA ROMNEY-LEUE.

HSBC International Trustee (BVI) Ltd: POB 916, Road Town, Tortola; tel. 494-5414; fax 494-5417; e-mail kenneth.morgan@rawlinson-hunter.vg; Man. K. W. MORGAN.

Hunte & Co Services Ltd: POB 3504, Road Town, Tortola; tel. 495-0232; fax 495-0229; internet www.hunteandco.com; Man. LEWIS HUNTE.

Maples Finance BVI Ltd: POB 173, Road Town, Tortola; tel. 494-3384; fax 494-4643; internet www.maplesandcalder.com; Man. ANTHONY LYNTON.

Moore Stephens International Services (BVI) Ltd: POB 3186, Road Town, Tortola; tel. 494-3503; fax 494-3592; e-mail moorestephens@surfbvi.com; internet www.moorestephens.com; Man. CRAIG MURPHY-PAIGE.

Midocean Management and Trust Services (BVI) Ltd: POB 805, Road Town, Tortola; tel. 494-4567; fax 494-4568; e-mail midocean@maitlandbvi.com; Man. ELIZABETH WILKINSON.

Totalserve Trust Company Ltd: POB 3200, Road Town, Tortola; tel. 494-7295; fax 494-7296; e-mail bvi@jerseytrustco.com; internet www.jerseytrustco.com; Man. MICHELLE D. CELESTINE.

TMF (BVI) Ltd: POB 964, Road Town, Tortola; tel. 494-4997; fax 494-4999; e-mail tmfbvi@surfbvi.com; Man. GRAHAM COOK.

Tricor Services (BVI) Ltd: POB 3340, Road Town, Tortola; tel. 494-6004; fax 494-6404; e-mail eybvi@surfbvi.com; Man. PATRICK A. NICHOLAS.

Trident Corporate Services (BVI) Ltd: POB 659, Road Town, Tortola; tel. 494-3215; fax 494-3216; e-mail tcbvi@tridenttrust.com; internet www.tridenttrust.com; Man. BARRY R. GOODMAN.

INSURANCE

AMS Insurance Management Services Ltd: POB 116, Road Town, Tortola; tel. 494-4078; fax 494-2519; e-mail amsins@amsbvi.com; Man. GREGORY M. TAYLOR.

Atlas Insurance Management (BVI) Ltd: POB 129, Road Town, Tortola; tel. 494-2728; fax 494-4393; e-mail cil@surfbvi.com; Man. JOHN WILLIAMS.

ATU Insurance Management (BVI) Ltd: POB 3463, Road Town, Tortola; tel. 494-1100; fax 494-1199; e-mail atu@atubvi.com; internet www.atubvi.com; Man. PETER REICHENSTEIN.

Belmont Insurance Management Ltd: POB 3443, Road Town, Tortola; tel. 494-5800; fax 494-6565; e-mail kpmginsurance@surfbvi.com; Man. PAUL MARTIN.

Captiva Global Ltd: POB 4428, Road Town, Tortola; tel. 494-4111; fax 494-4222; e-mail info@captiva.vg; internet www.captiva.vg; Man.Dir HARRY THOMPSON.

Caribbean Insurance Management: POB 129, Road Town, Tortola; tel. 494-8239; fax 494-4393; e-mail cil@surfbvi.com; Man. JOHN WILLIAMS.

Caribbean Insurers Ltd: POB 129, Road Town, Tortola; tel. 494-2728; fax 494-4393; e-mail cil@surfbvi.com; Man. JOHN WILLIAMS.

Codan Management (BVI) Ltd: POB 3140, Road Town, Tortola; tel. 494-2065; fax 494-4929; e-mail bvi@cdp.bm; Man. A. GUY ELDRIDGE.

Euro-American Insurance Management Ltd: POB 3161, Road Town, Tortola; tel. 494-4692; fax 494-4695; e-mail eamsbvi@surfbvi.com; Man. KAY REDDY.

HWR Insurance Management Services Ltd: POB 71, Road Town, Tortola; tel. 494-2233; fax 494-3547; e-mail mail@harneys.com; Man. CONNOR JENNINGS.

Marine Insurance Office (BVI) Ltd: POB 874, Road Town, Tortola; tel. 494-3795; fax 494-4540; e-mail marinein@surfbvi.com; Man. WESLEY WOODHOUSE.

Marsh Management Services (BVI) Ltd: POB 3140, Road Town, Tortola; tel. 494-4850; fax 494-7467; Man. A. GUY ELDRIDGE.

Osiris Insurance Management Ltd: POB 2221, Road Town, Tortola; tel. 494-8920; fax 494-6934; e-mail osiristrust@surfbvi.com; Man. TERRANCE M. ROLLINS.

R & H Insurance Services Ltd: POB 3162, Road Town, Tortola; tel. 494-5414; fax 494-5417; e-mail edith.steel@rawlinson-hunter.vg; Man. EDITH STEEL.

Trafford Insurance Management Services Ltd: POB 116, Road Town, Tortola; tel. 494-4078; fax 494-2519; e-mail amsims@amsbvi.com; Man. GREGORY M. TAYLOR.

Trident Insurance Management (BVI) Ltd: POB 146, Road Town, Tortola; tel. 494-2434; fax 494-3754; e-mail trident@surfbvi.com; Man. GREGORY M. TAYLOR.

TSA Insurance Management Ltd: POB 3443, Road Town, Tortola; tel. 494-5800; fax 494-6563; e-mail kpmginsurance@surfbvi.com; Man. PAUL MARTIN.

USA Risk Group (BVI) Inc: POB 3140, Road Town, Tortola; tel. 494-2065; fax 494-4929; Man. A. GUY ELDRIDGE.

Several US and other foreign companies have agents in the British Virgin Islands.

Trade and Industry

GOVERNMENT AGENCY

Trade and Investment Promotion Department: Office of the Chief Minister, Road Town, Tortola; tel. 494-3701; fax 494-6413; internet www.trade.gov.vg.

CHAMBER OF COMMERCE

British Virgin Islands Chamber of Commerce and Hotel Association: James Frett Bldg, Wickhams Cay 1, POB 376, Road Town, Tortola; tel. 494-3514; fax 494-6179; e-mail bviccha@surfbvi.com; internet www.bvihotels.org; f. 1986; Chair. NELDA FARRINGTON-BRYDON; Pres. (Business and Commerce) FRED COLVILLE; Pres. (Hotels and Tourism) LOUIS SCHWARTZ.

UTILITIES

Electricity

British Virgin Islands Electricity Corpn (BVIEC): Long Bush, POB 268, Road Town, Tortola; tel. 494-3911; fax 494-4291; e-mail bviecce@caribsurf.com; f. 1979; state-owned, privatization pending; Chair. MARGARET ALMYRA PENN.

Water

Water and Sewerage Dept: Baughers Bay, Road Town, Tortola; tel. 468-3701; fax 494-6746.

Transport

ROADS

In 2002 there were 82 miles of access roads, 48 miles of primary roads, 23 miles of secondary roads and 56 miles of tertiary roads. In 2001 11,313 vehicles were licensed, 3,490 of which were private vehicles.

Public Works Department: Baughers Bay, Tortola; tel. 468-2722; fax 468-4740; e-mail pwd@mailbvigovernment.com; responsible for road maintenance.

SHIPPING

There are two direct steamship services, one from the United Kingdom and one from the USA. Motor launches maintain daily mail and passenger services with St Thomas and St John, US Virgin Islands. A new cruise-ship pier, built at a cost of US $6.9m. with assistance from the Caribbean Development Bank, was opened in Road Town in 1994 and was later expanded.

British Virgin Islands Port Authority: Port Purcell, POB 4, Road Town, Tortola; tel. 494-3435; fax 494-2642; e-mail bviports@candwbvi.net; internet www.bviports.org; f. 1991; Man. Dir GENE E. CREQUE (acting).

Tropical Shipping: Pasea Estate, POB 250, Road Town, Tortola; tel. 494-2674; fax 494-3505; e-mail lmoses@tropical.com; internet www.tropical.com; Man. LEROY MOSES.

CIVIL AVIATION

Beef Island Airport, about 16 km (10 miles) from Road Town, has a runway with a length of 1,100 m (3,700 ft). A new US $65m. airport terminal was opened at the airport in March 2002. After a long delay (see History), in October 2003 work began to lengthen the runway to 1,500 m (4,700 ft). Upon completion of the renovation in May 2004 the airport was renamed Terrence B. Lettsome Airport. Captain Auguste George Airport on Anegada has been designated an international point of entry and was resurfaced in the late 1990s. The airport

runway on Virgin Gorda was to be extended to 1,200 m (4,000 ft) to allow larger aircraft to land.
Director of Civil Aviation: MILTON CREQUE; tel. 494-3701; fax 494-3437.

Tourism

The main attraction of the islands is their tranquillity and clear waters, which provide excellent facilities for sailing, fishing, diving and other water sports. In 1998 there 1,231 hotel rooms in the islands and 365 rooms in guest-houses and rented apartments. There are also many charter yachts offering overnight accommodation. There were some 337,100 stop-over visitors and approximately 449,200 cruise-ship passengers in 2005. The majority of tourists are from the USA. Receipts from tourism totalled US $368.0m. in 2003.

British Virgin Islands Tourist Board: 2nd Floor, AKARA Bldg, DeCastro St, Road Town, Tortola; tel. 494-3134; fax 494-3866; e-mail info@bvitourism.com; internet www.bvitourism.com; Dir KEDRICK MALONE.

British Virgin Islands Chamber of Commerce and Hotel Association: see Chamber of Commerce.

THE CAYMAN ISLANDS

Introductory Survey

Location, Climate, Language, Religion, Flag, Capital

The Cayman Islands lie about 290 km (180 miles) west-north-west of Jamaica and consist of three main islands: Grand Cayman and, to the north-east, Little Cayman and Cayman Brac. The climate is tropical but is tempered by the trade winds, with a cool season between November and March, when temperatures average 24°C (75°F). The rainy season lasts from May until October. Mean annual rainfall is 1,524 mm (60 ins). The official language is English. Many Christian churches are represented. The flag is the British 'Blue Ensign', with the islands' coat of arms (a golden lion on a red background above three stars in green, representing the three main islands, superimposed on wavy lines of blue and white, the shield surmounted by a torse of white and blue bearing a yellow pineapple behind a green turtle, and with the motto 'He hath founded it upon the seas' on a scroll beneath) on a white roundel in the fly. The capital is George Town, on the island of Grand Cayman.

Recent History

The Cayman Islands came under acknowledged British rule in 1670 and were settled mainly from Jamaica and by privateers and buccaneers. The islands of Little Cayman and Cayman Brac were permanently settled only in 1833, and until 1877 there was no administrative connection between them and Grand Cayman. A representative assembly first sat in 1832. The islands formed a dependency of Jamaica until 1959, and the Governor of Jamaica held responsibility for the Cayman Islands until Jamaican independence in 1962, when a separate administrator was appointed (the title was changed to that of Governor in 1971). The 1959 Constitution was revised in 1972, 1992 and 1994.

For many years there have been no formal political parties on the islands, despite the emergence of a nascent party political system during the 1960s with the formation, in 1961, of the National Democratic Party (NDP), as part of a campaign for self-government. The Christian Democratic Party was formed as a conservative opposition. Both parties disappeared within a few years despite the electoral success of the NDP, largely owing to the system of gubernatorial nomination to the Executive Council. In the 1970s elections for the 12 elective seats in the Legislative Assembly came to be contested by 'teams' of candidates, as well as by independents. Two such teams were formed, Progress and Dignity (the more conservative) and Unity, but all candidates were committed to augmenting the economic success of the Caymans, and favoured continued dependent status. There are no plans for independence, and the majority of the population wish to maintain the islands' links with the United Kingdom.

At elections in November 1980 the Unity team, led by Jim Bodden, took eight of the 12 seats. In the November 1984 elections opposition independents won nine seats, aided by public disquiet at the rapid growth of the immigrant work-force, and the implications of the recent US challenges to the Cayman Islands' bank secrecy laws. In 1987 the Legislative Assembly successfully sought stricter regulations of status and residency for those able to participate in elections, in an attempt to protect the political rights of native Caymanians (in view of the very large immigrant population). At a general election in November 1988 seven of the existing members were returned, and five new members were elected. Prior to the election the teams had regrouped into more informal coalitions, indicating the primacy of personal over 'party' affiliations.

In July 1990 the Legislative Assembly approved proposals to review the Constitution, and in January 1991 the British Government sent two commissioners to the Territory to discuss possible amendments. The implementation of most recommendations, including the appointment of a Chief Minister, was postponed pending a general election to be held in 1992. One of the amendments, however, which involved increasing the number of elective seats in the Legislative Assembly to 15, was adopted in March 1992. The proposed reforms had prompted the formation, in mid-1991, of the Territory's first political organization since the 1960s, the Progressive Democratic Party (PDP). During 1992 the organization developed into a coalition and was renamed the National Team. At the general election in November 1992 National Team members secured 12 of the elective seats in the newly enlarged Legislative Assembly, while independent candidates won the remaining three. In November of that year James Ryan was appointed Chief Secretary, following the retirement of Lemuel Hurlston. The new Government opted to revoke the provisions in the Constitution for a Chief Minister; however, in 1994 it introduced a ministerial system and created a fifth ministerial portfolio.

At a general election on 20 November 1996 the governing National Team remained in power, although with a reduced majority, winning nine seats in the Legislative Assembly. Two new groupings, the Democratic Alliance and Team Cayman (which had formed in opposition to the Government's alleged mismanagement of the public debt and of Cayman Airways) secured two seats and one seat, respectively. Independent candidates won three seats.

In November 1997 the Minister of Community Development, Sport, Youth Affairs and Culture, McKeeva Bush, was dismissed from his post after it was alleged that a bank of which he was a director had authorized fraudulent loans totalling some US $1.1m. Bush (who denied any knowledge of the alleged corruption) was replaced by Julianna O'Connor Connolly, the first female minister on the island.

In March 1999 the Government of the United Kingdom published draft legislation pertaining to its relationship with its Overseas Dependencies, which were to be renamed United Kingdom Overseas Territories (and had been referred to as such since February 1998). The legislation proposed the extension of British citizenship to the citizens of Overseas Territories, although it also required its Territories to amend their legislation on human rights and on the regulation of the financial services sector to meet international standards. The Cayman Islands were praised for the introduction in 1998 of laws on tax evasion, and for strengthening the regulatory powers of the Monetary Authority, although concern was expressed that homosexuality remained a criminal offence in the islands. The issue of the legal status of homosexuality in the Cayman Islands had been highlighted in January 1998 by the authorities' refusal to permit a stop-over by a US cruise liner whose 900 passengers were homosexual men.

In late April 1999 representatives of the European Union (EU, see p. 228) held meetings with the overseas territories of member states to discuss proposed reforms of legislation relating to the financial services sector. The Cayman Islands delegation defended the islands' standards of regulation, arguing that the islands had implemented some of the strictest laws in the world against money-laundering, and that proposals to abolish the Cayman Islands' laws on banking secrecy would place the islands at a disadvantage, compared with the financial centres of Switzerland and Luxembourg. In early June the Cayman Islands announced that it was to seek certification under the UN's Offshore Initiative, and that consequently a UN agency, the Global Programme against Money Laundering, was to undertake a review of the Territory's financial systems and regulations.

In August 1999 a US citizen, John Matthewson, was sentenced to five years' probation by a US court on charges of money-laundering in the Cayman Islands. Matthewson had reportedly escaped a prison sentence by revealing to US investigators the extent of his activities in the Cayman Islands and the extent to which the islands' financial system benefited those seeking to evade US taxation. The US Government subsequently charged several of Matthewson's clients with tax evasion, and it was widely believed that the case had seriously damaged the islands' reputation both for secrecy and as a reputable financial centre. However, the island authorities claimed that the Royal Cayman Islands Police had co-operated fully with the US investigators, and also observed that in 1998 the islands' policy of co-operation with US investigators in their efforts to prevent money-laundering had been singled out for praise in the US *International Narcotics Control Strategy Report*.

Drugs-related crime continued to be a serious problem in the 1990s, when an estimated 75% of all thefts and burglaries in the islands were attributed, directly or indirectly, to the drugs trade. The Mutual Legal Assistance Treaty (signed in 1986, and ratified by the US Senate in 1990) between the Cayman Islands and the USA provides for the mutual exchange of information for use in combating crime (particularly drugs-trafficking and the diversion of funds gained illegally from the drugs trade). Further legislation relating to the abuse of the financial sector by criminal organizations was approved in November 1996. In October 2005 the Government introduced tougher sentences for possession of illegal firearms or bullet-proof vests. Offenders would be sentenced to a minimum of 10 years in prison and fined CI $100,000.

In a general election held on 8 November 2000 the governing National Team suffered a heavy defeat, losing six of its nine seats, including that held by Truman Bodden, the Leader of Government Business. The newly elected Legislative Assembly appointed Kurt Tibbetts of the Democratic Alliance as Leader of Government Business.

In an unprecedented development in November 2001, several members of the Legislative Assembly, dissatisfied with the Government's leadership during the economic slowdown, formed the United Democratic Party (UDP). McKeeva Bush, the leader of the new party and Deputy Leader of Government Business and Minister of Tourism, Environment and Transport, claimed that at least 10 members of the 15-member Assembly were UDP supporters. Subsequently, the passing of a motion of 'no confidence' against the Leader of Government Business resulted in Tibbetts and Edna Moyle, the Minister of Community Development, Women's Affairs, Youth and Sport, leaving the Executive Council. Bush became the new Leader of Government Business, while two other legislators, Gilbert McLean and Frank McField, both members of the UDP, joined the Cabinet. In May 2002, at the UDP's inaugural convention, Bush was formally elected leader of the party. In the same month it was announced that the five opposition members of the legislative assembly had formed a new political party, the People's Progressive Movement (PPM), led by Tibbetts.

In March 2002 the three-member Constitutional Review Commission, appointed by the Governor in May 2001, submitted a new draft constitution. The proposed document had to be debated by the Legislative Assembly and then approved by the British Parliament before being formally adopted. The draft constitution included the creation of the office of Chief Minister, proposed a full ministerial government, and incorporated a bill of rights. The opposition demanded a referendum on the recommendations, on the grounds that the UDP had rejected several of the proposals, despite strong public support for the changes, but Bush forwarded the proposals to the British Foreign and Commonwealth Office (FCO), via the Governor's office. In December Bush and the leader of the opposition, Tibbetts, travelled to the United Kingdom in order to review the proposed constitution with FCO officials. Consensus, however, proved impossible to achieve. While the PPM called for a public referendum on issue, the UDP announced in February 2004 that it would not participate in the constitutional review process before the next election. These were originally scheduled to be held in November 2004, but were postponed, owing to the damage caused by 'Hurricane Ivan' in September 2004 (see below). In March 2006 an FCO delegation visited the Cayman Islands for informal discussions aimed at restarting the process of constitutional reform.

In May 2002 the British Overseas Territories Act, having received royal assent in the United Kingdom in February, came into force and granted British citizenship to the people of its Overseas Territories, including the Cayman Islands. Under the new law Caymanians would be able to hold British passports and work in the United Kingdom and elsewhere in the EU. Also in May, the Cayman Islands became an associate member of the Caribbean Community and Common Market (CARICOM, see p. 183). In the same month Bruce Dinwiddy succeeded Peter Smith as Governor.

In January 2003 Bush accused the United Kingdom of undermining the course of Cayman Islands' justice, after a routine money-laundering case was dismissed amid allegations of espionage and obstruction of justice by British intelligence agents. The trial collapsed after it was alleged that the Director of the Cayman Islands Financial Reporting Unit (and a key witness in the trial) had passed information about the case to an unnamed agency of the British Government, understood to be the Secret Intelligence Service (MI6). It was claimed that MI6 wished to protect the names of its sources within the Caribbean 'offshore' banking community. Bush demanded the British Government pay for the failed trial, estimated to cost some US $5m., and for any negative repercussions the affair might have for the reputation of the territory's banking sector. The United Kingdom, however, refused to compensate the Cayman Islands and maintained that although its intelligence agencies might have helped in the investigation, they had never interfered in the case. In March the Attorney-General, David Ballantyne, resigned amid accusations that he was aware that British intelligence agents were working covertly in the Cayman Islands; Samuel W. Bulgin, the erstwhile Solicitor-General, was appointed as Ballantyne's permanent successor in July.

The Cayman Islands were close to the eye of 'Hurricane Ivan', which caused an estimated CI $2,800m. of damage to the islands, or more than CI $63,000 per person, in September 2004; damage to housing alone accounted for 50% of this total, with the education and tourism sectors also suffering badly. The Cayman Islands Recovery Operation was established at the end of 2004, under the management of Cabinet Secretary Orrett Connor. In February 2006 the FCO pledged closer co-operation in disaster preparedness with the Cayman Islands Government.

The opposition PPM won a resounding victory at the general election of 11 May 2005, securing nine of the 15 legislative seats. The ruling UDP won only five seats, with the remaining seat going to an independent. The outgoing UDP Government had been criticized for its handling of the aftermath of 'Hurricane Ivan' and also for its decision, in September 2004, to grant 'belonger' status to some 3,000 people, a move interpreted by many as an attempt to increase the party's electoral support. The new Leader of Government Business, Kurt Tibbetts, pledged to hold a referendum on increased autonomy for the Territory. In November Tibbetts announced a Freedom of Information Bill, to be debated in the Legislative Assembly, prior to a public consultation exercise. The proposed legislation was intended to promote government transparency and accountability and thus increase constitutional democracy. Also in that month, Stuart Jack succeeded Bruce Dinwiddy as Governor.

An estimated 1,500 Jamaicans were thought to be living illegally in the Cayman Islands in 2005. The Government announced an immigration amnesty in December 2005–January 2006, during which illegal immigrants could leave without fear of prosecution. However, only 49 people took advantage of the amnesty, of whom 32 were Jamaican. The maximum fine for living illegally in the Cayman Islands was CI $20,000.

Government

Under the revised Constitution of 1994, the Governor, who is appointed by the British monarch, is responsible for external affairs, defence, internal security and the public service. The Governor is Chairman of the Cabinet, comprising three members appointed by the Governor and five members elected by the Legislative Assembly. The Legislative Assembly comprises three official members and 15 members elected by universal adult suffrage for a period of four years.

Defence

The United Kingdom is responsible for the defence of the Cayman Islands.

Economic Affairs

In 2003, according to official estimates, the Cayman Islands' gross domestic product (GDP) was CI $1,603m., equivalent to some $36,793 per head. During 1995–2004, according to estimates from the Caribbean Development Bank (CDB), the population increased at an average annual rate of 3.7%, while GDP increased, in real terms, by 3.4% per year during 1995–2004; growth was estimated at 0.9% in 2004.

Agriculture (which engaged only 1.4% of the employed labour force in 1995 and provided some 0.5% of GDP in 1997) is limited by infertile soil, low rainfall and high labour costs. The principal crops are citrus fruits and bananas, and some other produce for local consumption. Flowers (particularly orchids) are produced for export. Livestock-rearing consists of beef cattle, poultry (mainly for eggs) and pigs. The traditional activity of turtle-hunting has virtually disappeared; the turtle farm (the only commercial one in the world) now produces mainly for domestic consumption (and serves as a research centre), following the imposition of US restrictions on the trade in turtle products in 1979. Fishing is mainly for lobster and shrimp.

Industry, engaging 12.6% of the employed labour force in 1995 and providing some 15.5% of GDP in 1997, consists mainly of construction and related manufacturing, some food-processing and tourist-related light industries. The construction sector contributed an estimated 9.3% of GDP in 1999, while manufacturing activities accounted for only about 2.3% of the total in that year. Energy requirements are satisfied by the import of mineral fuels and related products (10.9% of total imports in 1996).

Service industries dominate the Caymanian economy, accounting for 86.0% of employment in 1995 and contributing 83.9% of GDP in 1999. The tourism industry is the principal economic activity, and in 1991 accounted for 22.9% of GDP and employed, directly and indirectly, some 50% of the working population. The industry earned an estimated US $607.0m. in 2002. Most visitors are from the USA (71.0% of tourist arrivals in 1999). The Cayman Islands is one of the largest 'offshore' financial centres in the world; at April 2005 there were 438 banks and trust companies and 6,268 mutual funds on the islands, according to the Cayman Islands Monetary Authority. In 1995 the financial services sector engaged 18.9% of the working population, and in 1999 contributed about 36.0% of GDP.

In 2003 the Cayman Islands recorded an estimated trade deficit of US $549.2m. (commodity exports continue to represent less than 1% of the value of total imports). Receipts from tourism and the financial sector, remittances and capital inflows normally offset the trade deficit. The principal source of imports is the USA (which provided some 76.7% of total imports in 1996), which is also one of the principal markets for exports (34.6% in 1994). Other major trading partners in 1996 included the United Kingdom, Japan and the Netherlands Antilles (which received 10.6% of total exports in that year). Principal exports in the 1990s were fish and cut flowers. The principal imports are machinery and transport equipment (26.0% of total imports in 1996), foodstuffs (18.6%), manufactured articles (18.5%) and basic manufactures (13.6%).

An estimated government budget surplus of CI $21.0m. was recorded in 2003. In 1998 official development assistance totalled US $0.2m. At the end of 1999 the public debt stood at US $114.8m. The average annual rate of inflation was 3.2% in 1995–2004; consumer prices increased by an annual average of 0.6% in 2003 and 4.4% in 2004. According to official census figures, only 63% of the resident population of the islands were Caymanian in 1994 (compared with 79% in 1980). Some 4.4% of the labour force were unemployed in 2004.

The United Kingdom is responsible for the external affairs of the Cayman Islands, and the dependency has the status of Overseas Territory in association with the European Union (EU, see p. 228). The Cayman Islands gained associate member status in Caribbean Community and Common Market (CARICOM, see p. 183) in 2002; the territory is also a member of CARICOM's CDB (see p. 188).

Both the principal economic sectors, 'offshore' finance and tourism, benefit from the Cayman Islands' political stability, good infrastructure and extensive development. Tourism continued to expand in the early 2000s, although the Government attempted to limit tourist numbers in order to minimize damage to the environment, particularly the coral reef, and to preserve the islands' reputation as a destination for visitors of above-average wealth. The sector, nevertheless, suffered severe set-backs from the damage caused by 'Hurricane Ivan' in September 2004. The financial sector, which benefits from an absence of taxation and of foreign exchange regulations, recorded consistently high levels of growth during the 1990s, and provided an estimated 30% of GDP in 1998. The banking sector was reckoned to be the world's fifth largest in 2000, owing to the absence of direct taxation, lenient regulation and strict confidentiality laws. The Cayman Islands have a policy of openly confronting the issues of financial transparency and of money-laundering, and an information exchange treaty with the USA was ratified in 1990. However, despite the efforts of the authorities, the vulnerability of the islands' financial services sector to exploitation by criminal organizations continued to cause concern. In June 2000 the Cayman Islands were included on a list of harmful tax regimes compiled by an agency of the Organisation for Economic Co-operation and Development (OECD, see p. 320) and were urged to make legislative changes, introducing greater legal and administrative transparency. The Government pledged to adopt international standards of legal and administrative transparency by 2005, and in 2001, following stricter regulation of the private banking sector, the Cayman Islands were removed from the blacklist. In November of that year, in a further move to increase international confidence in its financial regulation, the Government signed a tax information exchange agreement with the USA, designed to reduce the potential for abuse of the tax system. In 2001 the Chamber of Commerce linked an economic downturn to the negative impact of OECD pressure on the financial services sector, although the global economic slowdown and the adverse affects on the tourism industry of the September 2001 terrorist attacks in the USA were also regarded as factors in the decline. Moreover, the Government's decision to increase the annual licensing fee charged to 'offshore' financial institutions in the 2002 budget was widely criticized as being potentially damaging to the industry. In late 2002 the financial sector faced further disruption when the United Kingdom, under pressure from an EU investigation into tax evasion, demanded that the Cayman Islands disclose the identities and account details of Europeans holding private savings accounts on the islands. The Cayman Islands, along with some other British Overseas Territories facing similar demands, claimed it was being treated unfairly, and refused to make any concessions. Nevertheless, the Legislative Assembly, after the British Government pledged to safeguard the territory's interests, voted to accept British/EU demands by 1 January 2005. Economic growth was originally forecast to reach 2.8% in 2004, but the damage and losses caused by 'Hurricane Ivan' in September of that year meant that annual GDP expanded by just 0.9%. Although the annual rate of inflation rose to 8.4% in 2005, the Financial Secretary expected the rate to stabilize quickly. Growth was estimated at 2.0% in 2005 and forecast at 1.8% in 2006.

Education

Schooling is compulsory for children between the ages of five and 15 years. It is provided free in 10 government-run primary schools, and there are also three state secondary schools, as well as six church-sponsored schools (five of which offer secondary as well as primary education). Primary education, from five years of age, lasts for six years. Secondary education is for seven years. Some CI $94.5m. was allocated for education in the 2005/06 budget.

Public Holidays

2006: 1 January (New Year's Day), 23 January (National Heroes' Day), 1 March (Ash Wednesday), 14 April (Good Friday), 17 April (Easter Monday), 15 May (Discovery Day), 12 June (Queen's Official Birthday), 3 July (Constitution Day), 13 November (Remembrance Day), 25–26 December (Christmas).

2007: 1 January (New Year's Day), 26 January (National Heroes' Day), 21 February (Ash Wednesday), 6 April (Good Friday), 9 April (Easter Monday), 14 May (Discovery Day), 11 June (Queen's Official Birthday), 2 July (Constitution Day), 12 November (Remembrance Day), 25–26 December (Christmas).

Weights and Measures

The imperial system is in use.

Statistical Survey

Sources: Government Information Services, Cricket Sq., Elgin Ave, George Town, Grand Cayman; tel. 949-8092; fax 949-5936; The Information Centre, Economic and Statistics Office, Government Administration Bldg, Grand Cayman; tel. 949-0940; fax 949-8782; e-mail infostats@gov.ky; internet www.eso.ky.

AREA AND POPULATION

Area: 262 sq km (102 sq miles). The main island of Grand Cayman is about 197 sq km (76 sq miles), about one-half of which is swamp. Cayman Brac is 39 sq km (15 sq miles); Little Cayman is 26 sq km (11 sq miles).

Population: 39,410 (males 19,311, females 20,099) at census of 10 October 1999 (Grand Cayman 37,473, Cayman Brac 1,822, Little Cayman 115). *2003* (estimated population at 31 December): 44,144.

Density (31 December 2003): 168.5 per sq km.

Principal Towns (population at 1999 census): George Town (capital) 20,626; West Bay 8,243; Bodden Town 5,764. *Mid-2003* (UN estimate, incl. suburbs): George Town 23,940 (Source: UN, *World Urbanization Prospects: The 2003 Revision*).

Births, Marriages and Deaths (estimates, 2001): Live births 622 (birth rate 15.0 per 1,000); Marriage rate 9.7 per 1,000 (2000); Deaths 132 (death rate 3.2 per 1,000).

Expectation of Life (years at birth): 79.8 in 2004. Source: Pan-American Health Organization.

Economically Active Population (sample survey, persons aged 15 years and over, October 1995): Agriculture, hunting, forestry and fishing 270; Manufacturing 320; Electricity, gas and water 245; Construction 1,805; Trade, restaurants and hotels 5,555; Transport, storage and communications 1,785; Financing, insurance, real estate and business services 3,570; Community, social and personal services 5,295; Total employment 18,845 (males 8,930, females 9,910). Figures exclude persons seeking work for the first time, totalling 100 (males 60, females 40), and other unemployed persons, totalling 900 (males 455, females 445). Source: ILO. *2004* (sample survey of 20–27 November, Grand Cayman): Total employed 22,420; Unemployed 1,034 (males 368, females 666); Total labour force 23,453 (males 12,432, females 11,021) (Note: Totals may not be equal to the sum of their constituent parts, as figures are approximations based on a reduced sample.).

HEALTH AND WELFARE

Physicians (per 1,000 head, 2003): 2.2.

Health Expenditure: % of GDP (1997): 4.2.

Health Expenditure: public (% of total, 1997): 53.2.

Source: mainly Pan American Health Organization.

For definitions, see explanatory note on p. vi).

UNITED KINGDOM OVERSEAS TERRITORIES

The Cayman Islands

AGRICULTURE, ETC.

Livestock (FAO estimates, '000 head, 2004): Cattle 1.3; Goats 0.3; Pigs 0.4; Chickens 6.
Fishing (metric tons, live weight, 2003): Total catch 125 (all marine fishes).
Source: FAO.

INDUSTRY

Electric Energy (consumption, million kWh): 414.6 in 2002; 429.3 in 2003; 450.3 in 2004. Source: Caribbean Utilities Company Ltd.

FINANCE

Currency and Exchange Rates: 100 cents = 1 Cayman Islands dollar (CI $). *Sterling, US Dollar and Euro Equivalents* (30 December 2005): £1 sterling = CI $1.435; US $1 = 83.3 CI cents; €1 = CI $0.983; CI $100 = £69.69 = US $120.00 = €101.73. *Exchange rate:* Fixed at CI $1 = US $1.20.
Budget (CI $ million, 2003): *Revenue:* Taxes on international trade and transactions 117.6; Taxes on other domestic goods and services 153.4; Taxes on property 17.7; Other tax revenue 5.4; Other current revenue 32.1; Total 326.2. *Expenditure:* Current expenditure 283.7 (Personnel costs 138.9, Supplies and consumable goods 61.3, Subsidies 58.8, Transfer payments 18.8, Interest payments 5.9); Capital expenditure and net lending 21.5; Total 305.2.
Cost of Living (Consumer Price Index; base: 2000 = 100): 103.6 in 2002; 104.3 in 2003; 108.9 in 2004. Source: ILO.
Gross Domestic Product (estimates, CI $ million in current prices): 1,482.3 in 2001; 1,546.0 in 2002; 1,603.2 in 2003.
Gross Domestic Product by Economic Activity (CI $ million in current prices, 1991): Primary industries 5; Manufacturing 9; Electricity, gas and water 19; Construction 54; Trade, restaurants and hotels 138; Transport, storage and communications 65; Finance, insurance, real estate and business services 210; Community, social and personal services 42; Government services 63; Statistical discrepancy 1; *Sub-total* 606; Import duties less imputed bank service charge 11; *GDP in purchasers' values* 617.

EXTERNAL TRADE

Principal Commodities (US $ million, 1996): *Imports c.i.f.:* Food and live animals 70.3; Beverages and tobacco 15.2; Mineral fuels, lubricants, etc. 41.2 (Refined petroleum products 39.8); Chemicals 22.2; Basic manufactures 51.3; Machinery and transport equipment 98.4; Miscellaneous manufactured articles 69.9; Total (incl. others) 377.9. *Exports f.o.b.:* Total 3.96.
Principal Trading Partners (US $ million): *Imports c.i.f.* (1996): Japan 8.2; Netherlands Antilles 40.1; United Kingdom 6.8; USA 289.7; Total (incl. others) 377.9. *Exports f.o.b.* (1994): USA 0.9; Total 2.6. *2003* (CI $ million): Total imports 553.5 (Fuel 43.2); Total exports 4.3.
Source: mainly UN, *International Trade Statistics Yearbook*.

TRANSPORT

Road Traffic (2000): Motor vehicles in use 24,791.
Shipping: *International Freight Traffic* ('000 metric tons): Goods loaded 735 (1990); Goods unloaded 239,138 (2000). *Cargo Vessels* (1995): Vessels 15, Calls at port 266. *Merchant Fleet* (vessels registered at 31 December 2004): 156; Total displacement 2,608,796 grt. (Source: Lloyd's Register-Fairplay, *World Fleet Statistics*).

TOURISM

Visitor Arrivals ('000): 1,548.9 (arrivals by air 334.1, cruise-ship passengers 1,214.8) in 2001; 1,877.6 (arrivals by air 302.7, cruise-ship passengers 1,574.8) in 2002; 2,112.5 (arrivals by air 293.5, cruise-ship passengers 1,819.0) in 2003.
Visitor Expenditure (estimates, US $ million): 559.2 in 2000; 585.1 in 2001; 607.0 in 2002.
Source: Caribbean Development Bank, *Social and Economic Indicators*.

COMMUNICATIONS MEDIA

Radio Receivers: 36,000 in use in 1997.
Television Receivers: 23,239 in use in 1999.
Telephones: 32,967 main lines in use in 2003.
Facsimile Machines: 116 in use in 1993.
Mobile Cellular Telephones (subscribers): 11,370 in 2000.

Internet Connections: 9,909 in 2003.
Daily Newspapers: 1 (circulation 10,500) in 2000.

EDUCATION

Institutions (2001): 10 state primary schools (with 2,246 pupils); 9 private primary and secondary schools (2,238 pupils); 3 state high schools (1,750 pupils); 1 community college; 1 private college (519 pupils).

Directory

The Constitution

The Constitution of 1959 was revised in 1972, 1992 and 1994. Under its terms, the Governor, who is appointed for four years, is responsible for defence and internal security, external affairs, and the public service. The Cabinet (known as the Executive Council until 2003) comprises the Chairman (the Governor), the Chief Secretary, the Financial Secretary, the Attorney-General, the Cabinet Secretary (all four of whom are appointed by the Governor) and five other Ministers elected by the Legislative Assembly from their own number. The Governor assigns ministerial portfolios to the elected members of the Cabinet. There are 15 elected members of the Legislative Assembly (elected by direct, universal adult suffrage for a term of four years) and three official members appointed by the Governor. The Speaker presides over the Assembly. The United Kingdom retains full control over foreign affairs. In May 2001 the Governor appointed a Constitutional Review Commission to make recommendations on changes to the Cayman Islands' political structure and processes.

The Government

Governor: STUART JACK (assumed office November 2005).

CABINET
(April 2006)

Chairman: STUART JACK (The Governor).
Chief Secretary and Minister of Internal and External Affairs*: GEORGE A. MCCARTHY.
Attorney-General and Minister of Legal Affairs*: SAMUEL W. BULGIN.
Financial Secretary*: KEN JEFFERSON.
Cabinet Secretary*: ORRETT CONNOR.
Leader of Government Business and Minister for District Administration, Planning, Agriculture and Housing: D. KURT TIBBETTS.
Minister for Health and Human Services: ANTHONY S. EDEN.
Minister for Education, Employment Relations, Youth, Sports and Culture: ALDEN MCLAUGHLIN.
Minister for Communications, Works and Infrastructure: V. ARDEN MCLEAN.
Minister for Tourism, Environment, Investment and Commerce: CHARLES CLIFFORD.

A District Commissioner, Kenny Ryan, represents the Governor on Cayman Brac and Little Cayman.
* Appointed by the Governor.

LEGISLATIVE ASSEMBLY

Members: The Chief Secretary, the Financial Secretary, the Attorney-General, and 15 elected members. The most recent election to the Assembly was on 11 May 2005. In February 1991 a Speaker was elected to preside over the Assembly (despite provision for such a post in the Constitution, the functions of the Speaker had hitherto been assumed by the Governor).
Speaker: EDNA MOYLE.
Leader of Government Business: D. KURT TIBBETTS.

GOVERNMENT OFFICES

Office of the Governor: Government Administration Bldg, Elgin Ave, George Town, Grand Cayman; tel. 949-7900; fax 949-7544; e-mail staffoff@candw.ky; internet www.gov.ky.

All official government offices and ministries are located in the Government Administration Bldg, Elgin Ave, George Town, Grand Cayman.

Political Organizations

People's Democratic Alliance (PDA): George Town, Grand Cayman; internet www.pda.ky; f. 2005; Leader LINFORD PIERSON.

People's Progressive Movement (PPM): POB 10526 APO, Grand Cayman; tel. 945-1776; e-mail ppm@governmentyoucantrust.org; internet www.governmentyoucantrust.org; f. 2002; Leader D. KURT TIBBETTS; Chair. ANTONY DUCKWORTH.

United Democratic Party (UDP): POB 10009, Grand Cayman; e-mail info@udp.ky; internet www.udp.ky; f. 2001; Leader W. MCKEEVA BUSH; Chair. BILLY REID.

Judicial System

There is a Grand Court of the Islands (with Supreme Court status), a Summary Court, a Youth Court and a Coroner's Court. The Grand Court has jurisdiction in all civil matters, admiralty matters, and in trials on indictment. Appeals lie to the Court of Appeal of the Cayman Islands and beyond that to the Privy Council in the United Kingdom. The Summary Courts deal with criminal and civil matters (up to a certain limit defined by law) and appeals lie to the Grand Court.

Chief Justice: ANTHONY SMELLIE.
President of the Court of Appeal: EDWARD ZACCA.
Solicitor-General: CHERYLL RICHARDS.
Registrar of the Grand Court of the Islands: DELENE M. BODDEN, Court's Office, George Town, Grand Cayman; tel. 949-4296; fax 949-9856.

Religion

CHRISTIANITY

The oldest-established denominations are (on Grand Cayman) the United Church of Jamaica and Grand Cayman (Presbyterian), and (on Cayman Brac) the Baptist Church. Anglicans are adherents of the Church in the Province of the West Indies (Grand Cayman forms part of the diocese of Jamaica). Within the Roman Catholic Church, the Cayman Islands forms part of the archdiocese of Kingston in Jamaica. Other denominations include the Church of God, Church of God (Full Gospel), Church of Christ, Seventh-day Adventist, Wesleyan Holiness, Jehovah's Witnesses, Church of the Latter Day Saints, Bahá'í and Church of God (Universal). In 1999 there were an estimated 90 churches in the Cayman Islands, including seven churches on Cayman Brac, and a Baptist Church on Little Cayman.

The Press

Cayman Islands Journal: The Compass Centre, Shedden Rd, POB 1365, George Town, Grand Cayman; tel. 949-5111; fax 949-7675; internet www.cayjournal.com; monthly; broadsheet business newspaper; Publr BRIAN UZZELL.

Cayman Net News: 85 North Sound Rd, Alissta Towers, POB 10707, Grand Cayman; tel. 946-6060; fax 949-0679; e-mail caymanet@candw.ky; internet www.caymannetnews.com; internet news service; publ. weekly newspaper (f. 2006); Publr and Editor-in-Chief DESMOND SEALES.

Caymanian Compass: The Compass Centre, Shedden Rd, POB 1365, George Town, Grand Cayman; tel. 949-5111; fax 949-7675; internet www.caycompass.com; f. 1965; 5 a week; Publr BRIAN UZZELL; circ. 10,000.

Chamber in Action: POB 1000, George Town, Grand Cayman; tel. 949-8090; fax 949-0220; e-mail info@caymanchamber.ky; internet www.caymanchamber.ky; f. 1965; monthly; newsletter of the Cayman Islands Chamber of Commerce; Editor WIL PINEAU; circ. 5,000.

Key to Cayman: The Compass Centre, Shedden Rd, POB 1365GT; tel. 949-5111; fax 949-2698; e-mail info@cfp.ky; internet www.caymanfreepress.com; 2 a year; free tourist magazine.

The Executive: Crewe Rd, George Town, POB 173 GT; tel. 949-5111; fax 949-7033; e-mail cfp@candw.ky; quarterly; circ. 7,500.

The New Caymanian: Grand Cayman; tel. 949-7414; fax 949-0036; weekly; Publr and Editor-in-Chief PETER JACKSON.

Publishers

Caribbean Publishing Co (Cayman) Ltd: 1 Paddington Pl., Suite 306, North Sound Way, POB 688, George Town, Grand Cayman; tel. 949-7027; fax 949-8366; internet www.caribbeanwhitepages.com; f. 1978.

Cayman Free Press Ltd: The Compass Centre, Shedden Rd, POB 1365, George Town, Grand Cayman; tel. 949-5111; fax 949-7675; e-mail info@cfp.ky; internet www.caymanfreepress.com; f. 1965.

Progressive Publications Ltd: Economy Printers Bldg, POB 764, George Town, Grand Cayman; tel. 949-5780; fax 949-7674.

Tower Marketing and Publishing: tel. 946-6000; fax 946-6001; e-mail info@tower.com.ky; internet www.tower.com.ky.

Broadcasting and Communications

TELECOMMUNICATIONS

Cable & Wireless (Cayman Islands) Ltd: Anderson Sq., POB 293, George Town, Grand Cayman; tel. 949-7800; fax 949-7962; e-mail cs@candw.ky; internet www.candw.ky; f. 1966; Cable & Wireless' monopoly over the telecommunications market ended in 2004; Man. Dir TONEY HEART; Gen. Man. TIMOTHY ADAM.

Digicel: POB 700, George Town, Grand Cayman; tel. 345-9433; fax 945-1351; e-mail caycustomercare@digicelgroup.com; internet www.digicelcayman.com; f. 2003; owned by an Irish consortium; acquired the operations of Cingular Wireless (fmrly those of AT & T Wireless) in the country in 2005 (www.cingular.ky).

TeleCayman: 4th Floor, Cayman Corporate Centre, POB 704 GT, Grand Cayman; e-mail gilbert.chalifoux@telecaymen.com; internet www.telecayman.com; Man. GILBERT CHALIFOUX.

BROADCASTING

Radio

Radio Cayman: Elgin Ave, POB 1110 GT, George Town, Grand Cayman; tel. 949-7799; fax 949-6536; e-mail radiocym@candw.ky; internet www.gov.ky/radiocayman; started full-time broadcasting 1976; govt-owned commercial radio station; service in English; Dir LOXLEY E. M. BANKS.

Radio Heaven 97 FM: POB 31481 SMB, Industrial Park, George Town, Grand Cayman; tel. 945-2797; fax 945-2707; e-mail heaven97@candw.ky; internet www.heaven97.com; f. 1997; Christian broadcasting, music and news; commercial station.

Radio ICCI-FM: International College of the Cayman Islands, Newlands, Grand Cayman; tel. 947-1100; fax 947-1210; e-mail icci@candw.ky; f. 1973; educational and cultural; Pres. Dr ELSA M. CUMMINGS.

Radio Z99.9 FM: 256 Crewe Rd, Suite 201, Crighton Bldg, Seven Mile Beach, POB 30110, Grand Cayman; tel. 945-1166; fax 945-1006; e-mail info@z99.ky; internet www.z99.ky; Gen. Man. RANDY MERREN.

Television

Cayman Adventist Television Network (CATN/TV): George Town, Grand Cayman; tel. 949-2739; internet www.tagnet.org/cayman/tv.html; f. 1996; local and international programmes, mainly religious.

Cayman Christian TV Ltd: POB 30213, George Town, Grand Cayman; Vice-Pres. FRED RUTTY; relays Christian broadcasting from the Trinity Broadcasting Network (USA).

CITN Cayman 27: POB 55G, Sound Way, George Town, Grand Cayman; tel. 945-2739; fax 945-1373; e-mail citn@Cayman27.com.ky; internet www.cayman27.com.ky; f. 1992 as Cayman International Television Network; 24 hrs daily; local and international news and US entertainment; 10-channel cable service of international programmes by subscription; Mans COLIN WILSON, JOANNE WILSON.

Weststar TV Ltd: POB 30563 SMB, Grand Cayman; e-mail weststar@candw.ky; internet www.weststartv.net.ky; Man. ROD HANSEN.

Finance

(cap. = capital; res = reserves; dep. = deposits; m. = million; brs = branches)

Banking facilities are provided by commercial banks. The islands have become an important centre for 'offshore' companies and trusts. At the end of 2003 there were 68,078 companies registered in the Cayman Islands. In 2005 there were also 438 licensed banks and trusts and some 6,268 registered mutual funds. The islands were well-known as a tax 'haven' because of the absence of any form of direct taxation. In mid-June 2005 assets held by banks registered in the Cayman Islands totalled US $1,265,000m.

Cayman Islands Monetary Authority: 80E Shedden Rd, Elizabethan Sq., POB 10052 APO, George Town, Grand Cayman; tel. 949-7089; fax 945-2532; e-mail admin@cimoney.com.ky; internet www.cimoney.com.ky; f. 1997; responsible for managing the Territory's currency and reserves and for regulating the financial services sector; cap. CI $7.1m., res CI $8.1m., dep. CI $51.6m. (Dec. 2002); Chair. TIMOTHY RIDLEY; Man. Dir CINDY SCOTLAND.

UNITED KINGDOM OVERSEAS TERRITORIES   *The Cayman Islands*

PRINCIPAL BANKS AND TRUST COMPANIES

AALL Trust and Banking Corpn Ltd: AALL Bldg, POB 1166, George Town, Grand Cayman; tel. 949-5588; fax 949-8265; Chair. ERIC MONSEN; Man. Dir KEVIN DOYLE.

Ansbacher (Cayman) Ltd: POB 887, George Town, Grand Cayman; tel. 949-8655; fax 949-7946; e-mail info@ansbacher.com.ky; internet www.ansbacher.com; f. 1971; cap. US $10.0m., res US $3.8m., dep. US $198.3m. (June 2002); Regional Man. Dir and Chair. MICHAEL L. HODGSON.

Atlantic Security Bank: POB 10340, George Town, Grand Cayman; f. 1981 as Banco de Crédito del Peru International, name changed as above 1986; Chair. DIONISIO ROMERO; Pres. CARLOS MUÑOZ.

Julius Baer Bank and Trust Co Ltd: Windward Bldg 3, Safe Haven Corporate Centre, West Bay Rd, POB 1100, George Town, Grand Cayman; tel. 949-7212; fax 949-0993; internet www.juliusbaer.ch; f. 1974; Man. Dir CHARLES FARRINGTON.

Banca Unione di Credito (Cayman) Ltd: Anderson Sq. Bldg, POB 10182 APO, George Town, Grand Cayman; tel. 949-7129; fax 949-2168; internet www.buc.ch; cap. Sw Fr 10.0m., dep. Sw Fr 704.4m., total assets Sw Fr 733.1m. (Dec. 2002); Gen. Man. URS FREI.

Banco Português do Atlântico: POB 30124, Grand Cayman; tel. 949-8322; fax 949-7743; e-mail bcpjvic@candw.ky; Gen. Man. HELENA SOARES CARNEIRO.

Banco Safra (Cayman Islands) Ltd: c/o Bank of Nova Scotia, POB 501, George Town, Grand Cayman; tel. 949-2001; fax 949-7097; f. 1993; cap. US $60.0, res US $124.5m., dep. US $254.3m. (Dec. 2002).

BANIF-Banco Internaçional do Funchal (Cayman) Ltd: Genesis Bldg, 3rd Floor, POB 32338 SMB, George Town, Grand Cayman; tel. 945-8060; fax 945-8069; e-mail banifcay@candw.ky; internet www.banif.pt; Chair. and CEO Dr JOAQUIM FILIPE MARQUES DOS SANTOS; Gen. Man. VALDEMAR B. LOPES.

Bank of America Trust and Banking Corpn (Cayman) Ltd: Fort St, POB 1092, George Town, Grand Cayman; tel. 949-7888; fax 949-7883; f. 1999; Man. Dir CHARLES FARRINGTON.

Bank of Bermuda (Cayman) Ltd: 3rd Floor, British American Tower, POB 513, George Town, Grand Cayman; tel. 949-9898; fax 949-7959; internet www.bankofbermuda.bm; f. 1968 as a trust; converted to a bank in 1988; total assets US $1,041m. (July 2001); Chair. HENRY B. SMITH; Man. Dir ALLEN BERNARDO.

Bank of Butterfield International (Cayman) Ltd: 1 Butterfield Place, 7 Main St, George Town, Grand Cayman; tel. 949-7055; fax 949-7761; e-mail info@butterfieldbank.ky; internet www.butterfieldbank.ky; f. 1967; subsidiary of N. T. Butterfield & Son Ltd, Bermuda; cap. US $16.5m., res US $35.0m., dep. US $1,092.7m. (June 2002); Chair. ALAN THOMPSON; Man. Dir CONOR J. O'DEA; 3 brs.

Bank of Nova Scotia: 6 Cardinal Ave, POB 689, George Town, Grand Cayman; tel. 949-7666; fax 949-0020; e-mail scotiaci@candw.ky; internet www.scotiabank.com; also runs trust company; Man. Dir FARRIED SULLIMAN.

Bank of Novia Scotia Trust Company (Cayman) Ltd: Scotiabank Bldg, 6 Cardinal Ave, POB 501 GT, George Town, Grand Cayman; tel. 949-2001; fax 949-7097; e-mail cayman@scotiatrust.com; internet www.scotiabank.com; Man. JOHN FLETCHER.

BankBoston Trust Co (Cayman Islands) Ltd: The Bank of Nova Scotia Trust Co (Cayman) Ltd, Scotiabank Bldg, 6 Cardinal Ave, POB 501, George Town, Grand Cayman; tel. 949-8066; fax 949-8080; e-mail info@maples.candw.ky; internet www.bankbostoninternational.com; f. 1997.

Bermuda Trust (Cayman) Ltd: 5th Floor, Bermuda House, POB 513, George Town, Grand Cayman; tel. 949-9898; fax 949-7959; internet www.bankofbermuda.bm; f. 1968 as Arawak Trust Co; became subsidiary of Bank of Bermuda in 1988; bank and trust services; Chair. JOSEPH JOHNSON; Man. Dir KENNETH GIBBS.

BFC Bank (Cayman) Ltd: Trafalgar Pl., POB 1765, George Town, Grand Cayman; tel. 949-8748; fax 949-8749; e-mail bfc@candw.ky; f. 1985; FC Financière de la Cité, Geneva, 99.9%; cap. US $0.8m., res US $3.7m., dep. US $33.5m. (March 2001); Chair. SIMON C. TAY; Resident Man. CHERRYLEE BUSH.

Caledonian Bank and Trust Ltd: POB 1043, George Town, Grand Cayman; tel. 949-0050; fax 949-8062; e-mail info@caledonian.com; internet www.caledonian.com; f. 1970; Chair. WILLIAM S. WALKER; Man. Dir DAVID S. SARGISON.

Cayman National Bank Ltd: Cayman National Bank Bldg, 4th Floor, 200 Elgin Ave, POB 1097, George Town, Grand Cayman; tel. 949-4655; fax 949-7506; e-mail cnb@caymannational.com; internet www.caymannational.com; f. 1974; subsidiary of Cayman National Corpn; cap. CI $2.4m., res CI $41.4m., dep. CI $466.0m. (Sept. 2002); Chair. ERIC J. CRUTCHLEY; Pres. DAVID J. MCCONNEY; 6 brs.

Coutts (Cayman) Ltd: Coutts House, 1446 West Bay Rd, POB 707, George Town, Grand Cayman; tel. 945-4777; fax 945-4799; internet www.coutts.com; f. 1967; fmrly NatWest International Trust Corpn (Cayman) Ltd; Chair. GERALD C. WILLIAMS; Man. Dir ANDREW GALLOWAY.

Deutsche Bank (Cayman) Ltd: Elizabethan Sq., POB 1984, George Town, Grand Cayman; tel. 949-8244; fax 949-8178; e-mail dmg-cay@candw.ky; internet www.dboffshore.com; f. 1983 as Morgan Grenfell (Cayman) Ltd; name changed to Deutsche Morgan Grenfell (Cayman) Ltd in 1996; name changed as above in 1998; cap. US $5.0m., res US $20.3m., dep. US $129.3m. (Dec. 1998); Chair. HANS JUERGEN KOCH; Branch Man. JANET HISLOP.

Deutsche Bank International Trust Co (Cayman) Ltd: POB 1984, George Town, Grand Cayman; tel. 949-8244; fax 949-7866; f. 1999.

Deutsche Girozentrale Overseas Ltd: POB 852, George Town, Grand Cayman; tel. 914-1066; fax 914-4060.

Fidelity Bank (Cayman) Ltd: POB 914, George Town, Grand Cayman; tel. 949-7822; fax 949-6064; e-mail info@fidelitycayman.com; internet www.fidelitycayman.com; Pres. and CEO BRETT HILL.

FirstCaribbean International Bank Ltd: POB 68, George Town, Grand Cayman; tel. 949-7300; fax 815-2292; internet www.firstcaribbeanbank.com; f. 2002 following merger of Caribbean operations of Barclays Bank PLC and CIBC; Exec. Chair. MICHAEL MANSOOR; CEO CHARLES PINK.

Fortis Bank (Cayman) Ltd: POB 2003, George Town, Grand Cayman; tel. 949-7942; fax 949-8340; e-mail phil.brown@ky.fortisbank.com; internet www.fortis.com; f. 1984 as Pierson, Heldring & Pierson (Cayman) Ltd; name changed to Mees Pierson (Cayman) Ltd in 1993; present name adopted in June 2000; Man. Dir ROGER HANSON.

HSBC Financial Services (Cayman) Ltd: Strathvale House, 2nd Floor, 90 North Church St, POB 1109, George Town, Grand Cayman; tel. 949-7755; fax 949-7634; e-mail hfsc.info@ky.hsbc.com; internet www.hsbc.ky; f. 1982; Dirs TOM CLARK, DAVID A. WHITEFIELD.

IBJ Whitehall Bank and Trust Co: West Wind Bldg, POB 1040, George Town, Grand Cayman; tel. 949-2849; fax 949-5409; Man. ROGER HEALY.

Intesa Bank Overseas Ltd: c/o Coutts (Cayman) Ltd, Coutts House, West Bay Rd, POB 707, George Town, Grand Cayman; tel. 945-4777; fax 945-4799; f. 1994 as Ambroveneto International Bank; name changed as above in March 1999; cap. US $10.0m., total assets US $1,339.8m. (Dec. 1999); Chair. FRANCESCO DE VECCHI; Man. Dirs RICHARD AUSTIN, ANDREW GALLOWAY.

LGT Bank in Liechtenstein (Cayman) Ltd: UBS House, POB 852, George Town, Grand Cayman; tel. 949-7676; fax 949-8512; internet www.lgt-bank-in-liechtenstein.com.

Lloyds TSB Bank and Trust (Cayman) Ltd: Grand Cayman; tel. 949-7854; fax 949-0090; Man. ROGER C. BARKER.

Mercury Bank and Trust Ltd: POB 2424, George Town, Grand Cayman; tel. 949-0800; fax 949-0295; Man. VOLKER MERGENTHALER.

Merrill Lynch Bank and Trust Co (Cayman) Ltd: POB 1164, George Town, Grand Cayman; tel. 949-8206; fax 949-8895; internet www.ml.com.

Royal Bank of Canada: 24 Shedden Rd, POB 245, Grand Cayman; tel. 949-4600; fax 949-7396; internet www.royalbank.com; Man. HARRY C. CHISHOLM.

Royal Bank of Canada Trust Co (Cayman) Ltd: 24 Shedden Rd, POB 1586 GT, George Town, Grand Cayman; tel. 949-9107; fax 949-5777; internet www.rbcprivatebanking.com/cayman-islands.html; Man. Dir RALPH AWREY.

UBS (Cayman Islands) Ltd: UBS House, 227 Elgin Ave, POB 852, George Town, Grand Cayman; tel. 914-1060; fax 914-4060; internet www.ubs.com/cayman-funds; CEO WALTER EGGENSCHWILER.

Development Bank

Cayman Islands Development Bank: Cayman Financial Centre, 36B Dr Roy's Dr., POB 2576, George Town; tel. 949-7511; fax 949-6168; e-mail cidb@gov.ky; f. 2002; replaced the Housing Devt Corpn and the Agricultural and Industrial Devt Bd; Devt Finance Institution Gen. Man. ANGELA J. MILLER.

Banking Association

Cayman Islands Bankers' Association: Macdonald Sq., Fort St, POB 676, George Town, Grand Cayman; tel. 949-0330; fax 945-1448; e-mail ciba@candw.ky; Pres. TIMOTHY GODBER.

STOCK EXCHANGE

Cayman Islands Stock Exchange (CSX): 4th Floor, Elizabethan Sq., POB 2408, George Town, Grand Cayman; tel. 945-6060; fax 945-6061; e-mail csx@csx.com.ky; internet www.csx.com.ky; f. 1996; 872 cos listed, incl. 788 mutual funds (Feb. 2005); CEO VALIA THEODORAKI.

INSURANCE

Several foreign companies have agents in the islands. A total of 672 captive insurance companies were registered at the end of 2003. In particular, the islands are a leading international market for health insurance. Local companies include the following:

British Caymanian Insurance Agency Ltd: Elizabethan Sq., POB 74 GT, Grand Cayman; tel. 949-8699; fax 949-8411.

Caribbean Home Insurance: Commerce House 7, Genesis Close, POB 931, George Town, Grand Cayman; tel. 949-7788; fax 949-8422.

Cayman General Insurance Co Ltd: Cayman National Bank Bldg, 200 Elgin Ave, POB 2171, George Town, Grand Cayman; tel. 949-7028; fax 949-7457; e-mail cgi@caymannational.com; internet www.caymannational.com; Chair. BENSON O. EBANKS; Pres. DANNY A. SCOTT.

Cayman Insurance Centre: POB 10056, Cayman Business Park; tel. 948-1382; internet www.cic.com.ky; Pres. LINDA CHAPMAN-KY.

Cayman Islands National Insurance Co (CINICO): Phase 3, 1st Floor, Elizabethan Sq., POB 512 GT, Grand Cayman; tel. 949-8101; fax 949-8226; internet www.cinico.ky; CEO and Pres. RON SULISZ.

Island Heritage Insurance Co Ltd: POB GT, Grand Cayman; tel. 949-7280; fax 945-6765; e-mail info@islandheritage.com.ky; internet www.island-heritage.com; Chair. ROBERT CLEMENTS.

Global Life Assurance Co Ltd: Global House, North Church St, POB 1087, Grand Cayman; tel. 949-8211; fax 949-8262; f. 1992; Man. WINSOME RUDDOCK.

Sagicor Life of the Cayman Islands Ltd: 198 North Church St, George Town, Grand Cayman; tel. 949-8211; fax 949-8262; e-mail global@candw.ky; internet www.themutual.com; f. 2004 by merger between Global Life and Capital Life; Man. MICHEL TRUMBACH.

Trade and Industry

CHAMBER OF COMMERCE

Cayman Islands Chamber of Commerce: Macdonald Sq., Fort St, POB 1000, George Town, Grand Cayman; tel. 949-8090; fax 949-0220; e-mail info@caymanchamber.ky; internet www.caymanchamber.ky; f. 1965; Pres. MORGAN DACOSTA; Chief Exec. WIL PINEAU; 730 local mems.

TRADE ASSOCIATION

Cayman Islands Financial Services Association (CIFSA): POB 11048, Grand Cayman; tel. 946-6000; fax 946-6001; e-mail info@caymanfinances.com; internet www.caymanfinances.com; f. 2003; Dir EDUARDO D'ANGELO P. SILVA.

EMPLOYERS' ORGANIZATION

Labour Office: 4th Floor, Tower Bldg, Grand Cayman; tel. 949-0941; fax 949-6057; Dir DALE M. BANKS.

The Cayman Islands have had a labour law since 1942, but only three trade unions have been registered.

UTILITIES

Electricity

Caribbean Utilities Co. Ltd (CUC): Corporate HQ & Plant, North Sound Rd, POB 38, George Town, Grand Cayman; tel. 949-5200; fax 949-4621; e-mail info@cuc.ky; internet www.cuc-cayman.com; Pres. and CEO PETER A. THOMSON; Chair. DAVID RITCH.

Cayman Brac Power and Light Co. Ltd: Stake Bay Point, POB 95, Stake Bay, Cayman Brac; tel. 948-2224; fax 948-2204.

West Indies Power Corpn Ltd: CUC Corporate Centre, North Sound Rd, POB 38, George Town, Grand Cayman; tel. 949-2250.

Water

Cayman Islands Water Authority: 13G Red Gate Rd, POB 1104, George Town, Grand Cayman; tel. 949-6352; fax 949-0094; e-mail wac@candw.ky.

Consolidated Water Co Ltd (CWCO): Windward 3, 4th Floor, Regatta Office Park, POB 1114, George Town, Grand Cayman; tel. 945-4277; fax 949-2957; e-mail info@cwco.com; internet www.cwco.com; f. 1973; Pres. and CEO FREDERICK W. MCTAGGART; Chair. JEFFREY M. PARKER.

Transport

ROADS

There are some 406 km (252 miles) of motorable roads, of which 304 km (189 miles) are surfaced with tarmac. The road network connects all districts on Grand Cayman and Cayman Brac (which has 76 km (47 miles) of motorable road), and there are 27 miles of motorable road on Little Cayman (of which about 11 miles are paved).

SHIPPING

George Town is the principal port and a new port facility was opened in July 1977. Cruise liners, container ships and smaller cargo vessels ply between the Cayman Islands, Florida, Jamaica and Costa Rica. There is no cruise-ship dock in the Cayman Islands. Ships anchor off George Town and ferry passengers ashore to the North or South Dock Terminals in George Town. In February 2002 the Florida Caribbean Cruise Ship Association agreed to provide up to US $10m. for improvements to the port's cruise-ship facilities. In 1993 the Government limited the number of cruise-ship passengers to 6,000 per day. The port of Cayman Brac is Creek; there are limited facilities on Little Cayman. In December 2004 the shipping register comprised 156 vessels totalling 2,608,796 grt.

Port Authority of the Cayman Islands: Harbour Dr., POB 1358, George Town, Grand Cayman; tel. 949-2055; fax 949-5820; e-mail info@caymanport.com; internet www.caymanport.com; Port Dir PAUL HURLSTON.

Cayman Freight Shipping Ltd: Mirco Commercial Centre, 2nd Floor, Industrial Park, POB 1372, George Town, Grand Cayman; tel. 949-4977; fax 949-8402; e-mail cfssl@candw.ky; internet www.seaboardmarinecayman.ky; Man. Dir ROBERT FOSTER.

Cayman Islands Shipping Registry: Kirk House, 3rd Floor, 22 Albert Panton St, POB 2256, George Town, Grand Cayman; tel. 949-8831; fax 949-8849; e-mail cisrky@cishipping.com; internet www.cishipping.com; Dir A. JOEL WALTON.

Thompson Shipping Co Ltd: Terminal Eastern Ave, POB 188, George Town, Grand Cayman; tel. 949-8044; fax 949-8349; f. 1977.

CIVIL AVIATION

There are two international airports in the Territory: Owen Roberts International Airport, 3.5 km (2 miles) from George Town, and Gerrard Smith International Airport on Cayman Brac. Both are capable of handling jet-engined aircraft. Edward Bodden Airport on Little Cayman can cater for light aircraft. Several scheduled carriers serve the islands.

Civil Aviation Authority of the Cayman Islands: Unit 4, Cayman Grand Harbour, POB 10277 APO, George Town, Grand Cayman; tel. 949-7811; fax 949-0761; e-mail civil.aviation@caacayman.com; internet www.caacayman.com; f. 1987; Dir-Gen. RICHARD SMITH.

Cayman Airways Ltd: 233 Owen Roberts Dr., POB 10092 APO, Grand Cayman; tel. 949-8200; fax 949-7607; e-mail customerrelations@caymanairways.net; internet www.caymanairways.com; f. 1968; wholly govt-owned since 1977; operates local services and scheduled flights to Jamaica, Honduras and the USA; Chair. ROY MCTAGGART; CEO MIKE ADAM.

Island Air: Airport Rd, POB 2433, George Town, Grand Cayman; tel. 949-5252; fax 949-7044; e-mail iair@candw.ky; operates daily scheduled services between Grand Cayman, Cayman Brac and Little Cayman.

Tourism

The Cayman Islands are a major tourist destination, the majority of visitors coming from North America. The tourism industry was badly affected by the damage caused by 'Hurricane Ivan' in September 2004, and a major reconstruction effort was in progress in early 2005. The beaches and opportunities for diving in the offshore reefs form the main attraction for most tourists. Major celebrations include Pirates' Week in October and the costume festivals on Grand Cayman (Batabano), at the end of April, and, one week later, on Cayman Brac (Brachanal). In 1995 there were an estimated 7,648 hotel beds. In 2003 there were approximately 293,500 arrivals by air and some 1,819,000 cruise visitors. In 2002 the tourism industry earned an estimated US $607.0m.

Cayman Islands Department of Tourism: Cricket Sq., POB 67, George Town, Grand Cayman; tel. 949-0623; fax 949-4053; internet www.caymanislands.ky; f. 1965; Dir PILAR BUSH.

Cayman Islands Tourism Association (CITA): 73 Lawrence Blvd, Islander Complex, POB 31086 SMB, Grand Cayman; tel. and fax 949-8522; fax 946-8522; e-mail info@cita.ky; internet www.cita.ky; f. 2001 as a result of the amalgamation of the Cayman Tourism Alliance and the Cayman Islands Hotel and Condominium Asscn; Pres. MARK BASTIS.

Sister Islands Tourism Association: Stake Bay, POB 187, Cayman Brac; tel. and fax 948-1345; e-mail sita@candw.ky; internet www.sisterislands.com; Pres. MAX HILLIER.

THE FALKLAND ISLANDS

Introductory Survey

Location, Climate, Language, Religion, Flag, Capital

The Falkland Islands, comprising two large islands and about 200 smaller ones, are in the south-western Atlantic Ocean, about 770 km (480 miles) north-east of Cape Horn, South America. The climate is generally cool, with strong winds (mainly westerly) throughout the year. The mean annual temperature is 6°C (42°F), while average annual rainfall is 635 mm (25 ins). The language is English. Most of the inhabitants profess Christianity, with several denominations represented. The flag is the British 'Blue Ensign', with the colony's coat of arms (a shield showing a white and violet ram standing in green grass, on a blue background, above a sailing ship bearing red crosses on its pennants and five six-pointed stars on its central sail, on three white horizontal wavy lines, with the motto 'Desire the Right' on a scroll beneath) on a white disc in the centre of the flag. The capital is Stanley, on East Falkland Island.

Recent History

The first recorded landing on the islands was made from a British ship in 1690, when the group was named after Viscount Falkland, then Treasurer of the Royal Navy. French sailors named the islands 'Les Malouines' (after their home port of Saint-Malo, from which the Spanish name 'Islas Malvinas' is derived. A French settlement was established in 1764 on the island of East Falkland, but in 1767 France relinquished its rights to the territory to Spain, which then ruled the adjacent regions of South America. Meanwhile, a British expedition annexed West Falkland in 1765, and a garrison was established. The British settlement, formed in 1765–66, was recognized by Spain in 1771 but withdrawn in 1774. The Spanish garrison was withdrawn in 1811.

When the United Provinces of the River Plate (now Argentina) gained independence from Spain in 1816, the Falkland Islands had no permanent inhabitants, although they provided temporary bases for sealing and whaling activities by British and US vessels. In 1820 an Argentine ship was sent to the islands to proclaim Argentine sovereignty as successor to Spain. An Argentine settlement was founded in 1826 but most of its occupants were expelled by a US warship in 1831. The remaining Argentines were ejected by a British expedition in 1832, and British sovereignty was established in 1833.

The islands became a Crown Colony of the United Kingdom, administered by a British-appointed Governor. However, Argentina did not relinquish its claim, and negotiations to resolve the dispute began in 1966 at the instigation of the UN. The inhabitants of the islands, nearly all British by descent, consistently expressed their desire to remain under British sovereignty.

After routine talks between delegations of the British and Argentine Governments in New York in February 1982, the Argentine foreign ministry announced that it would seek other means to resolve the dispute. Rumours of a possible invasion had begun in the Argentine press in January, and Argentina's military regime took advantage of a British protest at the presence of a group of Argentine scrap merchants, who had made an unauthorized landing on South Georgia (q.v.) in March and had raised an Argentine flag, to invade the Falkland Islands on 2 April. A small contingent of British marines was overwhelmed, the British Governor, Rex (later Sir Rex) Hunt, was expelled and an Argentine military governorship was established. The USA and the UN attempted (unsuccessfully) to mediate, in an effort to prevent military escalation. British forces, which had been dispatched to the islands immediately after the Argentine invasion, recaptured South Georgia on 25 April. The Argentine forces on the Falklands formally surrendered on 14 June, after a conflict in the course of which about 750 Argentine, 255 British and three Falklanders' lives were lost.

The Governor returned to the islands as Civil Commissioner on 25 June 1982, and Britain established a 'protection zone' around the islands, extending 150 nautical miles (278 km) off shore, as well as a garrison of about 4,000 troops. The British Government began an investigation into the possibilities of developing the islands' economy, and in November agreed to grant the Falkland Islanders full British citizenship. In November 1983 the post of Chief Executive of the Falkland Islands Government was created, in combination with the executive vice-chairmanship of the newly formed Falkland Islands Development Corporation. The Civil Commissioner, Sir Rex Hunt, retired in September 1985, whereupon a new Governor was appointed.

The issue of the sovereignty of the Falkland Islands remained a major impediment to the normalization of relations between Argentina and the United Kingdom. The Argentine Government refused to agree to a formal declaration that hostilities were ended until the United Kingdom agreed to participate in negotiations over sovereignty, while the United Kingdom refused to negotiate until Argentina had formally ended hostilities.

Following the return to civilian rule in Argentina in December 1983, the newly elected President, Dr Raúl Alfonsín, stated his Government's desire to seek a negotiated settlement to the dispute over the Falkland Islands. In October 1984 the Argentine Government removed restrictions on British companies and interests in Argentina as a possible prelude to resuming negotiations.

The British Government's refusal to discuss the issue of sovereignty, and its insistence on the paramountcy of the Falkland Islanders' wishes, were reflected in the new Constitution for the Falklands (approved by the islands' Legislative Council in January 1985), which guaranteed the islanders' right to self-determination.

The number of British troops stationed on the islands was reduced, following the opening, in mid-1985, of a new military airport at Mount Pleasant, about 30 km south-west of Stanley, enabling rapid reinforcement of the garrison, if necessary. In July the British Government ended its ban on Argentine imports, which had been in force since 1982. In October elections took place on the Falklands for a new Legislative Council. In the same month, South Georgia and the South Sandwich Islands (see separate section) ceased to be dependencies of the Falkland Islands, although the Governor of the Falkland Islands was to be (ex officio) Commissioner for the territories.

In 1986 parliamentary delegations from the United Kingdom and Argentina conducted exploratory talks. However, the British Government remained intransigent on the issue of the sovereignty of the islands. In early 1986 Argentina's continued claim to the naval 'protection zone' was manifested in attacks on foreign fishing vessels by Argentine gunboats. In October Britain unilaterally declared a fisheries conservation and management zone extending 150 nautical miles (278 km) around the islands, with effect from February 1987, to prevent the over-fishing of the waters. The imposition of this zone, whose radius coincided with that of the naval protection zone, was condemned by the majority of UN members, as was Britain's rejection, in November 1986, of an offer by Argentina to declare a formal end to hostilities in exchange for the abolition of the protection zone. The resignation, in June 1989, of three members of the Legislative Council, in protest against a proposed agricultural grants scheme, prompted the dissolution of the legislative body. In the ensuing parliamentary elections in October, eight independent candidates, all of whom vigorously opposed renewing links, at any level, with Argentina, defeated 10 other candidates to take all the elective seats.

In October 1993 25 independent candidates contested elections to the eight elective seats of the Legislative Council. The successful candidates had all expressed a reluctance to develop closer contacts with Argentina as long as the Argentine Government continued to claim sovereignty over the islands.

At elections to the Legislative Council held on 9 October 1997, the eight elective seats were secured by independent candidates, all of whom expressed their determination not to enter into negotiations with Argentina regarding the islands' sovereignty.

On 22 November 2001 a general election took place to elect members to a new Legislative Council. Of the eight elected, only three members had not served on the Legislative Council before. In a concurrent referendum the electorate voted against changing the two-constituency system (the Stanley constituency and the Camp constituency) to a single constituency for legislative elections.

A general election was held on 17 November 2005 in which eight independent candidates, of whom five were new members, were elected to the Legislative Council.

Beginning in 1982 the UN General Assembly voted annually, by an overwhelming majority, in favour of the resumption of negotiations between Argentina and the United Kingdom. The British Government consistently declined to engage in such dialogue. However, relations between Argentina and the United Kingdom improved, following the election, in May 1989, of a new Argentine President, Carlos Saúl Menem, who initially indicated that his country would be willing to suspend temporarily its demand that the issue of the sovereignty of the Falkland Islands be discussed, in the interests of the restoration of full diplomatic and commercial relations with the United Kingdom. In October a meeting of British and Argentine representatives, which took place in Madrid, Spain, culminated in the formal cessation of all hostilities, and the re-establishment of diplomatic relations at consular level. Restrictions on Argentine merchant vessels with regard to the naval protection zone around the Falkland Islands were also eased. In the following month, however, the United Kingdom announced that it was to increase the extent of its territorial waters around the islands from three to 12 nautical miles, in spite of protests from the Argentine authorities. In February 1990 Argentina and the United Kingdom conducted further negotiations in Madrid, as a result of which the two countries re-established full diplomatic relations. It was also announced that the naval protection zone around the Falkland Islands was to be modified in March, and that mutually agreed military procedures, that would ensure the security of the region, would take effect. In mid-1993 the further reduction of military restrictions around the islands was announced by both Governments.

Following successful negotiations between Argentina and the United Kingdom in Madrid in November 1990, an agreement regarding the protection and conservation of the South Atlantic fishing area was announced, whereby a temporary ban on fishing was to be extended, from late December, to an area incorporating an additional 50-mile (93-km) semicircular region to the east of the islands, beyond the existing 150-mile fishing zone. (The agreement was renewed in December 1991 and 1992.) The two sides also agreed to establish a South Atlantic Fisheries Commission, which was to meet at least twice in every year that the ban remained in place, in order to discuss fishing activity and conservation in the region. Throughout 1990 the Falkland Islands Government had appealed to the British Government to exercise its legal right under international law to extend the fisheries conservation and management zone, claiming that over-fishing of the previously well-stocked waters just beyond the 150-mile limit by vessels from Taiwan and the Republic of Korea (ignoring previously agreed voluntary restraints on fishing in the area) had seriously depleted stocks and posed a threat to the islands' lucrative squid-fishing industry.

In May 1993 the British Government announced that it would extend from 12 to 200 nautical miles its territorial jurisdiction in the waters surrounding South Georgia and the South Sandwich Islands. In December the Argentine Government indicated its acceptance of the United Kingdom's proposed extension of fishing rights around the Falkland Islands from 150 to 200 miles, in order to allow the islanders to fulfil an annual squid-fishing quota of 150,000 metric tons (effective from January 1994). The Argentine quota was agreed at 220,000 tons (compared with an estimated catch of 130,000 tons in 1992). In August 1994 the British Government unilaterally decided to extend its fisheries conservation zone north of the islands, thereby annexing a small but lucrative fishing ground (not previously protected by British or Argentine legislation) that was being plundered by foreign fishing vessels. In January 1997 the United Kingdom and Argentina agreed to resume negotiations on a long-term fisheries agreement that would include the disputed waters around the islands. Following the release of a Joint Declaration between the two Governments on 14 July 1999, both Governments agreed to co-operate to combat illegal fishing in the South West Atlantic and to ensure the sustainability of fish stocks in the region.

In November 1991 the Governments of both Argentina and the United Kingdom claimed rights of exploration and exploitation of the sea-bed and the subsoil of the continental shelf around the Falkland Islands (which are believed to be rich in petroleum reserves). In April 1992 the Falkland Islands Government invited tenders for seismic reports of the region. In December 1993 the British Geological Survey reported that preliminary seismic investigations indicated deposits in excess of those located in British North Sea oilfields. A bilateral agreement on petroleum and gas exploration in an area of 18,000 sq km, south-west of the islands, was concluded in New York in September 1994. A joint hydrocarbons commission would regulate licensing in the area, examining bids from Anglo-Argentine joint ventures (in which case taxes would be levied on operators by the respective Governments) or by third countries (from which royalties on revenues would be exacted by the Falkland Islands Government at a rate expected to approach 9%). The successful conclusion of the agreement appeared to dissipate Argentine objections, voiced earlier in the year, to the Falkland Islands' unilateral offer of rights to drill in 19 areas (comprising 44,000 sq km not covered by the Anglo-Argentine agreement) to the north and south of the islands. Licences to explore for hydrocarbons were awarded to five international consortia in October 1996. The possibility that commercial quantities of petroleum might be discovered prompted renewed discussion as to the amount of any future royalties exacted by the Falkland Islands Government that should be returned to the Government of the United Kingdom. In early 1997 the British Government indicated that it expected to benefit considerably from any such royalties, while the Falkland Islands administration proposed that some of the revenue could be used to finance the islands' defence expenditure (currently funded by the United Kingdom). Meanwhile, the Argentine Government claimed that it should be entitled to benefit from the discovery of petroleum in the region: draft legislation presented to Congress provided for the imposition of sanctions on petroleum companies and fishing vessels operating in Falkland Islands waters without Argentine authorization, in addition to the levying of 3% royalties from the sale of petroleum discovered in the area.

In late 1996 the Argentine Government suggested, for the first time, that it might consider shared sovereignty of the Falkland Islands with the United Kingdom. The proposal was firmly rejected by the British Government and by the Falkland Islanders, who reiterated their commitment to persuading the UN Special Political and Decolonization Committee to adopt a clause granting the islanders the right to self-determination.

In May 1999 formal negotiations between the Falkland Islands and Argentina took place in the United Kingdom. Issues under discussion included co-operation in fishing and petroleum exploration, Argentine access to the islands and the resumption of air links with mainland South America. (In March Chile had ended its country's regular air services to the islands in protest at the British Government's continued detention of Gen. Pinochet; Uruguay subsequently agreed not to establish an air link with the islands unless flights were routed via the Argentine capital.) The sovereignty of the Falkland Islands was not scheduled for discussion. Four of the islands' councillors also attended the three days of talks, thereby occasioning the first direct talks between Falkland Islanders and the Argentine Government. The dialogue continued in July in New York and London. On 14 July a joint Argentine-British declaration was issued that eliminated the restrictions on travel by Argentine citizens to the Falkland Islands and re-established airline services by the Chilean carrier LanChile between South America and the Falkland Islands (with a stop-over in Argentina). It was also agreed to increase bilateral co-operation between Argentina and the Falkland Islands on combating illegal fishing and conservation of fish stocks. Symbolic gestures included allowing the construction of a monument to the Argentine war dead at their cemetery on the islands (permission was finally granted in March 2002), while in return the Argentine Government would cease to use the Spanish names given to Falklands locations during the 1982 occupation. The agreement did not affect claims to sovereignty. Even so, the round of talks provoked demonstrations by an estimated 500 people on the Falkland Islands. The protests resumed on 16 October when the first flights carrying Argentine visitors arrived in the Falklands. In July 2000 the Anglo-Argentine dialogue on joint petroleum and gas exploration was suspended by mutual agreement for an indefinite period of time.

On the 20th anniversary of the landing of Argentine troops on the Falkland Islands in April 2002, the new Argentine President, Eduardo Duhalde, promised to recover the Falkland Islands by non-violent means. On 3 December Howard Pearce succeeded Donald Lamont as Governor of the Falkland Islands and Commissioner of South Georgia and the Sandwich Islands. In March 2003 Chris Simpkins became the new Chief Executive; he replaced Michael Blanch, who had reached the end of his three-year contract.

In May 2003 the new Argentine President, Néstor Kirchner, promised in his inaugural speech to maintain his country's claim to the Falkland Islands; he reiterated that commitment in January 2005, and once more appealed for the resumption of bilateral negotiations. In November 2003 Argentina began to demand that the increasingly frequent air-charter services flying from the Falkland Islands to Chile obtain permission to use Argentine airspace. The decision was intended to pressure the British Government into reversing its policy of not allowing Argentine airlines to fly to the Falkland Islands. The services were suspended in January 2004 after the British Government lodged objections to the Argentine demands; the situation seemed likely to damage the territory's burgeoning tourism trade. In March a British proposal for the resumption of direct charter flights from Argentina to the Falkland Islands was rejected by the Kirchner Government, which continued to demand that an Argentine carrier be authorized to benefit from the increased passenger traffic between the Falkland Islands and mainland South America. A reference to the Islands was included in a draft of the constitutional treaty of the European Union, to which the Argentina strongly objected. At a meeting of the UN's Special Committee on Decolonization, held in mid-2005, the Falkland Islands appealed for the right to self-determination; the Committee requested that the Governments of Argentina and the United Kingdom resume negotiations. In July of the same year it was announced that Alan Huckle, Governor of Anguilla, would succeed Howard Pearce as Governor of the Falkland Islands from June 2006.

Government

Administration is conducted by the appointed Governor (who is the personal representative of the British monarch), aided by the Executive Council, comprising two *ex-officio* members and three members elected by the Legislative Council. The Legislative Council is composed of two *ex-officio* members and eight elected members. Voting is by universal adult suffrage.

Defence

In August 2005 there were approximately 1,200 British troops stationed on the islands (including 450 members of the army and 750 members of the air force). The total cost of the conflict in 1982 and of building and maintaining a garrison for four years was estimated at £2,560m. The current annual cost of maintaining the garrison is approximately £70m. Total expenditure in 1999/2000 was £71.1m. There is a Falkland Islands Defence Force, composed of islanders.

Economic Affairs

According to government estimates, gross domestic product (GDP) was some £70m. in 2001, with GDP per head of £24,030 and annual growth of an estimated 2%. Gross national income was estimated to have increased from £5m. in 1980 to more than £50m. in 2000.

Most of the agricultural land on the Falkland Islands is devoted to the rearing of sheep. However, the land is poor and more than four acres are required to support one animal. In the late 1990s annual exports of wool were valued at some £3.5m. Declining international wool prices encouraged agricultural diversification, such as the pursuit of organic farming, the breeding of cashmere goats and also the development of meat production (an abbattoir was constructed to meet European Union standards, incurring expenditure of £372,332 in 2002 and a further £678,371 in 2003). Some vegetables are produced (notably in a hydroponic market garden), and there are small dairy herds. From 1987, when a licensing system was introduced for foreign vessels fishing within a 150-nautical-mile conservation and management zone (see Recent History), the economy was diversified and the islands' annual income increased considerably. Although revenue from the sale of licences declined in the 1990s following the Argentine Government's commencement of the sale of fishing licences in 1993, licences (and transhipments) totalled £22.9m. in 2001/02, 51.5% of total budget revenue in that year. The revenue funds social provisions and economic development programmes. In the late 1980s about one-third of the world's total catch of *illex* and *loligo* squid was derived from this fishing zone. However, over-fishing in the area surrounding the conservation zone had a detrimental effect on stocks of fish in the islands' waters, and frequently the Government has been obliged to call an early halt to the exploitation of both squid types, as it did in both 2004 and 2005. The 2006 season for *illex* squid fishing began in mid-February and by the end of March approximately 40 licences had been sold. According to The Virement Report 2005/2006, revenues from fishing licences increased to approximately £14.1m. by March 2006, compared with the previous year's figure of £13.7m.

Manufacturing activity on the islands reflects the predominance of the agricultural sector: a wool mill on West Falkland produces yarns for machine knitting, hand knitting and weaving. Several small companies in the Falklands produce garments for local and export sales. Some fish-processing also takes place on East Falkland.

The Falkland Islands are heavily dependent on imports of all fuels, except peat; households primarily depend on kerosene and diesel for heating purposes. Wind power is used in many remote locations to offset this dependence and reduce pollution of the atmosphere. The Falkland Islands Government licensed five consortia to explore for hydrocarbons in waters north of the islands in 1996. These companies, including Shell, Amerada Hess and LASMO, drilled six exploration wells in 1998. Five of the six wells had minor traces of hydrocarbons present, but no commercial quantities of petroleum were found in the initial phase of drilling. A British prospecting company has been granted an exploration licence to search for minerals on the islands. Mineral sands including garnet and rutile were being appraised, while more valuable minerals such as gold were being sought. In July 2002 the Falkland Islands Government granted 10 petroleum exploration licences to the Falklands Hydrocarbon Consortium (comprising Global Petroleum Ltd, Hardman Resources Ltd and Falkland Islands Holdings) for an area covering 57,700 sq km to the south of the islands. Activity was renewed in both the minerals and hydrocarbons sectors in 2005.

The Falkland Islands Development Corporation oversees the islands' economic development on behalf of the Government. Since the 1980s the Government has sought to promote the development of the tourism sector. Tourism, and in particular 'eco-tourism', was developing rapidly in this century, and the number of visitors staying on the Falklands Islands had grown to some 3,000 a year, while around 40,000 tourists per year sail through Stanley harbour on their way to Antarctica and sub-antarctic islands such as South Georgia. The sale of postage stamps and coins represents a significant source of income; the value of sales of the former was £296,229 in 1996/97, while the value of sales of the latter totalled £49,351 in 1995/96.

In 2000 the islands recorded an estimated trade surplus of £28,041,897. Fish, most of which is purchased by the United Kingdom, Spain and Chile, is the islands' most significant export. The principal imports are fuel, provisions, alcoholic beverages, building materials and clothing. In early 2001 the Government brought 100 reindeer from the South Georgia Islands (with the aim of increasing the number to 10,000 over the following 20 years) in order to export venison to Scandinavia and Chile.

Ordinary budget estimates for the financial year 2001/02 envisaged revenue of £44.5m. and expenditure of £51.7m. The islands are self-sufficient in all areas except defence. The annual rate of inflation averaged 2.5% in 1995–2003; consumer prices increased by 0.7% in 2002 and by 1.2% in 2003. There is a significant shortage of local labour on the islands.

Since 1982 the economy of the Falkland Islands has enjoyed a period of strong and sustained growth, partly owing to substantial investment by the British Government during the 1980s, but primarily as a result of the introduction of the fisheries licensing scheme in 1987. It was anticipated that royalties derived from the sale of licences for the exploration and exploitation of hydrocarbons would strengthen the economy further. The services sector expanded rapidly during the late 1990s, while the importance of the agricultural sector has decreased, not least because of its reliance on direct and indirect subsidies. The revenues from the sale of fishing licences fund social provisions and economic development programmes, including subsidies to the wool industry, which is in long-term decline, owing to the oversupply of that commodity on the international market. The Government's development plan emphasized agricultural diversification and the promotion of tourism as its main economic aims; it also sought to develop services and to encourage the growth of industries related to the fishing industry (such as freezer plants and mussel farms). Following the early closure, for conservation reasons, of the *illex* fishery and a consequential reduction in licensing fees, the Falkland Islands Government presented an austere budget for the 2004/05 fiscal year; as a result, a budget deficit of £1.4m. was estimated by the end of the financial year, an improvement on the £3.0m. anticipated at the beginning of the year. The improved performance was attributed largely to a net increase in revenue of £3.9m., generated mainly by taxation and investment. Budget forecasts estimated the operating revenue for 2005/06 to be £43.5m., with a budget deficit of £0.5m.

Education

Education is compulsory, and is provided free of charge, for children between the ages of five and 16 years. Facilities are available for further study beyond the statutory school-leaving age. In 2003 203 pupils were instructed by 18 teachers at the primary school in Stanley, while 160 pupils received instruction from 18 teachers at the secondary school in the capital; further facilities existed in rural districts, with six peripatetic teachers visiting younger children for two out of every six weeks (older children boarded in a hostel in Stanley). Total expenditure on education and training was estimated at £3.5m. for 2001/02.

Public Holidays

2006: 1 January (New Year's Day), 14 April (Good Friday), 21 April (HM the Queen's Birthday), 14 June (Liberation Day), 2 October (Spring Holiday), 8 December (Anniversary of the Battle of the Falkland Islands in 1914), 25–29 December (Christmas).

2007: 1 January (New Year's Day), 6 April (Good Friday), 23 April (for HM the Queen's Birthday), 14 June (Liberation Day), 1 October (Spring Holiday), 10 December (for Anniversary of the Battle of the Falkland Islands in 1914), 25–29 December (Christmas).

Weights and Measures

Both the imperial and metric systems are in general use.

Statistical Survey

Source (unless otherwise stated): The Treasury of the Falkland Islands Government, Stanley, FIQQ 1ZZ; tel. 27143; fax 27144.

AREA AND POPULATION

Area: approx. 12,173 sq km (4,700 sq miles): East Falkland and adjacent islands 6,760 sq km (2,610 sq miles); West Falkland and adjacent islands 5,413 sq km (2,090 sq miles).

Population: 2,913 (males 1,598, females 1,315) at census of 8 April 2001. Note: Figures exclude 112 persons normally resident, but include 534 civilian personnel based at Mount Pleasant military base.

Density (2001): 0.24 per sq km.

Principal Town (2001 census): Stanley (capital), population 1,989.

Births and Deaths (2000): Live births 27; Deaths 6.

Economically Active Population (persons aged 15 years and over, 2001 census): 2,475 (males 1,370, females 1,105).

AGRICULTURE, ETC.

Livestock (FAO estimates, 2004): Sheep 690,000; Cattle 4,200; Horses 1,188; Poultry 3,000.

Livestock Products (FAO estimates, metric tons, 2004): Beef and veal 131; Mutton and lamb 774; Cow's milk 1,500; Sheepskins (fresh) 129; Wool (greasy) 2,340; Wool (scoured) 1,520.

Fishing ('000 metric tons, live weight of capture, 2003): Southern blue whiting 2.5; Patagonian grenadier 9.5; Patagonian squid 43.8; Total catch (incl. others) 60.6.

Source: FAO.

FINANCE

Currency and Exchange Rates: 100 pence (pennies) = 1 Falkland Islands pound (FI £). *Sterling, Dollar and Euro Equivalents* (30 December 2005): £1 sterling = FI £1.00; US $1 = 58.08 pence; €1 = 68.51 pence; FI £100 = £100.00 sterling = $172.18 = €145.96. *Average Exchange Rate* (FI £ per US dollar): 0.6125 in 2003; 0.5462 in 2004; 0.5500 in 2005. Note: The Falkland Islands pound is at par with the pound sterling.

Budget (FI £ million, 2001/02): *Revenue:* Operating revenue 44.0 (Sales and services 9.0, Fishing licences and transhipment 22.9, Investment income 6.7, Taxes and duties 5.4); Capital revenue 0.5; Total 44.5. *Expenditure:* Operating expenditure 33.6 (Public works 6.3, Fisheries 6.0, Health care 4.5, Education 3.5, Aviation 1.7, Police and justice 1.2, Agriculture 1.0, Central administration 2.6, Other 6.8); Capital expenditure 18.1; Total 51.7.

Cost of Living (Consumer Price Index for Stanley; base: 2000 = 100): 101.3 in 2001; 102.0 in 2002; 103.2 in 2003. Source: ILO.

EXTERNAL TRADE

2000 (estimates): Total imports £18,958,103; Total exports £47,000,000. Fish is the principal export. Trade is mainly with the United Kingdom, Spain and Chile.

TRANSPORT

Shipping: *Merchant Fleet* (at 31 December 2004): Vessels 29; Displacement 50,453 grt. Source: Lloyd's Register-Fairplay, *World Fleet Statistics*.

Road Traffic: 3,065 vehicles in use in 1995.

TOURISM

Day Visitors (country of origin of cruise-ship excursionists, 2000/01): Germany 1,842; United Kingdom 2,042; USA 14,938; Total (incl. others) 24,000.

EDUCATION

2003 (Stanley): *Primary:* Teachers 18; Pupils 203, *Secondary:* Teachers 18; Pupils 160.

Directory

The Constitution

The present Constitution of the Falkland Islands came into force on 3 October 1985 (replacing that of 1977) and was amended in 1997. The Governor, who is the personal representative of the British monarch, is advised by the Executive Council, comprising six members: the Governor (presiding), three members elected by the Legislative Council, and two *ex-officio* members, the Chief Executive and the Financial Secretary of the Falkland Islands Government, who are non-voting. The Legislative Council is composed of eight elected members and the same two (non-voting) *ex-officio* members. One of the principal features of the Constitution is the reference in the preamble to the islanders' right to self-determination. The separate post of Chief Executive (responsible to the Governor) was created in 1983. The electoral principle was introduced, on the basis of universal adult suffrage, in 1949. The minimum voting age was lowered from 21 years to 18 years in 1977.

The Government
(April 2006)

Governor: Howard J. S. Pearce (took office 3 December 2002).
Governor-designate: Alan Huckle (scheduled to take office in June 2006).
Chief Executive of the Falkland Islands Government: Chris Simpkins.
Government Secretary: Peter T. King.
Financial Secretary: Derek F. Howatt.
Attorney-General: David G. Lang.
Military Commander: Cdre Richard Ibbotson.

EXECUTIVE COUNCIL
The Council consists of six members (see Constitution, above).

LEGISLATIVE COUNCIL
Comprises the Governor, two *ex-officio* (non-voting) members and eight elected members.

GOVERNMENT OFFICES

Office of the Governor: Government House, Stanley, FIQQ 1ZZ; tel. 27433; fax 27434; e-mail gov.house@horizon.co.fk.
General Office: Secretariat, Stanley, FIQQ 1ZZ; tel. 27242; fax 27109; e-mail atomlinson@sec.gov.fk; internet www.falklands.gov.fk.
London Office: Falkland Islands Government Office, Falkland House, 14 Broadway, London SW1H 0BH, United Kingdom; tel. (020) 7222-2542; fax (020) 7222-2375; e-mail receptionist@falklands.gov.fk; internet www.falklandislands.com; f. 1983.

Judicial System

The judicial system of the Falkland Islands is administered by the Supreme Court (presided over by the non-resident Chief Justice), the Magistrate's Court (presided over by the Senior Magistrate) and the Court of Summary Jurisdiction. The Court of Appeal for the Territory sits in England and appeals therefrom may be heard by the Judicial Committee of the Privy Council.

Chief Justice of the Supreme Court: James Wood.
Judge of the Supreme Court and Senior Magistrate: Clare Faulds.
Courts Administrator: Lesley Titterington, Ross Rd, Stanley, FIQQ 1ZZ; tel. 27271; fax 2720.
Registrar-General: John Rowland, Town Hall, Stanley, FIQQ 1ZZ; tel. 27272; fax 27270.

FALKLAND ISLANDS COURT OF APPEAL
President: Sir Lionel Brett.
Registrar: Michael J. Elks.

Religion

CHRISTIANITY
The Anglican Communion, the Roman Catholic Church and the United Free Church predominate. Also represented are the Evangelist Church, Jehovah's Witnesses, the Lutheran Church, Seventh-day Adventists and the Bahá'í faith.

The Anglican Communion
The Archbishop of Canterbury, the Primate of All England, exercises episcopal jurisdiction over the Falkland Islands and South Georgia.
Rector: Rev. Alistair McHaffie, The Deanery, Christ Church Cathedral, Stanley, FIQQ 1ZZ; tel. 21100; fax 21842; e-mail deanery@horizon.co.fk; internet www.horizon.co.fk/cathedral.

The Roman Catholic Church
Prefect Apostolic of the Falkland Islands: Michael Bernard McPartland, St Mary's Presbytery, 12 Ross Rd, Stanley, FIQQ 1ZZ; tel. 21204; fax 22242; e-mail stmarys@horizon.co.fk; internet www.southatlanticrcchurch.com; f. 1764; 230 adherents (2003).

The Press

The Falkland Islands Gazette: Stanley, FIQQ 1ZZ; tel. 27242; fax 27109; e-mail atomlinson@sec.gov.fk; internet www.falklands.gov.fk; govt publication.
Falkland Islands News Network: POB 141, Stanley, FIQQ 1ZZ; tel. and fax 21182; e-mail finn@horizon.co.fk; internet www.falklandnews.com; relays news daily online and via fax as FINN(COM) Service; Man. Juan Brock; publishes:
  Teaberry Express: Stanley, FIQQ 1ZZ; tel. 21182; weekly.
Penguin News: Ross Rd, Stanley, FIQQ 1ZZ; tel. 22684; fax 22238; e-mail pnews@horizon.co.fk; internet www.penguin-news.com; f. 1979; weekly; independent newspaper; Man. Editor Jenny Cockwell; circ. 1,550.

Broadcasting and Communications

TELECOMMUNICATIONS
In 1989 Cable & Wireless PLC installed a £5.4m. digital telecommunications network covering the entire Falkland Islands. The Government contributed to the cost of the new system, which provides international services as well as a new domestic network. Further work to improve the domestic telephone system was completed in the late 1990s at a cost of £3,286,000.

Cable & Wireless PLC: Ross Rd, POB 584, Stanley, FIQQ 1ZZ; tel. 20801; fax 22207; e-mail info@cwfi.co.fk; internet www.horizon.co.fk; f. 1989; exclusive provider of national and international telecommu-

UNITED KINGDOM OVERSEAS TERRITORIES

nications services in the Falkland Islands under a licence issued by the Falkland Islands Government; CEO RICHARD HALL.

BROADCASTING

Radio

Falkland Islands Broadcasting Station (FIBS): Broadcasting Studios, Stanley, FIQQ 1ZZ; tel. 27277; fax 27279; e-mail fibs.fig@horizon.co.fk; 24-hour service, financed by local Govt in association with SSVC of London, United Kingdom; broadcasts in English; Broadcasting Officer TONY BURNETT (acting); Asst Producer CORINA GOSS.

British Forces Broadcasting Service (BFBS): BFBS Falkland Islands, Mount Pleasant, BFPO 655; tel. 32179; fax 32193; e-mail chris.pearson@bfbs.com; internet www.bfbs.com; 24-hour satellite service from the United Kingdom; Station Man. CHRIS PEARSON; Sr Engineer ADRIAN ALMOND.

Television

British Forces Broadcasting Service: BFBS Falkland Islands, Mount Pleasant, BFPO 655; tel. 32179; fax 32193; daily four-hour transmissions of taped broadcasts from BBC and ITV of London, United Kingdom; Sr Engineer COLIN MCDONALD.

KTV: 16 Ross Rd West, Stanley, FIQQ 1ZZ; tel. 22349; fax 21049; e-mail kmzb@horizon.co.fk; satellite television broadcasting services; Man. MARIO ZUVIC BULIC.

Finance

BANK

Standard Chartered Bank: Ross Rd, POB 597, Stanley, FIQQ 1ZZ; tel. 21352; fax 22219; e-mail standardchartered@horizon.co.fk; branch opened in 1983; Man. N. P. HUTTON.

INSURANCE

The British Commercial Union, Royal Insurance and Norman Tremellen companies maintain agencies in Stanley.

Consultancy Services Falklands Ltd: 44 John St, Stanley, FIQQ 1ZZ; tel. 22666; fax 22639; e-mail consultancy@horizon.co.uk; Man. ALISON BAKER.

Trade and Industry

DEVELOPMENT ORGANIZATION

Falkland Islands Development Corporation (FIDC): Shackleton House, Stanley, FIQQ 1ZZ; tel. 27211; fax 27210; e-mail develop@fidc.co.fk; internet www.fidc.co.fk; f. 1983; provides loans and grants; encourages private-sector investment, inward investment and technology transfer; Gen. Man. JULIAN MORRIS.

CHAMBER OF COMMERCE

Chamber of Commerce: POB 378, Stanley, FIQQ 1ZZ; tel. 22264; fax 22265; e-mail commerce@horizon.co.fk; internet www.falklandislandschamberofcommerce.com; f. 1993; promotes private industry; operates DHL courier service; runs an employment agency; Pres. TIM MILLER; 70 mems.

TRADING COMPANIES

Falkland Islands Co Ltd (FIC): Crozier Pl., Stanley, FIQQ 1ZZ; tel. 27600; fax 27603; e-mail fic@horizon.co.fk; internet www.the-falkland-islands-co.com; f. 1851; part of Falkland Islands Holding PLC; the largest trading co; retailing, wholesaling, shipping, insurance and Land Rover sales and servicing; operates as agent for Lloyd's of London and general shipping concerns; travel services and hoteliers; wharf owners and operators; Dir and Gen. Man. ROGER KENNETH SPINK.

Falkland Oil and Gas Ltd (FOGL): 56 John St, Stanley, F1QQ 1ZZ; e-mail info@fogl.co.uk; internet www.fogl.co.uk; f. 2004; Falkland Islands Holdings plc (18%), Global Petroleum (16%) and RAB Capital plc (31%); operates an offshore petroleum exploration programme with 8 licences covering 83,700 sq km; Chair. RICHARD LIDDELL; CEO TIM BUSHELL.

EMPLOYERS' ASSOCIATION

Sheep Owners' Association: Coast Ridge Farm, Fox Bay, FIQQ 1ZZ; tel. 42094; fax 42084; e-mail n.knight.coastridge@horizon.co.fk; asscn for sheep-station owners; Sec. N. KNIGHT.

TRADE UNION

Falkland Islands General Employees Union: Ross Rd, Stanley, FIQQ 1ZZ; tel. 21151; f. 1943; Sec. C. A. ROWLANDS; 100 mems.

CO-OPERATIVE SOCIETY

Stanley Co-operative Society: Stanley, FIQQ 1ZZ; tel. 21215; f. 1952; open to all members of the public; Man. NORMA THOM.

Transport

RAILWAYS

There are no railways on the islands.

ROADS

There are 29 km (18 miles) of paved road in and around Stanley. There are 54 km (34 miles) of all-weather road linking Stanley and the Mount Pleasant airport (some of which has been surfaced with a bitumen substance), and a further 37 km of road as far as Goose Green. There are 300 km of arterial roads in the North Camp on East Falkland linking settlements, and a further 197 km of road on West Falkland. An ongoing roads network project to link remote farms is in progress. Where roads have still not been built, settlements are linked by tracks, which are passable by all-terrain motor vehicle or motor cycle except in the most severe weather conditions.

SHIPPING

There is a ship on charter to the Falkland Islands Co Ltd which makes the round trip to the United Kingdom four or five times a year, carrying cargo. A floating deep-water jetty was completed in 1984. The British Ministry of Defence charters ships, which sail for the Falkland Islands once every three weeks. There are irregular cargo services between the islands and southern Chile and Uruguay.

The Falkland Islands merchant fleet numbered 29 vessels, with a total displacement of 50,453 grt, at December 2004; the majority of vessels registered are deep-sea fishing vessels.

Stanley Port Authority: c/o Dept of Fisheries, POB 598, Stanley, FIQQ 1ZZ; tel. 27260; fax 27265; e-mail jclark@fisheries.gov.fk; Harbour Master J. CLARK.

Private Companies

Byron Marine Ltd: 3 'H' Jones Rd, Stanley, FIQQ 1ZZ; tel. 22245; fax 22246; e-mail info@byronmarine.co.fk; internet www.byronmarine.com; f. 1992; additional activites include oil exploration support services, deep-sea fishing and property; contracted managers of the Falkland Islands Government Port Facility (email: portservices@byronmarine.co.fk); island-wide pilotage services; vessel agent; Man. LEWIS CLIFTON.

Darwin Shipping Ltd: Stanley, FIQQ 1ZZ; tel. 27629; fax 27626; e-mail darwin@horizon.co.fk; internet www.the-falkland-islands-co.com; subsidiary of the Falkland Islands Company Ltd; Man. EVA CLARKE.

Falkland Islands Co. Ltd: Crozier Pl., Stanley, FIQQ 1ZZ; tel. 27600; fax 27603; e-mail fic@horizon.co.fk; internet www.the-falkland-islands-co.com; Man. ROGER SPINK.

Seaview Ltd: 37 Fitzroy Rd, POB 215, Stanley, FIQQ 1ZZ; tel. 22669; fax 22670; e-mail polar.falklands@btinternet.com; internet www.fis.com/polar; Man. DICK SAWLE.

Sulivan Shipping Services Ltd: Davis St, Stanley, FIQQ 1ZZ; tel. 22626; fax 22625; e-mail sulivan@horizon.co.fk; internet www.sulivanshipping.com; f. 1987; provides port-agency and ground-handling services; Man. Dir JOHN POLLARD.

CIVIL AVIATION

There are airports at Stanley and Mount Pleasant; the latter has a runway of 2,590 m, and is capable of receiving wide-bodied jet aircraft. The British Royal Air Force operates three weekly flights from the United Kingdom. The Chilean carrier LanChile operates weekly return flights from Punta Arenas.

Falkland Islands Government Air Service (FIGAS): Stanley Airport, Stanley, FIQQ 1ZZ; tel. 27219; fax 27309; e-mail fwallace@figas.gov.fk; f. 1948 to provide social, medical and postal services between the settlements and Stanley; aerial surveillance for Dept of Fisheries since 1990; operates four nine-seater aircraft to over 35 landing strips across the islands; Gen. Man. VERNON R. STEEN.

Tourism

During the 2000/01 season some 24,000 day visitors from cruise ships (primarily US citizens, numbering 14,938) visited the islands. Wildlife photography, bird-watching and hiking are popular tourist activities. The Falkland Islands Development Corpn plans to develop the sector, which currently generates some £3m. in turnover annually.

Falkland Islands Tourism: Shackleton House, Stanley, FIQQ 1ZZ; tel. 22215; fax 22619; e-mail jettycentre@horizon.co.fk; internet www.tourism.org.fk; Man. CONNIE STEVENS.

GIBRALTAR

Introductory Survey

Location, Climate, Language, Religion, Flag

The City of Gibraltar lies in southern Europe. The territory consists of a narrow peninsula of approximately 4.8 km (3 miles) in length, running southwards from the south-west coast of Spain, to which it is connected by an isthmus. About 8 km (5 miles) across the bay, to the west, lies the Spanish port of Algeciras, while 32 km (20 miles) to the south, across the Strait of Gibraltar, is Morocco. The Mediterranean Sea lies to the east. The climate is temperate, and snow or frost are extremely rare. The mean minimum and maximum temperatures during the winter are 13°C (55°F) and 18°C (65°F), respectively, and during the summer they are 13°C (55°F) and 29°C (85°F) respectively; the average annual rainfall is 890 mm (35 ins). The official language is English, although most of the population are bilingual in English and Spanish. More than three-quarters of the population are Roman Catholic. The flag (proportions 1 by 2) bears the arms of Gibraltar (a red castle with a pendant golden key) on a background, the upper two-thirds of which are white and the lower one-third red.

Recent History

Since the Second World War, this Overseas Territory has achieved considerable social and economic progress, through intensive development of its social and economic infrastructure, and by the expansion of commerce and the encouragement of tourism. Gibraltar has exercised control over most internal matters since 1969.

The Spanish Government lays claim to Gibraltar as a part of its territory, while the United Kingdom maintains that the Treaty of Utrecht (1713) granted sovereignty over Gibraltar to the United Kingdom in perpetuity (with the stipulation that, if the United Kingdom relinquished the colony, it would be returned to Spain). In 1963 the Spanish Government began a campaign, through the UN, for the cession of Gibraltar to Spain. It also imposed restrictions against Gibraltar, culminating in the closure of the frontier in 1969, the withdrawal of the Spanish labour force, and the severing of transport and communication links with Spain.

Following a referendum held in the territory in 1967, in which the overwhelming majority voted in favour of retaining British sovereignty, a new Constitution, promulgated in 1969, contained a provision that the British Government undertook never to enter into arrangements whereby the people of Gibraltar would pass under the sovereignty of another state against their freely and democratically expressed wishes. Gibraltar joined the European Community (EC—now European Union—EU, see p. 228) with the United Kingdom in 1973, under the provisions of the Treaty of Rome that relate to European territories for whose external relations a member state is responsible.

By 1977, a more flexible attitude by Spain towards Gibraltar became apparent. At talks held between Spanish and British ministers in November representatives of the Gibraltar Government were included for the first time as part of the British delegation. In December 1979 Spain requested new negotiations, and at meetings in April 1980 it was agreed, in principle, to reopen the frontier by June. However, the reopening was delayed by the Spanish Government's insistence that Spanish workers in Gibraltar should be allowed equal status with nationals of EC countries. In October the British Parliament granted Gibraltarians the right to retain full British citizenship. Negotiations for the full opening of the frontier continued in 1982, but a change of attitudes in both countries, following the war between the United Kingdom and Argentina over the sovereignty of the Falkland Islands (q.v.), resulted in an indefinite postponement. In December Spain reopened the border to pedestrians of Spanish nationality and to British subjects resident in Gibraltar.

In a general election held in January 1984, the Gibraltar Labour Party—Association for the Advancement of Civil Rights (GLP—AACR), led by Sir Joshua Hassan, retained a majority of one seat in the House of Assembly. The Gibraltar Socialist Labour Party (GSLP), led by Joseph Bossano, secured the remaining seven seats, replacing the Democratic Party of British Gibraltar as the opposition party in the House of Assembly. (Under the terms of the Constitution, the party with the largest share of the vote obtained a maximum of eight seats in the House of Assembly.)

In November 1984 the British and Spanish Governments agreed to provide equal rights for Spaniards in Gibraltar and for Gibraltarians in Spain; to allow free movement for all traffic between Gibraltar and Spain; and to conduct negotiations on the future of the territory, including (for the first time) discussions on sovereignty. Border restrictions were finally ended in February 1985, and negotiations took place between the British and Spanish Governments to improve cross-border co-operation, especially in tourism and civil aviation. In December, however, Spanish proposals for an interim settlement of the territory's future were rejected by the British Government as unacceptable since they implied the eventual automatic cession of Gibraltar to Spain. Subsequent discussions concerning principally Spain's demands for access to the Gibraltar airport (which the Spanish Government claimed was situated on land not covered by the terms of the Treaty of Utrecht) were inconclusive, owing to the Gibraltar Government's insistence that the airport remain exclusively under the control of the British and Gibraltar authorities. In December 1987 negotiators concluded an agreement that recommended increased co-operation between Spain and Gibraltar in the area of transport, in particular the joint administration of Gibraltar's airport, which would exempt passengers travelling to and from Spain from Gibraltar frontier controls. It was announced that Gibraltar's inclusion in an EC directive concerning air transport regulation was subject to the Gibraltar Government's approval of the Anglo-Spanish agreement. However, Gibraltar's House of Assembly rejected the agreement, on the grounds that it would represent an infringement of British sovereignty, and voted unanimously to contest Gibraltar's exclusion from the EC directive. The Spanish Government announced that, if Gibraltar continued to reject the agreement, it would consider the construction of its own airport on the Spanish side of the border.

In December 1987 Hassan resigned as Chief Minister and leader of the GLP—AACR and was succeeded by Adolfo Canepa, the Deputy Chief Minister. At a general election held in March 1988, the GSLP received 58.2% of the votes cast, obtaining eight seats in the House of Assembly, and the GLP—AACR received 29.3% of the vote, securing seven seats. The newly formed Independent Democratic Party failed to obtain parliamentary representation. Bossano replaced Canepa as Chief Minister, at the head of Gibraltar's first socialist Government. Bossano announced that he would not participate in Anglo-Spanish negotiations concerning Gibraltar, on the grounds that the territory's sovereignty was not a matter for negotiation between Spain and the United Kingdom, and that the December 1987 agreement would, in his view, result in the absorption of Gibraltar into Spain.

In January 1989, in an unprecedented gesture of co-operation between Gibraltar and Spain, Bossano met the mayor of La Línea, the Spanish town bordering Gibraltar, and offered to assist in financing an economic revival in the region. In February 1990 the British and Spanish Governments agreed to contest a legal action that was to be brought by Gibraltar in the European Court of Justice against Gibraltar's exclusion from measures adopted to liberalize European air transport, which prevented the territory from expanding its air links with Europe. The decision to contest the action was considered to be a further attempt by the United Kingdom to persuade Gibraltar to co-operate with Spain. In March 1991 the United Kingdom withdrew the majority of British army personnel from Gibraltar, although the Royal Navy and Royal Air Force detachments remained.

In May 1991 the Spanish Prime Minister made an official visit to the United Kingdom, and was reported to have proposed a plan for joint sovereignty over Gibraltar, whereby the dependency would become effectively autonomous, with the British and Spanish monarchs as joint heads of state. Although it represented a significant concession by the Spanish Government (which had hitherto demanded full sovereignty over Gibraltar), the plan was rejected by the Gibraltar Government in July. At the EC summit meeting held at Maastricht, Netherlands, in December, Spain continued to refuse to recognize Gibraltar's status as a member of the EC, and remained determined to exclude it from the External Frontiers Convention (EFC), which was designed to strengthen common controls on entry into countries belonging to the EC. It was asserted by the Spanish Government that the inclusion of Gibraltar had to be subject to a separate bilateral agreement between the United Kingdom and Spain.

At a general election held in January 1992 the GSLP retained eight seats in the House of Assembly, and Bossano was returned for a second term as Chief Minister. The Gibraltar Social Democrats (GSD), an organization founded in 1989 that supported Gibraltar's participation in Anglo-Spanish negotiations, secured the remaining seven seats. In February 1992, prior to discussions with British ministers in London, Bossano announced that Gibraltar was to attempt to obtain a revision of the 1969 Constitution, with the aim of achieving self-determination within four years. The British Government, however, stated that it would not consider granting independence to Gibraltar, unless the Spanish Government was prepared to accept the agreement, and excluded the possibility of formal negotiations on the issue.

In May 1992 Spain announced that it would continue to exclude Gibraltar from the EFC, unless there was progress in the Anglo-Spanish negotiations regarding the restoration of Spain's sovereignty over Gibraltar. Further Anglo-Spanish negotiations, which were to take place in November, were postponed, however, and the continued failure to reach an agreement on the issue of the administration of Gibraltar airport prevented the ratification of the EFC.

In January 1993 Gibraltarians formally protested, after increasingly stringent monitoring of vehicles by Spanish customs officials resulted in severe delays at the border with Spain. In March an official meeting between the foreign ministers of the United Kingdom and Spain achieved little progress; it was agreed, however, that contacts between British and Spanish officials were to be maintained. In early 1994 Bossano accused the British Government of subordinating the interests of Gibraltar to the promotion of harmonious relations with Spain, and demanded a renegotiation of the 1987 airport agreement on the grounds that its provisions were redundant and contrary to EU law, following the implementation of the Third Air Liberalization Directives in 1993.

In September 1994 the Gibraltar Government began to come under pressure from the United Kingdom to implement EU directives governing health and safety regulations, public procurement procedures, environmental matters and the regulation of the banking and financial services sectors. In addition, it was alleged by Spain that insufficient action was being taken by Gibraltar to curtail the smuggling of tobacco from Gibraltar to Spain and of drugs between Morocco and Spain by Gibraltar-based fast launches. The imposition in October of stringent border inspections by Spain, leading to lengthy delays in commercial and visitor traffic, prompted a protest by the British Government. These border checks were eased following assurances that measures were being taken to curtail the activities of the fast launches operating from Gibraltar.

Spain reimposed frontier controls in March 1995 and was again criticized by the British Government. In May, however, it emerged that the Gibraltar Government had brought into effect only about one-quarter of the relevant EU directives, and Gibraltar was warned by the British Government that substantial progress should be made by late June. Bossano, however, declared that the House of Assembly had the right to interpret EU legislation as it saw fit, and that any interference by the United Kingdom would be challenged in the British courts. In July 1996 the Gibraltar authorities extended offences of money-laundering, hitherto applicable solely to proceeds from drugs-trafficking, to those from all crimes.

In July 1995, following the confiscation of more than 60 speed launches, alleged to be used in the transport of contraband, the Spanish Government eased the frontier controls imposed 16 months earlier. The seizures provoked two days of riots and looting in the City, followed, however, by a peaceful mass demonstration, organized by Gibraltar business interests and trade unions, in support of the continuing implementation of anti-smuggling measures. Although the British and Spanish Governments jointly agreed in September that the anti-smuggling measures were proving effective, the death of a Spanish civil guard in pursuit of smugglers in April 1996 led to the renewal of border controls by Spain, and in the following month the newly elected Spanish Government, alleging a resurgence of smuggling activity, threatened to impose a total closure of the frontier.

Campaign debates in advance of legislative elections in May 1996 focused on the single issue of the territory's external relations. Bossano and the GSLP proposed that Gibraltar's colonial status be replaced before the year 2000 by a form of 'free association' with the United Kingdom, while the GSD declared as its aims the achievement of improved relations both with Spain and the United Kingdom and the modernization of Gibraltar's Constitution. The GSD also stated its willingness to participate in negotiations with Spain on matters of mutual co-operation, excluding the issue of sovereignty. The election attracted an unusually high turn-out (88% of eligible voters), and resulted in the GSD receiving 48% of the vote and the maximum of eight seats in the House of Assembly; the GSD leader, Peter Caruana, became Chief Minister. The GSLP received 39% of the vote and the Gibraltar National Party obtained 13%.

In November 1996 the Spanish Government lodged a complaint with the EU Commission over a private visit to Gibraltar by the EU Commissioner responsible for Immigration and Home and Judicial Affairs to view the operation of Spanish border controls. In the same month Chief Minister Caruana renewed his demand that Gibraltar be accorded equal status with the United Kingdom in future negotiations concerning the territory's interests. On a visit to the EU Commission in January 1997, the Chief Minister cited a number of alleged abuses by Spain of EU treaty arrangements, including its imposition of a ban on maritime and air links and its refusal to recognize identity cards issued in Gibraltar. Caruana indicated that legal action would be instituted against the Spanish Government where violations of EU regulations could be established. In the same month Caruana refused to attend discussions on Gibraltar, held in Madrid, Spain, between the United Kingdom and Spain, on the grounds that Gibraltar would not be granted power of veto. A suggestion by Spain that sovereignty over Gibraltar be shared between Spain and the United Kingdom for a 100-year period, with full control then passing to Spain, was rejected by the British Government. In September the Government of Gibraltar opened an office in Brussels, Belgium, to promote the territory's financial services and tourism and to facilitate liaison with British representation at the EU.

In October 1997 Caruana informed the Decolonization Committee of the UN General Assembly that he was to seek from the British Government an extensive review of the territory's 1969 Constitution. It was to be proposed that Gibraltar would obtain additional autonomy in the conduct of its affairs while remaining in a close political and constitutional relationship with the United Kingdom, similar to that held by the Channel Islands and the Isle of Man (qq.v.). The Chief Minister stated his belief that such an arrangement would 'strengthen and modernize' Gibraltar's relationship with the United Kingdom, and that these proposals would, if accepted by the people of Gibraltar in a referendum, create a non-colonial relationship and constitute an effective and valid exercise of self-determination.

During 1997 new tensions arose between the United Kingdom and Spanish Governments over the long-standing refusal by Spain to permit military aircraft from the United Kingdom and the North Atlantic Treaty Organization (NATO, see p. 314) to cross Spanish airspace on their approach to Gibraltar airport. In July the British Secretary of State for Foreign and Commonwealth Affairs indicated that the United Kingdom would oppose the full incorporation of Spain into NATO unless the ban was lifted. An indication by Spain of its willingness to open its airspace to these flights in return for joint military control of the airport was strongly opposed by Caruana and rejected by the British Government. In July 1998 Spain reversed its long-standing refusal to participate in NATO manoeuvres that were based in, or passed through, Gibraltar. In that month the Spanish Government unsuccessfully requested the British Government to consider a revived proposal for the shared sovereignty of Gibraltar for a period of 50 years, to be followed by the territory's full integration into Spain.

In November 1998 complaints by the Gibraltar Government arose over the conduct of Spanish fishing vessels in the Bay of Gibraltar, which were stated to be operating in violation of the territory's nature protection ordinance. In January 1999 a Spanish trawler was arrested by the Gibraltar authorities, and Spain began to intensify delays in motor traffic crossing the frontier. An agreement reached in February between the Gibraltar authorities and the Spanish fishermen (at the Gibraltar Government's initiative) was not recognized by the Spanish Government. Border crossing delays were intensified, and Spain indicated that it was considering withdrawing its recognition of driving licences and other legal documents issued by the Gibraltar Government. Although relations with Spain were further complicated in March by an announcement that the British Government wished to obtain the right for Gibraltar residents to vote in EU elections, negotiations between the two countries continued throughout 1999.

At the general election held in February 2000 the GSD secured 58.7% of the vote, against 40.8% obtained by an electoral coalition of the GSLP and the Gibraltar Liberal Party (GLP). Caruana was reconfirmed as Chief Minister, again commanding eight seats in the House of Assembly. Immediately following the election, Caruana expressed his wish for improved relations with Spain.

The extended negotiations between the Spanish and British Governments were concluded in April 2000 with a compromise agreement whereby Spain was to recognize the validity of Gibraltar identity cards and of the Territory's financial institutions, provided that the 'competent authority' responsible for their supervision was the United Kingdom rather than the Gibraltar Government. It was also agreed that the British authorities would provide a facility, based in London, through which the Spanish and Gibraltar authorities could have indirect communication. An incidental effect of the agreement was to terminate the long-standing refusal by Spain to adopt any legislation by the EU that might have required it to deal directly with Gibraltar's police or financial regulatory authorities.

In February 2001 the Spanish Government issued a statement attacking British sovereignty over Gibraltar, criticizing the territory's monetary system and accusing the territory of being an 'economic parasite' financed by Spain. In March the Gibraltar political parties reached an agreement to request the previously proposed reforms to the 1969 Constitution, allowing self-determination, and to hold a referendum on decolonization. However, the move was condemned by Spain as a breach of the Treaty of Utrecht.

In July 2001 the British and Spanish Governments renewed discussions on Gibraltar's future status for the first time since 1998. In response, the Gibraltarian legislature requested that a UN declonization mission visit the territory. At a subsequent meeting in October, the British Secretary of State for Foreign and Commonwealth Affairs, Jack Straw, and his Spanish counterpart, Josep Piqué I Camps, agreed to work towards achieving a settlement on the issue by December 2002 (this was later modified to September 2002). Amid public criticism of proposals of joint British-Spanish sovereignty, Caruana rebuffed an invitation to attend the next round of negotiations in November, claiming that he would not be accorded equal status in the discussions. The Chief Minister also stated that the territory would not accept any change in sovereignty, the sharing of responsibility for its external affairs between Spain and the United Kingdom, nor Spanish military presence.

At the negotiations in November 2001, Piqué announced that Spain was prepared to increase the number of telephone lines available to Gibraltar from 35,000 to 100,000 and provide greater access to the Spanish health care system. However, the issue of the right of the citizens of Gibraltar to vote on the terms of an agreement regarding the future status of the territory remained one of the main points of contention between Spain and the United Kingdom. At the end of the month the British Government announced that Gibraltarians would be given the right to vote in elections to the European Parliament, but ruled out the possibility of the territory's further integration into the United Kingdom. Caruana continued to voice Gibraltar's opposition to a transfer of sovereignty and asserted its citizens' rights to self-determination. In an open letter published in the local press, Piqué attempted to allay Gibraltarians' fears of the implications of Spanish rule and urged Caruana to attend the negotiations. The following month, however, most of the territory's 300,000 citizens took part in a public demonstration against the proposals. Following further public protests in March 2002, EU leaders agreed to a joint British-Spanish request for a grant of £37m. to fund the development of Gibraltar's port, infrastructure and airport. Caruana rejected the proposals and threatened to organize a referendum.

Shortly before negotiations on the sovereignty issue were due to resume in May 2002, the Spanish Prime Minister, José María Aznar, asserted that Spain would never withdraw its territorial claim to Gibraltar. During a subsequent visit, Straw's efforts to persuade Gibraltar of the benefits of joint sovereignty, and to reassure its residents that any agreement would be subject to a referendum, were met with scepticism. Also in May, the Overseas Territories Act, having received royal assent in the United Kingdom in February, came into force, granting British citizenship rights to the people of its Overseas Territories, including Gibraltar. Under the new law Gibraltarians would be able to hold British passports and work in the United Kingdom and other EU countries.

Negotiations between the Spanish and British Governments progressed in mid-2002, although discussions stalled over Spain's claims to eventual sovereignty rather than permanent co-sovereignty and its refusal to allow British control over the military base. In response, Caruana called a referendum for November 2002. Talks recommenced in September, but with no certain deadline. The referendum, held on 7 November, in which 87.9% of the electorate voted, demonstrated overwhelming (98.97%) opinion against joint sovereignty with Spain; it was, however, not recognized, by either Spain or the United Kingdom, and the British Prime Minister, Tony Blair, refused to abandon discussions regarding joint sovereignty. Relations were strained later that month when the Spanish Minister of Foreign Affairs claimed that Gibraltar was partly responsible for the sinking of the oil tanker *Prestige* off the coast of Galicia in Spain, as Gibraltarian maritime officials had allegedly failed properly to examine the vessel when it had docked near the enclave in June. The British Government refuted these accusations, as the tanker had docked outside the port, and confirmed further that the final destination of the ship had been Singapore, and not Gibraltar as Spain claimed.

In January 2003 Caruana proposed constitutional reforms that would establish a decolonized status for the enclave but maintain its links with the United Kingdom. Meanwhile, further discussions between Spain and the United Kingdom were scheduled for that year. In June Dennis McShane, the British Minister of State for Europe, admitted the plan for joint sovereignty was practically unenforceable given the almost unanimous opposition of Gibraltar's population. Spain continued to exert pressure on the issue and in the same month asked the US President, George W. Bush, a close ally of both Blair and Aznar, to mediate in the dispute.

Sir Francis Richards took office as Governor and Commander-in-Chief in May 2003, in succession to David Durie.

At a general election held on 28 November 2003 the GSD secured 51.5% of the vote, a significant decrease from the 2000 election, against 39.7% secured by the GSLP-GLP coalition. The balance of seats in the House of Assembly, however, remained unchanged, with the GSD holding eight seats and the opposition seven seats, and Caruana retained the position of Chief Minister. Caruana effected a minor reorganization of the Government following the election; the most significant change was the appointment of Joe Holliday, hitherto Minister for Tourism and Transport, as Minister for Trade, Industry and Communications, a post that now also included responsibility for ports and shipping and for tourism.

For the purposes of the 2004 elections to the European Parliament, in late 2003 the British Parliament adopted legislation incorporating Gibraltar into the South-West region of the United Kingdom; for the first time, Gibraltarians were thus eligible to vote in European elections. Approximately 58% of the Gibaltarian electorate participated in the elections, which were held in mid-June 2004 and were won, with a decisive majority, by the Conservatives. As expected, following the elections the Spanish Government announced that it would legally challenge the results; the complaint was heard at the European Court of Justice in July 2005.

In February 2004 three Gibraltarian soldiers from the Royal Gibraltar Regiment were charged with attempting to smuggle a large amount of hashish into Spain. The allegations were a considerable embarrassment to the Gibraltarian authorities, which had repeatedly denied claims that the territory was extensively used as a conduit for illegal drugs-trafficking. Celebrations by the Government and people of Gibraltar of 300 years of British rule, held in mid-2004, further antagonized relations with Spain, particularly owing to the attendance of the British Secretary of State for Defence, Geoffrey Hoon.

In October 2004 Straw and his new Spanish counterpart, Miguel Ángel Moratinos (Minister of Foreign Affairs and Co-operation in the recently elected Government of José Luis Rodríguez Zapatero), held discussions in Madrid, at which they addressed the issue of the future format for talks on Gibraltar, which were to include Gibraltarian representation for the first time. Talks involving the three parties took place in the United Kingdom in December further to define this new forum, and in February 2005 the first official trilateral session took place in Málaga, Spain. As a result, a number of Technical Working Groups were established to focus on the most significant issues: the airport, border control, nuclear submarines, telecommunications and pensions. A further trilateral meeting was held in Faro, Portugal, in July.

Following lengthy negotiations between the United Kingdom and Gibraltar, it was announced in March 2006 that the two sides had finally reached agreement on the main provisions of a new draft constitution for the territory. The British authorities stressed that the proposals (which would be voted on at a national referendum later in the year) did not in any way diminish British sovereignty of Gibraltar, which would remain listed as a United Kingdom Overseas Territory. The United Kingdom was to retain its full international responsibility for Gibraltar, including for Gibraltar's external relations and defence, and as the member state responsible for Gibraltar in the EU. The preamble to the new constitution also made clear that the United Kingdom would uphold its longstanding commitment that Gibraltar would remain part of the Queen's dominions unless and until an Act of Parliament otherwise provided, and that the British Government would never enter into arrangements under which the people of Gibraltar would pass under the sovereignty of another state against their freely and democratically expressed wishes. The draft constitution confirmed that the people of Gibraltar had the right of self-determination (according to the provisions of the UN Charter); this right was not constrained by the Treaty of Utrecht except in so far as Spain would have the right of refusal should Britain ever renounce sovereignty. Thus, Gibraltarian independence would be an option only with Spanish consent. The remainder of the text introduced substantial reform and modernization. The main elements included limiting the responsibilities of the Governor to the areas of external affairs, defence, internal security and public services, thereby reversing the existing practice and giving Gibraltar much greater control over its internal affairs. The House of Assembly was to be restyled the Gibraltar Parliament and would be allowed to determine its own size. The Governor's powers to withhold assent on legislation passed by the Gibraltarian authorities would be streamlined and his power to disallow proposed new laws would be removed (although his mandate to make Orders in Council would be retained). New commissions were to be created to deal with appointments to the judiciary and to public services, and a new Police Authority for Gibraltar was to be established.

Government

Gibraltar is a United Kingdom Overseas Territory. Executive authority is exercised by the Governor, who is advised by the Gibraltar Council, which comprises four *ex officio* members and five elected members of the Gibraltar House of Assembly. The Council of Ministers, which is presided over by the Chief Minister, is responsible for domestic affairs, excluding defence and internal security. The House of Assembly comprises the Speaker (who is appointed by the Governor after consultation with the Chief Minister), two *ex officio* members, and 15 members who are elected for a four-year term. The party obtaining the largest share of the vote at a general election is restricted to a maximum of eight seats in the Assembly.

Defence

There is a local defence force, the Gibraltar Regiment, which, following the abolition of conscription, was reorganized as a predominantly volunteer reserve unit (comprising 175 members in August 2005. In August 2005 British army personnel stationed in Gibraltar numbered 60 and there was a total of about 105 Royal Air Force personnel. There is one Royal Navy base located in Gibraltar.

Economic Affairs

In 2002/03 Gibraltar's gross domestic product (GDP), measured at current prices, was £507.2m., equivalent to £17,770 per head.

Gibraltar's population totalled some 28,231 at the census of May 2001, and was estimated to be 28,759 in 2004.

Gibraltar lacks agricultural land and natural resources, and the territory is dependent on imports of foodstuffs and fuels. Foodstuffs were estimated to account for 6% of total imports (excluding petroleum products) in 2004.

The industrial sector (including manufacturing, construction and power) employed 15.7% of the working population at October 2004.

Manufacturing employed 2.8% of the working population at October 2004. The most important sectors are shipbuilding and ship-repairs, and small-scale domestic manufacturing (mainly bottling, coffee-processing, pottery and handicrafts).

Gibraltar is dependent on imported petroleum for its energy supplies. Mineral fuels (excluding petroleum products) accounted for about 55% of the value of total imports in 2004.

Tourism and banking make a significant contribution to the economy. In 2004 revenue from tourism was estimated at G£229m. Visitor arrivals by air in 2004 totalled some 134,497, according to official figures The number of visitor arrivals via the land frontier also reached a record high in 2004; 7,311,555 people crossed into Gibraltar during that year. These, primarily, cross-border day visitors come to the country with the purpose of shopping, thus investing a welcome economic stimulus. At October 2004 the financial sector employed about 8.3% of the working population. Several Spanish banks have established offices in Gibraltar, encouraging the growth of the territory as an 'offshore' banking centre, while the absence of taxes for non-residents has also encouraged the use of Gibraltar as a financial centre. The value of bank deposits increased by more than 480% in the period 1987–95. By March 2004 there were 17 banks and 39 licensed insurance companies operating in Gibraltar. In November 2002, however, the European Commission ruled that Gibraltar's tax-free status was illegal and ordered Gibraltar to close its tax 'haven', which was unique in the European Union (EU, see p. 228). In March 2005 the Commission ruled that Gibraltar could extend the tax-exempt status of 8,464 companies registered in the territory until December 2010. In the intervening period the Gibraltar Government was to introduce a new taxation structure. (Further contention arose in the meantime over the implementation of an EU directive regarding the taxation of royalty and interest payments between associated companies across Europe, which should have been in place at January 2004.)

In 2004 Gibraltar recorded a visible trade deficit of £183.6m. In that year the principal source of imports (excluding petroleum products) was the United Kingdom (accounting for 28.9% of the total). Other major trading partners included Spain (15.5%), Japan and the Netherlands. The principal imports in 2004 were mineral fuels and manufactured goods. The principal re-exports in that year were petroleum products, manufactured goods and wines, spirits, malt and tobacco.

In the year 2004/05 there was an estimated budgetary surplus of £2.9m. A surplus of £3.8m. was forecast for 2005/06. The annual rate of inflation averaged 1.3% during 1993–2002. The annual average rate was 2.9% in 2004. Less than 5.0% of the labour force was unemployed in 2004.

Gibraltar joined the European Community (now EU, see p. 228) with the United Kingdom in 1973.

The Gibraltar economy is based on revenue from the British defence forces, tourism, shipping, and banking and finance. In 1988 the Gibraltar Government declared its aim to develop the territory as an 'offshore' financial centre, to stimulate private investment, and to promote the tourism sector. A project to build a new financial and administrative centre on land reclaimed from the sea commenced in 1990, and in the same year a Financial Services Commission was appointed to regulate financial activities in Gibraltar. In 1994, following the reduction in British military personnel in Gibraltar, revenue from the British defence forces (which had accounted for some 60% of the economy in 1985) contributed only 10% to total government revenue. In 1999 there was a sudden increase in gambling outlets in Gibraltar, as leading operations transferred from the United Kingdom. By mid-2004 the Government had issued 11 new licences. The three main sectors of the economy in the early 2000s were financial services, tourism and shipping, and manufacturing. Gibraltar was to be the recipient of some €8m. in EU Structural Funds during 2000–06, the purpose of which was the encouragement of sustainable economic diversification.

Education

Education is compulsory between the ages of five and 15 years, and is provided free in government schools. The language of instruction is English. There are four nursery schools, 11 primary schools (of which one is private), one Service school (administered by the Ministry of Defence for the children of military personnel) and two secondary comprehensive schools—one for boys and one for girls. Scholarships for students in higher education are provided by both government and private sources. There is also one college providing technical and vocational training, and a special school for handicapped children.

Government expenditure on education, employment and training in 2004/05 was G£22.2m. (equivalent to 12.5% of total spending).

Public Holidays

2006: 1 January (New Year's Day), 13 March (Commonwealth Day), 14 April (Good Friday), 17 April (Easter Monday), 1 May (May Day), 29 May (Spring Bank Holiday), 19 June (Queen's Official Birthday), 28 August (Late Summer Bank Holiday), 10 September (Gibraltar National Holiday), 25–26 December (Christmas).

2007: 1 January (New Year's Day), 12 March (Commonwealth Day), 6 April (Good Friday), 9 April (Easter Monday), 28 May (Spring Bank Holiday), 18 June (Queen's Official Birthday), 27 August (Late Summer Bank Holiday), 10 September (Gibraltar National Day), 25–26 December (for Christmas).

Weights and Measures

Imperial weights and measures are in use, but the metric system is gradually being introduced.

Statistical Survey

Source (unless otherwise indicated): Statistics Office, 99 Harbours Walk, The New Harbours, Gibraltar; tel. 75515; fax 51160; e-mail gibstats@gibtelecom.net.

AREA AND POPULATION

Area: 6.5 sq km (2.5 sq miles).

Population (excl. armed forces): 27,495 (males 13,644, females 13,851) at census of 12 November 2001 (Gibraltarians 22,882, Other British 2,627, Non-British 1,986). *2004* (official figure): 28,759 (Gibraltarians 23,200, Other British 3,326, Non-British 2,233).

Density (2003): 4,424.5 per sq km.

Births, Marriages and Deaths (2004, excl. armed forces): Live births 421 (birth rate 14.6 per 1,000); Marriages 886 (marriage rate 5.5 per 1,000); Deaths 242 (death rate 8.4 per 1,000).

Expectation of Life (years at birth): Males 78.5; Females 83.3 at census of 2001.

Employment (October 2004): Manufacturing 453; Construction 1,788; Electricity, gas and water 275; Wholesale and retail trade, and repair of goods 2,697; Restaurants and hotels 974; Transport, storage and communications 945; Financial intermediation 1,332; Real estate, renting and business activities 1,793; Public administration and defence 2,179; Education 720; Health and social work 1,174; Other community, social and personal services 1,664; Total 15,994 (males 9,350, females 6,644). Figures cover only non-agricultural activities, excluding mining and quarrying.

INDUSTRY

Electric Energy (2004): 135.6m. kWh.

FINANCE

Currency and Exchange Rates: 100 pence (pennies) = 1 Gibraltar pound (G£). *Sterling, Dollar and Euro Equivalents* (30 December 2005): £1 sterling = G£1.0000; US $1 = 58.08 pence; €1 = 68.51 pence; G£100 = £100.00 sterling = $172.18 = €145.96. *Average Exchange Rate* (G£ per US dollar): 0.6125 in 2003; 0.5462 in 2004; 0.5500 in 2005. Note: The Gibraltar pound is at par with sterling.

Budget (forecasts, G£ '000, year ending 31 March 2005): *Recurrent Revenue:* Taxes 104,100; Duties 36,673; Gambling fees 4,643; Rates 14,400; Departmental fees and receipts 14,477; Government earnings 6,735; Total 181,028. *Recurrent Expenditure:* Education, employment and training 22,230; Heritage, culture, youth and sport 3,392; Housing 8,909; Environment, roads and utilities 24,440; Social and civic affairs 18,979; Trade, industry and communications 10,513; Health and civil protection 37,417; Administration 9,356; Finance 11,746; Law officers 597; Judiciary 912; House of Assembly 954; Office of Principal Auditor 541; Consolidated fund charges 28,091; Total 178,077.

Cost of Living (Retail Price Index at January; base: April 1998 = 100): 104.2 in 2002; 106.0 in 2003; 108.6 in 2004.

Gross National Product (G£ million, at factor cost): 401.44 in 2000/01; 429.65 in 2001/02; 458.94 in 2002/03.

Gross Domestic Product (G£ million, at factor cost): 433.61 in 2000/01; 470.18 in 2001/02; 570.17 in 2002/03.

EXTERNAL TRADE

Imports c.i.f. (G£ million, excluding petroleum products): 256.2 in 2002; 286.1 in 2003; 292.0 in 2004.

Exports f.o.b. (G£ million, excluding petroleum products): 98.5 in 2002; 90.1 in 2003; 108.4 in 2004.

Principal Trading Partners (G£ '000, 2004, excluding petroleum products): *Imports:* United Kingdom 84,424; Spain 45,206; Netherlands 6,340; Japan 3,022; USA 2,295; Total (incl. others) 291,981. Note: Figures for exports are not available.

TRANSPORT

Road Traffic (licences current at 31 December 2004): Private vehicles 12,395; Commercial vehicles 1,065; Motorcycles 5,358.

Shipping (merchant vessels, 2003): Tonnage entered ('000 grt) 170,700; Vessels entered 7,701.

Civil Aviation (2004): Passenger arrivals 157,061; Passenger departures 157,359; Freight loaded 61 metric tons; Freight unloaded 320 metric tons. Figures exclude military passengers and freight.

TOURISM

Visitor Arrivals ('000): 7,608.5 in 2002; 7,781.4 in 2003; 7,628.7 in 2004.

Tourism Receipts (G£ million): 177.38 in 2002; 202.58 in 2003; 229.15 in 2004.

COMMUNICATIONS MEDIA

Radio Receivers (1997): 37,000 in use (Source: UNESCO, *Statistical Yearbook*).

Television Licences (2004): 7,644.

Daily Newspapers (1999): 1.

Telephone Stations (2004): 34,476.

Facsimile Machines (1997): 322 in use (Source: UN, *Statistical Yearbook*).

Mobile Cellular Telephones (2000): 5,558 subscribers (Source: International Telecommunication Union).

Internet Connections (2003): 6,018.

EDUCATION

Primary (state schools, 2004, unless otherwise indicated): 11 schools (1999), 2,996 pupils.

Secondary (state schools, 2004, unless otherwise indicated): 2 schools (1999), 2,043 pupils.

Total Teaching Staff at Primary and Secondary Schools (state schools, 2004): 333.

Technical and Vocational (1999): 1 college, 201 full-time students.

Directory

The Constitution

Gibraltar is a United Kingdom Overseas Territory, and the supreme authority is vested in the Governor and Commander-in-Chief, who is the representative of the British monarch. Relations with the British Government are maintained through the Foreign and Commonwealth Office.

Gibraltar controls the majority of its domestic affairs, while the United Kingdom is responsible for matters of external affairs, defence and internal security. Following the referendum of 10 September 1967 (in which the people of Gibraltar voted in favour of retaining British sovereignty), a new Constitution was introduced on 11 August 1969. This Constitution contains a code of human rights and provides for its enforcement by the Supreme Court of Gibraltar. The other main provisions are as follows:

BRITISH SOVEREIGNTY

The Preamble to the Gibraltar Constitution Order contains assurances that Gibraltar will remain part of the dominions of the British Crown (unless these provisions are amended by further legislation adopted by the British Parliament), and that the United Kingdom will never enter into arrangements under which the people of Gibraltar would pass under the sovereignty of another State against their freely and democratically expressed wishes.

THE GOVERNOR AND COMMANDER-IN-CHIEF

As a representative of the British monarch, the Governor and Commander-in-Chief is responsible for matters which directly relate to external affairs, defence and internal security and certain other matters not specifically defined as domestic matters. The Governor is also head of the executive and administers Gibraltar, acting generally on the advice of the Gibraltar Council. In exceptional circumstances, the Governor has special powers to refuse any advice from the Gibraltar Council which, in the Governor's opinion, may not be in the interests of maintaining financial and economic stability. The Governor's formal assent, on behalf of the Crown, is required for all legislation. In some cases, the prior concurrence of the Crown, conveyed through the Secretary of State for Foreign and Commonwealth Affairs, is also required. The Crown may, through the Governor and Commander-in-Chief, disband the House of Assembly, introduce direct rule and enact legislation for the 'peace, order and good government of Gibraltar'.

THE GIBRALTAR COUNCIL

The Council consists of the Deputy Governor, the Land Forces Commander, the Attorney-General, the Financial and Development Secretary, *ex officio*, the Chief Minister, who is appointed by the Governor as the elected member of the House of Assembly most likely to command the confidence of the other elected members, and four other ministers designated by the Governor after consultation with the Chief Minister. The Council advises the Governor, who usually acts on its advice.

COUNCIL OF MINISTERS

The Council of Ministers comprises the Chief Minister and between four and eight other ministers appointed from the elected members of the Assembly by the Governor, in consultation with the Chief Minister. It is presided over by the Chief Minister and deals with domestic matters which have been defined as such by the Constitution. The Chief Minister is constitutionally responsible for the economy. Individual ministers may be given responsibility for specific business. Heads of Departments and other government officials appear before it when required.

HOUSE OF ASSEMBLY

The House of Assembly is composed of the Speaker, 15 elected members and two *ex officio* members (the Attorney-General and the Financial and Development Secretary). The Financial and Development Secretary is appointed by the Governor, normally after consultation with the Chief Minister. The Speaker is appointed by the Governor, after consultation with the Chief Minister and the Leader of the Opposition.

The normal term of the House of Assembly is four years. Elections are open to all adult British subjects and citizens of the Republic of Ireland who have been ordinarily resident in Gibraltar for a continuous period of six months prior to the date for registration as an elector. The minimum voting age is 18 years. The system of proportional representation, which was formerly used for elections to the Legislative Council, has been abandoned in favour of a new system, whereby each elector may vote for a maximum of eight candidates, and the party with the largest share of the vote is restricted to a maximum of eight seats.

The elected members of the House of Assembly elect the Mayor from among their number, and he carries out ceremonial and representational functions on behalf of the City of Gibraltar.

Note: In March 2006 Gibraltar and the United Kingdom finally reached agreement on the main provisions of a new draft constitution for the territory. The proposals (which were to be put to a national referendum later in the year) did not diminish British sovereignty of Gibraltar, but limited the responsibilities of the Governor, thereby giving the Gibraltar authorities greater control over the internal affairs of the territory (see Recent History).

The Government

Governor and Commander-in-Chief: Sir FRANCIS RICHARDS (took office 27 May 2003).

GIBRALTAR COUNCIL

President: Sir FRANCIS RICHARDS (The Governor).

Ex Officio Members: PAUL BARTON (Deputy Governor), Cdre ALLAN ADAIR WILLMETT (Commander British Forces), TIMOTHY BRISTOW (Financial and Development Secretary), R. RHODA (Attorney-General).

Elected Members: PETER CARUANA, Dr BERNARD LINARES, ERNEST BRITTO, JOE HOLLIDAY, JAIME NETTO, YVETTE DEL AGUA, CLIVE BELTRAN, FABIAN VINET.

Gibraltar

COUNCIL OF MINISTERS
(April 2006)

Chief Minister: Peter Caruana.
Minister for Trade, Industry, Communications, the Employment Service and Public Transport: Joe J. Holliday.
Minister for Education and Training, Civic and Consumer Affairs and Minority Issues: Dr Bernard Linares.
Minister for Health: Ernest Britto.
Minister for Housing: Clive Beltran.
Minister for Social Affairs and Children's, Single Parent and Women's Issues: Yvette Del Agua.
Minister for Heritage, Culture, Youth, Sport and Utilities: Fabian Vinet.
Minister for the Environment, Roads, Traffic and Urban Renewal: Jaime Netto.

MINISTRIES

Office of the Governor: The Convent, Main St; tel. 45440; fax 47823; e-mail enquiry.gibraltar@fco.gov.uk.
Office of the Chief Minister: 6 Convent Pl.; tel. 70071; fax 76396; e-mail govsec@gibnet.gi; internet www.gibraltar.gov.gi/chief_minister/chief_minister_index.htm.
Ministry of Education and Training, Civic and Consumer Affairs and Minority Issues: 40 Town Range; tel. 77486; fax 71564; e-mail teachers@gibnynex.gi.
Ministry of the Environment, Roads, Traffic and Urban Renewal: Joshua Hassan House, Secretary's Lane; tel. 59801; fax 76223; e-mail meru@gibtelecom.net.
Ministry of Heritage, Culture, Youth, Sport and Utilities: 6 Convent Pl.; tel. 70071; fax 76396.
Ministry of Housing: City Hall, John Mackintosh Sq.; tel. 75603; fax 52947.
Ministry of Social Affairs: 14 Governor's Parade; tel. 78566; fax 42509; e-mail dss@gibraltar.gov.gi.
Ministry of Trade, Industry, Communications, the Employment Service and Public Transport: Suite 771, Europort; tel. 52052; fax 71406; e-mail gibdti@gibtelecom.net; internet www.gibraltar.gov.gi.

Legislature

House of Assembly
156 Main St; tel. 78420; fax 42849; e-mail house@gibtelecom.net; internet www.gibraltar.gov.gi.
Speaker: Haresh K. Budhrani.

General Election, 28 November 2003

Party	% of votes cast	Seats
Gibraltar Social Democrats	51.5	8
Gibraltar Socialist Labour Party	39.7	7
Gibraltar Liberal Party		
Gibraltar Labour Party	8.3	—
Reform Party	0.5	—
Total	100.0	15

In addition to the 15 elected members, the House of Assembly has an appointed Speaker and two *ex officio* members (the Attorney-General and the Financial and Development Secretary). A Mayor of Gibraltar, with ceremonial and representational functions, is chosen from among their number by the elected members of the Assembly.

Political Organizations

All political organizations in Gibraltar advocate self-determination for the territory.

Gibraltar Liberal Party (GLP): 93 Irish Town, POB 225; tel. 76959; fax 74664; e-mail libparty@gibnet.gi; internet www.gib.gi/liberalparty; f. 1991 as the Gibraltar National Party; Leader Dr Joseph García; Chair. Jonathan Stagnetto; Sec.-Gen. Damon Bossino.
Gibraltar Social Democrats (GSD): 3/5 Horse Barrack Court; tel. and fax 70786; e-mail info@gsd.gi; internet www.gsd.gi; f. 1989; holds a majority of seats in the House of Assembly; absorbed the Gibraltar Labour Party in 2005; Leader Peter Caruana; Gen. Sec. Laura V. Correa.
Gibraltar Socialist Labour Party (GSLP): Suite 16, Block 3, Watergardens; tel. 50700; fax 78983; e-mail hqgslp@gibtelecom.net; internet www.gslp.gi; f. 1976; Leader Joseph Bossano.
Reform Party: POB 676; tel. 77655; e-mail info@reformpartygib.com; internet www.reformpartygib.com; f. 2000 as the Independent Liberal Forum; Leader Lyana Armstrong-Emery.

Judicial System

The 1969 Gibraltar Constitution provides for the protection of the fundamental rights and freedoms of the individual and the maintenance of a Supreme Court with unlimited jurisdiction to hear and determine any civil or criminal proceedings under any law. The Courts of Law of Gibraltar comprise a Court of Appeal, the Supreme Court and the Magistrates' Court.

The substantive law of Gibraltar is contained in Orders in Council which apply to Gibraltar, enactments of the Parliament of the United Kingdom which apply to or have been extended or applied to Gibraltar, locally enacted ordinances and subsidiary legislation, and common law and the rules of equity from time to time in force in the United Kingdom so far as they may be applicable and subject to all necessary modification.

COURT OF APPEAL
277 Main St; the Court of Appeal holds three sessions each year. The Justices of Appeal are drawn from the English Court of Appeal.
President: Sir Christopher Staughton.
Justices of Appeal: Sir Murray Stuart-Smith, Sir Philip Otton, Sir William Aldous.

SUPREME COURT
277 Main St; the Supreme Court includes the office of Admiralty Marshal.
Chief Justice: Derek Schofield.
Justice: Anthony E. Dudley.

MAGISTRATES' COURT
Stipendiary Magistrate: Charles Pitto.

Religion

At the 2001 census 78.1% of the population were Roman Catholic, 7.0% Church of England, 4.0% Muslim, 2.1% Jewish and 1.8% Hindu.

CHRISTIANITY
The Roman Catholic Church
Gibraltar forms a single diocese, directly responsible to the Holy See. At 31 December 2003 there were an estimated 21,470 adherents in the territory.
Bishop of Gibraltar: Rt Rev. Charles Caruana, 215 Main St; e-mail epis.carroca@gibnynex.gi; tel. 76688; fax 43112.

The Church of England
The diocese of Gibraltar in Europe, founded in 1980, has jurisdiction over the whole of continental Europe, Turkey and Morocco.
Bishop of Gibraltar in Europe: Rt Rev. Dr Geoffrey Rowell, Bishop's Lodge, Church Rd, Worth, RH10 7RT, United Kingdom; tel. (1293) 883051; fax (1293) 884479; e-mail bishop@eurobish.clara.co.uk; internet europe.anglican.org; in Gibraltar: Cathedral of the Holy Trinity, Cathedral Sq., Main St; tel. 75745; fax 78463.

Other Christian Churches
Church of Scotland (St Andrew's Presbyterian): Governor's Parade; tel. and fax 77040; e-mail lamont@gibraltar.gi; internet www.scotskirkgibraltar.com; f. 1800; Minister Rev. Stewart Lamont (St Andrew's Manse, 29 Scud Hill); 50 mems.
Methodist Church: Wesley House, 297 Main St; tel. and fax 40870; e-mail widor@gibnetmail.gi; Minister Rev. Wilf Pearce; f. 1769; 49 mems.

ISLAM
A mosque to serve the Islamic community in Gibraltar and financed by the Government of Saudi Arabia was constructed in the late 1990s.

JUDAISM
Jewish Community: Managing Board, 10 Bomb House Lane, POB 318; tel. 72606; fax 40487; e-mail mbjc@g.btelecom.net; Pres. H. J. M. Levy; Hon. Sec. M. Anahory (acting); Admin. Sec. E. Benady; 600 mems.

The Press

Gibraltar Chronicle: 2 Library Gardens, POB 27; tel. 78589; fax 79927; e-mail gibchron@gibnet.gi; internet www.chronicle.gi; f. 1801; daily (except Sunday); English; Man. Editor D. SEARLE; circ. 6,000.

Gibraltar Gazette: 6 Convent Pl.; tel. 47932; fax 74524; e-mail legisunit@gibnynex.gi; f. 1949; weekly; publ. by Gibraltar Chronicle; official notices; circ. 375.

Gibraltar Magazine: Suite 6377, Imossi House, Irish Town; tel. and fax 77748; e-mail gibmag@gibnet.gi; internet www.thegibraltarmagazine.com; f. 1995; monthly; English; Editor ANDREA MORTON.

Insight: tel. 40913; e-mail advert@insight-gibraltar.com; internet www.insight-gibraltar.com; f. 1992; print and internet magazine; circ. 6,000.

Panorama: 93–95 Irish Town; tel. 79797; fax 74664; e-mail gibnet@gibnews.gi; internet www.panorama.gi; f. 1975; weekly, on Monday; English; Editor JOE GARCÍA; circ. 4,000.

The New People: 6B Portland House, Glacis Rd, POB 484; tel. 79018; fax 50349; weekly; English with Spanish section; Editor C. GOLT; circ. 1,000.

Vox: Unit 101, Harbours Walk, New Harbours, POB 306; tel. 77414; fax 72531; e-mail vox@gibnynex.gi; f. 1955; weekly; bilingual (English and Spanish); Editor E. J. CAMPELLO; circ. 1,800.

Broadcasting and Communications

TELECOMMUNICATIONS

Gibraltar Regulatory Authority (GRA): Suite 811, Europort; tel. 74636; fax 72166; e-mail info@gra.gi; internet www.gra.gi; f. 2000; statutory body responsible for overseeing the regulation of the telecommunications sector and for the management of the non-military radio spectrum; Chief Exec. PAUL CANESSA.

GibNet Ltd: Suite 121, Eurotowers, POB 797; tel. 47200; fax 47272; e-mail enquiries@gibnet.net; internet www.gibnet.gi; f. 1994; internet service provider.

Gibtelecom Ltd: Suite 942, Europort; tel. 52200; fax 71673; e-mail info@gibtele.com; internet www.gibtele.com; f. 1990; jointly owned by Govt and Verizon Inc (USA); Gibraltar Nynex Communications Ltd (GNC), GNC Networks Ltd and Gibraltar Telecommunications International Ltd (Gibtel) merged in 2002 to form the above; GNC Networks Ltd (f. 1996) was renamed Gibconnect; operates local and international telephone and telecommunications services; provides range of digital, satellite, mobile and internet services.

BROADCASTING

Gibraltar Broadcasting Corporation (GBC): Broadcasting House, 18 South Barrack Rd; tel. 79760; fax 78673; e-mail gbc@gibraltar.gi; internet www.gbc.gi; f. 1963; responsible for television and radio broadcasting; Gen. Man. G. J. VALARINO.

Radio

GBC—Radio (Radio Gibraltar): 24 hours daily in English and Spanish, including commercial broadcasting. In addition to local programmes, the BBC World Service programme is relayed.

Television

GBC—TV: operates in English for 24 hours dailyGBC and relayed BBC programmes are transmitted.

Finance

(cap. = capital; res = reserves; dep. = deposits; m. = million; brs = branches; amounts in G£)

BANKING

There were 17 banks operating in Gibraltar in March 2004.

Regulatory Authority

Financial Services Commission: Suite 943, Europort, POB 940; tel. 40283; fax 40282; e-mail info@fsc.gi; internet www.fsc.gi; f. 1989; regulates the activities of the financial sector; Chair. MARCUS KILLICK.

Banks

ABN AMRO Bank (Gibraltar) Ltd: Sorte 731–734, Europort; tel. 74474; fax 78512; e-mail private.banking@gi.abnamro.com; internet www.abnamro.gi; f. 1964; cap. and res 1.8m., dep. 148m. (Dec. 1995); Chair. J. J. W. ZWEEGERS; Man. Dir HANS DIEDEREN.

BBVA Privanza International (Gibraltar) Ltd: 260–262 Main St, POB 488; tel. 79420; fax 73870; e-mail bbvpring@gibnet.gi; Man. TONINO LETO.

Barclays Bank PLC: Regal House, 3 Queensway, POB 187; tel. 78565; fax 795069; e-mail gibraltar@barclays.co.uk; Chief Man. DOUGLAS REYES.

Credit Suisse (Gibraltar) Ltd: 1st Floor, Neptune House, Marina Bay, POB 556; tel. 78399; fax 76027; e-mail csg.mail@cspb.com; f. 1987; cap. and res 5.0m., dep. 198.9m. (Dec. 2002); Chair. A. VAYLOYAN; Man. Dir PETER SCHUSTER.

EFG Bank (Gibraltar) Ltd: Eurolife Bldg, 1 Corral Rd, POB 561; tel. 40117; fax 40110; e-mail atlaco@gibnet.gi; formerly Banco Atlántico (Gibraltar) Ltd; Man. EMILIO MARTÍNEZ PRIEGO.

S. G. Hambros Bank & Trust (Gibraltar) Ltd: Hambro House, 32 Line Wall Rd, POB 375; tel. 74850; fax 79037; e-mail gibraltar@sghambros.com; internet www.sghambros.com; est. 1981; cap. 1.5m., res 10.2m., dep. 245.0m. (June 2005); Chair. WARWICK J. NEWBURY; Man. Dir FRANCO CASSAR.

Hispano Commerzbank (Gibraltar) Ltd: Don House, Suite 14, 30/38 Main St; tel. 74199; fax 74174; e-mail hcg@gibnynex.gi; f. 1991; cap. and res 5.0m., dep. 3.8m. (Dec. 2000); Pres. and Chair. JOSÉ REIG; CEO BERND VON OELFFEN; Gen. Man. JUAN ROSAS.

Jyske Bank (Gibraltar) Ltd: 76 Main St, POB 143; tel. 72782; fax 72732; e-mail jyskebank@jyskebank.ltd.gi; internet www.jbpb.com; f. 1855 as Galliano (A. L.) Bankers; in 1988 name changed as above; cap. 26.5m., res 0.2m., dep. 1,566.2m. (Dec. 2003); Chair. JENS LAURITZEN; Man. Dir TIM MARSHALL.

Lloyds TSB Bank PLC: 323 Main St, POB 482; tel. 77373; fax 70023; Man. ALBERT DOUGLAS LANGSTON.

Lombard Odier Private Bank (Gibraltar) Ltd: Suite 921, Europort, POB 407; tel. 73350.

NatWest Offshore Ltd: NatWest House, 57/63 Line Wall Rd, POB 707; tel. 77737; fax 74557; e-mail natwestgib@gibnynex.gi; internet www.natwestoffshore.com; f. 1988; Chief Man. PETE YEOMAN.

Royal Bank of Scotland (Gibraltar) Ltd: 1 Corral Rd; tel. 73200; fax 70152.

Turicum Private Bank Ltd: Turicum House, 315 Main St, POB 619; tel. 44144; fax 44145; e-mail turicum@gibnet.gi; internet www.turicumprivatebank.com; f. 1993; cap. and res €5.0m., dep. €15.7m. (Dec. 2003); Chair. Dr RAYMOND BISANG; Gen. Man. FRIEDRICH STUCKI.

Savings Bank

Gibraltar Savings Bank: Treasury Dept, Treasury Bldg, 23 John Mackintosh Sq.; tel. 48396; fax 74552; e-mail treasury@gibtelecom.net; dep. 182.98m. (March 2004); Dir D. D. TIRATHDAS.

Association

Gibraltar Bankers' Association: c/o S. G. Hambros Bank & Trust (Gibraltar) Ltd, 32 Line Wall Rd; tel. 74850; fax 79037; f. 1982; Pres. RAY LANGHAM; 20 mem. banks.

INSURANCE

There were 39 licensed insurance companies operating in Gibraltar in March 2004.

BMI Insurance Services Limited: Unit 7, Portland House, Glacis Rd, POB 469; tel. 51010.

Capurro Insurance and Investments Ltd: 20 Line Wall Rd, POB 130; tel. 40850; fax 40851; e-mail info@capurroinsurance.com; internet www.capurroinsurance.com.

Castiel Winser Insurance and Financial Consultants: Natwest House, 57/63 Line Wall Rd, POB 464; tel. 77723; fax 79257; e-mail financialservices@castielwinser.com; f. 1985; Man. Dir SYDNEY ATTIAS.

Eurolife Assurance (International) Ltd: Eurolife Bldg, 1 Corral Rd, POB 233; tel. 73495; fax 73120; e-mail eurolife@gibnet.gi; Man. A. SMITH.

Eurolinx (Gibraltar) Ltd: Suites 21–22, Victoria House, 26 Main St, POB 671; tel. 40240; fax 40241; e-mail eurolinx@sapphirenet.gi; f. 1990; Dir ALAN JOSEPH MONTEGRIFFO.

Gibro Insurance Services Ltd: Gibro House, 4 Giros Passage, POB 693; tel. 43777; fax 43538; e-mail gibroins@gibtelecom.net.

Middle Sea Insurance PLC: Suite 1A, 143 Main St, POB 502; tel. 76434.

Norwich Union International Insurance Ltd: Regal House, 3 Queensway, POB 45; tel. 79520; fax 70942; e-mail nugib@gibnet.gi; f. 1984; cap. 1,600,000; CEO. ERIC D. CHALONER; Chair. PAUL L. SAVIGNON.

Ophir Insurance Services Ltd: 123 Main St, POB 914; tel. 73871; fax 50411; e-mail ophir@gibtelecom.net.

UNITED KINGDOM OVERSEAS TERRITORIES

Association

Gibraltar Insurance Association: c/o NatWest House, 57/63 Line Wall Rd, POB 464; tel. 77723; fax 79257; f. 1995.

Trade and Industry

CHAMBER OF COMMERCE

Gibraltar Chamber of Commerce: Watergate House, Casemates Sq. 2/6, POB 29; tel. 78376; fax 78403; e-mail gichacom@gibnet.gi; internet www.gibraltarchamberofcommerce.com; f. 1882; Pres. PETER A. ISOLA; 300 mems.

EMPLOYERS' ORGANIZATIONS

Gibraltar Federation of Small Businesses: GFSB House, POB 115, Irish Town; tel. 47722; fax 47733; e-mail gfsb@gfsb.gi; internet www.gfsb.gi; f. 1996; Chair. MARILOU GUERRERO.

Gibraltar Hotel Association: c/o Caleta Hotel; tel. 76501; fax 71050; e-mail caleta@gibnynex.gi; internet www.caletahotel.com; f. 1960; Chair. FRANCO OSTUNI; seven mems.

Gibraltar Licensed Victuallers' Association: c/o Watergate Restaurant, Queensway Quay; tel. 74195; f. 1976; Chair. M. OTON; 120 mems.

Gibraltar Motor Traders' Association: POB 167; tel. 79004; f. 1961; Gen. Sec. G. BASSADONE; six mems.

Hindu Merchants' Association: POB 82; tel. 73521; fax 79895; e-mail budlaw@gibnynex.gi; f. 1964; Pres. H. K. BUDHRANI; 125 mems.

PRINCIPAL TRADE UNIONS

Gibraltar Taxi Association: 19 Waterport Wharf; tel. 70052; fax 76986; f. 1957; Pres. CLIVE ZAMMIT; 100 mems.

Gibraltar Trades Council: 7 Hargraves Ramp, POB 279; tel. 76930; fax 79646; e-mail prospect.ggca@gibtelecom.net; comprises unions representing 70% of the working population; affiliated to the United Kingdom Trades Union Congress; Sec. MICHAEL J. A. TAMPIN; Pres. EDWIN J. REYES.

Affiliated unions:

NASUWT (Gibraltar) (NASUWT): 40 Town Range; tel. 76308; fax 77608; e-mail gtateachers@gibtelecom.net; f. 1962; fmrly known as the Gibraltar Teachers' Association; Pres. MONICA RITCHIE; 350 mems.

Prospect/GGCA Branch: 7 Hargrave's Ramp, POB 279; tel. 76930; fax 79646; e-mail prospect.ggca@gibtelecom.net; internet www.prospectbranches.org.uk/gibraltar; f. 1967; Pres. JOSE LUIS GARCIA; Br. Sec. MICHAEL J. A. TAMPIN; 910 mems (2005).

Transport & General Workers' Union (United Kingdom) (Gibraltar District): tel. 74185; fax 71596; f. 1924; Dist. Officer LUIS MONTIEL; 4,239 mems.

UTILITIES

Electricity

Gibraltar Electricity Authority: Waterport Power Station, North Mole; tel. 48908; fax 77408; govt-owned; generation, distribution and supply of electricity.

Water

AquaGib Ltd: Leanse Pl., Suite 10B, 50 Town Range; tel. 40880; fax 40881; e-mail main.office@aquagib.gi; internet www.aquagib.gi; fmrly known as Lyonnais des Eaux (Gibraltar) Ltd; renamed as above Dec. 2003; Man. Dir P. LATIN.

Transport

There are no railways in Gibraltar. There are 12.9 km of highways in the City, and a total road length of 53.1 km, including 6.8 km of footpaths.

ROADS

Ministry of the Environment, Roads, Traffic and Urban Renewal: see Ministries.

SHIPPING

The Strait of Gibraltar is a principal ocean route between the Mediterranean and Black Sea areas and the rest of the world.

Gibraltar is used by many long-distance liners, and has dry dock facilities and a commercial ship-repair yard. Tax concessions are available to ship-owners who register their ships at Gibraltar. At 31 December 2004 170 vessels, with a combined total displacement of 1,142,448 grt, were registered at Gibraltar.

Office of the Maritime Administrator: Gibraltar Ship Registry, Duke of Kent House, Cathedral Sq.; tel. 47771; fax 47770; e-mail shipregistry@gibnynex.gi.

Gibraltar Port Authority: Port Office, North Mole; tel. 77254; fax 77011; e-mail davis@gibtelecom.net; internet www.gibraltarport.com; administers the Port of Gibraltar; CEO TONY DAVIES.

Cammell Laird (Gibraltar) Ltd: Main Wharf Rd, The Dockyard, POB 858; tel. 59400; fax 44404; e-mail mail@lairds.gi; drydock facilities and general ship repairing; Man. Dir MEL SMITH.

M. H. Bland & Co Ltd: Cloister Bldg, Market Lane, POB 554; tel. 75009; fax 71608; f. 1810; ship agents, salvage and towage contractors; Chair. JOHN G. GAGGERO.

Association

Gibraltar Shipping Association: c/o Inchcape Shipping Services, POB 194; tel. 46315; fax 46316; e-mail mark.porral@iss-shipping.com; f. 1957; Sec. P. L. IMOSSI; 11 mems.

CIVIL AVIATION

The airport is at North Front, on the isthmus, 2.5 km from the City centre.

Gibraltar Civil Aviation Advisory Board: Air Terminal, Winston Churchill Ave; tel. 73026; fax 73925; e-mail info@gibraltar-airport.com; Sec. JOHN GONÇALVES.

GB Airways Ltd: The Rotunda, Winston Churchill Ave; tel. 79300; fax 51562; internet www.gbairways.com; f. 1931 as Gibraltar Airways; private co; franchise operator for British Airways (United Kingdom) from 1995; Pres. JOSEPH J. GAGGERO; Man. Dir JOHN PATTERSON.

Tourism

Gibraltar's tourist attractions include its climate, beaches and a variety of amenities. Following the reopening of the border with Spain in February 1985, the resumption of traffic by day-visitors contributed to the expansion of the tourist industry. In 2004 visitor arrivals (by sea, air and land) numbered some 7.63m., while revenue from tourism totalled G£229.15m.

Gibraltar Tourist Board: Duke of Kent House, Cathedral Sq.; tel. 74950; fax 74943; e-mail tourism@gibraltar.gi; internet www.gibraltar.gov.uk; CEO PETER R. CANESSA.

MONTSERRAT

Introductory Survey

Location, Climate, Language, Religion, Flag, Capital

Montserrat is one of the Leeward Islands in the West Indies. A mountainous, volcanic island, it lies about 55 km (35 miles) north of Basse-Terre, Guadeloupe, and about 43 km (27 miles) south west of Antigua. The climate is generally warm, with a mean maximum temperature of 30°C (86°F) and a mean minimum of 23°C (73°F), but the island is fanned by sea breezes for most of the year. The average annual rainfall is about 1,475 mm (58 ins), although there is more rain in the central and western areas. English is the official language. Many Christian churches are represented, but the principal denominations are the Anglican, Roman Catholic and Methodist Churches. The flag is the British 'Blue Ensign', with the island's badge (a shield depicting a woman dressed in green holding a harp and a cross) on a white roundel in the fly. The capital is Plymouth.

Recent History

Montserrat was first settled by the British (initially Roman Catholic exiles) in 1632, by which time the few original Carib inhabitants had disappeared. It formed part of the federal colony of the Leeward Islands from 1871 until 1956, when the federation was dissolved and the presidency of Montserrat became a separate colony. Montserrat participated in the short-lived Federation of the West Indies (1958–62) and, from 1960, the island had its own Administrator (the title was changed to that of Governor in 1971). The Constitution (see below) came into force in 1960.

The first priority of successive legislatures has been to improve infrastructure and maintain a healthy economy. Between 1952 and 1970 William Bramble dominated island politics. His son, Austin Bramble, leader of the Progressive Democratic Party (PDP), opposed and succeeded him as Chief Minister. In November 1978 the People's Liberation Movement (PLM) won all seven elective seats in the Legislative Council, and the PLM's leader, John Osborne, became Chief Minister. In the general election of February 1983 the PLM was returned to government with five seats. The remainder were won by the PDP, whose commitment to development projects, agriculture and education complemented those of the PLM.

Attempts to form an opposition alliance between the PDP and the National Development Party (NDP—formed by business interests and former members of the PDP) were unsuccessful. Against a divided opposition, the PLM won four of the seven elective seats in the Legislative Council at an early general election in August 1987. The NDP won two seats, and the PDP one (Bramble lost his seat and announced his retirement from politics). Osborne was returned to office as Chief Minister.

Osborne was an advocate of independence from the United Kingdom, despite the apparent lack of popular support for this policy. A referendum on the issue was planned for 1990, but the devastation caused by 'Hurricane Hugo' in September 1989, meant that any plans for independence were postponed. Furthermore, the Osborne Government and the British authorities were embarrassed by controversy surrounding the hitherto lucrative 'offshore' financial sector. In early 1989 the Governor's office announced that the British police were investigating serious allegations against certain banks (involving the processing of illegal funds from a variety of criminal activities). Registration was suspended, several people were charged with criminal offences and, at the end of 1989, most banking licences were revoked. The Montserrat Government agreed to introduce recommended provisions for the regulation of the financial services industry, but Osborne objected strongly to a proposed amendment to the Constitution which transferred responsibility for the sector from the Chief Minister to the Governor. Agreement was subsequently reached, however, when Osborne acknowledged that 'offshore' finance was part of the British Government's responsibility for external affairs.

In late 1990 a dispute arose between the Chief Minister and his deputy, Benjamin Chalmers, who was reported to have accused Osborne of dishonesty in his relations with the Executive Council. Allegations of corruption continued in 1991, and in June an inquiry was undertaken by the British police to investigate the possible involvement of members of the Executive Council in the 1989 banking scandal, as well as in fraudulent land transfers.

The resignation of Chalmers in September 1991, following a further dispute with Osborne, resulted in the loss of the Government's majority in the Legislative Council. This prompted an early election in the following month, when the National Progressive Party (NPP), which had been formed only two months prior to the election, secured four seats. The PLM and the NDP retained one seat each, while an independent candidate won the remaining seat. The leader of the NPP, Reuben Meade, became Chief Minister.

In December 1991 the Legislative Council approved legislation allowing the re-establishment of a comprehensive 'offshore' financial centre. Despite considerably improved regulation, more than 90% of the island's 'offshore' and commercial banks were again closed down, following further investigations by British inspectors in mid-1992.

The eruption of Chance's Peak volcano in July 1995, which had been dormant for more than 100 years, caused severe disruption to the island and threatened to devastate Plymouth and surrounding areas in southern Montserrat. In late August the threat of a more serious eruption prompted the evacuation of some 5,000 people to the north of the island, and the declaration by the Government of a state of emergency and a night curfew. As volcanic activity subsided in September, evacuated islanders returned to Plymouth and villages near the volcano. However, by December the area was again deemed to be unsafe, and 4,000 people were evacuated for a further period of several weeks. The Governor and Chief Minister secured an agreement from the British Government for the provision of assistance with evacuation and rehabilitation programmes. A third evacuation took place in April 1996, following a further series of eruptions, and it was announced that some 5,000 evacuees living in 'safe areas' would remain there at least until the end of the year. In that month the British Government announced that Montserratians would be granted residency and the right to work in the United Kingdom for up to two years. In August the British Government announced that it was to provide assistance worth £25m. to finance housing construction projects, infrastructure development, the provision of temporary health and education facilities and other public services in the northern 'safe areas' of the island. By the end of 1996 it was estimated that some 5,000 islanders had left the Territory since the onset of volcanic activity in mid-1995.

In September 1996 the Government announced that the general election would take place, despite the continued disruption in the Territory. The Deputy Chief Minister, Noel Tuitt, resigned from his post and from the NPP later that month, stating that he was disillusioned with Meade's leadership. Disagreement over the Government's management of the volcano crisis and its handling of aid funds led to the proposal, by an opposition member in early October, of a motion of 'no confidence' in the Chief Minister. Meade, however, avoided a vote on the motion by dissolving the Legislative Council. No party won an overall majority at the election on 11 November 1996. The NPP secured only one seat (won by Meade). The recently formed People's Progressive Alliance (PPA), led by John Osborne, secured two seats, as did both the Movement for National Reconstruction (MNR), led by Austin Bramble, and independent candidates. A four-member coalition cabinet (which included Meade, but did not include either PPA member) was subsequently formed under the leadership of Bertrand Osborne, who was sworn in as Chief Minister on 13 November.

In June 1997 the scale of volcanic activity on the island increased dramatically with the eruption of the Soufrière Hills volcano, which left some two-thirds of the island uninhabitable, destroyed the capital and resulted in the deaths of 19 people. Islanders were evacuated to 'safe areas' in the north of the country. The British Government responded to the crisis by releasing emergency aid in order to finance the construction of emergency shelters for evacuees, and for repairs to temporary hospital facilities. In July it was announced that a package of options for Montserratians was being formulated, which would offer islanders resettlement grants and assisted passage either to other islands within the Caribbean or to the United Kingdom. The 'safe area' in the north was to be developed for those wishing to remain on the island. By the end of July the population of Montserrat was estimated to have declined to 5,800; in the month since the eruption of the Soufrière Hills volcano some 800 islanders had moved to Antigua, bringing the total number who had moved there since the onset of volcanic activity in 1995 to some 3,000. Many more had resettled on other Caribbean islands or in the United Kingdom.

On 21 August 1997 Bertrand Osborne resigned as Chief Minister following four days of public demonstrations in protest at his handling of the volcano crisis, in particular at uncertainty surrounding the future of the islanders and at poor conditions in emergency shelters. On the same day the British Government announced the financial details of its voluntary evacuation scheme for those wishing to leave Montserrat. The offer, which comprised a relocation grant of £2,400 for adults and £600 for minors, in addition to travel costs, provoked an angry response from islanders, who protested that the grants were severely inadequate. Osborne's successor as Chief Minister, David Brandt, an independent member of the Legislative Council, criticized the British Government's offer while also accusing it of attempting to depopulate Montserrat by showing insufficient commitment to the redevelopment of the island. The British Secretary of State for International Development, Clare Short, denied that the United Kingdom was encouraging people to leave Montserrat. However, accusations made by Short, to the effect that the island's leaders were making unreasonable demands, caused considerable offence to the island Government and the controversy was assuaged only when the British Secretary of State for Foreign and Commonwealth Affairs, Robin Cook, announced, on 25 August, the formation of a special inter-departmental committee charged with co-ordinating assistance to Montserrat. At the end of August George Foulkes, the Under-Secretary of State for International Development, visited the island for discussions with the Montserrat Government, during which he announced a five-year sustainable development plan for the north of the island, to include finance for new housing, social services and improved infrastructure. In September Tony Abbott was inaugurated as Governor of Montserrat, replacing Frank Savage.

In January 1998 Brandt renewed his accusations that the British Government was attempting to depopulate Montserrat by delaying the release of development funds. Prompted by these accusations, in February Cook made a formal visit to Montserrat and it was subsequently announced that the United Kingdom would provide further finance of £4.8m. for housing on the island. The new funding brought the total amount committed by the British Government in 1995–98, since the beginning of the volcano crisis, to £59m.

In May 1998 the British Government announced that all citizens of Montserrat, except those already resident in other countries, would be entitled to settle in the United Kingdom. The estimated 3,500 refugees already in the United Kingdom on temporary visas were to be allowed to apply for permanent residency. In early July, to the surprise of monitoring scientists, the Soufrière Hills volcano erupted again, covering much of the island in ash, and postponing plans to re-open parts of Plymouth to residents. In August part of the central zone of Montserrat was re-opened, following operations to remove ash and debris. Also in August a committee of British MPs investigating the situation in Montserrat criticized the Government's handling of the crisis, noting that neither the Foreign and Commonwealth Office nor the Department for International Development had taken full responsibility for the situation. In September the Chief Minister and the Governor met Baroness Symons, Under-Secretary of State in the Foreign and Commonwealth Office, to discuss the current aid package and the speed of aid delivery.

In January 1999 an inquest into the 19 deaths during the eruptions found that in nine cases, the British Government was in part to blame for the deaths. The jury criticized the public shelters provided, where conditions were described as 'deplorable', and the Government's failure to provide farming land in the 'safe area', which had led to some farmers' choosing to risk their lives rather than abandon their farms. The Department for International Development, which was accused of providing 'unimaginative, grudging and tardy' long-term aid, denied culpability for the deaths, and announced that it was to spend a further £75m. on a three-year redevelopment programme in the north of the island.

In February 1999 studies were published confirming that the volcanic ash covering much of Montserrat contained significant amounts of silica, the cause of the lung disease silicosis. It was suggested that the threat to health from long-term exposure to the ash might further limit the number of areas of the island suitable for redevelopment. In July a bulletin from the Montserrat Volcano Observatory noted that there were no signs of decline in residual volcanic activity, warning that it would take decades for the lava still present to cool to ambient temperatures. Further explosions of ash and minor eruptions of lava continued throughout the rest of the year.

In September 1999 public consultations took place to discuss government proposals to establish a new capital at Little Bay, in the north-west of the island. The new town would take an estimated 10 years to construct. In the same month the British Government announced further assistance for the construction of housing and expressed support for Government plans to establish Montserrat as a centre for international financial services. In March 2000 the dome of lava, which had been covering the Soufrière Hills volcano, collapsed, producing lava flows and mudslides in the west of the island, and covering much of the 'safe zone' with ash.

In May 2000 an advisory commission on electoral reform recommended the replacement of the constituency system, which was deemed to be redundant following the abandonment of much of the island, by a nine-member single constituency. It was intended that the new system would be in place prior to the general election, scheduled for late 2001. In June 2000 the Organisation for Economic Co-operation and Development (OECD, see p. 320) published a list, on which Montserrat was included, of countries which it believed were taking insufficient action against money-laundering. Brandt subsequently called Montserrat's inclusion an 'affront' and stated that he would provide OECD with no further information unless it could point to illegal activities on the island. In December Brandt declared his wish for responsibility for managing and monitoring Montserrat's financial services sector to be transferred to the Eastern Caribbean Central Bank, and for policy matters to fall under the Ministry of Finance portfolio. In March 2002 OECD declared that the Government had made sufficient commitments improve transparency and effective exchange of information on tax matters with OECD countries by 2005, and removed Montserrat from its blacklist.

In July 2001 there was a further partial collapse of the dome of lava covering the Soufrière Hills volanco. Hot ash and volcanic pebbles affected the communities of Salem and Olveston, and ash clouds severely disrupted air travel in the north-eastern Caribbean. In the following month Montserrat signed up to a British mortgage assistance programme, which would provide housing subsidies and loans to residents who had been made homeless as a result of volcanic activity. Many residents were still paying mortgages on homes in an off-limits zone of the island as well as paying rent for new accommodation.

In February 2001 Chief Minister Brandt's coalition Government collapsed following the resignations of Adelina Tuitt, the Minister of Education, Health and Community Services, and Rupert Weekes, the Deputy Chief Minister and Minister of Communications, Works and Sports. The two accused Brandt of making decisions, in particular about a proposed new airport, without consulting other ministers. Their resignations forced Brandt to dissolve the Executive Council and announce that an early general election would be held on 2 April, under the new system of the nine-member single constituency (see above). The main contestants in the election were former Chief Minister Reuben Meade's NPP, and former Chief Minister John Osborne's newly formed New People's Liberation Movement (NPLM). Brandt was not seeking re-election. There was anger following the announcement that Montserratians who had left the island following the volcanic eruptions would not be entitled to vote. At the election the NPLM won seven of the nine seats and 52% of the votes cast. The NPP won the remaining two seats. Turn-out was put at 77.6% of the 2,955 islanders registered to vote. Osborne was sworn in as Chief Minister on 5 April and an Executive Council was subsequently formed.

In May 2001 Anthony Longrigg was inaugurated as Governor of Montserrat, replacing Tony Abbott.

In February 2002 the Organisation of Eastern Caribbean States (OECS, see p. 397) countries, including Montserrat, agreed to allow nationals of member states to travel freely within the OECS area and to remain in a foreign territory within the area for up to six months. In May 2002 the British Overseas Territories Act, having received royal assent in the United Kingdom in February, came into force and granted British citizenship to the people of its 14 Overseas Territories, including Montserrat. Under the new law Montserratians would be able to hold British passports and work in the United Kingdom and anywhere else in the European Union. In October 2003 the British Government formally backed plans for Montserrat to to particpate fully in the Caribbean Single Market and Economy (CSME) proposed by the Caribbean Community and Common Market (CARICOM, see p. 183), of which Montserrat was a founder member. (As a United Kingdom Overseas Territory, Montserrat required prior approval from the British Government before undertaking international commitments.) The CSME came into force at the beginning of 2006, although Montserrat was not a founding member.

In March 2003 the resignation of the Minister of Communications and Works, Lowell Lewis, from the NPLM (and the Executive Council) reduced the Government's majority to a single seat. Lewis had challenged the leadership of Osborne earlier in the month and regarded his position as untenable after he considered supporting a vote of 'no confidence' in the Government, proposed by the leader of the opposition.

A massive volcanic eruption, reported to be the largest since 1995, occurred on 12 July 2003, causing infrastructural damage, and the destruction of numerous buildings in Salem, which is on the edge of the 'safe zone'. A further, minor eruption occurred in April 2005.

In May 2004 Deborah Barnes-Jones took over as Governor from Anthony Longrigg.

In September 2005 the Minister for Agriculture, Lands, Housing and the Environment, Ann Dyer Howe, resigned, citing dissatisfaction with the Government's leadership. However, the opposition did not, as anticipated, propose a motion of 'no confidence' in the legislature, which, if successful, would force the dissolution of the Executive Council. In consequence, days later Dyer-Howe withdrew her resignation. The Chief Minister continued to preside over a minority Government until the scheduled general election on 31 May 2006. In the weeks preceding the ballot, the popularity of the NPLM administration fell further following rumours, in March, that an agreement was to be signed between the Government and West Indian Power Ltd (WIPL), granting a 25-year monopoly to the WIPL on the exploitation and use of Montserrat's geothermal energy, in return for royalties equivalent to around 4% of total revenue. Those opposing the agreement claimed that the country's natural resources would be depleted as a result of the accord.

Government

Under the provisions of the 1960 Constitution and subsequent legislation, the Governor is appointed by the British monarch and is responsible for defence, external affairs and internal security. The Governor is President of the seven-member Executive Council. The Legislative Council comprises 12 members: a Speaker, two official members, two nominated and seven elected by universal adult suffrage. A constitutional review was begun in 2002 and was continuing in 2006.

Economic Affairs

In 2004 Montserrat's gross domestic product (GDP) at market prices was an estimated EC $110.9m., equivalent to approximately EC $21,169 per head. In 1996–2004 real GDP decreased by an annual average of 5.5%; however, it expanded by an estimated 6.8% in 2004.

Agriculture (including forestry and fishing) contributed an estimated 1.1% of GDP in 2004, and engaged 6.6% of the employed labour force in 1992. The sector was almost destroyed by the volcanic eruptions of 1997, which caused an 81.3% decline in agricultural production, and a return to subsistence farming. The sector's GDP contracted by a further 33.3% in 1998, in real terms, but increased by 7.6% in 1999 and by a massive 46.5% in 2000. A contraction of 17.3% in agricultural GDP in 2001 was followed, in 2002, by a 38.4% recovery. However, no growth was recorded in the sector in 2003, and the sector contracted by 17.8% in 2004, largely owing to a further eruption of the Soufrière Hills volcano in July 2003 that destroyed some 95% of that year's food crop. Prior to the volcanic eruption the principal crops grown were white potatoes, onions, rice and sea-island cotton. Cattle, goats, sheep and poultry were also farmed. Montserrat's fisheries are under-exploited, owing to the absence of a sheltered harbour. The sector declined by 7.7% in 2004.

Industry (including mining, manufacturing, construction and public utilities) contributed some 20.6% to GDP in 2004, and engaged some 30.9% of the employed labour force in 1987. Mining and quarrying contributed less than 1.0% of GDP in 2004. Manufacturing contributed 0.6% of GDP in 2004, engaged 5.6% of the employed labour force (together with mining) in 1992, and accounted for about 70% of exports in the early 1990s. Many industrial sites were destroyed in 1997, causing a decline in real manufacturing GDP of 45.2% in that year and of 85.0% in 1998. In 1999 the sector's GDP improved by 10.6%, but growth was static in 2000–04. Light industries comprise the processing of agricultural produce (also cotton and tropical fruits), as well as spring-water bottling and the manufacture of garments and plastic bags. The assembly of electrical components, which accounted for 69% of export earnings in 1993, ceased in 1998, following further volcanic activity. In May 2006 the Government signed a 25-year contract with a British plastics recycling company to supply volcanic ash, to be used in the blending of recycled plastics. Exports of digital data-processing machines comprised 16.7% of total exports in 2003.

Construction contributed an estimated 12.9% of GDP in 2004 and employed 17.5% of the working population in 1988. The sector enjoyed growth in the early 1990s, owing to reconstruction programmes in response to the devastation caused by 'Hurricane Hugo' in 1989. Activity in the sector declined in the mid-1990s, before increasing in the middle of the decade, as a result of further reconstruction work following the volcanic eruptions. In 2000, however, real construction GDP fell by 35.8%. It continued to decrease, by 7.7%, in 2001, before increasing by 40.9% in 2002, although there was a further contraction of 2.9% in 2003. The trend was reversed yet again in 2004 with the sector increasing by an estimated 2.4%. Energy requirements are dependent upon the import of hydrocarbon fuels (15.5% of total imports in 2003).

It is hoped to re-establish Montserrat as a data-processing centre, and as a centre for financial services, which previously provided an important source of government revenue. The tourism sector, which in 2004 contributed an estimated EC $23.2m. in gross visitor expenditure, remains important to the island, and it is hoped to establish Montserrat as a centre for environmental tourism, with the volcano itself as the premier attraction. The GDP of the hotel and restaurant sector increased by an annual average of 3.5% between 1996–2004, in spite of dramatic sectoral contractions (of 78.2% and 42.9%, respectively) in 1996 and 1997. The sector recorded a 31.6% contraction in 2003, followed by a 33.8% expansion in 2004. The real GDP of the services sector decreased by an annual average of 5.0% during 1996–2004, but increased by 1.4% in 2003 and by a further 5.3% in 2004. Services contributed 78.3% of GDP in 2004.

In 2004 Montserrat recorded an estimated trade deficit of EC $69.7m. Earnings from the services sector, mainly tourism receipts and net transfers (in particular, the remittances from Montserratians abroad and the income of foreign retired people), generally offset persistent trade deficits. There was an estimated deficit on the current account of the balance of payments of EC $18.2m. in 2004. The principal trading partner is the USA (58.4% of imports and 33.3% of exports in 2003). Other trading partners of importance include the United Kingdom, Japan, Trinidad and Tobago and Antigua and Barbuda. The export of rice and of electrical components, previously the most important of the island's few exports, ceased in 1998 following further volcanic activity. Export receipts were, however, estimated to have increased to some US $1.8m. by 2003. Food, beverage and tobacco imports constituted 11.6% of total imports in 2003; the principal imports are machinery and transport equipment and basic manufactures.

In 2004, according to preliminary figures, there was a budgetary deficit of EC $9.2m. The capital budget is funded almost entirely by overseas aid, notably from the United Kingdom and Canada. The United Kingdom initially provided aid worth £14.5m. for 1995–98 (additional assistance for emergency housing and other services necessitated by continued volcanic activity had brought this total to £59m. by the end of 1998). In 1999 official development assistance totalled US $65.6m, with British budgetary assistance of £75m. being made available for the three-year reconstruction programme agreed in January 1999. A £55m. programme for 2001–04 was followed by a further three-year £40m. programme extending to 2007. The aid programme for 2006 was valued at £14m., of which £10.2m. was a grant to cover the recurrent budget deficit. Montserrat's total external public debt was estimated to be around EC $11.01m., according to government figures. Consumer prices decreased in 2003, by 2.2%, but increased by 2.4% in 2004. The Caribbean Development Bank (see p. 188) estimated the unemployment rate to stand at some 13% of the labour force in 2001, compared with around 8.3% in 1994.

Montserrat is a member of the Eastern Caribbean Central Bank (ECCB), the Caribbean Community and Common Market (CARICOM, see p. 183), the Organisation of Eastern Caribbean States (OECS, see p. 397) and, as a dependency of the United Kingdom, has the status of Overseas Territory in association with the European Union (EU, see p. 228). The territory is also a member of the regional stock exchange, the Eastern Caribbean Securities Exchange (based in Saint Christopher and Nevis), established in 2001.

The eruption of the Soufrière Hills volcano in June 1997, and subsequent volcanic activity, rendered the southern two-thirds of Montserrat, including the capital, Plymouth, uninhabitable. Much of the country's infrastructure, including the main port and airport, was destroyed, and the island's agricultural heartland devastated. The implications for the island's principal industry, tourism, were extremely severe. In August the British Government announced a five-year reconstruction programme for the development of the 'safe areas' in the north of the island. However, by mid-February 1998 the population of Montserrat had declined to just 2,850 (the population was an estimated 11,581 in 1994), owing to the lack of employment prospects and to poor living conditions. Of the remaining work-force, some 25% were employed by the Government or statutory bodies. The population was enumerated at 4,482 in the census of May 2001, and it was hoped that a reduction in volcanic activity would encourage Montserratians resident abroad to return home, thereby stimulating the economy. By 2004, however, the population was estimated to have reached just 4,690. It was anticipated that the ongoing reconstruction efforts and the development of the island as a centre for environmental tourism would stimulate short-term economic growth, while in the long-term it was hoped to re-establish Montserrat as a centre for international financial services. At the end of 2003 some 22 International Business Companies and two banks were registered in the Territory. However, Montserrat's economic prospects depended entirely on the activity of the volcano, and although reconstruction work was in progress, other areas of the economy were likely to remain at extremely low levels of output for some years. The Government set aside EC $7m. of the 2004 budget for a three-year 'tourism repositioning strategy', aimed at capitalizing on Montserrat's considerable environmental assets; this amount was in addition to $9m. provided in October 2003 by the British Government for development of the local tourism industry. New port infrastructure was brought into operation during 2004 and an air terminal, which would include an airstrip of at least 600 m, capable of taking small aircraft for flights to neighbouring islands, and funded by the EU and the United Kingdom, was opened in early 2005. According to government estimates, economic growth in 2005 was around 3.5%.

Education

Education, beginning at five years of age, is compulsory up to the age of 14. In 1993 there were 11 primary schools, including 10 government schools. Secondary education begins at 12 years of age, and comprises a first cycle of five years and a second, two-year cycle. In 1989 there was one government secondary school and one private secondary school. In addition, in 1993 there were 12 nursery schools, sponsored by a government-financed organization, and a Technical College, which provided vocational and technical training for school-leavers. There was also an extra-mural department of the University of the West Indies in Plymouth. In 2002 the European Union (EU) and the United Kingdom contributed a total of EC $6m. to the construction of a further education college, the Montserrat Community College, which was completed in late 2003. A nursery school was constructed in 2002 with a further nursery school opened in Salem in September 2005 as part of the Government's commitment to providing increased access to early childhood education. Three 'offshore' medical schools were licensed in 2003. The Ministry of Education and Health was allocated a total of EC $4.3m. in the 2006 budget.

Public Holidays

2006: 1 January (New Year's Day), 17 March (St Patrick's Day), 14 April (Good Friday), 17 April (Easter Monday), 1 May (Labour Day), 5 June (Whit Monday), 10 June (Queen's Official Birthday), 7 August (August Monday), 23 November (Liberation Day), 25–26 December (Christmas), 31 December (Festival Day).

2007: 1 January (New Year's Day), 17 March (St Patrick's Day), 6 April (Good Friday), 9 April (Easter Monday), 7 May (Labour Day), 4 June (Whit Monday), 9 June (Queen's Official Birthday), 6 August (August Monday), 23 November (Liberation Day), 25–26 December (Christmas), 31 December (Festival Day).

Weights and Measures

The imperial system is in use but the metric system is being introduced.

Statistical Survey

Sources (unless otherwise stated): Government Information Service, Media Centre, Chief Minister's Office, Old Towne; tel. 491-2702; fax 491-2711; Eastern Caribbean Central Bank, POB 89, Basseterre, Saint Christopher; internet www.eccb-centralbank.org; OECS Economic Affairs Secretariat, *Statistical Digest*.

AREA AND POPULATION

Area: 102 sq km (39.5 sq miles).

UNITED KINGDOM OVERSEAS TERRITORIES *Montserrat*

Population: 10,639 (males 5,290, females 5,349) at census of 12 May 1991; 4,482 at census of 12 May 2001 (Source: UN, *Population and Vital Statistics Report*). *2004* (estimate): 4,690.

Density (2004): 46.0 per sq km.

Principal Towns: Plymouth, the former capital, was abandoned in 1997. Brades is the interim capital.

Births and Deaths (1986): 200 live births (birth rate 16.8 per 1,000); 123 deaths (death rate 10.3 per 1,000). *2003:* Crude birth rate 9.6 per 1,000; Crude death rate 12.3 per 1,000 (Source: Caribbean Development Bank, *Social and Economic Indicators*).

Expectation of Life (years at birth, estimates): 78.5 (males 76.4; females 80.8) in 2004. Source: Pan American Health Organization.

Employment (1992): Agriculture, forestry and fishing 298; Mining and manufacturing 254; Electricity, gas and water 68; Wholesale and retail trade 1,666; Restaurants and hotels 234; Transport and communication 417; Finance, insurance and business services 242; Public defence 390; Other community, social and personal services 952; *Total* 4,521 (Source: *The Commonwealth Yearbook*). *1998* (estimate): Total labour force 1,500.

HEALTH AND WELFARE

Physicians (per 1,000 head, 1999): 0.18.

Hospital Beds (per 1,000 head, 2003): 3.3.

Health Expenditure (public,% of GDP, 2000): 7.7.

Health Expenditure (public, % of total, 1995): 67.0.

Access to Water (% of persons, 2002): 100.

Access to Sanitation (% of persons, 2002): 96.

Source: Pan American Health Organization.

For definitions, see explanatory note on p. vi.

AGRICULTURE, ETC.

Principal Crops (FAO estimate, metric tons, 2004): Vegetables 475; Fruit (excl. melons) 710.

Livestock (FAO estimates, '000 head, 2004): Cattle 9.7; Sheep 4.7; Goats 7.0; Pigs 1.1.

Livestock Products (FAO estimates, '000 metric tons, 2004): Beef and veal 0.7; Cows' milk 2.3.

Fishing (FAO estimate, metric tons, live weight, 2003): Total catch 50 (all marine fishes).

Source: FAO.

INDUSTRY

Electric Energy (million kWh): 15 in 1999 (estimate); 12 in 2000 (estimate); 12 in 2001. Source: UN, *Industrial Commodity Statistics Yearbook*.

FINANCE

Currency and Exchange Rates: 100 cents = 1 East Caribbean dollar (EC $). *Sterling, US Dollar and Euro Equivalents* (30 December 2005): £1 sterling = EC $4.649; US $1 = EC $2.700; €1 = EC $3.185; EC $100 = £21.51 = US $37.04 = €31.40. *Exchange Rate*: Fixed at US $1 = EC $2.70 since July 1976.

Budget (EC $ million, preliminary figures, 2004): *Revenue:* Revenue from taxation 30.3 (Taxes on income and profits 12.8; Taxes on property 1.0; Taxes on domestic goods and services 3.2; Taxes on international trade and transactions 13.3); Non-tax revenue 2.0, Total 32.3 (excl. grants 92.7). *Expenditure:* Current expenditure 83.0 (Personal emoluments 25.9, Goods and services 29.8, Interest payments 0.2; Transfers and subsidies 27.1; Capital expenditure 32.8; Total 115.8.

International Reserves (US $ million at 31 December 2004): Foreign exchange 14.10. Source: IMF, *International Financial Statistics*.

Money Supply (EC $ million at 31 December 2004): Currency outside banks 12.96; Demand deposits at deposit money banks 31.51; *Total money* 44.47. Source: IMF, *International Financial Statistics*.

Cost of Living (Consumer Price Index; base: previous year = 100): 103.5 in 2002; 101.2 in 2003; 103.6 in 2004. Source: partly Caribbean Development Bank, *Social and Economic Indicators*.

Expenditure on the Gross Domestic Product (EC $ million at current prices, 2003, provisional figures): Government final consumption expenditure 58.32; Private final consumption expenditure 71.88; Gross fixed capital formation 63.66; *Total domestic expenditure* 193.86; Export of goods and services 39.44; *Less* Imports of goods and services 128.79; *GDP at market prices* 104.51.

Gross Domestic Product by Economic Activity (EC $ million at current prices, 2004, provisional figures): Agriculture, forestry and fishing 1.12; Mining and quarrying 0.09; Manufacturing 0.62; Electricity and water 7.10; Construction 13.19; Wholesale and retail trade 4.39; Restaurants and hotels 0.93; Transport 7.73; Communications 3.72; Banks and insurance 10.09; Real estate and housing 12.83; Government services 32.55; Other services 7.76; *Sub-total* 102.12; *Less* Financial intermediation services indirectly measured 7.22; *Gross value added at basic prices* 94.90; Taxes, less subsidies, on products 16.04; *GDP at market prices* 110.94.

Balance of Payments (EC $ million, 2004, provisional figures): Goods (net) –55.6; Services (net) –20.5; *Balance on goods and services* –76.1; Income (net) –4.9; *Balance on goods, services and income* –81.0; Current transfers (net) 62.8; *Current balance* –18.2; Capital account (net) 31.9; Direct investment (net) 6.6; Portfolio investment (net) 0.2; Public sector long term investment –0.9; Commercial banks –12.6; Other investment assets 0.9; Other investment liabilities (incl. net errors and omissions) –3.7; *Overall balance* 4.2.

EXTERNAL TRADE

Principal Commodities (US $ million, 2003): *Imports c.i.f.*: Food and live animals 3.3; Beverages and tobacco 1.4; Crude materials (inedible) except fuels 0.8; Mineral fuels, lubricants, etc. 4.4; Chemicals 1.4; Manufactured goods 4.7; Machinery and transport equipment 9.2; Miscellaneous manufactured articles 3.1; Total (incl. others) 28.4. *Exports f.o.b.*: Mineral fuels, lubricants, etc. 0.7; Manufactured goods 0.1; Machinery and transport equipment 0.5 (Complete digital data-processing machines 0.3); Miscellaneous manufactured articles 0.3; Total (incl. others) 1.8.

Principal Trading Partners (US $ million, 2003): *Imports c.i.f.*: Barbados 0.7; Canada 0.6; Dominica 0.3; Japan 1.3; Netherlands 0.3; Trinidad and Tobago 1.0; United Kingdom 5.7; USA 16.6; Total (incl. others) 28.4. *Exports f.o.b.*: Antigua and Barbuda 0.8; St Christopher and Nevis 0.1; United Kingdom 0.1; USA 0.6; Total (incl. others) 1.8.

Source: UN Statistics Division.

TOURISM

Tourist Arrivals (preliminary figures, 2004): Stay-over arrivals 9,569 (USA 1,871, Canada 334, United Kingdom 2,663, Caribbean 4,389, Others 312); Excursionists 5,106; Cruise-ship passengers 363; *Total visitor arrivals* 15,038.

Tourism Receipts (EC $ million): 23.4 in 2002; 19.8 in 2003; 23.2 in 2004 (preliminary figure).

TRANSPORT

Road Traffic (vehicles in use, 1990): Passenger cars 1,823; Goods vehicles 54; Public service vehicles 4; Motorcycles 21; Miscellaneous 806.

Shipping: ('000 metric tons, 1990): *International Freight Traffic*: Goods loaded 6; Goods unloaded 49. Source: UN, *Monthly Bulletin of Statistics*.

Civil Aviation (1985): Aircraft arrivals 4,422; passengers 25,380; air cargo 132.4 metric tons.

COMMUNICATIONS MEDIA

Radio Receivers (1997): 7,000 in use.

Television Receivers (1999): 3,000 in use.

Telephones (2000): 2,811 main lines in use.

Mobile Cellular Telephones (2000): 489 subscribers.

Non-daily Newspapers (1996): 2 (estimated circulation 3,000).

Sources: UNESCO, *Statistical Yearbook*; International Telecommunication Union.

EDUCATION

Pre-primary (1993/94): 12 schools; 31 teachers; 407 pupils.

Primary (1993/94, unless otherwise indicated): 11 schools; 85 teachers; 460 pupils (2003).

Secondary: 2 schools (1989); 80 teachers (1993/94); 308 pupils (2003).

Sources: UNESCO, *Statistical Yearbook*; Caribbean Development Bank, *Social and Economic Indicators*.

UNITED KINGDOM OVERSEAS TERRITORIES   *Montserrat*

Directory

The eruption in June 1997 of the Soufrière Hills volcano, and subsequent volcanic activity, rendered some two-thirds of Montserrat uninhabitable and destroyed the capital, Plymouth. Islanders were evacuated to a 'safe zone' in the north of the island.

The Constitution

The present Constitution came into force on 19 December 1989 and made few amendments to the constitutional order established in 1960. The Constitution now guarantees the fundamental rights and freedoms of the individual and grants the Territory the right of self-determination. Montserrat is governed by a Governor and has its own Executive and Legislative Councils. The Governor retains responsibility for defence, external affairs (including international financial affairs) and internal security. The Executive Council consists of the Governor as President, the Chief Minister and three other Ministers, the Attorney-General and the Financial Secretary. The Legislative Council consists of the Speaker (chosen from outside the Council), nine elected, two official and two nominated members. Owing to the disruption caused by evacuation from the south of the island, the 2001 general election was conducted according to a new 'at large' voting system, without constituencies, but still choosing nine members of the legislature.

The Government

Governor: DEBORAH BARNES-JONES (took office on 10 May 2004).

EXECUTIVE COUNCIL
(April 2006)

President: DEBORAH BARNES-JONES (The Governor).
Official Members:
Attorney-General: ESCO HENRY-GREER.
Financial Secretary: JOHN SKERRIT.
Chief Minister and Minister of Finance, Economic Development, Trade, Tourism and Media: JOHN A. OSBORNE.
Minister of Agriculture, Lands, Housing and the Environment: ANN DYER-HOWE.
Minister of Communications and Works: JOHN WILSON.
Minister of Education, Health and Community Services: IDABELLE MEADE.
Clerk to the Executive Council: CLAUDETTE WEEKES.

MINISTRIES

Office of the Governor: Lancaster House, Olveston; tel. 491-2688; fax 491-8867; e-mail govoff@candw.ag; internet www.montserrat-newsletter.com; internet www.gov.ms/index/governor.htm.
Office of the Chief Minister: Government Headquarters, POB 292, Brades; tel. 491-3378; fax 491-6780; e-mail ocm@gov.ms.
Ministry of Agriculture, Lands, Housing and the Environment: Government Headquarters, POB 292, Brades; tel. 491-2546; fax 491-9275; e-mail malhe@gov.ms; internet www.malhe.gov.ms.
Ministry of Communications and Works: Woodlands; tel. 491-2521; fax 491-3475; e-mail mcw@gov.ms; internet www.gov.ms/commsworks.
Ministry of Education, Health and Community Services: Government Headquarters, Brades; tel. 491-2880; fax 491-3131; e-mail mehcs@gov.ms; internet www.mehcs.gov.ms.
Ministry of Finance, Economic Development, Trade, Tourism and Media: Government Headquarters, POB 292, Brades; tel. 491-2777; fax 491-2367; e-mail minfin@gov.ms; internet minfin@gov.ms.

LEGISLATIVE COUNCIL

Speaker: Dr JOSEPH MEADE.
Election, 2 April 2001

Party	Seats
New People's Liberation Movement (NPLM)	7
National Progressive Party (NPP)	2
Total	**9**

There are also two *ex-officio* members (the Attorney-General and the Financial Secretary) and two nominated members.

Political Organizations

Movement for National Reconstruction (MNR): f. 1996; Leader AUSTIN BRAMBLE.
National Progressive Party (NPP): tel. 491-2444; f. 1991; Leader REUBEN T. MEADE.
New People's Liberation Movement (NPLM): f. 2001 as successor party to People's Progressive Alliance; Leader JOHN A. OSBORNE.

Judicial System

Justice is administered by the Eastern Caribbean Supreme Court (based in Saint Lucia), the Court of Summary Jurisdiction and the Magistrate's Court. A revised edition of the Laws of Montserrat came into force on 15 April 2005, following five years of preparation by a Law Revision Committee.

Puisne Judge (Montserrat Circuit): NEVILLE L. SMITH.
Magistrate: CLIFTON WARNER, Govt HQ, Brades; tel. 491-4056; fax 491-8866; e-mail magoff@candw.ag.
Registrar: SONYA YOUNG, Govt HQ, Brades; tel. 491-2129; fax 491-8866; e-mail courtreg@candw.ag.

Religion

CHRISTIANITY

The Montserrat Christian Council: St Peter's, POB 227; tel. 491-4864; fax 491-2813; e-mail 113057.1074@compuserve.com; Chair. Rev. SINCLAIR WILLIAMS.

The Anglican Communion

Anglicans are adherents of the Church in the Province of the West Indies, comprising eight dioceses. Montserrat forms part of the diocese of the North Eastern Caribbean and Aruba. The Bishop is resident in The Valley, Anguilla.

The Roman Catholic Church

Montserrat forms part of the diocese of St John's-Basseterre, suffragan to the archdiocese of Castries (Saint Lucia). The Bishop is resident in St John's, Antigua and Barbuda.

Other Christian Churches

There are Baptist, Methodist, Pentecostal and Seventh-day Adventist churches and other places of worship on the island.

The Press

Montserrat Newsletter: Unit 8, Farara Plaza, Brades; tel. 491-2688; fax 491-8867; e-mail monmedia@candw.ag; internet www.montserrat-newsletter.com; government information publication; Publicity Officer RICHARD ASPIN.
The Montserrat Reporter: POB 306, Davy Hill; tel. 491-4715; fax 491-2430; e-mail editor@montserratreporter.org; internet www.themontserratreporter.com; weekly on Fridays; circ. 2,000; Editor BENNETTE ROACH.
The Montserrat Times: POB 28; tel. 491-2501; fax 491-6069; weekly on Fridays; circ. 1,000.

Broadcasting and Communications

TELECOMMUNICATIONS

Cable & Wireless: POB 219, Sweeney's; tel. 491-1000; fax 491-3599; e-mail venus.george@cwnl.cwplc.com; internet www.cwmontserrat.com.

BROADCASTING

Prior to the volcanic eruption of June 1997 there were three radio stations operating in Montserrat. Television services can also be obtained from Saint Christopher and Nevis, Puerto Rico and from Antigua and Barbuda (ABS).

Radio

Gem Radio Network: Barzey's, POB 488; tel. 491-5728; fax 491-5729; f. 1984; commercial; Station Man. KEVIN LEWIS; Man. Dir KENNETH LEE.
Radio Antilles: POB 35/930; tel. 491-2755; fax 491-2724; f. 1963; in 1989 the Govt of Montserrat, on behalf of the OECS, acquired the station; has one of the most powerful transmitters in the region; commercial; regional; broadcasts in English and French; Chair. Dr H. FELLHAUER; Man. Dir KRISTIAN KNAACK; Gen. Man. KEITH GREAVES.

Radio Montserrat (ZJB): POB 51, Sweeney's; tel. 491-2885; fax 491-9250; e-mail zjb@gov.ms; internet www.zjb.gov.ms; f. 1952; first broadcast 1957; govt station; Station Man. ROSE WILLOCK; CEO LOWELL MASON.

Television

Cable Television of Montserrat Ltd: POB 447, Olveston; tel. 491-2507; fax 491-3081; Man. SYLVIA WHITE.

Finance

The Eastern Caribbean Central Bank, based in Saint Christopher and Nevis, is the central issuing and monetary authority for Montserrat.

Eastern Caribbean Central Bank—Montserrat Office: Farara Plaza, POB 484, Brades; tel. and fax 491-6877; e-mail eccbmni@candw.ag; internet www.eccb-centralbank.org; Resident Rep. CHARLES T. JOHN.

Financial Services Commission: Phoenix House, POB 188, Brades; tel. 491-6887; fax 491-9888; e-mail enquiries@fscmontserrat.org; internet www.fscmontserrat.org; f. 2002; the Commission consists of the Commissioner and three other mems appointed by the Governor; Chair. C. T. JOHN.

BANKING

Bank of Montserrat Ltd: POB 10, St Peters; tel. 491-3843; fax 491-3163; e-mail bom@candw.ag; Man. ANTON DOLDRON.

Montserrat Building Society: POB 101, Brades; tel. 491-2391; fax 491-6127; e-mail mbsl@candw.ms.

Royal Bank of Canada: POB 222, Brades; tel. 491-2426; fax 491-3991; e-mail rbcmont@candw.ms; Man. J. R. GILBERT.

St Patrick's Co-operative Credit Union Ltd: POB 337, Brades; tel. 491-3666; fax 491-6566; e-mail monndf@candw.ms.

STOCK EXCHANGE

Eastern Caribbean Securities Exchange: based in Basseterre, Saint Christopher and Nevis; e-mail info@ecseonline.com; internet www.ecseonline.com; f. 2001; regional securities market designed to facilitate the buying and selling of financial products for the eight member territories—Anguilla, Antigua and Barbuda, Dominica, Grenada, Montserrat, Saint Christopher and Nevis, Saint Lucia and Saint Vincent and the Grenadines; Gen. Man. TREVOR E. BLAKE.

INSURANCE

Caribbean Alliance Insurance Co Ltd: POB 185, Brades; tel. 491-2103; fax 491-6013; e-mail ismcall@candw.ag.

Insurance Services (Montserrat) Ltd: POB 185, Sweeney's; tel. 491-2103; fax 491-6013.

NAGICO: Ryan Investments, Brades; tel. 491-9301; fax 491-3403; e-mail ryaninvestments@candw.ag.

Nemwil: POB 287, Brades; tel. 491-3813; fax 491-3814.

United Insurance Co Ltd: Jacquie Ryan Enterprises Ltd, POB 425, Brades; tel. 491-2055; fax 491-3257; e-mail united@candw.ms.

Trade and Industry

GOVERNMENT AGENCY

Montserrat Economic Development Unit: POB 292; tel. 491-2066; fax 491-4632; e-mail devunit@gov.ms; internet www.devunit.gov.ms.

CHAMBER OF COMMERCE

Montserrat Chamber of Commerce and Industry: Vue Pointe Hotel, Old Towne, POB 384, Brades; tel. 491-3640; fax 491-3639; e-mail chamber@candw.ag; internet www.montserratcci.com; refounded 1971; 31 company mems, 26 individual mems; Pres. KENNETH A. CASSELL.

UTILITIES

Electricity

Montserrat Electricity Services Ltd (MONLEC): POB 16, St John's; tel. 491-3148; fax 491-3143; e-mail monlec@candw.ag; domestic electricity generation and supply.

Gas

Grant Enterprises and Trading: POB 350, Brades; tel. 491-9654; fax 491-4854; e-mail granten@candw.ag; domestic gas supplies.

Water

Montserrat Water Authority: POB 324; tel. 491-2527; fax 491-4904; e-mail mwa@candw.ag; f. 1972; domestic water supplies; Chair. ALIC TAYLOR; Gen. Man. EMILE DU BERRY.

TRADE UNIONS

Montserrat Allied Workers' Union (MAWU): POB 245, Dagenham, Plymouth; tel. 491-6049; fax 491-6145; e-mail bramblehl@candw.ag; f. 1973; private-sector employees; Gen. Sec. HYLROY BRAMBLE; 1,000 mems.

Montserrat Civil Service Association: POB 468, Plymouth; tel. 491-3797; fax 491-2367.

Montserrat Seamen's and Waterfront Workers' Union: tel. 491-6335; fax 491-6335; f. 1980; Sec.-Gen. CHEDMOND BROWNE; 100 mems.

Montserrat Union of Teachers: POB 460; tel. 491-7034; fax 491-5779; e-mail hcb@candw.ag; f. 1978; Pres. GREGORY JULIUS (acting); Gen. Sec. HYACINTH BRAMBLE-BROWNE; 46 mems.

Transport

The eruption in June 1997 of the Soufrière Hills volcano, and subsequent volcanic activity, destroyed much of the infrastructure in the southern two-thirds of the island, including the country's principal port and airport facilities, as well as the road network.

ROADS

Prior to the volcanic eruption of June 1997 Montserrat had an extensive and well-constructed road network. There were 203 km (126 miles) of good surfaced main roads, 24 km (15 miles) of secondary unsurfaced roads and 42 km (26 miles) of rough tracks. The 2006 budget allocated funds for continued road and infrastructure improvements.

SHIPPING

The principal port at Plymouth was destroyed by the volcanic activity of June 1997. An emergency jetty was constructed at Little Bay in the north of the island. Regular transhipment steamship services are provided by Harrison Line and Nedlloyd Line. The Bermuth Line and the West Indies Shipping Service link Montserrat with Miami, USA, and with neighbouring territories. A twice-daily ferry service is in operation between Montserrat and Antigua.

Port Authority of Montserrat: Little Bay; tel. 491-2791; fax 491-8063; Man. ROOSEVELT JEMMOTTE.

Montserrat Shipping Services: POB 46, Carr's Bay; tel. 491-3614; fax 491-3617.

CIVIL AVIATION

The main airport, Blackburne at Trants, 13 km (8 miles) from Plymouth, was destroyed by the volcanic activity of June 1997. A helicopter port at Gerald's in the north of the island was completed in 2000. A new, temporary international airport at Gerald's, financed at a cost of EC $42.6m. by the European Union and the British Department for International Development, was completed in 2005; a new terminal building was opened in February and the airport officially opened in July, to be serviced by Windward Islands Airways International (WINAIR). In the longer term, the Government intended to construct a permanent international airport at Thatch Valley. Montserrat is linked to Antigua by a helicopter service, which operates three times a day. The island is also a shareholder in the regional airline, LIAT (based in Antigua and Barbuda).

Montserrat Airways Ltd: tel. 491-6494; fax 491-6205; charter services.

Montserrat Aviation Services Ltd: POB 257, Nixon's, Cudjoe Head; tel. 491-2533; fax 491-7186; f. 1981; handling agent.

Tourism

Since the 1997 volcanic activity, Montserrat has been marketed as an eco-tourism destination. Known as the 'Emerald Isle of the Caribbean', Montserrat is noted for its Irish connections, and for its range of flora and fauna. In 2004 there were 9,569 stay-over tourist arrivals. In that year some 46% of tourist arrivals were from Caribbean countries, 28% from the United Kingdom, 20% from the USA and 3% from Canada. A large proportion of visitors are estimated to be Montserrat nationals residing overseas. In 2004 earnings from the sector amounted to a preliminary EC $23.2m.

Montserrat Tourist Board: POB 7, Brades; tel. 491-2230; fax 491-7430; e-mail info@montserrattourism.ms; internet www.visitmontserrat.com; f. 1961; Chair. JOHN RYAN; Dir of Tourism ERNESTINE CASSELL.

PITCAIRN ISLANDS

Introduction

The Pitcairn Islands consist of Pitcairn Island and three uninhabited islands, Henderson, Ducie and Oeno. Pitcairn, situated at 25°04′ S, and 130°06′ W, and about midway between Panama and New Zealand, has an area of 4.5 sq km (1.75 sq miles) and had a population of 44 in March 2003.

Discovered in 1767 and first settled by the British in 1790, Pitcairn officially became a British settlement in 1887. In 1893 a parliamentary form of government was adopted, and in 1898 responsibility for administration was assumed by the High Commissioner for the Western Pacific. Pitcairn came under the jurisdiction of the Governor of Fiji in 1952, and, from 1970 onwards, of the British High Commissioner in New Zealand acting as Governor, in consultation with an Island Council, presided over by the Island Magistrate (who is elected triennially) and comprising one *ex-officio* member (the Island Secretary), five elected and three nominated members. In 1987 the British High Commissioner in Fiji, acting on behalf of Pitcairn, the United Kingdom's last remaining dependency in the South Pacific, joined representatives of the USA, France, New Zealand and six South Pacific island states in signing the South Pacific Regional Environment Protection Convention, the main aim of which is to prevent the dumping of nuclear waste in the region.

In 1989 uninhabited Henderson Island was included on the UNESCO 'World Heritage List'. The island, 168 km (104 miles) east-north-east of Pitcairn, is to be preserved as a bird sanctuary. There are five species of bird unique to the island: the flightless rail or Henderson chicken, the green Henderson fruit dove, the Henderson crake, the Henderson warbler and the Henderson lorikeet. However, concern was expressed in 1994 following claims by scientists studying the island that its unique flora and fauna were threatened by the accidental introduction of foreign plant species by visitors and by an increase in the rat population.

Following some structural changes in the local government of Pitcairn, Steve Christian was elected to the position of Mayor in December 1999, presiding over the Island Council (a role previously fulfilled by the Island Magistrate).

In early 2000 British detectives began an investigation into an alleged rape case on the island. The British team was joined by the New Zealand police force in early 2001, when the case was widened to include 15 alleged sexual assaults, amid reports claiming that sexual abuse, particularly of children, was commonplace on the island. The trial, which was expected to take place in Auckland, New Zealand, would represent the first significant criminal case on Pitcairn since a murder trial in 1897. In November 2000 Auckland's Crown Solicitor, Simon Moore, was appointed Pitcairn's first Public Prosecutor, with the task of deciding whether to bring charges against 20 Pitcairn Islanders. His decision was delayed by the fact that many of the complainants now lived in New Zealand and by the logistical problems of a trial that could potentially involve the entire populace. However, in April 2003 a judicial delegation of eight people visited Pitcairn and nine men on the island were charged with a total of 64 offences, some of which dated back about 40 years. Many islanders expressed serious concern that their community would not be able to manage if the men (who constituted virtually the entire male workforce) were extradited to New Zealand to stand trial. In early June a further four men, all now resident in New Zealand, were charged with a total of 32 offences, including 10 charges of rape, which were alleged to have taken place on Pitcairn between five and 40 years previously. In April 2004 the Supreme Court of Pitcairn (sitting for only the second time in its history, at a special session in Auckland) rejected the accused men's application to be tried on Pitcairn, reiterating that they should stand trial in New Zealand. However, in late June Pitcairn's Court of Appeal (sitting for the first time in its history) overruled this decision and stated that, despite the logistical problems involved, the trial would be conducted on Pitcairn. Meanwhile, lawyers for the accused men argued that the trial should be abandoned as the islanders were all descendants of the *Bounty* mutineers, who had renounced all allegiance to the British Crown. Their claims that Pitcairn Islanders were not subject to British jurisdiction appeared to be supported by historical documents discovered in London. Moreover, a group of women from Pitcairn issued a public statement claiming that sexual relations between men and girls below the British legal age of consent were commonplace on the island, and not considered to be a criminal offence by either party or by the community as a whole. However, in late September 2004 the trial of seven of the defendants began in converted school premises on Pitcairn. Some 25 lawyers, police officers and journalists travelled to the island, and witnesses in New Zealand gave evidence via live satellite video link. The trial concluded in late October. Six of the seven defendants were found guilty of many of the 51 charges against them. One islander was acquitted of the charges against him. Among those convicted was the Mayor of Pitcairn, Steve Christian, who was found guilty of five counts of rape. The convicted men, four of whom were given prison sentences of between two and six years while two received non-custodial sentences, began a legal challenge against their convictions in February 2005. Their defence was based on a previous claim that Pitcairn Islanders were not subject to British jurisdiction. In May their appeal was rejected by the Pitcairn Supreme Court, sitting in Auckland, New Zealand, although the sentences were again deferred pending the outcome of an appeal to the Privy Council in London, which was expected to be announced in July 2006. Further legal debate with regard to the case took place in February 2006 in Auckland, concluding after two weeks when the judges agreed to reserve their decision.

At elections to the Island Council in December 2004 five new Council members were elected and Jay Warren, the only defendant to be acquitted in the recent trials, was elected as the island's Mayor.

The British Overseas Territories Act, which entered effect in May 2002, granted citizenship rights in the United Kingdom to residents of the Overseas Territories, including Pitcairn. The legislation also entitled Pitcairn Islanders to hold British passports and to work in the United Kingdom and elsewhere in the European Union.

The economy has been based on subsistence gardening, fishing, handicrafts and the sale of postage stamps. Attempts to increase revenue from the island's agricultural output by producing dried fruits (notably bananas, mangoes and pineapples) began in 1999. Diversification of this sector to include production of jam, dried fish and coffee was subsequently under consideration. In early 1999 the Pitcairn Island police and customs office requested that no honey or beeswax be sent to the Territory in order to protect from disease the island's growing honey industry, which was being developed as a source of foreign exchange. Pitcairn honey, which was pronounced to be 'exceptionally pure' by the New Zealand Ministry of Agriculture, began to be exported, largely through internet sales, in late 1999. A new stamp was issued to commemorate the launch of the industry.

A reafforestation scheme, begun in 1963, concentrated on the planting of miro trees, which provide a rosewood suitable for handicrafts. In 1987 the Governor of the islands signed a one-year fishing agreement with Japan, whereby the Japan Tuna Fisheries Co-operative Association was granted a licence to operate vessels within Pitcairn's EEZ. The agreement was subsequently renewed, but lapsed in 1990. In 1992 an exclusive economic zone (EEZ), designated in 1980 and extending 370 km (200 nautical miles) off shore, was officially declared.

In early 1992 it was reported that significant mineral deposits, formed by underwater volcanoes, had been discovered within the islands' EEZ. The minerals, which were believed to include manganese, iron, copper, zinc, silver and gold, could (if exploited) dramatically affect the Territory's economy.

New Zealand currency is used. There is no taxation (except for small licensing fees on guns and vehicles), and government revenue has been derived mainly from philatelic sales (one-half of current revenue in 1992/93), and from interest earned on investments. In 1998/99 revenue totalled $NZ492,000 and expenditure $NZ667,000. In the early 2000s revenue was estimated to total about $NZ415,000 annually. Capital assistance worth an average of £100,000 annually is received from the United Kingdom. In 2003/04 exports from Pitcairn to New Zealand were worth $NZ6,000, while imports from that country cost $NZ739,000. Exports to Australia totalled $A21,000 in 2000/01, while imports from Australia, consisting mainly of food, totalled $A7,000 in that year. Pitcairn's imports from the USA totalled US $5.5m. in 2001, while exports to the USA were worth US $0.2m. Hopes that Pitcairn might find an additional source of revenue through the sale of website addresses were boosted in early 2000 when the island won a legal victory to gain control of its internet domain name suffix '.pn'.

Development projects have been focused on harbour improvements, power supplies, telecommunications and road-building. Pitcairn's first radio-telephone link was established in 1985, and a modern telecommunications unit was installed in 1992. A new health clinic was established, with British finance, in 1996. Major improvements to the jetty and slipway at Bounty Bay and to the Hill of Difficulty road, which leads to the landing area, were carried out in 2005. In the same year a museum was constructed on the island to house some of Pitcairn's historical artefacts, including the Bounty cannon, which had been raised from Bounty Bay several years previously.

A steady decline in the population, due mainly to emigration to New Zealand, is a major problem. In March 2001 a New Zealand company expressed an interest in acquiring development rights on Pitcairn with the aim of establishing fishing and tourism projects. The company claimed that if the islands achieved self-sufficiency through the proposals within five years then Pitcairn could become an independent state within the Commonwealth. In May 2002 the company's director reportedly announced that the development would begin within the next 12 months, describing plans for a lodge on Pitcairn and for a floating hotel off Oeno Island. The British High Commission in Wellington, however, emphasized that any such developments remained subject to the approval of Pitcairn Island Council, but that the company was welcome to submit proposals.

In August 2004 the British Government announced the provision of US $6.5m. in emergency assistance for the Territory in order to avert a financial crisis. The aid programme included a grant (partly financed by the European Union) to fund improvements to the road between Bounty Bay and Adamstown, which were carried out in mid-2005, and to investigate the potential for ecotourism as a possible source of future revenue.

Statistical Survey

Source: Office of the Governor of Pitcairn, Henderson, Ducie and Oeno Islands, c/o British Consulate-General, Pitcairn Islands Administration, Private Box 105-696, Auckland, New Zealand; tel. (9) 366-0186; fax (9) 366-0187; e-mail pitcairn@iconz.co.nz.

AREA AND POPULATION

Area: 35.5 sq km. *By Island*: Pitcairn 4.35 sq km; Henderson 30.0 sq km; Oeno is less than 1 sq km and Ducie is smaller.

Population: 48 (April 2005).

Density (Pitcairn only, April 2005): 11.0 per sq km.

Employment (able-bodied men, 2002): 9.

FINANCE

Currency and Exchange Rates: 100 cents = 1 Pitcairn dollar. The Pitcairn dollar is at par with the New Zealand dollar ($NZ). New Zealand currency is usually used.

Budget ($NZ, 1998/99): Revenue 492,000; Expenditure 667,000.

EXTERNAL TRADE

Trade with New Zealand ($NZ '000, year ending 30 June): *Imports:* 32 in 2000/01; 342 in 2001/02; 100 in 2002/03. *Exports:* 134 in 2000/01; 85 in 2001/02; 38 in 2002/03.

TRANSPORT

Road Traffic (motor vehicles, 2002): Passenger vehicles 29 (two-wheeled 1, three-wheeled 6, four-wheeled 23); Tractors 3; Bulldozer 1; Digger 1.

Shipping: *Local Vessels* (communally-owned open surf boats, 2000): 3. *International Shipping Arrivals* (visits by passing vessels, 1996): Ships 51; Yachts 30.

COMMUNICATIONS

Telephones (2002): a party-line service with 15 telephones in use; 2 public telephones; 2 digital telephones. Most homes also have VHF radio.

Directory

THE CONSTITUTION AND GOVERNMENT

Pitcairn is a British settlement under the British Settlements Act 1887, although the islanders reckon their recognition as a colony from 1838, when a British naval captain instituted a Constitution with universal adult suffrage and a code of law. That system served as the basis of the 1904 reformed Constitution and the wider reforms of 1940, effected by Order in Council. The Constitution of 1940 provides for a Governor of Pitcairn, Henderson, Ducie and Oeno Islands (who, since 1970, is concurrently the British High Commissioner in New Zealand), representing the British monarch. A Mayor is elected every three years to preside over the Island Council. The Local Government Ordinance 1964 constituted an Island Council of 10 members: in addition to the Mayor, five members are elected annually; three are nominated for terms of one year (the Governor appoints two of these members at his own discretion); and the Island Secretary is an *ex-officio* member. In addition to the Island Council there is an Island Magistrate who presides over the Magistrate's Court of Pitcairn, and is appointed by the Governor. Liaison between the Governor and the Island Council is conducted by a Commissioner, usually based in the Office of the British Consulate-General in Auckland, New Zealand.

Customary land tenure provides for a system of family ownership (based upon the original division of land in the 18th century). Alienation to foreigners is not forbidden by law, but in practice this is difficult. There is no taxation, and public works are performed by the community.

Governor of Pitcairn, Henderson, Ducie and Oeno Islands: RICHARD FELL (British High Commissioner in New Zealand—took office December 2001).

Office of the Governor of Pitcairn, Henderson, Ducie and Oeno Islands: c/o British High Commission, 44 Hill St, POB 1812, Wellington, New Zealand; tel. (4) 924-2888; fax (4) 473-4982; e-mail ppa.mailbox@fco.gov.uk; internet www.britain.org.nz; Gov. RICHARD FELL; Deputy Gov. MATTHEW FORBES; Commissioner LESLIE JAQUES.

Pitcairn Islands Office: Private Box 105-696, Auckland, New Zealand; tel. (9) 366-0186; fax (9) 366-0187; e-mail admin@pitcairn.gov.pn; internet www.government.pn.

Island Council
(April 2006)

Mayor: JAY WARREN.

Island Secretary (ex officio): BETTY CHRISTIAN.

Government Treasurer: NADINE CHRISTIAN.

Island Auditor: MIKE CHRISTIAN.

Chairman of Internal Committee: MIKE WARREN.

Other Members: LEA BROWN, OLIVE CHRISTIAN, CAROL WARREN, MERALDA WARREN, BRENDA CHRISTIAN.

Elections to the Island Council take place each December. Meetings are held at the Court House in Adamstown.

Office of the Island Secretary: The Square, Adamstown.

JUDICIAL SYSTEM

Chief Justice: CHARLES BLACKIE.

Island Magistrate: LEA BROWN.

Public Prosecutor: SIMON MOORE.

Public Defender: PAUL DACRE.

RELIGION

Christianity

Since 1887 many of the islanders have been adherents of the Seventh-day Adventist Church.

Pastor: JOHN O'MALLEY, SDA Church, The Square, POB 24, Adamstown; fax 872-7620/9763.

THE PRESS

Pitcairn Miscellany: monthly four-page mimeographed news sheet; f. 1959; edited by the Education Officer; circulation 1,400 in 2002; Editor P. FOLEY.

FINANCE, TRADE AND INDUSTRY

There are no formal banking facilities. A co-operative trading store was established in 1967. Industry consists of handicrafts, honey and dried fruit.

TRANSPORT

Roads

There are approximately 14 km (9 miles) of dirt road suitable for two-, three- and four-wheeled vehicles. In 2002 Pitcairn had one conventional motor cycle, six three-wheelers and 22 four-wheeled motor cycles, one four-wheel-drive motor car, three tractors, a five-ton digger and a bulldozer; traditional wheelbarrows are used occasionally. In 1995 a total of £79,000 was received from individual donors for work to improve the road leading to the jetty at Bounty Bay. Work to concrete the road, known as the Hill of Difficulty, finally began in June 2005.

Shipping

No passenger ships have called regularly since 1968, and sea communications are restricted to cargo vessels operating between New Zealand and Panama, which make scheduled calls at Pitcairn three times a year, as well as a number of unscheduled calls. There are also occasional visits by private yachts. The number of cruise ships calling at Pitcairn increased in the late 1990s, and 10 such vessels visited the island in 2000 (compared with just two or three annually in previous years). Two cruise ships called at Pitcairn in April 2005 before stopping at Oeno Island for the tourists to witness a solar eclipse near the island. Bounty Bay, near Adamstown, is the only possible landing site, and there are no docking facilities. In 1993 the jetty derrick was refitted with an hydraulic system. The islanders have three aluminium open surf boats. Major work to repair the slipway and jetty was carried out by the islanders in mid-2005.

SAINT HELENA AND DEPENDENCIES

Saint Helena

Introduction

Saint Helena lies in the South Atlantic Ocean, about 1,930 km (1,200 miles) from the south-west coast of Africa. Governed by the British East India Co from 1673, the island was brought under the direct control of the British Crown in 1834. The present Constitution (see p. 4622) came into force in 1989. At general elections held in September 1976, the Saint Helena Progressive Party, advocating the retention of close economic links with the United Kingdom, won 11 of the 12 elective seats in the Legislative Council. This policy has been advocated by almost all members of the Legislative Council brought to office at subsequent general elections (normally held every four years) up to and including that held in August 2005.

In October 1981 a commission was established by the Governor to review the island's constitutional arrangements. The commission reported in 1983 that it was unable to identify any proposal for constitutional change that would command the support of the majority of the islanders. In 1988, however, a formal Constitution was introduced to replace the Order in Council and Royal Instructions under which Saint Helena had been governed since 1967. The Constitution entered into force on 1 January 1989.

Owing to the limited range of economic activity on the island (see below), Saint Helena is dependent on development and budgetary aid from the United Kingdom. Since 1981, when the United Kingdom adopted the British Nationality Act, which effectively removed the islanders' traditional right of residence in Britain, opportunities for overseas employment have been limited to contract work, principally in Ascension and the Falkland Islands. In 1992 an informal 'commission on citizenship' was established by a number of islanders to examine Saint Helena's constitutional relationship with the United Kingdom, with special reference to the legal validity of the 1981 legislation as applied to Saint Helena. In April 1997 the commission obtained a legal opinion from a former Attorney-General of Saint Helena to the effect that the application of the Act to the population of Saint Helena was in contravention of the Royal Charter establishing British sovereignty in 1673. The commission indicated that it intended to pursue the matter further. In July 1997 private legislation was introduced in the British Parliament to extend full British nationality to 'persons having connections with' Saint Helena. In the following month the British Government indicated that it was considering arrangements under which islanders would be granted employment and residence rights in the United Kingdom. In February 1998, following a conference held in London of representatives of the British Dependent Territories, it was announced that a review was to take place of the future constitutional status of these territories, and of means whereby their economies might be strengthened. It was subsequently agreed that the operation of the 1981 legislation in relation to Saint Helena would also be reviewed. As an immediate measure to ameliorate the isolation of Saint Helena, the British Government conceded permission for civilian air landing rights on Ascension Island, which, with the contemplated construction of a small airstrip on Saint Helena, could facilitate the future development of the island as a tourist destination. In March 1999 the British Government published draft legislation proposing that full British nationality, including the right of abode in the United Kingdom, was to be restored to the population of Saint Helena and its dependencies, under the reorganization of the British Dependent Territories as the United Kingdom Overseas Territories. However, this had still not been implemented by July 2000, when the citizens took their case to the UN Committee on Decolonization, seeking British passports, a new Constitution and administration as a Crown dependency rather than as a colony. In May 2002 the British Overseas Territories Act, which granted British citizenship to the people of the Overseas Territories, including Saint Helena and dependencies, came into effect, having received royal assent in February. Under the new legislation these citizens acquired the right to hold a British passport and to work in the United Kingdom, but not the other benefits of citizenship (such as reduced fees for education). The Act restored those rights removed by the British Nationality Act of 1981. In September 2002 an independent constitutional adviser visited Saint Helena and consulted extensively with the island's residents on the options for future constitutional development. A consultative poll on the draft for a new constitution, which, *inter alia*, proposed the creation of a ministerial form of government, took place on 25 May 2005. The draft document was rejected by 52.6% of voters. Concern was expressed at the low rate of voter participation, recorded at 43% of registered voters. Nevertheless, it was indicated that elements of the rejected constitution were expected to be adopted, including a change to the number of constituencies on Saint Helena. The British Government subsequently stated that it wished to identify any possible improvements to the existing Constitution in conjunction with the new Executive Council, which took office following the elections held on 31 August 2005.

On 4 February 2002 a referendum was held by the Government in Saint Helena, Ascension Island, the Falkland Islands and on RMS *Saint Helena* on future access to the island; 71.6% of votes cast were in favour of the construction of an airport (28.4% opting for a shipping alternative). Plans for the airport and associated commercial developments were cancelled in February 2003, on the grounds of unprofitability and environmental concerns; however, following protests by islanders, in April the Executive Council invited tenders for the construction of the airport. In late January 2006 the Airport Development Bill was presented to the Legislative Council for approval and the following month it was announced that three consortia had prequalified to contest for the contract to construct the airport. The project was expected to cost some £40m., of which the British Government was reported to have agreed to contribute some £26.3m., approximately equal to the cost of replacing the mail ship in 2010. The airport, to be located on the eastern coast of the island, was scheduled to be fully functional by 2010. It was hoped that the airport would bring strong benefits to the local economy, particularly through the development of tourism.

The economy of Saint Helena is heavily reliant on British aid. In 1996 the Saint Helena Government undertook a strategic review, which formed the basis of a three-year country policy plan, committing the British Government to provide a package of development assistance totalling some £26m. over the period 1997/98–1999/2000. The assistance consisted of direct budgetary aid (£5.7m. in 2004/05), an annual subsidy for the operation of the RMS *St Helena* (£2.5m. in 2004/05) and support for bilateral development assistance. In 1999/2000 the island received about £8.9m. in British aid. Budget revenue totalled £12.56m. in 2004/05, and expenditure in that year was £12.72m. The annual rate of inflation averaged 3.7% in 1990–2001. Consumer prices increased by an average of 1.4% in 2000 and by 3.5% in 2001. According to Foreign and Commonwealth Office figures, GDP (measured at current prices) was US $10.1m. in 2000/01 and GDP per capita was $2,291 in the same period. In 2001/02 the rate of unemployment was recorded at 12.7%.

Saint Helena's persistently high rate of unemployment has resulted in widespread reliance on welfare benefit payments and a concurrent decline in living standards for the majority of the population. Evidence of underlying social discontent emerged in April 1997, when minor public disorders broke out in Jamestown following the refusal of the Governor (who exercises full executive and legislative authority in Saint Helena) to accept the nomination of a prominent critic of government policy to the post of Director of the Department of Social Welfare. Two members of the Executive Council (which acts in an advisory capacity) resigned in protest at the action of the Governor, who subsequently announced that elections to the Legislative Council were to take place in July. Following the elections, held on 9 July, the Governor agreed to the nomination as Chairman of the Education Committee of the candidate he had previously refused to nominate to the Social Welfare Directorate. The newly elected Legislative Council became the first in which members were to receive a fixed salary to serve on a full-time basis, relinquishing any other employment during their term of office.

At the 1998 census 10.2% of the employed labour force were engaged in agriculture and fishing, 19.7% in industry (predominantly construction), 65.6% in services and 4.5% in unspecified activities. Employment in the public sector was estimated to be at 45% of the working population in 1999. Saint Helena's unemployment rate was 18.1% at the 1998 census, but decreased to around 15% in 1999. In 2000 exports of fish (which, apart from a small quantity of coffee, is the only commodity exported) totalled 43.1 metric tons (compared with 27.2 tons in 1985) and export earnings from this source amounted to £113,000. Timber production is being developed, with sales amounting to 390 cu m in 1999. However, a large proportion of the labour force (approximately 1,000) must seek employment overseas, principally on Ascension and the Falkland Islands. In March 2001 551 Saint Helenians were working on Ascension, and in December 1999 371 were working on the Falkland Islands; according to the British Foreign and Commonwealth Office, approximately 1,700 members of the work-force were employed offshore at the beginning of 2005.

Saint Helena is of interest to naturalists for its rare flora and fauna. The island has about 40 species of flora that are unique to Saint Helena.

Statistical Survey

Source: Development and Economic Planning Dept, Government of Saint Helena, Saint Helena Island, STHL 1ZZ; e-mail depd@helanta.sh.

AREA AND POPULATION

Area: 122 sq km (47 sq miles).

Population: 5,644 at census of 22 February 1987; 5,157 (males 2,612, females 2,545) at census of 8 March 1998; 4,299 in December 2004.

Density (December 2004): 35.3 per sq km.

Principal Town (UN estimate, incl. suburbs): Jamestown (capital), population 1,787 in mid-2003 (Source: UN, *World Urbanization Prospects: The 2003 Revision*).

Births and Deaths (2004): Registered live births 34; Registered deaths 33.

Economically Active Population (1998 census): Agriculture, hunting and related activities 187; Fishing 20; Manufacturing 87; Electricity, gas and water 48; Construction 267; Wholesale and retail trade 344; Hotels and restaurants 24; Transport, storage and communications 181; Financial intermediation 17; Real estate, renting and business activities 7; Public administration and defence 293; Education 187; Health and social work 196; Other community services 87; Private household 74; Extra-territorial organizations 11; *Total employed* 2,037 (males 1,146; females 891); Unemployed 449 (males 290; females 159); *Total labour force* 2,486 (males 1,436, females 1,050). *2000:* Employed 2,637 (males 1,527, females 1,110); Registered unemployed 273 (Source: ILO).

AGRICULTURE, ETC.

Livestock (2004): Cattle 996; Sheep 767; Pigs 751; Goats 1,190; Donkeys 134; Poultry 6,489.

Fishing (metric tons, live weight, including Ascension and Tristan da Cunha, 2003): Skipjack tuna 178; Yellowfin tuna 158; Tristan da Cunha rock lobster 534; Total catch (incl. others) 985. Figures include catches of rock lobster from Tristan da Cunha during the 12 months ending 30 April of the year stated. Source: FAO.

FINANCE

Currency and Exchange Rate: 100 pence (pennies) = 1 Saint Helena pound (£). *Sterling, Dollar and Euro Equivalents* (30 December 2005): £1 sterling = Saint Helena £1; US $1 = 58.08 pence; €1 = 68.51 pence; £100 = $172.18 = €145.96. *Average Exchange Rate* (£ per US dollar): 0.6125 in 2003; 0.5462 in 2004; 0.5500 in 2005. Note: The Saint Helena pound is at par with the pound sterling.

Budget (2004/05): *Revenue* £12.56m. (including local revenue of £5.8m.); *Expenditure* £12.72m.

Cost of Living (Consumer Price Index; base: 1990 = 100): 142.0 in 1999; 144.0 in 2000; 149.0 in 2001. Source: ILO.

EXTERNAL TRADE

Principal Commodities: *Imports* (1994/95, £ '000): Total 5,076 (Food and live animals 27.9%; Beverages and tobacco 8.5%; Mineral fuels, lubricants, etc. 8.5%; Chemicals and related materials 11.4%; Basic manufactures 12.7%; Machinery and transport equipment 11.7%; Miscellaneous manufactured articles 13.0%; Other commodities and transactions 3.3%); *Exports* (2000): fish £113,000; coffee n.a. Trade is mainly with the United Kingdom and South Africa. *2002/03* (trade with UK): Imports £4.9m.; Exports £0.9m.

TRANSPORT

Road Traffic (2002): 1,931 licensed vehicles.

Shipping (1999): Vessels entered 214; Merchant fleet (31 December 2004): 1 vessels; Total displacement 921 grt (Source: Lloyd's Register-Fairplay, *World Fleet Statistics*).

COMMUNICATIONS MEDIA

Radio Receivers ('000 in use, 1997): 3. Source: UNESCO, *Statistical Yearbook*.

Television Receivers ('000 in use, July 2001): 1.

Telephones ('000 main lines in use, July 2001): 2.

EDUCATION

Primary (2004/2005): 3 schools; 17 teachers; 171 pupils.

Intermediate (2004/2005): 3 schools; 23 teachers; 205 pupils.

Secondary (2004/2005): 1 school; 2 teachers; 368 pupils.

Directory

The Constitution

The Saint Helena Constitution Order 1988, which entered into force on 1 January 1989, replaced the Order in Council and Royal Instructions of 1 January 1967. Executive and legislative authority is reserved to the British Crown, but is ordinarily exercised by others in accordance with provisions of the Constitution. The Constitution provides for the office of Governor and Commander-in-Chief of Saint Helena and its dependencies (Ascension Island and Tristan da Cunha). The Legislative Council for Saint Helena consists of the Speaker, three *ex-officio* members (the Chief Secretary, the Financial Secretary and the Attorney-General) and 12 elected members; the Executive Council is presided over by the Governor and consists of the above *ex-officio* members and five of the elected members of the Legislative Council. The elected members of the legislature choose from among themselves those who will also be members of the Executive Council. Although a member of both the Legislative Council and the Executive Council, the Attorney-General does not vote on either. Members of the legislature provide the Chairmen and a majority of the members of the various Council Committees. Executive and legislative functions for the dependencies are exercised by the Governor (although an advisory Island Council was inaugurated on Ascension in November 2002).

The Government
(April 2006)

Governor and Commander-in-Chief: MICHAEL CLANCY.

Chief Secretary: ETHEL YON (acting).

Financial Secretary: LINDA CLEMETT.

Chairmen of Council Committees:

Agriculture and Natural Resources: STEDSON GRAHAM FRANCIS.

Education: ERIC WILLIAM BENJAMIN.

Employment and Social Security: BRIAN WILLIAM ISAAC.

Public Health and Social Services: WILLIAM ERIC DRABBLE.

Public Works and Services: BERNICE ALICIA OLSSON.

Speaker of the Legislative Council: JOHN WAINWRIGHT NEWMAN.

GOVERNMENT OFFICES

Office of the Governor: The Castle, Jamestown, STHL 1ZZ; tel. 2555; fax 2598; e-mail ocs@helanta.sh; internet www.sainthelena.gov.sh.

Office of the Chief Secretary: The Castle, Jamestown, STHL 1ZZ; tel. 2555; fax 2598; e-mail ocs@helanta.sh.

Political Organizations

There are no political parties in Saint Helena. Elections to the Legislative Council, the latest of which took place in August 2005, are conducted on a non-partisan basis.

Judicial System

The legal system is derived from English common law and statutes. There are four Courts on Saint Helena: the Supreme Court, the Magistrate's Court, the Small Debts Court and the Juvenile Court. Provision exists for the Saint Helena Court of Appeal, which can sit in Jamestown or London.

Chief Justice: B. W. MARTIN (non-resident).

Attorney-General: KEN BADDON.

Sheriff: G. P. MUSK.

Magistrates: J. BEADON, D. BENNETT, D. CLARKE, R. COLEMAN, J. CORKER, L. CROWIE, J. FLAGG, P. FRANCIS, B. GEORGE, E. W. GEORGE, I. GEORGE, H. LEGG, V. MARCH, G. P. MUSK, R. PRIDHAM, G. SIM, S. STROUD, D. WADE, C. YON, P. YON, S. YOUDE.

Religion

The majority of the population belongs to the Anglican Communion.

CHRISTIANITY

The Anglican Communion

Anglicans are adherents of the Church of the Province of Southern Africa. The Metropolitan of the Province is the Archbishop of Cape Town, South Africa. St Helena forms a single diocese.

Bishop of Saint Helena: Rt Rev. JOHN SALT, Bishopsholme, POB 62, Saint Helena, STHL 1ZZ; tel. and fax 4471; e-mail bishop@helanta.sh; diocese f. 1859; has jurisdiction over the islands of Saint Helena and Ascension.

The Roman Catholic Church

The Church is represented in Saint Helena, Ascension and Tristan da Cunha by a Mission, established in August 1986. There were an estimated 87 adherents in the islands at 31 December 2000.

Superior: Rev. Fr MICHAEL MCPARTLAND (also Prefect Apostolic of the Falkland Islands); normally visits Tristan da Cunha once a year and Ascension Island two or three times a year; Vicar Delegate Rev. Fr JOSEPH WHELAN, Sacred Heart Church, Jamestown, STHL 1ZZ; tel. and fax 2535.

Other Christian Churches

The Salvation Army, Seventh-day Adventists, Baptists, New Apostolics and Jehovah's Witnesses are active on the island.

BAHÁ'Í FAITH

There is a small Bahá'í community on the island.

The Press

St Helena News Media: Saint Helena News Media Board, Broadway House, Jamestown, STHL 1ZZ; tel. 2612; fax 2802; e-mail sthelena.herald@helanta.sh; internet www.news.co.sh; f. 1986; govt-sponsored, independent; weekly; includes the St Helena Herald and St Helena Radio; Chief Exec. and Editor STUART MOORS; circ. 1,600.

Broadcasting and Communications

TELECOMMUNICATIONS

Cable & Wireless PLC: POB 2, The Briars, Jamestown, STHL 1ZZ; tel. 2200; fax 2206; e-mail webmaster@helanta.sh; internet www.cw.com/sthelena; operates the Helanta internet and e-mail service.

BROADCASTING

Cable & Wireless PLC: The Moon, Jamestown, STHL 1ZZ; tel. 2200; f. 1995; provides a three channel television service 24 hours daily from five satellite channels.

Saint FM: Association Hall, Main St, Jamestown, STHL 1ZZ; tel. 2660; e-mail fm@helanta.sh; internet www.saint.fm; f. 2004; independent radio station; Station Man. MIKE OLSSON.

St Helena Radio: Saint Helena Information Office, Broadway House, Jamestown, STHL 1ZZ; tel. 4669; fax 4542; e-mail radio.sthelena@helanta.sh; independent service; providing broadcasts for 24 hours per day; local programming and relays of British Broadcasting Corporation World Service programmes; Station Man. RALPH PETERS.

Finance

BANK

Bank of Saint Helena: Post Office Bldg, Main St, Jamestown STHL 1ZZ; tel. 2390; fax 2553; e-mail info@sthelenabank.com; internet www.sainthelenabank.co.sh; f. 2004; replaced the Government Savings Bank; total deposits £8,782,269 (31 March 1996); 1 br. on Ascension; Chair. LYN THOMAS; Man. Dir JOHN TURNER.

INSURANCE

Solomon and Co PLC: Solomon and Co (Saint Helena) PLC, Jamestown, STHL 1ZZ; tel. 2682; fax 2755; e-mail insurance@solomons.co.sh; internet www.solomons-sthelena.com; Solomon and Co operated an insurance agency on behalf of Royal SunAlliance Insurance Group during 1933–2002, until the latter co withdrew its interest from Saint Helena; negotiations for the foundation of a mutual insurance company on the island commenced in 2004; Insurance Man. TRACEY THOMAS.

Trade and Industry

GOVERNMENT AGENCY

St Helena Development Agency: POB 117, Jamestown, STHL 1ZZ; tel. 2920; fax 2166; e-mail enquiries@shda.co.sh; internet www.shda.helanta.sh; f. 1995; Man. Dir TONY GREEN.

CHAMBER OF COMMERCE

St Helena Chamber of Commerce: Jamestown, STHL 1ZZ; internet www.chamber.co.sh.

CO-OPERATIVE

St Helena Growers' Co-operative Society: Jamestown, STHL 1ZZ; tel. and fax 2511; vegetable marketing; also suppliers of agricultural tools, seeds and animal feeding products; 108 mems (1999); Chair. STEDSON FRANCIS; Sec. PETER W. THORPE.

Transport

There are no railways in Saint Helena. In 2004 the Government conducted initial surveys for the construction of an airport, which was scheduled to be completed by 2008 and was to be situated on Prosperous Bay Plain.

ROADS

In 2002 there were 118 km of bitumen-sealed roads, and a further 20 km of earth roads, which can be used by motor vehicles only in dry weather. All roads have steep gradients and sharp bends.

SHIPPING

St Helena Line Ltd: Andrew Weir Shipping, Dexter House, 2 Royal Mint Court, London, EC3N 4XX, United Kingdom; tel. (20) 7265-0808; fax (20) 7481-4784; internet www.aws.co.uk; internet www.rms-st-helena.com; awarded the five-year government contract in May 2001; service subsidized by the British Government by £1.5m. annually; operates two-monthly passenger/cargo services by the RMS *St Helena* to and from the United Kingdom and Cape Town, South Africa, calling at the Canary Islands, Ascension Island and Vigo, Spain, and once a year at Tristan da Cunha; also operates programme of shuttle services between Saint Helena and Ascension Island and the St Helena Liner Shipping Service.

Tourism

Although Saint Helena possesses flora and fauna of considerable interest to naturalists, as well as the house (now an important museum) in which the French Emperor Napoleon I spent his final years in exile, the remoteness of the island, which is a two-day sea voyage from Ascension Island, has inhibited the development of tourism. The construction of an airport on Saint Helena, which was scheduled to be fully operational by 2010, should greatly increase the island's accessibility to the limited number of visitors that can currently be accommodated. A total of 8,968 tourists visited Saint Helena in 1997. There are three hotels and a range of self-catering facilities.

St Helena Tourist Office: The Canister, Main St, Jamestown, STHL 1ZZ; tel. 2158; fax 2159; e-mail sthelena.tourism@helanta.sh; internet www.sthelenatourism.com; f. 1998; provides general information about the island; Dir PAMELA YOUNG.

Ascension

The island of Ascension lies in the South Atlantic Ocean, 1,131 km (703 miles) north-west of Saint Helena, of which it is a dependency. Discovered by Portuguese navigators in 1501, the island is a semi-barren, rocky peak of purely volcanic origin. Britain took possession of Ascension in 1815, in connection with Napoleon's detention on Saint Helena. The island is famous for green turtles, and is also a breeding ground for the sooty tern. Under an agreement with the British Government, US forces occupy Wideawake Airfield, which is used as a tracking station for guided missiles. Ascension has no indigenous population, being inhabited by British and US military personnel, *émigré* workers and government administrative staff from Saint Helena, together with expatriate civilian personnel of Merlin Communications International (MCI), which operates the British Broadcasting Corporation (BBC) Overseas World Service Atlantic relay station, Cable and Wireless PLC, which provides international communications services and operates the 'Ariane' satellite tracking station of the European Space Agency, and staff providing the island's common services. The island is an important communications centre. The BBC operates a relay station on the island. Ascension does not raise its own finance; the costs of administering the island are borne collectively by the user organizations, supplemented by income from philatelic sales. The island is developing a modest eco-tourism sector. Some revenue, which is remitted to the Saint Helena administration, is derived from fishing licences (estimated to be around £1m. in 1999). Facilities on Ascension underwent rapid development in 1982 to serve as a major staging post for British vessels and aircraft on their way to the Falkland Islands (q.v.), and the island has continued to provide a key link in British supply lines to the South Atlantic. On 31 March 2001 the joint venture between the BBC and Cable and Wireless to provide public services to the island was dissolved. The Ascension Island Government took over responsibility for health and education, the Ascension Island Works and Services Agency, a statutory body, was established to maintain transport and infrastructure, and any remaining services were taken over by the new Ascension Island Commercial Services Ltd (AICS) company. AICS was jointly owned by the Ascension Islands Government, the BBC and Cable and Wireless and had the declared aim of privatizing the new enterprises by April 2002. This development was regarded as reorientating public-service provision towards the demands of the resident population rather than the needs of those organizations using the island.

Dissent developed among the resident population in June 2002, following the decision of the Foreign and Commonwealth Office to impose taxes for the first time on the island (including income tax, property tax and tax on alcohol and tobacco). The primary objection of the population was that this was 'taxation without representation', as the islanders do not possess the right to vote, to own property or even to live on the island. The Governor responded with plans to introduce a democratically elected council that would have a purely advisory function and no decision-making powers, claiming that the islanders initially needed to acquire experience of governance. On 22–23 August a vote on the democratic options took place on the island, with 95% of the votes cast being in favour of an Island Council, rather than an Inter-Island Council plus Island Council structure; 50% of those eligible to vote did so. The Council was to be chaired by the Administrator, on behalf of the Governor, and was to comprise seven elected members, the Attorney-General, the Director of Finance and one or two appointed members. Elections for councillors took place in October, and the Island Council was inaugurated in the following month. A joint consultative council was also to be established, with representatives from both Ascension and Saint Helena, in order to develop policy relating to economic development and tourism common to both islands.

The British Government subsequently stated its intention to enact legislation granting the islanders right of abode and the right to own property. However, following a visit to the island by a delegation of British officials in November 2005, it was announced that the proposed reforms would not be carried out. The British Government cited its reluctance to fundamentally change the nature of the territory and also maintained that granting such rights would impose greater financial liabilities on British taxpayers and would bring an unacceptable level of risk to the United Kingdom. In January 2006 The Island Council announced that it intended to seek clarification regarding the legality of the British Government's decision and reiterated its commitment to securing the islanders' right to abode and the right to purchase property.

As of early 2004 Ascension Island had a balanced fiscal budget, although with minimal reserves. Government expenditure funds one school, one hospital (offering limited services), police and judicial services; these services are provided without charge to local taxpayers. The Saint Helena-based firm Solomons has a primary role in the incipient private sector and a sports-fishing industry was in the process of being established.

In October 2003 the British Government concluded negotiations with the US authorities over the signing of an agreement to allow US air-charter access to the airfield.

Area: 88 sq km (34 sq miles).

Population: (March 2001): 982 (St Helenians 760, UK nationals 150, US nationals 65).

Budget: (estimates, £ million, for year ending 31 March 2004): Revenue 4.3; Expenditure 4.0 (Recurrent expenditure 3.3, Capital expenditure 0.7).

Government: The Governor of Saint Helena, in his capacity as Governor of Ascension Island, is represented by an Administrator. Two advisory groups, one comprising senior managers of resident organizations, and one comprising their employees' representatives, assist the Administrator, who also has professional financial and technical advisers. In November 2002 an advisory Island Council, chaired by the Administrator and comprising seven elected members, the Attorney-General, the Director of Finance and two appointed members, was inaugurated.

Administrator: MICHAEL HILL, The Residency, Georgetown Ascension, ASCN 1ZZ; tel. 7000; fax 6152; e-mail aigenquiries@ascension.gov.ac; internet www.ascension-island.gov.ac.

Magistrate: (vacant).

Justices of the Peace: G. F. THOMAS, A. FOWLER, J. PETERS, C. PARKER-YON.

Religion: Ascension forms part of the Anglican diocese of Saint Helena, which normally provides a resident chaplain who is also available to minister to members of other denominations. There is a Roman Catholic chapel served by visiting priests, as well as a small mosque.

Transport: (1998): *Road vehicles*: 830. *Shipping*: ships entered and cleared 105. The St Helena Line Ltd (q.v.) serves the island with a two-monthly passenger/cargo service between Cardiff, in the United Kingdom, and Cape Town, in South Africa. A vessel under charter to the British Ministry of Defence visits the island monthly on its United Kingdom–Falkland Islands service. A US freighter from Cape Canaveral calls at three-month intervals. *Air services*: A twice-weekly Royal Air Force Tristar service between the United Kingdom and the Falkland Islands transits Ascension Island both southbound and northbound. There is a weekly US Air Force military service linking the Patrick Air Force Base in Florida, USA, with Ascension Island, via Antigua.

Tourism: Small-scale eco-tourism is encouraged, although accommodation on the island is limited and all visits require written permission from the Administrator. Access is available by twice-weekly flights operated from the United Kingdom by the Royal Air Force (see above), and by the RMS *St Helena* (see Saint Helena—Shipping).

Tristan da Cunha

The island of Tristan da Cunha lies in the South Atlantic Ocean, 2,800 km (1,740 miles) west of Cape Town, South Africa. It comes under the jurisdiction of Saint Helena, 2,300 km (1,430 miles) to the north-east. Also in the group are Inaccessible Island, 37 km (23 miles) west of Tristan; the three Nightingale Islands, 37 km (23 miles) south; and Gough Island (Diego Alvarez), 425 km (264 miles) south. Tristan da Cunha was discovered in 1506, but remained uninhabited until occupied by US whalers during 1790–1811. The British Navy took possession of the island in 1817. Tristan's population was evacuated in 1961, after volcanic eruptions, but was resettled in 1963. The island's major source of revenue derives from a royalty for a crayfishing concession, supplemented by income from the sale of postage stamps and other philatelic items, and handicrafts. The fishing industry and the administration employ all of the working population. Some 20 power boats operating from the island land their catches to a fish-freezing factory built by the Atlantic Islands Development Corpn, whose fishing concession was transferred in January 1997 to a new holder, Premier Fishing (Pty) Ltd, of Cape Town. Premier also operates two large fishing vessels exporting the catch to the USA, France and Japan. Budget estimates for 2005/06 projected a deficit of £147,507. Development aid from the United Kingdom ceased in 1980; since then the island has financed its own projects. In June 2001 a hurricane in the main settlement of Edinburgh of the Seven Seas destroyed the hospital, community centre and numerous homes, and also killed many cattle; the satellite phone link was lost and the island was without electricity for one week, although no serious injuries were sustained. The British Department for International Development granted a £75,000 emergency aid package in response to the disaster. However, the cost of repairs surpassed that figure considerably. Furthermore, the problem of poaching in the island's waters resulted in much of Tristan da Cunha's limited resources being used to fund fishing patrols rather than swiftly restoring the damaged infrastructure.

Area: Tristan da Cunha 98 sq km (38 sq miles); Inaccessible Island 10 sq km (4 sq miles); Nightingale Islands 2 sq km (3/4 sq mile); Gough Island 91 sq km (35 sq miles).

Population: (April 2005): 276 (including 10 expatriates) on Tristan; there is a small weather station on Gough Island, staffed, under agreement, by personnel employed by the South African Government.

Fishing: (catch, metric tons, year ending 30 April): Tristan da Cunha rock lobster 425 in 2000/01; 301 in 2001/02; 534 in 2002/03. Source: FAO.

Budget: (estimates for 2005/06): Revenue £711,320; Expenditure £858,827 (with excess expenditure financed from capital reserves of £1.2m.).

Government: The Administrator, representing the Governor of Saint Helena, is assisted by an Island Council of eight elected members (of whom at least one must be a woman) and three appointed members, which has advisory powers in legislative and executive functions. The member receiving the largest number of votes at elections to the Council is appointed Chief Islander. The Council's advisory functions in executive matters are performed through 11 committees of the Council dealing with the separate branches of administration. Elections are held every three years. The last elections were held in November 2003.

Administrator: MIKE HENTLEY, The Administrator's Office, Edinburgh of the Seven Seas, Tristan da Cunha, TDCU 1ZZ; tel. (satellite) 874-1445434; fax (satellite) 874-1445435; e-mail admin@tristandc.com; internet www.tristandc.com/administator.php.

Legal System: The Administrator is also the Magistrate and Coroner.

Religion: Adherents of the Anglican church predominate on Tristan da Cunha, which is within the Church of the Province of Southern Africa, and is under the jurisdiction of the Archbishop of Cape Town, South Africa. There is also a small number of Roman Catholics.

Transport: The St Helena Line Ltd (q.v.), the MV *Hanseatic*, and MS *Explorer* and the SA *Agulhas* each visit the island once each year, and two lobster concession vessels each make three visits annually, remaining for between two and three months. Occasional cruise ships also visit the island. There is no airfield.

Tourism: Permission from the Administrator and the Island Council is required for visits to Tristan da Cunha. Facilities for tourism are limited, although some accommodation is available in island homes.

SOUTH GEORGIA AND THE SOUTH SANDWICH ISLANDS

South Georgia, an island of 3,592 sq km (1,387 sq miles), lies in the South Atlantic Ocean, about 1,300 km (800 miles) east-south-east of the Falkland Islands. The South Sandwich Islands, which have an area of 311 sq km (120 sq miles), lie about 750 km (470 miles) south-east of South Georgia.

The United Kingdom annexed South Georgia and the South Sandwich Islands in 1775. With a segment of the Antarctic mainland and other nearby islands (now the British Antarctic Territory), they were constituted as the Falkland Islands Dependencies in 1908. Argentina made formal claim to South Georgia in 1927, and to the South Sandwich Islands in 1948. In 1955 the United Kingdom unilaterally submitted the dispute over sovereignty to the International Court of Justice (based in the Netherlands), which decided not to hear the application in view of Argentina's refusal to submit to the Court's jurisdiction. South Georgia was the site of a British Antarctic Survey base (staffed by 22 scientists and support personnel) until it was invaded in April 1982 by Argentine forces, who occupied the island until its recapture by British forces three weeks later. The South Sandwich Islands were uninhabited until the occupation of Southern Thule in December 1976 by about 50 Argentines, reported to be scientists. Argentine personnel remained until removed by British forces in June 1982.

In mid-1989 it was reported that the British Government was considering the imposition of a conservation zone extending to 200 nautical miles (370 km) around South Georgia, similar to that which surrounds the Falkland Islands, in an attempt to prevent the threatened extinction of certain types of marine life.

Under the provisions of the South Georgia and South Sandwich Islands Order of 1985, the islands ceased to be governed as dependencies of the Falkland Islands on 3 October 1985. The Governor of the Falkland Islands is, *ex officio*, Commissioner for the territory.

In May 1993, in response to the Argentine Government's decision to commence the sale of fishing licences for the region's waters, the British Government announced an extension, from 12 to 200 nautical miles, of its territorial jurisdiction in the waters surrounding the islands, in order to conserve crucial fishing stocks.

In September 1998 the British Government announced that it would withdraw its military detachment from South Georgia in 2000, while it would increase its scientific presence on the island with the installation of a permanent team from the British Antarctic Survey to investigate the fisheries around the island for possible exploitation. The small military detachment finally withdrew in March 2001. The British garrison stationed in the Falkland Islands would remain responsible for the security of South Georgia and the South Sandwich Islands. In July 2005 it was announced that Alan Huckle would succeed Howard Pearce as Governor of the Falkland Islands and Commissioner of South Georgia and the South Sandwich Islands from 2006.

Previously thought to be dormant, increased volcanic activity on Montagu Island had been monitored closely by the British Antarctic Survey since 2001. In late 2005 Mount Belinda erupted, adding some 50 acres to the Island's land area in just one month. The Island is largely ice-covered and the eruption allowed scientists the rare opportunity to make direct observations of volcanic activity under ice sheets.

Commissioner: HOWARD PEARCE (assumed office 3 December 2002).

Commissioner-designate: ALAN HUCKLE (scheduled to take office in June 2006).

Assistant Commissioner and Director of Fisheries: HARRIET HALL (Stanley, Falkland Islands).

THE TURKS AND CAICOS ISLANDS

Introductory Survey

Location, Climate, Language, Religion, Flag, Capital

The Turks and Caicos Islands consist of more than 30 low-lying islands forming the south-eastern end of the Bahamas chain of islands, and lying about 145 km (90 miles) north of Haiti. Eight islands are inhabited: Grand Turk and Salt Cay (both in the smaller Turks group to the east of the Caicos), South Caicos, Middle (Grand) Caicos, North Caicos, Providenciales (Provo), Pine Cay and Parrot Cay. The climate is warm throughout the year but tempered by constant trade winds. The average annual temperature is 27°C (82°F) and rainfall ranges from 530 mm (21 ins) in the eastern islands to 1,000 mm (40 ins) in the west. The official language is English, though some Creole is spoken by Haitian immigrants. Many Christian churches are represented, the largest denomination being the Baptist Union (25.5% of the population at the census of May 1990). The flag is the British 'Blue Ensign', with the shield from the islands' coat of arms, bearing a shell, a lobster and a cactus, in the fly. The capital is Cockburn Town, on Grand Turk island.

Recent History

The Turks and Caicos Islands were first settled by Amerindian peoples. The islands were then inhabited by privateers, and were settled from Bermuda and by exiled 'Loyalists' from the former British colonies in North America. A Jamaican dependency from 1874 to 1959, the Turks and Caicos Islands became a separate colony in 1962, following Jamaican independence. After an administrative association with the Bahamas, the islands received their own Governor in 1972. The first elections under the present Constitution took place in 1976, and were won by the pro-independence People's Democratic Movement (PDM). In 1980 an agreement was made with the United Kingdom whereby, if the governing PDM won the 1980 elections, the islands would receive independence and a payment of £12m. However, lacking the leadership of J. A. G. S. McCartney, the Chief Minister (who had been killed in an aircraft accident in May 1980), the PDM lost the election in November to the Progressive National Party (PNP), which is committed to continued dependent status. At a subsequent general election, in May 1984, the PNP, led by the Chief Minister, Norman Saunders, won eight of the 11 elective seats.

In March 1985 the Chief Minister, the Minister for Development and Commerce and a PNP member of the Legislative Council were arrested in Miami, Florida, USA, on charges involving illicit drugs and violations of the US Travel Act. All three men were subsequently convicted and imprisoned (with Saunders receiving an eight-year sentence). Saunders resigned and was replaced as Chief Minister by Nathaniel Francis, hitherto the Minister of Public Works and Utilities.

In July 1986 a commission of inquiry into allegations of arson and administrative malpractice following the destruction by fire of a government building in December 1985 concluded that Francis and two of his ministers were unfit for ministerial office; all three ministers subsequently resigned. Two members of the PDM were also deemed to be unfit for public office. In the same month the Governor dissolved the Government, and the Executive Council was replaced by an interim advisory council, comprising the Governor and four members of the former Executive Council. A constitutional commission was appointed in September to review the future administration of the islands.

A general election, preceding the return to ministerial rule, took place in March 1988, following the British Government's acceptance of the principal recommendations of the constitutional commission in the previous year. Under a new multi-member system of representation (see Constitution, below), the PDM won 11 of the 13 seats on the Legislative Council, and the PNP won the remaining two. Oswald O. Skippings, the leader of the PDM, was appointed Chief Minister. The new Constitution strengthened the reserve powers of the Governor, but otherwise the form of government was similar to the provisions of the 1976 Constitution.

In April 1991 a general election took place, at which the PNP secured eight seats, defeating the PDM (which won the remaining five). Skippings was replaced as Chief Minister by C. Washington Misick, the leader of the PNP.

At a general election in January 1995 the PDM secured eight seats, while the PNP won four. Derek Taylor, leader of the PDM, was appointed Chief Minister.

A serious dispute arose between the Legislative Council and the Governor in August 1995, following the latter's decision to reappoint Kipling Douglas to the position of Chief Justice. Taylor, who claimed that Douglas did not enjoy the confidence of his Government, described the decision as provocative and disrespectful. Relations deteriorated in subsequent months, and in February 1996 a petition requesting the immediate removal of the Governor, signed by all members of the Government and opposition, was presented to the British Foreign and Commonwealth Office. The signatories accused Bourke of abusing his position, and were particularly angered by remarks he had made in an interview that portrayed the islands as lawless and unstable, with drugs-related crime and corruption at unprecedented levels. A delegation of politicians from the Territory travelled to the United Kingdom to reinforce the views of the Legislative Council, which were believed to be shared by a majority of islanders. In the following month, however, their demands were rejected by the British Government, which deployed a frigate in the islands' waters and ordered 100 police-officers to prepare for immediate transfer to the Territory in the event of civil disturbance. A climate of animosity between the Governor and the islanders persisted during 1996, and in September Bourke departed from the Territory, without formal ceremony, following the expiry of his term of office. He was replaced by John Kelly.

At a general election held on 4 March 1999 the PDM increased its representation in the Legislative Council to nine seats, after Norman Saunders, who had previously held a seat as an independent, successfully stood as a PDM candidate. The PNP won the other four seats.

In June 2000 the Turks and Caicos Islands were included on a list of territories regarded as operating harmful tax regimes. The Organisation for Economic Co-operation and Development (OECD), which compiled the list, urged the Government to make legislative changes, in order to introduce greater legal and administrative transparency to prevent companies using the country's tax system for money-laundering or tax-avoidance purposes. OECD removed the Turks and Caicos Islands from the list in March 2002, declaring that the Government had made sufficient commitments to improve transparency and effective exchange of information on tax matters by the end of 2005. In late 2002, however, the recovering financial sector faced further disruption when the United Kingdom, under pressure from a European Union (EU, see p. 228) investigation into tax evasion, demanded that the Turks and Caicos Islands disclose the identities and account details of Europeans holding private savings accounts on the islands. The Turks and Caicos Islands, along with some other British Overseas Territories facing similar demands, claimed it was being treated unfairly, but pledged to introduce the necessary legislation to implement the EU's Savings Tax Directive in 2004, provided it was given the same allowances as powerful European countries, such as Switzerland and Luxembourg.

In April 2002 the Governor established a Constitutional Modernisation Review Body to discuss changes to the Territory's Constitution. This all-party panel presented a report in September. Discussions on a new constitution took place in 2004 between representatives of the Turks and Caicos Islands and the British Governments. Following further negotiations between government ministers in October 2005, it was agreed that a draft text of a modernized constitution would be drawn up by the United Kingdom's Foreign and Commonwealth Office. This proposed document, expected in 2006, would be subject to approval by both the PDM and the PNP, after with a public consultation period would be held. Adoption of the amendments would be subject to approval by the Legislative Council.

In May 2002 the British Overseas Territories Act, having received royal assent in the United Kingdom in February, came into force and granted British citizenship rights to the people of its Overseas Territories, including the Turks and Caicos Islands. Under the new law Turks and Caicos Islanders would be able to hold British passports and work in the United Kingdom and anywhere else in the EU. In March 2005 a delegation from the Turks and Caicos Islands made an official visit to the Bahamas in a bid to forge closer ties between the two Governments.

In October 2002 capital punishment for treason and piracy, the only remaining capital crime in the United Kingdom Overseas Territories, was abolished in the Turks and Caicos Islands. In December Jim Poston replaced Mervyn Jones as Governor.

At the general election of 24 April 2003 the PDM won seven of the 13 seats in the Legislative Council, two fewer than in 1999. The PNP took the remaining six seats, but challenged the results in two of the more closely fought constituencies. In June the Supreme Court ruled in favour of the defeated PNP candidates in the two disputed constituencies; Chief Justice Ground found evidence of bribery by supporters of the PDM in one constituency and irregularities in voter-registration lists in the other. Following the judicial ruling, by-elections were held in the two constituencies on 7 August; the PNP secured victory in both ballots and therefore wrested overall control of the Legislative Council from the PDM. Taylor resigned as Chief Minister on 15 August and Misick was sworn in as his replacement on the same day. Misick's first Executive Council included Floyd Hall as the Minister of Finance and National Insurance. A new position of Minister of Housing (held, in addition to the immigration and labour portfolios, by Jeffrey Hall), was established as part of Misick's commitment to the provision of adequate housing for the whole population.

In mid-October 2004 Chief Minister Misick dismissed the Minister of Health, Social Services and Gender Affairs, Karen Delancy. Amendments were made to the portfolio of her successor, Galmo Williams, who was appointed Minister of Natural Resources and Social Services. In April 2005 Mahala Wynns was sworn in as the new Chief Secretary following the retirement of Cynthia Astwood. In the same month a new parliament building was inaugurated. On 11 July James Poston was succeeded by Richard Tauwhare as Governor.

In April 2006, in spite of ongoing discussions regarding a new constitution, the Chief Minister met with members of the UN's Special Committee on Decolonisation to discuss options for self-determination. Three directions were outlined: independence; independence by free association; or independence by way of integration. However, it was not clear how many islanders wanted independence, and the opposition questioned Misick's motives behind the talks.

Government

Under the provisions of the 1976 Constitution (amended in 1988), executive power is vested in the Governor, appointed by the British monarch. The Governor is responsible for external affairs, internal security, defence and the appointment of public officers. The Governor is President of the Executive Council, which comprises nine members: three *ex officio* and six appointed by the Governor from among the elected members of the Legislative Council. The Legislative Council comprises the Speaker, three nominated members, the *ex-officio* members of the Executive Council and 13 members elected by universal adult suffrage.

Economic Affairs

In 2002, according to estimates by the Caribbean Development Bank (CDB), the Turks and Caicos Islands' gross domestic product (GDP) was US $216.2m., equivalent to some $10,345 per head. During 1994–2003, it was estimated, the population increased at an average annual rate of 6.0%, while GDP increased, in real terms, by 5.8% per year during 1994–2002; growth in 2002 was 3.4%.

Agriculture is not practised on any significant scale in the Turks Islands or on South Caicos (the most populous island of the Territory). The other islands of the Caicos group grow some beans, maize and a few fruits and vegetables. There is some livestock-rearing, but the islands' principal natural resource is fisheries, which account for almost all commodity exports, the principal species caught being the spiny lobster (an estimated 247 metric tons in 2003) and the conch (an estimated 5,646 metric tons in that year). Conchs are now being developed commercially (on the largest conch farm in the world), and there is potential for larger-scale fishing. Exports of lobster and conch earned $3.4m. in 1995, which constituted an increase of more than 14% compared with the previous year's earnings.

Industrial activity consists mainly of construction (especially for the tourism industry) and fish-processing. The islands possess plentiful supplies of aragonite. The Territory is dependent upon the import of mineral fuels to satisfy energy requirements.

The principal economic sector is the service industry. This is dominated by tourism, which is concentrated on the island of Providenciales. The market is for wealthier visitors, most of whom come from the USA. Tourist arrivals increased from approximately 117,600 in 1999 to 165,400 in 2001 and this level was maintained with figures of 155,600 in 2002 and 163,600 in 2003, even in the face of weakened global demand in the aftermath of the September 2001 terrorist attacks on the USA and the subsequent US-led 'war on terror'. The depreciation in value of the US dollar, the official currency of the Turks and Caicos, in the 2003–04, prompted an increase in non-US visitors to the Islands. In January 2004 it was announced that a new US $35m. cruise-ship terminal would be constructed in Grand Turk, enabling, for the first time, large passenger liners to stop in the territory. The terminal was inaugurated in February 2006. An 'offshore' financial sector was encouraged in the 1980s, and new regulatory legislation was ratified at the end of 1989. In 2000 there were some 8,000 overseas companies registered in the islands.

In 2003 the Turks and Caicos Islands recorded a trade deficit of US $160.9m. (exports were 5.7% of the value of imports). This deficit is normally offset by receipts from tourism, aid from the United Kingdom and revenue from the 'offshore' financial sector. The USA is the principal trading partner, but some trade is conducted with the United Kingdom and with neighbouring nations.

According to figures from the CDB, there was an overall budget deficit of US $7.9m. in 2003. In the Government's 2005/06 budget plan, an overall budgetary surplus of $4.6m. was forecast. The islands received a total of $8.2m. in British development assistance in 1999/2000. The total external public debt was $20.0m. in 2003. The rate of inflation, which stood at about 4% in 1995, is dependent upon the movement of prices in the USA, the Territory's principal trading partner. Unemployment increased to an estimated 10% in the late 1990s. A large number of Turks and Caicos 'belongers' have emigrated, many to the Bahamas, especially in search of skilled labour (there is no tertiary education in the Territory). In July 2000 the CDB announced a loan to the Government of some US $4m. to assist the Turks and Caicos Investment Agency.

The Turks and Caicos Islands, as a dependency of the United Kingdom, have the status of Overseas Territory in association with the European Union (EU, see p. 228). The Territory is also a member of the CDB (see p. 188) and an associate member of the Caribbean Community and Common Market (CARICOM, see p. 183). The Territory became an associate member of the Association of Caribbean States (ACS, see p. 384) in April 2006.

The economy, and also the population, of the Turks and Caicos Islands were estimated to have doubled in size during the 1990s, making the islands one of the region's most dynamic economies. The remarkable economic growth experienced by the islands was chiefly owing to the increasing significance of the tourism and international financial services sectors, both of which benefited from the perceived stability of United Kingdom Overseas Territory status. In the past decade the 'offshore' financial sector successfully rehabilitated its international reputation through the introduction, in 2002, of a supervisory body, the Financial Services Commission, and the implementation of more stringent regulatory legislation based on the maxim of 'privacy not secrecy'. In early 2004 the financial sector faced further regulatory disruption when the territory came under pressure to implement the EU's Savings Tax Directive (see Recent History). Tourism also grew steadily in the late 1990s, and as a result many new hotels and resorts have been developed. Concern has, however, been expressed that the islands are in danger of becoming overdeveloped and thereby of damaging their reputation as an unspoilt tourist location. A further source of disquiet has been the exclusion of many inhabitants from the benefits of economic growth; it was estimated that the economic situation of the majority of 'belongers' improved only marginally during the 1990s, as newly created jobs were often taken by low-wage migrant workers or by highly skilled expatriate workers. It has also been noted that the Territory's growth, which is driven more by inward investment than by domestic production, is highly dependent on exterior factors, and international proposals to force comprehensive reforms of 'offshore' financial services centres are therefore of particular concern. A 10-year National Development Plan was launched in October 2005, an initiative between the Department of Planning and the Department of Economic Planning and Statistics.

Education

Primary education, beginning at seven years of age and lasting seven years, is compulsory, and is provided free of charge in government schools. Secondary education, from the age of 14, lasts for five years, and is also free. In 1997 there were 21 primary schools, and in 1990 one private secondary school and four government secondary schools. In 1997 the Caribbean Development Bank approved a loan of just under US $4m. to fund the establishment of a permanent campus for the Turks and Caicos Community College.

Public Holidays

2006: 1 January (New Year's Day), 13 March (Commonwealth Day), 14 April (Good Friday), 17 April (Easter Monday), 29 May (National Heroes' Day), 12 June (Queen's Official Birthday), 7 August (Emancipation Day), 29 September (National Youth Day), 9 October (Columbus Day), 24 October (International Human Rights Day), 25–26 December (Christmas).

2007: 1 January (New Year's Day), 12 March (Commonwealth Day), 6 April (Good Friday), 9 April (Easter Monday), 28 May (National Heroes' Day), 11 June (Queen's Official Birthday), 1 August (Emancipation Day), 28 September (National Youth Day), 8 October (Columbus Day), 24 October (International Human Rights Day), 25–26 December (Christmas).

Weights and Measures

The imperial system is in use.

Statistical Survey

Source: Chief Secretary's Office, South Base, Grand Turk; tel. 946-2702; fax 946-2886.

AREA AND POPULATION

Area: 430 sq km (166 sq miles).

Population: 7,435 at census of 12 May 1980; 12,350 (males 6,289, females 6,061) at census of 31 May 1990; *Mid-2002* (estimate): 20,900 (Source: Caribbean Development Bank, *Social and Economic*

Indicators). *By Island* (1980): Grand Turk 3,098; South Caicos 1,380; Middle Caicos 396; North Caicos 1,278; Salt Cay 284; Providenciales 977. *1990:* Grand Turk 3,761; Providenciales 5,586.

Density: 48.6 per sq km (mid-2002).

Principal Towns: Cockburn Town (capital, on Grand Turk), population 2,500 (estimate, 1987); Cockburn Harbour (South Caicos), population 1,000. *Mid-2003* (UN estimate, incl. suburbs): Grand Turk 5,680 (Source: UN, *World Urbanization Prospects: The 2003 Revision*).

Births and Deaths (2000): Live births 290; Deaths 67 (Source: UN, *Population and Vital Statistics report*). *2005:* Birth rate 22.2 per 1,000; Death rate 4.3 per 1,000 (Source: Pan American Health Organization).

Expectation of Life (years at birth, 2004): 74.3 (males 72.1; females 76.6). Source: Pan American Health Organization.

Economically Active Population (1990 census): 4,848 (males 2,306, females 2,542).

HEALTH AND WELFARE

Total Fertility Rate (children per woman, 2005): 3.1.
Under-5 Mortality Rate (per 1,000 live births, 1997): 22.0.
Hospital Beds (per 1,000 head, 2003): 94.7.
Physicians (per 1,000 head, 1999): 0.73.
Access to Water (% of persons, 2002): 100.
Access to Sanitation (% of persons, 2002): 96.

Source: Pan American Health Organization.

For definitions see explanatory note on p. vi.

AGRICULTURE, ETC.

Fishing (metric tons, live weight, 2003): Capture 6,093* (Marine fishes 200*, Caribbean spiny lobster 247, Stromboid conchs 5,646); Aquaculture 25; *Total catch* 6,118*. Figures exclude aquatic plants and mammals.
* FAO estimate.
Source: FAO.

INDUSTRY

Electric Energy (estimated production, million kWh): 5 in 1999; 5 in 2000; 5 in 2001. Source: UN, *Industrial Commodity Statistics Yearbook*.

FINANCE

Currency and Exchange Rate: United States currency is used: 100 cents = 1 US dollar ($). *Sterling and Euro Equivalents* (30 December 2005): £1 sterling = US $1.7219; €1 = US $1.1797; $100 = £58.08 = €84.77.

Budget (US $ million, 2003): Total revenue and grants 122.5 (current revenue 104.3, capital revenue and grants 18.2); Total expenditure 114.9 (current expenditure 93.5, capital expenditure 21.4). Source: Caribbean Development Bank, *Social and Economic Indicators*.

Gross Domestic Product (US $ million at current prices): 222.7 in 2000; 266.1 in 2001; 280.1 in 2002. Source: Caribbean Development Bank, *Social and Economic Indicators*.

Expenditure on the Gross Domestic Product (US $ million, 2002): Government final consumption expenditure 53.5; Public final consumption expenditure 339.9; Gross fixed capital formation 55.4; *Total domestic expenditure* 448.8; Exports of goods and services 8.7; *Less* Imports of goods and services 177.5; *GDP in market prices* 280.1.

Balance of Payments (US $ million, 2002): Exports of goods f.o.b. 8.7; Imports of goods f.o.b. −177.5; *Trade balance* −168.8; Exports of services 163.1; Imports of services −81.8; *Balance on goods and services* −87.5. Source: Caribbean Development Bank, *Social and Economic Indicators*.

EXTERNAL TRADE

Principal Trading Partners (US $ million, 2003): *Imports c.i.f.:* USA 167.7; Total 170.7. *Exports f.o.b.:* USA 9.2; Total 9.8. Source: Caribbean Development Bank, *Social and Economic Indicators*.

TRANSPORT

Road Traffic (1984): 1,563 registered motor vehicles.
Shipping: *International Freight Traffic* (estimates in '000 metric tons, 1990) Goods loaded 135; Goods unloaded 149. *Merchant Fleet* (vessels registered at 31 December 2004): 5; Total displacement 975 grt. Sources: UN, *Monthly Bulletin of Statistics*; Lloyd's Register-Fairplay, *World Fleet Statistics*.

TOURISM

Tourist Arrivals ('000): 165.4 in 2001; 155.6 in 2002; 163.6 in 2003.
Tourism Receipts (estimates, US $ million): 314 in 2000; 341 in 2001; 319 in 2002.

Source: Caribbean Development Bank, *Social and Economic Indicators*.

COMMUNICATIONS MEDIA

Radio Receivers (1997): 8,000 in use.
Telephones (1994): 3,000 main lines in use.
Facsimile Machines (1992): 200 in use.
Non-daily Newspapers (1996): 1 (estimated circulation 5,000).

Sources: UNESCO, *Statistical Yearbook*; UN, *Statistical Yearbook*.

EDUCATION

Pre-primary (2001/02): 21 schools (1996/97); 70 teachers; 886 pupils.
Primary (2003): 21 schools (1996/97); 119 teachers (2001/02); 3,003 pupils.
General Secondary (2003): 5 schools (1990); 141 teachers (UNESCO estimate, 2001/02); 1,391 pupils.
Vocational Education (1993/94): 30 teachers; 89 pupils.
Adult Literacy Rate (UNESCO estimates): 99% (males 99%; females 98%) in 1998.

Sources: UNESCO Institute for Statistics; Caribbean Development Bank, *Social and Economic Indicators*.

Directory

The Constitution

The Order in Council of July 1986 enabled the Governor to suspend the ministerial form of government, for which the Constitution of 1976 made provision. Ministerial government was restored in March 1988, following amendments to the Constitution, recommended by a constitutional commission.

The revised Constitution of 1988 provides for an Executive Council and a Legislative Council. Executive authority is vested in the British monarch and is exercised by the Governor (the monarch's appointed representative), who also holds responsibility for external affairs, internal security, defence, the appointment of any person to any public office and the suspension and termination of appointment of any public officer.

The Executive Council comprises: two *ex officio* members (the Chief Secretary and the Attorney-General); a Chief Minister (appointed by the Governor) who is, in the judgement of the Governor, the leader of the political party represented in the Legislative Council that commands the support of a majority of the elected members of the Council; and four other ministers, appointed by the Governor, on the advice of the Chief Minister. The Executive Council is presided over by the Governor.

The Legislative Council consists of the Speaker, the two *ex officio* members of the Executive Council, 13 members elected by residents aged 18 and over, and three nominated members (appointed by the Governor, one on the advice of the Chief Minister, one on the advice of the Leader of the Opposition and one at the Governor's discretion).

For the purposes of elections to the Legislative Council, the islands are divided into five electoral districts. In 1988 and 1991 a multiple voting system was used, whereby three districts elected three members each, while the remaining five districts each elected two members. However, from the 1995 election a single-member constituency system was used.

The Government

Governor: RICHARD TAUWHARE (sworn in 11 July 2005).

EXECUTIVE COUNCIL
(April 2006)

President: RICHARD TAUWHARE (The Governor).

UNITED KINGDOM OVERSEAS TERRITORIES

Chief Minister and Minister of Development, Planning, Tourism and District Administration: Dr MICHAEL EUGENE MISICK.
Deputy Chief Minister and Minister of Finance, Health and National Insurance: FLOYD BASIL HALL.
Minister of Communications, Works, Utilities and Housing: JEFFREY CHRISTOVAL HALL.
Minister of Education, Youth, Sports and Cultural Development: LILLIAN ELAINE BOYCE.
Minister of Natural Resources: MCALLISTER EUGENE HANCHELL.
Minister of Home Affairs: GALMO WILLIAMS.
Ex Officio **Members: Attorney-General:** KURT DE FREITAS.
Chief Secretary: MAHALA WYNNS.

GOVERNMENT OFFICES

Office of the Governor: Government House, Grand Turk; tel. 946-2308; fax 946-2903; e-mail govhouse@tciway.tc.
Office of the Chief Minister: Government Sq., Grand Turk; tel. 946-2801; fax 946-2777.
Chief Secretary's Office: South Base, Grand Turk; tel. 946-2702; fax 946-2886; e-mail cso@tciway.tc.
Office of the Permanent Secretary: Finance Dept, Chief Minister's Office, Government Bldgs, Front St, Grand Turk; tel. 946-1115; fax 946-2777.

LEGISLATIVE COUNCIL

Speaker: GLENNEVANS CLARKE.

Election, 24 April 2003

Party	Seats*
People's Democratic Movement (PDM)	7
Progressive National Party (PNP)	6
Total	**13**

* Following two by-elections on 7 August 2003, the PDM held five seats and the PNP held eight seats.

There are two *ex officio* members (the Chief Secretary and the Attorney-General), three appointed members, and a Speaker (assisted by a Deputy Speaker) chosen from outside the Council.

Political Organizations

People's Democratic Movement (PDM): POB 38, Grand Turk; favours internal self-govt and eventual independence; Leader DEREK H. TAYLOR.
Progressive National Party (PNP): Providenciales; tel. 941-4663; fax 946-3673; e-mail pnp@tciway.tc; internet www.votepnp.com; supports full internal self-govt; Chair. SANDRA GARLAND; Leader MICHAEL EUGENE MISICK.
United Democratic Party (UDP): Grand Turk; f. 1993; Leader WENDAL SWANN.

Judicial System

Justice is administered by the Supreme Court of the islands, presided over by the Chief Justice. There is a Chief Magistrate resident on Grand Turk, who also acts as Judge of the Supreme Court. There are also three Deputy Magistrates.
The Court of Appeal held its first sitting in February 1995. Previously the islands had shared a court of appeal in Nassau, Bahamas. In certain cases, appeals are made to the Judicial Committee of the Privy Council (based in the United Kingdom).

Judicial Department

Grand Turk; tel. 946-2114; fax 946-2720; e-mail court@gov.tc.
Chief Justice: (vacant).
Magistrate: DEREK REDMAN.
Attorney-General's Chambers: South Base, Grand Turk; tel. 946-2882; fax 946-2588; e-mail attorneygeneral@tciway.tc.
Attorney-General: KURT DE FREITAS.

Religion

CHRISTIANITY

The Anglican Communion

Within the Church in the Province of the West Indies, the territory forms part of the diocese of Nassau and the Bahamas. The Bishop is resident in Nassau. According to census results, there were 1,465 adherents in 1990.

Anglican Church: St Mary's Church, Front St, Grand Turk; tel. 946-2289; internet bahamas.anglican.org; Archbishop Rev. DREXEL GOMEZ.

The Roman Catholic Church

The Bishop of Nassau, Bahamas (suffragan to the archdiocese of Kingston in Jamaica), has jurisdiction in the Turks and Caicos Islands, as Superior of the Mission to the Territory (founded in June 1984).
Roman Catholic Mission: Leeward Highway, POB 340, Providenciales; tel. and fax 946-1888; e-mail rcmission@tciway.tc; internet www.catholic.tc; churches on Grand Turk, South and North Caicos, and on Providenciales; 132 adherents in 1990 (according to census results); Chancellor Fr PETER BALDACCHINO.

Other Christian Churches

Baptist Union of the Turks and Caicos Islands: South Caicos; tel. 946-3220; 3,153 adherents in 1990 (according to census results).
Jehovah's Witnesses: Kingdom Hall, Intersection of Turtle Cove and Bridge Rd, POB 400, Providenciales; tel. 941-5583.
Methodist Church: The Ridge, Grand Turk; tel. 946-2115; 1,238 adherents in 1990 (according to census results).
New Testament Church of God: Orea Alley, Grand Turk; tel. 946-2175.
Seventh-day Adventists: Grand Turk; tel. 946-2065; Pastor PETER KERR.

The Press

Times of the Islands Magazine: Southwind Plaza, POB 234, Providenciales; tel. and fax 946-4788; e-mail timespub@tciway.tc; internet www.timespub.tc; f. 1988; quarterly; circ. 10,000; Editor KATHY BORSUK.
Turks and Caicos Free Press: Market Pl., POB 179, Providenciales; tel. 941-5615; fax 941-3402; e-mail freepress@tciway.tc; internet www.freepress.tc; f. 1991; bi-weekly; circ. 2,000; Editor CINDI ROUSE; Man. KATHI BARRINGTON.
Turks & Caicos Islands Real Estate Association Real Estate Magazine: Southwind Plaza, POB 234, Providenciales; tel. and fax 946-4788; e-mail timespub@tciway.tc; internet www.timespub.tc; 3 a year; circ. 15,000; Editor KATHY BORSUK.
Turks and Caicos Weekly News: Leeward Highway, Cheshire House, POB 52, Providenciales; tel. 946-4664; fax 946-4661; e-mail tcnews@tciway.tc.
Where, When, How: POB 192, Providenciales; tel. 946-4815; fax 941-3497; e-mail wwh@provo.net; internet www.wherewhenhow.com; monthly; travel magazine.

Broadcasting and Communications

TELECOMMUNICATIONS

Cable & Wireless (Turks and Caicos) Ltd: Leeward Highway, POB 78, Providenciales; tel. 946-2200; fax 946-2497; e-mail cwtci@tciway.tc; internet www.cw.tc; f. 1973; monopoly ended in Jan. 2006.
Digicel: Providenciales; owned by an Irish consortium; granted licence in 2006 to provide mobile telecommunications services in Turks and Caicos; Chair. DENIS O'BRIEN.

Radio

Power 92.5 FM: Providenciales; e-mail kenny@power925fm.com; internet www.power925fm.com.
Radio Providenciales: Leeward Highway, POB 32, Providenciales; tel. 946-4496; fax 946-4108; commercial.
Radio Turks and Caicos (RTC): POB 69, Grand Turk; tel. 946-2007; fax 946-1600; e-mail rtc@tciway.tc; internet www.turksandcaicos.tc/rtc/; govt-owned; commercial; broadcasts 105 hrs weekly; Man. LYNETTE SMITH.
Radio Visión Cristiana Internacional: North End, South Caicos; tel. 946-6601; fax 946-6600; e-mail radiovision@tciway.tc; internet www.radiovision.net; commercial; Man. WENDELL SEYMOUR.

Television

Television programmes are available from a cable network, and broadcasts from the Bahamas can be received in the islands.
Turks and Caicos Television: Pond St, POB 80, Grand Turk; tel. 946-1530; fax 946-2896.
WIV Cable TV: Tower Raza, Leeward Highway, POB 679, Providenciales; tel. 946-4273; fax 946-4790.

Finance

REGULATORY AUTHORITY

Financial Services Commission (FSC): Harry E. Francis Bldg, Pond St, POB 173, Grand Turk; tel. 946-2791; fax 946-2821; e-mail fsc@tciway.tc; f. 2002; regulates local and 'offshore' financial services sector; Man. Dir NEVILLE CADOGAN.

BANKING

Belize Bank: Providenciales; tel. 941-5028; fax 941-5029.

Bordier International Bank and Trust Ltd: Caribbean Pl., Leeward Highway, POB 5, Providenciales; tel. 946-4535; fax 946-4540; e-mail enquiries@bibt.com; internet www.bibt.com; Man. ELISE HARTSHORN.

FirstCaribbean International Bank (Bahamas) Ltd: Leeward Highway, POB 698, Providenciales; tel. 946-2831; fax 946-2695; e-mail care@firstcaribbeanbank.com; internet www.firstcaribbeanbank.com; f. 2002 following merger of Caribbean operations of Barclays Bank PLC and CIBC; Exec. Chair. MICHAEL MANSOOR; CEO CHARLES PINK.

Scotiabank (Canada): Cherokee Rd, POB 15, Providenciales; tel. 946-4750; fax 946-4755; e-mail bns.turkscaicos@scotiabank.com; Man. Dir DAVID TAIT; br. on Grand Turk.

Turks and Caicos Banking Co Ltd: Duke St North, Cockburn Town, POB 123, Grand Turk; tel. 946-2368; fax 946-2365; e-mail tcbc@tciway.tc; internet www.turksandcaicosbanking.tc; f. 1980; cap. US $2.7m., dep. US $9.7m.; Man. Dir ANTON FAESSLER.

TRUST COMPANIES

Berkshire Trust Co Ltd: Caribbean Pl., POB 657, Providenciales; tel. 946-4324; fax 946-4354; e-mail berkshire.trust@tciway.tc; internet www.berkshire.tc; Pres. GORDON WILLIAMSON.

Chartered Trust Co: Town Centre Bldg, Butterfield Sq., POB 125, Providenciales; tel. 946-4881; fax 946-4041; e-mail reception@chartered-tci.com; internet www.chartered-tci.com; Man. Dir PETER A. SAVORY.

Meridian Trust Co Ltd: Caribbean Pl., Leeward Highway, POB 599, Providenciales; tel. 941-3082; fax 941-3223; e-mail mtcl@tciway.tc; internet www.meridiantrust.tc.

M & S Trust Co Ltd: Butterfield Sq., POB 260, Providenciales; tel. 946-4650; fax 946-4663; e-mail mslaw@tciway.tc; internet www.mslaw.tc/trusts.htm; Man. TIMOTHY P. O'SULLIVAN.

Temple Trust Co Ltd: 228 Leeward Highway, Providenciales; tel. 946-5740; fax 946-5739; e-mail info@templefinancialgroup.com; internet www.templefinancialgroup.com; f. 1985; CEO DAVID C. KNIPE.

INSURANCE

Turks and Caicos Islands National Insurance Board: Misick's Bldg, POB 250, Grand Turk; tel. 946-1048; fax 946-1362; e-mail nib@tciway.tc; internet www.nib.tc; 4 brs.

Several foreign (mainly US and British) companies have offices in the Turks and Caicos Islands. More than 2,000 insurance companies were registered at the end of 2002.

Trade and Industry

GOVERNMENT AGENCIES

Financial Services Commission (FSC): see Finance.

General Trading Company (Turks and Caicos) Ltd: PMBI, Cockburn Town, Grand Turk; tel. 946-2464; fax 946-2799; shipping agents, importers, air freight handlers; wholesale distributor of petroleum products, wines and spirits.

Turks Islands Importers Ltd (TIMCO): Front St, POB 72, Grand Turk; tel. 946-2480; fax 946-2481; f. 1952; agents for Lloyds of London, importers and distributors of food, beer, liquor, building materials, hardware and appliances; Dir H. E. MAGNUS.

DEVELOPMENT ORGANIZATION

Turks and Caicos Islands Investment Agency (TC Invest): Hon. Headley Durham Bldg, Church Folly, POB 105, Grand Turk; tel. 946-2058; fax 946-1464; e-mail tcinvest@tciway.tc; internet www.tcinvest.tc; f. 1974 as Devt Bd of the Turks and Caicos Islands; ; statutory body; devt finance for private sector; promotion and management of internal investment; Chair. LILLIAN MISICK; Pres. and CEO COLIN R. HEARTWELL.

CHAMBERS OF COMMERCE

Grand Turk Chamber of Commerce: POB 148, Grand Turk; tel. 946-2324; fax 946-2504; e-mail gtchamberofcommerce@tciway.tc; internet www.turksandcaicos.tc/GrandTurkChamber; f. 1974; Pres. and Exec. Dir GLENNEVANS CLARKE; Hon. Sec. SHERLIN WILLIAMS.

North Caicos Chamber of Commerce: tel. 231-1232; Pres. FRANKLYN ROBINSON.

Providenciales Chamber of Commerce: POB 361, Providenciales; tel. 231-2110; fax 946-4582; internet www.provochamber.com; Pres. DOUG PARNELL.

UTILITIES

Electricity and Gas

Atlantic Equipment and Power (Turks and Caicos) Ltd: New Airport Rd, Airport Area, South Caicos; tel. 946-3201; fax 946-3202.

PPC Ltd: Town Centre Mall, POB 132, Providenciales; tel. 946-4313; fax 946-4532.

Turks and Caicos Utilities Ltd: Pond St, POB 80, Grand Turk; tel. 946-2402; fax 946-2896.

Water

Provo Water Co: Grace Bay Rd, POB 124, Providenciales; tel. 946-5202; fax 946-5204.

Turks and Caicos Water Co: Provo Golf Clubhouse, Grace Bay Rd, POB 124, Providenciales; tel. 946-5126; fax 946-5127.

TRADE UNION

Turks and Caicos Workers' Labour Trade Union: Grand Turk; all professions; f. 2000; Leader CALVIN HANDFIELD.

Transport

ROADS

There are 121 km (75 miles) of roads in the islands, of which 24 km (15 miles), on Grand Turk, South Caicos and Providenciales, are surfaced with tarmac.

SHIPPING

There are regular freight services from Miami, Florida, USA. The main sea ports are Grand Turk, Providenciales, Salt Cay and Cockburn Harbour on South Caicos. A new US $35m. cruise-ship terminal in Grand Turk, which would enable large passenger liners to stop in the territory, opened in February 2006.

Cargo Express Shipping Service Ltd: South Dock Rd, Providenciales; tel. 941-5006; fax 941-5062.

Seacair Ltd: Churchill Bldg, Front St, POB 170, Grand Turk; tel. 946-2591; fax 946-2226.

Tropical Shipping: South Dock Rd, Providenciales; tel. 941-5006; fax 941-5062; e-mail nbeen@tropical.com; internet www.tropical.com; Pres. RICK MURRELL.

CIVIL AVIATION

There are international airfields on Grand Turk, South Caicos, North Caicos and Providenciales, the last being the most important; there are also landing strips on Middle Caicos, Pine Cay, Parrot Cay and Salt Cay.

Department of Civil Aviation: POB 168, Grand Turk; tel. 946-2138; fax 946-1185; e-mail cad@tciway.tc; Dir THOMAS SWANN.

Air Turks and Caicos (2003) Ltd: 1 InterIsland Plaza, Old Airport Rd, POB 191, Providenciales; tel. 941-5481; fax 946-4040; e-mail fly@airturksandcaicos.com; internet www.airturksandcaicos.com.

Caicos Caribbean Airlines: South Caicos; tel. 946-3283; fax 946-3377; freight to Miami (FL, USA).

Cairsea Services Ltd: Old Airport Rd, POB 138, Providenciales; tel. 946-4205; fax 946-4504; e-mail info@cairsea.com; internet www.cairsea.com.

SkyKing Ltd: POB 398, Providenciales; tel. 941-5464; fax 941-4264; e-mail king@tciway.tc; internet www.skyking.tc; f. 1985; daily inter-island passenger services, and services to Haiti and the Dominican Republic; CEO HAROLD CHARLES; Gen. Man. MALLORY MCCOMISH.

Turks Air Ltd: Providenciales; Head Office: 6111 North West 72nd Ave, Miami, FL 33166, USA; tel. 946-4504; fax 946-4504; tel. (305) 593-8847; fax (305) 871-1622; e-mail turksair@earthlink.net; twice-weekly cargo service to and from Miami (USA); Grand Turk Local Agent CRIS NEWTON.

Turks and Caicos Airways Ltd: Providenciales International Airport, POB 114, Providenciales; tel. 946-4255; fax 946-4438; f. 1976 as Air Turks and Caicos; privatized 1983; scheduled daily inter-island service to each of the Caicos Islands, charter flights; Chair. ALBRAY BUTTERFIELD; Dir-Gen. C. MOSER.

Tourism

The islands' main tourist attractions are the numerous unspoilt beaches, and the opportunities for diving. Salt Cay has been designated a World Heritage site by UNESCO. Hotel accommodation is available on Grand Turk, Salt Cay, South Caicos, Parrot Cay, Pine Cay and Providenciales. In 2003 there were some 163,600 tourist arrivals (an increase of 5.1% compared with the previous year). In 2000 73.9% of tourists were from the USA. In 1998 there were 1,522 hotel rooms (some 80% of which were on Providenciales). Revenue from the sector in 2002 totalled an estimated US $319m.

Turks and Caicos Hotel and Tourism Association: Ports of Call, Providenciales; tel. 941-5787; fax 946-4001; e-mail tchta@tciway.tc; internet www.tchta.com; fmrly Turks and Caicos Hotel Asscn; Chair. ANDRE NIEDERHAUSER; CEO CAESAR CAMPBELL.

Turks and Caicos Islands Tourist Board: Front St, POB 128, Grand Turk; tel. 946-2321; fax 946-2733; e-mail tci.tourism@tciway.tc; internet www.turksandcaicostourism.com; f. 1970; br. in Providenciales; Dir LINDSEY MUSGROVE.

THE UNITED STATES OF AMERICA

Introductory Survey

Location, Climate, Language, Religion, Flag, Capital

The United States of America comprises mainly the North American continent between Canada and Mexico. Alaska, to the north-west of Canada, and Hawaii, in the central Pacific Ocean, are two of the 50 States of the USA. There is considerable climatic variation, with mean annual average temperatures ranging from 29°C (77°F) in Florida to −13.3°C (10°F) in Alaska. Average annual rainfall ranges from 1,831 mm (72.1 in) in Arkansas to 191 mm (7.5 in) in Nevada. Much of Texas, New Mexico, Arizona, Nevada and Utah is desert. The official language is English, although there are significant Spanish-speaking minorities. Christianity is the predominant religion. The national flag (proportions 10 by 19) has 13 alternating stripes (seven red and six white) with a dark blue rectangular canton, containing 50 white five-pointed stars, in the upper hoist. The capital is Washington, DC.

Recent History

Concern at the spread of communist influence in Asia dominated US foreign policy during the 1960s and early 1970s. From 1961, until their termination in 1973 by President Richard Nixon, US military operations against communist forces in South Viet Nam led to considerable political division within the USA and were widely criticized internationally. Following a series of scandals involving Nixon and senior administration officials in allegations of corruption and obstruction of justice, known as the 'Watergate' affair, Nixon resigned in August 1974 and was replaced by the Vice-President, Gerald Ford. In November 1976 Jimmy Carter, a Democrat, was elected President. Efforts by the new Administration to resolve tensions in the Middle East culminated in the signing in 1979 of a peace treaty between Egypt and Israel. In 1978 the USA severed formal links with Taiwan and established diplomatic relations with the People's Republic of China. Domestically, economic recession and inflation preoccupied the Carter Administration, and the President's management of the economy was a decisive factor in his defeat by the Republican candidate, Ronald Reagan, in the 1980 presidential election. Although economic recession and high unemployment persisted in the early period of the new Administration, the Republicans retained their previous level of congressional representation in the November 1982 elections. With the resumption of economic growth in 1983, and its strong resurgence through 1984, unemployment and inflation fell, and in November Reagan was re-elected for a further four-year term, securing the largest majority of electoral votes in US history.

The conservative orientation of the Reagan Administration was expressed domestically in a programme aimed at transferring to the individual states the financial responsibility for many federal social programmes, while expanding expenditure on defence. In foreign affairs, the Government generally pursued a firmly anti-communist line, notably in its active support of right-wing regimes in Latin America, where the US military occupation of Grenada in November 1983 attracted considerable international criticism, and in Africa and the Middle East. Generally friendly relations were, however, maintained with the People's Republic of China. The change of leadership in the USSR in November 1982 was followed by a period of deterioration in contacts between the two countries. Formal disarmament negotiations were renewed following the assumption of leadership in the USSR by Mikhail Gorbachev in 1985. However, US–Soviet relations were overshadowed by Reagan's pursuit of his Strategic Defense Initiative (SDI). Initiated in 1983, this advanced-technology research programme aimed to create a space-based system of defences against nuclear attack. The Reagan Government consistently refused to negotiate the termination of SDI, which was viewed by the USSR as a potential source of arms escalation and a first step in the militarization of space. US–Soviet relations experienced further strain following Soviet military intervention in Afghanistan in 1979.

During the Reagan period the USA adopted a forceful stance (generally welcomed by other Western governments) on international air and sea terrorism. However, in 1985 a ban on trade with Libya, which Reagan alleged to be promoting terrorist activity, received little support from other Western countries. In April 1986, following a terrorist attack on US military personnel in West Berlin, Reagan ordered the selective bombing of government offices and military installations in Tripoli and Benghazi. Direct US military involvement in the Middle East, which had been minimized since its withdrawal in 1984 from peace-keeping operations in Lebanon, was reactivated in July 1987, when Reagan agreed to a request by Kuwait to provide military protection for its petroleum tankers in the Persian (Arabian) Gulf, following attacks on them by Iran. Subsequent incidents in the Gulf brought the USA and Iran into armed confrontations. In April 1988 the USA was a signatory, with the USSR, Afghanistan and Pakistan, of an agreement for the phased withdrawal of Soviet troops from Afghanistan, which was completed in February 1989.

Negotiations on the issue of arms control were maintained between the USA and the USSR during 1986. In November the USA abandoned the weapon deployment limits set by the 1979 Strategic Arms Limitation Treaty (SALT II), which, although never ratified by Congress, had been informally observed by both the USA and the USSR. In March 1987, however, the US Government responded favourably to an indication by the USSR of its willingness to expedite an agreement to eliminate medium-range nuclear missiles from Europe by 1992.

These discussions, which were subsequently extended to include short-range nuclear weaponry, were followed, in September 1987, by an agreement in principle on terms under which both countries would eliminate all stocks of medium- and short-range nuclear missiles. The resultant Intermediate Nuclear Forces (INF) treaty, the first to terminate an entire class of offensive nuclear weapon, was finalized in December, when the two leaders also agreed to pursue negotiations towards a new Strategic Arms Reduction Treaty (START) to reduce long-range nuclear weaponry by up to 50%. The INF treaty was ratified and activated in 1988. The further advancement of SDI, meanwhile, had become increasingly conjectural: the US Congress proved reluctant to allocate its high funding requirements, and during 1988 and 1989 expressed doubts about the feasibility of the project's goals. The USSR, while maintaining its objections to SDI, agreed in 1990 to exclude it from the ambit of negotiations on START.

In November 1986 details began to emerge of covert foreign policy operations by senior members of the Reagan Administration in relation to US contacts with the Government of Iran. The ensuing scandal, known as the 'Irangate' or 'Iran-Contra' affair, developed into a major political embarrassment for the President. Subsequent investigations by an independent commission, and by the US Congress, concluded that secret arms sales had been made to the Iranian Government, in return for an undertaking by Iran to help to secure the release of US hostages held by pro-Iranian Islamic groups in Lebanon, and that Reagan had been misled by officials of the security services into authorizing the arms transactions, and bypassing the required congressional consultative procedures. The report also upheld allegations that funds derived from the arms sales had been secretly diverted into bank accounts held by the Nicaraguan Contra rebels. Reagan, who accepted full personal responsibility for the 'Iran-Contra' affair, was exonerated of any deliberate attempt to misrepresent his role in the events. The closing months of Reagan's presidency were clouded by further political scandals involving senior presidential appointees.

At the November 1988 presidential election, Reagan was succeeded by his Vice-President, George Bush, although the Senate and House of Representatives both retained Democratic majorities. The initial months of the Bush Administration were dominated by concern over the formulation of effective measures to contain the federal budget deficit, and over the future course of arms reduction negotiations with the USSR. In June 1989, following an agreement to resume START discussions, President Bush proposed the initiation of new negotiations aimed at achieving substantial reductions in North Atlantic Treaty Organization (NATO) and Warsaw Pact countries' conventional ground forces in Europe. In September the USA and USSR finalized agreements on the monitoring of chemical weapons and procedures for the verification of limits on strategic forces and nuclear tests. A summit meeting between Bush and Gorbachev followed at Valletta, Malta, in December, which marked the opening of a new era in US–Soviet relations. Under discussion were the prospects for new agreements by the mid-1990s for reductions of 50% in nuclear strategic arms, together with substantial reductions in the size of conventional forces based in Europe.

The withdrawal by the USSR in late 1989 and early 1990 from the exercise of direct political influence on the internal affairs of the countries of Eastern Europe was accompanied by a further improvement in US–Soviet relations, and by the implementation of programmes of US economic aid for several of the former Soviet 'client' states. In September 1990 the USA and USSR, with France and the United Kingdom, the other powers that occupied Germany at the end of the Second World War, formally agreed terms for the unification of the two post-war German states, which took effect in the following month. US–Soviet relations came under some strain, however, following the assertion by Lithuania of independence from the USSR and subsequent Soviet measures to blockade the Lithuanian economy. In July the USA, together with the world's six largest industrial democracies, agreed to provide the USSR with economic and technical assistance in undertaking a change-over to a market economy. In the same month, a summit meeting of NATO members proposed that the USSR and the other members of the Warsaw Pact alliance join in a formal declaration that the two military groupings were no longer adversaries and would refrain from the threat or use of force. This initiative was followed in November by the signing in Paris, by members of NATO and the Warsaw Pact, of a Treaty on Conventional Armed Forces in Europe (CFE), which provided for bilateral limits to be placed on the number of non-nuclear weapons sited between the Atlantic Ocean and the Ural Mountains. Immediately following the signing of the CFE Treaty, Presidents Bush and Gorbachev were present at a meeting of the Conference on Security and Co-operation in Europe (CSCE, now the Organization for Security and Co-operation in Europe—OSCE, see p. 327), at which the USA, the USSR and 32 other countries signed a charter declaring the end of the post-war era of confrontation and division in Europe.

In September 1989 President Bush outlined the terms of a federal programme aimed at combating drug abuse, which in recent years had become a serious social problem in the USA. The initiative received co-operation from the governments of Bolivia, Colombia and Peru, but the activities of drugs-traffickers operating from Panama, allegedly with the collusion of the regime controlled by Gen. Manuel Noriega, had been unaffected by US sanctions. In December 1989, following the failure of an internal coup attempt that received non-military US support, the USA carried out an armed invasion of Panama and subsequently installed an elected government. US troops were withdrawn in February 1990. In Nicaragua the departure of the Sandinista government, as the result of a general election held in February 1990, was followed by the resumption of cordial relations with the US Government.

Following the invasion of Kuwait by Iraqi forces on 2 August 1990, and the subsequent annexation of that country by Iraq, the US Government assumed a leading international role in the implementation of political, economic and military measures to bring about an Iraqi withdrawal. The imposition of mandatory economic sanctions against Iraq by the UN Security Council on 6 August was quickly followed by 'Operation Desert Shield', in which US combat troops and aircraft were dispatched to Saudi Arabia, at that country's request, to secure its borders against a possible attack by Iraq. Tensions were heightened in mid-August by Iraq's detention of Western nationals resident in Kuwait and Iraq, and the harassment of Western diplomatic personnel in Kuwait. An offer, subsequently repeated, by President Saddam Hussain of Iraq to link withdrawal from Kuwait with a resolution of other outstanding Middle East problems, was rejected, and in late August the UN Security Council endorsed the use of military action to enforce its economic sanctions. Despite intense diplomatic activity, in which the USSR was prominent, the crisis deepened. In early September Presidents Bush and Gorbachev jointly demanded an Iraqi withdrawal, although the USSR expressed reluctance to support military operations by the UN. In late September the UN Security Council intensified its economic measures against Iraq. However, the ineffectiveness both of economic sanctions and of diplomatic negotiation had become evident by late November, and the USSR gave its assent to the use of force against Iraq, although it did not participate in the multinational force that was now arrayed in the Gulf region and included, under US command, air, sea and ground forces from the United Kingdom, France, Italy, Egypt, Morocco, Kuwait and the other Arab Gulf states. Jordan, which was active throughout the crisis in seeking to promote a negotiated settlement, was perceived by the US Government as sympathetic to Iraq, and US financial aid programmes to that country were suspended.

On 29 November 1990 the UN Security Council authorized the use of 'all necessary means' to force Iraq to withdraw from Kuwait, unless it did so by 15 January 1991. By early January the USA had established a considerable military presence in the Gulf region, and on 17 January 'Operation Desert Storm' was launched, with massive air and missile attacks against Iraqi positions, both in Iraq and Kuwait. In the course of the conflict, more than 110,000 attacking air missions were flown over Kuwait and Iraq by multinational air forces, while naval support operations were conducted from the Gulf. In the following weeks, severe damage was inflicted on Iraqi military and economic targets, while counter-attacks by its air force, and attempts to draw Israel into the conflict by launching missile attacks on population centres, proved ineffective. A ground offensive by the multinational force was launched on 23–24 February, and Iraqi positions were quickly overrun. Hostilities were suspended on 28 February. The Government of Iraq accepted cease-fire terms on 3 March, leaving the multinational forces in control of Kuwait, together with an area of southern Iraq, comprising about 15% of that country's total national territory. Troop withdrawals from the occupied area of Iraq commenced in March, with the remaining US troops evacuated in early May, to be replaced by a UN peace-keeping force.

Following the termination of hostilities, in which 148 US troops died in combat, internal rebellions broke out within Iraq by groups opposed to President Saddam Hussain. The severity with which these were suppressed, particularly in the northern region among the Kurdish ethnic group, and the subsequent flight of refugees into neighbouring areas of Turkey and Iran, prompted large-scale international relief operations. The US Government was widely criticized for its refusal to support the anti-Government insurgents and to take action to depose Saddam Hussain. In May 1991 the USA began airlifting troops to northern Iraq to establish 'safe' enclaves, to which Kurdish refugees were encouraged to return. The US military continued to monitor events in these Kurdish areas from operational bases in Turkey and other strategic points in the region. In September 1996 the USA launched missile strikes from naval vessels in the Gulf at military targets in Iraq, in retaliation for attacks by Iraqi forces against Kurds in northern Iraq.

In the period following the Gulf War, the US Government actively pursued initiatives to convene a regional conference, with joint and Soviet sponsorship, to seek a permanent solution to the wider problems of the Middle East. In August 1991 the US Secretary of State, James Baker, obtained the agreement of Egypt, Israel, Jordan, Lebanon and Syria to take part in such a conference, the opening session of which was convened in October. Successive negotiations failed to make any substantive progress, and traditionally close relations between Israel and the USA subsequently came under strain, following pressure by the US Government on Israel to suspend the construction of Jewish settlements in occupied territories, pending the eventual outcome of the peace negotiations.

During the second half of 1991 there was increasing concern by the US Government at the implications of economic dislocation and political unrest within the USSR. In June President Bush offered the USSR guarantees of up to $1,500m. in loans for grain purchases, together with assistance in restructuring the Soviet food distribution system. In late July the USA and USSR signed START, providing for a 30% reduction in long-range nuclear weapons over a seven-year period. Further moves towards bilateral disarmament followed in September, when the USA announced that it was to begin the phased elimination of sea and air tactical nuclear weapons in Europe and Asia; in October the USSR offered to reduce its holdings of nuclear weapons to below the levels agreed in START.

In December 1991, following the replacement of the USSR by the Commonwealth of Independent States (CIS) comprising 11 of the republics of the former Soviet Union, the independence of each republic was recognized by the USA. In January 1992 a meeting was held between President Bush and President Yeltsin of Russia, the dominant republic within the CIS. President Bush expressed concern that effective measures should be taken by the Russian Government to ensure that the nuclear weapons and related technical expertise of the former USSR did not become available to countries not in possession of nuclear weapons capability, or to nations in the Middle East or to the Democratic People's Republic of Korea (DPRK—North Korea). At a subsequent meeting held in February, the Russian leader assured President Bush that immediate safeguards were in force, and that all short-range nuclear warheads would be moved into Russia from sites in other CIS republics by July 1992. President Yeltsin also proposed that the USA and Russia should share in the joint future development of the SDI project (see above), and further reductions in nuclear arsenals were agreed by the two leaders.

At a summit meeting held between Presidents Bush and Yeltsin in June 1992 in Washington, DC, agreement was reached on further substantial reductions in nuclear arms, under which, by 2003, total holdings of nuclear warheads would be reduced to less than one-half of the quotas contained in START. Agreements covering other areas of co-operation, including the encouragement of US private-sector investment in Russia, arrangements for mutual assistance in the event of accidents in space, and the outline of a joint ballistic missiles protection system, were also signed.

In its relations with the former communist countries in Europe, the USA augmented its commitment to the CSCE with economic support, and promoted the membership of former members of the Warsaw Pact in the North Atlantic Co-operation Council, an offshoot of NATO. Contacts were also revived between the USA and Viet Nam, and in May 1992 there was a partial relaxation of a trade embargo in force since 1975. Relations with Iraq remained tense following the discovery, made in November 1991 by UN representatives, that President Saddam Hussain's regime was seeking to conceal its continuing development of nuclear weapons capability.

Following the conclusion of the Gulf War in early 1991, Bush's political popularity fell sharply, amid growing public perception that the Government was assigning greater priority to foreign affairs than to addressing the problems of the US economy, which had been in recession since early 1989. Criticism was also directed at the Administration's alleged neglect of other domestic issues, particularly in the areas of social welfare, medical costs and health care, and the interrelated issues of urban poverty and civil rights. In 1990 Bush vetoed legislation providing financial compensation for those victimized by discrimination in employment, although a compromise version was eventually approved in November 1991. In April 1992 serious rioting broke out in Los Angeles and spread briefly to several other cities. The underlying causes of the disorders were widely ascribed to the worsening economic and social plight of the impoverished urban black minority.

The 1992 presidential election campaign, in which Bush was opposed by Bill Clinton, a Democratic state governor, and Ross Perot, a populist independent, was dominated by social and economic issues. Bush's record of economic management, particularly in relation to the persistence of federal budget deficits, provided the major line of attack by the opposing candidates. The turn-out of voters, at 55%, was the highest at any presidential election since 1968, and gave a decisive majority, of 43% to 37%, to Clinton. Perot, whose campaign had concentrated on the question of federal deficit spending, obtained almost 19% of the popular vote.

Foreign affairs dominated the final months of the Bush Administration. In July 1992 contention arose between the Government of Iraq and the UN over the rights of UN observers to inspect Iraqi nuclear facilities, and in the following month the US Government sought to limit internal military operations by the Iraqi Government by imposing an air exclusion zone south of latitude 32°N. This was followed, in January 1993, by US participation in selective bombings of Iraqi missile sites. In December 1992 relations with the People's Republic of China, which had been strained since 1989 by the Chinese Government's persistent suppression of political dissent, were revived by the removal of a US embargo on sales of military equipment. In the same month President Bush launched 'Operation Restore Hope', under which 24,000 US troops were sent to Somalia, as part of an international force under US command, to protect shipments of food aid and to assist in the restoration of civil order. (In May 1993 the USA transferred command of operations in Somalia to the UN, although about 4,000 US troops remained until the termination of the peace-keeping operation in March 1994.)

Shortly before the transfer of the presidency to Bill Clinton in January 1993, Presidents Bush and Yeltsin met in Moscow to sign a second Nuclear Arms Reduction Treaty (START II), which provided for the elimination by 2003 of almost 75% of all US and CIS-held nuclear warheads. The implementation, however, of START I and START II could not begin until Belarus, Kazakhstan and Ukraine, the other former republics of the USSR which held stocks of nuclear weapons, had endorsed START I. Ukraine was the last of these republics (in December 1994) to ratify the START arrangements, and in March 1995 undertook that the transfer of its stocks of nuclear weapons to Russia would be completed by 1997. Clinton announced the termination of SDI, although there was subsequent discussion within the USA of its possible reactivation (see below). Although ratified by the US Senate in 1993, START II remained unratified by the Russian legislature until April 2000. However, arrangements agreed in late 1997 by the US and Russian Governments had extended by five years the period allowed for the elimination of Russia's long-range nuclear missiles.

The initial preoccupation of the Clinton Administration was the formulation of an economic recovery plan, to be phased over a five-year period, to reduce the federal budget deficit by means of increased taxation and economies in the cost of government, rather than by reduced levels of federal spending. Military expenditure was a particular area in which economies were proposed, while additional spending was planned for infrastructural projects and measures to stimulate economic activity. A major restructuring of the US health care system was also planned, and a commission to formulate proposals was placed under the chairmanship of President Clinton's wife, Hillary. Certain aspects of the economic recovery plan, particularly those relating to higher income tax and a new energy tax, encountered initial opposition in the Democrat-controlled Congress, but were eventually approved, in a modified form, by the House of Representatives in May 1993. Approval by the Senate, following further amendments, took place in June. By mid-1993, however, the President's initial popularity had fallen sharply, owing in part to perceptions of indecisiveness by Clinton in formulating effective policies. There was also widespread criticism of the competence of some of his advisers and appointees.

By mid-1993 the crisis in former Yugoslavia had assumed increased importance as a foreign policy issue, leading to disagreements between the USA and the Western European powers, which opposed US proposals to launch direct air strikes against military positions held by Bosnian Serbs. The US Administration, while avoiding any direct military commitment, gave its support, through NATO, to peace-keeping operations in Bosnia and Herzegovina. Clinton was unsuccessful, however, in efforts to secure the removal of the international embargo on arms sales to the Bosnian Muslims. In June 1994 the US Government endorsed proposals by the European Union (EU) countries for the tripartite partition of Bosnia and Herzegovina.

The Clinton Administration made renewed efforts to restore to power Fr Jean-Bertrand Aristide, the first democratically elected President of Haiti, who had taken refuge in the USA following his overthrow by a military junta in 1991. An economic embargo imposed by the Organization of American States (OAS, see p. 333), together with implied threats of military intervention by the US Government, had failed to displace the military regime, and conditions within Haiti had led large numbers of refugees to seek asylum in the USA, many of whom were forcibly repatriated by the US authorities. In June 1994, following the imposition in the previous month of international sanctions against Haiti by the UN Security Council, Clinton announced the suspension of all commercial and financial transactions with Haiti. In September, following a diplomatic mission led by former President Carter, a UN-sponsored multinational force, composed almost entirely of US troops, arrived in Haiti with the agreement of the military junta, which relinquished power in October. US troops were withdrawn from the UN force in March 1995. In January 2004 the Administration of George W. Bush (2001–) condemned attacks on thousands of demonstrators protesting against the Aristide Government. In early March, in the face of growing violence and under international pressure, Aristide resigned and went into exile, although he claimed that he had been unconstitutionally removed from office by the USA. Several hundred US marines were deployed in Haiti in March–June 2004 as the vanguard of 'a multinational UN Stabilization Mission in Haiti to disarm rebel forces and stabilize the country.

THE UNITED STATES OF AMERICA

Introductory Survey

During 1993 the Clinton Administration continued to foster efforts to promote a general resolution of tensions in the Middle East. With US assistance, but as a direct result of secret diplomatic mediation by Norway, the Palestine Liberation Organization (PLO) and the Government of Israel signed an agreement providing for Palestinian self-government in the Occupied Territories and for mutual recognition by Israel and the PLO. In January 1994, following a meeting held in Geneva, Switzerland, between Clinton and President Assad of Syria, negotiations were initiated for a settlement between Israel and Syria.

Political and economic contacts with Russia continued on a cordial level, with the two countries adopting a co-operative stance in many areas of foreign policy. In February 1994 the US Government lifted the remaining sanctions on trade with Viet Nam (see above) and in the following July the USA established full diplomatic relations with that country. Relations with the People's Republic of China improved in 1994, following a controversial decision by Clinton to extend enhanced trading privileges to that country until June 1995, despite China's continued suppression of free political debate. Little progress, however, was made in the resolution of the persistently adverse US balance of trade with Japan, despite an agreement between the two countries in July 1993 to implement measures to reduce the trade deficit.

The prevention of nuclear proliferation, which remained a prime objective of US foreign policy, led in 1993 and early 1994 to a serious confrontation between the USA and North Korea. In March 1993 the DPRK, which is a signatory of the Nuclear Non-Proliferation Treaty (NPT) and is subject, by virtue of its membership of the International Atomic Energy Agency (IAEA, see p. 98), to the monitoring of its nuclear installations, refused to grant the IAEA inspectorate full access to its nuclear power facility. It cited as its reasons the existence of joint military exercises between the Republic of Korea (South Korea) and the USA and 'unjust acts' by the IAEA. The US Government stated that it had reason to suspect that the DPRK had been diverting nuclear plant material for the development of atomic weapons. In July Clinton visited South Korea, and warned the DPRK that any use of nuclear weapons by them would be met with military force. He reiterated that the USA would maintain its military presence in the Republic of Korea. Despite increasing international pressure (from which the People's Republic of China remained aloof), and attempts at mediation by the UN, the DPRK repeatedly asserted its refusal to comply with the treaty's inspection requirements. The crisis steadily worsened during early 1994, and in June the US Government, after seeking unsuccessfully to offer the DPRK economic aid, investment and diplomatic recognition, began to seek support for the imposition of UN economic sanctions. Later in the same month, following a visit to the DPRK by former President Carter (acting as an unofficial representative of the Government), the DPRK agreed to a temporary suspension of its nuclear programme, pending formal discussions with the US Government. These meetings were convened in July. Negotiations aimed at improving relations between the USA and the DPRK, and at fostering a political settlement between the DPRK and the Republic of Korea, were pursued throughout both Clinton Administrations. In March 1999 the US and DPRK Governments agreed on terms whereby US officials would receive unrestricted access to inspect DPRK nuclear facilities.

During 1993 and 1994 the personal integrity of both President Clinton and his wife was challenged by accusations of financial irregularities in their alleged involvement in a savings bank and property development company that collapsed in 1989, during Clinton's tenure as Governor of Arkansas. These allegations, which came to be known as the 'Whitewater' affair, were strenuously denied by the Clintons, and were made the subject of official investigations. In May 1996 Clinton's successor as Governor of Arkansas resigned following his conviction for fraud in connection with the 'Whitewater' affair. In the following month a Senate committee alleged that Hillary Clinton and certain officials in the President's office had acted to obstruct a federal investigation into the Whitewater Corporation. These findings, however, were challenged by Democrat members of the committee.

The collapse of Clinton's plans for health care reform following congressional opposition in 1994, together with increasing public concern about the domestic economy and the effectiveness of Clinton's policies on social issues (notably in the areas of welfare expenditure, law enforcement and the protection of traditional social values), led to a sharp rise in support for the conservative doctrines of politicians representing the right wing of the Republican Party. At congressional elections in November 1994, the Republicans gained control both of the Senate (for the first time since 1986) and the House of Representatives (which had been controlled by the Democrats since 1954). As a result, in 1995 serious divisions began to emerge between President Clinton and Congress. In February Clinton threatened to veto foreign policy legislation on the grounds that it violated the President's constitutional prerogatives in foreign relations and defence. In June further tensions arose over proposals to achieve a balanced federal budget. Negotiations proved inconclusive, and in November Clinton, in an effort to resolve the deadlock, refused to renew the temporary funding arrangements, causing an eight-day shutdown of all non-essential operations of the federal government. Agreement on the 1995/96 budget was eventually reached in April 1996, although disagreements on the timetable for, and the method of achieving, a balanced budget remained unresolved.

The interlinked issues of political terrorism and the private possession of firearms (which is constitutionally guaranteed) came to the fore in April 1995, when 168 lives were lost in the terrorist bombing of a federal building in Oklahoma City. Subsequent investigations suggested the involvement of sympathizers of paramilitary groups whose supporters accused the federal Government of conducting a conspiracy to deprive them of individual and constitutional freedoms. One such sympathizer, Timothy McVeigh, was eventually convicted of the attack and was executed in June 2001.

In the presidential election that was held in November 1996, Clinton was decisively re-elected to the presidency, obtaining 49% of the popular vote, compared with 43% in the 1992 election. Robert Dole, the Republican nominee, obtained 41% of the votes, while Ross Perot, who was nominated by the Reform Party, an organization founded by him to seek radical reductions in federal government spending, attracted 8%. The Republicans retained control of the Senate and House of Representatives.

Following his inauguration for a second term in January 1997, Clinton declared the enhancement of educational standards to be a primary aim of his second term. Proposals were also announced to achieve further reductions in welfare dependency, by providing tax credits and other incentives to employers. Financial savings were to be achieved by further reductions in defence expenditure, and by the implementation of further cuts in spending on health care for the elderly. Clinton reiterated his intention, however, of seeking improved provisions for insured health care, and of achieving a balanced federal budget by 2002. Agreement between Clinton and the Republican congressional leadership on the general terms of these budgetary measures was reached in May 1997.

In foreign affairs, the Clinton Administration continued to support economic reform in Russia and the successor states of the former USSR, with particular emphasis on fostering the change-over from defence to consumer production. Prior to the cease-fire declared in August 1996, the US Government expressed disapproval of the scale of Russian military operations in Chechnya, and in May 1995 the Clinton Administration was refused Russian co-operation in its ban on US trade and investment in Iran, in retaliation for that country's alleged involvement in international terrorism. Concerns expressed by Russia at the proposed enlargement of NATO were addressed at a summit meeting of Presidents Yeltsin and Clinton in Helsinki, Finland, in March 1997. (See the chapter on Russia for details of the subsequent agreement between NATO and Russia.)

The reluctance of the Clinton Administration to participate directly in UN military operations in Bosnia and Herzegovina was modified in June 1995 with a statement by Clinton that US ground troops would be sent to Bosnia and Herzegovina in 'emergency' circumstances on a 'limited basis' if required to assist in the redeployment of existing UN forces, or to participate in monitoring an eventual peace settlement. In November, following US-sponsored negotiations held in Dayton, Ohio, a peace agreement was reached by the opposing sides. As part of its implementation, the US Government agreed to contribute 20,000 troops to a multinational supervisory force of 60,000 troops under the command of NATO. The USA committed about 8,500 troops in an extended NATO peace-keeping operation in Bosnia and Herzegovina until mid-1998 and about 1,000 soldiers served as part of NATO's Stabilization Force until December 2004. A small contingent of US troops remained in Bosnia and Herzegovina in 2005, serving at NATO's offices in the Bosnian capital, Sarajevo.

Relations with the People's Republic of China pursued an uneven course under the Clinton Administration, owing to disagreements over trade matters and criticism by the USA of alleged abuses by the Chinese Government of human rights. Relations between the two countries declined sharply in February 1996, following US protests over Chinese military operations near Taiwan. Relations between the two countries were enhanced in October 1997 by a state visit to the USA by President Jiang Zemin, following which the US Government revoked a ban, in force since 1989, on the export of US nuclear technology to China. China, together with Russia and the USA, refused in December 1997 to sign an international treaty—the Ottawa Convention—banning the manufacture and use of anti-personnel landmines; the US Government based its objection to the arrangements on its requirement for landmines to protect its troops stationed in the Republic of Korea. It was stated that the USA proposed to develop an alternative weapons technology to replace landmines by 2003. (Following a two and a half year review of landmine policy, in late February 2004 the Bush Administration announced that it would not sign the treaty and would continue to use, indefinitely, 'non-persistent' landmines that would self-destruct or self-deactivate after a certain period of time.) In mid-1998 President Clinton made a state visit to the People's Republic of China, the first to be undertaken by a US President since that country's violent suppression of political dissent in 1989. Following the settlement in June 1999 of a dispute over infringements of US copyright and other intellectual property rights, enhanced trading privileges were granted permanent status in May 2000, opening the way for the People's Republic of China to join the World Trade Organization (WTO, see p. 370).

Successive US Governments remained unwilling to restore relations with Cuba. Relations between the two countries deteriorated in March 1996, after two civilian aircraft carrying Cuban exiles protesting against the Castro Government were shot down by the Cuban air force over international waters. In response, Clinton acceded to congressional demands to strengthen the US commercial and economic embargo that has been in force since 1962. Under the new measure, the Cuban Liberty and Solidarity (Helms-Burton) Act, the USA was to penalize foreign investors whose business in any way involves property in Cuba that was confiscated from US citizens following the 1959 revolution. This measure, which was initially intended to enter into operation in August 1996, attracted strong protests from the EU, and from Mexico and Canada, which have substantial trading links with Cuba. In June legislation was approved by Congress to impose penalties on foreign companies investing in Iran and Libya, both of which were accused by the US Government of sponsoring international terrorism. In July a number of Canadian, Mexican and Italian companies were informed that sanctions were to be imposed on them under the Helms-Burton legislation, barring their senior executives and certain shareholders from visiting the USA. In response to intense international pressure, Clinton declared a temporary moratorium on certain provisions of the Helms-Burton Act, and in April 1997 the US Government and the EU, which had referred its complaint to the WTO, announced that a compromise had been agreed, subject to the abandonment by the US Government of certain sections of the Act. The moratorium on Title III of the Act was subsequently extended at six-monthly intervals and remained in operation in 2006. In March 1998 the US Government lifted bans (imposed in 1996) on civilian aircraft services to Cuba and on financial remittances to Cuba from the USA. In late 2001 the USA lifted temporarily the trade embargo against Cuba to allow the purchase of food and medicines necessary for the reconstruction and aid effort following the devastation caused by 'Hurricane Michelle'. In April 2004 a motion, supported by the USA, condemning Cuba for human rights violations, was approved by the UN General Assembly; similar US-backed motions had been passed by the UN in 2002 and 2003. In April 2005 a milder, US-proposed motion requesting that the mandate of the UN's Special Rapporteur on Human Rights in Cuba be extended was approved by the General Assembly. In July the US Secretary of State, Condoleezza Rice, appointed Caleb McCarry Cuba Transition Co-ordinator, a position created at the behest of a special panel charged with directing the US Government's actions 'in support of a free Cuba' and hastening the end to President Castro's premiership.

In January 1995 the USA led an international financial consortium to provide substantial loan guarantees to resolve a major financial crisis in Mexico. In the previous month President Clinton proposed the formation, by 2006, of a Free Trade Area of the Americas (FTAA), comprising 34 countries of the Western hemisphere. Proposals for the new free trade area were discussed at a two 'Summits of the Americas' held in Santiago, Chile, in April 1998, and Québec, Canada, in April 2001. Negotiations were scheduled to conclude by January 2005, but stalled in November 2004; in early November 2005, at a Fourth Summit of the Americas, in Mar del Plata, Argentina, an agreement was reached to resume talks in 2006.

At the end of 1998 President Clinton and the President of Colombia, Andrés Pastrana Arango, signed a Counter-Narcotics Alliance, in an attempt to address the ongoing war against drugs-trafficking. In January 2000 the Clinton Administration announced an aid package for the Andean region worth $1,300m., the largest ever aid programme for Latin America. The main portion of the programme, which became known as the 'Plan Colombia', was some $860m. to Colombia, three-quarters of which was allocated to the security forces in that country. The size of the military component of the Plan caused controversy internationally, as did the proposed aerial destruction of crops in the region. As a result, in 2001 the incoming Administration of George W. Bush proposed a modified Plan Colombia, to be known as the Andean Regional Initiative, the focus of which would be on improving social and economic conditions in the region. Nevertheless, the objective remained the same: to reduce significantly the flow of drugs from the Andean region into the USA.

International concern at the effects on world climate of emissions of carbon dioxide and other gases that have a warming effect on the atmosphere ('greenhouse gases') has, in recent years, brought the USA and other industrialized countries under pressure to implement measures to reduce the use of these substances. In December 1997, at the third Conference of the Parties to the Framework Convention on Climate Change (see UN Environment Programme, see p. 58), held in Kyoto, Japan, the USA undertook to implement reductions of its emissions of 'greenhouse gases' to 7% below 1990 levels by the year 2012. However, in view of the problems inherent in the cost-effective phasing-out of these substances, ratification of the Kyoto arrangements encountered strong opposition in Congress and among business leaders. Soon after taking office in 2001 President George W. Bush announced that his Government did not support the ratification of the agreement (see below).

In November 1997 the Government of Iraq demanded the immediate removal of US inspectors working in the UN Special Commission (UNSCOM, see p. 101) and see also the chapter on Iraq) carrying out the identification and elimination of biological, chemical and other weapons of mass destruction allegedly held by Iraq. This action was strongly resisted by the UN, amid increasing concern in the USA and internationally at subsequent actions by Iraq to disrupt the weapons inspection programme. Following repeated threats of military action by the USA against Iraq to enforce the inspections arrangements, substantial US military forces were dispatched to the Gulf region. Following extended negotiations, culminating in a meeting in February 1998 between President Saddam Hussain and the UN Secretary-General, Kofi Annan, the Government of Iraq agreed to restore unrestricted access to UN inspectors, and to withdraw its objection to the presence of US personnel. The US Government accepted the agreement, but warned of 'serious consequences' in the event of future violations by Iraq.

US policy continued to encourage political reform and economic development in the former communist countries of Eastern Europe, and in 1998 the Senate gave formal approval for the accession to NATO membership in 1999 of the Czech Republic, Hungary and Poland. Foreign policy concerns involving South Asia were revived in June, when successive tests of nuclear weapons were carried out by the Governments of India and Pakistan. The tests, which were condemned by the five states with nuclear armaments (the USA, France, Russia, the United Kingdom and the People's Republic of China), prompted Clinton to impose economic sanctions on both countries, while pursuing efforts to obtain their accession to the NPT.

During his second term as President, Clinton was confronted by a number of other allegations, which he consistently denied, dating from prior to 1992 and extending through his presidency, of perjury and obstruction of justice arising from accusations of sexual harassment. These matters, which related to Clinton's period as a state official in Arkansas, were brought within the ambit of a congressionally mandated independent counsel, Kenneth Starr, who began in 1994 to examine the legal ramifications of the 'Whitewater' affair (see above). In January 1998 a former junior employee on the presidential staff, Monica Lewinsky, was required to give evidence in a civil action by Paula Jones, who had alleged that she had been sexually harassed by Clinton in 1991. In that month Starr was authorized by the Attorney-General to investigate whether a sexual relationship alleged by Lewinsky had taken place with the President in 1995. Clinton vehemently denied any improper conduct with Lewinsky, and, following his private testimony to a grand jury, declared in late January 1998 that he had made no attempt to induce Lewinsky or others to give perjured testimony. In August, however, following an offer of immunity from prosecution by Starr to Lewinsky, the President submitted new testimony to the grand jury; he subsequently made a public statement to the effect that an inappropriate relationship had taken place with Lewinsky, and asked for forgiveness of his behaviour, although insisting that he had at no time sought to obstruct legal processes. Clinton's political prospects apparently worsened in September, when Congress received the completed Starr report, making public intimate details of the President's relationship with Lewinsky, and alleging that Clinton had committed 11 offences of perjury and obstruction of justice, constituting grounds for his removal from office. No evidence, however, was offered of wrongdoing by Clinton in relation to the 'Whitewater' affair.

In October 1998 the House of Representatives voted by 258–176 votes to commence an impeachment inquiry against the President. Following extensive committee hearings, the case was referred in late December to the Senate, which is constitutionally empowered to remove the President from office, subject to a majority vote of two-thirds (67 of 100 seats). However, ahead of the impeachment proceedings, which began in January 1999, it had become clear that the electorate was satisfied with the Clinton Administration's conduct of government, and largely indifferent to any personal shortcomings of the President. In the November 1998 mid-term elections, at which the voter turn-out was only 36%, the lowest figure since 1942, the Republicans, while retaining control of the Congress, sustained a net loss of five seats in the House of Representatives and made no gains in the Senate. The party also lost one state governorship. In mid-February 1999 the Senate acquitted Clinton by 55 votes to 45 on the first article of impeachment, alleging perjury before a grand jury, and by 50 votes to 50 on the second article, relating to alleged obstruction of justice. A subsequent attempt in the Senate to obtain a vote of censure on Clinton was unsuccessful. (In January 2001, shortly before he left office, Clinton agreed to admit giving misleading testimony to an Arkansas court regarding his relationship with Lewinsky and to make a contribution towards the cost of the investigation into his alleged obstruction of justice in the matter. In return, the investigation was discontinued.)

In August 1998 bomb attacks on US embassy buildings in Nairobi, Kenya, and Dar es Salaam, Tanzania, claimed 258 lives, and were followed by US air missile attacks on a factory site in Khartoum, Sudan (which was alleged to be a manufactory of chemicals for use in toxic gases), and on targets in Afghanistan, which were stated by the US Government to be operational centres for Osama bin Laden, a fugitive Saudi Arabian-born Islamist activist whom the USA believed to be responsible for past assaults on US forces and facilities in Somalia, Yemen and Saudi Arabia. Bin Laden was also held responsible for terrorist operations within the USA, including the 1993 bombing of the World Trade Center in New York. In October 2001 four associates of bin Laden were sentenced to life imprisonment by a US court for their involvement in the bomb attacks in Nairobi and Dar es Salaam.

In December 1998, following the termination by Iraq of international weapons inspections in its territory, the USA and the United Kingdom conducted a series of missile raids on Iraqi military sites. In March 1999 the US Government initiated and led, under NATO auspices, a sustained campaign of missile raids on military and related installations in Serbia and Montenegro, in support of international demands that the President of the Federal Republic of Yugoslavia, Slobodan Milošević, desist from the mass expulsion of members of the ethnic Albanian population of the Serbian province of Kosovo. NATO air attacks on Belgrade during May resulted in the accidental bombing by US aircraft of the diplomatic mission in the Yugoslav capital of the People's Republic of China, which, despite a subsequent apology and the payment of compensation by the US Government, led to a period of strained relations between the two countries. Following the military withdrawal of Serbian forces from Kosovo in June, US forces took a leading role in subsequent UN peace-keeping operations in the region.

Throughout Clinton's presidency the USA continued to pursue an active role in efforts to secure the settlement of conflicts in the Middle East, with particular reference to matters at issue between Israel, Syria and Lebanon, and in December 1999, under Clinton's auspices, the first substantive negotiations since 1996 between the Governments of Israel and Syria took place in Washington, DC. In March 2000 the US Government sought to move towards a *rapprochement* with Iran with the announcement that it was to ease some of the trade sanctions against Iran that had been in force since 1979.

In January 1999 the Clinton Administration indicated that it was considering an allocation of $7,000m. over a three-year period from 2000 for new research into the SDI programme (see above), which had been initiated by President Reagan in 1983 and on which an estimated $55,000m. had been spent prior to its termination by Clinton in 1995. Under the new proposals, which attracted considerable congressional support from Republicans, the original concept of a space-based missile defence system was to be replaced by a network of ground- or sea-based interceptor rockets with the capability of destroying intercontinental ballistic missiles either accidentally launched or fired by a hostile power. This modification of the SDI, which was redesignated as the National Missile Defence (NMD) system, would require the agreement of Russia to amend prior anti-nuclear treaties, and has been widely criticized as posing a possible threat to efforts to achieve further reductions in nuclear arms world-wide. In May 2000 the USA, together with the United Kingdom, France, Russia and the People's Republic of China, announced a commitment to global nuclear disarmament, although no timetable was set out for the eventual elimination of stockpiles of these weapons. In early September 2001, in return for China's acceptance of NMD, the USA pledged to keep China informed of its development and agreed to recognize that the Chinese might, in the future, want to resume nuclear weapons testing. The USA also urged China not to transfer ballistic missile technology to countries which the USA considered to be 'rogue states' (deemed by the Department of State to be those countries with the capabilities to use weapons of mass destruction without adherence to traditional international conventions).

A presidential election was held on 7 November 2000. Vice-President Al Gore was the Democratic Party candidate, while George W. Bush, the Governor of Texas and a son of former President Bush, was the Republican Party's nominee. Following voting, it emerged that the possession of an overall majority in the presidential Electoral College would depend on the 25 college mandates from the state of Florida, where the result of the ballot was in dispute. The state was initially declared in favour of Governor Bush by some 1,600 votes, giving him 271 of the 538 Electoral-College mandates, pending the result of a mandatory automated recount of the votes; however, the Democrats challenged the declaration (and the state government's refusal to permit the ballots to be recounted by electoral staff following the automated recount) in the Florida Supreme Court, claiming that a significant number of votes in certain counties had been incorrectly registered by the automated voting and counting system. The Court ruled that the ballots in the counties concerned should be recounted by electoral staff and allowed an additional 12 days for this process to be completed. The US Supreme Court disallowed this ruling, however, and returned the matter to the Florida Supreme Court for further consideration. Only one county completed its 'manual' recount and the result remained in Governor Bush's favour (by 537 votes).

The Democrats began further legal action, claiming that the recounting of all disputed ballots transcended time limits. A Florida judge rejected the claim, but the Florida Supreme Court upheld an appeal and ordered the recounting of some 45,000 disputed ballots. The Republicans challenged the verdict, claiming that no provision for such 'manual' recounts was made in the electoral legislation. The US Supreme Court upheld the Republican appeal, by a margin of five judges to four. With all legal recourses exhausted, and with the Florida legislature having voted to endorse a list of Republican electors irrespective of the outcome of further legal action, Vice-President Gore conceded defeat in Florida (and thereby nationally) on 13 December 2000.

Final results subsequently indicated that Vice-President Gore obtained 48.4% of the valid votes cast, compared with 47.9% obtained by Governor Bush. Thus, the latter became the first contender since 1876 to win a majority in the Electoral College while losing the national popular ballot. In the concurrently held elections to the Senate, the Democrats made a net gain of five seats, resulting in both parties holding 50 of the 100 seats (Hillary Rodham Clinton, the wife of President Clinton, was elected as a Democratic Senator representing New York). The Republicans retained their effective majority in the chamber, however, owing to the casting vote of the President of the Senate, the incoming Vice-President, Dick Cheney. In May 2001 Senator James Jeffords of Vermont left the Republican Party to sit in the Senate as an Independent, thus establishing a Democratic majority of one in the chamber. The Democrats also made net gains of three seats in the House of Representatives and one state governorship.

Governor Bush was inaugurated as President on 20 January 2001; his first Cabinet contained several individuals who had served in his father's Administration, as well as one member of Clinton's Cabinet. His Administration immediately suspended the implementation of a number of environmental regulations issued by Clinton shortly before his departure from office. The Administration's first budget, presented in February, included provisions for reductions in levels of personal taxation. Environmental campaigners (who had expressed reservations over President Bush's attitude to environmental issues) and numerous foreign governments and international organizations strongly criticized the new President in March when his Administration withdrew support for the ratification process of the Kyoto Protocol on climate change, claiming it would be detrimental to US economic interests. In February 2002 Bush proposed voluntary, less far-reaching, measures to reduce emissions of 'greenhouse gases'. The Bush Administration published a report on energy policy in May 2001, which included a proposal to introduce legislation authorizing exploratory drilling for oil in the Arctic National Wildlife Refuge in Alaska (ANWR). The plan prompted criticism from the environmental lobby. In August 2001 the House of Representatives voted in favour of the proposal by a narrow majority; however, the proposed legislation was rejected by the Senate in April 2002. The Administration subsequently introduced a provision to allow drilling to start in 2004, whereby federal revenue would be raised from the sale of leases to petroleum companies; however, in March 2003 Congress passed an amendment to remove the provision. In August the Government proposed further controversial amendments to regulations governing carbon emissions; under the new legislation, energy companies would no longer be required to install anti-pollution measures when upgrading equipment. The announcement prompted criticism from environmental groups, and legal contests against the proposals were immediately begun in 13 states. In March–April 2005 Congress narrowly approved a proposal to begin drilling in the ANWR. However, in its final version, the relevant legislation was part of a wider budget reconciliation bill that was only approved by both houses in late December once the ANWR provision had been removed. In what appeared to be a repetition of the previous year's events, in mid-March 2006 the Senate narrowly approved (by 51 votes to 49) legislation that was expected could lead to the opening of parts of the ANWR to drilling; however, the outcome was again contingent on congressional approval of another budget reconciliation bill. According to the US Geological Survey, recoverable oil reserves in the ANWR were estimated at 10,400m. barrels of oil in 2005; at that time the USA was consuming 20m. barrels per day.

President Bush's strong personal support for the NMD programme, expressed throughout the electoral campaign and in the period after his inauguration, caused further concern both within the USA and abroad. In November 2001, following a summit meeting in Washington, DC, President Bush and Russian President Vladimir Putin both pledged to reduce their nation's nuclear arsenals by approximately two-thirds over the following decade; a formal agreement was signed in May 2002. (Bush also pledged to repeal the Jackson-Vanik Amendment of 1974, which imposed trade sanctions on the former USSR). In June 2002 the USA formally withdrew from the Anti-Ballistic Missile Treaty (ABM), signed with the USSR in 1972, claiming that its adherence prevented the development of NMD. President Bush emphasized that the USA's withdrawal from the ABM would not undermine US–Russian relations. Putin described the withdrawal as a mistake, but insisted it would not damage Russian security. In December 2001, the USA received fierce criticism from EU member states after forcing the collapse of an international conference convened to reinforce the terms of the Biological and Toxic Weapons Convention, signed in 1972; the USA opposed plans which would have allowed international inspectors to monitor its military and industrial facilities. The USA attracted further international criticism by its refusal to sign up to the terms of the International Criminal Court (ICC), established to try war criminals, which was inaugurated at The Hague, Netherlands, in March 2003. The USA defended its position by claiming that members of its military could be put on trial on political grounds, and, in response, in the same month, Congress passed the American Service Member and Citizen Protection Act, which would enable the USA to free, by force if necessary, any member of its military arrested by the ICC. In mid-June the UN Security Council granted US forces exemption from prosecution by the ICC for one year. Early in the following month the USA reduced military aid to some 35 countries that refused to sign agreements that would give US citizens immunity from prosecution. Following allegations of abuse and torture of Iraqi prisoners by US soldiers (see below), in June 2004 the USA withdrew a proposed resolution at the UN Security Council to give US personnel immunity from prosecution at the ICC.

In February 2001 US and British aircraft were involved in the bombardment of a number of targets in Iraq, ostensibly to maintain the 'no-fly' zones imposed on that country. The action was condemned by numerous countries. A further bombardment took place in April, the USA stating that the missions were in response to anti-aircraft fire in the southern zone. Further bombardments were reported in June, August, September and October, during which three unmanned US surveillance planes were reportedly shot down over the 'no-fly' zones.

On 11 September 2001 four commercial passenger aircraft were hijacked shortly after take-off from Boston, New York and Washington, DC. The two aircraft originating in Boston, both bound for Los Angeles, were diverted to New York and each was flown into the two towers of the World Trade Center, both of which subsequently collapsed. The third aircraft was flown into the Pentagon building (the headquarters of the Department of Defense) in Washington, DC, and the fourth aircraft, also apparently heading for Washington, DC, crashed in farmland near Pittsburgh, Pennsylvania. The death toll was eventually put at 2,752, including 266 passengers and crew (including the hijackers) on the four aircraft, 190 at the Pentagon, and the remainder in New York, principally those unable to escape from the towers before they collapsed, and members of the emergency services. On 13 September the Secretary of State, Gen. Colin Powell, identified Osama bin Laden (see above) and his al-Qa'ida (Base) organization, a network of fundamentalist Islamist militants, as responsible for the attacks. However, bin Laden, who was believed to be in Afghanistan, where he was harboured by the extremist Islamist Taliban regime, had already denied accusations that he had ordered the hijackings, although he expressed his approval of the attacks. In late 2002 an independent bipartisan inquiry, the National Commission on Terrorist Attacks Upon the United States, was established to investigate the circumstances surrounding the attacks (see below). In early March 2003 security forces in Rawalpindi, Pakistan, arrested the Kuwaiti-born Khalid Sheikh Mohammed, accused of being the operational planner behind the attacks, and released him into US custody for interrogation. In late March 2006, in a court in Virginia, Moroccan-born Zacarias Moussaoui pleaded guilty to charges of conspiracy to commit acts of terrorism, in relation to the attacks. Moussaoui had pleaded guilty to conspiracy charges in July 2002, but subsequently retracted his plea. In early May 2006 he was sentenced to life imprisonment. Moussaoui remained the only person to have been charged as part of the investigation into the attacks.

In the immediate wake of the attacks, President Bush declared that those responsible should be captured 'dead or alive'. Both houses of Congress unanimously approved emergency anti-terrorism legislation, which made provision for increased military spending and US $20,000m. for reconstruction in New York, and approved a resolution authorizing the President to use 'all necessary and appropriate force' against those who organized the attacks. Congress also approved the so-called 'Patriot Act' (Uniting and Strengthening America by Providing the Appropriate Tools Required to Intercept and Obstruct Terrorism—PATRIOT—Act of 2001), which was signed into law in late October 2001, giving wide-ranging powers to the Government to investigate citizens and non-citizens alike. The Act was viewed by critics as a threat to civil liberties. (The Patriot Act was scheduled to expire at the end of 2005, but was temporarily extended by Congress until February 2006. In mid-December 2005 President Bush confirmed reports that he had authorized the warrantless surveillance of suspects as part of anti-terror

THE UNITED STATES OF AMERICA

Introductory Survey

investigations by the National Security Agency.) The Government began to form an international coalition against terrorism, for which most Western Governments pledged their support. NATO invoked Article Five of the NATO Charter (which states that an attack on a member state is an attack on all 19 members), which required members to assist the USA, according to judgement and resources; the Governments of the United Kingdom, France and Germany, among others, offered military and financial assistance. The Taliban regime in Afghanistan denied involvement in the terrorist attacks, and warned that it would retaliate if attacked. On 17 September the USA issued an ultimatum to the Taliban, via Pakistan (the only state with diplomatic links to the regime), to surrender bin Laden or face an imminent military assault. Several weeks of intense diplomatic activity ensued, during which time international support for the USA's so-called global 'war on terror' increased, and the US Government reportedly was able to gather further evidence of the al-Qa'ida network's involvement in the attacks. The Taliban reportedly requested to see evidence of bin Laden's involvement in the attacks, a request rejected by the USA. In the meantime, US military forces increased their presence in the region around Afghanistan. Pakistan and Uzbekistan agreed to grant the US-led forces access to their air bases for emergency operations and Russia allowed access to its airspace for humanitarian missions. Saudi Arabia, although it refused to allow the USA to use its military bases, granted access to its airspace.

On 2 October 2001 NATO declared that it had received evidence from the USA that confirmed bin Laden's responsibility for the terrorist attacks. On 7 October US and British armed forces commenced military operations ('Operation Enduring Freedom') against Taliban military targets and suspected al-Qa'ida training camps in Afghanistan. In addition to military strikes, aircraft released food and medicine parcels to Afghan civilians; leaflets were also dropped offering protection and a reward in return for information on the whereabouts of al-Qa'ida leaders. On 14 October a senior Taliban official offered to surrender bin Laden to a third country in return for a cessation of US bombing, if the USA provided evidence of his involvement in the terrorist attacks, an offer the USA rejected. The US-led forces co-ordinated operations with the military wing of the exiled Afghanistani Government, the United National Islamic Front for the Salvation of Afghanistan (UIFSA—also known as the Northern Alliance). During November the latter made substantial territorial gains in northern and western Afghanistan, including the Afghan capital, Kabul, and Mazar-i-Sharif, a strategically important town in the north. In late November US ground forces were deployed for the first time, near the southern city of Kandahar, in an attempt to locate bin Laden. Kandahar fell to the US-led forces in early December, leaving only pockets of Taliban resistance; US forces subsequently intensified their search for bin Laden, who was believed to be in the Tora Bora caves near Jalalabad, in the east of the country. US-led ground forces were still deployed in Afghanistan in May 2002, attempting to overcome a small number of Taliban and al-Qa'ida members who had not surrendered; bin Laden remained at large. The USA refused, however, to deploy peace-keeping troops in Afghanistan to support the interim administration of Hamid Karzai, which had replaced the Taliban regime in early December 2001, although it released previously withheld assets to his Government, and pledged financial aid to rebuild the country's infrastructure. In January 2002 the Bush Government pledged some $296.8m. in funds for the reconstruction of Afghanistan.

In mid-January 2002 the US military began transferring members of the Taliban and al-Qa'ida, who had been captured in battle, to the US naval base in Guantánamo Bay in Cuba. Initially, the USA refused to grant the detainees (numbering almost 300) prisoner-of-war status under the Geneva Convention of 1949 (which guaranteed trial by court martial or a civilian court, as opposed to a military tribunal), prompting criticism from its coalition partners, which intensified following the publication of photographs showing prisoners shackled and blindfolded. In February, following pressure from the British and French Governments, President Bush accorded partial protection of the Convention to captured Taliban fighters (he stopped short of full protection, however, claiming that the soldiers were members of an irregular militia); al-Qa'ida captives were offered no protection, as they were considered to be terrorists with no allegiance to any specific state or government. President Bush also abandoned an earlier demand to make the final judgment on a detainee's guilt or innocence. By March 2004 only two men had been charged. In late June the Supreme Court ruled that, while the President as Commander-in-Chief had the power to detain enemy combatants, they were entitled to legal representation in a US federal court. The following day the first three prisoners from Guantánamo Bay appeared before a military tribunal. At November 2005 179 detainees had been released and 73 had been transferred to continue their detention in their countries of origin; more than 500 detainees remained at Guantánamo Bay. (In February 2006 it was reported that there were also more than 500 detainees at the Bagram air base in Afghanistan.)

Also in November 2005, it was reported that US intelligence services maintained a network of secret prisons—referred to as 'black sites'—in locations which included eastern EU countries. It was further alleged that terrorist suspects were taken from these prisons to countries where torture was tolerated, in a practice known as 'extraordinary rendition'. The following month Secretary of State Condoleezza Rice acknowledged the existence of rendition but denied any toleration of the torture of suspects. However, in January 2005 it had been revealed that, three years previously, the chief legal counsel to the President, Alberto Gonzales (later Attorney-General), had issued a memorandum stating that the USA was not bound by the Geneva Conventions in its treatment of prisoners captured in Afghanistan. In another memorandum ordered by Gonzales in August 2002, it was proposed that Central Intelligence Agency (CIA) officers and other non-military personnel be exempted from a presidential directive for the humane treatment of prisoners. In mid-February 2006 the UN Commission on Human Rights published a report that concluded that the methods used by the US military to interrogate prisoners at Guantánamo Bay amounted to torture, and called on the US Government to close the base and try the remaining detainees before courts on the US mainland. A military report to the Senate's armed forces committee in mid-July found that treatment of the prisoners did not constitute torture, but that it was, however, abusive and degrading. In mid-December President Bush announced that he would approve an amendment proposed by Republican Senator John McCain to ban the 'cruel, inhuman and degrading' treatment of prisoners. Previously Bush had said that he would veto any such amendment and at the signing of the bill, in late December, he appended a presidential signing statement to the effect that the President's authority superseded the new legislation.

In late September 2001 the Bush Administration established the Office of Homeland Security, under Thomas J. Ridge, to develop and implement a strategy to prevent future terrorist attacks against the USA. The Office was upgraded to a federal Department in November 2002; in mid-February 2005 Michael Chertoff replaced Ridge as head of the Department. In October 2001 traces of anthrax (a toxic biological agent) were discovered in items of post sent to senior members of Congress, as well as to government buildings and media organizations in Washington, DC, New York and Florida. The House of Representatives was closed for several days in late October as a precautionary measure. Responsibility for the contamination was initially attributed to al-Qa'ida, although it was subsequently reported that the anthrax had originated in the USA; however, the perpetrators remained unknown. In total, five people died from exposure to anthrax spores (all in mainland USA), and some 300,000 postal workers and civil servants were given precautionary medical treatment in October and November.

In his State of the Union address in January 2002, President Bush described Iran, Iraq and the DPRK as forming an 'axis of evil' that supported international terrorism and sought to develop weapons of mass destruction, and hinted that the USA was considering pre-emptive strikes against them. US allies warned against attacking states unless firm evidence of a link to terrorism could be found. In February Bush faced protests on a visit to South Korea, and members of South Korean President Kim Dae-Jung's ruling party accused Bush of damaging the so-called 'sunshine policy' of reconciliation with North Korea. In the same month Secretary of State Powell made specific mention of removing Saddam Hussain from power in Iraq. In January it was announced that US troops were to be sent to the Philippines to fight against the Abu Sayyaf guerrilla group, which was believed to have links with al-Qa'ida network. In May the 'axis of evil' was extended to include Cuba, Libya and Syria. The Bush Administration accused Cuba of maintaining a biological warfare programme and offering weapons technology to 'rogue states', and claimed that Libya and Syria had violated international weapons treaties. In mid-December the Iranian Government denied US allegations of evidence of the secret manufacture of nuclear weapons. In mid-September 2003 the

USA supported an IAEA resolution establishing a deadline of the end of October for Iran to disclose full details of its nuclear programme and provide evidence that it was not developing nuclear weapons. In mid-December Libya agreed to disclose and dismantle its programme to develop weapons of mass destruction and long-range ballistic missiles, following nine months of secret negotiations between the Libyan leader, Col Muammar al-Qaddafi, and US and British diplomats. In January 2004 a US delegation visited Libya to discuss the weapons-dismantling process. As a result, in February the USA ended the restrictions on its citizens travelling to Libya, in place since 1981, and in late June diplomatic relations were officially re-established between the two countries for the first time in 23 years; however, Libya was not removed from the US list of state sponsors of terrorism until mid-May 2006. In mid-February 2005, in protest at what it believed to be Syria's role in the assassination of the Prime Minister of Lebanon, Rafiq Hariri, the USA removed its ambassador to Syria for consultations, and later demanded that all Syrian troops withdraw from Lebanon. In mid-March, for the first time, the USA agreed with France, Germany and the United Kingdom to offer Iran economic benefits if that country pledged to end its nuclear programme. However, in mid-April 2006 the Iranian President, Mahmoud Ahmadinejad, announced that Iran had successfully achieved the enrichment of uranium for civilian purposes. The Iranian Government claimed that the enriched uranium was not weapons-grade, but rather, to be used as nuclear fuel. In the same month the US Administration continued to deny reports that it was planning to attack sites in Iran involved in that country's nuclear programme.

In January 2002, following an escalation in the ongoing conflict in the Middle East, the USA brokered talks towards securing a cease-fire agreement between Israel and Palestine. In March the Israeli Prime Minister, Ariel Sharon, agreed to redeploy some Israeli troops from Palestinian areas. However, in early April, following a further escalation in the conflict, President Bush urged Sharon to withdraw Israeli forces from Palestinian towns and to adhere to the cease-fire recommendations proposed by former Senator George Mitchell and the CIA Director George Tenet in 2001. In mid-April Secretary of State Colin Powell visited Israel and held separate talks with Sharon and with Arafat in his besieged headquarters, in an attempt to bring an end to the crisis. However, the mission failed to bring about a cease-fire or the withdrawal of Israeli forces from Palestinian areas. At the end of April 2003 President Bush presented both the Israeli and Palestinian Prime Ministers with a internationally sponsored 'roadmap' for peace, envisaging the phased creation of a sovereign Palestinian state by 2005–06. However, despite acceptance of the plan, Israel continued work on the construction of a 'security fence' in the disputed West Bank region, begun in mid-2002. In July the US Administration threatened to withhold almost US $10,000m. in essential loan guarantees unless construction of the fence ceased. Following approval by the Israeli Government of a further phase of construction, in late November the US Congress cut US $290m. from a total $1,400m. in loan guarantees to Israel as a penalty for the continuing expansion of Jewish settlements in the West Bank and Gaza. At a meeting between Bush and Sharon in Crawford, Texas, in mid-April 2005, the President gave his support to Israel's planned withdrawal from the Gaza Strip, but criticized the continued expansion of Jewish settlements in the West Bank.

In December 2001 Enron Corporation, the largest energy company in the USA, filed for bankruptcy. This was the largest ever bankruptcy in US history, with the immediate loss of 4,000 jobs. It subsequently emerged that Enron's accounts had been falsified over several years, possibly with the approval of the Corporation's accountancy firm, Arthur Andersen. The firm was found guilty of obstructing justice in June 2002. (The ruling was overturned by the Supreme Court in late May 2005.) Furthermore, it was revealed that Enron had donated more than $500,000 to Bush's presidential campaign, and that Vice-President Cheney had met senior Enron executives on several occasions in 2001 while drafting the proposed national energy plan. An investigation into the bankruptcy was begun by the Department of Justice in early 2002. It was also reported that senior members of the Bush Administration had refused requests from Enron for financial assistance in 2001. Enron's former finance chief, Andrew Fastow, was arrested in early October 2002; he pleaded guilty to two counts of conspiracy in January 2004. In June 2002 WorldCom, Inc, the second largest long-distance telecommunications company in the USA, revealed that it too had manipulated its accounts to show figures for cash flow and profits that were higher than in reality; the disclosure prompted the Securities and Exchange Commission to announce that the regulation of listed companies and subsequent penalties would become more stringent. WorldCom's Chief Executive, Bernie Ebbers, was arrested in early March 2004 and charged with fraud. Both Enron and WorldCom filed for Chapter 11 bankruptcy protection and continued to trade. In April WorldCom, now part of a restructured MCI, Inc, left Chapter 11 protection following a restatement of its accounts. Ebbers was found guilty of nine criminal charges in mid-March 2005 and, in July, sentenced to 25 years in prison. The trials for fraud and conspiracy of Enron's founder, Kenneth Lay, and its former CEO, Jeffrey Skilling, began in late January 2006.

At mid-term elections held on 5 November 2002, the Republicans assumed control of the Senate and increased their majority in the House of Representatives. The Democrats gained three state governorships overall. Following his party's electoral success, in January 2003 President Bush announced a series of tax reductions worth US $726,000m. over 10 years. The 2004 budget, presented in the following month, included further requests for extensions to tax allowances. However, in March the proposals were vetoed by Congress, which was concerned over increased homeland security expenditure and the cost of the military operation in Iraq (see below). Eventually, in May Congress approved, by one vote, amended legislation that introduced tax cuts of some $350,000m. over the next decade. In early November Congress approved a presidential request for an additional $87,000m. in funding for reconstruction efforts in Iraq and Afghanistan. Also in November Congress enacted legislation extending Medicare (federal health care for the elderly) benefits to cover the cost of most prescription drugs.

In January 2004 the US-Visit programme was implemented, requiring that all visa-holders entering the USA were electronically fingerprinted and photographed on arrival. By January 2005 the programme had been extended to 50 land border crossings and was scheduled to reach a further 115 by the end of that year. In April 2006 some 500,000 people in Los Angeles participated in a march in protest at restrictive new immigration legislation; other protest marches took place in Phoenix, Denver and Milwaukee. The legislation, approved by the House of Representatives in the previous December, made illegal immigration a criminal offence, and approved the construction of a 1,130 km (700 miles) fence on the US–Mexican border. In early April the Senate failed to reach a compromise agreement on the proposed law that would provide 'non-immigrant visas' to some 11m. undocumented workers. The concession had the support of President Bush, but not of the Republican Party, which enjoyed a majority in the Senate.

In July 2004 the National Commission on Terrorist Attacks Upon the United States delivered its final report into intelligence failures in the months preceding the attacks of 11 September 2001. It did not lay the blame on either the Clinton or Bush Governments, but asserted that both Administrations had failed to realize the immediacy of the threat posed by the al-Qa'ida network. The report highlighted opportunities to uncover the plot that had been overlooked by both the CIA and the Federal Bureau of Investigation (FBI). However, it did not conclude that the attacks could have been prevented. It also found that, while Osama bin Laden had approved Khalid Sheikh Mohammed's plan in 1999, there was no evidence to link al-Qa'ida with Saddam Hussain (see below). The report recommended, *inter alia*: the creation of a national director of intelligence with overall responsibility for all of the intelligence services; the formation of a national counter-terrorism centre to co-ordinate intelligence-gathering; a reduction in the number of congressional intelligence oversight committees; the establishment of an international network of intelligence-sharing; and the implementation of a national policy to address the threat of militant Islamism. On 17 December 2004, following its approval earlier in the month by both houses of Congress, President Bush enacted the Intelligence Reform and Terrorism Act, which drew on some of the recommendations of the Commission's report. The legislation was designed to restructure the security services and provided for a cabinet-level Director of National Intelligence, to be responsible for co-ordinating the activities of 15 different agencies, including the CIA and the FBI. In April 2005 Bush's nominee to the new post, the erstwhile US ambassador to Iraq, John D. Negroponte, was confirmed by the Senate. An internal investigation by the CIA into intelligence failings, concluded in

THE UNITED STATES OF AMERICA

Introductory Survey

January of that year, was particularly critical of its former director, George Tenet, who had resigned in June 2004.

Presidential and legislative elections were held on 2 November 2004. The elections were notable for being the first in which unregulated, or so-called 'soft money' donations, to the electoral campaigns of political parties from individuals, businesses and unions were banned. These funds were ostensibly intended only for general activities, but had often been used to support the campaigns of particular candidates. In the presidential ballot, President Bush was returned for a second term of office, ultimately securing 286 Electoral College votes (270 votes were necessary to win the presidency). The Democratic challenger, John Kerry, conceded defeat before the final result was confirmed, making a public call for national unity. President Bush took some 51.02% of the popular votes and Kerry 48.07%. In the concurrent legislative elections the Republicans also increased their majority in both houses of Congress: following the ballot the party held 55 of the 100 seats in the Senate (where elections were conducted to renew one-third of the membership) and 232 of the 435 seats in the new House of Representatives. In gubernatorial elections in 11 states the parties' standings remained unchanged overall. More than 116m. voters participated in the ballots nation-wide, an increase of some 10m. on the turn-out at the 2000 elections. The President was sworn in on 20 January 2005. His new Cabinet included Condoleezza Rice, hitherto Assistant to the President for National Security Affairs, as Secretary of State, in succession to Colin Powell, who had stated his intention not to serve a second term in office, and Alberto Gonzales, the President's former chief legal counsel, as Attorney-General. In early February Bush presented a 2006 budget plan to Congress which proposed reductions in funding to 12 out of 23 government agencies. Spending cuts targeted subsidies to farmers, health care payments to the poor and military veterans, as well as education and environment programmes. The budget did not include the cost of a proposed restructuring of the social security system nor the additional cost of military operations overseas: to this last end, in early May a presidential request for a further US $82,000m., principally towards continued military involvement in Afghanistan and Iraq, was approved by Congress.

In late August 2005 'Hurricane Katrina' caused extensive damage to the Gulf coast states of Louisiana, Mississippi and Alabama. Louisiana was the worst affected state: an estimated 80% of the city of New Orleans was flooded. On 2 September President Bush declared a state of emergency in 13 states to release some US $10,500m. in emergency funding; on the same day Congress approved legislation for emergency aid amounting to $51,800m. Damage to infrastructure was blamed for delays in delivering relief to those affected by the hurricane: the first relief convoys took four days to arrive in New Orleans. The US Government appealed to the EU, NATO and the UN for crisis assistance. On 6 September the mayor of New Orleans ordered the evacuation of the entire city, some 480,000 people; however, an estimated 10,000 people, who were either unable or unwilling to move, remained in the city. More than 38,000 members of the National Guard were deployed in affected areas; 7,000 were deployed in New Orleans itself with orders to shoot to kill looters. They were joined by 8,500 soldiers on active duty. Meanwhile, the Government released oil supplies from the Strategic Petroleum Reserve to counter the disruption caused to the region's energy supply network, which accounted for almost one-third of domestic oil production. The closure of eight refineries reduced national oil-refining capacity by 10% and a Louisiana oil-import terminal, responsible for some 10% of overall imports, was also temporarily closed. The impact of another hurricane, 'Hurricane Rita', along the Gulf coast at the end of September, further affected relief efforts. By February 2006 the confirmed death toll as a result of the hurricane was over 1,300; a further 1,900 people remained missing.

The federal Government came under much criticism for its perceived slow reaction to 'Hurricane Katrina': on 9 September 2005 Michael Brown, the Director of the Federal Emergency Management Agency (FEMA), responsible for co-ordinating the relief effort, was relieved of his duties at the head of the recovery operation in Louisiana. Less than a week later, Brown resigned as FEMA Director. A report by the Government Accountability Office (GAO), published in February 2006, criticized government at all levels for its failure adequately to respond to the emergency. It found that relief efforts had been hampered by the absence of a clear chain of command, and compounded by insufficient planning and preparation; it also identified examples of waste and fraud in the appropriation of relief and reconstruction funds. A House of Representatives select committee delivered its own report in mid-February; it agreed with the GAO that overall responsibility for co-ordinating the response should have been assumed by the Secretary of Homeland Security, Michael Chertoff. Meanwhile, President Bush appealed to Congress for a further $19,600m. towards reconstruction along the Gulf coast, particularly the strengthening of the protective levees around New Orleans.

The Republican Party faced a series of corruption scandals throughout 2005. In late September the Republican Majority Leader in the House of Representatives, Tom DeLay, was indicted on charges of having illegally financed Republican candidates in the 2002 election campaign. DeLay stepped down temporarily as Majority Leader, but was replaced in a permanent capacity in February 2006 by John Boehner. DeLay resigned his congressional seat in April. In late October 2005 I. 'Scooter' Lewis Libby, chief of staff to Vice-President Dick Cheney, was indicted on charges that included obstruction of justice and perjury during an investigation into the leaking of the identity of CIA agent Valerie Plame in mid-2003. It was held that Plame's identity had deliberately been made public as a reprisal against her husband, Senator Joseph Wilson, who had publicly accused the Administration of making selective use of intelligence to justify the invasion of Iraq in 2003 (see below). In November 2005 Republican Representative Randy 'Duke' Cunningham resigned his seat in the House after pleading guilty to charges which included conspiracy to commit bribery and tax evasion for his role in influencing the allocation of defence contracts; he was sentenced to more than eight years' imprisonment in March 2006. In early January of that year, lobbyist Jack Abramoff pleaded guilty to charges which included conspiracy to bribe public officials, fraud and tax evasion. It was reported that Abramoff had entered a plea bargain to receive a more lenient sentence in return for information with the potential to implicate up to 60 members of Congress in abuse of their positions. Following Abramoff's plea some two dozen members of Congress returned campaign contributions they had received from him. Abramoff was sentenced to 70 months' imprisonment in late March.

In early February 2006 President Bush presented to Congress the 2007 federal budget, which proposed reductions in spending on social, health and welfare programmes, while calling for existing tax cuts to be made permanent. There were increases in expenditure on defence and homeland security (see Economic Affairs). However, the budget was criticized for omitting projected expenditure on reconstruction efforts in Iraq and Afghanistan after 2007 and reconstruction after 2005 in New Orleans following 'Hurricane Katrina'. The budget also included projected revenue from leasing drilling rights in the ANWR (see above), despite the fact that the required legislation had yet to be approved by Congress. It was anticipated that requests for additional funding for continued military operations in Iraq and Afghanistan would amount to US $120,000m. in 2006, bringing their total cost to around $350,000m. Funding of reconstruction in Iraq was scheduled to finish at the end of that year.

In September 2002 the Bush Administration issued a National Security Strategy for the United States, which set out the new threats faced by the USA internationally, and outlined the policies adopted to meet these challenges. In the same month the Republicans submitted a draft resolution to Congress which would authorize President Bush to use 'any means necessary' to enforce existing UN resolutions against the regime of Saddam Hussain in Iraq and to defend US national interests by depriving Iraq of weapons of mass destruction. It was the first tangible evidence that the Administration was willing to deploy unilateral military action if the UN Security Council did not pass a new resolution authorizing military action against the Iraqi regime. The resolution was approved in October by both houses of Congress, with the provision that the Administration should first exhaust all available channels at the UN and other diplomatic means. As a result of US-led pressure, in November the UN passed unanimously Resolution 1441, which obliged Iraq, *inter alia*, to declare all weapons of mass destruction within 30 days, to comply with the UN Monitoring, Verification and Inspection Commission (UNMOVIC—the UN weapons inspectors, and successor to UNSCOM), to allow UNMOVIC to resume its work within 45 days (UNSCOM had been expelled from Iraq in 1998—see above), and to allow inspectors unrestricted access within Iraq, including Saddam Hussain's palaces. Later that month UNMOVIC resumed its operations and reported that the

Iraqi Government was prepared to comply with Resolution 1441. In December Iraq presented its report on weapons of mass destruction to UNMOVIC; however, US officials declared Iraq to be in 'material breach' of Resolution 1441, for failing to comply with the demand for an accurate and complete account of its weapons programmes, and for resubmitting information that it had previously given to the UN. Following this development, the US and British Governments drew up a timetable to allow UNMOVIC to carry out intensified searches in early 2003, with the threat of military action against Saddam's regime for non-compliance.

In January 2003 some 70,000 US servicemen and -women joined the 60,000 troops already stationed in the Persian (Arabian) Gulf, and military exercises intensified. The French and German Governments expressed their opposition to any eventual conflict and called for a resolution to the problem by diplomatic means. In response, President Bush stated that the USA would lead a 'coalition of the willing' if support was withheld by other UN Security Council members and its traditional allies. The Administration took an increasingly uncompromising stance; the Secretary of Defense, Donald Rumsfeld, described France and Germany as 'old Europe' (as opposed to other more pro-US states in Southern and Eastern Europe), and the Secretary of State, Colin Powell, excluded the possibility of extending the time allocated to inspectors to find prohibited weapons in Iraq. However, Rumsfeld had also suggested the possibility of granting senior Iraqi leaders amnesty and avoiding conflict if they chose exile in a third country. In late January UNMOVIC reported that it had discovered substances and missiles which could be in contravention of UN resolutions. In February the USA, together with the United Kingdom, intensified its efforts to secure a second UN resolution which would authorize military intervention in Iraq; on 5 February Powell presented evidence of, *inter alia*, the alleged existence of weapons of mass destruction in Iraq, and possible links between Saddam Hussain's regime and al-Qa'ida. However, in mid-February UNMOVIC reported greater co-operation on the part of the Iraqi Government and that it had thus far failed to find any weapons of mass destruction. (On 13 February Saddam Hussain issued a presidential decree prohibiting weapons of mass destruction, although some al-Samoud missiles were found with a greater range than permitted under UN resolutions.) On 24 February the USA, with the United Kingdom and Spain, presented a draft resolution, reiterating that Iraq had been warned it would face serious consequences if it failed to disarm, and that it had failed to comply with Resolution 1441. In an effort to win the support of the 10 non-permanent members of the UN Security Council, the draft resolution contained no ultimatum to Iraq or explicit threat of attack. A few days later, however, President Bush insisted that only full disarmament could prevent war. In early March diplomatic efforts to resolve the crisis showed signs of breaking down when Russia and then France declared that they would employ their veto on any resolution leading to conflict, while the UN Secretary-General, Kofi Annan, questioned the legitimacy of a conflict in Iraq without UN approval. Nevertheless, Powell stated that the USA could go to war without a second UN resolution. UNMOVIC, meanwhile, reported that Iraq had destroyed part of its stock of al-Samoud missiles. An amended version of the draft for a second resolution was issued in mid-March and a deadline of 17 March given for Iraq to demonstrate full compliance with Resolution 1441. On 16 March President Bush, the British Prime Minister, Tony Blair, and the Spanish premier, José María Aznar, held an emergency summit in the Azores, Portugal, at the end of which the three leaders issued an ultimatum giving Saddam Hussain and his two sons 48 hours to leave Iraq or face invasion. The following day the USA, the United Kingdom and Spain decided not to seek a second UN resolution and condemned France for obstructing diplomatic efforts to reach a peaceful outcome. The President of France, Jacques Chirac, responded by criticizing the USA and the United Kingdom for making an 'unjustified' decision to resort to war, and for gravely undermining the UN. The USA announced that some 30 countries had expressed support for its 'coalition of the willing', although only the United Kingdom, Australia, the Czech Republic and Slovakia provided troops.

Shortly after the expiry of President Bush's 48-hour deadline, on 19 March 2003 US and British armed forces launched 'Operation Iraqi Freedom' to oust the regime of Saddam Hussain. A first wave of air-strikes against targets in the southern suburbs of Baghdad, apparently aimed at leading members of the Iraqi regime (including the President himself), failed to achieve their target. Soon afterwards British and US forces crossed into Iraq from Kuwait and generally made a swift advance towards the capital. At the same time, a concerted campaign of massive air-strikes was launched by US-led forces against the key symbols of the Iraqi regime in and around Baghdad, including selected military bases, communications sites, government buildings and broadcasting headquarters. Government and military sites in other prominent Iraqi cities were targeted by the US-led coalition in subsequent days. The US and British forces adopted a simultaneous campaign of issuing leaflets and broadcasting radio messages, in an attempt to persuade Iraqi citizens to abandon their support for Saddam Hussain: their declared intention was that 'Operation Iraqi Freedom' would precipitate the disintegration of the regime 'from within'. Some criticism was made within the US Administration of senior military officials for underestimating the determination of the Iraqi forces. However, by 9 April US forces reached the centre of Baghdad and on 1 May the conflict was officially declared over: Iraq did not formally offer its surrender. In mid-April US Gen. (retd) Jay Garner, Director of the USA's Office of Reconstruction and Humanitarian Service in Iraq (ORHA), was appointed Civil Administrator in Iraq, with the intention of overseeing the peaceful transition to civilian rule by Iraqi nationals. An Iraq Survey Group was established to investigate the presence of illegal weapons in the country. In early May a US diplomat, L. Paul Bremer, succeeded Garner as Civil Administrator in Iraq. In late July US special forces killed Saddam Hussain's sons, Uday and Qusay, in Mosul and on 13 December US special forces captured Saddam Hussain himself, in the village of Ad-Dawr near his birthplace, Tikrit: he was accorded prisoner-of-war status and held in US custody, pending his trial by a court to be convened by the Iraqi Governing Council. Legal custody of Saddam Hussain was transferred to the new Iraqi Interim Government in late June 2004 but he remained under US guard. His trial began in Baghdad in mid-October 2005.

In early July 2003 the US Administration admitted that claims, made in January, that the regime of Saddam Hussain had attempted to procure uranium from several African countries as part of its nuclear programme were 'possibly inaccurate'. The claims had formed part of the argument for declaring war on Iraq. In October the Iraq Survey Group published its first report; the report stated that although no weapons of mass destruction had been found thus far, there was evidence of weapons-related programmes. However, in late January 2004 David Kay, the head of the Iraq Survey Group, resigned, stating that he did not believe that any stockpiles of weapons of mass destruction ever existed. Kay proposed the establishment of an independent inquiry into US intelligence on Iraqi weapons capability. The Survey Group left Iraq in mid-January 2005. In an interim report to Congress in October 2004, Kay's successor, Charles Duelfer, concluded that Saddam Hussain had destroyed his stocks of weapons of mass destruction 10 years previously. In a report at the end of March 2005 the Survey Group was critical of the restructuring proposed at the CIA and FBI. It also criticized the agencies' failure to provide accurate information on the state of unconventional weapons in Iraq and highlighted weaknesses in their capacity accurately to report on nuclear programmes in Iran and the DPRK in particular. In July 2004 a Senate intelligence committee concluded that the CIA had provided the Bush Administration with flawed intelligence before the invasion of Iraq. At that time the Secretary of Energy, Spencer Abraham, announced that US officials had removed 1.77 metric tons of enriched uranium from Iraq in the previous month.

In late April 2004 photographs, taken in late 2003, were published of US soldiers allegedly abusing prisoners at the Abu Ghraib prison near Baghdad, Iraq. As further evidence of maltreatment continued to emerge, in early May the Department of Defense revealed that in September 2003 investigations had begun into some 20 cases of the death or alleged torture of prisoners in US custody in Iraq; however, the military denied that there was any evidence of systematic maltreatment of detainees. President Bush publicly condemned the abuse of prisoners. The first prosecution of one of the soldiers involved began in the USA in mid-June. In August an internal military investigation directly implicated 27 soldiers in abuse at Abu Ghraib. In the same month an independent civilian panel confirmed 66 out of some 300 reported cases of prisoner abuse in US-run prisons in Iraq, Afghanistan and at Guantánamo Bay (see above). However, it did not find any systematic policy of abuse or instructions from senior military or government officials. By February 2006 eight US soldiers had been found guilty of the abuse of detainees at Abu Ghraib prison or of dereliction of duty: these included army corporal Charles Graner, found guilty in January 2005 of nine charges of maltreatment of prisoners and sentenced to 10 years' imprisonment; and Private Lynndie England, who was sentenced to three years' imprisonment in September, also on charges including maltreatment of prisoners at Abu Ghraib. In May President Bush ordered the demotion of Brig.-Gen. Janis Karpinski, of the army reserve, who had been in command of the police brigade at Abu Ghraib and was found guilty of dereliction of duty by the US army inspector general. Colonel Thomas Pappas, the officer in charge of intelligence and interrogations at the prison, was also found guilty of dereliction of duty and relieved of his command. In early March it was announced that the USA was to hand over control of the prison to the Iraqi authorities. At that time in Iraq there were an estimated 10,000 prisoners at one British-run and three US-run prisons, including Abu Ghraib.

In late June 2004 L. Paul Bremer officially handed over sovereignty to the Interim Government of Iraq. The event took place in secret two days ahead of schedule, amid fears of terrorist attacks. Full diplomatic relations were restored. In the previous month the US Army had extended the period of duty of thousands of serving troops. In June the Army announced plans to call up 5,600 retired and discharged soldiers to compensate for a lack of trained specialists. As part of the Disabled Soldier Support System, it also hoped to retain soldiers who had been wounded; in December it was estimated that 900 out of 9,300 soldiers injured in Iraq would be eligible for the programme. In January 2005 the Department of Defense revealed that it planned to make cuts of US $60,000m. over the following six years and fundamentally to restructure the armed forces, diverting funds from costly weapons systems to manpower. At that time the cost of the military operation in Iraq had already exceeded $200,000m. At mid-April 2006 more than 2,300 US troops had died since the commencement of operations two years earlier. In mid-December 2005, for the first time, President Bush gave an official estimate of the number of Iraqi casualties—both military and civilian—as around 30,000. During 2005–06 the Administration came under increasing pressure to announce a timetable for the withdrawal of US troops from Iraq; speaking at a press conference in late March 2006 President Bush stated that US troops would remain in Iraq until at least 2009.

Relations with Turkey were strained in March 2003 following the Turkish National Assembly's rejection of a motion allowing the USA to use its military bases and territory for an eventual assault on northern Iraq. In early April the USA secured the use of Turkey as a route to transport humanitarian supplies and logistical aid to the US military in Iraq, following an offer of an US $8,500m. loan. In early March 2005, however, the USA withdrew the loan offer after the Turkish Government had shown no intention of taking it up. In the same week Turkey also announced that it would no longer need a $1,000m. grant from the USA intended to protect its economy from the impact of the war in Iraq.

Relations with the DPRK were severely strained in late 2002 when it emerged that the DPRK Government had resumed its nuclear energy programme, effectively breaking the accord signed with the USA in 1994. In October the DPRK demanded a treaty of non-aggression with the USA and asserted its right to possess nuclear weapons. In the following month the USA, the Republic of Korea, Japan and the EU suspended their supply of petroleum to the DPRK until its Government promised to terminate its nuclear weapons programme, although the DPRK denied it operated such a programme. However, in December it announced operations would resume at the Yongbyon nuclear plant, which was capable of producing weapons-grade plutonium. The USA considered that economic sanctions would be an effective means of containing North Korea, although this led to a more uncompromising stance from the DPRK, which said it would consider UN sanctions an 'act of war', and subsequently withdrew from the NPT in January 2003. In mid-July the DPRK claimed that it had made enough plutonium to produce six nuclear bombs. In late August six-party negotiations opened in the Chinese capital, Beijing, between the USA, the DPRK, the People's Republic of China, South Korea, Japan and Russia; however, little progress was achieved. In October President Bush announced that the USA would be prepared to offer security assurances to the DPRK in exchange for verifiable dismantling of any weapons programmes. In January 2004 a group of US nuclear scientists visited the Yongbyon plant, in an unofficial capacity, and announced that they had been shown plutonium but had seen no proof of a nuclear bomb. In February a further round of six-party talks took place in Beijing, but no significant resolutions were reached. Talks in June ended unsuccessfully and in February 2005 the DPRK admitted for the first time that it possessed nuclear weapons. The USA rejected a request in March to hold bilateral talks. Talks eventually resumed in August and the following month it appeared that a breakthrough had been made when the DPRK agreed in principle to end its weapons development programme in exchange for a civilian light-water reactor. However, the DPRK refused to begin dismantling its nuclear programme until it had received the reactor: the USA took the opposite position. Meanwhile, the US Administration alleged that the Banco Asia Delta in Macao, People's Republic of China, was laundering money on behalf of the DPRK Government and imposed a ban on transactions with the bank. The following month US authorities froze the assets of eight North Korean companies, which were accused of supporting the DPRK weapons programme. In October the US Department of Justice charged the DPRK with having forged millions of dollars worth of counterfeit $100 bills—so-called 'Supernotes'—since 1989. The DPRK Government insisted that six-party negotiations would not resume until the economic sanctions against it were lifted. In April 2006 the USA again rejected a request to hold bilateral talks.

Government

The USA is a federal republic. Each of the 50 constituent states and the District of Columbia exercises a measure of internal self-government. Defence, foreign affairs, coinage, posts, the higher levels of justice, and internal security are the responsibility of the federal Government. The President is head of the executive and is elected for a four-year term by a college of representatives elected directly from each state. The President appoints the other members of the executive, subject to the consent of the Senate. The Congress is the seat of legislative power and consists of the Senate (100 members) and the House of Representatives (435 members). Two senators are chosen by direct election in each state, to serve a six-year term, and one-third of the membership is renewable every two years. Representatives are elected by direct and universal suffrage for a two-year term. The number of representatives of each state in Congress is determined by the size of the state's population. Ultimate judicial power is vested in the Supreme Court, which has the power to disallow legislation and to overturn executive actions which it deems unconstitutional.

Defence

In August 2005 US armed forces totalled 1,433,600: army 502,000, air force 379,500, navy 376,650 and 175,350 marine corps; there was also a Coast Guard numbering 40,360 (not including civilians). There are also active reservists numbering 1,290,988. Military conscription ended in 1973. The Strategic Air Command and Polaris nuclear submarines are equipped with nuclear weapons. The USA is a member of the NATO alliance. Estimated federal defence expenditure for 2006 totalled $535,943m. (some 19.8% of total federal budgetary expenditure, equivalent to 4.1% of GDP).

Economic Affairs

In 2004, according to estimates by the World Bank, the USA's gross national income (GNI), measured at average 2002–04 prices, was US $12,150,931.2m., equivalent to $41,400 per head. During 1995–2004, it was estimated, the population increased at an annual average rate of 1.1%, while gross domestic product (GDP) per head increased, in real terms, by an average of 2.3% per year. During the same period overall GDP increased, in real terms, at an average annual rate of 3.4%; GDP grew by 4.2% in 2004.

Agriculture (including forestry and fishing) contributed 1.0% of GDP and employed 1.6% of the economically active civilian population in 2004. The principal crops are hay, potatoes, sugar beet and citrus fruit, which, together with cereals, cotton and tobacco, are important export crops. The principal livestock are cattle, pigs and poultry. Food and live animals provided 6.0% of total exports in 2003. The GDP of the sector increased, in real terms, by an average of 6.4% per year in 1995–2001. Real agricultural GDP increased by 7.6% in 2003 and by 1.8% in 2004.

Industry (including mining, manufacturing, construction and utilities) provided 20.7% of GDP and employed 20.8% of the civilian working population in 2004. Industrial GDP increased, in real terms, at an average annual rate of 2.3% in 1995–2001. GDP of the goods-producing industrial sector (including agriculture) increased by 1.2% in 2003 and by a further 3.9% in 2004.

THE UNITED STATES OF AMERICA

Mining and quarrying contributed 1.3% of GDP and employed 0.4% of the civilian working population in 2004. The USA's principal mineral deposits are of petroleum, natural gas, coal, copper, iron, silver and uranium. Crude materials (excluding fuels) accounted for 4.6% of total exports in 2003. Mineral fuels accounted for a further 2.0% of exports in that year. In real terms, the GDP of the sector decreased at an average annual rate of 2.6% during 2000–03. Real mining GDP decreased by 1.5% in 2003, but increased by 2.3% in 2004.

Manufacturing contributed 12.7% of GDP and the sector employed 11.8% of the civilian working population in 2004. In 2004 the principal branches of manufacturing (measured by value of output) were transport equipment (15.6% of the total), chemical products (12.4%), food products (12.0%), computer and electronic equipment (8.5%), and petroleum and coal products(7.3%). Manufacturing GDP increased, in real terms, by an average of 2.5% per year in 1995–2001. Sectoral GDP increased by 1.9% in 2003 and by 4.8% in 2003.

Energy is derived principally from domestic and imported hydrocarbons. In 2002 51.3% of total electricity production was provided by coal, 20.1% was provided by nuclear power, and 17.8% was derived from natural gas. In 2003 fuel imports amounted to 12.5% of total merchandise import costs.

Services (including government services) provided 78.3% of GDP and 77.6% of total civilian employment in 2004. The combined GDP of all service sectors rose, in real terms, at an average rate of 4.4% per year during 1995–2001. Services GDP increased by 3.2% in 2003 and by 4.9% in 2004.

In 2004 the USA recorded a visible trade deficit of $661,900m. (excluding military transactions); there was a deficit of $668,100m. on the current account of the balance of payments. The USA's principal export market and main source of imports in 2003 was Canada, which accounted for 23.4% of total US exports and 17.4% of total imports. Mexico was the second largest trading partner, taking 10.7% of US exports and providing 13.5% of US imports. Other major trading partners include the People's Republic of China, Japan, Germany, the United Kingdom and other members of the European Union (EU). In 2003 machinery and transport equipment constituted the principal category of exports (accounting for 48.6% of the total) and of imports (40.9%).

In the financial year ending 30 September 2005 there was an estimated federal budget deficit of $318,346m., equivalent to 2.5% of GDP. The annual rate of inflation averaged 2.1% in 1999–2005. The average annual rate was 2.7% in 2004 and 3.4% in 2005. The rate of unemployment averaged 5.5% in 2004.

The USA is a member of the Organisation for Economic Co-operation and Development (OECD, see p. 320), the North American Free Trade Agreement (NAFTA, see p. 312) and the World Trade Organization (WTO, see p. 370). Negotiations towards a free trade agreement, to be known as the Central American Free Trade Agreement (CAFTA), between the USA and Guatemala, Costa Rica, El Salvador, Honduras and Nicaragua were concluded in December 2003 and signed in May 2004 in Washington, DC. The Agreement, which was restyled DR-CAFTA following the inclusion of the Dominican Republic in 2004, was ratified by Congress in late July 2005 and signed by President Bush early in the following month. DR-CAFTA was scheduled to come into effect in 2006, once individual countries fulfilled the criteria for entry. Discussions to establish a Free Trade Area of the Americas, first proposed in 1995, stalled in late 2004, but were scheduled to recommence in 2006 (see above).

The US economy grew strongly throughout the 1990s, despite the persistence of many of the factors that had inhibited growth in the previous decade. The federal Government's level of foreign debt continued to increase until 1998, its reduction being a priority of the second Administration of President Bill Clinton (1993–2001). The deficits in trade and on the current account of the balance of payments increased throughout the decade. Trade with Canada, and particularly with Mexico, was facilitated by NAFTA, which entered into operation in January 1994 and provided for the progressive abolition (over a 15-year period) of tariffs between the three countries. In the second half of the decade the US dollar appreciated considerably in value against many major world currencies, enabling the Federal Reserve System to maintain low interest rates, thus stimulating growth, led by developments in the telecommunications and information-technology sectors. However, growth in these sectors began to decelerate in 2000, provoking fears of a recession in the economy as a whole. Under President Clinton the country's budget deficit was reduced and, from 1998–2001, a budget surplus was operated. The first budget of the Administration of President George W. Bush, which took office in 2001, included the largest single cut in federal taxation since 1981, amounting to $1,350,000m. in 2001–10. Concerns of a significant recession prompted a sharp cut in interest rates in this year, in an effort to sustain economic activity. The attacks of 11 September 2001 further undermined confidence in the US economy and placed new demands on federal budget expenditure for emergency aid and counter-terrorism measures. As a result, the federal budget recorded a deficit of US $157,797m. in 2002. This figure increased to $375,295m., in 2003, mainly owing to increases in defence spending. In January of that year the Administration presented plans to reduce taxes worth some $726,000m. over 10 years; however, in March Congress voted to reduce the cuts to $350,000m., owing partly to concerns about the cost of the US-led military conflict in Iraq and the eventual reconstruction of that country. In November Congress approved a presidential request for an additional $87,000m. in funding for reconstruction efforts in Iraq and Afghanistan; in early May 2005 Congress approved a further $82,000m. requested by the President. The federal budget deficit increased to an estimated $412,727m. in 2004. In November of that year Congress enacted legislation extending health care for the elderly to cover prescription drugs (the so-called Medicare Prescription Drug and Modernization Act), at an estimated cost of $400,000m. over the next 10 years. Provision for further agricultural subsidies over the same period was also made following the approval of legislation in 2002. In 2005 the federal deficit fell to $318,346m. following extensive reductions to government programmes. Further cuts to domestic programmes were proposed under the budget presented in 2006: expenditure on the Medicaid health insurance programme was to be reduced by $36,000m. over five years. Tax cuts were proposed amounting to $1,500,000m. over 10 years. Meanwhile, defence expenditure rose by $40,608m. to an estimated $535,943m., accounting for almost one-fifth of total outlay. As a result, the federal deficit was forecast to increase to a record $423,186m., equivalent to 3.2% of GDP. Economic growth was forecast at 3.5% in 2005.

Education

Education is primarily the responsibility of state and local governments, but some federal funds are available to help meet special needs at primary, secondary and higher education levels. Public education is free in every state from elementary school through high school. The period of compulsory education varies among states, but most states require attendance between the ages of seven and 16 years. In 2005 there were an estimated 33.5m. pupils enrolled in public primary schools and 14.8m. in public secondary schools. Private school enrolment was approximately 4.9m. at primary level and about 1.4m. at secondary level. In 2001 there were 4,197 two-year and four-year universities and colleges, with a total enrolment of an estimated 16.6m. students at the in 2005. Federal government expenditure on education (including training and employment programmes) totalled $109,651m. in 2004. Spending on education by all levels of government in 2002/03 was $621,335m. (28.7% of total public expenditure).

Public Holidays*

2006: 2 January (for New Year's Day), 16 January (Martin Luther King Day), 20 February (Presidents' Day), 29 May (Memorial Day), 4 July (Independence Day), 4 September (Labor Day), 9 October (Columbus Day), 10 November (for Veterans' Day), 23 November (Thanksgiving Day), 25 December (Christmas Day).

2007: 1 January (New Year's Day), 15 January (Martin Luther King Day), 19 February (Presidents' Day), 28 May (Memorial Day), 4 July (Independence Day), 3 September (Labor Day), 8 October (Columbus Day), 12 November (for Veterans' Day), 22 November (Thanksgiving Day), 25 December (Christmas Day).

* Federal legal public holidays are designated by presidential proclamation or congressional enactment, but need not be observed in individual states, which have legal jurisdiction over their public holidays.

Weights and Measures

With certain exceptions, the imperial system is in force. One US billion equals 1,000 million; one US cwt equals 100 lb; long ton equals 2,240 lb; short ton equals 2,000 lb. A policy of gradual voluntary conversion to the metric system is being encouraged.

THE UNITED STATES OF AMERICA

Statistical Survey

Source (unless otherwise stated): Statistical Information Office, Population Division, Bureau of the Census, US Dept of Commerce, Washington, DC 20233-0001; internet www.census.gov.

Area and Population

AREA, POPULATION AND DENSITY

Area (sq km)	
Land	9,161,923
Water*	664,706
	9,826,630†
Population (census results)‡	
1 April 1990	248,709,873
1 April 2000	
Males	138,053,563
Females	143,368,343
Total	281,421,906
Population (official estimates at mid-year)§	
2003	290,850,005
2004	293,656,842
2005	296,410,404
Density (per sq km) at mid-2005‖	32.4

* Comprises Great Lakes, inland, territorial, and coastal waters.
† 3,794,083 sq miles.
‡ Excluding adjustment for underenumeration; the adjusted total was 281,424,602.
§ Estimates of the resident population, based on adjusted 2000 census results.
‖ Based on land area only.

RACES
(2000 census)

	Number	%
White	211,460,626	75.14
Black	34,658,190	12.32
Asian	10,242,998	3.64
American Indian and Alaska Native	2,475,956	0.88
Native Hawaiian and Pacific Islander	398,835	0.14
Others*	22,185,301	7.88
Total	281,421,906	100.00

* Includes those of two or more races.

Hispanic or Latino population (all races): 35,305,818 (12.6%).

STATES
(population at census of 1 April 2000*)

State	Land area (sq km)	Residents ('000)	Density (per sq km)	Capital
Alabama	131,426	4,447	33.8	Montgomery
Alaska	1,481,347	627	0.4	Juneau
Arizona	294,312	5,131	17.4	Phoenix
Arkansas	134,856	2,673	19.8	Little Rock
California	403,933	33,872	83.9	Sacramento
Colorado	268,627	4,301	16.0	Denver
Connecticut	12,548	3,406	271.4	Hartford
Delaware	5,060	784	154.9	Dover
District of Columbia	159	572	3,596.7	Washington
Florida	139,670	15,982	114.4	Tallahassee
Georgia	149,976	8,186	54.6	Atlanta
Hawaii	16,635	1,212	72.9	Honolulu
Idaho	214,314	1,294	6.0	Boise
Illinois	143,961	12,419	86.3	Springfield
Indiana	92,895	6,080	65.5	Indianapolis
Iowa	144,701	2,926	20.2	Des Moines
Kansas	211,900	2,688	12.7	Topeka
Kentucky	102,896	4,042	39.3	Frankfort
Louisiana	112,825	4,469	39.6	Baton Rouge
Maine	79,931	1,275	16.0	Augusta
Maryland	25,314	5,296	209.2	Annapolis
Massachusetts	20,306	6,349	312.7	Boston
Michigan	147,121	9,938	67.5	Lansing
Minnesota	206,189	4,919	23.9	St Paul
Mississippi	121,488	2,845	23.4	Jackson
Missouri	178,414	5,595	31.4	Jefferson City
Montana	376,979	902	2.4	Helena

State—continued	Land area (sq km)	Residents ('000)	Density (per sq km)	Capital
Nebraska	199,099	1,711	8.6	Lincoln
Nevada	284,448	1,998	7.0	Carson City
New Hampshire	23,227	1,236	53.2	Concord
New Jersey	19,211	8,414	438.0	Trenton
New Mexico	314,309	1,819	5.8	Santa Fe
New York	122,283	18,976	155.2	Albany
North Carolina	126,161	8,049	63.8	Raleigh
North Dakota	178,647	642	3.6	Bismarck
Ohio	106,056	11,353	107.0	Columbus
Oklahoma	177,847	3,451	19.4	Oklahoma City
Oregon	248,631	3,421	13.8	Salem
Pennsylvania	116,074	12,281	105.8	Harrisburg
Rhode Island	2,706	1,048	387.2	Providence
South Carolina	77,983	4,012	51.4	Columbia
South Dakota	196,540	755	3.8	Pierre
Tennessee	106,752	5,689	53.3	Nashville
Texas	678,051	20,852	30.8	Austin
Utah	212,751	2,233	10.5	Salt Lake City
Vermont	23,956	609	25.4	Montpelier
Virginia	102,548	7,079	69.0	Richmond
Washington	172,348	5,894	34.2	Olympia
West Virginia	62,361	1,808	29.0	Charleston
Wisconsin	140,663	5,364	38.1	Madison
Wyoming	251,489	494	2.0	Cheyenne
Total	9,161,923	281,422	30.7	

* Includes armed forces residing in each State.

Note: Totals may not be equal to sum of components, owing to rounding.

PRINCIPAL TOWNS
(population at census of 1 April 2000)

New York	8,008,278	Oklahoma City	506,132
Los Angeles	3,694,820	Tucson	486,699
Chicago	2,896,016	New Orleans	484,674
Houston	1,953,631	Las Vegas	478,434
Philadelphia	1,517,550	Cleveland	478,403
Phoenix	1,321,045	Long Beach, CA	461,522
San Diego	1,223,400	Albuquerque	448,607
Dallas	1,188,580	Kansas City, MO	441,545
San Antonio	1,114,646	Fresno	427,652
Detroit	951,270	Virginia Beach, VA	425,257
San Jose	894,943	Atlanta	416,474
Indianapolis	791,926	Sacramento	407,018
San Francisco	776,733	Oakland	399,484
Jacksonville	735,617	Mesa City, AZ	396,375
Columbus, OH	711,470	Tulsa	393,049
Austin	656,562	Omaha	390,007
Baltimore	651,154	Minneapolis	382,618
Memphis	650,100	Honolulu	371,657
Milwaukee	596,974	Colorado Springs	360,980
Boston	589,141	St Louis	348,189
Washington, DC (capital)	572,059	Wichita	344,284
Nashville-Davidson	569,891	Santa Ana, CA	337,977
El Paso	563,662	Pittsburgh	334,563
Seattle	563,374	Arlington, TX	332,969
Denver	554,636	Cincinnati	331,285
Charlotte	540,828	Anaheim	328,014
Fort Worth	534,694	Toledo, OH	313,619
Portland, OR	529,121	Tampa	303,447

THE UNITED STATES OF AMERICA

BIRTHS, MARRIAGES, DEATHS

	Registered live births		Registered marriages		Registered deaths	
	Number ('000)	Rate (per 1,000)	Number ('000)	Rate (per 1,000)	Number ('000)	Rate (per 1,000)
1997	3,881	14.2	2,384	8.9	2,314	8.5
1998	3,942	14.3	2,244	8.4	2,337	8.5
1999	3,959	14.2	2,358	8.6	2,391	8.6
2000	4,059	14.4	2,329	8.2	2,403	8.5
2001	4,026	14.1	2,345	8.2	2,416	8.5
2002	4,022	13.9	2,254	7.8	2,444	8.5
2003	4,090	14.1	2,245*	7.7*	2,448	8.3
2004*	4,121	14.0	2,279	7.8	2,393	8.1

* Provisional figure(s).

Source: National Center for Health Statistics, US Department of Health and Human Services.

Expectation of life (WHO estimates, years at birth): 77 (males 75; females 80) in 2003 (Source: WHO, *World Health Report*).

IMMIGRATION
(year ending 30 September)

Country of birth	2001/02	2002/03	2003/04
Europe	174,209	100,769	127,669
Bosnia-Herzegovina	25,373	6,168	10,552
Poland	12,746	10,526	14,250
Russia	20,833	13,951	13,358
Ukraine	21,217	11,666	13,655
United Kingdom	16,421	9,601	14,915
Asia	342,099	244,759	330,004
China, People's Republic	61,282	40,659	51,156
India	71,105	50,372	70,116
Iran	13,029	7,251	10,434
Korea, Republic	21,021	12,512	19,766
Pakistan	13,743	9,444	12,086
Philippines	51,308	45,397	57,827
Viet Nam	33,627	22,133	31,514
Africa	60,269	48,738	66,309
Nigeria	8,129	7,892	9,374
North America, Central America and the Caribbean	404,437	250,726	341,242
Canada	19,519	11,446	15,567
Mexico	219,380	115,864	175,364
Caribbean	96,489	68,815	88,921
Cuba	28,272	9,304	20,488
Dominican Republic	22,604	26,205	30,492
Haiti	20,268	12,314	13,998
Jamaica	14,898	13,384	14,414
Central America	68,979	54,565	61,333
El Salvador	31,168	28,296	29,795
Guatemala	16,229	14,415	17,999
Nicaragua	10,850	4,174	4,000
South America	74,506	55,247	71,785
Brazil	9,474	6,357	10,504
Colombia	18,845	14,777	18,678
Ecuador	10,602	7,083	8,611
Peru	11,999	9,444	11,781
Total (incl. others)	1,063,732	705,827	946,142

Source: US Department of Homeland Security, *Yearbook of Immigration Statistics*.

ECONOMICALLY ACTIVE POPULATION
(annual averages, civilian labour force, '000 persons aged 16 years and over)

	2003	2004
Agriculture, hunting, forestry and fishing	2,275	2,232
Mining and quarrying	525	539
Manufacturing	16,902	16,484
Electricity, gas and water	1,193	1,168
Construction	10,138	10,768
Wholesale and retail trade; repair of motor vehicles, motorcycles and personal and household goods	20,706	20,869
Hotels and restaurants	9,021	9,131
Transport, storage and communications	5,758	5,844
Financial intermediation	6,834	6,940
Real estate, renting and business activities	16,793	17,137
Public administration and defence; compulsory social security	6,243	6,365
Education	11,826	12,058
Health and social work	16,434	16,661
Other services	13,089	13,056
Total employed	137,736	139,252
Unemployed	8,774	8,149
Total labour force	146,510	147,401
Males	78,238	78,979
Females	68,272	68,422

Source: ILO.

Health and Welfare

KEY INDICATORS

Total fertility rate (children per woman, 2003)	2.1
Under-5 mortality rate (per 1,000 live births, 2004)	8
HIV/AIDS (% of persons aged 15–49, 2003)	0.6
Physicians (per 1,000 head, 2000)	5.49
Hospital beds (per 1,000 head, 2000)	3.6
Health expenditure (2002): US $ per head (PPP)	5,274
Health expenditure (2002): % of GDP	14.6
Health expenditure (2002): public (% of total)	44.9
Access to water (% of persons, 2002)	100
Access to sanitation (% of persons, 2002)	100
Human Development Index (2003): ranking	10
Human Development Index (2003): value	0.944

For sources and definitions, see explanatory note on p. vi.

THE UNITED STATES OF AMERICA

Agriculture

PRINCIPAL CROPS
('000 metric tons)

	2002	2003	2004
Wheat	44,062	63,814	58,738
Rice (paddy)	9,569	9,034	10,470
Barley	4,933	6,059	6,091
Maize	228,805	256,905	299,917
Oats	1,722	2,096	1,679
Sorghum	9,392	10,446	11,555
Potatoes	20,856	20,766	20,686
Sweet potatoes	584	721	731
Sugar cane	32,253	30,715	26,320
Sugar beet	25,145	27,744	27,176
Dry beans	1,360	1,021	807
Soybeans (Soya beans)	74,825	66,778	85,013
Groundnuts (in shell)	1,506	1,880	1,945
Sunflower seed	1,129	1,209	960
Rapeseed	706	686	613
Cottonseed	5,610	6,046	7,477
Cabbages	1,968	1,981	2,156
Lettuce	4,541	4,755	4,977
Tomatoes	12,238	10,522	12,766
Cucumbers and gherkins	1,058	1,016	969
Onions (dry)	3,168	3,328	3,670
Green peas	793	1,061	885
String beans	991	918	1,013
Carrots	1,537	1,638	1,602
Green corn (Maize)	3,984	4,256	4,013
Watermelons	1,796	1,734	1,670
Cantaloupes and other melons	1,248	1,241	1,150
Oranges	11,226	10,473	11,677
Tangerines, mandarins, etc.	533	495	476
Lemons and limes	733	939*	732*
Grapefruit and pomelos	2,199	1,872	1,964
Apples	3,866	3,989	4,726
Pears	807	847	808
Peaches and nectarines	1,422	1,390	1,430
Plums	668	728	295
Strawberries	855	978	1,004
Grapes	6,658	6,027	5,653
Tobacco (leaves)	399	364	399
Cotton (lint)	3,747	3,975	5,062

* Unofficial figure.
Source: FAO.

LIVESTOCK
('000 head at 1 January)

	2002	2003	2004
Cattle	96,723	96,100	94,888
Pigs	59,721	59,554	6,105
Sheep	6,623	6,321	2,525*
Horses*	5,300	5,300	5,300
Chickens (million)	1,940†	1,950†	1,970*
Turkeys (million)*	87	87	88

* FAO estimate(s).
† Unofficial figure.
Source: FAO.

LIVESTOCK PRODUCTS
('000 metric tons)

	2002	2003	2004
Beef and veal	12,427	12,039	11,261
Mutton and lamb*	101	92	90
Pig meat	8,929	9,056	8,312
Chicken meat	14,701	14,924	15,514
Cows' milk	77,139	77,289	77,475
Eggs	5,165	5,169	5,278
Butter	615	564	567
Cheese	4,216	4,231	4,375

* Unofficial figures.
Source: FAO.

Forestry

ROUNDWOOD REMOVALS
('000 cubic metres)

	2002	2003	2004
Sawlogs and veneer logs	234,578	230,012	234,673
Pulp wood	161,391	166,596	171,024
Other industrial wood	8,989	9,005	9,005
Fuel wood	43,042	42,900	43,608
Total	448,000	448,513	458,310

Source: FAO.

SAWNWOOD PRODUCTION
('000 cubic metres)

	2002	2003	2004
Coniferous	60,913	61,190	65,212
Broadleaved	27,730	24,969	22,224
Total	88,643	86,159	87,436

Source: FAO.

Fishing

('000 metric tons, live weight)

	2001	2002	2003
Capture	4,944.3	4,937.3	4,939.0
Humpback salmon	173.1	116.0	151.6
Pacific cod	214.0	232.6	257.4
Walleye pollock	1,442.2	1,515.5	1,524.9
North Pacific hake	172.1	129.6	140.3
Atlantic menhaden	261.4	211.6	203.3
Gulf menhaden	528.5	582.5	522.2
American sea scallop	165.0	186.6	200.5
Atlantic surf clam	165.7	175.7	167.8
Aquaculture	479.3	497.3	544.3
Channel catfish	270.8	286.0	300.1
Total catch	5,423.6	5,434.7	5,483.3

Note: Figures exclude aquatic plants (metric tons): 37,165 in 2001; 47,183 in 2002; 49,496 in 2003. Also excluded are corals (metric tons): 8.5 in 2001; 1.9 in 2003 (2002 data not available). Also excluded are sponges (metric tons): 291.3 in 2001; 260.7 in 2002; 237.1 in 2003. Also excluded are aquatic mammals (generally recorded by number rather than weight). The number of whales and dolphins caught was: 883 in 2001; 506 in 2002; 40 in 2003. The number of seals and sea lions caught was: 2,229 in 2001; 2,019 in 2002 (2003 data not available). The number of American alligators caught was: 265,470 in 2001; 325,291 in 2002; 341,735 in 2003.

Source: FAO.

Mining

('000 metric tons, unless otherwise indicated)

	2003	2004	2005
Crude petroleum (million barrels)[1]	2,073	1,983	1,869
Natural gas (million cubic feet)[1,2]	19,974	19,684	19,115
Coal (million short tons)[1,3]	1,072	1,112	1,133
Iron ore[4]	48,600	54,700	55,000[5]
Copper[6]	1,120	1,160	1,150[5]
Lead[6]	460	445	440[5]
Zinc[6]	768	739	760[5]
Molybdenum (metric tons)[6]	33,500	41,500	56,900[5]
Silver (metric tons)[6]	1,240	1,250	1,300[5]
Uranium ('000 pounds)[1,7]	2,000[8]	2,282	2,701[9]
Gold (metric tons)[6]	277	258	250[5]
Platinum group metals (kilograms):[6]			
Platinum	4,170	4,040	4,200[5]
Palladium	14,000	13,700	14,200[5]
Lime	19,200	20,000	20,000[5]

THE UNITED STATES OF AMERICA

—continued

	2003	2004	2005
Sand and gravel (million metric tons):			
Construction	1,160	1,240	1,260[5]
Industrial	27,500	29,700	31,300[5]
Stone, crushed (million metric tons)	1,530	1,590	1,650[5]
Bentonite	3,770	4,060	4,430[5]
Fuller's Earth	3,610	3,260	3,170[5]
Kaolin	7,680	7,760	7,200[5]
Phosphate rock[2]	35,000	35,800	38,300[5]
Potash (a)[2,10]	1,100	1,300	1,200[5]
Soda ash	10,600	11,000	11,100[5]
Diatomite	599	620	635[5]
Boron (b)[10]	605	637	657[5]
Salt	43,700	46,500	45,900[5]
Bromine (c)[10]	216	222	212[5]

[1] Source: Energy Information Administration, US Department of Energy.
[2] Figures refer to marketable production.
[3] 1 short ton = 0.907185 metric tons.
[4] Figures refer to the gross weight of usable ore.
[5] Estimate.
[6] Figures refer to metal content of ores and concentrates.
[7] Figures refer to gross weight of uranium oxide ore.
[8] Figure is rounded to avoid disclosure of individual company data.
[9] Provisional.
[10] Figures refer to the content of (a) K_2O, (b) B_2O_3 or (c) bromine contained in minerals and compounds.

Source (unless otherwise indicated): US Geological Survey.

Industry

PRINCIPAL MANUFACTURES
(value of shipments in $ '000 million)

	2002	2003	2004
Food	458.1	483.2	511.5
Beverages and tobacco products	105.7	108.8	112.3
Wood products	89.1	92.1	103.4
Paper	153.7	151.1	154.0
Printing and related activities	95.6	92.7	93.2
Petroleum and coal products	215.5	247.3	312.9
Chemicals	461.5	486.6	528.2
Plastics and rubber products	174.6	178.3	182.5
Non-metallic mineral products	95.1	96.9	101.9
Primary metal industries	139.4	138.1	179.0
Fabricated metal products	247.1	245.6	259.9
Machinery	255.3	257.4	269.2
Computers and electronic products	357.6	352.6	361.9
Electric equipment, appliances and components	103.0	100.1	104.2
Transportation equipment	636.7	661.1	666.5
Total (incl. others)	3,914.6	4,015.1	4,265.8

Source: Bureau of the Census, US Department of Commerce, *Annual Survey of Manufactures*.

Finance

CURRENCY AND EXCHANGE RATES

Monetary Units
100 cents = 1 United States dollar ($).

Sterling and Euro Equivalents (30 December 2005)
£1 sterling = US $1.7219;
€1 = $1.1797;
US $100 = £58.08 = €84.77.

FEDERAL BUDGET
($ million, year ending 30 September)

Revenue	2004	2005	2006*
Individual income taxes	808,959	927,222	997,599
Corporation income taxes	189,371	278,282	277,122
Social insurance taxes and contributions	733,407	794,125	841,087
Excise taxes	69,855	73,094	73,511
Estate and gift taxes	24,831	24,764	27,523
Customs duties and fees	21,083	23,379	25,887
Miscellaneous receipts	32,773	32,993	42,762
Total	1,880,279	2,153,859	2,285,491

Expenditure	2004	2005	2006*
National defence	455,908	495,335	535,943
Education, training, employment and social services	87,948	97,526	109,651
Health	240,134	250,612	268,789
Medicare	269,360	298,638	342,987
Income security	333,059	345,847	360,632
Social security	495,548	523,305	554,740
Veterans' benefits and services	59,779	70,151	70,410
Energy	−166	429	2,621
Natural resources and environment	30,725	28,023	32,731
Commerce and housing credit	5,273	7,574	9,087
Transportation	64,627	67,894	71,637
Community and regional development	15,822	26,264	52,025
International affairs	26,891	34,592	34,750
General science, space and technology	23,053	23,674	23,996
Agriculture	15,440	26,566	26,846
Administration of justice	45,576	40,019	41,342
General government	22,321	16,994	19,085
Allowances	—	—	3,726
Net interest	160,245	183,986	220,053
Undistributed offsetting receipts	−58,537	−65,224	−72,374
Total	2,293,006	2,472,205	2,708,677

* Estimates.

Source: Office of Management and Budget, Executive Office of the President.

STATE AND LOCAL GOVERNMENT FINANCES
($ million, fiscal years*)

Revenue	2000/01	2001/02	2002/03
From Federal Government	324,033	360,534	389,264
From state and local governments	1,566,858	1,447,039	1,658,073
General revenue from own sources	1,323,128	1,324,241	1,373,948
Taxes	914,119	904,971	938,972
Property	263,689	279,122	296,683
Sales and gross receipts	320,217	324,040	337,787
Individual income	226,334	202,858	199,407
Corporation income	35,296	28,152	31,369
Other	52,135	70,800	73,726
Charges and miscellaneous	409,009	419,270	434,976
Utility and liquor stores	100,460	107,387	108,388
Insurance trust revenue	143,271	15,410	175,737
Employee retirement	102,692	−29,261	120,157
Unemployment compensation	23,341	27,086	35,335
Other	17,237	17,586	20,245
Total	1,890,891	1,807,573	2,047,337

THE UNITED STATES OF AMERICA

Statistical Survey

Expenditure	2000/01	2001/02	2002/03
General expenditure	1,621,757	1,730,809	1,817,513
Education	563,572	594,591	621,335
Elementary and secondary	392,278	411,073	428,503
Institutions of higher education	146,155	156,810	164,187
Other	25,139	26,707	28,645
Libraries	7,802	8,257	8,911
Public welfare	257,380	279,598	306,463
Hospitals	80,545	87,247	93,175
Health	53,465	59,132	61,703
Social insurance administration	4,359	5,082	5,267
Veterans' services	337	361	1,017
Highways	107,235	115,467	117,696
Other transportations	23,186	21,529	24,559
Police	59,584	64,492	67,361
Fire protection	24,970	25,978	27,854
Correction	52,370	54,687	55,471
Protective inspection	9,620	11,629	11,593
Natural resources	22,163	22,000	22,808
Parks and recreation	27,920	30,096	31,765
Housing and community development	27,402	31,610	35,275
Sewerage	28,061	31,238	32,540
Solid waste management	18,657	19,047	19,183
Financial administration	30,007	32,653	34,911
Judicial and legal services	29,204	31,236	32,460
General public buildings	9,854	10,898	11,951
Other government administration	16,844	18,003	19,336
Interest on general debt	73,836	75,303	77,277
Other and unallocable	93,382	100,674	97,602
Utility and liquor stores	133,544	143,851	148,996
Insurance trust expenditure	139,543	169,672	193,263
Unemployment compensation	22,986	42,166	51,547
Employee retirement	104,414	114,208	127,197
Other	12,142	13,298	14,520
Total†	1,899,150	2,048,719	2,164,176

* Figures refer to the fiscal year of individual state governments, normally ending 30 June, or, in the case of the following exceptions, ending on some date within the previous 12 months: the state government of Texas and Texas school districts (31 August); the state governments of Alabama and Michigan, all local governments in the District of Columbia, and Alabama school districts (30 September); all state and local governments of New York (31 March).
† Including intergovernmental expenditure ($ million): 4,306 in 2000/01; 4,387 in 2001/02; 4,404 in 2002/03.

Source: Governments Division, Bureau of the Census, US Department of Commerce, *Government Finances*.

INTERNATIONAL RESERVES
($ million at 31 December)

	2003	2004	2005
Gold (national valuation)	11,043.1	11,044.7	11,043.2
IMF special drawing rights	12,637.6	13,627.6	8,209.8
Reserve position in IMF	22,534.6	19,544.1	8,035.9
Foreign exchange	39,721.8	42,718.3	37,838.1
Total	85,937.2	86,934.7	65,127.0

Source: IMF, *International Financial Statistics*.

CURRENCY AND COIN IN CIRCULATION*
($ million at 31 December)

	2003	2004	2005
Total	693,371.3	733,171.0	764,628.2

* Currency outside Treasury and Federal Reserve banks, including currency held by commercial banks.

Source: Financial Management Service, US Department of the Treasury.

COST OF LIVING
(Consumer Price Index for all urban consumers, average of monthly figures. Base: 1982–84 = 100, unless otherwise indicated)

	2003	2004	2005
Food and beverages	180.5	186.6	191.2
Housing	184.8	189.5	195.7
Shelter	213.1	218.8	224.4
Fuels and utilities	154.5	161.9	179.0
Household furnishings and operations	126.1	125.5	126.1
Clothing	120.9	120.4	119.5
Transport	157.6	163.1	173.9
Medical care	297.1	310.1	323.2
Recreation*	107.5	108.6	109.4
Education and communication*	109.8	111.6	113.7
Other goods and services	298.7	304.7	313.4
All items	184.0	188.9	195.3

* Base: December 1997 = 100.

Source: Bureau of Labor Statistics, US Department of Labor.

NATIONAL ACCOUNTS
($ '000 million at current prices)

National Income and Product

	2002	2003	2004
Compensation of employees	6,096.6	6,326.7	6,693.4
Operating surplus	2,377.6	2,511.4	2,719.4
Domestic factor incomes	8,474.2	8,838.1	9,412.8
Consumption of fixed capital	1,292.0	1,331.3	1,435.3
Statistical discrepancy	−21.0	47.1	76.8
Gross domestic product (GDP) at factor cost	9,745.2	10,216.5	10,924.9
Taxes on production and imports	762.8	801.4	852.8
Less Subsidies on production and imports	38.4	46.7	43.5
GDP in purchasers' values	10,469.6	10,971.2	11,734.3
Factor income received from abroad	305.7	343.7	415.4
Less Factor income paid abroad	275.0	275.6	361.7
Gross national product (GNP)	10,500.2	11,039.3	11,788.0
Less Consumption of fixed capital	1,292.0	1,331.3	1,435.3
Net national product	9,208.3	9,708.0	10,352.8
Statistical discrepancy	21.0	−47.1	−76.8
National income in market prices	9,229.3	9,660.9	10,275.9

Expenditure on Gross Domestic Product

	2002	2003	2004
Government final consumption expenditure	1,616.9	1,736.7	1,843.4
Private final consumption expenditure	7,350.7	7,709.9	8,214.3
Increase in stocks	11.9	15.4	55.4
Gross fixed capital formation	1,914.5	2,010.2	2,245.1
Total domestic expenditure	10,894.0	11,472.2	12,358.2
Exports of goods and services	1,005.9	1,045.6	1,173.8
Less Imports of goods and services	1,430.3	1,546.5	1,797.8
GDP in purchasers' values	10,469.6	10,971.2	11,734.3
GDP at constant 2000 prices	10,048.8	10,320.6	10,755.7

Gross Domestic Product by Economic Activity*

	2002	2003	2004
Private industries	9,154.1	9,604.2	10,276.6
Agriculture, forestry, fishing and hunting	96.9	113.9	116.6
Agriculture	70.8	84.8	n.a.
Forestry, fishing and related activities	26.1	29.1	n.a.
Mining	104.9	130.3	147.5
Electricity, gas and water	210.7	222.2	241.2
Construction	479.1	501.3	541.4
Manufacturing	1,347.2	1,402.3	1,494.0
Wholesale trade	624.9	645.4	688.1
Retail trade	744.3	770.5	797.6

THE UNITED STATES OF AMERICA

—continued	2002	2003	2004
Transport and storage	304.4	319.3	338.6
Information	470.0	493.8	547.2
Finance and insurance	818.2	882.9	972.4
Real estate and rental and leasing	1,330.0	1,367.4	1,451.3
Professional and business services	1,190.0	1,244.3	1,341.4
Professional, scientific and technical services	712.9	743.3	792.1
Management of companies and enterprises	178.0	191.3	213.6
Administrative and waste management services	299.1	309.7	335.6
Education	91.5	94.5	99.5
Health care and social assistance	707.6	756.7	804.4
Arts, entertainment and recreation	102.5	106.6	111.8
Hotels and restaurants	279.8	289.8	308.1
Other private services	252.1	263.0	275.5
Government	1,332.9	1,399.9	1,458.4
Federal	415.8	447.1	465.4
General government	350.4	378.4	n.a.
Government enterprises	65.4	68.7	n.a.
State and local	917.1	952.8	993.0
General government	844.3	876.9	n.a.
Government enterprises	72.8	75.9	n.a.
Sub-total	10,487.0	11,004.0	11,735.0
Statistical discrepancy	−17.4	−32.8	−0.7
GDP in purchasers' values	10,469.6	10,971.2	11,734.3

*Estimates; distribution is based on the 1997 North American Industry Classification System (NAICS), which differs from ISIC.

Source: Bureau of Economic Analysis, US Department of Commerce.

BALANCE OF PAYMENTS
($ '000 million)

	2002	2003	2004
Exports of goods f.o.b.	685.9	716.7	811.0
Imports of goods f.o.b.	−1,164.7	−1,260.8	−1,473.0
Trade balance	−478.8	−544.0	−661.9
Exports of services	291.3	305.9	340.4
Imports of services	−233.7	−256.6	−296.1
Balance on goods and services	−421.2	−494.8	−617.6
Other income received	270.8	309.8	379.5
Other income paid	−260.8	−263.5	−349.1
Balance on goods, services and income	−411.2	−448.5	−587.1
Current transfers received	12.0	14.7	17.9
Current transfers paid	−76.0	−85.9	−98.9
Current balance	−475.2	−519.7	−668.1
Capital account (net)	−1.4	−3.2	−1.6
Direct investment abroad	−154.5	−140.6	−252.0
Direct investment from abroad	80.8	67.1	106.8
Portfolio investment assets	−48.6	−156.1	−102.4
Portfolio investment liabilities	427.6	538.8	762.7
Other investment assets	−87.3	−33.3	−503.9
Other investment liabilities	285.9	283.1	570.6
Net errors and omissions	−23.7	−37.8	85.1
Overall balance	3.7	−1.5	−2.8

Source: IMF, *International Financial Statistics*.

FOREIGN AID
($ million, year ending 30 September)

	2003/04*	2004/05*	2005/06†
Multilateral assistance	1,464.7	1,702.8	1,797.2
Bilateral assistance	15,554.7	31,546.9	14,364.0
Military assistance	6,285.4	4,848.3	5,151.2

* Appropriated.
† Requested.

Source: US Agency for International Development.

External Trade

The customs territory of the USA includes Puerto Rico and the US Virgin Islands. Figures exclude trade with other US possessions.

PRINCIPAL COMMODITIES
(distribution by SITC, $ million)

Imports c.i.f.	2001	2002	2003
Food and live animals	39,992.0	42,080.3	46,126.7
Mineral fuels, lubricants, etc.	129,086.9	122,023.7	163,370.1
Petroleum, petroleum products, etc.	106,479.0	105,713.5	136,728.1
Crude petroleum oils, etc.	79,288.9	82,588.5	106,989.1
Chemicals and related products	79,948.0	87,038.3	102,382.7
Basic manufactures	130,951.1	134,761.5	141,480.8
Machinery and transport equipment	508,043.2	514,835.6	533,668.3
Power-generating machinery and equipment	36,661.3	34,606.3	33,028.7
General industrial machinery, equipment and parts	34,328.3	36,440.4	39,919.4
Office machines and automatic data-processing machines	77,359.6	78,544.4	82,432.9
Automatic data-processing machines and units	48,492.2	51,012.8	52,984.5
Telecommunications and sound equipment	63,829.1	67,462.9	72,509.9
Other electrical machinery, apparatus, etc.	86,564.8	83,720.3	85,296.6
Electronic microcircuits	26,137.0	22,525.3	21,051.4
Road vehicles	159,916.3	170,770.5	175,390.7
Passenger motor vehicles (excl. buses)	108,187.8	115,629.9	115,967.6
Miscellaneous manufactured articles	206,825.1	214,640.6	229,929.1
Clothing and accessories (excl. footwear)	66,592.7	66,938.2	71,487.9
Total (incl. others)	1,180,073.8	1,202,284.5	1,305,091.6

Exports f.o.b.	2001	2002	2003
Food and live animals	41,135.9	40,291.8	43,283.9
Crude materials (inedible) except fuels	28,057.4	28,108.6	33,520.6
Mineral fuels, lubricants, etc.	13,297.6	12,159.1	14,575.9
Chemicals and related products	80,008.5	78,769.2	88,790.1
Organic chemicals	16,983.6	16,867.3	20,484.5
Medicinal and pharmaceutical products	15,421.3	16,144.4	19,197.5
Artificial resins, plastics, cellulose esters, etc.	17,373.0	17,802.7	19,358.7
Basic manufactures	67,993.8	65,909.7	68,589.4
Machinery and transport equipment	374,354.5	349,427.9	351,343.2
Power-generating machinery and equipment	36,180.6	34,381.0	33,620.2
Machinery specialized for particular industries	26,612.7	24,004.6	23,678.7
General industrial machinery, equipment and parts	34,840.3	33,137.1	33,671.1
Office machines and automatic data-processing machines	49,403.6	39,744.2	41,049.9
Automatic data-processing machines and units	27,386.3	21,812.1	21,591.2
Parts and accessories for office machines, etc.	20,868.8	17,174.8	18,741.7
Telecommunication equipment, parts and accessories	26,133.5	21,587.2	20,362.7
Other electrical machinery, apparatus, etc.	87,992.8	82,465.2	85,729.5

THE UNITED STATES OF AMERICA

Statistical Survey

Exports f.o.b.—*continued*	2001	2002	2003
Thermionic valves, tubes, etc.	47,621.9	44,518.4	47,769.4
Electronic microcircuits	39,242.0	36,896.2	40,777.7
Road vehicles (incl. air-cushion vehicles) and parts*	56,703.5	60,329.3	63,128.3
Passenger motor vehicles (excl. buses)*	18,043.8	20,800.8	22,385.9
Parts and accessories for cars, buses, lorries, etc.*	29,165.3	29,248.8	28,327.0
Other transport equipment*	48,025.0	46,148.5	42,470.5
Aircraft (incl. spacecraft), associated equipment and parts*	44,688.6	43,876.4	39,598.7
Miscellaneous manufactured articles	87,281.2	81,137.6	84,453.1
Professional, scientific and controlling instruments, etc.	32,530.8	29,620.5	31,598.0
Total (incl. others)	731,006.0	693,222.4	723,608.7

* Excluding tyres, engines and electrical parts.

Source: UN, *International Trade Statistics Yearbook*.

PRINCIPAL TRADING PARTNERS*
($ million)

Imports c.i.f.	2001	2002	2003
Australia	10,944.9	13,083.5	13,092.3
Belgium	13,522.7	13,342.3	15,216.5
Brazil	15,928.5	12,408.8	11,217.9
Canada	163,721.5	160,794.8	169,451.6
China, People's Republic	19,234.4	22,052.4	28,416.6
France (incl. Monaco)	20,124.7	19,347.1	17,340.1
Germany	30,113.2	26,627.7	28,845.9
Hong Kong	14,069.3	12,609.0	13,539.7
Ireland	7,149.6	6,748.7	7,689.7
Israel	7,482.3	7,039.3	6,878.3
Italy	9,922.5	10,097.6	10,578.3
Japan	57,637.1	51,438.3	52,061.6
Korea, Republic	22,196.6	22,595.8	24,097.3
Malaysia	9,380.2	10,348.1	10,920.4
Mexico	101,507.7	97,530.5	97,452.4
Netherlands	19,524.5	18,334.3	20,694.8
Philippines	7,664.5	7,270.1	7,992.1
Singapore	17,691.3	16,221.0	16,574.9
Switzerland-Liechtenstein	9,841.4	7,789.8	8,674.8
United Kingdom	40,796.3	33,252.4	33,893.8
Total (incl. others)	731,006.0	693,222.4	723,608.7

Exports f.o.b.	2001	2002	2003
Brazil	15,258.7	16,721.9	18,963.0
Canada	220,104.0	213,905.1	227,600.1
China, People's Republic	109,380.5	133,484.1	163,250.1
France (incl. Monaco)	30,980.4	29,024.4	29,897.5
Germany	60,490.6	63,879.8	69,613.2
India	10,290.4	12,449.5	13,752.1
Ireland	18,626.2	22,484.8	25,959.1
Israel	12,158.1	12,643.7	13,008.7
Italy	24,953.3	25,417.7	26,664.3
Japan	129,708.2	124,633.0	121,232.3
Korea, Republic	36,491.2	36,909.8	38,344.9
Malaysia	23,071.7	24,733.6	26,188.0
Mexico	132,774.6	136,142.5	139,700.4
Saudi Arabia	14,414.4	13,891.5	19,525.0
Singapore	15,261.4	15,093.2	15,459.5
Thailand	15,566.0	15,682.8	16,105.7
United Kingdom	42,347.1	41,811.6	43,741.6
Venezuela	16,140.6	15,828.4	18,074.3
Total (incl. others)	1,180,073.8	1,202,284.5	1,305,091.6

* Imports by country of origin; exports by country of destination.

Source: UN, *International Trade Statistics Yearbook*.

Transport

RAILWAYS
(revenue traffic on class I railroads only)

	2000	2001	2002
Passengers carried ('000)*	22,985	23,444	23,269
Passenger-miles (million)*	5,574	5,571	5,314
Freight carried (million short tons)	2,179	2,187	2,207
Freight ton-miles ('000 million)	1,466	1,495	1,507

* AMTRAK passenger traffic only.

Source: Association of American Railroads, Washington, DC.

ROAD TRAFFIC
('000 motor vehicles registered at 31 December)

	2001	2002	2003
Passenger cars	137,633	134,605	135,670
Buses and coaches	750	761	777
Lorries (Trucks) and vans	92,045	92,939	94,944
Motorcycles	4,862	4,963	5,328

Source: Federal Highway Administration.

INLAND WATERWAYS
(freight carried, million short tons)

	2001	2002	2003
Lake waterways	100.0	101.5	89.8
Coastal waterways	223.6	216.4	223.5
Internal waterways*	619.8	608.0	609.6
Total†	1,042.5	1,021.0	1,016.1

* Internal refers to freight moved solely within US boundaries, excluding traffic on the Great Lakes system. Figures also exclude waterway improvement materials and fish.
† Totals include intra-port and intra-territorial traffic.

Source: Waterborne Commerce Statistics Center, US Army Corps of Engineers.

OCEAN SHIPPING

Sea-going Merchant Vessels

	2001	2002	2003
Number:			
passenger	11	13	11
container	90	91	87
roll-on/roll-off	60	60	64
bulk	15	17	20
tanker	142	130	110
other*	136	132	124
Total	454	443	416
Capacity ('000 dwt):			
passenger	99	104	90
container	3,058	3,201	3,309
roll-on/roll-off	1,260	1,273	1,411
bulk	604	706	837
tanker	8,447	7,532	5,828
other*	2,362	2,162	1,818
Total	15,830	14,978	13,294

* Includes breakbulk, partial container, refrigerated cargo, barge carrier and specialized cargo vessels.

Source: Maritime Administration, US Department of Transportation.

Vessels Entered and Cleared in Foreign Trade in all Ports

	1998	1999	2000
Entered:			
number	61,417	58,374	60,064
displacement ('000 net tons)	619,071	621,204	672,834
Cleared:			
number	60,711	56,599	57,864
displacement ('000 net tons)	630,816	618,990	670,855

Source: Maritime Administration, US Department of Transportation.

THE UNITED STATES OF AMERICA

CIVIL AVIATION
(US airlines, revenue traffic on scheduled services)

	2003	2004	2005*
Number of departures ('000)	10,839	11,398	11,475
Domestic traffic:			
Passengers enplaned ('000)	592,412	640,683	670,152
Passenger-miles (million)	500,271	551,935	579,661
Freight ton-miles (million)†	12,342	12,756	12,634
Mail ton-miles (million)†	880	819	719
International traffic:			
Passengers enplaned ('000)	53,863	62,222	68,273
Passenger-miles (million)	156,638	181,743	199,326
Freight ton-miles (million)†	13,021	13,926	14,178
Mail ton-miles (million)†	492	477	476

* Provisional figures.
† Short tons (1 short ton = 0.907185 metric tons).
Source: Air Transport Association of America.

Tourism

FOREIGN VISITOR ARRIVALS
(by country of residence, '000)

	2003	2004	2005
Australia	406	520	582
Canada*	12,666	13,856	14,865
France	689	775	879
Germany	1,180	1,320	1,416
Italy	409	471	546
Japan	3,170	3,748	3,884
Korea, Republic	618	627	705
Mexico*	10,526	11,906	12,858
United Kingdom	3,936	4,303	4,345
Total (incl. others)	41,218	46,084	49,402

* Estimates based on survey research.

Tourism receipts (incl. passenger transport, $ million): 80,041 in 2003; 93,339 in 2004; 103,905 in 2005 (preliminary estimate).

Source: Office of Travel and Tourism Industries, International Trade Administration, US Department of Commerce.

Communications Media

	2002	2003	2004
Telephones ('000 main lines in use)	187,524	181,403	177,947
Mobile cellular telephones ('000 subscribers)	140,767	158,722	181,105
Personal computers ('000 in use)	190,000	n.a.	220,000
Internet users ('000)	159,000	161,632	185,000

Television receivers ('000 in use): 267,000 in 2001.
Radio receivers ('000 in use): 570,000 in 1996 (estimate).
Facsimile machines ('000 in use): 21,000 in 1997 (estimate).
Books published (number of titles): 96,080 in 2000.
Daily newspapers (2001): 1,468 titles with average circulation of 55,600.

Sources: International Telecommunication Union; UN, *Statistical Yearbook*.

Education

ENROLMENT
('000 students at September of each year, projections)

	2003	2004	2005
Public:			
elementary	33,917	33,686	33,528
secondary	14,296	14,584	14,847
higher	12,952	13,092	13,283
Private:			
elementary	4,935	4,910	4,910
secondary	1,384	1,414	1,439
higher	3,958	4,003	4,068

Total elementary and secondary school teaching staff (projections, full-time equivalents, '000): 3,472 (public 3,074, private 398) in 2003; 3,501 (public 3,100, private 401) in 2004; 3,526 (public 3,122, private 404) in 2005.

Source: National Center for Education Statistics, US Department of Education.

Directory

The Constitution

Adopted 4 March 1789.

PREAMBLE

We, the people of the United States, in order to form a more perfect Union, establish justice, insure domestic tranquility, provide for the common defence, promote the general welfare, and secure the blessings of liberty to ourselves and our posterity, do ordain and establish this Constitution for the United States of America.

ARTICLE I

Section 1

All legislative powers herein granted shall be vested in a Congress of the United States, which shall consist of a Senate and House of Representatives.

Section 2

1. The House of Representatives shall be composed of members chosen every second year by the people of the several States and the electors in each State shall have the qualifications requisite for electors of the most numerous branch of the State Legislature.

2. No person shall be a Representative who shall not have attained to the age of 25 years and been seven years a citizen of the United States and who shall not, when elected, be an inhabitant of that State in which he shall be chosen.

3. Representatives and direct taxes shall be apportioned among the several States which may be included within this Union according to their respective numbers, which shall be determined by adding to the whole number of free persons, including those bound to service for a term of years, and excluding Indians not taxed, three-fifths of all other persons. The actual enumeration shall be made within three years after the first meeting of the Congress of the United States, and within every subsequent term of 10 years, in such manner as they shall by law direct. The number of Representatives shall not exceed one for every 30,000, but each State shall have at least one Representative; and until such enumeration shall be made, the State of New Hampshire shall be entitled to choose 3; Massachusetts 8; Rhode Island and Providence Plantations 1; Connecticut 5; New York 6; New Jersey 4; Pennsylvania 8; Delaware 1; Maryland 6; Virginia 10; North Carolina 5; South Carolina 5; and Georgia 3.*

4. When vacancies happen in the representation from any State, the Executive Authority thereof shall issue writs of election to fill such vacancies.

5. The House of Representatives shall choose their Speaker and other officers and shall have the sole power of impeachment.

* See Amendment XIV.

Section 3

1. The Senate of the United States shall be composed of two Senators from each State, chosen by the Legislature thereof, for six years; and each Senator shall have one vote.

2. Immediately after they shall be assembled in consequence of the first election, they shall be divided as equally as may be into three classes. The seats of the Senators of the first class shall be vacated at the expiration of the second year, of the second class at the expiration of the fourth year, and of the third class at the expiration of the sixth year, so that one-third may be chosen every second year, and if vacancies happen by resignation or otherwise, during the recess of

the Legislature or of any State, the Executive therefore may make temporary appointment until the next meeting of the Legislature, which shall then fill such vacancies.

3. No person shall be a Senator who shall not have attained to the age of 30 years, and been nine years a citizen of the United States, and who shall not, when elected, be an inhabitant of that State for which he shall be chosen.

4. The Vice-President of the United States shall be President of the Senate, but shall have no vote unless they be equally divided.

5. The Senate shall choose their other officers, and also a President *pro tempore*, in the absence of the Vice-President, or when he shall exercise the office of the President of the United States.

6. The Senate shall have the sole power to try all impeachments. When sitting for that purpose, they shall be on oath or affirmation. When the President of the United States is tried, the Chief Justice shall preside; and no person shall be convicted without the concurrence of two-thirds of the members present.

7. Judgment of case of impeachment shall not extend further than to removal from office, and disqualification to hold and enjoy any office of honour, trust, or profit under the United States; but the party convicted shall nevertheless be liable and subject to indictment, trial, judgment, and punishment, according to law.

Section 4

1. The times, places and manner of holding elections for Senators and Representatives shall be prescribed in each State by the Legislature thereof; but the Congress may at any time by law make or alter such regulations, except as to places of choosing Senators.

2. The Congress shall assemble at least once in every year, and such meeting shall be on the first Monday in December, unless they shall by law appoint a different day.

Section 5

1. Each House shall be the judge of the elections, returns, and qualifications of its own members, and a majority of each shall constitute a quorum to do business; but a smaller number may adjourn from day to day, and may be authorized to compel the attendance of absent members in such manner and under such penalties as each House may provide.

2. Each House may determine the rules of its proceedings, punish its members for disorderly behaviour, and with the concurrence of two-thirds, expel a member.

3. Each House shall keep a journal of its proceedings, and from time to time publish the same, excepting such parts as may in their judgment require secrecy; and the yeas and nays of the members of either House on any question shall, at the desire of one-fifth of those present, be entered on the journal.

4. Neither House, during the session of Congress shall, without the consent of the other, adjourn for more than three days, nor to any other place than that in which the two Houses shall be sitting.

Section 6

1. The Senators and Representatives shall receive a compensation for their services to be ascertained by law, and paid out of the Treasury of the United States. They shall in all cases, except treason, felony, and breach of the peace, be privileged from arrest during their attendance at the session of their respective Houses, and in going to and returning from the same; and for any speech or debate in either House they shall not be questioned in any other place.

2. No Senator or Representative shall, during the time for which he was elected, be appointed to any civil office under the authority of the United States which shall have been created, or the emoluments whereof shall have been increased during such time; and no person holding any office under the United States shall be a member of either House during his continuance in office.

Section 7

1. All bills for raising revenue shall originate in the House of Representatives, but the Senate may propose or concur with amendments, as on other bills.

2. Every bill which shall have passed the House of Representatives and the Senate shall, before it becomes a law, be presented to the President of the United States; if he approve, he shall sign it, but if not he shall return it, with his objections to that House in which it shall have originated, who shall enter the objections at large on their journal and proceed to reconsider it. If after such reconsideration two-thirds of that House shall agree to pass the bill, it shall be sent, together with the objections, to the other House, by which it shall likewise be reconsidered; and if approved by two-thirds of that House it shall become a law. But in such cases the votes of both Houses shall be determined by yeas and nays, and the names of the persons voting for and against the bill be entered on the journal of each House respectively. If any bill shall not be returned by the President within 10 days (Sundays excepted) after it shall have been presented to him the same shall be a law in like manner as if he had signed it, unless the Congress by their adjournment prevent its return; in which case it shall not be a law.

3. Every order, resolution, or vote to which the concurrence of the Senate and House of Representatives may be necessary (except on a question of adjournment) shall be presented to the President of the United States, and before the same shall take effect shall be approved by him, or being disapproved by him shall be repassed by two-thirds of the Senate and the House of Representatives, according to the rules and limitations prescribed in the case of a bill.

Section 8

1. The Congress shall have power

To lay and collect taxes, duties, imposts, and excises, to pay the debts and provide for the common defense and general welfare of the United States; but all duties, imposts, and excises shall be uniform throughout the United States.

2. To borrow money on the credit of the United States.

3. To regulate commerce with foreign nations; and among the several States and with the Indian tribes.

4. To establish a uniform rule of naturalization and uniform laws on the subject of bankruptcies throughout the United States.

5. To coin money, regulate the value thereof, and of foreign coin, and fix the standard of weights and measures.

6. To provide for the punishment of counterfeiting the securities and current coin of the United States.

7. To establish post-offices and post-roads.

8. To promote the progress of science and useful arts by securing for limited times to authors and inventors the exclusive rights to their respective writings and discoveries.

9. To constitute tribunals inferior to the Supreme Court.

10. To define and punish piracies and felonies committed on the high seas, and offences against the law of nations.

11. To declare war, grant letters of marque and reprisal, and make rules concerning captures on land and water.

12. To raise and support armies, but no appropriation of money to that use shall be for a longer term than two years.

13. To provide and maintain a navy.

14. To make rules for the government and regulation of the land and naval forces.

15. To provide for calling forth the militia to execute the laws of the Union, suppress insurrections, and repel invasions.

16. To provide for organizing, arming and disciplining the militia, and for governing such part of them as may be employed in the service of the United States, reserving to the States respectively the appointment of the officers, and the authority of training the militia according to the discipline prescribed by Congress.

17. To exercise exclusive legislation in all cases whatsoever over such district (not exceeding 10 miles square) as may, by cession of particular States and the acceptance of Congress, become the seat of Government of the United States and to exercise like authority over all places purchased by the consent of the Legislature of the State in which the same shall be, for the erection of forts, magazines, arsenals, dry-docks, and other needful buildings.

18. To make all laws which shall be necessary and proper for carrying into execution the foregoing powers and all other powers vested by this Constitution in the Government of the United States, or in any department or officer thereof.

Section 9

1. The migration or importation of such persons as any of the States now existing shall think proper to admit shall not be prohibited by the Congress prior to the year 1808, but a tax or duty may be imposed on such importations, not exceeding 10 dollars for each person.

2. The privilege of the writ of habeas corpus shall not be suspended, unless when in cases of rebellion or invasion the public safety may require it.

3. No bill or attainder or *ex post facto* law shall be passed.

4. No capitation or other direct tax shall be laid, unless in proportion to the census or enumeration hereinbefore directed to be taken.

5. No tax or duty shall be laid on articles exported from any State.

6. No preference shall be given by any regulation of commerce or revenue to the ports of one State over those of another, nor shall vessels bound to or from one State be obliged to enter, clear, or pay duties to another.

7. No money shall be drawn from the Treasury but in consequence of appropriations made by law; and a regular statement and account of the receipts and expenditures of all public money shall be published from time to time.

8. No title of nobility shall be granted by the United States. And no person holding any office of profit or trust under them shall, without the consent of the Congress, accept of any present, emolument, office, or title of any kind whatever from any king, prince, or foreign state.

THE UNITED STATES OF AMERICA

Section 10

1. No State shall enter into any treaty, alliance or confederation, grant letters of marque and reprisal, coin money, emit bills of credit, make anything but gold and silver coin a tender in payment of debts, pass any bill of attainder, *ex post facto* law, or law impairing the obligation of contracts, or grant any title of nobility.

2. No State shall, without the consent of the Congress, lay any impost or duties on imports or exports, except what may be absolutely necessary for executing its inspection laws, and the net produce of all duties and imposts, laid by any State on imports or exports, shall be for the use of the Treasury of the United States; and all such laws shall be subject to the revision and control of the Congress.

3. No State shall, without the consent of Congress, lay any duty of tonnage, keep troops or ships of war in time of peace, enter into agreement or compact with another State, or with a foreign power, or engage in war, unless actually invaded, or in such imminent danger as will not admit of delay.

ARTICLE II

Section 1

1. The Executive power shall be vested in a President of the United States of America. He shall hold his office during the term of four years, and, together with the Vice-President chosen for the same term, be elected as follows

2. Each State shall appoint, in such manner as the Legislature thereof may direct, a number of electors equal to the whole number of Senators and Representatives to which the State may be entitled in the Congress; but no Senator or Representative or person holding an office of trust or profit under the United States shall be appointed an elector.

3. The electors shall meet in their respective States and vote by ballot for two persons, of whom one at least shall not be an inhabitant of the same State with themselves. And they shall make a list of all the persons voted for, and of the number of votes for each, which list they shall sign and certify and transmit, sealed, to the seat of the Government of the United States, directed to the President of the Senate. The President of the Senate shall, in the presence of the Senate and House of Representatives, open all the certificates, and the votes shall then be counted. The person having the greatest number of votes shall be the President, if such number be a majority of the whole number of electors appointed, and if there be more than one who have such a majority, and have an equal number of votes, then the House of Representatives shall immediately choose by ballot one of them for President; and if no person have a majority, then from the five highest on the list the said House shall in like manner choose the President. But in choosing the President, the vote shall be taken by States, the representation from each State having one vote. A quorum, for this purpose, shall consist of a member or members from two-thirds of the States, and a majority of all the States shall be necessary to a choice. In every case, after the choice of the President, the person having the greatest number of votes of the electors shall be the Vice-President. But if there should remain two or more who have equal votes, the Senate shall choose from them by ballot the Vice-President.*

4. The Congress may determine the time of choosing the electors and the day on which they shall give their votes, which day shall be the same throughout the United States.

5. No person except a natural born citizen, or a citizen of the United States, at the time of the adoption of the Constitution, shall be eligible to the office of President; neither shall any person be eligible to that office who shall not have attained to the age of 35 years and been 14 years a resident within the United States.

6. In case of the removal of the President from office, or of his death, resignation, or inability to discharge the powers and duties of the said office, the same shall devolve on the Vice-President, and the Congress may by law provide for the case of removal, death, resignation, or inability, both of the President and Vice-President, declaring what officer shall then act as President, and such officer shall act accordingly until the disability be removed or a President shall be elected.†

7. The President shall, at stated times, receive for his services a compensation which shall neither be increased nor diminished during the period for which he shall have been elected, and he shall not receive within that period any other emolument from the United States, or any of them.

8. Before he enter on the execution of his office he shall take the following oath or affirmation:

'I do solemnly swear (or affirm) that I will faithfully execute the office of President of the United States, and will, to the best of my ability, preserve, protect, and defend the Constitution of the United States.'

* This clause is superseded by Amendment XII.
† This clause is amended by Amendments XX and XXV.

Section 2

1. The President shall be Commander-in-Chief of the Army and Navy of the United States, and of the militia of the several States when called into the actual service of the United States; he may require the opinion, in writing, of the principal officer in each of the executive departments upon any subject relating to the duties of their respective offices, and he shall have the power to grant reprieves and pardons for offences against the United States except in cases of impeachment.

2. He shall have power by and with the advice and consent of the Senate to make treaties, provided two-thirds of the Senators present concur; and he shall nominate and by and with the advice and consent of the Senate shall appoint ambassadors, other public ministers and consuls, judges of the Supreme Court, and all other officers of the United States whose appointments are not herein otherwise provided for, and which shall be established by law; but the Congress may by law vest the appointment of such inferior officers as they think proper in the President alone, in the courts of law, or in the heads of departments.

3. The President shall have power to fill up all vacancies that may happen during the recess of the Senate by granting commissions, which shall expire at the end of their next session.

Section 3

He shall from time to time give to the Congress information of the state of the Union, and recommend to their consideration such measures as he shall judge necessary and expedient; he may, on extraordinary occasions, convene both Houses, or either of them, and in case of disagreement between them with respect to the time of adjournment, he may adjourn them to such time as he shall think proper; he shall receive ambassadors and other public ministers; he shall take care that the laws be faithfully executed, and shall commission all the officers of the United States.

Section 4

The President, Vice-President, and all civil officers of the United States shall be removed from office on impeachment for conviction of treason, bribery or other high crimes and misdemeanours.

ARTICLE III

Section 1

The judicial power of the United States shall be vested in one Supreme Court, and in such inferior courts as the Congress may from time to time ordain and establish. The judges, both of the Supreme and inferior courts, shall hold their offices during good behaviour, and shall at stated times receive for their services a compensation which shall not be diminished during their continuance in office.

Section 2

1. The judicial power shall extend to all cases in law and equity arising under this Constitution, the laws of the United States, and treaties made, or which shall be made, under their authority; to all cases affecting ambassadors, other public ministers and consuls; to all cases of admiralty and maritime jurisdiction; to controversies to which the United States shall be a party; to controversies between two or more States, between a State and citizens of another State, between citizens of different States, between citizens of the same State claiming lands under grants of different States, and between a State, or the citizens thereof, and foreign States, citizens, or subjects.

2. In all cases affecting ambassadors, other public ministers, and consuls, and those in which a State shall be party, the Supreme Court shall have original jurisdiction. In all the other cases before mentioned the Supreme Court shall have appellate jurisdiction both as to law and fact, with such exceptions and under such regulations as the Congress shall make.

3. The trial of all crimes, except in cases of impeachment, shall be by jury, and such trials shall be held in the State where the said crimes shall have been committed; but when not committed within any State the trial shall be at such place or places as the Congress may by law have directed.

Section 3

1. Treason against the United States shall consist only in levying war against them, or in adhering to their enemies, giving them aid and comfort. No person shall be convicted of treason unless on the testimony of two witnesses to the same overt act, or on confession in open court.

2. The Congress shall have power to declare the punishment of treason, but no attainder of treason shall work corruption of blood, or forfeiture except during the life of the person attained.

THE UNITED STATES OF AMERICA

ARTICLE IV

Section 1

Full faith and credit shall be given in each State to the public acts, records, and judicial proceedings of every other State. And the Congress may by general laws prescribe the manner in which such acts, records, and proceedings shall be proved, and the effect thereof.

Section 2

1. The citizens of each State shall be entitled to all privileges and immunities of citizens in the several States.

2. A person charged in any State with treason, felony, or other crime, who shall flee from justice, and be found in another State, shall, on demand of the Executive authority of the State from which he fled, be delivered up, to be removed to the State having jurisdiction of the crime.

3. No person held to service or labour in one State, under the laws thereof, escaping into another shall in consequence of any law or regulation therein, be discharged from such service or labour, but shall be delivered up on claim of the party to whom such service or labour may be due.

Section 3

1. New States may be admitted by the Congress into this Union; but no new State shall be formed or erected within the jurisdiction of any other State, nor any State be formed by the junction of two or more States, or parts of States, without the consent of the Legislatures of the States concerned, as well as of the Congress.

2. The Congress shall have the power to dispose of and make all needful rules and regulations respecting the territory or other property belonging to the United States; and nothing in this Constitution shall be so construed as to prejudice any claims of the United States, or of any particular State.

Section 4

The United States shall guarantee to every State in this Union a Republican form of government, and shall protect each of them against invasion, and on application of the Legislature, or of the Executive (when the Legislature cannot be convened) against domestic violence.

ARTICLE V

The Congress, whenever two-thirds of both Houses shall deem it necessary, shall propose amendments to this Constitution, or, on the application of the Legislature of two-thirds of the several States, shall call a convention for proposing amendments, which in either case, shall be valid to all intents and purposes, as part of this Constitution, when ratified by the Legislature of three-fourths of the several States, or by conventions in three-fourths thereof, as the one or the other mode of ratification may be proposed by the Congress, provided that no amendment which may be made prior to the year 1808 shall in any manner affect the first and fourth clauses in the Ninth Section of the First Article; and that no State, without its consent, shall be deprived of its equal suffrage in the Senate.

ARTICLE VI

1. All debts contracted and engagements entered into before the adoption of this Constitution shall be as valid against the United States under this Constitution as under the Confederation.

2. This Constitution and the laws of the United States which shall be made in pursuance thereof and all treaties made, or which shall be made, under the authority of the United States, shall be the supreme law of the land, and the judges in every State shall be bound thereby, anything in the Constitution or laws of any State to the contrary notwithstanding.

3. The Senators and Representatives before mentioned, and the members of the several State Legislatures, and all executives and judicial officers, both of the United States and of the several States, shall be bound by oath or affirmation to support this Constitution; but no religious test shall ever be required as a qualification to any office or public trust under the United States.

ARTICLE VII

The ratification of the Conventions of nine States shall be sufficient for the establishment of this Constitution between the States so ratifying the same.

Amendments to the Constitution

Ten Original Amendments, in force 15 December 1791:

AMENDMENT I

Congress shall make no law respecting an establishment of religion, or prohibiting the free exercise thereof; or abridging the freedom of speech or of the Press; or the right of the people peaceably to assemble and to petition the Government for a redress of grievances.

AMENDMENT II

A well-regulated militia being necessary to the security of a free State, the right of the people to keep and bear arms shall not be infringed.

AMENDMENT III

No soldier shall, in time of peace, be quartered in any house without the consent of the owner, nor in time of war but in a manner to be prescribed by law.

AMENDMENT IV

The right of the people to be secure in their persons, houses, papers, and effects, against unreasonable searches and seizures, shall not be violated, and no warrants shall issue but upon probable cause, supported by oath or affirmation, and particularly describing the place to be searched, and the persons or things to be seized.

AMENDMENT V

No person shall be held to answer for a capital or other infamous crime unless on a presentment or indictment of a Grand Jury, except in cases arising in the land or naval forces, or in the militia, when in actual service, in time of war or public danger; nor shall any person be subject for the same offense to be twice put in jeopardy of life or limb; nor shall be compelled in any criminal case to be a witness against himself, nor be deprived of life, liberty, or property, without due process of law; nor shall private property be taken for public use without just compensation.

AMENDMENT VI

In all criminal prosecutions, the accused shall enjoy the right to a speedy and public trial, by an impartial jury of the State and district wherein the crime shall have been committed, which districts shall have been previously ascertained by law, and to be informed of the nature and cause of the accusation; to be confronted with the witnesses against him; to have compulsory process for obtaining witnesses in his favour, and to have the assistance of counsel for his defense.

AMENDMENT VII

In suits at common law, where the value in controversy shall exceed 20 dollars, the right of trial by jury shall be preserved, and no fact tried by a jury shall be otherwise re-examined in any court of the United States than according to the rules of the common law.

AMENDMENT VIII

Excessive bail shall not be required, nor excessive fines imposed, nor cruel and unusual punishments inflicted.

AMENDMENT IX

The enumeration in the Constitution of certain rights shall not be construed to deny or disparage others retained by the people.

AMENDMENT X

The powers not delegated to the United States by the Constitution, nor prohibited by it to the States, are reserved to the States respectively, or to the people.

Subsequent Amendments:

AMENDMENT XI

(became part of the Constitution February 1795)

The judicial power of the United States shall not be construed to extend to any suit in law or equity, commenced or prosecuted against one of the United States, by citizens of another State, or by citizens or subjects of any foreign State.

AMENDMENT XII

(ratified June 1804)

The Electors shall meet in their respective States, and vote by ballot for President and Vice-President, one of whom at least shall not be an inhabitant of the same State with themselves; they shall name in their ballots the person voted for as President, and in distinct ballots the person voted for as Vice-President; and they shall make distinct list of all persons voted for as President, and of all persons voted for as Vice-President, and of the number of votes for each, which list they shall sign and certify, and transmit, sealed, to the seat of the Government of the United States, directed to the President of the Senate; the President of the Senate shall, in the presence of the Senate and House of Representatives, open all the certificates and the votes shall then be counted; the person having the greatest number of votes for President shall be the President, if such number be a majority of the whole number of Electors appointed; and if no person have such majority, then from the persons having the highest number, not exceeding three, on the list of those voted for as President, the House of Representatives shall choose immediately, by ballot, the President. But in choosing the President, the votes shall be taken by States, the representation from each State having one vote; a quorum for this purpose shall consist of a member or members from two-thirds of the States, and a majority of all the States shall be necessary to a choice. And if the House of Representatives shall not choose a President, whenever the right of choice shall devolve upon them, before the fourth day of March next following, then the Vice-President shall act as President, as in the case of the death or other constitutional disability of the President. The person having the greatest number of votes as Vice-President shall be the Vice-President if such number be a majority of the whole number of Electors appointed, and if no person have a majority, then, from the two highest numbers on the list the Senate shall choose the Vice-President; a quorum for the purpose shall consist of two-thirds of the whole number of Senators, and a majority of the whole number shall be necessary to a choice. But no person constitutionally ineligible to the office of President shall be eligible to that of Vice-President of the United States.

AMENDMENT XIII
(ratified December 1865)

1. Neither slavery nor involuntary servitude, except as a punishment for crime whereof the party shall have been duly convicted, shall exist within the United States, or any place subject to their jurisdiction.

2. Congress shall have the power to enforce this article by appropriate legislation.

AMENDMENT XIV
(ratified July 1868)

1. All persons born or naturalized in the United States, and subject to the jurisdiction thereof, are citizens of the United States and of the State wherein they reside. No State shall make or enforce any law which shall abridge the privileges or immunities of citizens of the United States, nor shall any State deprive any person of life, liberty, or property without due process of law, nor deny to any person within its jurisdiction the equal protection of the laws.

2. Representatives shall be apportioned among the several States according to their respective numbers, counting the whole number of persons in each State excluding Indians not taxed. But when the right to vote at any election for the choice of Electors for President and Vice-President of the United States, Representatives in Congress, the executive and judicial officers of a State, or the members of the Legislature thereof, is denied to any of the male inhabitants of such State, being 21 years of age, and citizens of the United States, or in any way abridged, except for participation in rebellion, or other crime, the basis of representation therein shall be reduced in the proportion which the number of such male citizens shall bear to the whole number of male citizens 21 years of age in such State.

3. No person shall be a Senator or Representative in Congress, or Elector of President and Vice-President or hold any office, civil or military, under the United States, or under any State, who, having previously taken an oath as member of Congress or as an officer of the United States, or as a member of any State Legislature, or as an executive or judicial officer of any State, to support the Constitution of the United States, shall have engaged in insurrection or rebellion against the same, or given aid and comfort to the enemies thereof. But Congress may, by vote of two-thirds of each House, remove such disability.

4. The validity of the public debt of the United States, authorized by law, including debts incurred for payment of pensions and bounties for services in suppressing insurrection and rebellion, shall not be questioned. But neither the United States nor any State shall assume or pay any debt or obligation incurred in aid of insurrection or rebellion against the United States, or any claim for the loss or emancipation of any slave; but all such debts, obligations, and claims shall be held illegal and void.

5. The Congress shall have power to enforce by appropriate legislation the provisions of this article.

AMENDMENT XV
(ratified March 1870)

1. The right of the citizens of the United States to vote shall not be denied or abridged by the United States or by any State on account of race, colour, or previous condition of servitude.

2. The Congress shall have power to enforce the provisions of this article by appropriate legislation.

AMENDMENT XVI
(ratified February 1913)

The Congress shall have power to lay and collect taxes on incomes, from whatever sources derived, without apportionment among the several States, and without regard to any census or enumeration.

AMENDMENT XVII
(ratified May 1913)

1. The Senate of the United States shall be composed of two Senators from each State, elected by the people thereof, for six years; and each Senator shall have one vote. The electors in each State shall have the qualifications requisite for electors of the most numerous branch of the State Legislature.

2. When vacancies happen in the representation of any State in the Senate, the executive authority of such State shall issue writs of election to fill such vacancies: provided that the Legislature of any State may empower the Executive thereof to make temporary appointment until the people fill the vacancies by election as the Legislature may direct.

3. This amendment shall not be so construed as to affect the election or term of any Senator chosen before it becomes valid as part of the Constitution.

AMENDMENT XVIII
(ratified January 1919*)

1. After one year from the ratification of this article the manufacture, sale, or transportation of intoxicating liquors within, the importation thereof into, or the exportation thereof from the United States, and all territory subject to the jurisdiction thereof for beverage purposes is hereby prohibited.

2. The Congress and the several States shall have concurrent power to enforce this article by appropriate legislation.

3. This article shall be inoperative unless it shall have been ratified as an amendment to the Constitution by the Legislatures of the several States, as provided in the Constitution, within seven years from the date of the submission hereof to the States by the Congress.
* Repealed by Amendment XXI.

AMENDMENT XIX
(ratified August 1920)

1. The right of citizens of the United States to vote shall not be denied or abridged by the United States or by any State on account of sex.

2. Congress shall have power, by appropriate legislation to enforce the provisions of this article.

AMENDMENT XX
(ratified January 1933)

Section 1
The terms of the President and Vice-President shall end at noon on the 20th day of January, and the terms of Senators and Representatives at noon on the third day of January, of the years in which such terms would have ended if this article had not been ratified; and the terms of their successors shall then begin.

Section 2
The Congress shall assemble at least once in every year, and such meetings shall begin at noon on the third day of January, unless they shall by law appoint a different day.

Section 3
If, at the time fixed for the beginning of the term of the President, the President elect shall have died, the Vice-President elect shall become President. If a President shall not have been chosen before the time fixed for the beginning of his term, or if the President elect shall have failed to qualify, then the Vice-President elect shall act as President until a President shall have qualified; and the Congress may by law provide for the case wherein neither a President elect nor a Vice-President elect shall have qualified, declaring who shall then act as President, or the manner in which one who is to act shall be selected, and such person shall act accordingly until a President or Vice-President shall have qualified.

Section 4
The Congress may by law provide for the case of the death of any of the persons from whom the House of Representatives may choose a President whenever the right of choice shall have devolved upon them, and for the case of the death of any of the persons from whom the Senate may choose a Vice-President whenever the right of choice shall have devolved upon them.

Section 5
Sections 1 and 2 shall take effect on the 15th day of October following the ratification of this article.

THE UNITED STATES OF AMERICA

Section 6
This article shall be inoperative unless it shall have been ratified as an amendment to the Constitution by the legislature of three-fourths of the several States within seven years from the date of its submission.

AMENDMENT XXI
(ratified December 1933)

Section 1
The 18th article of amendment to the Constitution of the United States is hereby repealed.

Section 2
The transportation or importation into any State, Territory or Possession of the United States for delivery or use therein of intoxicating liquors, in violation of the laws thereof, is hereby prohibited.

Section 3
This article shall be inoperative unless it shall have been ratified as an amendment to the Constitution by conventions in the several States, as provided in the Constitution, within seven years from the date of the submission hereof to the States by the Congress.

AMENDMENT XXII
(ratified February 1951)

No person shall be elected to the office of President more than twice, and no person who has held the office of President, or acted as President, for more than two years of a term to which some other person was elected President shall be elected to the office of President more than once. But this article shall not apply to any person holding the office of President when this Article was proposed by Congress, and shall not prevent any person who may be holding the office of President, or acting as President, during the term within which this Article becomes operative from holding the office of President or acting as President during the remainder of such term.

AMENDMENT XXIII
(ratified March 1961)

Section 1
The District constituting the seat of Government of the United States shall appoint in such manner as the Congress may direct:

A number of electors of President and Vice-President equal to the whole number of Senators and Representatives in Congress to which the District would be entitled if it were a State, but in no event more than the least populous State; they shall be in addition to those appointed by the States, but they shall be considered, for the purposes of the election of President and Vice-President, to be electors appointed by a State; and they shall meet in the District and perform such duties as provided by the 12th article of amendment.

Section 2
The Congress shall have power to enforce this article by appropriate legislation.

AMENDMENT XXIV
(ratified January 1964)

Section 1
The right of citizens of the United States to vote in any primary or other election for President or Vice-President, for electors for President or Vice-President, or for Senator or Representative in Congress, shall not be denied or abridged by the United States or any State by reason of failure to pay any poll tax or other tax.

Section 2
The Congress shall have power to enforce this article by appropriate legislation.

AMENDMENT XXV
(ratified February 1967)

Section 1
In the case of the removal of the President from office or of his death or resignation, the Vice-President shall become President.

Section 2
Whenever there is a vacancy in the office of the Vice-President, the President shall nominate a Vice-President who shall take office upon confirmation by a majority vote of both Houses of Congress.

Section 3
Whenever the President transmits to the President *pro tempore* of the Senate and the Speaker of the House of Representatives his written declaration that he is unable to discharge the powers and duties of his office, and until he transmits to them a written declaration to the contrary, such powers and duties shall be discharged by the Vice-President as Acting President.

Section 4
Whenever the Vice-President and a majority of either the principal officers of the executive departments or of such other body as Congress may by law provide, transmit to the President *pro tempore* of the Senate and the Speaker of the House of Representatives their written declaration that the President is unable to discharge the powers and duties of his office, the Vice-President shall immediately assume the powers and duties of the office as Acting President.

Thereafter, when the President transmits to the President *pro tempore* of the Senate and the Speaker of the House of Representatives his written declaration that no inability exists, he shall resume the powers and duties of his office unless the Vice-President and a majority of either the principal officers of the executive department or of such other body as Congress may by law provide, transmit within four days to the President *pro tempore* of the Senate and the Speaker of the House of Representatives their written declaration that the President is unable to discharge the powers and duties of his office. Thereupon Congress shall decide the issue, assembling within 48 hours for that purpose if not in session. If the Congress, within 21 days after receipt of the latter written declaration, or, if Congress is not in session, within 21 days after Congress is required to assemble, determines by two-thirds vote of both Houses that the President is unable to discharge the powers and duties of his office, the Vice-President shall continue to discharge the same as Acting President; otherwise, the President shall resume the powers and duties of his office.

AMENDMENT XXVI
(ratified July 1971)

Section 1
The right of citizens of the United States, who are 18 years of age or older, to vote shall not be denied or abridged by the United States or by any State on account of age.

Section 2
The Congress shall have power to enforce this article by appropriate legislation.

AMENDMENT XXVII
(ratified May 1992)

No law, varying the compensation for the services of the Senators and Representatives, shall take effect, until an election of Representatives shall have intervened.

By Article IV, Section 3 of the Constitution, implemented by vote of Congress and referendum in the territory concerned, Alaska was admitted into the United States on 3 January 1959, and Hawaii on 21 August 1959.

The Executive

HEAD OF STATE

President: GEORGE W. BUSH (took office 20 January 2001; re-elected 2 November 2004).
Vice-President: RICHARD B. CHENEY.

THE CABINET
(April 2006)

Secretary of State: Dr CONDOLEEZZA RICE.
Secretary of the Treasury: JOHN W. SNOW.
Secretary of Defense: DONALD H. RUMSFELD.
Attorney-General: ALBERTO R. GONZALES.
Secretary of the Interior: LYNN SCARLETT (acting).
Secretary of Agriculture: MIKE JOHANNS.
Secretary of Commerce: CARLOS GUTIERREZ.
Secretary of Labor: ELAINE L. CHAO.
Secretary of Health and Human Services: MICHAEL O. LEAVITT.
Secretary of Homeland Security: MICHAEL CHERTOFF.
Secretary of Housing and Urban Development: ALPHONSO R. JACKSON.

THE UNITED STATES OF AMERICA

Secretary of Transportation: NORMAN Y. MINETA.
Secretary of Energy: SAMUEL W. BODMAN.
Secretary of Education: MARGARET SPELLINGS.
Secretary of Veterans Affairs: JIM NICHOLSON.

Officials with Cabinet Rank

Vice-President: RICHARD B. CHENEY.
Chief of Staff to the President: JOSHUA B. BOLTEN.
Director of the Office of Management and Budget: ROBERT J. PORTMAN (designate).
US Trade Representative: SUSAN SCHWAB (designate).
Administrator of the Environmental Protection Agency: STEPHEN L. JOHNSON.
Director of the Office of National Drug Control Policy: JOHN P. WALTERS.
Director of National Intelligence: JOHN D. NEGROPONTE.

GOVERNMENT DEPARTMENTS

Department of Agriculture: 1400 Independence Ave, SW, Washington, DC 20250; tel. (202) 720-2791; fax (202) 720-6314; internet www.usda.gov; f. 1889.
Department of Commerce: 1400 Constitution Ave, NW, Washington, DC 20230-0001; tel. (202) 219-3605; fax (202) 219-4247; e-mail cgutierrez@doc.gov; internet www.doc.gov; f. 1913.
Department of Defense: 1000 Defense Pentagon, Washington, DC 20301; tel. (703) 428-0711; fax (703) 428-1982; internet www.defenselink.mil; f. 1947.
Department of Education: 400 Maryland Ave, SW, Washington, DC 20202; tel. (202) 401-2000; fax (202) 401-0596; internet www.ed.gov; f. 1979.
Department of Energy: Forrestal Bldg, 1000 Independence Ave, SW, Washington, DC 20585; tel. (202) 586-5000; fax (202) 586-4403; internet www.energy.gov; f. 1977.
Department of Health and Human Services: 200 Independence Ave, SW, Washington, DC 20201; tel. (202) 690-6343; internet www.os.dhhs.gov; f. 1980.
Department of Homeland Security: 1600 Pennsylvania Ave, NW, Washington, DC 20528; tel. (202) 282-8000; e-mail john.minnick@dhs.gov; internet www.dhs.gov; f. 2002.
Department of Housing and Urban Development: 451 Seventh St, SW, Washington, DC 20410; tel. (202) 708-1112; fax (202) 708-0299; internet www.hud.gov; f. 1965.
Department of the Interior: 1849 C St, NW, Washington, DC 20240; tel. (202) 208-3100; fax (202) 208-5048; internet www.doi.gov; f. 1849.
Department of Justice: 950 Pennsylvania Ave, NW, Washington, DC 20530-0001; tel. (202) 514-2000; fax (202) 307-6777; e-mail askdoj@usdoj.gov; internet www.usdoj.gov; f. 1870; incl. the Office of the Attorney-Gen.
Department of Labor: Frances Perkins Bldg, 200 Constitution Ave, NW, Washington, DC 20210; tel. (202) 219-7316; fax (202) 693-6111; internet www.dol.gov; f. 1913.
Department of State: 2201 C St, NW, Washington, DC 20520; tel. (202) 647-4000; fax (202) 647-6738; internet www.state.gov; f. 1789.
Department of Transportation: 400 Seventh St, SW, Washington, DC 20590; tel. (202) 366-4000; fax (202) 366-7202; e-mail dot.comments@dot.gov; internet www.dot.gov; f. 1967.
Department of the Treasury: 1500 Pennsylvania Ave, NW, Washington, DC 20220; tel. (202) 622-2000; fax (202) 622-6415; internet www.ustreas.gov; f. 1789.
Department of Veterans Affairs: 810 Vermont Ave, NW, Washington, DC 20420; tel. (202) 273-6000; internet www.va.gov; f. 1989.

EXECUTIVE OFFICE OF THE PRESIDENT

The White House Office: 1600 Pennsylvania Ave, NW, Washington, DC 20500; tel. (202) 456-1414; fax (202) 456-2461; e-mail vice_president@whitehouse.gov; internet www.whitehouse.gov; co-ordinates activities relating to the President's immediate office; Chief of Staff to the Pres. JOSHUA B. BOLTEN.
Central Intelligence Agency: Office of Public Affairs, Washington, DC 20505; tel. (703) 482-0623; fax (703) 482-1739; internet www.cia.gov; f. 1947; Dir Lt-Gen. MICHAEL HAYDEN (designate).
Council of Economic Advisers: Eisenhower Executive Office Bldg, 17th St and Pennsylvania Ave, NW, Washington, DC 20502; tel. (202) 395-5042; fax (202) 395-6958; internet www.whitehouse.gov/cea; f. 1946; Chair. Dr EDWARD LAZEAR.
Council on Environmental Quality: 722 Jackson Pl., Washington, DC 20503; tel. (202) 395-5750; fax (202) 456-6546; internet www.whitehouse.gov/ceq; f. 1969; Chair. JAMES L. CONNAUGHTON.
National Security Council: Eisenhower Executive Office Bldg, 17th St and Pennsylvania Ave, NW, Washington, DC 20504; tel. (202) 456-9371; internet www.whitehouse.gov/nsc; f. 1947; Asst to the Pres. for Nat. Security Affairs STEPHEN J. HADLEY.
Office of Administration: Eisenhower Executive Office Bldg, 17th St and Pennsylvania Ave, NW, Washington, DC 20503; tel. (202) 395-7235; fax (202) 456-6512; internet www.whitehouse.gov/oa; f. 1977; Dir (vacant).
Office of Faith-Based and Community Initiatives: The White House, Washington, DC 20502; tel. (202) 456-6708; fax (202) 456-7019; internet www.fbci.gov; f. 2001; Dir (vacant).
Office of Management and Budget: 725 17th St and Pennsylvania Ave, NW Washington, DC 20503; tel. (202) 395-3080; fax (202) 395-3888; internet www.whitehouse.gov/omb; Dir ROBERT J. PORTMAN (designate).
Office of National AIDS Policy: The White House, Rm 464 EEOB, Washington, DC 20502; tel. (202) 456-7320; fax (202) 456-7315; internet www.whitehouse.gov/onap/aids.html; Dir CAROL THOMPSON.
Office of National Drug Control Policy: 750 17th St, NW, Washington, DC 20006POB 6000, Rockville, MD 20849-6000; tel. (202) 395-6700; fax (202) 395-6708; e-mail ondcp@ncjrs.gov; internet www.whitehousedrugpolicy.gov; f. 1988; Dir JOHN P. WALTERS.
Office of Policy Development: Executive Office of the President, 1600 Pennsylvania Ave, NW, Washington, DC 20500; tel. (202) 456-6515; fax (202) 456-2878; internet www.whitehouse.gov/dpc; f. 1970; composed of the Domestic Policy Council (f. 1993) and the Nat. Economic Council; Asst to the Pres. for Economic Policy and Dir of the Nat. Economic Council ALLAN B. HUBBARD.
Office of Science and Technology Policy: 725 17th St, Rm 5228, NW, Washington, DC 20502; tel. (202) 456-7116; fax (202) 456-6021; e-mail info@ostp.gov; internet www.ostp.gov; f. 1976; Dir JOHN H. MARBURGER, III.
Office of the United States Trade Representative: Winder Bldg, 600 17th St, NW, Washington, DC 20508; tel. (202) 395-3230; fax (202) 395-4549; e-mail contactustr@ustr.eop.gov; internet www.ustr.gov; f. 1963; US Trade Rep. SUSAN SCHWAB (designate).
United States Mission to the United Nations: 799 United Nations Plaza, New York, NY 10017; tel. (212) 415-4404; fax (212) 415-4303; e-mail usa@un.int; internet www.un.int/usa; US Ambassador to the United Nations JOHN BOLTON.
USA Freedom Corps: 1600 Pennsylvania Ave, NW, Washington, DC 20500; e-mail info@usafreedomcorps.gov; internet www.usafreedomcorps.gov; f. 2002; Dir DESIREE T. SAYLE.
White House Military Office: Executive Office of the President, 1600 Pennsylvania Ave, NW, Washington, DC 20500; internet www.whitehouse.gov/whmo; areas of responsibility incl. Camp David (f. 1942) and Air Force One (f. 1962); Dir Rear-Adm. MARK I. FOX.

President and Legislature

PRESIDENT

Election, 2 November 2004

	Popular votes	% of Popular votes	Electoral College votes
George W. Bush (Republican)	61,872,711	50.57	286
John F. Kerry (Democrat)	58,894,584	48.14	252
Others*	1,582,185	1.29	—
Total	122,349,480	100.00	538

* Including write-in candidates, etc.

CONGRESS

Senate
(April 2006)

The Senate comprises 100 members. Senators' terms are for six years, one-third of the Senate being elected every two years.

President of the Senate: Vice-President RICHARD B. CHENEY.
President Pro Tempore: TED STEVENS.
Republicans: 55 seats.

THE UNITED STATES OF AMERICA

Democrats: 44 seats.
Independent: 1 seat.
Majority Leader: William H. Frist.
Minority Leader: Harry M. Reid.

Members
(With political party and year in which term expires—on 3 January in all cases)

Alabama		
Jeff Sessions	Rep.	2009
Richard C. Shelby	Rep.	2011
Alaska		
Ted Stevens	Rep.	2009
Lisa Murkowski	Rep.	2011
Arizona		
Jon Kyl	Rep.	2007
John McCain	Rep.	2011
Arkansas		
Mark Pryor	Dem.	2009
Blanche Lincoln	Dem.	2011
California		
Dianne Feinstein	Dem.	2007
Barbara Boxer	Dem.	2011
Colorado		
Wayne Allard	Rep.	2009
Ken Salazar	Dem.	2011
Connecticut		
Joe Lieberman	Dem.	2007
Chris Dodd	Dem.	2011
Delaware		
Thomas Carper	Dem.	2007
Joseph R. Biden, Jr	Dem.	2009
Florida		
Bill Nelson	Dem.	2007
Mel Martinez	Rep.	2011
Georgia		
Saxby Chambliss	Rep.	2009
Johnny Isakson	Rep.	2011
Hawaii		
Daniel K. Akaka	Dem.	2007
Daniel K. Inouye	Dem.	2011
Idaho		
Larry E. Craig	Rep.	2009
Michael Crapo	Rep.	2011
Illinois		
Richard J. Durbin	Dem.	2009
Barack Obama	Dem.	2011
Indiana		
Richard G. Lugar	Rep.	2007
Evan Bayh	Dem.	2011
Iowa		
Tom Harkin	Dem.	2009
Chuck Grassley	Rep.	2011
Kansas		
Pat Roberts	Rep.	2009
Sam Brownback	Rep.	2011
Kentucky		
Mitch McConnell	Rep.	2009
Jim Bunning	Rep.	2011
Louisiana		
Mary L. Landrieu	Dem.	2009
David Vitter	Rep.	2011
Maine		
Olympia J. Snowe	Rep.	2007
Susan M. Collins	Rep.	2009
Maryland		
Paul S. Sarbanes	Dem.	2007
Barbara Mikulski	Dem.	2011
Massachusetts		
Edward M. Kennedy	Dem.	2007
John F. Kerry	Dem.	2009
Michigan		
Debbie Stabenow	Dem.	2007
Carl Levin	Dem.	2009
Minnesota		
Mark Dayton	Dem.	2007
Norm Coleman	Rep.	2009
Mississippi		
Trent Lott	Rep.	2007
Thad Cochran	Rep.	2009
Missouri		
Jim Talent	Rep.	2009
Kit Bond	Rep.	2011
Montana		
Conrad Burns	Rep.	2007
Max Baucus	Dem.	2009
Nebraska		
Ben Nelson	Dem.	2007
Chuck Hagel	Rep.	2009
Nevada		
John Ensign	Rep.	2007
Harry M. Reid	Dem.	2011
New Hampshire		
John E. Sununu	Rep.	2009
Judd Gregg	Rep.	2011
New Jersey		
Robert Menéndez	Dem.	2007
Frank R. Lautenberg	Dem.	2009
New Mexico		
Jeff Bingaman	Dem.	2007
Pete V. Domenici	Rep.	2009
New York		
Hillary Rodham Clinton	Dem.	2007
Charles E. Schumer	Dem.	2011
North Carolina		
Elizabeth Dole	Rep.	2009
Richard Burr	Rep.	2011
North Dakota		
Kent Conrad	Dem.	2007
Byron L. Dorgan	Dem.	2011
Ohio		
Mike DeWine	Rep.	2007
George V. Voinovich	Rep.	2011
Oklahoma		
James M. Inhofe	Rep.	2009
Tom Coburn	Rep.	2011
Oregon		
Gordon Smith	Rep.	2009
Ronald L. Wyden	Dem.	2011
Pennsylvania		
Rick Santorum	Rep.	2007
Arlen Specter	Rep.	2011
Rhode Island		
Lincoln Chafee	Rep.	2007
Jack Reed	Dem.	2009
South Carolina		
Lindsey Graham	Rep.	2009
Jim DeMint	Rep.	2011
South Dakota		
Tim Johnson	Dem.	2009
John Thune	Rep.	2011
Tennessee		
Bill Frist	Rep.	2007
Lamar Alexander	Rep.	2009
Texas		
Kay Bailey Hutchison	Rep.	2007
John Cornyn	Rep.	2009
Utah		
Orrin G. Hatch	Rep.	2007
Bob. Bennett	Rep.	2011
Vermont		
Jim Jeffords	Ind.	2007
Patrick J. Leahy	Dem.	2011
Virginia		
George Allen	Rep.	2007
John W. Warner	Rep.	2009

THE UNITED STATES OF AMERICA

Washington
| Maria Cantwell | Dem. | 2007 |
| Patty Murray | Dem. | 2011 |

West Virginia
| Robert C. Byrd | Dem. | 2007 |
| Jay Rockefeller, IV | Dem. | 2009 |

Wisconsin
| Herb Kohl | Dem. | 2007 |
| Russell D. Feingold | Dem. | 2011 |

Wyoming
| Craig Thomas | Rep. | 2007 |
| Mike Enzi | Rep. | 2009 |

House of Representatives
(April 2006)

A new House of Representatives, comprising 435 members, is elected every two years.

Speaker: J. DENNIS HASTERT.
Republicans: 230 seats.
Democrats: 201 seats.
Independent: 1 seat.
Vacant: 3 seats.
Majority Leader: JOHN BOEHNER.
Minority Leader: NANCY PELOSI.

Election Commission

Federal Election Commission: 999 E St, NW, Washington, DC 20463; tel. (202) 694-1100; fax (202) 219-3880; e-mail webmaster@fec.gov; internet www.fec.gov; f. 1975; independent; Chair. MICHAEL E. TONER.

Independent Agencies

Advisory Council on Historic Preservation: 1100 Pennsylvania Ave, NW, Suite 809, Old Post Office Bldg, Washington, DC 20004; tel. (202) 606-8503; e-mail achp@achp.gov; internet www.achp.gov; f. 1966; Chair. JOHN L. NAU, III; Exec. Dir JOHN M. FOWLER.

African Development Foundation: 1400 Eye St, NW, 10th Floor, Washington, DC 20005-2248; tel. (202) 673-3916; fax (202) 673-3810; e-mail info@adf.gov; internet www.adf.gov; Chair. EDWARD ('WARD') BREHM.

American Battle Monuments Commission: Courthouse Plaza II, Suite 500, 2300 Clarendon Blvd, Arlington, VA 22201-3367; tel. (703) 696-6900; fax (703) 696-6666; internet www.abmc.gov; f. 1923; Chair. Gen. (retd) FREDERICK M. FRANKS, Jr; Sec. and CEO Brig.-Gen. (retd) JOHN W. NICHOLSON.

Appalachian Regional Commission: 1666 Connecticut Ave, NW, Washington, DC 20009-1068; tel. (202) 884-7700; fax (202) 884-7682; e-mail crea@arc.gov; internet www.arc.gov; f. 1965; Fed. Co-Chair. ANNE B. POPE; Alt. Fed. Co-Chair. RICHARD J. PELTZ.

Commission on Civil Rights: 624 Ninth St, NW, Washington, DC 20425; tel. (202) 376-8312; fax (202) 376-7672; e-mail wwwadmin@usccr.gov; internet www.usccr.gov; f. 1957; Chair. GERALD A. REYNOLDS.

Commission of Fine Arts: National Bldg Museum, Suite 312, 401 F St, NW, Washington, DC 20001-2728; tel. (202) 504-2200; fax (202) 504-2195; e-mail staff@cfa.gov; internet www.cfa.gov; f. 1910; Chair. EARL A. POWELL, III.

Commodity Futures Trading Commission (CFTC): 3 Lafayette Centre, 1155 21st St, NW, Washington, DC 20581; tel. (202) 418-5000; fax (202) 418-5521; internet www.cftc.gov; f. 1974; Chair. REUBEN JEFFERY, III.

Corporation for National and Community Service (CNS): 1201 New York Ave, NW, Washington, DC 20525; tel. (202) 606-5000; fax (202) 565-2799; internet www.nationalservice.gov; CEO DAVID EISNER.

Defense Nuclear Facilities Safety Board: 625 Indiana Ave, NW, Washington, DC 20004-2901; tel. (202) 694-7088; fax (202) 208-6518; e-mail mailbox@dnfsb.gov; internet www.dnfsb.gov; f. 1988; Chair. Dr A. J. EGGENBERGER.

Environmental Protection Agency: Ariel Rios Bldg, 1200 Pennsylvania Ave, NW, Washington, DC 20460; tel. (202) 272-0167; internet www.epa.gov; f. 1970; Admin. STEPHEN L. JOHNSON.

Equal Employment Opportunity Commission: 1801 L St, NW, Washington, DC 20507; tel. (202) 663-4900; fax (202) 663-4110; internet www.eeoc.gov; f. 1965; Chair. CARI M. DOMINGUEZ.

Export-Import Bank of the United States (Ex-Im Bank): see Finance—Banking.

Farm Credit Administration (FCA): 1501 Farm Credit Dr., McLean, VA 22102-5090; tel. (703) 883-4000; fax (703) 790-3260; e-mail info-line@fca.gov; internet www.fca.gov; f. 1933; Chair. and CEO NANCY C. PELLET.

Federal Communications Commission: see Broadcasting and Communications.

Federal Deposit Insurance Corporation (FDIC): 550 17th St, NW, Washington, DC 20429; tel. (202) 736-0000; internet www.fdic.gov; f. 1933; Chair. MARTIN J. GRUENBERG (acting); Dir THOMAS J. CURRY.

Federal Election Commission: see Election Commission.

Federal Emergency Management Agency: Federal Center Plaza, 500 C St, SW, Washington, DC 20472; tel. (202) 646-4600; fax (202) 646-2531; internet www.fema.gov; f. 1979; part of the Dept of Homeland Security; Dir R. DAVID PAULISON (acting).

Federal Housing Finance Board: 1777 F St, NW, Washington, DC 20006; tel. (202) 408-2500; fax (202) 408-1435; e-mail fhfb@fhfb.gov; internet www.fhfb.gov; Chair. DONALD A. ROSENFELD.

Federal Labor Relations Authority (FLRA): 1400 K St, 2nd Floor, NW, Washington, DC 20424-0001; tel. (202) 218-7910; fax (202) 482-6608; internet www.flra.gov; f. 1978; Chair. DALE CABANISS.

Federal Maritime Commission: see Transport—Ocean Shipping.

Federal Mediation and Conciliation Service: 2100 K St, NW, Washington, DC 20427; tel. (202) 606-8100; fax (202) 606-4251; internet www.fmcs.gov; f. 1947; Dir ARTHUR F. ROSENFELD.

Federal Reserve System: see Finance—Banking.

Federal Retirement Thrift Investment Board (FRTIB): 1250 H St, NW, Washington, DC 20005; tel. (202) 942-1600; fax (202) 942-1676; internet www.frtib.gov; f. 1986; Exec. Dir GARY A. AMELIO.

Federal Trade Commission: 600 Pennsylvania, NW, Washington, DC 20580; tel. (202) 326-2222; fax (202) 326-2396; internet www.ftc.gov; f. 1914; Chair. DEBORAH PLATT MAJORAS.

General Services Administration: 1800 F St, NW, Washington, DC 20405; tel. (202) 501-1231; fax (202) 501-1489; internet www.gsa.gov; f. 1949; Admin. DAVID L. BIBB (acting).

Inter-American Foundation: 901 North Stuart St, 10th Floor, Arlington, VA 22203; tel. (703) 306-4319; fax (703) 306-4365; e-mail info@iaf.gov; internet www.iaf.gov; f. 1969; provides grants to non-governmental and community-based orgs in Latin America and the Caribbean; Chair. ROGER W. WALLACE.

Medicare Payment Advisory Commission (MedPAC): 600 New Jersey Ave, NW, Washington, DC 2001; tel. (202) 220-3700; e-mail webmaster@medpac.gov; internet www.medpac.gov; Chair. GLENN M. HACKBARTH.

Merit Systems Protection Board: 1615 M St, NW, Washington, DC 20419; tel. (202) 653-7200; fax (202) 653-7130; e-mail mspb@mspb.gov; internet www.mspb.gov; f. 1979; Chair. NEIL A. G. MCPHIE.

National Aeronautics and Space Administration (NASA): 2 Independence Sq., 300 E St, SW, Washington, DC 20546; tel. (202) 358-2345; fax (202) 358-2810; internet www.hq.nasa.gov; f. 1958; Admin. MICHAEL D. GRIFFIN.

National Archives and Records Administration: 8601 Adelphi Rd, College Park, MD 20740-6001; tel. (301) 837-1600; fax (301) 837-3218; internet www.archives.gov; f. 1934; Archivist of the United States ALLEN WEINSTEIN.

National Capital Planning Commission: 401 Ninth St, NW, Suite 500 North Lobby, Washington, DC 20004; tel. (202) 482-7200; fax (202) 482-7272; e-mail info@ncpc.gov; internet www.ncpc.gov; f. 1924; Chair. JOHN V. COGBILL, III.

National Commission on Libraries and Information Science: 1800 M St, NW, Suite 350 North Tower, Washington, DC 20036; tel. (202) 606-9200; fax (202) 606-9203; e-mail info@nclis.gov; internet www.nclis.gov; f. 1970; Chair. BETH FITZSIMMONS.

National Council on Disability: 1331 F St, NW, Washington, DC 20004-1107; tel. (202) 272-2004; fax (202) 272-2022; internet www.ncd.gov; f. 1990; Chair. LEX FRIEDEN.

National Credit Union Administration: 1775 Duke St, Alexandria, VA 22314-3428; tel. (703) 518-6330; fax (703) 518-6319; e-mail boardmail@ncua.gov; internet www.ncua.gov; f. 1970; Chair. JoAnn Johnson.

National Endowment for the Arts: 1100 Pennsylvania Ave, NW, Washington, DC 20506; tel. (202) 682-5400; fax (202) 682-5611; e-mail webmgr@arts.gov; internet www.arts.gov; f. 1965; Chair. Dana Gioia.

National Endowment for the Humanities: 1100 Pennsylvania Ave, NW, Rm 503, Washington, DC 20506; tel. (202) 606-8310; e-mail info@neh.gov; internet www.neh.gov; f. 1965; Chair. Bruce Cole.

National Labor Relations Board: 1099 14th St, NW, Washington, DC 20570-0001; tel. (202) 273-1991; fax (202) 273-4266; internet www.nlrb.gov; f. 1935; Chair. Robert J. Battista.

National Mediation Board (NMB): 1301 K St, NW, Washington, DC 20572; tel. (202) 692-5000; fax (202) 523-5082; internet www.nmb.gov; f. 1934; Chair. Read Van De Water.

National Science Foundation (NSF): 4201 Wilson Blvd, Arlington, VA 22230; tel. (703) 292-5111; internet www.nsf.gov; f. 1950; Dir Arden L. Bement, Jr.

National Transportation Safety Board: see Transport.

Nuclear Regulatory Commission (NRC): 1 Office of Public Affairs, Washington, DC 20555; tel. (301) 415-8200; internet www.nrc.gov; Chair. Nils J. Diaz.

Occupational Safety and Health Review Commission (OSHRC): 1 Lafayette Centre, 1120 20th St, NW, Washington, DC 20036-3419; tel. (202) 606-5398; fax (202) 606-5050; e-mail lgravely@oshrc.gov; internet www.oshrc.gov; f. 1970; Chair. W. Scott Railton.

Office of Government Ethics: 1201 New York Ave, NW, Washington, DC 20005; tel. (202) 482-9300; internet www.usoge.gov; f. 1978; Dir (vacant).

Office of Personnel Management (OPM): Theodore Roosevelt Federal Bldg, 1900 E St, NW, Washington, DC 20415; tel. (202) 606-1212; fax (202) 606-2573; e-mail general@opm.gov; internet www.opm.gov; f. 1979; Dir Linda M. Springer.

Office of Special Counsel: 1730 M St, NW, Suite 218, Washington, DC 20036-4505; tel. (202) 254-3600; fax (202) 653-5151; internet www.osc.gov; Special Counsel Scott J. Bloch.

Peace Corps: 1111 20th St, NW, Washington, DC 20526; tel. (202) 692-2100; fax (202) 692-2101; e-mail webmaster@peacecorps.gov; internet www.peacecorps.gov; f. 1961; Dir Gaddi H. Vasquez.

Pension Benefit Guaranty Corporation: 1200 K St, NW, Washington, DC 20005-4026; tel. (202) 326-4000; fax (202) 326-4153; e-mail ask.pbgc@pbgc.gov; internet www.pbgc.gov; f. 1974; Exec. Dir Bradley D. Belt.

Postal Rate Commission: 901 New York Ave, NW, Suite 200, NW, Washington, DC 20268-0001; tel. (202) 789-6800; fax (202) 789-6861; e-mail prc-webmaster@prc.gov; internet www.prc.gov; f. 1970; Chair. George A. Omas.

Railroad Retirement Board: 844 North Rush St, Chicago, IL 60611-2092; tel. (312) 751-4777; fax (312) 751-7154; e-mail opa@rrb.gov; internet www.rrb.gov; f. 1935; Chair. Michael Schwartz.

Securities and Exchange Commission: 450 Fifth St, NW, Washington, DC 20549; tel. (202) 942-8088; fax (202) 942-9646; internet www.sec.gov; f. 1935; Chair. Christopher Cox.

Selective Service System: 1515 Wilson Blvd, Arlington, VA 22209-2425; tel. (703) 605-4100; fax (703) 605-4106; e-mail information@sss.gov; internet www.sss.gov; f. 1940; Dir William A. Chatfield.

Small Business Administration: 409 Third St, SW, Washington, DC 20416; tel. (202) 205-6650; fax (202) 205-6802; internet www.sba.gov; f. 1953; Admin. Hector V. Barreto, Jr.

Smithsonian Institution: 1000 Jefferson Dr., SW, Washington, DC 20560-0001POB 37012, SIB 153, MRC 010, Washington, DC 20013-7012 ; tel. (202) 633-1000; fax (202) 357-2116; e-mail info@si.edu; internet www.si.edu; f. 1846; Sec. Lawrence M. Small.

Social Security Administration: Office of Public Inquiries, Windsor Park Bldg, 6401 Security Blvd, Baltimore, MD 21235; tel. (410) 965-3120; fax (410) 966-1463; internet www.ssa.gov; Commr Jo Anne B. Barnhart.

Tennessee Valley Authority: 400 West Summit Hill Dr., Knoxville, TN 37902; tel. (865) 632-6263; e-mail tvainfo@tva.gov; internet www.tva.gov; f. 1933; Chair. William B. Sansom; Pres. Tom Kilgore.

United States Agency for International Development (USAID): Ronald Reagan Bldg, 1300 Pennsylvania Ave, NW, Washington, DC 20523-6100; tel. (202) 712-4810; fax (202) 216-3524; e-mail pinquiries@usaid.gov; internet www.usaid.gov; f. 1961; Dir Randall Tobias.

United States Consumer Product Safety Commission: 4330 East-West Hwy, Bethesda, MD 20814-4408; tel. (301) 504-0580; fax (301) 504-0124; e-mail info@cpsc.gov; internet www.cpsc.gov; f. 1972; Chair. Harold D. ('Hal') Stratton.

United States International Trade Commission: 500 E St, SW, Washington, DC 20436; tel. (202) 205-2000; fax (202) 205-2798; e-mail webmaster@usitc.gov; internet www.usitc.gov; f. 1916; Chair. Stephen Koplan.

United States Postal Service: 475 L'Enfant Plaza, SW, Washington, DC 20260-0010; tel. (202) 268-2000; fax (202) 268-4860; internet www.usps.com; f. 1970; Postmaster-Gen. and CEO John E. Potter.

United States Trade and Development Agency (USTDA): 1621 North Kent St, Suite 300, Arlington, VA 22209-2131; tel. (703) 875-4357; fax (703) 875-4009; e-mail info@ustda.gov; internet www.ustda.gov; Dir Thelma J. Askey.

State Governments
(with expiration date of Governors' current term of office; legislatures at March 2006)

Alabama: Governor Bob Riley (Rep.—Jan. 2007); Senate: Dem. 25, Rep. 10; House: Dem. 63, Rep. 42.

Alaska: Governor Frank Murkowski (Rep.—Dec. 2006); Senate: Dem. 8, Rep. 12; House: Dem. 14, Rep. 26.

Arizona: Governor Janet Napolitano (Dem.—Jan. 2007); Senate: Dem. 12, Rep. 18; House: Dem. 21, Rep. 39.

Arkansas: Governor Mike D. Huckabee (Rep.—Jan. 2007); Senate: Dem. 27, Rep. 8; House: Dem. 72, Rep. 28.

California: Governor Arnold Schwarzenegger (Rep.—Jan. 2007); Senate: Dem. 25, Rep. 15; Assembly: Dem. 48, Rep. 32.

Colorado: Governor Bill Owens (Rep.—Jan. 2007); Senate: Dem. 18, Rep. 17; House: Dem. 35, Rep. 30.

Connecticut: Governor M. Jodi Rell (Rep.—Jan. 2007); Senate: Dem. 24, Rep. 12; House: Dem. 99, Rep. 52.

Delaware: Governor Ruth Ann Minner (Dem.—Jan. 2009); Senate: Dem. 13, Rep. 8; House: Dem. 15, Rep. 25, Ind. 1.

Florida: Governor John Ellis ('Jeb') Bush (Rep.—Jan. 2007); Senate: Dem. 14, Rep. 26; House: Dem. 36, Rep. 84.

Georgia: Governor Sonny Perdue (Rep.—Jan. 2007); Senate: Dem. 22, Rep. 34; House: Dem. 78, Rep. 101, Ind. 1.

Hawaii: Governor Linda Lingle (Rep.—Jan. 2007); Senate: Dem. 20, Rep. 5; House: Dem. 41, Rep. 10.

Idaho: Governor Dirk Kempthorne (Rep.—Jan. 2007); Senate: Dem. 7, Rep. 28; House: Dem. 13, Rep. 57.

Illinois: Governor Rod R. Blagojevich (Dem.—Jan. 2007); Senate: Dem. 32, Rep. 26, Ind. 1; House: Dem. 65, Rep. 53.

Indiana: Governor Mitchell Daniels (Rep.—Jan. 2009); Senate: Dem. 17, Rep. 33; House: Dem. 48, Rep. 52.

Iowa: Governor Tom Vilsack (Dem.—Jan. 2007); Senate: Dem. 25, Rep. 25; House: Dem. 49, Rep. 51.

Kansas: Governor Kathleen Sebelius (Dem.—Jan. 2007); Senate: Dem. 10, Rep. 30; House: Dem. 42, Rep. 83.

Kentucky: Governor Ernie Fletcher (Rep.—Dec. 2007); Senate: Dem. 15, Rep. 22, Ind. 1; House: Dem. 56, Rep. 44.

Louisiana: Governor Kathleen Babineaux Blanco (Dem.—Jan. 2008); Senate: Dem. 24, Rep. 15; House: Dem. 65, Rep. 39, Ind. 1.

Maine: Governor John E. Baldacci, Jr (Dem.—Jan. 2007); Senate: Dem. 19, Rep. 16; House: Dem. 74, Rep. 73, Ind. 4.

Maryland: Governor Robert Ehrlich, Jr (Rep.—Jan. 2007); Senate: Dem. 33, Rep. 14; House: Dem. 98, Rep. 43.

Massachusetts: Governor W. Mitt Romney (Rep.—Jan. 2007); Senate: Dem. 34, Rep. 6; House: Dem. 137, Rep. 20, Ind. 3.

Michigan: Governor Jennifer M. Granholm (Dem.—Jan. 2007); Senate: Dem. 16, Rep. 22; House: Dem. 52, Rep. 58.

Minnesota: Governor Tim Pawlenty (Rep.—Jan. 2007); Senate: Dem. Farm. Lab. 357 Rep. 29, Ind. 1; House: Dem. Farm. Lab. 66, Rep. 68.

Mississippi: Governor Haley Barbour (Rep.—Jan. 2008); Senate: Dem. 27, Rep. 24, 1 vacancy; House: Dem. 75, Rep. 47.

Missouri: Governor Matt Blunt (Rep.—Jan. 2009); Senate: Dem. 11, Rep. 23; House: Dem. 66, Rep. 97.

Montana: Governor Brian Schweitzer (Dem.—Jan. 2009); Senate: Dem. 27, Rep. 23; House: Dem. 50, Rep. 50.

Nebraska: Governor Dave Heineman (Rep.—Jan. 2007); Legislature: unicameral body comprising 49 members elected on a non-partisan ballot and classed as senators.

THE UNITED STATES OF AMERICA

Nevada: Governor KENNY GUINN (Rep.—Jan. 2007); Senate: Dem. 9, Rep. 12; Assembly: Dem. 26, Rep. 16.

New Hampshire: Governor JOHN LYNCH (Rep.—Jan. 2009); Senate: Dem. 8, Rep. 16; House: Dem. 152, Rep. 246.

New Jersey: Governor JON S. CORZINE (Dem.—Jan. 2010); Senate: Dem. 22, Rep. 18; Assembly: Dem. 48, Rep. 32.

New Mexico: Governor BILL RICHARDSON (Dem.—Jan. 2007); Senate: Dem. 24, Rep. 18; House: Dem. 42, Rep. 28.

New York: Governor GEORGE E. PATAKI (Rep.—Jan. 2007); Senate: Dem. 27, Rep. 35; Assembly: Dem. 105, Rep. 45.

North Carolina: Governor MIKE EASLEY, Jr (Dem.—Jan. 2009); Senate: Dem. 29, Rep. 21; House: Dem. 63, Rep. 57.

North Dakota: Governor JOHN HOEVEN (Rep.—Jan. 2009); Senate: Dem. 15, Rep. 32; House: Dem. 27, Rep. 67.

Ohio: Governor BOB TAFT (Rep.—Jan. 2007); Senate: Dem. 11, Rep. 22; House: Dem. 38, Rep. 61.

Oklahoma: Governor BRAD HENRY (Dem.—Jan. 2007); Senate: Dem. 25, Rep. 22, 1 vacancy; House: Dem. 44, Rep. 57.

Oregon: Governor TED KULONGOSKI (Dem.—Jan. 2007); Senate: Dem. 18, Rep. 12; House: Dem. 27, Rep. 33.

Pennsylvania: Governor ED RENDELL (Dem.—Jan. 2007); Senate: Dem. 20, Rep. 30; House: Dem. 94, Rep. 109.

Rhode Island: Governor DONALD L. CARCIERI (Rep.—Jan. 2007); Senate: Dem. 33, Rep. 5; House: Dem. 60, Rep. 15.

South Carolina: Governor MARK SANFORD (Rep.—Jan. 2007); Senate: Dem. 20, Rep. 26; House: Dem. 50, Rep. 74.

South Dakota: Governor M. MICHAEL ROUNDS (Rep.—Jan. 2007); Senate: Dem. 10, Rep. 25; House: Dem. 19, Rep. 51.

Tennessee: Governor PHIL BREDESEN (Dem.—Jan. 2007); Senate: Dem. 15, Rep. 18; House: Dem. 53, Rep. 46.

Texas: Governor RICK PERRY (Rep.—Jan. 2007); Senate: Dem. 12, Rep. 19; House: Dem. 63, Rep. 87.

Utah: Governor JON HUNTSMAN, Jr (Rep.—Jan. 2009); Senate: Dem. 8, Rep. 21; House: Dem. 19, Rep. 56.

Vermont: Governor JIM DOUGLAS (Rep.—Jan. 2009); Senate: Dem. 21, Rep. 9; House: Dem. 83, Rep. 60, Ind. 7.

Virginia: Governor TIMOTHY M. KAINE (Dem.—Jan. 2010); Senate: Dem. 17, Rep. 23; House: Dem. 40, Rep. 57, Ind. 3.

Washington: Governor CHRISTINE O. GREGOIRE (Dem.—Jan. 2009); Senate: Dem. 26, Rep. 23; House: Dem. 56, Rep. 42.

West Virginia: Governor JOE MANCHIN, III (Dem.—Jan. 2009); Senate: Dem. 21, Rep. 13; House: Dem. 69, Rep. 31.

Wisconsin: Governor JAMES E. DOYLE (Dem.—Jan. 2007); Senate: Dem. 14, Rep. 19; Assembly: Dem. 39, Rep. 60.

Wyoming: Governor DAVE FREUDENTAHL (Dem.—Jan. 2007); Senate: Dem. 7, Rep. 23; House: Dem. 14, Rep. 46.

Political Organizations

Communist Party USA: 235 West 23rd St, 7th Floor, New York, NY 10011; tel. (212) 989-4994; fax (212) 229-1713; e-mail cpusa@cpusa.org; internet www.cpusa.org; f. 1919; mems in all 50 states, organized in over 40 states; Chair. SAM WEBB.

Democratic National Committee: 430 South Capitol St, SE, Washington, DC 20003; tel. (202) 863-8000; fax (202) 863-8174; internet www.democrats.org; f. 1848; Nat. Chair. HOWARD DEAN; Sec. ALICE TRAVIS GERMOND; Treas. ANDREW TOBIAS.

The Green Party of the United States: POB 57065, Washington, DC 20037; tel. (202) 319-7191; e-mail info@greenpartyus.org; internet www.gp.org; f. 2001; Sec. HOLLY HART.

The Greens/Green Party USA: POB 3568, Eureka, CA 95 5025; tel. (707) 444-3864; e-mail info@greenparty.org; internet www.greenparty.org; f. 1984 as Greens Cttee of Correspondence; present name adopted in 1991.

Libertarian Party: 2600 Virginia Ave, NW, Suite 100, Washington, DC 20037; tel. (202) 333-0008; fax (202) 333-0072; e-mail hq@lp.org; internet www.lp.org; advocates individual freedom, smaller govt and fewer taxes; f. 1971; Chair. MICHAEL DIXON.

Prohibition National Committee: POB 2635, Denver, CO 80201; tel. (303) 237-4947; e-mail earldodge@dodgeoffice.net; internet www.prohibition.org; f. 1869; opposes the manufacture and sale of alcoholic drinks; opposes abortion, drug abuse and euthanasia; Nat. Chair. EARL F. DODGE; Nat. Sec. PAUL B. SCOTT.

La Raza Unida Party: 483 Fifth St, POB 13, San Fernando, CA 91340; tel. (818) 365-6534; e-mail partido_nacional@yahoo.com; internet larazaunida.tripod.com; f. 1972; aims to achieve self-determination and greater govt representation for Latinos through electoral processes; four state groups, 100 local groups; Nat. Chair. JENARO G. AYALA.

Reform Party of the USA: POB 126437, Fort Worth, TX 76126; tel. (877) 467-3367; fax (817) 249-5201; e-mail info@reformparty.org; internet www.reformparty.org; f. 1996; advocates reform of political system and ethical govt; Nat. Chair. CHARLES FOSTER; Sec. DIONE ORMOND.

Republican National Committee: 310 First St, SE, Washington, DC 20003; tel. (202) 863-8500; fax (202) 863-8820; e-mail info@mc.org; internet www.rnc.org; f. 1854; Chair. Nat. Cttee KEN MEHLMAN; Co-Chair. JO ANN DAVIDSON.

Social Democrats, USA: 815 15th St, NW, Suite 921, Washington, DC 20005; tel. (202) 638-1515; fax (202) 347-5585; e-mail info@socialdemocrats.org; internet www.socialdemocrats.org; f. 1972 to succeed Socialist Party (f. 1901); Pres. DAVID JESSUP; Nat. Vice-Chair. NORMAN HILL.

Socialist Labor Party: POB 218, Mountain View, CA 94042; tel. (408) 280-7226; fax (408) 280-6964; e-mail socialists@slp.org; internet www.slp.org; f. 1877; Nat. Sec. ROBERT BILLS.

Socialist Party USA: 339 Lafayette St, Suite 303, New York, NY 10012; tel. and fax (212) 982-4586; e-mail socialistparty@sp-usa.org; internet www.sp-usa.org; f. 1901; Nat. Co-Chairs MARY CAL HOLLIS, ANTONIO SALAS; Nat. Sec. GREG PASON; 1,800 mems.

Socialist Workers Party: 306 West 37th St, 10th Floor, New York, NY 10018; tel. (212) 242-4094; fax (212) 727-3107; e-mail swpno@verizon.net; f. 1938; Nat. Sec. JACK BARNES.

Diplomatic Representation

EMBASSIES IN THE USA

Afghanistan: 2341 Wyoming Ave, NW, Washington, DC 20008; tel. 483-6414; fax 483-9523; e-mail info@embassyofafghanistan.org; internet www.embassyofafghanistan.org; Ambassador SAID TAYEB JAWAD.

Albania: 2100 S St, NW, Washington, DC 20008; tel. (202) 223-4942; fax (202) 628-7342; Chargé d'affaires a.i. KRESHNIK COLLAKU.

Algeria: 2118 Kalorama Rd, NW, Washington, DC 20008; tel. (202) 265-2800; fax (202) 667-2174; e-mail embalg.us@verizon.net; internet www.algeria-us.org; Ambassador AMINE KHERI.

Andorra: 2 United Nations Plaza, 25th Floor, New York, NY 10017; tel. (212) 750-8064; fax (212) 750-6630; Chargé d'affaires a.i. JELENA V. PIA-COMELLA.

Angola: 2108 16th St, NW, Washington, DC 20009; tel. (202) 785-1156; fax (202) 785-1258; e-mail angola@angola.org; internet www.angola.org; Ambassador JOSEFINA PERPÉTUA PITRA DIAKITÉ.

Antigua and Barbuda: 3216 New Mexico Ave, NW, Washington, DC 20016; tel. (202) 362-5122; fax (202) 362-5225; e-mail embantbar@aol.com; Ambassador DEBORAH MAE LOVELL.

Argentina: 1600 New Hampshire Ave, NW, Washington, DC 20009; tel. (202) 238-6400; fax (202) 332-3171; e-mail info@embajadaaargentinaeeuu.org; internet www.embajadaargentinaeeuu.org; Ambassador JOSÉ OCTAVIO BORDÓN GONZÁLEZ.

Armenia: 2225 R St, NW, Washington, DC 20008; tel. (202) 319-1976; fax (202) 319-2982; e-mail armecon@speakeasy.net; internet www.armeniaemb.org; Ambassador TATOUL MARKARIAN.

Australia: 1601 Massachusetts Ave, NW, Washington, DC 20036-2273; tel. (202) 797-3000; fax (202) 797-3168; e-mail library.washington@dfat.gov.au; internet www.austemb.org; Ambassador DENNIS RICHARDSON.

Austria: 3524 International Court, NW, Washington, DC 20008-3022; tel. (202) 895-6700; fax (202) 895-6750; e-mail obwas@sysnet.net; internet www.austria.org; Ambassador EVA NOWOTNY.

Azerbaijan: 2741 34th St, NW, Washington, DC 20008; tel. (202) 357-3500; fax (202) 357-5911; e-mail azerbaijan@azembassy.com; internet www.azembassy.com; Ambassador HAFIZ MIR JALAL PASHAYEV.

Bahamas: 2220 Massachusetts Ave, NW, Washington, DC 20008; tel. (202) 319-2660; fax (202) 319-2668; e-mail bahemb@aol.com; Ambassador JOSHUA SEARS.

Bahrain: 3502 International Dr., NW, Washington, DC 20008; tel. (202) 342-1111; fax (202) 362-2192; e-mail info@bahrainembassy.org; internet www.bahrainembassy.org; Ambassador NASSER MOHAMED AL-BALOOSHI.

Bangladesh: 3510 International Dr., NW, Washington, DC 20008; tel. (202) 244-0183; fax (202) 244-2771; e-mail bdootwash@bangladoot.org; internet www.bangladoot.org; Ambassador SHAMSHER M. CHOWDHURY.

THE UNITED STATES OF AMERICA

Barbados: 2144 Wyoming Ave, NW, Washington, DC 20008; tel. (202) 939-9200; fax (202) 332-7467; e-mail washington@foreign.gov.bb; Ambassador MICHAEL IAN KING.

Belarus: 1619 New Hampshire Ave, NW, Washington, DC 20009; tel. (202) 986-1604; fax (202) 986-1805; e-mail usa@belarusembassy.org; internet www.belarusembassy.org; Ambassador MIKHAIL KHVOSTOV.

Belgium: 3330 Garfield St, NW, Washington, DC 20008; tel. (202) 333-6900; fax (202) 333-3079; e-mail washington@diplobel.org; internet www.diplobel.org; Ambassador FRANS VAN DAELE.

Belize: 2535 Massachusetts Ave, NW, Washington, DC 20008; tel. (202) 332-9636; fax (202) 332-6888; e-mail chancery@embassyofbelize.org; internet www.embassyofbelize.org; Ambassador LISA M. SHOMAN.

Benin: 2124 Kalorama Rd, NW, Washington, DC 20008; tel. (202) 232-6656; fax (202) 265-1996; Ambassador CYRILLE OGUIN.

Bolivia: 3014 Massachusetts Ave, NW, Washington, DC 20008; tel. (202) 483-4410; fax (202) 328-3712; e-mail webmaster@bolivia-usa.org; internet www.bolivia-usa.org; Ambassador SACHA LLORENTI.

Bosnia and Herzegovina: 2109 E St, NW, Washington, DC 20037; tel. (202) 337-1500; fax (202) 337-1502; e-mail info@bhembassy.org; internet www.bhembassy.org; Ambassador BISERA TURKOVIĆ.

Botswana: 1531-1533 New Hampshire Ave, NW, Washington, DC 20036; tel. (202) 244-4990; fax (202) 244-4164; Ambassador LAPOLOGANG CAESAR LEKOA.

Brazil: 3006 Massachusetts Ave, NW, Washington, DC 20008; tel. (202) 238-2700; fax (202) 238-2827; e-mail webmaster@brasilemb.org; internet www.brasilemb.org; Ambassador ROBERTO ABDENUR.

Brunei: 3520 International Court, NW, Washington, DC 20008; tel. (202) 237-1838; fax (202) 885-0560; e-mail info@bruneiembassy.org; internet www.bruneiembassy.org; Ambassador Pengiran INDERA NEGARA P. A. PUTEH.

Bulgaria: 1621 22nd St, NW, Washington, DC 20008; tel. (202) 387-0174; fax (202) 234-7973; e-mail office@bulgaria-embassy.org; internet www.bulgaria-embassy.org; Ambassador ELENA POPTODOROVA.

Burkina Faso: 2340 Massachusetts Ave, NW, Washington, DC 20008; tel. (202) 332-5577; fax (202) 667-1882; e-mail ambawdc@rcn.com; internet www.burkinaembassy-usa.org; Ambassador TERTIUS ZONGO.

Burundi: 2233 Wisconsin Ave, NW, Suite 212, Washington, DC 20007; tel. (202) 342-2574; fax (202) 342-2575; e-mail burundiembassy@erols.com; Ambassador ANTOINE NTAMOBWA.

Cambodia: 4530 16th St, NW, Washington, DC 20011; tel. (202) 726-7742; fax (202) 726-8381; e-mail cambodia@embassy.org; internet www.embassy.org/cambodia; Ambassador SEREYWATH EK.

Cameroon: 2349 Massachusetts Ave, NW, Washington, DC 20008; tel. (202) 265-8790; fax (202) 387-3826; Ambassador JEROME MENDOUGA.

Canada: 501 Pennsylvania Ave, NW, Washington, DC 20001; tel. (202) 682-1740; fax (202) 682-7726; e-mail webmaster@canadianembassy.org; internet www.canadianembassy.org; Ambassador MICHAEL WILSON.

Cape Verde: 3415 Massachusetts Ave, NW, Washington, DC 20007; tel. (202) 965-6820; fax (202) 965-1207; e-mail ambacvus@verizon.net; internet www.virtualcapeverde.net; Ambassador JOSE BRITO.

Central African Republic: 1618 22nd St, NW, Washington, DC 20008; tel. (202) 483-7800; fax (202) 332-9893; e-mail car@ambarca.org; Ambassador EMMANUEL TOUABOY.

Chad: 2002 R St, NW, Washington, DC 20009; tel. (202) 462-4009; fax (202) 265-1937; e-mail info@chadembassy.org; internet www.chadembassy.org; Ambassador MAHAMOUD ADAM BECHIR.

Chile: 1732 Massachusetts Ave, NW, Washington, DC 20036; tel. (202) 785-1746; fax (202) 887-5579; e-mail embassy@embassyofchile.org; internet www.embassyofchile.org; Ambassador ANDRÉS BIANCHI.

China, People's Republic: 2300 Connecticut Ave, NW, Washington, DC 20008; tel. (202) 558-0032; fax (202) 232-7855; e-mail webmaster@china-embassy.org; internet www.china-embassy.org; Ambassador ZHOU WENZHONG.

Colombia: 2118 Leroy Pl., NW, Washington, DC 20008; tel. (202) 387-8338; fax (202) 232-8643; e-mail enwas@colombiaemb.org; internet www.colombiaemb.org; Ambassador ANDRÉS PASTRANA ARANGO.

Comoros: 336 East 45th St, 2nd Floor, New York, NY 10017; tel. (212) 972-8010; fax (212) 983-4712; e-mail comun@undp.org; Ambassador (vacant).

Congo, Democratic Republic: 1800 New Hampshire Ave, NW, Washington, DC 20009; tel. (202) 234-7690; fax (202) 237-0748; Ambasssador FAIDA MITIFU.

Congo, Republic: 4891 Colorado Ave, NW, Washington, DC 20011; tel. (202) 726-5500; fax (202) 726-1860; e-mail info@embassyofcongo.org; internet www.embassyofcongo.org; Ambassador SERGE MOMBOULI.

Costa Rica: 2114 S St, NW, Washington, DC 20008; tel. (202) 234-2945; fax (202) 265-4795; e-mail embassy@costarica-embassy.org; internet www.costarica-embassy.org; Ambassador TOMÁS DUENAS.

Côte d'Ivoire: 2424 Massachusetts Ave, NW, Washington, DC 20008; tel. (202) 797-0300; fax (202) 462-9444; Ambassador DAOUDA DIABATE.

Croatia: 2343 Massachusetts Ave, NW, Washington, DC 20008; tel. (202) 588-5899; fax (202) 588-8936; e-mail public@croatiaemb.org; internet www.croatiaemb.org; Ambassador NEVEN JURICA.

Cuba: 'Interests section' in the Embassy of Switzerland, 2630 16th St, NW, Washington, DC 20009; tel. (202) 797-8518; fax (202) 797-8521; e-mail consulcuba@sicuw.org; internet www.geocities.com/cubainte; Counselor DAGOBERTO RODRÍQUEZ BARRERA.

Cyprus: 2211 R St, NW, Washington, DC 20008; tel. (202) 462-5772; fax (202) 483-6710; e-mail cypembwash@earthlink.net; internet www.cyprusembassy.net; Ambassador EURIPIDES L. EVRIVIADES.

Czech Republic: 3900 Spring of Freedom St, NW, Washington, DC 20008; tel. (202) 274-9100; fax (202) 966-8540; e-mail washington@embassy.mzv.cz; internet www.mzv.cz/washington; Ambassador PETR KOLAR.

Denmark: 3200 Whitehaven St, NW, Washington, DC 20008-3616; tel. (202) 234-4300; fax (202) 328-1470; e-mail wasamb@um.dk; internet www.denmarkemb.org; Ambassador FRIIS ARNE PETERSEN.

Djibouti: 1156 15th St, NW, Suite 515, Washington, DC 20005; tel. (202) 331-0270; fax (202) 331-0302; Ambassador ROBLÉ OLHAYE.

Dominica: 3216 New Mexico Ave, NW, Washington, DC 20016; tel. (202) 364-6781; fax (202) 364-6791; e-mail embdomdc@aol.com; Ambassador (vacant).

Dominican Republic: 1715 22nd St, NW, Washington, DC 20008; tel. (202) 332-6280; fax (202) 265-8057; e-mail embassy@us.serex.gov.do; internet www.domrep.org; Ambassador FLAVIO DARIO ESPINAL.

Ecuador: 2535 15th St, NW, Washington, DC 20009; tel. (202) 234-7200; fax (202) 667-3482; e-mail embassy@ecuador.org; internet www.ecuador.org; Ambassador LUIS BENIGNO GALLEGOS CHIRIBOGA.

Egypt: 3521 International Court, NW, Washington, DC 20008; tel. (202) 895-5400; fax (202) 244-4319; e-mail embassy@egyptembdc.org; internet www.embassyofegyptwashingtondc.org; Ambassador NABIL M. FAHMY.

El Salvador: 2308 California St, NW, Washington, DC 20008; tel. (202) 265-9671; e-mail correo@elsalvador.org; internet www.elsalvador.org; Ambassador RENÉ ANTONIO LEÓN RODRÍGUEZ.

Equatorial Guinea: 2020 16th St, NW, Washington, DC 20009; tel. (202) 518-5700; fax (202) 518-5252; Ambassador PURIFICACIÓN ANGUE ONDO.

Eritrea: 1708 New Hampshire Ave, NW, Washington, DC 20009; tel. (202) 319-1991; fax (202) 319-1304; Ambassador GIRMA ASMEROM TESFAY.

Estonia: 2131 Massachusetts Ave, NW, Washington, DC 20008; tel. (202) 588-0101; fax (202) 588-0108; e-mail info@estemb.org; internet www.estemb.org; Ambassador JÜRI LUIK.

Ethiopia: 3506 International Dr., NW, Washington, DC 20008; tel. (202) 364-1200; fax (202) 587-0195; e-mail info@ethiopianembassy.org; internet www.ethiopianembassy.org; Ambassador SAMUEL ASSEFA.

Fiji: 2233 Wisconsin Ave, NW, Suite 240, Washington, DC 20007; tel. (202) 337-8320; fax (202) 337-1996; e-mail info@fijiembassy.org; internet www.fijiembassy.org; Ambassador JENSONI VITUSAGAVULU.

Finland: 3301 Massachusetts Ave, NW, Washington, DC 20008; tel. (202) 298-5800; fax (202) 298-6030; e-mail sanomat.was@formin.fi; internet www.finland.org; Ambassador PEKKA LINTU.

France: 4101 Reservoir Rd, NW, Washington, DC 20007; tel. (202) 944-6166; fax (202) 944-6072; e-mail info-washington@diplomatie.gouv.fr; internet www.ambafrance-us.org; Ambassador JEAN-DAVID LEVITTE.

Gabon: 2034 20th St, NW, Suite 200, Washington, DC 20009; tel. (202) 797-1000; fax (202) 332-0668; Ambassador JULES MARIUS OGOUEBANDJA.

The Gambia: 1156 15th St, NW, Suite 905, Washington, DC 20005-2076; tel. (202) 785-1399; fax (202) 785-1430; Ambassador DODOU BAMMY JAGNE.

Georgia: 1615 New Hampshire Ave, NW, Suite 300, Washington, DC 20009; tel. (202) 387-2390; fax (202) 393-4537; e-mail embassyofgeorgia@hotmail.com; internet www.georgiaemb.org; Ambassador VASIL SIKHARULIDZE.

Germany: 4645 Reservoir Rd, NW, Washington, DC 20007-1998; POB 40680, Washington, DC 20016-0680; tel. (202) 298-8140; fax

THE UNITED STATES OF AMERICA

(202) 298-4249; internet www.germany.info; Ambassador Klaus Scharioth.

Ghana: 3512 International Dr., NW, Washington, DC 20008; tel. (202) 686-4520; fax (202) 686-4527; e-mail ghemwash@ghanaembassy.org; internet www.ghana-embassy.org; Ambassador Fritz Kwabena Poku.

Greece: 2221 Massachusetts Ave, NW, Washington, DC 20008; tel. (202) 939-1300; fax (202) 939-1324; e-mail greece@greekembassy.org; internet www.greekembassy.org; Ambassador Alexandros P. Mallias.

Grenada: 1701 New Hampshire Ave, NW, Washington, DC 20009; tel. (202) 265-2561; fax (202) 265-2468; e-mail grenada@oas.org; Ambassador Denis G. Antoine.

Guatemala: 2220 R St, NW, Washington, DC 20008; tel. (202) 745-4952; fax (202) 745-1908; e-mail info@guatemala-embassy.org; internet www.guatemala-embassy.org; Ambassador José Guillermo Castillo.

Guinea: 2112 Leroy Pl., NW, Washington, DC 20008; tel. (202) 483-9420; fax (202) 483-8688; Ambassador Alpha Oumar Rafiou Barry.

Guinea-Bissau: POB 33813, Washington, DC 20033-3813; tel. and fax (301) 947-3958; Chargé d'affaires a.i. Henrique Adriano Da Silva.

Guyana: 2490 Tracy Pl., NW, Washington, DC 20008; tel. (202) 265-6900; fax (202) 232-1297; e-mail guyanaembassydc@verizon.net; internet www.guyana.org/govt/embassy.html; Ambassador Bayney Ram Karran.

Haiti: 2311 Massachusetts Ave, Washington, DC 20008; tel. (202) 332-4090; fax (202) 745-7215; e-mail embassy@haiti.org; internet www.haiti.org; Ambassador Raymond A. Joseph.

Holy See: 3339 Massachusetts Ave, NW, Washington, DC 20008-3687; tel. (202) 333-7121; fax (202) 337-4036; e-mail nuntius@worldnet.att.net; Apostolic Nuncio Most Rev. Pietro Sambi (Titular Archbishop of Bellicastrum).

Honduras: 3007 Tilden St, NW, Suite 4-M, Washington, DC 20008; tel. (202) 966-7702; fax (202) 966-9751; e-mail embassy@hondurasemb.org; internet www.hondurasemb.org; Ambassador Roberto Flores Bermudez.

Hungary: 3910 Shoemaker St, NW, Washington, DC 20008; tel. (202) 362-6730; fax (202) 966-8135; e-mail office@huembwas.org; internet www.huembwas.org; Ambassador Dr András Simonyi.

Iceland: 1156 15th St, NW, Suite 1200, Washington, DC 20005-1704; tel. (202) 265-6653; fax (202) 265-6656; e-mail icemb.wash@utn.stjr.is; internet www.iceland.org/us; Ambassador Helgi Ágústsson.

India: 2107 Massachusetts Ave, NW, Washington, DC 20008; tel. (202) 939-7000; fax (202) 483-3972; e-mail information@indiagov.org; internet www.indianembassy.org; Ambassador Ronen Sen.

Indonesia: 2020 Massachusetts Ave, NW, Washington, DC 20036-1084; tel. (202) 775-5200; fax (202) 775-5256; e-mail information@embassyofindonesia.org; internet www.embassyofindonesia.org; Ambassador Sudjadnan Parnohadiningrat.

Iran: 'Interests section' in the Embassy of Pakistan, 2209 Wisconsin Ave, NW, Washington DC 20007; tel. (202) 965-4990; e-mail requests@daftar.org; internet www.daftar.org; Dir Ali Jazini.

Iraq: 1801 P St, Washington, DC 20036; tel. (202) 483-7500; fax (202) 462-5066; e-mail admin@iraqiembassy.org; internet www.iraqiembassy.org; Ambassador Samir Shakir Mahmood al-Sumaidaie.

Ireland: 2234 Massachusetts Ave, NW, Washington, DC 20008; tel. (202) 462-3939; fax (202) 232-5993; e-mail embirlus@aol.com; internet www.irelandemb.org; Ambassador Noel Fahey.

Israel: 3514 International Dr., NW, Washington, DC 20008; tel. (202) 364-5590; fax (202) 364-5566; e-mail ask@israelemb.org; internet www.israelemb.org; Ambassador Daniel Ayalon.

Italy: 3000 Whitehaven St, NW, Washington, DC 20008; tel. (202) 612-4400; fax (202) 518-2154; e-mail stampa@itwash.org; internet www.italyemb.org; Ambassador Giovanni Castellaneta.

Jamaica: 1520 New Hampshire Ave, NW, Washington, DC 20006; tel. (202) 452-0660; fax (202) 452-0081; e-mail info@emjamusa.org; internet www.emjamusa.org; Ambassador Gordon Shirley.

Japan: 2520 Massachusetts Ave, NW, Washington, DC 20008-2869; tel. (202) 238-6700; fax (202) 238-2187; e-mail jicc@embjapan.org; internet www.us.emb-japan.go.jp; Ambassador Ryozo Kato.

Jordan: 3504 International Dr., NW, Washington, DC 20008; tel. (202) 966-2664; fax (202) 966-3110; e-mail hkjembassydc@aol.com; internet www.jordanembassyus.org; Ambassador Karim Tawfik Kawar.

Kazakhstan: 1401 16th St, NW, Washington, DC 20036; tel. (202) 232-5488; fax (202) 232-5845; e-mail kazakh.embusa@verizon.net; internet www.kazakhembus.com; Ambassador Kanat B. Saudabayev.

Kenya: 2249 R St, NW, Washington, DC 20008; tel. (202) 387-6101; fax (202) 462-3829; e-mail information@kenyaembassy.com; Ambassador Leonard Njogu Ngaithe.

Korea, Republic: 2450 Massachusetts Ave, NW, Washington, DC 20008; tel. (202) 939-5600; fax (202) 797-0595; e-mail information-usa@mofat.go.kr; internet www.koreanembassyusa.org; Ambassador Tae-Sik Lee.

Kuwait: 2940 Tilden St, NW, Washington, DC 20008; tel. (202) 966-0702; fax (202) 966-0517; internet www.kuwait-info.org; Ambassador Sheikh Salem Abdallah al-Jaber as-Sabah.

Kyrgyzstan: 1732 Wisconsin Ave, NW, Washington, DC 20007; tel. (202) 338-5141; fax (202) 338-5139; e-mail embassy@kyrgyzstan.org; internet www.kyrgyzstan.org; Ambassador Zamira Beksultanovna Sydykova.

Laos: 2222 S St, NW, Washington, DC 20008; tel. (202) 332-6416; fax (202) 332-4923; e-mail webmaster@laoembassy.com; internet www.laoembassy.com; Ambassador Phanthong Phommahaxay.

Latvia: 4325 17th St, NW, Washington, DC 20011; tel. (202) 726-8213; fax (202) 726-6785; e-mail embassy.usa@mfa.gov.lv; internet www.latvia-usa.org; Ambassador Maris Riekstins.

Lebanon: 2560 28th St, NW, Washington, DC 20008; tel. (202) 939-6300; fax (202) 939-6324; e-mail info@lebanonembassyus.org; internet www.lebanonembassyus.org; Ambassador Dr Farid Abboud.

Lesotho: 2511 Massachusetts Ave, NW, Washington, DC 20008; tel. (202) 797-5533; fax (202) 234-6815; e-mail lesothowashington@compuserve.com; Ambassador Prof. Molelekeng E. Rapolaki.

Liberia: 5201 16th St, Washington, DC 20011; tel. (202) 723-0437; fax (202) 723-0436; e-mail info@liberiaemb.org; internet www.liberiaemb.org; Ambassador Charles A. Minor.

Libya: Liaison Office, 2600 Virginia Ave, NW, Suite 705, Washington, DC 20037; tel. (202) 944-9601; fax (202) 944-9606; Chief of Office Ali Suleiman Aujali.

Liechtenstein: 1300 Eye St, Suite 550w, NW, Washington, DC 20005; tel. (202) 216-0460; fax (202) 216-0459; e-mail bettina.marxer@was.rep.llv.li; internet www.ilechtenstein.li; Ambassador Claudia Fritsche.

Lithuania: 2622 16th St, NW, Washington, DC 20009; tel. (202) 234-5860; fax (202) 328-0466; e-mail info@ltembassyus.org; internet www.ltembassyus.org; Ambassador Vygaudas Usackas.

Luxembourg: 2200 Massachusetts Ave, NW, Washington, DC 20008; tel. (202) 265-4171; fax (202) 328-8270; e-mail info@luxembourg-usa.org; internet www.luxembourg-usa.org; Ambassador Joseph Weyland.

Macedonia: 1101 30th St, NW, Suite 302, Washington, DC 20007; tel. (202) 337-3063; fax (202) 337-3093; e-mail usoffice@macedonianembassy.org; internet www.macedonianembassy.org; Ambassador Nikola Dimitrov.

Madagascar: 2374 Massachusetts Ave, NW, Washington, DC 20008; tel. (202) 265-3034; fax (202) 483-7603; e-mail malagasy.embassy@verizon.org; Ambassador Rajaonarivony Narisoa.

Malawi: 1156 15th St, NW, Suite 320, Washington, DC 20005; tel. (202) 721-0270; fax (202) 721-0288; e-mail malawidc@aol.com; Ambassador Henry Moto.

Malaysia: 3516 International Court, NW, Washington, DC 20008; tel. (202) 572-9700; fax (202) 572-9882; e-mail mwalsh@kln.gov.my; Ambassador Dato' Sheikh Abdul Khalid Ghazzali.

Maldives: 800 Second Ave, Suite 400E, New York, NY 10017; tel. (212) 599-6195; Ambassador Dr Mohamed Latheef.

Mali: 2130 R St, NW, Washington, DC 20008; tel. (202) 332-2249; fax (202) 332-6603; e-mail info@maliembassy.us; internet www.maliembassy.us; Ambassador Abdoulaye Diop.

Malta: 2017 Connecticut Ave, NW, Washington, DC 20008; tel. (202) 462-3611; fax (202) 387-5470; e-mail maltaembassy.washington@gov.mt; internet www.foreign.gov.mt; Ambassador John Lowell.

Marshall Islands: 2433 Massachusetts Ave, NW, Washington, DC 20008; tel. (202) 234-5414; fax (202) 232-3236; e-mail info@rmiembassyus.org; internet www.rmiembassyus.org; Ambassador Banny de Brum.

Mauritania: 2129 Leroy Pl., NW, Washington, DC 20008; tel. (202) 232-5700; fax (202) 319-2623; Ambassador Tijani Ould M. E. Kerim.

Mauritius: 4301 Connecticut Ave, NW, Suite 441, Washington, DC 20008; tel. (202) 244-1491; fax (202) 966-0983; e-mail mauritius.embassy@prodigy.net; internet www.maurinet.com/embasydc.html; Chargé d'affaires a.i. Shiu Ching Young Kim Fat.

Mexico: 1911 Pennsylvania Ave, NW, Washington, DC 20006; tel. (202) 728-1600; fax (202) 234-1698; e-mail mexembusa@sre.gob.mx; internet www.sre.gob.mx/eua; Ambassador Carlos de Icaza González.

THE UNITED STATES OF AMERICA
Directory

Micronesia: 1725 N St, NW, Washington, DC 20036; tel. (202) 223-4383; fax (202) 223-4391; e-mail fsm@fsmembassy.org; internet fsmembassy.org; Ambassador JESSE B. MAREHALAU.

Moldova: 2101 S St, NW, Suite 329, Washington, DC 20008; tel. (202) 667-1130; fax (202) 667-1204; Ambassador MIHAIL MANOLI.

Mongolia: 2833 M St, NW, Washington, DC 20007; tel. (202) 333-7117; fax (202) 298-9227; e-mail esyam@mongolianembassy.us; internet www.mongolianembassy.us; Ambassador RAVDAN BOLD.

Morocco: 1601 21st St, NW, Washington, DC 20009; tel. (202) 462-7979; fax (202) 265-0161; Ambassador AZIZ MEKOUAR.

Mozambique: 1990 M St, NW, Suite 570, Washington, DC 20036; tel. (202) 293-7146; fax (202) 835-0245; e-mail embamoc@aol.com; internet www.embamoc-usa.org; Ambassador ARMANDO ALEXANDRE PANGUENE.

Myanmar: 2300 S St, NW, Washington, DC 20008; tel. (202) 332-9044; fax (202) 332-9046; e-mail thuriya@aol.com; Chargé d'affaires a.i. LWIN MYINT.

Namibia: 1605 New Hampshire Ave, NW, Washington, DC 20009; tel. (202) 986-0540; fax (202) 986-0443; e-mail info@namibiaembassyusa.org; Ambassador HOPELONG U. IPINGE.

Nauru: 800 Second Ave, New York, NY 10017; tel. (212) 937-0074; fax (212) 937-0079; Ambassador MARLENE MOSES.

Nepal: 2131 Leroy Pl., NW, Washington, DC 20008; tel. (202) 667-4550; fax (202) 667-5534; e-mail info@nepalembassyusa.org; internet www.nepalembassyusa.org; Ambassador (vacant).

Netherlands: 4200 Linnean Ave, NW, Washington, DC 20008; tel. (202) 244-5300; fax (202) 362-3430; e-mail webmaster@netherlands-embassy.org; internet www.netherlands-embassy.org; Ambassador BOUDEWIJN JOHANNES VAN EENENNAAM.

New Zealand: 37 Observatory Circle, NW, Washington, DC 20008; tel. (202) 328-4800; fax (202) 667-5227; e-mail nz@nzemb.org; internet www.nzembassy.com; Ambassador ROY FERGUSON.

Nicaragua: 1627 New Hampshire Ave, NW, Washington, DC 20009; tel. (202) 939-6570; fax (202) 939-6545; e-mail nicaraguan.embassy@embanic.org; Ambassador SALVADOR STADTHAGEN.

Niger: 2204 R St, NW, Washington, DC 20008; tel. (202) 483-4224; fax (202) 483-3169; e-mail ambassadeniger@hotmail.com; internet www.nigerembassyusa.org; Ambassador AMINATA DJIBRILLA MAIGA TOURÉ.

Nigeria: 3519 International Court, NW, Washington, DC 20008; tel. (202) 986-8400; fax (202) 775-1385; internet www.nigeriaembassyusa.org; Ambassador GEORGE ACHULIKE OBIOZOR.

Norway: 2720 34th St, NW, Washington, DC 20008; tel. (202) 333-6000; fax (202) 337-0870; e-mail emb.washington@mfa.no; internet www.norway.org; Ambassador KNUT VOLLEBAEK.

Oman: 2535 Belmont Rd, NW, Washington, DC 20008; tel. (202) 387-1980; fax (202) 745-4933; Ambassador HUNAINA SULTAN AHMED AL-MUGHAIRY.

Pakistan: 3517 International Court, NW, Washington, DC 20008; tel. (202) 939-6200; fax (202) 387-0484; e-mail info@embassyofpakistan.org; internet www.embassyofpakistan.org; Ambassador JEHANGIR KARAMAT.

Palau: 1800 K St, NW, Suite 714, Washington, DC 20006; tel. (202) 452-6814; fax (202) 452-6281; e-mail info@palauembassy.com; internet www.palauembassy.com; Ambassador HERSEY KYOTA.

Panama: 2862 McGill Terrace, NW, Washington, DC 20008; tel. (202) 483-1407; fax (202) 483-8413; Ambassador FEDERICO A. HUMBERT ARIAS.

Papua New Guinea: 1779 Massachusetts Ave, NW, Suite 805, Washington, DC 20036; tel. (202) 745-3680; fax (202) 745-3679; e-mail info@pngembassy.org; internet www.pngembassy.com; Ambassador EVAN JEREMY PAKI.

Paraguay: 2400 Massachusetts Ave, NW, Washington, DC 20008; tel. (202) 483-6960; fax (202) 234-4508; Ambassador JAMES SPALDING HELLMERS.

Peru: 1700 Massachusetts Ave, NW, Washington, DC 20036; tel. (202) 833-9860; fax (202) 659-8124; e-mail webmaster@embassyofperu.us; internet www.peruvianembassy.us; Ambassador EDUARDO FERRERO COSTA.

Philippines: 1600 Massachusetts Ave, NW, Washington, DC 20036-2274; tel. (202) 467-9300; fax (202) 328-7614; e-mail info@philippineembassy-usa.org; internet www.philippineembassy-usa.org; Ambassador ALBERTO F. DEL ROSARIO.

Poland: 2640 16th St, NW, Washington, DC 20009; tel. (202) 234-3800; fax (202) 328-6271; e-mail polemb.info@earthlink.net; internet www.polandembassy.org; Ambassador JANUSZ REITER.

Portugal: 2125 Kalorama Rd, NW, Washington, DC 20008; tel. (202) 328-8610; fax (202) 462-3726; internet www.portugalemb.org; Ambassador PEDRO CATARINO.

Qatar: 2555 M St, NW, Washington, DC 20037-1305; tel. (202) 274-1600; fax (202) 237-0061; e-mail info@qatarembassy.net; internet www.qatarembassy.net; Ambassador NASSER BIN HAMAD AL-KHALIFA.

Romania: 1607 23rd St, NW, Washington, DC 20008; tel. (202) 232-4846; fax (202) 232-4748; e-mail office@roembus.org; internet www.roembus.org; Ambassador SORIN DUCARU.

Russia: 2650 Wisconsin Ave, NW, Washington, DC 20007; tel. (202) 298-5700; fax (202) 298-5735; e-mail rusembus@erols.com; internet www.russianembassy.org; Ambassador YURII VIKTOROVICH USHAKOV.

Rwanda: 1714 New Hampshire Ave, NW, Washington, DC 20009; tel. (202) 232-2882; fax (202) 232-4544; e-mail rwandemb@rwandemb.org; internet www.rwandemb.org; Ambassador Dr ZAC NSENGA.

Saint Christopher and Nevis: 3216 New Mexico Ave, NW, Washington, DC 20016; tel. (202) 686-2636; fax (202) 686-5740; e-mail info@stkittsnevis.org; internet www.stkittsnevis.org; Ambassador Dr IZBEN CORDINAL WILLIAMS.

Saint Lucia: OECS Bldg, 3216 New Mexico Ave, NW, Washington, DC 20016; tel. (202) 364-6792; fax (202) 364-6723; Ambassador SONIA MERLYN JOHNNY.

Saint Vincent and the Grenadines: 3216 New Mexico Ave, NW, Washington, DC 20016; tel. (202) 364-6730; fax (202) 364-6736; e-mail mail@embvsg.com; internet www.embvsg.com; Ambassador ELLSWORTH I. A. JOHN.

Samoa: 800 Second Ave, Suite 800D, New York, NY 10017; tel. (212) 599-6196; fax (212) 599-0797; e-mail samoa@un.int; Ambassador ALI'IOAIGA FETURI ELISAIA.

Saudi Arabia: 601 New Hampshire Ave, NW, Washington, DC 20037; tel. (202) 342-3800; fax (202) 944-5983; e-mail info@saudiembassy.net; internet www.saudiembassy.net; Ambassador Prince TURKI AL-FAISAL AL-SAUD.

Senegal: 2112 Wyoming Ave, NW, Washington, DC 20008; tel. (202) 234-0540; fax (202) 332-6315; Ambassador Dr AMADOU LAMINE BA.

Serbia and Montenegro: 2134 Kalorama Rd, NW, Washington, DC 20008; tel. (202) 332-0333; fax (202) 332-3933; e-mail info@yuembusa.org; internet www.yuembusa.org; Ambassador IVAN VUJACIC.

Seychelles: 800 Second Ave, Suite 900C, New York, NY 10017; tel. (212) 972-1785; fax (212) 972-1786; Ambassador EMILE P. J. BONNELAME.

Sierra Leone: 1701 19th St, NW, Washington, DC 20009; tel. (202) 939-9261; fax (202) 483-1793; Ambassador IBRAHIM M. KAMARA.

Singapore: 3501 International Pl., NW, Washington, DC 20008; tel. (202) 537-3100; fax (202) 537-0876; e-mail singemb.dc@verizon.net; internet www.mfa.gov.sg/washington; Ambassador HENG CHEE CHAN.

Slovakia: 3523 International Court, NW, Suite 210, Washington, DC 20008; tel. (202) 237-1054; fax (202) 237-6438; e-mail info@slovakembassy-us.org; internet www.slovakembassy-us.org; Ambassador RASTISLAV KACER.

Slovenia: 1525 New Hampshire Ave, NW, Washington, DC 20036-1203; tel. (201) 667-5363; fax (202) 667-4563; e-mail vwa@mzz-dkp.gov.si; internet www.gov.si/mzz-dkp/vwa; Ambassador SAMUEL ZBOGAR.

Solomon Islands: 800 Second Ave, Suite 400L, New York, NY 10017; tel. (212) 599-6192; fax (212) 661-8925; e-mail simny@solomons.com; Ambassador COLIN D. BECK.

South Africa: 3051 Massachusetts Ave, NW, Washington, DC 20008; tel. (202) 232-4400; fax (202) 232-3402; e-mail info@saembassy.org; internet www.saembassy.org; Ambassador BARBARA MASEKELA.

Spain: 2375 Pennsylvania Ave, NW, Washington, DC 20037; tel. (202) 452-0100; fax (202) 833-5670; e-mail embespus@mail.mae.us; internet www.spainemb.org; Ambassador CARLOS WESTENDORP Y CABEZA.

Sri Lanka: 2148 Wyoming Ave, NW, Washington, DC 20008; tel. (202) 483-4025; fax (202) 232-7181; e-mail slembassy@usa.org; internet www.slembassyusa.org; Ambassador BERNARD ANTON BANDARA GOONETILLEKE.

Sudan: 2210 Massachusetts Ave, NW, Washington, DC 20008; tel. (202) 338-8565; fax (202) 667-2406; e-mail info@sudanembassy.org; internet www.sudanembassy.org; Ambassador KHIDIR HAROUN AHMED.

Suriname: 4301 Connecticut Ave, NW, Suite 460, Washington, DC 20008; tel. (202) 244-7488; fax (202) 244-5878; e-mail esuriname@covad.net; internet www.surinameembassy.org; Ambassador HENRY L. ILLES.

Swaziland: 3400 International Dr., NW, Washington, DC 20008; tel. (202) 284-5002; fax (202) 234-8254; e-mail swaziland@compuserve.com; Ambassador EPHRAEM M. HLOPHE.

THE UNITED STATES OF AMERICA

Sweden: 1501 M St, NW, Suite 900, Washington, DC 20005; tel. (202) 467-2600; fax (202) 467-2699; e-mail ambassaden.washington@foreign.ministry.se; internet www.swedish-embassy.org; Ambassador GUNNAR W. LUND.

Switzerland: 2900 Cathedral Ave, NW, Washington, DC 20008; tel. (202) 745-7900; fax (202) 387-2564; e-mail vertretung@was.rep.admin.ch; internet www.swissemb.org; Ambassador URS ZISWILER.

Syria: 2215 Wyoming Ave, NW, Washington, DC 20008; tel. (202) 232-6313; fax (202) 234-9548; e-mail infosyremb@syrianembassy.org; Ambassador IMAD MOUSTAPHA.

Tajikistan: 1005 New Hampshire Ave, NW, Washington, DC 20037; tel. (202) 223-6090; fax (202) 223-6091; e-mail tajikistan@verizon.net; internet www.tjus.org; Ambassador KHAMROKHON ZARIPOV.

Tanzania: 2139 R St, NW, Washington, DC 20008; tel. (202) 939-6125; fax (202) 797-7408; e-mail balozi@tanzaniaembassy-us.org; internet www.tanzaniaembassy-us.org; Ambassador ANDREW MHANDO DARAJA.

Thailand: 1024 Wisconsin Ave, NW, Washington, DC 20007; tel. (202) 944-3600; fax (202) 944-3611; e-mail thai.wsn@thaiembdc.org; internet www.thaiembdc.org; Ambassador VIRASAKDI FUTRAKUL.

Timor-Leste: 3415 Massachusetts Ave, NW, Washington, DC 20008; tel. (202) 965-1515; fax (202) 965-1517; e-mail embtlus@earthlink.net; Ambassador JOSE LUIS GUTERRES.

Togo: 2208 Massachusetts Ave, NW, Washington, DC 20008; tel. (202) 234-4212; fax (202) 232-3190; Ambassador AKOUSSOULELOU BODJONA.

Tonga: 250 East 51st St, New York, NY 10022; tel. (917) 369-1025; fax (917) 369-1024; Ambassador FEKITAMOELOA UTOIKAMANU.

Trinidad and Tobago: 1708 Massachusetts Ave, NW, Washington, DC 20036; tel. (202) 467-6490; fax (202) 785-3130; e-mail info@ttembwash.com; Ambassador MARINA ANNETTE VALERE.

Tunisia: 1515 Massachusetts Ave, NW, Washington, DC 20005; tel. (202) 862-1850; fax (202) 862-1858; Ambassador MOHAMED NEJIB HACHANA.

Turkey: 2525 Massachusetts Ave, NW, Washington, DC 20008; tel. (202) 612-6700; fax (202) 612-6744; e-mail contact@turkishembassy.org; internet www.turkishembassy.org; Ambassador NABI SENSOY.

Turkmenistan: 2207 Massachusetts Ave, NW, Washington, DC 20008; tel. (202) 588-1500; fax (202) 588-0697; e-mail turkmen@mindspring.com; internet www.turkmenistanembassy.org; Ambassador MERET BAIRAMOVICH ORAZOV.

Uganda: 5911 16th St, NW, Washington, DC 20011; tel. (202) 726-7100; fax (202) 726-1727; e-mail ugembassy@aol.com; Ambassador EDITH GRACE SSEMPALA.

Ukraine: 3350 M St, NW, Washington, DC 20007; tel. (202) 333-0606; fax (202) 333-0817; e-mail infolook@aol.com; internet www.ukraineinfo.us; Ambassador OLEH SHAMSHUR.

United Arab Emirates: 3422 International Court, NW, Washington, DC 20008; tel. (202) 243-2400; fax (202) 243-2432; e-mail visas@uaeembassy-usa.org; internet www.uae-embassy.org; Ambassador SAQR GHOBASH SAEED GHOBASH.

United Kingdom: 3100 Massachusetts Ave, NW, Washington, DC 20008; tel. (202) 588-7800; fax (202) 588-7870; e-mail washi@fco.gov.uk; internet www.britainusa.com; Ambassador Sir DAVID MANNING.

Uruguay: 1913 Eye St, NW, Washington, DC 20006; tel. (202) 331-1313; fax (202) 331-8142; e-mail uruwashi@uruwashi.org; internet www.uruwashi.org; Ambassador CARLOS GIANELLI.

Uzbekistan: 1746 Massachusetts Ave, NW, Washington, DC 20036; tel. (202) 887-5300; fax (202) 293-6804; internet www.uzbekistan.org; Ambassador ABDULAZIZ KOMILOV.

Venezuela: 1099 30th St, NW, Washington, DC 20007; tel. (202) 342-2214; fax (202) 342-6820; e-mail apaiva@embavenez-us.org; internet www.embavenez-us.org; Ambassador BERNARDO ÁLVAREZ HERRERA.

Viet Nam: 1233 20th St, NW, Suite 400, Washington, DC 20036; tel. (202) 861-0737; fax (202) 861-0917; e-mail info@vietnamembassy-usa.org; internet www.vietnamembassy-usa.org; Ambassador TAM CHIEN NGUYEN.

Yemen: 2600 Virginia Ave, NW, Suite 705, Washington, DC 20037; tel. (202) 965-4760; fax (202) 337-2017; e-mail information@yemenembassy.org; internet www.yemenembassy.org; Ambassador ABDULWAHAB ABDULLA AL-HAJJRI.

Zambia: 2419 Massachusetts Ave, NW, Washington, DC 20008; tel. (202) 265-9717; fax (202) 332-0826; e-mail embzambia@aol.com; internet www.zambiaembassy.org; Ambassador Dr INONGE MBIKUSITA LEWANIKA.

Zimbabwe: 1608 New Hampshire Ave, NW, Washington, DC 20009; tel. (202) 332-7100; fax (202) 483-9326; e-mail info@zimbabwe-embassy.us; Ambassador MACHIVENYIKA TOBIAS MAPURANGA.

Judicial System

Each state has a judicial system structured similarly to the Federal system, with a Supreme Court and subsidiary courts, to deal with cases arising under State Law. These courts have jurisdiction in most criminal and civil actions. Each state has its own bar association of lawyers and its own legal code.

Supreme Court of the United States

Supreme Court Bldg, 1 First St, NE, Washington, DC 20543; tel. (202) 479-3000; fax (202) 479-2971; internet www.supremecourtus.gov.

The Supreme Court is the only Federal Court established by the Constitution. It is the highest court in the nation, comprising a Chief Justice and eight Associate Justices. Appointments, which are for life or until voluntary retirement, are made by the President, subject to confirmation by the US Senate.

Chief Justice: JOHN G. ROBERTS, Jr.

Associate Justices: JOHN PAUL STEVENS (1975), ANTONIN SCALIA (1986), ANTHONY M. KENNEDY (1988), DAVID H. SOUTER (1990), CLARENCE THOMAS (1991), RUTH BADER GINSBURG (1993), STEPHEN G. BREYER (1994), SAMUEL A. ALITO, Jr (2006).

US Courts of Appeal

Administrative Office of the US Courts, Washington, DC 20544; tel. (202) 273-1120; internet www.uscourts.gov.

The USA is divided into 12 judicial circuits, in each of which there is one Court of Appeals. The Court of Appeals for the Federal Circuit has nation-wide specialized jurisdiction.

Federal Courts hear cases involving federal law, cases involving participants from more than one state, crimes committed in more than one state and civil or corporate cases that cross state lines. Federal District Courts, of which there are 94, are the courts of first instance for most federal suits.

Federal Circuit: PAUL R. MICHEL (Chief Judge), ALAN D. LOURIE, PAULINE NEWMAN, RANDALL R. RADER, RAYMOND C. CLEVENGER, III, ALVIN A. SCHALL, WILLIAM CURTIS BRYSON, ARTHUR J. GAJARSA, RICHARD LINN, TIMOTHY B. DYK, SHARON PROST.

District of Columbia Circuit: DOUGLAS H. GINSBURG (Chief Judge), HARRY T. EDWARDS, DAVID B. SENTELLE, KAREN LeCRAFT HENDERSON, A. RAYMOND RANDOLPH, JUDITH W. ROGERS, DAVID S. TATEL, MERRICK B. GARLAND, JANICE ROGERS BROWN, THOMAS B. GRIFFITH.

First Circuit (Maine, Massachusetts, New Hampshire, Rhode Island, Puerto Rico): MICHAEL BOUDIN (Chief Judge), JUAN R. TORRUELLA, BRUCE M. SELYA, SANDRA L. LYNCH, KERMIT V. LIPEZ, JEFFREY R. HOWARD.

Second Circuit (Connecticut, New York, Vermont): JOHN M. WALKER, Jr (Chief Judge), DENNIS G. JACOBS, GUIDO CALABRESI, JOSÉ A. CABRANES, CHESTER J. STRAUB, ROSEMARY S. POOLER, ROBERT D. SACK, SONIA SOTOMAYOR, ROBERT A. KATZMANN, BARRINGTON D. PARKER, REENA RAGGI, RICHARD C. WESLEY, PETER W. HALL.

Third Circuit (Delaware, New Jersey, Pennsylvania, Virgin Islands): ANTHONY J. SCIRICA (Chief Judge), DOLORES K. SLOVITER, JANE R. ROTH, THEODORE A. McKEE, MARJORIE O. RENDELL, MARYANNE TRUMP BARRY, THOMAS L. AMBRO, JULIO M. FUENTES, D. BROOKS SMITH, D. MICHAEL FISHER, FRANKLIN S. van ANTWERPEN, MICHAEL A. CHAGARES.

Fourth Circuit (Maryland, North Carolina, South Carolina, Virginia, West Virginia): WILLIAM W. WILKINS (Chief Judge), H. EMORY WIDENER, Jr, J. HARVIE WILKINSON, III, PAUL V. NIEMAYER, J. MICHAEL LUTTIG, KAREN J. WILLIAMS, M. BLANE MICHAEL, DIANA GRIBBON MOTZ, WILLIAM B. TRAXLER, Jr, ROBERT B. KING, ROGER L. GREGORY, DENNIS W. SHEDD, ALLYSON K. DUNCAN.

Fifth Circuit (Louisiana, Mississippi, Texas): CAROLYN DINEEN KING (Chief Judge), THOMAS M. REAVLEY, WILL GARWOOD, E. GRADY JOLLY, PATRICK E. HIGGINBOTHAM, W. EUGENE DAVIS, EDITH H. JONES, JERRY E. SMITH, JACQUES L. WIENER, Jr, RHESA H. BARKSDALE, EMILIO M. GARZA, HAROLD R. DEMOSS, Jr, FORTUNATO P. BENAVIDES, CARL E. STEWART, JAMES L. DENNIS, EDITH BROWN CLEMENT, EDWARD C. PRADO, PRISCILLA RICHMAN OWEN.

Sixth Circuit (Kentucky, Michigan, Ohio, Tennessee): DANNY J. BOGGS (Chief Judge), BOYCE F. MARTIN, Jr, ALICE M. BATCHELDER, MARTHA CRAIG DAUGHTREY, KAREN NELSON MOORE, RANSEY GUY COLE, Jr, ERIC L. CLAY, RONALD LEE GILMAN, JULIA SMITH GIBBONS, JOHN M. ROGERS, JEFFREY S. SUTTON, DEBORAH L. COOK, DAVID W. McKEAGUE, RICHARD ALLEN GRIFFIN.

Seventh Circuit (Illinois, Indiana, Wisconsin): JOEL M. FLAUM (Chief Judge), THOMAS E. FAIRCHILD, WILLIAM J. BAUER, HARLINGTON WOOD, Jr, RICHARD D. CUDAHY, RICHARD A. POSNER, DANIEL A. MANION, KENNETH F. RIPPLE, FRANK H. EASTERBROOK, MICHAEL S. KANNE, JOHN L. COFFEY, ILANA DIAMOND ROVNER, DIANE P. WOOD, TERENCE T. EVANS, ANN C. WILLIAMS.

THE UNITED STATES OF AMERICA

Eighth Circuit (Arkansas, Iowa, Minnesota, Missouri, Nebraska, North Dakota, South Dakota): James B. Loken (Chief Judge), Roger L. Wollman, Morris S. Arnold, Diana E. Murphy, Kermit E. Bye, William J. Riley, Michael J. Melloy, Lavenski R. Smith, Steven M. Colloton, Raymond W. Gruender, Duane Benton.

Ninth Circuit (Alaska, Arizona, California, Guam, Hawaii, Idaho, Montana, Nevada, Northern Mariana Islands, Oregon, Washington): Mary M. Schroeder (Chief Judge), Harry Pregerson, Stephen Reinhardt, Alex Kozinski, Diarmuid F. O'Scannlain, Pamela Ann Rymer, Andrew J. Kleinfeld, Michael Daly Hawkins, Sidney R. Thomas, Barry G. Silverman, Susan B. Graber, M. Margaret McKeown, Kim McLane Wardlaw, William A. Fletcher, Raymond C. Fisher, Ronald M. Gould, Richard A. Paez, Marsha S. Berzon, Richard C. Tallman, Johnnie B. Rawlinson, Richard R. Clifton, Jay S. Bybee, Consuelo M. Callahan, Carlos T. Bea.

Tenth Circuit (Colorado, Kansas, New Mexico, Oklahoma, Utah, Wyoming): Deanell Reece Tacha (Chief Judge), Stephanie K. Seymour, David M. Ebel, Paul J. Kelly, Jr, Robert H. Henry, Mary Beck Briscoe, Carlos Lucero, Michael R. Murphy, Harris L. Hartz, Terrence L. O'Brien, Michael W. McConnell, Timothy M. Tymkovich.

Eleventh Circuit (Alabama, Florida, Georgia): J. L. Edmonson (Chief Judge), Gerald B. Tjoflat, R. Lanier Anderson, Stanley F. Birch, Jr, Joel F. Dubina, Susan H. Black, Edward E. Carnes, Rosemary Barkett, Frank M. Hull, Stanley Marcus, Charles R. Wilson, William H. Pryor, Jr.

United States Court of Federal Claims

717 Madison Pl., NW, Washington, DC 20005; tel. (202) 219-9657; fax (202) 219-9593; internet www.uscfc.uscourts.gov.

Judges: Edward J. Damich (Chief Judge), Christine Odell Cook Miller, Marian Blank Horn, Francis M. Allegra, Lawrence M. Baskir, Lynn J. Bush, Nancy B. Firestone, Emily C. Hewitt, Lawrence J. Block, Mary Ellen Coster Williams, Charles F. Lettow, Susan G. Braden, Victor J. Wolski, George W. Miller.

US Court of International Trade

1 Federal Plaza, New York, NY 10278-0001; tel. (212) 264-2800; fax (212) 264-1085; internet www.uscit.gov.

Judges: Jane A. Restani (Chief Judge), Gregory W. Carman, Donald C. Pogue, Evan J. Wallach, Judith M. Barzilay, Delissa A. Ridgway, Richard K. Eaton, Timothy C. Stanceu.

Senior Judges: Richard W. Goldberg, Nicholas Tsoucalas, R. Kenton Musgrave.

United States Tax Court

400 Second St, NW, Washington, DC 20217; tel. (202) 606-8754; internet www.ustaxcourt.gov.

Judges: Joel Gerber (Chief Judge), Carolyn P. Chiechi, Mary Ann Cohen, Maurice B. Foley, Joseph H. Gale, Joseph R. Goeke, Harry A. Haines, James S. Halpern, Mark V. Holmes, Diane L. Kroupa, David Laro, L. Paige Marvel, Stephen J. Swift, Michael B. Thornton, Juan F. Vasquez, Thomas B. Wells, Robert A. Wherry, Jr.

Religion

Christianity is the predominant religion. The largest single denomination is the Roman Catholic Church. Other major groups in terms of membership are the Baptist, Methodist, Lutheran and Orthodox churches. Numerous other beliefs are represented, the largest in terms of adherents being Judaism, Islam and Buddhism.

CHRISTIANITY

National Council of the Churches of Christ in the USA: 475 Riverside Dr., Rm 880, New York, NY 10115-0050; tel. (212) 870-2511; fax (212) 870-3112; e-mail webmaster@ncccusa.org; internet www.ncccusa.org; f. 1950; an ecumenical org. of 36 Protestant and Orthodox denominations, representing c.50m. mems; Pres. Elenie Huszagh; Gen. Sec. Dr Robert Edgar.

The Anglican Communion

The Episcopal Church in the USA: 815 Second Ave, New York, NY 10017-4564; tel. (212) 867-8400; fax (212) 490-6684; internet www.episcopalchurch.org; f. 1789; 7,342 churches (2000); 2.3m. mems (2000); Presiding Bishop and Pres. Exec. Council Most Rev. Frank Tracy Griswold, III; Exec. Officer Gen. Convention and Sec. Exec. Council Rev. Rosemari Sullivan.

The Baptist Church

Members (1998 estimate): 33.1m., in 15 bodies, of which the following have the greatest number of members:

American Baptist Association: 4605 North State Line Ave, Texarkana, TX 75503-2928; tel. (903) 792-2783; e-mail bssc@abaptist.org; internet www.abaptist.org; f. 1905; 1,760 churches; 275,000 mems; Pres. George Raley.

American Baptist Churches in the USA: POB 851, Valley Forge, PA 19482-0851; tel. (610) 768-2000; fax (610) 768-2320; e-mail richard.schramm@abc-usa.org; internet www.abc-usa.org; f. 1907; 5,775 churches; 1.5m. mems; Pres. Tinette V. McCray.

Conservative Baptist Association of America: 1501 West Mineral Ave, Suite B, Littleton, CO 80120; tel. (720) 283-3030; fax (720) 283-3333; e-mail cba@cbamerica.org; internet www.cbamerica.org; f. 1947; 1,200 churches; 200,000 mems; Exec. Admin. Rev. Ed Mitchell.

General Association of Regular Baptist Churches: 1300 North Meacham Rd, Schaumburg, IL 60173-4806; tel. (847) 843-1600; fax (847) 843-3757; e-mail garbc@garbc.org; internet www.garbc.org; 1,417 churches; Nat. Rep. Rev. John Greening.

National Baptist Convention, USA: White Rock Baptist Church Office, 5240 Chestnut St, Philadelphia, PA 19139; tel. (215) 474-5785; fax (215) 474-3332; e-mail info.nbcusa@verizon.net; internet www.nationalbaptist.com; f. 1880; 2,500 churches; 3.5m. mems; Pres. Dr. William J. Shaw; Gen. Sec. Rev. Roscoe Cooper.

Southern Baptist Convention: 901 Commerce St, Nashville, TN 37203-3629; tel. (615) 244-2355; fax (615) 742-8919; internet www.sbc.net; f. 1845; 42,000 churches; 16.3m. mems (2003); Pres. Dr. Bobby Welch; Pres. Exec. Cttee Dr Morris H. Chapman.

The Lutheran Church

Members (1998 estimate): 8.3m., in 10 bodies, of which the following have the greatest number of members:

Evangelical Lutheran Church in America: 8765 West Higgins Rd, Chicago, IL 60631; tel. (773) 380-2700; fax (773) 380-1465; e-mail info@elca.org; internet www.elca.org; f. 1988; 10,657 churches; 5m. mems; Head Bishop Rev. Dr Mark Stephen Hanson; Sec. Rev. Dr Lowell G. Almen.

Lutheran Church—Missouri Synod: 1333 South Kirkwood Rd, St Louis, MO 63122-7295; tel. (314) 965-9000; e-mail infocenter@lcms.org; internet www.lcms.org; f. 1847; 6,220 churches; 2.6m. mems; Pres. Dr Alvin L. Barry; Sec. Dr Raymond Hartwig.

The Methodist Church

Members (1998 estimate): 13.4m. in eight bodies, of which the following have the greatest number of members:

African Methodist Episcopal Church: 1134 11th St, NW, Washington, DC 20001; tel. (202) 371-8700; f. 1816; 86,200 churches, 2.5m. mems; Sr Bishop John H. Adams; Gen. Sec. Dr Cecil W. Howard.

African Methodist Episcopal Zion Church: POB 32843, Charlotte, NC 28232; tel. (704) 333-1769; f. 1796; 3,098 churches; 1.3m. mems; Pres. Samuel Chuka Ekenam, Sr.

The United Methodist Church: POB 320, Nashville, TN; tel. 37202; e-mail infoserve@umcom.umc.org; f. 1968; 35,102 pastoral charges and 8.3m. mems (2002); Pres. of Council of Bishops Bishop Peter Weaver; Sec. Gen. Conf. Carolyn M. Marshall.

The Orthodox Churches

Members (1998 estimate): 5.1m. in 12 bodies, of which the following have the greatest number of members:

Antiochian Orthodox Christian Archdiocese of North America (Greek Orthodox Patriarchate of Antioch and all the East): 358 Mountain Rd, Englewood, NJ 07631-3798; tel. (201) 871-1355; fax (201) 871-7954; e-mail archdiocese@antiochian.org; internet www.antiochian.org; f. 1895; 250 churches; 350,000 mems; Primate Metropolitan Philip (Saliba); Auxiliaries Bishop Joseph (Al-Zehlaoui), Bishop Basil (Essey), Bishop Demetri (Khouri), Bishop Thomas (Joseph), Bishop Mark (Maymon), Bishop Alexander (Mufarrij).

Armenian Apostolic Church of America: Eastern Prelacy: 138 East 39th St, New York, NY 10016; Western Prelacy: 6252 Honolulu Ave, La Crescenta, CA 91214; tel. (818) 248-7737; fax (818) 248-7745; e-mail prelacy@gis.net; internet www.armprelacy.org; tel. (323) 663-8273; fax (323) 663-0438; e-mail prelacy@aol.com; f. 1887; 32 churches; 150,000 mems; Prelate (Eastern Prelacy) Archbishop Oshagan Choloyan; Prelate (Western Prelacy) Archbishop Moushegh Mardirosian.

Armenian Church of America: Eastern Diocese, 630 Second Ave, New York, NY 10016; Western Diocese, 3325 North Glenoaks Blvd, Burbank, CA 91504; tel. (212) 686-0710; internet www.armeniandiocese.org; tel. (818) 558-7474; fax (818) 558-6333; f. 1889; 94 churches; 660,000 mems; Primate (Eastern Diocese) Archbishop Khajag Barsamian; Primate (Western Diocese) Archbishop Vatché Hovsepian.

THE UNITED STATES OF AMERICA

Greek Orthodox Archdiocese of North and South America: 10 East 79th St, New York, NY 10021-0191; tel. (212) 570-3500; fax (212) 861-8060; e-mail archdiocese@goarch.org; internet www.goarch.org; inc 1922; 600 churches; 2.5m. mems; Primate Archbishop DIMITRIOS; Chancellor Very Rev. SAVAS ZEMBILLAS (Troas).

Orthodox Church in America: POB 675, Syosset, NY 11791; tel. (516) 922-0550; fax (516) 922-0954; e-mail info@oca.org; internet www.oca.org; f. 1794; fmrly Russian Orthodox Greek Catholic Church of North America; 700 churches; 600,000 mems (2002); Primate Metropolitan HERMAN; Chancellor Archpriest ROBERT S. KONDRATICK; Dir of Communications Archpriest JOHN MATUSIAK.

The Albanian, Bulgarian, Coptic, Romanian, Russian, Serbian, Syrian and Ukrainian Orthodox Churches are also represented.

The Presbyterian Church

Members (1998 estimate): 4.1m. in nine bodies, of which the following have the greatest number of members:

Presbyterian Church in America: 1852 Century Pl., NE, Atlanta, GA 30345-4305; tel. (404) 320-3366; fax (404) 329-1275; e-mail ac@pcanet.org; internet www.pcanet.org; f. 1973; 1,340 churches; 280,000 mems; Moderator Rev. KENNEDY SMARTT; Stated Clerk Dr L. ROY TAYLOR.

Presbyterian Church (USA): 100 Witherspoon St, Louisville, KY 40202-1396; tel. (502) 569-5000; fax (502) 569-5018; e-mail presytel@pcusa.org; internet www.pcusa.org; f. 1983; 11,328 churches; 3.6m. mems; Moderator SYNGMAN RHEE; Stated Clerk Rev. CLIFTON KIRKPATRICK.

The Roman Catholic Church

At December 2003 there were 19,081 parishes in 195 dioceses and eparchies, with some 63.4m. mems.

United States Conference of Catholic Bishops: 3211 Fourth St, NE, Washington, DC 20017-1194; tel. (202) 541-3000; fax (202) 541-3322; internet www.usccb.org; f. 2001 by merger of the Nat. Conference of Catholic Bishops (f. 1966) and US Catholic Conference (f. 1966); Pres. Mgr WILLIAM S. SKYLSTAD (Bishop of Spokane); Gen. Sec. Mgr WILLIAM P. FAY.

Archbishops

Anchorage: ROGER L. SCHWIETZ.
Atlanta: WILTON D. GREGORY.
Baltimore: Cardinal WILLIAM H. KEELER.
Boston: SEAN PATRICK O'MALLEY.
Chicago: Cardinal FRANCIS E. GEORGE.
Cincinnati: DANIEL E. PILARCZYK.
Denver: CHARLES J. CHAPUT.
Detroit: Cardinal ADAM J. MAIDA.
Dubuque: JEROME G. HANUS.
Galveston-Houston: JOSEPH A. FIORENZA.
Hartford: HENRY J. MANSELL.
Indianapolis: DANIEL M. BUECHLEIN.
Kansas City in Kansas: JAMES P. KELEHER.
Los Angeles: Cardinal ROGER M. MAHONY.
Louisville: THOMAS C. KELLY.
Miami: JOHN C. FAVALORA.
Milwaukee: TIMOTHY M. DOLAN.
Mobile: OSCAR H. LIPSCOMB.
Newark: JOHN JOSEPH MYERS.
New Orleans: ALFRED C. HUGHES.
New York: Cardinal EDWARD MICHAEL EGAN.
Oklahoma City: EUSEBIUS J. BELTRAN.
Omaha: ELDEN F. CURTISS.
Philadelphia: Cardinal JUSTIN F. RIGALI, STEFAN SOROKA (Ukrainian, Byzantine Rite).
Pittsburgh: DONALD W. WUERL (until 22 June 2006); BASIL M. SCHOTT (Ruthenian, Byzantine Rite).
Portland in Oregon: JOHN G. VLAZNY.
Saint Louis: RAYMOND L. BURKE.
Saint Paul and Minneapolis: HARRY J. FLYNN.
San Antonio: JOSÉ H. GÓMEZ.
San Francisco: WILLIAM J. LEVADA.
Santa Fe: MICHAEL J. SHEEHAN.
Seattle: ALEXANDER J. BRUNETT.
Washington: Cardinal THEODORE E. MCCARRICK (until 22 June 2006), DONALD W. WUERL (from 22 June 2006).

Other Christian Churches

Assemblies of God: 1445 Boonville Ave, Springfield, MO 65802-1894; tel. (417) 862-2781; fax (417) 863-6614; e-mail info@ag.org; internet www.ag.org; f. 1914; 12,082 churches in USA; 2.6m. mems in USA; Gen. Supt THOMAS E. TRASK; Gen. Sec. GEORGE O. WOOD.

Christian Church (Disciples of Christ) in the USA and Canada: 130 East Washington St, POB 1986, Indianapolis, IN 46206-1986; tel. (317) 635-3100; fax (317) 635-3700; internet www.disciples.org; f. 1804; 3,750 congregations; 750,000 mems; Gen. Minister and Pres. Dr SHARON E. WATKINS.

Christian Reformed Church in North America: 2850 Kalamazoo Ave, SE, Grand Rapids, MI 49560; tel. (616) 224-0744; fax (616) 224-5895; e-mail engelhad@crcna.org; internet www.crcna.org; f. 1857; 1,021 churches; 273,220 mems (USA and Canada); Gen. Sec. Dr DAVID H. ENGELHARD.

Church of Christ: POB 472, Independence, MO 64051; e-mail cofctl@kcnet.com; f. 1830; Sec. Council of Apostles Apostle SMITH N. BRICKHOUSE.

Church of Christ, Scientist: 175 Huntington Ave, Boston, MA 02115; tel. (617) 450-2000; fax (617) 450-3554; internet www.tfccs.com; f. 1879; 2,400 congregations world-wide; Pres. JEAN STARK HEBENSTREIT; Clerk OLGA M. CHAFFEE.

Church of God in Christ: Mason Temple, 939 Mason St, Memphis, TN 38126; f. 1907; 15,300 churches; 5.5m. mems; Presiding Bishop CHANDLER D. OWENS.

Church of Jesus Christ of Latter-day Saints (Mormon): 47 East South Temple St, Salt Lake City, UT 84150-0001; tel. (801) 240-1000; fax (801) 240-2033; internet www.lds.org; f. 1830; 10,811 wards and brs (congregations) in USA; 4.9m. mems in USA; Pres. GORDON B. HINCKLEY.

Church of the Nazarene: 6401 The Paseo, Kansas City, MO 64131-1284; tel. (816) 333-7000; fax (816) 361-4983; f. 1908; 13,672 churches world-wide; 1.5m. mems world-wide; Gen. Sec. JACK STONE.

Friends United Meeting: 101 Quaker Hill Dr., Richmond, IN 47374-1980; tel. (765) 962-7573; fax (765) 966-1293; e-mail info@fum.org; internet www.fum.org; f. 1902; 44,000 mems (USA and Canada); Presiding Clerk BRENT MCKINNEY; Gen. Sec. RETHA MCCUTCHEN.

Mariavite Old Catholic Church—Province of North America: 2803 10th St, Wyandotte, MI 48192-4994; tel. and fax (734) 281-3082; fax (734) 281-3082; e-mail mariaviteocc@hotmail.com; f. 1930; 158 churches; 357,100 mems; Prime Bishop Most Rev. Archbishop Dr ROBERT R. J. M. ZABOROWSKI.

Reformed Church in America, General Synod: 475 Riverside Dr., New York, NY 10115-0001; tel. (212) 870-3071; fax (212) 870-2499; internet www.rca.org; f. 1628; 949 churches; 284,520 mems; Gen. Sec. Rev. WESLEY GRANBERG-MICHAELSON.

Seventh-day Adventists: 12501 Old Columbia Pike, Silver Spring, MD 20904-6600; tel. (301) 680-6400; fax (301) 680-6464; internet www.nadadventist.org; f. 1863; 5,026 churches; 998,450 mems (USA and Canada); Pres. JAN PAULSEN; Sec. ROSCOE J. HOWARD, III.

United Church of Christ: 700 Prospect Ave, Cleveland, OH 44115; tel. (216) 736-2100; fax (216) 736-2120; internet www.ucc.org; f. 1957; 5,923 churches; 1.4m. mems; Gen. Minister and Pres. Rev. JOHN H. THOMAS.

United Pentecostal Church International: 8855 Dunn Rd, Hazelwood, MO 63042-2212; tel. (314) 837-7300; fax (314) 837-4503; e-mail upcimain@aol.com; internet www.upci.org; f. 1945; 4,142 churches; 502,000 mems (USA and Canada); Gen. Supt Rev. KENNETH F. HANEY.

BAHÁ'Í FAITH

National Spiritual Assembly of Bahá'ís of the United States: 1320 19th St, NW, Suite 20, Washington, DC 20036-1610; tel. (202) 466-9870; fax (202) 466-9873; e-mail opi@usbnc.org; f. 1844 in Persia (Iran); 150,0000 mems; Chair. WILLIAM E. DAVIS; Sec.-Gen. Dr ROBERT C. HENDERSON.

BUDDHISM

There are an estimated 780,000 Buddhists in the USA.

American Buddhist Movement: 301 West 45th St, New York, NY 10036; tel. (212) 489-1075; e-mail kr_oneil@msn.com; internet www.buddhismonline.us; f. 1980; 15 regional groups; Pres. Dr KEVIN R. O'NEIL.

Buddhist Churches of America: 1710 Octavia St, San Francisco, CA 94109-4341; tel. (415) 776-5600; fax (415) 771-6293; e-mail bcahq@pacbell.net; f. 1899; Hongwanji-ha Jodo Shinshu denomination; c.230,000 mems; Presiding Bishop KOSHIN OGUI.

HINDUISM

There are an estimated 1.3m. Hindus in the USA.

THE UNITED STATES OF AMERICA

Ramakrishna–Vivekananda Center: 17 East 94th St, New York, NY 10128; tel. (212) 534-9445; fax (212) 828-1618; e-mail rvcnewyork@worldnet.att.net; internet www.ramakrishna.org; f. 1933; teachings based on the system of Vedanta; Minister and Spiritual Leader SWAMI ADISWARANANDA; Dir BARRY ZELIKOVSKY.

ISLAM

There are an estimated 4.0m. Muslims in the USA, of whom African-American Muslims are estimated to number 1.3m.

Council of Masajid of United States (CMUS): 45 Lilac St, Edison, NJ 08817; tel. (732) 985-3304; fax (732) 572-0486; e-mail dawud10@optonline.net; f. 1978; educational agency representing 650 local groups; Pres. DAWUD ASSAD.

Federation of Islamic Associations in the US and Canada: 25351 Five Mile and Aubery Rd, Redford Township, MI 48239; tel. (313) 534-3295; fax (313) 534-1474; f. 1951; co-ordinating agency for 45 affiliated orgs; Gen. Sec. NIHAD HAMED.

Islamic Center of New York: 1711 Third Ave, New York, NY 10029-7303; tel. (212) 722-5234; fax (212) 722-5936; f. 1966; Dir ZIYAD MONAYAIR.

Islamic Mission of America: 143 State St, Brooklyn, NY 11201; tel. (718) 875-6607; f. 1938; maintains an educational and training institute; 15,000 mems; Chair. MOHAMED KABBAJ.

JUDAISM

There are an estimated 6.2m. Jews in North America.

American Jewish Congress: 15 East 84th St, New York, NY 10028-0458; tel. (212) 879-4500; fax (212) 249-3672; internet www.ajcongress.org; f. 1918; 50,000 mems; Pres. JACK ROSEN.

Central Conference of American Rabbis: 355 Lexington Ave, New York, NY 10017; tel. (212) 972-3636; e-mail info@ccarnet.org; internet www.ccarnet.org; f. 1889; Reform; 1,840 mems; Pres. JANET MARDER.

The Rabbinical Assembly: 3080 Broadway, New York, NY 10027-4650; tel. (212) 280-6000; fax (212) 749-9166; e-mail info@rabbinicalassembly.org; internet www.rabassembly.org; f. 1901; 1,550 mems; Pres. Rabbi PERRY RAPHAEL RANK; Exec. Vice-Pres. Rabbi JOEL H. MEYERS.

Union of Orthodox Jewish Congregations of America: 11 Broadway, New York, NY 10004; tel. (212) 563-4000; fax (212) 564-9058; e-mail info@ou.org; internet www.ou.org; f. 1898; 1,000 affiliated congregations representing c. 1m. mems; Pres. HARVEY BLITZ; Exec. Vice-Pres. Rabbi Dr TZVI HERSH WEINVEB.

Union for Reform Judaism: 633 Third Ave, New York, NY 10017-6778; tel. (212) 650-4000; fax (212) 650-4169; e-mail urj@urj.org; f. 1873 as the Union of American Hebrew Congregations; present name adopted 2003; Reform; more than 900 affiliated congregations representing c. 1.5m. mems; Pres. Rabbi ERIC H. YOFFIE; Vice-Pres. Rabbi LEONARD R. THAL.

United Synagogue of Conservative Judaism: 155 Fifth Ave, New York, NY 10010-6802; tel. (212) 533-7800; fax (212) 353-9439; e-mail info@uscj.org; internet www.uscj.org; f. 1913; 760 affiliated congregations in North America representing c. 1.5m. mems; Pres. JUDY YUDOF; Exec. Vice-Pres. Rabbi JEROME EPSTEIN.

SIKHISM

There are an estimated 498,000 Sikhs in North America.

International Sikh Organization: 1901 Pennsylvania Ave, NW, Washington, DC 20006; Pres. Dr GURMIT SINGH AULAKH.

Sikh Center: 2514 West Warner Ave, Santa Ana, CA 92704; tel. (714) 797-9328; internet www.sikhcenter.org; Chief Admin. Siri Singh Sahib HARBHAJAN SINGH KHALSA YOGIJI; Sec.-Gen. SARDANI GURU AMRIT KAUR KHALSA.

The Press

The USA publishes more newspapers and periodicals than any other country. Most dailies give a greater emphasis to local news because of the strong interest in local and regional affairs and the decentralized structure of many government services. These factors, together with the distribution problem inherent in the size of the country, are responsible for the lack of national newspapers. In 2003 it was estimated that some 53.4% of the adult population read a daily newspaper.

Most influential and highly respected among the few newspapers with a national readership are the *New York Times* (which introduced a national edition in 1980), the *Washington Post*, *Los Angeles Times* and *The Wall Street Journal* (the financial and news daily with editions in New York City, California, Illinois and Texas, and a European and an Asian edition). In 1982 the first national general interest newspaper, *USA Today*, was introduced by Gannett. An international edition was launched in 1984.

In 2005 56 daily newspapers had circulations of over 250,000 copies. Among the largest of these, in order of daily circulation, were *USA Today*, *The Wall Street Journal*, *The New York Times*, *Los Angeles Times*, *The Washington Post*, *Chicago Tribune*, *New York Daily News*, *The Denver Post/Rocky Mountain News*, *The Philadelphia Inquirer* and *The Houston Chronicle*.

In 2004 there were 1,456 English-language daily newspapers, with a total circulation (in September of the previous year) of 55.2m. copies per day. The Sunday edition is an important and distinctive feature of US newspaper publishing; many Sunday newspapers run to over 300 pages. In 2004 there were 917 Sunday newspapers, with a total circulation of about 58.5m. (as of September 2003). In 2003 there were 6,704 weekly newspapers.

The famous tradition of press freedom in the USA is grounded in the First Amendment to the Constitution which declares that 'Congress shall make no law. . . abridging the freedom of speech or of the Press. . .' and confirmed in the legislations of many states which prohibit any kind of legal restriction on the dissemination of news.

Legislation affecting the Press is both state and federal. A source of controversy between the Press and the courts has been the threat of the encroachment by judicial decrees on the area of courtroom and criminal trial coverage. In 1972 the Supreme Court ruled that journalists were not entitled to refuse to give evidence before grand juries on information they have received confidentially. Since then the frequent issuing of subpoenas to journalists and the jailing of several reporters for refusing to disclose sources has led to many 'shield' bills being put before Congress and state legislatures calling for immunity for journalists from both federal and state jurisdiction.

In recent years, increased production costs have subjected the industry to considerable economic strain, resulting in mergers and take-overs, a great decline in competition between dailies in the same city, and the appearance of inter-city dailies catering for two or more adjoining centres. A consequence of these trends has been the steady growth of newspaper groups or chains.

The following are among the principal daily newspaper groups:

Advance Publications, Inc: 950 Fingerboard Rd, Staten Island; tel. (212) 286-2860; fax (718) 981-1456; Chair. SAMUEL I. ('SI') NEWHOUSE, Jr; Pres. DONALD E. NEWHOUSE; interests in cable television and internet websites; owns Condé Nast Publications, Parade Publications, and American City Business Journals.

Newhouse Newspapers: 711 Third Ave, 15th Floor, New York, NY 10017; tel. (212) 697-8020; fax (212) 972-3146; internet www.newhouse.com; Pres. DONALD E. NEWHOUSE; 25 daily newspapers incl. *The Star-Ledger*, *The Cleveland Plain Dealer* and *The Oregonian*; more than 40 weekly newspapers.

American Community Newspapers: 10917 Valley View Rd, Eden Prairie, MN 55344; tel. (952) 829-0797; e-mail webinfo@mnsun.com; internet www.americancommunitynewspapers.com; CEO GENE M. CARR; 2 daily and 68 weekly newspapers, incl. the Sun Newspapers group; combined circ. c. 900,000.

Block Communications, Inc (BCI): 541 North Superior St, Toledo, OH 43660; tel. (419) 724-6000; e-mail info@blockcommunications.com; internet www.blockcommunications.com; f. 1900; Chair. WILLIAM BLOCK, Jr; Man. Dir ALLAN BLOCK; 2 daily newspapers, *The Pittsburgh Post-Gazette* and *The Toledo Blade*; also owns 2 cable cos, 5 television stations and a telephone co; interests in security, cable construction and advertising.

The Copely Press, Inc: 7776 Ivanhoe Ave, La Jolla, CA 92037; tel. (858) 454-0411; fax (858) 729-7629; internet www.copleynewspapers.com; f. 1928; Chair., Pres. and CEO DAVID C. COPELY; 10 daily newspapers, incl. *The San Diego Union-Tribune*, 9 weekly newspapers and 1 bi-weekly newspaper; owns the Copley News Service syndicate (f. 1955).

Cox Newspapers, Inc: 6205 Peachtree Dunwoody Rd, Atlanta, GA 30328; tel. (678) 645-0000; e-mail christopher.caneles@cox.com; internet www.coxnews.com; f. 1898; Pres. JAY R. SMITH; 17 daily newspapers, incl. *The Atlanta Journal-Constitution*, and 24 weekly newspapers; combined weekday circ. 1.2m., combined Sun. circ. 1.6m.

Dow Jones & Co Inc: 1 World Financial Center, 200 Liberty St, New York, NY 10281; tel. (212) 416-2000; fax (212) 416-3478; internet www.dowjones.com; f. 1882; Chair. PETER R. KANN; CEO RICHARD ZANNINO; publs incl. *The Wall Street Journal*, the weekly financial magazine *Barron's* and the monthly *Far Eastern Economic Review*; also incl. the community newspaper subsidiary.

Ottaway Newspapers, Inc (ONI): POB 401, Campbell Hall, NY 10916; tel. (845) 294-8181; internet www.ottaway.com; f. 1936; merged with Dow Jones in 1970; Chair. and CEO DAN W. AUSTIN; Pres. JOHN N. WILCOX; 15 daily and 18 weekly newspapers; 18 other publs; combined weekday circ. 1.3m., combined Sun. circ. 1.4m.

Freedom Communications, Inc: 17666 Fitch, Irvine, CA 92614-6022; tel. (949) 253-2300; fax (949) 474-7675; e-mail info@link

THE UNITED STATES OF AMERICA

.freedom.com; internet www.freedom.com; Pres. ALAN J. BELL; 28 daily newspapers, incl. *The Orange County Register*, and 37 weekly publs; combined weekday circ. 1.2m.; owns 8 television stations.

Gannett Co Inc: 7950 Jones Branch Dr., McLean, VA 22107; tel. (703) 854-6000; fax (703) 854-2046; e-mail gcishare@info.gannett.com; internet www.gannett.com; f. 1906; Chair. DOUGLAS H. MCCORKINDALE; Pres. and CEO CRAIG A. DUBOW; largest US newspaper group in terms of total circ; 99 daily newspapers incl. *USA Today*, *Detroit Free Press* and *The Arizona Republic*; combined weekday circ. 7.6m.; owns 21 television stations broadcasting to 17.9% of the USA, and more than 130 internet websites.

Hearst Corpn: 959 Eighth Ave, New York, NY 10019; tel. (212) 649-2148; fax (212) 649-2108; internet www.hearstcorp.com; Chair. GEORGE R. HEARST, Jr; Pres. and CEO VICTOR F. GANZI; 12 daily newspapers, incl. the *Houston Chronicle* and *San Francisco Chronicle*, and 14 weekly newspapers; 18 magazines incl. *Good Housekeeping*, *Cosmopolitan*, *O, The Oprah Magazine* and *Redbook*; interests in television and radio broadcasting, cable networks, interactive media, and business information publishing.

Knight Ridder: 50 West San Fernando St, San Jose, CA 95113-2413; tel. (408) 938-7700; fax (408) 938-7755; internet www.knightridder.com; f. 1974 by merger of Knight Newspapers, Inc and Ridder Publications, Inc; Chair. and CEO P. ANTHONY RIDDER; 32 daily newspapers incl. the *Miami Herald* and the *Philadelphia Enquirer*; combined weekday circ. 8.5m., combined Sun. circ. 11.0m.

Lee Enterprises: 201 North Harrison St, Davenport, IA 52801-1939; tel. (563) 383-2100; internet www.lee.net; f. 1890; Chair., Pres. and CEO MARY E. JUNCK; 58 daily newspapers and more than 300 weekly newspapers and speciality publs; combined weekday circ. 1.7m., combined Sunday circ. 2.0m.; interests in publishing, and purchasing and distribution of raw materials.

The McClatchy Co: 2100 Q St, POB 15779, Sacramento, CA 95818; tel. (916) 321-1855; fax (916) 321-1869; e-mail contact@mcclatchy.com; internet www.mcclatchy.com; Publr JAMES B. MCCLATCHY; Chair., Pres. and CEO GARY B. PRUITT; 12 daily newspapers, incl. the *Star Tribune*, and 17 community newspapers; combined weekday circ. 1.4m., combined Sun. circ. 1.9m.

Media General, Inc: POB 85333, Richmond, VA 23293-0001; tel. (804) 649-6059; e-mail etucker@mediageneral.com; internet www.mediageneral.com; Pres. and CEO MARSHALL N. MORTON; 25 daily newspapers, incl. *The Tampa Tribune*, and c. 100 weekly newspapers and other publs; holds a 20% interest in *The Denver Post*; owns 26 television stations.

MediaNews Group: 1560 Broadway, Suite 2100, Denver, CO 80202; tel. (303) 563-6360; fax (303) 894-9327; internet www.medianewsgroup.com; Vice-Chair. and CEO WILLIAM DEAN SINGLETON; Pres. JODY LODOVIC; 40 daily newspapers incl. *The Denver Post* (under a jt operating agreement with *The Rocky Mountain News*, publ. by E. W. Scripps); combined weekday circ. 1.7m., combined Sun. circ. 2.3m.; owns a television station and a radio station.

New York Times Co: 229 West 43rd St, New York, NY 10036; tel. (212) 556-1234; internet www.nytco.com; Chair. ARTHUR SULZBERGER, Jr; Pres. and CEO JANET L. ROBINSON; 18 daily newspapers incl. *The New York Times*, *The International Herald Tribune* and *The Boston Globe*; owns 9 television stations, 2 radio stations, and 35 internet websites.

E. W. Scripps Co: 312 Walnut St, 2800 Scripps Center, Cincinnati, OH 45202; POB 5380, Cincinnati, OH 45201; tel. (513) 977-3000; fax (513) 977-3721; e-mail corpcomm@scripps.com; internet www.scripps.com; Chair. WILLIAM R. BURLEIGH; Pres. and CEO KENNETH W. LOWE; 21 daily newspapers, incl. *The Rocky Mountain News* (under a jt operating agreement with *The Denver Post*, publ. by MediaNews), and 5 community newspapers; owns the Scripps Howard News Service syndicate, 10 television stations, and 5 cable and satellite programming networks.

Tribune Publishing: 435 North Michigan Ave, Chicago, IL 60611; tel. (312) 222-9100; fax (312) 222-4760; internet www.tribune.com; f. 1847; subsidiary of Tribune Co; merged with the Times Mirror Co in 2000; Pres. SCOTT SMITH; 11 daily newspapers incl. *Newsday*, the *Chicago Tribune*, the *Los Angeles Times*, the *Baltimore Sun* and the Spanish-language newspaper *Hoy*; combined weekday circ. 8.0m., combined Sun. circ. 12.0m.

PRINCIPAL DAILY AND SUNDAY NEWSPAPERS
(m = morning; e = evening; d = all day; s = Sunday)

In general, only newspapers with circulations exceeding 50,000 are included, except in Wyoming, where the newspaper with the largest circulation is listed.

Alabama

Birmingham News: 2200 North Fourth Ave, POB 2553, Birmingham, AL 35202-2553; tel. (205) 325-2222; fax (205) 325-2410; internet www.bhamnews.com; f. 1888; Publr V. H. HANSON, II; Editor THOMAS SCARRITT; circ. 152,000 (e), 186,000 (s).

Huntsville Times: 2317 Memorial Parkway, Huntsville, AL 35801-5623; tel. (205) 532-4000; fax (205) 532-4420; internet www.htimes.com; f. 1910; Publr BOB LUDWIG; Editor JOE DISTELHEIM; circ. 60,000 (d), 67,000 (Sat.), 85,000 (s).

Mobile Register, Mobile Press-Register: 304 Government St, POB 2488, Mobile, AL 36630; tel. (334) 433-1551; fax (334) 434-8662; e-mail gtab@dibbs.net; internet www.al.com; f. 1813; Publr HOWARD BRONSON; Editor KEN BOOTH; circ. 100,000 (m, Mobile Register), 120,000 (s, *Mobile Press Register*).

Montgomery Advertiser: 200 Washington Ave, POB 1000, Montgomery, AL 36101-1000; tel. (334) 262-1611; fax (334) 261-1521; e-mail advertiser@compuserve.com; internet www.montgomeryadvertiser.com; f. 1828; Publr SCOTT M. BROWN; Exec. Editor PAULA MOORE; circ. 59,000 (m), 73,000 (s).

Alaska

Anchorage Daily News: 1001 Northway Dr., POB 149001, Anchorage, AK 99514-9001; tel. (907) 257-4200; fax (907) 258-2157; e-mail subscription@adn.com; internet www.adn.com; f. 1946; Publr MICHAEL SEXTON; Editor W. PATRICK DOUGHERTY; circ. 71,400 (m), 85,800 (s).

Arizona

Arizona Daily Star: 4850 South Park Ave, POB 26807, Tucson, AZ 85726-6807; tel. (520) 573-4220; fax (520) 573-4107; internet www.azstarnet.com; f. 1877; Publr and Editor JOHN M. HUMENIK; circ. 106,590 (m), 168,485 (s).

Arizona Republic: 120 East Van Buren St, Phoenix, AZ 85001; tel. (602) 271-8000; fax (602) 271-8044; internet www.arizonarepublic.com; f. 1890; Editor TOM CALLINAN; circ. 496,000 (m), 601,000 (s).

Tucson Citizen: 4850 South Park Ave, POB 26807, Tucson, AZ 85726-6807; tel. (520) 573-4560; fax (520) 573-4569; e-mail citizen@tucsoncitizen.com; internet www.tucsoncitizen.com; f. 1870; Publr and Editor MICHAEL CHIHAK; circ. 51,000 (e).

Arkansas

Democrat-Gazette: POB 2221, Little Rock, AR 72203; tel. (501) 378-3400; fax (501) 372-3908; e-mail news@ardemgaz.com; internet www.ardemgaz.com; f. 1819; Publr WALTER E. HUSSMAN, Jr; Exec. Editor GRIFFIN SMITH, Jr; circ. 172,223 (m), 285,731 (s).

California

Bakersfield Californian: POB 440, Bakersfield, CA 93302-0440; tel. (805) 395-7500; fax (805) 395-7519; internet www.bakersfield.com; f. 1866; Publr GINGER MOORHOUSE; Exec. Editor MIKE JENNER; circ. 77,000 (m), 92,000 (s).

Daily Breeze: Copley Los Angeles Newspapers, 5215 Torrance Blvd, Torrance, CA 90509; tel. (310) 540-5511; f. 1894; Mon. to Sat. evening, Sun. morning; Publr ART WIBLE; Exec. Editor SUE SCHMITT; circ. 82,372 (e), 120,302 (s).

Daily News: 21221 Oxnard St, Woodland Hills, POB 4200, CA 91367; tel. (818) 713-3000; fax (818) 713-0057; internet www.dailynews.com; f. 1911; morning; Publr JOHN SCHUELER; Editor DAVID J. BUTLER; circ. 207,421 (m), 192,326 (Sat.), 226,294 (s).

Fresno Bee: 3425 North First St, Suite 201, Fresno, CA 93726-6819; tel. (209) 441-6111; fax (209) 441-6436; f. 1922; Publr J. KEITH MOYER; Exec. Editor CHARLIE WATERS; circ. 155,000 (m), 192,000 (s).

Investor's Business Daily: 12655 Beatrice Ave, Los Angeles, CA 90066; tel. (310) 448-6000; fax (310) 577-7350; e-mail ibdcust@investors.com; internet www.investors.com; f. 1984; morning; Publr W. SCOTT O'NEILL; Editor WESLEY F. MANN; circ. 233,000.

Los Angeles Times: 202 West First St, Los Angeles, CA 90012-3645; tel. (213) 237-5000; fax (213) 237-4712; internet www.latimes.com; f. 1881; Pres. and Publr JOHN PUERNER; Editor JOHN CARROLL; circ. 1,111,000 (m), 1,384,000 (s).

Modesto Bee: 1325 H St, Modesto, CA 95354; tel. (209) 578-2000; fax (209) 578-2207; internet www.modbee.com; f. 1884; Publr LYNN DICKERSON; Exec. Editor MARK VASCHE; circ. 83,023 (m), 90,341 (s).

Oakland Tribune: 401 13th St, Alameda, CA 94612; tel. (510) 208-6400; fax (510) 208-6477; internet www.oaklandtribune.com; f. 1874; Editor MARIO DIANDA; circ. 77,000 (m), 75,000 (s).

Orange County Register: 625 North Grand Ave, POB 11626, Santa Ana, CA 92701-4347; tel. (714) 767-7000; fax (714) 796-3681; e-mail ocregister@link.freedom.com; internet www.ocregister.com; Publr CHRISTIAN ANDERSON; Editor TONNIE KATZ; circ. 358,654 (d), 412,553 (s).

Press Democrat: 427 Mendocino Ave, Santa Rosa, CA 95401; tel. (707) 546-2020; fax (707) 521-5330; internet www.pressdemocrat

THE UNITED STATES OF AMERICA

.com; f. 1857; Publr MICHAEL PARMAN; Exec. Editor CATHERINE BARNETT; circ. 99,363 (m), 102,985 (s).

Press Enterprise: 3512 14th St, POB 792, Riverside, CA 92501; tel. (714) 684-1200; fax (714) 782-7630; internet www.pe.com; f. 1878; publ. by Belo Corpn; morning; Publr WILLIAM D. RICH; Exec. Editor MARCIA MCQUERN; circ. 154,790 (m), 162,940 (s).

Press-Telegram: 604 Pine Ave, Long Beach, CA 90844-0001; tel. (562) 435-1161; fax (562) 437-7892; e-mail ptconnect@infi.net; internet www.ptconnect.com; Pres. and Publr IAN LAMONT; Exec. Editor RICH ARCHBOLD; circ. 106,000 (d), 125,000 (s).

Sacramento Bee: 2100 Q St, POB 15779, Sacramento, CA 95852; tel. (916) 321-1000; fax (916) 321-1109; e-mail jheapy@sacbee.com; internet www.sacbee.com; f. 1857; Pres. and Publr JANIS HEAPHY; Exec. Editor RICK RODRIGUEZ; circ. 293,973 (m), 352,629 (s).

San Bernardino County Sun: 399 North D St, San Bernardino, CA 92401-1518; tel. (909) 889-9666; fax (909) 381-3976; e-mail citydesk@sbsun.com; internet www.sbsun.com; f. 1894; Publr BOB GRAY; Editor STEVE LAMBERT; circ. 82,000 (m), 91,000 (s).

San Diego Union-Tribune: 350 Camino de la Reina, San Diego, CA 92112; tel. (619) 299-3131; fax (619) 293-1896; e-mail letters@uniontrib.com; internet www.uniontrib.com; f. 1868; Publr HELEN K. COPLEY; Editor KARIN WINNER; circ. 376,500 (d), 453,900 (s).

San Francisco Chronicle: 901 Mission St, San Francisco, CA 94103; tel. (415) 777-1111; fax (415) 896-1107; e-mail chronletters@sfgate.com; internet www.sfgate.com; f. 1865; Publr, Chair and CEO JOHN OPPEDAHL; Editor ROBERT S. CAUTHORN; circ. 600,000 (m), 704,000 (s).

San Francisco Examiner: 988 Market St, San Francisco, CA 94103-2918; tel. (415) 359-2600; fax (415) 359-2766; internet www.examiner.com; f. 1887; Publr TED FANG; Editor J. PIMENTEL; circ. 70,000 (m), 90,000 (s).

San Jose Mercury News: 750 Ridder Park Dr., San Jose, CA 95190-0001; tel. (408) 920-5000; fax (408) 288-8060; internet www.mercurynews.com; f. 1851; Publr and Pres. JOSEPH 'CHIP' VISCI; Exec. Editor SUSAN GOLDBERG; circ. 276,166 (m), 309,520 (s).

Stockton Record: 530 East Market St, POB 900, Stockton, CA 95202-3009; tel. (209) 943-6397; fax (209) 943-8246; e-mail newsroom@recordnet.com; internet www.recordnet.com; f. 1895; Publr VIRGIL L. SMITH; Man. Editor JIM GOLD; circ. 54,000 (m), 60,000 (s).

Colorado

Denver Post: 1560 Broadway, Denver, CO 80202; tel. (303) 820-1010; fax (303) 820-1369; e-mail newsroom@denverpost.com; internet www.denverpost.com; f. 1892; Publr KIRK MACDONALD; Editor GLENN GUZZO; circ. 370,423 (m), 523,324 (s).

The Gazette: 30 South Prospect, Colorado Springs, CO 80903; tel. (719) 632-5511; fax (719) 636-0202; e-mail gtnews@usa.net; internet www.gazette.com; f. 1872; Publr SCOTT A. FISCHER; Editor SHARON PETERS; circ. 104,000 (m), 125,000 (s).

Rocky Mountain News: 400 West Colfax Ave, POB 719, Denver, CO 80204; tel. (303) 892-5000; fax (303) 892-5081; e-mail subscribe@rockymountainnews.com; internet www.rockymountainnews.com; f. 1859; Publr, Pres. and Editor JOHN R. TEMPLE; circ. 394,000 (m), 504,000 (s).

Connecticut

Connecticut Post: 410 State St, Bridgeport, CT 06604-4501; tel. (203) 333-0161; fax (203) 366-8158; e-mail ctnews@snet.net; internet www.connpost.com; f. 1883; Pres. and Publr ROBERT H. LASKA; Editor FRANK J. KEEGAN; circ. 78,255 (m), 90,217 (s).

Hartford Courant: 285 Broad St, Hartford, CT 06115-2510; tel. (860) 241-6200; fax (860) 520-3176; e-mail custserv@courant.com; internet www.courant.com; f. 1764; Publr and CEO JACK DAVIS; Editor BRIAN P. TOOLAN; circ. 211,866 (m), 298,143 (s).

New Haven Register: 40 Sargent Dr., New Haven, CT 06511; tel. (203) 789-5200; fax (203) 865-7894; e-mail editor@ctcentral.com; internet www.nhregister.com; f. 1812; Publr KEVIN F. WALSH; Editor JACK KRAMER; circ. 100,000 (m), 114,000 (s).

Waterbury Republican-American: American-Republican, Inc, 389 Meadow St, POB 2090, Waterbury, CT 06722-3636; tel. (203) 574-3636; fax (203) 754-0644; f. 1844; morning; Publr WILLIAM J. PAPE, II; Exec. Editor JONATHAN F. KELLOGG, II; circ. 60,202 (m), 77,682 (s).

Delaware

News Journal: 950 West Basin Rd, New Castle, DE 19720; tel. (302) 324-2500; fax (302) 324-5509; e-mail newsroom@newsjournal.com; internet www.newszap.com; f. 1871; Publr SAL DE VIVO; Editor DEBORAH S. HENLEY; circ. 126,000 (d), 140,000 (s).

District of Columbia

Washington Post: 1150 15th St, NW, Washington, DC 20071; tel. (202) 334-6000; fax (202) 334-5693; internet www.washingtonpost.com; f. 1877; Chair. DONALD E. GRAHAM; Publr and CEO BOISFEUILLET JONES; Exec. Editor LEONARD DOWNIE, Jr; Man. Editor STEVE COLL; circ. 802,594 (m), 1,070,809 (s).

Washington Times: 3600 New York Ave, NE, Washington, DC 20002; tel. (202) 636-3000; fax (202) 832-2206; internet www.washingtontimes.com; f. 1982; Editor-in-Chief WESLEY PRUDEN; Man. Editor FRANCIS B. COOMBS, Jr; circ. 100,932 (m), 72,524 (Sat.), 61,856 (s).

Florida

Daytona Beach News-Journal: 901 Sixth St, Daytona Beach, FL 32120-2831; tel. (904) 252-1511; fax (904) 258-8470; internet www.news-journalonline.com; f. 1904; morning; Publr and Gen. Man. GEORGIA M. KANEY; Exec. Editor DON LINLEY; circ. 99,556 (m), 117,571 (s).

Diario Las Américas: 2900 NW 39th St, Miami, FL 33142; tel. (305) 633-3341; fax (305) 635-7668; internet www.diariolasamericas.com; f. 1953; Spanish; Publr and Editor HORACIO AGUIRRE; circ. 66,000 (m), 70,000 (s).

Florida Times-Union: Riverside Ave, Jacksonville, FL 32202-4904; POB 1949, Jacksonville, FL 322311; tel. (904) 359-4111; fax (904) 359-4478; internet www.jacksonville.com; f. 1864; Publr CARL N. CANNON; Exec. Editor PAT YACK; circ. 170,504 (m), 251,216 (s).

Florida Today: Cape Pubs, Inc, POB 419000, Melbourne, FL 32941-9000; tel. (407) 242-3500; fax (407) 242-6618; f. 1966; morning; Publr MICHAEL J. COLEMAN; Exec. Editor TERRY EBERLE; circ. 83,502 (m), 111,674 (s).

Ledger: POB 408, Lakeland, FL 33802; tel. (813) 687-7000; fax (813) 687-7090; f. 1924; morning; Publr JOHN FITZWATER; Exec. Editor LOUIS MICHAEL PEREZ; circ. 81,325 (m), 99,143 (s).

Miami Herald: 1 Herald Plaza, Miami, FL 33132-1693; tel. (305) 350-2111; fax (305) 376-5287; internet www.miami.com; f. 1910; Publr ALBERTO IBARGUEN; Exec. Editor MARTIN BARON; circ. 310,870 (m), 482,149 (s).

News-Press: 2422 Dr Martin Luther King, Jr Blvd, Fort Myers, FL 33901-3987; tel. (941) 335-0200; fax (941) 332-7581; internet www.news-press.com; f. 1884; morning; Publr CAROL HUDLER; Editor KATE MARYMONT; circ. 93,769 (m), 116,944 (s).

Orlando Sentinel: 633 North Orange Ave, Orlando, FL 32801-1300; tel. (407) 420-5000; fax (407) 420-5350; internet www.orlandosentinel.com; f. 1876; morning; Publr, Pres. and CEO KATHLEEN WALTZ; Editor ANTHONY MOOR; circ. 260,367 (d), 382,439(s).

Palm Beach Post: 2751 South Dixie Hwy, West Palm Beach, FL 33405; tel. (561) 820-4100; fax (561) 820-4407; internet www.pbpost.com; f. 1916; Publr TOM GIUFFRIDA; Man. Editor BILL ROSE; Editor JOHN BARTOSEK; circ. 187,000 (m), 237,000 (s).

Pensacola News Journal: 101 East Romana St, Pensacola, FL 32502; POB 12710, Pensacola, FL 32591; tel. (850) 435-8500; fax (850) 435-8633; e-mail pns@gulfsurf.infi.net; internet www.gulfcoastgateway.com; f. 1889; Publr DENISE IVEY; Exec. Editor RANDY HAMMER; circ. 62,000 (m), 85,000 (s).

Sarasota Herald-Tribune: 801 South Tamiami Trail, Sarasota, FL 34236; tel. (941) 953-7755; fax (941) 957-5276; internet www.newscoast.com; f. 1925; Publr DIANE MCFARLIN; Exec. Editor MIKE CONNELLY; circ. 120,000 (m), 149,000 (s).

St Petersburg Times: 490 First Ave South, POB 1121, St Petersburg, FL 33701; tel. (813) 893-8111; fax (813) 893-8200; e-mail letters@sptimes.com; internet www.sptimes.com; f. 1894; CEO ANDREW BARNES; Pres. and Editor PAUL TASH; circ. 331,905 (m), 415,766 (s).

Sun-Sentinel: 200 East Las Olas Blvd, Fort Lauderdale, FL 33301-2293; tel. (954) 356-4000; fax (954) 356-4559; internet www.sun-sentinel.com; f. 1960; Publr ROBERT GREMILLION; Editor JEFF GLICK; circ. 600,000 (m), 850,000 (s).

Tampa Tribune: 200 Parker St, Tampa, FL 33606; POB 191, Tampa, FL 33601; tel. (813) 259-7111; fax (813) 254-4952; internet www.tampatrib.com; f. 1893; morning; Publr and Pres. GIL THELEN; Editor FRANK M. DENTON; circ. 252,000 (m), 350,000 (s).

Georgia

Atlanta Journal-Constitution: 72 Marietta St, POB 4689, Atlanta, GA 30302-4689; tel. (404) 526-5151; fax (404) 526-5746; e-mail access@ajc.com; internet www.ajc.com; f. 1950; Sun. morning; Publr JOHN MELLOT; Editor JULIA WALLACE; circ. 703,590.

Augusta Chronicle: 725 Broad St, POB 1928, Augusta, GA 30913-1928; tel. (706) 724-0851; fax (706) 722-5746; internet www

THE UNITED STATES OF AMERICA

.augustachronicle.com; Pres. JULIAN MILLER; Exec. Editor DENNIS SODOMKA; circ. 75,000 (m), 100,000 (s).

Macon Telegraph: 120 Broadway, Macon, GA 31201-3444; POB 4167, Macon, GA 31208; tel. (912) 744-4200; fax (912) 744-4269; e-mail metro@mto.infi.net; internet www.macon.com; f. 1826; Publr JEANIE ENYHART; Exec. Editor SHERRIE MARSHALL; circ. 69,420 (m), 90,491 (s).

Savannah Morning News: 111 West Bay St, Savannah, GA 31401; POB 1088, Savannah, GA 31402-1088; tel. (912) 236-9511; fax (912) 234-6522; internet www.savannahnow.com; f. 1850; Publr DON HARWOOD; Exec. Editor REXANNA LESTER, Jr; circ. 56,000 (m), 82,000 (s).

Hawaii

Honolulu Advertiser: The News Bldg, 605 Kapi'olani Blvd, POB 3110, Honolulu, HI 96802; tel. (808) 525-8000; fax (808) 525-8037; e-mail hawaii@honoluluadvertiser.com; internet www.honoluluadvertiser.com; f. 1856; Pres. and Publr MICHAEL J. FISCH; Editor SAUNDRA KEYES.

Honolulu Star-Bulletin: The News Bldg, 605 Kapi'olani Blvd, Honolulu, HI 96802; tel. (808) 525-8000; fax (808) 525-8037; e-mail editor@starbulletin.com; internet www.starbulletin.com; f. 1882; Pres. DON KENDALL; Editor FRANK BRIDGEWATER; circ. 66,000.

Idaho

Idaho Statesman: 1200 North Curtis Rd, POB 40, Boise, ID 83707; tel. (208) 377-6400; fax (208) 377-6449; e-mail news@idstates.com; internet www.idahostatesman.com; f. 1864; Publr MARGARET BUCHANAN; Man. Editor CAROLYN WASHBURN; circ. 66,730 (m), 88,542 (s).

Illinois

Chicago Sun-Times: 401 North Wabash Ave, Chicago, IL 60611-3593; tel. (312) 321-3000; fax (312) 321-3084; e-mail letters@suntimes.com; internet www.suntimes.com; f. 1948; Publr DAVID HILLER; Editor-in-Chief JOHN CRUICKSHANK; circ. 600,988 (m), 445,000 (s).

Chicago Tribune: 435 North Michigan Ave, Chicago, IL 60611-4041; tel. (312) 222-3232; fax (312) 222-4674; internet www.chicagotribune.com; f. 1847; Publr, Pres. and CEO SCOTT C. SMITH; Editor ANN MARIE LIPINSKI; circ. 675,000 (m), 1,001,000 (s).

Daily Herald: POB 280, Arlington Heights, IL 60006; tel. (847) 870-3600; fax (847) 398-0172; internet www.dailyherald.com; f. 1872; owned by Paddock Publications Inc; Editor DOUGLAS K. RAY; circ. 130,000 (m), 128,000 (s).

Journal Star: 1 News Plaza, Peoria, IL 61643; tel. (309) 686-3000; fax (309) 686-3296; internet www.pjstar.com; f. 1855; Publr JOHN T. MCCONNELL; Editor JACK BRIMEYER; circ. 81,000 (m), 108,000 (s).

The Pantagraph: 301 West Washington, Bloomington, IL 61701-3803; tel. (309) 829-9000; fax (309) 829-9104; internet www.pantagraph.com; f. 1837; Publr HENRY BIRD; Editor TERRY GREENBERG; circ. 48,076 (m), 50,463 (s).

Rockford Register Star: 99 East State St, Rockford, IL 61104; tel. (815) 987-1200; fax (815) 987-1365; e-mail rrslibrary@smtp.registerstartower.com; internet www.rrstar.com; f. 1888; Publr MARY P. STIER; Exec. Editor LINDA G. CUNNINGHAM; circ. 78,000 (m), 90,000 (s).

State Journal-Register: 1 Copley Plaza, POB 219, Springfield, IL 62705-0219; tel. (217) 788-1300; fax (217) 788-1551; e-mail sjr@sj-r.com; internet www.sj-r.com; f. 1831; Publr PATRICK COBURN; Editor BARRY J. LOCHER; circ. 59,597 (m), 68,577 (s).

Indiana

Evansville Courier: 300 Walnut St, POB 268, Evansville, IN 47713; tel. (812) 424-7711; fax (812) 422-8196; e-mail courierpress@evansville.net; internet www.courierpress.com; f. 1845; Publr and Pres. JACK PATE; Exec. Editor J. BRUCE BAUMANN; circ. 73,000 (m), 107,000 (s).

Indianapolis News: 307 North Pennsylvania St, Indianapolis, IN 46204; tel. (317) 633-1240; fax (317) 633-1038; f. 1869; Mon. to Sat. evening; Publr EUGENE S. PULLIAM; Editor RUSSEL B. PULLIAM; circ. 93,000 (e).

Indianapolis Star: 307 North Pennsylvania St, Indianapolis, IN 46204; tel. (317) 633-1240; fax (317) 633-1038; internet www.indystar.com; Publr and Pres. BARBARA A. HENRY; Editor TERRY R. EBERLE; circ. 272,483 (m), 371,684 (s).

Journal-Gazette: 600 West Main St, Fort Wayne, IN 46801; tel. (219) 461-8335; fax (219) 461-8648; e-mail jgnews@jg.net; internet www.journalgazette.net; f. 1863; Publr JULIE INSKEEP; Editor CRAIG KLUGMAN; circ. 62,000 (m), 134,000 (s).

News-Sentinel: 600 West Main St, Fort Wayne, IN 46802; tel. (219) 461-8222; fax (219) 461-8649; internet www.fortwayne.com; f. 1833; Publr MARY JACOBUS; Exec. Editor RICHARD GRIFFIS; circ. 54,000 (e).

Post-Tribune: 1065 Broadway, Gary, IN 46402-2907; tel. (219) 881-3000; fax (219) 881-3232; f. 1907; Publr SCOTT BOSLEY; Editor MARK LETT; circ. 64,000 (m), 72,000 (s).

South Bend Tribune: 225 West Colfax Ave, South Bend, IN 46626; tel. (219) 235-6161; fax (219) 236-1765; e-mail mclein@sbt.sbtinfo.com; internet www.sbtinfo.com; f. 1872; Publr and Editor DAVID C. RAY; circ. 72,000 (e), 102,000 (s).

The Times: 601 45th Ave, Munster, IN 46325; tel. (219) 932-3100; fax (219) 933-3332; internet www.nwitimes.com; f. 1906; morning; Publr WILLIAM V. MONOPOLI; Exec. Editor WILLIAM NANGLE; circ. 65,494 (m), 63,896 (Sat.), 72,740 (s).

Iowa

Cedar Rapids Gazette: 500 Third Ave, SE, Cedar Rapids, IA 52401; tel. (319) 398-8333; fax (319) 398-5846; e-mail editorial@gazettecommunications.com; internet www.gazetteonline.com; f. 1883; Publr and Editor JOE F. HLADKY, III; Man. Editor MARK BOWDEN; circ. 71,000 (m), 85,000 (s).

Des Moines Register: 715 Locust St, POB 957, POB 907, Des Moines, IA 50304-0907; tel. (515) 284-8000; fax (515) 268-2504; internet www.desmoinesregister.com; f. 1849; Pres. and Publr MARY P. STIER; Editor PAUL ANGER; circ. 154,326 (m), 245,057 (s).

Quad-City Times: 500 East Third St, POB 3828, Davenport, IA 52801-1708; tel. (319) 383-2200; fax (319) 383-2433; internet www.qctimes.com; f. 1855; Publr ROBERT A. FUSIE; Editor DANIEL K. HAYES; circ. 54,000 (d), 85,000 (s).

Sioux City Journal: 515 Pavonia St, Sioux City, IA 51101; tel. (712) 279-5027; fax (712) 279-5059; e-mail scjournal@pronet.net; internet www.siouxcityjournal.com; f. 1864; Publr RON PETERSON; Editor LARRY MYHRE; circ. 50,000 (m).

Kansas

Topeka Capital-Journal: 616 SE Jefferson St, Topeka, KS 66607-1120; tel. (785) 295-1111; fax (785) 295-1198; internet www.cjonline.com; f. 1879; Publr JOHN FISH; Exec. Editor PETE GOERING; circ. 59,000 (m), 65,000 (s).

Wichita Eagle: 825 East Douglas Ave, POB 820, Wichita, KS 67201; tel. (316) 268-6000; fax (316) 268-6627; e-mail wenews@wichitaeagle.com; internet www.wichitaeagle.com; f. 1872; Publr PETER PITZ; Editor RICK THAMES, Jr; circ. 91,943 (m), 168,974 (s).

Kentucky

Courier-Journal: 525 West Broadway St, Louisville, KY 40202-2137; POB 740031, Louisville, KY 40201; tel. (502) 582-4011; fax (502) 582-4200; internet www.courier-journal.com; f. 1868; Publr EDWARD MANASSAH; Editor BENNY L. IVORY; circ. 231,630 (m), 301,426 (s).

Lexington Herald-Leader: 100 Midland Ave, Lexington, KY 40508-1999; tel. (606) 231-3100; fax (606) 231-3454; internet www.kentuckyconnect.com; f. 1860; Publr TIM KELLY; Man. Editor TOM EBLEN; circ. 121,034 (m), 165,352 (s).

Louisiana

Advocate: POB 588, Baton Rouge, LA 70821; tel. (504) 383-1111; fax (504) 388-0371; internet www.theadvocate.com; f. 1904; Publr DOUGLAS L. MANSHIP; Editor LINDA C. LIGHTFOOT; circ. 92,524 (m), 124,589 (s).

The Times: 222 Luke St, POB 30222, Shreveport, LA 71130; tel. (318) 459-3200; fax (318) 459-3301; f. 1872; Publr RICHARD STONE; Editor MIKE WHITEHEAD; circ. 77,000 (m), 94,000 (s).

Times-Picayune: 3800 Howard Ave, New Orleans, LA 70125-1429; tel. (504) 826-3279; fax (504) 826-3700; internet www.nola.com; f. 1880; Publr ASHTON PHELPS, Jr; Man. Editor PETER KOVACS; Editor JIM AMOSS; circ. 264,001 (d), 324,000 (s).

Maine

Bangor Daily News: 491 Main St, Bangor, ME 04401; POB 1329, Bangor, ME 04402-1329; tel. (207) 990-8000; fax (207) 941-9476; internet www.bangornews.com; f. 1834; Publr RICHARD J. WARREN; Exec. Editor A. MARK WOODWARD; circ. 72,000 (m).

Maine Sunday Telegram: 390 Congress St, POB 1460, Portland, ME 04104; tel. (207) 780-9000; fax (207) 791-6920; f. 1887; Publr JEAN GANNETT HAWLEY; Exec. Editor LOUIS A. URENECK; circ. 145,000.

Portland Press Herald: 390 Congress St, POB 1460, Portland, ME 04104; tel. (207) 780-9000; fax (207) 791-6931; e-mail herald@portland.com; internet www.pressherald.com; f. 1862; Publr JEAN GANNETT HAWLEY; Editor and Vice-Pres. JEANNINE A. GUTTMAN; circ. 76,000.

THE UNITED STATES OF AMERICA

Maryland

Baltimore Sun: 501 North Calvert St, Baltimore, MD 21278-0001; tel. (410) 332-6000; fax (410) 752-6049; e-mail imogene.lambie@baltsun.com; internet www.baltimoresun.com; f. 1837; Publr and CEO DENISE E. PALMER; Editor TIM FRANKLIN; circ. 320,000 (m), 490,692 (s).

Massachusetts

Boston Globe: 135 Morrissey Blvd, POB 55819 Boston, MA 02205-5819; tel. (617) 929-2000; fax (617) 929-3192; e-mail news@globe.com; internet www.boston.com; f. 1872; Publr RICHARD GILMAN; Editor MARTIN D. BARON; circ. 464,472 (m), 721,859 (s).

Boston Herald: 1 Herald Sq., POB 2096, Boston, MA 02106-2096; tel. (617) 426-3000; fax (617) 426-1896; e-mail library@bostonherald.com; internet www.bostonherald.com; f. 1825; Publr PATRICK PURCELL; Editor ANDREW F. COSTELLO; circ. 263,113 (m), 206,996 (s).

Christian Science Monitor: 1 Norway St, Boston, MA 02115-3195; tel. (617) 450-7160; internet www.csmonitor.com; f. 1908; Mon.–Fri.; Editor PAUL VAN SLAMBROUCK; circ. 60,723.

Lowell Sun: 15 Kearney Sq., POB 1477, Lowell, MA 01853; tel. (978) 458-7100; fax (978) 970-4600; internet www.newschoice.com; f. 1878; Pres. and Sr Editor JOHN H. COSTELLO, Jr; circ. 55,000 (e), 57,000 (s).

Patriot Ledger: 400 Crown Colony Dr., POB 699159, Quincy, MA 02269-9159; tel. (617) 786-7000; fax (617) 786-7298; e-mail delivery@ledger.com; internet www.southofboston.com; f. 1837; Publr JAMES PLUGH; Editor CHAZY DOWALIBY; circ. 77,000 (e).

The Republican: 1860 Main St, Springfield, MA 01101; tel. (413) 788-1000; fax (413) 788-1301; e-mail unews-news@union-news.com; internet www.masslive.com; f. 1824; fmrly Sunday Republican, merged with Union-News in 2003; Publr and CEO LARRY MCDERMOTT; Exec. Editor WAYNE E. PHANEUF; circ. 92,000 (d), 132,000 (s).

Worcester Telegram & Gazette: 20 Franklin St, POB 15012, Worcester, MA 01615-0012; tel. (508) 793-9100; fax (508) 793-9281; internet www.telegram.com; f. 1866; Publr BRUCE S. BENNETT; Editor HARRY T. WITHIN; circ. 112,000 (d), 142,000 (s).

Michigan

Detroit Free Press: 600 West Fort St, Detroit, MI 48226; tel. (313) 222-6400; fax (313) 222-5981; e-mail merriwe@freepress.com; internet www.freep.com; f. 1831; Publr HEATH J. MERRIWEATHER; Editor ROBERT MCGRUDER; circ. 362,841 (m), 1,173,000 (s).

Detroit News: 615 West Lafayette Blvd, Detroit, MI 48226-3197; tel. (313) 222-2300; fax (313) 222-2335; e-mail msilverman@detnews.com; internet www.detnews.com; f. 1873; Publr and Editor MARK SILVERMAN; circ. 246,638 (e), 830,000 (s).

Flint Journal: 200 East First St, Flint, MI 48502; tel. (810) 766-6100; fax (810) 767-7518; e-mail fj@flintjournal.com; internet www.flintjournal.com; f. 1876; Publr ROGER SAMUEL; Editor PAUL KEEP; circ. 102,000 (e), 124,000 (s).

Grand Rapids Press: 155 Michigan St, NW, Grand Rapids, MI 49503-2302; tel. (616) 459-1400; fax (616) 459-1502; f. 1890; Editor MICHAEL S. LLOYD; circ. 139,000 (e), 190,000 (s).

Kalamazoo Gazette: 401 South Burdick St, Kalamazoo, MI 49007-5279; tel. (616) 345-3511; fax (616) 345-0583; f. 1883; Publr GEORGE ARWADY; Editor REBECCA PIERCE; circ. 60,000 (e), 76,000 (s).

Lansing State Journal: 120 East Lenawee St, Lansing, MI 48919-0001; tel. (517) 377-1000; fax (517) 377-1298; f. 1855; Publr MICHAEL G. KANE; Exec. Editor MICHAEL HIRTEN; circ. 70,260 (m), 92,041 (s).

Oakland Press: 48 West Huron St, POB 436009, Pontiac, MI 48343; tel. (248) 332-8181; fax (248) 332-8294; f. 1843; Publr BRUCE H. MCINTYRE; Exec. Editor GARY GILBERT; circ. 86,000 (m), 103,000 (s).

Saginaw News: 203 South Washington Ave, Saginaw, MI 48607-1283; tel. (517) 752-7171; fax (517) 752-3115; e-mail thenews@thesaginawnews.com; internet www.thesaginawnews.com; f. 1859; Publr H. RENEE HAMPTON; Editor PAUL CHAFFEE; circ. 57,333 (e), 67,739 (s).

Minnesota

Duluth News-Tribune: 424 West First St, POB 169000, Duluth, MN 55816-9000; tel. (218) 723-5281; fax (218) 723-5339; f. 1869; morning; Publr MARTI BUSCAGLIA; Editor DON WYATT; circ. 58,565 (d), 84,518 (s).

Star Tribune: 425 Portland Ave South, Minneapolis, MN 55488; tel. (612) 673-4000; fax (612) 673-4359; internet www.startribune.com; f. 1920; Publr J. KEITH MOYER; Editor ANDERS GYLLENHAAL; circ. 375,807 (m), 669,290 (s).

St Paul Pioneer Press: 345 Cedar St, St Paul, MN 55101; tel. (612) 222-5011; fax (612) 228-5500; internet www.pioneerpress.com; f. 1849; Pres. RICK SADOWSKI; Editor VICKI GOWLER; circ. 207,624 (m), 275,057 (s).

Mississippi

Clarion-Ledger: 201 South Congress St, Jackson, MS 39201; tel. (601) 961-7000; fax (601) 961-7211; e-mail homesub@jackson-gannett.com; internet www.clarionledger.com; f. 1954; Publr and Pres. WILLIAM W. HUNSBERGER; Editor RONNIE AGNEW; circ. 112,000 (e), 130,000 (s).

Missouri

Kansas City Star: 1729 Grand Blvd, Kansas City, MO 64108; tel. (816) 234-4141; fax (816) 234-4926; e-mail subscriptions@kansascity.com; internet www.kansascity.com; f. 1880; Publr ARTHUR S. BRISBANE; Editor MARK ZIEMAN; circ. 275,336 (m), 434,000 (s).

News-Leader: 651 Boonville Ave, Springfield, MO 65806; tel. (417) 836-1100; fax (417) 836-1147; internet www.springfieldnewsleader.com; f. 1933; morning; Publr THOMAS A. BOOKSTAVER; Exec. Editor DAVID LEDFORD; circ. 61,623 (m), 101,612 (s).

St Louis Post-Dispatch: 900 North Tucker Blvd, St Louis, MO 63101; tel. (314) 340-8000; fax (314) 340-3050; internet www.stltoday.com; f. 1878; Pres. and Publr TERRENCE C. Z. EGGER; Gen. Man. MATTHEW C. KRANER; circ. 324,059 (d), 520,635 (s).

Montana

Billings Gazette: POB 36300, Billings, MT 59107; tel. (406) 657-1200; fax (406) 657-1208; internet www.billingsgazette.com; f. 1885; Publr MIKE GULLEDGE; Editor STEVE PROSINSKI; circ. 54,000 (m), 63,000 (s).

Nebraska

Lincoln Star: Journal Star Printing Co, 926 P St, POB 81609, Lincoln, NE 68501; tel. (402) 475-4200; fax (402) 473-7291; e-mail feedback@journalstar.com; internet www.journalstar.com; f. 1867; morning; Publr BILL JOHNSTON; Editor DAVID STOEFFLER; circ. 40,093 (m), 79,210 (Sat.), 84,699 (s).

Omaha World-Herald: 1334 Dodge St, Omaha, NE 68102-1122; tel. (402) 444-1000; fax (402) 345-0183; internet www.omaha.com; f. 1885; Publr and Pres. JOHN GOTTSCHALK; Editor LARRY KING; circ. 195,607 (d), 242,103 (s).

Nevada

Las Vegas Review-Journal: 1111 West Bonanza Rd, Las Vegas, NV 89106; tel. (702) 383-0211; fax (702) 383-4676; internet www.reviewjournal.com; f. 1908; Publr SHERMAN FREDERICK; Editor THOMAS MITCHELL; circ. 158,970 (m), 223,151 (s).

Reno Gazette-Journal: POB 22000, Reno, NV 89520-2000; tel. (702) 788-6200; fax (702) 788-6458; e-mail rgjfeedback@rgj.com; internet www.rgj.com; f. 1870; Publr FRED HAMILTON; Exec. Editor TONIA CUNNING; circ. 67,000 (m), 84,000 (s).

New Hampshire

Union Leader, New Hampshire Sunday News: Leader Corpn, 100 William Loeb Dr., POB 9555, Manchester, NH 03108-9555; tel. (603) 668-4321; fax (603) 668-0382; e-mail writeus@theunionleader.com; internet www.theunionleader.com; f. 1863; f. 1946; Pres. and Publr JOSEPH W. MCQUAID; Editor CHARLES PERKINS, III; circ. 65,250 (m, Union Leader), 88,000 (s, Sunday News).

New Jersey

Asbury Park Press: 3601 Hwy 66, POB 1550, Neptune, NJ 07754-1550; tel. (732) 922-6000; fax (732) 918-4818; e-mail editors@app.com; internet www.app.com; f. 1879; Publr and Pres. ROBERT T. COLLINS; Exec. Editor SKIP HIDLAY; circ. 160,069 (d), 224,800 (s).

Courier-News: 1201 Hwy 22 West, POB 6600, Bridgewater, NJ 08807; tel. (908) 722-8800; fax (908) 707-3252; e-mail cneditor@c-n.com; internet www.c-n.com; f. 1884; Publr CHARLES W. NUTT; Editor JAMES A. FLACHSENHAAR; circ. 42,000 (e), 43,000 (s).

Courier-Post: POB 5300, Cherry Hill, NJ 08034; tel. (856) 663-3000; fax (856) 663-2831; f. 1875; Pres. and Publr MARK J. FRISBY; Exec. Editor DEREK OSENENKO; circ. 87,000 (m), 99,000 (s).

Home News Tribune: 35 Kennedy Blvd, East Brunswick, NJ 08816; tel. (732) 246-5500; fax (732) 565-7208; e-mail hntmetro@thnt.com; internet www.thnt.com; f. 1879; Publr and Pres. ROBERT T. COLLINS; Exec. Editor CHARLES PAOLINO; circ. 70,000 (e), 77,500 (s).

Jersey Journal: 30 Journal Sq., Jersey City, NJ 07306; tel. (201) 653-1000; fax (201) 653-1414; internet www.thejerseyjournal.com; f. 1867; Editor JUDITH LOCORRIERE; circ. 55,000 (s).

The Record: 150 River St, Hackensack, NJ 07601-7172; tel. (201) 646-4000; fax (201) 646-4135; e-mail newsroom@northjersey.com; internet www.northjersey.com; f. 1895; Chair. MALCOLM A. BORG; Exec. Editor VIVIEN WAIXEL; circ. 158,000 (m), 213,000 (s).

Star-Ledger: 1 Star-Ledger Plaza, Newark, NJ 07101; tel. (973) 877-4141; fax (973) 877-5845; e-mail metro@starledger.com; internet

THE UNITED STATES OF AMERICA

www.nj.com/starledger; f. 1917; Publr LINDA DENNERY; Editor JIM WILLSE; circ. 407,537 (m), 608,015 (s).

The Times: 500 Perry St, Trenton, NJ 08605; tel. (609) 396-5454; fax (609) 396-3633; e-mail news@njtimes.com; internet www.nj.com/times; f. 1882; Publr RICHARD BILOTTI; Exec. Editor BRIAN S. MALONE; circ. 80,000 (m), 90,000 (s).

Trentonian: 600 Perry St, Trenton, NJ 08602; tel. (609) 989-7800; fax (609) 393-6072; internet www.trentonian.com; f. 1946; Publr DAVID BONFIELD; Editor PAUL MICKLE; circ. 48,342 (m), 43,749 (s).

New Mexico

Albuquerque Journal: 7777 Jefferson NE, NM 87103; tel. (505) 823-3800; fax (505) 823-3994; e-mail journal@abqjournal.com; internet www.abqjournal.com; f. 1880; Publr T. H. LANG; Editor KENT WALZ; circ. 108,931 (m), 168,818 (s).

Albuquerque Tribune: PO Drawer T, Albuquerque, NM 87103; tel. (505) 823-7777; fax (505) 823-3689; e-mail letters@abqtrib; internet www.abqtrib.com; f. 1922; evening; Editor PHILL CASAUS; circ. 18,000.

New York

Albany Times Union: News Plaza, POB 15000, Albany, NY 12212; tel. (518) 454-5420; fax (518) 454-5628; e-mail webmaster@timesunion.com; internet www.timesunion.com; f. 1856; Publr DAVID P. WHITE; Exec. Editor REX SMITH; circ. 100,401 (m), 146,723 (s).

Buffalo News: 1 News Plaza, POB 100, Buffalo, NY 14240; tel. (716) 849-3434; fax (716) 849-5150; internet www.buffalonews.com; f. 1880; Publr STANFORD LIPSEY; Editor STEVE BELL; circ. 232,926 (d), 340,000 (s).

Daily Gazette: 2345 Maxon Rd, Schenectady, NY 12308; POB 1090, Schenectady, NY 12301-1090; tel. (518) 374-4141; fax (518) 395-3089; e-mail gazette@dailygazette.com; internet www.dailygazette.com; f. 1894; Publr and Editor JOHN E. N. HUME, III; circ. 57,000 (m), 59,000 (s).

Democrat and Chronicle: 55 Exchange Blvd, Rochester, NY 14614-2001; tel. (716) 232-7100; fax (716) 258-3027; internet www.democratandchronicle.com; f. 1833; Publr DAVID L. HUNKE; Editor KAREN MAGNUSON; circ. 177,747 (m), 239,822 (s).

Newsday: 235 Pinelawn, Melville, NY 11747-4250; tel. (516) 843-4000; fax (516) 843-2953; e-mail ndstaff@newsday.com; internet www.newsday.com; f. 1940; Publr RAYMOND A. JANSEN; Editor DENNIS ELDER; circ. 576,345 (m), 657,559 (s).

Post-Standard, Herald-Journal: Clinton Sq., POB 4915, Syracuse, NY 13221; tel. (315) 470-0011; fax (315) 470-3081; internet www.syracuse.com; f. 1829; f. 1877; Publr STEPHEN A. ROGERS; Exec. Editor MICHAEL J. CONNOR; circ. 87,000 (m, *Post-Standard*), 83,000 (e, *Herald-Journal*).

Press & Sun-Bulletin: 4421 Vestal Pkwy East, POB 1270, Binghamton, NY 13850; tel. (607) 798-1234; fax (607) 798-0261; internet www.pressconnects.com; f. 1985; Publr WILLIAM V. MONOPOLI; Exec. Editor RICK JENSEN; circ. 65,000 (m), 80,000 (s).

Times Herald-Record, Record: 40 Mulberry St, POB 2046, Middletown, NY 10940; tel. (914) 341-1100; fax (914) 343-2170; internet www.recordonline.com; f. 1956; Publr JOHN M. SZEFC; Exec. Editor MIKE LEVINE; circ. 86,000 (m, *Times Herald-Record*), 102,000 (s, *Record*).

New York City

New York Daily News: 450 West 33rd St, New York, NY 10001; tel. (212) 210-2100; fax (212) 682-4953; internet www.nydailynews.com; f. 1919; Publrs FRED DRASNER, MORTIMER B. ZUCKERMAN; Editor-in-Chief EDWARD KOSNER; circ. 727,089 (m), 851,921 (s).

New York Post: 1211 Ave of the Americas, New York, NY 10036; tel. (212) 930-8000; fax (212) 930-8540; internet www.nypost.com; f. 1801; Chair. and Pres. RUPERT MURDOCH; Publr KEN CHANDLER; Editor-in-Chief STEVE CUOZO; circ. 443,951 (m), 382,000 (s).

New York Sun: 105 Chambers St, 2nd Floor, New York, NY 10007; tel. (212) 406-2000; internet www.nysun.com; f. 2002; Editor and Pres. SETH LIPSKY; circ. 40,483 (d).

New York Times: 229 West 43rd St, New York, NY 10036; tel. (212) 556-1234; internet www.nytimes.com; f. 1851; Chair. and Publr ARTHUR OCHS SULZBERGER, Jr; Pres. and CEO JANET ROBINSON; Exec. Editor BILL KELLER; circ. 1,097,180 (m), 1,698,281 (s).

Staten Island Advance: 950 Fingerboard Rd, Staten Island, New York, NY 10305; tel. (718) 981-1234; fax (718) 981-5679; internet www.silive.com; f. 1886; Publr RICHARD E. DIAMOND; Editor BRIAN J. LALINE; circ. 78,000 (e), 95,000 (s).

The Wall Street Journal: 200 Liberty St, New York, NY 10281; tel. (212) 416-2000; internet www.wsj.com; f. 1889; publ. by Dow Jones & Co Inc; morning; Chair. PETER R. KANN; CEO RICHARD F. ZANNINO; Man. Editor PAUL E. STEIGER; circ. 2,091,062.

North Carolina

Charlotte Observer: 600 South Tryon St, POB 32188-28232, Charlotte, NC 28202-1842; tel. (704) 358-5000; fax (704) 358-5036; internet www.charlotte.com/observer; f. 1886; Publr PETER RIDDER; Editor JENNIE BUCKNER; circ. 242,000 (m), 295,000 (s).

Citizen-Times: 14 O'Henry Ave, POB 2090, Asheville, NC 28802; tel. (704) 252-5611; fax (704) 251-2659; internet www.citizen-times.com; f. 1870; morning; Publr VIRGIL L. SMITH; Exec. Editor BOB GABORDI; circ. 66,564 (m), 79,302 (s).

Fayetteville Observer-Times: Fayetteville Publishing Co, 458 Whitfield St, POB 849, Fayetteville, NC 28302; tel. (919) 323-4848; fax (919) 486-3531; internet www.fayettevillenc.com; f. 1816; morning; Publr and Editor CHARLES BROADWELL; circ. 71,361 (m), 80,511 (s).

Greensboro News and Record: 200 East Market St, POB 20848, Greensboro, NC 27401-2910; tel. (919) 373-7000; fax (919) 373-7382; internet www.greensboro-record.com; f. 1905; Publr CARL MAGNUM, Jr; Exec. Editor JOHN ROBINSON; circ. 91,000 (m), 119,000 (s).

News and Observer: 215 South McDowell St, POB 191, Raleigh, NC 27602; tel. (919) 829-4500; fax (919) 829-4529; e-mail naostaff@nando.com; internet www.news-observer.com; f. 1872; Publr ORAGE QUARLES, III; Exec. Editor MELANIE SILL; circ. 161,604 (m), 208,676 (s).

Winston-Salem Journal: 418 North Marshall St, Winston-Salem, NC 27102-3159; tel. (336) 727-7211; fax (336) 727-4071; e-mail news@journalnow.com; internet www.wsjournal.com; Publr JON WITHERSPOON; Man. Editor JIM LAUGHRUN; circ. 90,344 (m), 102,878 (s).

North Dakota

The Forum: 101 Fifth St North, Box 2020, Fargo, ND 58107; tel. (701) 235-7311; fax (701) 241-5487; internet www.in-forum.com; f. 1878; Publr WILLIAM C. MARCIL; Editor WILLIAM JOSEPH DILL; circ. 53,634 (m), 67,750 (s).

Ohio

Akron Beacon Journal: 44 East Exchange St, POB 640, Akron, OH 44328-0001; tel. (330) 996-3000; fax (330) 376-9235; internet www.ohio.com; f. 1839; Publr JAMES N. CRUTCHFIELD; Editor DEBRA ADAMS SIMMONS; circ. 136,795 (m), 172,313 (s).

Canton Repository: 500 Market Ave South, Canton, OH 44711-2112; tel. (330) 454-5611; fax (330) 454-5610; internet www.cantonrep.com; f. 1815; Publr DAVID GREENFIELD; Editor DAVID KAMINSKI; circ. 61,000 (e), 80,000 (s).

Cincinnati Enquirer: 312 Elm St, Cincinnati, OH 45202; tel. (513) 721-2700; fax (513) 768-8340; internet www.enquirer.com; f. 1841; Publr HARRY M. WHIPPLE; Editor WARD H. BUSHEE; circ. 195,360 (m), 351,898 (s).

Cincinnati Post: 125 East Court St, Cincinnati, OH 45202; tel. (513) 352-2000; fax (513) 621-3962; internet www.cincypost.com; f. 1881; Publr ALAN HORTON; Editor MIKE PHILIPPS; circ. 55,800 (m).

Cleveland Plain Dealer: 1801 Superior Ave East, Cleveland, OH 44114; tel. (216) 999-5000; fax (216) 999-6354; e-mail circhepl@plaind.com; internet www.plaindealer.com; f. 1842; Publr ALEX MACHASKEE; Editor DOUGLAS C. CLIFTON; circ. 382,933 (m), 492,337 (s).

Columbus Dispatch: 34 South Third St, Columbus, OH 43215-4241; tel. (614) 461-5000; fax (614) 461-7580; e-mail letters@dispatch.com; internet www.dispatch.com; f. 1871; Publr JOHN F. WOLFE; Editor BEN MARRISON; circ. 244,177 (m), 393,757 (s).

Dayton Daily News: 45 South Ludlow St, Dayton, OH 45402; tel. (937) 225-2000; fax (937) 225-2489; internet www.daytondailynews.com; Publr J. BRADFORD TILSON; Editor JEFF BRUCE; circ. 134,494 (m), 212,128 (s).

Dayton Journal Herald: 45 South Ludlow St, Dayton, OH 45402; tel. (937) 225-2000; fax (937) 225-2489; Sun.; Publr J. BRADFORD TILSON; Editor MAX JENNINGS; circ. 225,000.

News-Herald: 38879 Mentor Ave, Willoughby, OH 44094; tel. (216) 951-0000; fax (216) 951-0917; f. 1880; Mon. to Sat. evening, Sun. morning; Publr RICK STENGER; Editor GLENN GILBERT; circ. 56,332 (e), 66,668 (s).

Toledo Blade: 541 North Superior St, Toledo, OH 43660-1000; tel. (419) 245-6000; fax (419) 245-6191; internet www.toledoblade.com; f. 1835; Publr JOHN ROBINSON BLOCK; Editor RON ROYHAB; circ. 146,334 (e), 207,352 (s).

The Vindicator: 107 Vindicator Sq., POB 780, Youngstown, OH 44501-0780; tel. (330) 747-1471; fax (330) 747-6712; e-mail news@vindy.com; internet www.vindy.com; Publr BETTY H. BROWN JAGNOW; Editor DON SHILLING; circ. 70,000 (e), 120,000 (s).

THE UNITED STATES OF AMERICA

Oklahoma

Daily Oklahoman: 9000 North Broadway, POB 25125, Oklahoma City, OK 73114; tel. (405) 475-3311; fax (405) 475-3183; internet www.newsok.com; f. 1894; Publr EDWARD L. GAYLORD; Editor SUE HALE; circ. 198,576 (m), 295,775 (s).

Tulsa Tribune: 315 South Boulder Ave, POB 1770, Tulsa, OK 74103; tel. (918) 581-8400; fax (918) 584-1037; f. 1904; evening; Publr JENKIN L. JONES; Editor JENK JONES, Jr; circ. 67,000.

Tulsa World: 315 South Boulder Ave, POB 1770, Tulsa, OK 74103; tel. (918) 581-8300; fax (918) 581-8353; e-mail tulsaworld@tulsaworld.com; internet www.tulsaworld.com; f. 1906; Publr ROBERT E. LORTON; Editor JOE WORLEY; circ. 145,697 (m), 207,000 (s).

Oregon

The Oregonian: 1320 SW Broadway, Portland, OR 97201-3469; tel. (503) 221-8327; fax (503) 227-5306; internet www.oregonian.com; f. 1850; Publr. FRED A. STICKEL; Editor PETER BHATIA; circ. 348,468 (d), 449,715 (s).

The Register-Guard: 975 High St, POB 10188-2188, Eugene, OR 97408; tel. and fax (541) 485-1234; fax (541) 683-7631; internet www.registerguard.com; f. 1867; Publr and Editor TONY BAKER; circ. 75,510 (m), 78,903 (s).

Statesman Journal: 280 Church St, NE, POB 13009, Salem, OR 97309; tel. (503) 399-6611; fax (503) 399-6706; e-mail newsroom@statesmanjournal.com; internet www.statesmanjournal.com; f. 1851; Publr SONIA SORENSEN CRAIG; Exec. Editor DAVID RISSER; circ. 57,000 (m), 66,000 (s).

Pennsylvania

Bucks County Courier Times: 8400 Route 13, Levittown, PA 19057-5198; tel. (215) 949-4000; fax (215) 949-4177; internet www.phillyburbs.com; f. 1910; owned by Beaver Newspapers Inc (Calkins Media); Editor PAT WALKER; circ. 71,000 (m), 77,000 (s).

Call Chronicle: POB 1260, Allentown, PA 18105; tel. (610) 820-6500; fax (610) 820-6693; f. 1921; Sun.; Publr GARY K. SHORTS; Exec. Editor LAWRENCE H. HYMANS; circ. 189,000.

Harrisburg Patriot: 812 Market St, POB 2265, Harrisburg, PA 17105; tel. (717) 255-8100; fax (717) 257-4796; f. 1854; daily (except Sat.) morning; Publr JOHN A. KIRKPATRICK; circ. 100,208 (d), 154,543 (s).

The Morning Call: POB 1260, Allentown, PA 18101-1403; tel. (610) 820-6500; fax (610) 820-6693; internet www.mcall.com; Publr GUY GILMORE; Exec. Editor DAVID ERDMAN; circ. 129,574 (m), 182,907 (s).

Patriot-News: 812 Market St, Harrisburg, PA 17105; tel. (717) 255-8100; fax (717) 255-8456; internet www.patriot-news.com; f. 1854; Publr JOHN KIRKPATRICK; Exec. Editor DAVID NEWHOUSE; circ. 102,467 (m), 154,021 (s).

Philadelphia Daily News: POB 7788, Philadelphia, PA 19101; tel. (215) 854-5900; fax (215) 854-5910; e-mail dailynews.opinion@phillynews.com; internet www.philly.com; f. 1925; Publr ROBERT J. HALL; Editor ZACHARY STALBERG; circ. 154,145 (e).

Philadelphia Inquirer: 400 North Broad St, POB 8623, Philadelphia, PA 19101; tel. (215) 854-2000; fax (215) 854-4974; e-mail inquirer.opinion@phillynews.com; internet www.philly.com; f. 1829; Publr ROBERT J. HALL; Editor AMANDA BENNETT; circ. 400,385 (m), 838,296 (s).

Pittsburg Post-Gazette: 34 Blvd of the Allies, Pittsburgh, PA 15222; tel. (412) 263-1100; fax (412) 391-8452; f. 1786; Publrs WILLIAM BLOCK, Jr, JOHN ROBINSON BLOCK; Editor JOHN G. CRAIG, Jr; circ. 240,245 (m), 431,000 (s).

Sunday News: Lancaster Newspapers, Inc, 8 West King St, Lancaster, PA 17603; tel. (717) 291-8733; fax (717) 399-6506; internet www.lancasteronline.com/sunnews; f. 1923; Editor DAVID HENNIGAN; Ind; circ. 105,000.

Tribune-Democrat: 425 Locust St, Johnstown, PA 15907; tel. (814) 532-5199; fax (814) 539-1409; internet www.tribune-democrat.com; f. 1853; morning; Publr PAMELA J. MAYER; Editor DAVID LEVINE; circ. 50,000 (m), 56,000 (s).

Rhode Island

Providence Journal: 75 Fountain St, Providence, RI 02902-0050; tel. (401) 277-7000; fax (401) 277-7461; e-mail letters@projo.com; internet www.projo.com; f. 1829; publ. by Belo Corpn; Publr HOWARD G. SUTTON; Exec. Editor JOEL RAWSON; circ. 162,099 (d), 250,000 (s).

South Carolina

Greenville News: 305 South Main St, POB 1688, Greenville, SC 29601-2605; tel. (864) 298-4395; fax (864) 298-4805; internet www.greenvilleonline.com; f. 1874; Publr STEVEN BRANDT; Editor JOHN S. PITTMAN; circ. 88,898 (m), 116,455 (s).

The Post and Courier: 134 Columbus St, Charleston, SC 29403-4800; tel. (843) 577-7111; fax (843) 937-5579; e-mail seima@postandcourier.com; internet www.charleston.net; f. 1803; Publr LARRY TARLETON, Jr; Editor JOHN C. HUFF; circ. 110,000 (m), 122,000 (s).

State Record: POB 1333, Columbia, SC 29202; tel. (803) 771-6161; fax (803) 771-8430; e-mail state@thestate.com; internet www.thestate.com; f. 1891; Publr FRED MOTT; Exec. Editor MARK LETT; circ. 135,000 (m), 175,000 (s).

South Dakota

Argus Leader: POB 5034, Sioux Falls, SD 57117-5034; tel. (605) 331-2200; fax (605) 331-2294; e-mail editor@argusleader.com; f. 1881; Publr ARNOLD GARSON; Editor RANDALL BECK; circ. 51,000 (m), 73,000 (s).

Tennessee

Chattanooga Times-Free Press: 400 East 11th St, POB 1447, Chattanooga, TN 37401-1447; tel. (423) 756-6900; fax (423) 757-6383; internet www.chattimesfreepress.com; f. 1888; Publr WALTER E. HUSSMAN; Man. Editor TOM GRISCOM; circ. 82,000 (e), 110,000 (s).

The Commercial Appeal: 495 Union Ave, Memphis, TN 38103; tel. (901) 529-2211; fax (901) 529-2522; internet www.commercialappeal.com; f. 1841; Pres. and Publr JOHN WILCOX; Man. Editor OTIS STANFORD; circ. Mon. to Weds. 165,484 (m), Thurs. to Sat. 189,961 (m), 240,712 (s).

Knoxville News-Sentinel: 2332 News Sentinel Dr., Knoxville, TN 37921-5731; tel. (865) 523-3131; fax (865) 342-8650; e-mail kns@knoxnews.com; internet www.knoxnews.com; f. 1886; Editor JACK MCELROY; circ. 117,948 (m), 168,075 (s).

The Tennessean: 1100 Broadway St, Nashville, TN 37203; tel. (615) 259-8800; fax (615) 259-8093; internet www.tennessean.com; f. 1812; Publr CRAIG MOON; Editor DAVID GREEN; circ. 190,000 (m), 285,000 (s).

Texas

Austin American-Statesman: POB 670, Austin, TX 78767; tel. (512) 445-3500; fax (512) 445-3679; e-mail editors@statesman.com; internet www.statesman.com; f. 1871; Publr MICHAEL LAOSA; Editor FRED ZIPP; circ. 193,258 (m), 245,000 (s).

Beaumont Enterprise: 380 Main St, POB 3071, Beaumont, TX 77701-2331; tel. (409) 833-3311; fax (409) 838-2857; internet www.ent-net.com; f. 1880; Publr GEORGE B. IRISH; Editor BEN HANSEN; circ. 61,000 (m), 74,000 (s).

Corpus Christi Caller-Times: 820 North Lower Broadway, POB 9136, Corpus Christi, TX 78469; tel. (512) 884-2011; fax (512) 886-3732; e-mail cteds@caller.com; internet www.caller.com; f. 1883; Publr STEPHEN W. SULLIVAN; Exec. Editor DAVID A. HOUSE; circ. 70,000 (m), 92,000 (s).

Dallas Morning News: POB 655237, Dallas, TX 75265; tel. (214) 977-8222; fax (214) 977-8319; internet www.dallasnews.com; f. 1885; publ. by Belo Corpn; Publr BURL OSBORNE; Editor GILBERT BAILON; circ. 495,957 (m), 809,552 (s).

El Paso Times: Times Plaza, El Paso, TX 79901-1470; tel. (915) 546-6104; fax (915) 546-6496; f. 1881; Publr MACK QUINTANA; Editor ROBERT MOORE; circ. 66,000 (m), 97,000 (s).

Fort Worth Star-Telegram: POB 1870, Fort Worth, TX 76101; tel. (817) 390-7400; fax (817) 390-7789; e-mail newsroom@star-telegram.com; internet www.star-telegram.com; f. 1909; Publr WESLEY R. TURNER; Exec. Editor JIM WITT; circ. 240,136 (d), 341,893 (s).

Houston Chronicle: 801 Texas Ave, Houston, TX 77002; tel. (713) 220-7171; fax (713) 220-6677; e-mail online@chron.com; internet www.houstonchronicle.com; f. 1901; Publr JACK SWEENEY; Editor TONY PEDERSEN; circ. 549,440 (m), 738,456 (s).

Lubbock Avalanche-Journal: 710 Ave J, POB 491, Lubbock, TX 79401-1808; tel. (806) 762-8844; fax (806) 744-9603; internet www.lubbockonline.com; f. 1900; Publr MARK E. NUSBAUM; Editor RANDY SANDERS; circ. 65,000 (m), 75,000 (s).

San Antonio Express-News: Ave E and Third St, POB 2171-7297, San Antonio, TX 78297-2171; tel. (210) 250-3000; fax (210) 250-3105; internet www.expressnews.com; f. 1864; Mon. to Fri. all day, Sat. and Sun. morning; Publr W. LAWRENCE WALKER, Jr; Exec. Editor ROBERT RIVARD; circ. 218,661 (Mon. to Thurs.), 273,889 (Fri.), 267,051 (Sat.), 366,402 (s).

Utah

Deseret Morning News: 30 East First St South, POB 1257, Salt Lake City, UT 84110; tel. (801) 236-6000; fax (801) 237-2121; e-mail letters@desnews.com; internet www.deseretnews.com; f. 1850; Publr JIM WALL; Editor JOHN HUGHES; circ. 62,140 (m), 67,574 (s).

THE UNITED STATES OF AMERICA

Salt Lake Tribune: 143 South Main St, POB 867, Salt Lake City, UT 84111; tel. (801) 237-2800; fax (801) 521-9418; e-mail reader.advocate@sltrib.com; internet www.sltrib.com; f. 1871; Publr DOMINIC A. WELCH; Exec. Editor VERNON WELCH; circ. 134,152 (m), 150,146 (s).

Standard-Examiner: 332 Standard Way, POB 12790, Ogden, UT 84412; tel. (801) 625-4200; fax (801) 625-4508; e-mail inquire@standard.net; internet www.standard.net; f. 1888; Publr and Editor RANDALL C. HATCH; circ. 55,127 (e), 56,541 (s).

Vermont

Burlington Free Press: 191 College St, Burlington, VT 05402-0010; tel. (802) 863-3441; fax (802) 660-1802; e-mail bfreepress@aol.com; internet www.burlingtonfreepress.com; f. 1827; Publr JAMES CAREY; Exec. Editor MIKE TOWNSEND; circ. 53,171 (m), 66,855 (s).

Virginia

Daily Press: 7505 Warwick Blvd, Newport News, VA 23607; tel. (757) 247-4600; fax (757) 245-8618; e-mail dpedit@aol.com; internet www.dailypress.com; f. 1896; Publr RONDRA J. MATTHEWS; Editor ERNIE GATES; circ. 104,000 (m), 127,000 (s).

Richmond Times-Dispatch: 300 East Franklin St, POB 85333, Richmond, VA 23293; tel. (804) 649-6000; fax (804) 775-8059; e-mail news@www.timesdispatch.com; internet www.timesdispatch.com; f. 1850; Publr J. STEWART BRYAN, III; Exec. Editor WILLIAM H. MILLSAPS; circ. 196,423 (m), 235,000 (s).

Roanoke Times: POB 2491, Roanoke, VA 24010-2491; tel. (540) 981-3100; fax (540) 981-3346; internet www.roanoke.com; Publr WENDY ZOMPARELLI; Exec. Editor MIKE RILEY; circ. 115,000 (m), 127,000 (s).

USA Today: 7950 Jones Branch Dr., McLean, VA 22108-0605; tel. (703) 276-3400; internet www.usatoday.com; f. 1982; Pres. and Publr CRAIG A. MOON; Editor KENNETH PAULSON; circ. 2,300,000 (m).

Virginian-Pilot: 150 West Brambleton Ave, POB 449, Norfolk, VA 23501; tel. (757) 446-2000; fax (757) 446-2414; internet www.pilotonline.com; f. 1876; Publr DEE CARPENTER; Editor KAY TUCKER ADDIS; circ. 197,574 (e), 230,000 (s).

Washington

The Herald: 1213 California St, Everett, WA 98201; tel. (425) 339-3000; fax (425) 339-3049; internet www.heraldnet.com; f. 1891; Publr ALLEN B. FUNK; Exec. Editor STAN STRICK; circ. 53,000 (m), 64,000 (s).

News Tribune: POB 11000, Tacoma, WA 98411-0008; tel. (253) 597-8742; fax (253) 597-8266; internet www.tribnet.com; f. 1883; Publr BETSY BRENNER; Exec. Editor DAVID ZEECK; circ. 128,000 (m), 148,000 (s).

Seattle Post-Intelligencer: 101 Elliott Ave West, POB 1909, Seattle, WA 98119-4220; tel. (206) 448-8000; fax (206) 448-8165; e-mail editor@seattlep-i.com; internet www.seattlep-i.com; f. 1863; Publr and Editor ROGER OGLESBY; circ. 191,169 (m); 482,978 (s).

Seattle Times: 1120 John St, Seattle, WA 98111-0070; tel. (206) 464-2111; fax (206) 464-2261; internet www.seattletimes.com; f. 1896; Publr FRANK A. BLETHEN; Exec. Editor MICHAEL R. FANCHER; circ. 225,687 (e), 482,978 (s).

Spokesman-Review: 999 West Riverside, POB 2160, Spokane, WA 99210; tel. (509) 459-5000; fax (509) 459-5234; e-mail editor@spokesman.com; internet www.spokane.net; f. 1883; Publr W. STANLEY COWLES; Editor STEVEN A. SMITH; circ. 150,550 (m), 137,568 (s).

West Virginia

Charleston Daily Mail: 1001 Virginia St East, Charleston, WV 25301-2895; tel. (304) 348-5140; fax (304) 348-4847; e-mail dmnews@dailymail.com; internet www.dailymail.com; f. 1973; Publr SAMUEL E. HINDMAN; Editor NANYA FRIEND; circ. 40,000 (e), 95,000 (s).

Wisconsin

Green Bay Press-Gazette: 435 East Walnut St, POB 19430, Green Bay, WI 54307-5001; tel. (920) 435-4411; fax (920) 431-8499; internet www.greenbaypressgazette.com; f. 1915; Publr W. T. NUSBAUM; Editor BARBARA JANESH; circ. 58,000 (m), 86,000 (s).

Milwaukee Journal Sentinel: 333 West State St, POB 661, Milwaukee, WI 53201; tel. (414) 224-2000; fax (414) 224-2047; internet www.jsonline.com; f. 1837; Publr ELIZABETH 'BETSY' BRENNER; Editor MARTIN KAISER; circ. 238,382 (m), 431,000 (s).

Post-Crescent: POB 59, Appleton, WI 54912; tel. (920) 733-4411; fax (920) 733-1983; e-mail pcnews@postcrescent.com; internet www.postcrescent.com; f. 1920; Publr ELLEN LEIFIELD; Editor ANDREW OPPMAN; circ. 58,000 (m), 76,000 (s).

Wisconsin State Journal: 1901 Fish Hatchery Rd, POB 8058, Madison, WI 53713; tel. (608) 252-6100; fax (608) 252-6119; e-mail wsjcity@madison.com; internet www.madison.com; f. 1839; Publr JAMES HOPSON; Editor FRANK DENTON; circ. 94,000 (m), 158,000 (s).

Wyoming

Star-Tribune: POB 80, Casper, WY 82602; tel. (307) 266-0500; fax (307) 266-0568; internet www.trib.com; f. 1891; Publr ROBIN W. HURLESS; Editor DAN NEAL; circ. 33,500 (m), 38,000 (s).

SELECTED PERIODICALS

AARP The Magazine: 601 E St, NW, Washington, DC 20049; tel. (202) 434-2560; e-mail aarpmagazine@aarp.org; internet www.aarpmagazine.org; f. 1958 following merger of *My Generation* and *Modern Maturity*; publ. of the American Assen of Retired Persons; 6 a year; general interest for the over-50s; Group Publr JIM FISHMAN; Editor-in-Chief JAMES TOEDTMAN; Editor STEVE SLON; circ. 22,559,956; AARP also publishes *AARP Bulletin* (11 a year, circ. 22,042,940).

Allure: 4 Times Sq., New York, NY 10036; tel. (212) 286-2458; fax (212) 286-4654; internet www.allure.com; f. 1991; publ. by Condé Nast Publications Inc; monthly; women's fashion and wellbeing; Vice-Pres. and Publr NANCY BERGER CARDONE; Editor-in-chief LINDA WELLS; circ. 1,048,497.

American Heritage: 90 Fifth Ave, New York, NY 10011-8882; tel. (212) 367-3100; fax (212) 367-3149; internet www.americanheritage.com; e-mail mail@americanheritage.com; internet www.americanheritage.com; f. 1954; 8 a year; US history; Publr RICH KARLGAARD; Editor RICHARD F. SNOW; circ. 344,797.

The American Legion Magazine: 700 North Pennsylvania St, POB 1055, Indianapolis, IN 46206-1055; tel. (317) 630-1200; fax (317) 630-1280; e-mail magazine@legion.org; internet www.legion.org; f. 1919; publ. of The American Legion; monthly; Editor JOHN B. RAUGHTER; circ. 2,531,867.

American Rifleman: NRA Publications, 11250 Waples Mill Rd, Fairfax, VA 22030; tel. (703) 267-1329; e-mail publications@nrahq.org; internet www.nrapublications.org; f. 1885; official journal of the Nat. Rifle Assen; monthly; Editor-in-Chief MARK A. KEEFE, IV; circ. 1,387,828; other publs include *American Hunter* (f. 1973, circ. 1,006,193).

American Teacher: 555 New Jersey Ave, NW, Washington, DC 20001-2079; tel. (202) 879-4430; fax (202) 783-2014; e-mail online@aft.org; internet www.aft.org; f. 1916; 8 a year; Editor ROGER GLASS; circ. 950,000.

Architectural Digest: Condé Nast Publications Inc, 6300 Wilshire Blvd, Los Angeles, CA 90048; tel. (213) 965-3700; fax (213) 937-1458; internet www.archdigest.com; f. 1920; monthly; Publr AMY CHURGIN; Editor PAIGE RENSE; circ. 850,000.

Arthritis Today: 1330 West Peachtree St, NW, Suite 100, Atlanta, GA 30309; tel. (404) 872-7100; fax (404) 872-9559; e-mail atmail@arthritis.org; internet www.arthritis.org/resources/arthritistoday; f. 1987; publ. by the Arthritis Foundation; 6 a year; health and lifestyle magazine for sufferers of arthritis; Publr CINDY MCDANIELS; Editor-in-Chief MARCY O'KOON MOSS; circ. 659,584.

Barron's The Dow Jones Business & Financial Weekly: 4300 North Route 1, South Brunswick, NJ; tel. (609) 520-4000; e-mail editors@barrons.com; internet www.barrons.com; f. 1921; weekly; Editor EDWIN A. FINN, Jr; circ. 300,158.

Better Homes and Gardens: 1716 Locust St, Des Moines, IA 50309-3023; tel. (515) 284-3000; fax (515) 284-3684; internet www.bhg.com; f. 1922; monthly; Publr JEANNINE SHAO; Editor-in-Chief KAREL DE WULF NICKELL; circ. 7,600,000.

Bon Appetit: 6300 Wilshire Blvd, 10th Floor, Los Angeles, CA 90048; tel. (323) 965-3600; fax (323) 937-1206; internet www.bonappetit.com; f. 1955; monthly; Publr LYNN W. HEILER; Editor-in-Chief BARBARA FAIRCHILD; circ. 1,280,105.

Boys' Life: 1325 West Walnut Hill Lane, POB 152079, Irving, TX 75015-2079; tel. (972) 580-2366; fax (972) 580-2079; f. 1911; monthly; Editor J. D. OWEN; circ. 1,300,000.

BusinessWeek: 2 Penn Plaza, New York, NY 10121-0101; tel. (212) 904-2000; e-mail webmaster@mcgraw-hill.com; internet www.businessweek.com; f. 1929; publ. by BusinessWeek Group, a subsidiary of The McGraw-Hill Cos Inc; weekly; business, finance and technology; Sr Vice-Pres. and Publr (North America) GEOFFREY DODGE; Editor-in-Chief STEPHEN J. ADLER; circ. 985,029.

Car and Driver: 2002 Hogback Rd, Ann Arbor, MI 48105; tel. (734) 971-3600; fax (734) 971-9188; e-mail editors@caranddriver.com; internet www.caranddriver.com; f. 1956; Editor-in-Chief CSABA CSERE; circ. 1,365,195.

Catholic Digest: POB 64090, St Paul, MN 55164-0090; tel. (612) 962-6739; fax (612) 962-6725; e-mail cdigest@stthomas.edu; internet www.catholicdigest.org; f. 1936; monthly; Editor RICHARD REECE; circ. 509,000.

THE UNITED STATES OF AMERICA

Child: 375 Lexington Ave, 9th Floor, New York, NY 10017-5514; tel. (212) 499-2000; fax (212) 499-2038; e-mail childmail@child.com; internet www.child.com; f. 1986; 10 a year; Publr DAVE MEVORAH; Editor-in-Chief MIRIAM AROND; circ. 1,020,000.

Condé Nast Traveler: 4 Times Sq., 14th Floor, New York, NY 10036-6561; tel. (212) 286-2860; fax (212) 286-2094; e-mail jason_wagenheim@cntraveler.com; internet www.concierge.com/cntraveler; f. 1954; monthly; Publr LISA HENRIQUES HUGHES; Editor-in-Chief KLARA GLOWCZEWSKA; circ. 783,762.

Congressional Digest: 3231 P St, NW, Washington, DC 20007-2772; tel. (202) 333-7332; fax (202) 625-6670; e-mail cdeditor@aol.com; internet www.congressionaldigest.com; f. 1921; 10 a year; Publr PAGE B. ROBINSON.

Consumer Reports: 101 Truman Ave, Yonkers, NY 10703-1057; tel. (914) 378-2000; fax (914) 378-2900; internet www.consumerreports.org; f. 1936; monthly; Editor JULIA KAGAN; circ. 4,500,000.

Consumers Digest: 8001 North Lincoln Ave, 6th Floor, Skokie, IL 60077-3657; tel. (847) 763-9200; fax (847) 763-0200; f. 1959; 6 a year; Editor RANDY WEBER; circ. 1,000,000.

Cosmopolitan: 224 West 57th St, New York, NY 10019-3203; tel. (212) 649-2000; fax (212) 207-5363; e-mail cosmo_letters@hearst.com; internet www.cosmomag.com; f. 1886; monthly; women's; Publr SUSAN PLAGEMANN; Editor-in-Chief KATE WHITE; circ. 2,800,000.

Country Home: 1716 Locust St, Des Moines, IA 50309; tel. (515) 284-2015; e-mail countryh@mdp.com; internet www.countryhome.com; f. 1979; publ. by Meredith Corpn; 10 a year; lifestyle; Publr CAREY WITMER; Editor-in-Chief CAROL SHEEHAN; circ. 1,265, 174.

Country Living: 224 West 57th St, New York, NY 10019-3203; tel. (212) 649-2000; fax (212) 956-3857; e-mail countryliving@hearst.com; internet www.countryliving.com; f. 1978; monthly; Publr STEVEN GRUNE; Editor-in-Chief NANCY MERNIT SORRIANO; circ. 1,600,000.

Discover: 114 Fifth Ave, New York, NY 10011; tel. (212) 633-4400; fax (212) 633-4817; e-mail editorial@discover.com; internet www.discover.com; f. 1980; publ. by Discover Media LLC; science and technology; Publr TERESA KENDREGAN; Editor-in-Chief STEPHEN L. PETRANEK; circ 859,225.

Ebony: 820 South Michigan Ave, Chicago, IL 60605-2191; tel. (312) 322-9200; fax (312) 322-9375; internet www.ebony.com; f. 1945; monthly; African-American general interest; Publr and CEO JOHN H. JOHNSON; Exec. Editor LERONE BENNETT; circ. 1,800,000.

Elks Magazine: 425 West Diversey Pkwy, Chicago, IL 60614-6196; tel. (773) 755-4894; e-mail elksmag@elks.org; f. 1922; monthly; Publr CHERYL T. STACHURA; circ. 1,036,157.

Elle: 1633 Broadway, 44th Floor, New York, NY 10019; tel. (212) 767-5800; fax (212)767-5980; internet www.elle.com; f. 1985; publ. by Hachette Filipacchi Media US Inc; monthly; women's fashion; Sr Vice-Pres. and Group Publishing Dir CAROL SMITH; Editor-in-Chief ROBERTA MYERS; circ. 1,031,108.

Endless Vacation: 9998 North Michigan Rd, Carmel, IA 46032; tel. (317) 805-8200; fax (317) 805-8229; f. 1975; publ. by Resort Condominiums Int.; 6 a year; Vice-Pres. RICHARD CAPRIO; circ. 1,712,564.

Entertainment Weekly: 1675 Broadway, 29th Floor, New York, NY 10019; tel. (212) 522-5600; fax (212) 522-0074; internet www.ew.com; f. 1990; Man. Editor JAMES W. SEYMORE, Jr; circ. 1,518,763.

ESPN The Magazine: 19 East 34th St, New York, NY 10016; tel. (212) 515-1000; fax (212) 515-1275; internet espn.go.com/magazine; f. 1998; fortnightly; subsidiary of Walt Disney DIS; men's sports and lifestyle; Editor-in-Chief GARY HOENIG; circ. 1,858,079.

Esquire: 250 West 55th St, New York, NY 10019-3203; tel. (212)649-2000; fax (212) 977-3158; e-mail esquire@hearst.com; internet www.esquire.com; f. 1933; monthly; Publr KEVIN O'MALLEY; Editor-in-Chief DAVID GRANGER; circ. 672,073.

Essence: 1500 Broadway, 6th Floor, New York, NY 10036-4071; tel. (212) 642-0600; fax (212) 921-5173; e-mail info@essence.com; internet www.essence.com; f. 1970; monthly; Editor-in-Chief DIANE MARIE WEATHERS; circ. 950,000.

Family Circle: 375 Lexington Ave, New York, NY 10017-5514; tel. (212) 499-2000; fax (212) 499-6740; f. 1932; every 3 weeks; Editor-in-Chief SUSAN KELLIHER UNGARO; circ. 5,213,000.

FamilyFun: 244 Main St, Northampton, MA 01060; tel. (212) 633-4485; e-mail ellen.antoville@disney.com; internet familyfun.go.com; f. 1991; publ. by Disney Publishing Worldwide; monthly; general interest for families with young children; Editor ANN HALLOCK; circ. 1,920,073.

Family Handyman: 7900 International Dr., Suite 950, Bloomington, MN 55425-1510; tel. (612) 854-3000; fax (612) 854-8009; f. 1951; 10 a year; Editor GARY HAVENS; circ. 1,123,000.

Fast Company: 375 Lexington Ave, New York, NY 10017; tel. (212) 499-2000; fax (212) 389-5496; e-mail loop@fastcompany.com; internet www.fastcompany.com; f. 1995; monthly; acquired by Mansueto Ventures LLC in 2005; global business practice; Editor-in-Chief JOHN BYRNE; circ. 767,900.

FHM: 110 Fifth Ave, New York, NY 10011; tel. (212) 201-6700; fax (212) 201-6965; e-mail andrew.ormson@emapmetrousa.com; internet www.fhmus.com; f. 2000; publ. by Emap Metro LLC; monthly; men's lifestyle, entertainment and fashion; Exec. Publr and Pres. DANA FIELDS; Editor-in-Chief SCOTT GRAMLING; circ. 1,292,233.

Field & Stream: 2 Park Ave, New York, NY 10016-5601; tel. (212) 779-5000; fax (212) 779-5114; e-mail fsletters@time4.com; internet www.fieldandstream.com; f. 1895; 11 a year; Editor SID EVANS; circ. 1.5m.

Fitness: 375 Lexington Ave, New York, NY 10017-5514; tel. (212) 499-2000; internet www.fitnessmagazine.com; f. 1992; acquired by Meredith Corpn in 2005; women's health and fitness; Publr KATHERINE RIZZUTO; Editor-in-Chief EMILY LISTFIELD; circ. 1,567,176.

Food & Wine: 1120 Ave of the Americas, New York, NY 10036; tel. (212) 382-5600; fax (212) 382-5879; e-mail lynn.m.yoong@aexp.com; internet www.foodandwine.com; f. 1978; publ. by American Express Publishing Corpn; monthly; Publr JULIE MCGOWAN; Editor-in-Chief DANA COWIN; circ. 933,219.

Forbes: 60 Fifth Ave, New York, NY 10011-8802; tel. (212) 620-2200; fax (212) 620-1875; internet www.forbes.com; f. 1917; fortnightly; Pres. and Editor-in-Chief STEVE FORBES; Editor WILLIAM BALDWIN; circ. 900,000.

Fortune: 1271 Ave of the Americas, New York, NY 10020; tel. (212) 522-1212; fax (212) 522-0810; internet www.fortune.com; f. 1930; Man. Editor ERIC POOLEY; circ. 933,000.

Game Informer: 724 North First St, 4th Floor, Minneapolis, MN 55401; tel. (612) 486-6100; fax (612) 486-6101; e-mail andy@gameinformer.com; internet www.gameinformer.com; f. 1991; owned by Sunrise Publs; monthly; computer gaming; Publr CATHY PRESTON; Editor-in-Chief ANDY MCNAMARA; circ. 2,036,751.

Glamour: 4 Times Sq., 16th Floor, New York, NY 10036; tel. (212) 286-2860; fax (212) 286-6922; e-mail letters@glamour.com; internet www.glamour.com; f. 1939; monthly; Editor CYNTHIA LEIVE; circ. 2,132,000.

Golf Digest: 5520 Park Ave, Trumbull, CT 06611-3426; tel. (203) 373-7000; fax (203) 371-2162; e-mail editor@golfdigest.com; internet www.golfdigest.com; f. 1950; monthly; Editor JERRY TARDE; circ. 1,500,000.

Golf Magazine: 2 Park Ave, New York, NY 10016-5601; tel. (212) 779-5000; fax (212) 779-5522; e-mail letters@golfonline.com; internet www.golfonline.com; f. 1959; monthly; Editor-in-Chief GEORGE PEPER; circ. 1,400,000.

Good Housekeeping: 959 Eighth Ave, New York, NY 10019-5203; tel. (212) 649-2000; fax (212) 265-3307; internet www.goodhousekeeping.com; f. 1885; monthly; Publr PATRICIA HAEGELE; Editor-in-Chief ELLEN LEVINE; circ. 5,032,901.

Gourmet—The Magazine of Good Living: 4 Times Sq., 9th Floor, New York, NY 10036; tel. (212) 286-2860; fax (212) 753-2596; internet www.gourmet.com; f. 1941; monthly; Editor RUTH REICHL; circ. 855,000.

GQ: 4 Times Sq., New York, NY 10036; tel. (212) 286-6410; fax (212) 286-7969; internet us.gq.com; f. 1957; publ. by Condé Nast Publications; monthly; men's lifestyle; Vice-Pres. and Publr PETER HUNSINGER; Editor-in-Chief JIM NELSON; circ. 824,334.

Guideposts: 39 Seminary Hill Rd, Carmel, NY 10512; tel. (212) 929-1300; fax (212) 929-9574; e-mail atyourservice@guideposts.org; internet www.guidepostsmag.com; f. 1945; monthly; personal and spiritual development; Publr JANINE SCOLPINO; Editor-in-Chief EDWARD GRINNAN; circ. 2,652,174; other publs incl. *Positive Thinking Magazine* (10 a year, circ. 335,000), *Angels on Earth* (6 a year, circ. 600,000) and *Guideposts Sweet 16* (6 a year).

HANDY: 12301 Whitewater Dr., Minnetonka, MN 55343; tel. (952) 988-7294; fax (952) 936-9169; e-mail lokrend@namginc.com; internet www.handymanclub.com; f. 1993; publ. by North American Media Group Inc; official publ. of the Handyman Club of America; 6 a year; home improvement; Publr TOM SWEENEY; Editor LARRY OKREND; circ. 915,355.

Harper's Bazaar: 1700 Broadway, New York, NY 10019-5970; tel. (212) 903-5000; fax (212) 262-7101; e-mail bazaar@hearst.com; internet www.bazaar411.com; monthly; Publr VALERIE SALEMBIER; Editor-in-Chief GLENDA BAILEY; circ. 746,000.

Health: 2100 Lakeshore Dr., Birmingham, AL 35209; tel. (205) 445-6476; fax (205) 445-5123; internet www.health.com; f. 1987; publ. by Southern Progress Corpn, a subsidiary of Time Inc; 10 a year; women's health and wellbeing; Publr JENNIFER DEANS; Editor-in-Chief DOUG CRICHTON; circ. 1,375,538.

Highlights for Children: 803 Church St, Honesdale, PA 18413; tel. (717) 253-1080; fax (717) 253-0179; f. 1946; monthly; Editor CHRISTINE FRENCH CLARK; circ. 2,500,000.

THE UNITED STATES OF AMERICA — Directory

Home: 1633 Broadway, 44th Floor, New York, NY 10019; tel. (212) 767-5518; e-mail homemag@hfnm.com; internet www.homemag.com; f. 1981; publ. by Hachette Filipacchi Media US Inc; home improvement and decoration; Vice-Pres. and Publr JOHN H. GRANT; Vice-Pres. and Editor-in-Chief DONNA SAPOLIN; circ. 1,029,695.

Hot Rod Magazine: 6420 Wilshire Blvd, Los Angeles, CA 90048; tel. (332) 782-2000; fax (323) 782-2223; e-mail hotrod@primediacmmg.com; f. 1948; monthly; Editor DAVID FREIBURGER; circ. 780,000.

House and Garden: 4 Times Sq., 8th Floor, New York, NY 10036; tel. (212) 286-2191; fax (212) 286-4549; internet www.houseandgarden.com; f. 1901; publ. by Condé Nast Publications Inc; monthly; Vice-Pres. and Publr JOSEPH LAGANI; Editor-in-Chief DOMINIQUE BROWNING; circ. 920,154.

House Beautiful: 1700 Broadway, New York, NY 10019-5970; tel. (212) 903-5000; fax (212) 765-8292; f. 1896; monthly; Publr DAVID ARNOLD; Editor-in-Chief MARK MAYFIELD; circ. 850,000.

Inc.: 375 Lexington Ave, New York, NY 10017; tel. (212) 499-2000; internet www.inc.com; f. 1987; acquired by Mansueto Ventures LLC in 2005; monthly; small business resources and advice; Vice-Pres. and Publr GORDON LEE JONES, III; Editor-in-Chief JOHN KOTEN; circ. 700,035.

In Style: 1271 Ave of the Americas, New York, NY 10020; tel. (212) 522-1212; internet www.instyle.com; f. 1994; publ. by Time Inc; celebrity, women's lifestyle and fashion; Man. Editor CHARLA LAWHON; circ. 1,793,902.

In Touch Weekly: 270 Sylvan Ave, Englewood Cliffs, NJ 07632; tel. (201) 569-6699; fax (201) 569-3584; e-mail mail@intouchweekly.com; internet www.intouchweekly.com; f. 2002; publ. by Bauer Publishing USA; weekly; celebrity and entertainment; Publr BOB DAVIDOWITZ; Editor-in-Chief RICHARD SPENCER; circ. 1,123,455.

Jane: 750 Third Ave, New York, NY 10017; tel. (212) 630-4192; e-mail carlos.lamadrid@fairchildpub.com; internet www.janemag.com; f. 1992; publ. by Fairchild Publications; monthly; women's lifestyle; Vice-Pres. and Publr CARLOS LAMADRID; Editor-in-Chief BRANDON HOLLEY; circ. 700,159.

Jet: 820 South Michigan Ave, Chicago, IL 60605-2191; tel. (312) 322-9200; fax (312) 322-0951; internet www.jetmag.com; f. 1951; weekly; African-American general interest; Man. Editor MALCOLM R. WEST; circ. 1,000,000.

Junior Scholastic: 555 Broadway, New York, NY 10012; tel. (212) 343-6295; fax (212) 343-6333; e-mail junior@scholastic.com; f. 1937; 18 a year; Editor LEE BAIER; circ. 615,000.

Kiplinger's Personal Finance Magazine: 1729 H St, NW, Washington, DC 20006-3904; tel. (202) 887-6400; fax (202) 331-1206; e-mail magazine@kiplinger.com; internet www.kiplinger.com; f. 1947; monthly; Editor FRED FRAILEY; circ. 1,400,000.

Ladies' Home Journal: 125 Park Ave, New York, NY 10017-5599; tel. (212) 557-6600; fax (212) 455-1010; f. 1883; monthly; Editor-in-Chief MYRNA BLYTH; circ. 4,500,000.

Lion Magazine: 300 22nd St, Oak Brook, IL 60523; tel. (630) 571-5466; fax (630) 571-1685; e-mail rkleinfe@lionsclubs.org; f. 1918; monthly; business and professional; Editor ROBERT KLEINFELDER; circ. 500,000.

Lucky: 4 Times Sq., 8th Floor, New York, NY 10036; tel. (212) 286-2860; fax (212) 286-4986; internet www.luckymag.com; f. 2000; publ. by Conde Nast Publications Inc; monthly; fashion and shopping; Vice-Pres. and Publr ALEXANDRA 'SANDY' GOLINKIN; Editor-in-Chief KIM FRANCE; circ. 1,037,939.

Marie Claire: 1790 Broadway, 3rd Floor, New York, NY 10019; tel. (212) 649-5000; fax (212) 501-5050; e-mail marieclaire@hearst.com; internet www.marieclaire.com; f. 1994; monthly; Publr KATHERINE RIZZUTO; Editor-in-Chief LESLEY JANE SEYMOUR; circ. 903,000.

Martha Stewart Living: 11 West 42nd St, New York, NY 10036; tel. (212) 827-8000; fax (212) 827-8204; e-mail mstewart@marthastewart.com; internet www.marthastewart.com; f. 1991; publ. by Martha Stewart Living Omnimedia Inc; monthly; lifestyle and general interest; Publr SALLY PRESTON; Editor-in-Chief MARGARET ROACH; circ. 1,928,627; other publs incl. *Everyday Food* (f. 2003, circ. 852,407).

Maxim: 1040 Ave of the Americas, New York, NY 10018; tel. (212) 302-2626; fax (212) 302-2631; e-mail editors@maximmag.com; internet www.maximonline.com; f. 1997; publ. by Dennis Publishing Inc; monthly; men's lifestyle and general interest; Group Publr ROB GREGORY; Editor-in-Chief ED NEEDHAM; circ. 2,531,681; other publs incl. *Stuff* (f. 1999, circ. 1,356,636).

MediZine Healthy Living: 298 Fifth Ave, 2nd Floor, New York, NY 10001; tel. (212) 695-2223; fax (212) 695-2936; e-mail info@medizine.com; internet www.remedyonline.com; f. 1994; health and well-being; Editor-in-Chief DIANE UMANSKY; circ. 3,500,000; other publs incl. *Remedy* (f. 1995, circ. 2,200,363).

Men's Fitness: 1 Park Ave, 10th Floor, New York, NY 10016; tel. (212) 545-4805; fax (212) 686-9032; internet www.mensfitness.com; f. 1985; publ. by AMI/Weider Publs; monthly; men's health, fitness and lifestyle; Publr MARC RICHARDS; circ. 650,017; Editor-in-Chief NEAL BOULTON.

Men's Health: 733 Third Ave, 15th Floor, New York, NY 10017; tel. (212) 573-0555; e-mail jon.hammond@rodale.com; internet www.menshealth.com; f. 1988; men's health and general interest; 10 a year; publ. by Rodale Inc; Vice-Pres. and Publr JACK ESSIG; Editor-in-Chief DAVID ZINCZENKO; circ. 1,773,612.

Men's Journal: 1290 Ave of the Americas, New York, NY 10104-0298; tel. (212) 484-1616; fax (212) 484-3429; e-mail eric.bizzak@mensjournal.com; internet www.mensjournal.com; f. 1992; publ. by Wenner Media, Inc; monthly; men's general interest and active lifestyle; Publr WILL SCHENCK; Editor-in-Chief (vacant); circ. 675,452.

Metropolitan Home: 1633 Broadway, New York, NY 10019-6741; tel. (212) 767-4500; fax (212) 767-5636; f. 1981; 6 a year; Editor-in-Chief DONNA WARNER; circ. 600,000.

Midwest Living: 125 Park Ave, New York, NY 10017; tel. (212) 551-7110; fax (212) 551-7051; e-mail peter.gross@meredith.com; internet www.midwestliving.com; f. 1987; publ. by Meredith Corpn; monthly; lifestyle with focus on US Midwest; Publr PETER GROSS; Editor-in-Chief DAN KAERCHER; circ. 941,161.

Money: 1271 Ave of the Americas, New York, NY 10020-1301; tel. (212) 522-1212; fax (212) 522-0189; internet www.money.com; f. 1972; monthly; Man. Editor ROBERT SAFIAN; circ. 1,929,347.

More: 125 Park Ave, New York, NY 10017; tel. (212) 557-6600; fax (212) 455-1244; internet www.more.com; f. 1998; publ. by Meredith Corpn; 10 a year; women's lifestyle; Publr BRENDA SAGET DARLING; Editor DONNA ARMSTRONG; circ. 1,051,049.

Motor Trend: 6420 Wilshire Blvd, Los Angeles, CA 90048; tel. (323) 782-2220; fax (323) 782-2355; e-mail motortrend@emapusa.com; internet www.motortrend.com; f. 1949; monthly; Editor-in-Chief C. VAN TUNE; circ. 1,285,178.

National Enquirer: 600 South East Coast Ave, Lantana, FL 33462-0001; tel. (561) 586-1111; fax (561) 540-1010; e-mail letters@nationalenquirer.com; internet www.nationalenquirer.com; f. 1926; weekly; Editor IAIN CALDER; circ. 2,717,000.

National Geographic Magazine: 1145 17th St, NW, Washington, DC 20036-4701; tel. (202) 857-7000; fax (202) 775-6141; e-mail ngm@nationalgeographic.com; internet www.ngm.com; f. 1888; monthly; Editor CHRIS JOHNS; circ. 8,974,000.

National News: American Legion Auxiliary, 777 North Meridian St, 3rd Floor, Indianapolis, IN 46204-1420; tel. (317) 955-3862; fax (317) 955-3884; e-mail tmiller@legion-aux.org; internet www.legion-aux.org; publ. of the American Legion Auxiliary (ALA); 6 a year; information about the ALA; Editor TONY MILLER; circ. 771,942.

The New Yorker: 4 Times Sq., New York, NY 10036-7448; tel. (212) 286-2860; fax (212) 536-5735; e-mail themail@newyorker.com; internet www.newyorker.com; f. 1925; weekly; Editor DAVID REMNICK; circ. 850,081.

Newsweek: Newsweek Bldg, 251 West 57th St, New York, NY 10019-1894; tel. (212) 445-4000; fax (212) 445-5068; f. 1933; weekly; Man. Editor MARK WHITAKER; circ. 3,156,000.

Nick Jr. Family Magazine: 1515 Broadway, New York, NY 10036; tel. (212) 258-8000; internet www.nickjr.com; f. 2000; subsidiary of Viacom Int. Inc; monthly; parenting; Editor-in-Chief FREDDI GREENBERG; circ. 1,106,811.

North American Hunter: 12301 Whitewater Dr., Minnetonka, MN 55343; fax (952) 936-9169; e-mail dswenson@namginc.com; internet www.huntingclub.com; f. 1979; publ. by North American Media Group Inc; 8 a year; official publ. of the North American Hunting Club; hunting and conservation; Publr RICH SUNDBERG; Editor GORDY KRAHN; circ. 776,849.

O, The Oprah Magazine: 1700 Broadway, New York, NY 10019; tel. (212) 903-5366; e-mail omail@hearst.com; internet www.oprah.com/omagazine; f. 2001; Publr AMY GROSS; Editor-in-Chief JILL SEELIG.

Organic Gardening: 33 East Minor St, Emmaus, PA 18098-0001; tel. (610) 967-8363; fax (610) 967-7722; e-mail organicgardening@vodale.com; internet www.organicgardening.com; f. 1942; 6 a year; Editor SCOTT MEYER; circ. 350,000.

Outdoor Life: 2 Park Ave, 10th Floor, New York, NY 10016-5601; tel. (212) 779-5000; fax (212) 779-5366; e-mail olmagazine@aol.com; internet www.outdoorlife.com; f. 1898; 10 a year; Editor-in-Chief TODD W. SMITH; Exec. Editor COLIN B. MOORE; circ. 925,700.

Outside: 400 Market St, Santa Fe, NM 87501; tel. (505) 989-7100; fax (505) 989-4700; e-mail outsideonline@outsidemag.com; internet outside.away.com; f. 1976 as Mariah; publ. by Mariah Media Inc; monthly; adventure travel and outdoor recreation; Chair. and Editor-in-Chief LAWRENCE J. BURKE; Vice-Pres. and Publr SCOTT PARMELEE; circ. 656932.

THE UNITED STATES OF AMERICA — Directory

Parenting: 530 Fifth Ave, 4th Floor, New York, NY 10036; tel. (212) 522-8989; internet www.parenting.com; f. 1987; owned by Time Inc; monthly; Editor-in-Chief Janet Chan; Publr Jeff Wellington; circ. 2,170,314; other pubs. incl. *Babytalk* (f. 1935, circ. 1,800,769).

Parents' Magazine: 685 Third Ave, New York, NY 10017; tel. (212) 878-8700; fax (212) 986-2656; f. 1926; monthly; Editor-in-Chief Ann Pleshette Murphy; circ. 1,740,000.

PC Magazine: 1 Park Ave, New York, NY 10016-5802; tel. (212) 503-5255; fax (212) 503-5799; internet www.pcmag.com; f. 1981; fortnightly; personal computer industry; Editors Michael Miller, Robin Raskin; circ. 1,154,000.

PC World: 501 Second St, San Francisco, CA 94107; tel. (415) 243-0500; fax (415) 442-1891; e-mail pcwletters@pcworld.com; internet www.pcworld.com; f. 1982; publ. by PC World Communications, Inc, a subsidiary of International Data Group; monthly; computer technology; Vice-Pres. and Publr Wayne Silverman; Vice-Pres. and Editor-in-Chief Harry McCracken; circ. 880,844.

People: Time and Life Bldg, 28th Floor, Rockefeller Center New York, NY 10020; tel. (212) 522-2028; fax (212) 522-0331; internet www.people.com; f. 1974; publ. by Time Inc; weekly; celebrity and entertainment; Publr Paul Caine; Man. Editor Mark Bautz; circ. 3,779,640; other publs incl. *Teen People* (f. 1998, circ. 1,550,699).

Playboy: 680 North Lake Shore Dr., Chicago, IL 60611-4402; tel. (312) 751-8000; fax (312) 751-2818; e-mail edit@playboy.com; internet www.playboy.com/magazine-toc.html; f. 1953; monthly; men's interest; Publr Michael Carr; Editor-in-Chief Hugh M. Hefner; circ. 3,172,000.

Popular Mechanics: 810 Seventh Ave, New York, NY 10019; tel. (212) 649-2000; fax (212) 586-5562; internet www.popularmechanics.com; f. 1902; monthly; Publr William Congdon; Editor-in-Chief Joe Oldham; circ. 1,239,654.

Popular Science: 2 Park Ave, 9th Floor, New York, NY 10016; tel. (212) 779-5000; fax (212) 481-8062; e-mail psletters@aol.com; internet www.popsci.com; f. 1872; monthly; Editor-in-Chief Cecilia Wessner; circ. 1,550,000.

Prevention: 33 East Minor St, Emmaus, PA 18098-0001; tel. (610) 967-5171; fax (610) 967-7654; e-mail preventiondm@aol.com; internet www.prevention.com; f. 1950; monthly; Editor-in-Chief Catherine Cassidy; circ. 3,221,000.

Progressive Farmer: 2100 Lakeshore Dr., Birmingham, AL 35202; tel. (205) 445-6000; fax (205) 445-6860; e-mail progressivefarmer@timeinccom; internet www.progressivefarmer.com; f. 1886; monthly; Editor Jack Odle; circ. 600,000.

Reader's Digest: Reader's Digest Rd, Pleasantville, NY 10570-7000; tel. (914) 238-1000; fax (914) 238-4559; internet www.readersdigest.com; f. 1922; monthly; Exec. Editor Jacqueline Leo; circ. 12,500,000.

Real Simple: 1271 Ave of the Americas, New York, NY 10020; tel. (212) 522-1212; fax (212) 467-1398; internet www.realsimple.com; f. 2000; owned by Time Inc; 11 a year; women's lifestyle and general interest; Publr Robin Domeniconi; Man. Editor Kristin van Ogtrop; circ. 1,947,004.

Redbook: 224 West 57th St, 6th Floor, New York, NY 10019-3203; tel. (212) 649-2000; fax (212) 581-8114; internet www.redbookmag.com; f. 1903; monthly; Publr Mary E. Morgan; Editor-in-Chief Ellen Kunes; circ. 2,250,000.

Road & Track: 1499 Monrovia Ave, Newport Beach, CA 92663-2752; tel. (949) 720-5300; fax (949) 631-2757; e-mail rtletters@hfmus.com; internet www.roadandtrack.com; f. 1947; monthly; Editor Thomas L. Bryant; circ. 742,000.

Rolling Stone: 1290 Ave of the Americas, 2nd Floor, New York, NY 10104; tel. (212) 484-1616; fax (212) 767-8209; e-mail feedback@rollingstone.com; internet www.rollingstone.com; f. 1967; fortnightly; Man. Editor Robert Love; circ. 1,229,000.

Scholastic Parent & Child: 557 Broadway, New York, NY 10012; tel. (212) 343-6100; e-mail news@scholastic.com; internet www.scholastic.com/earlylearner/parentandchild/; f. 1995; publ. by Scholastic Inc; 6 a year; Assoc. Publr Stefanie Angeli; Editor-in-Chief Pam Abrams; circ. 1,238,983.

SchoolSports Magazine: 971 Commonwealth Ave, Boston, MA 02215-1305; tel. (617) 779-9000; fax (617) 779-9100; e-mail jon@schoolsports.com; internet schoolsports.scout.com; f. 1997; publ. by Scout Publishing; 7 a year; 15 regional edns distributed to c. 4,000 schools; sports and teenage active lifestyle; Publr David Weiss; Editor-in-Chief Jonathan Segal; circ. 652,275.

Scientific American: 415 Madison Ave, New York, NY 10017-1179; tel. (212) 754-0550; fax (212) 755-1976; e-mail editors@sciam.com; internet www.sciam.com; f. 1845; monthly; Exec. Editor Mariette DiChristina; Editor John Rennie; circ. 683,970.

Scouting Magazine: 1325 West Walnut Hill Lane, POB 152079, Irving, TX 75015-2079; tel. (972) 580-2000; fax (972) 580-2079; e-mail scole@netbsa.org; internet www.scoutingmagazine.org; f. 1913; publ. by Boy Scouts of America; 6 a year; Editor Jon C. Halter; circ. 1,000,000.

SELF Magazine: 4 Times Sq., 5th Floor, New York, NY 10036; tel. (212) 286-2860; fax (212) 286-8110; e-mail comments@self.com; internet www.self.com; f. 1979; monthly; Editor-in-Chief Lucy Danziger; circ. 1,111,000.

Seventeen: 1140 Broadway, 13th Floor, New York, NY 10022; tel. (212) 407-9700; fax (212) 935-4237; e-mail seventeenm@ad.com; internet www.seventeen.com; f. 1944; monthly; Publr Jayne Jamison; Editor-in-Chief Atoosa Rubenstein; circ. 2,350,000.

Shape: 1 Park Ave, 10th Floor, New York, NY 10016; tel. (212) 545-4800; fax (212) 252-1131; internet www.shape.com; f. 1981; publ. by American Media Inc; women's health and fitness; Publr Sabine Feldman; Editor-in-Chief Valerie Latona; circ. 1,659,845.

Sierra: 85 Second St, 2nd Floor, San Francisco, CA 94105; tel. (415) 977-5500; fax (415) 977-5799; e-mail sierra.magazine@sierraclub.org; internet www.sierraclub.org/sierra; f. 1893; official publ. of the Sierra Club; 6 a year; nature and ecology; Editor-in-Chief Joan Hamilton; circ. 742,083.

SmartMoney: 1755 Broadway, 2nd Floor, New York, NY 10019; tel. (212) 373-9300; e-mail pr@smartmoney.com; internet www.smartmoney.com; f. 1992; jt venture of Dow Jones & Co, Inc and Hearst Communications, Inc; Pres. and Publishing Dir Jay McGill, Jr; Chair. and Editor-in-Chief Edwin A. Finn, Jr; circ. 817,746.

Smithsonian Magazine: MRC 951, POB 37012, Washington, DC 20013-7012; tel. (202) 275-2072; e-mail articles@simag.si.edu; internet www.smithsonianmag.si.edu; f. 1970; monthly; Editor Carey Winfrey; circ. 2,100,000.

Southern Living: 2100 Lakeshore Dr., Birmingham, AL 35209-6721; tel. (205) 877-6000; fax (205) 877-6085; internet www.southernliving.com; f. 1966; monthly; Editor John Alex Floyd, Jr; circ. 2,300,000.

Sporting News: 10176 Corporate Sq. Dr., Suite 200, St Louis, MO 63132; tel. (314) 997-7111; fax (314) 997-0765; e-mail tsnmail@aol.com; internet www.sportingnews.com; f. 1886; weekly; Editor John Rawlings; circ. 600,000.

Sports Illustrated: Sports Illustrated Bldg, 135 West 50th St, New York, NY 10020-1393; tel. (212) 522-1212; fax (212) 977-4540; internet www.cnssi.com; f. 1954; weekly; Editor Bill Colson; circ. 3,220,000.

Star: 660 White Plains Rd, Tarrytown, NY 10591; tel. (914) 332-5000; fax (914) 332-5044; f. 1974; weekly; Editor-in-Chief Phil Bunton; circ. 1,984,000.

Sunset Magazine: 80 Willow Rd, Menlo Park, CA 94025-3691; tel. (650) 321-3600; fax (650) 327-5737; internet www.sunset.com; f. 1898; monthly; Editor Katie Tamony; circ. 1,500,000.

Tennis: 79 Madison Ave, 8th Floor, New York, NY 10016; tel. (212) 636-2700; fax (212) 636-2730; e-mail jwilliams@tennismagazine.com; internet www.tennis.com; f. 1965; acquired. by Miller Publishing Group LLC in 1997; 10 a year; tennis, travel and lifestyle; Publr Jeff Williams; Editor-at-Large Mark Woodruff; circ. 700,035.

This Old House: 1185 Ave of the Americas, 27th Floor, New York, NY 10036; tel. (212) 522-9465; fax (212) 522-9435; e-mail contact@thisoldhouse.com; internet www.thisoldhouse.com; f. 1995; publ. by Time Inc; 10 a year; home improvement; Editor J. Scott Omelianuk; circ. 972,605.

Time: Time-Life Bldg, Rockefeller Center, 1271 Ave of the Americas, New York, NY 10020-1393; tel. (212) 522-1212; fax (212) 522-0323; e-mail letters@time.com; internet www.time.com; f. 1923; weekly; Editor-in-Chief John Huey; Man. Editor James Kelly; circ. 4,500,000.

Traditional Home: 125 Park Ave, New York, NY 10017; tel. (212) 557-6600; fax (212) 551-6914; e-mail ellen.cummings@meredith.com; internet www.traditionalhome.com; f. 1978; publ. by Meredith Corpn; 8 a year; Publr Pam Daniels; Editor-in-Chief Ann Omvig Maine (acting); circ. 976,032.

Travel Holiday: 1633 Broadway, 43rd Floor, New York, NY 10019; tel. (212) 767-5126; fax (212) 767-5115; e-mail travelhol@aol.com; internet www.travelholiday.com; f. 1901; monthly; Editor John Owens; circ. 650,000.

Travel & Leisure: 1120 Ave of the Americas, 10th Floor, New York, NY 10036-6770; tel. (212) 382-5600; fax (212) 382-5877; e-mail tlquery@amexpub.com; internet www.travelandleisure.com; f. 1971; monthly; Editor-in-Chief Nancy Novogrod; circ. 960,485.

True Story: 333 Seventh Ave, 11th Floor, New York, NY 10003; tel. (212) 979-4800; fax (212) 979-7342; f. 1919; monthly; Editors Heather Dalton, Tina Pappalardo; circ. 825,000.

TV Guide: 1211 Ave of the Americas, New York, NY 10036; tel. (212) 852-7500; fax (212) 852-7470; internet www.tvguide.com; f. 1953; weekly; Exec. Editor Steve Sonsky; circ. 13,077,000.

THE UNITED STATES OF AMERICA

US Weekly: 1290 Ave of the Americas, 2nd Floor, New York, NY 10104-0002; tel. (212) 484-1616; fax (212) 484-1621; f. 1977; monthly; Editor TERRY MCDONELL; circ. 850,000.

US News & World Report: 1050 Thomas Jefferson St, NW, Washington, DC 20007; tel. (202) 955-2000; fax (202) 955-2049; e-mail letters@usnews.com; internet www.usnews.com; f. 1933; weekly; Editor-in-Chief B. ZUCKERMAN; Editor BRIAN DUFFY; circ. 2,000,000.

Vanity Fair: 4 Times Sq., 7th Floor, New York, NY 10036; tel. (212) 286-8180; fax (212) 286-6707; e-mail vfmail@vf.com; internet www.vanityfair.com; f. 1983; monthly; Editor GRAYDON CARTER; circ. 1,120,000.

VFW Magazine: 406 West 34th St, Kansas City, MO 64111-2736; tel. (816) 756-3390; fax (816) 968-1169; internet www.vfw.org; e-mail pbrown@vfw.org; f. 1912; 11 a year; Editor RICHARD K. KOLB; circ. 1,813,000.

VIA: 150 Van Ness Ave, San Francisco, CA 94102-5208; tel. (415) 565-2451; fax (415) 863-4726; f. 1917; 6 a year; motoring; Editor BRUCE ANDERSON; circ. 2,585,000.

VIBE: 215 Lexington Ave, New York, NY 10016; tel. (212) 448-7300; fax (212) 448-7400; internet www.vibe.com; f. 1993; publ. by VIBE/Spin Ventures; monthly; urban music and culture; Publr LEN BURNETT; Editor-in-Chief MIMI VALDÉS; circ. 862,933.

Vogue: 4 Times Sq., 12th Floor, New York, NY 10036; tel. (212) 286-7351; fax (212) 286-8593; e-mail voguemail@aol.com; internet www.vogue.com; f. 1892; monthly; Editor ANNA WINTOUR; circ. 1,250,000; also publ. *Teen Vogue* (circ. 1,527,990).

Weight Watchers Magazine: 360 Lexington Ave, 11th Floor, New York, NY 10017; tel. (212) 370-0644; fax (212) 687-4398; f. 1968; monthly; Editor KATE GREER; circ. 1,060,000.

WHERE: c/o Miller Publishing Group, 11100 Santa Monica Blvd, Suite 600, Los Angeles, CA, 90025-3384; tel. (310) 893-5400; fax (310) 893-5457; e-mail rick.mollineaux@wheremagazine.com; internet www.wheremagazine.com; f. 1936; acquired by Miller Publishing Group LLC in 1997; monthly; int. visitor information; 23 regional edns; Group Publr PETER BLACKWELL; Editorial Dir MARQ DE VILLIERS; circ. 1,084,218.

Woman's Day: 1633 Broadway, New York, NY 10019; tel. (212) 767-6418; e-mail womansday@hfmus.com; internet www.womansday.com; f. 1931; owned by Hachette Filipacchi; 17 a year; women's general interest; Editor-in-Chief JANE CHESNUTT; circ. 4,015,392.

Woman's World: 270 Sylvan Ave, Englewood Cliffs, NJ 07632; tel. (201) 569-0006; fax (201) 569-3584; e-mail tstadnicki@bauer-usa.com; f. 1981; publ. by Bauer Publishing USA; weekly; women's general interest; Publr GREG SLATTERY; circ. 1,602,619; other publs incl. *First for Women* (circ. 1,489,373), *J-14* (circ. 559,594) and *Life & Style Weekly*, (circ. 471,792).

Working Mother: 60 East 42nd St, Suite 2700, New York, NY 10165; tel. (212) 351-6400; fax (212) 351-6487; e-mail joanne.ko@workingmother.com; internet www.workingmother.com; f. 1978; publ. by Working Mother Media, Inc; lifestyle magazine with focus on working mothers; Pres. and Publr JOAN SHERIDAN LABARGE; Editor-in-Chief SUSAN LAPINSKI; circ. 831,062.

NEWS AGENCIES

Associated Press (AP): 50 Rockefeller Plaza, New York, NY 10020-1666; tel. (212) 621-1500; fax (212) 621-1679; e-mail info@ap.org; internet www.ap.org; f. 1848; Pres. and CEO TOM CURLEY; c. 1,700 newspaper mems in the US, 6,000 broadcast mems and over 8,500 subscribers abroad.

Bloomberg News: 499 Park Ave, 15th Floor, New York, NY 10022; tel. (212) 318-2000; fax (212) 893-5999; internet www.bloomberg.com; Editor-in-Chief MATTHEW WINKLER.

Dow-Jones Newswires: Harborside Financial Center, 600 Plaza II, Jersey City, NJ 07311-3992; tel. (201) 938-5400; fax (201) 938-5600; internet www.djnewswires.com; Pres. PAUL INGRASSIA; Man. Editor RICK STINE.

Jewish Telegraphic Agency, Inc (JTA): 330 Seventh Ave, 17th Floor, New York, NY 10001; tel. (212) 643-1890; fax (212) 643-8498; e-mail info@jta.org; internet www.jta.org; f. 1917; world-wide coverage of Jewish news; offices in Washington, DC, and Jerusalem, Israel; Exec. Editor and Publr MARK J. JOFFE.

Religion News Service: 1101 Connecticut Ave, NW, Suite 350, Washington, DC 20036; tel. (202) 463-8777; fax (202) 463-0033; e-mail info@religionnews.com; internet www.religionnews.com; Editor DAVID E. ANDERSON.

United Media (UM): 200 Madison Ave, 4th Floor, New York, NY 10016; tel. (212) 293-8500; fax (212) 293-8717; internet www.unitedmedialicensing.com; f. 1978; licensing and syndication of news features; Pres. and CEO DOUGLAS R. STERN.

United Press International (UPI): 1510 H St, NW, Washington, DC 20005; tel. (202) 898-8000; fax (202) 898-8057; internet www.upi.com; f. 1907; Pres. and CEO DOUGLAS JOO; Editor-in-Chief JOHN O'SULLIVAN; serves c. 1,000 newspaper clients world-wide.

Foreign Bureaux

Agence France-Presse (AFP): 1015 15th St, NW, Suite 500, Washington, DC 20005; tel. (202) 289-0700; fax (202) 414-0624; Bureau Chief ERIC SCHERER; also office in New York.

Agencia EFE (Spain): 25 West 43rd St, Suite 1512, New York, NY 10036; tel. (212) 867-5757; fax (212) 867-9074; e-mail efe@efenews.com; Rep. RAFAEL MORENO; also offices in Washington, DC, Miami and Glendale.

Agenzia Nazionale Stampa Associata (ANSA) (Italy): National Press Bldg, Suite 1285, Washington, DC 20045; tel. (202) 628-3317; fax (202) 638-1792; e-mail answs@nationalpress.com; Bureau Chief GIAMPIERO GRAMAGLIA; also offices in New York and San Francisco.

Allgemeiner Deutscher Nachrichtendienst (ADN) (Germany): UN Secretariat Bldg, Rm 482, UN Plaza, New York, NY 10017; tel. (212) 421-5876; fax (212) 832-5140; Bureau Chief ANDREAS LINDNER.

Canadian Press: 1331 Pennsylvania Ave, NW, Suite 524, Washington, DC 20004; tel. (202) 638-3367; fax (202) 638-3369; Bureau Chief BOB RUSSO.

Central News Agency (CNA) (Taiwan): 1173 National Press Bldg, Washington, DC 20045; tel. (202) 628-2738; fax (202) 637-6788; e-mail cnausa@cna.com.tw; Bureau Chief JORGE LIU; also offices in New York, San Francisco and Los Angeles.

Deutsche Presse-Agentur (dpa) (Germany): 969 National Press Bldg, Washington, DC 20045; tel. (202) 662-1220; fax (202) 662-1270; e-mail dpausa@dpa.com; Bureau Chief LASZLO TRANKOVITS; also office in New York.

Informatsionnoye Telegrafnoye Agentstvo Rossii—Telegrafnoye Agentstvo Suverennykh Stran (ITAR—TASS) (Russia): 50 Rockefeller Plaza, Suite 501, New York, NY 10020-1605; tel. (212) 245-4250; fax (212) 245-4258; e-mail itar@aol.com; Bureau Chief ALEX BEREZHKOV; also office in Washington, DC.

Inter Press Service (IPS) (Italy): United Nations Bldg, Rm S-485, New York, NY 10017; tel. (212) 963-6156; fax (212) 888-6099; e-mail thalifdeen@aol.com; internet www.ipsnews.org; Bureau Chief THALIF DEEN; also office in Washington, DC.

Jiji Tsushin (Japan): 120 West 45th St, 14th Floor, New York, NY 10036; tel. (212) 575-5830; fax (212) 764-3950; f. 1945; Chief Rep. SUGURU SASAKI; also offices in Washington, DC, Los Angeles, San Francisco and Chicago.

Kyodo Tsushin (Japan): 50 Rockefeller Plaza, Suite 816, Washington, DC 1002020045; tel. (202) 347-5767; fax (202) 393-2342; e-mail kyodony@aol.com; Bureau Chief MITSUO SAKURAI; also offices in New York and Los Angeles.

Magyar Távirati Iroda (MTI) (Hungary): 8515 Farrell Dr., Chevy Chase, MD 20815; tel. (301) 565-2221; fax (301) 589-6907; e-mail karpmti@aol.com; Bureau Chief JÁNOS KÁRPÁTI.

Reuters (United Kingdom): 1333 H St, NW, Suite 600, Washington, DC 20005; tel. (202) 898-0056; fax (202) 898-1237; Editor ROBERT DOHERTY; also offices in New York, Chicago, San Francisco and five other cities.

Tlačová agentúra Slovenskej republiky (TASR) (Slovakia): 4501 Connecticut Ave, Apt 713, NW, Washington, DC 20008; tel. (202) 686-4710; fax (202) 537-0574; f. 1992; Chief Officer OTAKAR KOŘINEK.

Xinhua (New China) News Agency (People's Republic of China): 40-35 72nd St, Woodside, NY 11377; tel. (718) 335-8388; fax (718) 335-8778; Bureau Dir JIYONG DUAN; also office in Washington, DC.

Agence Belga (Belgium), Middle East News Agency (Egypt), Press Trust of India, Česká tisková kancelář (Czech Republic), and Notimex (Mexico) are also represented.

NATIONAL ASSOCIATIONS

American Business Press: 675 Third Ave, Suite 415, New York, NY 10017; tel. (212) 661-6360; fax (212) 370-0736; e-mail abp2@aol.com; f. 1906; Pres. GORDON T. HUGHES, III; mems: 160 publrs, 900 periodicals, 35 associates (suppliers).

American Society of Magazine Editors: 919 Third Ave, New York, NY 10022; tel. (212) 872-3700; fax (212) 906-0128; e-mail asme@magazine.org; internet asme.magazine.org; Exec. Dir MARLENE KAHAN; 900 mems.

Audit Bureau of Circulations: 900 North Meacham Rd, Schaumburg, IL 60173-4968; tel. (847) 605-0909; fax (847) 605-0483; internet www.accessabc.com; f. 1914; Chair. and Sec. ANTHONY M. GASPARRO; Pres. and Man. Dir MICHAEL J. LAVERY; 4,500 mems.

Council of Literary Magazines and Presses (CLMP): 154 Christopher St, Suite 3C, New York, NY 10014-2839; tel. (212) 741-9110; fax (212) 741-9112; e-mail info@clmp.org; internet www

THE UNITED STATES OF AMERICA

.clmp.org; f. 1967; provides services to non-commercial US literary magazines and presses; Exec. Dir PEGGY RANDALL; 350 mems.

Magazine Publishers of America: 919 Third Ave, 22nd Floor, New York, NY 10022; tel. (212) 872-3700; fax (212) 888-4217; internet www.magazine.org; f. 1919; Chair. DANIEL B. BREWSTER, Jr; Pres. NINA B. LINK; 380 mems.

National Newspaper Association: POB 7540 Columbia, MO 65205-7540; tel. (573) 882-5800; fax (573) 884-5490; e-mail info@nna.org; internet www.nna.org; f. 1885; Pres. MIKE BUFFINGTON; Exec. Dir BRIAN STEFFENS; 4,000 mems.

Newspaper Association of America: 1921 Gallows Rd, Suite 600, Vienna, VA 22182-3900; tel. (703) 902-1600; fax (703) 917-0636; internet www.naa.org; f. 1992; Chair. BO JONES; Pres. and CEO JOHN F. STURM; more than 2,000 mems in USA and Canada accounting for over 87% of US daily newspaper circulation.

The Newspaper Guild: 501 Third St, NW, Washington, DC 20001-2760; tel. (202) 434-7177; fax (202) 434-1472; internet www.newsguild.org; f. 1933; journalists' org., organ of the Communications Workers of America trade union; Pres. LINDA K. FOLEY; 36,000 mems.

Periodical & Book Association of America Inc: 481 Eighth Ave, Suite 826, New York, NY 10001; tel. (212) 563-6502; fax (212) 563-4098; internet www.pbaa.net; Exec. Dir LISA W. SCOTT; 60 mems.

Publishers

Abaris Books: 64 Wall St, Norwalk, CT 06850; tel. (203) 838-8625; fax (203) 857-0730; e-mail abaris@abarisbooks.com; internet www.abarisbooks.com; f. 1973; division of Opal Publishing Corpn; scholarly, fine art reference, philosophy; Publr ANTHONY S. KAUFMANN; Gen. Man. J. C. WEST.

Abbeville Publishing Group: 22 Cortland St, 32nd Floor, New York, NY 10007; tel. (212) 577-5555; fax (212) 577-5579; internet www.abbeville.com; f. 1977; fine arts and illustrated books; Pres. and Publr ROBERT E. ABRAMS.

Abingdon Press: 201 Eighth Ave South, Nashville, TN 37202; tel. (615) 749-6403; fax (615) 749-6512; e-mail holson@ampublishing.org; internet www.abingdon.org; f. 1789; religious; Gen. Man. HARRIET JANE OLSON.

Harry N. Abrams, Inc: 100 Fifth Ave, New York, NY 10011; tel. (212) 206-7715; fax (212) 645-8437; e-mail abrams@abramsbooks.com; internet www.abramsbooks.com; division of Times Mirror Co; art, architecture, natural history, popular culture; owned by La Martinière Group (France); Pres., CEO and Editor-in-Chief STEVE PARR.

Addison-Wesley-Benjamin-Cummings: 75 Arlington St, Suite 300, Boston, MA 02116; tel. (617) 848-6000; fax (617) 944-9338; internet www.aw-bc.com; f. 1988; owned by Pearson; educational, trade, scientific, engineering, and language teaching materials; Chair. and CEO J. LARRY JONES.

Andrews McMeel Publishing: 4520 Main St, Suite 700, Kansas City, MO 64111; tel. (816) 932-6700; fax (816) 932-6706; f. 1970; humour, general trade; Pres. HUGH T. ANDREWS.

Jason Aronson, Inc: 230 Livingston St, Northvale, NJ 07647; tel. (201) 767-4093; fax (201) 767-4330; e-mail editor@aronson.com; internet www.aronson.com; f. 1965; psychiatry, psychoanalysis and behavioural sciences; Judaica; Pres. JASON ARONSON.

Augsburg Fortress, Publishers: 100 South Fifth St, POB 1209, Minneapolis, MN 55440; tel. (612) 330-3300; fax (612) 330-3455; e-mail info@augsburgfortress.org; internet www.augsburgfortress.org; f. 1890; religious; Pres. MARVIN ROLOFF.

August House Inc, Publishers: POB 3223, Little Rock, AR 72203; tel. (501) 372-5540; fax (501) 372-5579; e-mail ahinfo@augusthouse.com; internet www.augusthouse.com; f. 1979; Southern regional, history, humour and folklore; Pres. TED PARKHURST.

Avery Publishing Group, Inc: 375 Hudson St, New York, NY 10014; internet www.penguinputnam.com; f. 1976; a division of Penguin Putnam Inc; trade books specializing in childbirth, child care, health, cookery, nutrition; Publr MEGAN NEWMAN.

Avon Books: 10 East St, New York, NY 10022; tel. (212) 207-7000; fax (212) 207-7203; internet www.harpercollins.com; f. 1941; division of HarperCollins; reprints and originals; Pres. JANE FRIEDMAN.

Baker Book House: POB 6287, Grand Rapids, MI 49516; tel. (616) 676-9185; fax (616) 676-9573; internet www.bakerbooks.com; f. 1939; religious (Protestant); Pres. DWIGHT BAKER.

Ballantine Publishing Group: 1745 Broadway, New York, NY 10019; tel. (212) 572-2713; fax (212) 572-4912; e-mail bfi@randomhouse.com; internet www.randomhouse.com/bb; f. 1952; division of Random House Inc; fiction, non-fiction, reprints; Pres. GINA CENTRELLO.

Directory

Barnes and Noble Books: 76 Ninth Ave, 9th Floor, New York, NY 10011; tel. (212) 633-3489; fax (212) 675-0413; internet www.barnesandnoble.com; f. 1873; division of Rowman and Littlefield Publrs, Inc; educational and general; Chair. LEONARD RIGGIO; CEO MARIE J. TOULANTIS.

Barron's Educational Series, Inc: 250 Wireless Blvd, Hauppauge, NY 11788; tel. (631) 434-3311; fax (631) 434-3723; e-mail info@barronseduc.com; internet www.barronseduc.com; f. 1945; general non-fiction, educational, juvenile; Chair. and CEO MANUEL H. BARRON; Pres. and Publr ELLEN SIBLEY.

Beacon Press: 25 Beacon St, Boston, MA 02108; tel. (617) 742-2110; fax (617) 723-3097; internet www.beacon.org; f. 1854; world affairs, religion, general non-fiction; Dir HELENE ATWAN.

Blackwell Futura, Inc: 350 Main St, Malden, MA 02148; tel. (781) 388-8200; fax (914) 593-0731; e-mail jlevine@blackwellpub.com; internet www.blackwellcardiology.com; f. 1970; medical and scientific; division of Blackwell Publrs; Exec. Vice-Pres. and Publishing Dir NIGEL FLETCHER-JONES.

R. R. Bowker: 630 Central Ave, New Providence, NJ 07974; tel. (908) 464-6800; fax (908) 464-3553; e-mail info@bowker.com; internet www.bowker.com; f. 1872; reference, bibliographies; Pres. MICHAEL CAIRNS.

Braille Inc: 184 Seapit Rd, POB 457, East Falmouth, MA 02536-0457; tel. (508) 540-0800; fax (508) 548-6116; e-mail info@bowker.com; internet www.bowker.com; f. 1971; fiction, non-fiction, mathematics, science, educational and computer materials in Braille transcription; CEO DREW MEYER.

Branden Publishing Co, Inc: Branden Books, POB 812094, Wellesley, MA 02482; tel. (781) 734-2046; fax (781) 790-1056; e-mail www.branden@branden.com; internet www.branden.com; f. 1907; art, music, classics, fiction, general non-fiction; Pres. JILL NEUSTADT; Editor and Treas. ADOLPH CASO.

George Braziller, Inc: 171 Madison Ave, New York, NY 10016; tel. (212) 889-0909; fax (212) 689-5405; internet www.georgebraziller.com; f. 1955; fiction and non-fiction, art; Publr GEORGE BRAZILLER.

Broadman and Holman Publishers: 127 North Ninth Ave, Nashville, TN 37234-0198; tel. (615) 251-5003; fax (615) 251-5004; e-mail kstephe@bssb.com; internet www.broadmanholman.com; f. 1891; religious (Protestant), fiction, non-fiction, juvenile; Publr KENNETH H. STEPHENS.

Brookings Institution Press: 1775 Massachusetts Ave, NW, Washington, DC 20036-2188; tel. (202) 797-6000; fax (202) 797-6004; e-mail bibooks@brookings.edu; internet www.brookings.edu; f. 1927; economics, government, foreign policy; Dir ROBERT L. FAHERTY.

Burnham Publishers: 111 North Canal St, Chicago, IL 60606; tel. (312) 930-9446; fax (312) 930-5903; e-mail publishers@burnhaminc.com; f. 1909; Pres. and Publr KATHLEEN KUSTA; general interest non-fiction and educational.

Cambridge University Press: 40 West 20th St, New York, NY 10011-4211; tel. (212) 924-3900; fax (212) 691-3239; internet www.cup.org; CEO STEPHEN BOURNE.

Catholic University of America Press: 620 Michigan Ave, NE, Washington, DC 20064; tel. (202) 319-5052; fax (202) 319-4985; e-mail cua-press@cua,edu; internet www.cuapress.cua.edu; f. 1939; scholarly; Dir DAVID J. MCGONAGLE.

Caxton Press: 312 Main St, Caldwell, ID 83605; tel. (208) 459-7421; fax (208) 459-7450; e-mail publish@caxtonprinters.com; internet www.caxtonprinters.com; f. 1903; Western Americana; Vice-Pres. and Publr SCOTT GIPSON.

Columbia University Press: 61 West 62nd St, New York, NY 10023; tel. (212) 459-0600; fax (212) 459-3677; e-mail sm2063@columbia.edu; internet www.columbia.edu/cu/cup; f. 1893; trade, educational, scientific, reference; Pres. and Dir JAMES D. JORDAN.

Concordia Publishing House: 3558 South Jefferson Ave, St Louis, MO 63118; tel. (314) 268-1000; fax (314) 268-1329; internet www.cpn.org; f. 1869; religious (Protestant) children's books, devotionals, bulletins, curriculum music; Pres. PAUL T. MCCAIN.

Congressional Quarterly Books: 1414 22nd St, NW, Washington, DC 20037; tel. (202) 887-8500; fax (202) 887-6706; f. 1945; business, education and government; directories; Publr ROBERT MERRY.

Cornell University Press: Sage House, 512 East State St, POB 250, Ithaca, NY 14850; tel. (607) 257-2338; fax (607) 277-2374; e-mail cupressinfo@cornell.edu; internet www.cornellpress.cornell.edu; f. 1869; scholarly, non-fiction; Dir JOHN G. ACKERMAN.

Creative Co: 123 South Broad St, POB 227, Mankato, MN 56001; tel. (507) 388-6273; fax (507) 388-2746; e-mail creativeco@aol.com; f. 1932; juvenile; Pres. TOM PETERSON.

F. A. Davis Co: 1915 Arch St, Philadelphia, PA 19103; tel. (215) 568-2270; fax (215) 568-5065; e-mail info@fadavis.com; internet www.fadavis.com; f. 1879; medical, nursing and allied health textbooks; Pres. ROBERT H. CRAVEN, Jr.

THE UNITED STATES OF AMERICA

Marcel Dekker, Inc: 270 Madison Ave, New York, NY 10016; tel. (212) 696-9000; fax (212) 685-4540; e-mail marketing@dekker.com; internet www.dekker.com; f. 1963; textbooks and reference; Pres. and CEO MARCEL DEKKER.

Dover Publications, Inc: 31 East Second St, Mineola, NY 11501; tel. (516) 294-7000; fax (516) 742-5049; internet www.doverpublications.com; f. 1941; trade, reprints, scientific, classics, language, arts and crafts; Pres. PAUL NEGRI.

Dufour Editions, Inc: POB 7, Chester Springs, PA 19425-0007; tel. (610) 458-5005; fax (610) 458-7103; e-mail info@dufoureditions.com; internet www.dufoureditions.com; f. 1949; literary, political science, humanities, music, history; Pres. CHRISTOPHER MAY.

Duke University Press: POB 90660, Duke University, Durham, NC 27708-0660; tel. (919) 687-3600; fax (919) 688-4574; internet www.dukeupress.edu; f. 1921; scholarly; Editor-in-Chief KEN WISSOKER.

Duquesne University Press: 600 Forbes Ave, Pittsburgh, PA 15282; tel. (412) 396-6610; fax (412) 396-5984; e-mail wadsworth@duq.edu; internet www.dupress.duq.edu; f. 1927; scholarly; Dir SUSAN WADSWORTH-BOOTH; Production Editor KATHY MEYER.

Ediciones Universal: 3090 South West Eighth St, Miami, FL 33135; tel. (305) 642-3234; fax (305) 642-7978; e-mail ediciones@ediciones.com; internet www.ediciones.com; f. 1965; Man. JUAN MANUEL SALVAT; Spanish language fiction and non-fiction.

Elsevier Science, Inc: 655 Ave of the Americas, New York, NY 10010; tel. (212) 989-5800; fax (212) 633-3965; f. 1962; scientific, medical, technical, multilingual technical journals; division of Reed Elsevier; Publishing Dir PAUL WEISLOGEL.

Encyclopaedia Britannica, Inc: 310 South Michigan Ave, Chicago, IL 60604; tel. (312) 347-7000; fax (312) 347-7399; internet www.eb.com; f. 1768; encyclopaedias, atlases, dictionaries; CEO JORGE CAUZ.

M. Evans & Co, Inc: 216 East 49th St, New York, NY 10017; tel. (212) 688-2810; fax (212) 486-4544; e-mail editorial@mevans.com; f. 1960; adult fiction and non-fiction; Pres. GEORGE C. DE KAY.

Facts On File Inc: 11 Penn Plaza, New York, NY 10001-2006; tel. (212) 967-8800; fax (212) 967-9196; internet www.factsonfile.com; f. 1940; division of Infobase Holdings, Inc; non-fiction, reference, electronic data bases; Publr MARK MCDONNELL.

Farrar, Straus & Giroux, Inc: 19 Union Sq. West, New York, NY 10003; tel. (212) 741-6900; fax (212) 633-9385; f. 1946; general trade; Chair. ROGER W. STRAUS; Pres. JONATHAN GALASSI.

Ferguson Publishing Co: 200 West Madison St, Chicago, IL 60606; tel. (312) 580-5480; fax (312) 580-7215; internet www.fergpubco.com; f. 1907; children's, encyclopedias; Pres. PETER EWING.

Fordham University Press: University Box L, Bronx, NY 10458-5172; tel. (718) 817-4780; fax (718) 817-4785; e-mail mnoonan@fordham.edu; internet www.fordhampress.com; f. 1907; scholarly; Dir ROBERT OPPEDISANO.

W. H. Freeman & Co, Publishers: 41 Madison Ave, New York, NY 10010; tel. (212) 576-9400; fax (212) 689-2383; internet www.whfreeman.com; f. 1946; textbooks; Pres. ELIZABETH WIDDICOMBE.

Samuel French, Inc: 45 West 25th St, New York, NY 10010; tel. (212) 206-8990; fax (212) 206-1429; f. 1830; plays; Man. Dir CHARLES R. VAN NOSTRAND.

Garland Science Publishing/Taylor & Francis Group, LLC: 270 Madison Ave, 4th Floor, New York, NY 10016; tel. (212) 216-7800; fax (212) 927-3027; e-mail science@garland.com; internet www.garlandscience.com; f. 1969; division of the Taylor & Francis Group; college textbooks; Publr DENISE SCHANCK.

Bernard Geis Associates: 500 Fifth Ave, Suite 3600, New York, NY 10110; tel. (212) 730-4330; fax (212) 730-4464; f. 1958; general fiction and non-fiction; Pres. BERNARD GEIS.

Genealogical Publishing Co: 1001 North Calvert St, Baltimore, MD 21202; tel. (410) 837-8271; fax (410) 752-8492; e-mail info@genealogical.com; internet www.genealogical.com; f. 1959; genealogy, immigration studies, heraldry, local history; Editor-in-Chief MICHAEL TEPPER.

The K. S. Giniger Co, Inc: 250 West 57th St, Suite 2602, New York, NY 10107; tel. (212) 570-7499; fax (212) 369-6692; f. 1965; general non-fiction; Pres. KENNETH S. GINIGER.

Warren H. Green, Inc: 8356 Olive Blvd, St Louis, MO 63132; tel. (314) 991-1335; fax (314) 997-1788; e-mail editorial@whgreen.com; internet www.whgreen.com; f. 1966; medical, science, technology, philosophy; Pres. JOYCE R. GREEN.

Greenwood Publishing Group: 88 Post Rd West, POB 5007, Westport, CT 06881; tel. (203) 226-3571; fax (203) 222-1502; e-mail bookinfo@greenwood.com; internet www.greenwood.com; f. 1967; division of Reed Elsevier; business reference and non-fiction; Pres. WAYNE SMITH.

Grolier Publishing Co, Inc: 90 Sherman Turnpike, Danbury, CT 06816; tel. (203) 797-3500; fax (203) 797-3720; internet www.publishing.grolier.com; f. 1946; juvenile educational; Pres. JOSEPH TESSITORE.

Grove/Atlantic: 841 Broadway, New York, NY 10003-4793; tel. (212) 614-7850; fax (212) 614-7886; e-mail mentrekin@groveatlantic.com; internet www.groveatlantic.com; fiction, non-fiction and poetry; Pres. MORGAN ENTREKIN.

Hammond World Atlas Corpn: 95 Progress St, Union, NJ 07083; tel. (908) 206-1300; fax (908) 206-1104; e-mail chuck@hammondmap.com; internet www.hammondmap.com; f. 1900; maps, atlases, cartography; Chair. and CEO STUART DOLGINS.

Harcourt Inc: 6277 Sea Harbor Dr., Orlando, FL 32887; tel. (407) 345-2000; fax (407) 352-3445; f. 1919; fiction, textbooks, general; Pres. and CEO JAMES LEVY.

HarperCollins Publishers: 10 East 53rd St, New York, NY 10022; tel. (212) 207-7000; fax (212) 207-7759; internet www.harpercollins.com; f. 1817; fiction, non-fiction, religious, children's, medical, general; Pres. and CEO JANE FRIEDMAN.

Harvard University Press: 79 Garden St, Cambridge, MA 02138; tel. (401) 495-2600; fax (617) 495-5898; internet www.hup.harvard.edu; f. 1913; classics, fine arts, philosophy, science, medicine, law, literature, politicial science, religion, history and government; Dir WILLIAM P. SISLER.

Hastings House/Daytrips Publishers: POB 908, Winter Park, FA 32790-0908; tel. (407) 339-3600; fax (203) 838-4084; e-mail hastings_daytrips@earthlink.net; internet www.hastingshousebooks.com; f. 1936; travel and general; Pres. PETER LEERS.

Holiday House, Inc: 425 Madison Ave, New York, NY 10017; tel. (212) 688-0085; fax (212) 421-6134; internet www.holidayhouse.com; f. 1935; juvenile; Pres. JOHN H. BRIGGS, Jr.

Holloway House Publishing Co: 8060 Melrose Ave, Los Angeles, CA 90046; tel. (323) 653-8060; fax (323) 655-9452; e-mail info@psiemail.com; internet www.hollowayhousebooks.com; f. 1960; Black experience and American Indian literature, gambling, fiction, non-fiction; CEO BENTLEY MORRISS.

Holmes & Meier Publishers, Inc: POB 943, Teaneck, NJ 07666; tel. (212) 374-0100; fax (212) 374-1313; e-mail info@holmesandmeier.com; f. 1969; history, political science, area studies, Judaica, foreign literature in translation, college texts and scholarly; Publr MIRIAM H. HOLMES.

Hoover Institution Press: Stanford University, Stanford, CA 94305-6010; tel. (650) 723-3373; fax (650) 723-8626; e-mail presley@hoover.stanford.edu; internet www.hoover.org; f. 1962; public policy, educational; Exec. Editor PATRICIA A. BAKER.

Houghton Mifflin Co: 222 Berkeley St, Boston, MA 02116; tel. (617) 351-5000; fax (617) 351-3604; internet www.hcmo.com; f. 1832; general and educational; Chair., Pres. and CEO NADER F. DARESHORI.

Indiana University Press: 601 North Morton St, Bloomington, IN 47404-3796; tel. (812) 855-8817; fax (812) 855-8507; e-mail iuporder@indiana.edu; internet iupress.indiana.edu; f. 1950; trade and scholarly non-fiction; Dir JANET RABINOWITCH.

International Universities Press, Inc: 59 Boston Post Rd, Madison, CT 06443; tel. (203) 245-4000; fax (203) 245-0775; e-mail orders@iup.com; internet www.iup.com; f. 1943; psychology, psychiatry, medicine, social sciences and journals; Pres. MARTIN V. AZARIAN; Exec. Vice-Pres. Dr MARGARET EMERY.

Iowa State University Press: 2121 State Ave, Ames, IA 50014-8300; tel. (515) 292-0140; fax (515) 292-3348; e-mail marketing@iowastatepress.com; internet www.iowastatepress.com; f. 1924; textbooks, reference; Publishing Dir PAUL BECKER.

Islamic Books/Tahrike Tarsile Qur'ān, Inc: POB 731115, Elmhurst, NY 11373-0115; tel. (718) 446-6472; fax (718) 446-4370; internet www.koranusa.org; f. 1978; Pres. AUNALI KHALFAN; Koran and Islamic religious texts.

Jewish Publication Society: 2100 Arch St, 2nd Floor, Philadelphia, PA 19103; tel. (215) 832-0600; fax (215) 568-2017; f. 1888; Pres. ELLEN FRANKEL.

Johns Hopkins University Press: 2715 North Charles St, Baltimore, MD 21218-4319; tel. (410) 516-6900; fax (410) 516-6998; f. 1878; social and physical sciences, humanities, health sciences, economics, literary criticism, history.

Kendall/Hunt Publishing Co: POB 1840, Dubuque, IA 52004-1840; tel. (563) 589-1000; fax (563) 589-1046; e-mail orders@kendallhunt.com; internet www.kendallhunt.com; f. 1944; business and educational; COO MARK FALB.

Kluwer Academic Publishers: 101 Philip Dr., Norwell, MA 02061; tel. (617) 871-6600; fax (617) 871-6528; e-mail kluwer@wkap.com; internet www.wkap.nl; f. 1978; scientific, technical, medical, scholarly and professional books and journals; Pres. JAY LIPPENCOTT.

THE UNITED STATES OF AMERICA — Directory

Krieger Publishing Co: POB 9542, Melbourne, FL 32902-9542; tel. (321) 724-9542; fax (321) 951-3671; e-mail info@krieger-pubishing.com; internet www.krieger-publishing.com; f. 1970; scientific and technical originals and reprints; Pres. DONALD E. KRIEGER.

Lippincott, Williams & Wilkins: 530 Walnut St, 7th Floor, Philadelphia, PA 19106; tel. (215) 521-8300; fax (215) 521-8902; e-mail orders@lww.com; internet www.lww.com; f. 1792; division of Wolters Kluwer; medical, dental, veterinary, scientific; Pres. and CEO JAY LIPPINCOTT.

Loyola Press: 3441 North Ashland Ave, Chicago, IL 60657; tel. (773) 281-1818; fax (773) 281-0885; e-mail lane@loyolapress.com; internet www.loyolapress.org; f. 1912; Dir GEORGE A. LANE.

McGraw-Hill, Inc: 1221 Ave of the Americas, New York, NY 10020; tel. (212) 512-2000; fax (212) 512-2821; internet www.mcgraw-hill.com; f. 1888; information texts and services for business, industry, government and the general public; Chair. and CEO HAROLD McGRAW, III.

Macmillan USA: 201 West 103rd St, Indianapolis, IN 46290; tel. (317) 581-3500; fax (317) 581-4657; internet www.mcp.com; division of Pearson; scientific, technical and medical; Pres. GARY JUNE.

Merriam-Webster Inc: 47 Federal St, POB 281, Springfield, MA 01102; tel. (413) 734-3134; fax (413) 731-5979; e-mail merriam_webster@merriam-webster.com; internet www.merriam-webster.com; f. 1831; subsidiary of Encyclopaedia Britannica Inc; dictionaries, reference; Pres. and Publr JOHN M. MORSE.

Michigan State University Press: 1405 South Harrison Rd, 25 Manly Miles Bldg, East Lansing, MI 48823-5245; tel. (517) 355-9543; fax (517) 432-2611; e-mail msupress@msu.edu; internet www.msupress.msu.edu; f. 1947; scholarly; Dir FRED C. BOHM.

The MIT Press: 5 Cambridge Centre, Cambridge, MA 02142; tel. (617) 253-5646; fax (617) 258-6779; internet www.mitpress.mit.edu; f. 1932; computer sciences, architecture, design, linguistics, economics, philosophy, general science, neuroscience, cognitive science and engineering; Dir FRANK URBANOWSKI.

Moody Press: 820 North LaSalle Blvd, Chicago, IL 60610; tel. (312) 329-2101; fax (312) 329-2144; e-mail gthornto@moody.edu; internet www.moodypublishers.org; f. 1894; religious; Man. GREG THORNTON.

William Morrow & Co Inc: 10 East 53rd St, New York, NY 10022; tel. (212) 207-7000; fax (212) 207-7633; internet www.harpercollins.com; f. 1926; division of HarperCollins; fiction, non-fiction, juvenile; Pres. and CEO JANE FRIEDMAN.

National Academy Press: 500 Fifth St, NW, POB 285, Washington, DC 20055; tel. (202) 334-3180; fax (202) 334-2793; internet www.nap.edu; f. 1863; division of Nat. Academy of Sciences; scientific and technical reports, abstracts, bibliographies, catalogues; Dir BARBARA KLINE POPE.

National Learning Corpn: 212 Michael Dr., Syosset, NY 11791; tel. (516) 921-8888; fax (516) 921-8743; internet www.passbooks.com; f. 1967; professional and vocational study guides; Pres. MICHAEL P. RUDMAN.

New Directions Publishing Corpn: 80 Eighth Ave, 19th Floor, New York, NY 10011; tel. (212) 255-0230; fax (212) 255-0231; e-mail nd@ndbooks.com; internet www.ndpublishing.com; f. 1936; modern literature, poetry, criticism, belles-lettres; Pres. and Publr GRISELDA J. OHANNESSIAN.

New York University Press: 838 Broadway, New York, NY 10003; tel. (212) 998-2575; fax (212) 995-3833; e-mail customerservice@nyupress.org; internet www.nyupress.org; f. 1916; scholarly, non-fiction, general; Dir STEVE MAIKOWSKI.

Northwestern University Press: 629 Noyes St, Evanston, IL 60208; tel. (847) 491-2046; fax (847) 491-8150; e-mail nupress@northwestern.edu; internet www.nupress.northwestern.edu; f. 1958; scholarly and trade; Dir DONNA SHEAR.

W. W. Norton & Co Inc: 500 Fifth Ave, New York, NY 10110; tel. (212) 354-5500; fax (212) 869-0856; internet www.wwnorton.com; f. 1924; general fiction and non-fiction, college textbooks, paperbacks; CEO STEPHEN KING; Pres. DRAKE McFEELY.

NOVA Publications: 7342 Lee Hwy, No. 201, Falls Church, VA 22046; tel. and fax (703) 280-5383; e-mail novapublic@aol.com; internet www.members.aol.com/novapublic/index.htm; f. 1993; military history, political science, Russian and Middle Eastern studies; Publr ARNOLD C. DUPUY.

Oceana Publications Inc: 75 Main St, Dobbs Ferry, NY 10522-1632; tel. (914) 693-5956; fax (914) 693-0402; e-mail info@oceanalaw.com; internet www.oceanalaw.com; f. 1957; international law and trade; Pres. DAVID R. COHEN.

The Ohio State University Press: 1070 Carmack Rd, Columbus, OH 43210; tel. (64) 292-6930; fax (64) 292-2065; e-mail ohiostatepress@osu.edu; internet www.ohiostatepress.org; f. 1957; general scholarly non-fiction; Dir MALCOLM LITCHFIELD.

Ohio University Press: Scott Quadrangle 220, Ohio University, Athens, OH 45701; tel. (740) 593-1154; fax (740) 593-4536; e-mail gilbert@ohio.edu; internet www.ohiou.edu/oupress; f. 1964; scholarly, regional studies; Dir DAVID SANDERS.

Open Court Publishing Co: 140 South Dearborn, Suite 1450, Chicago, IL 60603; tel. (312) 701-1720; fax (312) 701-1728; e-mail opencourt@caruspub.com; internet www.opencourtbooks.com; f. 1887; general non-fiction; Pres. and Publr ANDRE CARUS.

Orbis Books: Walsh Bldg, POB 308, Maryknoll, NY 10545-0308; tel. (914) 941-7590; fax (914) 945-0670; e-mail orbisbooks@maryknoll.org; internet www.orbisbooks.com; f. 1970; theology, religion and social concerns; Exec. Dir MICHAEL LEACH.

Oxford University Press: 198 Madison Ave, New York, NY 10016; tel. (212) 726-6000; fax (212) 726-6446; e-mail custserv.us@oup.com; internet www.oup.com/us; f. 1896; non-fiction, trade, religious, reference, bibles, college textbooks, medical, music; Pres. LAURA BROWN.

Paladin Press: POB 1307, Boulder, CO 80306; tel. (303) 443-7250; fax (303) 442-8741; e-mail service@paladin-press.com; internet www.paladin-press.com; f. 1970; military science and history; Chair. and Pres. PEDER C. LUND.

Paragon House: 1925 Oakcrest Ave, Suite 7, St Paul, MN 55413-2619; tel. (651) 644-3087; fax (651) 644-0997; e-mail paragon@paragonhouse.com; internet www.paragonhouse.com; f. 1982; academic non-fiction, university texts, reference; Exec. Dir GORDON L. ANDERSON.

Penguin Putnam Inc: 375 Hudson St, New York, NY 10014; tel. (212) 366-2000; fax (212) 366-2666; e-mail online@penguinputnam.com; internet www.penguinputnam.com; f. 1925; Pres. DAVID SHANKS.

Pennsylvania State University Press: University Support Bldg I, Suite C, 820 North University Dr., University Park, PA 16802; tel. (814) 865-1327; fax (814) 863-1408; internet www.psupress.org; f. 1956; scholarly non-fiction; Dir SANFORD G. THATCHER.

Praeger Publishers/Greenwood Publishing Group: 88 Post Rd West, POB 5007, Westport, CT 06881; tel. (203) 226-3571; fax (203) 222-1502; internet www.greenwood.com; f. 1950; general non-fiction, reference, scholarly, academic; Pres WAYNE SMITH.

Princeton University Press: 41 William St, Princeton, NJ 08540; tel. (609) 258-4900; fax (609) 258-6305; e-mail webmaster@pupress.princeton.edu; internet pupress.princeton.edu; f. 1905; scholarly; Dir WALTER H. LIPPINCOTT, Jr; Editor-in-Chief SAM ELWORTHY.

Quite Specific Media Group Ltd: 260 Fifth Ave, New York, NY 10001; tel. (212) 725-5377; fax (212) 725-8506; e-mail info@quitespecificmedia.com; internet www.quitespecificmedia.com; f. 1967; costume, design, fashion, performing arts; Publr RALPH PINE.

Rand McNally: 8255 Central Park Ave, Skokie, IL 60076; tel. (847) 329-8100; fax (847) 673-0539; internet www.randmcnally.com; f. 1856; maps, atlases, travel guides; Chair. ANDREW McNALLY, III; Pres. RICHARD DAVIS.

Random House Inc: 1745 Broadway, New York, NY 10019; tel. (212) 751-2600; fax (212) 572-8026; internet www.randomhouse.com; f. 1925; originals, reprints, paperbacks, juvenile, series, textbooks; CEO GAIL REBUCK.

Reader's Digest Association, Inc: Reader's Digest Rd, Pleasantville, NY 10570-7000; tel. (914) 238-1000; fax (914) 238-4559; internet www.readersdigest.com; reference and non-fiction; Chair. and CEO THOMAS RYDER.

Rizzoli International Publications Inc: 300 Park Ave South, New York, NY 10010-5399; tel. (212) 387-3400; fax (212) 3873535; f. 1975; fine arts, performing arts, architecture; Pres., CEO and Publr MARTA HALLETT.

Routledge: 29 West 35th St, New York, NY 10001-2299; tel. (212) 244-3336; fax (212) 563-2269; internet www.routledge-ny.com; f. 1977; division of Taylor and Francis Group; scholarly, professional, trade, humanities, social sciences; Vice-Pres., Editorial and Marketing MARY MACINNES.

Rutgers University Press: 100 Joyce Kilmer Ave, Piscataway, NJ 08854; tel. (732) 445-7762; fax (732) 445-7039; internet rutgerspress.rutgers.edu; f. 1936; scholarly and regional; Dir MARLIE WASSERMAN.

William H. Sadlier Inc: 9 Pine St, New York, NY 10005; tel. (212) 227-2120; fax (212) 267-8696; e-mail wsd@sadlier.com; internet www.sadlier.com; f. 1832; textbooks; Pres. WILLIAM SADLIER DINGER.

St Martin's Press Inc: 175 Fifth Ave, New York, NY 10010; tel. (212) 674-5151; fax (212) 420-9314; e-mail inquiries@stmartins.com; internet www.stmartins.com; f. 1952; general, scholarly, college textbooks, reference; Pres. JOHN SARGENT.

Scarecrow Press, Inc: 4501 Forbes Blvd, Suite 200, Lanham, MD 20706; tel. (301) 459-3366; fax (301) 429-5748; e-mail custserve@rowman.com; internet www.scarecrowpress.com; f. 1950; reference, textbooks, library and information science; Vice-Pres. EDWARD KURDYLA.

Scholastic, Inc: 555 Broadway, New York, NY 10012; tel. (212) 343-6100; fax (212) 343-6930; internet www.scholastic.com; f. 1920;

THE UNITED STATES OF AMERICA

children's periodicals, textbooks, educational materials; Chair., Pres. and CEO M. RICHARD ROBINSON.

Shoe String Press Inc: 2 Linsley St, North Haven, CT 06473; tel. (203) 239-2702; fax (203) 239-2568; e-mail books@shoestringpress.com; internet www.shoestringpress.com; f. 1952; scholarly, children's and general non-fiction; Pres. and Editorial Dir DIANTHA THORPE.

Silhouette Books: 233 Broadway, Suite 1001, New York, NY 10279; tel. (212) 553-4200; fax (212) 227-8969; internet www.eharlequin.com; f. 1979; romantic fiction; Publr and CEO DONNA HAYES.

Simon & Schuster, Inc: 1230 Ave of the Americas, New York, NY 10020; tel. (212) 698-7000; fax (212) 698-7007; internet www.simonsays.com; f. 1924; trade, juvenile, reference, educational, business and professional; Pres. and CEO JACK ROMANOS.

Peter Smith Publisher, Inc: 5 Lexington Ave, Magnolia, MA 01930; tel. (978) 525-3562; fax (978) 525-3674; reprints; Pres. MARY ANN LASH.

Smithsonian Institution Press: 750 Ninth St NW, Suite 4300, Washington, DC 20560-0950; tel. (202) 275-2243; fax (202) 275-2243; e-mail info@sipress.si.edu; internet www.sipress.si.edu; f. 1848; scholarly and general interest in American studies and culture, anthropology, archaeology, natural science, museum studies; Dir DON FEHR.

Southern Illinois University Press: POB 3697, Carbondale, IL 62902-3697; tel. (618) 453-2281; fax (618) 453-1221; e-mail jstetter@siu.edu; internet www.siu.edu/~siupress; f. 1953; scholarly non-fiction; Dir JOHN F. STETTER.

Springer-Verlag New York, Inc: 175 Fifth Ave, 19th Floor, New York, NY 10010; tel. (212) 460-1500; fax (212) 473-6272; internet www.springer-ny.com; f. 1964; scientific, technical and medical; Exec. Vice-Pres. and Publr RÜDIGER GEBAUER.

Stanford University Press: 1450 Page Mill Rd, Palo Alto, CA 94304; tel. (650) 723-9434; fax (650) 725-3457; e-mail info@www.sup.org; internet www.sup.org; f. 1925; Man. Dir GEOFFREY BURN.

State University of New York Press: 194 Washington Ave, Suite 305, Albany, NY 12210-2365; tel. (518) 472-5000; fax (518) 472-5038; e-mail info@sunypress.edu; internet www.sunypress.edu; f. 1966; scholarly; Dir JAMES PELTZ.

Sterling Publishing Co, Inc: 387 Park Ave South, New York, NY 10016; tel. (212) 532-7160; fax (212) 213-2495; f. 1949; non-fiction; Chair. BURTON H. HOBSON.

Summy-Birchard Inc: 15800 NW 48th Ave, Miami, FL 33014; tel. (305) 620-1500; fax (305) 521-1768; e-mail judi.gowe@warnerchappell.com; f. 1872; educational music, methods and texts; Dir JUDI GOWE BAGNATO.

Syracuse University Press: Suite 110, 621 Skytop Rd, Syracuse, NY 13244-5290; tel. (315) 443-5534; fax (315) 443-5545; e-mail supress@syr.edu; internet www.syracuseuniversitypress.syr.edu; f. 1943; scholarly; Dir PETER B. WEBBER.

Taplinger Publishing Co Inc: POB 175, Marlboro, NJ 07746; tel. (305) 256-7880; fax (305) 256-7816; e-mail taplingerpub@yahoo.com; f. 1955; general fiction and non-fiction; Pres. LOUIS STRICK.

Taylor & Francis Books: 270 Madison Ave, New York, NY 10016; tel. (212) 216-7800; fax (212) 564-7854; e-mail info@taylorandfrancis.com; internet www.taylorandfrancis.com; f. 1972; scientific, technical and reference; Pres. FENTON MARKEVICH.

Charles C. Thomas, Publisher: 2600 South First St, Springfield, IL 62794-9265; tel. (217) 789-8980; fax (217) 789-9130; e-mail books@ccthomasa.com; f. 1927; textbooks and reference on education, medicine, psychology and criminology; Pres. MICHAEL P. THOMAS.

Thomson Gale: 27500 Drake Rd, Farmington Hills, MI 48331-3535; tel. (248) 669-4253; fax (248) 669-8064; e-mail galeord@gale.com; internet www.gale.com; f. 1954; reference; Pres. and CEO ALLEN PASCHAL.

Time-Life Books Inc: 2000 Duke St, Alexandria, VA 22314; tel. (703) 838-7000; fax (703) 838-7474; f. 1961; general non-fiction; Pres. and CEO JIM NELSON.

Tuttle Publishing: 153 Milk St, 7th Floor, Boston, MA 02109; tel. (617) 951-4080; fax (617) 951-4045; e-mail info@tuttlepublishing.com; internet www.tuttlepublishing.com; f. 1832; the Far East, particularly Japan, languages, art, crafts, martial arts, culture, juvenile, cookery; Publishing Dir EDWARD WALTERS.

United Nations Publications: United Nations Plaza, Room DC2-0853, New York, NY 10017; tel. (212) 963-8302; fax (212) 963-3489; e-mail publications@un.org; internet www.un.org; f. 1946; world and national economies, international trade, social questions, human rights, international law; Chief of Section CHRISTOPHER WOODTHORPE.

University of Alabama Press: POB 870380, Tuscaloosa, AL 35487; tel. (205) 348-5180; fax (205) 348-9201; f. 1945; scholarly non-fiction; Dir DANIEL J. J. ROSS.

University of Alaska Press: 104 Eielson Bldg, Salcha Lane, POB 756240, University of Alaska, Fairbanks, AK 99775-6240; tel. (907) 474-5831; fax (907) 474-5502; e-mail fypress@uaf.edu; internet www.uaf.edu/press; f. 1967; history, anthropology of the circumpolar north.

University of Arizona Press: 355 South Euclid, Suite 103, Tucson, AZ 85719; tel. (520) 621-1441; fax (520) 621-8899; e-mail uapress@arizona.edu; internet www.uapress.arizona.edu; f. 1959; scholarly, popular, regional, non-fiction; Dir CHRISTINE SZUTER.

University of Arkansas Press: McIlroy House, 201 Ozark Ave, Fayetteville, AR 72701; tel. (479) 575-3246; fax (479) 575-6044; e-mail uapress@uark.edu; internet www.uapress.com; f. 1980; general humanities, literature, regional studies, natural history, Middle Eastern studies, poetry, civil rights studies, American history; Dir LARRY MALLEY.

University of California Press: 2120 Berkeley Way, Berkeley, CA 94704-1012; tel. (510) 642-4247; fax (510) 643-7127; e-mail ucpress@ucop.edu; internet www.ucpress.edu; f. 1893; academic, scholarly; Dir LYNNE WITHEY.

University of Chicago Press: 1427 East 60th St, Chicago, IL 60637; tel. (773) 702-7700; fax (773) 702-2705; e-mail general@press.uchicago.edu; internet www.press.uchicago.edu; f. 1891; scholarly books and journals, general; Dir PAULA BARKER DUFFY.

University of Georgia Press: Athens, GA 30602; tel. (706) 369-6130; fax (706) 369-6131; f. 1938; academic, scholarly, poetry, fiction, non-fiction, literary trade; Dir NICOLE MITCHELL.

University of Hawaii Press: 2840 Kolowalu St, Honolulu, HI 96822; tel. (808) 956-8255; fax (808) 988-6052; e-mail uhpbooks@hawaii.edu; internet www.uhpress.hawaii.edu; f. 1947; Asian, Pacific and Hawaiian studies; Dir WILLIAM H. HAMILTON.

University of Idaho Press: POB 4416, Moscow, ID 83844-4416; tel. (208) 885-3300; fax (208) 885-3301; e-mail uipress@uidaho.edu; internet www.uidaho.edu/uipress; f. 1972; scholarly, regional studies, folklore, natural history, literary criticism, native American studies, journals, incl. *Hemingway Review* and *Native Plant Journal*, biannuals; Dir IVAR NELSON.

University of Illinois Press: 1325 South Oak St, Champaign, IL 61820; tel. (217) 333-0950; fax (217) 244-8082; e-mail uipress@uillinois.edu; internet www.uillinois.edu; f. 1918; scholarly and poetry; Dir WILLIS REGIER.

University of Massachusetts Press: POB 429, Amherst, MA 01004-0429; tel. (413) 545-2217; fax (413) 545-1226; e-mail umpress@umass.edu; internet www.umass.edu/umpress; f. 1964; scholarly non-fiction; Dir BRUCE G. WILCOX.

University of Michigan Press: 839 Greene St, POB 1104, Ann Arbor, MI 48106; tel. (313) 734-4388; fax (313) 734-0456; e-mail um.press.bus@umich.edu; internet www.press.umich.edu; f. 1930; academic, textbooks, paperbacks; Dir PHILIP POCHODA.

University of Minnesota Press: 111 Third Ave South, Suite 290, Minneapolis, MN 55401-5250; tel. (612) 627-1970; fax (612) 627-1980; internet www.upress.umn.edu; f. 1927; scholarly, general; Dir DOUGLAS M. ARMATO.

University of Missouri Press: 2910 LeMone Blvd, Columbia, MO 65201; tel. (573) 882-7641; fax (573) 884-4498; internet www.umsystem-edu/upress; scholarly; Dir BEVERLY JARRETT.

University of Nebraska Press: 1111 Lincoln Mall, Lincoln, NE 68588-0630; tel. (402) 472-3581; fax (402) 472-6214; e-mail pressmail@unl.edu; internet www.nebraskapress.unl.edu; f. 1941; general interest and scholarly; Dir GARY DUNHAM.

University of New Mexico Press: 1720 Lomas Blvd, NE, Albuquerque, NM 87131-1591; tel. (505) 277-2346; fax (505) 277-9270; e-mail unmpress@unm.edu; internet www.unmpress.com; f. 1929; scholarly, regional studies; Dir LUTHER WILSON.

University of North Carolina Press: POB 2288, Chapel Hill, NC 27515-2288; tel. (919) 966-3561; fax (919) 966-3829; e-mail uncpress@unc.edu; internet www.uncpress.unc.edu; f. 1922; biographical, regional, scholarly non-fiction; Dir KATE D. TORREY.

University of Notre Dame Press: Notre Dame, IN 46556; tel. (574) 631-6346; fax (219) 631-8148; e-mail undpress.1@nd.edu; internet www.undpress.nd.edu; f. 1949; humanities and social sciences; Dir BARBARA J. HANRAHAN.

University of Oklahoma Press: 2800 Venture Dr., Norman, OK 73069-8216; tel. (405) 325-2000; fax (405) 325-4000; internet www.oupress.com; f. 1928; scholarly; Co-Dir and Editor-in-Chief CHARLES E. RANKIN; Co-Dir JOHN DRAYTON.

University of Pennsylvania Press: 3905 Spruce St, Philadelphia, PA 19104-4112; tel. (215) 898-6261; fax (215) 898-0404; e-mail custserv@pobox.upenn.edu; internet www.upenn.edu/pennpress; f. 1890; scholarly; Dir ERIC HALPERN.

University of Pittsburgh Press: 3400 Forbes Ave, 5h Floor, Pittsburgh, PA 15260; tel. (412) 383-2456; fax (412) 383-2466;

THE UNITED STATES OF AMERICA

e-mail press@pitt.edu; internet www.pitt.edu/~press; f. 1936; Dir CYNTHIA MILLER; scholarly.

University of South Carolina Press: 1600 Hampton St, 5th Floor, Columbia, SC 29208; tel. (803) 777-5243; fax (803) 777-0160; e-mail gsauer@sc.edu; internet www.sc.edu/uscpress; scholarly, regional studies; Dir CURTIS L. CLARK.

University of Tennessee Press: 293 Communications Bldg, Knoxville, TN 37996-0325; tel. (423) 974-3321; fax (423) 974-3724; e-mail gadair@utk.edu; internet www.sunsite.utk.edu/utpress; f. 1940; scholarly and regional; Editor JOYCE HARRISON.

University of Texas Press: POB 7819, Austin, TX 78713-7819; tel. (512) 471-7233; fax (512) 320-0668; internet www.utexas.edu/utpress; f. 1950; general, scholarly non-fiction; Dir JOANNA HITCHCOCK.

University of Utah Press: 1795 East South Campus Dr., 101, Salt Lake City, UT 84112; tel. (801) 581-6771; fax (801) 581-3365; e-mail info@upress.utah.edu; internet www.uofupress.com; f. 1949; scholarly, regional and Middle East studies; Dir JEFF GRATHWOHL.

University of Virginia Press: POB 400318, Charlottesville, VA 22904-4318; tel. (434) 924-3469; fax (877) 288-6400; internet www.upress.virginia.edu; f. 1963; scholarly non-fiction, literature, history, Victorian, African and Afro-American studies; Dir PENELOPE KAISERLIAN.

University of Washington Press: POB 50096, Seattle, WA 98145-5096; tel. (206) 543-4050; fax (206) 543-3932; e-mail uwpord@u.washington.edu; internet www.washington.edu/uwpress; f. 1920; general, scholarly, non-fiction, reprints; Dir PAT SODEN.

University of Wisconsin Press: 1930 Monroe St, 3rd Floor, Madison, WI 53711-2059; tel. (608) 263-1110; fax (608) 263-1120; e-mail uwiscpress@uwpress.wisc.edu; internet www.wisc.edu/wisconsinpress; f. 1936; scholarly non-fiction, trade; Dir ROBERT MANDEL.

University Press of America, Inc: 4501 Forbes Blvd, Suite 200, Lanham, MD 20706; tel. (301) 459-3366; fax (301) 459-2118; internet www.univpress.com; f. 1974; scholarly; Editorial Dir JUDITH ROTHMAN.

University Press of Florida: 15 NW 15th St, Gainesville, FL 32611-2079; tel. (352) 392-1351; fax (352) 392-7302; e-mail info@upf.com; internet www.upf.com; f. 1945; general, scholarly, regional; Dir KENNETH J. SCOTT.

University Press of Kansas: 2502 Westbrooke Circle, Lawrence, KS 66049-3905; tel. (785) 864-4154; fax (785) 864-4586; e-mail upress@ku.edu; internet www.kansaspress.ku.edu; f. 1946; scholarly; Dir FRED M. WOODWARD.

University Press of Kentucky: 663 South Limestone St, Lexington, KY 40508-4008; tel. (606) 257-2951; fax (606) 257-2984; internet www.kentuckypress.com; f. 1943; non-fiction, scholarly, regional; Dir STEPHEN M. WRINN.

University Press of Mississippi: 3825 Ridgewood Rd, Jackson, MS 39211; tel. (601) 432-6205; fax (601) 432-6217; e-mail press@ihl.state.ms.us; internet www.upress.state.ms.us; f. 1970; scholarly, non-fiction, regional; Dir SEETHA SRINIVASAN.

University Press of New England: 23 South Main St, Hanover, NH 03755-2048; tel. (603) 643-7100; fax (603) 643-1540; internet www.upne.com; f. 1970; general, scholarly; Dir RICHARD ABEL.

Vanderbilt University Press: VU Station B 351813, Nashville, TN 37235; tel. (617) 322-3585; fax (617) 343-8823; e-mail vupress@vanderbilt.edu; internet www.vanderbilt.edu/vupress; f. 1940; scholarly, trade; Dir MICHAEL AMES.

Warner Books Inc: 1271 Ave of the Americas, New York, NY 10020; tel. (212) 522-7200; fax (212) 522-7991; f. 1961; reprints, fiction and non-fiction, trade; Pres. MAUREEN EGEN.

Wayne State University Press: 4809 Woodward Ave, Detroit, MI 48201; fax (313) 577-6131; e-mail jane.hoehner@wayne.edu; internet wsupress.wayne.edu; f. 1941; Dir JANE HOEHNER.

Westminster John Knox Press: 100 Witherspoon St, Louisville, KY 40202-1396; tel. (502) 569-5081; fax (502) 569-5113; e-mail www.presbypub.com; internet www.wjkbooks.com; f. 1938; religious and scholarly; Pres. and Publr DAVIS PERKINS.

Westview Press Inc: 5500 Central Ave, Boulder, CO 80301; tel. (303) 444-3541; fax (303) 449-3356; e-mail westview.press@perseusbooks.com; scholarly, academic, general interest and scientific; Publr MARCUS BOGGS.

John Wiley and Sons, Inc: 111 River St, Hoboken, NJ 07030; tel. (201) 748-6000; fax (201) 748-6088; internet www.wiley.com; f. 1807; higher education, scientific, technical, medical and social science; Chair. PETER BOOTH WILEY, II; Pres. and CEO WILL PESCE.

H. W. Wilson Co: 950 University Ave, Bronx, NY 10452; tel. (718) 588-8400; fax (718) 538-2716; internet www.hwwilson.com; f. 1898; book and periodical indices, reference; Pres. and CEO HAROLD REGAN.

Yale University Press: 302 Temple St, New Haven, CT 06511; tel. (203) 432-0960; fax (203) 432-0948; internet www.yale.edu/yup; f. 1908; scholarly; Dir JOHN DONATICH.

GOVERNMENT PUBLISHING HOUSE

Government Printing Office: North Capitol and H Sts, NW, Washington, DC 20401; tel. (202) 512-1991; fax (202) 512-1293; internet www.access.gpo.gov; Public Printer MICHAEL F. DIMARIO.

ORGANIZATIONS AND ASSOCIATIONS

American Booksellers' Association (ABA): 828 South Broadway, Tarrytown, NY 10591; tel. (914) 591-2665; fax (914) 591-2720; e-mail editorial@bookweb.org; internet www.bookweb.org; f. 1900; 8,000 mems; CEO AVIN MARK DOMNITZ.

American Medical Publishers' Association: c/o Jill G. Rudansky, 14 Fort Hill Rd, Huntingdon, NY 11743; tel. (631) 423-0075; fax (631) 423-0075; e-mail jillrudansky-ampa@msn.com; internet www.ampaonline.org; f. 1960; 75 mems; Pres. BRIAN CRAWFORD.

Association of American University Presses, Inc: 584 Broadway, Suite 410, New York, NY 10012; tel. (212) 989-1010; fax (212) 989-0275; e-mail info@aaupnet.org; internet www.aaupnet.org; f. 1937; 125 mems; Exec. Dir PETER J. GIVLER.

The Children's Book Council, Inc: 12 West 37th St, New York, NY 10018; tel. (212) 966-1990; fax (212) 966-2073; e-mail info@cbcbooks.org; internet www.cbcbooks.org; f. 1945; 75 mems; Pres. PAULA QUINT.

Music Publishers' Association of the US: 101 Constitution Ave, NW, Suite 701 East, Washington, DC 20001; e-mail pr@nmpa.org; internet www.nmpa.com; tel. (202) 742-4375; fax (202) 742-4377; f. 1917; 600 mems; Pres. and CEO DAVID ISRAELITE.

National Association of Independent Publishers: POB 430, Highland City, FL 33846-0430; tel. (836) 648-4420; fax (836) 647-5951; e-mail naip@aol.com; internet www.publishersreport.com; f. 1985; 250 mems; Exec. Dir BETSY WRIGHT-LAMPE.

Publishers' Marketing Association (PMA): 627 Aviation Way, Manhattan Beach, CA 90266; tel. (310) 372-2732; fax (310) 374-3342; e-mail naip@aol.com; internet www.pma-online.org; 1,600 mems; Exec. Dir JAN NATHAN.

Broadcasting and Communications

Federal Communications Commission (FCC): 445 12th St, SW, Washington, DC 20554; tel. (202) 418-0200; fax (202) 418-0232; e-mail fccinfo@fcc.gov; internet www.fcc.gov; f. 1934; regulates inter-state and foreign communications by radio, television, wire and cable; Chair. KEVIN J. MARTIN.

TELECOMMUNICATIONS
Principal Telecommunications Networks

AT&T (American Telegraph and Telephone Corporation): 32 Ave of the Americas, New York, NY 10013; tel. (212) 387-5400; fax (212) 226-4935; internet www.att.com; f. 1885; bought by SBC Communications (q.v.) in Jan. 2005, merger ongoing in early 2006; Chair. and CEO DAVID W. DORMAN; Pres. WILLIAM J. HANNIGAN.

BellSouth Corporation: 1155 Peachtree St, NE, Atlanta, GA 30309; tel. (404) 249-2000; fax (404) 249-5599; internet www.bellsouth.com; f. 1983; serves 18.7m. customers in nine states; Chair. and CEO DUANE ACKERMAN; Vice-Pres. HERSCHEL L. ABBOTT, Jr.

Cingular Wireless: Gledridge Highlands Two, 5545 Glenridge Connector, Atlanta, GA 30342; tel. (866) 241-6567; internet www.cingular.com; 60% owned by SBC Communications, 40% by BellSouth Corpn; 24.6m. subscribers (2004); Pres. and CEO STANLEY T. SIGMAN.

Comcast Corpn: 1500 Market St, Philadelphia, PA 19102; internet www.comcast.com; f. 1963; 21.5m. cable subscribers in 35 states, more than 7.4m. internet customers, 1.2m. cable telephone subscribers; acquired AT&T Broadband in 2002 and a share in Adelphia Communications in 2005; Chair. BRIAN L. ROBERTS; Dir RALPH J. ROBERTS.

Commonwealth Telephone Enterprises (CTE): 100 CTE Dr., Dallas, PA 18612-9774; tel. (570) 631-2700; fax (570) 675-6058; e-mail info@ct-enterprises.com; internet www.ct-enterprises.com; name changed from C-Tec Corpn in 1997; Pres. and CEO MICHAEL J. MAHONEY; Exec. Vice-Pres. EILEEN O'NEILL ODUM.

GE American Communications, Inc (GE Americom): 4 Research Way, Princeton, NJ 08540-6684; tel. (609) 987-4000; Chair. and CEO JOHN F. CONNELLY.

THE UNITED STATES OF AMERICA

MCI Inc: 22001 Loudoun County Pkwy, Ashburn, VA; internet www.mci.com; f. 1968; long-distance carrier serving c. 10m. customers; merger with Verizon Communications, Inc ongoing in late 2005; Pres. and CEO MICHAEL D. CAPELLAS.

Qwest Communications International, Inc: 1801 California St, Denver, CO 80202-2614; tel. (303) 992-1400; fax (303) 896-8515; e-mail qnews@qwest.com; internet www.qwest.com; telephone and internet provider to 25m. customers in USA and abroad; acquired US West in 2000; Chair. and CEO RICHARD C. NOTEBAERT; Exec. Vice-Pres. of Operations BARRY K. ALLEN.

US West, Inc: 7800 East Orchard Rd, Englewood, CO 80111; tel. (303) 793-6500; fax (303) 793-6654; internet www.uswest.com; f. 1983; main operating subsidiary comprises the fmr Mountain Bell, Northwestern Bell and Pacific Northwest Telephone cos; provides telecommunications services in 14 Western states; Chair. and CEO RICHARD D. MCCORMICK.

SBC Communications: 175 East Houston St, San Antonio, TX 78205; tel. (210) 821-4105; fax (210) 351-2274; internet www.sbc.com; f. 1997; by merger of SBC Corpn (fmrly Southwestern Bell Corpn) and Pacific Telesis Group (PacTel); bought by AT&T in Jan. 2005; Chair. EDWARD E. WHITACRE, Jr; Pres. and CEO ROBERT G. POPE.

Verizon Communications: 1095 Ave of the Americas, 36th Floor, New York, NY 10036; tel. (212) 395-1525; fax (121) 921-2917; internet www.verizon.com; f. 2000 by the merger of Bell Atlantic Corpn and GTE Corpn; 36m. customers in the USA; Chair. and CEO IVAN G. SEIDENBERG; Pres. LAWRENCE T. BABBIO, Jr.

Associations

US Telecom Association (USTA): 607 14th St, NW, Suite 400, Washington, DC 20005; tel. (202) 326-7300; fax (202) 326-7333; e-mail aremsen@ustelecom.org; internet www.usta.org; Pres. and CEO WALTER B. MCCORMICK, Jr; Chair. BRIAN H. STROM.

UTC–The United Telecom Council: 1140 Connecticut Ave, NW, Suite 1140, Washington, DC 20036; tel. (202) 872-0030; fax (202) 872-1331; e-mail utc@utc.org; internet www.utc.org; f. 1948; non-profit asscn representing telecommunications and information interests of public utilities, natural gas pipelines and other infrastructure cos and their strategic business partners.

BROADCASTING

The USA constitutes the world's biggest market for communications and broadcasting systems. The USA has the highest ratio of radio and television receivers per head of population of any country in the world. In 2002 radio sets were in use in 99% of homes and there were an estimated 254m. television receivers in use. There were 9,339 cable systems in operation in the same year, serving an estimated 85.5m. subscribers. In 2002 91.2% of households with television receivers used video cassette recorders.

Radio

In September 2002 there were 10,965 licensed commercial radio stations operating in the USA. In 2000 the average US household had 5.6 radio sets in use.

Principal Domestic Networks

ABC Radio Networks (American Broadcasting Company Radio Networks): 13725 Montfort Dr., Dallas, TX 75240; tel. (214) 991-9200; fax (214) 991-1071; e-mail steve.jones@abc.com; internet www.abcradio.com; f. 1944; subsidiary of Disney; serves more than 4,500 radio stations broadcasting five full service line networks; Pres. TRAUG KELLER.

Clear Channel Radio: 200 East Basse Rd, San Antonio, TX 78209; tel. (210) 822-2828; e-mail pr@clearchannel.com; internet www.clearchannel.com/radio; over 1,200 radio stations; Pres. and CEO MARK MAYS.

Premiere Radio Networks, Inc: 15260 Ventura Blvd, 5th Floor, Sherman Oaks, CA 91403; tel. (818) 377-5300; fax (818) 377-5333; e-mail affiliaterelations@premiereradio.com; internet www.premrad.com; f. 1987; subsidiary of Clear Channel Communications; Pres. and COO KRAIG T. KITCHIN.

Infinity Radio: Infinity Broadcasting, 1515 Broadway, New York, NY 10036; tel. (212) 846-3939; internet www.infinityradio.com; division of Infinity Broadcasting Corpn; subsidiary of Viacom, Inc; 178 radio stations operated from 22 states; Chair. and CEO JOEL HOLLANDER.

National Public Radio (NPR): 635 Massachusetts Ave, NW, Washington, DC 20001; tel. (202) 513-2000; fax (202) 513-3329; e-mail www-info@npr.org; internet www.npr.org; f. 1970; private non-profit corpn providing programmes and support facilities to over 750 mem. stations nation-wide; also operates a global programme distribution service by radio, cable and satellite; Chair. JOHN A. HERRMANN, Jr; Pres. and CEO KEVIN KLOSE.

USA Radio Networks: 2290 Springlake Rd, Suite 107, Dallas, TX 75234; tel. (972) 484-3900; fax (972) 243-3489; e-mail mark@usaradio.com; internet www.usaradio.com; news and information programmes carried by 1,100 affiliates; also broadcasts on short-wave and to US Armed Forces Radio; Pres. MARLIN MADDOUX.

Westwood One Inc: 40 West 57th St, 5th Floor, New York, NY 10019; tel. (212) 641-2000; internet www.westwoodone.com; f. 1934; managed by Infinity Broadcasting Corpn; subsidiary of Viacom, Inc; largest domestic outsource provider of traffic reporting services; produces and distributes national news, sports, talk, music and special event programs, in addition to local news, sports, weather and other information programming; operates BLAISE, CBS, CNN Max, Navigator, NBC, NeXt, Source Max and WONE radio networks; Pres. and CEO SHANE COPPOLA.

Principal External Radio Services

Armed Forces Radio and Television Service (AFN AFRTS): Defense Media Center (DMC), AFN Broadcast Center, 23755 Z St, Riverside, CA 92518-2031; tel. (951) 413-2319; fax (951) 413-2234; e-mail affrel@dodmedia.osd.mil; internet www.myafn.net; f. 1945; operated by Dept of Defense; provides US radio and TV programming in English as American Forces Network; limited to Dept of Defense and US military/civilian personnel in 177 countries, US territories and aboard US Navy ships; Dir MEL RUSSELL (AFRTS); Exec. Dir JEFFREY WHITE (DMC).

RFE/RL (Radio Free Europe/Radio Liberty): 1201 Connecticut Ave, NW, Suite 1100, Washington, DC 20036; tel. (202) 457-6900; fax (202) 457-6913; e-mail web@rferl.org; internet www.rferl.org; f. 1950; private, non-profit corpn financed by the federal Govt; broadcasts from Prague, Czech Republic, to Central and Eastern Europe, Eurasia and the Middle East; c. 1,000 hours weekly in 28 languages; Chair. KENNETH Y. TOMLINSON; Pres. THOMAS A. DINE.

Voice of America: 330 Independence Ave, SW, Washington, DC 20237; tel. (202) 619-2538; fax (202) 619-1241; e-mail publicaffairs@voa.gov; internet www.voa.gov; f. 1942; govt-controlled; broadcasts c. 1,000 hours weekly in 44 languages to all areas of the world; Dir DAVID S. JACKSON.

Television

In 2002 commercial television stations numbered 1,333. In that year the average US household had 2.4 sets in use.

In October 2004 the FCC announced plans to end analogue broadcasting by the end of 2006 on the basis that 85% of US viewers would have converted to digital television sets by that time.

Principal Networks

ABC, Inc (American Broadcasting Co, Inc): 500 South Buena Vista St, Burbank, CA 91521-4551; tel. (818) 460-7477; e-mail netaudr@abc.com; internet abc.go.com; f. 1953; subsidiary of the Walt Disney Co since 1996; 10 owned and 226 affiliated stations; Pres. and CEO ROBERT A. IGER; Pres., Disney-ABC TV Group ANNE SWEENEY.

C-SPAN (Cable-Satellite Public Affairs Network): 400 North Capitol St, Suite 650, Washington, DC 20001; tel. (2) 737-3200; e-mail viewer@c-span.org; internet www.c-span.org; private, non-profit public service; earns its operating revenues through licence fees paid by cable systems offering the network to their customers; Pres. and CEO BRIAN LAMB.

Capital Cities/American Broadcasting Companies, Inc: 77 West 66th St, New York, NY 10023; tel. (212) 456-7777; fax (212) 887-7168; internet www.abctelevision.com; f. 1986; Pres. and CEO THOMAS S. MURPHY; Pres., Radio Network ROBERT F. CALLAHAN.

CBS, Inc (Columbia Broadcasting System, Inc): 524 West 57th St, New York, NY 10019-6165; tel. (212) 975-3615; fax (212) 975-6347; internet www.cbs.com; f. 1948; subsidiary of Viacom, Inc; 6 owned and operated and more than 200 affiliated stations; Pres. DANIEL MASON.

CNN (Cable News Network): 1 CNN Center, Atlanta, GA 30303; tel. (404) 827-1700; fax (404) 827-1099; internet www.cnn.com; subsidiary of Time Warner; Pres. JONATHAN KLEIN; Chair. and CEO WALTER ISAACSON.

FOX Broadcasting Co: 10201 West Pico Blvd, Los Angeles, CA 90035; tel. (310) 369-8471; fax (310) 369-3553; e-mail joe.earley@fox.com; internet www.fox.com; f. 1986; subsidiary of News Corpn; more than 900 cable affiliations; Pres. GAIL BERMAN; CEO MITCH STERN.

Multimedia Cablevision, Inc: 701 East Douglas, POB 3027, Wichita, KS 67201; tel. (316) 262-4270; fax (316) 262-2309; cable television system serving more than 400,000 subscribers; Pres. MICHAEL BURRUS.

NBC Universal Television Stations: 30 Rockefeller Plaza, New York, NY 10112; tel. (212) 664-4444; fax (212) 664-5830; internet www.nbcuni.com; f. 1926; subsidiary of NBC Universal; 14 owned and over 200 affiliated stations; Pres. and CEO BOB C. WRIGHT; Pres., NBC Universal Television Stations JAY IRELAND.

# THE UNITED STATES OF AMERICA — Directory

PBS (Public Broadcasting Service): 1320 Braddock Pl., Alexandria, VA 22314-1698; tel. (703) 739-5000; fax (703) 739-0775; internet www.pbs.org; f. 1969; non-profit-making; financed by private subscriptions and federal govt funds; owned and operated by the 349 public US television stations; Pres. and CEO PAT MITCHELL.

Time Warner Cable (TWC): 290 Harbor Dr., Stamford, CT 06902; tel. (203) 328-0600; fax (203) 328-0690; internet www.timewarnercable.com; cable television system serving c. 10.9m. subscribers; bought part of Adelphia Communications in 2005; 84% owned by Time Warner; Chair. and CEO GLENN A. BRITT; Pres. THOMAS G. BAXTER.

Univision Network: 9405 North West 41st St, Miami, FL 33178-2301; tel. (305) 471-3900; fax (305) 471-4065; internet www.univision.com; subsidiary of Univision Communications, Inc; Spanish-language television network; Chair. and CEO JERROLD A. PERENCHIO.

Associations

National Association of Broadcasters (NAB): 1771 N St, NW, Washington, DC 20036; tel. (202) 429-5300; fax (202) 429-4199; e-mail nab@nab.org; internet www.nab.org; f. 1922; trade asscn of radio and TV stations and networks; 7,500 mems; Chair. PHILIP J. LOMBARDO; Pres. and CEO EDWARD O. FRITTS.

National Cable and Telecommunications Association (NCTA): 1724 Massachusetts Ave, NW, Washington, DC 20036-1905; tel. (202) 775-3550; fax (202) 775-3695; e-mail webmaster@ncta.com; internet www.ncta.com; f. 1952 as National Cable Television Asscn; c. 3,100 mems; Pres. and CEO KYLE MCSLARROW.

Finance

BANKING

Commercial Banking System

The US banking system is the largest and, in many respects, the most comprehensive and sophisticated in the world. Banking has, however, been largely subject to state rather than federal jurisdiction, and this has created a structure very different from that in other advanced industrial countries. In general, no bank may open branches or acquire subsidiaries in states other than that in which it is based, although in June 1985 the US Supreme Court ruled that federal legislation prohibiting interstate banks does not preclude state governments from permitting regional interstate banking. A number of such mergers have followed, although some states continue to restrict banks to a single branch, or to operating only in certain counties of the state. Federal anti-trust laws also limit mergers of banks within a state. The effect of these measures has been to preserve the independence of a relatively large number of banks: 7,630 in 2004. Nevertheless, the dominant banks are the main banks in the big industrial states; of the 10 largest in 2002, three were based in New York, two in North Carolina and two in Illinois. The influence of these banks, however, has been increasingly challenged by the formation of several groupings of regional banks. Federal legislation permitting the operation of interstate branch banking networks and the provision of non-banking financial services was enacted in November 1999. In October 2003 the Bank of America announced the acquisition of FleetBoston Financial Corporation, in an agreement that was to create the second largest banking company in the world. In 2004 the restructured Bank of America operated 5,880 branch offices, and controlled total deposits of more than US $551,559m. (or 9.9% of all banking deposits in the USA). The merger in 2004 of JP Morgan Chase & Co and Bank One Corporation established the second largest bank in the USA, with 2,300 branches and total assets in June 2005 of $973,113m.

Following the failure of a number of banks in the late 1980s, the Federal Deposit Insurance Corporation, a government-sponsored body which insures deposits in banks and acts as receiver for national and state banks that have been placed in receivership, was obliged to provide assistance for a large number of institutions. Many banks, meanwhile, have expanded their 'fee income' activities (such as sales of mutual fund investments) to offset declines in customer borrowing, particularly from the industrial and commercial sectors.

The possession of bank accounts and the use of banking facilities are perhaps more widespread among all regions and social groups in the USA than in any other country. This has influenced the formulation of monetary theory and policy, as bank credit has become a more important factor than currency supply in the regulation of the economy. The use of current accounts and credit cards is so common that many authorities claim that the USA can be regarded as effectively a cashless society.

Bank Holding Companies

Since 1956 bank holding companies, corporations that control one or more banks in the USA, have become significant elements in the banking system. The proportion of banks owned by holding companies increased from 62% in 1984 to 76% in 2000. In 2004 there were some 5,151 bank holding companies, of which 12% had financial holding company status.

Banking Activities Overseas

From the mid-1960s, the leading banks rapidly expanded their overseas interests. At the end of 1960 there were only eight US banks operating foreign branches, mostly in Latin America and the Far East. The main factors behind this expansion were the geographical limitations imposed by law at home; the rapid expansion of US business interests abroad; the faster economic growth of certain foreign markets; and finally the profitability of the 'Eurodollar' capital markets. The expansion in the overseas activities of US banks reached a high point in 1984. Subsequently declining levels of profitability in this area have resulted in the closure of some overseas offices, although the aggregate total of assets held has continued to rise.

In 1981 the Federal Reserve Board sanctioned the establishment of domestic International Banking Facilities (IBF), permitting commercial banks within the US (including US branches and agencies of foreign banks) to transact certain types of foreign deposit and loan business free of reserve requirements and, in most cases, state income tax liability.

Federal Reserve System: 20th St and Constitution Ave, NW, Washington, DC 20551; tel. (202) 452-3000; fax (202) 452-3819; internet www.federalreserve.gov.

The Federal Reserve System, founded in 1913, comprises the Board of Governors, the Federal Open Market Committee, the Federal Advisory Council, the Consumer Advisory Council, the Thrift Institutions Advisory Council, the 25 branches of the 12 Federal Reserve Banks, together with all member banks.

The Board of Governors is composed of seven members appointed by the President of the United States with the advice and consent of the Senate.

The Reserve Banks are empowered to issue Federal Reserve notes fully secured by the following assets, alone or in any combination: (i) Gold certificates; (ii) US Government and agency securities; (iii) Other eligible assets as described by statute; and (iv) Special Drawing Rights certificates. The Reserve Banks may discount paper for depository institutions and make properly secured advances to depository institutions. Federal Reserve Banks were established by Congress as the operating arms of the nation's central banking system. Many of the services performed by this network for depository institutions and for the Government are similar to services performed by banks and thrifts for business customers and individuals. Reserve Banks hold the cash reserves of depository institutions and make loans to them. They move currency and coin into and out of circulation, and collect and process millions of cheques each day. They provide banking services for the Treasury, issue and redeem government securities on behalf of the Treasury, and act in other ways as fiscal agent for the US Government. The Banks also take part in the primary responsibility of the Federal Reserve System, the setting of monetary policy, through participation on the Federal Open Market Committee.

The Comptroller of the Currency (see below) has primary supervisory authority over all federally chartered banks, and the banking supervisors of the States have similar jurisdiction over banks organized under State laws. State member banks are examined by the Federal Reserve.

In 2004 some 2,200 commercial banks were members of the Federal Reserve System.

Board of Governors

Chairman: BEN S. BERNANKE.
Vice-Chairman: (vacant).
Governors: SUSAN SCHMIDT BIES, MARK W. OLSON, RANDALL S. KROSZNER, DONALD L. KOHN, KEVIN M. WARSH.
Secretary of the Board: JENNIFER J. JOHNSON.

Federal Reserve Banks

	Chairman	President
Boston	Samuel O. Thier	Cathy E. Minehan
New York	John E. Sexton	Timothy F. Geithner
Philadelphia	Doris M. Damm	William H. Stone, Jr
Cleveland	Robert W. Mahoney	Sandra Pianalto
Richmond	Wesley S. Williams, Jr.	Jeffrey M. Lacker
Atlanta	David M. Ratcliffe	Jack Guynn
Chicago	W. James Farrell	Michael H. Moskow
St Louis	Walter L. Metcalfe, Jr.	William Poole
Minneapolis	Frank L. Sims	Gary H. Stern
Kansas City	Robert A. Funk	Thomas M. Hoenig
Dallas	Ray L. Hunt	Richard W. Fisher
San Francisco	David K. Y. Tang	Janet L. Yellen

www.europaworld.com

4687

THE UNITED STATES OF AMERICA

Comptroller of the Currency
250 E St, SW, Washington, DC 20219; tel. (202) 874-4900; internet www.occ.treas.gov.
The Comptroller of the Currency has supervisory control over all federally chartered banks (see Federal Reserve System).
Comptroller: JOHN C. DUGAN.

Principal Commercial Banks
(cap. = total capital and reserves; dep. = deposits; m. = million; amounts in US dollars)
In general, only banks with a minimum of $2,000m. deposits are listed. In states where no such bank exists, that with the largest deposits is listed.

Alabama

AmSouth Bank NA: POB 11007, Birmingham, AL 35288; tel. (205) 801-0359; fax (205) 326-5015; e-mail 10312,1342@compuserve.com; internet www.amsouth.com; f. 1873; cap. 10,000, dep. 35,300.0m. (Dec. 2002); Chair., Pres. and CEO C. DOWD RITTER.

Regions Bank: 417 North 20th St, POB 10247, Birmingham, AL 35202-0247; tel. (205) 326-7697; fax (205) 326-7779; internet www.regionsbank.com; f. 1928; cap. 0.1m., dep. 39,795.5m. (Dec. 2002); Chair. and CEO CARL E. JONES, Jr.

SouthTrust Bank NA: 420 North 20th St, POB 2554, Birmingham, AL 35290; tel. (205) 254-5000; fax (205) 254-5656; internet www.southtrust.com; f. 1887; cap. 9.0m., dep. 44,099.4m. (Dec. 2002); Chair., Pres. and CEO JULIAN W. BANTON.

Alaska

Wells Fargo Bank Alaska NA: 301 West Northern Lights Blvd, Anchorage, AK 99503; tel. (907) 522-8888; fax (907) 267-5448; e-mail questions@nbak.com; internet www.nbak.com; f. 1916; fmrly National Bank of Alaska, present name adopted in June 2001; cap. 80m., dep. 2,808.8m. (Dec. 2002); Chair. EDWARD B. RASMUSON; Pres. RICHARD STRUTZ.

Arizona

Bank One, NA: 201 North Central Ave, 11th Floor, Phoenix, AZ 85004; tel. (602) 221-2900; fax (602) 221-4993; internet www.bankone.com; f. 1899; cap. 1,435.2m., dep. 18,215.2m. (Dec. 1998); CEO R. MICHAEL WELBORN.

Wells Fargo Bank NA: 3300 North Central Ave, Phoenix, AZ 85012; tel. (602) 504-1234; known as Wells Fargo Bank (Arizona) until Feb. 2000; total assets 3,700m. (Aug. 1999).

Arkansas

First Commercial Bank NA: 400 West Capitol St, POB 1471, Little Rock, AR 72201; tel. (501) 371-7000; fax (501) 371-7413; cap. 138.4m., dep. 1,726.1m. (Dec. 2000).

California

Bank of the West: 180 Montgomery St, San Francisco, CA 94104; tel. (415) 765-4800; fax (415) 434-3470; internet www.bankofthewest.com; f. 1874; cap. 16.4m., dep. 20,713.3m. (Dec. 2002); Chair. WALTER A. DODS, Jr; Pres. and CEO DON J. MCGRATH.

California Bank and Trust: 11622 El Camino Real, Suite 200, San Diego, CA 92130; tel. (858) 793-7400; fax (858) 793-7438; e-mail info@calbanktrust.com; internet www.calbanktrust.com; f. 1998; cap. 3.2m., dep. 7,544.7m. (Dec. 2002); Chair. and CEO DAVID BLACKFORD.

City National Bank: 400 Roxbury Dr. North, Beverly Hills, CA 90210; tel. (310) 888-6000; fax (310) 888-6045; e-mail contact@cnb.com; internet www.cnb.com; f. 1954; cap. 90.0m., dep. 10,320.8m. (Dec. 2002); Chair. and CEO RUSSELL GOLDSMITH; Pres. GEORGE H. BENTER, Jr; 45 brs.

Comerica Bank–California: 333 West Santa Clara St, San Jose, CA 95113; tel. (408) 244-1700; fax (408) 286-5242; internet www.comerica.com; f. 1955; cap. 107.3m., dep. 18,118.7m. (Dec. 2002); Chair. PHILIP R. BOYCE; Pres. and CEO MICHAEL FULTON.

Union Bank of California NA: 350 California St, 6th Floor, San Francisco, CA 94104; tel. (415) 705-7000; internet www.uboc.com; f. 1996; cap. 604.6m., dep. 35,067.0m. (Dec. 2002); Pres. and CEO NORIMICHI KANARI; 267 brs.

Wells Fargo Bank NA: 420 Montgomery St, San Francisco, CA 94163; tel. (415) 477-1000; fax (415) 975-6847; internet www.wellsfargo.com; f. 1852; cap. 520.0m., dep. 153,424.0m. (Dec. 2002); Chair. PAUL HAZEN; Pres. and CEO RICHARD KOVACEVICH.

Colorado

Bank One, NA: 1125 17th St, POB 5586, Denver, CO 80202-2025; tel. (303) 759-0111; fax (303) 297-4462; internet www.bankone.com; cap. 345m., dep. 2,600m. (Dec. 1999); Chair. and CEO WAYNE HUTCHENS.

US Bank NA: 1515 Arapahoe St, POB 5548, Denver, CO 80217; tel. (303) 585-5000; fax (303) 585-7346; f. 1862 as Colorado Nat. Bank; renamed 1998 following series of mergers in 1993–97; cap. 453m., dep. 6,078.8m. (Dec. 1996); Chair. ROBERT MALONE; Pres. DANIEL QUINN.

Connecticut

Citizens Bank of Connecticut: 63 Eugene O'Neill Dr., New London, CT 06320; tel. (860) 638-4419; fax (860) 638-4444; e-mail intbank@citizensbank.com; internet www.citizensbank.com; f. 1996; dep. 2, 659.7m., total assets 2,960.8m. (Dec. 2002); Pres. and CEO JOSEPH R. MARCAURELE.

Delaware

Bank One, NA: 201 North Walnut St, Wilmington, DE 19801; tel. (302) 594-4000; internet www.firstusa.com; f. 1983; name changed from First USA Bank NA in 2002; cap. 17.5m., dep. 12,956.6m. (Dec. 2002).

Chase Manhattan Bank USA NA: 200 White Clay Center Dr., 1st Floor, Newark DE 19711; tel. (302) 758-2600; fax (302) 758-2603; internet www.chase.com; cap. 49.0m., dep. 25,865.1m. (Dec. 2002); Pres. MICHAEL J. BARRETT.

MBNA America Bank NA: 1100 North King St, Wilmington, DE 19801; tel. (302) 453-9930; fax (302) 456-8541; internet www.mbna.com; cap. 600.0m., dep. 38,173.2m. (Dec. 2002); Chair. and CEO BRUCE L. HAMMONDS; Pres. JOHN R. COCHRAN.

PNC Bank, Delaware: 300 Delaware Ave, POB 791, Wilmington, DE 19899; tel. (302) 429-1011; fax (302) 429-1206; f. 1952; cap. 202.5m., dep. 2,232.1m. (Dec. 1999); Chair., Pres. and CEO CONNIE BOND STUART, Jr.

Florida

Northern Trust Bank of Florida: 700 Brickell Ave, Miami, FL 33131; tel. (305) 372-1000; fax (305) 789-1106; internet www.northerntrust.com; f. 1982; cap. 18.6m., dep. 4,583.9m. (Dec. 2002); CEO WILLIAM L. MORRISON.

Ocean Bank: 780 Northwest 42nd Ave, Miami, POB 441140, FL 33126; tel. (305) 442-2660; fax (305) 444-8153; internet www.oceanbank.com; f. 1982; cap. 8.5m., dep. 3,765.4m. (Dec. 2002); Pres. and CEO JOSE A. CONCEPCION; 23 brs.

Republic Bank: 111 Second Ave, NE, Suite 211, POB 33008, St Petersburg, FL 33701; tel. (727) 823-7300; internet www.republicbankfl.com; f. 1973; cap. 34.8m., dep. 2,386.7m. (Dec. 2003); Pres. WILLIAM R. KLICH.

Georgia

SunTrust Bank: 25 Park Pl., POB 4418, Atlanta, GA 30302; tel. (404) 588-7785; fax (404) 302-4782; internet www.suntrust.com; f. 1891; assumed all SunTrust Banks 2000; cap. 21.6m., dep. 100,896.6m. (Dec. 2002); Chair. and Pres. PHILLIP HUMANN.

Hawaii

Bank of Hawaii: 111 South King St, Honolulu, HI 96813; tel. (888) 643-3888; fax (808) 537-8440; e-mail info@boh.com; internet www.boh.com; f. 1897; cap. 14,908.0m., dep. 8,042.0m. (Dec. 2002); Chair. and CEO MICHAEL E. O'NEILL; Pres. RICHARD J. DAHL.

First Hawaiian Bank: 999 Bishop St, Honolulu, HI 96813; tel. (808) 525-7000; fax (808) 525-8182; internet www.fhb.com; f. 1858; cap. 1,845.4m., dep. 6,990.1m. (Dec. 2003); Chair. and CEO WALTER A. DODS, Jr; Pres. DONALD G. HORNER.

Idaho

West One Bank, Idaho, NA: 101 South Capitol Blvd, POB 8247, Boise, ID 83733; tel. (208) 383-7000; fax (208) 383-7563; f. 1891; cap. 231.4m., dep. 3,502.5m. (Dec. 1996); Chair. DANIEL R. NELSON; Pres. and CEO ROBERT LANE.

Illinois

Bank One NA: 1 Bank One Plaza, Chicago, IL 60670; tel. (312) 732-7053; fax (312) 732-5466; internet www.bankone.com; f. 1863; merger pending with J.P. Morgan, to become J.P. Morgan Chase; cap. 201.0m., dep. 188,336.0m. (Dec. 2002); Chair. and CEO JAMES DIMON; Pres. VERNE G. ISTOCK.

First Midwest Bank: 300 Park Blvd, Suite 400, Itasca, IL 60143; internet www.firstmidwest.com; cap. 40.0m., dep. 5,444.8m. (Dec. 2002); Chair. and CEO JOHN O'MEARA; 69 brs.

Harris Trust and Savings Bank: 111 West Monroe St, Chicago, IL 60603; tel. (312) 845-2028; fax (312) 845-2199; internet www

THE UNITED STATES OF AMERICA

.harrisbank.com; f. 1882; cap. 105.0m., dep. 16,859.5m. (Dec. 2002); Chair. and CEO ALAN G. MCNALLY.

LaSalle Bank NA: 135 South LaSalle St, Chicago, IL 60603; tel. (312) 904-2000; fax (312) 904-2819; internet www.lasallebank.com; f. 1927; cap. 676.6m., dep. 47,259.4m. (Dec. 2002); Chair., Pres. and CEO NORMAN BOBINS.

Northern Trust Co: 50 South LaSalle St, Chicago, IL 60675; tel. (312) 630-6000; fax (312) 444-5244; internet www.northerntrust.com; f. 1889; cap. 213.8m., dep. 27,911.3m. (Dec. 2002); Chair. WILLIAM A. OSBORN; Pres. BARRY G. HASTINGS.

Indiana

Bank One NA: 111 Monument Circle, Indianapolis, IN 46277-0188; tel. (317) 321-3000; fax (317) 321-7965; f. 1839; cap. 609.1m., dep. 6,991.2m. (Dec. 1998); Chair. and CEO JOSEPH D. BARNETTE, Jr.

National City Bank of Indiana: 1 Merchants Plaza, Indianapolis, IN 46255; tel. (317) 267-7147; fax (317) 267-7152; internet www.national-city.com; f. 1865; cap. 21.3m., dep. 42,088.9m. (Dec. 2002); Chair., Pres. and CEO STEPHEN A. STITLE.

Iowa

Wells Fargo Iowa NA: POB 837, Des Moines, IA 50304; tel. (515) 245-8212; fax (515) 245-3139; f. 1929; fmrly Norwest Bank Iowa NA; total assets 6.1m. (March 2000).

Kansas

Bank IV Kansas, NA: POB 4, Wichita, KS 67201; tel. (316) 261-4444; fax (316) 261-2243; f. 1887; cap. 367.6m., dep. 3,905m. (Dec. 1994); Chair. and Pres. K. GORDON GREER.

Kentucky

Bank One NA: POB 32500, Louisville, KY 40202; tel. (502) 566-2000; fax (502) 566-2016; internet www.bankone.com; f. 1935; fmrly Bank One, Kentucky NA; merged into Bank One NA in May 2003; cap. 345.1m., dep. 4,799.3m. (Dec. 1998); Chair. WILLIAM HARTMAN.

National City Bank of Kentucky: 3700 National City Tower, 101 South Fifth St, Louisville, KY 40202; tel. (502) 581-4200; fax (502) 581-7909; internet www.nationalcity.com; f. 1863; cap. 21.0m., dep. 7,095.8m. (Dec. 2002); Chair. LEONARD V. HARDIN; Pres. and CEO FREDERICK W. SCHANTZ.

Louisiana

First National Bank of Commerce: 201 Baronne St, POB 60279, New Orleans, LA 70160; tel. (504) 561-1371; fax (504) 561-7082; f. 1933; cap. 422.3m., dep. 5,447.1m. (Dec. 1997); Chair. HOWARD C. GAINES; Pres. and CEO ASHTON J. RYAN, Jr.

Hibernia National Bank: 313 Carondelet St, New Orleans, LA 70130; tel. (504) 533-3333; fax (504) 533-5739; e-mail mailus@hibernia.com; internet www.hiberniabank.com; f. 1933; cap. 23.6m., dep. 15,247.9m. (Dec. 2002); Chair. ROBERT H. BOH; Pres. J. HERBERT BOYDSTUN.

Whitney National Bank: 228 St Charles Ave, New Orleans, LA 70130; tel. (504) 586-7272; fax (504) 586-7412; e-mail rchamberlin@whitneybank.com; internet www.whitneybank.com; f. 1883; cap. 3.4m., dep. 6,409.0m. (Dec. 2002); Chair. and CEO WILLIAM L. MARKS; Pres. R. KING MILLING.

Maine

Fleet Bank of Maine: 2 Portland Sq., Portland, ME 04104-5091; tel. (207) 874-5000; fax (617) 874-5117; internet www.fleet.com; f. 1991; merged into Fleet National Bank in Oct. 2001; cap. 118.5m., dep. 1,855.7m. (Dec. 1999); Chair. LEO BREITMAN; Pres. and CEO DAVID OTT.

Maryland

Provident Bank: 114 East Lexington St, Baltimore, MD 21202-1725; tel. (410) 281-7000; fax (410) 277-2768; internet www.provbank.com; f. 1951; cap. 30.0m., dep. 4,467.1m. (Dec. 2002); Chair. and CEO PETER MARTIN.

Massachusetts

Citizens Bank of Massachusetts: 28 State St, Boston, MA 02109; tel. (617) 725-5500; fax (617) 725-5877; e-mail intbank@citizensbank.com; internet www.citizensbank.com; f. 1825; dep. 19,275.9m., total assets 22,812.0m. (Dec. 2002); Pres. and CEO THOMAS J. HOLLISTER.

State Street Bank and Trust Co: 225 Franklin St, POB 351, Suffolk, MA 02101; tel. (617) 786-3000; internet www.statestreet.com; f. 1955; cap. 2,683.8m., dep. 39,327.4m. (Dec. 1998); Chair. and CEO MARSHALL N. CARTER; Pres. DAVID A. SPINA.

Michigan

Citizens Bank: 328 South Saginaw St, Flint, MI 48502; tel. (313) 766-7500; fax (313) 768-6948; internet www.citizensonline.com; f. 1871; cap. 12.5m., dep. 4,619.1m. (Dec. 2002).

Comerica Bank: 500 Woodward Ave, Detroit, MI 48226; tel. (313) 222-3300; fax (313) 961-7349; e-mail info@comerica.com; internet www.comerica.com; f. 1849; cap. 278.5m., dep. 33,607.9m. (Dec. 2002; Chair., Pres. and CEO RALPH W. BABB.

National City Bank of Michigan/Illinois: 211 South Rose St, Kalamazoo, MI 49007; tel. (313) 396-4480; fax (313) 396-4496; f. 1949; cap. 198.6m., dep. 18,192.7m. (Dec. 2002); Chair., Pres. and CEO RICHARD F. CHORMANN.

Minnesota

US Bank NA: 601 Second Ave South, Minneapolis, MN 55402-4302; tel. (612) 973-0728; fax (612) 973-0838; e-mail international.banking@usbank.com; internet www.usbank.com; f. 1929; cap. 18.2m., dep. 145,343.5m. (Dec. 2002); Chair. JOHN F. GRUNDHOFER; Pres. and CEO JERRY F. GRUNDHOFER; 2,133 brs.

Wells Fargo Bank Minnesota NA: Wells Fargo Center, International Wires, Sixth St and Marquette Ave, Minneapolis, MN 55479; internet www.wellsfargo.com; f. 1872; cap. 100.0m., dep. 47,938.4m. (Dec. 2002); Chair. JON R. CAMPBELL; Pres. and CEO RICHARD KOVACEVICH.

Mississippi

Trustmark National Bank: 248 Capitol St, Jackson, MS 39205; tel. (601) 354-5863; fax (601) 949-2387; internet www.trustmark.com; f. 1889; cap. 13.4m., dep. 6,262.4m. (Dec. 2002); Chair. and CEO REGINALD G. HICKSON.

Missouri

Commerce Bank NA: 1000 Walnut St, Mailstop KCIN, Kansas City, MO 64106; tel. (816) 234-2000; fax (816) 234-2799; e-mail mymoney@commercebank.com; internet www.commercebank.com; f. 1865; cap. 10.2m., dep. 10,124.7m. (Dec. 2002); Chair. and CEO JONATHAN KEMPER.

Montana

First Interstate Bank of Montana NA: 2 Main St, POB 7130, Kalispell, MT 59904; tel. (406) 752-5001; internet www.firstinterstatebank.com; f. 1891; cap. 35m., dep. 257.1m. (Dec. 1996); Chair. JAMES CURRAN; Pres. BOB SCHNEIDER.

Nebraska

First National Bank of Omaha: 1620 Dodge St, Omaha, NE 68102; tel. (402) 341-0500; fax (402) 633-3554; e-mail firstnational@fnni.com; internet www.firstnational.com; f. 1857; cap. 5.3m., dep. 4,642.1m. (Dec. 2002); Chair. F. PHILLIPS GILTNER; Pres. BRUCE R. LAURITZEN; 24 brs.

Wells Fargo Bank Nebraska NA: 1919 Douglas St, POB 3408, Omaha, NE 68103; tel. (402) 536-2420; fax (402) 536-2531; Norwest Bank Nebraska NA until June 2000; total assets 2,300m. (March 2000).

Nevada

Citibank (Nevada) NA: 8725 West Sahara, POB 6800, Las Vegas, NV 89109; cap. 75.0m., dep. 7,091.4m. (Dec. 2002).

Wells Fargo Bank Nevada NA: 3800 Howard Hughes Pkwy, Las Vegas, NV 89109; tel. (702) 791-6500; internet www.wellsfargo.com; known as First Interstate Bank of Nevada until 1996; dep. 4,400m. (July 1999); Pres. and CEO LAURA SCHULTE.

New Hampshire

Citizens Bank New Hampshire: 875 Elm St, Manchester, NH 03101; tel. (603) 634-7418; fax (603) 634-7481; e-mail intbank@citizensbank.com; internet www.citizensbank.com; f. 1853; cap. 0.8m., dep. 6,249.6m. (Dec. 2002); Pres. and CEO KIM A. MEADER.

New Jersey

Summit Bank: 301 Carnegie Center, POB 2066, Princeton, NJ 08543-2066; tel. (609) 987-3200; internet www.summitbank.com; f. 1996; cap. 2,150.9m., dep. 28,569.7m. (Dec. 1999); Chair., Pres. and CEO T. JOSEPH SEMROD.

Trust Co of New Jersey: 35 Journal Sq., Jersey City, NJ 07306; tel. (201) 420-2500; fax (201) 420-2516; internet www.trustcompany.com; f. 1896; cap. 36.6m., dep. 4,109.0m. (Dec. 2002); Chair. and CEO SIGGI B. WILZIG.

THE UNITED STATES OF AMERICA

New Mexico

Wells Fargo Bank NA: 40 First Plaza, POB 1305, Albuquerque, NM 87103; tel. (505) 765-4000; fax (505) 766-9571; internet www.firstsecuritybank.com; f. 1933; known as First Security Bank of New Mexico NA until April 2001; merged with Wells Fargo Bank in Oct. 2000; cap. 206.3m., dep. 2,578.8m. (Dec. 1999).

New York

American Express Bank Ltd: American Express Tower, 200 Vesey St, 23rd Floor, New York, NY 10285-2300; tel. (212) 640-5000; fax (212) 693-1721; internet www.americanexpress.com; f. 1919; cap. 121.0m., res 826.0m., dep. 9,844.0m. (Dec. 2002); Chair. and CEO W. RICHARD HOLMES.

Bank of New York: 1 Wall St, New York, NY 10286; tel. (212) 495-1784; fax (212) 495-1398; e-mail comments@bankofny.com; internet www.bankofny.com; f. 1784; cap. 1,135.3m., dep. 59,926.2m. (Dec. 2002); Chair. and CEO THOMAS A. RENYI; Pres. GERALD L. HASSELL.

Bank of Tokyo–Mitsubishi UFJ Trust Co: 1251 Ave of the Americas, New York, NY 10020-1104; tel. (212) 782-4000; fax (212) 782-6415; internet www.btmna.com; f. 1955; cap. 444.4m., dep. 1,792.4m. (Dec. 2002); Chair. NAOTAKA OBATA; Pres. and CEO NOBORU TAKEUCHI.

Citibank NA: 399 Park Ave, New York, NY 10043; tel. (212) 559-1000; fax (212) 223-2681; internet www.citibank.com; f. 1812; cap. 2,701.0m., dep. 418,446.0m. (Dec. 2002); Chair. and CEO VICTOR J. MENEZES.

Deutsche Bank Trust Company Americas: New York, NY; tel. (212) 250-2500; fax (212) 250-4429; internet www.deutsche-bank.com; f. 1903; fmrly Bankers' Trust Co, present name adopted April 2002; cap. 3,627.0m., dep. 31,633.0m. (Dec. 2002); Chair. and CEO JOSEF ACKERMAN; Pres. JOHN A. ROSS.

HSBC Bank USA: 1 HSBC Center, Buffalo, NY 14203; tel. (716) 841-2424; fax (716) 841-5391; internet www.marinemidland.com; f. 1999 following acquisition of Marine Midland Bank by Hongkong & Shanghai Banking Corpn; acquired Republic National Bank of New York 2000; cap. 205.0m., dep. 70,463.3m. (Dec. 2001); Pres. and CEO YOUSSEF A. NASR.

Manufacturers' and Traders' Trust Co—M & T Bank: 1 M & T Plaza, Buffalo, NY 14203-2399; tel. (716) 842-4200; fax (716) 842-5021; internet www.mandtbank.com; f. 1856; cap. 120.6m., dep. 28,346.0m. (Dec. 2002); Chair. and CEO ROBERT G. WILMERS.

National Bank of Geneva: 2 Seneca St, Geneva, NY 14456; tel. (315) 789-2300; fax (315) 789-0381; internet www.nbgeneva.com; f. 1817; cap. 61.1m., dep. 63.9m. (Dec. 2002); Pres. RANDOLPH C. BROWN; 12 brs.

Trustco Bank NA: 192 Erie Blvd, POB 1082, Schenectady, NY 12301-1082; tel. (518) 377-3311; fax (518) 381-3668; internet www.trustcobank.com; cap. 29.4m., dep. 2,312.5m. (Dec. 2002); Pres. ROBERT A. MCCORMICK.

United States Trust Co of New York: 114 West 47th St, New York, NY 10036; tel. (212) 852-1000; fax (212) 995-5642; e-mail info@trust.com; internet www.ustrust.com; f. 1853; cap. 15.0m., dep. 4,973.8m. (Dec. 2002); Chair. and CEO JEFFREY S. MAURER.

North Carolina

Bank of America NA: Bank of America Corporate Center, 100 North Tryon St, Charlotte, NC 28255; tel. (704) 386-5000; fax (704) 386-0981; internet www.bankamerica.com; f. 1904; cap. 2,834.0m., dep. 488,241.0m. (Dec. 2002); Chair. and CEO HUGH L. MCCOLL, Jr; Pres. KENNETH D. LEWIS.

First Union Corporation: 1 First Union Center, Charlotte, NC 28288-0570; tel. (704) 374-6161; fax (704) 374-3420; internet www.firstunion.com; f. 1908; cap. 17,135m., dep. 200,262.0m. (Dec. 1999); Chair. and CEO EDWARD E. CRUTCHFIELD, Jr; Pres. and CEO KEN THOMPSON.

Wachovia Bank NA: 301 South College St, Suite 4000, Charlotte, NC 28288-0013; tel. (704) 374-1246; internet www.wachovia.com; f. 1866; cap. 455.0m., dep. 265,776.0m. (Dec. 2002); Chair. and CEO LESLIE M. BAKER, Jr; Pres. KENNEDY THOMPSON.

North Dakota

Wells Fargo Bank North Dakota NA: 406 Main Ave, Fargo, ND 58126; tel. (701) 293-4200; fax (701) 280-8821; known as Norwest Bank North Dakota NA until Sept. 2000; total assets 1,300m. (Dec. 1999).

Ohio

Bank One NA: 100 East Bond St, Columbus, OH 43215; tel. (614) 248-5931; fax (614) 248-5518; internet www.bankone.com; f. 1868; cap. 1,945.9m., dep. 26,976.9m. (Dec. 1998); Chair. and CEO FREDERICK CULLEN.

Fifth Third Bank: 38 Fountain Sq. Plaza, Cincinnati, OH 45263; tel. (513) 579-5300; fax (513) 579-4185; internet www.53.com; f. 1927; total assets 9,400m. (Feb. 2005); Pres. and CEO GEORGE A. SCHAEFER, Jr; 1,094 brs.

FirstMerit Bank NA: 3 Cascade Plaza, Akron, OH 44308; tel. (330) 996-6300; fax (330) 384-7008; internet www.firstmerit.com; cap. 57.6m., dep. 9,438.2m. (Dec. 2002); Chair. and CEO JOHN R. COCHRAN.

Huntington National Bank: 7 Easton Oval, Columbus, OH 43219; tel. (614) 480-4685; fax (614) 331-5900; e-mail international@huntington.com; internet www.huntington.com; f. 1866; cap. 40.0m., dep. 23,581.5m. (Dec. 2002); Chair. THOMAS HOAGLIN.

KeyBank NA: 127 Public Sq., Cleveland, OH 44114; tel. (216) 689-3000; fax (216) 689-3683; internet www.key.com; f. 1849; cap. 50.0m., dep. 64,575.8m. (Dec. 2002); Chair. and CEO HENRY L. MEYER.

National City Bank: 1900 East Ninth St, POB 94750, Cleveland, OH 44114-3484; tel. (216) 575-2000; fax (216) 575-9263; internet www.national-city.com; f. 1845; cap. 7.3m., dep. 36,820.9m. (Dec. 2002); Chair. DAVID DABERKO; Pres. and CEO WILLIAM E. MACDONALD, III.

Oklahoma

Bank of Oklahoma NA: Bank of Oklahoma Tower, POB 2300, Tulsa, OK 74192; tel. (918) 588-6829; fax (918) 588-6026; internet www.bankofoklahoma.com; f. 1933; cap. 52.9m., dep. 8,958.8m. (Dec. 2002); Chair. GEORGE B. KAISER; Pres. and CEO STANLEY A. LYBARGER; 56 brs.

Oregon

United States National Bank of Oregon: 321 South West Sixth Ave, Portland, OR 97204; tel. (503) 275-6111; fax (503) 275-5132; f. 1891; cap. 1,095m., dep. 12,225m. (Dec. 1996); Chair. ROGER BREEZLEY; CEO GERRY CAMERON; Pres. JOHN ESKILDSEN.

Pennsylvania

Mellon Bank, NA: 1 Mellon Bank Center, Pittsburgh, PA 15258-0001; tel. (412) 234-5000; fax (412) 234-4025; internet www.mellon.com; f. 1869; cap. 169.3m., dep. 21,542.6m. (Dec. 2002); Chair., Pres. and CEO MARTIN G. MCGUINN.

PNC Bank, NA: 1 PNC Plaza, 249 Fifth Ave, Pittsburgh, PA 15222-2707; tel. (412) 762-2000; fax (412) 762-5022; internet www.pnc.com; f. 1959; cap. 218.9m., dep. 48,751.5m. (Dec. 2002); Chair., Pres. and CEO JAMES E. ROHR; 760 brs.

Rhode Island

Citizens Bank of Rhode Island: 1 Citizens Plaza, Providence, RI 02903; tel. (401) 454-2441; fax (401) 455-5859; e-mail intbank@citizensbank.com; internet www.citizensbank.com; f. 1996; cap. 1.0m., dep. 8,783.4m. (Dec. 2002); Chair. ROBERT M. MAHONEY; Pres. and CEO JOSEPH J. MARCAURELE.

South Carolina

Carolina First Bank: 102 South Main St, POB 1029, Greenville, SC 29602; tel. (864) 255-7900; fax (864) 239-6401; e-mail customerassistance@carolinafirst.com; internet www.carolinafirst.com; cap. 7.9m., dep. 5,624.7m. (Dec. 2002); Chair. MACK I. WHITTLE, Jr; Pres. JAMES W. TERRY, Jr.

South Dakota

Citibank USA NA: 701 East 60th St, North, POB 6000, Sioux Falls, SD 57117; tel. (605) 331-2626; internet www.citibank.com; f. 1981; fmrly Citibank (South Dakota), present name adopted in Jan. 2002; cap. 100.0m., dep. 2,488.6m. (Dec. 2002); Gen. Sec. DAVID L. ZIMBECK; Pres. KENDALL E. STORK.

Wells Fargo Bank South Dakota NA: 101 North Phillips Ave, Sioux Falls, SD 57117; tel. (605) 575-7300; fax (605) 575-4815; fmrly Norwest Bank South Dakota NA, present name adopted in Sept. 2000; total assets 5,500m. (Dec. 1999).

Tennessee

First Tennessee Bank NA: 165 Madison Ave, 9th Floor, POB 84, Memphis, TN 38101-0084; tel. (901) 523-4420; fax (901) 523-4438; internet www.ftb.com; f. 1864; cap. 72.5m., dep. 19,670.5m. (Dec. 2002); Chair. and CEO RALPH HORN; Pres. CHARLES BURKETT; 183 brs.

Union Planters Bank NA: 6200 Poplar, POB 387, Memphis, TN 38147; tel. (901) 580-5970; fax (901) 580-5958; internet www.unionplanters.com; f. 1869; cap. 18.0m., dep. 28,738.5m. (Dec. 2002); Chair. and CEO BENJAMIN W. RAWLINS, Jr.

THE UNITED STATES OF AMERICA

Texas

Bank One NA: 1717 Main St, Dallas, TX 75201; tel. (214) 290-4130; fax (214) 290-2090; internet www.bankone.com; cap. 1,661.2m.; dep. 22,626.1m. (Dec. 1998); Chair. and CEO TERRY KELLEY.

Comerica Bank–Texas: Thanksgiving Tower, 1601 Elm St, Dallas, TX 75201; tel. (214) 841-1400; fax (214) 841-9298; internet www.comerica.com; f. 1988; cap. 2.5m., dep. 3, 883.4m. (Dec. 2002); Pres. and CEO CHARLES L. GUMMER.

Frost National Bank: 100 West Houston St, POB 1600, San Antonio, TX 78296; tel. (210) 220-4011; e-mail frostbank@frostbank.com; internet www.frostbank.com; f. 1899; cap. 8.5m., dep. 8,599.4m. (Dec. 2002); Chair. and CEO T. C. FROST.

Wells Fargo Bank of Texas: Suite 1000, 16414 San Pedro, San Antonio, TX 78232; tel. (210) 856-5000; internet www.wellsfargo.com; f. 1996; cap. 21.0m., dep. 22,530.5m. (Dec. 2002).

Utah

Wells Fargo Bank NA: 79 South Main St, Salt Lake City, UT 84111; tel. (801) 246-6000; fax (801) 246-5992; e-mail amanbei@fscnet.com; internet www.wellsfargo.com; f. 1996; fmrly First Security Bank NA; merged with Wells Fargo in Oct. 2000; cap. 1,428.3m., dep. 15,517.2m. (Dec. 1999).

Virginia

Branch Banking and Trust Co of Virginia: 823 East Main St, Richmond, VA 23219; tel. (757) 823-7890; fax (704) 954-1117; internet www.bbandt.com; f. 1978; cap. 6.9m., dep. 10,690.1m. (Dec. 2002).

Chevy Chase Bank, FSB: 7926 Jones Branch Dr., Mclean, VA 22101; internet www.chevychasebank.com; f. 1955; dep. 7,189.5m. (Dec. 2000).

Washington

Bank of America: 701 Fifth Ave, POB 3586, Seattle, WA 98124; tel. (206) 358-3000; fax (206) 358-3771; f. 1870; fmrly Seafirst Bank, present name adopted in Sept. 1999; cap. 1,681m., dep. 14,375m. (Dec. 1996).

Washington Mutual Bank: 1201 Third Ave, Suite 1000, Seattle, WA 98101; tel. (206) 490-8625; internet www.wamu.com; dep. 166,460.0m., total assets 286,720.0m. (Sept. 2003); Pres. and Chair. KERRY KILLINGER.

West Virginia

Bank One NA: 1000 Fifth Ave, Huntington, WV 25701; tel. (304) 526-4336; internet www.bankone.com; f. 1872; fmrly Bank One, West Virginia NA; merged into Bank One NA in Aug. 2003; cap. 140.9m., dep. 1,637.3m. (Dec. 1998); Chair. and CEO A. MICHAEL PERRY.

Wisconsin

Bank One NA: 111 East Wisconsin Ave, Milwaukee, WI 53202; tel. (414) 765-3000; fax (414) 765-0553; internet www.bankone.com; f. 1930; cap. 552.1m., dep. 7,521.5m. (Dec. 1997); Chair. RONALD C. BALDWIN; Pres. and CEO WILLIAM E. READ.

US Bank NA: 800 Nicollet Mall, Minneapolis, MN 55402; tel. (612) 303-0799; fax (612) 973-0838; f. 1853; fmrly Firstar Bank NA, present name adopted in Aug. 2001; cap. 18.2m., dep. 145,343.5m. (Dec. 2002); Chair. and CEO JERRY A. GRUNDHOFER; 2,419 brs.

Wyoming

Wells Fargo Bank Wyoming NA: POB 2799, Casper, WY 82601; tel. (307) 266-1100; fax (307) 235-7626; fmrly Norwest Bank Wyoming NA, present name adopted in Aug. 2000; total assets 1,700m. (Dec. 1999).

Co-operative Bank

CoBank: POB 5110, Denver, CO 80217; tel. (303) 740-4000; fax (303) 740-4366; internet www.cobank.com; f. 1933; provides loan finance and domestic and international banking services for agricultural and farmer-owned co-operatives; cap. 1,334.3m., dep. 24,250.8m. (Dec. 2002); Chair. J. ROY ORTON; CEO DOUGLAS D. SIMS; Pres. ROBERT B. ENGEL.

Trade Bank

Export-Import Bank of the United States (Ex-Im Bank): 811 Vermont Ave, NW, Washington, DC 20571; tel. (202) 565-3946; fax (202) 565-3380; e-mail bdd@exim.gov; internet www.exim.gov; f. 1934; independent agency since 1945; cap. subscribed by the US Treasury; finances and facilitates US external trade, guarantees payment to US foreign traders and banks, extends credit to foreign governmental and private concerns; cap. 1,000.0m. (2002); Chair. and Pres. PHILIP MERRILL.

BANKING ASSOCIATIONS

There is a State Bankers Association in each state.

American Bankers Association: 1120 Connecticut Ave, NW, Washington, DC 20036; tel. (202) 663-5000; fax (202) 828-4547; e-mail custserv@aba.com; internet www.aba.com; f. 1875; Pres. JAMES E. SMITH.

America's Community Bankers: 900 19th St, NW, Suite 400, Washington, DC 20006; tel. (202) 857-3100; fax (202) 296-8716; e-mail info@acbankers.org; f. 1992; 2,000 mems; Pres. and CEO DIANE M. CASEY.

Bank Administration Institute (BAI): 1 North Franklin St, Suite 1000, Chicago, IL 60606; tel. (312) 553-4600; fax (312) 683-2426; e-mail info@bai.org; internet www.bai.org; f. 1924; Pres. and CEO THOMAS P. JOHNSON, Jr.

Bankers' Association for Finance and Trade: 1120 Connecticut Ave, NW, 5th Floor, Washington, DC 20036; tel. (202) 663-7575; fax (202) 663-5538; e-mail baft@baft.org; internet www.baft.org; Pres. MADELEINE L. CHAMPION.

Independent Community Bankers of America: 1 Thomas Circle, NW, Suite 400, Washington, DC 20005; tel. (202) 659-8111; e-mail info@icba.org; internet www.icba.org; f. 1930; Pres. and CEO DALE L. LEIGHTY; 5,000 banks.

Mortgage Bankers Association of America: 1919 Pennsylvania Ave, Washington, DC 20006; tel. (202) 557-2700; e-mail info@mbaa.org; internet www.mbaa.org; f. 1914; Chair. ROBERT M. COUCH; 2,700 mems.

PRINCIPAL STOCK EXCHANGES

American Stock Exchange: 86 Trinity Pl., New York, NY 10006; tel. (212) 306-1000; fax (212) 306-1152; internet www.amex.com; f. 1849; Chair. SALVATORE SODANO; Pres. PETER QUICK; mems: 661 regular, 160 associate, 203 option principal, 13 limited-trading permit-holders.

Boston Stock Exchange Inc: 100 Franklin St, Boston, MA 02110; tel. (617) 235-2000; internet www.bostonstock.com; f. 1834; Chair. and CEO KENNETH R. LEIBLER; 190 mems.

Chicago Stock Exchange: 440 South LaSalle St, Chicago, IL 60605; e-mail info@chx.com; internet www.chx.com; f. 1882; Chair. LEE M. MITCHELL; CEO DAVID A. HERRON; 445 mems.

Nasdaq Stock Market Inc: 2500 Sand Hill Rd, Suite 220, Menlo Park, CA 94025; tel. (650) 233-2000; fax (650) 233-2099; internet www.nasdaq.com; f. 1998; by the American Stock Exchange and the Nat. Asscn of Securities Dealers (NASD); world-wide electronic trading market.

National Stock Exchange: 36 Fourth St, Suite 906, Cincinnati, OH 45202; tel. (513) 786-8898; e-mail info@cincinnatistock.com; internet www.cincinnatistock.com; f. 1885; fmrly Cincinnati Stock Exchange, name changed in Nov. 2003; Chair. DONALD L. CALVIN; Pres. and CEO DAVID COLKER.

New York Stock Exchange Inc: 11 Wall St, New York, NY 10005; tel. (212) 656-3000; fax (212) 656-5646; internet www.nyse.com; f. 1792; Chair. MARSHALL CARTER; CEO JOHN THAIN; 2,800 mems.

Pacific Exchange Inc: 115 Sansome St, San Francisco, CA 94104; tel. (415) 393-4000; fax (415) 393-5964; internet www.pacificex.com; f. 1882; Chair. and CEO PHILIP D. DEFEO; 552 mems.

Philadelphia Stock Exchange Inc: Stock Exchange Bldg, 1900 Market St, Philadelphia, PA 19103; tel. (215) 496-5000; fax (215) 496-5460; e-mail info@phlx.com; internet www.phlx.com; f. 1790; Chair. and CEO MEYER S. FRUCHER; 505 mems.

INSURANCE

Principal Companies

The Acacia Group: 7315 Wisconsin Ave, Bethesda, MD 20814-3202; tel. (301) 280-1000; f. 1869; Chair., Pres. and CEO CHARLES T. NASON.

Allstate Corpn: 2775 Sanders Rd, Northbrook, IL 60062-6127; tel. (708) 402-5000; fax (708) 402-2351; e-mail allstate@digiplanet.com; internet www.allstate.com; f. 1931; Chair., Pres. and CEO EDWARD LIDDY.

American National Insurance Co: 1 Moody Plaza, Galveston, TX 77550-7999; tel. (409) 763-4661; f. 1905; Chair., Pres. and CEO R. L. MOODY.

American United Life Insurance Co: 1 American Sq., POB 368, Indianapolis, IN 46206-0368; tel. (317) 285-1877; internet www.aul.com; f. 1877; Chair. and CEO JERRY D. SEMLER; Pres. R. STEPHEN RADCLIFFE.

AmerUS Life: 611 Fifth Ave, Des Moines, IA 50309; tel. (515) 283-2371; fax (515) 242-4692; f. 1896; Pres. D. T. DOAN.

THE UNITED STATES OF AMERICA

Baltimore Life Insurance Co: 10075 Red Run Blvd, Owings Mills, MD 21117-4871; tel. (410) 581-6600; fax (410) 581-6602; internet www.baltlife.com; f. 1882; Chair., Pres. and CEO L. J. PEARSON.

Bankers' Life & Casualty Co: 222 Merchandise Mart Plaza, Chicago, IL 60654; tel. (312) 396-6000; fax (312) 685-4296; internet www.bankerslife.com; f. 1880; Chair. and CEO R. T. SHAW; Pres. J. W. GARDINER.

Business Men's Assurance Co of America: BMA Tower, 700 Karnes Blvd, POB 419458, Kansas City, MO 64141; tel. (816) 753-8000; fax (816) 751-5717; e-mail kvincent@bma.com; internet www.bma.com; f. 1909; Chair. and CEO GIORGIO BALZER; Pres. R. T. RAKICH, Jr.

Central United Life Insurance Co: 4301 Sergeant Rd, Sioux City, IA 51106; tel. (712) 276 8000; Chair F. W. PURMORT, Jr.

CIGNA Group Insurance: 2 Liberty Pl., 31st Floor, Philadelphia, PA 19192; tel. (215) 761-4555; fax (215) 761-5588; internet www.cigna.com; f. 1982; Chair. and CEO H. EDWARD HANWAY.

Combined Insurance: 5050 North Broadway St, Chicago, IL 60640; tel. (773) 275-8000; fax (773) 769-8705; internet www.combined.com; f. 1949; Chair. and CEO RICHARD M. RAVIN.

Commercial Union Insurance Companies (CGU): 1 Beacon St, Boston, MA 02108-3106; tel. (617) 725-6000; fax (617) 725-6702; internet www.cgu-insurance.net; f. 1861; Pres. and CEO ROBERT C. GOWDY.

Continental American Life Insurance Co: 300 Continental Dr., Newark, DE 19713-4399; tel. (302) 454-5000; fax (302) 731-1101; f. 1907; Chair. WILLIAM G. COPELAND; Pres. and CEO JOHN T. UNIPAN.

Continental Assurance Co/Continental Casualty Co: CNA Plaza, 333 South Wabash Ave, Chicago, IL 60685-0001; tel. (312) 822-5000; fax (312) 822-6419; Chair. and CEO DENNIS H. CHOOKASZIAN.

The Continental Insurance Co: 180 Maiden Lane, New York, NY 10038-4925; tel. (212) 440-3000; fax (212) 440-3857; f. 1853; Chair. and CEO J. P. MASCOTTE.

The Equitable Companies Inc: 787 Seventh Ave, New York, NY 10019; tel. (212) 554-1234; fax (212) 262-9019; f. 1859; Chair. CLAUDE BEBEAR; Pres. and CEO JOSEPH J. MELLONE.

Farmers Insurance Exchange: 4680 Wilshire Blvd, Los Angeles, CA 90010-3807; tel. (213) 930-3200; fax (213) 932-3101; Pres. and CEO MARTIN D. FERNSTEIN.

Federal Insurance Co: POB 1615, Warren, NJ 07061; tel. (908) 903-2000; internet www.chubb.com; CEO DEAN R. O'HARE.

Fidelity and Guaranty Life Insurance Co: 1001 Fleet St, Baltimore, MD 21202; tel. (800) 445-6758; fax (410) 895-0132; internet www.fglife.com; CEO HARRY N. STOUT.

Franklin Life Insurance Co: 1 Franklin Sq., Springfield, IL 62713; tel. (217) 528-2011; fax (217) 528-9106; internet www.americangeneral.com; f. 1884; Chair., Pres. and CEO WILLIAM A. SIMPSON (acting).

General American Life Insurance Co: 700 Market St, POB 396, St Louis, MO 63166; tel. (314) 444-0605; fax (314) 444-0510; internet www.genam.com; f. 1933; Chair., Pres. and CEO KEVIN EICHNER.

Great Southern Life Insurance Co: POB 219040, Dallas, TX 75221; tel. (972) 954-8100; fax (972) 954-8148; f. 1909; Pres. and CEO GARY L. MULLER.

Guarantee Mutual Life Insurance Co: 8801 Indian Hills Dr., Omaha, NE 68114-4066; tel. (402) 390-7300; fax (402) 390-7577; f. 1901; Sr Vice-Pres. RANDY BIGGERSTAFF.

The Guardian Life Insurance Co of America: 7 Hannover Sq., New York, NY 10004; tel. (212) 598-8259; fax (212) 353-7034; internet www.glic.com; f. 1860; Pres. and CEO DENNIS J. MANNING.

Hanover Insurance Co: 100 North Parkway, Worcester, MA 01605; tel. (508) 853-7200; fax (508) 856-9092; f. 1973; Chair. JOHN F. O'BRIEN; Pres. MHAYSE SAMALYA.

Home Beneficial Life Insurance Co: POB 27572, Richmond, VA 23261; tel. (804) 358-8431; fax (804) 254-9601; f. 1899; Pres. and CEO R. W. WILTSHIRE, Jr.

Indianapolis Life Insurance Co: 2960 North Meridian St, Indianapolis, IN 46206; tel. (317) 927-6500; fax (317) 927-3326; e-mail corpcom@indianapolislife.com; internet www.indianapolislife.com; f. 1905; Pres. and CEO GARY R. McPHAIL.

Integon Corpn: 500 West Fifth St, Winston-Salem, NC 27102-3199; tel. (910) 770-2000; fax (910) 770-2122; f. 1920; Pres. and CEO PAMELA H. GODWIN.

John Hancock Life Insurance Co: POB 111, Boston, MA 02117; tel. (617) 572-6000; fax (617) 572-4539; CEO DAVID F. D'ALESSANDRO.

Kansas City Life Insurance Co: 3520 Broadway, Kansas City, MO 64141-6139; tel. (816) 753-7000; f. 1895; Chair. and Pres. JOSEPH R. BIXBY.

Liberty Life Insurance Co: POB 789, Greenville, SC 29602; tel. (864) 609-8111; fax (864) 292-4390; internet www.rblibertyinsurance.com; f. 1905; Chair. W. JAMES WESTLAKE; Pres. ROBERT E. EVANS.

Liberty Mutual Insurance Group: 175 Berkeley St, Boston, MA 02117-0140; tel. (617) 357-9500; fax (617) 350-7648; Chair. and CEO EDMUND F. KELLY.

Liberty National Life Insurance Co: POB 2612, Birmingham, AL 35202; tel. (205) 325-2722; fax (205) 325-2520; f. 1900; Pres. ANTHONY L. MCWHORTER.

Life Insurance Co of Virginia: 6610 West Broad St, Richmond, VA 23230; tel. (804) 281-6000; fax (804) 281-6929; f. 1871; CEO PAUL RUTLEDGE.

Lincoln American Life Insurance Co: 11815 North Pennsylvania St, Carmel, IN 46032; tel. (317) 817-6300; fax (317) 817-6102; f. 1957; Pres. D. F. GONGAWARE; CEO S. C. HILBERT.

Manhattan Life Insurance Co: 111 West 57th St, New York, NY 10019-2211; tel. (212) 484-9300; fax (212) 484-9541; f. 1850; Chair. and CEO D. M. FORDYCE.

Massachusetts Mutual Life Insurance Co: 1295 State St, Springfield, MA 01111-0001; tel. (413) 788-8411; fax (413) 744-6005; internet www.massmutual.com; f. 1851; Chair. THOMAS B. WHEELER; Pres. and CEO ROBERT J. O'CONNELL.

Metropolitan Life Insurance Co: 1 Madison Ave, New York, NY 10010-3681; tel. (212) 578-2211; fax (212) 689-1980; internet www.metlife.com; f. 1868; Chair., Pres. and CEO ROBERT H. BENMOSCHE.

Minnesota Mutual Life Insurance Co: 400 Robert St North, St Paul, MN 55101; tel. (651) 665-3500; fax (651) 665-4488; internet www.minnesotamutual.com; f. 1880; Chair., Pres. and CEO ROBERT L. SENKLER.

Monarch Life Insurance Co: 1 Monarch Pl., Springfield, MA 01144-1001; tel. (413) 784-2000; fax (413) 784-6271; f. 1901; CEO ROGER T. SERVISON.

Mutual Life Insurance Co of New York (MONY): 1740 Broadway, New York, NY 10019; tel. (212) 708-2000; fax (212) 708-2056; f. 1842; Chair. and CEO MICHAEL I. ROTH.

Mutual of Omaha Insurance Co: Mutual of Omaha Plaza, Omaha, NE 68175; tel. (402) 342-7600; internet mutualofomaha.com; f. 1909; operating in 50 states, the District of Columbia, the US Virgin Is, Puerto Rico and Guam; Chair. and CEO JOHN W. WEEKLY; Pres. and COO JOHN A. STURGEON.

Nationwide Mutual Insurance: 1 Nationwide Plaza, Columbus, OH 43215-2220; tel. (614) 249-7111; internet www.nationwide.com; f. 1925; CEO WILLIAM G. JURGENSEN; Chair. and COO GALEN R. BARNES.

New York Life Insurance Co: 51 Madison Ave, New York, NY 10010-1603; tel. (212) 576-7000; fax (212) 576-6794; e-mail infonyl@e-mail.com; internet www.newyorklife.com; f. 1845; Chair. and CEO SEYMOUR STERNBERG; Pres. FREDERICK J. SIEVERT.

Northwestern Mutual Life Financial Network: 720 East Wisconsin Ave, Milwaukee, WI 53202-4797; tel. (414) 271-1444; internet www.northwesternmutual.com; f. 1857; Pres. and CEO EDWARD J. ZORE.

Old Line Life Insurance Co of America: POB 401, Milwaukee, WI 53201; tel. (414) 271-2820; fax (414) 283-5556; f. 1910; Pres. and CEO JAMES A. GRIFFIN.

Pacific Life Insurance Co: 700 Newport Center Dr., Newport Beach, CA 92660-6397; tel. (949) 219-3011; fax (949) 219-7614; e-mail info@pacificlife.com; internet www.pacificlife.com; f. 1868; Chair. and CEO THOMAS C. SUTTON.

Penn Mutual Life Insurance Co: Independence Sq., Philadelphia, PA 19172; tel. (215) 956-8000; fax (215) 956-7508; internet www.pennmutual.com; f. 1847; Chair. ROBERT E. CHAPPELL.

Phoenix Companies Inc: 1 American Row, Hartford, CT 06115; tel. (860) 403-5000; e-mail webmaster@phoenixwm.com; internet www.phoenixwm.com; f. 1851; operating in all states, the District of Columbia, Puerto Rico, the US Virgin Is and Canada; Chair., Pres. and CEO DONA DAVIS YOUNG.

Principal Financial Group: 711 High St, Des Moines, IA 50392; tel. (515) 247 5111; internet www.principal.com; CEO BARRY GRISWELL.

Protective Life Insurance Co: 2801 Hwy 280 South, Birmingham, AL 35223-2488; tel. (205) 879-9230; fax (205) 868-3196; f. 1907; Chair. DRAYTON NABERS, Jr.

Provident Life and Accident Insurance Co of America: 1 Fountain Sq., Chattanooga, TN 37402-1389; tel. (423) 755-1011; fax (423) 755-7013; f. 1887; Pres. and CEO WINSTON W. WALKER.

The Prudential Insurance Co of America: 751 Broad St, Newark, NJ 07102-3714; tel. (973) 802-6000; fax (973) 802-7277; internet www.prudential.com; f. 1875; Chair. and CEO ARTHUR F. RYAN; Pres. RONALD D. BARBARO.

THE UNITED STATES OF AMERICA

Directory

SAFECO Property and Casualty Insurance Cos: Safeco Plaza, 4333 Brooklyn Ave, NE, Seattle, WA 98185-0001; tel. (206) 545-5000; fax (206) 548-7117; tel. (206) 545-5000; internet www.safeco.com; f. 1929; Chair., Pres. and CEO MICHAEL S. MCGAVICK.

Security Mutual Life Insurance Co of New York: Court House Sq., POB 1625, Binghamton, NY 13902; tel. (607) 723-3551; internet www.smlny.com; f. 1886; operating in all states; Pres. and Chair. and CEO B. W. BOYEA.

Southwestern Life Insurance Co: POB 2699, Dallas, TX 752221; tel. (972) 954-7111; fax (972) 954-7717; f. 1903; Pres. THOMAS J. BROPHY.

Standard Insurance Co: POB 711, Portland, OR 97207; tel. (503) 248-2700; fax (503) 321-7757; e-mail info@standard.com; internet www.standard.com; f. 1906; Chair. RONALD E. TIMPE.

State Farm Life Insurance Co: 1 State Farm Plaza, Bloomington, IL 61710-0001; tel. (309) 766-2311; fax (309) 766-6169; internet www.statefarm.com; f. 1929; Chair. MARVIN D. BOWER; Pres. EDWARD B. RUST, Jr.

State Life Insurance Co: 141 East Washington St, Indianapolis, IN 46204-3649; tel. (317) 681-5300; fax (317) 681-5492; internet www.statelife.com; f. 1894; Chair. and Pres. ARTHUR L. BRYANT.

Sun Life Insurance Co of America: 11601 Wilshire Blvd, Los Angeles, CA 90025; tel. (213) 312-5000; f. 1897; operating in 48 states and the District of Columbia; Chair. ELI BROAD; Pres. and CEO ROBERT P. SALTZMAN.

Transamerica Occidental Life Insurance Co: 1150 South Olive St, Los Angeles, CA 90015-2290; tel. (213) 741-7629; fax (213) 742-5280; f. 1906; Pres. RON WAGLEY; COO KAREN MCDONAL.

Travelers Property & Casualty Corporation: 1 Tower Sq., Hartford, CT 06183-0001; tel. (860) 277-0111; fax (860) 277-1970; internet www.travelers.com; f. 1893; Chair.and CEO ROBERT I. LIPP.

Unigard Security Insurance Co: 15805 NE 24th St, POB 90701, Bellevue, WA 98008; tel. (425) 641-4321; fax (425) 562-5256; internet www.unigard.com; f. 1901; Pres. and CEO PETER CHRISTEN.

Union Central Life Insurance Co: POB 40888, Cincinnati, OH 45240; tel. (513) 595-2200; fax (513) 595-2888; internet www.unioncentral.com; f. 1867; Pres and CEO JOHN H. JACOBS.

United Insurance Co of America: 1 East Wacker Dr., Chicago, IL 60601-1883; tel. (312) 661-4500; fax (312) 661-4731; f. 1955; Pres. RICHARD C. VIE; Chair. J. V. JEROME.

United States Fidelity & Guaranty Co: 100 Light St, Baltimore, MD 21202-1036; tel. (410) 547-3000; fax (410) 625-2829; f. 1896; Chair. and CEO JACK MOSELEY; Pres. PAUL SCHEEL.

UNUM Life Insurance Co of America: 2211 Congress St, Portland, ME 04122-0001; tel. (207) 770-2211; internet www.unum.com; f. 1848; Chair. and CEO JAMES F. ORR, III.

Washington National Corporation: 300 Tower Pkwy, Lincolnshire, IL 60069; tel. (847) 793-3000; fax (847) 793-3737; f. 1911; Chair. and CEO ROBERT PATIN.

Western National Life Insurance Co: 5555 San Felipe Rd, Suite 900, Houston, TX 77056; tel. (713) 888-7800; fax (713) 888-7893; CEO J. K. CLAYTON.

Western & Southern Life Insurance Co: 400 Broadway, Cincinnati, OH 45202-3341; tel. (513) 629-1800; fax (513) 629-1050; f. 1888; operating in 44 states; Chair. W. J. WILLIAMS; Pres. and CEO JOHN F. BARRETT.

Zenith National Insurance Corpn: 21255 Califer St, Woodland Hills, CA 91367; tel. (818) 894-5297; fax (818) 713-0177; Chair. and Pres. S. R. ZAX.

INSURANCE ORGANIZATIONS

American Council of Life Insurance: 101 Constitution Ave, NW, Washington, DC 20001-2133; tel. (202) 624-2000; fax (202) 624-2319; e-mail webadmin@acli.com; internet www.acli.com; f. 1976; 400 mem. cos; Pres. and CEO FRANK KEATING, Jr.

American Institute of Marine Underwriters: 14 Wall St, 21st Floor, New York, NY 10005-2145; tel. (212) 233-0550; fax (212) 227-5102; e-mail aimu@aimu.org; internet www.aimu.org; f. 1898; 105 mems; Pres. JAMES M. CRAIG.

American Insurance Association: 1130 Connecticut Ave, NW, Suite 1000, Washington, DC 20036; tel. (202) 828-7100; fax (202) 293-1219; e-mail info@aiadc.org; internet www.aiadc.org; f. 1964; 300 mems; Chair. ROBERT P. RESTREPO, Jr; Pres. ROBERT E. VAGLEY.

Casualty Actuarial Society: 1100 North Glebe Rd, Suite 600, Arlington, VA 22201; tel. (703) 276-3100; fax (703) 276-3108; e-mail office@casact.org; internet www.casact.org; f. 1914; 3,012 mems; Pres. GAIL M. ROSS.

Life Insurance Marketing and Research Association International, Inc (LIMRA Inc): 300 Day Hill Rd, Windsor, CT 06095; tel. (860) 688 3358; fax (860) 298 9555; internet www.limra.com; f. 1916; 850 mems; Chair. J. TORAN; Pres. RICHARD A. WECKER.

LOMA (Life Office Management Association): 2300 Windy Ridge Pkwy, Suite 600, Atlanta, GA 30339-8443; tel. (770) 951-1770; fax (770) 984-6417; internet www.loma.org; f. 1924; 1,250 mem. cos; Chair. HOWARD R. FRICKE; Pres. THOMAS P. DONALDSON.

National Association of Health Underwriters: 2000 North 14th St, Suite 450, Arlington, VA 22201; tel. (703) 276-0220; fax (703) 841-7797; e-mail info@nahu.org; internet www.nahu.org; Pres. THOMAS G. KAUFMAN; Pres. TREI WILD.

National Association of Life Underwriters: 1922 F St, NW, Washington, DC 20006-4387; tel. (202) 331-6000; fax (202) 331-2179; internet www.agents-online.com/nalu/naluhome.html; 108,000 mems; CEO WILLIAM V. REGAN, III.

National Association of Mutual Insurance Cos (NAMIC): 3601 Vincennes Rd, POB 68700, Indianapolis, IN 46268-0700; tel. (317) 875-5250; fax (317) 879-8408; e-mail publications@namic.org; internet www.namic.org; f. 1895; 1,400 mems; Pres. and CEO CHARLES M. CHAMNESS.

Reinsurance Association of America: 1301 Pennsylvania Ave, NW, Suite 900, Washington, DC 20004; tel. (202) 638-3690; fax (202) 638-0936; internet www.reinsurance.org; f. 1969; 35 mems; Pres. FRANKLIN W. NUTTER.

Trade and Industry

CHAMBER OF COMMERCE

Chamber of Commerce of the USA: 1615 H St, NW, Washington, DC 20062-2000; tel. (202) 659-6000; fax (202) 463-5836; f. 1912; mems: c. 215,000 cos, professional asscns and chambers of commerce; Pres. RICHARD L. LESHER.

EMPLOYERS' ORGANIZATIONS

Chemicals

American Chemistry Council (ACC): 1300 Wilson Blvd, Arlington, VA 22209; tel. (703) 741-5000; fax (703) 741-6000; e-mail helpline@americanchemistry.com; internet www.americanchemistry.com; f. 1872; c. 126 mems; Pres. and CEO JACK N. GERARD; Sec. JOHN P. CONNELLY.

American Pharmacists Association (APhA): 2215 Constitution Ave, NW, Washington, DC 20037-2985; tel. (202) 628-4410; fax (202) 783-2351; e-mail infocenter@aphanet.org; internet www.aphanet.org; f. 1852; over 50,000 mems; Exec. Vice-Pres. and CEO JOHN A. GANS.

American Plastics Council (APC): 1300 Wilson Blvd, Arlington, VA 22209; tel. (703) 741-5000; fax (703) 741-6093; internet www.americanplasticscouncil.org; 17 mem. cos; Pres. RODNEY W. LOWMAN.

Consumer Specialty Products Association (CSPA): 900 17th St, NW, Suite 300, Washington, DC 20006; tel. (202) 872-8110; fax (202) 872-8114; e-mail info@cspa.org; internet www.cspa.org; f. 1914; fmrly Chemical Specialities Manufacturers Asscn; f. 1914; over 250 mems; Pres. CHRISTOPHER CATHCART.

Drug, Chemical and Associated Technologies Association, Inc (DCAT): 1 Washington Blvd, Suite 7, Robbinsville, NJ 08691; tel. (609) 448-1000; fax (609) 448-1944; e-mail info@dcat.org; internet www.dcat.org; f. 1890; fmrly Drug, Chemical and Allied Trades Asscn; 350 mems; Exec. Dir MARGARET M. TIMONY.

The Fertilizer Institute: Union Center Plaza, 820 First St, NE, Suite 430, Washington, DC 20002; tel. (202) 962-0490; fax (202) 962-0577; e-mail webmaster@tfi.org; internet www.tfi.org; f. 1883; 300 mem. orgs; Pres. FORD B. WEST.

National Community Pharmacists Association (NCPA): 100 Daingerfield Rd, Alexandria, VA 22314; tel. (703) 683-8200; fax (703) 683-3619; e-mail info@ncpanet.org; internet www.ncpanet.org; f. 1898; fmrly Nat. Asscn of Retail Druggists; 25,000 mems; Exec. Vice-Pres. BRUCE ROBERTS.

Pharmaceutical Research & Manufacturers of America (PhRMA): 1100 15th St, NW, Suite 900, Washington, DC 20005-1797; tel. (202) 835-3400; fax (202) 785-4834; internet www.pharma.org; f. 1958; 87 mems; Pres. WILLIAM TAUZIN.

Soap and Detergent Association (SDA): 1500 K St, NW, Suite 300, Washington, DC, 20005; tel. (202) 347-2900; fax (202) 347-4110; e-mail info@cleaning101.com; internet www.cleaning101.com; f. 1926; 100 mems; Pres. and CEO ERNIE ROSENBERG.

Synthetic Organic Chemical Manufacturers' Association (SOCMA): 1850 M St, NW, Suite 700, Washington, DC 20036-5810; tel. (202) 721-4100; fax (202) 296-8120; e-mail info@socma.com; internet www.socma.com; f. 1921; 300 mem. cos; Pres. JOSEPH G. ACKER.

THE UNITED STATES OF AMERICA

Construction
(see also Electricity, and Engineering and Machinery)

American Institute of Constructors (AIC): POB 26334, Alexandria, VA 22314; tel. (703) 683-4999; fax (703) 683-5480; e-mail admin@aicnet.org; internet www.aicnet.org; f. 1971; 1,600 mems; Pres. STEVEN DESALVO.

Associated Builders and Contractors, Inc (ABC): 4250 North Fairfax Dr., 9th Floor, Arlington, VA 22203-1607; tel. (703) 812-2000; e-mail gotquestions@abc.org; internet www.abc.org; f. 1950; 20,000 mems; Pres. and CEO M. KIRK PICKEREL.

Associated General Contractors of America (AGC) (AGC of America): 333 John Carlyle St, Suite 200, Alexandria, VA 22314; tel. (703) 548-3118; fax (703) 548-3119; e-mail info@agc.org; internet www.agc.org; f. 1918; 33,000 mems; CEO STEPHEN SANDHERR.

Associated Specialty Contractors, Inc (ASC): 3 Bethesda Metro Center, Suite 1100, Bethesda, MD 20814-5372; tel. (301) 657-3110; fax (301) 215-4500; e-mail dgw@necanet.org; internet www.assoc-spec-con.org; f. 1955; 9 mem. asscns; Pres. DANIEL G. WALTER.

Building Stone Institute (BSI): 300 Park Blvd, Suite 335, Itasca, IL 60143; tel. (630) 775-9130; fax (630) 775-9134; e-mail jeff@buildingstoneinstitute.org; internet www.buildingstoneinstitute.org; f. 1919; 400 mems; Pres. JEFF BUCZKIEWICZ.

Construction Specifications Institute (CSI): 99 Canal Center Plaza, Suite 300, Alexandria, VA 22314; tel. (703) 684-0300; fax (703) 684-0465; e-mail csi@csinet.org; internet www.csinet.org; f. 1948; 17,000 mems; Exec. Dir KARL BORGSTROM.

Mechanical Contractors Association of America, Inc: 1385 Piccard Dr., Rockville, MD 20850-4340; tel. (301) 869-5800; fax (301) 990-9690; e-mail info@mcaa.org; internet www.mcaa.org; f. 1889; 2,200 mems; Exec. Vice-Pres. JOHN R. GENTILLE.

National Association of Home Builders of the US (NAHB): 1201 15th St, NW, Washington, DC 20005; tel. (202) 266-8200; fax (202) 266-8400; internet www.nahb.org; f. 1942; 800 mem. asscns; 220,000 mems; Exec. Vice-Pres. and CEO JERRY HOWARD.

National Association of Plumbing-Heating-Cooling Contractors (PHCC): 180 South Washington St, POB 6808, Falls Church, VA 22040; tel. (703) 237-8100; fax (703) 237-7442; e-mail naphcc@naphcc.org; internet www.naphcc.org; f. 1883; 3,700 mems; CEO DWIGHT L. CASEY.

National Ready-Mixed Concrete Association (NRMCA): 900 Spring St, Silver Spring, MD 20910; tel. (301) 587-1400; fax (301) 585-4219; e-mail info@nrmca.org; internet www.nrmca.org; f. 1930; 1,000 mems; Pres. ROBERT A. GARBINI.

National Tile Contractors Association (NTCA): POB 13629, Jackson, MS 39236; tel. (601) 939-2071; fax (601) 932-6117; internet www.tile-assn.com; f. 1947; Exec. Dir BART BETTIGA.

Tile Council of America Inc (TCA): 100 Clemson Research Blvd, Anderson, SC 29625; tel. (864) 646-8453; fax (864) 646-2821; e-mail literature@tileusa.com; internet www.tileusa.com; f. 1945; 130 mems; Exec. Dir ROBERT E. DANIELS.

US Green Building Council (USGBC): 1015 18th St, NW, Suite 508, Washington, DC 20036; tel. (202) 828-7422; fax (202) 828-5110; e-mail info@usgbc.org; internet www.usgbc.org; Pres. and CEO S. RICHARD FEDRIZZI.

Electricity
(see also Construction, Electronics and Technology, Engineering and Machinery, and Trade and Industry—Utilities)

Edison Electric Institute (EEI): 701 Pennsylvania Ave, NW, Washington, DC 20004-2696; tel. (202) 508-5000; e-mail feedback@eei.org; internet www.eei.org; f. 1933; mems: 190 investor-owned electric utility cos, 60 int. affiliates; mems generate 70% of electricity produced by US utilities and supply 70% of US customers; Pres. THOMAS R. KUHN.

National Association of Electrical Distributors (NAED): 1100 Corporate Sq. Dr., Suite 100, St Louis, MO 63132; tel. (314) 991-9000; fax (314) 991-3060; e-mail info@naed.org; internet www.naed.org; f. 1908; 2,900 mems; Pres. TOM NABER.

National Electrical Contractors Association (NECA): 3 Bethesda Metro Center, Suite 1100, Bethesda, MD 20814-5372; tel. (301) 657-3110; fax (301) 215-4500; internet www.necanet.org; f. 1901; 4,200 mems; CEO JOHN M. GRAU.

National Electrical Manufacturers Association (NEMA): 1300 North 17th St, Suite 1847, Rosslyn, VA 22209; tel. (703) 841-3200; fax (703) 841-5900; e-mail webmaster@nema.org; internet www.nema.org; f. 1926; 450 mem. cos; Pres. MALCOLM E. O'HAGAN.

Electronics and Technology

AeA: 5201 Great America Pkwy, Suite 520, Santa Clara, CA 95054; tel. (408) 987-4200; fax (408) 970-8565; e-mail csc@aeanet.org; internet www.aeanet.org; f. 1943; fmrly American Electronics Asscn; 3,000 mem. cos; Pres. and CEO WILLIAM T. ARCHEY.

Electronic Industries Alliance: 2500 Wilson Blvd, Arlington, VA 22201-3834; tel. (703) 907-7500; fax (703) 907-7501; internet www.eia.org; f. 1924; over 2,100 mems; Pres. DAVE MCCURDY.

Institute of Electrical and Electronics Engineers, Inc (IEEE): 445 Hoes Lane, Piscataway, NJ 08854-1331; tel. (732) 981-0060; fax (732) 981-1721; e-mail webmaster@ieee.org; internet www.ieee.org; f. 1963; 365,000 mems world-wide; Pres. IEEE-USA Dr GERARD A. ALPHONSE.

IPC (Association Connecting Electronics Industries): 3000 Lakeside Dr., Suite 3095, Bannockburn, IL 60015; tel. (847) 615-7100; fax (847) 615-7105; e-mail orderipc@ipc.org; internet www.ipc.org; f. 1957; Pres. DENNY MCGUIRK.

Telecommunications Industry Association (TIA): 2500 Wilson Blvd, Suite 300, Arlington, VA 22201; tel. (703) 907-7700; fax (703) 907-7727; e-mail tia@tiaonline.org; internet www.tiaonline.org; f. 1988; Pres. MATTHEW J. FLANIGAN.

Engineering and Machinery
(see also Electricity and Construction)

Air-Conditioning and Refrigeration Institute (ARI): 4301 North Fairfax Dr., Suite 200, Arlington, VA 22203; tel. (703) 524-8800; fax (703) 528-3816; e-mail ari@ari.org; internet www.ari.org; f. 1953; 220 mems; Pres. WILLIAM G. SUTTON.

American Council of Engineering Companies (ACEC): 1015 15th St, NW, 8th Floor, Washington, DC 20005-2605; tel. (202) 347-7474; fax (202) 898-0068; e-mail acec@acec.org; internet www.acec.org; f. 1905; 5,500 mem. cos; Pres. DAVID A. RAYMOND.

American Institute of Chemical Engineers (AIChE): 3 Park Ave, New York, NY 10016-5991; tel. (212) 591-8100; fax (212) 591-8888; e-mail xpress@aiche.org; internet www.aiche.org; f. 1908; over 6,000 mems; Exec. Dir JOHN A. SOFRANKO.

American Institute of Mining, Metallurgical and Petroleum Engineers, Inc: 8307 Shaffer Pkwy, Littleton, CO 80127-4012; tel. (303) 948-4256; fax (303) 948-4260; e-mail aime@aimehq.org; internet www.aimehq.org; f. 1871; five constituent socs representing 90,000 mems; Exec. Dir J. RICK ROLATER.

American Society of Civil Engineers (ASCE): 1801 Alexander Bell Dr., Reston, VA 20191-4400; tel. (703) 295-6000; fax (703) 295-6222; e-mail webmaster@asce.org; internet www.asce.org; f. 1852; 137,000 mems; Exec. Dir PATRICK J. NATALE.

American Society of Heating, Refrigerating and Air Conditioning Engineers (ASHRAE): 1791 Tullie Circle, NE, Atlanta, GA 30329; tel. (404) 636-8400; fax (404) 321-5478; e-mail ashrae@ashrae.org; internet www.ashrae.org; f. 1894; 50,000 mems; Exec. Vice-Pres. JEFF LITTLETON.

American Society of Naval Engineers, Inc: 1452 Duke St, Alexandria, VA 22314-3458; tel. (703) 836-6727; fax (703) 836-7491; e-mail asnehq@navalengineers; internet www.navalengineers.org; f. 1888; 6,000 mems; Exec. Dir Capt. (retd) DENNIS K. KRUSE.

Association of Coastal Engineers (ACE): c/o Patricia Ehrman, 2770 North West 43rd St, Suite B, Applied Technology and Management Inc, Gainesville, FL 32606; e-mail linn@coastal.ufl.edu; internet www.coastalengineers.org; f. 1999; Pres. BILLY L. EDGE.

Association of Home Appliance Manufacturers (AHAM): 1111 19th St, NW, Suite 402, Washington, DC 20036; tel. (202) 872-5955; fax (202) 872-9354; e-mail jmcguire@aham.org; internet www.aham.org; f. 1915; Pres. JOSEPH M. MCGUIRE.

AMT (The Association for Manufacturing Technology): 7901 Westpark Dr., McLean, VA 22102-4206; tel. (703) 893-2900; fax (703) 893-1151; e-mail amt@amtonline.org; internet www.amtonline.org; f. 1902; 370 mems; Pres. R. J. WESKAMP.

ASME International (American Society of Mechanical Engineers): 3 Park Ave, New York, NY 10016-5990; tel. (212) 591-722; fax (212) 591-7674; e-mail infocentrale@asme.org; f. 1880; 120,000 mems; Exec. Dir VIRGIL R. CARTER.

Manufacturers Alliance/MAPI, Inc (Manufacturers Alliance for Productivity and Innovation): 1600 Wilson Blvd, Suite 1100, Arlington, VA 22209-2411; tel. (703) 841-9000; fax (703) 841-9514; e-mail info@mapi.net; internet www.mapi.net; f. 1933; 500 cos; Pres. and CEO THOMAS J. DUESTERBERG.

Petroleum Equipment Institute (PEI): POB 2380, Tulsa, OK 74101-2380; tel. (918) 494-9696; fax (918) 491-9895; e-mail info@pei.org; internet www.pei.org; f. 1951; 1,600 mems; Exec. Vice-Pres. ROBERT N. RENKES.

SAE, International (Society of Automotive Engineers): 400 Commonwealth Dr., Warrendale, PA 15096-0001; tel. (724) 776-4841; fax (724) 772-7079; e-mail customerservice@sae.org; internet www.sae.org; f. 1905; 75,000 mems; Exec. Vice-Pres. RAYMOND A. MORRIS.

THE UNITED STATES OF AMERICA

Society of Naval Architects and Marine Engineers (SNAME): 601 Pavonia Ave, Suite 400, Jersey City, NJ 07306-2907; tel. (201) 798-4800; fax (201) 798-4975; e-mail ccali-poutre@sname.org; internet www.sname.org; f. 1893; over 10,000 mems; Exec. Dir PHILIP B. KIMBALL.

United Engineering Foundation: 3 Park Ave, 27th Floor, New York, NY 10016-5902; tel. (212) 591-7829; fax (212) 591-7441; e-mail engfnd@aol.com; internet www.engfnd.org; f. 1914; umbrella org. of engineering socs, incl. ASME International, the Institute of Electrical and Electronics Engineers and the American Institute of Chemical Engineers; Pres. SIDNEY F. SPAKE.

Food

American Bakers Association (ABA): 1350 I St, NW, Suite 1290, Washington, DC 20005-3300; tel. (202) 789-0300; fax (202) 898-1164; e-mail info@americanbakers.org; internet www.americanbakers.org; f. 1897; Pres. and CEO PAUL C. ABENANTE.

American Beverage Association (ABA): 1101 16th St, NW, Washington, DC 20036-4803; tel. (202) 463-6732; fax (202) 463-5349; e-mail info@ameribev.org; internet www.ameribev.org; f. 1919; fmrly Nat. Soft Drink Asscn; 1,700 mems; Pres. and CEO SUSAN K. NEELY.

American Farm Bureau Federation (FB): 600 Maryland Ave, SW, Suite 800, Washington, DC 20024; tel. (202) 406-3600; fax (202) 406-3604; e-mail webmaster@fb.org; internet www.fb.com; f. 1919; 50 mem. states and Puerto Rico; Pres. BOB STALLMAN; Chief Admin. Officer RICHARD NEWPHER.

American Meat Institute: 1150 Connecticut Ave, NW, 12th Floor, Washington, DC 20036; tel. (202) 857-4200; fax (202) 857-4300; e-mail webmaster@meatami.com; internet www.meatami.com; f. 1906; 1,060 mems; Pres. and CEO J. PATRICK BOYLE.

DFA of California: 710 Striker Ave, Sacramento, CA 95834; tel. (916) 561-5900; fax (916) 561-5906; e-mail richn@dfaofca.com; internet www.dfaofca.com; f. 1908; dried fruit and nut asscn; 42 mems; Pres. and CEO RICHARD W. NOVY.

Distilled Spirits Council of the US, Inc (DISCUS): 1250 I St, NW, Suite 400, Washington, DC 20005; tel. (202) 628-3544; internet www.discus.health.org; f. 1973; 12 active mems and 23 affiliates; Pres. and CEO Dr. PETER H. CRESSY.

Food Marketing Institute (FMI): 655 15th St, NW, Suite 700, Washington, DC 20005; tel. (202) 452-8444; fax (202) 429-4519; e-mail fmi@fmi.org; internet www.fmi.org; f. 1977; 1,500 mems; Pres. TIMOTHY M. HAMMONDS.

Foodservice Sales and Marketing Association (FSMA): 9192 Red Branch Rd, Suite 200, Columbia, MD 21045; tel. (410) 715-6672; fax (410) 997-9387; e-mail info@fsmaonline.com; internet www.fsmaonline.com; f. 2003; Pres. and CEO RICK ABRAHAM.

Grocery Manufacturers of America, Inc (GMA): 2401 Pennsylvania Ave, NW, 2nd Floor, Washington, DC 20037; tel. (202) 337-9400; fax (202) 337-4508; e-mail info@gmabrands.com; internet www.gmabrands.com; f. 1908; over 140 mems; Pres. and CEO C. MANLY MOLPUS.

International Foodservice Distributors Association (IFDA): 201 Park Washington Court, Falls Church, VA 22046; tel. (703) 532-9400; fax (703) 538-4673; internet www.ifdaonline.org; f. 1906; over 130 mems; Pres. and CEO MARK ALLEN.

National Association of Wheat Growers (NAWG): 412 Second St, NE, Suite 300, Washington, DC 20002-4993; tel. (202) 547-7800; fax (202) 546-2638; e-mail wheatworld@wheatworld.org; internet www.wheatworld.org; f. 1950; 22 mem. states; CEO DAREN COPPOCK.

National Beer Wholesalers Association (NBWA): 1101 King St, Suite 600, Alexandria, VA 22314-2944; tel. (703) 683-4300; fax (703) 683-8965; e-mail info@nbwa.org; internet www.nbwa.org; f. 1938; 2,200 mem. cos; Pres. DAVID K. REHR.

National Cattlemen's Beef Association (NCBA): 9110 East Nichols Ave, Suite 300, Centennial, CO 80112; tel. (303) 694-0305; e-mail tstokes@beef.org; internet www.beefusa.org; f. 1898; 33,000 mems, plus 45 cattle asscns and 40 breed and industry asscns; Pres. MIKE JOHN; CEO TERRY L. STOKES.

National Confectioners Association of the US (NCA): 8320 Old Courthouse Rd, Suite 300, Vienna, VA 22182; tel. (703) 790-5750; fax (703) 790-5752; e-mail info@candyusa.org; internet www.candyusa.org; f. 1884; includes Chocolate Manufacturers Asscn; 340 mems; Pres. LAWRENCE T. GRAHAM.

National Dairy Council (NDC): 10255 West Higgins Rd, Suite 900, Rosemount, IL 60018; tel. (847) 803-2000; fax (847) 803-2077; e-mail ndc@dairyinformation.com; internet www.nationaldairycouncil.org; f. 1915; 600 mems; Pres. M. F. BRINK.

National Farmers (NFO): 528 Billy Sunday Rd, Ames, IA 50010; tel. 800-247-2110; e-mail nfo@nfo.org; internet www.nfo.org; f. 1955; c. 35,000 mems; Pres. PAUL OLSON.

National Farmers Union (NFU): 5619 DTC Pkwy, Suite 300, Greenwood Village, CO 80011-3136; tel. (303) 337-5500; fax (303) 771-1770; e-mail dave.frederickson@nfu.org; internet www.nfu.org; f. 1902; 300,000 mems; Pres. DAVID J. FREDERICKSON.

National Frozen and Refrigerated Foods Association (NFRA): 4755 Linglestown Rd, Suite 300, POB 6069, Harrisburg, PA 17112; tel. (717) 657-8601; fax (717) 657-9862; e-mail info@nfraweb.org; internet www.nfraweb.org; f. 1945; 400 mem. cos; Pres. and CEO NEVIN B. MONTGOMERY.

National Grain Trade Council (NGTC): 1300 L St, NW, Suite 1020, Washington, DC 20005; tel. (202) 842-0400; fax (202) 789-7223; e-mail info@ngtc.org; internet www.ngtc.org; f. 1930; 64 mems; Pres. JULIA J. KINNAIRD.

National Grocers Association (NGA): 1005 North Glebe Rd, Suite 250, Arlington, VA 22201-5758; tel. (703) 516 0700; fax (703) 516 0115; e-mail info@nationalgrocers.org; internet www.nationalgrocers.org; f. 1982; 3,000 mems; Pres and CEO THOMAS K. ZAUCHA.

National Meat Association (NMA): (NMA East) 1400 16th St, NW, Suite 400, Washington, DC 20036; tel. (202) 667-2108; NMA West: 1970 Broadway, Suite 825, Oakland, CA 94612; tel. (510) 763-1533; fax (510) 763-6186; e-mail staff@nmaonline.org; internet www.nmaonline.org; f. 1946; over 600 mems; Exec. Dir ROSEMARY MUCKLOW.

North American Millers' Association (NAMA): 600 Maryland Ave, SW, Suite 450, Washington, DC 20024; tel. (202) 484-2200; fax (202) 488-7416; e-mail generalinfo@namamillers.org; internet www.namamillers.org; f. 1998; 48 mems and 28 assoc. mems; Pres. BETSY FAGA.

United Fresh Fruit & Vegetable Association: 1901 Pennsylvania Ave, NW, Suite 1100, Washington, DC 20006; tel. (202) 303-3400; fax (202) 303-3433; e-mail united@uffva.org; internet www.uffva.org; f. 1904; 1,300 mems; Pres. and CEO THOMAS E. STENZEL.

US Dairy Export Council (USDEC): 2101 Wilson Blvd, Suite 400, Arlington, VA 22201-3061; tel. (703) 528-3049; fax (703) 528-3705; e-mail info@usdec.org; internet www.usdec.org; f. 1995; 70 mems; Pres. THOMAS M. SUBER.

Wine and Spirits Wholesalers of America, Inc (WSWA): 805 15th St, NW, Suite 430, Washington, DC 20005; tel. (202) 371-9792; fax (202) 789-2405; e-mail juanita.duggan@wswa.org; internet www.wswa.org; f. 1943; c. 450 mem. cos; Pres. and CEO JUANITA DUGGAN.

Iron and Steel

American Hardware Manufacturers Association (AHMA): 801 North Plaza Dr., Schaumburg, IL 60173-4977; tel. (847) 605-1025; fax (847) 605-1093; e-mail info@ahma.org; internet www.ahma.org; f. 1901; 1,000 mems; Pres. and CEO TIMOTHY S. FARRELL.

American Iron and Steel Institute (AISI): 1140 Connecticut Ave, NW, Suite 705, Washington, DC 20036; tel. (202) 452-7100; e-mail webmaster@steel.org; internet www.steel.org; f. 1908; 31 mem. cos and 118 assoc. and affiliated mems; Pres. and CEO ANDREW G. SHARKEY, III.

American Institute of Steel Construction (AISC): 1 East Wacker Dr., Suite 700, Chicago, IL 60601-1802; tel. (312) 670-2400; fax (312) 670-5403; internet www.aisc.org; f. 1921; Pres. H. LOUIS GURTHET.

Steel Founders' Society of America (SFSA): 780 McArdle Dr., Unit G, Crystal Lake, IL 60014; tel. (815) 455-8240; fax (815) 455-8241; e-mail monroe@sfsa.org; internet www.sfsa.org; f. 1902; 80 mems; Exec. Vice-Pres. RAYMOND W. MONROE.

Steel Manufacturers Association (SMA): 1150 Connecticut Ave, NW, Suite 715, Washington, DC 20036; tel. (202) 296-1515; fax (202) 296-2506; e-mail stuart@steelnet.org; internet www.steelnet.org; 42 mem. cos and 104 mems world-wide; Pres. THOMAS A. DANJCZEK.

Leather
(see also Textiles)

Leather Apparel Association (LAA): 19 West 21st St, Suite 403, New York, NY 10010; tel. (212) 727-1210; fax (212) 727-1218; e-mail info@leatherassociation.com; internet www.leatherassociation.com; f. 1990; over 100 mems; Pres. MORRIS GOLDFARB.

Leather Industries of America (LIA): 3050 K St, NW, Suite 400, Washington, DC 20007; tel. (202) 342-8497; fax (202) 342-8583; e-mail info@leatherusa.com; internet www.leatherusa.com; f. 1917; 80 mems; Pres. JOHN WITTENBORN.

Travel Goods Association (TGA): 5 Vaughn Dr., Suite 105, Princeton, NJ 08640; tel. (609) 720-1200; fax (609) 720-0620; e-mail info@travel-goods.org; internet www.travel-goods.org; f. 1938; 400 mems; Pres. MICHELE MARINI PITTENGER.

THE UNITED STATES OF AMERICA

Lumber
(see also Paper)

American Forest and Paper Association (AF&PA): 1111 19th St, NW, Suite 800, Washington, DC 20036; tel. (202) 463-2700; fax (202) 463-2771; e-mail info@afandpa.org; internet www.afandpa.org; f. 1993; over 250 mems and trade asscns; Pres. W. HENSON MOORE.

APA–The Engineered Wood Association: 7011 South 19th St, Tacoma, WA 98466; tel. (253) 565-6600; fax (253) 565-7265; e-mail help@apawood.org; internet www.apawood.org; f. 1933; 109 mems; Pres. DAVID L. ROGOWAY.

Forest Resources Association Inc: 600 Jefferson Plaza, Suite 350, Rockville, MD 20852-1150; tel. (301) 838-9385; fax (301) 838-9481; e-mail rlewis@forestresources.org; internet www.forestresources.org; f. 1934; 1,300 mems; Pres. R. LEWIS.

National Lumber and Building Material Dealers Association (NLBMDA): 900 Second St, NE, Suite 205, Washington, DC 20002; tel. (202) 547-2230; fax (202) 547-7640; e-mail industrynews@dealer.org; internet www.dealer.org; f. 1915; 20 mem. orgs, representing 8,000 cos; Pres. SHAWN D. CONRAD.

National Wooden Pallet and Container Association (NWPCA): 329 South Patrick St, Alexandria, VA 22314-3501; tel. (703) 519-6104; fax (703) 519-4720; e-mail bscholnick@palletcentral.com; internet www.nwpca.com; f. 1916; Pres. BRUCE N. SCHOLNICK.

North American Wholesale Lumber Association (NAWLA): 3601 Algonquin Rd, Suite 400, Rolling Meadows, IL 60008; tel. (847) 870-7470; fax (847) 870-0201; e-mail info@lumber.org; internet www.lumber.org; f. 1893; 650 mems; Pres. and CEO NICHOLAS R. KENT.

Southern Forest Products Association: 2900 Indiana Ave, Kenner, LA 70065-4605; tel. (504) 443-4464; fax (504) 443-6612; e-mail mail@spfa.org; internet www.sfpa.org; f. 1915; c. 220 mem. orgs; Pres. LIONEL J. LANDRY.

Western Forest Industries Association: 14780 South West Osprey Dr., Suite 270, Beaverton, OR 97007-8424; f. 1947; 125 mems; Pres. DAVID A. FORD.

Western Wood Products Association (WWPA): Yeon Bldg, 522 South West Fifth Ave, Suite 500, Portland, OR 97204-2122; tel. (503) 224-3930; fax (503) 224-3934; e-mail info@wwpa.org; internet www.wwpa.org; f. 1964; 250 mem. orgs; Pres. and CEO MICHAEL R. O'HALLORAN.

Wood Products Manufacturers Association (WPMA): 175 State Rd East, Westminster, MA 01473; tel. (978) 874-5445; fax (978) 874-9946; e-mail woodprod@wpma.org; internet www.wpma.org; f. 1929; 664 mems; Exec. Dir PHILIP BIBEAU.

Metals and Mining
(see also Iron and Steel)

Aluminum Association, Inc: 1525 Wilson Blvd, Suite 600, Arlington, VA 22209; tel. (703) 358-2960; fax (703) 358-2961; e-mail lbenton@aluminum.org; internet www.aluminum.org; f. 1933; 82 mems; Pres. J. STEPHEN LARKIN.

American Zinc Association (AZA): 2025 M St, NW, Suite 800, Washington, DC 20036; tel. (202) 367-1151; fax (202) 367-2232; e-mail zincinfo@zinc.org; internet www.zinc.org; 17 mems; Exec. Dir GEORGE VARY.

ASM International: 9639 Kinsman Rd, Materials Park, OH 44073-0002; tel. (440) 338-5151; fax (440) 338-4634; e-mail customerservice@asminternational.org; internet www.asm-intl.org; f. 1913; fmrly the American Society for Materials; 40,000 mems world-wide; Man. Dir STANLEY C. THEOBALD.

Copper and Brass Fabricators Council, Inc: 1050 17th St, NW, Suite 440, Washington, DC 20036-5518; tel. (202) 833-8575; fax (202) 331-8267; e-mail copbrass@aol.com; f. 1964; 20 mem. cos; Pres. JOSEPH L. MAYER.

Copper Development Association, Inc (CDA): 260 Madison Ave, New York, NY 10016; tel. (212) 251-7200; fax (212) 251-7234; e-mail questions@cda.copper.org; internet www.copper.org; f. 1962; 65 mems; Pres. and CEO ANDREW G. KIRETA, Sr.

Fabricators and Manufacturers Association, International (FMA): 833 Featherstone Rd, Rockford, IL 61107; tel. (815) 399-8775; fax (815) 484-7701; e-mail info@fmanet.org; internet www.fmanet.org; f. 1970; 1,400 mems; Pres. and CEO GERALD M. SHANKEL.

Manufacturing Jewelers and Suppliers of America, Inc (MJSA): 45 Royal Little Dr., Providence, RI 02904; tel. (401) 274-3840; fax (401) 274-0265; e-mail mjsa@mjsainc.com; internet www.mjsainc.com; f. 1903; 1,800 mems; Pres. and CEO JAMES F. MARQUART.

Metal Powder Industries Federation (MPIF): 105 College Rd East, 1st Floor, Princeton, NJ 08540-6692; tel. (609) 452-7700; fax (609) 987-8523; e-mail info@mpif.org; internet www.mpif.org; f. 1944; 300 corporate mems; Exec. Dir and CEO C. JAMES TROMBINO.

Mining and Metallurgical Society of America (MMSA): 476 Wilson Ave, Novato, CA 94947-4236; tel. (415) 897-1380; e-mail info@mmsa.net; internet www.mmsa.net; f. 1908; 340 mems; Exec. Dir ALAN K. BURTON.

National Mining Association (NMA): 101 Constitution Ave, NW, Suite 500 East, Washington, DC 20001-2133; tel. (202) 463-2600; fax (202) 463-2666; e-mail craulston@nma.org; internet www.nma.org; f. 1995; over 325 mem. cos; Pres. and CEO KRAIG R. NASSZ.

Northwest Mining Association (NWMA): 10 North Post St, Suite 220, Spokane, WA 99201; tel. (509) 624-1158; fax (509) 623-1241; e-mail nwma@nwma.org; internet www.nwma.org; f. 1895; 1,500 mems; Exec. Dir LAURA E. SKAER.

The Silver Institute: 1200 G St, NW, Suite 800, Washington, DC 20005; tel. (202) 835-0185; fax (202) 835-0155; e-mail info@silverinstitute.org; internet www.silverinstitute.org; f. 1971; 53 mems; Exec. Dir MICHAEL DiRENZO.

Paper
(see also Lumber)

Association of Independent Corrugated Converters (AICC): 113 South West St, Alexandria, VA 22313; tel. (703) 836-2422; fax (703) 836-2795; e-mail info@aiccbox.org; internet www.aiccbox.org; mems: 724 box-makers, 382 suppliers; Pres. A. STEVEN YOUNG.

National Paper Box Association (NPA): 113 South West St, 3rd Floor, Alexandria, VA 22314; tel. (703) 684-2212; fax (703) 683-6920; e-mail npahq@paperbox.org; internet www.paperbox.org; f. 1918; Exec. Vice-Pres. SCOTT MILLER.

NPTA Alliance: 500 Bi-County Blvd, Suite 200E, Farmingdale, NY 11735; tel. (631) 777-2223; fax (631) 777-2224; e-mail joann@gonpta.com; internet www.gonpta.com; f. 1903; fmrly Nat. Paper Trade Asscn, Inc; 2,000 mems; Pres. WILLIAM FROHLICH.

Paperboard Packaging Council (PPC): 201 North Union St, Suite 220, Alexandria, VA 22314; tel. (703) 836-3300; fax (703) 836-3290; e-mail paperboardpackaging@ppcnet.org; internet www.ppcnet.org; f. 1967; Pres. JEROME T. VAN DE WATER.

Petroleum and Fuel

American Association of Petroleum Geologists (AAPG): POB 979, Tulsa, OK 74101-0979; tel. (918) 584-2555; fax (918) 560-2694; e-mail pjfginc@aol.com; internet www.aapg.org; f. 1917; 30,000 mems world-wide; Exec. Dir RICHARD D. FRITZ.

American Association of Petroleum Landmen (AAPL): 4100 Fossil Creek Blvd, Fort Worth, TX 76137-2791; tel. (817) 847-7700; fax (817) 847-7704; e-mail aashton@landman.org; internet www.landman.org; f. 1955; 8,500 mems; Exec. Vice-Pres. ROBIN FORTE.

American Petroleum Institute (API): 1220 L St NW, Washington, DC 20005-4070; tel. (202) 682-8000; internet www.api.org; f. 1919; 400 corporate mems; Pres. and CEO RED CAVANEY.

Association of Diesel Specialists (ADS): 10 Laboratory Dr., POB 13966, Research Triangle Park, NC 27709-3966; tel. (919) 406-8804; fax (919) 406-1306; e-mail info@diesel.org; internet www.diesel.org; more than 700 corporate and individual mems; Exec. Dir DAVID FEHLING.

Coal Exporters' Association of the US, Inc: 1130 17th St, NW, Washington, DC 20036; tel. (202) 463-2639; fax (202) 833-9636; e-mail cea@nma.org; f. 1945; 35 mems; Exec. Dir MOYA PHELLEPS.

Independent Petroleum Association of America (IPAA): 1201 15th St, NW, Suite 300, Washington, DC 20005; tel. (202) 857-4722; fax (202) 857-4799; e-mail rcarter@ipaa.org; internet www.ipaa.org; f. 1929; 6,000 mems; Pres. BARRY RUSSELL.

National Ocean Industries Association (NOIA): 1120 G St, NW, Suite 900, Washington, DC 20005; tel. (202) 347-6900; fax (202) 347-8650; e-mail noia@noia.org; internet www.noia.org; f. 1972; over 300 mem. cos; Pres. TOM FRY.

National Petrochemical and Refiners' Association (NPRA): 1899 L St, NW, Suite 1000, Washington, DC 20036-3896; tel. (202) 457-0480; fax (202) 457-0486; e-mail info@npradc.org; internet www.npradc.org; f. 1902; over 450 mems; Pres. BOB SLAUGHTER.

Petroleum Marketers Association of America (PMAA): 1901 North Fort Myer Dr., Suite 500, Arlington, VA 22209-1604; tel. (703) 351-8000; fax (703) 351-9160; e-mail info@pmaa.org; internet www.pmaa.org; f. 1943; 43 mem. asscns; Pres. DANIEL F. GILLIGAN.

Western States Petroleum Association (WSPA): 1415 L St, Suite 600, Sacramento, CA 95814; tel. (916) 444-9981; fax (916) 444-5745; internet www.wspa.org; f. 1907; 30 mems; Pres. JOSEPH SPARANO.

Printing and Publishing
(see also Publishers)

Association for the Suppliers of Printing, Publishing and Converting Technologies (NPES): 1899 Preston White Dr.,

THE UNITED STATES OF AMERICA

Reston, VA 22091-4367; tel. (703) 264-7200; fax (703) 620-0994; e-mail npes@npes.org; internet www.npes.org; f. 1933; over 400 mem. cos; Pres. RALPH J. NAPPI.

Binding Industries Association International (BIA): Printing Industries of America, 100 Daingerfield Rd, 4th Floor, Alexandria, VA 22314; tel. (703) 519-8137; fax (312) 704-5025; e-mail bia1@ixnetcom.com; internet www.bindingindustries.org; f. 1955; 340 mems; Exec. Dir BETH PARROTT.

National Association for Printing Leadership (NAPL): 75 West Century Rd, Paramus, NJ 07652-1408; tel. (201) 634-9600; e-mail information@napl.org; internet www.napl.org; f. 1933; 150 assoc. mems; Pres. and CEO JOSEPH P. TRUNCALE.

National Association of Printing Ink Manufacturers (NAPIM): 581 Main St, Woodbridge, NJ 07095; tel. (732) 855-1525; fax (732) 855-1838; e-mail napim@napim.org; internet www.napim.org; Exec. Dir JAMES E. COLEMAN.

Printing Industries of America, Inc (PIA): 200 Deer Run Rd, Sewickley, PA 15143; tel. (412) 741-6860; fax (412) 741-2311; e-mail piagatf@piagatf.org; internet www.gain.net; f. 1887; 12,000 mems; CEO MICHAEL MAKIN.

Public Utilities
(see also Trade and Industry—Utilities)

American Public Power Association (APPA): 2301 M St, NW, 3rd Floor, Washington, DC 20037-1484; tel. (202) 467-2900; fax (202) 467-2910; e-mail mrufe@appanet.org; internet www.appanet.org; f. 1940; over 2,000 mem. utilities; Pres. and CEO ALAN RICHARDSON.

American Public Works Association (APWA): 2345 Grand Blvd, Suite 500, Kansas City, MO 64108-2641; tel. (816) 472-6100; fax (816) 472-1610; e-mail apwa@apwa.net; internet www.apwa.net; f. 1937; 26,000 mems; Exec. Dir PETER B. KING.

Rubber

Rubber Manufacturers Association (RMA): 1400 K St, NW, Suite 900, Washington, DC 20005-2043; tel. (202) 682-4800; e-mail info@rma.org; internet www.rma.org; f. 1915; over 100 mem. cos; Pres. and CEO DONALD B. SHEA.

Rubber Trade Association of North America, Inc: 220 Maple Ave, POB 196, Rockville Centre, NY 11571-0196; tel. (516) 536-7228; fax (516) 536-2251; f. 1914; 39 mems; Sec. F. B. FINLEY.

Stone, Clay and Glass Products

Glass Association of North America (GANA): 2045 South West Wanamaker Dr., Suite A, Topeka, KS 66614-5321; tel. (785) 271-0208; fax (785) 271-0166; e-mail gana@glasswebsite.com; internet www.glasswebsite.com; f. 1994; 208 mems; Exec. Vice-Pres. STANLEY L. SMITH.

National Glass Association (NGA): 8200 Greensboro Dr., Suite 302, McLean, VA 22102-3881; tel. (703) 342-5642; fax (703) 442-0630; e-mail administration@glass.org; internet www.glass.org; f. 1948; c. 4,400 mem. cos; Pres. and CEO PHILIP J. JAMES.

National Stone, Sand and Gravel Association (NSSGA): 1605 King St, Alexandria, VA 22314; tel. (703) 525-8788; e-mail info@nssga.org; internet www.nssga.org; f. 2000 by merger of Nat. Aggregates Asscn and Nat. Stone Asscn; 950 mems; Pres. and CEO JENNIFER JOY WILSON.

Textiles

American Apparel and Footwear Association (AAFA): 1601 North Kent St, Suite 1200, Arlington, VA 22209; tel. (703) 524-2262; fax (703) 522-6741; e-mail mrust@apparelandfootwear.org; internet www.apparelandfootwear.org; f. 2000; Pres. and CEO KEVIN M. BURKE.

American Fiber Manufacturers Association, Inc (AFMA): 1530 Wilson Blvd, NW, Suite 690, Arlington, VA 22209; tel. (703) 875-0432; fax (703) 875-0907; e-mail afma@afma.org; internet www.fibersource.com; f. 1933; 34 mems; Pres. PAUL T. O'DAY.

Apparel Retailers of America: 325 Seventh St, Suite 1000, NW, Washington, DC 20004-2801; tel. (202) 347-1932; fax (202) 457-0386; f. 1916; 1,200 mems; Exec. Dir DOUGLAS W. WIEGAND.

Knitted Textile Association: 386 Park Ave South, Suite 901, New York, NY 10016; tel. (212) 689-3807; fax (212) 889-6160; e-mail kta386@aol.com; f. 1965; 140 mems; Exec. Dir PETER ADELMAN.

National Council of Textile Organizations (NCTO): 910 17th St, NW, Suite 1020, Washington, DC 20006; tel. (202) 822-8028; fax (202) 822-8029; e-mail info@ncto.org; internet www.ncto.org; f. 2004; Pres. CASS JOHNSON.

National Knitwear and Sportswear Association: 386 Park Ave South, New York, NY 10016; tel. (212) 683-7520; fax (212) 532-0766; f. 1918; 600 mems; Exec. Dir SETH M. BODNER.

National Textile Association (NTA): 6 Beacon St, Suite 1125, Boston, MA 02108-3812; tel. (617) 542-8220; fax (617) 542-2199; e-mail info@nationaltextile.org; internet www.nationaltextile.org; f. 1854; fmrly Northern Textile Asscn and Knitted Textile Asscn; over 200 mems; Pres. KARL SPILHAUS.

Northern Textile Association: 230 Congress St, Boston, MA 02110; tel. (617) 542-8220; fax (617) 542-2199; e-mail textilenta@aol.com; f. 1854; 300 mems; Pres. KARL SPILHAUS.

United Infants' and Children's Wear Association Inc: 1430 Broadway, Suite 1603, New York, NY 10018; tel. (212) 244-2953; f. 1933; 50 mems; Pres. ALAN D. LUBELL.

Tobacco

Tobacco Associates: 1725 K St, NW, Suite 512, Washington, DC 20006; tel. (202) 828-9144; fax (202) 828-9149; e-mail taw@tobaccoassociatesinc.org; internet www.tobaccoassociatesinc.org; f. 1947; Pres. C. N. WAYNE, Jr.

Tobacco Merchants Association of the United States (TMA): POB 8019, Princeton, NJ 08543-8019; tel. (609) 275-4900; fax (609) 275-8379; e-mail tma@tma.org; internet www.tma.org; f. 1915; 170 mems; Pres. FARRELL DELMAN.

Transport

Aerospace Industries Association of America, Inc (AIA): 1000 Wilson Blvd, Suite 1700, Arlington, VA 22209-3928; tel. (703) 358-1000; fax (703) 358-1012; e-mail webmaster@aia-aerospace.org; internet www.aia-aerospace.org; f. 1919; 105 mems and 170 assoc. mems; Pres. and CEO JOHN W. DOUGLASS.

Air Transport Association of America, Inc: see Civil Aviation—Associations.

American Bureau of Shipping: see Ocean Shipping—Associations.

American Bus Association (ABA): 700 13th St, NW, Suite 575, Washington, DC 20005-5923; tel. (202) 842-1645; fax (202) 842-0850; e-mail abainfo@buses.org; internet www.buses.org; f. 1926; c. 3,250 mems; Pres. and CEO PETER J. PANTUSO.

American Institute of Merchant Shipping: see Ocean Shipping—Associations.

American International Automobile Dealers' Association (AIADA): 211 North Union St, Suite 300, Alexandria, VA 22314; tel. (703) 519-7800; fax (703) 519-8100; e-mail goaiada@aiada.org; internet www.aiada.org; f. 1970; 10,000 mems; Pres. MARIANNE MCINERNEY.

American Public Transportation Association (APTA): 1666 K St, NW, Suite 1100, Washington, DC 20006; tel. (202) 496-4800; fax (202) 496-4321; e-mail info@apta.com; internet www.apta.com; f. 1882; 1,537 mems; Pres. WILLIAM W. MILLAR.

American Railway Engineering and Maintenance-of-Way Association (AREMA): 8201 Corporate Dr., Suite 1125, Landover, MD 20785; tel. (301) 459-3200; fax (301) 459-8077; e-mail fcramer@arema.org; internet www.arema.org; f. 1997; Exec. Dir and CEO Dr CHARLES EMELY.

American Short Line Railroad Association: see Principal Railways—Associations.

American Trucking Associations (ATA): 2200 Mill Rd, Alexandria, VA 22314-4654; tel. (703) 838-1700; e-mail membership@trucking.org; internet www.truckline.com; f. 1933; 3,000 mems; Pres. and CEO WILLIAM GRAVES.

Association of American Railroads: see Principal Railways—Associations.

Independent Truck Owner/Operator Association: POB 621, Stoughton, MA 02072; tel. (617) 828-7200; fax (617) 828-6606; f. 1981; 10,000 mems; Pres. MARSHALL SIEGEL.

National Automobile Dealers Association (NADA): 8400 Westpark Dr., McLean, VA 22102-3522; tel. (703) 821-7000; e-mail nadainfo@nada.org; internet www.nada.org; f. 1917; 19,700 mems; Pres. PHILLIP D. BRADY.

Owner/Operator Independent Drivers' Association (OOIDA): 1 North West OOIDA Dr., Grain Valley, MO 64029; tel. (816) 229-5791; e-mail webmaster@ooida.com; internet www.ooida.com; f. 1973; 126,000 mems; Pres. JIM JOHNSTON.

Shipbuilders Council of America (SCA): 1455 F St, NW, Suite 225, Washington, DC 20005; tel. (202) 347-5462; fax (202) 347-5464; e-mail mallen@dc.bjllp.com; internet www.shipbuilders.org; f. 1921; 43 mem. cos; Pres. ALLEN J. WALKER.

THE UNITED STATES OF AMERICA

Miscellaneous

American Advertising Federation (AAF): 1101 Vermont Ave, NW, Suite 500, Washington, DC 20005-6306; tel. (202) 898-0089; fax (202) 898-0159; e-mail aaf@aaf.org; internet www.aaf.org; f. 1967; 50,000 mems, 130 corporate mems; Pres. and CEO WALLACE S. SNYDER.

American Association of Exporters and Importers (AAEI): 1050 17th St, NW, Suite 810, Washington, DC 20036; tel. (202) 857-8009; fax (202) 857-7843; e-mail hq@aaei.org; internet www.aaei.org; f. 1921; 1,200 mems; Pres. and CEO HALLOCK NORTHCOTT.

American Marketing Association (AMA): 311 South Wacker Dr., Suite 5800, Chicago, IL 60606; tel. (312) 542-9000; fax (312) 542-9001; e-mail info@ama.org; internet www.marketingpower.com; f. 1937; 38,000 mems; CEO DENNIS L. DUNLAP.

American Society of Association Executives (ASAE): 1575 I St, NW, Washington, DC 20005-1103; tel. (202) 626-2723; fax (202) 371-8825; e-mail service@asaenet.org; internet www.asaenet.org; f. 1920; 25,000 mems; Pres. and CEO JOHN H. GRAHAM.

Association of Equipment Manufacturers (AEM): 111 East Wisconsin Ave, Suite 1000, Milwaukee, WI 53202-4806; tel. (414) 272-0943; fax (414) 272-1170; internet www.aem.org; f. 2002; Pres. DENNIS SLATER.

Consumer Healthcare Products Association (CHPA): 900 19th St, NW, Suite 700, Washington, DC 20006; tel. (202) 429-9260; fax (202) 223-6835; e-mail sdibartolo@chpa-info.org; internet www.chpa-info.org; f. 1881; 165 mem. and assoc. mem. cos; Pres. LYNDA A. SUYDAM.

Cosmetic, Toiletry and Fragrance Association (CTFA): 1101 17th St, NW, Suite 300, Washington, DC 20036-4702; tel. (202) 331-1770; fax (202) 331-1969; internet www.ctfa.org; f. 1894; 600 mem. cos; Pres. ED KAVANAUGH.

Institute for Supply Management (ISM): 2055 East Centennial Circle, POB 22160, Tempe, AZ 85285-2160; tel. (408) 752-6276; fax (408) 752-7890; e-mail pnovak@ism.ws; internet www.ism.ws; f. 1915; 44,000 mems; CEO PAUL NOVAK.

Motion Picture Association of America, Inc (MPAA): 1600 Eye St, NW, Washington, DC 20006; tel. (202) 378-9100; fax (202)452-9823; internet www.mpaa.org; f. 1922; Chair. and CEO DAN GLICKMAN.

National Association of Manufacturers (NAM): 1331 Pennsylvania Ave, NW, Suite 600, Washington, DC 20004-1790; tel. (202) 637-3000; fax (202) 637-3182; e-mail manufacturing@nam.org; internet www.nam.org; f. 1895; 14,000 mems; Pres. and CEO JOHN ENGLER.

National Association of Realtors (NAR): 430 North Michigan Ave, Suite 500, Chicago, IL 60611-4087; fax (312) 329-8960; e-mail infocentral@realtors.org; internet www.realtor.org; f. 1908; 800,000 mems; Exec. Vice-Pres. and CEO TERENCE M. MCDERMOTT.

National Center for Manufacturing Sciences (NCMS): 3025 Boardwalk, Ann Arbor, MI 48108-3230; tel. (734) 995-0300; fax (734) 995-1150; internet www.ncms.org; f. 1986; Pres. and CEO RICHARD F. PEARSON.

National Cooperative Business Association (NCBA): 1401 New York Ave, NW, Suite 1100, Washington, DC 20005-2160; tel. (202) 638-6222; fax (202) 638-1374; e-mail ncba@ncba.org; internet www.ncba.org; f. 1916; 450 mems; Pres. and CEO PAUL HAZEN.

National Retail Federation (NRF): 325 Seventh St, NW, Suite 1100, Washington, DC 20004-2802; tel. (202) 783-7941; fax (202) 737-2849; e-mail blackwellp@nrf.com; internet www.nrf.com; f. 1911; mems: more than 100 state, nat. and trade orgs; Pres. and CEO TRACY MULLIN.

Society of Manufacturing Engineers (SME): 1 SME Dr., Dearborn, MI 48121; tel. (313) 271-1500; fax (313) 425-3401; e-mail service@sme.org; internet www.sme.org; f. 1932; Exec. Dir NANCY S. BERG.

UTILITIES

Electricity

American Electric Power (AEP): 1 Riverside Plaza, Columbus, OH 43215-2373; tel. (614) 223-1000; internet www.aep.com; f. 1906 as the American Gas and Electricity Co; present name adopted 1958; electricity supplier to Arkansas, Indiana, Kentucky, Louisiana, Michigan, Ohio, Oklahoma, Tennessee, Texas, Virginia and West Virginia; Chair., Pres. and CEO MICHAEL G. MORRIS.

American Public Power Association: 2301 M St, NW, 3rd Floor, Washington, DC 20037-1484; tel. (202) 467-2900; fax (202) 467-2910; internet www.appanet.org; f. 1940; 1,750 mems; Exec. Dir ALAN H. RICHARDSON.

Association of Edison Illuminating Companies: 600 North 18th St, POB 2641, Birmingham, AL 35291-0992; tel. (205) 250-2530; fax (205) 250-2540; f. 1885; mems comprise 78 investor-owned public utilities; Exec. Dir ROBERT E. NUFFMAN.

Edison Electric Institute: 701 Pennsylvania Ave, NW, Washington, DC 20004-2696; tel. (202) 508-5000; fax (202) 508-5794; internet www.eei.org; f. 1933; mems comprise 190 investor-owned electric utility cos in the USA and 26 foreign mems; Chair. WAYNE BRUNETTI; Pres. THOMAS R. KUHN.

Electrification Council: 701 Pennsylvania Ave, NW, Washington, DC 20004; tel. (202) 508-5900; fax (202) 508-5335; f. 1951; electricity industry trade partnership; 50 mems; Man. STEVEN KOEP.

Energy Telecommunications and Electrical Association: 5005 West Royal Lane, Suite 190, Irving, TX 75063; tel. (888) 503-8700; fax (972) 915-6040; f. 1928; 170 mems; Pres. PHILIP J. GRAMMATICO; Exec. Man. BLAINE SISKE.

National Rural Electric Co-operative Association: 4301 Wilson Blvd, Arlington, VA 22203; tel. (703) 907-5500; fax (703) 907-5599; e-mail nreca@nreca.org; internet www.nreca.org; f. 1942; rural electric co-operative systems, public power, and public utility distribution in 46 states; 1,000 mems; CEO GLENN ENGLISH.

Gas

American Gas Association: 400 North Capitol St, NW, Washington, DC 20001; tel. (202) 824-7000; fax (202) 824-7115; e-mail ccussimainio@aga.org; internet www.aga.org; f. 1918; Pres. and CEO DAVID N. PARKER.

American Public Gas Association: 11094D Lee Hwy, Suite 102, Fairfax, VA 22030; tel. (703) 352-3890; fax (703) 352-1271; f. 1961; promotes efficiency among public gas systems; 430 mems; Exec. Dir ROBERT S. CAVE.

Gas Research Institute: 8600 West Bryn Mawr Ave, Chicago, IL 60631; tel. (312) 399-8100; fax (312) 399-8170; internet www.gri.org; f. 1976; 255 mems; Pres. and CEO STEPHEN D. BAN.

Natural Gas Supply Association: 805 15th St, NW, Suite 510, Washington, DC 20005-2207; tel. (202) 331-8900; internet www.ngsa.org; f. 1967; monitors legislation and economic issues affecting natural-gas producers; Pres. R. SKIP HORVATH.

Water

American Water Works Association: 6666 West Quincy Ave, Denver, CO 80235-3098; tel. (303) 794-7711; fax (303) 794-7310; internet www.awwa.org; f. 1881; 54,000 mems; Exec. Dir JACK W. HOFFBUHR.

Association of Metropolitan Water Agencies: 1717 K St, NW, Suite 1102, Washington, DC 20036; tel. (202) 331-2820; fax (202) 842-0621; f. 1981; 63 mems; Exec. Dir DIANE VAN DE HEI.

National Association of Water Companies: 1725 K St, NW, Suite 1212, Washington, DC 20006; tel. (202) 833-8383; fax (202) 331-7442; internet www.nawc.org; f. 1895; privately- and commercially-owned water cos, and individuals; 500 mems; Exec. Dir PETER COOK.

National Rural Water Association: POB 1428, Duncan, OK 73534; tel. (405) 252-0629; fax (405) 255-4476; e-mail NRWAinfo@NRWA.org; internet www.cais.com/nrwainfo.

TRADE UNIONS

In 2002 there were approximately 16.1m. union members in the USA, representing 11.7% of the civilian labour force.

Many trade unions based in the USA have members throughout North America. Approximately 30% of Canada's trade union members belong to unions having headquarters in the USA.

American Federation of Labor and Congress of Industrial Organizations (AFL-CIO): 815 16th St, NW, Washington, DC 20006; tel. (202) 637-5000; fax (202) 637-5058; internet www.aflcio.org; f. 1955; Pres. JOHN J. SWEENEY; Sec.-Treas. RICHARD L. TRUMKA; 54 affiliated unions with total membership of 9m. (2006).

AFL-CIO Affiliates
(with 50,000 members and over)

Aluminum, Brick and Glass Workers International Union: 3362 Hollenberg Dr., Bridgeton, MO 63044; tel. (314) 739-6142; fax (314) 739-1216; f. 1982; Pres. ERNIE J. LABAFF; 51,800 mems.

Amalgamated Clothing and Textile Workers' Union: 15 Union Sq. West, New York, NY 10003; tel. (212) 242-0700; fax (212) 255-7230; f. 1976; Pres. JACK SHEINKMAN; Sec.-Treas. ARTHUR R. LOEVY; 273,000 mems.

Amalgamated Transit Union: 5025 Wisconsin Ave, NW, Washington, DC 20016; tel. (202) 537-1645; fax (202) 244-7824; f. 1892; Int. Pres. JOHN W. ROWLAND; 165,000 mems.

American Federation of Government Employees: 80 F St, NW, Washington, DC 20001; tel. (202) 639-6419; fax (202) 639-6441; f. 1932; Nat. Pres. BOBBY L. HARNAGE; 210,000 mems.

THE UNITED STATES OF AMERICA

American Federation of Musicians of the United States and Canada: Paramount Bldg, Suite 600, 1501 Broadway, New York, NY 10036; tel. (212) 869-1330; fax (212) 764-6134; internet www.afm.org; f. 1896; Pres. THOMAS F. LEE; Sec.-Treas. FLORENCE NELSON; 120,000 mems.

American Federation of State, County and Municipal Employees: 1625 L St, NW, Washington, DC 20036; tel. (202) 429-1000; fax (202) 429-1293; f. 1936; Pres. GERALD W. MCENTEE; Sec.-Treas. WILLIAM LUCY; 1.3m. mems.

American Federation of Teachers (AFT-AFL-CIO): 555 New Jersey Ave, NW, Washington, DC 20001; tel. (202) 879-4400; fax (202) 879-4545; f. 1916; Pres. EDWARD J. MCELROY; Sec.-Treas. NAT LACOUR; 1.3m. mems.

American Federation of Television and Radio Artists: 260 Madison Ave, 7th Floor, New York, NY 10016-2401; tel. (212) 532-0800; fax (212) 921-8454; f. 1937; Exec. Dir BRUCE A. YORK; 80,000 mems.

American Postal Workers' Union: 1300 L St, NW, Washington, DC 20005; tel. (202) 842-4200; fax (202) 842-4297; internet www.apwu.org; f. 1971; Pres. WILLIAM BURRUS; 330,000 mems.

Associated Actors and Artistes of America: 165 46th St West, New York, NY 10036; tel. (212) 869-0358; fax (212) 869-1746; f. 1919; Pres. THEODORE BIKEL; 7 nat. unions representing 125,000 mems.

Automobile, Aerospace and Agricultural Implement Workers of America, United: 8000 East Jefferson Ave, Detroit, MI 48214; tel. (313) 926-5000; fax (313) 823-6016; internet www.uaw.org; f. 1935; Pres. RON GETTELFINGER; Sec.-Treas. ELIZABETH BUNN; 622,603 mems (2004).

Bakery, Confectionery, Tobacco Workers' and Grain Millers International Union: 10401 Connecticut Ave, Kensington, MD 20895; tel. (301) 933-8600; fax (301) 946-8452; f. 1886; Pres. FRANK HURT; Sec.-Treas. DAVID B. DURKEE; 125,000 mems (1999).

Boilermakers, Iron Ship Builders, Blacksmiths, Forgers and Helpers, International Brotherhood of: 753 State Ave, Suite 570, Kansas City, KS 66101; tel. (913) 371-2640; fax (913) 281-8101; e-mail pamd@boilermakers.org; f. 1880; Pres. CHARLES W. JONES; Sec.-Treas. JERRY Z. WILLBURN; 80,000 mems (1999).

Bricklayers and Allied Craftsmen, International Union of: 815 15th St, NW, Washington, DC 20005; tel. (202) 783-3788; fax (202) 393-0219; f. 1865; Pres. JOHN J. FLYNN; Sec.-Treas. L. GERALD CARLISLE; 100,000 mems (1999).

Bridge, Structural, Ornamental and Reinforcing Iron Workers, International Association of: 1750 New York Ave, NW, Suite 400, Washington, DC 20006; tel. (202) 383-4810; fax (202) 638-4856; internet www.ironworkers.org; f. 1896; Gen. Pres. JOSEPH HUNT; Gen. Sec. MICHAEL A. FITZPATRICK; 120,000 mems (1997).

Communications Workers of America: 501 Third St, NW, Washington, DC 20001; tel. (202) 434-1100; fax (202) 434-1279; e-mail cwa@capcon.net; internet www.cwa-union.org; f. 1939; Pres. MORTON BAHR; Sec.-Treas. BARBARA J. EASTERLING; 700,000 mems (2003).

International Union of Electronic, Electrical, Salaried, Machine and Furniture Workers (IUE): 501 Third St, NW, Suite 600, Washington, DC 20001; tel. (202) 434-1228; fax (202) 434-1461; e-mail kburson@cwa-union.org; internet www.iue-cwa.org; f. 1949; industrial division of the CWA following merger in 2000; Pres. JIM CLARK; 150,000 mems.

Electrical Workers, International Brotherhood of: 1125 15th St, NW, Washington, DC 20005; tel. (202) 833-7000; fax (202) 467-6316; e-mail journalmedia@compuserve.com; f. 1891; Pres. J. J. BARRY; Sec.-Treas. EDWIN D. HILL; 750,000 mems (1999).

United Food and Commercial Workers International Union: 1775 K St, NW, Washington, DC 20006; tel. (202) 223-3111; fax (202) 466-1562; internet www.ufcw.org; f. 1979; Pres. JOSEPH T. HANSEN; 1.4m. mems (1999).

Glass Molders, Pottery, Plastics & Allied Workers International Union, AFL-CIO, CLC: 608 East Baltimore Pike, POB 607, Media, PA 19063; tel. (610) 565-5051; fax (610) 565-0983; f. 1842; Pres. JOSEPH MITCHELL, SR; Sec.-Treas. JOHN P. RYAN, SR; 68,000 mems (1999).

Government Employees, American Federation of: 80 F St, NW, Washington, DC, 20001; tel. (202) 737-8700; fax (202) 639-6441; e-mail communications@afge.org; internet www.afge.org; f. 1932; Nat. Pres. BOBBY L. HARNAGE, SR; Nat. Sec.-Treas JIM DAVIS; 200,000 mems (2000).

Graphic Communications International Union: 1900 L St, NW, Washington, DC 20036; tel. (202) 462-1400; fax (202) 721-0600; internet www.gciu.org; f. 1983; Pres. GEORGE TEDESCHI; Sec.-Treas. GERALD DENEAU; 125,000 mems (2003).

Hotel Employees & Restaurant Employees International Union: 1219 28th St, NW, Washington, DC 20007; tel. (202) 393-4373; fax (202) 333-0468; f. 1891; Pres. JOHN W. WILHELM; Sec.-Treas. TED HANSEN; 350,000 mems (1999).

International Association of Fire Fighters: 1750 New York Ave, NW, Washington, DC 20006-5395; tel. (202) 737-8484; fax (202) 737-8418; internet www.iaff.org; f. 1918; Gen. Pres. HAROLD SCHAITBERGER; Sec.-Treas. VINCENT J. BOLLON; 195,000 mems.

International Longshoremen's Association: 17 Battery Pl., Rm 1530, New York, NY 10004; tel. (212) 425-1200; fax (212) 425-2928; f. 1892; Pres. JOHN BOWERS; Sec.-Treas. HARRY R. HASSELGREN; 65,000 mems (1999).

International Union of Painters and Allied Trades: 1750 New York Ave, NW, Washington, DC 20006; tel. (202) 637-0700; f. 1887; Gen. Pres. MICHAEL E. MONROE; Sec.-Treas. JAMES A. WILLIAMS.

Letter Carriers, National Association of: 100 Indiana Ave, NW, Washington, DC 20001; tel. (202) 393-4695; fax (202) 737-1540; e-mail nalcinf@access.digex.net; internet www.nalc.org; f. 1889; Pres. VINCENT R. SOMBROTTO; Sec.-Treas. WILLIAM R. YATES; 315,000 mems (2000).

Machinists and Aerospace Workers, International Association of: 9000 Machinists Pl., Upper Marboro, MD 20772; tel. (301) 967-4500; fax (301) 967-4588; internet www.iamaw.org; f. 1888; Int. Pres. R. THOMAS BUFFENBARGER; Gen. Sec.-Treas. DONALD WHARTON; 780,000 mems (1999).

Maintenance of Way Employees, Brotherhood of: 26555 Evergreen Rd, Suite 200, Southfield, MI 48076-4225; tel. (248) 948-1010; fax (248) 948-7150; f. 1887; Pres. MAC A. FLEMING; Sec.-Treas. WILLIAM E. LARUE; 50,000 mems (1999).

Marine Engineers' Beneficial Association: 444 North Capitol St, NW, Suite 800, Washington, DC 20001; tel. (202) 638-5355; fax (202) 638-5369; e-mail mebahq@d1meba.org; f. 1875; Pres. C. E. DEFRIES; 50,000 mems.

United Mine Workers of America, International Union (UMWA): 8315 Lee Highway, Fairfax, VA 22031; tel. (703) 208-7200; internet www.umwa.org; f. 1890; Int. Pres. CECIL ROBERTS; Sec.-Treas. DAN KANE; 130,000 mems (1999).

Musicians of the United States and Canada, American Federation of: 1501 Broadway, Suite 600, New York, NY 10036; tel. (212) 869-1330; fax (212) 764-6134; e-mail info@afm.org; internet www.afm.org; f. 1896; Pres. THOMAS F. LEE; Sec.-Treas. FLORENCE NELSON; 100,000 mems (1999).

Office and Professional Employees International Union: 265 West 14th St, Suite 610, New York, NY 10011; tel. (212) 675-3210; fax (212) 727-3466; f. 1945; Int. Pres. MICHAEL GOODWIN; Sec.-Treas. GILLES BEAUREGARD; 130,000 mems (1999).

Operating Engineers, International Union of: 1125 17th St, NW, Washington, DC 20036; tel. (202) 429-9100; fax (202) 778-2616; f. 1896; Gen. Pres. FRANK HANLEY; 360,000 mems (1999).

PACE International Union: POB 1475, Nashville, TN 37202; tel. (615) 834-8590; fax (615) 831-6791; internet www.paceunion.org; f. 1999; by merger of United Paperworkers' International Union and Oil, Chemical and Atomic Workers' International Union; Pres. BOYD YOUNG; Sec.-Treas. JAMES DUNN; 320,000 mems (2004).

Painters and Allied Trades, International Union of: 1750 New York Ave, NW, 8th Floor, Washington, DC 20006; tel. (202) 637-0700; fax (202) 637-0771; f. 1887; Gen. Pres. MICHAEL E. MONROE; Gen. Sec.-Treas. JAMES A. WILLIAMS; 133,000 mems (2000).

Journeymen and Apprentices of the Plumbing and Pipe Fitting Industry of the United States and Canada, United Association of: 901 Massachusetts Ave, NW, Washington, DC 20001; tel. (202) 628-5823; fax (202) 628-5024; internet www.ua.org; f. 1889; Pres. MARTIN J. MADDALONI; Sec.-Treas. MARION A. LEE; 304,000 mems (1999).

International Union of Police Associations: 1549 Ringling Blvd, 6th Floor, Sarasota, FL 34236; tel. (941) 487-2560; fax (941) 487-2570; Pres. SAM A. CABRAL; 50,000 mems (1999).

Postal Workers Union, American: 1300 L St, NW, Washington, DC 20005; tel. (202) 842-4200; fax (202) 842-4297; internet www.apwu.org; f. 1971; Pres. WILLIAM BURRUS; Sec.-Treas. TERRY STAPLETON; 330,000 mems (1999).

Retail, Wholesale and Department Store Union: 30 East 29th St, New York, NY 10016; tel. (212) 684-5300; fax (212) 779-2809; internet www.atbs.com/rwdsu.html; f. 1937; Pres. STUART APPELBAUM; Sec.-Treas. CHARLIE N. HALL, SR; 100,000 mems (1997).

Screen Actors Guild: 5757 Wilshire Blvd, Los Angeles, CA 90036; tel. (323) 954-1600; fax (323) 549-6656; internet www.sag.org; f. 1933; Pres. MELISSA GILBERT; Nat. Exec. Dir and CEO A. ROBERT PISANO; 120,000 mems (Feb. 2005).

Seafarers International Union of North America: 5201 Auth Way, Camp Springs, MD 20746; tel. (301) 899-0675; fax (301) 899-7355; f. 1938; Pres. MICHAEL SACCO; Sec.-Treas. JOHN FAY; 85,000 mems (1999).

THE UNITED STATES OF AMERICA

Sheet Metal Workers' International Association: 1750 New York Ave, NW, Washington, DC 20006; tel. (202) 783-5880; fax (202) 662-0894; e-mail info@smwia.org; internet www.smwia.org; f. 1888; Gen. Pres. MICHAEL J. SULLIVAN; Gen. Sec.-Treas. THOMAS J. KELLY; 150,000 mems (1999).

State, County and Municipal Employees, American Federation of: 1625 L St, NW, Washington, DC 20036; tel. (202) 452-4800; fax (202) 429-1293; internet www.afscme.org; f. 1936; Pres. GERALD W. MCENTEE; Sec.-Treas. WILLIAM LUCY; 1.3m. mems (1999).

United Steelworkers of America: 5 Gateway Center, Rm 802, Pittsburgh, PA 15222; tel. (412) 562-2400; fax (412) 562-2445; e-mail webmaster@uswa.org; internet www.uswa.org; f. 1936; Int. Pres. LEO GERARD; Int. Sec.-Treas. JIM ENGLISH; 600,000 mems (2004).

Teachers, American Federation of: 555 New Jersey Ave, NW, Washington, DC 20001; tel. (202) 879-4400; fax (202) 879-4556; internet www.aft.org; f. 1916; Pres. SANDRA FELDMAN; Sec.-Treas. EDWARD J. MCELROY; 1.0m. mems (1999).

Television and Radio Artists, American Federation of: 260 Madison Ave, 7th Floor, New York, NY 10016-2401; tel. (212) 532-0800; fax (212) 545-1238; e-mail nyfilm@ios.com; internet www.ios.com/~nyfilm/union/aftra.html; f. 1937; Pres. SHELBY SCOTT; 75,000 mems (1999).

Theatrical Stage Employees, Moving Picture Technicians, Artists and Allied Crafts of the US, its Territories and Canada, International Alliance of: 1515 Broadway, Suite 601, New York, NY 10036; tel. (212) 730-1770; fax (212) 921-7699; internet www.iatse.lm.com; f. 1893; Int. Pres. THOMAS C. SHORT; Gen. Sec.-Treas. MICHAEL W. PROSCIA; 100,000 mems (2000).

Amalgamated Transit Union: 5025 Wisconsin Ave, NW, Washington, DC 20016; tel. (202) 537-1645; fax (202) 244-7824; f. 1892; Int. Pres. JAMES LASALA; 165,000 mems (1999).

Transport Workers Union International: 80 West End Ave, 5th Floor, New York, NY 10023; tel. (212) 873-6000; fax (212) 721-1431; e-mail twu@twu.com; internet www.twu.com; f. 1934; Int. Pres. SONNY HALL; Sec.-Treas. GEORGE LEITZ; 125,000 mems (1999).

Transportation-Communications International Union: 3 Research Pl., Rockville, MD 20850; tel. (301) 948-4910; fax (301) 948-1369; f. 1899; Pres. ROBERT A. SCARDELLETTI; Sec.-Treas. HOWARD W. RANDOLPH JR; 46,576 mems (2005).

United Rubber, Cork, Linoleum and Plastic Workers of America: 570 White Pond Dr., Akron, OH 44320; tel. (330) 869-0320; fax (330) 869-5627; f. 1935; Pres. KENNETH L. COSS; Sec.-Treas. GLENN ELLISON; 100,000 mems.

United Steelworkers of America: 5 Gateway Center, Pittsburgh, PA 15222; tel. (412) 562-2400; fax (412) 562-2445; f. 1936; Int. Pres. LEO W. GERARD; Sec.-Treas. JAMES D. ENGLISH; 750,000 mems.

United Transportation Union (UTU): 14600 Detroit Ave, Lakewood, OH 44107-4250; tel. (216) 228-9400; fax (216) 228-5755; e-mail pr@utu.org; internet www.utu.org; f. 1969; Pres. PAUL C. THOMPSON; Gen. Sec. and Treas. DANIEL E. JOHNSON, III; 125,000.

Utility Workers Union of America: 815 16th St, NW, Washington, DC 20006; tel. (202) 974-8200; fax (202) 974-8201; internet www.uwua.net; f. 1945; Pres. DONALD E. WIGHTMAN; Sec.-Treas. GARY M. RUFFNER; 50,000 mems (2006).

Independent Unions
(with 50,000 members and over)

Change to Win: 1900 L St, NW, Suite 900, Washington, DC 20036; tel. (202) 721-0660; fax (202) 721-0661; e-mail info@changetowin.org; internet www.changetowin.org; f. 2005 following split in the AFL-CIO; Chair. ANNA BURGER; Sec.-Treas. EDGAR ROMNEY.

Affiliates with 50,000 mems and over include:

Carpenters and Joiners of America, United Brotherhood of: 101 Constitution Ave, NW, Washington, DC 20001; tel. (202) 546-6206; fax (202) 543-5724; f. 1881; withdrew from AFL-CIO in 2001; Pres. DOUGLAS J. MCCARRON; Sec.-Treas. DOUG BANES; 509,000 mems (1999).

Laborers' International Union of North America: 905 16th St, NW, Washington, DC 20006; tel. (202) 737-8320; fax (202) 737-2754; f. 1903; Pres. TERENCE M. O'SULLIVAN; Gen. Sec.-Treas. ARMAND E. SABATONI; 820,000 mems (2003).

Brotherhood of Locomotive Engineers and Trainmen (BLET): 1370 Ontario St, Mezzanine, Cleveland, OH 44113-1702; tel. (216) 241-2630; fax (216) 241-6516; e-mail webmaster@ble.org; internet www.ble.org; f. 1863; division of the Rail Conference of the Int. Brotherhood of Teamsters; Pres. DON M. HAHS; Sec.-Treas. WILLIAM C. WALPERT; 58,000 mems (2005).

Service Employees' International Union (SEIU): 1313 L St, NW, Washington, DC 20005; tel. (202) 898-3200; fax (202) 898-3304; internet www.seiu.org; f. 1921; withdrew from AFL-CIO in 2005; Pres. ANDREW L. STERN; Sec.-Treas. ANITA BURGER; 1.8m. mems (2005).

Teamsters, International Brotherhood of: 25 Louisiana Ave, NW, Washington, DC 20001; tel. (202) 624-6800; fax (202) 624-6918; internet www.teamster.org; f. 1903; withdrew from AFL-CIO in 2005; Pres. JAMES P. HOFFA; Gen. Sec.-Treas. TOM KEEGAL; 1.3m. mems (2004).

UNITE HERE: 275 7th Ave, New York, NY 10001-6708; tel. (212) 265-7000; e-mail acooper@unitehere.org; internet www.unitehere.org; f. 2004 by merger of the Union of Needletrades, Industrial and Textile Employees (UNITE—f. 1995) and Hotel Employees and Restaurant Employees Int. Union (HERE—f. 1891); Gen. Pres. BRUCE RAYNOR; Pres. (Hospitality Industries) JOHN WILHELM; c. 460,000 mems.

United Food and Commercial Workers International Union: 1775 K St, NW, Washington, DC 20006; tel. (202) 223-3111; f. 1979; Int. Pres. DOUGLAS H. DORITY; Int. Sec.-Treas. JOSEPH HANSEN; 1.3m. mems.

National Education Association of the United States: 1201 16th St, NW, Washington, DC 20036; tel. (202) 833-4000; fax (202) 822-7974; internet www.nea.org; f. 1857; Pres. BOB CHASE; Exec. Dir JOHN WILSON; 2.6m. mems (2001).

National Federation of Federal Employees: 1016 16th St, NW, Suite 300, Washington, DC 20036; tel. (202) 862-4400; fax (202) 862-4432; internet www.nffe.org; f. 1917; Pres. ALBERT SCHMIDT; Sec.-Treas. R. JOYCE JAMES; 120,000 mems (1999).

Longshore and Warehouse Union, International: 1188 Franklin St, 4th Floor, San Francisco, CA 94109; tel. (415) 775-0533; fax (415) 775-1302; internet www.ilwu.org; f. 1937; Pres. JAMES SPINOSA; Sec.-Treas. WILLIAM ADAMS; 59,500 mems (2002).

American Nurses Association: 600 Maryland Ave, SW, Suite 100-W, Washington, DC 20024-2571; tel. (202) 651-7000; fax (202) 651-7001; e-mail ana@ana.org; internet www.nursingworld.org; f. 1896; Pres. MARY E. FOLEY; Exec. Dir LINDA STIERLE; 53 constituent state asscns comprising 180,000 mems (1999).

National Fraternal Order of Police: 1410 Donelson Pike, A-17, Nashville, TN 37217-2933; Nat. Pres. GILBERT G. GALLEGOS; Nat. Sec. JERRY W. ATNIP; 280,000 mems (1999).

National Rural Letter Carriers' Association: 1630 Duke St, 4th Floor, Alexandria, VA 22314-3465; tel. (703) 684-5545; fax (703) 548-8735; f. 1903; Pres. STEVEN SMITH; 98,000 mems (1999).

Treasury Employees Union, National: 901 E St, NW, Suite 600, Washington, DC 20004; tel. (202) 783-4444; fax (202) 783-4085; internet www.nteu.org; f. 1938; Nat. Pres. ROBERT M. TOBIAS; 155,000 mems (1999).

Transport

Federal Transit Administration: US Dept of Transportation, 400 Seventh St, SW, Washington, DC 20590; tel. (202) 366-4043; fax (202) 366-9854; internet www.fta.dot.gov; Admin. JENNIFER L. DORN.

National Transportation Safety Board: 490 L'Enfant Plaza East, SW, Washington, DC 20594; tel. (202) 314-6000; fax (202) 314-6148; internet www.ntsb.gov; f. 1967; seeks to ensure that all types of transportation in the USA are conducted safely; carries out studies and accident investigations; Chair. ELLEN G. ENGLEMAN.

Surface Transportation Board: Mercury Bldg, 1925 K St, NW, Washington, DC 20423; tel. (202) 565-1500; fax (202) 565-9016; internet www.stb.dot.gov; f. 1995; exercises regulatory authority over domestic surface common carriers; jurisdiction extends over rail, inland waterways and motorized traffic; Chair. ROGER NOBER.

Transportation Security Administration: 601 South 12th St, Arlington, VA 22202-4220; internet www.tsa.gov; f. 2001; to ensure the security of the country's transport system against possible terrorist attacks; Dir KIP HAWLEY.

RAILWAYS

Federal Railroad Administration: Dept of Transportation, 1120 Vermont Ave, NW, Washington, DC 20005; tel. (202) 493-6000; fax (202) 493-6009; internet www.fra.dot.gov; part of the Dept of Transportation; formulates federal railway policies and administers and enforces safety regulations; f. 1966; Admin. JOSEPH H. BOARDMAN.

Principal Companies

Alaska Railroad Corporation: POB 107500, Anchorage, AK 99510-7500; tel. (907) 265-2414; fax (907) 265-2312; e-mail reservations@akrr.com; f. 1912; independent corpn owned by the State of Alaska; year-round freight service and summer passenger service; Pres. and CEO PATRICK GAMBLE; 846 track-km.

AMTRAK (National Railroad Passenger Corpn): 60 Massachusetts Ave, NE, Washington, DC 20002; tel. (202) 906-3860; fax (202) 906-3306; internet www.amtrak.com; f. 1970; govt-funded private corpn

THE UNITED STATES OF AMERICA

operating inter-city passenger services over 33,600 track-km in 45 states; Chair. David M. Laney; Pres. and CEO David L. Gunn.

Burlington Northern Santa Fe Corporation: 2650 Lou Menk Dr., Fort Worth, TX 76131; tel. (817) 333-7000; Chair., Pres. and CEO Robert D. Krebs; 49,879 track-km.

Conrail (Consolidated Rail Corporation): 2001 Market St, POB 41419, Philadelphia, PA 19101-1419; tel. (215) 209-2000; fax (215) 209-4822; e-mail info@conrail.com; internet www.conrail.com; f. 1975; by fed. govt merger of six bankrupt freight carriers; transfer of most operations to CSX Transportation Inc and Norfolk Southern Railway Co completed in June 1999; Chair. David M. LeVan; 19,040 track-km (1998).

CSX Transportation Inc (Rail Transport): 500 Water St, Jacksonville, FL 32202; tel. (904) 359-3100; fax (904) 359-1832; f. 1980; by merger; Pres. John Snow; 30,248 track-km.

Guilford Rail Systems: Iron Horse Park, North Billerica, MA 01862; tel. (978) 663-1130; fax (978) 663-1143; Pres. T. F. Steiniger; 3,516 track-km.

Illinois Central Railroad: 455 North Cityfront Plaza Dr., Chicago, IL 60611; tel. (312) 755-7500; fax (312) 755-7920; f. 1851; Pres. and CEO John D. McPherson; 4,452 track-km.

Kansas City Southern Railway Co: 114 West 11th St, Kansas City, MO 64105; tel. (816) 983-1537; fax (816) 983-1418; internet www.kcsi.com; Chair. L. H. Rowland; Pres. Michael R. Haverty; 2,561 track-km.

Long Island Rail Road Co: Jamaica Station, Jamaica, NY 11435; tel. (718) 558-7400; fax (718) 558-6824; f. 1834; Pres. Thomas Prendergast; 435 track-km.

Norfolk Southern Railway Co: NS Tower, 3 Commercial Pl., Norfolk, VA 23510-2191; tel. (757) 629-2600; fax (757) 629-2345; f. 1982; Chair., Pres. and CEO D. R. Goode; 35,084 track-km.

Union Pacific Railroad Co: 1416 Dodge St, Omaha NE 68179; tel. (402) 271-5000; fax (402) 271-2256; internet www.uprr.com; f. 1897; division of Union Pacific Corpn; Chair. and CEO Richard Davidson; Pres. Jerry Davis; 57,833 track-km.

Associations

American Short Line and Regional Railroad Association: 1120 G St, NW, Suite 520, Washington, DC 20005; tel. (202) 628-4500; fax (202) 628-6430; f. 1913; Pres. Frank K. Turner; 760 mems.

Association of American Railroads: 50 F St, NW, Washington, DC 20001; tel. (202) 639-2100; fax (202) 639-2558; e-mail information@aar.org; internet www.aar.org; f. 1934; membership represents virtually all major railroads in the USA, Canada and Mexico, as well as rail industry products and services; Pres. Edward R. Hamberger.

ROADS

In 2000 there were 3,936,229 miles of roads, of which 388,726 miles were classified as arterial systems and 2,707,940 miles were local roads. In 1999 an estimated 58.8% of all roads were paved.

Federal Highway Administration (FHWA): 400 Seventh St, SW, Washington, DC 20590; tel. (202) 366-0604; internet www.fhwa.dot.gov; part of the Dept of Transportation; implements federal highway policy and promotes road safety; Admin. J. Richard Capka (acting).

INLAND WATERWAYS

St Lawrence Seaway Development Corporation: US Dept of Transportation, 400 Seventh St, SW, Rm 5424, Washington, DC 20590; tel. (202) 366-0091; fax (202) 366-7147; internet www.dot.gov/slsdc; responsible for the operations and maintenance of sections of the St Lawrence Seaway within the territorial limits of the USA; Admin. Albert S. Jacquez.

Principal Companies

American Commercial Lines Inc: 1701 East Market St, Jeffersonville, IN 47130; tel. (812) 288-0100; fax (812) 288-1664; operates barge services along c. 24,000 km of the Mississippi and Ohio rivers and tributaries to the Gulf Intracoastal Waterway; Pres. and CEO H. Joseph Bobizen, Jr; fleet of 2,400 barges and 96 towboats.

Great Lakes Dredge & Dock Co: 2122 York Rd, Oak Brook, IL 60521; tel. (630) 574-3000; fax (630) 574-2909; f. 1890; dredging, marine construction and reclamation; operates tugboats, drillboats, carfloats, barges and dredges; Man. (Int. Business) William Hannum; 149 vessels.

Great Lakes Fleet, Inc: 227 West First St, Suite 400, Duluth, MN 55802-1990; tel. (218) 723-2401; fax (218) 723-2455; Gen. Man. Elliott M. Hughes, III; 8 vessels.

Midland Enterprises Inc: 580 Walnut St, POB 5323, Cincinnati, OH 45201; tel. (513) 943-7100; fax (513) 943-1502; river and inter-coastal transportation, towing and tugboat service and marine cargo handling; ship and barge building and repair; Pres. C. F. Raskin.

Oglebay Norton Co Marine Transportation Division: 1100 Superior Ave, Cleveland, OH 44114-2598; tel. (216) 861-8700; fax (216) 861-2315; services on the Great Lakes; Gen. Man. Michael J. Siragusa; 12 vessels.

Associations

American Waterways Operators: 1600 Wilson Blvd, Suite 1000, Arlington, VA 22209; tel. (703) 841-9300; fax (703) 841-0389; internet www.americanwaterways.com; f. 1944; 386 mems; Pres. Thomas A. Allegretti.

Lake Carriers' Association: 915 Rockefeller Bldg, Cleveland, OH 44113-1383; tel. (216) 621-1107; fax (216) 241-8262; e-mail ryan@lcaships.com; f. 1892; 11 mem cos; Pres. George J. Ryan.

National Waterways Conference: 1130 17th St, NW, Suite 200, Washington, DC 20036-4676; tel. (202) 296-4415; fax (202) 835-3861; e-mail worth@waterways; internet www.waterways.org; f. 1960; 500 mems; Pres. Worth Hager.

OCEAN SHIPPING

At 31 December 2004 6,414 vessels, with a total displacement of 10,744,126 grt, were registered in the USA.

Federal Maritime Commission: 800 North Capitol St, NW, Washington, DC 20573; tel. (202) 523-5725; fax (202) 523-3782; internet www.fmc.gov; f. 1961; to regulate the waterborne foreign commerce of the USA; comprises 5 mems; Chair. Steven R. Blust, Jr.

Maritime Administration: 400 Seventh St, SW, Washington, DC 20590; tel. (202) 366-5812; fax (202) 366-3890; internet www.marad.dot.gov; concerned with promoting the US Merchant Marine; also administers subsidy programme to ship operators; Admin. Clyde J. Hart, Jr.

Principal Ports

The three largest ports in the USA, in terms of traffic handled, are the Port of South Louisiana, handling 245m. tons in 2000, Houston (194m. tons in 2001) and New York (135m. tons in 1997). Many other large ports serve each coast, 24 of them handling between 25m. and 89m. tons of traffic annually. The deepening of channels and locks on the St Lawrence–Great Lakes Waterway, allowing the passage of large ocean-going vessels, has increased the importance of the Great Lakes ports, of which the largest, Duluth-Superior, handled an average annual 40m. tons.

Principal Companies

Alcoa Steamship Co, Inc: 1501 Alcoa Bldg, 24th Floor, Pittsburgh, PA 15219; tel. (412) 553-2545; fax (412) 553-2624; bulk services world-wide; Pres. R. S. Hospodar; 5 vessels.

American President Lines Ltd: 1111 Broadway, Oakland, CA 94607; tel. (510) 272-8000; fax (510) 272-7941; f. 1929; serves east and west coasts of North America, Mexico, Caribbean Basin, Middle East and Far East; Chair. G. Hayashi; Pres. and CEO Timothy J. Rhein; 19 vessels.

Amoco Corpn: 200 East Randolph Dr., Chicago, IL 60601; tel. (312) 856-4511; fax (312) 856-2460; Pres. C. D. Phillips.

Central Gulf Lines, Inc: 650 Poydras St, Suite 1700, POB 53366, New Orleans, LA 70153; tel. (504) 529-5461; fax (504) 529-5745; Chair. N. M. Johnsen; Pres. E. L. Johnsen; 8 vessels.

Chevron Shipping Co: 555 Market St, Suite 2025, San Francisco, CA 94105-2870; tel. (415) 894-7700; fax (415) 894-5659; world-wide tanker services; Pres. Thomas R. Moore; 37 tankers.

Colonial Marine Industries, Inc: 26 East Bryan St, POB 9981, Savannah, GA 31412; tel. (912) 233-7000; fax (912) 232-8216; e-mail administrator@colonialmarine.com; internet www.colonialmarine.com; Exec. Vice-Pres. Richard C. Wigger; 7 vessels.

Coscol Marine Corpn: 9 Greenway Plaza, Houston, TX 77046; tel. (713) 877-3370; fax (713) 877-3433; e-mail edward.knutsen@coastalcorp.com; Pres. Edward W. Knutsen; 4 tankers.

Crowley Maritime Corpn: 155 Grand Ave, Oakland, CA 94612; tel. (510) 251-7500; fax (510) 251-7625; internet www.crowley.com; f. 1895; Chair., Pres. and CEO Tom Crowley, Jr; 200 vessels.

Energy Transportation Corpn: 1185 Ave of the Americas, 24th Floor, New York, NY 10036; tel. (212) 642-9800; fax (212) 642-9890; Pres. K. C. Chen; 8 vessels.

Farrell Lines Inc: 1 Whitehall St, New York, NY 10004; tel. (212) 440-4200; fax (212) 440-4645; internet www.farrell-lines.com; f. 1925; freight services from US Atlantic to West Africa, Mediterranean, Middle East and Black Sea; Chair. and CEO John M. Wilson, Jr; Pres. Richard Gronda.

THE UNITED STATES OF AMERICA

Lasco Shipping Co: 3200 NW Yeon Ave, Portland, OR 97210; tel. (503) 323-2700; fax (503) 323-2794; e-mail lasco@schn.com; Pres. A. L. THEOHARIS; 25 vessels.

Lykes Lines Ltd: 401 East Jackson St, Suite 3300, POB 31244, Tampa, FL 33631-3244; tel. (813) 276-4600; fax (813) 276-4873; f. 1997; routes from US Gulf and Atlantic ports to United Kingdom and northern Europe, Mediterranean and Africa; Pres. and CEO FRANK J. HALLIWELL.

Maritime Overseas Corpn: 511 Fifth Ave, New York, NY 10017; tel. (212) 953-4100; fax (212) 536-3735; manages c. 60 tankers and dry bulk carriers.

Matson Navigation Co: 333 Market St, POB 7452, San Francisco, CA 94120; tel. (415) 957-4000; fax (415) 957-4559; e-mail matson-info@www.matson.com; internet www.matson.com; f. 1901; container and other freight services between US west coast and Hawaii; container leasing world-wide; Chair. R. J. PFEIFFER; Pres. C. B. MULHOLLAND.

Mobil Oil Corpn: 3225 Gallows Rd, Fairfax, VA 22037; tel. (703) 846-1520; fax (703) 846-3180; Chair. and CEO L. A. NOTO; 29 vessels.

OMI Corpn: 90 Park Ave, New York, NY 10016-1302; tel. (212) 602-6700; fax (212) 602-6701; e-mail info@omnicorp.com; internet www.omnicorp.com; Chair. J. GOLDSTEIN; Pres. and CEO C. STEVENSON; 32 vessels.

Sea-Land Service, Inc: 6000 Carnegie Blvd, Charlotte, NC 28209-4613; tel. (704) 571-2000; largest US-flag container shipping co; 100 vessels providing containerized services to 80 ports in 120 countries and territories; Pres. and CEO JOHN P. CLANCEY.

SeaRiver Maritime, Inc: POB 1512, Houston, TX 77251-1512; tel. (713) 758-5000; fax (713) 758-5091; Pres. A. ELMER; 9 tankers.

Stolt-Nielsen Transportation Group: Stolt-Nielsen Bldg, 8 Sound Shore Dr., POB 2300, Greenwich, CT 06836; tel. (203) 625-9400; fax (203) 661-7695; Chair. SAMUEL L. COOPERMAN; CEO REGINALD J. R. LEE; 142 tankers.

Waterman Steamship Corpn: 1 Whitehall St, New York, NY 10004; tel. (212) 747-8550; fax (212) 747-8588; e-mail waterman@intship.com; internet www.waterman-steamship.com; f. 1919; services to the Middle East and South-East Asia; Chair. C. S. WALSH; Pres. N. M. JOHNSEN.

Associations

American Bureau of Shipping: 16855 Northchase Dr., Houston, TX 77060; tel. (281) 877-5800; fax (281) 877-5803; e-mail abs-worldhq@eagle.org; internet www.eagle.org; f. 1862; Chair. ROBERT D. SOMMERVILLE; Pres. ROBERT E. KRAMEK; 814 mems.

American Maritime Congress: Franklin Sq., 1300 Eye St, Suite 250 West, NW, Washington, DC 20005-3314; tel. (202) 842-4900; fax (202) 842-3492; e-mail gloriatosi@americanmaritime.org; f. 1977; mems represent major US-flag ship operating cos; Exec. Dir GLORIA CATANEO TOSI.

Chamber of Shipping of America: 1730 M St, NW, Suite 407, Washington, DC 20036-4517; tel. (202) 775-4399; fax (202) 659-3795; e-mail kjmetcalf@msn.com; Pres. JOSEPH J. COX; represents 19 US-based cos.

CIVIL AVIATION

Federal Aviation Administration: 800 Independence Ave, SW, Washington, DC 20591; tel. (202) 366-4000; internet www.faa.gov; f. 1958; part of the Dept of Transportation; promotes safety in the air, regulates air commerce and assists in development of an effective national airport system; Admin. MARION C. BLAKEY.

Principal Scheduled Companies

In September 2005 Delta Air Lines and Northwest Air Lines filed for bankruptcy; at that time United Air Lines and US Airways were already operating under Chapter 11 bankruptcy regulations.

Alaska Airlines: POB 68900, Seattle, WA 98168-0900; tel. (206) 433-3200; fax (206) 433-7253; internet www.alaskaair.com; f. 1932; Chair. and CEO JOHN KELLY; scheduled services to 35 US destinations as well as Canada and Mexico.

American Airlines Inc: POB 619616, Dallas/Fort Worth Airport, TX 75261-9616; tel. (817) 967-1577; fax (817) 967-4162; internet www.aa.com; f. 1934; Chair. and CEO DONALD CARTY; coast-to-coast domestic routes and services to Canada, Hawaii, Mexico, the Caribbean, South America, Europe and the Far East; acquired Trans World Airlines in 2001.

Continental Airlines Inc: 2929 Allen Pkwy, POB 4607, Houston, TX 77210-4607; tel. (713) 324-5000; fax (713) 523-2831; internet www.continental.com; f. 1934; Chair. and CEO GORDON M. BETHUNE; serves 139 US destinations and 85 points in Mexico, Canada, Europe and the Far East.

Delta Air Lines Inc: Hartsfield Atlanta International Airport, Atlanta, GA 30320-9998; tel. (770) 715-2600; fax (770) 715-5494; internet www.delta.com; f. 1929; CEO GERALD GRINSTEIN; domestic and international services to 208 cities in 32 countries.

Hawaiian Airlines Inc: 30008, Honolulu International Airport, Honolulu, HI 96820; tel. (808) 835-3700; fax (808) 835-3690; internet www.hawaiianair.com; f. 1929; Pres. and CEO PAUL J. CASEY; inter-island, US mainland and South Pacific services.

Northwest Airlines, Inc: 2700 Lone Oak Parkway, Eagan, MN 55121; tel. (612) 726-2111; fax (612) 726-0622; internet www.nwa.com; f. 1926; Chair. GARY L. WILSON; 113 domestic destinations and 42 points in Canada, Europe and the Far East.

Southwest Airlines: POB 36611, Love Field, Dallas, TX 75235; tel. (214) 792-4000; fax (214) 792-4011; internet www.southwest.com; scheduled domestic carrier; CEO MARY C. KELLY KELLEHER.

United Airlines Corpn: POB 66100, Chicago, IL 60666-0100; tel. (847) 700-4000; fax (847) 700-7347; internet www.ual.com; f. 1934; Chair., Pres. and CEO GLENN F. TILTON, Jr; domestic and international services to 139 destinations in 26 countries.

US Airways, Inc: 2345 Crystal Dr., Arlington, VA 22227; tel. (703) 872-7000; fax (703) 872-7304; internet www.usairways.com; f. 1939; Chair. and Acting CEO STEPHEN M. WOLF; scheduled passenger services to 210 points in the USA and world-wide.

Associations

Air Freight Association of America: 1220 19th St, NW, Suite 400, Washington, DC 20036; tel. (202) 293-1030; fax (202) 293-4377; f. 1948; Exec. Vice-Pres. STEPHEN A. ALTERMAN; 27 mems.

Air Transport Association of America, Inc: 1301 Pennsylvania Ave, NW, Suite 1100, Washington, DC 20004-1707; tel. (202) 626-4000; fax (202) 626-4181; internet www.airlines.org; f. 1936; Pres. and CEO JAMES C. MAY; mems: 22 US airlines, 4 non-US assoc. mems.

National Air Carrier Association: 1000 Wilson Blvd, Suite 9700, Arlington, VA 22209; tel. (703) 358-8060; e-mail naca@erols.com; internet www.naca.cc; f. 1962; Pres. RONALD N. PRIDDY; 16 mems.

National Air Transportation Association: 4226 King St, Alexandria, VA 22302; tel. (703) 845-9000; fax (703) 845-8176; e-mail info@nata-online.org; internet www.nata.online.org; f. 1940; Pres. JAMES E. COYNE.

Regional Airline Association: 1200 19th St, NW, Suite 300, Washington, DC 20036; tel. (202) 857-1170; fax (202) 429-5113; e-mail raa@sba.com; internet www.raa.org; Pres. WALTER S. COLEMAN.

Tourism

American Society of Travel Agents Inc: 1101 King St, Alexandria, VA 22314; tel. (703) 739-2782; fax (703) 684-8319; internet www.astanet.com; f. 1931; Pres. and CEO RICHARD M. COPLAND; Exec. Vice-Pres. WILLIAM A. MALONEY; 27,000 mems.

Office of Travel and Tourism Industries: International Trade Administration, US Department of Commerce, Rm 7025, Washington, DC 20230; tel. (202) 482-0140; fax (202) 482-2887; internet www.tinet.doc.gov; f. 1996; fed. govt agency; collects and analyses data and develops US tourism policy; Dep. Asst Sec. for Services DOUGLAS B. BAKER.

Travel Industry Association of America: 1100 New York Ave, NW, Suite 450, Washington, DC 20005; tel. (202) 408-8422; fax (202) 255-1225; internet www.tia.org; f. 1941; Pres. and CEO WILLIAM NORMAN.

US National Tourism Organization: 1100 New York Ave, NW, Suite 450, Washington, DC 20005; tel. (202) 408-8686; fax (202) 255-1225; f. 1996; promotes travel within the USA; Exec. Dir MARK HOY.

UNITED STATES COMMONWEALTH TERRITORIES

There are two US Commonwealth Territories, the Northern Mariana Islands, in the Pacific Ocean, and Puerto Rico, in the Caribbean Sea. A Commonwealth is a self-governing incorporated territory that is an integral part of, and in full political union with, the USA.

THE NORTHERN MARIANA ISLANDS

Introductory Survey

Location, Climate, Language, Religion, Flag, Capital

The Commonwealth of the Northern Mariana Islands comprises 14 islands (all the Marianas except Guam) in the western Pacific Ocean, about 5,300 km (3,300 miles) west of Honolulu (Hawaii). The temperature normally ranges between 24°C (75°F) and 30°C (86°F) in June–November, but is generally cooler and drier from December to May. The average annual rainfall is about 2,120 mm (84 ins). English, Chamorro and Carolinian are the official languages. The population is predominantly Christian, mainly Roman Catholic. The national flag of the United States of America (q.v.) is used by the Northern Mariana Islands. Six islands, including the three largest (Saipan, Tinian and Rota), are inhabited; the principal settlement and the administrative centre are on Saipan.

Recent History

The islands which comprise the Northern Mariana Islands were first sighted by Europeans during the 1520s, and were claimed for Spain in 1565. They were sold to Germany in 1899, but control was transferred to Japan, which had taken the islands from Germany in 1914, by the League of Nations in 1921. The USA captured Saipan and Tinian from the Japanese after fierce fighting in 1944, and the Northern Mariana Islands became a part of the Trust Territory of the Pacific Islands in 1947. (See the chapter on the Marshall Islands.)

In June 1975 the Northern Mariana Islands voted for separate status as a US Commonwealth Territory, and in March 1976 US President Ford signed the Northern Marianas Commonwealth Covenant. In October 1977 President Carter approved the Constitution of the Northern Mariana Islands, which provided that, from January 1978, the former Marianas District was internally self-governing. In December 1977 elections took place for a bicameral legislature, a Governor and a Lieutenant-Governor. In July 1984 it was reported that the US President, Ronald Reagan, had signed a proclamation giving residents of the Northern Mariana Islands a broad range of civil and political rights in the USA, including equal employment opportunities within the federal government, civil service and armed forces. The Northern Marianas were formally admitted to US Commonwealth status in November 1986, after the ending of the Trusteeship in the Territory. At the same time a proclamation, issued by Reagan, conferred US citizenship on the islands' residents.

At elections in 1989 Republicans retained control of the governorship and ousted a Democrat from the position of Washington Representative. Larry Guerrero was elected Governor after Pedro Tenorio had decided to stand down. Democratic candidates, however, won a majority of seats in the House of Representatives.

In December 1990 the UN Security Council voted to end the Trusteeship of the Northern Marianas, as well as that of two other Pacific Trust Territories. Although the decision to terminate the relationship had been taken in 1986, voting had been delayed. Guerrero, however, opposed the termination on the grounds that the new relationship would leave the islands subject to US law while remaining unrepresented in the US Congress.

At elections to the House of Representatives (which had been enlarged by three seats) in 1991 Republicans regained a majority. Similarly, the party increased the number of its senators to eight. Republicans retained their majority at elections to the House of Representatives in 1993. However, in the gubernatorial election a Democrat, Froilan Tenorio, was successful. Similarly, a Democratic candidate, Jesús Borja, was elected as Lieutenant-Governor, while Juan Babauta remained as Washington Representative.

The Territory's reputation was marred in April 1995 when the Government of the Philippines introduced a ban on its nationals accepting unskilled employment in the islands, because of persistent reports of abuse and exploitation of immigrant workers. Meanwhile, the US Congress announced that it was to allocate US $7m. towards the enforcement of the islands' labour and immigration laws, following the publication of a report in late 1994 that alleged the repeated violations of these regulations, as well as widespread corruption among immigration officials and business leaders.

In May 1997 the US President, Bill Clinton, informed Tenorio of his intention to apply US immigration and minimum wage laws to the Territory, stating that labour practices in the islands were inconsistent with US values. In the previous month Democratic congressman George Miller had proposed legislation in the US House of Representatives (the Insular Fair Wage and Human Rights Act) that would equalize the minimum wage level in the islands with that of the US mainland by 1999. The Territory's Government, which denied many of the claims of exploitation of immigrant workers, responded to the proposed legislation by initiating a public relations campaign that persuaded the Republican majority in the US House of Representatives to oppose the bill; labour standards dominated the election campaign during late 1997.

In January 1999 the Office of Insular Affairs (OIA) of the US Department of the Interior published a report in which it concluded that the Government's attempts to eradicate abuses of labour and immigration laws had been unsuccessful. In particular, it had failed to reduce the Territory's reliance on alien workers, to enforce US minimum wage laws and to curb evasions of trade legislation governing the export of garments to the USA. In the same month former employees of 18 US clothing retailers initiated legal action against the companies, which were accused of failing to comply with US labour laws in Saipan. In April 2000 a settlement was reached with the garment manufacturers, providing some US $8m. in compensation for the workers. The companies also agreed to conform to regulations established by an independent monitoring system in Saipan.

At legislative elections on 1 November 1997 Republican candidates won 13 of the 18 seats in the House of Representatives and eight of the nine seats in the Senate. At the gubernatorial election, held concurrently, Pedro Tenorio was successful, securing 46% of total votes. Opponents of Pedro Tenorio subsequently initiated a legal challenge to his election on the grounds that it constituted his third term as Governor, thereby violating the Constitution, which states that a maximum of two gubernatorial terms may be served by any one individual (although the Constitution had been amended to include this provision only during Pedro Tenorio's second term in office).

Following legislative elections on 6 November 1999, Democratic candidates held two of the nine seats in the Senate and six of the 18 seats in the House of Representatives.

In February 2000 the US Senate approved a bill granting permanent residency in the Northern Marianas to some 40,000 immigrant workers. However, the bill also included provisions for limiting the stay of all future guest workers. In December 2000 Governor Tenorio announced that he was to oppose the decision by the US Government to bring the Northern Marianas' labour and immigration laws under federal control; Tenorio argued that this might have a negative impact on the Northern Marianas' economy. In May 2001, following intense lobbying by the Northern Marianas Government, the US Congress abandoned the bill.

Legislative elections were held on 3 November 2001, at which the Republican Party secured 12 seats in the House of Representatives, the Democratic Party won five and the Covenant Party took one. The Republican Party won six seats in the Senate, the Democratic Party two and the Covenant Party one. Gubernatorial elections were held concurrently, at which Juan Nekai Babauta, the Republican Party candidate and former Representative to Washington, won a convincing victory, securing 42.8% of the votes cast. Benigno Fitial, of the Covenant Party, received 24.4%. Babauta was inaugurated as Governor in January 2002, while Diego Benavente, his running mate and the former Speaker of the House of Representatives, became Lieutenant-Governor.

In January 2002 the Supreme Court suspended deportation proceedings against an immigrant labourer working in the Northern Marianas illegally, after he appealed to the office of the UN High Commissioner for Refugees. The Court warned the Government that it might not be able to order the deportation of up to 10,000 of the Chinese, Sri Lankan and Bangladeshi workers in the Northern

Marianas. In late 2002 the Government successfully resisted an attempt by the US Administration to place the Northern Mariana Islands' immigration and labour legislation under direct federal control. In September 2003 the Northern Mariana Islands announced a new immigration co-operation agreement with the US Department of the Interior, which removed the right of overseas political refugees in the territory to seek asylum in the USA.

In May 2002 the issue of the Northern Marianas' working conditions was raised again by US Senator Edward Kennedy, who proposed a bill that would incrementally increase the minimum wage. In late September 2002 seven further major US clothing retailers agreed to pay US $11.25m. in compensation to employees alleged to have suffered intolerable working conditions and poor rates of pay. The funds also included sponsorship of independent monitoring of labour conditions in the islands. The case was finally settled in April 2003, when a total of $20m. in compensation was ordered to be made to the claimants. The Garment Oversight Board was constituted in June, with the authority to withdraw certification of working conditions in garment factories supplying major US clothing companies. In March 2004 the Board decertified one of the 26 participating garment manufacturers. In April more than 400 garment workers were referred to the Division of Immigration for probable deportation as a result of their non-co-operation with a Fair Labor Standards Act civil action against garment manufacturers. Nevertheless, a delegate from the US Commission on Civil Rights concluded in May of that year that the situation of garment workers on Saipan appeared to be improving. However, owing to unfavourable external circumstances (see Economic Affairs), in 2005 several garment factories ceased operations or reduced their work-force. In early April the repatriation of migrant workers no longer in employment began. In mid-2005 the minimum hourly wage in the Northern Marianas stood at $3.05, some 40% less than the rate prevailing in the mainland USA. Legislation seeking to harmonize the minimum wage in the Northern Marianas with that of the USA was introduced to the US Senate in May. The legislation was criticized by the Speaker of the House, Benigno R. Fitial, who believed that the resultant rise in the minimum wage would place the Northern Marianas at a disadvantage with regional competitors.

A US court order filed by the Center for Biological Diversity, an environmental group, forced military training on the island of Farallon de Medinilla to be suspended for 30 days in mid-2002. Despite environmentalists' concerns about the impact and legality of US military activity—in particular the testing of ordnances—upon the island's wildlife, the Northern Marianas Chamber of Commerce feared that the substantial revenue generated by the visiting US military might be jeopardized.

In May 2002 the Government 'froze' the assets of the Bank of Saipan, pending auditing of its accounts, after the institution's former Chairman was arrested for allegedly attempting to defraud the bank of more than US $6.6m. The bank, which was reported to hold substantial uninsured US government deposits, was placed in receivership and remained closed for 11 months. Following the bank's reopening in April 2003 with assets of some $12m., customers were permitted to retrieve a limited monthly quota of savings deposits. Four defendants were convicted in relation to the case in June.

In September 2002 Babauta proposed reforms to reduce government expenditure. In November the Government announced plans for a US $40m. bond issue to cover the cost of compensating traditional landowners for the loss of property expropriated for government use, and in April 2003 draft legislation was proposed that would substantially reduce government personnel costs. However, in August credit ratings agencies expressed concerns that the Government's other outstanding debts, in particular those to the Northern Mariana Islands' Retirement Fund, would prevent full repayment of the bonds.

At the legislative election of 1 November 2003 the Covenant Party gained a majority in the House of Representatives, winning nine of the 18 seats. The Republican Party secured seven seats, the Democrat Party took one seat and an independent candidate won one seat. The Covenant Party won three seats in the Senate, the Republican Party took two and the Democratic Party won one; three independent candidates were also elected. The rate of voter participation was reported to be 77.3%.

Several instances of corruption in public office were reported in 2003; in April Senator Ricardo S. Atalig was found guilty of illegally employing relatives of another Senator, José M. de la Cruz. (De la Cruz was suspended from office following his own conviction in July.) In August 2004 the Superior Court convicted the chief financial officer of Tinian municipality, Romeo Atalig Diaz, in the first public corruption case lodged by the new anti-corruption unit of the Attorney-General's Office. However, the sentence imposed (fines totalling only US $2,800) was considered derisory by the local press.

Several typhoons badly damaged property and infrastructure in 2002–04. The cost of repairs was met largely by assistance from the US Federal Emergency Management Agency. In late 2002, following the suspension of Northern Mariana islanders' access to medical facilities in Hawaii, islanders became legally obliged to contribute to the rising costs of their health care, although in March 2003 the Bush Administration pledged US $15m. to assist the development of adequate health care infrastructure in the US Pacific territories. None the less, the health and welfare of the population remained a cause for concern in 2002 and 2003, following the publication of independent surveys that claimed that the Northern Marianas registered the world's third highest incidence of diabetes and a child poverty rate of some 38%.

Co-operation between the Northern Marianas and the USA continued to increase. In early 2004 the Northern Marianas' representative in Washington, Pete Tenorio, requested authorization for a non-voting delegate to the US Congress from the Northern Marianas. In May four members of the original team of Covenant negotiators considered publicly the possibility of the Northern Marianas becoming the 51st state of the USA. Congressional approval was expected for a bill introduced in February 2005 proposing the creation of a delegate seat for the Northern Marianas in the US House of Representatives. Conditional upon the bill's passage into law, which was pending in early 2006, the election for the first congressional delegate was scheduled to take place later that year.

At legislative elections held on 5 November 2005 the Covenant Party won eight seats in the House of Representatives, the Republican Party seven seats, the Democratic Party two seats and an independent candidate one seat. Following the election, the Covenant Party and the Republican Party each held three seats in the Senate, the Democratic Party had two seats and there was one independent senator. At the concurrent gubernatorial elections Benigno R. Fitial of the Covenant Party and the hitherto Vice-Speaker of the House, Timothy P. Villagomez, were elected Governor and Lieutenant-Governor, respectively, winning 3,809 votes (equivalent to 28.0% of valid votes cast). Independent Republican Heinz S. Hofschneider and his vice-gubernatorial candidate, David M. Apatang, came second with 3,710 votes (27.3%), while incumbent Governor Babauta and Lieutenant-Governor Diego Benavente came third with 3,610 votes (26.7%). Following his election, Governor Fitial said that the alleviation of the Marianas' economic problems would be the priority of his administration.

Government

Legislative authority is vested in the Northern Marianas Commonwealth Legislature, a bicameral body consisting of the Senate and the House of Representatives. There are nine senators, elected for four-year terms, and 18 members of the House of Representatives, elected for two-year terms. Executive authority is vested in the Governor, who is elected by popular vote.

Defence

The USA is responsible for the defence of the Northern Marianas.

Economic Affairs

The Commonwealth of the Northern Mariana Islands' gross national income (GNI) was estimated by the Bank of Hawaii (BOH) to be US $696.3m. in 1999. GNI per head was estimated at $8,582. The population increased at an estimated annual rate of more than 4.6% during 1990–2002. According to the BOH, the territory's gross domestic product (GDP) totalled $557.0m. in 2002.

Agriculture is concentrated in smallholdings, important crops being coconuts, breadfruit, tomatoes and melons. Cattle-ranching is practised on Tinian. Vegetables, beef and pork are produced for export. There is little commercial fishing in the islands (the total catch was 163 metric tons in 2003), although there is a major transhipment facility at Tinian harbour. Imports of fish products increased from 1990; fishing remains a potentially valuable but as yet unrealized commercial resource. Agriculture (including forestry, fishing and mining) engaged 1.5% of the employed labour force, according to the census of 2000, and its commercial value as a sector is minimal. In 2002 it accounted for only 0.1% of gross business revenues (total revenues generated by business transactions; the Government does not calculate gross domestic product figures).

Industry (including manufacturing and construction) engaged 47.2% of the employed labour force in 2000. Manufacturing alone engaged 40.7% of workers, while construction employed 6.5%. The principal manufacturing activity is the garment industry, which grew rapidly after its establishment in the mid-1980s to become the islands' chief export sector. Manufacturers benefit from US regulations that permit duty-free and quota-free imports from the Commonwealth. Garment manufacturing accounted for 23.6% of gross business revenues in 2002, and overall exports of garments were worth US $925.7m. in 2001, compared with $1,017m. in 2000. The Government's direct revenues from the industry were projected to reach $48.2m. in 2003. The terminal decline of this industry in the Northern Marianas was being widely predicted by 2004, owing to increased domestic regulation and taxation, the moratorium of the World Trade Organization (WTO, see p. 370) on garment quotas, which came into force in January 2005, and stronger global competition (not least since the People's Republic of China joined the WTO in

2001). Several garment factories closed or reduced their work-force in 2005. Other small-scale manufacturing activities include handicrafts and the processing of fish and copra. Construction is very closely related to the tourist industry and demand for additional hotel capacity. However, the number of building permits sold, both commercial and residential, declined each year during 1997–2001, although there was a slight improvement in 2002.

Service industries dominate the economy, particularly tourism. In 2000 services (including utilities) engaged 51.3% of the employed labour force, whilst accounting for 29.2% of gross business revenues. Tourist receipts, however, declined from an estimated US $430m. in 2001 to $225m. in 2002. Japan provided the majority (68.7%) of the islands' visitors in 2002. Other significant sources of tourists were the Republic of Korea, Guam, the USA and the People's Republic of China. Although tourist numbers increased by 5.3% in 2000, the industry was severely affected by the repercussions of the September 2001 terrorist attacks on the USA: the hotel occupancy rate declined to only 35% in December 2001, and arrivals decreased by 15.6% in the year as a whole. A total of 535,224 visitors travelled to the islands in 2004, an increase of 16.5% in relation to the previous year. It was reported that hotel occupancy in 2004 had increased by some 10% compared with 2003, to reach 71.75%. Prospects for tourism improved further following the decision of the Chinese Government, in October 2004, to accord the status of approved destination to the Northern Marianas from April 2005. However, in May 2005 Japan Airlines, which hitherto had carried some 14,300 passengers per month to the Northern Marianas from Japan, announced its decision to suspend its flights to Saipan from October. Furthermore, it was reported that many Japanese tourists, especially families, were deterred from visiting Saipan because of the high and visible prevalence of prostitution on the island. Meanwhile, direct flights from Beijing, which had operated on a twice-weekly basis in mid-2004, were also terminated, leading in 2005 to a reported year-on-year decline of 23% in visitors from the People's Republic of China to the islands during July. In December it was estimated that, year-on-year, Japanese tourist arrivals for that month had decreased by 29%. However, arrivals from the People's Republic of China and the Republic of Korea had reportedly increased, year-on-year, and in February 2006 Northwest Airlines announced the commencement in April of a second weekly Tokyo–Saipan flight. In mid-1995, meanwhile, a US company opened the Territory's first casino on Tinian (gambling being prohibited on other islands). The Northern Marianas were expected to receive some $12m. annually in revenue from this casino. In February 2005 it was announced that a South Korean company was shortly to commence construction of a new resort near Tinian International Airport. To comprise 1,000 rooms, the hotel complex was to incorporate a casino and a golf course. This major project, which was to cost $300m., had attracted investment from various Asian countries, including China, as well as from the USA. In late 2005 the Virgin Islands-based Bridge Investment Group, LLC announced a $150m. project to build a hotel and casino complex on Tinian.

The Northern Marianas are dependent on imports, the value of which totalled US $267.2m. in 2000. The principal imports in that year were clothing (which accounted for 27.6% of the total), beverages (2.8%), construction materials (2.8%) and automobiles and parts (2.2%). In 1991 there was a trade deficit of $126.9m. In 2001 remittances from overseas workers and investments reached $76.7m.

The annual rate of inflation averaged 0.7%% in 1995–2004. After declining in 2003, consumer prices increased by 0.9% in 2004.

Under the Covenant between the Commonwealth of the Northern Mariana Islands and the USA, the islands receive substantial annual development grants. Loans from the Commonwealth Development Authority totalled more than US $0.5m. in 2001.

The Territory is a member of the Pacific Community (see p. 350) and an associate member of the UN Economic and Social Commission for Asia and the Pacific (ESCAP, see p. 33).

Continued economic problems in the Territory have been largely attributed to the dramatic increase in the Northern Marianas' population (from some 17,000 in 1979 to 74,151 in 2002). The main constraints on development have included the inadequacy of the islands' infrastructure, labour shortages and the dependence on foreign workers, Filipino nationals in particular. However, owing to the resulting excess of immigrant workers (whose numbers increased by 655% between 1980 and 1989 and exceeded the permanent population by a margin of two to one in the early 2000s), wages remained relatively low, and there were widespread complaints of poor working conditions. In September 2002 a judgment on a lawsuit against garment manufacturers in Saipan awarded compensation to the affected workers and provided for independent monitoring of labour practices in the Northern Marianas (see Recent History). Although the islands' Government resisted legislative proposals to bring immigration and labour practices into line with the mainland USA, there was concern in the Territory that new WTO measures removing import quotas on clothing, which took effect in January 2005, represented a direct threat to the comparative advantage of the garment industry's location within an unincorporated US Territory. None the less, the Northern Mariana Islands have long benefited from their political association with the USA; US federal funding and development assistance totalled some US $13m. in 2001/02, and in January 2004 an agreement was signed whereby the Northern Mariana Islands were to receive some $5.1m. in federal funding in order to offset the impact of migration, under the Compact of Free Association, to the Territory from the Marshall Islands, the Federated States of Micronesia, and Palau. In November 2004 it was reported that the islands' Republican administration, inaugurated in 2002, had pledged to prioritize economic reform by promoting free, competitive markets with a minimum of government intervention. In March 2002 the Government introduced tax incentives for new businesses and developers, worth a potential 100% abatement of local taxes, or a 95% rebate of federal taxes. However, despite improved expenditure controls, the continued recession in the islands was estimated to have led to a deterioration in the Government's fiscal position and an increase in public debt. In January 2006 the Senate approved legislation allowing the Governor to amend budgeted government expenditure for 2005/06, which had been limited at $213m. Later that month Governor Fitial authorized substantial reductions in government spending, primarily in order to divert funds to the Commonwealth Utilities Corporation, in the hope of ending the frequent power failures in the territory. Government revenue for 2005/06 was projected at $198.5m.

Education

School attendance is compulsory from six to 16 years of age. In 2002/03 there were 12 state primary schools, with a total of 5,849 pupils enrolled, and there were nine state secondary schools, with a total enrolment of 4,705 pupils. There was a total of 18 private schools, with a total enrolment of 2,326 pupils. There was one college of further education, with 1,641 students in 2000/01. Budgetary expenditure on education totalled US $49.6m. in 2000, equivalent to 22.0% of total government expenditure.

Public Holidays

2006: 2 January (for New Year's Day), 9 January (Commonwealth Day), 20 February (Presidents' Day), 24 March (Covenant Day), 14 April (Good Friday), 29 May (Memorial Day), 4 July (Liberation Day), 4 September (Labor Day), 9 October (Columbus Day), 3 November (Citizenship Day), 10 November (Veterans' Day), 23 November (Thanksgiving Day), 8 December (Constitution Day), 25 December (Christmas Day).

2007: 9 January (Commonwealth Day), 15 January (Martin Luther King Day), 21 February (Presidents' Day), 24 March (Covenant Day), 25 March (Good Friday), 30 May (Memorial Day), 4 July (Liberation Day), 5 September (Labor Day), 10 October (Columbus Day), 4 November (Citizenship Day), 11 November (Veterans' Day), 24 November (Thanksgiving Day), 8 December (Constitution Day), 26 December (for Christmas Day).

Weights and Measures

With certain exceptions, the imperial system is in force. One US cwt equals 100 lb; one long ton equals 2,240 lb; one short ton equals 2,000 lb. A policy of gradual voluntary conversion to the metric system is being encouraged by the Federal Government.

Statistical Survey

Source: (unless otherwise stated): Department of Commerce, Central Statistics Division, POB 10007, Saipan, MP 96950; tel. 664-3000; fax 664-3001; internet www.commerce.gov.mp.

AREA AND POPULATION

Area: 457 sq km (176.5 sq miles). *By Island*: Saipan 120 sq km (46.5 sq miles); Tinian 102 sq km (39.2 sq miles); Rota 85 sq km (32.8 sq miles); Pagan 48 sq km (18.6 sq miles); Anatahan 32 sq km (12.5 sq miles); Agrihan 30 sq km (11.4 sq miles); Alamagan 11 sq km (4.4 sq miles); Asuncion 7 sq km (2.8 sq miles); Aguijan (Goat Is) 7 sq km (2.7 sq miles); Sarigan 5 sq km (1.9 sq miles); Guguan 4 sq km (1.5 sq miles); Farallon de Pajaros 3 sq km (1.0 sq miles); Maug 2 sq km (0.8 sq miles); Farallon de Medinilla 1 sq km (0.4 sq miles).

Population: 43,345 at census of 1 April 1990; 69,221 (males 31,984, females 37,237) at census of 1 April 2000. *By Island*: Saipan 62,392; Rota 3,283; Tinian 3,540; Northern Islands 6. *2002* (estimates): Saipan 67,011; Total 74,151.

Density (2002 census): 162 per sq km.

Ethnic Groups (2000 census): Filipino 18,141; Chinese 15,311; Chamorro 14,749; part-Chamorro 4,383; Total (incl. others) 69,221.

Principal Towns (2000 census): San Antonio 4,741; Garapan (capital) 3,588; Koblerville 3,543; San Vincente 3,494; Tanapag 3,318; Chalan Kanoa 3,108; Kagman 3,026. Source: Thomas Brinkhoff, *City Population* (internet www.citypopulation.de).

Births and Deaths (2002): Registered live births 1,289 (birth rate 17.4 per 1,000); Registered deaths 164 (death rate 2.2 per 1,000).

Employment (2000 census, persons aged 16 years and over): Agriculture, forestry, fisheries and mining 623; Manufacturing 17,398; Construction 2,785; Transport, communication and utilities 1,449; Trade, restaurants and hotels 9,570; Financing, insurance and real estate 1,013; Community, social and personal services 9,915; *Total employed* 42,753 (males 19,485, females 23,268); Unemployed 1,712 (males 888, females 824); *Total labour force* 44,465 (males 20,373, females 24,092). *Mid-2003* (estimates): Agriculture, etc. 9,000; Total labour force 35,000 (Source: FAO).

AGRICULTURE, ETC.

Livestock (1997): Cattle 1,789; Pigs 831; Goats 249; Poultry birds 29,409.

Fishing (metric tons, live weight, 2003): Total catch 163 (Skipjack tuna 71; Yellowfin tuna 12; Scads 6). Source: FAO.

FINANCE

Currency and Exchange Rates: United States currency is used: 100 cents = 1 United States dollar (US $). *Sterling and Euro Equivalents* (30 December 2005): £1 sterling = US $1.7219; €1 = US $1.1797; US $100 = £58.08 = €84.77.

Federal Direct Payments (US $ million, 2002, rounded figures): Social security 10.3; Retirement and disability 6.3; Veterans 0.5; Other direct payments 3.2; Total 21.0.

Budget (estimates, US $ million, year ending 30 September 2002): Total revenue 199.7 (Taxes 166.8, Service fees 28.7, Operating transfers 4.3); Total expenditure 212.1 (Wages, salaries and benefits 108.9; Other expenditure 103.2). Source: Bank of Hawaii, *Commonwealth of the Northern Mariana Islands Economic Report* (October 2003).

Cost of Living (Consumer Price Index for Saipan; base: 2000 = 100): 99.4 in 2002; 98.4 in 2003; 99.3 in 2004. Source: ILO.

Gross Domestic Product (US $ million in current prices, estimate): 557.0 in 2002. Source: Bank of Hawaii, *Commonwealth of the Northern Mariana Islands Economic Report* (October 2003).

EXTERNAL TRADE

Principal Commodities (US $ million): *Imports* (1997): Beverages 12.8; Tobacco 5.4; Automobiles (incl. parts) 42.1; Clothing 309.2; Total (incl. others) 836.2. *Exports* (2000): Total 1,000.

Principal Trading Partners (US $ million, 1997): *Imports*: Guam 298.0; Hong Kong 200.5; Japan 118.3; Korea, Republic 80.6; USA 63.3; Total (incl. others) 836.2.

Sources: UN, *Statistical Yearbook for Asia and the Pacific* and *Statistical Yearbook*.

TRANSPORT

Shipping: *Registered Fleet* (2001): 1,029 vessels (791 fishing vessels); *Traffic* ('000 short tons, 1997): Goods loaded 184.1; Goods unloaded 425.9.

Civil Aviation (Saipan Int. Airport, year ending September 1999): 23,853 aircraft landings; 562,364 boarding passengers. Source: Commonwealth Ports Authority.

Road Traffic (registered motor vehicles, 2001): 17,900.

TOURISM

Visitor Arrivals: 444,284 in 2001; 475,547 in 2002; 459,458 in 2003. Source: World Tourism Organization.

Visitor Arrivals by Country (2002): Japan 326,735; Korea, Republic 90,324; USA (incl. Guam) 35,858; China, People's Republic 10,471.

Tourism Receipts (US $ million): 407 in 1999; 430 in 2000; 225 in 2002 (approximate figure). Source: Bank of Hawaii, *Commonwealth of the Northern Mariana Islands Economic Report* (October 2003).

COMMUNICATIONS MEDIA

Radio Receivers (households with access, census of 2000): 10,684.

Television Receivers (estimate, 1995): 15,460 in use.

Telephones (main lines in use, 2001): 25,306.

Mobile Cellular Telephones (2000): 3,000 subscribers*.

Facsimile Machines (1996): 1,200 in use†.

* Source: International Telecommunication Union.
† Source: UN, *Statistical Yearbook*.

EDUCATION

Pre-primary (2002/03, state schools, Headstart programme): 12 schools; 98 teachers; 606 pupils.

Primary (2002/03, state schools): 12 schools; 283 teachers; 5,849 students.

Secondary (2002/03, state schools): 9 schools; 248 teachers; 4,705 students.

Higher (2000/01): 1 college; 1,641 students (full- and part-time students).

Private Schools (2002/03): 18 schools; 186 teachers; 2,326 students.

Directory

The Government
(April 2006)

Governor: BENIGNO R. FITIAL (took office 9 January 2006).
Lieutenant-Governor: TIMOTHY P. VILLAGOMEZ.

DEPARTMENT SECRETARIES

Secretary of the Department of Finance: FEMIN ATALIG.

Secretary of the Department of Community and Cultural Affairs: DAISY VILLAGOMEZ-BIER.

Secretary of the Department of Labor: GIL M. SAN NICOLAS.

Secretary of the Department of Lands and Natural Resources: IGNACIO DELA CRUZ.

Secretary of the Department of Public Works: JOSE S. DEMAPAN.

Secretary of the Department of Commerce: ANDREW S. SALAS.

Commissioner of the Department of Public Safety: JUAN I. WABOL (acting).

Secretary of the Department of Public Health: JOSEPH KEVIN P. VILLAGOMEZ (acting).

GOVERNMENT OFFICES

Office of the Governor: Caller Box 10007, Capitol Hill, Saipan, MP 96950; tel. 664-2276; fax 664-2290; e-mail gov.frosario@saipan.com; internet www.saipan.com/gov/index.htm.

Office of the Resident Representative to the USA, Commonwealth of the Northern Mariana Islands: 2121 R St, NW, Washington, DC 20008; tel. (202) 673-5869; fax (202) 673-5873; e-mail rep@resrep.gov.mp; the Commonwealth Govt also has liaison offices in Hawaii and Guam.

Department of the Interior, Office of Insular Affairs (OIA): Field Office of the OIA, Dept of the Interior, POB 2622, Saipan, MP 96950; tel. 234-8861; fax 234-8814; e-mail jeff.schorr@saipan.com; internet www.doi.gov/oia/Islandpages/cnmipage.htm; OIA representation in the Commonwealth; Field Representative JEFFREY SCHORR.

Department of Commerce: Capitol Hill, Saipan, MP 96950; tel. 664-3000; fax 664-3067; e-mail commercedept@vzpacifica.net; internet www.commerce.gov.mp.

Department of Community and Cultural Affairs: Capitol Hill, Saipan, MP 96950; tel. 664-2571; fax 664-2570; e-mail dccaadm@vzpacifica.net.

Department of Finance: Capitol Hill, Saipan, MP 96950; tel. 664-1100; fax 664-1115; e-mail procurement@gtepacifica.net; internet www.dof.gov.mp.

Department of Labor: Capitol Hill, Saipan, MP 96950; tel. 236-0900; fax 236-0990.

Department of Lands and Natural Resources: Capitol Hill, Saipan, MP 96950; tel. 322-9830; fax 322-2633; e-mail dlnrgov@vzpacifica.net.

Department of Public Health: Capitol Hill, Saipan, MP 96950; tel. 236-8201; fax 236-8390.

Department of Public Safety: Capitol Hill, Saipan, MP 96950; tel. 664-9022; fax 664-9027; internet www.dps.gov.mp.

Department of Public Works: Capitol Hill, Saipan, MP 96950; tel. 235-5827; fax 235-6346.

UNITED STATES COMMONWEALTH TERRITORIES — The Northern Mariana Islands

Legislature

Legislative authority is vested in the Northern Marianas Commonwealth Legislature, a bicameral body consisting of the Senate and the House of Representatives. There are nine senators, elected for four-year terms, and 18 members of the House of Representatives, elected for two-year terms. The most recent legislative election was held on 5 November 2005. The Covenant Party won eight seats in the House of Representatives, the Republican Party seven seats, the Democratic Party two seats and an independent candidate one seat. Following the election, the Covenant Party and the Republican Party each held three seats in the Senate, the Democratic Party had two seats and there was one independent senator.

Senate President: (vacant).
Speaker of the House: (vacant).
Commonwealth Legislature: Capitol Hill, Saipan, MP 96950; tel. 664-7757; fax 322-6344.

Election Commission

Commonwealth Election Commission: POB 500470, Saipan, MP 96950; tel. 664-8683; fax 664-8689; internet www.votecnmi.gov.mp; Exec. Dir GREGORIO C. SABLAN.

Political Organizations

Covenant Party: c/o Commonwealth Legislature, Capitol Hill, Saipan, MP 96950; Leader BENIGNO R. FITIAL; Chair. ELOY INOS.
Democratic Party of the Commonwealth of the Northern Mariana Islands, Inc: Saipan; tel. 234-7497; fax 233-0641; Pres. Dr CARLOS S. CAMACHO; Chair. LORENZO CABRERA.
Republican Party of the Northern Marianas: POB 500777, Saipan, MP 96950; tel. 233-1288; fax 233-1288; e-mail dpwpio@vzpacifica.net; internet www.gop.com/States/StateDetails.aspx?state=MP; Pres. DAVID M. SABLAN; State Chair. JUAN S. REYES; Exec. Dir FELIPE Q. ATALIG.

Judicial System

The judicial system in the Commonwealth of the Northern Mariana Islands (CNMI) consists of the Superior Court, the Commonwealth Supreme Court (which considers appeals from the Superior Court) and the Federal District Court. Under the Covenant, federal law applies in the Commonwealth, apart from the following exceptions: the CNMI is not part of the US Customs Territory; the federal minimum-wage provisions do not apply; federal immigration laws do not apply; and the CNMI may enact its own taxation laws.

Attorney-General: MATTHEW T. GREGORY.
Public Defender: ELISA LONG (acting).

Religion

The population is predominantly Christian, mainly Roman Catholic. There are small communities of Episcopalians (Anglicans—under the jurisdiction of the Bishop of Hawaii, in the USA) and Protestants.

CHRISTIANITY

The Roman Catholic Church

The Northern Mariana Islands comprise the single diocese of Chalan Kanoa, suffragan to the archdiocese of Agaña (Guam). The Bishop participates in the Catholic Bishops' Conference of the Pacific, based in Suva, Fiji. At 31 December 2003 there were 43,000 adherents, including temporary residents, in the Northern Mariana Islands.

Bishop of Chalan Kanoa: Most Rev. TOMAS AGUON CAMACHO, Bishop's House, Chalan Kanoa, POB 500745, Saipan, MP 96950; tel. 234-3000; fax 235-3002; e-mail tcamacho@vzpacifica.net.

The Press

The weekly *Focus on the Commonwealth* is published in Guam, but distributed solely in the Northern Mariana Islands.

Marianas Observer: POB 502119, Saipan, MP 96950; tel. 233-3955; fax 233-7040; weekly; Publr JOHN VABLAN; Man. Editor ZALDY DANDAN; circ. 2,000.
Marianas Review: POB 501074, Saipan, MP 96950; tel. 234-7160; f. 1979 as *The Commonwealth Examiner*; weekly; English and Chamorro; independent; Publr LUIS BENAVENTE; Editor RUTH L. TIGHE; circ. 1,700.
Marianas Variety News and Views: POB 500231, Saipan, MP 96950; tel. 234-6341; fax 234-9271; e-mail mvariety@vzpacifica.net; internet www.mvariety.com; Mon.–Fri.; English and Chamorro; independent; f. 1972; Publrs ABED E. YOUNIS, PAZ C. YOUNIS; Editor ZALDY DANDAN; circ. 7,500.
North Star: Chalan Kanoa, POB 500745, Saipan, MP 96950; tel. 234-3000; fax 235-2531; e-mail north.star@saipan.com; internet www.cnmicatholic.org/News/NorthStar/North.htm; weekly; English and Chamorro; Roman Catholic; f. 1946; Publr BISHOP TOMAS A. CAMACHO; Man. Editor RUY VALENTE M. POLISTICO.
Pacific Daily News (Saipan bureau): POB 500822, Saipan, MP 96950; tel. 234-6423; fax 234-5986; Publr LEE WEBBER; circ. 5,000.
Pacific Star: POB 505815 CHRB, Saipan, MP 96950; tel. 288-0746; fax 288-0747; weekly; Operational Man. NICK LEGASPI; circ. 3,000.
Pacifica: POB 502143, Saipan, MP 96950; monthly; Editor MIKE MALONE.
Saipan Tribune: POB 10001, PMB 34, Saipan, MP 96950-8901; tel. 235-8747; fax 235-3740; e-mail editor.tribune@saipan.com; internet www.saipantribune.com; 2 a week; Editor JAYVEE L. VALLEJERA; Publr JOHN PANGELINAN; circ. 3,500.

Broadcasting and Communications

TELECOMMUNICATIONS

Verizon Micronesia/Pacifica: POB 500306 CK, Saipan, MP 96950; tel. 682-1060; fax 682-4555; e-mail larry.knecht@vzpacifica.com; internet www.vzpacifica.net; owned by Verizon Corpn (USA); Regional Man. LARRY KNECHT.

BROADCASTING

Radio

Inter-Island Communications, Inc: POB 500914, Saipan, MP 96950; tel. 234-7239; fax 234-0447; f. 1984; commercial; station KCNM-AM, or KZMI-FM in stereo; Gen. Man. HANS W. MICKELSON; Programme Dir KEN WARNICK; CEO ANGEL OCAMPO.
Far East Broadcasting Co, Inc: POB 500209, Saipan, MP 96950; tel. 322-9088; fax 322-3060; e-mail saipan@febc.org; internet www.febc.org; f. 1946; non-commercial religious broadcasts; Exec. Dir ROBERT L. SPRINGER; Pres. GREGG HARRIS.
KSAI-AM: tel. 234-6520; fax 234-3428; e-mail ksai@febc.org; f. 1978; local service; mainly religious broadcasts; Station Man. CHRIS SLABAUGH.
KFBS-SW: POB 500209, Saipan, MP 96950; tel. 322-9088; e-mail saipan@febc.org; internet www.febc.org; international broadcasts in Chinese, Indonesian, Russian, Vietnamese, Burmese, Mongolian; Far East Broadcasting Company, Inc; f. 1946; Exec. Dir ROBERT SPRINGER.
Power 99: POB 10000, Saipan, MP 96950; tel. 235-7999; fax 235-7998; e-mail curtis@saipan.com; internet www.radiopacific.com; Man. TINA PALACIOS.
The Rock 97.9: POB 10000 Saipan, MP 96950; tel. 235-7996; fax 235-7998; e-mail cdancoe@spbguam.com; internet www.radiopacific.com; Man. CURTIS DANCOE.
Station KHBI-SW: POB 501837, Saipan, MP 96950; tel. 234-6515; fax 234-5452; fmrly KYOI; non-commercial station owned by the *Christian Science Monitor* (USA); Gen. Man. DOMINGO VILLAR.
Station KPXP: PMB 415, Box 10000, Saipan, MP 96950; tel. 235-7996; fax 235-7998; e-mail curtis@saipan.com; internet www.radiopacific.com/p99/; f. 1981; acquired Station KRSI in 2000, which also broadcasts on Saipan; Gen. Man. CURTIS DANCOE.

Television

Marianas CableVision: Nauru Bldg, 2°, Susupe, Saipan, MP 96950; tel. 235-4628; fax 235-0965; e-mail mcv.service@saipan.com; internet www.mcvcnmi.com; 55-channel cable service provider, broadcasting US and Pacific Rim programmes; Pres. JOHN CRUIKSHANK; Gen. Man. MARK BIRMINGHAM.
Tropic Isles Cable TV Corporation: POB 501015, Saipan, MP 96950; tel. 234-7350; fax 234-9828; 33-channel commercial station, with 5 pay channels, broadcasting 24 hours a day; US programmes and local and international news; 5,000 subscribers; Gen. Man. FRED LORD.
KMCV-TV: POB 501298, Saipan, MP 96950; tel. 235-6365; fax 235-0965; f. 1992; 52-channel commercial station, with 8 pay channels, broadcasting 24 hours a day; US programmes and local and international news; 5,650 subscribers; Gen. Man. WAYNE GAMBLIN.

Finance

BANKING

Bank of Guam (USA): POB 500678, Saipan, MP 96950; tel. 233-5000; fax 233-5003; internet www.bankofguam.com; Gen. Man. MARCIE TOMOKANE; brs on Tinian and Rota.

UNITED STATES COMMONWEALTH TERRITORIES

The Northern Mariana Islands

Bank of Hawaii: Bank of Hawaii Bldg, El Monte Ave, Garapan, POB 500566, Saipan, MP 96950; tel. 236-8451; fax 236-8490; internet www.boh.com; Man. JOHN SHEATHER; 2 brs.

Bank of Saipan: POB 500690, Saipan, MP 96950; tel. 234-6260; fax 235-6294; e-mail bankofsaipan@gtepacifica.net; three-year period of receivership ended Aug. 2005; dep. US $23m. (Dec. 2004); Pres. JON BARGFREDE.

City Trust Bank: Gualo Rai, POB 501867, Saipan, MP 96950; tel. 234-7701; fax 234-8664; e-mail citytrustbank@ctbsaipan.com; Asst Vice-Pres. and Acting Man. MARIA LOURDES JOHNSON.

First Hawaiian Bank: Oleai Centre, Beach Rd, Chalan Laulau, Saipan 96950; tel. 234-6559; fax 236-8936; internet www.fhb.com; Gen. Man. KEN KATO.

First Savings and Loan Association of America (USA): Beach Rd, Susupe, POB 500324, Saipan, MP 96950; tel. 234-6617; Man. SUZIE WILLIAMS.

Guam Savings and Loan Bank: POB 503201, Saipan, MP 96950; tel. 233-2265; fax 233-2227; Gen. Man. GLEN PEREZ.

HSBC Ltd: Middle Rd, Garapan, Saipan, MP 96950; tel. 234-2468; fax 234-8882.

INSURANCE

Allied Insurance/Takagi and Associates, Inc: PPP 602 Box 10000 Saipan, MP 96950; tel. 233-2554; fax 670-2553; Gen. Man. PETER SIBLY.

Aon Insurance: Aon Insurance Micronesia (Saipan) Inc, POB 502177, Saipan, MP 96950; tel. 234-2811; fax 234-5462; e-mail rod.rankin@aon.com.au; internet www.aon.com; Communications Officer RODNEY RANKIN.

Associated Insurance Underwriters of the Pacific, Inc: POB 501369, Saipan, MP 96950; tel. 234-7222; fax 234-5367; e-mail aiup@itecnmi.com; Gen. Man. MAGGIE GEORGE.

Calvo's Insurance Underwriters, Inc.: POB 500035, Saipan, MP 96950; tel. 234-5699; fax 234-5693; e-mail calvospc@vzpacifica.net; internet www.calvosinsurance.com; Man. ELI C. BUENAVENTURA.

Century Insurance (Tan Holdings Corpn): Century Insurance PMB 193, POB 10000, Saipan, MP 96950; tel. 234-0609; fax 234-1845; e-mail customer_service@cicspn.com; Gen. Man. JERRY TAN.

General Accident Insurance Asia Ltd (Microl Insurance): POB 502177, Saipan, MP 96950; tel. 234-2811; fax 234-5462; Man. Dir MICHAEL W. GOURLAY.

Marianas Insurance Co Ltd: POB 502505, Saipan, MP 96950-2505; tel. 234-5091; fax 234-5093; e-mail mic@itecnmi.com; Gen. Man. ROSALIA S. CABRERA.

Midland Insurance Underwriters, Inc.: PMB 219, POB 10000, Capitol Hill, Saipan, MP 96950; tel. 235-3598; fax 235-3597; e-mail midland@vzpacifica.net.

Mitsui Sumitomo Insurance Co Ltd (Japan): POB 502505, Saipan, MP 96950-2505; tel. 234-5091; fax 234-5093; Gen. Man. ANDREW M. HOWLETT.

Moylan's Insurance Underwriters (Int.), Inc: POB 500658, Saipan, MP 96950; tel. 234-6571; fax 632-3788; e-mail saipan@moylansinsurance.com; internet www.moylansinsurance.com; Branch Man. TAMARA TALALEMOTOU.

Nichido Insurance: Oleai Central Bldg, San Jose, Saipan, MP 96950; tel. 234-5690; fax 234-5693.

Pacifica Insurance Underwriters, Inc: POB 500168, Saipan, MP 96950; tel. 234-6267; fax 234-5880; e-mail piui@pacificains.com; internet www.pacificains.com; Pres. NORMAN T. TENORIO.

Primerica Financial Services: POB 500964, Saipan, MP 96950; tel. 235-2912; fax 235-7910; Gen. Man. JOHN SABLAN.

Royal Crown Insurance: Royal Crown Bldg, Beach Road, Chalan LauLau, POB 10001, Saipan, MP 96950; tel. 234-2256; fax 234-2258.

Staywell: POB 502050, Saipan, MP 96950; tel. 323-4260; fax 323-4263; e-mail stwspn@ite.net; Man. FRANNY PANGELINAN.

Trade and Industry

GOVERNMENT AGENCIES

Commonwealth Development Authority: POB 502149, Wakins Bldg, Gualo Rai, Saipan, MP 96950; tel. 234-7145; fax 234-7144; e-mail administration@cda.gov.mp; internet www.cda.gov.mp; govt lending institution; funds capital improvement projects and private enterprises; offers tax incentives to qualified investors; Chair. TOM GLENN A. QUITUGA; CEO OSCAR C. CAMACHO (acting).

Marianas Public Lands Authority: POB 500380, Saipan, MP 96950; tel. 234-3751; fax 234-3755; e-mail mpla@vzpacifica.net; manages public land, which constitutes 82% of total land area in the Commonwealth (14% on Saipan).

CHAMBER OF COMMERCE

Saipan Chamber of Commerce: Chalan Kanoa, POB 500806 CK, Saipan, MP 96950; tel. 233-7150; fax 233-7151; e-mail saipanchamber@saipan.com; internet www.saipanchamber.com; Pres. ALEXANDER A. SABLAN; Exec. Dir CHRISTINE PARKE.

EMPLOYERS' ASSOCIATIONS

Association of Commonwealth Teachers (ACT): POB 5071, Saipan, MP 96950; tel. and fax 256-7567; e-mail cnmiteachers@netscape.net; supports the teaching profession and aims to improve education in state schools.

Saipan Garment Manufacturers' Association (SGMA): POB 10001, Saipan, MP 96950; tel. 235-7699; fax 235-7899; e-mail sgmaemy@vzpacifica.net; internet www.sgma-saipan.org; Exec. Dir (vacant).

UTILITIES

Commonwealth Utilities Corporation: POB 501220, Saipan, MP 96950; tel. 235-7025; fax 235-6145; e-mail cucedp@gtepacifica.net; scheduled for privatization.

TRADE UNION AND CO-OPERATIVES

International Brotherhood of Electrical Workers: c/o Micronesian Telecommunications Corpn, Saipan, MP 96950; Local 1357 of Hawaii branch of US trade union based in Washington, DC.

The Mariana Islands Co-operative Association, Rota Producers and Tinian Producers Associations operate in the islands.

Transport

RAILWAYS

There have been no railways operating in the islands since the Japanese sugar industry railway, on Saipan, ceased operations in the Second World War.

ROADS

In 1991 there were 494 km (307 miles) of roads on the islands, 320 km (199 miles) of which are on Saipan. First grade roads constitute 135 km (84 miles) of the total, 99 km (62 miles) being on Saipan. There is no public transport, apart from a school bus system.

SHIPPING

The main harbour of the Northern Mariana Islands is the Port of Saipan, which underwent extensive renovation in the mid-1990s. There are also two major harbours on Rota and one on Tinian. Several shipping lines link Saipan, direct or via Guam, with ports in Japan, Asia, the Philippines, the USA and other territories in the Pacific.

Commonwealth Ports Authority: POB 501055, Saipan, MP 96950; tel. 664-3500; fax 234-5962; e-mail cpa.admin@saipan.com; internet net.saipan.com/cftemplates/cpa/index.cfm; Exec. Dir CARLOS H. SALAS; Chair. RAMÓN S. PALACIOS.

Mariana Express Lines: POB 501937, CTS Building, Saipan, MP 96950; tel. 322-1690; fax 323-6355; e-mail winnie_ong@mariana-express.com; services between Saipan, Guam, Japan and Hong Kong; Man. WINIE ONG.

Saipan Shipping Co Inc (Saiship): Saiship Bldg, Charlie Dock, POB 500008, Saipan, MP 96950; tel. 322-9706; fax 322-3183; e-mail saiship.general@vzpacifica.net; weekly barge service between Guam, Saipan and Tinian; monthly services to Japan and Micronesia; Gen. Man. DARLENE CABRERA.

Westpac Freight: POB 2048, Puerto Rico, Saipan, MP 96950; tel. 322-8798; fax 322-5536; e-mail westpac@gtepacifica.net; services between Saipan, Guam and the USA; Man. MICHIE CAMACHO.

CIVIL AVIATION

Air services are centred on the main international airport, Isley Field, on Saipan. There are also airports on Rota and Tinian.

Continental Micronesia: POB 508778, A.B. Won Pat International Airport, Tamuning, MP 96911; tel. 647-6595; fax 649-6588; internet www.continental.com; f. 1968, as Air Micronesia, by Continental Airlines (USA); name changed 1992; subsidiary of Continental Airlines; hub operations in Saipan and Guam; services throughout the region and to destinations in the Far East and the mainland USA; Pres. MARK ERWIN.

Freedom Air: POB 500239 CK, Saipan, MP 96950; tel. and fax 288-5663; scheduled internal flights.

Pacific Island Aviation: PMB 318, POB 10,000, Saipan, MP 96950; tel. 234-3600; fax 234-3604; e-mail piasaipan@saipan.com; internet www.pacificislandaviation.com; f. 1987; scheduled services to Rota and Guam in partnership with Northwest Airlines (USA); repair

UNITED STATES COMMONWEALTH TERRITORIES

station; flight instruction; Pres. and CEO ROBERT F. CHRISTIAN; Exec. Vice-Pres. PAZ PABALINAS.

Tourism

Tourism is one of the most important industries in the Northern Mariana Islands, earning some US $225m. in 2002. In that year there were 4,313 hotel rooms. Most of the islands' hotels are Japanese-owned, and in 2002 68.7% of tourists came from Japan. The Republic of Korea and the USA are also important sources of tourists. The islands received a total of 535,224 visitors in 2004 (an increase of some 16.4% on the figure for the previous year). The islands of Asuncion, Guguan, Maug, Managaha, Sariguan and Uracas (Farallon de Pajaros) are maintained as uninhabited reserves. Visitors are mainly attracted by the white, sandy beaches and the excellent diving conditions. There is also interest in the *Latte* or *Taga* stones (mainly on Tinian), pillars carved from the rock by the ancient Chamorros, and relics from the Second World War.

Hotel Association of the Northern Mariana Islands: POB 501983, Saipan, MP 96950; tel. 234-3455; fax 234-3411; e-mail rds@itecnmi.com; f. 1985; Pres. LYNN KNIGHT.

Marianas Visitors Authority: POB 500861 CK, Saipan, MP 96950; tel. 664-3200; fax 664-3237; e-mail mva@mymarianas.com; internet www.mymarianas.com; f. 1976; responsible for the promotion and development of tourism in the Northern Mariana Islands; Chair. DAVID M. SABLAN; Man. Dir VICKY I. BENAVENTE.

PUERTO RICO

Introductory Survey

Location, Climate, Language, Religion, Flag, Capital

The Commonwealth of Puerto Rico comprises the main island of Puerto Rico, together with the small offshore islands of Vieques and Culebra and numerous smaller islets, lying about 80 km (50 miles) east of Hispaniola (Haiti and the Dominican Republic) in the Caribbean Sea. The climate is maritime-tropical, with an average annual temperature of 24°C (75°F) and a normal range between 17°C (63°F) and 36°C (97°F). The official languages are Spanish and English. Christianity is the dominant religion, and about 73% of the population are Roman Catholics. The flag (proportions 3 by 5) has five alternating red and white horizontal stripes of equal width, with a blue triangle, in the centre of which is a five-pointed white star, at the hoist. The capital is San Juan.

Recent History

Puerto Rico, also known as Borinquen (after the original Arawak Indian name Boriquen), was ruled by Spain from 1509 until 1898, when it was ceded to the USA at the conclusion of the Spanish-American war, and administered as an 'unincorporated territory' of the USA. In 1917 Puerto Ricans were granted US citizenship, and in 1947 Puerto Rico obtained the right to elect its own Governor. A Constitution, promulgated in 1952, assigned Puerto Rico the status of a self-governing 'Commonwealth', or 'Estado Libre Asociado', in its relation to the USA.

The Partido Popular Democrático (PPD) held a majority in both chambers of the legislature from 1944 until 1968, when, following a split within the party, the Partido Nuevo Progresista (PNP), an advocate of statehood, won the governorship and legislative control. This followed a plebiscite in 1967, when 61% of voters had ratified a continuation of Commonwealth status in preference to independence (1%) or incorporation as a State of the USA (39%). In the general election of 1972 the PPD, under the leadership of Rafael Hernández Colón, regained the governorship and legislative control from the PNP, only to lose them again in 1976. The victorious PNP was led by Carlos Romero Barceló, who became Governor in January 1977.

Romero Barceló, who had promised a referendum on statehood if re-elected for a further term in 1980, abandoned this plan following the election, in which he narrowly defeated former Governor Hernández Colón. The PPD, however, gained control of the legislature. The 1984 gubernatorial election, which was contested mainly on economic issues, was won by Hernández Colón by only 50,000 votes, with the PPD retaining substantial majorities in both legislative chambers. In September 1985 Romero Barceló was succeeded as leader of the PNP by Baltasar Corrada del Río.

A gubernatorial election, held in November 1988, resulted in the re-election of Hernández Colón, who obtained 49% of the popular vote, compared with 46% for Corrada del Río and 6% for Rubén Berríos Martínez of the pro-independence Partido Independentista Puertorriqueño (PIP). Electoral participation was unusually high, at almost 90%.

The question of eventual independence for Puerto Rico has been a politically sensitive issue for over 50 years. With the PPD supporting the continuation and enhancement of Commonwealth status and the PNP advocating Puerto Rico's inclusion as a state of the USA, mainstream party encouragement of independence aims has come mainly from the PIP and other left-wing groups. There are two small, and occasionally violent, terrorist factions, the Ejército Popular Boricua (Macheteros), which operates in Puerto Rico, and the Fuerzas Armadas de Liberación Nacional (FALN), functioning principally on the US mainland.

In the 1988 election campaign, Corrada del Río, whose campaign was endorsed by the successful US presidential candidate, George Bush, advocated the admission of Puerto Rico as the 51st state of the USA, while Hernández Colón reiterated the traditional PPD policy of 'maximum autonomy' for Puerto Rico 'within a permanent union with the USA'. President Bush's open support of the statehood option was criticized by Hernández Colón and the PPD. In January 1989 Hernández Colón promised that a further plebiscite would be held. Although it was initially planned to hold this referendum in June 1991, in February the proposed legislation to make its result binding on the US Government failed to obtain sufficient support in the US Senate to allow it to proceed to full consideration by the US Congress.

In December 1991 the PPD Government organized a referendum on a proposal to adopt a charter of 'democratic rights', which included guarantees of US citizenship regardless of future change in Puerto Rico's constitutional status, and the maintenance of Spanish as the official language. The proposed charter was rejected by a margin of 53% to 45%. This result was widely interpreted as an indication that the majority of voters wished to retain Puerto Rico's Commonwealth status. Hernández Colón announced in January 1992 that he would not seek re-election in the gubernatorial election in November, and in the following month resigned as leader of the PPD. His successor as party leader, Victoria Muñoz Mendoza, was defeated in the election by the PNP candidate, Pedro Rosselló, by a margin of 50% of the popular vote to 46% for the PPD. The leadership of the PPD subsequently passed to Héctor Luis Acevedo.

Rosselló, who took office in January 1993, announced that a further referendum on Puerto Rico's future constitutional status would be held during the year. The Government proceeded with legislation rescinding the removal, in 1991, of English as an official language of the island. The referendum, which took place in November 1993, resulted in a 48% vote favouring the retention of Commonwealth status, with 46% of voters supporting accession to statehood and 4% advocating full independence.

In July 1996 a committee of the US House of Representatives unanimously recommended that Puerto Rican voters be given an opportunity, before 1998, to choose whether to retain the island's present status, or to proceed to statehood or full self-government. A preference for change would be followed by a 10-year 'Transition Plan' based on the result, during which time ballots would be held periodically to confirm the direction of the Plan. These proposals, however, were opposed by the Resident Commissioner representing the Puerto Rican Government in the House of Representatives, and were withdrawn in late 1996.

At elections held in November 1996 Rosselló was re-elected as Governor, receiving 51% of the votes, as against 45% obtained by Acevedo, representing the PPD. The PNP retained control of both chambers of the Legislature. During the campaign, the levels of minimum wages on the island, together with the recent abolition by US President, Bill Clinton, of federal tax exemptions for US companies establishing plants in Puerto Rico, formed the main political issues.

Debate on the Territory's constitutional future intensified during 1997. In November, following a decision by the US Supreme Court expressly recognizing Puerto Rican citizenship as distinct from US citizenship, a new political movement, the Pro Patria National Union, was formed to encourage Puerto Ricans formally to renounce their US nationality. In March 1998, by a majority of only one vote, the US House of Representatives passed legislation providing for a referendum to determine the island's future status. Under the referendum plan, a vote in favour of statehood would oblige the US Congress to legislate for a 51st state during 1999, with Puerto Rico's admission to the union following within a 10-year period. In December 1998, however, the Puerto Rican electorate rejected the statehood proposal by a margin of 50% to 47%; 71% of eligible voters participated in the referendum. Rosselló, however, described the result as a reflection of the PNP Government's decline in popularity over domestic issues, and indicated that he was to petition the US Congress to implement measures to facilitate the island's transition to statehood. In June 1999, however, Rosselló unexpectedly announced that he would not seek re-election in the gubernatorial election scheduled to take place in November 2000. In July 2001 the new Governor, María Sila Calderón, voiced support for a further referendum on the island's status during 2002. In July 2002 Calderón announced the creation of a 'Status Committee' to resolve the issue; the Committee was to consist of representatives of the PPD, PNP and PIP, including Colón and Barceló.

An extended period of public protest followed the accidental death, in April 1999, of a civilian security guard during routine US military exercises on the small offshore island of Vieques, the eastern section of which, covering a coastline of 32 km, was used by the US Navy as an ammunition testing range. With support from the PIP, groups of protesters promptly established camps on the firing range, compelling the US Navy temporarily to suspend these operations. Following extended negotiations between the Puerto Rican and US Governments, in January 2000 Rosselló and President Clinton announced a compromise plan to end the protesters' occupation by undertaking that, in return for the resumption of naval exercises in which only dummy ammunition would be used, the US Administration would provide immediate development aid to Vieques of $40m. This figure would rise to $90m. if residents of the island would agree in a referendum (provisionally scheduled for November 2001 but subsequently cancelled—see below) to allow the US Navy to resume live ammunition testing, in which event the Navy would undertake to leave Vieques permanently by 2003. In May 2000, prior to a proposed unilateral resumption of naval exercises (using dummy ammunition), protests on Vieques intensified, and several hundred federal Government agents were sent to remove the protesters forcibly. The US Navy subsequently declared a 5-km land and sea 'security area' around the island.

Gubernatorial and legislative elections were held on 7 November 2000. Sila María Calderón of the PPD won 49% of the votes cast and was elected Governor; Carlos Pesquera of the PNP obtained 46% of the ballot and Rubén Berríos Martínez of the PIP 5%. The PPD secured 19 seats in the Senate, its net gain of 12 being equivalent to the net loss of the PNP, which secured eight seats. The PPD also became the largest party grouping in the House of Representatives, securing 27 of the 51 seats, compared with 23 of the 54 in the previous legislature. The PNP won 23 seats, compared with 36 at the previous election. The PIP's representation was unchanged, with one member in each chamber of the legislature.

Upon taking office, Calderón announced her administration's repudiation of the agreement on military activity on Vieques signed in January 2000 by Clinton and Rosselló. Military exercises on the island were resumed in April 2001, despite legal challenges and protests. Operations were suspended in May, but resumed in mid-June. In the days following the resumption of exercises on Vieques (amid further protests), the new US President, George W. Bush, announced that the US Navy would end military activity on the island by May 2003. The Mayor of Vieques was sentenced to four months' imprisonment in August for trespassing on US Navy property during a protest. Exercises ceased temporarily from September 2001. Meanwhile, Calderón announced plans for a referendum on US military activity on Vieques to be held in late July; it was postponed until November, but subsequently cancelled by the US Congress, which ordered the US military to remain on Vieques until an alternative location was found. The US Congress claimed that on-going tests were necessary as part of the US-led 'war on terror' following the terrorist attacks on Washington, DC, and New York in September. (A non-binding referendum had been held in July, in which 68% of voters were in favour of the immediate departure from the island of the US Navy.) Tests resumed in early April 2002, amid protests from members of the PIP. In mid-2002 the PIP threatened to call a general strike and instigate a campaign of civil disobedience if the US Navy failed to leave the island by May 2003. The final scheduled bombing exercises took place in February 2003, and the US Navy withdrew from the island on 1 May. The firing range was to become a wildlife reserve. The last remaining base, at Ceiba, was closed on 31 March 2004. In 2006 there were environmental concerns over underwater detonations carried out by the US Navy as part of its ongoing clean-up operations.

In early 2002 Calderón proposed legislation to combat corruption, including the creation of a public fund to finance election campaigns. However, in March the PNP alleged that Calderón had used public funds to finance her gubernatorial campaign in 2000, while mayor of San Juan; an investigation into the charges by the Office of the Comptroller was subsequently launched. Several prominent PNP officials who had served in the Rosselló administration went on trial in 2002, and in December former education secretary Victor Fajardo was sentenced to 12 years' imprisonment after being convicted of diverting state funds to the PNP. In January 2003 the former Speaker of the House of Representatives under the Rosselló administration, Edison Misla Aldorano, was found guilty of extortion, money-laundering and perverting the course of justice; a former member of Rosselló's staff was sentenced to 18 months' imprisonment in the same month. In March 2004 a legislative ethics committee found Oscar Ramos, a PNP deputy, guilty of bribery charges. However, the party voted not to expel Ramos, prompting the PPD to claim that the PNP was not taking seriously the fight against corruption in public office.

Legislative and gubernatorial elections were held on 2 November 2004. Initial results showed that Aníbal Acevedo Vilá of the ruling PPD won the gubernatorial election by just 3,880 votes, a margin of only 0.2%. Under electoral law a victory by a margin of 0.5% or less was subject to a recount. This duly began on 7 November; however, owing to legal challenges, announcement of the result was delayed until late December. On 23 December it was announced that, with 99.9% of the votes recounted, Acevedo Vilá had won 48.40% of the ballot, while the PNP's candidate, former Governor Rosselló, attracted 48.22% of the votes cast. The third placed candidate, Rubén Berríos Martínez, once again representing the PIP, won 2.74%. Having achieved a sufficient margin of votes, Acevedo Vilá was declared the winner and was duly sworn in as Governor on 2 January 2005. In the concurrently held legislative election, the PNP gained control of both houses from the PPD, winning a majority of seats in both the Senate and the House of Representatives (17 and 32, respectively), while the PPD secured nine senate and 18 lower-house seats. The pro-independence PIP won one seat in each chamber. Voter turn-out was 81.6%.

In mid-March 2005 Governor Acevedo Vilá presented budget proposals for 2006 that included a spending reduction of US $370m. and the elimination of some 23,000 government jobs; the proposals were rejected by the House of Representatives. On 31 March both houses of the legislature unanimously approved legislation providing for a referendum in July on whether to petition the US Congress and President Bush to agree to honour the results of a further referendum on how the island's future status should be decided, to be held before the end of 2006. However, the following month, Governor Acevedo Vilá vetoed the legislation on the grounds that it did not make sufficient provision for the option of a constituent assembly, instead of a popular, binding referendum, to decide on the eventual status of the island. The PNP was seeking a two-thirds' legislative majority to overturn the Governor's veto.

Also in March 2005, there was widespread opposition to the decision by the US Territorial District Court of Puerto Rico to impose the death sentence on two convicted murderers. Capital punishment had been banned in the Territory in 1930, a decision that had been upheld in 2000 by a ruling of the Supreme Court of Puerto Rico that it violated the island's Constitution. However, the ruling was subsequently overturned by the US Court of Appeals, which found that Puerto Rico was subject to US federal law and that the death penalty was applicable in certain cases; this decision was upheld by the US Supreme Court. In early April Acevedo Vilá wrote to the US Attorney-General requesting that the death penalty should not apply to residents of Puerto Rico. In May the jury serving on the trial moved to sentence to two men to life imprisonment.

In late May 2005, at the PNP's general assembly, a majority of party members voted that Pedro Roselló should replace fellow party member Kenneth McClintock as President of the Senate. McClintock announced that he would refuse to stand down. He received the support of five PNP senators who were consequently suspended from the party, and finally expelled in mid-March 2006, as was McClintock. McClintock continued to serve as President of the Senate and stated that he still considered himself a PNP politician. In late July 2005 Acevedo Vilá vetoed the proposed budget on the grounds that expenses were greater than income and that it was therefore unconstitutional. The Government continued to operate using the previous year's budget.

In early September 2005 Filiberto Ojeda Ríos, the leader of the Ejército Popular Boricua (see above), was shot and killed during a raid on his home, in Hormigueros, by agents of the USA's Federal Bureau of Investigation (FBI). The FBI had considered Ojeda Ríos a fugitive since he fled the USA in 1990 while awaiting trial for an armed robbery in 1983. In early February 2006 the FBI raided a number of residences and businesses in San Juan as part of an anti-terrorism operation related to the Ejército Popular Boricua. No arrests were made, but the raids provoked public anger: the Government was not informed until the operation was in progress, and during one raid FBI agents used pepper spray against journalists. In late February it was reported that up to 1,000 people took part in a demonstration in San Juan against both the raids and the killing of Ojeda Ríos.

In December 2005 a US presidential task force on the status of Puerto Rico, commissioned by President Bush in December 2003, delivered its findings. It recommended that Congress approve legislation for a two-stage plebiscite to be held in Puerto Rico within a year. In the first stage, the people of Puerto Rico would be given the option to continue as part of the Commonwealth or to seek a change in status.

UNITED STATES COMMONWEALTH TERRITORIES

Puerto Rico

In the event that they chose the latter, a second vote would be held on whether to be incorporated as a state within the USA or become an independent country. Irrespective of the outcome, any decision would have to be approved mutually by the US Congress and the Government of Puerto Rico. While the PNP and the PIP welcomed the report, it was criticized by Governor Acevedo Vilá and the PPD because it omitted autonomy as an option. In mid-January 2006 both houses of the Puerto Rico legislature approved legislation calling on Congress to act on the recommendations of the task force.

Government

Executive power is vested in the Governor, elected for a four-year term by universal adult suffrage. The Governor is assisted by an appointed Cabinet. Legislative power is held by the bicameral Legislative Assembly, comprising the Senate (with 27 members) and the House of Representatives (51 members). Additional members may be assigned in each chamber to ensure adequate representation of minority parties. The members of both chambers are elected by direct vote for four-year terms. The Resident Commissioner, also elected for a four-year term, represents Puerto Rico in the US House of Representatives, but is permitted to vote only in committees of the House. Puerto Ricans are citizens of the USA, but those resident in Puerto Rico, while eligible to participate in national party primary elections, may not vote in presidential elections.

Defence

The USA is responsible for the defence of Puerto Rico. Puerto Rico has a paramilitary National Guard numbering about 11,000, which is funded mainly by the US Department of Defense.

Economic Affairs

In 2001, according to estimates by the World Bank, Puerto Rico's gross national income (GNI), measured at average 1999–2001 prices, was US $42,057.5m., equivalent to US $10,950 per head (or $16,230 per head on an international purchasing-power basis). During 1995–2004, it was estimated the population increased at an average annual rate of 0.7%. Gross domestic product (GDP) per head increased, in real terms, by an average of 3.0% per year during 1996–2004, while overall GDP increased, in real terms, by an average of 3.7% per year during the same period. According to government estimates, GDP increased by 3.1% in 2004.

Agriculture, forestry and fishing contributed an estimated 0.5% of GDP and employed 2.1% of the working population in 2004, according to official figures. Dairy produce and other livestock products are the mainstays of the agricultural sector. The principal crops are sugar cane, plantains, bananas and oranges. Cocoa cultivation has been successfully introduced, and measures to improve agricultural land use have included the replanting of some sugar-growing areas with rice and the cultivation of plantain trees over large areas of unproductive hill land. Commercial fishing is practised on a small scale. The GDP of the agricultural sector increased, in real terms, at an average rate of 2.1% per year between 1980/81 and 1990/91. Agricultural GDP rose by approximately 1.5% in 1993/94.

Industry (including manufacturing, construction and mining) provided an estimated 51.8% of GDP and employed 18.6% of the working population in 2004. Industrial GDP increased, in real terms, at an average annual rate of 2.9% between 1980/81 and 1990/91. It rose by 3.3% in 1993/94.

Quarrying and construction was estimated to provide about 2.2% of GDP in 2004 and employed 7.3% of the working population in 2003. Otherwise, Puerto Rico has no commercially exploitable mineral resources, although deposits of copper and nickel have been identified.

Manufacturing is the main source of income, accounting for an estimated 43.2% of GDP and employing 11.3% of the working population in 2004. From 1996 employment in the manufacturing sector declined at an average annual rate of 6%. The principal branch of manufacturing in 2002/03, based on the value of output, was chemical products (accounting for 72.4% of the total sector), mainly drugs and medicines. Other important products were computer, electronic and electrical products (12.6%) and food products (6.0%). The GDP of the manufacturing sector increased, in real terms, by 2.9% per year between 1980/81 and 1990/91. The rate of advance was 3.5% in 1993/94. In 2004 total electricity production stood at 24,100.1 kWh. In April 2005 the Puerto Rico Electric Power Authority announced that it would build two new gas-fired power-stations, with a combined capacity of 971 MW.

Services (including electricity, gas and water) provided an estimated 47.7% of GDP and engaged 79.5% of the employed labour force in 2004 (including 22.3% employed by the Government). In real terms, the GDP of all service sectors increased at an average rate of 4.9% per year between 1980/81 and 1990/91, and by 4.4% in 1993/94. Tourism is of increasing importance; in 2004 tourist arrivals were estimated at 4.9m. visitors, generating revenue totalling US $3,024.0m. Visitors from the US mainland comprised more than 75% of the total number of visitors in 2003. The Government planned to add some 5,000 hotel rooms by 2008.

In 2004/05 there was a budget deficit of US $2,744m. A budget for 2005/06 had not been enacted by July 2005 and the administration continued to apply the previous year's spending plan (see Recent History). Puerto Rico's total public debt at the end of the fiscal year to June 2003 was an estimated $30,781.2m. The debt service ratio in 2004 was 6.8%. US federal aid programmes are of central importance to the Puerto Rican economy, and the island has also received disaster relief in respect of hurricanes that widely disrupt the Puerto Rican economy intermittently. In 2003/04 Puerto Rico recorded a visible trade surplus of $14,732.9m., but there was a deficit of $3,655.4m. on the current account of the balance of payments. Mainland USA is the island's dominant trading partner, providing 48.9% of Puerto Rico's recorded imports and absorbing 82.5% of its recorded exports in 2004. In that year other significant export markets were the Netherlands (3.2%) and Belgium (2.3%); other significant sources of imports were Ireland (20.7%) and Japan (3.9%). The principal category of recorded exports in 2003/04 was chemical products (accounting for 49.6% of the total), mainly drugs and pharmaceutical preparations. Other major exports were computers and electronic and electrical equipment, and food. The main imports were chemical products, food, petroleum products and transport equipment.

The annual inflation rate averaged 15.0% in 1995–2004. Consumer prices increased by an average of 7.8% in 2003 and by an average of 11.9% in 2004. Puerto Rico is very densely populated, and unemployment has been a persistent problem, although assisted by the growth in the tourism industry, the jobless rate declined during the 1990s. The average rate of unemployment declined from 12.1% in 2003 to 11.4% in 2004.

Puerto Rico holds associate status in the UN Economic Commission for Latin America and the Caribbean (ECLAC, see p. 36) and has observer status in the Caribbean Community and Common Market (CARICOM, see p. 183). Puerto Rico declined to accept associate status in the Association of Caribbean States (ACS), formed in 1994, on the grounds of opposition by the US Government to the inclusion of Cuba. In July 2001 Puerto Rico applied for associate membership of CARICOM; the USA criticized the move, emphasizing that it had authority over the island's foreign policy as long as Puerto Rico held Commonwealth status.

Puerto Rico's economic growth has been inhibited by the lack of an adequate infrastructure. Government programmes of industrial and taxation incentives, aimed at attracting US and foreign investors and encouraging domestic reinvestment of profits and long-term capital investment, have generated growth in the manufacturing and services sectors. However, from 1996 the US Government progressively withdrew a number of important tax exemptions (collectively known as Section 936) enjoyed by US and foreign investors; the last vestiges of Section 936 were finally to end on 31 December 2006. The Government of Puerto Rico attempted to counteract the economic impact of their removal by seeking to establish the island as a centre for the finishing of Latin American manufactured goods destined for member states of the North American Free Trade Agreement (NAFTA, see p. 312). Following the closure of the Roosevelt Roads US naval base at Ceiba in March 2004 (see Recent History), the former base became the site of the US $6,700m. Portal del Futuro development. The development was expected to create 20,000 direct jobs and a further 50,000 jobs indirectly over the following 30 years. However, in the immediate future, the closure of the naval base resulted in an estimated loss to the local economy of $300m. annually and some 6,000 jobs. Economic growth slowed in 2005, to an estimated 0.8%.

Education

The public education system is centrally administered by the Department of Education. Education is compulsory for children between six and 16 years of age. In 2004 there were an estimated 584,900 pupils attending public day schools and an estimated 215,800 pupils attending private schools. The 12-year curriculum, beginning at five years of age, is subdivided into six grades of elementary school, three years at junior high school and three years at senior high school. Vocational schools at the high-school level and kindergartens also form part of the public education system. Instruction is conducted in Spanish, but English is a required subject at all levels. In 2004 there were five universities. The State University system consists of three principal campuses and six regional colleges. In 2004 there were some 206,800 students in higher education. In 2002 US $2,152,724m. of current government expenditure was spent on public elementary and secondary day schooling.

Public Holidays

2006: 1 January (New Year), 6 January (Epiphany), 9 January (Birthday of Eugenio María de Hostos), 16 January (Martin Luther King Day), 20 February (Presidents' Day), 22 March (Emancipation of the Slaves), 14 April (Good Friday), 17 April (Birthday of José de Diego), 29 May (Memorial Day), 24 June (Feast of St John the Baptist), 4 July (US Independence Day), 17 July (Birthday of Luis Muñoz Rivera), 25 July (Constitution Day), 27 July (Birthday of José

UNITED STATES COMMONWEALTH TERRITORIES

Puerto Rico

Celso Barbosa), 4 September (Labor Day), 9 October (Columbus Day), 10 November (for Veterans' Day), 20 November (for Discovery of Puerto Rico Day), 23 November (US Thanksgiving Day), 25 December (Christmas Day).

2007: 1 January (New Year), 6 January (Epiphany), 8 January (Birthday of Eugenio María de Hostos), 15 January (Martin Luther King Day), 19 February (Presidents' Day), 22 March (Emancipation of the Slaves), 6 April (Good Friday), 16 April (Birthday of José de Diego), 28 May (Memorial Day), 24 June (Feast of St John the Baptist), 4 July (US Independence Day), 16 July (Birthday of Luis Muñoz Rivera), 25 July (Constitution Day), 27 July (Birthday of José Celso Barbosa), 3 September (Labor Day), 8 October (Columbus Day), 12 November (for Veterans' Day), 19 November (Discovery of Puerto Rico Day), 22 November (US Thanksgiving Day), 25 December (Christmas Day).

Weights and Measures

The US system is officially in force. Some old Spanish weights and measures, as well as the metric system, are used in local commerce.

Statistical Survey

Source (unless otherwise stated): Puerto Rico Planning Board, POB 41119, San Juan, 00940-1119; tel. (787) 723-6200; internet www.jp.gobierno.pr.

Area and Population

AREA, POPULATION AND DENSITY

Area (sq km)	8,959*
Population (census results)	
1 April 1990	3,522,037
1 April 2000	
Males	1,833,577
Females	1,975,033
Total	3,808,610
Population (official estimates at mid-year)	
2002	3,859,000
2003	3,879,000
2004	3,887,000
Density (per sq km) at mid-2004	433.9

* 3,459 sq miles.

PRINCIPAL TOWNS
(population at census of 1 April 2000)

San Juan (capital)	421,958	Caguas	88,680
Bayamón	203,499	Guaynabo	78,806
Carolina	168,164	Mayagüez	78,647
Ponce	155,038	Trujillo Alto	50,841

Source: Bureau of the Census, US Department of Commerce.

BIRTHS, MARRIAGES AND DEATHS

	Registered live births		Registered marriages		Registered deaths	
	Number	Rate (per 1,000)	Number	Rate (per 1,000)*	Number	Rate (per 1,000)
1996	63,259	17.0	32,572	11.7	29,871	8.0
1997	64,214	16.9	31,493	11.0	29,119	7.7
1998	60,518	15.8	26,390	9.3	29,990	7.8
1999	59,684	15.4	27,255	9.3	29,145	7.5
2000	59,460	15.5	25,980	8.9	28,550	7.6
2001	55,983	14.6	28,598	7.4	28,794	7.5
2002	52,871	13.7	25,645	6.6	28,098	7.3

* Rates calculated using estimates of population aged 15 years and over.
Source: Department of Health, Commonwealth of Puerto Rico.

2003 (rounded figures): Births 56,000 (Birth rate 14.2 per 1,000); Deaths 32,000 (Death rate 8.1 per 1,000).

2004 (rounded figures): Births 56,000 (Birth rate 14.1 per 1,000); Deaths 32,000 (Death rate 8.2 per 1,000).

2005 (rounded): Births 55,000 (Birth rate 14.0 per 1,000); Deaths 33,000 (Death rate 8.2 per 1,000).

Expectation of life (years at birth): 76.5 (males 72.2; females 80.8) in 2005 (Source: Pan American Health Organization).

ECONOMICALLY ACTIVE POPULATION
('000 persons aged 16 years and over)

	2001/02	2002/03	2003/04
Agriculture, forestry and fishing	23	25	26
Manufacturing	139	136	139
Construction	86	83	90
Trade	240	257	259
Transportation	30	28	27
Communication	18	15	16
Finance, insurance and real estate	42	43	43
Other public utilities	14	14	13
Services	316	335	348
Government	261	274	275
Total employed*	**1,170**	**1,211**	**1,234**

* Includes sectors employing fewer than 2,000 people, not listed separately.
Source: Department of Labor and Human Resources Statistics, *Household Survey*.

Unemployed: 160 in 2002; 167 in 2003; 158 in 2004.

Total labour force: 1,330 in 2002; 1,378 in 2003; 1,392 in 2004.

Health and Welfare

KEY INDICATORS

Total fertility rate (children per woman, 2005)	1.9
Under-5 mortality rate (per 1,000 live births, 2004)	11.4
Physicians (per 1,000 head, 1999)	1.75
Hospital beds (per 1,000 head, 2002)	3.2
Health expenditure (1994): % of GDP	6.0

Source: Pan American Health Organization.

For definitions see explanatory note on p. vi.

Agriculture

PRINCIPAL CROPS
('000 metric tons)

	2002	2003	2004*
Sugar cane	40	—	—
Tomatoes	11.6	19.7	20.0
Pumpkins, squash and gourds	13.8	14.3	14.3
Bananas	49.9	52.4	52.4
Plantains	100.9	104.8	105.0
Oranges	16.8	18.0	18.0
Mangoes	10.6	12.1	12.2
Pineapples	21.1	19.1	19.1
Coffee (green)	7.6	10.3	10.0

* FAO estimates.
Source: FAO.

LIVESTOCK
('000 head, year ending September)

	2002	2003	2004*
Cattle	400.3	420.9	420.0
Sheep*	16	16	16
Goats*	9	9	9
Pigs	102.4	100.7	100.0
Horses*	26	26	26
Poultry	11,218	11,140	11,200

* FAO estimate(s).
Source: FAO.

UNITED STATES COMMONWEALTH TERRITORIES

Puerto Rico

LIVESTOCK PRODUCTS
('000 metric tons)

	2002	2003	2004*
Beef and veal	10.6	9.4	10.0
Pig meat	9.3	11.9	11.5
Poultry meat	54.1	46.8	50.0
Cows' milk	371.5	370.2	370.0
Hen eggs	12.0	11.9	11.9

* FAO estimates.

Fishing
(metric tons, live weight)

	2001	2002	2003
Capture	3,794	2,529	2,919
Snappers and jobfishes	744	512	603
Seerfishes	124	90	94
Marine fishes	173	126	104
Caribbean spiny lobster	190	158	196
Stromboid conchs	1,643	931	1,141
Aquaculture	414	441	269
Penaeus shrimps	205	225	69
Total catch	4,208	2,970	3,188

Source: FAO.

Industry

SELECTED PRODUCTS
(year ending 30 June)

	1995/96	1996/97	1997/98*
Distilled spirits ('000 proof gallons)	25,343	36,292	33,471

* Preliminary.

Electric energy (million kWh): 22,563.0 in 2002; 23,717.1 in 2003; 24,100.1 in 2004 (Source: Government Development Bank for Puerto Rico, *Puerto Rico in Figures*).

Cement ('000 metric tons): 1,660 in 2000; 1,550 in 2001; 1,540 in 2002 (estimate) (Source: US Geological Survey).

Beer ('000 hectolitres): 317 in 1997; 263 in 1998; 259 in 1999 (Source: UN, *Industrial Commodity Statistics Yearbook*).

Finance

CURRENCY AND EXCHANGE RATES
Monetary Units
United States currency: 100 cents = 1 US dollar (US $).

Sterling and Euro Equivalents (30 December 2005)
£1 sterling = US $1.7219;
€1 = US $1.1797;
$100 = £58.08 = €84.77.

BUDGET
(US $ '000, general government operations, year ending 30 June)

Revenue	2002/03	2003/04	2004/05
Income tax	4,874,795	5,061,761	5,564,672
Excise tax	1,894,729	1,924,610	2,101,216
Other taxes	3,055	19,211	8,752
Charges for services	780,905	750,978	702,691
Intergovernmental transfers	4,230,372	3,776,579	4,446,276
Interest	85,565	58,914	116,686
Other revenue	314,002	507,613	741,416
Total	12,183,423	12,099,666	13,681,709

Expenditure	2002/03	2003/04	2004/05
General government services	1,774,156	1,777,365	1,675,428
Public safety	1,424,846	1,765,199	2,409,668
Health	1,908,717	2,176,741	2,344,522
Public housing and welfare	2,953,189	2,738,016	3,320,849
Education	3,297,248	3,474,013	4,177,664
Economic development	428,621	868,926	706,066
Intergovernmental transfers	465,699	528,829	—
Capital outlays	1,184,976	581,788	665,630
Principal on debt servicing	330,346	526,572	391,554
Interest	1,158,749	737,502	733,931
Total	14,926,547	15,174,951	16,425,312

Source: Department of the Treasury, Commonwealth of Puerto Rico.

COST OF LIVING
(Consumer Price Index; base: 2000 = 100)

	2002	2003	2004
Food (incl. beverages)	127.8	145.8	176.3
Fuel and light	100.6	105.6	110.9
Rent	104.4	106.0	107.5
Clothing (incl. footwear)	97.0	95.5	95.2
All items (incl. others)	113.6	122.5	137.1

Source: ILO.

NATIONAL ACCOUNTS
(US $ million at current prices, year ending 30 June)

Expenditure on the Gross Domestic Product

	1997/98	1998/99	1999/2000*
Government final consumption expenditure	7,098.9	7,486.3	7,208.2
Private final consumption expenditure	32,194.2	34,620.1	36,592.7
Increase in stocks	31.2	484.5	347.2
Gross fixed capital formation	9,293.7	12,057.0	12,560.6
Total domestic expenditure	48,618.0	54,647.9	56,708.7
Exports of goods and services / *Less* Imports of goods and services	5,515.1	5,391.4	6,441.0
GDP in purchasers' values	54,133.1	60,039.3	63,149.7
GDP at constant 1954 prices	9,252.1	9,915.8	10,276.8

* Preliminary.

Gross Domestic Product by Economic Activity

	2001/02	2002/03	2003/04*
Agriculture	276.5	313.9	434.7
Manufacturing	31,242.9	32,500.6	34,077.5
Construction and mining†	1,647.6	1,614.3	1,740.7
Transportation and public utilities‡	4,948.3	5,205.4	5,349.5
Trade	8,622.8	9,005.3	9,581.7
Finance, insurance and real estate	11,211.9	12,425.4	13,024.2
Services	7,078.5	7,257.0	7,899.2
Government	6,302.8	7,005.8	7,388.5
Sub-total	71,331.3	75,327.7	79,496.0
Statistical discrepancy	292.3	–493.3	–653.7
Total	71,623.5	74,834.4	78,842.2

* Preliminary.
† Mining includes only quarries.
‡ Includes radio and television broadcasting.

UNITED STATES COMMONWEALTH TERRITORIES   *Puerto Rico*

BALANCE OF PAYMENTS
(US $ million, year ending 30 June)

	2001/02	2002/03	2003/04
Merchandise exports f.o.b.	49,610.1	56,334.7	59,449.4
Merchandise imports f.o.b.	−36,740.7	−42,512.8	−44,716.5
Trade balance	12,869.4	13,821.9	14,732.9
Investment income received	1,025.9	1,011.2	1,185.4
Investment income paid	−28,553.7	−29,392.1	−30,683.8
Services and other income (net)	1,175.7	1,107.1	1,243.1
Unrequited transfers (net)	9,723.5	10,144.1	10,245.9
Net interest of Commonwealth and municipal governments	−416.2	−421.0	−378.9
Current balance	−4,175.4	−3,728.8	−3,655.4

External Trade

PRINCIPAL COMMODITIES
(US $ million, year ending 30 June)

Imports	2001/02	2002/03	2003/04
Mining products	315.5	800.1	945.9
Manufacturing products	27,360.2	31,608.1	36,408.6
Food, beverages and tobacco	2,338.8	2,274.1	2,420.4
Clothing and textiles	960.4	931.4	888.3
Paper, printing and publishing	700.9	691.3	721.2
Chemical products	12,324.5	15,111.2	19,289.3
Petroleum refining and related products	1,592.7	1,923.1	2,070.0
Rubber and plastic products	521.9	637.9	547.9
Primary metal products	341.4	401.8	410.2
Machinery, except electrical	1,073.6	1,153.3	1,133.5
Computer, electronic and electrical products	2,889.3	3,432.0	3,881.8
Transport equipment	2,189.7	2,345.8	2,355.5
Total (incl. others)	29,984.6	33,749.7	38,897.6

Exports	2001/02	2002/03	2003/04
Manufacturing products	46,722.9	54,690.1	54,601.7
Food, beverages and tobacco	3,832.1	3,265.4	3,002.6
Clothing and textiles	621.2	537.3	442.8
Chemical products	33,307.1	39,603.9	37,632.6
Machinery, except electrical	508.7	616.8	614.6
Computer, electronic and electrical products	5,389.0	6,886.7	6183.0
Total (incl. others)	47,172.3	55,175.3	55,080.2

PRINCIPAL TRADING PARTNERS
(US $ million)*

	1994/95 Imports	1994/95 Exports	1995/96 Imports	1995/96 Exports
Belgium	53.2	165.2	122.9	205.9
Canada	187.5	74.2	197.8	75.5
Dominican Repub.	664.2	693.7	768.1	677.4
France	130.3	86.1	194.1	103.6
Germany	207.0	280.8	175.7	233.8
Ireland	180.8	27.4	278.8	19.6
Italy	203.8	58.3	279.0	56.7
Japan	1,278.5	91.1	1,222.8	184.5
Korea, Repub.	216.8	43.8	236.7	61.1
Mexico	202.2	90.7	181.3	106.0
Netherlands	93.1	157.2	100.2	119.1
United Kingdom	708.3	178.0	560.8	159.0
USA	12,158.1	21,106.9	11,909.3	20,148.6
US Virgin Islands	307.0	164.8	366.8	137.3
Venezuela	424.0	43.1	509.5	35.8
Total (incl. others)	18,816.6	23,811.3	19,060.9	22,944.4

* Recorded trade only.

1996/97 (US $ million): Imports: USA 13,317.8; Total (incl. others) 21,387.4. Exports: USA 21,187.3; Total (incl. others) 23,946.8.

1997/98 (US $ million): Imports: USA 13,225.9; Total (incl. others) 21,797.5. Exports: USA 27,397.4; Total (incl. others) 30,272.9.

Transport

ROAD TRAFFIC
(vehicles in use)

	1987/88	1988/89	1989/90
Cars: private	1,322,069	1,289,873	1,305,074
Cars: for hire	14,814	11,033	10,513
Trucks: private	15,790	13,273	12,577
Trucks: for hire	4,131	3,933	3,283
Light trucks	176,583	174,277	189,705
Other vehicles	75,155	74,930	60,929
Total	1,608,542	1,567,319	1,582,081

2001: Passenger cars 2,075,521; Trucks 33,803; Other vehicles (incl. motorcycles) 25,163 (Source: Federal Highway Administration, US Department of Transportation, *Highway Statistics 2001*).

SHIPPING
(year ending 30 June)

	1985/86	1986/87	1987/88
Passengers arriving	29,559	59,089	33,737
Passengers departing	33,683	63,987	35,627
Cruise visitors	448,973	584,429	723,724

Cruise visitors (calendar year): 1,300,075 in 2000; 1,349,630 in 2001.

Freight handled (short tons): 10,231,435 in 2000; 9,729,644 in 2001.

Source: Puerto Rico Ports Authority.

CIVIL AVIATION
(year ending 30 June)

	1988/89	1989/90	1990/91
Passengers arriving	4,064,762	4,282,324	4,245,137
Passengers departing	4,072,828	4,297,521	4,262,154
Freight (tons)*	173,126	208,586	222,172

* Handled by the Luis Muñoz Marin International Airport.

Passengers arriving (calendar year): 4,688,477 in 2001.

Passengers departing (calendar year): 4,707,829 in 2001.

Freight handled (calendar year): 235,880 tons in 2000; 215,603 tons in 2001.

Source: Puerto Rico Ports Authority.

Tourism

	2001	2002	2003
Total visitors ('000)	3,551.2	3,087.1	3,238.3
From USA	2,616.2	2,212.9	2,454.3
From US Virgin Islands	18.8	17.5	16.2
From other countries	916.2	856.7	767.8
Expenditure ($ million)	2,728	2,486	2,677

2004: Total visitors 4,889,000; Total expenditure US $3,024m.

UNITED STATES COMMONWEALTH TERRITORIES

Puerto Rico

Communications Media

	1999	2000	2001
Television receivers ('000 in use)	1,270	1,290	n.a.
Telephones ('000 main lines in use)	1,294.7	1,299.3	1,329.5
Mobile cellular telephones ('000 subscribers)	813.8	926.4	1,211.1
Internet users ('000)	200	400	600

Radio receivers ('000 in use): 2,840 in 1997.

Facsimile machines ('000 in use): 543 in 1993.

Daily newspapers (1996): 3; average circulation ('000 copies) 475.

Non-daily newspapers (1988 estimates): 4; average circulation ('000 copies) 106.

Sources: UNESCO, *Statistical Yearbook*; UN, *Statistical Yearbook*; International Telecommunication Union.

Education

	1993/94	1994/95	1995/96
Total number of students	933,183	934,406	947,249
Public day schools	631,460	621,370	627,620
Private schools (accredited)*	140,034	145,864	148,004
University of Puerto Rico†	53,935	54,353	62,341
Private colleges and universities	107,754	112,819	109,284
Number of teachers‡	39,816	40,003	39,328

* Includes public and private accredited schools not administered by the Department of Education.
† Includes all university-level students.
‡ School teachers only.

2002 (Public schools): Elementary students 415,715; Secondary students 167,151; Teachers 42,369.

Enrolment at schools (estimates): 799,933 in 2001; 792,284 in 2002; 875,831 in 2003 (Source: Government Development Bank for Puerto Rico, *Puerto Rico in Figures*).

Enrolment at public and private universities: 190,776 in 2002; 199,842 in 2003; 206,771 in 2004 (Source: Government Development Bank for Puerto Rico, *Puerto Rico in Figures*).

Adult literacy rate (UNESCO estimates): 94.1% (males 93.9%; females 94.4%) in 2002 (Source: UNESCO).

Directory

The Constitution

RELATIONSHIP WITH THE USA

On 3 July 1950 the Congress of the United States of America adopted Public Law No. 600, which was to allow 'the people of Puerto Rico to organize a government pursuant to a constitution of their own adoption'. This Law was submitted to the voters of Puerto Rico in a referendum and was accepted in the summer of 1951. A new Constitution was drafted in which Puerto Rico was styled as a commonwealth, or estado libre asociado, 'a state which is free of superior authority in the management of its own local affairs', though it remained in association with the USA. This Constitution, with its amendments and resolutions, was ratified by the people of Puerto Rico on 3 March 1952, and by the Congress of the USA on 3 July 1952; and the Commonwealth of Puerto Rico was established on 25 July 1952.

Under the terms of the political and economic union between the USA and Puerto Rico, US citizens in Puerto Rico enjoy the same privileges and immunities as if Puerto Rico were a member state of the Union. Puerto Rican citizens are citizens of the USA and may freely enter and leave that country.

The Congress of the USA has no control of, and may not intervene in, the internal affairs of Puerto Rico.

Puerto Rico is exempted from the tax laws of the USA, although most other federal legislation does apply to the island. Puerto Rico is represented in the US House of Representatives by a non-voting delegate, the Resident Commissioner, who is directly elected for a four-year term. The island has no representation in the US Senate.

There are no customs duties between the USA and Puerto Rico. Foreign products entering Puerto Rico—with the single exception of coffee, which is subject to customs duty in Puerto Rico, but not in the USA—incur the same customs duties as would be paid on their entry into the USA.

The US social security system is extended to Puerto Rico, except for unemployment insurance provisions. Laws providing for economic co-operation between the Federal Government and the States of the Union for the construction of roads, schools, public health services and similar purposes are extended to Puerto Rico. Such joint programmes are administered by the Commonwealth Government.

Amendments to the Constitution are not subject to approval by the US Congress, provided that they are consistent with the US federal Constitution, the Federal Relations Act defining federal relations with Puerto Rico and Public Law No. 600. Subject to these limitations, the Constitution may be amended by a two-thirds' vote of the Puerto Rican Legislature and by the subsequent majority approval of the electorate.

BILL OF RIGHTS

No discrimination shall be made on account of race, colour, sex, birth, social origin or condition, or political or religious ideas. Suffrage shall be direct, equal and universal for all over the age of 18. Public property and funds shall not be used to support schools other than State schools. The death penalty shall not exist. The rights of the individual, of the family and of property are guaranteed. The Constitution establishes trial by jury in all cases of felony, as well as the right of habeas corpus. Every person is to receive free elementary and secondary education. Social protection is to be afforded to the old, the disabled, the sick and the unemployed.

THE LEGISLATURE

The Legislative Assembly consists of two chambers, the members of which are elected by direct vote for a four-year term. The Senate is composed of 27 members, who must be over 30 years of age. The House of Representatives is composed of 51 members, of whom 40 are elected on a constituency basis, and a further 11 are at large members, elected by proportional representation. Representatives must be over 25 years of age. The Constitution guarantees the minority parties additional representation in the Senate and the House of Representatives, which may fluctuate from one quarter to one third of the seats in each House.

The Senate elects a President and the House of Representatives a Speaker from their respective members. The sessions of each house are public. A majority of the total number of members of each house constitutes a quorum. Either house can initiate legislation, although bills for raising revenue must originate in the House of Representatives. Once passed by both Houses, a bill is submitted to the Governor, who can either sign it into law or return it, with his reasons for refusal, within 10 days. If it is returned, the Houses may pass it again by a two-thirds' majority, in which case the Governor must accept it.

The House of Representatives, or the Senate, can impeach one of its members for treason, bribery, other felonies and 'misdemeanours involving moral turpitude'. A two-thirds' majority is necessary before an indictment may be brought. The cases are tried by the Senate. If a Representative or Senator is declared guilty, he is deprived of his office and becomes punishable by law.

THE EXECUTIVE

The Governor, who must be at least 35 years of age, is elected by direct suffrage and serves for four years. Responsible for the execution of laws, the Governor is Commander-in-Chief of the militia and has the power to proclaim martial law. At the beginning of every regular session of the Assembly, in January, the Governor presents a report on the state of the treasury, and on proposed expenditure. The Governor chooses the Secretaries of Departments, subject to the approval of the Legislative Assembly. These are led by the Secretary of State, who replaces the Governor at need.

LOCAL GOVERNMENT

The island is divided into 78 municipal districts for the purposes of local administration. The municipalities comprise both urban areas and the surrounding neighbourhood. They are governed by a mayor and a municipal assembly, both elected for a four-year term.

The Government

HEAD OF STATE

Governor: ANÍBAL ACEVEDO VILÁ (took office 2 January 2005).

EXECUTIVE
(April 2006)

Secretary of State: MARISARA PONT MARCHESE.

UNITED STATES COMMONWEALTH TERRITORIES

Puerto Rico

Secretary of the Interior: Aníbal José Torres.
Secretary of Justice: Roberto Sánchez Ramos.
Secretary of the Treasury: Juan Carlos Méndez Torres.
Secretary of Education: Gloria E. Baquero Lleras.
Secretary of Transportation and Public Works: Gabriel Alcaráz Emmanuelli.
Secretary of Health: Rosa Pérez Perdomo.
Secretary of Agriculture: José Orlando Fabré Laboy.
Secretary of Housing: Jorge Rivera Jiménez.
Secretary of Natural and Environmental Resources: Javier Vélez Arocho.
Secretary of Consumer Affairs: Alejandro García Padilla.
Secretary of Sports and Recreation: David E. Bernier Rivera.
Secretary of Economic Development and Commerce: Jorge P. Silva Puras.
Attorney-General: Salvador Antonetti Stutts.
Resident Commissioner in Washington: Luis Fortuño.

GOVERNMENT OFFICES

Office of the Governor: La Fortaleza, POB 9020082, PR 00909-0082; tel. (787) 721-7000; fax (787) 724-0942; internet www.fortaleza.gobierno.pr.

Department of Agriculture: POB 10163, Santurce, PR 00908-1163; tel. (787) 721-2120; fax (787) 723-9747; internet www.agricultura.gobierno.pr.

Department of Consumer Affairs: POB 41059, Minillas Station, San Juan, PR 00940-1059; tel. (787) 721-0940; fax (787) 726-007; internet www.daco.gobierno.pr.

RTSDepartment of Economic Development and Commerce: 355 Avda Roosevelt, Suite 401, Hato Rey, PR 00918; internet www.ddecpr.com; tel. (787) 765-2900; fax (787) 753-6874.

Department of Education: Avda Teniente César González, esq. Calle Juan Calaf, Urb. Industrial Tres Monjitas, Hato Rey, PR 00917; POB 190759, San Juan, PR 00919-0759; tel. (787) 759-2000; fax (787) 250-0275; internet eduportal.de.gobierno.pr.

Department of the Family: POB 11398, Santurce, San Juan, PR 00910; tel. (787) 722-7400; fax (787) 722-7910; internet www.familia.gobierno.pr.

Department of Health: POB 70184, San Juan, PR 00936-8184; tel. (787) 766-1616; fax (787) 250-6547; e-mail webmaster@salud.gov.pr; internet www.salud.gov.pr.

Department of Housing: 606 Avda Barbosa, Juan C. Cordero, San Juan, PR 00928-1365; Apdo 21365, Rio Piedras, PR 00928; tel. (787) 274-2525; fax (787) 758-9263; e-mail mcardona@vivienda.gobierno.pr; internet www.vivienda.gobierno.pr.

Department of Justice: POB 9020192, San Juan, PR 00902-0192; tel. (787) 721-2900; fax (787) 724-4770; internet www.justicia.gobierno.pr; incl. the Office of the Attorney-General.

Department of Labor and Human Resources: Edif. Prudencio Rivera Martínez, 505 Avda Muñoz Rivera, Hato Rey, PR 00918; tel. (787) 754-2159; fax (787) 753-4201; e-mail lortiz@dtrh.gobierno.pr; internet www.dtrh.gobierno.pr.

Department of Natural and Environmental Resources: Pda 3 1/2 Avda Muñoz Rivera, Puerta de Tierra, San Juan; POB 906660 Puerta de Tierra Station, San Juan, PR 00906-6600; tel. (787) 724-8774; fax (787) 723-4255; e-mail webmaster@drna.gobierno.pr; internet www.drna.gobierno.pr.

Department of Recreation and Sports: 1611 Antiguo Edif. del Fondo del Seguro del Estado, Avda Fernández Juncos, esq. Calle Bolívar, San Juan, PR 00902-3207; POB 9023207, Rio Piedras, PR 00909; tel. (787) 721-2800; fax (787) 728-0313; e-mail fgandara@drd.gobierno.pr; internet www.drd.gobierno.pr.

Department of State: Apdo 9023271, San Juan, PR 00902-3271; tel. (787) 721-1768; fax (787) 723-3304; e-mail estado@gobierno.pr; internet www.estado.gobierno.pr.

Department of Transportation and Public Works: POB 41269, San Juan, PR 00940; tel. (787) 722-2929; fax (787) 728-8963; e-mail servciud@act.dtop.gov.pr; internet www.dtop.gobierno.pr.

Department of the Treasury: POB 9024140, San Juan, PR 00902-4140; tel. (787) 721-2020; fax (787) 723-6213; e-mail infoserv@hacienda.gobierno.pr; internet www.hacienda.gobierno.pr.

Gubernatorial Election, 2 November 2004

Candidate	Votes	%
Aníbal Acevedo Vilá (PPD)	963,303	48.40
Pedro Rosselló González (PNP)	959,737	48.22
Rubén Berríos Martínez (PIP)	54,551	2.74
Total (incl. others)*	1,990,372	100.00

* Including 4,960 blank votes and 4,042 spoiled votes.

Legislature

LEGISLATIVE ASSEMBLY

Senate

President of the Senate: Kenneth McClintock Hernández.

Election, 2 November 2004

Party	Seats
PNP	17
PPD	9
PIP	1
Total	27

House of Representatives

Speaker of the House: José Aponte Hernández.

Election, 2 November 2004

Party	Seats
PNP	32
PPD	18
PIP	1
Total	51

Election Commission

Comisión Estatal de Elecciones de Puerto Rico (CEE): Calle Arterial B 500, POB 195552, San Juan, PR 00919-5552; tel. (787) 294-1190; e-mail hava@cee.gobierno.pr; internet www.ceepur.org; f. 1977; independent; Pres. Aurelio Gracia Morales.

Political Organizations

Frente Socialista: 103 Américo Miranda, POB 70359, San Juan, PR 00936; e-mail internacional@frentesocialista.org; internet members.tripod.com/frentesocialistapr; f. 2001; mem. orgs include the Partido Revolucionario de los Trabajadores Puertorriqueños (PRTP-Macheteros) and Movimiento Socialista de Trabajadores

Movimiento Socialista de Trabajadores (MST): Apdo 22699, Estación UPR, San Juan, PR 00931-2699; e-mail info@bandera.org; internet www.bandera.org; f. 1982 by merger of the Movimiento Socialista Popular and Partido Socialista Revolucionario; pro-independence; mainly composed of workers and university students.

Movimiento Independentista Nacional Hostosiano (MINH): f. 2004 by merger of the Congreso Nacional Hostosiano and Nuevo Movimiento Independentista (fmr mems of the Partido Socialista Puertorriqueño); pro-independence; Co-Pres Julio Muriente Pérez, Héctor Pesquera.

Partido Independentista Puertorriqueño (PIP) (Puerto Rican Independence Party): 963 F. D. Roosevelt Ave, Hato Rey, San Juan PR 00920-2901; e-mail pipnacional@independencia.net; internet www.independencia.net; f. 1946; advocates full independence for Puerto Rico as a socialist-democratic republic; Leader Rubén Berríos Martínez; Exec. Pres. Fernando Martín; Sec.-Gen. Juan Dalmau Ramírez; c. 6,000 mems.

Partido Nuevo Progresista (PNP) (New Progressive Party): POB 1992, Fernández Zuncos Station, San Juan 00910-1992; tel. (787) 289-2000; e-mail dannyls@caribe.net; internet www.pnp.org; f. 1967; advocates eventual admission of Puerto Rico as a federated state of the USA; Pres. Pedro Rosselló; Sec.-Gen. Thomas Rivera Schatz; c. 225,000 mems.

Partido Popular Democrático (PPD) (Popular Democratic Party): Comité Central PPD, Puerta de Tierra, San JuanPOB 9065788 San Juan, PR 00906-5788; e-mail lherrero@ppdpr.net; internet www.ppdpr.net; f. 1938; supports continuation and improvement of the present Commonwealth status of Puerto Rico;

Pres. and Leader ANÍBAL ACEVEDO VILÁ; Sec.-Gen. GERARDO CRUZ; c. 950,000 mems.

Pro Patria National Union: seeks independence for Puerto Rico; encourages assertion of distinct Puerto Rican citizenship as recognized by US Supreme Court in Nov. 1997; Leader FUFI SANTORI.

Puerto Rican Republican Party: Suite 203, 1629 Avda Piñero, San Juan, PR 00920; tel. (787) 793-8084; e-mail cchardon@goppr.org; internet www.goppr.org; Chair. Dr TIODY DE JESÚS DE FERRÉ; Exec. Dir ANNIE J. MAYOL.

Puerto Rico Democratic Party: POB 5788, San Juan, PR 00906; tel. (787) 722-4952; Pres. WILLIAM MIRANDA MARÍN.

Refundación Comunista: Organización RC, POB 13362, San Juan, PR 00908-3362; e-mail refundacionpcp@hotmail.com; internet refundacioncomunista.tripod.com; f. 2001; Marxist-Leninist; pro-independence; maintains close relations with the Frente Socialista.

Judicial System

The Judiciary is vested in the Supreme Court and other courts as may be established by law. The Supreme Court comprises a Chief Justice and up to six Associate Justices, appointed by the Governor with the consent of the Senate. The lower Judiciary consists of Superior and District Courts and Municipal Justices equally appointed.

There is also a US Federal District Court, whose judges are appointed by the President of the USA. Judges of the US Territorial District Court are appointed by the Governor.

Supreme Court of Puerto Rico

POB 2392, Puerta de Tierra, San Juan, PR 00902-2392; tel. (787) 724-3551; fax (787) 725-4910; e-mail buzon@tribunales.gobierno.pr; internet www.tribunalpr.org.

Chief Justice: FEDERICO HERNÁNDEZ DENTON.

Justices: FRANCISCO REBOLLO LÓPEZ, JAIME B. FUSTER BERLINGERI, EFRAÍN E. RIVERA PÉREZ, LIANA FIOL MATTA, ANABELLE RODRÍGUEZ RODRÍGUEZ.

US Territorial District Court for Puerto Rico

Federico Degetau Federal Bldg, Carlos Chardón Ave, Hato Rey, PR 00918; tel. (787) 772-3011; internet www.prd.uscourts.gov.

Judges: JOSÉ A. FUSTÉ (Chief Judge), JUAN M. PÉREZ-GIMÉNEZ, CARMEN C. CEREZO, HECTOR M. LAFITTE, DANIEL R. DOMÍNGUEZ, JAY A. GARCÍA-GREGORY.

Religion

About 73% of the population belonged to the Roman Catholic Church at the end of 2003. The Protestant churches active in Puerto Rico include the Episcopalian, Baptist, Presbyterian, Methodist, Seventh-day Adventist, Lutheran, Mennonite, Salvation Army and Christian Science. There is a small Jewish community.

CHRISTIANITY

The Roman Catholic Church

Puerto Rico comprises one archdiocese and four dioceses. At 31 December 2003 there were 2,800,581 adherents.

Bishops' Conference of Puerto Rico

POB 40682, San Juan, PR 00940-0682; tel. (787) 728-1650; fax (787) 728-1654; e-mail ceppr@coqui.net; f. 1960; Pres. Rt Rev. ROBERTO OCTAVIO GONZÁLEZ NIEVES (Archbishop of San Juan de Puerto Rico).

Archbishop of San Juan de Puerto Rico: ROBERTO OCTAVIO GONZÁLEZ NIEVES, Arzobispado, Calle San Jorge 201, Santurce, POB 00902-1967; tel. (787) 725-4975; fax (787) 723-4040; e-mail cancilleria@arqsj.org.

Other Christian Churches

Episcopal Church of Puerto Rico: POB 902, St Just, PR 00978; tel. (787) 761-9800; fax (787) 761-0320; e-mail iep@spiderlink.net; internet www.iepanglicom.org; diocese of the Episcopal Church in the USA, part of the Anglican Communion; Leader Bishop Rt Rev. DAVID ANDRÉS ALVAREZ.

Puerto Rico Council of Churches: Calle El Roble 54, Apdo 21343, Río Piedras, San Juan, PR 00928; tel. (787) 765-6030; fax (787) 765-5977; e-mail ceprpr@coqui.net; f. 1954 as the Evangelical Council of Puerto Rico; Pres. Rev. HÉCTOR SOTO; Exec. Sec. Rev. CRUZ A. NEGRÓN TORRES; 8 mem. churches.

BAHÁ'Í FAITH

National Spiritual Assembly: POB 11603, San Juan, PR 00910-2703; tel. (787) 763-0982; fax (787) 753-4449.

JUDAISM

Jewish Community Center: 903 Ponce de León Ave, San Juan, PR 00907; tel. (787) 724-4157; fax (787) 722-4157; f. 1953; conservative congregation with 250 families; Rabbi GABRIEL TRYDMAN.

There is also a reform congregation with 60 families.

The Press

Puerto Rico has high readership figures for its few newspapers and magazines, as well as for mainland US periodicals. Several newspapers have a large additional readership among the immigrant communities in New York.

DAILIES
(m = morning; s = Sunday)

El Nuevo Día: Parque Industrial Amelia, Carretera 164, Guaynabo; POB 9067512, San Juan, PR 00906-7512; tel. (787) 641-8000; fax (787) 641-3924; e-mail laferre@elnuevodia.com; internet www.endi.com; f. 1970; Chair. and Editor ANTONIO LUIS FERRÉ; Pres. MARÍA EUGENIA FERRÉ RANGEL; Dir LUIS ALBERTO FERRÉ RANGEL; circ. 214,441 (m), 246,765 (s).

Primera Hora: Parque Industrial Amelia, Calle Diana Lote 18, Guaynabo, PR 00966; POB 2009, Cataño, PR 00963-2009; tel. (787) 641-5454; fax (787) 641-4472; internet www.primerahora.com; Pres. and Editor ANTONIO LUIS FERRÉ; Dir JORGE CABEZAS; Gen. Man. JUAN MARIO ALVAREZ CARTAÑA; circ. 133,483 (m), 92,584 (Sat.).

The San Juan Star: POB 364187, San Juan, PR 00936-4187; tel. (787) 782-4200; fax (787) 783-5788; internet www.thesanjuanstar.com; f. 1959; English; Pres. and Publr GERARD ANGULO; Gen. Man. SALVADOR HASBÚN; circ. 50,000.

El Vocero de Puerto Rico: Apdo 7515, San Juan, PR 00906-7515; tel. (787) 721-2300; fax (787) 722-0131; e-mail opinion@vocero.com; internet www.vocero.com; f. 1974; Publr and Editor GASPAR ROCA; circ 143,150 (m), 123,869 (Sat.).

PERIODICALS

Buena Salud: 1700 Fernández Juncos Ave, San Juan, PR 00909; tel. (787) 728-7325; f. 1990; monthly; Editor IVONNE LONGUEIRA; circ. 59,000.

Caribbean Business: 1700 Fernández Juncos Ave, San Juan, PR 00909-2938; POB 12130, San Juan, PR 00914-0130; tel. (787) 728-9300; fax (787) 726-1626; e-mail cbeditor@casiano.com; internet www.casiano.com/html/cb.html; f. 1973; weekly; business and finance; Editor ELISABETH ROMÁN; circ. 45,000.

Educación: c/o Dept of Education, POB 190759, Hato Rey Station, San Juan, PR 00919; f. 1960; 2 a year; Spanish; Editor JOSÉ GALARZA RODRÍGUEZ; circ. 28,000.

La Estrella de Puerto Rico: 165 Calle París, Urb. Floral Park, Hato Rey, PR 00917; tel. (787) 754-4440; fax (787) 754-4457; e-mail editor@estrelladepr.com; internet www.estrelladepr.com; f. 1983; weekly; Spanish and English; Editor-in-Chief FRANK GAUD; circ. 123,500.

Imagen: 1700 Fernández Juncos Ave, Stop 25, San Juan, PR 00909-2999; tel. (787) 728-4545; fax (787) 728-7325; e-mail imagen@casiano.com; internet www.casiano.com/html/imagen.html; f. 1986; monthly; women's interest; Editor ANNETTE OLIVERAS; circ. 71,000.

Qué Pasa: Loiza St Station, POB 6338, San Juan, PR 00914; tel. (787) 728-3000; fax (787) 728-1075; internet www.casiano.com/html/quepasa.html; f. 1948; quarterly; English; publ. by Puerto Rico Tourism Co; official tourist guide; Editor YAHIRA CARO; circ. 120,000.

Resonancias: POB 9024184, San Juan, PR 00902-4184; tel. (787) 721-0901; e-mail revista@icp.gobierno.pr; internet www.icp.gobierno.pr; f. 2000; biannual; Spanish; Puerto Rican and general culture and music; Editor GLORIA TAPIA; circ. 3,000.

Revista Colegio de Abogados de Puerto Rico: POB 9021900, San Juan, PR 00902-1900; tel. (787) 721-3358; fax (787) 725-0330; e-mail abogados@prtc.net; f. 1914; quarterly; Spanish; law; Editor Lic. ALBERTO MEDINA; circ. 10,000.

Revista del Instituto de Cultura Puertorriqueña: POB 9024184, San Juan, PR 00902-4184; tel. (787) 721-0901; e-mail revista@icp.gobierno.pr; internet www.icp.gobierno.pr; f. 1958; weekly; Spanish; arts, literature, history, theatre, Puerto Rican culture; Editor GLORIA TAPIA; circ. 3,000.

La Semana: Calle Cristóbal Colón, esq. Ponce de León, Casilla 6527, Caguas 00725; tel. (787) 743-6537; e-mail lasemana@lasemana.com; internet www.lasemana.com/principal.html; weekly; f. 1963; Spanish; Gen. Man. MARJORIE M. RIVERA RIVERA.

La Torre: POB 23322, UPR Station, San Juan, PR 00931-3322; tel. (787) 758-0148; fax (787) 753-9116; e-mail ydef@hotmail.com; f. 1953; publ. by University of Puerto Rico; quarterly; literary criticism, linguistics, humanities; Editor YUDIT DE FERDINANDY; circ. 1,000.

Vea: POB 190240, San Juan, PR 00919-0240; tel. (787) 721-0095; fax (787) 725-1940; e-mail editor@veavea.com; f. 1969; weekly; Spanish; TV, films and celebrities; Editor ENRIQUE PIZZI; circ. 92,000.

El Visitante: POB 41305, San Juan, PR 00940-1305; tel. (787) 728-3710; fax (787) 268-1748; e-mail director@elvisitante.biz; internet www.elvisitante.biz; f. 1975; weekly; Roman Catholic; Dir JOSÉ R. ORTIZ VALLADARES; Editor Rev. EFRAÍN ZABALA; circ. 59,000.

FOREIGN NEWS BUREAUX

Agencia EFE (Spain): Cobian's Plaza, Suite 214, Santurce, PR 00910; tel. (787) 723-6023; fax (787) 725-8651; Dir ELÍAS GARCÍA.

Associated Press (USA): Metro Office Park 8, 1 St 108, Guaynabo, PR 00968.

Publishers

Ediciones Huracán Inc: 874 Baldorioty de Castro, San Juan, PR 00925; tel. (787) 763-7407; fax (787) 753-1486; e-mail edhucan@caribe.net; f. 1975; textbooks, literature, social studies, history; Pres. CARMEN RIVERA-IZCOA.

Editorial Académica, Inc: 67 Santa Anastacia St, El Vigía, Río Piedras, PR 00926; tel. (787) 760-3879; f. 1988; regional history, politics, government, educational materials, fiction; Dir FIDELIO CALDERÓN.

Editorial Coquí: POB 21992, UPR Station, San Juan, PR 00931.

Editorial Cordillera, Inc: POB 192363, San Juan, PR 00919-2363; tel. (787) 767-6188; fax (787) 767-8646; e-mail info@editorialcordillera.com; internet www.editorialcordillera.com; f. 1962; Pres. PATRICIA GUTIÉRREZ; Sec. and Treas. ADOLFO R. LÓPEZ.

Editorial Cultural Inc: POB 21056, Río Piedras, San Juan, PR 00928; tel. (787) 765-9767; e-mail cultural@editorialcultural.com; f. 1949; general literature and political science; Dir FRANCISCO M. VÁZQUEZ.

Editorial Edil, Inc: POB 23088, UPR Station, Río Piedras, PR 00931; tel. (787) 753-9381; fax (787) 250-1407; e-mail editedil@coqui.net; internet www.editorialedil.com; f. 1967; univ. texts, literature, technical and official publs; Man. Dir and Publr CONSUELO ANDINO ORTIZ.

Librería y Tienda de Artesanias Instituto de Cultura Puertorriqueña: POB 9024184, San Juan, PR 00902-4184; tel. (787) 724-4295; fax (787) 723-0168; e-mail www@icp.gobierno.pr; internet www.icp.gobierno.pr; f. 1955; literature, history, poetry, music, textbooks, arts and crafts; Man. Dir MAIRA PIAZZA.

University of Puerto Rico Press (EDUPR): POB 23322, UPR Station, Río Piedras, San Juan, PR 00931-3322; tel. (787) 250-0550; fax (787) 753-9116; f. 1932; general literature, children's literature, Caribbean studies, law, philosophy, science, educational; Dir CARLOS D'ALZINA.

Broadcasting and Communications

TELECOMMUNICATIONS

Junta Reglamentadora de Telecomunicaciones de Puerto Rico: Edif. Capital Center II, 235 Suite 1001, Avda Arterial Hostos, San Juan, PR 00918-1453; tel. (787) 756-0804; fax (787) 756-0814; e-mail correspondencia@jrtpr.gobierno.pr; internet www.jrtpr.gobierno.com; Pres. MIGUEL REYES DÁVILA.

Puerto Rico Telephone Co (PRTC): POB 360998, San Juan, PR 00936-0998; tel. (787) 782-8282; fax (787) 774-0037; internet www.telefonicapr.com; provides all telecommunications services in Puerto Rico; majority control transferred from govt to private-sector GTE Corpn in March 1999; Pres. and CEO JON E. SLATER.

BROADCASTING

There were 120 radio stations and 15 television stations operating in early 2002. The only non-commercial stations are the radio station and the two television stations operated by the Puerto Rico Department of Education. The US Armed Forces also operate a radio station and three television channels.

Asociación de Radiodifusores de Puerto Rico (Puerto Rican Radio Broadcasters' Asscn): Caparra Terrace, Delta 1305, San Juan, PR 00920; tel. (787) 783-8810; fax (787) 781-7647; e-mail prbroadcasters@centennialpr.net; internet www.radiodifusores.com; f. 1947; 90 mems; Pres. JOSÉ A. MARTÍNEZ GIRAUD; Exec. Dir JOSÉ A. RIBAS DOMINICCI.

Finance

(cap. = capital; res = reserves; dep. = deposits; brs = branches; amounts in US dollars)

BANKING

Government Bank

Government Development Bank for Puerto Rico (Banco Gubernamental de Fomento para Puerto Rico—BGF): POB 42001, San Juan, PR 00940-2001; tel. (787) 728-9200; fax (787) 268-5496; e-mail gdbcomm@prstar.net; internet www.gdb-pur.com; f. 1942; an independent govt agency; acts as fiscal (borrowing) agent to the Commonwealth Govt and its public corpns and provides long- and medium-term loans to private businesses; cap. 20.5m., res 46.8m., dep. 5,816.5m. (June 2001); Pres. WILLIAM LOCKWOOD; Chair. JUAN AGOSTO ALICEA; 350 employees.

Autoridad para el Financiamiento de la Vivienda de Puerto Rico: POB 213365, Hato Rey, San Juan, PR 00928-1365; tel. (787) 274-0000; fax (787) 764-8680; f. 1961; fmrly Banco y Agencia de Financiamiento de la Vivienda de Puerto Rico until Aug. 2001; subsidiary of the Government Development Bank for Puerto Rico; finance agency; helps low-income families to purchase houses; Exec. Dir JOSÉ CESTERO CASANOVA.

Commercial Banks

Banco Bilbao Vizcaya Argentaria Puerto Rico: 15th Floor, Torre BBVA, 258 Muñoz Rivera Ave, San Juan 00918; POB 364745, San Juan, PR 00936-4745; tel. (787) 777-2000; fax (787) 777-2999; internet www.bbvapr.com; f. 1967 as Banco de Mayagüez; taken over by Banco Occidental in 1979; merged with Banco Bilbao Vizcaya, S.A. in 1988; named changed from BBV Puerto Rico in 2000; cap. 138.7m., res. 215.6m., dep. 4,640.3m. (Dec. 2002); Pres. ANTONIO UGUINA; 65 brs.

Banco Popular de Puerto Rico: Popular Center, 209 Muñoz Rivera Ave, San Juan, PR 00918; tel. (787) 765-9800; fax (787) 758-2714; internet www.bppr.com; f. 1893; cap. 8.0m., res 1,504m., dep. 19,595m. (Dec. 2002); Chair., Pres. and CEO RICHARD L. CARRIÓN; 193 brs.

Banco Santander Puerto Rico: 207 Ponce de León Ave, Hato Rey, PR 00919; POB 362589, San Juan, PR 00936-0062; tel. (787) 759-7070; fax (787) 767-7913; internet www.santanderpr.com; f. 1976; cap. 106.2m., res 6,383.1m., dep. 6,656.0m. (Dec. 2002); Pres. JOSÉ RAMON GONZALEZ; Chair. and CEO MONICA APARICIO; 64 brs.

Scotiabank de Puerto Rico: Plaza Scotiabank, 273 Ponce de León Ave, esq. Calle Méjico, Hato Rey, PR 00918; POB 362230, San Juan PR 00936-2230; tel. (787) 758-8989; fax (787) 766-7879; f. 1910; cap. 23.2m., res 143.5m., dep. 1,164.3m. (Dec. 2002); Chair. BRUCE R. BIRMINGHAM; Pres. and CEO IVAN A. MÉNDEZ; 13 brs.

Savings Banks

FirstBank Puerto Rico: First Federal Bldg, 1519 Ponce de León Ave, POB 9146, Santurce, PR 00908-0146; tel. (787) 729-8200; fax (787) 729-8139; internet www.firstbancorppr.com; f. 1948; cap. and res 368.3m., dep. 3,363.0m. (Dec. 2000); Pres. ANGEL ALVAREZ-PÉREZ; 45 brs.

Oriental Bank and Trust: Ave Fagot, esq. Obispado M-26, Ponce; tel. (787) 259-0000; fax (787) 259-0700; e-mail jllantin@orientalfg.com; internet www.orientalonline.com; total assets 2,039m. (June 2001); Chair., Pres. and CEO JOSÉ ENRIQUE FERNÁNDEZ.

Ponce Federal Bank, FSB: Villa esq. Concordia, POB 1024, Ponce, PR 00733; tel. (787) 844-8100; fax (787) 848-5380; f. 1958; Pres. and CEO HANS H. HERTELL; 19 brs.

R & G Corporation: POB 2510, Guaynabo, PR 00970; tel. (787) 766-6677; fax (787) 766-8175; internet www.rgonline.com; total assets 4,676m. (Dec. 2001); Chair., Pres. and CEO VÍCTOR J. GALÁN.

US Banks in Puerto Rico

Chase Manhattan Bank NA: 254 Muñoz Rivera Ave, Hato Rey, PR 00918; tel. (787) 753-3400; fax (787) 766-6886; Man. Dir and Gen. Man. ROBERT C. DÁVILA; 1 br.

Citibank NA: 252 Ponce de León Ave, San Juan, PR 00918; tel. (787) 753-5619; fax (787) 766-3880; Gen. Man. HORACIO IGUST; 14 brs.

SAVINGS AND LOAN ASSOCIATIONS

Caguas Central Federal Savings of Puerto Rico: POB 7199, Caguas, PR 00626; tel. (787) 783-3370; f. 1959; total assets 800m.; Pres. LORENZO MUÑOZ FRANCO.

Westernbank Puerto Rico: 19 West McKinley St, Mayagüez, PR 00680; tel. (787) 834-8000; fax (787) 831-5958; internet www.wbpr.com; cap. and res 250.6m.; dep. 2,610.4m. (Dec. 2000); Chair. and CEO FRANK C. STIPES; 31 brs.

Banking Organization

Puerto Rico Bankers' Association: 208 Ponce de León Ave, Suite 1014, San Juan, PR 00918; tel. (787) 753-8630; fax (787) 754-6077; e-mail info@abpr.com; internet www.abpr.com; Pres. JUAN A. NET; Exec. Vice-Pres. ARTURO L. CARRIÓN.

INSURANCE

Atlantic Southern Insurance Co: POB 362889, San Juan, PR 00936-2889; tel. (787) 767-9750; fax (787) 764-4707; internet www.atlanticsouthern.com; f. 1945; Chair. DIANE BEAN SCHWARTZ; Pres. RAMÓN L. GALANES.

Caribbean American Life Assurance Co: 273 Ponce de Léon Ave, Suite 1300, Scotiabank Plaza, San Juan, PR 00917; tel. (787) 250-1199; fax (787) 250-7680; internet www.calac.com; Pres. IVÁN C. LOPÉZ.

Cooperativa de Seguros Multiples de Puerto Rico: POB 3846, San Juan, PR 00936; internet www.segurosmultiples.com; general insurance; Pres. EDWIN QUIÑONES SUÁREZ.

La Cruz Azul de Puerto Rico: Carretera Estatal 1, Km 17.3, Río Piedras, San Juan, PR 00927; POB 366068, San Juan, PR 00936-6068; tel. (787) 272-9898; fax (787) 272-7867; e-mail scliente@cruzazul.com; internet www.cruzazul.comhealth; Exec. Dir MARKS VIDAL.

Great American Life Assurance Co of Puerto Rico: POB 363786, San Juan, PR 00936-3786; tel. (787) 758-4888; fax (787) 766-1985; e-mail galifepr@galifepr.com; known as General Accident Life Assurance Co until 1998; Pres. ARTURA CARIÓN; Sr Vice-Pres. EDGARDO DIAZ.

National Insurance Co: POB 366107, San Juan, PR 00936-6107; tel. (787) 758-0909; fax (787) 756-7360; internet www.nicpr.com; f. 1961; subsidiary of National Financial Group; Chair., Pres. and CEO CARLOS M. BENÍTEZ, Jr.

Pan American Life Insurance Co: POB 364865, San Juan, PR 00936-4865; tel. (787) 724-5354; fax (787) 723-3860; e-mail mmunozguren@panamericanlife.com; internet www.panamericanlife.com; Gen. Man. MAITE MUÑOZGUREN.

Puerto Rican-American Insurance Co: POB 70333, San Juan, PR 00936-8333; tel. (787) 250-5214; fax (787) 250-5371; f. 1920; total assets 119.9m. (1993); Chair. and CEO RAFAEL A. ROCA; Pres. RODOLFO E. CRISCUOLO.

Security National Life Insurance Co: POB 193309, Hato Rey, PR 00919; tel. (787) 753-6161; fax (787) 758-7409; Pres. CARLOS FERNÁNDEZ.

Universal Insurance Group: Calle 1, Lote 10, 3°, Metro Office Park, Guaynabo; POB 2145, San Juan, PR 00922-2145; tel. (787) 793-7202; fax (787) 782-0692; internet www.universalpr.com; f. 1972; comprises Universal Insurance Co, Eastern America Insurance Agency and Caribbean Alliance Insurance Co; Chair. and CEO LUIS MIRANDA CASAÑAS.

There are numerous agents, representing Puerto Rican, US and foreign companies.

Trade and Industry

DEVELOPMENT ORGANIZATION

Puerto Rico Industrial Development Co (PRIDCO): POB 362350, San Juan, PR 00936-2350; 355 Roosevelt Ave, Hato Rey, San Juan, PR 00918; tel. (787) 758-4747; fax (787) 764-1415; internet www.pridco.com; public agency responsible for the govt-sponsored industrial devt programme; Exec. Dir JORGE P. SILVA PURAS.

CHAMBERS OF COMMERCE

Chamber of Commerce of Puerto Rico: 100 Calle Tetuán, POB 9024033, San Juan, PR 00902-4033; tel. (787) 721-6060; fax (787) 723-1891; e-mail ebigas@camarapr.net; f. 1913; 1,800 mems; Pres. MANUEL MEJÍA GÓMEZ; Exec. Vice-Pres. EDGARDO BIGAS.

Chamber of Commerce of Bayamón: POB 2007, Bayamón, PR 00619; tel. (787) 786-4320; Pres. IVÁN A. MARRERO; Exec. Sec. ANGELICA B. DE REMÍREZ; 350 mems.

Chamber of Commerce of Ponce and the South of Puerto Rico: 65 Calle Isabel, POB 7455, Ponce, PR 00732-7455; tel. (787) 844-4400; fax (787) 844-4705; e-mail info@camarasur.org; internet www.camarasur.org; f. 1885; Pres. Dr ERNESTO CÓRDOVA; 550 mems.

Chamber of Commerce of the West of Puerto Rico Inc: Edif. Doral Bank Plaza, 9°, Méndez Vigo, POB 9, Mayagüez, PR 00681; tel. (787) 832-3749; fax (787) 832-4287; e-mail ccopr@coqui.net; internet www.ccopr.com; f. 1962; Pres. JULIO CÉSAR SANABRIA; 300 mems.

Official Chamber of Commerce of Spain: POB 894, San Juan, PR 00902; tel. (787) 725-5178; fax (787) 724-0527; f. 1966; promotes Spanish goods; provides information for Spanish exporters and Puerto Rican importers; Pres. MANUEL GARCÍA; Gen. Sec. ANTONIO TRUJILO; 300 mems.

Puerto Rico/United Kingdom Chamber of Commerce: 1509 Calle López Landrón, Suite 100, San Juan, Puerto Rico 00911; tel. (787) 721-0160; fax (787) 721-7333; e-mail iancourt1@cs.com; Chair. Dr IAN COURT; 120 mems.

INDUSTRIAL AND TRADE ASSOCIATIONS

Home Builders' Association of Puerto Rico: 1605 Ponce de León Ave, Condominium San Martín, Santurce, San Juan, PR 00909; tel. (787) 723-0279; Pres. FRANKLIN D. LÓPEZ; Exec. Dir WANDA I. NAVAJAS; 150 mems.

Pharmaceutical Industry Association of Puerto Rico (PIAPR): City View Plaza, Suite 407, Guaynabo, PR 00968; tel. (787) 622-0500; fax (787) 622-0503; e-mail info@piapr.com; internet www.piapr.com; Chair. CÉSAR SIMICH; Sec. EDGARDO FÁBREGAS; 17 mem. cos.

Puerto Rico Farm Bureau: Condominium San Martín, 16054 Ponce de León Ave, Suite 403, San Juan, PR 00909-1895; tel. (787) 721-5970; fax (787) 724-6932; f. 1925; Pres. ANTONIO ALVAREZ; over 1,500 mems.

Puerto Rico Manufacturers' Association (PRMA): POB 195477, San Juan, PR 00919-5477; tel. (787) 759-9445; fax (787) 756-7670.

Puerto Rico United Retailers Center: POB 190127, San Juan, PR 00919-0127; tel. (787) 641-8405; fax (787) 641-8406; e-mail mhernandez@centrounido.org; internet www.centrounido.org; f. 1891; represents small and medium-sized businesses; Pres. ENID TORO; Gen. Man. IGNACIO T. VELOZ; 20,000 mems.

UTILITIES

Electricity

Autoridad de Energía Eléctrica de Puerto Rico (Puerto Rico Electric Power Authority): POB 364267, San Juan, PR 00936-4267; tel. (787) 289-3434; fax (787) 289-4690; e-mail director@prepa.com; internet www.aeepr.com; govt-owned electricity corpn, opened to private co-generators in the mid-1990s; installed capacity of 4,389 MW; Dir HÉCTOR ROSARIO.

TRADE UNIONS

American Federation of Labor–Congress of Industrial Organizations (AFL–CIO): San Juan; internet www.afl-cio.org; Regional Dir AGUSTÍN BENÍTEZ; c. 60,000 mems.

Central Puertorriqueña de Trabajadores (CPT): POB 364084, San Juan, PR 00936-4084; tel. (787) 781-6649; fax (787) 277-9290; f. 1982; Pres. FEDERICO TORRES MONTALVO.

Confederación General de Trabajadores de Puerto Rico: 620 San Antonio St, San Juan, PR 00907; f. 1939; Pres. FRANCISCO COLÓN GORDIANY; 35,000 mems.

Federación del Trabajo de Puerto Rico (AFL–CIO): POB S-1648, San Juan, PR 00903; tel. (787) 722-4012; f. 1952; Pres. HIPÓLITO MARCANO; Sec.-Treas. CLIFFORD W. DEPIN; 200,000 mems.

Puerto Rico Industrial Workers' Union, Inc: POB 22014, UPR Station, San Juan, PR 00931; Pres. DAVID MUÑOZ HERNÁNDEZ.

Sindicato Empleados de Equipo Pesado, Construcción y Ramas Anexas de Puerto Rico, Inc (Construction and Allied Trades Union): Calle Hicaco 95, Urb. Milaville, Río Piedras, San Juan, PR 00926; f. 1954; Pres. JESÚS M. AGOSTO; 950 mems.

Sindicato de Obreros Unidos del Sur de Puerto Rico (United Workers' Union of South Puerto Rico): POB 106, Salinas, PR 00751; f. 1961; Pres. JOSÉ CARABALLO; 52,000 mems.

Unión General de Trabajadores de Puerto Rico: Apdo 29247, Estación de Infantería, Río Piedras, San Juan, PR 00929; tel. (787) 751-5350; fax (787) 751-7604; f. 1965; Pres. JUAN G. ELIZA-COLÓN; Sec.-Treas. OSVALDO ROMERO-PIZARRO.

Unión de Trabajadores de la Industría Eléctrica y Riego de Puerto Rico (UTIER): POB 13068, Santurce, San Juan, PR 00908; tel. (787) 721-1700; e-mail utier@coqui.net; internet www.utier.org; Pres. RICARDOS SANTOS RAMOS; Sec.-Treas. LUIS MERCED; 6,000 mems.

Transport

In January 2004 a 17-km urban railway (Tren Urbano), capable of carrying some 300,000 passengers per day, was inaugurated in greater San Juan. The railway took eight years to build and cost some US $2,150m. An extension to Carolina and Minillas was proposed in March 2005, at a projected cost of $900m.

Ponce and Guayama Railway: Aguirre, PR 00608; tel. (787) 853-3810; owned by the Corporación Azucarera de Puerto Rico; transports sugar cane over 96 km of track route; Exec. Dir A. MARTÍNEZ; Gen. Supt J. RODRÍGUEZ.

ROADS

The road network totalled 24,431 km (15,181 miles) in 2003, of which some 94% was paved. A modern highway system links all cities and towns along the coast and cross-country. A highways authority oversees the design and construction of roads, highways and bridges. In April 2002 it was announced that some US $585.6m. was to be invested in projects to improve or expand the road network.

Autoridad de Carreteras: Centro Gubierno Minillas, Edif. Norte, Avda de Diego 23, POB 42007, Santurce, San Juan, PR 00940-2007; tel. (787) 721-8787; fax (787) 727-5456; internet www.dtop.gov.pr/act/actmain.html; Dir Dr FERNANDO FACUNDO.

SHIPPING

There are 11 major ports on the island, the principal ones being San Juan, Ponce and Mayagüez. Other ports include Guayama, Guayanilla, Guánica, Yabucoa, Aguirre, Aguadilla, Fajardo, Arecibo, Humacao and Arroyo. San Juan, one of the finest and longest all-weather natural harbours in the Caribbean, is the main port of entry for foodstuffs and raw materials and for shipping finished industrial products. In 2001 it handled 9.7m. tons of cargo. Under US cabotage laws all maritime freight traffic between the USA and Puerto Rico must be conducted using US-registered vessels. Passenger traffic is limited to tourist cruise vessels. Work on the US $700m. Las Américas 'megaport' was ongoing in 2006. In April 2005 a high-speed ferry service was launched, connecting San Juan to the islands of Vieques and Culebra.

Autoridad de los Puertos (Puerto Rico Ports Authority): POB 362829, San Juan, PR 00936-2829; tel. (787) 729-8805; fax (787) 722-7867; internet www.prpa.gobierno.pr; manages and administers all ports and airports; Exec. Dir FERNANDO J. BONILLA.

CIVIL AVIATION

There are 11 airports on the island, the principal ones being at San Juan (Luis Muñoz Marín international airport, Carolina), Aguadilla, Ponce and Mayagüez. There are also six heliports.

Tourism

An estimated 4.9m. tourists visited Puerto Rico in 2004, when revenue from this source was estimated at US $3,024m. More than three-quarters of all tourist visitors were from the US mainland. In 2004 there were approximately 12,864 hotel rooms. The Government planned to add a further 5,000 rooms by 2008.

Compañía de Turismo (Puerto Rico Tourism Co): Edif. La Princesa, 2 Paseo La Princesa, POB 9023960, San Juan, PR 00902-3960; tel. (787) 721-2400; fax (787) 722-6238; internet www.prtourism.com; f. 1970; Dir TERESTELLA GONZÁLEZ DENTON.

UNITED STATES EXTERNAL TERRITORIES

The External or Unincorporated Territories of the USA comprise the Pacific Territories of American Samoa and Guam, the Caribbean Territory of the US Virgin Islands, and a number of smaller islands.

AMERICAN SAMOA

Introductory Survey

Location, Climate, Language, Religion, Flag, Capital

American Samoa comprises the seven islands of Tutuila, Ta'u, Olosega, Ofu, Aunu'u, Rose and Swains. They lie in the southern central Pacific Ocean, along latitude 14°S at about longitude 170°W, about 3,700 km (2,300 miles) south-west of Hawaii. The temperature normally ranges between 21°C (70°F) and 32°C (90°F), and the average annual rainfall is 5,000 mm (197 ins), the greatest precipitation occurring between December and March. English and Samoan, a Polynesian language, are spoken. The population is largely Christian, more than 50% being members of the Christian Congregational Church. The flag has a dark blue field, on which is superimposed a red-edged white triangle (with its apex at the hoist and its base at the outer edge of the flag), containing an eagle, representing the USA, grasping in its talons a yellow *fue* (staff) and *uatogi* (club), Samoan symbols of sovereignty. The capital is Pago Pago, on Tutuila (the officially designated seat of government is the village of Fagatogo).

Recent History

The Samoan islands were first visited by Europeans in the 1700s, but it was not until 1830 that missionaries from the London Missionary Society settled there. In 1878 the Kingdom of Samoa, then an independent state, gave the USA the right to establish a naval base at Pago Pago. The United Kingdom and Germany were also interested in the islands, but the United Kingdom withdrew in 1899, leaving the western islands for Germany to govern. The chiefs of the eastern islands ceded their lands to the USA in 1904, and the islands officially became an Unincorporated Territory of the USA in 1922.

Until 1978 American Samoa was administered by a Governor, appointed by the US Government, and a legislature comprising the Senate and the House of Representatives. In November 1977 the first gubernatorial elections took place and, in January 1978, Peter Coleman was inaugurated as Governor. He was re-elected for a second term in November 1980, after three years in office instead of four, to allow synchronization with US elections in 1980. At elections in November 1984 A. P. Lutali was elected Governor and Eni Hunkin (who subsequently adopted the use of his chiefly name, Faleomavaega) was elected Lieutenant-Governor. The High Court of American Samoa had ruled earlier that Coleman was ineligible to stand for a third successive term as Governor, because a law restricted tenure by any individual to two successive terms. In October 1986 a constitutional convention completed a comprehensive rewriting of the American Samoan Constitution. The draft revision, however, had yet to be submitted to the US Congress in the early 2000s. In April 2004 it was announced that the Political Status Study Commission was to examine the the territory's situation and submit its recommendations prior to the holding of another constitutional convention in 2005.

In July 1988 the Territory's delegate to the US House of Representatives, Fofō Sunia, announced that he would not seek re-election, as he was then the subject of an official investigation for alleged financial mismanagement. In October he received a prison sentence for fraud. Eni F. H. Faleomavaega replaced Sunia as delegate in November. At gubernatorial elections, which took place in November, Coleman was elected Governor for a third term, while Galea'i Poumele replaced Faleomavaega as Lieutenant-Governor.

At gubernatorial elections in November 1992 Peter Coleman was defeated by A. P. Lutali. At elections to the House of Representatives in November 1994 about one-third of those members who sought re-election were defeated. Faleomavaega was re-elected as non-voting delegate.

In late 1994 and early 1995 American Samoa was one of a number of Pacific islands to express concern at the proposed passage through their waters of regular shipments of plutonium, *en route* from Europe to Japan. Moreover, the decision by France to resume nuclear-testing in the South Pacific in September 1995 was fiercely criticized by Lutali, who described the action as an affront to the entire Pacific community.

Gubernatorial and legislative elections took place in November 1996. An estimated 87% of eligible voters participated in the election, at which only eight of the 18 members seeking re-election to the Fono were successful. At a second round of voting the incumbent Lieutenant-Governor, the Democrat Tauese Sunia, was elected Governor with 51.3% of the vote, defeating Leala Peter Reid, Jr, who secured 48.7% of votes. Faleomavaega was re-elected as delegate to the US House of Representatives, with 56.5% of the vote, defeating Gus Hannemann, who won 43.5% of votes.

The decision in July 1997 by the Government of neighbouring Western Samoa to change the country's name to simply Samoa caused some controversy in the Territory. Legislation approved in March 1998 in the House of Representatives stated that American Samoa should not recognize the new name, which was viewed by many islanders as serving to undermine their own Samoan identity. Similarly, legislation prohibiting citizens of Samoa (formerly Western Samoa) from owning land in American Samoa was approved in response to the change of name. Nevertheless, moves towards *rapprochement* continued. In August 2004 plans were announced for greater economic co-operation. Also, in early November a twice-weekly air passenger service began operations. Concerns were expressed, however, at the decision of the Samoan Government in March 2005 to require of American Samoan citizens travelling to Samoa a permit and a passport. In early April a meeting was held by the two countries' leaders in the Samoan capital to begin negotiations over travel requirements. Meanwhile, in late March the Samoan Government announced plans to open a consulate in American Samoa in order to facilitate bilateral communications. In early June the US State Department gave preliminary approval to the proposed establishment of the consulate. However, although the consulate was scheduled to commence operations in March 2006, its opening was postponed indefinitely.

In November 1998 Faleomavaega was re-elected as delegate to the US House of Representatives. In the same month, following a dispute lasting several years, a legal settlement was reached by the five leading US tobacco companies and the 46 US states and several of its territories, including American Samoa. It was agreed that between 1998 and 2025 American Samoa was to receive a total of some US $29m. in compensation for the harmful effects of cigarette smoking suffered by its inhabitants.

At elections held on 7 November 2000, Tauese Sunia was narrowly re-elected as Governor, receiving 50.7% of votes cast, compared with 47.9% for the opposition candidate, Senator Lealaifuaneva. However, following the Chief Electoral Officer's refusal to allow a recount, as requested by Lealaifuaneva (who claimed that absentee ballots had not been properly handled), Lealaifuaneva filed a lawsuit against the Government, but this was dismissed by the High Court in early December. At congressional elections, held concurrently, no candidate received the necessary 50% majority, Faleomavaega winning 45.7% of votes cast, compared with 30.3% for Hanneman. A second round of polling took place on 21 November, when Faleomavaega won a reported 61.1% of the votes and Hanneman received 38.9%. Faleomavaega therefore returned to the US House of Representatives for a seventh two-year term.

The issue of US jurisdiction in the Territory was raised once more in September 2001, when the Senate approved a resolution urging discussion with the US Government regarding the conferral of limited federal jurisdiction to the High Court of American Samoa, the only US territory without a sitting federal judge. A congressional public survey, conducted in the same month, registered wide popular support for a Federal Court and Public Prosecutor. At a meeting of the UN General Assembly in January 2002, the UN accepted American Samoa's proposal of May 2001 to be removed from the list of colonized territories. The Governor had sent a resolution to the UN Committee on Decolonization affirming American Samoa's wish to remain a US territory.

In mid-September 2002 the Territory's immigration procedures were amended to give the Attorney-General, rather than the Immigration Board, the ultimate authority to grant permanent residency status to aliens. The House of Representatives also approved a resolution to repeal legislation automatically conferring US citizenship in the Territory to foreign parents. In the same month the Territory's intelligence agencies claimed that the Speaker of the House of Representatives, Tuanaitau Tuia, had used public funds to purchase a car and to finance private travel for his wife. Meanwhile, in early June, a former president of the Amerika Samoa Bank (now ANZ Amerika Samoa Bank) was convicted of fraud for his involvement in a scheme that had misappropriated US $75m. of investors' money. Further allegations of corruption in the banking sector followed in 2004. The government-owned Development Bank of American Samoa was being investigated in April of that year by an anti-corruption senate committee, after records suggested favouritism in the approval of loans.

In elections for American Samoa's delegate to the Federal Congress on 6 November 2002, Faleomavaega won 41.3% of the votes cast, Fagafaga Daniel Langkilde secured 32.1% and Aumua Amata Coleman won 26.6%. Since none of the candidates received the 50% of votes required, Faleomavaega and Langkilde entered a second round of voting on 19 November, at which Faleomavaega secured an eighth term in office.

In mid-December 2002 legislation was introduced that prohibited nationals of 23 countries thought to present a terrorist threat from entering the Territory, unless they were granted special permission. Opposition groups in Fiji expressed their displeasure at the neighbouring islands' inclusion on the list of countries, owing to its large Muslim population. In late March 2003 airlines also complained that the strict security measures introduced at the airport were damaging business. Also in March Tauese Sunia died while travelling to Hawaii for medical treatment. Lieutenant-Governor Togiola Tulafono became Governor and appointed Aitofele Sunia as his deputy.

In late January 2003 the Senate approved a motion to begin expulsion hearings against Senator Faamausili Pola. Members had already voted to remove Faamausili Pola in September 2002 when it was alleged that he had not been elected according to Samoan tradition. In March 2003 it was reported that Kil Soo Lee, the South Korean owner of the Daewoosa Samoa clothing factory, had been convicted by a US court of human trafficking. (In June 2005 Lee was sentenced to 40 years' imprisonment; Lee subsequently announced his intention to appeal against the verdict.) The mainly Vietnamese and Chinese factory employees had received very low wages and suffered appalling working conditions. The American Samoan High Court had previously ordered Daewoosa to pay workers US $3.5m. in compensation and fined the company an additional $290,000 in April 2002. In March 2004 Governor Tulafono announced plans for legislation that would allow prosecution of human-trafficking offences in the territory. In July it was announced that a US senate committee would hold a hearing on human trafficking at the site of the closed garment factory.

During 2003 several allegations of official corruption were made against American Samoan government officials. In September an employee of the Territory's Office of Procurement was allowed to return to work despite a recent conviction in an insurance fraud case. In the same month the Senate ordered an official investigation into contracts awarded by Tafua Faau Seumanutafa, the Chief Procurement Officer, and senior officials from the Department of Health and Social Security and the Department of Education. In May 2004 Seumanutafa pleaded guilty in the Hawaii Federal District Court to one count of conspiracy to defraud the US Government, in a case that also implicated senior officials from the Department of Health and Social Security and the Department of Education. Also in May the Senate Select Investigative Committee issued subpoenas to several senators to testify about alleged corruption in the allocation of government contracts. In early September the Committee recommended that, while under investigation for alleged corruption, Lieutenant-Governor Ipulasi Aitofele Sunia be placed on leave and have his name removed from the list of candidates for the forthcoming gubernatorial election. Governor Tulafono claimed that the charges were politically motivated. Meanwhile, in February 2004 the US Federal Bureau of Investigation (FBI) began a wide-ranging investigation into the alleged misuse of US government funds. In early March 2005 the FBI effected an unannounced search of the government offices in Pago Pago, forbidding entry to the Governor, Lieutenant-Governor and Attorney-General for the duration of the operation. In mid-March the Government announced its intention to challenge the legality of the search warrants. In October Dr Sili K. Satauaa and Patolo Mageo, the former Directors of the Education and Human Resources Departments, respectively, were sentenced in a federal court in Honolulu, Hawaii, to custodial sentences following their conviction on corruption charges. The FBI's investigations continued in early 2006.

In May 2003 severe flooding and landslides led to the deaths of five people, and in the following month President George W. Bush declared the Territory a federal disaster area. In January 2004 a state of emergency was declared when a cyclone damaged the islands. The USA allocated US $12.5m. towards the relief effort.

At the gubernatorial election held on 2 November 2004 incumbent Governor Tulafono received 48.4% of the votes cast in the first round of polling, while Afoa Moega Lutu obtained 39.4%. At the second round of voting, conducted on 16 November, Tulafono was re-elected, having secured 55.72% of the votes; Moega Lutu received 44.28%). Following his re-election, Governor Tulafono announced that during his term of office priorities would include improvements in infrastructure, social provision and tax collection, increases in public-sector salaries and the promotion of private enterprise.

Government

Executive power is vested in the Governor, who is elected by popular vote and has authority which extends to all operations within the Territory of American Samoa. He has the power of veto with respect to legislation approved by the Fono (Legislature). The Fono consists of the Senate and the House of Representatives, with a President and a Speaker presiding over their respective divisions. The Senate is composed of 18 members, elected, according to Samoan custom, from local chiefs, or Matai, for a term of four years. The House of Representatives consists of 20 members who are elected by popular vote for a term of two years, and a non-voting delegate from Swains Island. The Fono meets twice a year, in January and July, for not more than 45 days, and at such special sessions as the Governor may call. The Governor, who serves a four-year term, has the authority to appoint heads of government departments with the approval of the Fono. Local government is carried out by indigenous officials.

Defence

The USA is responsible for the defence of American Samoa.

Economic Affairs

In 2000, according to estimates by the American Samoa National Income and Product Accounts Task Force, American Samoa's gross national income (GNI), measured at constant 1999 prices, was about US $348.6m., equivalent to some $6,332 per head. Between 1973 and 1985, it was estimated, GNI increased, in real terms, at an average rate of 1.7% per year, with real GNI per head rising by only 0.1% per year. Gross domestic product (GDP) was estimated (at constant 1999 prices and allowing for statistical discrepancy) in 1999 at $444.2m. and in 2000 at $437.9m. In 1990–2000 the population increased by an average of 3.3% per year. An estimated 91,000 American Samoans live on the US mainland or Hawaii.

Agriculture, hunting, forestry, fishing and mining engaged only 3.1% of the employed labour force in 2000. Agricultural production provides little surplus for export. Major crops are coconuts, bananas, taro, pineapples, yams and breadfruit. Local fisheries are at subsistence level, but tuna-canning plants at Pago Pago process fish from US, Taiwanese and South Korean vessels. Canned tuna constituted some 90.1% of export revenue in 2003/04, when earnings reached US $401.6m.

Within the industrial sector, manufacturing activities engaged 35.3% of the employed labour force in 2000. Fish-canning is the dominant industry, and in 2001 some 70% of those employed in these factories were guest workers from Samoa (formerly Western Samoa). Other manufacturing activities include meat-canning, handicrafts, dairy farming, orchid-farming and the production of soap, perfume, paper products and alcoholic beverages. A garment factory began operations at Tafuna in 1995 and in the following year employed more than 700 people (although almost one-half of these employees were foreign workers). However, the island's garment manufacturing industry was adversely affected following a riot between local workers and Vietnamese employees at a clothing factory, during which a number of people were injured. The incident was widely condemned, and Governor Tauese Sunia stated that the future of the garment industry in American Samoa would require consideration. Exports of textiles and garments were valued at $7.3m. in 2000/01, accounting for 3.2% of total exports. In 2002 the management of the Daewoosa clothing manufacturer was ordered by the authorities to pay compensation to its employees, owing to the poor working conditions at the factory, and in early 2003 the factory's South Korean owner was convicted of human trafficking (See Recent History). The construction sector engaged 6.4% of the employed labour force in 2000.

Service industries engage a majority of the employed labour force in American Samoa (55.2% in 2000). The Government alone employs almost one-third of workers, although in the mid-1990s a series of reductions in the number of public-sector employees were introduced. The tourist industry is developing slowly, and earned some US $10m. in 1998. The number of tourist arrivals rose from 41,287 in 1999 to 44,158 in 2000, declining to 36,009 in 2001.

The visible trade deficit rose from US $108m. in 1998/99 to $158m. in 2003/04, when imports (including items imported by the Government and goods by the fish-canning sector) totalled $604m. and exports reached $402m. Most of American Samoa's trade is conducted with the USA. Other trading partners in 2003/04 included Australia, which supplied 9.1% of total imports (excluding items imported by the Government and goods by the fish-canning sector),

UNITED STATES EXTERNAL TERRITORIES

American Samoa

and New Zealand (8.3%). In March 2003 preliminary figures indicated that there had been a $121m. surplus on the balance of payments in 2002.

In 2001/02 a fiscal surplus of US $30,990 was recorded. Subsequently, the Government reportedly maintained the surplus, which reached some $2.5m. in 2003 and $4m. in 2004. Annual inflation averaged 2.9% in 1995–2004. Following an increase of 4.9% in 2003, the inflation rate reached 7.1% in 2004. An estimated 10.5% of the total labour force were unemployed in 2003.

American Samoa is a member of the Pacific Community (see p. 350), and is an associate member of the UN Economic and Social Commission for Asia and the Pacific (ESCAP, see p. 33).

American Samoa's controversial minimum wage structure, in which American Samoa has considerably lower minimum hourly rates of pay than the rest of the USA, has been largely attributed to the presence of the two tuna-canning plants on the islands, which employ almost half of the labour force, and consequently exert substantial influence over the setting of wage levels. A US recommendation for modest increases in wage levels, implemented in mid-1996, was strongly opposed by the American Samoan Government, which argued that, with higher costs, the Territory's tuna-canning industry would be unable to compete with other parts of the world. In 2004 the minimum hourly rates of pay for the garment and cannery sectors were, respectively, US $2.68 and $3.26. In October 2005 it was announced that the minimum hourly rates in several sectors, including tourism and government, were to be increased by 14–17 cents by October 2006; the rate for the cannery sector, however, was to remain unchanged. The next minimum-wage review was scheduled for 2007. American Samoa's financial problems have been compounded by the high demand for government services from an increasing population, the limited economic and tax base and natural disasters. Attempts to achieve a greater measure of financial security for the islands have included severe reductions in the number of public-sector employees, increased fees for government services and plans to diversify the economy by encouraging tourism and expanding manufacturing activity. Economic development, however, is hindered by the islands' remote location, the limited infrastructure and lack of skilled workers. In 2001 the territory's first budgetary surplus for more than 20 years was recorded. The fiscal surpluses of 2003 and 2004 were primarily attributable to improved tax collection. In May 2001, meanwhile, the Government waived the provision requiring foreign employees to perform domestic duties for a year prior to progressing to other work. The move was welcomed by the tuna canneries, which were experiencing difficulties in recruiting sufficient workers. In 2002 the tuna-canning companies expressed concern that an impending US free trade agreement with Central American countries, which included the removal of tariffs on canned tuna, would threaten their exports to the USA. Nevertheless, in March 2003 the Senate approved a bill to levy tax on foreign tuna meat sold to the Territory's canneries. In December 2003 the USA declared American Samoa eligible for financing from a $30m. regional fund to offset the economic impact of Marshallese and Micronesian migrants. The Interior Appropriations bill for 2005/06, approved by the US Congress in July 2005, was to provide some $33m. for American Samoa, of which $23.1m. was intended to assist government operations, representing an increase in funding of $331,000 compared with the previous financial year. The increase in funding was approved, however, despite the concerns of the congressional Government Accountability Office, expressed in its report of December 2004, relating to the auditing and efficiency of federal spending in American Samoa. Budgeted US funding for American Samoa totalled $22.9m. in 2006/07. A government budget of $279.6m. for 2005/06 was submitted to the Fono in August 2005. In March 2006 Governor Tulafono proposed the issue of government bonds worth $20m., in order to raise funds for infrastructural projects.

Education

Education is officially compulsory for 12 years between six and 18 years of age. Primary education begins at six years of age and lasts for eight years. Secondary education, beginning at the age of 14, lasts for a further four years. In 2004 there were 51 pre-primary schools, 32 primary schools and 12 secondary schools. There was also a community college of further education, with 1,550 students. In 2003, meanwhile, there were 2,218 enrolled pre-primary-school pupils, 11,165 primary-school pupils and 4,336 secondary-school pupils. Expenditure on education and culture in 2001/02 was US $51.3m., or 28.4% of total government expenditure.

Public Holidays

2006: 2 January (for New Year's Day), 16 January (Martin Luther King Day), 20 February (Presidents' Day), 17 April (Flag Day, commemorating the first raising of the US flag in American Samoa), 29 May (Memorial Day), 4 July (US Independence Day), 4 September (Labor Day), 23 November (Thanksgiving Day), 25 December (Christmas Day).

2007: 1 January (New Year's Day), 15 January (Martin Luther King Day), 19 February (Presidents' Day), 17 April (Flag Day, commemorating the first raising of the US flag in American Samoa), 28 May (Memorial Day), 4 July (Independence Day), 3 September (Labor Day), 12 November (for Veterans' Day), 22 November (Thanksgiving Day), 25 December (Christmas Day).

Weights and Measures

With certain exceptions, the imperial system is in force. One US cwt equals 100 lb; one long ton equals 2,240 lb; one short ton equals 2,000 lb. A policy of gradual voluntary conversion to the metric system is being encouraged by the Federal Government.

Statistical Survey

Source (unless otherwise indicated): Statistics Division, Department of Commerce, Pago Pago, AS 96799; tel. 633-5155; fax 633-4195; internet www.amsamoa.com.

AREA AND POPULATION

Area: 201 sq km (77.6 sq miles); *By Island* (sq km): Tutuila 137; Ta'u 46; Ofu 7; Olosega 5; Swains Island (Olohenga) 3; Aunu'u 2; Rose 1.

Population: 46,773 at census of 1 April 1990; 57,291 (males 29,264, females 28,027) at census of 1 April 2000. *Mid-2005* 65,500. *By Island* (2000): Tutuila 55,400; Manu'a District (Ta'u, Olosega and Ofu islands) 1,378; Aunu'u 476; Swains Island (Olohenga) 37.

Density (mid-2005): 325.9 per sq km.

Ethnic Groups (2000 census): Samoan 50,545; part-Samoan 1,991; Asian 1,631; Tongan 1,598; Total (incl. others) 57,291.

Principal Towns (population at 2000 census): Tafuna 8,409; Nu'uuli 5,154; Pago Pago (capital) 4,278; Leone 3,568; Fagatogo 2,096.

Births, Marriages and Deaths (2004, unless otherwise stated): Registered live births 1,713 (birth rate 26.7 per 1,000); Registered marriages 254 (2001); Registered deaths 289 (death rate 4.5 per 1,000).

Expectation of Life (years at birth, 1995): Males 68.0; Females 76.0. Source: UN Economic and Social Commission for Asia and the Pacific.

Economically Active Population (persons aged 16 years and over, 2000 census): Agriculture, hunting, forestry, fishing and mining 517; Manufacturing 5,900; Construction 1,066; Trade, restaurants and hotels 2,414; Transport, storage, communications and utilities 1,036; Financing, insurance, real estate and business services 311; Community, social and personal services 5,474; *Total employed* 16,718 (males 9,804, females 6,914); Unemployed 909 (males 494, females 415); *Total labour force* 17,627 (males 10,298, females 7,329). Source: US Department of Commerce, *2000 Census of Population and Housing*. 2003 (estimates): Total employed 14,319; Unemployed 1,681; Total labour force 16,000 (Source: US Department of State).

AGRICULTURE, ETC.

Principal Crops (FAO estimates, '000 metric tons, 2004): Coconuts 5; Taro 2; Bananas 1.

Livestock (FAO estimates, 2004): Pigs 10,500; Cattle 103; Chickens 38,000.

Fishing (metric tons, live weight, 2003): Total catch 4,977 (Albacore 3,925; Yellowfin tuna 496).

Source: FAO.

INDUSTRY

Production (2004): Electric energy 188 million kWh.

FINANCE

Currency and Exchange Rates: United States currency is used. For details, see section on the Northern Mariana Islands.

Budget (US $ '000, year ending September 2002): *Revenue:* Taxes 55,431; Licenses and permits 826; Charges for services 9,983; Fines and fees 1,778; Grants 75,865; Total (incl. others) 211,531. *Expenditure:* General government 55,759; Public safety 9,481; Public works 14,098; Health and welfare 26,841; Education and culture 51,291; Economic development 11,449; Capital projects 7,444; Debt-servicing 4,177; Total 180,541.

UNITED STATES EXTERNAL TERRITORIES   American Samoa

Cost of Living (Consumer Price Index; annual averages; base: July–Sept. 1997 = 100): All items 107.7 in 2002; 113.0 in 2003; 121.0 in 2004.

Gross Domestic Product (US $ million, constant 1999 prices, provisional estimates): 444.2 in 1999 (with a statistical discrepancy of 6.7%); 437.9 in 2000 (with a statistical discrepancy of 4.4%). Note: Recorded accounts are not available; figures represent the findings of the American Samoa National Income and Product Accounts Task Force, established to produce reliable economic statistics for the territory.

EXTERNAL TRADE

Principal Commodities: *Imports* (US $ million, year ending September 2001): Food 66.3 (Fish 27.4); Fuel and oil 25.8 (Diesel fuel 16.3); Textiles and clothing 7.3; Machinery and transport equipment 23.7 (Road motor vehicles and parts 12.7); Miscellaneous manufactured articles 85.4 (Tin plates 59.8); Construction materials 19.3; Total (incl. others) 231.0. *2004* (US $ million, year ending September): Total imports 604; Total exports 446 (Canned tuna 402).

Principal Trading Partners (US $ million, year ending September 2004): *Imports* (excl. government purchases and cannery goods): Australia 28.2; Fiji 16.2; Japan 3.3; Korea, Republic 21.8; New Zealand 25.6; Samoa 19.5; Singapore 12.8; USA 149.0; Total (incl. others) 308.8. *Exports:* Total 445.6 (almost entirely to the USA).

TRANSPORT

Road Traffic ('000 registered motor vehicles, 2004): Passenger cars 7.0; Total 8.1.

International Sea-borne Shipping (estimated freight traffic, '000 metric tons, 2004): Goods loaded 260; Goods unloaded 527.

Civil Aviation (Pago Pago Int. Airport, 2004): Flights 5,135; Passengers (excl. transit) 148,549 (Boarding 79,546, Disembarking 69,003); Transit 5,085; Freight and mail ('000 lb) 3,991 (Loaded 968, Unloaded 3,022).

TOURISM

Tourist Arrivals: 41,287 in 1999; 44,158 in 2000; 36,009 in 2001.

Tourist Arrivals by Country (2001): Australia 726; China, People's Republic 722; Fiji 354; New Zealand 3,883; Philippines 236; Samoa 21,358; Tonga 458; United Kingdom 183; USA 7,177; Total (incl. others) 36,009.

Tourism Receipts (US $ million): 9 in 1996; 10 in 1997; 10 in 1998.
Source: World Tourism Organization.

COMMUNICATIONS MEDIA

Daily Newspapers (1996): 2; estimated circulation 5,000*.
Non-daily Newspapers (1996): 1; estimated circulation 3,000*.
Radio Receivers (1997): 57,000* in use.
Television Receivers (1999): 15,000* in use.
Telephones (2004): 10,400 main lines in use.
Facsimile Machines (2001): 694 subscribers.
Mobile Cellular Telephones (2004): 2,250 subscribers.
* Sources: UNESCO, *Statistical Yearbook* and American Samoa Telecommunications Authority.

EDUCATION

Pre-primary (2003, unless otherwise stated): 51 schools (2004); 130 teachers; 2,218 pupils.

Primary (2003, unless otherwise stated): 32 schools (2004); 494 teachers; 11,165 pupils.

Secondary (2003, unless otherwise stated): 12 high schools (2004); 301 teachers; 4,336 pupils.

Higher (2004): American Samoa Community College 1,550 students.

Sources: American Samoa Department of Education.

Directory

The Constitution

American Samoa is an Unincorporated Territory of the USA. Therefore, not all the provisions of the US Constitution apply. As an unorganized territory it has not been provided with an organic act by Congress. Instead the US Secretary of the Interior, on behalf of the President, has plenary authority over the Territory and enabled the people of American Samoa to draft their own Constitution.

According to the 1967 Constitution, executive power is vested in the Governor, whose authority extends to all operations within the Territory of American Samoa. The Governor has veto power with respect to legislation passed by the Fono (Legislature). The Fono consists of the Senate and the House of Representatives, with a President and a Speaker presiding over their respective divisions. The Senate is composed of 18 members, elected, according to Samoan custom, from local chiefs, or Matai, for a term of four years. The House of Representatives consists of 20 members who are elected by popular vote for a term of two years, and a non-voting delegate from Swains Island. The Fono meets twice a year, in January and July, for not more than 45 days and at such special sessions as the Governor may call. The Governor has the authority to appoint heads of government departments with the approval of the Fono. Local government is carried out by indigenous officials. In August 1976 a referendum on the popular election of a Governor and a Lieutenant-Governor resulted in an affirmative vote. The first gubernatorial elections took place on 8 November 1977 and the second occurred in November 1980; subsequent elections were to take place every four years.

American Samoa sends one non-voting Delegate to the US House of Representatives, who is popularly elected every two years.

The Government
(April 2006)

Governor: TOGIOLA TULAFONO; (took office March 2003, re-elected 16 November 2004).
Lieutenant-Governor: IPULASI AITOFELE SUNIA.

GOVERNMENT OFFICES

Governor's Office: Executive Office Building, Third Floor, Utulei, Pago Pago, AS 96799; tel. 633-4116; fax 633-2269; e-mail governorsoffice@asg-gov.net; internet www.asg-gov.net.

Department of the Interior, Office of Insular Affairs (OIA): Field Office of the OIA, Dept of the Interior, POB 1725, Pago Pago, AS 96799; tel. 633-2800; fax 633-2415; internet www.doi.gov/oia/Islandpages/asgpage; Field Representative LYDIA FALEAFINE NOMURA.

Office of the Representative to the Government of American Samoa: Amerika Samoa Office, 1427 Dillingham Blvd, Suite 210, Honolulu HI 96817, USA; tel. (808) 847-1998; fax (808) 847-3420; e-mail hawaiioff@aol.com; Representative SOLOALI'I FAALEPO, Jr.

Department of Administrative Services: American Samoa Government, Executive Office Building, Utulei, Pago Pago, AS 96799; tel. 633-4158; fax 633-1841; internet www.asg-gov.com/departments/as.asg; Dir NU'UTAI SONNY THOMPSON.

Department of Agriculture: American Samoa Government, Executive Office Building, Utulei, Pago Pago, AS 96799; tel. 699-1497; fax 699-4031; internet www.asg-gov.com/departments/doa.asg; Dir APEFA'I TAIFANE.

Department of Commerce: American Samoa Government, Executive Office Building, 2nd Floor, POB 1147, Utulei, Pago Pago, AS 96799; tel. 633-5155; fax 633-4195; e-mail asgdoc@amsamoa.com; internet www.amsamoa.com; Dir ALI'IMAU H. SCANLAN, Jr.

Department of Education: American Samoa Government, Executive Office Building, Utulei, Pago Pago, AS 96799; tel. 633-5237; fax 633-4240; e-mail philoj@doe.as; internet www.doe.as; Dir Dr MALAETELE LUI TUITELE.

Department of Health: American Samoa Government, Pago Pago, AS 96799; tel. 633-4606; fax 633-5379; internet www.asg-gov.com/departments/doh.asg; Dir UTOOFILI ASOF'AFETAI MAGA.

Department of Human Resources: American Samoa Government, Executive Office Building, Utulei, Pago Pago, AS 96799; tel. 633-4485; fax 633-1139; internet www.asg-gov.com/departments/dhr.asg; Dir PUNI PENEI SEWELL.

Department of Human and Social Services: American Samoa Government, Pago Pago, AS 96799; tel. 633-1187; fax 633-7449; internet www.asg-gov.com/departments/dhss/dhss.asg; Dir TALIA FA'AFETAI I'AULUALO.

Department of Legal Affairs: American Samoa Government, Executive Office Building, Utulei, Pago Pago, AS 96799; tel. 633-4163; fax 633-1838; internet www.asg-gov.com/departments/dla.asg; Dir Attorney-General SIALEGA MALAETASI MAUGA TOGAFAU.

Department of Local Government (Office of Samoan Affairs): American Samoa Government, Pago Pago, AS 96799; tel. 633-5201; fax 633-5590; internet www.asg-gov.com/departments/osa.asg; Gen. Sec. SOTOA SAVALI.

Department of Marine and Wildlife Resources: American Samoa Government, Executive Office Building, Utulei, Pago Pago, AS 96799; tel. 633-4456; fax 633-5590; internet www.asg-gov.com/departments/dmwr.asg; Dir UFAGAFA RAY TULAFONO.

Department of Parks and Recreation: American Samoa Government, Pago Pago, AS 96799; tel. 699-9614; fax 699-4427; internet www.asg-gov.com/departments/dpr.asg; Dir TA'AMU IAKOPO.

Department of Port Administration: American Samoa Government, Pago Pago, AS 96799; tel. 633-4251; fax 633-5281; internet www.asg-gov.com/departments/dpa.asg; Dir FOFO TUITELE.

Department of Public Information: American Samoa Government, Territory of American Samoa, Pago Pago, AS 96799; tel. 633-4191; fax 633-1044; Dir PAOLO SIVIA SIVIA.

Department of Public Safety: American Samoa Government, Pago Pago, AS 96799; tel. 633-1111; fax 633-7296; internet www.asg-gov.com/departments/dps; Dir TUITELELEAPAGA PESETA FUE IONAE.

Department of Public Works: American Samoa Government, Executive Office Building, Utulei, Pago Pago, AS 96799; tel. 633-4141; fax 633-5958; internet www.asg-gov.com/departments/dpw.asg; Dir PUNAOFO TILEI.

Department of Treasury: American Samoa Government, Executive Office Building, Utulei, Pago Pago, AS 96799; tel. 633-4155; fax 633-4100; internet www.asg-gov.com/departments/dtr.asg; Dir AITOFELE SUNIA.

Department of Youth and Women's Affairs: American Samoa Government, Executive Office Building, Utulei, Pago Pago, AS 96799; tel. 633-2835; fax 633-2875; internet www.asg-gov.com/departments/dywa; Dir FIASILI PUNI E. HALECK.

Environmental Protection Agency: American Samoa Government, Office of the Governor, Pago Pago, AS 96799; tel. 633-2304; fax 633-5590; e-mail ppeshut@yahoo.com; Dir PETER PESHUT (acting).

Legislature

FONO

Senate

The Senate has 18 members, elected, according to Samoan custom, from local chiefs, or Matai, for a term of four years.
President: LOLO LETALU MOLIGA.

House of Representatives

The House has 20 members who are elected by popular vote for a term of two years, and a non-voting delegate from Swains Island.
Speaker: MATAGI MAILO RAY MCMOORE.

CONGRESS

Since 1980 American Samoa has been able to elect, for a two-year term, a Delegate to the Federal Congress, who may vote in committee but not on the floor of the House of Representatives. Elections to the post took place in November 2004.
Delegate of American Samoa: ENI F. HUNKIN FALEOMAVAEGA, US House of Representatives, 2422 Rayburn House Office Bldg, Washington, DC 20515, USA; tel. (202) 225-8577; fax (202) 225-8757; e-mail faleomavaega@mail.house.gov.

Judicial System

The judicial system of American Samoa consists of the High Court, presided over by the Chief Justice and assisted by Associate Justices (all appointed by the Secretary of the Interior), and a local judiciary in the District and Village Courts. The judges for these local courts are appointed by the Governor, subject to confirmation by the Senate of the Fono. The High Court consists of three Divisions: Appellate, Trial, and Land and Titles. The Appellate Division has limited original jurisdiction and hears appeals from the Trial Division, the Land and Titles Division and from the District Court when it has operated as a court of record. The Trial Division has general jurisdiction over all cases. The Land and Titles Division hears cases involving land or Matai titles.

The District Court hears preliminary felony proceedings, misdemeanours, infractions (traffic and health), civil claims less than US $3,000, small claims, Uniform Reciprocal Enforcement of Support cases, and *de novo* trials from Village Courts. The Village Courts hear matters arising under village regulations and local customs.

Chief Justice: MICHAEL KRUSE.
Associate Justice: LYLE L. RICHMOND.
Attorney-General: SIALEGA MALAETASI MAUGA TOGAFAU.

High Court

Office of the Chief Justice, High Court, Pago Pago, AS 96799; tel. 633-1261; fax 633-1318; e-mail hcourt@samoatelco.com.
Judge of the District Court: JOHN L. WARD II, POB 427, Pago Pago, AS 96799; tel. 633-1101.
Judge of the Village Court: FAISIOTA TAUANU'U, Pago Pago, AS 96799; tel. 633-1102.

Religion

The population is largely Christian, more than 50% being members of the Congregational Christian Church and about 20% being Roman Catholics.

CHRISTIANITY

American Samoa Council of Christian Churches: c/o CCCAS Offices, POB 1637, Pago Pago, AS 96799; f. 1985; six mem. churches; Pres. (vacant); Gen. Sec. Rev. ENOKA L. ALESANA (Congregational Christian Church in American Samoa).

The Roman Catholic Church

American Samoa comprises the single diocese of Samoa-Pago Pago, suffragan to the archdiocese of Samoa-Apia and Tokelau. At 31 December 2003 there were 12,000 adherents in the islands. The Bishop participates in the Catholic Bishops' Conference of the Pacific, based in Suva, Fiji.
Bishop of Samoa-Pago Pago: Rev. JOHN QUINN WEITZEL, Diocesan Pastoral Center, POB 596, Fatuoaiga, Pago Pago, AS 96799; tel. 699-1402; fax 699-1459; e-mail quinn@samoatelco.com.

The Anglican Communion

American Samoa is within the diocese of Polynesia, part of the Church of the Province of New Zealand. The Bishop of Polynesia is resident in Fiji.

Protestant Churches

Congregational Christian Church in American Samoa (CCCAS): POB 1537, Pago Pago, AS 96799; tel. 699-9810; fax 699-1898; e-mail cccasgensec@samoatelco.com; internet www.cwmission.org.uk/about/view_church.cfm?ChurchID=6; Gen. Sec. Rev SAMUEL TIALAVEA; 40,000 mems (incl. congregations in New Zealand, Australia and USA) in 2004.

Other active Protestant groups include the Baptist Church, the Christian Church of Jesus Christ, the Methodist Church, Assemblies of God, Church of the Nazarene and Seventh-day Adventists. The Church of Jesus Christ of Latter-day Saints (Mormons) is also represented.

The Press

News Bulletin: Office of Public Information, American Samoa Government, Utulei; tel. 633-5490; daily (Mon.–Fri.); English; non-commercial; Editor PHILIP SWETT; circ. 1,800.

Samoa Journal and Advertiser: POB 3986, Pago Pago, AS 96799; tel. 633-2399; weekly; English and Samoan; Editor MICHAEL STARK; circ. 3,000.

Samoa News: POB 909, Pago Pago, AS 96799; tel. 633-5599; fax 633-4864; e-mail administration@samoanews.com; internet www.samoanews.com; 6 a week; English and Samoan; Publr VERA M. ANNESLEY; circ. 4,500.

Broadcasting and Communications

TELECOMMUNICATIONS

American Samoa Telecommunications Authority: Box M, Pago Pago, AS 96799; tel. 633-1211; e-mail info@samoatelco.com; internet www.samoatelco.com.

Blue Sky Communications: Tafuna Industrial Pk, POB 478, Pago Pago, AS 96799; tel. 699-2759; e-mail sales@bluesky.as; internet www.bluesky.as; mobile-telecommunications provider.

BROADCASTING

Radio

KSBS-FM: POB 793, Pago Pago, AS 96799; tel. 633-7000; fax 622-7839; e-mail helpdesk@ksbsfm.com; internet www.ksbsfm.com; commercial; Gen. Man. ESTHER PRESCOTT.

WVUV: POB 4894, Pago Pago, AS 96799; tel. 688-7397; fax 688-1545; fmr govt-administered station leased to Radio Samoa Ltd in 1975; commercial; English and Samoan; 24 hours a day; Man. VINCENT IULI.

UNITED STATES EXTERNAL TERRITORIES

Television

KVZK-TV: Office of Public Information, POB 3511, Pago Pago, AS 96799; tel. 633-4191; fax 633-1044; f. 1964; govt-owned; non-commercial; English and Samoan; broadcasts 18 hours daily on two channels; Gen. Man. Pablo Sivia Sivia; Technical Dir Jeffrey Alwin.

Finance

(cap. = capital; dep. = deposits; m. = million; amounts in US dollars)

BANKING

Commercial Banks

ANZ Amerika Samoa Bank: POB 3790, Pago Pago, AS 96799; tel. 633-5053; fax 633-5057; e-mail decourtb@samoatelco.com; internet www.anz.com.au/americansamoa; f. 1979; fmrly Amerika Samoa Bank; joined ANZ group in April 2001; Pres. Gary Ayre; 4 brs.

Bank of Hawaii (USA): POB 69, Pago Pago, AS 96799; tel. 633-4226; fax 633-2918; f. 1897; Man. Brent A. Schwenke; 3 brs.

Development Bank

Development Bank of American Samoa: POB 9, Pago Pago, AS 96799; tel. 633-4031; fax 633-1163; f. 1969; govt-owned and non-profit-making; cap. 6.4m. (1989); Chair. Eugene G. C. H. Reid; Pres. Manutafea E. Meredith.

INSURANCE

American International Underwriters (South Pacific) Ltd: Pago Pago, AS 96799; tel. 633-4845.

Mark Solofa, Inc: POB 3149, Pago Pago, AS 96799; tel. 699-5902; fax 699-5904; e-mail marksalofainc@yahoo.com.

National Pacific Insurance Ltd: Centennial Bldg, POB 1386, Pago Pago, AS 96799; tel. 633-4266; fax 633-2964; e-mail npi@samoatelco.com; f. 1977; Man. Peter Miller.

Oxford Pacific Insurance Management: POB 1420, Pago Pago, AS 96799; tel. 633-4990; fax 633-2721; e-mail progressive_oxford@yahoo.com; f. 1977; represents major international property and life insurance cos; Pres. Gregg F. Duffy.

South Seas Financial Services Corporation: POB 1448, Pago Pago, AS 96799; tel. 633-7896; fax 633-7895; e-mail ssfs@samoatelco.com.

Trade and Industry

DEVELOPMENT ORGANIZATIONS

American Samoa Development Corporation: Pago Pago, AS 96799; tel. 633-4241; f. 1962; financed by private Samoan interests.

American Samoa Economic Advisory Commission: Pago Pago; Chair. John Waihee.

Department of Commerce: see Government Offices; Dir Aliimau H. Scanlan, Jr.

CHAMBER OF COMMERCE

Chamber of Commerce of American Samoa: POB 2446, Pago Pago, AS 96799; tel. 699-9377; fax 699-2206; Man. Salaia L. Gabbard.

Utilities

American Samoa Power Authority: Pago Pago, AS 96799; tel. 644-2772; fax 644-5005; e-mail abe@aspower.com; internet www.aspower.com; supplies water and electricity throughout the islands; also manages sewer and solid waste collection; Chair. Toetagata Albert Mailo; CEO Marc S. Roy.

Transport

ROADS

There are about 150 km (93 miles) of paved and 200 km (124 miles) of secondary roads. Non-scheduled commercial buses operate a service over 350 km (217 miles) of main and secondary roads. There were an estimated 5,900 registered motor vehicles in the islands in 1996.

SHIPPING

There are various passenger and cargo services from the US Pacific coast, Japan, Australia (mainly Sydney) and New Zealand, that call at Pago Pago, which is one of the deepest and most sheltered harbours in the Pacific. Inter-island boats provide frequent services between Samoa and American Samoa.

Hamburg Süd: Samoan Sports Building, No. 1 Main St, Fagatogo, POB 1417, Pago Pago, AS 96799; tel. 633-4665; fax 699-8110; e-mail spsi@samoatelco.com; internet www.hamburgsud.com.

PM&O Line: Suite 202, Fagatogo Sq., POB 5023, Pago Pago, AS 96799; tel. 633-4527; fax 633-4530; e-mail paige@blueskynet.as; internet www.pmoline.com; f. 1978.

Polynesia Shipping: POB 1478, Pago Pago AS 96799; tel. 633-1211; fax 633-1265; e-mail polyship@samoatelco.com.

CIVIL AVIATION

There is an international airport at Tafuna, 11 km (7 miles) from Pago Pago, and smaller airstrips on the islands of Ta'u and Ofu. International services are operated by Hawaiian Airlines and Polynesian Blue (formerly Polynesian Airlines).

Samoa Aviation: POB 280, Pago Pago Int. Airport, Pago Pago, AS 96799; tel. 699-9106; fax 699-9751; e-mail sales@samoair.com; internet www.samoaair.com; f. 1986; operates service between Pago Pago and Samoa, Tonga and Niue; Pres. Andre Lavigne.

Tourism

The tourist industry is encouraged by the Government, but suffers from the cost and paucity of air services linking American Samoa with its main sources of custom, particularly the USA. Pago Pago is an important mid-Pacific stop-over for large passenger aircraft. A total of 36,009 tourists visited the islands in 2001. In that year 19.9% of tourists came from the USA and 10.8% from New Zealand. In 1992 there were some 542 hotel beds available in the islands. The industry earned an estimated US $10m. in 1998.

Office of Tourism: Convention Center, POB 1147, Tafuna, Pago Pago, AS 96799; tel. 699-9411; fax 699-9414; e-mail asgtourism@samoatelco.com; e-mail amsamoa@amerikasamoa.info; internet www.amerikasamoa.info; Deputy Dir Virginia Samuelu.

Pago Pago Visitors Association (PPVA): f. 2004; Pres. Tom Drabble.

GUAM

Introductory Survey

Location, Climate, Language, Religion, Flag, Capital

Guam is the southernmost and largest of the Mariana Islands, situated about 2,170 km (1,350 miles) south of Tokyo (Japan) and 5,300 km (3,300 miles) west of Honolulu (Hawaii). The temperature normally ranges between 24°C (75°F) and 30°C (86°F) in June–November, but is generally cooler and drier from December to May. The average annual rainfall is about 2,000 mm (79 ins). English is the official language, but Japanese and Chamorro, the local language, are also spoken. The principal religion is Christianity, about 90% of the population being Roman Catholics. The national flag of the United States of America (q.v.) is used by Guam. The capital is Hagåtña (formerly Agaña).

Recent History

Members of a Spanish expedition, under the Portuguese navigator, Fernão Magalhães (Ferdinand Magellan), were the first Europeans to discover Guam, visiting the island in 1521, during a voyage that accomplished the first circumnavigation of the globe. The island was claimed by Spain in 1565, and the first Jesuit missionaries arrived three years later. The native Micronesian population is estimated to have fallen from 100,000 in 1521 to fewer than 5,000 in 1741, owing largely to a combination of aggression by the Spaniards and exposure to imported diseases. The intermarrying of Micronesians, Spaniards and Filipinos resulted in the people now called Chamorros. Guam was ceded to the USA after the Spanish–American War of 1898, but was invaded by Japan in 1941. Fierce fighting took place before the island was recaptured by US forces in 1944.

Guam became an Unincorporated Territory of the USA, under the jurisdiction of the US Department of the Interior, in 1950. In 1970 the island elected its first Governor, and in 1972 a new law gave Guam one Delegate to the US House of Representatives. The Delegate may vote in committee but not on the floor of the House. In 1976 an island-wide referendum decided that Guam should maintain close ties with the USA, but that negotiations should be held to improve the island's status. In a further referendum, in 1982, in which only 38% of eligible voters participated, the status of a Commonwealth, in association with the USA, was the most favoured of six options, supported by 48%

of the votes cast. In 1987, in a referendum on the provisions of a draft law aimed at conferring the status of Commonwealth on the Territory, voters approved the central proposal, while rejecting articles empowering the Guam Government to restrict immigration and granting the indigenous Chamorro people the right to determine the island's future political status. In a further referendum in late 1987 both outstanding provisions were approved. Negotiations between the Guam Commission for Self Determination and the USA continued throughout the late 1980s and early 1990s.

In February 1987 the former Governor of Guam, Ricardo Bordallo, was found guilty of charges of bribery, extortion and conspiracy to obstruct justice, and was sentenced to 30 years' imprisonment (later reduced to nine years) in April. In November Bordallo's wife, Madeleine, was elected to replace him in the Guam Legislature, and in October 1988 Bordallo won an appeal and his sentence was cancelled. Bordallo was liable for imprisonment in the USA on charges of obstruction and attempting to influence witnesses, but he committed suicide at the end of January 1990. Madeleine Bordallo was the Democratic candidate at gubernatorial elections in November 1990, when Ada was re-elected. Concurrent elections to the Guam Legislature resulted in a Democratic majority of one seat.

At legislative elections in November 1992 the Democrats increased their representation to 14 seats, while the Republicans secured only seven. Robert Underwood was elected as the new Democratic Delegate to the US House of Representatives, replacing the Republican, Ben Blaz.

In January 1994 the US Congress approved legislation providing for the transfer of 3,200 acres of land on Guam from federal to local control. This was a significant achievement for the Government of Guam, which had campaigned consistently for the return of 27,000 acres (some 20% of Guam's total area), appropriated by US military forces after the Second World War. Chamorro rights activists, however, opposed the move, claiming that land should not be transferred to the Government of Guam, but rather to the original landowners.

At gubernatorial elections in November 1994 the Democrat Carl Gutierrez, defeated his Republican opponent, Tommy Tanaka, winning 54.6% of total votes cast, while Madeleine Bordallo was elected to the position of Lieutenant-Governor. Legislative elections held concurrently also resulted in a Democratic majority, with candidates of the party securing 13 seats, while the Republicans won eight. Robert Underwood was re-elected unopposed as Delegate to the US House of Representatives.

Reports that Chamorro rights activists had initiated a campaign for independence from the USA were denied by the Governor in July 1995. In September, however, at the Fourth World Conference on Women in Beijing, People's Republic of China, the Lieutenant-Governor, Madeleine Bordallo, expressed her support for the achievement of full autonomy for Guam and for the Chamorro people's desire for decolonization.

It was reported in 1995 that the US President, Bill Clinton, had appointed a team of Commonwealth negotiators to review the draft Guam Commonwealth Act. Guam's self-styled Commission on Decolonization was established in 1997, headed by the Governor. A plebiscite on the political status of Guam was originally scheduled for November 2000 but was deferred to coincide with legislative and presidential elections scheduled for November 2004. However, in May 2004 legislation was drafted that would postpone the referendum until the number of Chamorro voters registered by the Guam Elections Committee had reached the requisite 50%.

At elections in November 1996 Republican members regained a majority in the Legislature, winning 11 seats, while Democratic candidates secured 10 seats. In a referendum held concurrently voters approved a proposed reduction in the number of Senators from 21 to 15 (effective from November 1998), and plans to impose an upper limit (2.5% of total budgetary expenditure) on legislative expenses. However, a proposal to restrict the number of terms that Senators can seek to serve in the Legislature was rejected by voters. Guam's Delegate to the US House of Representatives, Robert Underwood, was re-elected unopposed.

In June 1998 Underwood secured approval from the US authorities to change the spelling of Guam's capital from Agaña to Hagåtña. The change was effected in order to reflect more accurately the original Chamorro language name for the town.

Robert Underwood was re-elected, with 70.2% of the total votes cast, as Guam's Delegate to the US House of Representatives on 4 November 1998, defeating Manuel Cruz, who secured 20.1% of the votes. Concurrent gubernatorial and legislative elections resulted in the return to office, as Governor, of Carl Gutierrez and, as Lieutenant-Governor, of Madeleine Bordallo. (In December former Governor Joseph Ada alleged that Gutierrez's victory had been achieved by fraudulent means, and later in the month a Guam court invalidated the election result and ordered a new poll to be held. In February 1999, however, the Superior Court of Guam found that there had been no electoral malpractice and confirmed the appointments of Gutierrez and Bordallo.) In elections to the legislature, where the number of seats had been reduced from 21 to 15, 12 candidates of the Republican Party and three candidates of the Democratic Party were returned as Senators.

US President Clinton visited Guam in November 1998. During his visit President Clinton approved the transfer of some 1,300 ha of federal land to the local administration and undertook to hasten the transfer of a further 2,020 ha of former US air force and navy land. In August 2001 the US Army announced plans to move some combat weaponry and equipment from Europe to storage bases in Guam, as well as in Taiwan and Hawaii. Throughout late 2004 and early 2005 the US Air Force stationed several of its B-52 and B-2 bombers on Guam, following the construction of a new hangar on the island. In May 2005 the US Government announced plans substantially to increase military spending in 2005/06 in Guam, with some US $162m. allocated for new construction projects. Notwithstanding the concerns of some anti-war and Chamorro rights activists, the increased military presence on Guam was widely welcomed as a source of new investment and employment.

In mid-1999 it was announced that Guam was no longer able to support the growing numbers of illegal immigrants from the People's Republic of China, some 500 having arrived between April and June alone, seeking refugee status. The immigrants were to be diverted to and detained in the nearby Northern Mariana Islands, the immigration laws of which differ from those of Guam.

At elections held on 7 November 2000, Underwood was re-elected as Guam's delegate to the US House of Representatives, winning 78.1% of votes cast. At legislative elections, held concurrently, eight candidates of the Republican Party and seven candidates of the Democratic Party were returned as senators.

Robert Underwood secured the Democratic nomination for the gubernatorial elections of 5 November 2002, but was defeated by the Republican candidate, Felix Camacho, who received 55.4% of the votes cast. (Madeleine Bordallo was designated Guam's Delegate to the US Congress.) In the Legislature, nine Democratic candidates were elected as senators, while the Republican party's representation decreased to six seats. Governor Camacho pledged to halt the widely perceived rise in corruption and misallocation of public funds on Guam, and to improve public finances (see Economic Affairs).

Also in November 2002, the US Congress approved the Guam War Claims Review Commission Act, which provided for the creation of a body to investigate events on the island following its occupation by the Japanese during the Second World War. Furthermore, the Commission would determine whether the USA had offered the Islanders sufficient compensation for their mistreatment prior to Guam's liberation in 1944. The War Claims Review Commission, appointed in September 2003, acknowledged the hardship and suffering of the people of Guam, their 'courageous loyalty to the USA' and the inequality in compensation payments as regards similar claims. In May 2004 the US State Department's Radiation Exposure Compensation Program declared Guam eligible for compensation for the effects of nuclear tests carried out in the Pacific region during the long period of mutual hostility between the USA and the Soviet Union known as the 'Cold War'. In April 2005 the US Congressional Committee to Assess the Scientific Information for the Radiation Exposure Screening and Education Program published a report recommending, in accordance with the wishes of the Guam delegation, that scientific criteria (including radiation measurements and analyses of public health data) be used for assessing eligibility for compensation, rather than geographical proximity to nuclear testing, which had determined eligibility hitherto. The report concluded that, although Guam had been exposed to radiation through wind-borne particles, this exposure had not significantly increased the incidence of cancers and other radiation-related illnesses. Consequently, future claims for compensation were thought unlikely to succeed.

At legislative elections held on 2 November 2004 the Republican party secured a majority in the legislature, winning nine of the 15 seats; five Democrat incumbents were deposed. At a concurrently held plebiscite, a proposal to legalize casinos on the island was rejected by a margin of some 7,800 votes. Later in the month a group of campaigners for the proposal filed an appeal in the Superior Court against the result of the election, alleging electoral malpractice.

Numerous investigations into alleged official corruption were conducted in the early and mid-2000s. In April 2003 a former Republican Senator and gubernatorial candidate, Tommy Tanaka, pleaded guilty to charges of misprision of felony, which related to his alleged involvement in a fraudulent government contract. In the same month Joseph Mafnas, a former chief of the Guam police department, was indicted on forgery charges. The case against him collapsed in September 2004, however, because the key witness for the prosecution was absent from the island. In March 2004 former Governor Carl Gutierrez was tried for his involvement in a private property development scheme, which allegedly involved the misappropriation of public funds. All but two minor charges against him were dismissed by a Superior Court judge in late April. However, in late August charges ranging from theft by deception to official misconduct were filed against the former Governor; the charges were dismissed in early September. Gutierrez stood trial in June

2005 for alleged improper dealings relating to the island's retirement fund; he was acquitted of all charges in the following month and in August announced his intention to contest the next gubernatorial election, scheduled for November 2006. However, in December 2005 new corruption charges relating to the retirement fund were brought against Gutierrez and others responsible for its operation. In January 2006 further charges were brought against the former Governor relating to his administration of the Guam Memorial Hospital. Meanwhile, in October 2005 Gutierrez's former Chief of Staff, Gil Shinohara, was convicted of conspiracy to commit fraud.

In March 1998, meanwhile, delegates from several Pacific island nations and territories met in Hawaii to discuss possible methods of controlling the increasing population of brown tree snakes in Guam. The venomous reptile, which was accidentally introduced to the island from New Guinea after the Second World War, has been responsible for frequent power cuts, as a result of climbing electricity poles and short-circuiting the lines, as well as for major environmental problems (including the decimation of native bird, rodent and reptile populations). The US Geological Survey has estimated the density of tree snakes on Guam to be roughly 13,000 per sq mile (33,670 per sq km) of forested land. By 2004 a team of 25 full-time snake-trappers and nine dog-handlers were capturing an estimated 6,000 tree snakes annually at Guam's five main ports (air and sea), but in September of that year plans were announced to reduce funding to this programme by nearly one-half. In late September the US House of Representatives approved a bill allocating US $104m. of federal funds towards the eradication of Guam's tree snake population. In October, furthermore, the US Senate authorized expenditure of $77m., to be divided among Guam, Hawaii and other islands for the purposes of snake-eradication programmes.

The island remained vulnerable to the impact of extreme weather formations. President George W. Bush declared the island a federal disaster area on two occasions, following Typhoon Chata'an in July 2002 and Supertyphoon Pongsona in December 2002. Although no loss of life was reported as a direct consequence of the severe storms, some 35,000 islanders were homeless in early 2003 and the cost of the damage was estimated at US $226m. The US Government granted some $10m. towards the recovery effort. In July, in response to the high costs incurred by the recovery effort, the island's Delegate to the US Congress, Madeleine Bordallo, introduced a bill to amend the Organic Act of Guam. The legislation attempted to empower the US Secretary of the Interior to waive Guam's outstanding federal debt, in order to offset social costs caused by migration to Guam from Compact of Free Association countries. The measure was defeated, although the amended Compact of Free Association signed in December approved some $14m. to offset Guam's migration costs, and erased $157m. of debt owed to the US Federal Government. In February 2006 Governor Camacho announced his intention to restart negotiations on some $60.5m. of debt forgiveness for Guam. Also in that month, legislation seeking to amend the Organic Act of Guam, in order to grant the territory greater autonomy from the US federal government, was submitted to the legislature. The financial cost of migration since 1986 from associated countries was estimated to be $269.3m. ($178.3m. for education and $91.0m. for health, safety, welfare and labour) in a report submitted by Governor Camacho to the US Department of the Interior in April 2004.

Government

Guam is governed under the Organic Act of Guam of 1950, which gave the island statutory local power of self-government and made its inhabitants citizens of the United States, although they are not permitted to vote in national elections. Guam's non-voting Delegate to the US House of Representatives is elected every two years. Executive power is vested in the civilian Governor, who is elected by popular vote every four years. The Government has 48 executive departments, whose heads are appointed by the Governor with the consent of the Guam Legislature. The Legislature consists of 21 members elected by popular vote every two years. It is empowered to enact legislation on local matters, including taxation and fiscal appropriations.

Defence

Guam is an important strategic military base for the USA, with 2,100 members of the Air Force and 2,300 naval personnel stationed there in August 2005.

Economic Affairs

In 2000, according to estimates by the Bank of Hawaii (BOH), Guam's gross national income (GNI), at current prices, was US $2,772.8m., equivalent to $16,575 per head. Between 1988 and 1993, it was estimated, GNI increased, in real terms, at an average rate of some 10% per year, and by 3.9% in 1994. In 1990–2002, according to World Bank figures, the population increased at an average annual rate of 1.5%.

Agriculture (including forestry, fishing and mining) engaged only an estimated 0.5% of the employed labour force in 2002. The principal crops cultivated on the island include watermelons, coconuts, cucumbers, bananas, runner beans, aubergines, squash, tomatoes and papaya. Livestock reared includes pigs, cattle, goats and poultry. The fishing catch totalled an estimated 162 metric tons in 2003.

The industrial sector accounted for some 15% of gross domestic product (GDP) in 1993. Construction and manufacturing engaged an estimated 8.9% of the employed labour force in 2002. Construction is the dominant industrial activity and is closely related to the tourist industry, which declined significantly in the early 21st century. Construction engaged 6.1% of the employed labour force in 2002. Manufacturing industries, including textile and garment production and boat-building, engaged an estimated 2.8% of the employed labour force in 2002. Guam is a low-duty port and an important distribution point for goods destined for Micronesia. Re-exports constitute a high proportion of Guam's exports, major commodities being petroleum and petroleum products, iron and steel scrap, and eggs.

Service industries dominate the economy, engaging 90.6% of the employed labour force in 2002. The federal and territorial Governments alone employed 27.9% of workers in that year. Tourism is Guam's most important industry, providing 18% of GDP in 1994. In 2002 some 1,058,700 tourists (of whom 74% were Japanese) visited the island, a decrease of 8.7% compared with the previous year. The number of tourists visiting Guam increased from 857,432 in 2003 to 1,120,676 in 2004. In 1999 tourism earned an estimated US $1,908m.; the sector engaged an estimated 21.4% of the employed labour force in 1994.

The Territory consistently records a visible trade deficit. The cost of imports was US $46.6m. in 2003, while export revenue totalled $43.3m. in that year. Singapore supplied 39.1% of total imports in 2002. Japan purchased 51.3% of the island's exports in 2003.

In the year ending September 2004 total budgetary operational expenditure stood at US $685.3m. and revenue at $658.0m. In May 2005 it was reported that the fiscal deficit accumulated since the beginning of 2004/05 had reached more than $300m. and was likely to exceed $400m. by the end of the financial year. Also in May 2005 the Office of the Public Auditor reported that some $26m. of public money had been lost in 2004 either through fraud or inefficiency. The Government's total debt stood at $326.7m. at the end of the financial year 2003/04. The average annual rate of inflation was 1.3% in 1995–2003. Consumer prices increased by 3.3% in 2003 and by 7.4% in 2004. Guam's unemployment rate stood at 7.7% in 2004, according to the Office of Insular Affairs.

Guam is a member of the Pacific Community (see p. 350) and an associate member of the UN's Economic and Social Commission for Asia and the Pacific (ESCAP, see p. 33). In early 1996 Guam joined representatives of the other countries and territories of Micronesia at a meeting in Hawaii, at which a new regional organization, the Council of Micronesian Government Executives, was established. The body aimed to facilitate discussion of economic developments in the region and to examine possibilities for reducing the considerable cost of shipping essential goods between the islands.

In the 1990s Guam's economy benefited from increased foreign investment, notably from Japan and the Republic of Korea. Much of this investment resulted in the rapid expansion of the tourist industry. The island continues to receive considerable financial support from the USA. In 2002 federal expenditure on the territory totalled US $1,215.8m., comprising military spending of $561.7m., non-defence expenditure of $552.2m. and other federal assistance of $101.9m. Federal contributions totalled $219.0m. in 2003/04. Military spending was expected to rise substantially, following the announcement in May 2005 of several new military construction projects on Guam. Considerable interest in establishing an 'offshore' financial centre on Guam has been expressed; the development of such a centre, however, was dependent upon the achievement of Commonwealth status, which would allow the introduction of new tax laws. In November 2004 the US Congress approved some $90m. in funding for federal programmes, including infrastructure improvement and military construction. Also, in January 2005 the Department of the Interior approved a grant of $14.8m. for health, education and social provision. In the early 2000s a series of natural disasters, notably Typhoon Pongsona in December 2002, severely damaged the island's infrastructure. Moreover, the tourism sector was badly affected by the repercussions of the terrorist attacks on the USA in September 2001, compounded by the continued economic difficulties in Japan (the principal source of the island's visitors). In 2003 the industry continued to stagnate as a result of the conflict in Iraq and the outbreak of Severe Acute Respiratory Syndrome (SARS) in East Asia. However, in 2004 tourist arrivals rose by 31%, to exceed 1.1m.. Meanwhile, the Government faced a growing fiscal shortfall owing to declining private-sector employment and accelerated rates of emigration (GDP was reported to have contracted by some 25% since the late 1990s). Moreover, the island's new Republican administration was unable to reduce its own employment costs, despite a substantial decline in US federal employment on the island. A series of measures intended to stimulate economic activity and improve public finances, including exemptions in business taxes and increased import duties, were reported to have effected only a limited improvement. In April 2003 the Legislature approved the issuance of some $246m. in new debt aimed at refinancing the Government's pensions and public service provision system. The privatization of the Guam Telephone Authority was finalized in December 2004, following its sale to TeleGuam Holdings LLC for some $150m. In February 2005 Governor Camacho announced his intention to privatize the Guam Waterworks Authority. Government spending in 2006/07 was budgeted at $457m., with revenue projected at $435m. In 2006 efforts to diversify the island's economy continued.

Education

School attendance is compulsory from six to 16 years of age. There were 26 public elementary schools, seven junior high and four senior high schools, as well as a number of private schools operating on the island in 2003. Total secondary enrolment in public schools in 2004/05 was 16,046 students. Some 3,034 students were enrolled at the university of Guam in that year. In 2000 the rate of adult illiteracy was estimated at 1.0%. Government expenditure on education was US $2000m. in 2003/04 (equivalent to 29% of total expenditure).

Public Holidays

2006: 2 January (for New Year's Day), 16 January (Martin Luther King Day), 20 February (Presidents' Day), 3 March (Guam Discovery Day), 14 April (Good Friday), 29 May (Memorial Day), 4 July (US Independence Day), 21 July (Liberation Day), 4 September (Labor Day), 9 October (Columbus Day), 2 November (All Souls' Day), 10 November (for Veterans' Day), 23 November (Thanksgiving Day), 8 December (Immaculate Conception), 25 December (Christmas Day).

2007: 1 January (New Year's Day), 15 January (Martin Luther King Day), 19 February (Presidents' Day), 5 March (Guam Discovery Day), 6 April (Good Friday), 28 May (Memorial Day), 4 July (US Independence Day), 21 July (Liberation Day), 3 September (Labor Day), 8 October (Columbus Day), 2 November (All Souls' Day), 12 November (for Veterans' Day), 24 November (Thanksgiving Day), 8 December (Immaculate Conception), 25 December (Christmas Day).

Weights and Measures

With certain exceptions, the imperial system is in force. One US cwt equals 100 lb; one long ton equals 2,240 lb; one short ton equals 2,000 lb. A policy of gradual voluntary conversion to the metric system is being encouraged by the Federal Government.

Statistical Survey

Sources (unless otherwise stated): Department of Commerce, Government of Guam, 102 M St, Tiyan, GU 96913; tel. 475-0321; fax 477-9031; e-mail commerce@ns.gov.gu; internet www.admin.gov.gu/commerce/economy; Office of the Public Auditor, Pacific News Building, Suite 401, 238 Archbishop Flores St, Hagåtña, Guam 96910; tel. 475-0390; fax 472-7951; internet www.guamopa.com.

AREA AND POPULATION

Area: 549 sq km (212 sq miles).

Population: 133,152 at census of 1 April 1990; 154,805 (males 79,181, females 75,624) at census of 1 April 2000. *Mid-2004* (official estimate): 166,090.

Density (mid-2004): 302.5 per sq km.

Ethnic Groups (2000 census): Chamorro 57,297; Filipino 40,729; White 10,509; Other Asian 9,600; part-Chamorro 7,946; Chuukese 6,229; Total (incl. others) 154,805.

Principal Towns (population at 2000 census): Tamuning 10,833; Mangilao 7,794; Yigo 6,391; Astumbo 5,207; Barrigada 4,417; Hagåtña (capital) 1,122.

Births, Marriages and Deaths (2004, unless otherwise indicated): Registered live births 3,427 (birth rate 20.6 per 1,000); Registered marriages (2000) 1,499; Registered deaths 691 (death rate 4.2 per 1,000). Sources: mostly UN, *Population and Vital Statistics Report* and Office of Insular Affairs, *2004 Guam Statistical Yearbook*.

Expectation of Life (UN estimates, years at birth): 78 in 2004. (males 76; females 81). Source: Office of Insular Affairs, *2004 Guam Statistical Yearbook*.

Economically Active Population (persons aged 16 years and over, excl. armed forces, 2002 estimates): Agriculture, forestry, fishing and mining 290; Manufacturing 1,570; Construction 3,420; Transport, storage and utilities 4,590; Wholesale and retail trade 12,690; Finance, insurance and real estate 2,450; Public administration 16,500; Education, health and social services 14,510; Total *employed* 56,020; Unemployed 7,070; *Total labour force* 63,090. Source: Guam Department of Labor.

AGRICULTURE, ETC.

Principal Crops (estimates, metric tons, 2004): Coconuts 53,000; Cucumbers and gherkins 390; Roots and tubers 2,350; Watermelons 2,400; Bananas 345.

Livestock (estimates, head, 2004): Chickens 200,000; Pigs 5,100; Cattle 130; Goats 680; Horses 20; Buffaloes 65.

Livestock Products (metric tons, 2004): Poultry meat 43; Hen eggs 700; Pig meat 140.

Fishing (metric tons, live weight, 2003): Common dolphinfish 25; Wahoo 17; Skipjack tuna 38; Total capture (incl. others) 162.

Source: FAO.

INDUSTRY

Electric Energy (million kWh): 830 in 1999 (estimate); 830 in 2000 (estimate); 1,745 in 2001. Source: UN, *Industrial Commodity Statistics Yearbook*.

FINANCE

Currency and Exchange Rates: US currency is used. For details, see section on the Northern Mariana Islands.

Budget (US $ million, year ending September 2004): *Revenue*: Taxes 383.7, Licenses, fees and permits 34.5, Use of money and property 1.9, Federal contributions 219.0, Other 18.9, Total 658.0. *Expenditure*: General government 53.7, Public order 79.8, Public health 56.4, Community services 47.9, Recreation 4.0, Individual and collective rights 52.9, Transportation 7.4, Public education 200.0, Environmental protection 4.7, Economic development 9.7, Transfer to persons 1.0, Retirement fund 11.8, Payments to public agencies and authorities 79.0, Capital projects 19.6, Debt service 57.7, Total 685.3.

Cost of Living (Consumer Price Index; base: July–September 1996 = 100): All items 104.2 in 2002; 107.6 in 2003; 115.6 in 2004. Source: Office of Insular Affairs, *2004 Guam Statistical Yearbook*.

Gross Domestic Product (US $ million at current prices, estimates): 2,772.8 in 2000; 2,772.8 in 2001; 2,069.0 in 2002. Source: Office of Insular Affairs, US Department of the Interior.

EXTERNAL TRADE

Principal Commodities: *Imports* (US $ '000, 2004): Travel goods, handbags, etc. 2,641; Clothing 3,956; Water, containing sugar 1,390; Beer 1,580; Vehicles and transport equipment 5,264; Construction materials 2,603; Meat and edible offals 1,560; Total (incl. others) 37,738. *Exports* (US $ '000, 2001): Fish (chilled, fresh, frozen, dried and salted) 31,253; Tobacco, cigars, etc. 3,535; Petroleum oils and gases 3,759; Perfumes and toilet waters 3,667; Total (incl. others) 60,819. Note: Figures for imports do not include petroleum and petroleum products (totalling US $163,685,000 in 1994). Total Exports (US $ million): 49.4 in 2002; 43.3 in 2003 (Source: Office of Insular Affairs, *2004 Guam Statistical Yearbook*).

Principal Trading Partners (US $ '000, 2002): *Imports*: Hong Kong 36,240; Japan 96,450; Korea, Republic 9,688; Philippines 1,437; Singapore 180,076; Australia 9,770; New Zealand 5,520; Total (incl. others) 527,000. *Exports*: Philippines 1,440; Singapore 500; Korea, Republic 2,280; Japan 30,780; Total (incl. others) 49,380. Source: UN, *Statistical Yearbook for Asia and the Pacific*.

TRANSPORT

Road Traffic (registered motor vehicles, 1999): Private cars 65,887; Taxis 537; Buses 627; Goods vehicles 26,220; Motorcycles 633; Total (incl. others) 99,618. Source: Department of Revenue and Taxation, Government of Guam.

International Sea-borne Shipping (estimated freight traffic, '000 metric tons, 1991): Goods loaded 195.1; Goods unloaded 1,524.1; Goods transhipped 314.7. *Merchant Fleet* (total displacement, '000 grt at 31 December 1992): 1 (Source: Lloyd's Register-Fairplay, *World Fleet Statistics*).

Air Cargo ('000 lb): 36,691 in 1998.

TOURISM

Foreign Tourist Arrivals: 1,013,161 in 2002; 857,432 in 2003; 1,120,676 in 2004 (Source: Office of Insular Affairs, *2004 Guam Statistical Yearbook*).

Tourist Arrivals by Country of Residence ('000, 2004): Japan 906.1; Korea, Republic 89.9; Philippines 7.0; Taiwan 24.2; USA 46.2; Total (incl. others) 1,120.7 (Source: Office of Insular Affairs, *2004 Guam Statistical Yearbook*).

Tourism Receipts (US $ million): 2,361 in 1998; 1,908 in 1999.

Source: mostly World Tourism Organization.

COMMUNICATIONS MEDIA

Radio Receivers (1997): 221,000 in use.

Television Receivers (1999): 110,000 in use.

Telephones (2001): 80,000 main lines in use†.

Mobile Cellular Telephones (2001): 32,600 subscribers†.

Internet Users (estimate, 2001): 48,000†.

Daily Newspapers (1997): 1 (circulation 24,457).

Non-daily Newspapers (1988): 4 (estimated circulation 26,000).

† Sources: International Telecommunication Union and UN, *Statistical Yearbook for Asia and the Pacific*.

EDUCATION

Institutions (public schools only, 2003): Elementary 26; Middle school 7; Senior high 4; Business colleges (private) 1; Guam Community College; University of Guam.

Teachers (public schools only, 2000/01): Elementary 953; Secondary 927.

Enrolment (public schools only, 2004/05 unless otherwise indicated): Elementary 14,687; Middle school 6,932; Senior high 9,114; Guam Community College (2002/03) 3,656; University of Guam (2005/06) 3,034.

Sources: Department of Education, Guam Community College, Office of Insular Affairs, *2004 Guam Statistical Yearbook* and University of Guam.

Directory

The Constitution

Guam is governed under the Organic Act of Guam of 1950, which gave the island statutory local power of self-government and made its inhabitants citizens of the United States, although they cannot vote in presidential elections. Their Delegate to the US House of Representatives is elected every two years. Executive power is vested in the civilian Governor and the Lieutenant-Governor, first elected, by popular vote, in 1970. Elections for the governorship occur every four years. The Government has 48 executive departments, whose heads are appointed by the Governor with the consent of the Guam Legislature. The Legislature consists of 15 members elected by popular vote every two years (members are known as Senators). It is empowered to pass laws on local matters, including taxation and fiscal appropriations.

The Government

(April 2006)

Governor: Felix Camacho (Republican—took office January 2003).

Lieutenant-Governor: Kaleo S. Moylan.

GOVERNMENT OFFICES

Government offices are located throughout the island.

Office of the Governor: POB 2950, Hagåtña, GU 96932; tel. 472-8931; fax 477-4826; e-mail governor@mail.gov.gu; internet ns.gov.gu.

Department of the Interior, Office of Insular Affairs (OIA): Hagåtña, GU 96910; tel. 472-7279; fax 472-7309; Field Representative Keith A. Parsky.

Department of Administration: POB 884, Hagåtña, GU 96932; tel. 475-1110; fax 475-6788; e-mail doadir@mail.gov.gu.

Department of Agriculture: 192 Dairy Rd, Mangilao, GU 96913; tel. 734-3942; fax 734-6569; e-mail guamagriculture@yahoo.com.

Department of Commerce: 102 M St, Tiyan, GU 96913; tel. 475-0321; fax 477-9031; e-mail commerce@mail.gov.gu.

Department of Corrections: POB 3236, Hagåtña, GU 96932; tel. 734-4668; fax 734-4990.

Customs and Quarantine Agency: 13–16A Mariner Ave, Tiyan, Barrigada, GU 96913; tel. 475-6202; fax 475-6207; internet www.guamjustice.net/custom.

Department of Education: POB DE, Hagåtña, GU 96932; tel. 475-0457; fax 472-5003; e-mail juanpflores@doe.edu.gu; internet www.doe.edu.gu.

Environmental Protection Agency: 17-3304 Mariner Ave, Tiyan, GU 96913; tel. 475-1658; fax 477-9402; e-mail margaret.aguilar@guamepa.net; internet www.guamepa.govguam.net.

Housing and Urban Renewal Authority: 117 Bien Venida Ave, Sinajana, GU 96910; tel. 477-9851; fax 472-7565; e-mail rdeguzman@netpci.com; internet www.ghura.org.

Department of Labor: POB 9970, Tamuning, GU 96931; tel. 475-0101; fax 477-2988; e-mail labor@ns.gov.gu; internet www.labor.gov.gu.

Department of Land Management: POB 2950, Hagåtña, GU 96932; tel. 475-5252; fax 477-0883; e-mail dlm@mail.gov.gu; internet www.admin.gov.gu/dlm.

Department of Law: Suite 2-200E, Judicial Ctr. building, 120 West O'Brien Drive, Hagåtña, GU 96910; tel. 475-3324; fax 475-2493; e-mail law@ns.gov.gu; internet www.justice.gov.gu/dol.

Department of Parks and Recreation: POB 2950, 13-8 Seagull Ave, Tiyan, Hagåtña, GU 96932; tel. 475-6296; fax 472-9626; e-mail parks@ns.gov.gu; internet ns.gov.gu/dpr/.

Department of Public Health and Social Services: POB 2816, Hagåtña, GU 96932; tel. 735-7102; fax 734-5910; e-mail director@dphss.govguam.net; internet www.dphss.govguam.net.

Department of Public Works: 542 North Marine Drive, Tamuning, GU 96911; tel. 646-4388; fax 649-6178; e-mail dpwdir@ns.gov.gu.

Department of Revenue and Taxation: Bldg 13-1 Mariner Ave, Tiyan Barrigada, GU 96913; tel. 475-5000; fax 472-2643; e-mail revtax@ns.gov.gu; internet ns.gov.gu/revtax.

Department of the Treasury: PDN Bldg, Suite 404, 238 Archbishop Flores St, Hagåtña, GU 96910.

Department of Youth Affairs: POB 23672, Guam Main Facility, GU 96921; tel. 734-2597; fax 734-7536; e-mail ddell@ns.gov.gu.

Office of Civil Defense (Guam Homeland Security): 221-B Chalan Palasyo, Agana Heights, GU 96910; tel. 475-9600; fax 477-3727; internet www.guamhs.org; f. 1999; Administrator Charles H. Ada, II (acting).

Legislature

GUAM LEGISLATURE

The Guam Legislature has 15 members, directly elected by popular vote for a two-year term. Elections took place on 2 November 2004, when the Republican Party won nine of the 15 seats and the Democratic Party won six seats.

Speaker: Mark Forbes.

CONGRESS

Guam elects a non-voting Delegate to the US House of Representatives. An election was held on 2 November 2004, when the Democratic candidate, Madeleine Z. Bordallo, was re-elected unopposed as Delegate.

Delegate of Guam: Madeleine Z. Bordallo, Cannon House Office Bldg, 427, Washington, DC 20515–5301, USA; tel. (202) 225-1188; fax (202) 226-0341; e-mail madeleine.bordallo@mail.house.gov; internet www.house.gov/bordallo.

Election Commission

Guam Election Commission: Guam Capital Investment Corpn bldg, 414 W Soledad Ave, Suite 200, Hagåtña 96910; tel. 477-9791; fax 477-1895; e-mail gec@kuentos.guam.net; internet www.guamelection.org; Chair. Frederick J. Horecky; Exec. Dir Gerald A. Taitano.

Judicial System

Attorney-General: Douglas B. Moylan.

US Attorney: Leonardo M. Rapadas.

Supreme Court of Guam: Suite 300, Guam Judicial Center, 120 West O'Brien Drive, Hagåtña, GU 96910; tel. 475-3162; fax 475-3140; e-mail justice@guamsupremecourt.com; internet www.guamsupremecourt.com; Chief Justice F. Philip Cabullido.

District Court of Guam

4th floor, US Courthouse, 520 West Soledad Ave, Hagåtña, GU 96910; tel. 473-9180; fax 473-9118; e-mail judith_hattori@gud.uscourts.gov; internet www.gud.uscourts.gov.

Judge appointed by the President of the USA. The court has the jurisdiction of a Federal district court and of a bankruptcy court of the United States in all cases arising under the laws of the United States. Appeals may be made to the Court of Appeals for the Ninth Circuit and to the Supreme Court of the United States.

UNITED STATES EXTERNAL TERRITORIES

Magistrate Judge: JOAQUIN V. E. MANIBUSAN, Jr.

Superior Court of Guam
120 West O'Brien Drive, Hagåtña, GU 96910; tel. 475-3250; internet www.justice.gov.gu/SuperiorCourt.

Judges are appointed by the Governor of Guam for an initial eight-year term and are thereafter retained by popular vote. The Superior Court has jurisdiction over cases arising in Guam other than those heard in the District Court.

Presiding Judge: ALBERTO C. LAMORENA, III.

There are also Probate, Traffic, Domestic, Juvenile and Small Claims Courts.

Religion

About 81% of the population are Roman Catholic, but there are also members of the Episcopal (Anglican) Church, the Baptist churches and the Seventh-day Adventist Church. There are small communities of Muslims, Buddhists and Jews.

CHRISTIANITY

The Roman Catholic Church

Guam comprises the single archdiocese of Agaña. The Archbishop participates in the Catholic Bishops' Conference of the Pacific, based in Suva, Fiji, and the Federation of Catholic Bishops' Conferences of Oceania, based in Wellington, New Zealand.

At 31 December 2003 there were 131,584 adherents in Guam.

Archbishop of Agaña: Most Rev. ANTHONY SABLAN APURON, Chancery Office, Cuesta San Ramón 96910B, Hagåtña, GU 96910; tel. 472-6116; fax 477-3519; e-mail archbishop@mail.archdioceseofguam.com; internet www.archdioceseofagana.com.

BAHÁ'Í FAITH

National Spiritual Assembly: POB Box BA, Hagåtña, GU 96931; tel. 472-9100; fax 472-9101; e-mail nsamar@ite.net; mems resident in 19 localities in Guam and 10 localities in the Northern Mariana Islands.

The Press

NEWSPAPERS AND PERIODICALS

Bonita: POB 11468, Tumon, GU 96931; tel. 632-4543; fax 637-6720; f. 1998; monthly; Publr IMELDA SANTOS; circ. 3,000.

Directions: POB 27290, Barrigada, GU 96921; tel. 635-7501; fax 635-7520; f. 1996; monthly; Publr JERRY ROBERTS; circ. 3,800.

Hospitality Guahan: POB 8565, Tamuning, GU 96931; tel. 649-1447; fax 649-8565; e-mail ghra@ghra.org; internet www.ghra.org; f. 1996; quarterly; circ. 3,000.

Marianas Business Journal: POB 3191, Hagåtña, GU 96932; tel. 649-0883; fax 649-8883; e-mail glimpses@kuentos.guam.net; internet www.mbjguam.net; f. 2003; fortnightly; Publr STEPHEN V. NYGARD; Editor MAUREEN MARATITA; circ. 3,000.

Pacific Daily News and Sunday News: POB DN, Hagåtña, GU 96932; tel. 477-1736; fax 472-1512; e-mail cblas@guampdn.com; internet www.guampdn.com; f. 1944; Publr LEE P. WEBBER; Exec. Editor RINDRATY LIMTIACO; circ. 28,520 (weekdays), 26,237 (Sunday).

The Pacific Voice: POB 2553, Hagåtña, GU 96932; tel. 472-6427; fax 477-5224; f. 1950; Sunday; Roman Catholic; Gen. Man. TEREZO MORTERA; Editor Rev. Fr HERMES LOSBANES; circ. 6,500.

TV Guam Magazine: 237 Mamis St, Tamuning, GU 96911; tel. 646-4030; fax 646-7445; f. 1973; weekly; Publr DINA GRANT; Man. Editor EMILY UNTALAN; circ. 15,000.

NEWS AGENCY

United Press International (UPI) (USA): POB 1617, Hagåtña, GU 96910; tel. 632-1138; Correspondent DICK WILLIAMS.

Broadcasting and Communications

TELECOMMUNICATIONS

Guam Educational Telecommunication Corporation (KGTF): POB 21449, Guam Main Facility, Barrigada, GU 96921; tel. 734-2207; fax 734-5483; e-mail kgtfl2@ite.net; internet www.kgtf.org.

Guam Telephone Authority: 624 N. Marines Corps Dr., POB 9008, Tamuning, GU 96931; tel. 644-4482; fax 649-4821; e-mail ask@gta.net; internet www.gta.net; acquired by TeleGuam Holdings LLC in Dec. 2004; CEO and Pres. ROBERT C. TAYLOR; Exec. Vice-Pres ROBERT G. SMITH, DOUGLASS B. LEE.

Guam

BROADCASTING

Radio

K-Stereo: POB 20249, Guam Main Facility, Barrigada, GU 96921; tel. 477-9448; fax 477-6411; operates on FM 24 hours a day; Pres. EDWARD H. POPPE; Gen. Man. FRANCES W. POPPE.

KGUM/KZGZ: Suite 800, 111 Chalan Santo Papa, Hagåtña, GU 96910; tel. 477-5700; fax 477-3982; e-mail rex@spbguam.com; internet www.radiopacific.com; Chair. and CEO REX SORENSEN; Pres. JON ANDERSON.

KOKU-FM: 424 West O'Brien Drive, Julale Center, Hagåtña, GU 96910; tel. 477-5658; fax 472-7663; e-mail marketing@hitradio100.com; operates on FM 24 hours a day; Pres. KURT S. MOYLAN; Marketing and Sales Man. VINCE LIMUACO.

KPRG FM: KPRG, UoG Station Mangilao, GU 96923; tel. 734-8930; fax 734-2958; e-mail kprg@kprg.org; internet www.kprg.org; operated by the University of Guam; news and music; Chair. MARIE MESA-KERLIN; Chairs TOD THOMPSON, NICK CAPTAIN; Gen. Man. DENISE MENDIOLA (acting).

Radio Guam (KUAM): 600 Harman Loop, Dededo, GU 96912; tel. 637-5826; fax 637-9865; e-mail generalmanager@kuam.com; internet www.kuam.com; f. 1954; operates on AM and FM 24 hours a day; Pres. PAUL M. CALVO; Gen. Man. JOEY CALVO.

Trans World Radio Pacific (TWR): POB CC, Hagåtña, GU 96932; tel. 477-9701; fax 477-2838; e-mail ktwr@twr.org; internet www.guam.net/home/twr; f. 1975; broadcasts Christian programmes on KTWR and one medium-wave station, KTWG, covering Guam and nearby islands, and operates five short-wave transmitters reaching most of Asia, Africa and the Pacific; Chair. THOMAS J. LOWELL; Pres. Dr DAVID G. TUCKER; Station Dir MICHAEL DAVIS.

Television

Guam Cable TV: 530 West O'Brien Drive, Hagåtña, GU 96910; tel. 477-7815; fax 477-7847; f. 1987; Pres. LEE M. HOLMES; Gen. Man. HARRISON O. FLORA.

KGTF—TV: POB 21449 Guam Main Facility, Barrigada, GU 96921; tel. 734-3476; fax 734-5483; e-mail kgtf12@kgtf.org; internet www.kgtf.org; f. 1970; cultural, public service and educational programmes; Gen. Man. GERALDINE 'GINGER' S. UNDERWOOD; Operations Man. BENNY T. FLORES.

KTGM—TV: 692 Marine Dr., Tamuning 96911; tel. 649-8814; fax 649-0371.

KUAM—TV: 600 Harmon Loop, Dededo, Hagåtña, GU 96912; tel. 637-5826; fax 637-9865; e-mail csanagustin@kuam.com; internet www.kuam.com; f. 1956; operates NTSC colour service channel 8; News Dir SABRINA SALAS.

Finance

(cap. = capital; res = reserves; = dep. = deposits; m. = million; brs = branches; amounts in US dollars)

BANKING

Commercial Banks

Allied Banking Corpn (Philippines): Suite 104, Bejess Commercial Bldg, 719 South Marine Drive, Tamuning, GU 96913; tel. 649-5001; fax 649-5002; e-mail abcguam@kuentos.guam.net; Man. MARIO R. PALISOC; 1 br.

Bank of Guam: POB BW, 111 Chalan Santo Papa, Hagåtña, GU 96932; tel. 472-5300; fax 477-8687; e-mail customerservice@bankofguam.com; internet www.bankofguam.com; f. 1972; total assets $704.6m. (2003); Chair. ANTHONY A. LEON GUERRERO; Exec. Vice-Pres. WILLIAM D. LEON GUERRERO; 19 brs.

Bank of Hawaii (USA): PO Box BH, Hagåtña, GU 96932; tel. 479-3500; fax 479-3777; Vice-Pres. RODNEY KIMURA; 3 brs.

BankPacific, Ltd: 151 Aspinall Ave, Hagåtña, GU 96910; tel. 472-8160; fax 477-1483; e-mail philipf@bankpacific.com; internet www.bankpacific.com; f. 1954; Pres. and CEO PHILIP J. FLORES; Exec. Vice-Pres. MARK O. FISH; 4 brs in Guam, 1 br. in Palau; 1 br. in Northern Mariana Islands.

Citibank NA (USA): 402 East Marine Drive, POB FF, Hagåtña, GU 96932; tel. 477-2484; fax 477-9441; internet www.citibank.com/guam; Vice-Pres. RASHID HABIB; 2 brs.

Citizens Security Bank (Guam) Inc: POB EQ, Hagåtña, GU 96932; tel. 479-9000; fax 479-9090; Pres. and CEO DANIEL L. WEBB; 4 brs.

First Commercial Bank (Taiwan): POB 2461, Hagåtña, GU 96932; tel. 472-6864; fax 477-8921; Gen. Man. YAO DER CHEN; 1 br.

First Hawaiian Bank (USA): Compadres Mall 562, Harmon Loop Rd, Dededo GU 96912; tel. 475-7900; fax 637-9686; internet www.fhb.com; Regional Man. (Guam and Saipan) JOHN K. LEE; 2 brs.

UNITED STATES EXTERNAL TERRITORIES

First Savings and Loan Association (FSLA): 140 Aspinal St, Hagåtña, GU 96910; affiliated to Bank of Hawaii; 6 brs.

HSBC Ltd: POB 27C, Hagåtña, GU 96932; tel. 647-8588; fax 646-3767; CEO GUY N. DE B. PRIESTLEY; 2 brs.

Metropolitan Bank and Trust Co (Philippines): 665 South Marine Drive, Tamuning, Guam 96911; tel. 649-9555; fax 649-9558; e-mail mbguam@metrobank.com.ph; f. 1975; Sen. Man. BENNETH A. REYES.

Union Bank of California (USA): 194 Hernan Cortes Ave, POB 7809, Hagåtña, GU 96910; tel. 477-8811; fax 472-3284; Man. KINJI SUZUKI; 2 brs.

INSURANCE

American National Insurance Co: POB 3340, Hagåtña, GU 96910; tel. 477-9600.

Chung Kuo Insurance Co: GCIC Bldg, Suite 707, 414 W Soledad Ave, Hagåtña, GU 96910; tel. 477-7696; fax 477-4788; e-mail chungkuo@ite.net; internet www.cki.com.tw.

Midland National Life Insurance Co: Winner Bldg, Suite 20N, Tamuning, GU 96911; tel. 649-0330; internet www.mnlife.com; f. 1906 as Dakota Mutual Life Insurance Company; name changed as above in 1925.

Moylan's Insurance Underwriters, Inc: Suite 102 Julale Shopping Center, 424 West O'Brien Dr., Hagåtña, GU 96910; tel. 477-8613; fax 477-1837; e-mail agana@moylansinsurance.com; internet www.moylansinsurance.com; Pres. KURT S. MOYLAN; Admin. Man CECILIA ANAS.

Nanbo Insurance: POB 2980, Hagåtña, GU 96910; tel. 477-9754; internet www.nanbo.com.

Pioneer Pacific Financial Services, Inc of Guam: POB EM, Hagåtña, GU 96910; tel. 477-6400.

Trade and Industry

DEVELOPMENT ORGANIZATION

Guam Economic Development and Commerce Authority (GEDCA): Guam International Trade Center Bldg, Suite 511, 590 South Marine Drive, Tamuning, GU 96911; tel. 647-4332; fax 649-4146; internet www.investguam.com; f. 1965.

CHAMBER OF COMMERCE

Guam Chamber of Commerce: Ada Plaza Center, Suite 101, 173 Aspinall Ave, POB 283, Hagåtña, GU 96932; tel. 472-6311; fax 472-6202; e-mail gchamber@guamchamber.com; internet www.guamchamber.com.gu; f. 1924; Chair. MONTY A. MCDOWELL.

EMPLOYERS' ORGANIZATION

Guam Employers' Council: 718 North Marine Drive, Suite 201, East-West Business Center, Upper Tumon, GU 96913; tel. 649-6616; fax 649-3030; e-mail babauta@ecouncil.org; internet www.ecouncil.org; f. 1966; private, non-profit asscn providing management development training and advice on personnel law and labour relations; Exec. Dir BILL BORJA.

UTILITIES

Electricity

Guam Energy Office: 1504 East Sunset Boulevard, Tiyan, GU 96913; tel. 477-0538; fax 477-0589; e-mail guamenergy@kuentos.guam.net.

Guam Power Authority: POB 2977, Hagåtña, GU 96932; tel. 648-3225; fax 649-6942; e-mail customersfirst@guampowerauthority.com; internet www.guampowerauthority.com; f. 1968; autonomous government agency; supplies electricity throughout the island; Gen. Man. JOHN BENAVENTE.

Water

Guam Waterworks Authority: 578 North Marine Drive, Tamuning, GU 96913; tel. 647-2603; fax 646-2335; e-mail ymcruz@guamwaterworks.org; internet www.guamwaterworks.org; Gen. Man. DAVID CRADDICK.

Public Utility Agency of Guam: Hagåtña, GU 96910; supplies the majority of water on the island.

TRADE UNIONS

Many workers belong to trade unions based in the USA such as the American Federation of Government Employees and the American Postal Workers' Union.

Guam Federation of Teachers (GFT): Local 1581, POB 2301, Hagåtña, GU 96932; tel. 735-4390; fax 734-8085; e-mail webmaster@gftunion.com; internet www.gftunion.com; f. 1965; affiliate of American Federation of Teachers; Pres. MATT RECTOR; 2,000 mems.

Guam Hotel and Restaurant Association: POB 8565, Tamuning, GU 96931; tel. 649-1447; e-mail ghra@ghra.org; internet www.ghra.org; 37 mem. restaurants and hotels; Pres. DAVID B. TYDINGCO; Chair. BARTLY JACKSON.

Guam Landowners' Association: Hagåtña; Sec. RONALD TEEHAN.

Transport

ROADS

There are 885 km (550 miles) of public roads, of which some 675 km (420 miles) are paved. A further 685 km (425 miles) of roads are classified as non-public, and include roads located on federal government installations.

SHIPPING

Apra, on the central western side of the island, is one of the largest protected deep-water harbours in the Pacific.

Port Authority of Guam: 1026 Cabras Highway, Suite 201, Piti, GU 96925; tel. 477-5931; fax 477-2689; e-mail mphenderson@portofguam.com; internet www.portofguam.com; f. 1975; government-operated port facilities; Gen. Man. JOSEPH F. MESA; Chair. RICHARD NORTHEY.

Ambyth, Shipping and Trading, Inc: 1026 Cabras Highway, Piti, GU 96915; tel. 477-7250; fax 472-1264; e-mail ops@ambyth.guam.net; internet www.ambyth.com; agents for all types of vessels and charter brokers; Pres. LAM AKY; Operations Man. DESIREE JOHNSON.

Atkins, Kroll, Inc: 443 South Marine Dr., Tamuning, GU 96913; tel. 649-6410; e-mail atkins_kroll@akguam.com; internet www.akguam.com; f. 1914; vehicle distribution; Pres. ROBERT J. HERNANDEZ; Vice-Pres. and Gen. Man. DAN CAMACHO.

COAM Trading Co Ltd: PAG Bldg, Suite 110, 1026 Cabas Highway, Piti, GU 96925; tel. 477-1737; fax 472-3386.

Dewitt Moving and Storage: 240 S Biang St, POB 2788, Tamuning, GU 96931; tel. 646-4442; fax 646-0034; e-mail ezdewitt@dewittguam.com; internet www.dewittguam.com.

Guam Shipping Agency: PO Box GD, Hagåtña, GU 96932; tel. 477-7381; fax 477-7553; Gen. Man. H. KO.

Interbulk Shipping (Guam) Inc: Bank of Guam Bldg, Suite 502, 111 Chalan Santo Papa, Hagåtña, GU 96910; Man. S. GYSTAD.

Maritime Agencies of the Pacific Ltd: Piti, GU 96925; tel. 477-8500; fax 477-5726; e-mail rehmapship@kuentos.guam.net; f. 1976; agents for fishing vessels, cargo, dry products and construction materials; Pres. ROBERT E. HAHN.

Pacific Navigation System: POB 7, Hagåtña, GU 96910; f. 1946; Pres. KENNETH T. JONES, Jr.

Seabridge Micronesian, Inc: 1026 Cabras Highway, Suite 114, Piti, Guam 96925; tel. 477-7345; fax 477-6206; Gen. Man. J. L. CRUZ.

Sea-Land Service, Inc: POB 8897, Tamuning, GU 96931; tel. 475-8100; internet www.horizon-lines.com; CEO CHUCK RAYMOND.

Tucor Services: 180 Guerrero St, Harmon Industrial Park, POB 6128, Tamuning, GU 96911; tel. 646-6947; fax 646-6945; e-mail boll@tucor.com; general agents for numerous dry cargo, passenger and steamship cos; Pres. MICHELLE BOLL.

CIVIL AVIATION

Guam is served by A. B. Won Pat International Airport.

Guam International Airport Authority: POB 8770, Tamuning, GU 96931; tel. 646-0300; fax 646-8823; e-mail lizb@guamairport.net; internet www.guamairport.com; Chair. FRANK F. BLAS; Exec. Man. JESUS Q. TORRES.

Asia Pacific Airline (APA): POB 24858, Guam Main Facility, Barrigada, Guam 96921; tel. 647-8440; fax 647-1086; e-mail info@flyapa.com; internet www.flyapa.com; f. 1999; affiliate of Tan Holdings Corpn. (Commonwealth of the Northern Mariana Islands); cargo; serving Guam, Hawaii, Hong Kong, Marshall Islands, Federated States of Micronesia, Palau and the Philippines.

Continental Micronesia Airlines: POB 8778, Tamuning, GU 96931; tel. 649-6594; fax 649-6588; internet www.continental.com; f. 1968, as Air Micronesia, by Continental Airlines (USA); hub operations in Guam and Saipan (Northern Mariana Islands); services throughout the region and to destinations in the Far East and the mainland USA; Pres. and CEO LARRY KELLNER.

Freedom Air: POB 1578, Hagåtña, GU 96932; tel. 472-8009; fax 4728080; e-mail freedom@ite.net; f. 1974; Man. Dir JOAQUIN L. FLORES, Jr.

Tourism

Tourism is the most important industry on Guam. In the year ending September 2004 there were 1,153,406 visitor arrivals. In 2002 some 74.3% of arrivals by air were visitors from Japan, 12.1% from the Republic of Korea, 3.9% from the USA and 1.8% from Taiwan. Most of Guam's hotels are situated in, or near to, Tumon, where amenities for entertainment are well-developed. Numerous sunken wrecks of aircraft and ships from Second World War battles provide interesting sites for divers. There were 7,879 hotel rooms on Guam at July 2003. A total of US $16.2m. was collected in hotel occupancy taxes in 2002. The industry as a whole earned some $1,908m. in 1999.

Guam Visitors Bureau: 401 Pale San Vitores Rd, Tumon, GU 96913; tel. 646-5278; fax 646-8861; e-mail guaminfo@visitguam.org; internet www.visitguam.org; Chair. DAVID B. TYDINGCO; Gen. Man. ALBERTO 'TONY' A. C. LAMORENA, V.

THE UNITED STATES VIRGIN ISLANDS

Introductory Survey

Location, Climate, Language, Religion, Flag, Capital

The Territory consists of three main inhabited islands (St Croix, St Thomas and St John) and about 50 smaller islands, mostly uninhabited. They are situated at the eastern end of the Greater Antilles, about 64 km (40 miles) east of Puerto Rico in the Caribbean Sea. The climate is tropical, although tempered by the prevailing easterly trade winds. The temperature averages 26°C (79°F), with little variation between winter and summer. The humidity is low for the tropics. English is the official language, but Spanish and Creole are also widely used. The people of the US Virgin Islands are predominantly of African descent. There is a strong religious tradition, and most of the inhabitants are Christians, mainly Protestants. The flag (proportions 2 by 3) is white, with a modified version of the US coat of arms (an eagle holding an olive branch in one foot and a sheaf of arrows in the other, with a shield, comprising a small horizontal blue panel above vertical red and white stripes, superimposed), between the letters V and I, in the centre. The capital is Charlotte Amalie, on the island of St Thomas.

Recent History

The Virgin Islands, originally inhabited by Carib and Arawak Indians, were discovered by Europeans in 1493. The group subsequently passed through English, French, and Dutch control, before the western islands of St Thomas and St John, colonized by Denmark after 1670, and St Croix, purchased from France in 1733, became the Danish West Indies. In 1917 these islands, which are strategically placed in relation to the Panama Canal, were sold for US $25m. by Denmark to the USA. They now form an unincorporated territory of the USA. Residents of the US Virgin Islands are US citizens, but cannot vote in presidential elections, if resident in the islands. The US Virgin Islands is represented in the US House of Representatives by one popularly elected Delegate, who is permitted to vote only in committees of the House.

The inhabitants of the islands were granted a measure of self-government by the Organic Act, as revised in 1954, which created the elected 15-member Senate. Since 1970, executive authority has been vested in the elected Governor and Lieutenant-Governor. In the first gubernatorial election, in 1970, the Republican incumbent, Melvin Evans, retained office. In 1974 Cyril E. King, leader of the Independent Citizens Movement (a breakaway faction of the Democratic Party), was elected Governor. On King's death in 1978, the former Lieutenant-Governor, Juan Luis, was elected Governor. He was returned to power in the 1982 election. The governorship passed to the Democratic Party with the election of Alexander Farrelly in 1986. Farrelly was re-elected Governor in 1990, and in the 1994 elections was succeeded by an Independent, Dr Roy Schneider. The governorship was regained by a Democrat, Charles Turnbull, in the 1998 elections. Turnbull was re-elected to the post in 2000 and 2002.

Since 1954 there have been five attempts to redraft the Constitution to give the US Virgin Islands greater autonomy. Each draft has, however, been rejected by a referendum. The US Government has expressed the view that it would welcome reform, if approved by the residents, as long as it was economically feasible and did not affect US national security. A non-binding referendum on the islands' future status, which was to take place in November 1989, was postponed following the disruption caused by 'Hurricane Hugo'. Voting, which eventually took place in October 1993, produced support of 80% for retaining the islands' existing status, with 14% favouring full integration with the USA and 5% advocating the termination of US sovereignty. The result of the referendum was, however, invalidated by the low turn-out: only 27% of registered voters took part, falling short of the 50% participation required for the referendum to be valid. Subsequent legislation to create a constitutional convention was presented to the US Virgin Islands Senate, and in May 2000 a committee of the US House of Representatives began consideration of a range of measures to enlarge the scope of local self-government in the Territory. In November 2004 Governor Turnbull approved legislation allowing the creation of a further constituent assembly to redraft the Constitution.

In February 2005 a 7,000-signature petition was submitted to the US Congress by residents of St Croix, in support of making the island a separate US External Territory from St Thomas and St John. Organizers of the petition claimed that such a move would generate more federal funding for the island, which was affected by a higher unemployment rate than the other two islands, despite being the location for one of the world's largest petroleum refineries. In May the Territorial Government brought a court case against the owners of the Hovensa LLC oil refinery (see Economic Affairs) and the defunct St Croix Alumina plant for contaminating the sole groundwater supply on St Croix. Both companies had reached an agreement with the US Environmental Protection Agency (EPA) in 2001 to clean up petroleum spillages; according to the EPA some 2m. gallons of petroleum leaked into the local aquifer between 1978 and 1991.

In March 2002 the Territory was removed from the Organisation for Economic Co-operation and Development's list of tax 'havens', after pledging to improve the transparency of its financial services sector by the end of 2005.

Economic Affairs

According to estimates by the Territorial Government, the islands' gross national income (GNI) in 1989 was US $1,344m., equivalent to about $13,100 per head. Average personal income in 2003 was $17,581 per head, or about 55.6% of the US mainland average. GNI increased, in real terms, at an average rate of 2.5% per year during 1980–89. In 1995–2004 the population increased by an annual average of 0.6%.

Most of the land is unsuitable for large-scale cultivation, but tax incentives have encouraged the growing of vegetables, fruit and cereals, which are produced for local consumption. According to the 2000 census figures, 0.7% of the economically active population were engaged in agriculture, forestry, fishing and mining.

The islands are heavily dependent on links with the US mainland. There are no known natural resources, and, because of limited land space and other factors, the islands are unable to produce sufficient food to satisfy local consumption. Most goods are imported, mainly from the mainland USA.

Industry (including construction and mining) engaged some 12.0% of the non-agricultural labour force in 2002, according to official figures. The main branch of manufacturing is petroleum-refining.

Services (including public administration) employed some 88.0% of the non-agricultural labour force in 2002, according to official figures, of which about 33% was employed in public administration. Tourism, which is estimated to account for more than 60% of gross domestic product (GDP), is the mainstay of the islands' income and employment, and provides the major source of direct and indirect revenue for other service sectors (including trade and transport). The emphasis is on the visiting cruise-ship business and the advantages of duty-free products for tourist visitors. In 2004 visitor arrivals (including excursionists and cruise passengers) were an estimated 2.6m.; in 2003 visitor expenditures amounted to US $1,270.5m. In late 2005 the an agreement was signed to build a $500m. casino and resort on St Croix; construction was expected to begin in August 2007 and was scheduled for completion by 2022. In 2006 work was ongoing on a number of construction projects related to the tourism industry, including a $150m. hotel and marina complex and a $63m. recreation centre on St Thomas, and the addition of a cruise-ship dock at St Croix harbour.

St Croix has the world's second largest petroleum refinery, Hovensa LLC (a joint venture between the US oil company Amerada Hess and Petróleos de Venezuela, SA) produced some 484,000 barrels per day (b/d) in 2004. In 2003 Hovensa exported refined petroleum products to the USA worth US $4,800m. In response to stricter environmental controls, in September 2005 the company began work on a $400m. desulphurization unit; construction had been scheduled to begin in late 2002 but was delayed by industrial action in Venezuela (q.v.), the origin of more than 50% of the refinery's crude

UNITED STATES EXTERNAL TERRITORIES

The United States Virgin Islands

petroleum imports. Efforts have been made to introduce labour-intensive and non-polluting manufacturing industries. Rum is an important product; the industry, however, was expected to encounter increased competition from Mexico as a result of the North American Free Trade Agreement (NAFTA, see p. 312), which entered into operation in January 1994. In 2003 the industry was based around a single company, Virgin Islands Rum Industries Ltd, which, in that year alone, exported some 5,973.3m. gallons of rum to the USA.

The population increased dramatically from the 1960s. This inflow included people from neighbouring Caribbean countries, together with wealthy white settlers from the US mainland, attracted by the climate and the low taxes. At the 2000 census 31% of the population originated from other Caribbean islands, and 14.5% from the mainland USA.

Throughout the 1990s the budget deficit of the Territorial Government increased. By December 1999 the deficit was estimated to have risen to US $305m., and in that year the Territorial Government introduced a Five-Year Strategic and Financial Operating Plan to reduce government expenditure and enhance the effectiveness of procedures for revenue collection. By 2003/04 the budget deficit had been reduced to $4.6m.; however, the Government forecast that the deficit would rise to $9.6m. in 2004/05 and to $92.4m. in 2005/06. In 2003/04 the islands' debt amounted to some $1,000m. The average rate of unemployment rose from 5.2% in 1996 to 9.4% in 2003; by 2005 the average rate of unemployment had fallen to 6.7%. The islands were expected in the foreseeable future to continue to receive grants and other remittances from the US Government.

In 2003 the Territory recorded a trade deficit of $9.6m. In that year the USA provided 10.8% of imports and took 93.2% of exports. Venezuela was also a major source of imports. Of total exports to the USA in 2003, 92.6% were refined petroleum products. Crude petroleum accounted for 80.3% of the islands' total imports in that year.

Owing to the islands' heavy reliance on imported goods, local prices and inflation are higher than on the mainland, and the islands' economy, in contrast to that of the USA, remained in recession for most of the 1990s. 'Hurricane Hugo', which struck the islands in September 1989, was estimated to have caused $1,000m. in property damage, although subsequent work on rebuilding temporarily revitalized employment in the construction sector. 'Hurricane Marilyn' caused considerable damage in September 1995, destroying an estimated 80% of houses on St Thomas. Serious storm damage was again experienced in July 1996, from 'Hurricane Bertha', and in September 1998 from 'Hurricane Georges'. In August 2000 'Hurricane Debby' caused less serious damage. In October 2004 the US Congress approved legislation to reform corporate tax in the US Virgin Islands. There were concerns that the measures would deter companies from using the Territory as a tax 'haven', at a cost to the local economy of up to US $63m. in lost revenue and as many as 600 jobs.

The Territory is an associate member of the UN Economic Commission for Latin America and the Caribbean (ECLAC, see p. 36).

Education

Education is compulsory up to the age of 16 years. It generally comprises eight years at primary school and four years at secondary school. In 2002 there were 24,934 students enrolled at elementary and secondary schools. The University of the Virgin Islands, with campuses on St Thomas and St Croix, had 2,610 students in 2004.

Public Holidays

2006: 1 January (New Year's Day), 6 January (Three Kings' Day), 16 January (Martin Luther King Day), 20 February (Presidents' Day), 27 March (Transfer Day), 14–17 April (Easter), 29 May (Memorial Day), 19 June (Organic Act Day), 3 July (Danish West Indies Emancipation Day), 4 July (US Independence Day), 24 July (Hurricane Supplication Day), 4 September (Labor Day), 9 October (for Columbus Day/Puerto Rico Friendship Day), 16 October (Virgin Islands Thanksgiving Day), 1 November (Liberty Day), 10 November (for Veterans' Day), 23 November (US Thanksgiving Day), 25–26 December (Christmas).

2007: 1 January (New Year's Day), 6 January (Three Kings' Day), 15 January (Martin Luther King Day), 19 February (Presidents' Day), 6–9 April (Easter), 26 March (Transfer Day), 28 May (Memorial Day), 18 June (Organic Act Day), 3 July (Danish West Indies Emancipation Day), 4 July (US Independence Day), 23 July (Hurricane Supplication Day), 3 September (Labor Day), 8 October (for Columbus Day/Puerto Rico Friendship Day), 15 October (Virgin Islands Thanksgiving Day), 1 November (Liberty Day), 12 November (for Veterans' Day), 22 November (US Thanksgiving Day), 25–26 December (Christmas).

Statistical Survey

Sources (unless otherwise stated): Office of Public Relations, Office of the Governor, Charlotte Amalie, VI 00802; tel. (340) 774-0294; fax (340) 774-4988; Bureau of Economic Research, Dept of Economic Development and Agriculture, POB 6400, Charlotte Amalie, VI 00804; tel. (340) 774-8784; internet www.usviber.org.

AREA AND POPULATION

Area: 347.1 sq km (134 sq miles): St Croix 215 sq km (83 sq miles); St Thomas 80.3 sq km (31 sq miles); St John 51.8 sq km (20 sq miles).

Population: 101,809 at census of 1 April 1990; 108,612 (males 51,684, females 56,748) at census of 1 April 2000. *By Island* (2000 census): St Croix 53,234, St Thomas 51,181, St John 4,197. Source: US Bureau of the Census. *2003* (official figures): St Croix 54,277; St Thomas 52,184; St John 4,279; Total 110,740.

Density (2003): 319.0 per sq km.

Principal Towns (population at census of 1 April 2000): Charlotte Amalie (capital) 11,004; Christiansted 2,637; Frederiksted 732. Source: Thomas Brinkhoff, *City Population* (internet www.citypopulation.de).

Births and Deaths (2002): Registered live births 1,634 (birth rate 15.0 per 1,000); Registered deaths (preliminary) 623 (death rate 5.7 per 1,000). Source: US National Center for Health Statistics.

Expectation of Life (estimates, years at birth): 79.0 (males 75.1; females 82.9) in 2005 (Source: Pan American Health Organization).

Economically Active Population (persons aged 16 years and over, 2000 census): Agriculture, forestry, fishing, hunting and mining 324; Manufacturing 2,754; Construction 4,900; Wholesale trade 912; Retail trade 6,476; Transportation, warehousing and utilities 3,321; Information 931; Finance, insurance, real estate, rental and leasing 2,330; Professional, scientific, management, administrative and waste management services 3,058; Educational, health, and social services 6,742; Arts, entertainment, recreation, accommodation and food services 7,351; Public administration 4,931; Other services 2,535; *Total employed* 46,565. Source: US Bureau of the Census. *2004* (official figures): Total employed 46,101; Unemployed 3,965; Total labour force 50,066.

HEALTH AND WELFARE

Total Fertility Rate (children per woman, 2005): 2.2.

Under-5 Mortality Rate (per 1,000 live births, 2004): 10.3.

Physicians (per 1,000 head, 2003): 1.47.

Hospital Beds (per 1,000 head, 1996): 18.7.

Source: Pan American Health Organization.

For definitions, see explanatory note on p. vi.

AGRICULTURE, ETC.

Livestock (FAO estimates, 2004): Cattle 8,000; Sheep 3,200; Pigs 2,600; Goats 4,000; Chickens 35,000.

Fishing (metric tons, live weight, 2003): Total catch (all capture) 1,492 (Snappers, jobfishes, etc. 183; Parrotfishes 197; Caribbean spiny lobster 130; Stromboid conchs 493).

Source: FAO.

INDUSTRY

Production (estimates, '000 metric tons, unless otherwise indicated, 2001): Jet fuels 1,620; Motor spirit (petrol) 2,370; Kerosene 70; Gas-diesel (distillate fuel) oil 2,910; Residual fuel oils 3,825; Liquefied petroleum gas 240; Electric energy 1,090 million kWh. Source: UN, *Industrial Commodity Statistics Yearbook*.

FINANCE

Currency and Exchange Rates: 100 cents = 1 United States dollar (US $). *Sterling and Euro Equivalents* (30 December 2005): £1 sterling = US $1.722; €1 = US $1,797; US $100 = £58.08 = €84.77.

Budget (projections US $ million, year ending 30 September 2002): Operating budget 580.2 (Net revenues from taxes, duties and other sources 521.8); Rum excise taxes (Federal remittance) 70.9; Direct Federal expenditures 573. *2003* Operating budget 616.5 (Net revenues from taxes, duties and other sources 536.8); Rum excise taxes (Federal remittance) 69.9.

Cost of Living (Consumer Price Index; base: 2001 = 100): All items 104.1 in 2001; 106.3 in 2002; 108.7 in 2003.

EXTERNAL TRADE

Total (US $ million): *Imports*: 4,608.7 in 2001; 4,213.2 in 2002; 5,570.4 in 2003. *Exports*: 4,234.2 in 2001; 3,876.3 in 2002; 5,560.8 in 2003. Note: The main import is crude petroleum ($4,473.5m. in 2003), while the principal exports are refined petroleum products ($4,799.3m. in 2003).

Trade with the USA (US $ million): *Imports*: 4,608.7 in 2001; 4,213.2 in 2002; 5,570.4. *Exports*: 3,960.3 in 2001; 3,519.9 in 2002; 5,181.1 in 2003.

TRANSPORT

Road Traffic (registered motor vehicles, 2002): 69,642.

Shipping: *Freight Imports* ('000 metric tons) 1,032 in 2000; 993 in 2001; 1,056 in 2003. *Cruise-ship Arrivals:* 888 in 2003; 924 in 2004; 818 in 2005. *Passenger Arrivals:* 1,738,703 in 2002; 1,773,948 in 2003; 1,963,609 in 2004.

Civil Aviation (visitor arrivals): 598,019 in 2002; 620,814 in 2003; 658,638 in 2004.

TOURISM

Visitor Arrivals ('000, 2003): Total visitors 2,392.6 (tourists 538.2, excursionists 1,854.4).

2004 ('000): Total visitors 2,623.3 (air 658.6, cruise-ship 1,964.7).

Visitor Receipts (US $ million, 2003): Total receipts 1,270.5 (tourists 765.8, excursionists 504.7).

COMMUNICATIONS MEDIA

Radio Receivers (1997): 107,100 in use.
Television Receivers (1999): 71,000 in use.
Telephones (2002): 68,961 main lines in use.
Mobile Cellular Telephones (2000): 35,000 subscribers.
Internet Users (1999): 12,000.
Daily Newspapers (1996): 3; average circulation 42,000 copies.
Non-daily Newspapers (1988 estimates): 2; average circulation 4,000 copies.

Sources: mainly UNESCO, *Statistical Yearbook*; International Telecommunication Union.

EDUCATION

Pre-primary (1992/93): 62 schools; 121 teachers; 4,714 students (2000).
Elementary (1992/93): 62 schools; 790 teachers (public schools only); 13,421 students (2001).
Secondary: 541 teachers (public schools only, 1990); 5,359 students (2001).
Higher Education: 266 teachers (2003/04); 2,610 students (2004).

Sources: UNESCO, *Statistical Yearbook*; US Bureau of the Census.

Directory

The Constitution

The Government of the US Virgin Islands is organized under the provisions of the Organic Act of the Virgin Islands, passed by the Congress of the United States in 1936 and revised in 1954 and 1984. Subsequent amendments provided for the popular election of the Governor and Lieutenant-Governor of the Virgin Islands in 1970 and, since 1973, for representation in the US House of Representatives by a popularly elected Delegate. The Delegate has voting powers only in committees of the House. Executive power is vested in the Governor, who is elected for a term of four years by universal adult suffrage and who appoints, with the advice and consent of the legislature, the heads of the executive departments. The Governor may also appoint administrative assistants as his representatives on St John and St Croix. Legislative power is vested in the legislature of the Virgin Islands, a unicameral body comprising 15 Senators, elected for a two-year term by popular vote. Legislation is subject to the approval of the Governor, whose veto can be overridden by a two-thirds vote of the Legislature. All residents of the islands, who are citizens of the USA and at least 18 years of age, have the right to vote in local elections but not in national elections. In 1976 the Virgin Islands were granted the right to draft their own constitution, subject to the approval of the US President and Congress. A constitution permitting a degree of autonomy was drawn up in 1978 and gained the necessary approval, but was then rejected by the people of the Virgin Islands in a referendum in March 1979. A fourth draft, providing for greater autonomy than the 1978 draft, was rejected in a referendum in November 1981.

The Government

EXECUTIVE
(April 2006)

Governor: CHARLES WESLEY TURNBULL.
Lieutenant-Governor: VARGRAVE A. RICHARDS, II.
Commissioner of Agriculture: LAWRENCE LEWIS.
Commissioner of Education: NOREEN MICHAEL.
Commissioner of Finance: BERNICE TURNBULL.
Commissioner of Health: DARLENE CARTY.
Commissioner of Housing, Parks and Recreation: IRA M. HOBSON.
Commissioner of Human Services: SEDONIE HALBERT.
Commissioner of Labor: CECIL R. BENJAMIN.
Commissioner of Licensing and Consumer Affairs: ANDREW RUTNIK.
Commissioner of Planning and Natural Resources: DEAN C. PLASKETT.
Commissioner of Police: ELTON LEWIS.
Commissioner of Property and Procurement: MARC BIGGS.
Commissioner of Public Works: GEORGE PHILLIPS (acting).
Commissioner of Tourism: PAMELA C. RICHARDS.
Attorney-General: KERRY E. DRUE.
US Virgin Islands Delegate to the US Congress: DONNA M. CHRISTENSEN.

GOVERNMENT OFFICES

Office of the Governor: Government House, 21–22 Kongens Gade, Charlotte Amalie, VI 00802; tel. (340) 774-0001; fax (340) 774-1361.
Office of the Lieutenant-Governor: Government Hill, 18 Kongens Gade, Charlotte Amalie, VI 00802; tel. (340) 773-6449; fax (340) 773-0330; tel. (340) 774-2991; fax (340) 774-6953; internet www.ltg.vi.
Department of Agriculture: Estate Lower Love, Kingshill, St Croix, VI 00850; tel. (340) 774-0997; fax (340) 774-5182; internet www.usvi.org/agriculture.
Department of Economic Development: 81 AB Kronprindsens Gade, POB 6400, Charlotte Amalie, VI 00801; tel. (340) 774-8784; fax (340) 774-4390.
Department of Education: 44–46 Kongens Gade, Charlotte Amalie, VI 00802; tel. (340) 774-0100; fax (340) 779-7153; e-mail education@usvi.org; internet www.doe.vi.
Department of Finance: GERS Bldg, 2nd Floor, 76 Kronprindsens Gade, Charlotte Amalie, VI 00802; tel. (340) 774-4750; fax (340) 776-4028; internet www.usvi.org/finance.
Department of Health: 48 Sugar Estate, Charlotte Amalie, VI 00802; tel. (340) 774-0117; fax (340) 777-4001; internet www.usvi.org/health.
Department of Housing, Parks and Recreation: Property & Procurement Bldg No. 1, Sub Base, 2nd Floor, Rm 206, Charlotte Amalie, VI 00802; tel. (340) 774-0255; fax (340) 774-4600.
Department of Human Services: Knud Hansen Complex Bldg A 1303, Hospital Ground, Charlotte Amalie, VI 00802; tel. (340) 774-0930; fax (340) 774-3466; e-mail humanservices@usvi.org; internet www.usvi.org/humanservices.
Department of Justice: GERS Bldg, 2nd Floor, 48B–50C Kronprindsens Gade, Charlotte Amalie, VI 00802; tel. (340) 774-5666; fax (340) 774-9710; internet www.usvi.org/justice.
Department of Labor: POB 302608, St Thomas, VI 00803; tel. (340) 776-3700; fax (340) 774-5908; e-mail customersupport@vidol.gov; internet www.vidol.gov.
Department of Licensing and Consumer Affairs: Property & Procurement Bldg No. 1, Sub Base, Rm 205, Charlotte Amalie, VI 00802; tel. (340) 774-3130; fax (340) 776-0675; e-mail commissioner@dlca.gov.vi; internet www.dlca.gov.vi.
Department of Planning and Natural Resources: 396-1 Anna's Retreat–Foster Bldg, Charlotte Amalie, VI 00802; tel. (340) 774-3320; fax (340) 775-5706; e-mail stt-office@vidpnr-dep.org; internet www.dpnr.gov.vi.

UNITED STATES EXTERNAL TERRITORIES

Department of Police: 8172 Sub Base, St Thomas, VI 00802; tel. (340) 774-2211; fax (340) 778-2373; e-mail police@usvi.org; internet www.vipd.gov.vi.

Department of Property and Procurement: Property & Procurement Bldg No. 1, Sub Base, 3rd Floor, Charlotte Amalie, VI 00802; tel. (340) 774-0828; fax (340) 774-9704; e-mail pnp@usvi.org; internet www.usvi.org/pnp.

Department of Public Works: No. 8 Sub Base, Charlotte Amalie, VI 00802; tel. (340) 773-1290; fax (340) 774-5869; e-mail publicworks@usvi.org; internet www.usvi.org/publicworks.

Department of Tourism: POB 6400, St Thomas, VI 00804; tel. (340) 774-8784; fax (340) 774-4390; e-mail info@usvitourism.vi; internet www.usvitourism.vi.

Legislature

LEGISLATIVE ASSEMBLY

Senate
(15 members)

President of the Senate: LORRAINE BERRY.
Election, 2 November 2004

Party	Seats
Democrats	10*
Independent Citizens Movement	3
Independent	2
Total	**15**

* In late November 2004 three Democrat candidates defected to form a consensus majority coalition with the Independents and Independent Citizens Movement.

Political Organizations

Democratic Party of the Virgin Islands: POB 2033, St Thomas Democratic District, VI 00803; affiliated to the Democratic Party in the USA; Chair. CECIL R. BENJAMIN, Jr.

Independent Citizens Movement: Charlotte Amalie, VI 00801; Chair. USIE RICHON.

Republican Party of the Virgin Islands: POB 1532, St Thomas, VI 00804; tel. (340) 776-0583; affiliated to the Republican Party in the USA; Chair. JAMES M. OLIVER.

Judicial System

Legislation was approved in October 2004 to establish a Supreme Court in the US Virgin Islands. Discussions were ongoing in early 2006 as to where the court should be located.

US Federal District Court of the Virgin Islands: Federal Bldg and US Courthouse, 5500 Veteran's Dr., Charlotte Amalie, VI 00802; tel. (340) 774-0640; internet www.vid.uscourts.gov; jurisdiction in civil, criminal and federal actions; the judges are appointed by the President of the USA with the advice and consent of the Senate.

US Territorial District Court of the Virgin Islands: Alexander A. Farrelly Justice Center, POB 70, Charlotte Amalie, VI 00802; tel. (340) 774-6680; internet www.vid.uscourts.gov; exclusive jurisdiction in violations of police and executive regulations; original jurisdiction over all local criminal matters and civil actions, regardless of the amount in controversy; and concurrent jurisdiction with the US Federal District Court of the Virgin Islands over federal question and diversity cases, and over local Virgin Islands criminal offences based on the same act or transaction if the act or transaction also constitutes an offence against federal law. The Court is also vested with jurisdiction to promulgate rules and regulations governing its practice and procedure, and to regulate the admission of attorneys to the Virgin Islands Bar.
Judges: RAYMOND L. FINCH (Chief Judge), CURTIS V. GOMEZ.

Religion

The population is mainly Christian. The main churches with followings in the islands are Baptist, Roman Catholic, Episcopalian, Lutheran, Methodist, Moravian and Seventh-day Adventist. There is also a small Jewish community.

The United States Virgin Islands

CHRISTIANITY

The Roman Catholic Church

The US Virgin Islands comprises a single diocese, suffragan to the archdiocese of Washington, DC, USA. At 31 December 2003 there were an estimated 30,000 adherents in the territory (27.6% of the population).

Bishop of St Thomas: Most Rev. GEORGE V. MURRY, Bishop's Residence, 29A Princesse Gade, POB 301825, Charlotte Amalie, VI 00803-1825; tel. (340) 774-3166; fax (340) 774-5816; e-mail chancery@islands.vi.

The Anglican Communion

Episcopal Church of the Virgin Islands: Bishop: Rt Rev. THEODORE A. DANIELS, POB 10437, St Thomas, VI 00801; fax (340) 777-8485; e-mail tad@aol.com.

The Press

Pride Magazine: 22ANorre Gade, POB 7908, Charlotte Amalie, VI 00801; tel. (340) 776-4106; f. 1983; monthly; Editor JUDITH WILLIAMS; circ. 4,000.

St Croix Avis: La Grande Princesse, Christiansted, St Croix, VI 00820; tel. (340) 773-2300; f. 1944; morning; Editor RENA BROADHURST-KNIGHT; circ. 10,000.

St John Tradewinds: Tradewinds Bldg, Garden Level Unit 4, POB 1500, Cruz Bay, St John, VI 00831; tel. (340) 776-6496; fax (340) 693-8885; e-mail editor@tradewinds.vi; internet www.stjohntradewindsnews.com; f. 1972; fortnightly; Publr MALINDA NELSON; circ. 2,500.

Virgin Islands Business Journal: 69 Kronprindsens Gade, POB 1208, Charlotte Amalie, VI 00804; tel. (340) 776-2874; fax (340) 774-3636; internet www.vibj.com; f. 1986; weekly; Man. Editor CARTER HAGUE; circ. 10,000.

Virgin Islands Daily News: 9155 Estate Thomas, VI 00802; tel. (340) 774-8772; fax (340) 776-0740; e-mail dailynews@vipowernet.net; internet www.virginislandsdailynews.com; f. 1930; bought by Innovative Communication Corpn in 1997; morning; CEO and Exec. Editor J. LOWE DAVIS; circ. 15,000.

Broadcasting and Communications

TELECOMMUNICATIONS

Innovative Telephone: POB 1141, Charlotte Amalie, VI 00801; tel. (340) 774-5555; internet www.iccvi.com; f. 1959 as Virgin Islands Telephone Corpn (Vitelco); present name adopted in 2001; bought by Innovative Communication Corpn in 1987; provides telephone services throughout the islands; Chair. JEFFREY J. PROSSER; Pres. and CEO DAVID SHARP.

Innovative Wireless: St Croix, 4006 Estate Diamond, Christiansted, VI 00820; fax (340) 778-6011; internet www.vitelcellular.com; f. 1989 as Vitelcellular; owned by Innovative Communication Corpn; mobile cellular telephone services; Gen. Man. NEIL WILLIAMS.

RADIO

WAVI—FM: POB 25016, Gallows Bay Station, St Croix, VI 00824; tel. (340) 773-3693; commercial; Gen. Man. DOUG HARRIS.

WGOD: Crown Mountain, POB 5012, Charlotte Amalie, VI 00803; tel. (340) 774-4498; fax (340) 776-0877; commercial; Gen. Man. PETER RICHARDSON.

WJKC-WMNG-WVIQ: 5020 Anchor Way, POB 25680, Christiansted, St Croix, VI 00824; tel. (340) 773-0995; e-mail jkc95@aol.com; internet www.wjkcisle95.com; commercial; Gen. Man. JONATHAN COHEN.

WSTA: Sub Base 121, POB 1340, St Thomas, VI 00804; tel. (340) 774-1340; fax (340) 776-1316; e-mail addie@wsta.com; internet www.wsta.com; commercial; Gen. Man. ATHNIEL C. OTTLEY.

WVWI, WVJZ, WWKS (Knight Quality Stations): 13 Crown Bay Fill, POB 305678, Charlotte Amalie, VI 00803; tel. (340) 776-1000; fax (340) 776-5357; e-mail kqs@viaccess.net; f. 1962; commercial; Pres. and Gen. Man. RANDOLPH H. KNIGHT.

TELEVISION

Caribbean Communications Corporation: 1 Beltjen Pl., Charlotte Amalie, VI 00802-6735; tel. (340) 776-2150; fax (340) 774-5029; f. 1966; cable service, 72 channels; Gen. Man. ANDREA L. MARTIN.

St Croix Cable TV: Heron Commercial Park, POB 5968, Sunny Isle, St Croix, VI 00823; tel. (340) 778-6701; f. 1981; bought by Innovative Cable Television in 1997; 32 channels; Gen. Man. JACK WHITE.

UNITED STATES EXTERNAL TERRITORIES

TV2: 1 Beltjen Pl., St Thomas, VI 00802; tel. (340) 774-2200; fax (340) 776-1957; e-mail bbutler@tv2.vi; internet www.tv2.vi; f. 2000; owned by Innovative Communication Corpn; Gen. Man. BRENT A. BUTLER.

WSVI—TV: Sunny Isle, POB 8ABC, Christiansted, St Croix, VI 00823; tel. (340) 778-5008; fax (340) 778-5011; f. 1965; one channel and one translator; Gen. Man. BARAKAT SALEH.

WTJX—TV (Public Television Service): Barbel Plaza, POB 7879, Charlotte Amalie, VI 00801; tel. (340) 774-6255; fax (340) 774-7092; e-mail lelskoe@wtjx.org; internet www.wtjx.org; one channel; Gen. Man. OSBERT POTTER.

Finance

BANKING

Banco Popular of the Virgin Islands: 193 Altona and Welgunst, Charlotte Amalie, VI 00802; tel. (340) 693-2702; fax (340) 693-2702; Regional Man. VALENTINO I. MCBEAN; 7 brs.

Bank of Nova Scotia (Canada): 214C Altona and Welgunst, POB 420, Charlotte Amalie, VI 00804; tel. (340) 774-6393; fax (340) 693-5994; Man. R. HAINES; 10 brs.

Bank of St Croix: POB 24240, Gallows Bay, St Croix 00824; tel. (340) 773-8500; fax (340) 773-8508; Man. JAMES BRISBOIS; 1 br.

Chase Manhattan Bank, NA (USA): Waterfront, Charlotte Amalie, POB 6620, VI 00801; tel. (340) 776-2222; Gen. Man. WARREN BEER; brs in St Croix and St John.

Citibank, NA (USA): Grand Hotel Bldg, 43–46 Norre Gade, POB 5167, Charlotte Amalie, VI 00801; tel. (340) 776-353; fax (340) 774-6609; Vice-Pres. KEVIN SZOT.

FirstBank of Puerto Rico: POB 3126, St Thomas, VI 00803; tel. (340) 774-2022; fax (340) 776-1313; acquired First Virgin Islands Federal Savings Bank in 2000; Pres. and CEO JAMES E. CRITES; 4 brs.

Virgin Islands Community Bank: 12–13 King St, Christiansted, St Croix, VI 00820; tel. (340) 773-0440; fax (340) 773-4028; Pres. and CEO MICHAEL J. DOW; 2 brs.

INSURANCE

A number of mainland US companies have agencies in the Virgin Islands.

Trade and Industry

GOVERNMENT AGENCY

US Virgin Islands Economic Development Commission: 1050 Norre Gade, Government Development Bank Bldg, 1050 Norre Gade, POB 305038, St Thomas, VI 00803; tel. (340) 774-8104; e-mail edc@usvieda.org; internet www.usvieda.org/idc; offices in St Thomas and St Croix.

CHAMBERS OF COMMERCE

St Croix Chamber of Commerce: 3009 Orange Grove, Suite 12, Christiansted, St Croix, VI 00820; tel. and fax (340) 773-1435; fax (340) 773-8172; e-mail info@stxchamber.org; f. 1924; Pres. DIANE BUTLER; Exec. Dir RACHEL HAINES; 250 mems.

St Thomas–St John Chamber of Commerce: POB 324, Charlotte Amalie, VI 00804; tel. (340) 776-0100; fax (340) 776-0588; e-mail chamber@islands.vi; internet www.usvichamber.com; Pres. THADDEUS BAST; Exec. Dir JOSEPH S. AUBAIN; c. 700 mems.

UTILITIES

Electricity

Virgin Islands Energy Office: 45 Mars Hill, Frederiksted, St Croix, VI 00840; tel. (340) 773-3450; e-mail vieo0441@viaccess.net; internet www.vienergy.org; Dir VICTOR SOMME, III.

Water

Virgin Islands Water and Power Authority (WAPA): POB 1450, Charlotte Amalie, VI 00804; tel. (340) 774-3552; fax (340) 774-3422; f. 1964; public corpn; manufactures and distributes electric power and desalinated sea water; Chair. DARYL 'MICKEY' LYNCH; Exec. Dir ALBERTO BRUNO-VEGA; c. 50,000 customers.

Transport

ROADS

The islands' road network totals approximately 855.5 km (531.6 miles). Throughout 2004 the Department of Public Works implemented a programme, valued at US $17.5m., to repair roads damaged in storms in November 2003.

SHIPPING

The US Virgin Islands are a popular port of call for cruise ships. The bulk of cargo traffic is handled at a container port on St Croix. A passenger and freight ferry service provides frequent daily connections between St Thomas and St John and between St Thomas and Tortola (British Virgin Islands); a service to Vieques (Puerto Rico) was also planned for 2006. In June 2004 the Port Authority approved a US $9.3m. project to expand freight, vehicle and passenger facilities at Red Hook.

Virgin Islands Port Authority: POB 301707, Charlotte Amalie, VI 00803; also at POB 1134, Christiansted, St Croix, VI 00821; tel. (340) 774-1629; fax (340) 774-0025; tel. (340) 778-1012; fax (340) 778-1033; e-mail info@viport.com; internet www.viport.com; f. 1968; semi-autonomous govt agency; maintains, operates and develops marine and airport facilities; Exec. Dir DARLAN BRIN.

CIVIL AVIATION

There are airports on St Thomas and St Croix, and an airfield on St John. Seaplane services link the three islands. The runways at Cyril E. King Airport, St Thomas, and Alexander Hamilton Airport, St Croix, can accommodate intercontinental flights.

Tourism

The islands have a well-developed tourism infrastructure, offering excellent facilities for fishing, yachting and other aquatic sports. A National Park covers about two-thirds of St John. There were 4,983 hotel rooms in 2004. In that year there were some 2,623,300 visitors to the islands, of whom 658,600 were tourists and 1,964,700 were cruise-ship passengers. Tourism expenditure increased from US $1,195.3m. in 2002 to $1,270.5m. in 2003.

St Croix Hotel Association: POB 24238, St Croix, VI 00824; tel. (340) 773-7117; fax (340) 773-5883.

St Thomas–St John Hotel and Tourism Association: POB 2300, Charlotte Amalie, VI 00803; tel. (340) 774-6835; fax (340) 774-4993; e-mail stsjhta@vipowernet.net; internet www.stsjhta.com; Pres. and Exec. Dir BEVERLY NICHOLSON.

OTHER UNITED STATES TERRITORIES

Baker and Howland Islands

The Baker and Howland Islands lie in the Central Pacific Ocean, about 2,575 km (1,600 miles) south-west of Honolulu, Hawaii; they comprise two low-lying coral atolls without lagoons, and are uninhabited. Both islands were mined for guano in the late 19th century. Settlements, known as Meyerton (on Baker) and Itascatown (on Howland), were established by the USA in 1935, but were evacuated during the Second World War, owing to Japanese air attacks. The islands are National Wildlife Refuges, and since 1974 have been administered by the US Fish and Wildlife Service. In 1990 legislation before Congress proposed that the islands be included within the boundaries of the State of Hawaii. The islands are administered by the US Department of the Interior, Department of Fish and Wildlife and Parks, 1849 C St, NW, Washington, DC 20240; tel. (202) 208-3171; fax (202) 208-6965; internet www.doi.gov.

Jarvis Island

Jarvis Island lies in the Central Pacific Ocean, about 2,090 km (1,300 miles) south of Hawaii. It is a low-lying coral island and is uninhabited. The island was mined for guano in the late 19th century. A settlement, known as Millersville, including a weather station for the benefit of trans-Pacific aviation, was established by the USA in 1935, but was evacuated during the Second World War. Legislation before Congress in 1990 proposed that the island be included within the State of Hawaii. The island is a National Wildlife Refuge and is administered by the US Department of the Interior, US Fish and Wildlife Service (details as above, under Baker and Howland Islands).

UNITED STATES EXTERNAL TERRITORIES   *Other United States Territories*

Johnston Atoll

Johnston Atoll lies in the Pacific Ocean, about 1,319 km (820 miles) west-south-west of Honolulu, Hawaii. It comprises Johnston Island, Sand Island (uninhabited) and two man-made islands, North (Akua) and East (Hikina); area 2.6 sq km (1 sq mile). Johnston Atoll was designated a Naval Defense Sea Area and Airspace Reservation in 1941, and is closed to public access. In 1985 construction of a chemical weapons disposal facility began on the atoll, and by 1990 it was fully operational. In 1989 the US Government agreed to remove artillery shells containing more than 400 metric tons of nerve gas from the Federal Republic of Germany, and destroy them on Johnston Island. In late 1991, following expressions of protest to the US Government by the nations of the South Pacific Forum (now Pacific Islands Forum, see p. 352), together with many environmental groups, a team of scientists visited the chemical disposal facility to monitor the safety and environmental impact of its activities. In May 1996 it was reported that all nerve gases stored on the atoll had been destroyed. However, 1,000 tons of chemical agents remained contained in landmines, bombs and missiles at the site. In December 2000 it was announced that the destruction of the remaining stock of chemical weapons had been completed (the original deadline for the destruction of 40,000 weapons stored on the island had been August 1995). The closure and decontamination of the facility was completed in 2004 and, in June of that year, all military personnel left and control of the Atoll was transferred to the US Fish and Wildlife Service, which has reported its intention eventually to create a nature reserve on the atoll. In March 2005 the Department of Defense announced the termination of the Air Force mission in Johnston Atoll. A facility capable of performing atmospheric tests of nuclear weapons remains operational on the atoll. The atoll had an estimated population of 173 in 1990, although this increased to approximately 1,000, mainly military, personnel during weapons disposal operations in previous years. Johnston Atoll falls under the jurisdiction of the Department of the Interior, US Fish and Wildlife Service (details as above, under Baker and Howland Islands). Operational control is the responsibility of the Defense Threat Reduction Agency (DTRA), Office of the General Counsel, 6801 Telegraph Rd, Room 109, Alexandria, VA 22310-3398; tel. (703) 325-7681. Permission to land on Johnston Island must be obtained from the DTRA. The residing military commander of Johnston Island acts as the agent for the DTRA.

Kingman Reef

Kingman Reef lies in the Pacific Ocean, about 1,500 km (925 miles) south-west of Hawaii, and comprises a reef and shoal measuring about 8 km (5 miles) by 15 km (9.5 miles). In 2000 administrative control was transferred from the US Navy to the Department of the Interior. In 2001 the waters around the reef were designated a National Wildlife Refuge, under the jurisdiction of the US Fish and Wildlife Service (details as above, under Baker and Howland Islands).

Midway Atoll

Midway Atoll lies in the northern Pacific Ocean, about 1,850 km (1,150 miles) north-west of Hawaii. A coral atoll, it comprises Sand Island, Eastern Island and several small islets within the reef, has a total area of about 5 sq km (2 sq miles) and a population 2,200 in 1983, although by 1990 this had declined to 13. Since the transfer of the islands' administration from the US Department of Defense to the Department of the Interior in October 1996, limited tourism is permitted. There is a National Wildlife Refuge on the Territory, which is home to many species of birds. Legislation before Congress in 1990 proposed the inclusion of the Territory within the State of Hawaii. The islands are administered by the US Department of the Interior, US Fish and Wildlife Service (details as above, under Baker and Howland Islands).

Navassa Island

Navassa Island lies in the Caribbean Sea, about 160 km (100 miles) south of Guantánamo Bay, Cuba, and 65 km (40 miles) west of Haiti. It is a raised coral island with a limestone plateau and has an area of 5.2 sq km (2 sq miles). The island is uninhabited. Navassa became a US Insular Area in 1857, and was mined throughout the late 19th century, under the Navassa Phosphate Co. All mining activities were terminated in 1898. In 1996 the US Coast Guard ceased operations of the island's lighthouse, and in January 1997 the Office of Insular Affairs (under the control of the US Department of the Interior) assumed control of the island. A research expedition undertaken in mid-1998 revealed the presence of numerous undiscovered plant and animal species, many of which were thought to be unique to the island. Visits to the island and its surrounding waters were subsequently prohibited, pending further assessment of the island's environment. In December 1999 administrative responsibility for Navassa passed wholly to the US Department of the Interior, US Fish and Wildlife Service (details as above, under Baker and Howland Islands); however, control over political matters was retained by the Office of Insular Affairs.

Palmyra

Palmyra lies in the Pacific Ocean, about 1,600 km (1,000 miles) south of Honolulu, Hawaii. It comprises some 50 low-lying islets, has a total area of 100 ha, is uninhabited and is privately owned. Since 1961 the Territory has been administered by the US Department of the Interior. In 1990 legislation before Congress proposed the inclusion of Palmyra within the boundaries of the State of Hawaii. In mid-1996 it was announced that the owners (the Fullard-Leo family in Hawaii) were to sell the atoll to a US company, which, it was believed, planned to establish a nuclear waste storage facility in the Territory. The Government of neighbouring Kiribati expressed alarm at the proposal, and reiterated its intention to seek the reinclusion of the atoll within its own national boundaries. However, in June one of the Hawaiian Representatives to the US Congress proposed legislation in the US House of Representatives to prevent the establishment of such a facility, and a US government official subsequently announced that the atoll would almost certainly not be used for that purpose. Palmyra was purchased by The Nature Conservancy (internet www.tnc.org) in December 2000. Designated a National Wildlife Refuge, the lagoons and surrounding waters within the 12 nautical mile zone of US territorial seas were transferred to the US Fish and Wildlife Service (details as above, under Baker and Howland Islands) in January 2001; the US Fish and Wildlife Service subsequently undertook negotiations to purchase part of the 680 acres of emergent lands owned by The Nature Conservancy.

Wake Island

Wake Island lies in the Pacific Ocean, about 2,060 km (1,280 miles) east of Guam. It is a coral atoll comprising the three islets of Wake, Wilkes and Peale, with an area less than 8 sq km (3 sq miles) and a population estimated to be almost 2,000 in 1988. Legislation before Congress in 1990 proposed the inclusion of the islands within the Territory of Guam. However, the Republic of the Marshall Islands, some 500 km (310 miles) south of Wake, exerted its own claim to the atoll (called Enenkio by the Micronesians), which is a site of great importance for the islands' traditional chiefly rituals. Plans by a US company, announced in 1998, to establish a large-scale nuclear waste storage facility on the atoll were condemned by environmentalists and politicians in the region. Since 1972 the group has been administered by the US Department of Defense, Department of the Air Force (Pacific/East Asia Division), The Pentagon, Washington, DC 20330; tel. (202) 694-6061; fax (703) 696-7273; internet www.af.mil.

URUGUAY

Introductory Survey

Location, Climate, Language, Religion, Flag, Capital

The Eastern Republic of Uruguay lies on the south-east coast of South America, with Brazil to the north and Argentina to the west. The climate is temperate, with an average temperature of 14°C–16°C (57°F–61°F) in winter and 21°C–28°C (70°F–82°F) in summer. The language is Spanish. There is no state religion but Roman Catholicism is predominant. The national flag (proportions 2 by 3) has nine horizontal stripes (five white and four blue, alternating), with a square white canton, containing a yellow sun with 16 alternating straight and wavy rays, in the upper hoist. The capital is Montevideo.

Recent History

Since independence from Spain, gained in 1825, domestic politics in Uruguay traditionally has been dominated by two parties: the Colorados ('reds' or Liberals) and the Blancos ('whites' or Conservatives, subsequently also known as the Partido Nacional). Their rivalry resulted in frequent outbreaks of civil war in the 19th century: the names derive from the flags of the 1836 civil war. From 1880 to 1958 the governing Partido Colorado was led by the Batlle family. Owing to the progressive policies of José Batlle y Ordóñez, Colorado President in 1903–07 and in 1911–15, Uruguay became the first welfare state in Latin America. During 1951–66 the presidency was in abeyance, being replaced by a collective leadership.

In December 1967 Jorge Pacheco Areco assumed the presidency. His period in office was notable for massive increases in the cost of living, labour unrest and the spectacular exploits of the Tupamaro urban guerrilla movement. In March 1972 Pacheco was succeeded by Juan María Bordaberry Arocena, a Colorado, who won the presidential election in November 1971. The army took complete control of the campaign against the Tupamaros, and by late 1973 had suppressed the movement. Military intervention in civilian affairs led, in 1973, to the closure of the Congreso and its replacement by an appointed 25-member Council of State (subsequently increased to 35 members). The Partido Comunista and other left-wing groups were banned; repressive measures, including strict press censorship, continued. In September 1974 army officers were placed in control of the major state-owned enterprises.

President Bordaberry was deposed by the army in June 1976 because of his refusal to countenance any return, however gradual, to constitutional rule. In July the recently formed Council of the Nation elected Dr Aparicio Méndez Manfredini to the presidency for five years. Despite the Government's announcement that there would be a return to democracy, persecution of political figures continued, and the number of political prisoners held in 1976 was thought to have reached 6,000.

President Méndez introduced constitutional amendments, known as Institutional Acts, to consolidate the internal situation and to create a 'new order'. By 1980 severe economic problems made the army anxious to return executive responsibility to civilian politicians. A new constitution, under which the armed forces would continue to be involved in all matters of national security, was drafted and submitted to a plebiscite in November 1980, but was rejected by 58% of voters. The military leadership was therefore forced to amend the draft document in consultation with leaders of the recognized political parties, and, in September 1981, a retired army general, Gregorio Alvarez Armellino, was appointed by the Joint Council of the Armed Forces to serve as President during the transition period to full civilian government.

The Government's reluctance to permit greater public freedom and to improve observance of human rights caused serious unrest throughout 1983. Popular discontent was further aroused by the rapid deterioration of the economy and by the effect of events in Argentina. In August the authorities suspended all public political activity and reserved the right to impose a new constitution without consultation, insisting, however, that the original electoral timetable would be maintained. The political opposition responded by threatening to boycott the elections and by uniting with proscribed opposition groups to hold a national day of protest. In September the first organized labour protest for 10 years was supported by 500,000 workers.

Political agitation increased during 1984, and the Government threatened to postpone the elections, planned for 25 November, unless the political parties agreed to its proposals for constitutional reform. Tensions increased in June, following the return from exile and the subsequent arrest of Ferreira Aldunate, the proposed presidential candidate of the Partido Nacional. Talks between the Government, the Partido Colorado and the Unión Cívica (a Christian democratic party) resumed in July; the parties obtained several important concessions, including the right to engage in political activity. In August, encouraged by the Government's commitment to the restoration of the democratic process, the parties (with the exception of the Partido Nacional) agreed to the Government's proposals. The Government confirmed that elections would take place, and all restrictions on political activity were withdrawn.

At elections in November 1984 the Partido Colorado, led by Dr Julio María Sanguinetti Cairolo, secured a narrow victory over the opposition. In February 1985 the military regime relinquished power, one month earlier than originally planned. President Sanguinetti was inaugurated on 1 March, as was a Government of national unity, incorporating representatives of the other parties. Concurrently, various outlawed organizations, including the Partido Comunista, were legalized. All political prisoners were released under an amnesty law later in the month.

The new Government announced its commitment to reversing the economic recession; however, its efforts to address the crisis were hampered by frequent industrial stoppages. Discussions between the administration and trade union and business leaders began in August 1985. Although the Government suspended negotiations following another series of strikes, discussions were resumed in September.

A major political issue in 1986 was the investigation into alleged violations of human rights by the armed forces during the military dictatorship. In August the Government proposed legislation that would offer an amnesty for all military and police personnel accused of this type of crime, in accordance with a pact made with the armed forces that human rights trials would not take place. In October the draft legislation was rejected by opposition parties, but in December a revised law (the Ley de Caducidad, or Statute of Limitations Law) was approved, which brought an end to current military trials and made the President responsible for any further investigations. The law was widely opposed and in February 1987 a campaign was initiated to organize a petition containing the signatures of at least 25% of the registered electorate, as required by the Constitution, in order to force a referendum on the issue. The campaign was supported principally by human rights groups, trade unions and the centre-left coalition, the Frente Amplio (FA). A referendum duly took place in April 1989, at which a total of 53% of the votes were cast in favour of maintaining the amnesty law.

The presidential and legislative elections in November 1989 resulted in victory (for the first time since 1962) for the Partido Nacional. In the presidential election, Luis Alberto Lacalle, the party's main candidate (the electoral code permitted each party to present more than one candidate), received 37% of the votes, while his closest rival, Jorge Batlle Ibáñez of the Partido Colorado, won 30%. However, the Partido Nacional failed to obtain an overall majority in Congress, thus compelling the President-elect to seek support from a wider political base. Immediately before taking office, in March 1990, he announced the conclusion of an agreement, the 'coincidencia nacional', between the two principal parties, whereby the Partido Colorado undertook to support proposed legislation on economic reform, in return for the appointment of four of its members to the Council of Ministers.

Labour unrest intensified during the early 1990s. The trade union confederation, the Plenario Intersindical de Trabajadores—Convención Nacional de Trabajadores (PIT—CNT), organized a series of general strikes in support of demands for wage increases and in opposition to government austerity measures and privatization plans. Opposition from within the ruling coalition to the planned sale of state enterprises became apparent in May 1991, when former President Sanguinetti, the leader of the Foro Batllista faction of the Partido Colorado, withdrew his support from the Government, thus forcing the resignation of the Minister of Public Health, the faction's sole representative in the Council of Ministers. Reservations were also expressed by elements of the Partido Nacional. In September, none the less, the privatization legislation was narrowly approved by the Congreso. In response, the opposition FA, with the support of another political organization, Nuevo Espacio, and the trade unions, began a campaign to overrule the legislature by way of a referendum. In October 1992, in a special poll, some 30% of the electorate voted for a full referendum to be held on the partial amendment of the Government's privatization legislation. At the referendum, held in December, 72% of voters supported the proposal for a partial repeal of the legislation. The vote was also widely recognized as a vote of censure against the President's economic policy, and in particular his determination to keep public-sector wage increases to a minimum. While the result of the referendum did not affect all planned divestments, it was considered to be a serious reverse and served to undermine confidence in government economic policy. Notwithstanding, President Lacalle indicated that he would continue to pursue the privatization programme.

Industrial unrest in the public sector intensified in 1992, owing primarily to the Government's refusal to grant wage increases in line with inflation. In November, however, following a four-day strike by the police, the Government was forced to concede wage increases of up to 50% to the security forces. Encouraged by this concession, transport and public health workers initiated strikes in support of demands for wage increases.

The presidential and legislative elections of 27 November 1994 were notable for the emergence of a third political force to rival the traditional powers of the Partido Nacional and the Partido Colorado. The Encuentro Progresista (EP)—a predominantly left-wing alliance principally comprising the parties of the FA, as well as dissidents of the Partido Nacional and other minor parties—secured 31% of the votes, as did the Partido Nacional, while the Partido Colorado won a narrow victory with 33% of the vote. Subsequently, the leading presidential candidate of the Partido Colorado, Sanguinetti, was pronounced President-elect. Sanguinetti indicated that he planned to appoint a broadly based Council of Ministers in order to ensure legislative support for his administration. Two plebiscites, concerning education and social security, were conducted concurrently with the presidential and legislative elections. The education proposal, which was promoted by the teachers' unions, sought to have 27% of the national budget allocated to education. The social security proposal, which was supported by pensioners' organizations, sought the repeal of social security legislation enacted under the Lacalle administration. The education proposal was rejected by the electorate, while the social security proposal received approval. A resolution of the latter issue was later identified by the Sanguinetti administration as its main priority.

In early 1995, following talks with opposition parties, the Partido Colorado established a 'governability pact' with the Partido Nacional, providing for a coalition Government. The Council of Ministers contained six members of the Partido Colorado, four from the Partido Nacional, one Unión Cívica member, and one representative from the Partido por el Gobierno del Pueblo (Lista 99), which had contested the elections in alliance with Sanguinetti's Foro Batllista faction of the Partido Colorado, and whose leader, Hugo Batalla, had been elected as Sanguinetti's Vice-President.

Despite popular opposition and resistance in the legislature from the FA, the proposed legislation to restructure the social security system was approved in August 1995. The measure provided for the introduction of a mixed public and private pension scheme, replacing the supposedly unsustainable system of state provision whereby the contributions of those in employment financed payments to current pensioners. The reform of the social security system, which provided for a gradual increase in the retirement age and introduced compulsory personal savings plans for those earning more than 5,000 pesos per month, aimed to eliminate the system's structural deficit within 10 years.

In July 1995 the Government and the legislative opposition reached an agreement providing for the reform of the electoral system. Under the existing system, known as the Ley de Lemas, parties were permitted to present more than one presidential candidate, with the leading candidate in each party assuming the total number of votes for candidates in that party. According to the proposed reform, each party would present one candidate, selected by means of an internal election, and, in the event of no candidate securing an absolute majority, a second round of voting would be conducted. In March 1996 draft legislation for the reform was submitted to the legislature. However, certain details of the bill were opposed by elements of the FA. In February Gen. (retd) Líber Seregni Mosquera resigned as President of the FA, owing to the party's inability to reach a consensus on the issue; members of the Partido Comunista, the Partido Socialista del Uruguay and the Movimiento de Liberación Nacional—Tupamaros opposed the proposal providing for a second round of presidential elections, which, they contended, would allow supporters of the Partido Nacional and the Partido Colorado to unite in order to deny the presidency to the FA. Supporters of Seregni preferred to endorse the proposal and thereby ensure the abolition of the prevailing multi-candidate system.

In October 1996 President Sanguinetti secured the necessary two-thirds' support in the legislature for the reform of the Constitution. Besides abolishing the Ley de Lemas and introducing provision for second-round presidential elections (see above), the reform also accorded greater autonomy to municipal administrations, and established a framework for environmental protection. The amendments were approved by 51% of voters in a plebiscite held in December, and came into effect in January 1997.

In May 1997 some 20,000 civilians staged a rally in the capital to demand that the Government and the armed forces provide information on the whereabouts of as many as 140 people who had 'disappeared' during the military dictatorship. In December President Sanguinetti issued a decree that granted an amnesty to 41 former army officers who had been dismissed from service during the dictatorship, owing to their political beliefs. Lt-Gen. Raúl Mermot, the Commander-in-Chief of the Armed Forces, resigned from his post one month ahead of schedule, in protest at the decision. In May 1999 some 15,000 people participated in a further march in support of demands that the authorities account for the disappearance of friends and relatives during the military dictatorship.

In late April 1999, in the first primary elections to be held in Uruguay, Lacalle, Batlle and Tabaré Ramón Vázquez Rosas were selected as the presidential candidates for the Partido Nacional, the Partido Colorado and the EP (subsequently known as Encuentro Progresista—Frente Amplio, EP—FA), respectively. Vázquez, a former mayor of Montevideo, won a particularly convincing victory, securing 82% of the votes of his party's supporters, while Batlle defeated Sanguinetti's favoured candidate, Luis Hierro López, who was later nominated as the Partido Colorado's candidate for the vice-presidency.

The presidential and legislative elections of 31 October 1999 confirmed the end of the traditional dominance of the Partido Colorado and the Partido Nacional. The EP—FA became the largest single party in both the Cámara de Representantes and the Cámara de Senadores, winning 40 and 12 seats, respectively. The Partido Colorado largely maintained its representation, securing 33 and 10 seats, while support for the Partido Nacional declined considerably, with the party winning only 22 seats in the lower house and seven in the Cámara de Senadores, having held a combined total of 41 seats in the outgoing legislature. Vázquez gained 39% of the vote, compared with 31% for Batlle and 21% for Lacalle. Despite the convincing success of the EP—FA in the first round, Jorge Batlle defeated Vázquez in a second round of voting on 28 November, with 52% of the vote, aided by the support of the Partido Nacional (under a formal accord). Following his inauguration on 1 March 2000, President Batlle appointed a new Council of Ministers, allocating eight portfolios to the Partido Colorado and five to the Partido Nacional.

In early 2000 Batlle held several meetings with Vázquez, in an apparent attempt to achieve a degree of rapprochement with the left, and also committed himself to resolving the issue of the 'disappeared', in marked contrast to his predecessor, Sanguinetti, who had consistently resisted pressure to investigate their fate. In April 2000 Batlle dismissed Gen. Manuel Fernández, one of the country's most senior army officials, after he sought to justify the military repression of the 1970s. In August Batlle announced the formation of a commission, composed of representatives from the Government, the opposition, the Church and the victims' families, to investigate the fate of 164 people who 'disappeared' during the military dictatorship. The unexpected dismissal in January 2001 of Gen. Juan Geymonat, Commander-in-Chief of the Armed Forces, was interpreted as a first step in a military reform programme advocated by Batlle. In late October 2002 the Commission reported its preliminary findings that 26 of the 33 'disappeared' Uruguayan citizens under its investigation had been murdered by Argentine and Uruguayan military officers.

Against a background of ongoing economic recession, the Battle administration encountered opposition to its policies from organized labour groups from 1999. In June 2000 a general strike was organized by the PIT—CNT to demand increased action on unemployment and more finance for education and health care, as well as to protest against emergency legislation, passed that month, which would allow the partial privatization of some public services, including the railways and the ports. A more widespread strike was held in December to protest at the same issues. However, an attempt by the EP—FA to force a referendum on the controversial law in February 2001 failed, owing to a lack of public support.

The financial crisis in neighbouring Argentina of December 2001–January 2002 caused additional economic hardship in Uruguay, with continued rural unrest and political and trade-union opposition to the austerity measures introduced by the Government. There was an unprecedented rise in street violence and organized crime, along with accelerated rates of emigration. In May the Argentine Government's imposition of severe restrictions on bank withdrawals prompted many Argentine citizens holding assets in Uruguay to access their funds, precipitating a crisis in Uruguay's financial system. In late June the Government was forced to abandon exchange rate controls in order to maintain the peso uruguayo's competitiveness against the devalued Argentine and Brazilian currencies. However, by late July, following a 30% decline in the peso's value in relation to the US dollar, and amid rising concerns over the viability and transparency of the banking sector, substantial numbers of Uruguayans also began to withdraw their deposits. In an attempt to avert a financial collapse, the Government instructed all banking institutions in Uruguay to close for a period of four days and introduced emergency economic measures, which included an increase in taxation on salaries and pensions. Moreover, three state-owned banks were placed under direct government administration, and restrictions were imposed on their customers' access to long-term foreign exchange deposits. The Government successfully sought an immediate loan of US $1,500m. from the USA to prevent a severe deterioration in international reserves and in November agreement was reached with the IMF on stand-by loans totalling some $2,800m., to be disbursed in 2002 and 2003. Nevertheless, as a result of the financial crisis, in late July Alberto Bensión, the Minister of Economy and Finance, was forced to resign, having lost the support of the Partido Nacional. He was succeeded by Alejandro Atchugarry, a prominent member of the Partido Colorado.

The financial crisis, as well as popular resentment towards the Government's economic strategy and unprecedentedly high levels of unemployment in mid-2002 led to a greater willingness within the Partido Nacional to reconsider its association with the Partido Colorado. In November the Partido Nacional terminated discussions on a new 'governability pact' between the two parties, removed its five ministers from the Government and withdrew from the ruling coalition, leaving the FA as the largest political bloc in the Congreso. President Batlle subsequently appointed non-partisan ministers to the vacant posts and a limited rationalization of ministries was effected.

In November 2002 it was announced that the three suspended state-run banks were to be merged into one: in March 2003 the Nuevo Banco Comercial began operations (see Economic Affairs). The incorporation of the new bank coincided with the resumption of IMF disbursements, suspended in November owing to the Government's perceived lack of progress on the restructuring of the banking sector. (In January 2005 the International Court of Arbitration of the International Chamber of Commerce (ICC, see p. 288) ruled that Uruguay must pay US $100m., in addition to legal expenses and accrued interest, to foreign investors in the liquidated Banco Comercial.)

In August 2003 a series of strikes were held by public-sector workers to protest at the Government's reform programme, in particular, plans to increase private-sector participation in the economy. In June the EP—FA succeeded in gaining parliamentary approval for a referendum to be held on the proposed partial privatization of the state-run oil, cement and alcohol monopoly, ANCAP (Administración Nacional de Combustible, Alcohol y Portland). In the referendum, held on 7 December, some 62% voted to repeal the controversial legislation. The high level of opposition to the law was widely interpreted as a further expression of public dissatisfaction with the Batlle administration. Furthermore, the EP—FA pledged to maintain state control of public utilities if successful in the upcoming presidential and legislative elections of 2004.

At the presidential election that was held on 31 October 2004, Tabaré Ramón Vázquez Rosas, the candidate of the EP—FA, won the presidency in the first round of voting, with 50.70% of the ballot. His nearest rival, Jorge Larrañaga, the candidate of the Partido Nacional, obtained some 34.06% of votes, while the Partido Colorado's nominee, Guillermo Stirling, attracted 10.32% of the votes cast. The EP—FA coalition also made gains in the concurrent legislative elections, winning a majority in both chambers of the legislature, with 16 of the 30 seats of the Senado and 52 of the 99 seats of the Cámara de Representantes. By contrast, the Partido Colorado's legislative representation fell sharply: from 33 to 10 seats in the lower house, and from 10 to just three seats in the Senado. The Partido Nacional became the second largest party in both chambers, winning a total of 35 seats in the Cámara de Representantes and 11 seats in the Senado. The EP—FA's electoral campaign had centred on pledges to increase social spending dramatically, to reform radically the tax and pension systems, and to retain state control over utilities and services.

Also on 31 October 2004, a referendum was held over a proposal that the water industry remain under state control. The proposal was supported by the EP—FA, but opposed by the incumbent Colorado administration. In the poll, 64.5% of those voting were in favour of the water sector remaining under state control. However, following the result of the ballot, the outgoing Colorado Government propounded that all private-sector contracts in the water industry be rescinded in order to achieve full nationalization, a proposal that was opposed by President-elect Vázquez.

In mid-November 2004 Larrañaga (who was also the leader of the Alianza Nacional faction of the Partido Nacional) and Sanguinetti, leader of the Foro Battlista tendency within the Partido Colorado, indicated that neither the Partido Nacional nor the Partido Colorado would participate in the incoming Government; however, in early February 2005 it was announced that the new administration would receive cross-party support for its economic policies (in addition to the support already pledged for its policies on education and foreign affairs). President Vázquez, who took office on 1 March, notably appointed Danilo Astori of the Asamblea Uruguay as Minister of Economy and Finance. The appointment of Astori, an orthodox economist on the right-wing of the EP—FA, was widely interpreted as an attempt to strengthen investor confidence in a broadly left-wing administration.

An immediate priority of the new Governmnent was to eradicate poverty; to this end, on 2 March 2005 President Vázquez announced the Plan de Atención Nacional de Emergencia Social, a programme of social spending, expected to total some US $200m. over two years. The following day the new Minister of National Defence, Azucena Berruti (a former human rights lawyer), announced that the Government had begun investigations into the 'disappearances' that occurred during the years of military rule. In August the heads of Uruguay's armed forces submitted to the President a report admitting the kidnap, torture and murder of political dissidents, and purportedly detailing the whereabouts of their remains. Information in the report led to the exhumation in November of the bodies of two dissidents murdered by members of the air force. Earlier that month President Vásquez had proposed legislation seeking to amend the Ley de Caducidad (see above) in order to facilitate prosecution of members of the military for human rights abuses committed during military rule. In December 35 unidentified corpses were exhumed from a cemetery in a town near the Brazilian border.

Meanwhile, in mid-March 2005 both the Partido Nacional and the Partido Colorado withdrew their support for the Government's economic policies in protest at their allocation of positions on the governing bodies of state banks, companies and quasi-autonomous agencies, which, they considered, fell short of the number traditionally allocated to members of the opposition. At municipal elections, held on 8 May, the ruling EP—FA won control of eight of the 19 departments, having only held Montevideo hitherto. The Partido Nacional retained 10 departments, but lost three, while the Partido Colorado only retained one.

Following a summit conference in Paraguay in March 1991, the Governments of Argentina, Brazil, Paraguay and Uruguay agreed to create a common market of the 'Southern Cone' countries, the Mercado Común del Sur (Mercosur, see p. 363). The Treaty of Asunción allowed for the dismantling of trade barriers between the four countries, and entered full operation in 1995. However, in February 2002, following the drastic reduction in exports to other Mercosur member states as a result of the devaluation of the Argentine peso at the beginning of that year, President Batlle declared that Uruguay would begin bilateral free trade negotiations with the USA. In January 2006 it was reported that the Government believed Uruguay's interests were not always best served within Mercosur and that, consequently, it would seek negotiations with the USA on a bilateral free trade agreement. However, in March the US Department of State declared that the US Government had no plans to negotiate such an agreement with Uruguay. A series of trade agreements between Chile and overseas nations in 2002 and 2003 also prompted Uruguay to seek international commercial agreements on a unilateral basis.

In April 2002 Uruguay severed diplomatic relations with Cuba, citing insults by the Cuban Government after Uruguay sponsored a motion, which was passed by the UN Human Rights Commission, calling on Cuba to improve its civil and political rights record. Diplomatic relations were restored, however, following the inauguration of the Vázquez administration in March 2005.

Relations with Argentina were strained from April 2005, when a Finnish company began construction in Uruguay of a cellulose plant near the River Uruguay, which separates the two countries. The Argentine Government expressed concerns over the environmental impact of this plant and of a further mill scheduled to be built nearby. The two plants were expected to generate some US $1,800m. of investment in Uruguay. (Construction of a third plant, to be built by a Swedish-Finnish company at a cost of some $1,250m., was under consideration in early 2006.) In January 2006 Argentine demonstrators blocked passage across the three bridges spanning the river in protests that were tolerated by the Argentine authorities, drawing condemnation from the Uruguayan Government. Furthermore, in March reports appeared in Argentine media suggesting that Uruguayan officials had been bribed to approve the plants' construction; the Government denied the accusations. Construction of the mills was suspended in mid-March, in return for the Argentine authorities' agreement to reopen passage across the bridges. A meeting on the issue, scheduled for later that month, between the two countries' Presidents was cancelled, however, in the absence of any preliminary agreements.

Government

Uruguay is a republic comprising 19 departments. Under the 1966 Constitution, executive power is held by the President, who is directly elected by universal adult suffrage for a five-year term. The President is assisted by the Vice-President and the appointed Council of Ministers. Legislative power is vested in the bicameral Congreso, comprising the Cámara de Senadores (Senate) and the Cámara de Representantes (Chamber of Representatives), also directly elected for five years. The President, the Vice-President, the Senators (who number 31, including the Vice-President, who is automatically allocated a seat as President of the Cámara de Senadores) and the 99 Deputies are elected nationally.

Defence

In August 2005 Uruguay's active armed forces comprised an army of 15,200, a navy of 5,700 and an air force of 3,100. Paramilitary forces numbered 920 men. Defence expenditure in 2005 was budgeted at some 4,000m. pesos uruguayos.

Economic Affairs

In 2004, according to estimates by the World Bank, Uruguay's gross national income (GNI), measured at average 2002–04 prices, was US $13,414.3m., equivalent to $3,950 per head (or $9,070 per head on an international purchasing-power parity basis). During 1995–2004, it was estimated, the population increased by an annual average of 0.6%, while gross domestic product (GDP) per head increased, in real terms, by an annual average of 0.4% per year. According to preliminary figures, overall GDP increased, in real terms, at an average annual rate of 1.0% in 1995–2004; GDP increased by 12.3% in 2004.

Agriculture (including forestry and fishing) contributed a preliminary 11.4% of GDP in 2004. Some 4.5% of the active labour force were employed in the sector in 2003. The principal crops are rice, sugar cane, wheat, barley, potatoes, sorghum and maize. Livestock-rearing, particularly sheep and cattle, is traditionally Uruguay's major economic activity. Live animals and animal derivatives provided an estimated 36.0% of export revenues in 2005, while exports of skins and hides provided a further estimated 8.3% in the same year. According to preliminary figures, agricultural GDP increased by an annual average of 1.9% per year in 1995–2004. Agricultural GDP increased by 10.6% in 2003 and by a further 12.8% in 2004.

Industry (including mining, manufacturing, construction and power) contributed a preliminary 28.5% of GDP in 2004, and employed 21.5% of the working population in 2003. According to preliminary figures, industrial GDP increased by an annual average of 0.2% in 1995–2004; industrial GDP increased by a preliminary 0.9% in 2003 and by a dramatic 16.1% in 2004.

Uruguay has few mineral resources and no proven hydrocarbon reserves. Accordingly, mining and quarrying only contributed a preliminary 0.2% of GDP in 2004, and employed 0.1% of the working population in 2003. Apart from the small-scale extraction of building materials, industrial minerals and semi-precious stones, there has been little mining activity, although gold deposits are currently being developed. According to preliminary figures, the GDP of the mining sector increased by an annual average of 0.6% in 1995–2004; mining GDP increased by an estimated 14.1% in 2003 and by a further estimated 7.2% in 2004.

Manufacturing contributed a preliminary 20.6% of GDP in 2004 and employed 14.6% of the working population in 2003. The principal branches of manufacturing were food products, beverages and tobacco, chemicals, metal products, machinery and equipment, and textiles, clothing and leather products. According to preliminary figures, manufacturing GDP decreased by an annual average of 0.3% in 1995–2004. However, manufacturing GDP increased by an estimated 4.7% in 2003 and by an impressive estimated 21.6% in 2004.

Energy is derived principally from hydroelectric power (82.1% of total electricity production in 2004). The first natural gas pipeline between Uruguay and Argentina, with an operating capacity of 4.9m. cu ft per day, began operating in late 1998. A second natural gas pipeline between Uruguay and Argentina, the Gasoducto Cruz del Sur (GCDS—Southern Cross pipeline), with a transportation capacity of 180m. cu ft per day, was completed in 2002. In early 2006 plans were under consideration for a possible extension of the GCDS to reach Porto Alegre, Brazil. Imports of mineral products (including fuels) comprised 22.9% of the value of total imports in 2003. In August 2005 the Venezuelan President, Lt-Col (retd) Hugo Rafael Chávez Frías, agreed to supply Uruguay with petroleum on preferential terms for the next 25 years.

The services sector contributed a preliminary 60.0% of GDP in 2004, and engaged 73.9% of the working population in 2003. Tourism is a significant source of foreign exchange, earning US $406m. in 2003. The GDP of the services sector increased by an annual average of 1.4% in 1995–2004, according to preliminary figures. The GDP of the services sector decreased by an estimated 1.6% in 2003, but increased by an estimated 6.0% in 2004.

In 2004 Uruguay recorded an estimated visible trade surplus of US $31.1m., and there was a deficit of $102.9m. on the current account of the balance of payments. In 2005 the principal source of imports was, according to preliminary figures, Brazil (21.3%); other major suppliers were Argentina (20.3%), Venezuela (6.3%) and the People's Republic of China (6.2%). The USA was the principal market for exports (22.4%) in that year; other major recipients were Brazil (13.5%) and Argentina (7.8%). The main exports in 2005 were, according to preliminary figures, live animals and animal products, and plants and their products. The principal imports in that year were petroleum and distillates, machinery and transport equipment, and other consumer goods.

In 2003 there was a budgetary deficit of 23,831m. pesos uruguayos, equivalent to some 7.5% of GDP. At the end of 2003 Uruguay's total external debt was US $11,764m., of which $7,430m. was long-term public debt. In that year the cost of debt-servicing was equivalent to 26.3% of the value of exports of goods and services. The average annual rate of inflation was 12.7% in 1995–2004. Consumer prices increased by 19.4% in 2003 and by a further 9.2% in 2004. An estimated average of 12.1% of the urban labour force were unemployed in 2005.

Uruguay is a member of the Inter-American Development Bank (IDB, see p. 284), the Asociación Latinoamericana de Integración (ALADI, see p. 305), the Sistema Económico Latinoamericano (SELA, see p. 386) and the Mercado Común del Sur (Mercosur, see p. 363). In December 2004 Uruguay was one of 12 countries that were signatories to the agreement, signed in Cusco, Peru, creating the South American Community of Nations (Comunidad Sudamericana de Naciones), intended to promote greater regional economic integration, due to become operational by 2007.

The recession experienced in Uruguay in 1999–2002 was largely precipitated by external factors, notably the negative impact of the economic crisis in Argentina and Brazil, the devaluation of the Brazilian currency at the beginning of 1999 and low world prices for its principal export products. In January 2002, in response to the financial crisis in Argentina, which adversely affected Uruguay's exports, as well as its tourism industry, the Government announced a plan to reduce the fiscal deficit by increasing taxes and selling off some state-owned real estate (although progress on privatization subsequently stalled). In March the IMF approved a new stand-by credit worth about US $743m.; the programme was extended by a further year in March 2003. In the wake of the crisis in the banking sector in mid-2002 (see Recent History), new legislation was introduced in 2003 enhancing the supervisory powers of the Central Bank and reforming state-controlled lending. In May the Government also successfully issued new bonds to restructure its short-term external debt. In the same month the World Bank disbursed further loans, totalling $252m., intended to finance infrastructure and social-welfare projects. The funds were to complement assistance from the IDB, which had pledged some $160m., in addition to finance from other international financial institutions. Uruguay's economy finally registered growth, of 2.4%, in 2003. In 2004 the recovery continued, with growth estimated at an impressive 12.3%, owing primarily to improved export prices, banking-sector reforms and increased industrial output (by some 22%). However, the level of public debt remained very high, equivalent to some 90% of GDP. The economic priorities of the Government of Tabaré Vázquez, which took office in March 2005, included a dramatic increase in social welfare expenditure. This was partly to be funded by sustained economic growth and increased foreign investment, as well as by a radical reform of the taxation system. In February 2005 the IMF, on completion of its seventh and final review of Uruguay's stand-by arrangement, approved a final disbursement of $213.8m. A new stand-by arrangement with the IMF worth some $1,110m. was agreed in June, with positive reviews in September and in January and March 2006 leading to further disbursements (of $44.4m., $44.3m. and $123.6m., respectively). However, introduction of legislation that was a condition of the IMF arrangement, which included financial reform, increased private-sector participation and fiscal prudence, would meet with opposition from many in the ruling left-wing coalition. Owing primarily to increased industrial output, economic expansion of 6.5% was estimated in 2005, with further growth, of 3.7%, forecast for 2006.

Education

All education, including university tuition, is provided free of charge. Education is officially compulsory for six years between six and 14 years of age. Primary education begins at the age of six and lasts for six years. Secondary education, beginning at 12 years of age, lasts for a further six years, comprising two cycles of three years each. In 1996 the total enrolment at primary and secondary schools was equivalent to 97% of the school-age population. In that year primary enrolment included 93% of children in the relevant age-group (males 92%; females 93%), while secondary enrolment was equivalent to 85% of the population in the appropriate age-group (males 77%; females 92%). The programmes of instruction are the same in both public and private schools, and private schools are subject to certain state controls. There were six universities in 2003. Central government expenditure on education in that year was 10,558m. pesos uruguayos (11.8% of central government spending).

Public Holidays

2006: 1 January (New Year's Day), 6 January (Epiphany), 10–14 April (Holy Week), 19 April (Landing of the 33 Patriots), 1 May (Labour Day), 18 May (Battle of Las Piedras), 19 June (Birth of General Artigas), 18 July (Constitution Day), 25 August (National Independence Day), 12 October (Discovery of America), 2 November (All Souls' Day), 8 December (Blessing of the Waters), 25 December (Christmas Day).

2007: 1 January (New Year's Day), 6 January (Epiphany), 2–6 April (Holy Week), 19 April (Landing of the 33 Patriots), 1 May (Labour Day), 18 May (Battle of Las Piedras), 19 June (Birth of General Artigas), 18 July (Constitution Day), 25 August (National Independence Day), 12 October (Discovery of America), 2 November (All Souls' Day), 8 December (Blessing of the Waters), 25 December (Christmas Day).

Many businesses close during Carnival week (27 February–3 March 2006 and 19–23 February 2007).

Weights and Measures

The metric system is in force.

URUGUAY

Statistical Survey

Sources (unless otherwise stated): Instituto Nacional de Estadística, Río Negro 1520, 11100 Montevideo; tel. (2) 9027303; internet www.ine.gub.uy; Banco Central del Uruguay, Avda Juan P. Fabini, esq. Florida 777, Casilla 1467, 11100 Montevideo; tel. (2) 9017112; fax (2) 9021634; e-mail info@bcu.gub.uy; internet www.bcu.gub.uy; Cámara Nacional de Comercio y Servicios del Uruguay, Edif. Bolsa de Comercio, Rincón 454, 2°, Casilla 1000, 11000 Montevideo; tel. (2) 9161277; fax (2) 9161243; e-mail info@cncs.com.uy; internet www.cncs.com.uy.

Area and Population

AREA, POPULATION AND DENSITY

Area (sq km)	
Land area	175,016
Inland water	1,199
Total	176,215*
Population (census results)†	
22 May 1996	3,163,763
May–July 2004	
Males	1,565,533
Females	1,675,470
Total	3,241,003
Density (per sq km) at 2004 census	18.4

* 68,037 sq miles.
† Excluding adjustment for underenumeration.

DEPARTMENTS
(population at 2004 census)

	Area (sq km)	Population	Density (per sq km)	Capital
Artigas	11,928	78,019	6.6	Artigas
Canelones	4,536	485,240	107.0	Canelones
Cerro Largo	13,648	86,564	6.3	Melo
Colonia	6,106	119,266	19.5	Colonia del Sacramento
Durazno	11,643	58,859	5.1	Durazno
Flores	5,144	25,104	4.9	Trinidad
Florida	10,417	68,181	6.5	Florida
Lavalleja	10,016	60,925	6.1	Minas
Maldonado	4,793	140,192	29.2	Maldonado
Montevideo	530	1,325,968	2,501.8	Montevideo
Paysandú	13,922	113,244	8.1	Paysandú
Río Negro	9,282	53,989	5.8	Fray Bentos
Rivera	9,370	104,921	11.2	Rivera
Rocha	10,551	69,937	6.6	Rocha
Salto	14,163	123,120	8.7	Salto
San José	4,992	103,104	20.7	San José de Mayo
Soriano	9,008	84,563	9.4	Mercedes
Tacuarembó	15,438	90,489	5.9	Tacuarembó
Treinta y Tres	9,529	49,318	5.2	Treinta y Tres
Total	175,016*	3,241,003	18.5	

* Land area only.

PRINCIPAL TOWNS
(population at 22 May 1996 census)

Montevideo (capital)	1,378,707	Mercedes	50,800
Salto	93,420	Maldonado	50,420
Paysandú	84,160	Melo	47,160
Las Piedras	66,100	Tacuarembó	42,580
Rivera	63,370		

Mid-2003 (estimate): Montevideo 1,340,560 (Source: UN, *World Urbanization Prospects: The 2003 Revision*).

BIRTHS, MARRIAGES AND DEATHS

	Registered live births*		Registered deaths	
	Number	Rate (per 1,000)	Number	Rate (per 1,000)
1996	56,928	17.8	31,108	9.5
1997	58,032	18.0	30,459	9.3
1998	54,760	16.6	32,082	9.8
1999	54,055	16.3	32,430	9.8
2000	52,720	15.9	30,456†	9.2†
2001	51,959	15.5	31,228†	9.3†
2002	51,997	15.5	31,628†	9.4†
2003†	50,538	15.0	32,427	9.6

* Data are tabulated by year of registration rather than by year of occurrence (Source: mainly UN, *Demographic Yearbook*).
† Preliminary.

Registered marriages: 13,888 (marriage rate 4.2 per 1,000) in 2000; 13,988 in 2001; 14,073 in 2002.

Expectation of life (WHO estimates, years at birth): 75 (males 71; females 80) in 2003 (Source: WHO, *World Health Report*).

ECONOMICALLY ACTIVE POPULATION
(ISIC major divisions, '000 persons aged 14 years and over, urban areas)

	2001	2002	2003
Agriculture, hunting, forestry and fishing	45.4	43.7	46.9
Mining and quarrying	1.3	1.2	1.2
Manufacturing (incl. electricity, gas and water)	167.1	154.2	151.1
Construction	87.9	77.4	69.6
Trade, restaurants, hotels and repair of vehicles and household goods	240.8	228.9	225.4
Transport, storage and communications	66.8	62.4	61.1
Financing, insurance, real estate and business services	97.4	96.5	91.0
Public administration and defence, compulsory social security	85.1	86.9	91.2
Education	57.2	62.2	61.6
Health and social work	72.5	76.7	76.7
Community, social and personal services	56.2	52.2	54.8
Private households with employed persons	98.5	96.0	100.9
Activities not adequately defined	—	—	0.3
Total employed	1,076.2	1,038.3	1,032.0
Males	617.7	597.9	589.7
Females	458.5	440.4	442.3
Unemployed	193.2	211.3	208.5
Total labour force	1,269.4	1,250.1	1,240.5

Source: ILO.

URUGUAY

Health and Welfare

KEY INDICATORS

Total fertility rate (children per woman, 2003)	2.3
Under-5 mortality rate (per 1,000 live births, 2004)	17
HIV/AIDS (% of persons aged 15–49, 2003)	0.3
Physicians (per 1,000 head, 2002)	3.65
Hospital beds (per 1,000 head, 1996)	4.39
Health expenditure (2002): US $ per head (PPP)	805
Health expenditure (2002): % of GDP	10.0
Health expenditure (2002): public (% of total)	29.0
Access to water (% of persons, 2002)	98
Access to sanitation (% of persons, 2002)	94
Human Development Index (2003): ranking	46
Human Development Index (2003): value	0.840

For sources and definitions, see explanatory note on p. vi.

Agriculture

PRINCIPAL CROPS
('000 metric tons)

	2002	2003	2004
Wheat	205.8	326.0	532.6
Rice (paddy)	939.5	1,250.0	1,262.6
Barley	217.4	323.7	406.5
Maize	163.4	178.5	223.0
Oats	15.6	29.8	26.3
Sorghum	61.9	60.2	69.7
Potatoes	141.2	173.8	136.3
Sweet potatoes	63.5*	65.0	30.0*
Sugar cane	187.7	116.2	181.5
Sunflower seed	150.3	234.0	177.0
Tomatoes	41.2	46.7	60.0*
Dry onions	26.9	39.5	44.0*
Carrots	32.5	37.0	24.0
Oranges	115.8	122.0	124.1
Tangerines, mandarins, clementines and satsumas	74.5	75.0	77.3
Lemons and limes	38.5	40.0	33.5
Apples	73.8	66.7	72.5
Pears	14.2	19.2	17.6
Peaches and nectarines	10.6	14.1	14.0
Grapes	93.8	108.2	147.1

* FAO estimate.

Source: FAO.

LIVESTOCK
('000 head, year ending September)

	2002	2003	2004
Cattle	11,274	11,689	11,700*
Sheep	10,986	9,780	9,508
Pigs	270	240	240*
Horses*	390	380	380
Chickens	13,200*	13,300	13,300*

* FAO estimate(s).

Source: FAO.

LIVESTOCK PRODUCTS
('000 metric tons)

	2002	2003	2004
Beef and veal	411.8	424.2	496.5
Mutton and lamb	30.8	26.9	26.5
Pigmeat	19.5	16.8	16.0*
Poultry meat*	53.2	53.5	53.5
Cows' milk	1,490.0*	1,495.0	1,500.0
Eggs	38.7	34.5	36.2
Wool: greasy	39.4	34.9	36.0
Cattle hides*	52.0	55.2	66.4
Sheepskins*	10.8	10.0	9.9

* FAO estimate(s).

Source: FAO.

Forestry

ROUNDWOOD REMOVALS
('000 cubic metres, excl. bark)

	2002	2003	2004
Sawlogs and veneer logs	591	485	485*
Pulpwood	1,151	1,637	1,637*
Other industrial wood	90	10	10*
Fuel wood	1,607	1,607	4,267*
Total	3,439	3,739	6,399

* FAO estimate.

Source: FAO.

SAWNWOOD PRODUCTION
('000 cubic metres, incl. railway sleepers)

	2002	2003	2004*
Coniferous (softwood)	120	82	82
Broadleaved (hardwood)	104	148	148
Total	224	230	230

* FAO estimates.

Source: FAO.

Fishing

('000 metric tons, live weight)

	2001	2002	2003
Capture	105.1	108.8	116.9
Argentine hake	27.7	32.2	35.2
Striped weakfish	10.9	9.0	7.1
Whitemouth croaker	27.3	26.7	30.7
Patagonian toothfish	7.8	6.5	4.9
Argentine shortfin squid	7.4	11.8	6.4
Red crab	2.1	2.0	3.0
Aquaculture	0.0	0.0	0.0
Total catch	105.1	108.8	116.9

Source: FAO.

Mining

('000 metric tons, unless otherwise indicated)

	2001	2002	2003*
Gold (kg)	2,083	2,079	1,730
Gypsum	1,127	1,130*	1,130
Feldspar (metric tons)	4,722	4,700*	4,700

* Estimate(s).

Source: US Geological Survey.

URUGUAY

Industry

SELECTED PRODUCTS
('000 metric tons, unless otherwise indicated)

	2001	2002	2003
Raw sugar*	7.0	6.7	6.3
Wine	87.3	71.4	72.0†
Cigarettes (million)	9,616	n.a.	n.a.
Motor spirit (petrol) ('000 barrels)‡	2,200	2,200	2,200
Kerosene ('000 barrels)‡	500	500	500
Distillate fuel oils ('000 barrels)‡	4,100	4,100	4,200
Residual fuel oils ('000 barrels)‡	3,600	3,600	3,650
Cement (hydraulic)	1,015	1,000‡	1,050‡
Electric energy (million kWh)	9,259	n.a.	n.a.

* Unofficial figures.
† FAO estimate.
‡ US Geological Survey estimate(s).

Sources: FAO; US Geological Survey; UN, *Industrial Commodity Statistics Yearbook*.

Finance

CURRENCY AND EXCHANGE RATES

Monetary Units
100 centésimos = 1 peso uruguayo.

Sterling, Dollar and Euro Equivalents (30 December 2005)
£1 sterling = 41.4978 pesos;
US $1 = 24.1000 pesos;
€1 = 28.4308 pesos;
1,000 pesos uruguayos = £24.10 = $41.49 = €35.17.

Average Exchange Rate (pesos per US $)
2003   28.2087
2004   28.7037
2005   21.2570

Note: On 1 March 1993 a new currency, the peso uruguayo (equivalent to 1,000 former new pesos), was introduced.

BUDGET*
(million pesos uruguayos)

Revenue	2001	2002	2003
Tax revenue	40,923	43,825	54,921
Taxes on income, profits, etc.	9,539	11,568	13,560
Individual taxes	4,198	6,307	8,065
Corporate taxes	5,149	5,056	5,153
Taxes on property	3,913	5,162	7,095
Social security contributions	505	84	—
Domestic taxes on goods and services	23,820	23,791	30,309
General sales, take-over or value-added tax	15,443	15,827	21,106
Taxes on international trade and transactions	1,795	1,364	1,665
Taxes on leisure activities	470	120	26
Other taxes and rates	881	1,736	2,266
Non-tax revenue	3,645	4,410	7,034
Transfers	3,226	4,504	2,703
Other income	307	358	899
Total	48,102	53,098	65,558

Expenditure	2001	2002	2003
General public services	16,270	17,724	18,616
Government administration	8,551	9,819	9,564
Defence	3,303	3,332	4,157
Public order and safety	4,416	4,573	4,895
Special and community services	31,903	33,808	36,369
Education	8,597	8,890	10,558
Health	5,228	5,336	6,117
Social security and welfare	16,155	17,837	17,986
Housing and community amenities	1,260	1,126	1,084
Recreational, cultural and religious affairs	664	620	625
Economic affairs and services	4,696	4,318	8,140
Fuel and energy	178	143	175
Agriculture, fishing, forestry and hunting	1,008	1,057	1,096
Mining and mineral resources	244	221	231
Transport and communications	2,737	2,306	2,690
Other economic services	528	591	3,948
Debt-servicing and governmental transfers	8,175	13,893	26,263
Total	61,044	69,744	89,389

* Figures represent the consolidated accounts of the central Government, which include social security revenue and expenditure.

INTERNATIONAL RESERVES
(US $ million at 31 December)

	2002	2003	2004
Gold	3	3	4
IMF special drawing rights	6	4	1
Reserve position in the IMF	—	—	—
Foreign exchange	763	2,079	2,507
Total	772	2,086	2,512

Source: IMF, *International Financial Statistics*.

MONEY SUPPLY
(million pesos uruguayos at 31 December)

	2002	2003	2004
Currency outside banks	7,673.4	9,440.5	10,803.7
Demand deposits at commercial banks	6,556.6	9,706.8	10,928.0
Total money (incl. others)	14,278.4	19,177.4	22,225.4

Source: IMF, *International Financial Statistics*.

COST OF LIVING
(Consumer Price Index for Montevideo; base: 2000 = 100)

	2001	2002	2003
Food	103.1	117.2	142.5
Fuel and light	105.4	125.4	175.4
Clothing and footwear	100.1	108.0	127.5
Rent	101.9	103.0	100.8
All items	104.4	118.9	142.0

2004: Food 159.2; All items 155.0.

Source: ILO.

URUGUAY

Statistical Survey

NATIONAL ACCOUNTS
(million pesos uruguayos at current prices)

Expenditure on the Gross Domestic Product

	2002	2003	2004
Government final consumption expenditure	33,622	35,833	41,137
Private final consumption expenditure	192,167	235,348	281,324
Increase in stocks	3,707	9,947	7,173
Gross fixed capital formation	26,360	29,785	43,222
Total domestic expenditure	255,856	310,913	372,856
Exports of goods and services	57,325	82,301	112,461
Less Imports of goods and services	52,214	77,535	105,999
GDP in purchasers' values	260,967	315,681	379,317
GDP at constant 1983 prices	246	252	283

Source: IMF, *International Financial Statistics*.

Gross Domestic Product by Economic Activity

	2002	2003*	2004*
Agriculture	23,518.2	39,681.4	43,043.5
Fishing	724.2	1,201.8	1,415.0
Mining and quarrying	553.6	701.7	806.4
Manufacturing	45,599.8	58,610.8	80,191.4
Electricity, gas and water	12,567.5	15,433.0	16,896.1
Construction	10,994.2	10,924.6	13,127.1
Trade, restaurants and hotels	31,605.2	37,844.8	49,236.2
Transport, storage and communications	24,019.5	30,527.0	36,554.6
Finance and insurance	29,818.3	33,870.1	35,539.1
Real estate and business services	44,111.6	44,208.3	46,195.7
General government services	25,466.1	26,993.9	30,716.7
Other community, social and personal services	28,204.0	30,584.7	35,337.1
Sub-total	277,182.3	330,582.0	389,058.9
Import duties	9,359.2	13,824.2	20,381.1
Less Imputed bank service charge	25,574.8	28,725.5	30,123.3
GDP in purchasers' values	260,966.7	315,680.6	379,316.8

* Preliminary figures.

BALANCE OF PAYMENTS
(US $ million)

	2002	2003	2004
Exports of goods f.o.b.	1,922.1	2,281.2	3,021.3
Imports of goods f.o.b.	−1,873.8	−2,097.8	−2,990.2
Trade balance	48.3	183.3	31.1
Exports of services	753.7	802.8	986.9
Imports of services	−600.3	−635.8	−682.8
Balance on goods and services	201.7	350.3	335.2
Other income received	453.4	241.7	356.9
Other income paid	−405.1	−730.1	−884.2
Balance on goods, services and income	250.0	−138.1	−192.0
Current transfers received	83.7	94.9	97.8
Current transfers paid	−11.5	−12.3	−8.6
Current balance	322.2	−55.5	−102.9
Direct investment abroad	−53.8	−15.0	−11.1
Direct investment from abroad	174.6	416.5	310.8
Portfolio investment assets	95.2	−512.6	−694.8
Portfolio investment liabilities	204.5	201.6	291.1
Other investment assets	1,825.9	−1,254.8	−238.4
Other investment liabilities	−4,173.5	1,168.5	303.0
Net errors and omissions	−2,291.8	1,009.2	446.7
Overall balance	−3,897.1	957.9	304.4

Source: IMF, *International Financial Statistics*.

External Trade

PRINCIPAL COMMODITIES
(US $ million)

Imports c.i.f.	2004	2005*
Food and beverages	159.1	202.8
Vehicles	56.8	93.2
Durable goods	76.7	111.5
Other consumer goods	271.7	314.6
Machinery and equipment	288.8	431.7
Transport equipment	46.5	82.6
Petroleum and distillates	656.9	864.7
Electric Energy	56.6	41.6
Total (incl. others)	3,113.6	3,878.9

Exports f.o.b.	2004*	2005*
Live animals and animal derivatives	1,043.0	1,225.4
Plants and plant derivatives (incl. cereals)	452.9	499.3
Food, beverages and tobacco	105.8	139.6
Mineral products	137.2	170.8
Chemicals and manufactures thereof	131.3	151.8
Plastics, rubber and manufactures thereof	140.3	173.5
Hides and leather goods	280.2	283.4
Wood, plant fibres and manufactures thereof	106.4	141.8
Wood pulp, paper and cardboard	54.7	64.5
Textiles	236.9	252.0
Base metals and their manufactures	46.1	52.3
Machines and electrical equipment	27.8	33.1
Transport goods and materials	56.3	68.4
Total (incl. others)	2,930.8	3,404.5

* Preliminary figures.

PRINCIPAL TRADING PARTNERS
(US $ million, preliminary figures)

Imports c.i.f.	2003	2004	2005
Argentina	571.7	686.5	785.7
Brazil	459.8	676.5	824.7
Canada	10.5	12.0	21.6
Chile	41.5	58.4	69.6
China, People's Republic	86.0	172.7	242.3
Germany	61.7	82.6	87.8
Iran	0.1	114.9	0.7
Italy	50.2	66.2	75.7
Japan	28.1	42.8	42.9
Mexico	20.5	29.6	50.9
Spain	42.8	55.7	48.1
United Kingdom	25.0	34.1	18.6
USA	165.6	259.2	17.7
Venezuela	1.1	1.8	244.7
Total (incl. others)	2,157.9	3,113.6	3,878.9

Exports f.o.b.	2003	2004	2005
Argentina	155.2	223.3	266.9
Brazil	470.9	483.6	458.2
Canada	86.8	105.1	87.1
Chile	71.4	61.1	83.1
China, People's Republic	95.4	112.9	119.6
France (incl. Monaco)	19.9	32.6	30.9
Germany	145.3	151.5	143.3
Iran	15.8	43.4	80.7
Italy	89.0	89.3	92.6
Japan	12.5	15.1	32.1
Mexico	91.3	117.7	139.4
Netherlands	37.3	53.7	46.9
Paraguay	47.8	58.5	55.8
Spain	76.1	95.2	130.8
United Kingdom	78.8	91.4	84.7
USA	234.0	577.3	761.3
Venezuela	5.7	32.7	33.5
Total (incl. others)	2,204.7	2,930.8	3,404.5

Source: partly ALADI.

URUGUAY

Transport

RAILWAYS
(traffic)

	1998	1999	2000
Passenger-km (million)	14	10	9
Net ton-km (million)	244	272	239

Sources: UN, *Statistical Yearbook*.

ROAD TRAFFIC
(motor vehicles in use at 31 December)

	1995	1996	1997
Passenger cars	464,547	485,109	516,889
Buses and coaches	4,409	4,752	4,984
Lorries and vans	41,417	43,656	45,280
Road tractors	12,511	14,628	15,514
Motorcycles and mopeds	300,850	328,406	359,824

Source: International Road Federation: *World Road Statistics*.

2003: Passenger cars and vans 526,236; Coaches and minibuses 6,681; Lorries and road tractors 53,615; Motorcycles and mopeds 427,286; Taxis and hire cars 5,447.

SHIPPING
Merchant Fleet
(registered at 31 December)

	2002	2003	2004
Number of vessels	90	90	94
Total displacement ('000 grt)	74.7	75.6	76.0

Source: Lloyd's Register-Fairplay, *World Fleet Statistics*.

CIVIL AVIATION
(traffic on scheduled services)

	2001	2002	2003
Kilometres flown (million)	7.5	7.1	8.4
Passengers carried ('000)	558.6	525.0	463.9
Passenger-km (million)	582.3	576.5	1,028.8
Total ton-km (million)	13.3	11.7	23.2

Source: UN Economic Commission for Latin America and the Caribbean, *Statistical Yearbook*.

Tourism

ARRIVALS BY NATIONALITY*
('000)

	2001	2002	2003
Argentina	1,478.6	813.3	866.6
Brazil	121.9	118.4	151.4
Total (incl. others)	2,136.4	1,353.9	1,508.1

*Figures refer to arrivals at frontiers of visitors from abroad, including Uruguayan nationals permanently resident elsewhere.

Tourism receipts (US $ million, incl. passenger transport): 700 in 2001; 409 in 2002; 406 in 2003.

Source: World Tourism Organization.

Communications Media

	1999	2000	2001
Television receivers ('000 in use)	1,760	1,770	n.a.
Telephones ('000 main lines in use)	896.8	929.1	950.9
Mobile cellular telephones ('000 subscribers)	316.1	440.2	520.0
Personal computers ('000 in use)	330	n.a.	370
Internet users ('000)	330	370	400

2004: Telephones ('000 main lines in use) 1,000; Mobile cellular telephones ('000 subscribers) 600.0; Personal computers ('000 in use) 430; Internet users ('000) 680.

Radio receivers (1997): 1,970,000 in use.

Book production (1996): 934 titles.

Daily newspapers (1996): 36 (estimated average circulation 950,000).

Facsimile machines (1995): 11,000 in use.

Sources: UNESCO, *Statistical Yearbook*; UN, *Statistical Yearbook*; International Telecommunication Union.

Education
(2003)

	Institutions	Teachers	Students
Pre-primary	1,507	3,425	103,619
Primary	2,396	16,605	354,843
Secondary: general	413	25,168*	229,404
Secondary: vocational	124	n.a.	68,779
University and equivalent institutions*	6	7,723	72,100

*Public education only.

Adult literacy rate (UNESCO estimates): 97.7% (males 97.3%; females 98.1%) in 2002 (Source: UN Development Programme, *Human Development Report*).

Directory

The Constitution

The Constitution of Uruguay was ratified by plebiscite, on 27 November 1966, when the country voted to return to the presidential form of government after 15 years of 'collegiate' government. The main points of the Constitution, as amended in January 1997, are as follows:

GENERAL PROVISIONS

Uruguay shall have a democratic republican form of government, sovereignty being exercised directly by the Electoral Body in cases of election, by initiative or by referendum, and indirectly by representative powers established by the Constitution, according to the rules set out therein.

There shall be freedom of religion; there is no state religion; property shall be inviolable; there shall be freedom of thought. Anyone may enter Uruguay. There are two forms of citizenship: natural, being persons born in Uruguay or of Uruguayan parents, and legal, being people established in Uruguay with at least three years' residence in the case of those with family, and five years' for those without family. Every citizen has the right and obligation to vote.

LEGISLATURE

Legislative power is vested in the Congreso (Congress or General Assembly), comprising two houses, which may act separately or together according to the dispositions of the Constitution. It elects in joint session the members of the Supreme Court of Justice, of the

URUGUAY

Electoral Court, Tribunals, Administrative Litigation and the Accounts Tribunal.

Elections for both houses, the President and the Vice-President shall take place every five years on the last Sunday in October; sessions of the Assembly begin on 1 March each year and last until 15 December (15 September in election years, in which case the new Congress takes office on 15 February). Extraordinary sessions can be convened only in case of extreme urgency.

CHAMBER OF REPRESENTATIVES

The Chamber of Representatives has 99 members elected by direct suffrage according to the system of proportional representation, with at least two representatives for each Department. The number of representatives can be altered by law by a two-thirds' majority in both houses. Their term of office is five years and they must be over 25 years of age and be natural citizens or legal citizens with five years' exercise of their citizenship. Representatives have the right to bring accusations against any member of the Government or judiciary for violation of the Constitution or any other serious offence.

SENATE

The Senate comprises 31 members, including the Vice-President, who sits as President of the Senate, and 30 members elected directly by proportional representation on the same lists as the representatives, for a term of five years. They must be natural citizens or legal citizens with seven years' exercise of their rights, and be over 30 years of age. The Senate is responsible for hearing cases brought by the representatives and can deprive a guilty person of a post by a two-thirds' majority.

THE EXECUTIVE

Executive power is exercised by the President and the Council of Ministers. There is a Vice-President, who is also President of the Congress and of the Senate. The President and Vice-President are directly elected by absolute majority, and remain in office for five years. They must be over 35 years of age and be natural citizens.

The Council of Ministers comprises the office holders in the ministries or their deputies, and is responsible for all acts of government and administration. It is presided over by the President of the Republic, who has a vote.

THE JUDICIARY

Judicial power is exercised by the five-member Supreme Court of Justice and by Tribunals and local courts; members of the Supreme Court must be over 40 years of age and be natural citizens, or legal citizens with 10 years' exercise and 25 years' residence, and must be lawyers of 10 years' standing, eight of them in public or fiscal ministry or judicature. Members serve for 10 years and can be re-elected after a break of five years. The Court nominates all other judges and judicial officials.

The Government

HEAD OF STATE

President: Dr TABARÉ RAMÓN VÁZQUEZ ROSAS (took office 1 March 2005).
Vice-President: RODOLFO NIN NOVOA (AP).

COUNCIL OF MINISTERS
(April 2006)

Minister of the Interior: JOSÉ DÍAZ (PS).
Minister of Foreign Affairs: REINALDO GARGANO (PS).
Minister of National Defence: AZUCENA BERRUTI (PS).
Minister of Social Development: MARINA ARISMENDI (PCU).
Minister of Economy and Finance: DANILO ASTORI (AU).
Director of Planning and the Budget Office: CARLOS VIERA (VA).
Minister of Industry, Energy and Mining: JORGE LEPRA (Ind.).
Minister of Livestock, Agriculture and Fishing: JOSÉ (PEPE) MUJICA (MPP).
Minister of Tourism: HÉCTOR LESCANO (AP).
Minister of Transport and Public Works: VÍCTOR ROSSI (AP).
Minister of Labour and Social Security: EDUARDO BONOMI (MPP).
Minister of Education, Culture, Youth and Sport: JORGE BROVETTO (Ind.).
Minister of Public Health: Dr MARÍA JULIA MUÑOZ (VA).
Minister of Housing, Territorial Regulation and the Environment: MARIANO ARANA (VA).

MINISTRIES

Office of the President: Casa de Gobierno, Edif. Libertad, Avda Luis Alberto de Herrera 3350, Montevideo; tel. (2) 4872110; fax (2) 4809397; internet www.presidencia.gub.uy.
Ministry of Economy and Finance: Col. 1089, 3°, 11100 Montevideo; tel. (2) 7122910; fax (2) 7122919; e-mail seprimef@mef.gub.uy; internet www.mef.gub.uy.
Ministry of Education, Culture, Youth and Sport: Reconquista 535, 11000 Montevideo; tel. (2) 9161174; fax (2) 9161048; e-mail webmaster@mec.gub.uy; internet www.mec.gub.uy.
Ministry of Foreign Affairs: Avda 18 de Julio 1205, 11100 Montevideo; tel. (2) 9022132; fax (2) 9021349; e-mail webmaster@mrree.gub.uy; internet www.mrree.gub.uy.
Ministry of Housing, Territorial Regulation and the Environment: Zabala 1427, 11000 Montevideo; tel. (2) 9150211; fax (2) 9162914; e-mail computos@mvotma.gub.uy; internet www.mvotma.gub.uy.
Ministry of Industry, Energy and Mining: Rincón 723, 11000 Montevideo; tel. (2) 9002600; fax (2) 9021245; internet www.miem.gub.uy.
Ministry of the Interior: Mercedes 953, 11100 Montevideo; tel. (2) 9021665; fax (2) 9023142; e-mail webmaster@minterior.gub.uy; internet www.minterior.gub.uy.
Ministry of Labour and Social Security: Juncal 1511, 4°, 11000 Montevideo; tel. (2) 9162681; fax (2) 9162708; e-mail webmtss@mtss.gub.uy; internet www.mtss.gub.uy.
Ministry of Livestock, Agriculture and Fishing: Avda Constituyente 1476, 11200 Montevideo; tel. (2) 4126326; fax (2) 4184051; e-mail webmaster@mgap.gub.uy; internet www.mgap.gub.uy.
Ministry of National Defence: Edif. General Artigas, Avda 8 de Octubre 2628, Montevideo; tel. (2) 4809707; fax (2) 4809397.
Ministry of Public Health: Avda 18 de Julio 1892, 11100 Montevideo; tel. (2) 4000101; fax (2) 4085360; e-mail msp@msp.gub.uy; internet www.msp.gub.uy.
Ministry of Social Development: Uruguay 948, esq. Río Branco, 11100 Montevideo; tel. (2) 9003266; fax (2) 9023521; e-mail dirgeneral@mides.gub.uy; internet www.mides.gub.uy.
Ministry of Tourism: Rambla 25 de Agosto, 1825 esq. Yacaré s/n, Montevideo; tel. (2) 1885100; fax (2) 9021624; e-mail webmaster@mintur.gub.uy; internet www.turismo.gub.uy.
Ministry of Transport and Public Works: Rincón 575, 4° y 5°, 11000 Montevideo; tel. (2) 9150509; fax (2) 9162883; e-mail direcciongeneral@mtop.gub.uy; internet www.mtop.gub.uy.
Office of Planning and the Budget: Edif. Libertad, Luis A. de Herrera 3350, Montevideo; tel. (2) 4872110; fax (2) 2099730; e-mail webmaster@opp.gub.uy; internet www.opp.gub.uy.

President and Legislature

PRESIDENT

Election, 31 October 2004

Candidate	% of vote
Tabaré Ramón Vázquez Rosas (Encuentro Progresista—Frente Amplio)	50.70
Jorge Larrañaga (Partido Nacional)	34.06
Guillermo Stirling (Partido Colorado)	10.32
Others	2.53
Invalid votes	2.39
Total	100.00

CONGRESO

Cámara de Senadores
(Senate)

Election, 31 October 2004

Party	Seats
Encuentro Progresista—Frente Amplio	16
Partido Nacional	11
Partido Colorado	3
Total*	30

* An additional seat is reserved for the Vice-President, who sits as President of the Senate.

URUGUAY

Cámara de Representantes
(Chamber of Representatives)

President: JULIO CARDOZO.

Election, 31 October 2004

Party	Seats
Encuentro Progresista—Frente Amplio	52
Partido Nacional	35
Partido Colorado	10
Other parties	2
Total	99

Election Commission

Corte Electoral: Ituzaingó 1474, Montevideo; tel. (2) 9159626; fax (2) 9155087; internet www.corteelectoral.gub.uy; f. 1967; Pres. CARLOS A. URRUTY NAVATTA.

Political Organizations

Alianza Libertadora Nacionalista: Montevideo; extreme right-wing; Leader OSVALDO MARTÍNEZ JAUME.

Encuentro Progresista—Frente Amplio (EP—FA): Col. 1367, 2°, 11100 Montevideo; tel. (2) 9022176; e-mail prensaepfa@montevideo.com.uy; internet www.epfaprensa.org; f. 1971; left-wing grouping; Pres. Dr TABARÉ RAMÓN VÁZQUEZ ROSAS; Vice-Pres. JORGE BROVETTO; mems include:

Alianza Progresista 738 (AP): Col. 1831, Montevideo; tel. and fax (2) 4016365; e-mail a738@alianza738.org.uy; internet www.alianza738.org.uy; left-wing; Leader RODOLFO NIN NOVOA.

Asamblea Uruguay (AU): Carlos Quijano 1271, Montevideo; e-mail jmahia@parlamento.gub.uy; internet www.asamblea.org.uy; centre-left; Leader DANILO ASTORI.

Frente Izquierda de Liberación (FIDEL): Montevideo; f. 1962; socialist; Leader ADOLFO AGUIRRE GONZÁLEZ.

Grupo Pregón: Montevideo; left-wing liberal party; Leaders SERGIO PREVITALI, ENRIQUE MORAS.

Movimiento de Acción Nacionalista (MAN): Montevideo; left-wing nationalist org.; Leader JOSÉ DURÁN MATOS.

Movimiento Blanco Popular y Progresista (MBPP): Montevideo; moderate left-wing; Leader A. FRANCISCO RODRÍGUEZ CAMUSSO.

Movimiento de Participación Popular (MPP): Germán Barbato 1491; tel. (2) 9086948; e-mail correos@mppuruguay.org; internet www.mppuruguay.org; f. 1989 by the MLN—Tupamaros (see below); grouping of left-wing parties; Leader JOSÉ (PEPE) MUJICA; mems include:

Movimiento de Liberación Nacional (MLN)—Tupamaros: Tristán Narvaja 1578, CP 11.200, Montevideo; tel. (2) 4092298; fax (2) 4099957; e-mail mln@chasque.apc.org; internet www.chasque.net/mlnweb; f. 1962; radical socialist; during 1962–73 the MLN, operating under its popular name of the Tupamaros, conducted a campaign of urban guerrilla warfare until it was defeated by the Armed Forces in late 1973; following the return to civilian rule, in 1985, the MLN announced its decision to abandon its armed struggle; legally recognized in May 1989; Sec.-Gen. JOSÉ (PEPE) MUJICA.

Movimiento 26 de Marzo: Durazno 1118, 11200 Montevideo; tel. (2) 9011584; f. 1971; socialist; Pres. EDUARDO RUBIO; Sec.-Gen. FERNANDO VÁZQUEZ.

Partido Comunista de Uruguay (PCU): Río Negro 1525, 11100 Montevideo; tel. (2) 9017171; fax (2) 9011050; e-mail comitecentral@webpcu.org; internet www.webpcu.org; f. 1920; Sec.-Gen. MARINA ARISMENDI; 42,000 mems (est.).

Partido de Democracia Avanzada: Montevideo; Communist.

Partido Socialista del Uruguay (PS): Casa del Pueblo, Soriano 1218, 11100 Montevideo; tel. (2) 9013344; fax (2) 9082548; e-mail info@ps.org.uy; internet www.ps.org.uy; f. 1910; Pres. REINALDO GARGANO; Sec.-Gen. EDUARDO (LALO) FERNÁNDEZ.

Partido por la Victoria del Pueblo (PVP): Calle Mercedes 1551, esq. Tacuarembó, Montevideo; tel. (2) 4020370; e-mail cores567@adinet.com.uy; internet www.pvp.org.uy; f. 1975 in Buenos Aires, Argentina; left-wing; Sec.-Gen. HUGO CORES.

Vertiente Artiguista (VA): San José 1191, CP 11200, Montevideo; tel. (2) 9000177; e-mail vertiente@vertiente.org.uy; internet www.vertiente.org.uy; f. 1989; left-wing; Leader MARCELO MANO.

Directory

Nuevo Espacio: Eduardo Acevedo 1615, 11200 Montevideo; tel. (2) 4026989; fax (2) 4026991; e-mail internacionales@nuevoespacio.org.uy; internet www.nuevoespacio.org.uy; f. 1994; social-democratic; allied to the Encuentro Progresista—Frente Amplio since Dec. 2002; moderate left-wing; Leader RAFAEL MICHELINI; Sec. EDGARDO CARVALHO.

Partido Azul (PA): Paul Harris 1722, Montevideo; tel. and fax (2) 6016327; e-mail hablacon@partidoazul.s5.com; internet www.partidoazul.s5.com; liberal; f. 1993; Leader Dr ROBERTO CANESSA; Gen. Sec. Ing. ARMANDO VAL.

Partido Colorado: Andrés Martínez Trueba 1271, 11100 Montevideo; tel. (2) 4090180; f. 1836; Sec.-Gen. JORGE LUIS BATLLE IBÁÑEZ; factions include:

Foro Batllista: Col. 1243, 11100 Montevideo; tel. (2) 9030154; e-mail info@forobatllista.com; internet www.forobatllista.com; Leader Dr JULIO MARÍA SANGUINETTI CAIROLO.

Lista 15: Leader JORGE LUIS BATLLE IBÁÑEZ.

Unión Colorada y Batllista (Pachequista): Buenos Aires 594, 11000 Montevideo; tel. (2) 9164648; right-wing.

Vanguardia Batllista: Casa de Vanguardia, Paysandú 1333, entre Ejido y Curiales, Montevideo; tel. (2) 9027779; e-mail info@scavarelli.com; internet www.scavarelli.com; Leader Dr ALBERTO SCARAVELLI.

Partido Demócrata Cristiano (PDC): Aquiles Lanza 1318 bis, Montevideo; tel. and fax (2) 9030704; e-mail pdc@chasque.apc.org; internet www.chasque.apc.org/pdc; fmrly Unión Cívica del Uruguay; allied to the Alianza Progresista since 1999; f. 1962; Pres. Dr HÉCTOR LESCANO; Sec.-Gen. FRANCISCO OTTONELLI.

Partido Justiciero: Montevideo; extreme right-wing; Leader BOLÍVAR ESPÍNDOLA.

Partido Nacional (Blanco): Juan Carlos Gómez 1384, Montevideo; tel. (2) 9163831; fax (2) 9163758; e-mail partidonacional@partidonacional.com.uy; internet www.partidonacional.com.uy; f. 1836; Exec. Pres. LUIS ALBERTO LACALLE; Sec.-Gen. ALBERTO ZUMARÁN; tendencies within the party include:

Alianza Nacional: Leader JORGE LARRAÑAGA.

Consejo Nacional Herrerista: Leader LUIS ALBERTO LACALLE.

Desafío Nacional: Leader JUAN ANDRÉS RAMÍREZ.

Linea Nacional de Florida: Leader ARTURO HEBER.

Manos a la Obra: Plaza Cagancha 1145, 11100 Montevideo; tel. (2) 9028149; Leader ALBERTO VOLONTÉ.

Movimiento Nacional de Rocha—Corriente Popular Nacionalista: Avda Uruguay 1324, Montevideo; tel. (2) 9027502; Leader CARLOS JULIO PEREYRA.

Partido del Sol: Peatonal Yi 1385, 11000 Montevideo; tel. (2) 9001616; fax (2) 9006739; e-mail partidodelsol@adinet.com.uy; internet www.partidodelsoluruguay.org; ecologist, federal, pacifist; Leader HOMERO MIERES.

Partido de los Trabajadores: Convención 1196, 11100 Montevideo; tel. (2) 9082624; f. 1980; extreme left-wing; Leader JUAN VITAL ANDRADE.

Unión Cívica: Montevideo; tel. (2) 9005535; e-mail info@unioncivica.org; internet www.dreamsmaker.com.uy/trabajos/union-civica; f. 1912; recognized Christian Democrat faction, split from the Partido Demócrata Cristiano in 1980; Leader W. GERARDO AZAMBUYA.

Diplomatic Representation

EMBASSIES IN URUGUAY

Argentina: Cuareim 1470, 11800 Montevideo; tel. (2) 9028166; fax (2) 9028172; e-mail emargrou@adinet.com.uy; internet emb-uruguay.mrecic.gov.ar; Ambassador HERNÁN MARÍA PATIÑO MAYER.

Bolivia: Dr Prudencio de Peña 2469, 11300 Montevideo; tel. (2) 7083573; fax (2) 7080066; e-mail embolivia-montevideo@rree.gov.bo; Ambassador ARMANDO LOAYZA MARIACA.

Brazil: Blvr Artigas 1328, 11300 Montevideo; tel. (2) 7072119; fax (2) 7072086; e-mail montevideo@brasemb.org.uy; internet www.brasil.org.uy; Ambassador EDUARDO DOS SANTOS.

Canada: Plaza Independencia 749, Of. 102, 11100 Montevideo; tel. (2) 9022030; fax (2) 9022029; e-mail mvdeo@dfait-maeci.gc.ca; internet www.dfait-maeci.gc.ca/uruguay; Ambassador PATRICIA FULLER.

Chile: Calle 25 de Mayo 575, Montevideo; tel. (2) 9164090; fax (2) 9153804; e-mail echileuy@netgate.com.uy; Ambassador CARLOS ENRIQUE APPELGREN BALBONTIN.

China, People's Republic: Miraflores 1508, Carrasco, Casilla 18966, Montevideo; tel. (2) 6016126; fax (2) 6018508; e-mail

URUGUAY

chinaemb_uy@mfa.gov.cn; internet uy.chineseembassy.org/esp; Ambassador WANG XIAOYUAN.

Colombia: Edif. Tupí, Juncal 1305, 18°, 11000 Montevideo; tel. (2) 9161592; fax (2) 9161594; e-mail euruguay@minrelext.gov.co; Ambassador CLAUDIA DINORA OLGA MARIA TURBAY QUINTERO.

Costa Rica: CP 12242, Montevideo; tel. (2) 7083645; fax (2) 7089727; e-mail embarica@adinet.com.uy; Ambassador RUTH MERY SALAS SALAZAR.

Cuba: Cristobal Echevarriarza 3471, Montevideo; tel. (2) 6232803; fax (2) 6232805; e-mail cancilleria@netgate.com.uy; Ambassador MARIELENA RUIZ CAPOTE.

Czech Republic: Luis B. Cavia 2996, Casilla 12262, 11300 Montevideo; tel. (2) 7087808; fax (2) 7096410; e-mail montevideo@embassy .mzv.cz; internet www.mzv.cz/montevideo; Chargé d'affaires a.i. PAVEL SUSTÁK.

Dominican Republic: Tomás de Tezanos 1186, 11300 Montevideo; tel. (2) 6287766; fax (2) 6289655; e-mail embajadomuruguay@ hotmail.com; Ambassador RAFAEL ANTONIO JULIÁN CEDANO.

Ecuador: Pedro Berro 1217, entre Guayaquí y Pereira, Montevideo; tel. (2) 7076463; fax (2) 7076465; e-mail embajadaecuador@netgate .com.uy; Ambassador LEONARDO CARRIÓN EGUIGUREN.

Egypt: Avda Brasil 2663, 11300 Montevideo; tel. (2) 7096412; fax (2) 7080977; e-mail boustanemontevideo@easymail.com.uy; Ambassador Dr OHEIB ANWAR ELSOKARY.

El Salvador: Melitón González 1157, Apto 501, Montevideo 11300; tel. (2) 6222005; fax (2) 6226842; e-mail embasauy@dedicado.net.uy; Ambassador MARIO AVILA ROMERO.

France: Avda Uruguay 853, Casilla 290, 11100 Montevideo; tel. (2) 9020077; fax (2) 9023711; e-mail ambfra@adinet.com.uy; internet www.amb-montevideo.fr; Ambassador LAURENT-JOSEPH RAPIN.

Germany: La Cumparsita 1417/1435, Casilla 20014, 11200 Montevideo; tel. (2) 9025222; fax (2) 9023422; e-mail info@ embajadaalemana-montevideo.info; internet www .embajadaalemana-montevideo.info; Ambassador Dr VOLKER ANDING.

Greece: Edif. Artigas, Rincón 487, 2°, 11100 Montevideo; tel. (2) 9165191; fax (2) 9150795; e-mail gremb.mvd@mfa.gr; Ambassador NICOLAOS DICTAKIS.

Guatemala: Calle General French 1693, Montevideo; tel. and fax (2) 6000250; e-mail emguatur@netgate.com.uy; Ambassador FERNANDO GONZÁLEZ DAVISON.

Holy See: Blvr Artigas 1270, Casilla 1503, Montevideo (Apostolic Nunciature); tel. (2) 7072016; fax (2) 7072209; Apostolic Nuncio Most Rev. JANUSZ BOLONEK (Titular Archbishop of Madaurus).

Iran: Blvr Artigas 531, 11300 Montevideo; tel. (2) 7116657; fax (2) 7116659; e-mail emb.iran.secretaria@multitel.com.uy; Ambassador MOHAMMAD FARAJI.

Israel: Blvr Artigas 1585, 11200 Montevideo; tel. (2) 4004164; fax (2) 4095821; e-mail israelambassadorsec-montevideo@montevideo.mfa .gov.il; internet montevideo.mfa.gov.il; Ambassador YOEL BARNEA.

Italy: José Benito Lamas 2857, Casilla 268, 11300 Montevideo; tel. (2) 7084916; fax (2) 7084148; e-mail ambasciata.montevideo@esteri .it; internet www.ambmontevideo.esteri.it/ambasciata_montevideo; Ambassador GIORGIO MALFATTI DI MONTE TRETTO.

Japan: Blvr Artigas 953, 11300 Montevideo; tel. (2) 4187645; fax (2) 4187980; e-mail embjapon@adinet.com.uy; internet www.uy .emb-japan.go.jp; Ambassador YOSHIHIRO NAKAMURA.

Korea, Republic: Edif. World Trade Center, Avda Luis Alberto de Herrera 1248, Torre 2, 10°, Montevideo; tel. (2) 6289374; fax (2) 6289376; e-mail ecorea@adinet.com.uy; Ambassador TAE-SHIN JAN.

Lebanon: Avda General Rivera 2278, Montevideo; tel. (2) 4086640; fax (2) 4086365; e-mail embliban@adinet.com.uy; Ambassador VICTOR GEORGES BITAR GHANEM.

Mexico: Andes 1365, 7°, 11100 Montevideo; tel. (2) 9020791; fax (2) 9021232; e-mail embajada-mexico@techtelnet.com.uy; Ambassador PERLA MARÍA CARVALHO SOTO.

Netherlands: Leyenda Patria 2880, Of. 202, 2°, Casilla 1519, 11300 Montevideo; tel. (2) 7112956; fax (2) 7113301; e-mail mtv@minbuza .nl; internet www.holanda.org.uy; Ambassador R. H. MEYS.

Panama: Juan Benito Blanco 3388, 11300 Montevideo; tel. (2) 6230301; fax (2) 6230300; e-mail empanuru@netgate.com.uy; Ambassador ELVIRA BARRIOS ICAZAS.

Paraguay: Blvr Artigas 1256, Montevideo; tel. (2) 7072138; fax (2) 7083682; e-mail embapur@netgate.com.uy; internet www.geocities .com/embapur; Ambassador RICARDO CABALLERO AQUINO.

Peru: Obligado 1384, 11300 Montevideo; tel. (2) 7076862; fax (2) 7077793; e-mail emba8@embaperu.org.uy; internet www.angelfire .com/country/embaperu; Ambassador WILLIAM BELEVÁN MCBRIDE.

Poland: Jorge Canning 2389, Casilla 1538, 11600 Montevideo; tel. (2) 4801313; fax (2) 4873389; e-mail ambmonte@netgate.com.uy; internet www.embajadapoloniauruguay.com; Ambassador LECH KUBIAK.

Portugal: Avda Dr Francisco Soca 1128, Casilla 701, 11300 Montevideo; tel. (2) 7084061; fax (2) 7096456; e-mail portmont@netgate .com.uy; Ambassador Dr DOMINGO TOMAS VILA GARRIDO SERRA.

Romania: Echevarriarza 3452, Casilla 12040, 11000 Montevideo; tel. (2) 6220876; fax (2) 6220135; e-mail bcemontevideo@adinet.com .uy; Ambassador GHEORGHE PETRE.

Russia: Blvr España 2741, 11300 Montevideo; tel. (2) 7081884; fax (2) 7086597; e-mail embaru@montevideo.com.uy; internet www .uruguay.mid.ru; Ambassador SERGUEY N. KOSHKIN.

South Africa: Echevarriarza 3335, Casilla 498, 11000 Montevideo; tel. (2) 6230161; fax (2) 6230066; e-mail safem@netgate.com.uy; Ambassador PETER GOOSEN (resident in Argentina).

Spain: Avda Libertad 2738, 11300 Montevideo; tel. (2) 7086010; fax (2) 7083291; e-mail embespuy@correo.mae.es; Ambassador FERNANDO VALDERRAMA PAREJA.

Switzerland: Ing. Federico Abadie 2936/40, 11°, Casilla 12261, 11300 Montevideo; tel. (2) 7115545; fax (2) 7115031; e-mail vertretung@mtv.rep.admin.ch; Ambassador DANIEL VON MURALT.

United Kingdom: Marco Bruto 1073, Casilla 16024, 11300 Montevideo; tel. (2) 6223630; fax (2) 6227815; e-mail bemonte@internet .com.uy; internet www.britishembassy.org.uy; Ambassador Dr HUGH SALVESSEN.

USA: Lauro Muller 1776, 11200 Montevideo; tel. (2) 4187777; fax (2) 4188611; e-mail webmastermvd@state.gov; internet uruguay .usembassy.gov; Chargé d'affaires a.i. JAMES D. NEALON.

Venezuela: José Agustín Iturriaga 3589, Montevideo; tel. (2) 6221262; fax (2) 6282530; e-mail embaven@adinet.com.uy; Ambassador MARÍA LOURDES URBANEJA DURANT.

Judicial System

The Supreme Court of Justice comprises five members appointed at the suggestion of the executive, for a period of five years. It has original jurisdiction in constitutional, international and admiralty cases, and hears appeals from the appellate courts, of which there are seven, each with three judges.

Cases involving the functioning of the state administration are heard in the ordinary Administrative Courts and in the Supreme Administrative Court, which consists of five members appointed in the same way as members of the Supreme Court of Justice.

In Montevideo there are 19 civil courts, 10 criminal and correctional courts, 19 courts presided over by justices of the peace, three juvenile courts, three labour courts and courts for government and other cases. Each departmental capital, and some other cities, have a departmental court; each of the 224 judicial divisions has a justice of the peace.

The administration of justice became free of charge in 1980, with the placing of attorneys-at-law in all courts to assist those unable to pay for the services of a lawyer.

Supreme Court of Justice
H. Gutiérrez Ruiz 1310, Montevideo; tel. (2) 9001041; fax (2) 902350; e-mail secparga@poderjudicial.gub.uy; internet www.poderjudicial .gub.uy.

President of the Supreme Court of Justice: Dr DANIEL GUTIÉRREZ.

Supreme Administrative Court: Mercedes 961, 11100 Montevideo; tel. (2) 9008047; fax (2) 9080539.

Religion

Under the Constitution, the Church and the State were declared separate and toleration for all forms of worship was proclaimed. Roman Catholicism predominates.

CHRISTIANITY

Federación de Iglesias Evangélicas del Uruguay: Avda 8 de Octubre 3324, 11600 Montevideo; tel. and fax (2) 4875907; internet www.chasque.net/obra/skontakt.htm; f. 1956; eight mem. churches; Pres. OSCAR BOLIOLI; Sec. OBED BODYAJIAN.

The Roman Catholic Church

Uruguay comprises one archdiocese and nine dioceses. At 31 December 2003 there were an estimated 2,316,495 adherents in the country, representing about 61% of the total population.

Bishops' Conference

Conferencia Episcopal Uruguaya, Avda Uruguay 1319, 11100 Montevideo; tel. (2) 9002642; fax (2) 9011802; e-mail ceusecre@adinet

.com.uy; internet www.iglesiauruguaya.com; f. 1972; Pres. Mgr PABLO JAIME GALIMBERTI DI VIETRI (Bishop of San José de Mayo).

Archbishop of Montevideo: Most Rev. NICOLÁS COTUGNO FANIZZI, Arzobispado, Treinta y Tres 1368, Casilla 356, 11000 Montevideo; tel. (2) 9158127; fax (2) 9158926; e-mail vicario@arquidiocesis.net.

The Anglican Communion

Uruguay is the newest diocese in the Province of the Southern Cone of America, having been established in 1988. The presiding Bishop of the Iglesia Anglicana del Cono Sur de América is the Bishop of Northern Argentina.

Bishop of Uruguay: Rt Rev. MIGUEL TAMAYO ZALDÍVAR, Centro Diocesano, Reconquista 522, Casilla 6108, 11000 Montevideo; tel. (2) 9159627; fax (2) 9162519; e-mail mtamayo@netgate.com.uy; internet www.uruguay.anglican.org.

Other Churches

Baptist Evangelical Convention of Uruguay: Mercedes 1487, 11100 Montevideo; tel. and fax (2) 2167012; e-mail suspasos@adinet.com.uy; f. 1948; 4,500 mems; Pres Dr JUAN CARLOS OTORMÍN.

Iglesia Adventista (Adventist Church): Castro 167, Montevideo; f. 1901; 4,000 mems; Principal officers Dr GUILLERMO DURÁN, Dr ALEXIS PIRO.

Iglesia Evangélica Metodista en el Uruguay (Evangelical Methodist Church in Uruguay): San José 1457, 11200 Montevideo; tel. (2) 4136552; fax (2) 4136554; e-mail iemu@adinet.com.uy; internet www.gbgm-umc.org/iemu; f. 1878; 1,193 mems (1997); Pres. Rev. OSCAR BOLIOLI.

Iglesia Evangélica Valdense (Waldensian Evangelical Church): Avda 8 de Octubre 3039, 11600 Montevideo; tel. and fax (2) 4879406; e-mail ievm@internet.com.uy; f. 1952; 15,000 mems; Pastor ALVARO MICHELIN SALOMÓN.

Iglesia Pentecostal Unida Internacional en Uruguay (United Pentecostal Church International in Uruguay): Helvecia 4032, Piedras Blancas, 12200 Montevideo; tel. (2) 5133618; e-mail lrodrigu@montevideo.com.uy; internet members.tripod.com/~lrodrigu; Pastor LUIS RODRÍGUEZ.

Primera Iglesia Bautista (First Baptist Church): Avda Daniel Fernández Crespo 1741, Casilla 5051, 11200 Montevideo; tel. (2) 4098744; fax (2) 4094356; e-mail piebu@adinet.com.uy; f. 1911; 314 mems; Pastor LEMUEL J. LARROSA.

Other denominations active in Uruguay include the Iglesia Evangélica del Río de la Plata and the Iglesia Evangélica Menonita (Evangelical Mennonite Church).

BAHÁ'Í FAITH

National Spiritual Assembly of the Bahá'ís: Blvr Artigas 2440, 11600 Montevideo; tel. (2) 4875890; fax (2) 4802165; e-mail bahai@multi.com.uy; f. 1938; mems resident in 140 localities.

The Press

DAILIES

Montevideo

El Diario: Rincón 712, 11000 Montevideo; tel. (2) 9030465; fax (2) 9030637; e-mail joterom@adinet.com.uy; f. 1923; evening; independent; Editor JORGE OTERO; circ. 12,000.

El Diario Español: Cerrito 551–555, Casilla 899, 11000 Montevideo; tel. (2) 9159481; fax (2) 9157389; f. 1905; morning (except Monday); newspaper of the Spanish community; Editor MARCELO REINANTE; circ. 20,000.

Diario Oficial: Avda 18 de Julio 1373, Montevideo; tel. (2) 9085042; fax (2) 9023098; e-mail impo@impo.com.uy; internet www.impo.com.uy; f. 1905; morning; publishes laws, official decrees, parliamentary debates, judicial decisions and legal transactions; Dir ZAIN NASSIF DE ZARUMBE.

La Mañana: Casilla 5005, Suc. 2, Montevideo 11100; tel. (2) 9029055; fax (2) 9021326; f. 1917; supports the Partido Colorado; Editor Dr SALVADOR ALABÁN DEMARE; circ. 50,000.

Mundocolor: Cuareim 1287, 11800 Montevideo; f. 1976; evening (except Sunday); Dir DANIEL HERRERA LUSSICH; circ. 4,500.

El Observador: Cuareim 2052, 11800 Montevideo; tel. (2) 9247000; fax (2) 9248698; e-mail elobservador@observador.com.uy; internet www.observador.com.uy; f. 1991; morning; Editor RICARDO PEIRANO; circ. 26,000.

Observador Económico: Soriano 791, 11100 Montevideo; tel. (2) 9030690; fax (2) 9030691.

El País: Zelmar Michelini 1287, 4°, 11100 Montevideo; tel. (2) 9020115; fax (2) 9020464; e-mail cartas@elpais.com.uy; internet www.elpais.com.uy; f. 1918; morning; supports the Partido Nacional; Editor MARTÍN AGUIRRE; circ. 106,000.

La República: Avda Gral Garibaldi 2579, 11600 Montevideo; tel. (2) 4873565; fax (2) 4873823; e-mail redaccion@diariolarepublica.com; internet www.larepublica.com.uy; f. 1988; morning; Editor FEDERICO FASANO MERTENS; circ. 20,000.

Ultimas Noticias: Paysandú 1179, 11100 Montevideo; tel. (2) 9020452; fax (2) 9024669; e-mail avisos@ultimasnoticias.com.uy; internet www.ultimasnoticias.com.uy; f. 1981; evening (except Saturday); owned by Impresora Polo; Publr Dr ALPHONSE EMANUILOFF-MAX; circ. 25,000.

Florida

El Heraldo: Independencia 824, 94000 Florida; tel. (35) 22229; fax (35) 24546; e-mail elheraldo@elheraldo.com.uy; internet www.elheraldo.com.uy; f. 1919; morning; independent; Dir ALVARO RIVA REY; circ. 20,000.

Maldonado

Correo de Punta del Este: Zelmar Michelini 815 bis, 20000 Maldonado; tel. and fax (42) 35633; e-mail gallardo@adinet.com.uy; internet www.diariocorreo.com; f. 1993; morning; Editor MARCELO GALLARDO; circ. 2,500.

Minas

La Unión: Florencio Sánchez 569, Minas; tel. (442) 2065; fax (442) 4011; e-mail union@chasque.apc.org; f. 1877; evening (except Sunday); Dir LAURA PUCHET MARTÍNEZ; Editor ALEJANDRO MAYA SOSA; circ. 2,600.

Paysandú

El Telégrafo: 18 de Julio 1027, 60000 Paysandú; tel. (722) 3141; fax (722) 7999; e-mail correo@eltelegrafo.com; internet www.eltelegrafo.com; f. 1910; morning; independent; Dir FERNANDO M. BACCARO; circ. 8,500.

Salto

El Pueblo: 18 de Julio 15, Salto; tel. (733) 4133; e-mail dipueblo@adinet.com.uy; internet www.diarioelpueblo.com.uy; morning; Dir ADRIANA MARTÍNEZ.

Tribuna Salteña: Joaquín Suárez 71, Salto; f. 1906; morning; Dir MODESTO LLANTADA FABINI; circ. 3,000.

PERIODICALS

Montevideo

Aquí: Zabala 1322, Of. 102, 11000 Montevideo; weekly; supports the Encuentro Progresista—Frente Amplio; Dir FRANCISCO JOSÉ O'HONELLI.

Brecha: Avda Uruguay 844, 11100 Montevideo; tel. (2) 9008777; fax (2) 9020388; e-mail brecha@brecha.com.uy; internet www.brecha.com.uy; f. 1985; weekly; politics, current affairs; circ. 8,500; Dir IVONNE TRÍAS; Editor-in-Chief DANIEL GATTI.

Búsqueda: Avda Uruguay 1146, 11100 Montevideo; tel. (2) 9021300; fax (2) 9022036; e-mail busqueda@adinet.com.uy; f. 1972; weekly; independent; politics and economics; Dir DANILO ARBILLA FRACHIA; circ. 25,000.

Charoná: Gutiérrez Ruiz 1276, Of. 201, Montevideo; tel. (2) 9086665; internet www.charona.com; f. 1968; fortnightly; children's; Dir SERGIO BOFFANO; circ. 25,000.

Colorín Colorado: Dalmiro Costa 4482, Montevideo; f. 1980; monthly; children's; Dir SARA MINSTER DE MURNINKAS; circ. 3,000.

Crónicas Económicas: Avda Libertador Brig.-Gen. Lavalleja 1532, Montevideo; tel. (2) 9004790; fax (2) 9020759; e-mail cronicas@netgate.com.uy; internet www.cronicas.com.uy; f. 1981; weekly; independent; business and economics; Dirs JULIO ARIEL FRANCO, WALTER HUGO PAGÉS, JORGE ESTELLANO.

La Gaceta Militar Naval: Montevideo; monthly.

Guambia: Rimac 1576, 11400 Montevideo; tel. (2) 6132703; fax (2) 6132703; e-mail info@guambia.com.uy; internet www.guambia.com.uy; f. 1983; monthly; satirical; Dir and Editor ANTONIO DABEZIES.

Indice Industrial-Anuario de la Industria Uruguaya: Sarandí 456, 11000 Montevideo; tel. (2) 9151963; f. 1957; annual; Dir W. M. TRIAS; circ. 6,000.

La Justicia Uruguaya: 25 de Mayo 555, 11000 Montevideo; tel. (2) 9157587; fax (2) 9159721; e-mail lajusticiauruguaya@lju.com.uy; internet www.lajusticiauruguaya.com.uy; f. 1940; bimonthly; jurisprudence; Dirs EDUARDO ALBANELL, ADOLFO ALBANELL, SUSANA ARIAS; circ. 3,000.

La Juventud: 18 de Julio 1357, Of. 202, Montevideo; tel. (2) 9030305; e-mail weblajuve@yahoo.com.ar; internet www.chasque

URUGUAY

.apc.org/juventud; weekly; supports the Movimiento 26 de Marzo; Dir GUILLERMO FERNÁNDEZ; Editor JOSÉ L. BORGES.

Marketing Directo: Guaná 2237 bis, 11200 Montevideo; tel. (2) 4012174; fax (2) 4087221; e-mail consumo@adinet.com.uy; internet www.ciecc.org; f. 1988; monthly; Dir EDGARDO MARTÍNEZ ZIMARIOFF; circ. 9,500.

Mate Amargo: Tristán Narvaja 1578 bis, Montevideo; f. 1986; organ of the Movimiento de Liberación Nacional; circ. 22,500.

Opción: J. Barrios Amorín 1531, Casilla 102, 11100 Montevideo; f. 1981; weekly; Dir FRANCISCO JOSÉ OTTONELLI; circ. 15,000.

Patatín y Patatán: Montevideo; f. 1977; weekly; children's; Dir JUAN JOSÉ RAVAIOLI; circ. 3,000.

Patria: Montevideo; internet www.patria.com.uy; weekly; organ of the Partido Nacional; right-wing; Dir LUIS A. HEBER; Editor Dr JOSÉ LUIS BELLANI.

Revista Naval: Soriano 1117, 11100 Montevideo; tel. (2) 9087884; f. 1988; 3 a year; military; Editor GUSTAVO VANZINI; circ. 1,000.

PRESS ASSOCIATIONS

Asociación de Diarios del Uruguay: Río Negro 1308, 6°, 11100 Montevideo; f. 1922; Pres. BATLLE T. BARBATO.

Asociación de la Prensa Uruguaya: Col. 1086, Of. 903, Montevideo; tel. and fax (2) 9013695; e-mail apu@adinet.com.uy; f. 1944; Pres. MANUEL MÉNDEZ.

PRESS AGENCIES
Foreign Bureaux

Agence France-Presse (AFP): Plaza Independencia 831, 11100 Montevideo; tel. (2) 9005095; Chief JUPITER PUYO.

Agencia EFE (Spain): Wilson Ferreira Aldunate 1294, Of. 501, 11200 Montevideo; tel. (2) 9020322; fax (2) 9026726; e-mail mhurtado@efe.com.uy; Correspondent MARTA HURTADO GÓMEZ.

Agenzia Nazionale Stampa Associata (ANSA) (Italy): Florida 1408, Montevideo; tel. (2) 9011032; fax (2) 9081950; Bureau Chief JUAN ATELLA.

Associated Press (AP) (USA): Avda 18 de Julio 1076, Montevideo; tel. (2) 9018291; Correspondent DANIEL GIANELLI.

Deutsche Presse-Agentur (dpa) (Germany): Avda 18 de Julio 994, 4°, Montevideo; tel. (2) 9028052; fax (2) 9022662; e-mail dpaurc@montevideo.com.uy; Correspondent MARÍA ISABEL RIVERO DE LOS CAMPOS.

Inter Press Service (IPS) (Italy): Juan Carlos Gómez 1445, Of. 102, 1°, 11000 Montevideo; tel. (2) 9164397; fax (2) 9163598; e-mail ips@tips.org.uy; internet www.ips.org; f. 1964; Dir MARIO LUBETKIN.

Reuters (United Kingdom): Plaza Independencia 831, Of. 907-908, 11100 Montevideo; tel. (2) 9020336; fax (2) 9027912; Correspondent ANAHI RAMA.

Publishers

Autores Uruguayos: Paysandú 1561,11200 Montevideo; e-mail mensajes@autoresuruguayos.com.uy; internet www.autoresuruguayos.com; publishes works by Uruguayan authors; Man. ADRIANA DOS SANTOS.

Editorial Arca: Ana Monterroso 2231, Montevideo; tel. (2) 4099796; fax (2) 4099879; f. 1963; general literature, social science and history; Man. Dir ENRIQUE PIQUÉ.

Ediciones de la Banda Oriental: Gaboto 1582, 11200 Montevideo; tel. (2) 4083206; fax (2) 4098138; e-mail ebo@chasque.net; general literature; Man. Dir HEBER RAVIOLO.

CENCI—Uruguay (Centro de Estadísticas Nacionales y Comercio Internacional): Misiones 1361, Casilla 1510, 11000 Montevideo; tel. (2) 9152930; fax (2) 9154578; e-mail cenci@cenci.com.uy; f. 1956; economics, statistics; Dir KENNETH BRUNNER.

Editorial y Librería Jurídica Amalio M. Fernández SRL: 25 de Mayo 589, 11000 Montevideo; tel. and fax (2) 9151782; e-mail amflibrosjurid@movinet.com.uy; f. 1951; law and sociology; Man. Dir CARLOS W. DEAMESTOY.

Editorial La Flor del Itapebí: Luis Piera 1917/401, Montevideo; tel. and fax (2) 7109267; internet www.itapebi.com.uy; f. 1991; cultural, technical, educational.

Fundación de Cultura Universitaria: 25 de Mayo 568, Casilla 1155, 11000 Montevideo; tel. (2) 9152532; fax (2) 9152549; e-mail ventas@fcu.com.uy; internet www.fcu.com.uy; f. 1968; law and social sciences; Pres. Dr PABLO DONNÁNGELO.

Hemisferio Sur: Buenos Aires 335, Casilla 1755, 11000 Montevideo; tel. (2) 9164515; fax (2) 9164520; e-mail librperi@adinet.com.uy; f. 1951; agronomy and veterinary science.

Directory

Editorial Idea: Misiones 1424, 5°, 11000 Montevideo; tel. (2) 9165456; fax (2) 9150868; e-mail vescovi@fastlink.com.uy; law; Dir Dr GUILLERMO VESCOVI.

Librería Linardi y Risso: Juan C. Gómez 1435, 11000 Montevideo; tel. (2) 9157129; fax (2) 9157431; e-mail lyrbooks@linardiyrisso.com.uy; internet www.linardiyrisso.com.uy; f. 1944; general; Man. Dirs ALVARO RISSO, ANDRÉS LINARDI.

Editorial Medina SRL: Gaboto 1521, Montevideo; tel. (2) 4085800; f. 1933; general; Pres. MARCOS MEDINA VIDAL.

A. Monteverde & Cía, SA: Treinta y Tres 1475, Casilla 371, 11000 Montevideo; tel. (2) 9152939; fax (2) 9152012; f. 1879; educational; Man. Dir LILIANA MUSSINI.

Mosca Hermanos SA: Avda 18 de Julio 1578, 11300 Montevideo; tel. (2) 4093141; fax (2) 4088059; e-mail mosca@attmail.com.uy; f. 1888; general; Pres. Lic. ZSOLT AGARDY.

Librería Selecta Editorial: Guayabo 1865, 11200 Montevideo; tel. (2) 4086989; fax (2) 4086831; f. 1950; academic books; Dir FERNANDO MASA.

Ediciones Trilce: Durazno 1888, 11200 Montevideo; tel. (2) 4127662; fax (2) 4127722; e-mail trilce@trilce.com.uy; internet www.trilce.com.uy; f. 1985; science, politics, history.

Vintén Editor: Hocquart 1771, Casilla 11804, Montevideo; tel. (2) 2090223; internet vinten-uy.com; poetry, theatre, history, art, literature.

PUBLISHERS' ASSOCIATION

Cámara Uruguaya del Libro: Juan D. Jackson 1118, 11200 Montevideo; tel. (2) 4015732; fax (2) 4011860; e-mail camurlib@adinet.com.uy; f. 1944; Pres. ERNESTO SANJINÉS; Man. ANA CRISTINA RODRÍGUEZ.

Broadcasting and Communications
TELECOMMUNICATIONS

Administración Nacional de Telecomunicaciones (ANTEL): Complejo Torre de las Telecomunicaciones, Guatemala 1075, Montevideo; e-mail antel@antel.com.uy; internet www.antel.com.uy; f. 1974; state-owned; Pres. Ing. MARÍA SIMON; Gen. Man. Ing. JOSÉ LUIS SALDÍAS.

  ANCEL: Pablo Galarza 3537, Montevideo; internet www.ancel.com.uy; f. 1974; state-owned mobile telephone co; pending partial (40%) privatization; Pres. MARÍA SIMON.

Movistar Uruguay: Avda Constituyente, Edif. Torre el Gaucho, 1467 Montevideo; tel. (2) 4087502; internet www.movicom.com.uy; owned by Telefónica Móviles, SA (Spain); mobile telephone services.

Unidad Reguladora de Servicios de Comunicaciones (URSEC): Uruguay 988, Casilla 11100, Montevideo; tel. (2) 9028082; fax (2) 9005708; e-mail bergara@ursec.gub.uy; internet www.ursec.gub.uy; regulates telecommunications and postal sectors; Dir MARIO BERGERA.

BROADCASTING
Regulatory Authority

Asociación Nacional de Broadcasters Uruguayos (ANDEBU): Carlos Quijano 1264, 11100 Montevideo; tel. (2) 9021525; fax (2) 9021540; e-mail andebu@internet.com.uy; internet www.andebu.com.uy; f. 1933; 101 mems; Pres. CARLOS FALCO; Vice-Pres. Dr WALTER C. ROMAY.

Radio

El Espectador: Río Branco 1481, 11100 Montevideo; tel. (2) 9023531; fax (2) 9083192; e-mail ventas@espectador.com.uy; internet www.espectador.com; f. 1923; commercial; Gen. Man. ESTELA BARTOLIC.

Radio Carve: Mercedes 973, 11100 Montevideo; tel. (2) 9026162; fax (2) 9020126; e-mail carve@portalx.com.uy; internet www.carve.com.uy; f. 1928; commercial; Dir PABLO FONTAINA MINELLI.

Radio Montecarlo: Avda 18 de Julio 1224, 1°, 11100 Montevideo; tel. (2) 9030703; fax (2) 9017762; f. 1928; commercial; Dir DANIEL ROMAY.

Radio Sarandí: Enriqueta Compte y Riqué 1250, 11800 Montevideo; tel. (2) 2082612; fax (2) 2036906; e-mail direccion@sarandi690.com.uy; internet www.radiosarandi.com.uy; f. 1931; commercial; Pres. RAMIRO RODRÍGUEZ VALLAMIL RIVIERE.

Radio del Sol: (2) 6283314; e-mail comoestamos@fmdelsol.com; internet www.comoestamos.com.uy.

Radio Universal: Avda 18 de Julio 1220, 3°, 11100 Montevideo; tel. (2) 9026022; fax (2) 9026050; e-mail info@22universal.com; internet www.22universal.com; f. 1929; commercial; Pres. OSCAR IMPERIO.

Radiodifusión Nacional SODRE: Sarandí 430, 11000 Montevideo; tel. (2) 957865; fax (2) 9161933; f. 1929; state-owned; Pres. Julio César Ocampos.

In 2002 there were some 16 AM and six FM radio stations in the Montevideo area. In addition, there were approximately 41 AM and 56 FM radio stations outside the capital.

Television

The Uruguayan Government holds a 10% stake in the regional television channel Telesur (q.v.), which began operations in May 2005 and is based in Caracas, Venezuela.

Canal 4 Monte Carlo: Paraguay 2253, 11800 Montevideo; tel. (2) 9244444; fax (2) 9247929; e-mail secretarias@montecarlotv.com.uy; internet www.canal4.com.uy; f. 1961; Dir Hugo Romay Salvo.

SAETA TV—Canal 10: Dr Lorenzo Carnelli 1234, 11200 Montevideo; tel. (2) 4102120; fax (2) 4009771; internet www.canal10.com.uy; f. 1956; Pres. Jorge de Feo.

SODRE (Servicio Oficial de Difusión Radiotelevisión y Espectáculos): Blvr Artigas 2552, 11600 Montevideo; tel. (2) 4806448; fax (2) 4808515; e-mail direccion@tveo.com.uy; internet www.sodre.gub.uy; f. 1963; Pres. Dra Nelly Goitiño.

Teledoce Televisora Color—Canal 12: Enriqueta Compte y Riqué 1276, 11800 Montevideo; tel. (2) 2083555; fax (2) 2037623; e-mail latele@teledoce.com; internet www.teledoce.com; f. 1962; Gen. Man. Horacio Scheck.

TV Ciudad: Javier Barrios Amorín 1460, Montevideo; tel. (2) 4021908; fax (2) 4001908; e-mail tvciudad@tvciudad.imm.gub.uy; internet www.montevideo.gub.uy/teveciudad; f. 1996; state-owned.

In 1999 there were 21 television stations outside the capital.

Finance

BANKING

(cap. = capital; res = reserves; dep. = deposits; m. = million; amounts in pesos, unless otherwise indicated)

State Banks

Banco Central del Uruguay: Avda Juan P. Fabini 777, Casilla 1467, 11100 Montevideo; tel. (2) 9085629; fax (2) 9021634; e-mail info@bcu.gub.uy; internet www.bcu.gub.uy; f. 1967; note-issuing bank, also controls private banking; Pres. Walter Cancela; Vice-Pres. César Failache; Gen. Man. Andrés Pieroni; Gen. Sec. Dr Aureliano Berro.

Banco Hipotecario del Uruguay (BHU): Avda Daniel Fernández Crespo 1508, Montevideo; tel. (2) 4090000; fax (2) 4090782; e-mail info@bhu.net; internet www.bhu.net; f. 1892; state mortgage bank; in 1977 assumed responsibility for housing projects in Uruguay; Pres. Miguel Piperno.

Banco de la República Oriental del Uruguay (BROU): Cerrito y Zabala 351, 11000 Montevideo; tel. (2) 9150157; fax (2) 9162064; e-mail broupte@adinet.com.uy; internet www.brounet.com.uy; f. 1896; a state institution; cap. and res 10,848.1m., dep. 114,686.5m. (Dec. 2002); Pres. Daniel Cairo Vila; Gen. Man. Fernando Jorajuría; 107 brs.

Nuevo Banco Comercial (NBC): Casilla 34, Cerrito 400, 11000 Montevideo; tel. (2) 9160541; fax (2) 9168955; internet www.nbc.com.uy; f. 2003 by merger of Banco Comercial, Banco La Caja Obrera and Banco de Montevideo; state-run, scheduled for privatization; dep. US $667m., assets US $882m. (July 2003); privatization due by end 2005; Pres. Eduardo Arruabarrena; Gen. Man. José Fuentes; 46 brs.

Principal Commercial Banks

Banco Bilbao Vizcaya Argentaria Uruguay SA (BBVA): 25 de Mayo 401, esq. Zabala, 11000 Montevideo; tel. (2) 9161444; fax (2) 9162821; internet www.bbvabanco.com.uy; f. 1968; fmrly Unión de Bancos del Uruguay, and later Banesto Banco Uruguay, SA and Banco Francés Uruguay, SA; adopted current name in 2000 following merger with Banco Exterior de América, SA; cap. 1,299.8m., res 1,091.1m., dep. 13,377.4m. (Dec. 2002); Chair. Tomás Deane; Gen. Man. Vicente Bogliolo del Río; 14 brs.

Banco Galicia Uruguay, SA: World Trade Center, Luis A. Herrera 1248, 22°, Montevideo; tel. 6281230; e-mail contactenos@bancogalicia.com.uy; internet www.bancogalicia.com.uy; f. 1999.

Banco Surinvest SA: Rincón 530, 11000 Montevideo; tel. (2) 9160177; fax (2) 9160241; e-mail bancosurinvest@surinvest.com.uy; internet www.surinvest.com.uy; f. 1981 as Surinvest Casa Bancaria; name changed as above 1991; cap. 202.2m., res 90.6m., dep. 3,104.1m. (Dec. 2003); Gen. Man. Alberto A. Mello.

Foreign Banks

ABN AMRO Bank Uruguay NV (Netherlands): Julio Herrera y Obes 1365, Casilla 888, 11100 Montevideo; tel. (2) 9031073; fax (2) 9025011; internet www.abnamro.com.uy; f. 1952; Country Rep. Francisco Di Roberto, Jr; 24 brs.

Banco de la Nación Argentina: Juan Carlos Gómez 1372, 11000 Montevideo; tel. (2) 9158760; fax (2) 9164582; e-mail bna@bna.com.uy; f. 1961; Gen. Man. Dr Oscar Jorge Vissani; 2 brs.

Banco Santander, SA: Cerrito 449, esq. Misiones, 11000 Montevideo; tel. (2) 9160656; fax (2) 9163685; e-mail santander@santander.com.uy; internet www.santander.com.uy; 100% owned by Banco Santander Central Hispano (Spain); cap. 161.1m., res. 477.9m., dep. 9,283.8m. (Dec. 2000); Vice-Pres. Miguel Estrugo Santaeugenia; Dir Jorge Jourdán Peyronel; 28 brs.

Banco Sudameris (Brazil): Rincón 500, 11000 Montevideo; tel. (2) 9150095; fax (2) 9164292; e-mail suduruguay@sudameris.com.uy; internet www.sudameris.com.uy; acquired by Banco ABN AMRO Real of Brazil in 2003; Pres. Dr Sagunto Pérez Fontana; Gen. Man. Alejandro Suzacq; 6 brs.

BankBoston NA (USA): Zabala 1463, Casilla 90, 11000 Montevideo; tel. (2) 9160127; fax (2) 9162209; internet www.bankboston.com.uy; f. 1976; Gen. Man. Horacio Vilaró; 13 brs.

BNP Paribas (Uruguay) SA (France): Rincón 477, Of. 901/5, Montevideo; tel. (2) 9162768; fax (2) 9162609; e-mail uruguay@bnpparibas.com.ar; f. 1989 as BNP (Uruguay) SA; adopted present name in 2001.

Citibank NA (USA): Cerrito 455, esq. Misiones, Casilla 690, 11000 Montevideo; tel. (2) 91550374; fax (2) 9150374; internet www.citibank.com.uy/uruguay; Vice-Pres. Paola Feoli De Mello; 2 brs.

Discount Bank (Latin America), SA (USA): Rincón 390, 11000 Montevideo; tel. (2) 9164848; fax (2) 9160890; e-mail mensajes@discbank.com.uy; internet www.discbank.com.uy; f. 1978; cap. US $12.8m., res $0.62m., dep. $179.3m. (Dec. 2002); Pres. and Chair. Arie Sheer; Gen. Man. Valentin D. Malachowski; 4 brs.

HSBC Bank (Uruguay), SA (United Kingdom): Ituzaingó 1389, 11000 Montevideo; tel. (2) 9153395; fax (2) 9160125; f. 1995; fmrly Banco Roberts (Argentina); CEO Fernando Grassi.

Lloyds TSB Bank PLC (United Kingdom): Zabala 1500, Casilla 204, 11000 Montevideo; tel. (2) 9161370; fax (2) 9161262; e-mail lloydsm@lloydstsb-americas.com.uy; internet www.lloydstsb.com.uy; f. 1862; fmrly Bank of London and South America; Gen. Man. Eduardo Angulo.

Credit Co-operatives

There are several credit co-operatives, which permit members to secure small business loans at preferential rates.

Cooperativa Nacional de Ahorro y Crédito (COFAC): Zabala 1338, 11000 Montevideo; tel. (2) 9160100; fax (2) 9160826; e-mail mensajes@cofac.com.uy; internet www.cofac.com.uy; 200,000 mems; f. 1986; operations suspended in March 2005; Gen. Man. Gustavo Javier Marton Ameal; 37 brs.

Federación Uruguaya de Cooperativas de Ahorro y Crédito (FUCAC): Blvr Artigas 1472, Montevideo; tel. (2) 7088888; fax (2) 7088888; e-mail empresas@fucac.com.uy; internet www.fucac.com.uy; f. 1972; Pres. Carlos Alberto Icasuriaga Samano; Gen. Man. Javier Humberto Pi León.

Bankers' Association

Asociación de Bancos del Uruguay (Bank Association of Uruguay): Rincón 602, 5°, 11000 Montevideo; tel. (2) 9162342; fax (2) 9162329; e-mail uy34042@adinet.com.uy; internet www.abu.org.uy; f. 1945; 7 mem. banks; Dir Oscar Jorge Vissani.

STOCK EXCHANGE

Bolsa de Valores de Montevideo: Edif. Bolsa de Comercio, Misiones 1400, 11000 Montevideo; tel. (2) 9165051; fax (2) 9161900; e-mail info@bolsademontevideo.com.uy; internet www.bolsademontevideo.com.uy; f. 1867; 75 mems; Pres. Ignacio Rospide.

INSURANCE

From mid-1994, following the introduction of legislation ending the state monopoly of most types of insurance, the Banco de Seguros del Estado lost its monopoly on all insurance except life, sea transport and fire risks, which have been traditionally open to private underwriters.

AIG Uruguay Compañía de Seguros, SA (USA): Col. 993, 1°, Montevideo; tel. (2) 9000330; fax (2) 9084552; e-mail aig.uruguay@aig.com; internet www.aig.com; f. 1996; all classes; Gen. Man. Jorge Ferrante.

URUGUAY   *Directory*

Alico Compañía de Seguros de Vida, SA (USA): 18 de Julio 1738, Montevideo; tel. (2) 4033939; fax (2) 4033938; e-mail alico@alico.com.uy; internet www.alico.com; f. 1996; life; Gen. Man. JUAN ETCHEVERRY.

Axa Seguros Uruguay, SA (France): Misiones 1549, Montevideo; tel. (2) 9160850; fax (2) 9160847; e-mail gabriel.penna@axa-seguros.com.uy; internet www.axa-seguros.com.uy; f. 1998; general; fmrly UAP Seguros, SA; Gen. Man. GABRIEL PENNA.

Banco de Seguros del Estado: Avda Libertador 1465, Montevideo; tel. (2) 9089303; fax (2) 9017030; e-mail directorio@bse.com.uy; internet www.bse.com.uy; f. 1912; state insurance org.; all risks; Pres. ENRIQUE ROIG CURBELO; Gen. Man. CARLOS VALDÉS.

Compañía de Seguros Aliança da Bahia Uruguay, SA (Brazil): Río Negro 1394, 7°, Montevideo; tel. (2) 9021086; fax (2) 9021087; e-mail avivo@netgate.com.uy; f. 1995; transport; Gen. Man. BERNARDO VIVO.

Mapfre Compañía de Seguros, SA (Spain): Blvr Artigas 459, Montevideo; tel. (2) 7116595; fax (2) 7116595; e-mail info@mapfre.com.uy; internet www.mapfre.com.uy; f. 1994; general; Gen. Man. DIEGO SOBRINI.

Porto Seguro, Seguros del Uruguay SA (Brazil): Blvr Artigas 2025; tel. (2) 4028000; fax (2) 4030097; e-mail admin@portoseguro.com.uy; internet www.portoseguro.com.uy; f. 1995; property; Pres. LEANDRO SUÁREZ.

Real Uruguaya de Seguros SA (Netherlands): Avda 18 de Julio 988, Montevideo; tel. (2) 9025858; fax (2) 9024515; e-mail realseguros@abnamro.com; internet www.realseguros.com.uy; f. 1900; life and property; part of the ABN AMRO Group; Gen. Man. JOSÉ LUIZ TOMAZINI.

Royal & SunAlliance Seguros, SA (United Kingdom): Peatonal Sarandí 620, Montevideo; tel. (2) 9170505; fax (2) 9170490; internet www.royalsunalliance.com.uy; f. 1997; life and property; Dir Dr JUAN QUARTINO.

Surco, Compañía Cooperativa de Seguros: Blvr Artigas 1320, Montevideo; tel. (2) 7090089; fax (2) 7077313; e-mail surco@surco.com.uy; internet www.surco.com.uy; f. 1995; insurance co-operative; all classes; Gen. Man. ANDRÉS ELOLA.

INSURANCE ASSOCIATION

Asociación Uruguaya de Empresas Aseguradoras (AUDEA): Juncal 1305, Of. 1901, 11000 Montevideo; tel. (2) 9161465; fax (2) 9165991; e-mail audea@adinet.com.uy; Pres. MANUEL RODRÍGUEZ; Gen. Man. MAURICIO CASTELLANOS.

Trade and Industry

GOVERNMENT AGENCIES

Oficina de Planeamiento y Presupuesto de la Presidencia de la República: Edif. Libertad, Luis A. de Herrera 3350, Montevideo; tel. (2) 4872110; fax (2) 2099730; e-mail diropp@presidencia.gub.uy; internet www.opp.gub.uy; f. 1976; responsible for the implementation of devt plans; co-ordinates the policies of the various ministries; advises on the preparation of the budget of public enterprises; Dir CARLOS VIERA; Sub-Dir DANIEL MESA PELUFFO.

Uruguay XXI (Instituto de Promoción de Inversiones y Exportaciones de Bienes y Servicios): Yaguarón 1407, Of. 1103, 11100 Montevideo; tel. (2) 9002912; fax (2) 9008298; e-mail info@uruguayxxi.gub.uy; internet www.uruguayxxi.gub.uy; govt agency to promote economic investment; f. 1996; Exec. Dir VICTOR ANGENSCHEIDT.

DEVELOPMENT ORGANIZATIONS

Corporación Nacional para el Desarrollo (CND): Rincón 528, 7°, Casilla 977, 11000 Montevideo; tel. (2) 9162680; fax (2) 9159662; e-mail cnd01@adinet.com.uy; internet www.cnd.org.uy; f. 1985; national devt corpn; mixed-capital org.; obtains 60% of funding from state; Pres. ÁLVARO GARCÍA; Vice-Pres. RICARDO PUGLIA; Gen. Man. MARTÍN J. DIBARBOURE ROSSINI.

Asociación Nacional de Micro y Pequeños Empresarios (ANMYPE): Miguelete 1584, Montevideo; tel. (2) 9241010; e-mail anmype@anmype.net.uy; internet www.anmype.net.uy; promotes small businesses; f. 1988; Pres. RICARDO POSADA.

Asociación Nacional de Organizaciones No Gubernmentales Orientadas al Desarrollo: Avda del Libertador 1985 escalera 202, Montevideo; tel. and fax (2) 9240812; e-mail anong@anong.com.uy; internet www.anong.org.uy; f. 1992; umbrella grouping of devt NGOs; Pres. MARÍA ELENA MARTÍNEZ.

Centro Interdisciplinario de Estudios sobre el Desarrollo, Uruguay (CIEDUR): 18 de Julio 1645-7, Casilla 11200, Montevideo; tel. and fax (2) 408 4520; e-mail ciedur@chasque.net; internet www.chasque.net/ciedur; devt studies and training; Exec. Sec. ALFREDO BLUM.

Fundación Uruguaya de Cooperación y Desarrollo Solidario (FUNDASOL) (Uruguayan Foundation for Supportive Co-operation and Development): Blvr Artigas 1119, esq. Maldonado, Montevideo 11200; tel. (2) 4002020; fax (2) 4081485; e-mail consultas@fundasol.org.uy; internet www.fundasol.org.uy; f. 1979; Gen. Man. JORGE NAYA.

Programa Alianzas para el Desarrollo Local en América Latina (ALOP): Montevideo; tel. and fax (2) 9007194; e-mail info@desarrollolocal.org; internet www.desarrollolocal.org; umbrella grouping of local devt orgs; Dir ENRIQUE GALLICCHIO.

CHAMBERS OF COMMERCE

Cámara de Industrias del Uruguay (Chamber of Industries): Avda Italia 6101, Montevideo 11500; tel. (2) 6040464; fax (2) 6040501; e-mail ciu@ciu.com.uy; internet www.ciu.com.uy; f. 1898; Pres. WASHINGTON BURGHI.

Cámara Nacional de Comercio y Servicios del Uruguay (National Chamber of Commerce): Edif. Bolsa de Comercio, Rincón 454, 2°, Casilla 1000, 11000 Montevideo; tel. (2) 9161277; fax (2) 9161243; e-mail info@cncs.com.uy; internet www.cncs.com.uy; f. 1867; 1,500 mems; Pres. JOSÉ LUIS PUIG; Sec. and Man. Dr CLAUDIO PIACENZA.

Cámara Mercantil de Productos del País (Chamber of Commerce for Local Products): Avda General Rondeau 1908, 1°, 11800 Montevideo; tel. (2) 9240644; fax (2) 9240673; e-mail info@camaramercantil.com.uy; internet www.camaramercantil.com.uy; f. 1891; 180 mems; Pres. RICARDO SEIZER; Gen. Man. GONZALO GONZÁLEZ PIEDRAS.

EMPLOYERS' ORGANIZATIONS

Asociación de Importadores y Mayoristas de Almacén (Importers' and Wholesalers' Asscn): Edif. Bolsa de Comercio, Of. 317/319, Rincón 454, 11000 Montevideo; tel. (2) 9156103; fax (2) 9160796; e-mail fmelissori@nidera.com.uy; f. 1926; 52 mems; Pres. FERNANDO MELISSORI.

Asociación Rural del Uruguay (ARU): Avda Uruguay 864, 11100 Montevideo; tel. (2) 9020484; fax (2) 9020489; e-mail consultas@aru.com.uy; internet www.aru.com.uy; f. 1871; 1,800 mems; Pres. FERNANDO MATTOS COSTA; Vice-Pres. ROBERTO SYMONDS.

Comisión Patronal del Uruguay de Asuntos Relacionados con la OIT (Commission of Uruguayan Employers for Affairs of the ILO): Edif. Bolsa de Comercio, Rincón 454, 2°, Casilla 1000, 11000 Montevideo; tel. (2) 9161277; fax (2) 9161243; f. 1954; mem. of Cámara Nacional de Comercio y Servicios del Uruguay; 8,000 mems; Sec. and Man. Dr CLAUDIO PIACENZA.

Federación Rural del Uruguay: Avda 18 de Julio 965, 1°, Montevideo; tel. (2) 9005583; fax (2) 9004791; e-mail fedrural@adinet.com.uy; f. 1915; 2,000 mems; Pres. ALEJANDRO TEDESCO.

Unión de Exportadores del Uruguay (Uruguayan Exporters' Asscn): Edif. Nacional de Aduanas, Yacaré s/n, 11000 Montevideo; tel. (2) 9170105; fax (2) 9165967; e-mail info@uruguayexporta.com; internet www.uruguayexporta.com; Pres. DANIEL SOLODUCHO; Exec. Sec. TERESA AISHEMBERG.

UTILITIES

Electricity

Administración Nacional de Usinas y Transmisiones Eléctricas (UTE): Paraguay 2431, 10°, 11100 Montevideo; tel. (2) 2003424; fax (2) 2037082; e-mail ute@ute.com.uy; internet www.ute.com.uy; f. 1912; autonomous state body; sole purveyor of electricity until 1997; Pres. Ing. BENO RUCHANSKY; Gen. Man. CARLOS POMBO.

Gas

Conecta: Sanlúcar 1631, esq. Avda Rivera, Montevideo; tel. (2) 6008400; fax (2) 6006732; internet www.conecta.com.uy; gas distribution.

Gaseba Uruguay (Gaz de France): 25 de Mayo 702, 11000 Montevideo; tel. (2) 9017454; internet www.gaseba.com.uy; gas producers and service providers.

Petroleum

Administración Nacional de Combustibles, Alcohol y Portland (ANCAP): Paraguay 1598, 11100 Montevideo; tel. (2) 9020608; fax (2) 9021136; e-mail webmaster@ancap.com.uy; internet www.ancap.com.uy; f. 1931; deals with transport, refining and sale of petroleum products, and the manufacture of alcohol, spirit and cement; tanker services, also river transport; Pres. DANIEL MARTÍNEZ; Gen. Man. SERGIO LATTANZIO; Sec.-Gen. JORGE URRUTIA.

URUGUAY

Water

Aguas de la Costa: Maldonado; subsidiary of Aguas de Barcelona (Spain); operating in Uruguay since 1994, contract due to expire in 2019; management of water supply in Maldonado dept.

Obras Sanitarias del Estado (OSE): Carlos Roxlo 1275, 11200 Montevideo; tel. (2) 4001151; fax (2) 4088069; e-mail oserou@adinet.com.uy; internet www.ose.com.uy; f. 1962; processing and distribution of drinking water, sinking wells, supplying industrial zones of the country; Pres. Ing. JORGE CARLOS COLACCE MOLINARI; Vice-Pres. FERNANDO DANIEL NOPITSCH D'ANDREA.

TRADE UNION

Plenario Intersindical de Trabajadores—Convención Nacional de Trabajadores (PIT—CNT): Avda 18 de Julio 2190, Montevideo; tel. (2) 4096680; fax (2) 4004160; e-mail pitcnt@adinet.uy; internet www.chasque.net/icudu; f. 1966; org. comprising 83 trade unions, 17 labour federations; 320,000 mems; Pres. JORGE CASTRO; Exec. Sec. JUAN CASTILLO.

Transport

Dirección Nacional de Transporte: Rincón 575, 5°, 11000 Montevideo; tel. (2) 9162940; fax (2) 9163122; e-mail dntdinac@adinet.com.uy; internet www.dnt.gub.uy; co-ordinates national and international transport services.

RAILWAYS

Administración de los Ferrocarriles del Estado (AFE): La Paz 1095, Casilla 419, Montevideo; tel. (2) 9240805; fax (2) 9240847; e-mail affegg@adinet.com.uy; f. 1952; state org.; 3,002 km of track connecting all parts of the country; there are connections with the Argentine and Brazilian networks; passenger services ceased in 1988; passenger services linking Montevideo with Florida and Canelones were resumed in mid-1993; Pres. NILO OJEDA.

ROADS

In 2003 Uruguay had an estimated 8,733 km of motorways (forming the most dense motorway network in South America), connecting Montevideo with the main towns of the interior and the Argentine and Brazilian frontiers. There was also a network of approximately 40,000 km of paved roads under departmental control.

Corporación Vial del Uruguay, SA: Rincón 528, 7°, 11000 Montevideo; tel. (2) 9170114; e-mail cvu@cnd.org.uy; state road construction agency; 100% owned by the Corporación Nacional para el Desarrollo; Gen. Man. CRISTINA MONTES; Pres. ALDO BONSIGNORE.

INLAND WATERWAYS

There are about 1,250 km of navigable waterways, which provide an important means of transport.

Nobleza Naviera, SA: Avda General Rondeau 2257, Montevideo; tel. (2) 9243222; fax (2) 9243218; e-mail nobleza@netgate.com.uy; operates cargo services on the River Plate, and the Uruguay and Paraná rivers; Chair. AMÉRICO DEAMBROSI; Man. Dir DORIS FERRARI.

SHIPPING

Administración Nacional de Combustibles, Alcohol y Portland (ANCAP): Paraguay 1598, 11100 Montevideo; tel. (2) 9020608; fax (2) 9021136; e-mail webmaster@ancap.com.uy; internet www.ancap.com.uy; f. 1931; deals with transport, refining and sale of petroleum products, and the manufacture of alcohol, spirit and cement; tanker services, also river transport; Pres. DANIEL MARTÍNEZ; Gen. Man. SERGIO LATTANZIO; Sec.-Gen. JORGE URRUTIA.

Directory

Administración Nacional de Puertos (ANP): Rambla 25 de Agosto de 1825 160, Montevideo; tel. (2) 9151441; fax (2) 9161704; e-mail presidencia@anp.com.uy; internet www.anp.com.uy; f. 1916; national ports admin; Pres. LUIS E. LOUREIRO.

Prefectura Nacional Naval: Edif. Comando General de la Armada, 5°, Rambla 25 de Agosto de 1825 s/n, esq. Maciel, Montevideo; tel. (2) 9160741; fax (2) 9163969; internet www.armada.gub.uy/prena; f. 1829; maritime supervisory body, responsible for rescue services, protection of sea against pollution, etc.; Commdr Rear-Adm. OSCAR OTERO IZZI.

Navegación Atlántida, SA: Río Branco 1373, 11100 Montevideo; tel. (2) 9084449; f. 1967; ferry services for passengers and vehicles between Argentina and Uruguay; Pres. H. C. PIETRANERA.

Transportadora Marítima de Combustibles, SA (TRAMACO, SA): Rincón 540, Puerta Baja, 11000 Montevideo; tel. (2) 9165754; fax (2) 9165755; e-mail tramaco@tramaco.com.uy; Pres. J. FERNÁNDEZ BAUBETA.

CIVIL AVIATION

Civil aviation is controlled by the Dirección General de Aviación Civil and the Dirección General de Infraestructura Aeronáutica. The main airport is at Carrasco, 21 km from Montevideo, and there are also airports at Paysandú, Rivera, Salto, Melo, Artigas, Punta del Este and Durazno.

Primeras Líneas Uruguayas de Navegación Aérea (PLUNA): Col. 1013, 11000 Montevideo; tel. (2) 9030273; fax (2) 9023916; e-mail info@pluna.com.uy; internet www.pluna.aero; f. 1936; nationalized 1951; partially privatized in 1994; 49% stake acquired by Aerolíneas Argentinas in 2004; operates international services to Argentina, Brazil, Chile, El Salvador, Paraguay, Spain and the USA; Dir VÍCTOR MESA; Man. JORGE NEVES.

Aeromás, SA: Aeropuerto Internacional de Carrasco s/n, Of. 101, Montevideo; tel. (2) 6040294; fax (2) 6040013; e-mail aeromas@aeromas.com; internet www.aeromas.com; private hire, cargo, and air ambulance flights; internal mass transit services to Salto, Paysandú, Rivera, Tacuarembó and Artigas; f. 1983; Dir DANIEL DALMÁS.

Tourism

The sandy beaches and woodlands on the coast and the grasslands of the interior, with their variety of fauna and flora, provide the main tourist attractions. About 57% of tourists came from Argentina, and a further 10% from Brazil in 2003. Uruguay received 1.5m. visitors in that year. In 2003 tourism revenues totalled US $406m.; however, these figures represented a significant decrease from the the 2.1m. visitors received in 2001, when revenues totalled $700m. The decline was owing to economic difficulties in neighbouring Argentina, which accounted for over one-half of all tourist arrivals. Brazil accounted for a further 10% of tourists.

Asociación Uruguaya de Agencias de Viajes (AUDAVI): Río Branco 1407, Of. 205, 11100 Montevideo; tel. (2) 9012326; fax (2) 9021972; e-mail audavi@netgate.com.uy; f. 1951; 100 mems; Pres. FEDERICO GAMBARDELLA; Man. MÓNICA W. DE RAIJ.

Cámara Uruguaya de Turismo: La Paz 3052, 11800 Montevideo; tel. (2) 4016013; fax (2) 4016013.

Uruguay Natural: Rambla 25 de Agosto de 1825, esq. Yacaré s/n, Montevideo; tel. (2) 1885100; e-mail webmaster@mintur.gub.uy; internet www.uruguaynatural.com; f. 2003; state-run tourism promotion agency; Dir-Gen. MARTHA CASAL.

Uruguayan Hotel Association: Gutiérrez Ruiz 1213, Montevideo; tel. (2) 9080141; fax (2) 9082317; e-mail ahru@montevideo.com.uy; internet www.ahru.org; Pres. EDGARDO BENZO.

UZBEKISTAN

Introductory Survey

Location, Climate, Language, Religion, Flag, Capital

The Republic of Uzbekistan (formerly the Uzbek Soviet Socialist Republic) is located in Central Asia. It is bordered by Kazakhstan to the north, Turkmenistan to the south-west, Kyrgyzstan to the east, Tajikistan to the south-east and Afghanistan to the south. The climate is marked by extreme temperatures and low levels of precipitation. Summers are long and hot with average temperatures in July of 32°C (90°F); daytime temperatures often exceed 40°C (104°F). During the short winter there are frequent severe frosts, and temperatures can fall as low as −38°C (−36°F). The official language is Uzbek. Islam is the predominant religion. Most Uzbeks are Sunni Muslims, principally of the Hanafi school, although there are small communities of Salafis; Sufism is relatively well established in southern Uzbekistan. There are also Orthodox Christians among the Slavic communities. At the end of 1993 there were some 32,000 Jews in Uzbekistan; many Jews have since emigrated to Israel. The national flag (proportions 1 by 2) consists of five unequal horizontal stripes of (from top to bottom) light blue, red, white, red and light green, with a white crescent and 12 white stars near the hoist on the top stripe. The capital is Tashkent (Toshkent).

Recent History

Soviet power was first established in parts of Uzbekistan in November 1917. In April 1918 the Turkestan Autonomous Soviet Socialist Republic (ASSR), a vast region in Central Asia including Uzbekistan, was proclaimed, but Soviet forces withdrew against opposition from the nationalist *basmachi* movement, the White Army and a British expeditionary force. Soviet power was re-established in September 1919, although armed opposition continued until the early 1920s. The khanates of Boxora (Bukhara) and Xiva (Khiva) became nominally independent Soviet republics in 1920, but were incorporated into the Turkestan ASSR by 1924. On 27 October 1924 the Uzbek Soviet Socialist Republic (SSR) was established (including, until 1929, the Tajik ASSR). In May 1925 the Uzbek SSR became a constituent republic of the Union of Soviet Socialist Republics (USSR, which had been established in December 1922). In 1936 Qoraqalpog'iston (Karakalpakstan) was transferred from the Russian Federation to the Uzbek SSR, retaining its status as a nominally autonomous viloyat (oblast or region).

The National Delimitation of the Central Asian republics of 1924–25 established an Uzbek nation-state for the first time. Its formation was accompanied by the development of a new literary language (the ancient Uzbek literary language, Chagatai, was understood by only a small minority of the population). Literacy rose from 3.8% at the 1926 census to 52.5% in 1932, and there was an increase in the provision of educational facilities, which played a crucial role in the policy of secularization. Muslim schools, courts and mosques were closed, and Muslim clergy were persecuted.

There had been little industrial development in Central Asia under the Tsarist regime, other than the extraction of raw materials. Under the first two Five-Year Plans (1928–33 and 1933–38), however, there was considerable economic growth, aided by the immigration of skilled workers from other republics of the USSR. Although economic expansion continued at a significant rate after the Second World War (during which Uzbekistan's industrial base was enlarged by the transfer of industries from the war-zone), most Uzbeks continued to lead a traditional rural life-style, affected only by the huge increase in the amount of cotton grown in the republic.

There was a greater measure of freedom of the press in the late 1980s, facilitated by the policies of the Soviet leader, Mikhail Gorbachev, which allowed discussion of previously unexamined aspects of Uzbek history and contemporary ecological and economic problems. The over-irrigation of land to feed the vast cotton-fields had caused both salination of the soil and, most importantly, the desication of the Aral Sea, which is a vital element in the ecology of the entire region.

Environmental problems and the status of the Uzbek language were among the concerns on which Uzbekistan's first major non-communist political movement, Unity (Birlik), campaigned. Formed in 1988, it rapidly became the main challenger to the ruling Communist Party of Uzbekistan (CPU). However, the movement was not granted official registration, and its attempts to nominate a candidate in the 1989 elections to the USSR's Congress of People's Deputies were unsuccessful. Nevertheless, its campaign led to the adoption of legislation declaring Uzbek to be the official language of the republic in October of that year.

On 18 February 1990 elections were held to the 500-seat Uzbekistani Supreme Soviet (Supreme Council—legislature). Members of Unity were not permitted to stand as candidates, and many leading members of the CPU stood unopposed. The new Supreme Soviet convened in March and elected Islam Karimov, the First Secretary (leader) of the CPU, to the newly created post of executive President.

In April 1991 Uzbekistan agreed, together with eight other Soviet republics, to sign a new Union Treaty to redefine the state structure of the USSR. However, on 19 August, the day before the signing was to take place, there was an attempt to stage a *coup d'état* by conservative communists in Moscow, the Russian and Soviet capital. President Karimov only expressed his opposition to the coup once it became clear that it had failed. On 31 August an extraordinary session of the Supreme Soviet voted to declare the republic independent, as the Republic of Uzbekistan. The CPU voted to dissociate itself from the Communist Party of the Soviet Union, and in November the party was restructured as the People's Democratic Party of Uzbekistan (PDPU), with Karimov retaining the leadership.

On 21 December 1991 Karimov agreed, together with 10 other republican leaders, to dissolve the USSR and formally establish the Commonwealth of Independent States (CIS, see p. 201). On 29 December a direct presidential election was held for the first time in Uzbekistan, which was won by Karimov, with a reported 86% of the total votes cast. His sole rival (winning 12% of the votes) was the poet Muhammad Salih (Solikh), the leader of the Freedom (Erk) party, which had been established as an offshoot of Unity in 1990. (Unity was banned from contesting the election, as it had still not been granted official registration as a political party.) A referendum was held concurrently, in which 98.2% of participants endorsed Uzbekistan's independence.

The PDPU remained dominant both in the Supreme Council and the Cabinet of Ministers. Under Karimov's authoritarian leadership, there was widespread repression of opposition and Islamist groups. Uzbekistan's new Constitution, adopted on 8 December 1992, firmly enshrined the concept of state secularism. It also guaranteed a democratic multi-party system, freedom of expression and the observance of human rights. In addition, the Constitution provided for a new, smaller legislature, the 250-member Oly Majlis (Supreme Assembly), with effect from elections due to be held in late 1994.

Despite the Constitution's provisions, on the day of its adoption three leading opposition members, who were attending an international conference on human rights in the Kyrgyzstani capital, Bishkek, were seized by Uzbekistani security police on charges of sedition. (One of their number was put on trial.) On the following day Unity was banned for its allegedly subversive activities. Restriction of the media also intensified: in mid-1993 the Government instructed all newspapers and periodicals to be re-registered with the State Committee for the Press; only organs of state and government were permitted official registration. In October Freedom failed to receive registration as a political party and was subsequently banned.

Although Karimov pledged that all political parties would be free to contest the elections to the Oly Majlis in 1994, in the event only the PDPU and its ally, Progress of the Fatherland (PF), were permitted to register. At the elections, held on 25 December (with a second round of voting in January 1995), the PDPU won 69 of the 250 seats, and the PF secured 14. The remaining 167 deputies elected had been nominated by local councils rather than by political parties; however, the majority of these deputies (some 120) were members of the PDPU, and thus the party's domination of the Majlis was retained. Some 94% of eligible voters were reported to have participated in the election.

In January 1995 Karimov announced that the Government would welcome a diversification of opinions in the Oly Majlis and that it would permit the formation of blocs. In February a new political party, the Justice (Adolat) Social Democratic Party of Uzbekistan, was registered, and immediately declared its intention to establish such a parliamentary faction (it claimed to have the support of some 47 deputies within the Majlis). A referendum held in March produced a 99.6% vote in favour of extending Karimov's presidential term from 1997 to 2000, when parliamentary elections were due to be held. In May two new political formations emerged: the National Revival (Milliy Tiklanish) Democratic Party and the People's Unity (Xalq Birligi) Movement. Both were reported to be pro-Government, and were officially registered in June. In December 1995 Otkir Sultanov, hitherto the Minister of Foreign Economic Relations, replaced Abdulkhashim Mutalov as Prime Minister. In June 1996 Karimov resigned from his position as Chairman of the PDPU.

During 1996 Karimov began to advocate the creation of a political opposition to the PDPU, and in December a new law on political parties was approved by the Oly Majlis. The legislation prohibited the organization of parties on a religious or ethnic basis and compelled prospective parties to provide evidence of some 5,000 members drawn from a majority of Uzbekistan's administrative regions.

There was an upsurge of violence in eastern Uzbekistan, particularly in the densely populated Farg'ona (Fergana) valley (which Uzbekistan shares with Kazakhstan, Kyrgyzstan and Tajikistan), in late 1997: in November the deputy head of the local administration of Namangan Viloyat (region) was assassinated, and in the following month four police-officers were killed. The Government attributed the unrest to groups of Islamist activists, and in mid-December government troops were dispatched to the area, resulting in hundreds of arrests. The Government's campaign against Islamist extremism intensified in early 1998. In February the Ministry of Foreign Affairs appealed to the Pakistani Government to extirpate military training camps in that country, where Uzbeks were allegedly being trained in dissident activities. (Pakistan denied the existence of any such camps.) In May the Oly Majlis adopted legislation that severely limited the activities of religious organizations in Uzbekistan. Karimov declared to the Majlis that he would be prepared personally to execute members of Islamist groups found guilty of terrorism. In May–July several suspected militant Islamists were sentenced to terms of imprisonment, and a member of an Islamist organization was sentenced to death after having been found guilty of the murder of five people and of involvement in the training of militants in Afghanistan. Human rights groups claimed that the Government was attempting to create fear within the religious opposition prior to the forthcoming legislative and presidential elections. In January 1999 five men allegedly linked with a former *imam* of Tashkent's Tokhtoboy mosque, who had been in hiding since early 1998, were found guilty of attempting to overthrow the Government and establish an Islamist state. Meanwhile, in June 1998 new legislation was passed banning the purchase, sale or exchange of land.

In February 1999 a series of bombs exploded in the centre of Tashkent, killing an estimated 15 people. Government officials claimed that the explosions had been carried out in an attempt to assassinate President Karimov and destabilize the country. In mid-May the Government announced legislation imposing harsher punishment for members of 'religious, extremist, separatist and fundamentalist organizations', under an amendment to the Criminal Code. Following the trial, in June, of 22 people suspected of involvement in the bomb attacks, six of the accused were sentenced to death, and the other defendants received lengthy prison sentences. In mid-August six members of the banned Freedom party were also given prison sentences of between eight and 15 years for their alleged involvement in the bombings; it was reported that two of the defendants were brothers of Salih. In mid-November the Tashkent region was infiltrated by a group of about 15 armed militants, resulting in the shooting of three police-officers and three civilians. (It was alleged that the group, who were subsequently killed by security forces, had been trained in the separatist Chechen Republic, Russia, and had entered Uzbekistan from Kyrgyzstan.) Following the violence, Karimov demanded increased security in the capital and appealed to the Organization of Security and Co-operation in Europe (OSCE, see p. 327) to assist Uzbekistan in combating international terrorism.

At elections to the Oly Majlis, held on 5 and 19 December 1999, the PDPU was reported to have secured the largest representation of any single party in the legislature, winning 48 seats. Non-partisan local council nominees, however, obtained a combined total of 110 seats. The Self-Sacrificers' (Fidokorlar) National Democratic Party (founded in December 1998 with the support of Karimov) was the second largest party, with 34 seats, while the PF (with 20 seats), the Justice Social Democratic Party (11) and the National Revival Democratic Party (10) also achieved representation in the Oly Majlis. Of the 250 seats, only 184 were filled at the first round, on 5 December, which necessitated a second round of voting on 19 December, at which all but one deputy was elected. The rate of voter participation at the first round was reported to be some 93.5%. The OSCE had sent only a limited number of observers to the elections, claiming that Uzbekistan had reneged on earlier commitments to make them free and fair, since all of the parties participating were pro-Government and two opposition parties had been prevented from contesting.

President Karimov reportedly secured 91.9% of the votes cast at the presidential election held on 9 January 2000, compared with only 4.2% for his sole opponent, the leader of the PDPU, Abdulkhafiz Jalolov. He was duly inaugurated for another five-year term on 22 January. A reported 95% of the registered electorate participated in the poll. However, both the OSCE and the US Government criticized the election as undemocratic, as opposition parties had been barred from nominating candidates.

The trial of 12 defendants accused of involvement in the bomb attacks of February 1999 opened in October 2000. In mid-November the spiritual leader of the banned militant group the Islamic Movement of Uzbekistan (IMU), Takhir Yoldoshev, and his field commander, Jumaboy Khojiyev (known as Juma Namangoniy), were sentenced to death, *in absentia*. The remaining 10 defendants (including, *in absentia*, Salih) were sentenced to between 12 and 20 years' imprisonment. In June 2001 10 further Islamist militants were reported to have received prison sentences for attempting to overthrow the Government. In early December it was reported that Karimov had requested the extradition of Salih from the Czech capital, Prague. However, in mid-December Salih was released by a Czech court.

The Government's repression of minorities continued in 2001. During March, in the towns of Samarqand and Boxora (Bukhara), which had large ethnic Tajik populations and which had been incorporated into Uzbekistan at the formation of the SSRs, books in the Tajik language were removed from libraries and schools. At the end of April allegations emerged that the Ministry of Education had commanded the destruction of books in the Tajik language elsewhere in the country, including areas with large ethnic Tajik populations.

The perceived threat of the Islamist militant movement intensified in the latter half of 2001, following the suicide attacks in the USA on 11 September (see below), and Uzbekistan's decision to co-operate with the USA in its attempts to form an international coalition to combat the al-Qa'ida (Base) organization (harboured by Afghanistan's Taliban regime). It was widely believed that Karimov expected to secure strategic benefits from such co-operation, notably the suppression of the IMU and the moderation of international criticism of his Government's position on economic reforms and human rights. In the mean time, further restrictions were placed on the media, in an attempt to limit public reprisals against the country's co-operation with the USA. There were frequent allegations of the torture and arrest of suspected members of the IMU and Hizb-ut-Tahrir al-Islami (Hizb-ut-Tahrir—the Party of Islamic Liberation), a clandestine, transnational organization, which sought to re-establish a caliphate, apparently solely through peaceful means, and which was alleged to enjoy significant support in Uzbekistan and neighbouring countries, particularly in the Farg'ona valley region. In mid-October an estimated 5,000–7,000 members of the IMU (which both the UN and the USA identified as a terrorist organization) were reported to be fighting alongside forces of Afghanistan's Taliban regime.

On 27 January 2002 a referendum took place to seek approval for proposed constitutional amendments, which would extend the President's term of office for a further two years and change the legislative structure. Some 91.6% of the electorate participated, of whom 93.7% approved the establishment of a bicameral legislature and 91.8% endorsed the extension of the presidential term to seven years. In early April the Oly Majlis approved a resolution delaying the next presidential election by two years, until 2007. The legislature also endorsed a resolution on the election of a new, bicameral legislature in December 2004; the upper chamber, the Senat (Senate), was to be composed of members of local councils and 16 presidentially appointed citizens. In early March 2002 the Government registered the country's first domestic human rights group.

In December 2002 the Oly Majlis passed legislation on the formation of the new, bicameral legislature; Karimov announced that the Senat would assume some of the duties formerly performed by the President. In April 2003 the Oly Majlis approved constitutional amendments permitting the redistribution of authority within the Government, with effect from the next legislative elections. The changes were to separate responsibility for leading the cabinet from the role of the President, and to remove the right to occupy simultaneously the roles of president and prime minister. In addition, a law granting former presidents lifelong immunity from prosecution and permanent membership of the Senat was endorsed, and the judiciary was restructured.

On 11 December 2003 the Oly Majlis confirmed the appointment by Karimov of a new Prime Minister, Shavkat Mirziyoyev, who had substantial experience in the agricultural sector; O'tkir Sultonov, whose Government had been criticized for its focus on industry, became a Deputy Prime Minister, with responsibility for energy, petroleum and the chemicals sectors. In mid-March 2004 the Deputy Prime Minister and Minister of the Economy, Rustam Azimov, revealed plans to improve the efficiency of the Government, which was reorganized to comprise 13 ministries and 11 state committees.

In late March 2004 there was an outbreak of widespread violence, the motives for which were unclear. On 28–29 March three police-officers were reportedly killed in two separate shooting incidents in Tashkent; on 29 March further casualties were reported, following two apparent suicide bomb attacks in the city's Chorsu market. It was also reported that 10 people had been killed and 26 injured after bombs exploded in an apartment block in Buxoro, which police alleged was being used to manufacture explosives. On 30 March security forces carried out a raid in Tashkent, during which at least 16 suspected militants and three police-officers were reported to have been killed. Karimov attributed the violence to militant Islamist organizations, and at the end of the month the Uzbekistani authorities began to make widespread arrests. A further bomb attack on 1 April killed one person and prompted the Government to temporarily close its land borders. By late July some 85 people suspected of involvement in the attacks had been arrested. In August 13 Islamist militants were sentenced to between six and 16 years' imprisonment; a further two, Furkat Yusupov and Farkhad Kazakbayev, considered to be the most active members of Jamoat, a militant Islamic organization alleged to be associated with al-Qa'ida, each received gaol sentences of 18 years. In late October 23 of the accused were sentenced to between three and 18 years' imprisonment; officials dismissed allegations that torture had been used to obtain confessions. In July 2005 a further 20 men were sentenced to terms of imprisonment for their involvement in the attacks.

Meanwhile, in late July 2004 seven people were killed as a result of suicide bomb attacks in Tashkent outside the Israeli and US embassies and outside the Office of the Prosecutor-General. President Karimov rejected allegations of IMU involvement in the attacks and accused Hizb-ut-Tahrir of bearing primary responsibility, in collusion with other international militant Islamist groups. In early December the office of the Prosecutor-General declared that all three of the suicide bombers had been Kazakhstani citizens.

Further civil unrest had broken out in early November 2004, with riots in Qoqand in the Farg'ona valley, where some 5,000–10,000 people protested against the introduction of new laws affecting market traders; the protests spread to markets in other towns in Uzbekistan, including Farg'ona, Boxora and Margilan. In early December rights groups and opposition parties gathered outside the US embassy, urging the USA to encourage the Uzbekistani Government to promote democracy and respect for human rights in Uzbekistan, after three opposition parties (Unity, Freedom and the Free Peasants' Party) were refused permission to put forward candidates for the legislative elections scheduled for the end of the month; all five of the parties permitted to participate in the elections supported the Government. Ten days before the elections, security measures were tightened around the country, apparently in an attempt to forestall possible terrorist attacks.

Elections to the Qoqunchilik palatasi Kengashi (Legislative Chamber), as the lower chamber of the new bicameral legislature was designated, were held on 26 December 2004, with a second round of voting on 9 January 2005 in 58 of the 120 constituencies where no candidate had obtained an absolute majority of votes cast. A party established in late 1993 by allies of Karimov, and led by Muhammadjon Ahmadjonov, the Movement of Entrepreneurs and Businessmen—Liberal Democratic Party of Uzbekistan, obtained 41 seats, securing the largest representation of any single party in the legislature. The PDPU obtained 28 seats, the Self-Sacrificers' National Democratic Party 18, the National Revival Democratic Party 11, and the Justice Social Democratic Party 10. The rate of voter participation at the first round was estimated to be 85.1%. Although OSCE observers commented that the Government's refusal to register opposition groups and independent candidates had deprived citizens of a genuine choice, the Central Election Commission maintained that the ballot had been conducted freely, in accordance with democratic standards. On 14 January 2005 President Karimov announced the appointment of 16 members of the Senat (the upper chamber); regional council members elected 84 senators on 17–20 January. The Senat's inaugural session took place on 27 January. Meanwhile, a number of ministerial changes were effected in late 2004 and early 2005.

There were reports of heightened political tensions in early 2005, particularly in the Farg'ona valley, which were attributed to a number of factors, including dissatisfaction at widespread poverty, the influence of the political upheaval in neighbouring Kyrgyzstan in March (see the chapter on Kyrgyzstan), and discontent at restrictions on trade and on the freedom of association. From February daily peaceful protests, some of which were apparently attended by up to 1,000 people, were reported outside a court in Andijon, where 23 local business executives had been brought to trial on charges of belonging to a prohibited Islamist organization, referred to by the authorities as Akhramia, and alleged to have broken away from Hizb-ut-Tahrir. All 23 denied the charges brought against them. In the early hours of 13 May, several days before the trial of the alleged Islamists was due to conclude, a group of armed men (stormed the gaol in Andijon, and released as many as 2,000 prisoners, including the 23 people charged with belonging to Akhramia. Armed rebels were reported to have taken control of the regional administration building in the city later that day, and several thousand people gathered in the main city square, apparently to protest against both the trial of the alleged militants and economic difficulties. Heavily armed state security forces, including troops in tanks, entered the city and opened fire on the demonstrators. The exact number of people killed was disputed, in part because of the strict restrictions placed on media coverage and on access to the region by foreign diplomatic representatives or members of non-governmental organizations. Karimov blamed the violence on Islamist extremists who, he claimed, sought to establish a caliphate across Central Asia, although he denied that he had ordered troops to fire on the crowd. Protests continued in Andijon later in the month, and unrest was reported in Qorasuv, south-east of Andijon, on the border with Kyrgyzstan, where local Islamist rebels seized control of the local administration and re-opened a border crossing with Kyrgyzstan that had been closed in 2000. State forces subsequently surrounded the town and repulsed the militants. Meanwhile, Kyrgyzstan reported that it had registered more than 500 Uzbekistani refugees in the immediate aftermath of the violence in Andijon (see below).

President Karimov rejected requests by the international community for an independent investigation into the events in Andijon, although foreign diplomats were permitted a restricted tour of the city. In July 2005 the Prosecutor of Andijon Viloyat announced that 187 people had been killed as a result of the violence, including 94 'terrorists', 57 civilians, 20 law-enforcement officials and 11 soldiers (in contrast, according to some independent reports, as many as 1,000 people, mainly civilians, had been killed). In early September a report released by the Office of the Prosecutor-General stated that external Islamists had staged the violence. The report also claimed that in January–April instructors in Kyrgyzstan had trained some 70 religious fundamentalists in terrorist techniques. In August Karimov approved a decree abolishing capital punishment from 2008.

UZBEKISTAN

In September 2005 the First Deputy Prosecutor-General proposed that 'external forces' had instructed Western journalists to publish false information about the events in Andijon in the foreign media. Meanwhile, individuals and organizations providing accounts that undermined the credibility of the Government's version of events were subject to official harassment, and many were expelled from the country or imprisoned. In October the European Union (EU, see p. 228) imposed sanctions on Uzbekistan (including a ban on travel to EU states by officials suspected of involvement in the shooting of civilians in Andijon, and an embargo on the export of weapons and other equipment that could be used for internal repression), owing to the Government's refusal either to permit an international investigation into events at Andijon or to bring those who had perpetrated the killings to trial. By late December more than 150 people had been sentenced to terms of imprisonment for their involvement in the protests in Andijon; in November the UN High Commissioner for Human Rights and the USA expressed concern that defendants were being convicted without being permitted a fair trial, and the international human rights organization Human Rights Watch condemned the use of closed trials. There were also allegations of the use of torture to extract confessions. In February 2006 the Government approved a resolution that made journalists deemed to be interfering in internal affairs or insulting Uzbekistani citizens liable to prosecution. In March the authorities requested that the UN High Commissioner for Refugees vacate its offices in Uzbekistan, asserting that it was no longer required in the country.

Meanwhile, frequent government changes continued to be effected in 2005–06. Notably, in mid-November 2005 Karimov dismissed the Minister of Defence, Qodir G'ulomov; he was succeeded by Ruslan Mirzayev. Later in November, Rustam Azimov was appointed as Minister of Finance; Azimov, hitherto the Minister of Foreign Economic Relations, Investment and Trade, was replaced in that position by Alisher Shayxov. At the end of December the Minister of Internal Affairs, Zokirjon Almatov, resigned from his post, citing ill health (the EU held Almatov responsible for overseeing the violent repression of the protests in Andijon). He was replaced by Bahodir Matlyubov in early January 2006. In April Vyacheslav Golishev was dismissed from the position of Deputy Prime Minister, responsible for the Economic Sector and Foreign Economic Relations, and Minister of the Economy; he was replaced by Botir Hojayev.

Uzbekistan's closest relations are with the neighbouring Central Asian republics—Kazakhstan, Kyrgyzstan, Tajikistan and Turkmenistan—also CIS members. In September 1997 a Central Asian peace-keeping battalion participated, with troops from the USA and other countries, in military manoeuvres, which were held in Uzbekistan and elsewhere in the region under the auspices of NATO's 'Partnership for Peace' (see p. 316) programme of military co-operation. (Uzbekistan had joined the programme in 1994.) In October 1998 Uzbekistan and Kazakhstan signed a Treaty of Eternal Friendship and agreed on a seven-year programme of bilateral economic co-operation. In November 2001 Uzbekistan and Kazakhstan signed a treaty demarcating most of their border. However, the demarcation of certain areas, including the villages of Bagys and Turkestanets, remained unresolved. The majority of citizens in Bagys were ethnic Kazakhs, and it had been hoped that the land, hitherto leased to Uzbekistan, would be returned to Kazakhstan following independence. However, Uzbekistan had been reluctant to cede the land, and Kazakhstan did not pursue the matter, in order to maintain good diplomatic relations. As a sign of their frustration, in December residents declared an Independent Kazakh Republic of Bagys, and elected a president and legislature. The Uzbekistani security forces subsequently arrested a number of activists, and in late April 2002 it was reported that troops had barricaded the villages, after virtual martial law had been established in Bagys. In September a new agreement delimiting the Kazakhstani–Uzbekistani border was signed by the countries' Presidents. However, at the end of 2002 Uzbekistan unexpectedly closed its border with Kazakhstan, following the introduction of new import taxes. The creation of a working group to finalize the demarcation of the border between the two countries was announced in early August 2003. However, there was a reported increase in violent confrontations on the border between Uzbekistan and Kazakhstan following the arrests of Kazakhstani citizens in connection with a series of bombings in Uzbekistan in mid-2004 (see above), and in early January 2005 representatives from the Uzbekistani Ministry of Defence reportedly announced that they considered Kazakhstan to be a potential military adversary and a base for militant groups opposed to the Uzbekistani regime. In the same month the Uzbekistani authorities announced proposals for the demolition of settlements along the border, apparently in response to cross-border smuggling. Demonstrations in early February by residents demanding compensation for the destruction of their homes were met with a promise from the Khokim (Governor) of Tashkent Viloyat that an assessment of property values in the village would be conducted with the view of providing the residents with future compensation. In early March President Karimov and the President of Kazakhstan, Nursultan Nazarbayev, agreed to establish a working group to create a future free-trade zone.

In mid-1990 there was inter-ethnic tension in connection with clashes in Osh, a region in Kyrgyzstan in the Farg'ona valley with an ethnic Uzbek majority (see the chapter on Kyrgyzstan). Border crossings were closed to prevent up to 15,000 armed Uzbekistani citizens from joining the Uzbeks in Kyrgyzstan, and President Karimov declared a state of emergency in Andijon Viloyat (which borders Osh). Relations worsened in September 2000, when Uzbekistani government forces planted landmines along the Kyrgyzstani–Uzbekistani border, in order to prevent insurgents from entering Uzbekistan, apparently without having informed Kyrgyzstani border guards. Although it was announced in June 2001 that the mines were to be removed, there were claims in September that the laying of mines was continuing. As a result, the Kyrgyzstani legislature refused to ratify an agreement with Uzbekistan on arms supplies. Tension on the border increased in April, after the two Governments again failed to resolve territorial disputes. In March 2002 Uzbekistan agreed to supply natural gas to Kyrgyzstan in return for deliveries of water.

Relations with Kyrgyzstan were again strained in mid-2005, when the Kyrgyzstani Government refused to return a large number of refugees, who had fled there from Uzbekistan following the violence in Andijon in May (see above). In July more than 400 refugees were deported from Kyrgyzstan to Romania, which Uzbekistan condemned as a violation of international law. There were subsequent reports that refugees repatriated to Uzbekistan had been tortured, and in August 2005 Uzbekistan annulled a bilateral agreement to supply natural gas to Kyrgyzstan. The following month, Uzbekistan issued a report accusing Kyrgyzstan of having permitted religious extremists to use bases in the south of the country to prepare to foment unrest in Andijon. (Ethnic Kyrgyz had been among those arrested in connection with the violence.)

In September 2000 Turkmenistan and Uzbekistan signed a treaty demarcating their 1,867-km border. Tighter control of the border, however, exacerbated tension (see the Turkmenistan chapter). In mid-December 2002 Turkmen special forces entered the Uzbekistani embassy in the Turkmen capital, Aşgabat, purportedly in order to investigate reports that it was harbouring Boris Shikhmuradov, whom the Turkmenistani authorities blamed for an assassination attempt against that country's President, Saparmyrat Niyazov. Uzbekistan's ambassador to Turkmenistan was subsequently declared *persona non grata*, on the grounds that he had offered support to Shikhmuradov. The Uzbekistani authorities denied the allegations and reacted with hostility; open confrontation rapidly led to the deployment of troops from both countries along their mutual border, and an associated increase in border security. However, in mid-November 2004 Presidents Karimov and Niyazov met for their first presidential summit in more than four years, in Boxora, where they signed three bilateral agreements, pertaining to: friendship, mutual trust, and co-operation; simplifying regulations concerning cross-border travel for residents of border zones (where cross-border smuggling and related shooting incidents had become a problem in recent years); and a framework for sharing regional water resources. The Presidents declared that all bilateral issues had been resolved, and in January 2005 Uzbekistan appointed a new ambassador to Turkmenistan.

Uzbekistan dispatched troops to Tajikistan in 1992, as part of a CIS peace-keeping contingent, and it tightened border controls with Tajikistan in an attempt to prevent the Tajikistani civil conflict from extending into Uzbekistan (see the chapter on Tajikistan). It was reported that the Uzbekistani Government actively supported the communist regime in Tajikistan in its efforts to suppress opposition Islamist and democratic forces. This was attributed, in part, to Uzbek concerns for co-nationals in Tajikistan (who formed that republic's largest ethnic minority). The Tajikistani Government and opposition forces signed a peace accord in June 1997; however, Uzbekistan did not agree to act as one of the guarantor states of the accord until August. During a visit to Uzbekistan in January 1998, President Imamali Rakhmonov of Tajikistan met Karimov, and the two leaders expressed their opposition to religious extremism. In the following month an intergovernmental agreement on restructuring Tajikistan's debt to Uzbekistan was agreed. In mid-1998 Tajikistan joined the trilateral economic area established by Uzbekistan, Kazakhstan and Kyrgyzstan, which became the Central Asian Co-operation Organization (CACO) from March 2002. In February 1999 Uzbekistan announced its intention to withdraw from the CIS Collective Security Treaty, owing to its opposition to Russia's attempts at closer integration within the CIS and, in particular, Russia's military presence in Tajikistan. In August the Uzbekistani Government accused Tajikistan of allowing militant groups to operate from its territory. From August 2000 armed Islamist militants made a series of incursions into the section of the Farg'ona valley in Uzbekistan from Tajikistan, leading to armed conflict with government forces. By mid-September, however, the remaining militants were reported to have been killed by government troops. In the mean time, Uzbekistan, which had begun laying landmines along its border with Tajikistan from mid-2000, in an effort to prevent cross-border incursions by Islamist insurgents, officially informed Tajikistan of its actions only in early May 2001. However, relations between the two countries subsequently improved. President Rakhmonov met President Karimov in Uzbekistan in December 2001; although no border agreement was reached, it was announced that the crossing between the Penjakent district in Tajikistan and Samarqand Viloyat, in Uzbekistan, was to reopen. The leaders also agreed to collaborate to combat terrorism, crime and the illegal drugs trade. At a meeting of the Tajikistani and Uzbekistani Prime Ministers in February 2002, an agreement on border-crossing procedures was reached. The continued influx of illegal drugs from Tajikistan also threatened relations. However, following a summit of the CACO in October, the Presidents of the two countries agreed on the demarcation of over 85% of their shared border. (In October 2005 it was announced that the CACO intended to merge with the Eurasian Economic Community.)

Uzbekistan's concerns for the security of the Central Asian region, and the threat to stability caused by Islamist extremism, were augmented by the long-standing civil war in Afghanistan. In the early 1990s President Burhanuddin Rabbani of Afghanistan claimed that Uzbekistan was providing military and financial assistance to the Afghan militia leader, Gen. Abdul Rashid Dostam (an ethnic Uzbek), whose forces controlled parts of northern Afghanistan. In 1994 the Uzbekistani Government denied any military involvement in Afghanistan and declared that only humanitarian aid had been given. At a summit meeting attended by representatives of Russia and the Central Asian republics in October 1996, Karimov confirmed that no military assistance would be accorded to Gen. Dostam, but declared that Dostam's forces provided the only defence for the Central Asian republics against the Taliban militant Islamist grouping. Following the defeat of Dostam's forces in May 1997, increased numbers of troops were deployed on the Uzbekistani–Afghan border. In late 1997 the Uzbekistani Government denied having facilitated the return of Gen. Dostam to Afghanistan from exile in Turkey. In October 2000 Gen. Dostam rejected allegations that his troops fought alongside Uzbekistani government forces in August–September to repel incursions by Islamist militants. Relations with the *de facto* ruling Taliban regime in Afghanistan deteriorated after they granted political asylum to Jumaboy Khojiyev, the field commander of the IMU. Relations worsened further following reports in the Pakistani press in late August 2001 that Khojiyev had been appointed the deputy Commander-in-Chief of the Taliban forces.

The Islamist militant threat intensified following the suicide attacks on the USA of 11 September 2001 (see the chapter on the USA). At the same time, Uzbekistan's relationship with the USA became closer. (Relations had already improved noticeably in the latter half of the 1990s, and during a visit to Tashkent in April 2000, the US Secretary of State had affirmed the USA's willingness to assist Uzbekistan in combating the spread of Islamist extremism.) Uzbekistan's decision to support the US-led 'coalition against global terrorism' was of great strategic importance to the USA, which hoped to benefit from access to the country's transportation facilities. On 23 September the Uzbekistani Government confirmed that US military aircraft had landed at an airfield near Tashkent. On 7 October Uzbekistan and the USA signed a co-operation agreement, whereby Uzbekistan agreed to make its airbases available for use in humanitarian and 'search-and-rescue' operations during the US-led aerial bombardment of Taliban and terrorist bases in Afghanistan. The USA also agreed to enter into urgent negotiations, should Uzbekistan's security be threatened. In October 2001 Uzbekistan commenced the deployment of its troops on the Uzbekistani–Afghan border. The Uzbekistani Government was reluctant to accept refugees from Afghanistan, even though 1.5m. of them were ethnic Uzbeks, citing security concerns. Initially, the Government also refused to open the border to allow humanitarian aid to reach Afghanistan. Following the military successes of the anti-Taliban forces in November, however, the Government was persuaded to open the 'Friendship Bridge', the only transit point into Afghanistan, in early December. Khojiyev was reported to have been killed during the US-led military action in Afghanistan. At an official summit of the heads of the Central Asian states in Tashkent in late December 2001 (Turkmenistan was not represented), the leaders declared their support for the new Afghan Interim Administration, which was established following the defeat of the Taliban regime. In March 2002 the leaders of Uzbekistan and Afghanistan pledged jointly to combat terrorism and the drugs trade; the IMU, for example, continued to be a threat to both countries.

In late November 2001 Uzbekistan and the USA signed a number of agreements pledging to improve bilateral relations and to increase economic co-operation. The USA agreed to donate more than US $150m. in aid towards improving Uzbekistan's security and economic development. Further bilateral agreements on political, economic and military co-operation were signed in January and March 2002, and Karimov visited the USA in March. Disagreements over Uzbekistan's pace of democratization, however, remained, and in July 2004 Uzbekistan's lack of progress in democratic reform and human rights practices led the USA to reduce its aid programme by $18m. In October the US Drug Enforcement Agency and Uzbekistan's Ministry of Internal Affairs, together with Azerbaijan, Georgia, Kazakhstan, Kyrgyzstan, Moldova, Russia, Tajikistan and Ukraine, initiated an operation to control the flow of illegal drugs.

Following the violence in Andijon in May 2005, the USA urged Uzbekistan to allow an international inquiry to be undertaken. In June a spokesman from the US Department of State stated that witnesses had reported the killing of hundreds of civilians by Uzbekistani government forces. Uzbekistan subsequently imposed restrictions on the USA's use of the Qarshi-Khanabad ('K-2') military base, which had been used by the USA since October 2001 to support military and other operations in Afghanistan (see above); Uzbekistan also proposed that the USA withdraw from the airbase. Uzbekistan denied allegations that its decision to impose restrictions on the USA's use of the base was prompted by that country's stance on the events in Andijon. However, in July 2005 the Shanghai Co-operation Organization (SCO, see p. 398), prompted by Uzbekistan's allies Russia and the People's Republic of China, issued a statement demanding that deadlines be imposed on the use of military bases in Central Asia by Western countries for operations in Afghanistan. Later in the month, following discussions with the USA, Uzbekistan renounced the agreement under which the USA was permitted to use the Qarshi-Khanabad airbase, and demanded that it vacate the base within six months. The last US military aircraft left the Qarshi-Khanabad base in November.

Relations with Russia, the most influential member state of the CIS, have been intermittently strained by concerns regarding Uzbekistan's ethnic Russian population (which comprised an estimated 5.5% of the population in 1996, according to official figures). Uzbekistan has repeatedly refused to grant dual citizenship to its Russian minority, and since independence many thousands of these Russians have emigrated (Russians had comprised 8.3% of the population in 1989, according to census figures). In October 1998 Russia, Uzbekistan and Tajikistan signed a pact offering mutual military assistance, especially against 'the threat of religious extremism'; at the same time Russia and Uzbekistan signed a number of inter-governmental agreements. Russia supported the Uzbekistani Government's official report on the events in Andijon in May 2005. In June the Russian Minister of Foreign Affairs, Sergei Lavrov, alleged that Islamist militant groups had been involved in the violence. Uzbekistan forged closer relations with Russia in 2005 (as relations with Western countries notably worsened), and in November Karimov and the Russian President, Vladimir Putin, signed a bilateral agreement, which provided for co-operation in:

trade and security; the use of military facilities; and efforts to combat drugs-trafficking and terrorism. Notably, the two countries agreed to provide mutual support in the event that one of them came under attack.

In April 1999 Uzbekistan joined the GUAM grouping, comprising Azerbaijan, Georgia, Moldova and Ukraine, which envisaged implementing joint economic and transportation initiatives and establishing a sub-regional free-trade zone; the organization was therefore renamed GUUAM. However, Uzbekistan was not an active participant in the group, and in early May 2005 announced its intention to withdraw. In March 2006 President Karimov approved legislation passed by the Oly Majlis earlier in the year, which completed Uzbekistan's withdrawal from the organization.

Relations with the People's Republic of China improved in the 1990s, and in July 1996 Jiang Zemin became the first Chinese President to visit Uzbekistan; a joint declaration on bilateral relations and co-operation was signed. China and Uzbekistan signed further co-operation agreements in November 1999, including a joint communiqué on the development of bilateral relations. In October 2000 the two countries signed an agreement on combating terrorism. In June 2001 Uzbekistan joined the SCO, hitherto the Shanghai Forum—comprising China, Russia, Kazakhstan, Kyrgyzstan and Tajikistan—and signed the Shanghai Convention on Combating Terrorism, Separatism and Extremism. At an emergency meeting in October, members agreed to establish a regional anti-terrorism centre, which was to be located in Tashkent. In May 2005 China praised Uzbekistan's management of the outbreak of violence in Andijon earlier that month.

Government

Under the terms of the Constitution of 8 December 1992, Uzbekistan is a secular, democratic presidential republic. The directly elected President is Head of State and also holds supreme executive power. In April 2002 the Oly Majlis adopted a resolution extending the presidential term from five to seven years, with immediate effect. The Government (Cabinet of Ministers) is subordinate to the President, who appoints the Prime Minister, Deputy Prime Ministers and Ministers (subject to the approval of the legislature). The highest legislative body is the bicameral Oly Majlis (Supreme Assembly). The Majlis may be dissolved by the President (with the approval of the Constitutional Court). The Oly Majlis comprises the 120-member lower chamber, the Qoqunchilik palatasi Kengashi (Legislative Chamber), whose members are directly elected for a five-year term. The upper chamber, the Senat (Senate), is composed of 84 members indirectly elected by regional Council members and 16 citizens appointed by the President. Uzbekistan is divided into 12 Viloyats (regions), the city of Toshkent (Tashkent), and one sovereign republic (Qoraqalpog'iston—Karakalpakstan).

Defence

The establishment of Uzbekistani national armed forces was initiated in 1992, and by August 2005 they numbered some 55,000, including an army of 40,000 and an air force of some 10,000–15,000. There were also paramilitary forces numbering up to 20,000 (comprising a 1,000-strong National Guard attached to the Ministry of Defence and up to 19,000 troops attached to the Ministry of Internal Affairs). Compulsory military service lasts for 12 months. The budget for 2005 allocated an estimated 59,900m. sum (US $60m.) to defence. In July 1994 Uzbekistan joined the North Atlantic Treaty Organization's (NATO) 'Partnership for Peace' (see p. 316) programme of military co-operation. In April 1999 Uzbekistan withdrew its membership of the Collective Security Treaty of the Commonwealth of Independent States (CIS, see p. 201).

Economic Affairs

In 2004, according to the World Bank, Uzbekistan's gross national income (GNI), measured at average 2002–04 prices, was US $11,860m., equivalent to $460 per head (or $1,860 per head on an international purchasing-power parity basis). During 1995–2004, it was estimated, the population increased by an annual average of 1.4%, while gross domestic product (GDP) per head increased, in real terms, at an average annual rate of 2.9%. Overall GDP increased, in real terms, by an average of 4.4% per year in 1995–2004. According to the Asian Development Bank (ADB, see p. 169), growth was 7.7% in 2004 and 7.0% in 2005.

In 2004, according to the ADB, agriculture (including forestry) contributed 31.1% of GDP; the agricultural sector employed 31.0% of the working population in that year. Some 60% of the country's land is covered by desert and steppe, while the remainder comprises fertile valleys watered by two major river systems. The massive irrigation of arid areas has greatly increased production of the major crop, cotton, but has caused devastating environmental problems (most urgently the desiccation of the Aral Sea). Uzbekistan is among the five largest producers of cotton in the world, and the crop accounted for 27.5% of the value of total exports in 2000. Other major crops include grain, rice, vegetables and fruit. Since independence the Government has striven to reduce the area under cultivation of cotton in order to produce more grain. Private farming was legalized in 1992, and by 1996 more than 98% of agricultural production originated in the non-state sector. According to World Bank figures, during 1995–2004 agricultural GDP increased, in real terms, by an annual average of 3.3%. According to the ADB, agricultural GDP increased by 10.1% in 2004 and by 6.6% in 2005.

According to the ADB, industry (including mining, manufacturing, utilities and construction) contributed 25.2% of GDP in 2004, when it provided 13.0% employment. According to World Bank figures, during 1995–2004 industrial GDP increased by an average of 2.3% annually, in real terms. According to the ADB, sectoral GDP increased by 5.4% in 2004 and by 4.2% in 2005.

Uzbekistan is well endowed with mineral deposits, in particular gold, natural gas, petroleum and coal. It was estimated that Uzbekistan had sufficient reserves of crude petroleum to maintain output at mid-1990s levels for 30 years, and enough natural gas for 50 years. There are large reserves of silver, copper, lead, zinc and tungsten, and Uzbekistan is one of the world's largest producers of uranium and gold. In 2002 1,860 metric tons of uranium ore was produced; all uranium mined is exported. The Murantau mine, in the Kyzyl-kum desert, was reportedly the world's largest single open-cast gold mine, and produced a reported 74% of Uzbekistan's estimated output in 2003. In 2004 Oxus Gold (of the United Kingdom) and the Uzbekistani Government officially opened a further gold-mining complex in Amantaytau, 30 km from the Murantau mine. Each party had a 50% share in the mine, which had estimated reserves of some 1,400 tons, and was expected to produce some 14 tons of gold per year by 2007.

The manufacturing sector contributed 9.1% of GDP in 2004. In 2001 manufacturing activity focused largely on the machine-building and metal-working sub-sectors. This was owing, in part, to the development of an automobile-manufacturing plant. Production of consumer goods (such as textiles and rugs) declined in the late 1990s. However, significant investment has been directed to the expansion of the raw-materials processing industry.

Uzbekistan is self-sufficient in natural gas, crude petroleum and coal, and became a net exporter of crude petroleum in 1995. Energy products accounted for 4.2% of the value of imports in 2000. The opening of two petroleum refineries, which had a total refining capacity of 173,000 barrels per day (b/d), significantly increased Uzbekistan's hydrocarbons capacity. In 2002 71.8% of electricity was generated by natural gas, 12.8% was produced by hydroelectric power and 11.4% by petroleum.

According to the ADB, the services sector contributed 43.7% of GDP in 2004, when it employed 56.1% of the working population. According to World Bank figures, during 1995–2004 the GDP of the services sector increased, in real terms, by an average of 4.7% annually. According to the ADB, services GDP increased by 7.3% in 2004 and by 10.3% in 2004.

In 2003, according to the ADB, Uzbekistan recorded a visible trade surplus of US $761m., and there was a surplus of $881m. on the current account of the balance of payments. In 2004 the principal source of imports was Russia (accounting for 26.4% of the total value of imports). Other major suppliers were the Republic of Korea (South Korea)—accounting for 10.8%), Germany (9.4%), the USA (9.4%), the People's Republic of China (8.3%), Kazakhstan (6.0%) and Turkey (6.0%). Russia was also the main market for exports in that year (accounting for 21.2% of the total value of exports); other important purchasers were China (14.0%), Ukraine (7.0%), Turkey (6.3%) and Tajikistan (5.8%). The principal exports in 2000 were cotton fibre, energy products, metals and food products. The main imports in that year were machinery and equipment, chemicals and plastics, food products and metals. By 2000 trade with republics of the former USSR represented only some 35% of Uzbekistan's total trade, compared with about 83% in 1990.

In 2004 Uzbekistan's overall budget deficit (including extra-budgetary operations) was 43,950m. sum (equivalent to 0.4% of

GDP). At the end of 2003 Uzbekistan's total external debt was US $5,006m., of which $4,250m. was long-term public debt. In that year the cost of debt-servicing was equivalent to 21.3% of the value of exports of goods and services. The average annual rate of inflation declined from 1,568% in 1994 to 28% in 2000. The rate of inflation declined to 26.6% in 2001, and rose slightly, to 27.6%, in 2002, declining to 10.3% in 2003 and to just 1.6% in 2004. In 2004 some 35,000 people (0.4% of the economically active population) were officially registered as unemployed, although the actual level was believed to be considerably higher.

In 1992 Uzbekistan became a member of the IMF and the World Bank, also joining the European Bank for Reconstruction and Development (EBRD, see p. 224) as a 'Country of Operations'. In the same year Uzbekistan was admitted to the Economic Co-operation Organization (ECO, see p. 223). Uzbekistan became a member of the ADB in 1995, and in 2003 it joined the Islamic Development Bank (see p. 303). In early 2006 Uzbekistan became a member of the Eurasian Economic Community, a customs union founded in 2000 by the Presidents of Russia, Belarus, Kazakhstan, Kyrgyzstan, and Tajikistan. Uzbekistan is pursuing membership of the World Trade Organization (WTO, see p. 370).

Following the collapse of the USSR in 1991, GDP declined sharply and inflation increased rapidly. The economy returned to growth from 1996, although it was adversely affected by the Russian financial crisis of 1998. In 2002 Uzbekistan agreed to implement a structural-reform programme, but there was international concern that Uzbekistan's economic policies continued to further its economic isolation. The sum was finally made fully convertible in October 2003. In April 2004 the EBRD announced that it was to limit its activities in Uzbekistan, owing to the Government's failure to implement reform; in July 2005, following the violence in the city of Andijon in May, the EBRD announced that it would not participate in any further public-sector projects in Uzbekistan, and would only contribute to work in the private sector. Meanwhile, in 2004 the Russian state-controlled natural gas company Gazprom and the Uzbekistani company Uzbekneftgazkurilish agreed a 15-year production-sharing agreement at the Shakhpakhty gas and condensate field in Uzbekistan, where annual production was expected to reach 500m. cu m by 2006. In December 2004 a consortium of three companies from Iran, Ukraine and the United Kingdom won a tender to increase liquefied gas production at Uzbekneftgazkurilish's Shurtan gas complex; this, together with other planned projects, was expected to increase annual output of liquefied gas to 615,000 metric tons by 2010, compared with 119,000 tons in 2002. In January 2006 Uzbekistan signed a new production-sharing agreement with Gazprom for three further natural gas fields, and an agreement was also signed on joint exploration of the region for further resources; the entire project, the exact details of which were due to be finalized in July, was to cost some US $1,500m. Meanwhile, in 2005 Uzbekistan increased the export price for its sales of natural gas to Kazakhstan, Kyrgyzstan, and Tajikistan, with effect from 2006. In early 2006 Russia also agreed to pay increased prices for natural gas. Strong growth in GDP was recorded in 2004 and 2005, and in early 2006 it was reported that advances had been made in implementing fiscal reform. However, little progress had been made in the planned privatization of large enterprises, in reform of the banking sector or in improving the business environment. The Government was implementing a large-scale public-finance reform programme, which included measures to simplify the tax structure and administration, and a scheme to establish a single treasury system. Nevertheless, lack of structural reform was considered to be the main factor preventing the economy from achieving its potential and preventing growth led by the private sector.

Education

Primary education, beginning at seven years of age, lasts for four years. Secondary education, beginning at 11 years of age, lasts for seven years, comprising a first cycle of five years and a second cycle of two years. The gross primary enrolment ratio in 1999, according to the Asian Development Bank, was equivalent to 85% of females and 86% of males in the relevant age-group, while the overall gross secondary enrolment ratio in 1994 was 94%. In 2004 6.2m. pupils were enrolled in general secondary schools. Higher education was provided in 63 institutes in that year. Legislation adopted in May 1993 banned private educational establishments in Uzbekistan; those already in existence were reportedly to be transferred to state control. In 1999 the Tashkent Islamic University was established by presidential decree. In 2004 government expenditure on education was an estimated 765,384.8m. sum (27.4% of total budgetary expenditure). The 2006 budget allocated some 1,285,078.5m. sum to education (29.8% of total budgetary expenditure).

Public Holidays

2006: 1 January (New Year's Day), 10 January*† (Kurban Hayit, Id al-Adha or Feast of the Sacrifice), 8 March (International Women's Day), 21 March (Navruz Bairam, Uzbek New Year), 9 May (Victory Day), 1 September (Independence Day), 23 October* (Ruza Hayit, Id al-Fitr or end of Ramadan), 10 December (Constitution Day), 31 December*† (Kurban Hayit, Id al-Adha or Feast of the Sacrifice).

2007: 1 January (New Year's Day), 7–8 March (International Women's Day), 21 March (Navruz Bairam, Uzbek New Year), 9 May (Victory Day), 1 September (Independence Day), 13 October* (Ruza Hayit, Id al-Fitr or end of Ramadan), 10 December (Constitution Day), 20 December* (Kurban Hayit, Id al-Adha or Feast of the Sacrifice).

* These holidays are dependent on the Islamic lunar calendar and may vary by one or two days from the dates given.

† This festival occurs twice (in the Islamic years AH 1426 and 1427) within the same Gregorian year.

Weights and Measures

The metric system is in force.

UZBEKISTAN

Statistical Survey

Area and Population

AREA, POPULATION AND DENSITY

Area (sq km)	447,400*
Population (census results)†	
17 January 1979	15,389,307
12 January 1989	
Males	9,784,156
Females	10,025,921
Total	19,810,077
Population (UN estimates at mid-year)‡	
2002	25,452,000
2003	25,828,000
2004	26,209,000
Density (per sq km) at mid-2004	58.6

* 172,740 sq miles.
† Figures refer to *de jure* population. The *de facto* total at the 1989 census was 19,905,158.
‡ Source: UN, *World Population Prospects: The 2004 Revision*.

POPULATION BY ETHNIC GROUP
(1996, estimates, rounded)

	%
Uzbek	80.0
Russian	5.5
Tajik	5.0
Kazakh	3.0
Kara-Kalpak	2.5
Tatar	1.5
Others	2.5
Total	**100.0**

Source: Ministry of Health, Tashkent.

ADMINISTRATIVE DIVISIONS
(1996, official estimates, rounded figures)

	Area (sq km)	Population	Density (per sq km)	Capital city (with population)
Sovereign Republic:				
Qoraqalpog'iston	165,600	1,400,000	8.5	Nukus (236,700)
Viloyats				
Andijon	4,200	1,899,000	452.1	Andijon (303,000)
Buxoro (Bukhara)	39,400	1,384,700	35.2	Buxoro (263,400)
Farg'ona (Fergana)	6,800	2,597,000	381.9	Farg'ona (214,000)
Jizzax	20,500	910,500	44.4	Jizzax (127,200)
Namangan	7,900	1,862,000	235.7	Namangan (341,000)
Navoiy	110,800	767,500	6.9	Navoiy (128,000)
Qashqadaryo	28,400	2,029,000	71.4	Qarshi (177,000)
Samarqand	16,400	2,322,000	141.6	Samarqand (366,000)
Sirdaryo (Syrdarya)	5,100	648,100	127.1	Guliston (54,000)
Surxondaryo	20,800	1,676,000	80.6	Termiz (95,000)
Toshkent (Tashkent)*	15,300	4,450,000	290.9	Toshkent (2,100,000)
Xorazm (Khorezm)	6,300	1,200,000	190.5	Urgench (135,000)
Total	**447,400**	**23,145,800**	**51.7**	

* Including Toshkent (Tashkent) City, which subsequently assumed a separate administrative status.

Source: Government of Uzbekistan.

PRINCIPAL TOWNS
(estimated population at 1 January 2000)

Toshkent (Tashkent, the capital)	2,133,300	Margilan	156,800
Namangan	388,300	Chirchik	142,700
Samarqand	361,100	Urgench	139,000
Andijon	336,500	Jizzax	129,800
Buxoro (Bukhara)	238,800	Angren	129,100
Nukus	208,600	Navoiy	141,100
Qarshi	202,400	Termiz	114,400
Qoqand	198,000	Olmaliq	114,000
Farg'ona (Fergana)	184,800		

Source: UN, *Demographic Yearbook*.

Mid-2003 (UN estimate, incl. suburbs): Toshkent (Tashkent) 2,154,649 (Source: UN, *World Urbanization Prospects: The 2003 Revision*).

BIRTHS, MARRIAGES AND DEATHS

	Registered live births		Registered marriages		Registered deaths	
	Number	Rate (per 1,000)	Number	Rate (per 1,000)	Number	Rate (per 1,000)
1994	657,725	29.5	176,287	7.9	148,423	6.7
1995	677,999	29.9	170,828	7.5	145,439	6.4
1996	634,842	27.4	171,662	7.4	144,829	6.3
1997	602,694	25.6	181,126	7.7	137,331	5.8
1999*	553,745	23.1	170,525	7.1	140,526	5.9
2000	527,580	21.4	168,908	6.9	135,598	5.5
2001	512,950	20.5	170,101	6.8	132,542	5.3

* Figures for 1998 are not available.

Source: UN, *Demographic Yearbook*.

Expectation of life (WHO estimates, years at birth): 66 (males 63; females 69) in 2003 (Source: WHO, *World Health Report*).

EMPLOYMENT
(annual averages, '000 persons)

	1998	1999	2000
Agriculture*	3,467	3,213	3,083
Industry†	1,114	1,124	1,145
Construction	573	640	676
Transport and communications	362	370	382
Trade and catering‡	717	735	754
Other services	1,976	2,042	2,042
Housing, public utilities and personal services	235	240	246
Health care, social security, physical culture and sports	502	538	567
Education, culture and art	1,073	1,094	1,120
Banking and insurance	50	48	51
General administration	111	122	126
Information and computer services	5	—	—
Total (incl. others)	**8,800**	**8,885**	**8,983**

* Including forestry.
† Comprising manufacturing (except printing and publishing), mining and quarrying, electricity, gas, water, logging and fishing.
‡ Including material and technical supply.

Source: Centre for Economic Research, Tashkent, *Uzbek Economic Trends*.

2001 ('000 persons): Total employed 9,136 (Agriculture 3,062, Industry 1,160, Other 4,914) (Source: Asian Development Bank, *Key Indicators of Developing Asian and Pacific Countries*).

2002 ('000 persons): Total employed 9,333 (Agriculture 3,046, Industry 1,186, Other 5,101) (Source: Asian Development Bank, *Key Indicators of Developing Asian and Pacific Countries*).

2003 ('000 persons): Total employed 9,589 (Agriculture 3,063, Industry 1,223, Other 5,303) (Source: Asian Development Bank, *Key Indicators of Developing Asian and Pacific Countries*).

2004 ('000 persons): Total employed 9,911 (Agriculture 3,068, Industry 1,284, Other 5,559) (Source: Asian Development Bank, *Key Indicators of Developing Asian and Pacific Countries*).

Unemployed ('000 persons registered): 38 in 2001; 35 in 2002; 32 in 2003; 35 in 2004 (Source: Asian Development Bank, *Key Indicators of Developing Asian and Pacific Countries*).

UZBEKISTAN

Health and Welfare

KEY INDICATORS

Total fertility rate (children per woman, 2002)	2.4
Under-5 mortality rate (per 1,000 live births, 2004)	69
HIV/AIDS (% of persons aged 15–49, 2003)	0.1
Physicians (per 1,000 head, 2001)	2.89
Hospital beds (per 1,000 head, 2001)	5.34
Health expenditure (2002): US $ per head (PPP)	143
Health expenditure (2002): % of GDP	5.5
Health expenditure (2002): public (% of total)	45.5
Access to water (% of persons, 2002)	89
Access to sanitation (% of persons, 2002)	57
Human Development Index (2003): ranking	111
Human Development Index (2003): value	0.694

For sources and definitions, see explanatory note on p. vi.

Agriculture

PRINCIPAL CROPS
('000 metric tons)

	2002	2003	2004
Wheat	4,967	5,437	5,378
Rice (paddy)	175	334	181
Barley	221	155	108
Maize	147	146	156
Sorghum*	8	10	5
Potatoes	777	834	896
Dry broad beans*	6	4	4
Sunflower seed	10	12	11
Safflower seed	3	5	8
Sesame seed†	16	18	18
Cottonseed*	1,781	1,590	1,968
Other oilseeds†	3	3	3
Cabbages	231	219	274
Tomatoes	1,080	1,410	1,245
Cucumbers and gherkins	166	168	184
Dry onions	480	525	339
Garlic	28*	25	29
Carrots	38*	43*	40†
Other vegetables†	911	906	912
Watermelons	479	583	460†
Apples	544*	489*	500†
Pears	25*	22*	24†
Apricots	47*	42*	42†
Cherries	21*	20*	20†
Peaches and nectarines	51*	46*	45†
Plums	109*	98*	90†
Grapes	516	402	589
Other fruits and berries*	46	43	55
Tobacco (leaves)*	19	19	19
Jute†	20	20	20
Cotton (lint)	1,008	945	1,150

* Unofficial figure(s).
† FAO estimate(s).

Source: FAO.

LIVESTOCK
('000 head at 1 January)

	2002	2003	2004
Horses*	145	145	145
Asses*	160	155	150
Cattle	5,478	5,879	6,243
Camels*	25	25	25
Pigs	75	90	87
Sheep†	8,311	8,934	9,514
Goats†	923	995	1,066
Chickens	15,355	17,676	18,834
Turkeys	370†	377†	350*
Rabbits*	80,000	80,000	80,000

* FAO estimate(s).
† Unofficial figure(s).

Source: FAO.

LIVESTOCK PRODUCTS
('000 metric tons)

	2002	2003	2004
Beef and veal*	425.3	455.9	490.5
Mutton, lamb and goat meat	71.1	74.1	70.5
Pig meat	4.3	11.2	12.6
Poultry meat	10.1	16.0	16.7
Other meat	3.0*	3.1*	2.0†
Cows' milk*	3,631.1	3,924.3	4,165.0
Sheep's milk*	25.0	30.0	31.7
Goats' milk*	65.0	70.3	74.5
Cheese†	17.8	20.6	20.9
Butter†	3.1	3.1	3.1
Hen eggs*	75.2	89.6	102.8
Other poultry eggs*	1.8	1.4	1.6
Honey	2.5	2.3	2.2
Raw silk (incl. waste)†	1.2	1.2	1.2
Wool: greasy	16.6	17.4	18.6
Wool: scoured	10.0	10.4	11.2
Cattle hides (fresh)†	40.6	44.0	52.8
Sheepskins (fresh)†	7.2	7.7	7.3

* Unofficial figure(s).
† FAO estimate(s).

Source: FAO.

Fishing

(metric tons, live weight)

	2001	2002	2003*
Capture	4,070	2,009	2,000
Freshwater bream	540	72	80
Common carp	906	148	150
Crucian carp	331	38	40
Roach	1,300	1,457	1,430
Silver carp	544	75	80
Aquaculture	4,082	5,112	5,112
Common carp	840	580	580
Crucian carp	140	523	523
Silver carp	1,862	2,405	2,405
Bighead carp	1,240	1,604	1,604
Total catch	8,152	7,121	7,112

* FAO estimates.

Source: FAO.

Mining

(metric tons, unless otherwise indicated)

	2002	2003	2004
Coal ('000 metric tons)*	2,736	1,913	2,699
Crude petroleum ('000 metric tons)†	7,234	7,169	6,617
Natural gas ('000 million cu metres)	60	58	60
Copper ore‡§	80,000	80,000	n.a.
Molybdenum ore‡	500	500	500§
Silver ore (kilograms)‡	80,000	80,000	80,000§
Gold (kilograms)‡§	90,000	90,000	93,000
Kaolin ('000 metic tons)§	5,500	5,500	5,500
Feldspar§	4,300	4,300	4,300

* Including lignite and brown coal.
† Including gas condensate.
‡ Figures refer to the metal content of ores.
§ Estimated production.

Sources: Asian Development Bank, *Key Indicators of Developing Asian and Pacific Economies*, and US Geological Survey.

Uranium ore (metal content, metric tons): 2,350 in 2000; 1,962 in 2001; 1,860 in 2002.

Copper ore (metal content, metric tons, estimated production): 78,000 in 2001; 80,000 in 2002; 80,000 in 2003.

Industry

SELECTED PRODUCTS
('000 metric tons, unless otherwise indicated)

	1998	1999	2000
Beer ('000 hectolitres)	569	422	609
Cigarettes (million)	7,582	10,668	7,766
Wool yarn (pure and mixed)	2	3	3
Cotton yarn (pure and mixed)	105	105	135
Woven cotton fabrics (million sq m)	314	333	360
Sulphuric acid	856	897	823
Nitrogenous fertilizers (a)*	755	707	717
Phosphate fertilizers (b)*	141	169	117
Motor spirit (petrol)	1,603	1,638	1,709
Gas-diesel (distillate fuel) oils	2,227	2,220	1,900
Residual fuel oils	1,977	1,750	1,700
Lubricating oils	229	223	238
Cement	3,331	3,284	3,722
Domestic refrigerators ('000)	16	2	1
Domestic washing machines ('000)	5	—	—
Television receivers ('000)	192	50	26
Electric energy (million kWh)†	54,790	55,581	56,401

* Production in terms of (a) nitrogen; (b) phosphoric acid.
† Source: Asian Development Bank, *Key Indicators of Developing Asian and Pacific Countries*.
Source (unless otherwise indicated): UN, *Industrial Commodity Statistics Yearbook*.

2001: Cement ('000 metric tons) 3,722; Electric energy (million kWh) 47,961 (Source: Asian Development Bank, *Key Indicators of Developing Asian and Pacific Countries*).

2002: Cement ('000 metric tons) 3,927; Electric energy (million kWh) 49,398 (Source: Asian Development Bank, *Key Indicators of Developing Asian and Pacific Countries*).

2003: Cement ('000 metric tons) 4,062 (Source: Asian Development Bank, *Key Indicators of Developing Asian and Pacific Countries*).

2004: Cement ('000 metric tons) 4,805 (Source: Asian Development Bank, *Key Indicators of Developing Asian and Pacific Countries*).

Finance

CURRENCY AND EXCHANGE RATES

Monetary Units
100 teen = 1 sum.

Sterling, Dollar and Euro Equivalents (30 November 2005)
£1 sterling = 1,989.5 sum;
US $1 = 1,152.0 sum;
€1 = 1,355.8 sum;
10,000 sum = £5.03 = $8.68 = €7.38.

Average Exchange Rate (sum per US $)
2000   236.61
2001   423.31
2002   769.50

Note: Prior to the introduction of the sum (see below), Uzbekistan used a transitional currency, the sum-coupon. This had been introduced in November 1993 to circulate alongside (and initially at par with) the Russian (formerly Soviet) rouble. Following the dissolution of the USSR in December 1991, Russia and several other former Soviet republics retained the rouble as their monetary unit. The Russian rouble ceased to be legal tender in Uzbekistan from 15 April 1994.

On 1 July 1994 a permanent currency, the sum, was introduced to replace the sum-coupon at 1 sum per 1,000 coupons. The initial exchange rate was set at US $1 = 7.00 sum. Sum-coupons continued to circulate, but from 15 October 1994 the sum became the sole legal tender. On 15 October 2003 the sum became fully convertible.

STATE BUDGET*
(million sum)

Revenue	2004	2005	2006†
Direct taxes	729,697.0	865,830.2	1,045,920.6
Tax on income of legal entities	218,536.8	209,331.4	218,955.1
Personal income tax	336,878.9	465,641.1	603,416.7
Other direct taxes	174,281.3	190,857.7	223,548.8
Indirect taxes	1,540,086.2	1,627,909.5	1,986,656.3
Value-added tax	654,887.2	748,938.2	1,017,352.0
Excises	741,188.6	692,628.9	760,548.6
Other indirect taxes	140,010.4	186,342.4	208,755.7
Property, mining, land and resources taxes	316,758.3	629,770.4	768,184.1
Infrastructure development tax	46,463.7	52,169.4	69,614.5
Other	116,369.7	135,174.5	172,084.9
Total	2,749,374.9	3,310,854.0	4,042,460.4

Expenditure	2003	2004
Education	623,041.1	765,384.8
Health care	228,708.5	277,404.8
Culture, sport and mass media	51,359.2	65,280.7
Social protection	9,519.5	10,895.0
Social security	183,222.7	212,936.2
Economy	286,503.6	364,693.4
Centralized investments	322,963.1	342,083.8
State authority and administration	58,657.7	85,329.4
Reserve fund	55,940.7	37,714.0
Other	557,027.7	631,602.7
Total	2,376,943.9	2,793,324.8

* Excluding special budgetary funds.
† Preliminary.

2005 (million sum, preliminary, excl. special budgetary funds): Education 991,502.9; Health care 377,846.9; Culture, sport and mass media 59,381.6; Social security and welfare 13,873.2; Public utility subsidy 15,979.9; Family allowances 212,864.4; Other expenditure relating to the social sphere and social support 49,528.4; Economy and public investment 804,254.6; State authority and administration 95,085.7; Other 843,789.5; Total 3,464,107.1.

2006 (million sum, preliminary, excl. special budgetary funds): Education 1,285,078.5; Health care 494,675.1; Culture, sport and mass media 66,179.7; Science 22,549.3; Social security and welfare 16,872.4; Public utility subsidy 13,160.9; Family allowances 282,554.8; Other expenditure relating to the social sphere and social support 74,278.2; Economy and public investment 952,666.0; State authority and administration 115,963.0; Other 989,544.2; Total 4,313,522.1.

Source: Ministry of Finance.

INTERNATIONAL RESERVES
(US $ million at 31 December)

	2002	2003	2004
Total	1,216.4	1,659.3	2,146.5

Source: Asian Development Bank, *Key Indicators of Developing Asian and Pacific Countries*.

MONEY SUPPLY
(million sum at 31 December)

	2002	2003	2004
Currency outside banks	273,347	404,928	590,199
Demand deposits at deposit money banks	194,839	170,036	214,596
Total money	468,186	574,964	804,795

Source: Asian Development Bank, *Key Indicators of Developing Asian and Pacific Countries*.

UZBEKISTAN

COST OF LIVING
(Consumer Price Index; base: previous year = 100)

	2002	2003	2004
Food	128.0	105.4	95.3
Other goods	119.3	113.9	106.3
All items	127.6	110.3	101.6

Source: Asian Development Bank, *Key Indicators of Developing Asian and Pacific Countries*.

NATIONAL ACCOUNTS
(million sum at current prices)

Expenditure on the Gross Domestic Product

	2002	2003	2004
Government final consumption expenditure	1,339,170	1,717,376	2,081,460
Private final consumption expenditure	4,488,459	5,474,760	6,305,843
Changes in stocks	−69,615	−26,348	218,648
Gross fixed capital formation	1,648,530	2,069,070	2,694,452
Total domestic expenditure	7,406,544	9,234,858	11,300,403
Exports of goods and services	2,352,607	3,630,737	4,946,826
Less Imports of goods and services	2,308,916	3,027,754	4,057,774
GDP in purchasers' values	7,450,235	9,837,841	12,189,455

Gross Domestic Product by Economic Activity

	2002	2003	2004
Agriculture and forestry	2,244,241	2,812,623	3,260,946
Mining and quarrying			
Manufacturing	1,079,273	1,553,330	2,085,498
Electricity, gas and water			
Construction	365,163	442,392	551,021
Trade	735,202	921,116	1,101,772
Transport and communications	612,868	923,699	1,191,837
Finance	250,586	286,543	
Public administration	230,666	277,185	2,290,595*
Other services	994,219	1,275,871	
GDP at factor cost	6,512,218	8,492,759	10,481,669
Indirect taxes	938,016	1,345,081	1,707,786
Less Subsidies			
GDP in purchasers' values	7,450,235	9,837,841	12,189,455

* Figure obtained as a residual.

Source: Asian Development Bank, *Key Indicators of Developing Asian and Pacific Countries*.

BALANCE OF PAYMENTS
(US $ million)

	1996	1997	1998
Exports of goods f.o.b.	3,534	3,695	2,888
Imports of goods f.o.b.	−4,240	−3,767	−2,717
Trade balance	−706	−72	171
Services and other income (net)	−272	−540	−252
Balance on goods, services and income	−978	−612	−81
Current transfers (net)	−2	29	43
Current balance	−980	−584	−39
Direct investment (net)	90	167	176
Other capital (net)	80	−507	−802
Net errors and omissions	296	−185	—
Overall balance	−50	−480	1

Source: IMF, *Republic of Uzbekistan—Recent Economic Developments* (March 2000).

2001 (US $ million): Exports of goods f.o.b. 3,170.4; Imports of goods f.o.b. −3,136.9; Trade balance 33.5 (Source: Asian Development Bank, *Key Indicators of Developing Asian and Pacific Countries*).

2002 (US $ million): Exports of goods f.o.b. 2,988.4; Imports of goods f.o.b. −2,712.0; Trade balance 276.4 (Source: Asian Development Bank, *Key Indicators of Developing Asian and Pacific Countries*).

2003 (US $ million): Exports of goods f.o.b. 3,725.0; Imports of goods f.o.b. −2,964.2; Trade balance 760.8 (Source: Asian Development Bank, *Key Indicators of Developing Asian and Pacific Countries*).

External Trade

PRINCIPAL COMMODITIES
(US $ million)

Imports f.o.b.	1998	1999	2000
Chemicals and plastics	407.2	363.0	399.5
Metals	303.6	245.4	253.5
Machinery and equipment	1,553.7	1,393.5	1,044.1
Food products	512.2	408.1	361.1
Energy products	16.3	66.6	112.7
Total (incl. others)	3,288.7	3,110.7	2,696.4

Exports f.o.b.	1998	1999	2000
Cotton fibre	1,361.0	883.7	897.1
Chemicals and plastics	51.7	101.8	93.4
Metals	180.7	138.9	216.7
Machinery and equipment	146.6	103.2	111.8
Food products	111.9	206.7	176.4
Energy products	277.8	371.5	335.2
Total (incl. others)	3,528.2	3,235.8	3,264.7

Source: Center for Economic Research, Tashkent, *Uzbek Economic Trends*.

PRINCIPAL TRADING PARTNERS
(US $ million)

Imports	2002	2003	2004
China, People's Republic	114.6	161.5	220.9
France	38.7	48.5	43.2
Germany	224.5	235.7	251.4
Kazakhstan	111.1	151.7	161.2
Korea, Republic	207.3	271.9	288.9
Russia	498.7	553.6	703.3
Tajikistan	80.2	73.8	78.4
Turkey	103.1	152.3	159.7
Ukraine	74.9	92.0	97.7
USA	224.5	235.7	251.4
Total (incl. others)	2,081.9	2,487.4	2,667.2

Exports	2002	2003	2004
China, People's Republic	24.9	182.1	364.1
Italy	133.8	54.3	47.8
Japan	66.7	84.3	78.4
Kazakhstan	78.7	81.6	102.1
Korea, Republic	88.0	71.8	89.9
Russia	310.6	436.7	549.0
Tajikistan	120.3	120.6	151.1
Turkey	68.5	90.4	162.4
Ukraine	25.3	145.9	182.7
USA	74.0	79.5	87.9
Total (incl. others)	1,556.1	1,983.0	2,593.9

Source: Asian Development Bank, *Key Indicators of Developing Asian and Pacific Countries*.

Transport

RAILWAYS
(traffic)

	1999	2000	2001
Passenger-km (million)	2	2	2
Freight ton-km (million)	14	15	16

Source: UN, *Statistical Yearbook*.

CIVIL AVIATION
(estimated traffic on scheduled services)

	1999	2000	2001
Kilometres flown (million)	37	39	57
Passengers carried ('000)	1,658	1,745	2,256
Passenger-km (million)	3,328	3,732	5,268
Total ton-km (million)	370	417	580

Source: UN, *Statistical Yearbook*.

Tourism

FOREIGN VISITOR ARRIVALS
('000, incl. excursionists)

Region of origin	2001	2002	2003
Africa	1.0	1.0	1.0
Americas	10.0	4.1	4.1
East Asia and the Pacific	192.9	195.1	145.0
Europe	109.0	99.8	51.0
Middle East	24.0	23.5	24.0
South Asia	8.0	8.0	8.0
Total	344.9	331.5	231.0

Tourism receipts (US $ million, excl. passenger transport): 72 in 2001; 68 in 2002; 48 in 2003.

Source: World Tourism Organization.

Communications Media

	2001	2002	2003
Telephones ('000 main lines in use)	1,663.0	1,681.1	1,717.1
Mobile cellular telephones ('000 subscribers)	128.0	186.9	320.8
Internet users ('000)	150.0	275.0	492.0

Source: International Telecommunication Union.

2004: Mobile cellular telephones ('000 subscribers) 544.1; Internet users ('000) 880.0.

Book production: 1,003 titles and 30,914,000 copies in 1996 (Source: UNESCO, *Statistical Yearbook*).

Daily newspapers: 3 titles and 75,000 copies (average circulation) in 1996 (Source: UNESCO, *Statistical Yearbook*).

Non-daily newspapers: 350 titles and 1,404,000 copies (average circulation) in 1996 (Source: UNESCO, *Statistical Yearbook*).

Other periodicals: 81 titles and 684,000 copies (average circulation) in 1996 (Source: UNESCO, *Statistical Yearbook*).

Radio receivers ('000 in use): 10,800 in 1997 (Source: UNESCO, *Statistical Yearbook*).

Television receivers ('000 in use): 7,000 in 2001 (Source: International Telecommunication Union).

Facsimile machines (number in use): 3,325 in 2001 (Source: International Telecommunication Union).

Education

(2004, unless otherwise indicated)

	Institutions	Teachers	Students
Pre-primary	6,603	96,100*	575,100
Primary	} 9,835	92,400*	1,905,693*
Secondary:			
general		476,300	6,151,400
teacher training	n.a.	2,464†	35,411†
vocational	892	7,900*	214,500*
Higher	63	18,400*	263,600
Universities	20*	n.a.	131,100*

* 1994/95.
† 1993.
‡ 1992/93.

Sources: UNESCO, *Statistical Yearbook*; and Center for Economic Research, Tashkent.

Adult literacy rate (UNESCO estimates): 99.3% (males 99.6%; females 98.9%) in 2002 (Source: UN Development Programme, *Human Development Report*).

Directory

The Constitution

A new Constitution was adopted by the Supreme Council on 8 December 1992. It declares Uzbekistan to be a secular, democratic and presidential republic. Basic human rights are guaranteed. The principal features of the Constitution, as subsequently revised, are as follows:

THE OLY MAJLIS

The highest legislative body is the Oly Majlis (Supreme Assembly). The Oly Majlis comprises two chambers: the Qoqunchilik palatasi Kengashi (Legislative Chamber); and the Senat (Senate). The 120 deputies of the Qoqunchilik palatasi Kengashi are elected for a term of five years. Of the 100 members of the Senat, 84 members are indirectly elected by regional Council members, and 16 are appointed by the President of the Republic. Parliament may be dissolved by the President (by agreement with the Constitutional Court). The Oly Majlis enacts normal legislation and constitutional legislation, elects its own officials, the judges of the higher courts and the Chairman of the State Committee for Environmental Protection. It confirms the President's appointments to ministerial office, the procuracy-general and the governorship of the Central Bank. It must ratify international treaties, changes to borders and presidential decrees on emergency situations. Legislation may be initiated by the deputies, by the President, by the higher courts, by the Procurator-General and by the Autonomous Republic of Qoraqalpog'iston.

PRESIDENT OF THE REPUBLIC

The President of the Republic, who is directly elected by the people for a seven-year term, is Head of State and holds supreme executive power. (The term of office was extended, with immediate effect, from five to seven years in April 2002.) An individual may be elected President for a maximum of two consecutive terms. The President is required to form and supervise the Cabinet of Ministers, appointing the Prime Minister and Ministers, subject to confirmation by the Oly Majlis. The President also nominates the candidates for appointment to the higher courts and certain offices of state, subject to confirmation by the Oly Majlis. The President appoints the judges of the lower courts and the khokims (governors) of the regions. Legislation may be initiated, reviewed and returned to the Oly Majlis by the Pre-

UZBEKISTAN

sident, who must promulgate all laws. The President may dissolve the Oly Majlis. The President is also Commander-in-Chief of the Armed Forces and may declare a state of emergency or a state of war (subject to confirmation by the Oly Majlis within three days).

THE CABINET OF MINISTERS

The Cabinet of Ministers is the Government of the republic; it is subordinate to the President, who appoints its Prime Minister, Deputy Prime Ministers and Ministers, subject to the approval of the legislature. Local government is carried out by elected councils and appointed khokims, the latter having significant personal authority and responsibility.

JUDICATURE

The exercise of judicial power is independent of government. The higher courts, of which the judges are nominated by the President and confirmed by the Oly Majlis, consist of the Constitutional Court, the Supreme Court and the High Economic Court. There is also a Supreme Court of the Sovereign Republic of Qoraqalpog'iston. Lower courts, including economic courts, are based in the regions, districts and towns. The Procurator-General's office is responsible for supervising the observance of the law.

The Government

HEAD OF STATE

President of the Republic: ISLAM A. KARIMOV (elected by Supreme Soviet 24 March 1990; term of office extended by popular referendum 27 March 1995; re-elected 9 January 2000).

CABINET OF MINISTERS
(April 2006)

Prime Minister: SHAVKAT M. MIRZIYOYEV.

Deputy Prime Minister, responsible for the Economic Sector and Foreign Economic Relations, and Minister of the Economy: BOTIR HOJAYEV.

Deputy Prime Minister, responsible for Machine-construction, Metallurgy, Chemicals, Fuel, Energy and Geology: ERGASH R. SHOISMATOV.

Deputy Prime Minister, responsible for Information and Communications Technologies, Director-General of the Uzbekistani Agency for Communications and Technology: ABDULLA N. ARIPOV.

Deputy Prime Minister, responsible for the Social Sector, and Minister of Higher and Specialized Secondary Education: RUSTAM S. QOSIMOV.

Deputy Prime Minister, responsible for Construction, Industry, Construction Materials, Housing and Municipal Services and Transport: NODIRXON M. XANOV.

Deputy Prime Minister, Chairperson of the Committee for Women's Affairs: SVETLANA T. INAMOVA.

Minister of Foreign Affairs: ELYOR M. G'ANIYEV.

Minister of Justice: BO'RITOSH MUSTAFOYEV.

Minister of Internal Affairs: BAHODIR A. MATLYUBOV.

Minister of Foreign Economic Relations, Investment and Trade: ALISHER E. SHAYXOV.

Minister of National Education: TUROBJON I. JO'RAYEV.

Minister of Health: FERUZ G. NAZIROV.

Minister of Labour and Social Protection: OQILJON O. OBIDOV.

Minister of Culture and Sports: ALISHER A. AZIZHO'JAYEV.

Minister of Finance: RUSTAM S. AZIMOV.

Minister of Defence: RUSLAN E. MIRZAYEV.

Minister for Emergency Situations: BAHTIYOR J. SUBANOV.

Minister of Agriculture and Water Resources: SAYFIDDIN U. ISMOILOV.

Note: The Constitution provides for the Chairman of the Council of Ministers of the Republic of Qoraqalpog'iston to serve as an *ex officio* member of the Council of Ministers of the Republic of Uzbekistan. Since October 2002 this position has been held by TURSINBAI T. TANIPBERGENOV. The following are also members of the Cabinet of Ministers: chairmen of state committees and agencies and the Chairman of the Central Bank.

MINISTRIES

Office of the President: 700163 Tashkent, pr. Uzbekistanskii 43; tel. (71) 139-53-25; fax (71) 139-56-25; e-mail presidents_office@press-service.uz; internet www.press-service.uz.

Office of the Cabinet of Ministers: 700078 Tashkent, Mustaqillik maydoni 5; tel. (71) 139-82-95; fax (71) 139-84-63; internet www.gov.uz.

Agency of Foreign Economic Relations: 700029 Tashkent, Shevchenko ko'ch. 1; tel. (71) 138-51-00; fax (71) 138-52-00; e-mail secretary@mfer.uz; internet www.afer.uz.

Ministry of Agriculture and Water Resources: 700004 Tashkent, A. Navoiy ko'ch. 4; tel. (71) 241-13-53; fax (71) 241-87-87; e-mail qshv@intal.uz; internet www.msvx.uz.

Ministry of Culture and Sport: 700129 Tashkent, A. Navoiy ko'ch. 30; tel. (71) 144-26-23; fax (71) 144-18-30; e-mail mincult@dostlinc.net; internet www.mincult.uzpak.uz.

Ministry of Defence: 700000 Tashkent, Ak. Abdullayev ko'ch. 100; tel. (71) 169-82-43; fax (71) 169-82-28; internet www.mod.uz.

Ministry of the Economy: 700003 Tashkent, pr. Uzbekistanii 45A; tel. (71) 139-63-20; fax (71) 132-63-72; e-mail mineconomy@mmes.gov.uz; internet www.mineconomy.cc.uz; tel. (71) 139-86-64.

Ministry of Education: 700078 Tashkent, Mustaqillik maydoni 5; tel. (71) 139-41-11; e-mail yazdon@uzsci.net; internet www.mno.edu.uz.

Ministry for Emergency Situations: 700084 Tashkent, Yunus-Abadskii raion, ul. Kichik Khalka iuli-4; tel. (71) 139-16-85; fax (71) 133-09-55; e-mail mes@st.uz; internet www.mes.st.uz.

Ministry of Finance: 700008 Tashkent, Mustaqillik maydoni 5; tel. (71) 133-70-73; fax (71) 144-56-43; e-mail info@mf.uz; internet www.mf.uz.

Ministry of Foreign Affairs: 700029 Tashkent, ul. Uzbekistanskaya 9; tel. (71) 133-64-75; fax (71) 139-15-17; e-mail letter@mfa.uz; internet www.mfa.uz.

Ministry of Foreign Economic Relations, Investment and Trade: 700029 Tashkent, ul. Shevchenko 1; tel. (71) 138-51-00; fax (71) 138-52-00; e-mail secretary@mfer.uz; internet www.mfer.uz.

Ministry of Health: 700011 Tashkent, ul. Navoi 12; tel. (71) 139-48-08; fax (71) 144-10-33; e-mail minzdrav@uzpak.uz; internet www.mzr.uz.

Ministry of Higher and Specialized Secondary Education: 700078 Tashkent, Mustaqillik maydoni 5; tel. (71) 133-16-26; e-mail oliy@uzsci.net.

Ministry of Internal Affairs: 700029 Tashkent, Yu. Rajaby ko'ch. 1; tel. (71) 139-73-36; fax (71) 133-89-34; internet www.mvd.uz.

Ministry of Justice: 700047 Tashkent, Sailgoh ko'ch. 5; tel. and fax (71) 133-13-05; fax (71) 133-51-76; e-mail info@minjust.gov.uz; internet www.minjust.uz.

Ministry of Labour and Social Security: 700100 Tashkent, A. Avloni ko'ch. 20A; tel. (71) 46-99-04; fax (71) 139-41-13; e-mail mehnat@uzpak.uz.

President

Presidential election, 9 January 2000

Candidate	%
Islam Karimov	91.9
Abdulkhafiz Jalolov	4.2
Total*	100.0

*Including invalid votes.

Legislature

OLY MAJLIS
(Supreme Assembly)

**Qoqunchilik palatasi Kengashi
(Legislative Chamber)**

700008 Tashkent, Xalqlar Do'stligi shoh ko'ch. 1; tel. (71) 139-87-07; fax (71) 139-41-51; internet www.parliament.gov.uz.

Chairman: ERKIN H. HALILOV.

UZBEKISTAN

General Election, 26 December 2004 and 9 January 2005

Parties, etc.	Seats
Movement of Entrepreneurs and Businessmen—Liberal Democratic Party of Uzbekistan	41
People's Democratic Party of Uzbekistan	28
Self-Sacrificers' National Democratic Party (Fidokorlar)	18
National Revival Democratic Party of Uzbekistan (Milliy Tiklanish)	11
Justice Social Democratic Party of Uzbekistan (Adolat)	10
Citizens' groups	12
Total	**120**

Senat (Senate)

700029 Tashkent, Mustaqillik maydoni 6; tel. (71) 138-26-66; fax (71) 138-29-01; internet www.parliament.gov.uz.

Of the 100 members of the chamber, 84 members are indirectly elected by regional Council members, and 16 are appointed by the President of the Republic. The first presidential appointees to the Senat were announced on 14 January 2005, while the first indirect elections of senators were held on 17–20 January 2005. The inaugural session of the chamber convened on 27 January.

Chairman: Murat Sharifkhojaev.

Election Commission

Central Election Commission: Tashkent; tel. (71) 139-15-72; fax (71) 139-43-91; internet www.elections.uz; mems approved by the Oly Majlis; Mirza-Ulugbek E. Abdusalomov.

Political Organizations

Following Uzbekistan's independence (achieved in August 1991), the ruling People's Democratic Party of Uzbekistan (PDPU—the successor to the Communist Party of the Uzbek SSR) took increasingly repressive measures against opposition and Islamist parties. A new law on political parties was approved in 1996; among other provisions, the law prohibited the establishment of parties on a religious or ethnic basis and stipulated a minimum membership, per party, of 5,000 people (with stipulation that membership be distributed across the country's regions). From February 2004 the minimum membership requirement was increased to 20,000 people. Since independence a number of opposition elements have been based abroad, particularly in Russia.

Free Peasants' Party (Ozod Dehqonlar partiyasi—Ozod Dehqonlar): 700000 Tashkent; f. 2003; denied registration; Exec. Sec. of Political Council Nigora Hidoyatova; Ideological Leader Babur Malikov (in USA).

Freedom Democratic Party of Uzbekistan (O'zbekiston Erk Demokratik Partiyasi—Erk): Tashkent; e-mail info@uzbekistanerk.org; internet www.uzbekistanerk.org; f. 1990; banned in 1993; Chair. Muhammad Salih (based in Norway); 5,000 mems (1991).

Islamic Renaissance Party: Tashkent; banned in 1991; advocates introduction of a political system based on the tenets of Islam; leader Abdullah Utayev 'disappeared' in 1992.

Justice Social Democratic Party of Uzbekistan ('Adolat' Sotsial Demokratik Partiyasi—Adolat): 700047 Tashkent, Musahanov ko'ch. 103; tel. (71) 133-26-75; f. 1995; advocates respect of human rights, improvement of social justice and consolidation of democratic reform; supports President Karimov; First Sec. Turg'unpo'lat O. Daminov; 50,000 mems (2003).

Movement of Entrepreneurs and Businessmen—Liberal Democratic Party of Uzbekistan (Tadbirkorlar va Ishbilarmonlar Harakati—O'bekiston Liberal Demokratik Partiyasi—O'zlidep): 700015 Tashkent, Mirobod tumani, Nukus ko'ch. 73A; tel. (71) 133-28-46; e-mail uzlidep@intal.uz; f. 2003; supports President Karimov; Chair. Muhammadjon A. Ahmadjonov; 142,000 members (Dec. 2004).

National Revival Democratic Party of Uzbekistan (O'zbekiston Milliy Tiklanish Demokratik Partiyasi—Milliy Tiklanish): 700000 Tashkent, Navoiy ko'ch. 30; tel. (71) 144-81-28; f. 1995; supports President Karimov; Leader Aziz Kayumov; Chair. of Central Council Xurshid N. Do'stmuhammedov; 50,000 mems (2003).

People's Democratic Party of Uzbekistan (O'zbekiston Xalq demokratik partiyasi): 700029 Tashkent, Mustaqillik maydoni 5/1; tel. (71) 139-83-11; fax (71) 133-59-34; f. 1991; successor to Communist Party of Uzbekistan; Leader Asliddin A. Rustamov; c. 580,000 mems (2003).

People's Unity Movement (Xalq Birligi Harakati—Xalq Birligi): Tashkent; f. 1995; supports President Karimov; Chair. Turabek Dolimov.

Self-Sacrificers' National Democratic Party (Fidokorlar Milliy Demokratik Partiyasi—Fidokorlar): 700000 Tashkent, Xalqlar Do'stligi ko'ch. 1; tel. (71) 139-45-53; f. 2000; incorporates fmr Watan Taraqqioti (Progress of the Fatherland) party; supports President Karimov; First Sec. Axtam S. Tursunov; 61,000 mems (2003).

Unity People's Movement Party ('Birlik' Xalq Harakati Partiyasi—Birlik): c/o Union of Writers of Uzbekistan, 700000 Tashkent, Neru ko'ch. 1; tel. (71) 233-63-74; e-mail webmaster@birlik.net; internet www.birlik.net; f. 1988; leading opposition group, banned in 1992; registered as a social movement; refused registration as a political party 2004; Chair. Prof. Abdurakhim Pulat; Sec.-Gen. Vasila Inoyatova.

The militant Islamist group Islamic Movement of Uzbekistan (IMU) was founded in 1999. It was banned by the Uzbek Government in 1999 and its leaders sentenced to death *in absentia* in 2000. The IMU's activities were believed to have been seriously curtailed after the death of one its leaders during the US-led military campaign in Afghanistan that commenced in late 2001. The transnational militant Islamist Hizb-ut-Tahrir al-Islami (Party of Islamic Liberation) was believed to operate in Uzbekistan. In 2004 President Karimov accused the organization of instigating a series of suicide bomb attacks. As in neighbouring states, the organization was proscribed in Uzbekistan. A related organization, Akramiya, also banned, was founded in 1996 by Akram Yuldoshev, who was given a 17-year gaol sentence in 1999 for alleged involvement in terrorist activity. Akramiya apparently regards violence as an appropriate means of pursuing its goals.

Diplomatic Representation

EMBASSIES IN UZBEKISTAN

Afghanistan: 700047 Tashkent, Murtazoev ko'ch. 6; tel. (71) 134-84-32; fax (71) 134-84-65; e-mail afgemuz@mail.tps.uz; Ambassador Abdul Samad.

Algeria: 700000 Tashkent, Murtozayev ko'ch. 6; tel. (711) 34-17-74; fax (71) 20-62-75; Ambassador Hasen Laskri.

Azerbaijan: 700000 Tashkent, Sharq Tongi ko'ch. 25; tel. (71) 173-61-67; fax (71) 173-26-58; e-mail sefir@tps.uz; internet www.azembassy.uz; Ambassador Oydin Azimbekov.

Bangladesh: 700015 Tashkent, 1-chi Kunaev ko'ch. 17; tel. (71) 152-26-92; fax (71) 120-67-11; e-mail bdoot.tas@online.ru; Ambassador A. B. M. Abdus Salam.

Belarus: 700090 Tashkent, V. Vohidov ko'ch. 53; tel. (71) 120-72-52; fax (71) 120-72-53; e-mail uzbekistan@belembassy.org; Ambassador Dr Nikolai N. Demchuk.

Bulgaria: Tashkent, Rakatboshi ko'ch. 52; tel. (71) 56-48-88; fax (71) 152-39-52; Chargé d'affaires Stoyanka G. Rusinova.

China, People's Republic: 700047 Tashkent, Ya. G'ulomov ko'ch. 79; tel. (71) 133-80-88; fax (71) 133-47-35; e-mail chinaemb_uz@mfa.gov.cn; internet www.chinaembassy.uz; Ambassador Chan Chimin.

Czech Republic: 700041 Tashkent, Navnihol ko'ch. 6; tel. (71) 120-60-71; fax (71) 120-60-75; e-mail tashkent@embassy.mzv.cz; Ambassador Aleš Fojtík.

Egypt: 700115 Tashkent, Chilonzor ko'ch. 53A; tel. (71) 120-50-08; fax (71) 120-64-52; Ambassador Gamil Said Ibrahim Fayed.

France: 700041 Tashkent, Oxunboboev ko'ch. 25; tel. (71) 133-53-82; fax (71) 133-62-10; e-mail presse@ambafrance-uz.org; internet www.ambafrance-uz.org; Ambassador Jean-Bernard Harth.

Georgia: 700170 Tashkent, Asom Muhitdinov ko'ch. 6; tel. (711) 62-62-43; fax (71) 62-91-39; e-mail gruzemb@geo-embassy.co.uz; Ambassador David Zalkaniani.

Germany: 700017 Tashkent, Sh. Rashidov ko'ch. 15; tel. (71) 120-84-40; fax (71) 120-66-93; e-mail info@taschkent.diplo.de; internet www.taschkent.diplo.de; Ambassador Hans-Joachim Kiderlen.

India: Tashkent, A. Tolstoy ko'ch. 3; tel. (71) 133-82-67; fax (71) 136-19-76; e-mail indhoc@rol.ru; Ambassador Sharat Sabharval.

Indonesia: 700000 Tashkent, Ya.G'ulomov ko'ch. 73; tel. (71) 132-02-36; fax (71) 120-65-40; e-mail tashkent@indonesia.embassy.uz; internet www.indonesia.embassy.uz; Ambassador Hasyim Salih.

Iran: 700007 Tashkent, Parkent ko'ch. 20; tel. (71) 268-69-68; fax (71) 120-67-61; e-mail iriemuz@hotmail.com; Ambassador Husayn Narokiyon.

Israel: 700000 Tashkent, A. Kahhor ko'ch. 3; tel. (71) 120-58-08; fax (71) 120-58-12; e-mail operator@tashkent.mfa.gov.il; internet tashkent.mfa.gov.il; Ambassador Ami Mel.

Italy: 700031 Tashkent, Yusuf Xos Hojib koʻch. 40; tel. (71) 152-11-19; fax (71) 120-66-06; e-mail ambital@uzb.sarkor.com; Ambassador ANGELO FERRI PERSIANI.

Japan: 700047 Tashkent, S. Azimov 1-tor koʻch. 28; tel. (71) 120-80-60; fax (71) 120-80-77; Ambassador AKIO KAWATO.

Jordan: 700000 Tashkent, Farhod koʻch. 9; tel. (71) 74-64-83; fax (71) 120-66-44; Ambassador MUHAMMAD NOUR OTHMAN YOUSEF BALKAR.

Kazakhstan: 700015 Tashkent, Chekhov koʻch. 23; tel. (71) 152-16-54; fax (71) 152-16-50; e-mail kzembuz@silk.org; Ambassador TLEUKHAN KABDRAKHMANOV.

Korea, Democratic People's Republic: 700000 Tashkent, Usmon Nosir koʻch. 95A; tel. (71) 152-63-16; fax (71) 152-63-15; Ambassador RI THONG PAL.

Korea, Republic: 700000 Tashkent, Afrosiab koʻch. 7; tel. (71) 152-31-51; fax (71) 120-62-48; e-mail admin1@korea.anet.uz; Ambassador KIM SUNG-HWAN.

Kuwait: 700000 Tashkent, Batumi koʻch. 2; tel. (71) 120-58-88; fax (71) 120-84-96; Ambassador VALID AHMAD AL-KANDARI.

Kyrgyzstan: 700000 Tashkent, X. Samatov koʻch. 30; tel. (71) 137-47-94; fax (71) 120-72-94; e-mail krembas@globalnet.uz; Ambassador ULUKBEK K. CHINALIYEV.

Latvia: 700000 Tashkent, Murtazoev koʻch. 6/115–17; tel. (71) 134-92-13; fax (71) 120-70-36; e-mail amblatv@bcc.com.uz; Ambassador IGORS APOKINS.

Malaysia: 700031 Tashkent, M. Yaqubov koʻch. 28; tel. (71) 115-27-31; fax (71) 133-32-71; e-mail mwtskent@rol.uz; Ambassador MUHAMMAD ZAIN ABU BAKR.

Moldova: 700000 Tashkent, Maxatma Gandi koʻch., 1-chi proezd, 39-uy; tel. (71) 133-26-66; fax (71) 137-21-05; e-mail moldova@sarkor.uz; Ambassador EFIM CHILARI.

Pakistan: 700115 Tashkent, Abdurakhmonov koʻch. 15; tel. (71) 144-20-73; fax (71) 144-79-43; e-mail parepuzb@online.ru; Ambassador SAJJAD KAMRAN.

Poland: 700084 Tashkent, Firdavsiy koʻch. 66; tel. (71) 120-86-50; fax (71) 120-86-51; e-mail embassy@poland.uz; internet www.poland.uz; Ambassador ZENON KUCHCIAK.

Russia: 700015 Tashkent, Nukus koʻch. 83; tel. (71) 152-62-80; fax (71) 120-35-09; e-mail rusemb@albatros.uz; Ambassador FARIT MUKHAMETSHIN.

Slovakia: Tashkent, Yakkasaroy koʻch. 18; tel. (71) 120-68-52; fax (71) 120-68-51; e-mail slovakia@buzton.com; Chargé d'affaires PETER YUZA.

Switzerland: 700070 Tashkent, Usmon Nosyr koʻch., tupik 1/4; tel. (71) 120-67-38; fax (71) 120-62-59; e-mail vertretung@tas.rep.admin.ch; Ambassador PETER BURKHARD.

Tajikistan: 700000 Tashkent, A. Kahhor koʻch., 6-chi proezd, 61; tel. (71) 254-99-66; fax (71) 254-89-69; Ambassador GULOMJON MIRZAEV.

Turkey: 700000 Tashkent, Ya. Gʻulomov koʻch. 87; tel. (71) 133-21-07; fax (71) 136-35-25; e-mail turemb@bcc.com.uz; Ambassador RESHIT UMAN.

Turkmenistan: 700000 Tashkent, 1-chi Katta Mirobod koʻch. 10; tel. (71) 120-52-78; fax (71) 120-52-81; Ambassador SOLTAN PIRMUHAMEDOV.

Ukraine: 700000 Tashkent, Gʻulyamov koʻch. 68; tel. and fax (71) 136-08-12; fax (71) 133-10-89; e-mail emb_uz@mfa.gov.ua; internet www.ukraine.uz; Ambassador OLEG V. KLINCHENKO.

United Kingdom: 700000 Tashkent, ul. Ya. Gʻulomov koʻch. 67; tel. (71) 120-78-52; fax (71) 120-65-49; e-mail brit@emb.uz; internet www.britain.uz; Ambassador DAVID MORAN.

USA: 700093 Tashkent, Moyqorghon kʻoch. 3, Yunusobod District,; tel. (71) 120-54-50; fax (71) 120-63-35; e-mail consul_tashkent@yahoo.com; internet www.usembassy.uz; Ambassador JON R. PURNELL.

Viet Nam: 700000 Tashkent, Sh. Rashidov koʻch. 100; tel. (71) 134-03-93; fax (71) 120-62-65; e-mail dsqvntas@online.ru; Ambassador DO VAN DONG.

Judicial System

Supreme Court of the Republic of Uzbekistan
(Oʻzbekistan Respublikasi Oliy sud)
700000 Tashkent, A. Qodiriy koʻch. 1; tel. and fax (71) 144-62-93; internet www.supcourt.gov.uz.

Chairman: FARUHA F. MUHITDINOVA.

Office of the Procurator-General: 700000 Tashkent, Ya Gʻulomov koʻch. 66; tel. (71) 133-20-66; Prosecutor-General RASHIDJON H. QODIROV.

Constitutional Court (Konstitutsiyaviy sud): 700000 Tashkent, Mustaqillik maydoni 6; tel. (71) 139-80-20; fax (71) 139-86-36; e-mail interconcourt@sarkor.uz; Chairman MIRZO-ULUGʻBEK E. ABDUSALAMOV.

Supreme Economic Court (Oliy Xoʻjalik Sudi): 700097 Tashkent, Choʻp onota koʻch. 6; tel. (71) 367-36-18; fax (71) 173-84-78; e-mail economical-court@sarkor.uz; internet www.economical-court.uz; Chair. AMINDJAN D. ISHMETOV.

Religion

The Constitution of 8 December 1992 stipulates that, while there is freedom of worship and expression, there may be no state religion or ideology. A new law on religion was adopted in May 1998, which severely restricted the activities of religious organizations. The Government stated that the legislation was designed to curb the recent increase in militant Islamist activity (including terrorism) in Uzbekistan.

The most widespread religion in Uzbekistan is Islam; the majority of ethnic Uzbeks are Sunni Muslims (Hanafi school), but the number of Salafi (often referred to, inaccurately, as Wahhabi) communities is increasing. At 1 October 2002 there were 1,965 organizations concerned with the Islamic faith registered in Uzbekistan, including 11 educational institutions. Most ethnic Slavs in Uzbekistan are adherents of Orthodox Christianity: there were 36 organizations concerned with the Russian Orthodox faith registered in Uzbekistan at 1 October 2002. At the end of 1993 there were some 32,000 Jews in Uzbekistan; many Jews have since emigrated to Israel.

State Committee for Religious Affairs: 700069 Tashkent, 18-chi Zarqaynar koʻch., alleya 47A; tel. (71) 139-10-14; fax (71) 139-17-63; e-mail info@religions.uz; internet www.religions.uz; Chair. SHAAZIM SH. MINAVAROV.

ISLAM

Muslim Board of Central Asia: 700002 Tashkent, Madrese ʻBarakhan', Zarkainar koʻch. 103; tel. (71) 240-39-33; fax (71) 240-08-31; f. 1943; has spiritual jurisdiction over the Muslims in Kyrgyzstan, Tajikistan, Turkmenistan and Uzbekistan; Chair. ABDURASHID QORI BAKROMOV (Chief Mufti of Mowarounnahr—Central Asia).

CHRISTIANITY

Roman Catholic Church

The Church is represented in Uzbekistan by a Mission, established in September 1997. There were five organizations concerned with the Roman Catholic faith registered in Uzbekistan at 1 October 2002. There were an estimated 4,000 adherents at 31 December 2003.

Superior: Fr KRZYSZTOF KUKUŁKA, 700047 Tashkent, Musahanova koʻch. 80/1; tel. (71) 133-70-35; fax (71) 133-70-25; e-mail ordinary@agnuz.info.

Russian Orthodox Church (Moscow Patriarchate)

Eparchy of Tashkent and Central Asia: 700047 Tashkent, S. Azimov koʻch. 22; tel. (71) 133-14-65; Metropolitan of Tashkent and Central Asia VLADIMIR (IKIM); has jurisdiction over Kyrgyzstan, Tajikistan, Turkmenistan and Uzbekistan.

JUDAISM

Chief Rabbi: Rabbi DAVID GUREVICH Tashkent 700100, ul. Shokhzhakhon 30; tel. (71) 152-59-78; fax (71) 120-64-31; internet www.jewish.uz.

The Press

In 1997, according to official statistics, there were 495 newspapers published in Uzbekistan, including 385 published in Uzbek. The average daily circulation was 1,844,200 copies. There were 113 periodicals published, including 90 in Uzbek. Newspapers and periodicals were also published in Russian, Kazakh, Tajik, Korean, Arabic, English and Kara-Kalpak.

The publications listed below are in Uzbek, unless otherwise stated.

REGULATORY AUTHORITY

Uzbek Agency for Press and Information: 700129 Tashkent, Navoiy koʻch. 30; tel. (71) 133-65-03; fax (71) 133-66-45; e-mail info@aci.uz; internet aci.uz; f. 2002; Gen. Dir ABDULLA N. ARIPOV.

UZBEKISTAN

PRINCIPAL NEWSPAPERS

Adolat (Justice): 700000 Tashkent, Matbuotchilar ko'ch. 32; tel. (71) 133-41-89; f. 1995; organ of the Justice Social Democratic Party of Uzbekistan (Adolat); Editor TOHTAMUROD TOSHEV; circ. 5,900.

Biznes-vestnik Vostoka (Business Bulletin of the East): 700000 Tashkent, Matbuotchilar ko'ch. 32; tel. (71) 133-95-93; e-mail info@uzreport.com; f. 1991; weekly; in Russian and English; economic and financial news; Editor VADIM SIROTIN; circ. 20,000 (Russian), 1,000 (English).

Fidokor (Self-Sacrificer): 700000 Tashkent, Xalqlar Do'stligi ko'ch. 1; tel. (71) 139-45-53; weekly; organ of the Fidokorlar (Self-Sacrificers') National Democratic Party; Editor JALOLIDDIN SAFAYEV; circ. 32,000.

Hurriyat (Freedom): Tashkent; tel. (71) 144-25-06; fax (71) 144-36-16; e-mail amir@uzpac.uz; f. 1996; independent; circ. 5,000.

Inson va Qonun (Person and Law): Ministry of Justice, 700047 Tashkent, Sailgoh ko'ch. 5; internet www.minjust.uz/uz/group.scm?groupId=4146; weekly; organ of the Ministry of Justice; Editor-in-Chief SHODIQUL HAMROEV.

Ma'rifat (Enlightenment): 700000 Tashkent, Matbuotchilar ko'ch. 32; tel. (71) 133-50-55; e-mail mariat@ars-inform.uz; f. 1931; 2 a week; Editor KHALIM SAIDOV; circ. 33,000 (2006).

Menejer (Manager): 700000 Tashkent, Buyuk Turon ko'ch. 41; tel. (71) 136-58-85; f. 1997; weekly; in Russian and Uzbek; commercial information and advertising; Editor KHOTAM ABDURAIMOV; circ. 15,000.

Molodezh Uzbekistana (Youth of Uzbekistan): 700000 Tashkent, Matbuotchilar ko'ch. 32; tel. (71) 133-72-77; fax (71) 133-41-52; e-mail pressa@online.ru; f. 1926; weekly; in Russian; economic and social news; Editor-in-Chief IVAN N. KASACHEV; circ. 6,000.

Mulkdor (Property Owner): 700083 Tashkent, Buyuk Turon ko'ch. 41; tel. (71) 139-21-96; f. 1994; weekly; Editor-in-Chief MIRODIL ABDURAKHMANOV; circ. 10,000.

Postda/Na postu: 700029 Tashkent, Yunus Rajaby ko'ch. 1; f. 1930; in Uzbek and Russian; Editor Z. ATAYEV.

Novyi Vek (New Age): 700060 Tashkent, Movarounnaxr ko'ch. 19; tel. (71) 133-48-55; fax (71) 133-76-84; f. 1992; fmrly *Kommercheskii Vestnik* (Commerical Herald); in Russian; Editor VALERII NIYAZMATOV; circ. 22,000.

O'zbekiston Adabiyoti va San'ati (Literature and Art of Uzbekistan): 700000 Tashkent, Matbuotchilar ko'ch. 32; tel. (71) 133-52-91; f. 1956; weekly; organ of the Union of Writers of Uzbekistan; Editor AKHMAJON MELIBOYEV; circ. 10,300.

O'zbekiston ovozi/Golos Uzbekistana (Voice of Uzbekistan): 700000 Tashkent, Matbuotchilar ko'ch. 32; tel. (71) 133-65-45136–55-15; fax (71) 133-12-56133-65-45; e-mail uzbovozi@sarkor.uzinfo@uzbekistonovozi.uz; internet www.uzbovozi.cc.uzwww.uzbekistonovozi.uz; f. 1918; Uzbek and Russian edns; organ of the People's Democratic Party of Uzbekistan; Editor-in-Chief SAFAR OSTONOV.

Pravda Vostoka (Truth of the East): 700000 Tashkent, Matbuotchilar ko'ch. 32; tel. (71) 133-56-33; fax (71) 133-70-98; e-mail pvostok@tps.uz; internet www.pv.uz; f. 1917; 5 a week; in Russian; organ of the Cabinet of Ministers; in Russian; Editor BAKHTIYOR-ABBASKHAN KHASANOVUSMANOV; circ. 12,000.

Savdogar (Trader): 700000 Tashkent, Buyuk Turon ko'ch. 41; tel. (71) 133-34-55; f. 1992; Editor MUHAMMAD ORAZMETOV; circ. 17,000.

Soliq va Bojxona Xabarlari: 700000 Tashkent, Abaya ko'ch. 6; tel. (71) 144-02-01; f. 1994; Editor MIKHAIL PERPER; circ. 45,000.

Sport: 700000 Tashkent, pr. Uzbekistanskii 98A; tel. (71) 144-07-52; f. 1932; Editor HAYDAR AKBAROV; circ. 8,490.

Toshkent Xakikati/Tashkentskaya Pravda (Tashkent Truth): 700000 Tashkent, Matbuotchilar ko'ch. 32; tel. (71) 133-64-95; f. 1954; 2 a week; Uzbek and Russian edns; Editor FATKHIDDIN MUKHITDINOV; circ. 19,000 (Uzbek edn), 6,400 (Russian edn).

Turkiston (Turkestan): 700000 Tashkent, Matbuotchilar ko'ch. 32; tel. (71) 136-56-58; f. 1925 as *Yash Leninchy* (Young Leninist), renamed as above 1992; 2 a week; organ of the Kamolot Asscn of Youth of Uzbekistan; Editor GAFAR KHATOMOV; circ. 12,580.

Xalk Suzi/Narodnoye Slovo (People's Word): 700000 Tashkent, Matbuotchilar ko'ch. 32; tel. (712) 133-15-22; e-mail info@narodnoeslovo.uz; f. 1991; Uzbek and Russian edns; 5 a week (Uzbek), weekly (Russian); organ of the Oly Majlis and the Cabinet of Ministers; Editor ABBASKHON USMANOV; circ. 41,580 (Uzbek edn), 12,750 (Russian edn).

Xamkor (Business Partner): 700077 Tashkent, Buyuk Ipak Yuli 75; tel. (71) 68-72-04; fax (71) 34-64-82; f. 1991; in Uzbek, Russian and English; Editor ISMAT HUSHEV; circ. 20,000.

PRINCIPAL PERIODICALS

Monthly, unless otherwise indicated.

Fan va turmush (Science and Life): 700000 Tashkent, Ya. G'ulomov ko'ch. 70; tel. (71) 133-07-05; f. 1933; every 2 months; publ. by the Fan (Science) Publishing House; popular scientific; Editor MURAD SHARIFKHOJAYEV; circ. 28,000.

Gulhan (Bonfire): 700000 Tashkent, Buyuk Turon ko'ch. 41; tel. (71) 136-78-85; f. 1929; illustrated juvenile fiction; Editor SAFAR BARNOYEV; circ. 26,000.

Guliston: 700000 Tashkent, Buyuk Turon ko'ch. 41; tel. (71) 136-78-90; f. 1925; every 2 months; socio-political; Editor TILAB MAHMUDOV; circ. 4,000.

Guncha (Small Bud): 700000 Tashkent, Buyuk Turon ko'ch. 41; tel. (71) 136-78-80; f. 1958; illustrated; for pre-school-age children; Editor ERKIN MALIKOV; circ. 35,000.

Jakhon Adabiyoti (World Literature): 700129 Tashkent, A. Navoiy ko'ch. 30; tel. (71) 144-41-60; fax (71) 144-41-61; f. 1997; Editor OZOD SHARAFIDDINOV; circ. 2,000.

Mushtum (Fist): 700000 Tashkent, Buyuk Turon ko'ch. 41; tel. (71) 133-99-72; f. 1923; fortnightly; satirical; Editor ASHURALI JURAYEV; circ. 10,650.

Obshchestvennye Nauki v Uzbekistane (Social Sciences in Uzbekistan): 700047 Tashkent, Ya.G'ulomov ko'ch. 70; tel. (71) 136-73-29; f. 1957; publ. by the Fan (Science) Publishing House of the Academy of Sciences of Uzbekistan; history, oriental studies, archaeology, economics, ethnology, etc; in Russian and Uzbek; Editor A. MUKHAMEJANOV; circ. 500.

O'zbek Tili va Adabiyoti (Uzbek Language and Literature): 700000 Tashkent, Muminov ko'ch. 9; tel. (71) 262-42-47; f. 1958; every 2 months; publ. by the Fan (Science) Publishing House; journal of the Academy of Sciences of Uzbekistan; history and modern development of the Uzbek language, folklore, etc.; Editor AZIM KHAJIYEV; circ. 3,700.

Saodat (Happiness): 700083 Tashkent, Buyuk Turon ko'ch. 41; tel. (71) 133-68-10; f. 1925; 8 a year; women's popular; Editor OIDIN KHAJIYEVA; circ. 70,000.

Sharq Yulduzi/Zvezda Vostoka (Star of the East): 700000 Tashkent, Buyuk Turon ko'ch. 41; tel. (71) 133-09-18; f. 1932; journal of the Union of Writers of Uzbekistan; fiction; Uzbek and Russian edns; Editor (Uzbek edn) UTKUR KHASHIMOV; Editor (Russian edn) NIKOLAI KRASILNIKOV; circ. 10,000 (Uzbek edn), 3,000 (Russian edn).

Sikhat Salomatlik (Health): 700000 Tashkent, Parkent ko'ch. 51; tel. (71) 268-17-54; f. 1990; every 2 months; Editor DAMIN A. ASADOV; circ. 36,000.

Tong Yulduzi (Morning Star): 700129 Tashkent, A. Navoiy ko'ch. 30; tel. (71) 144-62-34; e-mail ijod@uzpak.uz; f. 1929; weekly; children's; Editor UMIDA ABDUAZIMOVA; circ. 60,000.

Yoshlik (Youth): 700000 Tashkent, Buyuk Turon ko'ch. 41; tel. (71) 133-09-18; f. 1932; literature and arts for young people; Editor SABIR UNAROV; circ. 10,000.

NEWS AGENCIES

Jahon (World) Information Agency: 700029 Tashkent, pr. Uzbekistanskii 9; tel. (71) 133-65-91; fax (71) 120-64-43; e-mail aajahon@mfa.uz; internet jahon.mfa.uz; information agency of Ministry of Foreign Affairs; Dir ABROR GULYAMOV.

Turkiston Press: 700047 Tashkent, Xorazm ko'ch. 51; tel. (71) 133-78-54; fax (71) 133-95-38; e-mail tpress@sarkor.uz; Dir-Gen. SAGDULA HAKIMOV.

Uzbekistan National News Agency (UzA): 700047 Tashkent, Musahanov ko'ch. 38; tel. (71) 133-16-22; fax (71) 133-24-45; internet www.uza.uz; Dir MAMATSKUL KHAZRATSKULOV.

Foreign Bureaux

Agence France-Presse (AFP): Tashkent; tel. (71) 132-02-93; e-mail galima@bcc.com.uz; Correspondent GALIMA BURHARBAYEVA.

Anadolu Ajansı (Turkey): Tashkent, 1–Center 47/37; tel. (71) 133-69-85; e-mail taskent@anadoluajansi.com.tr.

Associated Press (AP) (USA): Tashkent; tel. (71) 136-19-58; Correspondent TIMOFEY ZHUKOV.

Interfax (Russia): Tashkent; tel. (71) 133-70-69; Correspondent BAKHTIYOR KHASANOV.

Reuters (United Kingdom): Tashkent; tel. (71) 120-73-66; e-mail shamil.baygin@reuters.co.uz; Correspondent SHAMIL BAYGIN.

Publishers

In 1997 there were approximately 1,000 book titles published in Uzbekistan, of which some 70% were in Uzbek.

Uzbek Agency for Press and Information: 700129 Tashkent, A. Navoiy ko'ch. 30; tel. (71) 144-32-87; fax (71) 144-14-84; e-mail

UZBEKISTAN

Directory

ozmaa@uzpak.uz; internet www.uzapi.gov.uz; f. 2002; mass media, press and information exchange; printing, publishing and distribution of periodicals; Gen. Dir BABUR ALIMOV.

Abdulla Qadiri Publishers: 700129 Tashkent, A. Navoiy ko'ch. 30; tel. (71) 144-61-51; f. 1992; history, culture, literature; Dir D. I. IKRAMOVA.

Abu Ali ibn Sino Publishers: 700129 Tashkent, A. Navoiy ko'ch. 30; tel. (71) 144-31-45; fax (71) 144-51-72; e-mail ibnsino@glb.net; f. 1958; medical sciences; Dir OMONOV BAKHTIOR.

Chulpon (Morning Star) Publishers: 700129 Tashkent, A. Navoiy ko'ch. 30; tel. (71) 139-13-75; Dir N. KHOLBUTAYEV.

Fan (Science) Publishers: 700047 Tashkent, Ya. G'ulomov ko'ch. 70/102; tel. (71) 133-69-61; scientific books and journals; Dir N. T. KHATAMOV.

Gafur Gulom Publishing House: 700129 Tashkent, A. Navoiy ko'ch. 30; tel. (71) 144-22-53; fax (71) 41-35-47; f. 1957; fiction, the arts; books in Uzbek, Russian and English; Dir MIZROB M. BURONOV; Editor-in-Chief NAZIRA J. JURAYEVNA.

Mekhnat (Labour) Publishers: 700129 Tashkent, A. Navoiy ko'ch. 30; tel. (71) 144-22-27; f. 1985; Dir RUSTAM A. MIRZAYEV.

O'gqituvchi (Teacher) Publishing-Printing and Creative House: 700129 Tashkent, A. Navoiy ko'ch. 30; tel. (71) 144-26-89; fax (71) 144-26-89; f. 1936; literary textbooks, education manuals, scientific popular literature, juvenile; Dir R.O. MIRZAYEV.

O'zbekiston Milliy Entsiklopediyasi (Uzbekistan National Encyclopaedias): 700129 Tashkent, A. Navoiy ko'ch. 30; tel. (71) 144-34-38; f. 1997; encyclopedias, dictionaries and reference books; Dir N. TUKHLIYEV.

O'zbekiston (Uzbekistan) Publishing and Printing Creative House: 700129 Tashkent, A. Navoiy ko'ch. 30; tel. (71) 144-34-01; fax (71) 144-38-10; e-mail aptpk@ars-inform.uz; f. 2004; politics, economics, law, history and art, illustrated, manuals and textbooks for schools and higher educational institutes; Dir ZAIR T. ISADJANOV; Editor-in-Chief SHOMUKHITDIN SH. MANSUROV.

Yozuvchi (Writer) Publishers: 700129 Tashkent, A. Navoiy ko'ch. 30; tel. (71) 144-29-97; f. 1990; Dir M. U. TOICHIYEV.

WRITERS' UNION

Union of Writers of Uzbekistan: 700000 Tashkent, J. Neru ko'ch. 1; tel. (71) 133-63-74; Chair. ABDULLA ARIPOV.

Broadcasting and Communications

TELECOMMUNICATIONS

Communications and Information Agency of Uzbekistan: 700011 Tashkent, A. Navoiy ko'ch. 28A; tel. (71) 133-65-03; fax (71) 139-87-82; e-mail info@aci.uz; internet www.aci.uz; Dir-Gen. ABDULLA N. ARIPOV.

Service Providers

Coscom: 700031 Tashkent, V. Vaxidova ko'ch. 118; tel. (71) 152-15-51; fax (71) 120-72-65; e-mail inform@coscom.uz; internet www.coscom.uz; f. 1996; Uzbekistani-US jt venture; mobile cellular telecommunications.

Unitel (Daewoo GSM): 700000 Tashkent, Buxoro ko'ch. 1; tel. (71) 133-33-30; fax (71) 132-12-22; e-mail info@daewoounitel.com; internet www.unitel.uz; f. 1996; fmrly Daewoo Unitel; mobile cellular telecommunications.

Uzbektelecom: 700000 Tashkent, Amir Temur ko'ch. 24; tel. (71) 133-42-59; fax (71) 136-01-88; e-mail uztelecom@intal.uz; internet www.uztelecom.uz; f. 2000; provides local, regional and international telecommunications services; partial privatization pending; Gen. Dir KH. A. MUKHITDINOV.

Uzdunrobita: 700000 Tashkent, Amir Temur ko'ch. 24; tel. (97) 130-01-01; fax (97) 130-01-05; e-mail office@uzdunrobita.com.uz; internet www.uzdunrobita.uz; f. 1991 as an Uzbek-US jt venture; provides mobile cellular telecommunications services; 74% acquired by Mobile Telesystems (Russia) in 2004; Gen. Dir BEKHZOD AKHMEDOV.

BROADCASTING

State Television and Radio Broadcasting Company of Uzbekistan (UZTELERADIO): 700011 Tashkent, A. Navoiy ko'ch. 69; tel. (71) 133-81-06; fax (71) 144-16-60; e-mail uztele@tkt.uz; internet www.teleradio.uz; local broadcasts, as well as relays from Egypt, France, India, Japan, Russia and Turkey; Chair. ALISHER KHUJAYEV.

Radio

Radio Tashkent International: 700047 Tashkent, Xorazm ko'ch. 49; tel. (71) 133-38-94; fax (71) 133-60-68; e-mail ino@uzpak.uz; internet ino.uzpak.uz; f. 1947; broadcasts in Uzbek, Kazakh, Kyrgyz, Tajik, Turkmen, Arabic, Chinese, Dari, English, Farsi, German, Hindu, Pashto, Turkish, Uigur and Urdu; Dir SHERZOD GHULOMOV.

Television

Uzbekistan Television and Radio Company (Uzteleradio): 700011 Tashkent, A. Navoiy ko'ch. 69; tel. (71) 133-81-06; fax (71) 144-16-60; e-mail uztcint@hotmail.com; four local programmes as well as relays from Russia, Kazakhstan, Egypt, India and Turkey; Chair. ALISHER KHADJAYEV.

Kamalak Television: 700084 Tashkent, Amir Temur ko'ch. 109; tel. (71) 137-51-77; fax (71) 120-62-28; e-mail kam.tv@kamalak.co.uz; f. 1992; jt venture between State Television and Radio Broadcasting Company and a US company; satellite broadcasts; relays from France, Germany, India, Russia, the United Kingdom and the USA; Gen. Dir PULAT UMAROV.

Finance

(cap. = capital; res = reserves; dep. = deposits; m. = million; amounts in Uzbek sum, unless otherwise stated; brs = branches)

BANKING

A reform of the banking sector was begun in 1994. A two-tier system was introduced, consisting of the Central Bank and about 30 commercial banks. An association of commercial banks was established in 1995 to co-ordinate the role of commercial banks in the national economy. At the end of 2002 there were reported to be 35 banks in Uzbekistan, of which 13 were under private ownership.

Central Bank

Central Bank of the Republic of Uzbekistan: 700001 Tashkent, pr. Uzbekistanskii 6; tel. (71) 136-77-04; fax (71) 133-00-44; e-mail turgun@cbu.gov.uz; internet www.gov.uz/government/cbu/cbu_0e.htm; f. 1991; Chair. of Bd FAIZULLA M. MULLAJONOV.

State Commercial Bank

National Bank for Foreign Economic Activity of the Republic of Uzbekistan (O'zbekiston Respublikasi Tashqi Iqtisodiy Faoliyat Milliy Banki): 700084 Tashkent, Amir Temur ko'ch. 101; tel. (71) 137-59-70; fax (71) 133-32-00; e-mail webmaster@central.nbu.com; internet www.nbu.com; f. 1991; cap. 22,386m., res 385,567m., dep. 765,613m. (Dec. 2003); Chair. ZAINIDDIN S. MIRKHOJAYEV; 99 brs.

State Joint-Stock Commercial Banks

Asaka—Specialized State Joint-Stock Commercial Bank: 700015 Tashkent, Nukus ko'ch. 67; tel. (71) 120-81-11; fax (71) 120-86-91; e-mail contact@asakabank.com; internet www.asakabank.com; f. 1995; cap. US $153.5m., res $7.2m., dep. $102.5m. (Dec. 2003); Chair. SHOKIR J. JURAYEV; 26 brs.

Halk Bank (State Commercial People's Bank of the Republic of Uzbekistan): 700096 Tashkent, Katortol ko'ch. 46; tel. (71) 278-59-44; fax (71) 173-69-13; e-mail farhod_azizov@yahoo.com; f. 1995; fmrly Savings Bank of Uzbekistan; cap. 5,720m., res 519.9m., dep. 43,900m. (Jan. 2003); Chair. ADHAM HAYDAROV; 2,849 brs.

UzJilSberBank—Uzbek State Joint-Stock Housing Savings Bank: 700000 Tashkent, Pushkin ko'ch. 17; tel. (71) 132-12-96; fax (71) 132-13-23; e-mail uzjsbved@online.ru; internet www.uzujb.com; cap. 26,500m., total assets 145,000m. (2003); Chair. TIMUR S. AZIMOV.

Zaminbank State Joint-Stock Commercial Mortgage Bank: 700015 Tashkent, P. Rzhevskiy ko'ch. 3; tel. (71) 255-82-59; fax (71) 255-77-49; f. 1995; Chair. of Bd ODLI O. MAVLANOV.

Other Joint-Stock Commercial Banks

Alokabank: 700015 Tashkent, Oybek ko'ch. 30; tel. (71) 152-78-74; fax (71) 152-78-04; e-mail info@alokabank.uz; internet www.alokabank.uz; f. 1995; cap. 3,481m., res 1,031m., dep. 1,824m. (2004); Chair. FAKHRIDDIN T. YULDASHEV; 11 brs.

Avia Bank: 700015 Tashkent, Nukus ko'ch. 86A; tel. (71) 254-75-75; fax (71) 254-79-53; e-mail aviabank2002@mail.ru; f. 1989; cap. 1,700m., res 732.1m., dep. 3,205.8m. (Jan. 2003); Chair. SHUKURULLO IMAMALIYEV.

Galla Bank: 700060 Tashkent, Lakhuti ko'ch. 38; tel. and fax (71) 133-42-25; Chair. YULDASHBAI E. ERGASHEV.

HamkorBank: 710011 Andijon, Babura ko'ch. 85; tel. and fax (74) 24-70-39; e-mail hamkorbank@mail.ru; f. 1991; Chair. IKRAM IBRAGIMOV; 15 brs.

UZBEKISTAN

Ipak Yuli: 700135 Tashkent, Farkod koʻch. 12; tel. (71) 119-19-91; fax (71) 133-32-00; e-mail ipak@online.ru; f. 2000.

Oʻzsanoatkurilishbank (Uzpromstroibank) (Uzbek Industrial Construction Bank): 700000 Tashkent, Shaxrisab koʻch. 3; tel. (71) 136-75-41; fax (71) 132-06-14; internet www.uzpsb.com; f. 1922; Chair. KIYOMIDDIN RUSTAMOV; 46 brs.

Parvina Bank: 703005 Samarqand, ul. Uzbekistanskaya 82; tel. (66) 31-05-07; fax (66) 31-02-82; e-mail parvina@uol.uz; Chair. AKBAR S. KADIROV.

Paxta Bank (Pakhta Bank): 700096 Tashkent, Mukimi koʻch. 43; tel. (71) 278-21-96; fax (71) 120-88-18; e-mail pahtabnk@sovam.com; internet www.pakhtabank.com; f. 1995; cap. 12,500m., res 38,079.4m., dep. 100,514.2m. (Dec. 2004); Chair. ABDURAKHMAT BOYMURATOV; 184 brs.

Savdogarbank: 700060 Tashkent, S. Barak koʻch. 76; tel. (72) 254-19-91; fax (71) 256-56-71; internet www.savdogarbank.uz; Chair. MURSURMON N. NURMAMATOV.

Tadbirkor Bank: 700047 Tashkent, S. Azimov koʻch. 52; tel. (71) 133-18-75; fax (71) 136-88-32; Chair. MUZAFFARBEK SABIROV.

Trustbank: 700038 Tashkent, A. Navoiy koʻch. 7; tel. (71) 144-76-22; e-mail info@trustbank.uz; internet www.trustbank.uz; f. 1994; cap. US $1.9m., dep. $0.4m., res $2.1m. (Aug. 2005); Chair. ILHOM F. SOLIYEV; 2 brs.

Turonbank: 700011 Tashkent, A. Navoiy koʻch. 44; tel. (71) 144-34-66; fax (71) 144-72-99; e-mail turon@sarkor.uz; internet turonbank.sarkor.uz; f. 1990; Chair. of Bd DANIYOR B. ARIFJANOV; 40 brs.

Joint-Venture Banks

ABN-AMRO Bank NB Uzbekistan AO: 700000 Tashkent, Nosirov koʻch. 77; tel. (71) 120-61-41; fax (71) 120-63-67; e-mail aziz.mirjuraev@abnamro.com; internet www.abnamro.com/wholesale/docs/country/uzbekistan.asp; f. 1996 as jt venture between European Bank for Reconstruction and Development, ABN-AMRO (Netherlands), the World Bank and the Uzbek National Bank for Foreign Economic Relations; universal commercial bank; cap. US $8.5m.; Chair. and Gen. Man. HUGO MINDERHOUD.

Uzbekistan-Turkish UT Bank: 700043 Tashkent, Xalqlar Doʻstligi koʻch. 15B; tel. (71) 173-83-25; fax (71) 120-63-62; e-mail utbank@utbk.com; f. 1993; cap. 3,845.3m., res 1.711.1m., dep. 3,042.2m. (Dec. 2003); Chair. UTKIRBOY U SHUKUROV.

UzDaewoo Bank: 700000 Tashkent, Pushkin koʻch.; tel. (71) 120-80-00; fax (71) 120-69-70; e-mail office@daewoobank.com; internet www.daewoobank.com; f. 1997; total assets US $45m.; Chair. JOONG MYUNG-JUNG.

Uzprivatbank (Uzbek International Bank for Privatization and Investments): 700003 Tashkent, pr. Uzbekistanskii 51; tel. (71) 120-63-08; fax (71) 120-63-07; e-mail bank@uib.iz; internet www.uzprivatbank.com; f. 1994; cap. US $5.5m.; Chair. A. A. ERGASHEV.

INSURANCE

Oʻzbekinvest (Uzbekinvest) National Export–Import Insurance Co: 700017 Tashkent, Suleimanov koʻch. 49; tel. (71) 133-05-56; fax (71) 133-07-04; e-mail root@unic.gov.uz; internet www.unic.gov.uz; f. 1994, restructured 1997; jt venture with American International Group (AIG—USA); cap. US $60m.; Dir-Gen. SUNNAT A. UMAROV; Chief Exec. NODIR KALANDAROV.

COMMODITY EXCHANGE

Tashkent Republican Commodity and Raw Materials Exchange: 700003 Tashkent, pr. Uzbekistanskii 53; tel. (71) 139-83-77; fax (71) 139-83-92; Chair. of Bd NABIHON S. SAMATOV.

STOCK EXCHANGE

Tashkent Republican Stock Exchange (UZSE): 700047 Tashkent, Buxoro koʻch. 10; tel. (71) 136-07-40; fax (71) 133-32-31; e-mail info@uzse.com; internet www.uzse.com; f. 1994; stocks and securities; Chair. BAKHTIYOR RADJABOV.

Trade and Industry

GOVERNMENT AGENCIES

Foreign Investment Agency: 700077 Tashkent, Buyuyk Ipak Yulli koʻch. 75; tel. (71) 68-77-05; fax (71) 67-07-52; e-mail afi@mail.uznet.net; Gen. Dir SHAZIYATOV S. SHOAZIZ.

State Committee of the Republic of Uzbekistan for De-monopolization and the Development of Competition (Oʻzbekiston Respublikasi Monopoliadan Chiqarish va Raqobatni Rivojlantirish Davlat Qoʻmitasi): 700011 Tashkent, A. Navoiy koʻch. 18A; tel. (71) 139-15-42; fax (71) 139-83-42; e-mail devonhona@antimon.uz; internet www.antimon.uz; Chair. JAMSHED B. SAYFIDDINOV.

State Committee of the Republic of Uzbekistan for the Management of State Property and Support of Entrepreneurship (State Property Committee): 700003 Tashkent, pr. Uzbekistanskii 55; tel. (71) 139-44-46; fax 71 139-14-84; e-mail ves@spc.gov.uz; internet www.spc.gov.uz; Chair. MAKHMUDJON A. ASKAROV.

CHAMBER OF COMMERCE

Chamber of Commerce and Industry of Uzbekistan: 700047 Tashkent, Buxoro koʻch. 6; tel. (71) 133-06-99; fax (71) 132-09-03; e-mail info@chamber.uz; internet www.chamber.uz; f. 1996 as Chamber of Commodity Producers and Entrepreneurs of Uzbekistan; re-established and re-named as above by presidential decree 2004; provides assistance, consultancy and support for businesses; Chair. ALISHER SHAIKHOV.

EMPLOYERS' ORGANIZATIONS

Employers' Association of Uzbekistan: 700017 Tashkent, A. Qadiry koʻch. 2; tel. (71) 234-06-71; fax (71) 234-13-39.

STATE HYDROCARBONS COMPANY

Uzbekneftegaz (Uzbekistani Petroleum and Natural Gas Co): 700047 Tashkent, Akhunbabayev koʻch. 21; tel. (71) 133-57-57; fax (71) 136-77-71; e-mail nhk@uzneftegaz.uz; internet www.uzneftegaz.uz; f. 1999; national petroleum and gas corpn; Chair. ABDUSALOM A. AZIZOV; 90,000 employees.

TRADE UNIONS

Federation of Trade Unions of Uzbekistan: Tashkent; Chair. of Council KHULKAR JAMALOV.

Transport

RAILWAYS

Uzbekistan's railway network is connected to those of the neighbouring republics of Kazakhstan, Kyrgyzstan, Tajikistan and Turkmenistan, and to that of Russia. In 1994 Oʻzbekiston Temir Yoʻllari (the Uzbekistan State Railway Company) was established on the basis of the existing facilities of its predecessor, the Central Asian Railway. There were 3,986 km of standard-gauge track in 2001, of which 619 km was electrified. Another line, connecting central Uzbekistan with the north-western part of the country, was brought into operation in March 2001.

Oʻzbekiston Temir Yoʻllari (Uzbekistan State Railway Co): 700060 Tashkent, T. Shevchenko koʻch. 7; tel. (71) 138-80-00; fax (71) 133-45-49; e-mail uzrailway@uzpak.uz; internet www.uzrailway.uz; f. 1994; state-owned joint-stock co; Pres. ACHILBAY ZH. RAMATOV.

City Underground Railway

Tashgorpasstreans (Tashkent Metro): 700027 Tashkent, pr. Uzbekistanskii 93A; tel. (71) 232-38-52; fax (71) 133-66-81; e-mail metro@sarkor.uz; f. 1977; three lines with total length of 36 km, and fourth line due to open by 2010; Chair. M. A. ODILOV.

ROADS

In 1999 the total length of the road network was estimated at 81,600 km, of which approximately 87.3% was paved.

INLAND WATERWAYS

The extensive use of the waters of the Amu-Dar'ya and Syr-Dar'ya for irrigation lessened the flow of these rivers and caused the desiccation of the Aral Sea. This reduced a valuable transport asset. However, the Amu-Dar'ya Steamship Co still operates important river traffic.

CIVIL AVIATION

There is an international airport at Tashkent. From 1996 the airports at Samarqand, Urgench and Buxoro (Bukhara) were upgraded to stimulate tourism.

Uzbekistan Airways (Uzbekiston Havo Yollari): 700061 Tashkent, ul. Proletarskaya 41; tel. (71) 291-14-90; fax (71) 232-73-71; e-mail info@uzbekistan-airways.com; internet www.airways.uz; f. 1992; operates flights between Uzbekistan and destinations in Central Asia, South-East Asia, the USA, the Middle East and Europe; Dir-Gen. RAFIKOV GANIY; Gen. Dir VALERIY TYAN.

Tourism

Since independence Uzbekistan has sought to promote tourism as an important source of revenue. The republic has more than 4,000 historical monuments, many of which are associated with the ancient 'Silk Route', particularly the cities of Samarqand (Tamerlane's capital), Xiva (Khiva) and Buxoro (Bukhara), as well as other historic sites. Infrastructural limitations, however, have constrained development. In 2003 Uzbekistan received an estimated 231,000 foreign visitors (including excursionists). In that year tourism receipts totalled some US $48m.

Uzbektourism: 700027 Tashkent, Xorazm ko'ch. 47; tel. (71) 133-54-14; fax (71) 136-79-48; f. 1992; Chair. BAKHTIYOR M. HUSANBAYEV.

VANUATU

Introductory Survey

Location, Climate, Language, Religion, Flag, Capital

The Republic of Vanuatu comprises an irregular archipelago of 83 islands in the south-west Pacific Ocean, lying about 1,000 km (600 miles) west of Fiji and 400 km (250 miles) north-east of New Caledonia. The group extends over a distance of about 1,300 km (808 miles) from north to south. The islands have an oceanic tropical climate, with a season of south-east trade winds between May and October. Winds are variable, with occasional cyclones for the rest of the year, and annual rainfall varies between 2,300 mm (90 ins) in the south and 3,900 mm (154 ins) in the north. In Port Vila, in the centre of the group, mean temperatures vary between 22°C (72°F) and 27°C (81°F). The national language is Bislama, ni-Vanuatu pidgin. There are many Melanesian languages and dialects. English, French and Bislama are the official languages. Most of the inhabitants (about 80%) profess Christianity, of which a number of denominations are represented. The national flag (proportions 3 by 5) consists of two equal horizontal stripes, red above green, on which are superimposed a black-edged yellow horizontal 'Y' (with its base in the fly) and, at the hoist, a black triangle containing two crossed yellow mele leaves encircled by a curled yellow boar's tusk. The capital is Port Vila, on the island of Efate.

Recent History

During the 19th century the New Hebrides (now Vanuatu) were settled by British and French missionaries, planters and traders. The United Kingdom and France established a Joint Naval Commission for the islands in 1887. The two countries later agreed on a joint civil administration, and in 1906 the territory became the Anglo-French Condominium of the New Hebrides (Nouvelles-Hébrides). Under this arrangement, there were three elements in the structure of administration: the British National Service, the French National Service and the Condominium (Joint) Departments. Each power was responsible for its own citizens and other non-New Hebrideans who chose to be *'ressortissants'* of either power. Indigenous New Hebrideans were not permitted to claim either British or French citizenship. This resulted in two official languages, two police forces, three public services, three courts of law, three currencies, three national budgets, two resident commissioners in Port Vila (the capital) and two district commissioners in each of the four Districts.

Local political initiatives began after the Second World War, originating in New Hebridean concern over the alienation of native land. More than 36% of the New Hebrides was owned by foreigners. Na-Griamel, one of the first political groups to emerge, had its source in cult-like activities. In 1971 the leaders of Na-Griamel petitioned the UN to prevent further sales of land at a time when areas were being sold to US interests for development as tropical tourist resorts. In 1972 the New Hebrides National Party was formed, with support from Protestant missions and covert support from British interests. In response, French interests formed the Union des Communautés Néo-Hébridaises in 1974. Discussions in the United Kingdom in 1974 resulted in the replacement of the Advisory Council, established in 1957, by a Representative Assembly of 42 members, of whom 29 were directly elected in November 1975. The Assembly did not hold its first full working session until November 1976, and it was dissolved in early 1977, following a boycott by the National Party, which had changed its name to the Vanuaaku Pati (VP) in 1976. However, the VP reached an agreement with the Condominium powers on new elections for the Representative Assembly, based on universal suffrage for all seats.

In 1977 it was announced, at a conference in France involving British, French and New Hebridean representatives, that the islands would become independent in 1980, following a referendum and elections. The VP boycotted this conference, as it demanded immediate independence. The VP also boycotted the elections in November 1977, and declared a 'People's Provisional Government'. Nevertheless, a reduced Assembly of 39 members was elected, and a measure of self-government was introduced in early 1978. A Council of Ministers and the office of Chief Minister (occupied by Georges Kalsakau) were created, and the French, British and Condominium Services began to be replaced by a single New Hebrides Public Service. In December a Government of National Unity was formed, with Fr Gérard Leymang as Chief Minister and Fr Walter Lini (the VP President) as Deputy Chief Minister.

At elections in November 1979 the VP won 26 of the 39 seats in the Assembly. The outcome of the election led to rioting by supporters of Na-Griamel on the island of Espiritu Santo, who threatened non-Santo 'foreigners'. However, the new Assembly elected Lini as Chief Minister.

In June 1980 Jimmy Stevens, the leader of Na-Griamel, declared Espiritu Santo independent of the rest of the New Hebrides, styling it the 'Independent State of Vemarana'. Members of his movement, allegedly assisted by French *colons* and supported by private US business interests, moved to the coast and imprisoned government officers and police, who were later released together with other European and indigenous public servants. British Royal Marines were deployed as a peace-keeping force, prompting strong criticism by the French, who would not permit Britain's unilateral use of force on Espiritu Santo.

In mid-July 1980, however, agreement was reached between the two Condominium powers and Lini, and the New Hebrides became independent within the Commonwealth, under the name of Vanuatu, as planned, on 30 July. The first President was the former Deputy Chief Minister, George Kalkoa, who adopted the surname Sokomanu ('leader of thousands'), although the post is largely ceremonial. Lini became Prime Minister. The Republic of Vanuatu signed a defence pact with Papua New Guinea, and in August units of the Papua New Guinea Defence Force replaced the British and French troops on Espiritu Santo and arrested the Na-Griamel rebels.

At a general election in November 1983 the VP retained a majority in Parliament, taking 24 of the 39 seats. Sokomanu remained as President. Parliament was expanded to 46 seats for the general election held in December 1987. Of these, the VP won 26 seats, the Union of Moderate Parties (UMP) 19, and the Fren Melanesia one.

In May 1988 a government decision to abolish a local land corporation, which had been a principal source of patronage for Sope, prompted a demonstration in Port Vila by Sope's supporters. Serious rioting ensued, in which one person was killed and several others injured. Lini accused Sope of being instrumental in provoking the riots, and subsequently dismissed him from the Council of Ministers. In July Sope and four colleagues resigned from the VP, and were subsequently dismissed from Parliament at Lini's behest. In addition, 18 members of the UMP were dismissed after they had boycotted successive parliamentary sittings in protest at the expulsions. In September Sope and his colleagues announced the formation of a new political party, the Melanesian Progressive Pati (MPP), and in October the VP expelled 128 of its own members for allegedly supporting the new party. In October the Court of Appeal ruled as unconstitutional the dismissal from Parliament of Sope and his colleagues, and reinstated them, but upheld the expulsion of the 18 members of the UMP. In November Sope resigned from Parliament, citing loss of confidence in its Speaker. In December President Sokomanu dissolved Parliament and announced that Sope would act as interim Prime Minister, pending a general election scheduled to be held in February 1989. Lini immediately denounced Sokomanu's actions, and the Governments of Australia, New Zealand and Papua New Guinea refused to recognize the interim Government. The islands' police force remained loyal to Lini, and later in December Sokomanu, Sope and other members of the interim Government were arrested and charged with treason. In 1989 Sokomanu was sentenced to six years' imprisonment, and Sope and the then leader of the parliamentary opposition, Maxime Carlot Korman, were jailed for five-year terms, for seditious conspiracy and incitement to mutiny. However, representatives of the International Commission of Jurists, who had been present at the trials, criticized the rulings, and in April the Court of Appeal overturned the original judgment, citing insufficient evidence for the convictions. Fred Timakata, the former

Minister of Health, replaced Sokomanu as President in January 1989.

Diminishing support for Lini's leadership led to the approval in August 1991 of a motion of 'no confidence' in Lini as party leader at the VP's congress. Donald Kalpokas, the Secretary-General of the VP, was unanimously elected to replace Lini as President of the party. In September a motion of 'no confidence' in the premiership of Lini was narrowly approved in Parliament, and Kalpokas was elected Prime Minister. Subsequently, Lini, with the support of a substantial number of defectors from the VP, formed the National United Party (NUP). At a general election in December the UMP secured 19 seats, while the VP and NUP each won 10 seats, the MPP four and Tan Union, Fren Melanesia and Na-Griamel one each. The leader of the UMP, Maxime Carlot Korman, was appointed Prime Minister, and a coalition Government was formed between the UMP and the NUP.

At a presidential election in February 1994 neither the UMP's candidate, Fr Luc Dini, nor Fr John Bani, who was supported by the opposition, attained the requisite two-thirds of total votes cast. The election was rescheduled for March. The VP subsequently agreed to vote with the ruling UMP, in return for a guaranteed role in a future coalition government. As a result of this agreement, the UMP's candidate, Jean-Marie Leye, was elected to the presidency with 41 votes. The VP subsequently withdrew its support for the UMP when Carlot refused to offer the party more than one ministerial post; the VP had requested three.

In May 1994 Regenvanu, Tabisari and Sinker were expelled from the NUP. They subsequently formed a new grouping, the People's Democratic Party (PDP), and later that month signed an agreement with the UMP to form a new coalition Government, the third since the election of December 1991. The UMP-PDP coalition held a total of 26 legislative seats.

In October 1994 the Supreme Court granted the Government a restraining order against further actions by the President, pending the hearing of an application to the Supreme Court to overrule several of the President's recent decisions. Members of the Government and judiciary had become increasingly alarmed by Leye's exercise of his presidential powers, which had included orders to free 26 criminals (many of whom had been convicted on extremely serious offences) and to appoint a convicted criminal to the position of Police Commissioner (on the recommendation of the Prime Minister).

In April 1995 Carlot attracted severe criticism from the Vanuatu-based regional news agency, Pacnews, when he dismissed two senior government officials for making comments critical of the Government; moreover, the journalists who reported the comments were threatened with dismissal. The Prime Minister's increasing reputation for intolerance of criticism was compounded by allegations that, as part of his Government's policy of reducing the number of employees in the public service, civil servants believed to be opposition sympathizers were among the first to lose their jobs.

At a general election held in November 1995, the Unity Front coalition won 20 of the 50 seats in the newly enlarged Parliament and the UMP secured 17 seats. A period of intense political manoeuvring followed the election, as the two main parties sought to form coalitions with other members in an attempt to secure a parliamentary majority. The situation was compounded by the emergence of two factions within the UMP, one comprising the supporters of Carlot and another led by Serge Vohor (the party's President). The Carlot faction of the UMP and the Unity Front both sought the political allegiance of the NUP. The latter's decision to accept the offer of a coalition with the UMP effectively excluded the Unity Front (the grouping with the largest number of seats) from Government, and, in protest, its members boycotted the opening of Parliament in December, thus preventing a vote on the formation of a new government taking place. At a subsequent parliamentary session Vohor was elected as Prime Minister, despite continuing allegations of irregularities in the election of senior members of Government.

In early February 1996 seven dissident UMP members of Parliament proposed a motion of 'no confidence' in Vohor, supported by 22 other opposition members. However, Vohor announced his resignation as Prime Minister, thus preventing the vote from taking place. A parliamentary session to elect a new premier was abandoned as a result of a boycott by supporters of Vohor, who was reported to have retracted his resignation. However, at a further sitting, Carlot was elected Prime Minister.

In July 1996 a report published by the national ombudsman revealed that a serious financial scandal had occurred in the country, involving the issuing of 10 bank guarantees with a total value of US $100m. The Minister of Finance, Barak Sope, who had issued the guarantees in April, had been persuaded by an Australian financial adviser, Peter Swanson, that the scheme could earn the country significant revenue. Swanson, who left Vanuatu after securing the guarantees, was subsequently traced and charged with criminal offences relating to his dealings with Sope. (In February 1998 the Supreme Court found Swanson guilty on seven charges arising from the scandal, sentencing him to 18 months' imprisonment.) Carlot, meanwhile, rejected demands for his resignation for his compliance with the scheme and resisted considerable pressure to dismiss Sope and the Governor of the Reserve Bank of Vanuatu. In the following month, however, Sope was dismissed following his defection to the opposition.

In an attempt to restore a measure of political stability, Carlot appealed for reconciliation among the various political groups in the country in August 1996 and invited members of the opposition to join the Government. The opposition responded by reiterating its demand for Carlot's resignation, and in September a motion of 'no confidence' in the Government was approved and Vohor was elected Prime Minister. Vohor's coalition Government comprised the pro-Vohor faction of the UMP, the NUP, the MPP, Tan Union and Fren Melanesia. A new Council of Ministers, in which Sope was appointed Deputy Prime Minister, was announced in mid-October.

A dispute over unpaid allowances, dating from 1993, led members of the 300-strong Vanuatu Mobile Force (VMF—the country's paramilitary force) briefly to abduct the President and Deputy Prime Minister to demand a settlement. Both Leye and Sope expressed sympathy for the VMF members. Sope was replaced as Deputy Prime Minister by Donald Kalpokas, and Fr Walter Lini was appointed Minister of Justice. Following a further incident in November in connection with the pay dispute, in which an official from the Department of Finance was abducted and allegedly assaulted, Lini ordered the arrest of more than half of the members of the VMF. About 30 members were detained and charged with criminal offences. In June 1999 18 VMF members were charged with the alleged kidnapping of a number of government officers in 1996. One was found guilty and was to be referred to a court martial for sentencing.

In March 1997 a memorandum of agreement was signed between the VP, the NUP and the UMP, the three parties of the newly formed governing coalition. The defection in May, however, of five NUP members of Parliament, including two cabinet ministers, to the VP led to the party's expulsion from the Government. As a result, a new coalition, comprising the UMP, the MPP, Tan Union and Fren Melanesia, was formed. The subsequent designation of a new Cabinet was controversial for the appointment of Sope to the position of Deputy Prime Minister and Minister of Commerce, Trade and Industry. Sope had been described in January by the national ombudsman, Marie-Noëlle Ferrieux-Patterson (in a further report on the financial scandal of the previous year), as unfit for public office. Ferrieux-Patterson also criticized the recent appointment of Willie Jimmy as Minister of Finance.

In July 1997 legal action was initiated to recover the estimated US $300,000 of public funds paid in 1993 by Jimmy, together with Carlot, as compensation to the 23 members dismissed from Parliament following their boycott of the legislature in 1988. In the same month it was reported that the Government was preparing to amend legislation governing the powers of the ombudsman, in an attempt to contain her increasingly vociferous criticism of certain public figures.

In September 1997 Vohor dismissed Jimmy from his position as Minister of Finance, apparently owing to a dispute between Jimmy and the Prime Minister over the latter's decision to remove several areas of responsibility from the Finance portfolio. Meanwhile, further allegations of financial impropriety were published by the ombudsman, this time concerning the illegal sale of ni-Vanuatu passports to foreign nationals. In September the Prime Minister ordered an investigation into the matter. With both Vohor and Jimmy alleging the involvement of the other, the dispute intensified the disunity within the UMP, which had now come to comprise three factions, led respectively by Vohor, Carlot and Jimmy.

In November 1997 Parliament approved legislation to repeal the Ombudsman Act and the Government announced that it was to establish a commission of inquiry to determine if the ombudsman had exceeded her constitutional powers. However, President Leye refused to promulgate the new law on the grounds that it was unconstitutional, and he referred it to the Supreme Court. Later in the month Carlot filed a motion of 'no confidence' in Vohor's Government. When Vohor attempted to withdraw all proposed legislation in order to prevent debate on the motion, Leye announced the dissolution of Parliament. However, the Supreme Court revived the parliamentary session in December. The matter was referred to the Court of Appeal, and Vohor and Carlot agreed to co-operate temporarily pending its judgment, which was eventually delivered in January 1998 and which once again ordered the immediate dissolution of Parliament. Following Leye's announcement of a forthcoming general election, Carlot announced the formation of the Vanuatu Republikan Pati (VRP). Meanwhile, Ferrieux-Patterson released a report in December 1997 in which she recommended that Vohor be investigated for offences relating to the illegal sale of ni-Vanuatu passports. The release of outspoken reports by the ombudsman continued into early 1998 and was widely believed to have contributed significantly to the domination of the election campaign by allegations of government corruption.

At a general election held on 6 March 1998, the VP won 18 of the 52 seats in the newly enlarged Parliament, the UMP secured 12, the NUP won 11, the MPP obtained six, the John Frum Movement secured two, the VRP obtained one, and independent candidates won two seats. In mid-March the VP and the NUP agreed to form a coalition Government, with the support of Carlot (the VRP's sole representative) and one independent member. At the end of the month Kalpokas was elected Prime Minister with 35 parliamentary votes, defeating Vohor (who secured 17). Kalpokas also assumed three ministerial portfolios, including that for Foreign Affairs, while Lini, who was appointed to the revived post of Deputy Prime Minister, also became Minister of Justice and Internal Affairs.

In June 1998, despite strong opposition, notably from the UMP, Parliament approved a new 'leadership code'. Regarded as a key element in ensuring greater accountability and transparency in public life, the code defined clear guidelines for the conduct of state officials (including a requirement that all public figures submit an annual declaration of assets to Parliament), and laid down strict penalties for those convicted of corruption. Shortly before, the Supreme Court upheld the repeal of the Ombudsman Act, as approved by Parliament in November 1997. The Kalpokas Government emphasized its commitment to strengthening the role of the ombudsman, stating that new legislation governing the office would be prepared. Although the ombudsman was to continue to function in the mean time, in early August 1998 Ferrieux-Patterson issued a statement in which she expressed concern that her powers of jurisdiction had been diminished.

In October 1998 Kalpokas expelled the NUP from the governing coalition, following reports that Lini (who died in February 1999), the party's leader, had organized a series of meetings with prominent members of the opposition, with the aim of forming a new coalition government which would exclude the VP. NUP ministers were largely replaced by members of the UMP faction led by Jimmy, which included the Deputy President of the party, Vincent Boulekone, and its Secretary-General, Henri Taga; one ministerial post was allocated to the John Frum Movement. In March 1999 Fr John Bani was chosen by the electoral college to succeed Jean-Marie Leye as President of Vanuatu.

The issue of press freedom returned to the fore in May 1999 when the Pacific Islands News Association expressed concern at the alleged assault on a local newspaper publisher by an associate of the Deputy Prime Minister, Willie Jimmy. Jimmy was reportedly displeased with the newspaper's coverage of an election campaign. The news association urged the Government to act against the increasing number of cases of media intimidation on the island.

The governing coalition was threatened in August 1999 by a decision by the National Council of the UMP to oppose participation in the Government. The Council issued a directive to the 17 members of Jimmy's faction to resign from the Kalpokas administration. Following their refusal to comply with the directive, the National Council acted to suspend the members in October. However, later that month the suspensions were overruled by the Supreme Court. The two factions of the UMP had previously attempted reunification but negotiations had stalled over the demands of Vohor's faction for two of the four ministerial positions held by Jimmy's faction. (The UMP achieved reunification in November 2000.)

At the end of August 1999 four by-elections took place, three of which were won by opposition parties, thus eliminating the Government's majority in Parliament. In November the Government staged a boycott of Parliament to avoid a proposed vote of 'no confidence' by opposition parties against the Kalpokas administration. However, the subsequent defection to the opposition of an independent representative, followed by that of the Minister of Health, forced the resignation of Kalpokas prior to a 'no confidence' motion on 25 November. The Speaker, Edward Natapei, announced his resignation shortly afterwards and Paul Ren Tari of the NUP was elected as his replacement. The leader of the MPP, Sope, was elected to lead a new Government the same day; he secured 28 votes compared with the 24 votes gained by Natapei as the newly appointed President of the VP. Sope formed a five-party coalition Government, comprising the MPP, the NUP, the Vohor faction of the UMP, the VRP and the John Frum Movement. The composition of the new Council of Ministers was swiftly announced; it included Vohor as Minister of Foreign Affairs and Carlot as Minister of Lands and Mineral Resources, both of whom, with Sope, had been the subject of critical reports by the ombudsman. The new Government pledged to reduce the country's dependence on foreign advisers, review the recently introduced value-added tax and ensure that adequate services were delivered to rural communities.

In May 2000 Parliament approved controversial legislation (the Public Services Amendment Bill and the Government Amendment Bill) giving the Government direct power to appoint and dismiss public servants. The opposition criticized the changes, claiming that they contravened the principles of the Comprehensive Reform Programme (a range of economic measures supported by the Asian Development Bank—ADB). President John Bani subsequently referred both pieces of legislation to the Supreme Court, which, in August, ordered that he approve them. The ADB reacted angrily to the development, arguing that it allowed for political bias in the public sector, and threatened to withhold further funds from Vanuatu. The bank's stance served to perpetuate an ongoing dispute between the organization and the Vanuatu Government, which had often expressed the view that the bank imposed harsh conditions in return for its finance.

An incident in August 2000 in which the Deputy Prime Minister, Reginald Stanley, was allegedly involved in the serious assault of two people and in causing criminal damage to property while under the influence of alcohol led to Stanley's dismissal from the post. He was replaced by the Minister of Trade Development, James Bule.

In September 2000 the opposition leader, Edward Natapei, invited the Vohor faction of the UMP to join the opposition and form a new government. Vohor declined the offer, saying that his priority was the stability of the current Government. The resignation of a VP member in October prevented the success of a motion of 'no confidence' in the Prime Minister. Also in October the Government was forced to defend a controversial plan, which allowed a Thai company, Apex, to pay off a portion of government debt, allegedly in return for tax-haven privileges. The President of Apex, Amarendra Nath Ghosh, was also Vanuatu's recently appointed honorary consul to Thailand. In January 2001 the Government deported Mark Neil-Jones, the publisher of the independent newspaper, *Trading Post*, on the grounds of instigating instability in the country. (The *Trading Post* had recently published several critical articles about the Government, including reports on the Government's financial dealings with Nath Ghosh.) However, the Supreme Court reversed the decision, declaring that the deportation order was illegal, and Neil-Jones was allowed to return to the country. An investigation was subsequently launched into the circumstances of the deportation.

In late January 2001 three members of the UMP resigned from the party, further reducing the Government's majority. The Government's problems intensified in March after the withdrawal of the UMP from the ruling coalition. Opposition attempts to vote on a motion of 'no confidence' were delayed as Sope initiated legal action against the motion, and the Speaker, Paul Ren Tari, refused to allow the vote while legal action was pending. The Chief Justice, however, ordered the vote to proceed, and after further postponements by the Speaker, the Sope Government was voted out of office on 13 April. A new Government, led by Edward Natapei of the VP, was elected. The incoming administration, a coalition of the VP and UMP, was sworn in on 17 April and pledged to continue the reform programme and to restore investor confidence. One of the Government's first acts was to remove Nath Ghosh from his diplomatic position. Vohor was appointed Deputy Prime Minister. In early May Parliament held an extraordinary session to debate a motion to remove Ren Tari as Speaker because of his conduct during the political crisis. Ren Tari responded by suspending Natapei, along with five other Members of Parliament who held cabinet posts, for breaching parliamentary procedure. Despite an order by the Chief Justice that they be allowed to return to Parliament to continue the extraordinary session, Ren Tari refused to open the legislature while he appealed to the Supreme Court against the order. In response, Ren Tari and his two deputies were arrested and charged with sedition. A new Speaker, Donald Kalpokas, President of the UMP, was elected, thus reducing Matapei's majority in Parliament to one. In September 2001 opposition leader Sope tabled a motion of 'no confidence' against the ruling coalition but was defeated.

In November 2001 Sope was ordered to appear in court to answer charges that he had forged two government-supported Letters of Guarantee, worth US $23m., while he was Prime Minister. It was reported that police were also investigating the activities of the former Minister of Finance, Morkin Steven, whose signature appeared on the documents. Meanwhile, Sope was under investigation for possible involvement in the illegal issuing of diplomatic passports and in connection with allegations of bribery. The preliminary hearing of the forgery charges was postponed until February 2002, enabling Sope to contest the general election due to take place later in that year.

In March 2002 Parliament was dissolved after the Supreme Court ruled that its four-year term had expired. Prime Minister Natapei remained in charge of a 'caretaker' Government until the general election, scheduled for 2 May 2002. Also in March it was announced that the newly established People's Progressive Party (PPP) and Fren Melanesia were to form a coalition with the ruling NUP to contest the forthcoming election. The announcement contradicted a statement issued earlier in the same month by the NUP, in which the party had declared that it would stand independently. Meanwhile, the Government dismissed the board of the Vanuatu Broadcasting and Television Corporation (VBTC), claiming that the organization had failed to consult with it over a number of important decisions and that it had incurred unnecessary costs. Later in March 27 VBTC employees returned to work, having been dismissed in October 2001 for participating in a strike. They claimed to have been reinstated by the newly appointed government board—a claim denied by the board—and refused to leave. The individuals alleged to be responsible for the reinstatement subsequently resigned. Negotiations to settle the ongoing disputes began in April amid allegations of political interference into the affairs of the company by government appointees. It was reported that the general election was to be monitored by an independent group of observers. The future of the Comprehensive Reform Programme was widely perceived to be the main issue at stake in the electoral campaign.

The general election was held on 2 May 2002. A total of 327 candidates contested the 52 seats available in Parliament. A record 138 candidates stood as independents, prompting Natapei to comment prior to the election that if Vanuatu were to attain political stability the electoral constituency should vote only for party candidates. Bad weather and problems with ballot papers delayed voting in some constituencies. The two ruling coalition parties secured a sufficient number of seats in the new Parliament to claim victory. The NUP came third. After some initial uncertainty, it was announced that the UMP had won 15 seats in the new Parliament and that the VP had secured 14. In accordance with the terms of the coalition agreement, however, the VP was permitted to nominate the next Prime Minister. The new Government was formed on 3 June 2002, with Natapei duly re-elected Prime Minister.

In July 2002 former Prime Minister Barak Sope was convicted of fraud by the Supreme Court and sentenced to three years' imprisonment. It was alleged soon afterwards that New Zealand had interfered in Vanuatu's internal affairs by funding the investigation that had led to Sope's conviction. In early August, following the controversial appointment of Mael Apisai as Vanuatu's new Police Commissioner, disaffected police officers staged a raid during which they arrested Apisai, Attorney-General Hamilton Bulu and 14 other senior civil servants on charges of seditious conspiracy. Following an investigation, the charges were abandoned owing to a lack of evidence. Prime Minister Natapei subsequently assumed the police and VMF portfolios from the Minister of Internal Affairs, Joe Natuman, in what was thought to be an attempt to distance Natuman from some members of the police force, with whom he had reportedly become too closely involved. Later in the month members of the VMF surrounded the police headquarters in Port Vila to serve arrest warrants on 27 of those who had been involved in the raid, including the acting police commissioner, Holis Simon, and the commander of the VMF, Api Jack Marikembo. Shortly afterwards, in an attempt to bring an end to hostilities, the Government signed an agreement with representatives from the police department and the VMF during a traditional Melanesian reconciliation ceremony. The police officers involved, who had been suspended from their posts, were reinstated, the police and the VMF pledged to make no further arrests and it was agreed that Apisai's appointment would be reviewed by a newly appointed police services commission. At the same time it was decided that the allegations of conspiracy that had been brought against the 15 officials initially arrested would be considered by the judicial authorities. A new acting police commissioner, Lt-Gen. Arthur Coulton, was then appointed. In early October 2002 it was announced that the charges against 18 of those arrested in connection with the August raid would be abandoned, leaving eight senior officers to face trial on charges of mutiny and incitement to mutiny. Meanwhile, the UMP urged the removal of the Australian High Commissioner, Steve Waters, while reportedly accusing Australia of interference in Vanuatu's internal affairs and of destabilizing the coalition Government by communicating solely with the VP at the expense of the UMP. Deputy Prime Minister Serge Vohor alleged that the Australian Federal Police (AFP) had been engaged in the surveillance of government ministers and other officials in Vanuatu. The AFP denied the charges. In early December four of the eight senior police officers tried were found guilty by the Supreme Court on charges of mutiny, incitement to mutiny, kidnapping and false imprisonment and were given suspended two-year prison sentences. In the same month police intervened to prevent the former Prime Minister Barak Sope from reclaiming his seat in Parliament, claiming that this was nullified by his conviction for fraud in July, despite receiving a pardon in November from President Bani. The pardon, which Bani stated he had made on the grounds of Sope's poor health, provoked widespread public opposition and led the Government to announce the appointment of a commission of inquiry to investigate the President's decision. However, in November 2003, at a by-election to the seat vacated by his conviction for fraud, Barak Sope was re-elected.

In April 2003 the election of Ham Lini (brother of Walter Lini, the late founder of the NUP) as President of the NUP, led to the signing of a memorandum of understanding inviting that party to join the coalition Government. The NUP was expected to assume three ministerial portfolios (including finance) in a development which observers believed could signify the possible reunification of the NUP with the VP (which had been a single political organization until their split in 1991). However, in late April the NUP rejected the VP's offer and announced its intention to remove the Government in a motion of 'no confidence'. A further attempt to propose a motion of 'no confidence' in the Government led Natapei to remove the UMP from the ruling coalition in a reorganization of cabinet portfolios in November. The party was replaced in the coalition by members of the NUP, the PPP, the Green Party and independents. Continued instability within the governing coalition prompted three further cabinet reorganizations during the first three months of 2004.

In April 2004 Alfred Maseng Nalo was sworn in as Vanuatu's new President following a lengthy and closely contested election. Maseng defeated 31 other candidates during a total of four rounds of voting. However, the validity of the election was questioned when it was revealed, shortly after his appointment, that Maseng was serving a suspended sentence having been convicted of misappropriation and receiving property dishonestly. In May, only four weeks after his appointment to the presidency, the Supreme Court ruled that Maseng should be removed from office. The likelihood that the Government, which held a minority of seats in Parliament, would be removed in an imminent vote of 'no confidence' led to a decision by the Council of Ministers to dissolve Parliament in June.

A general election was held on 6 July 2004 at which no single party won an overall majority and 25 new members were elected, including many independent candidates. The validity of the election, however, was jeopardized by an incident on Tanna in which ballot boxes en route to Port Vila for counting were ambushed and burnt. More than 40 people were arrested in connection with the incident, including the acting Minister of Finance, Jimmy Nickelim of the VP. In late July Serge Vohor was elected Prime Minister defeating Ham Lini by 28 votes to 24. A Council of Ministers composed of five political groups and several independents was appointed shortly afterwards. However, the stability of the new administration was threatened by rumours of shifting allegiances and reports that several members were being persuaded to cross the floor of Parliament. Despite these suggestions, an opposition motion of 'no confidence' in the new Government, proposed in September, was defeated, with Vohor's administration securing the support of 31 of the 52 members. Further doubts over Vohor's ability to continue as Prime Minister were cast when the country's Police Commissioner attempted to arrest him on charges of contempt, following comments made in Parliament accusing the Chief Justice, Vincent Lunabeck, of being a 'pikinini blong white man' and therefore unduly influenced by a desire to please foreign interests in the country. The Supreme Court, however, dismissed the charges against Vohor during an appeal in late September.

The Prime Minister became the focus of further serious controversy in November 2004 when he announced the establishment of diplomatic relations with Taiwan. The announcement, which Vohor defended by claiming that Taiwan's assistance was necessary to cover the budgetary deficit, came only weeks after the Prime Minister had made an official visit to the People's Republic of China during which he had reiterated Vanuatu's allegiance to that country. The Council of Ministers, which had not given the necessary approval of the agreement with Taiwan, responded by demanding that Vohor renounce recognition of Taiwan or dismiss the entire cabinet. Controversy surrounding the situation increased following reports that Vohor had assaulted the Chinese ambassador when questioned over the legitimacy of the Taiwanese flag flying in Port Vila. A parliamentary vote of 'no confidence' in Vohor took place in early December, despite the Prime Minister's attempts to prevent the motion by means of a legal challenge, and was approved by 35 votes to 14. Ham Lini was elected Prime Minister and subsequently appointed a cabinet that included five former ministers who had crossed the floor of the legislature to vote against Vohor.

Lini's Government reversed the policy of the previous administration regarding Taiwan, and in July 2005 the Minister for Home Affairs made an official visit to China to sign a co-operation agreement providing for technical, logistical and financial support for the Vanuatu Police Force. Lini effected a cabinet reorganization in the same month. Further changes to the Council of Ministers reflected the decision of five opposition members to join the Green Party led by the Minister of Finance, Moana Carcasses Kalosil. Their defection resulted in the Green Party becoming Lini's most significant partner in the governing coalition. In November 2005 Moana Carcasses was replaced as Minister of Finance by Willie Jimmy, hitherto Minister of Lands, Geology and Mines. At the same time, Lui Etap was appointed Minister of Ni-Vanuatu Business Development, replacing Joshua Kalsakau. In a further reallocation of portfolios announced in March 2006, Dunstan Hilton replaced Barak Sope as Minister of Agriculture, following reports that the former Prime Minister had been conducting negotiations aimed at attempting to oust the incumbent Ham Lini from office. The Minister of Youth and Sports was also replaced. In the same month the Prime Minister defeated by 30 parliamentary votes to 20 a motion of 'no confidence', which had been presented by the opposition partly as a result of criticism of the Government's handling of the ban on the import of Fijian biscuits, which had been imposed in retaliation for Fiji's ban on kava from Vanuatu (see Economic Affairs)

As part of a programme of reform of the country's judicial system, in early 2006 a new building accommodating a magistrate's court was opened in Port Vila. New court buildings were also to be constructed on three other islands, thus improving the population's access to the justice system.

Meanwhile, Vanuatu has had an uneasy relationship with France. In 1981 the French Ambassador to Vanuatu was expelled, following the deportation from New Caledonia of the VP Secretary-General, who had been due to attend an assembly of the New Caledonian Independence Front. France immediately withdrew aid to Vanuatu but this was subsequently restored and a new Ambassador appointed. However, the French Ambassador was expelled again in 1987, for allegedly providing 'substantial financial assistance' to Vanuatu's opposition parties. In response to the expulsion, the French Government again announced that it would withdraw aid to Vanuatu. Carlot, Vanuatu's first francophone Prime Minister, made an official visit to France in May 1992, and the two countries fully restored diplomatic relations in October. In July, however, the Carlot Government reaffirmed its support for the Kanak independence movement on the French Territory of New Caledonia, following threats by Lini to withdraw from the Government unless Carlot's pro-French policies were modified. Improved relations with France were confirmed in 1993 with the signing of a bilateral co-operation agreement. In mid-1995 the Carlot Government was virtually alone in the region in failing to condemn France's resumption of nuclear tests in French Polynesia. The opposition criticized the Government's stance as not reflecting the views of the vast majority of ni-Vanuatu.

In March 1988 Vanuatu signed an agreement with Papua New Guinea and Solomon Islands to form the 'Spearhead Group', which aimed to preserve Melanesian cultural traditions and to lobby for independence for New Caledonia. In 1994 the Melanesian Spearhead Group concluded an agreement providing for the gradual establishment of a free-trade area encompassing the three countries. Fiji joined the group in 1996. In March 2006 the Melanesian Spearhead Group met in Port Vila to discuss several issues concerning regional trade and security. Vanuatu had been accused of breaching the group's agreement by restricting its markets through the imposition of export licences for the sale of kava and other commodities. Negotiations were also taking place regarding the construction in Vanuatu of a permanent headquarters for the Melanesian Spearhead Group Secretariat.

In August 2005 it was announced that discussions had taken place between the Prime Ministers of Solomon Islands and Vanuatu on the possibility of establishing an agreement governing border control and a patrol system. The issues were discussed amid concerns regarding drug- and people-trafficking, money-laundering and other border-related crime. It was hoped that a system of mutual co-operation similar to that operating between Solomon Islands and Papua New Guinea might be established.

Government

Vanuatu is a republic. Legislative power is vested in the unicameral Parliament, with 52 members who are elected by universal adult suffrage for four years. The Head of State is the President, elected for a five-year term by an electoral college consisting of Parliament and the Presidents of the Regional Councils. Executive power is vested in the Council of Ministers, appointed by the Prime Minister and responsible to Parliament. The Prime Minister is elected by and from members of Parliament. Legislation enacted in 1994 resulted in the replacement of the 11 local government councils by six provincial bodies, with greater executive powers. The six provincial authorities are Malampa, Penama, Sanma, Shefa, Tafea and Torba.

Economic Affairs

In 2004, according to estimates by the World Bank, Vanuatu's gross national income (GNI), measured at average 2002–04 prices, was US $287.5m., equivalent to $1,340 per head (or $2,790 per head on an international purchasing-power parity basis). During 1995–2004, it was estimated, the population increased at an average annual rate of 2.7%, while gross domestic product (GDP) per head decreased, in real terms, by an average of 2.1% per year. Overall GDP increased, in real terms, at an average annual rate of 0.6% in 1995–2004. According to the Asian Development Bank (ADB), GDP increased by 4.2% in 2004 and by 3.1% in 2005.

The agricultural sector (including forestry and fishing) contributed 15.0% of GDP in 2003, compared with some 40% in the early 1980s. According to figures from the ADB, the GDP of the agricultural sector was estimated to have increased by an average annual rate of 2.3% in 1995–2003. Compared with the previous year, the sector's GDP decreased by 2.6% in 2003, but increased by 5.5% in 2004 before decreasing again, by 0.8%, in 2005. About 35% of the employed labour force were engaged in agricultural activities in 2003, according to FAO. Coconuts, cocoa and coffee are grown largely for export (copra and cocoa being the most important of these), while yams, taro, cassava, breadfruit and vegetables are cultivated for subsistence purposes. Cattle, pigs, goats and poultry are the country's principal livestock, and beef is an important export commodity (contributing 8.8% of export earnings in 2003). Vanuatu has encouraged the development of a forestry industry. However, the Government caused considerable controversy in 1993, when it granted a Malaysian consortium a licence to log 70,000 cu m of timber annually; previous licences for all operators had permitted total logging of only 5,000 cu m per year. A complete ban on the export of round logs was subsequently introduced. The Government derives substantial revenue from the sale of fishing rights to foreign fleets: sales of licences to Taiwanese and South Korean vessels earned more than $A136,000 in 1997. In October 2005 the Government and the People's Republic of China signed an agreement that provided for the financing of the establishment of a new fish-processing plant near Port Vila. The facility was to have a processing capacity in excess of 3,000 tons of fish, with the potential ultimately to increase annual production to more than 10,000 tons. The plant was expected to create some 200 local jobs and would also be available for processing other products for export, such as beef. Upon completion of this plant, revenue from the fishing sector, which had hitherto been limited, was expected to increase substantially.

The industrial sector (including manufacturing, utilities and construction) contributed about 8.2% of GDP in 2003, although only 3.5% of the employed labour force were engaged in the sector in 1989. According to figures from the ADB, in 1995–2003 the GDP of the industrial sector was estimated to have decreased at an average annual rate of 2.3%. Compared with the previous year, industrial GDP decreased by 3.2% in 2003 before increasing by 3.5% in 2004 and by 3.4% in 2005. Manufacturing, which contributed about 3.6% of GDP in 2003, is mainly concerned with the processing of agricultural products. In 1995–2003, however, the GDP of the manufacturing sector decreased by an average annual rate of 3.4%. The country's first kava extraction plant (for the manufacture of alcoholic drink) was opened in 1998. It was feared that a ban imposed on kava imports in 2001 by several countries in Europe owing to health concerns would have a detrimental effect upon the kava industry; however, new markets for the product were subsequently discovered. Construction activity alone contributed 2.6% of GDP in 2003. During the 1990s several potential mining projects were identified. An Australian company announced plans to mine 60,000 metric tons of manganese per year on the island of Efate, while possible projects involving the extraction of gold, copper and petroleum around the islands of Malekula and Espiritu Santo were discussed. In March 2006 an agreement was signed by the Vanuatu Government to allow a Swiss-US company to extract manganese deposits and to export the commodity; it was envisaged that the project would create hundreds of new jobs.

Electricity generation is largely thermal. Long-term plans focus on the potential of renewable resources. Imports of mineral fuels comprised 13.1% of the value of total imports in 2004.

The economy depends heavily on the services sector, which accounted for 76.8% of GDP in 2003. According to figures from the ADB, in 1995–2003 the GDP of the services sector was estimated to have increased at an average annual rate of 1.4%. the GDP of the services sector declined by 5.1% in 2003 but increased by 3.7% in 2004 and by 3.9% in 2005. Tourism, offshore banking facilities and a shipping registry, providing a 'flag of convenience' to foreign-owned vessels, make a significant contribution to the country's income. In 2004 a total of 60,611 foreign tourists visited Vanuatu, compared with 50,400 in the previous year. Revenue from tourism was estimated to have increased from US $62m. in 2002 to $71m. in 2003. A further improvement in the tourism sector was envisaged following the completion of two new hotels, the continuation of an overseas advertising campaign and the launch of a new airline, Pacific Blue (a low-cost carrier based in New Zealand) in September 2004.

In 2005 Vanuatu recorded a visible trade deficit of US $86.0m., and a deficit of $22.0m. on the current account of the balance of payments. In 2004 the principal sources of imports were Australia (15.5%) and Japan (10.7%), while the principal markets for exports were Thailand (46.3%) and Malaysia (18.2%). The principal imports in 2004 were machinery and transport equipment (21.4% of total imports), food and live animals (19.3%) and basic manufactures (14.4%). Copra (which provided 10.7% of total export earnings), beef (6.9%), and timber (which provided 5.9%) were the main export commodities in 2004.

Budget estimates for 2004 projected an overall deficit of 241m. vatu. An overall deficit equivalent to 0.3% of GDP was anticipated in 2005, compared with a surplus equivalent to 1.3% in 2004. In 2002 Vanuatu received US $27.5m. of official development assistance, of which US $22.4m. was bilateral aid and US $5.1m. was multilateral assistance. Australia, New Zealand, France, the United Kingdom and Japan are significant suppliers of development assistance. In 2005/06 Australia budgeted for aid of some $A34.1m., and in the same year development assistance from New Zealand was projected at $NZ7.25m. In February 2002 the European Union (EU) allocated Vanuatu 2,000m. vatu of aid to be disbursed over a five-year period from the ninth European Development Fund; the aid was to be used principally for the development of education and human resources training. Vanuatu's total external debt was US $90.0m. at the end of 2004. In that year the cost of debt-servicing was equivalent to 1.7% of the value of exports of goods and services; this figure was projected to decrease to 1.5% in 2005. The annual rate of inflation averaged 2.5% in 1995–2004. Consumer prices increased by 1.8% in 2004 and by 2.6% in 2005.

Vanuatu is a member of the Pacific Community (see p. 350), the Pacific Islands Forum (see p. 352), the Asian Development Bank (ADB, see p. 169) and the UN Economic and Social Commission for Asia and the Pacific (ESCAP, see p. 33). The country is a signatory of the South Pacific Regional Trade and Economic Agreement (SPARTECA, see p. 354) and of the Lomé Conventions and the successor Cotonou Agreement (see p. 277) with the EU. Vanuatu is also a member of the Melanesian Spearhead Group; a free-trade agreement concluded by members grants most-favoured nation status for all trading transactions.

Vanuatu's economic development has been impeded by its dependence on the agricultural sector, particularly the production and export of copra, which is vulnerable to adverse weather conditions (such as Cyclone Ivy, which struck the islands in February 2004) and fluctuations in international commodity prices. Successive administrations, therefore, have attempted to encourage the diversification of the country's economy, notably through the development of the tourism sector, but such initiatives remain inhibited by a shortage of skilled indigenous labour and a weak infrastructure. The Government's implementation in 1998 of a Comprehensive Reform Programme (CRP), approved by the ADB, was expected to enhance Vanuatu's economic prospects. In mid-1999 the ADB reported that the Government had demonstrated a strong level of commitment to the CRP: the number of ministries had been reduced from 34 to nine, and the number of civil service personnel had been decreased by 7%; a value-added tax had been introduced; and the National Bank and the Development Bank had been restructured. The country's status as an offshore financial centre aroused controversy in June 2000 when the Paris-based Organisation for Economic Co-operation and Development (OECD, see p. 320) listed Vanuatu as one of a number of countries and territories operating as unfair tax havens. It was claimed that the country was being used to 'launder' the proceeds of illegal activities of the Russian mafia and drug cartels. Vanuatu remained on the OECD's list of unco-operative tax havens until May 2003, when the country's commitment to implement transparent tax and regulatory systems (by 2005) led to its removal from the list. In November 2001, meanwhile, after five years of negotiations, the World Trade Organization (WTO, see p. 370) offered Vanuatu membership. However, the Government rejected the offer on the grounds that it wished to delay its entry while it negotiated a more favourable tariff agreement. The ban on kava imports by Europe and subsequently by Fiji had a detrimental effect on Vanuatu's trade. The latter ban was imposed in March 2005, in retaliation for the ban placed on Fijian biscuits by Vanuatu, and remained in force until December of that year. Meanwhile, the political instability of 2004 (see Recent History) impeded the timely implementation of the Prioritized Action Agenda, whereby the CRP was to be linked to the Government's medium-term investment programme and annual budgetary plans. One of the principal challenges facing the incoming Government of Ham Lini following its assumption of office in December 2004 was the need to address the problem of rural hardship and to reverse the decline in income; the country's GDP per head was estimated to be below the level of 20 years previously. Observers noted that there had been little improvement in the performance of public enterprises. In April 2005 it was announced that the national minimum wage per week was to be increased from the equivalent of approximately from US $145 to $181. The decision followed a three-month study of national wage levels. However, by the end of 2005 some businesses were reported to be attempting to avoid paying employees the higher rates. The Government also began developing an effective regulatory framework for the utilities sector, in an effort to improve efficiency and to reduce costs in the fields of electricity, telecommunications and water supply. In rural areas access to such services had remained extremely limited. The proposed framework, however, did not include an extension of these facilities into unserviced areas. In March 2006 Vanuatu and the US Millennium Challenge Corporation, signed an agreement providing the country with a grant of $65.7m. for the purposes of financing various infrastructural projects. The compact envisaged that per caput income in Vanuatu would increase by 15% within the five years encompassed by the plan.

Education

The abolition of nominal fees for primary education following independence resulted in a significant increase in enrolment at

VANUATU

Statistical Survey

that level. Thus, at the beginning of the 1990s it was estimated that about 85% of children between the ages of six and 11 were enrolled at state-controlled primary institutions. Secondary education begins at 12 years of age, and comprises a preliminary cycle of four years and a second cycle of three years. Vocational education and teacher-training are also available. The relatively low level of secondary enrolment has been a cause of some concern to the Government, and a major programme for the expansion of the education system was inaugurated in 1989. The programme aimed to double secondary enrolment by 1996. Literacy rates are another cause of concern; it was estimated in 1997 that 64% of the population was illiterate.

An extension centre of the University of the South Pacific was opened in Port Vila in May 1989. Students from Vanuatu can also receive higher education at the principal faculties of that university (in Suva, Fiji), in Papua New Guinea or in France.

The 2002 budget allocated an estimated 2,062m. vatu to education (20.1% of total recurrent expenditure by the central Government).

Public Holidays

2006: 1 January (New Year's Day), 21 February (Father Walter Lini Day), 5 March (Custom Chief's Day), 14–17 April (Easter), 1 May (Labour Day), 5 May (Ascension Day), 24 July (Children's Day), 30 July (Independence Day), 15 August (Assumption), 5 October (Constitution Day), 29 November (Unity Day), 25 December (Christmas Day), 27 December (Family Day).

2007: 1 January (New Year's Day), 20 February (Father Walter Lini Day), 5 March (Custom Chief's Day), 6–9 April (Easter), 1 May (Labour Day), 25 May (Ascension Day), 24 July (Children's Day), 30 July (Independence Day), 15 August (Assumption), 5 October (Constitution Day), 29 November (Unity Day), 25 December (Christmas Day), 27 December (Family Day).

Statistical Survey

Source (unless otherwise indicated): Vanuatu Statistics Office, PMB 19, Port Vila; tel. 22110; fax 24583; e-mail stats@vanuatu.com.vu; internet www.spc.int/stats/vanuatu.

AREA AND POPULATION

Area: 12,190 sq km (4,707 sq miles); *By Island*: (sq km) Espiritu Santo 4,010; Malekula 2,024; Efate 887; Erromango 887; Ambrym 666; Tanna 561; Pentecost 499; Epi 444; Ambae 399; Vanua Lava 343; Gaua 315; Maewo 300.

Population: 142,419 at census of 16 May 1989; 186,678 (males 95,682, females 90,996) at census of 16–30 November 1999; 207,000 (UN estimate) at mid-2004 (Source: UN, *World Population Prospects: The 2004 Revision*). *By Island* (mid-1999, official estimates): Espiritu Santo 31,811; Malekula 19,766; Efate 43,295; Erromango 1,554; Ambrym 7,613; Tanna 26,306; Pentecost 14,837; Epi 4,706; Ambae 10,692; Vanua Lava 2,074; Gaua 1,924; Maewo 3,385.

Density (mid-2004): 17.0 per sq km.

Principal Town (mid-2003, UN estimate, incl. suburbs): Port Vila (capital) 33,987. Source: UN, *World Urbanization Prospects: The 2003 Revision*.

Births and Deaths (estimates, 1995–2000): Birth rate 34.1 per 1,000; Death rate 6.7 per 1,000. Source: UN, *World Population Prospects: The 2004 Revision*.

Expectation of Life (WHO estimates, years at birth): 68 (males 67; females 69) in 2003. Source: WHO, *World Health Report*.

Economically Active Population (census of May 1989): Agriculture, forestry, hunting and fishing 40,889; Mining and quarrying 1; Manufacturing 891; Electricity, gas and water 109; Construction 1,302; Trade, restaurants and hotels 2,712; Transport, storage and communications 1,030; Financing, insurance, real estate and business services 646; Community, social and personal services 7,891; Activities not adequately defined 11,126; *Total labour force* 66,597 (males 35,692, females 30,905). *Mid-2003* (estimates): Agriculture, etc. 33,000; Total labour force 94,000 (Source: FAO).

HEALTH AND WELFARE

Key Indicators

Total Fertility Rate (children per woman, 2003): 4.1.

Under-5 Mortality Rate (per 1,000 live births, 2004): 40.

Physicians (per 1,000 head, 1997): 0.12.

Health Expenditure (2002): US $ per head (PPP): 121.

Health Expenditure (2002): % of GDP: 3.8.

Health Expenditure (2002): public (% of total): 73.6.

Access to Water (% of persons, 2002): 60.

Access to Sanitation (% of persons, 2002): 50.

Human Development Index (2003): ranking: 118.

Human Development Index (2003): value: 0.659.

For sources and definitions, see explanatory note on p. vi.

AGRICULTURE, ETC.

Principal Crops ('000 metric tons, 2004): Coconuts 313 (Unofficial figure); Copra 34 (FAO estimate); Roots and tubers 42 (FAO estimate); Vegetables and melons 11 (FAO estimate); Bananas 14 (FAO estimate); Other fruit 5 (FAO estimate); Groundnuts (in shell) 2 (FAO estimate); Maize 1 (FAO estimate); Cocoa beans 1 (FAO estimate).

Livestock (FAO estimates, 2004): Cattle 150,000; Pigs 62,000; Goats 12,000; Horses 3,100; Chickens 340,000.

Livestock Products (FAO estimates, metric tons, 2004): Beef and veal 3,300; Pig meat 2,805; Cows' milk 3,000; Hen eggs 320; Cattle and buffalo hides 525; Goatskins 6.

Forestry ('000 cu m, 2004): *Roundwood Removals* (excl. bark): Sawlogs and veneer logs 28; Fuel wood 91; Total 119. *Sawnwood Production* (all broadleaved, incl. railway sleepers): Total 28.

Fishing (FAO estimates, metric tons, live weight, 2003): Skipjack tuna 16,720; Yellowfin tuna 4,930; Bigeye tuna 6,061; Albacore 1,823; Total catch (incl. others) 31,329.

Source: FAO.

FINANCE

Currency and Exchange Rates: Currency is the vatu. *Sterling, Dollar and Euro Equivalents* (31 October 2005): £1 sterling = 195.32 vatu; US $1 = 109.88 vatu; €1 = 132.11 vatu; 1,000 vatu = £5.12 = $9.10 = €7.57. *Average Exchange Rate* (vatu per US $): 139.20 in 2002; 122.19 in 2003; 111.79 in 2004.

Budget (million vatu, 2004): *Revenue:* Tax revenue 6,622; Non-tax revenue 823; Total 7,445, excluding grants from abroad (685). *Expenditure:* Current expenditure 7,273; Capital expenditure 413; Total 7,686. Source: Asian Development Bank, *Key Indicators of Developing Asian and Pacific Countries*.

International Reserves (US $ million at 31 December 2004): IMF special drawing rights 1.44; Reserve position in IMF 3.88; Foreign exchange 56.49; Total 61.81. Source: IMF, *International Financial Statistics*.

Money Supply (million vatu at 31 December 2004): Currency outside banks 2,490; Demand deposits at banks 10,243; Total money (incl. others) 12,869. Source: IMF, *International Financial Statistics*.

Cost of Living (Consumer Price Index for Port Vila; base: 2000 = 100): 105.7 in 2002; 108.9 in 2003; 110.4 in 2004. Source: IMF, *International Financial Statistics*.

Expenditure on the Gross Domestic Product (million vatu at current prices, 2002): Government final consumption expenditure 7,582; Private final consumption expenditure 20,035; Changes in stocks −15; Gross fixed capital formation 6,943; Statistical discrepancy 3,491; *Total domestic expenditure* 38,036; Exports of goods and services 13,891; *Less* Imports of goods and services 19,200; *GDP in purchasers' values* 32,729. Source: Asian Development Bank, *Key Indicators of Developing Asian and Pacific Countries*.

Gross Domestic Product at Constant 1983 Prices (million vatu): 16,650 in 2001; 15,832 in 2002; 16,290 in 2003. Source: Asian Development Bank, *Key Indicators of Developing Asian and Pacific Countries*.

Gross Domestic Product by Economic Activity (million vatu at current prices, 2003): Agriculture, forestry and fishing 5,082; Manufacturing 1,209; Electricity, gas and water 683; Construction 887; Wholesale and retail trade, restaurants and hotels 10,263; Trans-

VANUATU

Directory

port, storage and communications 4,261; Finance 2,677; Public administration 4,960; Other services 3,798; *GDP in purchasers' values* 33,820. Source: Asian Development Bank, *Key Indicators of Developing Asian and Pacific Countries*.

Balance of Payments (US $ million, 2003): Exports of goods f.o.b. 26.84; Imports of goods f.o.b. −91.80; *Trade balance* −64.96; Exports of services 94.78; Imports of services −54.23; *Balance on goods and services* −24.41; Other income received 24.21; Other income paid −35.96; *Balance on goods, services and income* −36.16; Current transfers received 4.82; Current transfers paid −9.90; *Current balance* −41.25; Capital account (net) −4.65; Direct investment abroad −0.67; Direct investment from abroad 15.45; Portfolio investment assets 2.11; Other investment assets 51.80; Other investment liabilities −29.12; Net errors and omissions −5.02; *Overall balance* −11.35. Source: IMF, *International Financial Statistics*.

EXTERNAL TRADE*

Principal Commodities (million vatu, 2004): *Imports:* Food and live animals 2,756; Beverages and tobacco 551; Mineral fuels, lubricants, etc. 1,871; Chemicals 1,558; Basic manufactures 2,057; Machinery and transport equipment 3,057; Miscellaneous manufactured articles 1,471; Total (incl. others) 14,306. *Exports:* Cocoa 30; Copra 446; Beef 286; Timber 247; Total (incl. others) 4,167. Source: Asian Development Bank, *Key Indicators of Developing Asian and Pacific Countries*.

Principal Trading Partners (US $ million, 2004): *Imports:* Australia 38.3; China, People's republic 8.6; Fiji 11.4; France 4.0; Japan 26.4; New Caledonia 8.3; New Zealand 14.9; Singapore 19.7; Total (incl. others) 247.1. *Exports:* Australia 2.4; Germany 4.4; Indonesia 11.0; Japan 15.3; Malaysia 37.7; Thailand 96.1; Total (incl. others) 207.5. Source: Asian Development Bank, *Key Indicators of Developing Asian and Pacific Countries*.

* Figures refer to domestic imports and exports only.

TRANSPORT

Road Traffic (estimates, '000 motor vehicles in use, 2001): 2.6 Passenger cars; 4.4 Commercial vehicles. Source: UN, *Statistical Yearbook*.

Shipping: *Merchant Fleet* (registered at 31 December 2004): Vessels 381; Total displacement ('000 grt) 1,756.5 (Source: Lloyd's Register-Fairplay, *World Fleet Statistics*). *International Sea-borne Freight Traffic* (estimates, '000 metric tons, 1990): Goods loaded 80; Goods unloaded 55 (Source: UN, *Monthly Bulletin of Statistics*).

Civil Aviation (traffic on scheduled services, 2001): Kilometres flown (million) 3; Passengers carried ('000) 97; Passenger-km (million) 212; Total ton-km (million) 21. Source: UN, *Statistical Yearbook*.

TOURISM

Foreign Tourist Arrivals: 49,463 in 2002; 50,400 in 2003; 60,611 in 2004.

Tourist Arrivals by Country of Residence (2003): Australia 29,492; New Zealand 7,729; New Caledonia 5,050; Other Pacific 2,034; Europe 3,003; North America 1,625; Total (incl. others) 50,400.

Tourism Receipts (US $ million, incl. passenger transport): 58 in 2001; 62 in 2002; 71 in 2003. Source: World Tourism Organization.

COMMUNICATIONS MEDIA

Radio Receivers (1997): 62,000 in use*.
Television Receivers (1999): 2,000 in use†.
Telephones (2004): 6,800 main lines in use‡.
Facsimile Machines (1996): 600 in use†.
Mobile Cellular Telephones (2004): 10,500 subscribers‡.
Internet Users (2004): 7,500‡.
Personal Computers (2004): 3,000 in use‡.
Non-daily Newspapers (1996): 2 (estimated circulation 4,000)*.

* Source: UNESCO, *Statistical Yearbook*.
† Source: UN, *Statistical Yearbook*.
‡ Source: International Telecommunication Union.

EDUCATION

Pre-primary (1992 unless otherwise indicated): 252 schools; 49 teachers (1980); 5,178 pupils.

Primary: 374 schools (1995); 852 teachers (1992); 34,333 pupils (1999).

Secondary (General): 27 schools (1995); 220 teachers (1992); 7,628 students (1999).

Secondary (Vocational): 50 teachers (1981); 444 students (1992).

Secondary (Teacher Training): 1 college (1989); 13 teachers (1983); 124 students (1991).

Source: mainly UNESCO, *Statistical Yearbook*.

Directory

The Constitution

A new Constitution came into effect at independence on 30 July 1980. The main provisions are as follows:

The Republic of Vanuatu is a sovereign democratic state, of which the Constitution is the supreme law. Bislama is the national language and the official languages are Bislama, English and French. The Constitution guarantees protection of all fundamental rights and freedoms and provides for the determination of citizenship.

The President, as head of the Republic, symbolizes the unity of the Republic and is elected for a five-year term of office by secret ballot by an electoral college consisting of Parliament and the Presidents of the Regional Councils.

Legislative power resides in the single-chamber Parliament, consisting of 39 members (amended to 46 members in 1987, to 50 in 1995 and further to 52 in 1998) elected for four years on the basis of universal franchise through an electoral system that includes an element of proportional representation to ensure fair representation of different political groups and opinions. Parliament is presided over by the Speaker elected by the members. Executive power is vested in the Council of Ministers which consists of the Prime Minister (elected by Parliament from among its members) and other ministers (appointed by the Prime Minister from among the members of Parliament). The number of ministers, including the Prime Minister, may not exceed a quarter of the number of members of Parliament.

Special attention is paid to custom law and to decentralization. The Constitution states that all land in the Republic belongs to the indigenous custom owners and their descendants. There is a National Council of Chiefs, composed of custom chiefs elected by their peers sitting in District Councils of Chiefs. It may discuss all matters relating to custom and tradition and may make recommendations to Parliament for the preservation and promotion of the culture and languages of Vanuatu. The Council may be consulted on any question in connection with any bill before Parliament. Each region may elect a regional council and the Constitution lays particular emphasis on the representation of custom chiefs within each one. (A reorganization of local government was initiated in May 1994, and resulted in September of that year in the replacement of 11 local councils with six provincial governments.)

The Constitution also makes provision for public finance, the Public Service, the Ombudsman, a leadership code and the judiciary (see Judicial System).

The Government

HEAD OF STATE

President: KALKOT MATASKELEKELE (appointed 16 August 2004).

COUNCIL OF MINISTERS
(April 2006)

Prime Minister: HAM LINI.

Deputy Prime Minister and Minister for Foreign Affairs: SATO KILMAN.

Minister for Home Affairs: GEORGES WELLS.

Minister of Agriculture, Forestry and Fisheries: DUNSTAN HILTON.

Minister for Health: MORKIN STEVEN.

Minister of Education: JOE NATUMAN.

VANUATU

Minister for Finance and Economic Development: WILLIE JIMMY.
Minister of Infrastructure and Public Utilities: EDWARD NATAPEI.
Minister of Lands, Geology and Mines: MAXIME CARLOT KORMAN.
Minister of Trade and Business Development: JAMES BULE.
Minister of the Comprehensive Reform Programme, Women's Affairs and Children's Rights: ISABELLE DONALD.
Minister of Ni-Vanuatu Business Development: LUI ETAP.
Minister of Youth and Sports: MARCELLINO PIPITE.

MINISTRIES AND DEPARTMENTS

Prime Minister's Office: PMB 053, Port Vila; tel. 22413; fax 22863; internet www.vanuatugovernment.gov.vu.
Deputy Prime Minister's Office: PMB 057, Port Vila; tel. 22750; fax 27714.
Ministry of Agriculture, Livestock, Forestry and Fisheries: PMB 39, Port Vila; tel. 23406; fax 26498.
Ministry of Civil Aviation, Meteorology, Postal Services, Public Works and Transport: PMB 057, Port Vila; tel. 22790; fax 27214.
Ministry of the Comprehensive Reform Programme: POB 110, Port Vila.
Ministry of Culture, Home Affairs and Justice: PMB 036, Port Vila; tel. 22252; fax 27064.
Ministry of Education, Youth and Sports: PMB 028, Port Vila; tel. 22309; fax 24569; e-mail andrews@vanuatu.com.vu.
Ministry of Energy, Lands, Mines and Rural Water Supply: PMB 007, Port Vila; tel. 27833; fax 25165.
Ministry of Finance: PMB 058, Port Vila; tel. 23032; fax 27937.
Ministry of Foreign Affairs, External Trade and Telecommunications: PMB 074, Port Vila; tel. 27045; e-mail depfa@vanuatu.com.vu.
Ministry of Health: PMB 042, Port Vila; tel. 22545; fax 26113.
Ministry of Trade, Industry, Co-operatives and Commerce: PMB 056, Port Vila; tel. 25674; fax 25677.
Ministry of Women's Affairs: PMB 9091, Port Vila; tel. 25099; fax 26353; e-mail emorris@vanuatu.gov.vu.

Legislature

PARLIAMENT

Speaker: SAM DAN AVOCK.
General Election, 6 July 2004

	Seats
National United Party	10
Union of Moderate Parties	8
Vanuaaku Pati	8
People's Progressive Party	4
Vanuatu Republikan Pati	4
Green Party	3
Melanesian Progressive Pati	3
National Community Association	2
Namangi Aute	1
People's Action Party	1
Independents	8
Total	**52**

Election Commission

Vanuatu Electoral Commission: PMB 033, Port Vila; tel. 23914; fax 26681.

Political Organizations

Efate Laketu Party: Port Vila; f. 1982; regional party, based on the island of Efate.
Green Party: Port Vila; f. 2001; est. by breakaway group of the UMP; Leader MOANA CARCASSES KALOSIL.
Independence Front: Port Vila; f. 1995; est. by breakaway group of the UMP; Chair. PATRICK CROWBY.
Melanesian Progressive Pati (MPP): POB 39, Port Vila; tel. 23485; fax 23315; f. 1988; est. by breakaway group from the VP; Chair. BARAK SOPE; Sec.-Gen. GEORGES CALO.
National Democratic Party (NDP): Port Vila; f. 1986; advocates strengthening of links with France and the UK; Leader JOHN NAUPA.
National United Party (NUP): Port Vila; f. 1991; est. by supporters of Walter Lini, following his removal as leader of the VP; Pres. HAM LINI; Sec.-Gen. WILLIE TITONGOA.
New People's Party (NPP): Port Vila; f. 1986; Leader FRASER SINE.
People's Democratic Party (PDP): Port Vila; f. 1994; est. by breakaway faction of the NUP.
People's Progressive Party (PPP): Port Vila; f. 2001; formed coalition with National United Party (NUP) and Fren Melanesia to contest 2002 elections; Pres. SATO KILMAN.
Tu Vanuatu Kominiti: Port Vila; f. 1996; espouses traditional Melanesian and Christian values; Leader HILDA LINI.
Union of Moderate Parties (UMP): POB 698, Port Vila; f. 1980; Pres. SERGE VOHOR; the UMP is divided into two factions, one led by SERGE VOHOR and the other by WILLIE JIMMY.
Vanuaaku Pati (VP) (Our Land Party): POB 472, Port Vila; tel. 22584; f. 1971; est. as the New Hebrides National Party; advocates 'Melanesian socialism'; Pres. EDWARD NATAPEI; First Vice-Pres. IOLU ABBIL; Sec.-Gen. SELA MOLISA.
Vanuatu Independent Alliance Party (VIAP): Port Vila; f. 1982; supports free enterprise; Leaders THOMAS SERU, GEORGE WOREK, KALMER VOCOR.
Vanuatu Independent Movement: Port Vila; f. 2002; Pres. WILLIE TASSO.
Vanuatu Labour Party: Port Vila; f. 1986; trade-union based; Leader KENNETH SATUNGIA.
Vanuatu Republikan Pati (VRP): Port Vila; f. 1998; est. by breakaway faction of the UMP; Leader MAXIME CARLOT KORMAN.

The Na-Griamel (Leader FRANKLEY STEVENS), Namaki Aute, Tan Union (Leader VINCENT BULEKONE) and Fren Melanesia (Leader ALBERT RAVUTIA) represent rural interests on the islands of Espiritu Santo and Malekula. The John Frum Movement represents interests on the island of Tanna.

Diplomatic Representation

EMBASSIES AND HIGH COMMISSIONS IN VANUATU

Australia: Hawkes Law House, POB 111, Port Vila; tel. 22777; fax 23948; e-mail australia_vanuatu@dfat.gov.au; internet www.vanuatu.embassy.gov.au; High Commissioner JOHN PILBEAM.
China, People's Republic: PMB 9071, Rue d'Auvergne, Nambatu, Port Vila; tel. 23598; fax 24877; e-mail publicinfo@chinese-embassy.com.vu; Ambassador BAO SHUSHENG.
France: Kumul Highway, POB 60, Port Vila; tel. 22353; fax 22695; e-mail ambafra@vanuatu.com.vu; internet www.ambafrance-vu.org; Ambassador PIERRE MAYAUDON.
New Zealand: BDO House, Lini Highway, POB 161, Port Vila; tel. 22933; fax 22518; e-mail kiwi@vanuatu.com.vu; High Commissioner PAUL WILLIS.

Judicial System

The Supreme Court has unlimited jurisdiction to hear and determine any civil or criminal proceedings. It consists of the Chief Justice, appointed by the President of the Republic after consultation with the Prime Minister and the leader of the opposition, and three other judges, who are appointed by the President of the Republic on the advice of the Judicial Service Commission.

The Court of Appeal is constituted by two or more judges of the Supreme Court sitting together. The Supreme Court is the court of first instance in constitutional matters and is composed of a single judge.

Magistrates' Courts have limited jurisdiction to hear and determine any civil or criminal proceedings. Island Courts have been established in several local government regions, and are constituted when three justices are sitting together to exercise civil or criminal jurisdiction, as defined in the warrant establishing the court. A magistrate nominated by the Chief Justice acts as Chairman. The Island Courts are competent to rule on land disputes.

In late 2001 legislation was introduced to establish a new Land Tribunal which was intended to expedite the hearing of land disputes. The tribunal was to have three levels, and no cases were to go beyond the tribunal and enter either the Supreme Court or the

VANUATU

Island Courts. The tribunal was to be funded by the disputing parties.

In 1986 Papua New Guinea and Vanuatu signed a memorandum of understanding, under which Papua New Guinea Supreme Court judges were to conduct court hearings in Vanuatu, chiefly in the Court of Appeal.

Supreme Court of Vanuatu
PMB 041, rue de Querios, Port Vila; tel. 22420; fax 22692.
Attorney-General: HAMILTON BULU (acting).
Chief Justice: VINCENT LUNABECK.
Chief Prosecutor: HEATHER LINI LEO.

Religion

Most of Vanuatu's inhabitants profess Christianity. Presbyterians form the largest Christian group (with about one-half of the population being adherents), followed by Anglicans and Roman Catholics.

CHRISTIANITY

Vanuatu Christian Council: POB 13, Luganville, Santo; tel. 03232; f. 1967; est. as New Hebrides Christian Council; five mem. churches, two observers; Chair. Rt Rev. MICHEL VISI; Sec. Rev. JOHN LIU.

The Roman Catholic Church

Vanuatu forms the single diocese of Port Vila, suffragan to the archdiocese of Nouméa (New Caledonia). At 31 December 2003 there were an estimated 29,500 adherents in the country. The Bishop participates in the Catholic Bishops' Conference of the Pacific, based in Fiji.

Bishop of Port Vila: Rt Rev. MICHEL VISI, Evêché, POB 59, Port Vila; tel. 22640; fax 25342; e-mail catholik@vanuatu.com.vu.

The Anglican Communion

Anglicans in Vanuatu are adherents of the Church of the Province of Melanesia, comprising eight dioceses: Vanuatu (which also includes New Caledonia), Banks and Torres and six dioceses in Solomon Islands. The Archbishop of the Province is the Bishop of Central Melanesia, resident in Honiara, Solomon Islands. In 1985 the Church had an estimated 16,000 adherents in Vanuatu.

Bishop of Vanuatu: Rt Rev. HUGH BLESSING BOE, Bishop's House, POB 238, Luganville, Santo; tel. 37065; fax 36026; expected to retire on 29 June 2006.

Bishop of Banks and Torres: Rt Rev. NATHAN TOME, Bishop's House, POB 19, Toutamwat, Torba Province.

Protestant Churches

Presbyterian Church of Vanuatu (Presbitirin Jyos long Vanuatu): POB 150, Port Vila; tel. 23008; fax 26480; f. 1948; 56,000 mems (1995); Moderator Pastor BANI KALSINGER; Assembly Clerk Pastor FAMA RAKAU.

Other denominations active in the country include the Apostolic Church, the Assemblies of God, the Churches of Christ in Vanuatu and the Seventh-day Adventist Church.

BAHÁ'Í FAITH

National Spiritual Assembly of the Bahá'ís of Vanuatu: POB 1017, Port Vila; tel. 22419; e-mail nsavanuatu@vanuatu.com.vu; f. 1953; Sec. CHARLES PIERCE; mems resident in 205 localities.

The Press

Hapi Tumas Long Vanuatu: POB 1292, Port Vila; tel. 23642; fax 23343; quarterly tourist information; in English; Publr MARC NEIL-JONES; circ. 12,000.

Logging News: Port Vila; environment and logging industry.

Pacific Island Profile: Port Vila; f. 1990; monthly; general interest; English and French; Editor HILDA LINI.

Port Vila Presse: 1st Floor, Raffea House, POB 637, Port Vila; tel. 22200; fax 27999; e-mail marke@presse.com.vu; internet www.presse.com.vu; f. 2000; daily; English and French; Publr MARKE LOWEN; Editor RICKY BINIHI.

Vanuatu Daily Post: POB 1292, Port Vila; tel. 23111; fax 24111; e-mail tpost@vanuatu.com.vu; internet www.vanuatudaily.com.vu; daily; English; Publr MARC NEIL-JONES; Editor LEN GARAE; circ. 2,000.

Directory

Vanuatu Weekly: PMB 049, Port Vila; tel. 22999; fax 22026; e-mail vbtcnews@vanuatu.com.vu; f. 1980; weekly; govt-owned; Bislama, English and French; circ. 1,700.

Viewpoints: Port Vila; weekly; newsletter of Vanuaaku Pati; Editor PETER TAURAKOTO.

Wantok Niuspepa: POB 1292, Port Vila; tel. 23642; fax 23343.

Broadcasting and Communications

TELECOMMUNICATIONS

Freedom Telecommunications Company (USA): Santo; f. 2000; provides services on Santo and islands in the north of Vanuatu.

Telecom Vanuatu Ltd (TVL): POB 146, Port Vila; tel. 22185; fax 22628; e-mail telecom@tvl.net.vu; internet www.vanuatu.com.vu; f. 1989; est. as a jt venture between the Government of Vanuatu, Cable & Wireless Ltd and France Câbles et Radio; operates all national and international telecommunications services in Vanuatu; Man. Dir RICHARD HALL.

BROADCASTING

Radio

Vanuatu Broadcasting and Television Corporation (VBTC): PMB 049, Port Vila; tel. 22999; fax 22026; e-mail vbtcnews@vanuatu.com.vu; internet www.vbtc.com.vu; fmrly Government Media Services, name changed in 1992; Gen. Man. JOE BOMAL CARLO; Chair. GODWIN LIGO; Dir of Programmes A. THOMPSON.

Radio Vanuatu: PMB 049, Port Vila; tel. 22999; fax 22026; f. 1966; govt-owned; broadcasts in English, French and Bislama; Dir JOE BOMAL CARLO.

Television

Vanuatu Broadcasting and Television Corporation (VBTC): see Radio

Television Blong Vanuatu: PMB 049, Port Vila; f. 1993; govt-owned; French-funded; broadcasts for four hours daily in French and English; Gen. Man. CLAUDE CASTELLY; Programme Man. GAEL LE DANTEC.

Finance

(cap. = capital; res = reserves; dep. = deposits; amounts in vatu unless otherwise indicated)

Vanuatu has no personal income tax nor tax on company profits and is therefore attractive as a financial centre and 'tax haven'.

BANKING

Central Bank

Reserve Bank of Vanuatu: POB 62, Port Vila; tel. 23333; fax 24231; e-mail resrvbnk@vanuatu.com.vu; internet www.rbv.gov.vu; f. 1981; est. as Central Bank of Vanuatu; name changed as above in 1989; govt-owned; cap. 100.0m., res 668.2m., dep. 2,880.8m. (Dec. 2002); Gov. ODO TEVI.

Development Banks

Development Bank of Vanuatu: rue de Paris, POB 241, Port Vila; tel. 22181; fax 24591; f. 1979; govt-owned; cap. 315m. (Nov. 1988); Man. Dir AUGUSTINE GARAE.

Agence Française de Développement: Kumul Highway, La Casa d'Andrea Bldg, BP 296, Port Vila; tel. 22171; fax 24021; e-mail afd.arep@vanuatu.com.vu; fmrly Caisse Française de Développement; provides finance for various development projects; Man. BERNARD SIRVAIN.

National Bank

National Bank of Vanuatu: POB 249, Air Vanuatu House, rue de Paris, Port Vila; tel. 22201; fax 27227; e-mail nationalbank@vanuatu.com.vu; f. 1991; est. upon assumption of control of Vanuatu Co-operative Savings Bank; govt-owned; cap. 600m., dep. 2,826m. (Dec. 2002); Chair. JOHN AHURUHI; Man. Dir BOB HUGHES; 19 brs.

Foreign Banks

ANZ Bank (Vanuatu) Ltd: Lini Highway, POB 123, Port Vila; tel. 22536; fax 23950; e-mail anzvanuatu@anz.com; internet www.anz.com/vanuatu; f. 1971; cap. 3.7m., res 317.7m., dep. 24,734.2m. (Sept. 2003); Man. Dir MICHAEL FLOWER; brs in Port Vila and Santo.

European Bank Ltd (USA): International Bldg, Lini Highway, POB 65, Port Vila; tel. 27700; fax 22884; e-mail info@europeanbank

VANUATU

.net; internet www.europeanbank.net; f. 1972, obtained a full banking licence in 1995; cap. US $0.8m., res US $1.3m., dep. US $38.4m. (Dec. 2003); 'offshore' and private banking; Chair. THOMAS MONTGOMERY BAYER; Pres. ROBERT MURRAY BOHN.

Westpac Banking Corporation (Australia): Kumul Highway, POB 32, Port Vila; tel. 22084; fax 24773; e-mail westpacv@vanuatu.com.vu; Man. R. B. WRIGHT; 2 brs.

Financial Institution

The Financial Centre Association: POB 1401, Port Vila; tel. 24619; fax 26008; e-mail fincen@vanuatu.com.vu; f. 1980; group of banking, legal, accounting and trust companies administering 'offshore' banking and investment; Chair. JIM BATTY; Sec. CHARLES KLEIMAN.

INSURANCE

Pacific Insurance Brokers: POB 229, Port Vila; tel. 23863; fax 23089.

QBE Insurance (Vanuatu) Ltd: La Casa D'Andrea Bldg, POB 186, Port Vila; tel. 22299; fax 23298; e-mail info.van@qbe.com; Gen. Man. GEOFFREY R. CUTTING.

Trade and Industry

GOVERNMENT AGENCY

Vanuatu Investment Promotion Authority: PMB 9011, Port Vila; tel. 24096; fax 25216; internet www.investinvanuatu.com; fmrly the Vanuatu Investment Board, name changed as above in 2000; CEO JOE LIGO.

CHAMBER OF COMMERCE

Vanuatu Chamber of Commerce and Industry: POB 189, Port Vila; tel. 27543; fax 27542; e-mail vancci@vanuatu.com.vu; Pres. JOSEPH JACOBE.

MARKETING BOARD

Vanuatu Commodities Marketing Board: POB 268, Luganville, Santo; e-mail vcmb@vanuatu.com.vu; f. 1982; sole exporter of major commodities, including copra, kava and cocoa; Gen. Man. GEORGE CALO.

UTILITIES

Electricity

Union Electrique du Vanuatu (Unelco Vanuatu Ltd): POB 26, rue Winston Churchill, Port Vila; tel. 22211; fax 25011; e-mail unelco@unelco.com.vu; private organization contracted for the generation and supply of electricity in Port Vila, Luganville, Tanna and Malekula, and for the supply of water in Port Vila; Dir-Gen. JEAN FRANÇOIS BARBEAU.

Village generators provide electricity in rural areas. The Department of Infrastructure, Utilities and Public Works provides recirculated water supplies to about 85% of urban and 30% of rural households.

CO-OPERATIVES

During the early 1980s there were some 180 co-operative primary societies in Vanuatu and at least 85% of goods in the islands were distributed by co-operative organizations. Almost all rural ni-Vanuatu were members of a co-operative society, as were many urban dwellers. By the end of that decade, however, membership of co-operatives had declined, and the organizations' supervisory body, the Vanuatu Co-operative Federation, had been dissolved, after having accumulated debts totalling some $A1m.

TRADE UNIONS

Vanuatu Council of Trade Unions (VCTU): PMB 89, Port Vila; tel. 24517; fax 23679; e-mail synt@vanuatu.com.vu; Pres. OBED MASINGIOW; Sec.-Gen. EPHRAIM KALSAKAU.

National Union of Labour: Port Vila.

The principal trade unions include:

Oil and Gas Workers' Union: Port Vila; f. 1984.

Vanuatu Airline Workers' Union: Port Vila; f. 1984.

Vanuatu Public Service Association: Port Vila.

Vanuatu Teachers' Union: Port Vila; Gen. Sec. CHARLES KALO; Pres. OBED MASSING.

Vanuatu Waterside, Maritime and Allied Workers' Union: Port Vila.

Transport

ROADS

There are about 1,130 km of roads, of which 54 km, mostly on Efate Island, are sealed. In early 1998 Japan granted more than 400m. vatu to finance the sealing of the main road around Efate. In January 2002 an earthquake caused significant damage to the transport infrastructure around Efate. Several foreign donors, including New Zealand, contributed to funding urgent repairs to roads and bridges in the area. Two bridges on Efate were rebuilt with Japanese finance in 2004.

SHIPPING

The principal ports are Port Vila and Luganville.

Vanuatu Maritime Authority: POB 320, Marine Quay, Port Vila; tel. 23128; fax 22949; e-mail vma@vanuatu.com.vu; domestic and international ship registry, maritime safety regulator; Commissioner of Maritime Affairs JOHN T. ROOSEN; Chair. LENNOX VUTI.

Ports and Harbour Department: PMB 9046, Port Vila; tel. 22339; fax 22475; e-mail nhamish@vanet.com; Harbour Master Capt. LUKE BEANDI; Dir NORRIS HAMISH.

Burns Philp (Vanuatu) Ltd: POB 27, Port Vila.

Ifira Shipping Agencies Ltd: POB 68, Port Vila; tel. 22929; fax 22052; f. 1986; Man. Dir CLAUDE BOUDIER.

Sami Ltd: Kumul Highway, POB 301, Port Vila; tel. 24106; fax 23405.

South Sea Shipping: POB 84, Port Vila; tel. 22205; fax 23304; e-mail southsea@vanuatu.com.vu.

Vanua Navigation Ltd: POB 44, Port Vila; tel. 22027; f. 1977; by the Co-operative Federation and Sofrana Unilines; Chief Exec. GEOFFREY J. CLARKE.

The following services call regularly at Vanuatu: Compagnie Générale Maritime, Kyowa Shipping Co, Pacific Forum Line, Papua New Guinea Shipping Corpn, Sofrana-Unilines, Bank Line, Columbus Line and Bali Hai Shipping. Royal Viking Line, Sitmar and P & O cruises also call at Vanuatu.

CIVIL AVIATION

The principal airports are Bauerfield (Efate, for Port Vila) and Pekoa (Espiritu Santo, for Luganville). There are airstrips on all Vanuatu's principal islands and an international airport at White Grass on Tanna was completed in 1998. The Civil Aviation Corporation Act, approved by Parliament in August 1998, provided for the transfer of ownership of Vanuatu's airports to a commercially-run corporation, in which the Government is to have a majority shareholding. In early 2000 it was announced that a further three airports were to be built on the islands of Pentecost, Malekula and Tanna. Major improvements providing for the accommodation of larger aircraft at both Bauerfield and Pekoa airports began in mid-2000. Moreover, in September 2000 plans for a new international airport at Teouma (Efate) were announced, with finance from a private Thai investor. In late 2003 plans for the construction of an international air terminal at Pekoa (Espiritu Santo) costing US $1.6m. were announced.

Air Vanuatu (Operations) Ltd: POB 148, Du Vanuatu House, rue de Paris, Port Vila; tel. 23838; fax 23250; e-mail service@airvanuatu.com.vu; internet www.pacificislands.com/airlines/vanuatu.html; f. 1981; govt-owned national carrier since 1987; regular services between Port Vila and Sydney, Brisbane and Melbourne (Australia), Nadi (Fiji), Nouméa (New Caledonia), Auckland (New Zealand) and Honiara (Solomon Islands); the frequency of flights from Auckland, Sydney, Brisbane and Honiara to Port Vila was increased in mid-2004; Man. Dir and CEO JEAN-PAUL VIRELALA.

Vanair: rue Pasteur, PMB 9069, Port Vila; tel. 22643; fax 23910; e-mail vias@vanuatu.com.vu; internet www.islandsvanuatu.com/vanair.htm; operates scheduled services to 29 destinations within the archipelago; management of the airline assumed by Air Vanuatu in Jan. 2005.

Dovair: Port Vila; privately owned; operates domestic services.

Tourism

Tourism is an important source of revenue for the Government of Vanuatu. Visitors are attracted by the islands' unspoilt landscape and rich local customs. The establishment of regular air services from Australia and New Zealand in the late 1980s precipitated a significant increase in the number of visitors to Vanuatu. In 2004 there were an estimated 60,611 foreign visitor arrivals in Vanuatu, compared with 50,400 in the previous year. In 1997 passengers on cruise ships visiting the islands numbered 30,530. In 2003 some 59% of visitors were from Australia and 15% were from New Zealand. In that year some 77% of visitor arrivals were tourists, 13% were

VANUATU

travelling on business and 8% were visiting family and friends. There were some 120 hotels and guest houses in 2003, providing more than 1,300 rooms. Receipts from tourism totalled some US $46m. in 2001. The development of the tourist industry has hitherto been concentrated on the islands of Efate, Espiritu Santo and Tanna; however, the promotion of other islands as tourist centres is beginning to occur.

Vanuatu Hotel and Resorts Association: POB 215, Port Vila; tel. 22040; fax 27579; Pres. JOHN GROCOCK.

Vanuatu Tourism Office: Lini Highway, POB 209, Port Vila; tel. 22685; fax 23889; e-mail tourism@vanuatu.com.vu; internet www.vanuatutourism.com; Gen. Man. LINDA KALPOI; Chair. GABRIEL ARU BANI.

THE VATICAN CITY
(THE HOLY SEE)

Introductory Survey

Location, Climate, Language, Religion, Flag

The State of the Vatican City is situated entirely within the Italian capital, Rome, on the right bank of the Tiber river. It covers an area of 0.44 sq km (0.17 sq mile). The climate is Mediterranean, with warm summers and mild winters (see Italy). Italian and Latin are the official languages. Roman Catholicism is the official religion. The state flag, which is square, consists of two vertical stripes of yellow and white, with the papal coat of arms superimposed on the white stripe.

History

For a period of nearly 1,000 years, dating roughly from the time of Charlemagne to the year 1870, the Popes ruled much of the central Italian peninsula, including the city of Rome. During the process of unification, the Kingdom of Italy gradually absorbed these States of the Church, the process being completed by the entry into Rome of King Victor Emmanuel's troops in September 1870. From 1860 to 1870 many attempts had been made to induce the Pope, Pius IX, to surrender his temporal possessions. Since, however, he regarded them as a sacred trust from a higher Power, to be guarded on behalf of the Church, he refused to do so. After the entry of the Royal Army into Rome, he retired to the Vatican from where no Pope emerged again until the ratification of the Lateran Treaty of 11 February 1929. By the Law of Guarantees of May 1871, Italy attempted to stabilize the position of the Papacy by recognizing the Pope's claim to use of the Palaces of the Lateran and the Vatican, the Papal villa of Castelgandolfo, and their gardens and annexes, and to certain privileges customary to sovereignty. This unilateral arrangement was not accepted by Pius IX, and his protest against it was repeated constantly by his successors.

In 1929 two agreements were made with the Italian Government—the Lateran Treaty and the Concordat. By the terms of the Lateran Treaty, the Holy See was given exclusive power and sovereign jurisdiction over the State of the Vatican City, which was declared neutral and inviolable territory. Financial compensation was also given for the earlier losses. Under the Concordat, Roman Catholicism became the state religion of Italy, with special privileges defined by law. The new Italian Constitution of 1947 reaffirmed adherence to the Lateran Treaty, but in 1967 negotiations began for a revision of the Concordat. In December 1978 the two sides agreed on a draft plan for a new Concordat, under which Catholicism would cease to be the official Italian state religion and most of the Catholic Church's special privileges in Italy would be removed. The revised version, finally agreed, was signed in February 1984.

In 1917 the first legal code, the Code of Canon Law (Codex Iuris Canonici), was devised for the Catholic Church. In 1963 a pontifical commission was inaugurated to investigate possible reforms to the law, and in 1981 the Pope received more than 70 cardinals and bishops who had prepared the new code's 1,752 rules. Revisions included a reduction in the number of cases meriting excommunication and a general relaxing of penalties, with increased emphasis on the importance of the laity within the church. The code was ratified in January 1983, and came into force in November.

In October 1978 Cardinal Karol Wojtyła (then Archbishop of Kraków, Poland) became the first non-Italian Pope since the 16th century, taking the name John Paul II. Security surrounding the Pontiff was considerably tightened after an attempt on the Pope's life in May 1981 and another in May 1982. An Italian parliamentary inquiry, which published its findings in March 2006, concluded that the 1981 attempt was orchestrated by the former USSR.

In April 1984 Pope John Paul II announced a major reshuffle of offices in the Roman Curia, which included the delegation of most of his responsibility for the routine administration of the Vatican to the Secretariat of State. In July 1988 a number of reforms to the Curia were introduced. These consolidated the power of the Secretariat of State, as well as reorganizing some of the Congregations and Pontifical Commissions.

In February 1987 Italian judges issued a warrant for the arrest of Archbishop Paul Marcinkus, the Chairman of the Istituto per le Opere di Religione ('Vatican Bank'), and two other bank officials for alleged involvement in the fraudulent bankruptcy of the Banco Ambrosiano in Milan, which collapsed in 1982. In July 1987, however, the Italian Supreme Court cancelled the warrants for the arrest of the three bank officials, stating that the Vatican stood outside Italian jurisdiction and that, according to the Lateran Treaty, Italy did not have the right to interfere in the affairs of the central organs of the Roman Catholic Church. In May 1988, after an appeal, the Archbishop's immunity was endorsed by the Constitutional Court. In March 1989 the Vatican announced a wide-ranging reorganization of the Istituto per le Opere di Religione, by abolishing the post of Chairman, held by Marcinkus, and appointing a commission of five cardinals, nominated by the Pope, to preside over the bank, assisted by a committee of financial experts. Archbishop Marcinkus retired from papal service in October 1990 and died in February 2006.

In March 1998 the Vatican released its long-awaited 'definitive statement' condemning anti-Semitism and anti-Judaism, and repenting for Roman Catholic passivity during the Nazi Holocaust. However, a number of high-ranking Jewish officials expressed disappointment in the document and demanded an explicit apology for the attitude of Pope Pius XII and the Roman Catholic Church's failure to speak out, at the time, against Nazi atrocities. In March 2000, during a service in St Peter's Basilica in Rome, despite misgivings expressed by some theologians that such a statement would undermine the Church's authority, the Pope made a comprehensive and unprecedented plea for forgiveness for the 'past sins of the Church', including racial and ethnic discrimination and Christian mistreatment of minorities, women and native peoples. However, in July 2001 a panel of Catholic and Jewish historians was forced to halt its study of the Church's role in the Holocaust when the Vatican refused it access to files on Pope Pius XII, prompting allegations that the Vatican was seeking to conceal potentially damaging evidence. Following further pressure, however, archives covering the years 1922–39 were released in February 2003.

In February 2001 it was announced that the Constitution, dating back to the Lateran Treaty of 1929, was to be replaced by a new Basic Law incorporating a number of constitutional amendments made over the years. The Basic Law clarified the distinction between the legislative, executive and judicial branches.

In November 2001 Pope John Paul II issued an apology to victims of sexual abuse perpetrated by members of the Catholic clergy. Furthermore, in January 2002 new regulations were published by the Vatican, outlining the appropriate method of dealing with cases of alleged sexual abuse, notably against children, by members of the clergy. However, in mid-2002, in the most significant scandal to affect the Roman Catholic Church in many years, it was revealed that Cardinal Bernard Law, the Archbishop of Boston, Massachusetts, USA, had protected a number of priests who faced accusations of sexual misconduct against children. Hundreds of priests in the USA resigned or were subsequently suspended or sued in the wake of more than 200 allegations of sexual abuse involving members of the clergy in the Boston area. In April the Pope summoned 13 US cardinals to the Vatican to discuss the crisis. A 'zero tolerance' policy adopted by the US Conference of Catholic Bishops in June was subsequently rejected by the Vatican; a somewhat altered charter, which provided for the eventual dismissal of any priests found guilty of sexual abuse in a church tribunal, was accepted by the Vatican in December. Victims' groups were disappointed with the revisions, however, which reintroduced a 10-year statute of limitation on accusations. Following the filing of 450 lawsuits against Cardinal Law's archdiocese and the petition of 58 Boston priests, Law resigned in December 2002.

The publication in March 2003 of a *Lexicon On Ambiguous and Colloquial Terms About Family Life and Ethical Questions* caused controversy by its reaffirmation of the Catholic Church's uncompromising stance regarding birth control and homosexuality. In July a document was circulated to all bishops confirming the Vatican's opposition to the legalization of same-sex unions. Further controversy arose in October following claims by certain Vatican officials that the AIDS virus could be transferred through condoms, provoking much criticism from the World Health Organization. At the ninth consistory of John Paul II's papacy, which took place on 21 October, 30 new cardinals were elevated, thus bringing the number of cardinals eligible to vote in the conclave to elect a new Pope to 135. Of the mostly conservative cardinals elevated, only six were Italian, and the representation from Africa and Latin America was increased. An additional cardinal was elevated *in pectore* (i.e. his name was not publicly divulged).

In August 2004, in an open letter to the bishops entitled 'On the collaboration of men and women in the Church and the World', the Pope criticized radical feminism for having created a culture of enmity between the sexes. In October the *Compendium of the Social Doctrine of the Church*, published by the Pontifical Council for Justice and Peace, called on Catholics to include their faith in the life and legislation of the State and reiterated the Church's oppositional stance on homosexuality and birth control.

Following a long period of ill health, Pope John Paul II died on 2 April 2005 at the age of 84. Only St Peter and Pius IX, in the mid-19th century, had enjoyed longer papacies. More than 3m. people visited the Vatican City in the period between the death of John Paul II and his funeral, which took place on 8 April and was attended by around 200 world leaders. By the time of his death, John Paul II had canonized 482 saints (more than all his predecessors combined since the 16th century), performed 1,338 beatifications and created 232 cardinals.

The conclave to elect a new Pope began on 18 April 2005 and was attended by 115 of the 117 cardinals of voting age (under 80 years old). On 19 April Cardinal Joseph Ratzinger was elected as the Supreme Pontiff, and took the name Benedict XVI. Ratzinger, who was aged 78, was hitherto the Dean of the College of Cardinals, the Prefect of the Congregation for the Doctrine of the Faith and President of the International Theological Commission and of the Pontifical Biblical Commission. He was widely viewed as a conservative theologian whose views were similar to those of his predecessor. On taking office, Pope Benedict XVI reinstated the majority of officials in the Roman Curia who had served under John Paul II. In May Benedict XVI announced the commencement of the process of beatification of John Paul II.

In October 2005 the first synod of Benedict XVI's papacy took place, at which the celibacy of the priesthood was reaffirmed, and in January 2006 his first encyclical, *Deus Caritas Est*, on the nature of love, was published. On 24 March Pope Benedict XVI appointed 15 new cardinals, bringing to 120 the number of cardinals of voting age. Notable among the appointees was Joseph Zen Ze-kiun, Bishop of Hong Kong and an outspoken critic of the Chinese Government.

The Vatican's prominence in international affairs increased from the late 1980s. In July 1989 diplomatic relations with Poland, severed in 1945, were restored. The Vatican had hitherto maintained no diplomatic relations with eastern European Governments under communist rule, except for Yugoslavia. During the early 1990s diplomatic relations were restored or established with many former communist states, including, in 1990 relations with the USSR. In 1992 full diplomatic relations were restored, after more than 120 years of discord, between the Vatican and Mexico. In December 1993 the Vatican and Israel signed a mutual-recognition agreement, which led to the establishment of full diplomatic ties and the exchange of ambassadors in September 1994. Meanwhile, in February 1994 the Vatican established diplomatic relations with Jordan, in an apparent move to strengthen links with the Arab world to counterbalance its recent recognition of Israel. Similarly, in October of that year the Vatican instituted 'official relations' with the Palestine Liberation Organization.

Diplomatic relations between the Vatican and China had been severed in 1951 following the communists' accession to power in Beijing. In August 1999 the People's Republic of China vetoed plans for Pope John Paul II to visit Hong Kong later that year, owing to the Vatican's diplomatic ties with Taiwan. Any hope of a reconciliation between China and the Vatican looked increasingly unlikely in January 2000, when the state-controlled Patriotic Church in Beijing rebuffed the Pope by ordaining five bishops in a ceremony timed to upstage official papal ordinations in the Vatican City. Relations further deteriorated following the Pope's announcement in September 2000 that he was to canonize 120 western and Chinese Catholics killed in China between 1648 and 1930. The controversy was exacerbated by the decision to hold the ceremony on China's National Day, the anniversary of the accession to power of communist rule (although the Vatican insisted that the date was merely coincidental). The canonizations were also denounced by Catholic organizations in China. However, in October 2001 Pope John Paul II issued an apology to China for the sins committed by Christians against the country; an appeal was also made for diplomatic relations between the two states to be restored. Informal talks recommenced in early 2003, but were adversely affected by the outspoken anti-Government stance of Hong Kong's Bishop (later Cardinal), Joseph Zen Ze-kiun. Relations were again strained in mid-2004, following allegations that some 23 Roman Catholics had been arrested in China. Following the accession of Benedict XVI, there appeared to be a growing emphasis on the need to improve Sino-Vatican relations. However, the ordination of a series of bishops by the Patriotic Church in April and May 2006 provoked criticism from the Pope.

In February 2000 the Vatican and the Palestinian (National) Authority signed an historic agreement on joint interests, which appealed for a peaceful solution, through dialogue, to the Israeli-Palestinian conflict and called for an internationally guaranteed special statute for the city of Jerusalem that safeguarded freedom of religion and conscience. The Israeli Government criticized the accord as representing unwelcome 'interference' by the Vatican in the ongoing Middle East peace talks. In early 2000 the Pope undertook a millennial pilgrimage to some of the principal biblical sites of the Middle East, including Mount Sinai in Egypt in February (the first visit by a pontiff to that country) and Israel, Jordan and the West Bank in March. Pope John Paul II's six-day visit to the politically volatile Holy Land constituted the first papal visit to that region for 36 years. In April 2002 an agreement was signed by the Vatican and the Turkish Government, promoting religious dialogue between Muslims and Christians.

In mid-2001 Pope John Paul II undertook visits to Greece and Syria, the first of these since the division of Christianity into eastern and western churches. During his visit to Greece, the Pope attempted to heal the historic rift between the Roman Catholic and Orthodox churches by presenting an apology to the Orthodox community for wrongs committed over the centuries by the Roman Catholic Church. The Pope, despite not being granted the consent of the Russian Orthodox Patriarch, also visited Ukraine, where he called for an end to the 1,000-year schism between Roman Catholicism and the Orthodox Church in Ukraine and, by extension, the Russian Orthodox Church. The leaders of the Orthodox Church in Ukraine refused to meet the Pope, although his visit attracted much popular support. In September Pope John Paul II visited Armenia, becoming the first pontiff to visit the country.

Tensions between the Roman Catholic Church and the Russian Orthodox Church increased in February 2002 when the Vatican announced that the four apostolic administrations in Russia (officially considered to be temporary) had become dioceses. This move was interpreted by representatives of the Russian Orthodox Church as the establishment of an alternative church within the country, and a few days later a visit to Russia by the Head of the Pontifical Council for the Promotion of Christian Unity, Cardinal Walter Kasper, was cancelled by the Russian Orthodox Church.

In November 2002 John Paul II became the first pontiff to address the Italian Parliament, symbolically closing the Vatican's territorial dispute with Italy. His speech advocated institutional recognition by the European Union (EU, see p. 228) of Europe's Christian heritage. This followed an ultimately unsuccessful call in October for Christianity to be enshrined in the proposed EU constitution. In June 2004 John Paul II publicly criticized the lack of reference to Christianity in the approved EU constitutional treaty, and in early 2005 the Vatican again criticized the increasing secularization of the EU states, with particular reference to reforms planned in Spain by the ruling socialist party.

THE VATICAN CITY

During late 2002 and early 2003 Pope John Paul II was prominent in opposing the prospect of US-led military intervention to remove the regime of Saddam Hussain in Iraq; he denounced the planned conflict as a 'defeat for humanity', and urged a diplomatic resolution to the crisis. During February and March the Pope granted a series of private audiences to important international figures, including Tareq Aziz, the Deputy Prime Minister of Iraq, Kofi Annan, the Secretary-General of the UN, the British Prime Minister, Tony Blair, and the Italian Prime Minister, Silvio Berlusconi. Papal envoys were also sent to Baghdad and Washington. This was followed in March by an historic five-day meeting with a delegation from Israel's Chief Rabbinate. Later in the year the Pope continued to receive government representatives from various countries, including the Iranian and Israeli ministers responsible for foreign affairs and the Palestinian Prime Minister, Ahmad Quray.

While the number of foreign visits undertaken by John Paul II was reduced in 2003 owing to his increasing frailty, he continued to receive foreign leaders in the Vatican, including President Vladimir Putin of Russia in November, in what was widely perceived as an attempt to improve relations with the Russian Orthodox Church. The Pope maintained his engagement with former Soviet bloc countries, visiting Slovakia in September and receiving the Prime Ministers of the former Yugoslav republic of Macedonia and Croatia. In September talks on an accord between Croatia and the Vatican stalled owing to differences of opinion over the Catholic Church's presence in the largely Orthodox country. The Dalai Lama, the head of the Tibetan Buddhist hierarchy, had a private audience with the Pope in November. By the end of 2003 John Paul II had made 102 overseas journeys to a total of 129 countries, making him by far the most widely travelled pontiff.

Pope John Paul II visited Switzerland in June 2004, and it was announced that diplomatic relations, which had been severed in 1873, were to be restored. In mid-2004 the Pope continued his policy of engagement with the Orthodox churches, with a visit by the Russian Minister of Foreign Affairs, Sergei Lavrov, and the return of a copy of the icon Our Lady of Kazan to Moscow. On 1 July the Pope issued a joint statement with Patriarch Bartolomeos I of Constantinople, the Orthodox Patriarch in Istanbul, Turkey, confirming their commitment to dialogue between the Roman Catholic and Orthodox churches.

The first major foreign visit of Benedict XVI's pontificate was to his native Germany in August 2005, during which he participated in events surrounding World Youth Day and made a symbolic visit to a synagogue. In October the Most Rev. Giovanni Lajolo, the Secretary for Relations with States, paid an official visit to Russia. In early 2006 it was reported that the Pope had decided to stop using one of his nine official titles, that of Patriarch of the West. This was regarded as a gesture of reconciliation towards the Orthodox churches.

The population of the Vatican City was around 900 in 2004. Its inhabitants are of many nationalities, representing the presence of the Roman Catholic Church throughout the world. The papal guards, who number some 110, are of Swiss nationality.

Finance

The Vatican has three main sources of income: the Istituto per le Opere di Religione (see Directory), voluntary contributions to the Church, known as 'Peter's Pence' (Obolo di San Pietro), and interest on financial investments, managed by the Administration of the Patrimony of the Holy See. The euro is used as currency. The Vatican first revealed budget figures for the Holy See in 1979, when it disclosed a deficit of US $20.1m. This was incurred through the normal operating expenses of the Vatican bureaucracy, including the newspaper and radio services and overseas diplomatic missions. The alleged mismanagement of investments, banking scandals and the decline in the value of the US dollar contributed to a deficit of $56.7m. in 1986, when annual income reached $57m. The deficit was met by the receipt of $32m. from the 'Peter's pence' levy, and by the withdrawal of $24.7m. from the 'Peter's pence' reserve fund. In March 1988 the Vatican published an independently audited annual balance sheet, thereby, for the first time in its history, revealing the church's financial affairs to public scrutiny. During 1988–1990 the budget deficit continued to grow, and in April 1991 more than 100 representatives of bishops' conferences from around the world attended an unprecedented meeting held in the Vatican City, at which they discussed ways of making local dioceses systematically share the burden of the Vatican's annual budgetary deficit. In that year, however, the budgetary deficit reached a peak of $87.5m. The establishment of new diplomatic missions in the late 1980s and early 1990s (see History) entailed considerable capital expenditure for the papacy. However, in 1992 the deficit fell substantially and in 1993, after 23 years of budgetary deficits, a modest surplus, of $1.5m., was recorded. A small annual budgetary surplus was maintained throughout the 1990s, cumulating in a surplus of $8.5m. in 2000, a 70% rise compared with 1999, which reflected the greater receipts generated by activities associated with the jubilee year. The budget for 2001, in contrast, showed the first deficit since 1993, of $3.1m., as a result of a general slowdown in the global economy following the terrorist attacks in the USA on 11 September 2001; 'Peter's pence' contributions for that year, not included in the consolidated budget, amounted to almost $52m. In 2002 another budget deficit, of $21m., was recorded (expenditure $358m.; income $337m.). The considerable increase in the deficit was largely attributed to losses in investments of $18.5m., compared with profits of $37m. from investments in 2001. 'Peter's pence' contributions, however, rose by almost 86%, compared with the previous year, to $96.6m. in 2002. In 2003 another budget deficit, of $22.5m., was recorded. In that year 'Peter's pence' contributions amounted to $79.6m. In 2004 a budget surplus of $3.7m. (€3.0m.) was recorded, the first since 2000. Expenditure amounted to €202.6m., while income was €205.6m. The surplus was due in part to the sale of properties outside the Vatican. It was anticipated that a surplus would also be achieved in 2005, despite the costs incurred in conducting the funeral of John Paul II and the election of Benedict XVI in April of that year.

The Istituto per le Opere di Religione has consistently returned an operating profit, although much of the revenue generated by it in the 1980s was used to repay the creditors remaining from the collapse of the Banco Ambrosiano in 1982.

Directory

Government

The State of the Vatican City came into existence with the Lateran Treaty of 1929. The Holy See (a term designating the papacy, i.e. the office of the Pope, and thus the central governing body of the Roman Catholic Church) is a distinct, pre-existing entity. Both entities are subjects of international law. Ambassadors and Ministers are accredited to the Holy See, which sends diplomatic representatives (nuncios and pro-nuncios) to more than 120 states, as well as having delegates or observers at the UN and other international organizations. The Vatican City is also a member of certain international organizations, including specialized agencies of the UN.

Both entities are indissolubly united in the person of the Pope, the Bishop of Rome, who is simultaneously ruler of the State and visible head of the Roman Catholic Church.

On 1 February 2001 a new Basic Law replaced the former Constitution dating back to the 1929 Lateran Treaty.

THE GOVERNMENT OF THE VATICAN CITY STATE

The Vatican City State is under the temporal jurisdiction of the Pope, the Supreme Pontiff elected for life by a conclave comprising members of the Sacred College of Cardinals. The Pope holds all legislative, executive and judicial power. Legislative power is vested in the Pontifical Commission for the Vatican State, which comprises a Cardinal President and six other cardinals, nominated by the Pope for a five-year period. Executive power is vested in the President of the Pontifical Commission (who is also the President of the Governorate of the Vatican City State), who is assisted by a Secretary-General. The State Councillors, including one General Councillor and eight other Councillors, are nominated by the Pope for a five-year period, and assist in the drawing-up of laws and report to the Pontifical Commission. Judiciary power is vested in a number of Tribunals and the Apostolic Penitentiary, who exercise their judicial authority in the name of the Pope. The Pontiff exclusively retains the right to grant pardons and amnesties.

THE VATICAN CITY

Head of State

His Holiness Pope BENEDICT XVI (elected 19 April 2005).

Pontifical Commission for the Vatican City State

Cardinal EDMUND CASIMIR SZOKA (President).
Cardinal ANGELO SODANO.
Cardinal GIOVANNI BATTISTA RE.
Cardinal JOZEF TOMKO.
Cardinal ANDRZEJ MARIA DESKUR.
Cardinal JAN PIETER SCHOTTE.
Cardinal AGOSTINO CACCIAVILLAN.

State Councillors

Marchese Dott. GIULIO SACCHETTI (General Councillor).
There are seven additional councillors.

Governorate of the Vatican City State

President: Cardinal EDMUND CASIMIR SZOKA.
Secretary-General: Rt Rev. RENATO BOCCARDO (Titular Bishop of Aquipendium).
Vice Secretary-General: Rev. GIORGIO CORBELLINI.

THE SUPREME PONTIFF

His Holiness Pope Benedict XVI (Joseph Ratzinger), Bishop of Rome, Vicar of Christ, Successor of the Prince of the Apostles, Supreme Pontiff of the Universal Church, Primate of Italy, Archbishop and Metropolitan of the Province of Rome, Sovereign of the Vatican City State, Servant of the Servants of God, acceded on 19 April 2005 as the 265th Roman pontiff.

THE SACRED COLLEGE OF CARDINALS AND THE ROMAN CURIA

Members of the Sacred College of Cardinals are created by the Pope. The cardinals are divided into three orders: Bishops (including the Cardinal of Patriarchal Sees of Oriental Rites), Priests and Deacons. Under the decree of November 1970, *Ingravescentem Aetatem*, only cardinals under 80 years of age have the right to enter the conclave for the election of the Pope. Cardinals who reside in Rome, Italy, as the Pope's immediate advisers are styled Cardinals 'in Curia'. The Roman Curia acts as the Papal court and the principal administrative body of the Church. The College of Cardinals derives from the Church's earliest days. In March 1973 Pope Paul VI announced that the number of cardinals permitted to participate in the conclave would be limited to 120. This was increased to 135 by Pope John Paul II in February 2001. At 18 April 2005, as the conclave to elect John Paul II's successor began, there were 183 cardinals, of whom 117 were under the age of 80; 115 cardinals participated in the conclave. On 24 March 2006 the number of cardinals increased to 193, of whom 120 were of voting age. There are usually six Cardinal Bishops who are in titular charge of suburban sees of Rome—Sabina-Poggio Mirteto and Ostia, Albano, Frascati, Palestrina, Porto and Santa Rufina, and Velletri and Segni. The order of Cardinal Bishops also includes three Cardinals of Patriarchal Sees of Oriental Rites. Cardinal Priests occupy titular churches in Rome, Italy, founded soon after Christianity originated. The administration of the Church's affairs is undertaken through the Secretariat of State and the Council for the Public Affairs of the Church, under the Cardinal Secretary of State, and through a number of Congregations, each under the direction of a cardinal or senior member of the Church, as well as through Tribunals, Offices, Commissions and Secretariats for special purposes.

The 'Apostolic Constitution' (*Regimini Ecclesiae Universae*), published in August 1967 and effective from 1 March 1968, reformed the Roman Curia. Among the changes were the creation of new organs and the restructuring of the Secretariat of State. In 1969 the Congregation of Rites was divided into two Congregations—one for Divine Worship and the other for the Causes of Saints. The Congregation for the Discipline of the Sacraments and the Congregation for Divine Worship were amalgamated in 1975, but separated again in 1984.

In July 1988 further reforms of the Curia were introduced. The Secretariat of State was divided into two sections: the first section dealing with 'General Affairs' and the second 'Relations with States'. The Congregation for Divine Worship was again amalgamated with the Congregation for the Discipline of the Sacraments.

Members in order of precedence:

Cardinal Bishops

ANGELO SODANO (Italy—Titular Bishop of Albano and Ostia, Secretary of State and Dean of the College of Cardinals).
BERNARDIN GANTIN (Benin—Titular Bishop of Palestrina and of Ostia).
ROGER ETCHEGARAY (France—Titular Bishop of Porto-Santa Rufina, Vice-Dean of the College of Cardinals).
ALFONSO LÓPEZ TRUJILLO (Colombia—Titular Bishop of Frascati, President of the Pontifical Council for the Family).
GIOVANNI BATTISTA RE (Italy—Titular Bishop of Sabina-Poggio Mirteto, Prefect of the Congregation for the Bishops and President of the Pontifical Commission for Latin America).
FRANCIS A. ARINZE (Nigeria—Titular Bishop of Velletri-Segni, Prefect of the Congregation for Divine Worship and the Discipline of the Sacraments).

Cardinals of Patriarchal Sees of Oriental Rites

NASRALLAH PIERRE SFEIR (Lebanon—Maronite Patriarch of Antioch).
STÉPHANOS II GHATTAS (Egypt—Coptic Patriarch Emeritus of Alexandria).
IGNACE MOUSSA I DAOUD (Syria—Prefect of the Congregation of Oriental Churches, Grand Chancellor of the Pontifical Oriental Institute).

Cardinal Priests

STEPHEN KIM SOU-HWAN (Republic of Korea).
EUGÊNIO DE ARAÚJO SALES (Brazil).
JOHANNES WILLEBRANDS (Netherlands).
LUIS APONTE MARTÍNEZ (Puerto Rico).
SALVATORE PAPPALARDO (Italy).
PAULO EVARISTO ARNS (Brazil).
WILLIAM WAKEFIELD BAUM (USA).
ALOÍSIO LORSCHEIDER (Brazil).
MARCO CÉ (Italy).
ERNESTO CORRIPIO AHUMADA (Mexico).
FRANCISZEK MACHARSKI (Poland).
MICHAEL MICHAI KITBUNCHU (Thailand—Archbishop of Bangkok).
ALEXANDRE DO NASCIMENTO (Angola).
GODFRIED DANNEELS (Belgium—Archbishop of Mechelen-Brussels).
THOMAS STAFFORD WILLIAMS (New Zealand).
CARLO MARIA MARTINI (Italy).
JEAN-MARIE LUSTIGER (France).
JÓZEF GLEMP (Poland—Archbishop of Warsaw).
JOACHIM MEISNER (Germany—Archbishop of Cologne).
D. SIMON LOURDUSAMY (India).
ANTONIO INNOCENTI (Italy).
MIGUEL OBANDO BRAVO (Nicaragua).
PAUL AUGUSTIN MAYER (Germany).
ANGEL SUQUÍA GOICOECHEA (Spain).
RICARDO JAMIN VIDAL (Philippines—Archbishop of Cebu).
HENRYK ROMAN GULBINOWICZ (Poland).
JOZEF TOMKO (Slovakia—President of the Pontifical Committee for International Eucharistic Congresses).
ANDRZEJ MARIA DESKUR (Poland).
PAUL JOSEPH JEAN POUPARD (France—President of the Pontifical Council for Culture; President of the Pontifical Council for Inter-Religious Dialogue).
LOUIS-ALBERT VACHON (Canada).
ROSALIO JOSÉ CASTILLO LARA (Venezuela).
FRIEDRICH WETTER (Germany—Archbishop of Munich and Freising).
SILVANO PIOVANELLI (Italy).
ADRIANUS JOHANNES SIMONIS (Netherlands—Archbishop of Utrecht).
EDOUARD GAGNON (Canada).
ALFONS MARIA STICKLER (Austria).
BERNARD FRANCIS LAW (USA—Archpriest of the Patriarchal Liberian Basilica of Santa Maria Maggiore).
GIACOMO BIFFI (Italy).
EDUARDO MARTÍNEZ SOMALO (Spain—Chamberlain of the Holy Roman Church).
ACHILLE SILVESTRINI (Italy).
ANGELO FELICI (Italy).

THE VATICAN CITY

José Freire Falcão (Brazil).
Michele Giordano (Italy).
Alexandre José Maria dos Santos (Mozambique).
Giovanni Canestri (Italy).
Antonio María Javierre Ortas (Spain).
Simon Ignatius Pimenta (India).
Edward Bede Clancy (Australia).
Edmund Casimir Szoka (USA—President of the Pontifical Commission for the Vatican City State, President of the Governorate of the State of the Vatican City).
László Paskai (Hungary).
Christian Wiyghan Tumi (Cameroon—Archbishop of Douala).
Jean Margéot (Mauritius).
Pio Laghi (Italy—Patron of the Supreme Military Order of Malta).
Edward Idris Cassidy (Australia).
Frédéric Etsou-Nzabi-Bamungwabi (Democratic Republic of the Congo—Archbishop of Kinshasa).
Nicolás de Jesús López Rodríguez (Dominican Republic—Archbishop of Santo Domingo).
José Tomás Sánchez (Philippines).
Virgilio Noè (Italy).
Fiorenzo Angelini (Italy).
Roger Michael Mahony (USA—Archbishop of Los Angeles).
Anthony Joseph Bevilacqua (USA).
Giovanni Saldarini (Italy).
Cahal Brendan Daly (Ireland).
Camillo Ruini (Italy—Vicar-General of His Holiness for the Diocese of Rome, Archpriest of the Lateran Patriarchal Arcibasilica, and Grand Chancellor of the Lateran Pontifical University).
Ján Chryzostom Korec (Slovakia).
Henri Schwéry (Switzerland).
Georg Maximilian Sterzinsky (Germany—Archbishop of Berlin).
Miloslav Vlk (Czech Republic—Archbishop of Prague).
Carlo Furno (Italy—Grand Master of the Equestrian Order of the Holy Sepulchre of Jerusalem).
Peter Seiichi Shirayanagi (Japan).
Adolfo Antonio Suárez Rivera (Mexico).
Julius Riyadi Darmaatmadja (Indonesia—Archbishop of Jakarta).
Jaime Lucas Ortega y Alamino (Cuba—Archbishop of San Cristóbal de la Habana).
Emmanuel Wamala (Uganda—Archbishop of Kampala).
William Henry Keeler (USA—Archbishop of Baltimore).
Jean-Claude Turcotte (Canada—Archbishop of Montreal).
Ricardo María Carles Gordó (Spain).
Adam Joseph Maida (USA—Archbishop of Detroit, and Superior of the Cayman Islands).
Vinko Puljić (Bosnia and Herzegovina—Archbishop of Vrhbosna).
Armand Gaétan Razafindratandra (Madagascar).
Paul Joseph Pham Dình Tung (Viet Nam).
Juan Sandoval Iñiguez (Mexico—Archbishop of Guadalajara).
Kazimierz Świątek (Belarus—Archbishop of Minsk and Mogilev and Apostolic Administrator of Pinsk).
Ersilio Tonini (Italy).
Salvatore De Giorgi (Italy—Archbishop of Palermo).
Serafim Fernandes de Araújo (Brazil).
Antonio María Rouco Varela (Spain—Archbishop of Madrid).
Aloysius Matthew Ambrozic (Canada—Archbishop of Toronto).
Dionigi Tettamanzi (Italy—Archbishop of Milan).
Polycarp Pengo (Tanzania—Archbishop of Dar-es-Salaam).
Christoph Schönborn (Austria—Archbishop of Vienna).
Norberto Rivera Carrera (Mexico—Archbishop of Mexico City).
Francis Eugene George (USA—Archbishop of Chicago).
Paul Shan Kuo-hsi (Taiwan).
Adam Kozłowiecki (Zambia).
Marian Jaworski (Ukraine—Archbishop of Lviv—Latin Rite).
Jānis Pujats (Latvia—Archbishop of Rīga).
Antonio José González Zumárraga (Ecuador).
Ivan Dias (India—Prefect of the Congregation for the Evangelization of Peoples).
Geraldo Majella Agnelo (Brazil—Archbishop of São Salvador de Bahia).
Pedro Rubiano Sáenz (Colombia—Archbishop of Santafé de Bogotá).
Theodore Edgar McCarrick (USA).
Desmond Connell (Ireland).
Audrys Juozas Bačkis (Lithuania—Archbishop of Vilnius).
Francisco Javier Errázuriz Ossa (Chile—Archbishop of Santiago de Chile).
Julio Terrazas Sandoval (Bolivia—Archbishop of Santa Cruz de la Sierra).
Wilfrid Fox Napier (South Africa—Archbishop of Durban).
Oscar Andrés Rodrígues Maradiaga (Honduras—Archbishop of Tegucigalpa).
Bernard Agré (Côte d'Ivoire).
Juan Luis Cipriani Thorne (Peru—Archbishop of Lima).
Francisco Alvarez Martínez (Spain).
Cláudio Hummes (Brazil—Archbishop of São Paulo).
Varkey Vithayathil (India—Major Archbishop of Ernakulam-Angamaly).
Jorge Mario Bergoglio (Argentina—Archbishop of Buenos Aires).
José da Cruz Policarpo (Portugal—Patriarch of Lisbon).
Severino Poletto (Italy—Archbishop of Turin).
Cormac Murphy-O'Connor (United Kingdom—Archbishop of Westminster).
Edward Michael Egan (USA—Archbishop of New York).
Lubomyr Husar (Ukraine—Archbishop-Major of Lviv, Byzantine Ukrainian Rite).
Karl Lehmann (Germany—Bishop of Mainz).
Jean Honoré (France).
Angelo Scola (Italy—Patriarch of Venice).
Anthony Olubunmi Okogie (Nigeria—Archbishop of Lagos).
Bernard Panafieu (France).
Gabriel Zubeir Wako (Sudan—Archbishop of Khartoum).
Carlos Amigo Vallejo (Spain—Archbishop of Seville).
Justin Francis Rigali (USA—Archbishop of Philadelphia).
Keith Michael Patrick O'Brien (United Kingdom—Archbishop of St Andrews and Edinburgh).
Eusébio Oscar Scheid (Brazil—Archbishop of São Sebastião do Rio de Janeiro).
Ennio Antonelli (Italy—Archbishop of Florence).
Tarcisio Bertone (Italy—Archbishop of Genoa).
Peter Kodwo Appiah Turkson (Ghana—Archbishop of Cape Coast).
Telesphore Placidus Toppo (India—Archbishop of Ranchi).
George Pell (Australia—Archbishop of Sydney).
Josip Bozanić (Croatia—Archbishop of Zagreb).
Jean-Baptiste Pham Minh Mân (Viet Nam—Archbishop of Ho Chi Minh City).
Rodolfo Quezada Toruño (Guatemala—Archbishop of Guatemala).
Philippe Barbarin (France—Archbishop of Lyons).
Péter Erdö (Hungary—Archbishop of Estergom-Budapest).
Marc Ouellet (Canada—Archbishop of Québec).
Jorge Liberato Urosa Savino (Venezuela—Archbishop of Caracas—Santiago de Venezuela).
Gaudencio Borbon Rosales (Philippines—Archbishop of Manila).
Jean-Pierre Ricard (France—Archbishop of Bordeaux).
Antonio Cañizares Llovera (Spain—Archbishop of Toledo).
Sean Patrick O'Malley (USA—Archbishop of Boston).
Carlo Caffarra (Italy—Archbishop of Bologna).
Joseph Zen Ze-kiun (Hong Kong—Bishop of Hong Kong).

Cardinal Deacons

Luigi Poggi (Italy).
Gilberto Agustoni (Italy).
Jorge Arturo Augustin Medina Estévez (Chile).
Darío Castrillón Hoyos (Colombia—Prefect of the Congregation for the Clergy, and President of the Pontifical Commission 'Ecclesia Dei').
Lorenzo Antonetti (Italy—Pontifical Delegate for the Patriarchal Basilica of St Francis in Assisi).
James Francis Stafford (USA—Pro Grand Penitentiary of the Apostolic Penitentiary).
Giovanni Cheli (Italy).
Dino Monduzzi (Italy).
Agostino Cacciavillan (Italy).

THE VATICAN CITY

SERGIO SEBASTIANI (Italy—President of the Prefecture of the Economic Affairs of the Holy See).

ZENON GROCHOLEWSKI (Poland—Prefect of the Congregation for Catholic Education and Grand Chancellor of the Università Gregoriana).

JOSÉ SARAIVA MARTINS (Portugal—Prefect of the Congregation for the Causes of Saints).

CRESCENZIO SEPE (Italy—Archbishop of Naples).

JORGE MARÍA MEJÍA (Argentina).

MARIO FRANCESCO POMPEDDA (Italy).

WALTER KASPER (Germany—President of the Pontifical Council for the Promotion of Christian Unity).

ROBERTO TUCCI (Italy).

AVERY DULLES (USA).

JEAN-LOUIS TAURAN (France—Titular Archbishop of Thelepte, Archivist and Librarian for the Holy Roman Church).

RENATO RAFFAELE MARTINO (Italy—Titular Bishop of Segerme, President of the Pontifical Council for Justice and Peace; President of the Pontifical Council for the Pastoral Care of Migrants and Itinerant People).

FRANCESCO MARCHISANO (Italy—Titular Archbishop of Populonia, Archpriest of St Peter's Basilica, Vicar-General to His Holiness for the Vatican City).

JULIÁN HERRANZ CASADO (Spain—Titular Archbishop of Vertara, President of the Pontifical Council for Legislative Texts, President of the Disciplinary Commission of the Roman Curia).

JAVIER LOZANO BARRAGÁN (Mexico—President of the Pontifical Council for Health Professionals).

STEPHEN FUMIO HAMAO (Japan).

ATTILIO NICORA (Italy—President of the Administration of the Patrimony of the Holy See).

GEORGE MARIE MARTIN COTTIER (Switzerland).

THOMÁŠ ŠPIDLÍK (Czech Republic).

STANISŁAW KAZIMIERZ NAGY (Poland).

WILLIAM JOSEPH LEVADA (USA—Prefect of the Congregation for the Doctrine of the Faith, Prefect of the Pontifical Biblical Commission, Prefect of the International Theological Commission).

FRANC RODÉ (Slovenia—Prefect of the Congregation for Institutes of Consecrated Life and for Societies of Apostolic Life).

NICHOLAS CHEONG JIN-SUK (Republic of Korea—Archbishop of Seoul).

STANISLAW DZIWISZ (Poland—Archbishop of Kraków).

ANDREA CORDERO LANZA DI MONTEZEMOLO (Italy).

PETER PROEKU DERY (Ghana).

AGOSTINO VALLINI (Italy—Prefect of the Supreme Tribunal of the Apostolic Signature).

ALBERT VANHOYE (France).

THE ROMAN CURIA

Secretariat of State: Palazzo Apostolico Vaticano, 00120 Città del Vaticano; tel. (06) 69883913; fax (06) 69885255; e-mail vati026@relstat-segstat.va; Sec. of State Cardinal ANGELO SODANO.

First Section—General Affairs: Segreteria di Stato, 00120 Città del Vaticano; tel. (06) 69883438; fax (06) 69885088; e-mail vati023@genaff-segstat.va; Asst Sec. of State Most Rev. LEONARDO SANDRI (Titular Archbishop of Aemona).

Second Section—Relations with States: Palazzo Apostolico Vaticano, 00120 Città del Vaticano; tel. (06) 69883014; fax (06) 69885364; e-mail vati032@relstat-segstat.va; Sec. Most Rev. GIOVANNI LAJOLO (Titular Archbishop of Caesariana).

Congregations

Congregation for the Doctrine of the Faith: Palazzo del Sant'Uffizio, Piazza del S. Uffizio 11, 00193 Rome, Italy; tel. (06) 69883357; fax (06) 69883409; concerned with questions of doctrine and morals; examines doctrines and gives a judgement on them; Prefect Cardinal WILLIAM JOSEPH LEVADA; Sec. Most Rev. ANGELO AMATO (Titular Archbishop of Sila).

Congregation for the Eastern Churches: Palazzo del Bramante, Via della Conciliazione 34, 00193 Rome, Italy; tel. (06) 69884293; fax (06) 69884300; f. 1862; exercises jurisdiction over all persons and things pertaining to the Oriental Rites; Prefect Cardinal IGNACE MOUSSA I DAOUD; Sec. Most Rev. ANTONIO MARIA VEGLIÒ (Titular Archbishop of Eclano).

Congregation for Divine Worship and the Discipline of the Sacraments: Palazzo delle Congregazioni, Piazza Pio XII 10, 00193 Rome, Italy; tel. (06) 69884316; fax (06) 69883499; e-mail cultdiv@ccdds.va; internet www.ccds.va; considers all questions relating to divine worship, liturgy and the sacraments; Prefect Cardinal FRANCIS ARINZE; Sec. Most Rev. ALBERT MALCOLM RANJITH PATABENDIGE DON.

Congregation for the Causes of Saints: Palazzo delle Congregazioni, Piazza Pio XII 10, 00193 Rome, Italy; tel. (06) 69884247; fax (06) 69881935; e-mail vati335@csaints.va; concerned with the proceedings relating to beatification and canonization; Prefect Cardinal JOSÉ SARAIVA MARTINS; Sec. Most Rev. EDWARD NOWAK (Titular Archbishop of Luni).

Congregation for the Bishops: Palazzo delle Congregazioni, Piazza Pio XII 10, 00193 Rome, Italy; tel. (06) 69884217; fax (06) 69885303; e-mail vati076@cbishops.va; designed for the preparation of matters for the erection and division of dioceses and the election of Bishops and for dealing with Apostolic Visitations; Prefect Cardinal GIOVANNI BATTISTA RE; Sec. Most Rev. FRANCESCO MONTERISI (Titular Archbishop of Alba maritima).

Congregation for the Evangelization of Peoples: Palazzo di Propaganda Fide, Piazza di Spagna 48, 00187 Rome, Italy; tel. (06) 69879299; fax (06) 69880118; e-mail cepsegreteria@evangel.va; exercises ecclesiastical jurisdiction over missionary countries; Prefect Cardinal IVAN DIAS; Sec. Most Rev. ROBERT SARAH.

Congregation for the Clergy: Palazzo delle Congregazioni, Piazza Pio XII 3, 00193 Rome, Italy; tel. (06) 69884151; fax (06) 69884845; e-mail clero@cclergy.va; internet www.clerus.org; has jurisdiction over the life and discipline of the clergy and its permanent formation; parishes, chapters, pastoral and presbyteral councils; promotes catechesis and the preaching of the Word of God; deals with economic questions related to the compensation of the clergy and the patrimony of the Church; Prefect Cardinal DARÍO CASTRILLÓN HOYOS; Sec. Most Rev. CSABA TERNYÁK (Titular Archbishop of Eminentiana).

Congregation for Institutes of Consecrated Life and for Societies of Apostolic Life: Palazzo delle Congregazioni, Piazza Pio XII 3, 00193 Rome, Italy; tel. (06) 69884128; fax (06) 69884526; e-mail civcsva@ccscrlife.va; promotes and supervises practice of evangelical counsels, according to approved forms of consecrated life, and activities of societies of apostolic life; Prefect Cardinal FRANC RODÉ; Sec. Most Rev. PIERGIORGIO SILVANO NESTI.

Congregation for Catholic Education: Palazzo delle Congregazioni, Piazza Pio XII 3, 00193 Rome, Italy; tel. (06) 69884167; fax (06) 69884172; e-mail cec@cec.va; f. 1588; concerned with the direction, temporal administration and studies of Catholic universities, seminaries, schools and colleges; Prefect Cardinal ZENON GROCHOLEWSKI; Sec. Most Rev. J. MICHAEL MILLER; C.S.B (Titular Archbishop of Vertara).

Tribunals

Apostolic Penitentiary: Palazzo della Cancelleria, Piazza della Cancelleria 1, 00186 Rome, Italy; tel. (06) 69887526; fax (06) 69887557; Pro Grand Penitentiary Cardinal JAMES FRANCIS STAFFORD; Regent Most Rev. GIANFRANCO GIROTTI.

Supreme Tribunal of the Apostolic Signature: Palazzo della Cancelleria, Piazza della Cancelleria 1, 00186 Rome, Italy; tel. (06) 69887520; fax (06) 69887553; Prefect Cardinal AGOSTINO VALLINI; Sec. Rt Rev. VELASIO DE PAOLIS (Titular Bishop of Telepte).

Tribunal of the Roman Rota: Palazzo della Cancelleria, Piazza della Cancelleria 1, 00186 Rome, Italy; tel. (06) 69887502; fax (06) 69887554; Dean (vacant).

Pontifical Councils

Pontifical Council for the Laity: Piazza S. Calisto 16, 00153 Rome, Italy; tel. (06) 69887322; fax (06) 69887214; e-mail vati089@laity.va; advises and conducts research, on lay apostolic initiatives; Pres. Most Rev. STANISLAW RYLKO (Titular Archbishop of Novica); Sec. Rt Rev. JOSEF CLEMENS (Titular Bishop of Segerme).

Pontifical Council for the Promotion of Christian Unity: Via dell'Erba 1, 00193 Rome, Italy; tel. (06) 69884083; fax (06) 69885365; e-mail office1@chrstuni.va; f. 1964; Pres. Cardinal WALTER KASPER; Sec. Rt Rev. BRIAN FARRELL (Titular Bishop of Abitinae).

Pontifical Council for the Family: Piazza S. Calisto 16, 00153 Rome, Italy; tel. (06) 69887243; fax (06) 69887272; e-mail pcf@family.va; Pres. Cardinal ALFONSO LÓPEZ TRUJILLO; Sec. Rt Rev. KARL JOSEF ROMER (Titular Bishop of Colonnata).

Pontifical Council for Justice and Peace: Piazza S. Calisto 16, 00153 Rome, Italy; tel. (06) 69879911; fax (06) 69887205; e-mail pcjustpax@justpeace.va; to promote social justice, human rights, peace and development in needy areas; Pres. Cardinal RENATO RAFFAELE MARTINO; Sec. Rt Rev. GIAMPAOLO CREPALDI (Titular Bishop of Bisarcio).

Pontifical Council 'Cor Unum': Cor Unum, Piazza S. Calisto 16, 00153 Rome, Italy; tel. (06) 69889411; fax (06) 69887301; e-mail corunum@corunum.va; f. 1971; Pres. Most Rev. PAUL JOSEF CORDES (Titular Archbishop of Naissus); Sec. Rt Rev. Mgr KAREL KASTEEL.

THE VATICAN CITY

Pontifical Council for the Pastoral Care of Migrants and Itinerant People: Piazza S. Calisto 16, 00153 Rome, Italy; tel. (06) 69887193; fax (06) 69887111; e-mail office@migrants.va; f. 1970; Pres. Cardinal RENATO RAFFAELE MARTINO; Sec. Most Rev. AGOSTINO MARCHETTO (Titular Archbishop of Astigi).

Pontifical Council for Health Professionals: Via della Conciliazione 3, 00193 Rome, Italy; tel. (06) 69883138; fax (06) 69883139; e-mail opersanit@hlthwork.va; internet www.healthpastoral.org; Pres. Cardinal JAVIER LOZANO BARRAGÁN; Sec. Rt Rev. JOSÉ LUIS REDRADO MARCHITE (Titular Bishop of Ofena).

Pontifical Council for Legislative Texts: Palazzo delle Congregazioni, Piazza Pio XII 10, 00193 Rome, Italy; tel. (06) 69884008; fax (06) 69884710; e-mail vati495@legtxt.va; f. 1984; publishes 'Communicationes' journal twice yearly; Pres. Cardinal JULIÁN HERRANZ CASADO; Sec. Most Rev. BRUNO BERTAGNA (Titular Bishop of Drivasto).

Pontifical Council for Inter-Religious Dialogue: Via dell'Erba 1, 00193 Rome, Italy; tel. (06) 69884321; fax (06) 69884494; e-mail dialogo@interrel.va; f. 1964; Pres. Cardinal PAUL JOSEPH JEAN POUPARD; Sec. Most Rev. PIER LUIGI CELATA (Titular Archbishop of Doclea).

Pontifical Council for Culture: Piazza S. Calisto 16, 00153 Rome, Italy; tel. (06) 69893811; fax (06) 69887368; e-mail cultura@cultr.va; merged with Pontifical Council for Dialogue with Non-Believers in 1993; promotes understanding and dialogue between the Church and both the arts and non-believers; Pres. Cardinal PAUL JOSEPH JEAN POUPARD; Sec. Fr BERNARD ARDURA.

Pontifical Council for Social Communications: Palazzo S. Carlo, 00120 Città del Vaticano; tel. (06) 69883197; fax (06) 69885373; e-mail pccs@vatican.va; f. 1948; to examine the relationship between the media and religious affairs; manages all radio, TV, film and photographic work in the Vatican; Pres. Most Rev. JOHN PATRICK FOLEY (Titular Archbishop of Neapolis); Sec. Rt Rev. RENATO BOCCARDO (Titular Bishop of Acquapendente).

Pontifical Commissions and Committees

Pontifical Commission for the Cultural Patrimony of the Church: Palazzo della Cancelleria Apostolica, Piazza della Cancelleria 1, 00186 Rome, Italy; tel. (06) 69887556; fax (06) 69887567; e-mail pcbcc@pcchc.va; f. 1988; Pres. Rt Rev. MAURO PIACENZA (Titular Bishop of Victoriana); Sec. Rev. Prof. CARLO CHENIS.

Pontifical Biblical Commission: Palazzo della Congregazione per la Dottrina della Fede, Piazza del S. Uffizio 11, 00193 Rome, Italy; tel. (06) 69884886; e-mail pcombiblica@cfaith.va; Prefect Cardinal WILLIAM JOSEPH LEVADA; Sec. Rev. Fr KLEMENS STOCK.

Pontifical Commission of Sacred Archaeology: Palazzo del Pontificio Istituto di Archeologia Cristiana, Via Napoleone III 1, 00185 Rome, Italy; tel. (06) 4465610; fax (06) 4467625; e-mail pcomm.arch@arcsacra.va; internet www.vatican.va/roman_curia; Pres. Rt Rev. MAURO PIACENZA (Titular Bishop of Victoriana); Sec. Prof. FABRIZIO BISCONTI.

Pontifical Commission 'Ecclesia Dei': Palazzo della Congregazione per la Dottrina della Fede, Piazza del S. Uffizio 11, 00120 Città del Vaticano; tel. (06) 69885213; fax (06) 69883412; e-mail eccdei@ecclsdei.va; Pres. Cardinal DARÍO CASTRILLÓN HOYOS; Sec. Mgr CAMILLE PERL.

Pontifical Commission for Latin America: Palazzo di San Paolo, Via della Conciliazione 1, 00193 Rome, Italy; tel. (06) 69883131; fax (06) 69884260; e-mail pcal@latinamer.va; Pres. Cardinal GIOVANNI BATTISTA RE; Vice-Pres. Most Rev. LUIS ROBLES DÍAZ (Titular Archbishop of Stefaniaco).

International Theological Commission: Palazzo della Congregazione per la Dottrina della Fede, Piazza del S. Uffizio 11, 00193 Rome, Italy; tel. (06) 69884727; Prefect Cardinal WILLIAM JOSEPH LEVADA; Sec.-Gen. Fr LUIS LADARIA.

Pontifical Committee for International Eucharistic Congresses: Piazza S. Calisto 16, 00153 Rome, Italy; tel. and fax (06) 69887366; e-mail eucharistcongress@org.va; internet www.vatican.va/roman_curia/pont-committees/eucharist-congr/index_it.htm; Pres. Cardinal JOZEF TOMKO; Sec. Rev. Fr FERDINAND PRATZNER.

Pontifical Committee of Historical Sciences: Palazzo delle Congregazioni, Piazza Pio XII 3, 00193 Rome, Italy; tel. (06) 69884618; fax (06) 69873014; e-mail semeraro@ups.urbe.it; Pres. Mgr WALTER BRANDEMÜLLER; Sec. Rev. Prof. COSIMO SEMERARO.

Archives of the Second Vatican Council: c/o Archivio Segreto Vaticano, 00120 Città del Vaticano; tel. (06) 69883314; fax (06) 69885574; e-mail asv@asv.va; Dir Fr SERGIO PAGANO.

Commission for Lawyers: Palazzo della Cancelleria, Piazza della Cancelleria 1, 00186 Rome, Italy; tel. (06) 69887523; fax (06) 698887557; f. 1988; Pres. Cardinal MARIO FRANCESCO POMPEDDA.

Disciplinary Commission of the Roman Curia: Palazzo delle Congregazioni, Piazza Pio XII 10, 00120 Città del Vaticano; tel. (06) 69884008; fax (06) 69884710; e-mail vati494@legtxt.va; Pres. Cardinal JULIÁN HERRANZ CASADO.

Offices

Apostolic Chamber: Palazzo Apostolico, 00120 Città del Vaticano; tel. (06) 69883554; e-mail kkasteel@corunum.va; Chamberlain of the Holy Roman Church Cardinal EDUARDO MARTÍNEZ SOMALO; Vice-Chamberlain Most Rev. PAOLO SARDI (Titular Archbishop of Sutri); Dean Rt Rev. KAREL KASTEEL.

Administration of the Patrimony of the Holy See: Palazzo Apostolico, 00120 Città del Vaticano; tel. (06) 69893403; fax (06) 69883141; e-mail apsa-ss@apsa.va; f. 1967; Pres. Cardinal ATTLIO NICORA; Sec. Most Rev. CLAUDIO MARIA CELLI (Titular Archbishop of Civitanova).

Labour Office of the Apostolic See: Via della Conciliazione 1, 00193 Rome, Italy; tel. (06) 69884449; fax (06) 69883800; e-mail ulsa1@ulsa.va; Pres. Cardinal FRANCESCO MARCHISANO.

Prefecture for the Economic Affairs of the Holy See: Palazzo delle Congregazioni, Largo del Colonnato 3, 00193 Rome, Italy; tel. (06) 69884263; fax (06) 69885011; f. 1967; Pres. Cardinal SERGIO SEBASTIANI; Sec. Most Rev. FRANCO CROCI (Titular Bishop of Potenza Picena).

Prefecture of the Papal Household: 00120 Città del Vaticano; tel. (06) 69883114; fax (06) 69885863; f. 1967; responsible for domestic administration and organization; Prefect Most Rev. JAMES MICHAEL HARVEY (Titular Archbishop of Memphis).

Office of the Liturgical Celebrations of the Supreme Pontiff: Palazzo Apostolico, 00120 Città del Vaticano; tel. (06) 69883253; fax (06) 69885412; Master of Pontifical Liturgical Celebrations Most Rev. PIERO MARINI (Titular Archbishop of Martirano).

Holy See Press Office: Palazzo dei Propilei, Via dei Corridori 32, 00193 Rome, Italy; tel. (06) 69892425; fax (06) 69883053; internet www.vatican.va; Dir Dr JOAQUÍN NAVARRO-VALLS; Vice-Dir Fr CIRO BENEDETTINI.

Central Statistical Office of the Church: Palazzo Apostolico, 00120 Città del Vaticano; tel. (06) 69883493; fax (06) 69883816; Dir Mgr VITTORIO FORMENTI.

Pontifical Administration of the Patriarchal Basilica of San Paolo Fuori-le-Mura: 00120 Città del Vaticano; tel. (06) 5410194; fax (06) 54074049; e-mail spbasilica@org.va; Archpriest Most Rev. ANDREA CORDERO DE MONTEZEMOLO; Sec. Rt Rev. LUIGI RUCO.

Diplomatic Representation

DIPLOMATIC MISSIONS IN ROME ACCREDITED TO THE HOLY SEE

Albania: Via Silla 7/1, 00192 Rome, Italy; tel. (06) 39754085; fax (06) 39733150; e-mail ambalbvatican@libero.it; Ambassador ZEF BUSHATI.

Angola: Palazzo Odeschalchi, Piazza SS. Apostoli 81, 00166 Rome, Italy; tel. (06) 69190650; fax (06) 69788483; Ambassador ARMINDO FERNANDES DO ESPÍRITO SANTO VIEIRA.

Argentina: Via del Banco di Santo Spirito 42, 00186 Rome, Italy; tel. (06) 68801701; fax (06) 6879021; e-mail emba.argentina@flashnet.it; Ambassador CARLOS LUIS CUSTER.

Australia: Via Paola 24/10, 00186 Rome, Italy; tel. (06) 6877688; fax (06) 6896255; internet www.embassy.gov.au/va; Ambassador ANNE PLUNKETT.

Austria: Via Reno 9, 00198 Rome, Italy; tel. (06) 8416262; fax (06) 8543058; e-mail vatikan-ob@bmaa.gv.at; Ambassador Dr HELMUT TÜRK.

Belgium: Via Giuseppe de Notaris 6A, 00197 Rome, Italy; tel. (06) 3224740; fax (06) 3226042; e-mail vatican@diplobel.be; Ambassador BENOÎT CARDON DE LICHTBUER.

Bolivia: Via di Porta Angelica 15/2, 00193 Rome, Italy; tel. (06) 6874191; fax (06) 6874193; e-mail embolivat@rdn.it; Chargé d'affaires a.i. WALTER RICO FRONTAURA.

Bosnia and Herzegovina: Piazzale le Clodio 12/11, 00195 Rome, Italy; tel. (06) 39742411; fax (06) 39742484; e-mail embvavat@tin.it; Ambassador MIROSLAV PALAMETA.

Brazil: Via della Conciliazione 22, 00193 Rome, Italy; tel. (06) 6875252; fax (06) 6872540; e-mail embaixada@vatemb.it; internet www.vatemb.it; Ambassador VERA BARROUIN MACHADO.

Bulgaria: Via Ferdinando Galiani 63, 00191 Rome, Italy; tel. (06) 36307712; fax (06) 3292987; e-mail vladimirgradev@yahoo.it; Ambassador VLADIMIR NIKOLAEV GRADEV.

Canada: Palazzo Pio, Via della Conciliazione 4D, 00193 Rome, Italy; tel. (06) 68307316; fax (06) 68806283; e-mail vatcn@international.gc.ca; Ambassador DONALD W. SMITH.

THE VATICAN CITY

Chile: Piazza Risorgimento 55/18–19, 00192 Rome, Italy; tel. (06) 6861232; fax (06) 6874992; e-mail echileva@uni.net; Ambassador Máximo Pacheco Gómez.

China (Taiwan): Via della Conciliazione 4D, 00193 Rome, Italy; tel. (06) 68136206; fax (06) 68136199; e-mail taiwan@embroc.it; Ambassador Chu-seng Tou.

Colombia: Via Cola di Rienzo 285/4B, 00192 Rome, Italy; tel. (06) 3211681; fax (06) 3211703; e-mail estasede@minrelext; Ambassador Guillermo León Escobar Herrán.

Congo, Democratic Republic: Via del Castro Pretorio 28/2, 00185 Rome, Italy; tel. (06) 45447860; Chargé d'affaires a.i. Edouard Kambembo Ngunza.

Congo, Republic: Rome, Italy; Ambassador Pierre-Claver Akouala.

Costa Rica: Via del Corso 47/4, 00186 Rome, Italy; tel. and fax (06) 3215528; e-mail embcr.vaticano@iol.it; Ambassador Javier Guerra Laspiur.

Côte d'Ivoire: Via Sforza Pallavicini 11, 00193 Rome, Italy; tel. (06) 6877503; fax (06) 6867925; e-mail ambco.va@flashnet.it; Ambassador Kouamé Benjamin Konan.

Croatia: Via della Conciliazione 44, 00193 Rome, Italy; tel. (06) 6877000; fax (06) 6877003; e-mail velrhvat@tin.it; Ambassador Emilio Marin.

Cuba: Via Aurelia 137/5A, 00165 Rome, Italy; tel. (06) 39366680; fax (06) 636685; e-mail cuba.ssede@libero.it; Ambassador Raúl Roa Kouri.

Czech Republic: Via Crescenzio 91/1B, 00193 Rome, Italy; tel. (06) 6874694; fax (06) 99701582; e-mail vatican@embassy.mzv.cz; internet www.mzv.cz/vatican; Ambassador Jajtner Pavel.

Dominican Republic: Lungotevere Marzio 3, 00186 Rome, Italy; tel. and fax (06) 6864084; e-mail embajadardss@tiscali.it; Ambassador Rafael Marion-Landais.

Ecuador: Via di Porta Angelica 64, 00193 Rome, Italy; tel. (06) 6897179; fax (06) 68892786; e-mail mecuadorsantasede@ecuamss.it; Ambassador Francisco Salazar.

Egypt: Piazza della Città Leonina 9, 00193 Rome, Italy; tel. (06) 6865878; fax (06) 6832335; e-mail ambegyptvatican@tiscali.it; Ambassador Nevine Simaika Halim Abdalla.

El Salvador: Via Panama 22/2, 00198 Rome, Italy; tel. (06) 8540538; fax (06) 85301131; e-mail embasalssede@iol.it; Ambassador Francisco Soler.

France: Villa Bonaparte, Via Piave 23, 00186 Rome, Italy; tel. (06) 42030900; fax (06) 42030968; e-mail ambfrssg@tin.it; internet www.france-vatican.org; Ambassador Bernard Kessedjian.

Gabon: Piazzale Clodio 12, 00195 Rome, Italy; tel. (06) 39721584; fax (06) 39724847; Ambassador Désiré Koumba.

Germany: Via di Villa Sacchetti 4–6, 00197 Rome, Italy; tel. (06) 809511; fax (06) 80951227; internet www.vatikan.diplo.de; Ambassador Dr Gerhard Westdickenberg.

Greece: Via Giuseppe Mercalli 6, 00197 Rome, Italy; tel. (06) 8070786; fax (06) 8079862; e-mail ambasciatedigr@tuttopmi.it; Ambassador Stavros Likidis.

Guatemala: Piazzale Gregorio VII 65A, 00165 Rome, Italy; tel. (06) 6381632; fax (06) 39376981; e-mail embsantasede@minex.gob.gt; Ambassador Juan Gavarrete Soberón.

Haiti: Via de Villa Patrizi 5B, 00161 Roma, Italy; tel. (06) 44242749; fax (06) 44236637; Chargé d'affaires a.i. Patrick Saint-Hilaire.

Honduras: Via Boezio 45, 00192 Rome, Italy; tel. and fax (06) 6876051; e-mail honvati@fastwebnet.it; Ambassador Alejandro Emilio Valladares Lanza.

Hungary: Piazza Girolamo Fabrizio 2, 00161 Rome, Italy; tel. (06) 4402167; fax (06) 4402312; Ambassador Gabór Erdödy.

Indonesia: Piazzale Roberto Ardigò 42, 00142 Rome, Italy; tel. (06) 5940441; fax (06) 5417931; e-mail indonesia.vat@agora.stm.it; internet www.kbrivatikan.org; Ambassador Bambang Prayitno.

Iran: Via Bruxelles 57, 00198 Rome, Italy; tel. (06) 8450443; e-mail chalac@libero.it; Ambassador Mahdi Fardi Zadeh.

Iraq: Via della Camilluccia 355, 00135 Rome, Italy; tel. (06) 3014508; fax (06) 35506416; e-mail ftkemb@iraqmofamail.net; Ambassador Albert Edward Ismail Yelda.

Ireland: Villa Spada, Via Giacomo Medici 1, 00153 Rome, Italy; tel. (06) 5810777; fax (06) 5895709; Ambassador Philip McDonagh.

Israel: Via Michele Mercati 12, 00197 Rome, Italy; tel. (06) 36198690; fax (06) 36198616; e-mail info-vat@holysee.mfa.gov.il; internet vatican.mfa.gov.il; Ambassador Oded Ben-Hur.

Italy: Palazzo Borromeo, Viale delle Belle Arti 2, 00196 Rome, Italy; tel. (06) 3264881; fax (06) 3201801; e-mail amb.scv@esteri.it; Ambassador Giuseppe Balboni Acqua.

Japan: Via Virgilio 30, 00193 Rome, Italy; tel. (06) 6875828; fax (06) 68807543; Ambassador Gunkatsu Kano.

Lebanon: Via di Porta Angelica 15, 00193 Rome, Italy; tel. (06) 6833512; fax (06) 6833507; Ambassador Assi Naji Abi.

Libya: Via Orazio 31B, 00193 Rome, Italy; tel. (06) 97605051; fax (06) 45433476; Sec. of the People's Bureau Abdulhafed Gaddur.

Lithuania: Via G. G. Porro 4, 00197 Rome, Italy; tel. (06) 8078259; fax (06) 8078291; e-mail amb.va@urm.lt; internet va.urm.lt; Ambassador Algirdas Saudargas.

Luxembourg: Via Casale di S. Pio V 20, 00165 Rome, Italy; tel. (06) 660560; fax (06) 66056309; Ambassador Georges Santer (resident in Luxembourg).

Macedonia, former Yugoslav Republic: Via di Porta Cavalleggeri 143, 00165 Rome, Italy; tel. (06) 635878; fax (06) 634826; e-mail emb-mac-holysee@libero.it; Ambassador Bartolomej Kajtazi.

Mexico: Via Ezio 49, 00192 Rome, Italy; tel. (06) 3230360; fax (06) 3230361; e-mail embamex-s.sede@mclink.it; internet portal.sre.gob.mx/vaticano; Ambassador Luis Felipe Bravo Mena.

Monaco: Largo Nicola Spinelli 5, 00198 Rome, Italy; tel. (06) 8414357; fax (06) 8414507; e-mail ambmonacovat@virgilio.it; Ambassador Jean-Claude Michel.

Morocco: Via delle Fornaci 203, 00165 Rome, Italy; tel. (06) 39388398; fax (06) 6374459; e-mail sifamavat@pronet.it; Ambassador Ali Achour.

Netherlands: Piazza della Città Leonina 9, 00193 Rome, Italy; tel. (06) 6868044; fax (06) 6879593; e-mail vat@minbuza.nl; Ambassador Monique P. A. Frank.

Nicaragua: Via Luigi Luciani 42/1, 00197 Rome, Italy; tel. (06) 32600265; fax (06) 3207249; e-mail embanicsantasede@tin.it; Ambassador Dr Armando Luna Silva.

Panama: Largo di Torre Argentina 11/28, 00186 Rome, Italy; tel. (06) 68809764; fax (06) 68809812; e-mail embapass@tiscalinet.it; Chargé d'affaires a.i. Javier Francisco Torres González.

Paraguay: Via Alpinismo 24, 4° int 1, Rome, Italy; tel. (06) 39751368; fax (06) 39745063; e-mail pyssede@mclink.it; Ambassador Geronimo Narvaez Torres.

Peru: Via di Porta Angelica 63, 00193 Rome, Italy; tel. (06) 68308535; fax (06) 6896059; e-mail embaperuva@tin.it; internet xoomer.virgilio.it/embaperuva; Ambassador José Pablo Morán Val.

Philippines: Via Paolo VI 29, 00193 Rome, Italy; tel. (06) 68308020; fax (06) 6834076; e-mail vaticanpe@philamsee.mysam.it; Ambassador Leonida L. Vera.

Poland: Via dei Delfini 16/3, 00186 Rome, Italy; tel. (06) 6990958; fax (06) 6990978; e-mail polamb.wat@agora.stm.it; Ambassador Hanna Suchocka.

Portugal: Villa Lusa, Via S. Valentino 9, 00197 Rome, Italy; tel. (06) 8077012; fax (06) 8084634; e-mail embportugalvatican@tiscalinet.it; Ambassador João Alberto Bacelar da Rocha Páris.

Romania: Via Panama 92, 00198 Rome, Italy; tel. (06) 8541802; fax (06) 8554067; e-mail ambvatican@libero.it; Ambassador Mihail Dobre.

Russia: Via della Conciliazione 10, 00193 Rome, Italy; tel. (06) 6877078; fax (06) 6877168; Ambassador Vitaly Litvin.

San Marino: Piazza G. Winckelmann 14, 00162 Rome, Italy; tel. (06) 86321798; fax (06) 8610814; e-mail amb-sanmarino@libero.it; Ambassador Giovanni Galassi.

Senegal: Via dei Monti Parioli 51, 00197 Rome, Italy; tel. (06) 3218692; fax (06) 3203624; e-mail senvat@iol.it; Ambassador Félix Oudiane.

Serbia and Montenegro: Via dei Monti Parioli 20, 00197 Rome, Italy; tel. (06) 3200099; fax (06) 3204530; e-mail ambscg.vat@flashnet.it; Ambassador Dr Darko Tanasković.

Slovakia: Via dei Prati della Farnesina 57, 00194 Rome, Italy; tel. (06) 33221132; fax (06) 33219582; e-mail slovakemvat@libero.it; Ambassador Dagmar Babčanová.

Slovenia: Via della Conciliazione 10, 00193 Rome, Italy; tel. (06) 6833009; fax (06) 68307942; e-mail vva@mzz-dkp.gov.si; Ambassador Dr Ludvik Toplak.

Spain: Palazzo di Spagna, Piazza di Spagna 57, 00187 Rome, Italy; tel. (06) 6784351; fax (06) 6784355; e-mail ambespvat@mail.mae.es; Ambassador Francisco Vázquez (designate).

Turkey: Via Lovanio 24/1, 00198 Rome, Italy; tel. (06) 8550454; fax (06) 8543986; Ambassador Osman Durak.

Ukraine: Via A. G. Barrili 68A, Int. 5, 00152 Rome, Italy; tel. (06) 39378800; fax (06) 45439216; e-mail emb_va@mfa.gov.ua; Ambassador Dott. Grygorii Khoruzhy Fokovych.

United Kingdom: Osborne House, Via XX Settembre 80A, 00187 Rome, Italy; tel. (06) 42204000; fax (06) 42204205; internet www.britishembassy.gov.uk/vatican; Ambassador Francis Martin-Xavier Campbell.

# THE VATICAN CITY

USA: Villa Domiziana, Via delle Terme Deciane 26, 00153 Rome, Italy; tel. (06) 46743428; fax (06) 5758346; internet http://vatican.usembassy.gov; Ambassador FRANCIS ROONEY.

Uruguay: Via Antonio Gramsci 9/14, 00197 Rome, Italy; tel. (06) 3218904; fax (06) 3613249; e-mail uruvati@tin.it; Ambassador DANIEL PÉREZ DE CASTILLO.

Venezuela: Via Antonio Gramsci 14, 00197 Rome, Italy; tel. (06) 3225868; fax (06) 36001505; e-mail evidano@iol.it; Ambassador IVAN GUILLERMO RINCÓN URDANETA.

Ecclesiastical Organization

The organization of the Church consists of:
  (1) Patriarchs, Archbishops and Bishops in countries under the common law of the Church.
  (2) Abbots and Prelates 'nullius dioceseos'.
  (3) Vicars Apostolic and Prefects Apostolic in countries classified as Missionary and under Propaganda, the former having Episcopal dignity.

The population of the world adhering to the Roman Catholic faith, according to official estimates, was 1,086m. in 2003, of whom 50% lived in the Americas, 26% in Europe and 13% in Africa.

Among the Pope's official titles until early 2006, when Pope Benedict XVI decided no longer to use it, was that of Patriarch of the West. There are five other Patriarchates of the Latin Rite—Jerusalem, the West Indies, the East Indies, Lisbon and Venice. The Eastern Catholic Churches each have Patriarchs: Alexandria for the Coptic Rite, Babylon for the Chaldean Rite, Cilicia for the Armenian Rite, and Antioch for the Syrian, Maronite and Melkite Rites.

At 31 December 2004 there were 2,755 residential sees—13 patriarchates, two senior archbishoprics, 526 metropolitan archbishoprics, 76 archbishoprics and 2,138 bishoprics. Of the 2,062 titular sees (92 metropolitan archbishoprics, 91 archbishoprics and 1,879 bishoprics), 1,058 are filled by bishops who have been given these titles, but exercise no territorial jurisdiction. Other territorial divisions of the Church include 49 prelacies, 12 territorial abbacies, seven apostolic administrations, 26 exarchates of the Eastern Church, 78 apostolic vicariates, 45 apostolic prefectures and 11 missions 'sui iuris'.

The Press

Acta Apostolicae Sedis: Periodical Dept, Libreria Editrice Vaticana, 00120 Città del Vaticano; tel. (06) 69883529; fax (06) 39884716; e-mail mariasic2@publish.va; internet www.libreriaetitricevaticana.com; f. 1909; official bulletin issued by the Holy See; monthly, with special editions on special occasions; the record of Encyclicals and other Papal pronouncements, Acts of the Congregations and Offices, nominations, etc; circ. 6,000.

Annuario Pontificio: Libreria Editrice Vaticana, Via del Tipografia, 00120 Città del Vaticano; tel. (06) 69883493; fax (06) 69885088; e-mail ufoimenti@statistica.va; official year book edited by Central Statistical Office; Dir Mgr VITTORIO FORMENTI.

L'Osservatore Romano: Via del Pellegrino, 00120 Città del Vaticano; tel. (06) 69883461; fax (06) 69883675; e-mail ornet@ossrom.va; internet www.vatican.va/news_services/or/home_ita.html; f. 1861; an authoritative daily newspaper in Italian; its special columns devoted to the affairs of the Holy See may be described as semi-official; the news service covers religious matters and, in a limited measure, general affairs; weekly editions in Italian, French, Spanish, Portuguese, German, English, monthly edition in Polish; Editor-in-Chief Prof. MARIO AGNES; Man. Editor CARLO DE LUCIA; circ. (Italian daily) 20,000.

Pro Dialogo: Via dell' Erba 1, 00193 Rome, Italy; tel. (06) 69884321; fax (06) 69884494; e-mail dialogo@interrel.va; three per year; publ. by the Pontifical Council for Inter-Religious Dialogue; Editor Most Rev. FELIX A. MACHADO.

Statistical Yearbook of the Church: c/o Secretariat of State, 00120 Città del Vaticano; tel. (06) 69883655; fax (06) 69885088; Dir Mgr VITTORIO FORMENTI.

NEWS AGENCY

Agenzia Internazionale FIDES: Palazzo di 'Propaganda Fide', Via di Propaganda 1C, 00187 Rome, Italy; tel. (06) 69880115; fax (06) 69880107; e-mail fides@fides.va; internet www.fides.org; f. 1926; handles news of missions throughout the world and publishes a weekly bulletin in six languages (circ. 3,000), provides a daily news service by e-mail; Dir LUCA DE MATA.

Publishers

Biblioteca Apostolica Vaticana: Cortile del Belvedere, 00120 Città del Vaticano; tel. (06) 69879411; fax (06) 69884795; e-mail bav@vatlib.it; internet www.vatican.va/library_archives/vat_library/index_it.htm; f. 1451; philology, classics, history, catalogues; Librarian of the Holy Roman Church Cardinal JEAN-LOUIS TAURAN; Prefect Rev. RAFFAELE FARINA.

Libreria Editrice Vaticana: Via della Tipografia, 00120 Città del Vaticano; tel. (06) 69885003; fax 69884716; e-mail lev@publish.va; internet www.libreriaeditricevaticana.com; f. 1926; religion, philosophy, literature, art, Latin philology, history; Pres. Mgr. GUISEPPE SCOTTI; Dir Rev. CLAUDIO ROSSINI.

Tipografia Vaticana (Vatican Press): Via della Tipografia, 00120 Città del Vaticano; tel. (06) 69883506; fax (06) 69884570; e-mail tipvat@tipografia.va; f. 1587; religion, theology, education, juveniles, natural and social sciences; prints Acta Apostolicae Sedis and L'Osservatore Romano; Dir-Gen. Rev. ELIO TORRIGIANI.

Broadcasting and Communications

RADIO

Radio Vaticana was founded in 1931 and situated within the Vatican City. A transmitting centre, inaugurated by Pius XII in 1957, is located at Santa Maria di Galeria, about 20 km north-west of the Vatican. Under a special treaty between the Holy See and Italy, the site of this centre, which covers 420 ha, enjoys the same extra-territorial privileges as are recognized by international law for the diplomatic headquarters of foreign states.

The station operates an all-day service, normally in 37 languages, but with facilities for broadcasting liturgical and other religious services in additional languages, including Latin.

The purpose of the Vatican Radio is to broadcast papal teaching, to provide information on important events in the Roman Catholic Church, to express the Catholic point of view on problems affecting religion and morality, but above all to form a continuous link between the Holy See and Roman Catholics throughout the world.

Radio Vaticana: Palazzo Pio, Piazza Pia 3, 00193 Rome, Italy; tel. (06) 69883551; fax (06) 69883237; e-mail dirgen@vatiradio.va; internet www.vaticanradio.org; f. 1931; Dir-Gen. Rev. Fr FEDERICO LOMBARDI (SJ); Administrative and Tech. Dir ALBERTO GASBARRI (SJ); Dir of Programmes Rev. Fr ANDREJ KOPROWSKI (SJ).

TELEVISION

Centro Televisivo Vaticano (Vatican Television Centre): Via del Pellegrino, 00120 Città del Vaticano; tel. (06) 69885467; fax (06) 69885192; e-mail vati119@ctv.va; f. 1983; produces and distributes religious programmes; Pres. Dott. EMILIO ROSSI; Dir-Gen. Fr FREDERICO LOMBARDI.

Finance

Istituto per le Opere di Religione (IOR): 00120 Città del Vaticano; tel. (06) 69883354; fax (06) 69883809; f. 1887; renamed in 1942; oversees the distribution of capital designated for religious works; its assets are believed to lie between US $3,000m. and $4,000m; it takes deposits from religious bodies and Vatican residents; administrative changes, announced in 1989, involved the appointment of a commission of five cardinals and of a Board of Superintendence comprising five financial experts; Pres. Prof. ANGELO CALOIA; Dir-Gen. Comm. LELIO SCALETTI; Commission mems Cardinals ANGELO SODANO, JOZEF TOMKO, ADAM JOSEPH MAIDA, JUAN SANDOVAL IÑIGUEZ, EDUARDO MARTÍNEZ SOMALO.

Lay Employees' Association

In 1989 Pope John Paul II agreed to establish a Labour Council to settle any disputes between the Holy See and its lay employees.

Associazione Dipendenti Laici Vaticani (Association of Vatican Lay Workers): Arco del Belvedere, 00120 Città del Vaticano; tel. (06) 69885343; fax (06) 69884400; f. 1979; aims to safeguard the professional, legal, economic and moral interests of its members; Sec.-Gen. ALESSANDRO CANDI; mems 2,000.

Transport

There is a small railway (862 m) which runs from the Vatican into Italy. It began to operate in 1934 and now carries supplies and goods. There is also a heliport used by visiting heads of state and Vatican officials.

VENEZUELA

Introductory Survey

Location, Climate, Language, Religion, Flag, Capital

The Bolivarian Republic of Venezuela lies on the north coast of South America, bordered by Colombia to the west, Guyana to the east and Brazil to the south. The climate varies with altitude from tropical to temperate; the average temperature in Caracas is 21°C (69°F). The language is Spanish. There is no state religion, but some 84% of the population is Roman Catholic. The national flag (proportions 2 by 3) has three horizontal stripes of yellow, blue and red, with eight five-pointed white stars, arranged in a semi-circle, in the centre of the blue stripe. The state flag has, in addition, the national coat of arms (a shield bearing a gold wheat sheaf, a panoply of swords, an indigenous bow and arrow quiver, a machete, flags and a lance, and a white running horse in its three divisions, flanked by branches of laurel and palm and with two cornucopias at the crest) in the top left-hand corner. The capital is Caracas.

Recent History

Venezuela was a Spanish colony from 1499 until 1821 and, under the leadership of Simón Bolívar, achieved independence in 1830. The country was governed principally by dictators until 1945, when a military-civilian coup replaced Isaías Medina Angarita by Rómulo Betancourt as head of a revolutionary junta. Col (later Gen.) Marcos Pérez Jiménez seized power in December 1952 and took office as President in 1953. He remained in office until 1958, when he was overthrown by a military junta under Adm. Wolfgang Larrazábal. Betancourt was elected President in the same year.

A new Constitution was promulgated in 1961. Three years later President Betancourt became the first Venezuelan President to complete his term of office. Dr Raúl Leoni was elected President in December 1963. Supporters of former President Pérez staged an abortive military uprising in 1966. Dr Rafael Caldera Rodríguez became Venezuela's first Christian Democratic President in March 1969. He achieved some success in stabilizing the country politically and economically, although political assassinations and abductions committed by underground organizations continued into 1974. At elections in December 1973 Carlos Andrés Pérez Rodríguez, candidate of Acción Democrática (AD), the main opposition party, was chosen to succeed President Caldera. The new Government invested heavily in agriculture and industrial development, creating a more balanced economy, and also undertook to nationalize important sectors. The presidential election of December 1978 was won by the leader of the Partido Social-Cristiano (Comité de Organización Política Electoral Independiente—COPEI), Dr Luis Herrera Campíns, who took office in March 1979.

In 1981 a deteriorating economic situation provoked social unrest and a succession of guerrilla attacks. At a presidential election conducted in December 1983, Dr Jaime Lusinchi, the candidate of the AD, was elected with 57% of the votes cast. The AD also won the majority of seats in the Congreso Nacional; Lusinchi assumed power in February 1984.

At presidential and legislative elections conducted in December 1988, AD candidate Carlos Andrés Pérez Rodríguez became the first former President to be re-elected (he previously held office in 1974–79). However, the AD lost its overall majority in the Congreso Nacional. Following his inauguration in February 1989 President Pérez implemented a series of adjustments designed to halt Venezuela's economic decline. These measures, which included increases in the prices of petrol and public transport, provoked rioting throughout the country in late February. The Government introduced a curfew and suspended various constitutional rights in order to quell the disturbances, but it was estimated that some 246 people had died during the protests. In early March the curfew was revoked, and all constitutional rights were restored, after wages had been increased and the prices of some basic goods were 'frozen'.

In May 1989 popular opposition to the Government's austerity programme became co-ordinated by the country's largest trade union, the Confederación de Trabajadores de Venezuela (CTV), which organized a 24-hour general strike (the first for 31 years) in favour of the introduction of pro-labour reforms. However, in July, despite its growing dissatisfaction with the stabilization plan then in progress, the CTV signed an agreement with the Government and the business sector to promote national harmony and to support the continuation of economic adjustment policies that had been agreed with the IMF in June.

In May 1991 a controversial new labour law came into effect, providing for a severance benefit scheme and a social security system. In the second half of that year a series of widespread demonstrations and strikes were staged to protest against monthly increases in the price of petrol, or to demand, *inter alia*, wage increases, the reintroduction of price controls on basic goods, and the suspension of planned public-sector redundancies. The protesters often clashed with security forces and there were several fatalities.

On 4 February 1992 an attempt to overthrow the President by rebel army units was defeated by armed forces loyal to the Government. The rebels, identified as members of the 'Movimiento Bolivariano Revolucionario 200' (MBR-200), attempted to occupy the President's office, the Miraflores Palace, and his official residence but were forced to capitulate. Simultaneous rebel action in the cities of Maracay, Valencia and Maracaibo ended when one of the leaders of the coup, Lt-Col Hugo Rafael Chávez Frías, broadcast an appeal for their surrender. More than 1,000 soldiers were arrested, and 33 officers were subsequently charged. A number of constitutional guarantees were immediately suspended, and press and television censorship was imposed to exclude coverage of Chávez, who had received considerable passive popular support. The rebels' stated primary reasons for staging the insurrection were the increasing social divisions and uneven distribution of wealth resulting from government economic policy, and widespread corruption in public life. In what was widely perceived as an attempt to appease disaffected sectors of society, immediately following the attempted coup Pérez authorized a 50% increase in the minimum wage and a 30% increase in the pay of middle-ranking officers of the armed forces. He also announced plans to bring forward a US $4,000m. social project, aimed at improving health care, social welfare and education.

In March 1992 Pérez announced a series of proposed political and economic reforms, including the introduction of legislation for immediate reform of the Constitution. In addition, the President announced the suspension of increases in the price of petrol and electricity, and the reintroduction of price controls on a number of basic foodstuffs and on medicine. In that month, in an effort to broaden the base of support for his Government, Pérez appointed two members of COPEI to the Council of Ministers. Full constitutional rights were finally restored in April. Nevertheless, widespread protests against government austerity measures and alleged official corruption continued in September and October. A series of bomb attacks, attributed to the rebel movements Los Justicieros de Venezuela and the Fuerzas Bolivarianos de Liberación (an organization claiming to have links with MBR-200), were directed at the residences of allegedly corrupt senior politicians.

On 27 November 1992 a further attempt by rebel members of the armed forces to overthrow the President was suppressed by forces loyal to the Government. The attempted coup, led by senior air force and navy officers, was reported to have been instigated by members of MRB-200. A videotaped statement by the imprisoned Lt-Col Chávez, transmitted from a captured government-owned television station, urged Venezuelans to stage public demonstrations in support of the rebels. Principal air force bases were seized, and rebel aircraft attacked the presidential palace and other strategically important installations. The Government introduced a state of emergency and suspended the Constitution. Sporadic fighting continued into the following day, but by 29 November order had been restored and some 1,300 rebel members of the armed forces had been arrested. President Pérez rejected demands from the press and opposition parties for his resignation. The curfew imposed during the coup was ended at the beginning of December, and further constitutional rights were restored later in the month.

Popular discontent with the Government was reflected further in regional and municipal elections held on 6 December 1992, which resulted in significant gains for COPEI as well as revealing increasing support for the left-wing Movimiento al Socialismo (MAS) and La Causa Radical (La Causa R), whose candidate, Aristóbulo Istúriz, was elected mayor of Caracas. In March 1993 the Supreme Court annulled the rulings of an extraordinary summary court martial, which had been established by presidential decree to try those implicated in the attempted coup of November 1992, on the grounds that the court was unconstitutional. Those sentenced by the court were to be retried by an ordinary court martial.

In May 1993 an extraordinary joint session of the Congreso Nacional voted to endorse a Supreme Court ruling that sufficient evidence existed for Pérez to be prosecuted on corruption charges. The charges concerned allegations that Pérez, and two former government ministers, had, in 1989, embezzled US $17m. from a secret government fund. Pérez was subsequently suspended from office and, in accordance with the terms of the Constitution, replaced by the President of the Senado, Octavio Lepage, pending the election by the Congreso Nacional of an interim President who would assume control until the expiry of the presidential term in February 1994, should Pérez be found guilty. On 5 June the Congreso Nacional elected Ramón José Velásquez, an independent senator, as interim President. Velásquez immediately undertook a broad-ranging reorganization of the Council of Ministers. In August the Congreso Nacional approved legislation enabling Velásquez to introduce urgent economic and financial measures by decree in order to address the growing economic crisis. In late August a special session of the Congreso Nacional voted in favour of the permanent suspension from office of Pérez, regardless of the outcome of the legal proceedings being conducted against him. (In May 1994 Pérez was arrested and imprisoned, pending trial by the Supreme Court on charges of corruption.)

On 5 December 1993 the presidential and legislative elections proceeded peacefully. Dr Rafael Caldera Rodríguez, the candidate of a newly formed party, the Convergencia Nacional (CN), was elected President (having previously held office in 1969–74). However, the CN and its electoral ally, the MAS, secured only minority representation in the Congreso Nacional. Caldera took office in February 1994. In that month the AD and the COPEI established a legislative pact using their combined majority representation in the Congreso Nacional in order to gain control of the major legislative committees. In response, Caldera warned that he would dissolve the legislature and organize elections to a Constituent Assembly should the government programme encounter obstructions in the Congreso Nacional. Also in February, in an attempt to consolidate relations with the armed forces, Caldera initiated proceedings providing for the release and pardon of all those charged with involvement in the coup attempts of February and November 1992.

In June 1994 the Government announced that it was to assume extraordinary powers, in view of the deepening economic crisis and the virtual collapse of the banking sector. Six articles of the Constitution were suspended concerning guarantees including freedom of movement and freedom from arbitrary arrest and the right to own property and to engage in legal economic activity. The Government also announced the introduction of price controls and a single fixed exchange rate, in order to address the problems of a rapidly depreciating currency and depleted foreign exchange reserves. Later in the month Caldera issued a decree placing the financial system under government control. Of those banks affected by the crisis, 10 were closed permanently; the majority of those still operational were to be returned to private control. In July the Congreso Nacional voted to restore five of the six constitutional guarantees suspended by the Government in June. Despite protest, the Government promptly reintroduced the suspensions. Later that month, however, the legislative opposition, with the exception of La Causa R, which withdrew from the legislature in protest, endorsed emergency financial measures, including an extension of price controls and the strengthening of finance-sector regulation, which were presented by the Government as a precursor to the restoration of full constitutional guarantees.

In March 1995 the arrest of some 500 alleged subversives (including activists of the MBR-200) by the security forces prompted demonstrations in the capital in support of demands for the release of those detained and in opposition to the deployment of the National Guard to patrol Venezuela's cities. In July the constitutional guarantees were restored, except in border areas with Brazil, in light of continued criminal activity there. In September 1997 the Congreso conferred extraordinary powers to enact legislation by an 'enabling law' ('ley habilitante') on President Caldera, in order to facilitate the implementation of emergency economic measures designed to reduce the huge fiscal deficit and to accelerate social security reforms.

In May 1996 former President Pérez was found guilty by the Supreme Court of misuse of public funds, although he was acquitted of charges of embezzlement. He was sentenced to two years and four months under house arrest, of which he had already served two years. In July the Senado voted to deny Pérez the seat-for-life in that chamber to which former Presidents of the country were normally entitled. In April 1998 Pérez was charged with misappropriation of public funds during his time in office, and was placed under house arrest pending full investigation of the charges. At legislative elections conducted in November (see below), however, he was successfully elected to the Senado, and was therefore entitled to parliamentary immunity from prosecution.

The legislative elections of 8 November 1998 were won by the Polo Patriótico, an alliance of small, mainly left-wing parties led by the Movimiento V República (MVR). The MVR had been founded in the previous year by the leader of the attempted coup of February 1992, Lt-Col (retd) Hugo Rafael Chávez Frías; its electoral success widely considered to reflect the popular rejection of apparent corruption in the country's major political parties. Proyecto Venezuela (PRVZL), the party created to support the presidential candidacy of the independent Henrique Salas Römer, also performed well. Success at the concurrent gubernatorial elections was shared equally between the Polo Patriótico and AD, who each secured approximately one-third of the governorships.

In the light of the MVR's success in the legislative poll, prior to the presidential election AD and COPEI withdrew their support for their respective candidates and united in support of Salas Römer, hoping to forestall the loss of their long-standing political predominance. However, Chávez, who had styled himself as a radical left-wing populist, promising social revolution and constitutional reform, was elected President on 6 December 1998, with 56% of the votes cast, ahead of Salas Römer, who received the support of some 40% of voters.

Chávez immediately announced plans for elections to a Constituent Assembly to draft a new constitution, and requested congressional permission to employ the 'ley habilitante' to implement an extensive restructuring of public administration and a comprehensive economic recovery programme. Chávez was inaugurated as President on 2 February 1999 and a new Council of Ministers was installed. At the end of February Chávez announced details of an ambitious emergency social improvement plan (the Plan Bolívar 2000) to rehabilitate public property and land through voluntary civil and military action. Such pledges (together with a promise that the armed forces would not be used against the civilian population) prompted a series of rural and urban public land occupations, none of which was forcibly ended.

In April 1999, following prolonged negotiation and compromise, Chávez received congressional endorsement of his proposed use of the 'ley habilitante'. On 25 April a national referendum, organized to ascertain levels of popular support for the convening of a Constituent Assembly and the regulations governing the election of such a body, demonstrated 82% support for the Assembly and 80% support for Chávez's proposals for electoral procedures. (The successful endorsement of the proposals was, however, qualified by the 60% rate of voter abstention.) Elections to the National Constituent Assembly (ANC) in late July resulted in an outright victory for Polo Patriótico, which won 120 out of the 131 seats. The leadership of COPEI and of AD subsequently resigned. The ANC was formally inaugurated on 3 August and by late August had assumed most functions of the opposition-controlled Congreso; the Congreso itself was put into recess indefinitely. In response, the opposition accused the Government of establishing a *de facto* dictatorship. Chávez justified the control of the legislature, executive and judiciary as necessary in order to eradicate corruption and implement social reforms. A Judicial Emergency Commission was appointed in August with the task of investigating the notoriously corrupt judicial system. (By November 1999 200 judges had been dismissed or suspended.) In response, the Supreme Court President resigned. On 9 September the ANC and the Congreso signed an agreement of political coexistence that guaranteed the full functioning of the legislative branch from

2 October until a new constitution entered into force. However, relations between the Government and the Congreso were further strained when Chávez ignored congressional objections to the 2000 budget proposal and asked the ANC to approve it instead.

The draft of the new Constitution was signed by the ANC on 19 November 1999 and was approved by 71% of the popular vote in a referendum held on 15 December. The low rate of voter participation (only 46%) was largely blamed on torrential rain in much of the country (which resulted in the deaths of 30,000 and left a further 200,000 homeless in the central state of Vargas). The 350-article Constitution, which renamed the country the Bolivarian Republic of Venezuela, was promulgated on 30 December. It extended the President's term from five to six years, eliminated the Senate, permitted more state intervention in the economy, reduced civilian supervisory powers over the military, guaranteed the Government's oil monopoly and strengthened minority rights. The Government's political opponents opposed the Constitution because of its centralization of power in the executive branch. The Constitution also promoted public participation by giving the electorate the right to remove elected officials from office by referendum and to annul all but a handful of key laws with an absolute majority. The monitoring of such election processes was to be carried out by an independent National Electoral Council (Consejo Nacional Electoral—CNE). The Constitution also granted far-reaching social security and labour benefits, including the reduction of the working week to 44 hours, which was strongly opposed by business leaders. The Congreso of the Republic was officially dissolved on 4 January 2000. A new post of executive Vice-President was created, and on 24 January Chávez appointed Isaías Rodríguez (ANC Vice-President) to the position. In the same month the ANC appointed many of Chávez's nominees to head state institutions, ranging from the Tribunal Supremo de Justicia to the Central Bank, and including the Ombudsman, the Attorney-General and the Comptroller-General (national auditor). There was criticism that they were appointed without wider consultation and that they were all close associates of the President.

New elections for the President, governors, legislators and mayors, as stipulated under the new Constitution, were scheduled for 28 May 2000. The ANC was dissolved in January after it formally delegated its powers to a newly created 21-member Legislative Commission, which was designated as an interim body until the formation of a new Asamblea Nacional. For the first time in the country's history, the military were authorized to vote. Francisco Arias Cárdenas, Governor of the state of Zulia, and one of the four commanders who had led the abortive coup against President Carlos Andrés Pérez, was the main presidential challenger to Chávez. On 25 May, three days before voting was scheduled to take place, the Tribunal Supremo de Justicia suspended the elections, citing technical faults with the electronic voting system. Elections for the President, national legislators and governors were eventually held on 30 July, separate from the local elections, which were postponed until December. Despite the poor economic situation, popular support for the President, especially from the poorest sections of society, remained strong: Chávez won 59.7% of the valid votes cast in the presidential poll, compared with the 37.5% of the ballot polled by Arias and the 2.7% secured by Claudio Fermín (a former mayor of Caracas and ANC member). At the concurrent election to the new, 165-seat Asamblea Nacional, the ruling MVR secured a majority of 93 seats. The AD came second with 32 seats, Salas Römer's PRVZL gained eight seats, MAS won six seats, while the once powerful COPEI secured only five seats. However, the MVR's 93 seats fell short of the three-fifths' majority required to appoint members of the judiciary and the Attorney-General and Comptroller-General. In gubernatorial elections the MVR-led Polo Patriótico alliance dominated, narrowly gaining control of 14 regional executives. Chávez was sworn in as President on 16 August. His new administration was largely unchanged from the previous one. The Asamblea Nacional was convened for the first time in the same month.

In November 2000 Chávez's powers were further enhanced when the Asamblea approved (despite all opposition parties voting against it) a 'ley habilitante', allowing the President to decree, without legislative debate, a wide range of laws (from public finance to land reform) for one year. In the same month the legislature also passed controversial legislation that assigned the power to appoint important government posts, such as Attorney-General, public ombudsman and senior judges, to a 15-member congressional committee that was dominated by members of the ruling party. Also in November, a government proposal to hold a referendum on whether the opposition-controlled CTV trade union should be suspended until new leadership elections could be held, also received parliamentary approval. Chávez accused the CTV leadership of corruption and undemocratic behaviour while his critics accused him of trying to eradicate a powerful opposition faction. In the previous month members of Fedepetrol, the petroleum workers' union, had gone on strike to demand a higher daily rate of pay. Their action proved successful and strikes by other unions swiftly followed. The trade unions declared the proposed referendum to be unconstitutional, but the Tribunal Supremo de Justicia rejected their arguments and the referendum proceeded on 3 December. In the event, the proposal to suspend trade union leaders for 180 days was approved by 65% of the vote, but the result was undermined by a very low rate of voter participation (23%). The MVR also performed well in municipal elections, held on the same day, although these were also affected by a high abstention rate.

In early February 2001 José Vicente Rangel became the first civilian to be appointed Minister of National Defence, to the consternation of many within the armed forces. However, tensions were eased the following day, when the President appointed Gen. Luis Amaya Chacón to the newly created post of Commander of the Armed Forces, effectively removing Rangel from the chain of military command.

In March 2001 a preliminary report by the Comptroller-General alleged widespread corruption within the Chávez administration's social programme, the Plan Bolívar 2000. In May thousands of petroleum and steel workers went on strike to demand recognition of trade union rights. By late November the Chávez administration had antagonized both the labour and business sectors sufficiently for them to find common cause. Earlier that month it was confirmed, amid government allegations of fraud and electoral malpractice, that Carlos Ortega had won the CTV leadership election, thus frustrating Chávez's efforts to establish a pro-Government trade union umbrella organization. The CTV allied itself with the country's largest business association, Fedecámaras (Federación Venezolana de Cámaras y Asociaciones de Comercio y Producción), to call for a nation-wide general strike. Fedecámaras was protesting against a recently decreed series of 49 laws (passed using the 'ley habilitante', thereby bypassing legislative scrutiny); these measures included land-reform legislation allowing the Government to expropriate land it deemed unproductive, and a hydrocarbons law, which increased royalties on the petroleum industry. The CTV leaders objected to the hydrocarbons law, claiming that it threatened foreign investment and jobs. In the same month thousands of AD supporters marched on the Asamblea Nacional to demand the resignation of the President. A one-day general strike paralysed the country on 11 December and garnered support from a broad range of sectors.

In January 2002 Chávez replaced his Vice-President, Adina Bastidas, with his conspirator in the 1992 military coup attempt, Diosdado Cabello. Another participant in the 1992 coup attempt, Rámon Rodríguez Chacín, was appointed Minister of the Interior and Justice, while later in the month another former army colleague, Francisco Usón, was named Minister of Finance. The cabinet reshuffle was interpreted by many as a move to the left that would increase political instability in the country. Also in February, four military officials, in separate statements, publicly demanded that Chávez resign, leading to further anti-Government protests and counter-demonstrations in support of the Government. In the same month, in the face of increasing economic uncertainty, the Government abandoned the fixed currency exchange regime and allowed the bolívar to float freely, in an attempt to halt mass capital flight. The bolívar subsequently lost nearly 19% of its value against the US dollar.

In early March 2002 business leaders, trade union leaders and representatives of the Catholic Church signed a pact calling for the installation of a government of national unity, and more transparency in government, as well as action against poverty and corruption. At the same time, industrial unrest continued to escalate. Following the appointment of a new management board of the state petroleum company Petróleos de Venezuela, SA (PDVSA), several thousand PDVSA managers marched through Caracas in protest; the managers claimed that the appointments were politically motivated. The demonstrators were supported by Fedepetrol, the petroleum workers' trade union, as well as by Fedecámaras. As petroleum production and exports began to be severely affected by a five-week slow-down staged by managers and workers, on 9 April a 48-hour general strike was organized by the CTV and Fedecámaras. It was subsequently announced that the strike would continue indefinitely, and on 11 April more than 150,000 people marched on the presidential palace to demand Chávez's resignation. In the subsequent clashes outside the Miraflores palace between protesters, government supporters and the security forces, 20 people were killed and more than 100 injured.

On 12 April 2002 a group of senior military officers announced that President Chávez had resigned amid allegations that pro-Government loyalists had fired on opposition protesters. It later emerged that Chávez had, in fact, refused to resign and that, in effect, a military coup had taken place. The military conspirators appointed Pedro Carmona, the President of Fedecámaras, interim President, while Chávez was held incommunicado. On assuming power, Carmona immediately dissolved the Asamblea Nacional, the Tribunal Suprema de Justicia and pronounced Chávez's Bolivarian Constitution to be null and void. The removal from office by the military of an elected head of state was immediately condemned by many Governments in the region; however, in contrast, the US Administration of George W. Bush blamed the crisis on Chávez and refused to call his ousting from power a coup (see below). Thousands of pro-Chávez and pro-democracy supporters immediately took to the streets to demand Chávez's reinstatement, while many senior military officers also expressed their continued loyalty to the deposed President. In the face of threats by officers loyal to Chávez to attack the presidential palace, Carmona immediately resigned; Vice-President Cabello was sworn in as interim President on 13 April, and Chávez returned to the Miraflores palace within hours and, in a televised ceremony, resumed his presidential powers, less than two days after his ouster.

On reassuming the presidency, as a gesture of reconciliation, Chávez announced the resignation of the disputed PDVSA board of directors (Alí Rodríguez Araque, the Secretary-General of the Organization of the Petroleum Exporting Countries (OPEC, see p. 344) and former Minister of Energy and Mines, was subsequently appointed President of PDVSA). He also declared that there would be no persecution of those who had supported his removal from office. Nevertheless, Carmona and 100 military personnel were arrested. (Carmona escaped from house arrest and was subsequently granted asylum in Colombia.) In late April 2002 the Asamblea Nacional approved the establishment of a Truth Commission to investigate the events surrounding the coup attempt. (In mid-October 2004 eight people, including workers, business leaders and students, were convicted and sentenced to prison sentences of between three and six years for their roles in the uprising of April 2002.)

The country's political and economic situation continued to worsen throughout mid-2002. In August the Supreme Court ruled that there was insufficient evidence to prosecute four senior members of the military who had participated in the failed coup attempt in April. (However, this ruling was overturned in mid-March 2005.) In late October the opposition and its allies in the CTV labour union and Fedecámaras called a one-day strike, intended to force President Chávez to accept early presidential and legislative elections. The strike brought much of Venezuela to a halt, although the country's important oil industry was not seriously affected. On 23 October a group of 14 senior military officers declared themselves in rebellion against the Chávez Government. The men, many of whom had been involved in April's failed coup, occupied a square in eastern Caracas, where they were joined by hundreds of opposition activists. More than 100 junior officers later also expressed their rejection of Chávez's policies and joined the protest. All of the officers involved were subsequently dismissed from the armed forces. In an attempt to find a constitutional solution to the ongoing political crisis, 12 representatives of the opposition and the Government began round-table discussions in early November. The negotiations were chaired by the Secretary-General of the Organization of American States (OAS, see p. 333), César Gaviria Trujillo, and were also attended by representatives of the Carter Center. The talks failed to make any immediate progress, however, and in late November the opposition, the CTV and Fedecámaras announced that a general strike would be held from 2 December to force President Chávez to call fresh elections or submit to a referendum. The general strike lasted a further nine weeks. The vast majority of large businesses and international companies observed the stoppage, although small shopkeepers and public transport continued to operate throughout. The strike had a particularly severe impact on Venezuela's crucial oil industry. The majority of managers and administrative staff at PDVSA staged a walk-out, and the company was obliged to declare *force majeure* on its exports of crude petroleum and petroleum products. The President of PDVSA, Alí Rodríguez Araque, sought to restart the industry by replacing the strikers with new staff, contract workers and retired employees. He eventually dismissed 18,000 of PDVSA's previous 33,000 full-time work-force for observing the strike, and production reportedly recovered to pre-strike levels by late March 2003. The strike caused enormous difficulties for the Venezuelan Government, which saw oil revenues collapse, while ordinary Venezuelans suffered from severe shortages of food and other basic products.

In mid-January 2003 President Chávez suspended trading in the national currency, the bolívar, in response to the economic crisis. Early in the following month it was announced that the bolívar was to be 'pegged' to the US dollar, and that price controls were to be introduced on basic food items. None the less, the Government refused to negotiate on the issue of early elections, although discussions between the two sides, suspended at the start of the strike, began once more in late January. The general strike focused international attention on the ongoing crisis in Venezuela, and in late January six countries formed the 'Group of Friends of Venezuela', to support a peaceful solution to the crisis. The Group was composed of the USA, Brazil, Chile, Mexico, Portugal and Spain, despite President Chávez's call for the inclusion of countries more sympathetic to his revolutionary project, such as Cuba.

In early February 2003 the opposition parties, CTV and Fedecámaras announced an end to the two-month general strike after failing to secure any concessions from the Government. The opposition, which had combined under the Co-ordinadora Democrática (CD) grouping, presented on 2 February an estimated 4m. signatures in support of early elections. The Government did not respond to the petition, and several days later the Venezuelan authorities announced new exchange rate rules, which critics alleged were designed to punish companies that had participated in the recent strike. On 18 February the Government and opposition representatives at the OAS-sponsored negotiations signed an agreement to seek to reduce political tension in Venezuela. The pact was immediately thrown into question, however, when the following day police arrested the President of Fedecámaras, Carlos Fernández Pérez, on charges including treason, relating to his role in organizing the recent general strike. A warrant was also issued for his fellow strike leader, the President of the CTV, Carlos Ortega, who went into hiding and later obtained political asylum in Costa Rica. (Ortega was expelled from that country in March 2004. In December 2005 Ortega was found guilty of insurrection, incitement and use of false documents and sentenced to 15 years' imprisonment.) The opposition immediately accused President Chávez of authoritarianism and observers expressed fears that a further deterioration in the political situation was likely. On 20 March an appeals court ordered the release without charge of Fernández Pérez, ruling that there was no evidence against him. At the same time, charges against six senior PDVSA managers who had supported the strike were also struck down.

On 11 April 2003, following further OAS-sponsored negotiations, the Government and opposition agreed in principle that a referendum on the Chávez Government could be held if the opposition succeeded in collecting 2.4m. signatures in support of a vote. The agreement was finalized in the following month. The signatures collected by the opposition were to be verified by the CNE. However, since the Asamblea Nacional was unable to agree on appointments to the electoral body, responsibility passed, as stipulated by the Constitution, to the Supreme Tribunal, which appointed on 27 August a new head of the electoral authority, as well as four other board members. One week earlier opposition parties had submitted a 2.4m.-signature petition to the CNE demanding a recall referendum. However, in early September the new board of the electoral authority ruled that the petition was not valid, as some of the signatures had been collected more than six months before the date on which a referendum could be held. Furthermore, in late September the CNE issued a new and more stringent set of referendum guidelines, which stipulated, notably, that, in the case of a binding presidential recall referendum, a President would then only be removed from office if a greater proportion of the electorate voted against him than had supported him in the most recent election (in the case of Chávez in the 2000 ballot, this would be greater than 59.7% of the votes). Also, if there were insufficient valid signatures collected (20% of the electorate, equivalent to some

2.4m. voters), no further recall petitions would be permitted during that President's term of office.

On 1 October 2003 the CD presented a new recall referendum request to the CNE. In response, the MVR announced that it intended to compile more than 40 recall petitions on opposition deputies and state governors. The CNE ruled that any recall referendums would be restricted to members of the Asamblea Nacional and federal Government. In mid-October the CNE announced that signature-gathering for the recall of 37 opposition politicians would take place on 21–24 November, while that for the presidential (plus 33 MVR deputies) recall would be held one week later.

The CNE was scheduled to announce the validity of both sets of petitions by the end of December 2003. However, a series of technical problems and doubts over the validity of some petitions led to delays, provoking civil unrest in which eight protesters were killed in February 2004. Later that month the CNE announced that there would be a further delay, to allow about 1.1m. signatures to be revalidated. To this effect, in mid-March signatories of the petitions were to present themselves at electoral centres nation-wide to verify their signatures. Finally, following a rechecking of signatures that had technical irregularities at the end of May, in June the CNE ruled that the number of valid signatures collected was sufficient to force a presidential recall referendum. The Government accepted this ruling and the poll was duly held on 15 August. The motion to recall the President was defeated, with 3,989,008 votes (40.74% of those voting) in favour of Chávez's removal from office and 5,800,629 (59.25%) against. There was a voter turn-out of 70.0%. Despite assertions by the Carter Center, the OAS and other international observers that the ballot had been conducted fairly, the CD disputed the result, claiming that large-scale electoral fraud had been perpetrated by the Government. In late September the CNE rejected the CD's appeal against the referendum result, citing a lack of evidence. The CD alliance suffered further setbacks following the withdrawal of three parties (Causa R, Alianza Bravo Pueblo and Primero Justicia).

Immediately following the referendum in August 2004 President Chávez effected several changes to his Council of Ministers. Notably, Lt (retd) Jesse Chacón Escamillo replaced Lucas Rincón as Minister of the Interior and Justice. In the following month Chávez created two new portfolios—for food and for the mass economy. In late November Chávez unexpectedly dismissed Jesús Arnoldo Pérez as foreign minister, appointing Alí Rodríguez Araque, hitherto President of PDVSA, to the post. In early December Nelson Merentes Díaz was moved from the Ministry of Economic and Social Development to Finance, succeeding Tobías Nóbrega.

Meanwhile, in July 2004 the Supreme Tribunal ratified a law that prohibited journalists from working if they did not hold a recognized qualification or belong to a recognized professional association. In mid-December Chávez promulgated a law imposing new broadcasting restrictions, ostensibly to protect children from unsuitable material and to prevent incitements to breaches of public order. Also in that month the Asamblea Nacional approved amendments to the criminal code which introduced prison sentences for those judged to have publicly insulted the President or other representatives of the state. The reforms, which took effect in mid-March 2005, were strongly criticized by a broad range of opposition groups, foreign governments and non-governmental organizations as a threat to civil liberties. In mid-April a journalist of the newspaper *El Nuevo País*, Patricia Poleo, was convicted of defaming interior minister Chacón Escamillo and sentenced to six months' imprisonment.

Nevertheless, popular support for the Chávez Government was demonstrated by the results of the gubernatorial elections of 31 October 2004. Candidates of the MVR and its allies were successful in 20 of the country's 22 states.

On 18 November 2004 state prosecutor Danilo Anderson, who had been investigating the failed coup of April 2002, with a view to bringing charges against those involved, was assassinated in Caracas. In late November a former police commissioner of Caracas, Iván Simonovis, was arrested on suspicion of involvement with the murder; two other suspects were killed by police while allegedly resisting arrest. In October 2005 Attorney-General Isaías Rodríguez Díaz accused the US and Colombian intelligence services and Colombian paramilitaries of colluding in Anderson's assassination; both countries denied the accusation and cited a lack of supporting evidence. In November Patricia Poleo and three others were named in connection with the case.

In mid-December 2004 the Asamblea Nacional approved the appointment of 12 more judges to the Supreme Tribunal, in addition to the appointment of five replacements, increasing the total number of sitting judges from 20 to 32. The Government justified the measure as necessary for increasing the efficiency of the supreme court, although opposition groups and international human rights agencies criticized it as an attack on the independence of the judiciary.

On 10 January 2005 President Chávez signed a decree initiating a 90-day review process into both the level of productivity on privately owned land and into the validity of its ownership. Local authorities were granted powers to expropriate estates deemed unproductive by the review for redistribution to 'landless' farmers. The number of 'unproductive' estates was estimated at over 500, according to a preliminary government survey published earlier that month. In September President Chávez vowed to accelerate the process of land expropriations. On 1 January 2006 the Government took control of 32 oilfields under private operation, in accordance with its policy of revising all private-sector contracts for hydrocarbon exploitation in order to give the government-owned PDVSA a majority stake.

At elections to the Asamblea Nacional on 4 December 2005 the ruling MVR secured 114 of a total 167 seats, with the remaining seats won by parties allied to the Government. The overwhelming government victory was primarily owing to the boycott of the ballot by the main opposition parties (including the AD, Primero Justicia and Proyecto Venezuela), which claimed that the electronic voting system could not guarantee voters' anonymity. As a result, voter participation was estimated at just 25%. However, observers from the European Union and the OAS declared the elections to be free and transparent.

In 1982 Venezuela refused to renew the 1970 Port of Spain Protocol, declaring a 12-year moratorium on the issue of Venezuela's claim to a large area of Guyana to the west of the Essequibo river, which expired in that year. Venezuela's border garrisons were strengthened and border violations were reported. In 1985 Venezuela and Guyana requested UN mediation in an attempt to resolve their dispute over the Essequibo region. A UN mediator was appointed in late 1989; however, negotiations remained deadlocked and the dispute resurfaced in 1999 when Guyana granted offshore oil concessions in the disputed waters to foreign oil firms. In October Chávez renewed Venezuela's claim to the Essequibo region. The tension escalated in March 2000 when Guyana gave preliminary approval to the installation of a US satellite-launching facility in the disputed area. In March 2004 President Chávez met his Guyanese counterpart, Bharrat Jagdeo; although no progress was made on resolving the dispute, the Venezuelan Government indicated its willingness to 'authorize' Guyanese mineral exploration in Essequibo region.

Venezuela also has a claim to some islands in the Netherlands Antilles, and a territorial dispute with Colombia concerning maritime boundaries in the Gulf of Venezuela. In March 1989 an agreement was reached with Colombia on the establishment of a border commission to negotiate a settlement for the territorial dispute. In March 1990 President Virgilio Barco of Colombia and President Pérez signed the 'San Pedro Alejandrino' document, by which they pledged to implement the commission's proposals. At a meeting of the Presidents of Colombia and Venezuela in Caracas in January 1992, Pérez publicly recognized that Colombia had legitimate territorial rights in the Gulf of Venezuela.

Periodic incursions into Venezuelan territory by Colombian combatants and criminal elements continuously strained relations with Colombia. Despite agreements signed by both countries in 1997 and 2000 to increase co-operation in policing the border area, clashes between the Venezuelan military and Colombian guerrillas were frequent. Tensions were exacerbated in 2000, owing to Chávez's public opposition to the military component of 'Plan Colombia' (Colombia's US-supported anti-drugs strategy) and accusations by Colombia that Venezuela was covertly aiding the guerrilla forces. In November 2000 Colombia briefly recalled its ambassador to Venezuela after a representative of the Fuerzas Armadas Revolucionarias de Colombia—Ejército del Pueblo (FARC—EP) was allowed to speak in the Venezuelan Asamblea Nacional. In March 2001 Venezuela refused to extradite to Colombia a member of a guerrilla group accused of hijacking an aircraft in 1999. Although the right-wing Government of Alvaro Uribe Vélez repeatedly criticized President Chávez for failing to classify the FARC—EP as a terrorist organization, in November there were indications of *rapprochement* following a meeting between the two Presidents to promote

VENEZUELA

bilateral trade and security co-operation. However, the Venezuelan Government continued to demand improvements to border security arrangements, following confrontations with armed Colombian groups in December 2003 and September 2004 that resulted in the deaths of several Venezuelan soldiers. In a public demonstration of amity, Presidents Uribe and Chávez met in Cartagena, Colombia, in early November 2004 to discuss border security and economic co-operation. However, relations were severely strained in mid-December following the arrest by the Colombian authorities of Rodrigo Granda Escobar, the supposed international spokesperson of the FARC—EP. It was subsequently alleged by the Venezuelan Government that Granda, although ultimately arrested in Cúcuta, Colombia, was first kidnapped in Caracas by Venezuelan and Colombian agents in the pay of the Colombian Government and with the collusion of US intelligence services; the Uribe Government initially denied all accusations of wrongdoing and the US Government denied all involvement. In consequence, in January 2005 the Venezuelan ambassador to Colombia was recalled and restrictions on trade and passage between the two countries were imposed by the Chávez Government. Following an expression of regret by the Colombian Government in late January and a visit to Caracas by President Uribe in mid-February, relations between the two countries were normalized. Relations were strengthened in September following the Colombian authorities' refusal of political asylum to seven Venezuelan military officials and one diplomat accused of participating in the failed coup attempt of April 2002. However, in 2005 and early 2006 the Colombian and US Governments repeatedly expressed concern over Venezuela's rapid military expansion, which, it was argued, would upset the military balance of the region.

Following his election in December 1998, President Chávez announced that his administration would seek greater integration in large regional organizations such as CARICOM (see p. 183) and Mercosur (see p. 363). In May 2005 Chávez launched PetroSur, an initiative to promote energy integration and offer preferential prices for petroleum in the Southern Cone region. In September Chávez unveiled similar initiatives for the Andean and Caribbean regions, called PetroAndina and PetroCaribe, respectively.

President Chávez made closer relations with Cuba a priority and in October 2000 Chávez and the Cuban head of state Fidel Castro Ruz signed a co-operation agreement allowing the export of oil to Cuba on the same preferential terms enjoyed by a number of Central American and Caribbean countries. In 2003–04 improved relations between the two countries led to increased Cuban assistance for the Government's social-welfare programmes, and Venezuela continued to support Cuba's integration into regional trade associations.

Venezuela's relations with Mexico deteriorated in November 2005 at the Summit of the Americas in Mar del Plata, Argentina, owing to President Chávez's strident denunciation of an initiative promoted by Mexican President Vicente Fox Quesada for a free trade area of the Americas. The Venezuelan ambassador to Mexico was recalled later that month, as was the Mexican ambassador to Venezuela. Meanwhile, from early 2005 the Mexican authorities accused Venezuela with increasing frequency of failing to police adequately its sea and air ports in order to prevent the transhipment of illegal narcotics, primarily from Colombia, to Mexico. In April 2006 Mexican officials reportedly discovered 5.5 metric tons of cocaine on an aircraft arrived from Venezuela; the ultimate destination of the drugs was believed to be the USA.

The relationship between Venezuela and the USA (the main purchaser of Venezuelan crude petroleum) deteriorated markedly following the election of Chávez. In 2000 Chávez refused to authorize US drugs-surveillance flights over Venezuela. Furthermore, the President's close relationship with Fidel Castro led to further estrangement from the USA. The Venezuelan Government also signed a number of bilateral trade and cultural agreements with the People's Republic of China, India, Iran and Russia in 2001. (Further agreements on energy sector co-operation were signed with China and India in December 2004 and January 2005, respectively, and a bilateral investment agreement worth US $200m. was signed with Iran in February 2006.) Bilateral relations further deteriorated after the US Administration of George W. Bush refused to condemn the short-lived military ouster of Chávez in April 2002. It was subsequently revealed that US officials had met with opposition figures shortly before the failed coup; however, the US Government denied it had encouraged or supported the coup. Venezuela was highly critical of the US-led military campaign against the regime of Saddam Hussain in Iraq from March 2003. Relations with the USA remained hostile in early 2006, owing in large part to Chávez's sustained personal criticism of President Bush and his outspoken rhetoric against US 'imperialism'. In February 2005 the US Secretary of State, Condoleezza Rice, criticized the perceived deterioration of civil liberties in Venezuela. In April Venezuela suspended its military exchange programmes with the USA. In August Chávez suspended co-operation with the US Drug Enforcement Agency (DEA), following its repeated criticism of Venezuela's counter-narcotics policies. None the less, in mid-January 2006 Venezuela agreed to renew some co-operation with the DEA. Also in January, the US Department of State intervened to prevent the sale to Venezuela of Spanish military aircraft worth some US $2,000m., ostensibly on the grounds that the aircraft contained US-built components requiring an export licence. However, in early February it was announced that the sale would proceed despite US opposition. In the same month Venezuela expelled a US naval attaché in Venezuela, Capt. John Correa, accusing him of espionage. The following day the USA expelled a Venezuelan diplomat in response. In early April President Chávez threatened to expel the US ambassador, William Brownfield, accusing him of abusing the principles of diplomatic protection after Brownfield had visited a poor neighbourhood of Caracas and distributed free baseball equipment, an act against which anti-US activists protested violently. Meanwhile, throughout 2005 and early 2006 members of the Government, including President Chávez, repeatedly alleged that the USA was planning to invade Venezuela in order to secure its supply of petroleum; the USA dismissed the allegation as without substance.

Venezuela has observer status in the Non-aligned Movement (see p. 397).

Government

Venezuela is a federal republic comprising 22 states, a Federal District (containing the capital) and 72 Federal Dependencies. Under the 1999 Constitution, legislative power is held by the unicameral Asamblea Nacional (National Assembly). Executive authority rests with the President. The President is elected for six years by universal adult suffrage. The President has extensive powers, and is assisted by a Council of Ministers. Each state has a directly elected executive governor and an elected legislature.

Defence

Military service is selective for two years and six months between 18 and 45 years of age. In August 2005 the armed forces numbered 82,300 men: an army of 34,000, a navy of 18,300 (including an estimated 7,800 marines), an air force of 7,000 and a National Guard of 23,000. In April 2005 President Chávez swore in the General Command of a new army reserve, projected to number some 1.5m. The defence budget for 2004 was 2,400,000m. bolívares.

Economic Affairs

In 2004, according to estimates by the World Bank, Venezuela's gross national income (GNI), measured at average 2002–04 prices, was US $104,957.6m., equivalent to $4,020 per head (or $5,760 per head on an international purchasing-power parity basis). During 1995–2004, it was estimated, the population increased by an annual average of 1.9%, while gross domestic product (GDP) per head decreased, in real terms, at an average of 1.2% per year. Overall GDP increased, in real terms, by an average annual rate of 0.6% in 1995–2004; according to World Bank estimates, GDP grew by 17.3% in 2004.

Agriculture (including hunting, forestry and fishing) contributed a preliminary 4.4% of GDP in 2003 and engaged an estimated 9.8% of the employed labour force in 2002. The principal crops are sugar cane, bananas, maize, rice, plantains, oranges, sorghum and cassava. Cattle are the principal livestock, but the practice of smuggling cattle across Venezuela's border into Colombia has had a severe effect on the livestock sector. According to the World Bank, agricultural GDP increased by an estimated annual average of 0.9% during 1995–2002. The sector's GDP increased, in real terms, by 2.6% in 2001, but declined by 1.7% in 2002.

Industry (including mining, manufacturing, construction and power) contributed a preliminary 50.2% of GDP in 2003 and engaged an estimated 20.9% of the employed labour force in 2002. According to the World Bank, industrial GDP decreased by an annual average of 1.0% during 1995–2002. Sectoral GDP increased, in real terms, by 3.3% in 2001, but decreased by 12.4% in 2002.

Mining and quarrying contributed a preliminary 24.1% of GDP in 2003, but engaged only 0.5% of the employed labour force in 2002. Petroleum production is the most important industry in Venezuela, providing 81.4% of export revenue in 2003. In January 2005 proven reserves totalled 77,200m. barrels. (However, if heavy and extra-heavy crude petroleum reserves are included, Venezuela's total reserves are considerably higher, estimated at some 502,000m. barrels in March 2006.) Aluminium and iron ore are also major sources of export revenue. Venezuela also has substantial deposits of natural gas, coal, diamonds, gold, zinc, copper, lead, silver, phosphates, manganese and titanium. The GDP of the mining sector increased by an average of 2.5% per year in 1995–2001; the sector increased by 4.7% in 2000 and by an estimated 1.1% in 2001.

Manufacturing (including petroleum refining) contributed a preliminary 17.6% of GDP in 2003 and engaged approximately 11.9% of the employed labour force in 2002. The most important sectors were refined petroleum products, food products, transport equipment, industrial chemicals and iron and steel. Manufacturing GDP decreased by an annual average of 3.0% during 1995–2002. The sector's GDP increased, in real terms, by 2.9% in 2001, but declined by 11.0% in 2002.

Energy is derived principally from domestic supplies of petroleum and coal, and from hydroelectric power. Hydroelectric power provided 62% of electricity production in 2003, according to the US Energy Information Administration, with thermal generation supplying the remainder. Imports of mineral fuels comprised 2.0% of the total value of merchandise imports in 2003.

The services sector contributed a preliminary 45.4% of GDP in 2003 and engaged some 69.1% of the employed labour force in 2002. The sector increased by an annual average of 0.5% in 1995–2002. Sectoral GDP increased, in real terms, by 3.1% in 2001, but decreased by 3.0% in 2002.

In 2005 Venezuela recorded a visible trade surplus of US $31,532m., and there was a surplus of $25,359m. on the current account of the balance of payments. In 2003 the principal source of imports (33.0%) was the USA; other major suppliers were Colombia, Brazil, Mexico and Germany. The USA was also the principal market for exports (44.4%) in 2003; other major purchasers were the Netherlands Antilles, the Netherlands, Colombia and Cuba. The principal exports in 2003 were petroleum and related products (81.4%), steel, aluminium and chemical products. The principal imports in 2003 were machinery and transport equipment (35.6%), basic manufactures, and chemicals.

There was projected budgetary deficit of 1,879,100m. bolívares in 2004. Venezuela's total external debt was US $34,851m. at the end of 2003, of which $24,491m. was long-term public debt. In that year the cost of servicing the debt was equivalent to 30.1% of the value of exports of goods and services. In late October 2005 the Minister of Finance, Nelson Merentes Díaz, announced that Venezuela would pay off some $4,500m. of its external debt in 2006. The average annual rate of inflation was 32.8% in 1995–2004. Consumer prices increased by an annual average of 31.1% in 2003 and by 21.8% in 2004. An estimated 12.6% of the labour force were unemployed in July 2005.

Venezuela is a member of the Andean Community of Nations (CAN, see p. 158), the Inter-American Development Bank (IDB, see p. 284), the Latin American Integration Association (Asociación Latinoamericana de Integración—ALADI, see p. 305), the Organization of the Petroleum Exporting Countries (OPEC, see p. 344), the Latin American Economic System (Sistema Económico Latinoamericano—SELA, see p. 386) and the Group of Three (G3, see p. 386). In July 2004 Venezuela became an associate member of Mercosur (see p. 363), and in December 2005 it was accorded the rights of full membership, prior to its formal acceptance scheduled for 2007, once certain legal and economic obligations had been fulfilled. In November 2005, at the Summit of the Americas in Mar del Plata, Argentina, President Chávez discounted the possibility of Venezuela joining a proposed free trade area of the Americas. In mid-April 2006 President Chávez announced his intention to withdraw Venezuela from the CAN. In December 2004 Venezuela was one of 12 countries that were signatories to the agreement, signed in Cusco, Peru, creating the South American Community of Nations (Comunidad Sudamericana de Naciones), intended to promote greater regional economic integration, due to become operational by 2007.

Venezuela's economy is largely dependent on the petroleum sector, which provided some 47.7% of government revenue in 2004, and is therefore particularly vulnerable to fluctuations in the world petroleum market. The Chávez administration, inaugurated in 1999, introduced new pension benefits and health programmes, to be financed by surplus petroleum profits, known as the oil stabilization fund. While there was a large increase in public-sector pay and in pensions in 2000, the non-petroleum private sector stagnated, partly because of an overvalued currency. In an attempt to reduce the growing fiscal deficit, a wide-ranging series of economic measures was approved by decree in November 2001. However, the controversial measures contained in the package (most notably, a hydrocarbons law that increased royalty taxes on the petroleum sector from 16.6% to 30%) led to widespread industrial unrest and political instability, which severely affected petroleum production rates in early 2002. The situation was compounded in February after a controlled devaluation plan was abandoned in favour of a floating exchange rate, in a bid to halt the flight of capital caused by the continuing political unrest. Investor confidence in Venezuela continued to deteriorate following the attempted coup against President Chávez in April 2002 and the protracted industrial and social unrest in early 2003 (see Recent History). After the collapse of the general strike in February 2003, it was announced that the bolívar would be 'pegged' to the US dollar, although at a much-reduced value. Further devaluations of 15.6% and 10.7% were carried out, respectively, in February 2004 and March 2005. Under the Chávez Government increases in petroleum taxes and royalties, combined with the state appropriation, in early January 2006, of 32 privately operated oilfields, was expected further to deter investment. However, the outlook for the country's external debt improved from 2004, as investors exploited bond issues in order to avoid the restrictions on access to foreign currency. Exports rose by an estimated 45% in 2004, owing principally to the sharp rise in world petroleum prices, but also to increased production in the non-petroleum sector. Government spending on social programmes was also reported to have risen considerably. The reserves of the state-run petroleum company's social investment fund were reported to total some US $3,500m. in 2005. In late October of that year President Chávez announced plans to withdraw some US $5,000m. of Venezuela's international reserves, in order to fund further social and infrastructural spending. In 2005 government expenditure reportedly totalled 73,600,000m. bolívares, representing a sharp increase on the previous year's total spending of 51,565,900m. bolívares. Devaluations of the bolívar and the imposition of price and capital controls had failed to curb significantly the persistent high levels of inflation, estimated at 14.4% in 2005. Following a sharp decline in the economy in 2003, of approximately 7.7%, GDP was estimated to have grown dramatically in 2004, by an estimated 17.3%. Owing primarily to continued high prices for petroleum, growth was put at a more modest 9.3% in 2005 and was forecast at 5.6% in 2006.

Education

Education is officially compulsory for 10 years, to be undertaken between six and 15 years of age. Primary education, which is available free of charge, begins at six years of age and lasts for nine years. Secondary education, beginning at the age of 15, lasts for a further two years. In 1996 the total enrolment at primary and secondary schools was equivalent to 83% of the school-age population (males 80%; females 85%). Of children in the relevant age-groups, primary enrolment in 1996 was equivalent to 91% (males 90%; females 93%), while secondary enrolment in that year was equivalent to 40% (males 33%; females 41%). In 2003/04 there were 48 universities. Expenditure by the central Government on education and sport was an estimated 29,601.6m. bolívares in 2004.

Public Holidays

2006: 1 January (New Year's Day), 24 February–1 March (Carnival), 10 March (La Guaira only), 14–17 April (Easter), 19 April (Declaration of Independence), 1 May (Labour Day), 24 June (Battle of Carabobo), 5 July (Independence Day), 24 July (Birth of Simón Bolívar and Battle of Lago de Maracaibo), 4 September (Civil Servants' Day), 12 October (Discovery of America), 24 October (Maracaibo only), 24–25 December (Christmas), 31 December (New Year's Eve).

2007: 1 January (New Year's Day), 16–21 February (Carnival), 10 March (La Guaira only), 6–9 April (Easter), 19 April (Declaration of Independence), 1 May (Labour Day), 24 June (Battle of Carabobo), 5 July (Independence Day), 24 July (Birth of Simón

VENEZUELA

Bolívar and Battle of Lago de Maracaibo), 4 September (Civil Servants' Day), 12 October (Discovery of America), 24 October (Maracaibo only), 24–25 December (Christmas), 31 December (New Year's Eve).

Banks and insurance companies also close on: 6 January (Epiphany), 19 March (St Joseph), Ascension Day (25 May 2006, 17 May 2007), 29 June (SS Peter and Paul), 15 August (Assumption), 1 November (All Saints' Day), and 8 December (Immaculate Conception).

Weights and Measures
The metric system is in force.

Statistical Survey

Sources (unless otherwise stated): Instituto Nacional de Estadística (formerly Oficina Central de Estadística e Informática), Edif. Fundación La Salle, Avda Boyacá, Caracas 1050; tel. (212) 782-1133; fax (212) 782-2243; e-mail ocei@platino.gov.ve; internet www.ine.gov.ve; Banco Central de Venezuela, Avda Urdaneta, esq. de las Carmelitas, Caracas 1010; tel. (212) 801-5111; fax (212) 861-0048; e-mail mbatista@bcv.org.ve; internet www.bcv.org.ve.

Area and Population

AREA, POPULATION AND DENSITY

Area (sq km)	916,445*
Population (census results)	
20 October 1990†	18,105,265
30 October 2001‡	
Males	11,402,869
Females	11,651,341
Total	23,054,210
Population (official postcensal estimates at mid-year)§	
2003	25,673,550
2004	26,127,351
2005	26,577,423
Density (per sq km) at mid-2005	29.0

* 353,841 sq miles.
† Excluding Indian jungle population and adjustment for underenumeration, estimated at 6.7%.
‡ Excluding Indian jungle population, enumerated at 183,143 in a separate census of indigenous communities in 2001. Also excluding adjustment for underenumeration, estimated at 6.7%.
§ Based on results of 2001 census, including Indian jungle population and adjustment for underenumeration.

ADMINISTRATIVE DIVISIONS
(official postcensal estimates, mid-2005)

	Area (sq km)	Population	Density (per sq km)	Capital
Federal District	433	2,073,768	4,789.3	Caracas
Amazonas	177,617	134,594	0.8	Puerto Ayacucho
Anzoátegui	43,300	1,428,269	33.0	Barcelona
Apure	76,500	452,369	5.9	San Fernando
Aragua	7,014	1,617,333	230.6	Maracay
Barinas	35,200	724,331	20.6	Barinas
Bolívar	240,528	1,475,527	6.1	Ciudad Bolívar
Carabobo	4,650	2,155,610	463.6	Valencia
Cojedes	14,800	288,168	19.5	San Carlos
Delta Amacuro	40,200	145,586	3.6	Tucupita
Falcón	24,800	869,269	35.1	Coro
Guárico	64,986	716,896	11.0	San Juan de los Morros
Lara	19,800	1,736,983	87.7	Barquisimeto
Mérida	11,300	811,655	71.8	Mérida
Miranda	7,950	2,765,442	347.9	Los Teques
Monagas	28,900	819,197	28.3	Maturín
Nueva Esparta	1,150	422,668	367.5	La Asunción
Portuguesa	15,200	839,881	55.3	Guanare
Sucre	11,800	889,141	75.4	Cumaná
Táchira	11,100	1,134,710	102.2	San Cristóbal
Trujillo	7,400	685,442	92.6	Trujillo
Vargas	1,497	328,293	219.3	La Guaira
Yaracuy	7,100	573,726	80.8	San Felipe
Zulia	63,100	3,486,850	55.3	Maracaibo
Federal Dependencies	120	1,715	14.3	—
Total	916,445	26,577,423	29.0	—

PRINCIPAL TOWNS
(city proper, estimated population at 1 July 2000)

Caracas (capital)	1,975,787	Mérida	230,101
Maracaibo	1,764,038	Barinas	228,598
Valencia	1,338,833	Turmero	226,084
Barquisimeto	875,790	Cabimas	214,000
Ciudad Guayana	704,168	Baruta	213,373
Petare	520,982	Puerto la Cruz	205,635
Maracay	459,007	Los Teques	183,142
Ciudad Bolívar	312,691	Guarenas	170,204
Barcelona	311,475	Puerto Cabello	169,959
San Cristóbal	307,184	Acarigua	166,720
Maturín	283,318	Coro	158,763
Cumaná	269,428		

BIRTHS, MARRIAGES AND DEATHS*

	Registered live births		Registered marriages		Registered deaths	
	Number	Rate (per 1,000)	Number	Rate (per 1,000)	Number	Rate (per 1,000)
1999	527,888	23.9	90,220	3.8	101,907	4.9
2000	544,416	23.5	91,088	3.8	103,255	4.9
2001	529,552	23.2	81,516	3.3	107,867	5.0
2002	492,678	22.9	73,163	2.9	105,388	5.0
2003	555,614	22.6	74,562	2.9	118,562	5.0
2004	637,799	22.3	74,103	n.a.	114,480	5.0

* Figures for numbers of births and deaths exclude adjustment for underenumeration. Rates are calculated using adjusted data.

2003: Marriages 74,562 (Marriage rate 2.9 per 1,000).

Expectation of life (WHO estimates, years at birth): 74 (males 71; females 77) in 2003 (Source: WHO, *World Health Report*).

VENEZUELA

ECONOMICALLY ACTIVE POPULATION
(household surveys, '000 persons aged 15 years and over)*

	2000	2001	2002
Agriculture, hunting, forestry and fishing	899.5	892.1	949.0
Mining and quarrying	54.6	49.7	47.3
Manufacturing	1,147.0	1,207.1	1,150.3
Electricity, gas and water	59.5	57.7	51.4
Construction	707.5	774.3	775.8
Wholesale and retail trade, restaurants and hotels	2,292.6	2,455.3	2,585.3
Transport, storage and communications	612.1	654.3	703.6
Financing, insurance, real estate business services	455.6	482.2	481.8
Community, social and personal services	2,583.5	2,820.7	2,932.7
Activities not adequately defined	9.7	11.2	21.8
Total employed	8,821.8	9,404.6	9,698.9
Unemployed	1,423.5	1,435.8	1,822.6
Total labour force	10,245.3	10,840.4	11,521.5

*Figures exclude members of the armed forces.
Source: ILO.

2003 ('000 persons aged 15 and over, as at July): Total employed 9,795.3; Unemployed 2,187.1; Total labour force 11,982.4 (males 7,174.0, females 4,808.5).

2004 ('000 persons aged 15 and over, as at July): Total employed 10,204.7; Unemployed 1,844.2; Total labour force 12,048.9 (males 7,301.5, females 4,747.3).

2005 ('000 persons aged 15 and over, as at July): Total employed 10,487.2; Unemployed 1,509.5; Total labour force 11,966.6 (males 7,349.8, females 4,646.9).

Health and Welfare

KEY INDICATORS

Total fertility rate (children per woman, 2003)	2.7
Under-5 mortality rate (per 1,000 live births, 2004)	19
HIV/AIDS (% of persons aged 15–49, 2003)	0.7
Physicians (per 1,000 head, 2001)	1.94
Hospital beds (per 1,000 head, 1996)	1.47
Health expenditure (2002): US $ per head (PPP)	272
Health expenditure (2002): % of GDP	4.9
Health expenditure (2002): public (% of total)	46.9
Access to water (% of persons, 2002)	83
Access to sanitation (% of persons, 2002)	68
Human Development Index (2003): ranking	75
Human Development Index (2003): value	0.772

For sources and definitions, see explanatory note on p. vi.

Agriculture

PRINCIPAL CROPS
('000 metric tons)

	2002	2003	2004
Rice (paddy)	668.2	678.9	974.1
Maize	1,392.0	1,823.2	2,176.2
Sorghum	508.7	614.2	563.3
Potatoes	350.6	321.6	350.1
Cassava (Manioc)	520.7	545.3	511.4
Yautia (Cocoyam)	56.7	42.4	50.0*
Yams	93.2	52.5	69.9
Sugar cane	8,525.8	9,950.1	8,814.2
Coconuts	175.1	194.4	163.6
Oil palm fruit	319.9	313.8	315.0*
Cabbages	61.5	67.8	78.4
Tomatoes	197.0	180.6	196.9
Green chillies and peppers	69.4	74.5	91.4
Dry onions	276.7	276.0	236.3
Carrots	184.6	199.4	184.8
Other vegetables	217.3	219.1*	226.9*
Watermelons	205.5	184.0	257.9

Statistical Survey

—continued	2002	2003	2004
Cantaloupes and other melons	181.6	228.5	232.1
Bananas	590.8	559.8	463.0
Plantains	460.9	438.9	426.3
Oranges	341.6	333.3	374.4
Tangerines, mandarins, etc.	195.0	139.1	144.9
Lemons and limes	85.2	58.2	56.3
Mangoes	73.6	68.7	68.6
Avocados	49.9	46.2	52.4
Pineapples	347.3	340.2	322.8
Papayas	152.7	148.0	131.8
Other fresh fruit*	222.3	224.9	217.8
Coffee (green)	76.9	64.3	71.5

*FAO estimate(s).
Source: FAO.

LIVESTOCK
('000 head, year ending September)

	2002	2003	2004
Horses*	500	500	500
Asses*	440	440	440
Cattle	15,791	15,989	16,232
Pigs	2,825	2,922	3,047
Sheep	512	520	528
Goats	1,251	1,280	1,311
Chickens*	147,000	110,000	110,000

*FAO estimates.
Source: FAO.

LIVESTOCK PRODUCTS
('000 metric tons)

	2002	2003	2004
Beef and veal	428.8	435.2	376.0
Pig meat	118.8	120.2	101.4
Poultry meat	893.2	675.5	685.6
Cows' milk	1,389.3	1,238.2	1,170.4
Cheese	103.1	100.4	111.6
Hen eggs	160.1	147.0	146.5
Cattle hides (fresh)*	47.9	50.2	48.1

*FAO estimates.
Source: FAO.

Forestry

ROUNDWOOD REMOVALS
('000 cubic metres, excl. bark)

	2002	2003	2004
Sawlogs, veneer logs and logs for sleepers	1,227	827	805
Pulpwood	184	231	721
Fuel wood*	3,697	3,745	3,793
Total	5,108	4,803	5,319

*FAO estimates.
Source: FAO.

SAWNWOOD PRODUCTION
('000 cubic metres, incl. railway sleepers)

	2002	2003	2004
Coniferous (softwood)	101	260	845
Broadleaved (hardwood)	263	241	102
Total	364	501	947

Source: FAO.

VENEZUELA

Fishing

('000 metric tons, live weight)

	2001	2002	2003
Capture	411.6	513.8	524.4
Round sardinella	71.2	158.1	141.9
Yellowfin tuna	122.4	127.2	98.1
Ark clams	43.7	44.7	45.9
Aquaculture	16.6	17.9	15.7
Total catch	428.3	531.7	540.2

Note: Figures exclude crocodiles, recorded by number rather than by weight. The number of spectacled caimans caught was: 19,215 in 2001; 20,349 in 2002; 31,636 in 2003.

Source: FAO.

Mining

('000 metric tons, unless otherwise indicated)

	2001	2002	2003
Hard coal	7,685	8,097	7,034
Crude petroleum ('000 barrels)	1,155,075	1,105,793	964,695
Natural gas (million cu metres)*	62,941	61,982	61,657
Iron ore: gross weight	16,902	16,684	17,954
Iron ore: metal content	10,817	11,092	11,936
Nickel ore (metric tons)†	13,600	18,600	20,700
Bauxite	4,585	5,191	5,446
Gold (kilograms)†	9,076	9,465	8,190
Phosphate rock	399	390	260
Salt (evaporated)‡	350	350	350
Amphilbolite	14,230	18,610	3,520
Diamonds (carats): Gem	14,321	45,707	11,080
Diamonds (carats): Industrial	27,826	61,060	23,710

* Figures refer to the gross volume of output. Marketed production (in million cu metres) was: 35,347 in 2001; 33,124 in 2002; 26,060 in 2003.
† Figures refer to the metal content of ores and concentrates.
‡ Estimated production.

Source: US Geological Survey.

Industry

PETROLEUM PRODUCTS
('000 barrels)

	2001	2002	2003*
Motor spirit (petrol)	74,128	68,565	55,000
Kerosene	157	—	125
Jet fuel	32,233	32,113	26,000
Distillate fuel oils	110,642	114,584	92,000
Residual fuel oils	92,914	81,475	65,000

* Estimated production.

Source: US Geological Survey.

Statistical Survey

SELECTED OTHER PRODUCTS
('000 metric tons, unless otherwise indicated)

	2001	2002	2003
Raw sugar*	612	637	736‖
Fertilizers†‡	525	576	n.a.
Cement§	8,700‖	7,000	7,000
Crude steel§	3,814	4,164	3,930
Aluminium§	571	605	601
Electric energy (million kWh)†	85,211	87,406	n.a.

* FAO figures.
† Data from UN Economic Commission for Latin America and the Caribbean.
‡ Including phosphatic, nitrogenous and potassic fertilizers, year beginning 1 July.
§ Data from US Geological Survey.
‖ Estimate.

Finance

CURRENCY AND EXCHANGE RATES

Monetary Units
100 céntimos = 1 bolívar.

Sterling, Dollar and Euro Equivalents (30 December 2005)
£1 sterling = 3,696.92 bolívares;
US $1 = 2,147.00 bolívares;
€1 = 2,532.82 bolívares;
10,000 bolívares = £2.70 = $4.66 = €3.95.

Average Exchange Rate (bolívares per US dollar)
2003   1,606.96
2004   1,891.33
2005   2,089.75

BUDGET
('000 million bolívares, preliminary figures)

Revenue	2002	2003	2004
Tax revenue	11,447.7	15,145.4	26,931.4
Petroleum	990.8	1,967.9	3,802.4
Other tax revenue	10,456.9	13,177.5	23,129.0
Non-tax revenue	12,441.5	16,239.6	22,755.4
Petroleum	10,331.9	13,586.4	19,915.9
Other non-tax revenue	2,109.6	2,653.2	2,839.5
Total revenue	23,889.2	31,384.9	49,686.8

Expenditure	2002	2003	2004
Current expenditure	20,704.2	27,888.0	40,536.1
Wages and salaries	4,507.1	5,709.1	9,496.5
Interest payments	4,950.7	6,300.1	7,061.6
Goods and services	1,740.9	2,064.4	1,906.5
Transfers	9,467.8	13,511.2	22,071.5
Other current expenditure	37.7	303.1	—
Capital expenditure	4,798.7	7,364.8	10,628.7
Acquisition of fixed capital	931.1	2,302.1	560.1
Capital transfers	3,867.6	5,062.7	10,068.5
Extrabudgetary expenditure	1,385.8	1,718.6	155.7
Total expenditure*	26,888.7	36,971.4	51,320.5

* Excluding net lending (preliminary figures): 846.6 in 2002; 315.3 in 2003; 245.4 in 2004.

Source: Central Office of Budget, Caracas.

CENTRAL BANK RESERVES
(US $ million at 31 December)

	2003	2004	2005
Gold (national valuation)	4,632	5,122	5,718
IMF special drawing rights	10	9	5
Reserve position in IMF	478	500	460
Foreign exchange	15,546	17,867	23,454
Total	20,667	23,497	29,637

Source: IMF, *International Financial Statistics*.

VENEZUELA

Statistical Survey

MONEY SUPPLY
('000 million bolívares at 31 December)

	2003	2004	2005
Currency outside banks	4,777.5	6,506.3	8,926.2
Demand deposits at commercial banks	13,651.2	20,036.5	32,393.7
Total (incl. others)	19,055.8	27,927.3	49,291.8

Source: IMF, *International Financial Statistics*.

COST OF LIVING
(Consumer Price Index for Caracas; Base: 2000 = 100)

	2002	2003	2004
Food	149.0	205.2	274.6
Clothing and footwear	114.9	142.9	168.6
Rent	135.9	153.4	168.1
All items (incl. others)	137.8	180.6	219.9

Source: ILO.

NATIONAL ACCOUNTS

National Income and Product
(million bolívares at current prices)

	2001	2002	2003*
Compensation of employees	31,261.0	35,636.6	41,187.3
Net operating surplus	33,024.0	41,474.9	57,035.0
Net mixed income	12,196.8	14,368.3	17,064.9
Domestic primary incomes	76,481.8	91,479.8	115,287.2
Consumption of fixed capital	5,367.0	7,113.0	8,284.6
Gross domestic product (GDP) at factor cost	81,848.8	98,592.8	123,571.9
Taxes on production and imports	7,386.0	9,669.2	12,484.7
Less Subsidies	289.3	421.8	1,839.3
GDP in market prices	88,945.6	107,840.2	134,217.3
Primary incomes received from abroad	1,882.0	1,781.3	2,771.8
Less Primary incomes paid abroad	3,351.0	4,973.0	6,659.2
Gross national income (GNI)	87,476.6	104,648.5	130,329.9
Less Consumption of fixed capital	5,367.0	7,113.0	8,284.6
Net national income	82,109.6	97,535.4	122,045.2
Current transfers from abroad	257.9	335.0	416.9
Less Current transfers paid abroad	365.8	525.6	388.7
Net national disposable income	82,001.7	97,344.9	122,073.4

* Preliminary figures.

Expenditure on the Gross Domestic Product
('000 million bolívares at current prices)

	2001	2002	2003*
Final consumption expenditure	61,502.2	71,767.3	90,772.0
Households	47,993.2	56,775.7	72,275.5
Non-profit institutions serving households	845.6	964.5	1,208.2
General government	12,663.4	14,027.2	17,288.3
Gross capital formation	24,481.5	22,817.8	20,885.0
Gross fixed capital formation	21,389.0	23,643.3	20,943.0
Changes in inventories	3,089.9	-826.6	-58.6
Acquisitions, less disposals, of valuables	2.6	1.0	0.6
Total domestic expenditure	85,983.7	94,585.1	111,657.0
Exports of goods and services	20,222.3	32,819.6	45,344.7
Less Imports of goods and services	17,260.5	19,564.5	22,784.4
GDP in market prices	88,945.6	107,840.2	134,217.3
GDP at constant 1997 prices	42,405.4	38,650.1	35,667.5

* Preliminary figures.

Gross Domestic Product by Economic Activity
('000 million bolívares at current prices)

	2001	2002	2003*
Agriculture, hunting and forestry	3,507.2	3,813.7	5,202.2
Fishing	256.5	335.0	556.0
Mining and quarrying†	12,482.0	20,243.1	31,443.9
Manufacturing‡	15,111.3	17,727.4	22,961.4
Electricity, gas and water	2,075.0	2,508.1	2,757.0
Construction	8,498.6	9,834.1	8,307.3
Wholesale and retail trade; repair of motor vehicles, motorcycles and personal and household goods	7,019.9	8,030.7	10,833.2
Hotels and restaurants	1,581.2	1,788.2	2,303.1
Transport, storage and communications	5,813.9	6,766.9	8,369.6
Financial intermediation	2,213.4	3,019.8	3,646.4
Real estate, renting and business activities	9,739.4	11,216.6	12,039.5
Public administration and defence; compulsory social security	5,065.0	5,456.3	6,451.0
Education	6,682.9	7,626.7	9,016.4
Health and social work	2,837.9	3,209.8	3,849.6
Other community, social and personal services	1,596.3	1,817.1	2,058.8
Private households with employed persons	517.3	594.2	703.0
Sub-total	84,997.8	103,987.7	130,498.4
Less Financial intermediation services indirectly measured	2,172.7	2,883.1	3,539.4
Gross value added in basic prices	82,824.9	101,104.6	126,959.0
Taxes on products	6,402.3	7,078.5	9,066.3
Less Subsidies on products	281.6	342.9	1,808.0
GDP in market prices	88,945.6	107,840.2	134,217.3

* Preliminary figures.
† Includes crude petroleum and natural gas production.
‡ Includes petroleum refining.

BALANCE OF PAYMENTS
(US $ million)

	2003	2004	2005
Exports of goods f.o.b.	27,170	38,748	55,487
Imports of goods f.o.b.	-10,687	-17,318	-23,955
Trade balance	16,483	21,430	31,532
Exports of services	878	1,098	1,334
Imports of services	-3,522	-4,724	-5,416
Balance on goods and services	13,839	17,804	27,450
Other income received	1,729	1,564	4,152
Other income paid	-4,140	-5,449	-6,136
Balance on goods, services and income	11,428	13,919	25,466
Current transfers received	257	180	213
Current transfers paid	-237	-269	-320
Current balance	11,448	13,830	25,359
Direct investment abroad	-1,318	348	-1,460
Direct investment from abroad	2,659	1,518	2,957
Portfolio investment assets	-812	-1,090	-641
Portfolio investment liabilities	-143	-853	3,378
Other investment assets	-4,328	-8,004	-18,851
Other investment liabilities	-1,000	-635	-1,555
Net errors and omissions	-1,052	-2,959	-3,762
Overall balance	5,454	2,155	5,425

Source: IMF, *International Financial Statistics*.

VENEZUELA

External Trade

PRINCIPAL COMMODITIES
(US $ million)

Imports f.o.b.	2001	2002	2003
Food and live animals	1,506.7	1,105.7	1,067.1
Cereals and cereal preparations	467.0	369.0	433.3
Mineral fuels	703.6	312.6	164.1
Petroleum and products	687.7	297.9	153.3
Animal and vegetable oils, fats and waxes	115.7	177.9	253.9
Chemicals and related products	2,315.2	1,821.7	1,694.2
Organic chemicals	459.4	295.5	259.0
Medicinal and pharmaceutical products	610.4	506.5	483.2
Medicaments (incl. vetinary)	477.6	418.9	391.8
Basic manufactures	2,475.1	1,594.1	1,058.2
Iron and steel	607.6	318.9	180.3
Machinery and transport equipment	6,847.4	5,025.1	2,972.1
Power generating equipment and machinery	410.9	287.1	317.6
Machinery specialized for particular industries	546.5	384.8	216.8
General industrial machinery equipment and parts	1,299.2	1,182.3	649.7
Heating and cooling equipment and parts	271.7	442.1	134.4
Telecommunications and sound recording and reproducing equipment	766.7	470.5	314.5
Telecommunications equipment parts and accessories	559.0	385.3	253.4
Other electrical machinery, apparatus, etc.	849.5	600.1	434.6
Road vehicles	2,293.7	1,225.9	590.9
Passenger motor vehicles (except buses)	1,535.6	801.7	261.2
Other transport equipment	222.1	604.6	252.4
Ships, boats and floating structures	139.3	361.9	103.2
Miscellaneous manufactured articles	1,913.3	1,221.7	791.5
Total (incl. others)	16,345.6	11,673.4	8,357.7

Exports f.o.b.	2001	2002	2003
Mineral fuels, lubricants and related materials	21,014.2	18,960.3	20,540.1
Petroleum, petroleum products and related materials	20,758.0	18,681.2	20,320.1
Crude petroleum	14,755.9	18,322.8	20,235.8
Petroleum products, refined	5,980.3	331.3	68.1
Chemicals and related products	944.2	854.2	777.1
Basic manufactures	2,065.8	2,143.3	2,243.7
Iron and steel	789.7	950.8	1,041.3
Aluminium	748.6	719.0	718.4
Total (incl. others)	25,304.3	23,293.3	24,974.3

Source: UN, *International Trade Statistics Yearbook*.

PRINCIPAL TRADING PARTNERS
(US $ million)

Imports f.o.b.	2001	2002	2003
Argentina	226.8	151.4	141.8
Bolivia	178.2	163.5	160.8
Brazil	975.0	755.5	555.5
Canada	473.2	320.2	219.7
Chile	281.9	189.9	135.2
China, People's Republic	335.8	224.8	176.0
Colombia	1,432.3	963.7	713.0
France (incl. Monaco)	302.7	221.7	222.1
Germany	579.0	583.0	347.9
Italy	549.5	505.0	272.1

Imports f.o.b.—continued	2001	2002	2003
Japan	749.2	435.9	194.6
Korea, Republic	352.4	226.3	82.6
Mexico	773.8	536.9	416.3
Netherlands	168.7	125.3	83.7
Netherlands Antilles	368.2	259.2	22.4
Panama	375.8	192.1	123.1
Spain	448.2	319.1	331.1
Switzerland-Liechtenstein	145.7	119.9	91.9
Trinidad and Tobago	41.0	141.4	24.5
United Kingdom	344.9	279.3	235.0
USA	5,572.2	3,845.0	2,754.0
Total (incl. others)	16,435.6	11,673.4	8,357.7

Exports f.o.b.	2001	2002	2003
Brazil	674.9	562.3	259.6
Canada	474.8	289.8	294.7
Colombia	730.7	751.9	650.8
Costa Rica	258.5	294.6	210.4
Cuba	16.2	11.6	642.0
Dominican Republic	715.4	675.2	187.7
Ecuador	211.6	324.0	198.5
India	461.7	355.8	4.4
Mexico	360.9	338.5	376.4
Netherlands	291.7	330.8	2,058.9
Netherlands Antilles	1,543.9	1,520.8	4,140.9
Peru	295.7	197.4	237.7
Spain	426.3	521.5	211.6
Trinidad and Tobago	420.2	317.3	384.3
United Kingdom	191.9	213.5	396.6
USA	14,280.3	13,115.8	11,074.9
Total (incl. others)	25,304.3	23,293.3	24,974.3

Source: UN, *International Trade Statistics Yearbook*.

Transport

RAILWAYS
(traffic)

	1994	1995	1996
Passenger-kilometres (million)	31.4	12.5	0.1
Freight ton-kilometres (million)	46.8	53.3	45.5

Freight ton-kilometres (million): 54.5 in 1997; 79.5 in 1998.

Source: UN Economic Commission for Latin America and the Caribbean.

ROAD TRAFFIC
('000 motor vehicles in use)

	1999	2000	2001
Passenger cars	1,420.0	1,326.2	1,372.0
Commercial vehicles	846.0	1,078.6	1,107.9

Source: UN, *Statistical Yearbook*.

SHIPPING

Merchant Fleet
(registered at 31 December)

	2002	2003	2004
Number of vessels	274	275	286
Total displacement ('000 grt)	865.4	847.0	1,010.9

Source: Lloyd's Register-Fairplay, *World Fleet Statistics*.

VENEZUELA

CIVIL AVIATION
(traffic on scheduled services)

	2001	2002	2003
Kilometres flown (million)	79.7	77.5	50.4
Passengers carried ('000)	4,051.7	5,446.8	3,823.7
Passenger-km (million)	3,680.5	3,301.5	2,042.8
Freight ton-km (million)	30.5	6.6	2.0

Source: UN Economic Commission for Latin America and the Caribbean.

Tourism

ARRIVALS BY NATIONALITY

	2001	2002	2003
Argentina	27,396	15,133	14,108
Belgium	11,798	11,300	7,660
Brazil	18,909	11,022	9,929
Canada	32,982	29,106	20,588
Chile	12,340	6,786	6,345
Colombia	20,029	11,855	10,576
Denmark	10,434	8,636	6,325
France	24,792	18,526	14,362
Germany	67,168	60,426	42,320
Italy	37,421	23,396	20,166
Mexico	13,730	8,722	7,447
Netherlands	56,341	52,310	36,039
Spain	20,060	14,288	11,389
United Kingdom	32,299	26,880	19,624
USA	121,135	80,007	66,711
Total (incl. others)	584,399	431,677	336,974

Tourism receipts (US $ million, incl. passenger transport): 677 in 2001; 484 in 2002; 368 in 2003.

Source: World Tourism Organization.

Communications Media

	2002	2003	2004
Telephones ('000 main lines in use)	2,841.8	2,842.6	3,346.5
Mobile cellular telephones ('000 subscribers)	6,463.6	7,015.7	8,421.0
Personal computers ('000 in use)	1,536	n.a.	2,145
Internet users ('000)	1,274.4	1,549.5	2,312.7

Facsimile machines ('000 in use, 1997): 70.
Radio receivers ('000 in use, 1997, estimate): 10,750.
Television receivers ('000 in use, 2001): 10,750.
Book production (titles, 1997): 3,851*.
Daily newspapers (1996): 86 (estimated average circulation 4,600,000).

* First editions only.

Sources: UNESCO Institute for Statistics; UN, *Statistical Yearbook*; International Telecommunication Union.

Education

(2003/04)

	Institutions	Teachers	Students*
Pre-school	14,857†	59,178	984,224
Basic education:			
grades 1–6	17,521†	172,322	3,449,579
grades 7–9	4,667†	109,437	1,383,891
Further education:			
general	} 3,362† {	56,458	501,243
professional		8,844	68,372
Adult education	2,402	43,660	506,301
Special needs	1,999	8,723	317,687
Universities	48	51,459	626,837
Other higher	120‡	30,664	447,513‡

* Excluding students in out-of-school education: 720,726 in 2003/04.
† Data may be duplicated for institutions where education is offered at more than one level. The total number of pre-school, basic and further educational establishments in 2003/04 was 24,634.
‡ Estimate.

Sources: Ministry of Education and Sport, Caracas; National Council of Universities, Caracas.

Adult literacy rate (UNESCO estimates): 93.0% (males 93.3%; females 92.7%) in 2003 (Source: UN Development Programme, *Human Development Report*).

Directory

The Constitution

The Bolivarian Constitution of Venezuela was promulgated on 30 December 1999.

The Bolivarian Republic of Venezuela is divided into 22 States, one Federal District and 72 Federal Dependencies. The States are autonomous but must comply with the laws and Constitution of the Republic.

LEGISLATURE

Legislative power is exercised by the unicameral National Assembly (Asamblea Nacional). This replaced the bicameral Congreso Nacional (National Congress) following the introduction of the 1999 Constitution.

Deputies are elected by direct universal and secret suffrage, the number representing each State being determined by population size on a proportional basis. A deputy must be of Venezuelan nationality and be over 21 years of age. Indigenous minorities have the right to select three representatives. Ordinary sessions of the Asamblea Nacional begin on the fifth day of January of each year and continue until the fifteenth day of the following August; thereafter, sessions are renewed from the fifteenth day of September to the fifteenth day of December, both dates inclusive. The Asamblea is empowered to initiate legislation. The Asamblea also elects a Comptroller-General to preside over the Audit Office (Contraloría General de la República), which investigates Treasury income and expenditure, and the finances of the autonomous institutes.

GOVERNMENT

Executive power is vested in a President of the Republic elected by universal suffrage every six years, who may serve one additional term. The President is empowered to discharge the Constitution and the laws, to nominate or remove Ministers, to take supreme command of the Armed Forces, to direct foreign relations of the State, to declare a state of emergency and withdraw the civil guarantees laid down in the Constitution, to convene extraordinary sessions of the Asamblea Nacional and to administer national finance.

JUDICIARY

Judicial power is exercised by the Supreme Tribunal of Justice (Tribunal Suprema de Justicia) and by the other tribunals. The Supreme Tribunal forms the highest court of the Republic and the Magistrates of the Supreme Tribunal are appointed by the Asamblea Nacional following recommendations from the Committee for Judicial Postulations, which consults with civil society groups. Magistrates serve a maximum of 12 years.

VENEZUELA

The 1999 Constitution created two new elements of power. The Moral Republican Council (Consejo Moral Republicano) is comprised of the Comptroller-General, the Attorney-General and the Peoples' Defender (or ombudsman). Its principal duty is to uphold the Constitution. The National Electoral Council (Consejo Nacional Electoral) administers and supervises elections.

The Government

HEAD OF STATE

President of the Republic: Lt-Col (retd) HUGO RAFAEL CHÁVEZ FRÍAS (took office 2 February 1999; re-elected 30 July 2000).

COUNCIL OF MINISTERS
(April 2006)

Vice-President: JOSÉ VICENTE RANGEL.
Minister of Finance: NELSON MERENTES DÍAZ.
Minister of the Interior and Justice: Lt (retd) JESSE CHACÓN ESCAMILLO.
Minister of National Defence: Adm. RAMÓN ORLANDO MANGLIA FERREIRA.
Minister of Basic Industry and Mining: VÍCTOR ALVAREZ RODRÍGUEZ.
Minister of Light Industry and Trade: MARÍA CRISTINA IGLESIAS.
Minister of Energy and Petroleum: RAFAEL DARÍO RAMÍREZ CARREÑO.
Minister of Foreign Affairs: ALÍ RODRÍGUEZ ARAQUE.
Minister of Labour: RICARDO DORADO.
Minister of the Mass Economy: ELÍAS JAUA.
Minister of Food: ERIKA FARÍAS.
Minister of Education and Sport: ARISTÓBULO ISTÚRIZ.
Minister of Tourism: WILMAR CASTRO SOTELDO.
Minister of Health: Dr FRANCISCO ARMADA.
Minister of Higher Education: SAMUEL MONCADA.
Minister of Infrastructure: RAMÓN ALFONSO CARRIZALES RENGIFO.
Minister of the Environment and Natural Resources: JACQUELINE COROMOTO FARÍA PINEDA.
Minister of Agriculture and Lands: ANTONIO ALBARRÁN MORENO.
Minister of Planning and Development: JORGE GIORDANI.
Minister of Science and Technology: MARLENE YADIRA CÓRDOVA.
Minister of Social Development and Popular Participation: Gen. JORGE LUIS GARCÍA CARNEIRO.
Minister of Communications and Information: YURI PIMENTEL.
Secretary of the Presidency: RODRIGO CHÁVEZ.

MINISTRIES

Ministry of Agriculture and Lands: Avda Lecuna, Torre Este, 7°, Parque Central, San Agustín, Caracas; tel. (212) 509-0405; internet www.mat.gov.ve.

Ministry of Basic Industry and Mining: Caracas.

Ministry of Communications and Information: Torre MCT, 10°, Avda Universidad, esq. 'El chorro', Caracas; tel. (212) 505-3207; e-mail contactenos@mci.gob.ve; internet www.minci.gov.ve.

Ministry of Education and Sport: Edif. Ministerio de Educación, Mezzanina, esq. de Salas, Parroquia Altagracia, Caracas 1010; tel. (212) 506-8211; e-mail atencion_al_publico@me.gob.ve; internet www.me.gov.ve.

Ministry of Energy and Petroleum: Edif. Petróleos de Venezuela, Torre Oeste, Avda Libertador con Avda Empalme, La Campiña, Porrocubo El Recreo, Caracas; tel. (212) 708-1299; fax (212) 708-7014; internet www.mem.gov.ve.

Ministry of the Environment and Natural Resources: Torre Sur, 25°, Centro Simón Bolívar, Caracas 1010; tel. (212) 408-1002; fax (212) 408-1009; e-mail jfaria@marn.gov.ve; internet www.marn.gov.ve.

Ministry of Finance: Edif. Ministerio de Finanzas, esq. de Carmelitas, Avda Urdaneta, Caracas; tel. (212) 802-1404; fax (212) 802-1413; e-mail consultapublica@mf.gov.ve; internet www.mf.gov.ve.

Ministry of Food: Antiguo Edif. Seguros Orinoco, 11°, Avda Fuerzas Armadas, esq. Socarras, Caracas 1010; tel. (212) 564-2415; e-mail oirp@minal.gob.ve; internet www.minal.gob.ve.

Ministry of Foreign Affairs: Torre MRE, esq. Carmelitas, Avda Urdaneta, Caracas 1010; tel. (212) 862-1085; fax (212) 864-3633; e-mail criptogr@mre.gov.ve; internet www.mre.gov.ve.

Ministry of Health: Torre Sur, 9°, Centro Simón Bolívar, El Silencio, Caracas 1010; tel. (212) 408-0000; e-mail msds.gov.ve@msds.gov.ve; internet www.msds.gov.ve.

Ministry of Higher Education: Torre MCT, 6°, Avda Universidad, esq. el Chorro, Caracas 1010; tel. (212) 596-5293; e-mail enlacesmes@mes.gov.ve; internet www.mes.gov.ve.

Ministry of Infrastructure: Torre Este, 50°, Parque Central, Caracas 1010; tel. (212) 509-1076; fax (212) 509-3682; internet www.infraestructura.gov.ve.

Ministry of the Interior and Justice: Edif. Ministerio del Interior y Justicia, esq. de Platanal, Avda Urdaneta, Caracas 1010; tel. (212) 506-1101; fax (212) 506-1559; e-mail webmaster@mij.gov.ve; internet www.mij.gov.ve.

Ministry of Labour: Torre Sur, 5°, Centro Simón Bolívar, Caracas 1010; tel. (212) 481-1368; fax (212) 483-8914; internet www.mintra.gov.ve.

Ministry of Light Industry and Trade: Torre Este, 18°, Avda Lecuna, Parque Central, Caracas 1010; tel. (212) 509-0445; fax (212) 574-2432; e-mail ministro@milco.gob.ve; internet www.milco.gov.ve.

Ministry of the Mass Economy: Edif. INCE, Avda Nueva Granada, Caracas; tel. (212) 603-1965; fax (212) 633-4932; e-mail visitantes@minep.gov.ve; internet www.minep.gov.ve.

Ministry of National Defence: Edif. 17 de Diciembre, planta baja, Base Aérea Francisco de Miranda, La Carlota, Caracas; tel. (212) 908-1264; fax (212) 237-4974; e-mail prensamd@mindefensa.gov.ve; internet www.mindefensa.gov.ve.

Ministry of Planning and Development: Torre Oeste, 22°, Avda Lecuna, Parque Central, Caracas 1010; tel. (212) 507-0811; fax (212) 573-3076; e-mail webmaster@mpd.gov.ve; internet www.mpd.gov.ve.

Ministry of Science and Technology: Edif. Maploca 1, planta baja, Final Avda Principal de los Cortijos de Lourdes, Caracas; tel. (212) 239-6475; fax (212) 239-6056; e-mail mct@mct.gov.ve; internet www.mct.gov.ve.

Ministry of Social Development and Popular Participation: Caracas.

Ministry of Tourism: Edif. Mintur, Avda Francisco de Miranda con Avda Principal de la Floresta, Municipio Chacao, Caracas; tel. (212) 208-4511; e-mail auditoria@mintur.gob.ve; internet www.mintur.gob.ve.

State Agencies

Consejo de Defensa de la Nación (Codena): Palacio Blanco, 3°, Avda Urdaneta frente del Palacio Miraflores, Caracas; tel. (212) 806-3104; fax (212) 806-3151; national defence council.

Contraloría General de la República (CGR): Edif. Contraloría, Avda Andrés Bello, Guaicaipuro, Caracas 1050; tel. (212) 508-3111; e-mail atencionciudadano@cgr.gov.ve; internet www.cgr.gov.ve; national audit office for Treasury income and expenditure, and for the finances of the autonomous institutes; Comptroller-Gen. CLODOSBALDO RUSSIÁN UZCÁTEGUI.

Defensoría del Pueblo: Edif. Defensoría del Pueblo, Plaza Morelos, Los Caobos, Caracas; tel. (212) 578-3862; fax (212) 578-3862; e-mail prensadefensoria@hotmail.com; internet www.defensoria.gov.ve; acts as an ombudsman and investigates complaints between citizens and the authorities; Defender of the People GERMÁN MUNDARAÍN.

Procuraduría General de la República: Paseo Los Ilustres con Avda Lazo Martí, Santa Mónica, Caracas; tel. (212) 693-0911; fax (212) 693-4657; e-mail webmaster@pgr.gov.ve; internet www.pgr.gob.ve; Procurator-Gen. MARISOL PLAZA IRIGOYEN.

President

Presidential Election, 30 July 2000

Candidates	% of valid votes
Lt-Col (retd) Hugo Rafael Chávez Frías (MVR)	59.7
Francisco Arias Cárdenas (La Causa R)	37.5
Claudio Fermín (Encuentro Nacional)	2.7
Others	0.1
Total	**100.0**

VENEZUELA

Legislature

ASAMBLEA NACIONAL
(National Assembly)

President: Nicolás Maduro Moros.
First Vice-President: Desirée Santos Amaral.
Second Vice-President: Roberto Manuel Hernández Wohnsiadler.

Election, 4 December 2005*

Party	Seats
Movimiento V República (MVR)	114
Por la Democracia (PODEMOS)	15
Patria para Todos (PPT)	11
Movimiento Electoral del Pueblo (MEP)	11
Partido Comunista de Venezuela (PCV)	8
Unión Popular Venezolana	8
Total	**167**

* The election was boycotted by opposition parties.

Election Commission

Consejo Nacional Electoral (CNE): Avda Washington, Quinta Adriana, El Paraíso, Caracas; tel. (212) 352-1032; fax (212) 352-6316; internet www.cne.gov.ve; f. 2002; 5 mems; Pres. Tibisay Lucena.

Political Organizations

Acción Democrática (AD): Casa Nacional Acción Democrática, Calle Los Cedros, La Florida, Caracas 1050; internet www.acciondemocratica.org.ve; f. 1936 as Partido Democrático Nacional; adopted present name and obtained legal recognition in 1941; social democratic; Sec-Gen. Henry Ramos Allup; Pres. Jesús Mendez Quijada.

Alianza Bravo Pueblo: Caracas; oppositionist; Pres. Antonio Ledezma.

Asamblea del Pueblo (Asamblea Popular): Caracas; e-mail coordinadorweb@aporrea.org; internet www.aporrea.org; f. 2005; opposition group formed by dissident left-wing mems of AD, Bandera Roja and CD; Leader Claudio Fermín.

Bandera Roja: Caracas; f. 1968; militant Marxist-Leninist grouping; Leader Gabriel Rafael Puerta Aponte.

Bloque Democrático: Caracas; e-mail contacto@bloquedemocratico.org; internet www.bloquedemocratico.org; hardline opposition grouping; split from Coordinadora Democrática in 2004; Dir Robert Alonso.

La Causa Radical (La Causa R): Santa Teresa a Cipreses, Residencias Santa Teresa, 2°, Ofs 21 y 22, Caracas; tel. (212) 545-7002; internet www.lacausar.org.ve; f. 1971; radical democratic; Leader Andrés Velásquez.

Convergencia Nacional (CN): Edif. Tajamar, 2°, Of. 215, Parque Central, Avda Lecuna, El Conde, Caracas 1010; tel. (212) 578-1177; fax (212) 578-0363; e-mail jjcaldera@convergencia.org.ve; internet www.convergencia.org.ve; f. 1993; Leader Dr Rafael Caldera Rodríguez; Gen. Co-ordinator Juan José Caldera.

Coordinadora Democrática (CD): Caracas; internet www.coordinadora-democratica.org; f. 2002; umbrella org. for 27 anti-Govt political parties and opposition groups; Leader Enrique Mendoza.

Fuerza Liberal: Caracas; e-mail alejandro@fuerzaliberalvenezuela.com.ve; e-mail fliberal@fuerzaliberalvenezuela.com.ve; internet www.fuerzaliberalvenezuela.com.ve; f. 2005; hard-line opposition party; right-wing; Pres. Haydée Deutsch; Sec.-Gen. José Rigoberto González.

Movimiento Electoral del Pueblo (MEP): Caracas; f. 1967 by left-wing AD dissidents; 100,000 mems; Pres. Dr Luis Beltrán Prieto Figueroa; Sec-Gen. Dr Jesús Ángel Paz Galarraga.

Movimiento Demócrata Liberal: 1°, Avda de Santa Eduvigis, entre 5° y 6° transversal, Quinta El Encuentro, Caracas; e-mail mpolesel@cantv.net; internet www.democrataliberales.org; liberal opposition party; Political Dir Marco Polesel.

Movimiento de Integración Nacional (MIN): Edif. José María Vargas, 1°, esq. Pajarito, Caracas; tel. (212) 563-7504; fax (212) 563-7553; f. 1977; Sec.-Gen. Gonzalo Pérez Hernández.

Movimiento de Izquierda Revolucionaria (MIR): c/o Fracción Parlamentaria MIR, Edif. Tribunales, esq. Pajaritos, Caracas; f. 1960 by splinter group from AD; left-wing; Sec.-Gen. Moisés Moleiro.

Directory

Movimiento Republicano: 4a transversal con Avda Andrés Bello, Residencia Guipelia, Apdo 4-A, Los Palos Grandes, Caracas 1060; tel. (212) 286-3137; e-mail movimientorepublicano@gmail.com; internet www.mrepublicano.unlugar.com; f. 1997; Pres. Carlos Pandilla; Sec.-Gen. Manual Rivas.

Movimiento al Socialismo (MAS): Quinta Alemar, Avda Valencia, Las Palmas, Caracas 1050; tel. (212) 793-7800; fax (212) 761-9297; e-mail asamblea07@cantv.net; internet www.mas.org.ve; f. 1971 by PCV dissidents; opposition democratic-socialist party; split in 1997 over issue of support for presidential campaign of Lt-Gen. (retd) Hugo Rafael Chávez Frías; Pres. Felipe Mujica; Sec.-Gen. Leopoldo Puchi.

Movimiento V República (MVR): Calle Lima, cruce con Avda Libertador, Los Caobos, Caracas; tel. (212) 782-3808; fax (212) 782-9720; f. 1998; promotes Bolivarian revolution; mem. of the Polo Patriótico (q.v.); Leader Lt-Col (retd) Hugo Rafael Chávez Frías.

Partido Comunista de Venezuela (PCV): Edif. Cantaclaro, esq. San Pedro, Apdo 20428, San Juan, Caracas; tel. (212) 484-0061; fax (212) 481-9737; internet www.pcv-venezuela.org; f. 1931; Sec.-Gen. Oscar Figuera.

Partido Social-Cristiano (Comité de Organización Política Electoral Independiente) (COPEI): esq. San Miguel, Avda Panteón cruce con Fuerzas Armadas, San José, Caracas 1010; f. 1946; Christian Democratic; more than 1,500,000 mems; Leader Enrique Mendoza; Sec.-Gen. César Pérez.

Partido Unión: Caracas; f. 2001; Leader Lt-Col (retd) Francisco Arias Cárdenas; Sec-Gen. Luis Manuel Esculpí.

Patria Para Todos (PPT): Caracas; tel. (212) 577-4545; e-mail ppt@cantv.net; f. 1997; breakaway faction of La Causa Radical; revolutionary humanist party; Leaders José Albornoz, Pablo Medina.

Polo Patriótico (PP): f. 1998; grouping of small, mainly left-wing and nationalist political parties, including the MVR (q.v.), in support of presidential election campaign of Lt-Col (retd) Hugo Rafael Chávez Frías.

Por la Democracia Social (PODEMOS): Caracas; e-mail contacto@podemos.org.ve; internet www.podemos.org.ve; f. 2001 by dissident mems of MAS (q.v.); Leader Ismael García.

Primero Justicia: Centro Comercial Chacaíto, Nivel sótano, local 26, Caracas; tel. (212) 952-9733; e-mail pjelhaltillo@cantv.net; internet www.primerojusticia.org.ve; f. 2000; no fixed ideological stance; Nat. Co-ordinator Julio Borges; Sec.-Gen. Gerardo Blyde.

Proyecto Venezuela (PRVZL): e-mail administrador@vpvonline.com; internet www.proyectovenezuela.org.ve; f. 1998; humanist party; ended alliance with Govt in Jan. 2002; Leader Jorge Sucre.

Solidaridad: Caracas; f. 2001; Leader Luis Miquilena.

Unión Popular Venezolana (UPV): Caracas; f. 2004; Pres. Lina Ninette Ron Pereira.

OTHER ORGANIZATIONS

Asociación Civil Queremos Elegir: Edif. Industrial, 4°, Avda Sucre, Los Dos Caminos, Municipio Sucre. Caracas; tel. (212) 286-9785; e-mail info@queremoselegir.org; internet www.queremoselegir.org; f. 1991; opposition grouping promoting citizens' rights; mem. of Alianza Cívica de la Sociedad Venezolana; Principal Co-ordinator Elías Santana.

COFAVIC: Edif. El Candil, 1°, Of. 1-A, Avda Urdaneta, esq. El Candilito, Apdo 16150, La Candelaria, Caracas 1011-A; tel. (212) 572-9631; fax (212) 572-9908; e-mail lortega@cofavic.org.ve; internet www.cofavic.org.ve; promotes human rights; Exec. Dir L. Ortega.

Movimiento 1011: tel. (414) 304-0432; e-mail contacto@movimiento1011.com; internet www.movimiento1011.com; civil asscn promoting educational reform; mem of Alianza Cívica de la Sociedad Venezolana.

Rumbo Propio para Zulia: Edif. Boyscouts de Venezuela, planta baja, Avda 3E con Calle 73, Maracaibo; tel. (414) 638-1657; e-mail rumbopropio@hotmail.com; internet rumbopropio.org.ve; f. 2005; right-wing autonomist grouping; Pres. Néstor Suárez.

Súmate: Caracas; e-mail info@sumate.org; internet www.sumate.org; f. 2002; opposition grouping promoting citizens' rights; Leader María Corina Machado.

Diplomatic Representation

EMBASSIES IN VENEZUELA

Algeria: 8va Transversal con 3ra Avda, Quinta Azahar, Urb. Altamira, Caracas 1060; tel. (212) 263-2092; fax (212) 261-4254; e-mail ambalgcar@cantv.net; Ambassador Mohammed Khelladi.

Argentina: Edif. Fedecámaras, 3°, Avda El Empalme, El Bosque, Apdo 569, Caracas; tel. (212) 731-3311; fax (212) 731-2659; e-mail

VENEZUELA

argentina@impsat.net.ve; internet www.embargentinacaracas.org.ar; Ambassador ALICIA CASTRO.

Australia: Avda Francisco de Miranda, cruce con Avda Sur Altamira, 1°, Caracas 1060-A; tel. (212) 263-4033; fax (212) 261-3448; e-mail caracas@dfat.gov.au; Ambassador JOHN MAGNUS L. WOODS.

Austria: Edif. Torre Las Mercedes, 4°, Of. 408, Avda La Estancia, Chuao, Apdo 61381, Caracas 1060-A; tel. (212) 991-3863; fax (212) 993-2753; e-mail caracas-ob@bmaa.gv.at; Ambassador MARIANNE DACOSTA.

Barbados: Edif. Los Frailes, 5°, Of. 501, Avda Principal con Calle La Guairita, Chuao, Caracas 1060; tel. (212) 992-0545; fax (212) 991-0333; e-mail caracas@foreign.gov.bb; Ambassador KEITH FRANKLIN.

Belgium: Quinta la Azulita, Avda 11, entre 6a y 7a Transversales, Apdo del Este 61550, Altamira, Caracas 1060; tel. (212) 263-3334; fax (212) 261-0309; e-mail caracas@diplobel.org; internet www.diplobel.org/venezuela; Ambassador BADOUIN VANDERHULST.

Bolivia: Avda Luis Roche con 6a Transversal, Altamira, Caracas; tel. (212) 263-3015; fax (212) 263-3386; e-mail embaboliviaven@hotmail.com; Ambassador RENÉ RECACOCHEA SALINAS.

Brazil: Avda Mohedano con Calle Los Chaguaramos, Centro Gerencial Mohedano, 6°, La Castellana, Caracas; tel. (212) 261-5505; fax (212) 261-9601; e-mail brasembcaracas@cantv.net; internet www.embajadabrasil.org.ve; Ambassador JOÃO CARLOS DE SOUZA-GOMES.

Bulgaria: Quinta Sofía, Calle Las Lomas, Urb. Las Mercedes, Apdo 68389, Caracas; tel. (212) 993-2714; fax (212) 993-4839; e-mail embulven@cantv.net; Ambassador LAZAR KOPRINAROV.

Canada: Edif. Embajada de Canadá, Avda Francisco de Miranda con Avda Sur, Altamira, Caracas 1060-A; Apdo 62302, Caracas 1060; tel. (212) 600-3101; fax (212) 261-8741; e-mail crcas@international.gc.ca; internet www.caracas.gc.ca; Ambassador RENATA WIELGOSZ.

Chile: Edif. Torre La Noria, 10°, Calle Paseo Enrique Eraso, Las Mercedes, Caracas; tel. (212) 992-3378; fax (212) 992-0614; e-mail echileve@cantv.net; internet www.embachileve.org; Ambassador FABIO VÍO UGARTE.

China, People's Republic: Avda El Paseo, Quinta El Oriente, Prados del Este, Caracas; tel. (212) 977-4949; fax (212) 978-0876; e-mail embcnven@cantv.net; internet ve.chineseembassy.org/esp; Ambassador JU YIJIE.

Colombia: Torre Credival, 11°, 2A Calle de Campo Alegre con Avda Francisco de Miranda, Apdo 60887, Caracas; tel. (212) 261-6596; fax (212) 261-1358; e-mail ecaracas@minrelext.gov.co; Ambassador ENRIQUE VARGAS RAMÍREZ.

Costa Rica: Edif. For You P.H., Avda San Juan Bosco, entre 1 y 2 transversal, Altamira, Apdo 62239, Caracas; tel. (212) 267-1104; fax (212) 265-4660; e-mail embaricavene@yahoo.com.mx; Ambassador WALTER RUBÉN HERNÁNDEZ JUÁREZ.

Croatia: Calle Río Ticoporo, Res. Patricia, Urb. La Ciudadela, Redoma de Prados del Este, Caracas 1080; tel. (212) 977-3967; fax (212) 979-0064; e-mail consuladocroacia@cantv.net; Ambassador ZDRAVKO SANCEVIC.

Cuba: Calle Roraima e Rio de Janeiro y Choroni, Chuao, Caracas 1060; tel. (212) 991-6611; fax (212) 993-5695; e-mail embacubavzla@cantv.net; Ambassador GERMÁN SÁNCHEZ OTERO.

Czech Republic: Calle Los Cedros, Quinta Isabel, Urb. Country Club, Altamira, Caracas 1060; tel. (212) 261-8528; fax (212) 266-3987; e-mail caracas@embassy.mzv.cz; internet www.mfa.cz/caracas; Ambassador Dr JIŘÍ JIRÁNEK.

Dominican Republic: Edif. Argentum, Ofs 1 y 2, 2a Tranversal, entre 1a Avda y Avda Andrés Bello, Los Palos Grandes, Caracas 1060; tel. (212) 283-3709; fax (212) 283-3965; e-mail embdomvenezuela@serex.gov.do; Ambassador JAIME DURÁN HERNÁNDEZ.

Ecuador: Centro Andrés Bello, Torre Oeste, 13°, Avda Andrés Bello, Maripérez, Apdo 62124, Caracas 1060; tel. (212) 265-0801; fax (212) 264-6917; e-mail embajadaecuador@cantv.net; internet www.embaecuador.org; Ambassador FRANCISCO SUÉSCUM OTTATI.

Egypt: Calle Caucagua con Calle Guaicaipuro, Quinta Maribel, Urb. San Román, Apdo 490007, Caracas; tel. (212) 992-6259; fax (212) 993-1555; e-mail egyptianembassy@cantv.net; Ambassador ESSAM SALEH AWAD MOUSTAFA.

El Salvador: Centro Comercial Ciudad Tamanaco (CCCT), Torre C, 4°, Of. 406, Chuao, Caracas; tel. (212) 959-0817; fax (212) 959-3920; e-mail embsalv@viptel.com; Chargé d'affaires RAFAEL HERNÁNDEZ.

Finland: Apdo 61118, Chacao, Caracas 1060; tel. (212) 952-4111; fax (212) 952-7536; e-mail sanomat.car@formin.fi; internet www.finland.org.ve/es; Ambassador MIKKO PYHÄLÄ.

France: Calle Madrid con Avda Trinidad, Las Mercedes, Apdo 60385, Caracas 1060; tel. (212) 909-6500; fax (212) 909-6630; e-mail infos@francia.org.ve; internet www.francia.org.ve; Ambassador PIERRE-JEAN VANDOORNE.

Germany: Torre La Castellana, 10°, Avda Eugenio Mendoza y Avda José Angel Lamas, La Castellana, Caracas 1010-A; tel. (212) 261-0181; fax (212) 261-0641; e-mail embajadaalemanacara@cantv.net; internet www.caracas.diplo.de; Ambassador HERMANN ERATH.

Greece: Quinta Maryland, Avda Principal del Avila, Alta Florida, Caracas 1050; tel. (212) 730-3833; fax (212) 731-0429; e-mail embgrccs@cantv.net; Ambassador ATHANASSIOS M. VALASSIDIS.

Grenada: Avda Norte 2, Quinta 330, Los Naranjos del Cafetal, Caracas; tel. (212) 985-5461; fax (212) 985-6391; e-mail egrenada@cantv.net; Chargé d'affaires a.i. DONALD MCPHAIL.

Guatemala: Avda de Francisco de Miranda, Torre Dozsa, 1°, Urb. El Rosal, Caracas; tel. (212) 952-1166; fax (212) 954-0051; e-mail embaguat@cantv.net; Ambassador IVAN ESPINOZA FARFÁN.

Guyana: Quinta 'Roraima', Avda El Paseo, Prados del Este, Apdo 51054, Caracas 1050; tel. (212) 977-1158; fax (212) 977-1158; fax (212) 976-3765; e-mail embaguy@caracas.org.ve; Ambassador BAYNEY RAM KARRAN.

Haiti: Quinta Flor 59, Avda Las Rosas, La Florida, Caracas; tel. (212) 730-7220; fax (212) 730-4605; Chargé d'affaires a.i. GANDY THOMAS.

Holy See: Avda La Salle, Los Caobos, Apdo 29, Caracas 1010-A (Apostolic Nunciature); tel. (212) 781-8939; fax (212) 793-2403; e-mail nunapos@cantv.net; Apostolic Nuncio Most Rev. ANDRÉ DUPUY (Titular Archbishop of Selsea).

Honduras: Edif. Excélsior, 5°, Avda San Juan Bosco, Altamira, Apdo 68259, Caracas; tel. (212) 263-3184; fax (212) 263-4379; e-mail honduven@cantv.net; Ambassador CARLOS ALBERTO TURCIOS OREAMUNO.

India: Quinta Tagore, No. 12, Avda San Carlos, La Floresta, Caracas, Venezuela; tel. (212) 285-7887; fax (212) 286-5131; e-mail info@embindia.org; internet www.embindia.org; Ambassador DEEPAK BHOJWANI.

Indonesia: Quinta La Trinidad, Avda El Paseo, Prados del Este, Apdo 80807, Caracas 1080; tel. (212) 976-2725; fax (212) 976-0550; e-mail kbri@telcel.net.ve; Ambassador CORNELIS MANOPPO.

Iran: Quinta Ommat, Calle Kemal Ataturk, Valle Arriba, Apdo 68460, Caracas; tel. (212) 992-3575; fax (212) 992-9989; e-mail embairanve@cantv.net; Ambassador AHMAD SOBHANI.

Iraq: Quinta Babilonia, Avda Nicolás Cópernico con Calle Los Malabares, Valle Arriba, Caracas; tel. (212) 991-1627; fax (212) 992-0268.

Israel: Centro Empresarial Miranda, 4°, Avda Principal de los Ruices cruce con Francisco de Miranda, Apdo 70081, Los Ruices, Caracas; tel. (212) 239-4511; fax (212) 239-4320; e-mail info@caracas.mfa.gov.il; internet caracas.mfa.gov.il; Ambassador SHLOMO COHEN.

Italy: Edif. Atrium, Calle Sorocaima, entre Avdas Tamanaco y Venezuela, El Rosal, Apdo 3995, Caracas; tel. (212) 952-7311; fax (212) 952-4960; e-mail ambcaracas@esteri.it; internet www.italamb.org.ve; Ambassador GERARDO CARANTE.

Jamaica: Edif. Los Frailes, 5°, Calle La Guairita, Urb. Chuao, Caracas 1062; tel. (212) 991-6741; fax (212) 991-5708; e-mail embjaven@cantv.net; Ambassador AUDLEY RODRÍQUEZ.

Japan: Edif. Bancaracas, 10°, Avda San Felipe con 2a Transveral, La Castellana, Caracas; tel. (212) 261-8333; fax (212) 261-6780; e-mail ajapon@genesisbci.net; internet www.ve.emb-japan.go.jp/esp/index.htm; Ambassador YASUO MATSUI.

Korea, Democratic People's Republic: Ambassador PAK TONG CHUN (resident in Cuba).

Korea, Republic: Avda Francisco de Miranda, Centro Lido, Torre B, 9°, Ofs 91-B y 92-B, El Rosal, Caracas; tel. (212) 954-1270; fax (212) 954-0619; e-mail venadmi@2net-uno.net; Ambassador SHIN SOONG CHULL.

Kuwait: Quinta El-Kuwait, Avda Las Magnolias con Calle Los Olivos, Los Chorros, Caracas; tel. (212) 239-4234; fax (212) 238-3878; Ambassador (vacant).

Lebanon: Edif. Embajada del Líbano, Prolongación Avda Parima, Colinas de Bello Monte, Calle Motatán, Caracas 1050; tel. (212) 751-5943; fax (212) 753-0726; e-mail emblibano@telcel.net.ve; Ambassador NICOLAS BECHARA KHAWAJA.

Malaysia: Centro Profesional Eurobuilding, 6°, Ofs 6F-G, Calle La Guairita, Apdo 65107, Chuao, Caracas 1060; tel. (212) 992-1011; fax (212) 992-1277; e-mail malcaracas@kln.gov.my; Ambassador RAMLI NAAM.

Mexico: Edif. Forum, Calle Guaicaipuro con Principal de las Mercedes, 5°, El Rosal, Apdo 61371, Caracas; tel. (212) 952-5777; fax (212) 952-3003; e-mail mexico@embamex.com.ve; internet www.embamex.com.ve; Ambassador ENRIQUE M. LOAEZA Y TOVAR (recalled in Nov. 2005).

Morocco: Torre Multinvest, Plaza Isabel La Católica, Avda Eugenio Mendoza, 2°, La Castellana, Caracas; tel. (212) 265-9573; fax (212) 266-4681; e-mail embamaroccaracas@cantv.net; Ambassador Dr IBRAHIM HOUSSEIN MOUSSA.

VENEZUELA

Netherlands: Edif. San Juan Bosco, 9°, San Juan Bosco con 2a Transversal de Altamira, Caracas; tel. (212) 263-3622; fax (212) 263-0462; e-mail car@minbuza.nl; internet www.mfa.nl/car-es; Ambassador H. Nijenhuis (designate).

Nicaragua: Avda Altamira Sur 1, Edif. Terepaima, 2°, Of. 207, Chacao, Caracas; tel. (212) 263-0904; fax (212) 263-8875; e-mail embanic@cantv.net; internet www.ibw.com.net; Ambassador Manuel Salvador Abauza.

Nigeria: Calle Chivacoa cruce con Calle Taría, Quinta Leticia, Urb. San Román, Apdo 62062, Chacao, Caracas 1060-A; tel. (212) 993-1520; fax (212) 993-7648; e-mail embnig@cantv.net; Ambassador A. Oyesola.

Norway: Centro Lido, Torre A-92A, Avda Francisco de Miranda, El Rosal, Apdo 60532, Caracas 1060-A; tel. (212) 953-0269; fax (212) 953-6877; e-mail emb.caracas@mfa.no; internet www.noruega.org.ve; Ambassador Martin Tore Bjørndal.

Panama: Edif. Los Frailes, 6°, Calle La Guairita, Chuao, Apdo 1989, Caracas; tel. (212) 992-9093; fax (212) 992-8107; Ambassador Carmen Gabriela Menéndez González.

Paraguay: Quinta Paraguay, Avda Principal Macaracuay 1960, entre Avda Cuicas y Carretera del Este, Caracas; tel. (212) 257-2747; fax (212) 257-7256; e-mail embaparven@cantv.net; internet www.mre.gov.py/paginas/representaciones/Embajadas.asp?CodRepresentacion=54=1; Ambassador Ana María Figueredo.

Peru: Andres Bello, 7°, Ofs 71-72 (Torre Oeste) y 73-74 (Torre Este), Mariperez, Caracas; tel. (212) 264-1483; fax (212) 265-7592; e-mail leprucaracas@cantv.net; Ambassador (vacant) (withdrawn in April 2006).

Philippines: 5a Transversal de Altamira, Quinta Filipinas, Altamira, Caracas 1060; tel. (212) 266-4725; fax (212) 266-6443; e-mail caracas@embassyph.com; Ambassador Ronald B. Allarey.

Poland: Quinta Ambar, Final Avda Nicolás Copérnico, Sector Los Naranjos, Las Mercedes, Apdo 62293, Caracas; tel. (212) 991-1461; fax (212) 992-2164; e-mail ambcarac@ambasada.org.ve; internet www.ambasada.org.ve; Ambassador Adam Skrybant.

Portugal: Edif. Fedecámaras, 1°, Avda El Empalme, El Bosque, Caracas 1062; tel. (212) 731-0320; fax (212) 731-0543; e-mail embajadaportugal@cantv.net; Ambassador José Manuel da Costa Arsénio.

Qatar: Avda Principal Lomas El Mirador, Alto Claro, Municipio Baruta, Caracas; tel. (212) 909-7800; fax (212) 993-2917; e-mail qatarven@cantv.net; Ambassador Naser Rashid Muhammad A. an-Nuami.

Romania: 4a Avda entre 8a y 9a Transversales, Quinta Guardatinajas 94-14, Altamira, Caracas; tel. (212) 261-9480; fax (212) 263-7161; e-mail ambasadaccs@cantv.net; Ambassador Ioan Les.

Russia: Quinta Soyuz, Calle Las Lomas, Las Mercedes, Caracas; tel. (212) 993-4395; fax (212) 993-6526; e-mail rusemb95@infoline.wtfe.com; Ambassador Aleksei Ermakov.

Saudi Arabia: Calle Andrés Pietri, Quinta Makkah, Los Chorros, Caracas 1071; tel. (212) 239-0290; fax (212) 239-6494; e-mail saudiembassycaracas@cantv.net; Ambassador Saleh A. al-Hegelan.

Serbia and Montenegro: 4a Avda de Campo Alegre 13, Urb. Campo Alegre, Caracas; tel. (212) 266-7995; fax (212) 266-9957; Chargé d'affaires Vera Mavrić.

South Africa: Centro Profesional Eurobuilding, 4°, Of. 4B-C, Calle La Guairita, Chuao, Apdo 2613, Caracas 1064; tel. (212) 991-6822; fax (212) 991-5555; e-mail rsaven@ifxnw.com.ve; Chargé d'affaires a.i. J. Swanepoel.

Spain: Avda Mohedano entre 1a y 2a Transversal, La Castellana, Caracas; tel. (212) 263-2855; fax (212) 261-0892; Ambassador Raúl Morodo Leoncio.

Suriname: 4a Avda entre 7a y 8a transversal, Quinta 41, Altamira, Caracas; Apdo 61140, Chacao, Caracas; tel. (212) 261-2724; fax (212) 263-9006; e-mail emsurl@cantv.net; Ambassador Glenn Antonius Alvares.

Sweden: Torre Phelps, 19°, Plaza Venezuela, Caracas; tel. (212) 781-6976; fax (212) 781-5932; e-mail consuladogensuecia@cantv.net; Ambassador Lena Nordström.

Switzerland: Centro Letonia, Torre Ing-Bank, 15°, La Castellana, Apdo 62555, Chacao, Caracas 1060-A; tel. (212) 267-9585; fax (212) 267-7745; e-mail vertretung@car.rep.admin.ch; Ambassador Walter Suter.

Syria: Avda Casiquiare, Quinta Damasco, Colinas de Bello Monte, Caracas; tel. (212) 753-5375; fax (212) 751-6146; Ambassador Mohammad Saleh Khafif.

Trinidad and Tobago: Quinta Serrana, 4a Avda entre 7 y 8 Transversales, Altamira, Caracas; tel. (212) 261-5796; fax (212) 261-9801; e-mail embtt@caracas.c-com.net; Ambassador Sheelagh Marilyn de Osuna.

Turkey: Calle Kemal Atatürk, Quinta Turquesa 6, Valle Arriba, Apdo 62078; Caracas 1060-A; tel. (212) 991-0075; fax (212) 992-0442; e-mail turquia@cantv.net; Ambassador Metin Göker.

United Kingdom: Torre La Castellana, 11°, Avda Principal La Castellana, Caracas 1061; tel. (212) 263-8411; fax (212) 267-1275; e-mail britishembassy@internet.ve; internet www.britain.org.ve; Ambassador Donald Alexander Lamont.

USA: Calle Suapure con Calle F, Colinas de Valle Arriba, Caracas; tel. (212) 975-6411; fax (212) 975-6710; e-mail embajada@state.gov; internet www.embajadausa.org.ve; Ambassador William R. Brownfield.

Uruguay: Torre Delta, 8°, Ofs A y B, Avda Francisco de Miranda, Altamira Sur, Apdo 60366, Caracas 1060-A; tel. (212) 261-7603; fax (212) 266-9233; e-mail uruvene@infoline.wtfe.com; Ambassador Juan José Arteaga Saenz de Zumarán.

Judicial System

The judicature is headed by the Supreme Tribunal of Justice, which replaced the Supreme Court of Justice after the promulgation of the December 1999 Constitution. The judges are divided into penal and civil and mercantile judges; there are military, juvenile, labour, administrative litigation, finance and agrarian tribunals. In each state there is a superior court and several secondary courts which act on civil and criminal cases. A number of reforms to the judicial system were introduced under the Organic Criminal Trial Code of March 1998. The Code replaced the inquisitorial system, based on the Napoleonic code, with an adversarial system in July 1999. In addition, citizen participation as lay judges and trial by jury was introduced, with training financed by the World Bank.

SUPREME TRIBUNAL OF JUSTICE

The Supreme Tribunal comprises 32 judges appointed by the Asamblea Nacional for 12 years. It is divided into six courts, each with three judges: political-administrative, civil, constitutional, electoral, social and criminal. When these act together the court is in full session. It has the power to abrogate any laws, regulations or other acts of the executive or legislative branches conflicting with the Constitution. It hears accusations against members of the Government and high public officials, cases involving diplomatic representatives and certain civil actions arising between the State and individuals.

Tribunal Supremo de Justicia

Final Avda Baralt, esq. Dos Pilitas, Foro Libertador, Caracas 1010; tel. (212) 801-9178; fax (212) 564-8596; e-mail cperez@tsj.gov.ve; internet www.tsj.gov.ve.

President: Omar Alfredo Mora Díaz.
President of the Constitutional Court: Luisa Estela Morales.
President of the Court of Administrative Policy: Evelyn Margarita Marrero Ortíz.
President of the Court of Civil Cassation: Carlos Oberto Vélez.
President of the Court of Penal Cassation: Eladio Ramón Aponte Aponte.
President of the Court of Social Cassation: Omar Alfredo Mora Díaz.
President of the Electoral Court: Juan José Núñez Calderón.
Attorney-General: Isaías Rodríguez Díaz.

Religion

Roman Catholicism is the religion of the majority of the population, but there is complete freedom of worship.

CHRISTIANITY

The Roman Catholic Church

For ecclesiastical purposes, Venezuela comprises nine archdioceses, 23 dioceses and four Apostolic Vicariates. There are also apostolic exarchates for the Melkite and Syrian Rites. At 31 December 2003 there were an estimated 23.8m. adherents, of whom 25,000 were of the Melkite Rite, accounting for 84% of the total population.

Latin Rite

Bishops' Conference
Conferencia Episcopal de Venezuela, Prolongación Avda Páez, Montalbán, Apdo 4897, Caracas 1010; tel. (212) 471-6284; fax (212) 472-7029; e-mail prensa@cev.org.ve; internet www.cev.org.ve; f. 1985;

VENEZUELA

statutes approved 2000; Pres. Most Rev. BALTAZAR ENRIQUE PORRAS CARDOZO (Archbishop of Mérida).

Archbishop of Barquisimeto: Most Rev. TULIO MANUEL CHIRIVELLA VARELA, Arzobispado, Venezuela con Calle 29 y 30 Santa Iglesia Catedral, Nivel Sótano, Barquisimeto 3001; tel. (251) 231-3446; fax (251) 231-3724; e-mail arquidiocesisdebarquisimeto@hotmail.com.

Archbishop of Calabozo: Most Rev. ANTONIO JOSÉ LÓPEZ CASTILLO, Arzobispado, Calle 4, No 11–82, Apdo 954, Calabozo 2312; tel. (246) 871-0483; fax (246) 871-2097; e-mail el.real@telcel.net.ve.

Archbishop of Caracas (Santiago de Venezuela): JORGE LIBERATO UROSA SAVINO, Arzobispado, Plaza Bolívar, Apdo 954, Caracas 1010-A; tel. (212) 542-1611; fax (212) 542-0297; e-mail arzobispado@cantv.net.

Archbishop of Ciudad Bolívar: Most Rev. MEDARDO LUIS LUZARDO ROMERO, Arzobispado, Avda Andrés Eloy Blanco con Calle Naiguatá, Apdo 43, Ciudad Bolívar 8001; tel. (285) 654-4960; fax (285) 654-0821; e-mail arzcb@cantv.net.ve.

Archbishop of Coro: Most Rev. ROBERTO LÜCKERT LEÓN, Arzobispado, Calle Federación esq. Palmasola, Apdo 7342, Coro; tel. (268) 251-7024; fax (268) 251-1636; e-mail dioceco@reaccium.ve.

Archbishop of Cumaná: Most Rev. DIEGO RAFAEL PADRÓN SÁNCHEZ, Arzobispado, Calle Bolívar 34 con Catedral, Apdo 134, Cumaná 6101-A; tel. (293) 431-4131; fax (293) 433-3413; e-mail dipa@cantv.net.

Archbishop of Maracaibo: Most Rev. UBALDO RAMÓN SANTANA SEQUERA, Arzobispado, Calle 95, entre Avdas 2 y 3, Apdo 439, Maracaibo; tel. (261) 722-5351; fax (261) 721-0805; e-mail ubrasan@hotmail.com.

Archbishop of Mérida: Most Rev. BALTAZAR ENRIQUE PORRAS CARDOZO, Arzobispado, Avda 4, Plaza Bolívar, Apdo 26, Mérida 5101-A; tel. (274) 252-5786; fax (274) 252-1238; e-mail arquimer@latinmail.com.

Archbishop of Valencia: Most Rev. JORGE LIBERATO UROSA SAVINO, Arzobispado, Avda Urdaneta 100-54, Apdo 32, Valencia 2001-A; tel. (241) 858-5865; fax (241) 857-8061; e-mail arqui_valencia@cantv.net.

Melkite Rite

Apostolic Exarch: Rt Rev. GEORGES KAHHALÉ ZOUHAÏRATY, Iglesia San Jorge, Final 3a Urb. Montalbán II, Apdo 20120, Caracas; tel. (212) 443-3019; fax (212) 443-0131; e-mail georges@cev.org.ve.

Syrian Rite

Apostolic Exarch: LOUIS AWAD, Parroquia Nuestra Señora de la Asunción, 1A Calle San Jacinto, Apdo 11, Maracay; tel. (243) 235-0821; fax (243) 235-7213.

The Anglican Communion

Anglicans in Venezuela are adherents of the Episcopal Church in the USA, in which the country forms a single, extra-provincial diocese attached to Province IX.

Bishop of Venezuela: Rt Rev. ORLANDO DE JESÚS GUERRERO, Avda Caroní 100, Apdo 49-143, Colinas de Bello Monte, Caracas 1042-A; tel. (212) 753-0723; fax (212) 751-3180; e-mail iglanglicanavzla@cantv.net.

Protestant Churches

Iglesia Evangélica Luterana en Venezuela: Apdo 68738, Caracas 1062-A; tel. and fax (212) 264-1868; e-mail ielv@telcel.net.ve; Pres. AKOS V. PUKY; 4,000 mems.

National Baptist Convention of Venezuela: Avda Santiago de Chile 12–14, Urb. Los Caobos, Caracas 1050; Apdo 61152, Chacao, Caracas 1060-A; tel. (212) 782-2308; fax (212) 781-9043; e-mail cnbv@telcel.net.ve; f. 1951; Pres. Rev. ENRIQUE DÁMASO; Gen. Man. Rev. DANIEL RODRÍGUEZ.

ISLAM

Mezquita Sheikh Ibrahim bin-Abdulaziz bin-Ibrahim: Calle Real de Quebrada Honda, Los Caobos, Caracas; tel. (212) 577-7382; internet www.mezquitaibrahim.org; f. 1994; Leader OMAR KADWA.

BAHÁ'Í FAITH

National Spiritual Assembly of the Bahá'ís: Colinas de Bello Monte, Apdo 49133, Caracas; tel. and fax (212) 751-7669; f. 1961; mems resident in 954 localities.

The Press

PRINCIPAL DAILIES

Caracas

Abril: Edif. Bloque DeArmas, final Avda San Martín cruce con Avda La Paz, Caracas; tel. (212) 406-4376; fax (212) 443-1575; e-mail ldelosreyes@dearmas.com; internet www.abril.com.ve; f. 1997; independent; morning; Mon. to Sat.; Pres. ANDRÉS DE ARMAS S.; Vice-Pres. MARTÍN DE ARMAS S.

Así es la Noticia: Maderero a Puente Nuevo, Caracas; tel. (212) 408-3444; fax (212) 408-3911; e-mail ipacheco@el-nacional.com; f. 1996; morning; Editor ERNESTINA HERRERA.

The Daily Journal: Avda Principal de Boleíta Norte, Apdo 76478, Caracas 1070-A; tel. (212) 237-9644; fax (212) 232-6831; e-mail redaccion@dj.com.ve; f. 1945; morning; in English; Chief Editor RUSSELL M. DALLEN, Jr.

Diario 2001: Edif. Bloque DeArmas, 2°, final Avda San Martín cruce con Avda La Paz, Caracas; tel. (212) 406-4111; fax 443-4961; e-mail contacto@dearmas.com; internet www.2001.com.ve; f. 1973; Pres. ANDRÉS DE ARMAS S.; Dir ISRAEL MÁRQUEZ.

El Diario de Caracas: Calle Los Laboratorios, Torre B, 1°, Of. 101, Los Ruices, Caracas 1070; tel. (212) 238-0386; e-mail editor@eldiariodecaracas.net; internet www.eldiariodecaracas.net; f. 2003; Editor JULIO AUGUSTO LÓPEZ.

El Globo: Avda Principal de Maripérez, Transversal Colón con Avda Libertador, Apdo 16415, Caracas 1010-A; tel. (2) 576-4111; fax (212) 576-1730; f. 1990; Dir ANÍBAL J. LATUFF.

Meridiano: Edif. Bloque DeArmas, final Avda San Martín cruce con Avda La Paz, Caracas 1010; tel. (212) 406-4040; fax (212) 442-5836; e-mail meridian@dearmas.com; internet www.meridiano.com.ve; f. 1969; morning; sport; Dir ANDRÉS DE ARMAS S.; Vice-Pres. MARTÍN DE ARMAS S.

El Mundo: Torre de la Prensa, 4°, Plaza del Panteón, Apdo 1192, Caracas; tel. (212) 596-1911; fax (212) 596-1478; e-mail dgomez@la-cadena.com; internet www.elmundo.com.ve; f. 1958; evening; independent; Pres. MIGUEL ANGEL CAPRILES LÓPEZ; Dir ENRIQUE RONDÓN.

El Nacional: Edif. El Nacional, Puente Nuevo a Puerto Escondido, El Silencio, Apdo 209, Caracas; tel. (212) 408-3111; fax (212) 408-3169; e-mail contactenos@el-nacional.com; internet www.el-nacional.com; f. 1943; morning; right-wing; independent; Pres. and Editor MIGUEL HENRIQUE OTERO; Asst Editor YELITZA LINARES; circ. 12,000.

El Nuevo País: Pinto a Santa Rosalía 44, Caracas; tel. (212) 541-5211; fax (212) 545-9675; e-mail enpais1@telcel.net.ve; f. 1988; Exec. Pres. ZORAIDA GARCÍA VARA; Dir and Editor FRANCISCO ORTA.

Puerto: Avda Soublette, Maiquetia, Caracas; tel. (212) 331-2275; fax (212) 331-0886; e-mail diariopuerto@telcel.net.ve; f. 1975; Pres. CARLOS PARMIGIANI.

La Religión: Edif. Juan XXIII, Torre a Madrices, Caracas; tel. (212) 563-0600; fax (212) 563-5583; e-mail religion@cantv.ve; internet www.iglesia.org.ve; f. 1890; morning; independent; Dir ENNIO TORRES.

Reporte (Diario de la Economía): Torre Británica, 12°, Of. B, Avda Luis Roche, Altamira Sur, Caracas; tel. (212) 264-0591; fax (212) 264-6023; e-mail reporte@reporte.com.ve; internet www.reporte.com.ve; f. 1988; Pres. TANNOUS GERGES; Editor WILLIAM BECERRA.

TalCual: Edif. Menegrande, 5°, Of. 51, Avda Francisco de Miranda, Caracas; tel. (212) 286-7446; fax (212) 232-7446; e-mail tpekoff@talcualdigital.com; internet www.talcualdigital.com; f. 2000; morning; right-wing; Pres. TEODORO PETKOFF; Editor-in-Chief EDMUNDO BRACHO.

Ultimas Noticias: Torre de la Prensa, 3°, Plaza del Panteón, Apdo 1192, Caracas; tel. (212) 596-1911; fax (212) 596-1433; e-mail edrangel@la-cadena.com; internet www.ultimasnoticias.com.ve; f. 1941; morning; independent; Pres. MIGUEL ANGEL CAPRILES LÓPEZ.

El Universal: Edif. El Universal, Avda Urdaneta, esq. de Animas, Apdo 1909, Caracas; tel. (212) 505-2314; fax (212) 505-3710; e-mail consejoeditorial@eluniversal.com; internet www.eluniversal.com; f. 1909; morning; Dir ANDRÉS MATA OSORIO; Chief Editor ELIDES ROJAS.

Vea: Sótano Uno, Edif. San Martín, Parque Central, Caracas 1010; tel. (212) 516-1004; fax (212) 578-3031; e-mail webmaster@diariovea.com.ve; internet www.diariovea.com.ve; f. 2003; morning; left-wing; Editor and Dir GUILLERMO GARCÍA PONCE; Asst Editor MANUEL PÉREZ RODRÍGUEZ.

La Voz: C. C. Nueva Guarenas, Mezzanina, Urb. Trapichito, Sector 2, Caracas; tel. (212) 362-9702; fax (212) 362-0851; e-mail diariolavoz@cantv.net; internet www.diariolavoz.net; morning; right-wing; Exec. Dir FREDDY BLANCO; Editor ALEXIS CASTRO BLANDÍN.

Barcelona

El Norte: Avda Intercomunal Andrés Bello, Sector Colinas del Neverí, Barcelona; tel. (281) 682-5694; fax (281) 286-2884; e-mail administrac@elnorte.com.ve; internet www.elnorte.com.ve; f. 1989; morning; Exec. Dir MARIELA DÁVILA; circ. 133,000.

Barquisimeto

El Impulso: Avda Los Comuneros, entre Avda República y Calle 1a, Urb. El Parque, Apdo 602, Barquisimeto; tel. (251) 250-2222; fax (251) 250-2129; e-mail reaccion@elimpulso.com; internet www.elimpulso.com; f. 1904; morning; independent; Dir and Editor JUAN MANUEL CARMONA PERERA.

El Informador: Edif. El Informador, Carrera 21, esq. Calle 23, Barquisimeto; tel. (251) 231-1811; fax (251) 231-0624; e-mail mauriciogomez@elinformador.com.ve; internet www.elinformador.com.ve; f. 1968; morning; Dir-Gen. MAURICIO GÓMEZ.

Ciudad Bolívar

El Bolivarense: Calle Igualdad 26, Apdo 91, Ciudad Bolívar; tel. (285) 632-2378; fax (285) 632-4878; e-mail abi28@unete.com.ve; f. 1957; morning; independent; Dir ALVARO NATERA.

El Expreso: Paseo Gáspari con Calle Democracia, Ciudad Bolívar; tel. (285) 632-0334; fax (285) 632-0334; e-mail webmaster@diarioelexpreso.com.ve; internet www.diarioelexpreso.com.ve; f. 1969; morning; independent; Dir LUIS ALBERTO GUZMÁN.

Maracaibo

Panorama: Avda 15, No 95–60, Apdo 425, Maracaibo; tel. (261) 725-6888; fax (261) 725-6911; e-mail editor@panodi.com; internet www.panodi.com; f. 1914; morning; independent; Pres. ESTEBAN PINEDA BELLOSO; Editorial Dir LUIS CAÑÓN; circ. 16,000.

Maracay

El Aragueño: Calle 3a Oeste con Avda 1 Oeste, Urb. Ind. San Jacinto, Maracay; tel. (243) 235-9018; fax (243) 235-7866; e-mail el-aragueno@cantv.net; internet www.el-aragueno.com.ve; f. 1972; morning; Editor EVERT GARCÍA.

El Siglo: Edif. 'El Siglo', Avda Bolívar Oeste 244, La Romana, Maracay; tel. (243) 554-9521; fax (243) 554-5154; e-mail direccion@elsiglo.com.ve; internet www.elsiglo.com.ve; f. 1973; morning; independent; Editor TULIO CAPRILES.

El Periodiquito: Calle Páez Este 178, Maracay; tel. (243) 321-422; fax (243) 336-987; e-mail farandula@elperiodiquito.com; internet www.elperiodiquito.com; f. 1986; Editorial Co-ordinator PACO FRANK; circ. 45,000.

Puerto la Cruz

El Tiempo: Edif. Diario El Tiempo, Avda Municipal 153, Puerto La Cruz; tel. (281) 260-0600; fax (281) 260-0660; e-mail buzon@eltiempo.com.ve; internet www.eltiempo.com.ve; f. 1958; independent; Dir JESÚS MÁRQUEZ; Editorial Dir GIOCONDA DE MÁRQUEZ.

San Cristóbal

Diario Católico: Carrera 4a, No 3–41, San Cristóbal; tel. (276) 343-2819; fax (276) 343-4683; e-mail catolico@truevision.net; f. 1924; morning; Catholic; Man. Dir Mgr NELSON ARELLANO.

Diario La Nación: Edif. La Nación, Calle 4 con Carrera 6 bis, La Concordia, Apdo 651, San Cristóbal; tel. (276) 346-4263; fax (276) 346-5051; e-mail lanacion@lanacion.com.ve; f. 1968; morning; independent; Editor JOSÉ RAFAEL CORTEZ.

El Tigre

Antorcha: Edif. Antorcha, Avda Francisco de Miranda, El Tigre; tel. (283) 235-2383; fax (283) 235-3923; e-mail yurbina@diarioantorcha.com; internet www.diarioantorcha.com; f. 1954; morning; independent; Pres. and Editor ANTONIO BRICEÑO AMPARÁN.

Valencia

El Carabobeño: Edif. El Carabobeño, Avda Universidad, Urb. La Granja, Naguanagua, Valencia; tel. (241) 867-2918; fax (241) 867-3450; e-mail website@el-carabobeno.com; internet www.el-carabobeno.com; f. 1933; morning; Dir EDUARDO ALEMÁN PÉREZ.

Notitarde: Avda Boyacá entre Navas Spínola y Flores, Valencia; tel. (241) 850-1666; fax (241) 850-1534; e-mail lauodr@notitarde.com; internet www.notitarde.com; evening; Dir LAURENTZI ODRIOZOLA ECHEGARAY.

PERIODICALS

Ambiente: Edif. Sur, Nivel Plaza Caracas, Local 9, Centro Simón Bolívar, Caracas; tel. (212) 408-1549; fax (212) 408-1546; e-mail fundamb@cantv.net; environmental issues; Gen. Man. AVRA MARINA SÁNCHEZ.

Artesanía y Folklore de Venezuela: C. C. Vista Mar, Local 20, Urbaneja, Lecherías, Estado Anzoátegui; tel. and fax (212) 286-2857; e-mail ismandacorrea@cantv.net; handicrafts and folklore; Dir ISMANDA CORREA.

Automóvil de Venezuela: Avda Caurimare, Quinta Expo, Colinas de Bello Monte, Caracas 1041; tel. (212) 751-1355; fax (212) 751-1122; e-mail ortizauto@cantv.net; internet www.automovildevenezuela.com; f. 1961; monthly; automotive trade; circ. 6,000; Editor MARÍA A. ORTIZ T.

Barriles: Centro Parque Carabobo, Torre B, 20°, Of. 2003, Avda Universidad, La Candelaria, Caracas; e-mail informaciones@camarapetrolera.org; publ. of the Cámara Petrolera de Venezuela; Editor HAYDÉE REYES.

Bohemia: Edif. Bloque DeArmas, Final Avda San Martín cruce con Avda La Paz, Apdo 575, Caracas; tel. (212) 406-4040; fax (212) 451-0762; e-mail bohemia@dearmas.com; f. 1966; weekly; general interest; Dir PEDRO RAMÓN ROMERA.

Business Venezuela: Torre Credival, Avda de Campo Alegre, Apdo 5181, Caracas 1010-A; tel. (212) 263-0833; fax (212) 263-2060; e-mail publicaciones@venamcham.org; internet www.bvonline.com.ve; every 2 months; business and economics journal in English published by the Venezuelan-American Chamber of Commerce and Industry; Gen. Man. ANTONIO HERRERA.

Computer World: Edif. Marystella, Avda Carabobo, El Rosal, Caracas; tel. (212) 952-7427; fax (212) 953-3950; e-mail cernic@cwv.com.ve; Editor CLELIA SANTAMBROGIO.

Contrapunto: Edif. Unión, 1°, Of. 2, Avda El Parque, Las Acacias Sur, Caracas; tel. (212) 690-0431; Dir VÍCTOR VERA MORALES.

Convenciones: Torre Nonza, 4°, Plaza Venezuela, Caracas; tel. (212) 793-1962; e-mail redacta@tutopia.com; Dir MARIO ERNESTO ARBELÁEZ.

El Corresponsal: Conj. Residencial El Naranjal, Torre D, 8°, No 82-D, Urb. Los Samanes, Caracas; tel. and fax (212) 941-0409; Editor DOMINGO GARCÍA PÉREZ.

Dinero: Edif. Aco, Entrada A, 7°, Avda Principal Las Mercedes, Caracas; tel. (212) 993-5011; fax (212) 991-3132; e-mail lomonaco@gep.com.ve; business and finance; Dir SALVATORE LOMONACO.

Exceso: Edif. Karam, Avda Urdaneta, 5°, Caracas; tel. (212) 564-1702; fax (212) 564-6760; e-mail baf-exceso@cantv.net; internet www.exceso.net; lifestyle; Dir BEN AMÍ FIHMAN; Editor ARMANDO COLL.

Gerente Venezuela: Avda Orinoco 3819, entre Muchuchies y Monterrey, Las Mercedes, Caracas 1060; tel. (212) 267-3733; fax (212) 267-6583; business and management; Editor LUIS RODÁN; circ. 15,000.

El Mirador: Edif. Pascal, Torre A, 1°, Of. 12-A, Avda Rómulo Gallegos, Santa Eduvigis, Caracas; tel. (212) 286-1661; fax (212) 283-5823; e-mail diarioelmirador@cantv.net; Dir JESÚS COUTO.

Mujer-Mujer: Centro Banaven, Nivel Sótano, No 13-A, Avda La Estancia, Chuao, Caracas; tel. (212) 959-5393; fax (212) 959-7864; e-mail ceciliapicon@hotmail.com.ve; women's interest; Dir and Editor CECILIA PICÓN DE TORRES.

Nueva Sociedad: Edif. IASA, 6°, Of. 606, Plaza La Castellana, Apdo 61712, Caracas; tel. (212) 265-9975; fax (212) 267-3397; e-mail nusoven@nuevasoc.org.ve; internet www.nuevasoc.org.ve; f. 1972; Latin American affairs; Editor DIETMAR DIRMOSER; Editor SERGIO CHEJFEC.

Primicia: Edif. El Nacional, 4°, Puente Nuevo a Puerto Escondido, Caracas; tel. (212) 408-3434; fax (212) 408-3485; e-mail primicia@el-nacional.com; current affairs and business; Editor FRANCHESCA CORDIDO.

La Razón: Edif. Valores, Sótano 'A', Avda Urdaneta, esq. de Urapal, Apdo 16362, La Candelaria, Caracas; tel. (212) 578-3143; fax (212) 578-2397; e-mail larazon@internet.ve; internet www.razon.com; weekly on Sundays; independent; Dir PABLO LÓPEZ ULACIO.

La Red: Urb. Vista Alegre, Calle 7, Quinta Luisa Amelia, Caracas; tel. (212) 472-0703; fax (212) 471-7749; e-mail ldavila@lared.com.ve; internet www.lared.com.ve; f. 1996; information technology; Editor LUIS MANUEL DÁVILA.

Reporte Petrolero: Torre Británica, 12°, Of. B, Altamira Sur, Caracas; tel. (212) 264-6023; fax (212) 266-9991; e-mail reporte2002@hotmail.com; journal of the petroleum industry; Dir ENRIQUE ROMAI; Editor MIGUEL LÓPEZ TROCELT.

Sic: Edif. Centro de Valores, esq. de Luneta, Centro Gumilla, Caracas; tel. (212) 564-9803; fax (212) 564-7557; e-mail sic@gumilla.org.ve; internet www.gumilla.org.ve/sic.htm; f. 1938; monthly; liberal Jesuit publication; Dir JESÚS MARÍA AGUIRRE.

Variedades: Edif. Bloque DeArmas, final Avda San Martín cruce con Avda La Paz, Caracas 1020; tel. (212) 406-43-90; fax (212) 451-

VENEZUELA *Directory*

0762; e-mail mgonzalez@dearmas.com; women's weekly; Dir GLORIA FUENTES DE VALLADARES.

VenEconomía: Edif. Gran Sabana, 1°, Avda Abraham Lincoln 174, Blvr de Sabana Grande, Caracas; tel. (212) 761-8121; fax (212) 762-8160; e-mail editor@veneconomia.com; internet www.veneconomia.com; f. 1982; monthly; Spanish and English; business and economic issues; Editor TOBY BOTTOME.

Venezuela Gráfica: Torre de la Prensa, Plaza del Panteón, Apdo 2976, Caracas 101; tel. (212) 81-4931; f. 1951; weekly; illustrated news magazine, especially entertainment; Dir DIEGO FORTUNATO; Editor MIGUEL ANGEL CAPRILES.

Zeta: Pinto a Santa Rosalía 44, Apdo 14067, Santa Rosalía, Caracas; tel. (212) 541-5211; fax (212) 545-9675; e-mail enpaiscolumna@hotmail.com; f. 1974; weekly; politics and current affairs; Dir JURATE ROSALES; Editor RAFAEL POLEO.

Zulia Deportivo: Torre Luali, 5°, Of. 3, Piñango a Muñoz, Avda Baralt, Maracaibo; tel. (261) 787-2809; sports; Dir MANUEL COLINA HIDALGO.

PRESS ASSOCIATIONS

Asociación de Prensa Extranjera en Venezuela (APEX): Hotel Caracas Hilton, Torre Sur, 3°, Of. 301, Avda México, Caracas; tel. (212) 503-5301; fax (212) 576-9284; e-mail caracashilton@hotmail.com; Pres. PHILIP GUNSON.

Bloque de Prensa Venezolano (BEV): Edif. El Universal, 5°, Of. C, Avda Urdaneta, Caracas; tel. (212) 561-7704; fax (212) 561-9409; e-mail luichi@telcel.net.ve; asscn of newspaper owners; Pres. MIGUEL ANGEL MARTÍNEZ.

Colegio Nacional de Periodistas (CNP): Casa Nacional del Periodista, 2°, Avda Andrés Bello, Caracas; tel. and fax (212) 781-7601; e-mail cnpjdn@cantv.net; journalists' asscn; Pres. LEVY BENSHIMOL; Sec.-Gen. NOEL MOLINA.

STATE PRESS AGENCY

Venpres: Torre Oeste, 16°, Parque Central, Caracas; tel. (212) 572-7175; fax (212) 571-0563; internet www.venpres.gov.ve; Dir ORLANDO UTRERA REYES.

FOREIGN PRESS AGENCIES

Agence France-Presse (AFP): Torre Provincial, Torre A, 14°, Of. 14-1, Avda Francisco de Miranda, Chacao, Caracas; tel. (212) 264-2945; fax (212) 267-7797; e-mail jorge.calmet@afp.com; Bureau Chief JACQUES THOMET.

Agencia EFE (Spain): Calle San Cristóbal, Quinta Altas Cumbres, Urb. Las Palmas, Caracas 1050; tel. (212) 793-7118; fax (212) 793-4920; e-mail efered1@cantv.net.

Agenzia Nazionale Stampa Associata (ANSA) (Italy): Centro Financiero Latino, 7°, Of. 2, Animas a Plaza España, Avda Urdaneta, Caracas; tel. (212) 564-2059; fax (212) 564-2516; e-mail ansaven@infoline.wtfe.com; Dir NATACHA SALAZAR.

Associated Press (AP) (USA): Edif. El Universal, 2°, Of. D, Avda Urdaneta, esq. Animas, Caracas; tel. (212) 564-1834; fax (212) 564-7124; e-mail janderson@ap.org; Chief JAMES ANDERSON.

BBC Latin Service: Res. Los Tulipanes, Torre A, 6°, No 6-B, Urb. Guaicai, Los Samanes; tel. (212) 941-7564; e-mail mariusareyes@hotmail.com; internet www.bbcmundo.com; Correspondent MARIUSA REYES.

Bloomberg: Torre Edicampo, 5°, Of. 1-2, Avda Francisco de Miranda, Caracas; tel. (212) 263-3355; fax (212) 264-2171; e-mail pewilson@bloomberg.net; Chief Correspondent PETER WILSON.

Deutsche Presse-Agentur (dpa) (Germany): Edif. El Universal, 4°, Of. 4-E, Avda Urdaneta, Caracas; tel. (212) 561-9776; fax (212) 562-9017; e-mail dpacaracas@tutopia.com; Correspondent NÉSTOR ROJAS.

Inter Press Service (IPS) (Italy): Edif. El Universal, 8°, Of. 3, Avda Urdaneta, Caracas; tel. (212) 564-6386; fax (212) 564-6374; e-mail caracas@ipsenespanol.org; Dir ANDRÉS CAÑIZÁLEZ.

Prensa Latina (Cuba): Edif. Fondo Común, Torre Sur, Of. 20-D, Avda de las Fuerzas Armadas y Urdaneta, Apdo 4400, Carmelitas, Caracas; tel. (212) 561-9733; fax (212) 564-7960; e-mail prelaccs@telcel.net.ve; Correspondent JAVIER RODRÍGUEZ.

Reuters (United Kingdom): Torre la Castellana, 4°, Avda Principal La Castellana, Caracas; tel. (212) 277-2700; fax (212) 277-2664; e-mail caracas.newsroom@reuters.com; Chief Correspondent PASCAL FLETCHER.

Xinhua (New China) News Agency (People's Republic of China): Quinta Xinjua, Avda Maracaibo, Prados del Este, Apdo 80564, Caracas; tel. (212) 8977-2489; fax (212) 978-1664; e-mail xinhua@c-com.ve; Bureau Chief QUANFU WUANC.

Publishers

Alfadil Ediciones: Calle Las Flores con Calle Paraíso, Sábana Grande, Apdo 50304, Caracas 1020-A; tel. (212) 762-3036; fax (212) 762-0210; f. 1980; general; Pres. LEONARDO MILLA A.

Armitano Editores, CA: Centro Industrial Boleita Sur, 4a Transversal de Boleita, Apdo 50853, Caracas 1070; tel. (212) 234-2565; fax (212) 234-1647; e-mail armiedit@telcel.net.ve; internet www.alfagrupo.com; art, architecture, ecology, botany, anthropology, history, geography; Pres. ERNESTO ARMITANO.

Ediciones La Casa Bello: Mercedes a Luneta, Apdo 134, Caracas 1010; tel. (212) 562-7100; f. 1973; literature, history; Pres. OSCAR SAMBRANO URDANETA.

Editorial El Ateneo, CA: Complejo Cultural, Plaza Morelos, Los Caobos, Apdo 662, Caracas; tel. (212) 573-4622; f. 1931; school-books and reference; Pres. MARÍA TERESA CASTILLO; Dir ANTONIO POLO.

Editorial Cincel Kapelusz Venezolana, SA: Avda Cajigal, Quinta K No 29, entre Avdas Panteón y Roraima, San Bernardino, Apdo 14234, Caracas 1011-A; f. 1963; school-books; Pres. DANTE TONI; Man. MAYELA MORGADO.

Colegial Bolivariana, CA: Edif. COBO, 1°, Avda Diego Cisneros (Principal), Los Ruices, Apdo 70324, Caracas 1071-A; tel. (212) 239-1433; f. 1961; Dir ANTONIO JUZGADO ARIAS.

Ediciones Ekaré: Edif. Banco del Libro, Final Avda Luis Roche, Altamira Sur, Apdo 68284, Caracas 1062; tel. (212) 264-7615; fax (212) 263-3291; e-mail editorial@ekare.com.ve; internet www.ekare.com; f. 1978; children's; Pres. CARMEN DIANA DEARDEN; Exec. Dir MARÍA FRANCISCA MAYOBRE.

Editora Ferga, CA: Torre Bazar Bolívar, 5°, Of. 501, Avda Francisco de Miranda, El Marqués, Apdo 16044, Caracas 1011-A; tel. (212) 239-1564; fax (212) 234-1008; e-mail ddex1@ibm.net; internet www.ddex.com; f. 1971; Venezuelan Exporters' Directory; Dir NELSON SÁNCHEZ MARTÍNEZ.

Fundación Biblioteca Ayacucho: Centro Financiero Latino, 12°, Ofs 1, 2 y 3, Avda Urdaneta, Animas a Plaza España, Apdo 14413, Caracas 1010; tel. (212) 561-6691; fax (212) 564-5643; e-mail biblioayacucho@cantv.net; f. 1974; literature; Pres. STEFANIA MOSCA.

Fundación Bigott: Casa 10-11, Calle El Vigia, Plaza Sucre, Centro Histórico de Petare, Caracas 1010-A; tel. (212) 272-2020; fax (212) 272-5942; e-mail contacto@fundacionbigott.com; internet www.fundacionbigott.com; f. 1936; Venezuelan traditions, environment, agriculture; Admin. Co-ordinator NELSON REYES.

Fundarte: Edif. Tajamar P. H., Avda Lecuna, Parque Central, Apdo 17559, Caracas 1015-A; tel. (212) 573-1719; fax (212) 574-2794; f. 1975; literature, history; Pres. ALFREDO GOSEN; Dir ROBERTO LOVERA DE SOLA.

Editorial González Porto: Sociedad a Traposos 8, Avda Universidad, Caracas; Pres. Dr PABLO PERALES.

Ediciones IESA: Edif. IESA, 3°, Final Avda IESA, San Bernardino, Apdo 1640, Caracas 1010-A; f. 1984; economics, business; Pres. RAMÓN PIÑANGO.

Ediciones María Di Mase: Caracas; f. 1979; children's books; Pres. MARÍA DI MASE; Gen. Man. ANA RODRÍGUEZ.

Monte Avila Editores Latinoamericana, CA: Avda Principal La Castellana, Quinta Cristina, Apdo 70712, Caracas 1070; tel. (212) 265-6020; fax (212) 263-8783; e-mail maelca@telcel.net.ve; f. 1968; general; Pres. MARIELA SÁNCHEZ URDANETA.

Nueva Sociedad: Edif. IASA, 6°, Of. 606, Plaza La Castellana, Apdo 61712, Chacao, Caracas 1060-A; Apdo 61712, Caracas 1060-A; tel. (212) 265-0593; fax (212) 267-3397; e-mail nuso@nuevasoc.org.ve; internet www.nuevasoc.org.ve; f. 1972; social sciences; Dir DIETMAR DIRMOSER.

Ediciones Panamericanas EP, SRL: Edif. Freites, 2°, Avda Libertador cruce con Santiago de Chile, Apdo 14054, Caracas; tel. (212) 782-9891; Man. JAIME SALGADO PALACIO.

Fundación Editorial Salesiana: Paradero a Salesianos 6, Apdo 369, Caracas; tel. (212) 571-6109; fax (212) 574-9451; e-mail administracion@salesiana.com.ve; internet www.salesiana.com.ve; f. 1960; education; Gen. Man. CLARENCIO GARCÍA.

Oscar Todtmann Editores: Avda Libertador, Centro Comercial El Bosque, Local 4, Caracas 1050; tel. (212) 763-0881; fax (212) 762-5244; science, literature, photography; Dir CARSTEN TODTMANN.

Vadell Hermanos Editores, CA: Edif. Golden, Avda Sur 15, esq. Peligro a Pele el Ojo, Caracas, (212) 572-3108; f. 1973; science, social science; Gen. Man. MANUEL VADELL GRATEROL.

Ediciones Vega S.R.L.: Edif. Odeon, Plaza Las Tres Gracias, Los Chaguaramos, Caracas 1050-A; tel. (212) 662-2092; fax (212) 662-1397; f. 1965; educational; Man. Dir FERNANDO VEGA ALONSO.

VENEZUELA   Directory

PUBLISHERS' ASSOCIATION

Cámara Venezolana del Libro: Centro Andrés Bello, Torre Oeste, 11°, Of. 112-0, Avda Andrés Bello, Caracas 1050-A; tel. (212) 793-1347; fax (212) 793-1368; f. 1969; Pres. HANS SCHNELL; Sec. ISIDORO DUARTE.

Broadcasting and Communications

TELECOMMUNICATIONS

Regulatory Authority

Comisión Nacional de Telecomunicaciones (CONATEL): Torre Este, 35°, Parque Central, Caracas; tel. (212) 993-5389; e-mail conatel@conatel.gov.ve; internet www.conatel.gov.ve; regulatory body for telecommunications; Dir-Gen. ALVIN REINALDO LEZAMA PEREIRA.

Service Providers

Compañía Anónima Nacional Teléfonos de Venezuela (CANTV): Edif. NEA, 20, Avda Libertador, Caracas 1010-A; tel. (212) 500-3016; fax (212) 500-3512; e-mail amora@cantv.com.ve; internet www.cantv.net; privatized in 1991; 49% state-owned, 40% owned by Verizon (USA); 11% owned by employees; Pres. GUSTAVO ROOSEN; Gen. Man. EDUARDO MENASCÉ.

Movilnet: Edif. NEA, 20, Avda Libertador, Caracas 1010-A; tel. (202) 705-7901; e-mail info@movilnet.com.ve; internet www.movilnet.com.ve; f. 1992; mobile cellular telephone operator; owned by CANTV; Pres. GUILLERMO OLAIZOLA.

CVG Telecomunicaciones, CA (CVG Telecom): Puerto Ordaz; f. 2004; state-owned telecommunications co.

Digicel CA: Caracas; internet www.digicel.com.ve; owned by Banco Santander Central Hispano of Spain; fixed-line telecommunications.

Digitel TIM: Caracas; e-mail 0412empres@digitel.com.ve; internet www.digitel.com.ve; f. 2000; mobile cellular telephone operator; owned by Telecom Italia Mobile (TIM) of Italy.

Intercable: Avda La Pedregosa Sur, cruce con Avda Los Próceres, Tapias; e-mail jguerrero@multimedios.net; internet www.intercable.net; cable, internet and telecommunications services; Dir JUAN GERARDO GUERRERO.

NetUno: Caracas; f. 1995; voice, data and video transmission services; Pres. GILBERT MINIONIS.

TelCel CA: Edif. Parque Cristal, Torre Este, 14°, Avda Francisco de Miranda, Caracas; tel. (212) 200-8201; internet www.telcel.net.ve; f. 1991; acquired by Telefónica Móviles, SA (Spain) in 2004; mobile cellular telephone operator; Pres. ENRIQUE GARCÍA VIAMONTE.

BROADCASTING

Regulatory Authorities

Cámara Venezolana de la Industria de Radiodifusión: Avda Antonio José Istúriz entre Mohedano y Country Club, La Castellana, Caracas; tel. (212) 263-2228; fax (212) 261-4783; e-mail camradio@camradio.org.ve; internet www.camradio.org.ve; Pres. MIGUEL ANGEL MARTÍNEZ.

Cámara Venezolana de Televisión: Edif. Venevisión, 4°, Colinas de Los Caobos, Caracas; tel. (212) 708-9223; fax (212) 708-9146; e-mail esalinas@cisneros.com; regulatory body for private stations; Pres. EDUARDO SALINAS.

Radio

Radio Nacional de Venezuela (RNV): Final Calle Las Marías, entre Chapellín y Country Club, La Florida, Caracas 1050; tel. (212) 730-6022; fax (212) 731-1457; e-mail ondacortavenezuela@hotmail.com; internet www.rnv.gov.ve; f. 1936; state broadcasting org.; 15 stations; Gen. Man. HELENA SALCEDO.

There are also 20 cultural and some 500 commercial stations.

Television

Government Stations

Telesur (Televisora del Sur): Edif. Anexo VTV, 4°, Avda Principal Los Ruices, Caracas; tel. (212) 716-5605; e-mail contactenos@telesurtv.net; internet www.telesurtv.net; f. 2005; jtly owned by govts of Venezuela (51%), Argentina (20%), Cuba (19%) and Uruguay (10%); regional current affairs and general interest; Pres. Lt (retd) ANDRÉS IZARRA; Vice-Pres. ARAM AHARONIAN.

Venezolana de Televisión (VTV)—Canal 8: Edif. VTV, Avda Principal Los Ruices, Caracas; tel. (212) 239-4870; fax (212) 239-8102; internet www.venezuela.gov.ve/vtv; 26 relay stations; Pres. VLADIMIR VILLEGAS POLJAK.

Private Stations

Corporación Televén—Canal 10: Edif. Televén, 4ta Transversal con Avda Rómulo Gallegos, Urb. Horizonte, Apdo 1070, Caracas; tel. (212) 280-0011; fax (212) 280-0204; e-mail aferro@televen.com; internet www.televen.com; f. 1988; Pres. OMAR CAMERO ZAMORA.

Corporación Venezolana de Televisión (Venevisión)—Canal 4: Edif. Venevisión, Final Avda La Salle, Colinas de los Caobos, Apdo 6674, Caracas; tel. (212) 708-9224; fax (212) 708-9535; e-mail mponce@venevision.com.ve; internet www.venevision.net; f. 1961; commercial; Pres. GUSTAVO CISNEROS.

Globovisión—Canal 33: Quinta Globovisión, Avda Los Pinos, Urb. Alta Florida, Caracas; tel. (212) 730-2290; fax (212) 731-4380; e-mail info@globovision.com; internet www.globovision.com; f. 1994; 24-hour news and current affairs channel; Pres. GUILLERMO ZULOAGA; Gen. Man. ALBERTO FEDERICO RAVELL.

Puma TV: Edif. Puma, Calle Sanatorio del Avila, Boleita Norte, Caracas 1070; tel. (212) 232-5656; fax (212) 237-8655; e-mail recheverria@pumatv.net; subscription TV channel; Pres. JOSÉ RODRÍGUEZ.

Radio Caracas Televisión (RCTV)—Canal 2: Edif. RCTV, Dolores a Puente Soublette, Quinta Crespo, Caracas; tel. (212) 401-2222; fax (212) 401-2647; e-mail marriaga@rctv.net; internet www.rctv.net; f. 1953; commercial station; station in Caracas and 13 relay stations throughout the country; Pres. MARCEL GRANIER.

Televisora Andina de Mérida (TAM)—Canal 6: Edif. Imperador, Entrada Independiente, Avda 6 y 7, Calle 23, Mérida 5101; tel. and fax (274) 251-0660; fax (274) 251-0660; f. 1982; Pres. Most Rev. BALTAZAR ENRIQUE PORRAS CARDOZO.

VALE TV (Valores Educativos)—Canal 5: Quinta VALE TV, Final Avda La Salle, Colinas de los Caobos, Caracas 1050; tel. (212) 793-9215; fax (212) 708-9743; e-mail webmaster@valetv.com; internet www.valetv.com; f. 1998; Pres. Mgr NICOLÁS BERMÚDEZ; Man. MARÍA ISABEL ROJAS.

Zuliana de Televisión—Canal 30: Edif. 95.5 América, Avda 11 (Veritas), Maracaibo; tel. (265) 641-0355; fax (265) 641-0565; e-mail elregionalredac@iamnet.com; Pres. GILBERTO URDANETA FIDOL.

Finance

(cap. = capital; res = reserves; dep. = deposits; m. = million; brs = branches; amounts in bolívares unless otherwise indicated)

BANKING

Regulatory Authority

Superintendencia de Bancos (SUDEBAN): Edif. SUDEBAN, Avda Universidad, Apdo 6761, Caracas 1010; tel. (212) 505-0933; e-mail sudeban@sudeban.gov.ve; internet www.sudeban.gov.ve; regulates banking sector; Supt TRINO A. DÍAZ.

Central Bank

Banco Central de Venezuela: Avda Urdaneta, esq. de Carmelitas, Caracas 1010; tel. (212) 801-5111; fax (212) 861-0048; e-mail info@bcv.org.ve; internet www.bcv.org.ve; f. 1940; bank of issue and clearing house for commercial banks; granted autonomy 1992; controls international reserves, interest rates and exchange rates; cap. 10.0m., res 9,662,937m., dep. 4,374,707m. (Dec. 2002); Pres. DIEGO LUIS CASTELLANOS ESCALONA.

Commercial Banks

Banco Capital, CA: Carrera 17 cruce con Calle 26, Frente a La Plaza Bolívar, Barquisimeto, Lara; tel. (251) 31-4979; fax (251) 31-1831; e-mail eximport@bancocapital.net; internet www.bancocapital.net; f. 1980; cap. 1,500.0m., res 1,854.7m., dep. 60,428.3m. (Dec. 1997); Chair. and Pres. JOSÉ REINALDO FURIATI; Gen. Man. VICENTE M. FURIATI; 13 brs.

Banco del Caribe, CA: Edif. Banco del Caribe, 1°, Dr Paúl a esq. Salvador de León, Apdo 6704, Carmelitas, Caracas 1010; tel. (212) 505-5103; fax (212) 562-0460; e-mail producto@bancaribe.com.ve; internet www.bancaribe.com.ve; f. 1954; cap. 10,666.7m., res 12,831.3m., dep. 425,340.7m. (Dec. 1999); Pres. JOSÉ ANTONIO ELOSEGUI; Gen. Man. Dr LUIS E. DE LLANO; 70 brs and agencies.

Banco Caroní: Edif. Multicentro Banco Caroní, Vía Venezuela, Puerto Ordaz, Estado Bolívar; tel. (286) 23-2230; fax (286) 22-0995; e-mail carupsis@telcel.net.ve; Pres. ARÍSTIDES MAZA TIRADO.

Banco de Comercio Exterior (Bancoex): Central Gerencial Mohedano, 1°, Calle Los Chaguaramos, La Castellana, Caracas 1060; tel. (212) 265-1433; fax (212) 265-6722; e-mail exports@bancoex.com; internet www.bancoex.com; f. 1997 principally to promote non-traditional exports; state-owned; cap. US $200m.; Pres. VÍCTOR ALVAREZ.

VENEZUELA
Directory

Banco Confederado: Edif. Centro Financiero Confederado, Blvd Gómez cruce con Calle Marcano, Porlamar, Estado Nuevo Esparta; tel. (95) 65-4230; fax (95) 63-7033; e-mail dbanel002@bancoconfederado.com; internet www.bancoconfederado.com; Pres. HASSAN SALEH SALEH.

Banco Exterior, CA—Banco Universal: Edif. Banco Exterior, 1°, Avda Urdaneta, esq. Urapal a Río, Candelaria, Apdo 14278, Caracas 1011-A; tel. (212) 501-0441; fax (212) 575-3798; e-mail presidencia@bancoexterior.com; internet www.bancoexterior.com; f. 1958; cap. 45,360m., res 80,492.9m., dep. 533,973.6m. (Dec. 2002); Chair. FRANCISCO LÓPEZ HERRERA; Pres. VÍCTOR ALVAREZ; 72 brs.

Banco Federal, CA: Avda Manaure, cruce con Avda Ruiz Pineda, Coro, Falcón; tel. (268) 51-4011; e-mail masterbf@bancofederal.com; internet www.bancofederal.com; f. 1982; cap. 50m., dep. 357m. (Dec. 1986); Pres. NELSON MEZERHANE; Exec. Pres. ROGELIO TRUJILLO.

Banco de Fomento Regional Los Andes, CA: Avda 8, La Concordia con Calle 4, San Cristóbal, Táchira; tel. (276) 43-1269; f. 1951; Pres. EDGAR A. HERNÁNDEZ; Exec. Vice-Pres. PEDRO ROA SÁNCHEZ.

Banco de Fomento Regional Coro, CA: Avda Manaure, entre Calles Falcón y Zamora, Coro, Falcón; tel. (268) 51-4421; f. 1950; transferred to private ownership in 1994; Pres. ABRAHAM NAÍN SENIOR URBINA.

Banco Guayana, CA: Edif. Los Bancos, Avda Guayana con Calle Caura, Puerto Ordaz, Bolívar; f. 1955; state-owned; Pres. OSCAR EUSEBIO JIMÉNEZ AYESA.

Banco Industrial de Venezuela, CA: Torre Financiera BIV, Avda Las Delicias de Sabana Grande, cruce con Avda Francisco Solano López, Caracas 1010; tel. (212) 952-4051; fax (212) 952-6282; e-mail webmaster@biv.com.ve; internet www.biv.com.ve; f. 1937; 98% state-owned; cap. 100,000m. (Dec. 2001); Pres. LEONARDO GONZÁLEZ DELLÁN; 60 brs.

Banco Mercantil, CA: Edif. Mercantil, 35°, Avda Andrés Bello 1, San Bernardino, Apdo 789, Caracas 1010-A; tel. (212) 503-1111; fax (212) 503-1075; e-mail mercan24@bancomercantil.com; internet www.bancomercantil.com; f. 1925; cap. 134,172.0m., res 216,594.0m., dep. 4,703,246.0m. (Dec. 2003); Chair. and CEO Dr GUSTAVO A. MARTURET; 293 brs.

Banco Occidental de Descuento, SACA: Avda 5 de Julio, esq. Avda 17, Apdo 695, Maracaibo 4001-A, Zulia; tel. (261) 759-3011; fax (261) 750-2274; e-mail oficina.virtual@bodinternet.com; internet www.bodinternet.com; f. 1957; transferred to private ownership in 1991; Pres. VÍCTOR VARGAS IRAUSQUIN; Exec. Dir CÁNDIDO RODRÍGUEZ LOSADA; 17 brs.

Banco Standard Chartered: Edif. Banaven, Torre D, 5°, Avda la Estancia A, Chuao, Caracas 1060; tel. (212) 993-3293; fax (212) 993-3130; internet www.standardchartered.com/ve; f. 1980 as Banco Exterior de los Andes y de España; current name adopted in 1998 following acquisition by Standard Chartered Bank (UK); representative office only; Chair. DAVID LORETTA.

Banco de los Trabajadores de Venezuela (BTV) CA: Edif. BTV, Avda Universidad, esq. Colón a esq. Dr Díaz, Caracas; tel. (212) 541-7322; f. 1968 to channel workers' savings for the financing of artisans and small industrial firms; came under state control in 1982; Pres. JOSÉ SÁNCHEZ PIÑA; Man. SILVERIO ANTONIO NARVÁEZ; 14 agencies.

Banco de Venezuela (Grupo Santander): Torre Banco de Venezuela, 16°, Avda Universidad, esq. Sociedad a Traposos, Apdo 6268, Caracas 1010-A; tel. (212) 501-2556; fax (212) 501-2546; internet www.bancodevenezuela.com; f. 1890; fmrly Banco de Venezuela CA, 93.38% share purchased by Banco Santander (Spain) in Dec. 1996; changed name to above in 1998; acquired Banco Caracas, CA in Dec. 2000; cap. 40,523.7m., res 319,642.9m., dep. 4,208,032.6m. (Dec. 2003); Pres. MICHEL J. GOGUIKIAN; 202 brs and agencies.

Banesco: Torre Banesco, Avda Guaicaipuro con Avda Principal de Las Mercedes, Caracas; tel. (212) 952-4972; fax (212) 952-7124; e-mail atcliente@banesco.com; internet www.banesco.com; Chair. JUAN CARLOS ESCOTET RODRÍGUEZ; Exec. Pres. LUIS XAVIER LUJÁN PUIGBÓ.

BBVA Banco Provincial, SA: Centro Financiero Provincial, 27°, Avda Vollmer con Avda Este O, San Bernardino, Apdo 1269, Caracas 1011; tel. (212) 504-5098; fax (212) 574-9408; e-mail calidad@provincial.com; internet www.provincial.com; f. 1952; 55.14% owned by Banco Bilbao Vizcaya Argentaria, 26.27% owned by Grupo Polar; cap. 91,945.4m., res 621,387.0m., dep. 4,586,027.8m. (Dec. 2003); Pres. HERNÁN ANZOLA GIMÉNEZ; Exec. Pres. JOSÉ CARLOS PLA ROYO.

Corp Banca, CA Banco Universal: Torre Corp Banca, Plaza la Castellana, Chacao, Caracas 1060; tel. (212) 206-3333; fax (212) 206-4950; e-mail calidad@corpbanca.com.ve; internet www.corpbanca.com.ve; f. 1969; fmrly Banco Consolidado, current name adopted in 1997; cap. 40,000m., res 36,842.2m., dep. 709,751.5m. (Dec. 2003); Chair. JORGE SELUME ZAROR; CEO MARIO CHAMORRO; 116 brs.

Unibanca Banco Universal, CA: Torre Grupo Unión, Avda Universidad, esq. El Chorro, Apdo 2044, Caracas; tel. (212) 501-7031; fax (212) 563-0986; internet www.unibanca.com.ve; f. 2001 by merger of Banco Unión (f. 1943) and Caja Familia; Pres. Dr IGNACIO SALVATIERRA; Vice-Pres. JOSÉ Q. SALVATIERRA; 174 brs.

Venezolano de Crédito SA—Banco Universal: Edif. Banco Venezolano de Crédito, Avda Alameda, San Bernadino, Caracas 1011; tel. (212) 806-6111; fax (212) 541-2757; e-mail jurbano@venezolano.com; internet www.venezolano.com; f. 1925, as Banco Venezolano de Crédito, SACA; name changed as above in 2001; cap. 42,000.0m., res 71,052.4m., dep. 974,008.3m. (Dec. 2003); Pres. Dr OSCAR GARCÍA MENDOZA; 59 brs.

Mortgage and Credit Institutions

Banco Hipotecario Unido, SA: Edif. Banco Hipotecario Unido, Avda Este 2, No 201, Los Caobos, Apdo 1896, Caracas 1010; tel. (212) 575-1111; fax (212) 571-1075; f. 1961; cap. 230m., res 143m., dep. 8,075m. (May 1990); Pres. ARTURO J. BRILLEMBOURG; Gen. Man. ALFONSO ESPINOSA M.

Banco Hipotecario de la Vivienda Popular, SA: Intersección Avda Roosevelt y Avda Los Ilustres, frente a la Plaza Los Símbolos, Caracas; tel. (212) 62-9971; f. 1961; cap. 100m., res 68.2m., dep. 259.3m. (Dec. 1987); Pres. HELY MALARET M.; First Vice-Pres. ALFREDO ESQUIVAR.

Banco Hipotecario del Zulia, CA: Avda 2, El Milagro con Calle 84, Maracaibo, Zulia; tel. (261) 91-6055; f. 1963; cap. 120m., res 133.5m., dep. 671.5m. (Nov. 1986); Pres. ALBERTO LÓPEZ BRACHO.

Development Banks

Banco de Desarrollo Económico y Social de Venezuela (BANDES): Torre Bandes, Avda Universidad, Traposos a Colón, Caracas 1010; tel. (212) 505-8010; fax (212) 505-8030; e-mail apublicos@bandes.gov.ve; internet www.bandes.gov.ve; state-owned devt bank; Pres. NELSON MERENTES; Gen. Man. MARITZA BALZA.

Banco del Pueblo Soberano CA: Edif. El Gallo de Oro, Gradillas a San Jacinto Parroquia Catedral, Caracas; tel. (212) 505-2800; fax (212) 505-2995; e-mail abarrera@bancodelpueblo.com.ve; internet www.bancodelpueblo.com.ve; f. 1999; microfinance; Pres. HUMBERTO ORTEGA DÍAZ; Dir JORGE GONZÁLEZ.

BANMUJER: Edif. Sudameris, planta baja, Avda Urdaneta con Avda Fuerzas Armadas, esq. Plaza España, Caracas 1010; tel. (212) 564-3015; e-mail banmujer@banmujer.gov.ve; internet www.banmujer.gov.ve; f. 2001; state-owned bank offering loans to women; Pres. NORA CASTAÑEDA.

Fondo de Desarrollo Microfinanciero (FONDEMI): Edif. Sudameras, 2°, Avda Urdaneta, esq. Fuerzas Armadas, Caracas 1030; tel. (212) 564-4327; fax 564-0170; e-mail promocion@fondemi.gov.ve; internet www.fondemi.gov.ve; f. 2001; microfinancing devt fund; Pres. ISA MERCEDES SIERRA FLORES.

Foreign Banks

ABN AMRO Bank NV (Netherlands): Edif. Centro Seguros Sud América, 1°, Avda Francisco de Miranda, El Rosal, Apdo 69179, Caracas 1060; tel. (212) 957-0300; fax (212) 953-5758.

Banco do Brasil SA (Brazil): Edif. Centro Lido, 9°, Of. 93A, Avda Francisco de Miranda, El Rosal, 1067-A Caracas; tel. (212) 952-2674; fax (212) 952-5251; e-mail caracas@bb.com.br; internet www.bb.com.br.

Citibank NA (USA): Edif. Citibank, esq. de Carmelitas a esq. de Altagracia, Apdo 1289, Caracas; tel. (212) 81-9501; fax (212) 81-6493; Pres. VÍCTOR J. MENEZES; 4 brs.

Banking Association

Asociación Bancaria de Venezuela: Torre Asociación Bancaria de Venezuela, 1°, Avda Venezuela, El Rosal, Caracas; tel. (212) 951-4711; fax (212) 951-3696; e-mail abvinfo@asobanca.com.ve; internet www.asobanca.com.ve; f. 1959; 49 mems; Pres. ARÍSTIDES MAZA TIRADO.

STOCK EXCHANGE

Bolsa de Valores de Caracas, CA: Edif. Atrium, Nivel C-1, Calle Sorocaima entre Avdas Tamanaco y Venezuela, Urb. El Rosal, Apdo 62724-A, Caracas 1060-A; tel. (212) 905-5511; fax (212) 952-2640; e-mail bvc@caracasstock.com; internet www.caracasstock.com; f. 1947; 65 mems; Pres. NELSON ORTIZ CUSNIER.

INSURANCE

Supervisory Board

Superintendencia de Seguros: Edif. Torre del Desarollo P.H., Avda Venezuela, El Rosal, Chacao, Caracas 1060; tel. (212) 905-1611; fax (212) 953-8615; e-mail sudeseg@sudeseg.gov.ve; internet www.sudeseg.gov.ve; Supt LUDMILA SOTO.

VENEZUELA

Principal Insurance Companies

Adriática, CA de Seguros: Edif. Adriática de Seguros, Avda Andrés Bello, esq. de Salesianos, Caracas; tel. (212) 571-5702; fax (212) 571-0812; e-mail adriatica@adriatica.com.ve; internet www.adriatica.com.ve; f. 1952; Pres. FRANÇOIS THOMAZEAU; Exec. Vice-Pres. GHISLAIN FABRE.

Avila, CA de Seguros: Edif. Centro Seguros La Paz, 7°, Avda Francisco de Miranda, Caracas; tel. (212) 239-7911; fax (212) 238-2470; f. 1936; Pres. RAMÓN RODRÍGUEZ; Vice-Pres. JUAN LUIS CASAÑAS.

Carabobo, CA de Seguros: Edif. Centro Empresarial Sábana Grande, 12°, Ofs 1 y 2, Calle Negrín, entre Avda Francisco Solano y Blvd de Sábana Grande, El Recreo, Caracas; tel. (212) 761-8514; fax (212) 761-5727; f. 1955; Pres. PAUL FRAYND; Gen. Man. ENRIQUE ABREU.

La Occidental, CA de Seguros: Edif. Seguros Occidental, Avda 4 (Bella Vista) esq. con Calle 71, No 10126, Maracaibo, Zulia; tel. (261) 798-4780; fax (261) 797-5422; e-mail relaciones@laoccidental.com; internet www.laoccidental.com; f. 1956; Pres. TOBÍAS CARRERO NÁCAR; Dir CARLOS MONÍZ ROCHA.

La Oriental, CA de Seguros: Torre Sede Gerencial La Castellana, Avda Francisco de Miranda, cruce con Avda Principal de la Castellana, Chacao, Caracas; tel. (212) 277-5000; fax (212) 263-1501; internet www.laoriental.com; f. 1975; Pres. GONZALO LAURÍA ALCALÁ.

Seguros Los Andes, CA: Edif. Seguros Los Andes, Avda Las Pilas, Santa Inés, San Cristóbal, Táchira; tel. (276) 340-2611; fax (276) 340-2596; Pres. RAMÓN RODRÍGUEZ.

Seguros Caracas de Liberty Mutual, CAV: Torre Seguros Caracas C-4, Centro Comercial El Parque, Avda Francisco de Miranda, Los Palos Grandes, Caracas; tel. (212) 209-9111; fax (212) 209-9556; f. 1943; Pres. ROBERTO SALAS.

Seguros Catatumbo, CA: Edif. Seguros Catatumbo, Avda 4 (Bella Vista), No 77–55, Apdo 1083, Maracaibo; tel. (261) 700-5555; fax (261) 216-0037; e-mail mercado@seguroscatatumbo.com; internet www.seguroscatatumbo.com; f. 1957; cap. 9,300m. (2003); Pres. ATENÁGORAS VERGEL RIVERA.

Seguros Mapfre La Seguridad, CA: Calle 3A, Frente a La Torre Express, La Urbina Sur, Apdo 473, Caracas 1010; tel. (212) 204-8000; fax (212) 204-8751; f. 1943; owned by Seguros Mapfre (Spain); Pres. ARISTÓBULO BAUSELA.

Seguros Mercantil, CA: Edif. Seguros Mercantil, Avda Libertador con calle Andrés Galarraga, Chacao, Caracas; tel. (212) 276-2000; fax (212) 276-2596; e-mail rcubillanb@segurosmercantil.com; internet www.segurosmercantil.com; f. 1988; acquired Seguros Orinoco in 2002; Pres. ALBERTO BENSHIMOL; Gen. Man. RAFAEL CUBILLÁN.

Seguros Nuevo Mundo, SA: Edif. Seguros Nuevo Mundo, Avda Luis Roche con 3 transversal, Altamira, Apdo 2062, Caracas; tel. (212) 201-1111; fax (212) 263-1435; internet www.nmbc.com.ve; f. 1856; cap. 100m. (2003); Pres. RAFAEL PEÑA ALVAREZ; Exec. Vice-Pres. RAFAEL VALENTINO.

Seguros La Previsora, CNA: Torre La Previsora, Avda Abraham Lincoln, Sábana Grande, Caracas; tel. (212) 709-1555; fax (212) 709-1976; internet www.previsora.com; f. 1914; Pres. ALBERTO QUINTANA; Exec. Vice-Pres. JUAN CARLOS MALDONADO.

Seguros Venezuela, CA: Edif. Seguros Venezuela, 8° y 9°, Avda Francisco de Miranda, Urb. Campo Alegre, Caracas; tel. (212) 901-7111; fax (212) 901-7218; e-mail carmen.guillen@segurosvenezuela.com; internet www.segurosvenezuela.com; part of American International group; Exec. Pres. ENRIQUE BANCHIERI ORTIZ.

Universitas de Seguros, CA: Edif. Impres Médico, 2°, Avda Tamanaco, El Rosal, Caracas; tel. (212) 951-6711; fax (212) 901-7506; e-mail tbarrera@universitasdeseguros.com; internet www.universitasdeseguros.com; cap. 6,500m; Pres. ANA TERESA FERRINI.

Insurance Association

Cámara de Aseguradores de Venezuela: Torre Taeca, 2°, Avda Guaicaipuro, El Rosal, Apdo 3460, Caracas 1010-A; tel. (212) 952-4411; fax (212) 951-3268; e-mail rrpp@camaraseg.org; internet www.camaraseg.org; f. 1951; 42 mems; Pres. CARLOS LUENGO; Exec. Pres. JUAN B. BLANCO-URIBE.

Trade and Industry

GOVERNMENT AGENCIES

Comisión de Administración de Divisas (CADIVI): Antiguo Edif. PDVSA Servicios, 6°, Avda Leonardo Da Vinci, Los Chaguaramos, Caracas; tel. (212) 606-3904; fax (212) 606-3026; e-mail info@cadivi.gov.ve; internet www.cadivi.gov.ve; f. 2003; regulates access to foreign currency; Pres. MARÍA ESPINOZA DE ROBLES.

Corporación Venezolana de Guayana (CVG): Edif. General, 2°, Avda La Estancia, Apdo 7000, Chuao, Caracas; tel. (212) 992-9764; fax (212) 993-0554; e-mail presidenciaccs@cvg.com; internet www.cvg.com; f. 1960; to organize devt of Guayana area, particularly its metal ore and hydroelectric resources; Pres. VÍCTOR ALVAREZ RODRÍGUEZ (Minister of Basic Industry and Mining).

Dirección General Sectorial de Minas y Geología: Avda Lecuna, Torre Oeste, 4°, Parque Central, Caracas; tel. (212) 708-7108; fax (212) 575-2497; division of Ministry of Energy and Mines responsible for formulating and implementing national policy on non-petroleum mineral reserves; Vice-Minister ORLANDO ORTEGANO.

Fondo Intergubermental para la Decentralización (FIDES): Avda Las Acacias, cruce con Avda Casanova, Torre Banhorient, Sábana Grande, Caracas; tel. (212) 708-0000; fax (212) 708-3642; e-mail info@fides.gov.ve; internet www.fides.gov.ve; f. 1993; part of the Ministry of Planning and Development; co-ordinates investment; Pres. RICHARD CANÁN.

Instituto Nacional de Nutrición (INN): Edif. INN, Avda Baralt, esq. El Carmen, Quinta Crespo, Caracas; tel. (212) 483-5142; Dir RHAITZA MENDOZA.

Instituto Nacional de Tierras (INTI): Avda Lecuna, Torre Oeste, 37°, Parque Central, Caracas; tel. (212) 574-8554; fax (212) 576-2201; internet www.inti.gov.ve; f. 1945, as Instituto Agrario Nacional (IAN); present name adopted in 2001; under Agrarian Law to assure ownership of the land to those who worked on it; now authorized to expropriate and reclassify idle or unproductive lands; Pres. RICHARD VIVAS.

Instituto Nacional de la Vivienda: Torre Inavi, Avda Francisco de Miranda entre Guaicaipuro y San Ignacio de Loyola, Chacao, Caracas; tel. (212) 206-9279; e-mail sugerencias@inavi.gov.ve; internet www.inavi.gov.ve; f. 1975; administers government housing projects; Pres. JESÚS HERNÁNDEZ GONZÁLEZ.

Mercal, CA: Edif. Torres Seguros Orinoco, Avda Fuerzas Armadas, esq. Socarras, Caracas; tel. (212) 564-3856; e-mail gestioncomunicacional@mercal.gov.ve; internet www.mercal.gov.ve; responsible for marketing agricultural products; fmrly Corporación de Mercadeo Agrícola; Pres. MARÍA MILAGROS TORO LANDAETA.

Superintendencia de Inversiones Extranjeras (SIEX): Edif. La Perla, Bolsa a Mercaderes, 3°, Apdo 213, Caracas 1010; tel. (212) 483-6666; fax (212) 484-4368; e-mail siexdespacho@cantv.net; internet www.siex.gov.ve; f. 1974; supervises foreign investment in Venezuela; Supt MIRIAM BEATRIZ AGUILERA DE BLANCO.

DEVELOPMENT ORGANIZATIONS

Corporación de Desarrollo de la Pequeña y Mediana Industria (Corpoindustria): Aragua; tel. (243) 23459; internet www.sain.org.ve/corpoind/cedinco.htm; promotes the devt of small and medium-sized industries; Pres. Dr CARLOS GONZÁLEZ-LÓPEZ.

CVG Bauxita Venezolana (Bauxivén): Caracas; f. 1978 to develop the bauxite deposits at Los Pijiguaos; financed by the FIV and the CVG which has a majority holding; Pres. JOSÉ TOMÁS MILANO.

Fondo de Desarrollo Agropecuario, Pesquero, Forestal y Afines (FONDAFA): Edif. FONDAFA, esq. Salvador de León a Socarras, La Hoyada, Caracas; tel. (212) 542-3570; fax (212) 542-5887; e-mail fondafa@fondafa.gov.ve; internet www.fondafa.gov.ve; f. 1974; devt of agriculture, fishing and forestry; Pres. ALIRIO RONDÓN.

Fondo de Desarrollo Microfinanciero (FONDEMI): see Finance—Development Banks.

CHAMBERS OF COMMERCE AND INDUSTRY

Federación Venezolana de Cámaras y Asociaciones de Comercio y Producción (Fedecámaras): Edif. Fedecámaras, Avda El Empalme, Urb. El Bosque, Apdo 2568, Caracas; tel. (212) 731-1711; fax (212) 730-2097; e-mail direje@fedecameras.org.ve; internet www.fedecamaras.org.ve; f. 1944; 307 mems; Pres. ALBIS MUÑOZ; Exec. Dir MARIO TEPEDINO RAVEN.

Cámara de Comercio de Caracas: Edif. Cámara de Comercio de Caracas, 8°, Avda Andrés Eloy Blanco 215, Los Caobos, Caracas; tel. (212) 571-3222; fax (212) 571-0050; e-mail comercio@ccc.com.ve; internet www.ccc.com.ve; f. 1893; 650 mems; Exec. Dir VLADIMIR CHELMINSKI.

Cámara de Industriales de Caracas: Edif. Cámara de Industriales, 3°, Avda Las Industrias, esq. Pte Anauco, La Candelaria, Apdo 14255, Caracas 1011; tel. (212) 571-4224; fax (212) 571-2009; e-mail ciccs@telcel.net.ve; internet www.cic.org.ve; f. 1939; Pres. ROBERTO J. BALL; 550 mems.

Cámara Venezolano-Americana de Industria y Comercio (Venamcham): Torre Credival, 10°, Of. A, 2a Avda Campo Alegre, Apdo 5181, Caracas 1010-A; tel. (212) 263-0833; fax (212) 263-2060; e-mail venam@venamcham.org; internet www.venamcham.org; f. 1950; Pres. IMELDA CISNEROS; Gen. Man. ANTONIO HERRERA VAILLANT.

VENEZUELA *Directory*

There are chambers of commerce and industry in all major provincial centres.

EMPLOYERS' ORGANIZATIONS
Caracas

Asociación Nacional de Comerciantes e Industriales: Plaza Panteón Norte 1, Apdo 33, Caracas; f. 1936; traders and industrialists; Pres. Dr HORACIO GUILLERMO VILLALOBOS; Sec. R. H. OJEDA MAZZARELLI; 500 mems.

Asociación Nacional de Industriales Metalúrgicos y de Minería de Venezuela: Edif. Cámara de Industriales, 9°, Puente Anauco a Puente República, Apdo 14139, Caracas; metallurgy and mining; Pres. JOSÉ LUIS GÓMEZ; Exec. Dir LUIS CÓRDOVA BRITO.

Asociación Textil Venezolana: Edif. Textilera Gran Colombia, Calle el Club 8, Los Cortijos de Lourdes, Caracas; tel. (212) 238-1744; fax (212) 239-4089; f. 1957; textiles; Pres. DAVID FIHMAN; 68 mems.

Asociación Venezolana de Exportadores (AVEX): Centro Comercial Coneresa, Redoma de Prados del Este 435, 2°, Prados del Este, Caracas; tel. (212) 979-5042; fax (212) 979-4542; e-mail directorejecutivo@avex.com.ve; internet www.avex.com.ve; Pres. FRANCISCO MENDOZA.

Cámara Petrolera: Torre Domus, 3°, Of. 3-A, Avda Abraham Lincoln con Calle Olimpo, Sábana Grande, Caracas; tel. (212) 794-1222; fax (212) 793-8529; e-mail informacion@camarapetrolera.org; internet www.camarapetrolera.org; f. 1978; asscn of petroleum-sector cos; Pres. ANTONIO VINCENTELLI.

Confederación Venezolana de Industriales (CONINDUSTRIA): Edif. CIEMI, Avda Principal de Chuao, Caracas 1061; tel. (212) 991-2116; fax (212) 991-7737; e-mail comunicaciones@conindustria.org; internet www.conindustria.org; asscn of industrialists; Pres. EDUARDO GÓMEZ SIGALA; Exec. Pres. JUAN FRANCISCO MEJÍA B.

Confederación Nacional de Asociaciones de Productores Agropecuarios (FEDEAGRO): Edif. Casa de Italia, planta baja, Avda La Industria, San Bernardino, Caracas 1010; tel. (212) 571-4035; fax (212) 573-4423; e-mail fedeagro@fedeagro.org; internet www.fedeagro.org; f. 1960; agricultural producers; 133 affiliated asscns; Pres. GUSTAVO MORENO LLERAS.

Federación Nacional de Ganaderos de Venezuela (FEDENAGA): Avda Urdaneta, Centro Financiero Latino, 18°, Ofs 18-2 y 18-4, La Candelaria, Caracas; tel. (212) 563-2153; fax (212) 564-7273; e-mail fedenagat@cantv.net; cattle owners; Pres. JOSÉ LUIS BETANCOURT.

Unión Patronal Venezolana del Comercio: Edif. General Urdaneta, 2°, Marrón a Pelota, Apdo 6578, Caracas; tel. (582) 561-7025; fax (582) 561-4321; trade; Sec. H. ESPINOZA BANDERS.

Other Towns

Asociación de Comerciantes e Industriales del Zulia (ACIZ): Edif. Los Cerros, 3°, Calle 77 con Avda 3C, Apdo 91, Maracaibo, Zulia; tel. (261) 91-7174; fax (261) 91-2570; f. 1941; traders and industrialists; Pres. JORGE AVILA.

Asociación Nacional de Cultivadores de Algodón (ANCA) (National Cotton Growers' Association): Edif. Portuguesa, Avda Los Pioneros, Sector Aspiga-Acarigua; tel. (255) 621-5111; fax (255) 621-4368; Sec. CONCEPCIÓN QUIJADA G.

Asociación Nacional de Empresarios y Trabajadores de la Pesca: Cumaná; fishermen's org.

Unión Nacional de Cultivadores de Tabaco: Urb. Industrial La Hamaca, Avda Hustaf Dalen, Maracay; tobacco growers.

STATE HYDROCARBONS COMPANIES

Corporación Petroquímica de Venezuela (CPV): Torre Pequiven, Avda Francisco de Miranda, Chacao, Apdo 2066, Caracas 1010-A; tel. (212) 201-4011; fax (212) 201-3189; e-mail webmaster@pdvsa.com; internet www.pequiven.com; f. 1956 as Instituto Venezolano de Petroquímica; became Pequiven in 1977; name changed as above in 2005 following independence from PDVSA; involved in many joint ventures with foreign and private Venezuelan interests for expanding petrochemical industry; active in regional economic integration; an affiliate of PDVSA from 1978 until 2005; Pres. SAÚL AMELIACH.

Petróleos de Venezuela, SA (PDVSA): Edif. Petróleos de Venezuela, Torre Este, Avda Libertador, La Campiña, Apdo 169, Caracas 1010-A; tel. (212) 708-4743; fax (212) 708-4661; e-mail saladeprensa@pdvsa.com; internet www.pdvsa.com; f. 1975; holding co for national petroleum industry; responsible for petrochemical sector since 1978 and for devt of coal resources in western Venezuela since 1985; Pres. RAFAEL DARÍO RAMÍREZ CARREÑO (Minister of Energy and Petroleum); Vice-Pres. of Exploration and Production LUIS VIERMA; Vice-Pres. of Refining ALEJANDRO GRANADO; The following are subsidiaries of PDVSA:

Bariven, SA: Edif. PDVSA Los Chaguaramos, 6°, Avda Leonardo Da Vinci, Urb. Los Chaguaramos, Apdo 1889, Caracas 1010-A; tel. (212) 606-4060; fax (212) 606-2741; handles the petroleum, petrochemical and hydrocarbons industries' overseas purchases of equipment and materials.

Bitúmenes Orinoco, SA (PDVSA-BITOR): Edif. PDVSA Exploración, Producción y Mejoramiento, 9°, Avda Ernesto Blohm, La Estancia, Chuao, Apdo 3470, Caracas 1010-A; tel. (212) 908-2811; fax (212) 908-3982; e-mail abreuew@pdvsa.com; plans, develops and markets the bitumen resources of the Orinoco belt; produces Venezuela's trademark boiler fuel Orimulsion.

Corporación Venezolana del Petróleo (CVP): Edif. Pawa, Calle Cali con Avda Veracruz, Las Mercedes, Caracas; internet www.pdvsa.com/index2.html; f. 1960, reformed 2003; responsible for PDVSA's negotiations with other petroleum cos.

Deltaven, SA: Edif. PDVSA Deltaven, Avda Principal de La Floresta, La Floresta, Caracas 1060; tel. (212) 208-1111; internet www.pdvsa.com/index2.html; f. 1997; markets PDVSA products and services within Venezuela.

INTERVEN Venezuela, SA: Edif. Chacofi II, planta baja, entrepiso y 2°, Avda del Libertador 602, Buenos Aires, Argentina; tel. (11) 4813-9652; f. 1986; manage PDVSA's interests in South America.

Intevep, SA: Centro de Investigación y Apoyo Tecnológico, Edif. Sede Central, Urb. Santa Rosa, Sector El Tambor, Los Teques, Apdo 76343, Caracas 1070-A; tel. (212) 330-6011; fax (212) 330-6448; internet www.intevep.pdvsa.com/index2.html; f. 1973 as Fundación para la Investigación de Hidrocarburos y Petroquímica; present name adopted in 1979; research and devt br. of PDVSA; undertakes applied research and devt in new products and processes and provides specialized technical services for the petroleum and petrochemical industries.

Palmaven: Edif. PDVSA La Floresta, Torre Palmaven, 7°, Avda Principal, Urb. La Floresta, Caracas; tel. (212) 204-4511; internet www.pdvsa.com/index2.html; sustainable devt agency of PDVSA; Man. Dir EDDIE RAMÍREZ.

PDV Marina: Edif. Petróleos de Venezuela Refinación, Suministro y Comercio, Torre Oeste, 9°, Avda Libertador, La Campiña, Apdo 2103, Caracas 1010-A; tel. (212) 708-1111; fax (212) 708-2200; internet www.pdvsa.com/index2.html; f. 1990; responsible for the distribution, by ship, of PDVSA products; Pres. FERNANDO CAMEJO ARENAS.

PDVSA Gas: Edif. Sucre, Avda Francisco de Miranda, La Floresta, Caracas; tel. (212) 208-6212; fax (212) 208-6288; e-mail messina@pdvsa.com; internet www.pdvsa.com/index2.html; f. 1998; gas exploration and extraction; Pres. NELSON MARTÍNEZ; Dir-Gen. JUAN JOSÉ GARCÍA.

UTILITIES
Electricity

CADAFE (Compañía de Administración y Fomento Eléctrico): Edif. Cadafe, 14°, Avda Sanz, El Marqués, Caracas; tel. (212) 280-8583; fax (212) 280-8667; e-mail dirgestion@cadafe.com.ve; internet www.cadafe.com.ve; f. 1958; electricity transmission; Pres. NERVIS VILLALOBOS; five subsidiaries:

CADELA (Compañía Anónima Electricidad de los Andes): San Cristóbal; tel. (276) 341-6128; fax (276) 300-3066; internet www.cadela.gov.ve; f. 1991; electricity transmission in Táchira, Mérida, Barinas and Trujillo; Pres. JHONNY CASTRO.

DESURCA (Desarrollo Uribante Caparo Compañía Anónima): Centro Comercial El Pinar, nivel sótano, Urb. Las Acacias, San Cristóbal; tel. (276) 347-1404; fax (276) 347-4428; f. 1990; oversees construction of the Uribante-Caparo hydroelectric complex.

ELECENTRO (Compañía Anónima Electricidad del Centro): Calle Mariño Sur, 45A, Maracay; tel. (243) 300-3062; internet www.elecentro.gov.ve; f. 1991; electricity transmission in Aragua, Miranda, Guárico, Apure and Amazonas.

ELEORIENTE (Compañía Anónima Electricidad de Oriente): Edif. Eleoriente, Avda Universidad, Cumana; tel. (293) 400-1177; fax (293) 400-1188; f. 1991; electricity transmission in Anzoátegui, Bolívar and Sucre.

ELEOCCIDENTE (Compañía Anónima Electricidad de Occidente): Edif. Centro Profesional MASCOLO, Calle 28, entre Avdas 30 y 31, Acarigua; tel. (255) 600-2026; fax (255) 600-2071; f. 1991; electricity transmission in Falcón, Lara, Yaracuy, Carabobo, Cojedes and Portuguesa.

Semda (Sistema Eléctrico de Monagas y Delta Amacuro): Edif. Nicamale, Calle Mariño con Piar, Maturín; tel. (291) 641-3654; fax (291) 641-3613; f. 1998; generation and transmission of electricity in Monagas and Delta Amacuro.

La Electricidad de Caracas (EDC): Edif. La Electricidad de Caracas, Avda Vollmer, San Bernadino, Caracas; tel. (212) 502-

VENEZUELA

2111; e-mail info@edc-ven.com; supplies electricity to capital; owned by AES Corpn; Pres. ANDRÉS GLUSKI.

Electrificación del Caroní, CA (Edelca): Edif. General, planta baja, Avda La Estancia, Chuao, Caracas; tel. (212) 950-2111; fax (212) 950-2808; e-mail wriera@edelca.com.ve; internet www.edelca.com.ve; affiliate of Corporación Venezolana de Guayana; supplies some 70% of the country's electricity; Pres. DANIEL MACHADO GÓMEZ.

Enelco (Energía Eléctrica de la Costa Oriental): tel. (264) 370-5555; e-mail atencionalcliente@enelco.com.ve; internet www.enelco.com.ve; electricity services to the eastern coast of the Lago de Maracaibo region.

Sistema Eléctrico de Nueva Esparta (Seneca): electricity co; privatized in Oct. 1998.

Gas

ENAGAS (Ente Nacional del Gas): Edif. PDVSA, Torre Sur, 9° y 10°, Avda Libertador, Caracas; tel. (212) 706-6654; fax (212) 706-6471; internet www.enagas.gov.ve; f. 1999; autonomous agency attached to the Ministry of Energy and Petroleum; regulatory body.

Water

Hidroven: Edif. Hidroven, Avda Augusto César Sandino con 9a Transversal, Maripérez, Caracas; tel. (212) 781-4778; fax (212) 781-6424; e-mail hvenpres@cantv.net; internet www.hidroven.gov.ve; national water co; owns Hidroandes, Hidrocapital, Hidrocaribe, Hidrofalcon, Hidrolago, Hidrollanos, Hidropaez, Hidrosuroeste, Aguas de Monagas, Aguas de Ejido, Hidrolara, Aguas de Anaco, Aguas de Cojedes, Aguas de Mérida, Aguas de Apure, Aguas de Yaracuy, Aguas de Portuguesa; Pres. CRISTÓBAL FRANCISCO ORTIZ; Vice-Pres. FRANCISCO DURÁN.

Compañía Anónima Hidrológica de la Región Capital (Hidrocapital): Edif. Hidroven, Avda Augusto César Sandino con 9a Transversal, Maripérez, Caracas; tel. (212) 793-1638; fax (212) 793-6794; e-mail 73070.2174@compuserve.com; internet www.hidrocapital.com.ve; f. 1992; owned by Hidroven; operates water supply in Federal District and states of Miranda and Vargas; Pres. ALEJANDRO HITCHER.

TRADE UNIONS

About one-quarter of the labour force in Venezuela belongs to unions, more than one-half of which are legally recognized. Venezuela's union movement is strongest in the public sector.

Confederación de Trabajadores de Venezuela (CTV) (Confederation of Venezuelan Workers): Edif. José Vargas, 17°, Avda Este 2, Los Caobos, Caracas; tel. (212) 575-0005; e-mail mcova@ctv.org.ve; internet www.ctv.org.ve; f. 1936; largest trade union confederation; principally active in public sector; Chávez Govt disputes legitimacy of election of CTV leadership; Pres. CARLOS ALFONSO ORTEGA CARVAJAL; Sec.-Gen. MANUEL JOSÉ COVA FERMÍN; 1,000,000 mems from 24 regional and 16 industrial feds.

Fedepetrol: union of petroleum workers; Pres. RAFAEL ROSALES.

Federación Campesina (FC): peasant union; CTV affiliate; Leader RUBÉN LANZ.

Fetrametal: union of metal workers; Leader JOSÉ MOLLEGAS.

Fuerza Bolivariana de Trabajadores (FBT): f. 2000; pro-Govt union.

Movimiento Nacional de Trabajadores para la Liberación (MONTRAL): Edif. Don Miguel, 6°, esq. Cipreses, Caracas; f. 1974; affiliated to CLAT and WFTU; Pres. LAUREANO ORTIZ BRAEAMONTE; Sec.-Gen. DAGOBERTO GONZÁLEZ; co-ordinating body for the following trade unions:

Central Nacional Campesina (CNC): Pres. REINALDO VÁSQUEZ.

Cooperativa Nacional de Trabajadores de Servicios Múltiples (CNTSM).

Federación Nacional de Sindicatos Autónomos de Trabajadores de la Educación de Venezuela (FENASATREV): Pres. LUIS EFRAÍN ORTA.

Federación de los Trabajadores de Hidrocarburos de Venezuela (FETRAHIDROCARBUROS).

Frente de Trabajadores Copeyanos (FTC): Sec.-Gen. DAGOBERTO GONZÁLEZ.

Movimiento Agrario Social-Cristiano (MASC): Sec.-Gen. GUSTAVO MENDOZA.

Movimiento Magisterial Social-Cristiano (MMSC): Sec.-Gen. FELIPE MONTILLA.

Movimiento Nacional de Trabajadores de Comunicaciones (MONTRAC).

Movimiento Nacional de Trabajadores Estatales de Venezuela (MONTREV).

Transport

RAILWAYS

In 1999 work began on lines linking Acarigua and Turén (45 km) and Morón and Riecito (100 km). Construction of the first section (Caracas–Cúa) of a line linking the capital to the existing network at Puerto Cabello (219 km in total) was also begun. Services on the underground system began in 1983 on a two-line system: east to west from Palos Verdes to Propatria; north to south from Capitolio/El Silencio to Zoológico. A southern extension from Plaza Venezuela to El Valle opened in 1995. Further extensions to the lines were under way in 2005.

CVG Ferrominera Orinoco, CA: Vía Caracas, Puerto Ordaz, Apdo 399, Bolívar; tel. (286) 30-3451; fax (286) 30-3333; e-mail 104721.2354@compuserve.com; f. 1976; state-owned; operates two lines San Isidro mine–Puerto Ordaz (316 km) and El Pao–Palua (55 km) for transporting iron ore; Pres. Ing. LEOPOLDO SUCRE FIGARELLA; Man. M. ARO G.

Ferrocarril de CVG Bauxilum—Operadora de Bauxita: Caracas; tel. (212) 40-1716; fax (212) 40-1707; f. 1989; state-owned; operates line linking Los Pijiguaos with river Orinoco port of Gumilla (52 km) for transporting bauxite; Pres. P. MORALES.

Instituto Autónomo de Ferrocarriles del Estado (IAFE): Edif. Torre Británica de Seguros, 7° y 8°, Avda José Féliz Sosa, Urb. Altamira, Chacao, Caracas 1062-A; tel. (212) 201-8911; e-mail relacp@cantv.net; state co; 336 km; Pres. RAFAEL ALVAREZ; Vice-Pres. INOVA CASTRO PÉREZ.

CA Metro de Caracas: Multicentro Empresarial del Este, Edif. Miranda, Torre B, 7°, Avda Francisco de Miranda, Apdo 61036, Caracas; tel. (212) 206-7111; fax (212) 266-3346; internet www.metrodecaracas.com.ve; f. 1976 to supervise the construction and use of the underground railway system; state-owned; Pres. DANIEL DAVIS.

ROADS

In 2004 there were an estimated 96,200 km of roads, of which 32,300 km were paved.

Of the three great highways, the first (960 km) runs from Caracas to Ciudad Bolívar. The second, the Pan-American Highway (1,290 km), runs from Caracas to the Colombian frontier and is continued as far as Cúcuta. A branch runs from Valencia to Puerto Cabello. The third highway runs southwards from Coro to La Ceiba, on Lake Maracaibo.

A new 'marginal highway' was under construction along the western fringe of the Amazon Basin in Venezuela, Colombia, Ecuador, Peru, Bolivia and Paraguay. The Venezuelan section now runs for over 440 km and is fully paved.

INLAND WATERWAYS

Instituto Nacional de Canalizaciones: Edif. INC, Calle Caracas, al lado de la Torre Diamen, Chuao, Caracas; tel. (212) 908-5106; fax (212) 959-6906; internet www.incanal.gov.ve; f. 1952; semi-autonomous institution connected with the Ministry of Infrastructure; Pres. Cmmdr WOLFGANG LÓPEZ CARRASQUEL; Vice-Pres. LUZKARIM CORNETT PABÓN.

Compañía Anónima La Translacustre: Maracaibo; freight and passenger service serving Lake Maracaibo, principally from Maracaibo to the road terminal from Caracas at Palmarejo.

SHIPPING

There are 13 major ports, 34 petroleum and mineral ports and five fishing ports. Formerly the main port for imports, La Guaira, the port for Caracas, was affected by mudslides caused by heavy rains in November 1999. Venezuela's main port is now Puerto Cabello, which handles raw materials for the industrial region around Valencia. Maracaibo is the chief port for the petroleum industry. Puerto Ordaz, on the Orinoco River, was also developed to deal with the shipments of iron from Cerro Bolívar.

Instituto Nacional de Puertos: Caracas; tel. (212) 92-2811; f. 1976; as the sole port authority; Pres. Vice-Adm. FREDDY J. MOTA CARPIO.

Consolidada de Ferrys, CA (CONFERRY): Torre Banhorient, 3°, Avda Las Acacias y Avda Casanova, Apdo 87, Sabana Grande, Caracas 1010-A; tel. (212) 781-9711; fax (212) 781-8739; f. 1970; Dir RAFAEL MATA.

Consorcio Naviero Venezolano (Conavén): Torre Uno, 4°, Avda Orinoco, Las Mercedes, Caracas; tel. (212) 993-2922; fax (212) 993-1636; e-mail conavent@conaven.com.ve.

Corpoven, SA: Edif. Petróleos de Venezuela, Avda Libertador, La Campiña, Apdo 61373, Caracas 1060-A; tel. (212) 708-1111; fax (212) 708-1833; Pres. Dr ROBERTO MANDINI; Vice-Pres. JUAN CARLOS GÓMEZ; 2 oil tankers.

VENEZUELA

Lagoven, SA: Edif. Lagovén, Avda Leonardo da Vinci, Los Chaguaramos, Apdo 889, Caracas; tel. (212) 606-3311; fax (212) 606-3637; f. 1978 as a result of the nationalization of the petroleum industry; fmrly Creole Petroleum Group; transports crude petroleum and by-products between Maracaibo, Aniba and other ports in the area; Pres. B. R. NATERA; Marine Man. P. D. CAREZIS; 10 tankers.

Tacarigua Marina, CA: Torre Lincoln 7A-B, Avda Lincoln, Apdo 51107, Sabana Grande, Caracas 1050-A; tel. (212) 781-1315; Pres. R. BELLIZZI.

Transpapel, CA: Edif. Centro, 11°, Of. 111, Centro Parque Boyaca, Avda Sucre, Los Dos Caminos, Apdo 61316, Caracas 1071; tel. (212) 283-8366; fax (212) 285-7749; e-mail nmaldonado@cantv.net; Chair. GUILLERMO ESPINOSA F.; Man. Dir Capt. NELSON MALDONADO A.

Transporte Industrial, SA: Edif. Anzoátegui, Planta Vencemos, Pertigalete, Carretera Guanta, Km 5, Apdo 4356, Puerto la Cruz; tel. (281) 68-5607; fax (281) 68-5683; f. 1955; bulk handling and cement bulk carrier; Chair. VÍCTOR ROMO; Man. Dir RAFAEL ANEE.

CIVIL AVIATION

There are two adjacent airports 13 km from Caracas; Maiquetía for domestic and Simón Bolívar for international services. There are 61 commercial airports, 11 of which are international airports.

National Airlines

Aeropostal (Alas de Venezuela): Torre Polar Oeste, 22°, Plaza Venezuela, Los Caobos, Caracas 1051; tel. (212) 708-6211; fax (212) 782-6323; internet www.aeropostal.com; f. 1933; transferred to private ownership in Sept. 1996, acquired by Venezuelan/US consortium Corporación Alas de Venezuela; domestic services and flights to destinations in the Caribbean, South America and the USA; Pres. and CEO NELSON RAMIZ.

Aerovías Venezolanas, SA (AVENSA): Torre Humboldt, 1°, Avda Rio Caura, Prados del Este, Caracas; tel. (212) 976-5240; fax (212) 563-0225; e-mail info@avensa.com.ve; internet www.avensa.com.ve; f. 1943; provides domestic services from Caracas and services to Europe and the USA; govt-owned; Pres. WILMAR CASTRO SOTELDO.

Aserca Airlines: Torre Exterior, 8°, Avda Bolívar Norte, Valencia, Carabobo 2002; tel. (241) 237-111; fax (241) 220-210; e-mail rsv@asercaairlines.com; internet www.asercaairlines.com; f. 1968; domestic services and flights to Caribbean destinations; Pres. SIMEÓN GARCÍA.

LASER (Línea Aérea de Servicio Ejecutivo Regional): Torre Bazar Bolívar, 8°, Avda Francisco de Miranda, El Marqués, Caracas; tel. (212) 202-0100; fax (212) 235-8359; internet www.laser.com.ve; f. 1994; scheduled and charter services to domestic and international destinations, passenger and cargo; Pres. INOCENCIO ALVAREZ; Gen. Man. JORGE ANDRADE HIDALGO.

Línea Turística Aereotuy, CA: Edif. Gran Sábana, 5°, Blvd de Sabana Grande, Apdo 2923, Carmelitas, Caracas 1050; tel. (212) 761-6231; fax (212) 762-5254; e-mail tuysales@etheron.net; internet www.tuy.com; f. 1982; operates on domestic and international routes; Pres. PETER BOTTOME; Gen. Man. JUAN C. MÁRQUEZ.

Santa Barbara Airlines: Avda 3H, No 78-51, Res. República, Local 01, Maracaibo; tel. (261) 922-090; fax (261) 927-977; internet www.sbairlines.com; f. 1996; domestic and international services; Pres. FRANCISCO GONZÁLEZ YANES.

Tourism

In 2003 Venezuela received 366,974 tourists. Receipts from tourism in that year amounted to US $368m. Venezuela's high crime levels, political instability and high prices relative to regional competitors have deterred tour operators. An estimated 90% of tourists visit the island of Margarita, while only 20% of tourists visit the mainland.

Corporación Nacional de Hoteles y Turismo (CONAHOTU): Caracas; f. 1969; govt agency; Pres. ERASTO FERNÁNDEZ.

INATUR: Hotel Caracas Hilton, Torre Sur, 4°, Of. 424, Caracas; tel. (212) 503-5423; fax (212) 503-5424; e-mail inatur@inatur.gov.ve; internet www.inatur.gov.ve; govt tourism devt agency; Exec. Dir SILVIA ARTEAGA.

Viceministerio de Turismo: c/o Central Information Office of the Presidency, Torre Oeste, 18°, Parque Central, Caracas; tel. (212) 509-0959; fax (212) 509-0941; e-mail vtur@mpc.gov.ve; Vice-Minister DALILA MONSERRATT.

VIET NAM

Introductory Survey

Location, Climate, Language, Religion, Flag, Capital

The Socialist Republic of Viet Nam is situated in South-East Asia, bordered to the north by the People's Republic of China, to the west by Laos and Cambodia, and to the east by the South China Sea. The climate is humid during both the hot summer and the relatively cold winter, and there are monsoon rains in both seasons. Temperatures in Hanoi are generally between 13°C (55°F) and 33°C (91°F). The language is Vietnamese. The principal religion is Buddhism. There are also Daoist, Confucian, Hoa Hao, Caodaist and Christian (mainly Roman Catholic) minorities. The national flag (proportions 2 by 3) is red, with a large five-pointed yellow star in the centre. The capital is Hanoi.

Recent History

Cochin-China (the southernmost part of Viet Nam) became a French colony in 1867. Annam and Tonkin (central and northern Viet Nam) were proclaimed French protectorates in 1883. Later all three were merged with Cambodia and Laos to form French Indo-China. Throughout the French colonial period, but especially after 1920, nationalist and revolutionary groups operated in Viet Nam. The best-organized was the Vietnamese Revolutionary Youth League, founded by Ho Chi Minh. The League was succeeded in 1930 by the Communist Party of Indo-China, also led by Ho Chi Minh.

In September 1940 Japanese forces began to occupy Viet Nam, although (Vichy) France retained administrative authority, and in June 1941 the nationalists formed the Viet Nam Doc Lap Dong Minh Hoi (Revolutionary League for the Independence of Viet Nam), or Viet Minh. In March 1945 French control was ended by a Japanese coup. Following Japan's surrender in August, Viet Minh forces entered Hanoi, and on 2 September the new regime proclaimed independence as the Democratic Republic of Viet Nam (DRV), with Ho Chi Minh as President. The Communist Party, formally dissolved in 1945, continued to be the dominant group within the Viet Minh Government. In March 1946, after French forces re-entered Viet Nam, an agreement between France and the DRV recognized Viet Nam as a 'free' state within the French Union. The DRV Government, however, continued to seek complete independence. Negotiations with France broke down, and full-scale hostilities began in December 1946.

In March 1949 the French established the State of Viet Nam in the South. Meanwhile, in the North the Viet Minh was dissolved in 1951, and the Communists formed the Dang Lao Dong Viet Nam (Viet Nam Workers' Party), with Ho Chi Minh as Chairman of the Central Committee. After the defeat of French forces at Dien Bien Phu in May 1954, terms for a cease-fire were settled in Geneva, Switzerland. Agreements signed in July provided for the provisional partition of Viet Nam into two military zones, with French forces south of latitude 17°N and DRV forces in the north. Later in 1954 the French withdrew from South Viet Nam. Ngo Dinh Diem became Prime Minister of the State of Viet Nam, and in 1955, following a referendum, proclaimed himself President of the Republic of Viet Nam. He thereby deposed Bao Dai, Emperor of Viet Nam from 1932 until his forced abdication in 1945, who had become Head of the State of Viet Nam in 1949. (The former Emperor died in exile in France in 1997.) Diem refused to participate in elections envisaged by the Geneva agreement. In the DRV Ho Chi Minh was succeeded as Prime Minister by Pham Van Dong in 1955, but remained Head of State and party Chairman.

The anti-communist Diem regime in the South was opposed by former members of the Viet Minh, who became known as the Viet Cong. Diem was overthrown by a coup in November 1963, and a series of short-lived military regimes held power until June 1965, when some stability was restored by the National Leadership Committee, with Lt-Gen. Nguyen Van Thieu as Chairman and Air Vice-Marshal Nguyen Cao Ky as Prime Minister. In 1967 Gen. Thieu was elected President, with Marshal Ky as Vice-President, and in 1971, after splitting with Ky, President Thieu was re-elected unopposed.

From 1959 the DRV actively assisted the insurgent movement in South Viet Nam, supporting the establishment there of the communist-dominated National Liberation Front (NLF) in December 1960. In 1961 the USA joined the war on the side of the anti-communist regime in the South, later bombing the North extensively from 1965 to 1968. In November 1968 peace talks between the four participants in the Viet Nam war began in Paris, France, but remained deadlocked as the fighting continued. In June 1969 the NLF formed the Provisional Revolutionary Government (PRG) in the South. Ho Chi Minh died in September 1969: he was succeeded as Head of State by Ton Duc Thang, while political leadership passed to Le Duan, First Secretary of the Viet Nam Workers' Party since 1960.

In 1972 PRG and North Vietnamese forces launched a major offensive in South Viet Nam, and US bombing of the North was renewed with greater intensity. In January 1973 a peace agreement was finally signed in Paris, providing for a cease-fire in the South, the withdrawal of US forces, the eventual peaceful reunification of the whole country, and US aid to the Government in the North to assist in reconstruction. US troops withdrew, and in December 1974 combined PRG and North Vietnamese forces began a final offensive, taking the southern capital, Saigon, in April 1975. By May the new regime was in complete control of the South.

While South Viet Nam, under the PRG, remained technically separate from the DRV, effective control of the whole country passed to Hanoi. In July 1976 the country's reunification was proclaimed under the name of the Socialist Republic of Viet Nam, and Saigon was renamed Ho Chi Minh City. A new Government was appointed, dominated by members of the former Government of the DRV but including some members of the PRG. In December Le Duan was appointed General Secretary of the Communist Party of Viet Nam (formerly the Viet Nam Workers' Party). President Ton Duc Thang died in March 1980. A new Constitution was adopted in December of that year. Truong Chinh was appointed President of the Council of State (Head of State) in July 1981, but real power remained with Le Duan.

Le Duan died in July 1986, and was succeeded as General Secretary of the Communist Party by Truong Chinh. At the Sixth Party Congress, held in December, the country's three most senior leaders, Truong Chinh, Pham Van Dong and Le Duc Tho, announced their retirement from the party Political Bureau (Politburo). However, they continued to attend politburo meetings in an advisory capacity. Truong Chinh and Pham Van Dong retained their respective posts as President of the Council of State and Chairman of the Council of Ministers (Prime Minister) until 1987, and Le Duc Tho continued to wield considerable political influence until his death in October 1990. The Congress appointed Nguyen Van Linh, a long-standing party official, as General Secretary of the Party.

In February 1987 an extensive government reshuffle involved the dismissal of 12 ministers, as well as the merger or restructuring of several ministries, apparently with a view to the implementation of economic reforms. An election to the National Assembly took place in April. There were 829 candidates for the 496 seats (compared with 613 candidates at the previous election). In June the new Assembly elected Vo Chi Cong and Pham Hung, both former Vice-Chairmen of the Council of Ministers, to the posts of President of the Council of State and Chairman of the Council of Ministers respectively. Although a veteran of the struggle with the South, and reputedly a strict conservative, Pham Hung gave his support to the programme of economic reform, referred to as doi moi (renovation), initiated by Nguyen Van Linh. The new liberalism of the regime was demonstrated by the release in September of 480 political prisoners from 're-education' camps, as part of an amnesty for more than 6,600 prisoners on the anniversary of independence from France in 1945. In February 1988 more than 1,000 political prisoners were released. In March Pham Hung died. The Council of State appointed Vo Van Kiet, a Vice-Chairman of the Council of Ministers and the Chairman of the State Commission for Planning, as acting Chairman of the Council of Ministers.

At the meeting of the National Assembly in June, members from the south took the unprecedented step of nominating the reformist Vo Van Kiet to oppose the Central Committee's more conservative candidate, Do Muoi (ranked third in the Politburo), in the election for the chairmanship of the Council of Ministers. Do Muoi was elected to the position, but Vo Van Kiet received unexpectedly strong support. Despite his reputation, Do Muoi declared his commitment to the advancement of reform. Widespread dissatisfaction with the condition of the economy and the slow progress of reform led to the removal of hundreds of cadres from government posts in a 'purification' of the party. In an attempt to improve international relations, and thus secure much-needed Western aid, Viet Nam amended its Constitution in December, removing derogatory references to the USA, the People's Republic of China, France and Japan. In March 1989 a reshuffle of senior economic ministers adjusted the balance further towards reform and strengthened the position of Nguyen Van Linh.

In August 1989 68 members of a US-based exiles' movement, the National Front for the Liberation of Viet Nam, were arrested while crossing from Thailand into Laos. Viet Nam formally protested to Thailand for supporting the group, which had allegedly attempted to incite a rebellion in southern Viet Nam, although the Thai Government denied involvement. In January 1990 38 suspected rebels were extradited to Viet Nam; they were later charged with attempting to overthrow the Government, and in October were sentenced to long terms of imprisonment.

Municipal elections to provincial and district councils took place in November 1989. Under new legislation, candidates who were not members of the Communist Party were allowed to participate for the first time. In December the National Assembly approved legislation imposing new restrictions on the press: the appointment of editors became subject to government approval, and journalists were required to reveal sources of information on request. Open dissension towards Communist Party policy also became a criminal offence. In late 1989 progress towards political reform under *doi moi* was adversely affected by government concern regarding the demise of socialism in Eastern Europe. At a meeting of the Central Committee in March 1990, disagreement on the issue of political pluralism resulted in the dismissal of a member of the Politburo, Tran Xuan Bach, who had openly advocated political reform. In April the Council of State announced an extensive ministerial reshuffle, in which four ministers were dismissed and several portfolios reorganized.

In the second half of 1990 the Government dismissed or brought charges against more than 18,000 officials, in an attempt to eradicate corruption. In December the Central Committee produced draft political and economic reports, reaffirming the party's commitment to socialism and to the process of economic liberalization, which were to be submitted to the next Party Congress. In the same month Bui Tin, the Deputy Editor of the official organ of the Communist Party, *Nhan Dan*, criticized government policy and demanded extensive political reform. He was subsequently expelled from the Politburo and dismissed as Deputy Editor. Following a request by the Central Committee for public comment on the reports, in early 1991 the party journal, *Tap Chi Cong San* (Communist Review), published articles by prominent intellectuals that severely criticized the reports and questioned the effectiveness of a socialist system in Viet Nam. The Communist Party subsequently increased surveillance of dissidents and instructed the press to publish retaliatory articles condemning party critics. In June the Communist Party Congress approved the reports. It elected Do Muoi to replace Nguyen Van Linh as General Secretary of the Party; seven members of the Politburo were removed from their posts, including Nguyen Van Linh, although he, together with Pham Van Dong and the President of the Council of State, Vo Chi Cong, remained in the Central Committee in an advisory capacity. At a session of the National Assembly held in late July and early August, the reformist Vo Van Kiet was elected to replace Do Muoi as Chairman of the Council of Ministers. The Ministers of Foreign Affairs and of the Interior (both formerly close associates of Le Duc Tho) were dismissed. In addition, the National Assembly studied proposals, made by a constitutional commission, for amendments to the Constitution.

A new draft Constitution was published in December 1991 and, after being reviewed in public discussions, was adopted by the National Assembly in April 1992. Like the previous (1980) Constitution, it emphasized the central role of the Communist Party; however, the new document stipulated that the party must be subject to the law. While affirming adherence to a state-regulated socialist economy, the new Constitution guaranteed protection for foreign investment in Viet Nam, and permitted foreign travel and overseas investment for Vietnamese. Land was to remain the property of the State, although the right was granted to procure long-term leases, which could be inherited or sold. The National Assembly was to be reduced in number, but was to have greater power. The Council of State was to be replaced by a single President as Head of State, to be responsible for appointing (subject to the approval of the National Assembly) a Prime Minister and senior members of the judiciary. The new Constitution was to enter into effect after the July 1992 general election.

In July 1992 a total of 601 candidates contested 395 seats in the National Assembly. Almost 90% were members of the Communist Party: although independent candidates (i.e. not endorsed by the Viet Nam Fatherland Front—the grouping of mass organizations, such as trade unions, affiliated to the Communist Party) were for the first time permitted to seek election, in the event only two were deemed to qualify, and neither was elected.

At the first session of the new National Assembly, in September 1992, the conservative Gen. Le Duc Anh (a member of the Politburo and a former Minister of Defence) was elected to the new post of executive President. Vo Van Kiet was appointed Prime Minister (the equivalent of his former post) by the Assembly in October. Only four ministers, all of whom had been implicated in corruption scandals, were not reappointed. During 1993 the Government emphasized its determination to continue progress towards a market-led economy and to encourage foreign investment. Despite the country's economic liberalization, however, there was no tolerance of political dissent. In August 14 people were sentenced to terms of imprisonment, after having been convicted of conspiring to overthrow the Government, and in November several Buddhist monks were imprisoned for allegedly inciting anti-Government demonstrations. At a Communist Party conference in January 1994 Do Muoi praised the country's recent economic achievements and its widening external relations, but denounced the continuing prevalence of poverty, the increase in corruption and crime, and the inadequacy of the educational system; he also strongly criticized the party for disunity and poor organization. Immediately before the conference four new members were appointed to the Politburo, including the Minister of Foreign Affairs, Nguyen Manh Cam, and during the conference 20 new members (all under the age of 55) were elected to the party's Central Committee. In June the National Assembly approved a labour law that guaranteed the right to strike (providing that the 'social life of the community' was not adversely affected). Strikes followed in some southern provinces, and in August the first incident of industrial action in Hanoi was reported. At the fourth Congress of the Fatherland Front, in August, a new, 200-member Central Committee was elected. Elections to provincial and district councils took place during December 1994.

In February 1995 a prominent human rights organization, Amnesty International, protested to the Vietnamese Government about the recent detention of members of the anti-Government Unified Buddhist Church of Viet Nam. In August the People's Court of Ho Chi Minh City sentenced nine political activists, who had attempted to organize pro-democracy conferences, to terms of imprisonment. (Two of those sentenced, who held joint US-Vietnamese nationality, were released in November following a request from the US Government.) In October the National Assembly adopted an extensive civil code (drafted over a period of 10 years), guaranteeing the rights of the individual and enshrining existing rights concerning land usage and inheritance of property. In November two former prominent members of the Communist Party, Do Trung Hieu and Hoang Minh Chinh, were sentenced to custodial terms on charges of damaging national security: Hieu had been involved with an organization demanding political pluralism, while Chinh had published articles urging the restoration of senior party officials removed in the 1960s.

In April 1996 the Central Committee of the Communist Party released draft reports on political and economic policy, which were to be submitted to the Eighth Communist Party Congress at the end of June, indicating that the party intended to maintain state control of the economy (while remaining committed to economic growth) and to continue to reject political pluralism. Also in April the Vice-Chairman of the National Assembly was dismissed from the Politburo and from the Communist Party; it was reported that he had been accused of treason in connection with the Viet Nam war. In June the Congress elected a new, 170-member Central Committee and an expanded (19-member) Politburo. A five-member Standing Board, which included Do Muoi, Le Duc Anh and Vo Van Kiet, was created. In November 12 ministers were dismissed in an extensive cabinet reorganization.

Later in the month Le Duc Anh withdrew temporarily from politics, owing to ill health: this prompted considerable speculation regarding the eventual leadership succession. In subsequent months Lt-Gen. Le Kha Phieu, a member of the new Standing Board, came to the fore as a likely successor to Do Muoi as General Secretary of the Communist Party. Widely seen as a conservative, Le Kha Phieu was expected to seek an increased political role for the military. Le Duc Anh returned to active politics in April 1997.

In December 1996 the Politburo issued a directive requiring the establishment of Communist Party cells in all foreign-invested enterprises, in order to increase party discipline. In January 1997 an unprecedentedly high-profile corruption case was brought to trial: the case involved former senior officials of Tamexco (an import-export company owned by the Communist Party), along with officials from Vietcombank (the state foreign trade bank) and the financial sector. The 20 defendants were accused of a range of financial crimes, principally embezzlement of socialist property. In late January four death sentences were pronounced, together with one sentence of life imprisonment, two suspended sentences and a combined total of 103 years' imprisonment for the remaining defendants. Appeals were lodged by 15 of those convicted in the Tamexco case; however, in March the Supreme People's Court upheld the sentences, and in January 1998 three of those sentenced to death were executed. In February 1997 a judge of the Supreme People's Court was sentenced to two years' imprisonment, having been found to have abused a position of influence for personal gain, and was thus the first member of Viet Nam's judiciary to be convicted of corruption.

In May 1997 substantial amendments to the criminal code were approved by the National Assembly in respect of corruption, bribery, child-abuse and drugs-trafficking. The acceptance of bribes in excess of 50m. dông, and possession of 5 kg of opium or 100 grams of heroin, became crimes punishable by death or life imprisonment; increased penalties were introduced for first-time offenders in cases of corruption. In the same month a group of 22 people, including police, customs and border officials, stood trial for drugs-trafficking: all were convicted, with eight sentenced to death and eight to life imprisonment. In July two people were sentenced to death, and three others to life imprisonment, following what was reported as Viet Nam's first terrorism trial, having been convicted of involvement in a bomb attack in Ho Chi Minh City in October 1994. Official reports stated that the defendants were members of the National Resistance Front for the Restoration of Viet Nam, which was alleged to have issued death threats to foreign nationals who had established businesses in Viet Nam.

Elections to the 10th National Assembly took place on 20 July 1997. A record 663 candidates contested 450 seats (expanded from 395 seats). Under a modified selection process, 112 non-Communist Party members registered as potential candidates. However, following rigorous screening procedures, only 11 independent ('self-nominated') candidates qualified to contest the elections, of whom three secured seats in the Assembly. Do Muoi was among senior figures who did not seek re-election, and, in total, fewer than one-third of the members of the outgoing Assembly returned to office. At the first session of the new National Assembly in late September, Tran Duc Luong, hitherto a Deputy Prime Minister, was elected as President in succession to Le Duc Anh, who, owing to continued ill health, did not seek re-election. The Assembly subsequently endorsed the appointment of Nguyen Thi Binh as Vice-President, Nong Duc Manh as Chairman of the National Assembly Standing Committee, and Phan Van Khai as Prime Minister. (Vo Van Kiet had also stepped down.) A reorganization of the Cabinet was approved at the end of September: the new Cabinet included an increased number of Deputy Prime Ministers, each of whom held a wide portfolio of responsibilities, and several new ministers. In October Do Que Luong was appointed acting Governor of the State Bank of Viet Nam (a cabinet post), following the refusal of the National Assembly to re-elect the incumbent Cao Si Kiem, deemed responsible for recent corruption scandals in the banking sector.

Reports emerged during September 1997 of violent unrest in the northern province of Thai Binh. The unrest, which had begun in May and intensified in June as hundreds of farmers protested against taxes and local corruption, had remained largely unreported earlier in the year as the province had been closed to foreign journalists. There was violence in November in the predominantly Roman Catholic province of Dong Nai, in southern Viet Nam, as thousands of protesters demonstrated against corruption in local government and attempts to confiscate church land. At the end of November the Government pledged to provide financial aid to Thai Binh province, and in February 1998 President Luong made an official tour of the province. In July 1998 more than 30 people were sentenced to terms of imprisonment for their involvement in the previous year's violent unrest in Thai Binh.

At the end of December 1997 Le Kha Phieu was elected to succeed Do Muoi as General Secretary of the Central Committee of the Communist Party. At the same time Do Muoi, Le Duch Anh and Vo Van Kiet resigned from the Politburo; all three were subsequently appointed as advisers to the Central Committee. Four new members were elected to the Politburo, and in early January 1998 the election by the Politburo of a new Standing Board, comprising Le Kha Phieu, Tran Duc Luong, Phan Van Khai, Nong Duc Manh and Pham The Duyet, was announced. The new appointments were widely perceived to reflect the consolidation of the conservative tendency within the leadership, and thus a cautious approach to reform, to the detriment of reformists, among them the Prime Minister. In March, in an illustration of the Government's commitment to countering corruption, the Communist Party announced that in 1997 it had disciplined and expelled some 18,000 members, and sentenced 469 to terms of imprisonment. Further members of the party were subsequently reported to have been disciplined over corruption-related offences in July. In August it was reported that a group of 11 veteran members of the Communist Party were responsible for a letter sent in May to the party's leadership accusing Pham The Duyet of corruption; the allegations were said to be under investigation by Communist Party leaders. In November it was announced that an investigation into allegations of corruption made against senior government officials had found the accusations to be unfounded; however, corruption among lower-level officials was acknowledged to represent a problem.

In a general amnesty announced by the Government to mark Viet Nam's National Day on 2 September 1998, more than 5,000 prisoners, including four of the country's most prominent dissidents—Doan Viet Hoat, Nguyen Dan Que, Thich Quang Do and Thich Tue Sy—were released from detention; however, the release of at least two of the dissidents was reported to be dependent upon their immediate exile from Viet Nam. In October 1998 amnesty was granted to a further 2,630 prisoners. Also in October, the former Editor-in-Chief of *Doanh Nghiep*, Nguyen Hoang Linh, was convicted of 'abusing freedom and democratic rights to violate the interests of the State', following the publication in his newspaper of articles detailing alleged government corruption; Nguyen Hoang Linh was sentenced to more than 12 months' imprisonment, but was released almost immediately as his sentence represented the exact time he had served in detention while awaiting trial. In October the Special Rapporteur on religious intolerance of the UN Commission on Human Rights, Abdelfattah Amor, visited Viet Nam to investigate assertions made by the Vietnamese authorities that greater freedom of religious expression was being afforded in the country. However, at the end of his visit, Amor stated that his investigation had been obstructed by government officials and that he had been prevented from meeting key religious dissidents.

In January 1999 the leadership of the Communist Party announced that it had expelled Gen. (retd) Tran Do from the party in response to his explicit criticism of the establishment in a series of letters to the leadership. His expulsion caused renewed speculation about divisions within the uppermost level of the leadership of the Communist Party and the Politburo, and also set the precedent for the continued suppression of political dissent throughout 1999. In March the prominent writer and geophysicist, Nguyen Thanh Giang, whose critiques of the Communist Party were reported to have been widely disseminated both within Viet Nam and abroad, was arrested on the grounds of 'propagandizing against the socialist regime'; he was released in May, but reportedly remained under house arrest. In September the trial opened of 24 members of the dissident People's Action Party, charged with 'exiting the country illegally for the purpose of undermining the people's administration'; all 24 defendants were subsequently convicted and sentenced to terms of imprisonment ranging from two to 20 years. Prior to the trial Le Kha Phieu, speaking at the Seventh Plenum of the Eighth Party Central Committee in August, had emphasized the Communist Party's opposition to 'political pluralism'.

In 1999 the issue of corruption remained a major source of concern for the Communist Party. At the Sixth Plenum of the Eighth Party Central Committee, which concluded in January, it was announced that the party was to renew its efforts to eliminate corruption from within its ranks. The trial of 74 people accused of smuggling (more than one-half of whom were reported to be former government officials) opened in March, with two of the defendants being subsequently sentenced to death, and the remainder to terms of imprisonment. In May 77 businessmen, bankers and government officials appeared in court charged with the fraudulent procurement of state loans; in August six of the defendants were sentenced to death (although two of these subsequently had their sentences commuted to life imprisonment), and the remainder to various terms of imprisonment. In December, in a further demonstration of the efforts of the Communist Party to address corruption, Deputy Prime Minister Ngo Xuan Loc was dismissed from the Cabinet following his implication in a corrupt land deal related to a private-sector project. However, in April 2000 he was reinstated to a government post and resumed responsibility for the sectors connected to the initial accusations against him, thus attracting speculation as to the extent of the Government's attempts to eliminate corruption. In September 2001 eight officials were tried on charges of fraud in Hanoi in connection with the land deal. One businessman received a 20-year prison sentence; the remaining defendants were either released or sentenced to prison terms of nine months or less.

Viet Nam experienced its worst flooding in more than 40 years in September 2000, as the Mekong River rose to exceptionally high levels. By late October more than 400 people had been killed, over 760,000 houses had been inundated, 40,000 families evacuated and 500,000 people left in need of emergency aid. Destruction of crops, schools and provincial roads was widespread. Viet Nam invited international relief agencies to help mitigate the disaster, and several western countries provided financial and humanitarian aid.

In October 2000 the Politburo issued orders to develop the country's information technology (IT) capabilities and raise them to a level comparable to other countries in the region by 2010. The order emphasized the application of IT for the development of economics, culture and society, along with defence and security. Also in October the Ministry of Public Security announced a nation-wide campaign against the use of illicit drugs. In November Communist Party documents divulged to the US-based human rights group, Freedom House, emphasized the leadership's level of concern regarding the increasing number of ethnic minorities converting to Christianity, and the fear that religion would be used by the USA and other countries to undermine communism in Viet Nam. In December the Minister of National Defence, Lt-Gen. Pham Van Tra, instructed the army not to become depoliticized, and to remain vigilant and safeguard the Communist Party and the socialist system. His directive was reiterated by the Party General Secretary, Le Kha Phieu, who in January 2001 urged the army to preserve political stability and guard against attempts to undermine socialism.

Ethnic violence broke out in the Central Highland provinces of Gia Lai and Dak Lak in February 2001, as local hill minorities (known as Montagnards) protested against perceived injustices caused by the migration of ethnic Vietnamese from the densely populated coastal regions and by the deforestation resulting from the establishment of coffee plantations. Some 5,000 protesters in the provincial capitals of Pleiku and Buon Ma Thuot respectively attacked state offices and blocked roads. The Vietnamese authorities deployed troops, riot police, water cannon and helicopters to quell the unrest, and injuries were reported on both sides. Some 20 people were arrested in connection with instigating the violence, which was attributed to 'extremists' seeking to use religion to foment unrest. The protesters had demanded autonomy, freedom to practise their Protestant religion, the return of ancestral lands confiscated for use as coffee plantations and the right to preserve their traditional way of life. The Ministry of Public Security accused the US-based Montagnard Foundation of organizing the violence, stating that several of those arrested were former members of the United Front for the Liberation of Oppressed Races (FULRO), a guerrilla unit that had close ties to the US Military and Central Intelligence Agency (CIA) during the Viet Nam war. The Vietnamese authorities also stated that during 2000 there had been several incursions into the country by agents of Free Viet Nam, a movement based in Thailand. The unrest coincided with a climate of increasing repression of religion, and it was feared that 'hardliners' in the Communist Party might use the incident to strengthen their position and to delay economic and political reforms. In March the authorities denounced a Catholic priest, Nguyen Van Ly, for writing to the US Congress and urging it not to ratify a bilateral trade agreement, owing to human rights abuses in Viet Nam. Nguyen Van Ly was accused of undermining Viet Nam's independence and was placed under house arrest. In October he was sentenced to 15 years in prison after a court convicted him of undermining national unity and contravening a detention order. (His sentence was reduced by five years in July 2003 and by a further five years in June 2004, and in February 2005 he was released from prison, having been granted amnesty.) Exiled Vietnamese Buddhist leaders also claimed that their followers in Viet Nam were routinely harassed. In September 2001 Ho Tan Anh, leader of the Buddhist Youth Movement, burnt himself to death in protest at the restrictions that had been imposed upon his organization.

The Ninth Party Congress was held in April 2001, and resulted in the election of a new 150-member Central Committee, 15-member Politburo and nine-member Secretariat. Nong Duc Manh was appointed General Secretary, replacing Le Kha Phieu, who was accused of using military intelligence against Party members and of slowing the pace of reforms. Phieu had agreed to step down under pressure from the Central Committee. Nong Duc Manh, who was rumoured to be the illegitimate son of Ho Chi Minh, was the first ethnic Tay to attain such a senior position. Some 84 members of the previous Central Committee were re-elected. President Tran Duc Luong and Prime Minister Phan Van Khai retained their party posts. However, former President Le Duc Anh, former Prime Minister Vo Van Kiet and former General Secretary Do Muoi lost their positions as senior advisers to the Central Committee upon the abolition of the posts. Manh was believed to favour economic reforms and greater democracy, the latter a major theme at the Congress. However, the Congress reiterated its commitment to socialism as a means to national industrialization and modernization. In June 2001 Nguyen Van An, a member of the Politburo, was elected to the chairmanship of the National Assembly, succeeding Nong Duc Manh.

In September 2001 14 Montagnards received sentences of between six and 12 years' imprisonment for participating in the protests of February of that year. In October a further six men were convicted of distributing propaganda and inciting ethnic unrest in the city of Buon Ma Thuot during the disturbances. No diplomats or foreign journalists were permitted to attend the trials. A critical report issued by the international organization Human Rights Watch in April 2002 warned of further violence in the Central Highlands if the Government continued to implement its repressive policies towards ethnic minorities. In November 2002 it was alleged that the Government had executed three Montagnards in the previous month, reportedly owing to their involvement in the violence of February 2001. In December a further eight people were convicted of charges of undermining national unity, having allegedly aided people attempting to leave the region following the violence. In January 2003, according to Human Rights Watch, 70 Montagnards were known to be imprisoned in Viet Nam owing to their political or religious beliefs. In April 2003 a report issued by Human Rights Watch claimed that government persecution of the Montagnards had escalated since January of that year. In May, following a one-day trial, 15 Montagnards were convicted of causing social disorder during the protests of February 2001. All were sentenced to lengthy prison terms. In April 2004 Human Rights Watch again accused the Vietnamese Government of repression, following reports that a rally held by Montagnards in that month in Dak Lak province, in protest against land confiscation and religious persecution, had been violently suppressed by government officials. Human Rights Watch claimed that at least 10 Montagnards had been killed, although the Vietnamese Government insisted that only two people had died. In May Human Rights Watch reported that the Vietnamese authorities had arrested a number of Montagnard church leaders, as well as Montagnards with relatives in the USA. In August nine Montagnards, who were alleged to be former members of the FULRO, were convicted of fomenting disorder and undermining national unity during the demonstrations of February 2001 and thereafter. They were sentenced to prison terms of between five and 12 years.

In December 2001 the National Assembly gave its approval to several constitutional amendments, including one allowing politicians to instigate mid-term votes of no confidence if they considered any minister to be performing unsatisfactorily. The amendments were intended to encourage the development of Viet Nam's market economy and improve democracy, thus facilitating the country's further integration into the international community.

It was reported in January 2002 that the Communist Party had passed a decree authorizing the police to engage in the destruction of publications that had not been approved by the party. Books written by several leading dissidents, including Gen. Tran Do, had subsequently been destroyed. In March the Politburo was reported to have established a special investigation into allegations that more than 50 government officials had colluded in organized crime. Several of those accused were reported to have accepted bribes to protect a gang whose alleged leader, Truong Van Cam, also known as Nam Cam, was undergoing investigation on murder charges. As the investigation continued, more than 100 government officials and an estimated 50 police-officers were implicated; two members of the Central Committee (the Director-General of the state radio station Voice of Viet Nam, Tran Mai Hanh, and Pham Sy Chien) were expelled from the Communist Party in July owing to their involvement. In November the Deputy Minister of Public Security, Maj.-Gen. Haong Ngoc Nhat, was dismissed from his position and demoted in rank, owing to his alleged complicity. In January 2003 the director of the Economic Commission of the Politburo, Truong Tan San, became the most senior member of the Communist Party to be punished in relation to the investigation; he was formally reprimanded for 'dereliction of duty' during his tenure as secretary of the party in Ho Chi Minh City in 1996–2000.

Meanwhile, in March 2002 the Communist Party decided that it would formally permit its members to engage in private business, indicating the Government's desire to encourage the expansion of the role of the private sector within the economy. In April 59 people went on trial in Ho Chi Minh City charged with embezzling state assets and violating commercial law in connection with the Chinese-owned Viet Hoa bank. The case proceeded despite the death, in 1997, of an alleged principal participant in the fraud, Tran Tuan Tai (the head of the bank), after which the bank's licence was revoked. In the following month all those tried were found guilty of the charges against them; 43 were sentenced to prison terms of varying lengths, while those remaining were given suspended sentences. The trial was widely perceived to constitute a further attempt on the part of the Government to take firm action against corruption.

Elections to the 11th National Assembly took place on 19 May 2002. The 498 seats available were contested by 759 candidates, only 13 of whom were independent. Non-Communist Party candidates won 51 seats and independents two, the remainder being secured by party members. In July and August the newly elected National Assembly held its first session, during which significant reorganizations of both the Standing Committee and the Cabinet were approved. Three new ministries were created during the extensive reshuffle, in which Vu Khoan, the former Minister of Trade, was promoted to the position of Deputy Prime Minister and former Minister of Public Security Le Minh Huong was replaced by Politburo member Le Hong Anh. President Tran Duc Luong, Prime Minister Phan Van Khai and the Chairman of the National Assembly, Nguyen Van An, were all formally re-elected to their posts, while Truong My Hoa succeeded Nguyen Thi Binh as Vice-President.

In November 2002 Le Chi Quang, a lawyer, was convicted of committing 'acts of propaganda' against the State, following his arrest in February of that year for allegedly publishing material critical of the Government on the internet. He was sentenced to a four-year prison term (but was released early, in June 2004, to serve a three-year term of house arrest). In December 2002 another dissident, Nguyen Khac Toan, was sentenced to 12 years in prison, having been convicted of using the internet for espionage purposes; he was subsequently granted amnesty and released in January 2006. In March 2003 the dissident Nguyen Dan Que, who had spent over 18 years in prison for campaigning for improved democracy and human rights in Viet Nam and had been freed five years previously, was arrested again after publishing an essay on the internet concerning Viet Nam's control of the media. In July 2004 he was sentenced to a 30-month prison term, but was granted amnesty and released in February 2005, one of an estimated 12 political or religious prisoners to be granted early release during the course of that year. Meanwhile, at the Seventh Plenum of the Central Committee of the Communist Party held in January 2003, a resolution was passed intended to increase the Party's control over religious affairs. At the Plenum Nguyen Van Chi was appointed to the Party Secretariat.

In February 2003 the trial of Nam Cam and 154 other defendants on a number of charges, including murder, organized gambling, bribery, drugs-trafficking and extortion, began in Ho Chi Minh City. Among the defendants were 21 former state and government officials. The hearings constituted Viet Nam's largest corruption trial to date. In June Nam Cam was convicted of all the charges against him and sentenced to death. In the same month many more defendants in the trial were convicted of the charges against them, including Tran Mai Hanh, who received a 10-year prison term, and Pham Sy Chien, who was to serve a six-year sentence. Five other defendants were given death sentences. In October an appeal by Nam Cam against his death sentence was rejected, and in June 2004 he was executed by firing squad, together with four of his co-defendants, the death sentence of the fifth having been commuted to life imprisonment.

In April 2003 Prime Minister Phan Van Khai held talks with Thich Huyen Quang, leader of the anti-Government Unified Buddhist Church of Viet Nam, who had been held under house arrest since the group was proscribed almost 20 years previously. While the meeting was welcomed by international diplomats, there was speculation that the Communist Party might use it to respond to continued criticism of its human rights record, while avoiding making any more substantial reforms. In May Thich Huyen Quang was permitted to meet with his deputy, Thich Quang Do, for only the third time in 21 years. In June Thich Quang Do was released from house arrest, two months before the end of his two-year sentence. In the same month, however, Pham Hong Son, a doctor, was sentenced to a 13-year prison term, to be followed by three years of house arrest, having been found guilty of charges of espionage and disseminating false information about the State on the internet. The Government later reduced the length of his sentence to five years in prison, followed by three years under house arrest. In October 2003 a 'stand-off' was reported to have taken place in Binh Dinh province between government security forces and supporters of the Unified Buddhist Church of Viet Nam, following an attempt by Thich Huyen Quang and Thich Quang Do to depart for Ho Chi Minh City; it ended on the next day. In November both the US House of Representatives and the European Parliament approved resolutions condemning the continuing official repression of non-recognized religious organizations in Viet Nam and calling for the release of Thich Huyen Quang.

In November 2003 the trial opened in Hanoi of two former junior agriculture ministers, Nguyen Thien Luan and Nguyen Quang Ha, together with La Thi Kim Oanh, the former director of a company controlled by the Ministry of Agriculture and Rural Development, and five other officials, on embezzlement charges. The opening of the trial was televised as part of the Government's ongoing campaign to combat corruption. In December all those tried were found guilty of the charges against them. La Thi Kim Oanh was sentenced to death, while the remaining defendants received prison sentences of various lengths. Meanwhile, in the same month former journalist Nguyen Vu Binh was sentenced to a seven-year prison term, having been convicted of espionage charges. In June 2004 the National Assembly approved the dismissal of the Minister of Agriculture and Development, Le Huy Ngo, on the grounds that he had failed adequately to monitor his subordinates and organizations under his administration in connection with the embezzlement case; he was replaced by Cao Duc Phat.

In March 2004 police arrested four members of the Mennonite Church, which was not officially recognized by the Government, after scuffles broke out when a number of Mennonites attempted to photograph police-officers who were posted outside the headquarters of the Church. In June Nguyen Hong Quang, the Secretary-General of the Mennonite Church in Viet Nam, was also arrested for his involvement in the incident, and a sixth church member was detained the following month. In November Quang was sentenced to three years' imprisonment for preventing officials from carrying out their duties, while the five other defendants received custodial sentences of between nine months and two years.

Two veteran dissidents, Tran Van Khue, a retired academic, and Pham Que Duong, a military historian, were sentenced to 19 months' imprisonment in July 2004, having been convicted of abusing democratic freedoms to undermine the interests of the State. Both men had posted articles critical of the Government on the internet. They were released at the end of the month, however, as they had been in detention since December 2002.

In late July 2004 the Minister of Posts and Telecommunications, Do Trung Ta, issued new regulations aimed at controlling access to the internet by allowing internet service providers to suspend contracts with cafés that allowed customers to view pornographic websites or those deemed to threaten national security. In the following month a special police unit was established to combat internet crime and prevent the spread of banned materials.

Also in July 2004 the President promulgated an Ordinance on Beliefs and Religions, which came into effect in mid-November. A coalition of non-recognized Protestant churches condemned the new law, which, while upholding the right of citizens to freedom of religious belief, decreed that only state-authorized clergy be entitled to preach and only within defined territorial jurisdictions. The ordinance also provided for the suspension of religious activities that were deemed to jeopardize national security, public order or national unity. In February 2005 it was reported that the Government had issued a decree allowing outlawed Protestant churches to operate if they renounced connections to the FULRO.

Details emerged in September 2004 of a major corruption scandal in which local textile companies had been allegedly obliged to pay large bribes to trade officials in order to secure export quotas to the USA. Some 19 people were subsequently arrested in connection with the case, the most prominent of whom was Deputy Minister of Trade Mai Van Dau; he was charged with abuse of power and dismissed from the Government in November. Meanwhile, in October Prime Minister Phan Van Khai announced plans to establish an anti-corruption agency; however, in early 2006 the plans had yet to be realized. In November the National Assembly approved new legislation on national security, which stipulated the principles of security policy and the powers and responsibilities of the agencies in charge of national security.

In December 2004 two retired state physicists, Tran Van Luong and Nguyen Thi Minh Hoan, were sentenced, respectively, to 21 months' and eight months' imprisonment for sending to state agencies documents and petitions that were critical of the Government and the Communist Party. The 11th plenary session of the Ninth Party Central Committee, which was convened in mid-January 2005, focused on preparations for the 10th Communist Party Congress, which was to take place in April 2006. Nong Duc Manh emphasized the need to achieve higher economic growth, to reduce poverty and to eliminate corruption, as well as to accelerate administrative and judicial reforms. At the end of January the Government announced that 8,323 prisoners, including six political dissidents and 33 foreigners, were to be released in an amnesty to mark Tet (the lunar New Year). In March the Government issued a decree aimed at tightening control over demonstrations and banning unauthorized gatherings. It was reported that the decree required the approval in advance of all gatherings not organized by the Communist Party or state organs.

In May 2005 Le Kha Phieu, the former General Secretary of the Communist Party claimed that he had been offered bribes while in office between 1997 and 2001, but he refused to identify publicly those allegedly involved. In November the National Assembly ratified a long-awaited Anti-Corruption Law, the terms of which required all officials, and their close relatives, to disclose fully their assets. There was considerable scepticism as to how effectively this would be enforced, especially in view of the protection given to the authorities by state control of the media. Earlier that month the deputy head of the State Inspectorate's department of economic inspection was arrested amidst claims that he had accepted bribes and had abused his position to supply relatives with employment; it was subsequently reported that Luong had offered a bribe of 110m. dông (US $6,875) to another senior official to interfere with investigation proceedings into the original alleged offences.

In April 2006 the Minister of Transport and Communications, Dao Dinh Binh, tendered his resignation from the Cabinet, following allegations concerning an apparent misappropriation of state funds by staff members within his ministry. It was claimed that officials had stolen money allocated to construction projects and had accepted numerous bribes. Binh announced that he was 'saddened' by the situation but would accept full responsibility for the actions of those employed in his ministry. The Deputy Minister of Transport and Communications, Nguyen Viet Tien, was arrested in connection with the embezzlement of state funds.

The 10th Communist Party Congress was held in late April 2006, during which elections were held for a new 160-member Central Committee, 14-member Politburo and eight-member Secretariat. Nong Duc Manh was retained as General Secretary of the Party; five other members of the previous Politburo also secured re-election. President Tran Duc Luong, Prime Minister Phan Van Khai and Chairman of the National Assembly Standing Committee, Nguyen Van An, all announced that they were to resign, thus preparing the way for a younger generation of officials to assume prominent positions within the party leadership. The Congress reaffirmed its commitment to socialism and announced its aim of Viet Nam achieving the status of a developed country by 2020. The issue of corruption within the party was also given considerable focus during the Congress. General Secretary Manh vowed in his opening speech to 'intensify' the fight against it. At its conclusion, the Congress was generally considered to have been a success, fulfilling the set agenda and adopting several important documents, including the Report and Five-Year Plan of Action on Socio-economic Development Goals for 2006–10. In May, as the National Assembly began its annual session, Prime Minister Phan Van Kai announced that he intended to retire, having served two five-year terms in office. He nominated First Deputy Prime Minister Nguyen Tan Dung as his successor.

By the end of 1976, meanwhile, Viet Nam had established diplomatic relations with many countries, including all of its South-East Asian neighbours. However, tension arose over the growing number of Vietnamese refugees (particularly ethnic Chinese) arriving in Thailand and other nearby countries. In 1979 more than 200,000 fled Viet Nam, and in July an international conference was convened in Geneva to discuss the situation. The Orderly Departure Programme, sponsored by the office of the UN High Commissioner for Refugees (UNHCR, see p. 62), whereby Viet Nam agreed to legal departures, was negotiated, and by the end of 1988 about 140,000 people had left the country in this way. Illegal departures continued, however, and the increasing reluctance of Western countries to provide resettlement opportunities led to a meeting in Malaysia in March 1989, at which representatives of 30 nations were present and a comprehensive programme of action was drafted. Members of the Association of South East Asian Nations (ASEAN, see p. 172) subsequently ceased to accept refugees for automatic resettlement and planned to institute a screening procedure to distinguish genuine refugees from economic migrants. A similar procedure had been in effect since June 1988 in Hong Kong, and an agreement had been signed in November, whereby Viet Nam agreed to accept voluntary repatriation of refugees from Hong Kong, funded by UNHCR and the United Kingdom, with UN supervision to protect the returning refugees from punitive measures by the Vietnamese Government.

In June 1989 a UN-sponsored conference adopted the so-called Comprehensive Action Plan that had been drafted in March, introducing the desired screening procedures to distinguish political refugees from economic migrants (who might be forcibly repatriated if efforts to secure their voluntary return proved unsuccessful). In December the United Kingdom forcibly repatriated a group of 51 Vietnamese from Hong Kong, provoking international criticism; this policy was abandoned as a result both of opposition by the USA and of Viet Nam's refusal to accept further deportations. In July 1990, however, the USA accepted in principle the 'involuntary' repatriation of refugees classed as economic migrants who did not actively oppose deportation. In September the United Kingdom, Viet Nam and UNHCR reached an agreement whereby the Vietnamese Government would no longer refuse refugees who had been repatriated 'involuntarily'. In May 1992 the United Kingdom and Viet Nam signed an agreement providing for the compulsory repatriation of all economic migrants from Hong Kong. In 1991–95 some 66,132 Viet-namese were voluntarily repatriated, while an additional 1,562 were forcibly returned. In January 1996 ASEAN member states, including Viet Nam (see below), agreed that all Vietnamese residing in South-East Asian refugee camps (apart from those in Hong Kong) would be repatriated by the end of June of that year. (China had already indicated that all Vietnamese refugees in Hong Kong should be returned prior to the transfer of the territory to Chinese sovereignty in June 1997.) In March 1996 UNHCR announced that it would suspend funding of Vietnamese refugee camps from the end of June. In April a new initiative, proposed by the US Government in an effort to accelerate the repatriation programme, whereby refugees who returned to Viet Nam would be eligible to apply for settlement in the USA under a new screening process, was received with caution by the Vietnamese authorities. In June both Malaysia and Singapore closed their camps, following the repatriation of all Vietnamese refugees from those countries. In September 1996 and February 1997 respectively Indonesia and Thailand also closed their camps, leaving Hong Kong as the only South-East Asian country with a significant number (12,000 in November 1996) of Vietnamese refugees. In December 1996 repatriates were prohibited from engaging in any type of political activity, and from January 1997 anti-communist activists and critics of the Government were banned from returning to Viet Nam. In mid-June the main Vietnamese detention centre in Hong Kong was closed. However, the scheduled repatriation of all remaining Vietnamese (estimated at some 1,600 people qualifying as refugees and 700 non-refugees) before the end of the month was not achieved. In January 1998 Hong Kong announced that it was to discontinue its policy of granting a port of first asylum to Vietnamese refugees. However, in July 1999 Hong Kong announced that the Vietnamese who remained in the territory—estimated to number around 1,400, some classed as refugees, others as 'stateless' persons—would be given permanent residency in Hong Kong; the last remaining camp for Vietnamese refugees in Hong Kong was closed in May 2000.

Following the unrest in the Central Highlands in February 2001 (see above), many Montagnards fled over the border into Cambodia, where they were accommodated in two camps situated in the provinces of Mondol Kiri and Rotanak Kiri. By December the camps housed 805 refugees, who sought a supervised return to the Highlands, accompanied by a guarantee that they would be given permission to reoccupy their ancestral lands. In January 2002 Viet Nam and Cambodia signed a joint repatriation agreement with UNHCR, and in February 15 refugees left the camps to return to their home in Kon Tum province. Later in the same month the Vietnamese Government criticized UNHCR for the delay in the repatriation of the refugees (of whom there were now more than 1,000). It had imposed a deadline of 30 April 2002 for the completion of the repatriation process. The programme was later suspended, as UNHCR claimed that by imposing the deadline the Government was undermining the voluntary nature of returns. In March 2002 UNHCR announced its withdrawal from the agreement, owing to the frequent intimidation of both refugees and UN staff at the camps. Its decision was precipitated by an incident in which more than 400 Vietnamese had crossed the border with Cambodia and threatened inmates and staff at the Mondol Kiri camp. Following the termination of the agreement, the US Government stated that it was prepared to offer asylum to the refugees who remained in Cambodia. The Cambodian Government announced in April that, while it would authorize the resettlement of the Montagnard refugees in the USA, it planned to close down the camps housing the refugees and cease its provision of asylum within one month. In April 2003 the Cambodian Government also announced its intention to shut the refugee transit centre operated by UNHCR in Phnom-Penh as soon as the remaining refugees housed there had been resettled. Following the repression of a protest rally in the Central Highland province of Dak Lak in April 2004 (see above), there was a further influx of Montagnards into Cambodia. In November UNHCR expressed concern that growing numbers of Montagnards were crossing into Cambodia in the mistaken belief that UNHCR could assist them to recover their confiscated lands. In January 2005 UNHCR and the Governments of Cambodia and Viet Nam signed an agreement on the resettlement to third countries or the repatriation to Viet Nam of some 750 Montagnards in Cambodia. The Vietnamese Government guaranteed that returnees would not be punished, discriminated against or prosecuted for their departure. In March the first group of 43 Montagnards who had opted for repatriation returned to Viet Nam; by that time a further 297 had decided to accept resettlement in third countries, including the USA, Finland and Canada. The Cambodian Government insisted that it would not allow the Montagnards to remain in Cambodia.

Relations with Kampuchea (known as Cambodia until 1976 and again from 1989) deteriorated during 1977, and in December Viet Nam launched a major offensive into eastern Kampuchea. Sporadic fighting continued, and in December 1978 Viet Nam invaded Kampuchea in support of elements opposed to the regime (see the chapter on Cambodia). By January 1979 the Government of Pol Pot had been overthrown and a pro-Vietnamese regime was installed. The invasion prompted much international criticism, and in February 1979 Chinese forces launched a punitive attack across the border into Viet Nam. Peace talks began in April but made little progress, and in March 1980 they were suspended by China. In March 1983 Viet Nam rejected a five-point peace plan, proposed by China, aimed at resolving the dispute over Kampuchea. In 1984 Chinese and Vietnamese troops engaged in heavy fighting, accusing each other of persistent border violations. China refused to normalize relations with Viet Nam until the withdrawal of Vietnamese troops from Kampuchea. Throughout 1986 and 1987 further armed clashes between Vietnamese and Chinese soldiers occurred on the Sino-Vietnamese border. Both sides denied responsibility for initiating the attacks. In early 1988 the tension between the two countries was exacerbated by the re-emergence of conflict over the Spratly Islands in the South China Sea, when the Vietnamese Government alleged that China had dispatched warships to the islands. (For many years the sovereignty of the islands had been contested, not only by Viet Nam and China, which engaged in military conflict over the issue in 1974, but also by the neighbouring states of Brunei, Malaysia, the Philippines and Taiwan.)

In March 1984 Viet Nam agreed in principle that it would eventually withdraw its troops from Kampuchea, and in August 1985 it was announced that all Vietnamese troops would be withdrawn by 1990. An eight-point peace plan, proposed by Kampuchean resistance leaders in March 1986 (involving the installation of a quadripartite government in Kampuchea, to be followed by UN-supervised elections), was rejected by Viet Nam. Viet Nam's urgent need of Western aid, together with increasing pressure from the USSR, prompted an announcement in May 1988 that Viet Nam would withdraw 50,000 (of an estimated total of 100,000) troops from Kampuchea by the end of the year. The Vietnamese military high command left Kampuchea in June, placing the remainder of the Vietnamese forces under Kampuchean control.

In April 1989 the Vietnamese Government and the Heng Samrin regime in Kampuchea declared that Vietnamese troops would withdraw by September even if a political settlement had not been reached, on condition that military assistance to the three other Kampuchean factions also ceased by that date. China responded that it would halt military aid to the Khmers Rouges only after a complete withdrawal of Vietnamese troops had been verified. The Vietnamese Government claimed that the withdrawal of troops had been completed by the end of September. However, the absence of a UN commission to verify the troops' departure led to claims by the Government-in-exile of Democratic Kampuchea that a number of troops remained in the country, while China, the ASEAN countries and the USA initially refused to recognize the alleged withdrawal. In July 1990 the USA finally acknowledged that all troops had been withdrawn.

In September 1990 secret negotiations took place between Viet Nam and China, during which the Vietnamese endorsed a new UN Security Council agreement to resolve the conflict in Cambodia (q.v.). It was widely believed that the Chinese had promised an improvement in Sino-Vietnamese relations in exchange for Vietnamese support for the UN plan. In October 1991 Viet Nam was a signatory to a peace agreement whereby an interim Supreme National Council was established in Cambodia, representing all four factions there, as a prelude to the holding of UN-supervised elections. The agreement allowed immediate progress towards ending Viet Nam's diplomatic and economic isolation (see below). During 1992–93 there were several massacres of civilians of Vietnamese origin living in Cambodia. In January 1995 the First Prime Minister of Cambodia, Prince Norodom Ranariddh, visited Viet Nam for discussions. In November of that year Viet Nam accused the Cambodian Government of supporting a dissident Vietnamese movement, based in Phnom-Penh. In January 1996 it was reported that Cambodian troops had opened fire in a southern border area; Cambodia subsequently claimed that Vietnamese forces had made incursions into Cambodian territory. Discussions between Vietnamese and Cambodian government officials on the border issue took place in April and May. In March 1997 Viet Nam and Cambodia signed an agreement on bilateral co-operation in combating crime and, during 2000, security officials from the two countries signed a number of agreements aimed at combating drugs-trafficking and strengthening border controls.

From the mid-1970s Viet Nam developed closer relations with the USSR, and became increasingly dependent on its support. In 1990–91 the USSR substantially reduced financial assistance to Viet Nam. After the dissolution of the USSR, the Vietnamese

Government pursued close relations with its successor states. In June 1994 Vo Van Kiet visited Ukraine, Kazakhstan and Russia to discuss economic and defence co-operation issues. During a visit by the Russian Minister of Foreign Affairs in July 1995, it was agreed that Russian vessels would continue to use the former Soviet naval base at Cam Ranh Bay, in central Viet Nam. In February 1997 Russia announced plans further to develop its defence ties with Viet Nam, and in November of that year the Russian Prime Minister, Viktor Chernomyrdin, paid an official visit to Viet Nam; Tran Duc Luong made a reciprocal visit to Russia in August 1998. The Russian Deputy Prime Minister, Viktor Khristenko, visited Viet Nam in July 2000 to discuss Russian involvement in oil and gas development, and Viet Nam's outstanding 11,000m. rouble Soviet-era debt. Agreement on the latter was reached in September, when it was arranged that Viet Nam would repay Russia US $1,700m. over 23 years, mostly in the form of business concessions. A major concern for Russia was its continued use of the naval base at Cam Ranh Bay. Under a 1978 agreement, Russia was to have access to the facilities until 2004. In February–March 2001 the Russian President, Vladimir Putin, became the first Russian (or Soviet) Head of State to visit Viet Nam. The two countries agreed to strengthen co-operation in economic, energy, and military and defence matters, and proclaimed a new 'strategic partnership'. The two leaders also supported non-involvement by other countries in their internal affairs, and expressed their opposition to the USA's planned military missile defence shield. In May 2002 control of the naval base at Cam Ranh Bay was formally transferred to the Vietnamese Government, two years ahead of the agreed date. President Tran Duc Luong visited Ukraine in April 2000 and pledged to increase bilateral economic and political co-operation. Viet Nam also signed a military co-operation agreement with Ukraine in May. In February 2004, during a visit by the Russian Deputy Prime Minister to Hanoi, Russia expressed interest in participating in the construction of Viet Nam's first nuclear power station. President Tran Duc Luong visited Russia in May of that year and held talks with President Putin on bilateral relations, focusing particularly on expanding economic co-operation. Both leaders confirmed their commitment to the 'strategic partnership'.

The collapse of communism in Eastern Europe prompted renewed efforts by Viet Nam to restore political and economic links with China. Relations between Viet Nam and China improved significantly in the second half of 1990, owing to the co-operation of the Vietnamese Government concerning Cambodia. After the conclusion of the Cambodian peace agreement in October 1991, Vo Van Kiet and Do Muoi paid an official visit to China in November, during which normal diplomatic relations were restored and agreements were concluded on trade and on border affairs, while in March 1992 further agreements were signed on the resumption of transport and communications links (severed in 1979), and on the reopening of border posts. In May 1992 Viet Nam protested to China when the latter unilaterally granted exploration rights to a US petroleum company in an area of the South China Sea regarded by Viet Nam as part of its continental shelf. Several more protests were lodged later in the year over the presence of Chinese vessels in disputed areas. In November the Chinese Premier, Li Peng, made an official visit to Viet Nam (the first visit by a Chinese head of government since 1971): new agreements on economic, scientific and cultural co-operation were signed, and the two Governments agreed to accelerate negotiations on disputed territory that had begun in the previous month. In October 1993 Viet Nam and China concluded an agreement to avoid the use of force when resolving territorial disputes. In November 1994 the two countries agreed to co-operate in seeking an early resolution to all border disputes. During an official visit by Do Muoi to China in November 1995, it was agreed that rail links between the two countries would be restored (they were subsequently reopened in February 1996). In April 1996 the state-owned petroleum company, Petrovietnam, signed a joint exploration contract with a US enterprise that covered part of the South China Sea where the Chinese Government had granted exploration rights in May 1992. In May 1996 China agreed to abide by the UN Convention on the Law of the Sea, which provided for international arbitration, but at the same time announced a new delineation of its sea border, attracting criticism from Viet Nam and other nations in the region.

In March 1997 Chinese vessels entered Vietnamese waters around the disputed Spratly Islands and were believed to be carrying out exploratory activities. China defended its actions, declaring a legitimate claim to the territory. In April China agreed to hold talks with Viet Nam over the issue; however, China withdrew the vessels before the discussions took place, stating that its operation in the area had been completed. In May China ratified the opening to traffic of a sea route between northeastern Viet Nam and China. In July Do Muoi visited China and met with President Jiang Zemin to discuss the development of bilateral relations. In October 1998 Phan Van Khai made an official visit to China, during which it was agreed that Viet Nam and China would increase efforts to reach a settlement on their various border disputes; in November, however, Viet Nam reiterated its territorial claim to the disputed Spratly Islands. In February 1999 Le Kha Phieu paid an official visit to China, and in December the Chinese Premier, Zhu Rongji, visited Viet Nam. Also in December a formal border treaty was signed by Viet Nam and China. Vietnamese leaders travelled to China in June 2000 to attend an ideological symposium on methods of introducing market reforms without incurring any loss of political control. The visit was regarded as a major improvement in bilateral relations, and was followed by a second symposium in Hanoi in November. The two countries also made further progress in delineating their mutual land border, which took effect from July 2000, and finalized their border in the Gulf of Tonkin in late December, the latter agreement demarcating their economic and fishing zones. Chinese military delegations visited Viet Nam in July 2000 and February 2001 to enhance military co-operation, and President Tran Duc Luong visited China in December 2000 and 2001. In February 2002 Chinese President Jiang Zemin paid an official visit to Viet Nam, his second since the restoration of normal bilateral relations in 1991. His visit coincided with campaigns mounted by several dissidents expressing concern over the agreements that had been signed to demarcate the Sino-Vietnamese border. An ongoing dispute over fishing rights in the Gulf of Tonkin prevented the ratification of any agreement to delineate the shared maritime boundary. During the Chinese President's visit modest agreements on technical and economic co-operation were signed, and the framework was agreed for a Chinese loan of US $12m. to Viet Nam. In April 2002 it was reported that the two countries had begun the three-year process of demarcating their land border. In November of that year, following an ASEAN summit meeting attended by China, a declaration was issued outlining a code of conduct to be observed by those countries contesting the Spratly Islands. It was hoped that the agreement would end Viet Nam's dispute with China over the issue. However, China strongly opposed Viet Nam's decision, in March 2004, to allow tourists to visit the Spratly Islands, claiming that the tours infringed its territorial sovereignty. Viet Nam and China accelerated efforts to delineate their border in early 2005, and an 11th round of talks was held on the issue in Hanoi in February and March. In October Viet Nam and China agreed to conduct joint military patrols of the Gulf of Tonkin. Later that month Chinese President Hu Jintao made a three-day state visit to Viet Nam, during which he met with President Tran Doc Luong and General Secretary of the Central Committee of the Communist Party Nong Duc Manh. Bilateral relations were discussed, as were issues of regional and international concern, and both countries pledged to work together to promote mutual trust and encourage further bilateral co-operation.

In the late 1990s Viet Nam developed closer links with India, ostensibly because of mutual concerns about China. The Indian Minister of Defence visited Viet Nam in March 2000 and signed a wide-ranging defence agreement that would allow Viet Nam to train the Indian army in jungle warfare and counter-insurgency methods, and India to assist in the modernization of the Vietnamese military. The two countries also agreed to take action to combat piracy in the South China Sea. The Indian Minister of External Affairs, Jaswant Singh, and Prime Minister Atal Bihari Vajpayee made separate visits to Viet Nam in November 2000 and January 2001 respectively and agreed to co-ordinate their positions in the Non-Aligned Movement (NAM), South-South Co-operation and regional forums. India's Oil and Natural Gas Company became an investor in Viet Nam's Nam Con Son gas field in 2000, and India pledged some US $238m. of investment in the Vietnamese petroleum and gas industries. In September 2001 the Minister of Foreign Affairs, Nguyen Dy Nien, visited India, and in March 2002 Vice-President Nguyen Thi Binh also visited the country to discuss the possibility of closer bilateral co-operation.

From 1984 Viet Nam indicated that it would welcome a return to normal diplomatic relations with the USA, but the latter rejected any re-establishment of relations until agreements were made concerning the return to the USA of the remains of US soldiers 'missing in action' (MIA) from Viet Nam, and the proposed resettlement in the USA of some 10,000 Vietnamese 'political prisoners'. A number of senior US officials visited Hanoi during 1985 and 1986 for discussions about missing soldiers (estimated to total 1,797), and Viet Nam arranged for the return of some of the remains. In September 1987 the Vietnamese Government agreed to investigate the fate of some 70 soldiers who were believed to have been captured alive, while the US Government, in turn, agreed to facilitate humanitarian aid for Viet Nam from US charities and private groups, which had hitherto been illegal. In July 1988 Viet Nam agreed in principle to the resettlement of former political detainees in the USA or elsewhere. In early 1991 a US representative was stationed in Hanoi to supervise inquiries into MIA, the first official US presence in Viet Nam since 1975. In April 1991 the USA proposed a four-stage programme for the resumption of normal diplomatic relations with Viet Nam, conditional on Vietnamese co-operation in reaching a diplomatic settlement in Cambodia and in accounting for the remaining MIA. Following the conclusion of the peace agreement on Cambodia in October, Viet Nam made a plea for the removal of the US economic embargo, and in November discussions on the establishment of normal trade relations began. In early 1992 the US Government agreed to provide humanitarian aid for Viet Nam, but refused to end the economic embargo, reiterating that relations would not fully return to normal until after the UN-supervised elections in Cambodia, due to take place in early 1993. The embargo was renewed for another year in September 1992, although in December the US Government announced that US companies would now be allowed to open offices and sign contracts in Viet Nam, in anticipation of a future removal of the embargo. In July 1993 the new administration of President Bill Clinton revoked the US veto on assistance from the IMF and the World Bank for Viet Nam. In September the USA permitted US companies to take part in projects in Viet Nam that were financed by international aid agencies. The trade embargo was finally removed in February 1994.

In January 1995 Viet Nam and the USA signed an agreement that permitted the two countries to establish liaison offices in each other's capitals (these were opened immediately), and which resolved a long-standing dispute concerning former US diplomatic properties seized by the Vietnamese authorities in 1975. The establishment of full diplomatic relations was announced in July 1995. In May 1996 Clinton formally ended Viet Nam's official classification as a combat zone. In March 1997 military relations were established between the two countries. In April Douglas Peterson was appointed as the first US ambassador to Viet Nam, and in May Le Van Bang was formally appointed the first Vietnamese ambassador to the USA. In June Madeleine Albright became the first US Secretary of State to visit the country since the end of the Viet Nam war. During a visit to Washington, DC, by the Vietnamese Minister of Planning and Investment, an agreement was signed to promote greater economic co-operation. This was facilitated in March 1998, when Clinton signed a waiver to the 'Jackson-Vanik amendment' to 1974 US trade legislation, which restricted trade with communist countries. (In August 1999 the US House of Representatives voted in favour of an extension of the waiver of the amendment for Viet Nam.) In September 1998 the Vietnamese Deputy Prime Minister and Minister of Foreign Affairs, Nguyen Manh Cam, made an official visit to the USA at the invitation of the US Secretary of State. In July 1999 Viet Nam and the USA reached agreement in principle on the establishment of normal trade relations. Madeleine Albright made another official visit to Viet Nam in September. In March 2000 the US Secretary of Defense, William Cohen, made the first visit to Viet Nam by a US Secretary of Defense since the end of the Viet Nam war.

Although in early 2000 the US Government continued to refuse to acknowledge the responsibility of the chemical defoliant Agent Orange, sprayed in large quantities over areas of Viet Nam by the USA during the Viet Nam war, for widespread health problems (including birth defects) among the Vietnamese, Cohen, during his visit in March, reportedly indicated that the US Government would be willing to conduct joint research with the Vietnamese Government into the effects of the chemical. In May the US House of Representatives passed a resolution calling for the release of all political and religious prisoners in Viet Nam, a motion that was criticized as 'impudent interference' by Viet Nam. A landmark bilateral trade agreement between the USA and Viet Nam was signed in Washington, DC, in July 2000, paving the way for an increase in exports to, and investment from, the USA. The agreement was subject to an annual review by the US Congress. In September the US Department of State released a report on religious freedom in 104 countries, which included strong criticism of Viet Nam. US President Bill Clinton made a highly significant visit to Viet Nam in November 2000, the first since a brief stop-over by Richard Nixon in 1969. Although warmly received by the Vietnamese people, Clinton's calls for greater freedoms were rebuffed by General Secretary Le Kha Phieu, who defended the socialist system. In March 2001 Viet Nam accused US-based groups of fomenting the recent unrest in the Central Highlands (see above). In April a helicopter carrying nine Vietnamese and seven US citizens, searching for the remains of MIA, crashed in the highlands, killing all on board. Some 1,498 US servicemen and 300,000 Vietnamese remained unaccounted for in Viet Nam.

Following the September 2001 attacks on the USA (see the chapter on the USA) the Vietnamese Government expressed its support for the US-led war on terrorism. In October the severe penalty imposed on the dissident Roman Catholic priest Father Nguyen Van Ly (see above) accelerated the passage of the Viet Nam Human Rights Act through the US House of Representatives. The act was intended to make US non-humanitarian aid to Viet Nam conditional upon the improvement of its human rights record, thus angering the Vietnamese Government, but was subsequently blocked and never voted on in the Senate. (The act was reintroduced and approved again by the US House of Representatives in July 2004, but subsequently stalled in the Senate.) In November 2001 the National Assembly finally ratified the bilateral trade agreement, marking the complete restoration of normal relations between the two countries. In March 2002 Vietnamese and US scientists attended an unprecedented joint conference in Hanoi, at which the effects of Agent Orange were discussed. As a result, the two countries formally agreed to conduct joint research into the effects of the defoliant. However, relations with the USA threatened to deteriorate once more when the US Government expressed its concern for the safety of refugees returning to the Central Highlands from Cambodia. In March 2002, following the collapse of Viet Nam's agreement with UNHCR, the USA offered asylum to those refugees who remained in Cambodia. In the same month relations were further strained when the US Government issued a critical report on Viet Nam's human rights record.

In 2003 relations with the USA remained somewhat strained. The Vietnamese Government condemned the US-led campaign to oust the regime of Saddam Hussain in Iraq early in that year and was reportedly angered by the approval by the US Congress of several items of legislation, including the Viet Nam Freedom of Information Bill and the Viet Nam Human Rights Bill, which it deemed an unacceptable interference in its internal affairs. However, in November relations improved when Minister of National Defence Lt-Gen. Pham Can Tra visited Washington, DC, and held talks with US Secretary of Defense Donald Rumsfeld. In the same month a US frigate spent four days in the port of Ho Chi Minh City, the first visit to Viet Nam by a US warship since the end of the Viet Nam war in 1975. In December 2003 an aviation agreement was signed with the USA, enabling direct flights between the two countries for the first time; the first US flight arrived in Ho Chi Minh City in December 2004. In February 2004, during a visit to the country, Adm. Thomas Fargo, head of the US Pacific Command, reportedly became the first foreign official to visit the naval base at Da Nang. Meanwhile, an independent organization, the Vietnam Association for Victims of Agent Orange, submitted a lawsuit to the US Federal Court, on behalf of three Vietnamese people who had been affected by the defoliant, against the US companies that were responsible for its manufacture. The lawsuit was the first of its kind to have been filed. In March 2005, however, the US Federal Court dismissed the lawsuit, ruling that there was no legal basis for the claims of the plaintiffs. The Vietnam Association for Victims of Agent Orange condemned the decision and announced that it was considering filing an appeal. In September 2004 the US Secretary of State designated Viet Nam as a 'country of particular concern' under the International Religious Freedom Act for particularly severe violations of religious freedom. The Department of State again urged the Vietnamese Government to release prisoners detained for their religious beliefs and to reopen churches closed in the Central Highlands. The designation was denounced by the Vietnamese Government, which lodged an official protest with the US Government. In June

2005 Prime Minister Phan Van Khai, accompanied by a delegation of government officials, made an official state visit to the USA. He thus became the most senior Vietnamese official to visit the USA since the end of the Viet Nam War three decades previously. During his visit, he met with US President George W. Bush. Among the issues discussed were Viet Nam's application to join the World Trade Organization (WTO, see p. 370), human rights, religious freedom and corporate development.

In October 1990 the European Community (now the European Union—EU, see p. 228) announced the restoration of diplomatic relations with Viet Nam. In October 1991 a group of industrialized countries, led by France, agreed to assist Viet Nam in paying its arrears to the IMF, thereby enabling it to qualify for future IMF loans (which were, however, still dependent on the approval of the USA, as the IMF's principal vote-holder). In February 1993 President Mitterrand of France made an official visit to Viet Nam (the first Western Head of State to do so since the country's reunification). France's Geopetrol oil company formed part of a consortium to develop Vietnamese offshore oil and gas deposits. In October 2002 President Tran Duc Luong paid the first visit to France by a Vietnamese leader since the establishment of diplomatic relations with France in 1973. President Jacques Chirac of France made an official visit to Viet Nam in early October 2004, attending the fifth biennial Asia-Europe Meeting, which took place in Hanoi. Several agreements on bilateral co-operation were signed during the visit, and President Chirac pledged his country's support for Viet Nam's bid to join the WTO. In January 1992 a Japanese government mission visited Viet Nam to negotiate the repayment of Vietnamese debts, and in November Japan (which—although a principal trading partner—had hitherto imposed a ban on official economic co-operation) began to provide financial assistance to Viet Nam. In March 1999 Prime Minister Phan Van Khai made an official visit to Japan. In August 2000 a Japanese consortium pledged to assist the construction of nuclear power plants in Viet Nam. During 2000 Viet Nam and Japan also strengthened their defence links, with the aim of promoting regional security. In June 2001 Phan Van Khai paid a further visit to Japan.

The Cambodian peace agreement of 1991 allowed Viet Nam to initiate closer relations with ASEAN member states: Vo Van Kiet visited Indonesia, Thailand and Singapore in October and November 1991 and Malaysia, Brunei and the Philippines in early 1992; agreements on economic co-operation were concluded with these countries, including guarantees of protection for future investment by them in Viet Nam. In July 1992 Viet Nam signed the ASEAN agreement (of 1976) on regional amity and co-operation, and in July 1995 became a full member of the organization. In September 1992 an agreement was signed with Singapore on the mutual provision of 'most-favoured nation' trading status. In April 1995 Viet Nam, Thailand, Laos and Cambodia signed an agreement providing for the establishment of the Mekong River Commission (see p. 387), which was to co-ordinate the sustainable development of the resources of the Lower Mekong River basin. In October 1997 Viet Nam and Thailand reached an agreement to demarcate their maritime boundary, following a series of incidents between Vietnamese and Thai fishing vessels. In December 1998 Viet Nam hosted the sixth summit meeting of the heads of state and government of the ASEAN grouping of countries. During 2000 Viet Nam reaffirmed sovereignty over the Spratly and Paracel Islands, but reassured ASEAN that it was committed to a peaceful solution to the territorial dispute through multilateral negotiations. It was hoped that the declaration of November 2002, which established a code of conduct to be adhered to by the claimants of the islands, would provide such a solution. Vietnamese and Laotian officials held several meetings during the course of 2000, and Viet Nam provided assistance to Laos in its fight against ethnic Hmong rebels. In November 2001 President Tran Duc Long held talks with President Gloria Macapagal Arroyo while on an official visit to the Philippines. The two countries agreed to the enhancement of economic relations and to co-operation in trade, investment and tourism. In February 2002 the Prime Minister met with the Prime Ministers of Cambodia and of Laos in Ho Chi Minh City. The three countries agreed to promote co-operation in the development of tourism and infrastructure within the 'development triangle'. In February 2004 the first joint meeting of the Cabinets of Viet Nam and Thailand took place. During the meeting, several co-operation agreements were signed concerning various social and economic issues. Prime Minister Phan Van Khai paid a four-day visit to Singapore (the largest foreign investor in Viet Nam) in March, during which a comprehensive co-operation framework document was signed. Following the announcement also in March that Viet Nam intended to allow tourists to begin visiting the Spratly Islands, the first tour took place in April, despite opposition from other claimants to the disputed islands. In May Viet Nam announced that it was renovating a disused runway on one of the islands to further its tourism plans.

In mid-November 1997 Viet Nam hosted the seventh summit meeting of francophone states (La Francophonie), which was attended by representatives of 49 countries. In April 2000 President Tran Duc Luong attended the Group of 77 (G-77) South Summit meeting of developing countries, held in Havana, Cuba.

Government

The 1992 Constitution declares the supremacy of the Communist Party. Legislative power is vested in the National Assembly, which is elected for a five-year term by universal adult suffrage and, from 2002, had 498 members. The President, elected by the National Assembly from among its members, is the Head of State and Commander-in-Chief of the armed forces. The President appoints a Prime Minister (from among the members of the National Assembly, and subject to their approval), who forms a government (again, subject to ratification by the National Assembly). The country is divided into provinces and municipalities, which are subordinate to the central government. Local government is entrusted to locally elected People's Councils.

Defence

In August 2005 the active ('Main Force') armed forces of Viet Nam had an estimated total strength of 484,000: an estimated 412,000 in the army, an estimated 42,000 in the navy, and 30,000 in the air and air defence forces. Military service is compulsory and usually lasts for two years. Paramilitary forces number in excess of 5m. and include the urban People's Self-Defence Force and the rural People's Militia. The defence budget for 2005 was estimated at US $3,470m.

Economic Affairs

In 2004, according to estimates by the World Bank, Viet Nam's gross national income (GNI), measured at average 2002–04 prices, was US $45,081.9m., equivalent to $550 per head (or $2,700 per head on an international purchasing-power parity basis). During 1995–2004, it was estimated, the population increased at an average annual rate of 1.3%, while gross domestic product (GDP) per head increased, in real terms, by an average of 5.6% per year. Overall GDP increased, in real terms, at an average annual rate of 7.0% in 1995–2004. According to the Asian Development Bank (ADB), GDP grew by 7.8% in 2004 and by 8.4% in 2005.

Agriculture (including forestry and fishing) contributed an estimated 21.8% of GDP in 2004, engaging 57.9% of the employed labour force in that year. The staple crop is rice, which also provided 3.6% of total export earnings in 2004. In addition, Viet Nam is a major world producer of coffee; this commodity accounted for 2.4% of export revenue in 2004. Other important cash crops include sugar cane, groundnuts, rubber, tea and cotton. In 1992, in an attempt to preserve Viet Nam's remaining forests, a ban was imposed on the export of logs and sawn timber, and in March 1997 a 10-year ban on all timber products except wooden artefacts was introduced. Following a successful planting programme undertaken between 1990 and 2000, by the latter year forest cover had risen to exceed 30% of Viet Nam's total land area. Exports of wood and wood products totalled US $1,139m. in 2004. Livestock-rearing and fishing are also important. In 2004 marine products accounted for some 9.1% of export revenues. According to figures from the ADB, agricultural GDP increased by an estimated annual average of 4.0% in 1995–2004. The sector's GDP expanded by 4.4% in 2004 and by 4.0% in 2005; growth in both years was impeded by prolonged drought in much of the country and by outbreaks of avian influenza ('bird flu').

In 2004 industry (comprising manufacturing, mining and quarrying, construction and utilities) contributed an estimated 40.1% of GDP. In that year the industrial sector engaged 17.4% of the labour force. In 2000 the non-state economic sector accounted for an estimated 22.4% of industrial production. According to figures from the ADB, industrial GDP increased by an annual average of 10.4% per year in 1995–2004. The sector's GDP expanded by 10.2% in 2004 and by 10.6% in 2005.

In 2004 mining and quarrying contributed an estimated 10.2% of GDP. In the same year the mining sector engaged 0.7% of the labour force. Viet Nam's principal mineral exports are petroleum and coal. Tin, zinc, iron, antimony, chromium, natural phosphates, bauxite and gold are also mined. Significant reserves of offshore natural gas were discovered in 1993. In 2004 exports of crude petroleum accounted for 22.0% of total merchandise exports. In 2005 the Vietnamese Government revised mining regulations in an attempt to increase the sector's attractiveness to potential investors. According to figures from the ADB, mining GDP increased by an annual average of 9.3% in 1995–2004. Mining GDP increased by 6.3% in 2003 and by 11.3% in 2004.

Manufacturing contributed an estimated 20.3% of GDP in 2004, and accounted for 11.7% of employment in the same year. The main manufacturing sectors in 2000, measured by gross value of output, included food-processing, cigarettes and tobacco, textiles, chemicals, and electrical goods. According to figures from the ADB, manufacturing GDP increased by an annual average of 11.2% in 1995–2004. Manufacturing GDP increased by 11.5% in 2003 and by 10.1% in 2004.

Energy is derived principally from hydroelectric installations, petroleum and coal. Although production of petroleum increased in the late 1980s and early 1990s, exports were mainly in the form of crude petroleum, and Viet Nam still relied on the import of refined products. Imports of mineral fuels accounted for 10.7% of total imports in 2003. Construction of Viet Nam's first petroleum refinery at Dung Quat commenced in late 2005 and was expected to be completed in early 2009. With a planned capacity of 6.5m. metric tons of crude petroleum per year, the refinery was expected to supply approximately one-third of domestic demand for petrol and oil. Meanwhile, Viet Nam would continue to depend on imports for its supplies of refined oil. Construction of the country's first nuclear power plant, to be built with Russian assistance, began in 2004.

The services sector contributed an estimated 38.2% of GDP in 2004 and employed 24.8% of the labour force in that year. Tourism is an important source of foreign exchange; receipts from tourism totalled 6,016.6m. dông in 2003. In 2005 approximately 3.5m. foreign tourists visited Viet Nam, an increase of 18.4% compared with the previous year; measures implemented during 2004, which included an easing of visa requirements for visitors from Japan and the Republic of Korea, together with the opening of more air routes and overseas representative offices by Viet Nam Airlines, were among the contributory factors. According to figures from the ADB, the GDP of the services sector increased by an average of 6.1% per year in 1995–2004. The sector's GDP rose by 7.3% in 2004 and by 8.5% in 2005.

In 2005 Viet Nam recorded a visible trade deficit of US $4,564m. The deficit on the current account of the balance of payments in that year was an estimated $1,885m. (equivalent to 3.6% of GDP). In 2004 the People's Republic of China was Viet Nam's principal source of imports, supplying 13.6% of total imports; other major sources Japan (11.5%), Singapore (also 11.5%) and the Republic of Korea (9.8%). The principal market for exports in that year was the USA (19.8%); other important purchasers were Japan (13.7%) and the People's Republic of China (8.4%). The principal exports in 2003 were miscellaneous manufactured goods (36.0%), food and live animals and mineral fuels. In 2003 the principal imports were machinery and transport equipment (31.4%), basic manufactures (26.4%), chemicals and related products and mineral fuels.

In 2005 a budgetary deficit of 42,000,000m. dông was forecast. The fiscal deficit was projected at the equivalent of 2.3% of GDP in that year. In 2005 Viet Nam's total external debt was estimated by the ADB at US $17,400m. In that year the cost of debt-servicing was equivalent to 5.2% of the value of exports of goods and services. According to the ADB, the annual rate of inflation averaged 3.4% in 1995–2003. Consumer prices increased by 3.2% in 2003 but, owing to the impact of avian influenza, drought and higher global rice prices, in 2004 food prices rose by 13.0%, and overall inflation increased to 7.7%. The ADB estimated that the rate of inflation increased to 8.3% in 2005. In 2005, according to the ADB, 5.1% of the labour force were unemployed.

Viet Nam is a member of the Asian Development Bank (ADB, see p. 169), the Association of South East Asian Nations (ASEAN, see p. 172), the Asia-Pacific Economic Co-operation (APEC, see p. 164), the UN Economic and Social Commission for Asia and the Pacific (ESCAP, see p. 33) and the Mekong River Commission (see p. 387). Viet Nam also joined the ASEAN Free Trade Area (AFTA) in 1996 and was granted until 2003 to comply with the requisite tariff reductions (to between 0% and 5%). The area was formally established on 1 January 2002. Viet Nam's application to become a member of the World Trade Organization (WTO, see p. 370) was well advanced in early 2006 (see below).

From 1990 the process of *doi moi* (renovation) aimed to transform Viet Nam from a centralized economy to a market-orientated system. New investment laws allowed the establishment of wholly foreign-owned enterprises. Agricultural production was stimulated by the removal of price controls, by a new system of land tenure and, from early 1998, by the relaxation of the state monopoly on rice exports, with the result that by the mid-1990s Viet Nam, formerly dependent on rice imports, had become one of the world's principal rice exporters. Despite a decline in performance precipitated by the regional economic crisis that originated in Thailand in mid-1997, from late 1999 the Vietnamese economy began to make a strong recovery. In December 2002 revisions to the Budget Law resulted in the delegation of a significant amount of power in budgetary management to provincial and city authorities. In 2004 rising global oil prices contributed to an increase of 30.3% in export revenues compared with the previous year; accordingly, the trade deficit declined moderately in that year. Further increases in global oil prices during 2005 led to an improvement in Viet Nam's fiscal balance. Oil-related tax receipts accounted for 21% of total government revenues in that year, while net oil exports contributed 4.8% of total GDP, compared with 3.5% in 2004. From 2004 foreign reserves strengthened as a result of increased capital inflows, particularly foreign investment and workers' remittances. Net private remittances reached an estimated US $3,200m. in 2005. In order to address the problem of the increasing budget deficit, in early 2005 the Government announced plans to raise $2,110m. through government bond issues in that year, an increase of 44% on the amount thus raised in 2004. In October 2005 the Vietnamese Government's first international bonds were released for sale, with revenue from these 10-year bonds amounting to approximately $750m. The establishment of the country's first stock exchange in July 2000 was also an important development; by early 2006 a total of 34 companies were listed on the exchange. Following improvements in legislation governing foreign investment in the country, levels of investment began to increase. During 2005 the National Assembly approved the implementation of several new laws intended to reduce administrative barriers to corporate development; it was hoped that these reforms would result in a further increase in levels of investment. Foreign direct investment rose from a total of $1,730m. in 2004 to $1,914m. in 2005. In May 2003 the USA significantly reduced Viet Nam's textile export quotas for that year, prompting fears that the country's expanding textile industry would be adversely affected (textiles constituted Viet Nam's primary source of export earnings in 2003). However, Vietnamese exports of textiles and garments to the USA totalled $4,300m. in 2004, an increase of 17.2% compared with the previous year. Despite the relatively weak performance in the first half of the year resulting from the removal of the quotas hitherto applicable to several competitor countries, exports of Vietnamese textiles and garments in 2005 increased by 9.6% compared with the previous year; textile and garment exports to the USA, however, increased by just 1.2% in that year. In November 2004 US President George W. Bush affirmed his country's support for the Vietnamese application to join the WTO, membership of which would significantly improve prospects for Viet Nam's textiles and garments industry since it would lead to the removal of the restrictive US quotas. Viet Nam's hopes of gaining entry to the WTO were bolstered by the conclusion of bilateral agreements with the European Union (EU) in October 2004, with Singapore in the following month and with Argentina, Brazil, Chile and Cuba by the end of December of that year. In the latter month, the ninth round of multilateral negotiations was completed successfully, and during the first three months of 2005 Viet Nam held bilateral discussions with 15 WTO members, including the USA, China and Japan. Further bilateral negotiations took place in conjunction with the 10th round of multilateral talks, held in the Swiss city of Geneva in May 2005. By the end of 2005 bilateral negotiations had been concluded with a further 15 countries, including China, India, Japan and the Republic of Korea. In early 2006 further agreements were formally concluded with Australia, the Dominican Republic, Honduras and New Zealand. At the 11th round of multilateral negotiations, held in March of that year, it was announced that agreements with the USA and Mexico—the two remaining countries with which Viet Nam needed to reach trade agreements in order to secure WTO membership—were also expected to be concluded shortly. The agreement with Mexico

VIET NAM

was subsequently signed in April, while that with the USA was concluded in May. In early 2006 the Government announced that 3,590 of the existing 5,655 state enterprises had been restructured between 2001 and 2005; 2,347 of these had undergone equitization. However, progress had been achieved principally among small companies; Viet Nam's continued economic development remained dependent upon the acceleration of equitization of larger enterprises and upon the implementation of further reforms within the banking and public administration sectors. The further development of the private sector and enhanced transparency of policy-making continued to be important. Widespread corruption amongst government officials also remained a significant problem, although in 2004 an additional 7,000,000m. đông was assigned for significant salary increases in an attempt to address the issue; a further 20,500,000m đông was allocated to this end for 2005. The regional outbreaks of avian influenza in 2004 affected Viet Nam particularly severely. Although this hindered agricultural performance in that year, GDP growth remained strong, driven by robust consumption and investment. Fears of a human pandemic mounted, however, and by April 2006 the virus had caused 106 known human fatalities in South-East Asia since late 2003, 42 of which had occurred in Viet Nam. No confirmed incidents of human-to-human transmission had been reported, and the impact on the economy in 2005 was offset by rising domestic demand and strong performance within both the industrial and service sectors, which contributed to that year's GDP growth rate of 8.4%. It was hoped that any impact of avian influenza on agriculture, tourism and foreign investment in 2006 would similarly be offset by strong performance in other sectors. At the Eighth National Assembly Session in November 2005 14 new, or amendments to existing, laws were ratified, including amendments to the Law on Special Consumption Tax and the Law on Value Added Tax (VAT). As of 1 January 2006 the rate of special consumption tax on automobiles, tobacco and alcoholic beverages was revised in accordance with international regulations, and unprocessed farm produce and certain aquatic products were added to the list of products exempted from VAT.

In a draft of its socio-economic development plan for 2006–10, the Government targeted annual GDP growth of 7.5%–8.0% during the five-year period covered by the plan; the draft also suggested that there was to be a continuation of efforts to transform Viet Nam's economy into a more market-orientated system. The ADB projected GDP growth of 7.8% for 2006 and of 8.0% for 2007.

Education

Primary education, which is compulsory, begins at six years of age and lasts for five years. Secondary education, beginning at the age of 11, lasts for seven years, comprising a first cycle of four years and a second cycle of three years. In 1997 total pre-primary enrolment was equivalent to 40% of children in the relevant age-group. In 2001 94.0% of children in the relevant age-group were enrolled in primary education and in the same year total secondary enrolment was equivalent to 70% of males and 64% of females in the relevant age-group. In 2003/04 there were 187 universities and colleges of higher education, with a total enrolment of 993,900 students. In 1989 Viet Nam's first private college since 1954 was opened in Hanoi; Thang Long College was to cater for university students. Of total planned budgetary expenditure by the central Government in 2002, 13,581,000m. đông (11.3%) was allocated to education.

Public Holidays

2006: 1 January (New Year's Day), 29–31 January* (Tet, lunar new year), 3 February (Founding of the Communist Party), 30 April (Liberation of Saigon), 1 May (May Day), 2 September (National Day).

2007: 1 January (New Year's Day), 3 February (Founding of the Communist Party), 18–20 February* (Tet, lunar new year), 30 April (Liberation of Saigon), 1 May (May Day), 2 September (National Day).

* Varies according to the lunar calendar.

Weights and Measures

The metric system is in force.

Statistical Survey

Sources (unless otherwise stated): General Statistics Office of Viet Nam, 2 Hoang Van Thu, Ba Dinh District, Hanoi; tel. (4) 7332997; e-mail banbientap@gso.gov.vn; internet www.gso.gov.vn; Communist Party of Viet Nam, 1 Hoang Van Thu, Hanoi; e-mail cpv@hn.vnn.vn; internet www.cpv.org.vn.

Area and Population

AREA, POPULATION AND DENSITY

Area (sq km)	329,315*
Population (census results)	
1 April 1989	64,411,713
1 April 1999	
Males	37,469,117
Females	38,854,056
Total	76,323,173
Population (official estimates, annual averages)	
2002	79,685,800
2003	80,902,400
2004†	82,032,300
Density (per sq km) at 2004	249.1

* 127,149 sq miles.
† Preliminary figure.

ADMINISTRATIVE DIVISIONS
(2004, annual averages)

	Area (sq km)	Population ('000)	Density (per sq km)
Red River Delta	14,812.5	17,836.0	1,204.1
Hanoi	921.0	3,082.8	3,347.2
Vinh Phuc	1,371.4	1,154.8	842.1
Bac Ninh	807.6	987.4	1,222.6
Ha Tay	2,192.1	2,500.0	1,140.5
Hai Duong	1,648.4	1,698.3	1,030.3
Haiphong	1,526.3	1,770.8	1,160.2
Hung Yen	923.1	1,120.3	1,213.6
Thai Binh	1,545.4	1,842.8	1,192.4
Ha Nam	852.2	820.1	962.3
Nam Dinh	1,641.3	1,947.1	1,186.3
Ninh Binh	1,383.7	911.6	658.8
North East	63,629.8	9,244.8	145.3
Ha Giang	7,884.3	660.7	83.8
Cao Bang	6,690.7	508.2	76.0
Bac Kan	4,857.2	296.2	61.0
Tuyen Quang	5,868.0	718.1	122.4
Lao Cai	6,357.0	565.7	89.0
Yen Bai	6,882.9	723.5	105.1
Thai Nguyen	3,542.6	1,095.4	309.2
Lang Son	8,305.2	731.7	88.1
Quang Ninh	5,899.6	1,067.3	180.9
Bac Giang	3,822.7	1,563.5	409.0
Phu Tho	3,519.6	1,314.5	373.5
North West	37,336.9	2,524.9	67.6
Dien Bien	9,560.0	440.8	46.1
Lai Chau	9,059.4	308.0	34.0
Son La	14,055.0	972.8	69.2
Hoa Binh	4,662.5	803.3	172.3

VIET NAM

Statistical Survey

—continued

	Area (sq km)	Population ('000)	Density (per sq km)
North Central Coast	51,510.8	10,504.5	203.9
Thanh Hoa	11,116.3	3,646.6	328.0
Nghe An	16,487.4	3,003.2	182.2
Ha Tinh	6,055.6	1,286.7	212.5
Quand Binh	8,051.8	831.6	103.3
Quang Tri	4,745.7	616.6	129.9
Thua Thien-Hué	5,054.0	1,119.8	221.6
South Central Coast	33,069.0	6,981.7	211.1
Da Nang	1,255.5	764.5	608.9
Quang Nam	10,407.4	1,452.3	139.5
Quang Ngai	5,137.6	1,259.4	245.1
Binh Dinh	6,025.0	1,545.3	256.5
Phu Yen	5,045.3	848.9	168.3
Khanh Hoa	5,198.2	1,111.3	213.8
Central Highlands	54,473.7	4,674.2	85.8
Kon Tum	9,614.5	366.1	38.1
Gia Lai	15,494.9	1,095.9	70.7
Dak Lak	13,085.0	1,687.7	129.0
Dak Nong	6,514.5	385.8	59.2
Lam Dong	9,764.8	1,138.7	116.6
South East	34,743.1	13,190.1	379.6
Ninh Thuan	3,360.1	554.7	165.1
Binh Thuan	7,828.4	1,135.9	145.1
Binh Phuoc	6,857.3	783.6	114.3
Tay Ninh	4,029.6	1,029.8	255.6
Binh Duong	2,695.6	883.2	327.7
Dong Nai	5,894.8	2,174.6	368.9
Ba Ria-Vung Tau	1,982.2	897.6	452.8
Ho Chi Minh City	2,095.2	5,730.7	2,735.2
Mekong River Delta	39,738.7	17,076.1	429.7
Long An	4,491.2	1,400.5	311.8
Tien Giang	2,366.6	1,681.6	710.6
Ben Tre	2,321.6	1,345.6	579.6
Tra Vinh	2,215.1	1,015.8	458.6
Vinh Long	1,475.2	1,044.9	708.3
Dong Thap	3,246.1	1,639.4	505.0
An Giang	3,406.2	2,170.1	637.1
Kien Giang	6,268.2	1,630.3	260.1
Can Tho	1,390.0	1,122.5	807.6
Hau Giang	1,608.0	781.0	485.7
Soc Trang	3,223.3	1,257.4	390.1
Bac Lieu	2,525.7	786.2	311.3
Ca Mau	5,201.5	1,200.8	230.9
Total	329,314.5	82,032.3	249.1

PRINCIPAL TOWNS
(estimated population, excl. suburbs, at mid-1992)

Ho Chi Minh City (formerly Saigon)	3,015,743*	Nam Dinh	171,699
Hanoi (capital)	1,073,760	Qui Nhon	163,385
Haiphong	783,133	Vung Tau	145,145
Da Nang	382,674	Rach Gia	141,132
Buon Ma Thuot	282,095	Long Xuyen	132,681
Nha Trang	221,331	Thai Nguyen	127,643
Hué	219,149	Hong Gai	127,484
Can Tho	215,587	Vinh	112,455
Cam Pha	209,086		

* Including Cholon.

Source: UN, *Demographic Yearbook*.

Mid-2003 (UN estimates, incl. suburbs): Ho Chi Minh City 4,850,717; Hanoi 3,977,202; Haiphong 1,754,537 (Source: UN, *World Urbanization Prospects: The 2003 Revision*).

BIRTHS AND DEATHS
(UN estimates, annual averages)

	1990–95	1995–2000	2000–05
Birth rate (per 1,000)	28.2	21.4	20.2
Death rate (per 1,000)	7.5	6.4	6.1

Source: UN, *World Population Prospects: The 2004 Revision*.

Expectation of life (WHO estimates, years at birth): 71 (males 68; females 74) in 2003 (Source: WHO, *World Health Report*).

ECONOMICALLY ACTIVE POPULATION
('000 persons aged 15 years and over)

	2002	2003	2004
Agriculture, hunting and forestry	23,645.4	23,236.7	23,068.6
Fishing	1,271.9	1,334.4	1,429.2
Mining and quarrying	244.4	322.1	294.9
Manufacturing	4,050.9	4,511.5	4,949.8
Electricity, gas and water	118.0	128.1	141.8
Construction	1,490.9	1,796.4	1,956.6
Wholesale and retail trade; repair of motor vehicles, motorcycles and personal and household goods	4,306.5	4,507.4	4,696.0
Hotels and restaurants	521.1	643.2	595.0
Transport, storage and communications	1,267.3	1,297.4	1,292.9
Financial intermediation	130.0	148.5	159.0
Real estate, renting and business activities	184.4	218.5	219.2
Public administration and defence; compulsory social security	590.0	620.1	698.9
Education	1,058.5	1,098.0	1,185.0
Health and social work	278.9	306.1	328.0
Other community, social and personal service activities	812.0	788.8	1,056.4
Private households with employed persons	190.2	217.0	241.1
Extra-territorial organizations and bodies	2.0	1.4	3.3
Total employed	40,162.3	41,175.7	42,315.6
Unemployed	871.0	949.0	926.4
Total labour force	41,033.3	42,124.7	43,242.0
Males	20,753.6	21,361.6	22,059.1
Females	20,279.7	20,763.1	21,182.9

Source: ILO.

Health and Welfare

KEY INDICATORS

Total fertility rate (children per woman, 2003)	2.3
Under-5 mortality rate (per 1,000 live births, 2004)	23
HIV/AIDS (% of persons aged 15–49, 2003)	0.40
Physicians (per 1,000 head, 2001)	0.53
Hospital beds (per 1,000 head, 1997)	1.67
Health expenditure (2002): US $ per head (PPP)	148
Health expenditure (2002): % of GDP	5.2
Health expenditure (2002): public (% of total)	29.2
Access to water (% of persons, 2002)	73
Access to sanitation (% of persons, 2002)	41
Human Development Index (2003): ranking	108
Human Development Index (2003): value	0.704

For sources and definitions, see explanatory note on p. vi.

Agriculture

PRINCIPAL CROPS
('000 metric tons)

	2002	2003	2004
Rice (paddy)	34,447	34,569	36,118
Maize	2,511	3,136	3,454
Potatoes	377	362	365*
Sweet potatoes	1,704	1,592	1,536
Cassava (Manioc)	4,438	5,229	5,688
Sugar cane	17,120	16,855	15,880
Dry beans	144	158	157
Cashew nuts†	515	658	826
Soybeans (Soya beans)	206	220	242
Groundnuts (in shell)	400	406	451
Coconuts	915	920	931
Cabbages	499	606	650*
Dry onions*	223	225	225
Other vegetables*	6,278	6,369	6,496

VIET NAM

—continued	2002	2003	2004
Watermelons	372	401	410*
Bananas	1,097	1,221	1,354
Oranges	435	500	538
Mangoes	227	306	314
Pineapples	374	338	422
Other fruit*	2,640	2,760	2,845
Coffee (green)	700	794	835
Tea (made)	94	100	108
Tobacco (leaves)	33	33	27
Natural rubber	373†	384†	400

* FAO estimate(s).
† Unofficial figure.
Source: FAO.

LIVESTOCK
('000 head, year ending September)

	2002	2003	2004
Horses	111	113	112*
Cattle	4,063	4,394	4,908
Buffaloes	2,814	2,835	2,870
Pigs	23,170	24,885	26,144
Goats	622	780	1,020
Chickens	163,100†	178,010†	159,233
Ducks	69,900†	69,000†	75,000*

* FAO estimate.
† Unofficial figure.
Source: FAO.

LIVESTOCK PRODUCTS
('000 metric tons)

	2002	2003	2004
Beef and veal	102.5	107.5	119.8
Buffalo meat*	98.9	99.5	101.1
Pig meat	1,653.6	1,800.4	2,012.0
Chicken meat	338.4	372.7	316.4
Duck meat*	81.6	82.8	88.2
Cows' milk	78.5	126.7	151.3
Buffaloes' milk*	31.0	31.0	31.0
Poultry eggs*	226.5	234.5	197.0
Cattle hides (fresh)*	16.8	18.2	20.2
Buffalo hides (fresh)*	18.4	18.5	18.8

* FAO estimates.
Source: FAO.

Forestry

ROUNDWOOD REMOVALS
('000 cubic metres, excl. bark)

	2002	2003	2004
Sawlogs, veneer logs and logs for sleepers*†	2,571	2,571	2,571
Pulpwood	1,262*	1,650	1,850
Other industrial wood	350*	550	650
Fuel wood	26,547*	21,500	21,250
Total	30,730*	26,271	26,321

* FAO estimate(s).
† Annual output assumed to be unchanged from 2000.
Source: FAO.

SAWNWOOD PRODUCTION
('000 cubic metres, incl. railway sleepers)

	2002	2003	2004
Total (all broadleaved)	2,667*	2,450	2,900

* Unofficial figure.
Source: FAO.

Fishing
('000 metric tons, live weight)

	2001	2002	2003
Capture*	1,490.3	1,507.4	1,666.9
Freshwater fishes	132.3	148.2	125.8
Marine fishes	1,033.6	1,025.8	1,213.4
Prawns and shrimps*	90.0	78.9	78.0
Cephalopods*	130.0	111.9	110.0
Aquaculture*	588.1	703.0	937.5
Freshwater fishes*	383.2	441.8	599.8
Total catch*	2,078.4	2,210.5	2,604.4

* FAO estimates.
Note: Figures exclude aquatic plants (FAO estimates, '000 metric tons, all aquaculture): 20 in 2001; 25 in 2002; 30 in 2003.
Source: FAO.

Mining
('000 metric tons)

	2002	2003	2004
Crude petroleum ('000 barrels)	117,753	125,281	142,844
Natural gas (million cubic metres)*	2,260	3,450	6,250
Coal (anthracite)	16,347	19,590	26,820
Chromium ore—gross weight†	80	120	150
Ilmenite—gross weight†	180	200	200
Gold (kilograms)†	2,000	2,000	2,000
Kaolin†	600	650	650
Barite (metric tons)	60,300†	81,500†	101,000
Phosphate rock: gross weight	680	823	800†
P^2O_5 content	204	247	240†
Salt (unrefined)	1,089	1,275†	1,300†

* Figures refer to gross production.
† Estimate(s).
Source: US Geological Survey.

Industry

SELECTED PRODUCTS
('000 metric tons, unless otherwise indicated)

	2002	2003	2004*
Raw sugar	1,069	1,360	1,371
Beer (million litres)	940	1,119	1,164
Cigarettes (million packets)	3,375	3,871	4,065
Fabrics (million metres)	470	496	518
Chemical fertilizers	1,158	1,294	1,453
Insecticides	34	41	44
Bricks (million)	11,365	12,810	14,501
Cement	21,121	24,127	25,329
Crude steel	2,503	2,954	2,929
Diesel motors (pieces)	107,433	184,418	192,838
Television receivers ('000)	1,597	2,188	2,479
Electric engines (pieces)	64,085	95,779	100,208
Bicycle tyres ('000)	22,778	26,686	27,000
Bicycle tubes ('000)	24,032	36,083	37,600
Rice milling equipment (pieces)	13,433	10,112	10,200
Transformers (pieces)	18,633	33,364	35,634
Electric energy (million kWh)	35,888	40,546	46,048

* Preliminary figures.

VIET NAM

Statistical Survey

Finance

CURRENCY AND EXCHANGE RATES

Monetary Units
100 xu = 1 new dông.

Sterling, Dollar and Euro Equivalents (30 September 2005)
£1 sterling = 28,075.4 dông;
US $1 = 15,895.0 dông;
€1 = 19,140.8 dông;
100,000 new dông = £3.56 = $6.29 = €5.22.

Average Exchange Rate (new dông per US $)
2001   14,725.2
2002   15,279.5
2003   15,509.6

Note: The new dông, equivalent to 10 former dông, was introduced in September 1985.

BUDGET
('000,000 million dông)

Revenue (incl. grants)	2003	2004*	2005†
Tax revenue	102.3	118.8	133.0
Corporate income tax	32.6	37.3	41.6
Individual income tax	2.9	3.7	4.1
Tax on the transfer of properties	1.8	2.0	2.2
Value-added tax (VAT)	32.7	41.1	47.2
Excises	8.9	12.5	14.7
Taxes on international trade	21.3	20.4	21.3
Non-tax and capital revenue	37.6	46.2	48.1
Fees and charges	6.2	4.4	8.7
Income from natural resources	10.6	12.2	12.5
Net profit after tax	10.6	12.6	12.8
Capital revenues	1.0	0.6	10.8
Grants	2.0	2.0	2.0
Total	**141.9**	**166.9**	**183.0**

Expenditure (cash basis)‡	2003	2004*	2005†
Current expenditure	103.2	117.8	135.8
General administrative services	11.3	12.5	12.0
Economic services	8.4	10.5	9.6
Social services	50.1	53.9	56.9
Education	17.7	19.1	20.5
Health	5.4	6.3	6.9
Pensions and social relief	16.6	17.3	17.4
Other services (incl. defence)	26.7	28.0	50.9
Interest on public debt	6.7	6.0	6.5
Capital expenditure	51.0	59.0	66.0
Onlending	17.8	13.3	23.2
Total	**172.1**	**190.2**	**225.0**

* Estimates.
† Forecasts.
‡ Excluding off-budget investment expenditure ('000,000 million dông): 13.9 in 2003; 8.5 in 2004 (estimate); 11.1 in 2005 (forecast).

Source: IMF, *Vietnam: Statistical Appendix* (February 2006).

INTERNATIONAL RESERVES
(US $ million at 31 December)

	2002	2003	2004
Gold (national valuation)	110.8	135.0	144.6
IMF special drawing rights	0.0	2.2	0.5
Foreign exchange	4,121.0	6,222.0	7,041.0
Total	**4,231.8**	**6,359.2**	**7,186.1**

Source: IMF, *International Financial Statistics*.

MONEY SUPPLY
('000 million dông at 31 December)

	2002	2003	2004
Currency outside banks	74,263	90,584	109,097
Demand deposits at banks	51,066	66,441	88,891
Total money	**125,329**	**157,025**	**197,989**

Source: IMF, *International Financial Statistics*.

COST OF LIVING
(Consumer Price Index; annual averages, base: 2001 = 100)

	2002	2003	2004
Staple foods	110.8	111.5	125.6
Other foods	107.3	110.9	125.7
Beverages and tobacco	101.4	105.8	110.0
Clothing (incl. footwear)	101.0	103.4	107.9
Household goods	100.8	102.0	105.2
Housing and construction	102.3	110.6	118.0
Transport and communications	97.2	98.8	97.1
All items (incl. others)	**104.0**	**107.3**	**115.6**

Source: IMF, *Vietnam: Statistical Appendix* (February 2006).

NATIONAL ACCOUNTS
('000 million dông at current prices)

Expenditure on the Gross Domestic Product

	2002	2003	2004
Government final consumption expenditure	33,390	38,770	45,715
Private final consumption expenditure	348,747	406,451	465,506
Increase in stocks	11,155	12,826	15,818
Gross fixed capital formation	166,828	194,654	236,991
Total domestic expenditure	**560,120**	**652,701**	**764,030**
Exports of goods and services	304,262	367,894	478,425
Less Imports of goods and services	331,946	411,119	534,321
Sub-total	532,436	609,476	708,134
Statistical discrepancy	3,326	3,966	4,937
GDP in purchasers' values	**535,762**	**613,443**	**713,072**
GDP at constant 1994 prices	**313,247**	**336,243**	**362,093**

Gross Domestic Product by Economic Activity

	2002	2003	2004
Agriculture, hunting, forestry and fishing	123,383	138,284	155,144
Mining and quarrying	46,153	57,326	72,492
Manufacturing	110,285	125,476	144,924
Electricity, gas and water	18,201	22,224	23,890
Construction	31,558	37,100	44,558
Trade	75,617	83,297	97,508
Transport, storage and communications	21,095	24,725	30,402
Finance	9,763	10,858	12,737
Public administration	44,940	54,016	61,255
Other community, social and personal services	54,767	60,137	70,162
Total	**535,762**	**613,443**	**713,072**

Source: Asian Development Bank, *Key Indicators of Developing Asian and Pacific Countries*.

VIET NAM

BALANCE OF PAYMENTS
(US $ million)

	2002	2003	2004
Exports of goods f.o.b.	16,706	20,176	26,503
Imports of goods f.o.b.	−17,760	−22,704	−28,759
Trade balance	−1,054	−2,528	−2,256
Exports of services	2,948	3,272	3,867
Imports of services	−3,698	−4,050	−4,739
Balance on goods and services	−1,804	−3,306	−3,128
Other income received	167	125	188
Other income paid	−888	−936	−1,079
Balance on goods, services and income	−2,525	−4,117	−4,019
Current transfers received	1,921	2,239	3,093
Current balance	−604	−1,878	−926
Direct investment from abroad	1,400	1,450	1,610
Other investment assets	624	1,372	35
Other investment liabilities	66	457	1,162
Net errors and omissions	−1,038	745	−946
Overall balance	448	2,146	935

Source: IMF, *International Financial Statistics*.

External Trade

SELECTED COMMODITIES
(distribution by SITC, US $ million)

Imports c.i.f.	2001	2002	2003
Food and live animals	834	939	1,262
Beverages and tobacco	108	149	153
Crude materials (inedible) except fuels	690	816	1,001
Mineral fuels, etc.	1,970	2,166	2,714
Animal and vegetable fats, and oils	83	131	152
Chemicals and related products	2,490	2,933	3,623
Basic manufactures	3,730	5,415	6,672
Machinery and transport equipment	4,865	5,758	7,922
Miscellaneous manufactured goods	1,447	1,427	1,575
Total (incl. others)	16,218	19,746	25,256

Exports f.o.b.	2001	2002	2003
Food and live animals	4,052	4,118	4,432
Beverages and tobacco	46	75	160
Crude materials (inedible) except fuels	413	517	631
Mineral fuels, etc.	3,469	3,568	4,151
Chemicals and related products	222	262	340
Basic manufactures	990	1,125	1,355
Machinery and transport equipment	1,399	1,337	1,793
Miscellaneous manufactured goods	4,408	5,691	7,260
Total (incl. others)	15,029	16,706	20,149

2004 (US $ million): Total imports c.i.f. 31,954; Total exports f.o.b. 26,504.

Source: Asian Development Bank, *Key Indicators of Developing Asian and Pacific Countries*.

PRINCIPAL TRADING PARTNERSS
(US $ million)

Imports c.i.f.	2002	2003	2004
China, People's Republic	2,158.8	3,496.4	4,139.7
Germany	558.1	732.5	1,089.7
Hong Kong	804.8	1,076.6	1,345.2
Indonesia	362.7	514.9	644.9
Japan	2,504.7	2,885.5	3,499.6
Korea, Republic	2,279.6	2,817.4	2,994.5
Malaysia	683.3	909.9	1,254.5
Singapore	2,533.5	2,653.2	3,496.7
Thailand	1955.2	1,393.4	2,060.3
USA	458.6	1,456.8	1,255.9
Total (incl. others)	19,744.4	25,742.5	30,524.3

Exports f.o.b.	2002	2003	2004
Australia	1,328.3	1,475.9	1,798.1
China, People's Republic	1,518.3	1,323.5	2,162.1
France	439.1	579.8	646.8
Germany	729.0	1,180.8	1,474.1
Japan	2,437.0	2,807.6	3,506.9
Korea, Republic	468.7	464.3	581.4
Netherlands	404.3	494.6	582.8
Singapore	961.1	930.9	1,228.7
United Kingdom	571.6	902.9	1,188.7
USA	2,453.2	4,463.2	5,077.1
Total (incl. others)	16,702.5	20,526.7	25,685.2

Source: Asian Development Bank, *Key Indicators of Developing Asian and Pacific Countries*.

Transport

RAILWAYS
(traffic)

	2002	2003	2004*
Passengers carried (million)	10.8	11.6	12.8
Passenger-km (million)	3,697.2	4,069.0	4,378.0
Freight carried ('000 metric tons)	7,051.9	8,385.0	8,829.4
Freight ton-km (million)	2,391.5	2,725.4	2,790.8

* Preliminary figures.

ROAD TRAFFIC

	2001	2002	2003*
Passengers carried (million)	655.4	699.3	718.3
Passenger-km (million)	24,237.7	26,010.2	26,582.8
Freight carried (million metric tons)	151.5	163.1	172.1
Freight ton-km (million)	8,095.4	8,650.1	9,219.4

* Preliminary figures.

Commercial vehicles ('000 in use): 49.4 in 1998; 57.8 in 1999; 69.9 in 2000 (Source: UN, *Statistical Yearbook*).

INLAND WATERWAYS

	2002	2003	2004*
Passengers carried (million)	137.7	161.7	166.2
Passenger-km (million)	2,481.4	3,282.4	3,440.0
Freight carried (million metric tons)	52.3	55.3	59.1
Freight ton-km (million)	4,968.2	5,140.5	5,591.8

* Preliminary figures.

VIET NAM

SHIPPING

Merchant Fleet
(registered at 31 December)

	2002	2003	2004
Number of vessels	721	735	797
Total displacement ('000 grt)	1,130.5	1,250.8	1,427.5

Source: Lloyd's Register-Fairplay, *World Fleet Statistics*.

International Sea-Borne Shipping
(freight traffic)

	2002	2003	2004*
Freight carried (million metric tons)	18.5	21.8	24.4
Freight ton-km ('000 million)	40.3	43.5	48.3

* Preliminary figures.

CIVIL AVIATION
(traffic on scheduled services)

	2002	2003	2004*
Domestic:			
Passengers carried ('000)	2,530.9	2,688.0	2,885.8
Passenger-km (million)	2,073.2	2,688.0	2,565.1
Freight carried ('000 metric tons)	39.5	48.2	53.7
Freight ton-km (million)	44.2	53.8	59.8
International:			
Passengers carried ('000)	1,914.1	1,831.0	2,646.2
Passenger-km (million)	4,241.2	5,028.2	4,424.0
Freight carried ('000 metric tons)	32.5	41.5	48.8
Freight ton-km (million)	127.6	156.9	178.1

* Preliminary figures.

Tourism

TOURIST ARRIVALS BY COUNTRY OF RESIDENCE

Country	2003	2004	2005
Australia	93,292	128,661	145,359
Cambodia	84,256	90,838	186,543
China, People's Republic	693,423	778,431	752,576
France	86,791	104,025	126,402
Japan	209,730	267,210	320,605
Korea, Republic	130,076	232,995	317,213
Laos	75,396	34,215	44,462
Malaysia	48,662	55,717	76,755
Singapore	36,870	50,942	77,676
Taiwan	207,866	256,906	286,324
Thailand	40,123	53,682	84,100
United Kingdom	63,348	71,016	80,884
USA	218,928	272,473	333,566
Total (incl. others)	2,428,735	2,927,876	3,467,757

Source: Vietnam National Administration of Tourism.

Tourism receipts ('000 million dông, accommodation establishments): 3,860.4 in 2001; 5,425.5 in 2002; 6,016.6 in 2003.

Communications Media

	2002	2003	2004
Telephones ('000 main lines in use)	3,929.1	4,402.0	10,124.9
Mobile cellular telephones ('000 subscribers)	1,902.4	2,742.0	4,960.0
Personal computers ('000 in use)	800	n.a.	1,044
Internet users ('000)	1,500	3,500	5,870

Facsimile machines ('000 in use): 31 in 1999.

Radio receivers ('000 in use): 8,200 in 1997.

Television receivers ('000 in use): 14,750 in 2000.

Book production: 11,455 titles (166,500,000 copies) in 2001.

Daily newspapers: 5 (with estimated circulation of 450,000 copies) in 1999.

Sources: partly International Telecommunication Union; UN, *Statistical Yearbook*; UNESCO, *Statistical Yearbook*.

Education

(2004/05)

	Institutions	Teachers ('000)	Students ('000)
Pre-primary	10,376	112.8	1,329.9
Primary	}	362.4	7,744.8
Lower secondary	26,817*	302.5	6,616.7
Upper secondary	}	106.1	2,761.1
Higher	230	47.6	1,319.8

* Of which: primary 14,518; lower secondary 9,041; upper secondary 1,828; primary and lower secondary 1,034; lower and upper secondary 396.

Adult literacy rate (UNESCO estimates): 90.3% (males 93.9%; females 86.9%) in 2003 (Source: UN Development Programme, *Human Development Report*).

Directory

The Constitution

On 15 April 1992 the National Assembly adopted a new Constitution, a revised version of that adopted in December 1980 (which in turn replaced the 1959 Constitution of the Democratic Republic of Viet Nam). The National Assembly approved amendments to 24 articles of the Constitution on 12 December 2001. The main provisions of the Constitution (which originally entered into force after elections in July 1992) are summarized as follows:

POLITICAL SYSTEM

All state power belongs to the people. The Communist Party of Viet Nam is a leading force of the state and society. All party organizations operate within the framework of the Constitution and the law. The people exercise power through the National Assembly and the People's Councils.

ECONOMIC SYSTEM

The State develops a multi-sectoral economy, in accordance with a market mechanism based on state management and socialist orien-

VIET NAM

tations. All lands are under state management. The State allots land to organizations and individuals for use on a stabilized and long-term basis: they may transfer the right to the use of land allotted to them. Individuals may establish businesses with no restrictions on size or means of production, and the State shall encourage foreign investment. Legal property of individuals and organizations, and business enterprises with foreign invested capital, shall not be subjected to nationalization.

THE NATIONAL ASSEMBLY

The National Assembly is the people's highest representative agency, and the highest organ of state power, exercising its supreme right of supervision over all operations of the State. It elects the President and Vice-President, the Prime Minister and senior judicial officers, and ratifies the Prime Minister's proposals for appointing members of the Government. It decides the country's socio-economic development plans, national financial and monetary policies, and foreign policy. The term of each legislature is five years. The National Assembly Standing Committee supervises the enforcement of laws and the activities of the Government. Amendments to the Constitution may only be made by a majority vote of at least two-thirds of the Assembly's members.

THE PRESIDENT OF THE STATE

The President, as Head of State, represents Viet Nam in domestic and foreign affairs. The President is elected by the National Assembly from among its deputies, and is responsible to the National Assembly. The President's term of office is the same as that of the National Assembly. He or she is Commander-in-Chief of the people's armed forces, and chairs the National Defence and Security Council. The President asks the National Assembly to appoint or dismiss the Vice-President, the Prime Minister, the Chief Justice of the Supreme People's Court and the Chief Procurator of the Supreme People's Organ of Control. According to resolutions of the National Assembly or of its Standing Committee, the President appoints or dismisses members of the Government, and declares war or a state of emergency.

THE GOVERNMENT

The Government comprises the Prime Minister, the Vice-Prime Ministers, ministers and other members. Apart from the Prime Minister, ministers do not have to be members of the National Assembly. The Prime Minister is responsible to the National Assembly, and the term of office of any Government is the same as that of the National Assembly, which ratifies the appointment or dismissal of members of the Government.

LOCAL GOVERNMENT

The country is divided into provinces and municipalities, which are subordinate to the central Government; municipalities are divided into districts, precincts and cities, and districts are divided into villages and townships. People's Councils are elected by the local people.

JUDICIAL SYSTEM

The judicial system comprises the Supreme People's Court, local People's Courts, military tribunals and other courts. The term of office of the presiding judge of the Supreme People's Court corresponds to the term of the National Assembly, and he or she is responsible to the National Assembly. The Supreme People's Organ of Control ensures the observance of the law and exercises the right of public prosecution. Its Chief Procurator is responsible to the National Assembly. There are local People's Organs of Control and Military Organs of Control.

The Government

HEAD OF STATE

President: TRAN DUC LUONG (elected by the 10th National Assembly on 24 September 1997; re-elected by the 11th National Assembly on 24 July 2002).
Vice-President: TRUONG MY HOA.

CABINET
(April 2006)

Prime Minister: PHAN VAN KHAI (announced imminent retirement on 16 May 2006).
First Deputy Prime Minister: NGUYEN TAN DUNG.
Deputy Prime Ministers: VU KHOAN, PHAM GIA KHIEM.
Minister of National Defence: Lt-Gen. PHAM VAN TRA.
Minister of Public Security: LE HONG ANH.
Minister of Foreign Affairs: NGUYEN DY NIEN.
Minister of Justice: UONG CHU LUU.
Minister of Finance: NGUYEN SINH HUNG.
Minister of Labour, War Invalids and Social Welfare: NGUYEN THI HANG.
Minister of Education and Training: Prof. NGUYEN MINH HIEN.
Minister of Public Health: TRAN THI TRUNG CHIEN.
Minister of Culture and Information: PHAM QUANG NGHI.
Minister of Construction: NGUYEN HONG QUAN.
Minister of Transport and Communications: (vacant).
Minister of Agriculture and Rural Development: CAO DUC PHAT.
Minister of Fisheries: Dr TA QUANG NGOC.
Minister of Industry: HOANG TRUNG HAI.
Minister of Trade: TRUONG DINH TUYEN.
Minister of Planning and Investment: VO HONG PHUC.
Minister of the Interior: DO QUANG TRUNG.
Minister of Science and Technology: HOANG VAN PHONG.
Minister of Natural Resources and the Environment: MAI AI TRUC.
Minister of Posts and Telecommunications: DO TRUNG TA.
State Inspector-General: QUACH LE THANH.
Minister, Chairman of the Ethnic Minorities and Mountain Region Commission: KSOR PHUOC.
Minister, Head of the Government Office: DOAN MANH GIAO.
Minister, Chairman of the Committee for Physical Training and Sports: NGUYEN DANH THAI.
Minister, Chairman of the Committee for Population, Family and Children: LE THI THU.

MINISTRIES AND COMMISSIONS

Ministry of Agriculture and Rural Development: 2 Ngoc Ha, Ba Dinh District, Hanoi; tel. (4) 7332160; fax (4) 8230381; e-mail icard@agroviet.gov.vn; internet www.agroviet.gov.vn.

Ministry of Construction: 37 Le Dai Hanh, Hai Ba Trung District, Hanoi; tel. (4) 9760271; fax (4) 8215591; e-mail bxd-vp@hn.vnn.vn.

Ministry of Culture and Information: 51–53 Ngo Quyen, Hoan Kiem District, Hanoi; tel. and fax (4) 9745846; internet www.cinet.gov.vn.

Ministry of Education and Training: 49 Dai Co Viet, Hai Ba Trung District, Hanoi; tel. (4) 8694795; fax (4) 8694085; e-mail intlaff@iupui.edu; internet www.edu.net.vn.

Ministry of Finance: 8 Phan Huy Chu, Hoan Kiem District, Hanoi; tel. (4) 8264872; fax (4) 8262266; e-mail support@mof.gov.vn; internet www.mof.gov.vn.

Ministry of Fisheries: 10 Nguyen Cong Hoan, Hanoi; tel. (4) 7716269; fax (4) 7716702; e-mail mofi@mofi.gov.vn; internet www.mofi.gov.vn.

Ministry of Foreign Affairs: 1 Ton That Dam, Ba Dinh District, Hanoi; tel. (4) 1992000; fax (4) 8445905; e-mail banbientap@mofa.gov.vn; internet www.mofa.gov.vn.

Ministry of Industry: 54 Hai Ba Trung, Hoan Kiem District, Hanoi; tel. (4) 8258311; fax (4) 8265303; internet www.moi.gov.vn.

Ministry of the Interior: 37A Nguyen Binh Khiem, Hanoi; tel. (4) 9780870; fax (4) 9781005; e-mail ngoc-hien@hn.vnn.vn.

Ministry of Justice: 25A Cat Linh, Dong Da District, Hanoi; tel. (4) 8438847; fax (4) 8430958; e-mail ttth@moj.gov.vn; internet www.moj.gov.vn.

Ministry of Labour, War Invalids and Social Welfare: 12 Ngo Quyen, Hoan Kiem District, Hanoi; tel. (4) 8246137; fax (4) 8248036; e-mail vvnd@fpt.vn.

Ministry of National Defence: 1A Hoang Dieu, Ba Dinh District, Hanoi; tel. (4) 8468101; fax (4) 8265540.

Ministry of Natural Resources and the Environment: 83 Nguyen Chi Thanh, Dong Da District, Hanoi; tel. (4) 8343911; fax (4) 8359221; e-mail webmaster@monroe.gov.vn; internet www.monre.gov.vn.

Ministry of Planning and Investment: 2 Hoang Van Thu, Ba Dinh District, Hanoi; tel. (4) 8453027; fax (4) 8234453; internet www.mpi.gov.vn.

Ministry of Posts and Telecommunications: 18 Nguyen Du, Hanoi; tel. (4) 9431368; fax (4) 9436736; e-mail tt_tt@mpt.gov.vn; internet www.mpt.gov.vn.

Ministry of Public Health: 138A Giang Vo, Ba Dinh District, Hanoi; tel. (4) 8464416; fax (4) 8464051; e-mail byt@moh.gov.vn; internet www.moh.gov.vn.

VIET NAM
Directory

Ministry of Public Security: 44 Yet Kieu, Hoan Kiem District, Hanoi; tel. (4) 8268131; fax (4) 8260774.
Ministry of Science and Technology: 39 Tran Hung Dao, Hoan Kiem District, Hanoi; tel. (4) 9439731; fax (4) 8252733; internet www.most.gov.vn.
Ministry of Trade: 21 Ngo Quyen, Hanoi; tel. (4) 8262538; fax (4) 8264696; e-mail webmaster@mot.gov.vn; internet www.mot.gov.vn.
Ministry of Transport: 80 Tran Hung Dao, Hoan Kiem District, Hanoi; tel. (4) 8254012; fax (4) 8267291; e-mail webmaster@mt.gov.vn; internet www.mt.gov.vn.
National Commission for Population, Family and Children: 35 Tran Phu, Ba Dinh District, Hanoi; tel. (4) 7473851; fax (4) 8237983; e-mail banbientap@vcfpc.gov.vn; internet www.vcpfc.gov.vn.
State Inspectorate: 220 Doi Can, Hanoi; tel. (4) 8325558; fax (4) 8325786; internet www.thanhtra.gov.vn.

NATIONAL DEFENCE AND SECURITY COUNCIL
President: TRAN DUC LUONG.
Vice-President: PHAN VAN KHAI.
Members: NGUYEN VAN AN, LE HONG ANH, Lt-Gen. PHAM VAN TRA, NGUYEN DY NIEN.

Legislature
QUOC HOI
(National Assembly)

Elections to the 11th National Assembly were held on 19 May 2002. The new Assembly comprised 498 members (compared with 450 in the previous Assembly), elected from among 759 candidates; 51 non-party candidates were elected.

Standing Committee
Chairman: NGUYEN VAN AN.
Vice-Chairmen: NGUYEN VAN YEU, NGUYEN PHUC THANH, TRUONG QUANG DUOC.

Political Organizations
COMMUNIST PARTY
Dang Cong San Viet Nam (Communist Party of Viet Nam): 1 Hoang Van Thu, Hanoi; e-mail cpv@hn.vnn.vn; internet www.cpv.org.vn; f. 1976; ruling party; fmrly the Viet Nam Workers' Party, f. 1951 as the successor to the Communist Party of Indo-China, f. 1930; c. 2.2m. mems (1996); Gen. Sec. of Cen. Cttee NONG DUC MANH.

Political Bureau (Politburo)
Members: NONG DUC MANH, LE HONG ANH, NGUYEN MINH TRIET, NGUYEN TAN DUNG, TRUONG TAN SANG, NGUYEN PHU TRONG, PHAM GIA KHIEM, PHAM QUANG NGHI, NGUYEN SINH HUNG, NGUYEN VAN CHI, HO DUC VIET, Sr Lt-Gen. PHUNG QUANG THANH, TRUONG VINH TRONG, LE THANH HAI.

Secretariat
Members: NONG DUC MANH, TRUONG TAN SANG, TRUONG VINH TRONG, NGUYEN VAN CHI, PHAM QUANG NGHI, Sr Lt-Gen. LE VAN DUNG, TONG THI PHONG, TO HUY RUA.

OTHER POLITICAL ORGANIZATIONS
Ho Chi Minh Communist Youth Union: 60 Ba Trieu, Hanoi; tel. (4) 9435709; fax (4) 9348439; e-mail cydeco@hn.vnn.vn; f. 1931; 4m. mems; First Sec. HOANG BINH QUAN.
People's Action Party (PAP): Hanoi; e-mail dang@ndhd.net; internet www.ndhd.net; Leader LE VAN TINH.
Viet Nam Fatherland Front: 46 Trang Thi, Hanoi; f. 1930; replaced the Lien Viet (Viet Nam National League), the successor to Viet Nam Doc Lap Dong Minh Hoi (Revolutionary League for the Independence of Viet Nam) or Viet Minh; in 1977 the original org. merged with the National Front for the Liberation of South Viet Nam and the Alliance of National, Democratic and Peace Forces in South Viet Nam to form a single front; 200-member Cen. Cttee; Pres. Presidium of Cen. Cttee PHAM THE DUYET; Gen. Sec. TRAN VAN DANG.
Vietnam Women's Union (VWU): 39 Hang Chuoi, Hanoi; tel. (4) 9713436; fax (4) 9713143; e-mail VWUnion@netnam.org.vn; internet hoilhpn.org.vn; f. 1930; 11.4m. mems; Pres. HA THI KHIET.

Diplomatic Representation
EMBASSIES IN VIET NAM

Algeria: 13 Phan Chu Trinh, Hanoi; tel. (4) 8253865; fax (4) 8260830; e-mail aldjazairvn@hn.vnn.vn; Ambassador TEWFIK ABADA.
Argentina: 8th Floor, Office Tower, Daeha Business Centre, 360 Kim Ma, Ba Dinh District, Hanoi; tel. (4) 8315262; fax (4) 8315577; e-mail embarg@hn.vnn.vn; internet www.embargentina.org.vn; Ambassador TOMÁS FERRARI.
Australia: 8 Dao Tan, Ba Dinh District, Hanoi; tel. (4) 8317755; fax (4) 8317711; e-mail austemb@fpt.vn; internet www.vietnam.embassy.gov.vn; Ambassador BILL TWEDDELL.
Austria: Prime Centre, 8th Floor, 53 Quang Trung, Hai Ba Trung District, Hanoi; tel. (4) 9433050; fax (4) 9433055; e-mail hanoi-ob@bmaa.gv.at; Ambassador Dr JOHANNES PETERLIK.
Bangladesh: 7th Floor, Daeha Business Centre, 360 Kim Ma, Ba Dinh District, Hanoi; tel. (4) 7716625; fax (4) 7716628; Ambassador SARWAR HOSSAIN MOLLAH.
Belarus: 52 Tay Ho, Tay Ho District, Hanoi; tel. (4) 8290494; fax (4) 7197125; e-mail vietnam@belembassy.org; Ambassador ALYAKSANDR KUTSALAY.
Belgium: 9th Floor, Somerset Grand Hanoi, 49 Hai Ba Trung, Hanoi; tel. (4) 9346179; fax (4) 9346183; e-mail ambabel@hn.vnn.vn; Ambassador PHILIPPE JOTTARD.
Brazil: 14 Thuy Khue, T72 Hanoi; tel. (4) 8430817; fax (4) 8432542; e-mail vetbrem@netnam.org.vn; Ambassador CHRISTIANO WHITAKER.
Brunei: 27 Quang Trung, Hoan Kiem District, Hanoi; tel. (4) 9435249; fax (4) 9435201; e-mail bruemviet@hn.vnn.vn; Ambassador Dato' Paduka Haji ALI Haji HASSAN.
Bulgaria: Van Phuc Quarter, Nui Truc, Hanoi; tel. (4) 8452908; fax (4) 8460856; e-mail bulemb@hn.vnn.vn; Ambassador GUEORGUI MIHOV.
Cambodia: 71 Tran Hung Dao, Hanoi; tel. (4) 9424788; fax (4) 9423225; e-mail arch@fpt.vn; Ambassador LONG KEM.
Canada: 31 Hung Vuong, Hanoi; tel. (4) 7345000; fax (4) 7345049; e-mail hanoi@international.gc.ca; internet www.dfait-maeci.gc.ca/vietnam; Ambassador RICHARD LECOQ.
China, People's Republic: 46 Hoang Dieu, Hanoi; tel. (4) 8453736; fax (4) 8232826; e-mail eossc@hn.vnn.vn; Ambassador QI JIANGUO.
Cuba: 65A Ly Thuong Kiet, Hanoi; tel. (4) 9424775; fax (4) 9422426; e-mail embacuba@netnam.org.vn; Ambassador FREDESMAN TURRÁ GONZÁLEZ.
Czech Republic: 13 Chu Van An, Hanoi; tel. (4) 8454131; fax (4) 8233996; e-mail hanoi@embassy.mzv.cz; internet www.mfa.cz/hanoi; Ambassador IVO ŽDÁREK.
Denmark: 19 Dien Bien Phu, Hanoi; tel. (4) 8231888; fax (4) 8231999; e-mail hanamb@um.dk; internet www.ambhanoi.um.dk; Ambassador PETER LYSHOLT HANSEN.
Egypt: 63 To Ngoc Van, Quang An, Tay Ho District, Hanoi; tel. (4) 8294999; fax (4) 8294997; e-mail arabegypt@ftp.vn; Ambassador ABDALLAH OMAR ALARNOSY.
Finland: 6th Floor, Central Bldg, 31 Hai Ba Trung, Hanoi; tel. (4) 8266788; fax (4) 8266766; e-mail sanomat.han@formin.fi; Ambassador KARI ALANKO.
France: 57 Tran Hung Dao, Hanoi; tel. (4) 9437719; fax (4) 9437236; e-mail ambafrance@hn.vnn.vn; internet www.ambafrance-vn.org; Ambassador JEAN-FRANÇOIS BLAREL.
Germany: 29 Tran Phu, Hanoi; tel. (4) 8453836; fax (4) 8453838; e-mail germanemb.hanoi@fpt.vn; internet www.hanoi.diplo.de; Ambassador CHRISTIAN-LUDWIG WEBER-LORTSCH.
Hungary: Daeha Business Centre, 12th Floor, 360 Kim Ma, Ba Dinh District, Hanoi; tel. (4) 7715714; fax (4) 7715716; e-mail hungemb@hn.vnn.vn; Ambassador Dr DÉNES SZÁSZ.
India: 58–60 Tran Hung Dao, Hanoi; tel. (4) 8244990; fax (4) 8244998; e-mail india@netnam.org.vn; Ambassador NEELAKANTAN RAVI.
Indonesia: 50 Ngo Quyen, Hanoi; tel. (4) 8253353; fax (4) 8259274; e-mail komhan@hn.vnn.vn; internet www.indonesia-hanoi.org.vn; Ambassador ARTAULI RATNA MENARA PANGGABEAN TOBING.
Iran: 54 Tran Phu, Ba Dinh District, Hanoi; tel. (4) 8232068; fax (4) 8232120; e-mail iriemb@fpt.vn; Ambassador HOSSEIN MOLLA-ABDOLLAHI.
Iraq: 66 Tran Hung Dao, Hanoi; tel. (4) 9424141; fax (4) 9424055; e-mail iraqyia@hn.vnn.vn; Ambassador SALAH AL-MUKHTAR (designate).
Israel: 68 Nguyen Thai Hoc, Hanoi; tel. (4) 8433141; fax (4) 8435760; e-mail infor@emisrael-vn.org; Ambassador AVRAHAM NIR.

VIET NAM

Italy: 9 Le Phung Hieu, Hoan Kiem District, Hanoi; tel. (4) 8256256; fax (4) 8267602; e-mail ambasciata.hanoi@esteri.it; internet www.ambhanoi.esteri.it; Ambassador ALFREDO MATACOTTA CORDELLA.

Japan: 27 Lieu Giai, Ba Dinh District, Hanoi; tel. (4) 8463000; fax (4) 8463043; Ambassador NORIO HATTORI.

Korea, Democratic People's Republic: 25 Cao Ba Quat, Hanoi; tel. (4) 8453008; fax (4) 8231221; e-mail emb.dprk@hn.vnn.vn; Ambassador PAK UNG-SOP.

Korea, Republic: 4th Floor, Daeha Business Centre, 360 Kim Ma, Ba Dinh District, Hanoi; tel. (4) 8315111; fax (4) 8315117; e-mail korembviet@mofat.go.kr; Ambassador YOO TAE-HYUN.

Laos: 22 Tran Binh Trong, Hanoi; tel. (4) 9424576; fax (4) 8228414; Ambassador VILAYVANH PHOMKEHE.

Libya: A3 Van Phuc Residential Quarter, Hanoi; tel. (4) 8453379; fax (4) 8454977; e-mail libpbha@yahoo.com; Secretary SALEM ALI SALEM DANNAH.

Malaysia: 16th Floor, Fortuna Tower, 6B Lang Ha, Hanoi; tel. (4) 8313400; fax (4) 8313402; e-mail mwhanoi@hn.vnn.vn; Ambassador Dato' AHMAD ANUAR ABDUL HAMID.

Mexico: 14 Thuy Khue, T-11, Hanoi; tel. (4) 8470948; fax (4) 8470949; e-mail embvietnam@sre.gob.mx; Ambassador FEDERICO URRUCHUA DURAND.

Mongolia: Villa 5, Van Phuc Quarter, Hanoi; tel. (4) 8453009; fax (4) 8454954; e-mail mongembhanoi@hn.vnn.vn; Ambassador GANBOLD BAASANJAV.

Myanmar: 298A Kim Ma, Hanoi; tel. (4) 8453369; fax (4) 8452404; e-mail myan.emb@fpt.vn; Ambassador U TIN LATT.

Netherlands: Daeha Office Tower, 6th Floor, 360 Kim Ma, Ba Dinh District, Hanoi; tel. (4) 8315650; fax (4) 8315655; e-mail han@minbuza.nl; internet www.netherlands-embassy.org.vn; Ambassador ANDRÉ HASPELS.

New Zealand: Level 5, 63 Ly Thai To, Hanoi; tel. (4) 8241481; fax (4) 8241480; e-mail nzembhan@fpt.vn; Ambassador MICHAEL CHILTON.

Norway: 7th Floor, Suite 701–702, Metropole Centre, 56 Ly Thai To, Hanoi; tel. (4) 8262111; fax (4) 8260222; Ambassador PER G. STAVNUM.

Pakistan: 8th Floor, Daeha Business Centre, 360 Kim Ma, Ba Dinh District, Hanoi; tel. (4) 7716420; fax (4) 7716418; e-mail parep-hanoi@hn.vnn.vn; Ambassador MUHAMMAD YOUSAF ALI.

Philippines: 27B Tran Hung Dao, Hanoi; tel. (4) 9437873; fax (4) 9435760; e-mail hanoipe@dfa.gov.ph; Ambassador VICTORIANO M. LECAROS.

Poland: 3 Chua Mot Cot, Hanoi; tel. (4) 8452027; fax (4) 8236914; e-mail polamb@hn.vnn.vn; Ambassador MIROSŁAW GAJEWSKI.

Romania: 5 Le Hong Phong, Hanoi; tel. (4) 8452014; fax (4) 8430922; e-mail rombcehan@fpt.vn; Ambassador CONSTANTIN LUPEANU.

Russia: 191 La Thanh, Hanoi; tel. (4) 8336991; fax (4) 8336995; e-mail moscow.vietnam@hn.vnn.vn; Ambassador ANDREI ALEXEEVICH TATARINOV.

Singapore: 41–43 Tran Phu, Hanoi; tel. (4) 8233965; fax (4) 7337627; e-mail singemb_hanoi@sgmfa.gov.sg; internet www.mfa.gov.sg/hanoi; Ambassador LIM THUAN KUAN.

Slovakia: 6 Le Hong Phong, Hanoi; tel. (4) 8454334; fax (4) 8454145; e-mail zuskemb@hn.vnn.vn; Ambassador ANTON HAJDUK.

South Africa: 3rd Floor, Central Bldg, 31 Hai Ba Trung, Hanoi; tel. (4) 9362000; fax (4) 9361991; e-mail hanoi@foreign.gov.za; Ambassador Maj.-Gen. LEONARD PITSO.

Spain: 15th Floor, Daeha Business Centre, 360 Kim Ma, Ba Dinh District, Hanoi; tel. (4) 7715207; fax (4) 7715206; e-mail embespvn@fpt.vn; Ambassador GONZALO ORTIZ Y DÍEZ-TORTOSA.

Sri Lanka: 55B Tran Phu, Ba Dinh District, Hanoi; tel. (4) 7341894; fax (4) 7341897; e-mail slembvn@fpt.vn; Ambassador MUSTHAFA M. JAFFEER.

Sweden: BP 9, Ba Dinh District, Hanoi; tel. (4) 7260400; fax (4) 8232195; e-mail ambassaden.hanoi@sida.se; internet www.swedenabroad.com/hanoi; Ambassador ANNA LINDSTEDT.

Switzerland: 44B Ly Thuong Kiet, 15th Floor, Hanoi; tel. (4) 9346589; fax (4) 9346591; e-mail vertretung@han.rep.admin.ch; Ambassador BÉNÉDICT DE CERJAT.

Thailand: 63–65 Hoang Dieu, Hanoi; tel. (4) 8235092; fax (4) 8235088; e-mail thaiemhn@netnam.org.vn; Ambassador KRIT KRAICHITTI.

Turkey: 4th Floor, North Star Bldg, 4 Da Truong, Hanoi; tel. (4) 8222460; fax (4) 8222458; e-mail turkeyhn@fpt.vn; Ambassador KAYNA INAL.

Ukraine: 49 Nguyen Dy, Hanoi; tel. (4) 9432764; fax (4) 9432766; e-mail ukraine@hn.vnn.vn; Ambassador PAVLO SULTANSKY.

United Kingdom: Central Bldg, 4th Floor, 31 Hai Ba Trung, Hanoi; tel. (4) 9360500; fax (4) 9360561; e-mail behanoi@hn.vnn.vn; internet www.uk-vietnam.org; Ambassador ROBERT GORDON.

USA: 7 Lang Ha, Ba Dinh District, Hanoi; tel. (4) 7721500; fax (4) 7721510; e-mail irchanoi@state.gov; internet usembassy.state.gov/vietnam; Ambassador MICHAEL W. MARINE.

Judicial System

Supreme People's Court
48 Ly Thuong Kiet, Hanoi.

The Supreme People's Court in Hanoi is the highest court and exercises civil and criminal jurisdiction over all lower courts. The Supreme Court may also conduct trials of the first instance in certain cases. There are People's Courts in each province and city which exercise jurisdiction in the first and second instance. Military courts hear cases involving members of the People's Army and cases involving national security. In 1993 legislation was adopted on the establishment of economic courts to consider business disputes. The observance of the law by ministries, government offices and all citizens is the concern of the People's Organs of Control, under a Supreme People's Organ of Control. The Chief Justice of the Supreme People's Court and the Chief Procurator of the Supreme People's Organ of Control are elected by the National Assembly, on the recommendation of the President.

Chief Justice of the Supreme People's Court: NGUYEN VAN HIEN.

Chief Procurator of the Supreme People's Organ of Control: HA MANH TRI.

Religion

Traditional Vietnamese religion included elements of Indian and all three Chinese religions: Mahayana Buddhism, Daoism and Confucianism. Its most widespread feature was the cult of ancestors, practised in individual households and clan temples. In addition, there were (and remain) a wide variety of Buddhist sects, the sects belonging to the 'new' religions of Caodaism and Hoa Hao, and the Protestant and Roman Catholic Churches. The Government has guaranteed complete freedom of religious belief.

BUDDHISM

In the North a Buddhist organization, grouping Buddhists loyal to the Democratic Republic of Viet Nam, was formed in 1954. In the South the United Buddhist Church was formed in 1964, incorporating several disparate groups, including the 'militant' An-Quang group (mainly natives of central Viet Nam), the group of Thich Tam Chau (mainly northern emigrés in Saigon) and the southern Buddhists of the Xa Loi temple. In 1982 most of the Buddhist sects were amalgamated into the state-approved Viet Nam Buddhist Church (which comes under the authority of the Viet Nam Fatherland Front; number of adherents estimated at 7% of total population in 1991). The Unified Buddhist Church of Viet Nam is an anti-Government organization.

Viet Nam Buddhist Church: Pres. Exec. Council Most Ven. THICH TRI TINH; Gen. Sec. THICH MING CHAU.

Unified Buddhist Church of Viet Nam: Patriarch THICH HUYEN QUANG.

CAODAISM

Formally inaugurated in 1926, this is a syncretic religion based on spiritualist seances with a predominantly ethical content, but sometimes with political overtones. A number of different sects exist, of which the most politically involved (1940–75) was that of Tay Ninh. Another sect, the Tien Thien, was represented in the National Liberation Front from its inception. There are an estimated 2m. adherents, resident mainly in the South.

Leader: Cardinal THAI HUU THANH.

CHRISTIANITY

In 1991 the number of Christian adherents represented an estimated 7% of the total population.

The Roman Catholic Church

The Roman Catholic Church has been active in Viet Nam since the 17th century, and since 1933 has been led mainly by Vietnamese priests. Many Roman Catholics moved from North to South Viet Nam in 1954–55, but some remained in the North. The total number of adherents was estimated at 5,667,398 in December 2003, representing 7.0% of the population. For ecclesiastical purposes, Viet Nam comprises three archdioceses and 22 dioceses.

VIET NAM
Directory

Bishops' Conference
Conférence Episcopale du Viêt Nam, 22 Tran Phu, Khank Hoa, Nha Trang; tel. (58) 822842; fax (58) 815494; e-mail vangia@dng.vnn.vn; f. 1980; Pres. Most Rev. PAUL NGUYEN VAN HOA (Bishop of Nha Trang).

Archbishop of Hanoi: Most Rev. JOSEPH NGO QUANG KIET, Archevêché, 40 Pho Nha Chung, Hanoi; tel. (4) 8254424; fax (4) 9285073; e-mail ttgmhn@hn.vnn.vn.

Archbishop of Ho Chi Minh City: Cardinal JEAN-BAPTISTE PHAM MINH MÂN, Archevêché, 180 Nguyen Dinh Chieu, Ho Chi Minh City 3; tel. (8) 9303828; fax (8) 9300598.

Archbishop of Hué: Most Rev. ETIENNE NGUYEN NHU THE, Archevêché, 6 Nguyen Truong To, Hué; tel. (54) 824937; fax (54) 833656; e-mail tgmhue@dng.vnn.vn.

Committee for Solidarity of Patriotic Vietnamese Catholics: 59 Trang Thi, Hanoi; Pres. Rev. VUONG DINH AI.

The Protestant Church
Introduced in 1920 with 500 adherents; the total number is estimated at 180,000.

HOA HAO
A new manifestation of an older religion called Buu Son Ky Huong, the Hoa Hao sect was founded by Nguyen Phu So in 1939, and at one time claimed 1.5m. adherents in southern Viet Nam.

ISLAM
The number of Muslims was estimated at 50,000 in 1993.

The Press

The Ministry of Culture and Information supervises the activities of newspapers, news agencies and periodicals.

DAILIES

Hanoi

Le Courrier du Viet Nam: 33 Le Thanh Tong, Hanoi; tel. (4) 9334587; fax (4) 8258368; e-mail courrier@vnagency.com.vn; internet lecourrier.vnagency.com.vn; French; publ. by the Viet Nam News Agency; Editor-in-Chief TRAN SON MACH.

Dan Tri (Intellectual People's Standard): 5 Ly Thuong Kiet, Hanoi; tel. (4) 7366491; fax (4) 7366490; e-mail info@dantri.com.vn; internet www.dantri.com.vn; f. 1982, fmrly known as Tin Tuc (News); publ. by the Viet Nam News Agency; afternoon; Vietnamese.

Hanoi Moi (New Hanoi): 44 Le Thai To, Hoan Kiem District, Hanoi; tel. (4) 8253067; fax (4) 8248054; e-mail hanoimoi@hanoimoi.com.vn; internet www.hanoimoi.com.vn/vn/; f. 1976; organ of Hanoi Cttee of the Communist Party of Viet Nam; Editor HO XUAN SON; circ. 35,000.

Lao Dong (Labour): 15/167 Tay Son, Hanoi; tel. (4) 5330305; fax (4) 5370141; e-mail laodong@fpt.vn; internet www.laodong.com.vn; f. 1929; organ of the Viet Nam General Confederation of Labour; Editor-in-Chief VUONG VAN VIET; circ. 80,000.

Nhan Dan (The People): 71 Hang Trong, Hoan Kiem District, Hanoi; tel. (4) 8254231; fax (4) 8255593; e-mail toasoan@nhandan.org.vn; internet www.nhandan.org.vn; f. 1946; official organ of the Communist Party of Viet Nam; Editor-in-Chief DINH THE HUYNH; circ. 180,000.

Quan Doi Nhan Dan (People's Army): 7 Phan Dinh Phung, Hanoi; tel. (4) 8254118; f. 1950; organ of the armed forces; Editor NGUYEN PHONG HAI; circ. 60,000.

Thanh Nien: 248 Cong Quynh St, District 1, Hanoi; tel. (8) 8394046; fax (8) 8322025; internet www.thanhniennews.com; f. 1986; flagship publication of the Viet Nam National Youth Federation; Chief Editor NGUYEN CONG KHE.

Viet Nam Economic Times: 96 Hoang Quoc Viet, Cau Giay District, Hanoi; tel. (4) 7552060; fax (4) 7552046; e-mail vet@hn.vnn.vn; internet www.vneconomy.com.vn; f. 1994; in Vietnamese (with monthly edn in English); Editor-in-Chief Prof. DAO NGUYEN CAT; Dep. Editor-in-Chief NGUYEN THI VAN ANH; circ 38,900.

Viet Nam News: 11 Tran Hung Dao, Hanoi; tel. (4) 9332316; fax 9332311; e-mail vnnews@vnagency.com.vn; internet vietnamnews.vnanet.vn; f. 1991; English; publ. by the Viet Nam News Agency; Editor-in-Chief TRAN MAI HUONG; circ. 25,000 (Mon.-Sat.), 20,000 Sun. edn (Viet Nam News Sunday); circ. 60,000.

Ho Chi Minh City

Sai Gon Giai Phong (Liberated Saigon): 432 Nguyen Thi Minh Khai, Ho Chi Minh City; tel. (8) 8395942; fax (8) 8324958; e-mail online@sggp.org.vn; internet www.sggp.org.vn; f. 1975; organ of Ho Chi Minh City Cttee of the Communist Party of Viet Nam; Editor-in-Chief DUONG TRONG DAT; circ. 100,000.

Saigon Times: 35 Nam Ky Khoi Nghia, District 1, Ho Chi Minh City; tel. (8) 8295936; fax (8) 8294294; e-mail sgt@hcm.vnn.vn; internet www.saigontimes.com.vn; f. 1991; Vietnamese and English; business issues; Editor-in-Chief VO NHU LANH.

PERIODICALS

Dai Doan Ket (Great Unity): 66 Ba Trieu, Hanoi; tel. (4) 8262420; f. 1977; weekly; organ of the Viet Nam Fatherland Front; Editor NGUYEN QUANG CANH.

Dau Tu: 175 Nguyen Thai Hoc, Hanoi; tel. (4) 8450537; fax (4) 8457937; e-mail vir@hn.vnn.vn; internet www.vir.com.vn; 3 a week business newspaper publ. in Vietnamese; Editor-in-Chief NGUYEN PHU KY; circ. 40,000.

Dau Tu Chung Khoan: 175 Nguyen Thai Hoc, Hanoi; tel. (4) 8450537; fax (4) 8457937; e-mail vir@hn.vnn.vn; internet www.vir.com.vn; weekly; stock market news publ. in Vietnamese; Editor-in-Chief NGUYEN PHU KY; circ. 40,000.

Giao Duc Thoi Dai (People's Teacher): 29B Ngo Quyen, Hoan Kiem District, Hanoi; tel. (4) 8241781; fax (4) 9345611; e-mail gdtd@fpt.vn; internet www.gdtd.com.vn; f. 1959; weekly; organ of the Ministry of Education and Training; Editor NGUYEN NGOC CHU.

Giao Thong-Van Tai (Communications and Transport): 1 Nha Tho, Hanoi; tel. (4) 8255387; f. 1962; weekly; Thursday; organ of the Ministry of Transport and Communications; Editor NGO DUC NGUYEN; circ. 10,000.

Hoa Hoc Tro (Pupils' Flowers): 5 Hoa Ma, Hanoi; tel. (4) 8211065; internet hhtonline.net; weekly; Editor NGUYEN PHONG DOANH; circ. 150,000.

Khoa Hoc Ky Thuat Kinh Te The Gioi (World Science, Technology and Economy): 5 Ly Thuong Kiet, Hanoi; tel. (4) 8252931; f. 1982; weekly.

Khoa Hoc va Doi Song (Science and Life): 70 Tran Hung Dao, Hanoi; tel. (4) 8253427; f. 1959; weekly; Editor-in-Chief TRAN CU; circ. 30,000.

Nghe Thuat Dien Anh (Cinematography): 65 Tran Hung Dao, Hanoi; tel. (4) 8262473; f. 1984; fortnightly; Editor DANG NHAT MINH.

Nguoi Cong Giao Viet Nam (Vietnamese Catholic): 59 Trang Thi, Hanoi; tel. (4) 8256242; f. 1984; weekly; organ of the Cttee for Solidarity of Patriotic Vietnamese Catholics; Editor-in-Chief SO CHI.

Nguoi Dai Bieu Nhan Dan (People's Deputy): 35 Ngo Quyen, Hanoi; tel. (4) 08046231; fax (4) 08046659; e-mail ndbnd@hn.vnn.vn; f. 1988; bi-weekly; disseminates resolutions of the National Assembly and People's Council; Editor-in-Chief HO ANH TAI (acting); circ. 2m..

Nguoi Hanoi (The Hanoian): 19 Hang Buom, Hanoi; tel. (4) 8255662; f. 1984; Editor VU QUAN PHUONG.

Nha Bao Va Cong Luan (The Journalist and Public Opinion): 59 Ly Thai To, Hanoi; tel. (4) 8253609; fax (4) 8250797; f. 1985; monthly review; organ of the Viet Nam Journalists' Asscn; Editor-in-Chief PHAN DUOC TOAN; circ. 40,000.

Nong Nghiep Viet Nam (Viet Nam Agriculture): 14 Ngo Quyen, Hanoi; tel. (4) 8256492; fax (4) 8252923; f. 1987; weekly; Editor LE NAM SON.

Outlook: 11 Tran Hung Dao, Hanoi; tel. (4) 8222884; fax (4) 9424908; e-mail vnnews@vnagency.com.vn; internet vietnamnews.vnanet.com.vn; f. 2002; monthly news magazine; Editor-in-Chief TRAN MAI HUONG; circ. 6,000.

Phu Nu (Woman): Vietnam Women's Union, International Relations Dept, 39 Hang Chuoi, Hanoi; e-mail VWunion@netnam.org.vn; f. 1997; fortnightly; women's magazine; circ. 100,000.

Phu Nu Thu Do (Capital Women): 72 Quan Su, Hanoi; tel. (4) 8247228; fax (4) 8223989; f. 1987; weekly; magazine of the Hanoi Women's Union; Editor-in-Chief MAI THUC.

Phu Nu Viet Nam (Vietnamese Women): 39 Hang Chuoi, Hanoi; tel. (4) 8253500; weekly; magazine of the Vietnamese Women's Union; Editor-in-Chief PHUONG MINH.

Suc Khoe Va Doi Song (Health and Life): 138 A Giang Vo, Hanoi; tel. (4) 8443144; weekly; published by the Ministry of Public Health; Editor LE THAU; circ. 20,000.

Tap Chi Cong San (Communist Review): 52 Nguyen Chi Thanh, Hanoi; tel. (4) 7753605; fax (4) 7753633; e-mail bbttccs@hn.vnn.vn; internet www.tapchicongsan.org.vn; f. 1955 as Hoc Tap; fortnightly; political and theoretical organ of the Communist Party of Viet Nam; Editor-in-Chief LE HUU NGHIA; circ. 50,000.

Tap Chi Nghiên Cuu Van Hoc (Literature Research Magazine): 20 Ly Thai To, Hanoi; tel. (4) 8252895; e-mail tcvapmail@vnn.vn; monthly; published by the Institute of Literature; Editor-in-Chief PHAN TRONG THUONG.

VIET NAM

Tap Chi San Khau (Theatre Magazine): 51 Tran Hung Dao, Hanoi; tel. (4) 9434423; fax (4) 9434293; e-mail trongkhoi@hn.vnn.vn; f. 1973; monthly; Editor NGO THAO.

Tap Chi Tac Pham Van Hoc: 65 Nguyen Du, Hanoi; tel. (4) 8252442; f. 1987; monthly; organ of the Viet Nam Writers' Asscn; Editor-in-Chief NGUYEN DINH THI; circ. 15,000.

Tap Chi Tu Tuong Van Hoa (Ideology and Culture Review): Hanoi; f. 1990; organ of the Central Committee Department of Ideology and Culture; Editor PHAM HUY VAN.

The Thao Van Hoa (Sports and Culture): 5 Ly Thuong Kiet, Hanoi; tel. (4) 8267043; fax (4) 8264901; f. 1982; weekly; Editor-in-Chief NGUYEN HUU VINH; circ. 100,000.

The Thao Viet Nam (Viet Nam Sports): 18 Ly Van Phuc, Hanoi; tel. (4) 7340217; fax (4) 7341494; e-mail baottvn@yahoo.com; internet www.thethaovietnam.com.vn; f. 1968; weekly; Editor NGUYEN HUNG.

Thieu Nhi Dan Toc (The Ethnic Young): 5 Hoa Ma, Hanoi; tel. (4) 9317133; bi-monthly; Editor PHAM THANH LONG; circ. 60,000.

Thieu Nien Tien Phong (Young Pioneers): 5 Hoa Ma, Hanoi; tel. (4) 9713133; fax (4) 8215710; e-mail toasoan@tntp.org.vn; internet www.tntp.org.vn; three a week; Editor PHAM THANH LONG; circ. 210,000.

Thoi Bao Kinh Te Viet Nam: 175 Nguyen Thai Hoc, Hanoi; tel. (4) 8452411; fax (4) 8432755; f. 1993; 2 a week; Editor-in-Chief PAVEF DAONGUYENCAT; circ. 37,000.

Thoi Trang Tre (New Fashion): 12 Ho Xuan Huong, Hanoi; tel. (4) 8254032; fax (4) 8226002; f. 1993; monthly; Editor VU QUANG VINH; circ. 80,000.

Thuong Mai (Commerce): 100 Lo Duc, Hanoi; tel. (4) 8263150; f. 1990; weekly; organ of the Ministry of Trade; Editor TRAN NAM VINH.

Tien Phong (Vanguard): 15 Ho Xuan Huong, Hanoi; tel. (4) 8264031; fax (4) 8225032; f. 1953; four a week; organ of the Ho Chi Minh Communist Youth Union and of the Forum of Vietnamese Youth; Editor DUONG XUAN NAM; circ. 165,000.

Van Hoa (Culture and Arts): 26 Dien Bien Phu, Hanoi; tel. (4) 8257781; f. 1957; fortnightly; Editor PHI VAN TUONG.

Van Nghe (Arts and Letters): 17 Tran Quoc Toan, Hanoi; tel. (4) 8264430; f. 1949; weekly; organ of the Vietnamese Writers' Union; Editor HUU THINH; circ. 40,000.

Van Nghe Quan Doi (Army Literature and Arts): 4 Ly Nam De, Hanoi; tel. (4) 8254370; f. 1957; monthly; Editor NGUYEN TRI HUAN; circ. 50,000.

Viet Nam Business Forum: 9 Dao Duy Anh, 4th Floor, Dong Da District, Hanoi; tel. (4) 5743985; fax (4) 5743063; e-mail vbfhn@hn.vnn.vn; internet vibforum.vcci.com.vn; f. 1995; weekly magazine in English; publ. by the Viet Nam Chamber of Commerce and Industry; Editor-in-Chief DOAN DUY KHUONG.

Viet Nam Courier: 5 Ly Thuong Kiet, Hanoi; tel. (4) 8261847; fax (4) 8242317; weekly; English; publ. by the Viet Nam News Agency; Editor-in-Chief NGUYEN DUC GIAP.

Viet Nam Cultural Window: 46 Tran Hung Dao, Hanoi; tel. (4) 8253841; fax (4) 8269578; e-mail vncw@hn.vnn.vn; f. 1998; every two months; English; Dir TRAN DOAN LAM.

Viet Nam Investment Review (VIR): 175 Nguyen Thai Hoc, Hanoi; tel. (4) 8450537; fax (4) 8235281; e-mail vir@hn.vnn.vn; internet www.vir.com.vn; f. 1990; weekly; business newspaper publ. in English; Editor-in-Chief Dr NGUYEN PHU KY; circ 40,000.

Vietnam Pictorial: 11 Tran Hung Dao, Hanoi; tel. (4) 9332303; fax (4) 9332291; e-mail vnpictorial@vnagency.com.vn; internet vietnam.vnanet.com.vn/vnp-website; f. 1954; monthly online, in Vietnamese, English, French, Chinese, Spanish and Russian; fmrly Viet Nam Review; Editor-in-Chief NGUYEN VINH QUANG; circ. 138,000.

Viet Nam Renovation: Hanoi; f. 1994; quarterly magazine on reform of the agricultural sector; in Vietnamese, Chinese and English.

Viet Nam Social Sciences: 27 Tran Xuan Soan, Hanoi; tel. (4) 9784578; fax (4) 9783869; e-mail 21.6.tapchikhxh@fpt.vn; f. 1983; every 2 months; publ. in English and Vietnamese; organ of Viet Nam Social Academy; Editor-in-Chief Dr LE DINH CUC.

Vietnamese Studies: 46 Tran Hung Dao, Hanoi; tel. (4) 8253841; fax (4) 8269578; e-mail thegioi@hn.vnn.vn; internet www.thegioipublishers.com.vn; f. 1964; quarterly; English and French edns; Dir and Chief Editor Dr TRAN DOAN LAM.

NEWS AGENCIES

Viet Nam News Agency (VNA): 5 Ly Thuong Kiet, Hoan Kiem District, Hanoi; tel. (4) 8255443; fax (4) 8252984; e-mail btk@vnanet.vn; internet www.vnanet.vn; f. 1945; mem. of Organization of Asian and Pacific News Agencies; Gen. Dir NGUYEN QUOC UY (acting).

Foreign Bureaux

Agence France-Presse (AFP): 76 Ngo Quyen, BP 40, Hanoi; tel. (4) 8252045; fax (4) 8266032; e-mail afphanoi@fpt.vn; Bureau Chief PHILLIPPE PERDRIAU.

Informatsionnoye Telegrafnoye Agentstvo Rossii—Telegrafnoye Agentstvo Suverennykh Stran (ITAR—TASS) (Russia): Trung Tam Da Nganh, Thanh Xuan Bac, Dong Da District, Hanoi; tel. and fax (4) 8541381; e-mail tassvn@mail.ru; Bureau Chief IOURI A. DENISSOVITCH.

Kyodo News Service (Japan): Room 304, 8 Tran Hung Dao, Hanoi; tel. (4) 8259622; fax (4) 8255848; Bureau Chief KAZUHISA MIYAKE.

Polska Agencja Prasowa (PAP) (Poland): B5 Van Phuc Residential Quarter, Hanoi; tel. (4) 8252601; Chief TOMASZ TRZCINSKI.

Prensa Latina (Cuba): 66 Ngo Thi Nham, Hanoi; tel. (4) 9434366; fax (4) 9434866; e-mail plvietnam@hn.vnn.vn; Correspondent MANUEL NAVARRO ESCOBEDO.

Reuters (UK): Room 402, 8 Tran Hung Dao, Hanoi; tel. (4) 8259623; fax (4) 8268606; e-mail hanoi.newsroom@reuters.com.

Rossiiskoye Informatsionnoye Agentstvo—Novosti (RIA—Novosti) (Russia): 55A Tran Phu, Hanoi; tel. (4) 8431607; fax (4) 8230001; e-mail riahanoi@hn.vnn.vn; internet www.rian.ru; f. 1955; Bureau Chief ANDREI P. SHAMSHIN.

Xinhua (New China) News Agency (People's Republic of China): 6 Khuc Hao, Hanoi; tel. (4) 8232521; fax (4) 8452913; Chief Correspondent ZHANG JIAXIANG.

PRESS ASSOCIATION

Viet Nam Journalists' Association: 59 Ly Thai To, Hanoi; tel. (4) 8269747; fax (4) 8250797; e-mail vja@hn.vnn.vn; f. 1950; asscn of editors, reporters and photographers working in the press, radio, television and news agencies; 11,000 mems (2000); Pres. HONG VINH; Vice-Pres. DINH PHONG.

Publishers

Am Nhac Dia Hat (Music) Publishing House: 61 Ly Thai To, Hoan Kiem District, Hanoi; tel. (4) 8256208; f. 1986; produces cassettes, videocassettes, books and printed music; Dir PHAM DUC LOC.

Cong An Nhan Dan (People's Public Security) Publishing House: 167 Mai Hac De, Hai Ba Trung District, Hanoi; tel. (4) 8260910; f. 1981; managed by the Ministry of the Interior; cultural and artistic information, public order and security; Dir PHAM VAN THAM.

Giao Thong Van Tai (Communications and Transport) Publishing House: 80B Tran Hung Dao, Hanoi; tel. (4) 8255620; f. 1983; managed by the Ministry of Transport and Communications; Dir TO KHANH THO.

Khoa Hoc Va Ky Thuat (Science and Technology) Publishing House: 70 Tran Hung Dao, Hanoi; tel. (4) 9424786; fax (4) 8220658; e-mail todanghai@hn.vnn.vn; internet www.nxbkhkt.com.vn; f. 1960; scientific and technical works, guide books, dictionaries, popular and management books; Dir Prof. Dr TO DANG HAI.

Khoa Hoc Xa Hoi (Social Sciences) Publishing House: 61 Phan Chu Trinh, Hanoi; tel. (4) 8255428; f. 1967; managed by the Institute of Social Science; Dir Dr NGUYEN DUC ZIEU.

Kim Dong Publishing House: 55 Quang Trung, Hanoi; tel. (4) 9434730; fax (4) 8229085; e-mail kimdong@hn.vnn.vn; internet www.nxbkimdong.com.vn; f. 1957; children's; managed by the Ho Chi Minh Communist Youth Union; Dir PHAM QUANG VINH; Editor-in-Chief LE THI DAT.

Lao Dong (Labour) Publishing House: 54 Giang Vo, Hanoi; tel. (4) 8515380; f. 1945; translations and political works; managed by the Viet Nam General Confederation of Labour; Dir LE THANH TONG.

My Thuat (Fine Arts) Publishing House: 44B Hamlong, Hanoi; tel. (4) 8253036; f. 1987; managed by the Plastic Arts Workers' Association; Dir TRUONG HANH.

Nha Xuat Ban Giao Duc (Education) Publishing House: 81 Tran Hung Dao, Hanoi; tel. (4) 8220554; fax (4) 8262010; f. 1957; managed by the Ministry of Education and Training; Dir PHAM VAN AN; Editor-in-Chief Prof. NGUYEN NHU Y.

Nha Xuat Ban Hoi Nha Van (Writers' Association) Publishing House: 65 Nguyen Du, Hoan Kiem District, Hanoi; tel. and fax (4) 8222135; f. 1957; managed by the Vietnamese Writers' Association; Editor-in-Chief and Dir (acting) NGO VAN PHU.

Nong Nghiep (Agriculture) Publishing House: DH 14, Phoung Mai Ward, Dong Da District, Hanoi; tel. (4) 8523887; f. 1976; managed by the Ministry of Agriculture and Rural Development; Dir DUONG QUANG DIEU.

Phu Nu (Women) Publishing House: 16 Alexandre De Rhodes, Hanoi; tel. (4) 8294459; f. 1957; managed by the Vietnamese Women's Union; Dir TRAN THU HUONG.

Quan Doi Nhan Dan (People's Army) Publishing House: 25 Ly Nam De, Hanoi; tel. (4) 8255766; managed by the Ministry of National Defence; Dir DOAN CHUONG.

San Khau (Theatre) Publishing House: 51 Tran Hung Dao, Hanoi; tel. (4) 8264423; f. 1986; managed by the Stage Artists' Association.

Su That (Truth) Publishing House: 24 Quang Trung, Hanoi; tel. (4) 8252008; fax (4) 8251881; f. 1945; managed by the Communist Party of Viet Nam; Marxist-Leninist classics, politics and philosophy; Dir TRAN NHAM.

Thanh Nien (Youth) Publishing House: 270 Nguyen Dinh Chieu, District 3, Hanoi; tel. and fax (4) 8222612; f. 1954; managed by the Ho Chi Minh Communist Youth Union; Dir BUI VAN NGOI.

The Duc The Thao (Physical Education and Sports) Publishing House: 7 Trinh Hoai Duc, Hanoi; tel. (4) 8256155; f. 1974; managed by the Ministry of Culture and Information; Dir NGUYEN HIEU.

The Gioi Publishers: 46 Tran Hung Dao, Hanoi; tel. (4) 8253841; fax (4) 8269578; e-mail thegioi@hn.vnn.vn; internet www.thegioipublishers.com.vn; f. 1957; foreign language publications; managed by the Ministry of Culture and Information; Dir and Chief Editor Dr TRAN DOAN LAM.

Thong Ke (Statistics) Publishing House: 96 Thuy Khe, Hanoi; tel. (4) 8257814; f. 1980; managed by the Gen. Statistics Office; Dir NGUYEN DAO.

Van Hoa (Culture) Publishing House: 43 Lo Duc, Hanoi; tel. (4) 8253517; f. 1971; managed by the Ministry of Culture and Information; Dir QUANG HUY.

Van Hoc (Literature) Publishing House: 19 Nguyen Truong To, Ba Dinh, Hanoi; tel. (4) 8294783; fax (4) 8294781; e-mail nxbvanhoc@hn.vnn.vn; f. 1948; managed by the Ministry of Culture and Information; Dir NGUYEN VAN CU.

Xay Dung (Building) Publishing House: 37 Le Dai Hanh, Hanoi; tel. (4) 8268271; fax (4) 8215369; f. 1976; managed by the Ministry of Construction; Dir NGUYEN LUONG BICH.

Y Hoc (Medicine) Publishing House: 4 Le Thanh Ton, Phan Chu Trinh, Hoan Kiem District, Hanoi; tel. (4) 8255281; e-mail xuatbanyhoc@netnam.vn; managed by the Ministry of Public Health; Dir HOANG TRONG QUANG.

Broadcasting and Communications

TELECOMMUNICATIONS

Directorate General for Posts and Telecommunications (DGPT): Department of Science-Technology and International Cooperation, 18 Nguyen Du, Hanoi; tel. (4) 8226580; fax (4) 8226590; industry regulator; Sec.-Gen. Dr MAI LIEM TRUC.

Board of the Technical and Economic Programme on Information Technology: 39 Tran Hung Dao, Hanoi; e-mail nyenet@itnet.gov.vn; Gen. Dir Dr DO VAN LOC.

Army Electronics and Communications Corporation: military-owned communications company; awarded a licence in 1998 to provide national telephone services, including a fixed network and mobile and paging systems.

Saigon Post and Telecommunications Service Corpn: 45 Le Duan, District 1, Ho Chi Minh City; tel. (8) 4040608; fax (8) 4040609; e-mail saigonpostel@saigonpostel.com.vn; internet www.saigonpostel.com.vn; f. 1995; partially owned by the State; nationwide post and telecommunications services; Chair. TRAN THI NGOC BINH; Gen. Dir PHAM NGOC TUAN.

Viet Nam Posts and Telecommunications Corporation (VNPT): 18 Nguyen Du, Hai Ba Trung District, Hanoi; tel. (4) 5113859; fax (4) 5182808; e-mail vnpt_website@vnpt.com.vn; internet www.vnpt.com.vn; f. 1995; state-owned communications company; Chair. VU VAN LUAN; Pres. and CEO PHAM LONG TRAN.

RADIO

In 1998 there were 390 FM stations, 567 district radio stations and 6,505 commune radio stations in Viet Nam. The Ministry of Culture and Information is responsible for the management of radio services.

Voice of Viet Nam (VOV): 58 Quan Su, Hanoi; tel. (4) 9344231; fax (4) 9344230; e-mail vovnews@hn.vnn.vn; internet www.vov.org.vn; f. 1945; four domestic channels in Vietnamese; two foreign service channels in English, Japanese, French, Khmer, Laotian, Spanish, Thai, Cantonese, Mandarin, Indonesian, Vietnamese and Russian; Dir-Gen. Dr VU VAN HIEN.

TELEVISION

At the end of 1994 there were 53 provincial television stations and 232 relay stations in Viet Nam. The Ministry of Culture and Information is responsible for the management of television services.

Viet Nam Television (VTV): 43 Nguyen Chi Thanh, Hanoi; tel. (4) 8354992; fax (4) 8350882; e-mail webmaster@vtv.org.vn; internet www.vtv.org.vn; television was introduced in South Viet Nam in 1966 and in North Viet Nam in 1970; broadcasts from Hanoi (via satellite) to the whole country and Asia region; Vietnamese, French, English; Dir-Gen. Dr VU VAN HIEN.

Finance

(cap. = capital; res = reserves; dep. = deposits; m. = million; brs = branches)

BANKING

In early 1990 the Government established four independent commercial banks, several joint-venture banks, and introduced legislation to permit the operation of foreign banks in Viet Nam. At the end of 1998 the Vietnamese banking system comprised six state-owned banks, four joint-venture banks, 24 foreign bank branches, 51 joint-stock commercial banks, 977 People's Credit Funds, two joint-stock finance companies, three corporation-subordinated finance companies and eight leasing companies. At the beginning of 2002 there were 27 foreign bank branches and 42 representative offices of foreign financial institutions in Viet Nam. From March 2006 foreign banks were for the first time allowed to offer a full range of banking services.

Central Bank

State Bank of Viet Nam: 47–49 Ly Thai To, Hanoi; tel. (4) 8242479; fax (4) 8268765; e-mail nhnn@sbv.gov.vn; internet www.sbv.gov.vn; f. 1951; central bank of issue; provides a national network of banking services and supervises the operation of the state banking system; Gov. LE DUC THUY; 61 brs and sub-brs.

State Banks

Bank for Agriculture and Rural Development: 2 Lang Ha, Ba Dinh District, Hanoi; tel. (4) 8313694; fax (4) 8313717; e-mail webmaster@vbard.com; internet www.vbard.com; f. 1988; cap. 3,844,915m. dông, res –4,215,110m. dông, dep. 82,607,320m. dông (Dec. 2002); Chair. NGUYEN QUOC TOAN; Gen. Man. VAN SO LE; 1,291 brs.

Bank for Foreign Trade of Viet Nam (Vietcombank): 198 Tran Quang Khai, Hanoi; tel. (4) 8251322; fax (4) 8269067; e-mail webmaster@vietcombank.com.vn; internet www.vietcombank.com.vn; f. 1963; authorized to deal in foreign currencies and all other international banking business; undergoing equitization in mid-2005; cap. 3,030,733m. dông, res 1,827,417m. dông, dep. 86,242,697m. dông (Dec. 2003); Chair. NGUYEN HOA BINH; Dir-Gen. VU VIET NGOAN; 23 brs.

Bank for Investment and Development of Vietnam (Vietinde Bank): Vincom City Tower, Block A, 191 Ba Trieu, Hai Ba Trung District, Hanoi; tel. (4) 2200422; fax (4) 2200399; e-mail bidv@hn.vnn.vn; internet www.bidv.com.vn; Chair. PHUNG THI VAN ANH; Gen. Dir TRINH NGOC HO.

Industrial and Commercial Bank of Viet Nam (VIETINCOMBANK): 108 Tran Hung Dao, Hanoi; tel. (4) 9421030; fax (4) 9421032; e-mail webteam@icbv.com; internet www.icb.com.vn; f. 1987; state-owned; authorized to receive personal savings, extend loans, issue stocks and invest in export-orientated cos and jt ventures with foreigners; cap. 2,100,000m. dông, res 898,174m. dông, dep. 59,283,956m. dông (Dec. 2002); Chair. NGUYEN VAN BINH; Gen. Dir PHAM HUY HUNG; 116 brs.

Saigon Bank for Industry and Trade: 2c Pho Duc Chinh, District 1, Ho Chi Minh City; tel. (8) 9143183; fax (8) 9143193; e-mail saigonbank@hcm.vnn.vn; internet www.saigonbank.com.vn; cap. 303,500m. dông, res 52,918m. dông, dep. 2,524,457m. dông (Dec. 2004); specializes in trade and industry activities; Dir-Gen. TRAN THI VIET ANH; 11 brs and 7 sub-brs.

Vietnam Export-Import Commercial Joint-Stock Bank (Vietnam Eximbank): 7 Le Thi Hong Gam, District 1, Ho Chi Minh City; tel. (8) 8210055; fax (8) 8296063; e-mail icbr.eximbank@hcm.vnn.vn; internet www.eximbank.com.vn; f. 1989 as Vietnam Export Import Bank, name changed as above 1992; authorized to undertake banking transactions for the production and processing of export products and export-import operations; cap. 300,000m. dông, res 31,585m. dông, dep. 5,521,704m. dông (Dec. 2003); Chair. NGUYEN THANH LONG; Dir-Gen. NGUYEN GIA DINH; 5 brs.

Viet Nam Technological and Commercial Joint-Stock Bank (Techcombank): 15 Dao Duy Tu, Hoan Kiem District, Hanoi; tel. (4)

VIET NAM

8243941; fax (4) 8250545; internet www.techcombank.com.vn; CEO Nguyen Duc Vinh.

Joint-Stock and Other Banks

CBD (Codo Rural Share Commercial Bank): Co Do, Thoi Dong, O Mon, Can Tho Province; tel. (71) 61642; Dir Tran Ngoc Ha.

Chohung Vina Bank: 3-5 Ho Tung Mau, District 1, Ho Chi Minh City; tel. (8) 8291581; fax (8) 8291583; e-mail hcmc.fvb@hcm.vnn.vn; f. 1993; jt venture between the Bank for Foreign Trade of Viet Nam and Korea First Bank; cap. US $20.0m., res US $1.2m., dep. US $71.9m. (Dec. 2001); Chair. Viet Ngoan Vu; Dir-Gen. Shin-Seong Kang.

DS Bank (Dongthap Commercial Joint-Stock Bank): 48 Rad 30/4, Cao Lanh Town, Dong Thap Province; tel. (67) 51441; fax (67) 51878; Dir Hoang Van Tu.

Ficombank (Denhat Joint-Stock Commercial Bank): 67A Le Quang Sung, District 6, Ho Chi Minh City; tel. (8) 8556066; fax (8) 8557093; Dir Van Duong.

Indovina Bank Ltd: 39 Ham Nghi, District 1, Ho Chi Minh City; tel. (8) 8224995; fax (8) 8230131; e-mail ivbhcm@hcm.vnn.vn; internet www.indovinabank.com.vn; f. 1990; jt venture of the Cathay United Bank (Taiwan) and the Industrial and Commercial Bank of Viet Nam; also has brs in Hanoi, Haiphong, Binh Duong, Can Tho and Dong Nai; cap. US $25m., res US $3.4m., dep. US $151m. (Dec. 2004); Chair. Roger Lee Ming Hsien; Gen. Dir Jan Yei Fong.

Maritime Bank: 5A Nguyen Tri Phuong, Haiphong; tel. (3) 1823076; fax (3) 1823063; e-mail msb@msb.com.vn; internet www.msb.com.vn; f. 1991; cap. 109,310m. dông (2003); Pres. Tran Ba Vinh; 9 brs.

Phuong Nam Bank (Phuong Nam Commercial Joint-Stock Bank): 279 Ly Thuong Kiet, District 11, Ho Chi Minh City; tel. (8) 8663890; fax (8) 8663891; e-mail ICSC-PNB@phuongnambank.com.vn; internet www.phuongnambank.com.vn; f. 1993; Chair. Truong Ty.

Quedo Joint-Stock Bank: 1-3-5 Can Giuoc, District 8, Ho Chi Minh City; tel. (8) 8562418; fax (8) 8553596; Dir Bao Lan.

VID Public Bank: Ground Floor, Hanoi Tungshing Square, 2 Ngo Quyen, Hanoi; tel. (4) 8268307; fax (4) 8268228; e-mail vpb.han@hn.vnn.vn; f. 1992; jt venture between the Bank for Investment and Development (Viet Nam) and the Public Bank Berhad (Malaysia); commercial bank; cap. US $20m. (2001); Chair. Tran Anh Tuan (acting); Gen. Dir Tay Hong Heng; 5 brs.

VinaSiam Bank: 2 Pho Duc Chinh, District 1, Ho Chi Minh City; tel. (8) 8210557; fax (8) 8210585; e-mail vsb@hcm.vnn.vn; internet www.vinasiambank.com; f. 1995; jt venture between Bank for Agriculture and Rural Development, Siam Commercial Bank (Thailand) and Charoen Pokphand Group (Thailand); cap. US $20m., dep. US $25.2m. (Dec. 2004), res US $2.8m. (2002); Chair. Le Van So; Gen. Man. Viroj Thanapitak.

VP Bank (Viet Nam Commercial Joint-Stock Bank for Private Enterprises): 18B Le Thanh Tong, Hanoi; tel. (4) 8245246; fax (4) 8260182; Chair. Lam Hoang Loc.

Foreign Banks

Australia and New Zealand Banking Group Ltd (Australia): 14 Le Thai To, Hanoi; tel. (4) 8258190; fax (4) 8258188; e-mail ahmada@anz.com; Gen. Man. Adil Ahmad; also has br. in Ho Chi Minh City.

Bangkok Bank Public Co Ltd (Thailand): Harbour View Tower, 35 Nguyen Hue, District 1, Ho Chi Minh City; tel. (8) 8214396; fax (8) 8213772; e-mail bblhcm@hcm.vnn.vn; Man. Wittaya Supatanakul.

Bank of Tokyo-Mitsubishi UFJ Ltd (Japan): The Landmark, 8th Floor, 5B Ton Duc Thang, District 1, Ho Chi Minh City; tel. (8) 8231560; fax (8) 8231559.

Calyon (France): Somerset Chancellor Court, 4th Floor, 21–23 Nguyen Thi Minh Khai, District 1, Ho Chi Minh City; tel. (8) 8295048; fax (8) 8296065; e-mail calyon-hcm@hcm.vnn.vn; Snr Country Officer Jean-Charles Belliol.

Natexis Banques Populaires (France): Rm 16-02, Prime Ctr, 53 Quang Trung, Hanoi; tel. (4) 9433667; fax (4) 9433665; e-mail natexis-vn@hcm.vnn.vn; Rep. Mme Ut.

Shinhan Bank (Republic of Korea): Yoco Bldg, 7th Floor, 41 Nguyen Thi Minh Khai, District 1, Ho Chi Minh City; tel. (8) 8230012; fax (8) 8230009; Gen. Man. Hae-Soo Kim.

United Overseas Bank Ltd (Singapore): Central Plaza Office Bldg, Ground Floor, 17 blvd Le Duan, District 1, Ho Chi Minh City; tel. (8) 8251424; fax (8) 8251423; e-mail UOB.HoChiMinhCity@UOBgroup.com; Gen. Man. Thng Tien Tat.

STOCK EXCHANGE

Securities Trading Centre: 45–47 Chuong Duong, Ho Chi Minh City; f. July 2000; by the State Securities Commission (see Development Organization).

INSURANCE

In January 1994 it was announced that foreign insurance companies were to be permitted to operate in Viet Nam and in 1995 it was announced that Baoviet's monopoly of the insurance industry was to be ended. A number of new insurance companies were subsequently established. By September 2003 there were 17 insurance companies operating in the country, of which three were state-owned, three were joint-stock, four were wholly foreign-owned and seven were joint ventures.

Allianz General Insurance Vietnam: Unit 4, 8th Floor, The Metropolitan, 235 Dong Khoi, District 1, Ho Chi Minh City; tel. (8) 8245050; fax (8) 8245054; e-mail jnr@allianzagf.com; f. 1999; fmrly Allianz–AGF Insurance Co Ltd; non-life.

Aon Inchibrok Insurance Services Co Ltd: Vietcombank Tower, 198 Tran Quang Khai, Hanoi; tel. (4) 8244828; fax (4) 8243983; f. 1994; fmrly Inchibrok Insurance; jt venture between Baoviet and Aon Corpn (USA).

Bao Long (Nha Rong Joint-Stock Insurance Co): 185 Dien Bien Phu, District 1, Ho Chi Minh City; tel. (8) 8239219; fax (8) 8239223; internet www.nharong.com; cap. 22,000m. dông (1994); Dir Tran Van Binh.

Bao Minh CMG Life Insurance Co Ltd: Level 3, Saigon Riverside Office Centre, 2A–4A Ton Duc Thang, District 1, Ho Chi Minh City; tel. (8) 8291919; fax (8) 8293131; e-mail bmcmg@baominhcmg.com.vn; internet www.baominhcmg.com.vn; f. 1999; jt venture between Bao Minh Insurance Co and CMG Colonial Mutual Life Assurance Society (Australia); Gen. Dir Rod Carkeet.

Bao Minh Insurance Co (Ho Chi Minh City Insurance Co): 26 Ton That Dam, District 1, Ho Chi Minh City; tel. (8) 8294180; fax (8) 8294185; e-mail baominh@baominh.com.vn; internet www.baominhvn.com.vn; f. 1995; non-life.

Baoviet (Viet Nam Insurance Co): 35 Hai Ba Trung, Hoan Kiem District, Hanoi; tel. (4) 8245935; fax (4) 8257188; e-mail service@baoviet.com.vn; internet www.baoviet.com.vn; f. 1965; property and casualty, personal accident, liability and life insurance; total assets 8,817,000m. dông (2004); CEO Trinh Thanh Hoan; Chair. Prof. Truong Môc Lâm.

Manulife (Vietnam) Ltd: 12th Floor, Diamond Plaza, 34 Le Duan, District 1, Ho Chi Minh City; tel. (8) 8257722; fax (8) 8257718; e-mail manulifevn_info@manulife.com; internet www.manulife.com.vn; f. 1999; fmrly Chinfon-Manulife Life Insurance Co Ltd; first wholly foreign-owned life insurance co to operate in Viet Nam; Gen. Dir David Matthews.

Petro Viet Nam Insurance Co (PV Insurance): 154 Hguyen Thai Hoc, Ba Dinh District, Hanoi; tel. (4) 7335588; fax (4) 7336284; e-mail info@pv-insurance.com; internet www.pv-insurance.com; f. 1996; non-life insurance; Man. Dir Le Van Hung.

Petrolimex Joint-Stock Insurance Co (PJICO Insurance): 22 Lang Ha, Dong Da District, Hanoi; tel. (4) 7760865; fax (4) 7760868; e-mail pjico@petrolimex.com.vn; internet www.pjico.com.vn; f. 1995; non-life insurance; Gen. Exec. Dir Tran Nghia Vinh.

Viet Nam International Assurance Co (VIA): 10th Floor, The Saigon Trade Center, 37 Ton Duc Thang, District 1, Ho Chi Minh City; tel. (8) 8221340; fax (8) 8221338; e-mail hcm@via.com.vn; internet www.via.com.vn; f. 1996; jt-venture co, 51% owned by Baoviet, 49% owned by Tokyo Marine and Fire Insurance Co (Japan); non-life insurance and reinsurance for foreign cos; Marketing Man. Peter Huy.

Trade and Industry

GOVERNMENT AGENCIES

State Financial and Monetary Council (SFMC): f. 1998; established to supervise, review and resolve matters relating to national financial and monetary policy.

Vietrade (Viet Nam Trade Promotion Agency): 20 Ly Thuong Kiet, Hanoi; tel. (4) 9347628; fax (4) 9344260; e-mail vietrade@vietrade.gov.vn; internet www.vietrade.gov.vn; part of the Ministry of Trade; responsible for state management, co-ordination and implementation of trade and trade-related investment promotion and development activities; Dir-Gen. Ngo Van Thoan.

Vinacontrol (The Viet Nam Superintendence and Inspection Co): 54 Tran Nhan Tong, Hanoi; tel. (4) 9433840; fax (4) 9433844; e-mail vinacontrolvn@hn.vnn.vn; internet www.vinacontrol.com.vn; f. 1957; brs in all main Vietnamese ports and trade centres; controls quality and volume of exports and imports and transit of goods, and conducts inspections of deliveries and production processes; price verification, marine survey, damage survey, claim settling and adjustment; consultant of international quality management system; Chair. Bui Duy Chinh; Gen. Dir Mai Tien Dung; 600 employees.

VIET NAM   Directory

DEVELOPMENT ORGANIZATION

State Securities Commission: 164 Tran Quang Khai, Hanoi; tel. (4) 9340750; fax (4) 9340739; internet www.ssc.gov.vn; f. 1997; responsible for developing the capital markets, incl. the establishment of a stock exchange; 14 mems; Chair. NGUYEN DUC QUANG.

CHAMBER OF COMMERCE

VCCI (Viet Nam Chamber of Commerce and Industry): 9 Dao Duy Anh, Hanoi; tel. (4) 5743985; fax (4) 5743063; e-mail vcci@fmail.vnn.vn; internet www.vcci.com.vn; f. 1963; offices in Ho Chi Minh City, Da Nang, Haiphong, Can Tho, Vung Tau, Nha Trang, Nghe An, Thanh Hoa and Vinh; promotes business and investment between foreign and Vietnamese cos; protects interests of businesses; organizes training activities, exhbns and fairs in Viet Nam and abroad; provides information about and consultancy in Viet Nam's trade and industry; represents foreign applicants for patents and trade mark registration; issues certificates of origin and other documentation; helps domestic and foreign businesses to settle disputes by negotiation or arbitration; in 1993 foreign businesses operating in Viet Nam and Vietnamese businesses operating abroad were permitted to become assoc. mems; Pres. and Chair. Dr VU TIEN LOC; Sec.-Gen. PHAM GIA TUC; associated organizations: Viet Nam International Arbitration Centre, Viet Nam General Average Adjustment Committee, Advisory Board.

Viet Nam International Arbitration Centre (VIAC): 6th Floor, International Trade Centre, 9 Dao Duy Anh, Dong Da District, Hanoi; tel. (4) 5742021; fax (4) 5743001; e-mail viac-vcci@hn.vnn.vn; internet www.viac.org.vn; f. 1993; adjudicates in disputes concerning both domestic and international economic relations.

INDUSTRIAL AND TRADE ORGANIZATIONS

Agrex Saigon (Agricultural Products and Foodstuffs Export Co): 58 Vo Van Tan, District 3, Ho Chi Minh City; tel. (8) 9306606; fax (8) 9303451; e-mail agrexsaigon@hcm.vnn.vn; internet www.agrexsaigon.com; f. 1976; exports agricultural produce, coffee, frozen foods and aquatic products; imports agricultural and industrial materials, machinery and equipment, and consumer goods; Gen. Dir DUONG KY HUNG.

Agrimex (Viet Nam National Agricultural Products Corpn): 173 Hai Ba Trung, District 3, Ho Chi Minh City; tel. (8) 8241049; fax (8) 8291349; e-mail agrimex@hcm.fpt.vn; f. 1956; imports and exports agricultural products; Gen. Dir NGUYEN BACH TUYET.

Airimex (General Civil Aviation Import-Export and Forwarding Co): 100 Nguyen Van Cu, Gia Lam, Long Bien District, Hanoi; tel. (4) 8271939; fax (4) 8271925; e-mail airimex@fpt.vn; f. 1989; imports and exports aircraft, spare parts and accessories for aircraft and air communications; Gen. Dir PHAM DOA HONG.

An Giang Afiex Co (An Giang Agriculture and Foods Import and Export Co): 34–36 Hai Ba Trung, Long Xuyen Town, An Giang Province; tel. (76) 841021; fax (76) 843199; e-mail xnknstpagg@hcm.vnn.net; f. 1992; mfr and sale of agricultural products, also beverages; Dir PHAM VAN BAY.

Artexport–Hanoi (Viet Nam Handicrafts and Art Articles Export-Import Corpn): 31–33 Ngo Quyen, Hanoi; tel. (4) 8252760; fax (4) 8259275; e-mail artexport.hn@fpt.vn; internet www.artexport.com.vn; f. 1964; deals in craft products and art articles; Gen. Dir DO VAN KHOI.

Barotex (Viet Nam National Bamboo and Rattan Export-Import Co): 15 Ben Chuong Duong, District 1, Ho Chi Minh City; tel. (8) 8295544; fax (8) 8295352; e-mail barotexsg@saigonnet.vn; f. 1971; specializes in art and handicrafts made from natural materials, sports shoes, ceramic and lacquer wares, gifts and other housewares, fibres, agricultural and forest products; Gen. Dir TA QUOC TOAN.

Bimson Cement Co: Lam Son Hamlet, Bim Con Town, Thanh Hoa Province; tel. (52) 824242; fax (37) 824046; mfr of cement; Dir LE VAN CHUNG.

Binh Tay Import-Export Co (BITEX): 78–82 Hau Giang, District 6, Ho Chi Minh City; tel. (8) 8559669; fax (8) 8557846; e-mail bitex@hcm.vnn.vn; trade in miscellaneous goods; Dir NGUYEN VAN THIEN.

B12 Petroleum Co: Cai Lan, Bay Chay Sub-District, Ha Long City, Quang Ninh Province; tel. (33) 846360; fax (33) 846349; distribution of petroleum products; Dir VU NGOC HAI.

Centrimex (Viet Nam National General Import-Export Corpn): 247 Giang Vo, Dong Da District, Hanoi; tel. (58) 8512986; fax (58) 8512974; e-mail centrimexhn@fpt.vn; internet www.centrimexhn.com.vn; f. 1986; exports and imports goods for five provinces in the south-central region of Viet Nam; Gen. Dir HOANG DINH DUNG.

Coalimex (Viet Nam National Coal Export-Import and Material Supply Corpn): 47 Quang Trung, Hanoi; tel. (4) 9423166; fax (4) 9422350; e-mail coalimex_gn@hn.vnn.vn; internet www.coalimex.com.vn; f. 1982; exports coal, imports mining machinery and equipment; Gen. Dir NINH XUAN SON.

Cocenex (Central Production Import-Export Corpn): 80 Hang Gai, Hanoi; tel. (4) 8254535; fax (4) 8294306; f. 1988; Gen. Dir BUI THI THU HUONG.

Coffee Supply, Processing and Materials Co: 38B Nguyen Bieu, Nha Trang City, Khanh Hoa Province; tel. (58) 21176; coffee producer.

Cokyvina (Post and Telecommunication Equipment Import-Export Service Corpn): 178 Trieu Viet Vuong, Hanoi; tel. (4) 9782362; fax (4) 9782368; e-mail cokyvina@hn.vnn.vn; f. 1987; imports and exports telecom equipment, provides technical advice on related subjects, undertakes authorized imports, jt ventures, jt co-ordination and co-operation on investment with foreign and domestic economic organizations; Dir NGUYEN KIM KY.

Constrexim (Viet Nam Construction Investment and Export-Import Holdings Corpn): 39 Nguyen Dinh Chieu, Hanoi; tel. (4) 9744836; fax (4) 9742701; e-mail constrexim@fpt.com; internet www.constrexim.com.vn; f. 1982; exports and imports building materials, equipment and machinery; undertakes construction projects in Viet Nam and abroad, and production of building materials with foreign partners; also involved in investment promotion and projects management, real estate development, and human resources development and training; Gen. Dir NGUYEN QUOC HIEP.

Culturimex (State Enterprise for the Export and Import of Works of Art and other Cultural Commodities): 22B Hai Ba Trung, Hanoi; tel. (4) 8252226; fax (4) 8259224; e-mail namson@fpt.vn; f. 1988; exports cultural items and imports materials for the cultural industry; Gen. Dir NGUYEN LAI.

Dau Tieng Rubber Corpn: Dau Tieng Townlet, Dau Tieng District, Binh Duong Province; tel. (650) 561847; fax (650) 561488; e-mail dtrubber@hcm.vnn.vn; f. 1981; planting, processing and export of natural rubber; Man. Dir LE VAN KHOA.

Epco Ltd (Export Import and Tourism Co Ltd): 1 Nyuyen Thuong Hien, District 3, Ho Chi Minh City; tel. (8) 8324392; fax (8) 8324744; f. 1986; processes seafood; tourism and hotel business; Gen. Dir NGUYEN LOC RI.

Foocosa (Food Co Ho Chi Min City): 57 Nguyen Thi Minh Khai, District 1, Ho Chi Minh City; tel. (8) 9309070; fax (8) 9304552; e-mail foocosa@hcm.vnn.vn; internet www.foocosa.com; mfr and distributor of food products (rice, instant noodles, porridge, sauces, biscuits); Dir NGO VAN TAN.

Forexco (Forest Products Export Co): Dien Ngoc Village, Dien Ban District, Quangnam Province; tel. (510) 843595; fax (510) 843619; e-mail forexcoqnam@dng.vnn.vn; internet www.forexcoqnam.com; f. 1986; mfr and exporter of furniture and other wood products; Gen. Dir DANG NGOC BA.

Garmex Saigon (Saigon Garment Manufacturing Import-Export Co): 213 An Duong Vuong, District 5, Ho Chi Minh City; tel. (8) 8557166; fax (8) 8557299; e-mail gmsg@hcm.fpt.vn; internet www.garmexsaigon.com; f. 1993; garment production and export; Gen. Dir LE QUANG HUNG.

Genecofov (General Co of Foods and Services): 64 Ba Huyen Thanh Quan, District 3, Ho Chi Minh City; tel. (8) 9325366; fax (8) 9325428; e-mail gecofov@hcm.fpt.vn; f. 1956; import and export of food products, handicrafts and ceramics, garage services, vehicle trading; under the Ministry of Commerce; Dir TO VAN PHAT.

Generalexim (Viet Nam National General Export-Import Corpn): 46 Ngo Quyen, Hoan Kiem, Hanoi; tel. (4) 8264009; fax (4) 8259894; e-mail gexim@generalexim.com.vn; f. 1981; export and import on behalf of production and trading organizations, also garment processing for export and manufacture of toys; Gen. Dir HOANG TUAN KHAI.

Generalimex (Viet Nam National General Import-Export Corpn): 66 Pho Duc Chinh, Ho Chi Minh City; tel. (8) 8292990; fax (8) 8292968; e-mail generalimex@hcm.fpt.vn; exports of agricultural products and spices, imports of machinery, vehicles, chemicals and fertilizers; Gen. Dir NGUYEN VAN HOANG.

Geruco (Viet Nam General Rubber Corpn): 236 Nam Ky Khoi Nghia, District 3, Ho Chi Minh City; tel. (8) 9325235; fax (8) 9327341; e-mail grc@vngeruco.com; internet www.vngeruco.com; merged with Rubexim (rubber export-import corpn) in 1991; manages and controls the Vietnamese rubber industry, including the planting, processing and trading of natural rubber and rubber wood products; also imports chemicals, machinery and spare parts for the industry; Dir-Gen. LE QUANG THUNG.

Haprosimex (Hanoi General Production and Import-Export Company): 22 Hang Luoc, Hanoi; tel. (4) 8266601; fax (4) 8264014; e-mail business@hapro.com.vn; internet www.hapro.com.vn; specializes in handicrafts, textiles, clothing and agricultural and forestry products; Gen. Dir NGUYEN CU TAM.

VIET NAM

Directory

Hatien Cement Co No 1: Km 8 Highway Hanoi, Thu Duc, Ho Chi Minh City; tel. (8) 8966608; fax (8) 8967635; mfr of cement; Dir NGUYEN NGOC ANH.

Hatien Cement Co No 2: Kien Luong Town, Ha Tien, Kien Giang Province; tel. (77) 53004; fax (77) 53005; mfr of cement; Dir NGUYEN MANH.

Haugiang Petrolimex (Haugiang Petrol and Oil Co): 21 Cach Mang Thang 8, Can Tho City, Can Tho Province; tel. (71) 21657; fax (71) 12746; distributor of fuel; Dir TRINH MANG THANG.

Hoang Thach Cement Co: Minh Tan Hamlet, Kim Mon, Hai Hung Province; tel. (32) 821092; fax (32) 821098; sale of construction materials; Dir NGUYEN DUC HOAN.

Intimex Import-Export Corpn: 96 Tran Hung Dao, Hanoi; tel. (4) 9423240; fax (4) 9424250; e-mail intimex@hn.vnn.vn; internet www.intimexco.com; f. 1979; exports mainly agricultural products and processed items; imports mainly consumer goods, motorcycles and raw materials, machinery and equipment for the construction industry; Gen. Dir VU ANH.

Lefaso (Viet Nam Leather and Footwear Assocn): Rm 120–2, Block 9, 7 Dao Duy Anh, Hanoi; tel. (4) 5770983; fax (4) 5770984; e-mail hhdg@hn.vnn.vn; internet www.lefaso.org.vn; f. 1990 to promote external trade relations, to provide technical support and technological training and to disseminate market information; Chair. NGUYEN GIA THAO; Gen. Sec. NGUYEN THI TONG.

Machinoimport (Viet Nam Machinery and Spare Parts Co): 8 Trang Thi, Hoan Kiem, Hanoi; tel. (4) 8253703; fax (4) 8254050; e-mail machino@hn.vnn.vn; internet www.machinoimport.com.vn; f. 1956 as Vietnam National Machinery Export-Import Corpn; reorganised in 2003; now controlled by Ministry of Trade; imports and exports machinery, spare parts and tools; consultancy, investment, jt-venture, and manufacturing services; comprises 12 cos; Chair. NGUYEN TRAN DAT; Gen. Dir TRAN DUC TRUONG.

Marine Supply (Marine Technical Materials Import-Export and Supplies): 276A Da Nang, Ngo Quyen, Haiphong; tel. (31) 847308; fax (31) 845159; f. 1985; imports and exports technical materials for marine transportation industry; Dir PHAN TRANG CHAN.

Mecanimex (Viet Nam National Mechanical Products Export-Import Co): 37 Trang Thi, Hoan Kiem District, Hanoi; tel. (4) 8257459; fax (4) 9349904; e-mail mecahn@fpt.vn; exports and imports mechanical products and hand tools; Gen. Dir TRAN BAO GIOC.

Minexport (Viet Nam National Minerals Export-Import Corpn): 28 Ba Trieu, Hanoi; tel. (4) 8253674; fax (4) 5532669; e-mail minexport@fpt.vn; f. 1956; 30% state-owned; exports minerals and metals, quarry products, chemical products and footwear; imports metals, chemical products, industrial materials, fertilizers and consumer goods; Gen. Dir ANH TRAN THI LAN.

Nafobird (Viet Nam Forest and Native Birds, Animals and Ornamental Plants Export-Import Enterprises): 64 Truong Dinh, District 3, Ho Chi Minh City; tel. (8) 8290211; fax (8) 8293735; f. 1987; exports native birds, animals and plants, and imports materials for forestry; Dir VO HA AN.

Naforimex (Hanoi Forest Products Export-Import and Production Corpn): 19 Ba Trieu, Hoan Kiem District, Hanoi; tel. (4) 8261255; fax (4) 8259264; e-mail naforimexhanoi@fpt.vn; f. 1960; imports chemicals, machinery and spare parts for the forestry industry and water supply network; exports oils, forest products, gum benzoin and resin; CEO NGUYEN BA HUNG.

Nitagrex (Ninh Thuan Agricultural Products Import-Export Co): 158 Bac Ai, Do Vinh Ward, Phan Rang Thap Cham, Ninh Thuan Province; tel. (68) 888779; fax (68) 888842; e-mail nitagrex@hcm.vnn.vn; internet www.nitagrex.com.vn; f. 1999; production and export of agricultural products; import of consumer goods, transport vehicles and agricultural materials and equipment; Gen. Dir DAO VAN CHAN.

Packexport (Viet Nam National Packaging Technology and Import-Export Co): 31 Hang Thung, Hanoi; tel. (4) 8262792; fax (4) 8269227; e-mail packexport-vn@vnn.vn; f. 1976; manufactures packaging for domestic and export demand, and imports materials for the packaging industry; Gen. Dir TRINH LE KIEU.

Petec-Trading and Investment Corpn: 70 Ba Huyen Thanh Quan, District 3, Ho Chi Minh City; tel. (8) 8299299; fax (8) 8299686; f. 1981; imports equipment and technology for oil drilling, exploration and oil production; exports crude petroleum, rice, coffee and agricultural products; invests in silk, coffee, financial and transport sectors; Gen. Dir TRAN HUU LAC.

Petrol and Oil Co (Zone 1): Duc Gliang Town, Gia Lam, Hanoi; tel. (4) 8271400; fax (4) 8272432; sales of oil and gas; Dir PHAN VAN DU.

Petrolimex (Viet Nam National Petroleum Corpn): 1 Kham Thien, Dong Da District, Hanoi; tel. (4) 8512603; fax (4) 8519203; e-mail xttm@petrolimex.com.vn; internet www.petrolimex.com.vn; f. 1956; import, export and distribution of petroleum products and liquefied petroleum gas; Chair. NGUYEN MANH TIEN; Dir-Gen. TRAN VAN DUC.

Petrolimex Saigon Petroleum Co (Zone 2): 15 Le Duan, District 1, Ho Chi Minh City; tel. (8) 8292081; fax (8) 8222082; sales of petroleum products; Dir TRAN VAN THANG.

Petrovietnam (The Viet Nam Oil and Gas Corpn): 22 Ngo Quyen, Hoan Kiem District, Hanoi; tel. (4) 8252526; fax (4) 8265942; e-mail webmaster@hn.pv.com.vn; internet www.petrovietnam.com.vn; f. 1975; exploration and production of petroleum and gas; Chair. Dr PHAM QUANG DU; Pres. and CEO Dr TRAN NGOC CANH.

Saigon Brewery Co: 187 Nguyen Chi Thanh, District 5, Ho Chi Minh City; tel. (8) 8396342; fax (8) 8296856; producer of beer; Dir HOANG CHI QUY.

Seaco (Sundries Electric Appliances Co): 64 Pho Duc Chinh, District 1, Ho Chi Minh City; tel. (8) 8210961; fax (8) 8210974; deals in miscellaneous electrical goods; Dir MAI MINH CUONG.

Seaprodex Hanoi (Hanoi Sea Products Export-Import Co): 20 Lang Ha, Hanoi; tel. (4) 8344437; fax (4) 8354125; e-mail seaprodexhn@hn.vnn.vn; Dir DANG DINH BAO.

Seaprodex Saigon (Ho Chi Minh City Sea Products Import-Export Corpn): 87 Ham Nghi, District 1, Ho Chi Minh City; tel. (8) 8293669; fax (8) 8224951; e-mail seasaigon@hcm.vnn.vn; internet www.seaprodexsg.com; f. 1978; exports frozen and processed sea products; imports machinery and materials for fishing and processing; Gen. Dir PHUNG QUOC MAN.

SJC (Saigon Jewellery Co): 115 Nguyen Cong Tru, District 1, Ho Chi Minh City; tel. (8) 9144056; fax (8) 9144057; e-mail sjc@hcm.vnn.vn; internet www.sjcvn.com; f. 1998; manufacturing, processing and trading of gold, gemstones, silver and jewellery; Man. Dir NGUYEN THANH LONG.

Technimex (Viet Nam Technology Export-Import Corpn): 70 Tran Hung Dao, Hanoi; tel. (4) 8256751; fax (4) 8220377; e-mail technimex@hn.vnn.vn; internet www.technimex.vn.com; f. 1982; exports and imports machines, equipment, instruments, etc.; Dir NGUYEN HUY BINH.

Technoimport (Viet Nam National Complete Equipment and Technics Import-Export Corpn): 16–18 Trang Thi, Hanoi; tel. (4) 8254974; fax (4) 8254059; e-mail technohn@netnam.vn; internet www.technoimport.com.vn; f. 1959; imports and exports equipment, machinery, transport equipment, spare parts, materials and various consumer commodities; exports products by co-investment and jt-venture enterprises; provides consulting services for trade and investment, transport and forwarding services; acts as import-export brokering and trading agents; Gen. Dir VU CHU HIEN.

Terraprodex (Corpn for Processing and Export-Import of Rare Earth and Other Specialities): 35 Dien Bien Phu, Hanoi; tel. (4) 8232010; fax (4) 8256446; f. 1989; processing and export of rare earth products and other minerals; Dir TRAN DUC HIEP.

Tocontap Saigon (Viet Nam National Sundries Import-Export Co): 35 Le Quy Don, District 3, Ho Chi Minh City; tel. (8) 9325687; fax (8) 9325963; e-mail tocontapsaigon@hcm.vnn.vn; internet www.tocontapsaigon.com; f. 1956; imports and exports apparel, agricultural products, art and handicrafts and sundries; Gen. Dir LE THI THANH HUONG.

Vama (Viet Nam Automobile Manufacturers' Association): 9 Dao Duy Anh St, Dong Da District, Hanoi; tel. (4) 5741785; fax (4) 5741778; Chair. and Pres. MAKOTO SASAGAWA.

Vasep (Viet Nam Asscn of Seafood Exporters and Producers): 10–1 Nguyen Cong Hoan, Ba Dinh District, Hanoi; tel. (4) 7715055; fax (4) 7715084; e-mail vasep@hn.vnn.vn; internet www.vasep.com.vn; f. 1998; exports seafood products; provides essential market information to Viet Nam's seafood industry; organizes and implements activities designed to develop and promote the industry; Chair. Dr HO QUOC LUC.

Vegetexco (Viet Nam National Vegetables and Fruit Export-Import Corpn): 2 Pham Ngoc Thach, Dong Da District, Hanoi; tel. (4) 5740779; fax (4) 8523926; e-mail vegetexcovn@fpt.vn; internet vegetexcovn.tripod.com; f. 1971; exports fresh and processed vegetables and fruit, spices and flowers, and other agricultural products; imports vegetable seeds and processing materials; Gen. Dir LE VAN ANH.

Vietrans (Viet Nam National Foreign Trade Forwarding and Warehousing Corpn): 13 Ly Nam De, Hoan Kiem District, Hanoi; tel. (4) 7333258; fax (4) 8455829; e-mail vietrans@hn.vnn.vn; internet www.vietrans.com.vn; f. 1970; agent for forwarding and transport of exports and imports, diplomatic cargoes and other goods, warehousing, shipping and insurance; Gen. Dir THAI DUY LONG.

Vietranscimex (Viet Nam Transportation and Communication Import-Export Co): 22 Nguyen Van Troi, Phu Nhuan District, Ho Chi Minh City; tel. (8) 8442993; fax (8) 8445240; exports and imports specialized equipment and materials for transportation and communication; Gen. Dir PHAM QUANG VINH.

Viettronimex (Viet Nam Electronics Import-Export Corpn): 74–76 Nguyen Hue, District 1, Ho Chi Minh City; tel. (8) 8298201; fax (8)

VIET NAM
Directory

8294873; e-mail vtr@hcm.vnn.vn; f. 1981; imports and exports electronic goods; Dir NGUYEN HUU THINH.

Vigecam (Viet Nam General Corpn of Agricultural Materials): 16 Ngo Tat To, Dong Da District, Hanoi; tel. (4) 8231972; fax (4) 7474647; exports and imports agricultural products; Gen. Dir TRAN VAN KANH.

Viglacera (Viet Nam Glass and Ceramics Corpn): 628 Hoang Hoa Tham, Ba Dinh District, Hanoi; tel. (4) 8326982; fax (4) 7613292; e-mail support@vinad.com; internet www.viglacera.com.vn; f. 1974; mfr of building materials; Gen. Dir NGUYEN TRAN NAM HUY.

Vimedimex II (Viet Nam National Medical Products Export-Import Corpn): 246 Cong Quynh, District 1, Ho Chi Minh City; tel. (8) 8398441; fax (8) 8325953; e-mail vietpharma@hcm.vnn.vn; internet www.vietpharm.com.vn; f. 1984; exports and imports medicinal and pharmaceutical materials and products, medical instruments; Gen. Dir NGUYEN TIEN HUNG.

Vimico (Viet Nam Minerals Corpn): 105 Nguyen Van Cu, Gia Lam District, Hanoi; tel. (8) 8770010; fax (8) 8770006; e-mail vimico@hn.vnn.vn; Chair. VU XUAN KHOAT; Gen. Dir NGO VAN TROI.

Vinacafe (Viet Nam National Coffee Import-Export Corpn): 5 Ong Ich Khiem, Ba Dinh District, Hanoi; tel. (4) 8235449; fax (4) 8456422; e-mail vinacafe@hn.vnn.vn; internet www.vinacafe.com.vn; f. 1995; exports coffee, and imports equipment and chemicals for coffee production; Pres. and CEO THAI DOAN LAI.

Vinachem (Viet Nam National Chemical Corpn): 1A Trang Tien, Hoan Kiem District, Hanoi; tel. (4) 8240551; fax (4) 8252995; e-mail vinachem@hn.vnn.vn; internet www.vinachem.com.vn; production, import and export of chemicals and fertilizers; Chair. DO QUANG CHIEU; Pres. and CEO DO DUY PHI.

Vinachimex (Viet Nam National Chemicals Import-Export Corpn): 4 Pham Ngu Lao, Hanoi; tel. (4) 8256377; fax (4) 8257727; f. 1969; exports and imports chemical products, minerals, rubber, fertilizers, machinery and spare parts; Dir NGUYEN VAN SON.

Vinafilm (Viet Nam Film Import, Export and Film Service Corpn): 73 Nguyen Trai, Dong Da District, Hanoi; tel. (4) 8244566; f. 1987; export and import of films and video tapes; film distribution; organization of film shows and participation of Vietnamese films in international film festivals; Gen. Man. NGO MANH LAN.

Vinafimex (Viet Nam National Agricultural Produce and Foodstuffs Import and Export Corpn): 58 Ly Thai To, Hanoi; tel. (4) 8255768; fax (4) 8255476; e-mail fime@hn.vnn.vn; f. 1984; exports cashews, peanuts, coffee, rubber and other agricultural products, and garments; imports malt, fertilizer, insecticide, seeds, machinery and equipment, etc.; Pres. NGUYEN TOAN THANG; Gen. Dir NGUYEN VAN THANG.

Vinafood Hanoi (Hanoi Food Import-Export Co): 6 Ngo Quyen, Hoan Kiem District, Hanoi; tel. (4) 8256771; fax (4) 8258528; f. 1988; exports rice, maize, tapioca; imports fertilizers, insecticides, wheat and wheat flour; Dir NGUYEN DUC HY.

Vinalivesco (Vietnam National Livestock Corporation): 519 Minh Khai, Hanoi; tel. (4) 8626763; fax (4) 8623645; f. 1996; imports and exports animal and poultry products, animal feeds and other agro-products, and foodstuffs; Gen. Dir NGUYEN VAN KHAC.

Vinamilk (Viet Nam Milk Co): 184–8 Nguyen Dinh Chieu, Ward 6, District 3, Ho Chi Minh City; tel. (8) 9304860; fax (8) 9304880; e-mail vinamilk@vinamilk.com.vn; internet www.vinamilk.com.vn; f. 1976; producer of dairy products; Dir MAI TRIUE LIEN.

Vinapimex (Viet Nam Paper Corpn): 25A Ly Thuong Kiet, Hanoi; tel. (4) 8260143; fax (4) 8260381; f. 1995; production and marketing of paper; Gen. Dir NGUYEN NGOC MINH.

Vinaplast (Viet Nam Plastics Corpn): 92–94 Ly Tu Trong, District 1, Ho Chi Minh City; tel. (8) 8238011; fax (8) 8237956; e-mail vnplast@hcm.vnn.vn; internet www.vinaplast.com.vn; f. 1976; import and export of products for plastic processing industry; production and trade of plastic products; Gen. Dir NGUYEN KHAC LONG.

Vinasteel (Viet Nam National Steel Corpn): D2 Ton That Tung, Dong Da District, Hanoi; tel. (4) 8525537; fax (4) 8262657; distributor of metal products; Dir NGO HUY PHAN.

Vinataba (Viet Nam National Tobacco Corpn): 25A Ly Thuong Kiet, Hoan Kiem District, Hanoi; tel. (4) 8265778; fax (4) 8265777; internet www.vinataba.com.vn; mfr of tobacco products; Chair. NGUYEN THAI SINH; Dir NGUYEN NAM HAI.

Vinatea (Viet Nam National Tea Development Investment and Export-Import Co): 46 Tang Bat Ho, Hanoi; tel. (4) 8212005; fax (4) 8212663; e-mail info@vinatea.com.vn; internet www.vinatea.com.vn; exports tea, imports tea-processing materials; Gen. Dir NGUYEN THIEN TOAN.

Vinatex (Viet Nam National Textile and Garment Corpn): 25 Ba Trieu, Hoan Kiem District, Hanoi; tel. (4) 8257700; fax (4) 8262269; e-mail vinatexhn@vinatex.com.vn; internet www.vinatex.com; f. 1995; imports raw material, textile and sewing machinery, spare parts, accessories, dyestuffs; exports textiles, ready-made garments, carpets, jute, silk; Gen. Dir VU DUC THINH.

Vitas (Viet Nam Tea Association): 92 Vo Thu Sau, Hai Ba Trung District, Hanoi; tel. (4) 6250908; e-mail vitas@fpt.vn; internet www.vitas.org.vn/vitas_english; f. 1988; promotes the trading and marketing of tea products; offers advice and information, both to the Govt and to farmers, regarding development schemes and policies; Chair. and Pres. NGUYEN KIM PHONG.

VNCC (Viet Nam National Cement Corpn—Vinacement): 228 Le Duan, Dong Da District, Hanoi; tel. (4) 8510593; fax (4) 8512778; f. 1980; manufactures and exports cement and clinker; Gen. Dir NGUYEN VAN HANH.

Vocarimex (National Co for Vegetable Oils, Aromas, and Cosmetics of Viet Nam): 58 Nguyen Binh Khiem, District 1, Ho Chi Minh City; tel. (8) 8294513; fax (8) 8290586; e-mail vocar@hcm.vnn.vn; f. 1976; producing and trading vegetable oils, oil-based products and special industry machinery; packaging; operating port facilities; Gen. Dir DUONG THI NGOC TRINH.

Xunhasaba (Viet Nam State Corpn for Export and Import of Books, Periodicals and other Cultural Commodities): 32 Hai Ba Trung, Hanoi; tel. (4) 8262989; fax (4) 8252860; e-mail xunhasaba@hn.vnn.vn; internet www.xunhasaba.com.vn; f. 1957; exports and imports books, periodicals, postage stamps, greetings cards, calendars and paintings; Dir HA TRIEU KIEN.

UTILITIES

Electricity

Electricity of Viet Nam (EVN): produces, transmits and distributes electrical power; Pres. and CEO DAO VAN HUNG.

Power Co No 1 (PC1): 20 Tran Nguyen Han, Hoan Kiem, Hanoi; tel. (4) 8255074; fax (4) 8244033; e-mail anhdn@pc1.com.vn; manages the generation, transmission and distribution of electrical power in northern Viet Nam; Dir DO VAN LOC.

Power Co No 2 (PC2): 72 Hai Ba Trung, District 1, Ho Chi Minh City; tel. (8) 8231303; fax (8) 8299680; manages the distribution of electrical power in southern Viet Nam; Dir NGUYEN THANH DUY.

Power Co No 3 (PC3): 315 Trung Nu Vuong, Hai Chau District, Da Nang; tel. (511) 621028; fax (511) 625071; f. 1975; manages the generation, transmission and distribution of electrical power in central Viet Nam; Gen. Dir TA CANH.

Water

Hanoi Water Business Co: 44 Yen Phu, Hanoi; tel. (4) 8292478; fax (4) 8294069; f. 1954; responsible for the supply of water to Hanoi and its five urban and two suburban districts; Dir-Gen. BUI VAN MAT.

Ho Chi Minh City Water Supply Co: 1 Cong Truong Quoc Te, District 3, Ho Chi Minh City; tel. (8) 8291974; fax (8) 8241644; e-mail hcmcwater@hcm.vnn.vn; f. 1966; manages the water services and water construction works of Ho Chi Minh City; Gen. Dir VO DUNG.

CO-OPERATIVES

Viet Nam Co-operative Alliance (VCA): 77 Nguyen Thai Hoc, Ba Dinh, Hanoi; tel. (4) 8431689; fax (4) 8431883; e-mail vca@vietnamcoop.org; internet www.vietnamcoop.org; f. 1993; fmrly Viet Nam Co-operatives Council; Pres. Dr NGUYEN TIEN QUAN.

TRADE UNIONS

Tong Lien doan Lao dong Viet Nam (Viet Nam General Confederation of Labour): 82 Tran Hung Dao, POB 627, Hanoi; tel. (4) 9421794; fax (4) 9423781; e-mail doingoaitld@hn.vnn.vn; f. 1929; merged in 1976 with the South Viet Nam Trade Union Fed. for Liberation; 4,000,000 mems; Pres. CU THI HAU; Vice-Pres NGUYEN HOA BINH, DANG NGOC CHIEN, DO DUC NGO, NGUYEN DINH THANG.

Cong Doan Nong Nghiep Cong Nghiep Thu Pham Viet Nam (Viet Nam Agriculture and Food Industry Trade Union): Hanoi; f. 1987; 550,000 mems.

National Union of Building Workers: 12 Cua Dong, Hoan Kiem, Hanoi; tel. (4) 8253781; fax (4) 8281407; f. 1957; Pres. NGUYEN VIET HAI.

Vietnam National Union of Industrial Workers: 54 Hai Ba Trung, Hanoi; tel. (4) 9344426; fax (4) 8245306; f. 1997; Pres. VU TIEN SAU.

Vietnam National Union of Post and Telecoms Workers: 30 Hang Chuoi, Hai Ba Trung, Hanoi; tel. (4) 9713514; fax (4) 9720236; f. 1947; Chair. HOANG DUY CAN.

Transport

RAILWAYS

Duong Sat Viet Nam (DSVN) (Viet Nam Railways): 118 Le Duan, Hanoi; tel. (4) 8220537; fax (4) 9422866; e-mail dsvn@hn.vnn.vn; internet www.vr.com.vn; 2,600 km of main lines (1996); lines in operation are: Hanoi–Ho Chi Minh City (1,726 km), Hanoi–Haiphong (102 km), Hanoi–Dong Dang (167 km), Hanoi–Lao Cai (296 km), Hanoi–Thai Nguyen (75 km), Thai Nguyen–Kep–Bai Chay (106 km); Chair. PHAM VAN GIAN; Gen. Dir Dr NGUYEN HUU BANG.

ROADS

In 1999 there were an estimated 93,300 km of roads, of which 25.1% were paved. In 1995 the Government announced plans to upgrade 430 km of the national highway, which runs from Hanoi in the north to Ho Chi Minh City in the south. In 1997 the Government announced plans to build a new 1,880-km north–south highway in the east of the country. In 2001 the Government also announced plans to upgrade the section of the national highway that runs between the northern provinces of Hoa Binh and Son La.

SHIPPING

The principal port facilities are at Haiphong, Da Nang and Ho Chi Minh City. In 2004 the Vietnamese merchant fleet (797 vessels) had a combined displacement totalling 1,427,500 grt. In 1994 there were 150 shipping companies with a combined capacity of 800,000 dwt.

Cong Ty Van Tai Duong Bien Viet Nam (VOSCO) (Viet Nam Ocean Shipping Co): 215 Tran Quoc Toan, Ngo Quyen District, Haiphong; tel. (31) 846951; fax (31) 845107; controlled by the Viet Nam Gen. Dept of Marine Transport; Dir TRAN VAN LAM; Dir-Gen. TRAN XUAN NHON.

Dai Ly Hang Hai Viet Nam (VOSA) (VOSA group of companies): Unit 1003, 10th Floor, Harbour View Tower, 35 Nguyen Hue, District 1, Ho Chi Minh City; tel. (8) 9140422; fax (8) 8214919; e-mail vosagroup@hcm.vnn.vn; internet www.vosagroup.com; f. 1957; fmrly the Viet Nam Ocean Shipping Agency; controlled by the Viet Nam National Shipping Lines (VINALINES); in charge of merchant shipping; arranges ship repairs, salvage, passenger services, air and sea freight forwarding services; main br. offices in Haiphong and Ho Chi Minh City; brs in Hanoi, Da Nang, Ben Thuy, Qui Nhon, Quang Ninh, Nha Trang, Vung Tau and Can Tho; Dir-Gen. HA CAM KHAI (acting).

Transport and Chartering Corpn (Vietfracht): 74 Nguyen Du, Hai Ba Trung, Hanoi; tel. (4) 9422355; fax (4) 9423679; e-mail vfhan@hn.vnn.vn; internet www.vietfracht.com.vn; f. 1963; ship broking, chartering, ship management, shipping agency, international freight forwarding; logistic and consultancy services, import-export services; Chair. NGUYEN QUANG THOAI; CEO TRAN VAN QUY.

Viet Nam Sea Transport and Chartering Co (Vitranschart): 428–432 Nguyen Tat Thanh, District 4, Ho Chi Minh City; tel. (8) 9404027; fax (8) 9404711; e-mail vitrans@fmail.vnn.vn; Dir VO PHUNG LONG.

CIVIL AVIATION

Viet Nam's principal airports are Tan Son Nhat International Airport (Ho Chi Minh City) and Thu Do (Capital) International Airport at Noi Bai (Hanoi). They cater for both overseas and domestic traffic. Airports at Da Nang, Hué, Nha Trang, Da Lat, Can Tho, Haiphong, Muong Thanh (near Dien Bien Phu), Buon Ma Thuot and Lien Khuong handle domestic traffic. In 1997 it was announced that numerous abandoned wartime airstrips were to be repaired and returned to service under a programme scheduled for completion in 2010, by which time the Government also aims to expand the annual capacity of Tan Son Nhat to 30m. passengers and 1m. tons of freight. In January 2004 plans were announced for the construction of a new international airport at Long Thang, in Dong Nai province. The airport was to have four runways and four terminals, the first of which were scheduled to become operational in 2011. Five further airports to handle domestic traffic were opened in 2004, at Ca Mau, Can Tho, Con Son, Chu Lai and Nha Trang. In early 2006 there were 20 domestic airports in Viet Nam.

Viet Nam Airlines: Gialem Airport, Hanoi; tel. (4) 8731484; fax (4) 8272291; internet www.vietnamairlines.com; fmrly the Gen. Civil Aviation Admin. of Viet Nam, then Hang Khong Viet Nam; wholly state-owned; operates domestic passenger services from Hanoi and from Ho Chi Minh City to the principal Vietnamese cities, and international services to 18 countries; Pres. and CEO NGUYEN XUAN HIEN; Chair. NGUYEN SY HUNG.

Pacific Airlines: 112 Hong Ha, Tan Binh District, Ho Chi Minh City; tel. (8) 8450090; fax (8) 8450085; e-mail quang.dongoc@pacificairlines.com.vn; internet www.pacificairlines.com.vn; f. 1991; operates charter cargo flights, also scheduled passenger and cargo services to Taiwan and Hong Kong; Chair. TRAN HUU TIEN; Man. Dir LUONG HOAI NAM.

Tourism

In the 1990s the Vietnamese Government encouraged tourism as a source of much-needed foreign exchange, with the objective of attracting some 4m. tourists annually by the year 2005. About 3.5m. foreign tourists visited Viet Nam in 2005. In 2003 revenue from tourism totalled 6,016.6m. dông.

Viet Nam National Administration of Tourism (VNAT): 80 Quan Su, Hanoi; tel. (4) 9423998; fax (4) 9424115; e-mail titc@vietnamtourism-info.com; internet www.vietnamtourism.com; f. 1960; Gen. Dir NGO HUY PHUONG.

Hanoi Tourism Service Company (HANOI TOSERCO): 8 To Hien Thanh, Hanoi; tel. (4) 9780004; fax (4) 8226055; e-mail hanoitoserco@hn.vnn.vn; internet www.tosercohanoi.com; f. 1998; manages the development of tourism, hotels and restaurants in the capital and other services including staff training; Dir TRAN TIEN HUNG.

Tong Cong ty Du lich Saigon (Saigon Tourist Co): 23 Le Loi, District 1, Ho Chi Minh City; tel. (8) 8225887; fax (8) 8291026; e-mail saigontourist@sgtourist.com.vn; internet www.saigon-tourist.com; f. 1975; holding co controlling 11 tour operators, 56 hotels, 10 resorts and 24 restaurants; Gen. Dir NGUYEN HUU THO.

Unitour (Union of Haiphong Tourist Co): 40 Tran Quang Khai, Haiphong; tel. (31) 8247295.

Viet Nam Tourism in Haiphong: 60A Dien Bien Phu, Haiphong; tel. and fax (31) 823651; f. 1960; hotel services, travel arrangements, visa service; Gen. Dir NGUYEN HUU BONG.

YEMEN

Introductory Survey

Location, Climate, Language, Religion, Flag, Capital

The Republic of Yemen is situated in the south of the Arabian peninsula, bounded to the north by Saudi Arabia, to the east by Oman, to the south by the Gulf of Aden, and to the west by the Red Sea. The islands of Perim and Kamaran at the southern end of the Red Sea, the island of Socotra, at the entrance to the Gulf of Aden, and the Kuria Muria islands, near the coast of Oman, are also part of the Republic. The climate in the semi-desert coastal strip is hot, with high humidity and temperatures rising to more than 38°C (100°F); inland, the climate is somewhat milder, with cool winters and relatively heavy rainfall in the highlands. The eastern plateau slopes into desert. The language is Arabic. The population is almost entirely Muslim, and mainly of the Sunni Shafi'a sect. The national flag (proportions 2 by 3) has three equal horizontal stripes, of red, white and black. The capital is San'a.

Recent History

The Republic of Yemen was formed in May 1990 by the amalgamation of the Yemen Arab Republic (YAR) and the People's Democratic Republic of Yemen (PDRY). The YAR (from 1967 also known as North Yemen) had formerly been a kingdom. When Turkey's Ottoman Empire was dissolved in 1918, the Imam Yahya, leader of the Zaidi community, was left in control. In 1948 Yahya was assassinated in a palace coup, when power was seized by forces opposed to his feudal rule. However, Yahya's son, Ahmad, defeated the rebel forces to become Imam. In 1958 Yemen and the United Arab Republic (Egypt and Syria) formed a federation called the United Arab States, though this was dissolved in 1961. The Imam Ahmad died in September 1962 and was succeeded by his son, Muhammad. Less than a week later, army officers, led by Col (later Marshal) Abdullah as-Sallal, removed the Imam and proclaimed the YAR. Civil war ensued between royalist forces, supported by Saudi Arabia, and republicans, aided by Egyptian troops. The republicans prevailed and Egyptian forces withdrew in 1967. In November President Sallal was deposed by a Republican Council.

The People's Republic of Southern Yemen, comprising Aden and the former Protectorate of South Arabia, was formed on 30 November 1967. Aden had been under British rule since 1839 and the Protectorate was developed by a series of treaties between the United Kingdom and local leaders. Prior to the British withdrawal, two rival factions, the National Liberation Front (NLF) and the Front for the Liberation of Occupied South Yemen, fought for control. The Marxist NLF eventually prevailed and assumed power as the National Front (NF). The country's first President, Qahtan ash-Sha'abi, was forced out of office in June 1969, when a Presidential Council, led by Salem Rubayi Ali, took power. Muhammad Ali Haitham became Prime Minister. In November 1970, on the third anniversary of independence, the country was renamed the PDRY. In May 1971 a provisional Supreme People's Council (SPC) was established as the national legislature. In August Haitham was replaced as Prime Minister by Ali Nasser Muhammad. Following the introduction of repressive measures against dissidents by the Government after independence, more than 300,000 Southern Yemenis fled to the YAR. Backed by Saudi Arabia and Libya, many of the refugees joined mercenary organizations, aimed at the overthrow of the Marxist regime in Southern Yemen, and conducted cross-border raids.

Intermittent fighting, beginning in early 1971, flared into open warfare between the two Yemens in October 1972, with the YAR receiving aid from Saudi Arabia and the PDRY being supplied with Soviet arms. A cease-fire was arranged in the same month, under the auspices of the League of Arab States (Arab League, see p. 306), and soon afterwards both sides agreed to the union of the two Yemens within 18 months. The union was not, however, implemented.

On 13 June 1974 a 10-member Military Command Council (MCC) seized power in the YAR, under the leadership of the pro-Saudi Lt-Col Ibrahim al-Hamadi. Mohsin al-Aini was appointed Prime Minister, but was replaced by Abd al-Aziz Abd al-Ghani in January 1975. An unsuccessful pro-royalist coup was reported in August. Al-Hamadi subsequently attempted to reduce the influence of the USSR, and endeavoured to re-equip the army with US weapons, making use of financial assistance from Saudi Arabia. In October 1977, however, al-Hamadi was killed by unknown assassins in San'a. Another member of the MCC, Lt-Col Ahmad bin Hussain al-Ghashmi, took over as Chairman, and martial law was imposed. In February 1978 the MCC appointed a Constituent People's Assembly, and in April the Assembly elected al-Ghashmi President of the Republic. The MCC was then dissolved.

In June 1978 the proposed union of the two Yemens was seriously hampered when President al-Ghashmi of the YAR was assassinated by a bomb carried in the suitcase of a PDRY envoy. In the following month the Constituent People's Assembly elected a senior military officer, Lt-Col (later Gen., and subsequently Field Marshal) Ali Abdullah Saleh, as President of the YAR. During recriminations that followed the assassination, President Rubayi Ali of the PDRY was deposed and executed by opponents within the ruling party, which had been known as the United Political Organization—National Front (UPO—NF), since its merger with two smaller parties in October 1975. The Prime Minister, Ali Nasser Muhammad, became interim Head of State. Two days after the overthrow of Rubayi Ali, it was announced that the UPO—NF had agreed to form a Marxist-Leninist 'vanguard' party. At the constituent congress of this Yemen Socialist Party (YSP), held in October 1978, Abd al-Fattah Ismail, who favoured uncompromising Marxist policies, became Secretary-General. A new SPC was elected in December and appointed Ismail to be Head of State. In April 1980 Ali Nasser Muhammad replaced Ismail as Head of State, Chairman of the Presidium of the SPC and Secretary-General of the YSP, while retaining the post of Prime Minister; his posts were confirmed at an extraordinary congress of the YSP in October.

Renewed fighting broke out between the YAR and the PDRY in February and March 1979, when the National Democratic Front (NDF), an alliance of disaffected YAR politicians, won the support of the PDRY and began a revolt. Later in the same month, however, at a meeting between the North and South Yemeni Heads of State in Kuwait, arranged by the Arab League, an agreement was signed pledging unification of the two states. Following a series of meetings, in December 1981 the two sides signed a draft Constitution for a unified state and established a joint YAR/PDRY Yemen Council to monitor progress towards unification. NDF forces rebelled again in 1982, but they were defeated and forced over the border into the PDRY.

Abd al-Aziz Abd al-Ghani was replaced as Prime Minister of the YAR in October 1980, but was reappointed in November 1983. Meanwhile, in May 1983 President Saleh submitted his resignation at an extraordinary meeting of the Constituent People's Assembly, declaring his intention to nominate himself for a presidential election. His five-year term of office was due to end in July. However, he was nominated and unanimously re-elected by the Assembly for a further five-year term. Elections to the Assembly itself, scheduled for early 1983, were postponed.

In the PDRY, President Muhammad relinquished the post of Prime Minister in February 1985, nominating the Minister of Construction, Haidar Abu Bakr al-Attas, as his successor (while retaining his other senior posts). The former President, Abd al-Fattah Ismail, returned from exile in the USSR in the same month, and was reappointed to the Secretariat of the YSP's Central Committee. At the party's third General Congress, in October, President Muhammad was re-elected to the posts of Secretary-General of the YSP and of its Political Bureau for a further five years. However, his control over the party was weakened by the enlargement of the Political Bureau from 13 members to 16 (including his rival, Ismail), and by an increase in membership of the Central Committee from 47 to 77, to incorporate a number of his critics.

On 13 January 1986 President Muhammad attempted to eliminate his opponents in the Political Bureau: his personal guard opened fire on six members who had assembled for a meeting with the President. Three were killed, and three escaped, including Ismail (who was, however, officially declared to have been killed in subsequent fighting). Muhammad was reported to have left Aden for his tribal stronghold in Abyan province, to the east of the city. In Aden itself, rival elements of the armed forces fought for control, causing widespread destruction, and the conflict quickly spread to the rest of the country, despite diplomatic efforts by the USSR. Apparently prompted by reports of massacres by President Muhammad's supporters, the army intervened decisively, turning back pro-Muhammad tribesmen from Abyan who were advancing on Aden. On 24 January al-Attas, the Prime Minister, who had been abroad when the troubles began, was named by the YSP Central Committee as head of an interim administration in Aden, and Muhammad was stripped of all his party and state posts; he reportedly fled to Ethiopia. An estimated 5,000 people died in the conflict. A new Government of the PDRY was formed in February. Al-Attas was confirmed as President, Chairman of the Presidium of the SPC and Secretary-General of the YSP Political Bureau. The former Deputy Prime Minister and Minister of Fisheries, Dr Yasin Said Numan, was named as Prime Minister. The new Council of Ministers contained only three members of the previous Government. In March a general amnesty was proclaimed, inviting supporters of Muhammad to return from the YAR, where some 10,000 of them had sought refuge. In October a general election took place for a 111-member SPC. Al-Attas was unanimously elected Chairman of the YSP. In December the Supreme Court sentenced Muhammad to death, *in absentia*, for treason; 34 other men received the same sentence, although it was only carried out in five cases.

In July 1988 the first general election took place in the YAR for 128 seats in the new 159-member Consultative Council, which replaced the non-elected Constituent People's Assembly. The remaining 31 seats were filled by presidential decree. Over 1m. people registered to vote and more than 1,200 candidates contested the poll. Approximately 25% of the elective seats were won by candidates sympathetic to the Muslim Brotherhood, a militant Islamist organization. Later in the month President Saleh was re-elected by the Consultative Council for a third five-year term, winning 96% of the votes, while the Vice-President, Abd al-Karim al-Arashi, was elected as Speaker of the Consultative Council. Al-Ghani was subsequently reappointed Prime Minister by President Saleh, and a new Council of Ministers was announced.

The first session of the joint YAR/PDRY Yemen Council (which had been established in 1981) was held in San'a in August 1983 and discussed the state of progress towards unification. These sessions were scheduled to take place every six months and to alternate between San'a and Aden. A joint committee on foreign policy met for the first time in March 1984 in Aden. In July 1986 Presidents Saleh of the YAR and al-Attas of the PDRY met for the first time in Libya to discuss unification. In early 1987 Kuwait acted as a mediator between the two Yemens in an effort to solve the problem of the thousands of refugees from the PDRY who had recently sought refuge in the north. In July it was reported that more than 50% of these refugees had returned to the PDRY.

In May 1988 the Governments of the YAR and the PDRY agreed to withdraw troops from their mutual border and to create a demilitarized zone, covering an area of 2,200 sq km, between Marib and Shabwah, where they intended to carry out joint projects involving exploration for petroleum. The movement of citizens between the two states was also to be facilitated. In July a programme of wide-ranging political and economic reforms was introduced in the PDRY, indicating the country's intention to create a free-market economy. In November President Saleh and the Secretary-General of the Central Committee of the YSP, Ali Salim al-Baid, signed an agreement to unify the two states. On 1 December a draft Constitution for the unified state was published: it was to be ratified by both countries within six months, and was subsequently to be approved by a referendum. At the end of December the Governments of the YAR and the PDRY agreed to release all political prisoners in their respective countries.

The first joint meeting of the two Councils of Ministers was held in San'a in January 1990 and resulted in restrictions on travel between the two countries being rescinded. In February President Saleh held talks with King Fahd of Saudi Arabia, who pledged his official support for the unification of the YAR and the PDRY. The growing atmosphere of democracy in the PDRY gave a large section of the work-force the confidence to stage an unprecedented series of strikes, which led to the granting by the Government of significant wage increases.

Opposition to unification developed in the YAR in early 1990. The Muslim Brotherhood, which believed that *Shari'a* (Islamic) law should be enshrined in the Constitution of the unified state (as in the YAR Constitution), condemned the draft Constitution, which was based principally, but not solely, on *Shari'a* law, and advocated a boycott of the referendum on the Constitution. In the PDRY, meanwhile, there were demonstrations by women, who feared that the increasing influence of Islamic militancy might jeopardize their freedom, and demanded that their existing rights in the secular Republic be guaranteed in the new Constitution.

In May 1990 the armed forces of the YAR and the PDRY were declared to be technically dissolved, prior to their unification, and it was announced that they were to be withdrawn from their respective capitals to designated military zones. In the same month a draft law embodying the freedom of the press was signed. The unification of the YAR and the PDRY was proclaimed on 22 May, six months ahead of the agreed deadline, apparently in order to counter the threat to the unification process posed by disruption in the north of the YAR. The unification agreement had been ratified on the previous day by both countries' legislatures. The new country was to be known as the Republic of Yemen, with San'a as its political capital and Aden its economic and commercial centre. President Saleh of the YAR became President of the new state, while al-Baid was elected Vice-President. The President of the PDRY, al-Attas, became Prime Minister, leading a transitional coalition Council of Ministers with 39 members, of whom 20 were from the YAR (members of the General People's Congress—GPC—a broad grouping of supporters of President Saleh) and 19 from the PDRY (all members of the YSP, under the continued leadership of al-Baid). A five-member Presidential Council (chaired by Saleh) was formed, together with a 45-member advisory council. The two legislatures were amalgamated to form the House of Representatives, pending elections to be held after a 30-month transitional period; an additional 31 members, including opponents of the YAR and PDRY governments, were nominated by President Saleh. In September it was reported that more than 30 new political parties had been formed since unification. The Yemeni Islah Party (YIP), an Islamic grouping with considerable support in the House of Representatives, was regarded as the most influential of the new parties.

In mid-May 1991 the people of Yemen voted in a referendum on the Constitution for the unified state. A few days earlier, religious fundamentalists and sympathizers, including YIP members, urged a boycott of the referendum, owing to the role of Islam under the proposed Constitution. Those who participated in the referendum approved the new Constitution by a large majority, although less than 50% of the electorate registered to vote. Members of the YIP and other opposition groups claimed that irregularities in the voting procedure had invalidated the result.

During late 1991 and early 1992 the deteriorating economic situation prompted domestic unrest. A shooting incident in San'a in October 1991 led to two days of rioting, in which nine people were believed to have died. In March 1992 workers in some parts of the country held a one-day strike, in support of demands for salary increases and the establishment of a job-creation programme for the estimated 850,000 returnees from Saudi Arabia (see below). In December riots in San'a, Taiz and Hodeida, apparently caused by a sharp rise in consumer prices, spread rapidly to Aden and other towns. It was officially reported that 15 people had been killed in the disturbances, and 661 arrested; opposition sources, however, estimated significantly higher figures.

In spite of the unrest, voter registration for the legislative elections, scheduled for 27 April 1993, took place during January and February. An estimated 4,730 candidates were to contest the 301 elective seats in the House of Representatives, of whom approximately 30% were affiliated to political parties. International observers were largely satisfied with the conduct of the elections, although there were reports of disturbances in several towns, and some complaints of irregularities. The GPC secured 123 of the 300 seats for which results were announced. The YIP won 62 seats, and the YSP 56, with independents securing 47 of the remaining seats. In May the two former ruling parties, the GPC and YSP, agreed to merge, thereby creating a single political group with an overall majority in the new House of Representatives. The subsequent election of the YIP's leader, Sheikh Abdullah bin Hussain al-Ahmar, as Speaker of the House was regarded as a concession to his party, whose influence had been weakened by the merger. At the end of the month, however, a 31-member coalition Government was announced, including representatives of all three leading parties. Al-Attas was reappointed Prime Minister.

In August 1993 the YSP leader, al-Baid, ceased to participate in the political process and withdrew from San'a to Aden. This followed a visit to the USA, apparently without the approval of President Saleh, for talks with the US Vice-President, Al Gore. Al-Baid claimed that Saleh had made no attempt to halt the numerous armed attacks by northern officials on southerners, and claimed that as many as 150 YSP members had been assassinated since unification. He also protested at what he perceived to be the increasing marginalization of the south, particularly with regard to the distribution of petroleum revenues. In October the House of Representatives elected a new five-member Presidential Council, and later in the month the Council, in the absence of al-Baid, re-elected Saleh as its Chairman, and, accordingly, as President of the Republic of Yemen, for a further four-year term. Al-Baid was unanimously re-elected as Vice-President, but was not sworn in.

The political deadlock persisted into November 1993, in spite of international mediation efforts. Reports emerged that the armed forces of the former YAR and the PDRY (which had failed to integrate since unification) were being deployed along the former frontier. In December, as a result of Jordanian mediation, GPC and YSP officials commenced negotiations with the aim of resolving the political crisis. In September al-Baid, who remained in Aden, had submitted an 18-point programme of conditions for his return to San'a. Although President Saleh accepted the programme in December, there was no indication of any improvement in the political situation. In January 1994 representatives of the main political parties signed a 'Document of Pledge and Agreement' designed to resolve the crisis. In February President Saleh and Vice-President al-Baid signed the document in Amman, Jordan. The agreement contained certain security guarantees, as well as providing for a degree of decentralization, and for a review of the Constitution and of the country's economic policies. Nevertheless, both leaders remained active in mustering support for their positions throughout the region. At the same time there were reports of clashes between rival army units.

In March 1994 Saleh and al-Baid held talks in Oman, but at the end of the month al-Baid, together with Salim Salih Muhammad, refused to attend a meeting of the Presidential Council, which he had boycotted since August 1993. In the last week of March 1994 two meetings of the Council of Ministers were held in Aden in an attempt to agree preliminary measures to implement the conciliation agreement. At the end of April the First Deputy Prime Minister, Hassan Muhammad Makki, was wounded during an assassination attempt in San'a. A series of pitched battles followed between battalions stationed in the territory of their former neighbour. On 5 May President Saleh declared a 30-day state of emergency, and dismissed al-Baid from his position as Vice-President, together with four other southern members of the Government, including Salim Muhammad. On the same day missile attacks were launched against economic and military targets, including San'a, Aden and other main airports. On 9 May Saleh announced that al-Attas had been replaced as Prime Minister by the Minister of Industry, Muhammad Said al-Attar, and that the Minister of Petroleum and Minerals had also been replaced. By this time fighting had become concentrated around Aden, and along the former north–south frontier. Several thousand southern reservists were mobilized, as the forces of the former YAR attempted to isolate and capture Aden. Meanwhile, President Saleh rejected appeals for a negotiated settlement to the civil war, and demanded that al-Baid surrender.

On 21 May 1994, the fourth anniversary of the unification of Yemen, al-Baid, in a televised address, declared the independence of a new Democratic Republic of Yemen (DRY), with Aden as its capital. He also announced the formation of a Presidential Council, with himself as President and Abd ar-Rahman al-Jifri, the leader of the League of the Sons of Yemen (LSY), as Vice-President. The composition of the Council reflected al-Baid's need to achieve a consensus of the different political and tribal groups of the former PDRY in opposition to the forces of President Saleh. Saleh himself immediately denounced the secession as illegitimate, and offered an amnesty to all in the PDRY who rejected it, with the exception of 16 YSP leaders (including al-Baid).

At the end of May 1994, with the northern army attacking Aden on three fronts to the north and east of the city, the UN Security Council met, at the instigation of Egypt and five of the Gulf states, to discuss the conflict. Resolution 924 was subsequently adopted, demanding a cease-fire and the resumption of dialogue in Yemen, and ordering the dispatch of a UN commission of inquiry to the region. Although welcomed by the authorities in Aden, the resolution was initially rejected by the Government in San'a, which urged the Arab League to support the unity of Yemen. Subsequently, however, the San'a Government declared itself positively disposed towards the resolution.

On 1 June 1994 the House of Representatives voted to extend the state of emergency for a further 30 days. On the following day al-Baid announced the composition of a DRY Government, in which al-Attas was to be Prime Minister and Minister of Finance. Although most of the ministers were from the YSP, the Government contained a range of religious, political and tribal representatives. As northern forces made further territorial gains around Aden, it was reported that al-Baid had transferred his centre of operations to Mukalla, east of Aden. Military pressure on Aden was maintained for the remainder of June, and on 7 July the town came under the control of Saleh's troops. Many of the southern secessionist leaders fled to neighbouring Arab states, and it was officially announced that the civil war had ended. Al-Baid was believed to have requested political asylum in Oman. In March 1998 al-Baid, together with al-Attas and three other rebel leaders, were sentenced to death *in absentia*.

According to official sources, 931 civilians and soldiers were killed, and 5,000 wounded, in the civil war, although this was generally regarded as a conservative estimate. President Saleh immediately undertook measures to consolidate his position and bring stability to the country, ending the state of emergency and reiterating the general amnesty; by August 1994, when the amnesty expired, more than 5,000 Yemenis had returned to the country. In the same month, in an attempt to undermine the strength of southern military units loyal to the YSP, President Saleh announced that party membership would no longer be permitted within the armed forces. In September, moreover, Saleh introduced amendments to the Constitution intended to strengthen his position further: the Presidential Council was abolished, and in future the President would be elected by universal suffrage. *Shari'a* would also serve as the basis of all legislation. On 1 October Saleh was re-elected President; he appointed Abd ar-Rabbur Mansur Hadi as his deputy, and Abd al-Aziz Abd al-Ghani (hitherto a member of the Presidential Council) as Prime Minister. In the new Council of Ministers, announced on 6 October, members of the GPC retained the key portfolios, the YSP was denied representation, and the YIP was rewarded for its allegiance during the civil war by the allocation of nine ministerial posts. In a reorganization of the Council of Ministers in June 1995, the GPC increased its share of portfolios at the expense of independents, leading to a Government composed entirely of GPC and YIP members. Also in June President Saleh was re-elected Chairman of the GPC at the party's first general assembly since 1988.

In July 1994 UN-sponsored negotiations between the Yemeni leadership and the secessionists proved inconclusive. President Saleh announced that any further discussions would have to be conducted in Yemen, effectively terminating dialogue, as the YSP leaders remained in exile. In August a faction of the YSP in Yemen declared itself the new party leadership, and selected a new leader and Political Bureau. In October, nevertheless, exiled leaders of the YSP announced the formation of a coalition, the National Opposition Front, which included former Prime Minister al-Attas and Abd ar-Rahman al-Jifri, leader of the LSY. The role of the YSP in Yemeni politics diminished considerably after the civil war, as it was deprived of military power, experienced leadership in the country, and its role in government. In February 1995 another opposition grouping, the Democratic Coalition of Opposition, was formed, embracing 13 political parties and organizations, including a faction of the YSP and the LSY.

The economic repercussions of the civil war on the population were significant, particularly in the south. During March and April 1994, following the devaluation of the riyal and the doubling of the price of fuel, demonstrators clashed with police in Aden, San'a and Dhamar, resulting in three deaths and more than 50 arrests. The activities of militant Islamists, meanwhile, posed an additional threat to internal stability. In September hundreds demonstrated in Abyan province to protest at water and electricity shortages and against an increase in the price of basic foodstuffs, while some 20 people were reportedly killed in clashes with the security forces there, following the destruction of three Muslim saints' shrines by Islamists who deemed them idolatrous. In September 1995 security forces arrested six alleged members of the Islamic Jihad group for their apparent involvement in acts of terrorism in Aden.

Tensions between the YIP and the GPC became increasingly evident during 1995. The YIP expressed its opposition to economic reforms recommended by the World Bank, and criticized the GPC for attending an economic summit meeting in Jordan, in October, at which Israeli officials were present. Moreover, in December the YIP Minister of Trade and Supply, Muhammad Ahmad Afandi, resigned from his post, citing political and economic differences with the GPC.

In June 1996 it was reported that the Government was considering a redefinition of the boundaries of several governorates in the former border region, prior to forthcoming parliamentary elections, in order to discourage further factionalism in the area. In December YIP deputies withdrew from parliamentary sessions dedicated to the endorsement of the 1997 budget, citing insufficient opportunity to discuss adequately the provisions of the budget prior to their passage to the House of Representatives for approval. Furthermore, 53 of the YIP's 62 parliamentary deputies boycotted the House of Representatives on 1 January 1997, when the budget was formally approved. There was speculation that the deputies had adopted this confrontational stance as a result of government proposals to merge future budget allocations for religious schools (previously administered by YIP members) with those for general expenditure on education. In April four cabinet ministers tendered their resignation in order to seek election at the forthcoming poll.

The results of elections, conducted on 27 April 1997, demonstrated a decisive victory for the GPC, which increased its parliamentary representation from 123 to 187 seats. The YIP secured 53 seats (compared with 62 seats in 1993), and independent candidates won 54 seats. The remaining seats were shared between Nasserite and Baathist parties. The GPC's position was further consolidated by the stated intention of 39 newly elected independent deputies to demonstrate parliamentary allegiance to the GPC.

Prime Minister al-Ghani presented his own resignation, and that of the Council of Ministers, to President Saleh on 12 May 1997. Two days later Faraj Said bin Ghanim, a political independent, was appointed Prime Minister and entrusted with the formation of a new Council of Ministers. All but four members of the new Cabinet, announced the following day, were drawn from the GPC. At the end of April 1998 bin Ghanim resigned; the Deputy Prime Minister and Minister of Foreign Affairs, Abd al-Karim al-Iryani, was appointed Prime Minister, and he announced his new Government in May. A substantial increase in the price of petrol and basic foodstuffs in June led to public demonstrations in which more than 50 people died. Further unrest was reported during 1998 and, in September, a series of explosions in Yemen was attributed by the Government to 'foreign elements'.

The suppression of lawlessness, which had been exacerbated by the widespread ownership of weapons dating from the period of internal unrest, was a persistent domestic problem in the late 1990s. A number of armed kidnappings, frequently of tourist visitors, attracted international attention during 1997 and 1998, and in December 1998 16 foreign tourists were taken hostage; four were later killed during an attempt to release them. Yemen was criticized for failing to warn foreign embassies of an increased terrorist threat to tourists and for its precipitate use of force to free the hostages. The trial of the kidnappers, who belonged to the Islamic Aden-Abyan Army, a small extremist Islamist movement, began in late January 1999. By the end of January 10 men, eight with British citizenship and two Algerians, had been arrested on suspicion of plotting terrorist attacks on British targets in Aden; they were also reported to have links to the Islamic Aden-Abyan Army. At their trial all denied the charges, claiming that their earlier confessions had been obtained under duress and that they had been tortured. Despite having no extradition treaty with the United Kingdom, Yemen also requested the extradition from that country of a prominent Muslim cleric, a relative of two of the defendants, who they claimed had funded and masterminded a series of terrorist incidents in Yemen, including the kidnapping of the tourists in December 1998. Relations with the United Kingdom had deteriorated as a result both of Yemeni actions to end the hostage situation (three of the tourists who died were British) and of Yemeni accusations of British support for international terrorism, which were vehemently denied. The lawyer representing the defendants was himself arrested in February 1999, shortly before he was due to publicize allegations of torture against them; he was subsequently expelled from the country. In May three of the kidnappers were sentenced to death, a fourth defendant received a 20-year prison sentence and the remainder were acquitted. Two of the death sentences were eventually commuted to life imprisonment and in October the leader of the Islamic Aden-Abyan Army, Ziene al-Abidine al-Mihdar, was executed. His was the first execution under legislation, enacted in August 1998, providing for the use of capital punishment in kidnapping cases. In August 1999 verdicts were delivered in the trial of the 10 men on terrorist charges. All 10 were found guilty of the charges; three of the Britons were sentenced to the time they had already served (and were released in September) and the remaining seven defendants were sentenced to between three and seven years' imprisonment. (In October 2002 the Islamic Aben-Abayan Army, using a small boat packed with explosives, attacked a French supertanker, the *Limburg*, transporting crude petroleum off the coast of Yemen. A spokesman for the group declared the attack, which killed a crew member and badly damaged the vessel, to be revenge for the execution of al-Mihdar.)

On 23 September 1999 the first direct presidential elections were held in Yemen. The incumbent President, Field Marshal Ali Abdullah Saleh, was re-elected, gaining 96.3% of the votes; his only opponent, Najib Qahtan ash-Sha'bi, a member of the GPC who stood as an independent, gained 3.7% of the votes. The elections, which were boycotted by the YSP, were criticized for their lack of a credible candidate to oppose President Saleh.

Some internal instability was reported in 1999, with a number of bomb explosions in San'a. In November security forces denied allegations that an assassination attempt had been carried out against the Minister of Culture and Tourism. In February 2000 clashes occurred between members of Islamic Jihad and the security forces, while three soldiers were killed in clashes with tribesmen in ad-Dali governorate, north of Aden. In March a demonstration was held in ad-Dali in protest at the detention of two YSP officials; at the end of April 15 YSP officials were arrested in Abyan governorate and the Secretary-General was arrested at San'a airport on his return to the country. Kidnappings continued throughout 1999 and early 2000, involving hostages from a number of Western nations; all were released unharmed. However, in June a Norwegian diplomat was killed during a police operation to release him and his son from kidnappers in San'a. In October Hatim Muhsin bin Farid, the alleged new leader of the Islamic Aden-Abyan Army, was granted a seven-year term of imprisonment, having been convicted of kidnapping charges. Owing to a lack of evidence, he was cleared of charges relating to his leadership of the movement and to the possession of heavy weapons. Meanwhile, clashes were reported in ad-Dali governorate between the police and supporters of the YSP, following a riot organized in protest at economic conditions in the country.

In mid-October 2000 a suicide bomb attack on a US destroyer, the USS *Cole*, in Aden harbour, as a result of which 17 US naval personnel were killed, was linked by many commentators to the escalating crisis in the Middle East. The Yemeni authorities responded by arresting several Islamist militants, including leading members of Islamic Jihad from Yemen, Egypt, Algeria and other Arab states. The USA blamed agents of Osama bin Laden, the Saudi-born fundamentalist Islamist believed at that time to be based in Afghanistan, for the attack, and claimed to have evidence that the two suicide bombers were Saudi nationals. Only days after the USS *Cole* bombing, the British embassy in San'a was the target of an attack, although it was unclear as to whether the two incidents were linked. (In July 2001 four Yemenis were found guilty of plotting and orchestrating the embassy bombing, and sentenced to between four and 15 years' imprisonment.) At the end of November 2000 Yemen and the USA signed an anti-terrorism agreement whereby the Yemeni authorities agreed to allow the US Federal Bureau of Investigation to assist in investigations into the USS *Cole* explosion, and to extradite any persons accused of involvement in terrorism against foreign targets. It was announced in early December that investigations into the bombing had been completed and that six Yemeni nationals were expected to stand trial in early 2001. At the end of January, however, the Yemeni Government agreed to a postponement of the trial, following a request by US officials for more time to gather additional evidence. A further two Yemenis entering the country from Afghanistan were detained in mid-February; another three suspects were reportedly arrested in April. In November a Yemeni newspaper published claims that the individual suspected of planning the attack had subsequently sought refuge in Afghanistan. The man was named as Muhammad Omar al-Harazi, and was also believed to have been one of the principal organizers of the 1998 attacks on the US embassies in Kenya and Tanzania. In February 2002 it was reported that the trial of eight of the suspects in the bombing of the USS Cole had been postponed at the request of the US authorities because of the possibility that new information about the case would be obtained during interrogation of al-Qa'ida (see below) and Taliban prisoners captured by US military forces in Afghanistan in late 2001. Two senior al-Qa'ida operatives believed to have been responsible for planning the attack on USS Cole were arrested by US forces and Pakistani police in November 2002 and April 2003, respectively. In April 2003 10 of the Yemenis accused of involvement in the USS Cole attack escaped from a high security prison; two of the fugitives were captured in May, and charged with the murder of US military personnel. The remaining eight, in addition to one further suspect, were reportedly captured in March 2004. In September two men (a Yemeni and a Saudi) were sentenced to death for their role in the attack. Four other Yemeni nationals received prison sentences of between five and 10 years. In February 2005 an appeal court ruling upheld one of the death sentences, but commuted the other to 15 years in prison and reduced the sentence of one of the other men from eight to five years.

In January 2001 the formation of a new opposition grouping, the Opposition Co-ordination Council, was announced in Yemen. The bloc, which included the YSP, was created in anticipation of the forthcoming municipal elections, in which it hoped to counter the political dominance of the GPC and the YIP. Yemen's first municipal elections since unification were held, as planned, on 20 February. A national referendum was held concurrently on proposed amendments to the Constitution that would extend the President's term of office from five to seven years and the duration of the House of Representatives from four to six years, abolish the right of the President to issue decree laws when parliament is not in session and provide for the creation of a 111-member Consultative Council. According to official sources, 77.5% of voters endorsed the constitutional changes. There were claims of electoral irregularities and harassment of opposition candidates, and violent clashes were reported (principally between supporters of the GPC and those of the YIP) in which, according to certain sources, up to 45 people were killed. The elections were boycotted by some opposition parties and were criticized by human rights groups, who claimed that the President and the GPC were seeking to consolidate their dominant position at the expense of further democratization.

At the end of March 2001 President Saleh dismissed Prime Minister Abd al-Karim al-Iryani and declared the formation of a new Government, to be led by the former Deputy Prime Minister and Minister of Foreign Affairs, Abd al-Qadir Bajammal. The new Council of Ministers was composed exclusively of GPC members; several new ministers were appointed (including Yemen's first female minister), with only 12 remaining from the previous administration. Commentators believed that al-Iryani's dismissal was an attempt to hasten the country's reform programme. At the end of April the President elected a new Consultative Council, which for the first time included three female politicians.

In early 2003 22 political parties were registered for a parliamentary election, which was held on 27 April. The GPC recorded another decisive victory, winning 228 of the 301 seats, while the YIP secured 47 seats, independents 14 and the YSP seven. (Final results were published following three by-elections held in July.) Voter turn-out was reported to total 76% of the electorate. The European Union (EU, see p. 228) expressed its satisfaction with the elections, although the US-based National Democratic Institute for International Affairs, which also monitored the voting, said the electoral process was flawed, and cited instances of under-age voting, ballot-buying and inappropriate behaviour by security forces. Moreover, opposition parties threatened to boycott the new Parliament after widespread claims of ballot-rigging, fraud and intimidation. None the less, on 10 May the President re-appointed Bajammal as Prime Minister and requested that he form a new Government. Bajammal's new Council of Ministers, which was sworn in on 19 May, included 17 new appointees, among them a Minister of Human Rights, Amat al-Alim as-Susua. The key portfolios of defence, the interior, petroleum and mineral resources, and foreign affairs, however, remained unchanged.

Meanwhile, also in May 2003 President Saleh declared an amnesty for five exiled southern secessionist leaders who had been sentenced to death in absentia in 1998. In June 2003 the House of Representatives endorsed a government proposal that Yemen's counter-terrorism organization should become a separate department overseen by the Ministry of Interior; the resources allocated to the unit were also increased. In July security forces killed six suspected Islamic militants during an operation in Abyan province where alleged members of the Islamic Aden-Abyan Army had taken refuge after attacking a military detachment earlier in the month; a cache of weapons and explosives was discovered during the raid. The Government had previously maintained that the Islamic Aden-Abyan Army had ceased to exist following the execution of its leader in 1999.

In mid-August 2003 it was reported that the Government was determined to remove imams suspected of affiliation to the YIP. A senior official accused the YIP of seeking to dominate the mosques and called on all political forces to fight against religious fanaticism. Later, the Minister of Religious Endowments and Guidance stated that the message from the mosques should advocate moderation and tolerance. He announced that the Government had formulated a programme to train imams to promote these values and was determined to prevent the preaching of jihad against the West or Israel. In June 2004 the Director of the Ministry of Religious Endowments and Guidance stated that the authorities would not allow Islamist parties to share control over state-controlled mosques and use them as platforms to preach extremism. Firm measures would be taken against imams who preached opposition to the Government and incited worshippers to violence. In late June the Council of Ministers gave orders to close down all unlicensed religious schools in an effort to combat extremism, and stated that an extensive review of religious education in public schools was urgently needed to ensure that teaching about Islam advocated moderation. Some commentators argued that the Government was merely responding to pressure from the US Administration.

As part of efforts to combat violence and extremism, the Government stated in 2003 that it had spent over US $32m since 2002 buying up weapons on sale on the open market and seeking to persuade ordinary citizens to sell their weapons to the authorities. (According to the Government, 60m.–80m. guns were owned by the country's population, which numbered some 19m.) Officials indicated, however, that they were unable to continue the scheme due to a lack of resources and had approached the USA for financial assistance. An initiative endorsed by President Saleh to prevent the public from carrying firearms resulted in riots in February 2005. Five people died and a further 10 were injured in the fighting between demonstrators and security forces in northern Yemen. Saudi Arabia had recently complained to Yemen over reports of the smuggling of arms into the kingdom, and in 2004 began the construction of a 'separation wall' along the Saudi–Yemen border in order to increase its security (see below).

In late June 2004 violent clashes took place in a mountainous region close to the northern town of Saada between the security forces and supporters of a militant cleric, Hussain al-Houthi, leader of Ash-Shabab al-Mo'men (Believing Youth). The authorities alleged that al-Houthi's movement had formed its own militia near the border with Saudi Arabia and had launched attacks against government buildings and mosques in Saada. Although the group appeared to be motivated by opposition to the USA and Israel and to have a militant Islamist agenda, it was not thought to have links to al-Qa'ida. Reports estimated that al-Houthi had some 3,000 armed supporters, of whom some 200–300 had been killed since the conflict began, with hundreds of rebels wounded or arrested. In early September al-Houthi was believed to have been killed by members of the security forces; the Government declared this development to have effectively ended the uprising. However, renewed fighting broke out with followers of the cleric in April 2005; five Yemeni soldiers and eight members of Ash-Shabab al-Mo'men were understood to have been killed. On 12 April it was reported that the conflict had decreased in intensity and that government forces were seeking al-Houthi's relatives: in particular his brother, Abd al-Malik al-Houthi, and his father, Badr ad-Din al-Houthi, who were believed to have acceded to the leadership of the movement. After several months of relative peace, fighting broke out again in late November when two days of conflict reportedly left 16 rebels and eight government soldiers dead. Further violent clashes occurred in February 2006.

In 2005 and early 2006 the President faced political pressure from the USA over the cleric and YIP politician Sheikh Abd al-Majid az-Zindani. Az-Zindani, the Chairman of the YIP's Shura Council, was described as a 'financier of terrorism' by the UN Security Council and as a 'global terrorist' by the USA; it was understood that the latter might increase the pressure on the Yemeni Government to arrest or extradite az-Zindani.

President Saleh announced in July 2005 that he would not seek re-election to the presidency in September 2006, despite the fact that he was permitted to serve a further term of office under the terms of the Constitution. Some observers suggested that a reference in his speech to 'young qualified leaders' indicated that President Saleh was preparing his son, Ahmad, head of the Republican Guard, to succeed him: however, this rumour was denied. President Saleh, however, was re-elected as Chairman of the GPC in December 2005, which, in the view of most commentators, increased the likelihood that he would in fact continue in office; many noted that the President had made a similar announcement about not contesting the 1999 presidential election, but changed his mind after state-orchestrated rallies urged him to remain in office. In December 2005 Sumayah Ali Rajah, the head of the Yemeni-French Forum, announced her candidature for the presidency, thereby potentially becoming the first woman in Yemeni history to stand for the office.

In late 2005 and early 2006 a series of kidnappings further undermined Yemen's image abroad. Meanwhile, in July 2005 at least 39 people were killed in severe riots in San'a, Aden and several other towns in protest at the Government's decision to remove subsidies on fuel and the consequent doubling in the price of petroleum products. The GPC accused opposition parties of instigating the riots after they publicly criticized the price increases. The opposition denied the allegations and condemned the killing of civilians by security forces. At the end of July the Government announced a partial reduction in fuel prices.

President Saleh effected a comprehensive reshuffle of the Council of Ministers, which was also increased in size, to 34 members (including two new female ministers), in February 2006. The ministers in charge of the key portfolios of defence, oil, finance and planning were all removed from their posts and a further 18 positions were altered; however, the Minister of the Interior, Gen. Rashid al-Alimi, who had been under pressure following the escape of 23 suspected al-Qa'ida sympathizers (including Jamal Badawi, who had been convicted for the bombing of USS Cole in 2000—see above) from a San'a prison earlier in the month, was promoted to Deputy Prime Minister. The President claimed that the changes would add new impetus to the process of economic and political reform, although the opposition suggested that the reorganization was targeted at strengthening the regime before the presidential and municipal elections, which were due in September.

Also in February 2006 the authorities charged three journalists (from separate publications) with denigrating Islam after they reprinted cartoons regarded as extremely offensive to Muslims that had been originally published in Denmark in late 2005. One of the men, Muhammad al-Asaadi, Editor-in-Chief of the Yemen Observer, was believed to be in danger of receiving the death penalty. The arrests came amid complaints that the freedom of the press was being reduced ahead of the 2006 presidential elections.

An agreement on the long-disputed former PDRY–Omani border was signed in San'a in October 1992 and ratified in December. Demarcation was completed in June 1995. Oman withdrew an estimated 15,000 troops from the last of the disputed territories on the Yemeni border in July 1996, in accordance with the 1992 agreement. In May 1997 officials from both countries signed the demarcation maps at a ceremony in Muscat, Oman. In January 2004 the two countries signed an agreement on their sea border during wider discussions over the establishment of a joint free-trade zone.

The Iraqi invasion of Kuwait in August 1990 proved problematic for the Yemeni Government, as the economy was heavily dependent on trade with, and aid from, Iraq, and also on aid from Saudi Arabia, which was host to a considerable number of Yemeni expatriate workers. In December Yemen assumed the chair of the UN Security Council (which rotates on a monthly basis), and the Government increased its efforts to mediate in the Gulf crisis. It was, however, unable to prevent the outbreak of war despite a peace plan, presented in January 1991, and further diplomatic initiatives. Following the US-led military offensive against Iraq, Yemen issued a statement condemning the action, and large demonstrations were held in support of Iraq. Later in January it was confirmed that US aid to Yemen was to be suspended indefinitely, apparently as a result of Yemen's policy towards Iraq, although reduced US economic aid was resumed in August. Yemen continued to support Iraq and in December 1998 it requested an Arab League summit on Iraq and called for an end to the sanctions. In April 2000 it was announced that the UN Sanctions Committee on Iraq, which had been considering a request from Yemen to remove, repair or sell eight Iraqi ships stranded at Aden port since 1990, had referred the issue to the International Maritime Organization (IMO, see p. 117). The Yemeni Government expressed its concerns regarding the US-led military operations against Iraqi air defence targets in 1999–2002.

Following the terrorist attacks apparently perpetrated by Osama bin Laden's al-Qa'ida (Base) network against New York and Washington, DC, USA on 11 September 2001, the Yemeni Government arrested a number of suspected Islamist militants and froze the assets of individuals and organizations deemed to have links with al-Qa'ida. In mid-December up to 30 people (including about 19 soldiers) were reportedly killed during clashes in the central Marib governorate when local residents apparently fought to prevent the Yemeni security forces from arresting a group of alleged militants. (President Saleh had, during a visit to Washington in late November, been presented with a list of suspected al-Qa'ida members residing in Yemen.) Meanwhile, at least 100 foreign students enrolled at the country's Islamic institutes were said to have been arrested on charges of violating residency requirements. In mid-January 2002 the US embassy at San'a was closed amid fears of an imminent terrorist attack; two grenades were thrown at the building in March, although no injuries were reported. There were reports in early March that the US Administration was considering the deployment of several hundred US troops to Yemen to assist the authorities in their struggle against militant Islamist organizations. In mid-April an explosion was reported close to the home of a leading security official involved in the search for al-Qa'ida militants; a previously unknown group styled the al-Qa'ida Sympathizers was suspected of having carried out the bombing. Despite increasing popular resentment towards US activities in the Middle East among Yemenis, President Saleh continued to co-operate with the USA over anti-terrorism initiatives throughout 2002, and in November an unmanned US aircraft killed six men in northern Yemen believed to have links with al-Qa'ida. Meanwhile, in December the Spanish navy intercepted a North Korean ship carrying Scud missiles, that was bound for Yemen. The vessel was handed over to the US authorities the next day, but, after protests by the Yemeni Government that the missiles were purchased legitimately, the shipment was released. In the same month three US missionaries were murdered by a Yemeni who confessed to having links with bin Laden's network. In November 2003 Muhammad Hamdi al-Ahdal, who, according to the USA, had been among the 20 most significant al-Qa'ida members still at large, was captured by security forces; al-Ahdal was suspected of having organized the bombings of the USS Cole in 2000 and the French petroleum tanker, the Limburg, in 2002 (see above). Another reported senior al-Qa'ida operative, who had apparently survived a US attempt to assassinate him in 2002, was arrested by security forces in March 2004.

In mid-February 2002 President Saleh was reported to have warned the US Government that a US-led attack on the regime of Saddam Hussain in Iraq, as part of its 'war on terror', would jeopardize the continued support of its traditional allies in the Arab region. However, Saleh was careful to emphasize his own ongoing efforts to persuade the Iraqi authorities to accept the return of UN weapons inspectors. When the military campaign in Iraq commenced, in March 2003, some 30,000 protesters, some of them armed, marched on the US embassy in San'a. Public resentment also continued to increase towards President Saleh's regime, as a result of its perceived co-operation with the USA. In June, however, the Director of the US Federal Bureau of Investigation, Robert Mueller, met Saleh in Aden to discuss further co-operation on security and intelligence. In September the human rights organization Amnesty International released a report claiming that the authorities were holding some 200 people without trial in an effort to assuage US concerns that Yemen was not co-operating fully with the 'war on terror'. In early 2004 the Government signed a memorandum of understanding with the USA, which was regarded as the first step towards a free-trade pact between the countries. The agreement also provided Yemen with an extra US $7.6m. in aid. In March

YEMEN

Introductory Survey

Yemen welcomed the signing of an interim constitution in Iraq, describing it as a step towards Iraq recovering its sovereignty, but continued to press for the USA and its allies to withdraw their forces from the country. In early August the Minister of Foreign Affairs confirmed that Yemen was preparing a peace-keeping force for Iraq under mandates from the Arab League and the UN, but would only send the troops should the US-led coalition forces withdraw from Iraq.

Relations with Saudi Arabia deteriorated as a result of Yemen's initially strong opposition to the presence of foreign armed forces in the Gulf and to the ambiguous stance it had subsequently adopted in this respect. In September 1990, apparently in retaliation, Saudi Arabia announced that it had withdrawn the privileges that Yemeni workers had previously enjoyed. This resulted in an exodus from Saudi Arabia of some 850,000 Yemeni workers during October and November, which caused widespread economic and social disruption. The expulsion and consequent return to Yemen of the workers not only caused a reduction in the country's income from remittances, but also led to a serious increase in unemployment. (During 1995, at negotiations proceeding from the February 1995 memorandum of understanding—see below, it was reported that the Saudi authorities had agreed to allow Yemenis sponsored by Saudi nationals to seek employment in the kingdom.) In 1998 Saudi Arabia began issuing visas to Yemeni workers.

The Governments of Yemen and Saudi Arabia held negotiations concerning the demarcation of their common border during 1992–94; however, in December 1994 Yemen accused Saudi Arabia of trespassing on Yemeni territory and alleged that three of its soldiers had been killed during clashes earlier in that month. Further clashes were reported in January 1995 following the failure of the two countries to renew the 1934 Ta'if agreement (renewable every 20 years), which delineated their existing frontier. Intense mediation by Syria culminated in a joint statement in mid-January 1995, in which Yemen and Saudi Arabia pledged to cease all military activity in the border area. It was subsequently announced that the demarcation of the disputed border would be undertaken by a joint committee. In February the Yemeni and Saudi Governments signed a memorandum of understanding that reaffirmed their commitment to the Ta'if agreement and provided for the establishment of six joint committees to delineate the land and sea borders and develop economic and commercial ties. In June President Saleh led a high-ranking delegation to Saudi Arabia, constituting the first official visit to that country since February 1990. The two Governments expressed their satisfaction with the memorandum of understanding and, in addition, pledged their commitment to strengthening economic, commercial and cultural co-operation.

Reports of an attempted incursion into Yemen by Saudi forces in December 1995 were denied by both sides. In July 1996 the two countries signed a bilateral security agreement which included provisions intended to counter the cross-border trafficking of illicit drugs. Friction over border claims, however, was revived in 1997, and in May 1998 it was reported that Saudi Arabia had occupied an uninhabited island in the Red Sea regarded by Yemen as within its national boundaries. In the same month Saudi Arabia sent a memorandum to the UN stating that it did not recognize the 1992 border agreement between Yemen and Oman and claiming that parts of the area involved were Saudi Arabian territory. The Saudi objection to the accord was widely believed to be related to its attempts to gain land access to the Arabian Sea, via a corridor between Yemen and Oman, which it had thus far been denied in its negotiations with Yemen. In July 1998 Yemen submitted a memorandum to the Arab League refuting the Saudi claim to the land, and stating that the Saudi protests contravened the Ta'if agreement signed by that country. In July three Yemeni troops were killed during fighting with a Saudi border patrol on the disputed island of Duwaima in the Red Sea; Saudi Arabia claimed its actions on the island were in self-defence and that, under the Ta'if agreement, three-quarters of the island belonged to Saudi Arabia. Meanwhile, bilateral discussions continued and the Saudi Minister of Foreign Affairs visited Yemen at the end of July. In October 1999 the Yemeni Prime Minister cancelled a planned visit to Saudi Arabia, reportedly owing to the failure of the two Governments to agree on the issues to be discussed. Despite reported clashes in the border area during 1999, however, relations continued to improve. In early June 2000, at a ceremony in Riyadh, Saudi Arabia, the Saudi Arabian and Yemeni ministers responsible for foreign affairs signed a final border treaty demarcating their joint land and sea border. The treaty incorporated both the 1934 Ta'if agreement and the 1995 memorandum of understanding, although it failed to define the eastern section of the Saudi–Yemeni land frontier. The two countries also agreed to further economic, commercial and cultural ties, and each pledged not to permit its territory to be used as a base for political or military aggression against the other. In the months following the signing of the treaty, however, clashes were reported between rival tribal groups near the border. In December 2000 a meeting was held of the Saudi-Yemeni Co-operation Council (the first since before the Gulf conflict), at which Saudi officials pledged financial assistance to Yemen for development projects. However, talks concerning the proposed construction of a petroleum pipeline between the two countries had reportedly been unsuccessful. In April 2001 Yemen and Saudi Arabia were said to have agreed on the location of four crossing-points on their joint border. At the same time reports suggested that the withdrawal of Yemeni and Saudi troops from their respective sides of the border was almost complete. Renewed tensions surfaced in early 2004 after the Saudi Government began construction of a 'separation wall' along the border that some considered to be in violation of the treaty of June 2000 on border demarcation. The construction of the wall reflected unease on the part of the Saudis regarding the capacity of the Yemeni authorities to maintain their own border security.

In November 1995 there were reports that Eritrean troops had attempted to land on the Red Sea island of Greater Hanish, one of three islands (the others being Lesser Hanish and Zuqar) claimed by both Yemen and Eritrea. The attempted invasion had apparently been prompted by Yemen's announced intention to develop Greater Hanish as a tourist resort, and its subsequent refusal to comply with an Eritrean demand that the island be evacuated. Negotiations in Yemen and Eritrea failed to defuse the crisis, and on 15 December fighting broke out between the two sides, resulting in the deaths of six Eritrean and three Yemeni soldiers. On 17 December Yemen and Eritrea agreed to a cease-fire, to be monitored by a commission comprising a senior official from each country and two US diplomats. None the less, fighting was renewed the following day and Eritrean forces succeeded in occupying Greater Hanish. The cease-fire was adhered to thenceforth, and some 180 Yemeni soldiers (captured during the fighting) were released at the end of the month. Attempts by the Ethiopian and Egyptian Governments to broker an agreement between the two sides proved unsuccessful. In January 1996 France assumed the mediatory role and in May it announced that Yemen and Eritrea would sign an arbitration agreement in Paris, France, whereby both countries would renounce the use of force and submit their dispute to an international tribunal. France subsequently undertook to observe and supervise military movements in the area around the disputed islands. In mid-August, however, Eritrean troops occupied Lesser Hanish, but these were withdrawn later in the month after representations by France and a UN Security Council edict to evacuate the island forthwith. At a meeting held in Paris in October, representatives of Eritrea and Yemen confirmed that they would submit the dispute to an international tribunal. In October 1998 the tribunal ruled that Yemen had sovereignty over Greater and Lesser Hanish, and all islands to their north-west, while Eritrea had sovereignty over the Mohabaka islands. The court recommended that the fishing traditions around the islands be maintained, thereby granting access to the Hanish islands to Eritrean and Yemeni fishermen. Both countries accepted the ruling, and shortly afterwards they agreed to establish a joint committee to strengthen bilateral co-operation. In May 1999 the Presidents of Eritrea and Yemen held talks to discuss bilateral relations. A final ruling on the Hanish islands, issued by the tribunal in December, delineated the joint maritime border as the median line between their mainland coastlines. This was welcomed by both countries and in January 2000 the Yemeni Vice-President made an official visit to Eritrea for talks with President Afewerki. In March Eritrea denied reports that it had appealed against the tribunal's decision on the islands. In June 2003 a number of Yemeni fishing boats and 133 crew members were arrested by Eritrean naval patrols in the area around the Hanish islands. Although the men were released in July, this latest development was an indication of increased tension between the countries since the decision of the tribunal.

Since the mid-1990s President Saleh has increasingly sought to widen the range of Yemen's international contacts, particularly in relation to aid and co-operation agreements. In November 1997 an accord was reached with the 'Paris Club' of official creditors for the amelioration of Yemen's burden of external debt. In the same month, on an official visit to the United Kingdom (during which a co-operation agreement was signed with the EU), President Saleh made a formal application for Yemen to join the Commonwealth (see p. 193). Saleh made a state visit to the People's Republic of China in February 1998, during which extensive agreements were negotiated for Yemen to receive technical and economic assistance. In early 2000 Saleh made official visits to Canada, the USA, Italy and Iran; at the same time Yemen repeatedly denied reports that it had had secret contacts with Israel and that it was seeking to normalize relations with that country. According to reports, in early 2004 the Government sought to borrow some US $700m. from Italy and Poland to finance sea patrols in order to improve coastal security. Meanwhile, in December 2003 Yemen concreted its improved relations with two of its neighbours to the west, Sudan and Ethiopia, with the establishment of the Tripartite San'a Co-operation Forum. Eritrea, however, accused the group of collaborating against it. In December 2005 Yemen offered to mediate between Ethiopia and Eritrea over the two countries' border demarcation dispute.

In September 2005 Yemen signed a security agreement with Bahrain; the two states agreed to co-operate on training, combating crime and terrorism, and exchanging intelligence.

Government

Legislative power is vested in the House of Representatives, with 301 members directly elected by universal adult suffrage. Under the revised Constitution, the President of the Republic (Head of State) is to be elected directly by voters for a period of seven years, renewable once. The President appoints a Council of Ministers, headed by a Prime Minister.

Defence

In August 2005 total armed forces of the Republic of Yemen were estimated to number 66,700: army 60,000; navy 1,700; air force 5,000. There was a paramilitary force with an estimated strength of 70,000. Tribal levies numbered at least 20,000. Military conscription was ended in May 2001. The defence budget for 2005 was forecast at 179,000m. riyals.

Economic Affairs

In 2004, according to estimates by the World Bank, Yemen's gross national income (GNI), measured at average 2002–04 prices, was US $11,218m., equivalent to $570 per head (or $820 per head on an international purchasing-power parity basis). During 1995–2004, it was estimated, the population increased at an average annual rate of 3.0%, while gross domestic product (GDP) per head increased, in real terms, by an average of 1.6% per year. Overall GDP increased, in real terms, at an average annual rate of 4.6% in 1995–2004; GDP growth in 2004 was estimated at 4.0%.

Agriculture (including forestry and fishing) contributed an estimated 12.9% of GDP in 2004, and the sector engaged some 54.2% of the working population in 2003. The principal cash crops are coffee, cotton and fruits. Subsistence crops include sorghum, potatoes, wheat and barley. Livestock-rearing (particularly in the east and north) and fishing are also important activities. Livestock, hides and skins and fish are all exported on a small scale. Estimates indicated growth averaging 5.7% annually in 1995–2004. Real agricultural GDP increased by 4.7% in 2004.

Industry (including mining, manufacturing, construction and power) contributed an estimated 43.8% of GDP in 2004, and 11.5% of the working population were employed in the sector in 2003. According to estimates, industrial GDP increased at an average annual rate of 3.9% in 1995–2004. Real growth in industrial GDP was estimated at 5.0% in 2004.

Mining and quarrying contributed some 31.1% of GDP in 2004 and employed 0.5% of the working population in 2003. Yemen's proven petroleum reserves totalled 2,900m. barrels at the end of 2004, sufficient to maintain production at that year's levels for 18 years. Petroleum production averaged 429,000 barrels per day (b/d) during 2004, considerably lower than the Government's planned output. The value of exports of petroleum and petroleum products accounted for 89.3% of the value of total exports in 2003. There are also significant reserves of natural gas: proven reserves at the end of 2004 were 480,000m. cu. m. Salt and gypsum are also exploited on a large scale. In addition, there are deposits of copper, lead, zinc, gold, sulphur and molybdenum. GDP of the mining sector increased at an estimated average annual rate of 13.3% in 1993–2002; real mining GDP rose by 2.1% in 2003.

The manufacturing sector contributed an estimated 5.6% of GDP in 2004; in 2003 3.8% of the working population were employed in the sector. The most important branches of manufacturing are food-processing, petroleum refining, construction materials (particularly cement and iron and steel), paper and paper products and traditional light industries (including textiles, leather goods and jewellery). The Aden oil refinery recommenced operations in 1994 and was being considered for partial privatization in the early 2000s; some imported crude oil is also refined. Plans for the construction of a new refinery at Hadramawt were completed in 2004; the facility was scheduled to commence supply of petroleum products to eastern Yemen in 2007. Real growth in manufacturing GDP was estimated at an average of 0.9% annually in 1995–2004; however, the sector's real GDP contracted by 5.3% in 2004.

Some domestic energy requirements are served by locally produced petroleum, but the country is somewhat reliant on fuel imports (particularly petroleum from other producers in the region). Imports of fuel and energy comprised 14.9% of the value of total imports in 2003. The northern and southern electricity grids were linked in mid-1997.

The services sector contributed some 43.3% of GDP in 2004, and employed 34.4% of the working population in 2003. A free-trade zone at Aden was inaugurated in May 1991. A series of kidnappings in late 2005 and early 2006 further damaged Yemen's image in the West (and consequently its likelihood of receiving tourists and investment). The real GDP of the services sector increased at an estimated average annual rate of 4.5% in 1995–2004. Real services GDP increased by 0.3% in 2004.

In 2004 Yemen recorded an estimated visible trade surplus of US $817.1m., and there was a surplus of $24.6m. on the current account of the balance of payments. In 2003 the principal source of imports (14.1%) was the United Arab Emirates. Other major suppliers were Saudi Arabia, Kuwait and the USA. In that year the main export destination (32.3%) was the Republic of China. Other important export markets were India, the Republic of Korea and Singapore. The principal exports in 2003 were petroleum and petroleum products (89.3%). The main imports in that year were food and live animals (especially cereals and cereal preparations), machinery and transport equipment, and basic manufactures.

A balanced budget was forecast for 2003. Total external debt at the end of 2003 was estimated to be US $5,377m., of which $4,746m. was long-term public debt. In that year the cost of debt-servicing was equivalent to 3.1% of the value of exports of goods and services. The annual rate of inflation averaged 7.1% in 1997–2003. Consumer prices increased by 12.5% in 2004. The rate of unemployment is estimated to be as high as 25% of the labour force.

Yemen is a member of the Arab Fund for Economic and Social Development (AFESD, see p. 161) and the Council of Arab Economic Unity (see p. 208).

Between the establishment of the Republic of Yemen in 1990 and the civil war of 1994, the economy declined substantially and in 1994 the annual rate of inflation averaged an estimated 55%, the budget deficit stood at 16.7% of GDP and the cost of servicing Yemen's external debt was equivalent to 186% of GNI. A programme of economic reform, implemented in 1995, achieved some success, particularly with regard to economic diversification, and Yemen's external debt was reduced by almost 50% following agreements with the 'Paris Club' of official creditors in 1996 and 1997. However, further problems were posed in 1998 both by the decline in international petroleum prices and by a lack of political consensus, which affected the Government's ability to implement economic reform. In order to minimize the effect of low petroleum prices on government revenue, budget expenditure was restricted and a number of government subsidies were reduced or abolished. The Government also encouraged the privatization of small state enterprises. Petroleum prices recovered strongly in late 1999, and Yemen's petroleum production capacity was increased, resulting in a more favourable environment for the Government to implement economic reforms. By 1999 inflation had been reduced, the budget deficit had narrowed and, according to the IMF, non-petroleum sector growth, in real terms, was an estimated 3.2% in that year. However, during 2000–04, the country's petroleum production declined, severely affecting the Government's main source of revenue. Nevertheless, GDP was estimated to have increased by 4.2% in 2002 and by 3.8% in 2003, bolstered by increasing

YEMEN

petroleum prices. Economic growth (estimated at 4.0% in 2004) was expected to decrease only slightly, to about 3.5%, in 2005 and 2006, despite a continued decline in crude petroleum production (the effect of which would again be masked by the high prices). The Government's third five-year development plan (for 2006–10) aimed to increase growth in the non-petroleum sectors, to improve economic partnerships with neighbouring countries and to attract foreign investment. The plan also aimed to reduce the rate of unemployment and to combat poverty. The Government's budget for 2006, approved by the Council of Ministers in late 2005, forecast a deficit equivalent to 4% of GDP (despite a projected 38% increase in public receipts), owing to increased spending (projected at 41% higher than the comparative figure in 2005), mainly on infrastructure projects and also on continued attempts at economic diversification. The World Bank expressed disappointment that the Government, which delayed for 18 months the implementation of a proposed sales tax, had not opted for greater fiscal caution in a period of high revenue owing to increasing petroleum prices. In 2005 the IMF had also criticized Yemen's efforts at economic reform, noting in particular the unsustainable fiscal position. The budgetary results for 2005 indicated that the projected revenue had severely underestimated the out-turn figures, owing to very high petroleum prices. The 2006 projections were reportedly based on a more realistic petroleum price (of US $40 per barrel) and there was, therefore, a danger that a year of unplanned expenditure or poor revenue collection could exacerbate Yemen's debt problem.

Education

Primary education, between the ages of six and 15, is compulsory. Secondary education, beginning at 15, lasts for a further three years. In 2002/03 enrolment at primary schools was equivalent to 72% of children in the relevant age-group (boys 84%; girls 59%). Enrolment at secondary schools, in 1999/2000, was equivalent to just 35% of students in the appropriate age-group (males 47%; females 21%). In 2003/04 some 184,072 students were enrolled at seven state-controlled institutions of higher education. In 2000 public expenditure on education was forecast at 90,054m. riyals, equivalent to 21.3% of total government spending. Enrolment in primary schools was estimated at 65% in 2004; a Basic Education Development project aimed to increase this figure to 85% over 40 years. The World Bank provided a loan of US $65m. to help fund the project.

Public Holidays

2006: 1 January (New Year's Day), 10 January*† (Id al-Adha, Feast of the Sacrifice), 31 January* (Muharram, Islamic New Year), 9 February* (Ashoura), 8 March (International Women's Day), 10 April* (Mouloud, Birth of the Prophet), 1 May (Labour Day), 13 June (Corrective Movement Anniversary), 21 August* (Leilat al-Meiraj, Ascension of the Prophet), 24 September* (Ramadan begins), 14 October (National Day), 23 October* (Id al-Fitr, end of Ramadan), 31 December*† (Id al-Adha, Feast of the Sacrifice).

2007: 1 January (New Year's Day), 20 January* (Muharram, Islamic New Year), 29 January* (Ashoura), 8 March (International Women's Day), 31 March* (Mouloud, Birth of the Prophet), 1 May (Labour Day), 13 June (Corrective Movement Anniversary), 10 August* (Leilat al-Meiraj, Ascension of the Prophet), 13 September* (Ramadan begins), 13 October* (Id al-Fitr, end of Ramadan), 14 October (National Day), 20 December* (Id al-Adha, Feast of the Sacrifice).

* These holidays are dependent on the Islamic lunar calendar and may vary by one or two days from the dates given.
† This festival occurs twice (in the Islamic years AH 1426 and 1427) within the same Gregorian year.

Weights and Measures

Local weights and measures are used, and vary according to location.

Statistical Survey

Sources (unless otherwise indicated): Republic of Yemen Central Statistical Organization, POB 13434, San'a; tel. (1) 250619; fax (1) 250664; internet www.cso-yemen.org; Central Bank of Yemen, POB 59, Ali Abd al-Mughni St, San'a; tel. (1) 274310; fax (1) 274360; e-mail info@centralbank.gov.ye; internet www.centralbank.gov.ye.

Area and Population

AREA, POPULATION AND DENSITY

Area (sq km)	536,869*
Population (census results)	
16 December 1994†	14,587,807
16 December 2004‡	
Males	10,036,953
Females	9,648,208
Total	19,685,161
Density (per sq km) at 16 December 2004	36.7

* 207,286 sq miles.
† Excluding adjustment for underenumeration.
‡ Population is *de jure*.

PRINCIPAL TOWNS
(population at 1994 census)

San'a (capital)	954,448	Hodeida	298,452
Aden	398,294	Mukalla	122,359
Taiz	317,571	Ibb	103,312

Source: UN, *Demographic Yearbook*.

Mid-2003 (UN estimate, incl. suburbs): San'a 1,469,072 (Source: UN, *World Urbanization Prospects: The 2003 Revision*).

BIRTHS, MARRIAGES AND DEATHS
(UN estimates, annual averages)

	1990–95	1995–2000	2000–05
Birth rate (per 1,000)	48.2	43.8	41.0
Death rate (per 1,000)	11.8	10.4	8.7

Source: UN, *World Population Prospects: The 2004 Revision*.

Expectation of life (WHO estimates, years at birth): 59 (males 57; females 61) in 2003 (Source: WHO, *World Health Report*).

EMPLOYMENT
(ISIC major divisions, '000 persons aged 15 years and over)

	2001	2002	2003
Agriculture, forestry and fishing	2,109	2,175	2,195
Mining and quarrying	19	20	19
Manufacturing	146	151	152
Electricity, gas and water	13	13	13
Construction	258	266	280
Trade, restaurants and hotels	468	483	504
Transport, storage and communications	129	133	140
Finance, insurance and real estate	32	33	33
Social and community services	251	259	268
Public administration	447	461	448
Total employed	**3,872**	**3,994**	**4,052**

Source: IMF, *Republic of Yemen: Statistical Appendix* (March 2005).

YEMEN

Health and Welfare

KEY INDICATORS

Total fertility rate (children per woman, 2003)	7.0
Under-5 mortality rate (per 1,000 live births, 2004)	111
HIV/AIDS (% of persons aged 15–49, 2003)	0.1
Physicians (per 1,000 head, 2001)	0.22
Hospital beds (per 1,000 head, 1998)	0.60
Health expenditure (2002): US $ per head (PPP)	58
Health expenditure (2002): % of GDP	3.7
Health expenditure (2002): public (% of total)	27.2
Access to water (% of persons, 2002)	69
Access to sanitation (% of persons, 2002)	30
Human Development Index (2003): ranking	151
Human Development Index (2003): value	0.489

For sources and definitions, see explanatory note on p. vi.

Agriculture

PRINCIPAL CROPS
('000 metric tons)

	2002	2003	2004
Wheat	132	104	105
Barley	40	28	22
Maize	41	33	32
Millet	58	41	66
Sorghum	289	213	263
Potatoes	211	213	213
Chick-peas	36	36*	36*
Other pulses	25	25*	25*
Sesame seed	18	19	19*
Cottonseed	19	19	19*
Tomatoes	267	273	200
Cucumbers and gherkins	15	16	8
Chillies and green peppers	13	13	20
Dry onions	80	82	203
Garlic*	12	12	12
Green beans	12	12	12*
Carrots	9	9	14
Okra	22	22	18
Watermelons	86	87	141
Cantaloupes and other melons	37	38	29
Other vegetables	73	68	67*
Bananas	97	99	99*
Oranges	163	166†	166*
Tangerines, mandarins, etc.	25	25†	26*
Grapes	165	168	169*
Mangoes*	28	28	28
Dates	32	33	33*
Papayas	72	74	74*
Other fruit	52	52*	52*
Coffee (green)	11	12	12*
Tobacco (leaves)	12	12	12*

* FAO estimate(s).
† Unofficial figure.

Source: FAO.

LIVESTOCK
('000 head, year ending September)

	2002	2003	2004*
Horses	3	3*	3
Asses*	500	500	500
Cattle	1,355	1,358	1,400
Camels	267	277	277
Sheep	6,548	6,589	6,600
Goats	7,318	7,311	7,300
Chickens (million)*	35	35	35

* FAO estimate(s).

Source: FAO.

Statistical Survey

LIVESTOCK PRODUCTS
('000 metric tons)

	2002	2003	2004*
Beef and veal	59.3	59.8	59.8
Mutton and lamb*	27.3	29.3	30.3
Goat meat*	24.7	26.0	26.0
Poultry meat	83.5	83.5	83.5
Camels' milk*	13.1	13.6	13.6
Cows' milk	192.6	192.6	192.6
Sheep's milk*	22.3	22.4	22.4
Goats' milk*	34.8	34.8	34.7
Cheese*	13.8	13.7	13.7
Butter*	5.1	5.1	5.1
Hen eggs	31.9†	32.0†	32.0
Wool (greasy)	6.0†	5.9†	6.8
Cattle hides	11.1	11.2	11.2
Goatskins (fresh)*	4.9	5.2	5.2
Sheepskins (fresh)*	5.4	5.8	6.0

* FAO estimates.
† Unofficial figure.

Source: FAO.

Forestry

ROUNDWOOD REMOVALS
('000 cubic metres, excl. bark, estimates)

	2002	2003	2004
Total (all fuel wood)	326	339	353

Source: FAO.

Fishing

('000 metric tons, live weight of capture)

	2001	2002	2003*
Demersal percomorphs	7.4	8.4*	8.3
Indian oil sardine*	5.5	6.2	6.2
Narrow-barred Spanish mackerel*	3.6	3.6	3.6
Pelagic percomorphs*	80.9	91.6	91.4
Sharks, rays and skates, etc.*	6.3	7.1	7.1
Cuttlefish and bobtail squids	9.3	10.4	10.4
Total catch (incl. others)*	142.2	159.3	159.0

* Estimate(s).

Source: FAO.

Mining

('000 metric tons, unless otherwise indicated)

	2002	2003	2004*
Crude petroleum ('000 barrels)	159,924	157,000	149,000
Natural gas (million cu m)†	29,991	30,000*	28,000
Salt	125	116	120
Gypsum (crude)	41	42	44

* Estimate(s).
† Gross production.

Source: US Geological Survey.

Industry

SELECTED PRODUCTS
('000 barrels, unless otherwise indicated)

	2001	2002	2003
Mineral water (million litres)	133	140	143*
Soft drinks (million litres)	94	103	105*
Cigarettes (million packets)	301	289	298*
Liquefied petroleum gas	910	1,100	1,100
Benzene	7,100	7,200	7,400
Kerosene	3,630	3,450	3,510
Distillate fuel oils	12,500	13,800	14,100
Residual fuel oils	9,320	6,770	6,910
Cement ('000 metric tons)	1,493	1,561	1,541
Paints ('000 litres)	7,479	7,554	7,667*
Plastic bags ('000 metric tons)	10,733	12,128	12,249*
Electric energy (million kWh)	3,643	3,769	4,094*

* Provisional figure.

Source: partly US Geological Survey.

2004 ('000 barrels, unless otherwise indicated): Liquefied petroleum gas 1,100 (estimate); Benzene 7,400 (estimate); Kerosene 3,600 (estimate); Distillate fuel oils 14,100 (estimate); Residual fuel oils 7,000 (estimate); Cement ('000 metric tons) 1,546 (Source: US Geological Survey).

Finance

CURRENCY AND EXCHANGE RATES

Monetary Units
100 fils = 1 Yemeni riyal.

Sterling, Dollar and Euro Equivalents (30 November 2005)
£1 sterling = 336.18 riyals;
US $1 = 194.66 riyals;
€1 = 229.10 riyals;
1,000 Yemeni riyals = £2.97 = $5.14 = €4.36.

Average Exchange Rate (Yemeni riyals per US $)
2002 175.625
2003 183.448
2004 184.776

Note: The exchange rate of US $1 = 9.76 Yemeni riyals, established in the YAR in 1988, remained in force until February 1990, when a new rate of $1 = 12.01 riyals was introduced. Following the merger of the two Yemens in May 1990, the YAR's currency was adopted as the currency of the unified country. In March 1995 the official exchange rate was amended from 12.01 to 50.04 riyals per US dollar. The rate has since been adjusted. From mid-1996 data refer to a market-determined exchange rate, applicable to most private transactions.

CENTRAL GOVERNMENT BUDGET
('000 million riyals)

Revenue*	2002	2003	2004†
Oil and gas	391.2	409.9	579.1
Exports	266.2	306.9	370.9
Domestic revenues	125.0	103.0	208.2
Non-oil revenues	169.6	254.0	223.3
Tax revenues	131.1	152.9	176.7
Non-tax revenues	38.5	101.1	46.6
Total	560.8	663.9	802.4

Expenditure	2002	2003	2004†
Current expenditure	485.0	526.3	626.3
Civil wages and salaries	134.5	143.2	159.5
Materials and services	45.2	51.7	58.1
Defence	129.5	98.3	105.5
Interest	34.7	38.0	55.6
Domestic	26.2	30.5	44.9
Foreign	8.5	7.5	10.7
Transfers and subsidies	126.4	177.2	225.5
Current transfers	69.4	66.6	77.2
Subsidies	57.0	110.6	148.3
Other current expenditure	14.7	17.9	22.1
Capital development expenditure	124.5	198.4	194.1
Total	609.5	724.7	820.4

* Excluding grants received ('000 million riyals): 28.0 in 2002; 8.3 in 2003; 1.8 in 2004 (preliminary).
† Preliminary.

INTERNATIONAL RESERVES
(US $ million at 31 December)

	2002	2003	2004
Gold (national valuation)	18.4	21.9	23.4
IMF special drawing rights	44.9	4.9	51.3
Foreign exchange	4,365.6	4,982.0	5,613.5
Total	4,428.9	5,008.8	5,688.2

Source: IMF, *International Financial Statistics*.

MONEY SUPPLY
(million riyals at 31 December)

	2003	2004	2005
Currency outside banks	268,813	297,939	330,620
Demand deposits at commercial banks	56,346	69,628	69,368
Total money (incl. others)	347,465	390,541	442,464

Source: IMF, *International Financial Statistics*.

COST OF LIVING
(Consumer Price Index; base: November 1999 = 100)

	2002	2003	2004
Food and non-alcoholic beverages	127.62	148.87	177.20
Housing and related items	120.46	133.51	136.48
Clothing and footwear	116.93	120.82	124.00
All items (incl. others)	131.37	145.60	163.81

NATIONAL ACCOUNTS
(million riyals at current prices, preliminary data)

National Income and Product

	2002	2003	2004
Domestic factor incomes*	1,774,608	2,084,309	2,410,358
Consumption of fixed capital	109,997	129,959	195,752
Gross domestic product (GDP) at factor cost	1,884,605	2,214,268	2,606,110
Indirect taxes, *less* subsidies	9,892	−36,805	−54,116
GDP in purchasers' values	1,894,497	2,177,463	2,551,994
Net factor income from abroad	−131,929	−175,709	−214,213
Gross national income (GNI)	1,762,568	2,001,754	2,337,781
Less Consumption of fixed capital	109,997	129,959	195,752
National income in market prices	1,652,571	1,871,795	2,142,029
Other current transfers received from abroad	243,217	253,497	262,075
Less Other current transfers paid abroad	19,507	13,072	8,675
National disposable income	1,876,281	2,112,220	2,395,429

* Compensation of employees and the operating surplus of enterprises; figure obtained as a residual.

YEMEN

Expenditure on the Gross Domestic Product

	2002	2003	2004
Government final consumption expenditure	283,281	311,493	344,336
Private final consumption expenditure	1,297,646	1,432,906	1,656,761
Changes in stocks	−4,591	19,541	−13,250
Gross fixed capital formation	332,072	446,068	497,562
Total domestic expenditure	1,908,408	2,210,008	2,485,409
Exports of goods and services	695,131	787,195	938,461
Less Imports of goods and services	709,042	819,740	871,876
GDP in purchasers' values	1,894,497	2,177,463	2,551,994
GDP at constant 1990 prices	270,193	280,436	291,718

Gross Domestic Product by Economic Activity

	2002	2003	2004
Agriculture, hunting, forestry and fishing*	265,170	296,420	330,440
Mining and quarrying	522,287	659,413	796,794
Manufacturing	91,480	100,841	142,196
Electricity, gas and water	14,414	15,784	24,134
Construction	79,406	86,597	157,398
Trade, restaurants and hotels	259,967	291,979	343,528
Transport, storage and communications	207,883	229,874	287,294
Finance, insurance, real estate and business services	144,036	165,614	190,324
Government services	208,356	221,742	250,864
Other community, social and personal services	17,969	19,854	33,184
Private non-profit services and services to households	806	855	2,584
Sub-total	1,811,774	2,088,973	2,558,740
Import duties	36,689	40,525	48,403
Less Imputed bank service charge	44,668	47,854	55,149
GDP in purchasers' values	1,803,795	2,081,644	2,551,994

* Including production of qat.

BALANCE OF PAYMENTS
(US $ million)

	2002	2003	2004
Exports of goods f.o.b.	3,620.7	3,934.3	4,675.7
Imports of goods f.o.b.	−2,932.0	−3,557.4	−3,858.6
Trade balance	688.7	376.9	817.1
Exports of services	166.2	317.7	369.7
Imports of services	−934.8	−1,003.6	−1,059.4
Balance on goods and services	−79.9	−308.9	127.3
Other income received	135.0	98.9	103.6
Other income paid	−900.6	−1,008.3	−1,450.1
Balance on goods, services and income	−845.6	−1,218.3	−1,219.1
Current transfers received	1,456.9	1,442.1	1,493.1
Current transfers paid	−73.1	−75.0	−49.4
Current balance	538.2	148.7	224.6
Capital account (net)	—	5.5	163.3
Direct investment from abroad	114.3	−89.1	143.6
Portfolio investment assets	−5.8	−0.4	−6.4
Other investment assets	−124.5	49.1	−25.4
Other investment liabilities	−140.8	60.2	−180.4
Net errors and omissions	43.3	156.4	53.3
Overall balance	424.7	330.3	372.5

Source: IMF, *International Financial Statistics*.

External Trade

PRINCIPAL COMMODITIES
(distribution by SITC, million riyals at current prices)

Imports c.i.f.	2001	2002	2003
Food and live animals	120,721.7	126,851.3	158,938.5
Dairy products and birds' eggs	14,940.1	14,374.6	18,763.0
Cereals and cereal preparations	55,490.6	56,007.2	61,468.3
Sugar, sugar preparations and honey	19,933.3	19,643.0	30,290.0
Beverages and tobacco	5,851.6	7,393.4	10,975.6
Mineral fuels, lubricants, etc.	50,021.5	75,173.1	100,202.6
Petroleum, petroleum products, etc.	50,007.7	75,160.6	100,178.4
Animal and vegetable oils and fats	8,061.8	9,200.6	12,774.9
Vegetable oils and fats	7,327.9	8,690.4	11,103.2
Chemicals and related products	38,378.5	44,449.5	52,932.0
Medical and pharmaceutical	14,980.1	18,282.4	22,024.7
Basic manufactures	66,828.4	77,636.7	108,386.0
Iron and steel	20,750.0	23,018.2	31,558.9
Machinery and transport equipment	95,243.5	134,835.5	177,938.7
Machinery specialized in particular industries	19,419.8	28,441.7	35,310.5
Road vehicles	29,637.6	29,370.0	32,091.4
Miscellaneous manufactured articles	19,517.1	25,999.9	37,152.3
Total (incl. others)	415,899.0	513,025.7	674,128.3

Exports f.o.b.*	2001	2002	2003
Food and live animals	19,853.1	27,933.4	29,699.9
Fish, crustacea and molluscs, and preparations thereof	9,537.5	16,161.9	16,307.6
Mineral fuels, lubricants, etc.	536,893.7	530,293.1	618,593.7
Petroleum, petroleum products, etc.	533,477.5	527,723.6	611,929.5
Total (incl. others)	569,007.5	585,946.0	684,907.7

* Including re-exports (47,378.5 in 2001; 45,213.9 in 2002; 25,431.3 in 2003).

PRINCIPAL TRADING PARTNERS
(million riyals at current prices)

Imports c.i.f.	2001	2002	2003
Argentina	6,699.5	9,225.4	6,307.0
Australia	7,474.4	5,769.7	5,331.7
Bahrain	1,964.4	5,343.9	604.6
Brazil	15,970.1	18,149.2	21,778.0
China, People's Republic	16,533.4	30,397.2	36,431.0
Djibouti	8,559.0	6,565.1	4,993.1
Egypt	4,593.0	7,706.9	12,998.2
France (incl. Monaco)	19,407.8	18,298.7	23,405.9
Germany	8,888.6	8,294.9	16,299.6
India	22,799.1	18,760.6	37,273.2
Indonesia	4,313.0	5,708.8	3,562.0
Italy	6,018.4	8,272.8	10,743.7
Japan	11,332.1	10,872.2	16,824.0
Korea, Republic	4,066.9	7,528.0	6,754.6
Kuwait	21,622.6	36,471.2	52,976.2
Malaysia	11,097.1	11,351.4	14,821.6
Netherlands	8,342.9	6,166.4	12,781.2
Oman	13,557.3	14,635.3	19,048.4
Saudi Arabia	51,611.3	61,862.1	75,042.5
Singapore	5,751.4	4,868.7	7,653.0
Switzerland	8,140.4	22,141.7	27,251.0
Thailand	6,932.8	10,330.4	14,590.4
Turkey	8,607.6	11,261.1	18,494.4
United Arab Emirates	51,896.7	84,702.0	95,086.2
United Kingdom	15,659.0	14,925.5	20,577.8
USA	20,559.8	23,038.3	42,285.5
Total (incl. others)	415,899.0	513,025.7	674,128.2

YEMEN

Exports f.o.b.	2001	2002	2003
China, People's Republic	54,288.4	87,830.1	213,295.5
India	104,320.0	95,876.2	68,332.1
Italy	12,153.8	1,857.9	1,828.9
Korea, Republic	75,110.9	71,502.0	36,256.8
Kuwait	2,593.4	10,715.2	26,814.1
Malaysia	36,374.4	35,022.9	11,001.5
Philippines	3,261.8	9,630.7	11,183.7
Saudi Arabia	10,907.3	15,400.8	15,881.8
Singapore	53,428.2	21,682.8	29,277.4
South Africa	18,611.4	10,170.7	6,446.6
Switzerland	124.3	2,575.6	11,630.6
Taiwan	6,912.2	9,650.8	561.0
Thailand	10,216.1	10,889.0	16,097.8
United Arab Emirates	1,000.1	1,457.2	12,519.5
USA	22,717.1	30,576.5	10,834.1
Total (incl. others)	521,629.0	540,732.2	659,476.4

Transport

ROAD TRAFFIC
(vehicles in use at 31 December)

	1994	1995	1996
Passenger cars	227,854	229,084	240,567
Buses and coaches	2,712	2,835	3,437
Goods vehicles	279,154	279,780	291,149

Source: IRF, *World Road Statistics*.

SHIPPING

Merchant Fleet
(registered at 31 December)

	2002	2003	2004
Number of vessels	47	50	49
Total displacement ('000 grt)	78.0	29.5	33.0

Source: Lloyd's Register-Fairplay, *World Fleet Statistics*.

International Sea-borne Freight Traffic
('000 metric tons unless otherwise indicated, excluding dhows)

	2001	2002	2003
Vessels called (number)	3,516	3,381	2,830
Dry cargo*:			
goods loaded	288	312	314
goods unloaded	5,966	6,809	7,500
Oil and petroleum products:			
goods loaded	11,368	10,441	10,472
goods unloaded	7,841	7,725	8,640

* Excluding livestock and vehicles.

CIVIL AVIATION
(traffic on scheduled services)

	1999	2000	2001
Kilometres flown (million)	15	16	18
Passengers carried ('000)	731	842	841
Passenger-km (million)	1,031	1,588	1,580
Total ton-km (million)	114	179	174

Source: UN, *Statistical Yearbook*.

Tourism

TOURISM ARRIVALS

	2001	2002	2003
Africa	4,867	3,045	8,627
Sudan	2,009	1,472	1,875
Americas	2,879	4,429	12,932
Europe	26,920	15,828	13,033
France	4,653	2,792	1,882
Germany	5,721	2,772	1,894
Italy	7,136	2,352	1,731
United Kingdom	1,468	1,951	4,640
Middle East	34,704	63,415	103,409
Egypt	2,517	2,509	3,677
Iraq	3,988	1,691	2,846
Jordan	2,569	2,385	2,689
Saudi Arabia	14,404	38,254	59,669
Syria	3,040	3,727	6,780
Total (incl. others)	75,579	98,020	154,667

Tourism receipts (US $ million, incl. passenger transport): 38 in 2001; 38 in 2002; 139 in 2003.

Source: World Tourism Organization.

Communications Media

	2002	2003	2004
Telephones ('000 main lines in use)	542.2	n.a.	798.1
Mobile cellular telephones ('000 subscribers)	411.1	700.0	1,072.0
Personal computers ('000 in use)	145	n.a.	300
Internet users ('000)	100	n.a.	5,870

Source: International Telecommunication Union.

Radio receivers ('000 in use): 1,050 in 1997.

Television receivers ('000 in use): 5,200 in 2000.

Facsimile machines ('000 in use, estimate): 2,784 in 1995.

Daily newspapers: 3 titles with total circulation of 50,000 copies in 2000.

Sources: UN, *Statistical Yearbook*; UNESCO, *Statistical Yearbook*.

Education

(2003/04, unless otherwise indicated)

	Schools	Teachers*	Males	Females	Total
Pre-primary†	42	532	3,274	2,822	6,156
Primary	11,013‡	113,812	2,541,000	1,454,000	3,995,000
Secondary	n.a.*	14,063	387,000	188,000	575,000
Higher†	7*	3,429§	138,291§	45,781§	184,072§

* 1999/2000.
† Public education only.
‡ 1993/94 (Source: UNESCO, *Statistical Yearbook*).
§ 2001/02.

Adult literacy rate (UNESCO estimates): 49.0% (males 69.5%; females 28.5%) in 2002 (Source: UN Development Programme, *Human Development Report*).

Directory

The Constitution

A draft Constitution for the united Republic of Yemen, based on that endorsed by the Yemen Arab Republic (YAR) and the People's Democratic Republic of Yemen (PDRY) in December 1981, was published in December 1989; it was approved by a popular referendum on 15–16 May 1991.

On 29 September 1994 52 articles were amended, 29 added and one cancelled, leaving a total of 159 articles in the Constitution. Further amendments to the Constitution were adopted by the House of Representatives in late November 2000 and approved in a national referendum on 20 February 2001.

The Constitution defines the Yemeni Republic as an independent and sovereign Arab and Islamic country. The document states that the Republic 'is an indivisible whole, and it is impermissible to concede any part of it. The Yemeni people are part of the Arab and Islamic nation'. The Islamic *Shari'a* is identified as the basis of all laws.

The revised Constitution provides for the election, by direct universal suffrage, of the President of the Republic; the President is elected for a seven-year term (increased from five years by the amendments approved in 2001). The President is empowered to appoint a Vice-President. The President of the Republic is, *ex officio*, Supreme Commander of the Armed Forces. The Constitution as amended in 2001 requires presidential candidates to obtain the endorsement of 5% of a combined vote of the appointed Consultative Council and the elected House of Representatives (in place of 10% of the latter chamber alone).

Legislative authority is vested in the 301-member House of Representatives, which is elected, by universal suffrage, for a six-year term (increased from four years by amendment in 2001). The role of the House of Representatives is defined as to 'monitor' the executive. The President is empowered to dissolve the legislature and call new elections within a period of 60 days.

The upper house of the legislature, the Consultative Council, has 111 members (increased from 59 by amendment in 2001), nominated by the President.

The President of the Republic appoints the Prime Minister and other members of the Government on the advice of the Prime Minister.

The Constitution delineates the separation of the powers of the organs of State, and guarantees the independence of the judiciary. The existence of a multi-party political system is confirmed. Serving members of the police and armed forces are banned from political activity.

The Government

HEAD OF STATE

President: Field Marshal Ali Abdullah Saleh (took office 24 May 1990; re-elected 1 October 1994, 23 September 1999).
Vice-President: Maj.-Gen. Abd ar-Rabbuh Mansur Hadi.

COUNCIL OF MINISTERS
(April 2006)

Prime Minister: Abd al-Qadir Bajammal.
Deputy Prime Minister and Minister of the Interior: Gen. Rashid al-Alimi.
Minister of Finance: Saif Mahyoub al-Asali.
Minister of Planning and International Co-operation: Abd al-Karim Ismail al-Arhabi.
Minister of Petroleum and Mineral Resources: Khalid Mahfouz Bahaj.
Minister of Social Affairs and Labour: Amat ar-Razzak Ali Hamad.
Minister of Local Government: Sadiq Amin Abduras.
Minister of Human Rights: Khadijah Ahmad al-Haisami.
Minister of Transport: Omar Mohsen al-Amoudi.
Minister of Information: Hassan Ahmad al-Lawzi.
Minister of Immigrants' and Foreign Affairs: Abu Bakr al-Kurbi.
Minister of Electricity: Ali Muhammad Majur.
Minister of Legal Affairs: Adnan Omar al-Jifri.
Minister of Religious Endowments and Guidance: Hamoud Muhammad Abbad.
Minister of Culture: Khalid Abdullah ar-Ruweishan.
Minister of Agriculture and Irrigation: Jalal Ibrahim Faqira.
Minister of Industry and Commerce: Khalid Rajeh Sheikh.
Minister of Public Health and Population: Abd al-Karim Ras'e.
Minister of Education: Abd as-Salam al-Jufi.
Minister of Fisheries: Mahmoud Ibrahim Sagheri.
Minister of Justice: Gazi Shayef al-Aghbari.
Minister of Higher Education and Scientific Research: Saleh Ali Basorra.
Minister of Technical Education and Vocational Training: Ali Mansour Safa'a.
Minister of Tourism: Nabil Hassan al-Faqih.
Minister of the Civil Service and Social Security: Omar Abdullah al-Kurshemi.
Minister of Communications and Information Technology: Abd al-Malik al-Maalami.
Minister of Defence: Muhammad Nasser Ahmad Ali.
Minister of Public Utilities and Urban Planning: Abdullah Hussain ad-Dafi.
Minister of Water and the Environment: Muhammad Lutf al-Iryani.
Minister of Youth and Sports: Abd ar-Rahman al-Akwaa.
Minister of State for Parliamentary Affairs: Rashid Ahmad ar-Rassas.
Minister of State and Mayor of San'a: Yehya Muhammad ash-Shaibi.
Minister of State: Muhammad Yasser.
Minister of State and Secretary-General for the Presidential Office: Abdullah al-Bashiri.

MINISTRIES

All ministries are in San'a.

Ministry of Communications and Information Technology: Airport Rd, al-Jiraf, POB 25237, San'a; tel. (1) 331456; fax (1) 331457.
Ministry of Defence: POB 4131, San'a; tel. (1) 252640; fax (1) 252375.
Ministry of Immigrants' and Foreign Affairs: San'a.
Ministry of Industry and Commerce: POB 22210, San'a; tel. (1) 252363; fax (1) 252337; e-mail most@y.net.ye; internet www.most.org.ye.
Ministry of Information: San'a; tel. (1) 274008; fax (1) 282004; e-mail yemen-info@y.net.ye; internet www.yemeninfo.gov.ye.
Ministry of Petroleum and Mineral Resources: POB 81, San'a; tel. (1) 202313.
Ministry of Planning and International Co-operation: POB 175, San'a; tel. (1) 250101; fax (1) 251503.

President and Legislature

PRESIDENT

Presidential Election, 23 September 1999

Candidates	Votes	% of votes
Field Marshal Ali Abdullah Saleh	3,445,608	96.3
Najib Qahtan ash-Sha'bi	132,532	3.7
Total	**3,577,960**	**100.0**

HOUSE OF REPRESENTATIVES

Speaker: Sheikh Abdullah bin Hussain al-Ahmar.
General Election, 27 April 2003

Party	Seats*
General People's Congress (GPC)	228
Yemeni Islah Party (YIP)	47
Independents	14
Yemeni Socialist Party (YSP)	7
Nasserite Unionist Popular Organization	3
Arab Socialist Baath Party	2
Total	**301**

* Includes the results of three by-elections held in July 2003.

Election Commission

Supreme Commission for Elections and Referendums (SCER): San'a; e-mail scer@y.net.ye; internet www.scer.org.ye; f. 1999; Chair. KHALED A. ASH-SHARIF.

Political Organizations

In the former PDRY the YSP was the only legal political party until December 1989, when the formation of opposition parties was legalized. There were no political parties in the former YAR. The two leading parties that emerged in the unified Yemen were the GPC and the YSP. During 1990 an estimated 30–40 further political parties were reported to have been formed, and in 1991 a law was passed regulating the formation of political parties. Following the civil war from May to July 1994, President Saleh excluded the YSP from the new Government formed in October 1994. There were 22 registered political parties in April 2003.

Democratic Coalition of Opposition: San'a; f. 1995 as a coalition of 13 political parties and organizations, including a splinter faction of the YSP and the LSY.

General People's Congress (GPC): San'a; e-mail gpc@y.net.ye; internet www.gpc.org.ye; a broad grouping of supporters of President Saleh; Chair. Field Marshal ALI ABDULLAH SALEH; Vice-Chair. Maj.-Gen. ABD AR-RABBUH MANSUR HADI; Sec.-Gen. Dr ABD AL-KARIM AL-IRYANI.

Al-Haq: San'a; conservative Islamic party; Sec.-Gen. Sheikh AHMAD ASH-SHAMI.

League of the Sons of Yemen (LSY): Aden; represents interests of southern tribes; Leader ABD AR-RAHMAN AL-JIFRI; Sec.-Gen. MOHSEN FARID.

Nasserite Unionist Popular Organization: Aden; f. 1989 as a legal party.

National Opposition Co-ordination Council: San'a; f. 2001 as a coalition of opposition parties, including the YSP.

Yemen Socialist Party (YSP): San'a; f. 1978 to succeed the United Political Organization—National Front (UPO—NF); fmrly Marxist-Leninist 'vanguard' party based on 'scientific socialism'; has Political Bureau and Cen. Cttee; Sec.-Gen. ALI SALEH OBAD.

Yemeni Islah Party (YIP): POB 23090, San'a; tel. (1) 213281; fax (1) 213311; f. 1990 by mems of the legislature and other political figures, and tribal leaders; seeks constitutional reform based on Islamic law; Leader Sheikh ABDULLAH BIN HUSSAIN AL-AHMAR; Sec.-Gen. Sheikh MUHAMMAD ALI AL-YADOUMI.

Yemeni Unionist Rally Party: Aden; f. 1990 by intellectuals and politicians from the fmr YAR and PDRY to safeguard human rights; Leader OMAR AL-JAWI.

Other parties in Yemen include the **Arab Socialist Baath Party**; the **Federation of Popular Forces**; the **Liberation Front Party**; the **Nasserite Democratic Party**; the **National Democratic Front**; the **National Social Party**; the **Popular Nasserite Reformation Party**; the **Social Green Party** and the **Yemen League**.

Diplomatic Representation

EMBASSIES IN YEMEN

Algeria: POB 509, 67 Amman St, San'a; tel. (1) 209689; fax (1) 209688; Ambassador BEN SAAD BIN AL-ABED.

Bulgaria: POB 1518, Asr, St 4, Residence 5, San'a; tel. (1) 207924; e-mail bgemb@y.net.ye; Chargé d'affaires ALEXI ALAXIEV.

China, People's Republic: POB 482, az-Zubairy St, San'a; tel. (1) 275337; fax (1) 275341; e-mail chinaemb@y.net.ye; internet ye.chineseembassy.org; Ambassador (vacant).

Cuba: POB 15256, St 6B, Block 9, House 3, Safia Zone, nr Amman St, San'a; tel. (1) 442321; fax (1) 442322; e-mail embacubayem@y.net.ye; Ambassador ROBERTO RODRÍGUEZ PEÑA.

Czech Republic: POB 2501, Safiya Janoobia, St 16, House 6, San'a; tel. (1) 247946; fax (1) 244418; e-mail sanaa@embassy.mzv.cz; internet www.mzv.cz/sanaa; Chargé d'affaires VÁCLAV MATOUŠEK.

Djibouti: San'a; Ambassador SUHAIL ISMAIL OMAR.

Egypt: POB 1134, Gamal Abd an-Nasser St, San'a; tel. (1) 275948; fax (1) 274196; Ambassador MUHAMMAD BADR ED-DIN ZAYED.

Eritrea: POB 11040, Western Safia Bldg, San'a; tel. (1) 209422; fax (1) 214088; Ambassador MAHMOUD ALI JABRA.

Ethiopia: POB 234, Al-Hamadani St, San'a; tel. (1) 208833; fax (1) 213780; e-mail ethoembs@y.net.ye; Ambassador ATO ABDI DOLAR.

France: POB 1286, Cnr Sts 2/21, San'a; tel. (1) 268888; fax (1) 269160; internet www.y.net.ye/ambafrancesanaa; Ambassador ALAIN MOUREAU.

Germany: POB 2562, Hadda, San'a; tel. (1) 413174; fax (1) 413179; e-mail info@sanaa.diplo.de; internet www.sanaa.diplo.de; Ambassador FRANK MARCUS MANN.

Hungary: POB 11558, As-Safiya al-Gharbiyya, St No. 6B, San'a; tel. (1) 441014; fax (1) 441012; e-mail hungemb@y.net.ye; Ambassador Dr TIBOR SZATMARI.

India: POB 1154, San'a; tel. (1) 508084; fax (1) 508105; e-mail indiaemb@y.net.ye; internet www.eoisanaa.com.ye; Ambassador A. KARUPPAIYAH (designate).

Indonesia: POB 19873, Beirut St, San'a; tel. (1) 427210; fax (1) 427212; e-mail indosan@y.net.ye; Ambassador KEMAS FACHRUDDIN.

Iran: POB 1437, Haddah St, San'a; tel. (1) 413552; fax (1) 414139; e-mail iriranemb@y.net.ye; internet www.iranyemen.com.ye; Ambassador HOSSEIN KAMALIAN.

Iraq: POB 498, South Airport Rd, San'a; tel. (1) 440184; fax (1) 440187; e-mail snaemb@iraqmofamail.net; Ambassador TALAL JAMEEL SALEH AL-OBAYDI.

Italy: POB 1152, No. 5 Bldg, St No. 29, San'a; tel. (1) 269164; fax (1) 266137; e-mail ambasciata.sanaa@esteri.it; internet www.ambitaliasanaa.org.ye; Ambassador MARIO BOFFO.

Japan: POB 817, San'a; tel. (1) 423700; fax (1) 417850; Ambassador YUICHI ISHII.

Jordan: POB 2152, San'a; tel. (1) 413276; fax (1) 414516; e-mail jaysem@y.net.ye; Ambassador AHMAD ALI JARADAT.

Korea, Democratic People's Republic: POB 1209, al-Hasaba, Mazda Rd, San'a; tel. (1) 232340; Ambassador CHANG MYONG SON.

Korea, Republic: San'a; tel. (1) 245959; Ambassador PAK HI-JOO.

Kuwait: POB 3746, South Ring Rd, San'a; tel. (1) 268876; fax (1) 268875; Ambassador ABD AR-RAHMAN SAYED AL-OTAEBI.

Lebanon: POB 2283, Haddah St, San'a; tel. (1) 203459; fax (1) 201120; Ambassador HASSAN BERRO.

Libya: POB 1506, Ring Rd, St No. 8, House No. 145, San'a; Secretary of Libyan Brotherhood Office A. U. HEFIANA.

Malaysia: POB 16157, San'a; tel. (1) 415605; fax (1) 416181; e-mail mwsanaa@y.net.ye; Ambassador Dato' MISRAN KARMAIN.

Mauritania: POB 19383, No. 6, Algeria St, San'a; tel. (1) 216770; fax (1) 215926; Ambassador AHMED OULD SIDY.

Morocco: Faj Attan, Hay Assormi, Ave Beyrouth, San'a; tel. (1) 426628; fax (1) 426627; Ambassador MUHAMMAD TOUHAMI.

Netherlands: POB 463, off 14th October St, San'a; tel. (1) 421800; fax 421035; e-mail holland@y.net.ye; internet www.holland.com.ye; Ambassador J. F. L. BLANKENBURG.

Oman: POB 105, Aser area, az-Zubairy St, San'a; tel. (1) 208933; Ambassador ABDULLAH BIN HAMAD AL-BADI.

Pakistan: POB 2848, Ring Rd, San'a; tel. (1) 248814; fax (1) 248866; e-mail pakembassy@yemen.net.ye; Ambassador NAWAB AMIR ABDUL REHMAN NOUSHERWANI.

Poland: POB 16168, Hadda St, San'a; tel. (1) 412243; fax (1) 413647; Ambassador KRZYSZTOF SUPROWICZ.

Qatar: POB 19717, San'a; tel. (1) 304640; fax (1) 304645; e-mail sanaa@mofa.gov.qa; Ambassador JASIM ABU AL-INAYN.

Russia: POB 1087, 26 September St, San'a; tel. (1) 278719; fax (1) 283142; Ambassador IGOR G. IVASHENKO.

Saudi Arabia: POB 1184, Zuhara House, Hadda Rd, San'a; tel. (1) 240429; Ambassador MUHAMMAD AL-QAHTANI.

Somalia: San'a; tel. (1) 208864; Ambassador ABD AS-SALLAM MU'ALLIM ADAM.

Sudan: POB 2561, 82 Abou al-Hassan al-Hamadani St, San'a; tel. (1) 265231; fax (1) 265234; Ambassador OMAR AS-SAID TAHA.

Syria: POB 494, Hadda Rd, Damascus St 1, San'a; tel. (1) 414891; Ambassador ABD AL-GHAFOUR SABOUNI.

Tunisia: POB 2561, Diplomatic area, St No. 22, San'a; tel. (1) 240458; Ambassador (vacant).

Turkey: POB 18371, as-Safiya, San'a; tel. and fax (1) 241395; Ambassador FUAT TANLAY.

United Arab Emirates: POB 2250, Ring Rd, San'a; tel. (1) 248777; Ambassador SAIF SULTAN AL-AWANI.

United Kingdom: POB 1287, 129 Hadda Rd, San'a; tel. (1) 264081; fax (1) 263059; e-mail britishembassysanaa@fco.gov.uk; internet www.britishembassy.gov.uk/yemen; Ambassador MICHAEL GIFFORD.

USA: POB 22347, Sheraton Hotel District, San'a; tel. (1) 238843; fax (1) 251563; e-mail usembassy08@y.net.ye; internet yemen.usembassy.gov; Ambassador THOMAS C. KRAJESKI.

YEMEN   Directory

Judicial System

Yemen's Constitution guarantees the independence of the judiciary and identifies Islamic law (*Shari'a*) as the basis of all laws.

Yemen is divided into 18 governorates, each of which is further divided into districts. Each district has a Court of First Instance in which all cases are heard by a single magistrate. Appeals against decisions of the Courts of First Instance are referred to a Court of Appeal. Each governorate has a Court of Appeal with four divisions: Civil, Criminal, Matrimonial and Commercial, each of which consists of three judges.

The Supreme Court of the Republic, which sits in San'a, rules on matters concerning the Constitution, appeals against decisions of the Courts of Appeal and cases brought against members of the Legislature. The Supreme Court has eight divisions, each of which consists of five judges.

The Supreme Judicial Council supervises the proper function of the courts and its Chairman is the President of the Republic.

Religion

ISLAM

The majority of the population are Muslims. Most are Sunni Muslims of the Shafi'a sect, except in the north-west of the country, where Zaidism (a moderate sect of the Shi'a order) is the dominant persuasion.

CHRISTIANITY

The Roman Catholic Church

Apostolic Vicariate of Arabia: POB 54, Abu Dhabi, United Arab Emirates; tel. (2) 4461895; fax (2) 4465177; e-mail vicapar@emirates.net.ae; responsible for a territory comprising most of the Arabian peninsula (including Saudi Arabia, the UAE, Oman, Qatar, Bahrain and Yemen), containing an estimated 1,300,500 Roman Catholics (31 December 2003); Vicar Apostolic PAUL FRIDOLIN HINDER (Titular Bishop of Macon, Georgia, resident in the UAE); Vicar Delegate for Yemen Rev. GEORGE PUDUSSERY.

The Anglican Communion

Within the Episcopal Church in Jerusalem and the Middle East, Yemen forms part of the diocese of Cyprus and the Gulf. The Anglican congregations in San'a and Aden are entirely expatriate; the Bishop in Cyprus and the Gulf is resident in Cyprus, while the Archdeacon in the Gulf is resident in Qatar.

HINDUISM

There is a small Hindu community.

The Press

Legislation embodying the freedom of the press in the unified Republic of Yemen was enacted in May 1990. The lists below include publications which appeared in the YAR and the PDRY prior to their unification in May 1990.

DAILIES

Al-Jumhuriya: Taiz Information Office, Taiz; tel. (4) 216748; Arabic; circ. 100,000.

Ar-Rabi' 'Ashar Min Uktubar (14 October): POB 4227, Crater, Aden; f. 1968; not published on Saturdays; Arabic; Editorial Dir FAROUQ MUSTAFA RIFAT; Chief Editor MUHAMMAD HUSSAIN MUHAMMAD; circ. 20,000.

Ash-Sharara (The Spark): 14 October Corpn for Printing, Publishing, Distribution and Advertising, POB 4227, Crater, Aden; Arabic; circ. 6,000.

Ath-Thawra (The Revolution): POB 2195, San'a; tel. (1) 262626; fax (1) 274139; e-mail contact@althawranews.net; internet www.althawranews.net; Arabic; govt-owned; Editor MUHAMMAD AZ-ZORKAH; circ. 110,000.

WEEKLIES AND OTHERS

Attijarah (Trade): POB 3370, Hodeida; tel. (3) 213784; fax (3) 211528; e-mail hodcci@y.net.ye; monthly; Arabic; commercial.

Al-Ayyam: POB 648, al-Khalij al-Imami, Crater, Aden; tel. (2) 255170; fax (2) 255692; e-mail editor@al-ayyam-yemen.com; Editor HISHAM BASHRAHEEL.

Al-Bilad (The Country): POB 1438, San'a; weekly; Arabic; centre-right.

Dar as-Salam (Peace): POB 1790, San'a; tel. (1) 272946; f. 1948; weekly; Arabic; political, economic and general essays; Editor ABDULLAH MUKBOOL AS-SICGUL.

Al-Fanoon: Ministry of Culture and Tourism, POB 1187, Tawahi 102, Aden; tel. (2) 23831; f. 1980; Arabic; monthly arts review; Editor FAISAL SOFY; circ. 15,500.

Al-Gundi (The Soldier): Ministry of Defence, Madinat ash-Sha'ab; fortnightly; Arabic; circ. 8,500.

Al-Hares: Aden; fortnightly; Arabic; circ. 8,000.

Al-Hikma (Wisdom): POB 4227, Crater, Aden; monthly; Arabic; publ. by the Writers' Union; circ. 5,000.

Al-Ma'in (Spring): Ministry of Information, San'a; monthly; general interest.

Majallat al-Jaish (Army Magazine): POB 2182, San'a; tel. (1) 231181; monthly; publ. by Ministry of Defence.

Al-Maseerah (Journey): Ministry of Information, POB 2182, San'a; tel. (1) 231181; monthly; general interest.

Al-Mithaq (The Charter): San'a; internet www.gpc.org.ye/mathak; weekly; organ of the General People's Congress.

Ar-Ra'i al-'Am (Public Opinion): POB 293, San'a; tel. (1) 242090; weekly; independent; Editor ALI MUHAMMAD AL-OLAFI.

Ar-Risalah: POB 55777, 26 September St, Taiz; tel. (4) 214215; fax (4) 221164; e-mail alaws@y.net.ye; f. 1968; weekly; Arabic.

As-Sahwa (Awakening): POB 11126, Hadda Road, San'a; tel. (1) 247892; fax (1) 269218; weekly; Islamic fundamentalist; Editor MUHAMMAD AL-YADDOUMI.

As-Salam (Peace): POB 181, San'a; tel. (1) 272946; weekly.

San'a: POB 193, San'a; fortnightly; Arabic; inclined to left.

Sawt al-'Ummal (The Workers' Voice): POB 4227, Crater, Aden; weekly; Arabic.

Sawt al-Yemen (Voice of Yemen): POB 302, San'a; weekly; Arabic.

Ash-Shura: POB 15114, San'a; tel. (1) 213584; fax (1) 213468; e-mail shoura@y.net.ye; Editor ABDALLAH SA'AD; circ. 15,000.

At-Ta'awun (Co-operation): at-Ta'awun Bldg, az-Zubairy St, San'a; weekly; Arabic; supports co-operative societies.

Ath-Thawri (The Revolutionary): POB 4227, Crater, Aden; weekly; published on Saturday; Arabic; organ of Cen. Cttee of YSP; Editor Dr AHMAD ABDULLAH SALIH.

26 September: 26 September Publishing, POB 17, San'a; tel. (1) 262626; fax (1) 234129; e-mail webmaster@26september.com; internet www.y.net.ye/26september; armed forces weekly; circ. 25,000.

Al-Wahda al-Watani (National Unity): Al-Baath Printing House, POB 193, San'a; tel. (1) 77511; f. 1982; fmrly Al-Omal; monthly; Editor MUHAMMAD SALEM ALI; circ. 40,000.

Al-Yemen: Yemen Printing and Publishing Co, POB 1081, San'a; tel. (1) 72376; f. 1971; weekly; Arabic; centre-right; Editor MUHAMMAD AHMAD AS-SABAGH.

Yemen Observer: POB 19183, Algeria St, San'a; tel. (1) 203393; fax (1) 207239; e-mail editor@yobserver.com; internet www.yobserver.com; f. 1996; independent weekly; English; Editor-in-Chief MUHAMMAD AL-ASAADI.

The Yemen Times: POB 2579, Hadda St, San'a; tel. (1) 268661; fax (1) 268276; e-mail editor@yementimes.com; internet www.yementimes.com; f. 1991; every Monday and Thursday; English; Editor-in-Chief NADIA AS-SAQQAF; circ. 30,000.

Yemeni Women: POB 4227, Crater, Aden; monthly; circ. 5,000.

NEWS AGENCIES

Aden News Agency (ANA): Ministry of Culture and Tourism, POB 1187, Tawahi 102, Aden; tel. (2) 24874; f. 1970; govt-owned; Dir-Gen. AHMAD MUHAMMAD IBRAHIM.

Saba News Agency: POB 881, San'a; tel. (1) 250078; fax (1) 250078; e-mail sabanews@y.net.ye; internet www.sabanews.gov.ye; f. 1970; Editor HUSSEIN AL-AWADI.

Publishers

Armed Forces Printing Press: POB 17, San'a; tel. (1) 274240.

14 October Corpn for Printing, Publishing, Distribution and Advertising: POB 4227, Crater, Aden; under control of the Ministry of Information; Chair. and Gen. Man. SALIH AHMAD SALAH.

26 September Publishing: POB 17, San'a; tel. (1) 274240.

Ath-Thawrah Corpn: POB 2195, San'a; fax (1) 251505; Chair. M. R. AZ-ZURKAH.

Yemen Printing and Publishing Co: POB 1081, San'a; Chair. AHMAD MUHAMMAD HADI.

YEMEN

Broadcasting and Communications

TELECOMMUNICATIONS

Public Telecommunications Corpn: POB 17045, Airport Rd, al-Jiraf, San'a; tel. (1) 250040; Dir-Gen. MUHAMMAD AL-KASSOUS.

BROADCASTING

Yemen Radio and Television Corpn: POB 2182, San'a; tel. (1) 230654; fax (1) 230761; state-controlled; Gen. Man. AHMAD T. SHAYANY.

Finance

(cap. = capital; res = reserves; dep. = deposits; m. = million; brs = branches; amounts in Yemeni riyals, unless otherwise indicated)

BANKING

Central Bank

Central Bank of Yemen: POB 59, Ali Abd al-Mughni St, San'a; tel. (1) 274310; fax (1) 274360; e-mail info@centralbank.gov.ye; internet www.centralbank.gov.ye; f. 1971; merged with Bank of Yemen in 1990; cap. 2,000.0m., res 81,089.4m., dep. 446,287.2m. (Dec. 2002); Gov. AHMAD ABD AR-RAHMAN AS-SAMAWI; Dep. Gov. MUHAMMAD AWAD BIN HUMAM; 22 brs.

Principal Banks

Arab Bank PLC (Jordan): POB 475, az-Zubairy St, San'a; tel. (1) 276585; fax (1) 276583; e-mail yam@arabbank.com.ye; internet www.arabbank.com; f. 1972; Man. MAHDI ALAWI; 10 brs.

Co-operative and Agricultural Credit Bank: POB 2015, Banks Complex, az-Zubairy St, San'a; tel. (1) 220090; fax (1) 220088; e-mail cacbank@y.net.ye; f. 1976; cap. 293m., total assets 4,930m. (Dec. 2000); Chair. Dr MUHAMMAD H. AL-WADAN; Dir-Gen. YAHIA AS-SABRI; 27 brs.

Crédit Agricole Indosuez (France): POB 651, az-Zubairy St, San'a; tel. (1) 274370; fax (1) 274501; e-mail caindosuezye@y.net.ye; internet www.ca-indosuez.com; f. 1978; Regional Man. ROBIN DE MOUXY; 6 brs.

International Bank of Yemen YSC: POB 4444, 106 az-Zubairy St, San'a; tel. (1) 273273; fax (1) 274127; e-mail ibyemen@ibyemen.com; internet www.ibyemen.com; f. 1980; commercial bank; cap. 1,014.6m., res 70.8m., dep. 23,913.8m. (Dec. 2002); Chair. ABDULLAH A. WALI NASHER; Gen. Man. AHMAD T. N. AL-ABSI; 4 brs.

Islamic Bank of Yemen for Finance and Investment: POB 18452, Mareb Yemen Insurance Co Bldg, az-Zubairy St, San'a; tel. (1) 206117; fax (1) 205679; e-mail ibr-islbk-yesan@y.net.ye; internet www.islamicbankymn.com; f. 1996; commercial, investment and retail banking; cap. 1,250.0m., res 349.7m., dep. 13,609.6m. (Dec. 2003); Chair. A. KARIM AR-RAHMAN AL-ASWADI; Gen. Man. ABDULMALIK THABET; 3 brs.

National Bank of Yemen: POB 5, Arwa Rd, Crater, Aden; tel. and fax (2) 253484; e-mail nby.ho@y.net.ye; internet www.natbankofyemen.com; f. 1970 as National Bank of South Yemen; reorg. 1971; cap. 2,100.0m., res 1,698.2m., dep. 44,532.8m. (Dec. 2003); Chair. and Gen. Man. ABD AR-RAHMAN MUHAMMAD AL-KUHALI; 27 brs.

Shamil Bank of Yemen and Bahrain: POB 19382, Hadah St, San'a; tel. (1) 264702; fax (1) 264703; e-mail shamilbank@y.net.ye; cap. and res 2,000.0m., dep. 4,780.0m. (Dec. 2002); Chair. AHMAD ABUBAKER OMER BAZARA; Gen. Man. MUHAMMAD NAJIB AHMAD SAAD.

Tadhamon International Islamic Bank: POB 2411, as-Saeed Commercial Bldg, az-Zubairy St, San'a; e-mail tib@y.net.ye; internet www.tib.com.ye; f. 1995 as Yemen Bank for Investment and Development; became Tadhamon Islamic Bank in 1996, name changed as above in 2002; cap. 2,250.0m., res 1,844.2m., dep. 72,287.4m. (Dec. 2003); Chair. ABD AL-GABBAR HAYEL SAID; Gen. Man. AMER M. TAWQAN.

United Bank Ltd (Pakistan): POB 1295, Ali Abd al-Mughni St, San'a; tel. (1) 272424; fax (1) 274168; e-mail ublsana@y.net.ye; Country Head MUHAMMAD ANWAR; 1 br.

Watani Bank for Trade and Investment: POB 3058, az-Zubairy St, San'a; tel. (1) 206613; fax (1) 205706; e-mail watanibank@y.net.ye; internet www.watanibank.com.ye; f. 1998; cap. 1,301.0m., res 55.9m., dep. 20,282.9m. (Dec. 2003); Chair. Dr AHMAD ALI AL-HAMDANI; Gen. Man.and CEO SHABIH S. MEHDI NAQVI.

Yemen Bank for Reconstruction and Development (YBRD): POB 541, 26 September St, San'a; tel. (1) 270481; fax (1) 271684; e-mail ybrdho@y.net.ye; internet www.ybrd.com.ye; f. 1962; cap. 2,000.0m., res 2,621.6m., dep. 47,890.3m. (Dec. 2004); Chair. ABDULLAH SALIM AL-GIFRI; Gen. Man. HUSSAIN FADHLE MUHAMMAD; 36 brs.

Yemen Commercial Bank: POB 19845, ar-Rowaishan Bldg, az-Zubairy St, San'a; tel. (1) 284272; fax (1) 284656; e-mail ycbho@y.net.ye; internet www.ycbank.com; f. 1993; cap. 1,234.1m., res 47.9m., dep. 29,807.6m. (Dec. 2003); Chair. Sheikh MUHAMMAD BIN YAHYA AR-ROWAISHAN; Chief Exec. and Gen. Man. SIKANDER MAHMOUD; 8 brs.

INSURANCE

Aman Insurance Co (YSC): POB 1133, San'a; tel. (1) 214104; fax (1) 209452; e-mail aman-ins@y.net.ye; internet www.y.net.ye/amaninsurance; all classes of insurance; Gen. Man. AKIL AS-SAKKAF.

Mareb Yemen Insurance Co: POB 2284, az-Zubairy St, San'a; tel. (1) 206115; fax (1) 206114; e-mail maryinsco74@y.net.ye; internet www.marebinsurance.com.ye; f. 1974; all classes of insurance; cap. 150m.; Chair. and Gen. Man. ALI M. HASHIM.

National Insurance and Re-insurance Co: POB 456, Aden; tel. (2) 51464; e-mail yireico@y.net.ye; f. 1970; Lloyd's Agents; cap. 5m. Yemeni dinars; Gen. Man. ABUBAKR S. AL-QOTI.

Saba Yemen Insurance Co: POB 19214, San'a; tel. (1) 240908; fax (1) 240943; e-mail info@saba-insurance.com; internet www.saba-insurance.com; f. 1990; all classes of insurance; Gen. Man. SABAH D. HADDAD.

Trust Yemen Insurance and Reinsurance Co: POB 18392, San'a; tel. (1) 425007; fax (1) 412570; all classes of insurance; Gen. Man. HUSSAIN AYYOUB.

United Insurance Co: POB 1883, az-Zubairy St, San'a; tel. (1) 555555; fax (1) 214012; e-mail uuicyemen@uicyemen.com; internet www.uicyemen.com; f. 1981; all classes of general insurance and life; cap. 400m. (2005); Gen. Man. TAREK A. HAYEL SAID.

Al-Watania Insurance Co (YSC): POB 15497, San'a; tel. (1) 272874; fax (1) 272924; e-mail alwatania@yenet.com; all classes of insurance.

Yemen General Insurance Co (SYC): POB 2709, YGI Bldg, 25 Algiers St, San'a; tel. (1) 442489; fax (1) 442492; e-mail ygi-san@y.net.ye; internet www.yginsurance.com; f. 1977; all classes of insurance; cap. 400m. (July 2004); Chair. ABD AL-GABBAR THABET; Gen. Man. BAKIR AL-MUNSHI.

Yemen Insurance Co: POB 8437, San'a; tel. (1) 272805; fax (1) 274177; e-mail ymnins@y.net.ye; f. 1990; all classes of insurance; Gen. Man. KHALID BASHIR TAHIR.

Trade and Industry

GOVERNMENT AGENCIES

General Corpn for Foreign Trade and Grains: POB 77, San'a; tel. (1) 202345; fax (1) 209511; f. 1976; Dir-Gen. ABD AR-RAHMAN AL-MADWAHI.

General Corpn for Manufacturing and Marketing of Cement: POB 1920, San'a; tel. (1) 215691; fax (1) 263168; Chair. AMIN ABD AL-WAHID AHMAD.

General Investment Authority (Yemen) (GIAY): POB 19022, San'a; tel. (1) 262962; fax (1) 262964; e-mail gias@y.net.ye; internet www.giay.org.

National Co for Foreign Trade: POB 90, Crater, Aden; tel. (2) 42793; fax (2) 42631; f. 1969; incorporates main foreign trading businesses (nationalized in 1970) and arranges their supply to the National Co for Home Trade; Gen. Man. AHMAD MUHAMMAD SALEH (acting).

National Co for Home Trade: POB 90, Crater, Aden; tel. (2) 41483; fax (2) 41226; f. 1969; marketing of general consumer goods, building materials, electrical goods, motor cars and spare parts, agricultural machinery, etc.; Man. Dir ABD AR-RAHMAN AS-SAILANI.

National Dockyards Co: POB 1244, Tawahi, Aden; tel. (2) 23837; f. 1969; Man. Dir ABDULLAH ALI MUHAMMAD.

National Drug Co: POB 192, Crater, Aden; tel. (2) 04912; fax (2) 21242; f. 1972; import of pharmaceutical products, chemicals, medical supplies, baby foods and scientific instruments; Chair. and Gen. Man. Dr AWADH SALAM ISSA BAMATRAF.

Public Corpn for Building and Housing: POB 7022, al-Mansoura, Aden; tel. (2) 342296; fax (2) 345726; f. 1973; govt contractors and contractors of private housing projects; Dir-Gen. HUSSAIN MUHAMMAD AL-WALI.

Public Corpn for Maritime Affairs (PCMA): POB 19396, San'a; tel. (1) 414412; fax (1) 414645; f. 1990; protection of the marine environment; registration of ships; implementation of international maritime conventions; Chair. SAID YAFAI.

YEMEN

Yemen Co for Industry and Commerce Ltd (YCIC): POB 5423, Taiz; tel. (4) 218058; fax (4) 218054; e-mail ycic@y.net.ye; internet www.ycic.com; f. 1970; Chair. ALI MUHAMMAD SAID.

Yemen Co for Investment and Finance Ltd (YCIF): POB 2789, San'a; tel. (1) 276372; fax (1) 274178; f. 1981; cap. 100m. riyals; Chair. and Gen. Man. ABDULLAH MUHAMMAD ISHAQ.

Yemen Drug Co for Industry and Commerce: POB 40, San'a; tel. (1) 234250; fax (1) 234290; Chair. MUHAMMAD ALI MUQBIL; Man. Dir ABD AR-RAHMAN A. GHALEB.

Yemen Economical Corpn: POB 1207, San'a; tel. (1) 262501; fax (1) 262508; e-mail info@yecoyemen.com; internet www.yecoyemen.com; f. 1973; Commercial Man. A. KARIM SAYAGHI.

Yemen Land Transport Corpn: POB 279, Taiz St, San'a; tel. (1) 268307; f. 1961; Chair. ABD AL-KADOOS AL-MASSRY; Gen. Man. SALEH ABDULLAH ABD AL-WALI.

Yemen Trading and Construction Co: POB 1092, San'a; tel. (1) 264005; fax (1) 240624; e-mail ytcc@y.net.ye; f. 1979; initial cap. 100m. riyals.

DEVELOPMENT ORGANIZATIONS

Agricultural Research and Extension Authority: POB 87148, Dhamar; e-mail muharram@y.net.ye.

General Board for Development of Eastern Region: San'a.

General Board for Development of Tihama: POB 49, Lufthansa Bldg, az-Zubairy St, San'a; tel. (1) 219436; fax (1) 219203; e-mail titra@y.net.ye; internet www.tihama-group.com; Dir ABBAS BAWAZIR.

Yemen Free Zone Public Authority: Aden; tel. (2) 241210; fax (2) 221237; supervises creation of a free zone for industrial investment; Chair. ABD AL-QADIR BAJAMMAL.

CHAMBERS OF COMMERCE

Chamber of Commerce and Industry—Aden: POB 473, Crater 101, Aden; tel. (2) 257376; fax (2) 255660; e-mail cciaden@y.net.ye; f. 1886; 5,000 mems; Pres. MUHAMMAD OMER BAMASHMUS; Dir G. AHMAD HADI SALEM.

Federation of Chambers of Commerce: POB 16992, San'a; tel. (1) 265038; fax (1) 261269; e-mail fucci@y.net.ye; Chair. MUHAMMAD ABDO SAID AN'AM.

Hodeida Chamber of Commerce: POB 3370, 20 az-Zubairy St, Hodeida; tel. (3) 217401; fax (3) 211528; e-mail hodcci@yemen.net.ye; f. 1960; 6,500 mems; cap. 10m. riyals; Dir NABIL AL-WAGEEH.

San'a Chamber of Commerce and Industry: Airport Rd, al-Hasabah St, POB 195, San'a; tel. (1) 232361; fax (1) 232412; f. 1963; Pres. Al-Haj HUSSAIN AL-WATARI; Gen. Man. ABDULLAH H. AR-RUBAIDI.

Taiz Chamber of Commerce: POB 5029, Chamber St, Taiz; tel. (4) 210580; fax (4) 212335; e-mail taizchamber@y.net.ye; Dir MOFID A. SAIF.

Yemen Chamber of Commerce and Industry: POB 16690, San'a; tel. (1) 223539; fax (1) 251555.

STATE HYDROCARBONS COMPANIES

General Corpn for Oil and Mineral Resources: San'a; f. 1990; state petroleum co; Pres. AHMAD BARAKAT.

Ministry of Petroleum and Mineral Resources: POB 81, San'a; tel. (1) 202313; responsible for the refining and marketing of petroleum products, and for prospecting and exploitation of indigenous hydrocarbons and other minerals; subsidiaries include:

Aden Refinery Co: POB 3003, Aden 110; tel. (2) 430743; fax (2) 76600; f. 1952; operates petroleum refinery; capacity 8.6m. metric tons per year; output 4.2m. tons (1990); operates one oil tanker; Exec. Dir FATHI SALEM ALI; Refinery Man. MUHAMMAD YESLAM.

Yemen National Oil Co: POB 5050, Maalla, Aden; sole petroleum concessionaire, importer and distributor of petroleum products; Gen. Man. MUHAMMAD ABD HUSSEIN.

UTILITIES

Electricity

Public Electricity Corpn: POB 11422, Government Complex, Haddah Rd, San'a; tel. (1) 264131; fax (1) 263115; Man. Dir AHMAD AL-AINI.

Water

National Water and Sanitation Authority (NWSA): (Taiz Branch) POB 5283, Taiz; tel. (4) 222628; fax (4) 212323.

TRADE UNIONS

Agricultural Co-operatives Union: POB 649, San'a; tel. (1) 270685; fax (1) 274125.

General Confederation of Workers: POB 1162, Maalla, Aden; f. 1956; affiliated to WFTU and ICFTU; 35,000 mems; Pres. RAJEH SALEH NAJI; Gen. Sec. ABD AR-RAZAK SHAIF.

Trade Union Federation: San'a; Pres. ALI SAIF MUQBIL.

Transport

RAILWAYS

There are no railways in Yemen.

ROADS

In 1996 Yemen had a total road network of 64,725 km, including 5,234 km of main roads and 2,474 km of secondary roads. In 1999 there were an estimated 67,000 km of roads, 11.5% of which were paved.

General Corpn for Roads and Bridges: POB 1185, az-Zubairy St, Asir Rd, San'a; tel. (1) 202278; fax (1) 209571; e-mail gcrb@y.net.ye; responsible for maintenance and construction.

Yemen Land Transport Co: Aden; f. 1980; incorporates fmr Yemen Bus Co and all other public transport of the fmr PDRY; Chair. ABD AL-JALIL TAHIR BADR; Gen. Man. SALEH AWAD AL-AMUDI.

SHIPPING

Aden is the main port. Aden Main Harbour has 28 first-class berths. In addition there is ample room to accommodate vessels of light draught at anchor in the 18-ft dredged area. There is also 800 ft of cargo wharf accommodating vessels of 300 ft length and 18 ft draught. Aden Oil Harbour accommodates four tankers of 57,000 metric tons and up to 40 ft draught. In March 1999 work was completed on a US $580m. programme to expand container handling facilities at Aden, with the aim of establishing the port as a major transhipment centre. A 35-year concession to operate Aden Container Terminal was signed by Dubai Ports World, of the United Arab Emirates, in late 2005. Hodeida port, on the Red Sea, was expanded with aid from the USSR and now handles a considerable amount of traffic; there are also ports at Maalla, Mocha, Nishtun and Salif.

At 31 December 2004 Yemen's merchant fleet comprised 49 vessels, with a combined displacement of 33,018 grt.

Yemen Ports Authority: POB 1316, Steamer Point, Aden; tel. (2) 201378; fax (2) 203521; e-mail info@portofaden.com; internet www.portofaden.com; f. 1888; Port Officer Capt. HUSSEIN AS-SAEDI.

Principal Shipping Companies

Aden Refinery Co: POB 3003, Aden 110; tel. (2) 430743; fax (2) 376600; f. 1952; two general tankers and one chemical tanker; Exec. Dir FATHI SALEM ALI.

Arabian Gulf Navigation Co (Yemen) Ltd: POB 3740, Hodeida; tel. (3) 2442; one general cargo vessel.

Elkirshi Shipping and Stevedoring Co: POB 3813, al-Hamdi St, Hodeida; tel. (3) 224263; operates at ports of Hodeida, Mocha and Salif.

Hodeida Shipping and Transport Co Ltd: POB 3337, Hodeida; tel. (3) 238130; fax (3) 211533; e-mail hodship_1969@y.net.ye; internet www.hodship.com; shipping agents, stevedoring, Lloyd's agents; clearance, haulage, land transportation, cargo and vessel surveys; Chair. MUHAMMAD ABDO THABET.

Al-Katiri Shipping Corpn: POB 716, Aden; tel. (2) 255538; fax (2) 251152; one general cargo vessel.

Middle East Shipping Co Ltd: POB 3700, Hodeida; tel. (3) 203977; fax (3) 203910; e-mail mideast@mideastshipping.com; internet www.mideastshipping.com; f. 1962; Chair. ABD AL-WASA HAYEL SAEED; Gen. Man. AHMAD GAZEM SAID; brs in Mocha, Aden, Taiz, Mukalla, San'a, Salif, Ras Isa, ash-Shihr.

National Shipping Co: POB 1228, Steamer Point, Aden; tel. (2) 204861; fax (2) 202644; e-mail natship@y.net.ye; shipping, bunkering, clearing and forwarding, and travel agents; Dir-Gen. MOHSEN SALEM BIN BREIK.

Yemen Navigation Line: POB 4190, Aden; tel. (2) 24861; fleet of three general cargo vessels.

Yemen Shipping Development Co Ltd: POB 3686, Hodeida; tel. (3) 224103; fax (3) 211584; one general cargo vessel; Shipping Man. FAHDLE A. KARIM.

Yeslam Salem Alshagga: POB 778, Aden; one general cargo vessel.

CIVIL AVIATION

There are six international airports—San'a International (13 km from the city), Aden Civil Airport (at Khormaksar, 11 km from the port of Aden), al-Ganad (at Taiz), Mukalla (Riyan), Seyoun and Hodeida Airport.

Yemen Airways (Yemenia): POB 1183, Airport Rd, San'a; tel. (1) 232380; fax (1) 252991; e-mail info@yemenia.com; internet www.yemenia.com; f. 1961 as Yemen Airlines; nationalized as Yemen Airways Corpn 1972; present name adopted 1978; merged with airlines of fmr PDRY in 1996; owned 51% by Yemeni Govt and 49% by Govt of Saudi Arabia; scheduled for privatization; supervised by a ministerial cttee under the Ministry of Transport; internal services and external services to more than 25 destinations in the Middle East, Asia, Africa, Europe and the USA; Chair. HASSAN ABDO SOHBI.

Tourism

The former YAR formed a joint tourism company with the PDRY in 1980. Yemen boasts areas of beautiful scenery, a favourable climate and towns of historic and architectural importance. UNESCO has named San'a and Shibam as World Heritage sites. However, the growth of tourism has, in recent years, been hampered by political instability. In 2003 some 154,667 tourists visited Yemen; in the same year tourist receipts US $139m.

Association of Yemen Tourism and Travel Agencies: San'a; internet www.aytta.org; Chair. YAHAYA M. A. SALEH.

General Authority of Tourism: POB 129, San'a; tel. (1) 252319; fax (1) 252316; e-mail mkt@yenet.com; Chair. ABD AR-RAHMAN MAHYOUB.

Yemen Tourism Promotion Board: POB 5607, 48 Amman St, San'a; tel. (1) 264057; fax (1) 264284; e-mail yementpb@y.net.ye; Man. ABDU LUTF.

ZAMBIA

Introductory Survey

Location, Climate, Language, Religion, Flag, Capital

The Republic of Zambia is a land-locked state in southern central Africa, bordered to the north by Tanzania and the Democratic Republic of the Congo, to the east by Malawi and Mozambique, to the south by Zimbabwe, Botswana and Namibia, and to the west by Angola. The climate is tropical, modified by altitude, with average temperatures from 18°C to 24°C (65°F–75°F). The official language is English. The principal African languages are Nyanja, Bemba, Tonga, Lozi, Lunda and Luvale. Christians comprise an estimated 50% of the population and are roughly divided between Protestants and Roman Catholics. A sizeable proportion of the population follow traditional animist beliefs. Most Asians are Muslims, although some are Hindus. The national flag (proportions 2 by 3) is green, with equal red, black and orange vertical stripes in the lower fly corner, and an orange eagle in flight in the upper fly corner. The capital is Lusaka.

Recent History

In 1924 control of Northern Rhodesia was transferred from the British South Africa Company to the Government of the United Kingdom. In 1953 the protectorate united with Southern Rhodesia (now Zimbabwe) and Nyasaland (now Malawi) to form the Federation of Rhodesia and Nyasaland. In 1962, following a campaign of civil disobedience organized by the United National Independence Party (UNIP), in support of demands that Northern Rhodesia be granted independence, the British Government introduced a new Constitution, which provided for a limited African franchise. In December 1963 the Federation was formally dissolved. Following elections in January 1964, the leader of UNIP, Dr Kenneth Kaunda, formed a Government. Northern Rhodesia, which was henceforth known as Zambia, became an independent republic within the Commonwealth on 24 October 1964, with Kaunda as the country's first President.

Following its accession to power, the Kaunda administration supported African liberation groups operating in Southern Rhodesia (then known as Rhodesia) and Mozambique; repeated clashes along the border with both countries were reported, while incidents of internal political violence, particularly in the Copperbelt region, also occurred. In December 1972 Zambia was declared a one-party state. In January 1973 the Rhodesian administration closed the border with Zambia.

Presidential and legislative elections took place in December 1978. Kaunda, who was the sole candidate, was returned for a fourth term as President. In October 1980 a coup was attempted, allegedly involving several prominent business executives, government officials and UNIP members. Kaunda accused South Africa and other foreign powers of supporting the attempt.

Kaunda was re-elected President in October 1983, with 93% of the votes cast. In March 1985 Kaunda adopted emergency powers to prohibit industrial action in essential services, following a series of strikes by public-sector employees and bank staff in support of demands for higher wages. In April several cabinet members and senior party officials were replaced, apparently as part of an ongoing campaign against corruption. During 1985–87 the Government introduced austerity measures in response to increasing economic decline, which precipitated sporadic civil unrest. In April 1987 Kaunda alleged that the South African Government, in collusion with Zambian business executives and military personnel, had conspired to overthrow his administration.

In August 1988 the Central Committee of UNIP was expanded from 25 to 68 members. In October nine people, six of whom were military officers, were arrested and accused of plotting to overthrow the Government. One of the civilians was subsequently released; four of the military officers were convicted of treason in August 1989 (but were released under the terms of a general amnesty in July 1990). Presidential and legislative elections took place later in October 1988. Kaunda, the only candidate, received 95.5% of the votes in the presidential election; however, only 54% of the electorate voted. At the legislative elections four cabinet ministers lost their seats in the National Assembly. In March Kebby Musokotwane, widely considered to be a potential rival to Kaunda, was replaced as Prime Minister.

In July 1989 the introduction of increases in the prices of essential goods provoked rioting in the Copperbelt region. In June 1990 Frederick Hapunda (believed to be a supporter of multi-party politics) was dismissed as Minister of Defence, and several other prominent state officials were replaced. Later in the month the introduction of austerity measures provoked violent rioting in the capital. At the end of June troops loyal to Kaunda suppressed a revolt by members of the armed forces.

In May 1990 Kaunda announced that a popular referendum on the subject of multi-party politics would take place in October of that year, and that supporters of such a system (which Kaunda and UNIP opposed) would be permitted to campaign and hold public meetings. Accordingly, in July the Movement for Multi-party Democracy (MMD), an unofficial alliance of political opponents of the Government, was formed. The MMD, which was led by a former government minister, Arthur Wina, and the Chairman of the Zambian Congress of Trade Unions (ZCTU), Frederick Chiluba, swiftly gained widespread public support. Later in July Kaunda announced that the referendum was to be postponed until August 1991, to facilitate the registration of a large section of the electorate. In September 1990, however, following the recommendation by Kaunda that a multi-party political system be reintroduced, that multi-party elections be organized by October 1991, that the national referendum be abandoned, and that a commission be appointed to revise the Constitution, the National Council of UNIP endorsed proposals for multi-party legislative and presidential elections, and accepted the recommendations of a parliamentary committee regarding the restructuring of the party.

In December 1990 Kaunda formally adopted constitutional amendments (which had been approved by the National Assembly earlier in the same month) that permitted the formation of other political associations to contest the forthcoming elections. The MMD was subsequently granted official recognition. In early 1991 several prominent members of UNIP resigned from the party and declared their support for the MMD, while the ZCTU officially transferred allegiance to the MMD. Several other opposition movements were also established. In February violent clashes between supporters of the MMD and members of UNIP were suppressed by the security forces.

In June 1991 the constitutional commission presented a series of recommendations, including the creation of the post of Vice-President, the expansion of the National Assembly from 135 to 150 members and the establishment of a constitutional court. Kaunda accepted the majority of the proposed constitutional amendments, which were subsequently submitted for approval by the National Assembly. The MMD, however, rejected the draft, and announced that it would boycott the forthcoming elections if the National Assembly accepted the proposals. In July, following discussions between Kaunda, Chiluba and delegates from seven other political associations, Kaunda agreed to suspend the review of the draft Constitution in the National Assembly pending further negotiations. It was also announced that state subsidies would be granted to all registered political parties. Subsequent discussions between the MMD and UNIP resulted in the establishment of a joint commission to revise the draft Constitution. In late July Kaunda conceded to opposition demands that ministers be appointed only from the National Assembly and that proposals for a constitutional court be abandoned. A provision granting the President the power to impose martial law was also rescinded.

On 2 August 1991 the National Assembly formally adopted the new Constitution. At the UNIP congress in the same month Kaunda was unanimously re-elected as President of the party. However, several prominent party officials, including the incumbent Secretary-General, refused to seek election to a new Central Committee. Kaunda also announced the dissociation of the armed forces from UNIP; senior officers in the armed forces were subsequently obliged to retire from the party's Central Committee. In September 1991 Kaunda officially dissociated UNIP from the State; workers in the public sector were henceforth prohibited from engaging in political activity.

On 31 October 1991 Chiluba, with 75.8% of votes cast, defeated Kaunda in the presidential election. In the concurrent legislative elections, contested by 330 candidates representing six political parties, the MMD secured 125 seats in the National Assembly, while UNIP won the remaining 25 seats; only four members of the previous Government were returned to the National Assembly. Kaunda's failure to secure re-election was attributed to widespread perceptions of economic mismanagement by his administration. On 2 November Chiluba was inaugurated as President. He appointed Levy Mwanawasa, a constitutional lawyer, as Vice-President and Leader of the National Assembly, and formed a new Cabinet. In addition, a government minister was appointed to each of the country's nine provinces, which had hitherto been administered by governors. Chiluba subsequently initiated a major restructuring of the civil service and of parastatal organizations, as part of efforts to reverse the country's significant economic decline and eradicate widespread corruption among officials.

In mid-1992 widespread opposition to government policies was reported. In May a dissident faction of academics within the MMD, the Caucus for National Unity (CNU), emerged. The CNU, which claimed to have the support of several government members, demanded that Chiluba review procedures for the appointment of cabinet ministers and heads of parastatal organizations, to ensure that all ethnic groups were represented. The CNU, together with other pressure groups, also advocated the establishment of a constitutional commission to curtail the executive power vested in the President and the Cabinet. In July two cabinet ministers (who reportedly supported the CNU) resigned in protest at what they alleged was the Government's failure to suppress corruption and to institute democratic measures, following the refusal of the National Assembly to accept a report that implicated several government members in alleged financial malpractice. Later that month the CNU registered as an independent political party. In September Kaunda formally resigned from active participation in UNIP; Musokotwane was subsequently elected as the party's President.

In March 1993 Chiluba declared a state of emergency, following the discovery of UNIP documents that allegedly revealed details of a conspiracy to destabilize the Government. Several prominent members of UNIP, including Kaunda's three sons, were subsequently arrested. Musokotwane admitted the existence of the documents, but denied that UNIP officials were involved in any plot, which he attributed to extreme factions within the party. Kaunda, however, claimed that the conspiracy had been fabricated by Zambian security forces, with the assistance of US intelligence services, in an attempt to undermine the opposition. Later in March diplomatic relations with Iran and Iraq were suspended, following allegations by the Zambian Government that the two countries had funded subversive elements within UNIP. Shortly afterwards the National Assembly approved the state of emergency, which was to remain in force for a further three months.

Divisions within the MMD became apparent in August 1993, when 15 prominent members (11 of whom held seats in the National Assembly) resigned from the party: they accused the Government of protecting corrupt cabinet ministers and of failing to respond to numerous reports linking senior party officials with the illegal drugs trade. Their opposition to the Government was consolidated later in the month by the formation of a new political group, the National Party (NP). In November Chiluba appointed a 22-member commission to revise the Constitution; it was announced that the draft document was to be submitted for approval by a Constituent Assembly, and subsequently by a national referendum.

In January 1994 two senior cabinet ministers announced their resignation, following persistent allegations of their involvement in drugs-trafficking. One of the ministers, Vernon Mwaanga (a founder member of the MMD), who had held the foreign affairs portfolio, had been implicated in the drugs trade by a tribunal in 1985, although he had not been convicted of the alleged offences. Two further ministers were dismissed in an ensuing government reorganization. At partial elections for 10 of the 11 vacated seats in the National Assembly, which took place in November 1993 and April 1994, the MMD regained five seats, while the NP secured four and UNIP took one. The remaining seat was secured by UNIP at a by-election in December.

Meanwhile, in July 1994 Mwanawasa resigned as Vice-President, citing long-standing differences with Chiluba, and was subsequently replaced by Brig.-Gen. Godfrey Miyanda. Also in July Kaunda stated that he intended to contest the presidential election due in 1996; however, UNIP officials indicated that he would only be allowed to resume the leadership of the party if he were officially elected by members. (Kaunda's decision to return to active politics subsequently resulted in factional division within UNIP.) In August Kaunda was apparently warned against inciting revolt, after he conducted a number of rallies in the Northern Province (where the MMD traditionally attracted considerable support). Later that month the Government announced that Kaunda had been placed under surveillance in the interests of national security, following reports that he had received support from foreign diplomatic missions in Zambia.

In June 1995 some members of the Constitutional Review Commission rejected a final draft of the Constitution, objecting, in particular, to restrictions on the independent press, and on public gatherings and demonstrations; they claimed that the four members of the Commission who had prepared the draft had taken payments from the Government, and accused the Chairman of complicity with the authorities. Later that month, however, the draft Constitution was submitted for approval. At the end of June Kaunda was elected President of UNIP, defeating Musokotwane; he reiterated his intention of seeking re-election to the state presidency, despite provisions in the draft Constitution that effectively debarred his candidature, on the grounds that he had already served two terms of office and that he was not of direct Zambian descent (his parents originated from Malawi). In August, following continued factional violence within UNIP, three parliamentary deputies resigned from the party: among them was the leader of the opposition in the National Assembly, who subsequently joined the MMD. At by-elections in 13 constituencies in September–October 1995, the MMD secured seven seats, and UNIP six; it was reported that Kaunda had been placed temporarily under house arrest following incidents of electoral violence. In October the Minister for Legal Affairs announced that Kaunda had not officially relinquished Malawian citizenship until 1970 (and had therefore governed illegally for six years), and that he had not obtained Zambian citizenship through the correct procedures. However, following widespread reports that the authorities intended to deport Kaunda, the Government ordered security forces to suspend investigations into the former President's citizenship (apparently owing to fears of civil unrest).

In January 1996 seven opposition parties, including UNIP and the NP, established an informal alliance to campaign in favour of democratic elections and the establishment of a Constituent Assembly to approve the draft Constitution by a process of national consensus. Opposition parties subsequently demanded that the Government abandon the draft Constitution and negotiate with them regarding electoral reform. Later that month UNIP deputies withdrew from a parliamentary debate on the draft, which was subsequently approved by a large majority in the National Assembly. On 28 May the Constitution was officially adopted by Chiluba. In early June Western donor Governments suspended aid to Zambia, in protest at the constitutional provisions that effectively precluded Kaunda from contesting the presidency, while Kaunda announced that he intended to defy the ban.

In August 1996 Chiluba and Kaunda met for discussions, as part of a programme of dialogue between the Government and opposition parties. Following Kaunda's decision to boycott a scheduled second round of discussions in September, the Government made minor concessions regarding the conduct of forthcoming elections, including assurances that votes would be counted at polling stations and that the Electoral Commission (appointed by Chiluba) would be independent; UNIP's request that the elections be conducted according to the 1991 Constitution was rejected. In mid-October 1996 Chiluba dissolved the National Assembly and announced that presidential and legislative elections would take place on 18 November. UNIP, still dissatisfied with the electoral system, announced its intention to boycott the elections and organize a campaign of civil disobedience; by early November a further six political parties had also decided to boycott the elections. There was widespread criticism of the voter registration process, in which fewer than one-half of the estimated 4.6m. eligible voters had been listed.

Despite appeals for a postponement, the elections were held as planned, and Chiluba and the MMD were returned to power by a large majority. In the presidential election Chiluba defeated the four other candidates with 72.5% of the valid votes cast. His nearest rival (with only 12.5%) was Dean Mung'omba of the Zambia Democratic Congress (ZADECO), an erstwhile opponent of Chiluba within the MMD. The MMD secured 131 of the 150 seats in the National Assembly. Of the eight other parties that contested the elections, only the NP (five seats), ZADECO (two seats) and Agenda for Zambia (AZ—two seats) won parliamentary representation, with independent candidates taking the remaining 10 seats.

Chiluba was inaugurated for a second presidential term on 21 November 1996. Amid demands for his resignation and for fresh elections to be held, Chiluba dissolved the Cabinet and placed the military on alert at the end of the month. In early December a new Government was appointed, although the main portfolios remained largely unchanged. Opposition parties continued their campaign of civil disobedience throughout that month, although nation-wide marches of solidarity with the Government were reported to have been widely supported. Four opposition parties filed petitions with the Supreme Court challenging Chiluba's citizenship (and therefore his eligibility as President), and accusing the Electoral Commission of conspiring with the MMD to commit electoral fraud; the petitions were dismissed in early 1997.

Political tension increased in the second half of 1997. In response to reports in June claiming that Kaunda and Roger Chongwe, the leader of the Liberal Progressive Front, were appealing for international assistance to overcome a political crisis in Zambia, the MMD denied that any such crisis existed. Later that month the MMD's chairman in Lusaka called for the declaration of a state of emergency, on the grounds that the opposition, by refusing to enter into talks with the MMD, were advocating a civil war. Chongwe insisted that the opposition would welcome dialogue, but only if the 1996 elections were annulled and the Constitution repealed. Meanwhile, the opposition's campaign of civil disobedience continued. In August 1997 Kaunda and Chongwe were shot and wounded (Chongwe seriously) when the security forces opened fire on an opposition gathering in Kabwe, north of Lusaka. Kaunda's subsequent allegation that the shooting was an assassination attempt organized by the Government was strongly denied by Chiluba.

On 28 October 1997 rebel army officers briefly captured the national television and radio station from where they proclaimed the formation of a military regime. The attempted coup was swiftly suppressed by regular military units; 15 people were arrested during the operation. Allegations by Kaunda that the Government had orchestrated the coup in order to be in a position to detain prominent members of the opposition were repeated by other opposition figures after Chiluba declared a state of emergency on 29 October, providing for the detention for 28 days without trial of people suspected of involvement in the attempted coup. Mung'omba was among 84 people arrested in the immediate aftermath of the coup.

Chiluba carried out an extensive cabinet reshuffle in early December 1997. Observers interpreted the transfer to lesser cabinet posts of Miyanda and of Benjamin Mwila, hitherto the Minister of Defence, as an attempt to forestall the emergence of potential rivals to Chiluba within the MMD. Lt-Gen. Christon Tembo, hitherto the Minister of Mines and Mineral Development, replaced Miyanda as Vice-President.

On 25 December 1997 Kaunda was arrested under emergency powers and imprisoned, shortly after his return to Zambia from more than two months abroad. Numerous regional and international Governments expressed serious concern at the detention of Kaunda, who refused food until the end of the month when he was visited by Julius Nyerere, the former President of Tanzania. On the following day Kaunda was placed under house arrest at his home in Lusaka. He was arraigned in court in January 1998, and in mid-February he was formally notified that he was to stand trial for 'misprision of treason', on the grounds that he had failed to report in advance to the authorities details allegedly known to him of the attempted coup of October 1997. Meanwhile, in late January 1998 the National Assembly voted to extend the state of emergency for a further three months; Chiluba eventually revoked the state of emergency on 17 March, following pressure from external donors. Also in March, Chiluba effected a minor cabinet reshuffle, most notably dismissing the Minister of Finance and Economic Development, Ronald Penza. In April 80 people who were being detained in connection with the attempted coup, including Kaunda and Mung'omba, were committed to summary trial in the High Court. Kaunda was released from detention in June, after charges against him were withdrawn, apparently owing to lack of evidence. He subsequently announced his intention to retire from active politics, and his resignation as UNIP President in July created a split within the party over the nomination of a replacement. The MMD was also reported to be divided over an eventual successor to Chiluba, despite a recent ban within the party on presidential campaigning, amid strongly denied suggestions that Chiluba might seek a third term of office in 2001, contrary to the Constitution.

In November 1998 Ronald Penza was murdered at his home by a gang of masked men. Shortly afterwards five of the six suspects were shot dead by police-officers, who claimed the motive for Penza's murder was robbery, although it was reported that nothing had been stolen. The police action, and Chiluba's subsequent approval of legislation providing for Zambia's intelligence service to be armed, were of considerable concern to human rights organizations. In December Mung'omba and Princess Nakatindi Wina, a former minister and the MMD's national chairperson for women, were granted bail, as no witnesses had provided evidence against them since their detention on charges of treason following the failed coup attempt of October 1997.

In mid-February 1999 opposition parties demanded the dismissal of Tembo and Benjamin Mwila, the Minister of Energy and Water Development (previously responsible for defence), who had been implicated, along with Kavindele, in Angolan claims that Zambia was supporting the Angolan rebel movement, União Nacional para a Independência Total de Angola (UNITA)—allegations that the Zambian authorities strongly denied. In late February a number of bombs exploded in Lusaka, one of which seriously damaged the Angolan embassy, killing a security guard, while several further explosive devices were discovered and defused. The security forces were placed on full alert, and an investigation into the bombings was instigated. In mid-March it was reported that two Zambians had been arrested, and two foreigners deported, in connection with the bombings. Twelve journalists were arrested and charged with espionage in March, after their newspaper printed a report claiming that Zambia's military capacity was inferior to that of Angola. In April the 12 were committed to trial by the High Court (but were all found not guilty in 2000). The Cabinet was reorganized in March 1999.

At the end of March 1999 the High Court delivered its judgment in a case concerning Kaunda's citizenship, declaring him to be a stateless person. The following day Kaunda appealed to the Supreme Court against the ruling, and later that day he escaped a reported assassination attempt, when a group of armed men opened fire on his car. In April five opposition parties, including the AZ and ZADECO, formed a new alliance, the Zambia Alliance for Progress (ZAP). However, the authorities refused to register the ZAP on the grounds that its constituent parties had not been dissolved. The ZAP initially disputed the ruling and announced its intention to appeal to the High Court, but in August ZADECO formally announced its dissolution, thus effectively losing its parliamentary seat. Meanwhile, in June Chiluba effected a minor cabinet reshuffle, notably appointing Katele Kalumba as Minister of Finance and Economic Development.

In September 1999 59 soldiers were sentenced to death for their part in the failed coup against the Chiluba administration in October 1997. A further soldier was sentenced to 21 years' imprisonment for concealing information regarding the coup attempt from the authorities, while another eight soldiers were acquitted of charges of treason, owing to lack of evidence. In October 1999 55 of the soldiers sentenced to death launched an appeal against the convictions.

In March 2000 Kaunda announced his resignation as President of UNIP and his retirement from active politics. At an extraordinary congress, which was convened in Ndola in May, Francis Nkhoma, a former governor of the Bank of Zambia, was elected to replace Kaunda as President of UNIP, while Kaunda's son, Tilyenji, became the party's new Secretary-General.

In May 2000 the Minister of the Environment and Natural Resources and MMD National Treasurer, Benjamin Mwila, announced that he intended to stand in the presidential election scheduled for 2001; Chiluba had previously prohibited members of his Cabinet from publicly discussing their potential candidacy for the presidency upon the expiry of the two terms permitted to him by the Constitution. Mwila was subsequently dismissed from the Government and expelled from the MMD. In July Mwila and a number of other MMD members formed a new political movement, the Republican Party (RP); Mwila reiterated his intention to seek election to the presidency. The RP merged with the ZAP in February 2001, Mwila becoming leader of the new movement, known as the Zambia Republican Party (ZRP).

In early 2001 a number of prominent figures in the MMD publicly advocated Chiluba's election to a third presidential term, despite such an event being prohibited by the Constitution. Chiluba, while declining to reveal his intentions, was reported to have expressed a willingness to listen to the outcome of any public debate on the issue. Opposition parties and some leading MMD members (including Tembo and several ministers) demanded that Chiluba announce that he would not seek re-election. In April, amid increasing controversy, a convention of the MMD approved a motion removing the stipulation that the party's President should serve a maximum of two five-year terms. Tembo, Miyanda and seven other ministers expressed their opposition to the convention's decision and were expelled from the party; their supporters subsequently alleged that intimidation by supporters of Chiluba had caused some who opposed the motion not to attend the conference. Several Western donor governments also expressed their opposition to Chiluba's re-election. In April Tilyenji Kaunda was adopted as the President of UNIP.

In May 2001 a motion to impeach Chiluba for misconduct, proposed by two MMD deputies, was signed by more than one-third of the members of the National Assembly. The following day Chiluba ended speculation regarding his potential third term by announcing that he would not seek re-election; he also announced the dissolution of the Cabinet. A new Cabinet was appointed some days later, with the ministers who had opposed Chiluba all being replaced—Tembo was succeeded as Vice-President by Kavindele, the Vice-President of the MMD and hitherto Minister of Health. Mwaanga returned to the Government as Minister of Information and Broadcasting Services. In July the FDD won a by-election in Lusaka, occasioned by the resignation of Tembo after his expulsion from the MMD; violent confrontations between rival supporters from the MMD and FDD were reported. Tembo was elected President of the FDD in October. Meanwhile, Miyanda had established a further opposition party, the Heritage Party (HP).

The MMD adopted former Vice-President Mwanawasa as its presidential candidate in August 2001. Later that month seven opposition parties, including UNIP and the FDD, agreed to form a government of national unity following the forthcoming legislative elections, in order to provide effective opposition in the event of the MMD securing the presidency. In September Michael Sata resigned as Minister without Portfolio and as National Secretary of the MMD, in protest at the nomination of Mwanawasa as presidential candidate. He subsequently formed a new political party, the Patriotic Front (PF). In October Tembo was elected as the FDD's presidential candidate.

The presidential and legislative elections took place on 27 December 2001. On 1 January 2002 (the scheduled date for the announcement of the election results) violent confrontations took place between anti-Government demonstrators and the security forces in Lusaka and Kitwe, amid allegations that the MMD had engaged in electoral fraud and voter intimidation. Mwanawasa was officially declared President on the following day, with 29.15% of the valid votes cast, narrowly defeating Anderson Mazoka, the leader of the United Party for National Development (UPND, established in 1998), who secured 27.20%, while Tembo won 13.17% and Tilyenji Kaunda 10.12%. The High Court had rejected a petition for the further postponement of the declaration of the results by opposition parties, which were demanding an investigation into their allegations. The MMD secured 69 of the 150 elective seats in the National Assembly (and subsequently all eight of the seats nominated by the President); the UPND became the second largest party in the National Assembly, with 49 seats. Other parties to gain legislative representation were UNIP (with 13 seats), the FDD (12 seats), the HP (four seats), and the PF and the ZRP (one seat each); one independent candidate was also elected.

Although the MMD held only 77 of the 158 seats in the National Assembly, Mwanawasa refused to form a coalition with any of the opposition parties to ensure a working majority, and appointed a new Cabinet in early January, retaining many ministers from the previous administration. Kavindele remained Vice-President, and Kalumba was appointed as Minister of Foreign Affairs, while Mwanawasa assumed the defence portfolio himself. A report published in February by an observer mission of the European Union criticized the Electoral Commission of Zambia for misadministration of the recent elections, and later in that month the Supreme Court began hearing a legal challenge to the election results from UNIP, the FDD and the HP, which alleged that the MMD had won the polls fraudulently. (In February 2005 the Supreme Court ruled that although there had been irregularities in the electoral process, the overall result of the elections had not been affected.) Meanwhile, Mwaanga was dismissed from the Cabinet in early March 2002, after allegedly undermining Mwanawasa's authority; he was replaced as Minister of Information and Broadcasting Services by Newstead Zimba. Later that month senior members of the FDD expressed their support for the new President, praising his stated commitment to curbing corruption and alleviating poverty.

In July 2002 the Minister of Foreign Affairs and the Chief Justice resigned, apparently in response to pressure from Mwanawasa, exerted in what was regarded as an attempt to rid the administration of corrupt officials. Later that month the National Assembly voted to remove Chiluba's immunity from prosecution, pending a review by the High Court, in order to allow his trial on charges of corruption against him to proceed. Mwanawasa offered Chiluba a full pardon a few days later, on condition that he return the assets he was alleged to have embezzled. The decision to remove his immunity was upheld by the High Court in August. In February 2003 the Supreme Court ruled that Chiluba's immunity could not be restored, and a few days later he was arrested and charged with stealing more than US $2m. of public funds while President. Also in February a cabinet reshuffle was effected, in which a number of members of opposition parties assumed ministerial portfolios; observers considered it an attempt to prevent opposition parties from uniting to threaten the MMD's weak position in the National Assembly.

In May 2003 the National Citizens' Coalition (NCC) disbanded in order to merge with the MMD, following the resignation of its leader, Nevers Mumba, to join the ruling party. In late May Mumba was appointed as Vice-President, replacing Kavindele, who had been dismissed in a cabinet reshuffle. Prior to the merger of the NCC and the MMD, UNIP and the MMD had indicated their intention to co-operate. In June a commission commenced a review of the Constitution with which it had been charged in April by President Mwanawasa. In July Peter Magande was appointed as Minister of Finance and Economic Development in place of Emmanuel Kasonde, who had also been dismissed from the Cabinet in late May. In early October 2004 Mumba was removed from the Cabinet following his refusal to retract allegations that the Democratic Republic of the Congo (DRC, formerly Zaire) was harbouring individuals who had financed illegal opposition-party activities in Zambia. Mumba was replaced as Vice-President by a former Minister of Transport and Communications, Lupando Mwape. In January 2005 Mwanawasa reorganized the Cabinet; most notably Ronnie Shikapwasha was appointed Minister of Home Affairs, while the foreign affairs portfolio vacated by Shikapwasha was assumed by Kalombo Mwansa.

Meanwhile, in August 2003 former President Chiluba, who had been released on bail following his arrest in February, was rearrested and charged with the theft of US $29.7m. while in office. In October, amid an intensification of demands for political reform, President Mwanawasa convened a four-day national conference. The principal opposition parties and reformist civil organizations refused to participate in the conference, however. In December two concurrent trials of Chiluba commenced. The former President was reportedly arraigned on 264 charges of stealing a total of some $40m., in collaboration, in some instances, with other former government officials. In January 2004, following allegations that the early stages of Chiluba's trial had been mismanaged, the Director of Public Prosecutions, Mukelebai Mukelebai, was ordered by the President to begin a period of forced leave. Mukelebai claimed that the President had no right effectively to suspend him from office on the basis of what he claimed were anonymous allegations. In March Vice-President Mumba announced that about 150 former government officials and businessmen linked to Chiluba's administration were under investigation in connection with the theft of public funds. By January 2005 the charges against Chiluba had been reduced to six counts of theft of some $488,000. In mid-2005 Chiluba's lawyers halted the trial for four months demanding access to confidential prosecution documents; however, the High Court rejected their claims and in November ordered proceedings be resumed. The trial was ongoing in 2006.

In early August 2004 the National Assembly approved legislation postponing local elections—scheduled to take place in November—until 2006, when they were to be held concurrent with legislative and presidential elections. The legislation also extended the terms of office for mayors and councillors from three to five years. In late September the Constitutional Review Commission made recommendations that included, inter alia, the appointment of a non-executive President and the adoption of an electoral process based on proportional representation. In October President Mwanawasa announced that the Constitution could only be amended with the support of at least two-thirds of the National Assembly. In early 2005 opposition political parties and civil groups launched a petition for the Government to implement constitutional changes before the 2006 elections; their demands included a reduction of executive power and a requirement for a presidential candidate to win more than 50% of the vote before being elected to that position. In late June the Constitutional Review Commission published its report and a draft constitution, which included, inter alia, an updated bill of rights, the requirement for a presidential candidate to win more than 50% of the vote and certain limitations on the President's statutory powers. After considering the draft, in mid-January 2006 it was reported that Mwanawasa was prepared to accept the recommendations and implement constitutional reform prior to that year's elections. However, in early February he announced that the elections would be held under the terms of the existing Constitution and that a referendum and a national census were necessary before a new constitution could be enacted. Meanwhile, minor government reorganizations were effected in August and October 2005, and in March 2006.

In 1986 South African troops launched attacks on alleged bases of the African National Congress of South Africa (ANC) in Zambia; a number of foreigners and Zambian citizens were subsequently arrested in Zambia on suspicion of spying for South Africa. In August of that year Zambia undertook to impose economic sanctions against South Africa, and the South African Government retaliated by temporarily enforcing trade restrictions on Zambia. Further attacks on ANC targets took place during 1987–89. During the 1980s President Kaunda's support for the Governments of Angola and Mozambique resulted in attacks on Zambian civilians by Angolan rebels (with assistance from the Governments of South Africa and the USA) and by Mozambican rebels (also allegedly supported by South Africa). In September 1992 the Governments of Zambia and Angola signed a security agreement providing for common border controls. In early 1996 Zambia contributed some 1,000 troops to the UN Angola Verification Mission. Zambia consistently denied allegations, made by the Angolan Government in 1997–98, that it was providing military and logistical support to UNITA rebels.

In early 1999, however, tension between the two countries intensified, as the accusations resurfaced and a bomb severely damaged the Angolan embassy in Lusaka (see above). Chiluba requested precise details from the Angolan President, José Eduardo dos Santos, regarding Zambia's alleged involvement in the Angolan conflict and invited the international community to send independent missions to investigate the claims. In March 1999 the Angolan Government delivered a letter to the UN explaining its accusations against Zambia. The Zambian Government again refuted all allegations against it. In April, however, relations appeared to have improved, when both countries were reported to have signed an agreement aimed at resolving their differences, under the mediation of Swaziland's King Mswati III. In June the Zambian and Angolan Governments signed a further agreement, which provided for the reactivation of the joint permanent commission on defence and security and the organization of a summit between Chiluba and dos Santos. In December it was reported that Angolan jets had bombed Zambian territory in pursuit of UNITA rebels, and in January 2000 it was announced that some 21,000 Angolan refugees had entered Zambia since October 1999. During January–February 2000 UNITA rebels carried out a series of raids on Zambian villages, which prompted Chiluba to announce that he would not permit UNITA troops to operate from Zambia. In February, following the convention of the joint permanent commission on defence and security to discuss the security situation along the common border, both sides resolved to strengthen measures against UNITA forces operating in the common border area. In September the Zambian Government declined a request from the Angolan Government for its forces to be allowed to use Zambian territory to attack UNITA positions near the frontier.

In February 2001 the Governments of Zambia, Angola and Namibia agreed to establish a tripartite mechanism for political and security co-operation in an attempt to improve security on their joint borders. However, armed Angolans raided three Zambian villages close to the border in November, reportedly abducting some 100 Zambians and subsequently killing seven of them; Zambian forces claimed to have killed 10 Angolans in retaliation. Reports in the Zambian press attributed the attacks on the villages to the Angolan armed forces, which admitted occupying UNITA bases in the area, but claimed to have observed UNITA rebels crossing the border shortly before the attacks. At the end of 2002 there were 188,436 Angolan refugees in Zambia, compared with 218,154 at the beginning of the year. The office of the UN High Commissioner for Refugees (UNHCR) had assisted in the repatriation of some 172,000 Angolan refugees by December 2004; the UNHCR programme was ongoing in 2006. The increased availability of firearms in Zambia and the presence gunmen-for-hire (known as 'karavinas') was attributed to the end of the civil war in Angola in 2002. An amnesty programme for illegal firearms was introduced that year, offering payment in exchange for guns; however, by February 2005 only 800 weapons had been handed over to police.

In early March 1997 the Zambian Government appealed for international assistance in coping with the influx of refugees fleeing the civil conflict in Zaire; by March some 6,000 Zairean refugees had arrived in Zambia. In January 1998 Zambia and the DRC agreed to establish a joint permanent commission on defence and security. During late 1998 and early 1999 the Zambian Government was involved in regional efforts to find a political solution to the conflict in the DRC, after a rebellion was mounted against the Government in August 1998; President Chiluba was appointed to co-ordinate peace initiatives on the crisis by the Southern African Development Community and the Organization of African Unity (OAU, now the African Union, see p. 153). Meanwhile, thousands of Congolese entered Zambia, fleeing the renewed fighting, prompting the Government to appeal to the international community for immediate assistance to cope with the refugees, which, by then, reportedly numbered more than 30,000. In addition, several hundred DRC soldiers crossed into Zambia seeking refuge, but were subsequently repatriated. At a summit held in Lusaka during June–July 1999 a cease-fire document was formulated, providing for the withdrawal of foreign forces from the DRC and for political reform in the country. The accord was signed by the President of the DRC and the leaders of the five other countries involved in the conflict in July, and by rebel leaders in August. Nevertheless, progress with its implementation was slow. Zambia's involvement in mediation efforts aimed at achieving a definitive end to the conflict in the DRC diminished in the early 2000s, although a number of regional summit meetings were held in Lusaka. In March 2004 it was reported that more than 1,000 DRC nationals had entered Zambia, fleeing renewed fighting between government and rebel forces in south-eastern DRC. At the end of 2004 there were more than 191,000 refugees in Zambia, of whom the majority were from Angola; some 55,000 were from the DRC and some 6,400 from Rwanda.

Government

Under the provisions of the Constitution, which was formally adopted in May 1996, Zambia is a multi-party state. Executive power is vested in the President, who is the constitutional Head of State. Legislative power is vested in a National Assembly, which comprises 158 members, of whom 150 are elected by universal adult suffrage, and eight nominated by the President. The President and the National Assembly are elected simultaneously by universal adult suffrage for a five-year term. The maximum duration of the President's tenure of office is limited to two five-year terms. The President governs with the assistance of a Vice-President and a Cabinet, whom he appoints from members of the National Assembly. The Constitution also provides for a 27-member House of Chiefs, which represents traditional tribal authorities. Each of Zambia's nine provinces has a minister, who is appointed by the President.

Defence

The total strength of armed forces at 1 August 2005 was 15,100, with 13,500 in the army and 1,600 in the air force. Paramilitary forces numbered 1,400. Military service is voluntary. There is also a National Defence Force responsible to the Government. The defence budget for 2005 was estimated at K223,000m.

Economic Affairs

In 2004, according to estimates by the World Bank, Zambia's gross national income (GNI), measured at average 2002–04 prices, was US $4,748m., equivalent to $450 per head (or $890 per head on an international purchasing-power parity basis). During 1995–2004, it was estimated, the population increased at an average annual rate of 1.9%, while gross domestic product

(GDP) per head increased, in real terms, by an average of 1.6% per year. Overall GDP increased, in real terms, at an average annual rate of 3.5% in 1995–2004; growth in 2004 was 4.6%.

Agriculture (including forestry and fishing) contributed 22.3% of GDP in 2004. About 67.5% of the labour force were employed in the sector in mid-2003. The principal crops are sugar cane, maize, cassava, wheat, sweet potatoes, cotton and groundnuts. Millet, rice, sorghum, tobacco, sunflower seeds and horticultural produce are also cultivated. Cattle-rearing remains important. An increase in the wheat and tobacco harvests during 2003–04 was attributed to the contribution of recently arrived Zimbabwean farmers who had been forced off the land in their own country. During 1995–2004, according to the World Bank, agricultural GDP increased by an average of 1.3% per year. Agricultural GDP increased by 4.5% in 2004.

Industry (including mining, manufacturing, construction and power) contributed 27.0% of GDP in 2004, and engaged 26.3% of all wage-earning employees in that year. According to the World Bank, industrial GDP grew at an average annual rate of 3.0% in 1995–2004. Industrial GDP increased 7.8% in 2004.

In 2004 mining and quarrying contributed 3.2% of GDP, according to official figures, and engaged 11.1% of wage-earning employees. Foreign sales of refined copper, the main mineral export, accounted for some 61.3% of the total value of exports in 2002. Cobalt is also an important export, while coal, gold, emeralds, amethyst, limestone and selenium are also mined. In addition, Zambia has reserves of phosphates, fluorspar and iron ore. A new copper mine in Kansanshi, operated by the Canadian company First Quantum Minerals, created 1,300 direct jobs; production began in August 2005 with a target of 145,000 metric tons for 2006. The company also owned a share of the country's second largest copper producer, Mopani Copper Mines plc (principally controlled by the Switzerland-based Glencore International AG), which aimed to triple its output by 2007; the production target for 2006 was over 200,000 tons. In late 2005 the Indian company Vedanta Resources plc invested some US $400m. in the Konkola deep mine project, the largest single investment to have been made in Zambia. The Government retained a 20% share in the mine, which employed some 10,000 workers and 4,000 contractors, and was estimated to contribute more than one-third of national export earnings. The Vedanta investment aimed to raise annual copper production from 180,000 tons to 300,000 tons in 2006. The Australian company, Equinox Minerals Ltd, expected to begin production at its Lumwana mine in late 2006; it was anticipated that the mine would produce 125,000 tons of copper per year. It was reported that copper production rose from 394,000 tons in 2004 to over 500,000 tons in 2005 and was forecast to rise to 600,000 tons in 2006. During 1998–2004, according to the IMF, mining GDP increased by an estimated average of 2.4% per year. Mining GDP increased by 13.9% in 2004.

Manufacturing contributed 11.2% of GDP in 2004, and engaged 10.9% of all wage-earning employees in that year. The principal manufacturing activities are food-processing, the smelting and refining of copper and other metals, vehicle assembly, petroleum-refining, and the production of fertilizers, explosives, textiles, bottles, batteries, bricks and copper wire. During 1995–2004, according to the World Bank, manufacturing GDP increased at an average annual rate of 4.6%. Manufacturing GDP increased by 5.1% in 2004.

Energy is derived principally from hydroelectric power (99.5% in 2002), in which Zambia is self-sufficient. Imports of mineral fuels accounted for 7.1% of the value of merchandise imports in 2002. In 1998 agreements were signed that provided for the export of electricity from Zambia to South Africa and Tanzania. In September 2004 a number of agreements were reached with foreign investors and development agencies with the aim of refurbishing existing power-generating facilities and constructing new facilities and thus increasing Zambia's potential to export energy. The first phase of the Zambia-Kenya-Tanzania power interconnector project was expected to begin in 2005; the project was scheduled to commence operations in 2007. Proposals to extending the scheme to Rwanda was under consideration.

The services sector contributed 50.7% of GDP in 2004, and engaged 58.0% of wage-earning employees in that year. According to the World Bank, the GDP of the services sector increased by an average of 5.5% per year in 1995–2004. Services GDP increased by 2.1% in 2004.

In 2004 Zambia recorded an estimated trade deficit of US $109m., while there was a deficit of $642m. on the current account of the balance of payments. In 2002 the principal source of imports (51.2%) was South Africa; other major suppliers were the United Kingdom and Zimbabwe. The principal market for exports in 2002 was the United Kingdom (accounting for 42.3% of the total); other significant purchasers were Tanzania and Switzerland-Liechtenstein. The principal export in 2002 was refined copper. The principal imports in 2002 were machinery and transport equipment, chemicals and related products, basic manufactures, food and live animals, printed matter, chemicals and related products, and basic manufactures.

In 2005 there was an estimated overall budgetary deficit of K765,000m. Zambia's total external debt was US $6,425m. at the end of 2003, of which US $5,439m. was long-term public debt. In that year the cost of debt-servicing was equivalent to 27.8% of the value of exports of goods and services. In 1990–2003 the average annual rate of inflation was 50.3%. Consumer prices increased by an average of 21.4% in 2003.

Zambia is a member of the Southern African Development Community (see p. 358) and the Common Market for Eastern and Southern Africa (see p. 191).

The Zambian Government implemented an economic reform programme in the late 1990s, which aimed to achieve significant GDP growth to reduce the exceptionally high rate of inflation., and in February 2000 the World Bank granted Zambia development assistance worth some US $375m. over three years, supporting the Government's priority of increasing investment in the country. The IMF, the World Bank and creditor governments pledged a further $3,800m. of debt relief under the initiative for heavily indebted poor countries (HIPCs) in December 2000. In February 2005 the IMF announced that Zambia had fulfilled the targets required to reach the HIPC completion point, thus qualifying for the $3,800m. pledged in 2000. Moreover, under the terms of the Multilateral Debt Relief Initiative agreed by the Group of Eight leading industrialized nations (G-8) in mid-2005, Zambia also qualified for cancellation of its debts to the IMF, the World Bank and the African Development Bank. In February President Mwanawasa announced that the country's total foreign debt would be reduced to some $500m. by the end of 2005 (from $7,200m. in 2004). In the early 2000s Zambia continued to derive some 50% of its export earnings from copper, the traditional mainstay of its economy and the problems confronting the economy were to a large extent a consequence of a decline in the international price of that commodity since the mid-1970s. However, prices had recovered in response to demand from the People's Republic of China in particular. Much-needed efforts to diversify the economy have focused on agriculture to date and, in particular, horticulture; Zambia has established a presence in remunerative European markets for cut flowers. Furthermore, exports of non-traditional goods—including tobacco, cotton lint, sugar, copper wire, electrical cables and scrap metal—were reported to have doubled during 2001–05, earning $581.9m. in 2005. Tourism is another sector with the potential to lead the diversification of the economy, but requires substantial investment. An increase in the number of tourists was largely attributed to political unrest in Zimbabwe deterring habitual visitors, who travelled to Zambia instead. Subsistence agriculture, meanwhile, has suffered from the effects of drought and the HIV/AIDS pandemic. An estimated one-quarter of the population was dependent on food aid in 2003, while it was feared that the pandemic would lead to the loss of an entire generation of agricultural producers. (Malaria, however, continues to cause the greatest number of deaths from disease, although efforts to combat its spread reduced the number of deaths from 50,000 in 2003 to 33,000 in 2004.) In June 2005 the Minister of Agriculture, Mundia Sikatana, announced that there was sufficient maize to satisfy national requirements without importing foreign grain. However, following drought in the south of the country, in mid-November President Mwanawasa declared a national disaster and appealed for international assistance as 1.7m. people faced starvation. The Government waived import duties on maize in an effort to ensure adequate commercial supplies were imported. In his budget speech in February 2006 the Minister of Finance announced that in 2005 the rate of inflation fell to 15.9%, the lowest rate since the liberalization of the economy in 1991. However, appreciation of the kwacha against the dollar by some 34%—attributed to increased foreign exchange earnings, driven by demand for copper—was expected to have a negative effect on agricultural exports in particular.

ZAMBIA

Education

Between 1964 and 1979 enrolment in schools increased by more than 260%. Primary education, which is compulsory, begins at seven years of age and lasts for seven years. Secondary education, beginning at the age of 14, lasts for a further five years, comprising a first cycle of two years and a second of three years. In 2000/01 66% of children (66% of boys; 65% of girls) in the relevant age-group attended primary schools, and, according to UNESCO estimates, enrolment at secondary schools included 19% of children (20% of boys; 18% of girls) in the relevant age-group. There are two universities: the University of Zambia at Lusaka, and the Copperbelt University at Kitwe (which is to be transferred to Ndola). There are 14 teacher training colleges. In 2005 expenditure on education was K1,062.0m. The 2006 budgetary allocation for 2006 was K1,647.0m., some 26.9% of the overall budget. The Government recruited an additional 8,000 teachers in 2005 and planned to recruit a further 4,500 in 2006.

Public Holidays

2006: 1 January (New Year's Day), 11 March (Youth Day), 14–17 April (Easter), 1 May (Labour Day), 25 May (African Freedom Day, anniversary of OAU's foundation), 3 July (Heroes' Day), 4 July (Unity Day), 7 August (Farmers' Day), 24 October (Independence Day), 25 December (Christmas Day).

2007: 1 January (New Year's Day), 11 March (Youth Day), 6–9 April (Easter), 1 May (Labour Day), 25 May (African Freedom Day, anniversary of OAU's foundation), 2 July (Heroes' Day), 3 July (Unity Day), 6 August (Farmers' Day), 24 October (Independence Day), 25 December (Christmas Day).

Weights and Measures

The metric system is in use.

Statistical Survey

Source (unless otherwise indicated): Central Statistical Office, POB 31908, Lusaka; tel. (1) 211231; internet www.zamstats.gov.zm.

Area and Population

AREA, POPULATION AND DENSITY

Area (sq km)	752,612*
Population (census results)	
20 August 1990	7,383,097
25 October 2000	
Males	4,946,298
Females	4,939,293
Total	9,885,591
Population (UN estimates at mid-year)†	
2002	11,102,000
2003	11,291,000
2004	11,479,000
Density (per sq km) at mid-2004	15.3

* 290,585 sq miles.
† Source: UN, *World Population Prospects: The 2004 Revision*.

PROVINCES
(2000 census)

	Area	Population	Density
Central	94,394	1,012,257	10.7
Copperbelt	31,328	1,581,221	50.5
Eastern	69,106	1,306,173	18.9
Luapula	50,567	775,353	15.3
Lusaka	21,896	1,391,329	63.5
Northern	147,826	1,258,696	8.5
North-Western	125,826	583,350	4.6
Southern	85,283	1,212,124	14.2
Western	126,386	765,088	6.1
Total	**752,612**	**9,885,591**	**13.1**

PRINCIPAL TOWNS
(population at 2000 census)

Lusaka (capital)	1,084,703	Lundazi	236,833
Kitwe	376,124	Petauke	235,879
Ndola	374,757	Choma	204,898
Chipata	367,539	Solwezi	203,797
Chibombo	241,612	Mazabuka	203,219

Mid-2003 (UN estimate, incl. suburbs): Lusaka 1,394,315 (Source: UN, *World Urbanization Prospects: The 2003 Revision*).

BIRTHS AND DEATHS
(UN estimates, annual averages)

	1990–95	1995–2000	2000–05
Birth rate (per 1,000)	45.7	43.0	41.3
Death rate (per 1,000)	19.2	22.1	22.8

Source: UN, *World Population Prospects: The 2004 Revision*.

Expectation of life (WHO estimates, years at birth): 39 (males 39; females 39) in 2003 (Source: WHO, *World Health Report*).

ECONOMICALLY ACTIVE POPULATION
(living conditions survey, '000 persons aged 12 years and over)

	1996
Agriculture, hunting, forestry and fishing	2,261
Mining and quarrying	60
Manufacturing	171
Electricity, gas and water	14
Construction	36
Wholesale and retail trade; restaurants and hotels	406
Transport, storage and communication	58
Financial, insurance, real estate and business services	48
Community, social and personal services	312
Total employed	**3,368**
Unemployed*	614
Total labour force	**3,982**

* Figure obtained as a residual.

Source: ILO Sub-Regional Office for Southern Africa.

Health and Welfare

KEY INDICATORS

Total fertility rate (children per woman, 2002)	5.6
Under-5 mortality rate (per 1,000 live births, 2004)	182
HIV/AIDS (% of persons aged 15–49, 2003)	16.5
Physicians (per 1,000 head, 1995)	0.07
Health expenditure (2002): US $ per head (PPP)	51
Health expenditure (2002): % of GDP	5.8
Health expenditure (2002): public (% of total)	51.6
Access to water (% of persons, 2002)	55
Access to sanitation (% of persons, 2002)	45
Human Development Index (2003): ranking	166
Human Development Index (2003): value	0.394

For sources and definitions, see explanatory note on p. vi.

ZAMBIA

Agriculture

PRINCIPAL CROPS
('000 metric tons)

	2002	2003	2004*
Wheat	75†	135†	135
Rice (paddy)*	12	12	12
Maize	602†	1,161†	1,161
Millet	38†	35†	35
Sorghum	16†	20†	19
Potatoes*	11	11	11
Sweet potatoes	53*	53†	53
Cassava (Manioc)	950*	950†	950
Sugar cane	2,000*	1,800†	1,800
Pulses*	17	17	17
Soybeans (Soya beans)	16†	15*	15
Groundnuts (in shell)*	42	42	42
Sunflower seed*	10	10	10
Cottonseed*	62	62	62
Dry onions*	27	27	27
Tomatoes*	25	25	25
Other fresh vegetables*	215.4	215.4	215.4
Fresh fruit*	101.2	101.2	101.2
Cotton (lint)*	22	22	22
Tobacco (leaves)*	4.8	4.8	4.8

* FAO estimate(s).
† Unofficial figure.

Source: FAO.

LIVESTOCK
('000 head, year ending September)

	1999	2000	2001*
Cattle	2,905	2,621	2,600
Sheep	120†	140†	150
Goats	1,069†	1,249†	1,270
Pigs	324†	309	340
Chickens*	28,000	29,000	30,000

* FAO estimates.
† Unofficial figure.

2002–04: Figures assumed to be unchanged from 2001 (FAO estimates).

Source: FAO.

LIVESTOCK PRODUCTS
(FAO estimates, '000 metric tons)

	1999	2000	2001
Beef and veal	46.5	40.8	40.8
Pig meat	10.6	10.1	11.0
Poultry meat	33.5	35.0	36.5
Other meat	37.4	38.6	38.8
Cows' milk	61.5	64.2	64.2
Hen eggs	44.8	46.4	48.0
Cattle hides	6.3	5.4	5.4

2002–04: Hen eggs 46.4, all other figures assumed to be unchanged from 2001 (FAO estimates).

Source: FAO.

Forestry

ROUNDWOOD REMOVALS
(FAO estimates, '000 cubic metres)

	1997	1998	1999
Sawlogs, veneer logs and logs for sleepers	319	319	319
Other industrial wood	492	504	515
Fuel wood	7,219	7,219	7,219
Total	8,030	8,042	8,053

2000–04: Production as in 1999 (FAO estimates).

Source: FAO.

SAWNWOOD PRODUCTION
(FAO estimates, '000 cubic metres, incl. railway sleepers)

	1995	1996	1997
Coniferous (softwood)	300	230	145
Broadleaved (hardwood)	20	15	12
Total	320	245	157

1998–2004: Annual production as in 1997 (FAO estimates).

Source: FAO.

Fishing

('000 metric tons, live weight)

	2001*	2002*	2003
Capture	65.0	65.0	65.0*
Dagaas	8.5	8.5	8.5*
Other freshwater fishes	56.5	56.5	56.5*
Aquaculture	4.5	4.6	4.5
Three-spotted tilapia	2.7	2.7	2.3
Total catch	69.5	69.6	69.5*

* FAO estimate(s).

Note: Figures exclude aquatic mammals, recorded by number rather than weight. The number of Nile crocodiles caught was: 20,900 in 2001; 22,259 in 2002; 28,019 in 2003.

Source: FAO.

Mining

	2002	2003	2004*
Coal ('000 metric tons)	71.7	71.8	240
Copper ore ('000 metric tons)†	341.0	348.0	426.9‡
Cobalt ore (metric tons)†	10,000*	11,300	13,000
Amethysts (metric tons)	1,064.6‡	1,000	1,100

* Estimated production.
† Figures refer to the metal content of ore.
‡ Reported figure.

Source: US Geological Survey.

Industry

SELECTED PRODUCTS
('000 metric tons, unless otherwise indicated)

	2002	2003	2004*
Cement	230.4	480	525
Copper (unwrought): smelter	253.5	268	280
Copper (unwrought): refined	336.8	349.8	398.2
Cobalt (refined, metric tons)	6,144	6,550	7,800

* Estimates.

Raw sugar ('000 metric tons): 189 in 2000; 279 in 2001; 232 in 2002.

Electric energy (million kWh): 7,797 in 2000; 8,179 in 2001.

Sources: FAO; US Geological Survey; UN, *Industrial Commodity Statistics Yearbook*.

Finance

CURRENCY AND EXCHANGE RATES

Monetary Units
100 ngwee = 1 Zambian kwacha (K).

Sterling, Dollar and Euro Equivalents (30 December 2005)
£1 sterling = 6,042.1 kwacha;
US $1 = 3,509.0 kwacha;
€1 = 4,139.5 kwacha;
10,000 Zambian kwacha = £1.66 = $2.85 = €2.42.

Average Exchange Rate (Zambian kwacha per US $)
2003 4,733.27
2004 4,778.88
2005 4,463.50

CENTRAL GOVERNMENT BUDGET
(K '000 million)

Revenue	2003	2004*	2005†
Tax revenue	3,548	4,546	5,523
Income tax	1,622	2,032	2,436
Excise taxes	482	607	720
Value-added tax (VAT)	1,034	1,362	1,588
Domestic VAT	393	453	609
VAT on imports	642	909	979
Customs duty	409	544	778
Non-tax revenue	132	194	217
Total‡	3,680	4,740	5,739

Expenditure	2003	2004*	2005†
Current expenditure	4,002	4,654	6,170
Wages and salaries	1,728	2,012	2,531
Public service retrenchment	10	20	66
Recurrent departmental charges	648	835	1,513
Transfers and pensions	361	446	760
Domestic interest (paid)	563	746	850
External interest (paid)	229	152	200
Other current expenditure	456	430	243
Contingency	6	13	8
Capital expenditure	2,335	2,265	2,203
Total	6,338	6,919	8,373

* Preliminary figures.
† Forecasts.
‡ Excluding grants received (K '000 million): 1,424 in 2003; 1,433 in 2004 (preliminary figure); 1,869 in 2005 (forecast).

Source: IMF, *Zambia: Second Review Under the Three-Year Arrangement Under the Poverty Reduction and Growth Facility and Request for Waiver and Modification of Performance Criteria, and Financing Assurances Review–Staff Report; Staff Statement; Press Release on the Executive Board Discussion; and Statement by the Executive Director for Zambia* (April 2005).

INTERNATIONAL RESERVES
(US $ million at 31 December)

	2003	2004	2005
IMF special drawing rights	0.5	24.8	15.7
Foreign exchange	247.2	312.2	544.0
Total	247.7	337.1	559.8

Source: IMF, *International Financial Statistics*.

MONEY SUPPLY
(K '000 million at 31 December)

	2003*	2004	2005
Currency outside banks	590.7	727.0	820.1
Demand deposits at commercial banks	921.2	1,131.4	1,345.0
Total money (incl. others)	1,513.8	1,860.4	2,167.1

* Data from January 2003 onwards are based on a revised accounting system, and therefore are not strictly comparable with previous years.

Source: IMF, *International Financial Statistics*.

COST OF LIVING
(Consumer Price Index; low-income group; base: 2000 = 100)

	2001	2002	2003
Food (incl. alcohol and tobacco)	118.9	151.1	184.5
Clothing and footwear	120.5	139.4	168.8
Fuel and rent	121.4	145.1	176.5
All items (incl. others)	121.4	148.4	180.1

Source: ILO.

NATIONAL ACCOUNTS
(K '000 million at current prices)

Expenditure on the Gross Domestic Product

	2002	2003	2004*
Final consumption expenditure	16,044	19,583	20,257
Households	14,108	16,603	16,528
General government	1,936	2,981	3,729
Gross capital formation	3,580	5,238	6,296
Gross fixed capital formation	3,361	4,968	5,961
Changes in stocks	219	270	335
Total domestic expenditure	19,623	24,822	26,553
Exports of goods and services	4,241	5,059	9,738
Less Imports of goods and services	7,604	9,401	10,375
GDP in purchasers' values	16,260	20,479	25,916
GDP at constant 1990 prices	2,708	2,847	3001

* Preliminary figures.

Gross Domestic Product by Economic Activity

	2002	2003	2004
Agriculture, forestry and fishing	3,247.4	4,244.6	5,568.2
Mining and quarrying	575.1	564.8	809.7
Manufacturing	1,693.6	2,241.0	2,802.9
Electricity, gas and water	488.3	595.1	694.7
Construction	1,067.7	1,590.0	2,443.3
Wholesale and retail trade, restaurants and hotels	3,004.1	3,873.8	4,827.3
Transport and communications	1,055.9	1,058.2	1,220.5
Finance and insurance	1,493.1	1,847.7	2,282.7
Real estate and business services	1,041.2	1,341.2	1,658.4
Restaurants and hotels	406.8	527.7	659.3
Community, social and personal services*	1,414.4	1,757.0	2,041.6
Sub-total	15,487.6	19,641.1	25,008.6
Import duties	1,630.8	1,899.9	2,219.1
Less imputed bank service charge	858.1	1,061.8	1,311.8
GDP in purchasers' values	16,260.4	20,479.2	25,915.9

* Includes public administration, defence, sanitary services, education, health, recreation, and personal services.

Source: IMF, *Zambia: Selected Issues and Statistical Appendix* (March 2006).

ZAMBIA

BALANCE OF PAYMENTS
(US $ million, estimates)

	2002	2003	2004
Exports of goods f.o.b.	916	1,052	1,588
Imports of goods f.o.b.	−1,204	−1,393	−1,727
Goods procured by airlines	28	29	31
Trade balance	**−259**	**−311**	**−109**
Services (net)	−245	−238	−254
Balance on goods and services	**−504**	**−549**	**−363**
Income (net)	−155	−148	−304
Interest payments	−137	−131	−121
Balance on goods, services and income	**−659**	**−697**	**−667**
Current transfers (net)	7	−3	25
Current account	**−652**	**−700**	**−642**
Capital and financial accounts (net)	238	380	260
Net errors and omissions	31	−2	97
Overall balance	**−383**	**−321**	**−285**

Source: IMF, *Zambia: Second Review Under the Three-Year Arrangement Under the Poverty Reduction and Growth Facility and Request for Waiver and Modification of Performance Criteria, and Financing Assurances Review—Staff Report; Staff Statement; Press Release on the Executive Board Discussion; and Statement by the Executive Director for Zambia* (April 2005).

External Trade

PRINCIPAL COMMODITIES
(US $ million)

Imports f.o.b.	2000	2001	2002
Food and live animals	51.4	75.9	148.5
Cereals and cereal preparations	22.1	37.7	100.5
Crude materials (inedible) except fuels	44.5	40.2	36.2
Mineral fuels, lubricants, etc.	178.4	117.2	89.0
Petroleum and petroleum products	171.3	110.1	80.2
Gasoline and other light oils	134.4	83.7	—
Chemicals and related products	132.9	200.8	186.2
Fertilizers (manufactured)	41.0	38.7	50.3
Basic manufactures	128.3	178.4	159.9
Iron and steel	26.7	42.1	37.7
Manufactures of metals	25.1	34.4	27.5
Machinery and transport equipment	302.2	466.2	389.7
Machinery specialized for particular industries	35.7	77.0	74.0
General industrial machinery, equipment and parts	41.2	103.4	74.7
Telecommunications and sound equipment	30.5	35.3	28.9
Other electrical machinery, apparatus, etc.	53.0	50.5	56.0
Road vehicles and parts	93.1	121.4	109.9
Passenger motor vehicles (excl. buses)	31.6	39.3	32.6
Goods vehicles (lorries and trucks)	35.8	50.0	43.4
Miscellaneous manufactured articles	130.0	200.5	209.3
Printed matter	71.9	125.7	141.3
Total (incl. others)	**993.4**	**1,306.8**	**1,252.7**

Exports f.o.b.	2000	2001	2002
Food and live animals	54.7	80.1	67.7
Sugar and honey	23.1	43.1	35.1
Crude materials (inedible) except fuels	49.9	32.7	49.9
Metal ores and scrap	22.3	4.9	16.0
Basic manufactures	462.2	778.5	685.1
Textile yarn, fabrics and related products	34.5	31.5	24.8
Cotton yarn	25.1	30.4	22.9
Non-metallic mineral manufactures	26.4	24.9	29.6
Non-ferrous metals	346.8	638.5	569.5
Refined copper, unwrought	284.8	513.2	464.4
Base metals and cermets	45.2	98.5	83.0
Manufactures of metals	50.4	68.4	55.1
Machinery and transport equipment	22.9	36.2	45.5
Miscellaneous manufactured articles	42.4	4.2	8.2
Clothing and accessories	31.0	0.1	0.1
Total (incl. others)	**665.6**	**984.6**	**929.5**

Source: UN, *International Trade Statistics Yearbook*.

PRINCIPAL TRADING PARTNERS
(US $ million)

Imports f.o.b.	2000	2001	2002
China, People's Repub.	10.9	38.3	34.5
France	8.4	7.2	25.6
Germany	11.5	22.8	15.1
India	16.4	24.2	45.5
Japan	34.8	37.7	40.6
South Africa	544.2	702.1	641.7
Tanzania	21.1	11.9	14.9
United Kingdom	139.5	203.2	153.6
Zimbabwe	69.1	104.1	97.9
Total (incl. others)	**993.4**	**1,306.8**	**1,252.7**

Exports f.o.b.	2000	2001	2002
Belgium	21.3	9.3	17.3
Congo, Democratic Repub.	—	—	39.8
Congo, Repub.	29.0	33.7	0.2
Germany	17.7	17.5	8.7
India	8.2	13.8	17.0
Italy	7.4	3.0	2.4
Kenya	4.1	12.6	4.7
Malawi	11.3	9.2	19.4
Netherlands	6.5	9.8	11.3
Switzerland-Liechtenstein	75.6	60.5	57.1
Tanzania	5.8	4.0	71.1
United Kingdom	258.9	520.6	393.6
Zimbabwe	15.4	26.4	14.1
Total (incl. others)	**665.6**	**984.6**	**929.5**

Source: UN, *International Trade Statistics Yearbook*.

Transport

ROAD TRAFFIC
(estimates, '000 motor vehicles in use at 31 December)

	1994	1995	1996
Passenger cars	123	142	157
Lorries and vans	68	74	81

Source: IRF, *World Road Statistics*.

ZAMBIA

CIVIL AVIATION
(scheduled services)

	1999	2000	2001
Kilometres flown (million)	1	1	0
Passengers carried ('000)	36	45	12
Passenger-km (million)	32	38	5
Total ton-km (million)	3	4	0

Source: UN, *Statistical Yearbook*.

Tourism

VISITOR ARRIVALS BY NATIONALITY
(provisional figures)

	2001	2002	2003
Australia	16,985	19,508	19,938
South Africa	76,258	87,578	89,506
Tanzania	29,372	33,735	34,478
United Kingdom	55,348	63,570	64,970
USA	18,836	21,634	22,111
Zimbabwe	125,263	143,872	147,040
Total (incl. others)	491,991	565,073	577,515

Tourism receipts (US $ million, incl. passenger transport): 117 in 2001; 134 in 2002; 149 in 2003.

Source: World Tourism Organization.

Communications Media

	2002	2003	2004
Telephones ('000 main lines in use)	87.7	88.4	n.a.
Mobile cellular telephones ('000 subscribers)	139.1	241.0	300.0
Personal computers ('000 in use)	80	95	113
Internet users ('000)	52.4	68.2	231.0

Radio receivers ('000 in use): 1,436 in 1999.

Television receivers ('000 in use): 540 in 2001.

Facsimile machines (number in use): 1,005 (estimate) in year ending 31 March 1999.

Daily newspapers (1996): 3; average circulation: 114,000 copies.

Sources: UNESCO, *Statistical Yearbook*; UN, *Statistical Yearbook*; International Telecommunication Union.

Education

(1998)

	Institutions	Teachers	Males	Females	Total
Pre-primary	443	700	13,737*	16,263*	30,000*
Primary	4,221	34,810	810,873	746,384	1,557,257
Secondary	n.a.	10,000	164,992	125,093	290,085
Tertiary	n.a.	n.a.	14,520	7,181	22,701

*Estimate.

Source: UNESCO Institute for Statistics.

Adult literacy rate (UNESCO estimates): 67.9% (males 76.1%; females 59.7%) in 1995–99 (Source: UN Development Programme, *Human Development Report*).

Directory

The Constitution

The Constitution for the Republic of Zambia, which was formally adopted on 28 May 1996 (amending the Constitution of 1991), provides for a multi-party form of government. The Head of State is the President of the Republic, who is elected by popular vote at the same time as elections to the National Assembly. The President's tenure of office is limited to two five-year terms. Foreign nationals and those with foreign parentage are prohibited from contesting the presidency. The legislature comprises a National Assembly of 158 members: 150 are elected by universal adult suffrage, while the remaining eight are nominated by the President. The President appoints a Vice-President and a Cabinet from members of the National Assembly.

The Constitution also provides for a House of Chiefs numbering 27: four from each of the Northern, Western, Southern and Eastern Provinces, three each from the North-Western, Luapula and Central Provinces and two from the Copperbelt Province. It may submit resolutions to be debated by the Assembly and consider those matters referred to it by the President.

The Supreme Court of Zambia is the final Court of Appeal. The Chief Justice and other judges are appointed by the President. Subsidiary to the Supreme Court is the High Court, which has unlimited jurisdiction to hear and determine any civil or criminal proceedings under any Zambian law.

The Government

HEAD OF STATE

President: LEVY PATRICK MWANAWASA (took office 2 January 2002).

THE CABINET
(March 2006)

President: LEVY PATRICK MWANAWASA.
Vice-President: LUPANDO MWAPE.
Minister of Home Affairs: BATES NAMUYAMBA.
Minister of Foreign Affairs: Lt-Gen. RONNIE SHIKAPWASHA.
Minister of Defence: WAMUNDILA MULIOKELA.
Minister of Finance and National Planning: NG'ANDU PETER MAGANDE.
Minister of Commerce, Trade and Industry: DIPAK PATEL.
Minister for Legal Affairs: GEORGE KUNDA.
Minister of Agriculture, Food and Fisheries: MUNDIA SIKATANA.
Minister of Communications and Transport: ABEL CHAMBESHI.
Minister of Energy and Water Development: FELIX MUTATI.
Minister of Tourism, the Environment and Natural Resources: KABINGA PANDE.
Minister of Education: Brig.-Gen. BRIAN CHITUWO.
Minister of Science, Technology and Vocational Training: JUDITH KAPIJIMPANGA.
Minister of Health: SYLVIA MASEBO.
Minister of Local Government and Housing: ANDREW MULENGA.
Minister of Works and Supply: MARINA NSINGO.
Minister of Community Development and Social Welfare: STEPHEN MANJATA.
Minister of Sport, Youth and Child Development: GEORGE CHULUMANDA.
Minister of Lands: GLADYS NYIRONGO.
Minister of Labour and Social Security: MUTALE NALUMANGO.
Minister of Mines and Mineral Development: KALOMBO MWANSA.

ZAMBIA

Minister of Information and Broadcasting Services: VERNON MWAANGA.
Minister of Women's Affairs: ROSEMARY BANDA.

MINISTRIES

Office of the President: POB 30208, Lusaka; tel. (1) 218282; internet www.statehouse.gov.zm.
Ministry of Agriculture, Food and Fisheries: Mulungushi House, Independence Ave, Nationalist Rd, POB RW50291, Lusaka; tel. (1) 213551.
Ministry of Commerce, Trade and Industry: Kwacha Annex, Cairo Rd, POB 31968, Lusaka; tel. (1) 213767.
Ministry of Communications and Transport: Fairley Rd, POB 50065, Lusaka; tel. (1) 251444; fax (1) 253260.
Ministry of Community Development and Social Welfare: Fidelity House, POB 31958, Lusaka; tel. (1) 228321; fax (1) 225327.
Ministry of Defence: POB 31931, Lusaka; tel. (1) 252366.
Ministry of Education: 15102 Ridgeway, POB RW50093, Lusaka; tel. (1) 227636; fax (1) 222396.
Ministry of Energy and Water Development: Mulungushi House, Independence Ave, Nationalist Rd, POB 36079, Lusaka; tel. (1) 252589; fax (1) 252589.
Ministry of Finance and National Planning: Finance Bldg, POB 50062, Lusaka; tel. (1) 253512; fax (1) 251078.
Ministry of Foreign Affairs: POB RW50069, Lusaka; tel. (1) 213822; fax (1) 222440.
Ministry of Health: Woodgate House, 1st–2nd Floors, Cairo Rd, POB 30205, Lusaka; tel. (1) 227745; fax (1) 228385.
Ministry of Home Affairs: POB 32862, Lusaka; tel. (1) 213505.
Ministry of Information and Broadcasting Services: Independence Ave, POB 32245, Lusaka; tel. (1) 228202; fax (1) 253457.
Ministry of Justice: Fairley Rd, POB 50106, 15101, Ridgeway, Lusaka; tel. (1) 228522.
Ministry of Labour and Social Security: Lechwe House, Freedom Way, POB 32186, Lusaka; tel. (1) 212020.
Ministry of Lands: POB 50694, Lusaka; tel. (1) 252288; fax (1) 250120.
Ministry of Local Government and Housing: Church Rd, POB 34204, Lusaka; tel. (1) 253077; fax (1) 252680.
Ministry of Mines and Mineral Development: Chilufya Mulenga Rd, POB 31969, 10101 Lusaka; tel. (1) 251402; fax (1) 252095.
Ministry of Science, Technology and Vocational Training: POB 50464, Lusaka; tel. (1) 229673; fax (1) 252951.
Ministry of Sport, Youth and Child Development: Memaco House, POB 50195, Lusaka; tel. (1) 227158; fax (1) 223996.
Ministry of Tourism, the Environment and Natural Resources: Electra House, Cairo Rd, POB 30575, Lusaka; tel. (1) 227645; fax (1) 222189.
Ministry of Women's Affairs: Lusaka.
Ministry of Works and Supply: POB 50003, Lusaka; tel. (1) 253088; fax (1) 253404.

President and Legislature

PRESIDENT

Presidential Election, 27 December 2001

Candidate	Votes	% of votes
Levy Patrick Mwanawasa (MMD)	506,694	29.15
Anderson Mazoka (UPND)	472,697	27.20
Christon Tembo (FDD)	228,861	13.17
Tilyenji Kaunda (UNIP)	175,898	10.12
Godfrey Miyanda (HP)	140,678	8.09
Benjamin Mwila (ZRP)	85,472	4.92
Michael Sata (PF)	59,172	3.40
Nevers Mumba (NCC)	38,860	2.24
Gwendoline Konie (SDP)	10,253	0.59
Inonge Mbikusita-Lewanika (AZ)	9,882	0.57
Yobert Shamapande (NLD)	9,481	0.55
Total	**1,737,948**	**100.00**

NATIONAL ASSEMBLY

Speaker: AMUSAA KATUNDA MWANAMWAMBWA.

General Election, 27 December 2001

Party	Votes	% of votes	Seats
Movement for Multi-party Democracy (MMD)	490,680	27.48	69
United Party for National Development (UPND)	416,236	23.31	49
Forum for Democracy and Development (FDD)	272,817	15.28	12
United National Independence Party (UNIP)	185,535	10.39	13
Heritage Party (HP)	132,311	7.41	4
Zambia Republican Party (ZRP)	97,010	5.43	1
Independents	59,335	3.32	1
Patriotic Front (PF)	49,362	2.76	1
Others	48,066	2.71	—
Invalid votes	34,133	1.91	—
Total	**1,785,485**	**100.00**	**150**

House of Chiefs

The House of Chiefs is an advisory body which may submit resolutions for debate by the National Assembly. There are 27 Chiefs, four each from the Northern, Western, Southern and Eastern Provinces, three each from the North Western, Luapula and Central Provinces, and two from the Copperbelt Province.

Election Commission

Electoral Commission of Zambia: Block 27, Independence Ave, POB 50274, Lusaka; tel. (1) 253789; fax (1) 253884; internet www.elections.org.zm; f. 1996; independent; Chair. IRENE MAMBILIMA.

Political Organizations

Democratic Party (DP): Plot C4, President Ave (North), POB 71628, Ndola; f. 1991; Pres. EMMANUEL MWAMBA.
Heritage Party (HP): POB 51055, Lusaka; f. 2001; by expelled mems of the MMD; Pres. Brig.-Gen. GODFREY MIYANDA.
Liberal Progressive Front (LPF): POB 31190, Lusaka; f. 1993; Pres. ROGER CHONGWE.
Movement for Multi-party Democracy (MMD): POB 30708, Lusaka; f. 1990; governing party since Nov. 1991; Nat. Chair. BONIFACE KAWIMBE; Nat. Sec. VERNON MWAANGA.
National Democratic Front: Lusaka; f. 2006 to contest the presidential election; Acting Chair. NEVERS MUMBA (RP).
Comprising:
  All People's Congress Party (APC): Lusaka; f. 2005 by fmr mems of the FDD; Pres. KEN NGONDO.
  Party for Unity, Democracy and Development (PUDD): Lusaka; f. 2004 by fmr mems of the MMD; Pres. CHITALU SAMPA.
  Reform Party: Lusaka; f. 2005 by fmr mems of the MMD; Pres. NEVERS MUMBA; Nat. Chair. EVA SANDERSON; Sec.-Gen. CLEMENT MICHELO.
  Zambia Democratic Conference (ZADECO): Lusaka; f. 1998 as the Zambia Democratic Congress Popular Front by fmr mems of the Zambia Democratic Congress; disbanded in 1999; reformed after 2001 election by fmr mems of the ZAP; Pres. Rev. Dr DAN PULE.
  Zambia Republican Party (ZRP): Lusaka; f. 2001 by merger of the Republican Party (f. 2000) the and Zambia Alliance for Progress (f. 1999); Gen. Sec. SILVIA MASEBO; Nat. Chair. BEN KAPITA.
National Leadership for Development (NLD): POB 34161, Lusaka; f. 2000; Pres. Dr YOBERT K. SHAMAPANDE.
Patriotic Front: f. 2001 by expelled mems of the MMD; Pres. MICHAEL C. SATA; Sec.-Gen. GUY SCOTT.
United Democratic Alliance (UDA): Kenneth Kaunda House, Cairo Rd, Lusaka; f. 2006 to contest that year's elections; Leader ANDERSON MAZOKA (UPND); Nat. Chair. NEWTON NG'UNI (FDD).
Comprising:
  Forum for Democracy and Development (FDD): POB 35868, Lusaka; f. 2001 by expelled mems of the MMD; Pres. EDITH NAWAKWI; Chair. SIMON ZUKAS.

ZAMBIA

United National Independence Party (UNIP): POB 30302, Lusaka; tel. (1) 221197; fax (1) 221327; f. 1959; sole legal party 1972–90; Pres. TILYENJI KAUNDA; Nat. Chair. KEN KAIRA.

United Party for National Development (UPND): POB 33199, Lusaka; internet www.upnd.org; f. 1998; incl. fmr mems of the Progressive People's Party and Zambia Democratic Party; Leader ANDERSON MAZOKA.

Unity Party for Democrats (UPD): POB RW28, Ridgeway, Lusaka; f. 1997; Pres. MATHEW PIKITI.

Zambia Alliance for Progress (ZAP): Lusaka; f. 1999; re-registered as ZAP in 2001 after splitting from Zambia Republican Party; Pres. (vacant).

Diplomatic Representation

EMBASSIES AND HIGH COMMISSIONS IN ZAMBIA

Angola: Plot 108, Great East Rd, Northmead, POB 31595, 10101 Lusaka; tel. (1) 34764; fax (1) 221210; Ambassador (vacant).

Botswana: 5201 Pandit Nehru Rd, Diplomatic Triangle, POB 31910, 10101 Lusaka; tel. (1) 250555; fax (1) 250804; High Commissioner LAPOLOGANG CAESAR LEKOA.

Brazil: 74 Anglo American Bldg, Independence Ave, POB 33300; tel. (1) 250400; fax (1) 251652; Chargé d'affaires a.i. PAULO M. G. DE SOUSA.

Canada: Plot 5199, United Nations Ave, POB 31313, 10101 Lusaka; tel. (1) 250833; fax (1) 254176; e-mail lsaka@international.gc.ca; High Commissioner JOHN DEYELL.

China, People's Republic: Plot 7430, United Nations Ave, Longacres, POB 31975, 10101 Lusaka; tel. (1) 251169; fax (1) 251157; Ambassador HU SHOUQIN.

Congo, Democratic Republic: Plot 1124, Parirenyatwa Rd, POB 31287, 10101 Lusaka; tel. and fax (1) 235679; Ambassador JEAN-MARIE DIKANGA KAZADI.

Cuba: 5574 Mogoye Rd, Kalundu, POB 33132, 10101 Lusaka; tel. (1) 291308; fax (1) 291586; Ambassador NARCISO MARTIN MORA DIAZ.

Denmark: 4 Manenekela Rd, POB 50299, Lusaka; tel. (1) 254277; fax (1) 254618; e-mail lunamb@um.dk; Ambassador ORLA BAKDAL.

Egypt: Plot 5206, United Nations Ave, Longacres, POB 32428, Lusaka 10101; tel. (1) 250229; fax (1) 254149; Ambassador MOHAMED TAMER SAAD ELDIN MANSOUR.

Finland: Haile Selassie Ave, opposite Ndeke House, Longacres, POB 50819, 15101 Lusaka; tel. (1) 251988; fax (1) 253783; e-mail sanomat.lus@formin.fi; internet www.finland.org.zm; Chargé d'affaires a.i. JORMA SUVANTO.

France: Anglo-American Bldg, 4th Floor, 74 Independence Ave, POB 30062, 10101 Lusaka; tel. (1) 251322; fax (1) 254475; e-mail france@ambafrance-zm.org; internet www.ambafrance-zm.org; Ambassador FRANCIS SAUDUBRAY.

Germany: Plot 5209, United Nations Ave, POB 50120, 15101 Ridgeway, Lusaka; tel. (1) 250644; fax (1) 254014; e-mail info@lusaka.diplo.de; internet www.lusaka.diplo.de; Ambassador Dr IRENE HINRICHSEN.

Holy See: 283 Los Angeles Blvd, POB 31445, 10101 Lusaka; tel. (1) 251033; fax (1) 250601; e-mail nuntius@coppernet.zm; Apostolic Nuncio Most Rev. ORLANDO ANTONINI (Titular Archbishop of Formia).

India: 1 Pandit Nehru Rd, POB 32111, 10101 Lusaka; tel. (1) 253159; fax (1) 254118; High Commissioner YOGESH K. GUPTA.

Ireland: 6663 Katima Mulilo Rd, Olympia Park, POB 34923, 10101 Lusaka; tel. (1) 290650; fax (1) 290482; Chargé d'affaires a.i. BILL NOLAN.

Italy: Plot 5211, Embassy Park, Diplomatic Triangle, POB 31046, 10101 Lusaka; tel. (1) 250781; fax (1) 254929; e-mail ambasciata.lusaka@esteri.it; internet go.to/ambasciatalusaka; Ambassador Dr TULLIO GUMA.

Japan: Plot 5218, Haile Selassie Ave, POB 34190, 10101 Lusaka; tel. (1) 251555; fax (1) 254425; e-mail jez@zamtel.zm; internet www.zm.emb-japan.go.jp; Ambassador MASAAKI MIYASHITA.

Kenya: 5207 United Nations Ave, POB 50298, 10101 Lusaka; tel. (1) 250722; fax (1) 253829; e-mail kenhigh@zamnet.zm; High Commissioner ESTHER MSHAI TOLLE.

Libya: 251 Ngwee Rd, off United Nations Ave, Longacres, POB 35319, 10101 Lusaka; tel. (1) 253055; fax (1) 251239; Ambassador KHALIFA OMER SWIEXI.

Malawi: 31 Bishops Rd, Kabulonga, POB 50425, Lusaka; tel. (1) 213750; fax (1) 265764; e-mail mhcomm@zamtel.zm; High Commissioner Dr CHRISSIE MUGHOGHO.

Mozambique: Kacha Rd, Plot 9592, POB 34877, 10101 Lusaka; tel. (1) 220333; fax (1) 220345; e-mail mozhclsk@zamnet.zm; High Commissioner SHAHARUDDIN MOHAMMED SOM.

Namibia: 30B Mutende Rd, Woodlands, POB 30577, 10101 Lusaka; tel. (1) 260407; fax (1) 263858; High Commissioner FRIEDA NANGULA ITHETE.

Netherlands: 5208 United Nations Ave, POB 31905, 10101 Lusaka; tel. (1) 253819; fax (1) 253733; e-mail lus@minbuza.nl; internet www.netherlandsembassy.org.zm; Ambassador EDDY MIDDELDORP.

Nigeria: 5208 Haile Selassie Ave, Longacres, POB 32598, 10101 Lusaka; tel. (1) 253177; fax (1) 253560; High Commissioner Chief IBIRONKE O. VAUGHAN-ADEFOPE.

Norway: cnr Birdcage Walk and Haile Selassie Ave, Longacres, POB 34570, 10101 Lusaka; tel. (1) 252188; fax (1) 253915; e-mail emb.lusaka@mfa.no; internet www.norway.info; Ambassador TERJE VIGTEL.

Russia: Plot 6407, Diplomatic Triangle, POB 32355, 10101 Lusaka; tel. (1) 252120; fax (1) 253582; e-mail embrus@zamnet.zm; internet www.russianembassy.biz/zambia-lusaka.htm; Ambassador ANVAR AZIMOV.

Saudi Arabia: 27BC Leopards Hill Rd, Kabulonga, POB 34411, 10101 Lusaka; tel. (1) 266861; fax (1) 266863; e-mail saudiemb@uudial.zm; Ambassador TALAT SALEM RADWAN.

Serbia and Montenegro: Plot 5216, Diplomatic Triangle, POB 31180, 10101 Lusaka; tel. (1) 250247; fax (1) 253843; e-mail yuemblus@zamnet.zm; Chargé d'affaires a.i. MIRKO MANOJLOVIC.

Somalia: G3/377A Kabulonga Rd, POB 34051, Lusaka; tel. (1) 262119; Ambassador Dr OMAN UMAL.

South Africa: D26, Cheetah Rd, Kabulonga, Private Bag W369, Lusaka; tel. (1) 260999; fax (1) 263001; e-mail sahc@zamnet.zm; High Commissioner MASALA MZIWANDILA.

Spain: Lusaka; Ambassador SANTIAGO MARTÍNEZ CARO.

Sudan: 31 Ng'umbo Rd, Longacres, POB RW179X, 15200 Lusaka; tel. (1) 215570; fax (1) 40653; Ambassador ABDALLAH KHIDIR BASHIR.

Sweden: Haile Selassie Ave, POB 50264, 10101 Lusaka; tel. (1) 251711; fax (1) 254049; e-mail ambassaden.lusaka@sida.se; internet www.swedenabroad.com/lusaka; Ambassador CHRISTINA REHLEN.

Tanzania: Ujamaa House, Plot 5200, United Nations Ave, POB 31219, 10101 Lusaka; tel. (1) 253222; fax (1) 254861; e-mail tzreplsk@zamnet.zm; High Commissioner GEORGE MWANJABALA.

United Kingdom: Plot 5201, Independence Ave, POB 50050, 15101 Ridgeway, Lusaka; tel. (1) 251133; fax (1) 253798; High Commissioner ALISTAIR HARRISON.

USA: cnr Independence and United Nations Aves, POB 31617, Lusaka; tel. (1) 250955; fax (1) 252225; internet zambia.usembassy.gov; Ambassador CARMEN M. MARTINEZ.

Zimbabwe: 11058, Haile Selassie Ave, Longacres, POB 33491, 10101 Lusaka; tel. (1) 254012; fax (1) 227474; Ambassador TIRIVAFI JOHN KANGAI.

Judicial System

The judicial system of Zambia comprises a Supreme Court, composed of a Chief Justice, a Deputy Chief Justice and five Justices; a High Court comprising the Chief Justice and 30 Judges; Senior Resident and Resident Magistrates' Courts, which sit at various centres; and Local Courts, which deal principally with customary law, but which also have limited criminal jurisdiction.

Supreme Court of Zambia

Independence Ave, POB 50067, Ridgeway, Lusaka; tel. (1) 251330; fax (1) 251743.

Chief Justice: ERNEST L. SAKALA.

Deputy Chief Justice: DAVID M. LEWANIKA.

Supreme Court Judges: LOMBE CHIBESAKUNDA, DENNIS CHIRWA, PETER CHITENGI, IREEN MAMBILIMA, SANDSON SILOMBA.

Religion

CHRISTIANITY

Council of Churches in Zambia: Church House, Cairo Rd, POB 30315, Lusaka; tel. (1) 229551; e-mail info@ccz.org.zm; f. 1945; Chair. Rt Rev. THUMA HAMUKANG'ANDU (Brethren in Christ Church); Gen. Sec. JAPHET NDHLOVU; 22 mem. churches and 18 affiliate mem. orgs.

The Anglican Communion

Anglicans are adherents of the Church of the Province of Central Africa, covering Botswana, Malawi, Zambia and Zimbabwe. The Church comprises 15 dioceses, including five in Zambia. The Archbishop of the Province is the Bishop of the Upper Shire of Malawi. There are an estimated 80,000 adherents in Zambia.

ZAMBIA

Bishop of Central Zambia: Rt Rev. D. G. KAMUKWAMBA, POB 70172, Ndola; tel. (2) 612431; e-mail adcznla@zamnet.zm.

Bishop of Eastern Zambia: Rt Rev. WILLIAM MUCHOMBO, POB 510154, Chipata; tel. and fax (6) 221294; e-mail dioeastzm@zamtel.zm.

Bishop of Luapula: Rt Rev. ROBERT MUMBI.

Bishop of Lusaka: Rt Rev. MEDARDO MAZOMBWE, Bishop's Lodge, POB 30183, Lusaka; fax (1) 250228.

Bishop of Northern Zambia: Rt Rev. ALBERT CHAMA, POB 22317, Kitwe; tel. (2) 223264; fax (2) 224778; e-mail angdiolu@zamnet.zm.

Protestant Churches

At mid-2000 there were an estimated 2.7m. Protestants.

African Methodist Episcopal Church: POB 31478, Lusaka; tel. (1) 264013; Presiding Elder Rev. L. SICHANGWA; 440 congregations, 880,000 mems.

Baptist Church: Lubu Rd, POB 30636, Lusaka; tel. (1) 253620.

Baptist Mission of Zambia: Baptist Bldg, 3062 Great East Rd, POB 50599, 15101 Ridgeway, Lusaka; tel. (1) 222492; fax (1) 227520; e-mail bmzambia@zamnet.zm; internet bmoz.org.

Brethren in Christ Church: POB 630115, Choma; tel. (3) 20228; fax (3) 20127; e-mail biccz@zamtel.zm; internet www.bic.org; f. 1906; Bishop Rev. E. SHAMAPANI; 165 congregations, 17,623 mems.

Reformed Church in Zambia: POB 38255, Lusaka; tel. (1) 295369; f. 1899; African successor to the Dutch Reformed Church mission; 147 congregations, 400,000 mems.

Seventh-day Adventist Church: Plot 9221, cnr Burma Rd and Independence Ave, POB 31309, Lusaka; tel. (1) 255197; fax (1) 255191; e-mail zbu@zamnet.zm; Pres. Dr CORNELIUS MULENGA MATANDIKO; Sec. HARRINGTON SIMUI AKOMBWA; 463,000 mems.

United Church of Zambia: Synod Headquarters, Nationalist Rd at Burma Rd, POB 50122, Lusaka; tel. (1) 250641; fax (1) 252198; e-mail uczsynod@zamnet.zm; f. 1965; Synod Bishop Rev. MUTALE MULUMBWA (acting); Gen. Sec. Rev. Prof. TEDDY KALONGO; c. 3m. mems.

Other denominations active in Zambia include the Assemblies of God, the Church of Christ, the Church of the Nazarene, the Evangelical Fellowship of Zambia, the Kimbanguist Church, the Presbyterian Church of Southern Africa, the Religious Society of Friends (Quakers) and the United Pentecostal Church. At mid-2000 there were an estimated 2m. adherents professing other forms of Christianity.

The Roman Catholic Church

Zambia comprises two archdioceses and eight dioceses. At 31 December 2003 there were an estimated 3,429,513 adherents in the country, equivalent to 28.2% of the total population.

Bishops' Conference

Zambia Episcopal Conference, Catholic Secretariat, Unity House, cnr Freedom Way and Katunjila Rd, POB 31965, Lusaka; tel. (1) 212070; fax (1) 220996; e-mail zec@zamnet.zm; f. 1984; Pres. Rt Rev. TELESPHORE GEORGE MPUNDU (Bishop of Mpika).

Archbishop of Kasama: Most Rev. JAMES SPAITA, Archbishop's House, POB 410143, Kasama; tel. (4) 221248; fax (4) 222202; e-mail archkasa@zamtel.zm.

Archbishop of Lusaka: Most Rev. MEDARDO JOSEPH MAZOMBWE, 41 Wamulwa Rd, POB 32754, 10101 Lusaka; tel. (1) 239257; fax (1) 237008; e-mail adl@zamnet.zm.

ISLAM

There are about 10,000 members of the Muslim Association in Zambia.

BAHÁ'Í FAITH

National Spiritual Assembly: Sekou Touré Rd, Plot 4371, Private Bag RW227X, Ridgeway 15102, Lusaka; tel. and fax (1) 254505; e-mail nsa@zamnet.zm; f. 1968; Sec.-Gen. CHUUNGU MALITONGA; mems resident in 1,456 localities.

The Press

DAILIES

The Post: 36 Bwinjimfumu Rd, Rhodespark, Private Bag E352, Lusaka; tel. (97) 788200; fax (1) 229271; e-mail post@zamnet.zm; internet www.post.co.zm; f. 1991; privately-owned; Editor-in-Chief FRED M'MEMBE; circ. 29,000.

The Times of Zambia: Kabelenga Ave, POB 70069, Ndola; tel. (2) 621305; fax (2) 617096; internet www.times.co.zm; f. 1943; govt-owned; English; Deputy Editor-in-Chief DAVEY SAKALA; circ. 25,000.

Zambia Daily Mail: Zambia Publishing Company, POB 31421, Lusaka; tel. (1) 225131; fax (1) 225881; internet www.daily-mail.co.zm; f. 1968; govt-owned; English; Man. Editor EMMANUEL NYIRENDA; circ. 40,000.

PERIODICALS

African Social Research: Institute of Economic and Social Research, University of Zambia, POB 32379, Lusaka; tel. (1) 294131; fax (1) 253952; f. 1944; 2 a year; Editor MUBANGA E. KASHOKI; circ. 1,000.

The Challenge: Mission Press, Chifubu Rd, POB 71581, Ndola; tel. (2) 680456; fax (2) 680484; e-mail missionpress@ofmconv.org.zm; f. 1999; quarterly; English; social, educational and religious; Roman Catholic; edited by Franciscan friars; circ. 9,000.

Chipembele Magazine: POB 30255, Lusaka; tel. (1) 254226; 6 a year; publ. by Wildlife Conservation Soc. of Zambia; circ. 20,000.

Chronicle: Lusaka; bi-weekly; independent.

Farming in Zambia: POB 50197, Lusaka; tel. (1) 213551; f. 1965; quarterly; publ. by Ministry of Agriculture, Food and Fisheries; Editor L. P. CHIRWA; circ. 3,000.

Imbila: POB RW20, Lusaka; tel. (1) 217254; f. 1953; monthly; publ. by Zambia Information Services; Bemba; Editor D. MUKAKA; circ. 20,000.

Intanda: POB RW20, Lusaka; tel. (1) 219675; f. 1958; monthly; publ. by Zambia Information Services; Tonga; Editor J. SIKAULU; circ. 6,000.

Journal of Adult Education: University of Zambia, POB 50516, Lusaka; tel. (1) 216767; f. 1982; Exec. Editor FRANCIS KASOMA.

Journal of Science and Technology: School of Natural Sciences, Dept of Biological Sciences, University of Zambia, POB 32379, Lusaka 10101; tel. (1) 293008; fax (1) 253952; e-mail press@admin.unza.zm; f. 1996; science and technology journal of the Univ. of Zambia; 2 a year; Editor-in-Chief Prof. J. N. ZULU (acting).

Leisure Magazine: Farmers House, Cairo Rd, POB 8138, Woodlands, Lusaka; monthly; general interest.

Liseli: POB RW20, Lusaka; tel. (1) 219675; monthly; publ. by Zambia Information Services; Lozi; Editor F. AMNSAA; circ. 8,000.

The Lowdown: Lusaka; internet www.lowdown.co.zm; f. 1995; monthly; English; Editor HEATHER CHALCRAFT.

Lukanga News: POB 919, Kabwe; tel. (5) 217254; publ. by Zambia Information Services; Lenje; Editor J. H. N. NKOMANGA; circ. 5,500.

Mining Mirror: Zambia Consolidated Copper Mines Ltd, PR Dept, POB 71505, Ndola; tel. (2) 640142; f. 1973; monthly; English; Editor G. MUKUWA; circ. 30,000.

National Mirror: Multimedia Zambia, 15701 Woodlands, POB 320199, Lusaka; tel. (1) 263864; fax (1) 263050; f. 1972; fortnightly; news, current affairs and foreign affairs; publ. by Multimedia Zambia; Editor FANWELL CHEMBO; circ. 40,000.

Ngoma: POB RW20, Lusaka; tel. (1) 219675; monthly; Lunda, Kaonde and Luvale; publ. by Zambia Information Services; Editor B. A. LUHILA; circ. 3,000.

Orbit: Printpak Zambia Ltd, POB RW18X, Lusaka; tel. (1) 254915; f. 1971; 9 a year; publ. by Ministry of Education; children's educational magazine; Editor ELIDAH CHISHA; circ. 65,000.

Outlook: TBM Publicity Enterprises Ltd, POB 40, Kitwe; f. 1971; monthly; general interest.

Search Magazine: The Times Newspaper Ltd, POB 70069; tel. (2) 611001; Ndola; monthly; general interest.

Speak Out!: POB 70244, Ndola; tel. (2) 612241; fax (2) 620630; e-mail speakout@zamnet.zm; f. 1984; bi-monthly; Christian; aimed at youth readership; Man. Editor CONSTANTIA TREPPE; circ. 30,000.

The Sportsman: POB 31762, Lusaka; tel. (1) 214250; f. 1980; monthly; Man. Editor SAM SIKAZWE; circ. 18,000.

The Sun: Lusaka.

Sunday Express: Lusaka; f. 1991; weekly; Man. Editor JOHN MUKELA.

Sunday Times of Zambia: Kabelenga Ave, POB 70069, Ndola; tel. (2) 614469; fax (2) 617096; e-mail times@zamtel.zm; internet www.times.co.zm/sunday/; f. 1965; owned by UNIP; English; Man. Editor ARTHUR SIMUCHOBA; circ. 78,000.

Tsopano: POB RW20, Lusaka; tel. (1) 217254; f. 1958; monthly; publ. by Zambia Information Services; Nyanja; Editor S. S. BANDA; circ. 9,000.

Voters' Voice: Lusaka; monthly; independent.

Weekly Post: Post Newspapers Ltd, Private Bag E352, Lusaka; tel. (1) 293791; fax (1) 293788; f. 1968.

Workers' Challenge: POB 270035, Kitwe; tel. and fax (2) 210904; f. 1981; 2 a month; publ. by the Workers' Pastoral Centre; English

ZAMBIA

and Bemba; Co-Editors Fr MISHECK KAUNDA, JUSTIN CHILUFYA; circ. 16,000.

Workers' Voice: POB 20652, Kitwe; tel. (2) 211999; f. 1972; fortnightly; publ. by Zambia Congress of Trade Unions.

Youth: POB 30302, Lusaka; tel. (1) 211411; f. 1974; quarterly; publ. by UNIP Youth League; Editor-in-Chief N. ANAMELA; circ. 20,000.

Zambia Government Gazette: POB 30136, Lusaka; tel. (1) 228724; fax (1) 224486; f. 1911; weekly; English; official notices.

NEWS AGENCY

Zambia News Agency (ZANA): Mass Media Complex, POB 30007, Lusaka; tel. (1) 219673; internet www.zana.gov.zm; Editor-in-Chief VILLIE LOMBANYA.

Foreign Bureaux

Agence France-Presse: POB 33805, Lusaka; tel. (1) 212959; Bureau Chief ABBE MAINE.

Informatsionnoye Telegrafnoye Agentstvo Rossii—Telegrafnoye Agentstvo Suverennykh Stran (ITAR—TASS) (Russia): POB 33394, Lusaka; tel. (1) 254201; Correspondent ANDREY K. POLYAKOV.

Reuters (UK): Woodgate House, 3rd Floor, Cairo Rd, Lusaka; tel. 97843609; tel. and fax (1) 235698; e-mail shapi@reuters.com.zm; Correspondent SHAPI K. SHACINDA.

Rossiiskoye Informatsionnoye Agentstvo—Novosti (RIA—Novosti) (Russia): Lusaka; tel. (1) 252849; Rep. VIKTOR LAPTUKHIN.

Xinhua (New China) News Agency (People's Republic of China): United Nations Ave, POB 31859, Lusaka; tel. (1) 252227; fax (1) 251708; e-mail xinhuana@zamnet.zm; Chief Correspondent CHAI SHIKUAN.

PRESS ASSOCIATION

Press Association of Zambia (PAZA): c/o The Times of Zambia, Kabelenga Ave, POB 70069, Ndola; tel. (2) 621305; fax (2) 617096; f. 1983; Pres. ANDREW SAKALA; Chair. ROBINSON MAKAYI.

Publishers

Africa: Literature Centre, POB 21319, Kitwe; tel. (2) 210765; fax (2) 210716; general, educational, religious; Dir JACKSON MBEWE.

African Social Research: Institute of Economic and Social Research, University of Zambia, POB 32379, Lusaka; tel. (1) 294131; fax (1) 253952; e-mail inesor@zamnet.zm; social research in Africa; Editor MUBANGA E. KASHOKI.

Bookworld Ltd: Lottie House, Cairo Rd, POB 31838, Lusaka; tel. (1) 225282; fax (1) 226710; e-mail bookwld@zamtel.zm.

Daystar Publications Ltd: POB 32211, Lusaka; f. 1966; religious; Man. Dir S. E. M. PHEKO.

Directory Publishers of Zambia Ltd: Mabalenga Rd, POB 30963, Lusaka; tel. (1) 237915; fax (1) 237912; f. 1958; trade directories; Gen. Man. W. D. WRATTEN.

Multimedia Zambia: Woodlands, POB 320199, Lusaka; tel. and fax (1) 261193; f. 1971; religious and educational books, audio-visual materials; Exec. Dir GOLDEN ZIBA.

University of Zambia Press (UNZA Press): POB 32379, 10101 Lusaka; tel. (1) 290740; fax (1) 290409; e-mail press@admin.unza.zm; f. 1938; academic books, papers and journals.

Zambia Educational Publishing House: Chishango Rd, POB 32708, 10101 Lusaka; tel. (1) 222324; fax (1) 225073; f. 1967; educational and general; Man. Dir BENIKO E. MULOTA.

Zambia Printing Co Ltd: POB 34798, 10101 Lusaka; tel. (1) 227673; fax (1) 225026; Gen. Man. BERNARD LUBUMBASHI.

GOVERNMENT PUBLISHING HOUSES

Government Printer: POB 30136, Lusaka; tel. (1) 228724; fax (1) 224486; official documents and statistical bulletins.

Zambia Information Services: POB 50020, Lusaka; tel. (1) 219673; state-controlled; Dir BENSON SIANGA.

PUBLISHERS' ASSOCIATION

Booksellers' and Publishers' Association of Zambia: POB 31838, Lusaka; tel. (1) 222647; fax (1) 225195; Chair. RAY MUNAMWIMBU; Sec. BASIL MBEWE.

Broadcasting and Communications

TELECOMMUNICATIONS

Mobile cellular telephone networks are operated by Telecel Zambia and Zamcell.

Zambia Telecommunications Co Ltd (ZAMTEL): Provident House, POB 71660, Ndola; tel. (2) 611111; fax (2) 611399; internet www.zamtel.zm; transfer to private sector abandoned in 2005; commercialization pending; operates Cell Z cellular network (f. 2006); Chair. BASIL SICHALI; Man. Dir SIMON TEMBO.

BROADCASTING

Radio

Zambia National Broadcasting Corporation: Mass Media Complex, Alick Nkhata Rd, POB 50015, Lusaka; tel. (1) 252005; fax (1) 254013; e-mail michael@microlink.zm; internet www.znbc.co.zm; f. 1961; state-controlled; radio services in English and seven Zambian languages; Dir-Gen. EDDY MUPESO.

Educational Broadcasting Services: Headquarters: POB 50231, Lusaka; tel. (1) 251724; radio broadcasts from Lusaka; audio-visual aids service from POB 50295, Lusaka; Controller MICHAEL MULOMBE.

Radio Phoenix: Private Bag E702, Lusaka; tel. (1) 226652; fax (1) 226839; e-mail rphoenix@zamnet.zm; commercial; Man. Dir ERROL HICKEY.

Christian Voice (Rlg.): Private Bag E606, Lusaka; tel. (1) 274251; fax (1) 274526.

Television

Zambia National Broadcasting Corporation: (see Radio); television services in English.

Educational Broadcasting Services: POB 21106, Kitwe; television for schools; Controller MICHAEL MULOMBE.

Finance

(cap. = capital; auth. = authorized; res = reserves; dep. = deposits; m. = million; br. = branch; amounts in kwacha)

BANKING

From 30 June 1996 all banks operating in Zambia were required to have capital of not less than K2,000m. in order to receive a banking licence or to continue to function.

Central Bank

Bank of Zambia: Bank Sq., Cairo Rd, POB 30080, 10101 Lusaka; tel. (1) 228888; fax (1) 221722; e-mail pr@boz.zm; internet www.boz.zm; f. 1964; bank of issue; cap. 10m., res 31,675m., dep. 2,459,106m. (Dec. 2002); Gov. and Chair. Dr CALEB FUNDANGA; br. in Ndola.

Commercial Banks

Finance Bank Zambia Ltd: 2101 Chanik House, Cairo Rd, POB 37102, 10101 Lusaka; tel. (1) 229733; fax (1) 227290; e-mail fbz@financebank.co.zm; internet www.financebank.co.zm; f. 1986; cap. 3,630m., res 31,526m., dep. 168,467m. (Dec. 2002); Chair. Dr R. L. MAHTANI; Man. Dir A. C. GRANT; 28 brs and 12 agencies.

National Savings and Credit Bank of Zambia: Plot 248B, Cairo Rd, POB 30067, Lusaka; tel. (1) 227534; fax (1) 223296; e-mail natsave@webnet.zm; internet www.webnet.co.zm/nscb.htm; f. 1972; total assets 6,598m. (Dec. 1998); Man. Dir REGINALD MFULA.

New Capital Bank PLC: Anchor House, Mezzanine Floor, Sapele Rd, POB 36452, Lusaka; tel. (1) 229508; fax (1) 224055; f. 1992; cap. and res 4,510m., total assets 18,538m. (Dec. 2001); Chair. WILA D. MUNG'OMBA; CEO and Gen. Man. GODFREY P. MSISKA.

Union Bank Zambia Ltd: Zimco House, Cairo Rd, POB 34940, Lusaka; tel. (1) 229392; fax (1) 221866; cap. and res 3,775m., total assets 35,506m. (Dec. 1998); Chair. J. R. NAYEE; Man. Dir L. CHONGO.

Zambia National Commercial Bank PLC (ZNCB): POB 33611, Lusaka; tel. (1) 228979; fax (1) 223106; e-mail support@zanaco.co.zm; internet www.zanaco.co.zm; f. 1969; partial privatization agreed in 2005: 25% to remain govt-owned; 25.8% to be sold to Zambian citizens through the Zambian Privatisation Trust Fund; cap. and res 63,370m., total assets 584,667m. (Dec. 2000); Chair. MBIKUSITA W. LEWANIKA; Man. Dir LIKOLO NDALAMEI; 43 brs.

Foreign Banks

Bank of China (Zambia) Ltd (China): Amandra House, Ben Bella Rd, POB 34550, Lusaka; tel. (1) 238711; fax (1) 235350; e-mail boc@zamnet.zm; cap. and res 5,731m., total assets 73,237m. (Dec. 2001); Chair. PING YUE; Gen. Man. HONG XINSHENG.

Barclays Bank of Zambia plc (United Kingdom): Kafue House, Cairo Rd, POB 31936, Lusaka; tel. (1) 228858; fax (1) 222519; e-mail barclays.zambia@barclays.com; internet www.africa.barclays.com; f. 1971; cap. and res 114,618m., total assets 809,515m. (Dec. 2001); Chair. A. BRUCE MUNYAMA; Man. Dir MARGARET MWANAKATWE; 5 brs.

Citibank Zambia Ltd (USA): Citibank House, Cha Cha Cha Rd, POB 30037, Southend, Lusaka; tel. (1) 229025; fax (1) 226264; f. 1979; cap. 521.2m., dep. 237,176m. (Dec. 2001); Man. Dir SURINIVASAN SRIDHAR; 1 br.

Indo-Zambia Bank (IZB): Plot 6907, Cairo Rd, POB 35411, Lusaka; tel. (1) 224653; fax (1) 225090; e-mail izb@zamnet.zm; internet www.izb.co.zm; f. 1984; cap. and res 34,312m., dep. 200,770m. (March 2002); Chair. ORLENE Y. MOYO; Man. Dir ALOK K. MISRA; 7 brs.

Stanbic Bank Zambia Ltd: Woodgate House, 6th Floor, Nairobi Place, Cairo Rd, POB 31955, Lusaka; tel. (1) 229071; fax (1) 221152; internet www.stanbic.co.zm; f. 1971; wholly-owned by Standard Bank Investment Corpn; cap. and res 55,064m., total assets 425,746m. (Dec. 2001); Chair. D. A. R. PHIRI; Man. Dir A. H. S. MACLEOD; 7 brs.

Standard Chartered Bank Zambia Ltd (United Kingdom): Standard House, Cairo Rd, POB 32238, Lusaka; tel. (1) 229242; fax (1) 222092; f. 1971; cap. 2,048m., res 75,575m., dep. 450,784m. (Dec. 2001); Chair. A. K. MAZOKA; Man. Dir J. A. H. JANES; 14 brs.

Development Banks

Development Bank of Zambia: Development House, Katondo St, POB 33955, Lusaka; tel. (1) 228576; fax (1) 222426; internet www.dbz.co.zm; f. 1973; 99% state-owned; provides medium- and long-term loans and administers special funds placed at its disposal; cap. and res 7,580.0m., total assets 145,976.6m. (March 1998); Chair. J. M. MTONGA; Man. Dir DIPAK MALIK; 2 brs.

Lima Bank: Kulima House, Cha Cha Cha Rd, POB 32607, Lusaka; tel. (1) 213111; fax (1) 228077; cap. 57m. (March 1986); Chair. N. MUKUTU; Man. Dir K. V. KASAPATU.

Zambia Agricultural Development Bank: Society House, Cairo Rd, POB 30847, Lusaka; tel. (1) 219251; f. 1982; loan finance for devt of agriculture and fishing; auth. cap. 75m.; Chair. K. MAKASA; Man. Dir AMON CHIBIYA.

Zambia Export and Import Bank Ltd: Society House, Cairo Rd, POB 33046, Lusaka; tel. (1) 229486; fax (1) 222313; f. 1987; cap. 50m. (March 1992), dep. 50.9m. (March 1990); Man. Dir LIKANDO NAWA.

STOCK EXCHANGE

Lusaka Stock Exchange: Farmers House, 3rd Floor, Cairo Rd, POB 34523, Lusaka; tel. (1) 228537; fax (1) 225969; e-mail luse@zamnet.zm; internet www.luse.co.zm; f. 1994; Chair. JOHN JANES; Gen. Man. JOSEPH CHIKOLWA.

INSURANCE

African Life Assurance Zambia: Mukuba Pension House, 4th Floor, Dedan Kimathi Rd, POB 31991; tel. (1) 225452; fax (1) 225435; e-mail customercare@african-life.com.zm; f. 2002; CEO STEVE WILLIAMS.

Cavmont Capital Insurance Corpn Ltd: Farmers House, 3rd Floor, POB 38474, Lusaka; tel. (1) 228929; e-mail info@cavmont.com.zm; f. 2003; subsidiary of Cavmont Capital Holdings Ltd; Man. Dir MOSES MALUNGA.

Goldman Insurance Ltd: Zambia Nat. Savings and Credit Bank Bldg, 2nd Floor, Cairo Rd, Private Bag W395, Lusaka; tel. (1) 235234; fax (1) 227262; f. 1992; Chair. BWALYA CHITI.

Madison Insurance Co Ltd: Plot 255, Kaleya Rd, Roma, POB 37013, Lusaka; tel. (1) 295311; fax (1) 295320; e-mail madison@zamnet.zm; internet www.madisonzambia.com; f. 1992; general insurance and micro-insurance; Chair. DAVID A. R. PHIRI; Man. Dir LAWRENCE S. SIKUTWA.

NICO Insurance Zambia Ltd (NIZA): 1131 Parirenyatwa Rd, Fairview, POB 32825, Lusaka; tel. (1) 222862; fax (1) 222863; e-mail nicozam@zamnet.zm; internet www.nicomw.com/zambia; f. 1997; subsidiary of NICO Group, Malawi; general insurance services; Chair. JOHN MWANAKATWE; Gen. Man. TITUS KALENGA.

Professional Insurance Corpn Zambia Ltd (PICZ): Professional Insurance House, Heroes Pl., POB 34264, Lusaka; tel. (1) 227509; fax (1) 222151; e-mail ho@picz.co.zm; internet www.picz.co.zm; f. 1992; Exec. Dir GEORGE SILUTONGWE; Man. Dir ASHOK CHAWLA.

Zambia State Insurance Corporation Ltd: Premium House, Independence Ave, POB 30894, Lusaka; tel. (1) 229343; fax (1) 222263; e-mail zsic@zsic.co.zm; internet www.zsic.co.zm; f. 1968; sole authorized insurance provider in Zambia during 1971–1992; transfer to private sector pending; Chair. ALBERT WOOD; Man. Dir IRENE MUYENGA.

ZIGI Insurance Co Ltd: Mukuba Pension House, 5th Floor, POB37782, Lusaka; tel. (1) 226835; fax (1) 231564; e-mail zigi@zamnet.zm; f. 1998; Chair. and CEO SAVIOUR H. KONIE.

Trade and Industry

In early 2006 the National Assembly was considering the Zambia Development Agency Bill, which proposed merging into one body the Export Board of Zambia, the Export Processing Zones Authority, the Small Enterprises Development Board, the Zambia Investment Centre and the Zambia Privatisation Agency.

GOVERNMENT AGENCIES

Export Board of Zambia (EBZ): Woodgate House, 5th Floor, Cairo Rd, Heroes Place, POB 30064, Lusaka; tel. (1) 228106; fax (1) 222509; e-mail ebzint@zamnet.zm; internet www.ebz.co.zm; f. 1985 to develop and promote non-traditional exports.

Export Processing Zones Authority (EPZA): Plot No. 18939, cnr Great East and Katima Mulilo Rds, POB 337110, Lusaka; tel. (1) 212403; fax (1) 212406; e-mail zepza@uudial.zm; f. 2002; Chair. LOVEMORE CHIHOTA.

Small Enterprises Development Board (SEDB): SEDB House, Cairo Rd (South End), POB 35373, Lusaka; tel. and fax (1) 222176; f. 1981 as the Small Industries Devt Org.; to promote devt of small and village industries.

Zambia Investment Centre: Los Angeles Blvd, POB 34580, 10101 Lusaka; tel. (1) 255240; fax (1) 252150; e-mail invest@zamnet.zm; internet www.zic.org.zm; f. 1991; Dir-Gen. JACOB LUSHINGA.

Zambia Privatisation Agency: Privatisation House, Nasser Rd, POB 30819, Lusaka; tel. (1) 223859; fax (1) 225270; e-mail zpa@zpa.org.zm; internet www.zpa.org.zm; f. 1992; responsible for the divestment of various state-owned enterprises; Chair. LUKE MBEWE; CEO ANDREW CHIPWENDE.

DEVELOPMENT ORGANIZATIONS

Industrial Development Corporation of Zambia Ltd (INDECO): Indeco House, Buteko Place, POB 31935, Lusaka; tel. (1) 228026; fax (1) 228868; f. 1960; auth. cap. K300m.; taken over by the Nat. Housing Authority in May 2005; Chair. R. L. BWALYA; Man. Dir S. K. TAMELE.

Mpongwe Development Company: Block 4450, Mpongwe, POB 90599, Luanshya; tel. (2) 510584; fax (2) 511713; promotes the production of crops for domestic and regional markets; CEO HENK MARMELSTEIN.

CHAMBERS OF COMMERCE

Lusaka Chamber of Commerce and Industry: Business Centre, Farmers House, POB 37887, Lusaka; tel. (1) 221266; fax (1) 224134; f. 1933; Chair. JUSTIN CHISULO; 400 mems.

Zambia Association of Chambers of Commerce and Industry: Great East Rd, Showgrounds, POB 30844, Lusaka; tel. (1) 253020; fax (1) 252483; internet www.zacci.org.zm; f. 1938; Chair. A. MKANDAWIRE; CEO P. J. ARMOND.

INDUSTRIAL AND TRADE ASSOCIATIONS

Copper Industry Service Bureau Ltd: POB 22100, Kitwe; tel. (2) 214122; f. 1941; as Chamber of Mines.

The Dairy Produce Board of Zambia: Kwacha House, Cairo Rd, POB 30124, Lusaka; tel. (1) 214770; f. 1964; purchase and supply of dairy products to retailers, manufacture and marketing of milk products.

Metal Marketing Corporation (Zambia) Ltd (MEMACO): Memaco House, Sapele Rd, POB 35570, Lusaka; tel. (1) 228131; fax (1) 223671; f. 1973; sole sales agents for all metal and mineral production; Chair. R. L. BWALYA; Man. Dir U. M. MUTATI.

Tobacco Board of Zambia: POB 31963, Lusaka; tel. (1) 288995; Sec. J. M. CHIZUNI.

Zambia Association of Manufacturers: POB 240312, Ndola; tel. (2) 619296; fax (2) 619297; f. 1985; Chair. RICHARD P. HEALEY; Sec. MIKE G. PURSLOW; 180 mems.

Zambia Farm Employers' Association: Farmers' Village, Lusaka Agricultural and Commercial Showgrounds, POB 30395, Lusaka; tel. (1) 252649; fax (1) 252648; e-mail znfu@zamnet.zm; Chair. R. DENLY; 350 mems.

Zambia Seed Producers' Association: POB 30013, Lusaka; tel. (1) 223249; fax (1) 223249; f. 1964; Chair. BARRY COXE; 300 mems.

ZAMBIA

UTILITIES

Electricity

Zambia Electricity Supply Corporation (Zesco): Stand 6949, Great East Rd, POB 33304, Lusaka; tel. (1) 226084; fax (1) 222753; internet www.zesco.co.zm; Man. Dir RHODNIE P. SISALA.

CO-OPERATIVES

Zambia Co-operative Federation Ltd: Co-operative House, Cha Cha Cha Rd, POB 33579, Lusaka; tel. (1) 220157; fax (1) 222516; agricultural marketing; supply of agricultural chemicals and implements; cargo haulage; insurance; agricultural credit; auditing and accounting; property and co-operative devt; Chair. B. TETAMASHIMBA; Man. Dir G. Z. SIBALE.

TRADE UNIONS

Zambia Congress of Trade Unions (ZCTU): POB 20652, Kitwe; tel. (2) 211999; f. 1965; Pres. LEONARD HIKAUMBA; Sec.-Gen. ALEC CHIORMA; c. 400,000 mems in 18 affiliated unions.

Affiliated Unions

Airways and Allied Workers' Union of Zambia: POB 30272, Lusaka; Pres. F. MULENGA; Gen. Sec. B. CHINYANTA.

Guards Union of Zambia: POB 21882, Kitwe; tel. (2) 216189; f. 1972; Chair. D. N. S. SILUNGWE; Gen. Sec. MICHAEL S. SIMFUKWE; 13,500 mems.

Hotel Catering Workers' Union of Zambia: POB 35693, Lusaka; Chair. IAN MKANDAWIRE; Gen. Sec. STOIC KAPUTU; 9,000 mems.

Mineworkers' Union of Zambia: POB 20448, Kitwe; tel. (2) 214022; Pres. ANDREW MWANZA; Sec.-Gen. ERNEST MUTALE; 50,000 mems.

National Union of Building, Engineering and General Workers: POB 21515, Kitwe; tel. (2) 213931; Chair. LUCIANO MUTALE (acting); Gen. Sec. P. N. NZIMA; 18,000 mems.

National Union of Commercial and Industrial Workers: 87 Gambia Ave, POB 21735, Kitwe; tel. (2) 228607; f. 1982; Chair. I. M. KASUMBU; Gen. Sec. G. F. MWASE; 16,000 mems.

National Union of Communication Workers: POB 70751, Ndola; tel. (2) 611345; fax (2) 614679; e-mail nucw@zamtel.zm; Pres. PATRICK KAONGA; Gen. Sec. CHELLA WELLINGTON; 5,000 mems.

National Union of Plantation and Agricultural Workers: POB 80529, Kabwe; tel. (5) 224548; Chair. ALEX MSANGO; Gen. Sec. BERNADETTE CHIMFWEMBE; 15,155 mems.

National Union of Public Services' Workers: POB 32523, Lusaka; tel. (1) 215167; Chair. W. CHIPASHA; Gen. Sec. WILLIE MBEWE.

National Union of Transport and Allied Workers: Lusaka; tel. (1) 214756; Chair. B. MULWE; Gen. Sec. L. K. MABULUKI.

Railway Workers' Union of Zambia: POB 80302, Kabwe; tel. (5) 224006; Chair. H. K. NDAMANA; Gen. Sec. BENSON L. NGULA; 10,228 mems.

University of Zambia and Allied Workers' Union: POB 32379, Lusaka; tel. (1) 213221; f. 1968; Chair. BERIATE SUNKUTU; Gen. Sec. SAINI PHIRI.

Zambia Electricity Workers' Union: POB 70859, Ndola; f. 1972; Chair. COSMAS MPAMPI; Gen. Sec. ADAM KALUBA; 3,000 mems.

Zambia National Farmers' Union: Lusaka Agricultural and Commercial Showgrounds, POB 30395, Lusaka; tel. (1) 252649; fax (1) 252648; e-mail znfu@zamnet.zm; internet www.znfu.org.zm; Exec. Dir SONGOWAYO ZYAMBO.

Zambia National Union of Teachers: POB 31914, Lusaka; tel. (1) 236670; Chair. RICHARD M. LIYWALII; Gen. Sec. KENNETH KASEHELA; 2,120 mems.

Zambia Typographical Workers' Union: Ndola; Chair. R. SHIKWATA; Gen. Sec. D. NAWA.

Zambia Union of Financial Institutions and Allied Workers (ZUFIAW): POB 31174, Lusaka 10101; tel. (1) 231364; fax (1) 231364; e-mail zufiaw@zamnet.zm; internet www.zufiaw.org.zm; Pres. CEPHAS MUKUKA; Gen. Sec. JOYCE NONDE.

Zambia Union of Local Government Officers: f. 1997; Pres. ISAAC MWANZA.

Zambia Union of Skilled Mineworkers: f. 1998; Chair. ALEX MOLOI.

Zambia United Local Authorities Workers' Union: POB 70575, Ndola; tel. (2) 615022; Chair. A. M. MUTAKILA; Gen. Sec. A. H. MUDENDA.

Zambia Union of Journalists: POB 70956, Ndola; tel. (2) 613290; fax (2) 614229; Gen. Sec. OFFERING KAJIMALWENDO.

Principal Non-Affiliated Unions

Civil Servants' Union of Zambia (CSUZ): Plot 4550A, Mumbwa Rd, POB 50160, Lusaka; tel. and fax (1) 287106; e-mail csuz@zamnet.zm; f. 1975; Chair. L. C. HIKAUMBA; Gen. Sec. DARISON CHAALA; 35,000 mems.

Zambian African Mining Union: Kitwe; f. 1967; 40,000 mems.

Transport

RAILWAYS

Total length of railways in Zambia was 2,162 km (including 891 km of the Tanzania–Zambia railway) in 2000. There are two major railway lines: the Zambia Railways network, which traverses the country from the Copperbelt in northern Zambia and links with the National Railways of Zimbabwe to provide access to South African ports, and the Tanzania–Zambia Railway (Tazara) system, linking New Kapiri-Mposhi in Zambia with Dar es Salaam in Tanzania. The Tazara railway line increased its capacity from 1976, in order to reduce the dependence of southern African countries on trade routes through South Africa. In April 1987 the Governments of Zambia, Angola and Zaire (now the Democratic Republic of the Congo) declared their intention to reopen the Benguela railway, linking Zambian copper mines with the Angolan port of Lobito, following its closure to international traffic in 1975 as a result of the guerrilla insurgency in Angola. In 1997 a programme of repairs was begun, and plans were announced in June 2002 to rebuild the Benguela railway. In April 2005 Northwest Railways undertook to develop a new line between Chingola, in the Copperbelt Province, and Lumwana, in the North-Western Province. It was anticipated that the line could eventually be linked to the Benguela railway.

Tanzania–Zambia Railway Authority (Tazara): POB T01, Mpika; Head Office: POB 2834, Dar es Salaam, Tanzania; tel. (4) 370684; fax (4) 370228; tel. 860340; e-mail tazara@zamnet.zm; f. 1975; operates passenger and freight services linking New Kapiri-Mposhi, north of Lusaka, with Dar es Salaam in Tanzania, a distance of 1,860 km, of which 891 km is in Zambia; jtly owned and administered by the Tanzanian and Zambian Govts; a 10-year rehabilitation programme, assisted by the USA and EC (now EU) countries, began in 1985; it was announced in 2003 that a line linking the railway with the Zambian port of Mpulungu was to be constructed; Chair. SALIM H. MSOMA; Man. Dir CLEMENT MWIYA.

Zambia Railways Ltd: cnr Buntungwa St and Ghana Ave, POB 80935, Kabwe; tel. (5) 222201; fax (5) 224411; f. 1967; management assumed in 1998 by Hifab International AB (Sweden) in consortium with DE Consult (Germany); concession of assets and operations to New Limpopo Bridge Project Investments Ltd agreed in early 2003; Chair. B. NONDE; Man. Dir GÖRAN MALMBERG.

ROADS

In 1999 there was a total road network of 66,781 km, including 7,081 km of main roads and 13,700 km of secondary roads. The main arterial roads run from Beit Bridge (Zimbabwe) to Tunduma (the Great North Road), through the copper-mining area to Chingola and Chililabombwe (hitherto the Zaire Border Road), from Livingstone to the junction of the Kafue river and the Great North Road, and from Lusaka to the Malawi border (the Great East Road). In 1984 the 300-km BotZam highway linking Kazungula with Nata, in Botswana, was formally opened. A 1,930-km main road (the TanZam highway) links Zambia and Tanzania. In 1998 the Government initiated a 10-year Road Sector Investment Programme with funding from the World Bank, and in its second phase the European Union.

Road Development Agency: POB 50003, Lusaka; tel. (1) 253088; fax (1) 253404; e-mail rda_hq@roads.gov.zm; internet www.roads.gov.zm; fmrly Dept of Roads; Dir of Roads W. NG'AMBI.

SHIPPING

Zambia National Shipping Line: Lusaka; f. 1989; state-owned; cargo and passenger services from Dar es Salaam in Tanzania to northern Europe; Gen. Man. MARTIN PHIRI.

CIVIL AVIATION

In 1984 there were 127 airports, aerodromes and air strips. An international airport, 22.5 km from Lusaka, was opened in 1967.

National Airports Corpn Ltd (NACL): Lusaka International Airport, POB 30175, Lusaka; tel. (1) 271281; fax (1) 224777; e-mail naclmd@zamnet.zm; f. 1973; air cargo services; Man. Dir CHILESHE M. KAPWEPWE.

Zambia Skyways (Eastern Air): Plot 6, Addis Ababa Rd, POB 32661, Lusaka; tel. (1) 250987; fax (1) 250767; e-mail zskyways@yahoo.com; internet www.zambiatourism.com/zambiaskyways/index.htm; f. 1995; operates scheduled passenger services to domestic destinations and South Africa; Man. Dir YOOSUF ZUMLA.

ZAMBIA

Zambia Airways: Lusaka International Airport, POB 310277, Lusaka; tel. (1) 271230; fax (1) 271054; e-mail roanhq@zamnet.zm; internet www.zambiaairways.co.zm; f. 1988 as Roan Air; changed to current name in 1999; operates domestic and regional routes; CEO STEVE SIMWANZA.

Tourism

Zambia's main tourist attractions, in addition to the Victoria Falls, are its wildlife, unspoilt scenery and diverse cultural heritage; there are 19 national parks and 36 game management areas. In 2004 610,109 tourists visited Zambia, and tourism receipts totalled an estimated US $153m.

Tourism Council of Zambia: Holiday Inn Cottage, Church Rd, Lusaka; tel. (1) 252859; fax (1) 255337; e-mail tcz@zamnet.zm; internet www.zambiatourism.com/travel/localnews/tcz.htm; Chair. BRUCE CHAPMAN.

Zambia National Tourist Board: Century House, Lusaka Sq., POB 30017, Lusaka; tel. (1) 229087; fax (1) 225174; e-mail zntb@zamnet.zm; internet www.zambiatourism.com; Chair. ERROL HICKEY; Man. Dir CHANDA CHARITY LUMPA.

ZIMBABWE

Introductory Survey

Location, Climate, Language, Religion, Flag, Capital

The Republic of Zimbabwe is a land-locked state in southern Africa, with Mozambique to the east, Zambia to the north-west, Botswana to the south-west and South Africa to the south. The climate is tropical, modified considerably by altitude. Average monthly temperatures range from 13°C (55°F) to 22°C (72°F) on the Highveld, and from 20°C (68°F) to 30°C (86°F) in the low-lying valley of the Zambezi river. The rainy season is from November to March. The official languages are English, Chishona and Sindebele. About 55% of the population are Christians. A large number of the African population follow traditional beliefs, while the Asian minority comprises both Muslims and Hindus. The national flag (proportions 1 by 2) has seven equal horizontal stripes, of green, gold, red, black, red, gold and green, with a white triangle, bearing a red five-pointed star on which a gold 'Great Zimbabwe bird' is superimposed, at the hoist. The capital is Harare.

Recent History

In 1923 responsibility for Southern Rhodesia (now Zimbabwe) was transferred from the British South Africa Company to the Government of the United Kingdom, and the territory became a British colony. It had full self-government (except for African interests and some other matters) under an administration controlled by European settlers. African voting rights were restricted.

In 1953 the colony united with two British protectorates, Northern Rhodesia (now Zambia) and Nyasaland (now Malawi), to form the Federation of Rhodesia and Nyasaland. Sir Godfrey Huggins (later Viscount Malvern), the Prime Minister of Southern Rhodesia from 1933 to 1953, became the first Prime Minister of the Federation, being succeeded by Sir Roy Welensky in 1956. In Southern Rhodesia itself, Garfield Todd was Prime Minister from 1953 until 1958, when Sir Edgar Whitehead came to power. A new Constitution, which ended most of the United Kingdom's legal controls and provided for a limited African franchise, came into effect in November 1962. At elections in December Whitehead lost power to the Rhodesian Front (RF), a coalition of white opposition groups committed to maintaining racial segregation. The leader of the RF, Winston Field, became Prime Minister.

As a result of pressure from African nationalist movements in Northern Rhodesia and Nyasaland, the Federation was dissolved in December 1963. African nationalists were also active in Southern Rhodesia. The African National Congress, founded in 1934, was revived in 1957, with Joshua Nkomo as President. Following the banning of the Congress in February 1959, some of its members formed the National Democratic Party (NDP) in January 1960. Nkomo, although in exile, was elected President of the NDP in October. When the NDP was banned in December 1961, Nkomo formed the Zimbabwe African People's Union (ZAPU), which was declared an unlawful organization in September 1962. ZAPU split in July 1963, and a breakaway group, led by the Rev. Ndabaningi Sithole, formed the Zimbabwe African National Union (ZANU) in August. Robert Mugabe became Secretary-General of ZANU.

In April 1964 Field was succeeded as Prime Minister of Southern Rhodesia by his deputy, Ian Smith. The new regime rejected British conditions for independence, including acceptance by the whole Rhodesian population and unimpeded progress to majority rule. In August ZANU was banned. After Northern Rhodesia became independent as Zambia in October, Southern Rhodesia became generally (although not officially) known as Rhodesia. At elections in May 1965 the RF won all 50 European seats in the legislature. On 5 November a state of emergency (to be renewed annually) was declared, and on 11 November Smith made a unilateral declaration of independence (UDI) and proclaimed a new Constitution, naming the country Rhodesia. The British Government regarded Rhodesia's independence as unconstitutional and illegal, and no other country formally recognized it. The United Kingdom terminated all relations with Rhodesia, while the UN applied economic sanctions. Both ZAPU and ZANU took up arms against the RF regime, and African guerrilla groups were frequently involved in clashes with Rhodesian security forces.

Following a referendum in June 1969, Rhodesia was declared a republic in March 1970. The 1969 Constitution provided for a bicameral Legislative Assembly, comprising a 23-member Senate and a 66-member House of Assembly (50 Europeans and 16 Africans). The President had only formal powers, and Smith remained Prime Minister. The RF won all 50 European seats in the House of Assembly in 1970, 1974 and 1977.

In November 1971 the British and Rhodesian Governments agreed on draft proposals for a constitutional settlement, subject to their acceptability to the Rhodesian people 'as a whole'. In December the African National Council (ANC), led by Bishop Abel Muzorewa, was formed to co-ordinate opposition to the plan. In December 1974, however, the Rhodesian Government and leaders of four nationalist organizations (including ZAPU, ZANU and the ANC) agreed the terms of a cease-fire, conditional on the release of African political detainees and on the convening of a constitutional conference in 1975. The African organizations agreed to unite within the ANC, with Muzorewa as President. Mugabe opposed the incorporation of ZANU into the ANC, and in mid-1975 left Rhodesia for neighbouring Mozambique, where he took control of ZANU's external wing, and challenged Sithole's leadership of the party. In September the ANC split into rival factions, led by Muzorewa and Nkomo. Constitutional talks between the Government and the Nkomo faction began in December 1975, but were abandoned in March 1976. In September, under pressure from South Africa, Smith announced his Government's acceptance of proposals leading to majority rule within two years. In late 1976 representatives of the RF, the African nationalists and the British Government met to discuss the transition to majority rule. The nationalists were led by Muzorewa, Sithole, Nkomo and Mugabe (by then the recognized leader of ZANU). Nkomo and Mugabe adopted a joint position as the Patriotic Front (PF).

In January 1977 Angola, Botswana, Mozambique, Tanzania and Zambia (the 'front-line' states) declared their support for the PF. Smith rejected British proposals for an interim administration, and received a mandate from the RF to repeal racially discriminatory laws and to seek agreement with such African factions as he chose. In July the PF demanded that power be handed directly to them by the Rhodesian Government. In November Smith accepted the principle of universal adult suffrage, and talks on an internal settlement were initiated with Muzorewa's United African National Council (UANC), the Rev. Sithole's faction of the ANC and the Zimbabwe United People's Organization, led by Chief Jeremiah Chirau. These talks led to the signing of an internal settlement on 3 March 1978, providing for an interim power-sharing administration to prepare for independence on 31 December. The proposals were rejected by the PF and by the UN Security Council. In May 1978 the newly created Executive Council, consisting of Smith, Sithole, Muzorewa and Chirau, ordered the release of all political detainees in an attempt to bring about a cease-fire.

In January 1979 a 'majority rule' Constitution, with entrenched safeguards for the white minority, was approved by the House of Assembly and endorsed by a referendum of European voters. In April elections to the new House of Assembly (the first by universal adult suffrage) were held in two stages: for 20 directly elected European members (chosen by non-African voters only) and then for 72 African members (chosen by the whole electorate). The elections were boycotted by the PF. The UANC emerged as the majority party, with 51 seats, while the RF won all 20 seats for whites. In May the new Parliament elected Josiah Gumede as President. Muzorewa became Prime Minister of the country (renamed Zimbabwe Rhodesia) in June. In accordance with the Constitution, Muzorewa formed a government of national unity, a coalition of parties in the new House, including European members (Smith became Minister without Portfolio). However, international recognition was not forthcoming, and UN sanctions remained in force.

New impetus for a lasting and internationally recognized settlement followed the Commonwealth Conference in Zambia

ZIMBABWE

Introductory Survey

in August 1979. In September a Rhodesian Constitutional Conference in London, United Kingdom, was attended by delegations under Muzorewa and the joint leaders of the PF. The PF reluctantly agreed to special representation for the whites under the proposed new Constitution, which was eventually accepted by both parties; complete agreement was reached on transitional arrangements in November, and the details of a cease-fire between the guerrillas of the PF and the Rhodesian security forces were finalized in the following month. On 11 December the Zimbabwe Rhodesia Parliament voted to renounce independence and to revert to the status of a British colony, as Southern Rhodesia. Illegal rule ended on the following day, when Parliament was dissolved, the President, Prime Minister and Cabinet resigned, and the British-appointed Governor, Lord Soames, was vested with full executive and legislative authority for the duration of the transition to legal independence. The United Kingdom immediately revoked economic sanctions.

Lord Soames ended the ban on the two wings of the PF (ZAPU and ZANU) and ordered the release of most of the detainees who were held under the 'emergency powers' laws. Elections to a new House of Assembly proceeded in February 1980 (again in two stages) under the supervision of a British Electoral Commissioner. Mugabe's ZANU—PF emerged as the largest single party, winning 57 of the 80 African seats; Nkomo's PF—ZAPU took 20 seats and the UANC only three. In a separate poll of white voters, Smith's RF secured all 20 reserved seats. The new state of Zimbabwe became legally independent, within the Commonwealth, on 18 April, with Rev. Canaan Banana as President (with largely ceremonial duties) and Mugabe as Prime Minister, at the head of a coalition Government.

Relations within the Government were strained, particularly between Mugabe and Nkomo. The latter was removed from the Cabinet, with two PF colleagues, in February 1982, under suspicion of plotting against Mugabe. In March 1982 several deputies of the RF, now restyled the Republican Front, resigned from the party and sat as independents. By May 1984 the RF retained only seven of the 20 seats reserved for whites, the remaining 13 being held by independents. In July the RF was renamed the Conservative Alliance of Zimbabwe (CAZ), and opened its membership to all races.

Many of the unpopular practices of the Smith regime, including 'emergency powers' and the detention of political opponents, continued after independence. (The state of emergency continued to be renewed at six-monthly intervals until August 1990.) In September 1983 legislation was introduced providing for increased press censorship and granting the security forces greater powers under the state of emergency. In February 1984, in a renewed anti-insurgency campaign, an estimated 10,000 troops were again sent into Matabeleland. It was subsequently alleged that some 20,000 civilians were killed by the army during the two campaigns (see below).

There were several outbreaks of violence prior to a general election in June–July 1985. ZANU—PF was returned to power with an increased majority, winning 63 of the 79 'common roll' seats in the House of Assembly (and an additional seat at a by-election in August). ZAPU won 15 seats, retaining its traditional hold over Matabeleland, and ZANU—Sithole took a single seat. The UANC failed to gain representation. Of the 20 seats reserved for whites, 15 were secured by Smith's CAZ. However, CAZ was not represented in the new Cabinet.

During mid-1985 a large number of ZAPU officials were detained for questioning about dissident activity in Matabeleland. Later in the year, however, ZANU and ZAPU reached broad agreement on the terms of a merger of the two parties, in the interests of national unity; negotiations continued during 1986, but were suspended in April 1987. A resurgence of violence in Matabeleland followed, and in June ZAPU, which was accused of fomenting the unrest, was banned from holding public meetings. The failure, in August, of further talks aimed at uniting ZANU and ZAPU led to renewed rebel activity, whereupon the Government took steps to prevent ZAPU from functioning effectively: in September all offices of the party were closed, six ZAPU-controlled district councils in Matabeleland were dissolved, and a number of prominent ZAPU officers were detained. Furthermore, ZANU declined to endorse seven ZAPU-nominated candidates for the parliamentary seats made vacant in September by the abolition of seats reserved for whites (see below). In November, however, the ban on public meetings by ZAPU was revoked, and the party was permitted to reopen its offices in Harare and Bulawayo. In December Mugabe and Nkomo finally signed an agreement of unity, which was ratified by both parties in April 1988 and implemented in December 1989 (see below). In January 1988 Nkomo was appointed as one of the Senior Ministers in the President's Office, and two other ZAPU officials were given government posts. Following the unity agreement there was a significant improvement in the security situation in Matabeleland. However, the state of emergency remained in force, owing to incursions into eastern Zimbabwe by the Mozambican rebel movement, the Resistência Nacional Moçambicana (Renamo, see below).

Two major constitutional reforms were enacted during 1987. In September the reservation for whites of 20 seats in the House of Assembly and 10 seats in the Senate was abolished, as permitted by the Constitution, subject to a majority vote in the House. (In anticipation of this reform, several white deputies joined ZANU. In May Smith resigned as President of CAZ.) In October the 80 remaining members of the House of Assembly elected 20 candidates, who were nominated by ZANU, including 11 whites, to fill the vacant seats in the House of Assembly until the next general election. In the same month Parliament approved the replacement of the ceremonial presidency by an executive presidency. The post of Prime Minister was to be incorporated into the presidency. President Banana (who, as the only candidate, had been sworn in for a second term of office as President in April 1986) retired in December 1987, and at the end of that month Mugabe (the sole candidate) was inaugurated as Zimbabwe's first executive President.

In April 1989 Edgar Tekere, a former Secretary-General of ZANU, founded the Zimbabwe Unity Movement (ZUM), intending to challenge ZANU at the next general election. In November the Government was accused by the Supreme Court of failing to respect judicial decisions. In December ZANU and ZAPU merged to form a single party, named the Zimbabwe African National Union—Patriotic Front (ZANU—PF). The united party aimed to establish a one-party state with a Marxist-Leninist doctrine. Mugabe was appointed President of ZANU—PF, while Nkomo became one of its two Vice-Presidents.

Presidential and parliamentary elections were held concurrently in March 1990; at these elections legislation approved in late 1989 came into effect, abolishing the Senate and increasing the number of seats in the House of Assembly from 100 to 150 (of which 120 were to be directly elected; 12 were to be allocated to presidential nominees, 10 to traditional Chiefs and eight to provincial governors). Mugabe won nearly 80% of all votes cast at the presidential election; his sole opponent was Tekere. At the parliamentary elections ZANU—PF secured 117 of the 120 elective seats in the House of Assembly; the ZUM (which had entered into an informal electoral alliance with CAZ) won only two seats, and the UANC took one seat. Although ZANU—PF won an outright victory, only 54% of the electorate voted, and representatives of the ruling party were accused of intimidating voters. Following the elections Nkomo was appointed as one of two Vice-Presidents (the other being Simon Muzenda, also a Vice-President of ZANU—PF), and remained one of the Senior Ministers in the President's Office. In August 1990 the state of emergency was finally revoked.

In March 1992 the House of Assembly approved legislation (the Land Acquisition Act) that permitted the compulsory acquisition of land by the Government; this was intended to facilitate the redistribution of land ownership from Europeans (who owned about one-third of farming land in early 1992) to Africans. In May 1993 the Government published a list of properties allotted for transferral to the State under the Act, provoking a strong protest from the white-dominated Commercial Farmers' Union (CFU). The High Court subsequently ruled against three white farmers who had attempted to prove that the confiscation of their land was unconstitutional. A lack of available funds impeded the progress of the Government's land resettlement programme.

In early July 1992 Mugabe reorganized the Cabinet. Later that month several opposition organizations, including CAZ, the UANC and the ZUM, formed an informal alliance, known as the United Front, which aimed to remove Mugabe from power. In January 1994 the UANC was incorporated into Tekere's ZUM; later in that year Muzorewa, the former UANC leader, founded a new opposition grouping, the United Parties (UP).

ZANU—PF won an overwhelming victory at legislative elections in April 1995, receiving more than 82% of the votes cast and securing 118 of the 120 elective seats in the House of Assembly (55 of which were uncontested). The remaining two elective seats were taken by ZANU—Ndonga (formerly ZANU—Sithole). Following the allocation of nominated and reserved seats, ZANU—

PF controlled 148 of the total 150 seats. However, only 54% of the electorate voted, and the elections were boycotted by eight opposition groups, including the ZUM and the UP. In mid-April Mugabe appointed a reorganized and enlarged Cabinet; Nkomo and Muzenda remained as Vice-Presidents.

Mugabe retained the presidency at an election in March 1996, winning 92.7% of the votes cast. Turn-out was, however, low. The election was also unwillingly contested by Muzorewa (who took 4.7% of the votes) and Sithole (2.4%); they had been denied permission to withdraw their candidacies prior to the ballot. In late March Mugabe was sworn in for a third term as President. He reorganized the Cabinet extensively in May.

Between August and November 1996 there were a number of national strikes by public-sector workers demanding pay increases. In October it was announced that ZANU—PF was abandoning Marxism-Leninism as its guiding principle. In May 1997 a report compiled by the Legal Resources Foundation and the Catholic Commission for Justice and Peace emerged (prior to official publication), detailing atrocities allegedly committed by security forces in Matabeleland in the early 1980s (see above). A reorganization of the Cabinet in July 1997, in which several ministries were merged, was attributed to pressure from international creditors. In August the Government announced that the independence war veterans (an increasingly powerful lobby) were to be awarded a number of substantial, unbudgeted benefits.

In October 1997 Mugabe announced that the pace of the land resettlement programme would be accelerated, declaring that the constitutional right of white commercial farmers to receive full and fair compensation for confiscated land would not be honoured and (unsuccessfully) challenging the United Kingdom, in its role as former colonial power, to take responsibility for assisting them. A list of 1,503 properties to be reallocated forthwith was published in November. In January 1998, however, the IMF stipulated an assurance from the Mugabe administration that it would respect the Constitution during the land resettlement procedure as a condition for the release of financial assistance; such an assurance was eventually given in March, when it was announced that 120 farms would be acquired in the near future in exchange for full and fair compensation. In June there was a series of illegal farm occupations by black families. In August Mugabe introduced the second phase of the programme, to resettle 150,000 families on 1m. ha of land each year for the next seven years. Under pressure from Western donors, the Government agreed to reduce its plans, and was restricted to using 118 farms that it had already been offered. In November, however, 841 white-owned farms were ordered to be confiscated by the state: compensation was to be deferred. Pressure exerted by the IMF in light of a forthcoming release of aid brought an assurance from Mugabe that his administration would not break agreements for a gradual land reform programme. At the end of March 1999 the President contravened the agreement when he announced a new plan to acquire a further 529 white-owned farms. He accused the USA and the United Kingdom of 'destabilizing' Zimbabwe through their alleged control over the IMF, which was delaying financial assistance to his country. In the following month Mugabe threatened that Zimbabwe would sever its relations with the IMF and the World Bank, although the Minister of Finance continued to hope that further aid would be released shortly. (The IMF approved a US $193m. loan in August.) In May the Government agreed a plan that aimed to resettle 77,700 black families on 1m. ha by 2001. Some of this land was to come from the 118 farms that had already been offered. The remainder would be the result of uncontested acquisitions under the Government's reduced list of 800 farms for compulsory purchase. The plan was to be partially funded by the World Bank, and was broadly accepted by the white landowners' association.

Meanwhile, labour unrest escalated in December 1997, when a general strike was organized by the Zimbabwe Congress of Trade Unions (ZCTU), in protest at the imposition by the Government of three unpopular new taxes in order to finance the provision of benefits to war veterans (see above); the authorities capitulated, withdrawing two of the taxes immediately. Shortly after the demonstrations had subsided, Morgan Tsvangirai, the Secretary-General of ZCTU, was brutally attacked in his office by unknown assailants. The weak Zimbabwe currency and soaring food prices aggravated the nation-wide mood of discontent. In January 1998 riots erupted in most of the country's urban areas in protest at rises in the price of maize meal, the staple food. In response Mugabe agreed to withdraw the most recent price increase. However, the army was deployed to suppress the disturbances and was authorized to open fire on protesters; nine people were reportedly killed and some 800 rioters were arrested. The ZCTU organized a further two-day strike in March, to protest against the continuing rise in living costs.

In September 1998 threats for a five-day stoppage in support of demands for tax cuts resulted in government concessions. Meanwhile, further consumer price increases were followed by renewed rioting. A series of one-day strikes over pay were called by unions, and action took place until banned by Mugabe. In February 1999, however, the ban was ruled to be illegal. In that month growing unrest followed an address to the nation by Mugabe in which he attacked the judiciary, the independent media and 'British agents'. He also accused whites of 'fomenting unrest'. Unrest resulting from declining standards of living continued throughout 1999.

Meanwhile, in October 1998 the Government embarked on discussions on changing Zimbabwe's Constitution with an opposition grouping, known as the National Constitutional Assembly (NCA). The administration affirmed its commitment to an open process that would not allow government domination, and wanted the new constitution to be in force by the elections due in 2000. However, the opposition withdrew from the negotiations in the following month after protesters calling for constitutional change were prevented from marching by riot police. In March 1999 Mugabe appointed a commission of inquiry to make recommendations on a new constitution. The NCA refused to participate, owing to the alleged high risk of presidential manipulation. Joshua Nkomo died in early July 1999. (Joseph Msika, hitherto a minister without portfolio, replaced him as Vice-President in December.) At Nkomo's funeral, Mugabe apologized for the atrocities committed against the Ndebele in Matabeleland in the early 1980s (see above), and issued a call for national unity. Nevertheless, there was a resurgence of ZAPU under new leadership, called ZAPU 2000. This new party declared that it wanted a federal system for Zimbabwe, with considerable powers devolved to Matabeleland and other regions. (In an attempt to regain support, in October the Government announced compensation for the families of those killed in the violence.) Another challenge to ZANU—PF emerged in September with the formation of the Movement for Democratic Change (MDC), led by Morgan Tsvangirai. Administrative chaos and almost total apathy in local elections held in that month cast severe doubts on the Government's ability to hold general elections due in April or May 2000.

An international constitutional conference was held in November 1999, but several experts suspected that the draft constitution had already been written, and that they had been invited primarily to give the process global credibility. In late November a document bearing no relation to that prepared by the 400-member constitutional commission, a drafting committee overseen by ZANU—PF having deleted crucial clauses (particularly relating to the reduction of the President's powers and the introduction of a parliamentary system), was declared to have been 'adopted by acclamation', despite vigorous protests. In January 2000 Mugabe announced that a referendum on the new constitution would take place on 12–13 February. Confusion before the polls over such issues as eligibility to vote and the location of polling stations was believed by the opposition to have been orchestrated by ZANU—PF to maximize Mugabe's chances of victory. Despite fears that a lack of supervision of the ballot had led to widespread irregularities on ZANU—PF's part, 54.6% of the 26% of the electorate who participated in the polls voted to reject the draft constitution. The level of participation was highest in urban areas where MDC support was strong, while voters in the Government's rural strongholds were apathetic, despite promises that the new constitution would grant them redistributed white land. In a televised address a few days later, Mugabe accepted the result.

Within ZANU—PF, however, there was mounting dissatisfaction with Mugabe's leadership, and, in the wake of the plebiscite defeat, fears grew that he was an electoral liability. The Government embarked on a campaign to restore its popularity to ensure victory over an increasingly confident opposition in the legislative elections, which, it was announced in March, were to be held in May rather than April. Illegal occupations of white-owned farms by black 'war veterans' (many of whom, too young to have taken part in the war of independence, were suspected of having been paid to participate), which began in late February, were rumoured to have been organized by the Government in an attempt to regain support through the land issue. The security forces refused to act against the occupiers, declaring that the 'political issue' lay outside their jurisdiction. Occupations increased, and the police also failed to take steps to evict the protesters, following a ruling by the High Court in mid-March in favour of the white farmers (which was ignored by the veterans). Mugabe repeatedly denied that his administration was behind the occupations, but made no secret of his support for them. The invasions became increasingly violent, and two farmers were killed in April. A few days earlier Mugabe had threatened war against farmers who refused to give up their land voluntarily, and following the violence he declared that they were 'enemies of the state'. The international community condemned this increasingly militant stance, which also extended to the treatment of the opposition, in particular the MDC, which was subjected to a campaign of intimidation and aggression. A constitutional amendment approved in April stated that white farmers dispossessed of their land would have to apply to the 'former colonial power', the United Kingdom, for compensation (see below). Many farmers were aggrieved, as their land had been purchased under Zimbabwean law. As chaos reigned, following worsening displays of aggression, which had prompted the MDC to threaten to boycott the elections, and amid signs that ZANU—PF had regained its rural support, in mid-May Mugabe called for an end to the violence. He met with war veterans and white farmers and announced the creation of a land commission to redistribute farmland. Shortly afterwards, however, he signed a law allowing the seizure of 841 white-owned farms without compensation. Political violence continued unabated throughout the month. In early June a list was published of 804 farms that were to be confiscated. Farmers were to be granted approximately one month to contest the list.

International aid to Zimbabwe was suspended in October 1999 because the Government had failed to meet reform targets. The IMF also investigated reports that Zimbabwe had submitted figures to it relating to military expenditure that were substantially lower than those used by the treasury. Zimbabwe denied the allegations. The budget deficit continued to increase and huge arrears to overseas suppliers for fuel, partly owing to a desperate shortage of foreign currency reserves, led to the suspension of oil supplies in December. In the following month fuel rationing caused unrest. In February 2000 the Minister of Transport and Energy resigned. The President's office took over the running of the ministry. As reserves fell, so political tensions increased, and Mugabe was obliged to look for new suppliers, signing a one-year agreement with Kuwait in March. In April white farmers called for the currency to be substantially devalued and threatened that they would not take their tobacco crop to auction until this happened. The banks agreed that devaluation was needed to avoid mass default. The Government, however, fearing that devaluing the currency might adversely affect its chances of retaining power, refused to act.

Prior to legislative elections, which took place on 24–25 June 2000, there were reports of violence towards observers, and a UN team, sent to co-ordinate the polls, was recalled following obstruction by the Government. The authorities also refused to permit the accreditation of some 200 foreign monitors. ZANU—PF secured 48.6% of the votes cast and 62 of the 120 elective seats in the House of Assembly, the MDC won 47.0% of the ballot and 57 seats, while ZANU—Ndonga received one seat. Morgan Tsvangirai failed to win his constituency, as did the Ministers of Justice and Home Affairs. There were reports of widespread irregularities in the polls, which international observers declared not to have been free and fair. The MDC announced that it was to submit 10 dossiers listing alleged incidents of electoral fraud to the High Court. In total, the MDC challenged the results in 37 constituencies. In April 2001 the Court announced that results in two constituencies, including that contested by Tsvangirai, were to be nullified and new elections held; the MDC had previously abandoned proceedings relating to two other constituencies, and had been defeated in its challenge to the result in another. In June one more result was nullified, and one upheld.

Political unrest continued after the elections, with a general strike organized by the country's main trade unions in August 2000 being widely observed. Unrest at increases in food and fuel prices continued throughout 2000 and early 2001; the most notable incidents occurred in Harare in October, when police attempted to quell violent demonstrations against increased prices for food and public transport.

In September 2000 the editors of two state-owned newspapers were dismissed, reportedly in connection with falling sales. In October the Government announced an amnesty for all people accused of politically motivated crimes in January–July 2000. The printing presses of *The Daily News*, which was frequently critical of the Government, were severely damaged in an explosion in January 2001. The editor of the newspaper (who had alleged that the security forces had conspired to kill him in 2000) and two journalists were charged with defamation in April, in connection with a report containing allegations of corruption against Mugabe and his associates.

In September 2000 Tsvangirai made a speech to an MDC rally in which he urged Mugabe to resign, allegedly predicting that if the President could not be removed by democratic means, the country risked a popular uprising that would remove him by force. In the same month a hand grenade damaged the headquarters of the MDC—the party blamed supporters of ZANU—PF. In October it was announced that Tsvangirai, who was out of the country, would be arrested and charged with incitement to treason upon his return. However, Tsvangirai was able to re-enter the country without attracting the attention of the security forces, and plans to detain him were delayed. In February 2001 Tsvangirai was charged with incitement to violence in connection with the speech. In May the High Court referred Tsvangirai's trial to the Supreme Court, accepting his argument that his constitutional right to free speech was material to the case. In November the Supreme Court withdrew the charges against him; following the ruling, however, the Government announced its intention to replace the Law and Order (Maintenance) Act, under which Tsvangirai had been charged, with a new public order bill, making it an offence to engender hostility to the President.

Shortly after the legislative elections, Mugabe announced that some 500 additional white-owned farms would be appropriated for resettlement. In December 2000 Mugabe declared that whites were the enemy of Zimbabwe; he was criticized by Western governments and by several African leaders. In the same month a court ruling upheld previous opinions that declared the appropriation of white-owned farms without compensation payments to be unlawful, and urged the Government to produce a feasible land-reform programme by June 2001; Mugabe announced that enough white-owned land had been appropriated for resettlement, but repeated his assertion that he would not accept court-imposed impediments to any further land-reform measures. Negotiations between the Government and farmers' representatives resumed in January 2001.

Zimbabwe's Chief Justice, Anthony Gubbay, announced in February 2001 that he would retire, some months ahead of schedule, in June, following allegations of government intimidation. However, he subsequently rescinded this announcement, and stated that he had no intention of retiring early. Following intensive negotiations, Gubbay agreed to retire with immediate effect in March, reportedly in exchange for an agreement by the Government not to seek reprisals against other judges who had opposed its actions. He was succeeded by Godfrey Chidyausiku, a former minister in the justice department, believed to be a close ally of Mugabe. In July the Government increased membership of the Supreme Court from five to eight judges; opposition groups suggested that the measure was taken in order to increase the number of judges who were sympathetic to the Government. (By April 2002, however, the number of judges was again five, owing to two resignations and the death of one sitting judge.)

In March 2001 the Commonwealth announced that it would send a delegation comprising the foreign ministers of Australia, Barbados and Nigeria to Zimbabwe for discussions with the Government. Mugabe refused to meet the delegation, however, claiming that the decision had been inspired by the United Kingdom. Similar criticisms were made of an attempt by the European Union (EU, see p. 228) to establish a dialogue with Zimbabwe regarding its record on human rights. In April Mugabe dismissed speculation that he would resign and arrange a presidential election for July, by stating that he intended to contest the election at its scheduled time in 2002. In the same month various foreign diplomatic missions in Harare reported receiving threats from war veterans; the Government refused to guarantee the safety of diplomatic personnel if they 'became involved in local politics'. The leader of the veterans' movement, Chenjerai Hunzvi, denied that he had threatened any diplomatic staff or missions. In the same month the Minister of Industry and International Trade, Nkosana Moyo, resigned, stating that he believed Zimbabwe needed to alter its approach to its problems and advocating the formation of a government of national unity. Two cabinet ministers, Border Gezi and Moven Mahachi, died in road accidents in mid-2001, prompting numerous unsubstantiated reports that their deaths had been brought about deliberately by rival members of ZANU—PF. Hunzvi died in early June; at his funeral, Mugabe urged war veterans to intensify the occupation of white-owned farms, and in the following days attacks against such farms throughout the country were reported to have increased, causing the death of at least one farm worker. The Zimbabwean Government criticized US and British media coverage of the events, and in mid-June it imposed severe restrictions on journalists visiting the country. Later that month the Government listed a further 2,030 farms for compulsory acquisition, and in early August Joseph Made, the Minister of Lands, Agriculture and Rural Development announced the Government's intention to appropriate 8.3m. ha of commercial farmland. Further unrest occurred later that month in the north of the country, where approximately 100 white-owned farms were reported to have been evacuated following attacks by war veterans. Meanwhile, the ZCTU organized a two-day general strike in early July in protest at a recent increase in the price of fuel. A minor cabinet reshuffle was effected in August.

In early September 2001 a meeting of Commonwealth ministers, including the Zimbabwean Minister of Foreign Affairs, Stan Mudenge, was convened in Abuja, Nigeria, to discuss Mugabe's land resettlement programme; it was agreed that illegal farm seizures would cease and that international donors would compensate white farmers for the distribution of their land to landless black families. The agreement was broadly supported by both ZANU—PF and the MDC. By the end of September, however, more than 20 new farm invasions were reported to have taken place, resulting in several deaths, and talks between the Government and the CFU collapsed. Mugabe's intention to disregard the terms of the Abuja agreement became apparent in early October, when he ordered the Supreme Court to recognize the land reform programme as legal, reversing the ruling of December 2000; widespread criticism was directed at the Government for its manipulation of the judiciary. Commonwealth ministers and officials visited Zimbabwe later in October 2001 to monitor the Government's adherence to the Abuja agreement, but failed to persuade the Government to comply with its terms. Government repression intensified in November, when it amended the Land Act by decree. According to the revised legislation, any farm issued with a 'notice of acquisition' would become the property of the state with immediate effect; previously, a farm owner had been served 90 days' notice.

In November 2001 the Government ordered *The Daily News* to close its offices, alleging financial irregularities; it was widely believed, however, that the measure was taken to suppress criticism of the Government. The editor of that newspaper was charged with false reporting and undermining the Government in October 2002, under the Public Order and Security Act (see below), and resigned in December. Meanwhile, also in November 2001 the Government announced plans to make the carrying of national identity cards mandatory. In December Mugabe was nominated as the presidential candidate of ZANU—PF and announced that the election would take place in March 2002.

International concern about the situation in Zimbabwe intensified at the end of 2001. South African President Thabo Mbeki expressed doubts about whether conditions were suitable for a free and fair election, and the Commonwealth Ministerial Action Group on the Harare Declaration, meeting in London, United Kingdom, in late December, warned the Zimbabwean Government that it risked suspension from the organization unless it ended violent land seizures and political intimidation of the media and opposition groups. Meanwhile, the US Congress approved legislation offering aid and economic incentives to Zimbabwe, on condition that its Government act to create an equitable land reform programme. Despite Zimbabwe's growing isolation in the international community, in January 2002 further controversial legislation, aimed at suppressing opposition to Mugabe, was introduced: the Public Order and Security Bill prohibited the publication of documents that incited public disorder or undermined the security services, and banned public gatherings that incited rioting; the General Laws Amendment Bill prohibited foreign and independent missions from monitoring the elections, and forbade voter education (the Bill was repealed by the Supreme Court in February, following a challenge from the MDC); and the Access to Information Bill made it an offence for foreign news services to report from Zimbabwe unless authorized by the Zimbabwean Government. The EU finally imposed so-called 'smart' sanctions on Zimbabwe in mid-February, after the leader of its electoral observer mission was expelled from the country. (Mugabe had previously attempted to ban certain EU member states, including the United Kingdom, from participating in the mission.) The sanctions included an embargo on the sale of arms to Zimbabwe, the suspension of €128m. of aid scheduled to be disbursed during 2002–07, and the freezing of the assets of 19 Zimbabwean officials, including Mugabe, who were also prohibited from visiting any EU state; the USA imposed similar measures several days later. In July the EU applied the sanctions to a further 53 people, including all cabinet members. The EU extended sanctions for a further 12 months in February 2003, although Mugabe attended the Franco-African summit in Paris, France, later that month. The USA also extended its sanctions to more than 70 senior officials in March.

Meanwhile, in late February 2002 Tsvangirai and two other senior members of the MDC were arrested and charged with treason for allegedly plotting to assassinate Mugabe, after an Australian television network broadcast footage that purportedly showed Tsvangirai suggesting the possibility of 'eliminating' Mugabe. The three men appeared in court in mid-March and were released on bail.

The presidential election took place on 9–10 March 2002, but voting was extended to 11 March by the High Court, in response to a request from the MDC, which had claimed that the number of polling stations in areas with strong MDC support was inadequate, and that certain stations had closed on 10 March before many people had been able to vote. Mugabe was declared the winner on 13 March, with 56.2% of the valid votes cast; Tsvangirai secured 42.0%. Independent observers were divided in their judgement of whether the election was free and fair; most observers from African countries declared the election result legitimate, while the Norwegian delegation (the only European representatives) and independent Zimbabwean observers condemned the result and reported widespread electoral fraud and intimidation of the electorate and of observers by members of ZANU—PF. The MDC claimed that a number of its agents had been abducted from certain polling stations and detained by the police. Tsvangirai mounted a legal challenge to have the results declared null and void; however, after a protracted case, the High Court eventually ruled against him in 2005 and the Supreme Court dismissed his application in mid-February 2006.

Prior to the presidential election the Commonwealth had nominated the Nigerian President, Olusegun Obasanjo, President Mbeki and the Australian Prime Minister, John Howard, to consider the conduct of the election and to formulate the organization's response. Mbeki and Obasanjo visited Zimbabwe following the election and urged Mugabe and the MDC to form a government of national unity; however, the MDC refused to co-operate unless the election was held again. The Commonwealth suspended Zimbabwe from meetings of the organization for one year in mid-March, stating that the election result had been undermined by politically motivated violence and that conditions did not permit the free will of the electorate to be expressed. (The suspension was extended for a further nine months in March 2003.) Immediately after the election the Government enacted the Access to Information and Protection of Privacy Act (AIPPA), which required all journalists reporting in Zimbabwe to be approved by the state; seven journalists had been detained under the Act by early May. In April the NCA organized demonstrations in support of demands for a new constitution and a rerun of the presidential election, at which more than 80 demonstrators were arrested. Violence directed at supporters of the MDC intensified following the election, allegedly committed by ZANU—PF supporters, and more than 50 people were reported to have been killed between the election and the end of April.

Land seizures also escalated, and in late March 2002 the Government listed almost 400 white-owned farms for compulsory acquisition, bringing the total land area scheduled for redistribution to the black population to around 85% of total commercial farmland. In June Mugabe issued an order listing some 2,900 white-owned farms for seizure; farmers were obliged to cease working their land on 25 June, or face up to two years' imprisonment, and to leave their properties by early August. Some 860 farmers had vacated their properties by the deadline, while 1,700 refused to leave. (Some 300 had left their farms temporarily to avoid confrontation.) In a speech in mid-August Mugabe stated that white farmers who were 'loyal' to the Government had the option of staying, although later that month it was reported that almost 200 farmers had been arrested for refusing to leave their properties, while others had gone into hiding. In September the Land Acquisition Act was amended to allow the eviction of white farmers within seven days, as opposed to the 90 days previously required.

In April 2002 ZANU—PF and the MDC engaged in talks in an effort to end the political crisis, but negotiations collapsed in the following month, when ZANU—PF withdrew, citing the MDC's petition to the High Court, seeking to overturn the election results, which ZANU—PF regarded as unlawful. In August Mugabe dissolved his Cabinet and appointed a new Government a few days later, retaining many ministers from the previous administration, although the Minister of Finance and Economic Development, Simba Makoni, who had urged restraint in land seizures, was replaced. In February 2003 the trial of Tsvangirai and two other senior MDC officials for allegedly plotting to assassinate Mugabe (see above) began in Harare, but was adjourned until May. In March the MDC led a 'mass action' against the Government, aimed at forcing it to repeal what the party called repressive legislation and to release political prisoners; the Government claimed that the MDC had detonated bombs in Kadoma, south-west of Harare, and it was reported that up to 500 members of the opposition had been arrested and many more driven from their homes and beaten. In early June Tsvangirai was arrested at the conclusion of further demonstrations against the Government organized by the MDC, reportedly in connection with statements he had made in May; he was released on bail in late June.

In August 2003 the Government demanded that international relief agencies transfer responsibility for the distribution of food aid in areas affected by famine to ZANU—PF officials. In local elections held at the end of August the MDC reportedly won 137 of 222 contested council seats, in spite of alleged violations of voting procedures by agents of the ruling party. In September the closure of *The Daily News*, owing to the failure of its publisher to register with the Government's Media and Information Commission (MIC), provoked international condemnation. A court ruling that the newspaper should be allowed to resume publication pending the result of an application that it had made to register with the MIC was initially disregarded by the police. Publication of *The Daily News* did subsequently resume, despite the refusal of the MIC to grant it a licence, but was suspended again in February 2004 when the Supreme Court confirmed that its unlicensed appearance was illegal. (By early 2005 four newspapers had been closed under the Act: *The Daily News*, the *Daily News on Sunday*, *The Tribune* and *The Weekly Times*.)

The death, in September 2003, of Simon Muzenda, one of Zimbabwe's two Vice-Presidents, reignited speculation regarding an eventual successor to President Mugabe. It was reported in December that leading ZANU—PF officials had persuaded Mugabe to retire before the expiry of his term of office in 2008, but the annual conference of the party, held in December, elicited no indication of the President's intentions in this respect. Nor was there any confirmation of speculation that ZANU—PF was willing to engage in dialogue with the MDC in order to resolve Zimbabwe's political crisis. At the annual conference of the MDC, also held in December, Tsvangirai predicted that the range of forces opposed to the Government would oblige it to engage in dialogue in 2004, and he announced the MDC's intention to organize further 'mass action' in pursuit of democratic change. In November 2003, meanwhile, the emergence of three new opposition political groups—MPA Ndadzoka, a New Voice of the Revolutionary Choice Freedom; the Zimbabwe Freedom Movement (ZFM); and a party styling itself ZAPU, with reference to the former Zimbabwe African People's Union—was reported, although the MDC expressed scepticism over the credentials of, in particular, the ZFM, which was suspected of having been covertly established by ZANU—PF. Strike action planned for November by the ZCTU, in response to the arrest of trade union officials and other opposition activists in October, was reportedly cancelled owing to a lack of popular support.

From October 2003 increased concern was expressed at divisions within the Commonwealth over the political crisis in Zimbabwe. The decision, taken at a meeting of Commonwealth Heads of Government held in Abuja, Nigeria, in December, to extend Zimbabwe's suspension from the organization indefinitely, until the country had restored democracy and the rule of law, confirmed the existence of a rift between African Commonwealth members and their Western counterparts. The 12 members from southern Africa criticized the decision, and, in a statement published via the internet shortly after the conclusion of the heads of government meeting, President Mbeki claimed that other Commonwealth members had failed to understand the question of land ownership in Zimbabwe and that they were mistaken in their belief that the presidential election held in Zimbabwe in 2002 had been unfair. Zimbabwe, for its part, announced its decision to withdraw from the Commonwealth shortly before the conclusion of the Heads of Government meeting.

At a news conference in January 2004 Mbeki claimed that the Zimbabwean Government had made a commitment to take part in formal negotiations with the political opposition. Neither ZANU—PF nor the MDC, however, confirmed that any such commitment had been made. In the same month, giving evidence for the first time in his trial for treason, Tsvangirai denied that he had ever plotted to assassinate President Mugabe or to overthrow the Government. Tsvangirai was acquitted of the assassination charges in mid-October 2004; the outstanding treason charge was finally dropped in August 2005. At the end of January 2004 legislation was enacted that would permit the Government to take possession of large plantations and estates, such as the Hippo Valley sugar estates belonging to Anglo American plc. In February a cabinet reshuffle was effected in which, among other changes, Herbert Murerwa was replaced as Minister of Finance and Economic Development by Chris Kuruneri. In late April, however, Kuruneri was arrested on charges of illegally trading foreign currency; his arrest was stated by the authorities to be part of an anti-corruption campaign inaugurated earlier in the year; Murerwa, who was now serving as the Minister of Higher Education and Technology, was subsequently appointed to replace Kuruneri on an acting basis. (Kuruneri's trial began in May 2005. The Governor of the Reserve Bank of Zimbabwe, Gideon Gono, gave evidence that the currency in question had been legitimately obtained by Kuruneri. Kuruneri was granted bail in late July but placed under house arrest.) Meanwhile, in February 2004 the EU renewed sanctions imposed upon the Mugabe regime, extending the travel ban and assets freeze to cover a total of 95 Zimbabwean officials, and in March the USA imposed a further series of sanctions on Zimbabwe, notably targeting government-owned enterprises.

In late 2004 a power struggle developed within ZANU—PF. There was speculation that Mugabe was actively assigning key posts in the administration to members of his own Zezuru clan, replacing members of the majority Karanga clan. At the annual ZANU—PF conference in December Joyce Mujuru, the incumbent Minister of Water Resources, Infrastructural Development and Small and Medium Enterprises, was appointed to the post of Vice-President, which had been vacant since the death of Muzenda in September 2003. Vice-President Msika was expected to step down in 2008 and Mujuru, also a Zezuru, was regarded as Mugabe's appointed successor to the presidency. However, it was revealed that during November 2004 a group of senior ZANU—PF officials had been involved in a 'plot' to install a rival candidate, the Speaker of the House of Assembly, Emerson Mnangagwa, as Vice-President. Six provincial party chairmen and the Minister of State for Information and Publicity, Jonathan Moyo, who were among those alleged to have been involved in the plot, were disqualified from standing in the legislative elections the following March and suspended from active politics for five years. The Chairman of the National Liberation War Veterans' Association was also suspended, as were three more party officials in mid-January 2005. In December 2004 the country's voting constituencies were redrawn, reportedly increasing the number of seats available in traditional ZANU—PF strongholds, while reducing those available in areas where the MDC commanded popular support.

In January 2005 Mugabe approved an amendment to the AIPPA that made it an offence for any journalist to work without accreditation from the MIC. In mid-February Mugabe dismissed Moyo from the Cabinet after Moyo had announced his intention to stand as an independent candidate at the legislative elections in March. Moyo was also expelled from ZANU—PF and barred from taking his seat in the House of Assembly. In mid-March the Supreme Court ruled that an estimated 3.4m. economic and political refugees living outside Zimbabwe would be ineligible to vote in the forthcoming elections.

According to provisional results of the legislative elections held on 31 March 2005, Mugabe's ruling ZANU—PF party won 78 out of the 120 seats available, taking 56.4% of the vote. The opposition MDC took 41 seats with 42.1% of the votes cast; Moyo, was elected as an independent candidate. Under the Constitution the President could allocate 12 seats in the House of Assembly to candidates of his choosing and appoint the eight provincial governors; a further 10 seats were reserved for tribal chiefs, also loyal to Mugabe. The overall result therefore gave ZANU—PF a two-thirds majority in the Assembly which would allow Mugabe to amend the Constitution. International observers from the African Union (AU, see p. 153) and the Southern African Development Community (SADC, see p. 358) endorsed the results; observers from the Commonwealth, the EU and the USA were not invited owing to their perceived hostility towards the Mugabe Government. The Governments of Malawi, Mozambique, South Africa and Zambia were among those who accepted the elections as free and fair; however, the results were dismissed by Australia, the EU and the USA. (The observers from the AU later reversed their opinion and called for investigations into allegations of electoral fraud.) The MDC contested the results citing electoral irregularities in 76 out of the 120 constituencies, and claimed that it should, in fact, have won 94 seats. In mid-April the MDC released a report alleging that some 134,000 people had been turned away from polling stations and that ballot boxes had been filled with votes for ZANU—PF after the polls had closed. The MDC filed petitions at the Electoral Court challenging the results in 13 constituencies. Meanwhile, the outgoing Minister responsible for Land Reform and Resettlement, John Nkomo, announced that white farmers who had lost their farms during the resettlement programme would be compensated for the value of assets and improvements but not for the land itself, which the Government maintained was the responsibility of the United Kingdom. It was estimated that the white population in Zimbabwe had fallen from 200,000 in 2000 to around 25,000 at March 2005; of these some 500 were farmers.

The EU renewed its sanctions against Zimbabwe in February 2005, but in early April Italy was obliged to allow Mugabe to travel through the country to the Vatican City in order to attend the funeral of the Supreme Pontiff of the Roman Catholic Church, Pope John Paul II. The Zimbabwe Government exploited international treaties which obliged countries to allow foreign government officials to travel to international organizations hosted within those countries. In July 2005 the Governor of the Reserve Bank, Gideon Gono, and the Minister of Finance, Herbert Murerwa, both attended a meeting of the IMF in New York, USA, despite sanctions which otherwise would have prevented them travelling to that country; in October Mugabe attended a conference of the Food and Agriculture Organization in Rome, Italy.

In mid-April 2005 ZANU—PF officials announced that they were considering an amendment to the Constitution that would extend Mugabe's presidential term until 2010, in order to hold the presidential and legislative elections concurrently. Also in mid-April Mugabe announced his new Government, which he described as a 'development Cabinet': the former Zimbabwean ambassador to the United Kingdom, Simbarashe Mumbengegwi, was appointed Minister of Foreign Affairs replacing Stanislaus Mudenge, who moved to head the Ministry of Higher and Tertiary Education; Tichaona Jokonya, formerly Zimbabwe's Permanent Representative to the United Nations, assumed the hitherto vacant post of Minister of State for Information and Publicity; Murerwa was confirmed as Minister of Finance; and the two newly created posts of Minister of Economic Development and Minister of Rural Housing and Social Amenities were awarded to Rugare Gumbo and Mnangagwa, respectively. Sixteen ministers retained their portfolios, including Patrick Chinamasa as Minister of Justice, Legal and Parliamentary Affairs. Didymus Mutasa was appointed Minister of State for National Security and head of the Central Intelligence Organization, and in mid-May also assumed overall responsibility for the land redistribution programme.

In late May 2005 the Government launched Operation Murambatsvina ('Sweep Away the Rubbish'), which targeted black market trading—principally in foreign currency and fuel—and 'general lawlessness'. The MDC claimed that it was a punitive action against the urban poor who had voted against ZANU—PF in the elections in March. Shanty towns were razed to the ground in Harare and other major cities, including Bulawayo and Gweru. The operation attracted widespread international condemnation and the Secretary-General of the UN, Kofi Annan, called for its immediate end. According to a report by UN-Habitat published in late July, some 700,000 people were made homeless, however, the Government refused offers of humanitarian aid. In late June President Mugabe announced that some Z.$3,000,000m. was to be spent on new housing and commercial premises under a three-year redevelopment programme entitled Operation Garikai/Hlalani Kuhle. In late July Vice-President Mujuru announced the official end of Operation Murambatsvina and appealed for humanitarian aid; nevertheless the Government reaffirmed that it would not make an official appeal to the UN for food aid. In early October, as part of Operation Siyapambili/Hatidzokereshure ('Going Forward/No Turning Back'), police arrested more than 14,000 people in Harare on charges of illegal street trading and foreign currency dealing.

In late August 2005 the House of Assembly approved a bill which provided for a number of changes to the Constitution. The bill also included legislation designed to conclude the land redistribution programme: courts would no longer be able to hear appeals on land acquisition and once listed for appropriation land would immediately become state property. (However, in early 2006 banks were still refusing to extend loans to resettled farmers because they were not in possession of the title deeds to the land.) Under the bill it became a criminal offence for Zimbabweans to endorse sanctions or military action against their country; and the Zimbabwe Electoral Commission was established in place of the Electoral Supervisory Commission. In addition, the bill provided for the reintroduction of a 66-member Senate (abolished in 1990) as the second chamber of the legislature; senatorial elections were held in late November 2005. The MDC was deeply divided over the issue of participating in the elections. Morgan Tsvangirai opposed electoral participation, advocating mass protests and 'democratic resistance'; however, a faction led by the party Secretary-General, Welshman Ncube, fielded 26 candidates. ZANU—PF won 43 of the 50 elected seats, receiving 73.7% of the vote; MDC candidates took the remaining seven seats with 20.3% of the vote. The MDC effectively split in two, a 'pro-Senate' faction electing Arthur Mutumbara as its leader in February 2006. The rump of the party re-elected Tsvangirai as its President in late March at a conference reportedly attended by some 15,000 supporters.

Zimbabwe severed diplomatic relations with South Africa in September 1980 and subsequently played an important role in international attempts to stabilize southern Africa and to end apartheid in South Africa. In July 1987 the Cabinet rejected a proposal by Mugabe to impose sanctions against South Africa, and the Government opted instead for less stringent economic measures. South Africa is believed to have been responsible for intermittent attacks during the 1980s against the then banned African National Congress of South Africa (ANC) in Zimbabwe. A meeting between President Mugabe and a South African government official in April 1991 (following the implementation of a programme of political reforms by President F. W. de Klerk of South Africa in February 1990) constituted the first direct contact between the Zimbabwean and South African Governments since 1980. The two countries re-established diplomatic relations following the holding of the first democratic elections in South Africa in April 1994, and in March 1997 a mutual defence co-operation agreement was concluded. Relations deteriorated in 1998 owing to South Africa's opposition to Zimbabwe's military intervention in the civil war in the DRC (see below). Relations were also strained from 1999, owing to Zimbabwe's increasingly negative economic and political circumstances (see above). In February 2000 South Africa denied reports that it had offered a substantial loan to Zimbabwe to help the country to resolve its financial crisis. However, President Mbeki offered to negotiate on Zimbabwe's behalf with the IMF and the World Bank for emergency aid to prevent the collapse of the economy. By May the increasingly turbulent land reform situation in Zimbabwe had adversely affected South Africa's economy, prompting Mbeki to appeal to foreign donors to fund the transfer of white-owned land to black farmers.

Zimbabwe and South Africa are members of SADC. However, at a meeting in December 1996 Zimbabwe, together with Malawi, Mozambique and Zambia (also SADC members), formally agreed to establish the Beira Development Corridor, in an effort to develop an alternative trade route to that via South African ports. Zimbabwe was a member of the troika (with Botswana and South Africa) that mediated in the conflict in Lesotho throughout mid-to-late-1998 following elections in May (see chapter on Lesotho). In November 1999 Zimbabwe denied reports that Zimbabwean troops were fighting alongside the Angolan army in that country's civil war.

During the 1980s and early 1990s Zimbabwe provided support to the Mozambican Government against Renamo rebels; in late 1992–early 1993, under the terms of the peace agreement in Mozambique (q.v.), Zimbabwean troops, who had been stationed in Mozambique since 1982, were withdrawn. During the mid-1990s a group of armed Zimbabwean dissidents, known as the

Chimwenjes, were reportedly active in western Mozambique (see above). In January 1996 the Mozambican Government announced its intention to expel the rebels, and in January 1997 an accord was signed by representatives of Mozambique and Zimbabwe on the co-ordination of activities against the rebels. Plans for the repatriation of some 145,000 Mozambican refugees were announced in March 1993; this scheme, co-ordinated by the office of the UN High Commissioner for Refugees, was completed by May 1995.

Following an SADC summit in Harare in August 1998, the Zimbabwean Government dispatched troops and arms to the DRC to support the regime of President Laurent-Désiré Kabila against advancing rebel forces. Despite repeated summits attempting to find a peaceful solution to the conflict, by May 1999 it was reported that Zimbabwe had spent at least $500m. on the continuing unpopular military action. In mid-1999 all armed forces were put on stand-by and retirements and resignations were banned in an attempt to keep the ranks at full strength. A cease-fire agreement was signed at Lusaka, Zambia, on 10 July and troop withdrawals were to follow within the next few months. However, a few days later, both the rebels and the allies of the DRC were accused of violating the accord. An SADC military commission was formed later that month to monitor the cease-fire. In late September the first observers arrived in the DRC. The cease-fire was in danger of collapse in December as fierce fighting continued. The Zimbabwe and DRC Governments unveiled a plan in September to establish a joint diamond and gold marketing venture to finance the war. However, in early 2000 the Zimbabwean Government was reportedly unable to pay allowances to its troops fighting in the region owing to the critical shortage of foreign currency (see above). Public opinion was further turned against the continuation of the conflict in February when heavy rains and a cyclone struck Mozambique and neighbouring provinces of eastern Zimbabwe. There was a desperate shortage of helicopters, which were needed to bring aid to those affected, owing to their deployment in the DRC. The war also caused tensions between Zimbabwe and the IMF, the latter suspending assistance partly because of Zimbabwe's false accounting of expenses relating to the conflict. In March Congolese rebels breached the cease-fire, capturing a town in the eastern DRC, and continued to advance westwards.

In August 2000 a further conference was held in Lusaka, at which all the governments involved reiterated their support for the accord agreed at the previous meeting; President Kabila subsequently stated that he had no confidence in the process, however. Kabila was assassinated in January 2001 and was succeeded by his son, Joseph. Efforts to agree a solution to the conflict increased, and all countries involved in the conflict agreed to withdraw their forces by May, pending the deployment of a UN force. Nevertheless, in April 2002 the Zimbabwean army announced that some 6,000–7,000 of its troops remained in the DRC, from an initial deployment of around 11,000. However, following a number of positive developments in the peace process, the last Zimbabwean troops withdrew from the DRC in October.

Relations with the United Kingdom centred on land reform in 1999–2001. In November 1999, while on a private visit to London, Mugabe was assaulted by protesters in support of homosexual rights. The President subsequently alleged at a Commonwealth summit that the British Government had organized the incident to register its disapproval of plans to redistribute land (see above), and declared Prime Minister Tony Blair unfit to govern. Mugabe's anger had been aroused by a speech by Blair criticizing certain African countries' inactivity concerning AIDS. Mugabe repeated his allegations in an outburst in March 2000, also accusing the United Kingdom of orchestrating an international hate campaign against Zimbabwe.

In January 2000 the Blair administration was strongly criticized for selling arms to Zimbabwe in light of the latter's abuses of human rights. The British Government cited contractual obligations. Arms exports were suspended a few months later, as the seizures of farmland became excessively aggressive (see above). Meanwhile, in early April the two sides took part in talks about land reform. Further negotiations later that month followed Zimbabwe's decision that the United Kingdom should pay compensation to white farmers for their land. The 'former colonial power' offered aid towards resettlement, but not in the form of compensation. It also stipulated conditions for its release: illegal farm seizures and political violence must stop, free and fair elections must be held and only the black rural poor should receive redistributed land (there had been reports that thus far close allies of Mugabe had been the principal beneficiaries). The Zimbabwean Government rejected these terms. Meanwhile, relations deteriorated sharply over a diplomatic incident in March concerning the opening of British diplomatic baggage at Harare airport, which resulted in the British Government briefly recalling its High Commissioner to London. Zimbabwe countered by condemning the United Kingdom for smuggling goods into the country.

Relations between the United Kingdom and Zimbabwe remained strained throughout 2000 and deteriorated further in February 2001, when an official at the British Embassy was accused of obstructing the investigation into the activities of a British journalist, who was subsequently expelled from the country. In September 2002, at the UN World Summit on Sustainable Development in South Africa, tensions increased when Mugabe criticized Blair for his part in imposing EU sanctions on Zimbabwe and for interfering in the country's domestic politics; later that month the Government informed British diplomats that they could not leave Harare without permission from the Ministry of Foreign Affairs. In November Mugabe imposed a ban on senior British officials, including Blair, from travelling to Zimbabwe; the measure was taken in response to the United Kingdom's introduction of a requirement for Zimbabwean nationals to apply for a visa in order to visit that country.

In March 2004, at the international airport in Harare, the Zimbabwean authorities detained 70 men alleged to be involved in a plot to overthrow the Government of Equatorial Guinea, after impounding the aircraft in which 67 of them had travelled from South Africa. South African government officials suggested that the suspected mercenaries had landed in Harare *en route* to Equatorial Guinea in order to collect weapons, although the company that had chartered the aircraft insisted that the men had stopped to obtain mining-related supplies before flying to Burundi and the DRC to work as security guards. Later that month the 70 defendants appeared in a prison court near Harare, charged with a number of offences including conspiring against the Government of Equatorial Guinea and violating immigration laws. In June Zimbabwe and Equatorial Guinea agreed to open embassies in their respective capitals and it was reported that President Mugabe had agreed to extradite the 70 men accused of involvement in the coup plot in exchange for petroleum to the value of US $1,200m.

Government

Under the terms of the 1980 Constitution (as subsequently amended), legislative power is vested in a bicameral Parliament, consisting of a House of Assembly and a Senate. The House of Assembly comprises 150 members, of whom 120 are directly elected by universal adult suffrage, 20 are nominated by the President, 10 are traditional Chiefs and eight are provincial governors. Members of the House of Assembly serve for five years. The Senate comprises 66 members, 50 of whom are directly elected by universal adult suffrage (five in each of the 10 Provinces), 6 are appointed by the President and 10 are traditional chiefs. Executive authority is vested in the President, elected by Parliament for six years. The President appoints, and acts on the advice of, a Cabinet, which comprises two Vice-Presidents and other Ministers and Deputy Ministers. The Cabinet must have the confidence of Parliament, to which it is responsible.

Defence

Total armed forces numbered about 29,000 in August 2005: 25,000 in the army and 4,000 in the air force. Paramilitary forces comprise a police force of 19,500 and a police support unit of 2,300. Defence expenditure was budgeted at Z.$2,300,000m. for 2005.

Economic Affairs

In 2001, according to the World Bank, Zimbabwe's gross national income (GNI), measured at average 1999–2001 prices, was US $6,165m., equivalent to $480 per head (or $2,300 per head on an international purchasing-power parity basis; in 2002 this figure declined to $2,180). During 1995–2004, it was estimated, the population increased at an average annual rate of 1.5%, while gross domestic product (GDP) per head decreased, in real terms, by an average of 2.5% per year during 1995–2002. Overall GDP decreased, in real terms, at an average annual rate of 0.7% in 1995–2002; GDP declined by 8.4% in 2001 and by 5.6% in 2002.

Agriculture (including forestry and fishing) contributed 17.4% of GDP and engaged 15.5% of the employed labour force in 2004.

The principal cash crops are tobacco (which accounted for an estimated 13.5% of export earnings in 2004), maize, cotton, coffee and sugar. Exports of horticultural produce are expanding rapidly. In addition, wheat, soybeans and groundnuts are cultivated. Beef production was traditionally an important activity, earning US $2,400m. per year. However at December 2004 the Cattle Producers' Association reported that the commercial beef herd number fewer than 125,000 head of cattle, down from 1.4m. in 2000. Production of tobacco and maize was severely affected by the farm invasions that took place from the late 1990s (see Recent History). During 1995–2002 agricultural GDP increased by an average of 1.9% per year. Agricultural GDP decreased by 12.0% in 2001 and by 7.0% in 2002.

Industry (including mining, manufacturing, construction and power) contributed 23.8% of GDP in 2002, and engaged 22.2% of the employed labour force in 2004. During 1995–2002 industrial GDP decreased at an average annual rate of 3.3%. Industrial GDP declined by 9.8% in 2001 and by 8.2% in 2002.

Mining contributed 1.8% of GDP and engaged 5.0% of the employed labour force in 2004. Gold, nickel and asbestos are the major mineral exports. Chromium ore, copper, silver, emeralds, lithium, tin, iron ore, cobalt, magnesite, niobium, tantalum, limestone, phosphate rock, coal and diamonds are also mined. In October 1999 the discovery of significant diamond deposits in Zimbabwe was announced; in 2003 Rio Tinto opened Zimbabwe's second diamond mine, at Murowa, near Zvishavane. Mining of platinum ore at Hartley in central Zimbabwe began in March 1996, reaching full production in June 1997; further platinum deposits have subsequently been developed. In 2003 Anglo Platinum announced its intention to mine reserves located at Unki, on the Great Dyke. Zimbabwe also has large reserves of kyanite and smaller reserves of zinc and lead. In 2004 the export of minerals comprised an estimated 36.0% of the value of total exports. Mining GDP declined by an estimated 11.0% in 2000. According to government figures, mining GDP increased by 11.6% in 2004.

Manufacturing contributed 13.0% of GDP in 2002, and engaged 13.6% of the employed labour force in 2004. The most important sectors, measured by gross value of output, are food-processing, metals (mainly ferrochrome and steel), chemicals and textiles. According to the Confederation of Zimbabwe Industries, 840 manufacturing companies closed between 2000 and 2003. During 1995–2002 manufacturing GDP decreased by an average of 5.6% per year. Manufacturing GDP declined by 19.0% in 2001 and by 12.0% in 2002.

In 2002 55.1% of Zimbabwe's electricity production was derived from coal, and 44.5% from hydroelectric power. In 1998 a new project was introduced to supply electricity to villages by solar energy systems, funded by Italy. The Italian Government cancelled the project in September 1999, however, owing to Zimbabwe's political and economic difficulties. Imports of fuel and electricity comprised an estimated 14.0% of the value of total imports in 2003. In 2002 Zimbabwe purchased 24.2% of its electrical energy from neighbouring countries.

The services sector contributed 58.8% of GDP in 2002, and engaged 62.4% of the employed labour force in 2004. During 1995–2002 the GDP of the services sector increased at an average annual rate of 0.1%. Services GDP declined by 5.3% in 2001 and by 4.2% in 2002.

In 2004, according to estimates, Zimbabwe had a visible trade deficit of US $310m., while there was a deficit of $421m. on the current account of the balance of payments. In 2004 South Africa was the principal source of imports (50.5%) and the principal market for exports (30.2%). Other major trading partners were Botswana, Switzerland, the People's Republic of China, Zambia, the United Kingdom, Germany, Japan and Malawi. The principal exports in 2004 were gold, tobacco, ferrous alloys, platinum, and cotton lint. The main imports in that year were fuel and electricity, machinery and transport equipment, chemicals and food.

In 2004 there was an estimated budgetary deficit of Z.$1,419,400m. At the end of 2003 Zimbabwe's external debt totalled US $4,445m., of which $3,367m. was long-term public debt. In 2004 external debt was estimated to be equivalent to 77% of GDP and the cost of debt-servicing to 8.3% of GDP. The rate of inflation averaged 102.3% annually in 1995–2004. Consumer prices increased by an average of 698.7% in 2003 and by 232.7% in 2004. According to official figures, 6.0% of the total labour force was unemployed in 1999, although the actual percentage was believed to be significantly greater (reportedly more than 70% in 2005).

Zimbabwe is a member of the Southern African Development Community (see p. 358), which aims to promote closer economic integration among its members, and also belongs to the Common Market for Eastern and Southern Africa (see p. 191).

During the 1980s and 1990s Zimbabwe benefited from a well-developed infrastructure, mineral wealth and a highly diversified manufacturing sector. However, from 1999 the country suffered a severe economic crisis. Business and investor confidence have fallen as a result of Zimbabwe's financial and political problems, notably the issue of enforced land redistribution (see Recent History). In February 2003, in the continued absence of international funding and direct foreign investment, the Government attempted to boost exports as a source of hard currency through a partial, 93% devaluation of the Zimbabwean dollar, pegging the currency for exporters' earnings at Z.$800 = US $1 (although the official exchange rate for other transactions remained unchanged, at Z.$55 = US $1). A requirement that one-half of all export proceeds should be paid into the central bank remained in force. In early 2004, as a result of a new system of foreign-exchange auctions, the Zimbabwean dollar effectively depreciated by a further 80%. In late May 2005 the Reserve Bank announced an effective devaluation of the Zimbabwean dollar by 45% and a further devaluation of 39% in late July. Zimbabwe has been dependent on assistance from the UN World Food Programme (WFP) since 2002. The seizure of commercial farms, in combination with drought, was reported in 2003 to have resulted in a decline of at least 60% in domestic food production. (Tobacco output was similarly affected, and in October of that year sales of tobacco at Zimbabwe's annual auction fell to their lowest level in almost 50 years.) In late 2003 WFP was reported to have reduced individual rations distributed in Zimbabwe by one-half in order to be able to meet the country's needs until May 2004. WFP claimed that it had been unable to raise sufficient funds to buy the necessary supplies of food owing to the Government's failure to quantify its needs in time, as well as to foreign donors' perception of the food crisis in Zimbabwe as being man-made. In mid-November 2004 a bipartisan parliamentary committee dismissed government forecasts of a harvest of 2.4m. metric tons of grain; the committee found that, including imports, the national grain supply would only reach 574,000 tons by the end of the year. Zimbabwe annually consumes 1.8m. tons of maize with strategic reserves of 500,000 tons. In late December the Grain Marketing Board (GMB) confirmed that it had ordered 300,000 tons of grain from South Africa. In March 2005 Mugabe admitted that it would be necessary to import food for an estimated 1.5m. people; according to NGO sources the figure was 4.8m. In late August the Government ended the monopoly of the GMB, liberalizing the trade in cereals and removing import duties on maize and wheat. After months of negotiation, in December Zimbabwe signed an agreement with the WFP to provide food to some 3m. people under restrictive terms that limited the agency's direct involvement to schools, certain HIV/AIDS programmes and food-for-work programmes. In early 2006 the Minister of Agriculture, Joseph Made, continued to promote 'contract farming' by which private companies and non-governmental agencies would provide farmers with capital inputs to grow crops which they also agreed to buy at harvest. Since 2004 companies, which included the telecommunications provider TelOne and the Zimbabwe Energy Supply Authority, had invested in contract farming as a means of generating foreign currency from sales of cotton, tobacco and horticultural produce. The Government also authorized contract farming of previously controlled crops including wheat and maize. Meanwhile, international aid has been suspended since late 1999, owing to Zimbabwe's inability to comply with requirements for economic reform. The IMF removed Zimbabwe from the list of countries eligible to borrow resources under the Poverty Reduction and Growth Facility (PGRF) in September 2001, in response to Zimbabwe's failure to make debt repayments. By the end of 2005 domestic debt was reported to have risen from Z.$3,200,000m. at the beginning of the year to Z.$15,800,000m., largely owing to Government expenditure on imports of food and fuel. In mid-2003 the IMF suspended Zimbabwe's voting rights within the Fund, noting that the authorities had not 'adopted the comprehensive and consistent policies needed to address Zimbabwe's serious economic problems'. In December the IMF initiated its procedure on the compulsory withdrawal of Zimbabwe from the Fund for lack of co-operation and non-payment of arrears totalling more than US $270m. However, Zimbabwe repaid some US $37m. between January 2004 and mid-2005, when the country pledged to increase quarterly payments from US $1.5m. to US $9m. In September 2005 Zimbabwe was once again facing the prospect of expulsion from the Fund until it made an extraordinary payment of US $120m., funded in part by export proceeds and foreign currency liquidations. Zimbabwe's total repayments for 2005 amounted to some US $163.5m.; a further payment of US $9.5m. was made in January 2006 leaving a debt to the Fund of US $136.6m. In mid-February the Reserve Bank revealed that it had printed some Z.$21,000,000m. to buy foreign currency with which to make IMF payments in 2005, which was also blamed for propelling inflation to more than 600% in early 2006. (In late 2005 Zimbabwe was reported to have unsuccessfully approached both the People's Republic of China and South Africa for loans to cover the IMF payments.) In March 2006 Zimbabwe's arrears to the separate PRGF Exogenous Shocks Facility Trust remained at US $119m. and the IMF decided not to restore either the country's voting rights or its access to IMF resources. Fiscal and monetary stabilization measures were introduced from late 2003, with the aim of reducing the rate of inflation to less than 100%. However, in early 2004 the measures were reported to have compounded a crisis in the banking sector and led to the exclusion from the daily clearing system of more than one-third of the country's commercial banks owing to lack of funds. The budget for 2005 forecast a deficit of Z.$4,500,000m., equivalent to about 5% of estimated GDP; however, while GDP contracted by 3.5% in 2004 it was forecast to grow by between 3.5% and 5% in 2005. Inflation stood at 622.8% in January 2004 but had declined to 209% by the following October; the Government announced its aim to reduce the rate of inflation to between 30% and 50% by the end of 2005. Nevertheless, when the 2006 budget was presented in December 2005 the rate of inflation remained at around 400% and forecasts that the rate of inflation would be stabilized at around 80% within the next 12 months appeared unrealistic.

Education

Primary education, which begins at six years of age and lasts for seven years, has been compulsory since 1987. Secondary education begins at the age of 13 and lasts for six years. In 2000/01 enrolment at primary schools included 80% of children in the relevant age-group (males 80%; females 80%), while the comparable ratio for secondary enrolment, according to UNESCO estimates, was 40% of children (males 42%; females 39%). In 1998 some 11,451 students were attending universities, while 36,830 students were enrolled at institutions of higher education. There are two state-run universities, the University of Zimbabwe, which is located in Harare, and the University of Science and Technology, at Bulawayo. There are also two private universities, Africa University in Mutare and Solusi University in Figtree. Education was allocated Z.$6,800,000m. by the central Government in the budget for 2005, equivalent to 24.7% of total expenditure for that year.

Public Holidays

2006: 1 January (New Year's Day), 14–17 April (Easter), 18 April (Independence Day), 1 May (Workers' Day), 25 May (Africa Day, anniversary of OAU's foundation), 11 August (Heroes' Day), 12 August (Defence Forces National Day), 22 December (National Unity Day), 25–26 December (Christmas).
2007: 1 January (New Year's Day), 6–9 April (Easter), 18 April (Independence Day), 1 May (Workers' Day), 25 May (Africa Day, anniversary of OAU's foundation), 11 August (Heroes' Day), 12 August (Defence Forces National Day), 22 December (National Unity Day), 25–26 December (Christmas).

Weights and Measures

The metric system is in use.

Statistical Survey

Source (unless otherwise stated): Central Statistical Office, Ministry of Finance and Economic Development, Blocks B, E and G, Composite Bldg, cnr Samora Machel Ave and Fourth St, Private Bag 7705, Causeway, Harare; tel. (4) 706681; fax (4) 728529; internet www.mofed.gov.zw.

Area and Population

AREA, POPULATION AND DENSITY

Area (sq km)	390,757*
Population (census results)	
18 August 1992	10,412,548
18 August 1997	
Males	5,647,090
Females	6,142,184
Total	11,789,274
Population (UN estimates at mid-year)†	
2002	12,786,000
2003	12,863,000
2004	12,936,000
Density (per sq km) at mid-2004	33.1

* 150,872 sq miles.
† Source: UN, *World Population Prospects: The 2004 Revision*.

PRINCIPAL TOWNS
(population at census of August 1992)

Harare (capital)	1,189,103	Masvingo	51,743
Bulawayo	621,742	Chinhoyi (Sinoia)	43,054
Chitungwiza	274,912	Hwange (Wankie)	42,581
Mutare (Umtali)	131,367	Marondera (Marandellas)	39,384
Gweru (Gwelo)	128,037	Zvishavane (Shabani)	32,984
Kwekwe (Que Que)	75,425	Redcliff	29,959
Kadoma (Gatooma)	67,750		

Mid-2003 (UN estimate, incl. suburbs): Harare 1,469,149 (Source: UN, *World Urbanization Prospects: The 2003 Revision*).

BIRTHS AND DEATHS
(UN estimates, annual averages)

	1990–95	1995–2000	2000–05
Birth rate (per 1,000)	36.1	32.1	30.0
Death rate (per 1,000)	10.5	17.3	22.7

Source: UN, *World Population Prospects: The 2004 Revision*.

Expectation of life (WHO estimates, years at birth): 37 (males 37; females 36) in 2003 (Source: WHO, *World Health Report*).

ECONOMICALLY ACTIVE POPULATION
(sample survey, persons aged 15 years and over, 1999)

	Males	Females	Total
Agriculture, hunting, forestry and fishing	1,215,661	1,584,839	2,800,500
Mining and quarrying	46,946	3,367	50,313
Manufacturing	283,090	94,667	377,757
Electricity, gas and water	10,158	n.a.	10,158
Construction	98,908	6,659	105,567
Trade, restaurants and hotels	154,198	178,341	332,539
Transport, storage and communications	93,289	8,288	101,577
Financing, insurance, real estate and business services	100,425	20,749	121,174
Community, social and personal services	320,020	258,505	578,525
Activities not adequately defined	63,052	124,286	187,338
Total employed	2,385,747	2,279,701	4,665,448
Unemployed	187,142	110,669	297,811
Total labour force	2,572,889	2,390,370	4,963,259

Mid-2003 (FAO estimates, '000 persons): Agriculture, etc. 3,577; Total labour force 5,878 (Source: FAO).

ZIMBABWE

Health and Welfare

KEY INDICATORS

Total fertility rate (children per woman, 2003)	3.9
Under-5 mortality rate (per 1,000 live births, 2004)	129
HIV/AIDS (% of persons aged 15–49, 2003)	24.6
Physicians (per 1,000 head, 1995)	0.14
Hospital beds (per 1,000 head, 1990)	0.51
Health expenditure (2002): US $ per head (PPP)	152
Health expenditure (2002): % of GDP	8.5
Health expenditure (2002): public (% of total)	51.6
Access to water (% of persons, 2002)	83
Access to sanitation (% of persons, 2002)	57
Human Development Index (2003): ranking	145
Human Development Index (2003): value	0.505

For sources and definitions, see explanatory note on p. vi.

Agriculture

PRINCIPAL CROPS
('000 metric tons)

	2002	2003	2004
Wheat	150	213	140*
Barley	17	30*	25*
Maize	498.5*	929.6	550.0*
Millet	14.6	44.8*	40.0*
Sorghum*	74.5	39.6	80.0
Potatoes†	35	35	35
Cassava (Manioc)†	175	190	190
Dry beans†	50	52	52
Sugar cane	4,200†	4,533*	4,121*
Soybeans (Soya beans)	83	83*	93*
Groundnuts (in shell)	120†	147*	150†
Sunflower seed	7.7	4.8*	5.0†
Vegetables (incl. melons)†	161.1	161.5	161.8
Oranges†	93	93	93
Other citrus fruits†	29.7	29.7	29.7
Bananas†	85	85	85
Coffee (green)	8.1	10	10†
Tea (made)†	22	22	22
Tobacco (leaves)	178.4	102.7	63.3*
Cotton (lint)*	73	85	100

* Unofficial figure(s).
† FAO estimate(s).
Source: FAO.

LIVESTOCK
('000 head, year ending September)

	2001	2002	2003
Horses*	27.0	27.0	27.5
Asses*	108	110	112
Cattle	5,752	5,600*	5,400*
Sheep	600	600*	610*
Pigs	604	605*	620*
Goats	2,968	2,950*	2,970*
Chickens	20,000	22,000*	22,000*

* FAO estimate(s).
2004: Figures assumed to be unchanged from 2003 (FAO estimates).
Source: FAO.

LIVESTOCK PRODUCTS
(FAO estimates, '000 metric tons)

	2002	2003	2004
Beef and veal	99.0	96.8	96.8
Goat meat	12.7	12.8	12.8
Pig meat	27.0	27.5	27.5
Poultry meat	35.2	36.6	36.6
Other meat	29.4	31.4	33.4
Cows' milk	280	248	248
Butter	1.8	1.8	1.8
Cheese	2.1	2.1	2.1
Poultry eggs	22	22	22
Cattle hides	8.8	8.6	8.6

Source: FAO.

Forestry

ROUNDWOOD REMOVALS
('000 cubic metres, excl. bark)

	2000	2001	2002*
Sawlogs, veneer logs and logs for sleepers	773	786	786
Pulpwood	93	94	94
Other industrial wood*	112	112	112
Fuel wood*	8,115	8,115	8,115
Total*	9,094	9,108	9,108

* FAO estimates.
2003–04: Figures assumed to be unchanged from 2002 (FAO estimates).
Source: FAO.

SAWNWOOD PRODUCTION
('000 cubic metres, incl. railway sleepers)

	1999	2000	2001
Coniferous (softwood)	395	343	354
Broadleaved (hardwood)	43	43*	43*
Total	438	386	397

* FAO estimate.
2002–04: Figures assumed to be unchanged from 2001 (FAO estimates).
Source: FAO.

Fishing

(FAO estimates, '000 metric tons, live weight)

	2001	2002	2003
Capture	13.0	13.0	13.0
Tilapias	0.8	0.8	0.8
Other freshwater fishes	1.8	1.8	1.8
Dagaas	10.4	10.4	10.4
Aquaculture	2.3	2.2	2.6
Total catch	15.3	15.2	15.6

Source: FAO.

ZIMBABWE

Mining

('000 metric tons, unless otherwise indicated)

	2002	2003	2004*
Asbestos	168	147	104
Chromium ore	749.3	637.1	668.4
Coal	3,721	2,872	2,476
Cobalt ore (metric tons)†	99	79	59
Copper ore‡	2.5	2.8	2.4
Gold (kilograms)	15,469	12,564	21,330
Iron ore	272	367	283
Limestone	3,169	922	41
Magnesite (metric tons)	2,366	1,333	749
Nickel ore (metric tons)	8,092	9,516	9,776
Phosphate rock	107.9	95.5	83.4
Silver (kilograms)	1,711	747	3,216

* Preliminary figures.
† Figures include metal content of compounds and salts and may include cobalt recovered from nickel-copper matte.
‡ Figures refer to the metal content of ores and concentrates.

Source: US Geological Survey.

Industry

SELECTED PRODUCTS

('000 metric tons, unless otherwise indicated)

	2002	2003	2004*
Coke (metallurgical)	224	228	180†
Cement†	600	400	400
Pig-iron	122	131	150†
Ferro-chromium	258.1	245.3	193.1
Crude steel	105	152	180†
Refined copper—unwrought (metric tons)	7,200	7,200	7,000†
Refined nickel—unwrought (metric tons)	17,577	12,657	14,200†

* Preliminary figures.
† Estimate(s).

Source: US Geological Survey.

Raw sugar ('000 metric tons): 585 in 2000; 639 in 2001 (Source: UN, *Industrial Commodity Statistics Yearbook*).

Electric energy (million kWh): 8,587 in 2002; 8,799 in 2003; 9,719 in 2004.

Finance

CURRENCY AND EXCHANGE RATES

Monetary Units
100 cents = 1 Zimbabwe dollar (Z.$).

Sterling, US Dollar and Euro Equivalents (30 December 2005)
£1 sterling = Z.$134,247.20;
US $1 = Z.$77,964.60;
€1 = Z.$91,974.85;
Z.$100,000 = £7.44 = US $12.83 = €10.87.

Average Exchange Rate (Z.$ per US dollar)
2003   697.4240
2004   5,068.6600
2005   22,363.6000

Statistical Survey

BUDGET
(Z.$ '000 million, year ending 30 June)

Revenue	2002	2003	2004
Taxation	284.6	1,325.8	7,763.0
Taxes on income and profits	158.3	734.7	4,076.9
Personal income	116.4	588.8	3,184.8
Companies	30.0	80.6	604.9
Domestic dividends and interest	4.5	22.2	206.3
Other income taxes	7.5	43.2	80.9
Customs duties	27.2	92.9	930.0
Excise duties	18.8	94.6	278.8
Sales tax / Value-added tax	76.2	382.3	2,377.0
Miscellaneous taxes	4.0	21.3	100.4
Revenue from investments and properties	1.2	1.8	3.0
Fees paid for departmental facilities and services	1.1	2.5	16.4
Other revenue	17.3	44.7	289.3
Total	**304.2**	**1,374.8**	**8,071.7**

Expenditure*	2002	2003	2004
Recurrent	320.7	1,233.2	8,410.7
Goods and services	216.0	924.3	5,016.3
Salaries, wages and allowances	123.9	528.0	3,657.6
Subsistence and transport	6.4	34.1	181.9
Incidental expenses	20.8	43.7	860.6
Maintenance of capital works	3.9	18.3	269.8
Other recurrent expenditure	61.1	300.3	46.7
Interest payments	49.5	69.2	1,302.1
Foreign	9.2	3.3	568.0
Domestic	40.3	65.9	734.0
Transfers and subsidies	55.2	239.7	2,092.4
Pensions	22.6	77.2	772.1
Capital	25.2	107.7	1,220.2
Total	**345.9**	**1,340.9**	**9,630.9**

* Excluding loans (Z.$ '000 million): 5.4 in 2002; 53.7 in 2003; 139.8 in 2004.

Source: IMF, *Zimbabwe: Selected Issues and Statistical Appendix* (October 2005).

INTERNATIONAL RESERVES
(US $ million at 31 December)

	2000	2001	2002
Gold*	45.4	27.5	22.7
IMF special drawing rights	0.2	—	—
Reserve position in IMF	0.4	0.4	0.4
Foreign exchange	192.5	64.3	82.9
Total	**238.5**	**92.2**	**106.0**

* Valued at a market-related price which is determined each month.

2003–04 (US $ million at 31 December): Reserve position in IMF 0.5.

Source: IMF, *International Financial Statistics*.

MONEY SUPPLY
(Z.$ '000 million at 31 December)

	2002	2003	2004
Currency outside banks	79.66	441.71	1,655.89
Demand deposits at deposit money banks	275.40	1,636.45	5,148.17
Total money (incl. others)	**356.64**	**2,086.70**	**6,856.61**

Source: IMF, *International Financial Statistics*.

ZIMBABWE

COST OF LIVING
(Consumer Price Index; base: 1995 = 100)

	2002	2003	2004
Food	3,725	27,399	60,592
Beverages and tobacco	5,551	38,246	84,806
Clothing and footwear	3,652	22,833	53,142
Rent, fuel and light	1,253	5,704	18,886
All items (incl. others)	**3,490**	**24,384**	**56,753**

Source: IMF, *Zimbabwe: Selected Issues and Statistical Appendix* (October 2005).

NATIONAL ACCOUNTS
(Z.$ million at current prices)

Expenditure on the Gross National Product

	2001	2002	2003
Government final consumption expenditure	64,538	85,709	120,211
Private final consumption expenditure	636,753	1,824,491	6,214,782
Changes in stocks	−12,201	−242,074	−892,526
Gross fixed capital formation	51,757	92,992	174,659
Total domestic expenditure	**740,847**	**1,761,118**	**5,617,126**
Exports of goods and services	105,235	93,022	84,118
Less Imports of goods and services	136,868	155,961	182,488
GDP in purchasers' values	**709,214**	**1,698,180**	**5,518,757**
Factor income received from abroad	755	799	863
Factor income paid abroad	−12,690	−9,729	−7,931
Gross national income	**697,280**	**1,689,251**	**5,511,689**

Source: IMF, *Zimbabwe: Selected Issues and Statistical Appendix* (October 2005).

Gross Domestic Product by Economic Activity
(at factor cost)

	1997	1998	1999
Agriculture, hunting, forestry and fishing	17,042	27,135	35,812
Mining and quarrying	1,400	2,400	3,380
Manufacturing	16,208	20,708	30,538
Electricity and water	2,849	3,139	5,171
Construction	2,544	3,640	5,132
Trade, restaurants and hotels	17,163	22,652	36,261
Transport, storage and communications	5,192	6,712	11,373
Finance, insurance and real estate	9,797	15,679	26,917
Government services	13,640	16,916	22,913
Other services	5,320	6,806	8,273
Sub-total	**91,155**	**125,762**	**185,770**
Less Imputed bank service charges	1,149	1,242	1,357
Total	**90,006**	**124,540**	**184,413**

BALANCE OF PAYMENTS
(US $ million)

	2002	2003	2004*
Exports of goods f.o.b.	1,802	1,670	1,680
Imports of goods f.o.b.	−1,821	−1,778	−1,989
Trade balance	**−18**	**−108**	**−310**
Exports of services	217	185	317
Imports of services	−398	−401	−424
Balance on goods and services	**−199**	**−324**	**−417**
Investment income (net)	−242	−191	−208
Balance on goods, services and income	**−441**	**−515**	**−625**
Private transfers (net)	228	169	204
Current balance	**−213**	**−346**	**−421**
Official transfers (net)	38	38	24
Direct investment (net)	23	4	9
Portfolio investment (net)	−2	4	2
Long-term capital (net)	−281	−228	−221
Short-term capital (net)	−94	−27	17
Net errors and omissions	74	79	344
Overall balance	**−456**	**−476**	**−247**

* Estimates.

Source: IMF, *Zimbabwe: Selected Issues and Statistical Appendix* (October 2005).

External Trade

PRINCIPAL COMMODITIES
(US $ million)

Imports f.o.b.	2002	2003	2004*
Food	337	206	161
Tobacco and beverages	39	36	44
Crude materials	87	79	96
Fuel and electricity	352	456	462
Petroleum products	149	110	342
Oils and fats	27	25	30
Chemicals	361	328	401
Machinery and transport equipment	375	341	417
Other manufactured goods	241	220	269
Total (incl. others)	**1,821**	**1,778**	**1,989**

Exports†	2002	2003	2004*
Agricultural exports	646.6	516.0	384.2
Tobacco	434.7	321.3	226.7
Sugar	64.2	54.8	53.9
Cold Storage Co. beef	2.3	0.2	—
Coffee	5.4	5.9	4.1
Horticulture	126.6	118.7	84.1
Mineral exports	297.8	390.8	604.2
Gold‡	159.5	152.3	262.8
Asbestos	39.3	42.4	19.4
Nickel	31.8	68.5	95.7
Platinum	14.5	77.4	174.4
Copper	8.9	4.6	2.6
Manufacturing exports	287.3	691.2	620.9
Ferrous alloys	106.8	119.8	185.1
Cotton lint	53.2	67.2	122.1
Iron and steel	22.3	39.9	22.9
Textiles and clothing	17.7	28.2	13.8
Machinery and equipment	5.2	12.8	1.9
Chemicals	3.5	5.1	9.6
Total (incl. others)§	**1,397.9**	**1,670.3**	**1,679.7**

* Estimates.
† Value of exports based on official exchange rates.
‡ Based on unit value of US dollar per ounce.
§ Excluding unidentified exports and internal freight.

Source: IMF, *Zimbabwe: Selected Issues and Statistical Appendix* (October 2005).

ZIMBABWE

PRINCIPAL TRADING PARTNERS
(US $ '000)

Imports f.o.b.	1999	2001*	2002
Botswana	—	33,600	447,300
Congo, Democratic Repub.	200	96,100	2,900
France (incl. Monaco)	62,600	27,700	31,900
Germany	113,300	47,700	134,300
Japan	88,000	29,500	72,500
Kuwait	700	6,900	54,100
Mozambique	13,600	89,900	46,700
SACU†	919,400	—	—
South Africa	—	802,600	1,297,800
United Kingdom	142,400	54,300	120,700
USA	101,300	48,400	87,000
Total (incl. others)	2,126,200	1,714,900	2,466,700

Exports f.o.b.	1999	2000	2002‡
Botswana	—	62,200	68,100
China, People's Repub.	103,300	99,200	13,300
Germany	149,900	149,700	109,600
Italy	74,300	67,200	47,100
Japan	134,500	139,800	122,300
Malawi	72,900	48,300	120,100
Mozambique	62,600	37,400	69,000
Netherlands	65,500	62,700	89,800
SACU†	301,400	—	—
South Africa	—	288,800	431,400
Spain	46,400	32,300	70,500
Switzerland (incl. Liechtenstein)	46,000	76,100	303,700
United Arab Emirates	11,900	286,500	8,900
United Kingdom	181,800	0	140,400
USA	109,800	0	104,700
Zambia	69,000	82,800	215,600
Total (incl. others)	1,887,200	1,925,000	2,327,400

* Figures for 2000 unavailable.
† Southern African Customs Union, comprising Botswana, Lesotho, Namibia, South Africa and Swaziland.
‡ Figures for 2001 unavailable.

Source: UN, *International Trade Statistics Yearbook*.

Transport

RAIL TRAFFIC
(National Railways of Zimbabwe, including operations in Botswana)

	1998	1999	2000
Total number of passengers ('000)	1,787	1,896	1,614
Revenue-earning metric tons hauled ('000)	12,421	12,028	9,422
Gross metric ton-km (million)	9,248	8,962	6,953
Net metric ton-km (million)	4,549	4,375	3,326

ROAD TRAFFIC
('000 motor vehicles in use, estimates)

	1998	1999	2000
Passenger cars	540	555	573
Commercial vehicles	37	38	39

Statistical Survey

CIVIL AVIATION
(traffic on scheduled services)

	1998	1999	2000
Kilometres flown ('000)	13,957	11,532	10,080
Passengers carried ('000)	526	461	409
Passenger-km (million)	95	73	60
Total ton-km (million)	225	292	225

Tourism

VISITOR ARRIVALS BY NATIONALITY

	2000	2001	2002
Australia and New Zealand	56,631	76,519	36,841
Canada and USA	79,941	91,714	55,180
Mozambique	117,735	191,392	242,154
United Kingdom and Ireland	136,808	156,519	77,262
Zambia	409,532	786,839	224,302
Total (incl. others)	1,966,582	2,217,429	2,041,202

2003 (visitor arrivals by nationality): Botswana 242,750; Malawi 71,968; Mozambique 295,103; South Africa 882,726; United Kingdom 58,354; USA 47,197; Zambia 313,954; Total (incl. others) 2,256,205.

Tourism receipts (US $ million, incl. passenger transport): 81 in 2001; 76 in 2002; 44 in 2003.

Source: World Tourism Organization.

Communications Media

	2002	2003	2004
Telephones ('000 main lines in use)	287.9	300.9	317.0
Mobile cellular telephones ('000 subscribers)	353.0	379.1	397.5
Personal computers ('000 in use)	600	620	1,000
Internet users ('000)	500.0	n.a.	820.0

Radio receivers ('000 in use): 4,488 in 1999.

Television receivers ('000 in use): 410 in 2000.

Facsimile machines: 4,100 in use in year ending 30 June 1995.

Daily newspapers (1996): 2; average circulation: 209,000 copies.

Sources: UNESCO, *Statistical Yearbook*; UN, *Statistical Yearbook*; International Telecommunication Union.

Education

(1998)

	Schools	Teachers	Students
Primary	4,699	64,538	2,488,939
Secondary	1,539	30,482	829,977
University	5	n.a.	11,451
Other:			
agricultural colleges	7	n.a.	566
technical and vocational centres	11	721	17,891
teachers' colleges	15	907	17,268
nurses	n.a.	n.a.	1,105

Adult literacy rate (UNESCO estimates): 90.0% (males 93.8%; females 86.3%) in 2002 (Source: UN Development Programme, *Human Development Report*).

Directory

The Constitution

The Constitution of the Republic of Zimbabwe took effect at independence on 18 April 1980. Amendments to the Constitution must have the approval of two-thirds of the members of the House of Assembly (see below). The provisions of the 1980 Constitution (with subsequent amendments) are summarized below:

THE REPUBLIC

Zimbabwe is a sovereign republic and the Constitution is the supreme law.

DECLARATION OF RIGHTS

The declaration of rights guarantees the fundamental rights and freedoms of the individual, regardless of race, tribe, place of origin, political opinions, colour, creed or sex.

THE PRESIDENT

Executive power is vested in the President, who acts on the advice of the Cabinet. The President is Head of State and Commander-in-Chief of the Defence Forces. The President appoints two Vice-Presidents and other Ministers and Deputy Ministers, to be members of the Cabinet. The President holds office for six years and is eligible for re-election. Each candidate for the Presidency shall be nominated by not fewer than 10 members of the House of Assembly; if only one candidate is nominated, that candidate shall be declared to be elected without the necessity of a ballot. Otherwise, a ballot shall be held within an electoral college consisting of the members of the House of Assembly.

PARLIAMENT

Legislative power is vested in a bicameral Parliament, consisting of a House of Assembly and a Senate. The House of Assembly comprises 150 members, of whom 120 are directly elected by universal adult suffrage, 12 are nominated by the President, 10 are traditional Chiefs and eight are Provincial Governors. The life of the House of Assembly is ordinarily to be five years. The Senate comprises 66 members, of whom 50 are directly elected by universal adult suffrage, six are nominated by the President and 10 are traditional Chiefs. The life of the Senate is ordinarily to be five years.

OTHER PROVISIONS

An Ombudsman shall be appointed by the President, acting on the advice of the Judicial Service Commission, to investigate complaints against actions taken by employees of the Government or of a local authority.

Chiefs shall be appointed by the President, and shall form a Council of Chiefs from their number in accordance with customary principles of succession.

Other provisions relate to the Judicature, Defence and Police Forces, public service and finance.

The Government

HEAD OF STATE

President: ROBERT GABRIEL MUGABE (took office 31 December 1987; re-elected March 1990, 16–17 March 1996 and 9–11 March 2002).

THE CABINET
(March 2006)

Vice-President: JOSEPH MSIKA.
Vice-President: JOYCE MUJURU.
Minister of Special Affairs in the President's Office, responsible for Lands, Land Reform and Resettlement: FLORA BHUKA.
Minister of Special Affairs in the President's Office, in charge of the Anti-Corruption and Anti-Monopolies Programme: PAUL MANGWANA.
Minister of Defence: SYDNEY SEKERAMAYI.
Minister of Home Affairs: KEMBO MOHADI.
Minister of Justice, Legal and Parliamentary Affairs: PATRICK ANTHONY CHINAMASA.
Minister of Public Service, Labour and Social Welfare: NICHOLAS GOCHE.
Minister of Local Government, Public Works and National Housing: Dr IGNATIUS MORGAN CHIMINYA CHOMBO.
Minister of Agriculture and Rural Resettlement: JOSEPH MADE.
Minister of Rural Housing and Social Amenities: EMMERSON MNANGAGWA.
Minister of Industry and International Trade: OBERT MPOFU.
Minister of Energy and Power Development: MICHAEL NYAMBUYA.
Minister of Mines and Mining Development: AMOS MIDZI.
Minister of the Environment and Tourism: FRANCIS NHEMA.
Minister of Foreign Affairs: SIMBARASHE MUMBENGEGWI.
Minister of Finance: HERBERT MURERWA.
Minister of Economic Development: RUGARE GUMBO.
Minister of Higher and Tertiary Education: I. STANISLAUS GORERAZVO MUDENGE.
Minister of Education, Sports and Culture: AENEAS CHIGWEDERE.
Minister of Health and Child Welfare: DAVID PARIRENYATWA.
Minister of Science and Technology: OLIVIA MUCHENA.
Minister of Transport and Communications: CHRIS MUSHOHWE.
Minister of Women Affairs, Gender and Community Development: OPPAH MUCHINGURI.
Minister of Small and Medium Enterprises Development: (vacant).
Minister of Youth Development, Gender and Employment Creation: Brig. (retd) AMBROSE MUTINHIRI.
Minister of State for Water Resources and Infrastructural Development: MUNACHO MUTEZO.
Minister of State for Information and Publicity: TICHAONA JOKONYA.
Minister of State for National Security: DIDYMUS MUTASA.
Minister of State for Policy Implementation: WEBSTER SHAMU.
Minister of State for Indigenization and Empowerment: (vacant).
Minister without Portfolio: ELLIOT MANYIKA.

MINISTRIES

Office of the President: Munhumutapa Bldg, Samora Machel Ave, Private Bag 7700, Causeway, Harare; tel. (4) 707091.
Office of the Vice-Presidents: Munhumutapa Bldg, Samora Machel Ave, Private Bag 7700, Causeway, Harare; tel. (4) 707091.
Ministry of Agriculture and Rural Resettlement: Ngungunyana Bldg, Private Bag 7701, Causeway, Harare; tel. (4) 792223; fax (4) 734646.
Ministry of Defence: Defence House, Union Ave and Third St, Private Bag 7713, Causeway, Harare; tel. (4) 700155; fax (4) 727501.
Ministry of Economic Development: Harare; internet www.mofed.gov.zw.
Ministry of Education, Sports and Culture: Ambassador House, Union Ave, POB CY121, Causeway, Harare; tel. (4) 734051; fax (4) 707599.
Ministry of Energy and Power Development: Karigamombe Centre, Private Bag 7753, Causeway, Harare; tel. (4) 751720; fax (4) 734075.
Ministry of the Environment and Tourism: Kaguvi Bldg, 12th Floor, cnr 4th St and Central Ave, Private Bag 7753, Causeway, Harare; tel. (4) 701681; fax (4) 252559; e-mail metlib@zarnet.ac.zw; internet www.met.gov.zw.
Ministry of Finance: Blocks B, E and G, Composite Bldg, cnr Samora Machel Ave and Fourth St, Private Bag 7705, Causeway, Harare; tel. (4) 738603; fax (4) 792750; internet www.mofed.gov.zw.
Ministry of Foreign Affairs: Munhumutapa Bldg, Samora Machel Ave, POB 4240, Causeway, Harare; tel. (4) 727005; fax (4) 705161.
Ministry of Health and Child Welfare: Kaguvi Bldg, Fourth St, POB CY198, Causeway, Harare; tel. (4) 730011; fax (4) 729154.
Ministry of Higher Education and Technology: Government Composite Bldg, cnr Fourth St and Samora Machel Ave, Union Ave, POB UA275, Harare; tel. (4) 796441; fax (4) 728730; e-mail thesecretary@mhet.ac.zw; internet www.mhet.ac.zw.
Ministry of Home Affairs: Mukwati Bldg, Fourth St, Private Bag 7703, Causeway, Harare; tel. (4) 703299; fax (4) 707231.
Ministry of Indigenization and Empowerment: Harare.
Ministry of Industry and International Trade: Mukwati Bldg, Fourth St, Private Bag 7708, Causeway, Harare; tel. (4) 702731; fax (4) 729311.
Ministry of Information and Publicity: Linquenda House, Baker Ave, POB CY825, Causeway, Harare; tel. (4) 703894; fax (4) 707213.

ZIMBABWE

Ministry of Justice, Legal and Parliamentary Affairs: Corner House, cnr Samora Machel Ave and Leopold Takawira St, Private Bag 7751, Causeway, Harare; tel. (4) 774620; fax (4) 772999.
Ministry of Local Government, Public Works and National Housing: Mukwati Bldg, Fourth St, Private Bag 7755, Causeway, Harare; tel. (4) 7282019; fax (4) 708493.
Ministry of Mines and Mining Development: Harare.
Ministry of National Security: Chaminuka Bldg, POB 2278, Harare; tel. (4) 700501; fax (4) 732660.
Ministry of Policy Implementation: Harare.
Ministry of Public Service, Labour and Social Welfare: Compensation House, cnr Central Ave and Fourth St, Private Bag 7707, Causeway, Harare; tel. (4) 790871.
Ministry of Transport and Communications: Kaguvi Bldg, POB CY595, Causeway, Harare; tel. (4) 700991; fax (4) 708225.
Ministry of Water Resources, Infrastructural Development, and Small and Medium Enterprises: Makombe Complex, Private Bag 7701, Causeway, Harare; tel. (4) 706081.
Ministry of Youth Development, Gender and Employment Creation: ZANU—PF Bldg, Private Bag 7762, Causeway, Harare; tel. (4) 734691; fax (4) 732709.

PROVINCIAL GOVERNORS
(March 2006)

Bulawayo: CAIN MATHEMA.
Harare: DAVID KARIMANZIRA.
Manicaland: TINAYE CHIGUDU.
Mashonaland Central: EPHRAIM MASAWI.
Mashonaland East: RAY KAUKONDE.
Mashonaland West: NELSON SAMKANGE.
Masvingo: WILLARD CHIWEWE.
Matabeleland North: THOKOZILE MATHUTHU.
Matabeleland South: ANGELINA MASUKU.
Midlands: CEPHAS MSIPA.

President and Legislature

PRESIDENT

Election, 9–11 March 2002

Candidate	Votes	% of votes
Robert Gabriel Mugabe	1,685,212	56.2
Morgan Tsvangirai	1,258,401	42.0
Wilson Kumbala	31,368	1.0
Shakespeare Maya	11,906	0.4
Paul Siwela	11,871	0.4
Total	**2,998,758**	**100.0**

HOUSE OF ASSEMBLY

Speaker: JOHN NKOMO.
Election, 31 March 2005

	Votes	% of votes	Seats*
ZANU—PF	1,569,867	59.59	78
MDC	1,041,292	39.52	41
Independents	16,223	0.62	1
ZANU—Ndonga	6,608	0.25	—
Others	655	0.02	—
Total	**2,634,645**	**100.00**	**120**

*In addition to the 120 directly elective seats, 12 seats are held by nominees of the President, 10 by traditional Chiefs and eight by Provincial Governors.

SENATE

Speaker: EDNA MADZONGWE.
Election, 26 November 2005

	Votes	% of votes	Seats*
ZANU—PF	449,860	73.71	43
MDC	123,628	20.26	7
Others	36,807	6.03	—
Total	**610,295**	**100.00**	**50**

*In addition to the 50 directly elective seats, 6 seats are held by nominees of the President, and 10 by traditional Chiefs.

Election Commissions

Electoral Delimitation Commission (EDC): Harare; appointed by and responsible to the President; establishes constituency boundaries; Chair. GEORGE CHIWESHE.
Zimbabwe Electoral Commission (ZEC): Harare; f. 2005; the President appoints six commrs and also the Chairman in consultation with the Judicial Service Commission; superseded and replaced the Electoral Supervisory Commission (abolished Aug. 2005); responsible for voter registration and conducting elections; Chair. GEORGE CHIWESHE.

Political Organizations

Committee for a Democratic Society (CODESO): f. 1993; Karanga-supported grouping, based in Matabeleland; Leader SOUL NDLOVU.
Conservative Alliance of Zimbabwe (CAZ): POB 242, Harare; f. 1962; known as the Rhodesian Front until 1981, and subsequently as the Republican Front; supported by sections of the white community; Pres. GERALD SMITH; Chair. MIKE MORONEY.
Democratic Party: f. 1991 by a breakaway faction from ZUM; Nat. Chair. GILES MUTSEKWA; Pres. DAVIDSON GOMO.
Forum Party of Zimbabwe (FPZ): POB 74, Bulawayo; f. 1993; conservative; Pres. WASHINGTON SANSOLE.
Front for Popular Democracy: f. 1994; Chair. Prof. AUSTIN CHAKAWODZA.
General Conference of Patriots: Harare; f. 1998; opposes the Govt; aims to organize and direct dissent; Leader OBEY MUDZINGWA.
Independent Zimbabwe Group: f. 1983 by a breakaway faction from the fmr Republican Front; Leader BILL IRVINE.
Movement for Democratic Change (MDC): Harvest House, 6th Floor, cnr Angwa St and Nelson Mandela Ave, Harare; e-mail mdcinfo@mdczimbabwe.org; internet www.mdczimbabwe.org; f. 1999; allied to Zimbabwe Congress of Trade Unions; opposes the Govt; a 'pro-Senate' splinter faction emerged in Dec. 2005 led by Prof. Arthur Mutambara and Sec.-Gen. Welshman Ncube; Pres. MORGAN TSVANGIRAI; Sec.-Gen. TENDAI BITI.
National Democratic Union: f. 1979; conservative grouping with minority Zezuru support; Leader HENRY CHIHOTA.
National Progressive Alliance: f. 1991; Chair. CANCIWELL NZIRAMASANGA.
United National Federal Party (UNFP): Harare; f. 1978; conservative; seeks a federation of Mashonaland and Matabeleland; Leader Chief KAYISA NDIWENI.
United Parties (UP): f. 1994; Leader Bishop ABEL MUZOREWA.
Zimbabwe Active People's Unity Party: Bulawayo; f. 1989; Leader NEWMAN MATUTU NDELA.
Zimbabwe African National Union—Ndonga (ZANU—Ndonga): POB UA525, Union Ave, Harare; tel. and fax (4) 481180; f. 1977; breakaway faction from ZANU, also includes fmr mems of United African National Council; supports free market economy; Pres. (vacant); Sec.-Gen. EDWIN C. NGUWA.
Zimbabwe African National Union—Patriotic Front (ZANU—PF): cnr Rotten Row and Samora Machel Ave, POB 4530, Harare; tel. (4) 753329; fax (4) 774146; e-mail zanupf@africaonline.co.zw; internet www.zanupfpub.co.zw; f. 1989 by merger of PF—ZAPU and ZANU—PF; Pres. ROBERT GABRIEL MUGABE; Vice-Pres SIMON VENGAYI MUZENDA, JOSEPH W. MSIKA; Nat. Chair. JOHN LANDAU NKOMO.
Zimbabwe Congress Party: Harare; f. 1994; Pres. KENNETH MANO.
Zimbabwe Democratic Party: Harare; f. 1979; traditionalist; Leader JAMES CHIKEREMA.
Zimbabwe Federal Party (ZFPO): Stand 214, Nketa 6, P.O. Nkulumane, Bulawayo; f. 1994; aims to create national federation of five provinces; Leader RICHARD NCUBE.
Zimbabwe Integrated Programme: f. 1999; seeks economic reforms; Pres. Prof. HENEDI DZINOCHIKIWEYI.
Zimbabwe National Front: f. 1979; Leader PETER MANDAZA.
Zimbabwe Peoples' Democratic Party: f. 1989; Chair. ISABEL PASALK.
Zimbabwe Union of Democrats: Harare; f. 1998; aims to create an effective opposition in the national parliament; Pres. MARGARET DONGO.

ZIMBABWE

Zimbabwe Unity Movement (ZUM): f. 1989 by a breakaway faction from ZANU—PF; merged with United African National Council in 1994; Leader EDGAR TEKERE.

Diplomatic Representation

EMBASSIES IN ZIMBABWE

Angola: 26 Speke Ave, POB 3590, Harare; tel. (4) 770075; fax (4) 770077; Ambassador ALBERTO RIBEIRO.

Argentina: Intermarket Life Towers, 15th Floor, 77 Jason Moyo Ave, POB 2770, Harare; tel. (4) 730075; fax (4) 730076; Ambassador CARLOS M. FORADORI.

Australia: 29 Mazowe St, The Avenue, POB 4541, Harare; tel. (4) 253661; fax (4) 253679; e-mail zimbabwe.embassy@dfat.gov.au; internet www.dfat.gov.au/missions/countries/zw.html; Ambassador JON SHEPPARD.

Austria: 216 New Shell House, 30 Samora Machel Ave, POB 4120, Harare; tel. (4) 702921; Ambassador Dr PETER LEITENBAUER.

Bangladesh: 9 Birchenough Rd, POB 3040, Harare; tel. (4) 727004; Ambassador HARUN AHMED CHOWDHURY.

Belgium: Tanganyika House, 5th Floor, cnr 23 Third St and Nkrumah Ave, POB 2522, Harare; tel. (4) 700112; fax (4) 703960; e-mail harare@diplobel.org; internet www.diplomatie.be/harare; Ambassador BOUDEWIJN DEREYMAEKER.

Botswana: 22 Phillips Ave, Belgravia, POB 563, Harare; tel. (4) 729551; fax (4) 721360; Ambassador PELOKGALE SELOMA.

Brazil: Old Mutual Centre, 9th Floor, Jason Moyo Ave, POB 2530, Harare; tel. (4) 790740; fax (4) 790754; e-mail brasemb@ecoweb.co.zw; Ambassador GEORGE NEY DE SOUZA FERNANDES.

Bulgaria: 15 Maasdorp Ave, Alexandra Park, POB 1809, Harare; tel. (4) 730509; Ambassador CHRISTO TEPAVITCHAROV.

Canada: 45 Baines Ave, POB 1430, Harare; tel. (4) 252181; fax (4) 252186; e-mail hrare@dfait-maeci.gc.ca; internet www.harare.gc.ca; Ambassador ROXANA DUBE.

China, People's Republic: 30 Baines Ave, POB 4749, Harare; tel. and fax (4) 794155; e-mail chinaemb_zw@mfa.gov.cn; internet www.chinaembassy.org.zw; Ambassador ZHANG XIANYI.

Congo, Democratic Republic: 5 Pevensey Rd, Highlands, POB 2446, Harare; tel. (4) 481172; fax (4) 796421; Ambassador Dr KIKAYA BIN KARUB (acting).

Cuba: 5 Phillips Ave, Belgravia, POB 4139, Harare; tel. (4) 720256; Ambassador COSME TORRES.

Czech Republic: 4 Sandringham Dr., Alexandra Park, GPO 4474, Harare; tel. (4) 700636; fax (4) 720930; e-mail czechemb@ecoweb.co.zw; internet www.mzv.cz/harare; Ambassador JAROSLAV OLŠA, Jr.

Denmark: Intermarket Centre, cnr 59 Union and First St, POB 4711, Harare; tel. (4) 758185; fax (4) 758189; e-mail olemoe@um.dk; Ambassador OLE EMIL MOESBY.

Egypt: 7 Aberdeen Rd, Avondale, POB A433, Harare; tel. (4) 303445; fax 303115; Ambassador MUHAMMAD FARED MONEIB.

Ethiopia: 14 Lanark Rd, Belgravia, POB 2745, Harare; tel. (4) 701514; fax (4) 701516; e-mail embassy@ecoweb.co.zw; Ambassador DINA MUFTI.

France: 74–76 Samora Machel Ave, Harare; tel. (4) 703216; fax (4) 730078; internet www.dree.org/zimbabwe; Ambassador MICHEL RAIMBAUD.

Germany: 30 Ceres Rd, Avondale, Harare; tel. (4) 308655; fax (4) 303455; e-mail germemb@ecoweb.co.zw; Ambassador ALEXANDER MUHLEN.

Ghana: 11 Downie Ave, Belgravia, POB 4445, Harare; tel. (4) 700982; fax (4) 701014; e-mail ghcom25@africaonline.co.zw; Ambassador JOHN K. GBENAH.

Greece: 8 Deary Ave, Belgravia, POB 4809, Harare; tel. (4) 793208; fax (4) 703662; e-mail grembha@ecoweb.co.zw; Ambassador DIMITRI M. ALEXANDRAKIS.

Holy See: 5 St Kilda Rd, Mount Pleasant, POB MP191, Harare (Apostolic Nunciature); tel. (4) 744547; fax (4) 744412; e-mail nunzim@zol.co.zw; Apostolic Nuncio Most Rev. EDWARD JOSEPH ADAMS (Titular Archbishop of Scala).

Hungary: 20 Lanark Rd, Belgravia, POB 3594, Harare; tel. (4) 733528; fax (4) 730512; Ambassador TAMÁS GÁSPÁR GÁL.

India: 12 Natal Rd, Belgravia, POB 4620, Harare; tel. (4) 795955; fax (4) 722324; e-mail ihchre@mweb.co.zw; Ambassador AJIT KUMAR.

Indonesia: 3 Duthie Ave, Belgravia, POB 3594, Harare; tel. (4) 251799; fax (4) 796587; Ambassador DADANG SUKANDAR.

Iran: 8 Allan Wilson Ave, Avondale, POB A293, Harare; tel. (4) 726942; Ambassador HAMID MOAYER.

Israel: 54 Jason Moyo Ave, POB CY3191, Harare; tel. (4) 756808; fax (4) 756801; Ambassador ITZHAK GERBERG.

Italy: 7 Bartholomew Close, Greendale North, POB 1062, Harare; tel. (4) 498190; fax (4) 498199; e-mail segreteria@ambitalia.co.zw; Ambassador MARIO BOLOGNA.

Japan: Karigamombe Centre, 18th Floor, 53 Samora Machel Ave, POB 2710, Harare; tel. (4) 757861; fax (4) 757864; Ambassador TAKEO YOSHIKAWA.

Kenya: 95 Park Lane, POB 4069, Harare; tel. (4) 704820; fax (4) 723042; e-mail kenhicom@africaonline.co.zw; Ambassador Prof. MARIA NZOMO.

Korea, Democratic People's Republic: 102 Josiah Chinamano Ave, Greenwood, POB 4754, Harare; tel. (4) 724052; Ambassador RI MYONG CHOL.

Kuwait: 1 Bath Rd, Avondale, POB A485, Harare; Ambassador SAUD FAISAL AL-DAWESS.

Libya: 124 Harare St, POB 4310, Harare; tel. (4) 728381; Ambassador MAHMOUD YOUSEF AZZABI.

Malawi: 9–11 Duthie Rd, Alexandra Park, POB 321, Harare; tel. (4) 798485; fax (4) 799006; e-mail malahigh@africaonline.co.zw; High Commissioner BENSON TEMBO.

Malaysia: 40 Downie Ave, Avondale, POB 5570, Harare; tel. (4) 334413; fax (4) 334415; e-mail mwharare@africaonline.co.zw; Ambassador SHAHARUDDIN MOHAMED SOM.

Mozambique: 152 Herbert Chitepo Ave, cnr Leopold Takawira St, POB 4608, Harare; tel. (4) 790837; fax (4) 732898; Ambassador CORREIA FERNANDES SUMBANA.

Netherlands: 2 Arden Rd, Highlands, POB HG601, Harare; tel. (4) 776701; fax (4) 776700; e-mail nlgovhar@samara.co.zw; Ambassador HANS HEINSBROEK.

Nigeria: 36 Samora Machel Ave, POB 4742, Harare; tel. (4) 253900; e-mail nigerian@africaonline.co.zw; Ambassador ANTHONY U. OSULA.

Norway: 5 Lanark Rd, Belgravia, POB A510, Avondale, Harare; tel. (4) 252426; fax (4) 252430; e-mail emb.harare@mfa.no; internet www.norway.org.zw; Ambassador PER GULLIK STAVNUM.

Pakistan: 11 Van Praagh Ave, Milton Park, POB 3050, Harare; tel. (4) 720293; fax (4) 722446; Ambassador RIFFAT IQBAL.

Poland: 16 Cork Rd, Belgravia, POB 3932, Harare; tel. (4) 253442; fax (4) 253710; Ambassador JAN WIELINSKI.

Portugal: 12 Harvey Brown Ave, Milton Park, Harare; tel. (4) 706220; fax (4) 253637; e-mail embport@icon.co.zw; Ambassador JOÃO CARLOS VERSTEEG.

Romania: 105 Fourth St, POB 4797, Harare; tel. (4) 700853; fax (4) 725493; e-mail romemb@africaonline.co.zw; Chargé d'affaires LUMINITA FLORESCU.

Russia: 70 Fife Ave, POB 4250, Harare; tel. (4) 720359; fax (4) 700534; e-mail russemb@africaonline.co.zw; Ambassador OLEG SHERBAK.

Serbia and Montenegro: 1 Lanark Rd, Belgravia, POB 3420, Harare; tel. (4) 738668; fax (4) 738660; Ambassador LJUBISA KORAC.

South Africa: 7 Elcombe Rd, Belgravia, POB A1654, Harare; tel. (4) 251851; fax (4) 757908; e-mail sahcomm@ecoweb.co.zw; Ambassador JEREMIAH NDOU.

Spain: 16 Phillips Ave, Belgravia, POB 3300, Harare; tel. (4) 250740; fax (4) 795261; e-mail hararesp@earth.co.zw; Ambassador SANTIAGO MARTÍNEZ-CARO DE LA CONCHA-CASTAÑEDA.

Sudan: 4 Pascoe Ave, Harare; tel. (4) 725240; Ambassador MOHAMED ELHASSAN.

Sweden: Pegasus House, 52 Samora Machel Ave, POB 4110, Harare; tel. (4) 790651; fax (4) 754265; Ambassador STEN RYLANDER.

Switzerland: 9 Lanark Rd, POB 3440, Harare; tel. (4) 703997; fax (4) 794925; Ambassador MARCEL STUTZ.

Tunisia: Harare; tel. (4) 791570; fax (4) 727224; Ambassador HAMID ZAOUCHE.

United Kingdom: Corner House, cnr Samora Machel Ave and Leopold Takawira St, POB 4490, Harare; tel. (4) 772990; fax (4) 774605; e-mail consularharare@fco.gov.uk; internet www.britishembassy.gov.uk/zimbabwe; Ambassador Dr ANDREW POCOCK.

USA: 172 Herbert Chitepo Ave, POB 3340, Harare; tel. (4) 2505931; fax (4) 796488; internet usembassy.state.gov/zimbabwe; Ambassador CHRISTOPHER W. DELL.

Zambia: Zambia House, cnr Union and Julius Nyerere Aves, POB 4698, Harare; tel. (4) 773777; fax (4) 773782; Ambassador Prof. E. C. MUMBA.

Judicial System

The legal system is Roman-Dutch, based on the system which was in force in the Cape of Good Hope on 10 June 1891, as modified by subsequent legislation.

The Supreme Court has original jurisdiction in matters in which an infringement of Chapter III of the Constitution defining fundamental rights is alleged. In all other matters it has appellate jurisdiction only. It consists of the Chief Justice and eight Judges of Appeal. A normal bench consists of any five of these.

The High Court consists of the Chief Justice, the Judge President, and 11 other judges. Below the High Court are Regional Courts and Magistrates' Courts with both civil and criminal jurisdiction presided over by full-time professional magistrates.

The Customary Law and Local Courts Act, adopted in 1990, abolished the village and community courts and replaced them with customary law and local courts, presided over by chiefs and headmen; in the case of chiefs, jurisdiction to try customary law cases is limited to those where the monetary values concerned do not exceed Z.$1,000 and in the case of a headman's court Z.$500. Appeals from the Chiefs' Courts are heard in Magistrates' Courts and, ultimately, the Supreme Court. All magistrates now have jurisdiction to try cases determinable by customary law.

Chief Justice: GODFREY CHIDYAUSIKU.

Judges of Appeal: W. SANDURA, ANELE MATIKA, TADIUS KARWI, SUSAN MAVANGIRA, LAVENDER MAKONI.

Judge President: PADDINGTON GARWE.

Attorney-General: SOBUZA GULA-NDEBELE.

Religion

AFRICAN RELIGIONS

Many Africans follow traditional beliefs.

CHRISTIANITY

About 55% of the population are Christians.

Zimbabwe Council of Churches: 128 Mbuya Nehanda St, POB 3566, Harare; tel. (4) 772043; fax (4) 773650; f. 1964; Pres. Rt Rev. KHUMBULANI PETER NEMAPARE; Gen. Sec. DENSEN MAFIYANI; 24 mem. churches, nine assoc. mems.

The Anglican Communion

Anglicans are adherents of the Church of the Province of Central Africa, covering Botswana, Malawi, Zambia and Zimbabwe. The Church comprises 15 dioceses, including five in Zimbabwe. The Archbishop of the Province is the Bishop of the Upper Shire of Malawi. The Church had an estimated 320,000 members at mid-2000.

Bishop of Central Zimbabwe: Rt Rev. ISHMAEL MUKUWANDA, POB 25, Gweru; tel. (54) 21030; fax (54) 21097; e-mail diocent@telconet.co.zw.

Bishop of Harare: Rt Rev. ROBERT CHRISTOPHER NDLOVU, Bishopsmount Close, POB UA7, Harare; tel. (4) 702253; fax (4) 700419.

Bishop of Manicaland: Rt Rev. Dr SEBASTIAN BAKARE, 115 Herbert Chitepo St, Mutare; tel. (20) 64194; fax (20) 63076; e-mail diomani@syscom.co.zw.

Bishop of Matabeleland: Rt Rev. WILSON SITSHEBO, POB 2422, Bulawayo; tel. (9) 61370; fax (9) 68353; e-mail angdiomat@telconet.co.zw.

The Roman Catholic Church

For ecclesiastical purposes, Zimbabwe comprises two archdioceses and six dioceses. At 31 December 2003 there were some 1,286,400 adherents, equivalent to an estimated 8.8% of the total population.

Zimbabwe Catholic Bishops' Conference (ZCBC)
ZCBC Secretariat, Africa Synod House, 29–31 Selous Ave, POB CY738 Causeway, Harare; tel. (4) 705368; fax (4) 704001; internet www.zcbc.co.zw; f. 1969; Pres. Rt Rev. MICHAEL DIXON BHASERA (Bishop of Masvingo).

Archbishop of Bulawayo: Most Rev. PIUS ALICK NCUBE, cnr Lobengula St and 9th Ave, POB 837, Bulawayo; tel. (9) 63590; fax (9) 60359; e-mail archdbyo@mweb.co.zw.

Archbishop of Harare: Most Rev. ROBERT C. NDLOVU, Archbishop's House, 66 Fifth St, POB CY330, Causeway, Harare; tel. (4) 727386; fax (4) 721598; e-mail hrearch@zol.co.zw.

Other Christian Churches

At mid-2000 there were an estimated 4.8m. adherents professing other forms of Christianity.

Dutch Reformed Church (Nederduitse Gereformeerde Kerk): 35 Samora Machel Ave, POB 503, Harare; tel. (4) 774738; fax (4) 774739; e-mail pvanvuuren@mango.zw; f. 1895; 16 parishes; Chair. Rev. P. F. J. VAN VUUREN; Sec. Rev. J. DE BRUYN; 1,500 mems.

Evangelical Lutheran Church: POB 2175, Bulawayo; tel. (9) 254991; e-mail elczhead@mweb.co.zw; f. 1903; Sec. Rt Rev. L. M. DUBE; 57,000 mems.

Greek Orthodox Church: POB 2832, Harare; tel. and fax (4) 744991; e-mail zimbabwe@greekorthodox-alexandria.org; internet www.greekorthodox-zimbabwe; Archbishop GEORGE.

Methodist Church in Zimbabwe: POB CY71, Causeway, Harare; tel. (4) 250523; fax (4) 723709; e-mail methodistcon@zol.co.zw; f. 1891; Presiding Bishop Rev. MARGARET M. JAMES; Sec. of Conference Rev. SIMON U. MADHIBA; 112,529 mems.

United Congregational Church of Southern Africa: 40 Jason Moyo St, POB 2451, Bulawayo; tel. (9) 63686; Chair. Rev. D. SIKHOSANA.

United Methodist Church: POB 3408, Harare; tel. (4) 704127; f. 1890; Bishop of Zimbabwe ABEL TENDEKAYI MUZOREWA; 45,000 mems.

Among other denominations active in Zimbabwe are the African Methodist Church, the African Methodist Episcopal Church, the African Reformed Church, the Christian Marching Church, the Church of Christ in Zimbabwe, the Independent African Church, the Presbyterian Church (and the City Presbyterian Church), the United Church of Christ, the Zimbabwe Assemblies of God and the Ziwezano Church.

JUDAISM

The Jewish community numbered 897 members at 31 December 1997.

Zimbabwe Jewish Board of Deputies: POB 1954, Harare; tel. (4) 702507; fax (4) 702506; Pres. P. STERNBERG; Sec. E. ALHADEFF.

BAHÁ'Í FAITH

National Spiritual Assembly: POB GD380, Greendale, Harare; tel. (4) 495945; fax (4) 744611; e-mail nsazim@mweb.co.zw; internet www.bahai.co.zw; Nat. Sec. DEREK SITHOLE; f. 1970; mems resident in 57 clusters.

The Press

DAILIES

The Chronicle: POB 585, Bulawayo; tel. (9) 888871; fax (9) 888884; e-mail editor@chronicle.co.zw; internet www.chronicle.co.zw; f. 1894; owned by Zimpapers; circulates throughout south-west Zimbabwe; English; Editor STEVEN NDLOVU; circ. 44,000.

The Daily News: 18 Sam Nujoma St and cnr Speke Ave, Harare; tel. (4) 753027; fax (4) 753024; e-mail editor@daily-news.co.za; internet www.daily-news.co.za; independent, owned by Associated Newspapers of Zimbabwe; publ. suspended Sept. 2003; Editor NQOBILE NYATHI; CEO SAM SIPEPA NKOMO; Chair. STRIVE MASIYIWA.

The Herald: POB 396, Harare; tel. (4) 795771; fax (4) 700305; internet www.herald.co.zw; f. 1891; owned by Zimpapers; English; Editor PIKIRAYI DEKETEKE; circ. 122,077.

WEEKLIES

Business Herald: Harare; Editor ANDREW RUSINGA.

Financial Gazette: Coal House, 5th Floor, cnr Nelson Mandela Ave and Leopold Takawira St, Harare; tel. (4) 781571; fax (4) 781578; e-mail schamunorwa@fingaz.co.zw; internet www.fingaz.co.zw; f. 1969; independent; Editor-in-Chief SUNSLEEY CHAMUNORWA; Gen. Man. JACOB CHISESE; circ. 40,000.

The Gweru Times: 71 7th St, POB 66, Gweru; tel. (54) 23285; fax (54) 21614; f. 1897; English; Editor CLIFFORD MUNYATI; circ. 5,000.

Kwayedza: POB 396, Harare; tel. (4) 795771; fax (4) 791311; owned by Zimpapers; Shona; Editor GERVAS M. CHITEWE; circ. 20,000.

Manica Post: POB 960, Mutare; tel. (20) 61212; fax (20) 61149; f. 1893; owned by Zimpapers; Editor MAKUWERERE BWITITI; circ. 20,000.

Masvingo Mirror: POB 1214, Masvingo; tel. (39) 64372; fax (39) 64484; independent; Editor NORNA EDWARDS.

Midlands Observer: POB 533, Kwekwe; tel. (55) 22248; fax (55) 23985; e-mail nelson_mashiri@yahoo.com; f. 1953; weekly; English; Editor R. JARINJARI; circ. 20,000.

North Midlands Gazette: POB 222, Kadoma; tel. and fax (68) 3731; e-mail kidia@pci.co.zw; e-mail ckidia@web.co.zw; f. 1912; Editor C. B. KIDIA.

ZIMBABWE

The Standard: 1st Block, 3rd Floor, Ernst and Young Bldg, 1 Kwame Nkrumah Ave, POB 661730, Kopje, Harare; tel. 1750401; fax 1773854; e-mail chakaodzab@standard.mweb.co.zw; internet www.thestandard.co.zw; f. 1997; independent; Sun.; Exec. Chair and CEO TREVOR NCUBE.

Sunday Gazette: POB 66070, Kopje, Harare; tel. (4) 738722; Editor FRANCIS MDLONGWA.

Sunday Mail: POB 396, Harare; tel. (4) 795771; fax (4) 700305; internet www.sundaymail.co.zw; f. 1935; owned by Zimpapers; English; Chair. THOMAS SITHOLE; Editor WILLIAM CHIKOTO; circ. 159,075.

Sunday News: POB 585, Bulawayo; tel. (9) 540071; fax (9) 540084; f. 1930; owned by Zimpapers; English; Editor BREZHNEV MALABA; circ. 50,035.

The Zimbabwean: POB 248, Hythe, SO45 4WX, United Kingdom; e-mail feedback@thezimbabwean.co.uk; internet www.thezimbabwean.co.uk; f. 2005; independent; publ. in the United Kingdom and South Africa; focus on news in Zimbabwe and life in exile; Publr and Editor WILF MBANGA.

Zimbabwe Independent: Zimind Publishers (Private) Ltd, Suites 23/24, 1 Union Ave, POB BE1165, Belvedere, Harare; e-mail trevorn@mg.co.za; internet www.theindependent.co.zw; f. 1996; Editor VINCENT KAHIYA; Publr TREVOR NCUBE; circ. 30,500.

Zimbabwean Government Gazette: POB 8062, Causeway, Harare; official notices; Editor L. TAKAWIRA.

PERIODICALS

Africa Calls Worldwide: POB BW1500, Harare; tel. (4) 728256; fax (4) 792932; f. 1960; 6 a year; travel; Man. Editor DONETTE KRUGER.

Central African Journal of Medicine: POB A195, Avondale, Harare; tel. (4) 791630; fax (4) 791995; e-mail cajm@pci.co.zw; f. 1955; monthly; Editor-in-Chief Prof. G. I. MUGUTI.

Chamber of Mines Journal: POB 1683, Harare; tel. (4) 736835; fax (4) 749803; journal of the Chamber of Mines of Zimbabwe; monthly; Editor M. ZHUWAKINYU.

Chaminuka News: POB 251, Marondera; f. 1988; fortnightly; English and Chishona; Editor M. MUGABE; circ. 10,000.

City Observer: POB 990, Harare; tel. (4) 706536; fax (4) 708544; monthly.

Commerce: POB 1683, Harare; tel. (4) 736835; fax (4) 749803; journal of the Zimbabwe Nat. Chambers of Commerce; monthly; Editor I. MILLS; circ. 1,500.

Computer and Telecom News: POB 1683, Harare; tel. (4) 736835; fax (4) 749803; monthly; Editor R. STEWART.

CZI Industrial Review: POB 1683, Harare; tel. (4) 736835; fax (4) 749803; journal of the Confed. of Zimbabwe Industries; monthly; Editor I. MILLS.

Economic Review: c/o Zimbabwe Financial Holdings, POB 3198, Harare; tel. (4) 751168; fax (4) 757497; 4 a year; circ. 3,000.

Executive: Harare; tel. (4) 755084; fax (4) 752162; Editor MICHAEL J. HAMILTON.

Hotel and Catering Gazette: POB 2677, Kopje, Harare; tel. (4) 738722; fax (4) 707130; monthly; Editor PAULA CHARLES; circ. 2,000.

Indonsakusa: Hwange; f. 1988; monthly; English and Sindebele; Editor D. NTABENI; circ. 10,000.

Jassa: University of Zimbabwe, POB MP203, Mount Pleasant, Harare; tel. (4) 303211; fax (4) 333407; e-mail uzpub@admin.uz.ac.zw; internet www.uz.ac.zw/publications; applied science journal of the Univ. of Zimbabwe; 2 a year; Editor-in-Chief Prof. C. F. B. NHACHI.

Journal of Social Development in Africa: School of Social Work, Bag 66022, Kopje, Harare; 2 a year; Editor CAROLE PEARCE.

Just for Me: POB 66070, Kopje, Harare; tel. (4) 704715; f. 1990; family and women's interest; Editor BEVERLEY TILLEY.

Karoi News: POB 441, Karoi; tel. 6216; fortnightly.

Look and Listen: POB UA589, Harare; tel. (4) 752144; fax (4) 752062; e-mail munn@samara.co.zw; f. 1965; fortnightly; radio and TV programmes, cookery, entertainment and reviews; Editor ALASDAIR J. MUNN; circ. 23,000.

Mahogany: POB UA589, Harare; tel. (4) 752063; fax (4) 752062; e-mail munn@samara.co.zw; f. 1980; 6 a year; English; women's interest; Editor TENDAI DONDO; circ. 240,000.

Makoni Clarion: POB 17, Rusape; monthly.

Masiye Pambili (Let Us Go Forward): POB 591, Bulawayo; tel. (9) 75011; fax (9) 69701; f. 1964; 2 a year; English; Editor M. N. NDLOVU; circ. 21,000.

Moto: POB 890, Gweru; tel. (54) 24886; fax (54) 28194; e-mail moto@telco.co.zw; f. 1959; Roman Catholic; Editor SYDNEY SHOKO; circ. 22,000.

Directory

Mukai-Vukani Jesuit Journal for Zimbabwe: 1 Churchill Ave, Alexandra Park, POB ST194, Southerton, Harare; tel. (4) 744571; fax (4) 744284; e-mail owermter@zol.co.zw; internet www.jescom.co.zw; 6 a year; Catholic; Editor Fr OSKAR WERMTER; circ. 1,500.

Nehanda Guardian: Hwange; f. 1988; monthly; English and Chishona; Editor K. MWANAKA; circ. 10,000.

Nhau Dzekumakomo: POB 910, Mutare; f. 1984; publ. by Mutare City Council; monthly.

On Guard: National Social Security Authority, POB 1387, Causeway, Harare; tel. (4) 728931; fax (4) 796320; Editor P. TAGARA.

The Outpost: POB HG106, Highlands; tel. (4) 724571; fax (4) 703631; e-mail theoutpostmag@yahoo.com; f. 1911; monthly; English; Editor ELVIS CHIPUKA; circ. 26,000.

Quarterly Guide to the Economy: First Merchant Bank of Zimbabwe, FMB House, 67 Samora Machel Ave, POB 2786, Harare; tel. (4) 703071; fax (4) 738810; quarterly.

Railroader: POB 596, Bulawayo; tel. (9) 363526; fax (9) 363543; f. 1952; monthly; Editor M. GUMEDE; circ. 10,000.

The Record: POB 179, Harare; tel. (4) 708911; journal of the Public Service Asscn; 6 a year; Editor GAMALIEL RUNGANI; circ. 30,000.

Southern African Political and Economic Monthly: POB MP111, Mt Pleasant, Harare; tel. (4) 252962; fax (4) 252964; monthly; incorporating *Southern African Economist*; Editor-in-Chief KHABELE MATLOSA; circ. 16,000.

The Star: POB 138, Chinhoyi; tel. (67) 21656; f. 1989; weekly; English.

Teacher in Zimbabwe: POB 350, Harare; tel. (4) 497548; fax (4) 497554; f. 1981; monthly; circ. 60,000.

Tobacco News: POB 1683, Harare; tel. (4) 736836; fax (4) 749803; monthly; Editor D. MILLER; circ. 2,000.

Transactions of the Zimbabwe Scientific Association: POB CY124, Causeway, Harare; f. 1903; journal of the Zimbabwe Scientific Asscn.

Vanguard: POB 66102, Kopje; tel. 751193; every 2 months.

The Worker: POB 8323, Causeway, Harare; tel. 700466.

World Vision News: POB 2420, Harare; tel. 703794; quarterly.

Zambezia: University of Zimbabwe, POB MP203, Mount Pleasant, Harare; tel. (4) 303211; fax (4) 333407; e-mail uzpub@admin.uz.ac.zw; internet www.uz.ac.zw/publications; journal of the Univ. of Zimbabwe; 2 a year; humanities and general interest; Editor Dr Z. MGUNI-GAMBAHAYA.

Zimbabwe Agricultural Journal: POB CY594, Causeway, Harare; tel. (4) 704531; fax (4) 728317; f. 1903; 6 a year; Editor R. J. FENNER; circ. 2,000.

Zimbabwe Defence Forces Magazine: POB 7720, Harare; tel. (4) 722481; f. 1982; 6 a year; circ. 5,000.

Zimbabwe Journal of Educational Research: HRRC, Faculty of Education, University of Zimbabwe, POB MP167, Mount Pleasant, Harare; 3 a year; Editor-in-Chief Prof. F. ZINDI.

Zimbabwe News: POB CY3206, Causeway, Harare; tel. (4) 790148; fax (4) 790483; monthly.

Zimbabwe Science News: POB CY124, Causeway, Harare; e-mail husseiny@ecoweb.co.zw; f. 1967; quarterly.

Zimbabwe Veterinary Journal: POB CY168, Causeway, Harare; f. 1970; journal of the Zimbabwe Veterinary Asscn; 2 a year; Editor-in-Chief S. MUKARATIRWA.

NEWS AGENCIES

New Ziana: POB CY511, Causeway, Harare; tel. (4) 730151; fax (4) 794336; f. 1981; owned and controlled by Zimbabwe Mass Media Trust; fmrly Zimbabwe Inter-Africa News Agency.

Foreign Bureaux

Agence France-Presse (AFP): Robinson House, Union Ave, POB 1166, Harare; tel. (4) 758017; fax (4) 753291; e-mail afphre@africaonline.co.zw; Rep. FRANÇOIS-BERNARD CASTÉRAN.

ANGOP (Angola): Mass Media House, 3rd Floor, 19 Selous Ave, POB 6354, Harare; tel. (4) 736849.

Agenzia Nazionale Stampa Associata (ANSA) (Italy): Harare; tel. (4) 723881; Rep. IAN MILLS.

Associated Press (AP) (USA): POB 785, Harare; tel. (4) 706622; fax (4) 703994; Rep. JOHN EDLIN.

Deutsche Presse-Agentur (dpa) (Germany): Harare; tel. (4) 755259; fax 755240; Correspondent JAN RAATH.

Informatsionnoye Telegrafnoye Agentstvo Rossii—Telegrafnoye Agentstvo Suverennykh Stran (ITAR—TASS) (Russia): Mass Media House, 19 Selous Ave, POB 4012, Harare; tel. (4) 790521; Correspondent YURII PITCHUGIN.

ZIMBABWE *Directory*

Inter Press Service (IPS) (Italy): 127 Union Ave, POB 6050, Harare; tel. (4) 790104; fax (4) 728415; e-mail ipshre@harare.iafrica.com; Rep. KENNETH BLACKMAN.

News Agency of Nigeria (NAN): Harare; tel. (4) 703041.

Pan-African News Agency (PANA) (Senegal): 19 Selous Ave, POB 8364, Harare; tel. (4) 730971; Bureau Chief PETER MWAURA.

Prensa Latina (Cuba): Mass Media House, 3rd Floor, 19 Selous Ave, Harare; tel. (4) 731993; Correspondent HUGO RIUS.

Press Trust of India (PTI): Mass Media House, 3rd Floor, 19 Selous Ave, Harare; tel. (4) 795006; Rep. N. V. R. SWAMI.

Reuters (United Kingdom): 901 Tanganyika House, Union Ave, POB 2987 Harare; tel. (4) 724299; Bureau Chief DAVID BLOOM.

Rossiiskoye Informatsionnoye Agentstvo—Novosti (RIA—Novosti) (Russia): 503 Robinson House, cnr Union Ave and Angwa St, POB 3908, Harare; tel. (4) 707232; fax (4) 707233; Correspondent A. TIMONOVICH.

United Press International (UPI) (USA): Harare; tel. (4) 25265; Rep. IAN MILLS.

Xinhua (New China) News Agency (People's Republic of China): 4 Earls Rd, Alexander Park, POB 4746, Harare; tel. and fax (4) 731467; Chief Correspondent LU JIANXIN.

Publishers

Academic Books (Pvt) Ltd: POB 567, Harare; tel. (4) 755408; fax (4) 781913; educational; Editorial Dir IRENE STAUNTON.

Amalgamated Publications (Pvt) Ltd: POB 1683, Harare; tel. (4) 736835; fax (4) 749803; f. 1949; trade journals.

Anvil Press: POB 4209, Harare; tel. (4) 751202; fax (4) 739681; f. 1988; general; Man. Dir PAUL BRICKHILL.

The Argosy Press: POB 2677, Harare; tel. (4) 755084; magazine publrs; Gen. Man. A. W. HARVEY.

Baobab Books (Pvt) Ltd: POB 567, Harare; tel. (4) 665187; fax (4) 665155; e-mail academic@africaonline.co.zw; general, literature, children's.

The Bulletin: POB 1595, Bulawayo; tel. (9) 78831; fax (9) 78835; fmrly Directory Publishers Ltd; educational; CEO BRUCE BEALE.

College Press Publishers (Pvt) Ltd: 15 Douglas Rd, POB 3041, Workington, Harare; tel. (4) 754145; fax (4) 754256; e-mail beniasm@collegepress.co.zw; f. 1968; educational and general; Man. Dir B. B. MUGABE.

Graham Publishing Co (Pvt) Ltd: POB 2931, Harare; tel. (4) 752437; fax (4) 752439; f. 1967; general; Dir GORDON M. GRAHAM.

Harare Publishing House: Chiremba Rd, Hatfield, Harare; tel. (4) 570342; f. 1982; Dir Dr T. M. SAMKANGE.

HarperCollins Publishers Zimbabwe (Pvt) Ltd: Union Ave, POB UA201, Harare; tel. (4) 721413; fax (4) 732436; Man. S. D. MCMILLAN.

Longman Zimbabwe (Pvt) Ltd: POB ST125, Southerton, Harare; tel. (4) 62711; fax (4) 62716; f. 1964; general and educational; Man. Dir N. L. DLODLO.

Mambo Press: Senga Rd, POB 779, Gweru; tel. (54) 24017; fax (54) 21991; f. 1958; religious, educational and fiction in English and African languages.

Modus Publications (Pvt) Ltd: Modus House, 27–29 Charter Rd, POB 66070, Kopje, Harare; tel. (4) 738722; Man. Dir ELIAS RUSIKE.

Munn Publishing (Pvt) Ltd: POB UA460, Union Ave, Harare; tel. (4) 481048; fax (4) 7481081; Man. Dir I. D. MUNN.

Standard Publications (Pvt) Ltd: POB 3745, Harare; Dir G. F. BOOT.

Southern African Printing and Publishing House (SAPPHO): 109 Coventry Rd, Workington, POB MP1005, Mount Pleasant, Harare; tel. (4) 621681; fax (4) 666061; internet www.zimmirror.co.zw; Editor-in-Chief Dr IBBO MANDAZA.

University of Zimbabwe Publications: University of Zimbabwe, POB MP203, Mount Pleasant, Harare; tel. (4) 303211; fax (4) 333407; e-mail uzpub@admin.uz.ac.zw; internet www.uz.ac.zw/publications; f. 1969; Dir MUNANI SAM MTETWA.

Zimbabwe Newspapers (1980) Ltd (Zimpapers): POB 55, Harare; tel. (4) 704088; fax (4) 702400; e-mail theherald@zimpapers.co.zw; internet www.herald.co.zw; f. 1981; state-owned; controls largest newspaper group; Chair. HERBERT NKALA; CEO JUSTIN MUTASA.

ZPH Publishers (Pvt) Ltd: 183 Arcturus Rd, Kamfinsa, GD510, Greendale, Harare; tel. (4) 497548; fax (4) 497554; f. 1982 as Zimbabwe Publishing House Ltd; Man. Dir IRENE NDAIZIENYI NYAMAKURA.

www.europaworld.com

Broadcasting and Communications

TELECOMMUNICATIONS

Econet Wireless Zimbabwe: Econet Park, No.2 Old Mutare Rd, POB BE1298, Belvedere, Harare; tel. (4) 486121; fax (4) 486120; e-mail info@econet.co.zw; internet www.econet.co.zw; f. 1998; mobile cellular telecommunications operator; Chair. TAWANDA NYAMBIRAI; CEO DOUGLAS MBOWENI.

Net.One Ltd: POB CY579, Causeway, Harare; tel. (4) 707138; e-mail marketing@netone.co.zw; internet www.netone.co.zw; f. 1998; state-owned; mobile cellular telecommunications operator; Chair. CALLISTUS NDLOVU; CEO REWARD KANGAI.

Posts and Telecommunications Corpn (PTC): POB CY331, Causeway, Harare; tel. (4) 728811; fax (4) 731980; Chair. Dr M. MHLOYI; CEO BRIAN MUTANDIRO.

Telecel Zimbabwe: 148 Seke Rd, Graniteside, POB CY232, Causeway, Harare; tel. (4) 748321; fax (4) 748328; e-mail info@telecelzim.co.zw; internet www.telecel.co.zw; f. 1998; 60% owned by Telecel International and 40% owned by Empowerment Corpn; mobile cellular telecommunications operator; Chair. JAMES MAKAMBA; Man. Dir JOHN SWAIM.

TelOne: Runhare House, 107 Union Ave, POBCY331, Causeway, Harare; tel. (4) 798111; e-mail webmaster@telone.co.zw; internet www.telone.co.zw; state-owned; sole fixed-line telecommunications operator.

BROADCASTING

There are four state-owned radio stations (National FM, Power FM, Radio Zimbabwe and Spot FM) and one television station. Radio Voice of the People was established as an alternative to state broadcasting. An independent radio station, SW Radio Africa, broadcasts to Zimbabwe from London, UK.

Radio

Voice of the People (VOP): POB 5750, Harare; tel. (4) 707123; e-mail voxpopzim@yahoo.co.uk; internet www.vopradio.co.zw; f. 2000 by fmr ZBC staff; broadcasts one hour per day; Chair. DAVID MASUNDA; Exec. Dir JOHN MASUKU.

Zimbabwe Broadcasting Corpn: Broadcasting Center, Pockets Hill, POB HG444, Highlands, Harare; tel. (4) 498610; fax (4) 498613; e-mail zbc@zbc.co.zw; internet www.zbc.co.zw; f. 1957; programmes in English, Shona, Ndebele and 14 minority languages, incl. Chichewa, Venda and Xhosa; broadcasts a general service (mainly in English), vernacular languages service, light entertainment, and educational programmes; Editor-in-Chief CHRISTINA TARUVINGA.

Television

Zimbabwe Broadcasting Corpn: (see Radio).

The main broadcasting centre is in Harare, with a second studio in Bulawayo; broadcasts on two commercial channels (one of which, Joy TV, serves the Harare area only) for about 95 hours per week.

Finance

(cap. = capital; res = reserves; dep. = deposits; m. = million; brs = branches; amounts in Zimbabwe dollars)

BANKING

Central Bank

Reserve Bank of Zimbabwe: 80 Samora Machel Ave, POB 1283, Harare; tel. (4) 703000; fax (4) 706450; e-mail lchitapi@rbz.co.zw; internet www.rbz.co.zw; f. 1964; bank of issue; cap. and res 8m., dep. 296,439m. (Dec. 2001); Gov. Dr GIDEON GONO.

Commercial Banks

Barclays Bank of Zimbabwe Ltd: Barclays House, cnr First St and Jason Moyo Ave, POB 1279, Harare; tel. (4) 758281; fax (4) 752913; internet www.africa.barclays.com/zimbabwe.htm; f. 1912; commercial and merchant banking; cap. and res 1,268m., total assets 117,546m. (Dec. 2002); Chair. Dr ROBBIE MATONGO MUPAWOSE; CEO CHARITY JINYA; 44 brs.

Jewel Bank: Union House, 60 Union Ave, POB 3313, Harare; tel. (4) 758081; fax (4) 758085; e-mail cbzinfo@africaonline.co.zw; state-owned; cap. and res 2,551m., total assets 36,057m. (Dec. 2001); f. 1980; fmrly Commercial Bank of Zimbabwe; present name adopted 2004; Chair. RICHARD V. WILDE; 9 brs.

Kingdom Bank Ltd: Mukuvisi Office Park, Transtobac Rd, Msasa, Private Bag 2007, Harare; internet www.kingsec.co.zw; f. 2000; Man. Dir MARK WOOD.

ZIMBABWE — Directory

Stanbic Bank Zimbabwe Ltd: Stanbic Centre, 1st Floor, 59 Samora Machel Ave, POB 300, Harare; tel. (4) 759480; fax (4) 751324; e-mail zimbabweinfo@stanbic.com; f. 1990; cap. and res 1,164.7m., total assets 32,624.6m. (Dec. 2002); Chair. NICHOLAS NYANDORO; Man. Dir PINDIE NYANDORO; 14 brs.

Standard Chartered Bank Zimbabwe Ltd: John Boyne House, cnr Inez Terrace and Speke Ave, POB 373, Harare; tel. (4) 752852; fax (4) 758076; internet www.standardchartered.com/zw; f. 1983; cap. and res 3,422.7m., total assets 558,124m. (2003); Chair. H. P. MKUSHI; CEO WASHINGTON MATSAIRA; 28 brs.

Trade and Investment Bank Ltd: Cabs Centre, 10th Floor, 74 Jason Moyo Ave, POB CY1064, Causeway, Harare; tel. (4) 703791; fax (4) 705491; e-mail tib@tibl.co.zw; f. 1997; cap. and res 32m., total assets 421m. (Dec. 1997); Chair. Dr BERNARD THOMAS CHIDZERO; CEO Dr KOMBO JAMES MOYANA.

Zimbabwe Banking Corporation Ltd (Zimbank): Zimbank House, Speke Ave and First St, POB 3198, Harare; tel. (4) 757471; fax (4) 757497; internet www.finhold.co.zw; f. 1951; state-owned; cap. 100m., res 1,292m., dep. 15,305m. (Sept. 2001); Group CEO ELISHA N. MUSHAYAKARARA; 48 brs.

Development Banks

African Export-Import Bank (Afreximbank): Eastgate Bldg, 3rd Floor, Gold Bridge (North Wing), Second St, POB 1600 Causeway, Harare; tel. (4) 729751; fax (4) 729756; e-mail gmadhlawo@africaonline.co.zw; internet www.afreximbank.com.

Infrastructure Development Bank of Zimbabwe (IDBZ): 99 Rotten Row, Harare; tel. (4) 774226; fax (4) 774225; e-mail enquiries@zdb.co.zw; internet www.zdb.co.zw; f. 2005.

Zimbabwe Development Bank (ZDB): ZDB House, 99 Rotten Row, POB 1720, Harare; tel. (4) 774226; fax (4) 774225; e-mail info@zdb.co.zw; internet www.zdb.co.zw; f. 1985; 33.3% state-owned; cap. and res 355m., total assets 2,317m. (Dec. 2001); Chair. Dr T. MASAYA; Man. Dir CORNELIUS MARADZA; 3 brs.

Merchant Banks

African Banking Corporation of Zimbabwe Ltd: ABC House, 1 Endeavour Crescent, Mount Pleasant Business Park, Mount Pleasant, POB 2786, Harare; tel. (4) 369260; fax (4) 369939; e-mail abcmail@africanbankingcorp.com; internet www.africanbankingcorp.com; f. 1956; subsidiary of ABC Holdings Ltd; fmrly First Merchant Bank of Zimbabwe Ltd; cap. and res 36.8m., total assets 475.6m. (Dec. 2001); Chair. O. M. CHIDAWU; Man. Dir F. M. DZANYA.

Merchant Bank of Central Africa Ltd: Old Mutual Centre, 14th Floor, cnr Third St and Jason Moyo Ave, POB 3200, Harare; tel. (4) 701636; fax (4) 708005; internet www.mbca.co.zw; f. 1956; cap. 62.0m., res 230.1m., dep. 3,156.7m. (Dec. 2002); Chair. E. D. CHIURA; Man. Dir DAVID T. HATENDI.

NMB Bank Ltd: Unity Court, 1st Floor, cnr Union Ave and First St, POB 2564, Harare; tel. (4) 759651; fax (4) 759648; e-mail enquiries@nmbz.co.zw; internet www.nmbz.com; f. 1992; fmrly Nat. Merchant Bank of Zimbabwe; cap. and res 2,870.5m., total assets 30,742.8m. (Dec. 2001); Chair. P. T. ZHANDA; CEO Dr JULIUS T. MAKONI; 1 br.

Standard Chartered Merchant Bank Zimbabwe Ltd: Standard Chartered Bank Bldg, cnr Second St and Nelson Mandela Ave, POB 60, Harare; tel. (4) 708585; fax (4) 725667; f. 1971; cap. and res 78m., dep. 83m. (Dec. 1998); Chair. BARRY HAMILTON; Man. Dir EBBY ESSOKA.

Discount Houses

African Banking Corporation Securities Ltd: 69 Samora Machel Ave, POB 3321, Harare; tel. (4) 752756; fax (4) 790641; cap. and res 68m. (Dec. 1999); fmrly Bard Discount House Ltd; Chair. N. KUDENGA; Man. Dir D. DUBE.

The Discount Co of Zimbabwe (DCZ): 70 Park Lane, POB 3424, Harare; tel. (4) 705414; fax (4) 731670; cap. and res 8.9m., total assets 377.4m. (Feb. 1995); Chair. S. J. CHIHAMBAKWE.

Intermarket Discount House: Unity Court, 5th Floor, Union Ave, POB 3290, Harare.

National Discount House Ltd: MIPF House, 5th Floor, Central Ave, Harare; tel. (4) 700771; fax (4) 792927; internet www.ndh.co.zw; cap. and res 168.4m., total assets 2,365.2m. (Dec. 2000); Chair. EDWIN MANIKAI; Man. Dir LAWRENCE TAMAYI.

Banking Organizations

Bankers' Association of Zimbabwe (BAZ): Kuwana House, 4th Floor, Union Ave and First St, POB UA550, Harare; tel. (4) 728646; Pres. ELISHA MUSHAYAKARA; Dir FRANK READ.

Institute of Bankers of Zimbabwe: Union Ave, POB UA521, Harare; tel. (4) 752474; fax (4) 750281; e-mail info@iobz.co.zw; internet www.iobz.co.zw; f. 1973; Chair. S. BIYAM; Pres. M. L. WOOD; Dir I. E. H. HELBY; 7,000 mems.

STOCK EXCHANGE

Zimbabwe Stock Exchange: Chiyedza House, 5th Floor, cnr First St and Kwame Nkrumah Ave, POB UA234, Harare; tel. (4) 736861; fax (4) 791045; e-mail zse@econet.co.zw; internet www.zse.co.zw; f. 1946; Chair. G. MHLANGA; CEO EMMANUEL MUNYUKWI.

INSURANCE

Export Credit Guarantee Corporation of Zimbabwe (Pvt): 6 Earles Rd, Alexandra Park, POB CY2995, Causeway, Harare; tel. and fax (4) 744644; e-mail ecgc@telco.co.zw; internet www.ecgc.co.zw; f. 1999 as national export credit insurance agency; also provides export finance guarantee facilities; 100% owned by Reserve Bank of Zimbabwe; Chair. J. A. L. CARTER; Man. Dir RAPHAEL G. NYADZAYO.

Credit Insurance Zimbabwe (Credsure): Credsure House, 69 Sam Nujoma St, POB CY1584, Causeway, Harare; tel. (4) 706101; fax (4) 706105; e-mail headoffice@credsure.co.zw; export credit insurance; Man. Dir BRIAN HILLEN-MOORE.

Fidelity Life Assurance of Zimbabwe (Pvt) Ltd: 66 Julius Nyerere Way, POB 435, Harare; tel. (4) 750927; fax (4) 751723; f. 1977; 52% owned by Zimre Holdings Ltd; pensions and life assurance; Chair. J. P. MKUSHI; Man. Dir SIMON B. CHAPAREKA.

Intermarket Life Assurance Ltd: Intermarket Life Towers, 77 Jason Moyo Ave, POB 969, Harare; tel. (4) 708801; fax (4) 703186; e-mail info@interlife.co.zw; internet www.intermarket.co.zw; f. 1964; life assurance; Man. Dir AMBROSE G. CHINEMBIRI.

NICOZ Diamond: Corner House, Samora Machel and Leopold Takawira Ave, POB 1256, Harare; tel. (4) 704911; fax (4) 704134; e-mail enquiries@nicozdiamond.co.zw; internet www.nicozdiamond.co.zw; f. 2003 by merger of National Insurance Co of Zimbabwe and Diamond Insurance of Zimbabwe; Chair. PHINEAS S. CHINGONO; Man. Dir GRACE MURADZIKWA.

Old Mutual PLC: Old Mutual Central Africa CABS Bldg, Northend Close, Northridge Park, Highlands, Harare; POB 1346, Harare; tel. (4) 851484-88; fax (4) 485480; e-mail info@oldmutual.co.zw; internet www.oldmutual.co.zw; f. 1845; life assurance, asset management, banking and general insurance; Chair. M. J. LEVETT; CEO J. H. SUTCLIFFE.

Zimnat Lion Insurance Co Ltd: Zimnat House, cnr Nelson Mandela Ave and Third St, POB CY1155, Causeway, Harare; ; tel. (4) 701177; fax (4) 735060; e-mail zimnat@harare.iafrca.com; f. 1998 by merger of Zimnat Insurance Co Ltd and Lion of Zimbabwe Insurance; merged with AIG Zimbabwe in 2005; short-term insurance; Chair. S. MUTASA; Man. Dir CARLSON CHISWO.

Trade and Industry

GOVERNMENT AGENCIES

Export Processing Zones Authority (EPZA): POB 661484, Kopje, Harare; tel. (4) 780147; fax (4) 773843; e-mail info@epz.co.zw; internet www.epz.co.zw; f. 1996; administers and regulates export processing zones established since 1994; Chair. LOVEMORE CHIHOTA; Chief Exec. WALTER CHIDHAKWA.

Industrial Development Corporation of Zimbabwe (IDC): 93 Park Lane, POB CY1431, Causeway, Harare; tel. (4) 706971; fax (4) 250385; e-mail administrator@idc.co.zw; internet www.idc.co.zw; f. 1963; state investment agency; Chief Exec. MIKE NDUDZO.

Privatization Agency of Zimbabwe (PAZ): Club Chambers, 9th Floor, cnr Nelson Mandela and Third St, Private Bag 7728, Causeway, Harare; tel. (4) 251620; fax (4) 253723; internet www.paz.co.zw; f. 1999; CEO ANDREW N. BVUMBE.

Zimbabwe Investment Centre (ZIC): Investment House, 109 Rotten Row, POB 5950, Harare; tel. (4) 757931; fax (4) 757937; e-mail info@zic.co.zw; internet www.zic.co.zw; f. 1993; promotes domestic and foreign investment; CEO RICHARD MBAIWA (acting).

ZimTrade: 904 Premium Close, Mount Pleasant Business Park, POB 2738, Harare; tel. (4) 369330; fax (4) 369244; internet www.zimtrade.co.zw; f. 1991; national export promotion org.; Chair. FLORENCE SIGUDU MATAMBO; CEO ELIZABETH NERWANDE.

DEVELOPMENT ORGANIZATIONS

Alternative Business Association (ABA): Stand No. 15295, cnr First St and Eighth Crescent, Sunningdale, Harare; tel. (4) 589625; fax (4) 799600; e-mail ired@africaonline.co.zw; f. 1999 to address urban and rural poverty; programme areas include, agriculture, micro-mining, cross-border trade, micro-enterprise devt and microfinance; Dir ISRAEL MABHOU.

Indigenous Business Development Centre (IBDC): Pocket Bldg, 1st Floor, Jason Moyo Ave, POB 3331, Causeway, Harare; tel. (4) 748345; f. 1990; Pres. BEN MUCHECHE; Sec.-Gen. ENOCH KAMUSHINDA.

Indigenous Business Women's Organisation (IBWO): 73B Central Ave, POB 3710, Harare; tel. (4) 702076; fax (4) 614012; Pres. JANE MUTASA.

Zidco Holdings: 88 Robert Mugabe Rd, POB 1275, Harare; tel. (4) 253682; fax (4) 704391; f. 1981; fmrly Zimbabwe Devt Corpn; privatized in 2001; CEO (vacant).

Zimbabwe Women's Bureau: 43 Hillside Rd, POB CR 120, Cranborne, Harare; tel. (4) 747809; fax (4) 707905; e-mail zwbtc@africaonline.co.zw; f. 1978; promotes entrepreneurial and rural community devt; Dir BERTHA MSORA.

CHAMBERS OF COMMERCE

Manicaland Chamber of Industries: 91 Third St, POB 92, Mutare; tel. (20) 61718; f. 1945; Pres. KUMBIRAI KATSANDE; 60 mems.

Mashonaland Chamber of Industries: POB 3794, Harare; tel. (4) 772763; fax (4) 750953; f. 1922; Pres. CHESTER MHENDE; 729 mems.

Matabeleland Chamber of Industries: 104 Parirenyatwa St, POB 2317, Bulawayo; tel. (9) 60642; fax (9) 60814; e-mail linksbyo@internet.co.zw; f. 1931; Pres. FELIX TSHUMA; 75 mems (2003).

Midlands Chamber of Industries: POB 213, Gweru; tel. (54) 2812; Pres. Dr BILL MOORE; 50 mems.

Zimbabwe National Chamber of Commerce (ZNCC): ZNCC Business House, 42 Harare St, POB 1934, Harare; tel. (4) 749335; fax (4) 750375; e-mail info@zncchq.co.zw; internet www.zncc.co.zw; f. 1983; represents small and medium businesses; Pres. LUXON ZEMBE; CEO CAIN MPOFU (acting); 2,500 mems; 8 brs.

INDUSTRIAL AND TRADE ASSOCIATIONS

Chamber of Mines of Zimbabwe: Stewart House, North Wing, 4 Central Ave, POB 712, Harare; tel. (4) 702841; fax (4) 707983; e-mail chamines@utande.co.zw; internet www.chamines.co.zw; f. 1939; Pres. IAN SAUNDERS; Chief Exec. and Sec. DAVID E. H. MURANGARI.

Confederation of Zimbabwe Industries (CZI): 31 Josiah Chinamano Ave, POB 3794, Harare; tel. (4) 772763; fax (4) 750953; internet www.czi.org.zw; f. 1957; Pres. PATTISON SITHOLE; CEO FARAI ZIZHOU (acting).

Specialized affiliate trade asscns include:

CropLife Zimbabwe: POB AY78, Amby, Harare; tel. (4) 620191; fax (4) 660590; e-mail maxm@ecomed.co.zw; fmrly the Agricultural Chemical Industry Asscn; Chair. MAX MAKUVISE.

Furniture Manufacturers' Association: c/o CZI, 31 Josiah Chinamano Ave, POB 3794, Harare; Pres. MATT SNYMAN.

Zimbabwe Association of Packaging: 17 Conventry Rd, Workington, Harare; tel. (4) 753800; fax (4) 882020; e-mail zap@africaonline.co.zw.

Construction Industry Federation of Zimbabwe: Conquenar House, 256 Samora Machel Ave East, POB 1502, Harare; tel. (4) 746661; fax (4) 746937; e-mail cifoz@africaonline.co.zw; Pres. GILBERT MATIKA; CEO MARTIN CHINGAIRA; c. 460 mems.

Grain Marketing Board (GMB): Dura Bldg, 179–187 Samora Machel Ave, POB CY77, Harare; tel. (4) 701870; fax (4) 251294; e-mail seedco@seedcogroup.com; f. 1931; responsible for maintaining national grain reserves and ensuring food security; CEO SAMUEL MUVUTI (acting).

Indigenous Petroleum Group of Zimbabwe (IPGZ): Harare; f. 2004 following split from Petroleum Marketers' Asscn of Zimbabwe; Chair. HUBERT NYAMBUYA; represents 68 importers.

Minerals Marketing Corporation of Zimbabwe (MMCZ): 90 Mutare Rd, Msasa, POB 2628, Harare; tel. (4) 487200; fax (4) 487161; e-mail administrator@mmcz.co.zw; internet www.mmcz.co.zw; f. 1982; sole authority for marketing of mineral production (except gold); Chair. MERCY MKUSHI (acting); Gen. Man. and CEO ONESIMO MAZAI MOYO.

Petroleum Marketers' Association of Zimbabwe (PMAZ): 142 Samora Machel Ave, Harare; tel. (4) 797556; represents private importers of petroleum-based products; Chair. GORDON MUSARIRA.

Timber Council of Zimbabwe: Conquenar House, 256 Samora Machel Ave, POB 3645, Harare; tel. (4) 746645; fax (4) 746013; Exec. Dir MARTIN DAVIDSON.

Tobacco Growers' Trust (TGT): POB AY331, Harare; tel. (4) 781167; fax (4) 781722; f. 2001; manages 20% of tobacco industry foreign exchange earnings on behalf of the Reserve Bank of Zimbabwe; affiliated orgs include Zimbabwe Tobacco Asscn and Zimbabwe Farmers' Union; Chair. WILFANOS MASHINGAIDZE; Gen. Man. ALBERT JAURE.

Tobacco Industry and Marketing Board: Union Ave, POB UA214, Harare; tel. (4) 613263; fax (4) 613264; e-mail timb@timb.co.zw; internet www.timb.co.zw; Chair. NJODZI MACHIRORI; Gen. Man. STANLEY MUTEPFA.

Tobacco Trade Association: c/o 4–12 Paisley Rd, POB ST180, Southerton, Harare; tel. (4) 773858; fax (4) 773859; e-mail tta@zol.co.zw; f. 1948; represents manufacturers and merchants.

Zimbabwe National Traditional Healers' Association (ZINATHA): Red Cross House, 2nd Floor, Rm 202, 98 Cameron St, POB 1116, Harare; tel. and fax (11) 606771; f. 1980; certifies and oversees traditional healers and practitioners of herbal medicine through the Traditional Medical Practitioners Council; promotes indigenous methods of prevention and treatment of HIV/AIDS; Pres. Prof. GORDON CHAVUNDUKA; 55,000 mems (2004).

Zimbabwe Tobacco Association (ZTA): 69 Josiah Chinamano Ave, POB 1781, Harare; tel. (4) 796931; fax (4) 791855; e-mail fctobacco@zta.co.zw; internet www.zta.co.zw; f. 1928; represents growers; Pres. JAMES DE LA FARGUE; CEO RODNEY AMBROSE; c. 5,500 mems.

EMPLOYERS' ASSOCIATIONS

Commercial Farmers' Union (CFU): Agriculture House, cnr Adylinn Rd and Marlborough Dr., Marlborough; POB WGT390, Westgate, Harare; tel. (4) 309800; fax (4) 309849; e-mail aisd3@cfu.co.zw; internet www.cfu.co.zw; f. 1942; Pres. DOUGLAS TAYLOR-FREEME; Dir HENDRIK W. OLIVIER; 1,200 mems.

Cattle Producers' Association (CPA): Agriculture House, cnr Adylinn Rd and Marlborough Dr., Marlborough; POB WGT390, Westgate, Harare; tel. (4) 309800; tel. and fax (4) 309837; e-mail livestock@cfu.co.zw; Chair. PETE DRUMMOND; CEO PAUL D'HOTMAN.

Coffee Growers' Association: Agriculture House, cnr Adylinn Rd and Marlborough Dr., Marlborough; POB WGT390, Westgate, Harare; tel. and fax (4) 750238; e-mail pres@cfu.co.zw; f. 1961; Chair. T. GIFFORD; Dir H. OLIVIER.

Commercial Cotton Growers' Association: Agriculture House, cnr Adylinn Rd and Marlborough Dr., Marlborough; POB WGT390, Westgate, Harare; tel. (4) 309800; fax (4) 309849; e-mail cotton@cfu.co.zw; f. 1951; Chair. NEVILLE BROWN.

Commercial Oilseed Producers' Association (COPA): Agriculture House, Rm SW07, cnr Adylinn Rd and Marlborough Dr., Marlborough; POB WGT390, Westgate, Harare; tel. (4) 309800; fax (4) 309843; e-mail copa@cfu.co.zw; Chair. J. J. ODENDAAL; represents c. 800 producers.

National Association of Dairy Farmers: Agriculture House, cnr Adylinn Rd and Marlborough Dr., Marlborough; POB WGT390, Westgate, Harare; tel. (4) 309800; fax (4) 309837; e-mail nadfres@cfu.co.zw; f. 1953; Chair. DEON THERON; CEO ROB J. VAN VUUREN; Livestock Man. PAUL D'HOTMAN; 174 mems.

Ostrich Producers' Association of Zimbabwe (TOPAZ): Agriculture House, cnr Adylinn Rd and Marlborough Dr., Marlborough; POB WGT390, Westgate, Harare; tel. (4) 309800; fax (4) 309862; Chair. CEDRIC WILDE; Exec. Dir CLARE DAVIES.

Zimbabwe Association of Tobacco Growers (ZATG): Agriculture House, cnr Adylinn Rd and Marlborough Dr., Marlborough; POB WGT390, Westgate, Harare; f. 2001; Pres. JULIUS NGORIMA; CEO CANAAN RUSHIZHA; 1,500 mems.

Zimbabwe Cereals Producers' Association (ZCPA): Agriculture House, cnr Adylinn Rd and Marlborough Dr., Marlborough; POB WGT390, Westgate, Harare; tel. (4) 309800; fax (4) 309843; Chair. J. J. ODENDAAL.

Zimbabwe Grain Producers' Association (ZGPA): Agriculture House, cnr Adylinn Rd and Marlborough Dr., Marlborough; POB WGT390, Westgate, Harare; tel. (4) 309800; fax (4) 309849; Chair. GORDON CRAIG; c. 1,400 mems.

Zimbabwe Poultry Association (Commercial Poultry Producers' Association): Agriculture House, cnr Adylinn Rd and Marlborough Dr., Marlborough; POB WGT390, Westgate, Harare; tel. (4) 309800; fax (4) 309849; e-mail cpa@cfu.co.zw; represents c. 200 producers.

Employers' Confederation of Zimbabwe (EMCOZ): Stewart House, 4 Central Ave, 2nd Floor, POB 158, Harare; tel. (4) 739647; fax (4) 739630; e-mail emcoz@emcoz.co.zw; Pres. MIKE C. BIMHA; Exec. Dir JOHN W. MUFUKARE.

Horticultural Promotion Council (HPC): 12 Maasdorp Ave, Alexandra Park; POB WGT290, Westgate, Harare; tel. (4) 745492; fax (4) 745480; Chief Exec. BASILIO SANDAMU; represents c. 1,000 producers.

Export Flower Growers' Association of Zimbabwe (EFGAZ): 12 Maasdorp Ave, Alexandra Park; POB WGT290, Westgate, Harare; tel. (4) 725130; fax (4) 795303; Dir MARY DUNPHY; c. 300 mems.

ZIMBABWE

National Employment Council for the Construction Industry of Zimbabwe: St Barbara House, Nelson Mandela Ave and Leopold Takawira St, POB 2995, Harare; tel. (4) 773966; fax (4) 773967; e-mail neccon@africaonline.co.zw; CEO STANLEY R. MAKONI; represents over 19,000 mem. cos (2002).

National Employment Council for the Engineering and Iron and Steel Industry: Adven House, 5th Floor, cnr Inez Terrace and Speke Ave, POB 1922, Harare; tel. (4) 775144; fax (4) 775918; f. 1943; Gen. Sec. E. E. SHARPE.

Zimbabwe Association of Consulting Engineers (ZACE): 16 Murandy Sq. East, POB HG836, Highlands, Harare; tel. (4) 746010; fax (4) 746010; e-mail zace@mango.zw.

Zimbabwe Building Contractors' Association: Caspi House, Block C, 4 Harare St, Harare; tel. (4) 780411; represents small-scale building contractors; CEO CONCORDIA MUKODZI.

Zimbabwe Commercial Farmers' Union (ZCFU): 53 Third St, Mutare; tel. (20) 67163; fmrly Indigenous Commercial Farmers' Union; Pres. DAVISON MUGABE; Dir. JOHN MAUTSA; represents c. 11,000 black farmers (2003).

Zimbabwe Farmers' Union (ZFU): POB 3755, Harare; tel. (4) 704763; fax (4) 700829; Pres. SILAS HUNGWE; Exec. Dir KWENDA DZAVIRA; represents c. 200,000 small-scale black farmers (2002).

UTILITIES

Electricity

Rural Electrification Agency (REA): Megawatt House, 6th Floor, 44 Samora Machel Ave Harare, POB 311, Harare; tel. (4) 770666; fax (4) 101661; e-mail emidzi@zesa.co.zw; f. 2002; manages Rural Electrification Fund to expand and accelerate the electrification of rural areas; Chair. Dr SYDNEY GATA; CEO EMMANUEL MIDZI.

Zimbabwe Electricity Regulatory Commission (ZERC): Harare; f. 2004 to oversee the unbundling from ZESA of the Zimbabwe Power Co, Zimbabwe Electricity Transmission Co and Zimbabwe Electricity Distribution Co; Dir-Gen. MAVIS CHIDZONGA.

Zimbabwe Electricity Supply Authority (ZESA): 25 Samora Machel Ave, POB 377, Harare; tel. (4) 774508; fax (4) 774542; operates one hydroelectric and four thermal power stations; Chair. and CEO Dr SIDNEY GATA; dependable generation capacity of 1700 MW.

Oil

National Oil Company of Zimbabwe (Pvt) Ltd (NOCZIM): NOCZIM House, 100 Leopold Takawira St, POB CY223, Causeway, Harare; tel. (4) 748543; fax (4) 748525; responsible for importing liquid fuels; Chair. CHARLES CHIPATO; Man. Dir ZVINECHIMWE CHURA.

Water

Zimbabwe National Water Authority (ZINWA): POB CY1215, Causeway, Harare; tel. and fax (4) 793139; e-mail mtetwa@utande.co.zw; f. 2001; fmrly Dept of Water, privatized in 2001; construction of dams, water supply, resources planning and protection; Chief Exec. ALBERT MUYAMBO.

TRADE UNIONS

All trade unions in Zimbabwe became affiliated to the ZCTU in 1981. The ZCTU is encouraging a policy of union amalgamations.

Zimbabwe Congress of Trade Unions (ZCTU): Chester House, 9th Floor, Speke Ave and Third St, POB 3549, Harare; tel. (4) 794742; fax (4) 728484; f. 1981; co-ordinating org. for trade unions; Pres. LOVEMORE MATOMBO; Sec.-Gen. WELLINGTON CHIBEBE; c. 163,000 mems in 39 affiliated unions (2002).

Affiliates with over 3,000 mems include:

Associated Mineworkers' Union of Zimbabwe (AMWUZ): St. Andrew's House, 4th Floor, Leopold Takawira St and Samora Machel Ave, POB 384, Harare; tel. (4) 700287; Nat. Pres. EDMUND TINAGO RUZIVE; 25,000 mems (2002).

Commercial Workers' Union of Zimbabwe (CWUZ): CWUZ House, 15 Sixth Ave, ParktownPOB 3922 Harare; tel. (4) 664701; Pres. LUCIA MATIBENGA (acting); Gen. Sec. ENDWELL TARINGA (acting); 22,000 mems (2003).

Communication and Allied Services Workers Union of Zimbabwe (CASWUZ): Morgan House, 4th Floor, G. Silundika Ave, POB 739, Harare; tel. (4) 794763; fmrly the Zimbabwe Post and Telecommunication Workers' Union; present name adopted 2002; Pres. MARTIN MATSA; Gen. Sec. GIFT CHIMANIKIRE; 5,320 mems (2002).

General Agricultural and Plantation Workers' Union (GAPWUZ): NCR House, 65 Samora Machel Ave, Harare; tel. (4) 734141; Gen. Sec. GERTRUDE HAMBIRA; 5,000 mems (2002).

National Engineering Workers' Union (NEWU): St Barbara House, Nelson Mandela Ave and Leopold Takawira St, Harare; tel. (4) 759957; Pres. I. MATONGO; Gen. Sec. JAPHET MOYO; 9,000 mems (2002).

National Union of Clothing Industry Workers' Union (NUCI): POB RY28, Railton, Bulawayo; tel. (9) 64432; Gen. Sec. FRED MPOFU; 4,500 mems (2002).

Progressive Teachers' Union of Zimbabwe (PTUZ): 14 McLaren Rd, Milton Park, Harare; POB CR620, Cranborne, Harare; tel. (4) 757746; fax (4) 741937; e-mail ptuz@mweb.co.zw; f. 1997; Sec.-Gen. RAYMOND MAJONGWE; 12,000 mems (2002).

United Food and Allied Workers' Union of Zimbabwe: Harare; tel. (4) 74150; f. 1962; Gen. Sec. I. M. NEDZIWE.

Zimbabwe Amalgamated Railwaymen's Union (ZARU): Unity House, 13th Ave, Herbert Chitepo St, Bulawayo; tel. (9) 60948; Gen. Sec. GIDEON SHOKO; 7,000 mems (2002).

Zimbabwe Banks and Allied Workers' Union (ZIBAWU): 1 Meredith Dr., Eastlea, POB 966, Harare; tel. (4) 703744; e-mail bankunion@zol.co.zw; Pres. GEORGE KAWENDA; Gen. Sec. COLLEN GWIYO; 4,560 mems (2002).

Zimbabwe Catering and Hotel Workers' Union (ZCHWU): Nialis Bldg, 1st Floor, Manyika, POB 3913, Harare; tel. (4) 753338; Gen. Sec. NICHOLAS E. MUDZENGERERE; 8,500 mems (2002).

Zimbabwe Chemical and Allied Workers' Union: St Andrew's House, 2nd Floor, Leopold Takawira St and Samora Machel Ave, POB 4810, Harare; tel. (4) 796533; Gen. Sec. REMUS MAKUVAZA; 3,723 mems (2002).

Zimbabwe Leather Shoe and Allied Workers' Union (ZLSAWU): POB 4450, Harare; tel. (4) 727925; e-mail zlsawa@telco.co.zw; Pres. LANGTON MUGEJI; Gen. Sec. ISIDORE MANHANDO ZINDOGA; 6,745 mems (2002).

Zimbabwe Textile Workers' Union (ZTWU): 4 Bradfield Rd, Hillside, POB UA245, Harare; tel. (4) 747890; e-mail ztwu@mweb.co.zw; Gen. Sec. SILAS KUVEYA; 11,000 mems (2004).

Zimbabwe Tobacco Industry Workers' Union (ZTIWU): St. Andrew's House, 2nd Floor, Samora Machel Ave, POB 2757, Harare; Gen. Sec. ESTEVAO CUMBULANE; 3,000 mems (2002).

Zimbabwe Federation of Trade Unions: Harare; f. 1996 as alternative to ZCTU; Co-ordinator CUTHBERT CHISWA; affiliated unions include:

Zimbabwe Teachers' Union (ZITU): POB GV1, Glen View, Harare; tel. (4) 692454; fax (4) 708929; f. 2002; Gen. Sec. SIMPLISIO MATUMBE.

Non-affiliated Union

Zimbabwe Teacher's Association (ZIMTA): POB 1440, Harare, Zimbabwe; tel. (4) 728438; fax (4) 791042; e-mail zimta@telco.co.zw; Pres. LEONARD NKALA; Sec.-Gen. DENNIS SINYOLO; represents 55,000 teachers.

Transport

RAILWAYS

In 1998 the rail network totalled 2,592 km, of which 313 km was electrified. Trunk lines run from Bulawayo south to the border with Botswana, connecting with the Botswana railways system, which, in turn, connects with the South African railways system; north-west to the Victoria Falls, where there is a connection with Zambia Railways; and north-east to Harare and Mutare connecting with the Mozambique Railways' line from Beira. From a point near Gweru, a line runs to the south-east, making a connection with the Mozambique Railways' Limpopo line and with the Mozambican port of Maputo. A connection runs from Rutenga to the South African Railways system at Beitbridge. A 320-km line from Beitbridge to Bulawayo was opened in 1999.

National Railways of Zimbabwe (NRZ): cnr Fife St and 10th Ave, POB 596, Bulawayo; tel. (9) 363716; fax (9) 363502; f. 1899; reorg. 1967; privatization under way; Chair. (vacant); Gen. Man. MIKE TICHAFA KARAKADZAI.

ROADS

In 1999 the road system in Zimbabwe totalled an estimated 18,338 km, of which 6,781 km were main roads and 1,668 km were secondary roads; some 47.4% of the total network was paved. In December 2005 tollgates were introduced at the borders to raise funds to maintain the road network.

CIVIL AVIATION

International and domestic air services connect most of the larger towns.

Air Zimbabwe (Pvt) Ltd (AirZim): POB AP2, Harare Airport, Harare; tel. (4) 575111; fax (4) 575068; internet www.airzimbabwe

.com; f. 1967; scheduled domestic and international passenger and cargo services to Africa, Australia and Europe; plans were announced in Apr. 2006 to separate operations, creating the new cos Air Zimbabwe Technical, Air Zimbabwe Cargo, Nat. Handling Services and Galileo Zimbabwe, in addition to Air Zimbabwe; Chair. MIKE BIMHA; CEO RAMBAI CHIGWENA.

Expedition Airline: Harare Airport, Harare; f. 1997; domestic services between Harare and Victoria Falls, Bulawayo, Masvingo and Mutare.

Majestic Air: 106 Lomagund Rd, Avondale West, POB 2426, Harare; f. 2001.

Manicaland Air Charter: f. 1996; operates charter service between Harare and Mutare.

Zimbabwe Express Airlines: Kurima House, Ground Floor, 89 Nelson Mandela Ave, POB 5130, Harare; tel. (4) 729681; fax (4) 737117; f. 1995; domestic routes and service to Johannesburg (South Africa); Man. Dir and CEO EVANS NDEBELE.

Tourism

The principal tourist attractions are the Victoria Falls, the Kariba Dam and the Hwange Game Reserve and National Park. Zimbabwe Ruins, near Fort Victoria, and World's View, in the Matapos Hills, are also of interest. There is trout-fishing and climbing in the Eastern Districts, around Umtali. In 2003 2,256,205 tourists visited Zimbabwe, up from 2,041,202 in the previous year; however, revenue from tourism over the same period fell from US $76m. to US $44m.

Zimbabwe Tourism Authority (ZTA): POB CY286, Causeway, Harare; tel. (4) 758748; fax (4) 758826; e-mail info@ztazim.co.zw; internet www.zimbabwetourism.co.zw; f. 1984; promotes tourism domestically and from abroad; Chair. EMMANUEL FUNDIRA; associations licensed by the ZTA include:

Zimbabwe Association of Tour and Safari Operators (ZATSO): 18 Walter Hill Ave, Eastlea, Harare; tel. (4) 702402; fax (4) 707306; e-mail enquiries@soaz.net; CEO PAUL MATAMISA (acting).

INDEX OF TERRITORIES IN VOLUMES I AND II

	Page
Abu Dhabi	4469
Afghanistan	447
Ajman	4469
Åland Islands	1714
Albania	472
Alderney	4564
Algeria	492
American Samoa	4721
Andorra	518
Angola	525
Anguilla	4572
Antarctic Territory, Australian	645
Antarctic Territory, British	4585
Antarctica	545
Antigua and Barbuda	547
Argentina	556
Armenia	585
Aruba	3198
Ascension	4623
Ashmore Islands	645
Australia	603
Australian Antarctic Territory	645
Austria	647
Azad Kashmir	3409
Azerbaijan	672
Bahamas	691
Bahrain	701
Baker Island	4737
Bangladesh	715
Barbados	739
Barbuda	547
Belarus	749
Belau (see Palau)	
Belgium	770
Belize	798
Benin	808
Bermuda	4578
Bhutan	826
Bolivia	840
Bosnia and Herzegovina	860
Botswana	885
Bouvetøya	3347
Brazil	899
Brecqhou	4564
British Antarctic Territory	4585
British Indian Ocean Territory	4586
British Virgin Islands	4587
Brunei	933
Bulgaria	944
Burkina Faso	966
Burma (see Myanmar)	
Burundi	983
Caicos Islands	4626
Cambodia	1001
Cameroon	1022
Canada	1040
Cape Verde	1078
Cartier Island	645
Cayman Islands	4593
Central African Republic	1086
Ceuta	4047
Chad	1101
Channel Islands	4561
Chile	1119
China, People's Republic	1145
China (Taiwan)	1233
Christmas Island	638

	Page
Cocos Islands	640
Colombia	1266
Comoros	1291
Congo, Democratic Republic	1303
Congo, Republic	1323
Cook Islands	3243
Coral Sea Islands Territory	646
Costa Rica	1340
Côte d'Ivoire	1357
Croatia	1381
Cuba	1401
Cyprus	1426
Czech Republic	1451
Democratic People's Republic of Korea	2545
Democratic Republic of the Congo	1303
Denmark	1471
Djibouti	1507
Dominica	1516
Dominican Republic	1524
Dronning Maud Land	3347
Dubai	4469
East Timor (see Timor-Leste)	
Ecuador	1542
Egypt	1564
El Salvador	1594
Equatorial Guinea	1612
Eritrea	1622
Estonia	1635
Ethiopia	1654
Falkland Islands	4600
Faroe Islands	1495
Federated States of Micronesia	2998
Fiji	1675
Finland	1691
Former Yugoslav republic of Macedonia	2799
France	1718
French Guiana	1769
French Polynesia	1797
French Southern and Antarctic Territories	1821
Fujairah	4469
Futuna Islands	1815
Gabon	1834
Gambia	1850
Georgia	1864
Germany	1886
Ghana	1935
Gibraltar	4605
Great Britain	4486
Greece	1955
Greenland	1501
Grenada	1978
Grenadines	3733
Guadeloupe	1776
Guam	4726
Guatemala	1987
Guernsey	4561
Guinea	2007
Guinea-Bissau	2023
Guyana	2037
Haiti	2050
Herm	4564
Herzegovina	860

INDEX OF TERRITORIES IN VOLUMES I AND II

Territory	Page
Holy See	4788
Honduras	2071
Hong Kong	1198
Howland Island	4737
Hungary	2087
Iceland	2109
India	2122
Indian Ocean Territory, British	4586
Indonesia	2181
Iran	2222
Iraq	2252
Ireland	2281
Isle of Man	4567
Israel	2308
Italy	2349
Ivory Coast (see Côte d'Ivoire)	
Jamaica	2390
Jan Mayen	3347
Japan	2406
Jarvis Island	4737
Jersey	4565
Jethou	4564
Johnston Atoll	4738
Jordan	2453
Kazakhstan	2493
Keeling Islands	640
Kenya	2515
Kingman Reef	4738
Kiribati	2537
Korea, Democratic People's Republic	2545
Korea, Republic	2574
Kuwait	2611
Kyrgyzstan	2630
Laos	2648
Latvia	2664
Lebanon	2683
Lesotho	2711
Liberia	2724
Libya	2741
Liechtenstein	2759
Lihou	4564
Lithuania	2767
Luxembourg	2787
Macao	1220
Macedonia, former Yugoslav republic	2799
Madagascar	2818
Malawi	2836
Malaysia	2852
Maldives	2890
Mali	2901
Malta	2918
Man, Isle of	4567
Marshall Islands	2929
Martinique	1783
Mauritania	2937
Mauritius	2952
Mayotte	1807
Melilla	4051
Mexico	2967
Micronesia, Federated States	2998
Midway Atoll	4738
Miquelon	1812
Moldova	3005
Monaco	3024
Mongolia	3030
Montenegro	3813
Montserrat	4612
Morocco	3053

Territory	Page
Mozambique	3077
Myanmar	3096
Namibia	3122
Nauru	3140
Navassa Island	4738
Nepal	3148
Netherlands	3172
Netherlands Antilles	3204
Nevis	3713
New Caledonia	1822
New Zealand	3216
Nicaragua	3256
Niger	3275
Nigeria	3294
Niue	3250
Norfolk Island	642
North Korea	2545
Northern Areas (Pakistan)	3409
Northern Ireland	4486
Northern Mariana Islands	4703
Norway	3321
Oman	3348
Pakistan	3362
Palau	3410
Palestinian Autonomous Areas	3417
Palmyra	4738
Panama	3440
Papua New Guinea	3458
Paraguay	3480
People's Republic of China	1145
Peru	3498
Peter I Øy	3347
Philippines	3522
Pitcairn Islands	4619
Poland	3560
Portugal	3586
Príncipe	3757
Puerto Rico	4709
Qatar	3613
Ras al-Khaimah	4469
Republic of China (Taiwan)	1233
Republic of the Congo	1323
Republic of Korea	2574
Réunion	1789
Romania	3624
Ross Dependency	3239
Russian Federation	3651
Rwanda	3696
Saint Christopher and Nevis	3713
Saint Helena	4621
Saint Lucia	3722
Saint Pierre and Miquelon	1812
Saint Vincent and the Grenadines	3733
Samoa	3742
San Marino	3751
São Tomé and Príncipe	3757
Sark	4564
Saudi Arabia	3767
Senegal	3788
Serbia and Montenegro	3813
Seychelles	3844
Sharjah	4469
Sierra Leone	3853
Singapore	3870
Slovakia	3896
Slovenia	3915
Solomon Islands	3933

4913

INDEX OF TERRITORIES IN VOLUMES I AND II

Territory	Page
Somalia	3946
South Africa	3964
South Georgia	4625
South Korea	2574
South Sandwich Islands	4625
Spain	3998
Spanish North Africa	4047
Sri Lanka	4056
St Kitts (Saint Christopher)	3713
Sudan	4084
Suriname	4109
Svalbard	3345
Swaziland	4121
Sweden	4135
Switzerland	4160
Syria	4186
Taiwan	1233
Tajikistan	4209
Tanzania	4228
Thailand	4248
Timor-Leste	4279
Tobago	4323
Togo	4295
Tokelau	3239
Tonga	4313
Trinidad and Tobago	4323
Tristan da Cunha	4624
Tunisia	4341
Turkey	4360
'Turkish Republic of Northern Cyprus'	1426

Territory	Page
Turkmenistan	4396
Turks and Caicos Islands	4626
Tuvalu	4413
Uganda	4420
Ukraine	4439
Umm al-Qaiwain	4469
United Arab Emirates	4469
United Kingdom	4486
United States of America	4632
United States Virgin Islands	4733
Uruguay	4739
Uzbekistan	4757
Vanuatu	4776
Vatican City	4788
Venezuela	4797
Viet Nam	4823
Virgin Islands, British	4587
Virgin Islands, US	4733
Wake Island	4738
Wallis and Futuna Islands	1815
Western Samoa (see Samoa)	
Yemen	4851
Yugoslavia (see Serbia and Montenegro)	
Zambia	4870
Zimbabwe	4888

The Europa Regional Surveys of the World 2006

'Europa's Regional Surveys of the World are justly renowned for their exceptionally high levels of production, content and accuracy.' - *Reference Reviews*

A nine-volume library of historical, political, geographical and economic data, providing an accurate and impartial overview of the major regions of the world.

These exhaustive surveys bring together a unique collection of information, from description and analysis of the principal issues affecting each region, to statistical data and directory information.

Meticulously researched and updated every year, these Surveys are an indispensable information source on which you can rely.

Available as a set or individually, the nine titles that make up the series are as follows: *Africa South of the Sahara; Central and South-Eastern Europe; Eastern Europe, Russia and Central Asia; The Far East and Australasia; The Middle East and North Africa; South America, Central America and the Caribbean; South Asia; The USA and Canada; Western Europe.*

Bibliographic Details
November 2005: 285x220mm: 9 volumes
Set: 1-85743-320-3: **£2,700.00**

To order your set or for further information about individual volumes please contact:
Tel: + 44 (0) 20 7017 6629
Fax: + 44 (0) 20 7017 6720
E-mail: sales.europa@tandf.co.uk

Also available online!

Europa World *Plus*

Europa World and the Europa Regional Surveys of the World online

www.europaworld.com

Europa World Plus enables you to subscribe to Europa World together with as many of the nine Europa Regional Surveys of the World online as you choose, in one simple annual subscription.

The Europa Regional Surveys of the World complement and expand upon the information in Europa World with in-depth, expert analysis at regional, sub-regional and country level.

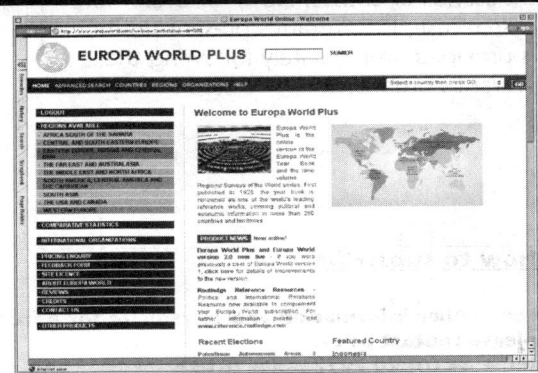

For further information and to register for a free trial please contact us at:
Tel: + 44 (0) 20 7017 6629; Fax: + 44 (0) 20 7017 6720
E-mail: reference.online@tandf.co.uk

Routledge
Taylor & Francis Group

The International Who's Who online
www.worldwhoswho.com

Free trial available!

All of the content of this exceptional reference source is available online. The added facilities of sophisticated search and browse functions and regular updates of content make www.worldwhoswho.com the premier source of information on the world's most influential people.

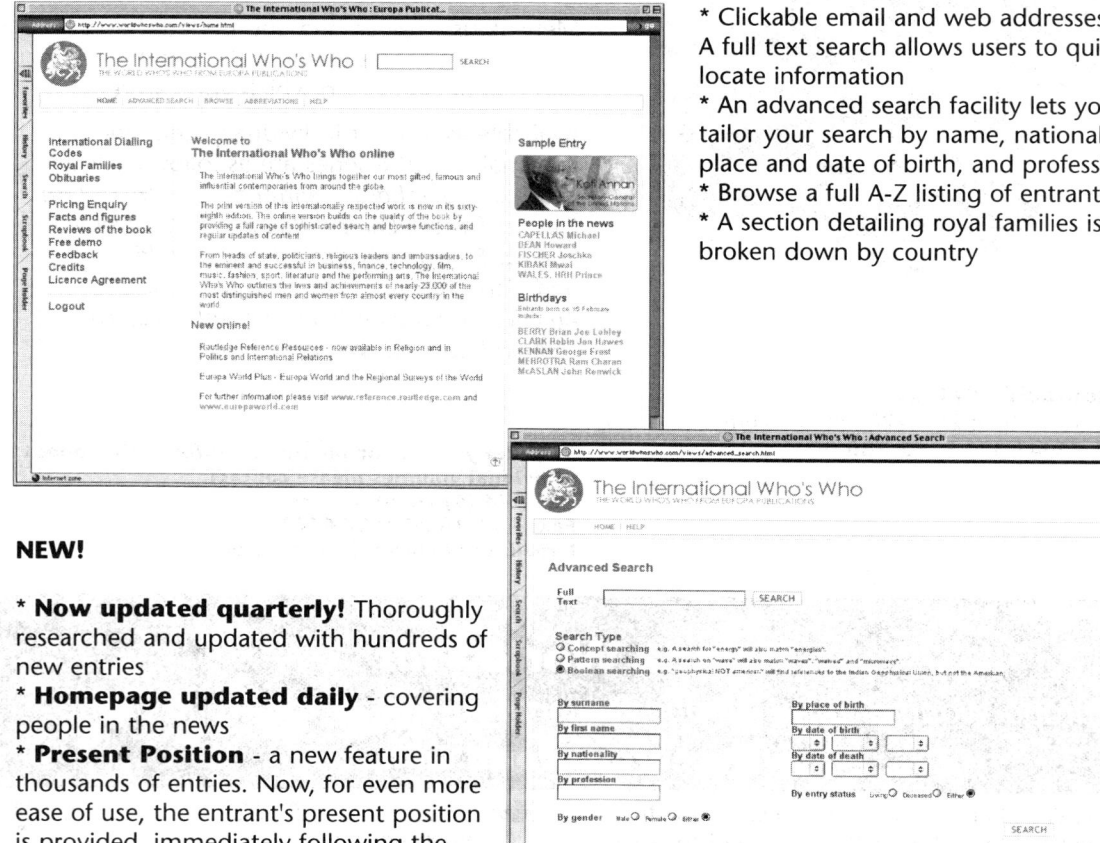

* Clickable email and web addresses
A full text search allows users to quickly locate information
* An advanced search facility lets you tailor your search by name, nationality, place and date of birth, and profession
* Browse a full A-Z listing of entrants
* A section detailing royal families is broken down by country

NEW!

* **Now updated quarterly!** Thoroughly researched and updated with hundreds of new entries
* **Homepage updated daily** - covering people in the news
* **Present Position** - a new feature in thousands of entries. Now, for even more ease of use, the entrant's present position is provided, immediately following the entrant's profession

How to subscribe

For further information and to register for a free trial please contact us at:
tel: + 44 (0) 20 7017 6608 /6131
fax: + 44 (0) 20 7017 6720
e-mail: reference.online@tandf.co.uk

The Europa World of Learning ONLINE
www.worldoflearning.com
Available Now

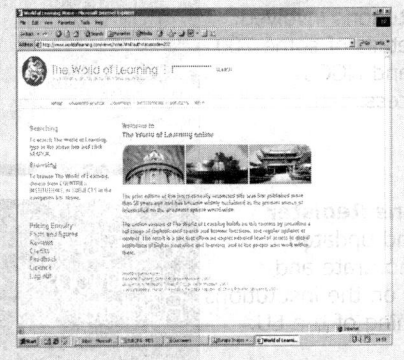

Locate academic institutions of every type, world-wide

- Universities and Colleges
- Schools of Art, Music and Architecture
- Learned Societies
- Research Institutes
- Libraries and Archives
- Museums and Art Galleries

Instant access to educational contacts around the globe

- Professors
- University Chancellors and Rectors
- Deans
- Librarians
- Curators
- Directors

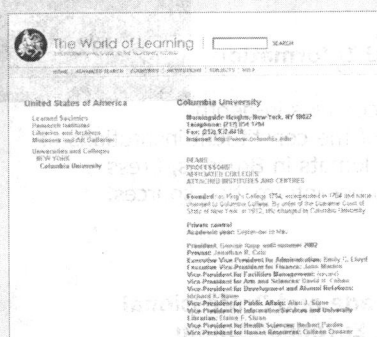

Additional features of The Europa World of Learning online

- Multiple-user facility available
- A full range of sophisticated search and browse functions
- Regularly updated

Free 30-day trial available
For further information e-mail: info.europa@tandf.co.uk

The European Union Information Series

6th Edition
European Union Encyclopedia and Directory 2006

Thoroughly updated, this extensive reference source provides in-depth information on all matters relating to the European Union: the expansion of the EU under the Nice Treaty is covered, and the future of the union is addressed.
November 2005

3rd Edition
A Dictionary of the European Union
David Phinnemore and Lee McGowan
Provides concise definitions and explanations on all aspects of the EU.
May 2006

3rd Edition
The Practical Guide to Foreign Direct Investment in the European Union
This title provides detailed coverage of national and EU financial incentives, and draws a comparison between each Member State's corporate and personal taxation, labour costs, social security charges and employment regulations.
December 2006

The Rome, Maastricht, Amsterdam and Nice Treaties: Comparative Texts
Highlights amendments and new Articles in the Nice Treaty compared with its precursors.
2003

3rd Edition
The Guide to EU Information Sources on the Internet
Divided thematically, this guide covers both institutional and non-institutional websites. Each entry includes: site name; web address; publisher's details; description of contents; languages; cost and useful notes.
July 2005

4th Edition
Lobbying in the European Union
A concise guide detailing the lobbying system of the European Union and the institutions involved. Contains contact details of some 700 trade associations and NGOs involved in the process.
October 2005

6th Edition
The EU Institutions Register
This fully revised and updated directory provides accurate and reliable information on the institutions involved in the running of the EU.
October 2005

15th Edition
The Directory of EU Information Sources
This major directory contains in-depth information on each of the constituent institutions of the EU, as well as diplomats in Brussels, Press Agencies and many other information sources.
March 2006

6th Edition
The Directory of Trade and Professional Associations in the European Union
Contact details, including e-mail and web addresses, of nearly 700 EU-level associations, and 11,700 national associations.
2004

2nd Edition
The EU Capital Guide
Facilitates rapid access to key Belgian and EU decision makers in government, foreign representations, services and other relevant fields.
2004

Influence and Interests in the European Union: the New Politics of Persuasion and Advocacy
Clearly discusses the impact and uses of interest representation in the EU.
2002

For further details please contact our marketing department:
Tel: +44 (0)20 7017 6649 Fax: +44 (0)20 7017 6720
E-mail: info.europa@tandf.co.uk Web: www.europapublications.com

	DATE DUE	
	SAINT MARY'S COLLEGE LIBRARY